The Grey House Performing Arts Directory

2015-16
Ninth Edition

The Grey House Performing Arts Directory

- Dance
- Instrumental Music
- Vocal Music
- Theatre
- Series & Festivals
- Facilities
- Information Resources
- Six Indexes

Grey House Publishing

PUBLISHER: Leslie Mackenzie
EDITOR: Richard Gottlieb
EDITORIAL DIRECTOR: Laura Mars

PRODUCTION MANAGER: Kristen Thatcher
PRODUCTION ASSISTANT: Katharine Hochswender
COMPOSITION: David Garoogian

MARKETING DIRECTOR: Jessica Moody

Grey House Publishing, Inc.
4919 Route 22
Amenia, NY 12501
518.789.8700
FAX 845.373.6390
www.greyhouse.com
e-mail: books@greyhouse.com

While every effort has been made to ensure the reliability of the information presented in this publication, Grey House Publishing neither guarantees the accuracy of the data contained herein nor assumes any responsibility for errors, omissions or discrepancies. Grey House accepts no payment for listing; inclusion in the publication of any organization, agency, institution, publication, service or individual does not imply endorsement of the editors or publisher.

Errors brought to the attention of the publisher and verified to the satisfaction of the publisher will be corrected in future editions.

Except by express prior written permission of the Copyright Proprietor no part of this work may be copied by any means of publication or communication now known or developed hereafter including, but not limited to, use in any directory or compilation or other print publication, in any information storage and retrieval system, in any other electronic device, or in any visual or audio-visual device or product.

This publication is an original and creative work, copyrighted by Grey House Publishing, Inc. and is fully protected by all applicable copyright laws, as well as by laws covering misappropriation, trade secrets and unfair competition.

Grey House has added value to the underlying factual material through one or more of the following efforts: unique and original selection; expression; arrangement; coordination; and classification.

Grey House Publishing, Inc. will defend its rights in this publication.

Copyright © 2014 Grey House Publishing, Inc.
All rights reserved

First edition published 2000
Ninth edition published 2014

Printed in Canada

The Grey House performing arts directory—9th ed.

1302 p.; 4.03 cm.
Bi-Annual
ISSN: 1540-8655

1. performing arts—United States—Directories. I. Grey House Publishing, Inc.,
II. Title: Performing arts directory

PN1561.G74
792
ISBN: 978-1-61925-290-5

Table of Contents

Introduction vii

DANCE
Listings by State 1

INSTRUMENTAL MUSIC
Listings by State 97

VOCAL MUSIC
Listings by State 260

THEATRE
Listings by State 340

SERIES & FESTIVALS
Listings by State 566

FACILITIES
Listings by State 767

INFORMATION RESOURCES
Listings by Resource Type 1048

INDEXES
Entry Name Index 1105
Executive Name Index 1133
Facilities Index 1239
Specialized Field Index 1249
Geographic Index 1271
Information Resources Index 1299

Introduction

This is the ninth edition of *The Grey House Performing Arts Directory*—a premier resource of performing arts organizations in America. It offers unequaled coverage of major performance categories, as well as resources for performers and artist managers alike.

Praise for previous edition:

> "...an impressive collection of material into one broadly useful resource for performing arts professionals, students, volunteers, and others..."
> —CHOICE, 2013

> "...this enormous and information-rich tome offers in-depth and comprehensive listings...a treasure trove for anyone looking for information on the performing arts in the United States..."
> —American Reference Books Annual, 2012

Arrangement

The Grey House Performing Arts Directory includes 9,452 performing arts organizations and resources—382 more than last edition—and 37,213 key contact names—8,000 more than last edition—both Artistic Management and Business titles. The listings are arranged first by performance category • **Dance** • **Instrumental Music** • **Vocal Music** • **Theatre** • **Series & Festivals** then by state and city, making it easy to research listings by both category and location. Following these five performing arts chapters are **Facilities** by state and **Information Resources** by type of resource—Associations, Newsletters, Magazines & Journals, Trade Shows, Directories & Databases, and Industry Web Sites.

Performing Arts Chapters

Each of these five chapters includes a vast range of listings in size, budget, and renown. From the *Alabama Ballet* to the *New York Metropolitan Opera*, from *Saratoga Performing Arts Series* to the *Pensacola Theater*, the scope of listings is unequalled. In addition to the range of listings, the number of listings in each chapter are impressive: 706 Dance; 1,131 Instrumental Music; 558 Vocal Music; 1,725 Theatre; and 1,727 Series & Festivals.

Each listing begins with important contact information—name, address, phone, fax, email and web site. You will find long lists of key staff—both Artistic Management and Business titles—and dozens of valuable details, such as: *Specialized Arts Fields; Number of Paid/Volunteer Staff; Income Sources; Budget; Year Founded; Affiliations; Annual Attendance; Seating Capacity; Guest Writers/Directors; Local Talent; Artists-in-Residence; Multimedia; Student Interns; Special Technical Talent,* and more.

Performance Facilities

This chapter includes 2,838 listings of venues for the performing arts. Organized first by state, then by city, many facilities listed are multi-purpose, such as arenas, stadiums, and college and university spaces. Some are devoted stages for dance or theater. All facilities listed include important contact information, most with key staff and important details, such as *Stage Dimensions, Seating Capacity,* and *Rental Contact*.

Information Resources

Taken from our popular *Directory of Business Information Resources*, this section includes 731 resources for the performing arts industry. Whether the need is educational or professional, users will find detailed listings for Associations, Newsletters, Magazines, Journals, Trade Shows, Directories, Databases, and Web Sites, with the contact information and key executive names needed for in depth research into the dynamic performing arts industry.

Introduction

Six Indexes

The Grey House Performing Arts Directory has six indexes to make it easy for researchers to locate the exact data they are looking for using a variety of criteria.

- **Entry Name Index:** An alphabetical listing of all performance organizations.

- **Executive Name Index:** An alphabetical listing of 37,213 key executives in the performing arts industry.

- **Facilities Index:** An alphabetical listing of 2,838 performance facilities.

- **Specialized Field Index:** An alphabetical listing of more than 250 performing arts categories within major categories of Dance, Vocal Music, Instrumental Music, Theatre, and Series & Festivals.

- **Geographic Index:** 8,685 performing arts listings and facilities listed by state

- **Information Resources Index:** An alphabetical listing of 731 performing arts Associations, Newsletters, Magazines, Journals, Trade Shows, Directories, Databases, and Web Sites.

Online Database

For even easier access to data, *The Grey House Performing Arts Directory* is available for subscription on G.O.L.D.—Grey House OnLine Database. Subscribers to G.O.L.D. have immediate access to 9,452 performing arts resources and 37,213 key industry contacts, and can search by dozens of criteria, including performance area, key staff, budget, keyword and so much more. Plus, subscribers can download contact sheets to create their own mailing list. Visit http:\\gold.greyhouse.com or call 800-562-2139 to demo the site.

DANCE / Alabama

Alabama

1
ALABAMA BALLET
2726 1st Avenue South
Birmingham, AL 35233
Phone: 205-322-4300
Fax: 205-322-4444
e-mail: information@alabamaballet.org
Web Site: www.alabamaballet.org
Management:
  Artistic Director: Tracey Alvey
  Associate Artistic Director: Roger Van Fleteren
  Executive Director: Megan Cottle
  Marketing & PR Director: AJ Roach
  Finance Manager: Islara Vazquez
  Production Director: Ed Zuckerman
  Technical Director: Atom Bennett
  Company Stage Manager: Joelle Linn
  Costume Director: Wendy Gamble
Mission: To promote and foster the development of classical and contemporary ballet through high-quality performances, dance education, and community outreach.
Utilizes: Choreographers; Dance Companies; Dancers; Educators; Guest Artists; Local Artists & Directors; Soloists; Theatre Companies
Founded: 1981
Specialized Field: Classical Ballet; Contemporary Ballet
Status: Non-Profit, Professional
Paid Staff: 10
Volunteer Staff: 4
Paid Artists: 22
Non-paid Artists: 13
Budget: $1.5 million
Income Sources: Ticket sales; donations; grants
Performs At: Samford Wright Center; Alabama Theatre; Ayls Stephens Center
Year Built: 1981
Organization Type: Performing; Touring

2
SOUTHEAST ALABAMA DANCE COMPANY
3010 Ross Clark Cir
Dothan, AL 36301-1122
Phone: 334-702-7139
Fax: 334-702-7139
e-mail: seadac@graceba.net
Web Site: www.southeastalabamadancecompany.org
Officers:
  President: Shane Sinquefield
Management:
  Executive Director: Tracy Solomon
  Legal Advisor: Paul Turner
  Costume Mistress: Cindi Tucker
  Office Manager: Rosa Kulik
  Bookkeeper: Rebecca McDonald
Mission: To provide performance opportunities and formal training to serious dance students, primarily in classical ballet.
Utilizes: Choreographers; Dance Companies; Dancers; Guest Accompanists; Guest Artists; Guest Ensembles; Guest Musicians; Original Music Scores; Resident Professionals; Scenic Designers; Singers; Soloists; Student Interns; Theatre Companies; Touring Companies; Volunteer Artists
Founded: 1978
Specialized Field: Jazz; Modern
Status: Non-Profit:Professional
Performs At: Dothan Civic Center

3
HUNTSVILLE BALLET COMPANY
800 Regal Drive
PO Box 373
Huntsville, AL 35804
Phone: 256-539-0961
Fax: 256-539-1837
e-mail: info@huntsvilleballet.org
Web Site: www.huntsvilleballetcompany.org
Officers:
  President: Dannye Drake
  First VP: Sherry Polk
  Second VP: Marion Merrell
  Treasurer: Lynn Kerkhof
Management:
  Artistic Director: Phillip Otto
  Ballet Mistress: Rachel Butler
Founded: 1964
Specialized Field: Ballet; Modern; Jazz; Tap; Pointe; Creative Movement
Status: Semi-professional; Nonprofit
Paid Staff: 20
Volunteer Staff: 100
Paid Artists: 20
Non-paid Artists: 100
Income Sources: Fundraising; Corporate Sponsorship; Individual Giving
Performs At: Ron Vaughn Center Concert Hall
Seating Capacity: 2,153
Year Built: 1975
Organization Type: Touring; Resident

4
MOBILE BALLET INC
4351 Downtowner Loop North
Mobile, AL 36609
Phone: 251-342-2241
Fax: 251-343-8289
e-mail: Info@mobileballet.org
Web Site: www.mobileballet.org
Officers:
  President: Becky S. Tate
  Vice President: Liz Kirby
  Secretary: Rhea Mostellar
  Chairman, Mobile Ballet Barre: Lenore Saget
Management:
  Artistic Director: Winthrop Corey
  Associate Director Mobile School: Pamela Thompson
  Associate Director: Zo‰ Lombard Todd
  Development Director, MD: Karen Kennedy
  Development Assistant: Kittrell Johnson
Mission: To provide superior dance education, to present quality performances, and to promote the ballet to the community as an expression of the human spirit.
Founded: 1987
Specialized Field: Ballet

5
ALABAMA DANCE THEATRE
Armory Learning Arts Center
1018 Madison Avenue
Montgomery, AL 36104
Mailing Address: PO Box 11327 Montgomery, AL 36111
Phone: 334-241-2590
Fax: 334-241-2504
e-mail: ADTDance1@aol.com
Web Site: www.alabamadancetheatre.com
Management:
  Artistic Director: Kitty Seale
  Ballet Master: Foye DuBose
  Director of Development: Brenda Robertson Dennis
  Public Relations, Ballet: Casey Vaughan
  Choreographer: Sara Sanford
  Choreographer: Jenny Plunkett Letner
  Choreographer: Janie Allen Atford
Mission: To train and educate students in the disciplined art of dance and to educate and develop the future audience for dance in central Alabama. ADT hosts a number of educational activities in the community which serve to build our audience and enhance the cultural life of our city.
Utilizes: Choreographers; Dance Companies; Dancers; Guest Accompanists; Guest Artists; Guest Ensembles; Soloists; Theatre Companies
Founded: 1986
Specialized Field: Classical Ballet; Modern Ballet; Jazz; Hip Hop; Tap
Performs At: Davis Theater
Seating Capacity: 1,200
Year Built: 1930

6
MONTGOMERY BALLET
2102 Eastern Boulevard
Suite 223
Montgomery, AL 36117
Mailing Address: PO Box 230097 Montgomery, AL 36123
Phone: 334-409-0522
Fax: 334-409-2311
e-mail: info@montgomeryballet.orgm
Web Site: www.montgomeryballet.org
Officers:
  President: Charlotte Meadows
  V.P. Special Events: Jenni Payne
  VP Development: Dottye Hannan
  Secretary: Clare Watson
  Treasurer: Ann Winbourne
  V.P. School: Jan Hodgson
Management:
  Artistic Director: Darren McIntyre
  Wardrobe Mistress/Costume Designer: Candace Love
  Set Designer/Props: Seay Earehart
  Lighting Designer/Production: Adam Stuart
  Principal Artist: Camilo Cardenas Herrera
  Principal Artist: Courtney Dressner
  Principal Artist: Lucas Athaide
  Soloist Artists: Nicole Miller
  Soloist Artists: Patrick Willison
Mission: To provide unparalleled excellence in training and annual performance opportunities.
Founded: 1958
Specialized Field: Ballet
Status: Professional; Nonprofit
Paid Staff: 4
Volunteer Staff: 10
Paid Artists: 55
Income Sources: Southeast Regional Ballet Association
Performs At: Alabama Shakesphere Festival
Seating Capacity: 700
Organization Type: Performing; Educational

7
MOMIX
35 Bell Hill Rd
Washington, AL 06793
Phone: 860-868-7454
e-mail: momix@snet.net
Web Site: www.mosespendleton.com
Management:
  Artistic Director: Moses Pendleton

DANCE / Alaska

Associate Director: Cynthia Quinn
Manager: Margaret Selby
Mission: To present work of exceptional inventiveness and physical beauty by creating surrealistic images using props, light, shadow, humor and the human body.
Founded: 1981
Specialized Field: Ilusion Dance
Budget: 1000000

Alaska

8
ALASKA DANCE THEATRE
550 E 33rd Avenue
Anchorage, AK 99503
Phone: 907-277-9591
Fax: 907-274-3078
e-mail: info@alaskadancetheatre.org
Web Site: www.alaskadancetheatre.org
Officers:
  President: Mark Musial
  Treasurer: Maryann Frazier
  Secretary: Suzanne La Pierre
  Vice President: Bettina Chastain
  Board Member: Ingrid Van Den Hoogen
Management:
  Artistic/School Director: Alice Bassler Sullivan
  Associate/Director: Coutland Weaver
  Interim Executive Director: Michelle Guisinger
Mission: To promote dance through performance, professional education and avocacy in Alaska and to provide a place within the dance comunity for local and visiting artists to expand their creative talent while nurturing discipline, confidence, fitness and the experience of movement. Alaska Dance Theatre strives to keeps its program affordable to a wide range of the population.
Utilizes: Choreographers; Collaborations; Dancers; Guest Accompanists; Guest Artists; High School Drama; Instructors; Local Artists; Multimedia; Music; Resident Artists; Soloists
Founded: 1981
Specialized Field: Ballet
Status: Nonprofit Organization
Paid Staff: 23
Volunteer Staff: 150
Paid Artists: 5
Non-paid Artists: 30
Budget: $50,000
Income Sources: Grants; Donations; Tuition
Performs At: Atwood Concert Hall
Type of Stage: Proscenium
Stage Dimensions: 120' wide by 52'deep
Seating Capacity: 2,000
Organization Type: Performing

9
PULSE DANCE COMPANY
2400 East Tudor Road #2422
Anchorage, AK 99503
Phone: 907-677-8573
e-mail: pulsedancecompany@gmail.com
Web Site: pulsedancecompany.org
Management:
  Artistic Director: Stephanie Wonchala
Mission: Community enrichment through dance. Pulse Dance Company provides ease of access to vibrant Alaskan arts and culture via training and performance opportunities, outreach programs, and collaborations. We cultivate the gifts of Alaskan dancers through continued professional development and nurture the budding artist in everyone.
Founded: 2013

Arizona

10
CROSSROADS PERFORMANCE GROUP
1870 W 5th Place
Mesa, AZ 85201
Phone: 480-969-6683
Fax: 480-692-1887
e-mail: lrchow@cox.net
Mission: The duo explore the merging of movement, sound, and drama to create new forms of performance art in its purest form. They strive to capture the imagination and intrigue the senses.
Specialized Field: Interdisciplinary; Collaborative Dance
Status: Non-Profit
Volunteer Staff: 5
Income Sources: Educational Programs; Performances

11
BALLET ARIZONA
2835 E. Washington Street
Phoenix, AZ 85034
Phone: 602-381-0184
Fax: 602-381-0189
e-mail: school@balletaz.org
Web Site: www.balletaz.org
Officers:
  Chairman: Ken Van Winkle
  Vice Chairman: Linda Perlich
  Treasurer: Dean Rennell
  Secretary: Mary Ehret
  School Manager: Alison Morse
  Marketing and Communications: Samantha Franck
Management:
  Artistic Director: Ib Andersen
  Executive Director: David Tompkins
  Director of Finance: Christopher J. Marsh
  Rehearsal Director: Maria Simonetti
  Director of Production: Michael Panvini
  Ballet Mistress: Lisbet Companioni
  School Director: Carlos Valcarcel
Mission: To creat, perform and teach classical and contemporary ballet.
Utilizes: Commissioned Composers; Commissioned Music; Dancers; Designers; Five Seasonal Concerts; Guest Accompanists; Guest Artists; Guest Conductors; Guest Instructors; Multimedia; Original Music Scores; Resident Professionals; Student Interns; Theatre Companies
Founded: 1986
Specialized Field: Dance
Status: Professional; Nonprofit
Paid Staff: 14
Volunteer Staff: 5
Paid Artists: 21
Budget: $5 million
Income Sources: Ticket Sales; Donations; Ballet School Tuition
Performs At: Orpheum Theatre
Facility Category: Performing Arts
Seating Capacity: 2,800
Year Built: 1927
Organization Type: Performing; Touring; Resident; Educational

12
DESERT DANCE THEATRE
PO Box 25332
Tempe, AZ 85285-5332
Phone: 480-962-4584
Fax: 480-962-1887
e-mail: Lisa@DesertDanceTheatre.org
Web Site: www.desertdancetheatre.org
Officers:
  Vice President: Lisa R Chow
  Secretary: Pualani Blackmon
  Treasurer: Thomas Bass
  Continuing Director: Marion K Jones
  Continuing Director: Margie Romero Wolf
  Continuing Director: Renee Davis
Management:
  Artistic Director/Choreographer: Lisa R Chow
  Associate Artistic Director: Renee Davis
  Artistic Director/Music Director: Step Raptis Lorena:
Mission: Performers, choreographers and educators who strive to bring the openness, spontaneity and diversity of dance to the public.
Utilizes: Actors; Choreographers; Collaborating Artists; Collaborations; Commissioned Music; Dance Companies; Dancers; Educators; Fine Artists; Five Seasonal Concerts; Guest Artists; Guest Choreographers; Guest Companies; Guest Ensembles; Guest Lecturers; Guest Musical Directors; High School Drama; Instructors; Multi Collaborations; Multimedia; Music; Organization Contracts; Original Music Scores; Sign Language Translators; Soloists; Student Interns
Founded: 1979
Specialized Field: Modern; Jazz; Ballet; Creative Movement
Status: Non-Profit
Volunteer Staff: 15
Paid Artists: 15
Budget: $50,000
Income Sources: Corporate Support; Private Sponsors
Performs At: Scottsdale Center For The Performing Arts
Seating Capacity: 838
Year Built: 1979
Organization Type: Performing; Educational

13
YUMA BALLET THEATRE & PERFORMING ARTS COMPANY
PO Box 6519
Yuma, AZ 85366
Phone: 928-341-1925
Fax: 928-341-1925
e-mail: ybt_dance@yahoo.com
Web Site: www.yumaballet.org
Officers:
  President: Carolyn Miller
  Vice President: Candice Orduno
  Secretary: Janet Chasse
  Treasurer: Juliea Gotsch
  Board Member: Aide Estrada
Management:
  Artistic Director: Erika Zabie Nields
  Executive Director: Lisa Mendez
Mission: To encourage and promote the excellence of dance in Yuma and Arizona by nurturing the highest artistic and moral values in our dancers, to showcase and support the work of emerging and established choreography, bring dance and its education to residents of Yuma and the surrounding areas, and fortify the artistic community of Yuma County through partnerships and resource sharing with art groups in the area.
Utilizes: Five Seasonal Concerts; Singers
Founded: 1979
Specialized Field: Ballet
Status: Non-Professional; Nonprofit; Part-Time Special Dancers

DANCE / Arkansas

Paid Staff: 6
Volunteer Staff: 20
Income Sources: Regional Dance America; Honor Company; Ticket Sales; Friends Of Ballet
Performs At: Snider Auditorium
Seating Capacity: 700
Organization Type: Performing; Educational

Arkansas

14
THE FOUNDATION OF ARTS
115 E Monroe Avenue
Jonesboro, AR 72401
Mailing Address: PO Box 310
Phone: 870-935-2726
Fax: 870-277-1683
e-mail: info@foajonesboro.org
Web Site: www.foajonesboro.org
Officers:
  Board Of Director, Chair: Dr. Rebecca Evans
  Vice Chair: Dana Kelley
  Treasurer: Robin Martin
  Secretary: Debra Sharp
Management:
  Executive/Artistic Director: Kristi Pulliam
  Education Programs Manager: LeeAnn Knierim
  Tech and Communications Coordinator: Wendeth Rauf
  Asst. Techical Director: Jonathan Stanley
  Customer Service Associate: Annie Clark
Mission: The Foundation of Arts for Northeast Arkansas is a regional non-profit organization that passionately strives to enhance the community's quality of life by providing and fostering arts programming that includes education, outreach and entertainment.
Utilizes: Actors; Choreographers; Educators; Guest Artists; Guest Designers; High School Drama; Instructors; Local Artists; Lyricists; Multimedia; Organization Contracts; Sign Language Translators; Soloists; Student Interns; Touring Companies
Founded: 1978
Specialized Field: Ballet, Hip-Hop, Tap Dance and Art and Painting Classes
Status: Non-Profit
Paid Staff: 15
Budget: $35,000-$100,000
Income Sources: Box Office; Grants; Private Donation; Class Tuition
Annual Attendance: 25,000
Facility Category: Theatre
Type of Stage: Proscenium
Seating Capacity: 670
Year Built: 1940
Year Remodeled: 2000
Rental Contact: Executive Director Sherri Beatty
Resident Groups: NEA Symphony; Theatre on the Ridge; Act Experience; Jonesboro City Ballet

15
BALLET ARKANSAS, INC.
PO Box 26203
Little Rock, AR 72221-6203
Phone: 501-223-5150
Fax: 501-227-0662
Web Site: balletarkansas.org
Officers:
  President: Karen Bassett
  Vice President: Todd Rice
  Treasurer: Cheddy Widdinton
  Secretary: Molly McGowan
  Guild President: Jammie Ziller
Management:
  Executive Director: Lauren Strother
  Ballet Mistress: Marla Edwards
  Artistic Director: Michael Bearden
  Associate Director: Guy Couch
  Production/Company Manager: Erin Anson
Mission: Ballet Arkansas is committed to enriching the community through development of its young performers and providing high caliber performances.
Utilizes: Guest Artists; Guest Companies; Singers
Founded: 1978
Specialized Field: Ballet
Status: Semi-Professional; Nonprofit
Paid Staff: 13
Income Sources: Southwest Regional Ballet Association; National Association for Regional Ballet
Performs At: Robinson Center Music Hall
Seating Capacity: 2,600
Organization Type: Performing; Touring; Educational; Sponsoring

California

16
ALAMEDA CIVIC BALLET
1402 Park Street
Alameda, CA 94501
Phone: 510-337-1929
e-mail: admin@alamedacivicballet.org
Web Site: alamedacivicballet.org
Management:
  Artistic Director: Abra Rudisill
Mission: Our mission is to create and present community accessible ballet performances while educating and engaging the community in the performing arts.
Founded: 2003
Specialized Field: Ballet
Status: Nonprofit

17
CENTRAL CALIFORNIA BALLET
Lively Arts Foundation
1379 Crown Drive
Alameda, CA 94501
Phone: 877-608-5883
e-mail: livelyarts2@aol.com
Web Site: www.livelyarts.org
Management:
  Artistic Director: Diane K Mosier
Mission: To help establish the Fresno metropolitan area as a major cultural force in California by providing a variety of world class music, dance and dramatic entertainment and by fostering a challenging and enriched environment for talented local students in the performing arts.
Founded: 1989
Specialized Field: Ballet
Paid Staff: 1
Volunteer Staff: 6
Performs At: Historic Tower Theatre
Seating Capacity: 900
Year Built: 1939
Organization Type: Performing; Touring

18
SUHAILA DANCE COMPANY & SUHAILA SALIMPOUR SCHOOL OF DANCE
425 San Pablo Avenue
Albany, CA 94706
Phone: 510-527-2400
e-mail: suhaila@suhailainternational.com
Web Site: www.therealsuhaila.com
Officers:
  Founder: Suhaila Salimpour
Management:
  Founder: Jamila Salimpour
  Master Instructor: Suhaila Salimpour
Mission: To create instructional and performance videos for all dance levels, as well as fully orchestrated middle eastern dance musicals and cd recordings of the latest percussion artists
Utilizes: Five Seasonal Concerts
Founded: 1996
Specialized Field: Belly Dance; Middle Eastern Dance
Status: Professional
Performs At: Zellerbach Hall; Berkeley Community Theater
Seating Capacity: 1,600
Organization Type: Performing; Educational

19
CLARITA & THE ARTE FLAMENCO DANCE THEATRE
Arte Flamenco Dance Theatre, Inc.
230 W Main Street
Alhambra, CA 91801
Phone: 626-458-1234
Fax: 626-458-0113
e-mail: info@clarita-arteflamenco.com
Web Site: www.clarita-arteflamenco.com
Officers:
  Founder/President/Artistic Director: Clarita
  VP/CFO/Managing Director: Art Jauregui
Management:
  Artistic Director: Clarita
  Administrative Assisstant: Renee Tabizon
  Managing Director: Art Jauregui
  Belly Dance Instructor: Aubre
  Hula Instructor: Christine
  Belly Dance Instructor: Kamala
Mission: Arte Flamenco is dedicated to promoting the value of dance In contemporary society by enthusiastically introducing the public to Spanish dance and its relevance as a positive way to develop appreciation of artistic and cultural diversity.
Utilizes: Artists-in-Residence; Choreographers; Dance Companies; Dancers; Educators; Grant Writers; Guest Artists; Guest Choreographers; Guest Ensembles; Guest Musical Directors; Guest Musicians; Guest Speakers; Original Music Scores; Paid Performers; Sign Language Translators; Soloists; Students
Founded: 1989
Specialized Field: Spanish; Flamenco
Status: Professional, Non-Profit
Paid Staff: 3
Volunteer Staff: 3
Paid Artists: 15
Organization Type: Performing

20
ANAHEIM BALLET
280 E Lincoln Avenue
Anaheim, CA 92805-3226
Phone: 714-520-0904
Fax: 714-520-0914
e-mail: info@anaheimballet.org
Web Site: www.anaheimballet.org
Management:
  Executive Director: Lawrence Rosenberg
  Administrator: Ashley Duree
  Director: Sarma Lapenieks Rosenberg
Mission: To enlighten and entertain audiences with classically rooted programming and contemporary presentation. Provides quality performances to audiences of balletomanes as well as novice

DANCE / California

ballet-goers and acts as a haven to talented Southern California artists and as a magnet to international talents.
Utilizes: Community Talent; Dance Companies; Dancers; High School Drama; Instructors; Original Music Scores; Resident Artists; Soloists
Founded: 1985
Specialized Field: Ballet; Jazz; Tap; Hip Hop
Status: Non-Profit
Budget: $326,000
Income Sources: Arts of Orange County; Discount Dance Supply; Anaheim Community Foundation; Pacific Life Foundation; Samueli Foundation; Target; Orange County Community Foundation
Affiliations: Anaheim Chamber of Commerce; Downtown Anaheim Association; Anaheim Arts Council
Organization Type: Performing

21
CRASH, BURN AND DIE DANCE COMPANY
Moving and Storage Performance Company
259 Rio Del Mar Boulevard
Aptos, CA 95003-4658
Phone: 831-688-3371
Web Site: www.ferrucci.com/crash
Officers:
   President: Darryl Ferrucci
Management:
   Artistic Director: Leslie Swaha
Mission: To enlighten the audience's point of view on the dancers' perspective of adventure, physical pleasure, and a sublime consciousness of the world.
Specialized Field: Contemporary
Status: Non-Profit
Budget: $280,000
Income Sources: Arts of Orange County; Discount Dance Supply; Anaheim Community Foundation; Pacific Life Foundation; Samueli Foundation; Target; Orange County Community Foundation
Affiliations: Anaheim Chamber of Commerce; Downtown Anaheim Association; Anaheim Arts Council
Organization Type: Performing

22
PLACER THEATRE BALLET
P.O. Box 6723
Auburn, CA 95604-6723
Phone: 916-630-7820
e-mail: shea.wing@placertheatreballet.org
Web Site: placertheatreballet.org
Management:
   Artistic Director: Shea Wing
Mission: Placer Theatre Ballet is a theatre ballet production company dedicated to the joy of storytelling through the art of dance. We offer high-caliber performances that are accessible to the community. From audition to rehearsal to final production, cast members and audiences are enriched through the art of theatrical dance.
Specialized Field: Ballet
Status: Publicly Funded Nonprofit

23
PROFESSIONAL BALLET SCHOOL
425 Harbor Boulevard
#3
Belmont, CA 94002
Phone: 650-598-0796
Fax: 650-598-0799
e-mail: info@professionalballetschool.com
Web Site: www.professionalballetschool.com
Management:
   Co-Director: Zoltan Peter
   Co-Director: Carmela Peter
   Staff: Brete Martin
   Staff - Jazz: Kimberly Drake
   Staff: Danielle Schmidt
   Staff - Contemporary: Tanya Bello
   Staff: Gail Zimmerman
Mission: To serve as a stepping stone for young committed people towards a professional career, along with providing enriching performance experiences to those young dancers who may not meet professional physical criteria or who are simply dancing for pleasure.
Founded: 1993
Specialized Field: Ballet
Status: Non-Profit; Semi-Professional
Affiliations: Joffrey Ballet; San Francisco Ballet; Boston Ballet; Pennsylvania Ballet; Kirov Ballet Institute

24
BERKELEY BALLET THEATER
2640 College Avenue
Berkeley, CA 94704
Phone: 510-843-4687
Fax: 510-843-2606
e-mail: idance@berkeleyballet.org
Web Site: www.berkeleyballet.org
Management:
   Director Emerita: Sally Streets
   Artistic Director: Ilona McHugh
   Associate Artistic Director: Susan Weber
   School Principal: Deborah Moss
   Office Manager: Ali Taylor Lange
Mission: Berkeley Ballet Theater believes that the joy of dance with all its physical, mental and aesthetic benefits should be available to everyone. Whatever a student's goal, we believe it is best achieved in a well-disciplined but positive and loving environment.
Founded: 1908
Specialized Field: Ballet
Status: Non-Profit
Paid Staff: 22
Volunteer Staff: 150
Performs At: Julia Morgan Theatre
Seating Capacity: 385
Year Built: 1908

25
SHA SHA HIGBY
PO Box 152
Bolinas, CA 94924
Phone: 415-868-2409
Fax: 415-868-2409
e-mail: shasha@shashahigby.com
Web Site: www.shashahigby.com
Officers:
   Founder: Sha Sha Higby
Mission: To approach dance through the medium of sculpture
Utilizes: Dance Companies; Dancers; Fine Artists; Guest Artists; Lyricists; Paid Performers; Resident Professionals; Touring Companies; Visual Arts
Founded: 1984
Specialized Field: Interpretive Dance
Paid Staff: 2
Paid Artists: 1
Performs At: Zellerbach Hall; Berkeley Community Theater
Seating Capacity: 500
Organization Type: Performing; Educational

26
LA DANSERIE
9759 Mason Avenue
Chatsworth, CA 91311
Phone: 818-341-0530
e-mail: jpgladanserie@yahoo.com
Web Site: www.ladanserie.com
Officers:
   President/CEO: Patricia Davis
Management:
   Artistic Director/Choreographer: Patrick Frantz
   Choreographer/Administrative Dir: Judy Pisarro-Grant
   Administrative Director: Judy Pisarro-Grant
Mission: To support and advance the art of dance. The company is guided by the belief that dance can act as a universal language to facilitate understanding among people of diverse cultures and backgrounds, and that dance has a tremendous potential to positively impact through an embodiment of positive values, including self respect, team work and persistence.
Utilizes: Collaborations; Dance Companies; Dancers; Designers; Five Seasonal Concerts; Guest Accompanists; Guest Artists; Organization Contracts; Resident Professionals
Founded: 1997
Specialized Field: Ballet
Paid Staff: 4
Volunteer Staff: 8
Paid Artists: 10
Non-paid Artists: 6

27
CAROLINA LUGO'S & CAROLE ACUNA'S BALLET FLAMENCO & DANCE CENTER
1301 Franquette Avenue
Concord, CA 94520
Phone: 415-933-9391
Fax: 925-939-9773
e-mail: carolinalugo1@msn.com
Web Site: www.carolinalugo.com
Management:
   Artistic Director: Carolina Lugo
   Co-Founder and Executive Director: Richard Tonkin
   Co-Artistic Director: Carole Acuna
Mission: The company represents a diversity of cultures from around the globe, appearing in a broad spectrum of creative mediums, including television, dinner theater, cabaret venues, opera and symphonic formats.
Founded: 1997
Specialized Field: Flamenco Dance
Status: Non-Profit

28
JANLYN DANCE COMPANY
Solo Concerts/Lecture Performances
18880 Tilson Avenue
Cupertino, CA 95014
Phone: 408-255-4114
Fax: 408-257-9080
e-mail: janlyndanc@aol.com
Management:
   Artistic Director: Jayne King
Mission: To excite audiences about the world of modern dance.
Founded: 1979
Specialized Field: Modern
Paid Artists: 1
Income Sources: Performance Fees
Performs At: Lecture Hall W/Stage, Informal & Formal Spaces
Affiliations: Young audiences of San Jose and Silicon Valley
Type of Stage: Wood
Stage Dimensions: 32'x20'

DANCE / California

29
SAMAHAN FILIPINO AMERICAN PERFORMING ARTS
1442 Hillsmont Drive
El Cajon, CA 92020
Phone: 619-286-8029
Fax: 619-470-6024
e-mail: samahaphildance@gmail.com
Web Site: www.samahaphilippinedance.com
Management:
    Executive Director: Lolita D Carter, PhD
    Artistic Director: Ruby Pearl B Chiong
    Music Coordinator: Juanita Caccam
Mission: To provide Filipino youth opportunity to gain knowledge and appreciation of their cultural heritage.
Utilizes: Dancers; Five Seasonal Concerts; Guest Accompanists; Guest Artists; Music; Soloists
Founded: 1974
Specialized Field: Filipino Dance
Status: Semi-Professional; Nonprofit
Volunteer Staff: 20
Paid Artists: 18
Budget: $50,000
Income Sources: Grants; Admissions; Individual Contributions; Fundraisers; Classes
Affiliations: Saville Theatre
Facility Category: Theaters, informal spaces
Seating Capacity: 500
Year Built: 1960
Organization Type: Performing; Touring; Educational; Sponsoring

30
REDWOOD CONCERT BALLET
426 F Street
Eureka, CA 95501
Mailing Address: PO Box 680 Eureka, CA 95501
Phone: 707-442-7779
Officers:
    President: Sally Biggin
    VP: Mary Glavich
    Secretary: Marie Boylan
    Treasurer: Kathy Ehnebuske
Management:
    Artistic Director: Virginia Niekrasz-Laurent
Mission: RCB's performances touch a wide range of styles, and give opportunity to experience the dedication ands skill required to successfully dance professionally.
Specialized Field: Ballet; Modern; Jazz
Volunteer Staff: 30
Non-paid Artists: 1
Income Sources: Trition

31
CHOOKASIAN ARMENIAN CONCERT ENSEMBLE
2511 W Browning Avenue
Fresno, CA 93711
Phone: 559-449-1777
Fax: 559-449-1777
e-mail: chook3@qnis.net
Web Site: www.chookasian.com
Management:
    Artistic Director/Founder: John Chookasian, chook3@qnis.net
Mission: To present, preserve and perpetuate traditional Armenian music, folkdance, and culture through tours, concerts, festivals, special events venues, and the sale and distribution of multi award-winning live concert and festival CD's for the general public at large.
Utilizes: Dance Companies; Dancers; Filmmakers; Grant Writers; Guest Accompanists; Guest Musical Directors; Guest Musicians; Multimedia; New Productions; Organization Contracts; Original Music Scores; Paid Performers; Sign Language Translators; Theatre Companies
Founded: 1994
Specialized Field: Armenian Folk Dance
Status: Professional, Nonprofit
Paid Artists: 12
Income Sources: Grants; Fundraisers; Concerts; Concert Halls; Museums; Arts Centers; Churches; Cultural Organizations; Festivals; Colleges & Universities; Corporations; Individuals; Touring
Annual Attendance: 4,000 - 10,000
Organization Type: Performing; Touring; Educational

32
THE MAPLE CONSERVATORY OF DANCE
1824 Kaiser Avenue
Irvine, CA 92614
Phone: 949-660-9930
e-mail: info@mapleconservatory.com
Web Site: www.mapleconservatory.com
Management:
    Conservatory Director: Charles Maple
    Administrative Director: Kathy Crade
    Director/Young Dancers Program: Phil Doheny
    Director/Student Management: Kim Olmos
Mission: The Maple Conservatory of Dance is committed to providing Irvine, Newport Beach and their surrounding communities with a ballet training conservatory of the highest international standards. Through excellence in the classical ballet tradition, we seek to attract and expose our diverse community to the wonder and value of the art of dance.
Utilizes: Arrangers; Artists-in-Residence; Choreographers; Collaborating Artists; Collaborations; Composers; Dancers; Educators; Guest Speakers; Lyricists; Scenic Designers; Soloists; Students
Specialized Field: Ballet Instruction
Status: Non-Profit
Income Sources: Corporate Sponsors, Grants
Season: Year Round
Performs At: Maple Conservatory

33
THE ANTELOPE VALLEY BALLET
2763 W Avenue L
Lancaster, CA 93536
Phone: 661-722-9702
e-mail: antelopevalleyballet@gmail.com
Web Site: www.antelopevalleyballet.org
Officers:
    President: Dr. Brad Boyd
    Secretary: Gina Rossall
    Treasurer: Kimberly Brouwer
Management:
    Artistic Director: Kathleen Burnett
    Ballet Mistress: Tracie Phillips
    Technical Director: Scott Hartzog
    Wardrobe Mistress: Linda Schasch
    Backstage Coordinator: Tricia Wohlers
    Financial Advisor: Scott Evans, CPA
Mission: To provide dancers from across the Antelope Valley region with professional quality performance opportunities in a company setting. To provide high quality performances locally and regionally, stimulating interest in and appreciation for dance as a performing art. To be a positive force in the cultural climate of Antelope Valley and the State of California.
Founded: 1998
Specialized Field: Ballet
Status: Nonprofit
Performs At: Lancaster Performing Arts Center
Seating Capacity: 720
Year Built: 1992

34
REGINA KLENJOSKI DANCE COMPANY
PO Box 7732
Long Beach, CA 90807
Phone: 310-292-7024
Fax: 801-335-2472
e-mail: info@rkdc.org
Web Site: www.rkdc.org
Officers:
    President: Hirofumi Kawano
    Treasurer/Marketing Director: Stephen Schmidt
    Secretary: Albertossy Espinoza
Management:
    Artistic Director: Regina Klenjoski
    Managing Director: Cory Nakasue
    Social Media Manager: Jeffrey Raschiatore
Mission: To promote the understanding of and to create a passion for the art of contemporary dance, making it accessible to both seasoned and new audiences.
Founded: 1999
Specialized Field: Modern; Ballet
Income Sources: Los Angeles County Arts Commision And The Cultural Services Division Of The City Of Torrance
Performs At: Torrance Cultural Arts Center
Seating Capacity: 120
Year Built: 1938

35
RHAPSODY IN TAPS
4812 Matney Avenue
Long Beach, CA 90807
Phone: 562-428-6411
e-mail: linda@rhapsodyintaps.com
Web Site: rhapsodyintaps.com
Management:
    Artistic Director/Choreographer: Linda Sohl-Ellison
    Rehearsal Dirceton: Pauline Hagino
    Marketing Director: Carolyn Clarke
Mission: To promote and perform the act of rhythm tap dance while exploring new choreographic directions.
Utilizes: Singers
Founded: 1981
Specialized Field: Tap Dance
Status: Nonprofit
Budget: $50,000-$100,000
Organization Type: Performing; Touring

36
AEOLIAN BALLET THEATRE
914 Westwood Boulevard
Suite 250
Los Angeles, CA 90024
Phone: 310-838-0849
e-mail: info@aeolianballet.org
Officers:
    Executive Director: Maria Serafica-Stermer
Management:
    Artistic Advisor: Marat Daukayev
    Artistic Advisor: Stefan Wenta
Mission: The company is dedicated to enriching the human experience through live dance performance, to the creation of new works and the revival of historical pieces.
Founded: 1998
Specialized Field: Ballet
Status: Nonprofit, Professional

DANCE / California

Volunteer Staff: 10
Paid Artists: 20
Budget: $500,000
Performs At: Ucla
Seating Capacity: 650
Year Built: 1919

37
AISHA ALI DANCE COMPANY

3270 Kelton Avenue
Los Angeles, CA 90034
Phone: 310-474-4867
e-mail: info@aisha-ali.com
Web Site: www.aisha-ali.com
Management:
   Artistic Director: Aisha Ali
Mission: To introduce the arts of Middle Eastern and North African dance to audiences around the globe.
Founded: 1973
Specialized Field: Belly Dance; Middle-Eastern; North African Dance
Status: Professional

38
HEIDI DUCKLER DANCE THEATRE

2934-1/2 Beverly Glen Circle
Suite 25
Los Angeles, CA 90077
Phone: 818-784-8669
Fax: 818-981-4116
e-mail: animating.the.landscape@heididuckler.org
Web Site: www.heididuckler.org
Officers:
   Managing Director: Emily Wanserski
   Marketing & Events Associate: Emily Simmons
   Project Manager: Sadie Yarrington
   Bookkeeper: Lyn Paz
Management:
   Artistic Director: Heidi Duckler
Mission: We actively seek collaborations with artists, arts organizations and community groups in order to forge a link between professional performance, public space and audience. We seek non-traditional venues and methods for creating contemporary dance theatre works that seek new forms of relationship between audience and performer.
Utilizes: Actors; Collaborating Artists; Collaborations; Dancers; Designers; Filmmakers; Five Seasonal Concerts; Instructors; Multi Collaborations; Multimedia; Organization Contracts; Original Music Scores; Playwrights; Resident Artists; Resident Professionals; Selected Students; Soloists; Touring Companies; Visual Arts
Founded: 1987
Specialized Field: Contemporary Dance
Status: Non-Profit
Paid Staff: 3
Volunteer Staff: 20
Budget: $100,000
Income Sources: Grants; Fundraising; Ticket Sales
Performs At: California Science Center
Annual Attendance: 5,000
Seating Capacity: 435
Year Built: 1989
Organization Type: Performing; Touring

39
DIAVOLO

616 Moulton Avenue
Los Angeles, CA 90031
Phone: 323-225-4290
e-mail: info@diavolo.org
Web Site: www.diavolo.org
Officers:
   Chair: Jeffrey Shapiro
   Vice President: Peter Lesnik
Management:
   Artistic Director: Jacques Heim
   Executive Director: Jennifer Cheng
   Performer / Company Archivist: Leandro Damasco
   Lighting Director/ Stage Manager: John E D Bass
   Performer / Production Assistant: Alicia Garrity
   Performer / Rehearsal Director: Shauna Martinez
   Performer /Institute Co-Director: Chisa Yamaguchi
   Production Manager/Tech Director: Renee Larsen Engmyr
   Business Manager: Ilona Piotrowska
Mission: Redefine dance through dynamic movement, enlightening communities through trust, teamwork and individual expression.
Founded: 1992
Specialized Field: Interdisciplinary Dance
Status: Profit
Paid Staff: 7
Volunteer Staff: 15
Non-paid Artists: 3
Income Sources: Friends Of Diavolo; California Arts Commission; City Of Los Angeles, Cultural Affairs Department; The James Irvine Foundation
Performs At: The Carpenter Center
Seating Capacity: 2,041
Year Built: 1928
Organization Type: Performing; Touring; Educational

40
JAPANESE AMERICAN CULTURAL AND COMMUNITY CENTER

244 S San Pedro Street
Suite 505
Los Angeles, CA 90012
Phone: 213-628-2725
Fax: 213-617-8576
e-mail: info@jaccc.org
Web Site: www.jaccc.org
Officers:
   Chair: Henry Y. Ota
   American Airlines Vice-Chair: Nancy Matsui
   President & CEO: Leslie A. Ito
   Director of Development: Liliane Ribeiro
   Director of Operations & HR: Keith Shiozaki
   Development Manager: Janet Hiroshima
   Wedding & Event Consultant: Anne Bagasao
   Director of Finance: Michael Yee
   Office Manager: Marlene Lee
Management:
   Artistic Director: Hirokazu Kosaka
   Director of Performing Arts: Anthony Jones
   General Manager, Aratani Theatre: Carolyn Onaga
   Media Art Director: Wakana Kimura
   Consultant, Aratani Theatre: Gerald Ishibashi
Mission: To present, perpetuate, transmit and promote Japanese and Japanese American arts and culture to diverse audiences and to provide a center to enhance community programs.
Founded: 1971
Specialized Field: Japanese Dance; Japanese Arts
Paid Staff: 25
Volunteer Staff: 15
Performs At: Sakaye Aratant Japan American Theatre
Seating Capacity: 840

41
JAZZ TAP ENSEMBLE

1416 Westwood Boulevard
Suite 207
Los Angeles, CA 90024
Phone: 310-475-4412
e-mail: jtensemble@aol.com
Web Site: www.jazztapensemble.org
Management:
   Artistic Director: Lynn Dally
   Managing Director: Gayle Hooks
   Music Director: Jerry Kalaf
Mission: The Ensemble brings together the virtuosic talents of itss several dancers and musicians in a spirited display of creativity and spontaneity to express its dedication to tap dancing and jazz music.
Utilizes: Dancers; Guest Accompanists; Guest Musical Directors; Instructors
Founded: 1979
Specialized Field: Tap; Jazz
Status: Nonprofit
Paid Staff: 2
Paid Artists: 15
Budget: $200,000-$500,000
Income Sources: Grants; Ticket Sales
Performs At: John F. Kennedy Center For The Performing Arts
Seating Capacity: 2,100
Year Built: 1968

42
LOS ANGELES BALLET

11755 Exposition Boulevard
Los Angeles, CA 90064
Phone: 310-477-7411
Fax: 310-477-7414
e-mail: contact@losangelesballet.org
Web Site: www.losangelesballet.org
Management:
   Artistic Director: Thordal Christensen
   Artistic Director: Colleen Neary
   Lighting Director: Ben Pilat, rib@losangelesballet.org
   Director Of Sales: Liz Highstrete
   Music Director: Michael Andreas
   Design Director: Catherine Kanner
   Executive Director: Julie Whittaker
   Director of Development: Kathy Highstrete, CFRE
   Costume Director: Marianne Parker
Mission: To passionately pursue innovation and creativity in performances. To preserve the best choreographic work of the past and become the impetus for the best choreography yet to come.
Founded: 2006
Specialized Field: Ballet
Status: Professional

43
LULA WASHINGTON DANCE THEATRE

3773 S Crenshaw Boulevard
Los Angeles, CA 90016
Phone: 323-292-5852
Fax: 323-292-5851
e-mail: luladance@aol.com
Web Site: www.lulawashington.org
Officers:
   President: Todd Reznik
   Chair: Lula Washington
   Board Member: Emma Pullen
   Board Member: Renee Bizer
   Development Associate: Gail Christian
   Board Member: Donald McKayle
   Board Member: Donald Stinson

DANCE / California

Board Member: David Moch
Management:
  Artistic Director: Lula Washington
  Executive Director: Erwin Washington
  Associate Director/Choreographer: Tamica Washington-Miller
  Bookkeeper: Andress Walker
  Booking Assistant: Kelley Norrington
  Administrative Assistants: Emily Young
  Studio Manager: Roshada Baldwin
  Administrative Assistants: Marelle Camel
Mission: To provide a creative outlet for minority artists in South Los Angeles. To build a world class, professional, contemporary modern dance company that reflects many aspects of African American culture and history.
Utilizes: Choreographers; Dance Companies; Dancers; Designers; Five Seasonal Concerts; Guest Artists; Resident Professionals
Founded: 1980
Specialized Field: African American Dance
Status: Professional, Nonprofit
Income Sources: Black Dance Companies Association
Performs At: John F. Kennedy Center For The Performing Arts
Seating Capacity: 2,100
Year Built: 1968
Organization Type: Performing; Touring; Educational; Sponsoring

44
VOX DANCE THEATER INC
PO Box 861481
Los Angeles, CA 90086
Phone: 310-403-6134
e-mail: sarahvox@earthlink.net
Web Site: www.voxdancetheatre.org
Management:
  Artistic Director/Choreographer: Sarah Swenson
  Associate Artistic Director: Tamsin Carlson
  Composer: Lloyd McNeill
  Lighting Designer: Andrew Milhan
  Choreographer: John Pennington
  Choreographer: Rudy Perez
  Composer: Yuval Ron
Mission: Vox Dance Theatre creates and performs classical American modern dance, and promotes, preserves, and educates and about its history and values, often with content that illuminates women's experience of life.
Utilizes: Arrangers; Choreographers; Collaborating Artists; Collaborations; Dance Companies; Dancers; Educators; High School Drama; Instructors; Local Artists & Directors; Multimedia; Music; Paid Performers; Special Technical Talent
Founded: 2004
Specialized Field: Classical Modern
Status: Non-Profit, Professional
Income Sources: Donors, Sponsors
Season: Year Round
Performs At: San Bernandino College, Scripps College, Performing Arts Exchange, Diavolo Dance Theater

45
LOS ANGELES CHOREOGRAPHERS AND DANCERS - ZAPPED TAPS
351 South Virgil Avenue
Los Angeles, CA 90020
Phone: 213-385-1171
e-mail: louisehr@LAChoreographersAndDancers.org
Web Site: www.lachoreographersanddancers.org
Management:
  Founder: Alfred Desio
  Director: Louise Reichlin
Mission: Los Angeles Choreographers & Dancers (LA C&D) has a mission to create high-quality, innovative concert work, communicate to a diverse audience by infusing dance with the cultural influences found in LA, and to enlarge an educated dance audience in populations typically underexposed to the arts, especially youth. By involving audiences with participatory activities we explore humanistic themes.
Utilizes: Arrangers; Artists-in-Residence; Choreographers; Collaborating Artists; Collaborations; Dance Companies; Dancers; Educators; Fine Artists; Lyricists; Multimedia; Paid Performers
Founded: 1979
Specialized Field: Contemporary, Tap
Status: Non-Profit, Professional
Income Sources: Grants, Donors, Sponsors
Season: Year Round

46
GROUNDING POINT DANCE COMPANY
PO Box 123
Manhattan Beach, CA 90267
Phone: 942-302-1208
e-mail: info@gpdance.com
Web Site: www.gpdance.com
Officers:
  President: Carrie A Smaczny
Management:
  Artistic Director: Carrie A Smaczny
  Principle Dancer: Crystal Truesdell
Mission: To showcase artistic and entertaining dance forms through outreach residencies, dance for the camera projects and multimedia stage performances.camera projects, and multimedia stage performances.
Founded: 1998
Specialized Field: Multidisciplinary Dance
Status: Non-Profit, Semi-Professional
Paid Staff: 1
Volunteer Staff: 10
Income Sources: Tuition; Performances
Performs At: Scottsdale Center For Performing Arts
Seating Capacity: 838
Organization Type: Performing

47
CENTRAL WEST BALLET
5039 Pentecost Dr.
Modesto, CA 95356
Phone: 209-576-8957
Fax: 209-576-1308
e-mail: info@cwballet.org
Web Site: www.cwballet.org
Officers:
  President: Hugh Ross III
  Vice President: Cindi Yates
  Secretary: Denise Crosby
  Board Member: Ann Endsley
  Board Member: Liz Robbins
  Board Member: Paul Lamandia
  Board Member: Vita McSherry
  Board Member: Karin Reenstierna
  Board Member: Royal Robbins
Management:
  Artistic Director: Rene Daveluy
  Ballet Mistress: Leslie Ann Larson
  Executive Director: Cynthia Coughlin
  Principle Dancer: Paige Brown
Mission: The company has a dedication to inspiring excellence in dance and infusing passion that fosters a high quality, financially supported, professional dance company.
Utilizes: Choreographers; Collaborating Artists; Collaborations; Dance Companies; Dancers; Five Seasonal Concerts; Guest Artists; Guest Composers; Guest Designers; Guest Ensembles; Instructors; Local Artists; Organization Contracts; Resident Professionals; Soloists; Student Interns; Touring Companies
Founded: 1987
Specialized Field: Ballet
Status: Non-Profit, Pre-Professional
Paid Staff: 3
Volunteer Staff: 100
Paid Artists: 2
Non-paid Artists: 40
Budget: $250,000
Income Sources: Ads; Ticket Sales; Fund-Raising; Grants; Donations
Performs At: High school auditorium
Affiliations: Regional Dance America/Pacific
Annual Attendance: 10,000-14,000

48
INLAND PACIFIC BALLET
5050 Arrow Highway
Montclair, CA 91763
Phone: 909-482-1590
Fax: 909-482-1589
e-mail: admin@ipballet.org
Web Site: www.ipballet.org/contact.php
Officers:
  President: Neal Archer
  Treasurer: C A Sheppard
Management:
  Artistic Director: Victoria Koenig
  Ballet Mistress: Sarah Spradlin
  Founder/Director: Kevin A Myers
  Ballet Mistress: Kelly Lamoureux
  Ballet Mistress: Stephanie Orza
  Admin Director: Lynn Klug
  Marketing / Admin: Annette Johnson
Mission: To build and sustain a professional ballet company of national stature in the Inland Empire of Southern California. Inland Pacific Ballet strives to introduce new audiences to the magic of ballet, and to make the experience more available and accessible to all.
Founded: 1993
Specialized Field: Ballet
Paid Staff: 7
Volunteer Staff: 20
Paid Artists: 3
Non-paid Artists: 11
Income Sources: Tickets Sales; Merchandise Contributed Income; Foundation; Corporate; Individual
Performs At: Bridges Auditorium
Annual Attendance: 20,000
Facility Category: Opera House
Type of Stage: Proscenium
Seating Capacity: 2,500
Year Built: 1931
Year Remodeled: 1975
Cost: $600,000

49
INLAND PACIFIC BALLET
5050 Arrow Highway
Montclair, CA 91763
Phone: 909-482-1627
Fax: 904-482-1589
e-mail: admin@ipballet.org
Web Site: www.ipballet.org/contact.php
Officers:
  President: Neal Archer
  Treasurer: C A Sheppard
Management:

DANCE / California

Founder/Director: Victoria Koenig
Founder/Director: Kevin A Myers
Ballet Mistress: Kelly Lamoureux
Ballet Mistress: Stephanie Orzaureux
Admin Director: Lynn Klug
Marketing / Admin: Annette Johnson
Mission: Inland Pacific Ballet's mission is to build and sustain a professional ballet company of national stature in the Inland Empire of Southern California.
Specialized Field: Ballet
Status: Professional, Nonprofit

50
WESTERN BALLET
The Mountain View Ballet Company and School
914 N Rengstorff Avenue
Unit A
Mountain View, CA 94043
Phone: 650-968-4455
Fax: 650-968-4465
e-mail: info@westernballet.org
Web Site: www.westernballet.org
Officers:
  President: Robin Ching
  Secretary: Sara Lake
  Treasurer: Julia Liu
Management:
  Artistic Director: Alexi Zubiria
  Assistant to the Artistic Director: Alison Share
  School Administrator: Andrea Diaz
  Scenery Designer: Peter Crompton
  Technical Director: Adam Puglieli
  Stage Manager: Jamie Abbleggan
  Lighting Designer: Robert Anderson
  Sound/Technical Director: Alan Ruberg
Mission: We strive to create an environment that grooms young artists for professional careers, providing the best possible training and performance experience, bringing out each dancer's personal best.
Founded: 1976
Specialized Field: Ballet

51
AXIS DANCE COMPANY
1428 Alice Street
Suite 200
Oakland, CA 94612
Phone: 510-625-0110
Fax: 510-625-0321
e-mail: info@axisdance.org
Web Site: www.axisdance.org
Officers:
  President: Deirdre Spencer
  Vice President: Jan Garrett
  Secretary: Anne Finger
  Treasurer: Kerline Astre
Management:
  Development Manager: Sarah Clautero Soto, mollie@axisdance.org
  Education Director: Annika Presley
  Artistic Director: Judith Smith
  Managing Director: Karl Cronin
  Guest Artistic Director: Marc Brew
  Associate Director: Sonsheree Giles
  Marketing/Administrative Associate: Christy Rotman
Mission: To create and perform contemporary dance that is developed through the collaboration of dancers with and without disabilities. AXIS teaches dance and educates about collaboration and disability through community education and outreach programs. AXIS is committed to promoting and supporting this form of dance locally and abroad.
Founded: 1987
Specialized Field: Contemporary Physically Integrated Dance
Status: Non-Profit
Paid Staff: 4
Paid Artists: 7
Budget: $489,900
Income Sources: Touring; Performances; Commissions; Education/Outreach Work; Government; Foundation; Corporate & Individual Donations
Performs At: The Malonga Casquelourd Center for Performing Arts
Seating Capacity: 350
Year Built: 1927
Organization Type: Educational; Performing

52
DIMENSIONS DANCE THEATER
Malonga Casquelourd Center for the Arts
1428 Alice Street
Suite 308
Oakland, CA 94612-4004
Phone: 510-465-3363
Fax: 510-465-3364
e-mail: dimensionsdance@prodigy.net
Web Site: www.dimensionsdance.org
Management:
  Artistic Director: Deborah B Vaughan
  Administrative Coordinator: Latanya D Tigner
Mission: To create, perform, and teach dance that reflects the historical experiences and contemporary lives of African Americans.
Founded: 1972
Specialized Field: Modern; African Dance; Jazz
Performs At: Calvin Simmons Theatre
Seating Capacity: 1,924
Year Built: 1914
Organization Type: Performing

53
OAKLAND BALLET
The Ronn Guidi Foundation
Oakland, CA
Mailing Address: 2201 Broadway, Suite 206 Oakland, CA 94612
Phone: 510-893-3132
Toll-free: 866-711-6037
e-mail: info@OaklandBallet.org
Web Site: www.oaklandballet.org
Officers:
  Chair/President: Roz Perazzo
  Secretary: Michelle Migdal Gee
  Treasurer: Elizabeth Marrama
  Director: Ricard Cowan
  Director: Eva Christie
  Director: America Foy
  Director: Daniel Lo
  Director: Catherine Haley
  Director: Bertha Roman
Management:
  Artistic Director: Graham Lustig
  Director of Operations: Leah Curran
  Marketing Communications Manager: Kate Fratar
  Administrative Associate: Lisa Machac
Mission: To administer the operation of the Oakland Ballet Company, and to offer ballet training for young dancers while preserving and presenting historically significant ballet, including works from the Diaghilev Ballet Russers era.
Utilizes: Choreographers; Commissioned Music; Dancers; Five Seasonal Concerts; Grant Writers; Guest Accompanists; Guest Artists; Guest Conductors; Guest Musical Directors; Guest Musicians; Instructors; Local Artists; Original Music Scores; Resident Professionals; Visual Arts
Founded: 1968
Specialized Field: Ballet
Status: Professional, Nonprofit
Paid Staff: 3
Volunteer Staff: 50
Paid Artists: 33
Budget: $1,000,000-$2,500,000
Income Sources: Fundraising; Donations
Annual Attendance: 42,000
Type of Stage: Proscenium
Seating Capacity: 3,000
Organization Type: Performing; Touring

54
INTERPLAYCE
2273 Telegraph Avenue
Oakland, CA 94612
Phone: 510-465-2797
Fax: 510-836-3312
e-mail: info@interplay.org
Web Site: www.interplay.org
Management:
  Co-Director: Cynthia Winton-Henry
  Administrator: Stephanie Pile
  Development Director: Theron Shaw
Founded: 1989
Specialized Field: Modern; Improvisation; Theatrical Dance
Status: Professional; Non-Profit
Paid Staff: 3
Volunteer Staff: 100
Budget: $500,000
Annual Attendance: 3,000

55
BACKHAUSDANCE
PO Box 5890
Orange, CA 92863
Phone: 714-497-3137
e-mail: info@backhausdance.org
Web Site: www.backhausdance.org
Officers:
  President: Proud Usahacharoenporn
  Founder/Chairman: Jennifer Backhaus
  Vice President: Jeremy Hunt
  Board Member: Harold Hunt
  Board Member: Mary Hunt
  Board Member: Nancy Dickson-Lewis
Management:
  Artistic Director/Founder: Jennifer Backhaus
  Executive Director: Jeremy Hunt
  Education Director: Jenn Bassage Bonfil
  Ballet Mistress/Rehearsal Assistant: Kim Olmos
  Photography: Tim Agler
  Production Manager: Tobi Becerra
  Costume Designer: Rhonda Earick
  Lighting Designer: Tom Durante
  Composer/Percussionist: Erik Lekrone
Mission: Artistic Director Jennifer Backhaus formed Backhausdance in January of 2003. The company is a 501(c)(3), not-for-profit corporation with the mission to create excellent art and expose and educate the community about the relevance and vitality of concert dance. The company currently consists of eight dancers, two of whom are original members.
Utilizes: Choreographers; Composers; Dance Companies; Dancers; Fine Artists; Guest Choreographers; Instructors; Multimedia; New Productions; Singers; Visual Designers
Founded: 2003
Opened: 2003
Specialized Field: Concert/Contemporary Dance
Status: Non-Profit
Income Sources: Donations

DANCE / California

Performs At: Dorothy Chandler Pavillion, Alex Theater
Affiliations: California Dance Educators Association, Dance Resource Center of Los Angeles, Studio Series at South Coast Repertory

56
DANZA FLORICANTO/USA
4232 Whiteside Street
Pasadena, CA 90063
Phone: 323-261-0385
e-mail: floricanto@att.net
Web Site: www.danzafloricantousa.com
Management:
 Founder: Gema Sandoval
Mission: Their purpose is to preserve Mexican culture, validate it as a cultural and artistic expression of the Latino people in the American Southwest, and create awareness and appreciation or it through live performance.
Utilizes: Choreographers; Dancers; Original Music Scores
Founded: 1975
Specialized Field: Mexican Folk Dance/Chicano Dance
Status: Professional; Non-Profit
Paid Staff: 20
Volunteer Staff: 6
Paid Artists: 20
Budget: $75,000
Income Sources: Foundations; Government; Corporate; Individual; Ticket Sales
Performs At: John Anson Ford Theatre; Luckman Fine Arts Complex
Annual Attendance: 10,000

57
PASADENA CIVIC BALLET, INC.
253 North Vinedo Avenue
Pasadena, CA 91107
Phone: 626-792-0873
e-mail: inforequest@pcballet.com
Web Site: www.pcballet.com
Management:
 Artistic Director: Diane De Franco Browne
 Artistic Director: Tania Grafos
 School Director: Zoe Vidalakis
Mission: Provides quality instruction in the art and technique of dance, with an emphasis on ballet as the foundation for discipline and vocabulary; to create performance opportunities to allow the dancers to grow as artists as well as develop self confidence, poise and presentation skills; to provide a nuturing, supportive environment the emphasizes dance as an avenue to growth as an individual.
Utilizes: Choreographers; Collaborations; Dance Companies; Dancers; Five Seasonal Concerts; Guest Accompanists; Guest Artists; Guest Teachers; High School Drama; Lyricists; Original Music Scores
Founded: 1980
Specialized Field: Modern; Ballet; Jazz; Tap; Musical Theater; Character Dance; Hip Hop
Status: Pre-Professional; Nonprofit
Paid Staff: 11
Income Sources: Pasadena Arts Council
Performs At: San Gabriel Civic Auditorium
Seating Capacity: 1,500
Year Built: 1927
Rental Contact: Diane Browne
Organization Type: Performing; Educational

58
PASADENA DANCE THEATRE
1985 E Locust Street
Pasadena, CA 91107
Phone: 626-683-3459
Fax: 626-683-3559
e-mail: info@pasadenadance.org
Web Site: www.pasadenadance.org
Officers:
 President: Richard Herrera
 Vice President: Gwen Whitson
 Treasurer & Secretary: Sue McGinnis
 Board Member: Diana Alcorace
 Board Member: Soyou Yamaguchi
 Board Member: Abigail Lawrence
Management:
 Artistic Director: Cynthia Young
 Associate Director: Laurence Blake
Mission: To provide classical and innovative contemporary choeography through professional dance performance and to offer a high caliber of dacne training through its conservatory.
Founded: 1958
Specialized Field: Ballet
Status: Semi-Professional, Nonprofit
Paid Staff: 12
Volunteer Staff: 4
Paid Artists: 2
Non-paid Artists: 20
Income Sources: National Association for Regional Ballet; California Arts Council; Los Angeles County Arts Commission
Performs At: San Gabriel Civic Auditorium
Seating Capacity: 1,500
Year Built: 1927
Organization Type: Performing; Touring; Resident

59
PETALUMA CITY BALLET
110 Howard Street
Petaluma, CA 94952
Phone: 707-765-2660
e-mail: petballet@aol.com
Web Site: www.petalumacityballet.org
Officers:
 President: Shauna Buck
 Vice President: Katherine Reiff
 Treasurer: Heather Strand
 Secretary: Barbara Fields
Management:
 Artistic Director: Ann Derby
 Co-Artistic Director: Zoura O'Neill
Mission: To be a part of Petaluma's growing cultural community, offering quality productions of classical and comtemporary works by local and guest choreographers.
Founded: 1981
Specialized Field: Ballet
Status: Non-Profit, Pre-Professional
Paid Staff: 2
Volunteer Staff: 10
Non-paid Artists: 20
Budget: $50,000
Income Sources: Fund Raising; Grants
Performs At: SSU Everet B. Person Theatre; Spreckel's Performing Arts Center
Affiliations: Reginal Dance Of America
Annual Attendance: 2,500
Type of Stage: Full
Stage Dimensions: 40' X 35'
Seating Capacity: 475-511

60
THE TRAVELING BOHEMIANS
PO Box 990667
Redding, CA 96099
Phone: 530-229-7818
e-mail: info@travelingbohemians.org
Web Site: www.travelingbohemians.org
Management:
 Artistic Director: Nadia Hava-Robbins
 Technical Director: Peter S. Robbins
 Asst Theater Director: David Alexander Robbins
Specialized Field: Ethnic Dance

61
CALIFORNIA RIVERSIDE BALLET
3700 6th Street
Riverside, CA 92501-3694
Phone: 909-787-7850
Fax: 951-787-0879
e-mail: crballet@sbcglobal.net
Web Site: www.crballet.com
Officers:
 President: Susan Anderson
 Secretary: Wendy Villa-Strack
 CFO: Josefina Gadzinski
 Vice President: Gary Christmas
Management:
 Artistic Director: Mario Nugara
 Artistic Advisor/Choreographer: David Allan
 Choreographer: Michael Gervais
 Ballet Mistress: Kathleen Riker
 Ballet Master: Damien Diaz
Mission: Promoting excellence and enriching life through its presentation of the finest in classical and contemporary ballet. California Riverside Ballet accomplishes this through community outreach and performances, which educate and provide artistic experience to dancers and patrons alike. The ballet cultivates awareness of this traditional art expression to benefit the community and the arts.
Utilizes: Singers
Founded: 1969
Specialized Field: Modern; Ballet
Status: Professional, Nonprofit
Paid Staff: 75
Performs At: Landis Auditorium
Organization Type: Performing; Educational; Sponsoring

62
MAGIC CIRCLE THEATER
241 Vernon Street
Roseville, CA 95678
Phone: 916-782-1777
Fax: 916-782-1766
e-mail: boxoffice@civicwest.org
Web Site: www.mcircle.org
Officers:
 President: Calvin Stevens
 Vice President: Mike Illic
 Treasurer: Allen Delbrouck
 Secretary: Dave Wooldridge
Management:
 Artistic Director: Rosemarie Gerould
 Executive Producer: Robert Gerould
 Managing Director: Rick Daniels
 Program Director: Michelle Raskey
 Technical Director: John Bowles
Mission: To educate and entertain people of all ages, thereby enriching the cultural life of our community at large.
Founded: 1987
Specialized Field: Theatrical Dance
Budget: $800,000
Income Sources: Ads in the Program; Grants; Donations; Ticket Sales; Concessions; Sponsorships; Workshop Fees; Acting Class Fees
Performs At: Community Theatre

DANCE / California

Affiliations: Roseville Theatre
Type of Stage: Proscenium
Seating Capacity: 500
Year Built: 1929
Year Remodeled: 2001
Rental Contact: Executive Director Robert Gerould

63
SACRAMENTO BALLET
1631 K Street
Sacramento, CA 95814-4019
Phone: 916-552-5800
Fax: 916-552-5815
e-mail: info@sacballet.org
Web Site: www.sacballet.org
Officers:
   President: Nancy Garton
   VP: Frankie McDermott
   Secretary: Gregg Josephson
   Treasurer: Jeffrey.T Clair
Management:
   Artistic Director: Carrine Binda
   Artistic Director: Ron Cunningham
   Executive Director: Gregory Smith
   General Manager: Bob Reich
   Marketing Director: Amy Rossi
   Production Manager: Caitlin Sapunor-Davis
   Wardrobe Assistant: LeeAnne Larsen
   Music Director: Henrik Jul Hansen
Mission: The Sacramento Ballet entertains, educates, inspires and engages people through the powerful vehicle of dance.
Utilizes: Artists-in-Residence; Choreographers; Collaborating Artists; Collaborations; Dance Companies; Dancers; Designers; Educators; Grant Writers; Guest Accompanists; Guest Artists; Guest Composers; Guest Conductors; Guest Ensembles; Guest Musical Directors; High School Drama; Lyricists; Multimedia; Original Music Scores; Resident Artists; Student Interns; Visual Arts
Founded: 1954
Specialized Field: Ballet
Status: Professional, Nonprofit
Paid Staff: 11
Volunteer Staff: 2
Paid Artists: 28
Non-paid Artists: 5
Budget: $2.1 million
Income Sources: Ticket Sales; Program Ads; Grants; Contributions
Performs At: Monclavi Center
Affiliations: Dance USA; NSFRE; Regional Dance Pacific America
Annual Attendance: 80,000
Facility Category: Community Center Theatre
Type of Stage: Proscenium
Seating Capacity: 2,426
Organization Type: Performing; Touring; Resident

64
SAN DIEGO BALLET COMPANY
Dance Place San Diego
2650 Truxtun Road
Ste. 102
San Deigo, CA 92106
Phone: 619-294-7378
Fax: 619-294-7315
Web Site: sandiegoballetdancecompany.org
Officers:
   Interim President: Carol Crocker
   Secretary: Julie Maiorano
Management:
   Co-Artistic/Executive Director: Robin Sherertz Morgan
   Co-Artistic Director/Choreographer: Javier Velasco
   Ballet Mistress: Maxim Tchernychev
   General Manager: Karen Foster
   PR Consultant and Freelance Grant W: Jasmine Rios
   Director of Communications: Matt Carney
Mission: To excite, enrich and entertain our diverse audience.
Founded: 1991
Specialized Field: Ballet
Status: Professional, Nonprofit

65
CALIFORNIA BALLET COMPANY
4819 Ronson Court
San Diego, CA 92111
Phone: 858-560-5676
Fax: 858-560-0072
e-mail: info@califoniaballet.org
Web Site: www.californiaballet.org
Officers:
   President: Leslie Levinson
   Vice President: Sanjeev K. Dhand
   Vice President: Brad Ross
   Membership Secretary: Sheila Ferguson-Webb
   Corresponding Secretary: John Stubbs
Management:
   Director: Maxine Mahon
   Marketing: Diane Grosman
   Music Director and Conductor: John Stubbs
   Ballet Mistress/ Education Director: Judith Sharp
   Technical Director/Stage Manager: Stephen Judson
   Production Manager: Oscar Burciaga
   Accountant: Susan Hadley
   Lighting Designers: Eric Keel
Mission: To perform, educate and create new ballets.
Utilizes: Choreographers; Collaborations; Dance Companies; Dancers; Five Seasonal Concerts; Local Artists; Resident Artists
Founded: 1968
Specialized Field: Ballet
Status: Semi-Professional, Nonprofit
Budget: $950,000
Income Sources: Membership; Tickets; CAC; San Diego City Commission for Arts and Culture; Sponsors
Performs At: San Diego Civic Theatre
Seating Capacity: 3,000
Year Built: 1965
Organization Type: Performing; Touring; Resident

66
CITY BALLET SAN DIEGO
941 Garnet Avenue
PO Box 99072
San Diego, CA 92169
Mailing Address: PO Box 99072 San Diego, CA 92169-1072
Phone: 858-274-6058
Fax: 858-272-8375
e-mail: artistic.director@cityballet.org
Web Site: www.cityballet.org
Management:
   Artistic Director: Steven Wistrich
   Choreographer: Elizabeth Wistrich
   Music Director: John Nettles
   Ballet Mistress: Emily Kirn
Mission: City Ballet is a non-profit organization committed to furthering the ballet art form.
Specialized Field: Ballet
Status: Nonprofit
Paid Staff: 2
Paid Artists: 10
Non-paid Artists: 9
Budget: $450,000
Income Sources: Ticket Sales; Donations
Performs At: Spreckels Theatre
Annual Attendance: 16,000
Type of Stage: Fly Theatre; Proscenium Stage
Seating Capacity: 120-150
Year Built: 1928

67
CIVIC DANCE COMPANY
2125 Park Boulevard
San Diego, CA 92101
Phone: 619-235-5255
Web Site: www.civicdancearts.org
Mission: To support and promote a premier dance arts program and an appreciation of the arts, in cooperation with the San Diego Park and Recreation Department Dance Arts Program.
Founded: 1983
Specialized Field: Ballet; Jazz; Tap
Status: Non-Profit
Paid Staff: 18
Volunteer Staff: 120
Paid Artists: 4
Non-paid Artists: 40
Income Sources: Scholarships; Box Office Sponsor; Patron of the Arts; Management Sponsor; Parnership Sponsor Board of Directors Sponsors; Corporate Sponsor; Private Sponsor

68
MALASHOCK DANCE
2650 Truxton Road
Suite 202
San Diego, CA 92106
Phone: 619-260-1622
Fax: 619-523-0603
e-mail: info@malashockdance.org
Web Site: www.malashockdance.org
Officers:
   President: Russell King
Management:
   Artistic Director: John Malashock
   Associate Artistic Director: Michael Mizerany
   Education Director: Molly Puryear
   Executive Director: Cynthia Dillon
   Development Director: Pat Rice
   Assistant to Artistic Director: Lara Binder
   Administrative Co-ordinator: Corina Presutti
Mission: To provide transformational experiences through the creation, performance, and teaching of dance that fire the imagination and celebrate the human spirit.
Utilizes: Artists-in-Residence; Choreographers; Collaborations; Commissioned Composers; Community Members; Dance Companies; Dancers; Educators; Filmmakers; Guest Artists; Guest Ensembles; Guest Speakers; High School Drama; Instructors; Multi Collaborations; Soloists; Theatre Companies
Founded: 1988
Specialized Field: Modern Dance Company and School
Status: Professional, Non-Profit
Paid Staff: 5
Volunteer Staff: 65
Paid Artists: 7-12
Budget: $500,000-$600,000
Income Sources: Government; Foundation; Corporate; Individuals
Affiliations: Dance/USA; SD Performing Arts League; TCG; CA Arts Council Touring Artists
Annual Attendance: 2000
Organization Type: Performing; Touring

69
SAN DIEGO DANCE THEATER
Dance Place San Diego
2650 Truxton Road
Suite 108
San Diego, CA 92106
Phone: 619-255-1803
Fax: 619-255-1803
e-mail: info@sandiegodancetheater.org
Web Site: www.sandiegodancetheater.org
Management:
  Artistic Director: Jean Isaacs
  Music Director: Steve Baker
  Administrative Assistant/Technical: Blythe Barton
  Marketing and Public Relations: Toni Robin
Mission: Create and perform intelligent dances that breathe life into the people of our region and beyond. Provide acces to viewing, training in and dancing of Isaacs' dances by people of many ages, nationalities, body types, sexual preferences and physical abilities.
Founded: 1972
Specialized Field: Ballet; Modern; Theatre Dance
Status: Professional, Non-Profit
Paid Staff: 2
Volunteer Staff: 10
Paid Artists: 9
Budget: $250,000-$300,000
Income Sources: Public Grants; Foundations; Individual Donors; Ticket Sales; The City of San Diego/Commission for Arts and Culture; County of San Diego; California Arts Council.
Annual Attendance: 5,000
Organization Type: Touring; Performing

70
SUSHI PERFORMANCE & VISUAL ART
390 Eleventh Avenue
San Diego, CA 92101
Mailing Address: PO Box 152761, San Diego CA 92115
Phone: 619-235-8466
Fax: 619-235-8552
e-mail: info@sushiart.org
Web Site: sushiart.org
Officers:
  President: Stephen Silverman
  Treasurer: Ed Koijane
  Secretary: Barbara Measelle
Management:
  Executive Director: Lynn Schuette
Mission: Sushi is commited to providing its artists and audiences with a laboratory where creative exploration, community engagement and new ideas flourish.
Founded: 1980
Specialized Field: Contemporary Dance
Status: Professional, Nonprofit
Paid Staff: 1
Budget: $200,000
Income Sources: Grants; Individual Donations; Membership; Admissions
Annual Attendance: 4,000 - 6,000
Facility Category: Alternative Loft Space
Organization Type: Performing; Touring; Educational

71
ALONZO KING LINES BALLET
26 Seventh Street
San Francisco, CA 94103
Phone: 415-863-3040
Fax: 415-863-1180
e-mail: info@linesballet.org
Web Site: www.linesballet.org
Officers:
  Executive Director/CEO: Ann Marie Nemanich
  Chair: Lucia Choi-Dalton
  Vice Chair: Amy Schoening
  Secretary: Nicola Pitchford
  Treasurer: Jean Marc Torre
Management:
  Artistic Director: Alonzo King
  Marketing Manager: Annette Muller, tdill@linesballet.org
  Executive Director: Janette Gitler
  Creative Director: Robert Rosenwasser
  Ballet Master: Arturo Fernandez
  Production and Lighting Director: G. Chris Griffin
  Development Director: Sheri Kuehl
  Finance Director: Cindy Bruneman
Mission: LINES Ballet nurtures dynamic artistry and the development of auhtentic, creative expression through dance. The company is dedicated to exploring the possibilities of movement from a global perspective.
Utilizes: Choreographers; Collaborating Artists; Collaborations; Commissioned Composers; Commissioned Music; Dancers; Designers; Filmmakers; Five Seasonal Concerts; Guest Accompanists; Guest Artists; Guest Companies; Guest Conductors; Guest Ensembles; Guest Musical Directors; Guest Musicians; High School Drama; Multimedia; Original Music Scores; Resident Artists; Resident Professionals; Soloists; Theatre Companies; Visual Arts
Founded: 1982
Specialized Field: Ballet; Modern Ballet
Paid Staff: 20
Volunteer Staff: 50
Paid Artists: 14
Budget: $2,000,000-$3,500,000

72
BALLET FOLCLORICO DO BRASIL
Gary Lindsey Artist Services
2700 15th Avenue
San Francisco, CA 94127
Phone: 415-759-6410
Fax: 415-681-9801
e-mail: lindseyart@aol.com
Management:
  Artistic Director: Amen Santo
Specialized Field: Afro-Brazilian Dance

73
BRENDA ANGIEL AERIAL DANCE COMPANY
Gary Lindsey Artist Services
2700 15th Avenue
San Francisco, CA 94127
Phone: 415-759-6410
Fax: 415-681-9801
e-mail: lindseyart@aol.com
Web Site: www.danzaerea.com.ar/home.html
Management:
  Artistic Director/Choreographer: Brenda Angiel
Mission: Brenda Angiel Aerial Dance Company is an important part of Argentina's avant-garde dance movement.
Founded: 1998
Specialized Field: Avant-Garde Aeriel Dance

74
CHINA DANCE SCHOOL & THEATRE
3055 Clement Street
San Francisco, CA 94121
Phone: 415-668-6785
Fax: 415-668-6785
e-mail: chinadancetheatre@yahoo.com
Web Site: www.chinadancetheatre.com
Officers:
  Founder: Kaiwen You
Management:
  Artistic & Exec Dir/Choreographer: Kaiwen You
  Assistant Artistic Director: Aiping Zhou
Mission: The mission of China Dance School & Theatre is to introduce, educate and celebrate the rich and colorful heritage of Chinese ethnic and folk dance.
Utilizes: Choreographers; Dancers; Designers; Educators; Filmmakers; High School Drama; Local Artists; Local Talent; Multimedia; Paid Performers; Singers; Soloists
Founded: 2004
Specialized Field: Theatrical Dance; Dramatic Dance; Chinese Classic; Ethnic Dance

75
CHITRESH DAS DANCE COMPANY
2325 3rd St.
Suite #320
San Francisco, CA 94107
Phone: 415-333-9000
Fax: 415-373-1731
e-mail: info@kathak.org
Web Site: www.kathak.org
Management:
  Artistic Director: Pandit Chitresh Das
Mission: Produce exemplary traditional, innovative, and collaborative works of North Indian classical Kathak dance, increase awareness of Kathak dance, to train future generations and build local, national and international community support for the Kathak tradition.
Founded: 1980
Specialized Field: Kathak Dance
Status: Professional
Paid Staff: 6
Volunteer Staff: 25
Paid Artists: 9
Budget: $285,000-$300,000
Income Sources: Touring; Performances; Tuition

76
DANCE BRIGADE
3316 24th Street
San Francisco, CA 94110
Phone: 415-826-4441
Fax: 415-826-4441
e-mail: dancebrigade1984@yahoo.com
Web Site: www.dancebrigade.org
Mission: To create and perform dance theater that addresses the complex problems of contemporary American women. The company has created, performed, presented and produced issue-oriented dance theater exploring socio-political issues such as voilence against women, class injustice, war, racism, breast cancer, sexual abuse and homophobia.
Utilizes: Five Seasonal Concerts; Guest Artists; Singers
Founded: 1984
Specialized Field: Contemporary Dance
Status: Professional, Non-Profit
Paid Staff: 3
Volunteer Staff: 18
Paid Artists: 8
Performs At: Mission Theatre
Organization Type: Performing; Touring; Resident; Sponsoring

DANCE / California

77
DANCE THROUGH TIME
Gary Lindsey Artist Services
2700 15th Avenue
San Francisco, CA 94127
Phone: 415-759-6410
Fax: 415-681-9801
e-mail: lindseyart@aol.com
Management:
   Executive Director: Lawrence Ewing

78
DANCERS' GROUP
44 Gough St
Suite 201
San Francisco, CA 94103
Phone: 415-920-9181
Fax: 415-920-9173
Web Site: www.dancersgroup.org
Officers:
   President: Mary Armentrout
   Vice President: Shakthi Ganeshan, MD, MPH
   Secretary: Dana Lawton
   Treasurer: Robin Nasatir
Management:
   Executive Director: Wayne Hazzard
   Outreach Director: Shae Colett
   Program Director: Michelle Lynch
   Program Assistant: Rosa Lisbeth Navarrete
   Guardian of Books: Evangel King
Mission: We strive to bring a variety of artists and organizations together that create engaging partnerships and civic collaborations and we work to build the quality and accessibility of dance in the San Fransisco Bay Area. Our presenting and co-presenting programs increase visibility for dance artists that engage in a diverse community in an effort to bring new audiences to dance.
Founded: 1982
Specialized Field: Contemporary Dance
Paid Staff: 2
Volunteer Staff: 5
Income Sources: Dance Bay Area; Donations; Sponsors
Performs At: ODC Theater
Organization Type: Performing; Educational; Sponsoring

79
JOE GOODE PERFORMANCE GROUP
499 Alabamab Street
Suite 150
San Francisco, CA 94110
Phone: 415-561-6565
Fax: 415-561-6562
e-mail: info@joegoode.org
Web Site: www.joegoode.org
Officers:
   President: Lynne Blair
   Treasurer: Sue Cosgrove
Management:
   Artistic Director: Joe Goode
   Managing Director: Maia Rosal
   Executive Director: Dave Archuletta
   Development Manager: Adriana Marcial
   Education Coordinator: Damara Vita Ganley
   Company Manager: Alexander Zendzian
   Rehearsal Director: Felipe Barrueto-Cabello
Mission: To promote understanding, compassion and tolerance among people through the innovative use of dance and theater, as interpreted by the artistic vision and work of Joe Goode.
Founded: 1986
Specialized Field: Theatrical Dance
Budget: $600,000
Income Sources: Donations; Fundraising

80
JOSE GRECO II FLAMENCO DANCE COMPANY
Gary Lindsey Artist Services
2700 15th Avenue
San Francisco, CA 94127
Phone: 415-759-6410
Fax: 415-681-9801
Toll-free: 800-949-2745
e-mail: LindseyArt@aol.com

81
KULARTS
474 Faxon Avenue
San Francisco, CA 94112
Phone: 415-239-0249
e-mail: info@kularts.org
Web Site: www.kularts.org
Officers:
   President: Francis Wong
   Director: Christine Balance, PhD
   Director: Marcella Pabros
Management:
   Artistic/Executive Director: Alleluia Panis
   Program Manager: Lovelie Faustino
   Graphic Design: Tina Besa
   Development: Tamara Johnston
Mission: To inform and expand the understanding of American Philippino culture and preserve the spirit and integrity of ancient Pilipino art forms.
Founded: 1985
Specialized Field: Presenter of Contemporary And Tribal Pilipino Dance
Paid Staff: 2
Volunteer Staff: 100
Paid Artists: 10
Non-paid Artists: 5
Budget: $130,000
Income Sources: California Arts Council; California Council for the Humanities, San Francisco Grants for the Arts; San Francisco Arts Commission-Cultural Equity,Zellerbach Foundation;LIA Fnd
Annual Attendance: 5,000
Seating Capacity: 80
Year Built: 2008

82
LILY CAI CHINESE DANCE COMPANY
Chinese Cultural Productions
Fort Mason Center
Landmark Building C-353
San Francisco, CA 94123
Phone: 415-474-4829
Fax: 415-651-9589
e-mail: info@lilycaidance.org
Web Site: www.lilycaidance.org
Officers:
   Chair: Frank Zhou
   Director: Diane Lee
   Director: Rolland Luo
Management:
   Artistic Director: Lily Cai
   Executive Director/Music Director: Gang Situ
   General Manager: Ann Lin
Mission: To promote greater public awareness of Chinese dance and music, to produce original contemporary work that is firmly rooted in Chinese cultural traditions, to challenge American conceptions of traditional Chinese and Chinese American culture and to encourage our community artists to explore new avenues of self expression.
Utilizes: Dance Companies
Founded: 1989
Specialized Field: Chinese Dance
Status: Nonprofit Organization
Paid Staff: 4
Volunteer Staff: 10
Paid Artists: 7
Income Sources: Funders; Corporate Sponsors; Donations
Performs At: Extensively throughout California and the United States; Major Performing Arts Venues; Festivals; University Theatres
Organization Type: Performing; Touring

83
MARGARET JENKINS DANCE COMPANY
507 Polk Street
Suite 320
San Francisco, CA 94102
Phone: 415-861-3940
Fax: 415-861-3872
e-mail: info@mjdc.org
Web Site: www.mjdc.org
Management:
   Artistic Director: Margaret Jenkins
   Studio Coordinator and Tour Manager: Michelle Fletcher
   Administrator: Benjamin Sisson
   General Manager: Todd Eckert
   Development Associate: Jessica Mitchell
Mission: To perform the work of choreographer Margaret Jenkins.
Founded: 1972
Specialized Field: Modern Dance
Status: Professional; Nonprofit
Paid Staff: 3
Paid Artists: 9
Affiliations: Margaret Jenkins Dance Laboratory
Annual Attendance: 2,000
Organization Type: Performing; Touring; Resident; Educational

84
MARK FOEHRINGER DANCE PROJECT
1388 Haight Street
#28
San Francisco, CA 94117
Phone: 415-640-2784
Fax: 650-506-3275
e-mail: gary@mfdpsf.org
Web Site: www.mfdpsf.org
Officers:
   President: John Rechtfertig
   Treasurer: Gary Lindsay
   Secretary: Susanna Douthit
Management:
   Artistic Director/Choreographer: Mark Foehringer
   Managing Director: Susanna Douthit
   Production Manager/Technical Dir: Frederic O Boulay
   Business Manager: Gary Lindsay
   Publicist: Shannon Atlas
Mission: It is made of a repertoire of contemporary ballet works created by founder and choreographer Mark Foehringer and professional dancers.
Founded: 1996
Specialized Field: Contemporary
Status: Professional

DANCE / California

85
NANCY KARP & DANCERS
The New Arts Foundation
60 Guy Place
San Francisco, CA 94105
Phone: 415-516-8575
Fax: 510-652-0898
e-mail: info@nancykarp.org
Web Site: www.nancykarp.org
Management:
    Artistic Director/Choreographer: Nancy Karp
Mission: The New Arts Foundation is dedicated to the creation and presentation of new work that reflects the artistic vision of director/choreographer Nancy Karp and her dance company, Nancy Karp & Dancers.
Utilizes: Choreographers; Collaborating Artists; Collaborations; Commissioned Composers; Dancers; Designers; Fine Artists; Guest Artists; Guest Companies; Guest Conductors; Guest Musical Directors; Instructors; Local Artists; Lyricists; Organization Contracts; Original Music Scores; Poets; Resident Artists; Resident Professionals; Singers; Student Interns; Visual Arts
Founded: 1981
Specialized Field: Interdisciplinary; Collaborative Dance
Status: Professional, Nonprofit
Performs At: Cowell Theater; Theater Artaud
Type of Stage: Proscenium
Organization Type: Performing; Touring

86
ODC THEATER
ODC Theater at Project Artaud Theater
351 Shotwell Street
San Francisco, CA 94110
Phone: 415-863-6606
Fax: 415-863-9833
e-mail: info@odctheater.org
Web Site: www.odctheater.org
Management:
    Theater Director: Rob Bailis
    Artistic Director: Brenda Way
    Institutional Giving Director: Brian Wiedenmeier
    Finance Manager : Charlene Folcomer
    Associate Director of Marketing: Jenna Glass
    Executive Director: Victor Gotesman
    Deputy Director: Christy Bolingbroke
    Finance Manager: Charlene Folcomer
Mission: To inspire audiences, cultivate artists, engage community and foster diversity and inclusion through dance.
Founded: 1971
Specialized Field: Modern Dance
Paid Staff: 6
Volunteer Staff: 2
Budget: $300,000
Performs At: The Kennedy Center; Jacob's Pillow; The Joyce Theater, NYC; The Olympic Arts Festival;, The Spoletto Festival
Annual Attendance: 18,000
Facility Category: Studio Theater
Type of Stage: Sprung Wood
Stage Dimensions: 48'x40'
Seating Capacity: 187
Year Built: 1920
Year Remodeled: 1980
Rental Contact: Director Andrew Wood
Organization Type: Performing; Touring; Resident; Educational

87
THE PURPLE MOON DANCE PROJECT
1385 Mission St.
Ste. 340
San Francisco, CA 94103
Phone: 415-552-1105
e-mail: project@purplemoondance.org
Web Site: purplemoondance.org
Management:
    Executive/Artistic Director: Jill Togawa
    Administrative Manager: Frances Gay Teves Sedayao
    Financial Manager: Marie Chang
    Marketing Specialist: Tyese M. Wortham
Mission: To increase the visability of lesbians and women of color and to encourage social change, peace and healing in our society through the medium of dance. Purple Moon's work is diversity made physical.
Founded: 1992
Specialized Field: Western; Non-Western; Multidisciplinary Collaboration Dance
Paid Staff: 5
Volunteer Staff: 32
Non-paid Artists: 2
Performs At: The Gay Games Cultural Festival in New York; Santa Monica, California; Oregon
Annual Attendance: 4,500

88
ROBERT FRIEDMAN PRESENTS
453 30th Avenue
San Francisco, CA 94121
Phone: 415-759-1992
Fax: 415-290-0573
e-mail: rf@rfpresents.com
Web Site: www.rfpresents.com
Officers:
    President: Robert Friedman
Mission: To bring variant forms of theatrical art to the San Francisco area.
Founded: 1973
Specialized Field: Theatrical Performance

89
SAN FRANCISCO BALLET
War Memorial Opera House
301 Van Ness Avenue
San Francisco, CA 94102
Mailing Address: 455 Franklin Street San Francisco, CA 94102
Phone: 415-861-5600
e-mail: sfbmail@sfballet.info
Web Site: www.sfballet.org
Officers:
    Chair: Richard Barker
    President: Karen Murphy
Management:
    Artistic Director/Choreographer: Helgi Tomasson
    Membership Officer: Jennifer Jordan
    Associate Director of Development: Jennifer Mewha
    Education Office Manager: Dina D. Toy
    Associate Director, Communications: Kyra Jablonsky
    Communications Associate: Lauren White
    Planned Giving Manager: Elizabeth Lani
Mission: The San Francisco Ballet Company is dedicated to sharing our love of dance with the broadest possible audience.
Founded: 1933
Specialized Field: Ballet
Status: Professional, Non-Profit
Paid Staff: 70
Volunteer Staff: 300
Paid Artists: 69
Performs At: The War Memorial Opera House
Annual Attendance: 100,000
Facility Category: War Memorial Opera House
Type of Stage: Dance; Opera
Seating Capacity: 3,200
Year Remodeled: 1996
Organization Type: Performing; Touring

90
SAN FRANCISCO ETHNIC DANCE FESTIVAL
World Arts West
Fort Mason Center
2 Marina Blvd., Bldg. D, #230
San Francisco, CA 94123-1284
Phone: 415-474-3914
Fax: 415-474-3922
e-mail: info@worldartswest.org
Web Site: www.worldartswest.org
Management:
    Executive Director: Julie Mushet
    Artistic Director: Carlos Carvajal
    Artistic Director: CK Ladzekpo
    Production Manager: Jack Carpenter
    Technical Director: Sean Riley
    Production Associate: Micaela A. Nerguizian
    Marketing & Communications Director: Terry Conway
    Bookkeeper: Meryl Larsen
Mission: To honor and celebrate culturally diverse dance forms through presentation, education and support of artists and their tradititons.
Specialized Field: Multicultural Dance
Status: Professional, Non-Profit
Paid Staff: 4
Volunteer Staff: 15
Budget: $60,000-$150,000
Income Sources: Sponsors; Donations
Season: June
Affiliations: Palace of Fine Arts
Annual Attendance: 7,600
Seating Capacity: 1,000

91
SMUIN BALLET
44 Gough Street
Suite 103
San Francisco, CA 94103
Phone: 415-556-5000
Fax: 415-556-5200
e-mail: info@smuinballet.org
Web Site: www.smuinballet.org
Officers:
    President: Pattie Hume
    Vice President: Bruce Braden
    Secretary: Allie Weissman
    Treasurer: Robert Challey
Management:
    Director: Celia Fushille
    Ballet Master: Amy London
    Production Director: Kathryn T. Graham
    Lighting Director: Michael Oesch
    Company Manager: JoEllen Arntz
    Audio Director: Ernie Trevino
    Marketing Director: Mary Hand
    Development Director: Paola Muggia Stuff
    Tech Director & Asst Stage Manager: Candice Moenich
Mission: To bring enjoyment of dance to new as well as to existing audiences through works of uncompromising originality and quality.
Founded: 1994

DANCE / California

Specialized Field: Ballet
Status: Non-Profit, Professional
Paid Staff: 12
Volunteer Staff: 36
Paid Artists: 18
Budget: $2.3 million
Income Sources: Ticket Sales; Donations
Performs At: Palace of Fine Arts; Mountain View Center for Performing Arts; Yerba Buena Novellus Theatre; Lesher Center-Walnut Creek
Annual Attendance: 50,000

92
THE LIVELY FOUNDATION
2565 Washington Street
Suite 4
San Francisco, CA 94115-1828
Phone: 415-346-8959
Fax: 650-964-6858
e-mail: livelyfoundation@sbcglobal.net
Web Site: livelyfoundation.org
Management:
    Artistic Director: Leslie Friedman
Mission: The foundation is devoted to the ptoduction of artistic and educational programs in dance, music and related arts.
Founded: 1983
Specialized Field: Contemporary Dance
Performs At: Herbst Theater; Vetrans' Building Green Room
Organization Type: Performing; Touring; Educational

93
PROJECT ARTAUD
499 Alabama Street
San Francisco, CA 94110
Phone: 415-621-4240
Fax: 415-621-3824
Web Site: www.projectartaud.org
Officers:
    President: Javier Manrique
    VP: Norman Rutherford
    Secretary: Sarah Kennedy
    Interim Treasurer: Laurie Anderson
Mission: To provide support for artists and arts activities and a model of how artist communities can be shelters for artisans and resources for a city.
Utilizes: Five Seasonal Concerts; Guest Artists; Guest Companies; Singers
Founded: 1971
Specialized Field: Performing Arts
Status: Professional
Income Sources: National Performance Network; California Presenters
Organization Type: Performing

94
WORLD ARTS WEST
Fort Mason Center
Landmark Building D
San Francisco, CA 94123-1382
Phone: 415-474-3914
Fax: 415-474-3922
e-mail: info@worldartswest.org
Web Site: www.worldartswest.org
Management:
    Executive Director: Julie Mushet
    Artistic Director: Carlos Carvajal
    Artistic Director: CK Ladzekpo
    Production Manager: Jack Carpenter
    Technical Director: Sean Riley
    Production Associate: Micaela A. Nerguizian
    Marketing & Communications Director: Terry Conway
    Bookkeeper: Meryl Larsen
Mission: To honor and celebrate culturally diverse dance forms through presentation, education and support of artists and their traditions.
Utilizes: Dance Companies; Dancers
Specialized Field: Multicultural Performing Arts
Status: Nonprofit, Professional
Paid Staff: 4
Volunteer Staff: 15
Income Sources: Sponsors; Donations
Performs At: Palace of Fine Arts; Cowell Theater; Other Venues
Annual Attendance: 7,600
Organization Type: Performing; Resident; Educational; Sponsoring

95
YAELISA AND CAMINOS FLAMENCOS
26th Seventh Street
5th Floor
San Francisco, CA 94103
Phone: 510-531-9986
e-mail: info@caminosflamencos.com
Web Site: www.caminosflamencos.com
Management:
    Artist Director: Yaelisa
    Music Director: Jason McGuire
Mission: To create and present contemporary, traditional and theatrical dance programs showcasing artists from Spain and the US which reflect the changing face of Flamenco in the 21st century.
Founded: 1993
Specialized Field: Spanish; Flamenco
Performs At: ODC Theater

96
ZACCHO DANCE THEATRE
1777 Yosemite Avenue
Studio 330
San Francisco, CA 94124
Phone: 415-822-6744
Fax: 415-822-6745
e-mail: office@zaccho.org
Web Site: www.zaccho.org
Officers:
    President: Sean Cullen
    Secretary/Treasurer: Arianne Dar
    Board President: Jane Sullivan
Management:
    Artistic Director: Joanna Haigood
    Development Director: Jennifer Ross
    Operations Manager: Delina P. Brooks
    Studio and Facilities Manager: Sandla Langlois
    Finance Officer: Ann Berman
    Production Manager: Alejandra Duque
    Program Manager: Lizzy Spicuzza
Mission: Zaccho dance theater creates and presents performance work that investigates dance as it relates to place.
Founded: 1979
Specialized Field: Contemporary Performing Arts
Paid Staff: 4
Non-paid Artists: 1
Income Sources: Ticket Sales; Performances; Fundraising; Class Fees
Performs At: Walker Art Center; Theatre Artaud

97
LILY CAI CHINESE DANCE COMPANY
Fort Mason Center
Building C-353
San Fransisco, CA 94123
Phone: 415-474-4829
Fax: 415-651-9589
e-mail: info@lilycaidance.org
Web Site: www.lilycaidance.org
Officers:
    Executive Director: Gang Situ
    Director: Rolland Luo
    Chairman: Frank Zhou
    Board Member: Lily Cai
    Board Member: Diane Lee
    Board Member: Rolland Luo
Management:
    Artistic Director/Choreographer: Lily Cai
    Music Director/Composer: Gang Situ
    General Manager: Ann Lin
Mission: Elegant, sensual, and captivating, the Lily Cai Chinese Dance Company melds ancient Chinese forms with modern dance in an artistic and inventive marriage of styles. The Company bridges the continuum from past to contemporary - from spectacular court dances of Chinese dynasties to contemporary works fusing classical Chinese movement and ballet, complemented by dazzling costumes, original music, and multi-media designs. Established in 1988.
Utilizes: Choreographers; Composers; Dance Companies; Dancers; Designers; Fine Artists; Guest Ensembles; Original Music Scores
Founded: 1988
Specialized Field: Chinese Dance, Performing Arts
Status: Non-Profit, Professional
Income Sources: Funding, Supporters

98
ABHINAYA DANCE COMPANY
4950 Hamilton Ave.
Ste. 105
San Jose, CA 95130
Phone: 408-871-5959
Fax: 408-871-5955
e-mail: abdanceco@gmail.com
Web Site: www.abhinaya.org
Officers:
    Chairperson: Sharada Bose
    Secretary/Treasurer: Bhaskar Vissa
    Board Member: Ann Malmuth-Onn
    Board Member: Ram Varadarajan
Management:
    Artistic Director/Founder: Mythili Kumar
Mission: The company is dedicated to promoting the classical dance forms of South India through instructional classes and professional performances.
Founded: 1980
Specialized Field: South Indian Dance
Status: Non-Profit, Professional
Paid Staff: 2
Volunteer Staff: 50
Income Sources: Corporate Sponsors; Grants
Performs At: Mexican Heritage Theater; Louis B Meyer Theater; Center For Performing Arts
Organization Type: Performing

99
BALLET SAN JOSE
40 N First Street
San Jose, CA 95113
Phone: 408-288-2820
Fax: 408-993-9570
e-mail: ikopp@balletsj.org
Web Site: www.balletsj.org
Management:
    Artistic Director: Dennis Nahat
    Marketing Director: Lee Kopp

Mission: To provide the South Bay with theatrically produced ballet and professional dance education in a manner that is in vision of the artists, meets the highest technical and artistic standards, contributes to the fulfillment of the cultural needs of the community, and is accessible to as wide an audience as possible.
Utilizes: Collaborating Artists; Contract Orchestras; Dancers; Guest Accompanists; Guest Artists; Guest Conductors; Guest Speakers; Original Music Scores; Resident Artists; Resident Professionals
Founded: 1983
Specialized Field: Ballet
Paid Staff: 23
Paid Artists: 44
Income Sources: Corporate Sponsors
Performs At: Performing Arts Center With Continental Seating
Affiliations: AGMA; Musicians Union
Annual Attendance: 50,000
Type of Stage: Proscenium
Stage Dimensions: 48'x35'
Seating Capacity: 2,600
Year Built: 1972

100
PENINSULA BALLET THEATRE
1880 S Grant Street
San Mateo, CA 94402
Phone: 650-342-3262
Fax: 650-342-3265
e-mail: marketing@penisulaballet.org
Web Site: peninsulaballet.org
Officers:
  President/CEO: Christine Leslie
  Chairman: Michael Berube
  Treasurer: Katherine Jones
  Secretary: Lance Huntley
Management:
  Artistic Director: David Fonnegra
  Music Director: Chris Christenson
  Company Manager: Sharon Torrano
  Marketing Director: Lance Huntley
  Company Manager: Sharon Torrano
  Development Manager: Patricia Dwyer
  Choreographer: Carlos Carvajal
  Ballet Mistress: Brittney Wassermann
  Production Coordinator: Andrea Diaz
Mission: To support and foster a vital arts community in the greater Bay area through educational outreach and by engaging local art talent in the production and presentation of professional, live dance performances at prices affordable to all segments of the population.
Utilizes: Artists-in-Residence; Choreographers; Commissioned Composers; Community Members; Community Talent; Composers-in-Residence; Contract Orchestras; Dancers; Guest Artists; High School Drama; Local Artists; Original Music Scores; Singers; Soloists
Founded: 1967
Specialized Field: Ballet
Status: Professional, Nonprofit
Paid Staff: 4
Volunteer Staff: 25
Paid Artists: 52
Income Sources: Corporate; Foundation; Individual; Merchant Donors
Performs At: San Mateo Performing Arts Center
Organization Type: Performing; Resident

101
PERSPECTIVE DANCE THEATRE/RENO BALLET
Peninsula Ballet Theatre School
333 S B Street
PO Box 1804
San Mateo, CA 94401
Phone: 650-340-9444
Fax: 650-340-9495
e-mail: marketing@peninsulaballet.org
Web Site: peninsulaballet.org
Officers:
  President: Christine Leslie
  Chairman: Judy David
  Secretary: William U Savage
  Treasurer: Keith Kaiser
Management:
  Artistic Director: David Fonnegra
  Music Director: Chris Christenson
  Company Manager: Sharon Torrano
  Marketing Director: Lance Huntley
  Company Manager: Sharon Torrano
  Development Manager: Patricia Dwyer
  Choreographer: Carlos Carvajal
  Ballet Mistress: Brittney Wassermann
  Production Coordinator: Andrea Diaz
Mission: To support and foster a vital arts community in the greater Bay Area through educational outreach and by engaging local art talent in the production and presentation of professional, live dance performances at prices affordable to all segments of the population.
Founded: 1967
Specialized Field: Modern
Income Sources: Corporate; Foundation; Individual; Merchant Donors

102
SAN PEDRO CITY BALLET
1231 S Pacific Avenue
San Pedro, CA 90731
Phone: 310-732-1861
Fax: 310-732-1543
e-mail: spballetschool@sbcglobal.net
Web Site: www.sanpedrocityballet.org
Management:
  Artist Director: Cynthia Bradley
  Artistic Director: Patrick Bradley
  Director: Mary Armor
  Director: Carolina Brown
  Director: Elayne Grgas
Mission: To identify, train and promote a world class pre-professional dance company from the diverse population of the Los Angeles Harbor area that is founded in the base of classical works and traditions, and goes beyond to explore new contemporary and original modern works and to provide training to schools throughout Los Angeles for arts education and after school programs.
Founded: 1994
Specialized Field: Ballet

103
MARIN BALLET/CENTER FOR DANCE
100 Elm Street
San Rafael, CA 94901
Phone: 415-453-6705
Fax: 415-453-5894
e-mail: info@marinballet.org
Web Site: www.marinballet.org
Management:
  Artistic Director: Cynthia Lucas
  Executive Director: Lawrence Ewing
  Music Director: David Shepard
  School Registrar & Office Manager: Marisa Redd
  Marketing & Special Project: Connie Zabokrtsky
  Artistic Coordinator: Becky Moore
Mission: To provide excellent dance training and education and to promote the art of dance.
Founded: 1963
Specialized Field: Ballet
Status: Nonprofit; Non-Professional
Paid Staff: 17
Volunteer Staff: 20
Paid Artists: 5
Budget: $500,000-$1,000,000
Performs At: The Marin Center Veteran Memorial Auditorium; Phyllis Thelen Studio Theatre
Annual Attendance: 300-350

104
STATE STREET BALLET
2285 Las Positas Road
Santa Barbara, CA 93105
Phone: 805-563-3262
e-mail: ssbdance@aol.com
Web Site: www.statestreetballet.com
Officers:
  President: Roger Thompson
  Treasurer: Benjamin Cohen
  Secretary: Lynn Stokes-Pena
  Managing Director: Tim Mikel
Management:
  Artistic Director: Rodney Gustafson
  Ballet Master: Gary Mckenzie
  Ballet Master: Marina Fliagnina
  Costume Designer: A. Christina Giannni
  Choreographer: William Soleau
  Director of Education: Megan Philipp
  Production Manager: Mark Somerfield
Mission: The compant is dedicated to presenting excellence in dance through public performances and educational outreach programs. By combining classical tradition with diversity and sophisticated style we are commited to exploring new avenues in dance while preserving the classics.
Founded: 1994
Specialized Field: Ballet
Paid Staff: 2
Volunteer Staff: 20
Budget: $1,000,000
Income Sources: Donations; Grants; Ticket Sales
Performs At: Palmdale Playhouse

105
SANTA CLARA BALLET
3123 Millar Avenue
Santa Clara, CA 95051
Phone: 408-247-9178
e-mail: info@santaclaraballet.com
Web Site: www.santaclaraballet.org
Officers:
  President: Dennis Mullen
Management:
  Artistic Director: Josefa Villanueva
  Artistic Director: Benjamin Reyes
Mission: To stimulate and promote interest in ballet, primarily as an art form, by providing high-quality ballet performances at a reasonable cost to the general public. To provide performing opportunities to local dancers by helping them develop their talents and achieve their goals. To enhance the quality of life in the South Bay/Silicon Valley community through cultural awareness and diversity.
Utilizes: Actors; AEA Actors; Arrangers; Artists-in-Residence; Choreographers; Collaborating Artists; Collaborations; Commissioned Composers; Commissioned Music; Community Members;

DANCE / California

Community Talent; Composers; Composers-in-Residence; Contract Actors; Contract Orchestras; Curators; Dance Companies; Dancers; Designers; Educators; Equity Actors; Fine Artists; Guest Accompanists; Guest Musicians; Guest Speakers; High School Drama; Local Artists; Original Music Scores; Paid Performers; Singers; Soloists
Founded: 1973
Specialized Field: Ballet
Paid Staff: 3
Volunteer Staff: 8
Paid Artists: 8
Non-paid Artists: 15
Income Sources: Partially funded by the City of Santa Clara; memberships; donations; fund-raising
Performs At: Santa Clara Convention Center Theatre
Type of Stage: Wood
Seating Capacity: 607
Organization Type: Performing; Touring; Resident

106
DANCING CAT PRODUCTIONS, INC
PO Box 4287
Santa Cruz, CA 95063
Phone: 831-429-5085
Fax: 831-423-7057
e-mail: ml@dancingcat.com
Web Site: www.dancingcat.com
Management:
   Marketing: Jennifer Gallacher
Specialized Field: Contemporary Dance
Status: Professional
Paid Staff: 5

107
DR. SCHAFFER AND MR. STERN DANCE ENSEMBLE
PO Box 8055
Santa Cruz, CA 95061
Phone: 831-335-1861
Fax: 831-335-1876
e-mail: schafferkarl@fhda.edu
Web Site: www.schafferstern.org
Management:
   Co-Artistic Director: Karl Schaffer
   Co-Artistic Director: Erik Stern
   Creative Collaborator: Gregg Lizenbery
   Designer: Scott Kim
Mission: Presents the artistic and educational work of Karl Schaffer and Erik Stern.
Utilizes: Collaborating Artists; Collaborations; Commissioned Music; Dancers; Educators; Lyricists; Original Music Scores; Resident Professionals; Scenic Designers; Sign Language Translators; Singers; Student Interns; Visual Arts; Visual Designers; Volunteer Artists; Volunteer Directors & Actors; Writers
Founded: 1987
Specialized Field: Modern
Status: Professional; Non-Profit
Paid Staff: 2
Paid Artists: 5
Budget: $20,000-$60,000
Income Sources: Grants; Fee for Service; Touring; Donations
Performs At: Center for the Arts; Henry J. Mello Center; The Mondavi Center; The John F. Kennedy Center for the Performing Arts
Annual Attendance: 5,000-25,000

108
ALLAN HANCOCK COLLEGE DANCE PROGRAM
800 S College Drive
Santa Maria, CA 93454
Phone: 805-922-6966
Fax: 805-928-7905
Toll-free: 866-354-5242
e-mail: dmcmahon@hancockcollege.edu
Web Site: www.hancockcollege.edu/programs_of_study/dance/index.php
Management:
   Dance Program Coordinator: Diane McMahon
   Dance Spectrum Director: Larissa Nazarenko
Mission: Students and faculty are given the opportunity to choreograph as well as perform.
Utilizes: Actors; Arrangers; Choreographers; Commissioned Music; Composers-in-Residence; Dance Companies; Dancers; Educators; Equity Actors; Guest Artists; Guest Choreographers; Guest Companies; Guest Directors; Guest Ensembles; Guest Instructors; Guest Lecturers; Guest Musical Directors; Guest Musicians; Guest Soloists; Guest Speakers; Guest Teachers; Guest Writers; Guild Activities; High School Drama; Organization Contracts; Original Music Scores; Soloists
Specialized Field: Ballet; Jazz
Paid Staff: 50
Volunteer Staff: 200
Paid Artists: 10
Budget: $100,000
Income Sources: Community College Budget; Box Office Receipts
Performs At: Marian Theatre; Severson Theatre
Facility Category: Theater
Type of Stage: Thrust stage
Stage Dimensions: 40' x 40'
Year Built: 1967

109
DONNA STERNBERG & DANCERS
911 9th Street
#206
Santa Monica, CA 90403
Phone: 310-260-1198
Fax: 310-260-1198
e-mail: contact@dsdancers.com
Web Site: www.dsdancers.com
Officers:
   President: Walter Kornbluh
   Vice President: Michael Caan
   Secretary: Chris M. Bradford
   Treasurer: Donna Sternberg
Management:
   Artistic Director: Donna Sternberg, dsdancers@earthlink.net
Mission: An interdisciplinary dance company whose mission is to build bridges and make connections between dance, science, philosophy and other art forms so that people and ideas come together in ways that expand human awareness leading audiences to envision the world as theirs to create in a unique way.
Utilizes: Choreographers; Collaborating Artists; Collaborations; Dance Companies; Dancers; Designers; Educators; Guest Accompanists; Guest Instructors; Guest Musical Directors; Guest Soloists; Instructors; Lyricists; Multi Collaborations; Organization Contracts; Original Music Scores; Theatre Companies
Founded: 1985
Specialized Field: Contemporary Dance
Status: Non-Profit; Professional
Paid Staff: 1
Volunteer Staff: 2
Paid Artists: 6
Budget: 38,000
Income Sources: Government Grants; Foundations; Business; Individuals; Ticket Sales; Contracted Performances and Teaching Programs; Touring
Annual Attendance: 3,000

110
BANAFSHEH SAYYAD AND NAMAH
1537 Berkeley Street
Suite 2
Santa Monica, CA 90404
Phone: 310-499-7100
Fax: 818-888-3484
e-mail: info@namah.net
Web Site: www.namah.net
Management:
   Artistic Director: Banafsheh Sayyad
Mission: To promote and educate the broadest possible public appreciation and interest in Iranian and world performing arts, including dance, music and theater, through public performances, educational outreach programs, workshops, lectures and studio instruction.
Founded: 1994
Specialized Field: Contemporary Persian Dance; Sufi Whirling; Flamenco
Paid Staff: 1
Volunteer Staff: 1
Paid Artists: 6

111
KESHET CHAIM DANCE ENSEMBLE
4155 Dixie Canyon Avenue
Sherman Oaks, CA 91423
Phone: 818-784-0344
Fax: 818-896-1496
e-mail: info@kcdancers.org
Web Site: www.kcdancers.org
Officers:
   President: Leah Bleiweis
   Secretary: Genie Benson
   Treasurer: Scott Cargle
Management:
   Executive Director: Genie Benson
   Artistic Director: Eytan Avisar
   Administrator: Leah Bleiweis
   Education Director: Cecilia Hanono
Mission: A non-profit American-Israeli contemporary dance troupe, mission is to express the global spirit of Judaism and Israeli culture throughout the world, and to combat prejudice through education and the arts.
Founded: 1983
Specialized Field: Israeli Contemporary Folk Dance
Status: Non-Profit; Professional
Paid Staff: 3
Volunteer Staff: 5
Non-paid Artists: 20
Budget: $1,170,000
Income Sources: Government; Foundations; Corporate; Private Donors
Performs At: Various; Concert; Festival; School
Annual Attendance: 10,000

112
SANTA CRUZ BALLET THEATRE
2800 S Rodeo Gulch Road
Suite C
Soquel, CA 95073
Phone: 831-477-1606
Fax: 831-464-1219
e-mail: info@scbt.org
Web Site: www.scbt.org

DANCE / Colorado

Officers:
- **President:** Mark Swan
- **VP:** Tony Crane
- **Treasurer:** Ellen Taylor
- **Secretary:** Beth Colehower

Management:
- **Artistic Director:** Diane Cypher
- **Artistic Director:** Robert Kelley
- **Administrative Manager:** Sara Wilbourne
- **Music Director and Conductor:** Pamela Martin
- **Orchestra Manager:** Norman Peck

Mission: To inspire the community and create opportunities for young artists through the advamcement of the art of ballet.
Founded: 1978
Specialized Field: Ballet
Status: Non-Profit, Pre-Professional

113
SOUTH BAY BALLET
1261 Sartori Avenue
Torrance, CA 90501
Phone: 310-533-1247
e-mail: southbayballet@yahoo.com
Web Site: www.southbayballet.org

Officers:
- **President:** Catherine Jacobson
- **VP:** Suzette Savard
- **CFO:** Lynn Hollister
- **Secretary:** Karla McGillivray
- **Director:** Patricia Zieg

Management:
- **Artistic Director:** Diane Lauridsen
- **Assistant Artistic Director:** Elijah S. Pressman
- **Executive Director:** Mary Simoens

Mission: To provide quality artistic performances to the community as well as outstanding training to young and pre-professional dancers.
Founded: 1987
Specialized Field: Ballet

114
MENDOCINO BALLET
205 S State Street
Ukiah, CA 95482
Phone: 707-463-2290
e-mail: balletoffice@sbcglobal.net
Web Site: www.mendocinoballet.org

Management:
- **Artistic/Executive Director:** Trudy McCreanor

Mission: To provide the highest professional dance instruction and performance opportunities in Mendocino County and the surrounding areas.
Founded: 1984
Specialized Field: Ballet

115
FRANCISCO MARTINEZ DANCE THEATRE
6723 Matilija Avenue
Valley Glen, CA 91405
Phone: 818-988-2192
e-mail: info@fmdt.org
Web Site: www.fmdt.org

Management:
- **Artistic Director:** Francisco Martinez
- **Executive Director:** David Allen Jones

Mission: Francisco Martinez's dances are as varied as his far ranging interests, yet all reflect his deep affection for movement, music and the intriguing possibilities for combining the two.
Founded: 1971
Specialized Field: Ballet
Status: Non-Profit, Professional

Paid Staff: 8
Volunteer Staff: 2
Budget: $40,000-$400,0000
Performs At: Government; Corporate; Individual; Foundations
Annual Attendance: 25,000
Organization Type: Performing; Touring

116
THE VENTURA COUNTY BALLET COMPANY
505 Poli Street
Suite 402
Ventura, CA 93001
Phone: 805-648-2080
Fax: 805-643-6771
e-mail: info@venturacountyballet.com
Web Site: www.venturacountyballet.com

Management:
- **Executive Director:** Kathleen Noblin
- **Artistic Director:** Colleen O'Callaghan
- **Ballet Staff:** Eileen Riddle
- **Ballet Staff:** Marina Filagina

Mission: To provide the community with a prestigious professional/pre-professional ballet company to reach audiences countywide. Our goal is also to offer the county's underserved population quality ballet performances without charge.
Founded: 1998
Specialized Field: Ballet
Paid Staff: 4
Volunteer Staff: 100

117
DIABLO BALLET
PO Box 4700
Walnut Creek, CA 94596
Phone: 925-943-1775
Fax: 925-943-1115
e-mail: diablo@diabloballet.org
Web Site: www.diabloballet.org

Officers:
- **President:** Jack Catton
- **Treasurer:** Barbara L. Gray
- **Secretary:** Carol Mather

Management:
- **Artistic Director:** Lauren Jonas
- **Artistic Advisor:** Sally Streets
- **Executive Director:** Lee Foster
- **Director of Marketing:** Dan Meagher
- **Technical Director:** David McCollum
- **Music Director:** Greg Sudmeier
- **Development Coordinator:** Erika Johnson
- **Stage Manager:** David Hartenstein
- **Lighting Designer:** Jack Carpenter

Mission: To train and provide professional performance opportunities to dancers who have outstanding potential through Diablo Ballet's Apprentice and Professional Intermediate Programs.
Founded: 1993
Specialized Field: Theatrical Dance
Income Sources: Corporate; Merchant; Individual Donors
Performs At: Zellerbach Hall, University of California at Berkeley; Yerba Buena Center for the Arts
Organization Type: Performing; Touring; Educational

Colorado

118
HELANDER DANCE THEATER
Dairy Center For the Arts
2590 Walnut Street
Boulder, CO 80302-5700
Phone: 303-589-2048
Fax: 303-449-4614
e-mail: danelle@helanderdancetheater.org
Web Site: www.helanderdancetheater.org

Management:
- **Artistic Director:** Danelle Helander
- **Executive Director:** Sean Owens
- **Musical Director:** Matt Powelson

Mission: To make a vital contribution to the community through dance as a vehicle for greater understanding, sharing and healing.
Founded: 1980
Specialized Field: Ballet
Status: Non-Profit; Professional
Paid Staff: 2
Volunteer Staff: 15
Paid Artists: 10
Non-paid Artists: 3
Budget: $30,000
Income Sources: Grants; Foundations; Classes
Performs At: Dairy Center For The Arts
Annual Attendance: 10,500-2,000

119
LE CENTRE DU SILENCE MIME SCHOOL
PO Box 745
Boulder, CO 80026
Phone: 303-661-9271
e-mail: info@bodyspeak.com
Web Site: www.bodyspeak.com

Management:
- **Director:** Samuel Avital

Mission: To surpass the normal means of communication offered by the entertainment industry and society's abuse of the spoken word.
Founded: 1971
Specialized Field: Mime
Status: Professional, Profit
Volunteer Staff: 2
Performs At: International
Annual Attendance: 15-20

120
ORMAO DANCE COMPANY
10 South Spruce Street
Colorado Springs, CO 80905
Phone: 719-471-9759
Web Site: ormaodance.org

Management:
- **Director:** Jan Johnson
- **Assistant Director:** Tiffany Tinsley
- **Ballet Mistress:** Debra Mercer

Mission: To provoke, challenge, and entertain those in our community and beyond through the creative language of dance. To encourage diversity and experimentation in the arts. To enrich and enhance cultural opportunities within southern Colorado's communities and schools by spear-heading initiatives that bring dance to the public and programs that educate people of all ages.
Founded: 1990
Status: Professional; Nonprofit

DANCE / Colorado

121

CLEO PARKER ROBINSON DANCE
119 Park Avenue W
Denver, CO 80205
Phone: 303-295-1759
Fax: 303-295-1328
e-mail: cleodance@aol.com
Web Site: www.cleoparkerdance.org
Officers:
   Chair: Harryette Johnson
   Treasurer: Al Walker
   Secretary: Kelly Hawthorne
Management:
   Executive Artistic Director: Cleo Parker Robinson
   Senior Director: Malik Robinson
   Booking & Sales: Mary Hart
Mission: Cleo Parker Robinson Dance is an international, cross-cultural, dance arts and educational institution rooted in African American traditions and dedicated to excellence in providing instruction, performances and community programs for intergenerational students, artists and audiences.
Utilizes: Five Seasonal Concerts
Founded: 1970
Specialized Field: African Dance; Ballet; Jazz; Break Dancing; Hip Hop
Paid Staff: 7
Volunteer Staff: 30
Paid Artists: 18
Budget: $1.5 million
Income Sources: Ensemble Performances; School; Government; Grants
Performs At: Theatre; 3 Studios
Affiliations: Denver Center for the Performing Arts
Facility Category: Concert Hall; Performance Center
Type of Stage: Proscenium
Seating Capacity: 300 plus 6 for special needs
Year Built: 1886
Rental Contact: Operations Director Mary Hart
Organization Type: Performing; Touring; Resident; Educational
Resident Groups: Cleo Parker Robinson Dance Ensemble

122

COLORADO BALLET
1278 Lincoln Street
Denver, CO 80203
Phone: 303-837-8888
Fax: 303-861-7174
e-mail: info@coloradoballet.org
Web Site: www.coloradoballet.org
Officers:
   Co-Chair: Holly Baroway
   Co-Chair: Henny Lasley
   Secretary: Jean Armstrong
   Development Chair: Gleneen Brienza
   Treasurer and Finance Chair: William J. Tryon
Management:
   Artistic Director: Gil Boggs
   Ballet Mistress: Lorita Travaglia
   Ballet Mistress: Sandra Brown
   Company Manager: Brandi Glass
   Managing Director: Mark Chase
   Technical Director and Production M: Pete Nielson
   Development Director: Claire Margolf
   Accounting Manager: Janina Blue
   Development Coordinator: Julia Symanski
Mission: To provide enriching, inspiring opportunities to people of all ages and backgrounds, fostering and appreciation of the artistry and athleticism of ballet, and making dance accsssible as a culturally important means of creativity and expression.
Utilizes: Dancers; Guest Companies; Singers
Founded: 1951
Opened: 1961
Specialized Field: Ballet
Status: Professional; Nonprofit
Paid Staff: 35
Volunteer Staff: 20
Budget: $5,000,000
Income Sources: Corporate; Individual; Auxiliary
Performs At: Denver Auditorium Theatre; Temple Hoyne Buell Theatre
Annual Attendance: 50,000
Organization Type: Performing; Touring; Resident; Sponsoring

123

HANNAH KAHN DANCE COMPANY
75 S Cherokee Street
Denver, CO 80223
Phone: 303-789-4181
e-mail: hannahkahndance@gmail.com
Web Site: www.hannahkahndance.org
Management:
   Artistic Director: Hannah Kahn, hannahkahndance@gmail.com
Mission: The Hannah Kahn Dance Company has been dedicated to making quality, innovative art and sharing it with the community.
Utilizes: Choreographers; Collaborating Artists; Collaborations; Dance Companies; Dancers; High School Drama; Instructors; Soloists; Visual Arts
Founded: 1992
Specialized Field: Modern Dance
Status: Professional; Non-Profit
Paid Staff: 12
Volunteer Staff: 1
Non-paid Artists: 1
Budget: $70,000
Income Sources: Grants; Contributions; Box Office; Performance & Teaching Fees; Classes
Annual Attendance: 11,000
Organization Type: Performing; Touring

124

KIM ROBARDS DANCE
The KRD Dance Loft
9990 East Colfax Avenue
Denver, CO 80010
Phone: 303-825-4847
Fax: 303-825-4846
e-mail: info@kimrobardsdance.org
Web Site: www.kimrobardsdance.org
Officers:
   CEO: ?Kim Robards
Management:
   Artistic Director: Kim Robards
   Associate Executive Director: LaRana Skalicky
   Outreach Coordinator: Rosemary Cleary-Hague
Mission: To expand awareness of modern dance as a unique art form that inspires and transforms lives through creating, performing and educating.
Founded: 1987
Specialized Field: Modern
Paid Staff: 4
Volunteer Staff: 30
Paid Artists: 15
Budget: $100,000-$200,000
Income Sources: Foundation; Grants; Ticket Sales
Performs At: Newman Performing Arts Center
Annual Attendance: 4,000

125

PDAC/ARTS FOR ALL
714 S. Pearl St
Denver, CO 80209
Phone: 303-722-1206
e-mail: PDACArts4All@aol.com
Web Site: www.bowendance.com
Officers:
   President: Linda Weiler
   VP: Tom Hobin
   Secretary: Diana Roth
   Treasurer: Gioia Cardelli
Management:
   Artistic Director: Gwen Bowen
Mission: To protect and promote the arts in the face of the threats that jeopardize arts programming in our schools and comunities today.
Founded: 1963
Specialized Field: Ballet; Tap; Modern; Jazz; Hip Hop; Flamenco
Income Sources: Fundraising; Performances; Ticket Sales
Performs At: The Metro Area

126

DAWSON WALLACE DANCE PROJECT
PO Box 140699
Edgewater, CO 80214
Phone: 303-789-2030
Fax: 720-335-6843
e-mail: info@dawsonwallace.org
Web Site: www.dawsonwallace.org
Officers:
   President: Allie White
   Director: Diana Burk Vickery
   Director: Jill Wayne
   Director: Lauren Schwartz
Management:
   Artistic Director: Gregory Dawson
   Executive Director: Lena Cazeaux
   Dancer Representative: Jackie McMenaman
   Company Class Teacher: Lizanne McAdams-Graham
Mission: To provide and present the highest standards in contemporary ballet performance, technical instruction and educational programs to the State of Colorado and throughout the Rocky Mountain Region.
Utilizes: Choreographers; Collaborating Artists; Collaborations; Commissioned Composers; Commissioned Music; Dance Companies; Dancers; Designers; Fine Artists; Grant Writers; Guest Accompanists; Guest Artists; Guest Choreographers; Guest Conductors; Guest Directors; Guest Ensembles; High School Drama; Instructors; Lyricists; Multi Collaborations; Multimedia; New Productions; Organization Contracts; Original Music Scores; Resident Professionals; Theatre Companies; Touring Companies; Visual Arts
Founded: 1979
Specialized Field: Contemporary Ballet
Status: Professional, Nonprofit
Paid Staff: 12
Volunteer Staff: 6
Paid Artists: 11
Non-paid Artists: 8
Budget: $500,000
Income Sources: Box Office; Grants; Individual Contributions
Performs At: Lakewood Cultural Center; Town Hall Arts Center; Auditorium Theatre
Annual Attendance: 70,000
Facility Category: Performance

Type of Stage: Proscenium
Stage Dimensions: 44' x 32'
Organization Type: Performing; Educational
Comments: Artist Management: Gary Lindsey Artist Services

127
CANYON CONCERT BALLET
4103 S Mason Street
Fort Collins, CO 80524-5313
Mailing Address: 1031 Conifer Street, Suite 3, Fort Collins CO 80524
Phone: 970-472-4156
Fax: 970-472-4158
e-mail: info@ccballet.org
Web Site: www.ccballet.org
Officers:
  President: Jim Frucci
  Treasurer: Melissa Clary
  Secretary: Tim Northburg
Management:
  Artistic Director: Jessica V. Freestone
  Executive Director: Kim Lang
  Office Manager: Teal Bosworth
  Ballet Mistress: Melissa Corr
  School Director: Teri English
  Bookkeeper: Judy Bejarno
Mission: To create and share the passion of dance through artistically enriching performances and dance education. Our vision is to provide a sustainable community forum for dance performance and education.
Founded: 1978
Specialized Field: Ballet
Paid Staff: 20
Volunteer Staff: 2
Income Sources: Friends of Canyon Concert Ballet Dance Fund; Ticket Sales
Performs At: Lincoln Center Performance Hall
Annual Attendance: 7,000

128
FIESTA COLORADO DANCE COMPANY
5 South Wadsworth Boulevard
Lakewood, CO 80226
Phone: 303-274-7844
e-mail: fiestacolorado@comcast.net
Web Site: fiestacolorado.org
Management:
  Artistic Director: Jeanette Trujillo-Lucero
Mission: The mission of Fiesta Colorado Dance Company is to preserve and present the cultural traditions of Mexican and Spanish dance and music arts for its community and to create an understanding and appreciation of the Latino culture through educational programs and professional performance.
Founded: 1972
Specialized Field: Mexican And Spanish Dance
Status: Nonprofit

Connecticut

129
ADAM MILLER DANCE PROJECT
94 Huntington Street
Hartford, CT 06105
Phone: 860-249-7748
e-mail: adamballet@aol.com
Web Site: www.adammillerdanceproject.com
Officers:
  President: Ken Warner Esq
  Chief Financial Officer: Michael J Giglio
  Board Member: Steven Kaufman
Management:
  Artistic Director: Adam Miller
  Associate Director: Natalie Koons
Mission: The mission of the Adam Miller Dance Project is to provide the greater Hartford area with a first rate professional dance organization which focuses on the creation and production of leading edge and ballet-based work.
Founded: 2001
Specialized Field: Ballet
Income Sources: Grants

130
MYSTIC BALLET
P.O. Box 429
Mystic, CT 06355
Phone: 860-536-3671
e-mail: info@mysticballet.org
Web Site: mysticballet.org
Management:
  Artistic Director: Goran Subotic
Specialized Field: Contemporary Ballet

131
CONNECTICUT BALLET
20 Acosta Street
Stamford, CT 06902
Phone: 203-964-1211
e-mail: ctballet@ix.netcom.com
Web Site: www.connecticutballet.com
Officers:
  President: Brett Raphael
  Vice President: Marie Seymour
  Secretary: Jeanne J. Hendrickson
  Treasurer: Thomas L. Kent, Esq.
  Chair: Leonard Vignola
Management:
  Artistic Director: Brett Raphael
  Ballet Mistress: Helen Coope
  Technical Director: Jon Curns
  Wardrobe Supervisor: Christina Giannini
  Production Stage Manager: Brian Westmoreland
  Lighting Designers: Kenneth Keith
  Wardrobe Assistant: Marjorie Tedesco
Mission: To be Connecticut's premier classical and contemporary ballet company, performing a diverse repertoire of new works, masterworks and great story ballets.
Utilizes: Five Seasonal Concerts
Founded: 1981
Specialized Field: Modern; Ballet
Status: Professional; Non-Profit
Paid Staff: 3
Volunteer Staff: 3
Budget: $500,000-$1,000,000
Performs At: Stamford Center For The Arts
Annual Attendance: 25,000
Organization Type: Performing; Touring; Educational

132
ZIG ZAG BALLET
20 Acosta Street
Stamford, CT 06902
Phone: 203-964-1211
Fax: 203-961-1928
e-mail: zigzagballet@hotmail.com
Web Site: www.connecticutballet.com
Officers:
  President: Brett Raphael
  Vice President: Marie Seymour
  Secretary: Jeanne J. Hendrickson
  Treasurer: Thomas L. Kent, Esq.
  Chair: Leonard Vignola
Management:
  Artistic Director: Brett Raphael
  Ballet Mistress: Helen Coope
  Technical Director: Jon Curns
  Wardrobe Supervisor: Christina Giannini
  Production Stage Manager: Brian Westmoreland
  Lighting Designers: Kenneth Keith
  Wardrobe Assistant: Marjorie Tedesco
Mission: To be Connecticut's premier classical and comtemporary ballet company, performing a diverse repertoire of new works, masterworks and great story ballets.
Specialized Field: Contemporary Dance
Status: Non-Profit; Professional
Paid Staff: 2
Paid Artists: 10
Budget: $250,000
Annual Attendance: 25,000

133
NUTMEG BALLET
Nutmeg Conservatory for the Arts
58 Main Street
Torrington, CT 06790
Phone: 860-482-4413
Fax: 860-482-7614
e-mail: info@nutmegconservatory.org
Web Site: www.nutmegconservatory.org
Officers:
  President: Susan Patterson
  Vice President: Marc Trivella
  Secretary: Joel Perlotto
  Treasurer: Joe Fazzino
Management:
  Artistic Director: Sharon Dante
  Senior Ballet Mistress: Denise Warner Limoli
  Teacher & Choreographer: Alexandre Proia
  Teacher & Choreographer: Brian Simerson
  Associate Director: Joan Kunsch
  Ballet Master: Alexel Tchernichov
  Ballet Master & Production Manager: Timothy Melady
Mission: To provide professional level ballet training to aspiring young dance artists.
Utilizes: Artists-in-Residence; Dance Companies; Dancers; Grant Writers; Guest Accompanists; Guest Artists; Guest Companies; High School Drama; Multimedia; Original Music Scores; Resident Artists; Singers; Soloists
Founded: 1969
Specialized Field: Ballet
Paid Staff: 40
Paid Artists: 20
Budget: $500,000-$1,000,000
Facility Category: Dance/Music Instruction
Year Built: 2001
Organization Type: Performing; Touring; Resident; Educational; Sponsoring

134
MOMIX
42 Bell Hill Road
Washington, CT 06793
Phone: 860-868-7454
Fax: 860-868-2317
e-mail: momix@snet.net
Web Site: www.momix.com
Management:
  Artistic Director: Moses Pendleton
  Associate Director: Cynthia Quinn
  Manager: Margaret Selby
Mission: To present work of exceptional inventiveness and physical beauty by creating surrealistic images using props, light, shadow, humor and the human body.
Founded: 1981

DANCE / Delaware

Specialized Field: Illusion Dance
Budget: $1,000,000
Performs At: Internationally
Organization Type: Performing; Touring

135
PILOBOLUS DANCE THEATRE
PO Box 388
Washington Depot, CT 06794
Phone: 860-868-0538
Fax: 860-868-0530
e-mail: info@pilobolus.com
Web Site: www.pilobolus.com
Officers:
  Treasurer: John Treacy Beyer
  Chair: Edward Klaris
  Vice Chair: David Mechlin
  President: Anne Hubbard
Management:
  Manager: Susan Mandler, info@pilobolus.org
  Artistic Director: Robby Barnett
  Artistic Co-Director: Michael Tracy
  Executive Director: Itamar Kubovy
  Associate Artistic Director: Matt Kent
  Co-Executive Director: Lily Binns
  General Manager: Susan Mandler
Mission: Pilobolus' mission is two-fold; to produce and perfect live and recorded dance theater works at the highest level to an increasing audience around the world, and through the Pilobolus Institute, to see our traditional background and collaborative creative methods in the most imaginative way to stimulate, educate, and broaden the audience for dance.
Utilizes: Choreographers; Collaborating Artists; Dancers; Educators; High School Drama; Students
Founded: 1971
Specialized Field: Modern
Status: Professional; Nonprofit
Income Sources: Individual Contributions; Grants; Commissions
Performs At: Schubert Performing Arts Center
Organization Type: Performing; Touring; Resident

136
THE HARTT SCHOOL
University of Hartford
200 Bloomfield Avenue
West Hartford, CT 06117-1599
Phone: 860-768-4454
e-mail: harttcomm@hartford.edu
Web Site: harttweb.hartford.edu
Officers:
  President, Dean: Aaron Flagg
Management:
  Public Relations: Sheri Ziccardi
Mission: The Hartt School seeks to enhance the practice and appreciation of all aspects of the performaing arts through professinal training in a conservatory environment, avocational programs & service and advocacy in its immediate and extended community.
Utilizes: Actors; Arrangers; Artists-in-Residence; Choreographers; Collaborating Artists; Collaborations; Composers; Composers-in-Residence; Dance Companies; Dancers; Designers; Educators; Fine Artists; Grant Writers; Guest Accompanists; Guest Artists; Guest Choreographers; Guest Companies; Guest Composers; Guest Conductors; Guest Designers; Guest Directors; Guest Ensembles; Guest Instructors; Guest Lecturers; Guest Musical Directors; Guest Musicians; Guest Soloists; Guest Speakers; High School Drama; Instructors; Local Artists; Local Unknown Artists; Lyricists; Multi Collaborations; Multimedia; Music; Organization Contracts; Paid Performers; Poets; Resident Companies; Resident Professionals; Sign Language Translators; Singers; Soloists; Students; Student Interns; Special Technical Talent; Visual Arts
Founded: 1920
Specialized Field: Theatrical Dance
Performs At: Millard Theatre; Lincoln Theatre
Annual Attendance: 689

Delaware

137
DELEWARE DANCE ALLIANCE, LLC
107 Maple Avenue
Milford, DE 19963
Phone: 302-422-2633
e-mail: dedancealliance@verizon.net
Web Site: dedancealliance.com
Management:
  Company Owner: Michelle Parisi
  Choreographer: Mark Parisi
Founded: 2010
Specialized Field: Dance, Martial Arts, Acting

138
DELAWARE DANCE COMPANY
168 Elkton Road
Suite 101 Madeline Crossing
Newark, DE 19711
Phone: 302-738-2023
Fax: 302-738-1820
e-mail: ddcoffice@verizon.net
Web Site: www.delawaredance.org
Officers:
  President: Allan Carlsen
  Vice-President: Brenda Cabrera-Nieves
  Secretary: Rebecca Coughenour
  Treasurer: Suzanne Fitzgerald
Management:
  Artistic Director: Sunshine Webster Latshaw
  Business Manager: Mary Roth
Mission: To advance the nowledge and appreciation of dance in the community and region through instruction, performances and outreach programs. To provide the highest quality educational opportunities possible in all aspects of dance to anyone desiring such education. To be viewed as a community and regional leader in preparing vocational students for a professional career in dance.
Utilizes: Five Seasonal Concerts; Singers
Founded: 1978
Specialized Field: Modern; Ballet; Tap; Theatre Dance
Paid Staff: 30
Income Sources: Fundraising; Private; Donations
Performs At: Dickinson Theatre; Delaware Theatre Company
Annual Attendance: 3,000
Organization Type: Performing; Touring; Educational

139
MID-ATLANTIC BALLET
104 E Main Street
PO Box 161
Newark, DE 19715
Phone: 302-266-6362
Fax: 302-266-6372
e-mail: mab5678@verizon.net
Web Site: www.midatlanticballet.org
Officers:
  President: Heather Uhlmann
  Vice-President: Chuck Halfen
  Treasurer: Stella Ng
  Secretary: Beth Evans
Management:
  Artistic Director: Patrick Korstange
  Founding Artistic Director: Sara Taylor Neal
  Ballet Mistress: Sandra Davis
  Resident Faculty: Carolyn Peck
  Executive Director: Dawn Alexis Calzada
  Office Manager?: Katie Bloom
Mission: Mid-Atlantic Ballet is dedicated to developing the minds and bodies of its students as well as promoting dance as an art form.
Founded: 1997
Specialized Field: Ballet

140
FIRST STATE BALLET THEATRE
818 N Market Street
Wilmington, DE 19801
Phone: 302-658-7897
Toll-free: 800-374-7263
e-mail: fsbt@firststateballet.com
Web Site: www.firststateballet.com
Officers:
  President: Robert Grenfell
  Vice-President: Virginia Harcke
  Treasurer: Rachael Mears
  Secretary: Mimi Link
Management:
  Artistic Director: Pasha Kambalov
  Assistant Artistic Director: Lev Assouliak
  School Director: Kristina Kambalov
  Executive Director: Robert Grenfell
  Development Director: Giovanna Saffos
  Resident Choreographer: Alex Buckner
  Business Manager: Mary Anne Grenfell
  Technical Director: Genevieve Fanelli
  Stage Manager: Paige Obara
Mission: To present professional quality ballet performances to audiences throughout Delaware, to provide performing opportunities to aspiring dancers and to educate the Delaware dance audience of the future.
Founded: 1999
Specialized Field: Ballet
Paid Staff: 3
Volunteer Staff: 36
Paid Artists: 10
Income Sources: Donations; Sponsors; Private; Fundraising
Performs At: The Grand Opera House
Annual Attendance: 4,000

District of Columbia

141
CITYDANCE ENSEMBLE
1111 16th Street NW
Suite 300
Washington, DC 20036
Mailing Address: 4908 Wisconsin Ave, Washington, DC 20016
Phone: 202-347-3909
Fax: 202-318-9191
e-mail: info@citydance.net
Web Site: www.citydance.net
Officers:
  Chairman: Karen Thomas
  Vice Chairman: Emily Lenzner
  Secretary: Kay Kendall
  Treasurer: Marcy Butler
  Board Member: Linda Potter
  Board Member: Scoot Logan
  Board Member: Lauren Talbott
  Board Member: Nancy Tartt

DANCE / District of Columbia

Management:
  Executive Director: Alexa Nowakowski, alexe@citydance.net
  Artistic Director: Lorraine Spiegler, lorraine@citydance.net
  Community Programs Director: Kelli Quinn, kelli@citydance.net
  Operations Director: Letitia Hayes
  Marketing/Sales Director: Julie Gerdes Becnel
  Education Adminsitration Director: Asanga Domask
  Community Programs Director: Sarah Levy
  Social Media: Megan Piluk
  Marketing Manager: Eve White
Mission: CityDance's mission is to advance the appreciation for and participation in contemporary dance through performance and education.
Utilizes: Choreographers; Dancers; Educators; Fine Artists; Guest Artists; Guest Companies; Guest Designers; Guest Directors; Guest Speakers; Scenic Designers; Soloists; Special Technical Talent
Founded: 1996
Specialized Field: Contemporary Dance Through Performance/Education
Paid Staff: 8
Income Sources: Contributions, Corporate Sponsors
Performs At: CityDance Center at Strathmore, CityDance Center at DC Dance Collective, The Madiera School
Stage Dimensions: 40 feet wide by 35 feet deep
Seating Capacity: 140
Year Head Theatre Renovated: 2011
Cost: $375,000.00

142
DANA TAI SOON BURGESS & COMPANY
2745 Arizona Avenue NW
Washington, DC 20016
Phone: 202-297-2436
Fax: 202-232-2786
e-mail: dtsbco@cs.com
Web Site: www.dtsbco.com
Officers:
  President: Jan Tievsky
  Vice-President: Bonnie Kogod
  Treasurer: Daniel Schuman
  Secretary: Mary Eccles
Management:
  Director/Founder: Dana Tai Soon Burgess
  Manager: Alyson Brokenshire
  MD, Educational Principal: Connie Lin Fink-Hammack
  Associate Artistic Director: Kelly Moss Southall
  Technical Coordinator: Felipe Oyarzun Moltedo
  Executive Director: Nicole Hollander
Founded: 1990
Specialized Field: Modern
Status: Non-Profit; Professional
Paid Staff: 3
Volunteer Staff: 25
Performs At: The Lincoln Center

143
DANCE PLACE
3225 Eighth Street NE
Washington, DC 20017
Phone: 202-269-1600
Fax: 202-269-4103
e-mail: ideas@danceplace.org
Web Site: www.danceplace.org
Officers:
  Chairman: Jannes Gibson
  President: Carla Perlo
  Vice Chair: Wendy Shapiro
  Treasurer: W. Christopher Hollinsed
  Secretary: Carol Bradwell
  Financial Director: Emily Crews
Management:
  Artistic Director: Carla Perlo
  Marketing Assistant: Amanda Blythe
  Marketing Associate: David Hopper
  Communications Director: Carolyn Kamrath
  Associate Technical Director: Bradley Porter
  Office Manager: Elizabeth Zinni
  Programming & Development Associate: Kiley Pogas
Mission: To transform lives through performing arts and creative education programs that inspire personal growth, professional success, physical wellness and community enegagement.
Utilizes: Dance Companies; Dancers; Five Seasonal Concerts; Guest Artists; Guest Choreographers; Guest Ensembles; Guest Musical Directors; Instructors; Local Artists; Sign Language Translators
Founded: 1980
Specialized Field: Modern; Ethnic Dance; Theatrical Dance
Paid Staff: 14
Volunteer Staff: 25
Budget: $900,000
Income Sources: Theater; Studio
Annual Attendance: 9,000
Facility Category: Studio/Theatre/Community Center
Type of Stage: Black Box
Seating Capacity: 165
Year Built: 1936
Year Remodeled: 2000
Organization Type: Performing; Touring; Resident; Educational; Sponsoring

144
DEBORAH RILEY DANCE PROJECTS
Dance Place
3255 8th Street NE
Washington, DC 20017-3502
Phone: 202-269-1600
Fax: 202-269-4103
e-mail: ideas@danceplace.org
Web Site: www.danceplace.org
Officers:
  Chairman: Jannes Gibson
  President: Carla Perlo
  Vice Chair: Wendy Shapiro
  Treasurer: W. Christopher Hollinsed
  Secretary: Carol Bradwell
  Financial Director: Emily Crews
Management:
  Artistic Director: Deborah Riley
  Marketing Assistant: Amanda Blythe
  Marketing Associate: David Hopper
  Communications Director: Carolyn Kamrath
  Associate Technical Director: Bradley Porter
  Office Manager: Elizabeth Zinni
  Programming & Development Associate: Kiley Pogas
Mission: To transform lives through performing arts and creative education programs that inspire personal growth, professional success, physical wellness and community engagement.
Founded: 1987
Specialized Field: Modern
Performs At: The Dance Place

145
GALLAUDET DANCE COMPANY
Gallaudet University
800 Florida Avenue NE
Washington, DC 20002
Phone: 202-651-5493
Web Site: www.gallaudet.edu
Officers:
  President: Dr. T. Alan Hurwitz
Management:
  Director: Diane Hottendorf
Mission: Gallaudet University is a bilingual, diverse. multicultural institution of higher education that ensures the intellectual and professional advancement of deaf and hard of hearing individuals through American Sign Language and English.
Founded: 1955
Specialized Field: Modern; Jazz; Tap; American Sign Language
Income Sources: Gallaudet University
Annual Attendance: 15-20
Organization Type: Educational; Performing

146
MAIDA WITHERS DANCE CONSTRUCTION COMPANY
800 21st Street NW
Suite 220
Washington, DC 20052
Phone: 703-300-4634
Fax: 202-994-9403
e-mail: m.withers@verizon.net
Web Site: www.maidadance.com
Officers:
  Board of Directors: Greg Hunter
  Board of Directors: Alison Beesley
  Board of Directors: Nancy Tartt
  Board of Directors: Aimee Fullman
Management:
  Founder/Artistic Director: Maida Withers
  Resident Composer and Musician: Steve Hilmy
  Visual Design and Dancer: Anthony Gongora
  Technical Production: Ayodamola Okunseinde
  Light Design: Michael A. Sperber
Mission: Project based company that creates/presents fresh and inspiring one of a kind dance works and films, conceived and choreographed by Maida Withers, that have social/political relevance in today's global society. Withers also creates site-specific works: recent projects include street performances in Washington, DC, the Lenin Museum in Krasnoyarsk, Siberia, Russia.
Founded: 1974
Specialized Field: Post-Modern Dance; New Media; Multi-Media Dance
Status: Non-Profit; Professional
Paid Staff: 2
Volunteer Staff: 15
Paid Artists: 10
Non-paid Artists: 10
Budget: $89,000
Income Sources: Box Office; US Department of State; Foundation/Corporation Support; Individual
Performs At: Betts Marvin Theatre
Affiliations: DC International Improvisation Plus Festival
Annual Attendance: 2000
Facility Category: Theatres; Sites; Festivals;
Type of Stage: Proscenium & Galleries/Museums

147
MOMENTUM DANCE THEATRE
651 E Street NE
Washington, DC 20002
Phone: 202-785-0035
e-mail: momentumdancetheatre@verizon.net
Web Site: momentumdancetheatre.com
Management:
  Artistic Director: Roberta Rothstein
  Associate Director: Kim Curtis

DANCE / Florida

Mission: To provide performance, training, and educational activities in the performing arts to entertain and challenge its audiences and to encourage dance training throughout the lifespan.

148
ST. MARK'S DANCE STUDIO
The Arts At St Mark's
St. Mark's Episcopal Church
301 A Street SE
Washington, DC 20003
Phone: 202-543-0053
Web Site: www.stmarks.net/arts/dance.html
Management:
    Artistic Director: Rosetta Brooks
    Ballet Mistress: Dorothy Rogers-Walker
    Director of Music: Jeff Kempskie
Mission: To support the arts in the St. Mark's community by providing opportunities for each parishioner to develop and expand his or her creativity as an expression of spiritual life.
Founded: 1991
Specialized Field: Ballet; Jazz
Paid Staff: 4
Volunteer Staff: 3
Budget: $40,000-$100,000
Income Sources: Tuition
Performs At: St. Mark's Church

149
WASHINGTON BALLET
3515 Wisconsin Avenue NW
Washington, DC 20016
Phone: 202-362-3606
Fax: 202-362-1311
e-mail: info@washingtonballet.org
Web Site: www.washingtonballet.org
Officers:
    Chairman: Sylvia A. de Leon
    Vice Chair: Eve Auchincloss Lilley
    President: Maureen Doyle Berk
    Treasurer: Armeane Choksi
    Secretary: Jean Marie Fernandez
    Finance Director: Shakira Segundo
Management:
    Artistic Director: Septime Webre
    Associate Artistic Director: David Palmer
    Ballet Master: Elaine Kudo
    Ballet Master: Scott Speck
    School Director: Kee Juan Han
    Managing Director: Arthur Espinoza
    Company Manager: Nick Mullikin
    Production Stage Manager: Edward R. Cucurello
    Marketing, Communications Manager: Elizabeth Chu
Mission: The company is dedicated to presenting the best in classical and contemporary ballet and is devoted to bringing ballet to broad communities throughout Washington DC.
Utilizes: Artists-in-Residence; Choreographers; Collaborating Artists; Commissioned Music; Dancers; Five Seasonal Concerts; Guest Artists; Guest Companies; Guest Conductors; High School Drama; Resident Professionals; Sign Language Translators; Soloists; Student Interns
Founded: 1976
Specialized Field: Ballet
Paid Staff: 25
Volunteer Staff: 15
Budget: $6 million
Income Sources: Earned; Donations
Performs At: John F Kennedy Center for the Performing Arts; Warner Theatre
Organization Type: Performing; Touring

Florida

150
BOCA BALLET THEATRE
7630 NW 6th Avenue
Boca Raton, FL 33487
Phone: 561-955-0709
Fax: 561-995-8356
e-mail: mail@bocaballet.org
Web Site: www.bocaballet.org
Officers:
    President: Seth A. Marmor
    Treasurer: Laurie Udine
    Vice President: Vanessa Boltz
    Secretary: Sharon Alpert
Management:
    Artistic/Executive Director: Dan Guin
    Co Artistic Director: Jane Tyree
    Director: Vanessa Boltz
    Director: Anne Henderson
Mission: To enrich the cultural landscape of our community and educate our youth in classical ballet and concert dance through focused training, interaction with professional dancers and participation in full-length ballets and contemporary choreography.
Founded: 1990
Specialized Field: Modern; Jazz; Ballet; Pilates
Status: Non-Profit; Non-Professional
Paid Staff: 6
Volunteer Staff: 50
Budget: $875,000
Performs At: FAU University Theatre
Annual Attendance: 5,000
Seating Capacity: 498

151
MOMENTUM DANCE COMPANY
PO Box 331973
Coconut Grove, FL 33233
Phone: 305-858-7002
e-mail: mdanceco@bellsouth.net
Web Site: www.mometumdance.com
Management:
    Artistic Director: Delma Iles
Mission: To develop and educate the audience for dance in South Florida, with emphasis on non-traditional and modern dance forms; and to educate and train students for the purposes of professional careers as well as personal appreciation and enjoyment of dance.
Utilizes: Five Seasonal Concerts; Singers
Founded: 1982
Specialized Field: Modern; Ballet; Jazz
Status: Professional; Non-Profit
Paid Staff: 2
Paid Artists: 10
Budget: $100,000-$200,000
Income Sources: Government; Earned; Foundations; Contributions
Annual Attendance: 5,000-7,000
Organization Type: Performing; Touring; Resident; Educational

152
NORTHWEST FLORIDA BALLET
310 Terry Avenue SE
Fort Walton Beach, FL 32548
Phone: 850-664-7787
Fax: 850-664-0130
Web Site: www.nfballet.org
Officers:
    President: Kevin Greene
    Treasurer: Paul Scarpulla
    VP: Denise Greene
    Board Member: Deedee Bruechner
    Secretary: Nia Kellogg
    CEO: Todd Allen
Management:
    Artistic Director: Todd Eric Allen
    Assistant Artistic Director: Sharon Allen
    Ballet Mistress: Dorothytte Daniels Lister
    Office Manager: Rhonda Starnes
    Bookkeeper: Cindy Hinton
    Marketing Assistant: Megan Fontaine
Mission: To provide quality dance performances and instruction for Northwest Florida, to identify and develop talented dancers and increase appreciation of the arts through public education and outreach.
Utilizes: Five Seasonal Concerts
Founded: 1969
Specialized Field: Ballet
Paid Staff: 12
Budget: $200,000-$500,000
Income Sources: Florida Dance Association
Performs At: The Sanger Theatre
Annual Attendance: 7,000-10,000
Organization Type: Performing; Touring; Resident; Educational; Sponsoring

153
DANCE ALIVE NATIONAL BALLET
1325 NW Second Street
Gainesville, FL 32601
Phone: 352-373-1166
Fax: 352-373-1166
e-mail: dance@pofahlstudios.com
Web Site: www.dancealive.org
Officers:
    President: Bryan da Frota
    VP: Weaver Gaines
    Secretary: Susan Scannella
    Treasurer: Tim Cannon
Management:
    Artistic Director: Kim Tuttle
    Residence Choreographer: Judy Skinner
    Office Manager: Sally McDonell
    Director of Development: Linda Rocha
Mission: Dance Alive National Ballet, State Touring Company of Florida is based in Gainesville. With a cast of superb international dancers, the Company presents ravishing classical and the most provocative of contemporary dance. From sensuality and athleticism to the neoclassical beauty of Balanchine with humor, passion and jazzy playfulness, this company does it all.
Specialized Field: Classical Ballet; Contemporary Dance
Season: October-December
Performs At: Curtis M Phillips Center
Type of Stage: Proscenium Hall, Black Box Theatre
Seating Capacity: 1,700, 200

154
FLORIDA BALLET AT JACKSONVILLE
300 E State Street
Suite E
Jacksonville, FL 32202
Phone: 904-353-7518
Fax: 904-353-7709
e-mail: floridaballet@floridaballet.org
Web Site: floridaballet.org
Officers:
    President: Marc Sellers
    VP: Leila LeVan
    Treasurer: Jim Monahan
    Secretary: Suzanne Jenkins
Management:
    Artistic Director: Laurie Picinich-Byrd

DANCE / Florida

Administrative Director: Linda Jenkins
Development Director: J. Stephen Jenkins
Mission: To take a contemporary approach to performance of classical guest choreographers' ballet.
Utilizes: Five Seasonal Concerts
Founded: 1978
Specialized Field: Ballet
Status: Professional; Nonprofit
Budget: $40,000-$100,000
Organization Type: Performing; Touring; Resident

155
JACKSONVILLE BALLET THEATRE
10131 Atlantic Boulevard
Jacksonville, FL 32225
Phone: 904-727-7515
e-mail: jaxballettheatre@yahoo.com
Web Site: jacksonvilleballettheatre.com
Officers:
   President: David R Sutton Jr MD
Management:
   Artistic Director: Duce Anaya
Mission: To Bgive Jacksonville dancers the opportunity to participate in original choreographies of full-length classical and modern works, present high quality ballet performances for the benefit of the community and to encourage appreciation for and enjoyment of the art of dance.
Founded: 1970
Specialized Field: Ballet
Performs At: Civic Auditorium
Organization Type: Performing; Educational

156
KEY WEST CONTEMPORARY DANCE COMPANY
916 Pohalski Street
Key West, FL 33040
Phone: 508-971-4695
e-mail: info@poorme.org
Web Site: dancekeywest.org
Mission: Dedicated to initiating, illuminating, and inspiring art in the physical form; building contemporary danceworks to regale, stimulate, and share with the public, serving as an educator, descendant and impetus to the continuance of contemporary dance in life.
Status: Nonprofit
Organization Type: Touring, Performing

157
DANCE NOW! MIAMI
212 NE 59 Terrace
Miami, FL 33137
Phone: 305-975-8489
e-mail: info@dancenowmiami.org
Web Site: dancenowmiami.org
Management:
   Artistic Director: Hannah Baumgarten
   Artistic Director: Diego Salterini
Mission: To promote the artistic vision of co-founders Hannah Baumgarten and Diego Salterini. The company creates, promotes, and produces contemporary dance of the highest caliber and makes the art accessible to diverse audiences locally, nationally, and internationally.
Founded: 2000

158
FLORIDA DANCE ASSOCIATION
PO Box 415818
Miami, FL 33141-7818
Phone: 305-547-1117
Fax: 786-472-4178
Web Site: www.floridadanceassociation.org
Officers:
   President: Ric Rose
   Vice President: Anjali Austin
Management:
   Director of Operations: Bill Doolin
Mission: To encourage excellence, support artistic and cultural diversity in dance, and increase opportunities for all people to experience dance and the arts.
Founded: 1972
Specialized Field: Ethnic Dance
Status: Professional, Nonprofit
Paid Staff: 2
Volunteer Staff: 10
Paid Artists: 40
Budget: $400,000
Income Sources: Sponsors; Foundations; Corporate; Community Partners
Affiliations: Dance/USA; National Performance Network; Florida Cultural Alliance; Association of Performing Arts Presenters
Organization Type: Educational; Sponsoring; Service

159
VLADIMIR ISSAEV'S SCHOOL OF CLASSICAL BALLET
15939 Biscayne Boulevard
Miami, FL 33160
Phone: 305-948-4777
Fax: 888-935-1035
Web Site: www.clasicalballetschool.com
Management:
   Artistic Director/Ballet Master: Vladimir Issaev
Mission: To enhance the lives of all who learn with us and while we shall demand from each student, whether or not a dance career is planned, the best effort of which he or she is capable, we shall give in return the care and attention that each student deserves.
Specialized Field: Ballet; Pointe; Jazz; Tap
Status: Professional
Affiliations: Arts Ballet Theatre of Florida
Facility Category: 2,200 Square Feet/2 Studios/Marley Covered Spring Floors

160
MIAMI CITY BALLET
2200 Liberty Avenue
Miami Beach, FL 33139
Phone: 305-929-7010
Web Site: www.miamicityballet.org
Officers:
   Chairman: Susan D. Kronick
   Vice Chairman: Ana Marie Codina Barlick
   Treasurer: Ron Esserman
   Chief Financial Officer: Jonah Pruitt, III
Management:
   Founding Artistic Director: Edward Villella
   Executive Vice President, Artistic: Pamela Gardiner
   Principal Ballet Mistress: Roma Sosenko
   Artistic Director: Lourdes Lopez
   Executive Director: Jonah Pruitt
   Company Manager: Anne Camille Hersh
   Ballet Mistress: Joan Latham
   Principal Conductor: Maestro Gary Sheldon
   Production Stage Manager: Nicole M. Mitchell
Mission: From Edward Villella, the creative inspiration and artistic soul of the company, to the dancers whose artistry and talent have awed a nation, Miami City Ballet brings a gold standard of excellence to the cultural landscape of our community.
Utilizes: Five Seasonal Concerts; Guest Artists; Singers
Founded: 1986
Specialized Field: Ballet
Status: Professional, Nonprofit
Budget: $10.7 million
Performs At: The Naples Philharmonic Center
Organization Type: Performing; Touring; Resident

161
SURFSCAPE CONTEMPORARY DANCE THEATRE
563 Caro Court
New Smyrna Beach, FL 32168
Phone: 386-366-5108
e-mail: contact@surfscapedance.org
Web Site: surfscapedance.org
Management:
   Artistic Director: Rachael Leonard
   Artistic Director: Kristin Polizzi
Founded: 2005
Specialized Field: Contemporary Dance
Status: Nonprofit
Paid Artists: 18

162
CENTRAL FLORIDA BALLET
3306 Maggie Boulevard, Suite B
Orlando, FL 32811
Phone: 407-849-9948
Fax: 407-203-8905
e-mail: vpetrutiu@centralfloridaballet.com
Web Site: centralfloridaballet.com
Management:
   Executive Director: Vasile Petrutiu
   Artistic Director: Vladimir Bykov
   Marketing Coordinator: Kailey Klopfenstein
Mission: To entertain, educate, and inspire through the universal art form of dance. With a diverse repertoire of dance productions and programs from classical to contemporary and beyond, each attendee is to be culturally enriched while developing an appreciation for the arts.
Founded: 2001
Specialized Field: Ballet
Status: Nonprofit

163
ORLANDO BALLET
1111 N Orange Avenue
Orlando, FL 32804
Phone: 407-426-1733
Fax: 407-426-1734
e-mail: jleon@orlandoballet.org
Web Site: www.orlandoballet.org
Officers:
   President: Ava Doppelt
   Executive VP: Jose Fajardo
   Treasurer: Matthew Ahearn
   Secretary: Judy Sandefur
Management:
   Artistic Director: Robert Hill
   Director of Production: Larry Rayburn
   Costume Director: Eddy Frank Fernandez
   Managing Director: Katherine Fabian
   Assistant to the Artistic Director: Joey Lynn Mann
   Ballet Mistress: Yan Chen
   Director of Development: Kathleen Berman
   Marketing Director: Rey Tabarrok
   Director of Finance and Personnel: Anna Miller
Mission: Orlando Ballet has grown to become Central Florida's only professional resident ballet company and is one of the few ballet companies of its size and budget that is performing the full length classical ballets.
Utilizes: Artists-in-Residence; Choreographers; Collaborations; Commissioned Composers; Commissioned Music; Dance Companies; Dancers; Educators; Five Seasonal Concerts; Grant Writers;

DANCE / Florida

Guest Accompanists; Guest Artists; Guest Companies; Guest Composers; Guest Conductors; Guest Ensembles; Guest Instructors; Guest Musical Directors; Guest Musicians; Guest Soloists; High School Drama; Instructors; Local Artists; Lyricists; Multimedia; Organization Contracts; Original Music Scores; Resident Artists; Resident Professionals; Soloists; Visual Arts
Founded: 1973
Specialized Field: Ballet
Status: Professional, Nonprofit
Paid Staff: 53
Volunteer Staff: 2
Paid Artists: 28
Budget: $4.5 million
Income Sources: State Dance Association of Florida
Annual Attendance: 100,000
Organization Type: Performing; Touring; Sponsoring

164
RUSSIAN BALLET OF ORLANDO
618 North Mills Ave.
Orlando, FL 32803
Phone: 407-896-0309
Fax: 407-275-2405
e-mail: info@russianacademyofballet.com
Web Site: www.russianballetoforlando.org
Officers:
   President: Michele Paymer
Management:
   Artistic Director: Irina Depler
Mission: To sponsor students of the Russian Academy of Ballet of all ages and levels, and to give them opportunity to perform in profesional quality performances.
Founded: 1989
Specialized Field: Russian Ballet

165
BALLET PALM BEACH
The Esther Center 10357 Ironwood Road
Palm Beach Garden, FL 33410
Phone: 561-630-8235
e-mail: company@balletpalmbeach.org
Web Site: balletpalmbeach.org
Management:
   Artistic Director: Colleen Smith
Specialized Field: Ballet

166
BALLET PENSACOLA
400 S Jefferson Street
Pensacola, FL 32502
Phone: 850-432-9546
Fax: 850-432-3297
e-mail: board@balletpensacola.com
Web Site: www.balletpensacola.com
Officers:
   President: Edward Sheffield
   Secretary: Terri Gatton
   Treasurer: Peter Heckathorn
   Vice President of Development: Lisa Greskovich
   Vice President of Marketing: Janice Cooper Holmes
Management:
   Artistic Director: Richard Steinert
   Interim Director, Dev, Marketing: Raven Holloway
   Ballet Mistress: Christine Duhon
   Production Designer: Lance Brannon
   Office Manager: Marsha Suarez
Mission: To enhance the cultural life of the community by developing an appreciation and knowledge of the art of dance through excellent dance training and quality performances.

Utilizes: Singers
Founded: 1978
Specialized Field: Dance
Status: Professional, Nonprofit
Income Sources: Private; Corporate; Fundraising; Grants; Foundations
Performs At: The Sanger Theatre
Annual Attendance: 8,000
Organization Type: Performing; Resident; Educational

167
FREDDICK BRATCHER & COMPANY
525 Jeffrey Drive
Saint Augustine, FL 32086
Phone: 305-302-8947
e-mail: fbcompany@att.net
Web Site: www.freddickbratcherandcompany.com
Management:
   Founding Artistic Director: Freddick Bratcher
Mission: To provide local audiences with superior quality jazz, modern, classical and narrative choreographic works and to offer local talent a challenging and rewarding opportunity to mature artistically in a creative environment.
Utilizes: Five Seasonal Concerts; Singers
Founded: 1980
Specialized Field: Contemporary Dance
Status: Professional, Nonprofit
Performs At: Gusman Center for the Performing Arts
Organization Type: Performing; Touring; Educational

168
FUZION DANCE ARTISTS INC.
8437 Tuttle Avenue #160
Sarasota, FL 34243
Phone: 941-345-5755
e-mail: fuziondance@gmail.com
Web Site: fuziondance.org
Management:
   Artistic Director: Leymis Bolanos Wilmott
Mission: To bring contemporary dance to the community through eclectic performance and educational programming while collaborating with artists and community groups to further enrich the human experience.
Founded: 2006
Status: Nonprofit

169
SARASOTA BALLET OF FLORIDA
5555 N Tamiami Trail
Sarasota, FL 34243
Phone: 941-359-0099
Fax: 941-358-1504
Toll-free: 866-722-5538
e-mail: maservian@sarasotaballet.org
Web Site: www.sarasotaballet.org
Officers:
   Chairman: Hillary Steele
   Founder: Jean Allenby-Weidner
   Vice Chair: Sally Yanowitz
   Secretary: Peggy Abt
   Treasurer: Robert Zabelle
   Governance Officer: John Simon
Management:
   Artistic Director: Iain Webb
   Assistant Director: Margaret Barbieri
   Development Director: Brenda Terris
   Managing Director: Mary Anne Servian
   Sales & Marketing Director: Mike Marraccini
   Stage Manager: Mark Noble
   Company Manager: Susan Reeves
   Director of Education: Dex Honea

Mission: To be committed to artistic excellence through the presentation of the highest quality of classical and contemporary dance, through the encouragement of choreographic talent, through the ongoing expansion of education programs and opportunities for community outreach and service.
Utilizes: Choreographers; Dancers; Lyricists; Organization Contracts
Founded: 1990
Specialized Field: Ballet
Paid Staff: 24
Volunteer Staff: 10
Paid Artists: 28
Budget: $2,500,000
Income Sources: Ticket Sales; Foundation and Corporate Grants; Individual Donations
Performs At: Van Wezel Performing Arts Hall; FSU Center for the Performing Arts
Affiliations: Sarasota Ballet Association
Annual Attendance: 35,000
Seating Capacity: 1700 and 500

170
THOMAS ARMOUR YOUTH BALLET
5818 SW 73rd Street
South Miami, FL 33143
Phone: 305-667-5543
Fax: 305-667-1024
e-mail: info@thomasarmouryouthballet.org
Web Site: www.thomasarmouryouthballet.org
Management:
   Program Administrator: Camila Escobar
   Director and Ballet Instructor: Ruth Wiesen
   Registrar & Operations: Marina Ilinskaya
   Office Administrator: Addyson Fonte
Mission: The Thomas Armour Youth Ballet puts an emphasis on community outreach, ballet education and making the world of ballet accessible to under privileged youth both as audience members and as performers.
Utilizes: Dancers; Educators; Five Seasonal Concerts; Guest Artists; Instructors; Local Talent; Students; Visual Designers
Founded: 1951
Specialized Field: Ballet; Tap
Status: Non-Professional, Non-Profit
Paid Staff: 30
Budget: $119,000
Income Sources: Private; Foundations; Corporate and Government
Performs At: Dade County Auditorium and Public Schools
Annual Attendance: 9,000
Organization Type: Performing; Resident

171
THE ACADEMY OF BALLET ARTS
2914 First Avenue N
St Petersburg, FL 33713
Phone: 727-327-4401
Web Site: www.academyofballetarts.org
Management:
   Artistic Director: Suzanne Pomerantzeff
Mission: To develop each student's creative potential by allowing them to express their individual ideas and emotions through the beauty of movement.
Founded: 1969
Specialized Field: Ballet
Status: Professional, Non-Profit
Paid Staff: 7
Volunteer Staff: 6
Non-paid Artists: 15
Income Sources: Tuition; Fundraising; Donations
Annual Attendance: 1,000

DANCE / Georgia

172
THE TALLAHASSEE BALLET
218 E Third Avenue
Tallahassee, FL 32303
Mailing Address: P.O. Box 772, Tallahassee, FL 32302
Phone: 850-224-6917
Fax: 850-224-7681
e-mail: info@TallahasseeBallet.org
Web Site: www.tallahasseeballet.org
Officers:
  President: Holly Edenfield
  Treasurer: Blaine Click
  Recording Secretary: Shelby Augustyniak
  Guild Chair: Marianne Brooks
Management:
  Executive Director: Janet Pichard
  Artistic Director: Tyrone Brooks
  Ballet Mistress, Artistic Associate: Lauren Owen
  Education & School Finance Director: Keisha Calderon
Mission: The Tallahassee Ballet is a non-profit dance company which provides an outstanding training ground for emerging professionals while stimulating appreciation of the dance arts through quality productions of classical and contemporary works.
Utilizes: Five Seasonal Concerts; Guest Companies; Singers
Founded: 1972
Specialized Field: Ballet
Status: Non-profit, Semi-Professional
Paid Staff: 4
Volunteer Staff: 3
Non-paid Artists: 55
Budget: $200,000-$500,000
Income Sources: Ticket Revenue; Advertising Sales; Memberships; Annual Fundraisers
Performs At: Ruby Diamond Auditorium; Opperman Music Hall
Affiliations: Florida Dance Association
Annual Attendance: 7,000-10,000
Organization Type: Performing; Resident; Educational

173
FIRETHORN DANCE ACADEMY
10630 N 56th Street
Suite 3
Temple Terrace, FL 33617
Phone: 813-985-2555
e-mail: info@firethorn-dance.com
Web Site: www.firethorn-dance.com
Management:
  Director/Instructor: Carine Puckett
Mission: Firethorn has provided quality dance training for dancers of all levels in a friendly and enjoyable environment.
Founded: 1979
Specialized Field: Modern; Ballet; Jazz; Tap; Hip Hop
Paid Staff: 2

174
BALLET FLORIDA
500 Fern Street
West Palm Beach, FL 33401
Phone: 561-659-1212
Fax: 561-659-2222
Web Site: www.balletflorida.com
Management:
  Founding Artistic Director: Marie Hale
  Ballet Mistress: Claudia Cravey
  Ballet Master: Steven Hoff
Mission: To produce and present ballets danced by professional dancers; create an eclectic repertoire choreographed by contemporary choreographers of note or of historical importance; maintain the highest levels of design and production; reach, expose and educate the widest audience possible with its programs.
Utilizes: Five Seasonal Concerts
Founded: 1986
Specialized Field: Ballet; Contemporary Ballet
Status: Professional, Nonprofit
Paid Staff: 60
Volunteer Staff: 8
Budget: $4,500,000
Income Sources: Grants; Foundations; Corporate; Private Sponsors
Performs At: Eissey Theatre; Kravis Center for the Performing Arts
Organization Type: Performing; Touring; Resident; Educational

175
FIRETHORN DANCE ACADEMY
10630 N 56th Street
Suite 208-211
indianapolis, FL 33617
Phone: 813-985-2555
e-mail: info@firethorn-dance.com
Web Site: www.firethorn-dance.com
Management:
  Director/Instructor: Carine Puckett
  Instructor of Acrobatics: Alison Jones
  Instructor of Jazz and Lyrical: Danielle Hargis
  Instructor of Modern: Victoria Heldreth
  Instructor of Tap: Kimberly Terenzi
  Instructor of Ballet, Jazz: Teal Trombetta
Mission: Firethorn has provided quality dance training for dancers of all levels in a friendly and enjoyable environment.
Founded: 1979
Specialized Field: Modern; Ballet; Jazz; Tap; Hip Hop
Paid Staff: 2

Georgia

176
REFUGE DANCE COMPANY
4566 Grove Park Way NW
Acworth, GA 30101
Phone: 678-630-9600
e-mail: info@refugedance.org
Web Site: refugedance.org
Management:
  Artistic Director: Katherine Gant
  Executive Director: David Gant
  Choreographer: Angella Foster
Mission: To present innovative works that display the dancer in an authentic manner as both a person and an artist with the goal of presenting dance in a way that is accessible for everyone, and to equip and train the next generation as leaders of the dance world.
Founded: 2006
Status: Nonprofit

177
UGA BALLET ENSEMBLE
University of Georgia
263 Dance Building
Athens, GA 30602-3653
Phone: 706-542-4415
Fax: 706-542-4084
e-mail: ugadance@uga.edu
Web Site: www.dance.uga.edu
Management:
  Associate Professor of Dance: Joan Buttram
  Associate Professor of Dance: Rebecca Gose Enghauser
  Professor of Dance: Lisa Fusillo
  Professor of Dance: Mark Wheeler
  Lecturer of Dance: Janet Robertson
  Professor of Dance: Lisa Fusillo
  Business Manager I: Betty Disharoon Prickett
  Technical Director: Christopher Fleming
Mission: The UGA Department of Dance provides a variety of performance company options focused towards pre-professional training, student choreography and student performance. These companies provide performances to local, community, state, national and international audiences.
Founded: 1993
Specialized Field: Ballet
Status: Non-Profit, Pre-Professional
Paid Staff: 3
Volunteer Staff: 3
Income Sources: UGA Foundation; Student Activities; Grant Support

178
UGA CORE CONCERT DANCE COMPANY
263 Dance Building, University of Georgia
Athens, GA 30602-3653
Phone: 706-542-4415
Fax: 706-542-4084
e-mail: ugadance@uga.edu
Web Site: www.coreconcertdance.edu
Management:
  Artistic Director: Bala Sarasvati
Mission: The UGA Department of Dance provides a variety of performance company options focused towards pre-professional training, student choreography and student performance. These companies provide performances to local, community, state, national, and international audiences.
Founded: 1991
Specialized Field: Modern; Ballet
Status: Non-Profit, Pre-Professional
Paid Staff: 3
Volunteer Staff: 3
Annual Attendance: 1,200

179
ATLANTA BALLET
1695 Marietta Boulevard NW
Atlanta, GA 30318
Phone: 404-873-5811
Fax: 404-874-7905
e-mail: jmcfall@atlantaballet.com
Web Site: www.atlantaballet.com
Officers:
  President & CEO: Arturo Jacobus
  Chief Operating Officer: Pamela Whitacre
  Accounting Manager: Ashley Reid
  Company Manager: Bradley Renner
  Marketing Assistant: Lauren Wilson
  Public Relations Manager: Sigele Winbush
  Marketing Coordinator: Kelly Pierce
  Group Sales Manager: Myredith Gonzales
Management:
  Artistic Director: John McFall
  Ballet Mistress: Sarah Hillmer
  Ballet Mistress: Rosemary Miles
  Ballet Mistress: Sharon Story
  Ballet Mistress: Dale Shields
  Costume Director: Tamara Cobus
  Director of Marketing: Tricia Ekholm
  Director of Development: Lisa Dabney
  Technical Director: John Beaulieu
Mission: To provide professional ballet performances for the people of metropolitan Atlanta and the surrounding area.

DANCE / Georgia

Utilizes: Choreographers; Dancers; Guest Artists; Guest Companies; Guest Conductors; Resident Artists; Singers
Founded: 1929
Specialized Field: Ballet
Status: Professional, Nonprofit
Paid Staff: 27
Paid Artists: 45
Budget: $6.6 million
Income Sources: National Association for Regional Ballet; Corporate; Tuition
Performs At: Fabulous Fox Theatre; Cobb Energy Performing Arts Centre
Annual Attendance: 60,000
Facility Category: Theatre
Seating Capacity: 4,500; 2,750
Rental Contact: Gene Conroy
Organization Type: Performing; Touring; Resident

180
BALLETHNIC DANCE COMPANY
2587 Cheney Street
PO Box 7749
Atlanta, GA 30344
Phone: 404-762-1416
Fax: 404-762-6319
e-mail: Karenid@ballethnic.org
Web Site: www.ballethnic.org
Management:
   Co-Founder/Co-Artistic Director: Nena Gilreath
   Co-Founder/Co-Artistic Director: Waverly Lucas
   Company Photographer: Kris Roberts
   Academy Administrator: Toren Steele
   Parent Organization President: Karen Rivers
   Marketing, Communications: Thomas Vanderbilt
   Official Fine Artist: Raymond Cody
   Rehearsal Instructor: Lydia Mitchell
   Technical Support Consultant: James Seals
Mission: Ballethnic Dance Company is a classically trained, culturally diverse professional performing company producing innovative performances of artistic excellence and is committed to providing opportunities to those who are overlooked because of race and ethnicity.
Founded: 1990
Specialized Field: Ballet
Status: Professional, Non-Profit
Paid Staff: 4
Volunteer Staff: 8
Paid Artists: 9
Non-paid Artists: 5
Income Sources: Foundations; Corporate
Performs At: Robert Far Center

181
DANCING ON COMMON GROUND
PO Box 88674
Atlanta, GA 30338
Phone: 770-454-8651
e-mail: top@america.net
Mission: Using exciting choreography and traditional and original music, Dancing on Common Ground takes the audience on a thrilling adventure from the arrival of the irish during the potato famine of 1848 through the evolution of irish dance and music into its present day american forms.
Specialized Field: Theatrical Dance; Traditional Dance

182
FULL RADIUS DANCE
PO Box 54453
Atlanta, GA 30308
Phone: 404-724-9663
Fax: 404-724-9663
e-mail: fullradiusdance@aol.com
Web Site: www.fullradiusdance.org
Officers:
   Chairman: Marcelo Roman
   Vice Chairman: David Cable
Management:
   Artistic/Executive Director: Douglas Scott
   Theatre Artist/Lighting Designer: Joseph Futral
Mission: To promote, advance and enhance the modern dance form for persons with disabilities, for dance artists and the general community.
Utilizes: Dancers; Original Music Scores
Founded: 1991
Specialized Field: Modern
Status: Non-Profit, Professional
Paid Staff: 1
Volunteer Staff: 8
Budget: $70,000
Income Sources: Private; Government; Corporations; Business; Earned
Annual Attendance: 9,000

183
THE MYSTICAL ARTS OF TIBET
1781 Dresden Drive
Atlanta, GA 30319
Phone: 404-982-6437
Fax: 404-982-6435
e-mail: mystical@drepung.org
Web Site: www.mysticalartsoftibet.org
Management:
   Director: Lobsang Tenzin
   Assistant Director: Irene S Lee
Mission: The Mystical Arts of Tibet is a world tour to promote peace and healing by sharing Tibet's rich and authentic sacred performing and visual arts with modern audiences. The two most requested programs are the Sacred Music Sacred Dance performance and Mandala Sand Painting exhibition.
Founded: 1991
Specialized Field: World Music
Status: Non-Profit; Professional
Paid Staff: 6
Income Sources: Performances
Organization Type: Performing; Touring

184
BEACON DANCE COMPANY
PO Box 1553
Decatur, GA 30031-1553
Phone: 404-377-2929
Fax: 404-377-2929
e-mail: info@beacondance.org
Web Site: www.beacondance.org
Officers:
   VP: Ann Ritter
   Secretary: Maggie Turlington
Management:
   Artistic Director: D Patton White, patton@beacondance.org
   Independent Stage Manager: Eleanor Brownfield
   Independent Landscape Designer: Susan Keller
   Writer, Designer: Lynn Hesse
   Community & Economic Development: Emelyne Williams
Mission: To develop peoples's understanding of the art of movement as a means of communication.
Utilizes: Actors; Artists-in-Residence; Choreographers; Collaborating Artists; Collaborations; Community Members; Dance Companies; Dancers; Educators; Filmmakers; Five Seasonal Concerts; Guest Accompanists; Guest Artists; Guest Companies; Guest Designers; Guest Soloists; Guest Speakers; Guest Teachers; Instructors; Lyricists; Multi Collaborations; Original Music Scores; Paid Performers; Sign Language Translators; Student Interns; Theatre Companies
Founded: 1952
Specialized Field: Modern; Ballet; Jazz
Status: Professional, Nonprofit
Volunteer Staff: 12
Non-paid Artists: 1
Budget: $20,000
Income Sources: Earned Income; Grants; Contributions
Performs At: Beacon Hill Arts Center Studio Theatre
Annual Attendance: 4,000
Organization Type: Performing; Educational

185
CORE PERFORMANCE COMPANY
PO Box 2045
Decatur, GA 30031-2045
Phone: 404-373-4154
Fax: 404-377-1815
e-mail: pattonw@COREdance.org
Web Site: www.coredance.org
Officers:
   Managing Director: Elizabeth Geiger
   Communications: Jenny Costantino
   Company and Production Manager: D. Patton White
Management:
   Artistic Director: Sue Schroeder
   Studio and Operations: Rose Caudle
   Technology Mgr: Claiborne White
   Outreach Coordinator: Juana Farfan
Mission: To create, present and produce contemporary dance.
Founded: 1980
Specialized Field: Contemporary Dance
Status: Non-Profit, Professional
Paid Staff: 3
Volunteer Staff: 2
Paid Artists: 6
Budget: $270,000
Income Sources: Foundations; Corporate; Individual
Affiliations: The Field
Annual Attendance: 80,000
Facility Category: Studio Theater

186
NORTHEAST ATLANTIC BALLET
4047 Darling Court
Lilburn, GA 30017
Phone: 770-921-7277
e-mail: balletensemble@yahoo.com
Web Site: www.northeastatlantaballet.org
Officers:
   President: Marsha Byokawski
   Treasurer: Teresa Klein
   Secretary: Patti Huggins
   Director: Debi Thomas
   Director: Rhonda Williams
   Director: Cheryl Thomas
   Director: Inessa Yavnel
Management:
   Artistic Director: Jennifer Byokawski-Gordon
Mission: Mission and purpose is to provide performing opportunities to talented young dancers and to provide quality arts programming at prices affordable to families of all socioeconomic groups.
Founded: 1996
Specialized Field: Ballet; Jazz; Tap
Status: Non-Profit

DANCE / Hawaii

187
GEORGIA BALLET
1255 Field Parkway
Marietta, GA 30066
Phone: 770-528-0881
Fax: 770-528-0891
e-mail: info@georgiaballet.org
Web Site: www.georgiaballet.com
  School Director:
Management:
  Artistic Director: Gina Hyatt-Mazon
  Executive Director/School Director: Michele Ziemann-Devos
  Ballet Mistress: Gina Hyatt Mazon
  Ballet Master: Janusz Mazon
  Assistant School Director: Kara Hill-Protos
Mission: Dedicated to promoting excellence in ballet performance and training, fostering an increased public awareness and appreciation for dance, and providing dedicated and talented dancers with the opportunity for advanced training and professional preforming venues.
Founded: 1960
Specialized Field: Ballet
Status: Non-profit
Paid Staff: 5
Volunteer Staff: 15
Performs At: The Anderson Theatre
Annual Attendance: 19,500

188
GEORGIA DANCE CONSERVATORY
49 West Park Square
Marietta, GA 30060-1923
Phone: 770-426-0007
e-mail: info@georgiadance.com
Web Site: www.georgiadance.com
Officers:
  President: Sandra Ratchford
  Vice President: Courtney Kennedy
  Treasurer: Carmen Dillard
  President of the Guild: Judy Freeman
Management:
  Artistic Director: Ruth Mitchell
  Production Manager: Courtney Kennedy
Mission: To provide the community with a small, eclectic company to perform in places not suited for large ballet companies.
Utilizes: Five Seasonal Concerts
Founded: 1956
Specialized Field: Modern; Ballet; Jazz
Status: Professional, Nonprofit
Income Sources: National Association for Regional Ballet; Dance Coalition of Atlanta; Young Audiences of Atlanta
Organization Type: Performing; Touring

189
SIDEWAYS CONTEMPORARY DANCE COMPANY
920 Woodstock Road Suite 200
Roswell, GA 30075
Phone: 404-955-7232
e-mail: charlotte@sidewaysdance.com
Web Site: sidewaysdance.org
Management:
  Artistic Director: Charlotte Foster
Founded: 2006
Status: Nonprofit

190
ATLANTA FESTIVAL BALLET COMPANY AND SCHOOL
416 Eagle's Landing Parkway
Stockbridge, GA 30281
Phone: 770-507-2775
Fax: 770-507-9182
e-mail: contactus@atlantafestivalballet.com
Web Site: www.atlantafestivalballet.com
Officers:
  President: Betty Hall
  Treasurer: Bill Buchanan
  Secretary: Karen Beth Buckley
Management:
  Artistic Director: Gregory Aaron
  Artistic Director: Nicolas Pacana
  Company Manager: Gesielle DiBlasi
  Artistic Director: Joceyln Buchanan
Mission: To thrill and move our audience, dancers, choreographers, students, supporters and staff with art and discipline to enrich and inspire lives.
Founded: 1989
Specialized Field: Ballet
Status: Non-Profit, Professional
Paid Staff: 12
Volunteer Staff: 12
Paid Artists: 19
Non-paid Artists: 12
Budget: $300,000
Income Sources: Partners in Education; Grants; Donations; Ticket Sales
Affiliations: Clayton County Schools; Henry County Schools
Annual Attendance: 20,000

Hawaii

191
CONVERGENCE DANCE THEATRE
1159 Nuuanu
Honolulu, HI 96817
Phone: 808-542-9442
e-mail: convergencedance@gmail.com
Web Site: convergencedance.org
Management:
  Artistic Director: Jenny Shannon
Specialized Field: Contemporary Modern

192
HONOLULU DANCE STUDIO
1030 Queen Street, Suite 2B
Honolulu, HI 96814
Phone: 808-699-4199
e-mail: honoluludanceco.7@gmail.com
Web Site: honoluludanceco.com
Management:
  Director: Cathy Izumi
Mission: The Honolulu Dance Studio nurtures the process of perfection, preserving in dance excellence and persisting in purity of character. Perfection is our goal. Excellence is tolerated.
Founded: 1986

193
WEST HAWAII DANCE THEATRE
74-5626 Alapa Street
Kailua-Kona, HI 96740
Phone: 808-329-8876
Fax: 808-329-1033
e-mail: whdtheatre@gmail.com
Web Site: www.whdt.org
Management:
  Artistic Director: Virginia Holte, vh2dns4@ilhawaii.net
  Teacher/Choreographer/Designer: Megan Hoyt Chapman
Mission: The dance company sponsors educational outreach programs, public performances, guest artists and workshops while the academy provides professional dance training from preschool through advanced.
Founded: 1989
Specialized Field: Classical Ballet, Contemporary Dance, Modern, Jazz, Hip Hop, Hula, Yoga, Pilates Mat, Gyrotonic Expansion System

Idaho

194
BALLET IDAHO
Esther Simplot Performing Arts Academy
501 S 8th Street
Boise, ID 83702
Phone: 208-343-0556
Fax: 208-424-3129
e-mail: info@balletidaho.org
Web Site: www.balletidaho.org
Officers:
  President: Chris Privon
  Secretary: Christine Nicholas
  Vice President: Kathryn Zimmerman
Management:
  Artistic Director: Peter Anastos
  Executive Director: Paul Kaine
  Ballet Master: Alex Ossadnik
  Business Manager: Kim Wegener
  Marketing Director: Kim Kaine
  Academy Director: Emily Wallace
  Marketing Director: Meredith Stead
  Development Manager: KC Driscoll
  Academy Administrator: Leslie Asin
Mission: To promote the value of classical and contemporary dance in Idaho through excellence in performance and education.
Utilizes: Artists-in-Residence; Choreographers; Dancers; Designers; Five Seasonal Concerts; Guest Accompanists; Guest Artists; Guest Ensembles; Lyricists; Multimedia; Original Music Scores; Resident Artists; Resident Professionals; Student Interns
Founded: 1972
Specialized Field: Modern; Ballet
Status: Professional, Non-Profit
Paid Staff: 6
Paid Artists: 23
Budget: $1,150,000
Income Sources: Corporate; Foundations; Individual; Business Alliance
Season: September-May
Performs At: Morrison Center for the Performing Arts
Affiliations: Eugene Ballet Company
Annual Attendance: 14000
Seating Capacity: 2090
Organization Type: Performing; Touring; Resident; Educational; Sponsoring

195
IDAHO DANCE THEATRE
405 South 8th Street, Suite 305
Boise, ID 83702
Phone: 208-331-9592
e-mail: info@idahodancetheatre.org
Web Site: idahodancetheatre.org
Management:
  Executive/Artistic Director: Carl Rowe
  Artistic Director: Marla Brattain Hansen

DANCE / Illinois

Technical Director: Alfred Hansen
Company Manager: Jynx Jenkins
Mission: To create and perform superb contemporary dance that is personal, innovative, and exciting.
Status: Nonprofit

196
OINKARI BASQUE DANCERS
P.O. Box 1011
Boise, ID 83701
Phone: 208-557-1960
e-mail: info@oinkari.org
Web Site: www.oinkari.org
Officers:
- President: Lael Uberuaga
- Vice-President: Tyler Smith
- Secretary: Alaina Gavica
- Women's Dance Director: Amaya Criswell
- Men's Dance Director: Ben Monasterio
- Public Relations: Marie Monasterio

Management:
- Girls Dance Director: Toni Ansotegui
- Boys Dance Director: Dan Ansotegui

Mission: The promotion and enhancement of our culture through dance, song, language and education.
Utilizes: Guest Companies; Singers
Specialized Field: Ethnic Dance; Folk Dance
Status: Nonprofit
Paid Staff: 70
Income Sources: Euskaldunak
Performs At: Boise Basque Center
Organization Type: Performing; Touring; Educational

197
TREY MCINTYRE PROJECT
PO Box 2698
2285 Warm Springs Avenue
Boise, ID 83701
Phone: 877-867-2320
e-mail: info@treymcintyre.com
Web Site: www.treymcintyre.com
Officers:
- Chairman: Blair Kutrow
- President: Trey McIntyre
- Vice Chair: Richard Raimondi
- Treasurer: Nancy Einhorn
- Secretary: Virginia Friend
- Board Member: John Michael Schert
- Board Member: Frankie Hoover Gibson
- Board Member: Mark Aronchick
- Board Member: Bert Johnson

Management:
- Artistic Director: Trey McIntyre
- Executive Director: John Michael Schert
- Managing Director: Brian Aune
- Rehearsal Director: Christina Johnson
- Sr Development Manager: Caty Solace
- Development Manager: Heather Roberts
- Development Coordinator: K C Driscoll
- Sr Manager for Brand: Jane Naillon
- Sr Manager for Programs: Kristine Aune

Mission: Boise-based nonprofit arts organization founded to nurture, support and produce the artistic vision of artist Trey McIntyre. We believe in the power of art and dance to transform, heal and enlighten. Through our groundbreaking and award-winning methods, we engage with communities and audiences across the globe every year. We are every person who has seen a TMP performance, donated time or money, or engaged with us in a meaningful way.

Utilizes: Arrangers; Choreographers; Collaborating Artists; Collaborations; Community Talent; Dance Companies; Dancers; Educators; Fine Artists; Lyricists; Multi Collaborations; Paid Performers; Special Technical Talent; Theatre Companies
Founded: 1985
Specialized Field: Ballet, Modern, Contemporary, Jazz
Status: Non-Profit, Professional
Income Sources: Sponors, Donors
Season: Year Round
Performs At: Thalia Mara Hall, Grand Sierra Resort Casino, Ted Shaw Theater, EJ Thomas Hall, Morrison Center, Harris Theater of Dance

Illinois

198
BALLET CHICAGO
17 N. State Street, 19th Floor
Chicago, IL 60602
Phone: 312-251-8838
Fax: 312-251-8840
e-mail: info@balletchicago.org
Web Site: www.balletchicago.org
Officers:
- President: Spencer Wood
- VP: Daniel Duell
- Treasurer: Jared L. Pitman
- Secretary: Carolyn Metnick

Management:
- Artistic Director: Daniel Duell
- School Director: Patricia Blair
- Operations Director: Robert Bondlow
- Co-Artistic Director: Sara Ford
- Stage Manager: Andrew Glasenhardt
- Finance Manager: Ryan Uecke
- Marketing Manager: Margo Ruter
- Production Manager: Margaret Nelson
- Technical Director: Jacob Snodgrass

Mission: To develop future career classical dancers for Chicago and the dance world at large through the study and performance of the aesthetic and repertory of George Balanchine, this century's most influential and widely performed choreographer.
Utilizes: Guest Accompanists
Founded: 1987
Specialized Field: Ballet
Status: Pre-Professional, Nonprofit
Paid Staff: 20
Volunteer Staff: 5
Income Sources: Tuition; Performances; Donations; Corporate; Individual; Foundations
Performs At: Athenaeum Theatre
Annual Attendance: 20,000
Organization Type: Performing;Educational

199
BREATRIZ RODRIGUEZ
10 E. Randolph St.
Chicago, IL 60601
Phone: 312-739-0120
Fax: 312-739-0119
e-mail: thejoffery@aol.com
Web Site: www.joffrey.com
Officers:
- Chair: Zachary D. Lazar, Jr
- Vice Chair: Sonia Florian
- Vice Chair: Anne Kaplan
- Secretary: Ronald.J Allen
- Treasurer: Adam DeWitt
- Women's Board President: Liz Sharp

Management:
- Artistic Director: Ashley C Wheater

Executive Director: Greg Cameron
Music Director: Scott Speck
Ballet Master: Nicolas Blanc
Ballet Master: Gerard Charles
Ballet Master/Principal Coach: Graca Sales
General Manager: Laurie Garwood
Director of Production: Claude Binder

Mission: Unique american vision of ballet. Associated with Joffrey Ballet.
Specialized Field: Ballet; Traditional Dance

200
THE CHICAGO MOVING COMPANY
3035 N Hoyne Street
Chicago, IL 60618
Phone: 773-880-5402
Fax: 773-880-5402
e-mail: cmc@enteract.com
Web Site: www.chicagomovingcompany.org
Officers:
- Board Director: Jeff Abell
- Board Director: Larry Blust
- Board Director: Chris Gent
- Board Director: Jeff Spahn
- Board Director: Lois Grossman
- Board Director: Nana Shineflug

Management:
- Artistic Co-Director: Nana Shineflug
- Managing Director: Kay Wendt Lasota
- Technical Director: Jacob Snodgrass
- Special Projects Coordinator: Suzy Grant

Mission: To perform art that speaks to life to touch the spirit of the audience, and engage them in feeling and reflections.
Utilizes: Singers
Founded: 1972
Specialized Field: Modern
Status: Professional, Nonprofit
Income Sources: Performances; Touring; Workshops; Grants
Performs At: Columbia Dance Center
Annual Attendance: 30,000
Organization Type: Performing; Touring; Educational

201
CHICAGO TAP THEATRE
601 Wood Street
4th Floor
Chicago, IL 60640
Mailing Address: 1624 West Winona, Suite 2, Chicago, IL 60640
Phone: 412-335-5293
Fax: 412-927-2873
e-mail: lreznik@rivercityartists.com
Web Site: www.chicagotaptheatre.com
Officers:
- President: Jason Ambramowitz
- Vice President: Kathleen Duckey
- Secretary: Adrienne Guldin
- Treasurer: Joe JaQuay
- Board Member: Rob Smith
- Board Member: Jillian Tattersall

Management:
- Artistic Director: Mark Yonally
- Marketing Director: Monte Rifkin
- Business Manager: Jennifer Yonally
- Company Manager: Danielle Whaley
- Graphic Design: Lynda Pasteur
- Performance Photography: Josh Hawkins
- Social Marketing Coordinator: Leah Martin
- Studio Photography: Kristie Kahns

Mission: Chicago Tap Theatre is a non-profit 501(c)3 with a multifaceted mission: to preserve America's indigenous dance form, to promote that dance through

DANCE / Illinois

story-based shows and innovative presentation, to educate the community and make tap dance accessible to a broad spectrum of people and to foster relationships with other arts organizations.
Utilizes: Choreographers; Dancers; Guest Artists; Paid Performers
Founded: 2002
Opened: 2002
Specialized Field: Dance, Tap
Status: Non-Profit, Professional
Income Sources: Donations, Gifts
Performs At: Academy of Dance Arts, Alvina Krauss Theatre, Blue Fugue, Chicago Cultural Center, Giordana Dance Center, Grant Park

202
DANCE CENTER OF COLUMBIA COLLEGE
1306 S Michigan Avenue
Chicago, IL 60605
Phone: 312-344-8300
Fax: 312-344-8036
e-mail: info@dum.edu
Web Site: www.dancecenter.org
Officers:
  Chair: Bonnie Brooks
  Associate Chair: Margi Cole
Management:
  Executive Director: Phil Reynolds
  Operations Manager: Shannon Epplett
  Marketing Director: Heather Hartley
  Music Director: Richard Woodbury
  Visiting Artist: Mariah Maloney
Mission: To provide dance instruction to a variety of people from culturally diverse backgrounds.
Utilizes: Artists-in-Residence; Choreographers; Collaborating Artists; Collaborations; Commissioned Music; Dance Companies; Dancers; Educators; Guest Accompanists; Guest Artists; Guest Choreographers; Guest Ensembles; Guest Instructors; Guest Soloists; High School Drama; Local Artists; Multi Collaborations; Original Music Scores; Selected Students; Theatre Companies
Founded: 1969
Specialized Field: Modern; Ballet; Jazz; Ethnic Dance; Improvisation
Status: Professional, Nonprofit
Paid Staff: 7
Paid Artists: 35
Budget: $2,100,000
Income Sources: Earned and Contributed Income
Performs At: The Harris Theatre
Affiliations: APAP; IPN; MADTC
Annual Attendance: 10,000
Facility Category: Black Box
Type of Stage: Dance
Seating Capacity: 272
Year Built: 2000
Cost: $3,500,000
Rental Contact: Shannon Epplett
Organization Type: Performing; Educational

203
HUBBARD STREET DANCE CHICAGO
1147 West Jackson Boulevard
Chicago, IL 60607
Phone: 312-850-9744
Fax: 312-455-8240
e-mail: general@hubbardstreetdance.com
Web Site: hubbardstreetdance.com
Management:
  Artistic Director: Glenn Edgerton
  Executive Director: Jason D. Palmquist
  Rehearsal Director: Lucas Crandall
  Resident Choreographer: Alejandro Cerrudo
Mission: To bring artists, art and audiences together to enrich, engage, educate, transform and change lives through the experience of dance.
Founded: 1977

204
JOEL HALL DANCER CENTER
5965 N. Clark St
Chicago, IL 60660
Phone: 773-293-0900
Fax: 773-293-1130
e-mail: info@joelhall.org
Web Site: www.joelhall.org
Officers:
  Chair: Margaret Thomas
  Vice President & Secretary: Craig Davis
  Acting Executive Director: Valerie Bushey
Management:
  Artistic Director: Joel Hall
  Managing Director: Susan Dickson
  Associate Director: Vanessa Truvillion
  Associate Artistic Director: Nancy Teinowitz
Mission: To build and serve a constituency that is racially, ethnically, culturally and socially diverse, to promote a philosophy of inclusiveness, and to enrich the lives of community members through dance education and performance.
Utilizes: Five Seasonal Concerts
Founded: 1974
Specialized Field: Jazz; Ballet; Modern; Hip Hop; Tap; Egyptian Dance; Educational Dance
Status: Professional, Nonprofit
Annual Attendance: 10,000
Facility Category: Dance Studio
Organization Type: Performing; Touring; Resident; Educational

205
JOFFREY BALLET
10 E. Randolph St.
Chicago, IL 60601
Phone: 312-739-0120
Fax: 312-739-0119
e-mail: information@joffrey.com
Web Site: www.joffrey.com
Officers:
  Chair: Zachary D. Lazar, Jr
  Vice Chair: Sonia Florian
  Vice Chair: Anne Kaplan
  Secretary: Ronald.J Allen
  Treasurer: Adam DeWitt
  Women's Board President: Liz Sharp
Management:
  Artistic Director: Ashley.C. Wheater
  Executive Director: Greg Cameron
  Music Director: Scott Speck
  Ballet Master: Nicolas Blanc
  Ballet Master: Gerard Charles
  Ballet Master/Principal Coach: Graca Sales
  General Manager: Laurie Garwood
  Director of Production: Claude Binder
Mission: To preserve, recreate and present historical masterpieces of the twentieth century and to nurture, commission and present works of young artists, particularly Americans, to audiences worldwide.
Founded: 1956
Specialized Field: Ballet
Status: Non-Profit, Professional
Budget: $2,500,000
Income Sources: Tickets Sales; Touting; Contributions
Performs At: Auditorium Theatre of Roosevelt University

206
THE LIRA ENSEMBLE
6525 N Sheridan Road
#CH-LL
Chicago, IL 60626
Phone: 773-508-7040
Fax: 773-508-7043
e-mail: lira@liraensemble.org
Web Site: www.liraensemble.org
Officers:
  President: Maria Ciesla
  Vice Chair: Frank A. Cizon
Management:
  Artistic Director/General Manager: Lucyna Migala
  Co-Conductor: Malgorzata Borysiewicz
  Conductor: Mina Zikri
  Choreographer: Iwona Puc
Mission: To help acquaint Polish Americans with the richness of their thousand year old heritage of music and dance and to help other Americans learn about and appreciate Polish culture and traditions.
Founded: 1975
Specialized Field: Polish Folk Dance
Status: Non-Profit, Professional
Non-paid Artists: 30
Budget: $200,000-$500,000
Organization Type: Performing

207
MORDINE AND COMPANY DANCE THEATRE
1016 N Dearborn Parkway
Chicago, IL 60610
Phone: 312-654-9540
Fax: 847-864-9730
e-mail: info@morfine.org
Web Site: www.mordine.org
Officers:
  Acting President: Jeannie Uzdawinnis
  Secretary/Treasurer: Kristen Klinger
  Vice President: Shirley Mordine
Management:
  Artistic /Executive Director: Shirley Mordine
  Assistant to the Artistic Director: Simone Baechle
  Managing Director: Suzy Grant
  Financial Manager: Philip Martini
  Graphic Design: Dennis Tuskan
  Website Designer: Tory Lawrence
Mission: To create innovative dance works and to collaborate with outstanding artists as well as conduct educational programs for high school students and young choreographers.
Utilizes: Community Members; Five Seasonal Concerts; Singers; Special Technical Talent
Founded: 1969
Specialized Field: Modern
Status: Professional, Nonprofit
Paid Staff: 3
Non-paid Artists: 2
Income Sources: Association for Performing Arts Presenters; Dance USA; Chicago Dance Coalition
Performs At: The Dance Center of Columbia College
Annual Attendance: 4,000
Organization Type: Performing; Resident; Educational

208
MUNTU DANCE THEATRE OF CHICAGO
1809 E. 71st Street
Suite 203
Chicago, IL 60649

DANCE / Illinois

Phone: 773-241-6080
Fax: 773-241-6089
e-mail: info@muntu.com
Web Site: www.muntu.com
Officers:
    Chairperson: Leana B. Flowers
    President: Joan Gray
    Vice-Chairperson: Abena J. Brown
    Vice-Chairperson: Al Perry
    Treasurer: Sidney Dillard
    Secretary: Barbara Jackson-Lee
Management:
    Artistic Director: Amaniyea Payne
    Assistant Artistic Director: Babu Atiba
    Assistant Artistic Director: Idy Ciss
    Musical Director: Clifton Robinson
    Resource Development Manager: Neffer Oduntunde A. Kerr
Mission: The performance of traditional and contemporary African and African American dance, music and folklore.
Founded: 1972
Specialized Field: Ethnic Dance
Status: Professional, Nonprofit
Budget: $500,000-$1,000,000
Organization Type: Performing; Touring; Resident

209
NAJWA DANCE CORPS
1900 W Van Buren Street
Room 0223
Chicago, IL 60612
Phone: 312-850-7224
e-mail: najwadancecorps@sbcglobal.net
Web Site: www.najwadance.org
Officers:
    Executive Director: Sheila Walker-Wilkens
Management:
    Artistic Director: Najwa, najwadancecorps@sbcglobal.net
Mission: To preserve dance styles and techniques of different era's as it relates to the African American dance experience. Najwa Dance Corps is dedicated to being a live historical dance archive.
Utilizes: Artists-in-Residence; Choreographers; Collaborating Artists; Collaborations; Dance Companies; Dancers; Educators; Guest Accompanists; Guest Ensembles; Guest Speakers; High School Drama; Instructors; Local Talent; Multimedia; Original Music Scores; Playwrights; Poets; Scenic Designers; Students; Theatre Companies
Founded: 1978
Opened: 1979
Specialized Field: African; Carribean; Tap; Jazz; Modern Dance
Status: Professional, Nonprofit
Paid Staff: 4
Volunteer Staff: 4
Paid Artists: 12
Budget: $40,000-$100,000
Income Sources: Chicago Dance Art Coalition; African-American Arts Alliance
Organization Type: Performing; Touring; Educational

210
NATYA DANCE THEATER
410 South Michigan Avenue
Suite 725
Chicago, IL 60605-1387
Phone: 312-212-1240
Fax: 312-224-8153
e-mail: info@natya.com
Web Site: www.natya.com
Officers:
    President & Founder: Hema Rajagopalan
    Chair: Jagriti Chander
    Vice-Chair: Payal Shah
    Secretary: Pushpa Satkunaratnam
    Treasurer: Rehmah Sufi
Management:
    Artistic Director: Hema Rajagopalan, hema@natya.com
    Associate Artistic Director: Krithika Rajagopalan
    Program Coordinator: Bill Jordon, bill@natya.com
Mission: To promote the dance theater of India in today's contemporary world.
Founded: 1975
Specialized Field: Indian Dance
Status: Non-Profit, Professional
Paid Staff: 3
Volunteer Staff: 8
Paid Artists: 15
Non-paid Artists: 25
Income Sources: Foundations; Corporations; Earned Income; Ticket Revenue
Annual Attendance: 40,000

211
RIVER NORTH CHICAGO DANCE COMPANY
1016 N Dearborn Parkway
Chicago, IL 60610
Phone: 312-944-2888
Fax: 312-944-2581
e-mail: info@rivernorthchicago.com
Web Site: www.rivernorthchicago.com
Officers:
    President: Marcus Boggs
    Treasurer: Timothy Sherck
    Vice President, Development: Joe Seigle
    Secretary: Alison Baldwin
Management:
    Artistic Director: Frank Chaves
    Executive Director: Gail Kalver
    Workshop Director/Artistic Administ: Sara Bibik
    Rehearsal Assistant: Hanna Brictson
    Director of Marketing: Alexis Jaworski
    Technical Director: Josh Weckesser
    Development Manager: Paula Petrini Lynch
    Interim Managing Director: Kate Piatt-Eckert
    Ballet Master: Patrick Simoniello
Mission: Established for the purpose of cultivating and promoting Chicago's wealth of jazz dance talent.
Founded: 1989
Specialized Field: Jazz; Contemporary Dance
Status: Professional, Non-Profit
Paid Staff: 3
Paid Artists: 24
Budget: $1.1 million
Income Sources: Performance Fees; Corporate, Foundation, and Government Contributions; Individual Contributions
Annual Attendance: 30,000

212
T DANIEL & LAURIE WILLETS
6619 N Campbell Street
Chicago, IL 60645
Phone: 773-743-0277
Fax: 773-743-0276
e-mail: info@tdanielcreations.com
Web Site: www.tdanielcreations.com
Officers:
    Co-Founder: T Daniel
    Co-Founder: Laurie Willets
Management:
    Artistic Co-Director: T Daniel
    Artistic Co-Director: Laurie Willets
Mission: To create, educate and tour theatrical productions, shows and concert programs dynamically based upon the Art of Mime for audiences of all ages.
Utilizes: Collaborations; Multi Collaborations
Founded: 1971
Specialized Field: Theatrical Dance
Status: Professional, Non-Profit
Paid Staff: 2
Paid Artists: 2

213
THODOS DANCE CHICAGO
860 West Blackhawk Street
Suite 305
Chicago, IL 60642
Phone: 312-266-6255
Fax: 312-266-6457
e-mail: info@thodosdancechicago.org
Web Site: thodosdancechicago.org
Officers:
    President: Elaine Rosenfeld Margulis
    Treasurer: Paula Bork
    Secretary: Lesli Babbs
    Board Member: Shannon Raglin Cecola
    Board Member: Bradley Dineen
    Board Member: Camille Goldberg
Management:
    Founder/Artistic Director: Melissa Thodos
    Executive Director: Gail Ford
    Grants/Booking Director: Rick Johnston
    Administrative Associate: Stephanie Cibler
    Education Associate: Carrie Patterson
    Administrative Associate: Annie Zahour
Mission: Breathtakingly athletic, powerfully beautiful, performing vibrant choreography are among the many critical accolades that Thodos Dance Chicago (TDC) has received. This ensemble of well-rounded artists who teach, choreograph, and perform brings contemporary dance to a wider audience with an appealing style incorporating a variety of dance forms created and performed with an innovative flair. The Company's highly unique mission of inspiring.
Utilizes: Arrangers; Choreographers; Collaborating Artists; Collaborations; Dance Companies; Dancers; Educators; Local Artists & Directors; Lyricists; Multimedia; Paid Performers; Special Technical Talent; Theatre Companies
Specialized Field: Contemporary Dance
Status: Non-Profit, Professional
Income Sources: Donors, Sponsors, Grants
Season: Year Round
Performs At: Galvin Fine Arts Theater, Harris Theeater, Ruth Page Center/Arts, Duke Performance Hall, Dorothy Menker Theater

214
ZEPHYR DANCE
2010 N. Damen
Chicago, IL 60647
Phone: 773-489-5069
Fax: 773-489-9930
e-mail: michelle@zephyrdance.com
Web Site: www.zephyrdance.com
Management:
    Artistic Director: Michelle Kranicke
    Associate Artistic Director: Emily Stein
Mission: To bring experiences in self-expression and creative development to diverse communities through its educational outreach programming.
Founded: 1989
Specialized Field: Ballet; Modern; Creative Movement
Status: Non-Profit; Professional
Paid Staff: 1
Volunteer Staff: 10

DANCE / Illinois

Performs At: Ruth Page Center
Annual Attendance: 500-1,000

215
JUDITH SVALANDER SCHOOL BALLET
83 E Woodstock Street
Crystal Lake, IL 60014
Phone: 815-455-2055
Fax: 815-477-0313
e-mail: info@jsvalander.com
Web Site: www.svalanderschool.org
Officers:
   Business Administrator: Nora Kay Belt
   Founder: Judith Svalander
Management:
   Artistic Director: Judith Svalander
   Creative Dance Director: Laura Bobkowski
   Resident Guest Artist: Greg Begley
   Assistant Director: Julie Fiore Hirsch
   Business Manager: Nora Kay Pelt
   Office Manager: Ashler Tesmer
   Ballet Instructor: Amanda Goerlitz
Mission: Dedication to the development of dance and the combination of skills and the joy of music.
Specialized Field: Ballet

216
TRINITY IRISH DANCE COMPANY
747 Church Rd
Elmhurst, IL 60126
Phone: 630-415-3382
Fax: 630-415-3383
Toll-free: 877-326-2328
e-mail: info@trinitydance.com
Web Site: www.trinity-dancers.com
Officers:
   Founder: Mark Howard
Management:
   Artistic Director: Mark Howard
   Company Manager: Michael Carr
Mission: Trinity Academy of Irish Dance is the most widely recognized dance program in the world. The program gives everyone the opportunity to embark on a unique journey of Irish dance.
Founded: 1990
Specialized Field: Irish Dance
Status: Professional, Non-Profit
Budget: $980,000
Income Sources: Touring Revenue; Individual Grants; Corporation Grants
Annual Attendance: 57,000

217
GIORDANO DANCE CHICAGO
1509 South Michigan Avenue, 2nd Floor
Evanston, IL 60605
Phone: 312-922-1332
Fax: 312-922-1335
e-mail: ggjdc@giordnojazzdance.com
Web Site: giordanodance.org
Officers:
   President: John Seeback
   Vice President: Beth Stephens
   Treasurer: A Steven Crown
   Secretary: Stephanie Weidenborner
   Founder: Gus Giordano
   Chair: Dina Gallay
Management:
   Artistic Director: Nan Giordano
   Executive Director: Michael McStraw
   Director: Gus Giordano
   Office Manager & Bookkeeper: Emily Nelson
Mission: To excite audiences about dance in general, specifically jazz dance.
Utilizes: Choreographers; Collaborations; Dancers; Designers; Guest Artists; Guest Conductors; High School Drama; Original Music Scores; Student Interns
Founded: 1962
Specialized Field: Jazz; Contemporary Dance
Status: Professional, Non-Profit
Paid Staff: 4
Paid Artists: 16
Budget: $200,000-$500,000
Income Sources: Illinois Arts Council; Foundations; Ticket Sales; Performing Fees; Government; Corporations; Individual Donations
Affiliations: Jazz Dance World Congress
Annual Attendance: 56,000
Organization Type: Performing; Touring; Educational

218
CHICAGO FESTIVAL BALLET
1239 S Naper Boulevard
Naperville, IL 60540
Phone: 630-527-1052
Fax: 630-527-8427
e-mail: general@chicagofestivalballet.org
Web Site: www.chicagofestivalballet.com
Officers:
   Chairman: Christopher Rosean
   Secretary: Sue Doser
   Tresurer: Ron Pavlacka
   Founder: Kenneth Von Heidecke
Management:
   Director: Kenneth Von Heidecke
   Artistic Honorary Advisor: Maria Tallchief
   Artistic Advisor: Nathalie Krassovska
   Studio Manager: Leslie Peterson
Mission: To maintain the highest artistic standards and uncompromising quality of spirited performances through the traditions of classical ballet.
Specialized Field: Ballet
Status: Nonprofit

219
MOMENTA
Academy of Movement and Music
605 Lake Street
Oak Park, IL 60302-2651
Phone: 708-848-2329
Fax: 708-848-2391
e-mail: info@momenta-dance.org
Web Site: www.momenta-dance.org
Management:
   Press Represetative/Artistic Dir: Stephanie Clemens
   Artistic Co-Director: Larry Ippel
   Lighting Design: Mike Dutka
   Balletmaster: Valery Dolgallo
Mission: To produce and present dance concerts.
Founded: 1983
Specialized Field: Historical Dance; Modern; Contemporary Dance
Paid Staff: 2
Volunteer Staff: 3
Paid Artists: 15
Non-paid Artists: 50
Budget: $175,000
Income Sources: Tickets; Memberships; Fundraising
Performs At: Doris Humphrey Memorial Theatre
Annual Attendance: 2500
Facility Category: Black Box Theatre
Type of Stage: Proscenium
Stage Dimensions: 45'x 30'x 125'
Seating Capacity: 150
Year Built: 1924
Year Remodeled: 1983
Cost: negotiable
Rental Contact: Stephanie Clemens

220
PEORIA BALLET
800 W Detweiller Drive
Peoria, IL 61615
Phone: 309-690-7990
Fax: 309-690-7991
e-mail: info@peoriaballet.com
Web Site: www.peoriaballet.com
Officers:
   President: Scot Fairfield
   Vice President: Laurie Pearl Cane
   Treasurer: Stephanie Rickets
   Secretary: Linda Hallman
Management:
   Artistic Director: Erich Yetter
   General Manager: Paula Sapinski
   Marketing/Advertising Director: Rachael Hamilton
   Office Manager: Laura Kessler
   Development Director: Amy Bearce
   Academy Director: Tamra Challacombe
Mission: To further the participation, education and appreciation of all disciplines of dance as a cultural art form with a particular emphasis in ballet.
Founded: 1965
Specialized Field: Ballet
Status: Professional, Nonprofit
Paid Staff: 11
Paid Artists: 6
Budget: $400,000
Income Sources: Corporate and Private Donations; Grants; Fundraising Events; Tuition; Illionis Arts Counsil
Performs At: Peoria Civic Center
Annual Attendance: 6,000
Organization Type: Performing; Touring; Resident

221
BALLET QUAD CITIES
613 17th Street
Rock Island, IL 61201
Phone: 309-786-3779
e-mail: jcookballetqc@mediacombb.net
Web Site: www.balletquadcities.com
Officers:
   President: Paul Van Duyne
   Vice President: Linda Bowers
   Secretary: Ruth Lee
   Treasurer: Dennis Miller
Management:
   Artistic Advisor: Dominic Walsh
   Artistic Affiliate: Stuart Loungway
   Artistic Director: Courtney Lyon
   Ballet Mistress: Erica Wood
   Resident Choreographer: Deanna Carter
   Guest Artist: Domingo Rubio
   Guest Choreographer: Elie Lazar
   Development Director: Diane Koster
Mission: Ballet Quad Cities provides classical and contemporary dance to the entire bi-state region through oustanding performances, entertainig lecture-demonstrations and innovative educational outreach programs for people of all ages.
Founded: 1996
Specialized Field: Ballet

222
ROCKFORD DANCE COMPANY
711 N Main Street
Rockford, IL 61103
Phone: 815-963-3341
Fax: 815-963-3541
e-mail: info@rockforddancecompany.com
Web Site: www.rockforddancecompany.com

DANCE / Indiana

Officers:
  President: Laura.D Mruk
  Vice President: Carole Newcomer
  Treasurer: Elizabeth.A Grabin
  Secretary: Melinda S. Lucchesi
  Board Member: Sue Brubakar
Management:
  Executive Director: Carm Cavallaro Rongere
  Artistic Director: Matthew Keefe
  Office Manager: Pam Parkinson
  School Coordinator: Brittany Keefe
  School and Outreach Coordinator: Meghan Baylor
  Registrar: Patty Parlee
Mission: Committed to serving as an arts resource in dance through its presentations, performances and education.
Utilizes: Five Seasonal Concerts
Founded: 1972
Specialized Field: Modern; Ballet; Jazz
Status: Semi-Professional, Nonprofit
Paid Staff: 15
Volunteer Staff: 10
Income Sources: Corporate; Foundations; Tuition; Ticket Sales
Performs At: The Cornado Theatre
Organization Type: Performing; Resident; Educational; Sponsoring

223
THE SPRINGFIELD BALLET COMPANY
420 S Sixth Street
Springfield, IL 62701
Phone: 217-544-1967
Fax: 217-544-1968
e-mail: info@springfieldballetco.org
Web Site: springfieldballetco.org
Officers:
  President: Sarah L. Beuning
  Vice President: Mindy Vance
  Treasurer: Linda Shaefer
  Secretary: Angie Bruce
  Finance Chair: Julie Davis
  Promotions Chair: Sarah Dietrich Yockey
Management:
  Artistic Director: Julie Ratz
  Ballet Mistress: Gina DeCroix Russell
  Administrative Director: Sally Hamilton
Mission: To use beauty, energy, and diversity of dance to speak to the community; to foster dance as the common language that encourages freedom of expression, bridges generations and cultures, and adds to the richness of life in Central Illinois.
Utilizes: Guest Companies; Singers
Founded: 1975
Specialized Field: Modern; Ballet; Jazz; Folk Dance
Status: Non-Professional, Nonprofit
Paid Staff: 3
Volunteer Staff: 150
Budget: $30,000
Income Sources: Corporate; Individual; Grants;
Performs At: The Sangamon Auditorium
Affiliations: Illionis Arts Counsil; Springfield Arts Counsil
Annual Attendance: 25,000
Organization Type: Performing; Touring; Educational; Sponsoring

224
SALT CREEK BALLET
98 E Chicago Avenue
Westmont, IL 60559
Phone: 630-769-1199
Fax: 630-769-0052
e-mail: saltcreek@saltcreekballet.org
Web Site: www.saltcreekballet.org
Officers:
  President: Ken Nelson
  Treasurer: Greg Sjullie
  Secretary: Joan Emery
Management:
  Artistic Director: Sergey Kozadayev
  Artistic Director: Zhanna Dubrovskaya
  Executive Director: Christina Salerno
  Founder: Patricia Sigurdson
  Communications Coordinator: Carmela Hoerman
  Outreach Coordintor/Teaching Artist: Dr. Kelly Stokes
Mission: to bring professional quality dance programming to area audiences
Utilizes: Choreographers; Collaborations; Dance Companies; Dancers; Educators; Guest Accompanists; Guest Artists; Guest Composers; Guest Conductors; Guest Musical Directors; Original Music Scores; Resident Professionals; Soloists; Student Interns
Founded: 1985
Specialized Field: Ballet
Status: Non-Profit; Non-Professional
Paid Staff: 15
Budget: $750,000
Income Sources: Grants; Contributions; Ticket Sales
Annual Attendance: 10,000
Organization Type: Touring Company

Indiana

225
ANDERSON YOUNG BALLET THEATRE
29 Young Drive
Anderson, IN 46016
Phone: 765-643-2184
e-mail: aybt@sbcglobal.net
Web Site: www.andersonyoungballet.org
Officers:
  President: Cheryl Shank
  VP: Bekah Snyder-Logan
  Secretary: Jennifer DeLillo
  Treasurer: Terra Skinner
Management:
  Executive Artistic Director: LouAnn Young
  Assistant Artistic Director: Kory Browder
  Instructor/Choreographer: Michael Worcel
  Co-Artistic Director: Jennifer Weatherburn-Thiemet
  Co-Artistic Director: Catherine Sparks-Petraits
Specialized Field: Ballet

226
CARMEL DANCE ARTS-INDY LATIN DANCE
575 W Carmel Drive
Carmel, IN 46032
Phone: 317-844-9131
e-mail: carmeldancearts@indylatindance.com
Mission: Our dance group offers typical folkloric dancing, salsa and latin dance performances.
Specialized Field: Folkloric Dance; Salsa; Latin

227
EVANSVILLE DANCE THEATRE
333 Plaza East Boulevard
Suite E
Evansville, IN 47715
Phone: 812-473-8937
Fax: 812-473-0392
e-mail: evvdance@cigecom.net
Web Site: www.edtdance.org
Officers:
  President: Mary Mably
  VP: Martha Alle
  Secretary: Kelly Gates
  Treasurer: Klara Stone
Management:
  Artistic Director: Keith J Martin
  Ballet Mistress: BJ Martin
  Guest Artist: Jason Keith Martin
Mission: Increase public awareness and appreciation of dance as a performing art as well as producing and presenting excellent dance performances, invrntive choreography and showcasing unique talents.
Utilizes: Collaborations; Dance Companies; Dancers; Five Seasonal Concerts; Guest Writers
Founded: 1981
Specialized Field: Ballet; Theatrical Dance
Status: Professional,Nonprofit
Paid Staff: 12
Paid Artists: 7
Income Sources: Corporate; Foundations; Grants
Performs At: Victory and Shankein Theatre
Organization Type: Performing; Touring; Educational

228
FORT WAYNE BALLET
300 East Main Street
Fort Wayne, IN 46802
Phone: 260-484-9646
Fax: 260-484-9647
e-mail: info@fortwayneballet.org
Web Site: www.fortwayneballet.org
Officers:
  President: Hope Huber
  Vice President: Bix Benson
  Treasurer: Vonda Yanez
  Secretary: Kathy Roudebush
Management:
  Artistic/Executive Director: Karen Gibbons Brown
  Director of Administration: Christy Sandmaier
  Business Manager: Becky Zulager
  Director of Visual Art: Tess Heet
  Development Coordinator: Marie Clifford
  Registrar: Lauren Slocum
  Musical Director: Nikolay Todorinov
  Artistic Associate: David Ingram
Mission: The mission of the Fort Wayne Ballet, Inc., is to inspire and nurture an appreciation for the art of dance through educational excellence, artistic achievement, performance experiences and outreach activities in the community and beyond.
Utilizes: Guest Companies; Singers
Founded: 1956
Specialized Field: Ballet; Jazz; Contemporary Dance; Character Dance
Status: Semi-Professional, Nonprofit
Paid Staff: 17
Volunteer Staff: 250
Budget: $897,000
Income Sources: Arts United of Greater Ft. Wayne
Performs At: Performing Arts Center
Affiliations: Arts United of Greater Ft. Wayne
Annual Attendance: 28,000
Organization Type: Performing; Educational

229
FORT WAYNE DANCE COLLECTIVE
437 E Berry Street
Suite 203
Fort Wayne, IN 46802

Phone: 260-424-6574
Fax: 260-424-2789
e-mail: info@fwdc.org
Web Site: www.fwdc.org
Officers:
   President: Kate Brogan
   VP: Megan Corcoran
   Secretary: Nathan Smith
   Treasurer: Jennifer McKinney
   Managing Director: Jarin Hart
Management:
   Artistic Director: Liz Monnier
   Managing Director: Cat Moors
   Outreach Director: Alison Gerardot
Mission: To promote and expand the development of human creativity and expression through movement, as well as to sustain and develop the Fort Wayne Dance Collective's traditions by presenting dance, inter- and multi-disciplinary arts, and educational programs of the highest quality to diverse audiences and student populations.
Utilizes: Artists-in-Residence; Choreographers; Collaborating Artists; Collaborations; Commissioned Music; Community Talent; Composers; Dance Companies; Dancers; Educators; Five Seasonal Concerts; Guest Accompanists; Guest Artists; Guest Choreographers; High School Drama; Instructors; Lyricists; Multi Collaborations; Original Music Scores; Soloists; Theatre Companies
Founded: 1979
Specialized Field: Modern; Jazz; Belly Dance; Yoga
Status: Professional; Nonprofit
Paid Staff: 3
Paid Artists: 16
Budget: $300,000
Income Sources: Earned Income; Local Foundations; State and National Grants
Affiliations: Arts United
Annual Attendance: 24,000
Organization Type: Performing; Educational; Sponsoring; Video Producer for Public Access

230
BALLET INTERNATIONALE
502 N Capitol Avenue
Suite B
Indianapolis, IN 46204
Phone: 317-637-8979
Fax: 317-637-1637
e-mail: info@balletinternational.org
Web Site: www.balletinternational.org
Officers:
   President: Clare D Coxey
   Treasurer: Patrick J Burley
Management:
   Artistic Director: Eldar Aliev
   Executive Director: Bill Wilson
   Company/Booking Manager: Carolyn Treebee
   Marketing/Public Relations Director: Kevin O'Donohue
Mission: To stimulate the evolution of our community in those ways only possible with world-class ballet.
Founded: 1973
Specialized Field: Classical Ballet
Status: Professional; Non-Profit
Paid Staff: 20
Volunteer Staff: 25
Paid Artists: 27
Budget: $2.5 million
Income Sources: Ticket Sales; Contributed Income; Touring; Residencies; Merchandise Sales; Production Rental
Performs At: Murat Centre

Affiliations: Association of Performing Arts Presenters; Arts Midwest; Western Arts Alliance
Annual Attendance: 40,000
Facility Category: Multi-use
Type of Stage: Proscenium
Seating Capacity: 2,500
Rental Contact: General Manager Terry Hennessey
Organization Type: Performing; Touring; Resident; Educational; Sponsoring

231
DANCE KALEIDOSCOPE
4603 Claredon Road
Room 32
Indianapolis, IN 46208
Phone: 317-940-6555
Fax: 317-940-6557
e-mail: dk@dancekal.org
Web Site: www.dancekal.org
Officers:
   Co-President: Tim Garnett
   Treasurer: Bernadette Fletcher
   Co-VP Development: Phyllis Feigenbaum
   VP Marketing: Lisa Hendrickson
Management:
   Artistic Director: David Hochoy
   Resident Lighting Designer: Laura Glover
   Executive Director: Janice Virgin
   Marketing Director: Paul Hansen
   Office Manager: Janie Snyder
   Director of Education & Touring: Lynn Webster
Mission: To inspire, educate and entertain through the experience of outstanding professional contemporary dance.
Founded: 1972
Specialized Field: Modern; Contemporary Dance
Status: Professional, Nonprofit
Paid Staff: 7
Paid Artists: 11
Budget: $1 million
Income Sources: Earned; Developed; Special Events
Performs At: Pike Performing Arts Center; Indiana Repertory Theatre
Affiliations: Indian Repretory
Annual Attendance: 10,000
Facility Category: Professional Theatre
Type of Stage: Proscenium
Seating Capacity: 600
Organization Type: Performing; Touring; Resident

232
INTO SALSA DANCE STUDIO
363 N. Illinois St.
Suite 202
Indianapolis, IN 46204
Phone: 317-658-6567
e-mail: mail@intosalsa.com
Web Site: www.intosalsa.com
Mission: Yang Xiao and Erin Lamb have performed and captivated thousands of audiences in Central America. In the spring of 2005 they opened IntoSalsa Latin Dance Studio.
Opened: 2005
Specialized Field: Ethnic Dance; Salsa

233
INDIANA BALLET THEATRE
8888 Louisiana
Merrillville, IN 46410
Phone: 219-755-4444
Fax: 219-226-0920
e-mail: info@ibtnw.org
Web Site: www.ibtnw.org
Officers:

   CEO: Gloria Tuohy
   President Executive: Dan Botich
   VP: Carol Highsmith
   Secretary: Anna Rominger
   Treasurer: Katie Holderby
Management:
   Office Manager: Jo Munro
   Studio Manager: Michelle Hartman
   Graphic Artist: Laura Herrera
Mission: Indiana Ballet Theatre Northwest is dedicated to the art of dance and to enriching the cultural life of our community.
Founded: 1980
Specialized Field: Ballet
Status: Professional, Nonprofit

234
MUNCIE BALLET STUDIO
118 S Walnut St.
Muncie, IN 47305
Phone: 765-216-5472
Web Site: www.muncieballet.org
Management:
   Director: Lisa Love
Mission: Muncie ballet studio is creating audiences for today, tomorrow and memories to last a lifetime.
Specialized Field: Ballet

Iowa

235
CO' MOTION DANCE THEATER
129 E Seventh Street
Ames, IA 50010
Phone: 515-232-7374
Fax: 515-233-9290
e-mail: dance@comotion.org
Web Site: www.comotion.org
Officers:
   President: Ronald Jackson
   VP: Beth Clarke
   Secretary: Brenda Witherspoon
   Treasurer: Larry Gleason
Management:
   Director: Valerie Williams
   General Manager: Susan Jackson
Mission: To bring high-caliber and professional dance to Midwestern sponsors at affordable prices and to offer the highest quality in dance education to its students.
Utilizes: Choreographers; Collaborating Artists; Dance Companies; Dancers; Guest Musical Directors; High School Drama; Instructors; Local Artists & Directors; Lyricists; Original Music Scores; Paid Performers; Poets; Student Interns
Founded: 1978
Specialized Field: Modern
Status: Professional, Nonprofit
Paid Staff: 1
Volunteer Staff: 6
Paid Artists: 3
Non-paid Artists: 3
Performs At: The Ames City Auditorium
Organization Type: Performing; Touring; Resident; Educational

236
IOWA DANCE THEATRE
6720 Hickman Rd
Des Moines, IA 50324
Phone: 515-979-6622
Fax: 515-276-2694
Web Site: www.iowadancetheatre.com
Officers:

DANCE / Kansas

President: Tom Moorhead
Vice President: Elizabeth Harano Adams
Treasurer: Martha Mile
Secretary: Sheri Soich
Management:
  Executive Director: Mary Joyce Lind
  Project Director: Janice Baker-Haines
  Co-Director: Lisa Hamilton
  Co-Director: Cathy Bergman
  Co-Director: Lana Lyddon-Hattan
  Head Chamber Dances: Kathleen Hurley
Mission: Dedicated to supporting a company of dancers who will perform and promote the art form of dance.
Founded: 1983
Specialized Field: Modern; Ballet; Jazz
Status: Semi-Professional; Nonprofit
Volunteer Staff: 15
Paid Artists: 12
Non-paid Artists: 15
Income Sources: Grants; Fundraisers
Performs At: Civic Center of Greater Des Moines
Annual Attendance: 5,000
Seating Capacity: 2,750
Year Built: 1979
Year Remodeled: 2000
Organization Type: Performing; Touring; Educational

Kansas

237
COHAN/SUZEAU DANCE COMPANY
University of Kansas Dept. of Dance
1301 Sunnyside Avenue
Room 251
Lawrence, KS 66045
Mailing Address: 1002 Avalon Road, Lawrence, KS 66044
Phone: 785-864-4264
e-mail: suzeau@ku.edu
Web Site: dance.ku.edu
Management:
  Co-Artistic Director: Patrick Suzeau
  Co-Artistic Director: Muriel Cohan
  Manager: Suan Whitfield
Founded: 1973
Specialized Field: Contemporary Dance; East Indian Classical Dance; Contemporary/Indian Fusion
Status: Professional; Non-Profit
Paid Staff: 1
Paid Artists: 12
Income Sources: Touring; Performing
Performs At: The Lied Center
Affiliations: University Of Kansas
Type of Stage: Proscenium

238
LAWRENCE BALLET THEATRE
940 New Hampshire Street
Lawrence, KS 66044
Phone: 785-218-7120
e-mail: cyncrews@gmail.com
Web Site: lawrenceartscenter.org/advanced-dance-companies/
Management:
  Artistic Director: Cynthia Crews
Mission: To provide training and performance opportunities for serious students who are seeking a collegiate or professional career in the field of dance, and to provide high quality, rich dance experiences for audiences in Lawrence and beyond.
Status: Pre-Professional

239
KANSAS REGIONAL BALLET
11728 Quivira Road
Overland Park, KS 66210
Phone: 913-451-9292
Fax: 913-498-2222
e-mail: krbdance@mindsping.com
Web Site: krb.homestead.com
Officers:
  President: Dennis Landsman
  Vice President: Kathy Landsman
  Secretary: Linda Smith
  Treasurer: Dennis Landsman
Mission: To introduce and educate all ages to the art form of dance.
Utilizes: Choreographers; Dancers; Guest Accompanists; Guest Artists; Multimedia; Soloists
Founded: 1979
Specialized Field: Ballet
Status: Pre-Professional; Nonprofit
Paid Staff: 2
Volunteer Staff: 27
Non-paid Artists: 27
Budget: $100,000
Income Sources: Fund Raisers; Grants; Ticket Sales
Performs At: Johnson Community College/The Carlson Center
Affiliations: Midstates Regional Dance America
Annual Attendance: 5,000
Facility Category: Community College
Type of Stage: Proscenium
Stage Dimensions: 55'x 45'
Seating Capacity: 1,300
Year Built: 1988
Rental Contact: Johnson County Community College
Organization Type: Performing; Touring; Educational

240
WICHITA CONTEMPORARY DANCE THEATRE
Witchita State University
1845 N Fairmount
Box 101
Wichita, KS 67260
Phone: 316-978-3456
e-mail: webmaster@wichita.edu
Web Site: www.wichita.edu/thisis/academics/finearts
Management:
  Director Dance: C Nicholas Johnson
  Choreographer: Denise A Celestin
Mission: To provide high quality entertaining dance performances and to foster understanding and appreciation for dance through educational programs as well as provide a venue for artists to live and work.
Founded: 1924
Specialized Field: Modern; Ballet; Jazz; Tap
Status: Non-Professional, Non-Profit
Paid Staff: 3
Budget: $20,000
Income Sources: Performances; Tuition; Foundations; Corporate; Individual
Annual Attendance: 2,500

Kentucky

241
KENTUCKY BALLET THEATRE
736 National Avenue
Lexington, KY 40502
Phone: 859-252-5245
Fax: 859-252-7925
e-mail: info@kyballet.com
Web Site: www.kyballet.com
Officers:
  President: Jan Foody
  Vice President: Rainey Hayes
  Secretary: Sandy Robinson
  Treasurer: Paul E. Holbrook
Management:
  Artistic Director: Norbe Risco
  Academy Director and Company Dancer: Rafaela Cento Munoz
  Principal Dancer: Orlando Viamontes
  Principal Dancer: Kelsey Van Tine
Mission: To establish through performance and education a professional company and academy committed to the art of dance.
Utilizes: Artists-in-Residence; Choreographers; Dance Companies; Dancers; Guest Artists; Guest Musical Directors; Guest Writers; High School Drama; Multimedia; Original Music Scores; Soloists
Founded: 1998
Specialized Field: Ballet; Theatrical Dance
Status: Non-Profit, Professional
Performs At: The Lexington Opera House

242
THE LEXINGTON BALLET
161 N Mill Street
4th Floor
Lexington, KY 40507
Phone: 859-233-3925
Fax: 859-252-0505
e-mail: info@lexingtonballet.org
Web Site: www.lexingtonballet.org
Officers:
  Executive Chair: Susan Zearfoss
  Vice-Chair: Melanie Mathis
  Treasurer: Thomas F. Western
  Secretary: Cynthia Kelly
  Development Chair: Marilee Varner
  Scholarship Chair: Linda Hollembaek
Management:
  School Director/Artistic Director: Luis Dominguez
  School Director: Nancy Dominguez
  Research Associate: Melissa Rucker
Mission: Committed to offering a variety of performances in contemporary and classical dance.
Utilizes: Five Seasonal Concerts
Founded: 1974
Specialized Field: Ballet
Status: Professional, Nonprofit
Paid Staff: 5
Volunteer Staff: 20
Budget: $200,000-$500,000
Income Sources: Donations; Tuition; Ticket Revenue
Annual Attendance: 9,500
Organization Type: Performing; Resident

243
LOUISVILLE BALLET
315 E Main Street
Louisville, KY 40202
Phone: 502-583-3150
Fax: 502-583-0006
e-mail: info@louisvilleballet.org
Web Site: www.louisvilleballet.org
Officers:
  President: Joel Stone
  VP: Philip D. Payne, Jr
  Treasurer: David Smith
  Secretary: Lisa.P Leet
  General Manager: Cara Hicks

DANCE / Louisiana

Director of Development: C. F. Callihan II
Director of Finance: Lora Limeberry
Management:
  Artistic Director: Bruce Simpson
  Senior Ballet Master: Harald Uwe Kern
  Lighting /Production Stage Manager: Michael T. Ford
  Director Operations: Michael Harris
  Costume Master: Dan Fedie
  Ballet Mistress: Mikelle Bruzina
  Technical Director: Ron Riall
  Director: Elena Diehl
  Stage Manager: Leslie K. Oberhausen
Mission: To bring to the broadest audience high-quality professional dance.
Utilizes: Guest Artists; Guest Companies; Singers
Founded: 1952
Specialized Field: Ballet
Status: Professional; Nonprofit
Paid Staff: 120
Budget: $3,000,000
Income Sources: Dance USA; Southeast Regional Ballet Association; Individual; Corporate; Foundations
Affiliations: Dance USA; Southeast Regional Ballet Association
Organization Type: Performing; Touring; Resident; Educational; Sponsoring

Louisiana

244
BATON ROUGE BALLET THEATER
10745 Linkwood Court
Baton Rouge, LA 70810
Mailing Address: PO Box 82288, Baton Rouge, LA 70884-2288
Phone: 225-766-8379
Fax: 225-766-8230
e-mail: BRBTInfo@batonrougeballet.org
Web Site: www.batonrougeballet.org
Officers:
  President: Lisa Broussard
  VP: Renee Puyau Stelzer
  Treasurer: Robbie Phillabaum
  Secretary: Susan Puyau
Management:
  Artistic Co-Director: Sharon Mathews
  Artistic Co-Director: Molly Buchmann
  Director Development/Communications: Nicole Naquin
  Ballet for Children Director: Michele Ball
  Youth Ballet Director: Susan Perlis
  Associate Director: Rebecca Acosta
  Administrative Director: Gayle Beard
  Costume Mistress: Polly Normand
  Costume Consultant: LaDawn Jones
Mission: To promote, aid and assist, in any manner whatsoever, the development, improvement and advancement of ballet by maintaining a performing dance company.
Utilizes: Choreographers; Dance Companies; Dancers; Guest Accompanists; Guest Artists; Guest Choreographers; Multimedia; Original Music Scores
Founded: 1963
Specialized Field: Dance
Status: Professional; Nonprofit
Paid Staff: 5
Budget: $200,000-$500,000
Income Sources: Ticket Sales; Grants; Donations
Performs At: Baton Rouge River Center; Performing Arts Theatre
Organization Type: Performing; Touring; Resident

245
DELTA FESTIVAL BALLET
3351 Severn Avenue
Suite 303B
Metairie, LA 70002
Mailing Address: P.O. Box 7425, Metairie, LA 70010-7425
Phone: 504-888-0931
Fax: 504-888-0941
e-mail: deltafestballet@aol.com
Web Site: www.deltafestivalballet.com
Officers:
  President: Joan Patrick
  Vice Pres., Memberships: Thomas Holley
  Vice Pres., Promotions: Linda Fried
  Treasurer: Scott Dessens
  Secretary: Jessica D. Van Vrancken
Management:
  Artistic Director: Joseph Giacobbe
  Artistic Director: Maria Giacobbe
  Ballet Master: Richard Rholdon
Mission: Advancing the art of dance through professional performance, education, cultural outreach and community involvement. Delta Festival Ballet is committed to arts-in-education.
Utilizes: Dancers
Founded: 1967
Specialized Field: Ballet
Status: Professional; Nonprofit
Paid Staff: 15
Budget: $300,000
Income Sources: National Association for Regional Ballet; Arts Counsil of New Orleans
Annual Attendance: 12,000
Organization Type: Performing; Touring; Resident; Educational

246
NEW ORLEANS BALLET ASSOCIATION
935 Gravier Street
Suite 800
New Orleans, LA 70112
Phone: 504-522-0996
Fax: 504-595-8454
e-mail: noba@nobadance.com
Web Site: www.nobadance.com
Officers:
  Chair: Charlotte Bollinger
  Vice Chair - Board Development: Carlos F. Mickan
  Vice Chair - Administration: Cynthia LeBreton
  Vice Chair - Governance: John M. Duck
  Secretary: Pamela M. Williams
  Treasurer: Guy P. Brierre
Management:
  Executive Director: Jenny R Hamilton
  Director of Finance/Operations: Sandra Q. Fank
  Director of Programming/Marketing: Laura Burkhart
  Administrative Coordinator: Wanda Fulton
  Development Manager: Caitlin Williams
  Education Coordinator: Millette White
  Education Coordinator: Susan Bensinger
  Education Administrative Associate: Diane Stengle
  Technical Director: Joan Long
Mission: To cultivate understanding, appreciation, and enjoyment of dance through performance, education, and community service.
Utilizes: Artists-in-Residence; Choreographers; Collaborating Artists; Collaborations; Dance Companies; Dancers; Educators; Grant Writers; Guest Accompanists; Guest Artists; Guest Choreographers; Guest Instructors; Guest Soloists; High School Drama; Instructors; Local Artists; Lyricists; Original Music Scores; Theatre Companies
Founded: 1969
Specialized Field: Dance
Status: Nonprofit, Professional
Paid Staff: 6
Volunteer Staff: 37
Paid Artists: 125
Non-paid Artists: 1
Budget: $1,500,000
Income Sources: Ticket Sales; Contributions
Performs At: Mahalia Jackson Theater for the Performing Arts
Affiliations: Dance/USA; National Guild of Community Schools of the Arts; National Dance Education Organization
Annual Attendance: 25,000
Facility Category: Concert Hall
Type of Stage: Proscenium
Seating Capacity: 2,317
Organization Type: Sponsoring; Presenting; Educational

247
SHREVEPORT METROPOLITAN BALLET
1324 North Hearne Avenue
Suite 202
Shreveport, LA 71107
Mailing Address: P.O. Box 78564, Shreveport, LA 71137
Phone: 318-221-8500
Fax: 318-221-8508
e-mail: info@shreveportmetroballet.org
Web Site: www.shreveportmetroballet.org
Officers:
  President: Dr. Margaret Crittell
  Vice-President: Sonja Nicolosi
  Secretary: Lucy Medvec
  Treasurer: David Steen
  President-Elect: Dr. Wanda Thomas
Management:
  Artistic Director: Kendra Feazel Meiki
  Executive Director: Kate Pedrotty
Mission: To promote the art of classical ballet in Shreveport-Bossier City.
Utilizes: Five Seasonal Concerts
Founded: 1973
Specialized Field: Classical Ballet
Status: Semi-Professional, Nonprofit
Paid Staff: 2
Income Sources: Memberships; Grants; Fundraising; Corporate; Foundations; Ticket Sales
Performs At: The Shreveport Civic Theatre
Annual Attendance: 5,000-12,000
Organization Type: Performing; Resident; Educational

Maine

248
BANGOR BALLET
14 State Street
Bangor, ME 04401
Phone: 207-945-3457
e-mail: bangorballet@gmail.com
Web Site: bangorballet.com
Management:
  Artistic Director: Ivy Clear-Forest
  Executive Director: Jane Bragg
Mission: Dedicated to creating performance opportunities for talented dancers and choreographers and to providing high quality live dance performances for audiences near and far.

DANCE / Maryland

Founded: 1994
Specialized Field: Ballet

249
MAINE STATE BALLET
348 US Route One
Falmouth, ME 04105
Phone: 207-781-7672
Fax: 207-781-3663
e-mail: info@mainestateballet.org
Web Site: www.mainestateballet.org
Officers:
   President: William McKinley
   Treasurer: Curtis Call
   Secretary: Zsuzsa Williams
   President and Owner: Steve Carter
Management:
   Artistic Director: Linda MacArthur Miele
   Associate Director: Gail Csoboth
   Conductor: Karla Kelley
   Production Manager: Fred Bernier
   Artistic Assistant: Janet Davis
   Technical Director: Dave Herrman
   Assistant Technical Director: Dan Switaj
   Lighting Director: Plato Skinascous
Mission: Maine State Ballet's mission is to enrich the Maine community through education, outreach and expanded enjoyment of dance and the performing arts.
Founded: 1986
Specialized Field: Ballet
Status: Professional, Nonprofit
Paid Artists: 25

250
BATES DANCE FESTIVAL
Bates College
Pettigrew Hall, 305 College St.
Lewiston, ME 04240-6016
Phone: 207-786-6381
Fax: 207-786-8332
e-mail: dancefest@bates.edu
Web Site: www.batesdancefestival.org
Management:
   Director: Laura Faure
   Associate Director/Registrar: Nancy Salmon
Mission: The Bates Dance Festival brings an artistically and ethnically diverse group of the best contemporary dance artists to Maine during the summer season to teach, perform, and create new work; encourages and inspires established and emerging artists by providing them with a creative, supportive environment in which to work; and actively engages people from the community and region in a full range of dance activities.
Founded: 1982
Specialized Field: Dance; Music
Status: Professional, Non-Profit
Paid Staff: 8
Volunteer Staff: 14
Paid Artists: 40
Budget: $600,000
Income Sources: Public; Private; and Earned Income
Performs At: Schaeffer Theatre
Affiliations: Bates College
Annual Attendance: 4,000
Type of Stage: Proscenium
Stage Dimensions: 28'x35'
Seating Capacity: 300
Year Built: 1952
Organization Type: Resident; Educational; Sponsoring

251
PORTLAND BALLET COMPANY
517 Forest Avenue, Suite 2
Portland, ME 04101
Phone: 207-772-9671
Fax: 207-772-3307
e-mail: info@portlandballet.org
Web Site: portlandballet.org
Management:
   Artistic Director: Eugenia L. O'Brien
Founded: 1985
Specialized Field: Ballet

252
BAY CHAMBER CONCERTS
18 Central Street
Rockport, ME 04856
Mailing Address: P.O. Box 599 Rockport, ME 04856
Phone: 207-236-2823
Fax: 207-230-0454
Toll-free: 888-707-2770
e-mail: info@baychamberconcerts.org
Web Site: www.baychamberconcerts.org
Officers:
   President: Edes Gilbert
   Vice President at Large: Luther Black
   Chair of Overseers: Alexandra Wolf Fogel
   Vice President Education: Eleanor Barlow
   Vice President for Marketing: Paul Cavalli
   Treasurer: Harris J. Bixler
   Secretary: Warren Schubert
Management:
   Executive Director: Monica Kelly
   Artistic Director: Manuel Bagorro
   Program and Events Coordinator: Shaunna Brown
   Marketing Coordinator: Peter Johnson
   Development Director: Laura Chaney
   Registrar and Ticketing Coordinator: Joan Kulle
Mission: To present a variety of music styles and educational programs to reach a diverse audience along the coast of Maine.
Utilizes: Commissioned Music; Dancers; Fine Artists; Grant Writers; Guest Accompanists; Guest Choreographers; Guest Directors; Guest Musical Directors; Guest Musicians; Lyricists; Multimedia; Original Music Scores; Resident Artists; Sign Language Translators; Singers; Special Technical Talent
Founded: 1960
Specialized Field: Music
Status: Non-Profit, Professional
Paid Staff: 9
Budget: $500,000
Performs At: Rockport Opera House
Facility Category: Opera House; Strom Auditorium
Type of Stage: Proscenium; Auditorium
Seating Capacity: 400; 800
Organization Type: Performing

Maryland

253
BALLET THEATRE OF MARYLAND
801 Chase Street
Annapolis, MD 21401
Phone: 410-224-5644
Fax: 410-224-5645
e-mail: btmmgr@balletmaryland.org
Web Site: www.balletmaryland.org
Officers:
   President: Kelly Shubic Weiner
   First Vice-President: Dee Ann Lombard, RN
   Second Vice-President: Gail Deutsch
   Treasurer: Dr. Albert Del Negro
   Secretary: Bill Shipp
Management:
   Artistic Director: Dianna Cuatto
   Office Manager/Admin Assistant: Charlotte McNutt
   Executive Administrative Assistant: Laura Lansing
   School Administrator: Nicole Kelsch
   Marketing & Business Development Co: Adrienne Westlake
Mission: To provide Maryland with a fully profesional ballet company and training academy that meets the aesthetic and recreational needs of Maryland through expressive movement. To promote interest in and enjoyment of the dance arts in the state of Maryland by providing dancers an opportunity to study, perform and grow artistically.
Utilizes: Actors; Collaborating Artists; Dancers; Five Seasonal Concerts; Resident Professionals
Founded: 1978
Specialized Field: Ballet
Status: Professional; Nonprofit
Paid Staff: 3
Volunteer Staff: 100
Paid Artists: 16
Non-paid Artists: 15
Budget: $200,000-$500,000
Annual Attendance: 10,000
Organization Type: Touring; Resident

254
NATIONAL BALLET COMPANY
1816 Margaret Ave.
Annapolis, MD 21401
Mailing Address: 6360 Franklin Gibson Rd, Tracey's Landing, MD 20779
Phone: 301-218-9822
Fax: 301-686-7040
e-mail: balletnbcoffice@aol.com
Web Site: www.nationalballet.com
Officers:
   Founder: Helen Moore
Management:
   Director: Pamela Moore
   Assistant Director: Bat Erdene Udval
   Ballet Mistress: Kirsten Koerner
   Ballet Mistress: Kimmary McLean
   Office Administrator: Elizabeth McLean
Mission: Performing a wide range of ballets from the full length classics to contemporary works. There is always something that appeals to the individual audience member that brings artistic satisfaction.
Founded: 1948
Specialized Field: Ballet

255
DANCE BALTIMORE
847 North Howard Street
Baltimore, MD 21201
Phone: 410-225-3130
e-mail: info@dancebaltimore.org
Web Site: dancebaltimore.org
Management:
   Director: Cheryl T. Goodman
Mission: The mission of Dance Baltimore is to enhance the role of dance in the Baltimore metropolitan community.
Founded: 2003
Status: Nonprofit

DANCE / Maryland

256
DOUG HAMBY DANCE
University of Maryland
Department of Dance UMBC
1000 Hilltop Circle
Baltimore, MD 21250
Phone: 410-455-2950
e-mail: hamby@umbc.edu
Web Site: www.umbc.edu
Officers:
  President: Freeman A Hrabowski,III
  VP: Nancy Young
Management:
  Artistic Director: Doug Hamby
Specialized Field: Ballet; Modern
Status: Non-Profit, Professional
Budget: $10,000-$25,000
Income Sources: Grants; Ticket Sales; Private Donations
Annual Attendance: 1,000

257
WORD DANCE THEATER
4938 Hampden Lane
Box 405
Bethesda, MD 20814
Phone: 301-785-9970
Fax: 443-782-0062
e-mail: info@worddance.org
Web Site: worddance.org
Officers:
  President: Stacy Yu
  Past President: Margaret Johnson
  Treasurer: Debrah Shaver
  Secretary: Heidi Sung
Management:
  Artistic Director: Cynthia Word
  Associate Director: Ingrid Zimmer
  Musical Director: Carlos Cesar Rodriguez
Mission: Word Dance Theater's mission is to create and perform modern dance productions and to provide educational experiences that preserve and illuminate the philosophy and choreography of Isadora Duncan, founder of Modern Dance. Through the artful blending of dance, music and theater, Word Dance Theater pays tribute to Duncan's philosophy as a rich foundation from which new dance experiences can emerge.
Utilizes: Arrangers; Choreographers; Collaborating Artists; Collaborations; Contract Orchestras; Dancers; Fine Artists; High School Drama; Instructors; Multimedia; Music; Paid Performers; Student Interns; Special Technical Talent
Founded: 2000
Specialized Field: Modern Dance
Status: Non-Profit, Professional
Income Sources: Donations, Corporate Sponsors
Season: Fall
Performs At: Sidney Harmon Hall

258
MARYLAND BALLET THEATRE
PO Box 4783
Crofton, MD 21114
Phone: 410-428-8099
e-mail: arleene@marylandballettheatre.org
Officers:
  Founder: Arleene Monahan
Management:
  Artistic Director: Arleene Monahan
Mission: To train and inspire students to further develop their performing capabilities through professionally oriented training.
Founded: 1989
Specialized Field: Ballet; Russian Classical

259
FROSTBURG STATE UNIVERSITY DANCE COMPANY
Frostburg State University
Department of Theatre and Dance
101 Braddock Road
Frostburg, MD 21532-2303
Phone: 301-687-4000
e-mail: nmattis@frostburg.edu
Web Site: www.frostburg.edu
Officers:
  President: Dr. Jonathan C. Gibralter
Mission: To prepare students for the theatre profession through pre-professional training and production experience.
Utilizes: Actors; AEA Actors; Artists-in-Residence; Choreographers; Dancers; Designers; Educators; Equity Actors; Five Seasonal Concerts; Grant Writers; Guest Artists; Guest Conductors; Guest Ensembles; Guest Lecturers; Guest Musical Directors; Guest Soloists; Guest Speakers; Guest Teachers; Instructors; Multi Collaborations; Music; Paid Performers; Performance Artists; Sign Language Translators
Specialized Field: Modern; Ballet; Jazz; Tap; Designing; Directing; Playwriting; Singing; Musical Theatre; Improv; Shakespeare; Stage Combat; Movement & Speech;Pilates
Paid Staff: 20
Performs At: Performing Arts Center
Affiliations: SAFD; AEA; SAG
Facility Category: Recital Hall, Studio Theatre, Large Drama Theatre

260
NATIONAL TAP ENSEMBLE
PO Box 4102
Hagerstown, MD 21741-2439
Phone: 301-790-1180
Fax: 270-964-1476
Toll-free: 800-683-8277
e-mail: pr1@usatap.org
Management:
  Public Relations Director: Miles Johnson
Mission: Over 2,000 programs performed worldwide.
Founded: 1989
Specialized Field: Tap; Jazz; American Vernacular Dance
Paid Staff: 3
Paid Artists: 12
Budget: $200,000-$500,000
Annual Attendance: 250,000

261
HARFORD BALLET COMPANY
701 Whitaker Road
Joppa, MD 21085
Phone: 410-877-0777
e-mail: info@harfordballetcompany.org
Web Site: harfordballetcompany.org
Officers:
  President: Anthony Gibbs
  Vice President: Gigi Devanney
  Treasurer: Rob Adkins
  Secretary: Chris Dumm
Management:
  Artistic Director: Barclay Gibbs
  Executive Director: Kaitlin Weber
Mission: HBC strives to provide the highest quality dance training and performance opportunities to its members and exceptional dance entertainment and education to the community.
Status: Nonprofit

262
METROPOLITAN BALLET THEATRE INC.
10076 Darnestown Road
Suite 202
Rockville, MD 20850
Phone: 301-762-1757
Fax: 301-762-1757
Web Site: www.mbtdance.org
Officers:
  President: Erica Hwang
  Vice President: Gretchen Fitzpatrick
  Secretary: Sharon Tharkur
  Treasurer: Leslie Wallace
Management:
  Artistic Director: Elizabeth Odell Catlett
  Ballet Master: Tyrone C. Walker
  Director of Development & Marketing: Paula Ross
  Business/Communications Manager: Brenda Lipowsky
  Ballet Instructor: Laura Wilson
Mission: Teaching dancers to be the best they can be.
Founded: 1989
Specialized Field: Ballet; Jazz
Status: Nonprofit; Professional
Paid Staff: 3
Volunteer Staff: 150
Budget: $350,000
Income Sources: Donation; Grants; Tuition; Ticket Revenue; Fundraisers
Performs At: Robert E. Parilla Performing Arts Center
Annual Attendance: 5,500

263
SACRED DANCE GUILD
550M Ritchie Highway
#271
Severna Park, MD 21146
Phone: 877-422-8678
Fax: 410-544-4640
e-mail: admin@sacreddanceguild.org
Web Site: www.sacreddanceguild.org
Officers:
  President: Wendy Morrell
  Co-Vice Presidents: Jessica Clark
  Co-Vice Presidents: Cherie Hill
  Secretary/Treasurer: Marcia Miller
Management:
  Executive Director: Karen Josephson
  Public Relations: Linda Telesco
  Programs Co-Director: Mary Kamp
  Programs Co-Director: Elaine Herg Sisler
  Public Relations Co-Director: Ann Pomeroy
Founded: 1958
Specialized Field: Ballet; Jazz; Tap; Hip Hop; Modern; Indigenous
Status: Non-Profit; Professional
Affiliations: American Dance Guild; IACD; ILDA/NPM; National Dance Association; American Alliance for Health
Annual Attendance: 150-300

264
CLANCYWORKS DANCE COMPANY
PO Box 3111
Silver Spring, MD 20918
Phone: 301-717-9271
e-mail: info@clancyworks.org
Web Site: www.clancyworks.org
Officers:
  President: Ed Burleson
  Treasurer: Fernando Silva
  Secretary: Glenna Blessing

DANCE / Massachusetts

Board Member: Nanci Brown
Board Member: Jennifer Clancy
Management:
Founding Artistic Director: Adrienne Clancy, adrienne@clancyworks.org
Program Coordinator: Erin Tunbridge, erin@clancyworks.org
Company Coordinator: Jasmine Booker, melissa@clancyworks.org
Marketing Coordinator: Bryonna Odhner
Artistic Advisor: Karen Bernstein
Administrative Consultant: Ilsa Bush
Mission: ClancyWorks Dance Company, founded in 2001 by Artistic Director Adrienne Clancy, is committed to enhancing the quality of life for individuals in various communities using the arts as a vehicle to develop understanding and to advance positive social action - we aim to shift perceptions through performance.
Utilizes: Choreographers; Collaborating Artists; Dancers; Educators; Fine Artists; Lyricists; Touring Companies
Specialized Field: Ballet, Performance Art
Status: Non-Profit
Income Sources: Contributions, Donations, Gifts
Performs At: Alvin Alley Center, Kennedy Center Millenium Stage

265
ARKA BALLET
P.O. Box 11561
Takoma Park, MD 20913-1561
Phone: 301-587-6225
Fax: 301-587-6225
e-mail: inquiries@arkaballet.org
Web Site: www.arkaballet.org
Officers:
President: Roudolf Kharatian
Management:
Artistic Director: Roudolf Kharatian
Executive Director: Tania J Chichmanian
Associate Artistic Director: Jonathan Jordan
Mission: ARKA Ballet's mission is to bring high level dance to diverse audiences and to nurture, develop and showcase international level dance talent through inspiring and challenging choreography.
Founded: 1999
Specialized Field: Ballet
Status: Non-Profit, Professional
Volunteer Staff: 5
Income Sources: Donations; Ticket Sales;
Performs At: The Kennedy Center

266
DANCE EXCHANGE
7117 Maple Avenue
Takoma Park, MD 20912
Phone: 301-270-6700
Fax: 301-270-2273
e-mail: mail@danceexchange.org
Web Site: www.danceexchange.org
Officers:
Co-chair: Martha S. Head
Co-chair: Ines Cifuentes, PhD
Treasurer: Charles Gravitz
Secretary: Elliot Maxwell
Management:
Artistic Director: Cassie Meador
Managing Director: Ellen Chenoweth
Communications and Development Dire: Emily Macel Theys
Partnerships and Production Manager: Ouida Maedel
Mission: A professional company of dance artists that creates, performs, teaches and engages people in making art. They provide groundbreaking new dance works performed by a cross-generational company on major stages both in the U.S and internationally.
Utilizes: Five Seasonal Concerts; Singers
Founded: 1976
Specialized Field: Contemporary Dance
Status: Professional, Nonprofit
Paid Staff: 8
Volunteer Staff: 4
Paid Artists: 7
Non-paid Artists: 6
Budget: $1.3 million
Income Sources: Corporate; Foundations; Grants; Private
Organization Type: Performing; Touring; Resident; Educational

267
DEEP VISION DANCE COMPANY
8000 York Road
Towson, MD
Phone: 443-567-0028
e-mail: nicolea.martinell@gmail.com
Web Site: deepvisiondancecompany.org
Management:
Artistic Director: Nicole A. Martinell
Assistant Director: Kelly Weckesser Hall
Company Manager/Treasurer: Paul M. Martinell
Mission: Our mission is to engage, inspire, and motivate the community through high quality dance performances and educational experiences.
Founded: 2011
Status: Nonprofit

Massachusetts

268
COMMONWEALTH BALLET COMPANY
PO Box 892
Acton, MA 01720-0892
Phone: 978-263-6533
e-mail: chip.morris@commonwealthballet.org
Web Site: www.commonwealthballet.org
Officers:
President: Eva Macarthur
Treasurer: Patricia M. Wilkey
Secretary & Clerk: John Bookis
Management:
Artistic Director: Chip Morris
Artistic Director Emerita: Kathryn Anderson
Mission: The purpose of the Commonwealth Ballet Company (CBC) is to develop, foster, and promote the performance and appreciation of classical and contemporary ballet among the citizens of Massachusetts. Specifically, the company's main objectives are to: maintain strong ties with the communities it serves, provide a substantial educational opportunity for young dancers and demonstrate the highest level of artistic quality.
Founded: 1992
Specialized Field: Classical Ballet; Contemporary Ballet
Status: Nonprofit
Income Sources: Acton-Boxborough Local Cultural Council; Corporate; Individual
Season: September-May

269
AMHERST BALLET THEATRE COMPANY INC
29 Strong Street
Amherst, MA 01002
Phone: 413-549-1555
e-mail: info@amherstballet.org
Web Site: www.amherstballet.org
Officers:
Founder: Therese Brady Donohue
President: Mark Harowitz
Vice President: Andrew Fisk
Treasurer: Michele Anderson
Secretary: Libby Stanworth
Management:
Executive Director: Sueann Townsend
Mission: A non-profit organization run by a volunteer Board of Directors is dedicated to dance education and professional training. Through nurturing and inspiring local young dancers, we help them strive toward an understanding of artistic excellence, discipline, leadership and a lifelong appreciation of dance.
Utilizes: Five Seasonal Concerts
Founded: 1971
Specialized Field: Ballet; Creative Movement; Jazz; Modern
Status: Nonprofit
Income Sources: Tuition; Grants; Donations

270
JACOB'S PILLOW DANCE
385 George Carter Road
Becket, MA 01223
Phone: 413-243-9919
e-mail: info@jacobspillow.org
Web Site: jacobspillow.org
Officers:
President: Christopher Jones
Chair: Mark A. Leavitt
Treasurer: Mark Williams
Secretary: Nurit Amdur
Management:
Executive/Artistic Director: Ella Baff
Mission: To support dance creation, presentation, education, and preservation; and to engage and deepen public appreciation and support for dance.
Founded: 1933

271
BOSTON BALLET
19 Clarendon Street
Boston, MA 02116-6100
Phone: 617-695-6950
Fax: 617-695-6995
Toll-free: 800-447-7400
e-mail: pr@bostonballet.com
Web Site: www.bostonballet.org
Officers:
Chair: Jack R. Meyer
Vice-Chair: Alison A. Quirk
Company Manager: Kirsten Hwang
Management:
Artistic Director: Mikko Nissien
Music Director/Principal Conductor: Jonathan McPhee
Resident Choreographer: Jorma Elo
Production Stage Manager: Craig Margolis
Executive Director: Barry Hughson
Ballet Master: Larissa Ponomarenko
Assistant Artistic Director: Russell Kaiser
Ballet Master: Anthony Randazzo

Mission: Boston Ballet's mission is to bring new levels of excellence to ballet both on and offstage. We will accomplish this through a process that is inclusive in scope, educational and creative.
Founded: 1963
Specialized Field: Ballet
Status: Professional, Nonprofit
Income Sources: Corporate; Foundations; Grants; Donations
Season: October-May
Performs At: Boston Opera House; Wang Theatre

272
DANCE PRISM
23 Hastings Road
Boston, MA 02421-6806
Phone: 978-371-1038
e-mail: dance_prism@verizon.net
Web Site: www.danceprism.com
Management:
  Artistic Director: Mary Demaso
Mission: A Boston area ballet company dedicated to making affordable professional ballet available to the secondary communities of New England.
Founded: 1982
Specialized Field: Ballet
Season: November-December
Performs At: Bristol Community College; Performing Arts Center; Mechanics Hall; The Collins Center

273
JEANNETTE NEILL DANCE STUDIO
261 Friend Street
5th Floor
Boston, MA 02114
Phone: 617-523-1355
Fax: 617-557-4404
e-mail: info@jndance.com
Web Site: www.jndance.com
Officers:
  Founder: Jeannette Neill
Management:
  Artistic Director: Jeannette Neill
  Music Director: J. Allen Collier
  Work/Study Coordinator: Susan Savoy
Mission: The Jeannette Neill Dance Studio has provided personalized and comprehensive dance training to both the professional and recreational adult dancer.
Founded: 1979
Specialized Field: Hip Hop; Jazz; Theatre Dance
Paid Staff: 3
Volunteer Staff: 10
Performs At: Tsai Performance Center
Type of Stage: Proscenium
Stage Dimensions: 41 1/2 W x 17 91/2 H

274
URBANITY DANCE
280 Shawnut Avenue #1
Boston, MA 02118
Phone: 617-572-3727
e-mail: ask@urbanitydance.org
Web Site: urbanitydance.org
Management:
  Director: Betsi Graves
Mission: To push the limits of contemporary dance technique, striving to inspire audiences with its edgy artistry and startling unpredictability of movement. Building on a rich foundation of classical ballet and modern dance, the company seeks to combine lyrical fluidity with a jazzy economy of expression.
Founded: 2008
Specialized Field: Contemporary Dance

275
ANNA MYER AND DANCERS
536 Massachusetts Ave.
Cambridge, MA 02139
Phone: 617-513-9314
e-mail: annamyerdancers@gmail.com
Web Site: annamyeranddancers.org
Management:
  Director/Performer: Anna Myer
  Composer: Jakov Jakoulov
Mission: Since its founding in 1992 Anna Myer and Dancers has performed Anna Myer's innovative choreography to a steadily growing audience throughout the Northeast, most notably in Boston and New York City, and to the acclaim of some of the country's most prominent dance critics. Myer's unique language of movement is a fusion of her classical, modern, and postmodern background. Her dances are emotionally charged and infused with a keen formal intelligence
Utilizes: Arrangers; Artists-in-Residence; Choreographers; Collaborating Artists; Collaborations; Dance Companies; Dancers; Educators; Fine Artists; Instructors; Lyricists; Multi Collaborations; Multimedia; Music; Playwrights; Singers; Soloists; Special Technical Talent; Volunteer Directors & Actors; Writers
Founded: 1992
Specialized Field: Classical, Modern, Post Modern, Ballet, Hip Hop
Status: Non-Profit
Income Sources: Sponors, Donors
Season: Year Round
Performs At: Institute of Contemporary Art

276
BOSTON DANCE COMPANY
550 Massachusetts Avenue, 3rd Floor
Cambridge, MA 02139
Phone: 617-491-8615
Web Site: bostondancecompany.net
Management:
  Artistic Director: James Reardon
  Associate Artistic Director: Clyde Nantais
  Ballet Mistress: Erika Wolf
Mission: To develop a diverse company and school which provides professional dancers, as well as children, the opportunity to study and perform the works of many different choreographers, and to provide high quality dance productions.
Founded: 1992
Specialized Field: Classical Ballet
Status: Nonprofit
Season: Spring; Winter
Organization Type: Performing; Educational

277
INCA SON: MUSIC AND DANCE OF THE ANDES
P.O. Box 381899
Cambridge, MA 02238-1899
Phone: 781-284-4622
Fax: 781-284-9365
e-mail: CIncaSonV@aol.com
Web Site: www.incason.com
  Chair: Jack R. Meyer
  Vice Chair: Alison.A Quirk
Management:
  Founder/Creative Director: Cesar Villalobos
  Manager: Marianne Ruggiero
Mission: To introduce and educate peoples to the riches of Andean Culture.
Founded: 1988
Specialized Field: Andean Music and Dance
Status: Professional
Performs At: Festivals; Museums; University; Private Parties; Theatre; Schools
Annual Attendance: 1,000,000

278
JOSE MATEO BALLET THEATRE
400 Harvard Street
Cambridge, MA 02138
Phone: 617-354-7467
Fax: 617-354-7856
Web Site: www.ballettheatre.org
Officers:
  Chair: Richard.P Shea
  Board of Directors: Brad Bellows
  Board of Directors: Erline Belton
  Board of Directors: Michelle Caldeira
Management:
  Artistic Director/Choreographer: Jose Mateo
  Managing Director: Scott Fraser
  Director of Development and Institu: Kelly Delekta
  Associate Director of Performance: Andrew Kelley
  Director of Communications: Julie Hayen-Miller
  Development Associate: Katie Epstein
  Studio Programs Manager: Liz Smith
  Accountant: Harvey Soolman
  School Principal: Mary Thompson
Mission: Our mission is to create new ballets of excellence that are stimulating and culturally relevant to diverse audiences and reposition the role of dance in our culture and expand its purpose in the education of youth and enrichment of community locally and beyond.
Founded: 1986
Specialized Field: Ballet
Status: Professional, Nonprofit
Income Sources: Corporate; Foundations, Gifts; Grants; Individuals
Season: October-December
Performs At: The Sanctuary Theatre
Annual Attendance: 10,000

279
SNAPPY DANCE THEATER
720 Massachusetts Avenue
#2
Cambridge, MA 02139
Mailing Address: PO Box 400075, Cambridge, MA 02140
Phone: 617-718-2497
Fax: 775-248-4980
e-mail: info@snappydance.com
Web Site: www.snappydance.com
Officers:
  President: Ellen Grossman
  Treasurer: Jerry Boos
Management:
  Artistic Director: Martha Mason
  General Manager: Philippe Naulot
  Executive Director: Jurgen Weiss
Mission: The group is dedicated to creating compelling performances which work the edge of oxymoron-emotions and images which contradict themselves in art, as in real life.
Founded: 1997
Specialized Field: Contemporary; Modern
Status: Nonprofit

280
ALBANY BERKSHIRE BALLET
116 Fenn Street
Pittsfield, MA 01201

DANCE / Michigan

Mailing Address: 25 Monroe Street, Albany, NY 12210
Phone: 413-445-5382
e-mail: abballet@verizon.net
Web Site: www.berkshireballet.org
Officers:
Founder: Madeline Cantarella Culpo
President: Victile Donahue
Treasurer: Janine Maschino
Secretary: Claire Dalton
Management:
Artistic Director: Madeline Cantarella Culpo
Stage Manager: Laura Claus
Choreographer: Philip Jerry
Choreographer: Francis Patrelle
Mission: The Albany Berkshire Ballet is nationally recognized for its versatility in performing both classical and contemporary dance works with excellence.
Founded: 1960
Specialized Field: Classical; Contemporary

281
THE ART OF BLACK DANCE AND MUSIC
32 Cameron Avenue
Somerville, MA 02144
Phone: 617-666-1859
Fax: 617-666-1859
e-mail: Deamabattle@abdm.net
Web Site: www.abdm.net
Officers:
Founder: DeAma Battle
Management:
Artistic/Executive Director: DeAma Battle
Mission: Our mission is to bridge cultural gaps by teaching the common history of humankind through African-rooted dance, music and folklore, and to entertain audiences of all ages with culturally diverse expressions of African-American heritage.
Utilizes: Five Seasonal Concerts; Singers
Founded: 1975
Specialized Field: Folk Dance
Paid Staff: 1
Volunteer Staff: 2
Paid Artists: 7
Non-paid Artists: 3
Performs At: Veterans War Memorial Auditorium
Annual Attendance: 30,000 - 50,000

Michigan

282
ANN ARBOR DANCE WORKS
University of Michigan Dance Department
1100 Baits Dr.
Ann Arbor, MI 48109-2085
Phone: 734-764-0583
Fax: 734-763-5097
e-mail: cmicklez@umich.edu
Web Site: www.music.umich.edu
Officers:
Chair: Angela Kane
Management:
Dance Administrator: Carla Mickler-Konz
Mission: Our mission is to bridge dance practice and scholarship and to foster interdisciplinary inquiry. As an internationally renowned faculty, we bring a challenging range of perspectives to our teaching and research and we continually reexamine our curriculum in order to prepare both young and mature dancers for careers in an ever-evolving field.
Utilizes: Choreographers; Collaborating Artists; Collaborations; Commissioned Music; Dance Companies; Dancers; Designers; Filmmakers; Five Seasonal Concerts; Grant Writers; Guest Accompanists; Guest Artists; Guest Choreographers; Guest Companies; Guest Conductors; Guest Directors; Guest Musical Directors; Guest Musicians; Instructors; Lyricists; Multi Collaborations; Multimedia; Organization Contracts; Touring Companies
Founded: 1984
Specialized Field: Modern
Status: Professional, Nonprofit
Paid Artists: 9
Non-paid Artists: 10
Budget: $20,000
Income Sources: Corporate; Endowments; Individal; Matching Gifts, Planned Giving
Performs At: Power Center for the Performing Arts
Affiliations: University of Michigan
Annual Attendance: 800
Type of Stage: Proscenium
Stage Dimensions: 55'3-3/4 x 28'
Orchestra Pit: y
Seating Capacity: 1368
Resident Groups: Dance Company of the University of Michigan.

283
MICHIGAN CLASSIC BALLET COMPANY
782 Denison Court
Bloomfield Hills, MI 48302
Phone: 248-334-6964
e-mail: admin@michiganclassicballet.org
Web Site: michiganclassicballet.org
Management:
Artistic Director: Mary C. Geiger
Mission: The purpose of the Michigan Classic Ballet Company is to provide superior performance training for young dancers and to cultivate a public awareness and appreciation of ballet.
Founded: 1989
Specialized Field: Ballet
Status: Nonprofit
Organization Type: Performing; Educational

284
THE MICHIGAN DANCE PROJECT
101 Appian Way, Suite 104
Brighton, MI 48116
Phone: 810-229-5678
e-mail: michigandanceproject@yahoo.com
Web Site: michigandanceproject.com
Management:
Director: Kathy King
Mission: Michigan Dance Project is committed to strengthening the dance community throughout Michigan. By holding regular rehearsals, frequent and affordable classes, and unique performances, MDP is creating excitement about professional dance and the arts within our community.
Founded: 2006
Specialized Field: Contemporary
Status: Nonprofit

285
GRAND RAPIDS BALLET COMPANY
Meijer-Royce Center for Dance
341 Ellsworth
Grand Rapids, MI 49503
Phone: 616-454-4771
Fax: 616-454-0672
e-mail: info@grballet.com
Web Site: www.grballet.com
Officers:
President Spectrum Health: Steffany Dunker
President Elect: Steve Wert
Secretary: Anda Vizulis
Treasurer: Michael P. Kling
Management:
Artistic Director/Choreographer: Patricia Barker
Associate Artistic Director: Laura Schwenk-Berman
Executive Director: Glenn Del Vecchio
Mission: Original programming, innovative choreography, and a commitment to excellence are hallmarks of the Grand Rapids Ballet Company. With artists invested in the community and a community that supports the arts, the Grand Rapids Ballet Company has created a flourishing arts center for all of Michigan and continues to provide the highest level of excellence in dance theatre and education for all individuals.
Utilizes: Choreographers; Collaborations; Commissioned Music; Dancers; Educators; Grant Writers; Guest Accompanists; Guest Artists; Guest Composers; Guest Conductors; Guest Musical Directors; Guest Musicians; High School Drama; Local Unknown Artists; Lyricists; Multimedia; Resident Professionals; Sign Language Translators
Founded: 1971
Specialized Field: Ballet
Status: Professional, Nonprofit
Paid Artists: 16
Budget: $1-$2.5 million
Income Sources: Corporate; Endowment; Individual
Season: October-May
Performs At: DeVos Performance Hall; Peter Martin Wege Theatre
Seating Capacity: 300

286
INTERLOCHEN CENTER FOR THE ARTS
PO Box 199
Interlochen, MI 49643-0199
Phone: 231-276-7200
Fax: 231-276-7464
Toll-free: 800-681-5912
e-mail: admission@interlochen.org
Web Site: www.intelochen.org
Officers:
Chair: Steve Hayden
President: Jeffrey Kimpton
Management:
Dance Director: Mark Borchelt
Mission: Interlochen Center for the Arts engages and inspires people worldwide through excellence in educational, artistic and cultural programs, enhancing the quality of life through the universal language of the arts.
Founded: 1928
Specialized Field: Ballet; Modern
Status: Nonprofit
Income Sources: Corporate; Employer Match; Individual
Season: September-May
Performs At: Corson Auditorium; Dendrinos Chapel; Harvey Theatre; Kresge Auditorium
Annual Attendance: 5,000+
Type of Stage: Proscenium, Amphitheater
Seating Capacity: 952, 200, 4,000, 200

287
BULLARD SCHOOL OF DANCE
431 E South Street
Kalamazoo, MI 49007
Phone: 269-343-3027
Fax: 269-342-8788
Web Site: www.bullardschool.com
Officers:
Founder: Therese Bullard
Management:
Artistic Director: Terry Bullard
Finance Director: Christy Spoehr

DANCE / Minnesota

Marketing / Box Office Director: Misty Hendricks
Mission: The company's artistic philosophy focuses on excellence in professional performance together with fine arts education, coupled with a commitment to developing and maintaining a varied repertoire consisting of traditional (including Highland), classical and innovative dance works.
Utilizes: Five Seasonal Concerts; Guest Artists; Singers
Founded: 1969
Specialized Field: Ballet; Classical; Traditional Ballet
Income Sources: Corporate; Fundraisers; Grants; Individuals
Performs At: Kalamazoo Civic Theatre; Miller Auditorium
Affiliations: Mid-States Regional Dance America Association
Organization Type: Performing; Touring; Educational

288
WELLSPRING/CORI TERRY & DANCERS
359 S Kalamazoo Mall
Suite 204
Kalamazoo, MI 49007
Phone: 269-342-4354
Fax: 269-342-4245
e-mail: wellspring@wellspringdance.org
Web Site: www.wellspringdance.org
Officers:
   President: Matthew Downey
   Treasurer: Kimberley Roberts
   Secretary: Kathie Tomlinson
   VP: Charlie Tomlinson
Management:
   Artistic Director: Cori Terry
   Executive Director: Maria Suszynski
   Artistic Associate: Michael Miller
   Assistant of Operations: Leslie Boughton
Mission: Exists to offer a unique and authentic voice in modern dance, which serves to move, challenge and inspire the community.
Utilizes: Actors; Arrangers; Collaborating Artists; Collaborations; Dance Companies; Dancers; Guest Accompanists; Guest Artists; Guest Lecturers; Guest Musical Directors; Guest Musicians; Instructors; Lyricists; Resident Professionals; Soloists; Touring Companies; Visual Arts
Founded: 1981
Specialized Field: Modern Dance
Status: Professional
Paid Staff: 9
Volunteer Staff: 13
Income Sources: Grants, Donations, Tickets Sales, Rentals
Performs At: Dance/Music
Annual Attendance: 6,000
Facility Category: Stadium Seating
Type of Stage: Sprung Wood
Stage Dimensions: 36' x 26'
Seating Capacity: 140
Year Built: 2000

289
RIVER RAISIN BALLET COMPANY
114 South Monroe Street
Monroe, MI 48161
Phone: 734-242-7722
e-mail: info@riverraisinballet.org
Web Site: riverraisinballet.org
Management:
   Company Director: Gail Choate-Pettit
   Assistant Company Director: Melissa Moore
Founded: 2001
Specialized Field: Ballet
Status: Nonprofit

290
MICHIGAN BALLET THEATRE
1800 S Livernois
Rochester, MI 48307
Phone: 248-652-3117
Web Site: michiganballettheatre.com
Officers:
   President: Pam Kaczmarek
   Vice President: Michelle Stuhlreyer
   Secretary: Joni Christie
   Treasurer: Fran Rossi
Management:
   Executive/Artistic Director: Cornelia Sampson
Mission: To promote and foster dance in Michigan by presenting programs of professional quality thereby giving students and dancers in pursuit of professional careers the opportunity to participate in such programs.
Founded: 1985
Specialized Field: Ballet
Status: Nonprofit

291
EISENHOWER DANCE ENSEMBLE
1541 W Hamlin Road
Rochester Hills, MI 48309
Phone: 248-852-5850
Web Site: www.ededance.org
Officers:
   Founder: Laurie Eisenhower
Management:
   Artistic Director: Laurie Eisenhower
   Associate Artistic Director: Stephanie Pizzo
   Executive Director: Maury Okun
   Vice President for Marketing and De: Natalie Bruno
   Communications Manager: Margo Strebig
Mission: To educate and inform the public about the art of dance through concert performances, educational residencies and workshops.
Founded: 1991
Specialized Field: Contemporary Dance
Paid Staff: 5
Volunteer Staff: 15
Paid Artists: 9
Non-paid Artists: 2

Minnesota

292
CONTINENTAL BALLET COMPANY
Bloomington Civic Plaza
1800 West Old Shakopee Road
Bloomington, MN 55431
Phone: 952-563-8562
Fax: 952-563-8561
e-mail: cbcinfo@continentalballet.com
Web Site: www.continentalballet.com
Management:
   Founder/Director: Riet Velthuisen
   Assistant Director: Jenny Spooner
   Stage Manager: Jacob Edholm
   Assistant Stage Manager: Barbara Torkelson
   Registrar: Alicia Smith
   Production Manager: Joseph Bingham
   Costume Manager: Sharon Jacobson
Mission: Continental Ballet Company's mission is to promote the integrity of classical ballet while bringing the ballet into the community. This is accomplished through public performances, studio classes and educational programs. Every effort is made to make the art of ballet accessible to a greater audience and to share knowledge and passion for the art of classical ballet.
Utilizes: Choreographers; Dancers; Grant Writers; Guest Accompanists; Soloists; Special Technical Talent; Theatre Companies
Founded: 1988
Specialized Field: Classical Ballet
Status: Non-Profit
Income Sources: Donations, Sponsorship

293
MINNESOTA BALLET
301 W First Street
Suite 800
Duluth, MN 55802
Phone: 218-529-3742
Fax: 218-529-3744
e-mail: office@minnesotaballet.org
Web Site: www.minnesotaballet.org
Officers:
   President: Harvey Plasch
   First VP: Susan Johnson
   Second VP: Carole Turner
   Treasurer: Ken Kolquist
   Secretary: Betsy Holcomb
Management:
   Artistic Director: Robert Gardner
   Production/Tour Manager: Kenneth Pogin
   Managing Director: Willy McManus
   Stage Manager/Projects Coordinator: Cheryl Vander Heyden
   Office Assistant: Tracy Colclough
   Company Photographer: Jeff Frey
Mission: To maintain a high-quality school of ballet and a company of professional dancers; to present a regular series of performances.
Utilizes: Choreographers; Dance Companies; Dancers; Designers; Five Seasonal Concerts; Guest Accompanists; Guest Artists; Guest Ensembles; Guest Musical Directors; High School Drama; Instructors; Local Artists; Multimedia; Original Music Scores; Resident Artists; Resident Professionals; Soloists; Theatre Companies
Founded: 1965
Specialized Field: Ballet; Jazz; Tap; Modern
Status: Professional, Nonprofit
Paid Staff: 4
Volunteer Staff: 30
Paid Artists: 12
Budget: $500,000-$600,000
Income Sources: Foundations; Corporate; Individual
Performs At: Duluth Entertainment & Convention Center
Type of Stage: Proscenium
Stage Dimensions: 60'x45'
Seating Capacity: 2,400
Organization Type: Performing; Touring; Resident; Educational; Sponsoring

294
HAUSER DANCE COMPANY
1750 Hennepin Avenue
Minneapolis, MN 55403
Phone: 612-375-7670
e-mail: info@mnartists.org
Web Site: www.mnartists.org/article.do?rid=14323
Management:
   Artistic Director/Choreographer: Heidi Hauser Jasmin, nhdc@tcinternet.net
   Project Director: Scott Stulen
   Project Coordinator: Jehra Patrick
   Program Director: Jehra Patrick
   Program Assistant: Emily Gastineau

DANCE / Minnesota

Mission: The mission of Houser Dance is to promote and sustain the living language of music and dance. Our mission is accomplished by performing and teaching the constantly evolving Houser aesthetics and to provide opportunities for people of all ages and abilities to participate in and appreciate the art form. We are commited to presenting the highest quality of music dance performance and educational programming for the broadest possible audience
Utilizes: Choreographers; Collaborating Artists; Commissioned Composers; Composers; Dance Companies; Dancers; Designers; Educators; Grant Writers; Guest Ensembles; Guest Speakers; High School Drama; Original Music Scores; Resident Artists; Selected Students
Founded: 1961
Specialized Field: Modern
Status: Professional, Nonprofit
Paid Staff: 2
Volunteer Staff: 20
Paid Artists: 6
Non-paid Artists: 15
Budget: $55,000
Income Sources: Foundations; Corporations; Individuals
Performs At: Small Theatre
Annual Attendance: 1,000
Facility Category: Dance studio; Small black box theater
Stage Dimensions: 28'x40'
Seating Capacity: 100
Year Built: 1925
Year Remodeled: 1989
Organization Type: Performing; Touring; Educational; Sponsoring

295
JAMES SEWELL BALLET
528 Hennepin Avenue
Suite 215
Minneapolis, MN 55403-1810
Phone: 612-672-0480
e-mail: info@jsballet.org
Web Site: www.jsballet.org
Officers:
   Co-Founder: James Sewell
   Co-Founder: Sally Rousse
Management:
   Artistic Director/Choreographer: James Sewell
   Artistic Associate: Penelope Freeh
   Lighting Designer/Production Mgr: Kevin A Jones
   Executive Director: George Sutton
   Operations Director: Mary Jo Peloquin
Mission: James Sewell Ballet's mission is to create and perform works that connect artists with audiences and to advance contemporary ballet.
Founded: 1990
Specialized Field: Ballet

296
MINNESOTA DANCE THEATRE & DANCE INSTITUTE
528 Hennepin Avenue
6th Floor
Minneapolis, MN 55403
Phone: 612-338-0627
Fax: 612-338-5160
e-mail: info@mndance.org
Web Site: www.mndance.org
Officers:
   Managing Director: Marsha Walker
Management:
   Artistic Director: Lise Houlton
   Managing Director: Marsha Walker
   Business Manager: Tefera Kassa
   Office Manager: Denise Culshaw
Mission: Minnesota Dance Theatre & the Dance Institute is renowned as one of Minnesota's cultural treasures with an eclectic international voice performing dance.
Utilizes: Singers
Founded: 1962
Specialized Field: Theatrical Dance; Traditional Dance; Contemporary Dance
Status: Professional, Nonprofit
Paid Staff: 140
Volunteer Staff: 150
Paid Artists: 35
Budget: $1,000,000
Income Sources: Ticket Revenue; Donations; State Funding; Grants
Performs At: State Theatre; Illusion Theater; Fitzgerald Theater
Annual Attendance: 23,000
Organization Type: Performing; Touring; Resident; Educational

297
NORTHROP DANCE SEASON
84 Church Street Se
Minneapolis, MN 55455
Phone: 612-625-6600
Fax: 612-626-1750
e-mail: northrop@umn.edu
Web Site: www.northrop.umn.edu/events/northrop-dance
Management:
   Artistic Director: Ben Johnson
   Event Manager: Eileen May
   Stage Manager: Mike Damman
   Stage Manager: Justin Burke
   Operations Director: Sally Dischinger
   Business Manager: Robin Sauerwein
Mission: To offer an annual season featuring six to eight of the finest national and international dance companies.
Utilizes: Students
Founded: 1928
Specialized Field: Jazz
Status: Professional, Nonprofit
Paid Staff: 13
Volunteer Staff: 20
Budget: $4,000,000
Income Sources: Association of Performing Arts Presenters; International Society of Performing Arts Administrators
Performs At: Northrop Memorial Auditorium
Annual Attendance: 235,560
Organization Type: Sponsoring

298
STUART PIMSLER DANCE & THEATER
528 Hennepin Ave S.
Suite 707
Minneapolis, MN 55403
Phone: 763-521-7738
e-mail: spdanth@gmail.com
Web Site: www.stuartpimsler.com
Management:
   Co-Artistic Director: Stuart Pimsler
   Co-Artistic Director: Suzanne Costello
   Associate Professor of Dance: Heather Klopchin
Mission: Stuart Pimsler Dance and Theater's work stands apart in the field of contemporary performance for its vast emotional range, intellectual provocations and stunning visual environments.
Utilizes: Guest Companies; Singers
Founded: 1978
Specialized Field: Modern
Status: Professional
Budget: $200,000-$500,000
Income Sources: Ohio Dance; Association for Performing Arts Presenters; Alliance for Dance & Movement Arts
Organization Type: Performing

299
ZENON DANCE COMPANY AND SCHOOL
528 Hennepin Avenue
Suite 400
Minneapolis, MN 55403
Phone: 612-338-1101
Fax: 612-338-2479
e-mail: info@zenondance.org
Web Site: www.zenondance.org
Management:
   Artistic Director: Linda Andrews
   Managing Director: Danielle Robinson-Prater
   Development Director: Mara Winke
   School Coordinator: Lauren Holmes
   Business Assistant: Adia Morris
   Workstudy Coordinator: Patty Lefaive
   External Relations & Media: Camille LeFevre
Mission: Our mission is to sustain an artistically excellent, professional dance company in the Twin Cities by commissioning the works of emerging and locally, nationally and internationally recognized modern and jazz choreographers and to present this work to diverse communities, including those with disabilities.
Utilizes: Commissioned Composers; Commissioned Music; Dance Companies; Dancers; Five Seasonal Concerts; Guest Artists; Guest Companies; High School Drama; Local Artists; Multimedia; Original Music Scores; Resident Artists; Selected Students
Founded: 1983
Specialized Field: Modern; Jazz
Status: Professional, Nonprofit
Paid Staff: 5
Volunteer Staff: 30
Paid Artists: 8
Facility Category: 2 Dance Studios
Stage Dimensions: 54'x46'; 56'x27'
Organization Type: Performing; Touring; Resident; Educational

300
ZORONCO FAMENCO DANCE THEATER AND SCHOOL
3012 Minnehaha Ave South
Minneapolis, MN 55406-1932
Phone: 612-234-1653
e-mail: zorongoflamenco@gmail.com
Web Site: www.zorongo.oeg
Management:
   Choreographer/Artistic Director: Susana Di Palma
   Director/Composer/Guitarist: Pedro Cortes Jr
Mission: One of the few American Spanish dance companies that present both traditional flamenco programs as well as original theater flamenco works. The company is comprised of an ensemble of international artists, dancers and musicians - renowned for bringing the power, passion and virtuosity of the art of flamenco to American audiences.
Utilizes: Arrangers; Artists-in-Residence; Choreographers; Collaborating Artists; Collaborations; Composers; Dancers; Lyricists; Multi Collaborations; Multimedia; Music; Paid Performers
Founded: 1982
Specialized Field: American Spanish Dance
Status: Non-Profit
Income Sources: Donors, Sponsors

Season: November
Performs At: James J Hill Reference Library

301
ETHNIC DANCE THEATRE
3507 Clinton Ave South
New Hope, MN 55408
Phone: 763-545-1333
e-mail: info@ethnicdancetheatre.com
Web Site: www.ethnicdancetheatre.com
Officers:
   Founder: Donald LaCourse
   Chair: Eva Maria Kish
   Vice Chair: Rita Schultz
   Secretary: Jeanne Schultz
Management:
   Artistic Director: Donald LaCourse
   Volunteer Managing Director: Eva Kish
   Chief Financial Officer: Zinta Pone
Mission: Our mission is to foster understanding and awareness of world cultures through the re-creation and presentation of traditional ethnic dance and music.
Founded: 1974
Specialized Field: Ethnic Dance
Status: Professional, Nonprofit
Budget: $154,000
Income Sources: Grants; Federal; Government; Corporation; Individual; Ticket Sales
Performs At: Concordia University
Annual Attendance: 40,000
Organization Type: Performing; Touring; Resident; Educational

Mississippi

302
BALLET MISSISSIPPI
201 East Pascagoula Street
Suite 106
Jackson, MS 39215
Phone: 601-960-1560
Fax: 601-960-2135
e-mail: keary@balletms.com
Web Site: www.balletms.com
Management:
   Artistic Director: David Keary
Mission: Ballet Mississipi has continued the tradition begun by the founders, by reestablishing the Ballet Mississippi School which focuses on classical technique, discipline and performance opportunities.
Utilizes: Five Seasonal Concerts; Singers
Founded: 1983
Specialized Field: Classical
Status: Professional, Nonprofit
Budget: $100,000-$200,000
Organization Type: Performing; Touring; Resident; Educational

303
HINGE DANCE COMPANY
2580 West Jackson Avenue, Suite 35
Oxford, MS 03865
Phone: 770-655-1352
e-mail: lydiasiniard@gmail.com
Web Site: hingedancecompany.com
Management:
   Artistic Director: Lydia Siniard
   Artistic Director: Lindsay Fine

Missouri

304
ALEXANDRA BALLET
68 E Four Seasons Center
Chesterfield, MO 63017
Phone: 314-469-6222
Fax: 314-469-6222
e-mail: alexandraballet@msn.com
Web Site: www.alexandraballet.com
Officers:
   President: Peter Karutz
   Vice President: Donnagail Carr
   Secretary: Sally Duncan
   Treasurer: Juliet Chayat
Management:
   Artistic Director: Alexandra Zaharias
   Company Administrator: CiCi Houston
   Marketing/Communications: Lisa Howe
   Ballet Mistress: Norma Winslow Gabriel
   Ballet Mistress: Lauren Trerice
Mission: Repertoire ranges from classic to contemporary. Performance showcases original works through the restaging of classics by locally and internationally known choreographers and the collaboration of professional guest artists.
Utilizes: Choreographers; Collaborations; Dancers; Educators; Guest Artists
Founded: 1984
Specialized Field: Ballet
Status: Non-Profit; Semi-Professional
Paid Staff: 3
Volunteer Staff: 56
Income Sources: Foundations; Fundraising; Corporate; Missouri Arts Council; Regional Arts Commission-St. Louis; Arts & Education Council of Greater St. Louis
Performs At: Touhill Performing Arts Center; Purser Center; Sheldon Concert Hall, Edison Theatre
Affiliations: Regional Dance America
Annual Attendance: 8,000
Resident Groups: Dance

305
SAINT LOUIS BALLET
218 THF Boulevard
Chesterfield, MO 63005
Phone: 636-537-1998
e-mail: info@stlouisballet.org
Web Site: www.stlouisballet.org
Officers:
   President: Chris Grahn-Howard
   VP: Lisa Forsyth
   Treasurer: Lawrence Miller
   Secretary: Cathie Hernandez
Management:
   Artistic/Executive Director: Gen Horiuchi
   Ballet Mistress: Heather Iler
   Principal Guest Choreographer: Christopher d'Amboise
   Development Manager: Becky Goff
   Finance Manager: Julie Abernathie
   Associate Administrator: Jennifer Warren
   Lighting Director: Don Guy
   Stage Manager: Amy Soll
Mission: Dedicated to bringing audiences quality performances through a diverse repertoire that is both classical and contemporary.
Specialized Field: Classical; Contemporary
Status: Professional, Nonprofit

306
MISSOURI CONTEMPORARY BALLET
110 Orr Street, Suite 102
Columbia, MO 65201
Phone: 573-219-7134
e-mail: info@missouricontemporaryballet.com
Web Site: missouricontemporaryballet.com
Management:
   Artistic/Executive Director: Karen Mareck Grundy
   Ballet Mistress: Joanne Sandorfi
   Ballet Mistress: Julie Atremova-Schauwecker
   Resident Choreographer: Shannon West
   Ballet Master/Rehearsal Director: Ken Braso
Mission: Missouri Contemporary Ballet (MCB) is a professional dance company committed to creating and presenting high-quality productions and educational opportunities through the art of contemporary ballet.
Founded: 2010
Specialized Field: Contemporary Ballet
Status: Nonprofit; Professional

307
BALLET NORTH
6308 N Prospect Avenue
Gladstone, MO 64119-1825
Phone: 816-454-4859
e-mail: ballet.north@gmail.com
Web Site: www.balletnorth.com
Officers:
   Co-Founder: Laura Luzicka Reinschmidt
   Co-Founder: Matthew Reinschmidt
Management:
   Artistic Director: Laura Luzicka Reinschmidt
   Artistic Director: Mathew Reinschmidt
Mission: Perform rarely seen full-length classical ballets and modern works in theatre.
Founded: 1986
Specialized Field: Classical
Status: Nonprofit
Paid Staff: 4
Volunteer Staff: 12
Paid Artists: 8
Non-paid Artists: 20
Budget: $55,000
Income Sources: Performance revenue; Fund raisers; Grants
Affiliations: Independent
Facility Category: Professional theater

308
KANSAS CITY BALLET
1616 Broadway Street
Kansas City, MO 64108-1208
Mailing Address: 500 W. Pershing Road, Kansas City, MO 64108-2430
Phone: 816-931-2232
Fax: 816-931-1172
Toll-free: 888-968-2538
e-mail: info@kcballet.org
Web Site: www.kcballet.org
Officers:
   President: Jean Paul Wong
   Chairperson: Julia I. Kauffman
   Vice-President: Jack Rowe, J.D.
   Treasurer: Barbara Storm
   Secretary: Claire Brand
Management:
   Artistic Director: William Whitener
   Ballet Master: James Jordan
   Ballet Mistress: Karen Brown
   Production Manager: Amy Taylor
   Stage Manager: Heather O'Mara
   Executive Director: Jeffrey J Bentley

DANCE / Montana

Marketing Director: Mike Allen
General Manager: Kevin Amey
Director of Community Programs: Linda Martin
Mission: To establish Kansas City Ballet as an indispensable asset of the Kansas City community through exceptional performances, excellence in dance training and community education for all ages.
Utilizes: Sign Language Translators; Students
Founded: 1957
Specialized Field: Ballet
Status: Professional
Paid Artists: 25
Budget: $5,000,000
Performs At: Lyric and Midland Theatre
Affiliations: MAC, National Endowment for the Arts
Annual Attendance: 48,000

309
WYLLIAMS/HENRY CONTEMPORARY DANCE COMPANY (WHCDC)
209 South Olive
Kansas City, MO 64124
Phone: 816-241-4511
Web Site: www.wylliams-henry.org
Management:
  Artistic Director: Mary Pat Henry
  Co-Founder: Leni Wylliams
  Co-Artistic Director/Atlanta: Lonnie Davis
  Assistant Director: Paula Weber
  Choreographer: Amber Ann Perkins
  Choreographer: Anna Sokolow
  Choreographer: Bill Jones
  Choreographer: Charles Moulton
  Coreographer: David Parsons
Mission: The Wylliams/Henry Contemporary Dance Company has been hailed by critics and audiences alike as one of the most exciting, captivating dance troupes in the Midwest. WHCDC is known for its beautiful, athletic style in a repertory ranging from the lyric to the avant garde. Performances are given in both conventional and non-traditional spaces — often in partnership with community organizations — to introduce contemporary dance to new audiences.
Utilizes: Arrangers; Artists-in-Residence; Choreographers; Collaborating Artists; Collaborations; Dancers; Educators; Local Artists; Local Artists & Directors; Multimedia; Paid Performers; Student Interns
Founded: 2001
Specialized Field: Contemporary
Status: Donors, Sponsors
Income Sources: Donors, Sponsors
Season: September
Performs At: White Hall

310
DANCE SAINT LOUIS
3547 Olive Street
Suite 301
Saint Louis, MO 63103
Phone: 314-534-5000
Fax: 314-534-5001
e-mail: bmacrobie@dancestlouis.org
Web Site: www.dancestlouis.org
Officers:
  Founder: Annelise Mertz
  Chairman: Ken Kranzberg
  President: Mark Lindgren
  Secretary: Connie Schnuck
  Treasurer: Jesika Barnes
Management:
  Artistic/Executive Director: Michael Uthoff
  Finance Director: Berrien Tedford
  Development Director: Richard.M Dee
  Box Office Manager: Rachel Lampert
  Grants Manager: Alex Klein
  Director of Operations & Education: Janet Brown
  Director of Marketing: Julie Kruempel
  Marketing Coordinator: Miranda Donley
Mission: Dance Saint Louis' mission is to provide the Saint Louis region with the world's best dance and to develop an appreciation of dance as an art form. Dance Saint Louis fulfills this mission through dance presentation, creation and education outreach.
Utilizes: Singers
Founded: 1966
Specialized Field: Classical Ballet; Contemporary Ballet; Modern; Ethnic Dance; Ballroom; Tap; Jazz; Hip Hop
Status: Nonprofit
Income Sources: Dance USA; Individual; Corporate
Performs At: Kiel Opera House; Edison Theatre; Washington University
Organization Type: Resident; Educational; Sponsoring

311
THE SPRINGFIELD BALLET COMPANY
420 S Sixth Street
Springfield, MO 62701
Phone: 217-544-1967
Fax: 217-544-1968
e-mail: info@springfieldballetco.org
Web Site: www.springfieldballetco.org
Officers:
  President: Sarah L. Beuning
  Vice President: Mindy Vance
  Treasurer: Linda Shaefer
  Secretary: Angie Bruce
  Finance Chair: Julie Davis
  Promotions Chair: Sarah Dietrich Yockey
Management:
  Artistic Director: Julie Dunn
  Ballet Mistress: Gina DeCroix
  Administrative Director: Sally Hamilton
Mission: Dance is the language of movement that gives voice to the human spirit. The Springfield Ballet Company uses the beauty, energy and diversity of dance to speak to the community. It is this common language that encourages freedom of expression, bridges generations and cultures and adds to the richness of life in central Illinois.
Utilizes: Choreographers; Collaborations; Dance Companies; Dancers; Designers; Guest Artists; Guest Choreographers; Guest Companies; Guest Conductors; Guest Writers; High School Drama; Local Artists; Resident Professionals; Soloists
Founded: 1975
Specialized Field: Classical; Contemporary; Jazz; Modern; Tap; Theatre Dance
Status: Nonprofit
Paid Staff: 3
Paid Artists: 30

Montana

312
THE MONTANA BALLET COMPANY
521 E. Peach Street
Bozeman, MT 59715
Phone: 406-582-8702
Fax: 406-586-9659
Web Site: www.montanaballet.com
Officers:
  Founder: Ann Bates
  Board Chair: Kirsten Smith
  Treasurer: Donna Murphrey
Management:
  Artistic Director: Ann Bates
  Co-Artistic Director: Amy Lynn Stoddart
  Co-Artistic Director: Elizabeth DeFanti
Mission: The mission of Montana Ballet Company has been to produce top quality dance performances from a variety of cultural and ethnic traditions and to provide outstanding education outreach opportunities to the underserved populations.
Utilizes: Collaborating Artists; Composers; Dance Companies; Dancers; Five Seasonal Concerts; Guest Accompanists; Guest Choreographers; Guest Musical Directors; Guest Musicians; Guest Speakers; Guest Writers; Organization Contracts; Theatre Companies
Founded: 1984
Specialized Field: Ballet
Status: Pre-Professional, Nonprofit
Paid Staff: 3
Volunteer Staff: 75
Budget: $210,000
Income Sources: Grants; Donations; Ticket Sales
Performs At: Willson Auditorium
Annual Attendance: 7,000-10,000
Facility Category: School
Stage Dimensions: 32'x 26'
Seating Capacity: 1,100
Organization Type: Performing; Touring; Educational; Sponsoring

313
BALLET MONTANA
1601 North Benton Avenue
Helena, MT 59625
Phone: 406-447-5508
e-mail: smulcahy@carroll.edu
Web Site: balletmontana.us
Management:
  Director: Sallyann Mulcahy
Founded: 1995
Specialized Field: Ballet
Status: Nonprofit

314
HEADWATERS DANCE COMPANY
P.O. Box 9356
Missoula, MT 59807
Phone: 406-728-1131
e-mail: info@headwatersdance.org
Web Site: headwatersdance.org
Management:
  Director: Amy Ragsdale
Mission: The mission of Headwaters Dance Co. is to develop and showcase thought-provoking, contemporary, socially relevant dance and to increase audience appreciation for this kind of dance.
Founded: 2004
Specialized Field: Contemporary
Status: Professional

315
ROCKY MOUNTAIN BALLET THEATRE
2704 Brooks Street
Missoula, MT 59801
Phone: 406-549-5155
e-mail: rmbts@aol.com
Web Site: www.rmbt.org
Officers:
  President: Honore Bray
  Vice President: Donald Carey
  Secretary: Ernese Vitalis
  Board Member: Nancy Matthews
  Board Member: Susie Risho
  Board Member: Katie Davis
  Advisory Board: Stanley Holden
  Advisory Board: Michael Smuin
Management:

DANCE / Nebraska

Artistic Director: Charlene Campbell Carey
Music Director: Karen Carreno
Director: Brandy Reinhardt
Assistant to the Director: Jenifer Kerber
Mission: Rocky Mountain Ballet Theatre (RMBT) and Rocky Mountain Ballet Theatre School were founded 1998 by Artistic Director Charlene Campbell Carey. RMBT is one of the few schools in Montana that has a music director who provides live piano accompaniment for classes. RMBT School opened with 40 students and has now tripled in size. The school offers classes in ballet, pointe, jazz, tap, kick line, and contemporary repertoire for ages 3 to adult.
Utilizes: Choreographers; Collaborating Artists; Dance Companies; Dancers; Educators; Fine Artists; Guest Artists; Guest Ensembles; High School Drama; Local Artists; Scenic Designers; Soloists; Special Technical Talent; Theatre Companies
Founded: 1998
Specialized Field: Ballet, Pointe, Jazz, Tap, Creative Movement
Income Sources: Corporate Giving, Class Fees
Affiliations: Pasadena Civic Ballet, Debut Dance Company, Broadway Dance Center, All Heart Boxing Foundation. University of Montana

Nebraska

316
BALLET NEBRASKA
P.O. Box 6413
Omaha, NE 68106
Phone: 402-541-6946
e-mail: info@balletnebraska.org
Web Site: balletnebraska.org
Management:
  Artistic Director: Erika Overturff
  Ballet Master: Matthew Carter
Mission: Enriching the communities of Nebraska and Iowa through professional dance performance, educational programs, and community outreach.
Specialized Field: Ballet
Status: Nonprofit

317
NEBRASKA THEATRE CARAVAN
Omaha Community Playhouse
6915 Cass Street
Omaha, NE 68132-2696
Phone: 402-553-4890
Fax: 402-553-6288
Web Site: www.nebraskatheatrecaravan.com
Officers:
  MD: Greg Scheer
Management:
  Artistic Director: Carl Beck
  Executive Director: Tim Schmad
  Technical Director: Don Hook
  House Manager: Matt Bross
  Artistic Coordinator: Lara Marsh
  Producing Director: Beau Bisson
  Managing Director: Greg Scheer
Mission: To provide quality theatrical experiences and educational opportunities to communities in which they would not otherwise be available. The Nebraska Theatre Caravan is the professional touring wing of the Omaha Community Playhouse.
Founded: 1975
Specialized Field: Theatrical Dance; Educational Dance

Nevada

318
LAS VEGAS BALLET COMPANY
1350 South Jones Boulevard Suite 110
Las Vegas, NV 89117
Phone: 702-240-3262
e-mail: info@lasvegasballet.org
Web Site: lasvegasballet.org
Management:
  Artistic Director: Kyudong Kwak
Mission: Las Vegas Ballet Company aims to educate the people of the community in classical ballet, thereby promoting and nurturing the city's growing artistic culture.
Specialized Field: Classical Ballet
Status: Nonprofit

319
NEVADA BALLET THEATRE
1651 Inner Circle
Las Vegas, NV 89134
Phone: 702-243-2623
Fax: 702-804-0365
e-mail: info@nevadaballet.com
Web Site: www.nevadaballet.com
Officers:
  President: Madeleine Andress
  Co-Chair: Nancy Houssels
  Co-Chair: Wendy Plaster
  Vice-President: Kari Halkyard
  CFO & General Manager: Lorin Wolfe
  Secretary: Lauri Thompson
  Treasurer: Craig Cavileer
Management:
  Artistic Director: James Canfield
  Company Instructor: Clarice Rathers
  Executive Director/CEO: Beth Barbre
  Assistant to the Executive Director: Jackie Wolf
  Ballet Mistress: Peggy Dolkas
  Production/Stage Manager: Tom Mehan
  Director of Development: Angela Quick
  Director of Public Relations: Jenn Kratochwill
  Director of External Affairs: Jennifer Cornet
Mission: Our mission is to educate and inspire regional, statewide and national audiences and vitally impact community life through professional company productions, dance training, education and outreach.
Founded: 1972
Specialized Field: Ballet
Status: Nonprofit
Budget: $1-$2,5 million

320
THE LAS VEGAS CONTEMPORARY DANCE THEATER
9920 Garamound Avenue
Las Vegas, NV 89117
Phone: 702-878-1227
e-mail: info@lvdance.org
Web Site: lvcontemporarydancetheater.org
Management:
  Artistic Director: Bernard H. Gaddis
Mission: Dedicated to preserving and presenting the work of generations of great artists, choreographers and teachers, as well as, showcasing the work of emerging talent in a broad spectrum of dance styles.
Founded: 1990
Specialized Field: Contemporary
Status: Nonprofit

321
NEVADA FESTIVAL BALLET
1790 W Fourth Street
Suite B
Reno, NV 89503
Phone: 775-785-7915
Fax: 775-785-7918
e-mail: leann@gbis.com
Officers:
  President: Michael McKeno
Management:
  Business Manager: Leann Pinguelo
Utilizes: Choreographers; Collaborating Artists; Collaborations; Dance Companies; Dancers; Guest Artists; Guest Composers; Guest Ensembles; Guest Musical Directors; High School Drama; Instructors; Lyricists; Original Music Scores; Soloists; Student Interns; Theatre Companies
Founded: 1984
Specialized Field: Ballet

322
THE RENO IRISH DANCE COMPANY
3005 Skyline Boulevard Suite 150
Reno, NV 89509
Phone: 775-745-0820
e-mail: ridco@gmail.com
Web Site: renoirishdanceco.org
Management:
  Artistic Director/Choreographer: Amanda Coulson
Mission: The company provides a platform for young aspiring, pre-professional dancers, singers and musicians in the performing arts, in a professional environment. Their mission in the community is to reach, educate and entertain all ages with the traditional and the new age of Irish and Celtic Music and Dance.
Founded: 1997
Specialized Field: Irish Dance
Status: Nonprofit

New Hampshire

323
NORTHERN BALLET THEATRE DANCE CENTER
36 Arlington Street
Nashua, NH 03060
Phone: 603-889-8408
Web Site: nbtdc.com
Officers:
  Founder: Doreen Cafarella
  President: Andrew Piela
  VP: Rhonda Rendina
  Treasurer: Patricia Lavoie
  Secretary: Janice Bauer
Management:
  Founder: Doreen Cafarella
  Artistic Director: Tina Cassidy
Mission: Northern Ballet Theatre is dedicated to providing world class dancers, exciting sets and breathtaking choreography.
Founded: 1986
Specialized Field: Ballet
Status: Professional, Nonprofit

324
GREAT BAY ACADEMY OF DANCE
1 Raynes Avenue
Suite 203
Portsmouth, NH 03801

DANCE / New Jersey

Phone: 603-433-4200
Web Site: www.gbadance.com
Management:
  Artistic Director: Barbara Pontecorvo
  Executive Director: Martha Lemire
  Director: Elisa Gerasin
  Administrative Manager: Elissa Cummings
  Tap, Contemporary: Rebecca Waitt
  Ballet, Rehearsal Mistress: Elyssa Bigos
  Ballet, Lyrical: Crystal Lisbon
Mission: Dedicated to producing the highest standard in excellence in professional dance performance, educating dancers of all ages and levels and providing outreach programming throughout the New England area.
Specialized Field: Ballet
Status: Pre-Professional, Nonprofit
Budget: $200,000-$500,000

New Jersey

325
NEW JERSEY TAP ENSEMBLE
590 Bloomfield Avenue
Suite 383
Bloomfield, NJ 07003
Phone: 973-743-0600
Fax: 973-743-3899
e-mail: njtapinfo@njtap.org
Web Site: njtap.org
Officers:
  Treasurer: Sonia Vance
  Chairman: Donald Kalfus
  Board Chair: Barbara Hoffman
Management:
  Artisitc Director: Deborah Mitchell
  Business Manager: Kenneth MacDonald
  Creative Director: Christina Balas
  Bookkeeper: Ann Kern
Mission: This touring dance company's mission is to preserve and celebrate the american art form of rythym tap dancing through public performances.
Founded: 1994
Specialized Field: Rythym Tap
Status: Non-Profit

326
ATLANTIC CITY BALLET
2301 Boardwalk
Egg Harbor City, NJ 08401
Phone: 609-348-7201
e-mail: apieroni@acballet.org
Web Site: www.acballet.org
Officers:
  President: Dr J Zimmerman
  Vice President: Diane DeLuca
  Treasurer: Ted De Ment
  Secretary: Sandra Kahn
Management:
  Artistic Director/Choreographer: Phyllis Papa
  Company Pianist: Steve Huber
  Wardrobe Mistress: Regina Silver
  Marketing Manager: Alexandria Pieroni
  Company Photographer: Craig Billow
  Booking Agent: Larry McCoy
  Accountant?: L. Robin Macmillan
  Development: Peter Marro
Mission: The Atlantic City Ballet (ACB) is a 501 c (3) not-for-profit organization dedicated to bringing the highest quality classical and contemporary dance to audiences of all ages and cultures, with a primary focus on audiences in Southern New Jersey and the surrounding region. Promotes this mission through access to fully-staged performances by a skilled resident company of professional dancers, educational programs suitable for all skill levels.
Utilizes: Artists-in-Residence; Choreographers; Collaborations; Dance Companies; Dancers; Fine Artists; Lyricists; Multimedia; Paid Performers; Poets; Resident Artists
Founded: 1982
Specialized Field: Ballet, Classical, Contemporary Dance
Status: Non-Profit, Professional
Paid Artists: 25
Non-paid Artists: 11
Income Sources: Sponsors, Donations
Performs At: Atlantic City's Boardwalk Hall, Keswick Theatre in Glenside, Pennsylvania
Affiliations: Atlantic City Convention and Visitors Authority

327
ATLANTIC CONTEMPORARY BALLET
713 W Moss Mill Road
Egg Harbor City, NJ 08205
Phone: 609-804-1995
e-mail: acbt@acbt.org
Web Site: www.acbt.org
Officers:
  Founder: Phyllis Papa
Management:
  Artistic Director: Phyllis Papa
  Staff: Mark McCormack
  Administration: Alexandria Pieroni
Mission: The Atlantic City Ballet is a unique chamber ballet company with an exciting repertoire which cherishes the great tradition of classical ballet and explores the contemporary. The Atlantic City Ballet is in residence at the Atlantic Contemporary Ballet.
Utilizes: Actors; Dancers; Five Seasonal Concerts; Guest Ensembles; Guest Musical Directors; Guest Musicians; High School Drama; Original Music Scores; Sign Language Translators; Soloists
Founded: 1982
Specialized Field: Chamber Ballet
Paid Artists: 9
Budget: $40,000-$100,000

328
NAI-NI CHEN DANCE COMPANY
PO Box 1121
Fort Lee, NJ 07024
Toll-free: 800-650-0246
e-mail: info@nainichen.org
Web Site: www.nainichen.org
Officers:
  Chair: Nai-Ni Chen
  President: Regina Andriolo
Management:
  Artistic Director/Choreographer: Nai-Ni Chen
  Executive Director: Andrew Chiang
  Company Manager: Heather Wallace
Mission: Nai-Ni Chen's distinctive style blends the discipline of Chinese classical movement with the freedom of American modern dance. Her work finds inspiration in everything from the flowing lines of calligraphy to the thunderous motion of martial arts to the grace and beauty of nature itself.
Founded: 1988
Specialized Field: Contemporary; Traditional Ballet
Status: Professional, Nonprofit
Paid Staff: 3
Paid Artists: 09
Income Sources: New Jersey State Council of the Arts; Corporate; Foundations; Grants
Annual Attendance: 100,000

329
MOSAIC DANCE THEATER COMPANY
7 Columbus Ave
Glen Ridge, NJ 07028
Phone: 973-783-2395
e-mail: mosaicdtc@att.net
Web Site: www.mosaicdancetheaterco.org
Officers:
  President: Celeste Varricchio
  Secretary: Robert Greenwald
  Treasurer: Karen Lindsay
Management:
  Artistic Director: Morgiana Celeste
  Artisitc Director/Choreographer: Samara
  Producing Artistic Director: Morgiana Celeste Varricchio
  Education & Outreach Coordinator: Adriana Rosa
Mission: This performing and touring dance company presents original dance, theater, and educational programs celebratinbg the rich diversity of cultures and folkloric traditions of the Mediterranean, including the Middle East, North Africa, Turkey, Greece, Italy and spain.
Founded: 2003
Specialized Field: Middle Eastern; Mediterranean Dance
Status: Non-Profit

330
RANDY JAMES DANCE WORKS
PO Box 4452
Highland Park, NJ 08904
Phone: 732-247-2653
Fax: 732-247-5353
e-mail: rjdwed@aol.com
Web Site: www.dancenj.org/ob/dancenj/directory/randyjames.shtml
Officers:
  President: Dr Philip Levy
  Vice President: Dorothy Bitetto
  Treasurer: Marvin Auerbach
Management:
  Artistic Director/Choreographer: Randy James
  Executive Director: Ruth Lanza
Mission: The company is deeply committed to dance education and providing a forum for nurturing creative thoughts and ideas and exposing the public to physical, emotional, mental and spiritual benefits of dance through the production of dance performances and workshops.
Founded: 1993
Specialized Field: Modern
Paid Staff: 8
Volunteer Staff: 20
Paid Artists: 12
Budget: $100,000-$200,000
Income Sources: State Government; Foundations; Individual Supporters; Earned Income
Affiliations: Member of Dance USA, Dance NJ, DTW

331
THE KENNEDY DANCERS
79 Central Avenue
Jersey City, NJ 07306
Phone: 201-659-2190
e-mail: kennedydancers@aol.com
Web Site: www.kennedydancers.org
Officers:
  President: Diane Dragone
  Chairman: Guy Catrillo
Management:

Artistic Director: Diane Dragone
Mission: This contemporary performing and touring dance company offers outreach programs, lectures, demonstrations and a cable tv series with a mission of bringing high quality dance to the New york/New Jersey metro area.
Founded: 1976
Specialized Field: Contemporary Dance
Status: Non-Profit; Professional

332
SHUA GROUP
340 Summit Avenue #1
Jersey City, NJ 07306
Phone: 201-993-9668
e-mail: joshua@shuagroup.org
Web Site: shuagroup.org
Management:
   Director: Joshua Bisset
   Director: Laura Quattrocchi
Status: Nonprofit

333
ROXEY BALLET
243 N Union Street
Lambertville, NJ 08530
Phone: 609-397-7616
Fax: 609-397-6889
e-mail: info@roxeyballet.org
Web Site: www.roxeyballet.org
Officers:
   President: Barry Jackson
   Vice President: Melissa Roxey
   Treasurer: Cory Sparks
   Secretary: Laura McMillian
Management:
   Artistic Director: Mark Roxey
   Assistant to the Director: Fiona Jackson
   Finance: Donna Merkel
   Ballet Master: Giovanni Ravelo
   Rehearsal Assistant: Tara Seymour
   Rehearsal Assistant: Julie Cobble
   Teaching Artist/Education: Kristen Smith
   Costume Designer: Alicia Worden
   Costumes Designer: Nilda Roxey - Jone
Mission: Through touring and performing, Roxey Ballet delivers artistic and cultural excellence through professional dance.
Founded: 1995
Specialized Field: Ballet
Status: Non-Profit

334
NEW JERSEY BALLET COMPANY
15 Microlab Road
Suite 102
Livingston, NJ 07039
Phone: 973-597-9600
Fax: 973-597-9442
e-mail: info@njballet.org
Web Site: www.njballet.org
Officers:
   Chairman: Donald A Robinson Esq
   President: Peter Maloff Esq
   Executive Vice President: Carolyn Clark
   Treasurer: Scott T Tross Esq
   Secretary: Gale Difabio Raffield
Management:
   Director: Carolyn Clark
   Assistant Artistic Director: Paul Hilliard McRae
   Ballet Mistress: Marina Bogdanova
   Ballet Mistress: Luba Gulyaeva
   Production Manager: Brian Coakley
   Marketing: Nancy Hartmann

Mission: The Company brings the magic of dance theatre to thousands every year in every part of the state. It makes ballet accessible to New Jersey seniors and families with children through subsidized low-cost tickets.
Utilizes: Five Seasonal Concerts; Guest Artists; Guest Companies
Founded: 1958
Specialized Field: Ballet
Status: Professional, Nonprofit
Budget: $1-$2.5 million
Organization Type: Performing; Touring; Educational

335
NEW JERSEY DANCE CENTER
202 Maplewood Avenue
Maplewood, NJ 07040
Phone: 973-762-3033
e-mail: info@newjerseydancecenter.com
Web Site: www.newjerseydancecenter.com
Management:
   Artistic Director: Anne Krohley
Mission: Dedicated to giving students the highest quality dance training with a curriculum based program from ages 3 to 18 at all levels of experience in a friendly, nurturing environment.
Founded: 1982
Specialized Field: Ballet
Status: Semi-Professional, Commercial
Performs At: New Jersey Dance Theatre
Organization Type: Resident

336
ARGEN TANGO DANCERS
Dance Time Studio of New Jersey
36 West Highway Route 70, Room 201
Marlton, NJ 08053-3014
Phone: 856-751-2770
Fax: 856-574-4018
e-mail: tangodancers@comcast.net
Web Site: www.argen-tango.com
Management:
   Argen Tango Manager: Vittoria Natale
   Argen Tango Company Manager: Guillermo Elkhouse
Mission: Argentine Tango is among the most beautiful dance forms in history, and possibly the most passionate. The dance has a rich history that spans several lifetimes, and has infatuated more than its fair share of avid disciples. So much has already been written about Argentine Tango, and we've come across some fantastic articles where you can learn more about Argentine Tango, its music, history, and influences.
Utilizes: Choreographers; Dancers; Guest Ensembles; Soloists
Founded: 1999
Specialized Field: Authentic Argentine Tango Dance
Paid Staff: 4
Income Sources: Argen Tango Dance Classes
Performs At: Dance Time Studio of New Jersey

337
ST. JOHN'S RENAISSANCE DANCERS
239 Midland Avenue
Montclair, NJ 07042
Phone: 201-783-9845
Fax: 201-783-0001
Mission: The presentation of high quality dance and music of the Renaissance and the recreation of the splendor of 15th and 16th-century Europe.
Utilizes: Guest Ensembles
Founded: 1979
Specialized Field: Historical Dance
Status: Professional

Organization Type: Performing; Touring; Educational

338
NATIONAL BALLET OF NEW JERSEY
5113 Church Road
Mount Laurel, NJ 08054
Phone: 856-235-5342
Fax: 856-235-6343
e-mail: balletnj@aol.com
Management:
   Artistic Director: Kenna McAdams-Connor
   Co-Administrator: Gayle Gardiner
   Founder: Lorraine McAdams
Mission: To provide training and special coaching to young artists through a trainee and apprentice program, thereby providing exposure and professional appearances, performance opportunities and an introduction to dance as a profession.
Specialized Field: Ballet
Budget: $500,000-$1,000,000

339
AMERICAN REPERTORY BALLET
7 Livingston Ave.
New Brunswick, NJ 08903
Mailing Address: P.O. Box 250, New Brunswick, NJ 08903
Phone: 732-249-1254
Fax: 732-249-8475
Web Site: www.americanrepertoryballet.org
Officers:
   Chairman: Patrick Bradley
   Treasurer: Robin Moscato
   Secretary: Jo-Ann Munoz
   Vice Chair/Development Chair: Joan Barry McCormick
Management:
   Artistic Director: Douglas Martin
   Executive Director: Marvin Preston
   Ballet Master: Bat Abbitt
   Company Teacher: Kathleen Moore
   Stage Manager: Peter C. Cook
   Business Manager: Dawn Dell'Omo
   Director of PR and Communications: Alexis Branagan
   Bookkeeper: Arlene Mastrocola
   Lighting Designer: Christopher Chambers
Mission: American Repertory Ballet is committed to helping ensure the survival and accountability of dance as an art form through educational initiatives.
Utilizes: Actors; AEA Actors; Arrangers; Artists-in-Residence; Choreographers; Collaborating Artists; Collaborations; Commissioned Composers; Commissioned Music; Community Members; Community Talent; Composers; Composers-in-Residence; Contract Actors; Contract Orchestras; Dance Companies; Dancers; Designers; Educators; Five Seasonal Concerts; Grant Writers; Guest Accompanists; Guest Artists; Guest Conductors; Guest Ensembles; Guest Musical Directors; Instructors; Local Artists; Lyricists; Multi Collaborations; Multimedia; Resident Professionals; Selected Students; Soloists; Student Interns; Visual Arts
Founded: 1987
Specialized Field: Ballet
Status: Professional, Nonprofit
Budget: $2.5 million
Organization Type: Performing; Resident; Touring; Educational

340
LKB DANCE
9 Livingston Avenue
New Brunswick, NJ 08901

DANCE / New Mexico

Phone: 732-742-1523
e-mail: info@lkbdance.org
Web Site: www.lkbdance.org
Management:
    Artistic Director: Leah Kreutzer Barber
    Assistant Artistic Director: Emily Edwards
Mission: Dedicated to the creation and performance of new modern dance works by Leah Kreutzer Barber with an emphasis on collaborations with living composers and other artists.
Founded: 1999
Specialized Field: Modern
Status: Professional, Nonprofit
Volunteer Staff: 3
Paid Artists: 8
Budget: $30,000
Income Sources: Foundations; Corporations; Individual; Government
Performs At: George Street Playhouse
Affiliations: Dance USA; Dance Theatre Workshop
Annual Attendance: 2,000
Seating Capacity: 350

341
DANCEVISION INC.
116 Rockingham Row
Princeton, NJ 08540
Phone: 609-520-1020
e-mail: info@dancevisionnj.org
Web Site: dancevisionnj.org
Officers:
    President: Kathy Azaro
    Vice President: Martha Easton
    Treasurer: Laura Pronesti
    Secretary: Melissa Ackerman
Management:
    Artistic Director: Risa Gary Kaplowitz
    Program Director: Marie Alonzo Snyder
Mission: DanceVision's mission is to enrich the community with quality dance experiences, including performances, school residencies, and dance festivals. DanceVision has two components: community outreach and professional quality performances.
Founded: 2005
Status: Nonprofit

342
ART OF MOTION INC.
17 Chesnut Street, 2nd Floor
Ridgewood, NJ 07450
Phone: 201-652-5800
Fax: 201-652-3347
e-mail: artofmotion.inc@gmail.com
Web Site: artofmotion.org
Management:
    Artistic Director: Lynn Needle
    Artistic Director: Olivia Galgano
    Studio Manager: Linda Combs
Mission: AOM believes in developing an individual's range of movement to his or her fullest capacity, and we emphasize the history and artistry of dance as a discipline and an art form.
Status: Nonprofit
Organization Type: Educational; Performing

343
CAROLYN DORFMAN DANCE COMPANY
2780 Morris Avenue
Suite 1-A
Union, NJ 07083
Phone: 908-687-8855
Fax: 908-686-5245
Toll-free: 800-887-9322
e-mail: info@cddc.info
Web Site: cddc.info
Officers:
    Chair: Don Jay Smith
    President: Betsy Vaden
    Vice President: Robin Aubrey
Management:
    Artistic Director/Choreographer: Carolyn Dorfman
    Stage Manager: Jennifer Mesce
    Production Manager: Sean Perry
    Executive Director: Anita Thomas
    Office Administrator: Wilfredo Hernandez
    Associate Artistic Director: Jacqueline Dumas Albert
    Communication/Development Manager: Anna Shaffner
    Company Manager/Office Assistant: Stephanie Cathey
Mission: With cohesive artistic and educational programming, the Carolyn Dofrman Dance Company works on and off the stage to bring contemporary dance to its audiences.
Utilizes: Choreographers; Commissioned Composers; Commissioned Music; Dancers; Designers; Five Seasonal Concerts; Guest Accompanists; Guest Artists; Guest Conductors; Guest Musical Directors; Lyricists; Multi Collaborations; Organization Contracts; Original Music Scores; Resident Artists; Resident Professionals; Sign Language Translators
Founded: 1982
Specialized Field: Modern
Status: Professional, Nonprofit
Budget: $500,000
Income Sources: New Jersey State Council on the Arts; Foundation; Corporate; Individual

344
MOE-TION DANCE THEATRE
90 Pine Street
Verona, NJ 07044
Phone: 973-477-1938
e-mail: moeglennon@aol.com
Web Site: moetiondancetheater.org
Management:
    Artistic Director: Maureen Glennon
Mission: Moe-tion dance theater's mission is to present a wide range of programs that educate, enrich and entertain. It seeks to promote an inclusive vision of the arts through the language of modern dance, painting, sculpture, photography, literature, and live music. It strives to include people of all ages, backgrounds, and abilities. It wishes to create productions that expose the community to multiple art forms in one event.
Founded: 2007
Specialized Field: Contemporary Modern Dance

New Mexico

345
KESHET DANCE COMPANY
4121 Cutler Ave NE
Albuquerque, NM 87110
Phone: 505-224-9808
Fax: 505-842-0309
e-mail: info@keshetdance.org
Web Site: www.keshetdance.org
Officers:
    Founder: Shira Greenberg
    President: Emily Thaler
    Vice President: Randy Trask
    Treasurer: Maria Castellano
    Secretary: Samantha Updegraff
Management:
    Artistic Director: Shira Greenberg
    General Manager: Kelsey Ann O'Keefe
    Director: Kelsey Paschich
    Operations Coordinator: Jane Hogland
    Advancement Coordinator: Cece Shantzek
Mission: Keshet Dance Company is a professional company of dance artists committed to inspiring passion and opening unlimited possibilities through the experience of dance. Keshet dancers use movement, music and spoken word to connect people with art and to build a stronger community.
Founded: 1996
Specialized Field: Modern
Status: Professional, Non-Profit
Paid Staff: 3
Volunteer Staff: 200
Paid Artists: 10
Non-paid Artists: 20
Budget: $250,000
Income Sources: Tickets; Foundations; Government; Private
Annual Attendance: 6,000

346
NEW MEXICO BALLET COMPANY
4200 Wyoming Boulevard NE
PO Box 21518
Albuquerque, NM 87154
Phone: 505-292-4245
e-mail: jolie@newmexicoballet.org
Web Site: newmexicoballet.org
Officers:
    Managing Director: Emily Fine
Management:
    Artistic Director: Jolly Sutton-Simballa
    Executive Director: Emily Fine
    Associate Artistic Director: Amy Duda
    Founder/Artistic Associate: Suzanne M. Johnston
    Company Manager: Desirae Anslover
    Technical Director: Mimi Peavy
Mission: Our mission is to create and produce unique, innovative ballet and classical ballet performances for the people of New Mexico through dance education, ticket sales, major contributors, grants and a strong volunteer Board and Guild.
Founded: 1972
Specialized Field: Classical
Status: Nonprofit
Budget: $100,000-$200,000
Income Sources: Ticket Sales; Major Contributors; Grants
Organization Type: Performing; Touring

347
ASPEN SANTA FE BALLET
550B Saint Michael's Drive
Suite 1
Santa Fe, NM 87505
Mailing Address: 0245 Sage Way, Aspen, CO 81611
Phone: 505-983-5591
Fax: 505-992-1027
e-mail: jp@aspensantafeballet.com
Web Site: www.aspensantafeballet.com
Officers:
    Founder: Bebe Schweppe
    President: Judith Zee Steinberg
    Vice President: Leigh Moiola
    Treasurer: Denise Jurgens
    Asst. Treasurer: Michael Hauger
    Secretary: A. Charles Forte

Management:
    Artistic Director: Tom Mossbrucker
    Executive Director: Jean-Philippe Malaty
    Development Director: Zander Higbie
    Development: Kaitlin Windle
    Marketing Manager: Andre Bouchard
    Controller: Berry Hurst
    Business Development: Zander Higbie
    Technical Director: Danny Bacheldor
    Lighting Supervisor: Seah Johnson
Mission: A company of eleven classically trained dancers who perform an eclectic repertoire by some of the world's foremost choreographers. Performs year-round at home in Aspen and Santa Fe and on tour throughout the United States.
Founded: 1990
Specialized Field: Ballet
Status: Professional, Non-Profit
Budget: $2.5 million
Income Sources: Ticket Revenue; Earned Income; Foundations
Annual Attendance: 45,000

348
MARIA BENITEZ TEATRO FLAMENCO
Institute for Spanish Arts
1604 Agua Fria
Santa Fe, NM 87501
Mailing Address: P.O Box 8418, Santa Fe NM, 87501
Phone: 505-467-3773
Toll-free: 888-435-2636
e-mail: flamenco@mariabenitez.com
Web Site: www.institutespanisharts.org
Officers:
    Co-Founder: Cecilio Benitz
    Co-Founder: Maria Benitez
Management:
    Artistic Director: Maria Benitez
Mission: The mission of Maria Benitez Teatro Flamenco is to preserve, strengthen, and disseminate our rich and diverse artistic Spanish heritage as expressed through music, dance, visual arts and other art forms which are deeply rooted in New Mexico's traditional legacies.
Utilizes: Scenic Designers; Sign Language Translators
Founded: 1970
Specialized Field: Flamenco
Status: Nonprofit
Paid Staff: 6
Paid Artists: 18
Income Sources: Ticket Sales; Contributed Income
Performs At: Santa Fe: Maria Benitez Theatre
Annual Attendance: 30,000
Facility Category: Cabaret-Style
Type of Stage: Sprung Wood Floor
Stage Dimensions: 22x14
Seating Capacity: 200
Resident Groups: Maria Benitez Teatro Flamenco

349
SANTA FE FESTIVAL BALLET
PO Box 1595
Santa Fe, NM 87504-1595
Phone: 505-983-3362
Fax: 505-982-6718
e-mail: info@santafeballet.org
Management:
    General Director: Henry Holth
    Executive Director: Jean-Philippe Malaty
    Artistic Director: Tom Mossbrucker
    Development Director: Robin Cole
    Development Associate/Aspen: Andrea Sprick
Mission: Company of eleven, classically trained dancers who perform an eclectic repertoire by some of the world's foremost choreographers.
Specialized Field: Ballet
Budget: $200,000-$500,000

New York

350
THE EBA THEATRE
EBA Inc
351 Hudson Avenue
Albany, NY 12210
Phone: 518-465-9916
Fax: 518-465-9916
e-mail: ebadance@eba-arts.org
Web Site: www.eba-arts.org
Officers:
    Chief Executive Officer: Maude Baum
Management:
    Artistic Director: Maude Baum
    Technical Director: Matt Murphy
    Building Superintendent: Alain Roullier
    School Receptionist: Courtney Blackwell
    Bookkeeper: Michele Sweet
    Company Photographers: A. Roullier
Mission: With a mission to bring the best of American Modern Dance Theatre choreography and performance to audiences and to inspire creativity, Maude Baum & Company Dance Theatre creates, performs and tours acclaimed American Modern Dance works and offers a superb repertoire of dance theatre works.
Founded: 1972
Specialized Field: Modern
Status: Professional, Nonprofit
Budget: $200,000-$500,000
Income Sources: Grants; Contributions; Tuition; Foundations
Annual Attendance: 40,000

351
AMY MARSHALL DANCE COMPANY
28-43 41st Street
Second Floor
Astoria, NY 11103
Phone: 917-647-9477
e-mail: amy@amymarshall.con
Web Site: www.amymarshall.com
Officers:
    President: Chad Levy
    Vice President: Linda Hodes
    Secretary: Leigh Kearney
    Board Member: Elizabeth Flynn
    Board Member: Gregory Gulia
    Board Member: Susan Woodham
    Advisor: Amy Marshall
Management:
    Artistic Director/Choreographer: Amy Marshall
    Executive Director: Chad Levy
    Lighting Designer: Donalee Katz
    Lighting Director: Kathleen Scott
    Composer: Kevin Keller
    Composer: Marlon Cherry
    Promotions: Ava Savitsky
Mission: Choreographer Amy Marshall and Executive Director Chad Levy co-founded the Amy Marshall Dance Company in 2000 in order to realize a vision of dance theater as a visual metaphor for the human spirit. Ms. Marshall's choreography pays tribute to both the beauty and tribulations of life's experiences through dramatic movement. The work's emotional structure explodes across the stage with dramatic confrontation and then suddenly resolves itself.
Utilizes: Arrangers; Choreographers; Collaborating Artists; Collaborations; Community Members; Composers; Dancers; Designers; Grant Writers; Instructors; Lyricists; Multi Collaborations; Multimedia; Music; Original Music Scores; Paid Performers; Touring Companies
Founded: 2000
Specialized Field: Classical Contemporary, Modern
Status: Non-Profit, Professional
Income Sources: Donors
Season: July through August
Performs At: Plymouth State University Silver Center for the Arts

352
EGLEVSKY BALLET
700 Hicksville Road
Suite 102
Bethpage, NY 11714
Phone: 516-746-1115
Fax: 516-746-1117
e-mail: info@eglevskyballet.com
Web Site: www.eglevskyballet.org
Officers:
    President: Janine Racanelli
    VP: Gary Limoncelli
    Treasurer: Jennifer Gilooley
    Secretary: Pamela Shaddock
Management:
    Artistic Director: Lazlo Berdo
    Executive Director: Marnie Katzman
    Bookkeeper: JoEllen Gillooley
    Receptionist: John Ferrantino
    Receptionist: Catherine Fowle
Mission: The Eglevsky Ballet endeavors to develop a distinct artistic identity through performance and outreach programs furthering the appreciation of the art form. The company aspires to develop a unique and innovative repertoire of classical and contemporary works to enrich the Long Island community and to strive for national and international recognition.
Founded: 1961
Specialized Field: Contemporary; Classical
Status: Professional

353
BILL EVANS DANCE COMPANY
3920 Lake Road North
Brockport, NY 14420
Phone: 585-391-3756
Fax: 585-385-5134
e-mail: billevansdance@hotmail.com
Web Site: www.billevansdance.org
Officers:
    Founder: Bill Evans
Management:
    Artistic Director/Choreographer: Bill Evans
Mission: To support the creation and performance of contemporary dance and rhythm tap dance work.
Utilizes: Soloists
Founded: 1975
Specialized Field: Contemporary Dance; Jazz
Status: Professional, Nonprofit
Paid Staff: 2
Volunteer Staff: 2
Budget: $100,000
Income Sources: Ticket sales; grants
Annual Attendance: 7,000
Facility Category: Theatre
Type of Stage: Proscenium
Stage Dimensions: 40'x 35'
Seating Capacity: 420
Year Built: 1969
Year Remodeled: 1996

DANCE / New York

Resident Groups: Bill Evans Dance Company

354
LES GUIRIVOIRES DANCE COMPANY
Guiraud-McDonald Cultural Exchange Inc
2195 Grand Concourse
Suite 6B
Bronx, NY 10453
Phone: 718-562-8656
Fax: 917-792-4237
e-mail: info@guiraudmredec.org
Web Site: www.guiraudmredec.org
Officers:
   Founder: Rose Marie Guiraud
   Treasurer/Secretary: Emmett O McDonald
Management:
   Artistic/Executive Director: Rose Marie Guiraud
   Choreographer: Christal Brown
   Educational/Artistic Dir. Assistant: Anthony Craig
Mission: Les Guirivoires Dance Theatre Company is the New York based professional performance organ of Guiraud-McDonald Cultural Exchange whose mission is to provide inter-cultural performances which include African traditional and contemporary dance, modern and jazz dance, music concerts and theater.
Founded: 1973
Specialized Field: African Traditional; Contemporary; Modern; Jazz
Status: Profesional, Nonprofit
Performs At: Throughout New York

355
MERIAN SOTO DANCE & PERFORMANCE
1001 Grand Concourse #10F
Bronx, NY 10452
Phone: 267-625-1513
e-mail: meriansoto@gmail.com
Web Site: www.meriansoto.com
Management:
   Artistic Director: Merian Soto
   Associate Director: Jane Gabriels
Founded: 1983
Specialized Field: Traditional Dance; Ethnic Dance
Paid Staff: 2
Paid Artists: 10

356
STREB LABORATORY FOR ACTION MECHANICS (SLAM)
51 North First Street
Brooklyn, NY 11249
Phone: 718-384-6491
Fax: 718-384-6490
e-mail: info@streb.org
Web Site: www.streb.org
Management:
   Artistic Director: Elizabth Streb, elizabeth@strb.org
   Managing Director: Susan Meyers, mea@strb,org
   Managing Director: Cathy Eihorn
   Producing Director: Kim Cukken
   Associate Artistic Director: Fabio Tavarres
   Marketing Director: Millie Li
   Education Director: Ashley Waters
   Educational Liason: Cassandre Joseph
   Technical Director: Matthew McAdon
Mission: Founded in 1985, STREB tours extensively throughout the United States and internationally presenting performances and residencies and conducts year-round activity at its home studio/laboratory, the STREB LAB for ACTION MECHANICS (S.L.A.M.), located in Williamsburg, Brooklyn.

Utilizes: Arrangers; Choreographers; Collaborating Artists; Collaborations; Community Talent; Dance Companies; Five Seasonal Concerts; Grant Writers; Guest Accompanists; High School Drama; Multi Collaborations; Multimedia; Original Music Scores; Paid Performers; Scenic Designers; Student Interns; Special Technical Talent; Theatre Companies; Touring Companies; Visual Arts
Founded: 1985
Opened: 2003
Specialized Field: Contemporary, Modern
Status: Non-Profit, Professional
Income Sources: Donors, Sponsors, Educational Grants
Season: Year Round

357
BIG DANCE THEATER INC
303 Clinton Street
Brooklyn, NY 11231
e-mail: aaron@bigdancetheater.org
Web Site: www.bigdancetheater.org
Management:
   Choreographer/Co-Director: Annie B Parson
   Co-Director: Paul Lazar
   Founding Member: Molly Hickok
Mission: Big Dance Theater is known for its inspired use of dance, music, text and visual design. The company often works with wildly incongruent source material, weaving and braiding disparate strands into multi-dimensional performance.
Utilizes: Arrangers; Choreographers; Composers; Dance Companies; Dancers; Fine Artists; High School Drama; Local Artists & Directors; Local Unknown Artists; Original Music Scores; Paid Performers; Special Technical Talent; Touring Companies; Visual Arts
Founded: 1991
Specialized Field: Interpretive Dance, Theater, Visual Arts
Status: Non-Profit
Income Sources: Donors
Performs At: Brooklyn Academy of Music, Dance Theater Workshop, The Kitchen, Classic Stage Company, Japan Society, Yerba Buena

358
BRIGHTON BALLET THEATRE COMPANY, INC.
The School Of Russian American Ballet
Kingsborough Community College
2001 Oriental Boulevard Building T7
Brooklyn, NY 11235
Phone: 718-769-9161
Fax: 866-812-7646
Toll-free: 866-812-7646
e-mail: brightonballet@gmail.com
Web Site: www.brightonballet.org
Officers:
   Founder: Irina Roizin
Management:
   Artistic Director/Choreographer: Irina Zaharias
   Executive Director: Irina Roizin
Mission: Brighton Ballet Theater was created to preserve and further the tradition of Russian classical and folk dance in New York City.
Utilizes: Artists-in-Residence; Choreographers; Collaborating Artists; Collaborations; Community Members; Community Talent; Dance Companies; Dancers; Educators; Five Seasonal Concerts; Grant Writers; Guest Accompanists; Guest Artists; Guest Musicians; High School Drama; Instructors; Local Artists & Directors; Original Music Scores; Paid Performers; Resident Artists; Resident Companies; Soloists; Students; Visual Designers; Volunteer Artists
Founded: 1987
Specialized Field: Classical Ballet; Folk Dance
Status: Nonprofit

359
BROOKLYN ARTS EXCHANGE
421 Fifth Avenue
3rd Floor
Brooklyn, NY 11215
Phone: 718-832-0018
Fax: 718-832-9189
e-mail: info@bax.org
Web Site: www.bax.org
Officers:
   Founder: Marya Warshaw
   President: Oliver Fein
   Treasurer: Steven Flax
   Board of Directors: Rosio Amodio
   Board of Directors: Gene Russianoff
   Board of Directors: Any Sumner
   Managing Director: Vanessa Adato
   Secretary: Suzanne Blezard
Management:
   Artistic Director/Executive Dir: Marya Warshaw
   Technical Director: Emma Rivera
   Operations Manager: Sara Roer
   Marketing & Communications Director: Fernando Maneca
   Education Director: Lucia Scheckner
   Education Manager: Joie Golomb
   Education Assistant: Dana O'Brien
Mission: Our mission is to provide a nurturing, year-round performance, rehearsal and educational venue in Brooklyn that encourages artistic risk-taking and stimulates dialogue among diverse constituencies.
Utilizes: Artists-in-Residence; Curators; Dance Companies; Guest Artists
Founded: 1991
Specialized Field: Theatrical Dance; Educational Dance
Status: Nonprofit
Paid Staff: 5
Budget: $200,000-$500,000
Income Sources: Individual; Foundation; Corporate
Facility Category: Theatre and rehearsal studios
Stage Dimensions: 25'X 30'
Seating Capacity: 75

360
BROOKLYN BALLET
160 Schermerhorn Street
Brooklyn, NY 11201
Phone: 718-245-0146
e-mail: info@brooklynballet.org
Web Site: brooklynballet.org
Management:
   Artistic Director: Lynn Parkerson
   Development Director: Roxana Vadia
   Development Manager: Nellie Rainwater
Mission: The company continues to create and perform new repertory bringing Brooklyn audiences the artistic excellence they've come to expect.
Founded: 2002
Specialized Field: Contemporary Ballet
Status: Professional; Nonprofit

361
THE CHARLES MOORE DANCE THEATRE
Dances & Drums of Africa
397 Bridge Street
2nd Floor
Brooklyn, NY 11201

DANCE / New York

Mailing Address: 635 Carroll Street, Suite #2, Brooklyn, NY 11215
Phone: 718-638-4878
Fax: 718-638-4878
e-mail: susangoldbetter@gmail.com
Web Site: www.circuitproductions.org/artists/dance/cmdt.html
Officers:
  Co-Founder: Ella Thompson-Moore
  Co-Founder: Charles Moore
Management:
  Artistic Director/Choreographer: Ella Thompson-Moore
  Member: Jarbean Gilkes
  Member: Wayne Daniels
Mission: To demonstrate the beauty and great variety of African, Caribbean and African-American culture, the company also proves that multiculturalism and traditional black American arts are inseparable.
Utilizes: Singers
Founded: 1974
Specialized Field: African Dance; Caribbean
Status: Professional, Nonprofit
Paid Staff: 2
Volunteer Staff: 15
Paid Artists: 12
Income Sources: New York State Council Dance Arts; Department of Cultural Affairs; New York Division of the Humanities Education Department
Performs At: Charles Moore Center for Ethnic Studies
Organization Type: Performing; Touring; Educational

362
COVENANT BALLET THEATRE OF BROOKLYN
4119 Avenue T
Brooklyn, NY 11234
Mailing Address: 2718A East 21 Street, Brooklyn, NY 11235
Phone: 718-891-6199
Fax: 718-891-0259
e-mail: info@covenantballet.com
Web Site: covenantballet.org
Officers:
  President: Lucie G. Santoro
  Treasurer: Pasquale Santoro
  Secretary: Geovanni Este
Management:
  Artistic Director: Marla A. Hirokawa
  Program Director: Lucie G. Santoro
  General Manager: Dawn C. Wortman
Mission: Committed to providing excellent professional standard performances, pre-professional dance instruction, and educational programs in Brooklyn and beyond, CBT seeks to foster an intelligent, holistic appreciation of dance as an art form offering educational and cultural experiences to the younger generations. Activities are designed to reflect Christian and wholesome family values and ethics in the arts.
Founded: 1987
Specialized Field: Ballet
Status: Nonprofit

363
DANCEWAVE
45 4th Avenue
Brooklyn, NY 11217
Phone: 718-522-4696
Fax: 718-522-4769
e-mail: info@dancewave.com
Web Site: www.dancewave.org
Officers:
  Chair: Saundra Thomas
  Secretary: Hanna Edwards
  Board of Directors: Melissa Shurkin
  Board of Directors: James.A. Roth
Management:
  Executive/Artistic Director: Diane Jacobowitz
  Education/Marketing Manager: Veronica Carnero
  Associate Director of Development: Lauren Elicks
  Director of Marketing & Production: Jeso O'Neill
  School Administrator: Audrey Lowry
Mission: A unique dance troupe in which boys and girls perform works by world choreographers such as Mark Morris, Twyla Tharp, David Dorfman and others.
Utilizes: Choreographers; Commissioned Composers; Dance Companies; Grant Writers; Guest Accompanists; Guest Choreographers; Guest Companies; Guest Ensembles; Singers
Founded: 1979
Specialized Field: Modern
Status: Semi-Professional, Non-Profit
Paid Staff: 3
Paid Artists: 25
Budget: $150,000
Performs At: NYC theaters
Annual Attendance: 5,000
Organization Type: Performing; Touring; Resident; Educational; Sponsoring

364
DUSON TYNEK DANCE THEATRE
415 Ninth Street
Suite 54
Brooklyn, NY 11215
Phone: 718-249-7708
e-mail: dance@dusantynek.org
Web Site: www.dusantynek.org
Officers:
  President: Dwayne Linville
  Secretary: Dusan Tynek
  Associate: Jessica P'An
Management:
  Artistic Director/Choreographer: Dusan Tynek
  Company Manager: Dwayne Linville
  Writer: Cynthia Polutanovich
  Voice Coach: Lucinda Child
  Stage Manager: Elite Rabinowitz
  Publicist: William Murray
  Composer: Ted Reichman
  Composer: Aleksandra Vrebalov
Mission: It is a sign of the skill, range and taste of the Czech-born choreographer Dusan Tynek that a new dance of his will often recall the work of a great choreographer ... dance with uncommon poetry .... With the help of good musicians, Mr. Tynek's work breathes.
Utilizes: Arrangers; Choreographers; Collaborating Artists; Collaborations; Dance Companies; Dancers; Fine Artists; Guest Directors; Lyricists; Multimedia; Music; Paid Performers
Founded: 2003
Specialized Field: Contemporary Dance
Status: Non-Profit
Income Sources: Donors, Sponsors
Season: Year Round
Performs At: Various

365
ERICA ESSNER PERFORMANCE CO-OP
26 Berkeley Place
Suite #1
Brooklyn, NY 11217
Phone: 646-335-5264
e-mail: essner@eecop.org
Web Site: www.eecop.org
Management:
  Director/Choreographer: Erica Essner
  Composer: Erik Walker
Mission: Striving for the essence of individuality, the cooperative process is revealed in the merging of unique and idiosyncratic movement styles based on each member of the company.
Founded: 1990
Specialized Field: Modern
Paid Staff: 3
Volunteer Staff: 10
Paid Artists: 6

366
EVA DEAN DANCE COMPANY
725 Union Street
Brooklyn, NY 11215
Phone: 718-857-8368
Web Site: evadeandance.org
Management:
  Director: Eva Dean
Mission: To support and strengthen the presence of dance as a performing art form in New York City, to develop and reach diverse audiences for dance, to support the work of other choreographers and dancers, to create and perform the choreography of Eva Dean, and to teach Eva Dean Dance technique and repertory to students representing a wide range of ages, abilities, and cultural backgrounds.
Founded: 1985
Specialized Field: Neo-Contemporary

367
GALLIM DANCE
520 Clinton Avenue
Brooklyn, NY 11238
Phone: 718-622-2165
e-mail: info@gallimdance.com
Web Site: gallimdance.com
Management:
  Artistic Director: Andrea Miller
  Executive Director: Meredith (Max) Hodges
Mission: To create, to play inside the imagination, to find juxtapositions of the mind and body that resonate in the soul, to investigate our limitations and pleasures, and to realize the endless human capacity for inspiration.
Founded: 2007
Specialized Field: Contemporary

368
MARK MORRIS DANCE GROUP
3 Lafayette Avenue
Brooklyn, NY 11217-1415
Phone: 718-624-8400
Fax: 718-624-8900
e-mail: info@mmdg.org
Web Site: www.markmorrisdancegroup.org
Officers:
  Chair: David Resnicow
  Vice Chairman: Mark Selinger
  Chief Financial Officer: Elizabeth Fox
  Secretary: Isaac Mizrahi
Management:
  Artistic Director: Mark Morris
  Production/Facilities Manager: Peter Gorneault
  Executive Director: Nancy Umanoff
  General Manager: Huong Hoang
  Company Manager: Sarah Horne
  Director of Development: Michelle Amador
  Director of Marketing: Karyn LeSuer
  Technical Director: Johan Henckens
Mission: Mark Morris Dance Group's mission is to develop, promote and sustain dance, music and opera productions by Mark Morris and serve as a cultural resource to engage and enrich the community.

All listings are in alphabetical order by state, then city, then organization within the city.

DANCE / New York

Utilizes: Singers
Founded: 1980
Specialized Field: Dance
Status: Professional, Nonprofit
Budget: $4 million
Organization Type: Performing; Touring

369
DANCE THEATRE ETCETERA
480 Van Brunt Street
Room 3
Brooklyn, NY 11231
Phone: 718-643-6790
Fax: 718-643-6733
Web Site: www.dancetheatreetcetera.org
Officers:
  Board of Directors: Audrey Anastasi
  Board of Directors: Martha Bowers
  Board of Directors: Sam Sills
  Board of Directors: Mark Philips
Management:
  Executive Director: Martha Bowers
  Director of Finance and Operations: Michael Levinton
  Education Program Manager: Jasmin Jenoure
Mission: Premised on the belief that the arts are an effective vehicle for social transformation, Dance Theatre Etcetera unites artists and community members as co-creators in dynamic cultural activities. Through site-specific performances, festivals, parades, and performing arts and media education programs, Dance Theatre Etcetera stimulates the social imagination through acts of informed expression.
Founded: 1981
Specialized Field: Theatrical Dance; Street Theatre
Status: Professional, Nonprofit
Budget: $40,000-$100,000
Income Sources: Foundations; Corporations; Individual
Performs At: Throughout Brooklyn
Annual Attendance: 5,000

370
POLISH AMERICAN FOLK DANCE COMPANY
261 Driggs Avenue
Brooklyn, NY 11222
Phone: 718-907-6199
Web Site: www.pafdc.org
Officers:
  Vice President: Andrzej Buczek
  Vice President: Richard Mazur
  Treasurer: Margaret Pasanowic
  Secretary: Marta Statucka
Management:
  Artistic Director: Ryszard Sudol
  Executive Director: Mariusz Bernatowicz
Mission: Our mission is to stimulate public interest in Polish culture primarily through presentation of authentic Polish songs and dances.
Founded: 1938
Specialized Field: Polish American Folk Dance
Status: Nonprofessional, Nonprofit
Budget: $75,000
Performs At: The Lincoln Center
Annual Attendance: 300,000
Organization Type: Performing; Touring

371
TIFFANY MILLS COMPANY
129 Columbia Heights
Suite 45
Brooklyn, NY 11201
Phone: 917-767-6350
e-mail: tiffany@tiffanymillscompany.org
Web Site: tiffanymillscompany.org
Officers:
  Board Member: Robert Burr
  Board Member: Rebecca Gupte
  Board Member: Megan Kennedy
  Board Member: Julie Lemberger
  Board Member: Mike Lonardo
  Advisory Board: Richard Gaples
  Advisory Board: Kay Cummings
  Advisory Board: Kristin Marting
  Advisory Board: Martha Myers
Management:
  Artistic Director/Choreographer: Tiffany Mills
  Company Manager: Megan Kennedy
  Lighting Designer: Chris Hudacs
  Company Manager: Megan Kennedy
  Special Projects: Alexjo Natale
Mission: Tiffany Mills is making a name for herself as a young modern-dance innovator. Her work favors a boldly physical vocabulary, where vivid partnering plays a prime role in detailing human relations. In her crafted world of gesture, touch, and fluid form, Mills' dancers partner in three-dimensional explosions, syncopating space. The Tiffany Mills Company strikes a nerve - triggered by instinct - driven out of raw physicality.
Utilizes: Arrangers; Choreographers; Collaborating Artists; Collaborations; Dance Companies; Dancers; Designers; Educators; High School Drama; Instructors; Lyricists; Paid Performers; Theatre Companies
Founded: 1995
Specialized Field: Modern, Jazz
Status: Non-Profit, Professional
Income Sources: Donors, Ticket Sales
Season: Year Round
Performs At: BAM Fisher Theater, Alfred University Residency, Temple University Residency, Baryshnikov Arts Center

372
URBAN BUSH WOMEN
138 S Oxford Street
Suite 4B
Brooklyn, NY 11217
Phone: 718-398-4537
Fax: 718-398-4783
e-mail: info@urbanbushwomen.org
Web Site: www.urbanbushwomen.org
Officers:
  Chair: Tammy Bormann
  Treasurer: Cristal Baron
  Secretary: Jennifer Smith
  Finance Committee Chair: Lorrie A. Warner
Management:
  Program Manager: Pia Murray
  Executive Director: Jana Le Sorte
  Director of Education and Community: Maria Bauman
  Finance Manager: Henry Liles
  Lighting Designer and Technical Dir: Susan Hamburger
  Manager of Daily Operations: Lai-Lin Robinson
Mission: Urban Bush Women seeks to bring the untold and under-told histories and stories of disenfranchised people to light through dance. We do this from a woman-centered perspective, as members of the African Diaspora community, in order to create a more equitable balance of power in the dance world and beyond.
Founded: 1984
Specialized Field: African Dance
Status: Professional, Nonprofit
Paid Staff: 12
Volunteer Staff: 24
Budget: $600,000-$700,000
Income Sources: Earned; Government; Individual; Foundations
Organization Type: Performing; Touring

373
YOUNG DANCERS IN REPERTORY
Sunset Station
PO Box 205037
Brooklyn, NY 11220
Phone: 347-702-7155
Fax: 347-702-7157
e-mail: ydr@youngdancersinrep.org
Web Site: www.youngdancersinrep.org
Officers:
  CEO/Artistic Director: Maude Baum
  Administrator: JuliAnn Goronkin
  Chair: Michael Spinner
  Board Member: Yvette Morales
  Vice Chair: Tara Regan
  Board Member: Ashley Murray
Management:
  Technical Director: Richard Chafin
  Executive Director: Craig Gabrian
  Deputy Director: June December
  Program Director: Malika Henriques
  Program Director: Steven Gerleit
Mission: Classical modern dance
Specialized Field: Modern; Ballet; Ethnic Dance

374
AFRICAN-AMERICAN CULTURAL CENTER
350 Masten Avenue
Buffalo, NY 14209
Phone: 716-884-2013
Fax: 716-885-2590
e-mail: africancultural350@gmail.com
Web Site: www.aaccbuffalo.org
Officers:
  Secretary: Gwendolyn Bassett
  Treasurer: Paulette S. Counts
  Board Of Directors, Chairperson: Harry Stokes
  Board Of Director, Vice Chairperson: Emma Bassett
  Board of Directors: Earl Smith
Management:
  Artistic Director: Paulette D Harris
  Dance Director: Linda Barr
  Assistant Director: Alicia Banner
  Executive Director: Agnes.M Bain
  Assistant Director: Alicia. Banner
Mission: Committed to promoting a positive sense of self among the community it was founded to serve. Its programs and services are still structured to motivate personal growth, stimulate untapped potential and facilitate a better understanding of cultural diversity among all people.
Founded: 1958
Specialized Field: African Dance; Ethnic Dance
Status: Semi-Professional, Nonprofit

375
MID-HUDSON BALLET COMPANY
Estelle & Alfonso, Inc.
738 Route 9, Shoprite Plaza
Fishkill, NY 12524
Phone: 845-897-2667
Fax: 845-897-7052
e-mail: director@estelleandalfonso.com
Web Site: www.estelleandalfonso.com
Management:
  Artistic Director: Alfonso Weinlein

DANCE / New York

Artistic Director: Estelle Weinlein
Mission: To promote interest in the art of dance including but not limited to ballet and to foster, promote all activities and movements for the social and educational benefits of its members and public.
Utilizes: Dance Companies; Dancers; Educators; Fine Artists; Guest Artists
Founded: 1959
Specialized Field: Ballet
Status: Nonprofit
Income Sources: Northeast Regional Ballet; Dutchess County Arts Council
Performs At: Mid-Hudson Civic Center
Affiliations: Eisenhower Hall Theatre
Organization Type: Performing; Educational

376
ITHACA BALLET
PO Box 4341
Ithaca, NY 14852-4341
Phone: 607-277-1967
Web Site: www.ithacaballet.org
Officers:
  President: Elmer Fairbank
Management:
  Artistic Director: Alice Reid
  Associate Director: Cindy Reid
  Lighting Designer: Craig Eagleson
  Stage Manager: Jeff Franzese
  Production & Stage Manager: Courtney McGuire
  Marketing Director: Amy Operman Cash
  Technical Director: Mike Garrett
Mission: The ballet is a professional ensemble corps, having a varied repertoire of classical and contemporary works. The Ithaca Ballet is Upstate New York's only repertory company and is the resident ballet company at State Theatre.
Utilizes: Singers
Founded: 1961
Specialized Field: Classical; Contemporary
Status: Professional
Budget: $40,000-$100,000
Organization Type: Performing; Touring

377
DINIZULU AFRICAN DANCERS, DRUMMERS AND SINGERS
Dinizula Ctr for African Culture & Research
11562 Sutphin Boulevard
Jamaica, NY 11434
Phone: 718-843-6213
Fax: 718-528-3065
e-mail: dancecompany@dinizulu.org
Management:
  Executive Director: Alice Dinizulu
  Artistic Director: Kiamati Dinizulu
Mission: Dedicated to presenting the beauty and majesty of African culture through dance.
Founded: 1950
Specialized Field: Ethnic Dance; African Dance
Status: Professional; Nonprofit
Organization Type: Performing; Touring; Resident; Educational; Sponsoring

378
AMERICAN BOLERO DANCE COMPANY
42-24 9th Street
Long Island City, NY 11101
Phone: 718-392-8888
Fax: 718-392-3840
e-mail: info@ambolero.com
Web Site: www.ambolero.com
Officers:
  Founder: Gabriela Granados
Management:
  Artistic Director/Choreographer: Gabriela Granados
  Ballet Master: Debra Anich
Mission: American Bolero Dance Company's primary goal is to bring the music, history and tradition of Spanish Dance to the United States.
Founded: 1996
Specialized Field: Flamenco; Spanish; Bolero

379
THE CONSTRUCTION COMPANY
10 East 18th Street
3rd Floor
Manhattan, NY 10001
Phone: 212-924-7882
e-mail: constructioncompany@earthlink.net
Web Site: www.theconstructioncompany.org
Officers:
  Fundraiser/Volunteer: Pauline Fleming
  Board Member/Marketing Consultant: Lauri Goldberg
  Chairperson/President: Enid Ringer
  Board Member: Robert Taylor
  Board Member: Rhonda Weiss
  Advisor/Artistic Director: Maurice Edwards
  Advisor/Radio Network Producer: Ellen Godfrey
  Advisor: Charles Kaufmann
Management:
  Choreographer: Ariane Anthony
  Choreographer: Scott Caywood
  Choreographer: Rachel Cohen
  Choreographer: Bryan Hayes
Mission: Dance Under Construction presents a festival each year of music and dance collaborations. Talented choreographers are given the opportunity of working with original music in live performances. Dance Under Construction also presents the work of individual choreographers including Bryan Hayes, Carolyn Lord, Beth Leonard, Christopher Caines and others.
Utilizes: Choreographers; Collaborating Artists; Composers; Dance Companies; Dancers; Grant Writers; Local Unknown Artists; Multimedia; Special Technical Talent; Touring Companies; Visual Designers
Founded: 1970
Opened: 1972
Specialized Field: Contemporary Dance, Visual Arts
Status: Non-Profit
Income Sources: Donations

380
VANAVER CARAVAN
10 Main Street
Suite 322
New Paltz, NY 12561
Phone: 845-256-9300
Fax: 845-256-9400
e-mail: vcoffice@vanavercaravan.org
Web Site: www.vanavercaravan.org
Officers:
  Co-Founder: Bill Vanaver
  Co-Founder: Livia Vanaver
  Board of Directors: Terrence Fister
  President: Philip Rose
  Secretary: Carol Jordan
Management:
  Artistic Director: Bill Vanaver
  Artistic Director: Livia Drapkin Vanaver
  Administrative Director: Jennifer Cottingham
  Administrative Assistant: Marina Lopez
Mission: To mision of The Vanaver Caravan is to enlighten, educated and inspire diverse audiences through performances of traditional dance and music at concerts, festivals, workshops and school presentations. Our work is based on concepts of ancestry, ethnic/cultural & spiritual origins. We create and perform work that celebrates and promotes international (multi-cultural) understandiing and appreciation of the global family tree.
Utilizes: Selected Students; Sign Language Translators; Soloists; Theatre Companies
Founded: 1972
Specialized Field: Modern; Ethnic Dance; Folk Dance
Status: Professional, Nonprofit
Paid Staff: 5
Volunteer Staff: 10
Paid Artists: 25
Budget: $50,000-$100,000
Income Sources: New York State Counsil for the Arts; Grants
Organization Type: Performing; Touring; Educational

381
AILEY II
Alvin Ailey Dance Foundation
Joan Weill Center for Dance
405 W 55th Street
New York, NY 10019
Phone: 212-405-9000
Fax: 212-405-9001
e-mail: info@alvinailey.org
Web Site: www.alvinailey.org
Officers:
  Chair: Joan H. Weill
  Senior Director: Calvin Hunt
  Chief Financial Officer: Pamela Robinson
  President: Daria L. Wallach
  VP: Simin.N Allison
Management:
  Artistic Director: Robert Battle
  Associate Artistic Director: Masazumi Chaya
  Executive Director: Bennett Rink
  Rehearsal Director: Matthew Rushing
  Deputy Director of Marketing: Ashley Pitman
  Associate Director of Marketing: Lynette P. Rizzo
  Controller: Prital Chohan
  Public Relations Associate: Amanda Householder
  Program Editor: PennyMaria Jackson
Mission: Ailey II couples the energy of young dance talent with emerging choreography, thus bringing exciting dance and innovative outreach programs to diverse communities throughout the country.
Founded: 1974
Specialized Field: Modern

382
AJKUN BALLET THEATRE
193 Cross Street
New York, NY 10464-1225
Phone: 914-235-2265
e-mail: AJKUN@aol.com
Web Site: www.ajkunbt.org
Management:
  Artistic Director: Leonard Ajkun
  Artistic Director: Chiara Ajkun
  Company Scheduler: Ichiko Nakajama, artisticstaff@arkunbt.org
  Office Manager: Aimira Bubesi
Mission: Professional company with a repertoire of traditional ballets and contemporary creations performed during its 48 week season. Part of the company mission is the goal to open the avenues of opportunities to youngest artists thru funding, summer intensives in New York and Italy, and arts in education programs.
Utilizes: Artists-in-Residence; Choreographers; Community Members; Community Talent; Contract Orchestras; Dance Companies; Dancers; Educators;

DANCE / New York

Filmmakers; Five Seasonal Concerts; Guest Accompanists; Guest Artists; Guest Musicians; Instructors; Original Music Scores; Resident Companies; Students
Founded: 2000
Opened: 2001
Specialized Field: Ballet
Status: Non-Profit
Paid Staff: 15
Paid Artists: 35
Income Sources: Public & Private Funding
Affiliations: The Field; LUDT

383
ALLNATIONS DANCE COMPANY
Performing Arts Foundation
500 Riverside Drive
New York, NY 10027
Phone: 212-316-8431
Management:
   Artistic Director: Sophia Pachecano
   Executive Director: Herman Rottenberg
Mission: The troupe is composed of dynamic ethnic dancers, who present their own cultures through music and dance and unite with each other to perform dances from around the world.
Utilizes: Singers; Student Interns
Founded: 1967
Specialized Field: Ethnic Dance
Status: Professional, Nonprofit
Budget: $100,000
Performs At: International House
Organization Type: Performing; Touring; Educational

384
ALPHA OMEGA THEATRICAL DANCE COMPANY
711 Amsterdam Avenue
Suite 4E
New York, NY 10025
Phone: 212-749-0095
Fax: 212-749-0095
e-mail: info@alphaomegadance.org
Web Site: www.alphaomegadance.org
Officers:
   Board of Directors: Paul Kwame Johnson
   Board of Directors: Coran James
   Board of Directors: Walter Grandberry
   Board of Directors: Warren Smith
Management:
   Artistic Director: Enrique Cruz De Jesus
   Executive Director: Dolores Vanison-Blakely
   Associate Director: Donna Clark
Mission: The company was founded with the purpose of expanding opportunities for minority choreographers and dancers and to work with a variety of art forms. It is committed to promoting knowledge and appreciation of artistic activities related to dance through schools, repertory ensembles and a professional company.
Utilizes: Artists-in-Residence; Choreographers; Commissioned Music; Dance Companies; Dancers; Designers; Educators; Five Seasonal Concerts; Guest Artists; Original Music Scores; Singers
Founded: 1972
Specialized Field: Modern; Jazz; Ballet
Status: Professional, Nonprofit
Paid Staff: 3
Volunteer Staff: 5
Paid Artists: 12
Budget: $69,000
Income Sources: Individual, NYSCA
Organization Type: Performing

385
ALVIN AILEY AMERICAN DANCE THEATER
Alvin Ailey Dance Foundation
Joan Weill Center for Dance
405 W 55th Street
New York, NY 10019
Phone: 212-405-9000
Fax: 212-405-9001
e-mail: info@alvinailey.org
Web Site: www.alvinailey.org
Officers:
   Chair: Joan H. Weill
   President: Daria L. Wallach
   VP: Simin.N Allison
   Senior Director: Calvin Hunt
   Chief Financial Officer: Pamela Robinson
Management:
   Artistic Director: Robert Battle
   Associate Artistic Director: Masazumi Chaya
   Executive Director: Bennett Rink
   Rehearsal Director: Matthew Rushing
   Deputy Director of Marketing: Ashley Pitman
   Associate Director of Marketing: Lynette P. Rizzo
   Controller: Prital Chohan
   Public Relations Associate: Amanda Householder
   Program Editor: PennyMaria Jackson
Mission: Alvin Ailey American Dance Theater is dedicated to the preservation of unique Black cultural expression and the enrichment of the American modern dance heritage.
Utilizes: Choreographers; Dancers; Grant Writers; Guest Artists; Guest Companies; Guest Conductors; Singers; Soloists
Founded: 1958
Specialized Field: Modern; Ballet; Jazz; Ethnic Dance
Status: Professional, Nonprofit
Budget: $18 million
Income Sources: Earned Revenue; Contributed
Performs At: City Center
Annual Attendance: 450,000
Organization Type: Performing; Touring; Educational

386
AMERICAN BALLET THEATRE
890 Broadway
3rd Floor
New York, NY 10003
Phone: 212-477-3030
Fax: 212-254-5938
Web Site: www.abt.org
Officers:
   CEO: Rachel Moore
   Vice President and Treasurer: Brian J. Heidtke
   Chairman: Donald Kramer
   President: Sharon Patrick
   Secretary: Nancy Havens-Hasty
Management:
   Artistic Director: Kevin McKenzie
   Ballet Masters: Susan Jones
   Associate Artistic Director: Victor Barbee
   Artistic Administrator: Cristina Escoda
   General Manager: David G. Lansky
   Company Manager: Kyle Pickles
   Rehearsal Coordinator: Miki Shintani La
   Director of Production: N. James Whitehill III
   Lighting Director: Brad Fields
Mission: To develop a repertoire of the best ballets from the past and to encourage the creation of new works by gifted young choreographers, wherever they might be found.
Founded: 1940
Specialized Field: Ballet
Status: Professional, Non-Profit
Budget: $2.5 million
Performs At: Metropolitan Opera House
Affiliations: Dance/Usa; The Arts and Business Council
Organization Type: Performing; Touring

387
AMERICAN TAP DANCE FOUNDATION
154 Christopher Street
#2B
New York, NY 10014
Phone: 646-230-9564
Fax: 646-230-7777
e-mail: info@atdf.org
Web Site: www.atdf.org
Officers:
   Board Chair: Deb Beard
   Board Member, Artistic Mentor: Brenda Bufalino
   Board C-Chair, Producer: Hoagy B Carmichael
Management:
   Artistic/Executive Director: Tony Waag
   Choreographer/Director: Mercedes Ellington
   Technical Director: Tony Mayes
   Operations Director: Hjordis Linn
   Producer: Pamela Koslow Hines
   Director of Strategic Partnerships: Lisa.M Scotto
   Director of Youth Programs: Susan Hebach
   Registrar/Education Associate: Courtney Runft
   Education Advisor: Margaret Morrison
Mission: A nonprofit tap dance company dedicated to celebrating, preserving and perpetuating one of America's few indigenous art forms and tap dance.
Utilizes: Singers
Founded: 1986
Specialized Field: Jazz; Tap
Status: Professional, Nonprofit
Performs At: American Tap Dance Center
Organization Type: Performing; Touring; Educational

388
ANNABELLA GONZALEZ DANCE THEATER
4 E 89th Street
Suite #P-C
New York, NY 10128-0645
Phone: 212-722-4128
Fax: 718-701-1777
e-mail: agdt@mindspring.com
Web Site: www.agdt.org
Officers:
   Board of Directors: Lutecia Gonzalez
   Board of Directors: Wanda Ruggiera
   Board of Directors: Vincent Samat
   Board of Directors: Sidney.B Joyner
Management:
   Artistic Director/Choreographer: Annabella Gonzalez, agdt@mindspring.com
   Board Chair: Richard Grimm, richard.grimm@mindspring.com
Mission: To create excellent and original dances; to educate individuals of all ages and circumstances on modern dance, Mexican dance, jazz and creative improvisations.
Utilizes: Choreographers; Collaborations; Commissioned Composers; Dancers; Designers; Five Seasonal Concerts; Guest Accompanists; Guest Artists; Guest Companies; Guest Conductors; Guest Musical Directors; Multimedia; Original Music Scores
Founded: 1976
Opened: 1976
Specialized Field: Modern; Ethnic Dance
Status: Professional, Nonprofit
Paid Staff: 1

DANCE / New York

Volunteer Staff: 2
Paid Artists: 6
Budget: $80,000-$100,000
Income Sources: Government Foundations, Corporate Support; Individual Contributions; Fall Galas
Affiliations: Dance Theater Worshop; ART/New York; The Association of Hispanic Arts
Annual Attendance: 8,500
Facility Category: Rental theatres, school theatres, libraries, etc.
Organization Type: Performing; Touring; Educational

389
APOLLO'S BANQUET
Grand Central Station
PO Box 523
New York, NY 10163
Phone: 203-838-1904
Fax: 203-838-1904
e-mail: louixiv203@aol.com
Web Site: www.apollosbanquet.com
Officers:
    Founder: Thomas Baird
    Co-Founder: Hugh Murphy
Management:
    Founder: Thomas Baird
    Founder: Hugh Murphy
Mission: To present baroque dance and music of the highest quality possible in concert venues.
Founded: 1995
Specialized Field: Eighteenth-Century Dance

390
ASIAN AMERICAN ARTS CENTRE
111 Norfolk Street
New York, NY 10002
Phone: 212-233-2154
Fax: 360-283-2154
e-mail: aaacinfo@artspiral.org
Web Site: www.artspiral.org
Management:
    Artistic Director: Eleanor Yung
    Manager: Ananya Chatterjea
    Executive Director: Robert Lee
Mission: To advance traditional Asian dance and its synthesis with traditional dance through performing and visual art programs, concerts, exhibitions, a research center and a forum for critical exchange.
Founded: 1974
Specialized Field: Modern; Ethnic Dance; Folk Dance
Status: Professional; Nonprofit
Organization Type: Performing; Touring; Educational

391
AVODAH DANCE ENSEMBLE
C/O HUC-JIR
1 West 4th Street
New York, NY 10012
Phone: 917-822-9665
e-mail: avodahdance@gmail.com
Web Site: www.avodahdance.org
Officers:
    Founding Director: JoAnne Tucker
Management:
    Artistic Director: Julie Gayer
    Outreach and Development Assistant: Meredith Lyn Avey
    Musician: Newman Taylor Baker
    Dancers: Sarah Zitnay
Mission: Avodah is a modern dance company that uses ancient sacred texts to connect and reconnect our spiritual selves to god and community, reaching deep within the jewish tradition, using dance, music and movement.
Utilizes: Artists-in-Residence; Choreographers; Collaborating Artists; Dancers; Five Seasonal Concerts; Guest Accompanists; Guest Artists; Local Artists; Lyricists; Original Music Scores; Singers
Founded: 1973
Specialized Field: Modern
Status: Professional, Nonprofit
Paid Staff: 2
Paid Artists: 6
Budget: $75,000
Income Sources: Bookings; Grants; Individual Contributions; Foundations
Annual Attendance: 2,000-10,000
Organization Type: Performing; Touring; Resident; Educational

392
BALLET ACADEMY EAST
1651 Third Avenue
New York, NY 10128
Phone: 212-410-9140
Fax: 212-369-2723
e-mail: info@baenyc.com
Web Site: balletacademyeast.com
Management:
    Director: Julia Dubno
    Administrative Director: Diane Miller-Chapman
Founded: 1979
Specialized Field: Ballet
Performs At: Gerald W. Lynch Theater, 524 West 59th Street, NYC
Organization Type: Educational; Performing

393
BALLET HISPANICO OF NEW YORK
167 W 89th Street
New York, NY 10024
Phone: 212-362-6710
Fax: 212-362-7809
e-mail: info@ballethispanico.org
Web Site: www.ballethispanico.org
Officers:
    Chair: Kate B. Lear
    President: David Perez
    Vice President: Vin Cipolla
    Secretary: James F. McCoy
    Treasurer: Charles J. Wortman
Management:
    Artistic Director: Eduardo Vilaro
    Executive Director: Lee Koonce
    Company Manager: Gregory Stuart
    General Manager: Derek R Munson
    Wardrobe Supervisor: Diana Ruettiger
    Rehearsal Director: Michelle Manzanales
    Ballet Master: Juan-Carlos Penuela
    Production Manager: Joshua Preston
    Stage Manager: Nathan K. Claus
Mission: Providing performances and training in traditional and contemporary Hispanic-American dance.
Utilizes: Artists-in-Residence; Dance Companies; Educators; Five Seasonal Concerts; Guest Artists; Touring Companies; Visual Arts
Founded: 1970
Specialized Field: Latin; Contemporary; Classical; Concert
Status: Professional, Nonprofit
Paid Artists: 39
Budget: $3 million
Income Sources: Earned Revenue; Public and Private Sector Contributions
Affiliations: Dance/USA; Association of Performing Arts Presenters
Organization Type: Performing

394
BALLET TECH
890 Broadway
New York, NY 10003
Phone: 212-777-7710
Fax: 646-537-2629
e-mail: questions@ballettech.org
Web Site: www.ballettech.org
Officers:
    President/Artistic Director: Eliot Feld
    Vice President: Carol Zerbe Hurford
    Treasurer: Robert Freedman
    Secretary: Yvette Neier
    Board of Directors: Philip E. Aarons
    Board of Directors: Lorraine Cooper
Management:
    Operations Director: Maggie Christ
    Facilities Manager: Patrick Crowson
    Director of Development: Jessica Banks
    Development Assistant: Ellen Potenza
    Finance Associate: Russell Murphy
Mission: Ballet Tech is dedicated to seeking out talented New York City public school students and provides a continuum of training from introductory through professional level training.
Utilizes: Dancers; Designers; Guest Artists; Guest Conductors; Multimedia; Original Music Scores; Resident Professionals; Visual Arts
Founded: 1974
Specialized Field: Ballet
Status: Nonprofit
Budget: $3 million
Income Sources: Individual; Corporate; Foundation
Performs At: Joyce Theater
Affiliations: The Ballet Tech School

395
BATTERY DANCE COMPANY
380 Broadway
5th Floor
New York, NY 10013-3518
Phone: 212-219-3910
Fax: 212-219-3911
e-mail: peggy@batterydance.org
Web Site: www.batterydance.org
Management:
    Artistic/Executive Director: Jonathan Hollander
    Production Designer: Barry Steele
    Project Coordinator: Gabrielle Hoffman
    Deputy Director For Domestic Progra: Elena Ryabova
    Deputy Director for International P: Emad Salem
    Project Coordinator: Natalia Mesa
Mission: Battery Dance Company performs on the world's stages, teaches, presents and advocates for the field of dance.
Founded: 1976
Specialized Field: Modern; Contemporary Dance
Status: Professional, Non-Profit
Budget: $200,000-$500,000
Income Sources: Pace University
Performs At: Tribeca Performing Arts Center
Annual Attendance: 100,000
Organization Type: Performing; Touring; Resident; Educational; Sponsoring

396
BEBE MILLER COMPANY
PO Box 82484
New York, NY 43202
Phone: 646-298-1108
e-mail: Nicole@bebemillercompany.org
Web Site: www.bebemillercompany.org

DANCE / New York

Officers:
  President: Michael Mazzola
  Secretary and Treasurer: Dana Whitco
Management:
  Artistic Director: Bebe Miller
  Company Director: Caterina Bartha
Mission: The mission of Bebe Miller Company is to support the artistic vision of choreographer Bebe Miller in creative, cross-disciplinary explorations and in creating and performing new works.
Founded: 1985
Specialized Field: Modern
Status: Professional, Nonprofit
Paid Staff: 2
Paid Artists: 6
Budget: $200,000-$500,000
Organization Type: Performing; Touring; Resident

397
BILL T JONES/ARNIE ZANE DANCE COMPANY
219 W 19th Street
New York, NY 10011
Phone: 212-691-6500
Fax: 212-633-1974
e-mail: info@newyorklivearts.org
Web Site: www.newyorklivearts.org
Officers:
  Executive Director: Jean Davidson
Management:
  Artistic Director: Bill T Jones
  Associate Artistic Director: Janet Wong
  Producing Director: Michael Lonergan
  Creative Director: Bjorn G Amelan
  Resident Costume Designer: Liz Prince
  Resident Lighting Designer: Robert Wierzel
  Band Leader: Christopher Lancaster
  Artistic Consultant: Bill Katz
  Program Director: David Archuletta
Mission: The 10 member company has performed worldwide in over 200 cities and 30 countries. The Harlem based company is recognized as one of the most innovative and powerful forces in the modern dance world.
Specialized Field: Modern

398
BILL YOUNG/COLLEEN THOMAS AND DANCERS
100 Grand Street
2nd Floor
New York, NY 10013
Phone: 212-925-6573
e-mail: wgy@panix.com
Web Site: www.panix.com/~wgy/
Management:
  Artistic Director: Bill Young
Mission: Abstract and extremely physical dance performed by a group of international dancers.
Specialized Field: Modern

399
BLANCO PERFORMING ARTS FOUNDATION
Old Chelsea Station
PO Box 985
New York, NY 10011
Phone: 212-362-6061
Fax: 212-877-0814
e-mail: blancoarts@aol.com
Web Site: www.blancoarts.org
Management:
  Co-Artistic Director: Carol Blanco
  Co-Artistic Director: R Michael Blanco
Mission: Produces innovative cross-media performances in dance, theater, music and visual design.
Founded: 1993
Specialized Field: Theatre Dance; Dramatic Dance
Status: Professional, Nonprofit
Income Sources: Donations; Grants; Earned Income

400
BUGLISI DANCE THEATRE
229 West 42nd Street, Suite 502
New York, NY 10036
Phone: 212-719-3301
Fax: 212-719-3302
e-mail: buglisi@buglisidance.org
Web Site: buglisidance.org
Management:
  Artistic Director: Jacqulyn Buglisi
  Executive Director: Suzanne Konowitz
Mission: Threshold Dance Projects, Inc., and Buglisi Dance Theatre will be recognized globally as a flag bearer of American Contemporary Dance through the innovative choreography of its founding directors, performance excellence, worldwide collaborations, touring, and educational outreach.
Founded: 1994
Organization Type: Touring; Performing

401
CAROLYN LORD AND COMPANY
10 E 18th Street
3rd Floor
New York, NY 10003
Phone: 212-924-7882
Fax: 212-989-6112
e-mail: info@miltonfletcher.com
Web Site: www.theconstructioncompany.org
Management:
  Artistic Director: Carolyn Lorde
  Choreographer: Ariane Anthony
  Choreographer: Cedric Neugebauer
  Choreographer: Christopher Caines
Founded: 1972
Specialized Field: Modern

402
CEDAR LAKE DANCE
547 West 26th Street
New York, NY 10001
Phone: 212-244-0015
Fax: 212-244-0982
e-mail: info@cedarlakedance.com
Web Site: cedarlakedance.com
Management:
  Artistic Director: Alexandra Damiani
  Executive Director: Gerald Halpern
  Technical Director: Kurtis Rutherford
  Production Manager: Andy Cappelli
  Manager Of External Affairs: Ally Duffey
  Company Manager: Jen De Santo
  Director Of Operations: Barbara Myers
Mission: Dedicated to the continued development of dance by providing choreographers a comprehensive environment for creation as well as curating work for presentation to a worldwide audience.
Founded: 2003
Specialized Field: Contemporary Ballet
Status: Nonprofit

403
CELEBRATION TEAM
National Dance Institute
217 West 147th Street
New York, NY 10039
Phone: 212-226-0083
Fax: 212-226-0761
e-mail: cgriffin@nationaldance.org
Web Site: www.nationaldance.org
Officers:
  Chair: Karhy Mele
  Vice Chair: Edith Fassberg
  Secretary: Carole Sobin
  Treasurer: Robert D. Krinsky
Management:
  Artistic Director: Ellen Weinstein
  Associate Artistic Director: Tracy Straus
  Music Director: Jerry Korman
  Program Director: Aileen Barry
  Founder: Jacques d'Amboise
  Executive Director: Kathy Landau
  Associate Music Director: David Marck
  Director of Development: Michele O'Mara
  Director of Advanced Programs: Samantha Belth
Mission: National Dance Institute was founded in the belief that the arts have a unique power to engage children and motivate them toward excellence.
Founded: 1976
Specialized Field: Ballet; Modern; Jazz
Status: Semi-Professional

404
CHEN DANCE CENTER
70 Mulberry Street, 2nd Floor
New York, NY 10013
Phone: 212-349-0126
e-mail: info@chendancecenter.org
Web Site: chendancecenter.org
Management:
  Choreographer: H.T. Chen
Founded: 1978
Specialized Field: Asian American Modern Dance
Status: Nonprofit

405
CHINESE FOLK DANCE COMPANY
NY Chinese Cultural Center
390 Broadway 2nd Floor
New York, NY 10013
Phone: 212-334-3764
Fax: 212-334-3768
e-mail: info@chinesedance.org
Web Site: www.chinesedance.org
Officers:
  President: Geoffrey R. Sant
  Secretary: Arnold Chu
  Treasurer: Jeffrey Lee
  Vice President: Jackie Quan
Management:
  Artistic Director: Jiang Qi
  Executive Director: Cathy Hung
  Operations Manager: Janie Wong
  Education Programs Manager: Angela Tam
  Special Projects & Administrative A: Nico Li
  Education Associate: Jessie Jiayan Yong
Mission: To inspire and educate through Chinese cultural arts.
Founded: 1973
Specialized Field: Chinese Dance
Status: Professional, Nonprofit
Paid Staff: 5
Volunteer Staff: 2
Paid Artists: 20

DANCE / New York

Budget: $500,000
Annual Attendance: 150,000
Facility Category: Dance Studio
Rental Contact: Belle Lam
Organization Type: Performing; Touring; Educational

406
CHRISTOPHER CAINES DANCE COMPANY
639 West 204th Street SE
New York, NY 10034-3913
Phone: 646-623-4433
e-mail: info@christophercainesdance.org
Web Site: www.christophercainesdance.org
Officers:
  President: Jock Ireland
  Tresurer: Andrew Clearfield
  Secretary: Christopher Woodrell
  Board Member: Joan Duddy
  Advisor/Assoc Professor of Dance: Mindy Aloff
  Advisor/Assoc Professor of Dance: Beth Genne
  Advisor/Esquire/Executive Director: Elena Paul
  Director of Research: Nancy Reynolds
Management:
  Artistic Director: Christopher Caines
  Development: Fran Kirmser
  Public Relations: Diane Tedesco
Mission: n 2000, after a decade of making dances, evening-length dance-theater pieces with his own music, two full-length solos, and numerous scores for other choreographers and directors, Christopher Caines got together a pianist, two singers, and six of his dancer friends, and made ARIAS, a suite of dances set to vocal music ranging from Italian Baroque arias to songs by Faur?, Schoenberg, and Gershwin.
Utilizes: Choreographers; Collaborating Artists; Composers; Contract Orchestras; Dancers; Grant Writers; Lyricists; Multimedia; Music; Singers
Founded: 2000
Opened: 2002
Specialized Field: Interpretive Dance to Vocal and Choral Music
Income Sources: Donations, Performances
Season: Fall

407
BERNARD SCHMIDT PRODUCTIONS, INC
16 Penn Plaza
Suite 545
New York, NY 10001
Phone: 212-564-4443
Fax: 212-397-2459
e-mail: bschmidtpd@aol.com
Web Site: www.bernardschmidtproductions.com
Management:
  Artists Representative: Bernard Schmidt
Mission: Performers from around the world at the crossroads of innovation and tradition.
Specialized Field: Contemporary Dance; Moorish Dance; Spanish Dance
Paid Staff: 2
Paid Artists: 8

408
CREACH/COMPANY
238 W 20th Street
Suite 1D
New York, NY 10011-5805
Phone: 212-924-5443
Fax: 212-924-5443
e-mail: TLCreach@aol.com
Management:
  Director: Terry Creach
Utilizes: Choreographers; Collaborations; Dancers; Designers; Guest Companies; Guest Conductors; Original Music Scores; Visual Arts
Founded: 1980
Specialized Field: Contemporary Dance; Traditional Dance
Income Sources: New York Council for the Arts; Harkness Foundation for Dance; Meet the Composer; Joyce Mertz-Gilmore Foundations

409
DANCE COLLECTIVE NEW YORK
463 West Street #953H
New York, NY 10014
Phone: 212-627-4275
Fax: 212-627-4275
e-mail: cnolte2344@aol.com
Web Site: www.dancecollectiveny.com
Management:
  Artistic Director/Choreographer: Carol Nolte
Mission: Comprised of dancers from a variety of ethnic and cultural backgrounds, creative artists in their own right, the company is committed to both community involvement and the expansion of creative potential.
Founded: 1974
Specialized Field: Modern
Status: Professional, Nonprofit
Paid Staff: 1
Volunteer Staff: 4
Paid Artists: 6
Affiliations: Dance Theatre Workshop; The Field
Organization Type: Performing; Touring

410
DANCE JUNE LEWIS AND COMPANY
PO Box 2025
New York, NY 10159
Phone: 212-741-3044
Fax: 718-996-1433
Web Site: www.dancejunelewis.wordpress.com
Management:
  Publicity Manager: Mel Leifer
  Artistic Director: June Lewis
  Associate Artistic Director: Claudio Assante
Founded: 1968
Specialized Field: Modern; Contemporary Dance
Status: Professional
Organization Type: Performing; Touring; Resident; Educational

411
DANCE THEATRE OF HARLEM
466 W 152nd Street
New York, NY 10031-1814
Phone: 212-690-2800
Fax: 212-690-8736
e-mail: info@dancetheatreofharlem.org
Web Site: www.dancetheatreofharlem.org
Officers:
  Chairman: Kendrick F. Ashton Jr.
  Vice-Chairman: Michael Armstrong
  Treasurer: Frank Baker
  Secretary: Don Tellock
Management:
  Artistic Director: Virginia Johnson
  Executive Director: Laveen Naidu
  Marketing Manager: Keyana K. Patterson
  Development Consultant: Lisa Van Putten
  Sr. Development Officer: JoAnn Wong
  Marketing Consultant: Melissa Y. Hudnell
  Public Relations: Simone Cooper
  Media Relations: Gilda Squire
  Ballet Master: Keith Saunders
Mission: A leading dance institution as unparalleled global acclaim, encompassing a Classically American dance company, a leading arts education center and Dancing Through Barriers an International outreach program.
Founded: 1969
Specialized Field: Dance
Status: Professional, Nonprofit
Organization Type: Touring; Performing; Educational

412
DANCES PATRELLE
139 Fulton Street
Suite 310
New York, NY 10038
Mailing Address: PO Box 286189 New York, NY 10128
Phone: 212-722-7933
Fax: 212-966-2978
e-mail: director@dancespatrelle.org
Web Site: www.dancespatrelle.org
Officers:
  Managing Director: Kirk Sprinkles
Management:
  Artistic Director: Francis Patrelle
  Rehearsal Director: Leda Meredith
  Co-Managing Director: Lisa Iannacito
  Co-Managing Director: Hana Ginsburg
  Principal: Jennifer Ringer
  Principal: Jared Angle
Mission: Dances Patrelle's mission has been to bring dramatic ballet, with an emphasis on societal and historical concerns, to the stage. We strive to address all elements of the human condition and by so doing, make ballet accessible to a wider audience.
Founded: 1998
Specialized Field: Ballet

413
DANCING IN THE STREETS
2500 Westchester Avenue
New York, NY 10461
Phone: 718-589-2230
Fax: 718-842-4622
e-mail: info@dancinginthestreets.org
Web Site: www.dancinginthestreets.org
Officers:
  Founder: Elise Bernhardt
  President: Carl Stoll
  Secretary: Ellen Gesmer
  Treasurer: Betsy O'Brien
Management:
  Artistic/Executive Director: Aviva Davidson
  Assistant to the Executive Director: Tori Swedin
  Social Media Manager: Nitzan Nickie Levy
  Bookkeeper: Darin Webb
Mission: Dancing in the Streets strives to illuminate the urban experience with free public performances and site-specific installations that examine the kinetic life and history of natural and architectural public spaces.
Founded: 1984
Specialized Field: Street Theatre
Status: Professional, Nonprofit
Organization Type: Producing

414
DANSPACE PROJECT
131 E 10th Street
New York, NY 10003
Phone: 212-674-8112
Fax: 212-529-2318
e-mail: info@danspaceproject.org
Web Site: www.danspaceproject.org
Officers:

DANCE / New York

President: David Fanger
First Vice President: Frances Milberg
Second Vice President: Ann Tuomey-DePiro
Treasurer: Sam Miller
Secretary: David Parker
Officer-at-Large: Helen Warwick
Management:
  Program Manager: Abby Harris Holmes
  Technical Director: Leo Janks
  Executive Director: Judy Hussie-Taylor
  Finance and HR Manager: Jodi Bender
  Development Director: Peggy.H Chang
  Communications Associate: Lily Cohen
  Lighting Designers: Kathy Kaufmann
  Lighting Designers: Carol Mullins
  Development Assistant: Michael DiPietro
Mission: The mission of the Danspace Project is to stimulate, promote and present challenging new work in dance from a broad range of artistic voices within a distinguished and nurturing environment.
Utilizes: Curators; Dance Companies; Theatre Companies
Founded: 1974
Specialized Field: Modern; Experimental Dance; Post-Modern Dance
Status: Professional, Nonprofit
Paid Staff: 5
Volunteer Staff: 15
Paid Artists: 30
Budget: $1 million
Performs At: Sanctuary Performance Space at St. Mark's Church
Annual Attendance: 15,000
Stage Dimensions: 36'x48'
Seating Capacity: 200
Year Built: 1799
Year Remodeled: 1980
Organization Type: Performing; Artists Services

415
DONALD WILLIAMS
Dube Zakin Management
67 Riverside Drive
New York, NY 10024
Phone: 212-877-3388
Fax: 212-799-8420
Specialized Field: Contemporary Dance; Traditional Dance

416
DONNA UCHIZONO COMPANY
140-42 Second Avenue, Suite 501
New York, NY 10003
Phone: 917-570-6120
e-mail: ladonnadance@gmail.com
Web Site: donnauchizono.org
Management:
  Artistic Director: Donna Uchizono
Mission: Committed to fostering public awareness and appreciation of the performing and visual arts. DUC's goal is to remain a viable, non-profit entity that creates active and permanent contributions to New York City's cultural community as well as the national and international dance community.
Founded: 1990
Specialized Field: Contemporary
Status: Nonprofit

417
DOUG ELKINS DANCE COMPANY
506 Fort Washington Avenue
1 H
New York, NY 10033
Phone: 212-928-6517
e-mail: dougelkinsdance@aol.com
Web Site: www.dougelkinsdance.com
Management:
  Artistic Director: Doug Elkins
  Managing Director: Ken Maldonado
  Financial Director: Lisa Hicks
  Booking: Cathy Zimmerman
Mission: Established to create and present the work of Doug Elkins and to provide dance education for all levels and ages.
Founded: 1987
Specialized Field: Modern; Street Theatre
Status: Professional; Nonprofit
Organization Type: Performing; Educational

418
DOUG VARONE AND DANCERS
Doug Varone and Dancers/DOVA, Inc.
260 W Broadway
Suite 4
New York, NY 10013
Phone: 212-279-3344
Fax: 212-279-6397
e-mail: info@dougvaroneanddancers.org
Web Site: www.dougvaroneanddancers.org
Officers:
  Executive Director: Thomas Ward
  Chair: Naomi Grabel
  Board of Directors: Richard Caples
  Board of Directors: Lida Orzeck
  Board of Directors: Elizabeth Geiger
Management:
  Artistic Director: Doug Varone
  Interim Executive Director: Sarah Bodley
  Company Manager: Alex Springs
  Technical Director: Tricia Tolliver
  Public Relations: Jenny Lerner
  Technical Director: Dan Feith
Mission: A dance performance company headed by Doug Varone, performs at such venues as London's Queen Elizabeth Hall and at the Jacob's Pillow Dance festival in western Massachusettes. It also performs an annual season in New York City at the Joyce theatre and other venues.
Specialized Field: Dance

419
DOUGLAS DUNN AND DANCERS
Rio Grande Union, Inc.
541 Broadway
3rd Floor
New York, NY 10012
Phone: 212-966-6999
Fax: 212-274-1804
e-mail: admin@douglasdunndance.com
Web Site: www.douglasdunndance.com
Management:
  Artistic Director: Douglas Dunn
Mission: Dedicated to producing and promoting the works of contemporary choreographer Douglas Dunn.
Utilizes: Singers
Founded: 1976
Specialized Field: Modern
Status: Professional; Nonprofit
Organization Type: Performing; Touring; Educational

420
EIKO AND KOMA
246 W 38th Street
4th Floor
New York, NY 10018-5805
Phone: 212-278-8111
Fax: 212-278-8555
e-mail: ivans@pentacle.org
Web Site: www.eikoandkoma.org
Management:
  Artistic Director/Choreographer: Eiko Otake
  Artistic Director/Choreographer: Koma Otake
Mission: Established to perform the theater choreography of Eiko and Koma.
Specialized Field: Contemporary Dance
Status: Professional, Nonprofit
Organization Type: Performing; Touring; Resident; Educational

421
ELISA MONTE DANCE
481 8th Avenue
Suite 543
New York, NY 10001
Phone: 212-868-4488
Fax: 212-868-4494
e-mail: info@elisamontedance.org
Web Site: www.elisamontedance.org
Officers:
  Chair: Rima Vargas-Vetter
Management:
  Artistic Director: Elisa Monte
  Associate Artistic Director: Tiffany Rea Fisher
  Director of Finance: Nicholas Reich
  Creative & Communications Associate: Jordan Gehley
  Development Associate: Caroline Yost
Mission: In order to advance and enrich the art of dance, Elisa Monte Dance will present the choreography of Elisa Monte to an American and international audience to bridge cultures.
Founded: 1981
Specialized Field: Modern
Status: Professional, Nonprofit
Income Sources: Dance USA
Performs At: The Joyce Theater
Organization Type: Performing; Touring; Educational

422
ERNESTA CORVINO'S DANCE CIRCLE COMPANY
451 W 50th Street
New York, NY 10019
Phone: 212-247-2564
e-mail: ecdoesit3@att.net
Web Site: www.corvinoballet.org
Management:
  Director: Ernesta Corvino
  Ballet Mistress: Andra Corvino
Mission: To provide the public with high quality and affordable dance performances, as well as workshops and lecture demonstrations.
Founded: 1981
Specialized Field: Ballet
Status: Professional, Nonprofit
Performs At: Marymount Manhattan Theatre
Organization Type: Performing

423
ETHAN BROWN
67 Riverside Drive
New York, NY 10024
Phone: 212-877-3388
Fax: 212-799-8420
Specialized Field: Contemporary Dance; Traditional Dance

DANCE / New York

424
EUGENE JAMES DANCE COMPANY
PO Box 2504
New York, NY 10116
Phone: 212-564-1026
Fax: 212-564-1026
Management:
    Manager: Richard Williams
    Artistic Director: Eugene James
Mission: Dedicated to extending the contributions of Afro-American rhythms to dance.
Founded: 1967
Specialized Field: Modern; Ethnic Dance
Status: Professional; Nonprofit
Volunteer Staff: 3
Organization Type: Performing; Touring; Resident

425
FELICE LESSER DANCE THEATER
484 W 43rd Street
#9T
New York, NY 10036
Phone: 212-594-3388
Fax: 215-594-3388
e-mail: fldtny@aol.com
Web Site: www.fldt.org
Management:
    Artistic/Executive Director: Felice Lesser
Mission: Creates and performs multi-disciplinary works-mixing dance with video, computer animation, contemporary music, drama and art. Committed to education as well as performance, it has developed an extensive program of lecture-demonstrations, classes, residencies and workshops to develop audiences and bring the general public and students into the creative process.
Utilizes: Singers
Founded: 1975
Specialized Field: Modern; Ballet
Status: Professional, Nonprofit
Affiliations: Dance USA
Organization Type: Performing; Touring; Resident; Educational

426
FLY-BY-NIGHT DANCE THEATER
116 Seaman Avenue #4E
New York, NY 10034
Phone: 212-304-3791
e-mail: julie@flybynightdance.org
Web Site: flybynightdance.org
Management:
    Artistic Director: Julie Ludwick

427
GILMA BUSTILLO
67 Riverside Drive
New York, NY 10024
Phone: 212-877-3388
Fax: 212-799-8420
Specialized Field: Traditional Dance

428
GINA GIBNEY DANCE
890 Broadway
Studio 5-2
New York, NY 10003
Phone: 212-677-8560
Fax: 212-777-8653
e-mail: info@gibneydance.org
Web Site: www.gibneydance.org
Officers:
    General Administrator: Courtney Drasner
    Chair: Thomas Scott
    1st Vice Chair: James W. Kennedy
    Treasurer: Lynn Gitlitz
    Secretary: Katherine Wickham
    Officer-at-Large: Lauren DiPaolo
    Second Vice Chair: Marcia L. Worthing
Management:
    Artistic Director, CEO: Gina Gibney
    Operations Manager: Jit Seneviratne
    Operations Associate: Allie Pfeffer
    Operations Assistant: Andy Chapman
    Finance Manager: George Cochran
    Marketing Manager: Elena Light
    Associate Artistic Director: Amy Miller
    Chief Development Manager: Liz Montgomery
Mission: Gina Gibney Dance maintains an active schedule that includes an annual New York season and touring engagements throughout the US and abroad.
Founded: 1991
Specialized Field: Traditional Dance

429
H.T. CHEN DANCE COMPANY, INC.
Chen Dance Center
70 Mulberry Street 2nd Floor
New York, NY 10013
Phone: 212-349-0126
Fax: 212-349-0494
e-mail: info@chendancecenter.org
Web Site: www.chendancecenter.org
Officers:
    Founder: H.T. Chen
    Chairperson: Rita Gail Johnson
    Honorary Chair: Shirley Ubell
    Board Member: Ernest Abuba
    Board Member: Kevin Benson
Management:
    Artistic Director: HT Chen
    Associate Director: Dian Dong
Mission: Chen Dance Center (CDC) is a not-for-profit organization that provides for the cultural vitality of the performing arts community through its company, theater and school. All of CDC's programs and activities reflect its ongoing mission to provide moving experiences in Asian-American and contemporary dance through artistic creation, arts education, and presentation.
Utilizes: Artists-in-Residence; Choreographers; Collaborations; Community Members; Dance Companies; Dancers; Five Seasonal Concerts; High School Drama; Paid Performers; Soloists; Students; Theatre Companies
Founded: 1978
Specialized Field: Modern; Asian American Dance
Status: Professional, Nonprofit
Paid Staff: 5
Volunteer Staff: 3
Paid Artists: 25
Non-paid Artists: 2
Budget: $600,000
Income Sources: Association for Performing Arts Presenters
Performs At: Black box theater for Modern Dance only
Affiliations: Dance/USA, Dance Theater Workshop, Asian American Arts Alliance
Annual Attendance: 20,000
Facility Category: Marley flooring over wood
Type of Stage: Marley floor for Modern Dance
Stage Dimensions: 24 x 22
Seating Capacity: 70
Year Built: 1892
Year Remodeled: 2010
Cost: $1,800
Rental Contact: Artistic Director H.T. Chen

430
DANCE THEATRE OF HARLEM
466 West 152nd Street
New York, NY 10031
Phone: 212-690-2800
e-mail: jtyrus@dancetheatreofharlem.org
Web Site: dancetheatreofharlem.org
Management:
    Executive Director: Laveen Naidu
    Artistic Director: Virginia Johnson
Mission: To maintain a world-class school that trains young people in classical ballet and the allied arts; to provide arts education, community outreach programs and positive role models for all; to present a ballet company of African American and other racially diverse artists who perform the most demanding repertory at the highest level of quality.
Founded: 1969

431
ICE THEATRE OF NEW YORK
62 Chelsea Piers
Suit 308
New York, NY 10011
Phone: 212-929-5811
Fax: 212-929-0105
e-mail: itny@icetheatre.org
Web Site: www.icetheatre.org
Management:
    Founder/Artistic Director: Moira North
    Executive Director: Jirina Ribbens
Mission: Committed to developing figure skating as a performing art. They build an artistic repertory of ice skating performance pieces; to allow professional skaters from various backgrounds to collaborate with choreographers, musicians and visual artists.
Utilizes: Choreographers; Collaborations; Commissioned Composers; Commissioned Music; Dancers; Guest Artists; Guest Companies; High School Drama; Lyricists; Original Music Scores
Founded: 1984
Specialized Field: Modern
Status: Professional; Nonprofit
Paid Staff: 4
Volunteer Staff: 30
Paid Artists: 65
Non-paid Artists: 10
Budget: $450,000
Income Sources: Performances; Ticket Sales
Performs At: The Rink at Rockefeller Plaza
Annual Attendance: 2,189,300
Organization Type: Performing; Touring; Educational

432
ISADORA DUNCAN DANCE FOUNDATION
141 W 26th Street
3rd Floor
New York, NY 10001
Phone: 212-691-5040
Fax: 212-627-0774
e-mail: info@isadoraduncan.org
Web Site: www.isadoraduncan.org
Officers:
    Founder: Lori Belilove
    Board Member: Jim Belilove
    Board Member: Bernadette Carr
    Board Member: Reba Palker
Management:
    Artistic Director: Lori Belilove
    Associate Artistic Director: Cherlyn Smith
    Music Director: John Link
    Office Administrator: Julienne Vicens

DANCE / New York

Principal Dancer: Elizabeth Disharoon
Principal Dancer: Mary Staub
Mission: The Isadora Duncan Dance Foundation's mission is to preserve, present and teach the work of Isadora Duncan through the perfomance and educational programs.
Founded: 1979
Specialized Field: Traditional Dance; Educational Dance
Status: Professional, Non-Profit
Paid Staff: 6
Volunteer Staff: 20
Paid Artists: 12
Non-paid Artists: 5
Budget: $200,000
Income Sources: Grants; Individual & Corporate Contributions

433
JANIS BRENNER AND DANCERS
123 W 93rd Street
Suite #3E
New York, NY 10025-7554
Phone: 212-864-3874
Fax: 212-864-3874
e-mail: janis@janisbrenner.com
Web Site: www.janisbrenner.com
Management:
    Artistic Director/Choreographer: Janis Brenner
    Principal Dancer: Aaron Selissen
Mission: Established to perform the work of Janis Brenner and to conduct teaching workshops in technique, improvisation, composition, repertory and sounding.
Utilizes: Collaborations; Commissioned Composers; Dancers; Educators; Soloists; Students
Founded: 1985
Specialized Field: Modern; Contemporary
Status: Professional, Nonprofit
Paid Staff: 1
Volunteer Staff: 1
Paid Artists: 7
Organization Type: Performing; Touring; Educational

434
JENNIFER MULLER: THE WORKS
131 W 24th Street
4th Floor
New York, NY 10011
Phone: 212-691-3803
Fax: 212-206-6630
e-mail: jmuller@jmtw.org
Web Site: www.jmtw.org
Officers:
    Chairman: Deborah S. Greenhut, Ph.D
    Board of Directors: Anna Lascar
    Board of Directors: Alison Price Becker
    Board of Directors: Cindy Cook
Management:
    Artistic Director/Choreographer: Jennifer Muller
    Artistic Council: Rosie Lani Fiedelman
    Administrative Associate: Rachel Gorman
    Lighting Director: Jeff Croiter
    Wardrobe Supervisor: Keiko Voltaire
Mission: Jennifer Muller: The Works' mission is to create work through a multi-discipline approach combining technical virtuosity with dance and theater, to subject matter that is accessible and communicates directly to audiences about issues that touch their lives.
Utilizes: Actors; Collaborating Artists; Collaborations; Dancers; Designers; Educators; Filmmakers; Fine Artists; Five Seasonal Concerts; Guest Companies; Guest Conductors; Guest Directors; Guild Activities;

Lyricists; Multi Collaborations; Multimedia; New Productions; Organization Contracts; Original Music Scores; Resident Professionals
Founded: 1974
Specialized Field: Contemporary Dance
Status: Professional, Nonprofit
Paid Staff: 4
Volunteer Staff: 2
Paid Artists: 12
Budget: $200,000-$700,000
Income Sources: Individual; Corporate; Foundations; Government
Performs At: The Joyce Theatre
Annual Attendance: 10,000
Organization Type: Performing; Touring; Resident

435
JOAN MILLER DANCE PLAYERS
1380 Riverside Drive
Suite 10B
New York, NY 10033
Phone: 212-568-8854
Fax: 212-795-5212
Management:
    Artistic Director/Choreographer: Joan Miller
Mission: A unique, multi-ethnic, street smart, mixed media company with a zany sense of humor, a slightly off-beat point of view and an eclectic sense of dance theater.
Utilizes: Singers
Founded: 1970
Specialized Field: Modern; Ballet; Jazz; Ethnic Dance
Status: Professional; Non-Profit
Paid Staff: 5
Budget: $60,000-$100,000
Income Sources: Grants; Foundations; Bronx Counsil For The Arts
Annual Attendance: 5,000-6,000
Organization Type: Performing; Touring

436
JODY OBERFELDER DANCE PROJECTS
455 FDR Drive B902
New York, NY 10002
Phone: 212-777-6227
e-mail: jody@jodyoberfelder.com
Web Site: www.jodyoberfelder.com
Management:
    Artistic Director: Jody Oberfelder
    Co-Director: David Lachman
    Company Manager: Dana Florin-Weiss
    Intern: Hendryx Silva
Mission: Jody Oberfelder Dance Projects endeavors to bring boldly physical dance to both a traditional and a non-traditional dance audience.
Founded: 1989
Specialized Field: Contemporary Dance
Status: Professional, Nonprofit
Budget: $45,000
Annual Attendance: 6,000

437
JOHN GARDNER
67 Riverside Drive
New York, NY 10024
Phone: 212-877-3388
Fax: 212-799-8420
Specialized Field: Traditional Dance

438
JOLINDA MENENDEZ
67 Riverside Drive
New York, NY 10024

Phone: 212-877-3388
Fax: 212-799-8420
Specialized Field: Traditional Dance

439
THE JOSE LIMON DANCE FOUNDATION
307 W 38th Street
Suite 1105
New York, NY 10018
Phone: 212-777-3353
Fax: 212-777-4764
e-mail: info@limon.org
Web Site: www.limon.org
Officers:
    Executive Director: Gabriela Poler-Buzali
    Chair: Tomas J. Rossant
    Board Member: Paula Carrico
    Secretary: Fernando Bohorquez
    Treasurer: Rebeca Vargas
Management:
    Artistic Director: Carla Maxwell
    Associate Artistic Director: Roxane D'Orleans Juste
    Institute Director: Ann Vachon
    Business Manager: Alex Gonzalez
    School Director: Alan Danielson
    Program Manager: Becky Brown
Mission: Presents modern classics, jazz works and other contemporary works through performances and residencies throughout the United States and abroad. The foundation also offers a variety of educational programs.
Founded: 1946
Specialized Field: Modern
Status: Nonprofit, Professional
Budget: $1.5 million
Income Sources: Corporate; Foundation; Government Grants; Individual Donations; Performance Fees; Liscensing Fees

440
JUILLIARD SCHOOL
Dance Division
60 Lincoln Center Plaza
New York, NY 10023-6588
Phone: 212-799-5000
Fax: 212-724-0263
e-mail: admissions@juilliard.edu
Web Site: www.juilliard.edu
Officers:
    Vice President for Library and IR: Jane Gottlieb
    Associate VP for Production: Kent McKay
    Vice Chair: Katheryn.C Patterson
    Board of Directors: Pierre.T Bastid
    Board of Directors: Pamela Daley
Management:
    Artistic Director: Lawrence Rhodes
    Administrative Director: Sarah Adriance
    Director: Courtney Blackwell
    Director: Nicholas Saunders
    Administrative Director: Katherine Hood
Mission: Juilliard's central mission is to educate talented performing musicians, dancers and actors so that they may achieve the highest artistic standards, as well as become leaders in their professions.
Founded: 1951
Specialized Field: Contemporary Dance
Status: Pre-professional, Nonprofit
Paid Staff: 30
Budget: $500,000-$1,000,000
Organization Type: Performing; Resident

DANCE / New York

441
KATHAK ENSEMBLE & FRIENDS/CARAVAN
141 E 3rd Street
#12H
New York, NY 10009
Phone: 212-673-1282
Fax: 212-673-1282
e-mail: info@kathakensemble.com
Web Site: www.kathakensemble.com
Management:
    Artistic/Administrative Director: Janaki Patrik
Mission: To teach and perform classical Northern Indian Kathak dance with live musical accompaniment, to create new repertoire inspired by classical and modern Indian music and dance.
Founded: 1978
Specialized Field: North Indian Dance
Status: Professional, Nonprofit

442
KATHY ROSE
10 Stuyvsant Oval
New York, NY 10009-2421
Phone: 212-353-9891
e-mail: kabukimenco@gmail.com
Web Site: www.krose.com
Management:
    Artistic Director: Kathy Rose
Founded: 1983
Specialized Field: Theatrical Dance; Educational Dance

443
KEI TAKEI'S MOVING EARTH
28 Vesey Street
#2200
New York, NY 10007-2906
Phone: 212-459-4383
Fax: 212-732-3926
e-mail: kei@keitakei.org
Web Site: http://keitakei.org/
Officers:
    Chairperson: Kei Takei
    President: Louise Roberts
    VP: Maldwyn Pate
    Secretary/Treasurer: Lawrence Brezer
Management:
    Executive Director: Laz Brezer
Mission: To perform the internationally acclaimed, award-winning choreography of Kei Takei.
Founded: 1968
Specialized Field: Modern
Status: Professional
Paid Staff: 8
Organization Type: Performing; Touring

444
KEIGWIN + COMPANY
143 West 29th Street, 5th Floor
New York, NY 10001
Phone: 212-278-0691
e-mail: larry@keigwinandcompany.com
Web Site: keigwinandcompany.com
Management:
    Artistic Director: Larry Keigwin
    Executive Director: Andrea Lodico Welshons
    Associate Director: Nicole Wolcott
    Business Manager: Salena M. Watkins
    Marketing Associate: Marisha Johnson
Mission: Keigwin + Company's commitment to variety allows for cross-pollination of audiences and encourages harmony between uptown and downtown, professional and amateur, high-brow and low-brow, all while maintaining a vision of dance that is both artistically driven and entertaining.
Founded: 2003
Specialized Field: Contemporary

445
LABAN/BARTENIEFF INSTITUTE OF MOVEMENT STUDIES
138 South Oxford Street
Suite 2D
New York, NY 11217
Phone: 212-643-8888
Fax: 347-422-0948
e-mail: info@limsonline.org
Web Site: www.limsonline.org
Officers:
    President: Virginia Reed
    Executive Director: Karen Bradley
    Financial Manager: Lorraine Benjamin
Management:
    Executive Director: Karen Bradley
    Arts & Culture Director: Regina Miranda
    Certification Programs Administrato: Corinne Cappelletti
    Financial Manager: Lorraine Benjamin
Mission: To teach Laban movement analysis, Bartenieff fundamentals on the introductory and professional level. Devoted to the study, exploration and teaching of movement as a human fundamental experience.
Founded: 1978
Specialized Field: Laban Movement Analyis; Bartenieff Fundamentals; Anatomy & Kinesiology; Bartenieff X-Class for Fitness
Status: Professional; Nonprofit
Paid Staff: 6
Paid Artists: 12
Budget: $350,000
Income Sources: National Association of Schools of Dance; Emergency Fund for Student Dancers; Dance Theatre Workshop: American Dinner Theatre Association; International Movement Therapists
Organization Type: Performing; Educational; Sponsoring

446
LAR LUBOVITCH DANCE COMPANY
229 W 42nd Street
8th Floor
New York, NY 10036-7201
Phone: 212-221-7909
Fax: 212-221-7938
e-mail: lubovitch@aol.com
Web Site: www.lubovitch.org
Officers:
    President: Virginia Kinzey
    Vice President: Maxine Pollak
    Vice President: Dale L. Ponikvar
    Treasurer: Lewis Steinberg
    Secretary: Jeffery Sholeen
Management:
    Executive Director: Richard J Caples
    Artistic Director: Lar Lubovitch
    Company Manager: Leticia D Baratta
    Office Manager: Jill Frere
Mission: To create, perform and teach modern dance throughout the United States and the world.
Founded: 1968
Specialized Field: Modern
Status: Professional; Nonprofit
Paid Staff: 4
Volunteer Staff: 20
Paid Artists: 20
Budget: $1,000,000-$2,500,000
Affiliations: Dance USA; Association of Performing Arts Presenters
Annual Attendance: 85,000
Type of Stage: Sprung Floor
Stage Dimensions: 40'x42'

447
LES BALLETS GRANDIVA
101 W 67th Street
Suite 49 E
New York, NY 10023
Phone: 212-875-0951
Fax: 212-875-0952
e-mail: grandiva01@aol.com
Web Site: www.balletsgrandiva.com
Officers:
    President: Suguru Aito
Management:
    Artistic Director: Victor Trevino
Mission: To develop sance audiences by performing comedic parodies of a wide range of choreographic styles both classical and contemporary.
Founded: 1996
Specialized Field: Comedy; Classic; Contemporary
Status: Non-Profit, Professional
Paid Staff: 2
Paid Artists: 19
Budget: $600,000
Income Sources: Performance Fees; Donations
Annual Attendance: 80,000

448
LES BALLETS TROCKADERO DE MONTE CARLO
Cathedral Station
Box 46
New York, NY 10025
Mailing Address: Box 1325 Gracie Station, New York City, NY 10028
Phone: 212-865-7925
Fax: 212-865-7925
e-mail: les.ballets.trockadero@aol.com
Web Site: www.trockadero.org
Management:
    General Director: Eugene McDougle
    Artistic Director: Tory Dobrin
    Associate Director: Isabel Martinez Rivera
    Ballet Master: Paul Gheslin
    Associate Ballet Master: Raffaela Mora
    Associate Production Manager: Barbara Domue
Mission: The original concept of Les Ballets Trockadero De Monte Carlo has not changed. It is a company of professional male dancers performing the full range of the ballet and modern dance repertoire, including classical and original works in faithful renditions of the manners and conceits of those dance styles.
Founded: 1974
Specialized Field: Ballet
Status: Professional, Nonprofit
Budget: $500,000-$1,000,000
Organization Type: Performing; Touring

449
LES GRANDS BALLETS DE LOONY
484 W 43rd Street
#32H
New York, NY 10036
Phone: 212-279-5169
Fax: 212-279-5169
e-mail: nephties@earthlink.net
Management:
    Artistic Director/Choreographer: Marco Galante

DANCE / New York

Mission: Marco Galantes goal is to present a show in which the work is solid, clever and very funny, a show which is diverse in its programming and is audience friendly.
Founded: 1992
Specialized Field: Ballet

450
LOTUS MUSIC & DANCE
336 West 37th Street
Suite 315
New York, NY 10018
Phone: 212-627-1076
Fax: 212-675-7191
e-mail: info@lotusmusicanddance.org
Web Site: www.lotusmusicanddance.org
Officers:
   Chair: Malabika Biswas
   Treasurer: Rupal Shankar
   Board of Directors: David Eastman
   Board of Directors: Michael Lent
   Board of Directors: Richard Turner
Management:
   Artistic Director: Kamala Cesar
   Development Director: Simmi Malhotra Degenemark
   Studio Manager: Angelina Hines-Jones
   Marketing and Publicity Coordinator: Carol Leogite
   Arts In Education Coordinator: Makalina Gallagher
Mission: Our mission is to protect, promote and celebrate the music and dance traditions of all world cultures.
Founded: 1989
Specialized Field: Ethnic Dance
Status: Nonprofit
Performs At: Throughout New York City

451
MARJORIE LIEBERT
New York, NY 10025
Mailing Address: PO Box 20456, Parkwest Station
Phone: 212-724-3238
Fax: 212-724-3238
Mission: To nurture and develop artistry and help healthy artists develop proper alignment. Rehabilitates injuries. Prevents future injuries. Reduces stress and develops muscles without stress.
Founded: 1980
Specialized Field: Ballet; Educational Dance
Status: Professional
Paid Staff: 1

452
MARK DEGARMO AND DANCERS
Dynamic Forms Inc
107 Suffolk Street
Suite 310
New York, NY 10002
Phone: 212-375-9214
Fax: 212-375-9216
e-mail: info@markdegarmoarts.org
Web Site: www.markdegarmoarts.org
Officers:
   President: Lawrence Holodak
   Treasurer: Jimmy Ren Zhao
   Executive Director: Mark DeGarmo, PhD
   Secretary: Karen DeLuca Stephens, MA
Management:
   Development Associate: Karen Stephens, MA
   Assistant to the Executive Director: Jes Osrow, BA
   Executive and Artistic Director: Mark DeGarmo
   Development Director: Daryl Sprague
   Education Director: Hawley Hussey
Mission: Established to develop and perform the original choreography of Mark DeGarmo.
Founded: 1982
Specialized Field: Modern
Status: Professional, Nonprofit
Income Sources: Dance USA
Organization Type: Performing; Touring; Resident; Educational

453
MARK KAPPEL
252 W 76th Street
Suite 6E
New York, NY 10023
Phone: 212-724-3889
Fax: 212-874-5039
e-mail: markkapl1@aol.com
Web Site: www.markkappeldance.com
Mission: Presents an international array of dancers and choreographers.
Specialized Field: Ballet

454
MARTHA GRAHAM DANCE COMPANY
55 Bethune Street
New York, NY 10014
Phone: 212-229-9200
Fax: 212-838-0339
e-mail: info@marthagraham.org
Web Site: www.marthagraham.org
Officers:
   President: Inger K. Witter
   Interim Chairman: Laura J. Gordon
Management:
   Executive Director: LaRue Allen
   Artistic Director: Janet Eilber
   Senior Artistic Associate: Denise Vale
   General Manager: Faye Rosenbaum
   Director: Virginie Mecene
   Marketing Manager: Brigid Pierce
   Company Manager: Simona Ferrara
   Lighting Supervisor: Lauren Libretti
   Costume Supervisor: Karen Young
Mission: Established to perform the original works of Martha Graham.
Founded: 1926
Specialized Field: Contemporary Dance
Status: Professional, Nonprofit
Performs At: Citi Centre
Organization Type: Performing; Touring; Educational

455
MARY ANTHONY DANCE THEATRE
Mary Anthony Dance Theatre Foundation, Inc.
736 Broadway
7th Floor
New York, NY 10003
Phone: 212-674-8191
Fax: 212-674-8191
e-mail: info@madt.org
Web Site: www.maryanthonydance.tripod.com
Management:
   Artistic Director/Choreographer: Mary Anthony
   Associate Artistic Director: Kun-Yang Lin
   Choreographer: Bertam Ross
Mission: To present modern dance through performances, lecture demonstrations and technique classes.
Founded: 1956
Specialized Field: Modern
Status: Professional, Nonprofit
Organization Type: Performing; Touring; Educational

456
MERCE CUNNINGHAM DANCE COMPANY
130 W 56th Street
Suite 707
New York, NY 10019
Phone: 212-255-8240
Fax: 212-633-2453
e-mail: lwichern@mercecunningham.org
Web Site: www.mercecunningham.org
Officers:
   Chair: Molly Davies
   Co-Chair: Loyd Lewis
   Vice Chairman: Alvin Chereskin
Management:
   Director of Choreography: Robert Swinston
   Executive Director: Lynn Wichern
   Trustee: Trevor Carlson
   Patricia: Robert Swinston
Mission: Committed to developing, understanding and public interest in dance through performances, dance instruction and videotapes.
Utilizes: Singers; Special Technical Talent
Founded: 1964
Specialized Field: Modern
Status: Professional; Nonprofit
Budget: $5,000,000
Income Sources: American Guild of Musical Artists; National Association of Schools of Dance; Dance USA
Performs At: Merce Cunningham Studio
Organization Type: Performing; Touring; Educational

457
MICHAEL MAO DANCE
1841 Broadway
Suite 1008
New York, NY 10023
Phone: 212-757-9669
Fax: 212-757-4198
e-mail: admin@michaelmaodance.org
Web Site: www.michaelmaodance.org
Management:
   Marketing Director: Vadim Ghin
   Choreographer: Michael Mao
Mission: Dance Performance; Touring; Community Outreach; Arts-in-Education; WSL Dance
Utilizes: Choreographers; Collaborations; Commissioned Composers; Commissioned Music; Dancers; Designers; Educators; Five Seasonal Concerts; Grant Writers; Multimedia; Music; Original Music Scores; Performance Artists; Resident Professionals; Selected Students; Student Interns; Touring Companies; Visual Arts
Specialized Field: Modern
Status: 501c3
Paid Staff: 3
Paid Artists: 15
Budget: $200,000-$500,000
Income Sources: NEA; NYSCA; DCA; Foundations; Corporations; Fees; Tickets
Affiliations: ISPA; DTN; APAP

458
MIMI GARRARD DANCE COMPANY
Two Penn Plaza
Suite 1500
New York, NY 10121
Phone: 212-674-6868
Fax: 845-386-4883
e-mail: mimi@mimigarrarddance.com
Web Site: www.mimigarrarddance.com
Management:
   Director/Choreographer: Mimi Garrard

Mission: Established to present original, professional dance theatre productions to the public and offer classes and workshops for individuals of all ages.
Founded: 1965
Specialized Field: Modern
Status: Professional, Nonprofit
Budget: $40,000-$100,000
Income Sources: Dance Theatre Workshop
Performs At: Mimi Garrard Dance Company
Organization Type: Performing; Touring; Resident

459
MOLISSA FENLEY AND DANCERS
Momenta Foundation
260 Broadway
Suite 1
New York, NY 10013
Phone: 212-941-8911
Fax: 212-334-5149
e-mail: artservicesinc@mindspring.com
Web Site: www.molissafenley.com
Management:
  Artistic Director/Choreographer: Molissa Fenley
  Administration: Mimi Johnson
  Choreographer: Judene Jean-Louis
  Choreographer: Peling Kao
Mission: Molissa Fenley is noted for incorporating quotes from classical and traditional dance worldwide into her choreography and for using unmediated physicality to convey emotional and psychic intensity.
Founded: 1977
Specialized Field: Ballet; Modern
Budget: $100,000-$200,000

460
MOMIX
1790 Broadway
16th Floor
New York, NY 10019
Phone: 212-841-9554
Fax: 212-841-9771
e-mail: momix@snet.net
Web Site: www.momix.com
Management:
  Artistice Director/Choreographer: Moses Pendleton
  Associate Director: Cynthia Quinn
Mission: Known internationally for presenting work of exceptional inventiveness and physical beauty, MOMIX is a company of dancer-illusionists under the direction of Moses Pendleton. In addition to stage performances world-wide.
Utilizes: Choreographers; Collaborations; Dance Companies; Dancers; Lyricists; Original Music Scores; Paid Performers
Specialized Field: Classical, Modern, Contemporary, Jazz, Ballet
Status: Non-Profit, Professional
Income Sources: Donors, Sponsors
Season: Year Round
Performs At: Teatro Olimpico, Shepaug Valley Highschool, Baker Hall, Stadtheater

461
MORPHOSES LTD
800 Fifth Avenue
Suite 18B
New York, NY 10065
Phone: 212-813-9818
Fax: 888-391-1110
e-mail: info@morphoses.org
Web Site: morphoses.org
Officers:
  Trustee: Lourdes Lopez
  Trustee: Charles Adelman
  Trustee: Shane Adler
  Trustee: Stan DiCicco
  Trustee: Catherine Gildor
  Trustee: Michael Ginsberg
  Trustee: Gail Hashimoto
  Trustee: George Skouras
Management:
  Artistic Director/Co-Founder: Lourdes Lopez
  Operations Director: Elizabeth Johanningermeier
Mission: Morphoses' mission is to revitalize the artform of dance by fostering cutting-edge artistry and collaboration among various media to present theatrical experiences that challenges assumptions and moves ballet forward into the 21st century. We believe in the transformative nature of dance, and therefore exist to continually contribute to growth in the artform.
Utilizes: Arrangers; Choreographers; Collaborating Artists; Collaborations; Dance Companies; Dancers; Educators; Lyricists; Music; Paid Performers
Founded: 2001
Specialized Field: Modern, Ballet
Status: Non-Profit, Professional
Income Sources: Donors, Sponsors
Season: Year Round
Performs At: Jacob's Pillow Dance, The Joyce Theater, Danses Hus, Norrlandsoperan

462
MUNA TSENG DANCE PROJECTS
115 Christopher Street
4th Floor
New York, NY 10014
Phone: 212-627-5638
Fax: 212-645-5319
e-mail: info@munatseng.org
Web Site: www.munatseng.org
Officers:
  Chairman: Christopher Gray
  President: Muna Tseng
  Secretary: Ray Tseng
Management:
  Artistic Director/Choreographer: Muna Tseng
Mission: Muna Tseng Dance Projects was founded to produce art in a culture of creative ideas, with collaborators bringing a gesture, a text, a melody, a picture or a story. We work through live performances, books, visual art installations, exhibitions and media projects such as video, film and DVD.
Utilizes: Actors; Choreographers; Collaborating Artists; Collaborations; Commissioned Composers; Composers; Curators; Dancers; Designers; Educators; Fine Artists; Guest Artists; Lyricists; Multi Collaborations; Multimedia; Organization Contracts; Original Music Scores; Paid Performers; Performance Artists; Playwrights; Resident Professionals; Scenic Designers; Students; Theatre Companies; Touring Companies; Visual Arts; Volunteer Directors & Actors; Writers
Founded: 1988
Specialized Field: Dance; Visual Art; Contemporary Photography
Status: Professional, Non-Profit
Paid Staff: 2
Paid Artists: 6
Budget: $100,000
Annual Attendance: 5,000

463
NATIONAL DANCE INSTITUTE
217 West 147th Street
New York, NY 10039
Phone: 212-226-0083
Fax: 212-226-0761
e-mail: cgriffin@nationaldance.org
Web Site: www.nationaldance.org
Officers:
  Chair: Karhy Mele
  Vice Chair: Edith Fassberg
  Secretary: Carole Sobin
  Treasurer: Robert D. Krinsky
Management:
  Artistic Director: Ellen Weinstein
  Associate Artistic Director: Tracy Straus
  Technical Director/Producer: Kit Westerman
  Program Director: Aileen Barry
  Founder: Jacques d'Amboise
  Executive Director: Kathy Landau
  Finance and Human Resources Manager: Rachel Lee
  Associate Music Director: David Marck
  Director of Development: Michele O'Mara
Mission: To make the arts a foundation of children's education through the medium of dance to reach children who would otherwise not have the opportunity to become involved in the arts.
Utilizes: Singers
Founded: 1976
Specialized Field: Modern; Jazz; Tap
Status: Professional, Nonprofit
Paid Staff: 20
Volunteer Staff: 100
Income Sources: Grants; Foundations; Government
Performs At: LaGuardia High School
Annual Attendance: 17,000
Seating Capacity: 1,000
Organization Type: Performing; Educational

464
NETA DANCE COMPANY
Our Children's Foundation
449 W 125th Street
Apt # 5D
New York, NY 10027
Phone: 212-866-4626
e-mail: neta@ufl.edu
Web Site: www.netacompany.org
Management:
  Artistic Director: Neta Pulvermacher
Mission: To present contemporary performance arts to the public.
Founded: 1986
Specialized Field: Modern; Ballet; Contemporary
Status: Professional
Paid Staff: 2
Budget: $40,0000-$200,000
Income Sources: Dance Theatre Workshop; Circum Arts
Organization Type: Performing; Touring; Resident; Educational; Sponsoring

465
NEUER TANZ
Bernard Schmidt Productions
461 W 49th Street, E Office
New York, NY 10019
Phone: 212-307-5046
Fax: 212-397-2459
e-mail: bschmidtpd@aol.com
Web Site: www.bernardschmidtproductions.com
Management:
  Artists Representative: Bernard Schmidt
Mission: Performers from around the world at the crossroads of innovation and tradition.
Founded: 1986
Specialized Field: Modern; German Dance

DANCE / New York

Paid Staff: 3
Paid Artists: 10

466
NEW YORK CITY BALLET
David H Koch Theatre
20 Lincoln Center
New York, NY 10023
Phone: 212-870-4060
e-mail: NYChoreoInst@nycballet.com
Web Site: www.nycballet.com
Officers:
- Founder: George Balanchine
- Founder: Lincoln Kirstein
- Chairman: Jay Fisherman
- President: Robert Lipp
- Treasurer: Gordon B Pattee
- Secretary: Kristin Kennedy Clark
- Counsel: Randal R. Craft. Jr.

Management:
- Chief Ballet Master: Peter Martins
- Co-Chief Ballet Master: Jerome Robbins
- Ballet Mistress: Rosemary Dunleavy
- Music Director: Faycal Karoui
- Associate Artistic Director: Richard Tanner
- Managing Director: Ellen Sorrin
- Manager: Renee Rossi
- Executive Director: Katherine E. Brown

Mission: The goal of producing and performing a new ballet repertory that would reimagine the principles of classical dance.
Utilizes: Singers
Founded: 1948
Specialized Field: Ballet
Status: Professional, Nonprofit
Volunteer Staff: 350
Paid Artists: 350
Budget: $2,500,000
Performs At: New York State Theater
Facility Category: Proscenium
Seating Capacity: 2,779
Organization Type: Performing; Touring; Resident; Educational

467
NEW YORK THEATRE BALLET/BALLET SCHOOL OF NY
30 E 31st Street
5th Floor
New York, NY 10016
Phone: 212-679-0401
Fax: 212-679-8171
e-mail: admin@nytb.org
Web Site: www.nytb.org
Officers:
- COO: Richard Berman
- Senior VP: Kas Rigas
- Advisory Board: Alexandra Damiani
- Advisory Board: Gail Spangenberg
- Chair: Sarah Frank
- Treasurer: Alan R. Kusinitz, Esq.
- Secretary: Mary McLarnon, M.D.

Management:
- Artistic Director: Diana Byers
- Grants Officer: Paula Jarowski
- Finance Manager: Liliane Berley
- Ballet Mistress: Sallie Wilson
- Production Manager: Pepper Fajans
- Publicist: Michelle Tabnick

Mission: New York Theatre Ballet provides an intimate environment for the performance, study and appreciation of classical and contemporary dance, with a commitment to cultural enrichment and enjoyment for all.
Utilizes: Choreographers; Dancers; Guest Artists; Original Music Scores
Founded: 1978
Specialized Field: Ballet; Theatrical Dance
Status: Professional, Nonprofit
Paid Staff: 12
Paid Artists: 14
Budget: $500,000-$1,000,000
Annual Attendance: 40,000

468
NINA WINTHROP AND DANCERS
161 Sixth Avenue
14th Floor
New York, NY 10013
Fax: 212-255-2053
e-mail: mail@ninawinthropdancers.org
Web Site: www.ninawinthropdancers.org
Management:
- Artistic Director/Choreographer: Nina Winthrop
- Managing Director: Taimi Strehlow
- Cosume Designer: Naoko Nagata
- Costume Designer: Naomi Luppescu
- Composer: Jon Gibson
- Collaborator: Maria Antelmann

Mission: Nina Winthrop and Dancers was founded in 1991 and incorporated in 2000 as NW&D Inc. The Company's mission is to create and produce original, multidisciplinary contemporary dance pieces, commission artists of various media for artistic collaboration, and increase awareness and accessibility of contemporary dance.
Utilizes: Arrangers; Artists-in-Residence; Choreographers; Collaborating Artists; Collaborations; Dancers; Educators; Fine Artists; High School Drama; Local Artists & Directors; Lyricists; Multimedia; Music; Original Music Scores; Paid Performers
Founded: 1991
Specialized Field: Mutidisciplinary, Contemporary
Status: Non-Profit, Professional
Income Sources: Grnats, Donors, Sponsors
Season: Year Round
Performs At: The Flea Theater

469
NYC BHANGRA DANCE COMPANY
520 8th Avenue 16th Floor
New York, NY 10018
Phone: 212-371-8001
e-mail: info@nycbhangra.com
Web Site: nycbhangra.com
Management:
- Artistic Director: Megha Kalia

Mission: Spreading joy and awareness through dance.
Specialized Field: Indian Dance
Status: Public Charity

470
PARSONS DANCE COMPANY
229 W 42nd Street
8th Floor
New York, NY 10036
Phone: 212-869-9275
Fax: 212-944-7417
e-mail: info@parsonsdance.org
Web Site: www.parsonsdance.org
Officers:
- President: Steven Morris
- VP: Froma Benerofe
- VP Finance, Development, Treasurer: Chris Yegen
- Secretary: Stephanie French

Management:
- General & Stage Manager: Rebecca Josue
- Program, Marketing & Development: Colleen Cashman
- Executive Director: David Harrison
- Assistant Technical Director: Marco Gavezzoli
- Technical Director & Lighting Super: Chris Chambers
- Office Administrator: Brendan Spieth

Mission: Parsons Dance is an internationally renowned contemporary dance company under the artistic direction of choreographer David Parsons. Parsons Dance creates and performs contemporary American dance of extraordinary artistry that is entertaining and enriching to diverse audiences.
Founded: 1985
Specialized Field: Modern; Contemporary Dance
Status: Professional, Non-Profit
Budget: $1,000,000-$2,500,000
Income Sources: Individual; Foundations; Corporate
Performs At: Nationally; Internationally
Organization Type: Performing; Touring; Resident; Educational

471
PAUL TAYLOR DANCE COMPANY
551 Grand Street
New York, NY 10012-3947
Phone: 212-431-5562
Fax: 212-966-5673
e-mail: jt@ptdc.org
Web Site: ptdc.org
Officers:
- Chairman: Paul Taylor
- President: Robert E Aberlin
- Treasurer: Joseph A Smith
- Secretary: Joan C Bowman
- Vice President: Elise Jaffe
- Vice President: Carol Strickland
- Vice President: C F Stone, III

Management:
- Executive Director: Martin Kagan
- General Manager: John Tomlinson
- Development Director: Kim Chan
- Director of Marketing and Communica: Alan Olshan
- Director of Finance:: Sarah Schindler
- Artistic Director: Paul Taylor

Mission: The Paul Taylor Dance Foundation generates the resources Mr. Taylor needs to create new works; maintains the Paul Taylor Dance Company as one of the finest ensembles in the world; ensures that Mr. Taylor's work is seen by the largest possible audience; promotes the Taylor style through education initiatives; and preserves Mr. Taylor's dances for future generations.
Utilizes: Dancers; Singers
Founded: 1954
Specialized Field: Modern Dance
Status: Professional; Nonprofit
Paid Staff: 15
Volunteer Staff: 8
Paid Artists: 25
Budget: $6,200,000
Income Sources: Grants; Individual Donations; Ticket Sales; Matching Gifts; In Kind Donations; Touring Fees
Facility Category: Dance Studio/Dance School/Offices
Organization Type: Performing; Touring; Resident

472
PERIDANCE CONTEMPORARY DANCE COMPANY
126 East 13th Street
New York, NY 10003

DANCE / New York

Phone: 212-505-0886
Fax: 212-674-2239
e-mail: info@peridance.com
Web Site: peridance.com
Management:
    Artistic Director: Igal Perry
    Executive Director: Yarden Ronen
Mission: Committed to leadership and creative collaboration in both dance performance and dance education. The company aspires to advance the performing arts by offering the public visionary choreography and strongly executed performances, nationally and internationally, and by fostering an intelligent appreciation of dance as an art form.
Founded: 1985
Specialized Field: Contemporary
Status: Nonprofit

473
PHYLLIS ROSE DANCE COMPANY
Dance Vectors, Inc.
102-00 Shore Front Parkway
Suite 10P
New York, NY 11694
Mailing Address: Rockaway Park
Phone: 718-474-1672
Fax: 718-634-0348
e-mail: dvi7@verizon.net
Web Site: www.phyllisrosedance.com
Officers:
    President: Phyllis Rose
    Secretary: Miriam Bird
    Treasurer: Richard Lambert
Management:
    Company Director: Phyllis Rose
    Engagement Coordinator: Morgayne West
Mission: To provide arts-in-education experiences in the areas of dance, music, and folklore to young audiences, via performances, workshops and residency programs special focus on young audiences.
Utilizes: Singers
Founded: 1969
Specialized Field: Modern; Jazz; Ethnic Dance; Folk Dance; Novelty Dance; Theatrical Dance
Status: Professional; Nonprofit
Paid Staff: 3
Volunteer Staff: 1
Paid Artists: 15
Budget: $100,000-200,000
Income Sources: Earned; Donations
Performs At: Touring
Organization Type: Performing; Resident; Educational; Sponsoring

474
PICK UP PERFORMANCE COMPANY
520 8th Street
3rd Floor, Room 303
New York, NY 10018
Phone: 212-244-7622
Fax: 917-591-8452
e-mail: gordon@pupcs.org
Web Site: www.pickupperformance.org
Officers:
    Founder: David Gordon
Management:
    Director: David Gordon
    Co-Director: Ain Gordon
    Producer: Alyce Dissette
Mission: Dedicated to producing and promoting the work of David Gordon and Ain Gordon.
Founded: 1971
Specialized Field: Modern; Theatrical Dance
Status: Professional, Nonprofit

Income Sources: Dance USA; Association for Performing Arts Presenters; Western Alliance of Arts Administrators
Organization Type: Performing; Touring; Resident

475
POPPO & THE GOGO BOYS
165 W 26th Street
6th Floor
New York, NY 10001
Phone: 212-989-4819
Fax: 212-989-4819
e-mail: mikopop@gis.net
Management:
    Artistic Director: Poppo Shiraishi
    Manager: Miko Otake
Specialized Field: Modern

476
REBECCA KELLY BALLET
579 Broadway
Suite 4B
New York, NY 10012
Phone: 212-431-8489
e-mail: rkballet1@verizon.net
Web Site: www.rebeccakellyballet.com
Officers:
    Founder: Rebecca Kelly
    Executive Director: Craig D. Brashear
    Secretary: Eve S Wolfsohn
Management:
    Artistic Director/Choreographer: Rebecca Kelly
    Founder: Craig Brashear
Mission: Rebecca Kelly creates abstract and narrative ballets which convey her humanistic outlook. The works features Kelly's vibrant expression, fusing classical dance with modern forms resulting in an arresting lyrical yet earthy quality.
Founded: 1979
Specialized Field: Contemporary Ballet
Status: Professional, Nonprofit
Paid Artists: 8
Budget: $180,000-$220,000
Income Sources: Grants; Contributions; Foundations; Classes; Performances
Performs At: The Duke Theater; Kaye Playhouse; Tribeca Performing Arts Center
Annual Attendance: 1,000-2,000

477
REBECCA STENN COMPANY
425 West 24th Street
Suite 1-B
New York, NY 10011
Phone: 917-501-5239
e-mail: rstenn@verizon.net
Web Site: rebeccastenncompany.com
Management:
    Artistic Director/Choreographer: Rebecca Stenn
    Assistant Choreographer: Eric Jackson Bradley
    Resident co-composer/cellist: Dave Eggar
    Resident co-composer: Jay Weissman
    Set design: Jodi Kaplan
Mission: Since its inception, the company has toured to over 35 cities in the US and abroad, performing, creating commissioned works and holding residencies. The group is devoted to bringing together new music, rock, jazz and classical with evocative, athletic dance to create distinctive pieces that challenge the ways these two mediums interact.
Utilizes: Arrangers; Artists-in-Residence; Choreographers; Collaborating Artists; Collaborations; Composers; Composers-in-Residence; Dancers; Fine Artists; High School Drama; Instructors; Lyricists;

Multimedia; Music; Student Interns; Special Technical Talent; Theatre Companies; Touring Companies; Visual Arts
Founded: 1996
Specialized Field: Classical, Modern, Contemporary, Hip Hop, Jazz
Status: Non-Profit, Professional
Income Sources: Donors, Contributors
Season: Year Round
Performs At: All Across the Country

478
RIOULT
246 W 38th Street
11th Floor
New York, NY 10018
Phone: 212-398-5901
Fax: 212-398-5902
e-mail: info@rioult.org
Web Site: www.rioult.org
Officers:
    Founder: Pascal Rioult
    Company Manager: Holly Evans
    Board Chair: Hope Greenfield
Management:
    Executive Director: Lonnie Cooper
    Lead Teaching Artist: Anastasia Soroczynski
    Artistic Director: Pascal Rioult
    Associate Artistic Director: Joyce Herring
    Associate Artistic Director: Judy Boomer
    Managing Director: Amy Harrison
    Production Manager: Spencer Anderson
    Marketing Director: Penelope Gonzalez
    Education Director: Nicole Philippidis
Mission: Educating and expanding audiences for modern dance at home and throuh touring nationally and internationally.
Specialized Field: Modern Dance

479
RISA JAROSLOW AND DANCERS
65 Greene Street, 5th Floor
Suite 310
New York, NY 10012
Phone: 917-922-0936
e-mail: risajaroslowanddancers@gmail.com
Web Site: www.risajaroslowdance.org
Officers:
    President: Mark Elliott
Management:
    Artistic Director/Choreographer: Risa Jaroslow
    Managing Director: Chantel Bell
Mission: Dedicated to merging performance and community work and to including diverse communities as participants and audience.
Founded: 1985
Specialized Field: Modern
Status: Professional, Nonprofit
Paid Staff: 3
Volunteer Staff: 1
Paid Artists: 6
Budget: $170,000-$180,000
Income Sources: Foundations; Government; Private Donors; Earned Income
Affiliations: Dance Theater Workshop
Annual Attendance: 2,000-3,000
Organization Type: Performing; Touring; Resident; Educational

480
ROD RODGERS DANCE COMPANY & STUDIOS
62 E 4th Street
New York, NY 10003

All listings are in alphabetical order by state, then city, then organization within the city.

DANCE / New York

Phone: 212-674-9066
Fax: 212-674-9068
e-mail: rodrodgers.dance@verizon.net
Web Site: www.rodrodgersdance.org
Officers:
 Founder: Rod Rodgers
Management:
 Artistic Director: Kim Grier
Mission: Rod Rodgers Dance Company considers use of dance as a vehicle for human development, including helping people realize their positive potential and inner beauty, to provide information and stimulate dialogues about our and about historic contributions of landmark figures, are considered central to the Rod Rodgers Dance Company mission.
Utilizes: Guest Artists
Founded: 1960
Specialized Field: Modern; Theatrical Dance
Budget: $100,000-$200,000

481
SAEKO ICHINOHE DANCE COMPANY
159 W 53rd Street
New York, NY 10019
Phone: 212-757-2531
e-mail: info@ichinohedance.org
Web Site: www.ichinohedance.org
Officers:
 Founder: Saeko Ichinohe
Management:
 Artistic Director/Choreographer: Saeko Ichinohe
 Technical Director: Chenault Spence
Mission: Saeko Ichinohe has been creating dance by merging traditional Japanese movement, music and costumes with modern Western movement continuously since 1970.
Founded: 1970
Specialized Field: Contemporary Western Dance
Volunteer Staff: 3
Paid Artists: 6
Budget: $20,000-$60,000
Income Sources: Grants; Contributions; Foundations; Corporate; Individual
Performs At: The Alley Citigroup Theater

482
SALIA NI SEYDOU
Bernard Schmidt Productions
461 W 49th Street, E Office
New York, NY 10019
Phone: 212-307-5046
Fax: 212-397-2459
e-mail: bschmidtpd@aol.com
Web Site: www.bernardschmidtproductions.com
Management:
 Executive Director: John Hassle
Mission: Performers from around the world at the crossroads of innovation and tradition.
Specialized Field: African Dance; West African Dance
Paid Staff: 3
Volunteer Staff: 5

483
SENSEDANCE
1425 3rd Avenue
Suite 3C
New York, NY 10028
Phone: 212-717-6869
Fax: 212-717-6869
e-mail: sensedance@sensedance.org
Web Site: www.sensedance.org
Management:
 Artistic Director/Choreographer: Henning Rubsam
Mission: Sensedance has been created in the hope that through the senses for a moment we can still all meet.
Founded: 1991
Specialized Field: Modern
Status: Nonprofit
Paid Staff: 2
Volunteer Staff: 2
Paid Artists: 9
Budget: $40,000-$100,000

484
SOLARIS DANCE THEATRE & VIDEO
2100 Chestnut Street
2nd Floor
New York, NY 10011
Phone: 215-563-8108
Fax: 212-242-2201
e-mail: solaris@libertynet.org
Web Site: www.lakotasolarisdancetheatre.org
Management:
 Artistic Director: Henry Smith
Mission: To create experimental dance theatre through the workshop process and through cross-cultural performance; to create bonds with people otherwise unrecognized in our society.
Utilizes: AEA Actors; Artists-in-Residence; Choreographers; Collaborating Artists; Collaborations; Commissioned Composers; Commissioned Music; Composers-in-Residence; Dancers; Designers; Educators; Filmmakers; Five Seasonal Concerts; Guest Accompanists; Guest Artists; Guest Ensembles; Guest Lecturers; Guest Musical Directors; Guest Musicians; Guest Soloists; Instructors; Lyricists; Multi Collaborations; Multimedia; Organization Contracts; Original Music Scores; Poets; Resident Professionals; Touring Companies
Founded: 1976
Specialized Field: Modern; Ethnic Dance; Folk Dance; Martial Arts
Status: Professional; Nonprofit
Paid Staff: 4
Volunteer Staff: 6
Paid Artists: 12
Budget: $165,000
Income Sources: Grants; Performances
Performs At: Professional Theatre Venues, as well as Non-Theatre Situations
Affiliations: Arts; Business Council
Organization Type: Performing; Touring; Resident; Educational

485
PETRONIO
140 2nd Avenue
Suite 504
New York, NY 10003
Phone: 212-473-1660
Fax: 212-477-3471
e-mail: info@stephenpetronio.com
Web Site: petron.io
Officers:
 Board of Directors: Jill Brienza
 Board of Directors: Karen Ericson
 Board of Directors: Claire P. Flack
 Board of Directors: Jean-Marc Flack
Management:
 Executive Director: Laurie Uprichard
 Artistic Director: Stephen Petronio
 General Manager: Yvan Greenberg
 Assistant to Artistic Director: Gino Greenek
 Marketing & Tour Coordinator: Yvan Greenberg
Mission: Stephen Petronio Dance Company creates an expansive body of work marked by an unmistakable movement language and groundbreaking choreography in collaboration with contemporary innovators in the fields of music, visual arts and fashion.
Founded: 1984
Specialized Field: Modern
Status: Professional; Nonprofit
Performs At: The Joyce Theatre
Organization Type: Performing; Touring

486
STEPS BEYOND
2121 Broadway At 64th Street
New York, NY 10023
Phone: 212-874-2410
e-mail: info@stepsnyc.com
Web Site: stepsnyc.com
Management:
 Artistic Director: Diane Grumet
 Production Manager: Bradley Shelver
Founded: 1979

487
SUSAN MARSHALL AND COMPANY
120 West 28th Street
Studio 4L
New York, NY 10001
Phone: 212-219-0005
Fax: 212-966-2978
e-mail: dance@sumac.org
Web Site: www.sumac.org
Management:
 Managing Director: Desiree van Rensburg
 Executive Director: Jeremy Olson
Mission: Susan Marshall's choreography illuminates the contemporary condition by interweaving movement, structure, imagery and drama.
Founded: 1982
Specialized Field: Modern
Status: Professional, Nonprofit
Paid Staff: 4
Volunteer Staff: 1
Paid Artists: 21
Budget: $450,000
Income Sources: Dance USA
Annual Attendance: 30,000
Organization Type: Performing; Touring

488
THE AMERICAN MIME THEATRE
61 Fourth Avenue
New York, NY 10003
Phone: 212-777-1710
e-mail: mime@americanmime.org
Web Site: www.americanmime.org
Officers:
 Board Member: Phillip Horvath
 Board Member: Jim Crowe
 Board Member: Elizabeth Kirby
Management:
 Director: Paul J Curtis
Mission: American Mime is a unique performing art created by a particular balance of playwriting, acting, moving, pantomime, and theatrical equipment. It is entirely different from the pantomime of the French Schools and the dance of the Eastern Mime disciplines. American Mime is a complete theatre medium defined by its own aesthetic laws, terminology, techniques, script material and teaching methods.
Utilizes: Actors; Arrangers; Choreographers; Collaborating Artists; Dance Companies; Lyricists; Multi Collaborations; Selected Students; Special Technical Talent; Theatre Companies; Touring Companies

DANCE / New York

Founded: 1952
Opened: 1970
Specialized Field: Interpretive Dance, Mime
Status: Non-Profit
Income Sources: Sponsors, Donations
Affiliations: American Academy of Dramatic Arts, Circle in the Square Theatre School

489
TRISHA BROWN DANCE COMPANY
341 West 38th Street
Suite 801
New York, NY 10018
Phone: 212-977-5365
Fax: 212-925-8687
e-mail: b.dufty@trishabrowncompany.org
Web Site: www.trishabrowncompany.org
Officers:
    Founder: Tricia Brown
    Chairman: Robert Rauschenberg
    President: Kirk Radke
    VP: Jeanne Linnes
    Treasurer: Michael Hecht
    Secretary: David Blasband
Management:
    Artistic Director/Choreographer: Trisha Brown
    Executive Director: Barbara Dufty
    Assistant Artistic Director: Dorothy Alemany
    Company Manager: Carrie Brown
    Development Associate: Heather Wigmore
    Finance Manager: Adriane Medina
Mission: The Trisha Brown Dance Company has initiated the Legacy and Preservation Program, to ensure that future generations have access to the artistry of Trisha Brown.
Founded: 1970
Specialized Field: Modern
Status: Professional, Nonprofit
Paid Staff: 6
Paid Artists: 17
Budget: $1,000,000-$2,500,000
Income Sources: Foundation; Corporate; Grants; Performance Fees; Individual Contribution
Organization Type: Performing; Touring; Resident; Educational

490
WOFA! PERCUSSION AND DANCE FROM GUINEA, WEST AFRICA
Bernard Schmidt Productions
461 W 49th Street, E Office
New York, NY 10019
Phone: 212-307-5046
Fax: 212-397-2459
e-mail: bschmidtpd@aol.com
Web Site: www.bernardschmidtproductions.com
Management:
    Artists Representative: Bernard Schmidt
Mission: Performers from around the world at the crossroads of innovation and tradition.
Specialized Field: African Dance; Contemporary Dance
Paid Staff: 2
Paid Artists: 10

491
WORLD MUSIC INSTITUTE
101 Lafayette Street
Suite 801
New York, NY 10013
Phone: 212-545-7536
Fax: 212-889-2771
e-mail: chris@worldmusicinstitute.org
Web Site: www.heartheworld.org
Officers:
    Chair: Paul Palmer
    Secretary: Zette Emmons
    Board of Directors: Andrew Faulkner
    Board of Directors: Nancy Hager
    Board of Directors: Sandhya Malhotra
Management:
    Executive/Artistic Director: Robert H Browning
    Promotion Director: Helene Browning
    Finance/Administration Director: Elias El-Hage
    Development Director: Jennifer Rajotte
    Produciton Coordinator: Song Lee
    Senior Director: Alexa Burneikis
Mission: Dedicated to the research and presentation of the finest in traditional and contemporary music and dance from around the world. World Music Institute supports and encourages musicians from immigrant communities and collaborates with universities, cultural organizations and other presenting organizations that have similar goals.
Founded: 1985
Specialized Field: Ethnic Dance; Folk Dance; World Music
Status: Nonprofit
Paid Staff: 10
Volunteer Staff: 20
Income Sources: Ticket Sales; Grants
Performs At: Symphony Space; Town Hall; Merkin Hall; Zankel Hall
Annual Attendance: 35,000
Organization Type: Touring

492
YOSHIKO CHUMA AND THE SCHOOL OF HARD KNOCKS
201 E 4th Street
New York, NY 10009
Phone: 212-533-9473
Fax: 915-773-3891
Web Site: www.yoshikochuma.org
Officers:
    Managing Director: Bonnie Stein
Management:
    Artistic Director/Choreographer: Yoshiko Chuma
Mission: Yoshiko Chuma has been building unique structures in the liminal area between her native Japanese culture and her adopted American one. Using trained and pedestrian movers, virtuoso instrumentalists (whose playing she often conducts), film, video and sculptural forms by collaborating artists, she develops unusual time based art works that blend the live and the recorded, the flat and the three-dimensional, people and things.
Founded: 1984
Specialized Field: Post-Modern Dance
Status: Professional, Nonprofit
Income Sources: Grants; Foundations; Corporations
Organization Type: Performing; Touring

493
ZENDORA DANCE COMPANY
34 Watts Street #30
New York, NY 10013
Phone: 212-431-5155
e-mail: zendoradancecompany@earthlink.net
Web Site: zendoradancecompany.com
Management:
    Artistic Director: Nancy Zendora
Founded: 1977

494
POSEY DANCE COMPANY
57 Main Street
Northport, NY 11768
Phone: 631-757-2700
e-mail: PoseySchoolOfDance@gmail.com
Web Site: www.poseyschool.com
Management:
    Founder/Director: Elsa Posey
    Administrative Manager: Kimberly M. Wager
    Music Program Director: Allison Savitz
Mission: Education.
Founded: 1953
Specialized Field: Modern; Ballet; Jazz
Status: Professional, Nonprofit
Income Sources: American Dance Guild
Organization Type: Performing; Touring; Educational

495
DEBRA WEISS DANCE COMPANY
51 Summit Street
Nyack, NY 10960
Phone: 914-572-2126
Fax: 845-353-3860
e-mail: info@debraweissdance.org
Web Site: www.debraweissdance.org
Officers:
    President: Debra Weiss
Management:
    Artistic Director: Debra Weiss
Mission: We use dance as a medium for storytelling and living history programs for children, teens and adults. Much of our work is in schools and museums, where we supplement and enrich existing cirricula and exhibits with our programming.
Utilizes: Actors; Artists-in-Residence; Choreographers; Collaborations; Commissioned Music; Dancers; Grant Writers; Guest Lecturers; Guest Musical Directors; Guild Activities; High School Drama; Instructors; Local Artists; Lyricists; Original Music Scores; Singers; Students
Founded: 1983
Specialized Field: Storytelling; Educational Dance
Status: Professional, Nonprofit
Paid Artists: 3
Organization Type: Performing; Touring; Resident; Educational

496
THE WESTCHESTER BALLET COMPANY
PO Box 694
Ossining, NY 10562
Phone: 914-941-4532
Fax: 941-923-7693
e-mail: info@westchesterballet.org
Web Site: westchesterballet.wordpress.com
Officers:
    President: Barbara Chandler
    VP: Beth Marchant
    Treasurer: Jackie Dyer
    Secretary: Diana Bohrman
    Board Member: Amy Bogusz
    Board Member: Jeanne Carroll
    Board Member: Marianne Leblanc
Management:
    Artistic Director: Beth Fritz-Logrea
    Co-Artistic Director: Jean Logrea
Mission: To promote the awareness and appreciation of dance through all the communitites of Westchester County. Westchester Ballet Company has become known for excellence in performance and dance education.
Utilizes: Singers
Founded: 1950
Specialized Field: Ballet
Status: Professional, Nonprofit
Paid Staff: 70
Performs At: Westchester County Center For The Arts

All listings are in alphabetical order by state, then city, then organization within the city.

DANCE / New York

Organization Type: Performing; Educational

497

BALLET NY
4445 Post Road
Suite 3H
Riverdale, NY 10471
Phone: 718-543-2760
Fax: 718-543-2760
e-mail: balletny.directors@gmail.com
Web Site: www.balletny.org
Officers:
   Chair: Lauren B Cramer
Management:
   Artistic Director: Judith Fugate
   Co-Artistic Director: Medhi Bahiri
Mission: Foremost in Ballet New York's mission is to offer emerging choreographers the opportunity to create new works on accomplished dancers. The company is also committed to keeping ticket prices affordable in an effort to attract, cultivate and educate new audiences for dance.
Founded: 1997
Specialized Field: Ballet

498

GARTH FAGAN DANCE
50 Chestnut Street
Rochester, NY 14604
Phone: 585-454-3260
Fax: 585-454-6191
e-mail: info@garthfagandance.org
Web Site: www.garthfagandance.org
Officers:
   Founder/President: Garth Fagan
   Chairman: Carmen Allen
   Treasurer: Jesse Dudley
   Secretary: Louise H Klinke
Management:
   Artistic Director/Choreographer: Garth Fagan
   Rehearsal Director: Norwood Pennewell
   Controller: Susanna Kreilick
   Company Manager: Bit Knighton
   Marketing Coordinator: Johanna M Lester
   Production Stage Manager: Bets Quackenbush
   Assistant Rehearsal Director: Natalie Roger-Cropper
Mission: To perform modern dance and compete on a national level with original choreography by Garth Fagan.
Founded: 1970
Specialized Field: Modern; Ethnic Dance
Status: Professional, Nonprofit
Budget: $1,000,000-$2,500,000
Income Sources: Grants; Performances; Foundations
Performs At: Nazareth College Arts Center
Organization Type: Performing; Touring; Resident; Educational

---
499

ROCHESTER CITY BALLET
1326 University Avenue
Rochester, NY 14607
Phone: 585-461-5850
Fax: 585-473-8847
e-mail: info@rochestercityballet.com
Web Site: www.rochestercityballet.org
Officers:
   Chair: Katherine Rogala
   Vice Chair: Ray Brown
   Secretary: Elaine Del Monte
   Treasurer: Aaron Byrd
Management:
   Artistic Director: Jamey Leverett
   Executive Director: Kathy Ertsgaard
   Ballet Master: Fidel Orrillo
   Ballet Mistress: Beth Bartholomew
   Senior Marketing Manager: Katie Olsen
   Development Manager: Kylee Fassler
   Acting Production Manager: Stephanie Mellinger
   Director of Finance & Operations: Andea Ferrari
   Wardrobe Mistress: Kathleen Kittelberger
Mission: Rochester City Ballet will nuture, promote and demonstrate the art of dance through education and performances of the highest technical exellence.
Specialized Field: Ballet

500

BALLET LONG ISLAND
1863 Pond Road
Ronkonkoma, NY 11779
Phone: 631-737-1964
e-mail: balletlongisland@aol.com
Web Site: www.balletlongisland.com
Management:
   Artistic Director: Debra Punzi
Mission: Our mission is to make dance available and affordable to everyone.
Utilizes: Artists-in-Residence; Choreographers; Collaborating Artists; Commissioned Music; Dancers; Guest Artists; High School Drama; Local Artists; Original Music Scores; Poets
Founded: 1985
Specialized Field: Ballet
Status: Professional, Nonprofit
Budget: $200,000-$500,000
Performs At: Islip Town Hall West; Long Island Ballet Center Performance Space
Affiliations: Ballet Center
Annual Attendance: 40,000
Seating Capacity: 500

501

PICK OF THE CROP DANCE
2344 Lake Road
Silver Creek, NY 14136
Phone: 716-934-0515
e-mail: info@poc.org
Web Site: www.poc.org
Management:
   Artistic Director: Elaine Gardner
   Music Director/Executive Director: Curt Steinzor
Mission: Pick of the Crop Dance's mission is to produce and promote excellence in contemporary dance through community performances, educational programs and the training of young dancers.
Founded: 1979
Specialized Field: Contemporary Dance
Budget: $100,000-$200,000

502

PAT CANNON'S FOOT & FIDDLE DANCE COMPANY
115 Johnsontown Road
Sloatsburg, NY 10974
Phone: 845-753-6950
Fax: 845-753-6949
e-mail: info@footandfiddle.org
Web Site: www.footandfiddle.org
Officers:
   Founder/President: Pat Cannon
Management:
   Artistic Director: Pat Cannon
Mission: Pat Cannon's Foot & Fiddle Dance Company is a versatile ensemble of dancers and musicians who present American dance and music in creative new ways.
Utilizes: AEA Actors; Choreographers; Dancers; Original Music Scores
Founded: 1981
Specialized Field: Tap; Square Dance; Appalachian Clogging; Swing Dance; Irish Dance
Status: Professional, Nonprofit
Paid Staff: 2
Budget: $125,000
Income Sources: Concert venues, Arts In Education, Square Dancers
Performs At: throughout the Northeast
Organization Type: Performing; Touring; Resident; Educational

---
503

STATEN ISLAND BALLET
460 Brielle Avenue
Staten Island, NY 10314
Phone: 718-980-0500
Web Site: siballettheater.org
Founded: 1993
Specialized Field: Ballet
Status: Nonprofit
Organization Type: Educational; Performing

504

MOWHAWK VALLEY BALLET
Mohawk Valley Performing Arts Inc
The Mohawk Valley Ballet, One Hopper Street
Utica, NY 13501
Phone: 315-738-7646
e-mail: info@mvperformingarts.org
Web Site: www.mvperformingarts.org
Officers:
   President: Byron W. Elias
   VP: Glade Cook
   Secretary: Lisa Burline-Roser
   Treasurer: Nicole Trificana
Management:
   Artistic Director: Delia Foley
   Assistant Artistic Director: Melissa Larish
   Choreography: William Starrett
Mission: The Mohawk Valley Ballet offers a subscription series including The Nutcracker and an Education through Experience Series for students and teachers.
Founded: 1973
Specialized Field: Ballet
Year Built: 1920

505

MANHATTAN TAP
PO Box 571
Valley Cottage, NY 10989
Phone: 845-480-1396
e-mail: hcornell@manhattantap.org
Web Site: www.manhattantap.org
Officers:
   Founder: Heather Cornell
Management:
   Artistic Director/Choreographer: Heather Cornell, hcornell@manhattantap.org
Mission: Manhattan Tap continues to create a new style of concert tap that has never lost the art of improvisation or the individual strengths of its members.
Utilizes: Singers
Founded: 1986
Specialized Field: Tap
Status: Professional, Non-Profit
Paid Staff: 2
Paid Artists: 9
Budget: $100,000-$250,000
Facility Category: Theater
Seating Capacity: 5,000

DANCE / North Carolina

North Carolina

506
TERPSICORPS THEATRE OF DANCE
339 Old Lyman St
Asheville, NC 28801
Phone: 828-231-8618
e-mail: info@terpsicorps.org
Web Site: www.terpsicorps.org
Officers:
   Chair: Karen Ramshaw
   President: Stephanie Biziewski
   Treasurer: Elizabeth Bright
   Secretary: Alison Watson
   Board of Directors: Elizabeth Bright
   Board of Directors: Lara Hanes
   Board of Directors: Lauren Ling
Management:
   Artistic Director: Heather Maloy
   Managing Director: Lucia Del Vecchio
   Ballet Master: Timothy Rinehart Yeager
   Company Staff: Jeff Cravota
   Director of Outreach: Joseph Curry
   Ballet Master: Christopher Bandy
Mission: A summer season from June to mid-August gives Terpsicorps the chance to introduce it's innovative style of dance to the citizens of Asheville through two concert performances at Pack Place.
Founded: 2003
Specialized Field: Contemporary Ballet
Status: Professional, Nonprofit

507
CHARLOTTE BALLET
701 N.Tryon St.
Charlotte, NC 28202
Phone: 704-372-0101
Fax: 704-375-0260
e-mail: awright@ncdance.org
Web Site: charlotteballet.org
Officers:
   President: Jean-Pierre Bonnefoux
   Chair: Thomas Brydon
   Treasurer: Stephen Hasty Jr
   Secretary: Stuart Goldstein
   Chair: Pat Bechdol
Management:
   Artistic Director: Jean-Pierre Bonnefoux
   Associate Artistic Director: Patricia McBride
   Executive Director: Doug Singleton
   Program Director NC Dance Theatre 2: Mark Diamond
   Associate Artistic Director: Sasha Janes
   Musical Associate/Facilities Mgr: Gene Gledsoe
   Resident Choreographer: Dwight Rhoden
   Development Director: Anthony M Wright
   Marketing Manager: Marketing Ralon
Mission: The North Carolina Dance Theatre's mission is to provide artistically excellent programming to diverse audiences in its home city of Charlotte, the Southeast region and to the varied communities it serves while on tour across the nation.
Utilizes: Choreographers; Commissioned Composers; Dancers; Designers; Educators; Five Seasonal Concerts; Guest Accompanists; Guest Artists; Guest Composers; Guest Conductors; Guest Ensembles; Guest Instructors; Guest Musical Directors; Guest Musicians; Instructors; Resident Artists; Resident Professionals; Sign Language Translators; Soloists; Visual Arts
Founded: 1970
Specialized Field: Modern; Ballet
Status: Professional, Nonprofit
Budget: $4.2 million
Income Sources: Arts and Science Council of Charlotte; Corporate; Individual
Performs At: North Carolina Blumenthal Performing Arts Center
Type of Stage: Proscenium
Stage Dimensions: 44'x34'
Seating Capacity: 1920
Year Built: 1992
Organization Type: Performing; Touring

508
AFRICAN AMERICAN DANCE ENSEMBLE, INC.
120 Morris Street
Durham, NC 27701
Phone: 919-560-2729
Fax: 919-560-2743
e-mail: AADENSEMBLE@gmail.com
Web Site: www.africanamericandanceensemble.org
Officers:
   Founder: Chuch Davis
   Chair: Edward Gomes Jr.
   Vice-Chair: Kimberly Monroe
   Secretary: Tim McGloin
   Treasurer: Armeer Kenchen
Management:
   Artistic Director: Chuck Davis
   Associate Artistic Director: Stafford C Berry Jr
   Executive Director: B. Angeloe Burch Sr.
   Musical Director: Kwabena Osei Appiagyei
   Program Director/Tour Manager: Normadien Gibson-Woolbright
   Technical Director: Elizabeth Droessler
Mission: The African American Dance Ensemble seeks to preserve and share the finest traditions of African and African American dance and music through research, education and entertainment.
Utilizes: Choreographers; Collaborating Artists; Collaborations; Dance Companies; Dancers; Guest Accompanists; Guest Musical Directors; Instructors; Lyricists; Original Music Scores; Sign Language Translators; Student Interns; Theatre Companies
Founded: 1984
Specialized Field: African Dance; African American Dance
Status: Professional, Non-Profit
Paid Staff: 12
Volunteer Staff: 10
Paid Artists: 9
Budget: $500,000
Income Sources: Federal, State and Private Funding; Earned Income from Performances
Performs At: Nationally; Internationally
Annual Attendance: 150,000

509
GREENSBORO BALLET
200 N Davie Street
Box 12
Greensboro, NC 27401
Phone: 336-333-7480
Fax: 336-333-7482
e-mail: greensboroballet@yahoo.com
Web Site: www.greensboroballet.org
Officers:
   CEO: Maryhelen Mayfield
Management:
   Artistic Director: Maryhelen Mayfield
   School Director: John Dennis
   Ballet Mistress: Elissa Fuchs
   Director of Children's Dance: Becky Turner
   Marketing Director: Jennifer Gentry
Mission: The Greensboro Ballet provides professional ballet performances and training to the people of Greensboro and surrounding communities.
Utilizes: Choreographers; Dance Companies; Dancers; Educators; Five Seasonal Concerts; Guest Artists; Guest Choreographers; Guest Musicians; Guest Speakers; High School Drama; Original Music Scores; Paid Performers; Resident Companies; Singers; Soloists; Volunteer Artists
Founded: 1980
Specialized Field: Classical Ballet
Status: Professional, Nonprofit
Paid Staff: 10
Volunteer Staff: 22
Paid Artists: 4
Non-paid Artists: 2
Budget: $325,000
Income Sources: Performances; Tuition; Foundations
Performs At: throughout Greensboro
Annual Attendance: 8,000-10,000

510
JAN VAN DYKE DANCE GROUP
NC Dance Project Inc
200 N. Davie Street #7
Greensboro, NC 27401
Phone: 336-373-2727
Fax: 336-334-3238
e-mail: jevandyk@uncg.edu
Web Site: www.janvandykedance.org
Officers:
   President: Tracie Foster
   Treasurer: Peggy Markham
Management:
   Artistic Director/Choreographer: Jan Van Dyke
Mission: To present the work of Jan Van Dyke through a variety of professional performances and educational programs to all ages.
Utilizes: Artists-in-Residence; Choreographers; Collaborations; Commissioned Composers; Commissioned Music; Community Talent; Composers; Dance Companies; Dancers; Designers; Filmmakers; Guest Companies; Guest Musical Directors; Instructors; Multi Collaborations; Multimedia; Organization Contracts; Original Music Scores; Playwrights; Resident Artists
Founded: 1989
Specialized Field: Modern
Status: Professional, Nonprofit
Paid Staff: 2
Paid Artists: 5
Budget: $20,000
Income Sources: Grants; Fundraising; Donations; Ticket Sales
Affiliations: North Carolina Dance Project; UNC Greensboro Department of Dance; United Arts Council of Greensboro
Organization Type: Performing; Touring
Resident Groups: University of North Carolina at Greensboro

511
CAROLINA BALLET
3401-131 Atlantic Avenue
Raleigh, NC 27604
Phone: 919-719-0900
Web Site: carolinaballet.com
Management:
   Artistic Director: Robert Weiss
   Ballet Master: Debra Austin
   Ballet Master: Marin Boieru
   Ballet Master: Melissa Podcasy
   Principal Guest Choreographer: Lynne Taylor-Corbett

DANCE / Ohio

Mission: Carolina Ballet's mission is to perform world-class professional ballet, entertaining and enlightening audiences in Raleigh, the Triangle region, the state of North Carolina, and beyond.
Founded: 1997
Specialized Field: Ballet
Performs At: Duke Energy Center For The Performing Arts, 2 E. South Street, Raleigh, NC

Ohio

512
OHIO BALLET
354 E Market Street
Akron, OH 44325
Phone: 330-972-7900
Fax: 330-972-7902
Web Site: www.ohioballet.org
Management:
  General Manager: Stephan Newenhisen
  Artistic Director: Jeffrey Graham Hughes
Mission: Delivering the magic of dance. To be a driving force creating a passion for dance.
Utilizes: Five Seasonal Concerts
Founded: 1968
Specialized Field: Ballet
Status: Professional; Nonprofit
Budget: $1,500,000
Performs At: Akron; Cleveland; Youngstown
Organization Type: Performing; Touring

513
CANTON BALLET
1001 N Market Avenue
Canton, OH 44702
Phone: 330-455-7220
Fax: 330-455-6977
e-mail: cantonballet@cantonballet.com
Web Site: www.cantonballet.com
Management:
  Artistic Director/Executive Directo: Cassandra Crowley
  Manager: Deby Barath
  Choreographer In Residence: Angelo Lemmo
  Assistant to Artistic Director: Jennifer Catazaro Hayward
  Marketing and Development Director: Jeanne Coen
  Costume Designer: Dianne Helaney
  Wardrobe Mistress: Kiki Kalos
  Office Coordinator: Cyndi Halter
  Resident Costume Designer: Elizabeth Kaplan
Mission: Committed to offering progressive levels of dance training of the highest quality and providing performance opportunities for dancers.
Utilizes: Singers
Founded: 1965
Specialized Field: Ballet
Status: Pre-professional; Nonprofit
Paid Staff: 15
Volunteer Staff: 100
Paid Artists: 10
Non-paid Artists: 150
Budget: $600,000
Income Sources: Tuition; Performance Admissions; Memberships; Foundations; Arts In Starks; Ohio Arts Council
Performs At: Palace Theatre
Affiliations: Regional Dance America; Ohio Citizens for the Arts; Ohio Dance
Annual Attendance: 7,000
Type of Stage: Proscenium
Seating Capacity: 1500
Year Built: 1929
Organization Type: Performing; Touring; Resident; Educational

514
BI-OKOTO CULTURAL INSTITUTE
5601 Montgomery Road
Cincinnati, OH 45212
Phone: 513-221-6112
Fax: 330-238-0023
e-mail: bi-okoto@bi-okoto.com
Web Site: www.bi-okoto.com
Officers:
  Chair: Elizabeth Kitchell
  Acting Secretary: Anna Burrage
  Treasurer: Nadine Pequignot
Management:
  Artistic/Executive Director: Adebola T Olowe Sr
  Company Manager: Jeaunita Ifewande Olowe
  Community Development Coordinator: David Choate
  Wardrobe Manager: Hamidou Koivoigue
  Admistrative Assistant: Joy Biggers
Mission: Our mission is to preserve, promote and share the rich cultural heritage of Africa and Africans using drums, music, dance, food, languages and other arts.
Founded: 1996
Specialized Field: Edo Dance; Apepe; Koroso; Jameba; Apeja Dance
Status: Nonprofit
Paid Staff: 5
Volunteer Staff: 7
Paid Artists: 20
Income Sources: Corporate; Grants; Individuals
Rental Contact: Courtney Smith

515
CINCINNATI BALLET
1555 Central Parkway
Cincinnati, OH 45214
Phone: 513-621-5219
Fax: 513-621-4844
Web Site: www.cballet.org
Officers:
  CEO: Victoria Morgan
  Chair: Otto M Budig Jr
  President: Kathy Selker
  VP: Rhonda Sheakley
  VP: Russ Shelton
  Treasurer: Michael J Sewell
  Secretary: Judy Dalambakis
Management:
  Artistic Director: Victoria Morgan
  Associate Artistic Director: Devon Carney
  Music Director: Carmon DeLeone
  Principal Ballet Mistress: Johanna Bernstein Wilt
  Finance/Operations Director: Craig Lattarulo
  Development Director: Rasheda Malcolm
  Marketing Director: Allie Honebrink
Mission: Cincinnati Ballet continues to thrill audiences with unparalleled performances. From excellence on stage to outreach in local schools and community Cincinnati Ballet takes pride in the fact that it is an integral part of the culture of the city.
Utilizes: Five Seasonal Concerts; Guest Companies
Founded: 1958
Specialized Field: Ballet
Status: Professional, Nonprofit
Budget: $5,000,000
Income Sources: Foundations; Earned; Government
Performs At: Music Hall
Annual Attendance: 9,000
Organization Type: Performing; Touring; Resident; Educational

516
CONTEMPORARY DANCE THEATER
College Hill Town Hall
1805 Larch Avenue
Cincinnati, OH 45224
Phone: 513-591-1122
Fax: 513-591-1222
e-mail: info@cdt-dance.org
Web Site: www.cdt-dance.org
Officers:
  Founder: Jefferson James
Management:
  Artistic/Executive Director: Jefferson James
  Assistant Director: Jeannes.S Mam-Luft
Mission: Our mission is moving bodies moving souls, the essence of contemporary dance. Connecting the community with diverse and socially relevant dance and performance art.
Utilizes: Actors; Choreographers; Collaborating Artists; Collaborations; Commissioned Composers; Community Members; Community Talent; Dance Companies; Dancers; Guest Accompanists; Guest Artists; Guest Choreographers; Guest Ensembles; Guest Musical Directors; Guest Speakers; Instructors; Local Artists; Local Artists & Directors; Original Music Scores; Paid Performers; Scenic Designers; Soloists; Visual Designers
Founded: 1972
Specialized Field: Modern; Jazz; Ballet; Tap; Improvisation; Hip Hop
Status: Professional, Nonprofit
Paid Staff: 2
Paid Artists: 7
Non-paid Artists: 12
Income Sources: Ohio Dance; Cincinnati Commission of the Arts; Dance Action
Performs At: The Dance Hall
Organization Type: Performing; Touring; Resident; Educational; Sponsoring

517
DE LA DANCE COMPANY
3905 Eastern Avenue
Cincinnati, OH 45226
Phone: 518-871-0914
e-mail: delaartsplace@earthlink.net
Web Site: deladancecompany.org
Management:
  Director: Meridith Benson
  Director: Mario De La Nuez
Mission: de la Dance Company's mission is to offer high quality, professional performances and a diverse repertory varying from contemporary to full length classical works, to encourage creativity, experimentation, and cooperation within the dance community;&present dance that is at once compelling, entertaining and relevant.
Status: Professional

518
BALLET IN CLEVELAND
1621 Euclid Avenue
Cleveland, OH 04415
Phone: 330-285-5779
e-mail: info@balletcleveland.org
Web Site: balletincleveland.org
Management:
  Founding Director: Jessica Wallis
  Business Manager: Jim Sebastian

Mission: Ballet in Cleveland is revolutionizing ballet in Cleveland and beyond by highlighting the unique and passionate artistry of ballet. Through multi-faceted presentations of exceptional professional ballet, Ballet in Cleveland promotes the presence, power, and relevance of the arts in our lives.
Specialized Field: Ballet

519
CLEVELAND STATE UNIVERSITY DANCE COMPANY
Dance Program
2121 Euclid Avenue PE 214
Cleveland, OH 44115-2214
Phone: 216-687-2000
Fax: 216-687-5410
e-mail: dance@csuohio.edu
Web Site: www.csuohio.edu
Officers:
  Chairman: Robert H. Rawson, Jr.
  Vice Chairman: Bernardo F. Moreno
  Treasurer: Morton Q. Levin
  Secretary: William J. Napier, Ph.D.
Management:
  Chief of Staff: Michael Artbauer
  Executive Assistant to President: Shane Connor
  Director Special Events: Barbara E. Smith
  Administrative Coordinator: Brenda Darkovich
Mission: Cleveland State University Dance Company offers students the opportunity to rehearse and perform their own work, as well as works by nationally renowned artists in the Greater Cleveland Area.
Founded: 1979
Specialized Field: Contemporary Dance
Status: Pre-Professional, Nonprofit

520
DANCECLEVELAND
13110 Shaker Square
Suite 106
Cleveland, OH 44120
Phone: 216-991-9000
Fax: 216-991-9001
e-mail: dex@dancecleveland.org
Web Site: www.dancecleveland.org
Officers:
  VP: Palmela Barr
  VP, Chair of Development: Sue Peay
Management:
  Executive Director: Pam Young
  Marketing Director: Heather Greer-Sikora
  Development Manager: Barbara Badalamenti
  Administrative Coordinator: Sarah Durham
  Projects Coordinator: Kitty McWilliams
  Grants Manager: Wendy Leatherberry
Mission: Our mission is to bring the passion and verve of modern and contemporary dance to Northeast Ohio.
Founded: 1956
Specialized Field: Dance
Status: Nonprofit
Income Sources: National Endowment for the Arts; Association for Performing Arts Presenters; International Society of Performing Arts Administrators; Arts Midwest; Dance USA; Arts Presenters
Performs At: Ohio Theatre; Playhouse Square Center
Organization Type: Educational; Sponsoring

521
DANCEVERT
71 East 214 Street
Cleveland, OH 44123
Phone: 216-269-6984
e-mail: tom@dancevert.org
Web Site: www.dancevert.org
Management:
  Artistic Director/Choreographer: Susana Weingarten
  Co-Artistic Director: Tom Evert
Mission: To share the innate vitality of movement as a form of expression and the body as an instrument connected with the mind and spirit.
Utilizes: Musical Directors; Singers
Founded: 1986
Specialized Field: Modern
Status: Professional, Nonprofit
Budget: $150,000
Income Sources: Association for Performing Arts Presenters; Arts Midwest; Arts Presenters Network; Ohio Dance; Ohio Citizens Committee for the Arts
Performs At: Cleveland Play House
Annual Attendance: 20,000
Organization Type: Performing; Touring; Resident; Educational; Special Events

522
GROUNDWORKS DANCE THEATER
13125 Shaker Square, Suite 102
Cleveland, OH 44120
Phone: 216-751-0088
e-mail: info@groundworksdance.org
Web Site: groundworksdance.org
Management:
  Executive Artistic Director: David Shimotakahara
  General Manager: Beth Rutkowski
Mission: GROUNDWORKS creates and presents groundbreaking work in contemporary dance that embraces risk and imagination, explores human experience, encourages interdisciplinary collaboration, expands the parameters of how and where dance is presented, and by doing so, engages with and enlivens the community of which it is part.
Founded: 1998
Specialized Field: Contemporary

523
INLET DANCE THEATRE
11125 Magnolia Drive
Cleveland, OH 44106
Phone: 216-721-8580
Fax: 216-721-8580
e-mail: info@inletdance.org
Web Site: www.inletdance.org
Officers:
  Founder: Bill Wade
  Chairperson: Matt Anderson
  Vice Chair: Lisa Boyko
  Treasurer: Linda Merriam
  Secretary: Judy Richner
Management:
  Artistic Director: Bill Wade
Mission: Inlet Dance Theatre is one of the region's most exciting professional contemporary dance companies dedicated to performing with a high level of quality, skill, innovation and purpose. Inlet utilizes the art form of dance to bring about personal development in the lives of individuals through training and mentoring, and to speak creatively about life and the issues we face.
Utilizes: Artists-in-Residence; Choreographers; Composers; Dancers; Educators; Filmmakers; Guest Artists; Local Talent; Theatre Companies
Founded: 2001
Specialized Field: Contemporary Dance
Season: November-December

524
MORRISONDANCE
4201 Lorain Avenue
Cleveland, OH 44113
Phone: 216-496-3536
e-mail: sarah@morrisondance.com
Web Site: www.morrisondance.com
Officers:
  Founder: Sarah Morrison
  Treasurer: Jennifer Bennett
  VP, Secretary: Kimi Nose
  Board Member: Bill Schmitz
  Board Member: Pat Rehm
Management:
  Artistic Director/Choreographer: Sarah Morrison
  Artist/Visual Designer: Scott Radke
Mission: To inspire and cultivate public awareness of the art of dance through performances, crossdisciplinary collaborations, in combination with various other art forms and disciplines. To provide, promote and participate in educational and outreach programs that increase the awareness of dance and that assist and encourage community cultural and artistic endeavors.
Founded: 1997
Specialized Field: Modern
Status: Professional, Nonprofit

525
BALLETMET DANCE CENTRE
322 Mount Vernon Avenue
Columbus, OH 43215
Phone: 614-229-4860
Fax: 614-229-4858
e-mail: shunt@balletmet.org
Web Site: www.balletmet.org
Officers:
  Chair: Susan Porter
  Chair-Elect: Randall Walters
  Treasurer: Thomas H Brinker
  Secretary: Trish Cadwallader
Management:
  Artistic Director: Gerard Charles
  Executive Director: Cheri Mitchell
  Resident Music Director: Mikhail Popov
  Ballet Mistress: Rebecca Rodriguez-Hodory
  Ballet Master: Hisham Omardien
  Development Director: Pam Bishop
  Marketing/Communications Director: Sheila Hunt
  Production Manager: Jaime Gross
Mission: BalletMet will celebrate dance by engaging the community through quality performances, instruction, education programs and creation of new work.
Utilizes: Singers
Founded: 1978
Specialized Field: Ballet
Status: Professional, Nonprofit
Income Sources: National Association for Regional Ballet; Dance USA
Performs At: Ohio Theatre
Organization Type: Performing; Touring; Resident; Educational; Sponsoring

526
HIXON DANCE
P.O. Box 82630
Columbus, OH 43235
Phone: 614-382-2787
e-mail: hixondance@gmail.com
Web Site: hixondance.com
Management:
  Music Director: Jacob Reed

DANCE / Ohio

Artistic Director: Sarah Hixon
Mission: To create and present works of fine art that touch and enrich the lives and experiences of audiences. Hixon dance believes that modern dance can belong in the realm of high art while still engaging and entertaining audiences of all backgrounds.
Founded: 2007
Specialized Field: Modern

527
OHIO STATE UNIVERSITY OF DANCE
1813 N High Street
Columbus, OH 43210
Phone: 614-292-7977
Fax: 614-292-0939
e-mail: dance@osu.edu
Web Site: www.dance.osu.edu
Officers:
  Chair: Susan Van Pelt Petry
Management:
  Music Director: Susan Chess
  Production Manager: David Covey
  Production Manager: Carrie Cox
  Academic Program Coordinator: Amy Esther Schmidt
  Program Assistant: Allegra Angelini
Mission: The department of dance at the Ohio State University is a community of diverse individuals trained on a common nexus of inquiry, the rich and complex phenomenon of dance.
Specialized Field: Traditional Dance; Educational Dance

528
SEVEN DANCE COMPANY
7878 Gilston Ct.
Columbus, OH 43235
Phone: 419-236-0641
e-mail: colleenbcreamer@gmail.com
Web Site: sevendancecompany.com
Management:
  Director: Cassia N. Cramer
Mission: Seven Dance Company is a contemporary dance company with a goal to inspire, encourage, and create a new way of thinking through movement exploration. We bring together a collaboration of artists who share the same vision and believe in sharing what we love.
Specialized Field: Contemporary

529
BALLET EXCEL OHIO
C/o Excellence In Dance Studio, 2315 State Ro
Cuyahoga Falls, OH 44223
Phone: 330-524-3400
e-mail: lakulwicki@yahoo.com
Web Site: www.balletexcelohio.org
Officers:
  Founder: Mia Klinger
  President: Larissa Malone
  Treasurer: Stephanie Gallagher
  Secretary: Stephanie Lallement
Management:
  Artistic Director: Mia Klinger Welch
  Artistic Consultant: Lori Klinger
  Administration: Larissa Malone
  Operations: Stephanie Lallement
  Marketing/Promotions: Mary Mitchell
Mission: To provide performing experience for talented young dancers, educating them in the realities of professional ballet to educate area children and families in the appreciation of ballet as an art form at affordable prices.
Utilizes: Five Seasonal Concerts

Founded: 1975
Specialized Field: Modern; Ballet
Status: Pre-Professional, Nonprofit
Paid Staff: 33
Income Sources: Ohio Arts Council; Foundations; Corporate; Individual
Performs At: Akron Civic Theatre; EJ Thomas Hall
Organization Type: Performing; Resident; Educational

530
CONTEMPORARY DANCE OF SINCLAIR
444 W 3rd Street
Sinclair Community College
Dayton, OH 45402
Phone: 937-512-2751
Fax: 937-512-2054
Toll-free: 800-315-3000
e-mail: info@sinclair.edu
Web Site: www.sinclair.edu
Management:
  Artistc Advisor: Patricia Fox
  Artistic Director: Rodney Veal
  Artistic Director: Denise Miller
Mission: Contmeporary Dance of Sinclair is a modern dance company for the performing aspiring adult trained dancers of the community college environment.
Founded: 1978
Specialized Field: Contemporary Dance

531
DAYTON BALLET
Dayton Ballet Association
140 N Main Street
Dayton, OH 45402
Phone: 937-449-5060
Fax: 934-461-8353
e-mail: info@daytonballet.org
Web Site: daytonperformingarts.org
Officers:
  Chairman: Craig Jennings
  Treasurer: Craig Brown
  Vice Chair: Rebecca Appenzeller
  Secretary: Richard M. DeLon
  President & CEO: Paul Helfrich
Management:
  Artistic/Executive Director: Karen Russo Burke
  Ballet Mistress: Katy Bowlby
  Ballet Mistress: Sharon Lancaster
  Resident Designer/Costumer: Lowell A Mathwich
  Marketing Director: Diane Schoeffler-Warren
  Production Manager: Stacie R Bigl
Mission: Dayton Ballet's mission is to educate, enlighten and entertain the widest audience possible with the very best in performance, outreach and community service.
Utilizes: Artists-in-Residence; Choreographers; Collaborating Artists; Collaborations; Commissioned Music; Dance Companies; Dancers; Fine Artists; Guest Artists; Guest Choreographers; Guest Conductors; Local Artists; Organization Contracts; Original Music Scores; Resident Artists; Resident Professionals; Soloists; Theatre Companies
Founded: 1927
Specialized Field: Ballet; Contemporary Dance
Status: Professional, Nonprofit
Paid Staff: 32
Budget: $2,000,000
Income Sources: Ticket Revenue; Community Support; State and Local Government
Performs At: The Victoria Theatre; Schuster Performing Arts Center
Annual Attendance: 30,000
Seating Capacity: 1,100
Year Built: 1866

Year Remodeled: 1989
Organization Type: Performing

532
DAYTON CONTEMPORARY DANCE COMPANY
840 Germantown Street
Dayton, OH 45402
Phone: 937-228-3232
Fax: 937-223-6156
e-mail: contactus@dcdc.org
Web Site: www.dcdc.org
Officers:
  Chair: Richard Lapedes
Management:
  Artistic Director: Debbie Blunden-Diggs
  Executive Director: Ro Nita Hawes-Saunders
  Touring/Production Manager: Teri Fritze
Mission: Dayton Contemporary Dance Company's mission is to deliver contemporary dance of the highest quality to the broadest possible audience. Dayton Contemporary Dance Company reaches this audience with local performances, through national and international touring and through the company's educational programs in the Miami Valley and on tour.
Utilizes: Actors; AEA Actors; Artists-in-Residence; Choreographers; Collaborating Artists; Collaborations; Community Members; Dance Companies; Dancers; Educators; Five Seasonal Concerts; Guest Artists; Guest Composers; Guest Writers; High School Drama; Multi Collaborations; Multimedia; Original Music Scores; Resident Professionals; Singers
Founded: 1968
Specialized Field: Contemporary Dance; Jazz; Modern
Status: Professional, Nonprofit
Paid Staff: 12
Paid Artists: 11
Non-paid Artists: 15
Budget: $1,300,000
Income Sources: Government; Corporate; Foundations; Individuals
Performs At: The Victoria Theatre
Annual Attendance: 4,500
Type of Stage: Proscenium
Organization Type: Performing; Touring; Resident

533
LEAHY GOOD
126 N Main Street
Suite 420
Dayton, OH 45402
Phone: 937-226-7463
Fax: 937-910-1048
Web Site: www.leahygood.com
Management:
  Artistic Director/Choreographer: Sharon Leahy
  Artistic Director/Composer: Rick Good
  Executive Director: Noreen Willhelm
  General Manager: Maggie Cooper
Mission: Rooted in traditional forms of american music and dance swing tunes, tap, hoedowns and clogging the varied repertoire of Rhythm in Shoes directed by choreographer Sharon Leahy and composer Rick Good is at once original and recognizable.
Utilizes: Actors; AEA Actors; Choreographers; Composers-in-Residence; Dancers
Founded: 1987
Specialized Field: Swing Dance; Tap; Clogging
Paid Staff: 2
Paid Artists: 15
Budget: $200,000-$500,000

DANCE / Ohio

534
SINCLAIR DANCE
Sinclair Community College
444 West Third Street
Dayton, OH 45402-1460
Phone: 937-512-2751
Fax: 937-512-2054
Toll-free: 800-315-3000
e-mail: info@sinclair.edu
Web Site: www.sinclair.edu/academics/lcs/departments/dan/
Management:
   Artistic Director: Patricia Fox
   Artistic Director: Dawn Quigley
Specialized Field: Ballet; Modern; Tap

535
ZIVILI DANCE COMPANY
1753 Loudon Street
Granville, OH 43023
Phone: 740-587-7715
Toll-free: 877-906-8314
e-mail: mobenauf@alltel.net
Officers:
   Founder/President: Melissa Pintar Obenauf
   Co-Founder/VP: Pamela Lacko Kelley
Management:
   Artistic Director: Pamela Lacko Kelley
   Dance/Executive Director: Melissa Pintar Obenauf
Mission: Zivili Dance Company was created to help preserve a strong cultural legacy of primarily Croatian dance and music.
Utilizes: Five Seasonal Concerts; Singers
Founded: 1973
Specialized Field: Croatian Dance
Status: Professional, Nonprofit
Budget: $250,000
Income Sources: Performances; Arts Counsil Grants; Individual Contributions
Performs At: Southern Theatre
Annual Attendance: 50,000
Organization Type: Performing; Touring; Educational

536
DEMETRIUS KLEIN DANCE COMPANY
575 Main Street
Hamilton, OH 45013
Phone: 513-869-9207
e-mail: demetrius.klein@gmail.com
Web Site: www.demetriuskleindancecompany.com
Management:
   Artistic Director: Kathleen Klein
Mission: Klein Dance has served South Florida by making the art of dance accessible for all who wish to be a part of it. In 2009 the Demetrius Klein Dance Company relocated to Ohio where Demetrius is resident choreographer at the Miami Valley ballet theatre.
Utilizes: Actors; Artists-in-Residence; Choreographers; Collaborating Artists; Collaborations; Dance Companies; Dancers; Five Seasonal Concerts; Grant Writers; Guest Artists; Guest Choreographers; Guest Conductors; Guest Ensembles; Guild Activities; Instructors; Local Artists; Lyricists; Organization Contracts; Original Music Scores; Resident Professionals; Soloists
Founded: 1987
Paid Staff: 4
Volunteer Staff: 10
Paid Artists: 10
Budget: $200,000-$500,000
Income Sources: Grants; Earned Income; Donations
Affiliations: Dans USA; Florida Dance Association

Annual Attendance: 10,000
Type of Stage: Sprung
Stage Dimensions: 30'x 40'
Seating Capacity: 500-700

537
BALLET THEATRE OF OHIO
265 North Main Street
Suite 13
Munroe Falls, OH 44262
Phone: 330-688-6065
Fax: 330-688-7781
e-mail: info@ballettheatreohio.org
Web Site: www.ballettheatreohio.org
Officers:
   Founder: Christine Meneer
Management:
   Artistic Director: Christine Meneer
Mission: Ballet Theatre of Ohio will present repertory performances and extensive educational outreach programs for the youth and the Akron area community.
Utilizes: Five Seasonal Concerts; Singers
Founded: 1993
Specialized Field: Ballet
Status: Professional, Nonprofit
Income Sources: Corporate; Foundation; Individual
Performs At: Akron Civic Theatre
Organization Type: Performing; Touring; Resident

538
OHIO DANCE THEATRE
39 S Main Street
Suite 241
Oberlin, OH 44074
Phone: 440-774-6077
Fax: 440-774-6160
e-mail: odt@oberlin.net
Web Site: www.ohiodancetheatre.org
Officers:
   Founder: Denise Gula
Management:
   Artistic Director: Denise Gula
   Faculty Coordinator/Dir Summer Prog: Nancy Brenstuhl
   Teacher: Kat Siroka Hilton
   Dance Faculty: Carol Hageman
Mission: Ohio Dance Theatre will encourage the growth and support of serious dance through the presentation of exceptional performances, instruction and educational programs that enhance the community's quality of life.
Specialized Field: Classical; Contemporary Dance; Theatre Dance
Income Sources: Community Foundation; Corporate; Fundraising; Individual; Matching Gifts; Nord Family Foundation; Ohio Arts Council; Stocker Foundation
Season: October-May

539
OBERLIN THEATER AND DANCE PROGRAM
Oberlin College
30 N Professor Street
Oberlin, OH 44074
Phone: 440-775-8152
Fax: 440-775-8340
e-mail: communications@oberlin.edu
Web Site: home.oberlin.edu
Officers:
   Associate Chair: Nusha Martynuk
Management:
   Dance Professor: Ann Cooper Albright
   Assistant Technical Director: David Bugher

Mission: The Theater and Dance Program offers students an interrelated series of courses and performance activities designed to provide a sound liberal arts grounding in the theory and practice of the arts of theater and dance.
Specialized Field: Modern
Performs At: Finney Chapel; Hall Auditorium; Warner Center

540
MIAMI UNIVERSITY DANCE THEATRE
106 E Phillips Hall
Oxford, OH 45056
Phone: 513-529-2730
Fax: 513-529-5006
e-mail: rosenblk@muohio.edu
Web Site: www.units.miamioh.edu/dancetheatre
Officers:
   President: Kristin Bell
   Vice President: Jessica Saponaro
   Treasurer: Carly Kennell
   Publicity Chair: Beth Seither
   Secretary: Danielle Sadler
Management:
   Artistic Director/General Manager: Lana Kay Rosenberg, rosenblk@umohio.edu
Founded: 1933
Specialized Field: Contemporary/Modern; Ballet; Jazz; Tap
Status: Semi-Professional; Non-Profit
Income Sources: Ticket Sales; Miami University
Performs At: Hall Auditorium
Affiliations: Ohio Dance; ACDFA
Annual Attendance: 1,100
Type of Stage: Proscenium
Seating Capacity: 730

541
VERB BALLETS
3445 Warrensville Center Rd.
Shaker Hts, OH 44122
Phone: 216-397-3757
Fax: 216-397-7872
e-mail: info@verbballets.org
Web Site: www.verbballets.org
Officers:
   President: Jeri Chaikin
   Treasurer: Robert M Shwab
   Secretary: Ann Levin
   VP: Richard Rinehart
Management:
   Director: Margaret Carlson
   Outreach Coordinator: Katie Gnagy
   Rehearsal Director: Richard Dickinson
   Finance: Michelle Gregorczyk
   Administration: M Haas
Mission: The mission of Verb Ballets is to promote and develop interest in and appreciation for contemporary dance nationally, regionally and locally through performance, programs that promote learning and nurture wellness, audience and community dialogue and advocacy efforts to support the art form.
Founded: 1987
Specialized Field: Dance
Status: Professional, Non-Profit
Paid Staff: 5
Volunteer Staff: 3
Paid Artists: 15
Budget: $400,000
Income Sources: Ticket Sales; Grants; Foundations; Coroprate

DANCE / Oklahoma

542
TRAVESTY DANCE GROUP CLEVELAND
2196 Swartz Road
Sheffield, OH 44260
Phone: 330-618-7334
e-mail: kkdance@aol.com
Web Site: www.travestydancegroupcleveland.com
Management:
  Co-Founder/Artistic Director: Kimberly Karpanty
  Co-Founder: Rebecca Malcolm-Naib
  Co-Founder: Karen Stokes
Mission: TRAVESTY DANCE GROUP was conceived to support and produce the creative projects of its founding members, Kimberly Karpant, Rebecca Malcolm-Naib and Karen Stokes. Enriched by collaborative process, Travesty Dance Group seeks to bring diverse original dance work to a variety of communities. The founders believe in dance as a basic human art, embracing both the complexities of contemporary society and the life a affirming essence of movement.
Utilizes: Arrangers; Choreographers; Collaborating Artists; Collaborations; Dancers; Fine Artists; Local Artists & Directors; Multimedia; Music; Original Music Scores; Paid Performers; Student Interns; Special Technical Talent
Founded: 1996
Specialized Field: Modern Dance, Contemporary, Ballet
Status: Non-Profit, Professional
Income Sources: Donors
Season: May
Performs At: Cleveland Public Theater

543
LEAVEN DANCE COMPANY
2292 Lynnwood Drive
Stow, OH 44224
Phone: 330-688-8806
Fax: 330-686-6103
e-mail: kmleaven@neo.rr.com
Web Site: faculty-l.slis.kent.edu/~tfroehli/leaven/index.php
Officers:
  Founder: Kathryn Mihelick
  President: Thomas J Froehlich PhD
  VP/Secretary: Robert Stadulis PhD
  Treasurer: Judith Denardo
Management:
  Artistic Director/Choreographer: Kathryn Mihelick
  Associate Artistic Director: Andrea Tecza Shearer
Mission: Leaven Dance Company is a professional dance ensemble whose work addresses spiritual, ethical, social and wholeness issues through performance and worship venues and educational, motivational workshops.
Founded: 1992
Specialized Field: Liturgical Dance; Experimental Dance
Status: Professional, Nonprofit
Paid Staff: 1
Volunteer Staff: 8
Paid Artists: 6
Budget: 10,000
Annual Attendance: 8,000

544
ALMA DANCE EXPERIENCE
10 Holland-Sylvania Road, Studio #205
Toledo, OH 43615
Phone: 419-810-2800
e-mail: almadance03@hotmail.com
Web Site: almadancetoledo.com
Management:
  Director: Allison Kodeih
  Artistic Director: Yaya Kabo
Mission: ALMA exists to celebrate dance and music, to bring dance and music to everyone, and to capitalize on the talents each individual artist brings to the group, to the stage, and to the classroom. ALMA is committed to artistic excellence through continuous study, performance, sharing of art form, and collaboration-working with other artists to build a larger dance and music community.
Specialized Field: West African Drum And Dance Ensemble
Status: LLC; Professional

545
TOLEDO BALLET ASSOCIATION
5001 Monroe Street
Suite R20
Toledo, OH 43623
Phone: 419-471-0049
Fax: 419-471-9005
e-mail: info@toledoballet.net
Web Site: www.toledoballet.net
Officers:
  Founder: Marie Bollinger Vogt
  President: Robert Koenig
  VP: James Hill
  Treasurer: William A. Southern
  Secretary: David Saygers
Management:
  Executive Director: Mari Davies
  Artistic Director Emerita: Marie Bollinger Vogt
  School Director: Lisa Mayer
  Marketing/Outreach Coordinator: Michael Lang
  Business Coordinator: Elizabeth White
  Grants Coordinator: Kelby Sodeman
  Office Assistant: Anthony Piercefield
Mission: The Toledo Ballet is dedicated to providing the highest quality of training, from the earliest stages and progressing through the pre-professional level, by blending the discipline of classical ballet with the respect for the entire spectrum of dance.
Utilizes: Collaborations; Dance Companies; Dancers; Educators; Five Seasonal Concerts; Guest Accompanists; Guest Artists; Guest Composers; Guest Writers; Theatre Companies
Founded: 1958
Specialized Field: Ballet
Status: Professional, Nonprofit
Paid Staff: 10
Volunteer Staff: 2
Budget: $633,000
Income Sources: Various
Performs At: Stranahan Theater; Franciscan Center
Annual Attendance: 15,000
Organization Type: Performing; Touring; Resident; Educational; Sponsoring

546
BALLET WESTERN RESERVE
218 W Boardman Street
Youngstown, OH 44501-1684
Phone: 330-744-1934
Fax: 330-744-2631
e-mail: info@balletwesternreserve.org
Web Site: www.balletwesternreserve.org
Officers:
  President: Don Foley
  VP: Aundrea Cika Heschmeyer
  Treasurer: Robert Smith
  Secretary: Amy Gelfand
Management:
  Artistic Director: Virginia Hartman
  Director Emeritus: Anita S Lin
  Business Manager: James McClellan
  Children's Dance Coordinator: Jackie Cunningham
  Ballet Instructor: Kara Kaplin Reider
Mission: Ballet Western Reserve students are offered the opportunity to develop the skills, experience and discipline that provide the necessary foundation for a professional career in dance.
Utilizes: Five Seasonal Concerts; Singers
Founded: 1962
Specialized Field: Modern; Ballet; Jazz
Status: Nonprofessional, Nonprofit
Income Sources: Tuition; Fundraising
Performs At: Youngstown State University; Powers Auditorium
Annual Attendance: 5,000-6,000
Organization Type: Performing; Educational

Oklahoma

547
WESTERN OKLAHOMA BALLET THEATRE
711 Frisco Avenue
Clinton, OK 73601
Phone: 580-323-7400
e-mail: debbie.brown@swosu.edu
Web Site: www.western-oklahoma-ballet.org
Officers:
  Founder: Candance Jones Smalley
Management:
  Artistic/Executive Director: Penny Askew
Mission: Western Oklahoma Ballet Theatre is dedicated to bringing quality dance performances and instruction to Western Oklahoma, focusing on the fine art of classical ballet.
Utilizes: Five Seasonal Concerts
Founded: 1977
Specialized Field: Classical Ballet
Status: Nonprofessional, Nonprofit
Paid Staff: 9
Income Sources: Regional Dance America; Southwestern Regional Ballet Association
Performs At: Southwestern Oklahoma State University Fine Arts
Organization Type: Performing; Educational

548
DUNCAN LAWTON CITY BALLET
1006 SW E Avenue
Lawton, OK 73501
Mailing Address: PO Box 3714 Lawton OK, 73502
Phone: 580-357-2700
Fax: 580-353-3527
e-mail: dlcballet@hotmail.com
Officers:
  Chair: Dr. Lloyd A Dawe
Management:
  Artistic Director/Founder: Margaret Gray
  Managing Director: Roger Gray
Mission: Dedicated to the presentation of ballet.
Founded: 1994
Specialized Field: Ballet
Status: Nonprofit
Volunteer Staff: 3
Non-paid Artists: 16
Income Sources: Local Foundations
Performs At: Simon Center Theatre
Annual Attendance: 7,200

DANCE / Oklahoma

549
CONTEMPORARY DANCE OKLAHOMA
University of Oklahoma School of Dance
660 Parrington Oval
Room 1000
Norman, OK 73019-0319
Phone: 405-325-4051
Fax: 405-325-7024
e-mail: dance@ou.edu
Web Site: www.ou.edu/finearts/dance
Officers:
   Chair: Mary Margaret Holt
Management:
   School Dance Director: Mary Margaret Holt
   Artistic Director: Austin Hartel
   Assistant to the Director: Rhonda Hill
   Associate Professor of Dance: Steve Brule
   Staff Assistant: Peggy Chafin
Mission: To present an eclectic repertoire of modern and contemporary dance works presented by a company of young, talented dancers.
Founded: 1961
Specialized Field: Modern
Status: Semi Professional, Non-Profit
Paid Staff: 6
Non-paid Artists: 24
Budget: $40,000
Income Sources: University Of Oklahoma; Tours
Performs At: The Rupel Jones Theatre; Donald W Reynolds Performing Arts Center Theatre (Holmberg Hall)
Annual Attendance: 5,500
Type of Stage: Proscenium Arch Stage (Both)
Stage Dimensions: 4,935sq ft(Jones); 5,000sq ft (Hall
Seating Capacity: 700;677
Year Built: 1965
Year Remodeled: 2002

550
OKLAHOMA FESTIVAL BALLET
660 Parrington Oval
Room 1000
Norman, OK 73019-0319
Phone: 405-325-4051
Fax: 405-325-7024
e-mail: dance@ou.edu
Web Site: www.ou.edu
Officers:
   Chair: Mary Margaret Holt
Management:
   School of Dance Director: Mary Margaret Holt
   Assistant to the Director: Rhonda Moore
   Associate Professor of Dance: Steve Brule
   Staff Assistant: Peggy Chafin
Mission: To present an eclectic repertoire through a classical ballet company of young dancers.
Utilizes: Choreographers; Collaborations; Dancers; Designers; Grant Writers; Guest Accompanists; Guest Artists; Original Music Scores; Soloists
Founded: 1961
Specialized Field: Ballet
Status: Semi-Professional, Non-Profit
Paid Staff: 6
Non-paid Artists: 30
Budget: $200,000-$500,000
Income Sources: University of Oklahoma; Tours
Performs At: The Rupel Jones Theatre; Donald W Reynolds Performing Arts Center Theatre(Holmberg Hall)
Annual Attendance: 5,500
Type of Stage: Proscenium arch stage (Both)
Stage Dimensions: 4,935sq ft(Jones);5,000sq ft(Hall)
Seating Capacity: 700;677
Year Built: 1965
Year Remodeled: 2002
Organization Type: Performing; Touring; Resident; Educational

551
ANN LACEY SCHOOL OF AMERICAN DANCE AND ARTS MANAGEMENT
Oklahoma City University
2501 N Blackwelder Avenue
Oklahoma City, OK 73106
Phone: 405-208-5000
Fax: 405-208-5588
Toll-free: 405-208-5588
e-mail: telecom@okcu.edu
Web Site: www.okcu.edu
Officers:
   Chairman: Jo Rowan
   Dean: John Bedford
   Associate Dean: Melanie Shelley
Management:
   External Affairs/Special Projects: Jennifer Polvado
   Dance Faculty: Melanie Shelley
   Dance Faculty: Diana Brooks
   Dance Faculty: John Bedford
   Dance Faculty: Susan Cosby
   Dance Faculty: Paul Gebb
Mission: A single place within a respected university where American dance art forms and arts management can be nurtured and developed to their highest level and properly recognized for their contributions to art and culture throughout the world.
Founded: 1981
Specialized Field: Jazz; Tap; Musical Theater Dance; Rhythm Tap and Ballet

552
OKLAHOMA CITY BALLET
7421 N Classen
Oklahoma City, OK 73116
Phone: 405-843-9898
Fax: 405-843-9894
e-mail: info@okcballet.com
Web Site: www.okcballet.com
Officers:
   President: Lea Morgan
   Treasurer: Nancy Hyde
   Secretary: Elaine DeGiusti
Management:
   Artistic Director: Robert Mills
   Executive Director: Shane Jewell
   Ballet Master: Jacob Sparso
   Company Teacher/Coach: Alexa Fioroni
   Technical/Lighting Director: Richard Weil
   Stage Manager: Courtney DiBello
   Company Manager: Lynna Schneider
   Company Teacher/School Director: Jane Vorburger
   Development Director: Ethan Hong
Mission: Continues to provide superb training for students interested in becoming professional ballet dancers as well as for others who want recreational ballet classes.
Utilizes: Five Seasonal Concerts; Singers
Founded: 1972
Specialized Field: Ballet; Jazz
Status: Professional, Non-Profit
Paid Staff: 7
Volunteer Staff: 5
Paid Artists: 18
Budget: $1,000,000-$2,500,000
Income Sources: Ticket Sales; Grants
Performs At: Oklahoma City Civic Center
Annual Attendance: 20,000
Organization Type: Performing; Touring; Resident; Educational; Sponsoring

553
PRAIRIE DANCE THEATRE
PO Box 16079
Oklahoma City, OK 73111
Phone: 405-922-0134
e-mail: pdtokc@gmail.com
Web Site: www.prairiedanceokc.org
Officers:
   President: Eugene King, Jr.
   Treasurer: Karon Jeter
   Secretary: Leslie Billetter
Management:
   Executive Director: Beth Shumway
   Artistic Director: Tonya Kilburn
Mission: Prairie Dance Theatre offers full concerts of contemporary dance and is known for original works based on Southwestern and Native American themes.
Utilizes: Five Seasonal Concerts; Guest Companies; Singers
Founded: 1978
Specialized Field: Modern; Ethnic Dance; Folk Dance
Status: Professional; Nonprofit
Budget: $100,000-$200,000
Income Sources: Kirpatrick Center Museum; MidAmerica Dance Network
Organization Type: Performing; Touring; Resident; Educational

554
TULSA BALLET
1212 E 45th Place
Tulsa, OK 74105
Phone: 918-749-6030
Fax: 918-749-0532
e-mail: admin@tulsaballet.org
Web Site: www.tulsaballet.org
Officers:
   President: Billie Barnett
   Vice President Finance/Treasurer: Dennis Cameron
Management:
   Artistic Director: Marcello Angelini
   Music Director: Nathan Fifield
   Ballet Mistress: Daniela Buson
   Ballet Mistress: Susan Frei
   Resident Choreographer: Val Caniparoli
   Production/Stage Manager: Jessica Flores
   Music Coordinator: Andrew Lahti
Mission: The artistic mission of the Tulsa Ballet has remained constant throughout the years to combine the beauty and joy expressed by dance with the drama and entertainment of the theatre.
Utilizes: Collaborations; Dancers; Five Seasonal Concerts; Guest Accompanists; Guest Artists; Guest Conductors; Guest Ensembles; Guest Writers; Multimedia; Music; Resident Professionals; Sign Language Translators
Founded: 1956
Specialized Field: Ballet
Status: Professional, Nonprofit
Paid Staff: 15
Paid Artists: 30
Budget: $2,700,000
Income Sources: Contributions; Ticket Sales
Performs At: Tulsa Performing Arts Center
Annual Attendance: 60,000
Organization Type: Performing; Touring

DANCE / Oregon

Oregon

555
DANCING PEOPLE COMPANY
310 Oak Street, Suite 5
Ashland, OR 97520
Phone: 541-488-9683
e-mail: info@dancingpeople.com
Web Site: dancingpeople.com
Management:
   Artistic Director: Robin Stiehm
Founded: 1994
Specialized Field: Modern
Status: Professional

556
DANCE THEATRE OF OREGON
815 Dorris Street
Eugene, OR 97404
Phone: 541-689-5189
Fax: 541-688-9235
e-mail: dto@efn.org
Web Site: www.dtodance.org
Officers:
   Founder: Marc Siegel
   Co-Founder: Pamela Lehan Siegel
Management:
   Co-Artistic/Managing Director: Marc Siegel
   Co-Artistic Director: Pamela Lehan-Siegel
Mission: Dance Theatre of Oregon is known for its daring, exuberant, entertaining and intriguing brand of dance theater, packed with emotion and humor for audience of all ages.
Founded: 1991
Specialized Field: Modern
Status: Professional, Nonprofit
Performs At: Hult Center For The Arts

557
EUGENE BALLET COMPANY
1590 Willamette Street
Eugene, OR 97401
Phone: 541-485-3992
Fax: 541-687-5745
e-mail: info@eugeneballetacademy.org
Web Site: www.eugeneballet.org
Officers:
   President: Anne DeLaney
   VP: Margot McDonnell
   Secretary: Hannah Bulkley
   Treasurer: Ken Singer
Management:
   Artistic Director/Choreographer: Toni Pimble
   Assoc Artistic Dir/Ballet Master: Peter Pawlyshynor
   Managing Director: Riley Grannan
   Development/Education Director: Jaclyn LaRue
   Marketing Director: Rob Bean
   Production Manager: Josh Neckles
   Ballet Mistress: Jennifer Amy-Cordero
   Finance Manager: Sandy Naishtat
   Technical Director: Barry Rodgers
Mission: To provide quality professional dance productions and innovative educational services to a broad based audience throughout the United States.
Utilizes: Choreographers; Collaborations; Dance Companies; Dancers; Designers; Guest Accompanists; Guest Artists; Guest Companies; Guest Composers; Guest Conductors; Resident Professionals
Founded: 1978
Specialized Field: Classical; Contemporary
Status: Professional, Nonprofit
Paid Artists: 21

Budget: $1,500,000
Income Sources: Individuals; Corporations; Foundations
Performs At: Hult Center for the Performing Arts
Annual Attendance: 25,000
Facility Category: Performing Arts Center
Type of Stage: Proscenium
Stage Dimensions: 52'x48'
Seating Capacity: 2,460
Year Built: 1982
Cost: $23 million
Organization Type: Performing; Touring; Resident; Sponsoring

558
UNIVERSITY OF OREGON DEPARTMENT OF DANCE
161 Gerlinger Annex
1214 University of Oregon
Eugene, OR 97403-1214
Phone: 541-346-3386
Fax: 541-346-3380
e-mail: Dance@uoregon.edu
Web Site: dance.uoregon.edu
Officers:
   President: Dave Frohnmayer
Management:
   Director: Rita Honka
   Assistant Professor: Brad Garner
   Assistant Professor: Shannon Mockli
   Office Coordinator: Marian Moser
Mission: The primary aim of the department of dance is to enrich the lives of majors, non majors and the Oregon community with diverse dance experiences.
Founded: 1993
Specialized Field: African Dance
Status: Pre-Professional, Non-Profit
Budget: $3,000
Income Sources: Donations; Performances
Annual Attendance: 500

559
RAINBOW DANCE THEATRE
345 North Monmouth Avenue
Monmouth, OR 97361
Phone: 503-623-9320
Fax: 503-623-9321
e-mail: valnoa@yahoo.com
Web Site: www.rainbowdancetheatre.com
Management:
   Artistic Director: Valerie Bergman
   Artistic Director: Darryl Thomas
Mission: Rainbow Dance Theatre's ensemble of eight virtuoso dancers transforms the concert stage into a world of mystery, pathos and humor. Delighting audiences of all ages with its athletic pull-out-the-stops celebration of dancing that pays homage to world-dance and music influences. RDT's repertory features modern works with roots in the traditions of many world cultures. Combined with innovative aerial choreography.
Utilizes: Choreographers; Collaborating Artists; Collaborations; Dance Companies; Dancers; Designers; Fine Artists; Guest Companies; High School Drama; Multi Collaborations; Multimedia; Student Interns; Special Technical Talent; Theatre Companies; Touring Companies; Visual Arts; Volunteer Artists
Founded: 1991
Opened: 1998
Specialized Field: Virtuosic Dance, Haitian Dance, Martial Arts, Hip Hop, American Modern Dance

560
BODYVOX
1201 NW 17th Ave.
Portland, OR 97209
Phone: 503-229-0627
Fax: 503-224-8227
e-mail: info@bodyvox.com
Web Site: www.bodyvox.com
Management:
   Artistic Director: Jamey Hampton
   Artistic Director: Ashley Roland
   Artistic Associate: Eric Skinner
   General Manager: Una Loughran
   Studio Class Manager: Heather Jackson
   Marketing Manager: Jonathan Krebs
   Director: Zacharey Carroll
Mission: BodyVox contemporary dance company performs and creates innovative multidisciplinary dance works.
Utilizes: Collaborating Artists; Dancers; Guest Accompanists; Guest Artists; Lyricists; Multimedia
Founded: 1997
Specialized Field: Contemporary Dance
Status: Professional, Non-Profit
Paid Staff: 4
Volunteer Staff: 20
Paid Artists: 13
Budget: $400,000
Income Sources: Artistic Fees; Private & Foundation Support
Annual Attendance: 10,000-15,000

561
METRO DANCERS
Portland Metro Arts
9003 SE Stark Street
Portland, OR 97216-1664
Phone: 503-408-0604
e-mail: info@pdxmetroarts.org
Web Site: www.pdxmetroarts.org
Officers:
   Chair: Dan Hess
   Treasurer: Tamara Larison
Management:
   Artistic/Executive Director: Nancy Yeamans
Mission: To create an avenue for gifted advanced dancers to perform traditional full length ballets, as well as modern, jazz, character and contemporary ballet pieces.
Founded: 1978
Specialized Field: Classical; Ballet; Modern; Jazz; Character Dance; Contemporary Ballet
Status: Pre-Professional, Nonprofit
Paid Staff: 10
Volunteer Staff: 30
Income Sources: Grants; Performances
Type of Stage: Sprung Floor
Stage Dimensions: 50'x50'
Seating Capacity: 165
Year Built: 2000
Year Remodeled: 2010
Rental Contact: Artistic/Executive Director Nancy Yeamans
Organization Type: Performing

562
NORTHWEST DANCE PROJECT
833 North Shaver Street
Portland, OR 97227
Phone: 503-421-7434
e-mail: info@newdanceproject.org
Web Site: nwdanceproject.org
Management:

DANCE / Pennsylvania

Director: Sarah Slipper
Executive Director: Scott Lewis
Company Manager: Katie Holliday
Mission: To close the chasm between the best emerging dancers and the field's leading dance creators and mentors by drawing them together to work in an open, collaborative and creative environment. We perform, educate, create, cultivate and champion diversity while engaging and deepening public appreciation and support of dance.
Founded: 2004
Specialized Field: Contemporary

563
OBO ADDY MASTER DRUMMER
7725 N Fowler Avenue
Portland, OR 97211
Phone: 503-810-0496
e-mail: susanjaddy@yahoo.com
Web Site: www.oboaddy.com
Management:
  Artistic Director/Master Drummer: Obo Addy
  Booking Manager: Susan Addy
Mission: To bring traditional and popular Ghana music to Europe and America.
Founded: 1980
Specialized Field: Ghana Dance; Ghana Music

564
OREGON BALLET THEATRE
818 SE Sixth Avenue
Portland, OR 97214
Phone: 503-227-0977
Fax: 503-227-4186
Toll-free: 888-922-5538
e-mail: info@obt.org
Web Site: www.obt.org
Officers:
  Chairman: Ken Hick
  Treasurer: Bradley Miller
  Secretary: Harold Goldstein
  Vice Chair: Nancy Locke
Management:
  Artistic Director: Kevin Irving
  Music Director/Conductor: Niel DePonte
  Rehearsal Director: Lisa Kipp
  Lighting Director: Michael Mazzola
  Director of Artistic Operations: Anne Mueller
  Ballet Master: Jeffrey Stanton
  Director of Production: Bill Anderson
  Stage Manager: Victoria A. Epstein
Mission: To entertain and educate audiences and to encourage the creative talents of dancers, choreographers, composers and musicians.
Utilizes: Choreographers; Dancers; Guest Artists
Founded: 1989
Specialized Field: Modern; Ballet; Jazz
Status: Professional, Nonprofit
Paid Artists: 18
Budget: $4.5 million
Income Sources: Public and Private Funding Organizations; Individual Donations; Ticket Sales; Gift Boutique
Season: October - June
Performs At: Keller Auditorium, Newmark Theatre, Portland Center
Organization Type: Performing; Touring; Resident; Educational; Sponsoring

565
WHITE BIRD
P.O. Box 99
Portland, OR 97207
Phone: 503-245-1600
e-mail: info@whitebird.org
Web Site: whitebird.org
Officers:
  President: Paul King
  Co-Vice President: Nancy Thorn
  Co-Vice President: George Thorn
  Secretary/Treasurer: Walter Jaffe
Management:
  General Manager: Walter Jaffe
  Development Manager: Paul King
  Marketing Manager: Sarah Toor
Mission: White Bird is committed to bringing the best Portland-based, regional, national, and international dance companies to Portland, Oregon and to fostering the growth of dance in the region.
Founded: 1997
Status: Nonprofit

566
LITTLE BALLET THEATRE
Maddox Dance Studio
389 S Main Avenue
Warrenton, OR 97146
Phone: 503-861-1971
Fax: 503-861-2350
e-mail: maddoxdancers@opusnet.com
Web Site: www.maddoxdancers.com
Officers:
  Founder: Jeanne Maddox Peterson
Management:
  Artistic Director: Jeanne Maddox Peterson
  Conductor: Lee Stromquist
Mission: Promote and foster dance in Lower Columbia Coastal area by presenting programs of professional quality and thereby giving dancers opportunities to participate in quality programs.
Founded: 1974
Specialized Field: Ballet
Status: Pre-Professional, Nonprofit
Performs At: Astoria High School Auditorium
Organization Type: Performing; Educational

Pennsylvania

567
ALLEGHENY BALLET COMPANY
1003 N. 4th Avenue
Suite D
Altoona, PA 16601
Phone: 814-941-9944
Fax: 814-943-6081
e-mail: info@alleghenyballet.com
Web Site: www.alleghenyballet.org
Management:
  Artistic Director: Connor Weigand
  Executive Director: Kristina M. Zlupko
Mission: Provides audiences the opportunity to experience a professional ballet in their own community.
Founded: 1981
Specialized Field: Ballet
Status: Pre-Professional, Nonprofit
Income Sources: Business Community, Individuals Patrons, Foundations, And Grants
Performs At: Mishler Theatre
Organization Type: Performing; Resident

568
PENNSYLVANIA YOUTH BALLET
Ballet Guild of the Lehigh Valley Inc
556 Main Street
Bethlehem, PA 18018
Phone: 610-865-0353
Fax: 610-865-2698
e-mail: pyb@rcn.com
Web Site: www.bglv.org
Officers:
  President: Jennifer L. Altemose, Esq.
  VP: Michelle Stringer
  Treasurer: Stephen E Prange
  Secretary: Tjasa Crofoot-Ritchey
  Board of Directors: Susan Blobe
Management:
  Artistic Director: Karen Kroninger Knerr
Mission: Dedicated to fostering the art of theatre dance, primarily classical ballet, through education and performances.
Utilizes: Dancers; Guest Accompanists; High School Drama; Original Music Scores
Founded: 1958
Specialized Field: Classical Ballet; Theatre Dance
Status: Semi-Professional, Nonprofit
Paid Staff: 6
Budget: $200,000 - $250,000
Performs At: Zoellner Arts Center, Lehigh University
Organization Type: Performing; Educational

569
CENTRAL PENNSYLVANIA YOUTH BALLET
5 N Orange Street
Suite 3
Carlisle, PA 17013
Phone: 717-245-1190
Fax: 717-245-1189
e-mail: info@cpyb.org
Web Site: www.cpyb.org
Officers:
  President: Hugh Aberman
  VP: Marissa J. Shollenberger
  Treasurer: John Steffee
  Secretary: Teresa.N Slocomb
Management:
  Artistic Director: Marca Dale Weary
  Associate Artistic Director: Darla Hoover
  Executive Director: Maurinda C Wingard
  Resident Choreographer: Alan Hineline
  Public Relations Director: Sarah Kopac
  Production Manager: David Nash
Mission: Central Pennsylvania Youth Ballet continues to provide exceptional dance training for beginning to pre-professional dancers, with many alumni going on to perform with top companies throughout the world.
Founded: 1956
Specialized Field: Ballet; Jazz; Hip Hop; Tap
Status: Pre-Professional, Nonprofit
Income Sources: The Allied Arts Fund; The Pennsylvania Council Of The Arts; The Greater Harrisburg Foundation; Generous Support From Many Individuals; Corporations; Foundations.
Performs At: The Whitaker Center; The Hershey Theatre
Affiliations: Resident Ballet Company

570
DANCE DELBELLO
1458 County Line Road, Suite G
Huntingdon Valley, PA 19006
Phone: 215-322-1137
e-mail: dancedelbello@gmail.com
Web Site: dancedelbello.org
Management:
  Artistic Director: Delphine Del Bello Spencer
  Associate Artistic Director: Stephanie Mumbauer
  Ballet Mistress: Tara George
  Ballet Regissuer: Thomas Gant, Jr.

DANCE / Pennsylvania

Mission: To provide high quality professional ballet and modern dance performances to Deleware Valley audiences; work daily to display and inspire a genuine love and appreciation for the performing arts.
Founded: 1982
Specialized Field: Ballet, Modern
Status: Nonprofit

571
VOLOSHKY UKRAINIAN DANCE ENSEMBLES
700 Cedar Avenue
Jenkintown, PA 19046
Phone: 215-663-0294
Fax: 215-763-8503
e-mail: info@voloshky.com
Web Site: www.voloshky.com
Management:
  Artistic Director: Taras Lewckyj
  Assistant Artistic Director: Oleg Goudimiak
Mission: The Voloshky Ukrainian Dance Ensemble is committed to sharing the wealth of Ukrainian dance and folklore.
Founded: 1973
Specialized Field: Classical Ballet; Ukrainian Dance
Income Sources: Federal; State; Local Organizations; Pennsylvania Arts Counsil

572
PITTSBURGH YOUTH BALLET COMPANY & SCHOOL
St Petersburg Center
210 Valley Brook Road
McMurray, PA 15317
Phone: 724-969-6000
Fax: 724-969-6900
e-mail: info@pybco.com
Web Site: www.pybco.com
Officers:
  Founder: Jean Gedeon
  President: Mary Roman
  VP: Leslie Borandi
  VP: Cara Strock
  Treasurer: Mohylyn Yocca
Management:
  Artistic Director: Jean Gedeon
  Ballet Mistress: Tamar Rachelle
  Ballet Master: Steven Annegarn
  Choreographer: Andrew Blight
  Faculty: Dana Arey
  Faculty: Sherry Mascio
  Faculty: Cynthia.K Ridley
Mission: The Pittsburgh Youth Ballet Company's mission is to train, inspire and nurture young dancers towards artistic excellence, perform works by choreographic masters and to bring the art of dance, through outreach efforts, to new multi-generational audiences.
Founded: 1983
Specialized Field: Contemporary Ballet
Status: Professional, Nonprofit

573
PENNSYLVANIA ACADEMY OF BALLET
29 N Narberth Avenue
Narberth, PA 19072
Phone: 610-664-3455
Fax: 610-664-6733
e-mail: info@paacademyofballet.com
Web Site: www.paacademyofballet.com
Officers:
  Founder: John White
  Founder: Margarita De Saa
Management:
  Director: Melinda Pendleton
  Founder and Teacher: John White
  Founder and Teacher: Margarita de Saa White
  Ballet Master: Bryan Koulman
Mission: To provide essential training for talented students with professional aptitudes and interest in pursuing careers in classical ballet.
Utilizes: Choreographers; Dancers; Scenic Designers; Touring Companies
Founded: 1974
Specialized Field: Classical Ballet
Affiliations: Pennsylvania Academy of Ballet Society

574
NEW CASTLE REGIONAL BALLET
210 W Washington Street
New Castle, PA 16105
Phone: 724-658-7122
e-mail: ncrb@verizon.net
Web Site: www.newcastleregionalballet.org
Officers:
  President: Lorree Houk
  Treasurer: Casey Carbone
  Secretary: Lori Scheidemantle
  Vice President: Sheryl DeSimone
Management:
  Artistic Director: Debbie Menichino Parou
  Faculty: Elissa Houk
  Faculty: Megan Trambley
  Faculty: Jordan Hall
Mission: A professional program using dance as the vehicle to teach children respect, commitment, honesty, teamwork and discipline. To educate a child's mind, body and to develop character on a professional level that will be useful in aspects of their life whether or not they choose dance as a profession.
Founded: 1987
Specialized Field: Ballet; Jazz; Tap
Status: Nonprofit
Income Sources: Pennsylvania Counsil Of The Arts

575
DANCE AFFILIATES
4701 Bath Street
Building 46B
Philadelphia, PA 19137
Phone: 215-636-9000
Fax: 267-672-2912
e-mail: info@danceaffiliates.org
Web Site: danceaffiliates.org
Officers:
  President: Ira S Lefton Esq
  VP: Nancy Purcell
  VP: Nicole D Galli Esq
  Treasurer: Christine M Lussier
  Secretary: Nila G. Betof
Management:
  Artistic Director: F Randolph Swartz
  Development Director: Jane Bensignor
  Bookkeeper: Kathleen Weller
  Staff Associate: Siobhan Hagan
  Artistic Director: F. Randolph Swartz
Mission: The mission of Dance Affiliates is to advance the growth, development and well being of the art of dance.
Utilizes: AEA Actors; Artists-in-Residence; Choreographers; Collaborating Artists; Commissioned Composers; Commissioned Music; Composers-in-Residence; Curators; Dance Companies; Dancers; Designers; Educators; Filmmakers; Five Seasonal Concerts; Grant Writers; Guest Accompanists; Guest Artists; Guest Choreographers; Guest Companies; Guest Conductors; Guest Ensembles; Guest Lecturers; Guest Soloists; High School Drama; Instructors; Lyricists; New Productions; Original Music Scores; Poets; Resident Professionals; Sign Language Translators; Soloists; Theatre Companies
Founded: 1979
Specialized Field: Modern; Ballet; Jazz; Ethnic Dance; Folk Dance
Status: Professional, Nonprofit
Paid Staff: 4
Volunteer Staff: 20
Budget: $1,000,000
Income Sources: Ticket Sales; Public & Private Funding
Performs At: Annenberg Center for the Performing Arts; Univ. of the Arts
Annual Attendance: 30,000
Facility Category: Theatre
Stage Dimensions: 48'x31'
Seating Capacity: 911
Year Built: 1972
Organization Type: Sponsoring

576
KORESH DANCE COMPANY
2020 Chestnut Street
Philadelphia, PA 19103
Phone: 215-751-0959
Fax: 215-665-0805
e-mail: info@koreshdance.org
Web Site: www.koreshdance.org
Officers:
  President: Steve Lazin
  VP: David Cooper
  Treasurer: Cary Borish
  Board Member: Leslie Baker Boris
  Board Member: Niza Davidson
Management:
  Artistic Director: Ronen Koresh
  Executive Director: Alon Koresh
  Assistant Artistic Director: Melissa Rector
  Development Director: Deborah Crocker
  Education & Outreach Director: Emily O'Rourke
  Company Manager: Dara Schmoyer
  Lighting Designer: Robb Andersen
Mission: Dedicated to the enrichment of the cultural landscape and artistic reputation of Philadelphia.
Founded: 1991
Specialized Field: Traditional Dance
Paid Staff: 5
Volunteer Staff: 15
Paid Artists: 31

577
PENNSYLVANIA BALLET
1819 JFK Boulevaard
Suite 210
Philadelphia, PA 19103
Phone: 215-551-7000
Fax: 215-551-7224
e-mail: info@paballet.org
Web Site: www.paballet.org
Officers:
  Chairman: David Hoffman
  Vice Chair: Janet Averill
  Treasurer: John Wolak
  Secretary: Elizabeth Luening Long, Esq.
Management:
  Artistic Director: Roy Kaiser
  Executive Director: Michael Scolamiero
  Assistant Artistic Director: Michael Sheridan
  Development Director: Hilary Alger
  Marketing/Communications Director: Shawn D Stone

DANCE / Pennsylvania

Production Director: John Hoey
Artistic Staff: Tamara Hadley
Mission: Our mission is to maintain and nurture a financially sound, Philadelphia-based ballet company that presents the finest in artistry and performance to the widest possible audience. To expand & diversify its classical and contemporary repertoire, and provide the highest caliber of instruction for aspiring professional dancers. The ballet strives to enrich and expand the cultural lives of children and adults through the art of ballet.
Founded: 1963
Specialized Field: Ballet
Status: Professional, Nonprofit
Paid Staff: 30
Paid Artists: 44
Budget: $8,000,000
Income Sources: Earned; Unearned; Corporate; Foundation
Performs At: The Merriam Theatre
Organization Type: Performing; Touring; Resident

578
PHILADELPHIA DANCE COMPANY
Philadanco
9 N Preston Street
Philadanco Way
Philadelphia, PA 19104-2210
Phone: 215-387-8200
Fax: 215-387-8203
e-mail: shaughton@philadanco.org
Web Site: www.philadanco.org
Officers:
  Founder: Joan Myers Brown
  Chairman: Spencer Wertheimer Esq
  President: Angela M. Brown
  VP: Stephanie Mays Boyd
  Treasurer: Danielle Pierre
  Secretary: Colette deChalus Lee, CCTE
Management:
  Artistic/Executive Director: Joan Myers Brown
  Assistant Artistic Director: Kim Bears-Bailey
  General Manager: Vanessa Thomas-Smith
  Development Director: Sandra N Haughton
  Marketing Director: Gail Bennett
Mission: To perform, instruct and train offering tuition-free instruction and performing opportunities to young dancers.
Utilizes: Actors; Choreographers; Collaborations; Commissioned Composers; Commissioned Music; Community Members; Dancers; Designers; Five Seasonal Concerts; Guest Accompanists; Guest Artists; Guest Companies; Guest Conductors; Guest Ensembles; Guest Writers; High School Drama; Instructors; Organization Contracts; Original Music Scores; Selected Students
Founded: 1970
Specialized Field: Modern; Contemporary Dance
Status: Professional, Nonprofit
Paid Staff: 6
Volunteer Staff: 4
Paid Artists: 19
Budget: $1,000,000-$2,500,000
Income Sources: Dance USA; International Association for Blacks in Dance; American Dance Guild; Greater Philadelphia Cultural Alliance; PDA; Philadelphia C.C.
Affiliations: IABD; GRCA; Dance/USA; PDA; American Dance Guild
Annual Attendance: 60,000
Facility Category: Performing Arts Center
Type of Stage: Proscenium
Seating Capacity: 990

Organization Type: Performing; Touring; Resident; Educational

579
DANCE ALLOY THEATER
5530 Penn Avenue
Pittsburgh, PA 15206
Phone: 412-363-4321
Fax: 412-363-4320
e-mail: info@dancealloy.org
Web Site: www.dancealloy.org
Officers:
  President: Thomas K Whitford
  VP: J Nicole Wilson
Management:
  Artistic Director: Beth Corning
  Managing Director: Susan Sparks
Mission: We are a performing professsional company, a studio open for dance and movement classes as well as a provider of dance education in the Pittsburgh Public Schools.
Utilizes: Choreographers; Commissioned Music; Curators; Dance Companies; Dancers; Educators; Five Seasonal Concerts; Grant Writers; Guest Artists; Guest Companies; Guest Conductors; High School Drama; Original Music Scores; Poets; Soloists
Founded: 1976
Specialized Field: Modern
Status: Professional, Nonprofit
Paid Staff: 6
Paid Artists: 5
Budget: $700,000
Income Sources: Foundations; Corporations; Government
Performs At: Kelly Strayhorn Theatre
Annual Attendance: 4,500
Organization Type: Performing; Touring; Educational

580
LABCO DANCE
1113 E Carson Street
3rd Floor
Pittsburgh, PA 15203
Toll-free: 800-607-0857
e-mail: labcodance@penn.com
Web Site: www.lightingdance.com
Officers:
  President: Eric A Stroud
  VP: Michael J Forlenza PhD
  Treasurer: Timothy W Garland
  Secretary: Marla N Stayduhar
Management:
  Co-Artistic Director: Evelyn Palleja-Vissicchio
  Co-Artistic Director: Elizabeth Brownlee-Sager
  Lighting Designer: Barb Thompson
Mission: A company committed to its mission of passionately advancing the daring art of movement while nurturing unity within the dance community.
Founded: 1996
Specialized Field: Contemporary Dance
Status: Professional, Nonprofit
Paid Staff: 1
Volunteer Staff: 50
Paid Artists: 6
Non-paid Artists: 20
Performs At: Kelly Strayhorn Performing Arts Center

581
MARY MILLER DANCE COMPANY
601 Wood Street
Pittsburgh, PA 15222-2503
Phone: 412-434-1169
e-mail: marymillerdanceco@netzero.net
Web Site: www.marymillerdanceco.org

Officers:
  President: William Lafe
  Treasurer: Debora Brenner Brown
  Secretary: Sheila Collins
  Board of Directors: Bobbi Deem
  Board of Directors: Christy Tarconish
Management:
  Artistic Director/Choreographer: Mary Miller
Mission: Our mission is to create, develop and present modern dance works that reflect on our daily life and today's social, psychological and political issues.
Founded: 1985
Specialized Field: Modern
Status: Professional, Non-Profit

582
PITTSBURGH BALLET THEATRE
2900 Liberty Avenue
Pittsburgh, PA 15201-1500
Phone: 412-281-0360
Fax: 412-281-9901
e-mail: inquiry@pittsburghballet.org
Web Site: www.pbt.org
Officers:
  Chairperson: James E. Crockard III
  Treasurer: Michael.J Haver
  Secretary: Kathleen Miclot
  Vice Chair: Michael C. LaRocco
Management:
  Artistic Director: Terrence S Orr
  Executive Director: Harris N Ferris
  Assistant Artistic Director: Robert Vickrey
  Ballet Mistress: Marianna Tcherkassky
  Ballet Master: Steven Annegarn
  Marketing/Communications Director: Aimee DiAndrea
  Music Director and Conductor: Charles Barker
  Director of Operations and Finance: Jay Romano
  Director of Development: Lois Wholey
Mission: Pittsburgh Ballet Theatre, the professional and classical ballet company of Western Pennsylvania.
Utilizes: Five Seasonal Concerts; Guest Artists
Founded: 1969
Specialized Field: Ballet
Status: Professional, Nonprofit
Budget: $2,500,000
Income Sources: National Endowment for the Arts; Dance USA
Organization Type: Performing; Touring; Resident; Educational

583
PITTSBURGH DANCE COUNCIL
Pittsburgh Cultural Trust
803 Liberty Avenue
Pittsburgh, PA 15222
Phone: 412-471-6070
Web Site: www.trustarts.org
Officers:
  President: J Kevin McMahon
Management:
  Executive Director: Paul Organisak
  Operations Manager: Jacob Bacharach
Mission: Committed to expanding the visibility, appreciation and presentation of dance as an art form in the Pittsburgh area while nurturing the field of dance on national and international levels.
Utilizes: Singers
Founded: 1969
Specialized Field: Modern; Ballet
Status: Professional, Nonprofit
Income Sources: Ticket Sales; Grants; Sponsorships
Performs At: Benedum Center; Byham Theater
Organization Type: Sponsoring; Presenting

DANCE / Rhode Island

584
PENNSYLVANIA DANCE THEATRE
PO Box 792
State College, PA 16801
Phone: 814-883-6907
Fax: 814-865-3039
e-mail: info@pdtdance.org
Web Site: www.tanztheater-ak.com
Management:
    Artistic Director/Choreographer: Andre Koslowski
Mission: Pennsylvania Dance Theatre provides dance enrichment through performance and educational outreach.
Utilizes: Five Seasonal Concerts; Singers
Founded: 1979
Specialized Field: Modern; Contemporary Dance
Status: Professional, Nonprofit
Paid Staff: 1
Budget: $100,000-$200,000
Organization Type: Performing; Touring; Educational

585
NOTARA DANCE THEATRE
700 Phillips Street
Stroudsburg, PA 18360
Phone: 570-421-1718
e-mail: sally@notara.net
Web Site: www.notara.net
Management:
    Co-Artistic Director: Sally Notara
    Co-Artistic Director: Darrell Notara
Specialized Field: Ballet; Modern; Jazz; Tap
Status: Nonprofit

586
BRANDYWINE BALLET
700 S High Street
317 Westtown Road, Suite 5
West Chester, PA 19382
Phone: 610-692-6402
e-mail: info@brandywineballet.org
Web Site: brandywineballet.com
Management:
    Artistic Director: Donna L. Muzio
    Ballet Mistress: Nancy Page
Founded: 1979
Specialized Field: Ballet; Contemporary
Status: Nonprofit; Professional; Pre-Professional
Season: May, October, December
Performs At: Emilie K. Asplundh Concert Hall, 700 S High Street

587
GREATER YORK YOUTH BALLET
Greater York Center for Dance Education
3524 E Market Street
York, PA 17402
Phone: 717-755-6683
Fax: 717-755-6688
e-mail: info@gydance.org
Web Site: gydance.org
Officers:
    Founding Director: Shana Garling
    President: Verna Stilwell
    VP: Jill Snell
Management:
    Artistic Director: Lori Pergament
    Executive Director: Melinda Fritz
    Business Director: Steve Pergament
    Asst to Business Director: Nan Taylor
Mission: The Greater York Youth Ballet provides intensive training, individual coaching, performance opportunities and the discipline of a pre-professional dance environment to aspiring dancers.
Founded: 1971
Specialized Field: Ballet
Status: Pre-Professional, Nonprofit
Performs At: Strand Capital Performing Arts Center

Rhode Island

588
FUSIONWORKS DANCE COMPANY
PO Box 402
Lincoln, RI 02865-0402
Phone: 401-334-3091
e-mail: fusionwk@cox.net
Web Site: www.fusionworksdance.org
Officers:
    President: Kate Dickson
    Vice President: Ann Sasso
    Secretary: Karen Dickson
    Treasurer: Greg Rieben
Management:
    Artistic Director: Deb Meunier
Mission: Fusionworks Dance Company provides access to and an understanding of contemporary dance through the presentation of high quality professional dance with an emphasis on direct audience experience. This is accomplished in an educational framework of concerts, public performances and school-based programming intended to introduce audiences to both the beauty that inspires and the processes behind the dances performed.
Founded: 1987
Specialized Field: Contemporary Dance
Status: Nonprofit
Income Sources: Individual; Corporate
Season: November-April

589
STATE BALLET OF RHODE ISLAND
52 Sherman Avenue
Lincoln, RI 02865
Phone: 401-334-2560
Fax: 401-334-0412
e-mail: info@stateballet.com
Web Site: www.stateballet.com
Officers:
    Chairperson: Herci Marsden
    Treasurer: Ana Mardsen Fox
    Recording Secretary: Barbara Ann Marsden
    VP of The State Ballet of RI: Mark Marsden
Management:
    Artistic Director: Herci Marsden
    Executive Director: Ana Marsden Fox
    Email Correspondant: Mia Nocera Godbout
    VP/Coordinator: Shana Fox Marceau
Mission: To create, present, preserve and extend the great repertoire of classical dancing through exciting performances and educational programming of the highest quality, presented to the widest possible audience
Utilizes: Guest Artists
Founded: 1959
Specialized Field: Classical Ballet
Status: Semi-Professional; Nonprofit; Civic; Regional Ballet Comp
Paid Staff: 2
Volunteer Staff: 35
Paid Artists: 13
Non-paid Artists: 60
Budget: $110,000
Income Sources: Admission; Benefactors; Members Contributor; Fund Raisers
Performs At: Roberts Auditorium; Rhode Island College
Affiliations: Brae Crest School of Ballet
Annual Attendance: 10,000
Facility Category: College Theatreium
Stage Dimensions: 45x60
Seating Capacity: 1,100
Rental Contact: Michael Dusharme
Organization Type: Performing; Touring; Resident; Educational

590
RHODE ISLAND'S BALLET THEATRE
20 Loring Street
Middletown, RI 02842
Phone: 401-847-5301
e-mail: ribt-nm@cox.net
Web Site: www.riballet.org
Officers:
    President: Warren McAuliffe
    VP/Secretary: Lisa Ross
    Board Member: Paul Boivin
    Board Member: Ellie Lupo
Management:
    Artistic Director: Nancy McAuliffe
    Executive Director: Warren McAuliffe
Specialized Field: Ballet

591
ISLAND MOVING COMPANY
3 Charles Street
Newport, RI 02840
Mailing Address: P.O. Box 746, Newport, RI 02840
Phone: 401-847-4470
e-mail: info@islandmovingco.org
Web Site: www.islandmovingco.org
Officers:
    Chair: John M. La Rocca, Sr.
    Vice President: John Brooks, Jr.
    Secretary: Ellen Barnes
    Treasurer: Kate Spinella
Management:
    Artistic Director: Miki Ohlsen
    Executive Director: Dominique Alfandre
    Technical Director: Roy K Omori
Mission: Island Moving Company is a classically trained contemporary ballet company founded on the belief that collaboration and a supportive environment enhance the creative process, producing great works of art representing profound expressions of the human spirit and experience.
Utilizes: Choreographers; Collaborating Artists; Commissioned Music; Dance Companies; Dancers; Guest Artists; Guest Choreographers; Instructors; Local Artists; Original Music Scores; Playwrights; Resident Artists
Founded: 1982
Specialized Field: Contemporary Ballet
Status: Professional, Nonprofit
Paid Staff: 6
Paid Artists: 15
Budget: $250,000
Income Sources: Admissions; Foundations; Grants; Membership
Affiliations: Newport Academy of Ballet
Annual Attendance: 4,000
Organization Type: Performing; Touring; Resident; Educational

DANCE / South Carolina

592
EVERETT DANCE THEATRE
9 Duncan Avenue
Providence, RI 02906
Phone: 401-831-9479
Fax: 401-455-0581
e-mail: info@everettdancetheatre.org
Web Site: www.everettri.org
Officers:
  Co-Founder: Dorothy Jungels
  Co-Founder: Aaron Jungels
  President: Shauna Duffy
  VP: Susan Joyce
  Treasurer: Nicole Turner
  Secretary: Susan Hradil
Management:
  Artistic Director: Dorothy Jungels
  Director of Ballet Program: Rachael Jungels
  Director of Hip-Hop Program: Sokeo Ros
  Operations Manager: Robyn Duffy
  Executive Director: Aaron Jungels
Founded: 1986
Specialized Field: Theatrical Dance
Status: Professional, Non-Profit
Paid Staff: 3
Paid Artists: 15
Income Sources: Performances, Foundations; Government; Individual
Annual Attendance: 20,000

593
FESTIVAL BALLET PROVIDENCE AND SCHOOL
Center for Dance Educaiton
825 Hope Street
Providence, RI 02906
Phone: 401-353-1129
Fax: 401-353-8853
e-mail: info@festivalballetprovidence.org
Web Site: www.festivalballet.com
Officers:
  President: Toots Zynsky
  VP: Edward M. Fogarty, Esq.
  Treasurer: Erica Guatieri
  Secretary: Kerry Altman
Management:
  Artistic Director: Milhailo Djuric
  Ballet Mistress: Milica Bijelic
  Managing Director: Lisa LaDew
  Marketing/Public Relations Manager: Mark Morin
  Office Administrator: Daphne Oman
  Development Director: Frazier Bell
  Marketing Director: Dylan Giles
Mission: Festival Ballet Providence enriches the community by expanding dance awareness through education and performance.
Utilizes: Collaborations; Dancers; Guest Accompanists; Guest Artists; Guest Ensembles; High School Drama
Founded: 1977
Specialized Field: Ballet
Status: Professional, Nonprofit
Paid Staff: 20
Paid Artists: 12
Non-paid Artists: 3
Budget: $1,500,000
Income Sources: Ticket Sales; School Tuition; Donations; Grants
Performs At: Providence Performing Arts Center; Veterans Memorial Aud.
Affiliations: The Festival Ballet Center for Dance Education
Annual Attendance: 35,000

Facility Category: Dance School; Performing Company
Type of Stage: Rent Providence Area Stages
Organization Type: Performing; Touring; Resident

South Carolina

594
DANCE STATION
1632 Chapin Road
Chapin, SC
Phone: 803-932-9999
e-mail: tjdancestation@aol.com
Web Site: www.dancestationinc.com
Management:
  Artistic Director: Tammy Johns
Specialized Field: Dance

595
ROBERT IVEY BALLET
College of Charleston School of the Arts
1910 Savannah Highway
Charleston, SC 29407-9679
Phone: 843-556-1343
Fax: 843-757-0960
e-mail: info@robertiveyballet.net
Web Site: www.robertiveyballet.net
Management:
  Artistic Director: Michael Wise
  Assistant Artistic Director: Olga Wise
  Business Manager: Sudie Alexander
Mission: To promote and educate in the art of dance.
Utilizes: Five Seasonal Concerts
Founded: 1977
Specialized Field: Modern; Ballet; Jazz
Paid Staff: 50
Volunteer Staff: 3
Paid Artists: 3
Non-paid Artists: 30
Income Sources: Grants; Fundraiser; Donations; Addmission Sales
Performs At: Sottioe Theatre
Annual Attendance: 7,000
Facility Category: Rental Theatre
Type of Stage: Proscenium
Stage Dimensions: 48' x 32'
Seating Capacity: 785
Organization Type: Resident

596
SPOLETO FESTIVAL USA
14 George Street
Charleston, SC 29401-1524
Phone: 843-722-2764
Fax: 843-723-6383
e-mail: info@spoletousa.org
Web Site: www.spoletousa.org
Officers:
  Chairman: Carlos.E Evans
  President: M.Edward Sellers
  VP: Jennie L. DeScherer
  VP: Lou Rena Hammond
  VP: John.M Palms
  Secretary: John B. Hagerty
Management:
  Artistic Director-Choral Activities: Joseph Flummerfelt
  Director, Chamber Music: Geoff Nuttall
  General Director: Nigel Redden
  Producer: Nunally Kersh
  Director Of Development: Julia Forster
  Director Marketing/Public Relations: Jennifer Scott
  Director of Finance: Tasha Gandy
Mission: To present opera, dance, theater, symphonic, choral and chamber music, jazz and visual arts exhibits of the highest quality; to serve as an educational environment for young artists and audiences alike.
Utilizes: Singers
Founded: 1977
Specialized Field: Jazz; Theatrical Dance
Status: Professional; Semi-Professional; Non-Profit
Paid Staff: 18
Budget: $7,000,000
Income Sources: Ticket Revenues; Contributions
Performs At: Gaillard Municipal Auditorium; Dock Street Theater
Annual Attendance: 70,000-80,000
Organization Type: Performing; Educational; Sponsoring

597
COLUMBIA CITY BALLET
1545 Main Street
Columbia, SC 29201
Phone: 803-799-7605
Fax: 803-799-7928
e-mail: marketing@columbiacityballet.com
Web Site: www.columbiacityballet.com
Officers:
  President: Fred Sheheen
  Vice President: Coralee Harris
  Treasurer: Chris Ray
Management:
  Artistic/Executive Director: William Starrett
  Ballet Mistress: Patricia Miller
  Ballet Mistress: Mariclare Miranda
  Technical Director/Lighting: Ryan Stender
  Marketing/Public Relations Manager: Skot Garrick
  Director of Development and Members: Kaytina Haack
  Director of Finance: Robert DeBerry
Mission: Columbia City Ballet's mission is to offer South Carolina and Southeastern audiences the highest quality ballet and to provide dancers with only the best professional dance training.
Utilizes: Artists-in-Residence; Dance Companies; Dancers; Five Seasonal Concerts; Guest Artists; Guest Conductors; High School Drama; Lyricists; Organization Contracts; Resident Professionals; Student Interns
Founded: 1961
Specialized Field: Ballet
Status: Professional, Nonprofit
Paid Staff: 9
Paid Artists: 34
Non-paid Artists: 7
Budget: $1,000,000
Income Sources: Box Office; Grants; Corporate Support
Performs At: Koger Center for the Arts
Annual Attendance: 125,000
Facility Category: Opera
Type of Stage: Proscenium
Seating Capacity: 2,100
Year Built: 1989
Rental Contact: Michael Taylor
Organization Type: Performing; Touring; Resident; Educational

598
THE COLUMBIA CITY JAZZ DANCE COMPANY & SCHOOL
550 River Drive
Columbia, SC 29210

DANCE / South Carolina

Phone: 803-252-0252
Fax: 803-779-6291
Web Site: www.columbiacityjazz.com
Management:
    Choreographer/Artistic Director: Dale Lam
    Ballet Faculty: Kiyomi Mercadante Marple
    Ballet Faculty: Talin Kenar
    Ballet Faculty: Bonnie Boiter-Jolley
Mission: Internationally known not-for-profit pre-professional jazz dance troupe.
Specialized Field: Dance
Status: Nonprofit

599
COLUMBIA COMMUNITY ARTS CENTRE
1001 Piney Woods Road
Columbia, SC 29210
Phone: 803-772-1462
Fax: 803-772-1462
e-mail: colacommac2010@att.net
Web Site: www.colacommarts.com
Management:
    Founder/Director: Gail Faust
Mission: To encourage and develope the worship of god through dance.
Utilizes: Artists-in-Residence; Collaborations; Community Talent; Dancers; Guest Artists; Guest Ensembles; Multimedia; Soloists
Founded: 2010
Specialized Field: Dance; Music; Drama
Income Sources: Donations; Grants; Fundraisers

600
COLUMBIA'S BALLROOM COMPANY
125D Outlet Point Blvd
Columbia, SC 29210
Phone: 803-750-0181
Fax: 803-750-0181
Web Site: www.columbiasballroom.com
Mission: Beginner to advance ballroom dancing.
Specialized Field: Dance

601
SC CHRISTIAN DANCE THEATER
736 St Andrews Road
Columbia, SC 29210
Phone: 803-609-4777
e-mail: admin@scchristiandance.com
Web Site: www.scchristiandance.com
Management:
    Director: Cynthia Dewar
    Faculty: Patty Graham
    Faculty: Shirly Crew
    Faculty: Kelley Connell
Mission: Offers dancers more opportunities for performance workshops and understanding what it means to worship through dance.
Specialized Field: Dance

602
SOUTHEASTERN SCHOOL OF BALLET
220 Business Park Blvd.
Columbia, SC 29203
Phone: 803-419-5512
Toll-free: 866-411-5512
e-mail: ssb@southeasternschoolofballet.com
Web Site: www.southeasternschoolofballet.com
Management:
    Director: Hillary Krieger
    Director: Gabor Toth
    Choreographer: Terrance Henderson
    Choreographer: Erika Shaw
    Choreographer: Joey Mock
Mission: Offer the highest quality of instruction in the various disciplines of ballet.
Specialized Field: Dance

603
UNBOUND DANCE COMPANY
701 Gervais Street
Columbia, SC 29201
e-mail: info@unbounddance.com
Web Site: unbounddance.com
Officers:
    President: Tom Chinn
    Secretary: Jessica Trotter
    Treasurer: Marsha Harris
    Company Manager: Joanna Lewis
Mission: UNBOUND is a new way of moving with no boundaries, raw, undefined, athletic, meaningful, literal, passionate. It gives dancers the artistic freedom to express themselves through movement without feeling constrained to any specific genre of dance. We want our audience to leave us wanting to live stronger, love harder and desire a better existence.
Status: Professional

604
VISTA BALLROOM
604 Meeting St
Columbia, SC 29201
Phone: 803-546-3705
e-mail: vistaballroom@gmail.com
Web Site: www.vistaballroom.net
Management:
    Director: Erin Bolshakov
Mission: Offering instruction in argentine tango, salsa, ballroom, latin, shag and swing dancing.
Specialized Field: Dance

605
GILBERT STUDIO OF DANCE ARTS
311 Broad Street
PO Box 191
Gilbert, SC 29054
Phone: 803-309-0887
e-mail: info@gilbertstudioofdance.com
Web Site: www.gilbertstudioofdance.com
Management:
    Owner/Director/Instructor: Linelle Yates
    Office Assistant: Kelly Brown
Mission: Ballet, tap, jazz, clogging, pom pon and praise dance.
Specialized Field: Dance

606
CAROLINA BALLET THEATRE
872 Woodruff Road
Greenville, SC 29607
Mailing Address: PO Box 135, Greenville, SC 29602
Phone: 864-421-0940
Fax: 864-297-1635
e-mail: info@carolinaballet.org
Web Site: www.carolinaballet.org
Officers:
    President: Jamie Prince
    Secretary: Dawn Koffskey
    Treasurer: Robert Cromley
Management:
    Artistic Director: Hernan Justo
    Executive Director: Anita Sleeman
    Ballet Mistress/Principal Dancer: Anita Sun Pacylowski Justo
    Production Manager: Louise M. Ochart
Mission: Carolina Ballet Threatre strives to offer quality performances that will educate and entertain a wide variety of audiences in the art of ballet.
Founded: 1972
Specialized Field: Classical Ballet; Contemporary
Status: Professional, Nonprofit
Paid Staff: 8
Volunteer Staff: 40
Budget: $250,000
Income Sources: Private; Grants; Ticket Sales; Community Outreach
Performs At: The Peace Center For The Performing Arts

607
GREENVILLE BALLET SCHOOL AND COMPANY
105 Woodruff Industrial Lane
Greenville, SC 29607-4101
Phone: 864-234-5677
Fax: 864-268-5653
e-mail: info@greenvilleballet.com
Web Site: www.greenvilleballet.com
Management:
    Director: Andrew Kuharsky
    Director: Merry Kuharsky
Mission: To provide the finest quality dance instruction in a fun and loving environment in order to promote life-long learning, fitness, and appreciation of the arts.
Specialized Field: Ballet
Status: Semi-Professional, Nonprofit
Budget: $20,000
Income Sources: Individual; Foundations; Ticket Sales
Performs At: Furman University
Annual Attendance: 3,000
Stage Dimensions: 35x45
Seating Capacity: 1900

608
THE SOUTHERN STRUTT STUDIO
90 Ashbourne Road
Irmo, SC 29063
Phone: 803-781-3980
e-mail: ngiles1055@aol.com
Web Site: www.southernstruttdance.com
Management:
    Owner/Director: Nancy Giles
    Office Manager: Dawn Edwards
    Performing Teams Director/Instructo: Jenny Davidson
Mission: To build individuals self confidence and to help them learn discipline and team work
Specialized Field: Dance

609
DANCE 1 STUDIO
3819 Mineral Springs Road
Lexington, SC 29073
Phone: 803-356-8400
e-mail: lizard120@msn.com
Specialized Field: Dance

610
CAROLINA BALLET THEATRE
872 Woodruff Road
Raleigh, SC 27607
Phone: 864-421-0940
Fax: 864-297-1635
e-mail: info@carolinaballet.org
Web Site: www.carolinaballet.com
Officers:
    President: Jamie Prince
    Secretary: Dawn Koffskey
    Treasurer: Robert Cromley
    Vice Chair: Larry Robins
Management:
    Artistic Director: Hernan Justo

DANCE / Tennessee

Executive Director: Anita Sleeman
Ballet Mistress/Principal Dancer: Anita Sun Pacylowski Justo
Production Manager: Louise M. Ochart
Resident Guest Choreographer: Lynne Taylor-Corbett
Sales Manager: Jim Casey
Wardrobe Manager: Sydney De Briel
Mission: Carolina Ballet's mission is to perform world-class professional ballet, entertaining and enlightening audiences in Raleigh and beyond.
Founded: 1984
Specialized Field: Ballet
Status: Pre-Profesisonal, Nonprofit
Paid Staff: 6
Volunteer Staff: 22
Paid Artists: 8
Non-paid Artists: 45
Budget: $180,000
Income Sources: Grants; Memberships; Earned; Unearned
Performs At: The Township Auditorium; Cmfa Black Box Theatre
Annual Attendance: 15,000

Tennessee

611
BALLET TENNESSEE
John A Patten Center
3202 Kelly's Ferry Road
Chattanooga, TN 37419
Phone: 423-821-2055
Fax: 423-821-2156
e-mail: anna@ballettennessee.org
Web Site: www.ballettennessee.org
Officers:
　President: Stacy Goodwin-Lightfoot
　Treasurer: Julia Sanford
　Secretary: Shonda Caines
Management:
　Artistic Director: Anna Baker-VanCura
　Executive Director: Barry VanCura
　Associate Director: Laurel Shastri
Mission: Strives to make a positive impact on people of all ages, races, abilities and economic levels through the art of ballet by providing professional quality performance and instruction.
Founded: 1987
Specialized Field: Classical Ballet; Contemporary Ballet
Status: Professional, Nonprofit
Budget: $200,000-$500,000
Income Sources: Allied Arts Of Greater Chattanooga, Tennessee Arts Commission, National Endowment For The Arts, Corporate Grants, Individual Contributions.
Performs At: The Tivoli Theatre
Annual Attendance: 20,000

612
CHATTANOOGA BALLET
PO Box 6175
Chattanooga, TN 37401
Phone: 423-265-0617
e-mail: chattballet@gmail.com
Web Site: www.chattanoogaballet.net
Officers:
　President: Stefanie Crowe
　Vice President: Blair Waddell
　Treasurer: David Binder
　Secretary: Becky McMahon
Management:
　Executive Director: Bob Willie
　Assistant Director: Laurne Abney
　Ballet Master: Frank Hay
Mission: The mission of the Chattanooga Ballet is to stimulate artistic growth and to increase public awareness and participation in the art of dance in our community and region.
Utilizes: Guest Companies; Singers
Founded: 1980
Specialized Field: Classical Ballet
Status: Professional, Nonprofit
Paid Staff: 11
Volunteer Staff: 100
Paid Artists: 11
Non-paid Artists: 110
Budget: $450,000
Income Sources: Corporations; Individual; Foundations; Government
Performs At: Fine Arts Center; University of Tennessee-Chattanooga; Tivoli Theatre
Affiliations: Tennessee Association of Dance; University of Tennessee
Annual Attendance: 36,000
Organization Type: Performing; Touring; Resident; Educational; Sponsoring

613
TENNESSEE ASSOCIATION OF DANCE
PO Box 3295
Chattanooga, TN 37602
Phone: 423-920-3317
e-mail: info@tennesseedance.org
Web Site: www.tennesseedance.org
Officers:
　President: Marcus Hayes
　VP: Morgan Fleming
　Treasurer: Eva Turbyville
　Secretary: Heidi Ehle
Management:
　Executive Director: Elizabeth Roemer
Mission: Tennessee Association of Dance is a statewide network of organizations and individuals dedicated to artistic excellence and committed to ensuring that dance is a vital and respected part of life for all Tennesseans.
Founded: 1971
Specialized Field: Modern; Ballet; Jazz; Tap
Status: Professional, Nonprofit
Performs At: Middle Tennessee State University
Organization Type: Educational

614
ZION DANCE COMPANY
280 West Old Andrew Johnson Highway
Jefferson City, TN 37760
Phone: 865-245-9466
e-mail: info@ziondance.com
Web Site: ziondance.com
Management:
　Artistic Director: Kara Price Moss
　Director: MacKenzie Price Meyers
Mission: As a Christian dance company our heart is to increase, expand, and enlarge, the Kingdom of God through dance.
Founded: 2012
Organization Type: Touring; Performing

615
CITY BALLET
PO Box 1664
Knoxville, TN 37901
Phone: 865-544-0495
Fax: 865-522-3043
e-mail: cityballet@nxs.net
Officers:
　President: John King
Management:
　Executive Director: John King
Mission: To raise the calibre of dance in this area through public performances; to build technically proficient dancers through the use of professional teachers, choreographers, and performers brought in by the company.
Utilizes: Five Seasonal Concerts; Guest Artists
Founded: 1988
Specialized Field: Modern; Ballet; Jazz
Status: Semi-Professional; Nonprofit
Paid Staff: 2
Budget: $550,000
Income Sources: Grants; Donations
Performs At: The Tennessee Theatre; Civic Coliseum
Organization Type: Educational; Sponsoring

616
TENNESSEE CHILDREN'S DANCE ENSEMBLE
4216 Sutherland Avenue
Knoxville, TN 37919
Phone: 865-584-9636
Web Site: tcdedance.org
Officers:
　Founder: Dorothy Floyd
　President: Kathy H. Reed
　VP: Wayne Kline
　Treasurer: Linda Wilson
　Secretary: Gail Powell
Management:
　Artistic Director: Irena Linn
　Managing Director: Judy Robinson
　Ballet Master/Choreographer: Lenette Perra
　Director of Education: Marti Mowery Bolton
　Ballet Mistress & Resident Choreogr: Dr. Lenette Perra
　Associate Artistic Director: Amy Renee Wilson
　Rehearsal Assistant: Lindsey Kline
Utilizes: Five Seasonal Concerts; Singers
Founded: 1981
Specialized Field: Modern
Status: Professional, Nonprofit
Paid Staff: 5
Paid Artists: 22
Budget: $200,000-$500,000
Income Sources: Corporations; Foundations; Grants; Individuals
Annual Attendance: 10,000-15,000
Type of Stage: 7
Organization Type: Performing; Touring; Resident; Educational

617
APPALACHIAN BALLET COMPANY
215 W Broadway
Maryville, TN 37801
Phone: 865-982-8463
Fax: 865-982-8463
Web Site: www.appalachianballet.com
Management:
　Artistic Director: Amy Moore Morton
Mission: To promote and foster a love and appreciation of the arts through performances and lecture demonstrations within the community.
Utilizes: Singers
Founded: 1972
Specialized Field: Classical Ballet
Status: Semi-Professional, Nonprofit
Paid Staff: 1
Volunteer Staff: 60
Performs At: Knoxville Civic Auditorium; Tennessee Theater

DANCE / Texas

Affiliations: Southeast Regional Ballet Association
Organization Type: Performing; Touring; Resident; Educational

618
BALLET MEMPHIS
Ballet Memphis Studios
7950 Trinity Road
Memphis, TN 38018
Phone: 901-737-7322
Fax: 901-737-7037
e-mail: callen@balletmemphis.org
Web Site: www.balletmemphis.org
Officers:
  Founder: Dorothy Gunther Pugh
  President: Clarence Davis
Management:
  Artistic Director: Dorothy Gunther Pugh
  Associate Artistic Director: Karl Condon
  Managing Director: Philip West
  Ballet Mistress: Tamara Hoffmann
  Development Director: Roger Johnson
  Production Manager: Allan Kerr
  Artistic Associate: Julia Adam
  Choreographic Associate: Steven Mcahon
Mission: Ballet Memphis is a creative resource to the nation as a maker and interpreter of the South's cultural legacy through dance, production and training.
Founded: 1986
Specialized Field: Ballet
Status: Professional, Non-Profit
Paid Artists: 19
Budget: $3,100,000
Performs At: Orpheum Theatre
Organization Type: Performing; Resident; Touring; Educational

619
DANCE THEATRE OF TENNESSEE
2710 Old Lebanon Road, 25B
Nashville, TN 37214
Phone: 615-391-5500
e-mail: info@dancetheatretn.org
Web Site: dancetheatretn.org
Management:
  Artistic Director: Christopher Mohnani
Mission: Expose new audiences to the diversity and beauty of dance, provide affordable, accessible professional performances, offer superior academy training, foster enlightened outreach programs, bring eminent national/international artists, choreographers, and premiere works to the mid-state area.
Status: Nonprofit

620
NASHVILLE BALLET
3630 Redman Street
Nashville, TN 37209-4827
Phone: 615-297-2966
Fax: 615-297-9972
e-mail: info@nashvilleballet.com
Web Site: www.nashvilleballet.com
Officers:
  President: Patricia B. Eastwood
  VP: Neil B. Krugman
  Treasurer: Gerard M. Hayden, Jr.
  Secretary: James F. Turner, Jr.
Management:
  Artistic Director/CEO: Paul Vasterling
  Executive Director: Angie Adams
  Director of Artistic Operations: Sharyn Mahoney
  Artistic Staff: Allison Zamorski
  Ballet Master: Timothy Rinehart Yeager
  Principal Guest Conductor: Nathan Fifield
  Executive Director: Angie Adams
  Director Finance, Administration: Martha Aus
  Business Associate: Rachel Norfleet
Mission: Create, perform, teach and promote dance as an essential and inspiring element of our community.
Utilizes: Community Members; Curators; Dancers; Five Seasonal Concerts; Guest Artists; Singers
Founded: 1986
Specialized Field: Ballet
Status: Professional, Nonprofit
Paid Staff: 15
Paid Artists: 15
Budget: $1,000,000-$2,500,000
Organization Type: Performing; Touring; Educational

Texas

621
BALLET AUSTIN
Ballet Austin Academy
501 W Third Street
Austin, TX 78701
Phone: 512-476-9151
Fax: 512-476-3973
Web Site: www.balletaustin.org
Officers:
  Chairperson: Sarah Butler
  President: Dan Byrne
  Board Member: Mark Adams
  Board Member: Stephen Adler
  Board Member: Lorrie Garcia
Management:
  Artistic Director: Stephen Mills
  Executive Director: Cookie Gregory Ruiz
  Associate Artistic Director: Michelle Martin
  Production Director: Bill Sheffield
  Marketing Director: Lance Johnson
Mission: As distinctive and dynamic as the city calls home, welcomes people near and far to participate in it's Classically Innovative vision of dance.
Utilizes: Artists-in-Residence; Collaborating Artists; Collaborations; Commissioned Composers; Commissioned Music; Dancers; Designers; Five Seasonal Concerts; Grant Writers; Guest Accompanists; Guest Artists; Guest Companies; Guest Conductors; Guest Directors; Guest Instructors; Guest Lecturers; Local Artists; Resident Artists; Touring Companies
Founded: 1956
Specialized Field: Ballet
Status: Professional, Nonprofit
Paid Staff: 16
Paid Artists: 47
Income Sources: Corporate; Foundation
Performs At: Performing Arts Center; University of Texas at Austin
Organization Type: Performing; Touring; Educational

622
CHADDICK DANCE THEATER
2410 E. Cesar Chavez, Suite 202
Austin, TX 78731
Phone: 512-371-7146
e-mail: chaddickdt@gmail.com
Web Site: chaddickdancetheater.com
Management:
  Artistic Director/Choreographer: Cheryl Chaddick
Mission: To create works that reflect the social, emotional, and physical experiences of our dancers, our audience and our community, and in so doing, reveal the fundamental humanity that connects us all. In our performance and education programs, we encourage freedom, humor and playfulness in the creative process while validating personal risk-taking with both physical and emotional expression.
Founded: 2008
Status: Nonprofit

623
JOHNSON/LONG DANCE COMPANY
PO Box 516
Austin, TX 78767
Phone: 512-467-0704
Fax: 512-475-3908
e-mail: along@bga.com
Management:
  Co-Artistic Director: Darla Johnson
  Co-Artistic Director: Andrew Long
Specialized Field: Ballet; Modern

624
KATHY DUNN HAMRICK DANCE COMPANY
Cafe Dance 3307-B Hancock Drive
Austin, TX 78731
Phone: 512-934-1082
e-mail: kathy@kdhdance.com
Web Site: kdhdance.com
Management:
  Artistic Director: Kathy Dunn Hamrick
Founded: 1999
Specialized Field: Contemporary
Status: Nonprofit

625
TAPESTRY DANCE COMPANY
2302 Western Trails
Austin, TX 78745
Phone: 512-474-9846
Fax: 512-474-9212
e-mail: dance@tapestry.org
Web Site: www.tapestry.org
Officers:
  Co-Founder: Acia Gray
  Co-Founder: Deirdre Strand
  President: Judy Witkin
Management:
  Artistic/Executive Director: Acia Gray
Mission: Created with the goal of cross discipline choreography and training, the company supports the artistic development in the mixture of tap, modern and jazz creating new works.
Founded: 1989
Specialized Field: Ballet; Tap; Jazz; Modern
Status: Pre-Professional, Nonprofit
Paid Artists: 7

626
CORPUS CHRISTI BALLET
1621 N Mesquite Street
Corpus Christi, TX 78401
Phone: 361-882-4588
Fax: 361-881-9291
e-mail: ccballet@sbcglobal.net
Web Site: www.corpuschristiballet.com
Officers:
  President: Robin Murray
  VP: Elias Cavazos
  Treasurer: Shay Raymond
  Secretary: Jim Kirkpatrick
  Board Member: Sue Connor
Management:
  Artistic Director: Cristina Stirling Munro
Mission: Dedicated to providing professional ballet productions for the South Texas community.
Utilizes: Five Seasonal Concerts; Guest Artists

DANCE / Texas

Founded: 1974
Specialized Field: Ballet
Status: Non-Professional, Nonprofit
Income Sources: Grants
Performs At: Bayfront Plaza Auditorium
Organization Type: Performing; Touring; Resident; Educational; Sponsoring

627
CONTEMPORARY BALLET DALLAS
5400 E Mockingbird, Ste. 207
Dallas, TX 75206
Phone: 214-821-2066
Web Site: contemporaryballetdallas.com
Management:
  Artistic Director: Valerie Shelton Tabor
Mission: The mission of Contemporary Ballet Dallas is to present innovative dance performances and educational programs to a broad audience, while cultivating emerging dance artists and choreographers in North Texas.
Founded: 2000
Specialized Field: Contemporary Ballet
Status: Nonprofit

628
DALLAS BLACK DANCE THEATRE
2700 Flora Street
Dallas, TX 75201
Phone: 214-871-2376
Fax: 214-871-2842
e-mail: e.flood@dbdt.com
Web Site: www.dbdt.com
Officers:
  Founder: Ann M Williams
  President: Georgia Scaife
  Treasurer: Lee McKinney
  Secretary: Paulette Turner
  Chairman: Gilbert Gerst
Management:
  Artistic Director: Ann M Williams
  Executive Director: Zenetta S Drew
  Associate Artistic Director: Melissa M Young
  Sr Marketing/Public Relations Dir: Sonya Spencer
  Lighting Designer/ Technical Direct: Milton Tatum
  Outreach Director: Galen Johnson
Mission: The mission of Dallas Black Dance Theatre is to create and produce contemporary modern dance at its highest level of artistic excellence.
Founded: 1976
Specialized Field: Modern; Jazz; Ethnic Dance
Status: Professional, Nonprofit
Paid Staff: 12
Paid Artists: 12
Budget: $1.7 million
Income Sources: Corporate Sponsorship; City of Dallas; Individuals Donations; Ticket Sales/Touring
Performs At: Majestic Theater
Affiliations: City of Dallas OCA; TCA; National Endowment for the Arts; IABA
Annual Attendance: 125,000
Facility Category: Dee and Charles Wyly Theater
Seating Capacity: 556
Year Built: 2009
Organization Type: Performing; Touring; Educational

629
DALLAS METROPOLITAN BALLET
6815 Hillcrest Avenue
Dallas, TX 75205
Phone: 214-361-0278
e-mail: dallasballet@msn.com
Web Site: www.dallasmetroballet.com

Officers:
  Founder: Ann Etgen
  Founder: Bill Atkinson
Management:
  Artistic Director: Ann Etgen
  Artistic Director: Bill Atkinson
Mission: The aims and focus of the company have remained consistent, to encourage and support ambitious, talented young dancers pursuing professional careers in ballet and to provide an opportunity for the serious student to continue quality dancing as an avocation.
Utilizes: Choreographers; Dancers; Guest Accompanists; Guest Artists; Original Music Scores
Founded: 1964
Specialized Field: Ballet
Status: Semi-Professional, Nonprofit
Paid Staff: 48
Volunteer Staff: 10
Paid Artists: 8
Non-paid Artists: 14
Income Sources: Ticket Sales; Donations; Grants; Fund Raisers
Performs At: McFarlin Auditorium; Southern Methodist University
Affiliations: Regional Dance America/Southwest
Organization Type: Performing; Touring; Resident; Educational

630
BALLET CONCERTO
3803 Camp Bowie Boulevard
Fort Worth, TX 76107-3355
Phone: 817-989-7168
e-mail: balletconcerto@hotmail.com
Web Site: www.balletconcerto.com
Officers:
  Founder: Margo Dean
  President: Howard Rattliff
  VP: Fielding Chandler
  Treasurer: Lynn Sudbury
  Recording Secretary: Margaret Prud'homme
Management:
  Artistic Director: Margo Dean
  Associate Artistic Director: Webster Dean
  Principal F.I.N.D. Instructor: Caradee Cline
Mission: Ballet Concerto is dedicated to continuing this tradition with a focus on providing lecture, demonstrations and other dance programs to school-aged children.
Utilizes: Guest Artists; Guest Companies; Singers
Founded: 1969
Specialized Field: Ballet
Status: Semi-Professional, Nonprofit
Paid Staff: 2
Volunteer Staff: 5
Paid Artists: 10
Non-paid Artists: 10
Organization Type: Performing

631
CONTEMPORARY DANCE/FORT WORTH
PO Box 11652
Fort Worth, TX 76110
Phone: 817-922-0944
e-mail: cdfw@cdfw.org
Web Site: www.cdfw.org
Officers:
  Founder: Susan Douglas Roberts
Management:
  Artistic Advisor: Susan Douglas Roberts
  Co-Artistic/Executive Director: Kerry Kreiman
  Associate Artistic Director: Tina N. Mullone

Mission: Contemporary Dance/Fort Worth was formed with the mission of promoting and producing modern dance in the Fort Worth and Tarrant County area.
Specialized Field: Modern
Status: Professional
Affiliations: Dance USA

632
TEXAS BALLET THEATER
1540 Mall Circle
Fort Worth, TX 76116
Phone: 817-763-0207
Fax: 817-763-0624
e-mail: margo@texasballettheater.org
Web Site: www.texasballet.org
Officers:
  Chairman: Cary Turner
  Chairman Elect: Courtney Marcus
  Secretary: Denise Mullins
  Treasurer: David Porter
  VP Development: Lisa Grady
Management:
  Artistic Director: Ben Stevenson, O.B.E.
  Associate Artistic Director: Tim O'Keefe
  Managing Director: Margo McCann
  Assistant Artistic Director: Li Anlin
  Principal Ballet Master: Anna Donovan
  Company Manager: Tammy Ballew
  Special Events Manager: Jeanne Cassidy
  Human Resource Manager: Louise Sall
Mission: To bring a world class ballet to North Texas in order to engage in the community, contribute to cultural knowledge and inspire an appreciation for the art of dance; to educate and train the next generation of world class dancers; to encourage creativity; collaboration and expression by creating a nationally recognized environment for dancers and choreographers to develop and showcase their talent.
Founded: 1961
Specialized Field: Ballet; Modern
Status: Professional, Nonprofit
Budget: $5,000,000

633
ALLEGRO BALLET OF HOUSTON
Allegro Academy
12680 Goar Road
Houston, TX 77077
Phone: 281-496-4670
Fax: 281-496-1007
e-mail: info@allegroballetofhouston.com
Web Site: www.allegroballetofhouston.com
Management:
  Artistic Director: Glenda Brown
  Artistic Director: Vanessa Brown
  Teacher: Thom Clower
  Teacher: Carla Capetillo
Mission: Dedicated to offering a performing outlet for gifted dancers by presenting them in performances both at home and abroad in both classical and contemporary repertoire.
Utilizes: Dance Companies; Dancers; Guest Artists; Singers
Founded: 1951
Specialized Field: Classical; Contemporary
Status: Semi-Professional, Nonprofit
Paid Staff: 2
Volunteer Staff: 6
Non-paid Artists: 15
Income Sources: Private Donations
Performs At: Wortham Center
Affiliations: Regional Dance America
Annual Attendance: 10,000
Organization Type: Performing; Resident; Educational

All listings are in alphabetical order by state, then city, then organization within the city.

DANCE / Texas

634
BAY AREA HOUSTON BALLET & THEATRE
PO Box 580466
Houston, TX 77258
Phone: 281-480-1617
e-mail: office@babt.org
Web Site: www.bahbt.org
Officers:
　Founder: Lynette Mason Gregg
　Chairperson: Ellen King
　Vice Chairperson: J.Pamela Culpepper
　Treasurer: Judith Blanchard
　Secretary: Tina Farrell
Management:
　Artistic/Executive Director: Lynette Mason Gregg
　Associate Artistic Director: Heather Steele
Mission: Bay Area Houston Ballet & Theatre strives to enhance cultural awareness through performing arts and develop aspiring performers with diversified performing skills as well as stimulate public participation and regional involvement.
Utilizes: AEA Actors; Artists-in-Residence; Choreographers; Dancers; Designers; Guest Accompanists; Guest Artists; Guest Choreographers; Guest Ensembles; Guest Musicians; High School Drama; Original Music Scores; Resident Professionals
Founded: 1976
Specialized Field: Theatrical Dance
Status: Semi-Professional, Nonprofit
Paid Staff: 10
Volunteer Staff: 200
Paid Artists: 20
Non-paid Artists: 75
Budget: $800,000
Income Sources: Grants; Patrons; Government; Cities; Foundations
Performs At: University of Houston at Clear Lake
Annual Attendance: 11,000
Facility Category: University
Type of Stage: Proscenium
Stage Dimensions: 50'x60'
Seating Capacity: 500
Year Built: 1975
Rental Contact: Tyler Gavin
Organization Type: Performing

635
CHRYSALIS REPERTORY DANCE COMPANY
PO Box 980398
Houston, TX 77098-0398
Phone: 713-661-9855
Fax: 713-664-0643
e-mail: drjsbak@gateway.net
Officers:
　President: Harold Eisenmann
　VP: Elin Grossman, Esquire
　Secretary: Kay Warhol
　Treasurer: Christine Lindall
Management:
　Artistic Associate: Christine Lidvall
　Director: Linda Phenix
Mission: To present innovative, quality dance to enhance Houston and other communities.
Utilizes: Five Seasonal Concerts; Singers
Founded: 1883
Specialized Field: Modern; Post-Modern Dance
Status: Professional; Nonprofit
Paid Staff: 3
Paid Artists: 7+
Budget: $100,000
Income Sources: Individuals; Foundations; Corporations; Performances; Government; Private
Performs At: Heinen Theatre; Houston Community College
Facility Category: Proscenium and Black Box Theaters
Organization Type: Performing; Touring; Resident; Educational; Sponsoring

636
CITY BALLET OF HOUSTON
9902 Long Point Road
Houston, TX 77055
Phone: 713-468-3670
Fax: 713-468-8708
e-mail: mmarshall9902@houston.rr.com
Web Site: www.cityballethouston.com
Management:
　Artistic Director: Margo Marshall
　Artistic Advisor: Dennis Marshall
　Associate Artistic Director: Mary Elizabeth Arrington
Mission: City Ballet of Houston is recognized as a company that brings quality performances to the community and prepares young dancers for professional careers.
Utilizes: Five Seasonal Concerts
Founded: 1958
Specialized Field: Ballet
Status: Semi-Professional, Nonprofit
Volunteer Staff: 10
Paid Artists: 4
Non-paid Artists: 20
Income Sources: Fundraising; Grants; Donations
Performs At: Galveston Grand Opera House; Music Hall
Organization Type: Performing

637
DOMINIC WALSH DANCE THEATER
2311 Dunlavy Street, Suite 210
Houston, TX 77006-1899
Phone: 713-652-3938
e-mail: info@dwdt.org
Web Site: dwdt.org
Mission: DWDT is a Houston-based contemporary ballet company that inspires and entertains audiences and artists with visually stunning performances. Dominic Walsh Dance Theater presents innovative, thought-provoking works by its founder and other leading U.S. and international choreographers.
Founded: 2002
Specialized Field: Contemporary
Organization Type: Performing; Touring

638
HOUSTON BALLET
601 Preston St
Houston, TX 77002
Phone: 713-523-6300
Fax: 713-523-4038
Toll-free: 800-828-2787
e-mail: nutcrackermarket@houstonballet.org
Web Site: www.houstonballet.org
Officers:
　Chairman: Karl S. Stern
　President: James M. Jordan
　Secretary: Russell C. Joseph
Management:
　Artistic Director: Stanton Welch
　Managing Director: Cecil C Conner Jr
　Music Director: Ermanno Florio
　Artistic Coordinator: Kelly Ann Vitacca
　Associate Choreographer: Christopher Bruce
　Production Director: Thomas Boyd
　Ballet Master: Steven Woodgate
　Artistic Director Emeritus: Ben Stevenson, O.B.E.
　Executive Director: James Nelson
Mission: To inspire a lasting love and appreciation for dance through artistic excellence, exhilarating performances, innovative choreography and superb educational programs.
Founded: 1969
Specialized Field: Ballet
Status: Professional, Nonprofit
Budget: $13,000,000
Income Sources: Corporate; Foundation; Individual Contributions
Performs At: Wortham Center for the Performing Arts
Annual Attendance: 250,000
Organization Type: Performing; Touring; Resident; Educational

639
METDANCE
2808 Caroline
PO Box 980457
Houston, TX 77098
Mailing Address: P.O. Box 980457, Houston, TX 77098
Phone: 713-522-6375
Fax: 713-849-2766
Web Site: www.metdance.org
Officers:
　President: Adam Nelson Walker
　Vice President: Janis Hansen Mecklenburg
　Treasurer: Cecilia Winters-Morris
　Secretary: Marcela Arroyave
Management:
　Executive Director: Michelle Smith
　Artistic Director & METtoo Director: Marlana Doyle
　METtoo Director: Kiki Lucas
　METtoo Assistant: Terrill Mitchell
　Stage Manager: Natasha Manley
　Lighting Designer: Kris Phelps
　Stage Manager: Natasha Manley
Mission: To enhance the quality of life for individuals and society through instruction in, and the performance of dance. Committed to the development of dance using movement as a learning tool.
Utilizes: Artists-in-Residence; Choreographers; Collaborations; Dancers; Guest Artists; Guest Choreographers; Guest Ensembles; Guest Speakers; High School Drama; Original Music Scores; Resident Artists; Soloists
Founded: 1995
Specialized Field: Contemporary Dance
Status: Professional; Nonprofit
Paid Staff: 25
Volunteer Staff: 50
Paid Artists: 15
Non-paid Artists: 15
Income Sources: Grants; Foundation; Corporations
Performs At: The Wortham Center
Annual Attendance: 10,000
Organization Type: Performing; Touring; Resident; Educational

640
EARTHEN VESSELS
PO Box 130936
Houston, TX 77219-0936
Phone: 713-701-7798
Fax: 713-222-1426
e-mail: sorgansodc@aol.com
Web Site: www.evsdance.org
Officers:

DANCE / Texas

Founder: Sandra Organ Solis
VP: Nicole Montgomery
Secretary: Mazella Boulden
Board Member: Camille Scott
Board Member: Andis Applewhite
President: Arneita McKinney
Treasurer: Terence Washington
Management:
Artistic Director: Sandra Organ Solis
Mission: To promote contemporary dance, educate the public and attract a diverse audience.
Founded: 1997
Specialized Field: Contemporary Dance

641
IRVING BALLET COMPANY
3333 N McArthur Boulevard
Irving, TX 75062
Phone: 972-717-3926
Fax: 972-254-0802
Web Site: www.irvingartscenter.com
Management:
Artistic Director: Dale Riley
Executive Director: Richard Huff
Assistant Executive Director/Admini: Rosie Meng
Mission: Dedicated to expanding ballet audiences in the Irving area and establishing a permanent base for future dance audiences.
Utilizes: Five Seasonal Concerts; Guest Companies
Founded: 1982
Specialized Field: Ballet; Jazz
Status: Semi-Professional; Professional
Paid Staff: 25
Income Sources: Irving Symphony; Cultural Affairs Council
Performs At: Irving Arts Center
Organization Type: Performing

642
MOMENTUM DANCE COMPANY
4121 Village Green Drive
Irving, TX 75038
Phone: 972-255-2338
e-mail: jaforcher@momentumdancecompany.org
Web Site: www.momentumdancecompany.org
Officers:
President: Jacquelyn Ralls Forcher
VP: Jerry Forcher
Secretary: Maria Lenzen
Board Member: Rose Blake
Board Member: Lorrie Falcone
Management:
Artistic Director: Jacquelyn Ralls Forcher
Mission: The Momentum Dance Company's goal is to bring the highest quality dance to the North Texas area.
Founded: 2005
Specialized Field: Ballet
Status: Nonprofit
Paid Staff: 3
Volunteer Staff: 12
Non-paid Artists: 15
Budget: $47,000
Income Sources: Grants; Donations; Ticket Sales
Performs At: Dance
Affiliations: Irving Arts Center

643
KERRVILLE PERFORMING ARTS SOCIETY
PO Box 291884
Kerrville, TX 78029-1884
Phone: 830-896-5727
e-mail: info@kpas.org
Web Site: www.kpas.org

Officers:
President: Tom Murray
Treasurer: Bettye Warnock
Mission: To promote and present professional level performing artists, to provide outreach workshops to community schools and organizations, and to offer scholarship aid to area students pursuing higher education in the performing arts.
Utilizes: Singers
Founded: 1983
Status: Non-Profit
Income Sources: Tickets; Donations; Sponsorships; Grants
Performs At: Auditorium
Annual Attendance: 10,000
Facility Category: Municipal Auditorium
Seating Capacity: 8000
Organization Type: Performing

644
RIO GRANDE VALLEY BALLET
5240 N Tenth Street
McAllen, TX 78504
Phone: 956-682-2721
Fax: 956-686-7672
e-mail: deborah@dcda.com
Web Site: www.dcda.com
Management:
Artistic Director: Deborah Case
Mission: Dedicated to promoting the enjoyment and art of dance in all its forms in the Rio Grande Valley and all across the State of Texas.
Utilizes: Five Seasonal Concerts; Singers
Founded: 1972
Specialized Field: Ballet; Jazz; Ethnic Dance; Folk Dance
Status: Semi-Professional, Nonprofit
Paid Staff: 10
Volunteer Staff: 30
Paid Artists: 15
Non-paid Artists: 50
Budget: $40,000-$100,000
Organization Type: Performing; Touring; Resident; Educational; Sponsoring

645
PAMPA CIVIC BALLET
315 N Nelson Street
Pampa, TX 79065
Phone: 806-669-6361
Management:
Artistic Director: Jeanne M Willingham
Assistant Director: Glennette Goode
Mission: To provide encouragement and performance opportunities to the more gifted and dedicated dancers in the area.
Utilizes: Choreographers; Community Talent; Dance Companies; Dancers; Five Seasonal Concerts; Guest Accompanists; Guest Artists; Guest Companies; Guest Musicians; Guest Speakers; High School Drama; Instructors; Local Artists; Multimedia; Resident Artists; Singers
Founded: 1972
Specialized Field: Ballet
Status: Non-Professional, Nonprofit
Income Sources: Contributions; Ticket Sales
Performs At: M.K. Brown Auditorium
Annual Attendance: 300
Facility Category: Civic Auditorium
Type of Stage: Proscenium
Stage Dimensions: 51x22
Seating Capacity: 1,200
Organization Type: Performing; Resident; Educational; Sponsoring

646
GUADALUPE DANCE ACADEMY
Guadalupe Cultural Arts Center
1300 Guadalupe Street
San Antonio, TX 78207
Phone: 210-271-3151
Fax: 210-271-3480
e-mail: info@guadalupeculturalarts.org
Web Site: www.guadalupeculturalarts.org
Officers:
Chairman: Sammy Nieto
Treasurer: Fernando Garcia
Management:
Interim Executive Director: Dan Gonzalez
Dance Program Director: Belinda Menchaca
Mission: The mission of the Guadalupe Dance Academy is to preseve, present and promote cultural heritage through traditional and contemporary styles of music and dance.
Founded: 1992
Specialized Field: Folkloric Dance; Flamenco
Status: Professional, Nonprofit
Paid Staff: 23
Budget: $1,700,000
Income Sources: Federal; State; Local; Private
Performs At: Guadalupe Theater
Annual Attendance: 190,000
Type of Stage: Proscenium; Thrust
Seating Capacity: 379
Year Built: 1940
Year Remodeled: 1984
Cost: $1,000,000
Organization Type: Resident

647
TYLER CIVIC BALLET
PO Box 9494
Tyler, TX 75711-0494
Phone: 903-596-0224
e-mail: email@ballettyler.org
Web Site: www.ballettyler.org
Officers:
President: Beth Price
VP: Mary Wright
Treasurer: Monique Dominguez
Secretary: LeAnn Murphy
Management:
Artistic Director: Kym Lanier
Assistant Artistic Director: Jennifer Bailey
Company Director: Shurrell Wiebe
Ballet Director: Patti Patterson
Stage Manager: Ann Russell
Mission: Our mission is to promote education in the art of dance and to provide performing experience and scholarships for promising young dancers in East Texas.
Founded: 1988
Specialized Field: Ballet
Status: Professional, Nonprofit

648
WICHITA FALLS BALLET THEATRE
1501 Midwerstern Parkway
Suite 116
Wichita Falls, TX 76308
Phone: 940-636-2861
e-mail: info@wichitafallsyouthballet.com
Web Site: wichitafallsyouthballet.com
Officers:
President: SueAnn Altman
Vice President: Mary Ferguson
Marketing: Joey Wilson
Board Member: SueAnn Altman

DANCE / Utah

Treasurer: Rebecca Reeves
Secretary: Michael Hicks
Management:
Artistic Director: Gari Boehm
Artistic Director: Patricia Thornton
Development: Chris Marvel Loskot
Mission: Dedicated to the creation of dance repertory and the advancement of the arts for the community.
Utilizes: Singers
Founded: 1963
Specialized Field: Modern; Ballet
Status: Semi-Professional, Nonprofit
Paid Staff: 18
Budget: $120,000
Income Sources: Southwest Regional Ballet Association
Performs At: Memorial Auditorium
Annual Attendance: 80,000
Seating Capacity: 2,717
Organization Type: Performing; Touring; Resident

Utah

649
ODYSSEY DANCE THEATRE
11537 S Berryknoll Circle
Draper, UT 84020
Phone: 801-495-3262
Fax: 801-998-3445
e-mail: avanalstyne@odysseydance.com
Web Site: www.odysseydance.com
Officers:
Treasurer/Secretary: Tori Lima
President & CEO: Derryl Yeager
Board Chair: Lance Schiffman
Management:
Artistic Director: Derryl Yeager
Associate Artistic Directors: Christina Bluth
Executive Director: Annie Van Alstyne
Mission: To provide quality entertainment and artistic excellence in theatrical dance as a professional dance company as well as creating and recreating classical and full length works that are exciting to young and old alike.
Founded: 1994
Specialized Field: Theatrical Dance; Ballet; Jazz
Status: Professional, Nonprofit
Income Sources: Ticket Sales

650
UTAH REGIONAL BALLET
Utah Valley State College
493 N 1030 W
Lindon, UT 84042
Phone: 801-796-7323
e-mail: shauna@jacquelinesballet.com
Web Site: www.utahregionalballet.org
Officers:
President: Ellen Christenson
Treasurer: Lawrence B. Larsen
Secretary: Mandi Winn
Management:
Founder/Artistic Director: Jacqueline P Colledge
Mission: One of the goals of Utah Regional Ballet is to bring world class ballet to Utah audiences as well as those nationally and even abroad.
Founded: 1980
Specialized Field: Ballet
Status: Professional, Nonprofit
Volunteer Staff: 50
Paid Artists: 11
Non-paid Artists: 20
Performs At: Covey Center for the Arts

Annual Attendance: Over 8,000 children
Year Built: 2005
Organization Type: Performing; Touring

651
BALLET WEST
304 Trolley Square
Salt Lake City, UT 84102
Phone: 801-323-6900
Fax: 801-359-3504
e-mail: info@balletwest.org
Web Site: www.balletwest.org
Officers:
Chairman: Victor S. Rickman
Treasurer: Scott M. Huntsman
Secretary: Barbara Clark
Board Member: Dr. Vilija Avizonis
Management:
Artistic Director: Adam Sklute
Executive Director: Scott Altman
Assistant Artistic Director: Nick Mullikin
Principal Ballet Mistress: Pamela Robinson-Harris
Ballet Master: Mark Goldweber
Ballet Master: Bruce Caldwell
Development Director: Denise Begue
Assistant to Executive Director: Pama Rejali
Mission: Dedicated to presenting high quality ballet performances.
Utilizes: Five Seasonal Concerts; Guest Artists; Singers
Founded: 1963
Specialized Field: Ballet
Status: Professional, Non-Profit
Paid Staff: 30
Budget: $6,500,000
Income Sources: Contributions; Ticket Sales
Organization Type: Performing; Touring; Resident; Educational

652
INTERNATIONAL DANCE THEATER
Eastern Arts
PO Box 526362
Salt Lake City, UT 84152
Phone: 801-485-5824
e-mail: kstjohn@burgoyne.com
Web Site: www.easternartists.com
Management:
Artistic Director/Choreographer: Katherine St John
Mission: Presenting traditional dance from many nations and ethnicities.
Founded: 1960
Specialized Field: Ethnic Dance
Status: Professional, Nonprofit
Paid Staff: 10
Income Sources: Western Alliance of Arts Administrators; Society for Ethno-Musicology; Middle East Studies Association; Society for Dance Ethnology
Organization Type: Performing; Educational; Sponsoring

653
REPERTORY DANCE THEATRE
PO Box 510427
Salt Lake City, UT 84151-0427
Phone: 801-534-1000
Fax: 801-534-1110
e-mail: rdt@rdtutah.org
Web Site: www.rdtutah.org
Officers:
President: Jon Daich
Treasurer: Joanna Johnston
Vice President: Hadley Rampton

Secretary: Cynthia Yeo
Management:
Artistic/Executive Director: Linda C Smith
Development Director: David Pace
Director Public Relations, Marketing: Stephanie Perkins
Director Of Education: Lynne Larson
Booking Director: Ricklen Nobis
Bookkeeper: Pamela Smith
Mission: Repertory Dance Theatre is dedicated to the creation, performance, perpetuation and appreciation of modern dance.
Founded: 1966
Specialized Field: Modern
Status: Professional, Non-Profit
Paid Staff: 4
Paid Artists: 9
Budget: $500,000-$1,000,000
Income Sources: Grants; Foundations; Ticket Sales
Organization Type: Performing; Touring; Resident; Educational; Sponsoring

654
RIRIE WOODBURY DANCE COMPANY
138 W Broadway
Salt Lake City, UT 84101
Phone: 801-297-4241
Fax: 801-297-4235
e-mail: info@ririewoodbury.com
Web Site: www.ririewoodbury.com
Officers:
Chairman: Joan Woodbury
Vice Chairman: Rhees Ririe
Secretary: Jeff Paris
President: Joel L. Deaton
Management:
Marketing/Public Relations: Jessica Ballard
Managing Director: Jena Woodbury
Development Director: David Hodges
Artistic Director: Daniel Charon
Director of Education: Gigi Arrington
Director of Marketing/PR: Dennis Busch
Booking Manager: Sara Taylor
Accountant: Phil Falkowski
Mission: Furthers contemporary dance as an accessible and valued art form though performance and dance education that raises the standards, deepens the understanding and promotes personal connections with contemporary dance.
Utilizes: Choreographers; Collaborating Artists; Dancers; Educators; Five Seasonal Concerts; Guest Artists; Guest Companies; Singers; Soloists
Founded: 1964
Specialized Field: Modern
Status: Professional; Nonprofit
Budget: $900,000
Income Sources: Government; Foundations; Corporations
Performs At: The Rose Wagner Performing Arts Center; Capital Theatre
Annual Attendance: 50,000
Organization Type: Performing; Touring; Resident; Educational; Sponsoring

655
CLOG AMERICA
Worldwide Association of Performing Artists
6645 Castleview Drive
West Valley City, UT 84128
Phone: 801-968-2411
Fax: 801-981-8222
e-mail: iae123@comcast.net
Web Site: www.wwapa.org
Officers:

DANCE / Vermont

Founder: Shawnda Bishop
President: Duane Bishop
Management:
  Artistic/Executive Director: Shawnda Bishop
  Assistant Director: Bonnie Romney
Mission: The promotion of clogging workshops, festivals, tours and performances throughout the USA and abroad.
Founded: 1990
Specialized Field: Folk Dance
Status: Semi-Professional, Commercial
Income Sources: Utah Arts Council; National Clogging Leaders Organization
Performs At: Scera Shell Amphitheatre
Organization Type: Performing; Touring; Educational

Vermont

656
BURKLYN BALLET THEATRE
Johnson State College
337 College Hill
Johnson, VT 05656
Mailing Address: P.O. Box 923, Denville, NJ 07834
Phone: 973-625-9300
Fax: 973-625-9304
Toll-free: 877-287-5596
e-mail: info@burklynballet.com
Web Site: www.burklynballet.com
Officers:
  President: James Whitehall
Management:
  Artistic Director: Joanne Whitehill
  Teacher: John Gardner
  Teacher: Arthur Leeth
Mission: Burklyn Ballet Theatre's goal is to bring to the world of dance a program of the highest artistic caliber and give performance opportunities to all participating dancers in a beautiful and safe environment.
Utilizes: Artists-in-Residence; Choreographers; Dancers; Educators; Guest Artists; Guest Ensembles; Guest Musical Directors; Guest Soloists; Guest Speakers; High School Drama; Resident Companies; Scenic Designers; Soloists; Students; Student Interns; Theatre Companies
Founded: 1976
Opened: 1976
Specialized Field: Ballet; Dance
Status: Pre-Professional
Paid Staff: 12
Paid Artists: 20
Non-paid Artists: 55
Budget: $500,000
Income Sources: Box Office; Tuition
Performs At: Dibden Center for the Arts
Affiliations: Burklyn Youth Ballet
Annual Attendance: Jan-00
Type of Stage: Proscenium
Stage Dimensions: 42'x 39'
Seating Capacity: 600
Year Built: 1968
Year Remodeled: 1992
Organization Type: Performing; Touring; Educational

Virginia

657
REV. J. BRUCE STEWART
Center for Literacy and the Arts
4327 Ravensworth Road
Suite 210
Annandale, VA 22003
Phone: 703-584-4750
e-mail: artwithyou@aol.com
Management:
  Artistic/Executive Director: Rev Stewart
Mission: Teaching, performing and consulting services on the use of arts in worship, community building and personal spiritual development.
Founded: 1981
Specialized Field: Dramatic Dance; Storytelling; Mime; Visual Arts

658
ARLINGTON DANCE THEATRE
PO Box 3091
Arlington, VA 22205
Phone: 703-524-4750
e-mail: adt@arlingtondance.org
Web Site: www.arlingtondance.org
Officers:
  President: Andrew Rylyk
  VP: Susan Tyson
  Secretary/Treasurer: Cheryl Scannell
Management:
  Youth Ballet Company Director: Martha Rutter
  Administrative Director: Amanda Smith
  School Director: Ann Kelly
Mission: To promote excellence in the performance and teaching of dance.
Utilizes: Singers
Founded: 1956
Specialized Field: Ballet; Jazz; Tap
Status: Semi-Professional, Nonprofit
Paid Staff: 16
Income Sources: Arlington County Cultural Affairs Office
Performs At: Thomas Jefferson Community Theatre
Organization Type: Performing; Educational

659
JANE FRANKLIN DANCE
3700 S Four Mile Run Drive
Arlington, VA 22206
Phone: 703-933-1111
e-mail: info@janefranklin.com
Web Site: www.janefranklin.com
Officers:
  President: Charlotte Hollister
  Treasurer: Cheryl Stevens
  Secretary: Christina Friedl
  Board Member: Emily Haggerty
Management:
  Artistic Director: Jane Franklin
  Admin. Associate: Abigail Wallace
  Admin. Associate: Kerry Doyle
  Marketing Associate: Alison Waldman
Mission: Jane Franklin Dance celebrates movement and makes dance accessible to a wide range of audiences through public performances, community engagement, dance education and collaborations with artists from other disciplines.
Founded: 1997
Specialized Field: Movement; Educational Dance; Traditional Dance
Status: Professional, Nonprofit
Paid Staff: 3
Volunteer Staff: 15
Budget: $65,000
Income Sources: Government; Foundations; Individual
Performs At: The Gunston Theatre
Annual Attendance: 9,000
Organization Type: Performing; Touring; Educational

660
VIRGINIA BALLET COMPANY
5595 Guinea Road
Fairfax, VA 22032
Phone: 703-249-8227
e-mail: virginia@virginiaballetcompany.org
Web Site: virginiaballetcompany.org
Officers:
  Chief Executive Officer: Tish Cordova
  President: Robert Mirabello
  Vice President: Terrance Walsh
  Treasurer: Barbara Mirabello
  Secretary: Colleen Stockmann
Management:
  Artistic Director: Tish Cordova
Mission: To enhance the cultural interests of Northern Virginia and the Metropolitan area through the institution of a ballet school that performs and brings an artistic force to the community, adding a dimension to the education of the community's youth.
Specialized Field: Ballet
Status: Nonprofit
Organization Type: Educational; Performing

661
HAMPTON ROADS CIVIC BALLET
Academy of Ballet
4218 Victoria Boulevard
Hampton, VA 23669
Phone: 757-722-8216
e-mail: info@hrcivicballet.org
Web Site: www.hamptonroadscivicballet.com
Officers:
  Founder: Muriel Shelley Evans
  President: Karen Page
  VP: Paula Hogg
  Treasurer: Debbie Scott
  Secretary: Frances Brown
Management:
  Artistic Director: Muriel Shelley Evans
Mission: Provides students with differing goals the opportunity to grow artistically and technically in a supportive, dynamic environment.
Founded: 1959
Specialized Field: Ballet
Status: Professional, Nonprofit
Organization Type: Performing; Resident; Educational

662
LOUDOUN BALLET COMPANY
PO Box 916
Leesburg, VA 20178
Phone: 703-771-1522
e-mail: info@loudounballet.org
Web Site: www.loudounballet.org
Officers:
  Founder: Sheila Hoffmann-Robertson
  Chairman: Steve Spaseff
  Treasurer: Cherilynne Pipert
  Secretary: Sarah Etro
  Vice Chairman: Mark Nachajski
Management:
  Artistic Director: Maureen Miller
  Ballet Mistress: Caitlin Jordan
Mission: The Loudoun Ballet Company's purpose is to support a professional dance company and offer a performing season for the Loudoun community.
Founded: 1978
Specialized Field: Ballet
Status: Professional, Nonprofit

DANCE / Virginia

663
DANCE THEATRE OF LYNCHBURG
722 Commerce Street
Lynchburg, VA 24504
Phone: 434-846-6272
e-mail: info@dancelynchburg.org
Web Site: dancelynchburg.org
Management:
  Artistic Director: Keith Lee
Mission: To share and spread the joy, passion and understanding of classical and contemporary dance with all interested students, supporters, and the community at large and to transcend any and all financial, cultural or other barriers to achieve these goals.
Founded: 1999

664
MALINI'S DANCES OF INDIA TROUPE
1510 Bordeaux Place
Norfolk, VA 23509
Phone: 757-533-5594
Fax: 757-533-4616
e-mail: malinidance@hotmail.com
Web Site: www.danceofindia.org
Management:
  Artistic Director: Malini Srirama
  Choreographer: Bharatha Natyam
Mission: The programs have been crafted to offer western audiences an understanding of the historical background and cultural development of India's art forms.also provides instructional classes in Virginia and Bangalore, India.
Specialized Field: Ethnic Dance/Cultural Indonesian Dance
Status: Professional, Nonprofit
Volunteer Staff: 7
Income Sources: Donors

665
MALINI'S DANCES OF INDIA
Malini's Dances of India Troupe
1510 Bordeaux Place
Norfolk, VA 23509
e-mail: malinidance@hotmail.com
Web Site: www.dancesofindia.org
Management:
  Dancer/Choreographer/Teacher: Bharatha Natyam
Mission: Malini Srirama and Malini's Dances of India, her classical Indian dance troupe, provides instructional classes in Virginia and in Bangalore, India.
Utilizes: Choreographers; Collaborations; Dancers; Educators; Fine Artists; Scenic Designers; Soloists
Specialized Field: Cultural Indonesian Dance
Status: Non-Profit
Income Sources: Donors

666
THEATRE ARTS DANCE PROGRAM
Old Dominion University
5115 Hampton Boulevard
Norfolk, VA 23529
Mailing Address: 1 Old Dominion University, Norfolk, VA 23529
Phone: 757-683-3000
Fax: 757-683-6098
e-mail: mmarloff@odu.edu
Web Site: www.odu.edu
Officers:
  President: John R Broderick
Management:
  Artistic Director: Marilyn Marloff
Mission: Focuses on intellectual understanding of the systems of motion, performance opportunities for creative expression and collaborative efforts that create synergy.
Specialized Field: Ballet; Jazz; Modern
Status: Nonprofit

667
VIRGINIA BALLET THEATRE
Virginia Ballet Academy
134 W Olney Road
Norfolk, VA 23510
Phone: 757-622-4822
Fax: 757-622-7904
e-mail: virginiaballettheatre@gmail.com
Web Site: www.virginiaballettheatre.com
Officers:
  President: Angela Martin Blackwell
  Treasurer: Gregory French
  Secretary: Michael Morisi
Management:
  Artistic Director: Jurijs Safonovs
  Executive Director: Thom Prevette
Mission: Professional ballet dance theatre bringing dance and dance education to Virginia and beyond.
Founded: 1961
Specialized Field: Ballet
Status: Non-Professional, Nonprofit
Paid Staff: 4
Volunteer Staff: 20
Paid Artists: 20
Organization Type: Performing; Resident

668
THE CONCERT BALLET OF VIRGINIA
Box 25501
Richmond, VA 23260
Phone: 804-798-0945
e-mail: concertballetofvirginia@yahoo.com
Web Site: www.concertballet.com
Officers:
  President: Susan McCoy
  VP: Kim Gangloff
  Treasurer: Amy Christopher
  Board Member: Susan Daly
  Board Member: Lucy Smith
  Corresponding Secretary: Lynn Fellenstein
  Recording Secretary: Stacie Baird
Management:
  Artistic Director: Robert Watkins
  Artistic Director: Scott Boyer
  Executive Director: Eleanor Rennie
  Production Manager: Tim Ryder
  Designer & Technical Director: Riddick deVeaux
  Crew Coordinator: Elizabeth Gosack-Fleming
  Wardrobe Coordinator: Kim Gangloff
Mission: To foster an appreciation of classical and contemporary dance by staging affordable productions at convenient locations throughout the state, while providing excellent training and challenging creative opportunities within a professional dance company.
Utilizes: Five Seasonal Concerts; Guest Artists
Founded: 1976
Specialized Field: Classical; Contemporary Dance
Status: Professional, Nonprofit
Paid Staff: 15
Income Sources: Fundraising; Foundations; Individual
Performs At: The Woman's Club Auditorium; Blackwell Auditorium
Organization Type: Performing; Touring; Educational

669
K DANCE
10601 Three Chopt Road
Richmond, VA 23233
Phone: 804-270-4944
Fax: 804-282-2301
e-mail: kdanceinc@gmail.com
Web Site: kdance.org
Management:
  Artistic Director: Kaye Weinstein Gary
Mission: This professional dance company presents concerts, lectures and educational residencies for the purpose of educating and informing the public about the art of dance, particularly contemporary modern dance and theatre. K Dance focuses on the creative process of dance, both in its educational programs and in developing concerts for the viewing public.
Specialized Field: Contemporary; Modern
Status: Nonprofit; Professional
Organization Type: Educational; Performing

670
RICHMOND BALLET
407 E Canal Street
Richmond, VA 23219
Phone: 804-344-0906
Fax: 804-344-0903
e-mail: smckinney@richmondballet.com
Web Site: www.richmondballet.com
Officers:
  Chairman: Selina Rainey
  President: Donna Ransone
  Vice President: Donald E. Steeber
  Treasurer: Kathleen Holman
  Secretary: Kathleen Luke
Management:
  Artistic Director: Stoner Winslett
  Operations Director: Sue McKinney
  Artistic Associate/Ballet Master: Malcolm Burn
  Ballet Master: Jerri Kumery
  Resident Artist: Igor Antonov
  Development Director: Susan Coogan
  Marketing/Communications Director: Aaron Sutten
  Managing Director: Brett Bonda
  Operations Director: Sue McKinney
Mission: Dedicated to the promotion, preservation and continuing evolution of the art form of ballet according to specific aesthetic and institutional values established by the vision of the artistic director.
Utilizes: Choreographers; Commissioned Music; Dance Companies; Dancers; Five Seasonal Concerts; Grant Writers; Guest Artists; Guest Companies; Guest Conductors; Original Music Scores
Founded: 1957
Specialized Field: Ballet
Status: Professional, Nonprofit
Paid Artists: 19
Budget: $2,500,000
Organization Type: Performing; Touring; Resident; Educational

671
VIRGINIA SCHOOL OF THE ARTS
Virginia University
1315 Floyd Avenue
PO Box 843007
Richmond, VA 23284
Phone: 804-828-0100
Fax: 804-828-7356
e-mail: dance@vcu.edu
Web Site: www.vcu.edu
Officers:

Chair: Richard E Toscan
Secretary: Kamlesh N. Dave
Management:
   Assistant Professor: Lea Marshall
   Senior Executive Director: Brian Shaw
Mission: Offers a vibrant, stimulating atmosphere where students are prepared for careers in the field of dance.
Founded: 1981
Specialized Field: Educational Dance; Theatrical Dance
Paid Staff: 6
Paid Artists: 24
Affiliations: NASD; CODA
Annual Attendance: 9,167
Facility Category: Theater
Seating Capacity: 225
Year Built: 1934
Year Remodeled: 1996
Rental Contact: Grace Street Theater House Manager Cynthia Theakston

672
MUSIC IN MOTION
629 N Lynnhaven Road
Virginia Beach, VA 23452
Phone: 757-340-1534
e-mail: dsdancer1@yahoo.com
Web Site: www.musicinmotionva.com
Management:
   Artistic Director: Darlene Stephens
Mission: Music in Motion® has an ongoing program of performances with public school systems and young audiences in Virginia.
Founded: 1987
Specialized Field: Ballet; Modern; Jazz
Status: Pre-Professional
Annual Attendance: 750

673
WILLIAMSBURG BALLET THEATRE
Institute for Dance
3356 Ironbound Road
Suite 501
Williamsburg, VA 23188
Phone: 757-229-1717
Fax: 757-229-4953
e-mail: bygorman@gmail.com
Web Site: www.institutefordance.org
Officers:
   Founder: Heidi Robitshek
   Board Member: John Thompson
   VP: Kate Gunter
   Treasurer: Kimberley Smith
   Secretary: Lori Gronbeck
   Board Member: Kathy Palmo
Management:
   Artistic Director: Kristine Antis
   Studio Director/Instructor: Kathy Martin-Palmo
   President: Heather Pedersen
Mission: Our mission is to bring cultural enrichment to Williamsburg and surrounding areas by presenting to our audiences professional quality performances.
Founded: 1968
Specialized Field: Ballet
Status: Nonprofit

Washington

674
VELA LUKA CROATIAN DANCE ENSEMBLE
PO Box 635
Anacortes, WA 98221
Phone: 360-299-2525
e-mail: info@velaluka.org
Web Site: www.velaluka.org
Management:
   Executive Director: Maria Franulovic Petrish
   Artistic Director: Maria Planich Kesovija
   Director: Alma Planich
Mission: The Vela Luka Croatian Dance Ensemble, founded in 1975, perform music and dance of Croatia and the United States. The performers in Vela Luka represent four generations of Croatian Americans who have introduced their culture's extraordinary choreography, music, and instruments to people all over the world. Forming a cross-cultural link between the Puget Sound region and Croatia, the company strives to preserve Croatian folkways.
Utilizes: Arrangers; Choreographers; Collaborating Artists; Collaborations; Dancers; Guest Directors; Multimedia; Music; Original Music Scores; Paid Performers
Founded: 1975
Specialized Field: Dance of Croatia
Status: Profit
Income Sources: Paid Performances
Season: Year Round

675
PENINSULA DANCE THEATRE
515 Chester Avenue
Bremerton, WA 98377
Phone: 360-377-6214
e-mail: pdtpresident@gmail.com
Web Site: www.peninsuladancetheatre.org
Officers:
   President: Scott Dempski
Management:
   Artistic Director: Lawan Morrison
   Junior Company Assistant Director: Diana Lau
   Music Director: Alan Futterman
   Assistant Director: Mallory Morrison
Mission: Peninsula Dance Theatre is dedicated to furthering classical and contemporary forms of dance in the Kitsap county region.
Founded: 1973
Specialized Field: Classical; Contemporary Dance
Status: Professional, Nonprofit
Performs At: Win Graulund Performing Arts Center
Organization Type: Performing; Resident

676
OLYMPIC BALLET THEATRE
Olympic Ballet School
700 Main Street
Edmonds, WA 98020
Phone: 425-774-7570
Fax: 425-672-1152
e-mail: dance@olympicballet.com
Web Site: www.olympicballet.com
Officers:
   Founder: Helen Wilkins
   Founder: John Wilkins
Management:
   Artistic Director: Mara Vinson
   Artistic Director: Oleg Gorboulev
   Administration/Marketing: Nancy Gottwald
Mission: Olympic Ballet Theatre seeks to develop and sustain professional dance, promote dance as a creative performing art and engage the widest possible audience with a stimulating repertoire of classical contemporary and dramatic ballets.
Utilizes: Singers
Founded: 1981
Specialized Field: Ballet
Status: Semi-Professional, Nonprofit
Paid Staff: 21
Budget: $200,000-$500,000
Performs At: The Moore Theatre; Everett Performing Arts Center
Organization Type: Resident

677
ARIA DANCE COMPANY
9th Avenue Performing Arts Center
33639 Ninth Avenue South
Federal Way, WA 98003
Phone: 253-242-3296
e-mail: aria@ninthavenuedance.com
Web Site: www.ariadancecompany.org
Officers:
   President: Martha Lawson
   VP: Carol Karalus
   Treasurer: Guy Pittman
   Secretary: Susan Rao
Management:
   Artistic/Executive Director: Christina Vandenberg-Suju
   Teacher: Laura Chang
   Teacher: Tesse George
   Teacher: Ula Jun
Mission: Aria is dedicated to helping dancers achieve self-discipline and artistic expression through dance.
Founded: 1996
Specialized Field: Ballet; Modern; Jazz; Folk; Character Dance
Status: Nonprofit

678
EVERGREEN CITY BALLET
2230 Lind Avenue SW, Suite 109
Renton, WA 98057
Phone: 425-228-6800
Fax: 425-228-0478
e-mail: info@evergreencityballet.org
Web Site: evergreencityballet.org
Officers:
   President: Keith Cline
   Vice President: Christopher Ferris
   Secretary: Wendy Kirchner
Management:
   Artistic/Executive Director: Kevin Kaiser
   Administrator: Sue Stevens
Mission: To provide the highest quality performances for audiences in the Puget Sound region, while developing dancers and educating a diverse public and its youth in the art of dance.
Founded: 1994
Specialized Field: Ballet
Status: Nonprofit

679
CHAMBER DANCE COMPANY
University of Washington
Box 351150
Seattle, WA 98195-1150
Phone: 206-543-4882
Fax: 206-685-2759
Web Site: www.meany.org
Officers:
   Founder: Hannah C Wiley

DANCE / Washington

Management:
- **Managing Director:** Rita Calabro
- **Director of Patron Services:** Rosa Alvarez
- **Director Finance, Administration:** Scott Coil
- **Technical Director:** Tom Burke
- **Audience Services Manager:** Nancy Hautala
- **Director Marketing, Communications:** Teri Mumme
- **Director of Philanthropy:** Cristi Benefield

Mission: The Chamber Dance Company's mission is to present and record works of historical and artistic significance.
Founded: 1990
Specialized Field: Educational Dance; Theatrical Dance
Status: Professional
Paid Artists: 6

680
DANCE PROGRAM
University of Washington
Box 351150
Seattle, WA 98195-1150
Phone: 206-543-0550
Fax: 206-543-8610
e-mail: uwdance@uw.edu
Web Site: dance.washington.edu
Management:
- **Marketing & Com Manager:** Kris Bain
- **Lecturer, Staff Musician:** Paul Moore
- **Production Manager:** Peter Bracilano
- **Academic Counselor:** George Kenneth Morell
- **Administrator:** Risa Morgan-Lewellyn

Mission: The mission of the University of Washington Dance Program is to educate performers, educators, arts advocates and cultural leaders.
Specialized Field: Ballet; Modern
Status: Professional, Nonprofit
Paid Staff: 10
Paid Artists: 30
Income Sources: University of Washington; Private; Corporations; Foundations
Performs At: Meany Hall
Organization Type: Sponsoring; Presenting

681
OCHEAMI AFRICAN DANCE COMPANY
PO Box 31635
Seattle, WA 98103
Phone: 206-329-8876
e-mail: ocheami@earthlink.net
Web Site: www.ocheami.org
Officers:
- **Founder:** Amma Anang
- **Founder:** Kofi Anang

Management:
- **Artistic Director:** Kofi Anang
- **Manager:** Amma Anang

Mission: Ocheami's purpose is to share West African culture by providing authentic, quality instruction and performances in African Arts and to have these experiences accessible to all.
Utilizes: Five Seasonal Concerts
Founded: 1978
Specialized Field: Historical Dance; African Dance
Status: Professional, Nonprofit
Organization Type: Performing; Touring; Educational

682
PACIFIC NORTHWEST BALLET
Pacific Northwest Ballet School
301 Mercer Street
Seattle, WA 98109
Phone: 206-441-9411
Fax: 206-441-2420
e-mail: tickets@pnb.org
Web Site: www.pnb.org
Officers:
- **Chairman:** Aya Hamilton
- **President:** David Hadley
- **Treasurer:** W Daniel Heidt
- **Secretary:** Lynn Lindsay

Management:
- **Artistic Director:** Peter Boal
- **Executive Director:** David Brown
- **Music Director:** Stewart Kershaw
- **Ballet Master:** Otto Neubert
- **Ballet Master:** Anne Dabrowski
- **Ballet Master:** Paul Gibson
- **Technical Director:** Norbert Herriges
- **Resident Lighting Designer:** Randall G. Chiarelli
- **Costume Shop Manager:** Larae Theige Hascall

Mission: Dedicated to maintaining a professional ballet company and school.
Utilizes: Choreographers; Collaborations; Commissioned Composers; Commissioned Music; Dancers; Designers; Educators; Fine Artists; Five Seasonal Concerts; Grant Writers; Guest Accompanists; Guest Artists; Guest Companies; Guest Conductors; Guest Ensembles; Guest Musical Directors; Guest Musicians; Guest Writers; High School Drama; Instructors; Lyricists; Multimedia; New Productions; Organization Contracts; Original Music Scores; Poets; Resident Professionals; Singers; Soloists; Student Interns
Founded: 1974
Specialized Field: Ballet
Status: Professional, Nonprofit
Paid Artists: 51
Budget: $12,000,000
Performs At: The McCaw Hall
Organization Type: Performing; Touring; Resident

683
THE PAT GRANEY COMPANY
PO Box 22868
Seattle, WA 98122-0868
Phone: 206-329-3705
Fax: 206-329-3730
e-mail: staff@patgraney.org
Web Site: www.patgraney.org
Officers:
- **Founder:** Pat Graney

Management:
- **Artistic/Executive Director:** Pat Graney

Mission: The mission of the Pat Graney Company is to create and perform new dance and performance works and to conduct arts education programming.
Utilizes: Collaborating Artists; Dancers; Designers; Educators; Guest Companies; Instructors; Local Artists; Multimedia; Original Music Scores; Student Interns
Founded: 1990
Specialized Field: Contemporary Dance
Status: Professional, Nonprofit
Volunteer Staff: 10
Paid Artists: 5
Budget: $200,000
Income Sources: Individual Donors; Foundations; Corporate Grants

684
THE RADOST FOLK ENSEMBLE
PO Box 31295
Seattle, WA 98103
Phone: 206-860-5251
e-mail: info@radost.org
Web Site: www.radost.org
Officers:
- **Founding Artistic Director:** Glenn Nielsen
- **President:** Ramona Wijayratne
- **Board of Trustee:** Tom Deering
- **Board of Trustee:** Lori Linenko

Management:
- **Co-Director:** Sidney Deering
- **Finance Director:** Margo Reich
- **Artistic Director:** Sidney Deering

Mission: Radost Folk Ensemble is an ethnic dance company dedicated to teaching, preserving and presenting the dance traditions of Eastern Europe.
Utilizes: Scenic Designers; Sign Language Translators; Singers; Students; Theatre Companies
Founded: 1976
Specialized Field: Ethnic Dance; Eastern Europe Dance
Status: Semi-Professional, Nonprofit
Paid Staff: 1
Volunteer Staff: 4
Paid Artists: 8
Non-paid Artists: 12
Budget: $20,000
Income Sources: Touring Concerts; Teaching; Grants; Private Donations
Organization Type: Performing; Touring; Educational; Sponsoring

685
SEATTLE EARLY DANCE
2366 Eastlake Avenue E. Suite #335
Seattle, WA 98102-3399
Phone: 206-528-1605
e-mail: info@seattleearlydance.org
Web Site: seattleearlydance.org
Management:
- **Artistic Director:** Anna Mansbridge

Mission: This dance company is dedicated to presenting dances that reflect the styles of European Courts between the 16th and 18th centuries. Dances are performed in elaborate costumes based on historical designs.

686
SPECTRUM DANCE THEATER
800 Lake Washington Blvd
Seattle, WA 98122
Phone: 206-325-4161
Fax: 206-325-3056
e-mail: staff@spectrumdance.org
Web Site: spectrumdance.org
Officers:
- **President:** Barbara Lewis
- **Vice President:** Kathy Lindenmayer
- **Secretary:** JoAnna Lau
- **Treasurer:** Steve Fellows
- **Director:** Anthony DiSalvo
- **Director:** Patricia Conover
- **Director:** Kathy Lindenmayer

Management:
- **Artistic Director:** Donald Byrd
- **Executive Director:** Susie Purves
- **Schhol Programs Director:** Shawn Roberts
- **Studio Manager:** Shirley Wong
- **Company/Production Manager:** Krina Turner
- **Communications Manager:** Van Diep
- **Development Coordinator:** Hayley Shannon
- **Interim Marketing Manager:** Katherine Spink

Mission: Spectrum Dance Theater's mission is: to produce and present contemporary dance of global caliber that challenges expectations and calls forth strong emotions, deep feelings and thoughtful responses, to provide expert dance instruction in

DANCE / West Virginia

diverse dance forms to all, to educate the community about dance as an art form and as a social/civic instrument.
Utilizes: Arrangers; Choreographers; Collaborating Artists; Collaborations; Community Talent; Dance Companies; Dancers; High School Drama; Lyricists; Multimedia; Music; Soloists; Special Technical Talent
Founded: 2002
Specialized Field: Contemporary Dance
Status: Non-Profit
Income Sources: Donations, Sponsors, Sales
Season: October through June
Performs At: DeBartolo Performing Arts Center, Texas Performing Arts, Redfern Arts Center, Cascia Performing Arts Center

687
PIONEER DANCE ARTS
172 Bell Meadow Lane
PO Box 238
Sequim, WA 98382
Phone: 360-683-3693
e-mail: mpirouette@earthlink.net
Officers:
  Secretary: Stacey Forshaw
  Treasurer: Kathy Clark
Management:
  Academy Director: Kathleen Moore
Mission: The mission of the company is to raise the dance art awareness on the North Olympic Penninsula.
Utilizes: Five Seasonal Concerts
Founded: 1974
Specialized Field: Classical Ballet; Modern; Contemporary Jazz; Tap
Status: Non-Professional, Nonprofit
Volunteer Staff: 100
Performs At: Port Angeles High School Auditorium
Organization Type: Performing; Resident; Educational; Sponsoring

688
FILIPINIANA DANCE COMPANY
569 N 166th Street
Shoreline, WA 98133
Phone: 206-542-7245
e-mail: rogervidal2005@yahoo.com
Officers:
  Founder/President: Roger Del Rosario
Management:
  Director: Roger Del Rosario
Mission: Traditional Filipino dance group that combines rich pageantry, elegant costumes, music and dance to create an exciting intermingling of very different cultures.
Utilizes: Five Seasonal Concerts; Singers
Founded: 1969
Specialized Field: Philippino Dance
Status: Semi-Professional, Nonprofit
Volunteer Staff: 30
Non-paid Artists: 50
Budget: $25,000
Income Sources: Festivals
Performs At: Shoreline Arts Center
Annual Attendance: 10,000
Organization Type: Performing; Touring; Resident; Educational; Sponsoring

689
TACOMA CITY BALLET
508 6th Avenue
Tacoma, WA 98402
Phone: 253-272-4219
Fax: 253-572-5624
e-mail: tcb@tacomacityballet.com
Web Site: www.tacomacityballet.com
Officers:
  Chairman: John Hodder
Management:
  Artistic Director: Erin M Ceragioli
  Executive Director: Nikki Smith
  Administrator: Leah Taff
  Ballet Mistress: Melissa Lovejoy Goldman
  Assistant Artistic Director: Joel Myers
Mission: To provide quality, fully-staged classical ballets for the Southern Puget Sound area.
Founded: 1955
Specialized Field: Ballet
Status: Semi-Professional
Paid Staff: 20
Income Sources: National Association for Regional Ballet; Pacific Regional Ballet Association
Performs At: Pantages Theater
Organization Type: Performing

690
TACOMA PERFORMING DANCE COMPANY
Jo Emery Ballet School
5212 D S Washington Street
Tacoma, WA 98409
Phone: 253-627-8272
e-mail: jo@joemeryballet.com
Web Site: www.tacomaperformingdance.org
Officers:
  Founder: Jo Emery
  President: Bernie Plancich
  VP: Sarah Heckman
  Treasurer: Helene Cox
  Secretary: Tom Kimpel
Management:
  Artistic Director: Jo Emery
Mission: The mission of Tacoma Performing Dance Company is to provide outstanding, versatile dance presentations to the greater south Puget Sound region at an affordable price for the enjoyment of all.
Utilizes: Guest Companies
Founded: 1967
Specialized Field: Modern; Ballet; Jazz
Status: Semi-Professional, Nonprofit
Performs At: Pantages Centre
Organization Type: Performing; Touring; Resident

691
NEXT STAGE DANCE THEATRE
PO Box 283
Tracyton, WA 98398
e-mail: info@nextstagedance.org
Web Site: nextstagedance.org
Officers:
  President: Michael Thatcher
  Vice President: Shirley Wong
  Secretary: Sherene Huntzinger
  Treasurer: Dominique Gabella
  Trustee: Evelyn Thatcher
Management:
  Artistic Director/Founder: Dominique Gabella
  Lighting Designer: Gwen Maksym
  Costume Designer: Val Mayse
  Rehearsal Director: Vacant
  Public Relations Coordinator: Sylvie Lytart
  Fundraising/Grant Writer: Anne Durieux
Mission: Next Stage Dance Theatre inspires people to recognize creativity in life, through performances and partnerships. Provides an arena for mature dancers to express themselves. Inspire audiences to accept life changes with grace. Connects people of all ages, cultures and conditions through performances and partnerships.
Utilizes: Choreographers; Collaborating Artists; Collaborations; Dancers; Designers; Lyricists; Paid Performers
Founded: 1985
Specialized Field: Modern, Contemporary
Status: Non-Profit, Professional
Income Sources: Fundraisers, Donors, Grants
Season: Year Round
Performs At: Dance Fremont Studio

West Virginia

692
WEST VIRGINIA DANCE COMPANY
110 Ellison Avenue
Beckley, WV 25801
Phone: 304-252-0030
e-mail: info@wvdanceco.com
Web Site: wvdanceco.com
Management:
  Managing Artistic Director: Toneta Akers-Toler
  Producing Artistic Director: Donald Laney
Mission: We're empowering students through the art of dance, with the truth that they are born with great imaginations that can produce creativity and shape innovative artists.
Founded: 1977
Specialized Field: Modern
Status: Nonprofit
Organization Type: Educational; Performing

693
THE CHARLESTON BALLET
100 Capital Street
Suite 302
Charleston, WV 25301
Phone: 304-342-6541
e-mail: info@thecharlestonballet.com
Web Site: www.thecharlestonballet.com
Management:
  Artistic Director/CEO: Kim R Pauley
  Office Manager: Elaine Baldwin
  Development: Harry Mills
  Production: Becky Tulley
Mission: To present ballet concerts for professional and talented young dancers.
Utilizes: Artists-in-Residence; Collaborating Artists; Collaborations; Composers; Contract Orchestras; Dancers; Educators; Filmmakers; Grant Writers; Guest Accompanists; Guest Artists; Guest Choreographers; Guest Ensembles; Guest Speakers; Instructors; Local Talent; Organization Contracts; Original Music Scores; Students
Founded: 1956
Specialized Field: Modern; Ballet; Contemporary
Status: Semi-Professional, Nonprofit
Paid Staff: 3
Volunteer Staff: 20
Paid Artists: 20
Non-paid Artists: 30
Season: October-March
Performs At: Charleston Civic Center Theater; Maier Performance Hall at Clay Center; Walker Theater at Clay Center
Organization Type: Performing; Touring

DANCE / Wisconsin

694

MID OHIO VALLEY BALLET COMPANY
Nash School
1311 Ann Street
PO Box 4204
Parkersburg, WV 26101
Mailing Address: P.O. Box 4204, Parkersburg, WV 26104
Phone: 304-422-5538
Fax: 304-422-6730
Toll-free: 800-882-1148
e-mail: movdance@suddenlink.net
Web Site: www.movballet.com
Management:
   Artistic Director: Suzy Gunter
   Executive Director: Norma J Gunter
   Music Director: Joy Held
   Educational Director: Terry Donne Gunter
   Artistic Advisor: Mark Jelks
   Artistic Advisor: Brian Palmer
Mission: Mid Ohio Valley Ballet is dedicated to quality performances, training and education and the preservation of classical ballet.
Founded: 1994
Specialized Field: Ballet; Modern
Status: Professional, Nonprofit
Paid Staff: 6
Budget: $1,000,000-$2,500,000
Income Sources: Artsbridge
Season: October-May

695

APPALACHIAN YOUTH JAZZ-BALLET COMPANY
605 D Street
South Charleston, WV 25303
Phone: 304-343-1076
Toll-free: 800-409-4646
Officers:
   President: Ricklin Brown
   VP: John Breed
   Secretary: Catherine Halloran
   Treasurer: Carol Velasquez
Management:
   Artistic Director: Nina Denton
Mission: To provide talented aspiring dancers liaisons between the classroom and the professional stage; to enrich the community through concerts and lecture demonstrations; to provide inspiration to youngsters in the audience.
Founded: 1982
Specialized Field: Ballet; Jazz
Status: Nonprofit
Paid Staff: 2
Income Sources: Washington Community Education
Performs At: Charleston Civic Center; Municipal Auditorium
Organization Type: Performing; Touring; Educational

Wisconsin

696

DANCE PROGRAM
University of Wisconsin
1050 University Avenue
Lathrop Hall
Madison, WI 53706
Phone: 608-262-1691
Fax: 608-265-3841
e-mail: uwdance@education.wisc.edu
Web Site: www.dance.wisc.edu
Officers:
   Dean: Julie K Underwood
Management:
   Professor: Jin-Wen Yu
   Professor: Li Chiao-Ping
   Professor/Music Director: Joseph N Koykkar
   Academic Department Associate: Jill Carlsen
Mission: To create and maintain high standards for dance in the Midwest and to bring quality modern dance to the largest public eye possible.
Utilizes: Singers
Founded: 1985
Specialized Field: Modern
Status: Professional, Nonprofit
Paid Staff: 1
Income Sources: University of Wisconsin-Madison
Organization Type: Performing; Touring

697

KANOPY DANCE COMPANY
341 State Street
Madison, WI 53703
Phone: 608-255-2211
e-mail: info@kanopydance.org
Web Site: www.kanopydance.org
Officers:
   President: Suzanne Voeltz
   VP: Richard Zillman
   Treasurer: Sue Gardner
   Secretary: Chuck Hahn
Management:
   Artistic Director/Choreographer: Lisa Andrea Thurrell
   Artistic Director/Choreographer: Robert E Cleary
Mission: To promote, encourage and increase the public's knowledge of and appreciation for the arts including the art of dance.
Utilizes: Singers
Founded: 1976
Specialized Field: Modern; Jazz
Status: Professional
Income Sources: Wisconsin Dance Council
Season: November-May
Performs At: Kanopy Studio; Wisconsin Union Theatre
Organization Type: Performing; Touring; Resident; Educational; Sponsoring

698

MADISON SCOTTISH COUNTRY DANCERS
318 South Owen Dr
Madison, WI 53705
Phone: 608-232-0512
e-mail: Madison_Scottish_Country_Dancers@yahoogroups.com
Web Site: sprott.physics.wisc.edu
Officers:
   Chair: Nancy McClements
   Treasurer: Dyan Steenport
   Secretary: Kate Deck
Management:
   Teacher: Norma Briggs
   Teacher: Chuck Snowdon
Mission: Madison Scottish Country Dancers is a social group that enjoys learning and dancing the traditional reels, jigs and strathspeys of Scotland.
Founded: 1977
Specialized Field: Ethnic Dance
Status: Non-Professional, Nonprofit
Paid Staff: 60
Income Sources: Royal Scottish Country Dance Society (Scotland)
Performs At: University of Wisconsin; Memorial Union
Organization Type: Performing; Educational

699

MM COLBERT
1321 E Johnson Street
Madison, WI 53703
Phone: 608-257-9807
Officers:
   Chairperson: Nancy Idaka Sheran
Management:
   Director/Choreographer: MM Colbert
Mission: To present original modern ballets in collaboration with other living artists.
Utilizes: Singers
Founded: 1980
Specialized Field: Modern; Ballet; Jazz
Status: Nonprofit
Organization Type: Performing

700

TAPIT/NEW WORKS ENSEMBLE THEATER
1957 Winnebago Street
Madison, WI 53704
Phone: 608-244-2938
Fax: 608-244-9114
e-mail: info@tapitnewworks.org
Web Site: www.tapitnewworks.org
Officers:
   President: Steve Holtzman
   Treasurer: Larry Lundy
   Vice President: Mary Beth Gaffney
   Acting Secretary: Kim Baker
Management:
   Producing Artistic Director: Danielle Dresden
   Producing Artistic Director: Donna Peckett
   Treasurer: Larry Lundy
Mission: Creates, produces and performs original works, collaborating with artists working in the disciplines of theater, tap dance, visual arts and music; brings the arts to audiences of all ages and backgrounds; encourages participation in the arts through outreach; and enriches the lives of individuals and communities.
Utilizes: Actors; Artists-in-Residence; Collaborating Artists; Collaborations; Commissioned Composers; Educators; Equity Actors; Grant Writers; Guest Companies; Guest Conductors; Guest Designers; Guest Ensembles; Guest Instructors; Guest Musical Directors; Guest Speakers; Guild Activities; High School Drama; Instructors; Local Artists; Local Talent; Original Music Scores; Playwrights; Selected Students; Students; Touring Companies; Visual Arts
Founded: 1985
Specialized Field: Theatre Dance; Multi-Disciplinary Work; Tap; Residencies; Workshops
Paid Staff: 3
Volunteer Staff: 3
Paid Artists: 15
Budget: $50,000-$120,000
Income Sources: Public; private; fees; tickets
Performs At: Perform in their storefront venue and tour throughout the US and abroad.
Annual Attendance: 12,000
Seating Capacity: 50
Year Remodeled: 1994
Rental Contact: Producing Artistic Director Donna Peckett

701

DANCECIRCUS
527 N 27th Street
Milwaukee, WI 53208

DANCE / Wisconsin

Phone: 414-277-8151
e-mail: info@dancecircus.org
Web Site: www.dancecircus.org
Officers:
  VP: Jean Dean
  Treasurer: Robert Lamb
Management:
  Artistic Director: Betty Salamun
Mission: With concern for the people and the land we bring affordable accessible programs to the entire community creating original works in music, dance and theatre true to our midwestern heritage.
Utilizes: Actors; Artists-in-Residence; Collaborating Artists; Collaborations; Commissioned Composers; Commissioned Music; Dance Companies; Dancers; Educators; Filmmakers; Guest Accompanists; Guest Artists; Guest Companies; Guest Musical Directors; Guest Musicians; Guest Teachers; Guild Activities; Instructors; Local Artists; Lyricists; Multimedia; Organization Contracts; Original Music Scores; Poets; Selected Students; Soloists; Touring Companies; Visual Arts
Founded: 1975
Specialized Field: Modern Dance
Status: Professional, Nonprofit
Paid Staff: 1
Volunteer Staff: 2
Paid Artists: 14
Budget: $62,000
Income Sources: Grants; Earned; Donations
Affiliations: Dance USA
Annual Attendance: 45,000-50,000
Organization Type: Performing; Touring; Educational

702
KO-THI DANCE COMPANY
PO Box 1093
Milwaukee, WI 53201
Phone: 414-273-0676
Fax: 414-273-0727
Toll-free: 800-442-8274
e-mail: kkothi@aol.com
Web Site: www.ko-thi.org
Officers:
  Chair-Board: Sheree Dallas
  Treasurer: Ann Terrell
  Secretary: Twyla McGhee
  Vice Chair: Dr. Katheryn D. Gilbert
  Board Member: Ferne Caulker
Management:
  Artistic Director: Ferne Yangyeitie Caulker
  Associate Artistic Director: Valencia Turner
  Managing Director: Una Van Duvall
Mission: To promulgate and preserve the African, African American and Caribbean art forms.
Utilizes: Choreographers; Collaborating Artists; Collaborations; Dance Companies; Dancers; Five Seasonal Concerts; Guest Artists; Guest Musical Directors; Guest Musicians; Local Artists; Lyricists; Multimedia; New Productions; Organization Contracts; Original Music Scores; Playwrights; Student Interns; Special Technical Talent; Touring Companies
Founded: 1969
Specialized Field: African Dance
Paid Staff: 6
Volunteer Staff: 10
Paid Artists: 28
Budget: $294,000
Income Sources: Instruction; Tickets
Performs At: UWM Deck School Of The Arts

703
MILWAUKEE BALLET COMPANY
504 W National Avenue
Milwaukee, WI 53204
Phone: 414-643-7677
Fax: 414-649-4066
e-mail: 2thepointe@milwaukeeballet.org
Web Site: www.milwaukeeballet.org
Officers:
  Chair: Mary Leahy
  Treasurer: Dorinda Floyd
Management:
  Artistic Director: Michael Pink
  Executive Director: Dennis Buehler
  Ballet Mistress: Nadia Thompson
  Ballet Master: Denis Malinkine
  Production Director: Steve Vallee
  Business Manager: Sam Bahr
  Operations Manager: Andrew Nielsen
  Marketing Manager: Chris Allen
Mission: Representing traditional and contemporary ballet performances expressing the highest aspirations and deepest emotions of the human spirit.
Utilizes: Dancers; Guest Artists; Guest Conductors; Singers
Founded: 1970
Specialized Field: Traditional Ballet; Contemporary Ballet
Status: Professional, Nonprofit
Budget: $4,800,000
Income Sources: Corporate; Individual; Donation
Performs At: Uihlein Hall; Milwaukee Performing Arts Center
Annual Attendance: 70,000
Organization Type: Performing; Touring; Resident; Educational

704
WILD SPACE DANCE COMPANY
Lincoln Center Middle School of the Arts
820 E Knapp Street
PO Box 511665
Milwaukee, WI 53202
Phone: 414-271-0307
Fax: 414-271-6087
e-mail: info@wildspacedance.org
Web Site: www.wildspacedance.org
Officers:
  President: Anne Wing Hamilton
  Vice President: Kirsten Mulvey
  Treasurer: Tricia Knight
  Secretary: Karen Campbell
Management:
  Founder/Artistic Director: Debra Loewen, DebLoewen@wildspacedance.org
  Managing Director: Sheri Urban, rick@wildspacedance.org
Mission: Its mission is to expand the audience for contemporary dance through inventive performances and innovative outreach programs throughout southeastern Wisconsin.
Utilizes: Actors; Artists-in-Residence; Choreographers; Collaborating Artists; Collaborations; Community Members; Composers; Dance Companies; Dancers; Educators; Five Seasonal Concerts; Grant Writers; Guest Accompanists; Guest Artists; Guest Designers; Guest Directors; Guest Lecturers; Guest Musical Directors; Guest Musicians; Guest Soloists; High School Drama; Instructors; Local Artists; Local Artists & Directors; Lyricists; Multi Collaborations; Multimedia; Music; Organization Contracts; Original Music Scores; Paid Performers; Poets; Resident Artists; Resident Companies; Scenic Designers; Sign Language Translators; Singers; Soloists; Students; Student Interns; Touring Companies; Visual Arts; Volunteer Artists
Founded: 1986
Specialized Field: Contemporary/Modern Dance
Status: Nonprofit
Paid Staff: 3
Volunteer Staff: 40
Paid Artists: 12
Non-paid Artists: 2
Budget: $175,000
Income Sources: Donations; Foundations; Ticket Sales; Partnerships; Contracted Residencies
Annual Attendance: 15,000+
Type of Stage: Warehouse
Seating Capacity: 175-400

705
DANCE WISCONSIN
6332 Monona Drive
Monona, WI 53716
Phone: 608-221-4535
Fax: 608-221-9632
e-mail: DanceWisconsin@gmail.com
Web Site: www.dancewisconsin.com
Officers:
  President: Roger White
  VP: Jean Adams
Management:
  Artistic Director: JoJean Retrum
Mission: To promote and foster dance in Wisconsin and develop appreciation of the arts including dance, music and theatre by creating productions of the highest caliber geared towards entertaining, educating and enriching our diversified audience.
Utilizes: Sign Language Translators
Founded: 1999
Specialized Field: Ballet
Status: Pre-Professional, Nonprofit
Volunteer Staff: 6
Paid Artists: 4
Non-paid Artists: 20
Budget: $100,000
Income Sources: Regional Dance America
Performs At: Madison Civic Center; Wisconsin Union Theatre; Milby Theatre
Seating Capacity: 2,000
Organization Type: Performing; Resident; Educational

706
LI CHIAO-PING DANCE
5973 Purcell Road
Oregon, WI 53575
Phone: 608-835-6590
Fax: 608-835-6592
e-mail: mgr@lichiaopingdance.org
Web Site: www.lichiaopingdance.org
Officers:
  Founder/President: Li Chiao-Ping
  VP: Blair Mathews
  Treasurer: David Johnsen
  Secretary: Kelly Rupp
Management:
  Artistic Director/Choreographer: Li Chiao-Ping
  Visual Artist: Douglas Rosenberg
  Communications Manager: Demetrios Lallas
  Costume Designer: Kristen Ginther
  Composer: Matan Rubinstein
  Costume Designer: Suzanne Rubinstein
  Communications Coordinator: Kelsey Manders
  Company Manager: Spencer McAfee-Gundrum
Mission: Dedicated to offering programs of emotionally charged and athletic works with striking visual design and the music of contemporary composers.

DANCE / Wisconsin

Utilizes: Choreographers; Collaborating Artists; Collaborations; Commissioned Composers; Dancers; Guest Accompanists; Guest Artists; Guest Companies; Guest Conductors; Multi Collaborations; Original Music Scores; Soloists
Founded: 1990
Specialized Field: Modern
Paid Staff: 1
Volunteer Staff: 9
Paid Artists: 10
Budget: $80,000
Income Sources: Grants; Fees; Ticket Revenue

INSTRUMENTAL MUSIC / Alabama

Alabama

707
ALABAMA SYMPHONY ORCHESTRA
3621 6th Avenue S
Birmingham, AL 35222
Phone: 205-251-6929
Fax: 205-251-6840
e-mail: orchestra@alabamasymphony.com
Web Site: www.alabamasymphony.org
Officers:
 President: Charles Perry
 Vice Chairman: H Corbin Day
 Vice Chairman: Gloria N Moody
 VP: William A. Bowron, Jr.
 Treasurer: James S. Snow
 Secretary: K Wood Herren
Management:
 Executive Director: Curtis Long
 Development Director: John Stone
 Artistic Coordinator: Seth Noble
 Artistic Administration Director: Pierre Ruhe
 Finance Director: Rick Atkerson
 Ticket Services & Analytics Manager: Smith Williams
 Operations Director: Mark Patrick
 Director Marketing, Communication: Britney Elliott
Mission: To provide high quality, professional musical performances and educational opportunities for the Central Arkansas community.
Utilizes: Fine Artists; Grant Writers; Guest Composers; Guest Lecturers; Guest Musical Directors; Guest Musicians; Instructors; Multimedia; Original Music Scores; Sign Language Translators; Singers
Founded: 1933
Specialized Field: Symphony; Orchestra
Status: Nonprofit
Paid Staff: 25
Volunteer Staff: 300
Paid Artists: 54
Budget: $7 million
Income Sources: Box Office; Grants; Corporate; Private Donations; Sponsorships
Performs At: Alys Stephens Center; Performing Arts Center; Indian Springs School Concert Hall; BJCC Concert Hall; Alabama Theatre
Affiliations: American Symphony Orchestra League; American Federation of Musicians
Annual Attendance: 100,000+
Type of Stage: Proscenium
Stage Dimensions: 28x88
Seating Capacity: 3,000
Year Built: 1996
Organization Type: Performing

708
RED MOUNTAIN CHAMBER ORCHESTRA
868 6th Street W
Birmingham, AL 35204
e-mail: suzanne@rmco.org
Web Site: www.rmco.org
Officers:
 Founder: Robert Markush
 President: Suzanne Beaudry
 Secretary: Gwen Knowlton
 Treasurer: Nancy Watson
Management:
 General Manager: Oliver Roosevelt
Mission: To educate and give pleasure to the public by performing music not otherwise heard in Birmingham.
Utilizes: Guest Lecturers; Guest Musical Directors; Guest Musicians; High School Drama; Local Artists; Multimedia; Sign Language Translators; Singers
Founded: 1980
Specialized Field: Classical Orchestra
Budget: $35,000
Income Sources: State and Local Grants; Private Donors
Performs At: Colleges; Churches; Birmingham Museum of Art
Affiliations: Birmingham Southern College
Annual Attendance: 1,200
Facility Category: Concert Hall
Type of Stage: Small Performance Space
Seating Capacity: 300

709
GADSDEN SYMPHONY ORCHESTRA
P.O. Box 13
Gadsden, AL 35902
Phone: 256-543-9187
e-mail: mdupont@bellsouth.net
Web Site: www.gadsdensymphony.org
Officers:
 President: Norman.R Dasinger
 VP: Christopher Word
 Conductor: Les Fillmer
 Treasurer: R. Marie Akin
Founded: 1991
Specialized Field: Symphony
Volunteer Staff: 20
Budget: $20,000-$30,000
Income Sources: Local Contributions; Grants
Affiliations: American Symphony Orchestra League
Annual Attendance: 1,100
Facility Category: Concert Hall; Outdoor Ampitheatre
Seating Capacity: 800
Year Built: 1960
Year Remodeled: 1999

710
HUNTSVILLE CHAMBER MUSIC GUILD
607 Airport Road
Huntsville, AL 35802
Phone: 256-489-7415
e-mail: info@hcmg.us
Web Site: www.hcmg.us
Officers:
 President: Bibi B. Pride
 Treasurer: Robert Fletcher
 Secretary: Jennifer Penfield
 VP: Douglas Fees
Management:
 Program Director: Wilson Luquire
Mission: To provide the community of Huntsville and the region of Northern Alabama with a season of performances of the highest quality musicianship.
Specialized Field: Classical Music
Income Sources: Jane K Lowe Foundation; Marilyn Horne Foundation; Alabama State Council on the Arts; National Endowment for the Arts
Season: October-April
Performs At: Trinity United Methodist Church; Roberts Recital Hall-University of Alabama

711
HUNTSVILLE SYMPHONY ORCHESTRA
Von Braun Center
700 Monroe Street SW
Huntsville, AL 35801
Mailing Address: PO Box 2400, Huntsville, AL 35804
Phone: 256-539-4818
Fax: 256-539-4819
e-mail: hso@hiwaay.net
Web Site: www.hso.org
Officers:
 President/CEO: Daniel Halcomb
 Chairman: Frances K. Huffman
 Vice Chairman: Patrick Robbins
 Treasurer: Ivor Fredrickson
 Secretary: Donna Shergy
Management:
 Music Director: Gregory Vajda
 Symphony School Director: Joe Lee
 Finance Director: Courtney Gattis
 Patron Engagement Manager: Sabrina Dillman
 Marketing and Development Director: Jennifer Doss
 Operations Director: Cindy Reaves
 Production Manager: Gary Boggs
 Director of Education: Julie Noles
Mission: To serve the community as an aid to industrial development. Huntsville Symphony strives to perform high quality performances to satisfy the community's high standards for leisure time activities.
Utilizes: Guest Artists; Sign Language Translators
Founded: 1954
Specialized Field: Symphony
Status: Non-Professional, Nonprofit, Commercial
Paid Staff: 75
Budget: $1,050,000-$3,600,000
Income Sources: American Symphony Orchestra League; Sponships and Gifts from local corporations; Ticket Sales
Performs At: Von Braun Civic Center - Concert Hall
Organization Type: Performing; Educational; Sponsoring

712
HUNTSVILLE YOUTH ORCHESTRA
PO Box 2532
Huntsville, AL 35804
Phone: 256-880-0622
e-mail: HYOmanager@yahoo.com
Web Site: huntsvilleyouthorchestra.org
Officers:
 President: Ellie Lienau
 Secretary: Kelly Manley
 Treasurer: Jim Chafin
Management:
 HYO Music Director: Joseph Lee
 Executive Director: Deborah Brown
 Chamber Coordinator: Marlies Sarette
Mission: To provide a rewarding and challenging experience for its members by means of active participation in the performance of good music
Utilizes: Guest Artists
Specialized Field: Youth Orchestra; Classical Music
Paid Staff: 270
Income Sources: American Symphony Orchestra League (Youth Orchestra Division); Alabama Federation of Music; Alabama Arts Council
Performs At: Von Braun Civic Center
Organization Type: Performing; Touring; Educational; Sponsoring

713
MOBILE CHAMBER MUSIC SOCIETY
University of Alabama Music Department
P.O. Box 3121
Mobile, AL 36652-3121

INSTRUMENTAL MUSIC / Alaska

Phone: 251-476-8794
Fax: 334-460-7328
e-mail: music@mobilechambermusic.org
Web Site: www.mobilechambermusic.org
Officers:
    President: Gordon Moulton
Management:
    Director: Dr Greg Turner
Mission: to present the best in Chamber Music to the Southern Alabama region
Specialized Field: Chamber Music
Volunteer Staff: 4
Income Sources: Mobile Arts Council; Alabama State Council on the Arts
Season: October-April
Performs At: Alabama School of Mathematics and Science Auditorium; Laidlaw Performing Arts Center Recital Hall

714
MOBILE SYMPHONY
257 Dauphin Street
Mobile, AL 36602
Mailing Address: PO Box 3127 Mobile AL 36652-3127
Phone: 251-432-2010
Fax: 251-432-6618
Web Site: www.mobilesymphony.org
Officers:
    Chair: Jimmy Hatcher
    Secretary: Karen Outlaw Atchison
    Treasurer: John Klotz
    Vice Chair, Board Development: Celia Mann Baehr
Management:
    Director: Scott Speck
    General Manager: Greg Gordon
    Development Director: Mary Hadley
    Marketing Director: Diana Brewer
    Director of Artistic Operations: J.C. Barker
    Music Director: Robert. J. Seebacher
    Accountant: Verna Richard
    Media Specialist: Ben Harper
Mission: To enhance the lives of every member of the community by achieving the highest standards in live symphonic music and music education
Specialized Field: Classical Music
Paid Staff: 10
Paid Artists: 65
Budget: $900,000-$1,050,000
Income Sources: Ticket Sales; Corporate Sponsors; Grants; Individual Donations
Performs At: Mobile Civic Center Theatre; Larkins Music Center
Annual Attendance: 3,000
Stage Dimensions: 90x60
Seating Capacity: 2,000

715
MONTGOMERY SYMPHONY ORCHESTRA
301 N Hull Street
Montgomery, AL 36104
Mailing Address: PO Box 1864, Montgomery, AL 36102
Phone: 334-240-4004
Fax: 334-240-4034
e-mail: montgomerysymphony@gmail.com
Web Site: www.montgomerysymphony.org
Officers:
    President: Bruce Crawford
    First VP: Wilbur Hill
    Second VP: Joe Mussafer
    Secretary: Hattie Boo Johnston
    Treasurer: George A Kent
    Board Member: Sam Adams
    Board Member: Jim Levy
Management:
    Orchestra Manager: Helen Steineker
    Assistant: Sherry Culver
    Assistant: Nicole Akers
    Executive Director: Kimberly C. Wolfe
    Office Manager: Sherry Culver
    Project Coordinator: Katherine Rodman
Mission: To perform great orchestral works by invested volunteers in the community.
Founded: 1976
Specialized Field: Symphony; Orchestra; Pops; Classical
Status: Semi-Professional, Volunteer
Non-paid Artists: 75
Budget: $70,000
Income Sources: American Symphony Orchestra League; Corporate and Patrol Sponsorships; Program Advertising
Performs At: Davis Theater for the Performing Arts
Type of Stage: Flexible Backbox Studio Theatre
Seating Capacity: 1250
Year Built: 1938
Organization Type: Performing; Educational

716
TUSCALOOSA SYMPHONY ORCHESTRA
PO Box 20001
Tuscaloosa, AL 35402-0001
Phone: 205-752-5515
Fax: 205-345-2787
e-mail: tso@tsoonline.org
Web Site: www.tsoonline.org
Officers:
    President: Gay Burrows
    Secretary: Camilla Huxford
    Treasurer: Bruce Burrows
    President Elect: Kirsten Hicks
    Vice President: Skip Snead
Management:
    Executive Director: Jessica Davis
    Operations Manager: David Bradley
    Interim Administrative Assistant: Marcelyn Morrow
    Box Office Agent: Ryan Landis
    Stage Manager: Leslie Sheppard
Mission: To enrich the livelihood of the community through high quality musical performances
Founded: 1979
Specialized Field: Instrumental Music
Paid Staff: 5
Volunteer Staff: 75
Paid Artists: 70
Budget: $260,000-$1,050,000
Income Sources: Sponsorships; Donations; Gloria Moody Narramore Foundation; City of Tuscaloosa; Corporate Gifts
Performs At: Moody Concert Hall
Seating Capacity: 1,000
Year Built: 1926
Organization Type: Performing; Educational

Alaska

717
ANCHORAGE SYMPHONY ORCHESTRA
400 D Street
Suite 230
Anchorage, AK 99501
Phone: 907-274-8668
Fax: 907-272-7916
e-mail: aso@youraso.org
Web Site: www.anchoragesymphony.org
Officers:
    President: Walter Featherly
    Secretary: Jan Cawvey
    Treasurer: Caren Mathis
    President-Elect: Bill Bernier
Management:
    Music Director: Randall Craig Fleischer
    Executive Director: Sherri Burkhart Reddick
    Marketing Director: Jennifer Cargile
    Associate Director: Darleen Fernandez
    Office Manager and Patron Services: Alana Williamson
    Production Manager: Lauren MacKenzie Miller
    Personnel Manager: Steven Alvarez
Mission: To inspire, engage and educate our community through the live performance of great music
Utilizes: Collaborations; Guest Accompanists; Guest Artists; Guest Companies; Guest Composers; Guest Musical Directors; Guest Musicians; Instructors; Multimedia; Original Music Scores; Poets; Selected Students; Singers; Student Interns
Founded: 1948
Specialized Field: Classical Music; Ballet
Paid Staff: 4
Paid Artists: 90
Budget: $1.2 million
Income Sources: ASL
Performs At: Evangeline Atwood Concert Hall
Annual Attendance: 240,000
Type of Stage: Proscenium
Stage Dimensions: 120x52
Seating Capacity: 2,000
Year Built: 1988
Organization Type: Performing; Educational

718
ANCHORAGE YOUTH SYMPHONY
PO Box 240541
Anchorage, AK 99524
Phone: 907-566-7297
Fax: 907-333-0576
e-mail: youthsymphony@gmail.com
Web Site: www.anchorageyouthsymphony.org
Officers:
    President: Tanguy Libbrecht
    Secretary: Jeanne Larsen
    Treasurer: Nancy Sopp
    Vice President: Patrick Rumley
Management:
    Music Director/Conductor: Linn Weeda
    General Manager: Ron Flugum
    Executive Director: Tracy Orakpo
    Conductor: William Reese Waag
Mission: To train young musicians through concert experience, tours and community involvement which produces high quality orchestra performances.
Founded: 1965
Specialized Field: Symphony; Orchestra
Status: Non-Professional, Non-Profit
Paid Staff: 2
Income Sources: American Symphony Orchestra League (Youth Orchestra Division)
Performs At: Discovery Theatre/ACPA West High Auditorium; Atwood Concert Hall; Alaska Center for the Performing Arts (three theatres)
Facility Category: Theatre
Seating Capacity: 750; 2,000; 300
Year Built: 1988
Cost: $87,000,000
Organization Type: Performing; Touring; Educational

INSTRUMENTAL MUSIC / Arizona

719
FAIRBANKS RED HACKLE PIPE BAND
PO Box 82782
Fairbanks, AK 99708-2782
Phone: 907-479-0807
e-mail: fairbanksredhacklepipeband.org
Web Site: www.fairbanksredhacklepipeband.org
Officers:
- President: Liam Forbes
- Treasurer: Rocky Janiro
- Secretary: D'Shaynna Anderson
- Vice President: Steve Stephens

Management:
- Staff: Dennis Stephens

Mission: Promoting the Scottish arts and traditions in the North
Utilizes: Community Members; Dance Companies; Dancers; Guest Ensembles; Guest Musical Directors; High School Drama; Soloists
Founded: 1974
Specialized Field: Scottish Music; Bag Pipes and Drums; Highland Dance
Performs At: Weddings; Parades; Picnics; Civic Events; Funerals
Organization Type: Performing; Educational

720
FAIRBANKS SYMPHONY ASSOCIATION
312 Tanana Dr, Room 234
Fairbanks, AK 99775
Mailing Address: PO Box 82104, Fairbanks, AK 99708
Phone: 907-474-5733
Fax: 907-474-5147
e-mail: symphony@fairbankssymphony.org
Web Site: www.fairbankssymphony.org
Officers:
- President: Chuck Lemke
- Treasurer: David McDowell
- Secretary: Martha Springer
- VP: Paul Schneider

Management:
- Executive Director: Laura Bergh
- Director: Eduard Zilberkant
- Marketing Director: George Rydlinski
- Operations Director: Jenni Warren

Mission: To provide a significant positive cultural and educational influence to its region by fostering, promoting, and developing the musical knowledge and appreciation of the public for symphonic music and the arts
Utilizes: Artists-in-Residence; Commissioned Music; Guest Accompanists; Guest Artists; Guest Musical Directors; Guest Musicians; Multimedia; Singers
Specialized Field: Symphony; Orchestra; Chamber; Classical
Paid Staff: 4
Volunteer Staff: 70
Income Sources: American Symphony Orchestra League; Alaska Alliance on the Arts; Individual Patrons; Foundations; Corporations; Fairbanks Symphony Endowment Fund
Performs At: Concert Hall
Affiliations: University of Alaska, Fairbanks
Annual Attendance: 7,000-10,000
Type of Stage: Concert
Seating Capacity: 910
Year Built: 1974
Organization Type: Performing; Touring; Resident; Educational; Sponsoring
Resident Groups: Fairbanks Symphony Orchestra; Arctic Chamber Orchestra

721
KENAI PENINSULA ORCHESTRA
315 W Pioneer Avenue
Homer, AK 99603
Phone: 907-235-4899
Fax: 907-235-5633
e-mail: kpoalaska@gmail.com
Web Site: www.kpoalaska.org
Officers:
- Board President: Jack Will

Management:
- Artistic Director: Tammy Vollom-Matturro
- Production Manager: Laura Norton

Mission: To provide the Kenai Peninsula community enriched, educational opportunities and cultural experiences through the study and performance of the Orchestral Arts.
Founded: 1983
Specialized Field: Symphony Orchestra
Status: Non-Profit, Non-Professional
Paid Staff: 3
Volunteer Staff: 3
Paid Artists: 8
Non-paid Artists: 80
Budget: $35,000
Seating Capacity: 200-450

722
JOCELYN CLARK
1109 C Street
Juneau, AK 99801
Phone: 907-586-9601
e-mail: jocelyn@jocelynclark.com
Web Site: www.jocelynclark.com
Officers:
- President: Jocelyn Clark

Mission: Solo performances and collaboration with non-Western musical ensembles
Specialized Field: Non-Western Music; Korean Music
Performs At: Meyerson Hall; Renee Weiler Concert Hall; Springstep Center

723
JUNEAU JAZZ AND CLASSICS
Juneau Arts & Culture Center
350 Whittier Street, Suite 105
Juneau, AK 99802
Mailing Address: PO Box 22152 Juneau AK 99801
Phone: 907-463-3378
Fax: 907-586-2148
e-mail: info@jazzandclassics.org
Web Site: www.jazzandclassics.org
Officers:
- Chair: Kathy Kolkhurst Ruddy
- Treasurer: Adam Sycks
- Secretary: Hal Geiger
- Board of Directors: Kathleen Donohoe
- Board of Directors: Christy Hartman
- Vice Chair: Vicki Van Fleet

Management:
- Artistic Director: Linda Rosenthal
- Executive Director: Sandy Fortier
- Administrator/Production Manager: Reggie Schapp

Mission: To provide a rich musical experience to music lovers in Juneau, the remote towns of Southeast Alaska and the entire state
Specialized Field: Classical; Jazz; Blues
Volunteer Staff: 100
Budget: $250,000
Income Sources: Private Donations
Season: May
Performs At: Alaska Native Brotherhood Hall
Seating Capacity: 1,000; 250; 250
Organization Type: Educational; Sponsoring

724
JUNEAU SYMPHONY
522 W. 10th St.
Juneau, AK 99801
Mailing Address: PO Box 21236, Juneau, Alaska 99802-1236
Phone: 907-586-4676
Fax: 907-463-2555
e-mail: info@juneausymphony.org
Web Site: www.juneausymphony.org
Officers:
- President: Bev Smith
- VP: Tamara Cook
- Secretary: Jetta Whittaker
- Treasurer: Mary Lou Madden

Management:
- Music Director: Kyle Wiley Pickett
- Concertmaster: Steve Tada
- Executive Director: Sara Radke Brown
- Project Coordinator: Tom Paul

Mission: Dedicated to give local musicians a platform to perform and develop musically, to provide live symphonic music for the community, and to offer musical opportunities and support for youth.
Founded: 1962
Specialized Field: Symphony
Status: Semi-professional; Volunteer
Paid Staff: 2
Paid Artists: 1
Non-paid Artists: 55
Budget: $185,000
Performs At: Juneau Douglas High School, Juneau Arts And Humanities Council
Seating Capacity: 900

Arizona

725
CHANDLER SYMPHONY ORCHESTRA
P.O. Box 6475
Chandler, AZ 85246
Phone: 480-899-3447
e-mail: info@chandlersymphony.net
Web Site: www.chandlersymphony.net
Officers:
- President: Pamela Hahn
- Secretary: Michael Wallick
- Treasurer: Catherine Nowell
- Lega Counsel: John Friedeman
- Director: Bob Koepke
- Director: Kathy Koepke
- Director: Ken Dodson
- Advisor: Alan Wilkie

Management:
- Music Director: Jack Herriman
- Associate Conductor: Alex Xiaozhong Zheng

Mission: The symphony's mission is to serve, the greater Chandler community by providing a series of classical concerts, free of charge to the general public, performed by professionally trained musicians who volunteer their time and talents.
Utilizes: Arrangers; Collaborating Artists; Collaborations; Commissioned Music; Composers; Composers-in-Residence; Grant Writers; Guest Directors; Lyricists; Multimedia; Music; Paid Performers; Sign Language Translators; Singers
Founded: 1991
Opened: 1993
Specialized Field: Symphony Orchestra
Status: Non-Profit, Professional

INSTRUMENTAL MUSIC / Arizona

Income Sources: Sopnsors, Donations, Fundraisers
Season: September through May
Performs At: Chandler Center for the Arts

726
FLAGSTAFF SYMPHONY ORCHESTRA
113 E Aspen Avenue
Suite A
Flagstaff, AZ 86001
Mailing Address: PO Box 122 flagstaff AZ 86002-0122
Phone: 928-774-5107
Fax: 928-774-5109
e-mail: info@flagstaffsymphony.org
Web Site: www.flagstaffsymphony.org
Officers:
   President: Carl Taylor
   Treasurer: Hann Cortner
   Secretary: Beatrice Cooley
Management:
   Music Director: Elizabeth Schulze
   Outreach Coordinator: Emily Wells
   Librarian / Office Manager: Cindy Gould
   Executive Director: Laura Kelly
   Orchestra Personnel: Sheila White
Mission: To enrich the cultural life of northern Arizona and expand the understanding, appreciation and love of music in people of all ages
Utilizes: Educators
Specialized Field: Symphony; Orchestra
Status: Nonprofit
Paid Staff: 3
Volunteer Staff: 65
Paid Artists: 65
Budget: $260,000-$1,050,000
Income Sources: Individual; Private Donations
Season: September-May
Performs At: Ardrey Auditorium
Annual Attendance: 1,500
Type of Stage: proscenium
Stage Dimensions: 26x54
Seating Capacity: 1,941
Organization Type: Educational; Performing

727
SYMPHONY OF THE SOUTHWEST
213 N. Morris
Mesa, AZ 85201
Phone: 480-827-2143
Fax: 480-827-2070
e-mail: symphonyofthesouthwest@gmail.com
Web Site: www.symphonyofthesouthwest.org
Officers:
   President: Virginia Ikeda
   Treasurer: Dawn Cain
Management:
   Executive Director: Alycia De Mesa
   Director: Cal Stewart Kellogg
   Marketing Director: Paul Dlouhy
Mission: To present the highest quality live, professional, orchestral and chamber concerts that compete in impact and significance with commerical productions
Utilizes: Collaborations; Guest Accompanists; Guest Companies; Guest Composers; Guest Directors; Guest Lecturers; Guest Musical Directors; Guest Musicians; Lyricists; Multimedia; Organization Contracts; Original Music Scores; Sign Language Translators; Soloists
Specialized Field: Symphony
Paid Staff: 3
Volunteer Staff: 20
Paid Artists: 70
Budget: $150,000-$260,000
Income Sources: American Symphony Orchestra League
Performs At: Chandler Central Arts
Annual Attendance: 60,000
Facility Category: 2 Halls, 1 Amphitheatre
Type of Stage: Proscenium
Stage Dimensions: 82x69
Seating Capacity: 1,550
Organization Type: Performing; Educational

728
PHOENIX CHAMBER MUSIC SOCIETY
Scottsdale Center for the Arts
5517 N Thrid Street
Phoenix, AZ 85012
Phone: 602-252-0095
e-mail: PCMSociety@aol.com
Web Site: www.phoenixchambermusicsociety.org
Officers:
   President: Janet Green
Management:
   Co-Founder: Lewis J. Ruskin
Mission: To bring the finest chamber music in the world to the valley
Founded: 1961
Specialized Field: Chamber
Status: Nonprofit
Income Sources: Private Donations; Ticket Sales; American Symphony Orchestra League
Performs At: Scottsdale Center for the Arts - Virginia Piper Theatre
Affiliations: Culture Finder.Com; Northwest Valley Chamber of Commerce; Chamber Music America
Type of Stage: Flexible
Seating Capacity: 838
Organization Type: Sponsoring; Performing; Educational

729
PHOENIX SYMPHONY
One North First Street
Suite 200
Phoenix, AZ 85004
Phone: 602-495-1117
Fax: 602-253-1772
e-mail: info@phoenixsymphony.org
Web Site: www.phoenixsymphony.org
Officers:
   President & CEO: James K. Ward
   Chairman: John Graham
   Vice Chair: David Bornemann
   Vice Chair & Secretary: Linda Hunt
   Vice Chair: Malcolm Jozoff
Management:
   Assistant to the President: Joan Hosey, president@phoenixsymphony.org
   Executive Vice President, COO: Katie Cobb
   General Manager: Jeff Hunsinger, operations@phoenixsymphony.org
   Marketing Director: Todd Vigil
   Development Director: Lauren Bouchard
   Artistic Planning Associate: Alan J. Tomasetti
   Head Librarian: Heather Jackson
   Orchestra Personnel Manager: Damien Shindelman
   Asst Personnel Manager: Karen Bea
Mission: The Phoenix Symphony will be the arts leader in the revitalization of a thriving Arizona. The Phoenix Symphony will be a cultural icon and a reason people will like to live in Arizona whether they attend concerts or not. And, the Symphony will be one of the many compelling reasons people will want to move to Arizona. This will happen because our community will recognize that the Symphony provides unparalleled civic value.
Utilizes: Commissioned Composers; Commissioned Music; Dancers; Educators; Guest Accompanists; Guest Composers; Guest Directors; Guest Lecturers; Guest Musical Directors; Guest Musicians; Local Artists; Original Music Scores; Sign Language Translators; Singers; Theatre Companies
Founded: 1947
Specialized Field: Symphony
Paid Artists: 75
Budget: $8,600,000
Income Sources: Private Donations; Institutional Supporters
Season: September-May
Performs At: Phoenix Symphony Hall; Orpheum Theatre; Sedona Cultural Park
Annual Attendance: 140,000
Facility Category: Symphony Hall
Stage Dimensions: 60x100
Seating Capacity: 2,587
Year Built: 1972
Organization Type: Performing; Touring; Educational

730
YAVAPAI SYMPHONY ASSOCIATION
228 N Alarcon Street
PO Box 2333
Prescott, AZ 86301
Phone: 928-776-4255
Fax: 928-778-5286
e-mail: ysa1@cableone.net
Web Site: yavapaisymphony.org
Officers:
   President: Arlon Inman
   Founding President: Mary Brooke
   Founding Vice President: Ted Liese
   Secretary: Lester Ward Ruffner
   Treasurer: Harold Wolfinger
   Board Member: Frederic B James
   Board Member: Raymond Henderson
   Board Member: Harold James
   Board Member: Charles Orme
Management:
   General Manager: Andres Kipe
   Office Manager: Pat Forrest
Mission: The initial purpose of the association was to sponsor, provide and promote musical concerts and programs, and cultural activities and events of every character intended to enrich both individual and community life and enjoyment, primarily for the citizens of Yavapai County.
Utilizes: Arrangers; Choreographers; Collaborating Artists; Collaborations; Community Talent; Dancers; Fine Artists; Guest Accompanists; Guest Artists; Guest Choreographers; Guest Companies; Guest Directors; Guest Instructors; Guest Lecturers; Guest Musical Directors; Lyricists; Multimedia; Paid Performers
Founded: 1966
Specialized Field: Classical
Status: Nonprofit; Professional
Volunteer Staff: 400
Paid Artists: 75
Income Sources: American Symphony Orchestra League; Private Donations
Season: November-June
Performs At: Yavapai College Performance Hall
Annual Attendance: 1,100
Stage Dimensions: 60x100
Seating Capacity: 2,587
Year Built: 1972
Organization Type: Sponsoring; Performing

INSTRUMENTAL MUSIC / Arizona

732
SCOTTSDALE SYMPHONY ORCHESTRA
8524 E Thomas Road
Scottsdale, AZ 85251
Phone: 480-945-8071
Fax: 480-946-8770
e-mail: sso@scotsymph.org
Web Site: www.scotsymph.org
Management:
    Music Director: Irving A Fleming
Mission: Provide the community with cultural entertainment and education through music.
Founded: 1975
Specialized Field: Classical; Symphony; Pops
Status: Nonprofit
Budget: $150,000-$260,000
Season: November-June
Performs At: Grace Chapel Auditorium
Seating Capacity: 700

733
CHAMBER MUSIC SEDONA
1487 W Highway 89A
Suite 9
Sedona, AZ 86336
Phone: 928-204-2415
Fax: 928-282-0893
e-mail: info@chambermusicsedona.org
Web Site: www.chambermusicsedona.org
Officers:
    President: John Steinbrunner
    Treasurer: Dwight Kadar
    Secretary: Mary Lee Warner
    VP: Pamela Fazzini
    Chair: Edward Ingraham
    Vice Chair: Marion Maby
Management:
    Executive Director: Bert Harclerode
    General Manager: Anna Cates
    Operations Director: Susan Saxton
    Marketing Coordinator: Kristine Follett
    Volunteer Coordinator: Marisol Molina
Mission: To enrich the lives of Northern Arizona residents and visitors by presenting the finest international, national, and regional performing artists and to promote a love of the performing arts through arts education programs.
Utilizes: Artists-in-Residence; Collaborating Artists; Commissioned Music; Five Seasonal Concerts; Grant Writers; Guest Companies; Guest Directors; Guest Lecturers; Guest Musical Directors; Local Artists; Multimedia
Specialized Field: Chamber Music, Bluegrass, The Met: Live In HD
Paid Staff: 3
Volunteer Staff: 65
Paid Artists: 52
Budget: $300,000
Income Sources: Contributions, Grants, Ticket Sales, Advertising Sales
Performs At: St. John Vianney Church; Sedona Performing Arts
Affiliations: CMA, ACA, SWAP
Annual Attendance: 4000
Facility Category: Catholic Church
Seating Capacity: 250; 750
Organization Type: Performing; Educational; Presenters

734
ARIZONA JAZZ FESTIVAL
P.O. Box 87947
Sedona, AZ 85080
Phone: 602-244-8444
e-mail: general@arizonajazzfestival.com
Web Site: www.arizonajazzfestival.com
Officers:
    President, Board of Directors: Bettye Wilson
Management:
    President: Bettye Wilson, president@sedonajazz.com
Mission: To celebrate jazz as a living art form through education and performance programs
Utilizes: Guest Accompanists; Instructors; Original Music Scores; Sign Language Translators; Soloists
Specialized Field: Jazz
Status: Non-Profit, Non-Professional
Volunteer Staff: 200
Budget: $400,000
Income Sources: Box Office; Corporate Sponsors; Grants
Season: September
Performs At: Poco Diablo Resort (Festival Site)
Affiliations: Sedona Arts & Culture Commission; Greater Sedona Community Foundation; Arizona Commission on the Arts; National Endowment for the Arts
Annual Attendance: 2,000
Facility Category: Various Venues
Seating Capacity: 200-4,000
Organization Type: Performing; Sponsoring

735
WEST VALLEY SYMPHONY
P O Box 7328
Sun City, AZ 85374-7328
Phone: 623-236-6781
e-mail: admin@westvalleysymphoney.org
Web Site: www.westvalleysymphony.org
Officers:
    President: Leslie Fountain
    Vice-President/President-Elect: Catherine Leas
    Treasurer: Mary Dehn Van Dessel
    Secretary: Carol Sailer
Management:
    Business Manager: Mona Myhre
    Ticket Manager: June McNamee
    Marketing Manager: Juliana Brutsche
Mission: To continue our presentations of the finest classical music to our many valuable patrons
Founded: 1968
Specialized Field: Symphony; Classical
Paid Staff: 4
Budget: $260,000-$1,050,000
Income Sources: Individual Contributions; Corporate Contributions; Grants
Season: November-March
Performs At: Various locations in the Northwest Valley of Phoenix Metro Area
Annual Attendance: 7,169
Organization Type: Performing

736
UNIVERSITY CHAMBER ORCHESTRA
Arizona State University
Herberger College of the Arts
PO Box 870405
Tempe, AZ 85287-0405
Phone: 480-965-3371
Web Site: music.asu.edu
Officers:
    President: Michael M Crow
    Secretary: Yvonne Delgado
Management:
    Interim Director, School of Music: Heather Landes
    Interim Dean and Director: Michael Underhill
    Director of Development: Shawn Richards
    Director of Institute Facilities: Leslie Robert Beres
    Director, School of Art: Adriene Jenik
Mission: To provide the highest level of instruction and research fo music professionals in the fields of performance, conducting, pedagogy, music education, music therapy, music history, music theory and composition.
Utilizes: Guest Musicians; Singers
Specialized Field: Orchestra; Ensemble; Classical
Volunteer Staff: 100
Budget: $100,000-$150,000
Performs At: Grady Gammage Auditorium
Annual Attendance: 15,000
Facility Category: Auditorium
Seating Capacity: 3000
Year Built: 1963

737
UNIVERSITY SYMPHONY ORCHESTRA
Arizona State University
Herberger College of the Arts
PO Box 870405
Tempe, AZ 85287-0405
Phone: 480-965-3371
Web Site: music.asu.edu
Officers:
    President: Michael M Crow
    Secretary: Yvonne Delgado
Management:
    Interim Dean and Director: Michael Underhill
    Director of Development: Shawn Richards
    Interim Director, School of Music: Heather Landes
    Director of Institute Facilities: Leslie Robert Beres
    Director, School of Art: Adriene Jenik
Mission: To provide the highest level of instruction and research for music professionals in the fields of performance, conducting, pedagogy, music education, music therapy, music history, music theory and composition.
Utilizes: Guest Musicians; Singers
Specialized Field: Orchestra; Ensemble; Classical
Volunteer Staff: 100
Budget: $100,000-$50,000
Performs At: Grady Gammage Auditorium
Annual Attendance: 15,000
Facility Category: Auditorium
Seating Capacity: 3000
Year Built: 1963

738
EASTERN ARIZONA COLLEGE- COMMUNITY ORCHESTRA
615 N Stadium Avenue
Thatcher, AZ 85552
Phone: 928-428-8472
Toll-free: 800-678-3808
e-mail: webmaster@eac.edu
Web Site: www.eac.edu
Officers:
    President: Mark Bryce, J.D.
    Chairman: Lois Ann Moody
    Secretary: Richard W. Mattice
Management:
    Director: Franklin Alvarez
    Marketing Director: Todd Haynie
    Associate Director: Jody Rockmaker
    Interim Director: Heather Landes
Mission: To display a passion for music that manifests into a lively and entertaining performance
Specialized Field: Symphony; Chamber
Budget: $35,000
Income Sources: Private Donations

INSTRUMENTAL MUSIC / Arizona

Performs At: Fine Arts Auditorium
Seating Capacity: 960
Organization Type: Performing; Educational

739
ARIZONA EARLY MUSIC SOCIETY
4440 N Campbell Avenue
Tucson, AZ 85737
Mailing Address: P.O. Box 44172 Tucson AZ 85733-4172
Phone: 520-721-0846
Fax: 520-297-3448
e-mail: aems@azearlymusic.org
Web Site: www.azearlymusic.org
Officers:
   President: Jeffri Sanders
   Treasurer: Laurie Camm
   Recording Secretary: J. Scott Mason
   Vice President: Christina Jarvis
Mission: Dedicated to the enrichment of contemporary life with the music of the past
Founded: 1982
Specialized Field: Medieval; Renaissance; Baroque
Status: Nonprofit
Budget: $10,000-20,000
Income Sources: Ticket Sales; Grants; National Endowment for the Arts; Western States Arts Federation; Arizona Commission on the Arts; Tucson/Pima Arts Council; Private Donations
Season: October-April
Performs At: St. Philip's in the Hills Episcopal Church
Seating Capacity: 500

740
ARIZONA FRIENDS OF CHAMBER MUSIC
PO Box 40845
Tucson, AZ 85717
Phone: 520-577-3769
Fax: 520-881-2009
e-mail: office@arizonachambermusic.org
Web Site: www.arizonachambermusic.org
Officers:
   President: Bryan Daum
   Vice President: Ted Buchholz
   Corresponding Secretary: Joseph Tolliver
   Recording Secretary: Helmut Abt
   Treasurer: Wes Addison
Management:
   Office Manager: Cathy Anderson
Mission: Presenters of chamber music concerts.
Founded: 1951
Specialized Field: Chamber
Status: Nonprofit
Paid Staff: 2-Ja
Volunteer Staff: 15
Paid Artists: 50
Budget: $200,000
Income Sources: Audience; AZ Commission on the Arts
Performs At: Leo Rich
Annual Attendance: 8,400
Facility Category: Concert Hall
Type of Stage: Proscenium
Stage Dimensions: 130x40
Seating Capacity: 511
Year Built: 1970
Organization Type: Performing; Sponsoring

741
CHAMBER MUSIC PLUS SOUTHWEST
5020 North Campana DR
Tucson, AZ 85718
Phone: 520-400-5439
Fax: 866-400-5439
e-mail: info@chambermusicplus.org
Web Site: www.chambermusicplus.org
Officers:
   President: Eric Abrams
Management:
   Artistic Director: Harry Clark
   Executive Director: Sanda Schuldmann
Utilizes: Actors; Artists-in-Residence; Collaborating Artists; Commissioned Music; Composers-in-Residence; Guest Companies; Guest Directors; Guest Instructors; Guest Musical Directors; Guest Soloists; Multimedia; Original Music Scores
Budget: $400,000
Income Sources: Private and Corporate Donations, Ticket Sales
Season: October-April
Annual Attendance: 200 per performance

742
CIVIC ORCHESTRA OF TUCSON
PO Box 42764
Tucson, AZ 85733-2764
Phone: 520-730-3371
Fax: 520-818-6584
e-mail: civicorchestra@att.net
Web Site: www.cotmusic.org
Officers:
   President: Dorothy Fitch
   Vice President: Marilyn McNamara
   Secretary: Elaine Walter
   Treasurer: John Munier
   Assistant Treasurer: Sylvia Payne
Management:
   Music Director: Dr. Herschel Kreloff
   General Manager: Bob Kovitz
   Webmaster: Lori Fitzsimmons
   Stage Manager: Ethan Beasley
Mission: Dedicated to continue the tradition of presenting free symphonic concerts.
Founded: 1975
Specialized Field: Symphony; Pops
Volunteer Staff: 60
Budget: $10,000-$15,000
Season: August-May
Performs At: UA Crowder Hall
Annual Attendance: 800
Seating Capacity: 544
Year Built: 1957
Year Remodeled: 1991

743
SOUTHERN ARIZONA SYMPHONY ORCHESTRA
PO Box 43131
Tucson, AZ 85733
Phone: 520-308-6226
e-mail: info@sasomusic.org
Web Site: www.sasomusic.org
Officers:
   President: Dee Schroer
   Treasurer: Julie Wypych
   Secretary: Heidi Crosby
   Second VP: Tim Secomb
Management:
   Music Director: Linus Lerner
   Co-Concertmaster: Erika Roush
   Co-Concertmaster: Jessamyn Schertz
Mission: Dedicated to exploring the classical repertoire and introducing new works to the community
Specialized Field: Classical
Status: Nonprofit
Budget: $35,000
Income Sources: Private Donations; Art Groups; Advertisers
Season: October-May
Seating Capacity: 60
Organization Type: Performing; Educational

744
TUCSON CHAMBER ORCHESTRA
PO Box 13925
Tucson, AZ 85732
Phone: 520-401-4369
e-mail: patrickgibbons@cox.net
Officers:
   President: Patrick Gibbons
Management:
   Director: Enrique Lasansky
Mission: To provide high quality, live performances of orchestral music in Tucson as well as throughout southern Arizona and northern New Mexico
Specialized Field: Chamber
Volunteer Staff: 60
Budget: $35,000-$100,000
Season: October-May
Performs At: Catalina High Magnet School Auditorium
Affiliations: Tucson Pima Arts Council; Arizona Commission on the Arts

745
THE TUCSON JAZZ SOCEITY
2777 N. Campbell Avenue
Suite 206
Tucson, AZ 85719
Phone: 520-903-1265
Fax: 520-903-1266
e-mail: info@tucsonjazz.org
Web Site: www.tucsonjazz.org
Officers:
   President: Mark P. Slivinski
   Vice President: Marty Dr. Jazz Dresner
   Treasurer: Clif Wickstrom
   Secretary: Ray Mott
Management:
   Office Manager: Pat Young, development@tucsonjazz.org
   Executive Director: Sandy Riser
   TJS Marketing Director: Kris Basel
   Fundraising Director: Lou Salute
Mission: Dedicated to promoting and preserving America's original music-jazz.
Founded: 1977
Specialized Field: Jazz
Status: Nonprofit
Volunteer Staff: 65
Income Sources: National Jazz Service Organization; International Association of Jazz Educators
Performs At: Berger Perfoming Arts Center
Type of Stage: Proscenium
Stage Dimensions: 48x28
Seating Capacity: 500
Year Built: 1990
Organization Type: Sponsoring

746
TUCSON PHILHARMONIA YOUTH ORCHESTRA
P.O. Box 41882
Tucson, AZ 85717
Phone: 520-623-1500
e-mail: info@tpyo.org
Web Site: www.tpyo.org
Management:
   Music Director: Suzette Battan

Mission: To provide the finest quality symphonic training and performance opportunities for young musicians in a professional environment that promotes advanced musical education, performance competition and responsibility
Founded: 1953
Specialized Field: Classical
Season: November-March
Performs At: Tucson Convention Center Music Hall; Armory Park Center
Type of Stage: Proscenium
Stage Dimensions: 128Wx49.5D
Seating Capacity: 2,289
Organization Type: Performing; Educational

747
TUCSON SYMPHONY ORCHESTRA
2175 N Sixth Avenue
Tucson, AZ 85705
Phone: 520-882-8585
Web Site: www.tucsonsymphony.org
Officers:
  Chair: Barbara R. Levy
  First Vice Chair: Bonnie Kampa
  Secretary: George Miraben
  Treasurer: David C. Carney
  Vice Chair Development: Meredith K. Marder
Management:
  Acting Executive Director: George Steele
  Director of Development: Jerusha Schmalzel
  Assoc Director of Marketing & PR: Terry Marshall
  General Manager & VP of Operations: Ian Harwood
  Operations Manager: Kayla Bording
Mission: To present live symphonic performances and music education at the highest level of artistic excellence, enriching and entertaining the people of Southern Arizona
Utilizes: Guest Composers; Guest Musicians
Specialized Field: Symphony
Paid Staff: 30
Paid Artists: 85
Budget: $4,098,500
Performs At: Tucson Convention Center Music Hall
Affiliations: ASOL, BMI, ASCAP
Facility Category: Music hall

748
TUCSON WINTER CHAMBER MUSIC FESTIVAL
PO Box 40845
Tucson, AZ 85717
Phone: 520-577-3769
e-mail: office@arizonachambermusic.org
Web Site: www.arizonachambermusic.org
Management:
  Artistic Director: Peter Rejto
Mission: To be one of the country's most active commissioning programs
Specialized Field: Chamber
Volunteer Staff: 15
Paid Artists: 20
Budget: $60,000-$150,000
Income Sources: Arizona Chamber Association
Season: February - March
Performs At: Leo Rich Theatre - Tucson Convention Center
Type of Stage: Proscenium
Seating Capacity: 560
Organization Type: Performing; Sponsoring

Arkansas

749
ARKANSAS STATE MUSIC PROGRAMS
Arkansas State University- Beebe
Howell Music Center
1000 Iowa Street
Beebe, AR 72012-1000
Mailing Address: PO Box 1000 Beebe AR 72012-1000
Phone: 501-882-3600
Fax: 501-882-8970
Web Site: www.asub.edu
Officers:
  President: Dr Les Wyatt III
  Chair: Mike Gibson
  Secretary: Florine Tousant Milligan
  Chair: Tom O'Connor
Management:
  Director: Neale Bartee
  University Police: Mark Adams
  Executive Assistant to Chancellor: Joe Berry
Mission: To provide students the opportunity to seek success in many different areas of the music profession through varied degree offerings
Specialized Field: Orchestra
Status: Nonprofit
Income Sources: Ticket Sales; Donations
Organization Type: Performing; Educational

750
CONWAY SYMPHONY ORCHESTRA
PO Box 1307
Conway, AR 72033
Phone: 501-269-1066
e-mail: symphony@conwaycorp.net
Web Site: www.conwaysymphonyorchestra.org
Officers:
  Past President: Carolyn Brown
  President: Mike Binko
  Vice President: Kelli Gordon
  Treasurer: Carrick Patterson
Management:
  Conductor/Music Director: Israel Getzof
  General Manager: Vicki Crockett
  UCA Music Department: Jeffery Jarvis
Mission: To create meaningful experiences through performances and education.
Founded: 1984
Specialized Field: Orchestra
Status: Pre-Professional, Professional
Paid Staff: 1
Affiliations: League Of American Orchestras
Seating Capacity: 1,000
Year Built: 2000

751
SOUTH ARKANSAS SYMPHONY
217 S. Jefferson
Suite 100
El Dorado, AR 71730-5876
Phone: 870-862-0521
Toll-free: 800-792-0521
e-mail: sasomail@sbcglobal.net
Web Site: www.southarkansassymphony.org
Management:
  Music Director: Kermit Poling
  Executive Director: Scott Watkins
  Operations Director: Virginia Matthews
  Operations Manager: Stephanie Mitchell
  Technical Director: Russell Wingfield
Mission: To promote symphonic music to the area and to introduce this music to children.
Founded: 1956
Specialized Field: Orchestra
Status: Professional
Paid Staff: 2
Volunteer Staff: 23
Paid Artists: 100
Budget: $100,000-$150,000
Income Sources: Corporate; Private Donations
Season: September-May
Performs At: Municipal Auditorium; Harton Theatre
Annual Attendance: 2,500
Type of Stage: Proscenium
Seating Capacity: 500
Year Built: 1924
Organization Type: Performing; Educational

752
NORTH ARKANSAS SYMPHONY SOCIETY
605 W Dickson Street
Fayetteville, AR 72702
Mailing Address: PO Box 1243 Fayetteville AR 72702
Phone: 479-521-4166
Officers:
  Chairman: Bob Gaddy
  Secretary: Joan Campbell
  Treasurer: Tom Garrison
Management:
  Director: Jeannine Wagar
  General Manager: Aldee Marquis
Mission: To provide north Arkansas with a fully professional regional orchestra presenting quality music, education and programs to enrich the communities
Utilizes: Guest Artists
Founded: 1954
Specialized Field: Symphony
Status: Semi-Professional; Nonprofit
Paid Staff: 6
Income Sources: University of Arkansas
Season: October-April
Performs At: Walton Arts Center
Seating Capacity: 1,200
Year Built: 1992
Organization Type: Performing; Educational

753
SYMPHONY OF NORTHWEST ARKANSAS
217 E. Dickson Street
Suite 106
Fayetteville, AR 72701
Mailing Address: PO Box 1243 Fayetteville AR 72702
Phone: 479-521-4166
Web Site: www.sonamusic.org
Officers:
  Chairman: Daymara Baker
  Secretary: Mary Benjamin
  Treasurer: Kathryn Birkhead
  Advisory Board: Ed Clifford
  Advisory Board: Cynthia Coughlin
  Advisory Board: Mary Ann Greenwood
  Advisory Board: Reed Greenwood
Management:
  Music Director: Paul Haas
  Executive Director: Karen Kapella
  Associate Director: Doug Cummins
  Orchestra Contractor: Ronnamarie Jensen
  Production Manager: Ben Harris
  Singers Director: Terry Hicks
Mission: The Symphony of Northwest Arkansas (SoNA) is the new name for the North Arkansas Symphony (NASO), which was founded in 1954 and has provided more than 50 years of musical

INSTRUMENTAL MUSIC / California

performances and educational opportunities. Under the musical direction of Paul Haas, SoNA presents classical and pops performances for symphonic music lovers in Northwest Arkansas, and is engaged in a partnership with the Walton Arts Center. SoNA brings great music to life.
Utilizes: Guest Artists; Singers
Founded: 1954
Specialized Field: Symphony
Status: Non-Profit, Professional
Paid Staff: 2
Paid Artists: 70
Performs At: Walton Arts Center
Organization Type: Educational; Sponsoring

754
FORT SMITH SYMPHONY
PO Box 3151
Fort Smith, AR 72913
Phone: 479-452-7575
Fax: 479-452-8985
e-mail: fssymphony@fortsmithsymphony.org
Web Site: www.fortsmithsymphony.org
Officers:
  Chair: Marilyn Patterson
  President: Kathy M. Babb
  Vice President Artistic Development: Lori Fay
  Treasurer: Sal Salamone
  Secretary: Carl Davis
Management:
  Music Director: John Jeter
  Development Director: Dr. Sandi Sanders
  Marketing Director: Becky Yates
  Financial Coordinator: Bonnie Scowden
  Director of Development: Dr. Sandi Sanders
Mission: Bringing wonderful music to the youth in our community- Kids first.
Utilizes: Artists-in-Residence; Commissioned Music; Composers-in-Residence; Educators; Fine Artists; Guest Accompanists; Guest Composers; Guest Lecturers; Guest Musicians; Local Artists; Multimedia; Original Music Scores; Singers
Specialized Field: Classical; Symphony
Paid Staff: 4
Volunteer Staff: 60
Budget: $260,000-$1,050,000
Income Sources: Arkansas Arts Council; National Endowment for the Arts
Performs At: Arkansas Best Corporation Performing Arts Center - Fort Smith Civic Center
Facility Category: Performing Arts Center
Seating Capacity: 1,400
Year Remodeled: 2000
Organization Type: Performing; Educational

755
ARKANSAS SYMPHONY ORCHESTRA
2417 N Tyler
PO Box 7328
Little Rock, AR 72207
Mailing Address: P.O. Box 7328, Little Rock, AR 72217
Phone: 501-666-1761
Fax: 501-666-3193
e-mail: gwixson@arkansassymphony.org
Web Site: www.arkansassymphony.org
Officers:
  Chair: Michael Shelley
Management:
  Music Director: Philip Mann
  Associate Conductor: Geoffrey Robson
  Executive Director: Christina Littlejohn
  Public Relations: Tamara Clement
  Director of Finance: Meagan Adams
  Staff Accountant: Linda Macon
Mission: To create a positive environment for the musical education of youth throughout Arkansas.
Founded: 1966
Specialized Field: Classical; Pops; Symphony
Status: Nonprofit
Paid Staff: 14
Volunteer Staff: 2000
Paid Artists: 60
Budget: $1,050,000-$3,600,000
Income Sources: Individual; Corporate; Foundation Donations
Season: September-May
Performs At: Robinson Center Music Hall
Affiliations: Arkansas Symphony Orchestra Society Guild, ASO Ovation
Annual Attendance: 250,000
Type of Stage: Proscenium
Stage Dimensions: 60Wx42Dx35H
Seating Capacity: 2,609
Organization Type: Performing; Educational

756
PINE BLUFF SYMPHONY ORCHESTRA
211 W 3rd Avenue
Pine Bluff, AR 71601
Mailing Address: P.O. Box 8725, Pine Bluff, AR 71611-8725
Phone: 870-536-7666
e-mail: pbsymphony@pbreynoldscenter.org
Web Site: www.pinebluffsymphony.com
Officers:
  President: James Cathy
  VP: Yvonne Glien
  Secretary: Donna Davis
  Treasurer: Robert Hart, Jr.
Management:
  Director: William H. Fox, Jr.
  Director Emeritus: Bennye H. Clemmons
  Advisory Board: Dr. Michael Bates
  Advisory Board: Ellen Nuckolls
  Advisory Board: Ron Stahara
Mission: To enlarge the symphony's demographic audience, supporting the health and wellness of the region's community and enbedding the educational value of classical music within every aspect of the new and emerging cultural infrastructure
Founded: 1987
Specialized Field: Orchestra; Symphony
Paid Staff: 3
Paid Artists: 70
Budget: $225,000
Income Sources: Private and Corporate Donations
Season: October-April
Annual Attendance: 25,000
Seating Capacity: 1,900
Year Built: 1987
Organization Type: Performing; Educational

California

757
BAKERSFIELD SYMPHONY ORCHESTRA
1328 34th Street
Suite A
Bakersfield, CA 93301
Phone: 661-323-7928
Fax: 661-323-7331
e-mail: info@BSOnow.org
Web Site: www.bakersfieldsymphony.org
Officers:
  President/CEO: M. Bryan Burrow
  Chairman: Jim Bell
  Secretary/Treasurer: Ira Cohen
  VC: Wayn Deats
  VP: Elaine LeCain
Management:
  Director: John Farrer
  Operations Director: Kari H. Heilman
  Orchestra Operations Manager: Mary Moore
  Artistic Consultant: Jerry Kleinsasser
  Sales & Advertising: Alice Oden
Mission: To provide the best possible performances of great music for the widest possible audience and provide musical education for the young people of Kern County
Founded: 1932
Specialized Field: Classical; Symphony
Paid Staff: 7
Volunteer Staff: 25
Paid Artists: 60
Budget: $260,000-$1,050,000
Income Sources: Indvidual and Corporate Donations, Foundations, Symphony Associates, Bakersfield Symphony Orchestra Endowment Foundation
Season: October-May
Performs At: Rabobank Theater
Affiliations: Bakersfield Masterworks Chorale, Bakersfield Youth Symphony, Bakersfield Summer Band
Annual Attendance: 5,000
Facility Category: Convention Center & Theater
Type of Stage: Full with Pit
Seating Capacity: 2,800
Year Built: 1965
Rental Contact: Ed Dorsey

758
BERKELEY SYMPHONY ORCHESTRA
1942 University Avenue
Suite 207
Berkeley, CA 94704
Phone: 510-841-2800
Fax: 510-841-5422
e-mail: info@berkeleysymphony.org
Web Site: www.berkeleysymphony.org
Officers:
  President: Thomas Z. Reicher
  Treasurer: Ed Osborn
  Secretary: Tricia Swift
  Vice President for Development: Janet McCutcheon
  Vice President for Community Engage: Stuart Gronningen
Management:
  Director: Kent Nagano
  Executive Director: Rene Mandel
  Operations Director: Theresa Gabel
  Development Director: Marissa Phillips
  Director of Communications: Jenny Lee
Mission: Ensuring that our programming continues to touch the lives of many, inside and outside the concert hall
Utilizes: Guest Artists; Singers
Founded: 1969
Specialized Field: Symphony; Contemporary
Status: Semi-Professional
Paid Staff: 37
Volunteer Staff: 20
Budget: 1 million
Income Sources: Private and Corporate Donations
Season: September-April
Performs At: Zellerbach Hall; University of California at Berkeley, Roda Theatre, St John's Presbyterian Church
Affiliations: Ameican Symphony Orchestra League
Annual Attendance: 20,000
Seating Capacity: 2,089

Year Built: 1968
Organization Type: Performing

759
SAN FRANCISCO EARLY MUSIC SOCIETY
PO Box 10151
Berkeley, CA 94709-1516
Phone: 510-528-1725
e-mail: sfems@sfems.org
Web Site: www.sfems.org
Officers:
  Chair, Board Of Directors: John Phillips
  VP: Yuko Tanaka
  VP: Robert Cole
  Treasurer: Marilyn Marquis
  Secretary: Sally Blaker
Management:
  Executive Director: Harvey Malloy, hmalloy@sfems.org
  Operations Director: Dorothy Manly, dorothy@sfems.org
  Festival and Workshop Administrator: Katie Hagen
  Publications Editor: Jonathan Harris
  IT Manager: Jody Ames
Mission: Seeks to create an appreciative and supportive environment for the study and performance of medieval, renaissance, and baroque music by both amateurs and professionals in Northern California
Utilizes: Contract Orchestras; Educators; Guest Directors; Multimedia; Original Music Scores
Founded: 1975
Specialized Field: Chamber; Ensemble
Status: Professional; Nonprofit
Paid Staff: 2
Budget: 1/4 million
Income Sources: Private and Corporate Donations, Grants
Season: October-May
Performs At: First Lutheran Church, St. John's Presbyterian Church; First Congregational Church; St. Mark's Lutheran Church
Affiliations: Early Music America; Chamber Music America
Year Built: 1920
Year Remodeled: 1991
Organization Type: Performing; Touring, Presenters

760
SAN FRANCISCO CHAMBER ORCHESTRA
PO Box 591566
Berkeley, CA 94119-1564
Mailing Address: PO Box 191564
Phone: 415-692-3367
Fax: 510-524-3683
e-mail: info@sfchamberorchestra.org
Web Site: www.sfchamberorchestra.org
Officers:
  Treasurer: John R. Houghton
  Secretary: Frederick J. Isaac
  Chair: Kathie Sollers
  Vice Chair: Giorgio Sorani
Management:
  Music Director: Benjamin Simon
  Personnel Manager: Robin May
  Executive Director: Kristen Steiner
Mission: Dedicated to bringing immediacy and intimacy of music for small orchestra and chamber ensemble to audiences of all ages by presenting classical, contemporary, and commissioned works as well as to educate and enlighten the next generation of music lovers through outreach programs.
Utilizes: Theatre Companies
Founded: 1952
Specialized Field: Classical
Status: Professional
Budget: $260,000-$1,050,000
Income Sources: Private Donations
Season: December-May
Performs At: Louise M Davies Symphony Hall, Florence Gould Theatre, Various Venues
Seating Capacity: 2,741, 316
Year Built: 1980
Organization Type: Performing; Educational

761
SAN FRANCISCO EARLY MUSIC SOCIETY
PO Box 10151
Berkeley, CA 94709-1516
Mailing Address: P.O. Box 27495, San Francisco, CA 94127-0495
Phone: 510-528-1725
e-mail: sfems@sfems.org
Web Site: www.sfems.org
Officers:
  Chair. Board of Directors: John Phillips
  VP: Yuko Tanaka
  VP: Robert Cole
  Treasurer: Marilyn Marquis
  Secretar: Sally Blaker
Management:
  Executive Director: Harvey Malloy, hmalloy@sfems.org
  Operations Manager: Dorothy Manly
  Festival and Workshop Administrator: Katie Hagen
  Jody: Harris Publications Editor
Mission: The San Francisco Early Music Society seeks to create an appreciative and supportive environment for the study and performance of Medieval, Renaissance, and Baroque music by both amateurs and professionals of Northern California.
Founded: 1975
Specialized Field: Chamber; Ensemble
Status: Professional; Nonprofit
Paid Staff: 2
Budget: $250,000
Income Sources: Private and Corporate Donations; Grants
Performs At: First Lutheran Church; St. John's Presbyterian Church; St. Mark's Lutheran Church
Seating Capacity: 400
Year Built: 1920
Year Remodeled: 1991

762
YOUNG PEOPLE'S SYMPHONY ORCHESTRA
PO Box 5593
Berkeley, CA 94705
Phone: 510-849-9776
Fax: 510-654-0274
e-mail: ypsomusic@yahoo.com
Web Site: www.ypsomusic.net
Officers:
  President: David Wolf
  VP: Meredith Montgomery
  Secretary: Lynn Mackay
  Treasurer: Brian Frazier
Management:
  Executive Director: Wendy Cilman
  Director: David Ramadanoff
  YPSO Orchestra Manager: David Davis
Mission: To provide orchestra education to young adults ranging from 13 to 21 living in the Bay Area
Utilizes: Soloists
Founded: 1935
Specialized Field: Symphony; Chamber
Paid Staff: 2
Paid Artists: 10
Budget: $100,000
Income Sources: Private and Corporate Donations, Grants
Performs At: Dean Lesher Regional Center for the Arts
Seating Capacity: 580
Rental Contact: Operations Manager David Davis
Organization Type: Performing; Educational

763
LOREN L ZACHARY SOCIETY FOR THE PERFORMING ARTS
2250 Gloaming Way
Beverly Hills, CA 90210
Phone: 310-276-2731
Fax: 310-275-8245
e-mail: infoz@zacharysociety.org
Web Site: www.zacharysociety.org
Officers:
  President: Nedra Zachary
Management:
  Conductor: Frank Fetta
  Competition Director: Nedra Zachary
Mission: Dedicated to producing the National Vocal Competition for Young Singers and Grand Finals Concert.
Utilizes: Guest Composers; Multimedia; Original Music Scores; Sign Language Translators
Founded: 1972
Specialized Field: Opera Singing
Status: Non-profit
Volunteer Staff: 100
Paid Artists: 35
Non-paid Artists: 1
Income Sources: Private Donations
Performs At: Wilshire Ebell Theatre
Annual Attendance: 1,260
Facility Category: Theatre
Type of Stage: Proscenium
Stage Dimensions: 28Dx48Wx60H
Seating Capacity: 1,270
Year Built: 1973
Year Remodeled: 1989

764
YOUNG MUSICIANS FOUNDATION DEBUT ORCHESTRA
244 South San Pedro Street
Suite 506
Beverly Hills, CA 90012
Phone: 213-617-7707
Fax: 213-617-7706
e-mail: info@ymf.org
Web Site: www.ymf.org
Officers:
  Chairman: David Weiss
  Secretary: Gunther Schiff
  Treasurer: Dave Regan
  Chairperson: Margot Smith Thomas
  Honorary President: Gregor Piatigorsky
Management:
  Executive Director: Julia Gaskill
  Director: Case Scaglione
  Artistic Director: Delores Stevens
  Development Associate: Omega Medina

INSTRUMENTAL MUSIC / California

Operations & Social Media Manager: Kimmie Fadem
Mission: To preserve the classical music heritage by providing performance opportunities, financial assistance and community outreach programming that contributes to the personal, academic and artistic development of youth from all socio-economic and ethnic backgrounds
Founded: 1955
Specialized Field: Chamber; Classical
Status: Professional
Budget: $260,000-$1,050,000
Income Sources: Private and Corporate Donations, Grants, Ticket Sales
Season: November-August
Performs At: Wilshire Ebell Theatre
Annual Attendance: 17,000
Stage Dimensions: 28Dx48Wx60H
Seating Capacity: 1,270
Year Built: 1955
Organization Type: Performing; Educational

765
SOUTHEAST SYMPHONY
1985 Rolling Vista Drive
Suite 55
Burbank, CA 91508
Phone: 323-293-7372
e-mail: cedickersoniii@sbcglobal.net
Web Site: www.southeastsymphony.org
Officers:
- **President/CEO:** Sheryl Harris
- **VP:** Morris O'Kelly
- **Treasurer:** Rosemarie Cook Glover
- **Secretary:** Allison Cook
- **Board Member:** Opal Carter

Management:
- **Music Director/Conductor:** Charles Dickerson

Mission: To perform concerts for the diverse community and to foster musical training for aspiring musicians, most of whom are African American.
Founded: 1948
Specialized Field: Symphony
Status: Nonprofit
Paid Staff: 14
Volunteer Staff: 30
Paid Artists: 60
Budget: $100,000-$150,000
Income Sources: Grants; Memberships; Donations
Affiliations: Association of California Symphony Orchestras
Seating Capacity: 1,100

766
CARMEL BACH FESTIVAL
Cottage 16, NW Corner of 10th & Mission
Carmel, CA 93921
Mailing Address: PO Box 575, Carmel, CA 93921
Phone: 831-624-1521
Fax: 831-624-2788
e-mail: info@bachfestival.org
Web Site: www.bachfestival.org
Officers:
- **Board President:** Betsey Pearson
- **First Vice President:** Alan Carlson
- **VP:** Lynn Evans
- **Treasurer/CFO:** Howard Fisher
- **Secretary:** Fran Lozano

Management:
- **Music Director/Conductor:** Bruno Weil
- **Associate Conductor:** William Jon Gray
- **Artistic Director:** Nana Fardiany
- **Managing Director:** Jesse Read
- **Concertmaster:** Elizabeth Wallfisch

General Manager: Elizabeth Pasquinelli
Ticket Manager: Luisa Cardoza
Mission: We celebrate the genius of Johann Sebastian Bach, as well as his contemporaries and musical heirs, through performances and educational activities of the highest caliber.
Founded: 1935
Specialized Field: Bach; Ensemble; Educational
Status: Professional; Nonprofit
Paid Staff: 35
Paid Artists: 100
Non-paid Artists: 30
Budget: $1.5 million
Income Sources: Private and Corporate Donations, Sponsors
Season: July-August
Performs At: All Saints Church, Sunset Theatre, Historic Carmel Mission Basilica, Church in the Forest in Pebble Beach
Affiliations: Various Sites in the vicinity of Carmel-by-the-Sea
Annual Attendance: 17,000
Facility Category: Community Auditorium
Type of Stage: Proscenium
Seating Capacity: 259
Year Built: 1928
Organization Type: Performing; Educational

767
CHAMBER MUSIC MONTEREY BAY
3785 Via Nona Marie
Suite 307
Carmel, CA 93923
Mailing Address: PO Box 221458 Carmel CA 93922
Phone: 831-625-2212
Fax: 831-625-3555
e-mail: info@chambermusicmontereybay.org
Web Site: www.chambermusicmontereybay.org
Officers:
- **President:** Barbara Babcock
- **First Vice President:** Ann Flower
- **Treasurer:** Janet Brennan
- **Secretary:** Ken Wanderman
- **President Emeritus:** Amy Anderson

Management:
- **Director:** John Newkirk, dana@chambermusic.org
- **Adminstrative Assistant:** Diane Lewis
- **Executive Director:** Dana Werdmuller

Mission: Enrich the cultural life of the community by producing an annual concert series of world renowned chamber ensembles, developing and delivering a variety of outreach and educational programs
Utilizes: Guest Directors; Guest Musical Directors; Multimedia
Founded: 1966
Specialized Field: Chamber
Status: Nonprofit
Paid Staff: 2
Volunteer Staff: 14
Paid Artists: 5
Budget: $105,000
Income Sources: Donations; Ticket Sales; Grants
Season: September-April
Performs At: Sunset Theatre
Annual Attendance: 3,000
Facility Category: Theatre and Community Center
Type of Stage: Proscenium
Seating Capacity: 700
Year Built: 1940
Year Remodeled: 2002
Organization Type: Sponsoring

768
MONTEREY BAY SYMPHONY
PO Box 146
Carmel, CA 93921
Phone: 831-373-8450
e-mail: ronweitzman@redshift.com
Web Site: www.montereybaysymphony.org
Officers:
- **President:** Ron A Weitzman
- **Secretary:** Dr John Castagna
- **Treasurer:** Robert Lee
- **VP:** Morley Brown
- **VP:** Bert Babcock

Management:
- **Director:** Dr Carl Christensen

Mission: To bring pops and patriotic orchestral music performed by professional musicians to the residents and visitors of Monterey County free of charge, while providing musical support to local arts organizations
Founded: 1985
Specialized Field: Pops; Patriotic Orchestral Music
Status: Nonprofit
Volunteer Staff: 20
Paid Artists: 56
Budget: $35,000-$100,000
Performs At: Naval Postgraduate School

769
MONTEREY SYMPHONY
2560 Garden Road
Suite 101
Carmel, CA 93940
Phone: 831-624-8511
Fax: 831-644-0669
Toll-free: 800-698-1138
e-mail: info@montereysymphony.org
Web Site: www.montereysymphony.org
Officers:
- **President:** Janet McDaniel
- **Secretary:** Susan Britton
- **Treasurer:** Pinkie Terry
- **Chair:** Lee E. Rosen
- **Vice Chairman:** Bruce Lindsen

Management:
- **Executive Director:** Edmund Feingold
- **Director of Finance & Administratio:** Leo Keech
- **Development Director:** Michelle Lange
- **Education Outreach Coordinator:** Carol Rein

Mission: To bring music of high quality to the people of Monterey and San Benito Counties and to foster and encourage the appreciation of it by people of all ages.
Utilizes: Guest Accompanists; Guest Companies; Guest Composers; Guest Musical Directors; Guest Musicians; Guest Writers; Organization Contracts; Original Music Scores
Founded: 1947
Specialized Field: Symphony; Orchestra;
Status: Professional; Nonprofit
Paid Staff: 6
Volunteer Staff: 7
Paid Artists: 80
Budget: $1,500,000
Income Sources: Association of California Symphony Orchestras, American Symphony Orchestra League, Cultural Council, Grants
Season: October-May
Performs At: Sunset Theatre; Sherwood Hall; Pacific Grove Middle School
Affiliations: ACSO; American Symphony Orchestra League
Annual Attendance: 20,000
Seating Capacity: 733; 1511
Year Remodeled: 2002

INSTRUMENTAL MUSIC / California

Organization Type: Performing

770
SACRAMENTO SYMPHONIC WINDS
PO Box 1503
Carmichael, CA 95608
Phone: 916-489-2576
Fax: 916-489-2576
e-mail: michr@sbcglobal.net
Web Site: www.sacwinds.org
Officers:
    President: Doug Hoffman
    VP: Cristine Hancock
    Secretary: Les Corbin
    Director: Les Lehr
    Founder: Dr.Les Lehr
Management:
    Conductor: Lester E Lehr
    Director: Dr.Les Lehr
Utilizes: Collaborations; Educators; Five Seasonal Concerts; Guest Accompanists; Guest Companies; Guest Musicians; Local Artists; Lyricists; Multimedia; Organization Contracts; Sign Language Translators; Singers
Volunteer Staff: 65
Non-paid Artists: 4
Annual Attendance: 1,500
Seating Capacity: 500

771
CARSON-DOMINGUEZ HILLS SYMPHONY
California State University at Dominguez Hills
1000 E Victoria Street
Carson, CA 90747
Phone: 310-243-3389
Fax: 310-516-4268
Web Site: cah.csudh.edu
Officers:
    President: Mildred Garcia
    Chair: Richard Kravchak PhD
Management:
    Director: David Bradfield MM
    Dean of Students: Munashe Furusa, Ph.D.
    Acting Associate Dean: Sheela Pawar, Ph.D.
    Academic Resource Manager: Gwendolyne D. Taylor
Mission: To provide music students with career-oriented skills for use in the music industry
Founded: 1976
Specialized Field: Orchestra
Status: Nonprofit; Professional
Budget: $148,000
Income Sources: Fundraising, Donations, National Endowment for the Arts
Season: December-May
Performs At: University Theatre; California State University of Los Angeles

772
CALIFORNIA E.A.R. UNIT
29654 Driver Avenue
Castaic, CA 91384
Phone: 661-775-9975
Fax: 661-775-3855
e-mail: altmuse@earthlink.net
Web Site: www.earunit.org
Officers:
    Founder: Dorothy Stone
Management:
    Artistic Director: Vicki Ray
    Executive Director: Amy Knoles
Mission: Dedicated to the performance, promotion, and creation of some of the most exciting music of our time
Founded: 1981
Specialized Field: Contemporary
Status: Professional; Nonprofit
Paid Staff: 2
Volunteer Staff: 2
Paid Artists: 6
Performs At: Los Angeles County Museum of Art
Organization Type: Performing; Touring; Resident; Educational
Resident Groups: New Chamber Music

773
CLAREMONT SYMPHONY ORCHESTRA
PO Box 698
Claremont, CA 91711
Phone: 909-593-5620
Web Site: www.claremontso.org
Officers:
    President: Dr. Cecilia Cloughly
    VP: Laura Jaoui
    Secretary: Gina Shaw
    Treasurer: Dr. David Sykes
    Concertmaster: Gloria Cangahuala
Management:
    Director: Dr James Fahringer
    Music Director: Robert Sage
    Associate Conductor: Ruth Charloff
    Associate Conductor: Gary Iida
Mission: To provide free concerts for the community that features an exciting variety of musical experiences
Founded: 1953
Specialized Field: Symphony
Status: Nonprofit
Budget: $18,000
Income Sources: Private Donations
Season: October-July
Performs At: Bridges Hall of Music
Affiliations: Association of California Symphony Orchestras
Seating Capacity: 600
Year Built: 1915
Year Remodeled: 1972
Organization Type: Performing; Educational

774
POMONA COLLEGE ORCHESTRA
Pomona College Department of Music
333 N. College Way
Claremont, CA 91711
Mailing Address: Pomona College, Music, 340 N. College Avenue, Claremont, CA
Phone: 909-621-8155
Fax: 909-621-8645
e-mail: music@pomona.edu
Web Site: music.pomona.edu
Officers:
    Chair: Eric Lindholm
Management:
    Director: Eric Lindholm
    Concert Production Manager: Elizabeth D. Champion
    Academic Department Coordinator: Cathy Endress
Mission: To meet the needs of both students who choose one of the concentration programs and students who wish to explore music one course at a time
Specialized Field: Orchestra
Status: Nonprofit
Paid Staff: 2
Volunteer Staff: 5
Budget: $15,000
Income Sources: Private and Corporate Donations
Season: October-April
Performs At: Bridges Hall of Music
Affiliations: Association of California Symphony Orchestras, Los Angeles County Arts Commission
Annual Attendance: 2,500-3,000
Seating Capacity: 600
Year Built: 1915
Year Remodeled: 2001
Organization Type: Performing

775
DIABLO SYMPHONY ASSOCIATION
PO Box 2222
Concord, CA 94595
Phone: 925-676-5888
Web Site: www.diablosymphony.org
Officers:
    President: Patrick Campbell
    Secretary: Ann Nelson
    Treasurer: Ron Cassano
    Board Member: Eileen Benway
Management:
    Director: Joyce Johnson-Hamilton
    Marketing Director: Bob Rezak
    Music Director & Conductor: Matilda Hofman
Mission: Provide great concerts in the Diablo/Walnut Creek area
Founded: 1962
Specialized Field: Orchestra
Status: Professional; Nonprofit
Paid Staff: 7
Volunteer Staff: 15
Paid Artists: 12
Budget: $125,000
Income Sources: Tickets; Sponsors; Members; American Symphony Orchestra League; Association of California Symphony Orchestras
Performs At: Dean Lesher Center for the Performing Arts
Annual Attendance: 7,000
Facility Category: Art Center Music Hall
Type of Stage: 3 Stage Music Hall
Stage Dimensions: 40x50
Seating Capacity: 297
Year Built: 1989
Organization Type: Performing; Sponsoring

776
MOZART CLASSICAL ORCHESTRA
Renee and Henry Segerstrom Concert Hall
600 Town Center Drive
Costa Mesa, CA 92626
Mailing Address: Mozart Classical Orchestra PO Box 54404 Irvine CA
Phone: 949-387-9197
Fax: 714-556-8984
e-mail: info@mozartorchestra.org
Web Site: www.mozartorchestra.org
Officers:
    President: Jack Teberg
Management:
    Director: Ami Porat
Founded: 1985
Status: Non-Profit; Professional
Budget: $328,000
Income Sources: Individual and Corporate Donations
Performs At: Zipper Hall; Colburn School for the Performing Arts
Seating Capacity: 415
Year Built: 1998
Organization Type: Performing

INSTRUMENTAL MUSIC / California

777
CULVER CITY SYMPHONY ORCHESTRA
Westchester Symphony Society
PO Box 4846
Culver City, CA 90231
Phone: 310-717-5500
e-mail: info@culvercitysymphony.org
Web Site: www.culvercitysymphony.org
Officers:
  President: Matthew Hetz
  Manager: Helene Mirich-Spear
Management:
  Director: Frank Fetta
Mission: Dedicated to providing the highest artistic standards in presenting music to our loyal audience
Utilizes: Educators; Multimedia
Founded: 1963
Specialized Field: Symphony; Orchestra
Status: Nonprofit; Professional
Budget: $35,000-$100,000
Income Sources: Membership in Symphony Society, Donations, and Grants
Performs At: Veterans Memorial Auditorium
Annual Attendance: 1,800-2,400
Seating Capacity: 1,000
Year Built: 1950
Organization Type: Performing; Educational

778
CYPRESS POPS ORCHESTRA
PO Box 434
Cypress, CA 90630
Phone: 714-527-4276
e-mail: cjm1@cypresspops.org
Web Site: www.thecypresspops.org
Officers:
  President: Rick Bemis
  Treasurer: Allyson Davis
  Secretary: Liz Royce
  VP: Steven.K Mauss
Management:
  Music Director: John E Hall III
Mission: Dedicated to providing quality performances at no cost to the public
Founded: 1988
Specialized Field: Pops
Status: Nonprofit
Budget: $75,000-$125,000
Income Sources: Audiences; Patrons; Corporate Sponsors; City of Cypress; Orchestra's Guild
Season: June-November
Performs At: Cypress Civic Center Green
Seating Capacity: 1,000
Year Built: 1967
Organization Type: Educational; Performing

779
CAPISTRANO VALLEY SYMPHONY
24681 La Plaza
Suite 360
Dana Point, CA 92629
Phone: 949-240-8540
Fax: 949-847-6828
e-mail: info@capovalleysymphony.com
Web Site: www.capovalleysymphony.com
Officers:
  President: Patti Short
Management:
  Director: David Matthies
Mission: To provide concerts and educational programs of the highest quality symphonic music for the residents of South Orange County and to make this music affordable and accessible to the broadest possible audience.
Utilizes: Five Seasonal Concerts; Guest Accompanists; Guest Companies; Singers
Founded: 1984
Specialized Field: Symphony
Status: Nonprofit
Paid Staff: 1
Budget: $260,000
Income Sources: Grants from local goverments and corporations; Individual Sponsors
Season: May-September
Performs At: Mission San Juan Capistrano
Annual Attendance: 100,000
Year Built: 1776
Organization Type: Educational; Performing

780
TASSAJARA SYMPHONY ORCHESTRA
696 San Ramon Valley Boulevard
Suite 104
Danville, CA 94526
Phone: 925-820-2494
e-mail: greatmusic@tassajarasymphony.org
Officers:
  President: Cheryl Williamson
Management:
  Founding Musical Director/Conductor: Sara Jobin
  Artistic Director: Dawn Wade
Mission: Aims to provide an exciting and enjoyable playing environment that encourages camradery and emphasizes fine ensemble playing.
Utilizes: Collaborations; Commissioned Composers; Commissioned Music; Dance Companies; Educators; Fine Artists; Five Seasonal Concerts; Guest Instructors; Guest Lecturers; Guest Musicians; Guest Writers; Multimedia; Original Music Scores; Sign Language Translators; Singers; Soloists
Founded: 1998
Specialized Field: Orchestra; Symphony
Paid Staff: 2
Volunteer Staff: 10
Paid Artists: 45
Budget: $140,000
Income Sources: Donors; Grants
Performs At: Community Church and Regional Center for the Arts
Annual Attendance: 1500

781
DOWNEY SYMPHONY ORCHESTRA
Downey Symphonic Society
PO Box 763
Downey, CA 90241-0763
Phone: 562-403-2944
Fax: 562-861-9499
Web Site: www.downeysymphony.org
Officers:
  President: Nick Frankart
  VP: Larry Lewis
  Secretary: Ruth Hillecke
  Treasurer: William Hare
Management:
  Music Director: Sharon Lavery
Mission: Provides leadership in bringing symphonic music to the community, encouraging and supporting the orchestra's artistic, organizational and fiscal development. The Society fosters accessibility, diversity, and excellence in its programs and promotes, to the public, the value and importance of symphonic music.
Founded: 1962
Specialized Field: Symphony
Status: Professional, Nonprofit
Paid Staff: 3
Volunteer Staff: 16
Paid Artists: 60
Budget: $150,000
Income Sources: Donations; Ticket Sales; Grants
Performs At: Downey Civic Center
Affiliations: ASCO
Annual Attendance: 3,000
Seating Capacity: 740
Year Built: 1961
Organization Type: Performing

782
IMPERIAL VALLEY SYMPHONY
1904 Johnson Lane
PO Box 713
El Centro, CA 92243-9547
Phone: 760-355-6287
Fax: 760-355-6398
e-mail: joel@imperial.cc.ca.us
Management:
  Music Director/Conductor: Gregory Van Sudmeier
Founded: 1974
Specialized Field: Symphony; Orchestra
Status: Nonprofit
Paid Staff: 1
Volunteer Staff: 4
Paid Artists: 25
Non-paid Artists: 35
Budget: $20,000
Affiliations: American Symphony Orchestra League
Annual Attendance: 1950
Seating Capacity: 1050
Year Built: 1996

783
FREMONT SYMPHONY ORCHESTRA
PO Box 104
Fremont, CA 94537
Phone: 510-371-4860
Fax: 510-794-1658
Toll-free: 877-938-9240
e-mail: info@fremontsymphony.org
Web Site: www.fremontsymphony.org
Officers:
  President: Steve Pietkiewicz
  Vice-President: Merna Morse
  Treasurer: Jean Louise
  Secretary: Caryl Dockter
Management:
  Music Director: Gregory Van Sudmeier
  Orchestra Personnel Manager: Carole Klein
  Orchestra Librarian: Marcella Schantz
  Executive Director: Eman Isadiar
  Patron Services: Lynne Siebert
Mission: To provide and develop, for the greater Fremont area, a professional symphony orchestra. The orchestra will fulfill the community's needs and wants by offering a balanced program of established symphonic repertoire.
Utilizes: Collaborations; Commissioned Composers; Dance Companies; Five Seasonal Concerts; Guest Composers; Guest Musicians; Guest Writers; Instructors; Local Artists & Directors; Organization Contracts; Original Music Scores; Paid Performers; Scenic Designers; Singers
Founded: 1964

INSTRUMENTAL MUSIC / California

Specialized Field: Symphony; Orchestra; Ensemble; Educational
Status: Professional
Paid Staff: 5
Volunteer Staff: 45
Paid Artists: 70
Budget: $270,000
Income Sources: Ticket Sales; Government; Corporate & Foundation Grants; Individual Contributions; Fundraising Events
Season: September-May
Performs At: Smith Center; Ohlone College
Affiliations: American Symphony Orchestra League; ACSO; Fremont Chamber; American Society of Composers, Authors and Publishers
Annual Attendance: 2,500-6,000
Facility Category: Theatre
Type of Stage: Proscenium
Stage Dimensions: 30x50
Seating Capacity: 405
Year Built: 1998
Rental Contact: Christopher Boorasa
Organization Type: Performing; Educational

784
CHOOKASIAN ARMENIAN CONCERT ENSEMBLE

2511 W Browning Avenue
Fresno, CA 93711-2508
Phone: 559-449-1777
Fax: 559-432-6666
e-mail: chook3@qnis.net
Web Site: www.chookasian.com
Management:
  Armenian Ensemble Director: John Chookasian
Mission: To preserve, present, and promote the traditional Armenian music, dance and culture through our concert and festival presentations around the world and our live concert/festival cD albums. Secondly, we have presented numerous educational programs that has broadened the understanding and appreciation of traditional Armenian music and culture to the students and general public at large.
Utilizes: Dancers; Filmmakers; Grant Writers; Guest Musical Directors; Organization Contracts; Paid Performers; Theatre Companies
Founded: 1994
Specialized Field: Armenia Music
Status: Professional
Paid Staff: 15
Paid Artists: 15
Income Sources: Grants; Concert Halls; University/College Concert Halls, Museums, Institutions, Art Center, Corporations, Churches, Festivals, Films, Individuals
Performs At: California State University Performing Arts Center
Seating Capacity: 600
Year Built: 1987

785
FRESNO PHILHARMONIC

2377 West Shaw Lane
Suite 101
Fresno, CA 93711
Phone: 559-261-0600
Fax: 559-261-0700
e-mail: info@fresnophil.org
Web Site: www.fresnophil.org
Officers:
  President: J.D. Northway, MD
  VP: Dr. Bernard K. Karian, D.D.S.
  Treasurer: Wayne Boos
  Secretary: Kay Whitten

Management:
  Music Director: Theodore Kuchar
  Executive Director: Stephen Wilson
  Marketing Director: Stacy Woods
  Finance Director: Lona Kiggins
  Patron Services Manager: Connie Miranda
Mission: To present high quality, live orchestral music to audiences throughout the San Joaquin Valley.
Utilizes: Collaborations; Guest Accompanists; Guest Artists; Guest Composers; Guest Lecturers; Guest Musical Directors; Guest Musicians; Multimedia; Singers
Founded: 1954
Specialized Field: Symphony; Orchestra
Status: Nonprofit
Paid Artists: 80
Budget: $1.8 million
Income Sources: Association of California Symphony Orchestras
Season: September-May
Performs At: William Saroyan Theatre; Fresno Convention Center
Seating Capacity: 2,353
Year Built: 1966
Organization Type: Performing; Touring; Resident

786
JOHN CHOOKASIAN INTERNATIONAL FOLK ENSEMBLE

2511 W Browning Avenue
Fresno, CA 93711-2508
Phone: 559-449-1777
Fax: 559-432-6666
e-mail: chook3@qnis.net
Web Site: www.chookasian.com
Management:
  Artistic Director: John Chookasian, chook3@qnis.net
Mission: To promote the folk music, folk dance, and folk instruments of the Near & Middle East, including: Armenian, Arabic, and Greek culture & traditions. Available for tours, concerts, festivals, conventions, corporate events, concert halls, colleges & universities, weddings, dances, private parties, night clubs and films.
Utilizes: Collaborating Artists; Dance Companies; Dancers; Grant Writers; Guest Accompanists; Guest Artists; Guest Musical Directors; Guest Musicians; Lyricists; Multimedia; Original Music Scores; Paid Performers; Poets; Sign Language Translators; Theatre Companies
Founded: 1964
Specialized Field: Near-East Music; Middle-Eastern Music
Status: Professional; Nonprofit
Paid Artists: 12
Income Sources: Grants; Concerts; Festivals; Arts Councils; Corporations; Cultural Institutions; Organizations; Individuals; Art Centers; Colleges & Universities; Churches
Annual Attendance: 4,000 - 6,000
Seating Capacity: 600
Year Built: 1987
Organization Type: Performing; Touring; Educational

787
PHILIP LORENZ MEMORIAL KEYBOARD CONCERTS

PO Box 14162
Fresno, CA 93650
Phone: 559-278-2337
Fax: 559-278-6800
e-mail: andreasw@csufresno.edu
Web Site: www.keyboardconcerts.com

Officers:
  Vice-President: Dr. James Prochazka
  Treasurer: Maria Prochazka
  Secretary: George Gianopulos
  President: Andreas Werz
Management:
  Artistic Director: Andreas Werz
Mission: Memorial Keyboard Concerts presents eight to ten pianists/organists from around the world.
Founded: 1971
Opened: 1971
Specialized Field: Piano
Status: Nonprofit
Paid Staff: 5
Volunteer Staff: 5
Paid Artists: 10
Budget: $60,000
Income Sources: Private and Corporate Donations, Ticket Sales
Performs At: Concert Hall; Callifornia State University, Fresno
Seating Capacity: 400

788
SOUTH VALLEY SYMPHONY

PO Box 1347
Gilroy, CA 95021-1347
Phone: 408-842-3934
Fax: 408-842-9776
e-mail: bbottini@verizon.net
Web Site: www.southvalleysymphony.org
Officers:
  President: Christine Hopwood
  VP: John Graham
  Secretary: Jenny Redfern
  Treasurer: Kay Spencer
Management:
  Music Director/Conductor: Anthony Quartuccio
Mission: To provide music from Verdi, Vivaldi, Mandel, Copeland, Donizetti, and much more. South Valley Symphony performs a series of 6 concerts.
Founded: 1974
Specialized Field: Symphony
Status: Nonprofit
Volunteer Staff: 10
Non-paid Artists: 40
Budget: $30,000-$35,000
Income Sources: Fundraisers, Advertising
Season: October-May
Performs At: Gavilian College Theatre
Annual Attendance: 275-425

789
GLENDALE SYMPHONY ORCHESTRA ASSOCIATION

PO Box 1986
Glendale, CA 91209-1986
Phone: 818-500-8720
Fax: 818-500-8721
e-mail: info@glendalesymphony.org
Web Site: www.glendalesymphony.org
Officers:
  President: Patrick Shahijanian
  VP: Jack Kabateck
  VP: Edna Karinski
  VP: Mary Ann Plumley
  Recording Secretary: Sheila Farrell Murray
  Corresponding Secretary: Jane Garcin
  Treasurer: Rita Burns
Management:
  Music Director: Olivia Tsui
  COO: Jack Kabateck

INSTRUMENTAL MUSIC / California

Mission: To contribute to the diversity of the community and to encourage an appreciation of music for future generations.
Utilizes: Guest Companies
Founded: 1924
Specialized Field: Symphony; Orchestra
Status: Professional, Nonprofit
Paid Staff: 1
Income Sources: American Symphony Orchestra League, Grants
Performs At: Alex Theater
Organization Type: Performing; Educational

790
GLENDALE YOUTH ORCHESTRA
PO Box 4401
Glendale, CA 91222-0401
Phone: 818-321-3083
Fax: 818-552-2043
e-mail: GYO@earthlink.net
Web Site: www.glendaleyouthorchestra.com
Officers:
  President: Mara Kelly
  VP: Thomas Metzler
  Treasurer: Alan Kleinsasser
  Recording Secretary & Hospitality: Relinda Beesemyer
  VP Fundraising/Solicitations: Eitan Sadeg
  VP Fundraising Events: Sue Kelly
  VP Publicity: Tom Metzler
  VP Recruiting: Helen Crosby
  Corresponding Secretary: Tim Kelley
Management:
  Music Director: Brad Keimach
  Advisor: Jennifer Babcock
Mission: To provide qualified young musicians an environment in which to explore, comprehend, appreciate and develop a lasting interest in music in a quality orchestral setting. As orchestra members, to perform concerts of standard symphonic music; to learn the value of achievement, teamwork, and discipline; to work with top teaching professionals as coaches.
Founded: 1989
Specialized Field: Youth Symphony
Status: Nonprofit
Budget: $35,000-$100,000
Income Sources: Individual and Corporate Donations, Fundraisers
Season: December-June
Performs At: Alex Theatre

791
RUSSIAN RIVER CHAMBER MUSIC
401 Center St.
#100
Healdsburg, CA 95448
Phone: 707-524-8700
Fax: 707-431-7622
e-mail: admin@russianriverchambermusic.org
Web Site: www.russianrivermusic.org
Officers:
  President: Scott Daley
  Treasurer: Jane Oriel
Management:
  Artistic Director: Gary McLaughlin
Mission: To promote the appreciation of chamber music in Sonoma County
Founded: 1992
Specialized Field: Chamber
Status: Nonprofit
Paid Staff: 1
Income Sources: Private and Corporate Donations, Ticket Sales, Grants
Season: October-May
Performs At: Healdsburg Community Church
Facility Category: Church
Seating Capacity: 300

792
HOLLYWOOD BOWL ORCHESTRA
The Hollywood Bowl
2301 N Highland Avenue
PO Box 1951
Hollywood, CA 90078-1951
Phone: 323-850-2000
Fax: 323-850-2155
Web Site: www.hollywoodbowl.com
Officers:
  Chairman: Deborah Borda Bohnett
  President: Deborah Borda
  Secretary: Alan Wayte
  Chair: Diane B. Paul
Management:
  Artistic Director: Chad Smith
  Director: Laura Connelly
  Manager: Johanna Rees
  Director: Wallis Annenberg
Founded: 1922
Status: Professional
Income Sources: Private and Corporate Donations
Performs At: Hollywood Bowl
Affiliations: Los Angeles Philharmonic
Annual Attendance: 18,000
Seating Capacity: 17,680

793
MOZART CLASSICAL ORCHESTRA
PO Box 54404
Irvine, CA 92619
Phone: 949-387-9197
e-mail: info@mozartorchestra.org
Web Site: www.mozartorchestra.org
Officers:
  Founder: Ami Porat
Management:
  Music Director/Conductor: Ami Porat
Mission: To encourage greater audience appreciation of the music from the great masters of chamber orchestra music.
Founded: 1980
Specialized Field: Chamber; Orchestra
Budget: $150,000-$260,000
Income Sources: Ticket Sales; Private and Corporate Donations
Performs At: St. Andrews Presbyterian Church; Irvine Barclay Theatre
Year Built: 1990

794
PHILHARMONIC SOCIETY OF ORANGE COUNTY
2082 Business Center Drive
Suite 100
Irvine, CA 92612
Phone: 949-553-2422
Fax: 949-553-2421
e-mail: contactus@philharmonicsociety.org
Web Site: www.philharmonicsociety.org
Officers:
  Chairman/CEO: Noel Hamilton
  Secretary/Treasurer: Douglas H. Smith
  Board of Directors: Elizabeth An
  Board of Directors: Jerry Harrington
  Board of Directors: David Koontz
Management:
  Artistic Director: Dean Corey
  Marketing: Chantel Chen
  Operations: Jeffrey Mistri
  Artistic Administrator: Sean Samimi
  Piano Technician: Kathy Smith
  Director of Finance: Chau Schwendimann
Founded: 1954
Status: Non-Profit
Budget: $3.7 million
Income Sources: Fundraising; Gifts from Individuals; Ticket Sales
Season: September-June
Performs At: Orange County Performing Arts Center
Seating Capacity: 2900
Year Built: 1969
Organization Type: Presenters

795
COLLEGE OF MARIN
Department of Performing Arts
835 College Avenue
Kentfield, CA 94904
Phone: 415-485-9460
Fax: 415-485-0135
e-mail: commusic@marin.edu
Web Site: www.marin.edu
Officers:
  Superintendent/President: Stephanie O'Brien
  Vice President: Eva Long, Ph.D.
Management:
  Co-Chair, Performing Arts: Tara Flandreau, tara.flandreau@marin.edu
  Clerk: Philip Kranenburg
Utilizes: Actors; Collaborations; Community Members; Community Talent; Dance Companies; Dancers; Educators; Guest Instructors; Guest Musical Directors; Guest Musicians; Guest Soloists; High School Drama; Local Artists; Multimedia; Music; Resident Professionals; Sign Language Translators; Singers; Soloists; Student Interns; Special Technical Talent
Specialized Field: Music, Drama & Dance
Status: Non-Profit
Performs At: Fine Arts Theatre
Affiliations: Association of California Symphony Orchestras, American Symphony Orchestra League, Theatre Bay Area
Seating Capacity: 600
Rental Contact: Cheryl Carlson
Organization Type: Performing; Educational

796
LA JOLLA MUSIC SOCIETY
7946 Ivanhoe Street
Suite 309
La Jolla, CA 92037
Phone: 858-459-3724
Fax: 858-459-3727
e-mail: lrosenthal@ljms.org
Web Site: www.ljms.org
Officers:
  Board Chairman: Clifford Schireson
  Vice Chair: Martha Dennis, Ph.D.
  Treasurer: Elaine Bennett Darwin
  Secretary: Angelina Kleinbub
Management:
  Artistic Administrator: Leah Z Rpsenthal
  Productions Manager: Hannes Kling
  President and Artistic Director: Christopher Beach
  SummerFest Music Director: Cho-Liang Lin
  Marketing Director: Kristen Sakamoto
Mission: To enhance the vitality and deepen the cultural life of San Diego by presenting and producing a dynamic range of performing arts for our increasingly diverse community.
Founded: 1941

INSTRUMENTAL MUSIC / California

Specialized Field: Symphony; Chamber; Ensemble; Piano; Jazz; Family Programming
Status: Professional, Nonprofit
Paid Staff: 25
Budget: $3.6 Million
Income Sources: Ticket Sales; Contributions
Performs At: Sherwood Auditorium; Civic Theatre; Copley Symphony Hall; Qualcomm Hall; Birch North Park Theatre; Neuroscience Institute
Annual Attendance: 35,000
Organization Type: Performing, Presenting

797
LA JOLLA SYMPHONY & CHORUS
9500 Gilman Drive
La Jolla, CA 92093-0361
Phone: 858-534-4637
Fax: 858-534-9947
e-mail: boxoffice@lajollasymphony.com
Web Site: www.lajollasymphony.com
Officers:
  President: Stephen L. Marsh
  Treasurer: Jennifer Smerud
  Secretary: Ida Houby
  VP: Paul E. Symczak
Management:
  Executive Director: Diane Salisbury
  Manager: Ted Bietz
  Patron Services Manager: Adam Perez
  Development Associat: Beth Sonnet
  Music Director: Steven Schick
Utilizes: Educators; Multimedia
Status: Non-Profit
Budget: $150,000-$260,000
Season: October-January
Performs At: Mandeville Center for the Performing Arts, Neurosciences Institute Auditorium
Affiliations: University of California, San Diego, City of San Diego Commission for Arts and Culture; County of San Diego; California Arts Council
Seating Capacity: 788, 350
Organization Type: Educational; Performing

798
LIVERMORE AMADOR SYMPHONY
Livermore Valley Performing Arts Center
2400 First Street
Livermore, CA 94550
Phone: 925-373-6100
Fax: 925-373-6097
e-mail: lalexander@livermoreperformingarts.org
Web Site: www.livermoreperformingarts.org
Officers:
  Chairman: Philip R Wente
  President: Joan K Seppala
  Secretary: Tom Reitter
  Treasurer: Michael Bocchicchio
  Director: Nancy Bankhead
Management:
  Executive Director: Len Alexander
  Development Director: Kimberly Moore
  Marketing Director: Nancy Mueller
  Productions Manager: Ed Estrada
  Operations Manager: Jole Mendoza
Status: Nonprofit
Budget: $35,000-$100,000
Income Sources: Fundraisers, Grants, Corporate Donations, Estate Sales
Season: September-May
Performs At: First Presbyterian Church, Amador Theatre
Seating Capacity: 450

799
LONG BEACH SYMPHONY ORCHESTRA
555 E. Ocean Blvd
Suite 106
Long Beach, CA 90802
Phone: 562-436-3203
Fax: 562-491-3599
e-mail: lbso@lbso.org
Web Site: www.lbso.org
Officers:
  President: John DiCarlo
  Vice President: Paulette Matson
  Treasurer: Rob Bellevue
  Secretary: Paulette Matson
  Community Leader: Barbara Blackwell
Management:
  Music Director: Enrique Diemecke
  Executive Director: Robert Jones
  General Manager: Janet Nyquist
  Production/Stage Manager: Ryan Lee
  Special Events Manager: Kari Regan
Mission: To provide high quality symphonic music for the entertainment and education of the community.
Founded: 1935
Specialized Field: Symphony; Orchestra
Status: Nonprofit, Professional
Paid Staff: 13
Volunteer Staff: 300
Paid Artists: 83
Income Sources: Ticket Sales, Individual and Corporate Donations, Conductor's Circle, Corporate Circle, Sponsorships, Fundraisers
Season: October-May
Performs At: Terrace Theater, Long Beach Arena; Long Beach Performing Arts Center
Annual Attendance: 40,000
Seating Capacity: 3,000, 7,000
Organization Type: Performing

800
PENINSULA SYMPHONY ORCHESTRA
146 Main Street
Suite 102
Los Altos, CA 94002
Phone: 650-941-5291
Fax: 650-941-5292
e-mail: info@peninsulasymphony.org
Web Site: www.peninsulasymphony.org
Officers:
  Chair: Dick Bennett
  Vice Chair: Frank Rahn
  Treasurer: Roy Bukstein
Management:
  Executive Director: Steve Carlton
  Marketing/Outreach Coordinator: Katie Bartholomew
  Development Associate: Angela Ragni
  Music Director & Conductor: Mitchell Sardou Klein
  Assistant Conductor: Nathaniel Berman
Mission: To enrich the lives of our community with the highest quality musical presentations at modest prices, inspire greater appreciation for music and promote music education.
Utilizes: Educators; Music
Founded: 1949
Status: Non-Profit, Professional
Paid Staff: 6
Paid Artists: 2
Budget: 600,000
Income Sources: Private and Corporate Donations, Sponships
Season: October-May

Performs At: Flint Center, Fox Theatre; Redwood City, San Mateo Performing Arts Center
Type of Stage: Proscenium
Stage Dimensions: 89.9Wx39.2Dx40H
Seating Capacity: 2,500, 1,460

801
AMERICAN YOUTH SYMPHONY
3424 Wilshire Boulevard
Suite 830
Los Angeles, CA 90010
Phone: 310-470-2332
Fax: 310-470-2772
e-mail: info@aysymphony.org
Web Site: www.aysymphony.org
Officers:
  Chairman: Kevin Dretzka
  President: David Newman
  Treasurer: David Papale
  Secretary: Peter Mandel
  VC: Steven A. Linder
Management:
  Executive Director: Varina Bleil
  Manager: Mason Dille
  Orchestra Manager: Isabel Thiroux
  Development & Audience Relations Co: Alice Dutton
Utilizes: Educators; Five Seasonal Concerts; Guest Composers; Guest Lecturers; Guest Musical Directors; High School Drama; Multimedia; New Productions; Organization Contracts; Singers; Soloists
Founded: 1959
Status: Non-Professional, Non-Profit
Budget: $700,000
Income Sources: American Symphony Orchestra League; Youth Orchestra Division, Private and Corporate Donations, Foundation and Government Support
Season: October-June
Performs At: Royce Hall; UCLA
Annual Attendance: 12,000
Type of Stage: Proscenium
Seating Capacity: 1,818
Year Built: 1929
Year Remodeled: 1994
Organization Type: Performing; Educational

802
LOS ANGELES BACH FESTIVAL
First Congregational Church
540 S Commonwealth Avenue
Los Angeles, CA 90020-1298
Phone: 213-385-1341
Fax: 213-487-0461
e-mail: jtalberg@fccla.org
Web Site: www.fccla.org
Officers:
  Interim Chief Program Minister and: Dr. R. Scott Colglazier
Management:
  Director: Jonathan Talberg
  Finance Coordinator: Stacey Brown
  Executive Assistant to Senior Minis: Laura Butt
  Organist-in-Residence: Dr. Christoph Bull
  Chief Administrative Officer: Ms. Susan Leary
Budget: $20,000-$35,000
Affiliations: First Congregational Church of Los Angeles
Seating Capacity: 150
Year Built: 1867

INSTRUMENTAL MUSIC / California

803
LOS ANGELES CHAMBER ORCHESTRA
350 S. Figueroa St.
Ste 183
Los Angeles, CA 90071
Phone: 213-622-7001
Fax: 213-626-2157
e-mail: info@laco.org
Web Site: www.laco.org
Officers:
  Chairman: Gregory J Soukup
  President: Michael Rosen
  Treasurer: Titus Brenninkmeijer
  Secretary: Debra Gastler
Management:
  Executive Director: Andrea Laguni
  Marketing: Nicolette Atkins
  Operations: Devin Thomas
  Music Director: Jeffrey Kahane
Utilizes: Collaborations; Commissioned Composers; Commissioned Music; Composers-in-Residence; Guest Composers; Guest Designers; Guest Lecturers; Guest Musical Directors; Guest Musicians; Guest Soloists; Local Artists; Music; Selected Students; Singers
Founded: 1968
Status: Professional; Non-Profit
Budget: $2.2 million
Income Sources: Ticket Sales; Contributed Income from Foundations; Corporations; Government Agencies; Individual Donations
Season: October-May
Performs At: Alex Theatre; Glendale, Royce Hall; UCLA
Affiliations: American Symphony Orchestra League; Association of California Symphony Orchestras; Western Arts Alliance; International Society of Performing Art
Annual Attendance: 1,500
Organization Type: Performing; Touring; Resident

804
LOS ANGELES DOCTORS SYMPHONY ORCHESTRA
PO Box 642949
Los Angeles, CA 90064
Phone: 323-364-4826
e-mail: info@ladso.org
Web Site: www.ladso.org
Officers:
  President/Orchestra Council: Richard Chen
  Vice President: Louis Fantasia
  Treasurer: Ken Alexander
Management:
  Music Director/Conductor: Ivan Shulman
Mission: To provide for the comradeship of music for its musicians, to contribute culturally to the community, to help raise funds for medical and other charities and provide concerts at low cost to the public.
Utilizes: Commissioned Music; Guest Musical Directors; Guest Musicians; Multimedia; Singers; Soloists
Founded: 1953
Specialized Field: Orchestra
Status: Nonprofit
Volunteer Staff: 10
Non-paid Artists: 3
Budget: $25,000
Income Sources: Dues; Grants; Donations
Season: October-July
Performs At: No Official Base
Annual Attendance: 2,500

805
LOS ANGELES PHILHARMONIC ASSOCIATION
135 N Grand Avenue
Los Angeles, CA 90012
Phone: 323-850-2000
Fax: 323-850-2155
Web Site: www.laphil.org
Officers:
  Chairman: David C Bohnett
  President: Myles Lee, MD
  VP: Joseph Braun, PhD
  Director: Julie Andrews
  Director: Mari.L Danihel
Management:
  Director: Esa-Pekka Salonen
  Artistic Director: Chad Smith
  Manager: Johanna Rees
Founded: 1919
Status: Nonprofit
Income Sources: Private and Corporate Donations, Ticket Sales, Grants
Season: October-June
Performs At: Walt Disney Concert Hall; Hollywood Bowl (summer)
Seating Capacity: 3,189, 20,000
Year Built: 1999
Organization Type: Educational; Performing; Touring

806
SANTA CECILIA ORCHESTRA
2759 W Broadway
Los Angeles, CA 90041
Phone: 323-259-3011
Fax: 323-257-0889
e-mail: info@scorchestra.org
Web Site: www.scorchestra.org
Management:
  Artistic Director: Sonia Marie De Leon De Vega
Founded: 1993
Status: Non-Profit
Budget: $7,000
Income Sources: Private and Corporate Donations, Foundations
Performs At: Greystone Mansion

807
THORNTON SYMPHONY
University of Southern California
Bovard Auditorium
3551 Trousdale Parkway
Los Angeles, CA 90089 1
Phone: 213-740-6935
Fax: 213-740-3217
e-mail: bovprod@usc.edu
Web Site: www.usc.edu
Officers:
  Chair: Wallis Annenberg
  Chair: Ian White Thomson
  President: Wanda M. Austin
  Founder: Thomas J. Barrack Jr.
  Chief Investment Officer: Lisa Mazzocco
Management:
  Operations: Pamela Hopson
  Manager: Michelle Maestas
Status: Non-Profit
Budget: $35,000
Season: September-December
Performs At: Bovard Auditorium
Seating Capacity: 1,544

808
PEPPERDINE UNIVERSITY ORCHESTRA
Pepperdine University
Fine Arts Division
24225 Pacific Coast Highway
Malibu, CA 90263-4966
Phone: 310-506-4000
Fax: 310-506-4077
e-mail: tony.cason@pepperdine.edu
Web Site: seaver.pepperdine.edu
Officers:
  Chair: Dr. Gary Cobb
  President: Andrew.K Benton
Management:
  Director: Tony Cason
Status: Semi-Professional
Performs At: mothers Theatre; Pepperdine University
Organization Type: Performing

809
MILL VALLEY CHAMBER MUSIC SOCIETY
38 Miller Avenue
Suite 521
Mill Valley, CA 94941
Mailing Address: PO Box 1907, Mill Valley CA 94942-1907
Phone: 415-381-4453
Fax: 415-381-2039
e-mail: mychambermusicsociety@yahoo.com
Web Site: www.chambermusicmillvalley.org
Officers:
  President: William Horne
  VP: Fred W Taylor
  Treasurer: Robert Glasson
  Secretary: John Cutler
  Chair: William Home
Management:
  Artist Relations Coordinator: Sylvia Gang
  Programs Coordinator: Tina Kun
  Box Office: Ruth Rosen
  Publicity and Telephone: Elizabeth Stone
  Hospitality: Betty Musser
Mission: To promote an appreciation of classical music for the next generation to enjoy.
Founded: 1974
Specialized Field: Chamber; Ensemble
Status: Nonprofit
Season: September-April
Performs At: Mt Tamalpais United Methodist Church
Organization Type: Educational; Sponsoring

810
MODESTO SYMPHONY ORCHESTRA
911 Thirteenth Street
Modesto, CA 95354
Phone: 209-523-4156
Fax: 209-523-0201
e-mail: info@modestosymphony.org
Web Site: www.modestosymphony.org
Officers:
  Chair: Brian McCaffrey MD
  President: Paul Jan Zdunek
  Treasurer: Lisa Finer
  Secretary: Robert Saunders
Management:
  Director: David Lockington
  Marketing: Caroline Nickel
  Development Director: Cathy Mendoza
  Senior Marketing Associate: Maureen Quinn
  Director of Finance: Lauren Bennett
  Director of Education: Katye Leonard

INSTRUMENTAL MUSIC / California

Utilizes: Guest Directors; Guest Instructors; Guest Musicians; Guest Writers; Instructors; Multimedia; Music; Original Music Scores; Singers
Founded: 1931
Status: Professional, Non-Profit
Budget: $1.7 million
Income Sources: Association of California Symphony Orchestras; American Symphony Orchestra League; Fundraising; Private and Corporate Donations; Ticket Sales
Season: September-December
Performs At: Modesto Junior College Auditorium
Seating Capacity: 940
Organization Type: Performing; Educational

811
MUSIC IN THE VINEYARDS
Napa Valley Chamber Music Festival
PO Box 6297
Napa, CA 94581
Phone: 707-258-5559
Fax: 707-258-5566
e-mail: mitv@sonic.net
Web Site: www.musicinthevineyards.org
Officers:
   VP: Lona Hardy
   President: Anne Golden
   Treasurer: Rick Boland
   Secretary: Diane Flyr
   Secretary: Paul Cantey
Management:
   Artistic Directors: Michael & Daria Adams
   Executive Director: Evie Ayers
   Marketing: Christy Bors
   Public Relations: Natasha Biels
   Marketing Manager: Chris Bors
   Finance Manager: Nancy Sellers
Mission: Music in the vineyards is dedicated to bringing together outstanding artists to perform in the unique vineyard settings of the Napa Valley so that both the performers and the audience can experience the intimacy of chamber music as it was intended to be performed.
Utilizes: Multimedia; Original Music Scores; Poets
Founded: 1995
Specialized Field: Chamber Music Festival
Status: Non-Profit
Paid Staff: 3
Volunteer Staff: 120
Paid Artists: 45
Budget: $140,000
Season: August
Performs At: Napa Valley; Festival Site, San Gabriel Civic Auditorium
Affiliations: Various vineyards and related venues
Seating Capacity: 150 - 250

812
PACIFIC CHAMBER SYMPHONY
Napa Valley Opera House
1030 Main Street
Napa Valley, CA 94559
Phone: 707-226-7372
Fax: 707-226-5392
Toll-free: 800-630-7836
e-mail: info@pacificchambersymphony.org
Web Site: www.pacificchambersymphony.org
Officers:
   Board Member: Chelle Clements
   Board Member: Walter Davies
   Board Member: Valerie Jonas
Management:
   Director: Lawrence Kohl
Founded: 1989
Status: Non=Profit
Budget: $260,000-$1,050,000
Performs At: Kanbar Hall; Jewish Community Ctr, Hofman Theatre; Dean Lesher Regional Ctr, Neighborhood Theater; Valley Community Theater

813
CSUN YOUTH ORCHESTRAS
California State University Northridge
18111 Nordhoff Street
Northridge, CA 91330-8314
Phone: 818-677-3074
e-mail: yhorch@csun.edu
Web Site: www.csunyouthorchestra.org
Management:
   Manager: Cari Craig
Budget: $100,000
Income Sources: Private and Corporate Donations, Fundraisers, Ticket Sales
Season: August-May
Performs At: Performing Arts Community Center
Annual Attendance: 5,000-6,000
Type of Stage: Proscenium
Year Built: 1994

814
BERKELEY YOUTH ORCHESTRA
1587 Franklin Street
Oakland, CA 94612
Mailing Address: PO Box 11607, Berkeley CA 94712
Phone: 510-663-3296
e-mail: president@byoweb.org
Web Site: www.berkeley-youth-orchestra.org
Officers:
   President: David Sutton
   Treasurer: Tina Huang
   Secretary: Lynn Mackay
Management:
   Executive Director: Al Maitland
   Conductor: Jay Lehmann
   Manager: Leah Maddock
   Director: Kent Brandenberg
Mission: BYO is an exceptional full symphonic orchestra fostering a musical community for dedicated young musicians grades 5-10+ from the greater Bay Area
Utilizes: Community Members; Music; Paid Performers
Founded: 1969
Specialized Field: Symphony; Orchestra
Status: Nonprofit
Volunteer Staff: 70
Budget: $55,000
Income Sources: Member Tuition Fees, Ticket Sales, Donations, Fundraising
Season: September-May
Performs At: Laney College Theatre
Affiliations: American Symphony Orchestra League
Annual Attendance: 1,500
Seating Capacity: 350
Organization Type: Performing; Educational

815
OAKLAND EAST BAY SYMPHONY
2201 Broadway
Suite 300
Oakland, CA 94612
Phone: 510-444-0801
Fax: 510-444-0863
e-mail: admin@oebs.org
Web Site: www.oebs.org
Officers:
   President: Paul E Garrison Esq
Management:
   Music Director/Conductor: Michael Morgan
   Assistant Conductor: Bryan Nies
   Executive Director: Jennifer Duston
   Development Director: Ken Ingraham
Mission: Oakland East Bay Symphony aims to make classical music accessible, particulary to those individuals in the community who might otherwise never hear live symphonic music.
Founded: 1988
Specialized Field: Classical; Folk Music
Paid Staff: 7
Volunteer Staff: 40
Paid Artists: 64
Budget: $2,000,000
Income Sources: Donations
Season: November-May
Performs At: Paramount Theatre
Annual Attendance: 75,000
Year Built: 1931
Year Remodeled: 1973

816
OAKLAND YOUTH ORCHESTRA
Malonga Casquelourd Center for Performing Arts
1428 Alice Street
Room 202M
Oakland, CA 94612
Phone: 510-832-7710
Fax: 510-832-2571
e-mail: manager@oyo.org
Web Site: www.oyo.org
Officers:
   President: Debbra Wood Schwartz
   Chairman: Conway B Jones Jr
   Treasurer: Kathleen Pickard
   Secretary: Janett Edrington
Management:
   Artistic Director: Michael Morgan
   General Manager: Gail Edwards
   Principal Conductor: John Kendall Bailey
Utilizes: Instructors
Founded: 1964
Status: Non-Profit
Paid Staff: 3
Volunteer Staff: 20
Paid Artists: 2
Budget: $250,000
Income Sources: Private and Corporate Donations, Tuition, Foundation and Government Grants
Season: September-June

817
CHAPMAN UNIVERSITY SYMPHONY ORCHESTRA & CHAMBER ORCHESTRA
Chapman University Conservatory of Music
One University Drive
Orange, CA 92866
Phone: 714-997-6815
Fax: 714-744-7671
e-mail: burba@chapman.edu
Web Site: www.chapman.edu
Officers:
   Chair: Doy B. Henley
   VC: David A. Janes, Sr
   Secretary: Scott Chapman
   Officer: Virgil Zuniga
   Officer: Josie Wright
Management:
   Music Director and Conductor: Daniel Alfred Wachs
Utilizes: Theatre Companies
Budget: $100,000-$150,000
Income Sources: Private and Corporate Donations, Fundraisers, Grants
Season: January-May

INSTRUMENTAL MUSIC / California

Performs At: Chapman Auditorium
Facility Category: Concert Hall
Seating Capacity: 1,100
Organization Type: Performing; Educational; Touring

818
ORANGE COUNTY YOUTH SYMPHONY ORCHESTRA
Chapman University Conservatory of Music
One University Drive
Orange, CA 92866
Phone: 714-744-7927
Fax: 714-744-7671
e-mail: info@ocyso.org
Web Site: www.ocyso.org
Management:
   Executive Director: Heather Ter-Jung
   Music Director and Conductor: Daniel Alfred Wachs
   Operations: John Acosta
   General Manager & Associate Conduct: Teren Shaffer
   Director of Artistic & Orchestra Op: Jacob Vogel
   Personnel Manager: Danielle Culhane
   Production/Stage Manager: Kevin Baker
Utilizes: Educators; Theatre Companies
Status: Non-profit, Pre-Professional
Budget: $35,000-$100,000
Income Sources: Private and Corporate Donations, Fundraisers, Grants, Ticket Sales
Season: December-March
Performs At: Chapman Auditorium
Seating Capacity: 1,100
Organization Type: Performing; Educational; Touring

819
DESERT SYMPHONY
72925 Fred Waring Drive
Suite 101
Palm Desert, CA 92260
Phone: 760-773-5988
Fax: 760-773-5652
e-mail: admin@desertsymphony.org
Web Site: www.desertsymphony.org
Officers:
   President: Nancy Tapick
   Secretary: Rhona S Kauffman
Management:
   Manager: Shane A Bitner
   Business Manager: Mariyn Benachowski
   Conductor: Gary Berkson
Founded: 1989
Status: Nonprofit, Professional
Seating Capacity: 1,127
Year Built: 1988

820
CALIFORNIA YOUTH SYMPHONY
441 California Avenue
Suite 5
Palo Alto, CA 94306
Phone: 650-325-6666
Fax: 650-325-1243
e-mail: californiayouthsymphony@gmail.com
Web Site: www.cys.org
Officers:
   President: Dave Morley
   Secretary: Ken Chu
   Treasurer: Bob Srinivas
   Vice-President Development: Shirley Yang
   Vice-President Senior Orchestra: Judy Chan
   Vice-President Junior Strings: Pam Lowe
   Scrip Coordinator: Lily Huang
Management:
   Executive Director: Jim Hogan
   Director: Leo Eylar
   Marketing: Elizabeth Frazier
   String Training Director: Katherine Kyme
   Wind Training Director: Rosita Amador
   Office Manager: Ching Ying Pang
   Orchestra Manager: Carmina Chua
Founded: 1952
Status: Non-Professional, Non-Profit
Season: November-May
Performs At: Flint Center for Performing Arts, San Mateo Performing Arts, Spangenber Theater; Gunn High School, Smithwick Theater
Affiliations: American Symphony Orchestra League, Youth Orchestra Division; Association of California Symphony Orchestras
Annual Attendance: 8,000
Organization Type: Performing; Educational; Touring

821
EL CAMINO YOUTH SYMPHONY
4055 Fabian Way
Palo Alto, CA 94303
Phone: 650-213-7111
Fax: 650-493-1525
e-mail: ecys@ecys.org
Web Site: www.ecys.org
Officers:
   President: Helen Zhang
   Vice President: Peter Farmer
   Secretary: Cindy Fan
   Treasurer: Rachael Tsong
Management:
   Executive Director: Cathy Spieth
   Development Director: Chiung Chi Chen
   Artistic Operations Manager: Emily Frank
Mission: To nurture, train and develop young musicians from culturally diverse backgrounds, encouraging their appreciation of music.
Utilizes: Artists-in-Residence; Collaborations; Community Members; Educators; Guest Composers; Guest Musical Directors; Instructors; Theatre Companies
Founded: 1963
Specialized Field: Orchestra; Chamber
Status: Non-Profit
Budget: $900,000
Income Sources: Private and Corporate Donations, Grants
Season: November-May
Performs At: Flint Center
Type of Stage: Proscenium
Seating Capacity: 2300
Organization Type: Performing; Educational; Touring

822
COLEMAN CHAMBER MUSIC ASSOCIATION
225 S Lake Avenue
Suite 300
Pasadena, CA 91101
Phone: 626-793-4191
e-mail: info@colemanchambermusic.org
Web Site: www.coleman.caltech.edu
Officers:
   VP & Treasurer: Susan Grether
   VP: Robert Winter
   Secretary: Donna Swayze
   President: Jerome Hamburger, M.D.
   Secretary: Phyllis Hudson
   Secretary: Priscilla Moorman
   Founder: Alice Coleman
Management:
   Executive Director: Kathy Freedland
Mission: To present international chamber ensembles and to reach local children with demonstration performances.
Utilizes: Guest Directors
Founded: 1904
Specialized Field: Chamber
Status: Nonprofit
Paid Staff: 1
Volunteer Staff: 50
Income Sources: Western Alliance of Arts Administrators; Chamber Music America; California Presenters; Ticket Sales, Membership Dues, Endowment Income and Gifts from Organizations
Season: October-April
Performs At: Caltech Beckman Auditorium
Stage Dimensions: 24x43x16
Seating Capacity: 1,150
Year Built: 1964
Organization Type: Sponsoring

823
PASADENA CONSERVATORY OF MUSIC
100 North Hill Avenue
Pasadena, CA 91106
Phone: 626-683-3355
Fax: 626-683-3303
e-mail: music@pasadenaconservatory.org
Web Site: www.pasadenaconservatory.org
Officers:
   Chairman: Henry O Eversole
   Treasurer: Stephen A Kanter
   Secretary: Karen Stracka
   Executive Director: Stephen McCurry
Management:
   Program Coordinator/Facilities Mgr: Jeannie Robbins
   Director of Operations: Amelia Firnstahl
   Director of Development: Melissa Froehlich
Mission: We provide an independent nonprofit community music school that is proud to provide a comprehensive curriculum of music study to students in and around Pasadena, California.
Founded: 1983
Specialized Field: Instrumental
Status: Nonprofit

824
PASADENA POPS ORCHESTRA
2 North Lake Ave
Suite 1080
Pasadena, CA 91101
Phone: 626-793-7172
Fax: 626-793-7180
e-mail: info@pasadenasymphony-pops.org
Web Site: www.pasadenasymphony-pops.org
Officers:
   President: Melinda Shea
   CEO: Paul Jan Zdunek
   Secretary: Priscilla McClure
   VP Finance: Robert Michero
   VP Governance: Ronald M LaBran
   Campbell: Clay
Management:
   Director: Rachael Worby
   General Manager: Lora Unger
   Personnel Manager: Polly Sweeney
   Artistic Advisor: James DePreist
   Pasadena POPS: Michael Feinstein
Status: Non-Profit
Income Sources: Private and Corporate Donations, Grants
Season: June-September
Annual Attendance: 16,000

INSTRUMENTAL MUSIC / California

825
PASADENA SYMPHONY
2 North Lake Ave
Suite 1080
Pasadena, CA 91101
Phone: 626-793-7172
Fax: 626-793-7180
e-mail: info@pasadenasymphony-pops.org
Web Site: www.pasadenasymphony-pops.org
Officers:
- President: Melinda Shea
- CEO: Paul Jan Zdunek
- Secretary: Priscilla McClure
- VP Finance: Robert Michero
- VP Governance: Ronald M LaBran
- Campbell: Clay

Management:
- Director: Jorge Mester
- General Manager: Lora Unger
- Personnel Manager: Polly Sweeney
- Artistic Advisor: James DePreist
- Pasadena POPS: Michael Feinstein

Utilizes: Guest Accompanists; Guest Musicians
Status: Professional
Budget: $2.3 million
Income Sources: Private and Corporate Donations, Ticket Sales, Foundations
Season: October-June
Performs At: Pasadena Civic Auditorium
Annual Attendance: 100,000
Seating Capacity: 3,000
Year Built: 1931
Organization Type: Performing

826
SOUTHWEST CHAMBER MUSIC
638 E. Colorado Boulevard
Suite 201
Pasadena, CA 91101-2006
Phone: 626-685-4455
Fax: 626-685-4458
Toll-free: 800-726-7147
e-mail: mail@swmusic.org
Web Site: www.swmusic.org
Officers:
- President: Jay Belloli
- VP: Betsy Tyler
- Secretary: Natalie Poole
- Treasurer: Peter Mandell
- Founder: Fritzie Culick

Management:
- Artistic Director: Jeff von der Schmidt
- Executive Director: Jan Karlin
- General Manager: Heidi Lesemann
- Production Manager: Joan Quinto

Mission: To provide multiculutral music through concert, recording and educational programming.
Founded: 1987
Specialized Field: Chamber
Status: Nonprofit
Season: September-May
Performs At: Norton Simon Museum; Colburn School of Performing Arts, Huntington Library
Annual Attendance: 100,000
Seating Capacity: 300; 400; 250

827
VILLAGE CENTER FOR THE ARTS
1720 Linda Drive
Pleasant Hill, CA 94523
Phone: 925-676-8400
e-mail: villagemusicschool@gmail.com
Web Site: www.villagemusicschool.net

Management:
- CEO: Robert Konkle
- Program Director: Liz Beggs

Mission: We believe that when music is fun and presented in a supportive environment using materials that inspire practice and commitment students develop a love and understanding for music that will last a lifetime.
Specialized Field: Music

828
SHASTA SYMPHONY ORCHESTRA
11555 Old Oregon Trail
PO Box 496006
Redding, CA 96049 - 60
Phone: 530-242-7500
Fax: 530-225-3942
e-mail: Business.Office@shastacollege.edu
Web Site: www.shastacollege.edu
Officers:
- Superintendent/President: Joe Wyse
- VP of Academic Affairs: Meridith Randall

Management:
- Music Director: Dr. Richard Allen Fiske
- General Manager: Ralph Perrin

Mission: To provide a symphony orchestra for the college and the community.
Utilizes: Guest Artists; Guest Companies
Founded: 1950
Specialized Field: Symphony
Status: Nonprofit
Budget: $10,000
Income Sources: Private and Corporate Donations, Tuition, Grants
Performs At: Shasta College Theater
Affiliations: ASOL; ACSO
Annual Attendance: 1,600-2,000
Seating Capacity: 474
Year Remodeled: 2008

829
REDLANDS SYMPHONY ASSOCIATION
1200 E Colton
PO Box 3080
Redlands, CA 92373-0999
Phone: 909-748-8018
Fax: 909-335-5213
e-mail: symphony@redlands.edu
Web Site: www.RedlandsSymphony.com
Officers:
- Board President: Zack Tucker
- Board VP: Bruce Satzger
- Board Secretary: Nancy Spencer
- Board Treasurer: Phillip Doolittle

Management:
- Music Director/Conductor: Jon Robertson
- Operations Manager: Rachel Wade
- Development Manager: Julie Nichols
- Executive Director: Karen Idmes

Mission: Developing and maintaining an excellent symphony orchestra which offers an annual series of concerts and coordinating outreach programs.
Founded: 1950
Specialized Field: Symphony
Status: Professional, Nonprofit
Paid Staff: 6
Paid Artists: 60
Budget: $800,000
Income Sources: Grants; Ticket Sales; Annual Fund Raising Gala
Season: September-April
Performs At: Memorial Chapel; University of Redlands
Affiliations: American Symphony Orchestra League, Association of California Symphony Orchestras
Seating Capacity: 1,486
Organization Type: Performing, Educational

830
BEACH CITIES SYMPHONY ASSOCIATION
PO Box 248
Redondo Beach, CA 90277-0248
Phone: 310-379-9725
Fax: 310-798-2834
e-mail: inquiryATbeachcitiessymphony.org
Web Site: www.beachcitiessymphony.org
Officers:
- Chairman: Pat Chavez
- President: Robert L Peterson
- Treasurer: Yong Reuter
- Secretary: Bill Malcolm
- Publicity: Jennifer Floto

Management:
- Music Director/Conductor: Barry Brisk
- Concertmaster: Rebecca Rutkowski
- Assistant Concertmaster: Joanne Satterburg

Mission: The Beach Cities Symphony Association believes that music enriches individuals whether performers or members of the audience and community at large.
Founded: 1949
Specialized Field: Symphony; Classical
Status: Semi-Professional, Nonprofit
Income Sources: American Symphony Orchestra League; Symphony League of Los Angeles County; Private and Corporate Donations
Season: October-May
Performs At: Marsee Auditorium; El Camino College
Annual Attendance: 4,000
Organization Type: Performing

831
REDWOOD SYMPHONY
1031 16th Avenue
Redwood City, CA 94063
Phone: 650-366-6872
e-mail: info@redwoodsymphony.org
Web Site: www.redwoodsymphony.org
Officers:
- Chair: Stephen Ruppenthal
- Treasurer: Richard Steinberg

Management:
- Director: Eric Kujawsky

Status: Non-Profit
Budget: $35,000
Income Sources: Private and Corporate Donations
Season: October-May
Performs At: Bayside Performing Arts Center, Notre Dame de Namur University Theatre, San Mateo Performing Arts Center & Theatre

832
RIVERSIDE COUNTY PHILHARMONIC
Riverside Municipal Auditorium
3700 Sixth Street
Suite 201
Riverside, CA 92501
Phone: 909-787-0251
Toll-free: 877-744-5849
e-mail: info@thephilharmonic.org
Web Site: www.thephilharmonic.org
Officers:
- President: Jeffry Kaatz
- VP: J. Sergio Bohon
- Secretary: Marcia McQuern
- Executive Director: Barbara Lohman

Management:
- Director: Patrick Flynn

INSTRUMENTAL MUSIC / California

Executive Director: Wayne Hinton
General Manager: Katherine Wilson
Personnel Manager: Geoffrey Osika
Stage Manager: Dave Hennager
Music Director: Tomasz Golka
Founded: 1959
Status: Professional, Non-Profit
Budget: $260,000-$1,050,000
Income Sources: Ticket Sales; Contributions; Grants
Season: October-May
Performs At: Riverside Municipal Auditorium; Gardiner W Spring Auditorium
Annual Attendance: 1,500
Seating Capacity: 1,776
Organization Type: Performing

833
ASIA AMERICA SYMPHONY ORCHESTRA
608 Silver Spur Road
Suite 320
Rolling Hills Estates, CA 90274
Phone: 310-377-8977
Fax: 310-377-8949
e-mail: aasa@asiaamericasymphony.org
Web Site: www.asiaamericasymphony.org
Officers:
  President: Randall Tamura
  Secretary: Valena Noguchi
  Chief Financial Officer: Tomoko Iwakawa
  Executive Director: Darryl W Tanikawa
  VP: Robert Pacifici
Management:
  Director: David Benoit
  Concertmaster: Yun Tang
Utilizes: Community Talent; Multimedia
Founded: 1961
Budget: $150,000-$260,000
Performs At: Norrise Center for the Performing Arts, Japanese American Cultural Center
Affiliations: Norris Center for the Performing Arts
Seating Capacity: 450
Organization Type: Performing; Educational

834
CHAMBER ORCHESTRA OF THE SOUTH BAY
Norris Theatre for the Performing Arts
27570 Norris Center Drive
Rolling Hills Estates, CA 90274
Phone: 310-544-0403
Fax: 310-544-0403
e-mail: jgruessing@norriscenter.com
Web Site: www.norristheatre.org
Officers:
  President: David Diestel
  Trustee: Joan Moe
Management:
  Director: Frances Steiner
  Artistic Director: Joan Moe
  Operations: Gilbert Cheng
  Executive Director: James W Gruessing
  Finance and HR Director: Susan Henry
Utilizes: Guest Musicians; Original Music Scores; Resident Artists; Singers
Status: Professional
Budget: $170,000
Income Sources: National Endowment for the Arts, Los Angeles County Arts Comission, Norris Foundation Cooperatives, Ticket Sales And Industrial Contributions
Season: October-April
Performs At: Norris Center for the Performing Arts

Affiliations: American Symphony Orchestra League; Association of California Symphony Orchestra
Annual Attendance: 2,200
Facility Category: Theatre
Type of Stage: Proscenium
Seating Capacity: 450
Year Built: 1983

835
CAMELLIA SYMPHONY ORCHESTRA
1545 River Park Drive
Suite 506
Sacramento, CA 95815
Mailing Address: P.O. Box 19786, Sacramento, CA 95819
Phone: 916-929-6655
Fax: 916-929-4292
e-mail: camelliaorch@aol.com
Web Site: camelliasymphony.org
Officers:
  President: Barbara Tracy
  VP: Mark Luhdorff
  Treasurer: Linda Killick
  Secretary: Davood Mesbah
Management:
  Conductor: Allan Pollack
  Music Director and Conductor: Christian Baldini
  Executive Director: Roberta McClellan
Mission: To expand the growth of music in the Sacramento area by presenting unique repertoire at reasonable prices, as well as provide opportunities for area musicians and composers.
Utilizes: Multimedia; Singers
Founded: 1962
Specialized Field: Orchestra
Status: Volunteer, Nonprofit
Paid Staff: 2
Budget: $175,000
Income Sources: Private and Corporate Donations; Ticket Sales; Grants
Performs At: Memorial Auditorium, Sacramento
Affiliations: Numerous Community Affiliations
Annual Attendance: 6,000
Facility Category: Community Center Theater
Seating Capacity: 2400
Year Built: 1925
Year Remodeled: 2008
Organization Type: Performing

836
SACRAMENTO PHILHARMONIC ORCHESTRA
2617 K Street
Suite 200
Sacramento, CA 95816
Phone: 916-732-9045
Fax: 916-732-9049
e-mail: orchestra@sacphil.org
Web Site: www.sacphil.org
Officers:
  President: David K. Nystrom
  Chief Financial Officer: Marta Quinn
  Treasurer: David R Motes
  Secretary: Sandra R Smoley
  VP: Susan Carson
  Chief Financial Officer: Marta Quinn
Management:
  Music Director & Principal Conducto: Michael Morgan
  Executive Director: Marc Feldman
  Interim Executive Director: Jane Hill
Status: Non-Profit
Budget: $1.4 million

Income Sources: Sacramento Philharmonic Orchestra Foundation; Sacramento Metropolitan Arts Commission; Private and Corporate Donations; Ticket Sales
Season: October-April
Performs At: Sacramento Convention Center, Community Center Theater
Annual Attendance: 9,540

837
SACRAMENTO YOUTH SYMPHONY & ACADEMY OF MUSIC
3443 Ramona Avenue
Suite 22
Sacramento, CA 95826
Phone: 916-731-5777
Fax: 916-736-3874
e-mail: cathytaylor@sacramentoyouthsymphony.org
Web Site: www.sacramentoyouthsymphony.org
Officers:
  President: Jack Holmes
  Secretary: Dwayne Slavin
  Treasurer: Hal Weber
Management:
  Artistic Director: Michael Neumann
  Executive Director: Cathy Taylor
  Programs Manager: Robert Vann
Mission: To educate and advance the musical skills of youth in our communities in ways that engage, challenge and inspire them to reach their highest potential.
Founded: 1956
Status: Non-Profit
Budget: $400,000
Season: September-May
Performs At: CSUS Music Recital Hall, Memorial Auditorium; Various Venues
Annual Attendance: 7,500
Organization Type: Performing; Educational; Touring

838
CHAMBER MUSIC IN NAPA VALLEY
4375 Atlas Peak Road
Saint Helens, CA 94558
Phone: 707-226-2190
Fax: 707-226-2936
e-mail: cmnv@napanet.net
Web Site: www.chambermusicnapa.org
Management:
  Director: John Kongsgaard
  Director: Maggy Kongsgaard
Status: Non-Profit
Income Sources: Private and Corporate Donations, Ticket Sales, Grants
Season: October-May
Performs At: United Methodist Church, Napa Valley Opera House
Seating Capacity: 320

839
SAN BERNARDINO SYMPHONY ORCHESTRA
198 N. Arrowhead Ave
San Bernardino, CA 92408
Phone: 909-381-5388
Fax: 909-883-6428
e-mail: sbsymphony1@aol.com
Web Site: sanbernardinosymphony.org
Officers:
  President: Judith Valles
  Treasurer: Lisa Doherty
  Secretary: Grace Baldwin
  VP: Earleen Ferguso Dudley

INSTRUMENTAL MUSIC / California

Management:
   Director: Carlo Pointi Jr
   Executive Director: Dr. Anne L. Viricel
Utilizes: Actors; Grant Writers; Guest Lecturers; Guest Musicians; Guest Soloists; Guest Writers; Instructors; Music; New Productions; Original Music Scores; Singers; Soloists
Founded: 1929
Status: Non-Profit
Budget: $500,000
Income Sources: Box Office; Donations; Special Events; Fundraising
Season: October-May
Performs At: California Theatre for the Arts
Affiliations: American Symphony Council Orchestra; Broadcast Music, Inc.
Annual Attendance: 10,000
Facility Category: Theatre
Type of Stage: Wood
Stage Dimensions: 28'x56'
Seating Capacity: 1,728
Year Built: 1928

840
MAINLY MOZART
444 West Beech Street
Suite 220
San Diego, CA 92101
Phone: 619-239-0100
Fax: 619-233-4292
e-mail: admin@mainlymozart.org
Web Site: www.mainlymozart.org
Officers:
   President: Jack McGrory
   Chairman: Alexander Pearson
   Treasurer: Steven Hart
   Secretary: Linda Satz
Management:
   Artistic Director: David Atherton
   Executive Director: Nancy Laturno Bojanic
Utilizes: Educators; Guest Accompanists; Guest Musical Directors; Guest Musicians; Multimedia
Founded: 1988
Status: Non-Profit
Budget: $1.4 million
Income Sources: Box Office; Grants; Donations; Ticket Sales; Fundraisers
Season: January-May
Performs At: Neurosciences Institute; Copley Symphony Hall
Annual Attendance: 19,000
Seating Capacity: 352;2247

841
SAN DIEGO CHAMBER ORCHESTRA
11772 Sorrento Valley Road
Suite 212
San Diego, CA 92121
Phone: 858-350-0290
Fax: 858-350-0297
Toll-free: 888-848-7326
e-mail: stella.karl@orchestranova.org
Web Site: www.sdco.org
Officers:
   President: Gay Hugo Martinez
   CEO: Beverly Lambert
Management:
   Executive Director: Tyler Hewes
   Customer Relations Manager: Erin Oleno
   Director of Development & Marketing: Joan Cumming
   Accountant: Elaine Standring
Mission: To provide a resident orchestra of the highest professional caliber for the greater San Diego area.
Utilizes: Guest Artists
Founded: 1984
Specialized Field: Symphony; Orchestra; Chamber
Status: Professional, Nonprofit
Paid Staff: 5
Volunteer Staff: 1
Paid Artists: 60
Budget: $1.3 million
Income Sources: Ticket Sales; Donations; Sponsors
Season: October-May
Performs At: Sherwood Auditorium, St Paul's Cathedral; La Jolla, Rancho Santa Fe; Fairbanks Ranch Country Club
Affiliations: American Symphony Orchestra League; Association of California Symphony Orchestras
Annual Attendance: 15,000
Seating Capacity: 100-3,000
Organization Type: Performing
Resident Groups: Chamber Orchestra

842
SAN DIEGO EARLY MUSIC SOCIETY
PO Box 82008
San Diego, CA 92138
Phone: 619-291-8246
Fax: 619-688-1684
e-mail: sdems@sdems.org
Web Site: www.sdems.org
Officers:
   President: Mark Lester
   Secretary: Angela Quinn
   Treasurer: Martha Altus-Buller
   VP: Laurent Planchon
Management:
   Director: Diemet Rose
Utilizes: Guest Musical Directors; Instructors; Multimedia; Original Music Scores; Sign Language Translators
Founded: 1981
Status: Non-Profit
Budget: $65,000
Income Sources: Box Office; Members; Ads; Grants
Season: October-April
Performs At: St. James-by-the-Sea; Sherwood Auditorium At S.D. Museum of Contemporary Art, La Jolla; S.D. Museum of Art
Affiliations: Early Music America; San Diego Performing Arts League
Annual Attendance: 2,500
Seating Capacity: 400; 500; 100

843
SAN DIEGO SYMPHONY ORCHESTRA
1245 7th Avenue
San Diego, CA 92101
Phone: 619-235-0800
Fax: 619-235-0005
e-mail: marketing@sandiegosymphony.org
Web Site: www.sandiegosymphony.com
Officers:
   Chairman: Evelyn Olsen Lamden
   Vice Chairman: Paul Hering
   Vice Chairman: Andrew Clark
   Vice Chairman: David Snyder
   Treasurer: Douglas Bradley
   Secretary: John Zygowicz
Management:
   Music Director: Jahja Ling
   Concertmaster: Jeff Thayer
   Assistant Concertmaster: Nick Grant
   Artistic Administrator: Tommy Phillips
   Production Manager: Jennifer Ringle
   Executive Director: Edward B Gill
Mission: To present the highest quality performances of classical music to the San Diego community.
Utilizes: Guest Artists
Founded: 1910
Specialized Field: Symphony; Orchestra
Status: Professional; Nonprofit
Income Sources: American Symphony Orchestra League; Association of California Symphony Orchestras; Private and Corporate Donations; Ticket Sales; Foundations
Season: October-May
Performs At: Copley Symphony Hall
Seating Capacity: 2,245
Year Built: 1929
Organization Type: Performing; Educational; Sponsoring

844
SAN DIEGO YOUTH SYMPHONY
1650 El Prado
Suite 207A
San Diego, CA 92101
Phone: 619-233-3232
Fax: 619-233-3236
e-mail: contactus@sdys.org
Web Site: www.sdys.org
Officers:
   Chair: Mark Bennett
   President/CEO: Dalouge Smith
   Treasurer: Joel Sollender
   Secretary: Anni Lipper
   Governance Vice Chair: Ernie Smith
Management:
   Music Director: Jeff Edmons
   Operations: Alexis Alfaro
   Marketing: Molly Clark
   Conductor: Michael Gray
Founded: 1945
Status: Semi-professional
Budget: $150,000-$260,000
Income Sources: Private and Corporate Donations, Ticket Sales, Grants, Foundations
Season: November-June
Performs At: Copley Symphony Hall
Annual Attendance: 600-4,000
Seating Capacity: 2,400

845
TIFERETH ISRAEL COMMUNITY ORCHESTRA
6660 Cowles Mountain Boulevard
San Diego, CA 92119
Phone: 619-697-6001
Fax: 619-697-1102
e-mail: tifereth@tiferethisrael.com
Web Site: www.tiferethisrael.com
Officers:
   Administrative Vice-President: Jerry Hermes
   Secretary: Sheila Korn
   Congregational Services Vice-Presid: Dr. Stuart Karasik
Management:
   Director: David Amos
   Executive Director: Nivi Rahm
   Program Director: Beth Klareich
   Office Manager: Linda Marus
Utilizes: Commissioned Composers; Composers-in-Residence; Guest Accompanists; Guest Companies; Guest Lecturers; Guest Musical Directors; Guest Musicians; Singers; Touring Companies
Founded: 1974
Budget: $15,000
Income Sources: Tickets, donations
Season: Novembr-July

INSTRUMENTAL MUSIC / California

Performs At: Tifereth Israel Synagogue
Affiliations: Tifereth Israel Synagogue
Annual Attendance: 4000
Facility Category: Social Hall
Seating Capacity: 400-1500

846
KRONOS QUARTET
PO Box 225340
San Francisco, CA 94122-5340
Phone: 415-731-3533
Fax: 415-664-7590
e-mail: talk@kronosquartet.org
Web Site: www.kronosquartet.org
Officers:
  Chairman: Curtis Smith
Management:
  Managing Director: Janet Cowperthwaite
  Artistic Administrator: Sidney Chen
  Development: Laird Rodet
  Associate Director: Laird Rodet
  Production Director: Laurence Neff
  Business Operations Manager: Lucinda Toy
Utilizes: Choreographers; Collaborating Artists; Collaborations; Commissioned Composers; Commissioned Music; Composers; Filmmakers; Guest Accompanists; Guest Choreographers; Guest Companies; Guest Musical Directors; Guest Musicians; Multimedia; Organization Contracts; Original Music Scores; Paid Performers; Sign Language Translators; Singers; Visual Arts
Founded: 1973
Status: Professional, Non-Profit
Budget: $1.5 million
Income Sources: Earned; Contributions; Individual; Foundations; Government Sources
Season: July-May
Performs At: Various Venues
Affiliations: Association of Performing Arts Presenters; Western Arts Alliance; Chamber Music America; National Academy of Recording Arts Sciences
Annual Attendance: 1,000,000
Organization Type: Performing; Touring; Sponsoring

847
MIDSUMMER MOZART FESTIVAL
760 Market Street
Suite 749
San Francisco, CA 94102
Phone: 415-627-9141
Fax: 415-627-9142
e-mail: peter@midsummermozart.org
Web Site: www.midsummermozart.org
Officers:
  Chair: Behzad Khosrovi
  Secretary: Tom Bria
Management:
  Executive Director: Marcy Straw
  Music Director: George Cleve
  Concert Master: Robin Hansen
  Executive Director: Peter Susskind
Mission: To present the music of Wolfgang Amadeus Mozart to expanding Bay Area audiences through performances of unparalleled excellence.
Founded: 1974
Specialized Field: Mozart; Ensemble
Status: Professional; Nonprofit
Budget: $10,000
Income Sources: American Symphony Orchestra League; California Confederation of the Arts; Association of California Symphony Orchestras; Private and Corporate Donations; Ticket Sales
Season: July-August

Performs At: Berkeley's First Congregational Church; San Farncisco's Palace of the Legion of Honor; Various Venues
Annual Attendance: 800
Organization Type: Performing

848
NEW CENTURY CHAMBER ORCHESTRA
665 Third Street
Suite 345
San Francisco, CA 94107
Phone: 415-357-1111
Fax: 415-357-1101
e-mail: info@ncco.org
Web Site: www.ncco.org
Officers:
  Chairman: Gordon P Getty
  President: Mark Salkind
  Treasurer: Richard Lonegran
  Secretary: Jerry Voight
  Vice President: Lucinda Lee Katz
Management:
  Music Director: Nadja Salemo Sonnenberg
  Executive Director: Parker E Monroe
  Operations Director: Everett L Doner
  Busse: Tom
  Vardigans: Interim Directo Sarah
Mission: To communicate vibrant orchestral music to the audience, blending each instrument harmoniously together without the guidance of a conductor.
Founded: 1992
Specialized Field: Chamber
Paid Staff: 7
Paid Artists: 19
Budget: $1.4 million
Income Sources: Private and Corporate Donations; Foundations; Goverment Agencies
Season: September-June
Performs At: Herbst Theatre; First Congregational Church; First United Methodist Church; Osher Marin JCC
Annual Attendance: 4,000
Seating Capacity: 926
Year Built: 1991

849
PAUL DRESHER ENSEMBLE
Musical Traditions Inc
333 Valencia Street
Suite 301
San Francisco, CA 94103-3552
Phone: 415-558-9540
Fax: 415-843-4140
e-mail: info@dresherensemble.org
Web Site: www.dresherensemble.org
Officers:
  Director: John Heller
Management:
  Artistic Director: Paul Dresher
  Operations: Sarah Lockhart
  Development: Michele Fromson
Utilizes: Commissioned Music; Theatre Companies
Status: Professional, Non-Profit
Budget: $150,000
Income Sources: Private and Corporate Donations, Donations of Stock or other Appreciated Items
Season: October-May
Performs At: Various Venues
Organization Type: Performing; Touring; Educational

850
PHILHARMONIA BAROQUE ORCHESTRA
414 Mason Street
Suite 606
San Francisco, CA 94102
Phone: 415-252-1288
Fax: 415-252-1488
e-mail: info@philharmonia.org
Web Site: www.philharmonia.org
Officers:
  President: Ross Armstrong
  Treasurer: E Paul Swatek
  Secretary: Douglas Tanner
  VP: David Low
  Treasurer: Donna Williams
Management:
  Executive Director: Cindi Hubbard
  Artistic Director: Jeff Phillips
  Development: Courtney Beck
  Executive Director: Michael Costa
  Patron Services Manager: David Challinor
  Graphic Designer: Jenna Hazlett
Utilizes: Guest Artists
Founded: 1981
Status: Professional, Non-Profit
Budget: $2.8 million
Income Sources: Ticket Sales, Private and Corporate Donations
Season: August-June
Performs At: Performs throughout the Bay area, US and in Europe
Annual Attendance: 30,000
Organization Type: Performing; Touring

851
ROVA SAXAPHONE QUARTET
333 12th Street
San Francisco, CA 94103
Phone: 415-487-1701
Fax: 415-487-1501
e-mail: rova@rova.org
Web Site: www.rova.org
Management:
  Manager: Julia Melancon
Utilizes: Collaborating Artists; Collaborations; Commissioned Composers; Commissioned Music; Dance Companies; Dancers; Educators; Five Seasonal Concerts; Grant Writers; Guest Companies; Guest Directors; Guest Instructors; Guest Musical Directors; Instructors; Lyricists; Multimedia; Organization Contracts; Sign Language Translators
Founded: 1978
Status: Professional, Non-Profit
Income Sources: Ticket Sales, Members of Rova Arts, Private and Corporate Donations, William and Flora Hewlett Foundation
Season: September-October
Annual Attendance: 5,000
Organization Type: Performing; Touring

852
SAN FRANCISCO COMMUNITY MUSIC CENTER
544 Capp Street
San Francisco, CA 94110
Phone: 415-647-6015
Fax: 415-647-3890
e-mail: info@sfcmc.org
Web Site: www.sfcmc.org
Officers:
  President: Patricia Taylor Lee
  VP: Catharine L Kalin
  Treasurer: Paul Sussman

INSTRUMENTAL MUSIC / California

Secretary: David J Neuman
Management:
  Executive Director: Stephen R Shapiro PhD
  Development: Fran Hildebrand
  Marketing: Sonia Caltvedt
  Executive Director: Christopher Borg
  Program Director: Chus Alonso
  Marketing Director: Sonia Caltvedt
Mission: To make high quality music accessible to all people, regardless of their financial status.
Founded: 1921
Opened: 1921
Specialized Field: Music Education
Status: Non-Profit
Paid Staff: 11
Budget: $2 million
Income Sources: Endowment; Planned Giving Program; Private and Corporate Donations; Tuition
Performs At: Music Center Recital Hall
Affiliations: National Guild of Community of the Arts, California Arts Council
Annual Attendance: 18,000
Seating Capacity: 250
Rental Contact: Linda Hitchcock
Organization Type: Performing; Educational

853
SAN FRANCISCO CONTEMPORARY MUSIC PLAYERS
55 New Montgomery
Suite 708
San Francisco, CA 94105
Phone: 415-278-9566
Fax: 415-778-6402
e-mail: info@sfcmp.org
Web Site: www.sfcmp.org
Officers:
  President: Susan Hartzell
  Executive Director: Adam L Frey
  VP/Treasurer: Donald Blais
  Secretary: George Bosworth
  President: Richard Diebold Lee
Management:
  Music Director/Conductor: David Milnes
  Operations Director: Carrie Blanding
  Executive Director: Rozella Floranz Kennedy
Mission: To professionally perform contemporary chamber music using a mixed ensemble.
Utilizes: Collaborations; Commissioned Composers; Five Seasonal Concerts; Guest Composers; Guest Musicians; Multimedia; Original Music Scores
Founded: 1971
Specialized Field: Chamber; Ensemble
Status: Professional; Nonprofit
Paid Staff: 3
Paid Artists: 45
Budget: $400,000
Income Sources: Government and Foundation Grants; Individual Donations; Ticket Sales; Stock Gift, Corporate Match, Planned Giving
Season: September-April
Performs At: Yerba Buena Center for the Arts
Annual Attendance: 2,000
Facility Category: Arts Center
Seating Capacity: 335
Organization Type: Performing; Touring

854
SAN FRANCISCO CONSERVATORY OF MUSIC
50 Oak Street
San Francisco, CA 94102-6011
Phone: 415-864-7326
Fax: 415-503-6299
e-mail: jseaman@sfcm.edu
Web Site: www.sfcm.edu
Officers:
  President: Colin Murdoch
  Dean: Mary Ellen Poole
  Executive Assistant to the Presiden: Jennifer Seaman
  Registrar: Jonas Wright
Management:
  Concert Operations Manager: Seth Ducey
  Assist Concert Operations Manager: Lauren Brown
  Accounting Manager: Whitney Valentine
  Payroll Manager: Jennifer Chang
Mission: The training of classical musicians for professional careers in performing, composing, conducting and teaching.
Utilizes: Singers
Founded: 1917
Specialized Field: Orchestra; Chamber; Ensemble; Electronic; Live Electronic
Status: Nonprofit
Season: September-March
Performs At: Three performance spaces
Affiliations: Western Association of Colleges and Schools, National Association of Schools of Music
Annual Attendance: 22,000
Seating Capacity: 350
Organization Type: Performing; Educational

855
SAN FRANCISCO JAZZ ORGANIZATION
201 Franklin Street (at Fell)
San Francisco, CA 94102
Phone: 415-398-5655
Fax: 415-398-5569
Toll-free: 866-920-5299
e-mail: info@sfjazz.org
Web Site: www.sfjazz.org
Officers:
  Founder/President: Randall Kline
  Chair: Bannus Hudson
  Interim Vice Chair: Mark Edmunds
  Secretary: Charles Charnas
  Treasurer: Brian E. Hollins
Management:
  Artistic Director: Randall Kline
  Artistic Producer: Lilly Schwartz
  Marketing Director: Patty Gessner
  Operations Director: Mount V. Allen III CFE
  Production Manager: Cecilia Engelhart
Mission: To feature the jazz performers from the local Bay Area as well as performers from around the country in San Francisco venues.
Utilizes: Poets
Founded: 1983
Specialized Field: Ensemble; Jazz; World Music
Status: Professional, Nonprofit
Paid Staff: 25
Volunteer Staff: 300
Paid Artists: 40
Non-paid Artists: 25
Budget: $6 million
Income Sources: Private and Corporate Donations, Organizations
Season: June-March
Performs At: Various Venues
Annual Attendance: 100,000
Organization Type: Performing; Resident; Educational; Presenter

856
SAN FRANCISCO SYMPHONY
Davies Symphony Hall
201 Van Ness Avenue
San Francisco, CA 94102
Phone: 415-864-6000
Fax: 415-554-0108
e-mail: patronservices@sfsymphony.org
Web Site: www.sfsymphony.org
Officers:
  President: John D Goldman
  Secretary: Robert R Tufts
  Chief Financial Officer: James Kirk
  Chair: Claire N Barnes
Management:
  Executive Director: Brent Assink
  Artistic Director: Gregg Gleasner
  Development: Robert W Lasher
  Chorus Manager: Elaine Robertson
  HR Director: Ken Auletta
  Conductor: Michael Tilson Thomas
Utilizes: Guest Artists
Founded: 1911
Status: Professional, Non-Profit
Income Sources: Private and Corporate Donations, Ticket Sales, Advertising
Performs At: Louise M Davies Symphony Hall, Flint Center
Affiliations: American Symphony Orchestra League; Association of California Symphony Orchestras
Annual Attendance: 600,000
Seating Capacity: 2,700, 2,500
Organization Type: Performing; Touring; Resident; Educational

857
SAN FRANCISCO SYMPHONY YOUTH ORCHESTRA
Davies Symphony Hall
201 Van Ness Avenue
San Francisco, CA 94102
Phone: 415-864-6000
Fax: 415-554-0108
e-mail: patronservices@sfsymphony.org
Web Site: www.sfsymphony.org
Officers:
  Chair: Claire N Barnes
  Chief Financial Officer: James Kirk
  Secretary: Robert R Tufts
  President: John D Goldman
Management:
  Director: Benjamin Shwartz
  Manager: Jefferson Packer
  Executive Director: Brent Assink
  Chorus Manager: Elaine Robertson
  HR Director: Ken Auletta
Utilizes: Guest Artists
Founded: 1981
Status: Non-Professional, Non-Profit
Income Sources: American Symphony Orchestra League; Youth Orchestra Division, Private and Corporate Donations
Performs At: Louise M Davies Symphony Hall
Annual Attendance: 25,000
Seating Capacity: 2,700
Organization Type: Performing; Touring; Resident; Educational; Sponsoring

858
EAST WEST MUSIC AND DANCE
7283 Coronado Drive
San Jose, CA 95129

INSTRUMENTAL MUSIC / California

Phone: 408-865-0654
Web Site: www.eastwestmusicanddance.com
Mission: All we do is teach. We do not sell or rent instruments of music. This leaves us free to specialize in one thing - providing the highest quality of music instruction.
Specialized Field: Instrumental

859
SAN JOSE CHAMBER MUSIC SOCIETY
PO Box 108
San Jose, CA 95103-0108
Phone: 408-286-5111
Fax: 510-651-0389
e-mail: sjcm@sjchambermusic.org
Web Site: www.sjchambermusic.org
Management:
 Artistic Director: Ted Lorraine
Founded: 1986
Status: Non-Profit
Budget: $100,000
Income Sources: Private and Corporate Donations, Ticket Sales
Season: October-April
Performs At: Le Petit Trianon Theatre
Annual Attendance: 2,600
Seating Capacity: 348
Year Built: 1920
Organization Type: Performing

860
SAN JOSE JAZZ SOCIETY
145 W San Carlos
San Jose, CA 95113
Phone: 408-288-7557
Fax: 408-288-7598
e-mail: info@sanjosejazz.org
Web Site: www.sanjosejazz.org
Officers:
 Chairman: Mike Warner
 Secretary: David Kennedy
 Treasurer: Henry Wang
Management:
 Acting Executive Director: Brendan Rawson
 Marketing Director: Massimo Chisessi
 Festival Director: Bruce Labadie
Founded: 1986
Status: Non-Profit
Income Sources: Grants; Donations; Sponsors; Members
Season: January-March
Performs At: Main Stage; Plaza de Cesar Chavez
Annual Attendance: 165,000
Seating Capacity: 200

861
SAN JOSE TAIKO GROUP
565 N 5th Street
PO Box 26895
San Jose, CA 95159
Phone: 408-293-9344
Fax: 408-293-9366
e-mail: taiko@taiko.org
Web Site: www.taiko.org
Officers:
 Executive Director: Wisa Uemura
 President: Marie Yoshidome
 Treasurer: Dan Sueyoshi
 Secretary: Ryan Yoshida
Management:
 General Manager: Wisa Uemura
 Artistic Director: Franco Imperial
 Performing Member: Rina Chang

Mission: San Jose Taiko, with a deep respect of cultural traditions and a commitment to artistic excellence, is dedicated to the advancement of the taiko art form through the development of its world-class Performing Ensemble and the San Jose Taiko Conservatory.
Utilizes: Artists-in-Residence; Choreographers; Collaborating Artists; Collaborations; Commissioned Music; Five Seasonal Concerts; Guest Artists; Guest Companies; Guest Directors; Guest Musical Directors; Local Artists; Multimedia; Original Music Scores; Poets; Singers; Soloists; Student Interns
Founded: 1973
Specialized Field: Traditional Folk Arts/Music
Status: Professional, Nonprofit
Paid Staff: 1
Volunteer Staff: 20
Paid Artists: 5
Non-paid Artists: 4
Income Sources: Private and Corporate Donations, CD's, Ticket Sales, Performance Fees
Season: May-October
Performs At: Various Venues
Organization Type: Performing; Touring; Educational

862
SOUTH BAY GUITAR SOCIETY
72 North Fifth Street
Suite 18
San Jose, CA 95112
Phone: 408-292-0704
Fax: 408-280-0407
e-mail: sbgs@sbgs.org
Web Site: www.sbgs.org
Officers:
 President: Jerry Snyder
 VP: Tom Ingalz
 Treasurer: Suzanne Patrick
 Secretary: Bob Orr
Management:
 Artistic Director: Jerry Snyder
 Managing Director: Tom Ingalz
Mission: To make classical guitar music accessible to people of diverse cultures, ages, abilities and economic means by offering performance opportunities to professional and amateur musicians, providing classical guitar music education, and by presenting the music of many cultures to the public.
Founded: 1986
Specialized Field: Classical Guitar
Status: Nonprofit
Income Sources: Local Government Arts Grants, Ticket Sales, Member Dues, Concert Subscriptions
Season: September-April
Performs At: Le Petit Trianon Theatre, Espresso Garden & Cafe
Seating Capacity: 348
Organization Type: Presenters

863
SAN LUIS OBISPO MOZART FESTIVAL
2050 Broad Street
San Luis Obispo, CA 93401
Mailing Address: PO Box 311, San Luis Obispo, CA 93406
Phone: 805-781-3009
Fax: 805-781-3011
e-mail: kathy@festivalmozaic.com
Web Site: www.mozartfestival.com
Officers:
 President: Dwyne Willis
 VP: Charles Myers
 Secretary: Peter Zaleski
 Treasurer: Rodger Mastako

Management:
 Music Director: Scott Yoo
 Executive Director: Curtis Pendleton
 Project Manager: Cary Woll
 Executive Director: Bettina Swigger
 Operations Manager: Janet Hillson
 Ticketing Manager: Prudy Lovtang
Mission: To present a classical music festival highlighting Mozart and other classical and contemporary composers.
Utilizes: Commissioned Composers; Commissioned Music; Guest Composers; Guest Lecturers; Guest Musical Directors; Multimedia; Original Music Scores; Singers
Founded: 1971
Specialized Field: Mozart; Ensemble; Jazz; Children's Concerts; Educational
Status: Professional, Nonprofit
Volunteer Staff: 200
Budget: $150,000-$400,000
Income Sources: Private and Corporate Donations, Ticket Sales
Season: July-August
Performs At: Throughout San Luis Obispo County (Festival Sites)
Affiliations: San Luis Performing Arts Center; Wineries; Chapels
Seating Capacity: 1,300
Organization Type: Performing; Educational

864
SAN LUIS OBISPO SYMPHONY
PO Box 658
San Luis Obispo, CA 93406
Phone: 805-543-3533
Fax: 805-781-3534
e-mail: staff@slosymphony.com
Web Site: www.slosymphony.com
Officers:
 President: June McIvor
 Treasurer: Cle Van Beurden
Management:
 Music Director/Conductor: Michael Nowak
 Co-Concertmaster: Pam Dassenko
 Co-Concertmaster: Paul Severtson
 Music Education Director: Andrea Stoner
 Executive Director: Jim Black
Mission: To support an outstanding community orchestra, to foster symphonic and chamber music education and to contribute to the cultural and economic vitality of the central coast community.
Utilizes: Collaborations; Commissioned Composers; Community Members; Five Seasonal Concerts; Local Unknown Artists; Original Music Scores; Singers; Soloists; Students
Founded: 1961
Specialized Field: Orchestra
Paid Staff: 7
Paid Artists: 83
Budget: $260,000-1,300,000
Income Sources: Ticket Sales; Donations; Grants; Fundraisers; Tuition
Season: October-June
Performs At: Performing Arts Center, Clark Center for the Performing Arts, United Methodist Church of Los Osos, Avila Beach Resort
Annual Attendance: 10,000
Seating Capacity: 1100 (Center) 3000 (Avila) 300-600 (sm. venu)
Organization Type: Performing, Touring

INSTRUMENTAL MUSIC / California

865
CALIFORNIA PHILHARMONIC ORCHESTRA
400 S. Baldwin Ave
Suite 2160
San Marino, CA 91007
Phone: 626-304-0333
Fax: 626-304-0038
e-mail: info@calphil.org
Web Site: www.calphil.org
Officers:
  President/CEO: Victor Vener
  Chairman Emeritus: Robert Kessel
  Chairman: Roger Ward
  Controller: Curtis Morris
  Treasurer: David Brooks
Management:
  Music Director: Victor Vener
  Artistic Administrator: Roger Allen Ward
Mission: To bring excellent professional performances of great music to the widest possible audience.
Founded: 1997
Specialized Field: Classical
Paid Staff: 10
Volunteer Staff: 500
Paid Artists: 70
Income Sources: Ticket Sales; Gifts from Corporate Sponsors; Community Foundations and Private Donations
Season: January-May
Performs At: Los Angeles County Arboretum and Botanic Garden
Annual Attendance: 170,000
Facility Category: Outdoor Amphitheatre

866
MARIN SYMPHONY ORCHESTRA
4340 Redwood Highway
Suite 409C
San Rafael, CA 94903 - 21
Phone: 415-479-8100
Fax: 415-479-8110
e-mail: greatmusic@marinsymphony.org
Web Site: www.marinsymphony.org
Officers:
  President and Chairman: Dr. Frances L. White
  VP: Stephen Goldman
  Secretary: Steven Machtinger
Management:
  Artistic Director: Alasdair Neale
  Executive Director: Noralee Monestere
  Marketing: Suzanne Crawford
  Executive Director: Jeff vom Saal
  Orchestra Personnel Manager: Craig McAmis
Mission: Dr. Frances L.
Utilizes: Commissioned Composers; Composers-in-Residence; Grant Writers; Guest Accompanists; Guest Companies; Guest Designers; Guest Lecturers; Instructors; Multimedia; Music; Organization Contracts; Original Music Scores; Poets; Sign Language Translators; Singers
Budget: $1.2 million
Season: October-May
Performs At: Marin Veterans' Memorial Auditorium in San Rafael
Affiliations: Association of California Symphony Orchestra, Americany Symphony Orchestra League
Annual Attendance: 24,000
Seating Capacity: 2,000
Architect: Frank Lloyd Wright

867
MARIN SYMPHONY YOUTH ORCHESTRA
4340 Redwood Highway
Suite 409C
San Rafael, CA 94903 - 21
Phone: 415-479-8100
Fax: 415-479-8110
e-mail: greatmusic@marinsymphony.org
Web Site: www.marinsymphony.org
Officers:
  President and Chairman: Dr. Frances L. White
  VP: Stephen Goldman
  Secretary: Steven Machtinger
Management:
  Artistic Director: George Thompson
  Executive Director: Noralee Monestere
  Marketing: Suzanne Crawford
  Executive Director: Jeff vom Saal
  Orchestra Personnel Manager: Craig McAmis
Mission: Dr. Frances L.
Income Sources: American Symphony Orchestra League, Youth Orchestra Division; Private and Corporate Donations; Ticket Sales; Tuition
Season: September-June
Performs At: San Rafael High School Auditorium
Annual Attendance: 3,000
Organization Type: Performing; Touring; Educational; Sponsoring

868
PACIFIC SYMPHONY
3631 S Harbor Blvd
Suite 100
Santa Ana, CA 92704 - 89
Phone: 714-755-5788
Fax: 714-755-5789
e-mail: info@pacificsymphony.org
Web Site: www.pacificsymphony.org
Officers:
  Chairman: Sally Anderson
  President: John E Forsyte
  Vice Chairman, Finance and Treasure: Mark Nielsen
  Secretary: Susan Anderrson
  Executive VP & C.O.O: Sean Sutton
Management:
  Music Director: Carl St Clair
  Principal Pops Conductor: Richard Kaufman
  Assistant Conductor: Maxim Eshkenazy
  Concertmaster: Raymond Kobler
  Production/Stage Manager: Will Hunter
  Office Manager: Billie Jo Spearing
Mission: Offers moving musical experiences with repertoire ranging from the great orchestral masterworks to music from today's most prominent composers, highlighted by the annual American Composers Festival.
Founded: 1978
Specialized Field: Orchestra
Volunteer Staff: 400
Budget: $3,600,000-$10,000,000
Income Sources: Private and Corporate Donations, Ticket Sales, Foundations, Luncheons, Fundraisers
Season: All Year
Performs At: Orange County Performing Arts Center, Summer Concerts in the park in Santa Ana and Anaheim
Annual Attendance: 18,000

869
MUSIC ACADEMY OF THE WEST
1070 Fairway Road
Santa Barbara, CA 93108-2899
Phone: 805-969-4726
Fax: 805-969-0686
e-mail: admissions@musicacademy.org
Web Site: www.musicacademy.org
Officers:
  President: Scott Reed
  VP Finance: Barbara Robertson
  VP Marketing/Communications: Susan Gwynne Jonathan:
  Jonathan E: Bishop VP for Institutional
Management:
  VP Artistic Programs: Richard Feit
  Dean of Students: Tiffany Schoemaker
  Special Events Manager: Brooke E Jacobs
  Director Operations: Leslie Kelleher
  Manager of Buildings & Grounds: Jim Pettit
Mission: The Music Academy of the West is dedicated to advancing the development of gifted young classical musicians and classical music professionals through a unique combination of intensive personal instruction, educational programs and performance opportunities, all of the highest quality.
Utilizes: Artists-in-Residence; Collaborating Artists; Grant Writers; Guest Artists; Guest Companies; Guest Composers; Guest Musical Directors; Guest Musicians; Multimedia
Founded: 1947
Specialized Field: Chamber; Classical; Opera; Orchestra
Paid Staff: 25
Budget: $5,000,000-$6,000,000
Income Sources: Individual Contributions; Foundations; Corporations; Stock Gifts; Planned Giving
Season: June-August
Performs At: Campus and City Venues
Affiliations: Association of California Symphony Orchestra, League of American Orchestras
Annual Attendance: 36,000
Facility Category: Recital Hall
Rental Contact: Leslie Kelleher

870
SANTA BARBARA CHAMBER ORCHESTRA
1330 State Street
Santa Barbara, CA 93101
Mailing Address: PO Box 90903, Santa Barbara, CA 93190
Phone: 805-966-2441
Fax: 805-966-2448
e-mail: info@sbco.org
Web Site: www.sbco.org
Officers:
  President: Donald Lafler
  Chairman: Pamela Taylor
  Treasurer: Robert Hanrahan
  Secretary: Peter Favero
  Chairman: Joe Campanelli
Management:
  Music Director/Conductor: Heiichiro Ohyama
  Concertmaster: Amy Hershberger
  General Manager: Daniel Kepl
  Artistic Operations Manager: Rachel Galvin
  Development Director: Leslie Bisno
  Taylor: Pamela
Mission: To present the Santa Barbara community with high quality music by skilled musicians and soloists.
Founded: 1978
Specialized Field: Chamber; Orchestra
Paid Staff: 4
Paid Artists: 30
Budget: $450,000-$500,000
Income Sources: Private and Corporate Donations, Matching Gifts, Donations of Stock, Planned Giving

INSTRUMENTAL MUSIC / California

Season: October-March
Performs At: Lobero Theatre, Natural History Museum
Annual Attendance: 11,000
Seating Capacity: 680

871
SANTA BARBARA SYMPHONY ASSOCIATION
1330 State Street
Suite 102
Santa Barbara, CA 93101
Phone: 805-898-9386
Fax: 805-898-9326
e-mail: info@thesymphony.org
Web Site: www.thesymphony.org
Officers:
   President: Paksy Plackis-Cheng
   VP: Arthur Swalley
   Treasurer: Gene Sinser
   Secretary: David Chernof
   Chairman: Joe Campanelli
Management:
   Music & Artistic Director: Nir Kabaretti
   Conductor Laureate: Gisele Ben-Dor
   Executive Director: David Grossman
   Director: Peter Madlem
Mission: To be a highly respected symphony orchestra performing great works with passion and excellence.
Founded: 1953
Specialized Field: Orchestra
Paid Staff: 11
Volunteer Staff: 3
Budget: $1,050,000-3,600,000
Income Sources: Sustaining Funds; Endowment Fund; Private and Corporate Donations ;Planned Giving; Foundations
Season: October-May
Performs At: Arlington Theatre
Annual Attendance: 40,000
Seating Capacity: 1,550

872
WEST COAST CHAMBER ORCHESTRA
1812 La Coronilla Drive
Santa Barbara, CA 93109
Phone: 805-962-6609
Fax: 805-962-6609
e-mail: info@westcoastsymphony.com
Officers:
   President: Christopher Story IV
   VP: Jacqueline Sarrgeri
   Secretary: Lawrence Hilton
   Treasurer: Gary Gray
Management:
   Music Director/Conductor: Christopher Story VI
Mission: To present the finest music from local musicians.
Utilizes: Guest Artists
Founded: 1987
Specialized Field: Symphony; Orchestra; Chamber
Status: Professional, Nonprofit
Volunteer Staff: 1
Paid Artists: 20
Non-paid Artists: 2
Budget: $40,000
Income Sources: Private and Corporate Donations, Ticket Sales
Performs At: Trinity Episcopal Church
Annual Attendance: 800
Facility Category: Church
Organization Type: Performing

873
SANTA CRUZ BAROQUE FESTIVAL
PO Box 482
Santa Cruz, CA 95061
Phone: 831-457-9693
e-mail: info@scbaroque.org
Web Site: www.scbaroque.org
Officers:
   Founder: Linda Burman-Hall
   President: Kathryn Tobish
   VP: Donald Wilson
   Treasurer: David Copp
   Secretary: Sophy Chou
   Secretary: Judy Foreman
Management:
   Artistic Director: Linda Burman-Hall
   General Manager: Alissa Roedig
Mission: The Santa Cruz Baroque Festival has brought to life a broad spectrum of music written by composers of centuries past.
Founded: 1974
Specialized Field: Ensemble; Baroque
Status: Professional, Nonprofit
Budget: $40,000
Income Sources: Private and Corporate Donations, Government Agencies, Advertisers, Media, Grants
Season: February-May
Performs At: Various Auditoriums
Annual Attendance: 1,500
Facility Category: Various auditoriums
Organization Type: Performing; Sponsoring

874
SANTA CRUZ COUNTY SYMPHONY
307 Church Street
Santa Cruz, CA 95060
Phone: 831-462-0553
Fax: 831-426-1193
e-mail: info@santacruzsymphony.org
Web Site: www.santacruzsymphony.org
Officers:
   President: Owen Brown
   Executive Director: Virginia Wright
   Ard: Pegi
   Henderson: Treasurer Edy
Management:
   Music Director: John Larry Granger
   Executive Director: Jan Derecho
   Production Manager: Rick Larsen
   Stage Manager: Eileen Flynn
Utilizes: Collaborations; Guest Artists; Guest Musical Directors; Guest Musicians; Guest Writers; Instructors; Resident Artists
Founded: 1957
Specialized Field: Classical
Status: Professional
Paid Staff: 4
Paid Artists: 80
Budget: $260,000-$1,050,000
Income Sources: Private and Corporate Donations, Ticket Sales, Sponsoring a Concert
Season: September-February
Performs At: Santa Cruz Civic Auditorium, Henry J Mello Center
Annual Attendance: 15,000
Facility Category: Civic Auditorium
Seating Capacity: 1,300
Year Built: 1930

875
BRENTWOOD-WESTWOOD SYMPHONY ORCHESTRA
11960 Sunset Blvd
Santa Monica, CA 90049-4228
Mailing Address: PO Box 956, Santa Monica, CA 90406
Phone: 310-940-9876
e-mail: TheBWSO@gmail.com
Web Site: www.brentwoodwestwoodsymphony.org
Officers:
   Founder: Alvin Mills
   Chairman: Bob Engelman
   President: Deborah Kim
   Treasurer: James Lee
   Secretary: Grusha Paterson-Mills
Management:
   Music Director/Conductor: Alvin Mills
   General Manager: Grusha Paterson-Mills
   Associate Conductor: Diego Miralles
Mission: In these times of turmoil and unrest music is still the universal language that enriches our lives. Let us share this treasure with each other.
Founded: 1952
Specialized Field: Symphony
Status: Nonprofit
Budget: $100,000-$150,000
Income Sources: Grants, Foundations, Private and Corporate Donations
Season: October-May
Performs At: Paul Revere Middle School Auditorium
Annual Attendance: 12,000

876
SANTA MONICA SYMPHONY ORCHESTRA
PO Box 3101
Santa Monica, CA 90408-3101
Phone: 310-395-6330
e-mail: office@smsymphony.org
Web Site: www.smsymphony.org
Officers:
   Chairman: David Bendett
   Treasurer: Paul Dolid
   Secretary: Ian McIlraith
   VP: Michael Miller
Management:
   Music Director/Conductor: Allen Gross
   Concertmaster: David Stenske
   Operations Manager: Ryan Bullard
   Stage Manager: Robert Godfrey
   Office Manager: Niklas Bertani
   House Manager: Chloe Jenkins
Mission: To provide high-quality admission-free concerts from the classical and contemporary symphony repertoire to Santa Monica and West Lost Angeles.
Founded: 1945
Specialized Field: Orchestra
Status: Nonprofit
Budget: $35,000-$100,000
Income Sources: Private and Corporate Donations, Grants from City of Santa Monica, County of Los Angeles, Friends of the Santa Monica Symphony
Season: October-May
Performs At: Santa Monica Civic Auditorium
Affiliations: Association of California Symphony Orchestra, American Symphony Orchestra League, Santa Monica Chamber of Comemrce
Annual Attendance: 5,600
Seating Capacity: 3,000
Year Built: 1958

INSTRUMENTAL MUSIC / California

877
SANTA ROSA JUNIOR COLLEGE CHAMBER CONCERT SERIES
1501 Mendocino Avenue
Music Department
Santa Rosa, CA 95401- 439
Phone: 707-527-4685
Fax: 707-521-7988
Toll-free: 800-564-SRJC
e-mail: ljohns@santarosa.edu
Web Site: www.santarosa.edu
Officers:
   Department Chair: Bennett Friedman
Mission: Santa Rosa Junior College's Chamber Concert Series has been delighting audiences with wonderful music performed by superb musicians in an intimate environment.
Specialized Field: Classical; Chamber
Income Sources: Private and Corporate Donations, Ticket Sales
Season: October-December
Performs At: Burbank Auditorium, Randolph Newman Auditorium
Annual Attendance: 1,200
Seating Capacity: 700, 350

878
SANTA ROSA SYMPHONY
50 Santa Rosa Avenue
Suite 410
Santa Rosa, CA 95404
Phone: 707-546-7097
Fax: 707-546-0460
e-mail: info@santarosasymphony.com
Web Site: www.santarosasymphony.com
Officers:
   President: Eric Rossin
   VP: James Hinton
   Treasurer: Harry Rubins
   Secretary: Peggy Elliott
Management:
   Music Director: Bruno Ferrandis
   Executive Director: Alan Silow
   Conductor Laureate: Jeffrey Kahane
   Choral Director: Robert Worth
   Concertmaster: Joseph Edelberg
   Artistic Operations Director: Tim Beswick
   Marketing Director: Sara Obuchowski
   Director of Artistic Operations: Timothy L Beswick
   Director of Education: Ben Taylor
Mission: To inspire and engage people with the highest quality musical performances and educational programs.
Utilizes: Collaborations; Commissioned Composers; Composers-in-Residence; Guest Artists; Guest Directors; Guest Musicians; Original Music Scores; Resident Artists; Sign Language Translators; Singers
Founded: 1928
Specialized Field: Symphony; Orchestra; Chamber; Ensemble
Status: Nonprofit
Paid Staff: 13
Volunteer Staff: 100
Paid Artists: 225
Budget: $20 million
Income Sources: Underwriters, Grants, Donations, Endowments, Ticket Sales
Season: October-May
Performs At: Wells Fargo Center for the Arts
Affiliations: Association of California Symphony Orchestras, American Symphony Orchestra League
Annual Attendance: 50,000
Seating Capacity: 1,500
Organization Type: Performing; Resident; Educational

879
STANFORD SYMPHONY ORCHESTRA
Department of Music Stanford University
Braun Music Center
541 Lasuen Mall
Stanford, CA 94305-3076
Phone: 650-724-6738
Fax: 650-725-2686
e-mail: marioch@stanford.edu
Web Site: www.music.stanford.edu
Officers:
   Chairman: Stephen M Sano
   Financial Officer: Velda Williams
Management:
   Administrative Director: Mario Champagne
   Facilities/Production Manager: Scott Kepley
   Publicist: Delane Haro
   Academic Administrator: Debbie Barney
   Recording Engineer: Mark Dalrymple
   Technical Services Manager: Scott Kepley
   Office Manager: Ardis Walling
Mission: The Stanford Symphony Orchestra is an on campus student organization supported by the Music Department and the Associated Students of Stanford University.
Utilizes: Theatre Companies
Founded: 1891
Paid Staff: 2
Volunteer Staff: 5
Budget: $35,000-$100,000
Income Sources: Friends of Music at Stanford, Private and Corporate Donations, Ticket Sales
Season: October-June
Performs At: Dinkelspiel Auditorium, Campbell Recital Hall
Facility Category: Recital Hall (Campbell)
Seating Capacity: 221
Year Built: 1985
Organization Type: Performing, Educational, Touring

880
CONSERVATORY OF MUSIC
University of the Pacific
3601 Pacific Avenue
Stockton, CA 95211
Phone: 209-946-2285
Web Site: www.pacific.edu
Officers:
   Interim Dean: William Hipp
Management:
   Development Director: Renna Beninoris
   Stage/Technical Direcgtor: James Gonzales
   Operations Manager: Stephen Perdicaris
Mission: We are dedicated to the education and training of musicians for the highest levels of artistic performance, creative endeavor and intellectual inquiry.
Specialized Field: Symphony
Budget: $35,000
Income Sources: Ticket Sales, Private and Corporate Donations, Grants
Season: October-April
Performs At: Faye Spanos Concert Hall
Annual Attendance: 12,000
Seating Capacity: 1,000

881
FRIENDS OF CHAMBER MUSIC
University of the Pacific
PO Box 4874
Stockton, CA 95204
Phone: 209-946-0540
e-mail: info@chambermusicfriends.org
Web Site: www.chambermusicfriends.org
Officers:
   VP: Carole Gilbertson
   President: Dwane Milnes
   Treasurer: Sara milnes Milnes
   Secretary: Marie Medford
Mission: The mission of the Friends of Chamber Music of Stockton is to develop, sustain and advance an interest in professional quality chamber music for the citizens of Stockton and surrounding communities.
Founded: 1955
Specialized Field: Chamber
Status: Nonprofit
Volunteer Staff: 8
Paid Artists: 19
Income Sources: Ticket Sales, Private and Corporate Donations
Season: September-March
Performs At: Faye Spanos Concert Hall in the Conservatory of Music, University of the Pacific
Seating Capacity: 1,000

882
STOCKTON SYMPHONY ASSOCIATION
1024 W. Robinhood Drive
Suite 1
Stockton, CA 95207
Phone: 209-951-0196
Fax: 209-951-1050
e-mail: jkenworthy@stocktonsymphony.org
Web Site: www.stocktonsymphony.org
Officers:
   President: Nancy Schneider
   Treasurer: Daniel Terry, Jr
   Secretary: Maury Marengo
   VP of Marketing: Gene Acevedo
Management:
   Music Director/Conductor: Peter Jaffe
   Executive Director: Jane E Kenworthy
   Orchestra Personnel Manager: Joanna Pinckney
Mission: The mission of the Stockton Symphony is to engage, educate and inspire the community through a commitment to excellence in its performances and programs.
Utilizes: Commissioned Composers; Guest Artists; Guest Musical Directors; Guest Musicians; Instructors; Multimedia; Music; Original Music Scores; Sign Language Translators; Soloists
Founded: 1926
Specialized Field: Symphonic Music
Status: Professional, Nonprofit
Paid Staff: 90
Paid Artists: 6
Budget: $1.3 million
Income Sources: Ticket Sales, Contributions, Grants
Season: September-April
Performs At: Atherton Auditorium, San Joaquin Delta College, Stockton Memorial Civic Auditorium, Stockton's Weber Point Event Center
Affiliations: American Symphony Orchestra League, Association of California Symphony Orchestras
Annual Attendance: 35,000
Type of Stage: Proceisum
Seating Capacity: 1,456
Year Built: 1976
Organization Type: Performing; Educational

883
NOVA VISTA SYMPHONY
PO Box 60312
Sunnyvale, CA 94088 - 03

INSTRUMENTAL MUSIC / California

Phone: 408-624-1492
e-mail: info@novavista.org
Web Site: www.novavista.org
Officers:
   President: Jeff Wachtel
   President/Nova Vista Board Of Dir.: Alayne Gyetvai
   VP: Mike Hamilton
   Treasurer: Wei-Lin Chang
   Secretary: Scott Hartman
Management:
   Marketing Director: Carolyn Hughes, ckhughes@msn.com
   Music Director: Anthony Quartuccio
Mission: Makes live orchestral music appealing and accessible to Santa Clara county residents at reasonable cost; educates young people on classical music and performs outreach to the local community; provides a showcase for local soloists and composers.
Founded: 1966
Specialized Field: Symphony Orchestra
Volunteer Staff: 20
Budget: $50,000
Income Sources: Private and Corporate Donations, Fundraisers
Season: November-April
Performs At: DeAnza Visual & Performing Arts Center
Affiliations: Art Council Silicon Valley; Foothill College Performing Arts Alliance
Seating Capacity: 550

884
CONEJO POPS ORCHESTRA
3648 Mountclef Boulevard
Thousand Oaks, CA 91360
Phone: 805-492-2764
Fax: 805-498-7092
Management:
   Music Director/Conductor: Elmer Ramsey
Mission: Dedicated to maintaining a nonprofit corporation for the education and enhancement of the musical, cultural and social interests of the community, through the medium of a symphony orchestra.
Utilizes: Guest Artists; Singers
Founded: 1961
Specialized Field: Symphony; Chamber
Status: Semi-Professional; Nonprofit
Paid Staff: 37
Income Sources: American Symphony Orchestra League, Private and Corporate Donations, Ticket Sales
Performs At: Preus-Brandt Forum; California Lutheran University
Seating Capacity: 246
Organization Type: Performing

885
NEW WEST SYMPHONY ASSOCIATION
2100 E Thousand Oaks Boulevard
Suite D
Thousand Oaks, CA 91362
Phone: 805-497-5800
Fax: 805-497-5839
e-mail: symphony@newwestsymphony.org
Web Site: www.newwestsymphony.org
Officers:
   President: Leonard Linton
   Interim VP: Judith Linton
   Treasurer: Harry Croner
   Secretary: Miriam Wille
   Chairman: Karl Klessig
Management:
   Music Director/Conductor: Boris Brott
   Executive Director: Natalia Staneva
   Concertmaster: Charles Stegeman
   Concertmaster: Elizabeth Pitcairn
   Communications Manager: Kerrie Sadler
   Music Van Manager: Erin Boskovich
Mission: To present concerts of classical music for the community and to promote an increased public knowledge and appreciation of concert music.
Utilizes: Commissioned Composers; Commissioned Music; Composers-in-Residence; Educators; Guest Accompanists; Guest Artists; Guest Companies; Guest Composers; Guest Conductors; Guest Lecturers; Guest Musical Directors; Guest Musicians; Instructors; Local Artists; Multimedia; Music; Original Music Scores; Sign Language Translators; Singers
Founded: 1995
Specialized Field: Symphony; Chamber; Ensemble
Status: Professional, Nonprofit
Paid Staff: 9
Budget: $2 million
Season: October-May
Performs At: Oxnard Performing Arts Center
Annual Attendance: 37,000
Facility Category: Multi-Purpose Theatre
Type of Stage: Proscenium
Seating Capacity: 528
Organization Type: Performing

886
SYMPHONY ORCHESTRA
El Camino College
Center for the Arts
16007 Crenshaw Boulevard
Torrance, CA 90506
Phone: 310-532-3670
Fax: 310-660-3734
Toll-free: 800-832-2787
e-mail: dteter@elcamino.edu
Web Site: www.elcamino.edu
Officers:
   President: Mary E Combs
   VP: Nathaniel Jackson
   Secretary: Maureen O'Donnell
Management:
   Music Director: Dane Teter
   Executive Director: Bruce Spain
   Production Manager: Nancy Adler
   Stage Manager: Jerry Root
Mission: The mission of the El Camino College Center for the Arts is to present high quality performing arts in a positive environment for the education and entertainment of the student, faculty, staff and communities.
Utilizes: Poets
Founded: 1949
Specialized Field: Orchestra
Status: Non-Professional, Nonprofit
Paid Staff: 1
Income Sources: Ticket Sales, Private and Corporate Donations, Grants
Season: September-June
Performs At: Marsee Auditorium
Annual Attendance: 700
Seating Capacity: 2,000
Organization Type: Performing; Educational

887
VALLEJO SYMPHONY ASSOCIATION
3467 Sonoma Boulevard
Suite 10
Vallejo, CA 94590
Mailing Address: PO Box 568
Phone: 707-643-4441
Fax: 707-643-5746
e-mail: vallejosymphony@gmail.com
Web Site: www.vallejosymphony.org
Officers:
   President: Suzie Peterson
   VP: Rosemary Thurston
   Recording Secretary: Mary Eichbauer
   Treasurer: Bonnie Bernhardt
Management:
   Music Director/Conductor: David Ramadanoff
   Concertmaster: Kathleen Comalli Dillon
   Personnel Manager: Melanie Keller
   Orchestra Librarian: Quelani Penland
   Stage Manager: David Rodgers
   Third Vice-President: Terri Hanley
Mission: To enjoy year round entertainment from this symphony that performs everything from classical to pops.
Utilizes: Guest Accompanists; Guest Musical Directors
Founded: 1931
Specialized Field: Symphony; Orchestra
Paid Staff: 6
Volunteer Staff: 25
Paid Artists: 85
Budget: $150,000-$200,000
Income Sources: Donors, Subscribers, Vallejo Symphony League, Fundraisers
Season: September-April
Performs At: Hogan Auditorium
Annual Attendance: 800

888
TULARE COUNTY SYMPHONY
208 W Main Street
Suite D
Visalia, CA 93291
Phone: 559-732-8600
Fax: 559-732-8617
e-mail: tcsymph@sbcglobal.net
Web Site: www.tcsymphony.org
Officers:
   President: Phil Bourdette
   Executive Director: Francie Levy
   VP: Ellen Gorelick
   Secretary: Roger Hall
   Treasurer: Fred Heumann
Management:
   Music Director: Bruce Kielsing
Mission: To educate the community and introduce people to symphonic music.
Utilizes: Guest Artists; Guest Companies
Founded: 1959
Specialized Field: Symphony; Orchestra
Status: Professional, Nonprofit
Paid Staff: 2
Volunteer Staff: 20
Paid Artists: 75
Budget: $350,000
Income Sources: Ticket Sales; Sponsorships; Grants; Donations
Season: September-April
Performs At: Visalia Fox Theatre
Annual Attendance: 8,000
Facility Category: Fox Theatre
Seating Capacity: 1,200
Year Built: 1929
Year Remodeled: 1999
Rental Contact: Paul Fry
Organization Type: Performing; Resident; Educational

889
CALIFORNIA SYMPHONY
1475 North Broadway
Suite 420
Walnut Creek, CA 94596

INSTRUMENTAL MUSIC / California

Phone: 925-280-2490
Fax: 925-280-2494
e-mail: info@californiasymphony.org
Web Site: www.californiasymphony.org
Officers:
   Founder: Barry Jekowsky
   Chairman: Gordon Getty
   President: Thomas G Overhoff
   Treasurer: Jesus Guijarro
   Secretary: Carlotta Dathe
Management:
   Music Director: Barry Jekowsky
   Executive Director: Walter Collins
   Concertmaster: Roy Malan
   Development Director: Jenna Ervice
   Operations & Education Director: Elaina Birnbaum
   Orchestra Personnel Manager: Ellen Pesavento
Mission: The California Symphony is passionately committed to providing music education programs to children and adults in the San Francisco East Bay.
Founded: 1986
Specialized Field: Symphony
Status: Professional
Paid Staff: 6
Volunteer Staff: 62
Paid Artists: 5
Budget: $1,050,000-$3,600,000
Income Sources: Private and Corporate Donations
Season: September-April
Performs At: Concord Pavilio; Dean Lesher Regional Center for the Arts, Hofmann Theatre; Todos Santos Plaza
Annual Attendance: 33,000
Seating Capacity: 12,000
Year Built: 1970

890
SACRAMENTO JAZZ JUBILEE

106 K Street
Suite 1
West Sacramento, CA 95814
Phone: 916-444-2004
e-mail: viviana@sacjazz.com
Web Site: www.sacjazz.com
Officers:
   President: Jim Roberson
   VP: Molly Greene
   Treasurer: Lisa Negri
   Secretary: Alicia Fullbright
Management:
   Executive Director: Jill Harper
Mission: The mission of the Sacramento Jazz Jubilee is to preserve and promote traditional jazz, Dixieland and classic jazz music.
Founded: 1974
Specialized Field: Jazz
Status: Nonprofit
Paid Staff: 4
Volunteer Staff: 2500
Budget: $1.8 million
Income Sources: Admissions, Sponsorships, Grants, Food Concession Sales, Souvenir Sales, Private and Corporate Donations, Memberships, Ticket Sales
Season: September-June
Performs At: Old Sacramento and Midtown
Affiliations: 30 Sacramento Area Venues (Indoor & Outdoor)
Annual Attendance: 65,000 +/-
Seating Capacity: 250-1,800

891
RIO HONDO SYMPHONY ASSOCIATION

PO Box 495
Whittier, CA 90608
Phone: 562-698-8626
e-mail: riohondosymphony@verizon.net
Web Site: www.riohondosymphony.org
Officers:
   President: Leighton Anderson
   VP: Randy Miller
   Secretary: Madeline Shapiro
   Treasurer: Charles Barth
Management:
   General Manager: Sue Walker
   Orchestra Manager: Lue Ann Barth
   Orchestra Manager: Kathleen Egbert
   Manager: Dorothea Cummings
Mission: To provide free concerts of symphonic music for the residents in the Rio Hondo Area and to encourage young talented artists with musical pursuits.
Founded: 1933
Specialized Field: Symphony; Orchestra
Status: Nonprofit
Paid Staff: 5
Income Sources: Rio Hondo Symphony Guild, Private and Corporate Donatins, Grants, Endowment, Tuition
Season: October-April
Performs At: Victor Lopez Auditorium, Whittier Union High School
Annual Attendance: 5,000
Organization Type: Performing; Resident

892
WHITTIER COLLEGE BACH FESTIVAL

Whittier College
13406 E Philadelphia Street
PO Box 634
Whittier, CA 90608
Phone: 562-907-4200
Fax: 562-907-4592
e-mail: dlozano@whittier.edu
Web Site: www.whittier.edu
Management:
   Director: Danilo Lozano
Mission: To present diverse, high quality music in appropriate venues throughout the San Gabriel Valley.
Specialized Field: Bach; Ensemble
Budget: $10,000
Season: October-June
Performs At: Whittier College Campus; Skyrose Chapel, Various Venues
Annual Attendance: 900
Facility Category: Whittier College Memorial Chapel & other venues
Seating Capacity: 300

893
SAN FERNANDO VALLEY SYMPHONY ORCHESTRA

20210 Haynes Street
Winnetka, CA 91306
Phone: 818-347-4807
e-mail: sfvsymphony@sfvsymphony.com
Web Site: www.sfvsymphony.com
Officers:
   President: Gloria Pollack
   VP: Gary Thomas
   Founder: James Elza Domine
Management:
   Music Director/Conductor: James Elza Domine
   Publicity Manager: Roberta Hoffman
Mission: To present classical concerts.
Utilizes: Guest Artists; Poets; Singers; Theatre Companies
Founded: 1980
Specialized Field: Symphony
Status: Professional, Nonprofit
Income Sources: Individual and Corporate Donations
Season: September-June
Performs At: Pierce College Performing Arts Theatre
Affiliations: Valley Cultural Center, American Symphony Orchestra League, Association Of California Symphony Orchestras
Seating Capacity: 400
Year Built: 1981
Organization Type: Performing; Touring; Resident; Educational; Sponsoring

894
HARMONIA BAROQUE PLAYERS

19795 Villager Circle
Yorba Linda, CA 92886-4452
Phone: 714-970-8545
e-mail: harmoniabaroque@sbcglobal.net
Management:
   Director: Marika Frankl
Mission: Harmonia Baroque has been established to perform rich and plentiful repertoire written for small ensembles in the Renaissance and Baroque period. The ensemble is committed to perform not only the popular works, but also the lesser known masterpieces of these times. The groups is also deeply committed to providing affordable and high quality performances.
Utilizes: Guest Musical Directors; Multimedia
Founded: 1981
Specialized Field: Baroque
Volunteer Staff: 15
Non-paid Artists: 6
Income Sources: Box Office; Private Donations
Season: October-May
Performs At: Oneonta Congregational Church; Concordia University; Peninsula Community Church; Norton Simon Museum; San Diego Art Museum
Affiliations: Arts Orange County
Annual Attendance: 700

895
NAPA VALLEY SYMPHONY

100 California Drive
Yountville, CA 94599
Mailing Address: 3379 Solano Ave., Suite 1000, Napa CA 94558
Phone: 707-944-9910
Fax: 707-944-9912
e-mail: info@napavalleysymphony.org
Web Site: www.napavalleysymphony.org
Officers:
   President: Kent Kuhlmann
   VP: Cookie Deckter
   Secretary: Marissa Schleicher
Management:
   Production Manager: James Collins
   Executive Director: Richard Aldag
   Operations Manager: Karen Frost
   Development Director: Andrea Lyons
Mission: To provide the Napa Valley with Symphonic music performances and education programs.
Founded: 1933
Specialized Field: Symphony
Status: Non-Profit
Paid Staff: 10
Paid Artists: 55
Budget: $1 million
Income Sources: Fundraisers, Private and Corporate Donations, Grants, Foundations
Performs At: Lincoln Theatre; Yountville

INSTRUMENTAL MUSIC / Colorado

Annual Attendance: 15,000
Seating Capacity: 1,200
Organization Type: Performing; Educational

Colorado

896
AURORA SYMPHONY ORCHESTRA
PO Box 441481
Aurora, CO 80044
Phone: 303-873-6622
e-mail: info@aurorasymphony.org
Web Site: www.aurorasymphony.org
Officers:
　Chairman: E Dwight Taylor Esq
　Treasurer: Angela Cho
　Secretary: Lori Hanson
　Vice Chairman: Gary Wheat
　President: Rich Duston
Management:
　Music Director/Conductor: Richard Niezen
　Executive Director: Rich Duston
　Concertmaster: Samuel Baker
　Assistant Concertmaster: Magdalena Lesniak
　Operations Manager: Sylvia Bowen
　Marketing Manager: Susana Mendez
Mission: The Aurora Symphony Orchestra have a strong commitment to educating the young musicians in the community to develop a lifelong love of music.
Founded: 1978
Specialized Field: Orchestra

897
BOULDER BACH FESTIVAL
PO Box 1896
Boulder, CO 80306
Phone: 303-776-9666
Fax: 303-682-9888
e-mail: info@boulderbachfestival.org
Web Site: www.boulderbachfestival.org
Officers:
　Co-President: Eileen O'Neill
　Co-President: Frederick Denny
　Executive Director: Carol Bartel
　Treasurer: Thurston Manning
　Production Manager: Jeff Rusnak
　Secretary: Albert Lundell
Management:
　Music Director: Rick Erickson
　Concertmaster: William Terwilliger
　Assistant Concertmaster: Annamaria Karacson
　Chorus Manager: Dan Seger
　Board Member/Volunteer Coordinator: Judy Barkley
　Executive Director: Marcia Schirmer
　Chorus Master: Gregg Cannady
Mission: To present the music of Johann Sebastian Bach and to encourage knowledge and appreciation of the Baroque master. Provides a three day festival each year, featuring an orchestra, chorus, and soloists drawn from the pool of area musicians, with a few nationally-known artists from other parts of the country.
Founded: 1981
Specialized Field: Bach; Ensemble
Status: Professional, Nonprofit
Paid Staff: 1
Volunteer Staff: 200
Paid Artists: 40+
Budget: $100,000
Income Sources: Admissions, Grants, Private and Corporate Donations, Foundations
Season: October-May

Performs At: University Lutheran Church, Mountain View Methodist Church, St John's Episcopal Church, Boulder High School
Affiliations: First Prebyterian Church
Annual Attendance: 2,500
Seating Capacity: 800

898
BOULDER PHILHARMONIC ORCHESTRA
Dairy Center for the Arts
2995 Wilderness Place Suite 100
Boulder, CO 80301-5700
Phone: 303-440-7826
Fax: 303-440-7104
e-mail: info@boulderphil.org
Web Site: www.peakarts.org
Officers:
　President: Robert McAllister
Management:
　Executive Director: Sue Levine
　Director Of Marketing And Sales: Melissa Vargas
　Director Of Operations: Glenn Ross
　Chorale Director: Timothy Kreuger
Mission: To offer music, classical dance and arts education experiences.
Status: Nonprofit

899
BOULDER PHILHARMONIC ORCHESTRA
2590 Walnut Street
Boulder, CO 80302
Phone: 303-449-1343
Fax: 303-443-9203
e-mail: info@boulderphil.org
Web Site: www.boulderphil.org
Officers:
　President: Kyle Heckman
　VP: Mary Street
　Secretary: Patricia Butler
　Treasurer: Erma Mantey
Management:
　Executive Director: Kevin Shuck
　Director: Michael Butterman
　Concert Manager: Glenn Ross
　Marketing: Jillian Crandall
　Development: Maegan Ball
　Assistant Conductor: Travis Jurgens
Mission: Connectng people to orchestral music with emphasis on education, outreach and a focus on collaborations with local artists.
Founded: 1958
Status: Non-Professional, Non-Profit
Budget: $1 million
Income Sources: American Symphony Orchestra League; Western Alliance of Arts Administrators, Endowment
Season: September-October
Performs At: Macky Auditorium Concert Hall
Organization Type: Performing; Sponsoring

900
BRECKENRIDGE MUSIC INSTITUTE ORCHESTRA
PO Box 1254
217 S Ridge Street
Breckenridge, CO 80424
Phone: 970-453-9142
Fax: 970-453-9143
e-mail: admin@breckenridgemusicfestival.com
Web Site: www.breckenridgemusicfestival.com
Officers:
　President: Laura Dziedzic
　VP: Samantha Morris
　Executive Director: Jeff D Braum
　Treasurer: Wally Ducayet
　Secretary: Sue Carver
Management:
　Music Director/Principal Conductor: Gerhardt Zimmermenn
　Co-Concertmaster: Nicholas DiEugenio
　Co-Concertmaster: Elbert Tsai
　Assistant Concertmaster: Helen Liu
　Assistant Concertmaster: Brent Price
　Executive Director: Marcia Kaufmann
　Orchestra Personnel Manager: Mike Koscso
　Stage Manager: Julia Lochra
Mission: Provide musicians the experience necessary to enhance their skills through an intense repertory performance experience.
Founded: 1960
Specialized Field: Jazz; Folk Music; Educational
Status: Nonprofit
Paid Staff: 16
Volunteer Staff: 35
Budget: $260,000-$1,050,000
Income Sources: Grants, Private and Corporate Donations
Season: June-August
Performs At: Riverwalk Center
Facility Category: Amphitheater
Seating Capacity: 750
Year Built: 1993

901
BRECKENRIDGE MUSIC FESTIVAL ORCHESTRA
PO Box 1254
Breckenridge, CO 80424
Phone: 970-453-9142
Fax: 970-453-9143
e-mail: bmi@breckenridgemusicfestival.com
Web Site: www.breckenridgemusicfestival.com
Officers:
　President: Laura Dziedzic
　VP: Samantha Morris
　Executive Director: Jeff D Braum
　Treasurer: Wally Ducayet
　Secretary: Sue Carver
Management:
　Music Director/Principal Conductor: Gerhardt Zimmermenn
　Co-Concertmaster: Nicholas DiEugenio
　Co-Concertmaster: Elbert Tsai
　Assistant Concertmaster: Helen Liu
　Assistant Concertmaster: Brent Price
　Executive Director: Marcia Kaufmann
　Orchestra Personnel Manager: Mike Koscso
　Stage Manager: Julia Lochra
Mission: The Breckenridge Music Festival's mission is to provide performing arts programs and arts education to the communities of Summit, Park and Lake Counties.
Utilizes: Guest Artists
Founded: 1980
Specialized Field: Jazz; Folk Music; Educational
Status: Professional, Nonprofit
Performs At: Breckenridge Event Tent
Seating Capacity: 750
Year Built: 1993
Organization Type: Performing; Educational

902
WALDEN PIANO QUARTET/WALDEN CHAMBER MUSIC SOCIETY
P.O. Box 5237
Buena Vista, CO 81211

INSTRUMENTAL MUSIC / Colorado

Phone: 214-750-1561
Fax: 214-369-4711
e-mail: admin@waldenchambermusic.org
Web Site: www.waldenchambermusic.org
Officers:
  President: James Culbertson
Management:
  Management Consultant: Clara Lau
  Artistic Director: Joe Boatright
Founded: 1981
Specialized Field: Chamber
Status: Professional
Paid Staff: 1
Volunteer Staff: 1
Paid Artists: 5
Budget: $20,000-$35,000
Income Sources: Private; City; Foundations
Performs At: Sanctuary, First Unitarian Church
Annual Attendance: 1,200
Stage Dimensions: 15 x 20
Year Built: 1965

903
COLORADO SPRINGS PHILHARMONIC
111 South Tejon Street
Suite 102
Colorado Springs, CO 80903- 224
Mailing Address: PO Box 1266,Colorado Springs CO 80901-1266
Phone: 719-575-9632
Fax: 719-575-9656
e-mail: constance@csphilmonic.org
Web Site: www.csphilmonic.org
Officers:
  President: Doug Adams
  Chairman: Alfred P Buettner
  vice chairman: Janine Musholt
  treasurer: Jerry Ellis
Management:
  Music Director: Josep Caball,-Domenech
  Associate Conductor: Thomas Wilson
  Executive Directror: Nathan Newbrough
  Concertmaster: Michael Hanson
  Associate Concertmaster: Lydia Svyatlovskaya
  Development Director: Constance Gelvin
Mission: To spread the joy of classical music beyond its traditional boundaries.
Utilizes: Guest Artists
Founded: 2003
Specialized Field: Symphony; Orchestra; Chamber
Status: Professional, Nonprofit
Budget: $1.12 million
Income Sources: Private and Corporate Donations, Foundations, Ticket Sales
Performs At: Pikes Peak Center
Annual Attendance: 45,000
Organization Type: Performing; Educational; Sponsoring

904
CRESTED BUTTE MUSIC FESTIVAL
308 3rd Street
PO Box 2117
Crested Butte, CO 81224
Phone: 970-349-0619
e-mail: swan@rmii.com
Web Site: www.cbmountaintheatre.org
Officers:
  Director Development/Marketing: Emily Bond
  COO: Barbara Chistian
  President: Jo Ann Macy
  Treasurer: Kristi Hargrove
Management:
  Co-Artistic Director/CEO: Debra Ayers
  Co-Artistic Director: Alexander Scheirle
  Principal Guest Conductor: Roland Kluttig
  Opera Director: David Malis
  Artistic Director: Harry Woods
  Administrative Director: Michele Simpson
Mission: We are proud to have carried on the tradition of presenting a broad spectrum of performing arts here in Crested Butte. Our goal is to create a unique festival for a unique town.
Founded: 1997
Specialized Field: Ensemble; Folk Music; Ethnic Music
Status: Nonprofit
Budget: $20,000-$35,000
Income Sources: Funding from Colorado Council on the Arts, Colordo General Assembly, National Endowment for the Arts
Season: July
Performs At: Crested Butte, CO (Festival Site)
Facility Category: Crested Butte Chamber Music Festival
Seating Capacity: 250

905
COLORADO SYMPHONY ORCHESTRA
Boettcher Concert Hall
1000 14thn Street Suite 15
Denver, CO 80202- 233
Phone: 303-292-5566
Fax: 303-293-2649
e-mail: admin@coloradosymphony.org
Web Site: www.coloradosymphony.org
Officers:
  Interim President: Kevin Duncan
  Treasurer: Tensie Homan
  Secretary: Abby Raymond
  Co - Chairman: Jerome H Kern
  Co - Chairman: Mary Rossick Kern
Management:
  Music Director: Jeffrey Kahane
  Conductor Laureate: Marin Alsop
  Resident Conductor: Scott O'Neil
  Concertmaster: Yumi Hwang-Williams
  Associate Concertmaster: Claudia Sim
  Artistic Advisor: Andrew litton
  Chorus Director: Duain Wolfe
Mission: The Colorado Symphony Orchestra embraces a tradition of musical excellence by presenting a wide variety of symphonic performances from classical repertoire to innovative new forms in Boettcher Concert Hall.
Utilizes: Guest Artists
Founded: 1990
Specialized Field: Symphony; Orchestra
Status: Professional, Nonprofit
Paid Staff: 30
Volunteer Staff: 1
Paid Artists: 804
Non-paid Artists: 250
Budget: $11 million
Income Sources: Ticket Revenue, Donations From Individuals, Foundations; Businesses, Public Agencies, Grants
Performs At: Denver Performing Arts Complex; Boettcher Concert Hall
Annual Attendance: 202,000
Facility Category: Concert hall, performance center
Type of Stage: In the round
Stage Dimensions: 35 x 80
Orchestra Pit: 1
Seating Capacity: 2,650
Year Built: 1974
Organization Type: Performing; Touring; Resident; Educational; Sponsoring
Resident Groups: Colorado Symphony Orchestra

906
DENVER MUNICIPAL BAND
2253 Bellaire Street
Denver, CO 80207
Phone: 303-322-8608
Fax: 303-322-8608
e-mail: gendsley@ecentral.com
Web Site: www.dmamusic.org
Management:
  Music Director/Conductor: Gerald Endsley
Mission: Presenting free summer concerts in Denver parks.
Founded: 1860
Specialized Field: Band; Folk Music
Status: Professional
Income Sources: Association of Concert Bands, Individuals, Foundations, Businesses
Season: May-December
Performs At: Various Venues, Parks
Organization Type: Performing

907
DENVER YOUNG ARTISTS ORCHESTRA
1245 E Colfax Avenue
Suite 302
Denver, CO 80218
Phone: 303-433-2420
Fax: 720-836-3335
e-mail: info@dyao.org
Web Site: www.dyao.org
Officers:
  President: Rayna Godfrey
  VP: Eileen Griffin
  Treasurer: Michael Proett
  Secretary: Donna Bloomer
Management:
  Music Director/Conductor: Jurgen de Lemos
  Assistant Conductor: Warren Deck
  Executive Director: Peter Hellyer
  Assistant Director: Deborah De La Torre
  Orchestra Manager: Alexander George
Mission: Its mission is to provide the finest possible youth orchestra programs inspiring and educating young musicians through the performance of great works of music and offering valuable cultural opportunities to the community.
Utilizes: Commissioned Composers; Five Seasonal Concerts; Guest Accompanists; Guest Composers; Instructors; Multimedia; Organization Contracts; Soloists
Founded: 1977
Specialized Field: Symphony
Status: Nonprofit
Paid Staff: 2
Volunteer Staff: 10
Paid Artists: 2
Non-paid Artists: 85
Budget: $150,000
Income Sources: Grants, Ticket Sales, Member Fees, Individuals, Foundations and Corporations, Fundraisers
Season: October-May
Performs At: Boettcher Concert Hall
Affiliations: Colorado Chamber Players
Annual Attendance: 5,000

908
SAN JUAN SYMPHONY
PO Box 1073
Durango, CO 81302
Phone: 970-382-9753
Web Site: www.sanjuansymphony.com
Officers:
  President: Sheri Rochford Figgs

All listings are in alphabetical order by state, then city, then organization within the city.

INSTRUMENTAL MUSIC / Colorado

VP: Denise Lakey
Treasurer: Melissa Zureich
Secretary: Julia Dodd
Management:
  Music Director: Arthur Post
  Executive Director: Kathy Myrick
  Personnel Manager: Julie Appelhanz
Mission: The San Juan Symphony is a regional orchestra uniting the Four Corners area by nurturing the art of music through education and high quality performances that touch the soul.
Founded: 1973
Specialized Field: Symphony; Orchestra
Status: Nonprofit
Budget: $35,000- $100,000
Income Sources: Grants from Regional and National Foundations, Private and Corporate Donations
Season: September-April
Performs At: Farmington Civic Center, Community Concert Hall; Fort Lewis College
Affiliations: American Symphony Orchestra League
Annual Attendance: 4000
Seating Capacity: 900, 600

909
COLORADO STATE UNIVERSITY ORCHESTRA

Music Department
1778 Campus Delivery
Fort Collins, CO 80523
Phone: 970-491-5529
e-mail: mtdinfo@colostate.edu
Web Site: www.music.colostate.edu
Officers:
  Chair: Michael H Thaut
Management:
  Music Director/Conductor: Wes Kenney
  Co-Executive Director: Michaelh Thaut
Mission: To prepare students to become highly skilled music educators, music therapists, performers, composers and conductors.
Specialized Field: Symphony
Status: Nonprofit
Income Sources: Private and Corporate Donations, Grants, Ticket Sales
Performs At: Edna Rizley Griffin Concert Hall
Annual Attendance: 2,000
Seating Capacity: 567

910
FORT COLLINS SYMPHONY ORCHESTRA

214 S. College Avenue
Fort Collins, CO 80524
Phone: 970-482-4823
Fax: 970-482-4858
e-mail: note@fcsymphony.org
Web Site: www.fcsymphony.org
Officers:
  President: Bev Donnelley
  Treasurer: Roxanne Slayden
  Secretary: Marilyn Cockburn
  VP: Luis Ramirez
Management:
  Music Director/Conductor: Wes Kenney
  Executive Director: Carrie Newman
  Orchestra Manager: April Johannesen
  Concertmaster: Stacy Lesartre
  Assistant Concertmaster: Hee-Jung Kim
  Production Manager: Jeff Lee
Mission: To provide orchestral music of the highest artistic standard for the purposes of entertainment, education and enhancement of the cultural environment.
Utilizes: Guest Accompanists; Guest Composers; Guest Lecturers; Guest Writers; Lyricists
Founded: 1949
Specialized Field: Symphony
Status: Professional
Paid Staff: 4
Volunteer Staff: 100
Paid Artists: 100
Budget: $391,000
Income Sources: Individual and Corporate Donations, Foundations, Ticket Sales, Matching Gifts, Planned Giving, Endowment
Performs At: Edna Rizley Griffin Concert Hall; Lincoln Center Auditorium
Affiliations: American Symphony Orchestra League
Annual Attendance: 10,000
Facility Category: City Auditorium Concert Hall
Type of Stage: Proscenium
Seating Capacity: 567
Year Remodeled: 1979

911
JEFFERSON SYMPHONY ORCHESTRA

PO Box 546
Golden, CO 80402-0546
Phone: 303-278-4237
e-mail: info@jeffersonsymphony.org
Web Site: jeffersonsymphonyorchestra.org
Officers:
  Chairman: Calvin Winn
  Treasurer: JoAnne Nadalin
  Secretary: Cheryl McEachran
  Vice Chairman: James Everson
Management:
  Music Director/Conductor: William Morse
  Associate Conductor: David Ackerman
  Assistant Conductor: J Stephen Mallinson
  Director: Michelle Haney
Mission: To achieve our vision we enrich the greater Jefferson County community through quality musical experiences and educational programs.
Utilizes: Collaborations; Guest Artists; Guest Musical Directors; Guest Musicians; Guest Writers; Multimedia; Organization Contracts; Original Music Scores; Sign Language Translators; Singers; Touring Companies
Founded: 1953
Specialized Field: Symphony; Orchestra; Ensemble
Status: Semi-Professional, Nonprofit
Paid Staff: 2
Volunteer Staff: 150
Budget: $275,000
Income Sources: Chamber of Commerces, Supported by Scientific and Cultural Facilities District, Fundraisers, Private and Corporate Donations
Season: October-May
Performs At: Green Centre; Colorado School of Mines
Annual Attendance: 10,000
Facility Category: auditorium
Seating Capacity: 1,100
Year Built: 1973
Organization Type: Performing

912
GRAND JUNCTION MUSICAL ARTS ASSOCIATION

225 N 5th St
Suite 120
Grand Junction, CO 81501
Mailing Address: PO Box 3039
Phone: 970-243-6787
Fax: 970-243-6792
e-mail: info@gjsymphony.org
Web Site: www.gjsymphony.org
Officers:
  President: Michael McCormick
  VP: Cara Golden
  Secretary: Laura Soucie
  Treasurer: Michael Philipp
Management:
  Music Director: Kirk Gustafson
  Concertmaster: Carlos Elias
  Executive Director: Kelly Anderson
  Technical Director: Gordon Rhoades
  Marketing Director: Jeremy Herigstad
Mission: To provide symphonic music for the enjoyment and enrichment of the Grand Junction area community.
Founded: 1978
Specialized Field: Symphony; Orchestra; Band
Status: Nonprofit
Paid Staff: 6
Volunteer Staff: 10
Paid Artists: 60
Budget: $400,000
Season: May-August
Performs At: Grand Junction High School Auditorium
Annual Attendance: 20,000
Facility Category: High School
Type of Stage: Proscenium
Stage Dimensions: 45x55
Seating Capacity: 1,500
Year Built: 1951
Organization Type: Performing; Touring; Educational; Sponsoring

913
GREELEY PHILHARMONIC ORCHESTRA

PO Box 1535
Greeley, CO 80632-1535
Phone: 970-356-6406
Fax: 970-352-8761
e-mail: greeleyphil@gmail.com
Web Site: www.greeleyphilharmonic.com
Officers:
  President: Kathy Christman
  Treasurer: Tony McCune
  Secretary: Phyllis Sandstedt
Management:
  Music Director/Conductor: Glen Cortese
  Executive Director: Dr Timothy Fleming
  Concertmaster: Chris Jusell
  Associate Concertmaster: Aaron Lande
  Administrative Coordinator: Gerry Helse
Mission: To develop, foster and promote a professional orchestra that satisfies the various musical needs of Greeley and the surrounding area.
Utilizes: Commissioned Music; Guest Composers; Guest Lecturers; Guest Musicians; Multimedia; Original Music Scores; Soloists
Founded: 1911
Specialized Field: Symphony; Orchestra
Status: Professional
Paid Staff: 4
Paid Artists: 80
Budget: $260,000-1,050,000
Income Sources: Tickets; Grants; Fund Drives; Sponsors
Season: September-April
Performs At: Union Colony Civic Auditorium
Annual Attendance: 12,000
Facility Category: Performance Hall
Seating Capacity: 1,665

INSTRUMENTAL MUSIC / Connecticut

Year Built: 1984

914
SYMPHONY ORCHESTRA
University of Northern Colorado
College of Performing and Visual Arts
Guggenheim Hall Room 204, Campus Box 30
Greeley, CO 80639
Phone: 970-351-2515
Fax: 970-351-2699
e-mail: info@arts.unco.edu
Web Site: www.arts.unco.edu
Officers:
 Dean: Andrew Jay Svedlow
Management:
 Music Driector: Russell Guyver
Mission: Provides rich and well founded tradition of excellence and has developed into a program that has received national and international recognition.
Utilizes: Educators; Guest Composers; Guest Musical Directors; Guest Musicians; High School Drama; Multimedia; Singers
Specialized Field: Orchestra
Budget: $35,000
Performs At: Union Colony Civic Center; Foundation Hall

915
ARAPAHOE PHILHARMONIC
2100 W Littleton Boulevard
Suite 250
Littleton, CO 80120
Phone: 303-781-1892
Fax: 303-781-4918
e-mail: ame@arapahoe.phil.org
Web Site: www.arapahoe-phil.org
Officers:
 Chair: Bert Glandon
 Treasurer: Gail Sindelar
 VP: John Leininger
 Secretary: Beth Dickinson
Management:
 Music Director/Conductor: Vincent C LaGuardia
 Associate Conductor: Steve Asheim
 Symphonic Strings/Symphony Director: Tracy LaGuardia
 Assistant Concertmaster: Giga Romero
 Administrator: Ame Leonard
 Administrative Director/APYO: John Leiniger
Mission: Dedicated to providing quality live orchestra performances for the community's enjoyment, appreciation and education.
Founded: 1954
Specialized Field: Symphony
Status: Nonprofit
Paid Staff: 1
Volunteer Staff: 75
Paid Artists: 15
Non-paid Artists: 60
Budget: $245,000
Income Sources: Box Office; Donations; Grants
Season: September-May
Performs At: South Suburban Christian Church
Annual Attendance: 5,000
Facility Category: Church

916
LONGMONT SYMPHONY ORCHESTRA
519 Main Street
Longmont, CO 80501
Phone: 303-772-5796
e-mail: info@photographymaestro.com
Web Site: www.longmontsymphony.org
Management:
 Music Director/Conductor: Robert Olson
 Associate Conductor: Brian St John
Mission: Dedicated to providing the highest possible classical music.
Utilizes: Educators; Fine Artists; Guest Companies; Guest Composers; Guest Designers; Guest Lecturers; Guest Musical Directors; Guest Musicians; Guest Writers; Instructors; Local Artists; Multimedia; Music; Original Music Scores; Singers; Soloists
Founded: 1966
Specialized Field: Classical
Status: Nonprofit
Budget: $150,000-$260,000
Season: October-May
Performs At: Vance Brand Civic Auditorium
Annual Attendance: 15,000

917
PUEBLO SYMPHONY
301 N Main Street
Suite 106
Pueblo, CO 81003
Phone: 719-545-7967
Web Site: www.pueblosymphony.com
Officers:
 President: Donna Seilheimer
 Conductor: Dr. Jacob Chi
Management:
 Music Director/Conductor: Jacob Chi
 Concertmaster: Daniel Brandt
Mission: The purpose of the Pueblo Symphony is to provide a quality musical experience for the people of the City and County of Pueblo by recognizing that music is a vital feature of the artistic, cultural and educational life of a community.
Founded: 1928
Specialized Field: Orchestra
Status: Nonprofit
Budget: $300,000
Income Sources: American Symphony Orchestra League, Private and Corporate Donations, Fundraisers
Season: October-February
Performs At: Hoag Recital Hall; CSU Pueblo Campus
Annual Attendance: 7,000
Organization Type: Performing

918
STRINGS IN THE MOUNTAINS
900 Strings Road
Steamboat Springs, CO 80487
Mailing Address: P.O. Box 774627, Steamboat Springs, CO 80477
Phone: 970-879-5056
Fax: 970-879-7460
Web Site: www.stringsinthemountains.com
Officers:
 Chairman: Darlinda Baldinger
 Treasurer: Ron Whaley
Management:
 Music Director: Andres Cardenes
 Music Director: Monique Mead
 Music Director/Chamber: Katherine Collier
 Music Director/Chamber: Yizhak Schotten
 Executive Director: Kay Clagett
 Operations and Non-Classical Progra: Betse Grassby
 Finance Director: Anne DeGroff
 Advertising/Marketing Director: Cristin Frey
Mission: Presents innovative programs of distinctive classical and popular contemporary music in an intimate and friendly setting to audiences of all ages, enhancing the cultural, educational and entertainment experiences of the community of Northwest Colorado and its visitors.
Utilizes: Artists-in-Residence; Guest Musical Directors; Guest Musicians; Multimedia; Music; Original Music Scores
Founded: 1988
Specialized Field: String Ensemble; Jazz; Children's Chamber Music
Status: Professional, Nonprofit
Paid Staff: 5
Volunteer Staff: 125
Paid Artists: 170
Budget: $1,000,000
Income Sources: American Symphony Orchestra League, Chamber Music America, Western Arts Alliance, Private and Corporate Donations, Grants, Ticket Sales, Festival Program Advertising
Season: July - August
Performs At: Tensile Fabric Structure
Facility Category: Strings Music Tent
Stage Dimensions: 13'x30'
Seating Capacity: 540
Year Built: 1982
Rental Contact: Facility Manager Jessie Burns
Organization Type: Performing

919
TELLURIDE CHAMBER MUSIC FESTIVAL
PO Box 115
Telluride, CO 81435
Phone: 970-728-8686
Toll-free: 800-525-3455
e-mail: info@telluridechambermusic.org
Web Site: www.telluridechambermusic.org
Officers:
 Founder: Roy Malan
 President: Warner Paige
 Treasurer: Lene Andersen
 Secretary: Susannah Smith
 VP: Andrew Molloy
Management:
 Artistic Director: Roy Malan
Mission: Our festival creates a spontaneous connection between audience and musicians which lifts the human spirit.
Founded: 1973
Specialized Field: Chamber
Status: Professional
Budget: $10,000
Income Sources: Individual Donations, Grants, Telluride Foundation
Season: August
Performs At: Telluride; Festival Site
Facility Category: Sheridan Opera House
Seating Capacity: 240

Connecticut

920
HARTFORD JAZZ SOCIETY
116 Cottage Grove Road
Room 202
Bloomfield, CT 06002-3200
Phone: 860-242-6688
Fax: 860-243-3130
e-mail: hartjazzsocinc@aol.com
Web Site: www.hartfordjazzsociety.com
Officers:
 President: Ronald Lyles
 Treasurer: Robert Pernell
 Secretary: Leslie Manselle
 VP: Daniel Feingold

INSTRUMENTAL MUSIC / Connecticut

Mission: To foster interest, understanding, and appreciation of jazz by presenting a variety of live jazz events and by nurturing new generations of jazz performers and audiences.
Founded: 1960
Specialized Field: Jazz
Status: Professional
Paid Staff: 2
Income Sources: Ticket Sales; Fund Raisers; Grants; Private and Corporate Donations
Performs At: Wadsworth Atheneum Museum of Art
Facility Category: Theater
Seating Capacity: 284
Year Built: 1842
Organization Type: Sponsoring

921
GREATER BRIDGEPORT SYMPHONY ORCHESTRA
446 University Avenue
Bridgeport, CT 06604
Phone: 203-576-0263
Fax: 203-367-0064
e-mail: GBSED@GBS.org
Web Site: www.gbs.org
Officers:
  Chairman: Robert S Tellalian
  President: Peter Guenther
  VP: Christine Kudravy
  Treasurer: Richard Hiendlmayr
  Secretary: Preston Tisdale
Management:
  Music Director/Conductor: Gustav Meier
  Executive Director: Alex Morr
  Concertmaster: Deborarh Wong
  Assistant Concertmaster: Nina Crothers
  Production Manager: Matt Maraffi
Mission: Dedicated to enriching the lives of young people within a musical community.
Utilizes: Guest Accompanists; Guest Composers; Guest Musicians; Original Music Scores; Singers
Founded: 1945
Specialized Field: Symphony
Status: Professional, Nonprofit
Budget: $260,000-$1,050,000
Income Sources: Private and Corporate Donations, Foundations, Grants, Ticket Sales
Season: October-April
Performs At: Klein Memorial Auditorium
Annual Attendance: 7,500
Facility Category: Auditorium
Seating Capacity: 1,468

922
ASTON MAGNA FOUNDATION
PO Box 3167
Danbury, CT 06813-3167
Phone: 203-792-4662
Fax: 203-744-7244
Toll-free: 800-875-7156
e-mail: info@astonmagna.org
Web Site: www.astonmagna.org
Officers:
  Chairman: Robert B Strassler
  Treasurer: Ronald Bernstein
  Secretary: Alexia Lalli
Management:
  Artistic Director: Daniel Stepner
  Acadmey Director: Raymond Erickson
  Executive Director: Ronnie Boriskin
  Artistic Administrator: Joseph Orchard

Mission: The mission of the Aston Magna Foundation is to enrich the appreciation of music of the past and the understanding of the cultural, political and social contexts in which it was composed and experienced.
Utilizes: Educators
Founded: 1972
Specialized Field: Chamber; Early Music
Status: Professional, Nonprofit
Paid Staff: 4
Volunteer Staff: 6
Income Sources: Massachusetts Cultural Council, Grants
Season: July-August
Performs At: St James Church Festival in Great Barrington, Daniel Arts Center at Simon's Rock College
Organization Type: Performing; Touring; Educational; Sponsoring

923
GREATER BRIDGEPORT SYMPHONY YOUTH ORCHESTRA
80 Maryanne Drive
Fairfield, CT 06468
Mailing Address: PO Box 645, Fairfield, CT 06824-0645
Phone: 203-459-4249
Fax: 203-459-4249
e-mail: gbyo@gbyo.org
Web Site: www.gbyo.org
Officers:
  President: Mark Halstead
Management:
  Music Director: Christopher Hisey
  Symphony Orchestra Conductor: Leo Ficks
  Concert Orchestra Conductor: Jeff Albright
  String Orchestra Conductor: Erica Messian
  Wind Ensemble Conductor: Aaron Barkon
  Executive Director: Barb Upton
Mission: To offer young musicians in the Greater Bridgeport area a quality orchestral experience.
Founded: 1961
Specialized Field: Symphony; Orchestra
Status: Non-Professional
Income Sources: Private and Corporate Donations, Foundations, Grants, Ticket Sales, Membership fees
Season: November-May
Performs At: Klein Auditorium
Organization Type: Performing; Educational

924
AMERICAN CLASSICAL ORCHESTRA
133 West 70th Street
Greenwich, CT 10023-4410
Mailing Address: PO Box 441
Phone: 212-362-2727
Fax: 212-362-2729
e-mail: info@aconyc.org
Web Site: www.americanclassicalorchestra.org
Officers:
  President: Lynne Flexner
  Treasurer: Victor Germack
  Secretary: Pamela Rabinovici
  Founder: Thomas Crawford
Management:
  Music Director: Thomas Crawford
  Development Associate: Glen Askin
  Executive Director: Vincent A Gardino
  President: Christopher D Stevens
  Public Relations: Jay Hoffman
Mission: To recreate classical music in its original form to revive and preserve period instrumentation.
Founded: 1985
Specialized Field: Classical
Paid Staff: 2

Volunteer Staff: 29
Paid Artists: 45
Budget: $260,000-$700,000
Income Sources: Private and Corporate Donations, Ticket Sales, American Classical Orchestra Guild, Advertising
Season: October-April
Performs At: Halls; Museums; Private Residences
Annual Attendance: 3,000
Seating Capacity: 1,062

925
GREENWICH SYMPHONY ORCHESTRA
299 Greenwich Avenue
PO Box 35
Greenwich, CT 06836
Phone: 203-869-2664
Fax: 203-869-2664
e-mail: gsorch@verizon.net
Web Site: www.greenwichsym.org
Officers:
  President: Mary J Radcliffe
  VP: Richard J Slagle
  Treasurer: Richard Chase
  Secretary: Lenore de Csepel
Management:
  Music Director/Conductor: David Gilbert
  Associate Conductor: Tara Simoncic
Mission: To offer a subscription series, youth concert series and chamber players series.
Founded: 1958
Specialized Field: Classical
Status: Professional
Budget: $260,000-$1,050,000
Income Sources: Ticket Sales; Private and Corporate Donations; Greenwich Symphony Guild; Endowment Fund
Performs At: Dickerman Hollister Auditorium; Greenwich High School
Annual Attendance: 11,000
Facility Category: Greenwich High School Auditorium
Seating Capacity: 850

926
SYMPHONY ON THE SOUND
RD 1, 18 Zygmont Lane
Greenwich, CT 06830
Phone: 203-661-7413
Fax: 203-661-7413
Officers:
  Executive Director: P Steinborn
  General Manager: P M Lewis
Management:
  Music Director/Conductor: Joseph Leniado-Chira
Specialized Field: Symphony
Status: Professional, Nonprofit
Annual Attendance: 20,000

927
CONNECTICUT CLASSICAL GUITAR SOCIETY
PO Box 1528
Hartford, CT 06114-1528
Phone: 860-249-1132
e-mail: info@ctguitar.org
Web Site: www.ctguitar.org
Officers:
  President: H Vivero
Management:
  Artistic Director: David Giardina
  Executive Director: Joyce Magee
Founded: 1985
Status: Non=Profit
Budget: $150,000

INSTRUMENTAL MUSIC / Connecticut

Income Sources: Funded in part by the Connecticut Commission of the Arts; The Greater Hartford Arts Council; Takamine Guitar; The Roberts Foundation: The D'Addario Foundation
Season: September-May
Performs At: Carol Autorino Center; St Joseph College, Autorino Great Hall, Belding Theater; Bushnell
Annual Attendance: 6,500

928
HARTFORD SYMPHONY ORCHESTRA
100 Pearl Street, 2nd Floor, East Tower
Hartford, CT 06103
Phone: 860-246-8742
Fax: 860-247-1720
e-mail: info@hartfordsymphony.org
Web Site: www.hartfordsymphony.org
Officers:
  President/CEO: Carrie Hammond
  VP: James S Remis
  VP: Pierre H Guertin
  Chairman: David M Roth
  Director of Development: April M Paterno
Management:
  Music Director/Conductor: Edward Cumming
  Executive Director: Kristin M Phillips
  Assistant Director: Karen L Degrace
  Director of Finance & Human Resourc: Cheryl Anderson
  Director of Artistic Operations: Grant Meachum
Mission: To bring music and educational programs of the highest artistic standards to the widest possible audience.
Utilizes: Actors; Collaborating Artists; Collaborations; Commissioned Composers; Commissioned Music; Dancers; Five Seasonal Concerts; Grant Writers; Guest Accompanists; Guest Companies; Guest Composers; Guest Lecturers; Guest Musical Directors; Guest Musicians; Instructors; Lyricists; Multi Collaborations; Multimedia; Original Music Scores; Sign Language Translators; Singers; Theatre Companies
Founded: 1934
Specialized Field: Orchestra
Budget: $6.1 million
Income Sources: Subscribers, Donors, Ticket Sales
Season: October-May
Performs At: Bushnell Center for the Performing Arts
Annual Attendance: 173,000
Seating Capacity: 2,805

929
MANCHESTER SYMPHONY ORCHESTRA/CHORALE
PO Box 861
Manchester, CT 06045-0861
Phone: 860-228-2921
e-mail: musicsix@cox.net
Web Site: www.msoc.org
Officers:
  President: Pete Bradley
  Treasurer: John Belbruno
  VP Orchestra: Sean McDonald
  VP Chorale: Lydia Messerschmidt
  Vice President - Orchestra: Jody Danielson
Management:
  Orchestra Director: Lewis J Buckley
  Chorale Director: Kevin L Mack
  Orchestra Conductor: Joseph Hodge
  Chorale Artistic Director: Kevin L Mack
Mission: To enhance the enjoyment and enrichment of members while furthering performing arts in the community.
Utilizes: Artists-in-Residence; Guest Artists
Founded: 1960
Specialized Field: Symphony; Orchestra; Chorus
Status: Non-Professional, Nonprofit, Volunteer, Community
Paid Staff: 4
Volunteer Staff: 100
Income Sources: Private and Corporate Donations, Ticket Sale, Endowment
Season: Octber-May
Performs At: Manchester Community College
Affiliations: Greater Manchester Chamber of Commerce, Association of Connecticut Choruses
Organization Type: Performing; Resident

930
NEW BRITAIN SYMPHONY ORCHESTRA
PO Box 1253
New Britain, CT 06050
Phone: 860-826-6344
Fax: 860-826-6344
e-mail: newbritainsymphony@gmail.com
Web Site: www.newbritainsymphony.org
Officers:
  President: Nancy Judd
  Secretary: Barbara Miller
  Treasurer: Soll Levine
  Executive VP: Peter Knaus
Management:
  Director: Elizabeth Elia
Founded: 1950
Status: Non-Profit
Income Sources: Private and Corporate Donations, Endowment Fund
Season: October-September
Performs At: Darius Miller Shell; Walnut Hill Park
Seating Capacity: 3,000
Organization Type: Performing

931
SILVERMINE GUILD SUMMER MUSIC SERIES
1037 Silvermine Road
New Canaan, CT 06840
Phone: 203-966-9700
Fax: 203-996-2763
e-mail: sgac@silvermineart.org
Web Site: www.silvermineart.org
Officers:
  Chairman: Roger Mudre
  Secretary: Marcia Harris
  Treasurer: LaVern Burton
  Vice-Chairman: Leslie Giuliani
Management:
  Executive Director: Leslee Asch
  Marketing: Robin Axness
  Finance Manager: LaWanza Holder
  Gallery Director: Jeffrey Mueller
Status: Non-Profit
Income Sources: Ticket Sales, Fundraisers
Performs At: Gillford Hall
Annual Attendance: 800

932
NEW HAVEN SYMPHONY ORCHESTRA
105 Court Street
New Haven, CT 06511
Phone: 203-865-0831
Fax: 203-865-0845
Toll-free: 800-292-6476
e-mail: boxoffice@newhavensymphony.org
Web Site: www.newhavensymphony.com
Officers:
  President: Burton Alter
  Executive Committee Chair: David W Benfer
  VP: Mario Zangari
  Treasurer: Tracey Scheer
  Treasurer: Robert Santy
  Recording Secretary: Carol von Pressentin Wright
Management:
  Executive Director: Natalie Forbes
  Principal Conductor/Music Director: William Boughton
  Associate Conductor: Gerald Steichen
Mission: Our mission is to reach a diverse audience and promote excellence in the performing arts. Our orchestra consists of 70 professionals.
Founded: 1894
Specialized Field: Orchestra
Status: Professional, Nonprofit
Paid Staff: 6
Paid Artists: 70
Budget: $1.8-$2 million
Income Sources: Box Office, Sponsorship, Private and Corporate Donations, Commemorative Gifts, Foundations, Grants
Season: September-April
Performs At: Woolsey Hall

933
ORCHESTRA NEW ENGLAND
PO Box 200123
New Haven, CT 06520
Phone: 203-777-4690
Fax: 203-772-0578
e-mail: info@orchestranewengland.org
Web Site: www.orchestranewengland.org
Management:
  Director: James Sinclair
Founded: 1974
Budget: $35,000-$100,000

934
YALE SYMPHONY ORCHESTRA
PO Box 201945
New Haven, CT 06520
Phone: 203-432-4140
Fax: 203-432-7642
e-mail: brian.s.robinson@yale.edu
Web Site: www.yale.edu
Officers:
  Dean: Robert L Blocker
  President: Larua Britton
  VP: Matthew Smith
Management:
  Music Director/Conductor: Toshiyuki Shimada
  Concertmaster: Kensho Watanabe
  Manager: Brian Robinson
Mission: To present diverse and high quality music.
Specialized Field: Orchestra; Symphony
Paid Staff: 1
Non-paid Artists: 200
Income Sources: Private and Corporate Donations, Endowment, Grants, Foundations, Ticket Sales
Season: October-February
Performs At: Woolsey Hall, Morse Recital Hall; Sprague Memorial Hall
Affiliations: ASOL
Annual Attendance: 8,000-10,000
Seating Capacity: 2,695
Year Built: 1901

935
EASTERN CONNECTICUT SYMPHONY
289 State Street
New London, CT 06320
Phone: 860-443-2876
Fax: 860-444-7601
e-mail: ectsymphony@snet.net
Web Site: www.ectsymphony.com

INSTRUMENTAL MUSIC / Connecticut

Officers:
   President: Thomas Castle
   VP: Barbara Richards
   Treasurer: Robert Salmonsen
   Secretary: Lois Andrews
Management:
   Executive Director: Isabelle G Singer
   Music Director: Toshiyuki Shimada
Mission: The mission of the Eastern Connecticut Symphony is to enrich the cultural life of the region by performing high quality music and by conducting educational outreach programs.
Founded: 1946
Specialized Field: Symphony; Orchestra; Ensemble
Status: Professional, Nonprofit
Paid Staff: 7
Paid Artists: 75
Budget: $795,000
Income Sources: Ticket Sales; Grants; Corporate Sponsorships; Individual Donations; Fundraising Events
Season: October-May
Performs At: Garde Arts Center
Annual Attendance: 8,400
Facility Category: Restored theater at Garde Arts Center
Seating Capacity: 1440
Year Built: 1926
Year Remodeled: 1998
Organization Type: Performing; Educational

936
NORFOLK CHAMBER MUSIC FESTIVAL
Yale Summer School of Music
PO Box 545
Norfolk, CT 06058
Phone: 860-542-3000
Fax: 860-542-3004
e-mail: norfolk@yale.edu
Web Site: www.yale.edu
Officers:
   Dean: Robert L Blocker
Management:
   Artistic Director: Paul Hawkshaw
   General Manager: James Nelson
   Associate Manager: Deanne Chin
   Associate Administrator: Ashley Starkins
Mission: To provide chamber music performances and professional training.
Utilizes: Artists-in-Residence; Composers-in-Residence; Guest Instructors; Guest Musical Directors; Guest Musicians; Multimedia; Singers; Soloists
Founded: 1941
Specialized Field: Chamber; Folk Music; Educational
Status: Professional, Nonprofit
Paid Staff: 12
Paid Artists: 70
Budget: $60,000-$150,000
Income Sources: Ticket Sales, Grants, Private and Corporate Donations
Season: Late June-Late August
Performs At: The Music Shed
Annual Attendance: 17,500
Facility Category: Indoor
Seating Capacity: 1,000
Year Built: 1906
Organization Type: Performing; Educational

937
NORWALK SYMPHONY ORCHESTRA
83 Wall Street
Suite 1
Norwalk, CT 06850
Phone: 203-847-8844
Fax: 203-847-2455
e-mail: info@norwalksymphony.org
Web Site: www.norwalksymphony.org
Management:
   Manager: Kate Altman
   Music Director/Conductor: Johnathan Yates
   President, Board of Governors: Emil Albanaese
Founded: 1939
Status: Professional
Budget: $500,000
Income Sources: Ticket Sales, Private and Corporate Donations, Grants
Season: October-May
Performs At: Norwalk Concert Hall
Annual Attendance: 5,000
Seating Capacity: 1,062

938
NORWALK YOUTH SYMPHONY
71 E Avenue
Suite N
Norwalk, CT 06851
Mailing Address: PO Box 73
Phone: 203-866-4100
Fax: 203-866-0012
e-mail: nysweb@norwalkyouthsymphony.org
Web Site: www.norwalkyouthsymphony.org
Officers:
   Chairman: Lisa Petno
   Vice President: Victoria Goodrick
   Treasurer: Suzanne Stawiasz
   Secretary: Don Steiner
Management:
   Executive Director: Sara Watkins
Utilizes: Artists-in-Residence; Commissioned Composers; Educators; Fine Artists; Guest Companies; High School Drama; Multimedia; Theatre Companies
Founded: 1956
Status: Non-Profit
Budget: $800,000
Income Sources: Tuition; Box Office; Donations; Grants
Season: November-May
Performs At: Norwalk Concert Hall
Affiliations: ASOL; MCNC; ASCAP; BMI
Annual Attendance: 5,500
Seating Capacity: 1,062
Organization Type: Performing; Educational

939
RIDGEFIELD SYMPHONY ORCHESTRA
90 East Ridge Road
Ridgefield, CT 06877
Phone: 203-438-3889
Fax: 203-438-0222
Web Site: www.ridgefieldsymphony.org
Officers:
   President: Donna Case
   Treasurer: Suzanne Escola
   Secretary: Mary Kaletta
Management:
   Executive Director: Sarah Miller
   Music Director: Gerald Steichen
   Operations Manager: Catherine da Cruz
Mission: To present high quality classical music programs in the communities surrounding Ridgefield.
Utilizes: Fine Artists; Guest Accompanists; Guest Musicians; Multimedia; Original Music Scores; Sign Language Translators; Singers
Founded: 1964
Specialized Field: Symphony
Status: Professional, Nonprofit
Paid Staff: 1
Volunteer Staff: 34
Paid Artists: 70+
Budget: $500,000
Income Sources: American Symphony Orchestra League; Broadcast Music Incorporated; American Society of Composers, Authors and Publishers, Private and Corporate Donations, Ticket Sales
Season: September-April
Performs At: Ann S Richardson Auditorium; Ridgefield High School, Ridgefield Playhouse
Annual Attendance: 6,000
Organization Type: Performing

940
STAMFORD SYMPHONY ORCHESTRA
263 Tresser Boulevard
Stamford, CT 06901
Phone: 203-325-1407
Fax: 203-325-8762
e-mail: office@stamfordsymphony.org
Web Site: www.stamfordsymphony.org
Officers:
   Chair: Michael Puleo
   President/CEO: Barbara J Soroca
   Vice Chairman: Alan McIntyre
   Treasurer: Michael Mayone
   Secretary: Juliet H Forrester
Management:
   General Manager: Elaine C Carroll
   Operations Manager: Susan Oetgen
   Director: Peter Anker
   Director: Jeff Ford
Mission: To develop an appreciation for classical music through diverse programming on a professional level.
Utilizes: Collaborations; Guest Accompanists; Guest Musical Directors; Guest Musicians; Multimedia; Resident Artists
Founded: 1968
Specialized Field: Symphony; Orchestra; Ensemble
Status: Professional, Nonprofit
Paid Staff: 7
Paid Artists: 70
Budget: $1.3 million
Income Sources: Ticket Sales, Contributions, Grants, Friends of SSO
Performs At: Palace Theatre
Annual Attendance: 15,000
Seating Capacity: 1,586
Organization Type: Performing; Resident; Educational

941
STAMFORD YOUNG ARTISTS PHILHARMONIC
Ridgeway Station
PO Box 3301
Stamford, CT 06905
Phone: 203-532-1278
e-mail: executivedirector@syap.org
Web Site: www.syap.org
Officers:
   President: John Colbert
   Secretary: Robin Edelston
   Co-Treasurer: Gloria Sinaguglia
   Co-Treasurer: Kathleen Kuberka
Management:
   Executive Director: Joyce DiCamillo, executivedirector@syap.org
Mission: To create an outlet for young musicians to perform, developing their skills and abilities, while exposing the community to this cultural art.
Founded: 1960
Specialized Field: Orchestra; Flute and Jazz Ensemble; Summer Jazz Workshop
Status: Non-Professional, Nonprofit

INSTRUMENTAL MUSIC / Delaware

Paid Staff: 150
Season: September-May
Performs At: Stamford High School
Organization Type: Performing; Educational

942
WILLIMANTIC ORCHESTRA
192 Plains Road
Tolland, CT 06084
Phone: 860-429-0865
e-mail: dhvaughan@charter.net
Web Site: www.willimanticorchestra.org
Officers:
- President: Fred Wengrzynek
- Treasurer: Paul Navratil

Management:
- Conductor: David Vaughan

Mission: To encourage college musicians to continue their musical pursuits and to stretch the abilities of more seasoned musicians.
Specialized Field: Orchestra
Budget: $35,000
Season: October-May
Performs At: Shafer Auditorium; Eastern Connecticut State University

943
WALLINGFORD SYMPHONY ORCHESTRA
Choate Rosemary Hall- Paul Mellon Arts Center
P.O. Box 6023
Wallingford, CT 06492
Phone: 203-697-2261
e-mail: csrodenhizer@yahoo.com
Web Site: www.wallingfordsymphony.org
Officers:
- President: Carl S Rodenhizer
- Treasurer: Donald Kirschbaum
- Secretary: Karen Grava

Management:
- Music Director: Philip T Ventre

Mission: To provide professional quality orchestral performances to reach and inspire the greater Wallingford community.
Founded: 1974
Specialized Field: Symphony; Orchestra
Status: Nonprofit
Paid Artists: 65
Budget: $35,000-$100,000
Income Sources: Subscription, Individual and Corporate Donations, Grants, Fundraisers
Facility Category: Theater
Seating Capacity: 780
Year Built: 1972

944
WATERBURY SYMPHONY ORCHESTRA
110 Bank Street
Waterbury, CT 06702
Phone: 203-574-4283
Fax: 203-755-6948
e-mail: waterbury.symphony@snet.net
Web Site: www.waterburysymphony.org
Officers:
- President: Kristen Jacoby
- Vice President: Malcolm H Forbes
- Recording Secretary: Estelle Mackenzie
- Corresponding Secretary: Maureen Donnarumma
- Treasurer: William Miller

Management:
- Executive Director: Steve Collins
- Marketing Director: Kathryn Dennen
- Operations Manager: Andrew Goldstein

Mission: To bring a diverse audience together through live symphonic music.
Utilizes: Artists-in-Residence; Choreographers; Collaborating Artists; Collaborations; Commissioned Composers; Commissioned Music; Dance Companies; Dancers; Educators; Five Seasonal Concerts; Grant Writers; Guest Accompanists; Guest Artists; Guest Choreographers; Guest Companies; Guest Composers; Guest Designers; Guest Directors; Guest Lecturers; Guest Musical Directors; Guest Musicians; Guest Soloists; High School Drama; Instructors; Local Artists; Lyricists; Multi Collaborations; Multimedia; Music; Organization Contracts; Original Music Scores; Resident Artists; Sign Language Translators; Singers; Soloists
Specialized Field: Classical; Pops
Status: Professional, Nonprofit
Paid Staff: 2
Volunteer Staff: 50
Paid Artists: 70
Budget: $260,000-$1,050,000
Income Sources: Annual Fund, Corporate Sponsors, Memberships, Grants
Performs At: Main Stage; Naugatuck Valley Community College
Annual Attendance: 15,000
Facility Category: Community College
Type of Stage: Proscenium
Stage Dimensions: 38x34
Seating Capacity: 800

945
CONNECTICUT YOUTH SYMPHONY
Hartt School Community Division
200 Bloomfield Avenue
West Hartford, CT 06117
Phone: 860-768-4100
Fax: 860-768-4777
e-mail: harttcomm@hartford.edu
Web Site: www.hartford.edu
Management:
- Music Director: Dan D'Addio

Mission: To provide programs for talented young musicians.
Founded: 1930
Specialized Field: Youth Symphony
Budget: $35,000
Income Sources: Tuition; Fundraising
Performs At: Lincoln Theater
Affiliations: Hartt School
Annual Attendance: 2,000
Seating Capacity: 700

946
ORCHESTRA NEW ENGLAND
University of New Haven
PO Box 200123
West Haven, CT 06520
Phone: 203-777-4690
Fax: 203-934-8379
e-mail: info@orchestranewengland.org
Web Site: www.orchestranewengland.org
Officers:
- President: Lydia Bornick

Management:
- Music Director: James Sinclair
- Executive Director: Darron McNutt
- Personnel Manager: Joseph Russo

Mission: To present exciting and versatile performances to enhance music appreciation in the community.
Founded: 1974
Specialized Field: Orchestra
Status: Professional, Nonprofit
Paid Staff: 3
Non-paid Artists: 25
Budget: $200,000
Income Sources: Fundraising, Ticket Sales, Private and Corporate Donations
Season: November-May
Performs At: Battell Chapel; Yale University, Dodds Hall Auditorium; University of New Haven Campus
Annual Attendance: 3,000
Seating Capacity: 850

Delaware

947
NEWARK SYMPHONY ORCHESTRA
PO Box 7775
Newark, DE 19714-7775
Phone: 302-369-3466
e-mail: info@newarksymphony.org
Web Site: www.newarksymphony.org
Officers:
- President: Philip Fuhrman
- VP: Carolyn Fuhrman
- Secretary: Debra Kenaley

Management:
- Music Director: Simeone Tartaglione
- Personnel Manager: Jennifer Hugh
- Business Manager: Denice Grawe
- Director: Stover Babcock
- Personnel Manager: Jen Hugh

Mission: To give volunteer musicians the opportunity to play symphonic literature and to provide live performances for the community.
Utilizes: Community Talent; Five Seasonal Concerts; Guest Directors; Guest Musicians
Founded: 1966
Specialized Field: Symphony
Status: Non-Professional, Nonprofit
Paid Staff: 3
Volunteer Staff: 80
Budget: $55,000
Income Sources: University of Delaware, Grants, National Endowment for the Arts, Delaware Division of the Arts
Season: October-April
Performs At: Newark United Methodist Church; The Independence School
Annual Attendance: 2,000-2,500
Organization Type: Performing

948
BRANDYWINE BAROQUE
1205 North Orange Street
Wilmington, DE 19801
Phone: 877-594-4546
Web Site: www.brandywinebaroque.org
Management:
- Artistic Director: Karen Flint
- Director: Robert Munsell

Mission: To provide lively Baroque music on period instruments to make the chamber music accessible to the modern audience.
Specialized Field: Chamber
Budget: $100,000-$150,000
Income Sources: Ticket Sales, Private and Corporate Donations
Performs At: Christ Church Christiana Hundred; Wilmington, St Peter's Church; Lewes

949
DELAWARE SYMPHONY ORCHESTRA
818 N.Market St, Floor 2R
Wilmington, DE 19801

INSTRUMENTAL MUSIC / District of Columbia

Mailing Address: PO Box 1870, Wilmington, DE 19889-1870
Phone: 302-656-7442
Fax: 302-656-7754
e-mail: lucindaw@delawaresymphony.org
Web Site: www.delawaresymphony.org
Officers:
    Chairman: Tatiana Copeland
    Secretary: Mary Jo Anderson
    Vice Chairman: Betty Duncan
Management:
    Executive Director: Lucinda Williams
    Development Director: Christopher Van Bergen
    Music Director: David Amando
    General Manager: Diana Milburn
Mission: Seeks to enrich the quality of life through live orchestral music by pursuing artistic excellence in symphonic and chamber music performances and cultivating a life-long love of orchestral music through education and community engagement programs.
Utilizes: Guest Artists
Founded: 1929
Specialized Field: Symphony; Orchestra; Classical; Pops; Chamber
Status: Professional, Nonprofit
Paid Staff: 10
Volunteer Staff: 100
Paid Artists: 86
Budget: $2.5 million
Income Sources: American Symphony Orchestra League, Ticket Sales, Private and Corporate Donations, Advertising, Grants
Season: October-May
Performs At: Grand Opera House, Gold Ballroom; Hotel duPont
Organization Type: Performing; Educational

950
DICKINSON THEATRE ORGAN SOCIETY
1801 Milltown Road
PO Box 7263
Wilmington, DE 19803-0296
Phone: 302-995-2603
e-mail: president@dtoskimball.org
Web Site: www.dtoskimball.org
Officers:
    President: Robert E Dilworth
Mission: To present theatre pipe organ concerts on the pipe organ located in the Dickinson High School Auditorium.
Utilizes: Guest Accompanists; Guest Directors; Guest Musical Directors; Instructors; Local Talent; Original Music Scores
Founded: 1973
Opened: 1969
Specialized Field: Organ Music
Status: Professional, Semi-Professional, Nonprofit
Volunteer Staff: 60
Paid Artists: 6
Budget: $75,000
Income Sources: Tickets; Donations
Season: September-July
Performs At: Dickinson High School Auditorium
Affiliations: American Theatre Organ Society
Annual Attendance: 5,000
Type of Stage: Proscenium
Stage Dimensions: 48'x35'
Organization Type: Sponsoring

District of Columbia

951
UNITED STATES AIR FORCE BAND
201 McChord Street
Bolling AFB, DC 20332-0202
Phone: 202-767-4225
Fax: 202-767-0686
Web Site: www.usaband.af.mil
Officers:
    Commander: Col Dennis M Layendecker
    Deputy Commander: Lt Col Alan C Sierichs
Management:
    Manager: CM Sgt Jerry Thomas
    Operations Director: Maj. Scott Guidry
    Marketing Director: CM Sgt Elizabeth Campeau
    Band Manager: Sgt. Craig LeDoux
Mission: To provide music support for American troops, to encourage service in the Air Force and to increase the public awareness and reputation of the armed forces.
Utilizes: Singers
Founded: 1941
Specialized Field: Symphony; Orchestra; Chamber; Ensemble; Chorus; Band
Status: Professional, Nonprofit
Paid Staff: 230
Volunteer Staff: 2
Budget: $1,800,000
Income Sources: Department of Defense Funds
Season: October-December
Performs At: DAR Constitution Hall
Organization Type: Performing; Touring

952
CAPITAL CITY SYMPHONY
1333 H Street NE
Washington, DC 20002
Phone: 202-399-7993
e-mail: information@capitalcitysymphony.org
Web Site: www.capitalcitysymphony.org
Officers:
    Chair: Sharon Hannon
    Vice Chair: Mattie Cohan
    Treasurer: Richard Strange
    Recording Secretary: Howard Spendelow
Management:
    Music Director: Victoria Gau
    Associate Conductor: David Grandis
    General Manager: Debbie Grossman
Mission: To present affordable programs with a relaxed atmosphere to make orchestral music approachable to the metropolitan DC community.
Founded: 1967
Specialized Field: Orchestra

953
CONTEMPORARY MUSIC FORUM
500 17th Street NW
Washington, DC 20006
Phone: 877-263-8431
e-mail: executivedirector@VERGEensemble.com
Web Site: www.contemporarymusic.org
Officers:
    Chair: Steve Antosca
    Vice Chair: Steve Soderberg
    Treasurer: Fred Weck
    Secretary: Michael Stover
Management:
    Executive Director: Lina Bahn
    Artistic Advisor: Steve Antosca
    Artistic Director: dan Visconti
Mission: To provide the Greater Washington area with quality contemporary music performances.
Founded: 1973
Specialized Field: Chamber
Status: Nonprofit
Income Sources: Private and Corporate Donations, Ticket Sales
Season: May-November
Performs At: Armand Hammer Auditorium; Corcoran Gallery of Art; Millennium Stage; CMF at the Kennedy Center
Organization Type: Performing; Resident

954
DC YOUTH ORCHESTRA PROGRAM
Brightwood Station
1700 E. Capitol Street
Washington, DC 20003
Phone: 202-698-0123
Fax: 202-723-4555
e-mail: info@dcyop.org
Web Site: www.dcyop.org
Officers:
    President: Victor L Reid
    Secretary: Robert Pullen
    Treasurer: Laura Price
Management:
    Executive Director: Joshua Simonds
    Interim Education Director: Claudine Nash
    Operations Manager: Rashida Coleman
Mission: To facilitate a creative outlet for young people, regardless of experience level, to practice and perform music.
Founded: 1960
Specialized Field: Symphony; Orchestra; Chamber
Status: Nonprofit
Budget: 642,000
Income Sources: American Symphony Orchestra League Youth Orchestra Division, Private and Corporate Donations, Ticket Sales, Matching Gifts, Planned Gifts
Performs At: Various Venues
Organization Type: Performing; Touring; Educational

955
GEORGE WASHINGTON UNIVERSITY SYMPHONY ORCHESTRA
George Washington University Music Department
801 22nd Street NW
Washington, DC 20052
Phone: 202-994-6245
e-mail: gwmusic@gwu.edu
Web Site: www.gwu.edu
Officers:
    Chair: Karen Ahlquist
Management:
    Director: Nancia D'Alimonte
Mission: To rehearse and perform diverse orchestral music ranging from contemporary music to traditional.
Founded: 1961
Specialized Field: Orchestra
Budget: $35,000
Income Sources: Private and Corporate Donations, Ticket Sales
Performs At: Lisner Auditorium

956
KENNEDY CENTER OPERA HOUSE ORCHESTRA
John F Kennedy Center
2700 F Street NW
Washington, DC 20566

INSTRUMENTAL MUSIC / District of Columbia

Phone: 202-467-4600
Toll-free: 800-444-1324
Web Site: www.kennedy-center.org
Officers:
  President: Michael Kaiser
  Founding Chair: Roger L Stevens
  Chair: David M Rubenstein
  Secretary: Jean Kennedy Smith
  Treasurer: Roland Betts
Management:
  Artistic Director: Heinz Fricke
  Manager: Kristy Dolbeare
  Music Director: Christoph Eschenbach
Mission: To accompany opera performances with orchestral music.
Founded: 1978
Specialized Field: Orchestra
Volunteer Staff: 500
Budget: $1,050,000-$3,600,000
Income Sources: Private and Corporate Donations, Charitable Estate Planning
Season: September-May
Performs At: John F Kennedy Center for the Performing Arts

957
NATIONAL GALLERY ORCHESTRA

National Gallery Of Art
4th and Constitution Avenue NW
Washington, DC 20565
Mailing Address: 2000B South Club Drive, Landover, MD 20785
Phone: 202-737-4215
e-mail: G-Manos@nga.gov
Web Site: www.nga.gov
Officers:
  Chair: John C Fontaine
  President: Victoria P Sant
Management:
  Music Director: George Manos
Mission: To provide the public with free concerts at the National Gallery of Art.
Utilizes: Commissioned Composers; Curators; Educators; Fine Artists; Guest Accompanists; Guest Directors; Guest Musical Directors; Multimedia; Original Music Scores
Founded: 1941
Specialized Field: Symphony; Orchestra; Chamber; Ensemble
Status: Nonprofit
Paid Staff: 8
Season: October-June
Performs At: Museum Garden Courts; National Gallery
Annual Attendance: 500
Seating Capacity: 500
Organization Type: Performing

958
NATIONAL SYMPHONY ORCHESTRA ASSOCIATION

Kennedy Center for the Performin Arts
2700 F Street NW
Washington, DC 20566
Phone: 202-467-4600
Toll-free: 800-444-1324
Web Site: www.kennedy-center.org
Officers:
  Founding Chairman: Robert L Stevens
  Chair: David M Rubenstein
  President: Michael M Kaiser
  Secretary: Jean Kennedy Smith
  Treasurer: Roland Betts
Management:
  Artistic Director: Nigel Boon
  Manager: Cynthia Pickett Steele
  Music Director: Christoph Eschenbach
Mission: To fulfill President Kennedy's vision to produce and present a diverse selection of performing arts for all ages.
Utilizes: Guest Artists
Founded: 1930
Specialized Field: Symphony; Orchestra; Chamber
Status: Nonprofit
Income Sources: American Symphony Orchestra League; John F. Kennedy Center for the Performing Arts
Performs At: John F. Kennedy Center for the Performing Arts
Organization Type: Performing; Touring

959
WASHINGTON BACH CONSORT

1010 Vermont Avenue NW
Suite 202
Washington, DC 20005
Phone: 202-429-2121
Fax: 202-429-2269
e-mail: creifel@bachconsort.org
Web Site: www.bachconsort.org
Officers:
  President: Charles Kinney
  VP: Jill Kent
  Secretary: David Condit
  Treasurer: Charles Reifel
Management:
  Executive Director: Charles Reifel
  Music Director: J Reilly Lewis
  Assistant Conductor: Scott Dettra
  Concertmaster: Andrew Fouts
Mission: To perform the music of Johan Sebastian Bach and his contemporaries to the highest standards to expand the appreciation of Bach in the community.
Founded: 1977
Specialized Field: Chorus; Classical
Status: Professional
Paid Staff: 6
Budget: $260,000-$1,050,000
Income Sources: Private and Corporate Donations, Ticket Sales, Appreciated Stock, Membership
Season: September-June
Performs At: National Presbyterian Church, Basilica of the Shrine of the Immaculate Conception, Clarice Smith Performing Arts Center
Organization Type: Performing, Touring

960
COMMODORES

United States Navy Band
617 Warrington Avenue SE
Washington Navy Yard, DC 20374-5054
Phone: 202-433-2525
e-mail: navybandwebmaster@navy.mil
Web Site: www.navyband.navy.mil
Officers:
  Executive Officer: Lt. Cmdr.Walt Cline
  Commanding Officer: Captain Brian O Walden
Management:
  Senior Chief Musician: Philip M Burlin
  Administrative Chief: Paul E Johnson
  Senior Chief Musician: Christopher J Raifsnider
Mission: To provide musical support to the President, Navy and government officials to inspire patriotism and increase troop morale.
Founded: 1969
Specialized Field: Jazz
Income Sources: Private Donations
Performs At: Official Military Ceremonies, Special Events
Annual Attendance: 1,300
Organization Type: Performing; Touring; Educational

961
COUNTRY CURRENT/US NAVY BAND

617 Warrington Ave SE
Washington Navy Yard, DC 20374-5054
Phone: 202-433-3676
Fax: 202-433-4108
e-mail: navybandwebmaster@navy.mil
Web Site: www.navyband.navy.mil
Officers:
  Commanding Officer: Captain Brian O Walden
  Executive Officer: Lt. Cmdr.Walt Cline
Management:
  Associate Conductor: LT Michael S Grant
  Operations Chief: MUCM Mark C Cochran
  Administrative Chief: Paul E Johnson
  Senior Chief Musician: Christopher J Raifsnider
Mission: Provides musical support to the President of the United States, the Departmnont of the Navy and other senior military and government officials.
Founded: 1973
Specialized Field: Country/Bluegrass
Performs At: Official Military Ceremonies, Special Events
Annual Attendance: 1,300
Organization Type: Performing; Touring

962
CRUISERS

617 Warrington Avenue SE
Washington Navy Yard, DC 20374-5054
Phone: 202-433-3676
Fax: 202-433-4108
e-mail: navybandwebmaster@navy.mil
Web Site: www.navyband.navy.mil
Officers:
  Executive Officer: Lt. Cmdr.Walt Clino
  Commanding Officer: Captain Brian O Walden
Management:
  Senior Chief Musician: John L Fisher
  Administrative Chief: Paul E Johnson
  Senior Chief Musician: Christopher J Raifsnider
Mission: To provide music for such ceremonies, functions and other occasions as may be directed by proper authority in order to best represent the Navy in a musical capacity at the seat of government and elsewhere as directed.
Founded: 1973
Specialized Field: Contemporary; Rock; Rythym; Blues
Performs At: Official Military Ceremonies, Special Events
Annual Attendance: 1,300
Organization Type: Performing; Touring

963
UNITED STATES NAVY BAND

617 Warrington Avenue SE
Washington Navy Yard, DC 20374-5054
Phone: 202-433-3676
Fax: 202-433-4108
e-mail: navybandwebmaster@navy.mil
Web Site: www.navyband.navy.mil
Officers:
  Lieutenant/Assistant Leader: Melvin P Kessler
  Lieutenant/Third Officer: Issac Daniel, Jr
  Executive Officer: Lt. Cmdr.Walt Cline
  Commanding Officer: Captain Brian O Walden
Management:
  Commander/Directr/Officer in Charge: Ralph Gambone
  Master Chief Musician: Jeffrey C Myers

All listings are in alphabetical order by state, then city, then organization within the city.

INSTRUMENTAL MUSIC / Florida

Chief Musician: John L Fisher
Chief Musician: Earl E Powers
Administrative Chief: Paul E Johnson
Senior Chief Musician: Christopher J Raifsnider
Mission: To provide music for such ceremonies, functions and other occasions as may be directed by proper authority in order to best represent the Navy in a musical capacity at the seat of government and elsewhere as directed.
Founded: 1925
Specialized Field: Ceremonial Music; Classical Rock; Jazz; Country
Status: Professional
Performs At: Official Military Ceremonies, Special Events
Annual Attendance: 1,500,000
Organization Type: Performing; Touring; Educational

Florida

964
MIAMI INTERNATIONAL PIANO FESTIVAL
20191 E Country Club Drive
Suite 709
Aventura, FL 33180
Phone: 305-935-5115
Fax: 305-935-9087
e-mail: info@miamipianofest.com
Web Site: www.miamipianofest.com
Officers:
  Founder: Giselle Brodsky
  President and CEO / Chairman: Jack Brodsky
  Treasurer: Steven Grant
Management:
  Artistic Director: Giselle Brodsky
  Executive Director: Barbara Muze
  Director: Mark Patrick
Mission: To discover, promote and support the great masters of the keyboard while providing audiences with a unique musical experience.
Founded: 1998
Specialized Field: Classical
Status: Nonprofit
Paid Staff: 2
Volunteer Staff: 10
Paid Artists: 15
Budget: $360,000
Income Sources: Private Donations; Grants; Ticket Sales; Merchandise
Season: February
Performs At: Lincoln Theatre
Annual Attendance: 5,000
Facility Category: Lincoln Theatre
Seating Capacity: 700

965
TAMPA BAY SYMPHONY
PO Box 4653
Clearwater, FL 33758
Phone: 727-827-8087
e-mail: info@tampabaysymphony.com
Web Site: www.tampabaysymphony.com
Officers:
  President: James R Parady
  VP: Kurt M Klotz
  Treasurer: Victoria G Patterson
  Secretary: Carol M Skey
Management:
  Musica Director/Conductor: Jack Heller
Mission: To promote interest in classical music in the Tampa Bay area and to encourage and educate youth throughout Florida with a Young Artist Competition.
Specialized Field: Orchestra

966
MIAMI BACH SOCIETY/TROPICAL BAROQUE MUSIC FESTIVAL
PO Box 4034
Coral Gables, FL 33114
Phone: 305-669-1376
e-mail: info@miamibachsociety.org
Web Site: miamibachsociety.org
Officers:
  Chairman: Volker Anding
  Treasurer: Kingsley Bewley
  Secretary: Claire Veater
  vice-chairman: Thomas Abbott
Management:
  Artistic Director: Donald Oglesby
  Executive Director: Kathryn B Gaubatz
  director: Jay Bernfeld
  Co-Artistic Director: Miles Morgan
Mission: To perform and present the music of Johann Sebastian Bach.
Utilizes: Guest Directors; Guest Musical Directors; Guest Musicians; Multimedia; Original Music Scores
Founded: 1984
Specialized Field: Baroque
Status: Nonprofit
Paid Staff: 4
Budget: $300,000
Income Sources: Corporations; Government; Indivdual Donations; Ticket Sales
Season: October-January
Performs At: Plymouth Congregational Church; First United Methodista Church of Coral Gables
Annual Attendance: 5,000
Organization Type: Performing, Touring and Presenting Musical Organization
Resident Groups: MBS Chorus and Orchestra

967
DAYTONA BEACH SYMPHONY SOCIETY
PO Box 2
Daytona Beach, FL 32115
Phone: 386-253-2901
Fax: 386-253-5774
e-mail: info@dbss.org
Web Site: www.dbss.org
Officers:
  President: Skip Diegel
  VP: Catherine Bauerle
  Secretary: Mary E Duckett
  Treasurer: John Phelps
  Chair: Dallas Weekley
Management:
  Executive Director: Carol Anderson McLean
  Operations Manager: Christine Gerhardt
Mission: To present diverse musical and cultural programs to stimulate the community with an appreciation for music.
Utilizes: Composers; Five Seasonal Concerts; Guest Soloists; Multimedia
Founded: 1952
Specialized Field: Symphony; Orchestra; Chamber
Status: Nonprofit
Paid Staff: 2
Budget: $35,259
Income Sources: Grants; Donations; Ticket Sales
Season: November-March
Performs At: Peabody Auditorium
Affiliations: None
Annual Attendance: 20,000
Organization Type: Sponsoring, Presenters

968
SYMPHONY OF THE AMERICAS
2425 East Commercial Blvd
Suite 405
Fort Lauderdale, FL 33308
Phone: 954-335-7002
Fax: 945-335-7008
e-mail: info@sota.org
Web Site: www.symphonyoftheamericas.org
Officers:
  President: Beth Holland
  Secretary: Sherill Capi
  Treasurer: Eric Handis
  Chairman: Debra Vogel
Management:
  Artistic Director: James Brooks-Bruzzese
  Executive Director: Renee LaBonte
Mission: To present diverse orchestral music to enrich the cultural environment of South Florida and the Americas.
Utilizes: Contract Orchestras; Guest Soloists
Founded: 1988
Specialized Field: Classical
Status: Nonprofit
Paid Staff: 4
Volunteer Staff: 2
Paid Artists: 60
Budget: $260,000-$1,050,000
Income Sources: Sponsers; Grants; Donations; Program Ads
Performs At: Broward Performing Arts Center-Lmetoro Theater
Annual Attendance: 2.7
Seating Capacity: 2,700

969
SOUTHWEST FLORIDA SYMPHONY ORCHESTRA & CHORUS ASSOCIATION
12651 McGregor Blvd. #4-403
Fort Myers, FL 33919
Phone: 239-418-0996
Fax: 239-418-0725
e-mail: info@swflso.org
Web Site: www.swflso.org
Officers:
  President: Christine Lacroix
  VP: Don King
  Secretary: Bruce Galbraith
  Treasurer: John Hudson
Management:
  Development Director: Tiffany Doer
  Marketing: Andrew Bassila
  Operations: Heidi Kelley
  Executive Director: Frances H Goldman
  Orchestra Operations Manager: Alex Albanese
Mission: Sharing the gift of classical music to more people in the communities through the Sanibel Series and the Around Town concerts.
Utilizes: Collaborations; Commissioned Composers; Composers; Contract Orchestras; Educators; Grant Writers; Guest Accompanists; Guest Companies; Guest Composers; Guest Directors; Guest Lecturers; Guest Musical Directors; Guest Musicians; Local Unknown Artists; Lyricists; Multimedia; Music; Resident Companies; Sign Language Translators; Soloists; Students
Founded: 1962
Specialized Field: Classical
Status: Professional
Volunteer Staff: 450
Budget: $1.3 million
Income Sources: Ticket Sales, Private and Corporate Donations, Fundraising, Symphony Society

INSTRUMENTAL MUSIC / Florida

Season: November-April
Performs At: Barbara B. Mann Performing Arts Hall
Annual Attendance: 22,000
Organization Type: Performing

970
GAINESVILLE CHAMBER ORCHESTRA
PO Box 357011
Gainesville, FL 32635-7011
Phone: 352-336-5448
Web Site: www.gcomusic.org
Officers:
   President: Lynn Noffsinger
   VP: Rebecca Micha
   VP: Greg Johnson
   Treasurer: Tim Hoskinson
   Secretary: Lispbeth Gets
Management:
   Music Director/Conductor: Evans Haile
   Orchestra Representative: Terence Muir
   Orchestra Representative: Grace Kang
   Personnel Director: Virginia Lamboley
Mission: To provide to Alachua County and surrounding areas quality programs of traditional and contemporary repertoire, which will entertain, enrich and educate a diverse and broad-based audience.
Founded: 1983
Specialized Field: Classical
Status: Professional
Budget: $200,000
Income Sources: Private and Corporate Donations, Ticket Sales
Performs At: Center for the Performing Arts; University of Florida and Santa Fe Community College
Annual Attendance: 15,000

971
MELBOURNE CHAMBER MUSIC SOCIETY
PO Box 033403
Indialantic, FL 32903
Phone: 321-213-5100
Fax: 321-956-8775
e-mail: mcms@cfl.rr.com
Web Site: www.melbournechambermusicsociety.com
Officers:
   President: Scott Apelgren
   Secretary: Peggy Snead
   Asst.Treasurer: Irene Quilleux
   VP: Sally Cook
Mission: To showcase international chamber artists for the Brevard community.
Founded: 1997
Specialized Field: Chamber
Income Sources: Private and Corporate Donations, Ticket Sales
Season: October-March
Performs At: St Mark's United Methodist Church
Organization Type: Presenters, Sponsors

972
JACKSONVILLE SYMPHONY ORCHESTRA
300 Water Street
Suite 200
Jacksonville, FL 32202
Phone: 904-354-5479
Fax: 904-354-9238
Toll-free: 877-662-6731
e-mail: frontdesk@jaxsymphony.org
Web Site: www.jaxsymphony.org
Officers:
   Chair: Richard H Pierpont
   Treasurer: James A Heinz
   Secretary: Halcyon E Skinner
   Treasurer: Kay Nichols
   VP: Matthew McAfee
Management:
   Exeucutive Director: Stacy Ridenour
   Operations: Kevin Roberts
   Development Director: Kaye Glover
   Orchestra Personnel Manager: Christopher Dwyer
   Stage Manager: Ray Klaase
Mission: To contribute to the artistic culture of the community by performing high quality music to Florida audiences.
Utilizes: Commissioned Composers; Composers; Guest Artists; Guest Musical Directors; Poets; Singers
Founded: 1949
Specialized Field: Symphony; Orchestra
Status: Professional, Nonprofit
Paid Staff: 25
Volunteer Staff: 1700
Paid Artists: 52
Budget: $6.2 million
Income Sources: Ticket sales, Private donations, Grants, Fundraisers, Jacksonville Symphony Guild
Season: October-May
Performs At: Robert E Jacoby Symphony Hall; Times Union Center For The Performing Arts
Annual Attendance: 220,000
Type of Stage: Platform
Seating Capacity: 1800
Year Built: 1997
Year Remodeled: 1999
Rental Contact: Director Adina Alford
Organization Type: Performing; Touring; Educational

973
KEY WEST SYMPHONY
Josephine S. Leiser Opera Center, 221 SW 3rd
Key West, FL 33312
Phone: 954-522-8445
Fax: 954-522-8430
e-mail: info@southfloridasymphony.org
Web Site: www.southfloridasymphony.org
Officers:
   Founder: Sebrina Alfonso
Management:
   General Manager: Susan Collins
   Conductor: Sebrina Maria Alfonso
Mission: To reach, entertain and educate the community with live symphonic music.
Founded: 1997
Specialized Field: Symphony
Status: Professional, Nonprofit
Paid Staff: 3
Paid Artists: 80
Budget: $700,000
Income Sources: Private and Corporate Donations, Ticket Sales, Grants
Season: December-April
Performs At: Tennessee Williams Fine Arts Center
Annual Attendance: 2,000

974
IMPERIAL SYMPHONY ORCHESTRA
1035 S Florida Avenue
Suite 205
Lakeland, FL 33803
Phone: 863-688-3743
Fax: 863-937-0292
e-mail: info@imperialsymphony.org
Web Site: www.imperialsymphony.org
Officers:
   President: Lu Fitzwater
   Secretary: Monique Quick
   Treasurer: R. Jeffrey Kincart
   Chair: Martha Linder
Management:
   Music Director/Conductor: Mark Thielen
Mission: To serve the community by providing touching musical performances.
Founded: 1965
Specialized Field: Symphony; Orchestra
Status: Professional, Nonprofit
Budget: $260,000-$1,050,000
Income Sources: Private and Corporate Donations, Ticket Sales, Grant from National Endowment for the Arts
Season: September-May
Performs At: Youkey Theater; Lakeland Center

975
BREVARD SYMPHONY ORCHESTRA
1500 Highland Avenue
Melbourne, FL 32935
Mailing Address: PO Box 361965, Melbourne, FL 32936
Phone: 321-242-2024
Fax: 321-259-4716
e-mail: info@brevardsymphony.com
Web Site: www.brevardsymphony.com
Officers:
   Treasurer: Travis Proctor
   Chairman: Brian Nemeroff
   Secretary: Keith Lundquist
Management:
   Music Director/Principal Conductor: Christopher Confessore
   Executive Director: Fran Detsie
   Personnel Manager: Antoinette Cook
Mission: The Brevard Symphony Orchestra shall inspire and enhance the quality of life within our community by providing exceptional orchestral music.
Utilizes: Resident Artists
Founded: 1954
Specialized Field: Musical
Status: Professional
Paid Staff: 6
Volunteer Staff: 250
Paid Artists: 50
Budget: $620,020
Income Sources: Private and Corporate Donations, Memorial Gift Contributions, Endowment Fund
Season: October-April
Performs At: King Center for the Performing Arts
Annual Attendance: 40,000+
Facility Category: In Residence

976
FRIENDS OF CHAMBER MUSIC OF MIAMI
2665 S Bayshore Drive
Miami, FL 33133
Phone: 305-372-2975
Fax: 305-381-8734
e-mail: juliankreeger @ gmail.com
Web Site: www.miamichambermusic.org
Officers:
   President: Julian H Kreeger
Mission: To present exemplary chamber musicians to preserve and develop appreciation for chamber music.
Founded: 1955
Specialized Field: Chamber
Status: Nonprofit
Income Sources: Private and Corporate Donations, Ticket Sales
Season: December-May
Performs At: Gusman Concert Hall, University of Miami
Organization Type: Presenters, Performing

INSTRUMENTAL MUSIC / Florida

977
GREATER MIAMI YOUTH SYMPHONY
5275 Sunset Drive
Miami, FL 33143
Phone: 305-667-4069
Fax: 305-402-0272
e-mail: info@gmys.org
Web Site: www.gmys.org
Officers:
- President: Laurie Hill
- Vice President: Walter Busse
- Tresurer: Dinora Cassanova
- Secretary: Jennifer Mendoza
- Past President: Wallace Glenn Kerrick
- Board Member: Jill Sharon White
- Board Member: Glenn Basham
- Board Member: Ross Harbaugh
- Board Member: Terry Bonnelli

Management:
- Music Director, Conductor: Huifang Chen
- Executive Director, Conductor: Melissa Lesniak PhD
- Strings Chamber Coach, Conductor: Vivian Ventura
- Young Mozarts Conductor: Besnick Hashani
- Concert, Jazz Band Instructor: Eugene Timmons
- Young Sousas Conductor: Oliver Diez

Mission: The mission of the Greater Miami Youth Symphony is 1) to instill life-long values of discipline, teamwork, responsibility, respect, and cultural appreciation in young musicians, ages five through eighteen, through learning, rehearsing, and performing in a professional, positive environment. 2) to enrich the cultural foundation of our community by reaching out to young musicians from different cultural, ethnic and economic backgrounds.
Utilizes: Arrangers; Collaborating Artists; Collaborations; Commissioned Music; Educators; Fine Artists; Guest Speakers; Instructors; Local Artists & Directors; Lyricists; Multimedia; Music; Paid Performers; Scenic Designers; Singers; Soloists
Founded: 1958
Specialized Field: Classical Instrumental, Jazz. Modern
Status: Non-Profit
Income Sources: Donors, Sponsors, Fundraisers
Season: Year Round
Performs At: North Shore Youth Center, Coral Gables Library, Pinecrest Gardens, Coral Gables Museum, ArtCenter

978
MIAMI CLASSICAL GUITAR SOCIETY
PO Box 0725
Miami, FL 33265
Phone: 305-412-2494
e-mail: info@miamiguitar.org
Web Site: www.miamiguitar.org
Officers:
- Founder/President: Carlos Molina

Mission: To promote appreciation for classical guitar music performed by local, national and international artists.
Utilizes: Composers; Guest Accompanists; Guest Musical Directors; Multimedia; Singers
Founded: 1987
Specialized Field: Classical Guitar
Volunteer Staff: 4
Paid Artists: 6
Budget: $45,000
Income Sources: Grants; Sponsors; Members; Ticket Sales
Performs At: Theaters; Churches

Annual Attendance: 2,000
Seating Capacity: 300

979
SOUTH FLORIDA YOUTH SYMPHONY
12645 SW 114 Avenue
Miami, FL 33176
Phone: 305-238-2729
e-mail: foertter@gmail.com
Web Site: www.sfys.net
Officers:
- President: Patricia Fernandez
- VP: Marcio Larsh
- Treasurer: Susy Larsh

Management:
- Executive & Musical Director: Marjorie Hahn
- Director: Ira Suzuki
- Piano Instructor: Dr. Pamela Schultz

Mission: To foster the musical growth of young people.
Utilizes: Actors; Artists-in-Residence; Collaborating Artists; Collaborations; Commissioned Music; Dancers; Educators; Guest Accompanists; Guest Companies; Guest Composers; Guest Designers; Guest Directors; Guest Ensembles; Guest Musical Directors; High School Drama; Instructors; Lyricists; Multi Collaborations; Multimedia; Organization Contracts; Selected Students; Soloists; Special Technical Talent; Theatre Companies
Founded: 1964
Specialized Field: Orchestra; Ensemble
Status: Nonprofit
Paid Staff: 1
Volunteer Staff: 6
Budget: $160,000
Income Sources: Grants, Private and Corporate Donations, Tuition, Fundraisers, Grant National Endowment for the Arts
Season: December-May
Performs At: Local Halls; Parks; Schools
Annual Attendance: 3,500
Organization Type: Performing; Educational
Resident Groups: All

980
NEW WORLD SYMPHONY
500 17th Street
Miami Beach, FL 33139
Phone: 305-673-3330
Fax: 305-673-6749
Toll-free: 800-597-3331
e-mail: pr@nws.edu
Web Site: www.nws.edu
Officers:
- Founder: Michael Tilson Thomas
- President/CEO: Howard Herring
- Executive VP: Victoria Rogers

Management:
- Artistic Senior Vice President: Douglas Merilatt
- Marketing Director: Sabrina Anico
- Development: Paul Woehrle

Mission: To prepare young music graduates for orchestral leadership with an advanced, three year training program.
Utilizes: Collaborations; Five Seasonal Concerts; Guest Accompanists; Guest Artists; Guest Companies; Guest Composers; Guest Ensembles; Guest Instructors; Guest Musical Directors; Guest Musicians; Guest Soloists; High School Drama; Instructors; Local Artists; Multimedia; Organization Contracts; Original Music Scores; Sign Language Translators; Singers; Soloists; Visual Arts
Founded: 1987
Specialized Field: Symphony; Orchestra; Chamber; Educational; Ensemble

Status: Professional, Nonprofit
Paid Staff: 48
Budget: $7.5 million
Income Sources: Endowment, Ticket Sales, Private and Corporate Donations
Season: August-May
Annual Attendance: 22,000
Facility Category: Theatre
Type of Stage: Sprung Beech
Stage Dimensions: 49'32 x 42'4 x 25
Seating Capacity: 705
Year Built: 1936
Year Remodeled: 1988
Organization Type: Performing; Touring

981
PHILHARMONIC CENTER FOR THE ARTS
5833 Pelican Bay Boulevard
Naples, FL 34108-2740
Phone: 239-597-1900
Fax: 239-597-7856
Toll-free: 800-597-1900
e-mail: info@thephil.org
Web Site: www.thephil.org
Officers:
- Founder: Myra Janco Daniels
- CEO and President: Kathleen van Bergen

Mission: To enlighten, educate and entertain people of all ages and backgrounds in Southwest Florida by presenting the very best of the visual and performing arts.
Founded: 1989
Opened: 1989
Specialized Field: Orchestra; Show Tunes
Status: Professional
Paid Staff: 412
Annual Attendance: 500,000
Seating Capacity: 1,425

982
OCALA SYMPHONY ORCHESTRA
820 SE Fort King Street
Ocala, FL 34471
Phone: 352-351-1606
Toll-free: 800-435-7352
e-mail: toni.james@embarqmail.com
Web Site: www.ocalasymphony.com
Officers:
- President: Cindy Van Heyde
- Treasurer: Bill Nassal
- Vice-President: Robert Reilly

Management:
- Music Director/Conductor: Matthew Wardell
- General Manager: Dorothy Pitone
- Kristina: Sameed S Afghani

Mission: To present orchestral music performances for the community.
Founded: 1975
Specialized Field: Orchestra
Budget: $200,000
Performs At: CFCC Fine Arts Auditorium; Lecanto Auditorium
Annual Attendance: 5,000

983
FLORIDA SYMPHONY YOUTH ORCHESTRA
812 E Rollins Street
Suite 300
Orlando, FL 32803
Phone: 407-999-7800
Fax: 407-898-5250
e-mail: kerry@fsyo.org
Web Site: www.fsyo.org

INSTRUMENTAL MUSIC / Florida

Officers:
  President: Donna McCue
  Treasurer: Roxanne Huber Weber
  Secretary: Stephen Schenck
  VP: Michael Parks
Management:
  Executive Director: Heide Evans Waldron
  Production Manager: Carl Rendek
  Director: Andrew Lane
  Member Relationship Coordinator: Briana Scales
  Director: Matthew Davis
Mission: To educate young musicians, strengthening their skills and appreciation of music.
Founded: 1957
Specialized Field: Symphony
Status: Nonprofit
Paid Staff: 3
Volunteer Staff: 50
Paid Artists: 3
Budget: $150,000-$260,000
Income Sources: Private and Corporate Donations, Box Office, Grants, United Arts and Florida Arts
Season: October-May
Performs At: Performing Arts Centre
Annual Attendance: 5,000
Seating Capacity: 2,359
Organization Type: Performing Arts Center

984
ORLANDO PHILHARMONIC ORCHESTRA
812 E Rollins Street
Suite 300
Orlando, FL 32803
Phone: 407-896-6700
Fax: 407-896-5512
e-mail: info@orlandophil.org
Web Site: www.orlandophil.org
Officers:
  President: Carol Connor
  Secretary: Susan M Curran
  Treasurer: Christopher Ranck
Management:
  Executive Director: David Schillhammer
  General Manager: Mark Fischer
  Operations: Sally Carter
  Marketing Director: Sandy Rendek
  Music Director: Christopher Wilkins
Mission: To share symphonic music with the community through performance, education and cultrual leadership.
Founded: 1993
Specialized Field: Orchestra; Classical; Pops
Budget: $1,050,000-$3,600,000
Income Sources: Private and Corporate Donations, State of Florida, Philharmonic's Endowment, Foundations, Grants
Season: October-April
Performs At: Margeson Theater; Lowndes Shakespeare Center, Community Presbyterian Church
Seating Capacity: 2,500

985
UNIVERSITY OF CENTRAL FLORIDA ORCHESTRA
UCF Music Department
4000 Central Florida Boulevard
Orlando, FL 32816-1354
Phone: 407-823-2869
Fax: 407-823-3378
e-mail: ucfmusic@ucf.edu
Web Site: www.music.cah.ucf.edu
Officers:
  Chair: Jeffrey Moore
Management:
  Director: Jeff More
  Director of Coral Activities: David Brunner
  Associate Director of Bands: Ryan Kelly
  Director of Jazz Studies: Jeff Rupert
  Director of Bands: Scott Tobias
Mission: To give students an artistic outlet to perform for the public in an orchestral setting.
Founded: 1929
Specialized Field: Ensemble; Chamber
Status: Nonprofit
Income Sources: University Of Central Florida
Performs At: Music Rehearsal Hall; University of Central Florida
Annual Attendance: 3,200
Seating Capacity: 500

986
PALM BEACH SYMPHONY
Palm Beach Towers
44 Cocoanut Row
Suite M207B
Palm Beach, FL 33480
Phone: 561-655-2657
e-mail: info@palmbeachsymphony.org
Web Site: www.palmbeachsymphony.com
Officers:
  Chair: Leslie Rose
  President: Dale McNulty
  Secretary: Jeannine Merrien
Management:
  Music Director: Ramon Tebar
  Artistic: Ray Robinson
Mission: To bring quality music programs to the Palm Beach community.
Utilizes: Guest Artists
Founded: 1963
Specialized Field: Symphony
Status: Nonprofit
Volunteer Staff: 2
Paid Artists: 60
Budget: $200,000
Income Sources: Private and Corporate Donations, Ticket Sales
Season: November-April
Performs At: Flagler Museum, Society of the Four Arts, Bethesda by the Sea Church, Colony Pavilion
Annual Attendance: 2,500-3,000
Facility Category: multi-venues
Seating Capacity: 1,000

987
JAZZ SOCIETY OF PENSACOLA
PO Box 18337
Pensacola, FL 32523-8337
Phone: 850-433-8382
Fax: 850-433-8790
e-mail: jsop1@juno.com
Web Site: www.jazzpensacola.com
Officers:
  President: Crystal Joy Albert
Management:
  Administrator: Kathy Lyon
Mission: The Jazz Society of Pensacola aspires to be the premier Jazz Society on the Central Gulf Coast dedicated to promoting all forms of jazz-America's Music. We endeavor to provide a social forum for jazz performance, education and enjoyment for listeners and musicians.
Founded: 1983
Specialized Field: Jazz
Status: Non-Profit
Paid Staff: 1
Volunteer Staff: 50
Budget: $40,000
Income Sources: Individual Donors, Corporate Sponsors, NWFL, Florida Arts Councils, Volunteers
Season: April
Performs At: Annual Pensacola JazzFest held in outdoor park; Seville Square; Monthly Concerts/Jam sessions In Local Venues
Affiliations: Charter Member; Jazz Education Network
Annual Attendance: 14,000
Facility Category: City Park
Type of Stage: Gazebo, Tented Stage

988
PENSACOLA SYMPHONY ORCHESTRA
205 E Zaragoza Street
PO Box 1752
Pensacola, FL 32502
Phone: 850-435-2533
e-mail: info@pensacolasymphony.com
Web Site: www.pensacolasymphony.com
Officers:
  President: Roger Webb
  Treasurer: Charles Beall
  Secretary: Rosilan Leahy Duckworth
  VP: Mark Lee
Management:
  Executive Director: Bret Barrow
  Development: John O'Connor
  Marketing Director: Crystal Lohman
  Music Director: Peter Rubardt
Mission: To educate and enrich the Pensacola community through music.
Utilizes: Guest Artists
Founded: 1926
Specialized Field: Symphony
Status: Nonprofit
Budget: $260,000-$1,050,000
Income Sources: Grants, Private and Corporate Supporters, Ticket Sales, Endowment Fund
Season: Octobor May
Performs At: Saenger Theatre
Annual Attendance: 43,000

989
SARASOTA YOUTH ORCHESTRAS
709 N Tamiami Trail
Sarasota, FL 34236
Phone: 941-953-4252
Fax: 941-953-3059
Toll-free: 866-508-0611
e-mail: rmccabe@sarasotaorchestra.org
Web Site: www.sarasotaorchestra.org
Officers:
  CFO: Douglas Shanley
  CMO: Gordon Greenfield
  Chair: Anne Folsom Smith
  Secretary: Lois Stulberg
  President & CEO: Joe McKenna
Management:
  Executive Director: Arnold Hoffman
  Education Director: Rose Ann McCabe
  Concertmaster: Daniel Jordan
Mission: The Sarasota Youth Orchestras consist of five orchestras, affording students the opportunity to participate in an orchestra comparable to their skill level.
Utilizes: Composers-in-Residence; Educators; Fine Artists; Guest Composers; Multimedia; Poets; Resident Artists; Resident Companies; Soloists
Founded: 1959
Specialized Field: Youth Philharmonic; Youth Symphony; String Ensemble
Status: Non-Professional, Nonprofit

All listings are in alphabetical order by state, then city, then organization within the city.

INSTRUMENTAL MUSIC / Florida

Income Sources: Ticket Sales; Sponsorships; Special Gifts; Scholarships; Endowment Gifts; Planned Giving; Fundraisers
Performs At: Sarasota Opera House; Van Wezel Performing Arts Hall; Holley Hall
Facility Category: Performing; Resident; Touring
Organization Type: Performing; Educational

990
JAZZ CLUB OF SARASOTA
330 S Pineapple Avenue
Suite 111
Sarasota, FL 34236
Phone: 941-366-1552
Fax: 941-366-1553
e-mail: admin@jazzclubsarasota.com
Web Site: www.jazzclubsarasota.org
Officers:
    VP: Wes Bearden
Management:
    Volunteer Artistic Director: Gordon Garrett
Mission: To promote, preserve, perform and educate people about jazz the original American art form.
Utilizes: Original Music Scores; Sign Language Translators
Founded: 1980
Specialized Field: Jazz
Paid Staff: 1
Volunteer Staff: 60
Paid Artists: 100
Non-paid Artists: 10
Income Sources: Membership Dues, Grants
Season: October-April
Performs At: Van Wezel Performing Arts Hall, Holley Hall, Bayfront Community Center
Annual Attendance: 8,000

991
SARASOTA ORCHESTRA STRING QUARTET
709 N Tamiami Trail
Sarasota, FL 34236
Phone: 941-953-4252
Fax: 941-953-3059
Toll-free: 866-508-0611
e-mail: rmmcabe@sarasotaorchestra.org
Web Site: www.sarasotaorchestra.org
Officers:
    President/CEO: Joseph McKenna
    CFO: Douglas Shanley
    CMO: Gordon Greenfield
    Chair: Anne Folsom Smith
    Secretary: Lois Stulberg
    President & CEO: Joe McKenna
Management:
    Executive Director: Arnold Hoffman
    Education Director: Rose Ann McCabe
    Concertmaster: Daniel Jordan
    Concertmaster: Daniel Jordan
    Artistic Director: Leif Bjaland
Mission: To provide a showcase for new, young string players in the Sarasota Orchestra.
Utilizes: Multimedia; Original Music Scores
Founded: 1967
Specialized Field: Ensemble
Status: Professional, Nonprofit
Paid Artists: 4
Income Sources: Ticket Sales, Sponsorships, Special Gifts, Scholarships, Endowment Gifts, Planned Giving, Fundraisers, Florida West Coast Symphony Association
Season: October-May
Performs At: Holley Hall
Organization Type: Performing; Touring; Resident

992
SARASOTA ORCHESTRA
709 N Tamiami Trail
Sarasota, FL 34236
Phone: 941-953-4252
Fax: 941-953-3059
Toll-free: 866-508-0611
e-mail: rmccabe@sarasotaorchestra.org
Web Site: www.sarasotaorchestra.org
Officers:
    President/CEO: Joseph McKenna
    CFO: Douglas Shanley
    CMO: Gordon Greenfield
    Chair: Anne Folsom Smith
    Secretary: Lois Stulberg
Management:
    Artistic Director: Leif Bjaland
    Operations Director: Patricia Joslyn
    Executive Director: Arnold Hoffman
    Education Director: Rose Ann McCabe
    Concertmaster: Daniel Jordan
Mission: To build an orchestra of resident musicians with talented musical skills, to present diverse music programming in Florida and to attract visiting soloists of international accclaim. The orchestra also strives to involve as many people as possible in classical and symphonic music, providing lifelong learning opportunities for the community.
Utilizes: Collaborations; Fine Artists; Five Seasonal Concerts; Grant Writers; Guest Companies; Guest Musical Directors; Guest Musicians; Guest Writers; Local Artists; Multimedia; Organization Contracts; Original Music Scores; Singers; Student Interns
Founded: 1956
Specialized Field: Symphony
Status: Nonprofit, Professional
Budget: $4 million
Season: September-May
Seating Capacity: 1,736
Year Built: 1968
Organization Type: Performing; Resident

993
SARASOTA ORCHESTRA NEW ARTISTS PIANO QUARTET
709 N Tamiami Trail
Sarasota, FL 34236
Phone: 941-953-4252
Fax: 941-953-3059
Toll-free: 866-508-0611
e-mail: rmmcabe@sarasotaorchestra.org
Web Site: www.sarasotaorchestra.org
Officers:
    President/CEO: Joseph McKenna
    CFO: Douglas Shanley
    CMO: Gordon Greenfield
    Chair: Anne Folsom Smith
    Secretary: Lois Stulberg
    President & CEO: Joe McKenna
Management:
    Artistic Director: Leif Bjaland
    Operations Director: Patricia Joslyn
    Executive Director: Arnold Hoffman
    Concertmaster: Daniel Jordan
    Education Director: Rose Ann McCabe
Mission: To promote classical music locally, statewide and nationally by presenting high quality music programs.
Utilizes: Artists-in-Residence; Multimedia; Poets; Resident Artists; Resident Companies
Founded: 1991
Specialized Field: String Ensemble
Status: Professional, Nonprofit
Paid Artists: 4
Income Sources: Ticket Sales, Sponsorships, Special Gifts, Scholarships, Endowment Gifts, Planned Giving, Fundraising, Florida West Coast Symphony Association
Season: October-May
Performs At: Holley Hall
Organization Type: Performing; Resident; Touring

994
SARASOTA ORCHESTRA WIND QUINTET
709 N Tamiami Trail
Sarasota, FL 34236
Phone: 941-953-4252
Fax: 941-953-3059
Toll-free: 866-508-0611
e-mail: rmmcabe@sarasotaorchestra.org
Web Site: www.sarasotaorchestra.org
Officers:
    President/CEO: Joseph McKenna
    CFO: Douglas Shanley
    CMO: Gordon Greenfield
    Chair: Anne Folsom Smith
    Secretary: Lois Stulberg
    President & CEO: Joe McKenna
Management:
    Artistic Director: Leif Bjaland
    Operations Director: Patricia Joslyn
    Executive Director: Arnold Hoffman
    Concertmaster: Daniel Jordan
Mission: To promote classical music locally, statewide and nationally by presenting high quality music programs.
Utilizes: Artists-in-Residence; Poets; Resident Artists; Resident Companies
Founded: 1984
Specialized Field: Wind Ensemble
Status: Professional, Nonprofit
Income Sources: Ticket Sales, Sponsorships, Special Gifts. Scholarships, Endowment Gifts, Planned Giving, Fundraising, Florida West Coast Symphony Association
Season: October-May
Performs At: Holley Hall
Facility Category: Performing; Resident; Touring

995
SARASOTA ORCHESTRA BRASS QUINTET
709 N Tamiami Trail
Sarasota, FL 34236
Phone: 941-953-4252
Fax: 941-953-3059
Toll-free: 866-508-0611
e-mail: rmmcabe@sarasotaorchestra.org
Web Site: www.sarasotaorchestra.org
Officers:
    President/CEO: Joseph McKenna
    CFO: Douglas Shanley
    CMO: Gordon Greenfield
    Chair: Anne Folsom Smith
    Secretary: Lois Stulberg
    President & CEO: Joe McKenna
Management:
    Artistic Director: Leif Bjaland
    Operations Director: Patricia Joslyn
    Executive Director: Arnold Hoffman
    Concertmaster: Daniel Jordan
Mission: To promote classical music locally, statewide and nationally by presenting high quality music programs.
Utilizes: Multimedia; Original Music Scores
Founded: 1967
Specialized Field: Ensemble
Status: Professional, Nonprofit
Paid Artists: 4

INSTRUMENTAL MUSIC / Florida

Income Sources: Ticket Sales, Sponsorships, Special Gifts, Scholarships, Endowment Gifts, Planned Giving, Fundraisers, Florida West Coast Symphony Association
Season: October-May
Performs At: Holley Hall
Organization Type: Performing; Touring; Resident

996
PINELLAS YOUTH SYMPHONY
PO Box 4106
Seminole, FL 33775
Phone: 727-438-3149
e-mail: pysdirector@yahoo.com
Web Site: www.pysmusic.org
Officers:
   President: Leo Meirose
   Secretary: John Creveling
   Treasurer: Wayne Raymond
Management:
   Executive Director: Jane Hine
   Conductor: Dr Susan Robinson
   Serenade String Orchestra: Lei Liu
   Operations Director: Wayne Raymond
Mission: To enhance the music education of the youth in Pinellas County.
Founded: 1958
Specialized Field: Orchestra; Ensemble
Status: Professional
Income Sources: Tuition, Grants, Contributions
Performs At: Murray Studio; Ruth Eckerd Hall
Organization Type: Performing

997
FLORIDA ORCHESTRA
244 Second Avenue N
Suite 420
St Petersburg, FL 33701
Phone: 727-892-3331
Fax: 727-892-3338
e-mail: admin@floridaorchestra.org
Web Site: www.floridaorchestra.org
Officers:
   Chairman: Thomas Farquhar
   President: Michael Pastreich
   Secretary: Susan B. Betzer, MD
   Finance Director: Diane Hinckley
   COO: Stephanie Gonthier
Management:
   Music Director: Stefan Sanderling
   Coffee Concert Conductor: Allistair Willis
   Artistic Administrator: David Rogers
   Development Director: Emily McClain
   Marketing and Communications Direct: Sherry Powell
Mission: To enrich the life of the Tampa Bay area as it inspires, entertains and educates a wide and diverse audience with the unique experience of live symphonic music ensuring that future generations will continue to enjoy this legacy that so magnificently celebrates the human spirit.
Founded: 1968
Specialized Field: Symphony; Orchestra
Status: Professional, Nonprofit
Paid Staff: 21
Paid Artists: 72
Budget: 8 Million
Income Sources: Ticket Sales; Private & Corporate Donations; Fundraising Events
Performs At: Progress Energy Center For The Arts; Mahaffey Theatre; Stroz Center For The Performing Arts; Ruth Eckerd Hall
Annual Attendance: 150,000
Organization Type: Performing; Touring; Resident; Educational

998
BIG BEND COMMUNITY ORCHESTRA
The Artist Series
690 Industrial Drive
Tallahassee, FL 32310
Phone: 850-224-9934
Fax: 850-224-1730
e-mail: hopkinsrs@comcast.net
Web Site: www.bbcorch.org
Officers:
   Board Chair: Richard Hopkins
   co-founder: Ginny Densmore
   co-founder: Waldie Anderson
Management:
   Conductor: Shleby Chipman
   Associate Conductor: Ed Kawakami
   Assistant Director: Jame Mick
Mission: All volunteer community orchestra provides area with The Artist Series.
Utilizes: Community Members; Community Talent; Educators; Guest Composers; Guest Designers; Guest Musical Directors; Guest Musicians; Instructors; Local Artists & Directors; Multimedia; Scenic Designers; Singers; Soloists
Founded: 1994
Specialized Field: Orchestra
Status: Nonprofit
Budget: $6,000
Income Sources: Funded by members of the Orchestra, City of Tallahassee, Leon County, Private and Corporate Donations
Season: October-April
Performs At: Lee Hall Auditorium
Affiliations: American Symphony Orchestra League
Annual Attendance: 600
Facility Category: FAMU Lee Hall Auditorium/TCC Turner Aud
Seating Capacity: 1,200

999
TALLAHASSEE SYMPHONY ORCHESTRA
1020 East Lafayette Street
Tallahassee, FL 32301
Phone: 850-224-0461
Fax: 850-222-9092
e-mail: operations@tallahasseesymphony.org
Web Site: www.tallahasseesymphoony.org
Officers:
   President: Mary Bedford
   Treasurer: Sean Singleton
   Secretary: Chris Sloan
Management:
   Music Director: Alexander Jimenez
   Executive Director: Lois D Griffin
   VP Artistic Affairs: Don Gibson
   Assistant Concertmaster: Rang Hee Kim
   Operations Director: Laura Figo
   Conductor: Yaniv Dinur
Mission: To maintain and further develop a resident, professional symphony orchestra to produce musical performances of the highest artistic quality and to provide cultural and educational opportunities in the Tallahassee, North Florida and South Georgia communities.
Founded: 1979
Specialized Field: Symphony
Status: Professional; Nonprofit
Paid Staff: 3
Income Sources: American Symphony Orchestra League, Private and Corporate Donations, Grants, Ticket Sales
Season: September-April
Performs At: Ruby Diamond Auditorium; Florida State University
Organization Type: Performing; Resident; Presenters

1000
VENICE SYMPHONY
PO Box 1561
Venice, FL 34284-1561
Phone: 941-488-1010
Fax: 941-488-7074
e-mail: venicesymphony@aol.com
Web Site: www.thevenicesymphony.org
Management:
   Artistic Director/Conductor: Kenneth Bowermeister
   Personnel Manager: Michael Fiore
   Executive Director: Jean Peters
Mission: To cultivate, promote and sponsor an appreciation of musical arts in the community, secure patrons of these arts, and perform concerts
Utilizes: Guest Accompanists; Guest Companies; Guest Musicians; Guest Writers; Local Unknown Artists; Multimedia; Original Music Scores; Sign Language Translators; Singers; Soloists
Founded: 1974
Specialized Field: Classical
Status: Professional
Paid Staff: 5
Paid Artists: 75
Budget: $450,000
Income Sources: Tickets; Contributions; Grants
Performs At: Church of the Nazarene
Annual Attendance: 11,875
Facility Category: Church
Seating Capacity: 625
Organization Type: Performing

1001
PALM BEACH POPS
Palm Beach Pops, Inc.
500 S Australian Avenue
Suite 100
West Palm Beach, FL 33401
Phone: 561-832-7677
Fax: 561-832-9686
Toll-free: 800-448-2472
e-mail: info@palmbeachpops.org
Web Site: www.palmbeachpops.org
Officers:
   President/Chairman/Founder: Jon Lappin
Management:
   Executive Director: Charlotte Laurent-Ottomane, dquilleon@palmbeachpops.org
   Music Director/Conductor: Robert Lappin
Mission: To provide artistic excellence and education with each performance.
Utilizes: Guest Accompanists; Guest Musicians; Multimedia; Original Music Scores; Paid Performers; Singers; Students
Founded: 1991
Specialized Field: Symphony; Pops; Orchestra
Status: Nonprofit
Paid Staff: 12
Season: November-April
Performs At: Kravis Center for the Performing Arts; Florida Atlantic University Center Auditorium; Palm Beach Gardens Eissey Campus
Annual Attendance: 65,000
Organization Type: Presenters, Performing

INSTRUMENTAL MUSIC / Georgia

Georgia

1002
ALBANY SYMPHONY ORCHESTRA
PO Box 70065
Albany, GA 31708
Phone: 229-430-8933
Fax: 229-430-8934
e-mail: info@albanysymphony.org
Web Site: www.albanysymphony.org
Officers:
   President: Jim Bullion
   General Manager: Marie Galamba-Pierce
   Publicity/Marketing: Robert M Drake
   Assistant Publicity Director: Richard H Waller
   Operations Manager: Edward J Trammell
   VP: Julian Price
   Secretary: Lynn Kennedy
   Treasurer: Frances Gahagan
Management:
   Music Director/Conductor: Claire Fox Hillard
   Concertmaster: Matson Topper
   Assistant Concertmaster: Alicija Vsarek
   Executive Director: Lark Ledbetter
Mission: Dedicated to providing and promoting quality symphonic music for Southwest Georgia through the maintenance of a symphony orchestra and related educational activities.
Utilizes: Artists-in-Residence; Collaborations; Composers-in-Residence; Guest Accompanists; Guest Companies; Guest Musicians; Instructors; Organization Contracts; Original Music Scores; Singers; Soloists
Founded: 1965
Specialized Field: Symphony; Orchestra
Status: Nonprofit
Paid Staff: 4
Volunteer Staff: 10
Budget: $275,000
Income Sources: American Symphony Orchestra League, Albany Arts Council, Private and Corporate Donations, Ticket Sales, Grants
Season: August-May
Performs At: Albany Municipal Auditorium, Albany Civic Center, Parks at Chehaw, Mount Zion Baptist Church, Veterans Park Amphitheater
Facility Category: Municipal Auditorium
Seating Capacity: 980
Year Built: 1915
Year Remodeled: 1993
Organization Type: Performing; Educational

1003
GEORGIA SOUTHWESTERN STATE UNIVERSITY CHAMBER CONCERT SERIES
Georgia Southwest State University
800 Wheatley Street
Americus, GA 31709-4693
Phone: 229-931-2204
Fax: 229-931-2527
e-mail: jem@canes.gsw.edu
Management:
   Director: Dr Julie Megginson
   Conductor: Dr Herschel Beazley
Mission: The series features a variety of chamber ensembles including string quartets and trios. Six classical performances are held each year.
Specialized Field: Chamber
Status: Nonprofit
Income Sources: Private and Corporate Donations, Ticket Sales, Grants
Season: October-April
Performs At: Jackson Performance Hall
Seating Capacity: 250

1004
ATLANTA CHAMBER PLAYERS
PO Box 5438
Atlanta, GA 31107
Phone: 404-872-4952
Fax: 404-872-4952
e-mail: paulapeace@bellsouth.net
Web Site: www.atlantachamberplayers.com
Officers:
   President, Board Of Advisors: James Throckmorton
   Secretary: Brian Hailes
   Treasurer: Charlie Chitwood
Management:
   Founder/Artistic Managing Director: Paula Peace
Mission: Atlanta Chamber Players is a professional ensemble of musicians committed to offering audiences world class traditional and contemporary masterpieces as well as commissioned new works.
Founded: 1976
Specialized Field: Chamber
Status: Professional; Nonprofit
Paid Staff: 3
Paid Artists: 11
Season: September-March
Performs At: Walter Hill Auditorium; High Museum Of Art
Organization Type: Performing; Touring; Resident; Educational

1005
ATLANTA SYMPHONY ORCHESTRA
1280 Peachtree Street NE
Atlanta, GA 30309-3552
Phone: 404-733-4900
Fax: 404-733-4901
e-mail: aso-info@woodruffcenter.org
Web Site: www.atlantasymphony.org
Officers:
   President/CEO: Stanley E Romanstein
   Chair: Jim Abrahamson
   Vice Chair: Clayton F Jackson
   Treasurer: Mark D Wasserman
   Secretary: Joni Winston
Management:
   Music Director: Robert Spano
   Orchestral Manager: Julie Fish
   Artistic Planning Director: Evans Mirageas
   Project Director: Tom Tomlinson
   Stage Manager: Richard Carvlin
Mission: To serve audiences with performances and educational opportunities, while striving for excellence.
Utilizes: Actors; Artists-in-Residence; Choreographers; Collaborating Artists; Collaborations; Commissioned Composers; Commissioned Music; Composers-In-Residence; Dancers; Designers; Educators; Five Seasonal Concerts; Guest Accompanists; Guest Artists; Guest Choreographers; Guest Companies; Guest Composers; Guest Designers; Guest Directors; Guest Instructors; Guest Musical Directors; Guest Musicians; Guest Soloists; Guest Writers; High School Drama; Instructors; Local Artists; Lyricists; Multi Collaborations; Multimedia; Music; New Productions; Organization Contracts; Original Music Scores; Resident Artists; Resident Professionals; Sign Language Translators; Singers; Soloists; Student Interns; Theatre Companies; Touring Companies; Visual Arts
Founded: 1945
Specialized Field: Symphony; Orchestra; Chamber
Status: Professional, Nonprofit
Paid Staff: 50
Paid Artists: 99
Income Sources: American Symphony Orchestra League, Private and Corporate Donations, Grants, Ticket Sales
Performs At: Symphony Hall; Chastain Park Amphitheatre
Annual Attendance: 500,000 +
Facility Category: Concert Hall
Type of Stage: Full Theater Facilities
Seating Capacity: 1749 / 82
Year Built: 1968
Rental Contact: Operations Manager Sandra Schaffer
Organization Type: Performing

1006
ATLANTA SYMPHONY YOUTH ORCHESTRA
1280 Peachtree Street NE
Atlanta, GA 30309
Phone: 404-733-4900
Fax: 404-733-4901
e-mail: aso-info@woodruffcenter.org
Web Site: www.atlantasymphony.org
Officers:
   Parents Association President: Bill Cecil
   Treasurer: Mark D Wasserman
   Secretary: Nancy Musselwhite
   President/CEO: Stanley E Romanstein
   Chair: Jim Abrahamson
Management:
   Music Director/Conductor: Jere Flint
   Music Director: Robert Spano
   Music Director/Conductor: Jere Flint
   Orchestral Manager: Julie Fish
   Stage Manager: Richard Carvlin
Mission: Atlanta Symphony Youth Orchestra plays a larger role in promoting the arts and arts education.
Utilizes: Guest Artists
Founded: 1974
Specialized Field: Youth Orchestra; Educational
Status: Nonprofit
Paid Staff: 60
Volunteer Staff: 22
Paid Artists: 100
Non-paid Artists: 120
Budget: $35,000-$100,000
Income Sources: Lanie and Ethel Foundation, Halle Foundation, Private and Corporate Donations, Grants, Ticket Sales
Season: November-February
Performs At: Robert W Woodruff Arts Center
Annual Attendance: 9,600
Seating Capacity: 1748
Rental Contact: Sandi Schaffer

1007
CHASTIAN PARK AMPHITHEATRE ATLANTA SYMPHONY ORCHESTRA FESTIVAL POPS
4469 Stella Drive
Atlanta, GA 30327
Phone: 404-733-4900
Fax: 404-733-4901
e-mail: aso-info@woodruffcenter.org
Web Site: www.classicchastian.org
Officers:
   Executive Director: Allison Vulgamore
   Director Public Relations: Minde Herbert
   Staff Accountant: April Satterfield
Management:
   Music Director: Robert Spano
   Conductor: Jere Flint
   Conductor: Michael Krajewski

INSTRUMENTAL MUSIC / Georgia

Principal Guest Conductor: Donald Runnicles
Mission: Provides young instrumentalists an opportunity to perform orchestral masterworks under the city's finest conductors.
Founded: 1945
Specialized Field: Orchestra
Status: Nonprofit
Paid Staff: 40
Volunteer Staff: 200
Budget: $6 million
Income Sources: Donations and Sponsors.
Season: June - August
Performs At: Atlanta Symphony Hall; Woodruff Arts Center
Affiliations: Atlanta Symphony Orchestra
Annual Attendance: 160,000
Facility Category: Chastian Park Amphitheatre
Type of Stage: Plywood/ Shell
Seating Capacity: 6,291
Year Built: 1933
Year Remodeled: 1989
Resident Groups: Atlanta Symphony Orchestra

1008
EMORY SYMPHONY ORCHESTRA
Emory University
Dept Of Music., Donna & Marvin Schwartz Cntr.
1700 N Decatur, Suite 206
Atlanta, GA 30322
Phone: 404-727-6280
Fax: 404-727-0074
e-mail: music@emory.edu
Web Site: www.music.emory.edu
Officers:
  Senior Secretary: Annie Carey
  Chairman: Kevin Karnes
Management:
  Conductor: Richard Prior
  Managing Director: Robert McKay
  Assoc. Director For Programming: Tracy Clark
  Stage Manager: Mark Teague
  Production Manager: Lewis Fuller
  Department Of Music Chair: Kevin Karnes
  Coordinator: Colin Bragg
Mission: Provides works selected from the rich heritage of symphonic literature and symphonic choral literature. Each spring their concert features a guest soloist the winner of the Music Department's Student Concerto Competition.
Utilizes: Artists-in-Residence; Educators; Guest Accompanists; Guest Composers; Guest Designers; Guest Directors; Guest Ensembles; Guest Instructors; Guest Musical Directors; Local Artists; Multimedia; Sign Language Translators; Soloists
Founded: 1836
Specialized Field: Symphony; Chamber
Status: Nonprofit
Budget: $5,104,801
Income Sources: Grants, Tuition, Ticket Sales, Private and Corporate Donations
Season: October
Performs At: Performing Arts Studio
Seating Capacity: 220

1009
SYMPHONY ORCHESTRA OF AUGUSTA
Augusta Symphony, Inc.
1301 Greene Street, Suite 200
PO Box 579
Augusta, GA 30903-0579
Phone: 706-826-4705
Fax: 706-826-4735
e-mail: sandraesoaugusta.org
Web Site: www.soaugusta.org
Officers:
  President: Joseph H. Huff
  VP: W.L. Fletcher
  Executive Director: Sandra Self
  Treasurer: Alicia Markyna
  Finance Manager: Martha Robinson
Management:
  Music Director/Conductor: Shizuo Kuwahara
  Production Manager: Arthur Ross III
Mission: To share the joy of great performance with our audience. Together we are music.
Utilizes: Artists-in-Residence; Collaborating Artists; Collaborations; Commissioned Composers; Commissioned Music; Dance Companies; Fine Artists; Guest Accompanists; Guest Composers; Guest Musical Directors; Guest Musicians; Guest Writers; Instructors; Lyricists; Multimedia; New Productions; Original Music Scores; Sign Language Translators; Singers
Founded: 1954
Specialized Field: Music; Orchestra
Status: Nonprofit
Paid Staff: 14
Volunteer Staff: 3
Paid Artists: 250
Budget: $1,200,000
Income Sources: Tickets; Contributions
Season: September-May
Performs At: First Baptis Of Augusta Bell Auditorium
Annual Attendance: 50,000
Facility Category: Symphony; Pops;Chamber;Outdoor & Educational Concerts
Seating Capacity: 800; 2,000; 300; 686
Year Built: 1950
Year Remodeled: 2000
Organization Type: Performing, Touring.
Resident Groups: Augusta Symphony String Quartet; Augusta Symphony Woodwind Trio

1010
COLUMBUS SYMPHONY ORCHESTRA
101 13th Street
PO Box 1499
Columbus, GA 31902
Phone: 706-323-5059
Fax: 706-323-7051
e-mail: sarak@csoga.org
Web Site: www.csoga.org
Officers:
  Executive Director: Sara Ketcham
  Marketing Director: Becky Young
  Development Director: Timothy R Watkins
  President: Steve Adams
Management:
  Music Director/Conductor: George Del Gobbo
  Personnel Manager/Operations: Jeanette Ross
  Marketing Director: Becky Young
  Finance Director: Tammy Zitzelberger
Mission: To provide quality music to area residents.
Utilizes: Commissioned Music; Grant Writers; Guest Accompanists; Guest Companies; Guest Musical Directors; Multimedia
Founded: 1855
Specialized Field: Symphony
Status: Semi-Professional
Paid Staff: 8
Volunteer Staff: 3
Budget: $715,000
Income Sources: American Symphony Orchestra League, Private and Corporate Donations, Ticket Sales
Performs At: River Center Bill Heard Theatre
Annual Attendance: 25,000
Facility Category: Theatre
Seating Capacity: 2,000
Organization Type: Performing; Touring; Resident; Educational; Sponsoring

1011
GAINESVILLE SYMPHONY ORCHESTRA
Brenau University
422 Brenau Avenue
PO Box 162
Gainesville, GA 30503
Phone: 770-532-5727
Fax: 770-535-0554
e-mail: info@gainesvillesymphony.com
Web Site: www.gsomusic.com
Officers:
  Executive Director: Pam Slaton
Management:
  Music Director/Conductor: Larry Sims
Mission: Dedicated to the promotion and appreciation of music throughout Alachua County and the State of Florida through performance and education.
Utilizes: Collaborations; Fine Artists; Grant Writers; Guest Companies; Local Artists; Lyricists; Original Music Scores; Touring Companies
Founded: 1981
Specialized Field: Symphony
Status: Professional, Nonprofit
Paid Staff: 2
Volunteer Staff: 30
Non-paid Artists: 80
Budget: $35,000-$100,000
Income Sources: Grants, National Endowment for the Arts, Private and Corporate Donations, Ticket Sales
Season: October-July
Performs At: Pearce Auditorium; Brenau University
Annual Attendance: 10,000

1012
MACON SYMPHONY ORCHESTRA
400 Poplar Street
Macon, GA 31201
Phone: 478-301-5300
Fax: 478-301-5505
e-mail: marian@maconsymphony.com
Web Site: www.maconsymphony.com
Officers:
  President: Blake Sharpton
  VP Development/Marketing: Eugene Cox Dunwody
  VP Audience Development: Susan T McDuffie
  General Manager: Doris Wood
  Treasurer: Frank Gaudry
  Secretary: Janet Tidwell
  CEO: Sheryl Towers
Management:
  Music Director/Conductor: Ward Stare
  Personnel Manager: Connie Davis
  Director of Operations: Marian Porter
Mission: To offer live quality classical music performances for the enjoyment of the community; to foster the appreciation of music through educational programs.
Utilizes: Artists-in-Residence; Collaborating Artists; Collaborations; Commissioned Music; Composers-in-Residence; Educators; Fine Artists; Five Seasonal Concerts; Guest Accompanists; Guest Companies; Guest Composers; Guest Lecturers; Guest Musical Directors; Guest Musicians; Guest Writers; Instructors; Local Artists; Lyricists; Multimedia; Organization Contracts; Original Music Scores; Sign Language Translators; Singers; Soloists
Founded: 1976
Specialized Field: Orchestra
Status: Professional; Nonprofit
Paid Staff: 6

INSTRUMENTAL MUSIC / Hawaii

Volunteer Staff: 1
Paid Artists: 75
Budget: $650,000
Income Sources: Ticket Sales, Donations, Grants
Performs At: Grand Opera House
Annual Attendance: 12,000+
Seating Capacity: 1,025
Year Built: 1887
Year Remodeled: 2000
Organization Type: Performing; Resident; Educational

1013
COBB SYMPHONY ORCHESTRA
PO Box 680993
Marietta, GA 30068-0017
Phone: 770-426-1509
Fax: 770-424-5541
e-mail: executivedirector@cobbsymphony.com
Web Site: www.cobbsymphony.com
Officers:
    Executive Director: Sherry M Roedl
Management:
    Music Director/Conductor: Michael Alexander
    Head Music Education Program: Nate Casey
Mission: To enrich the cultural life of Cobb County and surrounding communities by performing and promoting music of the highest quality and to provide an opportunity for local musicians to perform in a professional symphony orchestra that serves a culturally diverse population and aids in the music education of the community.
Founded: 1951
Specialized Field: Classical
Status: Nonprofit
Budget: $150,000-$260,000
Income Sources: Fundraising, Ticket Sales, Private and Corporate Donations
Season: August-May
Performs At: Stillwell Theatre

1014
ROME SYMPHONY ORCHESTRA
540 Broad Street
PO Box 533
Rome, GA 30162-0533
Phone: 706-291-7967
Fax: 706-291-3840
e-mail: symphony@romesymphony.org
Web Site: www.romesymphony.org
Officers:
    President: Barbara L Beninato
    VP: Larry Caywood
    Executive Director: MaryAnn Kelly Bray
    Treasurer: Evie McNiece
    Secretary: Suzanne Smith
    Secretary: George Awsumb
Management:
    Music Director/Conductor: Philip O Rice
    Personnel Manager: Steve Karp
    Executive Director: Debra M Cook
Mission: Promoting and providing quality musical programs.
Founded: 1921
Specialized Field: Symphony
Paid Staff: 2
Volunteer Staff: 5
Paid Artists: 65
Budget: $35,000-$100,000
Income Sources: Donations, Ticket Sales, Program Sales, Fund Raisers, Rome Symphony Women's Association
Season: October-September
Performs At: Rome City Auditorium
Seating Capacity: 1,094

1015
DEKALB SYMPHONY ORCHESTRA
PO Box 1313
Tucker, GA 30085
Phone: 678-891-3565
Fax: 678-891-3575
e-mail: Fyodor@DeKalbSymphony.com
Web Site: www.dekalbsymphony.com
Officers:
    Orchestra Manager: Richard Rogers
    Board President: Stanton J Shapiro
    Treasurer: Nancy Jacobson
    Secretary: Allyson Gevertz
Management:
    Music Director & Conductor: Fyodor Cherniavsky
    Orchestra Manager: Richard Rogers
Mission: Provides outstanding soloists and polished orchestral playing.
Founded: 1964
Specialized Field: Orchestra
Paid Staff: 2
Volunteer Staff: 4
Paid Artists: 12
Budget: $140,000
Income Sources: Private and Corporate Donations, Ticket Sales, Grants, Fundraisers
Season: November-July
Performs At: Marvin Cole Auditorium
Annual Attendance: 8,000
Facility Category: College Auditorium
Seating Capacity: 500

1016
VALDOSTA SYMPHONY ORCHESTRA
Valdosta State University
1500 N Patterson St
Valdosta, GA 31698-0115
Phone: 229-333-5800
Fax: 229-259-5578
e-mail: jploendue@valdosta.edu
Web Site: www.valdosta.edu/music
Officers:
    Executive Director: Taylor Harding
Management:
    Artistic Director: Dr J Plondke
    Concertmaster: Nina Lutz
    Stage Manager: Andy Baxter
Mission: Provides both the cultural life of the community and the regional academic mission of Valdosta State University.
Founded: 1990
Specialized Field: Symphony
Status: Nonprofit, Professional
Income Sources: Fundraisers, Ticket Sales, Private and Corporate Donations, Valdosta Symphony Guild, Valdosta State University
Season: September-April
Performs At: Whitehead Auditorium
Type of Stage: Proscenium
Seating Capacity: 774

Hawaii

1017
CHAMBER MUSIC HAWAII
P.O. Box 61939
Honolulu, HI 96839
Phone: 808-372-8236
Fax: 808-738-0202
e-mail: info@chambermusichawaii.com
Web Site: www.chambermusichawaii.com
Officers:
    President: James Moffitt
    VP: Robert Berssenbrugge
    Executive Director: David S Wallerstein
    Treasurer: Paul Lemcke
    Secretary: Norma Nichols
Management:
    General Manager: Jonathan Parrish
    Box Office Manager: Rochelle Uchibori
Mission: To provide the people of Hawaii with chamber music through support of resident chamber music ensembles.
Founded: 1982
Specialized Field: Chamber; Ensemble
Status: Professional; Nonprofit
Income Sources: Grants, State Foundation on Culture and the Arts, Hawaii Community Foundation, Cooke, Atherton & McInerny Foundations, National Endowment for the Arts, Michael Paul Foundation
Season: September-May
Performs At: Paliku Theatre; Windward Community College, Doris Duke Theatre; Honolulu Academy of Arts
Organization Type: Presenting

1018
HAWAII CHAMBER ORCHESTRA SOCIETY
3810 Maunaloa Avenue
Honolulu, HI 96816-4199
Phone: 808-734-0397
Fax: 808-926-8004
Officers:
    General Manager: Jacqueline Ward
Mission: To increase interest in and appreciation of classical music.
Founded: 1992
Specialized Field: Chamber; Ensemble
Status: Professional; Nonprofit
Income Sources: Ticket Sales, Grants
Performs At: Unity Church
Annual Attendance: 1,000+
Organization Type: Performing; Educational

1019
HAWAII YOUTH SYMPHONY ASSOCIATION
1110 University Avenue
Suite 200
Honolulu, HI 96826-1508
Phone: 808-941-9706
Fax: 808-941-4995
e-mail: admin@hiyouthsymphony.org
Web Site: www.hiyouthsymphony.org
Officers:
    President: Chris Yuen
    Executive Director: Selena Ching
    Treasurer: Jean Tsukamoto
    VP Resource Development: Tina Lau
    VP Operations: Les Murata
    Operations Manager: Judy Vierck
    Secretary: Richard Ing
Management:
    Music Director/Conductor: Henry Miyamura
    Conductor Youth Symphony II: Michael Nakasone
    Conductor Concert Orchestra: Derrick Yamane
    Conductor Concert String Orchestra: Joan Doike
    Executive Director: Randy Wong
    Programs Manager: Ann Doike
Mission: Dedicated to nurturing the educational and artistic development of student musicians.
Utilizes: Commissioned Composers; Commissioned Music; Educators; Five Seasonal Concerts; Guest Companies; Guest Composers; Guest Musical

Directors; Guest Musicians; High School Drama; Instructors; Multimedia; Music; Original Music Scores; Soloists
Founded: 1964
Specialized Field: Youth Symphony; Youth Orchestra
Status: Nonprofit
Paid Staff: 13
Volunteer Staff: 50
Paid Artists: 6
Budget: $600,000
Income Sources: Registration; Grants; Donations; Sponsorships; Tickets
Performs At: Venues range from shopping malls to the professional concert hall
Affiliations: American Symphony Orchestra League, HAAE
Annual Attendance: 15,000
Organization Type: Performing; Educational

1020
HONOLULU CHAMBER MUSIC SERIES
University of Hawaii
Box 2233
Honolulu, HI 96804
Phone: 808-528-8226
Fax: 808-956-9422
e-mail: panpac@lava.net
Web Site: www.honoluluchambermusicseries.org
Officers:
  President: Richard Lachmann
  Board Director: Andrew Bunn
Mission: Dedicated to providing chamber music.
Founded: 1954
Specialized Field: Chamber
Status: Professional, Nonprofit
Performs At: Orvis Auditorium

1021
HONOLULU SYMPHONY ORCHESTRA
650 Iwilei Road
Suite 202
Honolulu, HI 96817
Phone: 808-524-0815
Fax: 808-524-1507
e-mail: jmancuso@honolulusymphony.com
Web Site: www.honolulusymphony.com
Officers:
  Chair: Carolyn A Berry
  President: Steve Bloom
  Interim Executive Director: John Graham
  VP Finance/Administration: Suzanne Ruiz
  Marketing Manager: Ryan Lum
  Public Relations Manager: Suzanne Lee
  VP Development: Angela Smith
  Personnel Manager: Jennifer Lovejoy
Management:
  Music Director: Samuel Wong
  Pops Conductor: Matt Catingub
  Assistant Conductor: Joan Landry
  Chorus Director: Karen Kennedy
  Artistic Advisor: Maestro JoAnn Falletta
  Concertmaster: Ignace Jang
  Associate Concertmaster: Claire Sakai Hazzard
  Assistant Concertmaster: Judy Barrett
  Orchestra Operations Manager: Jim Mancuso
Mission: To enhance the quality of life of the people of Hawaii by sustaining a symphony orchestra of the highest artistic quality.
Founded: 1900
Specialized Field: Symphony
Status: Nonprofit
Budget: $3,600,000-$10,000,000
Income Sources: Private and Corporate Donations, Ticket Sales, Grants
Performs At: Neal Blaisdell Concert Hall

1022
MUSIC AT MANOA/UNIVERSITY OF HAWAII AT MANOA OUTREACH COLLEGE
2411 Dole Street
Honolulu, HI 96822
Phone: 808-956-7756
Fax: 808-956-9657
e-mail: uhmmusic@hawaii.edu
Web Site: www.hawaii.edu/uhmmusic
Officers:
  Chairman: Laurence Paxton
  Associate Chair: Thomas Yee
Management:
  Director: Tim Slaughter
Mission: Dedicated to presenting quality musical, dance, theater and special attractions to Hawaii audiences, including the Honolulu Chamber Music Series.
Founded: 1907
Specialized Field: Chamber; Ensemble; Ethnic Music; Soloists
Status: Professional
Income Sources: Western Alliance of Arts Administrators, Association for Performing Arts Presenters, Private and Corporate Donations, Ticket Sales
Season: January-December
Performs At: Blaisdell Concert Hall; Orvis Auditorium
Organization Type: Sponsoring

Idaho

1023
BOISE CHAMBER MUSIC SERIES
Boise State University
1910 University Drive
Boise, ID 83725-1560
Phone: 208-426-1216
Fax: 208-426-1771
e-mail: jbelfy@boisestate.edu
Web Site: www.boisechambermusicseries.org
Officers:
  Media Contact: Pat Pyke
  President: Dave Spencer
  Board Member: Jeanne Belfy
Management:
  Artistic Director: Dr Jeanne Belfy
Mission: To provide quality chamber music.
Specialized Field: Chamber
Season: September-February
Performs At: Morrison Center Recital Hall

1024
BOISE PHILHARMONIC ASSOCIATION
516 S 9th Street
Boise, ID 83702
Phone: 208-344-7849
Fax: 208-336-9078
Toll-free: 888-300-7849
e-mail: info@boisephilharmonic.org
Web Site: www.boisephilharmonic.org
Officers:
  President: Bill Drake
  VP: Ray Stark
  Treasurer: Eric Nadeau
  Director Finance: Gordon Swenson
  Education Coordinator: Jamey Lamar
  Secretary: Helen Carter
Management:
  Music Director/Conductor: Robert Franz
  Concertmaster: Geoffrey Trabichoff
  Associate Concertmaster: Jill Rowley
  Orchestra Personnel Manager: Marilyn Goerrich
  Stage Manager: Forrest Hartvigsen
  Artistic Director: Dr. James Jirak
Mission: Provide an opportunity to share the passion and talent of the members of teh Boise Philharmonic as they celebrate the great music of all ages.
Utilizes: Guest Artists
Founded: 1887
Specialized Field: Orchestra
Status: Nonprofit
Paid Staff: 10
Volunteer Staff: 50
Paid Artists: 72
Budget: $1.3 million
Income Sources: Private and Corporate Donations, Ticket Sales
Season: October-May
Performs At: Morrison Center for the Performing Arts
Annual Attendance: 58,000

1025
BOISE STATE UNIVERSITY CLASSICAL GUITAR SOCIETY
Boise State University
1910 University Drive
Boise, ID 83725
Phone: 208-426-1596
Fax: 208-426-1771
Toll-free: 800-824-7017
e-mail: musicadmissions@boisestate.edu
Web Site: www.boisestate.edu/music
Officers:
  Chairman: Mark R Hansen
Management:
  Director: Dr Joseph Baldassarre
Specialized Field: Classical Guitar
Status: Nonprofit
Performs At: Morrison Center for the Performing Arts
Seating Capacity: 2,000

1026
IDAHO FALLS SYMPHONY
450 A Street
Suite A
Idaho Falls, ID 83402
Phone: 208-529-1080
Fax: 208-529-1097
Web Site: www.ifsymphony.org
Officers:
  President: Dr. Arthur Kull
  VP: Ann Howell
  Treasurer: Joseph R Call
  Marketing: Karen Cornwell
  Development: Mary Lynn Hartwell
  Education: Renie Clements
  Secretary: Linda Neeley
Management:
  Music Director/Conductor: Thomas Heuser
  Concertmaster: Rick Hansen
  Associate Concertmaster: Myrna South
  Orchestra Representative: Linda Neeley
  Executive Director: Tally Adler
  Personnel Manager: Bill Crocker
Mission: Instrumental music.
Founded: 1950
Specialized Field: Symphony; Orchestra
Status: Semi-Professional; Nonprofit
Paid Staff: 3
Volunteer Staff: 50
Budget: $250,000

INSTRUMENTAL MUSIC / Illinois

Income Sources: American Symphony Orchestra League, Private and Corporate Donations, Ticket Sales, Endowment Fund
Season: October-May
Performs At: Colonial Theater, Civic Auditorium
Annual Attendance: 10,000+
Seating Capacity: 948
Organization Type: Performing; Resident; Educational

1027
IDAHO STATE CIVIC SYMPHONY
Campus Box 8099
Pocatello, ID 83209-0009
Phone: 208-234-1587
Fax: 208-236-4884
e-mail: symphony@isu.edu
Web Site: www.thesymphony.us
Officers:
    President: Carol Burnett
    VP: Jedd Thomas
    Treasurer: David Green
    Director: Faye Booth
    Secretary: Rayna Valentine
Management:
    Music Director/Conductor: George Adams
    Executive Director: Heather Sandy
Mission: To build and maintain a symphony orchestra which performs musical programs of high artistic quality.
Founded: 1954
Specialized Field: Symphony
Status: Nonprofit
Budget: $100,000-$150,000
Income Sources: Friends of Symphony, Fundraising, Ticket Sales, Private and Corporate Donations
Season: September-April
Performs At: Goranson Hall, Pocatello High School Auditorium
Annual Attendance: 12,000
Seating Capacity: 450
Year Built: 1965

1028
MAGIC VALLEY SYMPHONY
PO Box 1805
315 Falls Avenue
Twin Falls, ID 83301
Phone: 208-734-6549
Fax: 208-733-6161
e-mail: thadley@cableone.net
Web Site: www.mvsymphony.org
Officers:
    President: Paula Brown Sinclair
    Symphony League President: Elaine Bowen
    Business Manager: H Richard Cook
    VP: Doug Wangen
    Secretary: Annette Barnum
Management:
    Music Director/Conductor: H. Richard Cook
Mission: Committed to enhancing the cultural life of the community and providing an outlet for performers.
Utilizes: Guest Composers; Guest Musicians
Founded: 1959
Specialized Field: Symphony; Orchestra
Status: Non-Professional; Nonprofit
Paid Staff: 3
Budget: $25,500
Income Sources: Ticket Sales; Donations
Performs At: College of Southern Idaho Fine Arts Auditorium
Affiliations: American Society of Composers, Authors and Publishers
Annual Attendance: 2,000
Facility Category: Junior College
Seating Capacity: 900
Year Built: 1970
Organization Type: Performing

Illinois

1029
BELLEVILLE PHILHARMONIC ORCHESTRA
116 N Jackson Street
Belleville, IL 62220
Phone: 618-235-5600
Fax: 618-235-4975
e-mail: nfo@bellevillephilharmonic.org
Web Site: www.bellevillephilharmonic.org
Officers:
    Executive Director: Kathleen J AuBuchon
Management:
    Music Director: Robert Howard
    Assistant Conductor: Dr Leon Burke
    Personnel Manager: Philharmonic Chorale
Mission: Committed to serving the interests of music and musicians in the Greater Belleville area.
Founded: 1867
Specialized Field: Symphony; Orchestra
Status: Non-Professional; Nonprofit
Paid Staff: 100
Budget: $61,600
Income Sources: Advertising, Sponsor a Concert, Private and Corporate Donations, Ticket Sales
Season: October-May
Performs At: St Henry's Catholic Church, Scottish Rite Cathedral, Our Lady of the Snows, Union United Methodist Church, St Teresa Church
Annual Attendance: 1,500-1,800
Organization Type: Performing; Educational

1030
CENTRALIA PHILHARMONIC ORCHESTRA
1250 E Rexford Street
Centralia, IL 62801
Phone: 618-532-2951
Fax: 618-532-2964
e-mail: artcntr@msn.com
Web Site: www.centraliaarts.org
Officers:
    Administrative Coordinator: Jane Pacey
    President: Karen Crouse
    VP: Bronson Meyer
    Treasurer: Helmuth Harms
    Secretary: Sheri Sauer
Mission: To connect arts with the community and the community with the arts.
Utilizes: Artists-in-Residence; Touring Companies
Founded: 1961
Specialized Field: Orchestra; Show Tunes
Status: Nonprofit
Paid Staff: 1
Budget: $120,000
Income Sources: Ticket Sales, Patrons, Trust Funds, Illinois Arts Council, Private and Corporate Donations
Season: October-August
Annual Attendance: 25,000
Seating Capacity: 300
Year Built: 1971
Year Remodeled: 1981

1031
CHAMPAIGN-URBANA SYMPHONY ORCHESTRA
701 Devonshire Drive, C-24
Champaign, IL 61820
Phone: 217-351-9139
Fax: 217-351-1698
e-mail: marketing@cusymphony.org
Web Site: www.cusymphony.org
Officers:
    President: Kip Pope
    VP: Susan Feldman
    Treasurer: Peggy Schneider
    Secretary: Susan Feldman
    Development Director: Wayne Nagy
    Operations Director: Kevin McGuire
Management:
    Music Director/Conductor: Steven Larsen
    Orchestra Representative: Marina Antoline
    Executive Director: Jeffrey Farlow-Cornell
Mission: To provide live, symphonic music performances of the highest quality and music education for our community's children.
Founded: 1960
Specialized Field: Symphony
Status: Nonprofit, Professional
Budget: $150,000-$260,000
Income Sources: Private and Corporate Donations, Ticket Sales, Champaign-Urbana Symphony Guild
Season: September-April
Performs At: Krannert Center for the Performing Arts
Annual Attendance: 7,000

1032
EASTERN SYMPHONY ORCHESTRA
600 Lincoln Avenue
Charleston, IL 61920
Phone: 217-581-3010
Fax: 217-581-7137
e-mail: music@io.eiu.edu
Web Site: www.eiu.edu/~music
Management:
    Music Director: Richard Robert Rossi
Mission: To provide the finest symphony music.
Utilizes: Collaborations; Commissioned Composers; Commissioned Music; Educators; Fine Artists; Five Seasonal Concerts; Guest Accompanists; Guest Companies; Guest Composers; Guest Designers; Guest Directors; Guest Ensembles; Guest Instructors; Guest Lecturers; Guest Musical Directors; Guest Musicians; Guest Soloists; High School Drama; Instructors; Local Artists; Local Unknown Artists; Lyricists; Multi Collaborations; Multimedia; New Productions; Organization Contracts; Original Music Scores; Playwrights; Sign Language Translators; Singers; Soloists; Touring Companies
Specialized Field: Symphony
Status: Nonprofit
Volunteer Staff: 20
Paid Artists: 15
Non-paid Artists: 60
Budget: $50,000
Income Sources: Private and Corporate Donations, Ticket Sales
Performs At: Dvorak Hall

1033
CHICAGO CHAMBER ORCHESTRA
65 West Jackson Blvd. #133
Chicago, IL 60604
Phone: 312-357-1551
e-mail: koberdieter@aol.com
Web Site: www.chicagochamberorchestra.org
Management:
    Founder/Music Director/Conductor: Dieter Kober, jsherer@fourthchurch.org
    Assoc Conductor/Music Dir Designate: Edward Benyas, rloeckel#fourthchurch.org
    Concertmaster: Charles Pikler

INSTRUMENTAL MUSIC / Illinois

Assistant Concertmaster: Steven Boe
Mission: Dedicated to bringing great music directly to the community, to people from many different backgrounds, and to all ages. All concerts are presented admission free.
Founded: 1952
Specialized Field: Chamber Orchestra; Classic Repertory; New Music
Income Sources: Private and Corporate Donations, Governmental Subsidies, Grants
Season: September-May
Performs At: Chicago Cultural Center, First United Methodist Church; Oak Park, Second Presbyterian Church, Fourth Presbyterian Church

1034
CHICAGO SINFONIETTA
70 East Lake Street
Suite 226
Chicago, IL 60601
Phone: 312-236-3681
Fax: 312-235-5429
Web Site: www.chicagosinfonietta.org
Officers:
  Chairperson: Cheri Chappelle
  President: Roger G Wilson
  VP: Weldon Rougeau
  Secretary: Anita Wilson
  Treasurer: Mark Williams
Management:
  Music Director: Mei-Ann Chen
  General Manager: Thomas De Walle
  Development Administrator: Maria Mowbray
  Director Marketing: Ferris O'Shaughnessy
  Executive Director: Jim Hirsch
  Finance Director: Delores Williams
Mission: Offering classical music in original orchestration and promoting ethnic diversity in the concert hall.
Utilizes: Guest Artists
Founded: 1986
Specialized Field: Classical; Jazz; World Music
Status: Nonprofit
Paid Staff: 16
Volunteer Staff: 120
Paid Artists: 65
Non-paid Artists: 1
Income Sources: Chicago Music Alliance
Performs At: Lund Auditorium; Rosary College
Organization Type: Performing; Touring; Educational

1035
CHICAGO SYMPHONY ORCHESTRA
220 S. Michigan Ave.
Chicago, IL 60604
Phone: 312-294-3000
Fax: 312-294-3329
Toll-free: 800-223-7114
Web Site: www.cso.org
Officers:
  Chairman: William A. Osborn
  Vice Chairman: Paul C. Gignilliat
  President: Deborah R. Card
Management:
  Concertmaster: Robert Chen
  Music Director: Riccardo Muti
  Stage Manager: Kelly Kerins
  Mead Composer-in-Residence: Mason Bates
  Judson&Joyce Green Creative Consult: Yo-Yo Ma
  Helen Regenstein Conductor Emeritus: Pierre Boulez
Utilizes: Composers; Composers-in-Residence; Guest Artists; Guest Companies; Student Interns
Founded: 1890
Specialized Field: Symphony; Orchestra
Status: Nonprofit
Income Sources: American Symphony Orchestra League
Organization Type: Performing

1036
CHICAGO YOUTH SYMPHONY ORCHESTRA
410 S Michigan Avenue
Suite 833
Chicago, IL 60605
Phone: 312-939-2207
Fax: 312-939-2015
e-mail: sdodson@cyso.org
Web Site: www.cyso.org
Officers:
  Secretary: Lisa Klein
  Executive Director: Holly H. Hudak
  Director Development: R. Scott Dodson
  Chairman: Gary W Burns
Management:
  Music Director: Allen Tinkham
  Associate Conductor: Terrance Malone-Gray
  Director Chamber Music: Kathie Johnson
Mission: To provide the finest quality orchestral training and performance opportunities for Chicagoland musicians 8 - 18
Utilizes: Commissioned Composers; Educators; Fine Artists; Guest Artists; Guest Companies; Guest Composers; Guest Directors; Guest Instructors; Guest Musical Directors; Instructors; Multimedia; Original Music Scores; Singers; Soloists
Founded: 1946
Specialized Field: Orchestra
Status: Nonprofit
Paid Staff: 12
Budget: $848,450
Income Sources: Government; Foundations/Corporations; Benefit; Individuals
Performs At: Orchestra Hall
Facility Category: Large Rehearsal/Performance Hall
Organization Type: Performing; Touring; Sponsoring

1037
CLASSICAL SYMPHONY ORCHESTRA & THE PROTEGE PHILHARMONIC
218 South Wabash Avenue
Suite 260
Chicago, IL 60604-2445
Phone: 312-341-1521
Fax: 312-341-1835
e-mail: theorchestras@classicalsymphonyorchestra.org
Web Site: www.classicalsymphonyorchestra.org
Management:
  Music Director: Joseph Glymph
Specialized Field: Orchestra
Budget: $150,000-$260,000
Performs At: Preston Bradley Hall

1038
CSO PRESENTS
220 S Michigan Avenue
Chicago, IL 60604
Phone: 312-294-3000
Fax: 312-294-3329
Web Site: www.cso.org
Officers:
  Chairman: William A. Osborn
  Vice Chairman: Paul C. Gignilliat
  President: Deborah R. Card
Management:
  Concertmaster: Robert Chen
  Music Director: Riccardo Muti
  Stage Manager: Kelly Kerins
  Judson&Joyce Green Creative Consult: Yo-Yo Ma
  Helen Regenstein Conductor Emeritus: Pierre Boulez
  Mead Composer-in-Residence: Mason Bates
Specialized Field: Orchestra
Budget: $400,000-$1,000,000
Performs At: Orchestra Hall at Symphony Center

1039
LIRA DANCERS OF THE LIRA ENSEMBLE
6525 N Sheridan Road
Chicago, IL 60626
Phone: 773-508-7040
Fax: 773-508-7043
e-mail: lira@liraensemble.org
Web Site: www.liraensemble.com
Officers:
  Co-Conductor: Philip Seward
  Choreographer: Iowna Puc
  President: Lucyna Migala
  Secretary: Frances Weit
  Treasurer: Bernard Tresnowski
  Founder: Alice Stephens
Management:
  Artistic Director/General Manager: Lucyna Migala
  Co-Conductor: Paul Dijkstra
  Conductor: Mina Zikri
Mission: To help acquaint Polish Americans with the richness of their thousand-year-old heritage of music and dance, and to help other Americans learn about and appreciate Polish culture and traditions.
Founded: 1975
Specialized Field: Polish Music
Status: Non-Profit; Professional
Non-paid Artists: 30
Budget: $200,000-$500,000
Organization Type: Performing

1040
NEW BLACK MUSIC REPERTORY ENSEMBLE
Center for Black Music Research
Columbia College, 600 S Michigan
Chicago, IL 60605
Phone: 312-344-7559
Fax: 312-344-8029
Web Site: www.cbmr.org
Officers:
  Director: Resita M Sands, Jr
Management:
  Coordinator of Perf. Activities: Coleridge Parkinson
Mission: To perform works by black composers from 1700 to the present.
Founded: 1988
Specialized Field: Chamber; Ensemble; Ethnic Music
Status: Professional; Nonprofit
Paid Staff: 13
Paid Artists: 40
Income Sources: Columbia College, Federal and State Grants, Foundation and Corporate Grants
Organization Type: Performing; Touring

INSTRUMENTAL MUSIC / Illinois

1041
PERFORMING ARTS CHICAGO
410 S Michigan Avenue
#911
Chicago, IL 60605
Phone: 312-663-1628
Fax: 312-663-1043
Web Site: www.pachicago.org
Officers:
- Chair: Helyn Goldenberg
- President Director: Maya Polsky
- President: Judy Neisser
- Treasurer: David Ellis

Management:
- Executive Director: Susan Lipman
- Programs Manager: CJ Mitchell
- Director: Christy Uchida
- Operations Manager: Laurell Zahrobsky
- Development Assistant: Brigid Flynn

Mission: Performing Arts Chicago is dedicated to the presentation of new work by local, national, and international artists from a wide cultural spectrum, and in doing so, reaching out in collaboration with the Chicago arts and education communities to challenge our diverse urban audience.
Utilizes: Actors; Artists-in-Residence; Choreographers; Collaborating Artists; Dance Companies; Dancers; Local Artists; Multimedia; Original Music Scores; Special Technical Talent
Founded: 1959
Specialized Field: Chamber
Status: Professional; Nonprofit
Paid Staff: 6
Budget: $1,000,000
Performs At: The Civic Theater
Organization Type: Performing; Resident; Educational; Sponsoring

1042
ROOSEVELT UNIVERSITY ORCHESTRA: CHICAGO COLLEGE OF PERFORMING ARTS
430 S Michigan Avenue
Chicago, IL 60605
Phone: 312-341-3500
Fax: 312-341-6358
Web Site: www.roosevelt.edu
Officers:
- President: Charles R Middleton
- Chairman: James J Mitchell
- Secretary: William J Kirby

Management:
- Chief Resident Conductor: Steven Squires

Utilizes: Artists-in-Residence; Guest Directors; High School Drama; Soloists
Specialized Field: Orchestra
Performs At: Rudolph Ganz Memorial Hall

1043
UNIVERSITY OF CHICAGO SYMPHONY ORCHESTRA
1010 E 59th Street
Chicago, IL 60637
Phone: 773-702-8484
Fax: 773-753-0558
e-mail: musicdept@uchicago.edu
Web Site: www.music.uchicago.edu
Officers:
- President: Gilberto Zaldivar
- VP: Rene Buch
- Secretary/Treasurer: Robert Weber Federico
- Chairman: Lawrence Zbikowski

Management:
- Music Director/Conductor: Barbara Schubert
- Director Public Relations: Kristine Kohler-Hall

Specialized Field: Orchestra
Budget: $100,000
Performs At: Leon Mandel Hall
Affiliations: University of Chicago

1044
DANVILLE SYMPHONY ORCHESTRA
149 N Vermillion Street
Danville, IL 61832
Phone: 217-443-5300
Fax: 217-443-5313
e-mail: info@danvillesymphony.org
Web Site: www.danvillesymphony.org
Officers:
- President: Dr. Alice Marie Jacobs
- VP: Dr. Shawn Mallady
- Executive Director: Meda Bateman

Management:
- Music Director/Conductor: Jeremy Swerling
- Orchestra Manager: Stuart A. de Haro

Mission: To serve our community and to inspire it to achievement and excellence by presenting music at the highest possible levels of artistic excellence.
Utilizes: Dancers; Grant Writers; Guest Accompanists; Guest Choreographers; Guest Musical Directors; Guest Musicians; Guest Writers; Instructors; Multimedia; Sign Language Translators; Singers; Soloists
Founded: 1967
Specialized Field: Symphony; Orchestra; Chamber
Status: Semi-Professional; Nonprofit
Paid Staff: 2
Paid Artists: 80
Budget: $190,000
Income Sources: Illinois Council of Orchestras; Illinois Presenters Network
Performs At: High School Auditorium; David Palmer Civic Center
Seating Capacity: 1,700
Organization Type: Performing; Educational

1045
MILLIKIN-DECATUR SYMPHONY ORCHESTRA
Millikin University
1184 W Main
Decatur, IL 62522
Phone: 217-424-6300
Fax: 217-420-6652
Toll-free: 800-373-7733
e-mail: mluxner@mail.millikin.edu
Web Site: www.millikin.edu
Management:
- Music Director/Conductor: Michael Luxner
- Artistic Administrator: Nancy Freeman

Specialized Field: Orchestra
Budget: $150,000-$60,000
Performs At: Kirkland Center Theatre

1046
ELGIN SYMPHONY ORCHESTRA
20 DuPage Court
Elgin, IL 60120
Phone: 847-888-0404
Fax: 847-888-0400
e-mail: d.gallant@elginsymphony.org
Web Site: www.elginsymphony.org
Officers:
- President: Dr Jerry Cain
- Interim CEO: David Bearden

Management:
- Music Director: Robert Hanson
- Associate Conductor: Stephen Squires, ssquires@roosevelt.edu
- Education Coordinator: Randal Swiggum, rswiggum@wisc.edu
- Director of Business Administration: Doris Gallant
- Stage Manager: David Goldman

Founded: 1950
Specialized Field: Symphony; Orchestra

1047
ELMHURST SYMPHONY ORCHESTRA
PO Box 345
Elmhurst, IL 60126
Phone: 630-941-0202
Fax: 630-941-0627
e-mail: boxoffice@elmhurstsymphony.org
Web Site: www.elmhurstsymphony.org
Management:
- Music Director: Stephen Alltop
- Symphony Manager: Jennifer Thompson
- Executive Director: Cynthia Kraine

Founded: 1959
Specialized Field: Symphony; Orchestra
Paid Staff: 3
Volunteer Staff: 35
Paid Artists: 27
Non-paid Artists: 53
Budget: $250,000
Performs At: Hammerschmidt Memorial Chapel at Elmhurst College
Annual Attendance: 4,500
Facility Category: Chapel
Type of Stage: Closed Proscenium
Seating Capacity: 853

1048
CHICAGO PHILHARMONIC
1123 Emerson Street
Suite 207
Evanston, IL 60201
Phone: 847-866-6888
Fax: 847-866-6896
e-mail: info@chicagophilharmonic.org
Web Site: www.chicagophilharmonic.org
Officers:
- President: Dr. James Berkenstock
- Chairman: Paul Judy

Management:
- Music Director: Larry Rachleff
- Artistic Administrator: Barbara Haffner
- Executive Director: Donna Milanovich
- Bublik: Guillermo

Mission: The ensemble is dedicated to building new audiences for serious music by offering moderately priced concerts, at the highest professional level, in convenient venues. Its presentations of the full range symphonic works embody the excitement of live performances and exemplify a special relationship between performers and audiences.
Specialized Field: Orchestra
Budget: $260,000-$1,050,000
Performs At: Pick - Staiger Concert Hall

1049
DUPAGE SYMPHONY
PO Box 844
Glen Ellyn, IL 60566
Phone: 630-778-1003
Fax: 630-637-0230
e-mail: info@dupagesymphony.org
Web Site: www.dupagesymphony.org
Management:
- Music Director/Conductor: Barbara Schubert

INSTRUMENTAL MUSIC / Illinois

Business Manager: Doris Purdie
Mission: To provide area citizens an opportunity to hear live music; to offer a performance outlet for musicians.
Utilizes: Guest Artists
Founded: 1954
Specialized Field: Symphony; Orchestra; Chamber; Ensemble
Status: Non-Professional; Nonprofit
Paid Staff: 65
Income Sources: Illinois Council of Orchestras
Performs At: Dupage County Auditorium
Organization Type: Performing; Touring

1050
NEW PHILHARMONIC
College of DuPage
Fawell and Park Boulevards
Glen Ellyn, IL 60137
Phone: 630-942-4000
Fax: 630-790-9806
e-mail: raffel@cdnet.cod.edu
Web Site: www.home.cod.edu/atthemac
Management:
  Music Director: Kirk Muspratt
  Marketing Coordinator: Roland Raffel
Specialized Field: Orchestra
Budget: $150,000-$260,000
Seating Capacity: 800

1051
WHEATON SYMPHONY ORCHESTRA
344 Spring Avenue
Glen Ellyn, IL 60137-4826
Phone: 630-790-1430
Fax: 630-790-9703
e-mail: info@wheatonsymphony.org
Web Site: www.wheatonsymphony.org
Management:
  General Manager: Donald C Mattison
  Music Director: Kevin McMahon
Mission: Dedicated to performing the music of 19th and 20th-century composers which was composed for large orchestras.
Utilizes: Guest Musicians; Organization Contracts
Founded: 1959
Specialized Field: Symphony
Status: Non-Professional
Volunteer Staff: 2
Income Sources: American Symphony Orchestra League
Performs At: Auditorium
Type of Stage: Large In An Auditorium
Stage Dimensions: Large Holds Chorus & Orchestra
Seating Capacity: 700
Year Built: 1995
Organization Type: Performing

1052
CHAMBER MUSIC SOCIETY OF THE NORTH SHORE
319 Park Ave
Glencoe, IL 60022
Phone: 847-436-0587
e-mail: info@cms-ns.org
Web Site: www.cms-ns.org
Officers:
  President: Iris Cosnow
  Administrator: Sandra Weiss
Founded: 1984
Specialized Field: Chamber
Performs At: Pick-Staiger Concert Hall
Seating Capacity: 900

1053
ALTON SYMPHONY ORCHESTRA
PO Box 1205
Godfrey, IL 62002
Phone: 618-463-6933
Fax: 618-465-7435
e-mail: info@altonsymphony.org
Web Site: www.altonsymphony.org
Officers:
  President: Jerre Honke
  VP: Gayle Hill
  Treasurer: Anne Cacciottoli
  President Public Relations: Lynden Schuyler
  Secretary: Tom Johnson
Management:
  Music Director/Conductor: Leon Burke III
  Pops Concert Director: William Shane Williams
  Concertmaster: Deberah Haferkamp
  Concert Manager: Mark Landon
  Orchestra Manager: Elizabeth Zenk
  Stage Manager: Brian McKinney
Mission: To provide a training ground for the development of instrumental abilities of area musicians; to increase interest in orchestral music; to present concerts to the public.
Founded: 1945
Specialized Field: Symphony
Status: Non-Professional; Nonprofit
Budget: $2,000
Income Sources: Illinois Council of Orchestras, Private and Corporate Donations, Ticket Sales
Season: October-April
Performs At: Hatheway Hall; Lewis & Clark Community College
Organization Type: Performing

1054
MIDWEST YOUNG ARTISTS
878 Lyster Road
Highwood, IL 60040
Phone: 847-926-9898
Fax: 847-926-4787
e-mail: mya@mya.org
Web Site: www.mya.org
Officers:
  President: Richard Sugar
  VP: John Chipman
  Secretary: Tom Sharp
  Treasurer: Tom Drake
  Founder and Executive Director: Allan Dennis
Management:
  Director: Dr. Allan Dennis
  Director Administration: Karen Dennis
  Director Development: Richard Gage
  Auditions Coordinator: Chelsa Peterson
  Music Director: Robert Bassill
Founded: 1993
Specialized Field: Orchestra; Ensemble; Chamber; Jazz
Paid Staff: 6
Paid Artists: 18
Budget: $260,000-$1,050,000
Income Sources: Tuition; Ticket Sales; Program Ad Revenues
Performs At: Pick - Staiger Concert Hall
Affiliations: Illinois Council of Orchestras

1055
WEST SUBURBAN SYMPHONY
PO Box 565
Hinsdale, IL 60522
Phone: 630-887-7464
e-mail: info@westsubsymphony.org
Web Site: www.westsubsymphony.org
Management:
  Music Director: Peter Lipari
Mission: Offers Chicago-area audiences both intimate chamber music and grand works for symphony orchestra. Has inspires thousands of young people annually with the power of live music through special educational concerts and free concert admission for preteens. Provides a stage for outstanding local soloists and gives rewarding performance opportunities to volunteer players and singers annually.
Founded: 1947
Specialized Field: Orchestra

1056
LAKE FOREST SYMPHONY
900 North Shore Drive
Lake Forest, IL 60044
Phone: 847-295-2135
Fax: 847-295-2747
e-mail: info@lakeforestsymphony.org
Web Site: www.lakeforestsymphony.com
Officers:
  Treasurer: G Christopher Coffin
Management:
  Music Director: Alan Heatherington
  Interim Executive Director: Joanne Bernstein
  Controller: Gayle Heatherington
  Director Marketing: Pat Nissen
  Concertmaster: Ilya Kaler
Mission: Present five classical concerts during the regular season.
Utilizes: Guest Accompanists; Guest Musicians; Multimedia; Original Music Scores; Sign Language Translators; Singers
Founded: 1956
Specialized Field: Symphony; Orchestra
Paid Staff: 5
Volunteer Staff: 1
Budget: $1.3 million
Income Sources: Donations; Ticket Sales
Performs At: James Lumber Center For The Perfoming Arts
Annual Attendance: 4,000-5,000
Type of Stage: Thrust
Seating Capacity: 600

1057
CEDARHURST CHAMBER MUSIC
PO Box 923
Mount Vernon, IL 62864
Phone: 618-242-1236
Fax: 618-242-9530
e-mail: Shar@midwest.net
Web Site: www.cedarhurst.org
Management:
  Executive Director: Sharon Bradham
Mission: To generate enthusiastic participation in and support for the performing arts in Southern Illinois and surrounding region.
Utilizes: Artists-in-Residence; Collaborating Artists; Collaborations; Commissioned Composers; Commissioned Music; Curators; Educators; Five Seasonal Concerts; Guest Writers; Multimedia; Organization Contracts; Original Music Scores; Sign Language Translators; Special Technical Talent; Theatre Companies; Touring Companies
Founded: 1979
Specialized Field: Orchestra; Chamber; Ensemble; Ethnic Music
Status: Professional; Nonprofit
Paid Staff: 4

INSTRUMENTAL MUSIC / Illinois

Volunteer Staff: 12
Income Sources: Chamber Music America; Illinois Presenters Network
Performs At: Main Gallery; Mitchell Art Museum
Annual Attendance: 1,000
Facility Category: Museum
Type of Stage: Permanent
Stage Dimensions: 16' x 24'
Seating Capacity: 350
Year Remodeled: 2008
Rental Contact: Brett Gibbs
Organization Type: Sponsoring

1058
NORTHBROOK SYMPHONY ORCHESTRA
899 Skokie Boulevard
#LL12
Northbrook, IL 60062
Phone: 847-272-0755
Fax: 847-729-5606
e-mail: info@northbrooksymphony.org
Web Site: www.northbrooksymphony.org
Officers:
   President: Mehdi Alister
   Treasurer: Martin Zeidman
   VP: Paul Mathis
   VP Marketing: James Kahan
   Secretary: Linda Wachtel
Management:
   Music Director: Lawrence Rapchak
   General Manager: JC Wacholz
   VP Development: Judith Gelleerd
   Director: Elsa Fischer
Mission: To offer classical music concerts at an affordable price as well as outreach programs.
Utilizes: Collaborations; Educators; Guest Accompanists; Guest Composers; Guest Instructors; Guest Writers; Instructors; Multimedia; Original Music Scores; Sign Language Translators; Singers; Soloists
Founded: 1980
Specialized Field: Classical; Symphony; Orchestra; Educational
Paid Staff: 2
Volunteer Staff: 30
Paid Artists: 75
Non-paid Artists: 25
Budget: $260,000-$1,050,000
Income Sources: Ticket Sales; Foundations; Corporate & Individual Donations; Special Events
Performs At: Sheely Center for the Performing Arts
Affiliations: CHG Music Alliance; Illinois Council of Orchestra; American Symphony Orchestra League
Annual Attendance: 10,000
Seating Capacity: 1,484

1059
SYMPHONY OF OAK PARK & RIVER FOREST
PO Box 3564
Oak Park, IL 60303
Phone: 708-218-2648
Fax: 708-524-9892
e-mail: KCM908@aol.com
Web Site: www.symphonyoprf.com
Officers:
   Board President: David Leehey
Management:
   Music Director: Jay Friedman
   General Manager: Beth Gavriel
   Personnel Manager: Beth Gavriel
Specialized Field: Orchestra
Budget: $35,000-$100,000

1060
ILLINOIS PHILHARMONIC ORCHESTRA
377 Artists Walk
Park Forest, IL 60466
Phone: 708-481-7774
Fax: 708-481-7998
e-mail: ED@ipomusic.org
Web Site: www.ipomusic.org
Management:
   Music Director: Carmon DeLeone
   Executive Director: Edmund Feingold
Specialized Field: Orchestra; Jazz
Budget: $260,000-$1,050,000

1061
PEORIA SYMPHONY ORCHESTRA
101 State Street
Peoria, IL 61602
Phone: 309-671-1096
Fax: 309-637-7388
e-mail: arobertson@peoriasymphony.org
Web Site: www.peoriasymphony.org
Officers:
   President: Pam Johnson
   VP: Bob Parkhurst
   Treasurer: Kent Malone
   Secretary: Katharine Francis
   Board of Director: Sharon Amdall
Management:
   Music Director: George Stelluto
   Executive Director: Susan Hoffman
   Development Manager: Gloria Dearborn
   Stage Manager: Greg Etzel
   Director of Development: Andrea Robertson
Mission: We provide excellent performances of fine music to a large and diverse audience in a variety of settings. Through a team effort of musicians, volunteers, staff and boards, we develop aggressive programs of education, marketing, and development. Cooperative efforts with local organizations enable us to enrich the mind, life, and culture which is the soul of our community.
Utilizes: Guest Musicians; Guest Writers; Multimedia
Specialized Field: Orchestra
Budget: $950,000
Performs At: Peoria Civic Center

1062
QUINCY SYMPHONY ORCHESTRA
200 N 8th Street
Suite 102
Quincy, IL 62301
Phone: 217-222-2856
Fax: 217-222-2869
e-mail: qsoa@adams.net
Web Site: www.qsoa.org
Officers:
   President: Alan Steigelman
   VP: Ron Davis
   Secretary: Barbara Mitchell
   Treasurer: Lucas King
Management:
   General Manager: Jane Pollet
   Managerial Assistant: Sandi Terford
   Officer Assistant: Laura Kammerer
   Office Assistant: Laura Kammerer
Mission: To provide the area with fine orchestral music; to offer local musicians the opportunity to perform; to provide educational programs.
Utilizes: Fine Artists; Guest Composers; Guest Musical Directors; Guest Musicians; Guest Writers; Instructors; Lyricists; Multimedia; Sign Language Translators; Singers
Founded: 1947
Specialized Field: Symphony; Orchestra; Chamber
Status: Non-Professional; Nonprofit
Paid Staff: 45
Volunteer Staff: 40
Budget: $130,000
Income Sources: Grants; Donations; Tickets
Performs At: Quincy Junior High School Auditorium
Organization Type: Performing; Resident; Educational

1063
AUGUSTANA SYMPHONY ORCHESTRA
639 38 Street
Rock Island, IL 61201-2296
Phone: 800-798-8100
Fax: 309-794-7678
e-mail: webmaster@augustana.edu
Web Site: www.augustana.edu
Management:
   Music Director/Conductor: Daniel Culver
   Department Chair: Jon Hurty
Specialized Field: Orchestra; Chamber; Band; Ensemble
Budget: $35,000
Performs At: Centennial Hall

1064
MENDELSSOHN CLUB
406 N. Main Street
Rockford, IL 61103-6810
Phone: 815-964-9713
Fax: 815-964-9929
e-mail: info@mendelssohnpac.org
Web Site: www.mendelssohnclub.org
Officers:
   Executive Director: Kathleen Montgomery
   Marketing Coordinator: Elise Houck
Management:
   Executive Director: Beverly Broyles
   Finance Director: Gordon Pierson
   Music Director: Stephen Squires
   Personnel Manager: Scott Metlicka
   Assistant Director: Linda Smith
Mission: To promote, support and present quality music for all.
Founded: 1884
Specialized Field: Classical
Paid Staff: 5
Volunteer Staff: 45
Paid Artists: 41
Non-paid Artists: 406
Affiliations: Rockford Area Arts Council; Illinois Arts Council
Facility Category: Auditorium with Stage
Stage Dimensions: 18'x 40'
Seating Capacity: 220
Year Built: 1952
Year Remodeled: 2002

1065
ROCKFORD AREA YOUTH SYMPHONY ORCHESTRA
711 N Main Street
Rockford, IL 61103
Phone: 815-965-0049
Fax: 815-965-0642
e-mail: info@rockfordsymphony.com
Web Site: www.rockfordsymphony.com
Officers:
   President: Stephen Martin
   VP: Steven Nailor
   Treasurer: Greg Harlan
   Secretary: Thomas Sandquist
   Executive Director: Julie Thomas

INSTRUMENTAL MUSIC / Illinois

Management:
- **RSO Musical Director/Conductor:** Steven Larsen
- **RSO Youth Orchestra Conductor:** Daniel Black
- **Production Manager:** Curt Johnsen
- **Personnel Manager:** Matthew Cataladi

Utilizes: Soloists
Founded: 1965
Specialized Field: Youth Symphony; Educational
Paid Staff: 1
Paid Artists: 6
Non-paid Artists: 65
Budget: $260,000-$1,050,000
Income Sources: Grants; Ticket sales; Individual gifts; Sponsorshipos
Performs At: Coronado Theatre

1066
ROCKFORD SMYPHONY ORCHESTRA
711 North Main Street
Rockford, IL 61103
Phone: 815-965-0049
Fax: 815-965-0642
e-mail: info@rockfordsymphony.com
Web Site: www.rockfordsymphony.com
Officers:
- **President:** Stephen Martin
- **VP:** Steven Nailor
- **Treasurer:** Greg Harlan
- **Secretary:** Thomas Sandquist
- **Executive Director:** Julie Thomas

Management:
- **RSO Musical Director/Conductor:** Steven Larsen
- **RSO Youth Orchestra Conductor:** Daniel Black
- **Production Manager:** Curt Johnsen
- **Personnel Manager:** Matthew Cataladi

Mission: Committed more than ever to fulfilling its mission to educate and to entertain the people of northern Illinois through symphonic music performances of the highest artistic excellence.
Founded: 1943
Specialized Field: Orchestra

1067
SKOKIE VALLEY SYMPHONY ORCHESTRA
9501 Skokie Boulevard
Skokie, IL 60077
Phone: 847-679-9501
Fax: 847-679-1879
e-mail: customerservice@northshorecenter.org
Web Site: www.northshorecenter.org
Officers:
- **President Board Of Directors:** Kathryn Canny
- **Artistic VP:** Karen Frost
- **Administrative VP:** Sara Diaguardi

Management:
- **Music Director:** Francesco Miliato
- **General Manager:** Michael Pauken
- **Office Manager:** Carolyn Adams
- **Technical Director:** Frank Rose

Mission: Our community symphony, the Skokie Valley Symphony Orchestra, was founded in 1962 by musicians who wanted to enrich the lives of others through music.
Founded: 1962
Specialized Field: Symphony Music
Budget: $35,000-$100,000
Income Sources: Ticket sales; Donations; Grants
Affiliations: Illinois Council of Orchestra's
Facility Category: Concert Hall
Type of Stage: Proscenium
Seating Capacity: 839
Year Built: 1996

1068
ILLINOIS SYMPHONY ORCHESTRA
524 « E. Capitol Avenue
Springfield, IL 62701
Phone: 217-522-2838
Fax: 217-522-7374
Toll-free: 800-401-7222
e-mail: info@ilsymphony.org
Web Site: www.ilsymphony.org
Management:
- **Executive Director:** Trevor Orthmann
- **Director of Development & Marketing:** Theresa Lage
- **Development & Marketing Associate:** Jenna Hahn
- **Operations Manager:** Victoria J.Moore
- **Admin Assistant:** Linda Prince

Utilizes: Collaborations; Commissioned Composers; Grant Writers; Guest Accompanists; Guest Companies; Guest Musicians; Guest Writers; Instructors; Original Music Scores; Singers
Specialized Field: Orchestra
Budget: $260,000-$1,050,000

1069
ILLINOIS CHAMBER SYMPHONY
12 S 1st Avenue
St Charles, IL 60174
Phone: 630-377-6423
Fax: 630-377-3105
Officers:
- **President:** Charles Brown
- **VP:** Jeffrey Hunt
- **Secretary/Treasurer:** William Simmons

Management:
- **Music Director:** Stephen Squires
- **Marketing Director:** Robert Murphy
- **Executive Director:** Catherine Squires
- **Personnel Manager:** Amy Scarlato

Mission: Promoting live classical music of the highest artistic caliber and furthering cultural growth in the state of Illinois.
Founded: 1983
Specialized Field: Orchestra; Chamber
Status: Professional; Nonprofit
Income Sources: Indiana Orchestra Consortium; Kane County Tourism Association; American Symphony Orchestra League; Fox Valley Arts Council
Performs At: Norris Cultural Arts Center; Baker Methodist Church
Organization Type: Performing

1070
SINFONIA DA CAMERA
909 W Oregon
Suite 202
Urbana, IL 61801
Phone: 217-244-4350
Fax: 217-244-8419
e-mail: sinfonia@illinois.edu
Web Site: www.sinfonia.illinois.edu
Officers:
- **Secretary:** Jonathan Goodwin
- **Co-Chair:** Rick Murphy

Management:
- **Music Director:** Ian Hobson
- **General Manager:** Rebecca Hill Riley

Specialized Field: Orchestra
Budget: $150,000-$260,000
Performs At: Foellinger Great Hall

1071
WAUKEGAN SYMPHONY ORCHESTRA & CONCERT CHORUS
2000 Belvidere Street
Waukegan, IL 60085
Phone: 847-360-4700
Fax: 847-662-0592
Web Site: www.waukeganparks.org
Management:
- **Music Director:** Stephen Blackweldor

Specialized Field: Symphony
Paid Staff: 2
Paid Artists: 6
Non-paid Artists: 60
Budget: $100,000-$150,000
Income Sources: Waukegan Park District; Corporation; Grants
Performs At: Orlin D. Trapp Auditorium
Affiliations: Waukegan Park District
Annual Attendance: 1500
Facility Category: Auditorium
Type of Stage: Proscenium
Seating Capacity: 1800

1072
CHINESE CLASSICAL ORCHESTRA AND EDUCATIONAL PROGRAM
PO Box 5275
Woodridge, IL 60517-0275
Phone: 630-910-1551
Fax: 630-910-1561
Web Site: www.chinesemusic.net
Officers:
- **President:** Dr. Sin-yan Shen
- **VP:** Kok-Koon Ng

Management:
- **Director Concert Lecture Department:** Dr. Yuan-Yuan Lee
- **Music Director:** Shen Sin-yan

Mission: The music society is the largest Chinese music educational service institution in North America; publishes the Chinese Music Monograph Series, the international journal of Chinese Music, and educational material on music and acoustics.
Utilizes: Guest Artists; Guest Companies; Singers
Founded: 1976
Specialized Field: Symphony; Orchestra; Chamber; Ensemble; Ethnic Music; Folk Music; Electronic; Live Electronic
Status: Professional; Nonprofit
Budget: $260,000-$1,050,000
Organization Type: Performing; Touring; Resident; Educational; Sponsoring

1073
SILK AND BAMBOO ENSEMBLE
Chinese Music Society of North America
PO Box 5275
Woodridge, IL 60517-0275
Phone: 630-910-1551
Fax: 630-910-1561
Web Site: www.chinesemusic.net
Management:
- **Music Director/Conductor:** Dr. Sin-yan Shen
- **Manager:** Johson Hsu

Mission: To create chamber music of the 21st century; to perform works utilizing silk and bamboo instrumentation and just intervals; to tour internationally and in the US year round.
Utilizes: Guest Artists; Guest Companies; Singers
Founded: 1981
Specialized Field: Chamber; Ensemble; Ethnic Music
Status: Professional; Nonprofit

INSTRUMENTAL MUSIC / Indiana

Budget: $260,000-$1,050,000
Organization Type: Performing; Touring; Educational

1074
WOODSTOCK MOZART FESTIVAL
PO Box 734
Woodstock, IL 60098
Phone: 630-983-7072
Fax: 630-717-7782
e-mail: mozartfest@aol.com
Web Site: www.mozartfest.org
Officers:
   Interim President: Edward L. Streit
Management:
   General Director: Anita Whalen
   Artistic Advisor: Mark Peskanov
   Conductor: Arthur Arnold
Utilizes: Guest Accompanists; Guest Composers; Guest Musicians; Multimedia; Original Music Scores
Founded: 1987
Specialized Field: Mozart
Paid Staff: 1
Budget: $185,000
Income Sources: Individuals, Corporations, Foundations
Facility Category: Woodstock Opera House (121 Van Buren Street)
Seating Capacity: 412
Year Built: 1889
Year Remodeled: 1977

Indiana

1075
ANDERSON SYMPHONY ORCHESTRA ASSOCIATION
1124 Meridian Plaza
Anderson, IN 46016
Phone: 765-644-2111
Fax: 317-642-1477
Toll-free: 888-644-9490
e-mail: aso@andersonsymphony.org
Web Site: www.andersonsymphony.org
Officers:
   Adminisrative Assistant: RuthAnn Ginder
   President: David Shade
   Secretary: Cindy Lanane
   Treasurer: Brett Spangler
Management:
   Music Director: Richard Sowers
   Executive Director: Dana Stone, dana@andersonsymphony.org
Founded: 1967
Specialized Field: Orchestra
Paid Staff: 74
Budget: $150,000-$260,000
Performs At: Paramount Theatre Centre

1076
BLOOMINGTON SYMPHONY ORCHESTRA
718 N. Walnut Street
Bloomington, IN 47402
Mailing Address: PO Box 1823
Phone: 812-331-2320
Fax: 812-331-2320
e-mail: bso@bloomingtonsymphony.com
Web Site: www.bloomingtonsymphony.com
Officers:
   President: Joseph R. Carr
Management:
   Music Director: Charles Latshaw
   Office Manager: Kathy Barton
   Concertmaster: Juli Enzinger
   Office Manager: Anna Coogan
   Production Manager: Erik Hitchcock
Mission: Strives to provide serious music to the community; to encourage interest in hearing and participating in serious music; and to offer a professional environment for performing that music for both amateurs and professionals.
Utilizes: Arrangers; Collaborations; Community Members; Composers; Grant Writers; Guest Composers; Guest Musical Directors; Guest Musicians; Instructors; Local Artists & Directors; Local Talent; Multimedia; Music; Organization Contracts; Sign Language Translators; Soloists; Students; Student Interns; Visual Designers
Specialized Field: Orchestra
Paid Staff: 2
Non-paid Artists: 70

1077
CARMEL SYMPHONY ORCHESTRA
760 3rd Avenue SW
Suite 102
Carmel, IN 46032
Mailing Address: PO Box 761, Carmel, Indiana 46082-0761
Phone: 317-844-9717
Fax: 317-844-9916
e-mail: info@carmelsymphony.org
Web Site: www.carmelsymphony.org
Officers:
   President & CEO: Alan Davis
   Chairman: Lawrence E. Lawhead
   Secretary: Bradford S. Grabow
   Treasurer: A. Ridgeway Miller
   Past Chair: Paul G. Reis
Management:
   Artistic Director: Dr. David Bowden
   Office Manager: Denise Ryan
   Personnel Manager: Rachel Gries
Mission: Committed to enhancing our community's quality of life in a fically responsible manner through creative, artistically excellent performances and educational experiences for diverse audiences of all ages.
Founded: 1975
Specialized Field: Symphony
Status: Nonprofit
Paid Staff: 3
Volunteer Staff: 14
Paid Artists: 13
Non-paid Artists: 60
Budget: $150,000-$175,000
Income Sources: Box Office; Grants; Donations
Affiliations: American Symphony Orchestra League
Annual Attendance: 31,000
Organization Type: Performing; Educational

1078
COLUMBUS INDIANA PHILHARMONIC
315 Franklin St
Columbus, IN 47201
Phone: 812-376-2638
Fax: 812-376-2567
e-mail: info@columbus-in-phil.org
Web Site: www.thecip.org
Officers:
   President: Kaye Ellen Conner
   VP: Ronald F Sewell
   Treasurer: Robert Williamson
   Secretary: Bruce Pollert
   Immediate Past President: Jane B. Hoffmeister
Management:
   Communication Manager: Christopher Gordon
   Administration Manager: Laura Baker
   Music Director: David Bowden
   Executive Director: Margaret Powers
   Artistic Director: Ruth Dwyer
Mission: To enhance the quality of life in our community so that all citizens have the opportunity to be touched by live, classical music in a manner and style meaningful to them.
Founded: 1986
Specialized Field: Symphony
Status: Semi-Professional; Nonprofit
Budget: $260,000-$1,050,000
Income Sources: American Symphony Orchestra League; Indiana Orchestra Consort; Indiana Arts Commission; Columbus Area Arts Council
Performs At: Columbus North Erne Auditorium
Facility Category: Orchestra Professional
Organization Type: Performing; Educational; Sponsoring

1079
EVANSVILLE PHILHARMONIC ORCHESTRA
401 S.E. Sixth Street
Suite 105
Evansville, IN 47708
Mailing Address: PO Box 84, Evansville, IN 47701-0084
Phone: 812-425-5050
Fax: 812-426-7008
e-mail: evphil@evansvillephilharmonic.org
Web Site: www.evansvillephilharmonic.org
Officers:
   President: Chris Wolking
   VP: Sharon Kazee
   Secretary: Susan Vaughn
   Treasurer: Susan Elkington
   Board of Director: Danny Bateman
Management:
   Executive Director: Glenn Roberts
   Director Marketing: Lynette McClusky
   Sales Manager: Leslie Brown
Mission: To provide the Tri-State Area of Southern Indiana, Illinois and Kentucky with symphonic music of the highest quality; to present programs for adult audiences and students in the school systems.
Founded: 1934
Specialized Field: Symphony; Orchestra; Chamber; Ensemble
Status: Professional
Paid Staff: 18
Budget: $2,000,000
Income Sources: American Symphony Orchestra League; Indiana Orchestra Consortium; Evansville Arts & Education Council
Performs At: Victory Theatre
Seating Capacity: 1,800
Year Remodeled: 1998
Organization Type: Performing; Educational

1080
FORT WAYNE PHILHARMONIC ORCHESTRA
4901 Fuller Dr.
Fort Wayne, IN 46835
Phone: 260-481-0777
Fax: 219-456-8555
e-mail: info@fwphil.org
Web Site: www.FortWaynePhilharmonic.com
Officers:
   Chairman: Carol Lindquist
   Secretary: Jan Wilhelm

INSTRUMENTAL MUSIC / Indiana

Treasurer: Jeff Sebeika
VC: Eleanor Marine
Vice Chair: Alan Riebe
Management:
  Music Director: Andrew Constantine
  Assistant Conductor: David Borsnold
  Director Concert Operations: Laura Bordner
  Director Finance: Beth Conrad
Founded: 1924
Specialized Field: Orchestra; Educational
Paid Staff: 22
Paid Artists: 88
Budget: $4,100,000
Income Sources: Box office, grants, private donations
Performs At: Embassy Theatre
Affiliations: America Symphony Orchestra League, Indiana Orchestra Consortium
Annual Attendance: 220,000
Type of Stage: Proscenium
Seating Capacity: 2434
Year Built: 1928

1081
DEPAUW UNIVERSITY CHAMBER SYMPHONY
PO Box 37
Greencastle, IN 46135-0037
Phone: 765-658-4800
Fax: 765-658-4401
Toll-free: 800-447-2495
e-mail: music@depauw.edu
Management:
  Conductor: Orcenith Smith
Specialized Field: Orchestra; Band; Jazz
Budget: $6,000
Performs At: Kresge Auditorium
Type of Stage: Concert Stage
Stage Dimensions: 60'x 40'
Year Built: 1976
Rental Contact: 765-658-4828 Byron Craft

1082
BUTLER UNIVERSITY SYMPHONY ORCHESTRA
4600 Sunset Ave
Indianapolis, IN 46208
Phone: 800-368-6852
Fax: 317-940-9258
Toll-free: 800-368-6852
e-mail: info@butler.edu
Officers:
  Admissions Representative: Kathy Lang
  President: James M Danko
Management:
  Conductor and Orchestra Director: Richard Auldon Clark
  Music Chair: Andrea Gullickson
Specialized Field: Orchestra; Jazz; Ensemble
Performs At: Clowes Memorial Hall

1083
INDIANAPOLIS CHAMBER ORCHESTRA
32 East Washington Street
Suite 600
Indianapolis, IN 46204
Phone: 317-639-4300
Fax: 317-262-1159
e-mail: iso@indianapolis Symphony.org
Web Site: www.indianapolissymphony.org
Officers:
  Chairman: John R Thornburgh
  Secretary: Carolyn S Hardman
  Treasurer: Holly M Pantzer
  VP/General Manager: Thomas R Ramsey
  VP Finance/Administration: Susan L Prenatt
  VP Marketing: Ellen Schantz
Management:
  Music Director: Krzysztof Urbanski
  Principal Pops Conductor: Jack Everly
Specialized Field: Orchestra
Budget: $260,000-$1,050,000
Seating Capacity: 2,200

1084
INDIANAPOLIS SYMPHONY ORCHESTRA
45 Monument Circle
Indianapolis, IN 46204
Phone: 317-639-4300
Fax: 317-262-1159
e-mail: iso@indianapolis Symphony.org
Web Site: www.indianapolissymphony.org
Officers:
  Chairman: John R Thornburgh
  Secretary: Carolyn S Hardman
  Treasurer: Holly M Pantzer
  Music Director: Krzysztof Urbanski
  Principal Pops Conductor: Jack Everly
Management:
  VP/General Manager: Thomas R Ramsey
  VP Finance/Administration: Susan L Prenatt
  VP Marketing: Ellen Schantz
  VP Development: Kevin Garvey
  Director Public Relations: Thomas N Akins
  Music Director: Krzysztof Urbanski
  Conductor: Jack Everly
Mission: To perform live symphonic music at the highest artistic level; to promote, support and sustain interest in symphonic music in Indiana; to present programs that enrich, entertain and challenge all audiences.
Utilizes: Guest Artists; Singers
Founded: 1930
Specialized Field: Symphony; Orchestra; Chamber; Ensemble
Status: Professional; Nonprofit
Paid Staff: 60
Paid Artists: 90
Budget: $23 million
Income Sources: Ticket Sales; Contributions; Endowment
Performs At: Hilbert Circle Theatre
Affiliations: ASOL
Annual Attendance: 500,000+
Type of Stage: Proscenium
Stage Dimensions: 50x40
Seating Capacity: 1786
Year Built: 1916
Year Remodeled: 2002
Organization Type: Performing; Touring; Resident; Educational

1085
INTERNATIONAL VIOLIN COMPETITION OF INDIANAPOLIS
32 E Washington Street
Suite 1320
Indianapolis, IN 46204
Phone: 317-637-4574
Fax: 317-637-1302
e-mail: ivci@violin.org
Web Site: www.violin.org
Management:
  Executive Director: Glen Kwok
  Operations Director: Mindy Miller
  Development Director: Mary Jane Sobera
Mission: Recognizes, rewards and promote's the world's finest young classical violinists and encourages understanding, appreciation and support of the violin repertoire by a large and diverse audience. Utilizes its world prominence to bring international attention to Indianapolis, and maintains its efforts to be a visible and collaborative member of the arts communities in Indianapolis and Indiana.
Founded: 1979
Specialized Field: Chamber; International
Paid Staff: 4

1086
NEW WORLD YOUTH SYMPHONY ORCHESTRA
32 East Washington Street
Suite 950
Indianapolis, IN 46204
Phone: 317-408-4492
Fax: 317-236-4902
Web Site: www.nwyso.org
Officers:
  President: Gregory L. Pemberton
  VP Sales: Kerry Drake
  Artistic Director: Susan Kitterman
  Owner: Gabriel Harley
  Board Member: Matthew Rhea
Management:
  Founder & Artistic Director: Susan Kitterman
  Music Director: Nanna G Vaughn
  Executive Director: Adam Bodony
  Page: Jennifer
Specialized Field: Orchestra; Chamber; Ensemble
Budget: $100,000-$150,000
Performs At: Circle Theater

1087
PHILHARMONIC ORCHESTRA OF INDIANAPOLIS
32 East Washington Street
Suite 900
Indianapolis, IN 46204
Phone: 317-229-2367
Fax: 317-229-7087
e-mail: info@philharmonicindy.org
Web Site: www.philharmonicindy.org
Officers:
  President: Deana Slater
  VP: Charlie Mullen
  Treasurer: David Holets
  Secretary: Laurel Bronson
Management:
  Concertmaster: Anne Bryant
  Artistic Director: Orcenith Smith
Mission: We provide educational opportunities to the community and enhance the musical growth of volunteer membership.
Utilizes: Guest Artists
Founded: 1940
Specialized Field: Symphony; Orchestra; Chamber
Status: Non-Professional; Nonprofit
Paid Staff: 3
Paid Artists: 7
Non-paid Artists: 80
Budget: $100,000-$150,000
Performs At: Caleb Mills Hall
Organization Type: Performing; Resident; Educational

1088
KOKOMO SYMPHONY
1216 W. Sycamore Street
Kokomo, IN 46904-1659

All listings are in alphabetical order by state, then city, then organization within the city.

INSTRUMENTAL MUSIC / Indiana

Mailing Address: PO Box 6115, Kokomo, IN 46901
Phone: 765-236-0251
Fax: 765-453-0048
e-mail: kokomosymphony@sbcglobal.net
Web Site: www.kokomosymphony.org
Officers:
  President: Ray Biederman
  Secretary: Barbara Lennon
  Treasurer: Amy Lucas
Management:
  Executive Director: Paul L Wood
  Music Director: Jos, Valencia
Mission: To maintain a local orchestra, chorus and youth orchestra; to provide the highest quality of music under the direction of a capable conductor; to provide musical education programs in underserved areas.
Utilizes: Collaborations; Commissioned Music; Dance Companies; Guest Accompanists; Guest Directors; Guest Musicians; Instructors; Lyricists; Multimedia; Sign Language Translators; Singers
Founded: 1971
Specialized Field: Symphony; Orchestra; Chamber
Status: Nonprofit
Paid Staff: 2
Volunteer Staff: 460
Paid Artists: 65
Budget: $239,000
Income Sources: American Symphony Orchestra League; Indiana Orchestra Consortium; Indiana Advocates for the Arts
Performs At: Havens Auditorium
Affiliations: ASOL
Annual Attendance: 5400
Facility Category: Auditorium
Seating Capacity: 905
Organization Type: Performing; Touring; Resident; Educational; Sponsoring

1089
LAFAYETTE SYMPHONY
111 N 6th Street
Lafayette, IN 47901
Mailing Address: PO Box 52, Lafayette, IN 47902-0052
Phone: 765-742-6463
Fax: 765-742-2375
e-mail: executivedirector@lafayettesymphony.org
Web Site: www.lafayettesymphony.org
Officers:
  President: Phillip Fiorini
  VP: Cara Hines-Pham
  Treasurer: John Thieme
  Secretary: Shirley West
Management:
  Executive Director: Sara Mummey
  Music Director & Conductor: Nick Palmer
  Operations Manager: Debra Steinhauer
  Business Manager/Ticket Sales: Rockie Allee
  Development Director: Ken Bootsma
  Education Director: Allison Edberg
  Personnel Manager: Kara Stolle
Mission: The mission of the Lafayette Symphony Orchestra is to enrich the community by engaging audiences and inspiring a love of music through exciting live symphony performances, innovative programming, and educational outreach.
Utilizes: Guest Artists; Multimedia
Founded: 1951
Specialized Field: Symphony; Orchestra
Status: Semi-Professional; Nonprofit
Budget: $260,000-$1,050,000
Income Sources: American Symphony Orchestra League; Indiana Orchestra Consortium
Performs At: Long Center for the Performing Arts

Organization Type: Performing; Educational

1090
TIPPECANOE CHAMBER MUSIC SOCIETY
638 N Street
Lafayette, IN 47901
Phone: 765-409-3516
Fax: 765-583-2386
Web Site: www.tippecanoechambermusic.org
Management:
  Artistic Director: Verna Aloe
Mission: Fosters and promotes the appreciation of chamber music. Promotes the pursuit of musical excellence in the area's youth through diverse educational programs, including master classes, coaching and special school programs.
Founded: 1997
Specialized Field: Chamber
Status: Nonprofit

1091
MARION PHILHARMONIC ORCHESTRA
428 S. Washington Street
Suite 201
Marion, IN 46952
Mailing Address: PO Box 272, Marion, IN 46952
Phone: 765-662-0012
Fax: 765-662-0012
e-mail: mpo@marionphil.org
Web Site: www.marionphil.org
Officers:
  President: Dr. Shederick Whipple
  First VP: Dr. Todd Guy
  Secretary: Dr. Tammie Huntington
  Treasurer: Luke Mitchell
Management:
  Music Director: Alexander Platt
  Executive Director: Mary Kirby
Utilizes: Guest Artists
Founded: 1969
Specialized Field: Orchestra
Paid Staff: 80
Budget: $150,000-$260,000
Performs At: Marion High School Auditorium

1092
MUNCIE SYMPHONY ORCHESTRA
2000 W. University Ave
AC 112
Muncie, IN 47306
Phone: 765-285-5531
Fax: 765-285-9128
e-mail: munciesymphonyorchestra@gmail.com
Web Site: www.munciesymphony.com
Officers:
  President: Roberto J A Darroca
  VP: Don Whitaker
  Past President: Paul C Powers
  Secretary/Treasurer: TJ Bush
Management:
  Executive Director: Alena McKenzie
  Administrative Coordinator: Judy Cowling
  Concertmaster: Mary Kothman
Mission: To stimulate, educate, and entertain audiences in East Central Indiana, and to provide meaningful musical experience for professional, community, and student musicians, through the performance of fine music and other activities.
Utilizes: Guest Artists
Founded: 1948
Specialized Field: Symphony
Status: Semi-Professional; Nonprofit
Paid Staff: 11

Paid Artists: 80
Income Sources: American Symphony Orchestra League; American Society of Composers, Authors and Publishers; Broadcast Music Incorporated; Indiana Orchestra Consortium
Performs At: Emens Auditorium
Affiliations: Ball State University
Organization Type: Performing; Educational

1093
NORTHWEST INDIANA SYMPHONY ORCHESTRA AND SOCIETY
1040 Ridge Road
Munster, IN 46321
Phone: 219-836-0525
Fax: 219-836-0690
e-mail: info@NISOrchestra.org
Web Site: NISOrchestra.org
Officers:
  President: Christopher Morrow
  Treasurer/Secretary: Rick Suetanoff
Management:
  Music Director/Conductor: Kirk Muspratt
  Executive Director: John M Cain
  Marketing Director: Tricia Hernandez
  Orchestra Manager: Phil Bauman
  Director of Finance: Chris McCabe
Mission: Dedicated to presenting subscription, special, and children's concerts and maintaining the Youth Orchestra and Chorus.
Utilizes: Guest Musicians
Founded: 1941
Specialized Field: Symphony; Orchestra; Chamber; Ensemble
Status: Professional; Nonprofit
Paid Staff: 14
Paid Artists: 75
Non-paid Artists: 120
Budget: $1.2 million
Income Sources: Grants; Donations; Ticket Sales
Performs At: Star Plaza Theatre; Merrillville
Organization Type: Performing; Resident; Educational

1094
CHANTICLEER STRING QUARTET
944 Woods Road
Richmond, IN 47374
Phone: 765-966-6214
Fax: 765-973-4570
e-mail: cklemp @ hotmail .com
Web Site: www.portlandworkshop.com
Mission: Sharing in creative ways with people in all walks of life and of all ages the beauty of chamber music.
Founded: 1977
Specialized Field: Chamber
Status: Professional; Nonprofit
Organization Type: Performing; Touring; Educational

1095
RICHMOND SYMPHONY ORCHESTRA
612 East Grace Street,
Richmond, IN 47374
Mailing Address: PO Box 982
Phone: 765-966-5181
Fax: 765-973-3346
e-mail: rso@richmondsymphony.org
Officers:
  First VP: Karen Roeper
  Second VP: Sue Miller
  VP: Diana Pappin
  Secretary: Bobbi Whitlock
  Treasurer: Carol Smyth
Management:

INSTRUMENTAL MUSIC / Iowa

Music Director/Conductor: Guy Victor Bordo
President: Diiana Pappin
Utilizes: Dance Companies; Guest Accompanists; Guest Companies; Guest Directors; Guest Musical Directors; Guest Musicians; Multimedia; Original Music Scores; Sign Language Translators; Singers; Theatre Companies
Founded: 1957
Specialized Field: Orchestra
Budget: $260,000-$1,050,000
Performs At: Civic Hall Performing Arts Center

1096
SOUTH BEND SYMPHONY ORCHESTRA
127 N. Michigan Street
South Bend, IN 46601
Phone: 219-232-6343
Fax: 219-232-6627
e-mail: executive@southbendsymphony.org
Web Site: sbsymphony.org
Officers:
   President: George Soper
   VP: Harriet Hamer
   Secretary: Suzanne Cole
Management:
   Music Director/Conductor: Tsung Yeh
   Executive Director: Jane E Hunter
   Director of Operation: Earle Perez
Mission: To perform classical, pops, chamber orchestra, and educational programs.
Utilizes: Actors; Artists-in-Residence; Choreographers; Collaborating Artists; Collaborations; Commissioned Composers; Commissioned Music; Composers-in-Residence; Dance Companies; Dancers; Educators; Fine Artists; Grant Writers; Guest Accompanists; Guest Artists; Guest Choreographers; Guest Composers; Guest Directors; Guest Musical Directors; Guest Musicians; Guest Soloists; Instructors; Local Artists; Lyricists; Multimedia; Original Music Scores; Poets; Resident Professionals; Sign Language Translators; Singers; Soloists; Student Interns; Special Technical Talent
Founded: 1932
Specialized Field: Symphony; Orchestra
Paid Staff: 11
Paid Artists: 95
Budget: $1,050,000-$3,600,000
Income Sources: Sales; Contributions; Investments
Performs At: Morris Performing Arts Center
Affiliations: ASOL
Annual Attendance: 150,000
Type of Stage: Proscenium
Seating Capacity: 2,500
Year Built: 1920
Year Remodeled: 2000
Cost: 16,000,000
Rental Contact: Dennis Andres

1097
TERRE HAUTE SYMPHONY ORCHESTRA
25 N 6th Street
Terre Haute, IN 47807
Phone: 812-242-8476
Fax: 812-234-6060
Toll-free: 800-878-8476
e-mail: thsymphony@aol.com
Web Site: www.terrehautesymphony.org
Officers:
   President: Wieke Benjamin
   Secretary: Ted Piechocinski
   Treasurer: David Mitchell
Management:
   Executive Director: Jean Elliott Williams
   Music Director: David Bowden
   Librarian/Resident Composer: Daniel Powers
   Personnel Manager: Laura Q Savage
   Personnel Manager: Chad Roseland
   Bloomington Contractor: Gesa Kordes
   Stage Manager: Alice Yuritic
   House Manager: Emily L Fisher
   Concertmaster: Matvey Lapin
Mission: To increase the enjoyment and cultural enrichment of audiences in the Wabash Valley area by maintaining an orchestra dedicated to excellent performances of symphonic literature.
Utilizes: Collaborations; Dance Companies; Five Seasonal Concerts; Guest Accompanists; Guest Companies; Guest Musical Directors; Guest Musicians; Instructors; Lyricists; Multimedia; Organization Contracts; Original Music Scores; Sign Language Translators; Singers; Soloists; Special Technical Talent
Founded: 1926
Specialized Field: Symphony
Status: Professional
Paid Staff: 8
Paid Artists: 80
Budget: $345,000
Income Sources: Private; Corporate; State
Performs At: Tilson Auditorium; Indiana State University
Annual Attendance: 7,500
Facility Category: Music hall
Seating Capacity: 1478
Year Remodeled: 2002
Rental Contact: 812-237-3737 Hulman Center
Organization Type: Performing; Educational; Run-Outs

1098
VALPARAISO UNIVERSITY SYMPHONY ORCHESTRA
VU Center for the Arts
Valparaiso, IN 46383
Phone: 219-464-5455
Fax: 219-464-5244
e-mail: joseph.bognar@valpo.edu
Web Site: www.valpo.edu
Officers:
   Department Chair: Joseph Bognar
Management:
   Conductor: Dennis Friesen-Carper
Specialized Field: Orchestra
Budget: $35,000

Iowa

1099
AMES TOWN AND GOWN CHAMBER MUSIC ASSOCIATION
3222 Oakland Street
Ames, IA 50014
Phone: 515-292-3891
e-mail: ForrestPS@aol.com
Web Site: www.amestownandgown.org
Officers:
   President: Kevin Amidon
   VP: David Giese
   Secretary: Janet Alcorn
   Treasurer: Tom Jackson
Management:
   Artistic Director: Paula Forrest Helmuth
Mission: The presentation of four to six chamber music concerts annually.
Founded: 1950
Specialized Field: Chamber; Ensemble
Status: Nonprofit
Income Sources: Iowa State University Music Department
Performs At: Iowa State University Music Hall Recital Hall
Organization Type: Sponsoring

1100
CENTRAL IOWA SYMPHONY
PO Box 1080
Ames, IA 50014-1080
Phone: 641-269-4916
Fax: 515-292-4115
e-mail: info@cisymphony.org
Web Site: www.cisymphony.org
Officers:
   VP: Julie Stroud
   General Manager: Jamie Nieman
   Treasurer: Tom Jackson
   President: Sam Wormley
Management:
   Music Director/Conductor: Eric L McIntyre
   Personnel Manager: Brian Bunn
Mission: To foster quality performance of orchestral music for the people of the Central Iowa communities; to offer satisfying musical experience for its musicians; and to provide leadership in the arts community.
Specialized Field: Orchestra
Budget: $35,000-$100,000
Performs At: Ames City Hall Auditorium

1101
WATERLOO-CEDAR FALLS SYMPHONY ORCHESTRA
Gallagher-Bluedorn Center
Cedar Falls, IA 50614
Phone: 319-273-3373
Fax: 319-273-3363
e-mail: information@wcfsymphony.org
Web Site: www.wcfsymphony.org
Officers:
   President: Dave Braton
   Past President: Mike McCrary
   Secretary: David Mason Jr
   Treasurer: Louis Fettkether
Management:
   Executive Director: Rachel Ford
   Artistic Director & CEO: Jason Weinberger
   Finance Manager: Judy Hughes
   Concertmaster: Anita Tucker
   VP Planning: Thomas Romanin
Mission: To educate, entertain, and enrich listeners by presenting performances of the highest quality.
Utilizes: Collaborations; Guest Accompanists; Guest Artists; Guest Composers; Guest Musical Directors; Guest Musicians; Instructors; Multimedia; Original Music Scores; Sign Language Translators; Soloists
Founded: 1929
Specialized Field: Symphony; Orchestra; Chamber; Ensemble
Status: Nonprofit
Paid Staff: 7
Income Sources: American Symphony Orchestra League; American Society of Composers, Authors and Publishers; Broadcast Music Incorporated
Performs At: Kersenbrock Auditorium
Annual Attendance: 15,000
Facility Category: Performing Arts Center
Seating Capacity: 1,500
Year Built: 2000
Organization Type: Performing

INSTRUMENTAL MUSIC / Iowa

1102
CEDAR RAPIDS SYMPHONY ORCHESTRA
119 Third Avenue SE
Cedar Rapids, IA 52401
Phone: 319-366-8206
Fax: 319-366-5206
Web Site: www.crsymphony.org
Management:
  Executive Director: Marc D Levy
  Music Director/Conductor: Christian Tiemeyer
Founded: 1922
Specialized Field: Symphony; Orchestra; Chamber; Ensemble
Status: Professional; Nonprofit
Budget: $1,050,000-$3,600,000
Income Sources: American Symphony Orchestra League
Performs At: Paramount Theatre
Organization Type: Performing; Educational

1103
CLINTON SYMPHONY ORCHESTRA
PO Box 116
Clinton, IA 52733-0116
Phone: 319-243-2049
e-mail: execdirector@clinsonsymphony.org
Web Site: www.clintonsymphony.org
Officers:
  President: Richard J Phelan
Management:
  Executive Director: Robert Whipple
  Concertmaster: Jerry Henry
Specialized Field: Orchestra; Chamber
Budget: $35,000-$100,000

1104
QUAD CITY SYMPHONY ORCHESTRA ASSOCIATION
327 Brady Street
Davenport, IA 52801
Mailing Address: PO Box 1144
Phone: 563-322-0931
Fax: 563-322-6864
e-mail: info@qcsymphony.com
Web Site: www.qcsymphony.com
Officers:
  President: R Scott Vooren
  Executive VP: Susan Honsen
  Secretary: Gary L. Medd
  Treasurer: Peter McAndrews
  Honorary Chairman: Isador I. Katz
Management:
  Executive Director: Lance O Willett
  Orchestra Manager: Dennis Loftin
  Music Director/Conductor: Mark Russell Smith
  Marketing Director: Karen Brooke
  Interim Executive Director: Amy Best
  Stage Manager: Ryan Kinney
Mission: Dedicated to supporting symphonic performances; committed to fostering, stimulating and encouraging orchestral ensemble and other music through developmental programs and scholarships.
Utilizes: Guest Companies; Guest Musicians; Multimedia; Original Music Scores; Singers
Founded: 1915
Specialized Field: Symphony; Orchestra
Status: Professional; Nonprofit
Paid Staff: 6
Volunteer Staff: 375
Paid Artists: 90
Budget: $1,600,000
Income Sources: Ticket Sales; Contributions; Fund-raising
Performs At: Centennial Hall; Rock Island; Adler Theater; Davenport
Affiliations: American Symphony Orchestra League; Illinois Council of Orchestra
Annual Attendance: 40,000
Facility Category: Theatres
Type of Stage: Proscenium
Seating Capacity: 2,350; 1,620
Year Built: 1931
Year Remodeled: 1984
Organization Type: Performing; Educational

1105
QUAD CITY YOUTH STRING ENSEMBLE
327 Brady Street
Davenport, IA 52801
Mailing Address: PO Box 1144, Davenport, IA. 52805
Phone: 563-322-0931
Fax: 563-322-6864
e-mail: info@qcsymphony.com
Web Site: www.qcsymphony.com
Officers:
  President: R Scott Vooren
  Executive VP: Susan Honsen
  Secretary: Gary L. Medd
  Treasurer: Peter McAndrews
  Honorary Chairman: Isador I. Katz
Management:
  Executive Director: Lance O Willett
  Orchestra Manager: Dennis Loftin
  Music Director/Conductor: Mark Russell Smith
  Marketing Director: Karen Brooke
  Interim Executive Director: Amy Best
  Stage Manager: Ryan Kinney
Utilizes: Multimedia
Specialized Field: Youth Orchestra; Ensemble; Chamber
Paid Staff: 1
Budget: $5,000
Performs At: Adler Theatre; Centennial Hall
Annual Attendance: 500
Facility Category: Recital Hall

1106
LUTHER COLLEGE SYMPHONY ORCHESTRA
Luther College
700 College Drive
Decorah, IA 52101-1045
Phone: 563-387-1209
Fax: 563- 38—107
Toll-free: 800-369-8863
e-mail: selfje01@luther.edu
Management:
  Director/Choral: Arnold Craig
  Director/Orchestra: Daniel Baldwin
Specialized Field: Orchestra; Ensemble; Jazz
Budget: $35,000
Performs At: Center for Faith & Life

1107
DES MOINES SYMPHONY
221 Walnut Street
Des Moines, IA 50309
Phone: 515-280-4000
Fax: 515-280-4005
e-mail: info@dmsymphony.org
Web Site: www.dmsymphony.org
Officers:
  President: Audrey Rosenberg
  VP: Dr. John Ghrist
  Treasurer: Lawrence K Hedlin
Management:
  Music Director/Conductor: Joseph Giunta
  Executive Director: Richard L Early
  Artistic Administrator: John Roloff
  Managing Director, Symphony Academy: Joshua Barlage
Mission: To create and engage our community in extraordinary musical experiences and outstanding educational opportunities.
Utilizes: Guest Artists
Founded: 1937
Specialized Field: Symphony; Orchestra; Chamber; Ensemble
Status: Professional; Nonprofit
Paid Staff: 9
Budget: $1,700,000
Income Sources: Ticket Sales; Grants; Private Donations
Performs At: Civic Center of Greater Des Moines
Affiliations: American Symphony Orchestra League
Annual Attendance: 80,000
Facility Category: Civic Center
Type of Stage: Proscenium
Stage Dimensions: 61'x30'
Seating Capacity: 2,653
Year Built: 1979
Organization Type: Performing; Educational

1108
DRAKE SYMPHONY ORCHESTRA
2507 University Avenue
Des Moines, IA 50311
Phone: 515-271-2011
Fax: 515-271-2558
Toll-free: 800-44 -3725
e-mail: Clarence.Padilla@drake.edu
Web Site: www.drake.edu/artsci
Management:
  Orchestral Studies Director: John Canarina
  Muisc Chair: Clarence Padilla
Specialized Field: Orchestra; Ensemble; Jazz
Budget: $35,000
Performs At: Sheslow Auditorium

1109
DUBUQUE SYMPHONY ORCHESTRA
2728 Asbury Road
Suite 900
Dubuque, IA 52004
Phone: 563-557-1677
Fax: 563-557-9841
Toll-free: 866-803-9280
e-mail: info@dubuquesymphony.org
Web Site: www.dubuquesymphony.org
Officers:
  President: Keith Bibelhausen
  Preseident-Elect: Alan Avery
  Executive Director: Jeff Goldsmith
  Director Development: Jean Tucker
Management:
  Music Director: William Intriligator
Mission: To provide quality performances; to offer educational programs in the field of classical music.
Founded: 1959
Specialized Field: Symphony; Orchestra; Chamber; Ensemble
Status: Semi-Professional; Nonprofit
Income Sources: Symphony League
Performs At: Five Flags Center Theatre
Organization Type: Performing; Resident; Educational; Sponsoring

INSTRUMENTAL MUSIC / Kansas

1110
DES MOINES COMMUNITY ORCHESTRA
PO Box 1796
Johnston, IA 50306
Phone: 515-964-4562
e-mail: webmaster@desmoinescommunityorchestra.org
Web Site: www.desmoinescommunityorchestra.org
Officers:
  President: Steve Urion
  VP: Josh Whitver
  Treasurer: Laura Valle
  Secretary: Kendall Childs
  Social: Deb Gordley
  Music Acquisition: Rich Gordley
  Fund Raising: George Mosley
Management:
  Music Director/Conductor: Carl Johnson
Specialized Field: Orchestra
Budget: $35,000
Performs At: Hoyt Sherman Place

1111
SOUTHEAST IOWA SYMPHONY ORCHESTRA
601 N Main St
Mount Pleasant, IA 52641
Phone: 319-385-6352
Fax: 319-385-6286
e-mail: seiso@iwc.edu
Web Site: www.seiso.us
Officers:
  Treasurer: Ed VanderLinden
  VP: Margaret Hansen
  Secretary: Ed Kropa
  President: Ruth Seim
Management:
  Conductor/Music Director: Robert McConnell
  Manager: Joy Rayman Anderson
Mission: Dedicated to educating, encouraging and performing orchestral music in Southeast Iowa.
Founded: 1950
Specialized Field: Symphony; Orchestra
Status: Non-Professional; Nonprofit
Paid Staff: 40
Income Sources: American Symphony Orchestra League; Broadcast Music Incorporated; American Society of Composers, Authors and Publishers
Performs At: James Madison Auditorium; Iowa Wesleyan Chapel Auditorium
Organization Type: Performing

1112
OTTUMWA SYMPHONY ORCHESTRA
PO Box 173
Ottumwa, IA 52501
Phone: 641-682-4812
Fax: 515-682-8255
e-mail: theottumwasymphonyorchestra@gmail.com
Web Site: www.ottumwasymphonyorchestra.net
Officers:
  President: Maggie Morrissey
  Secretary: Diana Dowling
  Treasurer: Mick Lawson
  Associatev Treasurer: Kim Ardueser
  Manager: Patty Babb
Management:
  Manager: Patricia Babb
  Music Director: Dr. Eric McIntyre
  Conductor: Dr. Carey H. Bostian II
  Music Director: Dr. Carey H. Bostian II
Specialized Field: Orchestra
Budget: $35,000-$100,000
Performs At: St. John Auditorium

1113
CENTRAL COLLEGE COMMUNITY ORCHESTRA
Central College, Music Department
812 University
Pella, IA 50219
Phone: 877-462-3687
Fax: 641-628-5316
e-mail: lawsone@central.edu
Management:
  Director of Music Connection: Rita Burghart
Specialized Field: Orchestra; Ensemble
Budget: $1,000
Performs At: Douwstra Performing Arts Center
Facility Category: Auditorium
Seating Capacity: 650
Rental Contact: Lowell Olivier

1114
NORTHWEST IOWA SYMPHONY ORCHESTRA
498 4th Avenue NE
Sioux Center, IA 51250
Phone: 712-722-6230
e-mail: niso@dordt.edu
Web Site: www.niso.dordt.edu
Officers:
  Development Director: James Koldenhoven
Management:
  Music Director: Henry Duitman
  General Manager: Norman Gaines
Specialized Field: Orchestra
Budget: $35,000
Seating Capacity: 1,200

1115
SIOUX CITY SYMPHONY ORCHESTRA
520 Pierce Street
Suite 375
Sioux City, IA 51101
Mailing Address: PO Box 754, Sioux City, IA 51102-0754
Phone: 712-277-2111
Fax: 712-252-0224
e-mail: info@siouxcitysymphony.org
Web Site: www.siouxcitysymphony.org/
Officers:
  President: Juliet Everist
  Board VP: Dr. James Rossiter
  Board Treasurer: Rusty Clark
  Board Secretary: Marilyn Hagberg
  Director at Large: Eunice Acker
Management:
  Music Director/Conductor: Ryan Haskin, ryan@scsym.org
  Executive Director: David G. Krogh, dkrogh@scsym.org
  Operations Manager: Richard Bogenrief
Mission: To enhance the quality of life in Siouxland through symphonic music
Founded: 1915
Specialized Field: Symphony; Orchestra; Ensemble
Status: Professional; Nonprofit
Paid Staff: 5
Paid Artists: 100
Budget: $800,000
Income Sources: Sponsors; Grants; Individual Giving; Ticket Sales
Performs At: Orpheum Theatre
Seating Capacity: 2,500
Year Built: 1927
Year Remodeled: 2001
Cost: $9,200,000
Rental Contact: Orpheum Theatre Jennifer Canny
Organization Type: Performing; Resident; Educational

1116
SIOUXLAND YOUTH SYMPHONY ORCHESTRA
520 Pierce Street
Suite 375
Sioux City, IA 51101
Mailing Address: PO Box 754, Sioux City, IA 51102-0754
Phone: 712-277-2111
Fax: 712-252-0224
e-mail: info@siouxcitysymphony.org
Web Site: www.siouxcitysymphony.org
Officers:
  President: Juliet Everist
  Board VP: Dr. James Rossiter
  Board Treasurer: Rusty Clark
  Board Secretary: Marilyn Hagberg
  Director at Large: Eunice Acker
Management:
  Music Director/Conductor: Ryan Haskin
  Executive Director: David G. Krogh
  Operations Manager: Richard Bogenrief
Founded: 1955
Specialized Field: Youth Orchestra
Facility Category: College Auditorium

1117
WARTBURG COMMUNITY SYMPHONY ORCHESTRA
Wartburg College
222 9th Street NW
Waverly, IA 50677-0903
Phone: 319-352-8370
Fax: 319-352-8501
e-mail: daniel.kaplunas@wartburg.edu
Web Site: www.wartburg.edu/symphony
Management:
  Music Director/Conductor: Dr. Daniel Kaplunas
Founded: 1952
Specialized Field: Symphony; Orchestra
Volunteer Staff: 20
Paid Artists: 5

Kansas

1118
EMPORIA SYMPHONY ORCHESTRA
Emporia State University
105 Beach Hall Campus Box 4029
Emporia, KS 66801
Phone: 620-341-5431
Fax: 620- 34—560
Management:
  Music Director: Allan Comstock
  Chairman: Marie Miller
Specialized Field: Orchestra

1119
HAYS SYMPHONY ORCHESTRA
Fort Hays State University
Hays, KS 67601
Phone: 913-628-5360
Fax: 913-628-4096
Web Site: www.ellisco.org/symphony.htm
Officers:
  Chairman: David Thomas
  Secretary: Jenny Lomas

INSTRUMENTAL MUSIC / Kentucky

President: John Georgiadis
VP: Andrew Condon
Chairman: David Thomas
Treasurer: Stephen Gates
Management:
    Conductor/Music Director: Christine Webber
Mission: Offering Western Kansas musical and cultural activities and providing music students with artistic and educational opportunities.
Utilizes: Singers
Founded: 1920
Specialized Field: Symphony; Orchestra
Status: Nonprofit
Paid Staff: 2
Income Sources: American Society of Composers, Authors and Publishers; American Symphony Orchestra League
Performs At: Beach/Schmidt Performing Arts Center
Organization Type: Performing; Educational

1120
HUTCHINSON SYMPHONY ASSOCIATION
PO Box 1241
Hutchinson, KS 67504-1241
Phone: 620-728-0246
Fax: 620-728-8157
e-mail: keithtematt@sbcglobal.net
Web Site: www.hutchsymphony.org
Management:
    Conductor: Richard Koshgarian
Specialized Field: Orchestra
Budget: $100,000

1121
NEWTON MID-KANSAS SYMPHONY ORCHESTRA
Bethel College
PO Box 245
North Newton, KS 67117
Phone: 316-772-3265
Fax: 316-284-5286
e-mail: info@nmkso.org
Web Site: www.nmkso.org
Officers:
    President: Bonnie Tandoc
    Treasurer: Keith Neufeld
    Secretary: Rachel Newell
Management:
    Principal Conductor: Diego Sanchez Haase
    Music Director: Thomas W Douglas
    General Manager: Jill Gatz
    Assistant Manager: Parker Stanley
    General Manager: Jill Gatz
Founded: 1956
Specialized Field: Orchestra
Paid Staff: 1
Volunteer Staff: 20
Paid Artists: 2

1122
YOUTH SYMPHONY ASSOCIATION OF KANSAS
7301 Mission Road
Suite 333
Prairie Village, KS 66208
Phone: 913-722-6810
Fax: 913-722-6806
e-mail: ysymph@crn.org
Officers:
    Program Manager: Ingrid Stolzel
    President: Stephen Kort
Management:
    Music Director/Conductor: Dr. Glenn Block
    Executive Director: Mary Corneil
Mission: To provide educational opportunities for young musicians by performing before community-wide audiences and by inspiring excellence in performance.
Specialized Field: Youth Orchestra; Ensemble; Chamber
Budget: $260,000-$1,050,000

1123
TOPEKA SYMPHONY
PO Box 2206
Topeka, KS 66601-2206
Phone: 785-232-2032
Fax: 785-232-6204
e-mail: tso@TopekaSymphony.org
Web Site: www.topkeasymphony.org
Officers:
    President: Michael Lennen
    Treasurer: Eric Rea
    Secretary: Jayne Cafer
Management:
    Music Director/Conductor: John Strickler
    General Manager: Kathy Maag
    Admin. Assistant: Charles Baker
Mission: To encourage and cultivate appreciation and support for fine music in northeast Kansas by presenting performances of high quality and by providing educational and performance opportunities for youth.
Founded: 1946
Specialized Field: Orchestra
Paid Staff: 3
Paid Artists: 88

1124
WICHITA SYMPHONY
Century II Concert Hall
225 W Douglas
Wichita, KS 67202
Mailing Address: Suite 207
Phone: 316-267-7658
Fax: 316-267-1937
e-mail: info@wso.org
Web Site: www.wso.org
Officers:
    President: Phillip S Frick
    Secretary: Kurt A Harper
    Treasurer: Daniel A Flynn
Management:
    General Manager: Mitchell Berman
    Music Director/Conductor: Daniel Hege
    Executive Director: Don Reinhold
    Operations Manager: Anne Marie C Brown
    Business Manager: Linda Marshall
Mission: To rpovide Southcentral Kansas with the highest quality of cultural, educational and entertainment presentations through the maintencance of a symphony orchestra and related activities.
Utilizes: Guest Accompanists; Guest Lecturers; Guest Musicians; Multimedia; Singers
Founded: 1944
Specialized Field: Symphony; Orchestra; Chamber
Status: Professional; Nonprofit
Paid Staff: 6
Volunteer Staff: 350
Paid Artists: 95
Budget: $2.15 million
Income Sources: Ticket Sales; Donations; Program Advertising; Performance Fees; Investment Income
Performs At: Century II Concert Hall
Facility Category: Convention Center
Stage Dimensions: 49'x60'x29'
Seating Capacity: 2,250
Year Built: 1969
Organization Type: Performing; Touring; Educational; Sponsoring

Kentucky

1125
BOWLING GREEN-WESTERN SYMPHONY ORCHESTRA
416 E Main Street
Bowling Green, KY 42101
Phone: 270-782-2787
Fax: 270-782-2894
Web Site: www.wku.edu/Dept/Academic/AHSS/Music/
Management:
    Music Director/Conductor: Jooyong Ahn
Mission: Offering the people of Southern Kentucky classical music.
Founded: 1982
Specialized Field: Symphony; Orchestra; Chamber
Status: Semi-Professional; Nonprofit
Paid Staff: 35
Income Sources: American Symphony Orchestra League
Performs At: Van Meter Auditorium
Organization Type: Performing; Resident; Educational

1126
CENTRAL KENTUCKY YOUTH ORCHESTRAS
161 N Mill Street
Lexington, KY 40507
Phone: 859-254-0796
Fax: 859-254-9466
e-mail: ckyo@ckyo.org
Web Site: www.ckyo.org
Officers:
    President: Tracy Lovan
    Past President: Julie Quick
    Secretary: Jackie Sugarman
    Treasurer: Bob Stadleman
    Board Member: Lester Diaz
Management:
    Music Director: Daniel Chetel
    General Manager: Amelia Groetsch
Mission: Dedicated to the musical education and growth of its student members. Provides performance opportunities, motivational workshops, small group instruction, travel, mentoring and social interaction.
Specialized Field: Youth Orchestra

1127
CHAMBER MUSIC SOCIETY OF CENTRAL KENTUCKY
University of Kentucky
Lexington, KY 40506
Mailing Address: Box 12032
Phone: 859-278-3245
e-mail: wcthompson@insightbb.com
Web Site: www.cmsck.org
Officers:
    President: Charles Thompson
    VP: Roger Chesser
    Treasurer: Pat Lawrence
    Secretary: E. Randy Daniel
Mission: The purpose of this society is to foster and promote chamber music in Central Kentucky and the organization remains the only one in the area devoted exclusively to the presentation of music written for small ensembles.
Founded: 1950
Specialized Field: Chamber

INSTRUMENTAL MUSIC / Kentucky

Status: Nonprofit

1128
LEXINGTON PHILHARMONIC SOCIETY
161 N Mill Street
Lexington, KY 40507
Phone: 859-233-4226
Fax: 859-233-7896
Toll-free: 888-494-4226
e-mail: tickets@lexphil.org
Web Site: www.lexingtonphilharmonic.org
Officers:
  President: Gregory K Jenkins
  President Elect: Larry Deener
  Foundation Chairman: John Burrus
  Secretary: Ronald Saykaly
  Guild President: Doris King Shepherd
  Guild President Elect: Cindy Leveridge
  Chamber of Commerce: Barbara Wagner
Management:
  Music Director/Conductor: Scott Terrell
  Executive Director: Allison Kaiser
  Orchestra Representative: Elaine Cook
  General & Personnel Manager: Kelly Whelan
Mission: To offer entertainment and enjoyment to the local community.
Utilizes: Guest Accompanists
Founded: 1961
Specialized Field: Symphony; Chamber; Ensemble
Status: Nonprofit
Income Sources: Lexington Arts & Cultural Council; Kentucky Arts Council
Performs At: Singletary Center for the Arts
Organization Type: Performing; Educational
Comments: Special Seating and Facilities; Program in Large Type: Assistive Listening Devices

1129
LOUISVILLE BACH
4607 Hanford Lane
Louisville, KY 40207
Phone: 502-585-2224
Fax: 502-893-7954
Web Site: www.louisvillebachsociety.org
Management:
  Music Director: Melvin Dickinson
Mission: To perform the choral and orchestral music of Bach, as well as other baroque, modern, classical and romantic composers.
Founded: 1964
Specialized Field: Orchestra
Status: Nonprofit
Paid Staff: 80
Income Sources: Kentucky Arts Council; Greater Louisville Fund for the Arts; American Federation of Musicians
Performs At: University of Louisville
Organization Type: Performing; Touring; Resident; Educational

1130
LOUISVILLE CHAMBER MUSIC SOCIETY
University of Louisville
School of Music
Louisville, KY 40292
Phone: 502-852-6907
Fax: 502-852-0520
Toll-free: 800-334-UOFL
e-mail: gomusic@louisville.edu
Web Site: http://www.louisvillechambermusic.org/
Officers:
  Artist/Program Committee Chairman: Dr. Acton Ostling, Jr
Specialized Field: Chamber
Performs At: Recital Hall

1131
LOUISVILLE ORCHESTRA
323 West Broadway
Suite 700
Louisville, KY 40202
Phone: 502-587-8681
Fax: 502-589-7870
e-mail: info@louisvilleorchestra.org
Web Site: www.louisvilleorchestra.org
Officers:
  Chairman of the Board: Joe Pusateri
  President: Chuck Maisch
  CEO: Robert A Birman
Management:
  Operations Director: Toni M Robinson, Esq
  Music Director: Jorge Mester
  Principal Pops Coordinator: Robert Bernhardt
  Concertmaster: Michael Davis
Mission: To educate, enlighten, entertain, excite and enrich listeners of all ages by presenting live orchestral performances of the highest possible quality to audiences in Louisville, throughout the Commonwealth of Kentucky, and in the surrounding states.
Founded: 1937
Specialized Field: Symphony; Orchestra; Chamber
Status: Professional; Nonprofit
Paid Artists: 70
Budget: $7,000,000
Performs At: Whitney Hall; Brown Theatre; Olge Center; Louisville Palace
Organization Type: Performing; Touring; Educational; Sponsoring

1132
LOUISVILLE YOUTH ORCHESTRA
PO Box 997
Louisville, KY 40201-0997
Phone: 502-896-1851
Fax: 502-896-1862
e-mail: info@lyo.org
Web Site: www.lyo.org
Management:
  Music Director: Jason Seber
  Executive Director: Melody Welsh
  Conductor: Frederick C Speck
Mission: To provide high quality musical experiences and the opportunity of performing for the benefit of the community and its young musicians regardless of race, creed, or economic circumstances.
Utilizes: Guest Artists
Founded: 1958
Specialized Field: Youth Orchestra
Status: Nonprofit
Income Sources: Greater Louisville Fund for the Arts; Youth Performing Arts Council
Performs At: Youth Performing Arts Center
Organization Type: Performing; Educational

1133
KENTUCKY SYMPHONY ORCHESTRA
540 Linden Avenue
PO Box 72810
Newport, KY 41071
Mailing Address: PO Box 72810, Newport, KY 41072
Phone: 859-431-6216
Fax: 859-431-3097
e-mail: info@kyso.org
Web Site: www.kyso.org
Officers:
  President: Jeffrey Rosenstiel
  Secretary: Paula Steiner
  Treasurer: Paul Houston
Management:
  Music/Executive Director: James R Cassidy
  General Manager: Angela Williamson
  Personnel Manager: Jennifer King
Mission: To culturally enrich, educate and entertain the residents of Northern Kentucky and Greater Cincinnati through unique and innovative presentations designed to make symphonic music and the concert experience, accessible and affordable.
Utilizes: Guest Accompanists; Multimedia
Founded: 1992
Specialized Field: Orchestra
Paid Staff: 5
Volunteer Staff: 79
Paid Artists: 96
Non-paid Artists: 10
Budget: $600,000
Income Sources: Sponsorship; Grant; Ticket Sales; Gala Proceeds
Performs At: Performing Arts Center And Amphitheatre
Annual Attendance: 35,000
Seating Capacity: 405-6,000

1134
OWENSBORO SYMPHONY ORCHESTRA
211 East Second Street
Owensboro, KY 42303
Phone: 270-684-0661
Fax: 270-683-0740
e-mail: info@owensborosymphony.org
Web Site: www.owensborosymphony.org
Officers:
  President: David T Reynolds
  President Elect: Leslie Hines
  Secretary: Laura Ruth Edge
  Treasurer: Rodney Ellis
Management:
  Executive Director: Bill Price
  Music Director/Conductor: Nicholas Palmer
  General Manager: Paula Knott
  Operations Manager: Carl Davis
Mission: To enhance the cultural environment of Western Kentucky through performances of symphonic music.
Utilizes: Artists-in-Residence; Collaborations; Commissioned Composers; Commissioned Music; Dance Companies; Fine Artists; Guest Accompanists; Guest Artists; Guest Choreographers; Guest Companies; Guest Composers; Guest Directors; Guest Instructors; Guest Lecturers; Guest Musical Directors; Guest Musicians; Guest Writers; Instructors; Local Artists; Lyricists; Multimedia; Organization Contracts; Original Music Scores; Sign Language Translators; Singers; Soloists; Touring Companies
Founded: 1966
Specialized Field: Symphony; Orchestra
Status: Professional; Nonprofit
Paid Staff: 5
Volunteer Staff: 3
Paid Artists: 75
Budget: $759,000
Income Sources: American Symphony Orchestra League
Performs At: River Park Center
Annual Attendance: 7,400
Facility Category: Performing Arts Center
Seating Capacity: 1,482
Year Built: 1991
Rental Contact: Assistant Director Roxi Witt
Organization Type: Performing; Touring; Resident; Educational; Recording

INSTRUMENTAL MUSIC / Louisiana

1135
PADUCAH SYMPHONY ORCHESTRA
201 Broadway
Box 1763
Paducah, KY 42001
Mailing Address: PO Box 1763
Phone: 270-444-0065
Fax: 270-444-0456
Toll-free: 800-738-3727
e-mail: info@paducahsymphony.org
Web Site: www.paducahsymphony.org
Officers:
  President: Roger Truitt
  Jr. Past President: John Williams
  VP Finance: Lennis Thompson
  VP Education: Catherine Trampe
  Secretaty: Dick Holland
Management:
  Music Director & Conductor: Jordan Tang
  Artistic Director & Conductor: Raffaele Ponti
  Executive Director: Daniel Sene
  Patron Service Manager: Christey Brindley
  Marketing Manager: Craig Felker
Utilizes: Guest Musical Directors; Guest Musicians; High School Drama; Local Artists; Multimedia; Original Music Scores
Specialized Field: Orchestra
Paid Staff: 12
Volunteer Staff: 75
Paid Artists: 100
Budget: $400,000

Louisiana

1136
RAPIDES SYMPHONY ORCHESTRA
1101 Fourth Street
Suite 201
Alexandria, LA 71301
Phone: 318-442-9709
Fax: 318-484-4499
e-mail: manager@rapidessymphony.org
Web Site: www.rapidessymphony.org
Officers:
  President: Michael Truelove
  Vice President: Maggie Martin
  Treasurer: Terry Aubin
  Secretary: Kim Brady
Management:
  Conductor: William Kushner
  Music Director: Joshua Zona
Founded: 1967
Specialized Field: Orchestra
Paid Staff: 1
Volunteer Staff: 30
Non-paid Artists: 50

1137
BATON ROUGE SYMPHONY ORCHESTRA
7300 Highland Road
Baton Rouge, LA 70808
Mailing Address: PO Box 14209
Phone: 225-383-0500
Fax: 225-767-4609
Toll-free: 877-800-4099
e-mail: info@brso.org
Web Site: www.brso.org
Officers:
  President: Johnny Tate
  President Elect: Anthony Kurlas
  Director Marketing: Allen Wagner
  Chairman: John D'Angelo
  Secretary: Gwen Redding
  Treasurer: Harvey Schwartzberg
Management:
  Executive Director: Alan T. Hopper, ahopper@brso.org
  Director Operations/Education: Derrien Tolden, dtolden@brso.org
  Marketing & Development: Miriam Overton, moverton@brso.org
  Music Director / Conductor: Dr. Timothy W Muffitt
Mission: The mission of the Baton Rouge Symphony Orchestra is to develop and maintain a financially sound, first-class symphony orchestra with a regional and national profile which will provide education and cultural enrichment for the people of the Baton Rouge region and neighboring communities.
Founded: 1947
Specialized Field: Symphony; Orchestra; Chamber; Ensemble
Status: Nonprofit
Paid Staff: 6
Paid Artists: 84
Budget: $1.5 million
Income Sources: Individual And Corporate Gifts; Ticket Sales
Performs At: Riverside/Centroplex Theatre for Performing Arts
Affiliations: Louisiana Youth Orchestra; Baton Rouge Symphony League
Annual Attendance: 36,000
Seating Capacity: 1,905
Organization Type: Performing

1138
ACADIANA SYMPHONY ORCHESTRA
412 Travis Street
Lafayette, LA 70503
Mailing Address: PO Box 53632
Phone: 337-232-4277
Fax: 337-237-4712
e-mail: info@acadianasymphony.org
Web Site: www.acadianasymphony.org
Officers:
  Conservatory Director: Denise Melancon
Management:
  Music Director: Mariusz Smolij
  Executive Director: Timothy J Bergman
Mission: To promote music and music education with focus on the youth throughout the entire region of Acadiana.
Founded: 1984
Specialized Field: Orchestra
Paid Staff: 5
Paid Artists: 9

1139
LAKE CHARLES SYMPHONY
809 Kirby Street
Suite 210
Lake Charles, LA 70601
Phone: 337-433-1611
Fax: 337-433-1615
e-mail: info@lcsymphony.org
Web Site: www.lcymphony.org
Officers:
  President: Lucie Earhart
Management:
  Executive Director: Debbie Reed
  Fruge: Ashly
Founded: 1958
Specialized Field: Symphony; Orchestra
Status: Nonprofit
Paid Staff: 2
Volunteer Staff: 50
Paid Artists: 70
Affiliations: Southwest Regional Ballet Association

1140
MONROE SYMPHONY ORCHESTRA
PO Box 4353
Monroe, LA 71211-4353
Phone: 318-812-6761
Fax: 318-435-6761
e-mail: info@monroesymphonyorchestra.com
Web Site: www.bayou.com/symphony
Management:
  Music Director: Dr. Roger Jones
  Executive Director: Vicki Valenzano Pampe
  Executive Director: Mary Napoli
Mission: To provide the region with live symphonic music of quality and to educate the public about its music.
Founded: 1971
Specialized Field: Symphony; Orchestra

1141
LOUISIANA PHILHARMONIC ORCHESTRA
1010 Common Street
Suite 2120
New Orleans, LA 70112
Phone: 504-523-6530
Fax: 504-595-8468
e-mail: info@lpomusic.com
Web Site: www.lpomusic.com
Management:
  Managing Director: James Boyd
  Director of Artistic Planning: Jihyun Kim
  Operations Manager: Ron Bermingham
  Production and Stage Manager: Cherie Pons-Gunther
Mission: Strives to continue its artistic growth, continue its financial success, provide cultural enrichment to the community, as the only player-owned ochestra in the country.
Utilizes: Actors; Artists-in-Residence; Collaborating Artists; Collaborations; Educators; Five Seasonal Concerts; Grant Writers; Guest Accompanists; Guest Choreographers; Guest Companies; Guest Composers; Guest Directors; Guest Lecturers; Guest Musical Directors; Guest Musicians; Instructors; Lyricists; Multi Collaborations; Multimedia; Music; Organization Contracts; Original Music Scores; Resident Artists; Sign Language Translators; Singers; Soloists; Student Interns; Special Technical Talent; Theatre Companies; Touring Companies; Visual Arts
Founded: 1991
Specialized Field: Symphony; Orchestra
Paid Staff: 15
Volunteer Staff: 100
Paid Artists: 70
Budget: $4 million
Income Sources: Ticket Sales, Contributions, Grants
Season: September-May
Performs At: Orpheum Theater
Annual Attendance: 50,000
Facility Category: Theatre
Type of Stage: Orchestra
Seating Capacity: 1800
Year Built: 1921
Rental Contact: Jeff Montalbaro

1142
NEW ORLEANS CONCERT BAND
UNO Box 522
New Orleans, LA 70148-0522

Phone: 504-455-9380
e-mail: nocb@email.com
Web Site: www.neworleansconcertband.org
Officers:
President: Tiffany Adler
Management:
Conductor: Dr. Richard Dugser
Mission: An adult community band providing quality music at free concerts.
Founded: 1915
Specialized Field: Band; Wind Ensemble
Status: Professional; Non-Professional
Paid Artists: 80
Budget: $5,000
Income Sources: Dues, grants
Performs At: University of New Orleans Recital Hall
Affiliations: Association of Concert Bands
Annual Attendance: 10,000
Facility Category: University owned
Seating Capacity: 85
Year Built: 1965
Organization Type: Resident

1143
NEW ORLEANS JAZZ AND HERITAGE FOUNDATION
1205 N Rampart Street
New Orleans, LA 70116
Phone: 504-558-6100
Fax: 504-558-6122
Toll-free: 888-652-8751
e-mail: dmarshall@jazzandheritage.org
Web Site: www.nojhf.org
Officers:
Chief Administrative Officer: Marsha A. Boudy
Chief Financial Officer: Sheri LaBranche
Management:
Program Director: Sharon Martin
Executive Director: Don Marshall
Director of Programs: Scott Aiges
Development Associate: Ann DeLorenzo
Mission: The presentation and preservation of Louisiana's culture and music.
Founded: 1970
Specialized Field: Band; Jazz; Historical Music
Status: Nonprofit
Paid Staff: 12
Organization Type: Performing

1144
SHREVEPORT SYMPHONY ORCHESTRA
619 Louisiana Avenue
Suite 400
Shreveport, LA 71101
Mailing Address: PO Box 205
Phone: 318-222-7496
Fax: 318-222-7490
e-mail: office@shreveportsymphony.com
Web Site: www.shreveportsymphony.com
Officers:
President: Elizabeth Siskron
VP: Robert Rhoads
Secretary: Laura McLemore
Treasurer: Chris Haskew
Chairperson: Virginia Shehee
VP Education/Outreach: Janie Samuels
VP Development: Donald A Webb
Member-At-Large: Debbie Rathburn
Executive Director: Lois Robinson
Management:
Music Director/Conductor: Michael Butterman
Marketing Director: Lois Baldwin
Finance Director: Debbie Graham
Personnel Manager: Theresa Bridges

Mission: Dedicated to providing the three-state area with the highest possible quality musical performances.
Utilizes: Choreographers; Collaborations; Commissioned Music; Dance Companies; Dancers; Educators; Guest Accompanists; Guest Artists; Guest Composers; Guest Musical Directors; Guest Writers; Instructors; Local Artists; Lyricists; Multimedia; Organization Contracts; Sign Language Translators; Singers; Student Interns
Founded: 1947
Specialized Field: Symphony; Orchestra; Chamber; Ensemble
Status: Professional; Nonprofit
Paid Staff: 12
Budget: $1.2 million
Income Sources: American Symphony Orchestra League, Annual Fund, Ticket Sales
Performs At: Civic Theatre
Affiliations: American Symphony Orchestra League; Chamber of Commerce
Type of Stage: Proscenium
Seating Capacity: 1,737
Year Built: 1963
Organization Type: Performing; Touring; Educational

Maine

1145
BANGOR SYMPHONY ORCHESTRA
PO Box 1441
Bangor, ME 04402-1441
Phone: 207-942-5555
Fax: 207-990-1272
Toll-free: 800-639-3221
e-mail: symphony@bangorsymphony.com
Web Site: www.bangorsymphony.com
Officers:
Executive Director: Susan Jonason
Management:
Concertmaster: Trond Saeverud
Co-Concertmaster: Lynn Brubaker
Mission: The Bangor Symphony Orchestra performs locally as well as on tour.
Utilizes: Collaborations; Commissioned Composers; Guest Artists; Guest Companies; Guest Composers; Guest Musical Directors; Instructors; Multimedia; Original Music Scores; Sign Language Translators; Soloists
Founded: 1896
Specialized Field: Symphony; Orchestra; Chamber; Ensemble
Status: Professional; Nonprofit
Paid Staff: 7
Paid Artists: 90
Income Sources: American Symphony Orchestra League; Greater Bangor Arts Council
Performs At: Bangor Opera House
Annual Attendance: 12,000
Organization Type: Performing; Touring; Resident; Sponsoring

1146
ARCADY MUSIC SOCIETY
PO Box 780
Bar Harbor, ME 04609
Phone: 207-288-3151
Fax: 207-288-3151
e-mail: arcady@arcady.org
Management:
Artistic Director: Masanobu Ikemiya
Mission: To offer the finest contemporary and classical music to Maine residents, particularly chamber music and presentations for youth.

Utilizes: Guest Artists
Founded: 1981
Specialized Field: Ensemble; Classical Music
Status: Professional; Nonprofit
Paid Staff: 2
Volunteer Staff: 30
Paid Artists: 70
Budget: $307,000
Income Sources: Chamber Music America
Organization Type: Performing; Educational; Sponsoring

1147
MAINE MUSIC SOCIETY
221 Lisbon Street
Lewiston, ME 04240
Phone: 207-782-7228
Fax: 207-782-8192
e-mail: info@mainemusicsociety.org
Web Site: www.mainemusicsociety.org
Officers:
President: David M Blocher
Secretary: Susan.F Trask
Treasurer: Anne M Jarvis
Account Executive Promotions Mgr: Kevin Mitchell
Management:
Artistic Director: John Corrie
Mission: To support the artistic and educational activities of the professional Maine Chamber Ensemble and the auditioned, mixed-voice Androscoggin Chorale.
Founded: 1991
Specialized Field: Chamber; Ensemble
Status: Professional
Income Sources: Maine Community Foundation; Davis Family Foundation; Helen & George Ladd Charitable Foundation; Maine Arts Commision; Maine Humanities Commission
Performs At: Orchestral; Chamber and Coral Music; Educational Programs
Affiliations: American Symphony Orchestra League; Maine Arts Sponsors Association; Androscoggin County Chamber of Commerce; Maine Association Of Non-Profits

1148
LARK SOCIETY FOR CHAMBER MUSIC
PO Box 11
Portland, ME 04112
Phone: 207-761-1522
Fax: 207-780-6554
e-mail: lark@larksociety.org
Web Site: www.portlandstringquartet.org/lark
Management:
Executive Director: Giselle A/ Auger
Conductor: Paul Ross
Mission: Committed to supporting and presenting a Portland concert series and educational presentations by the Portland String Quartet. Presenters of the Portland Concert Series, and supporters of the PSQ's outreach activities, we promote chamber music and music education in the state of Maine.
Specialized Field: Chamber; Ensemble
Status: Professional
Income Sources: Chamber Music America
Organization Type: Performing; Touring; Resident; Educational

1149
PORTLAND STRING QUARTET CONCERT SERIES/WORKSHOP
The Lark Society
PO Box 11
Portland, ME 04112-4866

INSTRUMENTAL MUSIC / Maryland

Phone: 207-774-5144
Fax: 207-780-6554
e-mail: lark1@prexar.com
Management:
   LARK Society Executive Director: Giselle A Auger
Founded: 1969
Specialized Field: Chamber; String Ensemble

1150
PORTLAND SYMPHONY ORCHESTRA
50 Monument Square, 2nd Floor
Portland, ME 04104
Mailing Address: PO Box 3573
Phone: 207-773-6128
Fax: 207-773-6089
e-mail: psobox@portlandsymphony.org
Web Site: www.portlandsymphony.org
Officers:
   President: Sam Parkhill
   VP: Eleanor M. Baker
   Trustee: Ken Blaschke
   Chair: Colleen Khoury
Management:
   Executive Director: Lisa M. Dickson
   Finance Director: Beth Ansheles
   Concert Manager: Joe Boucher
   Finance Coordinator: Jody Plummer
   Education/Community Engagement Mngr: Heather Kienow
   Associate Director, Development: Leah Robertson
   Concert Manager: Joe Boucher
Mission: The PSO is a professional orchestra aspiring to the highest artistic quality; serving its city, state, and Northern New England. Its mission is to engage diverse audiences in the enjoyment of live orchestral music.
Founded: 1924
Specialized Field: Symphony; Orchestra
Status: Nonprofit
Paid Staff: 12
Volunteer Staff: 150
Budget: $2.5 million
Performs At: Merrill Auditorium
Organization Type: Performing

1151
BAY CHAMBER CONCERTS
18 Central Street
Rockport, ME 04856
Mailing Address: PO Box 599
Phone: 207-236-2823
Fax: 207-230-0454
Toll-free: 888-707-2770
e-mail: info@baychamberconcerts.org
Web Site: www.baychamberconcerts.org
Officers:
   President: Carole Brand
   VP: Luther Black
   Treasurer: Laurence Novotney
   Secretary: Warren Schubert
Management:
   Executive Director: Monica Kelly
   Artistic Director: Manuel Bagorro
Mission: To present a variety of music styles and educational programs to reach a diverse audience along the coast of Maine.
Utilizes: Commissioned Music; Dancers; Fine Artists; Grant Writers; Guest Accompanists; Guest Choreographers; Guest Directors; Guest Musical Directors; Guest Musicians; Lyricists; Multimedia; Original Music Scores; Resident Artists; Sign Language Translators; Singers; Special Technical Talent
Founded: 1960
Specialized Field: Music

Status: Non-Profit, Professional
Paid Staff: 9
Budget: $500,000
Performs At: Rockport Opera House
Facility Category: Opera House; Strom Auditorium
Type of Stage: Proscenium; Auditorium
Seating Capacity: 400; 800
Organization Type: Performing

Maryland

1152
ANNAPOLIS CHAMBER ORCHESTRA
Maryland Hall for the Creative Arts
801 Chase Street
Annapolis, MD 21401
Phone: 410-263-1906
Fax: 410-263-5989
e-mail: annapolischorale@closecall.com
Web Site: www.annapolischorale.org
Officers:
   President: Lisa Sherwood
   VP: Nancy Grisham
   Secretary: Corby Zeren
   Treasurer: Marilyn Rhodovi
Management:
   Music Director: J Ernest Green
   Artistic Administrator: Jim Dickey
   Accompanist: Erik Apland
   Director: Katherine Hilton
   Artistic Associate: Kari Shea
Founded: 1973
Specialized Field: Chamber; Orchestra
Annual Attendance: 12,000

1153
BALTIMORE CHAMBER ORCHESTRA
5807 Hartford Road
Baltimore
Baltimore, MD 21214
Phone: 410-426-0157
Fax: 410- 42—016
e-mail: info@baltchamberorch.org
Officers:
   Executive Director: Lockwood Hoehl
Management:
   Music Director: Markand Rhakar
   Concertmaster: Jonathan Carney
Utilizes: Actors; Guest Companies; Guest Composers; Guest Lecturers; Guest Musicians; Multimedia; Singers
Founded: 1984
Specialized Field: Orchestra
Income Sources: Legg Mason; Lockheed Martin; The Rouse Company
Annual Attendance: 8,000

1154
BALTIMORE CLASSICAL GUITAR SOCIETY
4607 Maple Avenue
Baltimore, MD 21227
Phone: 443-296-2247
Web Site: www.bcgs.org
Officers:
   President: David Hepple
Management:
   Composers: Kevin Cope
   Composers: Andy Mitchell
Mission: To promote awareness of the classical guitar as an art form.
Specialized Field: Classical Guitar

1155
BALTIMORE SYMPHONY ORCHESTRA
1212 Cathedral Street
Baltimore, MD 21201
Phone: 410-783-8000
Fax: 410-783-8077
e-mail: tweber@baltimoresymphony.org
Web Site: www.baltimoresymphony.org
Officers:
   President: Barbara Bozzuto
   Secretary: Kathleen A. Chagnon
   Secretary: Lainy LeBow
   Treasurer: Steven R.Schuh
Management:
   Concertmaster: Jon Carney
   VP Artistic/Education Programming: Williamsch
   Music Director: Marin Alsop
   Principal Pops Conductor: Jack Everly
   Music Director Emeritus: Yuri Temirkanov
Utilizes: Commissioned Composers; Commissioned Music; Dance Companies; Grant Writers; Guest Accompanists; Guest Artists; Guest Companies; Guest Composers; Guest Musical Directors; Guest Musicians; Multimedia; Original Music Scores
Founded: 1916
Specialized Field: Symphony
Status: Professional
Income Sources: American Symphony Orchestra League; American Arts Alliance
Performs At: Joseph Meyerhoff Symphony Hall
Organization Type: Performing

1156
CONCERT ARTISTS OF BALTIMORE
1114 St. Paul Street
Baltimore, MD 21202-2615
Phone: 410-625-3525
Fax: 410-625-9343
e-mail: info@cabalto.org
Web Site: www.cabalto.org
Officers:
   President: Barry.F Williams
   VP: Barbara.J Cox
   Secretary: Mitchell Nelson
Management:
   Artistic Director: Edward Polochick
   General Manager: Rod Clark, cheryl@cabalto.org
   Development Director: Nan Rosenthal, bfw53@aol.com
Mission: To present varied classical music programs, featuring an all professional orchestra and vocal ensemble.
Founded: 1987
Specialized Field: Chamber; Orchestra; Vocal Ensemble
Paid Staff: 4
Volunteer Staff: 10
Paid Artists: 70
Budget: $300,000
Income Sources: Grants; Ticket Sales; Corporate Foundations; Individual Giving
Annual Attendance: 7,500-10,000

1157
PEABODY CONSERVATORY OF MUSIC
1 E Mount Vernon Place
Baltimore, MD 21202
Phone: 410-234-4500
Fax: 410-659-8140
e-mail: m.bell@jhu.edu
Web Site: www.peabody.jhu.edu
Officers:
   Dean of the Conservatory: Carolee Stewart

INSTRUMENTAL MUSIC / Maryland

Management:
  Concert Manager: Elizabeth Pollack
  Director: Jeffrey Sharkey
  Registrar: Dobson James
  Orchestra Coordinator: Gajger Melina
Specialized Field: Orchestra
Performs At: Miriam A. Friedberg Concert Hall

1158
UNIVERSITY OF MARYLAND BALTIMORE COUNTY SYMPHONY
1000 Hilltop Circle
Baltimore, MD 21250
Phone: 410-455-2942
Fax: 410-455-1181
e-mail: music_info@umbc.edu
Web Site: www.umbc.edu/music
Management:
  Music Department Chair: Linda Dusman
  Associate Chair: Joseph Morin
  Department Manager: Susan Velli
  Multimedia Assistant: Mike Jeffries
Specialized Field: Orchestra; Electronic
Performs At: Fine Arts Building

1159
MONTGOMERY COUNTY YOUTH ORCHESTRA
508 Harry Street
Bethesda, MD 19428
Phone: 610-564-6153
e-mail: mcyoinfo@gmail.com
Officers:
  President: Titi Lakeru-Rivers
  Tresurer: Ginny Jacoby
  Secretary: Georganne Larsen
Management:
  Artistic Director: Olivia W Cutoff
  Operations Manager: Cheryl Jukes
Mission: Mission of the orchestras is to nurture, develop, and advance young, talented musicians in a quality orchestral program.
Founded: 1946
Specialized Field: Youth Orchestra; Chamber

1160
NATIONAL ORCHESTRAL INSTITUTE
2110 Clarice Smith Performing Arts Center
University of Maryland
College Park, MD 20742-1620
Phone: 301-405-5549
Fax: 301-314-9504
e-mail: umbands@umd.edu
Web Site: www.nationalorchestralinstitute.com
Officers:
  Chairman: Janet Montgomery
Management:
  Assistant Manager: Phil Kancianic
  Manager: Richard Scerbo
  Aristic Director: James Ross
  Artistic Director: Christopher Kendall
  Director: Robert Gibson
  Associate Director: Lori DeBoy
Mission: The NOI offers an intensive three-week training experience in orchestral musicianship and professional development for musicians on the threshold of their careers.
Founded: 1987
Specialized Field: Orchestra
Paid Staff: 2
Paid Artists: 41
Budget: $380,000
Income Sources: University Funds, Ticket Revenue

Performs At: University Performing Arts Facility
Annual Attendance: 3500
Facility Category: Concert Hall
Type of Stage: Open
Seating Capacity: 1100
Year Remodeled: 2001

1161
UNIVERSITY OF MARYLAND: INTERNATIONAL WILLIAM KAPELL PIANO COMPETITION & FESTIVAL
Clarice Smith Performing Arts Center
University of Maryland
College Park, MD 20742
Phone: 301-405-8174
Fax: 301-405-5977
Web Site: www.claricesmithcenter.umd.edu
Founded: 1971
Specialized Field: Piano
Status: Nonprofit
Income Sources: University of Maryland
Season: 2003
Performs At: Clarice Smith Performing Arts Center
Organization Type: Educational; Sponsoring

1162
CANDLELIGHT CONCERT SOCIETY
8950-A Route 108
Suite 115 A
Columbia, MD 21045
Phone: 410-997-2324
Fax: 410-997-2325
e-mail: info@candlelightconcerts.org
Web Site: www.candlelightconcerts.org
Management:
  Executive Director: Bonita J Bush
  Creative Strategy Sr. Manager: Kelly Andrews
  Associate Director: Bobby Asher
  Guest Appreence Coordinator: Lindsey Barr
  Stage Operation: Bill Brandwein
Mission: To offer Central Maryland audiences professional chamber music.
Founded: 1974
Specialized Field: Ensemble; Chamber; Children's Concerts
Status: Professional; Nonprofit
Paid Staff: 1
Volunteer Staff: 75
Budget: $178,000
Income Sources: Columbia Foundations; MSAC; HCAC; Chamber Music America; Contributions
Season: October - May
Performs At: Smith Theatre; Howard Community College
Annual Attendance: 16,000
Type of Stage: Proscenium
Seating Capacity: 417
Organization Type: Performing; Sponsoring

1163
COLUMBIA ORCHESTRA
8510 High Ridge Road
Ellicott City
Ellicott City, MD 21043
Phone: 410-465-8777
Fax: 461-465-8778
e-mail: execdir@columbiaorchestra.org
Web Site: www.columbiaorchestra.org
Officers:
  President: Bruce Kuehne
  VP: Anne Ward
  Tresurer: Brandi Healey
  Secretary: Viviana Acosta

Management:
  Music Director: Jason Love
  Concertmaster: Brenda Anna
  Personnel/Strings: Annette Szawan
  Personnel/Winds: Ann Ward
  Operations Manager: Katherine Keefe
  Executive Director: Tedd Griepentrog
Mission: The Columbia Orchestra is dedicated to serving local audiences, musicians, and students. This is accomplished by: providing the community with high-quality musical performances , providing area students, teachers and educational institutions witha classical music resource and providing local classical musicians with an opportunity to explore and perform orchestral literature and chamber music.
Founded: 1977
Specialized Field: Orchestra

1164
SUSQUEHANNA SYMPHONY ORCHESTRA
PO Box 963
Forest Hill, MD 21009
Phone: 410-838-6465
Fax: 410- 83—082
e-mail: susan73@yahoo.com
Web Site: www.ssorchestra.org
Officers:
  Orchestra Manager: Susan Burdette
  Marketing and Publicity: Tonya Woody
  Vp: Diane Sengstacke
  Secretary: Shannon Raum
  Treasurer: Jim Weed
Management:
  Music Director: Sheldon Bair
  Orchestral Manager: Kathy Frawley
  Personnel Manager: Amy Wilkinson
  Student Personnel Manager: Anne Lehman
  Donor Development: Colleen Grotke
Mission: The Susquehanna Symphony Orchestra is a nonprofit community orchestra, providing education and entertainment for Harford County, Maryland.
Founded: 1978
Specialized Field: Orchestra

1165
MARYLAND YOUTH SYMPHONY ORCHESTRA
800 South Rolling Road
Glenwood, MD 21228-5317
Phone: 410-442-5645
Fax: 410-489-7268
e-mail: mgattomyso@aol.com
Web Site: www.myso.info
Officers:
  President: Bruce Miller
  VP: Sharon Saunders
  Secretary: Clare Keating-Sladic
  Treasurer: Gary Sladic
Management:
  Conductor: Angelo Gatto
  General Manager: Margaret Gatto
Mission: The symphony provides the opportunity for talented young musicians to learn and perform major symphonic repertoire at a high professional level, thus providing cultural enrichment for both performer and audience
Founded: 1964
Specialized Field: Youth Symphony
Paid Staff: 3
Paid Artists: 6

INSTRUMENTAL MUSIC / Maryland

1166
MUSIC AT PENN ALPS
PO Box 668
Grantsville, MD 21536
Phone: 240-382-0903
Fax: 301-895-4603
e-mail: musicatpennalps@gmail.com
Web Site: www.musicatpennalps.org
Officers:
   President: Fred C Bolton
   VP: Bernice Friedland
   Tresurer: Joe McDaniel
Management:
   Program Director: Nancy Salmon
   Administrator: Julyen Norman
   House Manager: Dave Bohnert
Mission: To present high-quality classical chamber music to the communities of rural Western Maryland.
Founded: 1992
Specialized Field: Chamber Music
Paid Staff: 1
Volunteer Staff: 8
Budget: $40,000
Income Sources: Corporate Sponsors; Individual Contributions; Ticket Sales
Performs At: Informal Small Halls, Good Accoustics

1167
MARYLAND SYMPHONY ORCHESTRA
30 West Washington Street
Hagerstown, MD 21740
Phone: 301-797-4000
Fax: 301-797-2314
e-mail: info@marylandsymphony.org
Web Site: http://www.marylandsymphony.org/
Officers:
   President: James G Piern,
   Secretary: Barbara Henderson
   Tresurer: Kim Reno
   Assistant Treasurer: wILLIAM L. McGovern
   VP: Brendan Fitzsimmons
Management:
   Music Director: Elizabeth Schulze
   Orchestra Manager: Sharon Buck-Ahrens
   Director: Teresa Barr
Utilizes: Commissioned Composers; Commissioned Music; Fine Artists; Five Seasonal Concerts; Guest Accompanists; Guest Musicians; Local Artists; Multimedia; Music; New Productions; Organization Contracts; Original Music Scores; Sign Language Translators; Singers
Founded: 1982
Specialized Field: Symphony
Status: Professional
Paid Staff: 5
Budget: $1,000,000
Income Sources: Donors; Grants
Performs At: Maryland Theatre
Annual Attendance: 20,000
Seating Capacity: 1377
Organization Type: Performing

1168
NATIONAL MUSICAL ARTS
9506 Culver Street
PO Box 39162
Kensington, MD 20895-3628
Phone: 301-946-0355
Fax: 336-855-8494
e-mail: pgraypiano@msn.com
Officers:
   Chairman: Jane Siena
   Executive Director: Anne Taylor
   General Manager: Joe Ragan
   Secretary: Christopher Griner
Management:
   Artistic Director: Patricia Gray
   Orchestra Manager: Kate Gorecki
Mission: To revolutionize the way audiences experience musically innovative live performances and outreach projects, and by exploring music's role throughout the biosphere via transdisciplinary projects.
Utilizes: Collaborations; Commissioned Composers; Commissioned Music; Composers; Composers-in-Residence; Educators; Five Seasonal Concerts; Guest Accompanists; Guest Artists; Guest Companies; Guest Composers; Guest Instructors; Guest Musical Directors; Guest Musicians; Guest Soloists; Lyricists; Multi Collaborations; Multimedia; Organization Contracts; Original Music Scores; Resident Artists; Singers; Student Interns
Founded: 1980
Specialized Field: Chamber; Ensemble
Status: Professional; Nonprofit
Paid Staff: 2
Paid Artists: 20
Budget: $150,000
Income Sources: Grants, Ticket Sales, Private and Corporate Donations
Annual Attendance: 3,000
Facility Category: Auditorium
Type of Stage: Speaker Stage
Seating Capacity: 650
Year Built: 1970
Organization Type: Performing; Touring; Resident
Resident Groups: National Music Arts

1169
THE NATIONAL PHILHARMONIC
Music Center at Strathmore
5301 Tuckerman Lane
North Bethesda, MD 20852-3385
Phone: 301-493-9283
Fax: 301-493-9284
e-mail: office@nationalphilharmonic.org
Web Site: http://www.nationalphilharmonic.org/
Officers:
   President: Kenneth Oldham, Jr.
Management:
   Music Director/Conductor: Piotr Gajewski, plotr@nationalphilharmonic.org
   Chorale Artistic Director: Stan Engebretson
Mission: To be the dynamic organization of choice providing the highest quality orchestral, choral, and other musical experiences to enrich and inspire the lives of people in Montgomery County, the Washington DC metroploitan area and beyond through conecerts and educational programs for all ages.
Utilizes: Commissioned Composers; Commissioned Music; Composers-in-Residence; Educators; Five Seasonal Concerts; Guest Companies; Guest Composers; Guest Lecturers; Guest Musical Directors; Guest Musicians; Multimedia; Music; Organization Contracts; Original Music Scores; Sign Language Translators; Singers; Soloists
Specialized Field: Orchestra; Chamber
Status: Professional; Nonprofit
Paid Staff: 7
Volunteer Staff: 10
Paid Artists: 32
Budget: $350,000
Performs At: Duke Ellington School of the Arts; F. Scott Theatre
Annual Attendance: 8,000
Facility Category: Theatre
Organization Type: Resident

1170
PRINCE GEORGE'S PHILHARMONIC
PO Box 1111
Riverdale, MD 20738
Phone: 310-446-3245
Fax: 301-446-3233
Web Site: www.pgphilharmonic.org
Officers:
   VP: Blake Lorenz
Management:
   Music Director: Charles Ellis
   Executive Director: Brenton Benfield
   Associate Conductor: Shawn Storer
   VP: Blake Lorenz
   Secretary: Elisa L Hill
   Treasurer: Richard Dalton
Mission: The Philharmonic's partnership with Prince George's County schools helps cultivate a new generation of musicians and audiences. With a focus on helping children develop to their fullest potential, the schools and orchestra together clarify the best role for each to play.
Specialized Field: Orchestra
Organization Type: Performing; Educational

1171
JEWISH COMMUNITY CENTER SYMPHONY
6125 Montrose Road
Rockville, MD 20852
Phone: 301-881-0100
Fax: 301-881-5512
e-mail: info@jccso.org
Web Site: www.jccgw.org
Officers:
   President: Bradley C.Stillman
   VP: Brian Pearlstein
   VP Development: Heidi H.Brodsky
   VP Programming: Arthur Polott
   Secretary: Matthew Weinberg
Management:
   Music Director: Joel Lazar
   Director of Music JCCGW: Sarah N Schallern
   Assistant Secretary: Andrew Chod
   Assistant Treasurer: Darryl Shrock
   Ombudsperson: Monique Buckles
Specialized Field: Orchestra

1172
WASHINGTON JEWISH THEATRE
6125 Montrose Road
Rockville, MD 20852
Phone: 301-230-3775
Fax: 301-881-5512
e-mail: info@jccgw.org
Web Site: www.jccgw.org
Officers:
   President: Bradley C.Stillman
   VP: Brian Pearlstein
   VP Development: Heidi H.Brodsky
   VP Programming: Arthur Polott
   Secretary: Matthew Weinberg
Management:
   Music Director: Joel Lazar
   Director of Music JCCGW: Sarah N Schallern
   Assistant Secretary: Andrew Chod
   Assistant Treasurer: Darryl Shrock
   Ombudsperson: Monique Buckles
Founded: 1969
Specialized Field: Orchestra
Status: Nonprofit

INSTRUMENTAL MUSIC / Massachusetts

Massachusetts

1173
BOSTON BAROQUE
10 Guest Street
Suite 290
Belmont, MA 02135
Phone: 617-987-8600
Fax: 617-987-8603
e-mail: info@bostonbaroque.org
Web Site: www.bostonbaroque.org
Officers:
  Founder/Music Director: Martin Pearlman
  Executive Director: David Gaylin
  President: David Friend
  VP: Lee Carl Bromberg
  Treasurer: Julian Bullitt
Management:
  Operations Manager: Laurie Szablewski
  Music Director: Martin Pearlman
Mission: To present performances of Baroque and classical music on period instruments with a chorus.
Utilizes: Collaborations; Contract Orchestras; Guest Accompanists; Guest Soloists; Multimedia; Paid Performers
Founded: 1973
Specialized Field: Orchestra; Baroque
Status: Professional; Nonprofit
Income Sources: Memberships
Performs At: Jordan Hall; Sanders Theatre
Organization Type: Performing; Touring; Resident

1174
NORTH SHORE PHILHARMONIC ORCHESTRA
P.O. Box 461
Beverly, MA 01915-0095
Phone: 781-286-0024
Fax: 617-247-3087
e-mail: nsphil@hotmail.com
Web Site: www.nspo.org
Officers:
  President: Robert Marra, Jr
  VP: Mary Miller
  Treasurer: Irene Leamon
  Secretary: Thad Coverdale
Management:
  Manager: Herbert A Cohen
  Music Director: Robert Lehmann
Mission: Committed to providing access to quality music at an affordable price to communities on Boston's North shore; to developing, training and providing opportunities for young musicans; and to providing a large range of programs.
Founded: 1948
Specialized Field: Symphony; Orchestra
Status: Semi-Professional; Nonprofit
Paid Staff: 35
Organization Type: Performing; Resident

1175
ALEA III
855 Commonwealth Avenue
Boston, MA 02215
Phone: 617-353-3340
Fax: 781-793-8903
e-mail: aleaiii@bu.edu
Web Site: www.aleaiii.com
Officers:
  Chairman: Andra de Quadros
  President: George Demeter
  Co-President: Ellen Demeter
  Treasurer: Samuel Headrick
Management:
  Executive Administrator: Alexandros Kalogeras
  Music Director: Theodore Antoniou
Mission: Dedicated to performing and promoting twentieth and twenty first century classical music and supporting the work of contemporary composers.
Utilizes: Guest Artists; Guest Companies; Guest Lecturers
Founded: 1979
Specialized Field: Chamber; Ensemble; Electronic; Live Electronic
Status: Professional; Nonprofit
Income Sources: Boston University
Performs At: Tsai Performance Center
Organization Type: Performing; Resident

1176
BOSTON POPS ORCHESTRA
301 Massachusetts Avenue
Boston, MA 02115
Phone: 617-266-1492
Fax: 617-638-9493
e-mail: customerservice@bso.org
Web Site: www.bso.org
Management:
  Conductor: Keith Lockhart
  Manager: Tony Beadle
  Artistic Administrator: Dennis Alves
  Sales & Marketing Director: Kim Noltemy
  Director Finance: Thomas D May
  Operations Manager: Christopher W Ruigomez
  Chorus Manager: Felicia A Burrey
  Production Coordinator: Jana Gimenez
  Music Director: Seiji Ozawa
Opened: 1885
Specialized Field: Orchestra; Pops
Status: Professional; Nonprofit
Income Sources: Memberships
Performs At: Symphony Hall
Organization Type: Performing; Touring

1177
BOSTON SYMPHONY CHAMBER PLAYERS
301 Massachusetts Avenue
Boston, MA 02115
Phone: 617-266-1492
Fax: 617-638-9367
Web Site: www.bso.org
Officers:
  Managing Director: Mark Volpe
  Director Development: Bart Reidy
  Director Media Relations: Bernadette Horgan
Management:
  Orchestra Manager: Ray F Wellbaum
  Artistic Administrator: Anthony Fogg
  Music Director Laureate: Seiji Ozawa
  Music Director: James Levine
Mission: The Chamber Players comprise the 12 first-chair players of the Boston Symphony Orchestra. They present programs of standard and contemporary literature not only in Boston and at Tanglewood, but on tour throughout this country and abroad, especially to audiences in locations which would not ordinarily be able to hear the Boston Symphony Orchestra in person.
Founded: 1964
Specialized Field: Chamber; Ensemble
Status: Professional; Commercial
Income Sources: Boston Symphony Orchestra
Performs At: Jordan Hall; Tanglewood
Organization Type: Performing; Touring

1178
BOSTON SYMPHONY ORCHESTRA
301 Massachusetts Avenue
Boston, MA 02115
Phone: 617-266-1492
Fax: 617-638-9367
Toll-free: 888-266-1200
Web Site: www.bso.org
Officers:
  Managing Director: Mark Volpe
  Director Development: Bart Reidy
  Director Media Relations: Bernadette Horgan
Management:
  Music Director: James Levine
  Music Director Laureate: Seiji Ozawa
  Artistic Administrator: Anthony Fogg
  Orchestra Manager: Ray F Wellbaum
  Music Director: James Levine
Mission: To bring great music to the widest possible audience; the Boston Symphony Orchestra, Inc. is the parent organization of the Boston Symphony Orchestra, the Boston Pops, the Boston Symphony Chamber Players, Tanglewood and the Tanglewood Music Center. To foster and maintain an organization dedicated to the making of music consonant with the highest aspirations of musical art.
Utilizes: Guest Artists; Singers
Founded: 1881
Specialized Field: Symphony; Orchestra; Chamber; Ensemble
Status: Professional; Nonprofit
Performs At: Symphony Hall Tanglewood
Organization Type: Performing; Touring; Resident; Educational

1179
DINOSAUR ANNEX MUSIC ENSEMBLE
PO Box 400752
Boston, MA 02140
Phone: 617-482-3852
Fax: 617-482-4972
e-mail: manager@dinosaurannex.org
Web Site: www.dinosaurannex.org
Officers:
  Chairman: Kate Lowrie
  Treasurer: Diane Ota
Management:
  Artistic Director: Yu-Hui Chang
  GeneralManager: Jeremy Spindler
  Music Director: James Levine
Mission: Presenting the best in contemporary music for chamber ensemble.
Founded: 1975
Specialized Field: Orchestra; Chamber; Ensemble; Electronic; Live Electronic
Status: Professional; Nonprofit
Paid Staff: 1
Paid Artists: 22
Performs At: First and Second Church; Boston
Organization Type: Performing

1180
GREATER BOSTON YOUTH SYMPHONY ORCHESTRAS
855 Commonwealth Avenue
Boston, MA 02215
Phone: 617-353-3348
Fax: 617-353-5205
e-mail: byso@bu.edu
Web Site: www.gbyso.org
Officers:
  President: George Keches
  VP: Joe Grimaldi

INSTRUMENTAL MUSIC / Massachusetts

Secretary: Mark Fleming
Treasurer: Doris Fritz Welch
Management:
Executive Director: Catherine Weiskel
Music Director: Federico Cortese
Orchestra Manager: Ed Feingold
Director Public Relations/Marketing: Jessica Tanner
Director of Development: Ryan Losey
General Manager: Mathew Ritter
Operational Manager: Patricia Driscoll
Mission: To organize and promote a youth orchestra program that provides the highest quality musical education, training and performance opportunities for young people.
Founded: 1958
Specialized Field: Youth Symphony; Chamber
Status: Non-Professional; Nonprofit
Paid Staff: 5
Volunteer Staff: 25
Budget: $800,000
Income Sources: Boston University; Public/Private Grants; Tuition
Affiliations: Boston University
Organization Type: Performing; Touring; Resident; Educational

1181
HANDEL AND HAYDN SOCIETY
300 Massachusetts Avenue
Boston, MA 02115
Phone: 617-262-1815
Fax: 617-266-4217
e-mail: info@handelandhaydn.org
Web Site: www.handelandhaydn.org
Officers:
Chairman: Nicholas Gleysteen
VP: Julia D Cox
CEO: Marie-H,IŠne Bernard
Management:
Music Director: Grant Llewellyn
Conductor Laureate: Christopher Hogwood
Executive Director: Mary Deissler
Artistic Director: Harry Christophers
Mission: Dedicated to promoting the performance, study, composition and appreciation of music.
Utilizes: Commissioned Composers; Guest Composers; Guest Directors; Guest Musical Directors; Guest Musicians; Multimedia; Music; Original Music Scores; Sign Language Translators; Singers
Founded: 1815
Specialized Field: Chamber; Ensemble
Status: Professional; Nonprofit
Paid Staff: 16
Budget: $2,600,000
Performs At: Symphony Hall; Jordan Hall
Annual Attendance: 40,000
Organization Type: Performing; Touring; Educational; Sponsoring

1182
MASSACHUSETTS YOUTH WIND ENSEMBLE
290 Huntington Avenue
Boston, MA 02115
Phone: 617-585-1130
Fax: 617-585-1135
e-mail: prep@newenglandconservatory.edu
Management:
Music Director/Conductor: Michael Mucci
Extension Division Dean, NE: Mark Churchill
Mission: Providing exceptionally talented high school musicians with an opportunity to study and perform the quality literature written for wind, brass, and percussion instruments.
Utilizes: Guest Artists; Guest Companies; Singers
Founded: 1970
Specialized Field: Youth Orchestra; Chamber; Ensemble; Band
Status: Nonprofit
Income Sources: New England Conservatory
Performs At: Jordon Hall
Organization Type: Performing; Touring; Educational

1183
NEW ENGLAND PHILHARMONIC
6 Hemenway Street
Boston, MA 02140
Phone: 617-868-1222
Fax: 617-868-1222
Web Site: www.nephilharmonic.org
Officers:
President: Michele Sullivan
VP: Jennifer Snodgrass
Secretary/Director of Development: Timothy Alexander
Treasurer: John Guthrie
Management:
General Manager: Brian Ritter
Music Director: Richard Pittman
Personnel Manager: Elizabeth Dinwiddie
Stage Manager: John Kessen
Mission: To nurture and encourage the enjoyment and appreciation of new and unusual orchestral music and perform standard orchestral literature in community locations.
Utilizes: Community Talent
Founded: 1976
Specialized Field: Orchestra
Status: Non-Professional
Paid Staff: 65
Income Sources: American Symphony Orchestra League
Performs At: Sanders Theatre; Cambridge; Dwight Hall
Organization Type: Performing; Resident

1184
BROCKTON SYMPHONY ORCHESTRA
156 West Elm Street
Brockton, MA 02301
Phone: 508-588-3841
Fax: 508- 58—381
e-mail: brocktonsymphony1@gmail.com
Web Site: www.brocktonsymphony.org
Officers:
Chairman: Torben Hansen
VP: Andrea Delaney
Seceratary: Maureen Jardin
Treasurer: Susan Caplan
Management:
Board of Directors Chair: Paul J Carchidi
Executive Director: Andrea Bates
Music Director: James Orent
Founded: 1948
Specialized Field: Orchestra

1185
BOSTON CHAMBER MUSIC SOCIETY
60 Gore Street
Cambridge, MA 02141
Phone: 617-349-0086
Fax: 617-349-0080
e-mail: info@bostonchambermusic.org
Web Site: www.bostonchambermusic.org
Officers:
President: Eli Rosenbaum
VP: Michele Sullivan
Treasurer: Timothy Alexander
Secretary: Ann Teixeria
Board of Director: John Kessen
Management:
Artistic Director: Ronald Thomas
Executive Director: Alan Mann
Managing Director: Wen Huang
Mission: To provide Boston's concert-going public with exceptional performance of the great chamber music repertoire of the 18th, 19th, and 20th centuries while fostering understanding and appreciation of the artform.
Utilizes: Guest Accompanists; Guest Musical Directors; Multimedia
Founded: 1982
Specialized Field: Chamber
Paid Staff: 3
Budget: $520,000
Income Sources: Box Office; Grants; Contributions
Performs At: Concert Hall

1186
BOSTON MUSICA VIVA
353 Beacon Street
4th Floor
Cambridge, MA 02143
Phone: 617-354-6910
Fax: 617-354-8513
e-mail: bmv@pobox.com
Web Site: www.bmv.org
Officers:
President: Nicholas Altenbernd
Treasurer: Grant Anderson
Clerk: Robert Soorian
Management:
General Manager: Miguel A Rodriguez
Music Director: Richard Pittman
Executive Director: Alison LaRosa Montez
Mission: To promote the work of living American composers as well as comtemporary classics.
Founded: 1969
Specialized Field: Chamber; New Music
Status: Professional
Paid Staff: 2
Volunteer Staff: 4
Paid Artists: 10
Budget: $450,000
Income Sources: Box Office; Grants; Donations
Performs At: Edward Pickman Hall; Blackman Auditorium; Tsai Performance Center
Affiliations: Chamber Music America
Organization Type: Performing; Touring; Educational

1187
BOSTON PHILHARMONIC ORCHESTRA
295 Huntington Avenue
Suite 210
Cambridge, MA 02116
Phone: 617-236-0999
Fax: 617-236-8613
e-mail: info@bostonphil.org
Web Site: www.bostonphil.org
Management:
General Manager: Elisabeth Christensen
Outreach & Publications Manager: Pamela Feo
Conductor: Benjamin Zander
Mission: Committed to reaching and educating a wide audience in fine arts.
Founded: 1979
Specialized Field: Symphony; Orchestra
Status: Professional; Semi-Professional; Nonprofit
Paid Staff: 4

INSTRUMENTAL MUSIC / Massachusetts

Paid Artists: 60
Non-paid Artists: 25
Budget: $1,000,000
Income Sources: Arts Boston
Performs At: Jordan Hall; Sanders Theater; Symphony Hall
Annual Attendance: 7,000
Organization Type: Performing; Touring

1188
CAMBRIDGE SOCIETY FOR EARLY MUSIC: CHAMBER MUSIC SERIES
PO Box 380-336
Cambridge, MA 02238-0336
Phone: 617-489-2062
Fax: 617-489-0686
e-mail: info@csem.org
Web Site: www.csem.org
Officers:
   General Manager: Flynn Warmington
Mission: To entertain, enlighten, educate, and in general promote the rich musical culture of five centuries of Western music occuring up to the early nineteenth century.
Specialized Field: Chamber; Early Music

1189
HARVARD-RADCLIFFE ORCHESTRA
Harvard University
Music Building
Cambridge, MA 02138
Phone: 617-496-6276
Fax: 617-496-8081
e-mail: hro@hcs.harvard.edu
Management:
   Music Director/Conductor: Dr. James Yannatos
   President: Chrix Finne
Specialized Field: Orchestra

1190
KLEZMER CONSERVATORY BAND
83 Inman Street
Cambridge, MA 02139
Phone: 617-354-2884
Fax: 617-776-0955
Web Site: www.klezmerconservatory.com
Management:
   Business Manager Aaron Concert Man: James Guttmann
   Director: Hankus Netsky
   Managing Director: Jim Guttmann
Mission: To offer Yiddish instrumental and vocal music with many influences (Jazz, Dixieland, Ragtime, Latin and Broadway).
Founded: 1980
Specialized Field: Ethnic Music; Folk Music; Band
Status: Professional
Organization Type: Performing; Touring

1191
PRO ARTE CHAMBER ORCHESTRA
75 Arlington Street
Suite 500
Cambridge, MA 02116
Phone: 617-779-0900
Fax: 617-492-6596
Web Site: www.proarte.org
Officers:
   Chairman: Eugenia Ware
   Treasurer: John Barstow
   Secretary: Sandra Winslow Sherwood
   Executive Director: Larry Hill
Management:
   Executive Director: Nina Moe
   Music Director: Kevin Rhodes
   General Manager: Meena Malik
   Orchestra Manager: Susan Gottschalk
Mission: Seeks to make classical music accessible to the entire community. Through our Access to the Best Music program, low income, at-risk, disabled, and elderly individuals experience fine music.
Utilizes: Guest Accompanists
Founded: 1978
Specialized Field: Orchestra; Chamber
Status: Professional; Nonprofit
Paid Staff: 9
Volunteer Staff: 510
Paid Artists: 40
Budget: $550,000
Income Sources: Ticket Sales; Contributed Sources
Performs At: Sanders Theater
Annual Attendance: 6,500
Seating Capacity: 1,200
Year Built: 1870
Year Remodeled: 1994
Organization Type: Performing

1192
CONCORD BAND
PO Box 302
Concord, MA 01742
Phone: 978-897-9969
Fax: 978-369-1367
e-mail: trustees@concordband.org
Web Site: www.concordband.org
Officers:
   President: BP Troup
   Treasurer: J Grace
Management:
   Music Director: James O'Dell
   Manager/Librarian: J Kemson
   Fundraising: L Matson
   Assistant Director: Steven Barbas
Utilizes: Guest Artists
Founded: 1959
Specialized Field: Band
Status: Non-Professional; Nonprofit
Paid Staff: 70
Income Sources: Association of Concert Bands
Organization Type: Performing

1193
CONCORD ORCHESTRA
PO Box 381
Concord, MA 01742
Phone: 978-369-4967
e-mail: info@concordorchestra.com
Web Site: www.concordorchestra.com
Officers:
   President: Avril Waye
   VP: Dan Schrager
   Treasurer: Jane Bailey
Management:
   Conductor: Richard Pittman
Mission: Dedicated to providing our amateur musicians the enjoyment of playing music and offering good music to the community.
Founded: 1952
Specialized Field: Symphony; Orchestra
Status: Non-Professional; Nonprofit
Paid Staff: 70
Income Sources: American Symphony Orchestra League
Organization Type: Performing

1194
INTERNATIONAL MUSIC NETWORK
278 Main Street
Gloucester, MA 01930
Phone: 978-283-2883
Fax: 978-283-2330
e-mail: info@imnworld.com
Web Site: www.imnworld.com
Management:
   Co-Director/Co-Owner: AnneMarie Southard
   Co-Director/Co-Owner: Scott Southard
   International Agent: Scott Southard
   European Agent: Katherine McVicker
   International Coordinator: Kristen Teixeria
   Accountant: Pat Lefebvre
   Contract Administrator: Carey McGovern
   Midwest Agent: Michael Fox
Mission: Booking agency
Founded: 1989
Specialized Field: Jazz; World Music; International

1195
CAPE ANN SYMPHONY ORCHESTRA
PO Box 1343
Gloucester
Gloucester, MA 01930
Phone: 978-281-0543
Fax: 508-362-7916
e-mail: info@capeannsymphony.org
Web Site: www.capeannsymphony.org
Officers:
   Treasurer: Philip Chambers
Management:
   Music Director & Conductor: Yoichi Udagawa
   Business Manager: David Benjamin
Specialized Field: Orchestra

1196
PIONEER VALLEY SYMPHONY
91 Main Street
Greenfield, MA 01301
Phone: 413-773-3664
Fax: 413-772-6800
Toll-free: 800-681-7870
e-mail: pvsoffice@pvso.org
Web Site: www.pvso.org
Officers:
   President: Mandi J.Hanneke
   Treasurer: Michael Mandile
   Orchestra Liason: David Glassberg
   Secretary: David Glassberg
Management:
   Music Director: Paul Phillips
   Executive Director: Constance Clark
   Managing Director: Bela Breslau
   Production Manager: Cecilia Berger
Mission: To serve the Pioneer Valley.
Founded: 1939
Specialized Field: Orchestra

1197
SYMPHONY PRO MUSICA
PO Box 332
Hudson, MA 01749-0332
Phone: 978-562-0939
Fax: 978-562-0939
e-mail: spm@symphonypromusica.org
Web Site: www.symphonypromusica.org
Officers:
   President: Dan Sweeney
   VP: Ruth Washington Mayhew
Management:
   Music Director: Mark Churchill

INSTRUMENTAL MUSIC / Massachusetts

General Manager: Alison Doherty
Mission: Symphony Pro Musica have enriched the cultural life of our communities with live performances of the best symphonic music from the eighteenth, nineteenth, and twentieth centuries.
Founded: 1983
Specialized Field: Classical
Paid Staff: 2
Volunteer Staff: 15
Paid Artists: 6
Non-paid Artists: 65

1198
THAYER SYMPHONY ORCHESTRA
14 Monument Square
Suite 406
Leominster, MA 01453
Phone: 978-466-1800
Fax: 978-466-1000
e-mail: info@thayersymphony.org
Web Site: www.thayersymphony.org
Officers:
- **President:** Michael A Mahan
- **VP:** Robert Gallo
- **Treasurer?:** J. Paul H Gauvin

Management:
- **General Manager:** Francis Wada
- **Conductor/ Artistic Director:** Toshimasa Wada
- **Director:** Michael Bernatchez
- **Concertmaster:** Khanh Trinh
- **Personnel Manager:** Bruce Hopkins

Mission: To sustain and develop a symphony orchestra of the highest quality for the education, enrichment, and pleasure of the citizens and musicians of Central Massachusetts.
Founded: 1973
Specialized Field: Symphony
Status: Semi-Professional; Nonprofit
Paid Staff: 20
Income Sources: American Symphony Orchestra League; North Central Massachusetts Chamber of Commerce
Organization Type: Performing; Educational

1199
INDIAN HILL SYMPHONY
36 King Street
PO Box 1484
Littleton, MA 01460
Phone: 978-486-9524
Fax: 978-486-9844
Toll-free: 800-439-2370
e-mail: Info@indianhillmusic.org
Web Site: www.indianhillmusic.org
Officers:
- **Chairman:** Ralph Brown
- **VP:** Jeffrey Fuhrer
- **Treasurer:** Thomas Rosa

Management:
- **Artistic Director & Conductor:** Bruce Hangen
- **Executive Director:** Susan Randazzo
- **Director of Education:** Jo-Ann Wangh
- **Director of Performance:** Cheryl DaSilva

Utilizes: Artists-in-Residence; Collaborations; Composers-in-Residence; Educators; Guest Companies; Guest Composers; Guest Directors; Guest Lecturers; Guest Musical Directors; Guest Musicians; Multimedia; Original Music Scores
Founded: 1974
Specialized Field: Orchestra
Paid Staff: 75
Annual Attendance: 7,000
Facility Category: various venues

1200
BOSTON MODERN ORCHESTRA PROJECT
376 Washington Street
Malden, MA 02148
Phone: 781-324-0396
Fax: 781-324-0397
e-mail: bmop@bmop.org
Web Site: www.bmop.org
Officers:
- **Publicist:** April Thibeault

Management:
- **Artistic Director:** Gil Rose
- **Development Director:** Margaret Lias
- **Box Office Associate:** Jen Simons
- **GM:** Sissie Cohen
- **Production Associate:** Steve Giles

Mission: Boston Modern Orchestra project's mission is to illuminate the connections that exist naturally between contemporary music and contemporary society by reuniting composers and audiences in a shared concert experience.
Specialized Field: Orchestra

1201
MELROSE SYMPHONY ORCHESTRA
PO Box 760715
Melrose, MA 02176
Phone: 781-662-0641
Fax: 781-662-0641
e-mail: jessi@melrosesymphony.org
Web Site: melrosesymphony.org
Officers:
- **President:** Kathy Radley
- **First VP:** Anne Fremont-Smith
- **Second VP:** Katherine Radley
- **Secretary:** Rita Moore
- **Treasurer:** Debi Walsh

Management:
- **Executive Director:** Millie Rich
- **General Manager:** Jessi Eisdorfer
- **Music Director:** Yoichi Udagawa

Mission: To give the citizens of Melrose and surrounding area an opportunity to participate in the joy of music.
Utilizes: Commissioned Composers; Commissioned Music; Composers; Educators; Guest Accompanists; Guest Companies; Guest Composers; Guest Directors; Guest Instructors; Guest Lecturers; Guest Musical Directors; Guest Musicians; Lyricists; Multi Collaborations; Multimedia; Music; Organization Contracts; Scenic Designers; Singers
Founded: 1918
Specialized Field: Symphony; Orchestra
Status: Nonprofit
Volunteer Staff: 17
Paid Artists: 1
Non-paid Artists: 72
Performs At: Memorial Building (590 Main Street, Melrose)
Annual Attendance: 5,000
Facility Category: Auditorium Performance Center
Type of Stage: Performance Stage
Stage Dimensions: 30x40
Seating Capacity: 900
Year Built: 1912
Rental Contact: 7189794185 Millie Rich
Organization Type: Performing

1202
BOSTON CLASSICAL ORCHESTRA
PO Box 152
Newton, MA 02468-0002
Phone: 617-423-3883
Fax: 815-301-5541
Web Site: www.bostonclassicalorchestra.org
Officers:
- **President:** Herbert A Fox
- **VP:** Richards L Edwards
- **Treasurer:** Rand Folta

Management:
- **Executive Director:** Carolyn Copp
- **Music Director:** Steven Lipsitt

Mission: To offer outstanding performances of the chamber orchestra repertoire in an intimate setting, concentrating on music of the Classical period. Through imaginatively presented live concerts in a relaxed atmosphere, the BCO seeks to foster a sense of connection between audience and performers and to strengthen its appeal to a growing and varied public.
Founded: 1980
Specialized Field: Symphony; Orchestra; Chamber
Status: Professional; Nonprofit
Paid Staff: 3
Volunteer Staff: 25
Budget: $300,000
Performs At: Faneuil Hall
Organization Type: Performing

1203
NEWTON SYMPHONY ORCHESTRA
61 Washington Park
Newton, MA 02460
Phone: 617-965-2555
Fax: 617-965-0450
e-mail: newtonsymphony@compuserve.com
Web Site: www.newtonsymphony.org
Officers:
- **President:** Walter F Carter
- **VP:** Andris Vizolis
- **Secretary:** Nancy O'Brien
- **Treasurer:** Joel Corman

Management:
- **Administrative Coordinator:** Arks Smith
- **Music Director/Conductor:** Jeffrey Rink
- **Personnel Manager:** Mark Perreovlt

Mission: To provide area volunteer musicians the opportunity to maintain and develop their skills, and to enhance music appreciation, promote cross-cultural understanding, and build community through outreach programs for students and seniors.
Founded: 1965
Specialized Field: Symphony; Orchestra
Status: Nonprofit; Volunteer
Paid Staff: 3
Volunteer Staff: 7
Paid Artists: 10
Non-paid Artists: 60
Budget: $100,000
Income Sources: Box office; grants; private donations
Performs At: Rashi Auditorium
Annual Attendance: 3,000 - 4,000
Seating Capacity: 852
Organization Type: Performing

1204
CAPE COD CHAMBER MUSIC FESTIVAL
3 Main Street
Main Street Mercantile Unit 14
North Chatham, MA 02651
Phone: 508-247-9400
Fax: 508-247-9450
Toll-free: 800-229-5739
e-mail: info@capecodchambermusic.org
Web Site: www.capecodchambermusic.org
Officers:
- **President:** David B Farer

INSTRUMENTAL MUSIC / Massachusetts

Treasurer: Inez D'Arcangelo
Secretary: Lawrence M Handley
VP: Susan Hamilton
VP: Regina M. Mullen
Management:
   Artistic Director: Jon Manasse
   Executive Directoror: Elaine Lipton
   Artistic Administrator: Margo Garrett
Mission: To present the finest classical and contemporary chamber music by both world-class ensembles and exceptional young emerging artists to Cape Cod audiences; to develop new and younger audiences for chamber music; to commission new chamber works whenever possible; and to provide educational activities and programs which encourage, broaden and deepen appreciation of the chamber music art form.
Founded: 1979
Specialized Field: Chamber
Status: Professional; Nonprofit
Paid Staff: 3
Paid Artists: 30
Facility Category: Usually churches
Seating Capacity: 250 - 300
Organization Type: Performing; Educational

1205
SMITH COLLEGE ORCHESTRA
Smith College Musical Department
Sage Hall, Smith College
Northampton, MA 01063
Phone: 413-584-2700
Fax: 413-585-3180
e-mail: jhirsh@email.smith.edu
Web Site: www.sophia.smith.edu
Officers:
   President: Keisha Cassel
   VP: Celeste Pritchard
   Treasurer: Alana Sennett
Management:
   Conductor: Jonathan Hirsh
Utilizes: Original Music Scores; Soloists
Specialized Field: Orchestra
Performs At: Concert Halls

1206
STOCKBRIDGE CHAMBER CONCERTS AT SEARLES CASTLE
68 Kenilworth Street
Pittsfield, MA 01201
Phone: 413-442-7711
Fax: 413-442-7711
Toll-free: 888-528-7728
e-mail: elizabethhagenah@altavista.com
Officers:
   President: Elizabeth A Hagenah
   VP: Dr. David Anderegg
   Treasurer: Dr. Norma Thompson
Management:
   Artistic Director/Founder: Elizabeth A Hagenah
   Clerk: Eunice Agar
Mission: To promote cultural activities and help outstanding young talents by giving them scholarship performances with mature artists.
Utilizes: Sign Language Translators; Students
Founded: 1975
Specialized Field: Ensemble; Chamber
Status: Professional; Nonprofit
Paid Artists: 15
Budget: $16,000-$22,000
Income Sources: Ticket sales, contributions
Performs At: Searles Castle
Affiliations: Chamber Music America (member)
Annual Attendance: 175
Facility Category: Concert hall and reception atrium
Type of Stage: Small elevated
Seating Capacity: 175, 250 childrens programs
Year Built: 1886
Rental Contact: At John Dewey Academy Dr. Thomas Bratter
Organization Type: Performing; Touring; Resident; Educational; Sponsoring
Resident Groups: Stockbridge Chamber Concerts (summer)

1207
PLYMOUTH PHILHARMONIC ORCHESTRA
16 Court Street
Plymouth, MA 02360
Mailing Address: PO Box 3174, Plymouth, MA 12361
Phone: 508-746-8008
Fax: 508-746-0115
e-mail: thephil@adelphia.com
Web Site: www.plymouthphilharmonic.com
Officers:
   President: Louise Woodruff
   VP: Thomas Hurley
   VP: Michael Coleman
   Secretary/Clerk: Donna Frugoli
   Treasurer: Paul Kiley
   VP: N. Thompson Bosanquet
Management:
   Executive Director: Roberta J Otto
   Office Manager: Linda Hurley
   Development Manager: Christine Wells
   Marketing Specialist: Judith Ingram
   Music Director/Conductor: Steven Karidoyanes
Mission: To present excellent, professional symphonic music to the broadest possible audience and to encourage a life-long love of music through a variety of educational programs.
Utilizes: Collaborations; Commissioned Music; Educators; Five Seasonal Concerts; Guest Musical Directors; Guest Musicians; Local Artists; Multi Collaborations; Multimedia; Music; Organization Contracts; Original Music Scores; Sign Language Translators; Singers; Volunteer Artists
Founded: 1913
Specialized Field: Symphony; Orchestra; Chamber; Ensemble
Status: Professional; Semi-Professional; Nonprofit
Paid Staff: 8
Paid Artists: 75
Budget: $519,468
Income Sources: Ticket Sales; Grants; Contributions
Performs At: Memorial Hall - Plymouth, Massachusetts
Affiliations: American Symphony Orchestra League; Plymouth County Development Council; Plymouth Area Chamber of Commerce
Annual Attendance: 15,500
Facility Category: Municipal Auditorium
Seating Capacity: 1285
Year Built: 1926
Year Remodeled: 2002
Organization Type: Performing; Educational; Sponsoring

1208
ROCKPORT CHAMBER MUSIC FESTIVAL
21 Broadway
Suite B
Rockport, MA 01966
Mailing Address: PO Box 312, Rockport, MA 01966
Phone: 978-546-7391
Fax: 978-546-8351
e-mail: info@rockportmusic.org
Web Site: www.rcmf.org
Officers:
   President: Phillip D Cutter MD
   VP: Dianne Anderson
   VP: Barbara Sparks
   Treasurer: William Hausman
   Clerk/Secretary: Mollie Byrnes
Management:
   Artistic Director: David Deveau
   Executive Director: Tony Beadle
   Box Office Manager: Carol Ciulla
Mission: The presentation of a 16-concert series in June, featuring chamber ensembles performing alone and in collaboration.
Specialized Field: Chamber
Status: Professional; Nonprofit
Performs At: Rockport Art Association
Organization Type: Presenting

1209
MUSICORDA FESTIVAL & SUMMER STRING PROGRAM
PO Box 557
South Hadley, MA 01075
Phone: 413-538-2590
Fax: 413-538-3021
e-mail: musicorda@aol.com
Management:
   Artistic Director: Leopold Teraspulsky
   Executive Director: Jacqueline Melnick
Mission: To forge an international community of artists and students dedicated to sharing their joy in making music and to enriching the lives of diverse audiences through excellence in performance and education.
Founded: 1987
Specialized Field: String Ensemble
Status: Professional; Nonprofit
Paid Staff: 4
Volunteer Staff: 4
Performs At: Chapin Auditorium, Mount Holyoke College
Facility Category: Concert Hall
Seating Capacity: 800
Organization Type: Performing; Touring; Resident; Educational

1210
SPRINGFIELD ORCHESTRA ASSOCIATION
1350 Main Street
Suite 12
Springfield, MA 01103
Phone: 413-733-0636
Fax: 413-781-4129
e-mail: Info@springfieldsymphony.org
Web Site: www.springfieldsymphony.org
Officers:
   Chairman: Kris Houghton
   President: John Chandler
   Vice President: David Gang
   Treasurer: Michael Gregory
   Clerk & General Counsel: Atty. Ronald Weiss
Management:
   Music Director & Conductor: Kevin Rhodes
   Executive Director: Audrey J Jonnes
   Box Office Manager: Danny Boyle
   Production Stage Manager: Shari Guyer
Mission: To provide symphonic music and other musical entertainment to the residents of Western Massachusetts; to nurture music appreciation.
Specialized Field: Symphony
Status: Professional; Nonprofit
Performs At: Springfield Symphony Hall
Organization Type: Performing; Touring; Educational

INSTRUMENTAL MUSIC / Massachusetts

1211
SPRINGFIELD SYMPHONY ORCHESTRA
1350 Main Street
Suite 12
Springfield, MA 01103
Phone: 413-733-2291
Fax: 413-781-4129
e-mail: Info@springfieldsymphony.org
Web Site: www.springfieldsymphony.org
Officers:
  Chairman: Kris Houghton
  President: John Chandler
  Vice President: David Gang
  Treasurer: Michael Gregory
  Clerk & General Counsel: Atty. Ronald Weiss
Management:
  Music Director & Conductor: Kevin Rhodes
  Executive Director: Audrey J Jonnes
  Box Office Manager: Danny Boyle
  Production Stage Manager: Shari Guyer
Mission: To sponsor, promote and assist in the presentation of symphonic concerts; encourage and develop a desire for symphonic music; instruct, assist and develop musical abilities; assist in training and education; provide concerts, musical programs and other entertainment.
Founded: 1921
Specialized Field: Symphony; Orchestra; Chamber; Ensemble
Status: Professional; Nonprofit
Income Sources: American Symphony Orchestra League; Chamber Music America; Illinois Arts Alliance
Performs At: Braden Auditorium at Illinois State University
Organization Type: Performing; Touring; Resident; Educational

1212
MARTHA'S VINEYARD CHAMBER MUSIC SOCIETY
PO Box 4189
Vineyard Haven, MA 02568
Phone: 508-696-8055
Fax: 508-696-8055
e-mail: mvcms@vineyard.net
Web Site: www.mvcms.org
Officers:
  President: David Rhoderick
  VP: Dr. Sofia Anthony
  Treasurer: Max Skj"Idebrand
  Secretary: David Stanwood
Management:
  Executive Director: Jane Coakley
  Artistic Director: Delores Stevens
Mission: To produce chamber music concerts, promote and support classical music learning opportunities and create awareness of the value and significance of fine music on the island.
Utilizes: Collaborations; Commissioned Composers; Guest Musical Directors; Multimedia; Original Music Scores; Sign Language Translators
Founded: 1971
Specialized Field: Chamber
Status: Professional; Nonprofit
Paid Staff: 1
Paid Artists: 30
Budget: $100,000
Income Sources: Box Office; Grants; Private Donations
Performs At: Old Wharling Church; Chilmark Community Center
Annual Attendance: 2,800
Facility Category: Historic Church; Peformance & Community Center
Type of Stage: Proscenium
Seating Capacity: 500; 200

1213
NEW ENGLAND STRING ENSEMBLE
599 N Avenue, Suite 8
su
Wakefield, MA 01880
Phone: 781-224-1117
Fax: 781-224-3547
e-mail: info@nese.net
Web Site: www.nese.net
Officers:
  President: Gordon Conrad
  VPresident: James Wisdom
  Tresurer: Bob Sanferrare
  Clerk: John Wall
Management:
  Music Director: Susan Davenny Wyner
  Executive Director: Peter Stickel
  Orchestra Manager: John Bumstedd
Mission: The New England String Ensemble was founded to bring string music both to the concertgoing public and to those who might not overwise have the opportunity to hear a professional string orchestra.
Founded: 1994
Specialized Field: Classical; String Ensemble
Paid Staff: 3
Volunteer Staff: 2
Paid Artists: 30
Annual Attendance: 390,000
Facility Category: Concet Hall
Seating Capacity: 1,000

1214
BRANDEIS SYMPHONY ORCHESTRA
Slosberg Musical Building MS 051
Waltham, MA 02454
Phone: 781-736-3328
Fax: 781-736-3320
e-mail: brocksym@email.msn.com
Web Site: www.brandeis.edu/departments/music
Officers:
  Department Chair: Yu-Hui Chang
  Graduate Program Chair (Musicology): Eric Chafe
Management:
  Conductor: Neal Hampton
  Senior Academic Administrator: Mark Kagan
  Piano Technician: Deb Cyr
  Concert Program Manager: Deborah Rosenstein
  Director, Improv Collective: Tom Hall

1215
BRANDEIS UNIVERSITY DEPARTMENT OF MUSIC
415 South Street
Waltham, MA 02453
Phone: 781-736-3310
Fax: 781-736-3320
e-mail: music@brandies.edu
Web Site: www.brandeis.edu/departments/music
Officers:
  Department Chair: Yu-Hui Chang
  Graduate Program Chair (Musicology): Eric Chafe
Management:
  Conductor: Neal Hampton
  Senior Academic Administrator: Mark Kagan
  Piano Technician: Deb Cyr
  Concert Program Manager: Deborah Rosenstein
  Director, Improv Collective: Tom Hall
Mission: Pesenting a university concert series including Professional Series, Concerts at Noon and student performances.
Utilizes: Guest Artists
Founded: 1940
Specialized Field: Orchestra; Chamber; Ensemble; Electronic; Live Electronic
Status: Professional; Non-Professional; Nonprofit
Performs At: Slosberg Recital Hall
Organization Type: Performing; Resident

1216
BOSTON CIVIC SYMPHONY ORCHESTRA OF BOSTON
P.O. Box 1082
Westwood, MA 02446
Phone: 617-923-6333
Fax: 781-329-7293
e-mail: info@csob.org
Web Site: www.csob.org
Officers:
  President: Richard Blacher
Management:
  Music Director/Conductor: Max Hobart
  Orchestra Manager: Jane Zanichkowsky
  Personnel Manager: Mona Chang
Founded: 1924
Specialized Field: Orchestra

1217
WILLIAMS CHAMBER PLAYERS
54 Chaplin Hall Drive
Williamstown, MA 01267-2687
Phone: 413-597-2127
Fax: 413-597-3100
e-mail: Marilyn.Cole.Dostie@williams.edu
Web Site: music.williams.edu/node/1161
Officers:
  Chair/Department Music: Douglas B Moore
  Assisitant Director to Chair: Marilyn Cole Dostie
Management:
  Concert and Event Manager: Jonathan Myers
  Concert Manager: Ernest Clark
  Artist Associate in Jazz Piano: John Nazarenko
  Artist Associate: Susan Martula
  Artist Associate in Jazz Drums: Conor Meehen
Mission: To bring high-quality performance of chamber music repertoire to Williams students and the community-at-large.
Founded: 1999
Specialized Field: Chamber
Status: Professional; Nonprofit
Performs At: Brooks-Rogers Recital Hall; Bernhard Music Center
Organization Type: Performing; Touring; Resident

1218
QUINCY SYMPHONY ORCHESTRA
PO Box 2
Wollaston, MA 02170
Phone: 800-579-1618
Fax: 617-376-1297
Toll-free: 800-579-1618
e-mail: info@quincysymphonyorchestra.org
Web Site: www.quincysymphonyorchestra.org
Officers:
  President: Helenann Wright
  1st Vice President: Barbara Clement
  Second VP: Roberta Kopelman
  Secretary: Janet Petkun
  Treasurer: Arleen Greene
Management:
  Music Director: Yoichi Udagawa
  Concertmaster: Anne Hopper Webb

INSTRUMENTAL MUSIC / Michigan

Personnel Manager: Bruce Norian
Founded: 1954
Specialized Field: Orchestra

1219
CAPE COD SYMPHONY ORCHESTRA
712A Main Street
Yarmouth Port, MA 02675
Phone: 508-362-1185
Fax: 508-326-7916
e-mail: info@capesymphony.org
Web Site: www.capesymphony.org
Officers:
  Acting Executive Director: Jerome Karter
Management:
  Artistic Director/Conductor: JUNG-HO PAK
  Assocciate Conductor & Education Mu: Joan Landry
  Vice Chair: Jerome Karter
Mission: The program is designed to encourage appreciation and to futher develop the students understanding of classical music.
Specialized Field: Symphony

Michigan

1220
ADRIAN SYMPHONY ORCHESTRA
110 S Madison Street
Adrian, MI 49221
Phone: 517-264-3121
Fax: 517-264-3833
e-mail: info@adriansymphony.org
Web Site: www.adriansymphony.org
Officers:
  Chair: Michael Olsaver
  Vice Chair: Bronna Kahle
  Treasurer: Millie Pruett
  Secretary: Ann Hinsdale-Knisel
  Board Member: Larry Bogusz
Management:
  Executive Director: Libby Watson
  Music Director: John Thomas Dodson
  Director of Donor & Community Relat: Cindy Farnham
  Stage & Concert Operations Manager: Jee Pinsoneault
  Audience Services: Sharon Taylor
Mission: To remain Lenawee County's premiere musical ensemble and Adrian College's professional orchestra-in-residence; to perform classical, family, holiday, pops, chamber and young peoples' concerts.
Utilizes: Grant Writers; Guest Accompanists; Guest Artists; Guest Composers; Guest Musicians
Founded: 1981
Specialized Field: Symphony; Orchestra; Chamber; Ensemble
Status: Professional; Nonprofit
Paid Staff: 5
Budget: $350,000
Income Sources: American Symphony Orchestra League; Michigan Orchestra Association
Performs At: Dawson Auditorium
Affiliations: Adrian College
Organization Type: Performing; Touring; Resident; Educational

1221
ALMA SYMPHONY ORCHESTRA
614 W Superior Street
Alma, MI 48801
Phone: 989-463-7111
Fax: 517-463-7277
Toll-free: 800-321-2562
e-mail: kitzmillersm@alma.edu
Web Site: www.alma.edu/academics/music/alma-symphony-orchestra.php
Management:
  Music Director: Murray Gross
  Director of Percussion Ensemble: David Zerbe
  Department Secretary: Shirley Kitzmiller
Specialized Field: Orchestra; Ensemble; Band

1222
ANN ARBOR SYMPHONY ORCHESTRA
220 East Huron
Suite 470
Ann Arbor, MI 48104
Phone: 734-994-4801
Fax: 734-994-3949
e-mail: a2so@a2so.com
Web Site: www.a2so.com
Officers:
  President: J. Robert Gates
  First Vice President: Ann T. Hollenbeck
  Secretary: Steven C. Pierce
  Treasurer: Richard Hendricks
  Vice President - Artistic Affairs: Roderick Little
Management:
  Executive Director: Mary Steffek Blaske
  Conductor: Arie Lipsky
  Business Manager: Lori Zupan
  Education Dir & General Manager: Zac Moore
  Marketing Manager: Emily Fromm
Mission: Enrich musical culture of Ann Arbor and surrounding area, foster growing appreciation for orchestral music.
Utilizes: Collaborations; Commissioned Music; Guest Accompanists; Guest Musical Directors; Guest Musicians; Instructors; Multimedia; Organization Contracts; Original Music Scores; Sign Language Translators; Singers; Soloists
Founded: 1928
Specialized Field: Symphony; Orchestra
Status: Professional
Paid Staff: 8
Volunteer Staff: 3
Paid Artists: 220
Budget: $979,000
Income Sources: Tickets; Contributions; Grants
Performs At: Historic Theater
Annual Attendance: 18,000
Organization Type: Performing; Educational

1223
UNIVERSITY OF MICHIGAN SYMPHONY ORCHESTRAS
1100 Baits Drive
E V Moore Building
Ann Arbor, MI 48109-2085
Phone: 734-764-0583
Fax: 734-763-5097
e-mail: aderente@umich.edu
Web Site: www.music.umich.edu/special_programs/youth/mye/MYEsymphonyorch.htm
Officers:
  Dean: Christopher Kendall
  Assistant to the Dean: Terri Glazier
  Secretary to the Dean: Tracy Goetz
  Associate Dean for Administration: John Ellis
Management:
  Music Director: Kenneth Kiesler
  Ensembles Manager: David R Aderente
  Conductor: Anthony Elliott
Specialized Field: Orchestra
Budget: $35,000
Performs At: Hill Auditorium

1224
BATTLE CREEK SYMPHONY ORCHESTRA
PO Box 1613
Battle Creek, MI 49016
Phone: 269-963-1911
Fax: 269-966-2547
e-mail: execdirector@musiccenterscmi.com
Web Site: www.musiccenterscmi.com
Officers:
  President: Penny DeGarmo
Management:
  Music Director/Conductor: Anne Harrigan
  Executive Director: Stacy Little
  Marketing and Public Relations Mana: Heather Stratton
  Operations Manager: Megan Yankee
  Bookkeeper: Becky Rohrig
Mission: The performance of classical and pops concerts.
Utilizes: Collaborations; Commissioned Music; Guest Accompanists; Guest Composers; High School Drama; Multimedia; Sign Language Translators; Singers
Founded: 1899
Specialized Field: Symphony; Orchestra; Chamber
Status: Professional; Nonprofit
Paid Staff: 6
Paid Artists: 80
Budget: $500,000
Income Sources: American Symphony Orchestra League; Michigan Council for Arts and Cultural Affairs; United Arts Council
Performs At: WK Kellogg Auditorium
Organization Type: Performing; Educational

1225
MUSIC CENTER OF SOUTH CENTRAL MICHIGAN
PO Box 1613
Battle Creek, MI 49016
Phone: 269-963-1911
Fax: 269-966-2547
e-mail: execdirector@musiccenterscmi.com
Web Site: www.musiccenterscmi.com
Management:
  Music Director/Conductor: Anne Harrigan
  Executive Director: Stacy Little
  Marketing and Public Relations Mana: Heather Stratton
  Operations Manager: Megan Yankee
  Bookkeeper: Becky Rohrig
Mission: Your nonprofit resource for learning and performance in the Battle Creek region, featuring the symphony, music schools and choruses.
Specialized Field: Concert Band; Folk Music; Orchestra
Status: Nonprofit
Income Sources: Individual
Performs At: W K Kellogg Auditorium; Lakeview High School; First Presbyterian Church; First Congregational Church
Type of Stage: Black Box

1226
BIRMINGHAM-BLOOMFIELD SYMPHONY
PO Box 1925
Birmingham, MI 48012-1925

All listings are in alphabetical order by state, then city, then organization within the city.

INSTRUMENTAL MUSIC / Michigan

Phone: 248-645-2276
Fax: 248-645-2276
e-mail: bbso@bbso.org
Web Site: www.bbso.org
Officers:
   Chairman: Rich Tropea
   President: Carl Cleland
   Vice President and Orchestra Progra: Bill Close
   Young Artist Competition Chair: Millicent Berry
   Board Member: Shel Green
Management:
   Executive Director: Brandon Faber
   Accountant: Sharon Million
   Music Director: John Thomas Dodson
Mission: To foster an appreciation of the musical arts.
Utilizes: Guest Artists
Founded: 1975
Specialized Field: Symphony; Orchestra; Ensemble
Status: Professional; Nonprofit
Income Sources: American Society of Composers, Authors and Publishers; Michigan Orchestra Association; Michigan Orchestra Volunteer Association
Performs At: Temple Beth El
Organization Type: Performing; Educational

1227
MACOMB SYMPHONY ORCHESTRA
44575 Garfield Road
Clinton Township, MI 48038-1139
Phone: 586-286-2045
Fax: 248-643-0808
e-mail: thomusic@prodigy.net.
Web Site: www.macombsymphony.org
Management:
   Music Director: Thomas Cook
   Personnel Manager: Michele Demski
Utilizes: Multimedia
Founded: 1974
Specialized Field: Orchestra
Paid Staff: 2
Volunteer Staff: 28
Paid Artists: 82
Non-paid Artists: 6
Budget: $35,000-$100,000
Seating Capacity: 1,230
Year Built: 1981
Year Remodeled: 2002

1228
DEARBORN ORCHESTRAL SOCIETY / DEARBORN SYMPHONY
PO Box 2063
Dearborn, MI 48123
Phone: 313-565-2424
Fax: 313-982-1978
e-mail: info@dearbornsymphony.org
Web Site: www.dearbornsymphony.org
Officers:
   President: Sandra Butler
   Vice President: Ben Bachrach
   Vice President: John Matthews
   Treasurer: Brenda Lemecha
   Secretary: Linda Freitag
Management:
   Music Director: Kypros Markou
   Office Manager: Debora Brazakis
Utilizes: Guest Companies; Guest Lecturers; Local Artists; Multimedia; Sign Language Translators; Singers
Specialized Field: Orchestra
Paid Staff: 3
Income Sources: Donations; Corporate Support
Annual Attendance: 5,000
Facility Category: Ford Community and Performing Arts Center

Seating Capacity: 1,201
Year Built: 2001

1229
DETROIT SYMPHONY ORCHESTRA
3711 Woodward Avenue
Detroit, MI 48201
Phone: 313-576-5100
Fax: 313-576-5101
Web Site: www.detroitsymphony.com
Officers:
   Chairman: Stanley Frankel
   VP: Bruce D Peterson
   Treasurer: Arthur A Weiss
   Secretary: Glenda D Price
Management:
   Music Director: Leonard Slatkin
   Managing Director of Special Events: Anne Wilczak
   Senior Director of Accounting & Fin: Jeremiah Hess
   Director of Digital Media: Erica Woodhams
   Orchestra Manager: Alice Sauro
Utilizes: Guest Artists
Founded: 1914
Status: Non-Profit, Professional
Performs At: Orchestra Hall; Meadow Brook Music Festival
Organization Type: Performing; Touring; Resident; Educational; Sponsoring

1230
PRO MUSICA OF DETROIT
P.O. Box 15369
Detroit, MI 48215
Phone: 248-851-1673
Fax: 313-885-6685
e-mail: info@promusicadetroit.com
Web Site: www.promusicadetroit.com
Officers:
   First VP: Alice Haidostian
   Second VP: Dr. Hershel Sandberg
   Secretary: Ann Kondak
   Treasurer: James Diamond
   President: Alexander Suczek
Budget: $60,000
Income Sources: Ticket Sales; Membership; Endowment; Corporate Sponsors
Performs At: Recital Hall of the Detroit Institute of the Arts
Annual Attendance: 3,000
Seating Capacity: 1,100
Year Built: 1927

1231
CHAMBER MUSIC SOCIETY OF DETROIT
27655 Middlebelt Road
Suite 160
Farmington Hills, MI 48334
Phone: 248-737-9980
Fax: 248-737-9981
e-mail: Tickets@ChamberMusicDetroit.org
Web Site: www.chambermusicdetroit.org
Officers:
   Chairman: Wendy Zimmer Cox
   President: Stephen Wogaman
   Secretary: Paul J Blizman
   Treasurer: Robert D Hicks
   Vice President, Concert Division: Willa R. Walker
Management:
   Patron Services Manager: Christine Blair
   Development Consultant: Kirsten Mason
Utilizes: Collaborations; Commissioned Music; Guest Directors; Multimedia; Original Music Scores; Singers

Founded: 1944
Specialized Field: Chamber Music; Recitals
Performs At: Seligman Performing Arts Center; Orchestra Hall
Affiliations: Chamber Music America
Seating Capacity: 715; 2,035

1232
FLINT SCHOOL OF PERFORMING ARTS: YOUTH ENSEMBLES
1025 E Kearsley
Flint, MI 48503
Phone: 810-238-1350
Fax: 810-238-6385
e-mail: ptorre@thefim.org
Web Site: www.thefim.com
Officers:
   Chair: Howard S. Shand
   President and CEO: Paul Torre
   Chair Elect: Vince Lorraine
   Treasurer: Robert S. Fuller
   Secretary: James Spangler
Management:
   Music Director and Conductor: Enrique Diemecke
   Director of Donor Relations: Sheila Zorn
   Director of Human Resources and Adm: Desiree Smith
   Director of Business Operations: Marianne Stuckwisch
   Executive Artistic Director: Jeremy Winchester
Specialized Field: Orchestra; Youth Orchestra
Annual Attendance: 3500

1233
FLINT SYMPHONY ORCHESTRA
1025 E Kearsley Street
Flint, MI 48503
Phone: 810-238-1350
Fax: 810-238-6385
e-mail: ptorre@thefim.org
Web Site: www.thefim.com
Officers:
   Chair: Howard S. Shand
   President and CEO: Paul Torre
   Chair Elect: Vince Lorraine
   Treasurer: Robert S. Fuller
   Secretary: James Spangler
Management:
   Music Director and Conductor: Enrique Diemecke
   Director of Donor Relations: Sheila Zorn
   Director of Human Resources and Adm: Desiree Smith
   Director of Business Operations: Marianne Stuckwisch
   Executive Artistic Director: Jeremy Winchester
Utilizes: Guest Artists
Founded: 1917
Specialized Field: Symphony; Orchestra
Status: Professional; Nonprofit
Budget: $260,000-$15,000,000
Performs At: James H. Whiting Auditorium
Organization Type: Performing; Resident; Educational

1234
GRAND RAPIDS SYMPHONY
300 Ottawa Avenue
Suite 100
Grand Rapids, MI 49503
Phone: 616-454-9451
Fax: 616-454-7477
e-mail: grsinfo@grsymphony.org
Web Site: www.grsymphony.org
Officers:
   Chairperson: Peter M. Perez

Chairperson Elect: Kate Pew Wolters
Secretary: Karen Henry Stokes
Treasurer: Rosa L. Caswell
Vice Chairperson: Michael Ellis
Management:
  Music Director: David Lockington
  Chorus Director: Pearl Shangkuan
  Director of Education: Claire Van Brandeghen
  Operations Manager: Julie Nystedt
  Production Stage Manager: Kyle Viana
Mission: The purpose of the Grand Rapids Symphony Society is to provide concerts of orchestral and chamber music and educational programs of the highest quality to the widest possible audience.
Utilizes: Guest Artists; Guest Companies
Founded: 1929
Specialized Field: Symphony; Orchestra; Chamber; Ensemble
Status: Nonprofit
Paid Staff: 25
Paid Artists: 75
Budget: $6.2 million
Income Sources: Concert and Event Income; Grants; Private Donations
Annual Attendance: 200,000
Organization Type: Performing; Touring; Resident; Educational

1235
GRAND RAPIDS YOUTH SYMPHONY
220 Lyon Street NW
Suite 415
Grand Rapids, MI 49503
Phone: 616-454-9451
Fax: 616-454-7477
Management:
  Conductor: John Varineau
  Outreach Director: Pam French
Mission: The Grand Rapids Youth Symphony affords the area's finest young musicians the opportunity to perform orchestal compositions ats a high standard.
Founded: 1959
Specialized Field: Youth Symphony; Orchestra
Status: Non-Professional; Nonprofit
Paid Staff: 80
Income Sources: American Symphony Orchestra League (Youth Orchestra Division); Grand Rapids Symphony
Performs At: Forest Hills Northern High School Auditorium
Organization Type: Performing; Educational

1236
ST. CECILIA MUSIC SOCIETY
24 Ransom Avenue NE
Grand Rapids, MI 49503
Phone: 616-459-2224
Fax: 616-459-2997
e-mail: scms_pwp@iserv.net
Web Site: www.scmsonline.org
Officers:
  President: Scott Huizinga
  Vice President: Dan Persinger
  Secretary: Tim Raymer
  Treasurer: Jennifer Tyler
  Board Member: Kerry Akred
Management:
  Executive Director: Catherine Holbrook
  Development Director: Ricki L. Levine
  Facility and Event Director: Carla Messing
  Business Manager: Christy Spoehr
  Facility and Event Assistant Manage: Kalena Meyers Heibeck

Mission: To promote and support chamber music performance in Western Michigan, specifically Grand Rapids.
Utilizes: Actors; AEA Actors; Artists-in-Residence; Choreographers; Collaborating Artists; Collaborations; Dance Companies; Dancers; Educators; Fine Artists; Grant Writers; Guest Accompanists; Guest Choreographers; Guest Companies; Guest Directors; Guest Instructors; Guest Musical Directors; Guest Musicians; Guest Soloists; High School Drama; Instructors; Local Artists; Lyricists; Multi Collaborations; Multimedia; Organization Contracts; Original Music Scores; Selected Students; Sign Language Translators; Singers; Soloists; Student Interns; Theatre Companies
Founded: 1883
Specialized Field: Educational; Classical Music
Status: Nonprofit
Paid Staff: 20
Volunteer Staff: 300
Paid Artists: 50
Non-paid Artists: 100
Budget: $700,000
Income Sources: Membership, Grants, Corporate Funding
Performs At: Royce Auditorium
Annual Attendance: 35,000
Facility Category: Historic Landmark Building
Type of Stage: Proscenium
Seating Capacity: 650
Year Built: 1894
Year Remodeled: 1998
Organization Type: Sponsoring

1237
PRO MUSICA OF DETROIT
29069 Utley Rd
Grosse Pointe Farms, MI
Phone: 248-851-1673
Fax: 313-885-6685
e-mail: info@promusicadetroit.com
Web Site: www.promusicadetroit.com
Officers:
  First VP: Alice Haidostian
  Second VP: Dr. Hershel Sandberg
  Secretary: Ann Kondak
  Treasurer: James Diamond
  President: Alexander Suczek
Mission: To present world-class emerging performers in debut recitals; to offer performances of composers.
Utilizes: Guest Companies; Guest Directors; Guest Musical Directors; Guest Musicians; Multimedia; Original Music Scores; Sign Language Translators; Singers
Founded: 1927
Specialized Field: Ensemble; New Music; World Music; Classical Music
Status: Professional; Nonprofit
Volunteer Staff: 40
Paid Artists: 30-M
Budget: $60,000
Income Sources: Ticket Sales; Membership; Endowment; Corporate Sponsors
Performs At: Recital Hall of the Detroit Institute of the Arts
Annual Attendance: 3,000
Facility Category: Auditorium; Concert Hall
Seating Capacity: 1,100
Year Built: 1927
Organization Type: Performing

1238
HILLSDALE COLLEGE COMMUNITY ORCHESTRA
33 E College Street
Hillsdale, MI 49242
Phone: 517-437-7341
Fax: 517-437-3923
e-mail: jholleman@hillsdale.edu
Web Site: www.hillsdale.edu/academics/departments/music/ensembles#Orchestra
Officers:
  President: Larry P Arnn
Management:
  Music Director/Conductor: James A Holleman
Founded: 1844
Specialized Field: Orchestra; Ensemble
Budget: $35,000
Performs At: Markel Auditorium; Sage Center for the Arts

1239
HOLLAND CHAMBER ORCHESTRA
583 Riley
Holland, MI 49424
Mailing Address: PO Box 8084, Holland, MI. 49422-8084
Phone: 616-786-3172
Fax: 616-393-7616
e-mail: hco@macatawa.org
Management:
  Music Director: Mihai Craioveanu
  Orchestra Director: Thomas Working
Mission: Belongs to the community and allows adult musicians to share their love of music and further develop their talents; provides enjoyable and informative programs to promote classical music and inspire our listeners.
Specialized Field: Chamber
Budget: $35,000

1240
HOLLAND SYMPHONY ORCHESTRA
150 E. 8th Street
Holland, MI 49423
Mailing Address: PO Box 2685, Holland, MI 49422-2685
Phone: 616-494-0256
Fax: 616-392-7871
e-mail: hso@hollandsymphony.org
Web Site: www.hollandsymphony.org
Officers:
  Chairman: Doug Rasmussen
  Board Member: Susan Boersma
  Board Member: Sandy Chrispell
  Board Member: Robert Gamble
  Board Member: Brendan Bohnhorst
Management:
  Music Director & Conductor: Johannes M ller-Stosch
  Operations-Personnel Manager: Judy Meyer
  Bookkeeper: Millie Robbert
  Project Director: Lori Gramer
  Concertmaster/Program Notes/Librari: Amanda Dykhouse
Utilizes: Artists-in-Residence; Collaborating Artists; Collaborations; Commissioned Composers; Commissioned Music; Fine Artists; Guest Accompanists; Guest Composers; Guest Lecturers; Guest Musical Directors; Guest Musicians; Multimedia; Music; Original Music Scores; Singers
Founded: 1990
Specialized Field: Orchestra

INSTRUMENTAL MUSIC / Michigan

Paid Staff: 4
Volunteer Staff: 30
Paid Artists: 1
Non-paid Artists: 80
Budget: $100,000
Income Sources: Donations; Ticket Sales; Grants; Corporate Sponsorships
Performs At: Zeeland High School Dewitt Auditorium
Annual Attendance: 4000
Facility Category: Performing Arts Center
Seating Capacity: 942

1241
HOPE COLLEGE ORCHESTRA
127 E. 12th St.
Holland, MI 49423
Phone: 616-395-7650
Fax: 616-395-7182
e-mail: waterstone@hope.edu
Web Site: www.hope.edu/academic/music/ensembles/instrumental.html
Officers:
   President: James E Bultman
   VP/CFO: Tom Bylsma
Management:
   Conductor: Robert Ritsema
Mission: The presentation of concerts on campus as well as in other cities.
Utilizes: Guest Artists; Guest Companies
Founded: 1949
Specialized Field: Orchestra; Chamber
Status: Non-Professional; Nonprofit
Paid Staff: 60
Budget: $35,000
Income Sources: American Symphony Orchestra League; Michigan Orchestra Association
Performs At: Dimnent Chapel
Organization Type: Performing; Touring; Resident; Educational

1242
KEWEENAW SYMPHONY ORCHESTRA OF MICHIGAN TECHNOLOGICAL UNIVERSITY
Michigan Technological University
1400 Townsend Drive 209 Walker
Houghton, MI 49931-1295
Phone: 906-487-2067
Fax: 906-487-1841
Toll-free: 888-MTU-1885
e-mail: Fineart@mtu.edu
Web Site: www.mtu.edu/vpa/events/13-14/kso-color
Management:
   Director of Orchestra and Chorus: Milton Olsson
   Administrator: Shane Crist
Utilizes: Commissioned Music; Guest Companies; Guest Composers; Guest Musical Directors; Guest Musicians; Instructors; Multimedia; Original Music Scores; Singers
Founded: 1971
Specialized Field: Orchestra
Budget: $35,000-$100,000
Performs At: Rozsa Center for the Performing Arts
Affiliations: ASOL

1243
FONTANA CHAMBER ARTS
359 S. Kalamazoo Mall
Suite 200
Kalamazoo, MI 49007
Phone: 269-382-7774
Fax: 269-382-0812
e-mail: bwong@fontanachamberarts.org
Web Site: www.fontanachamberarts.org
Officers:
   Chairman: Thomas C. Bailey
   Vice Chairman: Thomas Seiler
   Treasurer: Dave Rozelle
   Secretary: Lee Kirk
   Board Member: Jane Baley
Management:
   Executive and Artistic Director: David Baldwin
   General Manager: Jill Perney
   Operations Coordinator: Charlie Tomlinson
   Accounting Assistant: Terri Hunter
   Intern: Carrie Brannen
Mission: Offering diverse, high quality chamber music programs in a relaxed rural setting.
Founded: 1980
Specialized Field: Chamber; Ensemble
Status: Professional; Nonprofit
Performs At: The Art Emporium
Organization Type: Performing; Sponsoring

1244
KALAMAZOO SYMPHONY ORCHESTRA
359 South Kalamazoo Mall
Suite 100
Kalamazoo, MI 49007
Phone: 269-349-7759
Fax: 269-349-9229
e-mail: jbarlament@kalamazoosymphony.com
Web Site: www.kalamazoosymphony.com
Officers:
   President: Doug Phillips
   President-Elect: Dr. Janice M. Brown
   Treasurer: Steven P. Kreider
   Secretary: Pamela Enslen
   Member-at-Large: Dave Mange
Management:
   Music Director: Raymond Harvey
   Assistant Conductor: Barry Ross
   Executive Director: Peter H. Gistelinck
   Stage Manager: Evan Menz
   Director of Artistic Operations: Sarah Clapp
Mission: To support a professional symphony orchestra and staff; to present concerts of symphonic music and related programs of the highest possible artistic level; to support effective regional music education; to serve and involve the people of the greater Kalamazoo area in the Symphony Society.
Utilizes: Artists-in-Residence; Collaborating Artists; Commissioned Composers; Commissioned Music; Educators; Five Seasonal Concerts; Guest Accompanists; Guest Artists; Guest Composers; Guest Directors; Guest Instructors; Guest Musical Directors; Guest Musicians; Local Artists; Multimedia; Original Music Scores
Founded: 1921
Specialized Field: Symphony; Orchestra; Chamber; Ensemble
Status: Professional; Nonprofit
Paid Staff: 12
Paid Artists: 85
Budget: $2,000,000
Income Sources: Individual & Corporate Sponsors; Local; State & National Grants
Performs At: Miller Auditorium
Annual Attendance: 25,000
Seating Capacity: 3,496
Organization Type: Performing; Educational

1245
LANSING SYMPHONY ORCHESTRA
501 S. Capitol Avenue
Suite 400
Lansing, MI 48933
Phone: 517-487-5001
Fax: 517-487-0210
e-mail: info@lansingsymphony.org
Web Site: www.lansingsymphony.org
Officers:
   President: Brian J. Lefler
   President-Elect: Michael Rhodes
   Secretary: Joseph H. Anthony
   Treasurer: Jonathan Riekse
   Board Member: Robert Hood
Management:
   Executive Director: Courtney Millbrook
   Director of Finance & Operations: Karen Dichoza
   Director of Marketing & Communicati: Rachel Santorelli
   Program Coordinator: Meredith Brown
   Communications Coordinator: Rachel Santorelli
Mission: Enriching lives through excellence in music and in educational outreach
Utilizes: Guest Musical Directors; Multimedia
Founded: 1929
Specialized Field: Symphony; Orchestra; Chamber; Ensemble
Status: Professional; Nonprofit
Performs At: Wharton Center for Performing Arts
Affiliations: League Of American Orchestras
Seating Capacity: 2,800
Organization Type: Performing; Educational

1246
LIVONIA SYMPHONY ORCHESTRA
37637 5 Mile Road
Livonia, MI 48154
Phone: 734-421-1111
Fax: 734-464-8713
e-mail: info@livoniasymphony.org
Web Site: www.livoniasymphony.org
Officers:
   President: Rose Kachnowski
   1st Vice President: Patrick Beckley
   Vice President-Finance: William C. Fried
   Treasurer: Ronald T Laing
   Secretary: Heather Gladden
Management:
   Conductor/Music Director Music Comm: Volodymyr Schesiuk
   Assistant Conductor/Music Committee: Carl Karoub
   Personnel Manager/Music Committee: Linda J. Ignagni
   Tax Accountant: Jack VanAssche
Specialized Field: Orchestra
Budget: $100,000-$150,000

1247
MIDLAND SYMPHONY ORCHESTRA
1801 W. St. Andrews Rd.
Midland, MI 48640-2695
Phone: 989-631-5930
Fax: 989-631-7890
e-mail: info@mcfta.org
Web Site: www.mcfta.org
Officers:
   Chair: Lee Rose
   Vice-Chair: Bill Collins
   Treasurer: Brian Rodgers
   Secretary: Melissa Barnard
   President & CEO: Mike Hayes

INSTRUMENTAL MUSIC / Michigan

Management:
   Managing Director: Kimberly Dimond
   Music Director: Bohuslav Rattay
   Symphony Librarian & Personnel Mana: Robin Von Wald
   Director of Visitor Services: David Kepler
   Facilities Director: Larry Salva
Mission: Encouraging and supporting the Midland Symphony Orchestra in its pursuit of artistic excellence.
Utilizes: Guest Artists
Founded: 1936
Specialized Field: Symphony; Orchestra; Chamber; Ensemble
Status: Professional; Semi-Professional; Non-Professional; Nonprofit
Income Sources: Michigan Orchestra Association; American Symphony Orchestra League
Performs At: Midland Center for the Arts
Organization Type: Performing; Touring; Educational; Sponsoring

1248
MUSIC SOCIETY: MIDLAND CENTER FOR THE ARTS
1801 W. St. Andrews Rd.
Midland, MI 48640-2695
Phone: 989-631-5930
Fax: 517-631-7890
e-mail: info@mcfta.org
Web Site: www.mcfta.org
Officers:
   Chair: Lee Rose
   Vice-Chair: Bill Collins
   Treasurer: Brian Rodgers
   Secretary: Melissa Barnard
   President & CEO: Mike Hayes
Management:
   Managing Director: Kimberly Dimond
   Music Director: Bohuslav Rattay
   Symphony Librarian & Personnel Mana: Robin Von Wald
   Director of Visitor Services: David Kepler
   Facilities Director: Larry Salva
Mission: Committed to providing performing and educational opportunities that would not otherwise exist.
Utilizes: Guest Artists; Guest Companies; Singers
Founded: 1943
Specialized Field: Orchestra; Chamber; Ensemble; Folk Music; Band
Status: Nonprofit
Performs At: Midland Center for the Arts
Organization Type: Performing; Educational; Sponsoring

1249
WEST MICHIGAN SYMPHONY
360 W. Western Ave.
Suite 200
Muskegon, MI 49440
Phone: 231-726-3231
Fax: 231-457-4033
e-mail: chill@westmichigansymphony.org
Web Site: www.wsso.org
Officers:
   President and CEO: Carla Hill
   VP Operations/Orchestra Personnel M: Gabe Slimko
   Chair: Susan Bissell
   Treasurer: Tom Ladd
   Secretary and Past Chair: David F. Gerdes
Management:
   Director of Operations/Guest Artist: Perry Newson
   Art Director/Marketing Coordinator: Keely Payne
   Business Development Manager: Cathleen M. Dubault
   Patron Services Manager/Tickets: Rita Smith
   Finance Manager: Emma Torresen
Mission: To bring fine live music to the West Michigan area.
Utilizes: Actors; AEA Actors; Artists-in-Residence; Choreographers; Dance Companies; Dancers; Guest Accompanists; Guest Companies; Guest Conductors; Guest Designers; Guest Directors; Instructors; Local Artists; Multimedia; Music; Original Music Scores; Performance Artists; Resident Professionals; Sign Language Translators; Singers; Soloists; Special Technical Talent; Theatre Companies
Founded: 1940
Specialized Field: Youth Symphony; Orchestra; Chamber
Status: Professional; Nonprofit
Paid Staff: 5
Budget: $12,500
Type of Stage: thrust
Stage Dimensions: 30' x 50'
Seating Capacity: 1,700
Year Remodeled: 1999
Organization Type: Performing

1250
PLYMOUTH SYMPHONY
470 Forest Place, Suite 18
PO Box 6349
Plymouth, MI 48170-0379
Phone: 734-451-2112
Fax: 734-451-3458
e-mail: plymouthsymphony@aol.com
Web Site: www.plymouthsymphony.com
Officers:
   President: The Lord Mayor
   VP: Vera Pearce
   Secretary: Denise Hasshill
   Treasurer: Ivan Sidgreaves
   Chairman: Michael Stone
Management:
   Executive Director: Darlene A Dreyer
   Music Director/Conductor: Nan Washburn
   Office Manager: Pat Derderian
Mission: To provide high quality orchestral and music education experiences for the surrounding community.
Utilizes: Choreographers; Collaborating Artists; Collaborations; Commissioned Music; Dance Companies; Educators; Fine Artists; Five Seasonal Concerts; Grant Writers; Guest Companies; Guest Directors; Guest Musicians; Guest Soloists; Guest Writers; Instructors; Local Artists; Lyricists; Multi Collaborations; Multimedia; Music; New Productions; Original Music Scores; Poets; Sign Language Translators; Soloists
Founded: 1875
Specialized Field: Orchestra
Paid Staff: 8
Volunteer Staff: 50
Paid Artists: 80
Budget: $271,000
Income Sources: Ticket Sales; Grants; Donations; Auction; Raffle
Performs At: Variety of Public Venues
Affiliations: ASOL
Facility Category: Churches, Auditoriums, Banquet Halls

1251
SAGINAW BAY SYMPHONY ORCHESTRA
201 S Washington Avenue
Saginaw, MI 48607
Phone: 989-755-6471
Fax: 989-755-1420
Toll-free: 877-755-7276
e-mail: info@saginawbayorchestra.com
Web Site: www.saginabayorchestra.com
Officers:
   President: Floyd P. Kloc
   Vice President: Michael Brush
   Secretary / Treasurer: Samuel Tilmon
   Past President: Michael Elliott
Management:
   Music Director/Conductor: Brett Mitchell
   Executive Director: Daniel McGee
   Office Manager: Kelly Belcher
   Production Manager: Anna Leppert-Largent
Founded: 1935
Specialized Field: Orchestra
Paid Staff: 3

1252
SOUTHWEST MICHIGAN SYMPHONY ORCHESTRA
513 Ship Street
Saint Joseph, MI 49085
Phone: 269-982-4030
Fax: 269-982-4181
e-mail: info@smso.org
Web Site: www.smso.org
Officers:
   President: Norma Tirado
   Secretary: Elizabeth Sexton
   Treasurer: Terry W Malone
   VP-Administration: Karen Johnson
   VP-Development: Michael Damschroder
Management:
   Executive Director: Sue Kellogg
   Music Director: Robin Fountain
   Marketing/Education Coordinator: Loretta Holmes
   Office Manager: Jean Bloomquist
Mission: To present concerts and sponsor an orchestra; to provide music educational activities.
Founded: 1950
Specialized Field: Symphony; Orchestra
Status: Professional
Performs At: Mendel Center; Lake Michigan College
Organization Type: Performing; Educational

1253
DETROIT CHAMBER WINDS & STRINGS
20300 Civinc Center Drive
Suite 100
Southfield, MI 48076-4166
Phone: 248-559-2095
Fax: 248-559-2098
e-mail: info@detroitchamberwinds.org
Web Site: www.detroitchamberwinds.org
Officers:
   Board Chair: Douglas Cale
   Trustee: William Duffy
   Trustee: Mary Jarman
   Trustee: Victoria King
   Trustee: Gerald Conway
Management:
   Artistic Advisor: H. Robert Reynolds
   Executive Director: Maury Okun
   Controller: Erica Battle
   Director of Communications: Margo Strebig
   Development Officer: Alison Gaudreau
Mission: To offer performances of works featuring between 6 and 20 winds.

INSTRUMENTAL MUSIC / Minnesota

Utilizes: Collaborating Artists; Collaborations; Commissioned Music; Dance Companies; Guest Companies; Guest Musicians; Instructors; Multimedia; Organization Contracts; Original Music Scores; Singers
Founded: 1982
Specialized Field: Chamber; Wind Ensemble; String Ensemble
Status: Professional; Nonprofit
Organization Type: Performing

1254
METROPOLITAN YOUTH SYMPHONY
4800 SW Macadam Avenue
Suite 105
Southfield, MI 97239
Phone: 503-239-4566
Fax: 503-239-4426
Toll-free: 888-752-9697
e-mail: alopera @ playmys.org
Web Site: www.playmys.org
Officers:
  President: David R. Ludwig
  Vice President: Andrea Cano
  Treasurer: Justin Ottman
  Secretary: Ryan Lowe
  Member-at-large: David Doerner
Management:
  Conductor: Andres Lopera
  Music Director: Andres Lopera
  Production Manager: Andrea Mgebroff
  Development Manager: Jessica Stern
  Excutive Director: Diana Scoggins
Specialized Field: Youth Orchestra

1255
LAKE ST. CLAIR SYMPHONY ORCHESTRA
PO Box 806249
St. Clair Shores, MI 48080
Phone: 586-777-8944
Fax: 810-776-1012
e-mail: tulrich@home.com
Web Site: www.lscso.com
Officers:
  President: Jack Lawrence
Management:
  Music Director: Zeljko Milicevic
Mission: To promote and provide a symphony orchestra for the residents of the communities adjacent to Lake St. Clair; to provide a continuing educational program in symphonic music for students of the various school districts in the communities served by the Orchestra; and to provide a community-based organization for the expression and enjoyment of the music.
Founded: 1962
Specialized Field: Symphony; Orchestra
Status: Semi-Professional; Nonprofit
Budget: $35,000-$100,000
Income Sources: American Symphony Orchestra League; Michigan Orchestra Association
Performs At: Schaublin Auditorium
Organization Type: Performing

1256
TRAVERSE SYMPHONY ORCHESTRA
300 E Front
Suite 230
Traverse City, MI 49684
Phone: 231-947-7120
Fax: 231-947-8118
e-mail: vschneider@tso-online.org
Web Site: www.traversesymphony.org
Officers:
  President: Thomas Haase
  Vice President: Carla Lamphere
  Treasurer: Patrick Kessel
  Secretary: Karen Smith
  Immediate Past President: J. Kermit Campbell
Management:
  Music Director: Kevin Rhodes
  Executive Director: Krista Cooper
  Annual Campaign Manager: Gary Gatzke
  Manager of Operations: Rick Jaissle
  Marketing Coordinator and Office Ma: Kelsey Lauer
Utilizes: Guest Musical Directors; Guest Musicians
Founded: 1951
Specialized Field: Symphony; Orchestra; Chamber
Status: Professional
Budget: $5,00,000
Income Sources: Ticket Sales; Grants; Donations; Sponserships
Annual Attendance: 7,000
Organization Type: Performing; Touring; Sponsoring

Minnesota

1257
BEMIDJI SYMPHONY ORCHESTRA
Bemidji State University
PO Box 3136
Bemidji, MN 56619
Phone: 218-751-0665
Fax: 218-755-4369
e-mail: Podium314@aol.com
Web Site: www.bemidjisymphony.org
Officers:
  Chair: Ann Long-Voelkner
  Secretary: Nancy Haugen
  Treasurer: Julia Conlon
  Board Member: Mary Auger
  Board Member: Stu Rosselet
Management:
  Conductor/Music Director: Dr Beverly Everett
  Executive Director: MaryAnne Wilimek
  Music Personnel Manager & Librarian: Gretchen Rusch
Mission: Dedicated to communicating the richness of a variety of African cultures and customs through dance, rythm, and song in an exciting, energetic and colorful manner.
Specialized Field: Orchestra
Budget: $35,000
Performs At: Bangsberg Fine Arts Complex Theatre & Recital Hall

1258
DULUTH-SUPERIOR SYMPHONY ORCHESTRA
130 W. Superior Street
Suite LL2
Duluth, MN 55802
Phone: 218-623-3776
Fax: 218-623-3789
e-mail: tickets@dsso.com
Web Site: www.dsso.com
Officers:
  Board Chair: Patrick Spott
  Board Chair Elect: Jeffrey Cadwell
  Treasurer: Jeffrey L. Tucker
  Board Member: Sandra Barkley
  Board Member: Jill Kaiser
Management:
  Executive Director: Rebecca Lynn Petersen
  Music Director: Dirk Meyer
  Concertmaster: Erin Aldridge
  Director of Sales: Mary Sheilds
  Concert Production Director: Heidi Lord
Mission: To generate the required financial and artistic resources to maintain the finest possible symphony orchestra as well as related programs and services; to develop future musicians and audiences.
Utilizes: Collaborations; Commissioned Music; Composers-in-Residence; Fine Artists; Guest Accompanists; Guest Composers; Guest Directors; Guest Musical Directors; Guest Musicians; Instructors; Multimedia; Music; New Productions; Original Music Scores; Singers
Founded: 1932
Specialized Field: Symphony; Orchestra; Chamber; Ensemble
Status: Professional; Nonprofit
Budget: $10,000,000
Income Sources: American Symphony Orchestra League; Saint Louis County Heritage & Arts Center
Performs At: Duluth Auditorium
Annual Attendance: 40,000
Facility Category: DECC Auditorium
Type of Stage: Normal Stage
Seating Capacity: 2,400
Year Built: 1966
Organization Type: Performing; Educational

1259
DULUTH-SUPERIOR YOUTH ORCHESTRAS & SINFONIA
331 West Superior Street
Suite LL2
Duluth, MN 55802
Phone: 218-623-3776
Fax: 218-623-3789
e-mail: tickets@dsso.com
Web Site: www.dsso.com
Officers:
  Board Chair: Patrick Spott
  Board Chair Elect: Jeffrey Cadwell
  Treasurer: Jeffrey L. Tucker
  Board Member: Sandra Barkley
  Board Member: Jill Kaiser
Management:
  Executive Director: Rebecca Lynn Petersen
  Music Director: Dirk Meyer
  Concertmaster: Erin Aldridge
  Director of Sales: Mary Sheilds
  Concert Production Director: Heidi Lord
Mission: To offer a learning and performing experience for students in the Youth Orchestra (high school) and Sinfonia (junior and senior high school).
Founded: 1940
Specialized Field: Youth Orchestra; Chamber; Ensemble
Status: Non-Professional; Nonprofit
Paid Staff: 100
Income Sources: American Symphony Orchestra League (Youth Orchestra Division); Duluth-Superior Symphony Orchestra
Organization Type: Performing; Educational

1260
HEARTLAND SYMPHONY ORCHESTRA
122 SE 1st Street
BOBox 241
Little Falls, MN 56345
Phone: 320-632-0960
Fax: 320-632-9025
Toll-free: 800-826-1997
e-mail: info@heartlandsymphony.org
Web Site: www.heartlandsymphony.org
Officers:
  President: Tom Kotval

INSTRUMENTAL MUSIC / Minnesota

Vice President: Leslie Zander
Treasurer: Ramona Steinke
Secretary: Helen O'Brien
Board Member: Betty Alderman
Management:
   Music Director & Conductor: Sergey Bogza
   Business Manager: Jeanne Bielejeski
   Orchestra Manager: Fran Dosh
Mission: To bring orchestral music to concert-goers in our area, to aquaint young people with the beauty of classical music, and to provide an opportunity for trained musicians to play together.
Utilizes: Guest Musicians
Founded: 1977
Specialized Field: Orchestra
Status: Nonprofit
Budget: $35,000-$100,000
Performs At: Tornstrom Auditorium; Charles Martin Auditorium

1261
MANKATO SYMPHONY ORCHESTRA
523 S. Second Street
Mankato, MN 56001
Mailing Address: PO Box 645 Mankato MN, 56002
Phone: 507-625-8880
Fax: 507-625-5792
e-mail: mso@hickorytech.net
Web Site: www.mankatosymphony.com
Officers:
   President: Herb Kroon
   Vice President: Jim Santori
   Secretary: Tricia Stenberg
   Treasurer: Eric Plath
   Board Member: Keith Balster
Management:
   Executive Director: Sara Buechmann
   Personnel Manager: John Clapham
Mission: The orchestra plays five subscription concerts each year plus three Youth Concerts, and provides many educational and artistic opportunities to area students, including the Young artist and Young Composer contests. The orchestra also plays one free outdoor concert in June.
Utilizes: Collaborating Artists; Collaborations; Guest Accompanists; Guest Musical Directors; Guest Musicians; Guest Writers; Instructors; Multimedia; Organization Contracts; Original Music Scores; Singers; Soloists; Theatre Companies
Founded: 1952
Specialized Field: Symphony; Orchestra
Status: Non-Professional; Nonprofit
Paid Staff: 1
Volunteer Staff: 65
Paid Artists: 90
Budget: $190,000
Income Sources: Grants; Sponsors; Contributions
Performs At: Mankato West High School Auditorium
Facility Category: High school auditorium
Organization Type: Performing; Resident; Educational

1262
CIVIC ORCHESTRA OF MINNEAPOLIS
PO Box 50604
Minneapolis, MN 55405-0604
Phone: 612-332-4842
Fax: 612-649-1288
e-mail: info@civicorchestrampls.org
Web Site: www.civicorchestrampls.org
Officers:
   President: Sylvia Wilson
   Vice President: Dorota Baczynska
   Board Member: Mary Josefson
   Treasurer: John Litch

   Board Member: Doug Overland
Management:
   Music Director: Cary John Franklin
   Orchestra Manager: Rachel Hest
Specialized Field: Orchestra
Budget: $35,000

1263
GREATER TWIN CITIES YOUTH SYMPHONIES
408 St. Peter Street
The Historic Hamm Building, Suite 300
Minneapolis, MN 55102
Phone: 651-602-6800
Fax: 651-292-3281
e-mail: mail@gtcys.org
Web Site: www.gtcys.org
Officers:
   President: Cathy Schmidt
   Vice President: Tami Schwerin
   Secretary: Bonnie Turpin
   Treasurer: Dennis D. Thonvold
   Board Member: Lisa Ashley
Management:
   Artistic Director & Symphony Conduc: Mark Russell Smith
   Executive Director: Megan Balda
   Program Assistant: Miranda Bryan
   Development Manager: Jeni Gregory
Mission: In the conviction that music nourishes the mind, body, and spirit of the individual and enriches the community, the Greater Twin Cities Youth Symphonies provides a rigorous and inspiring orchestral experience for qualifying young muscians.
Utilizes: Educators; Multimedia; Soloists
Founded: 1972
Specialized Field: Youth Symphony; Chamber; Ensemble
Status: Non-Professional; Nonprofit
Paid Staff: 6
Paid Artists: 8
Non-paid Artists: 5
Budget: $645,000
Performs At: Orchestra Hall; Landmark Center
Organization Type: Performing; Touring; Educational

1264
METROPOLITAN SYMPHONY ORCHESTRA
PO Box 581213
Minneapolis, MN 55458-1213
Phone: 651-698-1540
e-mail: msomailing@msomn.org
Web Site: www.msomn.org
Officers:
   Personnel Manager: David Wall
   VP: Terry Wilson
   Treasurer: Scott Simmons
   Secretary: Scott Simmons
Management:
   Music Director: William Schrickel
   General Manager: Mark Warhol
Specialized Field: Orchestra
Budget: $35,000

1265
MINNESOTA ORCHESTRA
1111 Nicollet Mall
Minneapolis, MN 55403
Phone: 612-371-5600
Toll-free: 800-292-4141
e-mail: info@mnorch.org
Web Site: www.minnesotaorchestra.org

Officers:
   Chair: Gordon M. Sprenger
   President/CEO: Michael Henson
   Vice Chair: Karen Himle
   Vice Chair: Nancy Lindahl
   Board Member: Marilyn Carlson Nelson
Management:
   General Manager: Robert Neu
   Principal Librarian: Paul Gunther
   Artistic Administrator: Kari Marshall
   Music Director: Osmo V„nsk„,
Mission: To enrich lives with great music.
Utilizes: Guest Artists; Guest Companies; Sign Language Translators; Singers
Founded: 1903
Status: Non-Profit; Professional
Paid Staff: 150
Paid Artists: 100
Budget: $28,000,000
Annual Attendance: 400,000
Type of Stage: Proscenium
Seating Capacity: 2,450
Year Built: 1974
Organization Type: Performing; Touring; Resident; Educational; Sponsoring

1266
MINNESOTA SINFONIA
901 N Third Street
Suite 112
Minneapolis, MN 55401
Phone: 612-871-1701
Fax: 612-871-1701
e-mail: mnsinfonia@aol.com
Web Site: www.mnsinfonia.org
Officers:
   Chairperson: Mary Weber
   Treasurer: David Haynes
Management:
   Artistic Director: Jay Fishman
   Managing Director: Raphael Fishman
   Matejcek: Emily
Specialized Field: Orchestra

1267
FARGO-MOORHEAD SYMPHONY ORCHESTRA
WDAY Office Tower
808 3rd Ave. S, Suite #300
Moorhead, MN 58103
Phone: 701—47-8-36
Fax: 218-236-1845
e-mail: fmsymphony@i29.net
Web Site: fmsymphony.org
Officers:
   Chair: Dan Mahli
   Vice Chair: Marv Degerness
   Treasurer: John Stern
   Secretary: Rebecca Sundet-Schoenwald
Management:
   Executive Director: Linda Boyd
   Development Director: Sara Granger
   Bookkeeper: Brenda Bohmert
   Librarian/Personnel Manager: Joan Covington
Mission: To provide our region with the opportunity to experience live orchestral music, including performances by local, regional, national, and international guest artists; to provide musicians in the community with the opportunity to perform.
Utilizes: Fine Artists; Guest Accompanists; Guest Companies; Guest Composers; Guest Lecturers; Guest Musicians; Multimedia; Music; Original Music Scores; Sign Language Translators; Singers
Founded: 1931

INSTRUMENTAL MUSIC / Mississippi

Specialized Field: Orchestra
Paid Staff: 8
Paid Artists: 75
Budget: $260,000-$1,050,000
Income Sources: Individual; Corporate; Foundations
Performs At: Reineke Fine Arts Center
Annual Attendance: 15,000
Facility Category: Concert hall- University
Stage Dimensions: 987
Seating Capacity: 1,000
Year Built: 1990
Rental Contact: 7012817932 Division of Fine Arts

1268
SAINT OLAF COLLEGE ORCHESTRA

Saint Olaf College
1520 St. Olaf Avenue
Northfield, MN 55057
Phone: 507-786-3179
Fax: 507-786-3125
e-mail: music@stolaf.edu
Web Site: wp.stolaf.edu/stolaf-orch
Management:
    Conductor: Steven Amundson
    Manager: Terra Widdifield, widdifie@stolaf.edu
    Assistant to Music Organizations/Bu: Christine Hanson, hansonc@stolaf.edu
    Assistant Director: Kevin Stocks
    Mechanical Rights Administrator: Mary Davis
Utilizes: Arrangers; Artists-in-Residence; Choreographers; Collaborations; Composers; Dancers; Educators; Guest Composers; Guest Directors; Guest Musical Directors; Guest Speakers; High School Drama; Multimedia; New Productions; Sign Language Translators; Singers; Soloists; Students; Theatre Companies
Founded: 1900
Specialized Field: Orchestra; Ensemble
Budget: $35,000-100,000
Performs At: Skoglund Center Auditorium
Seating Capacity: 4,000

1269
ST. CLOUD SYMPHONY ORCHESTRA

PO Box 234
Saint Cloud, MN 56302
Phone: 320-252-7276
e-mail: snadeau@stcloudsymphony.com
Web Site: www.stcloudsymphony.com
Officers:
    Co-President: David Haugen
    Co-President: Jane Schulzetenberg
    Vice President: Mark Springer
    Treasurer: Lori Johnson
    Secretary: Sharon Cogdill
Management:
    Executive Director: Sandy Nadeau
    Artistic Dir/Principal Conductor: Clinton Smith
    Assistant Conductor: Daniel O'Bryant
    Stage Manager: Derrick Johnson
    Librarian/Personnel Manager: David Peterson
Mission: The mission is to present high quality performance of orchestral music and educational outreach activities to Central Minnesota, to encourage participation by local and area musicians, and to further the understanding and appreciation of this music.
Founded: 1975
Specialized Field: Orchestra
Paid Staff: 4
Paid Artists: 85

1270
451ST ARMY BAND

506 Roeder Circle
Saint Paul, MN 55111-4009
Phone: 612-713-3339
Fax: 612-713-3519
Web Site: www.bands.army.mil
Management:
    Commander/Band Master: CW4 Bruce J Hedblom
    Assistant Conductor: SSG Robert A Lake
Mission: Representing the 88th United States Army Reserve Command to the military and to the general public as well as promoting and encouraging the performing arts.
Utilizes: Guest Artists; Guest Companies
Founded: 1923
Specialized Field: Ensemble; Ethnic Music; Folk Music; Band
Status: Professional; Nonprofit
Organization Type: Performing; Touring; Educational

1271
MINNESOTA STATE BAND

PO Box 130033
Saint Paul, MN 55113
Phone: 651-282-4077
e-mail: info@minnesotastateband.org
Web Site: www.minnesotastateband.org
Officers:
    Treasurer: Donna Hogenson
Management:
    Conductor: Charles Boody
    Public Relations: Neil Danielson
    Stage Manager: Pete Farm
    Concert Coordinator: Helmut Kahlert
    Webmaster: Fred Larson
Mission: Dedicated to furthering the musical development and appreciation of America's concert band and wind ensemble movement.
Utilizes: Guest Artists; Guest Companies; Singers
Founded: 1898
Specialized Field: Ensemble; Ethnic Music; Band
Status: Professional; Nonprofit
Paid Staff: 70
Income Sources: Association of Concert Bands
Organization Type: Performing; Touring; Educational

1272
SAINT PAUL CHAMBER ORCHESTRA

408 Saint Peter Street
Saint Paul, MN 55102
Phone: 651-291-1144
Fax: 651-292-3281
e-mail: pr@spcomail.org
Web Site: www.thespco.org
Officers:
    President: Bruce Coppock
    Artistic Operations Manager: Natalie Hokanson
    General Manager: Jean Parish
    Senior Director of Artistic Plannin: Kyu-Young Kim
    Orchestra Personnel Assistant: Paul Finkelstein
Mission: To present a world-class professional chamber orchestra in the Twin Cities, dedicated to superior performance and artistic innovation, for the enrichment of community life and world audiences.
Utilizes: Actors; Artists-in-Residence; Collaborations; Composers-in-Residence; Dance Companies; Educators; Fine Artists; Guest Accompanists; Guest Artists; Guest Choreographers; Guest Companies; Guest Composers; Guest Directors; Guest Instructors; Guest Musical Directors; Guest Musicians; Instructors; Multi Collaborations; Multimedia; Organization Contracts; Original Music Scores; Sign Language Translators; Singers; Soloists; Special Technical Talent; Touring Companies
Founded: 1959
Specialized Field: Orchestra; Chamber; Ensemble
Status: Professional; Nonprofit
Paid Artists: 33
Budget: $9,200,000
Income Sources: Government & Corporate Donors; Sales
Season: 38 weeks
Performs At: Ordway Center for the Performing Arts
Affiliations: American Symphony Orchestra League; Association of Performing Arts Presenters
Organization Type: Performing; Touring; Resident; Educational; Recording

Mississippi

1273
GULF COAST SYMPHONY

11975 Seaway Road
Biloxi, MS 39503
Phone: 228-896-4276
Fax: 228-435-9807
e-mail: gcso@worldnet.att.net
Web Site: www.gulfcoastsymphony.net
Officers:
    President: John Folding
    Vice President: Lauren Clark
    Secretary: Hugh Hanna
    Treasurer: Dr. Ron Schmidtling
    Board Member: Jamie Bates
Management:
    Executive Director: Whitney Sumrall
    Development Director: Signe Cutrone
    Music Director/Conductor: Dr. John Wesley Strickler
    Office Manager: Wendy Shade
    Operations Manager: Gaius Medley
Mission: The presentation of symphonic music to Gulf Coast residents.
Utilizes: Artists-in-Residence; Collaborating Artists; Collaborations; Commissioned Composers; Commissioned Music; Composers-in-Residence; Guest Companies; Guest Composers; Guest Lecturers; Guest Musicians; Local Artists; Multimedia; Organization Contracts; Original Music Scores; Singers; Soloists; Student Interns; Special Technical Talent
Founded: 1962
Specialized Field: Symphony
Status: Professional; Nonprofit
Paid Staff: 3
Volunteer Staff: 150
Paid Artists: 4
Budget: $460,000
Performs At: Saenger Theatre; Biloxi
Annual Attendance: 20,000
Facility Category: Theater
Seating Capacity: 1,050
Rental Contact: Lee Hood
Organization Type: Performing; Touring; Educational

1274
UNIVERSITY OF SOUTHERN MISSISSIPPI SYMPHONY

College Of Arts And Letters
118 College Drive #5081
103 South 30th Street
Hattiesburg, MS 39401
Mailing Address: 118 College Drive #5081, Hattiesburg, MS 39406-0001
Phone: 601-266-4001

INSTRUMENTAL MUSIC / Missouri

Fax: 601-266-4039
e-mail: symphony@usm.edu
Web Site: www.usm.edu/music/symphony
Officers:
   Secretary: Lynn Beach
Management:
   Director of Orchestral Activities: Dr. Jay Dean
   Marketing and Education Outreach Co: Jennifer Hart
   Public Relations/Recruiting Manager: Tearanny Street
Mission: Founded in 1910, The University of Southern Mississippi is a comprehensive doctoral and research-driven university with a proud history and an eye on the future. Our primary mission is to cultivate intellectual developmental creativity through the generation, dissemination, application and preservation of knowledge. The arts programs are internationally regarded as some of the finest ranking among only 31 fully accredited in all four discipline
Founded: 1910
Specialized Field: Art; Dance; Music; Theatre
Budget: $100,000-$150,000
Performs At: Bennett Auditoirum
Seating Capacity: 1,000

1275
MISSISSIPPI SYMPHONY ORCHESTRA
201 E Pascagoula Street
Jackson, MS 39201
Mailing Address: PO Box 2052,Jackson, MS 39225-2052
Phone: 601-960-1565
Fax: 601-960-1564
Toll-free: 800-898-5050
e-mail: mbeattie@msorchestra.com
Web Site: www.msorchestra.com
Officers:
   Chairman of the Board: Deidra S. Bell
   Vice-Chairman, Chairman-elect: Michael Cottingham
   President and Executive Director: Michael Beattie
   Secretary: Marth Ross Thomas
   Treasurer: Lesly Gaynor Murray
Management:
   Director of Marketing and Box Offic: Jim Moritsugu
   Music Director and Conductor: Crafton Beck
   Director of Finance: Charlotte Smith
   Director of Development: Phoebe Smith-Porter
   Director of Operations and Personne: Richard Hudson
Utilizes: Collaborations; Commissioned Composers; Commissioned Music; Dance Companies; Dancers; Educators; Filmmakers; Five Seasonal Concerts; Grant Writers; Guest Companies; Guest Composers; Guest Directors; Guest Lecturers; Guest Musical Directors; Guest Musicians; High School Drama; Instructors; Lyricists; Multi Collaborations; Multimedia; Music; Organization Contracts; Original Music Scores; Sign Language Translators; Singers; Soloists; Touring Companies
Founded: 1944
Specialized Field: Symphony; Orchestra; Chamber; Pops
Paid Staff: 7
Volunteer Staff: 1
Budget: $13,000,000
Performs At: Brianwood Presbyterian; Thalia Mara Hall; Galloway United Methodist Church
Seating Capacity: 2430

1276
MISSISSIPPI YOUTH SYMPHONY ORCHESTRA
201 E Pascagoula Street
Jackson, MS 39201
Mailing Address: PO Box 2052,Jackson, MS 39225-2052
Phone: 601-960-1565
Fax: 601-960-1564
Toll-free: 800-898-5050
e-mail: mbeattie@msorchestra.com
Web Site: www.msorchestra.com
Officers:
   Chairman of the Board: Deidra S. Bell
   Vice-Chairman, Chairman-elect: Michael Cottingham
   President and Executive Director: Michael Beattie
   Secretary: Marth Ross Thomas
   Treasurer: Lesly Gaynor Murray
Management:
   Music Director and Conductor: Crafton Beck
   Director of Marketing and Box Offic: Jim Moritsugu
   Director of Finance: Charlotte Smith
   Director of Development: Phoebe Smith-Porter
   Director of Operations and Personne: Richard Hudson
Mission: To promote education and appreciation of classical music through participation in the junior or senior youth orchestras.
Specialized Field: Youth Symphony
Status: Non-Professional; Nonprofit
Income Sources: American Symphony Orchestra League(Youth Orchestra Division)
Performs At: Chastain Junior High School
Organization Type: Performing; Touring; Educational

1277
MERIDIAN SYMPHONY ORCHESTRA
1921 24th Ave.
Meridian, MS 39301
Mailing Address: P.O. Box 2171, Meridian, MS 39302
Phone: 601-693-2224
Fax: 601-482-8824
e-mail: meridiansymphony@att.net
Web Site: www.meridianso.org
Officers:
   President: R Condon Hughes, III, MD
   Vice President: Cecil Johnson, MD
   Treasurer: Lee Moseley
   Secretary: Kacey Bailey
Management:
   Music Director: Peter Rubardt, PhD.
   General Manager: Carolyn Abdella
   Executive Director: Susie Johnson
   Chorus Director: Robert Hermetz, PhD.
Specialized Field: Orchestra
Budget: $260,000-$1,050,000
Performs At: Meridian Community College Auditorium
Seating Capacity: 600

1278
TUPELO SYMPHONY ORCHESTRA ASSOCIATION
1800 West main street
Tupelo, MS 38801
Phone: 662-842-8433
Fax: 662-842-9565
e-mail: tso@tupelosymphony.com
Web Site: www.tupelosymphony.com
Officers:
   Board Chairman: Rob Rice
   Vice Chair: Ted Moll
   Secretary: Ann Blair Huffman
   Treasurer: Cathy Robertson
   Board Member: George Booth
Management:
   Music Director & Conductor: Steven Byess
   President/Executive Director: Margaret Anne Murphy
Mission: To offer high quality performances of symphonic works.
Utilizes: Educators; Fine Artists; Five Seasonal Concerts; Guest Accompanists; Guest Composers; Guest Lecturers; Multimedia; Original Music Scores; Sign Language Translators; Singers
Founded: 1971
Specialized Field: Symphony; Orchestra
Status: Professional
Paid Staff: 1
Volunteer Staff: 3
Budget: $300,000
Income Sources: Ticket Sales; Contributors; Corporate Sponsors; Grants
Performs At: Tupedo Civic Auditorium
Affiliations: American Symphony Orchestra League
Facility Category: Concert Hall
Seating Capacity: 535
Year Built: 1965
Year Remodeled: 2000
Organization Type: Performing; Touring

Missouri

1279
MISSOURI SYMPHONY SOCIETY
203 S 9th Street
Columbia, MO 65201
Mailing Address: PO Box 841, Columbia, MO 65205-0841
Phone: 573-875-0600
Fax: 573-449-4214
e-mail: motheatre@socket.net
Web Site: mosymphonysociety.org
Officers:
   President: Lili Vianello
   President Elect: Lawrence Babcock
   Secretary: Pat Hostetler
   Treasurer: Cheryl Edington
   Board Member: Alice Harward
Mission: The enhancement of the cultural environment through fine music, education and the nurturing of young musicians.
Utilizes: Guest Composers; Guest Ensembles; Guest Musical Directors; Guest Musicians; Multimedia
Founded: 1971
Specialized Field: Symphony; Orchestra; Chamber
Status: Professional; Nonprofit
Paid Staff: 40
Budget: $375,000
Income Sources: Pops Orchestra; Chamber Orchestra Festival Symphony
Performs At: Missouri Theatre
Type of Stage: Proscenium
Seating Capacity: 1,220
Year Built: 1928
Rental Contact: Executive Director David A White
Organization Type: Performing; Touring; Educational; Sponsoring

1280
INDEPENDENCE SYMPHONY ORCHESTRA
PO Box 2276
Independence, MO 64063

INSTRUMENTAL MUSIC / Missouri

Phone: 816-373-8151
Fax: 816-220-6511
e-mail: LynnP12@juno.com
Officers:
  VP: Cathy Lawrey
  House Manager: Dave Mayta
  Treasurer: Helen Newlin
  Secretary: Betty Liston
Management:
  Conductor/Music Director: James Murray
  President: Jeff Quibell
Specialized Field: Orchestra
Budget: $35,000
Seating Capacity: 1500-5000

1281
FRIENDS OF CHAMBER MUSIC
4635 Wyandotte Street
Suite 201
Kansas City, MO 64112-1542
Phone: 816-561-9999
Fax: 816-561-8810
Toll-free: 877-697-3287
e-mail: marketing@chambermusic.org
Web Site: www.chambermusic.org
Officers:
  Chairman of the Board: Nancy Lee Kemper
  Vice Chairman & Treasurer: David M Eisenberg
  President and Founder: Cynthia Siebert
  Board Member: Dwight Arn
  Board Member: Richard Bruening
Management:
  Director of Development: Tricia Kyler Bowling
  Director of Marketing & Public Rela: Marcy Chiasson
  Manager of Production & Artists Ser: Robert Holland
  Graphic Designer: Laura Schneider
Specialized Field: Chamber
Status: Not-for-profit

1282
KANSAS CITY CHAMBER ORCHESTRA
11 East 40th Street
Kansas City, MO 64111
Phone: 816-960-1324
Fax: 816-960-1325
e-mail: kcco@earthlink.net
Web Site: www.kcchamberorchestra.org
Management:
  Music Director/Conductor: Bruce Sorrell
Utilizes: Guest Accompanists; Guest Musicians; Instructors; Local Artists; Original Music Scores; Sign Language Translators; Singers; Soloists
Founded: 1987
Specialized Field: Chamber; Ensemble
Budget: $150,000-$200,000
Income Sources: Donations, Grants, Ticket sales

1283
KANSAS CITY SYMPHONY
1703 Wyandotte
Suite 200
Kansas City, MO 64108
Phone: 816-471-1100
Fax: 816-471-0976
e-mail: tkutey@kcsymphony.org
Web Site: www.kcsymphony.org
Officers:
  Chair Emerita: Shirley Bush Helzberg
  Vice Chair: Robert A Kipp
  Vice Chair: Michael D Fields
  Vice Chair: Ann Kaufmann Baum
  Vice Chair & Secretary/Treasurer: William B. Taylor
Management:
  Music Director: Michael Stern
  Executive Director: Frank Byrne
  General Manager: Emma Kail
  Director of Artistic Operations: Rebecca Martin
Specialized Field: Orchestra

1284
NORTHLAND SYMPHONY ORCHESTRA
P.O. Box 11193
Kansas City, MO 64119
Phone: 816-316-0477
Fax: 816-759-9084
e-mail: northlandsymphonyorchestra@yahoo.com
Web Site: www.northlandsymphony.org
Officers:
  President: Erica Mason
  Vice President: Kristin Niederberger
  Co-treasurer: Mary Duren
  Co-treasurer: Matt Kendrick
  Secretary: Kathy Burgon
Management:
  Music Director/Conductor: James Murray III
Mission: To offer professional, amateur and student musicians an opportunity to preform fin orchestral music and free public concerts fir diverse audiences.
Specialized Field: Orchestra
Budget: $35,000
Performs At: Park Hill South School Auditorium
Seating Capacity: 950

1285
LIBERTY SYMPHONY ORCHESTRA
500 College Hill
Box 1137
Liberty, MO 64068
Phone: 816—86-6-05
Fax: 816-415-5012
e-mail: cory@libertysymphony.org
Web Site: www.libertysymphony.org
Officers:
  President: Mark Ellebracht
  President-Elect: Diane Karius
  Secretary: Chris Gregoire
  Treasurer: Mary Sousley
  Board Member: Bob Litle
Management:
  Conductor/Music Director: Dr Tony Brandolino
  Office Manager: Florence Cunningham
  Executive Director: Cory Unrein
Mission: Contributes to the cultural life of the Kansas City community by performing four concerts a season in the Liberty Performing Arts Theatre. In addition, two educational concerts for school-aged children are performed. More than 3,000 citizens in the area are reached through these programs. The Orchestra is transitioning through founder leadership and artistic direction to more active, hands-on participation by the Board of Directors.
Utilizes: Guest Musicians; Multimedia; Original Music Scores; Singers; Soloists
Founded: 1970
Specialized Field: Orchestra
Paid Staff: 2
Volunteer Staff: 50
Non-paid Artists: 58
Budget: $50,000
Income Sources: Sponsors; Patrons; Donors; Grants; Box Office
Performs At: Liberty Performing Arts Theatre; Liberty Community Center
Affiliations: Missouri Citizens for the Arts; American Symphony Orchestra League; Missouri Arts Council; Liberty Chamber of Commerce
Annual Attendance: 4,200
Facility Category: Performing Arts Theatre
Seating Capacity: 700
Year Built: 1991
Organization Type: Performing; Educational

1286
SAINT JOSEPH SYMPHONY SOCIETY
120 S Eighth Street
Saint Joseph, MO 64501-2231
Phone: 816-233-7701
Fax: 816-233-6704
e-mail: info@saintjosephsymphony.org
Web Site: www.saintjosephsymphony.org
Officers:
  President: Byron D Myers
  Vice President: Bradley Weil
  Treasurer: Charles Salanski
  Secretary: Mary Jo Hornaday
  Legal Advisor: Michael Insco
Management:
  Managing Director: Ann Brock
  Personnel Manager: Richard Yeager
  Stage Manager: Frank Polleck
Mission: To present symphonic concerts and educational activities for the citizens of Northwest Missouri and Eastern Kansas.
Founded: 1959
Specialized Field: Symphony
Status: Professional; Nonprofit
Performs At: Missouri Theatre
Organization Type: Performing; Educational

1287
KIRKWOOD SYMPHONY ORCHESTRA
PO Box 410053
Saint Louis, MO 63141
Phone: 314-569-3220
Fax: 314-569-3220
e-mail: violinist@claytonsymphony.org
Officers:
  President: Rusell A Willis
Management:
  Artistic Direcor: Edward Dolbashian
Specialized Field: Orchestra
Budget: $35,000
Performs At: St. John's Lutheran Church
Seating Capacity: 500

1288
NEW MUSIC CIRCLE
PO Box 9337
Saint Louis, MO 63117
Phone: 314-432-6073
Fax: 314-567-5384
Toll-free: 888-NMC-STL
e-mail: newmusiccircle.info@gmail.com
Web Site: www.newmusiccircle.org
Officers:
  President: John Newman
  Vice President: Fred Tompkins
  Treasurer: Sherri Lyss
  Secretary: Gary Gronau
  Board Member: Dave Cheli
Management:
  Music Director: Rich O'Donnell
Mission: To advocate for new music; to commission new works; to promote promising composers and ensembles.
Specialized Field: Electronic; Live Electronic; New Music; Avant Garde

Status: Professional; Nonprofit
Organization Type: Presenting

1289
SAINT LOUIS CLASSICAL GUITAR SOCIETY
PO Box 11425
Saint Louis, MO 63105
Phone: 314-567-5566
e-mail: info@guitarstlouis.net
Web Site: www.guitarstlouis.net
Officers:
   President: William Ash
Mission: To promote and foster an understanding and appreciation of the guitar, to encourage a high standard in instruction and performance, to encourage the creation and preservation of music for the guitar to sponsor the society.
Specialized Field: Classical Guitar
Status: Nonprofit
Budget: $100,000
Performs At: The Ethical Society

1290
SAINT LOUIS PHILHARMONIC ORCHESTRA
PO Box 220437
Saint Louis, MO 63122
Phone: 314-421-3600
e-mail: info@stlphilharmonic.org
Web Site: www.stlphilharmonic.org
Officers:
   President: Marilyn K Humiston
   VP: Stephen Larmore
   Secretary: Doug Kenner
   Treasurer: David Lyon
Management:
   Conductor: Robert Hart Bakor
Mission: To offer musicians an opportunity to play good music under the direction of an able conductor.
Utilizes: Guest Artists
Founded: 1860
Specialized Field: Symphony
Status: Non-Professional; Nonprofit
Performs At: Scottish Rite Cathedral
Organization Type: Performing

1291
SAINT LOUIS SYMPHONY ORCHESTRA
718 N Grand Boulevard
Saint Louis, MO 63103
Phone: 314-533-2500
Fax: 314-286-4142
e-mail: SymphonyINFO@stlsymphony.org
Web Site: www.slso.org
Officers:
   Chairman: Barry H. Beracha
   Vice Chairman: Kimberley Ann Eberlein
   Vice Chairman: Jo Ann Taylor Kindle
   Vice Chairman: David Steward
   Secretary: Donna Wilkinson
Management:
   Executive Director: Randy Adams
   Chorus Director: Amy Kaiser
   Artistic Administration Director: Jeremy Geffen
   Stage Manager: Mike Lynch
   Director Marketing: Stephen Duncan
   Concertmaster: David Halen
   Music Director: David Robertson
Utilizes: Guest Artists
Founded: 1879
Specialized Field: Symphony
Status: Professional; Nonprofit
Paid Staff: 150
Volunteer Staff: 200
Paid Artists: 97
Budget: $22,000,000
Income Sources: Ticket Sales, Sponsorships, Donations
Performs At: Powell Symphony Hall at Grand Center
Seating Capacity: 2,700
Year Built: 1925
Year Remodeled: 1966
Rental Contact: Melissa Lange
Organization Type: Performing; Touring; Educational

1292
SAINT LOUIS SYMPHONY YOUTH ORCHESTRA
718 N Grand Boulevard
Saint Louis, MO 63103
Phone: 314-533-2500
Fax: 314-286-4142
e-mail: SymphonyINFO@stlsymphony.org
Web Site: www.stlsymphony.org/youthorchestra
Officers:
   Chairman: Barry H. Beracha
   Vice Chairman: Kimberley Ann Eberlein
   Vice Chairman: Jo Ann Taylor Kindle
   Vice Chairman: David Steward
   Secretary: Donna Wilkinson
Management:
   Manager: Margaret Neilson
   Music Director: David Robertson
   Founder: Leonard Slatkin
Mission: The Saint Louis Symphony Youth Orchestra was founded in 1970 by Leonard Slatkin to acquaint young instrumentalists with the atmosphere of a professional orchestra, to introduce them to the environment of the Saint Louis Symphony and to provide them with the opportunity of investigating and performing a wide spectrum of symphonic music.
Utilizes: Guest Artists
Founded: 1970
Specialized Field: Youth Orchestra; Chamber
Status: Non-Professional; Nonprofit
Paid Staff: 100
Income Sources: American Symphony Orchestra League (Youth Orchestra Division)
Performs At: Powell Symphony Hall at Grand Center
Organization Type: Performing; Touring; Educational; Sponsoring

1293
KANSAS CITY YOUTH SYMPHONY ASSOCIATION OF KANSAS
7301 Mission Road
Suite 143
Shawnee Mission, MO 66208
Phone: 913-722-6810
Fax: 913-722-6806
e-mail: ysymph@crn.org
Web Site: www.crn.org/kcys
Management:
   Music Director/Conductor: Glenn Block
   Music Director: David Robertson
Mission: To provide educational opportunities for young musicians by performing before community-wide audiences and by inspiring excellence in performance.
Specialized Field: Youth Symphony

1294
SPRINGFIELD SYMPHONY ORCHESTRA
411 N. Sherman Parkway
Springfield, MO 65802
Phone: 417-864-6683
Fax: 417-864-8967
Web Site: www.springfieldmosymphony.org
Officers:
   President: Bryan N. Musgrave
   VP: Bill Nesbitt
   Treasurer: Irwin Cohen
   Secretary: Judith A. Hellam
   Guild President: Linda Peacock
Management:
   Executive Director: Janice Bennett
   Executive Secretary: Karrah Duckworth
   Operations Manager: Ned Horner
   Marketing Manager: Jeana Varney
   Music Director & Conductor: Kyle Wiley Pickett
Mission: To provide the highest level of symphonic music and music education to all of Southwest Missouri, commensurate with sound fiscal policies.
Utilizes: Guest Artists; Guest Companies; Singers
Founded: 1934
Specialized Field: Symphony
Status: Semi-Professional
Income Sources: American Symphony Orchestra League; Missouri Arts Council
Performs At: Juanita K. Hammons Hall for the Performing Arts
Organization Type: Performing

1295
CENTRAL MISSOURI STATE UNIVERSITY SYMPHONY ORCHESTRA
Utt Music Building, Room 109
Warrensburg, MO 64093
Phone: 660-543-4530
Fax: 660-543-8271
e-mail: admit@ucmo.edu
Web Site: www.ucmo.edu/music/groups/orchestra.cfm
Officers:
   Interim Chair Department of Music: Scott Lubaroff
Management:
   Music Director/Conductor: John Rutland
Mission: To give university students and community members exposure to the standard orchestral repertoire and serve as a cultural force within the greater Warrensburg area.
Founded: 1871
Specialized Field: Symphony
Paid Staff: 2
Paid Artists: 1
Non-paid Artists: 55
Budget: $35,000
Performs At: Hart Recital Hall
Seating Capacity: 350

Montana

1296
BILLINGS SYMPHONY SOCIETY
2721 2nd Avenue North
Suite 350
Billings, MT 59103
Phone: 406-252-3610
Fax: 406-252-3353
e-mail: symphony@billingssymphon.org
Web Site: www.billingssymphony.org/
Management:
   Music Director: Ann Harrigan
   Chorale Director: Steven Hart
   Executive Director: Darren Rich
   Director of Education: Candy Holzer
   Director of Marketing and Public Re: Michelle Tracy

INSTRUMENTAL MUSIC / Nebraska

Mission: To offer the community and the region live symphonic music.
Utilizes: Guest Artists
Founded: 1951
Specialized Field: Symphony; Orchestra
Status: Semi-Professional; Nonprofit
Budget: $260,000-$1,050,000
Income Sources: American Symphony Orchestra League; Montana Association of Symphony Orchestras
Performs At: The Alberta Bair Theater for the Performing Arts
Seating Capacity: 1,200
Organization Type: Performing

1297
YELLOWSTONE CHAMBER PLAYERS
1204 Rimhaven Way
Billings, MT 59102
Phone: 406-248-2832
Fax: 406-248-2832
e-mail: musician@yellowstonechamberplayers.org
Web Site: www.yellowstonechamberplayers.org
Officers:
  Board Member: Mary LaMonaca
  President: Elizabeth Adcock
  Secretary: Lisa Lombardy
  Treasurer: Ramona Turnbull
  VP: Delores Vigessa
Management:
  Ticket Manager: Caron Schultz
Mission: The performance of a wide variety of chamber music, from string quartets and piano quintets, to small ensembles employing clarinet, flute and guitar.
Utilizes: Artists-in-Residence; Collaborating Artists; Educators; Guest Companies; Guest Musical Directors; Multimedia; Original Music Scores; Sign Language Translators
Founded: 1980
Specialized Field: Chamber; Ensemble
Status: Professional; Nonprofit
Volunteer Staff: 20
Paid Artists: 15
Income Sources: Friends of YCP; Donations; Business Sponsors
Performs At: Churches; Small Recital Halls
Annual Attendance: 1,000
Organization Type: Performing; Touring; Resident

1298
GREAT FALLS SYMPHONY ASSOCIATION
11 3rd Street N
Great Falls, MT 59401
Mailing Address: PO Box 1078, Great Falls, MT 59403
Phone: 406-453-4102
Fax: 406-453-9779
e-mail: info@gfsymphony.org
Web Site: www.gfsymphony.org
Officers:
  President: Joan Schmidt
  Past President / VP Personnel: Roberta Boylan
  Vice President Elect: Sue Ann Stephenson-Love
  Treasurer: Darryl Stevens
  Secretary: Sharon Nalivka Hancock
Management:
  Executive Director: Carolyn Valacich
  Music Director/Conductor: Gordon J Johnson
  Choir Director: Paul Ritter
  Executive Director: Carolyn Valacich
  Patron Services: Donna Hoey
Mission: To produce and present symphonic, chamber and choral music and to serve as a s resource for education and outreach for the people of Montana.
Utilizes: Collaborations; Grant Writers; Guest Companies; Guest Directors; Multimedia; Organization Contracts; Original Music Scores; Theatre Companies
Founded: 1959
Specialized Field: Symphony; Orchestra; Chamber; Youth Orchestra
Status: Professional; Nonprofit
Paid Staff: 8
Paid Artists: 65
Non-paid Artists: 80
Budget: $450,000-$500,000
Income Sources: American Symphony Orchestra League; Montana Association of Symphony Orchestras; Tickets
Performs At: Great Falls Civic Center
Annual Attendance: 35,000
Seating Capacity: 1,776
Organization Type: Performing; Touring; Resident; Educational; Sponsoring

1299
HELENA SYMPHONY SOCIETY
2 N Last Chance Gulch
Suite 1
Helena, MT 59601
Mailing Address: PO Box 1073, Helena, Montana 59624
Phone: 406-442-1860
Fax: 406-443-6620
e-mail: helenasymphony@hotmail.com
Web Site: www.helenasymphony.org
Officers:
  President: Susan Brookhart, Ph.D.
  Treasurer: Ronald Baldwin
  Secretary: Eleanor Parker, Esq.
  Board Member: Sisi Carroll
  Board Member: Christa Tarver
Management:
  Music Director & Conductor: Allan R. Scott
  Assistant Conductor: Breanne Cepeda
  Director of Artistic Planning: Teak Hoiness
  Operations Manager: Scott Kall
Mission: The presentation of classical and popular symphony concerts, including choral and chamber concerts.
Utilizes: Composers-in-Residence; Guest Composers; Guest Musical Directors; Guest Musicians; Singers; Soloists
Founded: 1955
Specialized Field: Symphony; Orchestra; Chamber; Ethnic Music
Status: Nonprofit
Paid Staff: 4
Volunteer Staff: 20
Non-paid Artists: 140
Budget: $175,000
Income Sources: American Society of Composers; Authors and Publishers; Broadcast Music Incorporated; Donations; Tickets
Performs At: Helena Civic Center
Affiliations: American Symphony Orchestra League; Montana Association of Symphony Orchestra
Organization Type: Performing; Educational

1300
MISSOULA SYMPHONY ASSOCIATION
320 East Main Street
Missoula, MT 59807
Phone: 406-721-3194
Fax: 406-541-3194
e-mail: info@missoulasymphony.org
Web Site: www.missoulasymphony.org
Officers:
  President: Tom Copley
  VP: Doug Klein
  President-Elect: Sharon Snavely
  Treasurer: Keith Kuhn
  Secretary: Lila Bahin
Management:
  Music Director: Darko Butorac
  Choral Director: Dean Peterson
  Executive Director: John Driscoll
  Director of Operations: Peter McKenzie
  Patron Services Coordinator: Linnea Stanhope
Mission: To present artistic programs of excellence to Missoula and the surrounding areas, provide an opportunity for young persons and develop an interest in the arts through concerts and master classes.
Utilizes: Commissioned Composers; Commissioned Music; Composers-in-Residence; Educators; Guest Accompanists; Guest Directors; Guest Lecturers; Guest Writers; Instructors; Original Music Scores; Singers; Theatre Companies
Founded: 1954
Specialized Field: Symphony
Status: Nonprofit
Paid Staff: 4
Paid Artists: 10
Non-paid Artists: 60
Budget: $200,000
Income Sources: American Symphony Orchestra League
Performs At: University Theatre
Annual Attendance: 7,500
Facility Category: University Theatre
Stage Dimensions: 37'x 36'
Seating Capacity: 1,040
Year Built: 30's
Year Remodeled: 1997
Organization Type: Performing; Sponsoring

Nebraska

1301
HASTINGS SYMPHONY ORCHESTRA
Hastings College
PO Box 597
Hastings, NE 68902
Phone: 402-469-9396
Fax: 402-469-9396
e-mail: hso@hastingssymphony.com
Web Site: www.hastingssymphony.com
Officers:
  President: Dale Duensing
  Executive Secretary: Jodi Mackin
Management:
  Conductor/Artistic Director: Dr. Bryon Jensen, PhD
Mission: To enrich the cultural environment for people of all ages by providing quality, live performances of music in a symphonic setting, music education, and performance opportunities for talented musicians.
Utilizes: Artists-in-Residence; Commissioned Music; Guest Companies; Guest Composers; Guest Musicians; Local Artists; Multimedia; Original Music Scores; Sign Language Translators; Soloists
Founded: 1926
Specialized Field: Symphony; Orchestra
Status: Non-Professional; Nonprofit
Paid Staff: 2
Volunteer Staff: 40
Paid Artists: 6
Non-paid Artists: 4
Budget: $90,000
Income Sources: Tickets; Contributions; Grants
Performs At: Auditorium at Masonic Center
Annual Attendance: 2,500-3,500

INSTRUMENTAL MUSIC / Nebraska

Facility Category: City Auditorium
Seating Capacity: 850
Year Built: 1920
Organization Type: Performing; Touring; Resident; Educational
Resident Groups: American Symphony Orchestra League

1302
KEARNEY AREA SYMPHONY ORCHESTRA
University of Nebraska at Kearney
Music Department, 2506 12th Avenue
Kearney, NE 68849
Phone: 308-865-8618
Fax: 308-865-8806
e-mail: freedmand2@unk.edu
Web Site: www.unk.edu/academics/music/ensembles.php
Officers:
  President: Vernon Plambeck
  VP: John Johnson
  Secretary: C J Sabah
  Treasurer: Steven J Lind
Management:
  Conductor: Dr. Ron Crocker
Mission: Provides quality symphonic concerts for University and community members in Central Nebraska
Founded: 1905
Specialized Field: Orchestra
Paid Staff: 1
Volunteer Staff: 16
Budget: $25,000
Income Sources: Donations; Ads
Performs At: Auditorium
Affiliations: University Of Nebraska @ Kearney
Annual Attendance: 2000
Seating Capacity: 500
Year Built: 1970
Year Remodeled: 2005

1303
LINCOLN CIVIC ORCHESTRA
Nebraska Wesleyan University
5000 St. Paul
Lincoln, NE 68504
Phone: 402-465-2269
e-mail: jjc@nebrwesleyan.edu
Web Site: www.lincolncivicorchestra.org/concerts/concert-locations/
Management:
  Music Director: Dr. Pat Fortney
  Executive Director: Dean W Haist
  Conductor: Rob Salistean
  Associate Conductor: Brett Noser
Mission: Offering community members an opportunity to perform serious music.
Utilizes: Singers
Specialized Field: Orchestra
Status: Nonprofit
Paid Staff: 130
Budget: $35,000
Performs At: O'Donnell Aud.; Rogers Arts Center; Nebraska Wesleyan Univ.
Organization Type: Resident

1304
LINCOLN FRIENDS OF CHAMBER MUSIC
5211 W Chadderton Circle
Lincoln, NE 68521
Phone: 402-472-5121
Fax: 402-472-8962
e-mail: jkraus1@unl.edu
Web Site: www.lfcm.org
Officers:
  President: Joe Kraus
  Head Artists Subcommittee: Anne Chang-Barnea
Mission: Presenting chamber music; promoting community appreciation of chamber music; aiding talented local chamber music artists.
Utilizes: Guest Directors; Multimedia
Founded: 1965
Specialized Field: Chamber; Ensemble
Status: Nonprofit
Volunteer Staff: 15
Budget: $25,000
Income Sources: Ticket Sales; Donations; Grants
Performs At: Sheldon Art Gallery Auditorium
Annual Attendance: 1250
Facility Category: Art Gallery Auditorium
Stage Dimensions: 25'W x 10'D
Seating Capacity: 300
Year Built: 1963
Rental Contact: P.J. Jacobs
Organization Type: Sponsoring

1305
LINCOLN SYMPHONY ORCHESTRA
233 S 13th Street
Suite 1702
Lincoln, NE 68508
Phone: 402-476-2211
Fax: 402-476-2236
e-mail: info@lincolnsymphony.com
Web Site: lincolnsymphony.com
Officers:
  Interim President: Roxann Brennfoerder
  President-Elect: Marilyn Moore
  Treasurer: Cynthia Love
  Secretary: Reginald S. Kuhn
  VP Governance: James Griesen
Management:
  Music Director: Edward Polochick
  Executive Director: Barbara Zach
  Box Office Manager: Brittany Downey
  Operations/Personnel Manager: Travis Kulnicki
  Development Director: Tari Hendrickson Svvzency
  Orchestra Manager: Caleb Bailey
  Executive Coordinator: Lindsay Bartlett
Mission: Will enrich, educate and entertain current and potential audiences through the performances and advancement of symphonic music.
Founded: 1927
Specialized Field: Symphony; Orchestra
Status: Professional; Nonprofit
Paid Staff: 7
Paid Artists: 60
Budget: $260,000-$1,050,000
Performs At: Lied Center for the Performing Arts; Kimball Recital Hall
Affiliations: American Symhpony Orchestra League
Seating Capacity: 2285/ 850
Organization Type: Performing; Sponsoring

1306
LINCOLN YOUTH SYMPHONY
7201 Woody Creek Lane
Lincoln, NE 68501
Phone: 402-423-5343
Fax: 435-797-3150
e-mail: cpotter1@unl.edu
Web Site: www.lincolnyouthsymphony.org
Officers:
  Co-Presidents: Thomas Srb
  Co-Presidents: Paula Srb
  Treasurer: Carl Olson
  Administrator: Richard Scott
  Business Manager: Micheal Swartz
Management:
  Conductor: Clark Potter
  Assistant Conductor: Terry Rush
  Percussion Coach: Joe Holmquist
Mission: The Lincoln Youth Symphony Orchestra was organized to perform symphonic literature unable to be played within regular school instruction through participation in the Youth Orchestra or the Junior Youth Orchestra.
Founded: 1953
Specialized Field: Youth Symphony
Status: Non-Professional; Nonprofit
Paid Staff: 76
Income Sources: American Symphony Orchestra League (Youth Orchestra Division); Lincoln Public Schools
Performs At: Kimball Recital Hall; University of Nebraska
Organization Type: Performing; Touring; Educational; Sponsoring

1307
NEBRASKA JAZZ ORCHESTRA
315 South 9th Street
Suite 110
Lincoln, NE 68508-228
Phone: 402-477-8446
Fax: 402-477-8222
e-mail: njo@artsincorporated.org
Web Site: www.artsincorporated.org/njo
Officers:
  President: Del Smith
  Vice President - Performance: Craig Kingery
  Treasurer: Hank Van den Berg
Management:
  Music Director: Ed Love
  Executive Director: Dean Haist
Founded: 1975
Specialized Field: Jazz
Budget: $35,000-$100,000
Performs At: Embassy Suites;Joslyn Art Museum, Omaha
Seating Capacity: 450/ 1500
Organization Type: Performing

1308
OMAHA AREA YOUTH ORCHESTRAS
PO Box 34518
Omaha, NE 68134-0518
Phone: 402-238-2044
Fax: 402-238-2310
e-mail: oayo@radiks.net
Web Site: www.oayo.org
Officers:
  President: Sara McClure
  VP Development: Marian Kaiser
  Advisor: Jeremy Baguyos
  Advisor: Nancy Ayoub
  Advisor: Llinda Egger
Management:
  Music Director & Conductor: Aviva Segall
  Executive Director: Rana Scarlett-Johnson
  Director of Operations: Abby Bogenrief
  Coordinator: Hanna Mayer
  Assistant Conductor, Youth Conserva: Brittany Rom
Mission: To enhance the musical education of aspiring and talented young musicians through the medium of orchestral performance; to help them become

INSTRUMENTAL MUSIC / Nevada

appreciative listeners; and to build discipline, cooperation, and other skills necessary for a group accomplishment.
Founded: 1958
Specialized Field: Youth Orchestra; Chamber; Ensemble
Status: Non-Professional; Nonprofit
Paid Staff: 6
Volunteer Staff: 250
Budget: $200,000
Income Sources: American Symphony Orchestra League; Omaha Symphony Guild; ASTA; Music Educators National Conference; Nebraska Arts Council
Performs At: University Recital Hall
Annual Attendance: 7,000-8,000
Organization Type: Performing; Educational; Sponsoring

1309
OMAHA SYMPHONY
1605 Howard Street
Omaha, NE 68102
Phone: 402-342-3560
Fax: 402-342-3819
e-mail: info@omahasymphony.org
Web Site: www.omahasymphony.org
Officers:
  Chairman: William A. Fitzgerald
  President/CEO: James M Johnson
  Vice President of Finance & Adminis: Pamela Cleary
  Vice President of Development: Amy E. Jenson
  Vice President of Marketing: Teresa Ancona
Management:
  Music Director: Thomas Wilkins
  Resident Conductor: Ernest Richardson
  General Manager: Rachel Sepulveda
  Operations Manager: Jennifer Kreitz
  Artistic Manager: Kristin Patch
  Sales Manager: David Johnson
  Stage Manager: Rick Jones
  Art Director: Missy Ragatz
  Public Relations Manager: Stephanie Ludwig
Utilizes: Collaborations; Commissioned Music; Five Seasonal Concerts; Guest Accompanists; Guest Artists; Guest Composers; Guest Musical Directors; Guest Musicians; Guest Writers; Lyricists; New Productions; Organization Contracts; Resident Professionals
Founded: 1921
Specialized Field: Symphony; Orchestra; Chamber; Ensemble
Status: Professional; Nonprofit
Paid Staff: 27
Paid Artists: 70
Budget: $45,000,000
Income Sources: American Symphony Orchestra League; National Endowment for the Arts; Nebraska Arts Council
Organization Type: Performing; Touring; Resident; Educational; Sponsoring

1310
OMAHA SYMPHONY CHAMBER ORCHESTRA
1605 Howard Street
Omaha, NE 68102
Phone: 402-342-3560
Fax: 402-342-3819
e-mail: bravo@omahasymphony.org
Web Site: www.omahasymphony.org
Officers:
  Chairman: William A. Fitzgerald
  President/CEO: James M Johnson
  Vice President of Finance & Adminis: Pamela Cleary
  Vice President of Development: Amy E. Jenson
  Vice President of Marketing: Teresa Ancona
Management:
  Music Director: Thomas Wilkins
  Resident Conductor: Ernest Richardson
  General Manager: Rachel Sepulveda
  Operations Manager: Jennifer Kreitz
  Artistic Manager: Kristin Patch
  Sales Manager: David Johnson
  Stage Manager: Rick Jones
  Art Director: Missy Ragatz
  Public Relations Manager: Stephanie Ludwig
Specialized Field: Orchestra
Budget: $1,050,000-$3,600,000
Performs At: Orpheum Theatre; Joslyn Art Museum; Witherspoon Concert Hall
Seating Capacity: 2750/ 1174

Nevada

1311
CARSON CITY SYMPHONY ASSOCIATION
PO Box 2001
Carson City, NV 89702-2001
Phone: 775-883-4154
Fax: 775-883-4371
e-mail: dcbugli@aol.com
Web Site: CCSymphony.com
Officers:
  President: Elinor Bugli
  Vice President, Stage Manager: Grant Mills
  Treasurer: Charlotte Tucker
  Recording Secretary: Edith Isidoro-Mills
  Trustee: Becky Crowe
Management:
  Music Director/Conductor: David C. Bugli
  Chamber Singers Accompanists: Michael Langham
  Youth Orchestra Director: Sue Jesch
  Volunteer Coordinator: Betty Young
Mission: To provide amateur and volunteer professional musicians with opportunity to learn and perform various musical styles to entertain and educate the community.
Utilizes: Arrangers; Commissioned Composers; Community Members; Community Talent; Composers; Guest Choreographers; Guest Companies; Guest Directors; Guest Musical Directors; Guest Musicians; High School Drama; Instructors; Local Artists & Directors; Music; Soloists
Founded: 1984
Opened: 1984
Specialized Field: Educational; Symphony; Chorus; Youth Strings
Status: Nonprofit
Volunteer Staff: 10
Non-paid Artists: 55
Budget: $25,000
Income Sources: Memberships; Ticket sales; Grants; Donations
Performs At: Concert Hall at Carson City Community Center
Affiliations: Carson Chamber Singers, Strings In The School
Annual Attendance: 2,500
Facility Category: Concert hall in community center
Type of Stage: Proscenium
Seating Capacity: 800

1312
LAS VEGAS CIVIC SYMPHONY
821 Las Vegas Boulevard N
Las Vegas, NV 89101
Phone: 702-385-2838
Fax: 702-382-5199
Management:
  Cultural Supervisor: Patricia L Harris
  Cultural Center Coordinator: Ellis Rice
  Cultural Publicist: Stephanie Fosse
Mission: Provide culturally enriched performances and classes to the Greater Las Vegas area.
Specialized Field: Symphony
Paid Staff: 20
Paid Artists: 50
Non-paid Artists: 200
Budget: $260,000-$1,050,000
Performs At: Reed Whipple Cultural Arts Center
Seating Capacity: 300

1313
LAS VEGAS PHILHARMONIC
1412 S. Jones Blvd.
Las Vegas, NV 89146
Phone: 702-258-5438
Fax: 702-893-7757
e-mail: lvpinfo@lvphil.com
Web Site: www.lvphil.com
Officers:
  President & Chief Executive Officer: Jeri Crawford
  VP Director of Marketing, Secretary: Patricia Pieper Fink
  Treasurer: Ellis Landau
  Vice President of Development: Amy Wiles
  Trustee: Michael Bolognini
Management:
  Music Director/Conductor: Donato Cabrera
  Concertmaster: DeAnn Letourneau
  Finance/Personnel Manager & Librari: Doug Van Gilder
  Education Director: Connie Beisner Warling
  Project Manager: Sabrina Cozine
Mission: To provide live symphony music at the highest artistic standards. Encourage and build appreciation of music to all through educaitonal programming and community initiatives.
Founded: 1998
Specialized Field: Orchestra
Paid Staff: 4
Volunteer Staff: 2
Paid Artists: 76

1314
NEVADA SYMPHONY ORCHESTRA
4505 Maryland Parkway
VNLV Department of Music
Las Vegas, NV 89154
Phone: 702-895-3332
Fax: 702-895-4239
Web Site: www.nevadasymphony.org
Officers:
  President: M Rex Baird
  VP: Bruce B Borgelt
  Secretary: Collen Schoeder
  Treasurer/ President Elect: B. Michl Lloyd
Management:
  Artistic Director: Virko Baley
  Executive Doroctor: Judith Markham
  Director Operations: Timothy Bonenfant
  Chairman: Paul Kreider

INSTRUMENTAL MUSIC / New Hampshire

Mission: To offer symphonic performances, services and educational opportunities to the Las Vegas community.
Founded: 1980
Specialized Field: Orchestra; Ensemble
Status: Professional; Nonprofit
Organization Type: Performing; Educational; Sponsoring

1315
RENO CHAMBER ORCHESTRA
925 Riverside Drive Reno
Reno, NV 89503
Phone: 775-348-9413
Fax: 775-34—064
e-mail: info@renochamberorchestra.org
Web Site: www.renochamberorchestra.org
Officers:
   President: Karen Penner-Johnson
   First Vice President: Carol Parkhurst
   Second Vice President: Karen Vibe
   Secretary: Kathy Jakolat
   Treasurer: Patrick Ellingsworth
Management:
   Music Director/Conductor: Theodore Kuchar
   Executive Director: Scott Faulkner
   Associate Executive Director: Chris Morrison
   Office Manager: Fifi Day
   Librarian/Personnel Manager: Dustin Budish
Mission: To provide the highest quality performance of repertoire written for the smaller orchestra and educate and promote the appreciation of the music among diverse audiences.
Specialized Field: Chamber; Orchestra
Paid Staff: 4
Volunteer Staff: 45
Paid Artists: 40 +
Budget: $400,000-$425,000
Income Sources: Individual contributions; Tickets sales; Foundations; Grants; Corparate soliciations
Performs At: Nightingale Concert Hall
Facility Category: Concert Hall
Seating Capacity: 615

1316
RENO PHILHARMONIC
925 Riverside Drive
Suite 3
Reno, NV 89503
Phone: 775-323-6393
Fax: 775-323-6711
e-mail: renophil@renophil.com
Web Site: www.renophil.com
Officers:
   Chair: Keith Burrowes
   Chair-Elect: Gigi Turville
   President/CEO: Tim Young
   Secretary: Moira Lieberman
   Treasurer: Lori Tuntland
Management:
   Music Director/Conductor: Laura Jackson
   Orchestra Personnel Manager: Mary Miller
   Box Office Manager: Michael Higgs
   Marketing Director: Tracy Tootell
   Development Director: Jane Raley
Mission: To bring the best of symphonic music to the Truckee Meadows and surrounding communities; to ensure a high quality musical experience; to bring that musical experience to the youth of our community; to foster strong individual and corporate support for the Reno Philharmonic; to engage in sound business and fiscal planning and execution; to work in cooperation with the other local arts groups.
Founded: 1969
Specialized Field: Orchestra
Paid Staff: 7
Paid Artists: 150
Non-paid Artists: 300
Budget: $1.9 million
Income Sources: Earned Revenue/Contributions
Annual Attendance: 60,000

New Hampshire

1317
NEVERS' 2ND REGIMENT BAND
110 South State Street
P O Box 2352
Concord, NH 03301
Phone: 603-642-6623
e-mail: info@neversband.org
Web Site: www.neversband.org
Officers:
   Treasurer: Doug Osborne
   Secretary: Karie Swift
   Member-at-Large: Deborah C. Lincoln
Management:
   Executive Board: Priscilla Giles
   Director: Philip K. Martin
   Business Manager: Tom Cusano
Mission: To perpetuate its tradition of live, high quality performances of music for the benefit and enjoyment of all people; to promote and demonstrate the continuing relevance of modern and traditional concert band music and to preserve the history of the Band's regimental origins.
Utilizes: Community Talent; Guest Artists; Guest Musical Directors; Guest Musicians; Instructors; Lyricists; Multimedia; Scenic Designers; Singers; Students
Founded: 1861
Specialized Field: Band
Status: Semi-Professional; Nonprofit
Paid Staff: 6
Paid Artists: 30
Income Sources: City of Concord
Affiliations: American Federation of Musicians
Facility Category: Outdoors; Wagner Bandwagon
Seating Capacity: unlimited
Year Built: 1968
Organization Type: Performing

1318
APPLE HILL CENTER FOR CHAMBER MUSIC
410 Apple Hill Road
East Sullivan, NH 03457
Mailing Address: P.O. Box 217, Sullivan, NH 03445
Phone: 603-847-3371
Fax: 603-847-9734
Toll-free: 800-472-6677
e-mail: info@applehill.org
Web Site: www.applehill.org
Officers:
   President: John Woodbury
   Vice President: Mark Meess
   Secretary: Lindsay Dearborn
   Treasurer: Fred Hadlow
   Board Member: Lynette Blake
Management:
   Executive and Artistic Director: Leonard Matczynski
   Buildings and Grounds Manager: Richard Anderson
   Development Coordinator: Elizabeth Brown
   Grant Writer: Gail Malitas
   Summer Coordinator: Amelia Perro
Mission: To further the performing and teaching of chamber music at the highest standard and in so doing to play for peace. It pursues these goals through the internationally celebrated performance and coaching of its Artists-in-Residence, the Apple Hill Chamber Players.
Founded: 1971
Specialized Field: Chamber; Ensemble
Status: Professional; Semi-Professional; Non-Professional; Nonprofit
Paid Staff: 6
Paid Artists: 5
Performs At: Louise Shonk Kelly Concert Barn
Organization Type: Performing; Resident; Educational; Sponsoring

1319
NEW HAMPSHIRE PHILHARMONIC ORCHESTRA
83 Hanover Street
4th Floor
Manchester, NH 03101
Phone: 603-647-6476
Fax: 603-647-4130
e-mail: info@nhpo.com
Web Site: www.nhphilharmonic.org
Officers:
   President: Walter Zanchuk
   VP: Adele Baker
   Secretary: George Jobel
   Treasurer: John Gunther
Management:
   Executive Director: Steven A Olans
Mission: To offer classical concerts; to enhance music education; to provide opportunities for nonprofessionals to work with music professionals.
Founded: 1905
Specialized Field: Symphony; Orchestra
Status: Professional; Non-Professional, Nonprofit
Paid Staff: 2
Volunteer Staff: 2
Paid Artists: 2
Non-paid Artists: 65
Budget: $100,000
Income Sources: Box office; donations; foundations
Performs At: Palace Theatre
Annual Attendance: 10,000
Facility Category: Concert Hall
Type of Stage: Proscenium
Seating Capacity: 850
Year Built: 1920
Year Remodeled: 1975
Organization Type: Performing; Resident; Educational

1320
NEW HAMPSHIRE SYMPHONY ORCHESTRA
1087 Elm Street #306
Manchester, NH 03105-1298
Phone: 603-669-3559
Fax: 603-623-1195
Toll-free: 800-639-9320
e-mail: info@nhso.org
Web Site: www.nhso.org
Management:
   Music Director: Kenneth Kiester
   Executive Director: Douglas Barry CAE
   Director Development: George Regan
Founded: 1974
Specialized Field: Symphony; Orchestra
Status: Professional; Nonprofit

INSTRUMENTAL MUSIC / New Jersey

Performs At: Palace Theatre and Music Hall in Portsmouth, NH/ Capitol Center For The Arts in Concord
Affiliations: American Symphony Orchestra League
Organization Type: Performing; Touring; Educational

New Jersey

1321
COLONIAL SYMPHONY
246 B Madisonville Road
Basking Ridge, NJ 07920
Phone: 908-766-7555
Fax: 908-953-9799
e-mail: colonialsy@verizon.net
Web Site: www.colonialsymphony.org
Officers:
  President: Mark C Rosenblum
  VP: Carol Wead
  VP: Daniel H Olmsted
  Vice-President: Ross Longfield
  Treasurer: Thomas P. Bintinger
  Secretary: Lawrence J. Hunt
Management:
  Music Director/Conductor: Yehuda Gilad
  Executive Director: Suzanne Samson
Mission: Dedicated to nurturing and sustaining a superior orchestra performing a balance of classical and contemporary music and enhancing the understanding of music through education.
Utilizes: Choreographers; Collaborations; Commissioned Composers; Composers-in-Residence; Dancers; Guest Composers; Guest Musical Directors; Guest Musicians; Instructors; Singers
Founded: 1950
Specialized Field: Symphony
Status: Professional; Nonprofit
Paid Staff: 2.5
Volunteer Staff: 12
Paid Artists: 50
Budget: $500,000
Income Sources: Corporate Donations; Individual Donations; Government Endowments; Foundations
Performs At: Community Theatre in Morristown, N.J.
Affiliations: American Symphony Orchestra League
Annual Attendance: 5,000
Facility Category: Community Theatre of Morristown
Organization Type: Performing; Educational

1322
ORCHESTRA OF ST. PETER BY THE SEA
2456 Hooper Avenue
PO Box 215
Bay Head, NJ 08742
Phone: 732-920-4444
Fax: 732-477-6277
e-mail: seasymphonyinc@aol.com
Web Site: www.orchsp.com
Management:
  Music Director/Manager: Father Alphonse Stephenson
Founded: 1986
Specialized Field: Orchestra; Ensemble
Performs At: Touring Orchestra
Annual Attendance: 2,500

1323
BLOOMFIELD MANDOLIN ORCHESTRA
Bloomfield Recreation Commission
PO Box 1776
Bloomfield, NJ 07003
Phone: 973-748-0424
Fax: 973-743-0343
e-mail: nj.mandolins@worldnet.att.net
Web Site: www.mandolin.bloomfieldfm.org
  Treasurer: Filomena Peloro
Management:
  Musical Director: Gabriel Nevola
  Manager: Russell Kelner
  Orchestra Librarian: Yugo Re
Mission: To promote the mandolin by way of entertainment as well as instruction.
Utilizes: Singers
Founded: 1941
Specialized Field: Mandolin Orchestra
Status: Nonprofit
Non-paid Artists: 35
Performs At: Presbyterian Church on the Green
Organization Type: Performing, Touring, Educational

1324
GARDEN STATE PHILHARMONIC SYMPHONY YOUTH ORCHESTRA
1 College Drive
PO Box 2001
Brick, NJ 08754
Phone: 732-255-0460
Fax: 732-255-0478
e-mail: info@gardenstatephilharmonic.org
Web Site: www.gardenstatephilharmonic.com
Officers:
  President: Kenneth J. Malagiere
  Vice President: Mario A. Marano
  Vice President, Interim Treasurer: James Buffum
  Secretary: Lynda E. Rabens
Management:
  Artistic Director/Conductor: Anthony LaGruth
  Managing Director: Thomas L. Stephens
  Business Manager: Sandra Campbell
Specialized Field: Youth Orchestra
Budget: $250,000-$1,050,000
Performs At: Toms River H.S. Auditorium/ Ocean County College Arts Center
Seating Capacity: 1,266/ 604

1325
BAY-ATLANTIC SYMPHONY
59 East Commerce Street
Bridgeton, NJ 08302
Phone: 856-451-1169
Fax: 856-451-4380
e-mail: info@bayatlanticsymphony.org
Web Site: www.bayatlanticsymphony.org
Officers:
  President: Robert Watters
  Vice President: Alyce Parker
  Secretary: David Iams
  Treasurer: Robert Woodruff
  Trustee: Aaron Cohen
Management:
  Music Director/Conductor: Jed Gaylin
  Concertmaster: Ruotao Mao
  Executive Director: Paul D. Her-ron
  Personnel Manager: Christopher Di Santo
Founded: 1983
Specialized Field: Orchestra
Budget: $514,000
Income Sources: Geraldine R Dodge Foundation, New Jersey State Council Of Arts, Fleet Bank, Bergen Family Foundation, Silento Family Foundation, Basile Tesa, LLC
Performs At: Richard Stockton PAC in Atlanta, Performing Arts Center in Vinland, Cap May Music

1326
SOLID BRASS
5 Sunset Drive
Chatham, NJ 07928-1141
Phone: 973-701-0674
Fax: 973-701-0674
e-mail: haislip@solidbrass.com
Web Site: www.solidbrass.com
Management:
  Artistic Director: Douglas Haislip
  Management: Lois Scott, lsminc@aol.com
Mission: Preserving and perpetuating brass chamber music through performance, recording, composing and related activities.
Utilizes: Multimedia
Founded: 1982
Specialized Field: Chamber; Brass Ensemble
Status: Professional
Non-paid Artists: Yes
Annual Attendance: 1,500
Organization Type: Performing; Touring; Educational

1327
NEW JERSEY INTERGENERATIONAL ORCHESTRA
570 Central Avenue
Cranford, NJ 07974
Phone: 908-603-7691
Fax: 908-665-0929
e-mail: info@njio.org
Web Site: njio.org
Officers:
  President: Susan Peterson
  Vice President: Len Avdey
  Vice President: Judy Jacobson, Ph.D.
  Treasurer: Alan Campell
  Treasurer: Sue Davis
Management:
  Administrator: Mary Beth Sweet
Mission: To nurture the belief that senior citizens can share their wisdom and become vital resources for children by bringing youth and the elderly together to share experiences that promote mutual growth and understanding between generations.
Founded: 1994
Specialized Field: Orchestra
Status: Non-Professional
Paid Staff: 3
Volunteer Staff: 10
Paid Artists: 30
Non-paid Artists: 100

1328
ALL SEASONS CHAMBER PLAYERS
115 Orchard Road
Demarest, NJ 07627
Phone: 201-768-1331
e-mail: jeanstri@bellatlantic.net
Web Site: www.allseasonschamberplayers.org
Mission: A leading chamber music ensemble in New Jersey performing music from baroque to contemporary periods in mixed ensembles
Founded: 1981
Specialized Field: Baroque; Contemporary

1329
HADDONFIELD SYMPHONY
41 S Haddon Avenue
Suite 7
Haddonfield, NJ 08033

Phone: 856-429-1880
Fax: 856-428-5634
e-mail: symphony@haddonfield-symphony.org
Web Site: www.haddonfield-symphony.org
Officers:
  President: Trevor Orthmann
Management:
  Music Director/Conductor: Rossen Milanov
  Assistant Conductor: Benjamin Loeb
  Director Marketing/Public Relations: Michele Holcomb
  Director Development: Eileen K Myers CFRE
  Director Educational Artistic Oper.: Erin Bewsher
  Marketing /Development Assistant: Erica Heyer
Mission: Dedicated to enriching the musical lives of the residents of the state of New Jersey.
Utilizes: Guest Artists; Guest Companies; Singers
Founded: 1952
Specialized Field: Symphony; Orchestra
Status: Professional; Nonprofit
Paid Staff: 6
Organization Type: Performing; Educational

1330
NEW JERSEY CITY UNIVERSITY ORCHESTRA
2039 Kennedy Boulevard
New Jersey University/Music Department
Jersey City, NJ 07305-1597
Phone: 201-200-3111
Fax: 201-200-2352
e-mail: eraditz@njcu.edu
Web Site: www.njcu.edu
Management:
  Music Director: Edward Raditz
Utilizes: Guest Musical Directors; Guest Musicians; Multimedia; Soloists
Specialized Field: Orchestra; Ensemble
Paid Staff: 2
Volunteer Staff: 10
Paid Artists: 3
Budget: $35,000
Performs At: Margaret William Auditorium, New Jersey City University
Annual Attendance: 3000
Facility Category: Theatre\Auditorium
Seating Capacity: 1,000
Year Built: 1960
Year Remodeled: 1975

1331
NEW JERSEY MUSIC SOCIETY
311 Claremont Avenue
Montclair, NJ 07042
Phone: 973-746-6068
Fax: 973-746-0685
e-mail: njchambermusicsociety@att.net
Web Site: www.njmta.com
Management:
  Executive Director: Michael Lawson
  Assistant Executive Director: Marie Figueredo
  Artist in Residence: Paquito D'Rivera
Mission: To create, produce and maintain a repertoire of outstanding musical performances in classical, jazz and world music with core artists-in-residence and frequent nationally prominent guest artists. To provide new opportunities to a wider audience through innovative and stimulating children's programs, family concerts and workshops in area school system.
Founded: 1974
Specialized Field: Chamber
Status: Professional; Nonprofit
Performs At: Montclair Art Museum; Union Congregatinal Church
Organization Type: Performing; Touring; Resident; Educational

1332
PHILHARMONIC OF SOUTHERN NEW JERSEY
PO Box 768
Moorestown
Moorestown, NJ 08057
Phone: 856-779-2600
Fax: 609-654-8792
e-mail: Contact@psnj.org
Web Site: www.psnj.org
Officers:
  President: Tricia McCunney-Thomas
  Vice President: Michelle White
  Secretary: Eric M. Hurwitz
  Treasurer: Anthony Campione
  Board Member: Lisa Miller
Management:
  Music Director: Mathew Oberstein
  Personnel Manager: Barbara Travaline
  Concert/Production Manager: William Joyce
Mission: Provides quality classical music for the community; and offer rehearsal/performance opportunities for the talented musician.
Founded: 1991
Specialized Field: Orchestra
Budget: $35,000-$100,000
Income Sources: Grants and Contributions
Performs At: Forrest Rowland Auditorium
Affiliations: American Symphony Orchestra League; South Jersey Cultural Alliance
Seating Capacity: 1,300

1333
WEST JERSEY CHAMBER MUSIC SYMPHONY & SOCIETY
101 Bridgeboro Road
Moorestown, NJ 08057
Phone: 856-778-1899
Fax: 856-234-3666
e-mail: kiteandkeydesign@comcast.net
Web Site: www.wjcms.org
Management:
  Music Director: Joel Krott
Utilizes: Guest Artists; Guest Companies
Founded: 1980
Specialized Field: Orchestra; Chamber
Status: Professional; Nonprofit
Paid Staff: 2
Volunteer Staff: 15
Paid Artists: 40
Budget: $35,000-$100,000
Performs At: Various churches and schools
Organization Type: Performing; Touring

1334
NEW JERSEY YOUTH SYMPHONY
570 Central Avenue
Murray Hill, NJ 07974
Phone: 908-771-5544
Fax: 908-771-9839
e-mail: office@njys.org
Web Site: www.njys.org
Management:
  Executive Director: Linda Abrams
  Artistic Director: Barbara Barstow
  Executive Director: Susan Cauldwell
  Operations Manager: Robert Varner
  Conductor: Bryan Rudderow
Mission: To provide talented young musicians with orchestral and related music education experiences that will enable them to reach their highest potential as performers and listeners.
Founded: 1979
Specialized Field: Youth Symphony
Status: Non-Professional; Nonprofit
Non-paid Artists: 95
Budget: $500,000
Organization Type: Performing; Touring; Educational

1335
CATHEDRAL BASILICA OF THE SACRED HEART CONCERT SERIES
89 Ridge Street
Newark, NJ 07104
Phone: 973-484-2400
Fax: 973-497-9336
e-mail: jmiller@cathedralbasilica.org
Web Site: www.cathedralbasilica.org/concert/
Management:
  Director Music Ministry: John J Miller
  Associate Organist: Vincent Carr
  Coordinator of Hispanic Music Minis: Olfary Gutierrez
  Music Office Assistant: Carol Resch
Mission: Offering quality musical programs to Newark area residents.
Founded: 1983
Specialized Field: Symphony; Orchestra; Chamber; Ensemble

1336
NEW JERSEY SYMPHONY ORCHESTRA
60 Park Place
9th Floor
Newark, NJ 07102
Phone: 973-624-3713
Fax: 973-624-2115
e-mail: information@njsymphony.org
Web Site: www.njsymphony.org
Officers:
  Co-Chair of the Board: Stephen Sichak, Jr.
  Co-Chair of the Board: Ruth C. Lipper
  Chairman: Dr. Victor Parsonnet
  Treasurer: David R. Huber
  Secretary: Alan L. Danzis
Management:
  Music Director: Jacques Lacombe
  Office Manager: Karen Duda
  Controller: Denise Jaffe
  Stage Technician: Brian Donelly
  Artistic Operations Coordinator: Amanda Fischer
Mission: To engage the people of New Jersey by performing the full symphonic repertoire at the highest caliber in a variety of settings for diverse audiences.
Utilizes: Guest Artists
Founded: 1922
Specialized Field: Symphony; Orchestra; Chamber; Ensemble
Status: Professional; Nonprofit
Paid Staff: 43
Volunteer Staff: 76
Budget: $14.5 million
Performs At: New Jersey Performing Arts Center; John Harms Center for the Arts/Englewood; Community Theatre/Morristown; State Theatre
Affiliations: War Memorail Trenton
Seating Capacity: 2,600/1,900
Organization Type: Performing

INSTRUMENTAL MUSIC / New Jersey

1337
NEW JERSEY SYMPHONY ORCHESTRA
60 Park Place
9th Floor
Newark, NJ 07102
Phone: 973-624-3713
Fax: 973-624-2115
e-mail: information@njsymphony.org
Web Site: www.njsymphony.org
Officers:
- Co-Chair of the Board: Stephen Sichak, Jr.
- Co-Chair of the Board: Ruth C. Lipper
- Chairman: Dr. Victor Parsonnet
- Treasurer: David R. Huber
- Secretary: Alan L. Danzis

Management:
- Music Director: Neeme Jarvi
- Office Manager: Karen Duda
- Controller: Denise Jaffe
- Stage Technician: Brian Donelly
- Artistic Operations Coordinator: Amanda Fischer

Specialized Field: Orchestra
Budget: $35,000-$100,000
Performs At: New Jersey Performing Arts Center
Seating Capacity: 2,700

1338
OCEAN CITY POPS
P.O Box 931
Ocean City, NJ 08226
Phone: 609-525-9291
Fax: 609-339-0374
e-mail: oceancitypops@aol.com
Web Site: www.oceancitypops.com
Officers:
- Board Chair: John S Gabel
- Vice Chair/Finances: Janey Perotti

Management:
- Music Director: William Scheible
- Executive Director: Michael Dattilo

Specialized Field: Orchestra; Pops
Budget: $250,000-$1,050,000
Performs At: auditorium
Seating Capacity: 930

1339
PLAINFIELD SYMPHONY
PO Box 5093
Plainfield, NJ 07061
Phone: 908-561-5140
e-mail: info@plainfieldsymphony.org
Web Site: www.plainfieldsymphony.org
Officers:
- President: Peter Lomonaco
- Vice President: Liz Adam
- Treasurer: Lesley Rogers
- Secretary: Rrichard Tang
- Board Member: Harry Ailster

Management:
- Music Director: Charles Prince
- Executive Director: James Rowland

Mission: To prepare and present musical programs of a symphonic type; to stimulate interest in symphonic music in the Central New Jersey area; to provide educational opportunities through youth and family concerts; and to provide a medium of performance for talented nonprofessional musicians.
Founded: 1919
Specialized Field: Symphony; Ensemble
Paid Staff: 2
Paid Artists: 40
Non-paid Artists: 40
Budget: $100,000-$125,000

Performs At: Crescent Avenue Presbyterian Church
Seating Capacity: 600

1340
GREATER PRINCETON YOUTH ORCHESTRA
120 John Street Princeton
Princeton, NJ 08542
Mailing Address: PO Box 3037, Princeton, NJ 08543
Phone: 609-936-0150
Fax: 908- 87—017
e-mail: gpyo@patmedia.net
Web Site: www.gpyo.org
Officers:
- President: Richard Bilotti
- Trustee: Carl Carabelli
- Trustee: Michael Donahue
- Trustee: Andi Sjamsu

Management:
- Music Director: Kawika Kahalehoe
- Conductor: Dr. Arvin Gopal
- Administrative Director: Mini Krishnan
- Rehearsal Manager: Adam Warshawsky
- Concert and Recruitment Manager: Mark Morris

Mission: To provide exciting and unique educational opportunites for many of our community's young people. Through their involvement in the Orchestra, gifted young musicians from across Central New Jersey and Pennsylvania hone their skills as performers in a large orchestra and in chamber music groups, and learn to work with others in pursuing common goals.
Founded: 1961
Specialized Field: Youth Orchestra
Budget: $35,000-$100,000
Performs At: Richard Auditorium, Princeton University
Seating Capacity: 868

1341
PRINCETON SYMPHONY ORCHESTRA
PO Box 250
Princeton, NJ 08542
Phone: 609-497-0020
Fax: 609-497-0904
e-mail: info@princetonsymphony.org
Web Site: www.princetonsymphony.org
Officers:
- President: David A. Tierno
- Vice President: Richard J. Levine
- Treasurer: Yvonne Marcuse
- Secretary: Rachel D. Gray
- Board Member: Robert L. Annis

Management:
- Music Director/Conductor: Rosen Milanov
- Executive Director: Melanie Clarke
- General Manager and Artistic Admini: Kiri Murakami
- Manager: Carolyn Dwyer
- Development Coordinator: Niki Spruill

Mission: To present the finest classical compositions from the widest range, including unusual and seldom heard works; to enhance audience appreciation of the often unfamiliar works through lectures and presentations; to create an outstanding performance opportunity for the many excellent musicians in the New Jersey region; and to reach out to new audiences both geographically and demographically.
Founded: 1980
Specialized Field: Orchestra
Paid Artists: 55
Budget: $250,000-$1,050,000
Performs At: Richardson Auditorium
Seating Capacity: 850

1342
RIDGEWOOD SYMPHONY ORCHESTRA
PO Box 176
Ridgewood, NJ 07451-0176
Phone: 201-612-0118
Fax: 201-445-2762
e-mail: info@ridgewoodsymphony.org
Web Site: www.ridgewoodsymphony.org
Officers:
- President: E Sosinsky
- Treasurer: Richard A. Marri
- Secretary: Alfred Paranay
- Treasurer: Richard A. Macri

Management:
- General Manager: Karin A Todd
- House Manager: Brian Burns
- Personnel Manager: Donna Dixon-Olson
- Personnel Manager: Louise Butler
- Conductor/Music Director: Gary S Fagin

Founded: 1940
Specialized Field: Symphony; Orchestra
Paid Staff: 4
Volunteer Staff: 10
Non-paid Artists: 90
Budget: $90,000
Income Sources: Box Office; Grants; Private Donations; Fundraising
Performs At: Benjamin Franklin Middle School Auditorium
Annual Attendance: 3,700
Seating Capacity: 775

1343
SUMMIT SYMPHONY
P.O. BOX 352
Summit, NJ 07901
Phone: 816-401-5251
Fax: 908-277-2978
e-mail: office@lssymphony.org
Web Site: www.lssymphony.org
Officers:
- President: Bob White
- President-Elect: Shannon Lawrence
- Secretary: Carol Rothwell
- Treasurer: Gary Fruits
- Board Member: John Clabaugh

Management:
- Music Director: Russell E. Berlin, Jr.
- Manager Orchestra Personnel: Barry Davidson

Mission: To offer orchestra music to Summit and surrounding communities and provide an opportunity for nonprofessionals to perform major works.
Founded: 1937
Specialized Field: Symphony
Status: Non-Professional; Nonprofit
Income Sources: Summit Board of Recreation; New Jersey Council on the Arts
Performs At: Summit Senior High School; Summit Middle School
Organization Type: Performing

1344
BERGEN PHILHARMONIC ORCHESTRA
PO Box 174
Teaneck, NJ 07666
Phone: 201-837-1980
e-mail: bergenphil.orchestra@gmail.com
Web Site: www.bergenphilharmonic.org
Management:
- Music Director: David Gilbert

Specialized Field: Orchestra

INSTRUMENTAL MUSIC / New Jersey

1345
GARDEN STATE PHILHARMONIC SYMPHONY ORCHESTRA
1 College Drive
PO Box 2001
Toms River, NJ 08754
Phone: 732-255-0460
Fax: 732-255-0478
e-mail: info@gardenstatephilharmonic.org
Web Site: www.gardenstatephilharmonic.org
Officers:
   President, Board of Directors: Kenneth James Malagiere
   Vice President: Mario A. Marano
   Vice President, Interim Treasurer: James Buffum
   Secretary, Past President: Lynda E. Rabens
   Member-at-Large: Ann Marie Baker
Management:
   Artistic Director/Conductor: Anthony LaGruth
   Managing Director: Thomas Stephens
Mission: Dedicated to maintaining a professional orchestra in Ocean County and surrounding NJ counties, that will give concerts of the highest cultural and educational value for the community and to providing both educational and training programs as well as fostering activities to encourage appreciation of music.
Utilizes: Multi Collaborations
Founded: 1956
Specialized Field: Symphony; Orchestra
Status: Professional; Nonprofit
Paid Staff: 30
Volunteer Staff: 2
Paid Artists: 70
Income Sources: Grants
Performs At: Toms River High School North; The Strand Theatre
Seating Capacity: 1200
Organization Type: Performing

1346
GREATER TRENTON SYMPHONY ORCHESTRA
28 W State Street
Suite 202
Trenton, NJ 08608
Phone: 609-394-1338
Fax: 609-394-1394
e-mail: info@trentonsymphony.org
Web Site: www.trentonsymphony.org
Management:
   Executive Director/Conductor: John Peter Holly
Mission: To offer residents of the greater Trenton area high-quality performances of classical music for orchestra.
Utilizes: Artists-in-Residence; Guest Writers; Local Artists; Multimedia; Original Music Scores
Founded: 1921
Specialized Field: Symphony; Orchestra
Status: Professional; Nonprofit
Performs At: War Memorial Theater
Organization Type: Performing; Educational

1347
MONMOUTH SYMPHONY ORCHESTRA
P O Box 1302
Wall, NJ 07719
Phone: 732-747-2063
Fax: 732-747-2063
e-mail: veep@monsym.org
Web Site: www.monmouthsymphony.org
Officers:
   Membership Chairperson: Karen Slobodin
   President: Joan M Berzansky
Management:
   Music Director: Roy D Gussman
Founded: 1948
Specialized Field: Orchestra
Performs At: Count Basie Theatre, Red Bank
Annual Attendance: 500
Seating Capacity: 1,700

1348
DISCOVERY ORCHESTRA
PO Box 4064
Warren, NJ 07059
Phone: 908-226-7300
Fax: 908-226-7337
e-mail: info@discoveryorchestra.org
Web Site: www.discoveryorchestra.org
Officers:
   President: Stephen Reynolds
   Secretary: Rachel Weinberger
   Treasurer: Kelli Christensen
   Board Member: Mary G. Horn
   Board Member: Wilma Nurse
Management:
   Artistic Director: George Marriner Maull
   Executive Director: Virgina Johnson
   Events Director: Jeanne Maass
   Administrative Director: Diane Lester
Mission: In response to the cultural forces that regelate music to a background presence in people's lives, the mission of the Discovery Orchestra is to sensitize people to the difference between listening and hearing music through meaningful and compelling music educational experiences.
Founded: 1987
Specialized Field: Orchestra
Paid Staff: 95
Budget: $250,000-$1,050,000
Performs At: New Jersey Performing Arts Center
Seating Capacity: 2,800/785

1349
WILLIAM PATERSON UNIVERSITY PERFORMING & VISUAL ARTS
300 Pompton Road
Wayne, NJ 07470
Phone: 973-720-3271
Fax: 973-720-3592
e-mail: boxoffice@wpunj.edu
Web Site: www.wpunj.edu/wppresents/boxoffice.dot
Management:
   Executive Director of Performing Ar: Jane B. Stein
   Director of Operations: Al Schaefer
   Director of Audience Services/Box O: Lou Hamel
   Marketing Coordinator: Craig Woelpper
   Program Assistant: Lavene Gass-Youmans
Mission: To increase arts offerings and education within New Jersey's Tri-County area and present dynamic performances of great music, lectures and art.
Founded: 1986
Specialized Field: Orchestra
Status: Professional
Paid Staff: 10
Budget: $100,000
Performs At: Shea Center for the Performing Arts
Seating Capacity: 960
Year Built: 1967
Rental Contact: Operations Director (973)720-2384 Al Schaefer
Organization Type: Performing

1350
ARBOR CHAMBER MUSIC SOCIETY
PO Box 2901
Westfield, NJ 07091
Phone: 908-232-1116
Fax: 908-232-2423
e-mail: arbormusic@comcast.net
Web Site: westfieldnj.com/arbormusic
Management:
   Founder & Artistic Director: Lenore Fishman Davis
Mission: To bring the highest artistic standards of chamber music performance to New Jersey's audiences, to educate audiences and to develop the next generation of listeners and musicians.
Founded: 1991
Specialized Field: Chamber
Status: Professional
Income Sources: Private Foundations; Business/Corporate Donations; Box Office; Individual Donations
Performs At: Union City Arts Center; St. Paul's Episcopal Church-Westfield
Organization Type: Performing; Touring; Educational

1351
NEW JERSEY WORKSHOP FOR THE ARTS
150-152 E Broad Street
Westfield, NJ 07090
Phone: 908-789-9696
Fax: 908-789-9101
e-mail: njwa2@aol.com
Web Site: www.njworkshopforthearts.com
Officers:
   Chairman: Lowell Schantz
   Vice Chairman: Walter Metzger
   Secretary: Janet Elby
   Treasurer: Dennis Simon
   Board Member: Soori Ahamparam
Management:
   NJWA Concert Band: Howard Toplansky
   Music Director Big Band: Jon Paterson
   Symphony Director: Janet Lyman
   International Alphorn Ensemble: Dr. Ted Schlosberg
   Founder and Executive Director: Dr. Theodore K. Schlosberg
Mission: Where talent develops and creativity thrives, to enrich lives by providing opportunities to develop creative talents and encourage a greater appreciation of the arts through both instruction and performance.
Founded: 1972
Specialized Field: Music; Dance; Arts; Crafts
Status: Nonprofit
Budget: $1,000,000
Income Sources: Tuition, Grants
Performs At: Recital Hall

1352
NEW JERSEY FESTIVAL ORCHESTRA
224 E Broad Street
Suite 6
Westfield, NJ 07090
Phone: 908-232-9400
Fax: 908-232-2446
e-mail: ldoyle@njfestivalorchestra.org
Web Site: www.njfestivalorchestra.org
Officers:
   President: Norman Luka, MD
   Vice Chairman: Barry Zucker
   Treasurer: Alan Smith
   Secretary: Fred Malley

INSTRUMENTAL MUSIC / New Mexico

Charter President: Ann Allen
Management:
   Executive Director: Linda Doyle
   Music Director: David Wroe
   Orchestra Contractor: Vince Carano
   Stage Manager: Jim Reed
Mission: Westfield Symphony Orchestra is one of New Jersey's premiere fully professional regional symphonies. It's mission is to promote the world's legacy of symphonic and operatic music to audiences involving them in the rich heritage through a diversity of professional musical experience, including performance education and mentoring.
Utilizes: Guest Musicians; Original Music Scores; Singers
Founded: 1983
Specialized Field: Symphony
Status: Professional; Nonprofit
Paid Staff: 5
Volunteer Staff: 5
Paid Artists: 106
Budget: $600,000
Income Sources: Government Grants; Box Office; Corporate Donations; Foundation Contributions; Individual Donations
Performs At: Union County Arts Center; The Presbyterian Church, Westfield; Westfield High School; Kean University; PNC Arts Center
Affiliations: American Symphony Orchestra League; Westfield Area Chamber of Commerce; Center for Nonprofits
Organization Type: Performing; Resident; Touring; Educational
Comments: For information concerning accessibility for special needs, call (908) 232-9400

New Mexico

1353
CHAMBER ORCHESTRA OF ALBUQUERQUE
PO Box 35081
Albuquerque, NM 87176-5081
Phone: 505-881-2078
Fax: 505-881-2634
e-mail: coaoch@aol.com
Management:
   Music Director/Conductor: David Oberg
   Operations Manager: Diane Bonnell
   Personnel Manager: Carol Swift-Matton
   Stage Manager: Karla Simmet
Mission: To provide a broad range of listening and participatory musical opportunities to the State of New Mexico; to maintain a professional orchestra whose work enriches the quality of community life.
Founded: 1976
Specialized Field: Orchestra; Chamber
Status: Professional; Nonprofit
Paid Staff: 3
Paid Artists: 1
Performs At: St. John's United Methodist Church
Organization Type: Performing

1354
NEW MEXICO SYMPHONY ORCHESTRA
4407 Menaul Boulevard North East
Suite 4
Albuquerque, NM 87107
Mailing Address: PO Box 30208, Albuquerque, NM. 87190-0208
Phone: 505-881-9590
Fax: 505-881-9456
e-mail: postmaster@nmso.org

Management:
   Principal Pops Conductor: Michael Krajewski
   Resident Conductor/Choral Director: Roger Melone
   Music Director: Guillermo Figueros
   Marketing/Public Relations: Colleen Harris-Kistner
   Development Director: Joan Allen
Mission: To present live concerts of music for small ensembles through full orchestra in both educational and concert settings.
Utilizes: Singers
Founded: 1932
Specialized Field: Symphony; Orchestra
Status: Professional; Nonprofit
Paid Staff: 22
Paid Artists: 80
Income Sources: American Symphony Orchestra League; American Arts Alliance
Performs At: Popejoy Hall; National Hispanic Cultural Center
Organization Type: Performing; Educational

1355
SOUTHWEST SYMPHONY
215 W Broadway
Suite 6
Hobbs, NM 88240
Mailing Address: PO Box 101, Hobbs, NM 88241
Phone: 505-738-1041
Fax: 505-433-1041
e-mail: swshobbs@hotmail.com
Web Site: swsymphony.org/
Officers:
   Board Member: Sharon Sagerty
Management:
   Music Director: Dr. Mark Jelinek
   Executive Director: Genevieve S. Cavanaugh
   Orchestra Manager: Cindy Walker
   Marketing /Youth Series Coor: Abby Holmes
Utilizes: Dancers; Guest Directors; Local Artists; Multimedia; Original Music Scores; Theatre Companies
Founded: 1983
Specialized Field: Orchestra
Paid Staff: 2
Volunteer Staff: 120
Budget: $100,000-$150,000
Income Sources: Fund Drives: Season Tickets, Grants, Donations
Performs At: Auditorium
Seating Capacity: 2,000

1356
LAS CRUCES SYMPHONY ORCHESTRA
1075 N Horseshoe St
Suite 210
Las Cruces, NM 88003
Mailing Address: Post Office Box 1622, Las Cruces, NM 88004
Phone: 505-646-3709
Fax: 505-646-1086
e-mail: info@lascrucessymphony.com
Web Site: www.lascrucessymphony.com
Officers:
   Board President: Carolyn M Stolberg
   VP: Nita Swartz
   Treasurer: Tom Tate
   Secretary: Nancy Carlson
Management:
   Music Director/Conductor: Dr. Lonnie Klein
   Executive Director: Debra Medoff Marks
Utilizes: Five Seasonal Concerts; Guest Accompanists; Guest Musicians; Guest Writers; Instructors; Multimedia; Original Music Scores; Singers; Soloists
Specialized Field: Orchestra

Paid Staff: 1
Volunteer Staff: 70
Paid Artists: 8
Non-paid Artists: 1
Budget: $100,000-$150,000
Income Sources: Box Office; Grants; Private Donations
Performs At: NMSU Performance Center
Affiliations: American Symphony Orchestra League
Annual Attendance: 8,000
Facility Category: Music Hall
Type of Stage: Thrust
Seating Capacity: 540
Year Built: 1985

1357
ROSWELL SYMPHONY ORCHESTRA
W Office Plaza
1717 W Second, Suite 205
Roswell, NM 88201
Phone: 505-623-5882
Fax: 505-623-5882
Toll-free: 800-300-9822
e-mail: rso@dfn.com
Web Site: www.roswellsymphony.org
Officers:
   President: Sam Pettit
Management:
   Director of Financial Operations: Melynda Roberson
   Director of Concert Operations: Rhonda Robinson
   Music Director: John Farrer
Mission: To provide Roswell and Southeast New Mexico with the best orchestral literature by providing an annual concert season, music education programs for children, and a multi cultural chamber concert series.
Utilizes: Guest Accompanists; Guest Musicians; Guest Writers; Multimedia; Music; Original Music Scores
Founded: 1960
Specialized Field: Symphony; Orchestra
Paid Staff: 2
Paid Artists: 84
Budget: $150,000-$260,000
Income Sources: Tickets; Grants; Gifts; Fund Raising
Performs At: Pearson Auditorium
Affiliations: American Symphony Orchestra League
Annual Attendance: 11,000
Facility Category: Auditoriums
Seating Capacity: 930

1358
MUSIC FROM ANGEL FIRE
130 Grant Avenue
Suite 202
Santa Fe, NM 87501
Mailing Address: PO Box 502, Angel Fire, NM 87710
Phone: 575-377-3233
Fax: 505-820-2539
Toll-free: 888-377-3300
e-mail: info@musicfromangelfire.org
Web Site: www.musicfromangelfire.org
Management:
   Artistic Director: Ida Kavafian
   Executive Director: Elizabeth Harcombe
   Associate Director: Lynne S Mazza
   Education Coordinator: Jean Kenin
   Executive Administrator: Jean Lehman
Mission: To bring world-class chamber music performed by international artists to the Northern New Mexico communities of Angel Fire, Taos, Raton and Las Vegas
Founded: 1984

INSTRUMENTAL MUSIC / New York

Specialized Field: Chamber
Status: Professional; Nonprofit
Paid Staff: 2
Volunteer Staff: 40
Paid Artists: 40
Budget: $650,000
Affiliations: Chamber Music America; Classical Music Festivals Of The West; New Mexico Arts
Annual Attendance: 15,000
Facility Category: Concert Hall; Venues in Taos, Angel Fire, Raton, Las Vegas
Organization Type: Performing

1359
SANTA FE PRO MUSICA
1405 Luisa Street- Suite 2
Santa Fe, NM 87505
Mailing Address: PO Box 2091, Santa Fe, NM 87504
Phone: 505-988-4640
Fax: 505-984-2501
Toll-free: 800-960-6680
e-mail: info@santafepromusica.com
Web Site: www.santafepromusica.com
Officers:
  President: M. Carlota Baca
  Vice President: Donald Tashjian
  Treasurer: C. Byron Kohr
  Secretary: Bernard van der Hoeven
  Board Member: Don Close
Management:
  Executive Director: Linda Armer
  Artistic Director: Tom O'Connor
  Operations Manager: Toni Pittman
Mission: To provide the highest quality chamber music possible and make youth programs available to the public.
Utilizes: Guest Accompanists; Original Music Scores; Sign Language Translators
Founded: 1980
Specialized Field: Symphony; Orchestra; Chamber; Classical Music
Status: Professional; Nonprofit
Paid Staff: 5
Volunteer Staff: 35
Paid Artists: 80
Budget: $900,000
Performs At: Lensic Theatre
Annual Attendance: 14,000
Organization Type: Performing; Touring; Educational

1360
SANTA FE SYMPHONY
551 W Cordova Road, Suite D
Santa Fe, NM 87505
Mailing Address: Post Office Box 9692, Santa Fe, NM 87504
Phone: 505-983-3530
Fax: 505-982-3888
Toll-free: 800-480-1319
e-mail: symphony@santafesymphony.org
Web Site: www.sf-symphony.org
Officers:
  President: David L. Brown
  Vice President: Gregory W. Heltman
  Vice President: Dr. Penelope Penland
  Vice President: Dana Winograd
  Vice President: Michael E. Melody
Management:
  Founder/General Director: Gregory Heltman
  Operations Manager: Fallon Grafe
  Choral Director: Dr. Linda Raney
  Personnel Manager: Nicolle Maniaci
Utilizes: Sign Language Translators
Founded: 1984
Specialized Field: Symphony; Orchestra; Chamber
Status: Professional; Nonprofit
Paid Staff: 5
Volunteer Staff: 40
Paid Artists: 100
Non-paid Artists: 80
Budget: $950,000
Income Sources: Ticket Sales; Grants; Contributions
Performs At: Lensic Performing Arts Center
Affiliations: American Symphony Orchestra League; Santa Fe Performing Arts Association
Annual Attendance: 11,000
Facility Category: Theatre
Type of Stage: Proscenium
Stage Dimensions: 40' x 50'
Seating Capacity: 791
Year Built: 1927
Year Remodeled: 2000
Organization Type: Performing; Resident; Educational; Sponsoring

New York

1361
ALBANY SYMPHONY ORCHESTRA
19 Clinton Avenue
Albany, NY 12207
Phone: 518-465-4755
Fax: 518-465-3711
e-mail: info@albanysymphony.com
Web Site: www.albanysymphony.com
Officers:
  Chair: Marisa Eisemann
  Vice-Chair: Jerel Golub
  Vice-Chair: Marc H. Paquin
  Vice-Chair: Beth Beshaw
  Vice-Chair: Christine Standish
Management:
  Artistic Director: David Alan Miller
Mission: One of their major programs is Key's American Music Festival featuring new American Composers. The Albany Symphony Orchestra is committed to the live presentation and recording of top quality musical programming, with an emphasis on the creation and promotion of contemporary or overlooked American works and its dissemination to a broad-based regional audience from all cultural and economic backgrounds.
Utilizes: Artists-in-Residence; Commissioned Composers; Commissioned Music; Composers-in-Residence; Guest Accompanists; Guest Companies; Guest Musical Directors; Guest Musicians; Multi Collaborations; Multimedia; Organization Contracts; Original Music Scores; Sign Language Translators; Singers; Soloists
Founded: 1931
Specialized Field: Symphony; Ensemble
Status: Professional; Nonprofit
Paid Staff: 6
Volunteer Staff: 250
Paid Artists: 68
Budget: $1.4 million
Income Sources: American Symphony Orchestra League
Season: September-May
Performs At: Albany's Palace Theatre, Troy Savings Bank Music Hall, Canfield Casino, Saratoga Springs, NY
Annual Attendance: 18,000
Seating Capacity: 2,800; 1,200
Organization Type: Performing

1362
CAPITOL CHAMBER ARTISTS
263 Manning Boulevard
Albany, NY 12206
Phone: 518-458-9231
Fax: 518-458-9231
e-mail: info@capitolchamberartists.com
Web Site: www.capitolchamberartists.com
Management:
  Co-Founder/Director/Violinist: Mary Lou Saetta
  Co-Founder/Flutist: Irvin E Gilman
  Cellist: Andr, Laurent O'Neil
Mission: Performing the highest quality chamber music and educating a new audience.
Founded: 1969
Specialized Field: Chamber
Status: Professional; Nonprofit
Season: October-June
Performs At: First Congregational Church, Albany; Community Hall, Benson VT
Annual Attendance: 15,000
Organization Type: Performing; Touring; Resident; Educational

1363
GOLIARD CHAMBER SOLOISTS
Goliard Concerts
21-65 41st Street
Astoria, NY 11105
Phone: 718-728-8927
Fax: 718-728-8927
e-mail: info@goliardconcerts.com
Web Site: http://www.goliardconcerts.com
Officers:
  Executive Director: James Blanton
Management:
  Artistic Director: Arielle Levioff
  Development Associate: Gregg Lauterbach
Mission: Performing eclectic chamber music in various vocal and instrumental combinations.
Founded: 1983
Specialized Field: Chamber; Soloists
Status: Professional; Nonprofit
Paid Staff: 3
Volunteer Staff: 1
Paid Artists: 40
Performs At: Merkin Concert Hall at the Abrahman Goodman House
Organization Type: Performing; Touring; Presenting

1364
AUBURN CHAMBER ORCHESTRA
Willard Memorial Chapel 17 Nelson Street
PO Box 985
Auburn, NY 13021-0339
Phone: 315-252-0065
e-mail: info@auburnchamberorchestra.com
Web Site: www.auburnchamberorchestra.com
Officers:
  Board Member: Carolyn Becker
  Board Member: Deborah Geer
  Board Member: Kat Jenks
  Board Member: Karen Macier
  Board Member: Joe Salzone
Management:
  Conductor/Music Director: Steven Frackenpohl
  Personnel: Chris Gutelius
Founded: 1997
Specialized Field: Chamber
Budget: $4,000
Performs At: Willard Chapel
Seating Capacity: 300

INSTRUMENTAL MUSIC / New York

1365
ONONDAGA CIVIC SYMPHONY ORCHESTRA
3667 Woodland Drive
Baldwinsville NY
Baldwinsville, NY 13027
Phone: 315-622-3933
e-mail: sgmoore47@gmail.com
Web Site: www.onondagaorchestra.org
Officers:
   President: Lindsey Grant Burdick
   Vice President: John Harmon
   Treasurer: Sally Greenfield
   Secretary: Brenna Gillette
   Past President: Charles Moore
Management:
   Music Director: Erik Kibelsbeck
   Personnel Manager: Tom Cox
   Concertmaster: Stephen Levine
   Librarian Emeritus: Harold Britton
Specialized Field: Orchestra

1366
GENESEE SYMPHONY ORCHESTRA
PO Box 391
Batavia, NY 14021
Phone: 585-343-9313
Toll-free: 800-774-7372
e-mail: GeneseeSymphonyOrchestra@gmail
Web Site: www.geneseesymphony.com
Officers:
   President: Paul Saskowski
   Treasurer: David Boyle
   Secretary: Michael Rrivers
   Board Member: Ken Pike
   Board Member: David Porter
Management:
   Conductor/Music Director: Raffaele Ponti
   Orchestra Manager: Jeanette Partis
   Personnel Manager: Roxie Choate
Specialized Field: Orchestra
Season: October-April
Performs At: Stuart Steiner Theater, Genesee Community College

1367
BINGHAMTON PHILHARMONIC ORCHESTRA
168 Water Street
Binghamton, NY 13901
Phone: 607-722-6717
Fax: 607-722-6526
e-mail: info@binghamtonphilharmonic.org
Web Site: www.binghamtonphilharmonic.org
Officers:
   President: Susan Burtis
   Vice President: Charles Cesaretti
   Treasurer: John May
   Secretary: Barbara Bank
   Board Member: Linda Biemer
Management:
   Executive Director: Heidi J. Kelley
   Music Director: Jose-Luis Novo
   Development Director: Brittany Hall
   Operations Manager: Colin Bunnell
   Patron Services Manager: Nancy Murray
   Accounts/Office Manager: June M Christensen
Mission: Presentation of classical and pops concerts.
Utilizes: Commissioned Composers; Commissioned Music; Guest Accompanists; Guest Directors; Guest Musical Directors; Guest Musicians; Multimedia; Music; Organization Contracts; Original Music Scores
Founded: 1996
Specialized Field: Orchestra; Pops
Status: Professional; Nonprofit
Paid Staff: 6
Paid Artists: 76
Budget: $260,000-$1,050,000
Income Sources: Ticket sales, Grants, Donations
Season: October-April
Performs At: Forum Theatre; Anderson Center for Performing Arts at Binghamton University
Annual Attendance: 17,000
Seating Capacity: 1,188; 1,590
Organization Type: Performing

1368
BRONX ARTS ENSEMBLE
80 Van Cortlandt Park South
Suite 7D-1
Bronx, NY 10463
Phone: 718-601-7399
Fax: 718-549-4008
e-mail: info@bronxartsensemble.org
Web Site: www.bronxartsensemble.org
Officers:
   Chairman: E. Heidi Jerome, M.D.
   Vice-Chairman: Paula Luria Caplan
   Secretary: John W Freeman
   Treasurer: Michael J. Sulla
   Board Member: Susan Baldwin
Management:
   Executive/Artistic Director: William Scribner
   Production and Office Manager: Susan Fishman-Klopman
   Fundraising Consultant: Eboni Banks
   Coordinator: Maggie Krupka
   Fiscal Assistant: Kathleen McDermott
Mission: Offering chamber music programs and chamber orchestras at a variety of locations in the Bronx at affordable prices.
Utilizes: Guest Musical Directors; Guest Musicians; Multimedia; Original Music Scores; Singers
Founded: 1972
Specialized Field: Symphony; Chamber
Status: Professional; Nonprofit
Paid Staff: 5
Volunteer Staff: 10
Budget: $260,000-$1,050,000
Income Sources: Various
Season: Year-round
Performs At: Fordham University
Organization Type: Performing; Resident; Educational
Resident Groups: Fordham University

1369
BARGEMUSIC
Fulton Ferry Landing
Brooklyn, NY 11201
Phone: 718-624-4924
Fax: 718-624-1155
e-mail: info@bargemusic.org
Web Site: www.bargemusic.org
Officers:
   Founder: Olga Bloom
   President, Executive & Artistic Dir: Mark Peskanov
Management:
   Business Manager: Angela Nahagian
Mission: Presenting year-round chamber music concerts on a permanently moored barge in New York Harbor.
Founded: 1977
Specialized Field: Chamber
Status: Nonprofit
Budget: $1.5 million
Income Sources: Ticket Sales; Individual; Foundations; Contributions
Seating Capacity: 125
Organization Type: Performing

1370
BROOKLYN FRIENDS OF CHAMBER MUSIC
85 S. Oxford Street
140 Bond Street
Brooklyn, NY 11217-2242
Phone: 718-855-3053
Fax: 212-308-2442
e-mail: wflecknaf@aol.com
Web Site: www.brooklynfriendsofchambermusic.com
Management:
   Manager: Wanda Fleck
Mission: Six chamber music concerts, commissioning of new work.
Founded: 1988
Specialized Field: Chamber
Volunteer Staff: 10
Paid Artists: 50
Season: September-April
Performs At: Lafayette Avenue Presbyterian Church at 85 S Oxford Street

1371
BROOKLYN PHILHARMONIC ORCHESTRA
55 Washington Street
Suite 656
Brooklyn, NY 11201
Phone: 718-488-5700
Fax: 718-488-5901
e-mail: info@brooklynphilharmonic.org
Web Site: www.brooklynphilharmonic.org
Management:
   Operations Director: Sarah Stephens
   Executive Director: Greg Pierson
   Production Manager: Kathleen Coughlin
Mission: To be a nationally recognized symphony orchestra, introducing the best new music of our time while shining light on the great repertoire of the past. The Brooklyn Philharmonic is committed to education and serving the needs of diverse communitites of New York's most popular borough.
Founded: 1954
Specialized Field: Symphony; Orchestra; Chamber; Ensemble; Ethnic Music
Status: Professional; Nonprofit
Paid Staff: 5
Paid Artists: 80
Budget: $1.5 million
Annual Attendance: 24,000
Organization Type: Performing; Educational

1372
BROOKLYN SYMPHONY ORCHESTRA
PO Box 020-334
Brooklyn, NY 11202-0334
Phone: 718-852-0677
Fax: 718-951-5412
e-mail: info@brooklynsymphonyorchestra.org
Web Site: www.brooklynsymphonyorchestra.org
Officers:
   President: John Riedel
   Vice President: Kate Stocker
   Treasurer: Dan Strumpf
   Board Member: Emily Malinowski
   Board Member: Stephen Painter
Management:
   Music/Artistic Director: Nicholas Armstrong

INSTRUMENTAL MUSIC / New York

Concert Mistress: Judy Spokes
Designer/Developer: Alex Kale
Founded: 1973
Specialized Field: Orchestra; Chamber
Status: Professional; Semi-Professional
Budget: $35,000
Season: September-April
Performs At: Saint Ann's Church in Brooklyn Heightst; Park Slope
Seating Capacity: 500

1373
SEM ENSEMBLE
25 Columbia Place
Brooklyn, NY 11201
Phone: 718-488-7659
Fax: 718-488-7659
e-mail: info@semEnsemble.org
Web Site: www.semensemble.org
Officers:
  President: Noni Pratt
  Secretary: Paula Cooper
  Board Member: Sheldon M. Berlow
  Board Member: Thomas Buckner
  Board Member: Don Gillespie
Management:
  Artistic director: Peter Kotik
  Managing Director: Martina Perry
Mission: To offer performances of and education in new music.
Founded: 1970
Specialized Field: Orchestra; Chamber
Status: Professional
Performs At: Willow Place Auditorium
Organization Type: Performing; Touring; Resident; Educational

1374
ARS NOVA MUSICIANS CHAMBER ORCHESTRA
6820 E Quaker Road
Buffalo, NY 14127
Phone: 716-896-2515
e-mail: arsnovamusicians@aol.com
Web Site: www.arsnovamusicians.com
Management:
  Music Director/Conductor: Marylouise Nanna
  Manager Director: Susan Willet
Founded: 1974
Specialized Field: Chamber; Orchestra
Budget: $35,000- $100,000
Performs At: various locations

1375
BUFFALO CHAMBER MUSIC SOCIETY
PO Box 349
Buffalo, NY 14207
Phone: 716-462-4939
e-mail: bcms@bflochambermusic.org
Web Site: www.bflochambermusic.org
Management:
  Executive Director: Clementina Fleshler, bcms@bflochambermusic.org
Mission: Present world renowned chamber ensembles in Western New York.
Utilizes: Guest Directors; Guest Ensembles
Founded: 1924
Specialized Field: Chamber
Budget: $60,000-$150,000
Income Sources: Subscriptions
Performs At: Kleinhans Music Hall
Annual Attendance: 7,000
Seating Capacity: 700

1376
BUFFALO PHILHARMONIC ORCHESTRA
499 Franklin Street
Buffalo, NY 14202
Phone: 716-885-0331
Fax: 716-885-9372
e-mail: dianam@bpo.org
Web Site: www.bpo.org
Officers:
  Chair: Louis P. Ciminelli
  Vice-Chair: Dennis Black
  Treasurer: Stephen Swift
  Secretary: Randall Odza
  Board Member: Martin Anderson
Management:
  Executive Director: Daniel Hart
  Director of Development: Jennifer Barbee
  Director of Education & Community E: Robin Parkinson
  Teaching Artist Coordinator: Beth Donohue Templeton
  Director of Finance: Kevin James
  Special Events Coordinator: Lauren Piekarski
Mission: Perhaps the Orchestra's greatest accomplishment is its contribution to the artistic life of Western New York, made possible by more than six decades of support from its dedicated patrons. The Orchestra has performed over a thousand Youth Concerts for more than two million students as well as many concerts at campuses across the United States.
Specialized Field: Orchestra

1377
PUTNAM SYMPHONY ORCHESTRA
P O Box 534
Carmel, NY 10512
Phone: 914-299-6646
Fax: 845-228-4415
e-mail: putnamsymphonyorchestra@yahoo.com
Web Site: www.putnamsymphony.homestead.com
Management:
  Conductor: Christine Smith
  Assistant To The Conductor: Kyle Kayler
Mission: To expand opportunities for cultural entertainment within the community and to provide an opportunity to perform for community musicians.
Founded: 1976
Specialized Field: Music; Entertainment
Volunteer Staff: 12
Non-paid Artists: 100

1378
CHAUTAUQUA SYMPHONY ORCHESTRA
Chautauqua Institution
PO Box 28
Chautauqua, NY 14722
Phone: 716-357-6217
Fax: 716-357-9014
Toll-free: 800-836-2787
e-mail: cso@ciweb.org
Web Site: www.ciweb.org/entertainment/symphony
Officers:
  VP/Program Director: Marty Merkley
Management:
  Business/Personnel Manager: Jason Weintraub
Mission: To provide orchestral music to summer residents and attendees of Chautauqua Institution
Founded: 1929
Specialized Field: Summer Festival Orchestra
Status: Professional; Nonprofit
Budget: $1.7 million
Income Sources: Chautauqua Institution
Season: July-August
Affiliations: Chautauqua Institution
Annual Attendance: 100,000
Facility Category: Outdoor Roofed Ampitheater
Type of Stage: Thrust
Stage Dimensions: 50' x 40'
Seating Capacity: 5,000
Year Built: 1893
Year Remodeled: 1984
Organization Type: Performing; Resident; Educational

1379
MAMADOU DIABATE
On Queue Performing Artists
PO Box 145
Cooperstown, NY 13439
Phone: 607-264-2626
Fax: 607-435-2045
e-mail: info@onqueueartists.com
Web Site: www.onqueueartists.com/diabate
Management:
  Founder/Agent: Sandra Bernegger
Mission: To perform music from Mali, touring with balafon, ngoni, guitar, players and singer, Abdoulaye Diabate.
Founded: 1997
Specialized Field: World Music; Ethnic Music
Paid Staff: 4

1380
MATAPAT
PO Box 145
Cooperstown, NY 13326
Phone: 607-547-9494
Fax: 607-547-9494
e-mail: info@matapat.com
Web Site: www.onqueueartists.com
Management:
  Founder/Agent: Sandra Bernegger
Mission: To perform the traditional music, song and dance of Quebec with contempoary and world music influences.
Founded: 1997
Specialized Field: Ethnic Music
Paid Staff: 3
Paid Artists: 3

1381
QUINTET OF THE AMERICAS
15 Circle Road
Douglaston, NY 11363
Phone: 718-230-5189
Fax: 718-398-2737
e-mail: quintet@rcn.com
Web Site: www.quintet.org
Officers:
  Chair: Kenneth Thomas, Esq
  Board Member: James Cohn
  Board Member: Richard Levitz
  Board Member: Marta Noguera
  Board Member: Jane Rubinsky
Management:
  Director: Barbara Oldham
Mission: The presentation of chamber music and contemporary music, with an emphasis on North and South America.
Founded: 1976
Specialized Field: Chamber; Ethnic Music
Status: Professional; Nonprofit
Paid Staff: 3
Paid Artists: 5
Performs At: Center for Inter-American Relations
Organization Type: Performing; Touring; Resident; Educational

All listings are in alphabetical order by state, then city, then organization within the city.

INSTRUMENTAL MUSIC / New York

1382
ISLIP ARTS COUNCIL CHAMBER MUSIC SERIES
50 Irish Lane
East Islip, NY 11730
Phone: 631-224-5420
Fax: 631-224-5440
e-mail: iacouncil@aol.com
Web Site: www.islipartscouncil.org
Officers:
    President: Helene Katz
    VP: Nicholas Wartella
    Secreatary: Jean Lipshie
    Treasurer: Edward E. Wankel
Management:
    Executive Director: Lynda A. Moran
    Program Assistant: Victoria Berger
    Finance Assistant: Rosa Ramos
    Adminstrative Assistant: Catherine Dale
Mission: To present a variety of disciplines ranging from fine classical music to young persons' programs to avant garde performance art; to enable and emerging art organizations to gain information and assistance from the Arts Council library and staff in applying for not-for-profit status, funding, computer services, publicity, mailing lists, etc.
Utilizes: Singers
Founded: 1974
Specialized Field: Chamber; Ensemble
Status: Professional; Nonprofit
Budget: $250,000
Income Sources: Town of Islip; Suffolk County
Performs At: David Jones Concert Hall; Sayville Schools; Dowling College
Type of Stage: Semi-Thurst
Seating Capacity: 400
Organization Type: Performing

1383
SOUND SYMPHONY ORCHESTRA
PO Box 499
East Setauket, NY 11733
Phone: 631-827-9022
Fax: 631-632-8717
e-mail: mail@soundsymphony.org
Web Site: soundsymphony.org
Officers:
    Chairman: Daniel F. Millheiser
    Vice Chairman: Charles Kinder
    Treasurer: Cheryl Keenan
    Board Member: Elizabeth Jaklitsch
    Board Member: Joseph Dornicik
    Board Member: Wendy Fogal
Management:
    Music Director, Conductor: Dorothy Savitch
    General Manager: Lynda Reynolds
    Personnel Manager: Jennifer Haley
    Historian: Ira Kocivar
    Recording Secretary: Elizabeth Jaklitsch
    Recording Secretary: Christine Desiderio
Mission: The Sound Symphony is a unique and exciting orchestra that presents a series of concerts of great music, performed by members of the community, for the community. The Sound Symphony presents a series of outstanding programs, both of classical and contemporary composers. The orchestra seeks to encourage talented young musicians with its annual Solo Competition and provides three in-school programs.
Utilizes: Arrangers; Choreographers; Collaborating Artists; Composers; Educators; Fine Artists; Lyricists; Multimedia; Music; Original Music Scores; Paid Performers; Singers
Specialized Field: Classical/Contemporary Classical
Status: Non-Profit, Professional
Income Sources: Donors, Sponsors
Season: September through January
Performs At: Mastic Beach Property, Middle Country Public Library, Riverhead Highschool, Stony Brook Village Green

1384
FOREST HILLS SYMPHONY ORCHESTRA
107-23 71 Road
Suite 240
Forest Hills, NY 11375
Phone: 718-374-1627
Fax: 516-785-2532
e-mail: fermatasym64@aol.com
Web Site: www.fhso.org
Management:
    Music Director/Conductor: Franklin Verbsky
    Assistant Conductor: Michele Denton
    Flute Solo: Leslie Grazi
    Oboe Solo: Ed Flowers
    Violinist: Neal Wachenheimer
Mission: The QFO/FHSO is a non-profit, tax-exempt, educational organization whose philosophy is, in practice, as well as by charter, an educational organization. Our primary aims are: to teach the young and offer them skills necessary for an eventual career in music; to offer adults of varying musical abilities a place to improve their musical skills; for everyone, to create music in the positive social experience of community service.
Utilizes: Arrangers; Collaborating Artists; Collaborations; Composers; Lyricists; Multimedia; Music; Paid Performers; Resident Artists
Founded: 1964
Opened: 1969
Specialized Field: Instrumental Concert
Status: Non-Profit, Professional
Income Sources: Donors, Sponsors
Season: Year Round
Affiliations: New Horizons String Orchestra, Queens Festival Orchestra

1385
WESTERN NEW YORK CHAMBER ORCHESTRA
Mason Hall
State University College
Fredonia, NY 14063
Phone: 716-673-3463
Fax: 716-673-3154
Web Site: www.fredonia.edu/music/chamberorch.asp
Officers:
    President: James Merrins
    VP: Lydia Evans
    Secretary: Ruth Mohoney
    Treasurer: John Wrigley
Management:
    Executive Director: James East
    Artistic Director: Joel Revzen
    Business/Orchestra Manager: Signe Rominger
    Director: Dr. David Rudge
Mission: To present concerts throughout Western New York, Pennsylvania and on tour; to sponsor a chamber orchestra and chamber music series; to sponsor an ensemble-in-residence at the State University of New York, Fredonia School of Music.
Founded: 1981
Specialized Field: Orchestra; Chamber
Status: Professional; Nonprofit
Paid Staff: 3
Volunteer Staff: 1
Paid Artists: 55
Income Sources: Arts Council for Chautauqua County; Fund for the Arts in Chautauqua County
Performs At: King Concert Hall at State University of New York
Organization Type: Performing; Touring; Resident; Educational; Sponsoring

1386
FRIENDS OF MUSIC ORCHESTRA
Brodie Fine Arts Building
State University of New York - Geneseo
Geneseo, NY 14454
Phone: 716-243-2958
Fax: 716-245-5826
e-mail: jwalker@geneseo.edu
Web Site: www.geneseo.edu
Management:
    Music Director/Conductor: James Walker
Mission: To provide to the Geneseo Valley region a wide range of repertoire on a professional level, with emphasis on new music for chamber orchestra.
Founded: 1970
Specialized Field: Orchestra
Status: Professional; Profit
Volunteer Staff: 12
Paid Artists: 38
Non-paid Artists: 1
Performs At: Saint Michael's Church
Organization Type: Performing; Educational; Sponsoring

1387
GENESEO SYMPHONY ORCHESTRA
Brodie Fine Arts Building
State University of New York-Geneseo
Geneseo, NY 14454
Mailing Address: 1 College Circle, Geneseo, NY 14454
Phone: 716-245-5824
Fax: 716-245-5826
e-mail: jwalker@geneseo.edu
Web Site: www.geneseo.edu
Management:
    Music Director/Conductor: James Walker, jameswalker@frontiernet.net
Mission: Committed to providing younger performers an opportunity to interact with respected, established artists in performance as well as educational environments.
Founded: 1970
Specialized Field: Chamber
Status: Semi-Professional; Nonprofit
Paid Staff: 39
Performs At: Wadsworth Auditorium
Organization Type: Performing; Educational; Sponsoring

1388
TREMONT STRING QUARTET
1 College Circle
Geneseo, NY 14454
Phone: 585-245-5211
Fax: 716-245-5005
e-mail: jwalker@geneseo.edu
Web Site: www.geneseo.edu
Officers:
    President: Suny Geneso
Management:
    Music Director/Conductor: Richard Balkin
    Executive Director: James Kirkwood
Mission: Performing the best contemporary and standard chamber music repertory in venues throughout the world.
Specialized Field: Chamber; String Ensemble

INSTRUMENTAL MUSIC / New York

Status: Professional; Nonprofit
Organization Type: Performing; Touring; Resident; Educational; Sponsoring

1389
QUEENS SYMPHONY ORCHESTRA
c/o Queens College
65-30 Kissena Blvd.
Glendale, NY 11367
Phone: 718-570-0909
Fax: 718-570-0912
e-mail: qso@queenssymphony.org
Web Site: www.queenssymphony.org
Officers:
   President: Herbert M. Chain
   Executive Vice President: Elsi Levy
   Secretary: Joseph Murphy
   Treasurer: Tania Broschart
   Board Member: Mark Mantell
Management:
   Executive Director: Lynda Herndon
   Music Director: Constantine Kitsopoulos
   Marketing & Communications Manager: Kate Oberjat
Mission: To provide world-class music and education to the international community of Queens.
Founded: 1953
Specialized Field: Orchestral Music
Status: Professional; Nonprofit
Paid Staff: 5
Volunteer Staff: 45
Paid Artists: 65
Budget: $600,000
Income Sources: Government, Foundations, Corporate, Individuals
Performs At: Varies/Concert Halls
Facility Category: Queensborough Community College Performing Arts Center
Seating Capacity: 875
Organization Type: Performing

1390
GLENS FALLS SYMPHONY ORCHESTRA
7 Lapham Place
PO Box 2036
Glens Falls, NY 12801-2036
Phone: 518-793-1348
Fax: 518- 79—912
e-mail: info@gfso.org
Web Site: www.gfso.org
Officers:
   President: Joann Searles
   2nd Vice President: Suzanna M. Bernd
   Secretary: James Mathis
   Treasurer: Robert Oreschnick
   Board Member: Chris Detmer
Management:
   Music Director/Conductor: Charles Peltz
   Executive Director: Shay S. Mason
   Children's Chorus Director: Carol Ann Elze-Sussdorff
   Personnel Contractor: Stephani Emery
Specialized Field: Orchestra

1391
GREAT NECK PHILHARMONIC
38 Hicks Lane
Great Neck, NY 11024
Phone: 516-482-4225
Web Site: www.greatneck.patch.com
Management:
   Music Director: Mark Russell Amsterdam
   Executive Director: Susan Amsterdam
Specialized Field: Orchestra

1392
FOUNDATION FOR BAROQUE MUSIC
165 Wilton Road
Greenfield Center, NY 12833-1704
Phone: 518-893-7527
Fax: 518-893-2351
e-mail: baroquefestival@yahoo.com
Web Site: www.baroquefestival.org
Officers:
   President: Robert Conant
   VP: Nancy Conant
   Secretary/Treasurer: James P Ketterer
Management:
   Co-Artistic Director: Robert Conant
   Co-Artistic Director: Kenneth Slowik
   Artistic Advisor: Judson Griffin
Mission: Promoting 17th and 18th century music by performing with historically accurate techniques on period instruments.
Utilizes: Commissioned Music; Educators; Guest Accompanists; Guest Artists; Guest Composers; Guest Ensembles; Guest Musical Directors; Guest Musicians; Instructors; Multimedia; Original Music Scores; Sign Language Translators; Singers
Founded: 1959
Specialized Field: Baroque; Ensemble
Status: Professional; Nonprofit
Paid Staff: 1
Volunteer Staff: 2
Paid Artists: 28
Budget: $32,000
Income Sources: New York State Council on Arts; Private & Business Donations
Performs At: Baroque Festival Studio; Saratoga Springs City Center
Affiliations: ALA; SCAC; Early Music America; Chamber Music America; Greater Saratoga Chamber of Commerce
Annual Attendance: 800
Facility Category: Chamber music hall - all wood
Stage Dimensions: 25'x40'
Seating Capacity: 110
Year Built: 1973
Year Remodeled: 1996
Rental Contact: President Robert Conant
Organization Type: Performing; Resident; Educational

1393
WESTCHESTER PHILHARMONIC
123 Main Street
Lobby Level
Hartsdale, NY 10601
Phone: 914-682-3707
Fax: 914-682-3716
e-mail: info@Westchesterphil.org
Web Site: www.westchesterphil.org
Officers:
   Chair: Millicent Kaufman
   Vice Chair: Mary Neumann
   Vice Chair: Murray Stahl
   Board Member: Peter Brady
   Board Member: Tony Aiello
Management:
   Artistic & Executive Director: Joshua Worby
   Principal Conductor: Jaime Laredo
   Principal Conductor: Ted Sperling
   Director, Marketing and Development: Lenore Eggleston
   Manager, Education and Operations: Jennifer Kugelmas
Mission: The New Orchestra of Westchester is committed to bringing the highest quality music to the Westchester area with a goal of featuring music by living American composers as part of annual programming.
Utilizes: Artists-in-Residence; Commissioned Composers; Commissioned Music; Guest Musicians; Guest Soloists; Multimedia; New Productions; Original Music Scores; Playwrights; Singers
Founded: 1983
Specialized Field: Classical Music
Status: Professional; Nonprofit
Paid Staff: 3
Volunteer Staff: 25
Paid Artists: 100
Budget: $1,450,000
Income Sources: Westchester Council for Arts; New York State Coucil on Arts; National Endowment for the Arts
Performs At: Performing Arts Center; State University of New York
Annual Attendance: 27,650
Organization Type: Performing; Educational

1394
CAYUGA CHAMBER ORCHESTRA
171 East State Street Ithaca
Ford Hall, Ithaca College
Ithaca, NY 14850
Phone: 607-273-8981
Fax: 607-273-4816
e-mail: cco.orch@verizon.net
Web Site: www.ccoithaca.org
Officers:
   President: Toni Murdough
   Secretary: Angela Early
   Treasurer: Jari Poulin
   Board Member: Jim Orcutt
   Board Member: Lisa Fenwlck
Management:
   Music Director: Kimbo Ishii-Eto
   Executive Director: Sheila Ossit
   Conductor: Lanfranco Marcelletti, Jr.
   Personnel Manager: Susan Spafford
Specialized Field: Orchestra; Chamber

1395
NEW DIRECTIONS CELLO FESTIVAL
501 Linn Street
Ithaca, NY 14850
Phone: 607-277-1686
Fax: 607-277-1686
Toll-free: 877-665-5815
e-mail: info@newdirectionscello.com
Web Site: www.newdirectionscello.com
Management:
   Director: Chris White
   Education Director: Sera Surslen
Mission: To bring together cellists and others interested in nonclassical uses of cello (jazz, blues, folk, rock, etc.). Workshops, jams, concerts.
Utilizes: Artists-in-Residence; Collaborations; Guest Accompanists; Guest Directors; Guest Musical Directors; Guest Musicians; Multimedia; Organization Contracts; Original Music Scores; Soloists
Founded: 1995
Specialized Field: Cello Ensemble
Paid Staff: 2
Volunteer Staff: 10
Paid Artists: 12
Budget: $10,000
Income Sources: Sponsors, Participants, Donations
Season: July 11 - 13, 1999

INSTRUMENTAL MUSIC / New York

Performs At: University of Connecticut, Storrs [Festival Site]
Annual Attendance: 100
Facility Category: Mehden Auditorium/Recital Hall
Stage Dimensions: 50x25
Seating Capacity: 500
Year Built: 1985
Cost: $150 - 3 day

1396
JAMESTOWN CONCERT ASSOCIATION
315 N Main Street
Suite 200
Jamestown, NY 14701-5124
Phone: 716-487-1522
e-mail: icamusic@excite.com
Web Site: www.seasonsgreeters.org/JCA/index.htm
Officers:
   President: Richard Corbin
   VP: Sally Ulrich
   Treasurer: F John Fuchs
   Secretary: Mary Weeden
Management:
   Programming: Sally Ulrich
Mission: Purpose of presenting live classical performances in the Jamestown area.
Founded: 1934
Specialized Field: Orchestra; Band; Ensemble
Volunteer Staff: 16
Income Sources: Arts Association Chautauqua County
Performs At: Civic Center
Organization Type: Educational; Sponsoring

1397
LAKE GEORGE JAZZ WEEKEND
Lake George Arts Project
1 Amherst Street
Lake George, NY 12845
Phone: 518-668-2616
Fax: 518-668-3050
e-mail: mail@lakegeorgearts.org
Web Site: www.lakegeorgearts.org/lakegeorge-jazz.htm
Officers:
   President: Ed Ostberg
Management:
   Executive Director: John Strong
   Music Director: Paul Pines
Mission: Sponsoring a two-day jazz festival every September featuring nationally acclaimed as well as emerging jazz artists.
Founded: 1984
Specialized Field: Ensemble; Jazz
Status: Professional; Nonprofit
Income Sources: Grants; Donations; Patrons
Performs At: Shepard Park Bandstand
Organization Type: Performing; Touring

1398
BEETHOVEN FESTIVAL
Friends of the Arts
Locust Valley, NY 11560-0702
Mailing Address: PO Box 702
Phone: 516-922-0061
Fax: 516-922-0770
e-mail: info@fotapresents.org
Web Site: www.FOTApresents.org
Officers:
   President: Gary Andersen
   Vice President: Mitchell Rechler
   Treasurer: George M Simeone
Management:
   Executive Director: Maryann K Beaumont
   Director Marketing/Development: Debbie Honorof
   Director Arts Education: Lois Kipris
   Director Audience Services: Elisabeth Sinniger
   Finance Manager: Mariann Fresiello
   Conductor: Richard Owen Jr
Mission: Presenting Beethoven's lifetime body of work during one spectacular weekend.
Founded: 1981
Specialized Field: Ensemble; Classical Music
Status: Professional; Nonprofit
Income Sources: Sponsors
Performs At: Planting Fields Arboretum
Organization Type: Performing

1399
LONG ISLAND BAROQUE ENSEMBLE
48 Marshall Road Yonkers
Locust Valley, NY 10705
Phone: 914-965-7926
Fax: 631-864-4426
e-mail: mjlutzke@gmail.com
Web Site: www.longislandbaroqueensemble.com
Officers:
   President: Vipin Barathan
   Treasurer: Alfred Zoller
   Secretary: Bernice Kudysch
   VP: Alice Ross
Management:
   Founder, Director Emeritus: Sonia Gezairlian Grib
   Administator: Patricia Berman
   Artistic Director: Myron Lutzke
Mission: Performing early music on period instruments in conjunction with vocal specialists.
Founded: 1970
Specialized Field: Chamber; Ensemble; Baroque
Status: Professional; Nonprofit
Paid Staff: 2
Volunteer Staff: 10
Budget: $40,000
Income Sources: Government; Counties; Private; Ticket Sales
Season: October-April
Performs At: St. Andrews Lutheran Church, Smithtown; Christ Church, Oyster Bay
Annual Attendance: 2,000
Organization Type: Performing; Touring; Educational

1400
LONGISLAND MANDOLIN & GUITAR ORCHESTRA
Long Island, NY
Mailing Address: 3925 30th Avenue South, Minneapolis, MN 55406
Phone: 516-520-4477
e-mail: info@limago.home.comcast.net
Web Site: limago.home.comcast.net
Officers:
   President: Roz Kuras
   1st Chair: Vicki Gleicher
   1st Chair: Rosalba Malozzi
   1st Chair: Goldie Nessenoff
   1st Chair: Chris Ross
Management:
   Artistic Director, Conductor: Antonina Nigrelli
   Assistant Conductor: Charles Sloan
   Vocals: Lucille DiBello
Mission: The Orchestra is comprised of mandolins, mandolas, mandocellos, a mandobass, guitars an accordion and vocalists. Although the members span various age groups, come from all walks of life and enjoy diverse occupations, they are bound together by a desire to increase the popularity of the mandolin and by a love of music.
Utilizes: Arrangers; Collaborating Artists; Collaborations; Composers; Contract Orchestras; Fine Artists; Lyricists; Multimedia; Music; Paid Performers; Sign Language Translators; Singers
Founded: 1950
Specialized Field: International Folk, Ethnic, Light Classics, Classical, Popular
Status: Non-Profit
Income Sources: Donors, Fundraisers
Season: Year Round

1401
LONG ISLAND PHILHARMONIC
One Huntington Quadrangle
Suite 2C21
Melville, NY 11747-4401
Phone: 631-293-2223
Fax: 631-293-2655
e-mail: liphil@liphilharmonic.org
Web Site: www.liphilharmonic.com
Officers:
   Chairman: Larry Austin
   President: John T. Russell
   First Vice President: Jane Shalam
   Second Vice President: Robert C. Creighton
   Treasurer: Michael L. Desautels
Management:
   General Manager: Llinda M. Morrisey
   Music Director: David Wiley
   Orchestra/Production Manager: Matthew E Flood
   Concertmaster: Erica Kiesewetter
   Personnel Manager: Jonathan Taylor
   General Manager: Linda Morrisey
Utilizes: Sign Language Translators; Singers; Soloists; Special Technical Talent; Touring Companies
Founded: 1979
Specialized Field: Symphony; Orchestra; Chamber
Status: Professional
Budget: $1.7 million
Income Sources: Ticket Sales; Fundraisers; Private Contributions; Grants
Performs At: Tilles Center; Staller Center
Organization Type: Performing; Resident; Educational

1402
NOMADICS
PO Box 1073
Millbrook, NY 12545
Phone: 845-677-3319
Fax: 845-677-3319
e-mail: flautist107@yahoo.com
Web Site: www.thenomadics.com
Officers:
   Public Relations: Lynnette Benner
Mission: To expose people, children in particular, to ethnic music from countries other than our own. We perform Ethnic Folk Music, discuss its history, performance practices and traditional instruments. Some of the countries we touch on are Sweden, Austria, The British Isles, Turkey, Argentina and many others. Our concerts are interactive and informative.
Founded: 2001
Specialized Field: World Music; Folk Music; Celtic; Classical Music; Colonial
Paid Staff: 2
Paid Artists: 2
Performs At: Various Venues
Affiliations: American Federation of Musicians

INSTRUMENTAL MUSIC / New York

1403
DEL-SE-NANGO OLDE TYME FIDDLERS ASSOCIATION
RD #3
PO Box 61679
New Berlin, NY 27715-1679
Phone: 607-843-6745
e-mail: webmaster@oldtimeherald.org
Web Site: www.oldtimeherald.org
Officers:
   Editor-in-Chief:: Sarah Bryan
   Director: Peter Honig
   Founding Editor: Alice Gerrard
   Art Director: Steve Terrill
Mission: Dedicated to the preservation, promotion and perpetuation of the art of olde tyme fiddling, its music and dances.
Founded: 1978
Specialized Field: Folk Music
Status: Nonprofit
Paid Staff: 40
Organization Type: Performing; Educational; Sponsoring

1404
TANNERY POND CONCERTS
PO Box 446
New Lebanon, NY 12125
Phone: 888-820-9441
Fax: 413-442-7813
Toll-free: 800-820-9441
e-mail: info@tannerypondconcerts.org
Web Site: www.tannerypondconcerts.org
Officers:
   President: Leslie Teicholz
   Vice President: Frank Heller
   Vice President: Barbar Dobbs Mackenzie
   Vice President: Andrew Humphrey
   Treasurer/Secretary: Steven T. Atkins
Management:
   Artistic Director: Christian Steiner
   Administrative Director: Linda McGinley Papas
Specialized Field: Chamber; Ensemble; Classical Music
Performs At: Tannery Pond
Seating Capacity: 300

1405
AEOLIAN CHAMBER PLAYERS
173 Riverside Drive
New York, NY 10024
Phone: 212-595-4688
Fax: 212-595-8431
e-mail: Lewiskap@aol.com
Web Site: www.lewiskaplan.net
Officers:
   President: Leslie Teicholz
   VP: Frank Heller
   Treasurer: Andrew Humphrey
   Secretary: Charles E. Jenkins
Management:
   Director: Lewis Kaplan
   General Manager: Clellie Lynch
Mission: Committed to performing a broad repertoire of music from the classical to the contemporary.
Founded: 1961
Specialized Field: Chamber
Status: Professional
Income Sources: National Endowment for the Arts; New York State Council on Arts; Bowdoin Summer Music Festival
Organization Type: Performing; Touring; Resident

1406
AMERICAN COMPOSERS ORCHESTRA
240 W 35th Street
Suite 405
New York, NY 10019
Phone: 212-977-8495
Fax: 212-977-8995
e-mail: acoinfo@americancomposers.org
Web Site: www.americancomposers.org
Officers:
   Co-Chair: Astrid R. Baumgartner
   Co-Chair: Annette McEvoy
   Vice Chair: James S. Marcus
   President & Executive Director: Michael Geller
   Treasurer: Anthony B. Creamer III
Management:
   Director of Development: Barbara Burch, michael@americancomposers.org
   Director of Operations: Gregory D. Evans, john@americancomposers.org
   Director of Education: Kevin James, jenny@americancomposers.org
   Operations Associate: Alisa Herrington
   Public Relations: Christina Jensen
Mission: The ACO's purpose is to discover, produce and present the widest possible spectrum of American repertoire, past and present, in performances of the highest quality, thereby focusing national awareness and support of American composers and their music.
Utilizes: Collaborations; Commissioned Composers; Commissioned Music; Educators; Guest Accompanists; Guest Choreographers; Guest Companies; Guest Directors; Guest Instructors; Guest Lecturers; Guest Musical Directors; Guest Musicians; Guild Activities; Instructors; Multi Collaborations; Multimedia; Organization Contracts; Original Music Scores; Singers
Founded: 1977
Specialized Field: Symphony; Orchestra
Status: Professional; Nonprofit
Paid Staff: 7
Paid Artists: 84
Budget: $1,900,000
Income Sources: American Symphony Orchestra League
Season: November-May
Performs At: Carnegie Hall
Annual Attendance: 20,000
Organization Type: Performing

1407
AMERICAN SYMPHONY ORCHESTRA
263 West 38 Street
10th Floor
New York, NY 10018
Phone: 212-868-9276
Fax: 212-868-9277
e-mail: info@americansymphong.org
Web Site: www.americansymphony.org
Officers:
   Chair: Dimitri B. Papadimitriou
   Vice-Chair: Thurmond Smithgall
   Trustee: Miriam R. Berger
   Trustee: Michael Dorf
   General Manager: Jack Kliger
Management:
   Executive Director: Lynne Meloccaro
   Music Director: Leon Botstein
   Composer in Residence: Richard Wilson
   General Manager: Oliver Inteeworn
   Assistant Conductor: Geoffrey McDonald
   Director of Marketing: Brian J. Heck
   Orchestra Librarian: Marc Cerri
   Production Assistant: Ben Oatmen
   Orchestra Personnel Manager: Ann Yarbrough Guttman
Mission: American Symphony Orchestra is the only self-governing orchestra in the United States with a subscription series at Carnegie Hall. It is also a resource organization providing musical service to communities nurturing young artists.
Utilizes: Guest Musical Directors; Guest Musicians; Instructors; Multimedia; Singers
Founded: 1962
Specialized Field: Symphony; Orchestra; Ensemble
Status: Professional; Nonprofit
Paid Staff: 8
Season: October-April
Performs At: Carnegie Hall
Organization Type: Performing

1408
BACHANALIA CHAMBER ORCHESTRA
400 W 43rd Street
Suite 7D
New York, NY 10036
Phone: 212-239-5906
Fax: 212-239-5906
e-mail: info@bachanalia.org
Web Site: www.bachanalia.org
Officers:
   Chairman Emeritus: Daryl D. Smith
   President: Dr. Harvey J. Stein
   Vice President and Treasurer: Philip A. Mousin
   Secretary: Elizabeth Pinkhasov, PhD
Management:
   Founder/Artistic Director: Nina Beilina
   Assistant To Artistic Director: Marvette Henderson
   Composer-in-Residence: Steve Cohen
   General Manager: Paola Tiberi
   Advisor: Robert Sherman
Mission: The consort of professional musicians dedicated to innovative programming, a high level of performance, and a collaborative philosophy that does away with a conductor.
Specialized Field: Chamber; Ensemble

1409
BLOOMINGDALE SCHOOL OF MUSIC
323 W 108th Street
New York, NY 10025
Phone: 212-663-6021
Fax: 212-932-9429
e-mail: info@bsmny.org
Web Site: www.bsmny.org
Officers:
   President: Kenneth Michaels
   Vice President: Paul Ness
   Secretary: Susan Lanter Blank
   Treasurer: Brian Upbin
   Board Member: Evangeline Benedetti
Management:
   Project Manager: Margalit Cantor
   Assistant Director: Brandon Vazquez
   Director of Student Services: James McCain
   Director of Education: Naho Parrini
   Business Manager: Chen Chu
Mission: To promote, foster and develop the love of and interest for the musical arts.
Founded: 1964
Specialized Field: Orchestra; Chamber; Ensemble; Ethnic Music; Folk Music; Electronic; Live Electronic
Status: Professional; Nonprofit
Income Sources: National Guild of Community Schools of the Arts
Organization Type: Performing; Educational; Sponsoring

INSTRUMENTAL MUSIC / New York

1410
CARNEGIE CHAMBER PLAYERS
514 W 110th Street
Suite 41
New York, NY 10025
Phone: 212-645-7424
Management:
   Artistic Director: Richard Goldsmith
   Artistic Director: Yari Bond
Mission: The promotion of chamber music in a mixed string and woodwind ensemble; the commissioning of new works; the performing of a traditional chamber music repertoire.
Specialized Field: Chamber; Ensemble
Status: Professional; Nonprofit
Performs At: Montshire Science Museum; Norwich VT
Organization Type: Performing; Touring; Resident; Educational

1411
CHAMBER MUSIC AMERICA
99 Madison Avenue
5th Floor
New York, NY 10016
Mailing Address: UPS Box 458, 243 Fifth Avenue, New York, NY 10016
Phone: 212-242-2022
Fax: 646-430-5667
Web Site: www.chamber-music.org
Officers:
   Chair: Louise K. Smith
   President: Andrew Appel
   Vice President: Steven Ovitsky
   Vice President: Rusfus Reid
   Treasurer: John R. Kirk
Management:
   Program Director: Susan Dadian, sdadian@chamber-music.org
   Consulting Editor: Fred Cohn, fcohn@chamber-music.org
   Publications Director: Ellen Goldensohn, egoldensohn@chamber-music.org
   Development Manager: Elena Ryabova
   Conference and Events Manager: Sherry Robinson
Mission: To make chamber music a vital part of American cultural life through promoting professional chamber music.
Founded: 1977
Specialized Field: Chamber
Status: Professional; Nonprofit
Organization Type: Educational; Service Organization

1412
CHAMBER MUSIC SOCIETY OF LINCOLN CENTER
70 Lincoln Center Plaza
New York, NY 10023-6582
Phone: 212-875-5775
Fax: 212-875-5799
e-mail: info@chambermusicsociety.org
Web Site: www.chambermusicsociety.org
Officers:
   Chairman: James P. O'Shaughnessy
   Vice Chairman: Charles H. Hamilton
   Vice Chairman: Elinor L. Hoover
   Treasurer: Robert Hoglund
   Secretary: Anthony C. Gooch
Management:
   Executive Director: Suzanne Davidson
   Director of Marketing and Communica: Lauren Bailey
   Director of Education: Derek Balcom
   Director of Artistic Planning and T: Adriaan Fuchs
Mission: To present chamber music concerts.
Founded: 1969
Specialized Field: Chamber; Ensemble; Classical Music
Status: Professional; Nonprofit
Performs At: Alice Tully Hall
Organization Type: Performing; Touring; Resident; Educational

1413
CHINESE MUSIC ENSEMBLE OF NEW YORK
PO Box 1062
New York, NY 10002
Phone: 212-925-6110
e-mail: info@chinesemusic.org
Web Site: sites.google.com/site/chinesemusicensembleofnewyork1
Management:
   Director: Yu-chiung Teng
   Associate Director: Terence Yeh
   Associate Director: Oiman Chan
Mission: To introduce the music of China to Western audiences.
Founded: 1961
Specialized Field: Chinese Music; Ensemble; Ethnic Music; Folk Music
Status: Semi-Professional; Nonprofit
Organization Type: Performing; Touring; Educational

1414
CLASSICAL QUARTET
225 W 99th Street
New York, NY 10025
Phone: 604-219-2581
e-mail: ndradzi@yahoo.ca
Web Site: www.classicalquartet.com
Officers:
   President: Nancy Wilson
   Treasurer: David Miller
Management:
   Artist Representative: Beverly Simmons
Mission: The Classical Quartet was founded to present masterpieces of the Classic Era, string quartets of Hayden, Mozart, Beethoven and their contemporaries, on period instruments.
Founded: 1979
Specialized Field: Chamber; Brass Ensemble
Status: Professional
Performs At: Saint Michael's Church
Organization Type: Performing; Touring; Resident; Educational

1415
COLUMBIA UNIVERSITY ORCHESTRA
Music Department
116th Street and Broadway
New York, NY 10027
Phone: 212-854-5409
Fax: 212-854-8191
e-mail: cuoinfo@gmail.com
Web Site: www.columbia.edu/cu/cuo/
Officers:
   Board President: Alexandra Rice
   Provost: John H Coatsworth
   Secretary: Jerome Davis
Management:
   Assistant Conductor/Librarian: Mahir Cetiz, mc2765@columbia.edu
   Assistant Manager: Charlene Lee, cjl2144@columbia.edu
Mission: As a course in the department of music, students are given the opportunity to perform in a challenging ensemble.
Founded: 1896
Opened: 1899
Specialized Field: Orchestra

1416
EARLY MUSIC NEW YORK (EM/NY)
10 West 68 Street
New York, NY 10023
Phone: 212-749-6600
Fax: 212-749-2848
e-mail: info@EarlyMusicNY.org
Web Site: www.earlymusicny.org
Officers:
   President/Co-Treasurer: Edward Whitney
Management:
   Founder/Director: Frederick Renz, f.renz@EarlyMusicNY.org
   Operations Manager: Aaron Smith, admin@EarlyMusicNY.org
Mission: To foster historically informed performances
Utilizes: Collaborations; Dance Companies; Five Seasonal Concerts; Guest Directors; Instructors; Multimedia; Music; Original Music Scores; Paid Performers; Resident Companies
Founded: 1974
Specialized Field: Early Music; Dance & Music Drama; Medieval; Renassiance; Baroque;Classical
Status: Professional; Nonprofit
Paid Staff: 4
Paid Artists: 100
Budget: $300,000
Income Sources: Ticket Sales; CD Sales; Private Contributions & Grants; Government Awards
Performs At: Cathedral of Saint John the Divine
Affiliations: Early Music Foundation; New York Early Music Central (NYEMC)
Organization Type: Performing; Touring; Resident

1417
ENSEMBLE 21 ARTISTS
500 W 111th Street
Suite 3E
New York, NY 10025-1910
Web Site: www.ensemble21.com
Management:
   Artistic Director: Marilyn Nonken
   Executive Director: Jason Eckardt
Mission: Ensemble 21, the contemporary classical music performance group is recognized for its top caliber performances and has earned a reputation as a champion of innovative European composers rarely heard in America, specifically those associated with the new complexity and spectral movements.
Founded: 1993
Specialized Field: Instrumental Music

1418
GRAMERCY BRASS ORCHESTRA OF NEW YORK
Madison Square Station
PO Box 1974
New York, NY 10159
Phone: 212-229-7607
e-mail: info@gramercybrass.org
Web Site: gramercybrass.org
Officers:
   President: John Henry Lambert
   Chairman: Dr Marcella Halpert
   Vice President: Max Morden
   Secretary: Dr Morton Glickman
   Treasurer: Robertson H Bennett

INSTRUMENTAL MUSIC / New York

Board Member: Molly Alger
Board Member: Carla Hendra
Management:
   Founder, Music Director: John Henry Lambert
   Assistant Conductor: Max Morden
   Principal Horn: Lee Ann Newland
   Concerts, Corporate Events: Ellis Berger
   Director: John Henry Lambert
   Director, Operations & Webmaster: David Marden
Mission: Gramercy Brass Orchestra of NY develops and promotes an appreciation for the joy of the spirited music, artistry, and unique blend of instrumentation and sound, known in the brass orchestra traditions, to audiences of all ages. Diverse musical styles and repertoire of all genres make the Gramercy Brass Orchestra experience uplifting for both the listener and orchestra members, leading to positive benefits and values for the betterment of society.
Utilizes: Arrangers; Collaborating Artists; Collaborations; Composers; Contract Orchestras; Educators; Fine Artists; Lyricists; Multimedia; Music; Paid Performers; Singers
Founded: 1982
Specialized Field: Big Brass Band, Jazz Instrumental
Status: Non-Profit, Professional
Income Sources: Donors, Corporate Sponsors
Season: Year Round
Performs At: Varies

1419
INTERNATIONAL SEEJONG SOLOISTS
Seejong Soloists
163 Amsterdam Avenue
Suite 184
New York, NY 10023
Mailing Address: 119 West 72 Street, Suite 183, New York, NY 10023
Phone: 212-689-1731
Fax: 212-689-1953
e-mail: sejong@seejongsoloists.org
Web Site: www.sejongsoloists.org
Officers:
   Chair: Maureen Kim
   Vice Chair: Hahn Kang
   Board Member: Sung Chai
   Board Member: Geoffrey Fushi
   Advisory Board: Leon Fleisher
   Advisory Board: Lynn Harrell
   Advisory Board: Koichiro Harada
   Advisory Board: Sharon Isban
Management:
   Artistic Director, Conductor: Hyo Kang
   Executive Director: Kyung Kang
   Business Adminstrator: Christopher Brymer
   Program Manager: Ahran Cho
   Finance Manager: Mi-Hwa Chang
   Administration: Sora Hwang
Mission: To make a cultural and social contribution by enriching and expanding audience's lives through the beauty of music. To act as a cultural ambassador by performing concerts of the highest artistic level to diverse communities around the globe. To foster, nurture, develop, and educate the next generation of musicians to ensure the continued enrichment of our society through classical music.
Utilizes: Arrangers; Collaborating Artists; Contract Orchestras; Fine Artists; Lyricists; Multimedia; Music; Paid Performers; Singers
Founded: 1995
Specialized Field: Classical, Modern Instrumental
Status: Non-Profit, Professional
Income Sources: Donors, Sponsors
Season: January through April
Performs At: Seoul Women's Plaza Art Hall, Seongnam Arts Center, Gangreung Art Hall, HOAM Art Hall

1420
INTERSCHOOL ORCHESTRAS OF NEW YORK
121 West 27th Street
Suite 902
New York, NY 10001
Phone: 212-410-0370
Fax: 212-410-1606
e-mail: info@isorch.org
Web Site: www.isorch.org
Officers:
   Founder: Annabelle F. Prager
   President: Barbara B. Tracy
   Executive Vice President: Jane Ross
   Treasurer: Cynthia Mencher
   Secretary: Jacob Bousso
Management:
   Executive Director: Waddy Thompson, ngibson@isorch.org
   Artistic Director: Jeffrey Grogan, gtigner@isorch.org
   Program Director: Gary Tigner, bsimon@isorch.org
   Director of Administration: Sarah Koop
   Orchestra Administrator: Mitchell McCarthy
Mission: To provide a graded, systematic orchestral education program for children of all ages and abilities, bringing together students from all economic, cultural and racial backgrounds to play orchestral and chamber music.
Founded: 1972
Specialized Field: Chamber; Concert Band; Folk Music; Orchestra; Symphony
Income Sources: Individual; Corporate
Season: November-June
Performs At: Avery Fisher; Alice Tulley Halls; Symphony Space; New York Botanical Garden; Carnegie Hall

1421
JAZZ AT LINCOLN CENTER'S ESSENTIALLY ELLINGTON JAZZ FESTIVAL
Broadway at 60th Street
5th Floor
New York, NY 10019
Mailing Address: 3 Columbus Circle, 12th Floor, New York, New York 10019
Phone: 212-258-9800
Fax: 212-258-9900
e-mail: customerservice@jalc.org
Web Site: www.jazzatlincolncenter.org
Officers:
   Chairman: Robert J. Appel
   Vice Chair: Shahara Ahmad-Llewellyn
   Treasurer: John Arnhold
   Director Emeritus: Jonathan F. P. Rose
   Board Member: George Wein
Management:
   Managing and Artistic Director: Wynton Marsalis
   Executive Director: Greg Scholl
   Program Director: Gary Tigner
Mission: To promoting the appreciation and understanding of jazz through performance, education and preservation.
Founded: 1991
Specialized Field: Jazz
Status: Not-for-Profit
Performs At: Lincoln Center of Performing Arts
Organization Type: Performing; Touring; Education; Residence

1422
LITTLE ORCHESTRA SOCIETY OF NEW YORK
330 W 42nd Street
12th Floor
New York, NY 10036-6902
Phone: 212-971-9500
Fax: 212-971-9501
e-mail: info@littleorchestra.org
Web Site: www.littleorchestra.org
Officers:
   Co-Chair: William S Ohlemeyer Esq
   Co-Chair: Carol D Schaefer
   Treasurer: David Adelman
   Secretary: Sharon L. Volckhausen
   Vice President: Lawrence R. Bailey, Jr., Esq,
Management:
   Music Director: James Judd
   Executive Director: Joanne Bernstein-Cohen
   Director of Development: Peter Shavitz
   Director: Dan Lobel
   Director of Education: Juliana Han
Mission: Shares the vitality of live classical music and seeks to build future audiences by presenting innovative concerts that incorporate multiple art forms with a variety of artists to foster a deeper understanding and enjoyment of music.
Founded: 1947
Specialized Field: Music Performance
Paid Staff: 13
Volunteer Staff: 12
Paid Artists: 60

1423
LYRIC CHAMBER MUSIC SOCIETY OF NEW YORK
20 W 64th Street
Suite 27H
New York, NY 10023
Phone: 212-239-9190
Fax: 212-496-9927
e-mail: info@lyricny.org
Web Site: www.lyricny.org
Officers:
   Board President: Dr. Joan Thompson Kretschmer
   Treasurer: Taylor Hanex
   Secretary: Ambrose Richardson
   Board Member: Dr. Len Horovitz
   Board Member: Julia C. Reinhart
   Board Member: Dr. Irwin Rappaport
Management:
   Artistic Director: Dr. Joan Thomson Kretschmer
   Managing Director: Reggie Bahl
Mission: To provide exceptionally gifted musicians an opportunity to perform chamber music.
Utilizes: Artists-in-Residence; Composers-in-Residence; Educators; Five Seasonal Concerts; Guest Musical Directors; Instructors; Local Talent; Multimedia; Music; Organization Contracts; Original Music Scores; Sign Language Translators; Students; Volunteer Artists
Founded: 1997
Specialized Field: Chamber
Status: Non-Profit
Paid Staff: 2
Paid Artists: 15

INSTRUMENTAL MUSIC / New York

1424
MARGOT ASTRACHAN MUSIC
1050 5th Avenue
New York, NY 10028
Phone: 212-722-6394
Fax: 212-828-9026
Officers:
  Auction Chair: Vicki Downey
Management:
  Owner: Margot Astrachan
  Marketing Director: Sol Lieberman
  Event Producer: Margot Astrachan
  Director of Development: Nancy Barry
Founded: 1994
Specialized Field: Show Tunes; Traditional Classics

1425
MUSIC BEFORE 1800
Music Before 1800, Inc.
Corpus Christi Church
529 W 121st Street
New York, NY 10027
Phone: 212-666-9266
Fax: 212-666-9266
e-mail: mb1800@aol.com
Web Site: www.mb1800.org
Officers:
  Board Member: Oliver Allen
  Board Member: George Basbas
  Board Member: Louise Basbas
  Board Member: Nancy Hager
  Board Member: Stephen Jacobs
Management:
  Founder and Executive Director: Louise Basbas, mb1800@aol.com
  Program editor: Margaret Panofsky
  Graphic designer: Jane O'Wyatt
  Concert manager: Maryam Parhizkar
  Recording Engineer: Michael P. Hesse Zumoff
Mission: Offering performances of vocal and instrumental chamber music from before 1800 on historic instruments
Founded: 1975
Opened: 1975
Specialized Field: Chamber; Early Music
Status: Professional
Paid Staff: 2
Volunteer Staff: 20
Paid Artists: 60
Budget: $150,000
Performs At: Corpus Christi Church
Affiliations: Chamber Music America; Early Music America
Annual Attendance: 2,600
Seating Capacity: 500
Year Built: 1935
Year Remodeled: 2007
Organization Type: Performing; Sponsoring

1426
NATIONAL ORCHESTRAL ASSOCIATION
Po Box 7016
New York, NY 10150-7016
Phone: 212-208-4691
Fax: 212-208-4691
e-mail: info@nationalorchestral.org
Web Site: www.nationalorchestral.org
Officers:
  Chairman, President and Chief Execu: Matthew J Trachtenberg
  Vice President: David Levitman
  Vice President and Assistant Treasu: Reka Souwapawong
  Secretary and Assistant Treasurer: Joanne T. Hassler
  Assistant Secretary: Grace R. Vance
Management:
  Music Director and Conductor: John Barnett
  Director of Public Affairs: Steven B Allnatt
  Marketing/Special Events Consultant: Laurie Stokes Bott
  Director: Bright M Judson
  Executive Director: Eric Kuttner
  Founder: Louise Basbas
Mission: Trains American musicans in orchestral technique and repertoire, providing them with necessary experience for professional orchestral careers.
Founded: 1930
Specialized Field: Orchestra; Chamber
Status: Nonprofit
Performs At: Carnegie Hall
Organization Type: Educational

1427
NEW YORK CITY SYMPHONY ORCHESTRA
481 Eight Avenue
New York, NY 10001
Phone: 212-967-7538
Fax: 212-465-2367
e-mail: nycsym@aol.com
Web Site: www.nycsymphony.org
Management:
  Music Director: David Eaton
Mission: The presentation of young performers at the major concert halls in New York City; the presentation of performances and music by artists of different ethnic backgrounds.
Specialized Field: Symphony; Chamber
Status: Professional; Nonprofit
Performs At: Carnegie Hall; Alice Tully Hall
Organization Type: Performing

1428
NEW YORK CONSORT OF VIOLS
201 W 86th Street
Suite 905
New York, NY 10024
Phone: 212-580-9787
e-mail: info@nyconsortofviols.org
Web Site: www.nyconsortofviols.org
Management:
  Artistic Director: Judith Davidoff
Mission: Performing the vast repertoire of music for violas from the Renaissance and Baroque periods; encouraging the composition of new works for the viola.
Founded: 1972
Specialized Field: Chamber
Status: Professional; Nonprofit
Paid Staff: 1
Paid Artists: 4
Organization Type: Performing; Touring; Educational

1429
NEW YORK HARP ENSEMBLE
140 W End Avenue
Suite 3K
New York, NY 10023
Phone: 212-799-5989
Fax: 212-799-5989
Management:
  Music Director: Dr. Aristid von Wurtzler
Mission: To perform concerts worldwide; to offer new contemporary compositions for four harps; to provide master classes; to produce recordings and appear in television performances.
Founded: 1970
Specialized Field: Harp Ensemble
Status: Professional; Nonprofit
Organization Type: Performing; Touring; Resident; Educational

1430
NEW YORK PHILHARMONIC
Avery Fisher Hall
10 Lincoln Center Plaza
New York, NY 10023-6990
Phone: 212-875-5656
Fax: 212-875-5717
Web Site: nyphil.org
Officers:
  President: Zarin Mehta
  Assistant to President: Susan O'Dell
  Assistant to Chairman of the Board: Shelia Smith
  Manager: Daniel Boico
Management:
  Artistic Administrator: Pamela Walsh
  Director, Facilities and Operations: Michele Balm
  Director of Publications: Monica Parks
  Director of Leadership Gifts: Susan Ebersole
  Director, Institutional Giving: Nancy Kingston
  Director of Marketing: Julii Oh
  Director, Concert Production: Alex Johnston
Founded: 1842
Specialized Field: Symphony; Orchestra; Chamber
Status: Professional
Income Sources: American Symphony Orchestra League
Performs At: Avery Fisher Hall
Organization Type: Performing; Touring; Resident; Educational

1431
NEW YORK PHILOMUSICA CHAMBER ENSEMBLE
105 W 73rd Street
Suite 4C
New York, NY 10023
Phone: 212-580-9933
Fax: 212-580-3902
e-mail: info@ntphilomusica.org
Web Site: www.nyphilomusia.org
Officers:
  President: A. Robert Johnson
  Vice President: Margaret L. Evans
  Secretary: Kathleen Moore
  Treasurer: John Masten
  Advisory Board of Director: Lee Balter
Management:
  Artistic Director: A. Robert Johnson
  Press Contact: Kim Stanford
Mission: Performing and recording the music written from 1750 to the present for wind, strings and piano, with guest soloists.
Founded: 1971
Specialized Field: Chamber; Ensemble
Status: Professional; Nonprofit
Performs At: American Concert Hall; Merkin Concert Hall
Organization Type: Performing; Recording

1432
NEW YORK POPS
333 West 52nd Street
Suite 900
New York, NY 10019-6238
Phone: 212-765-7677
Fax: 212-315-3199
e-mail: info@newyorkpops.org
Web Site: www.newyorkpops.org

INSTRUMENTAL MUSIC / New York

Officers:
Chairman: James A. Read
Treasurer: Paul J. Massey, Jr.
Secretary: June Freemanzon
Board Member: James N. Blake
Management:
Artistic and Operations Manager: Nicholai Joaquin
Executive Director: Anne M Swanson
Director of Development: Lindsey Warford
Marketing Manager: Melissa L. Pelkey
Education Advisor: Dr. Sherrie Maricle
Associate Director of Development: Stacy Bauerlein
Mission: Publicly-supported, not-for-profit corporation dedicated to broadening public awareness and enjoyment of America's rich popular music heritage through presentation of orchestral concerts of the highest quality in traditional and non-traditional settings.
Founded: 1983
Specialized Field: Symphony; Pops
Status: Professional; Nonprofit
Paid Staff: 5
Paid Artists: 79
Budget: $2.1 million
Income Sources: Concert Fees, Ticket Sales, and Institutional Support From Individuals, Corporations, Foundations, and Government Sources.
Performs At: Carnegie Hall
Affiliations: American Syphony Orchestra League, NYC & Company
Facility Category: Concert Hall
Organization Type: Performing; Touring

1433
NEW YORK YOUTH SYMPHONY
110 West 40th Street
Suite 1503
New York, NY 10019-5230
Phone: 212-581-5933
Fax: 212-582-6927
e-mail: info@nyyouthsymphony.org
Web Site: www.nyyouthsymphony.org
Officers:
Chair: Leslie J Garfield
Vice Chair: A. Slade Mills Jr
Vice Chair: Robert L Poster
President: Melissa B. Eisenstat
Treasurer: Jed H. Garfield
Secretary: Susan S Rai
Management:
Music Director: Joshua Gersen
Orchestra Manager: Sarah Haines
Executive Director: Shauna Quill
Director of Artistic Operations: Robbi Kearns
Administrative Manager: Jillian Flexner
Marketing and Development Associate: Louise Lau
Mission: New York Youth Symphony is established as the premier orchestra in metropolitan New York offering a unique learning experience and musical showcase for the gifted, young musician, conductor, soloist and composer.
Utilizes: Singers
Founded: 1963
Specialized Field: Youth Symphony; Chamber; Jazz Ensemble
Status: Non-Professional; Nonprofit
Paid Staff: 5
Volunteer Staff: 60
Budget: $1,000,000
Income Sources: Contributions; Ticket Sales
Performs At: Carnegie Hall

Affiliations: American Symphony Orchestra League; Chamber Music America
Annual Attendance: 14,000
Seating Capacity: 2,800
Organization Type: Performing; Educational; Sponsoring

1434
NOONDAY CONCERTS
74 Trinity Place
New York, NY 10006-2088
Phone: 212-602-0800
Fax: 212-602-9630
Web Site: www.trinitywallstreet.org
Management:
Director Trinity Concerts: Earl Tucker
Founded: 1933
Specialized Field: Ensemble; Jazz; Classical Music
Paid Staff: 2

1435
NORTH/SOUTH CONSONANCE
Cathedral Station
PO Box 698
New York, NY 10025-0698
Phone: 212-663-7566
e-mail: ns.concerts@att.net
Web Site: www.northsouthmusic.org
Management:
Director: Max Lifchitz, ns.concerts@att.net
Mission: Performing and furthering the music of living composers with particular emphasis on music from the Americas.
Founded: 1980
Specialized Field: Chamber; Ensemble; Electronic; Live Electronic; New Music
Status: Professional; Nonprofit
Volunteer Staff: 2
Budget: $35,000
Income Sources: Chamber Music America
Performs At: Christ & St. Stephen's Church; Merkin Hall; Weil Recital Hall
Annual Attendance: 1,750
Organization Type: Performing; Touring; Resident; Educational

1436
ORCHESTRA OF ST. LUKE'S
450 West 37th Street
Suite 502
New York, NY 10018
Phone: 212-594-6100
Fax: 212-594-3291
e-mail: senelow@oslmusic.org
Web Site: http://www.oslmusic.org/home
Officers:
Chairman: Norma S Benaquen
President & Executive Director: Katy Clark
Vice-Chairman: Georgia Frasch
Board Member: Joseph Anderer
Board Member: Robert Appel
Management:
Director of Marketing & Public Rela: Bill Rhoads
Director of Operations: Angela DeGregoria
Director of Finance & Administratio: David Webber
Director of Community & Education: Jennifer Kessler
Artistic Administrator: Jose Rincon
Manager of Youth Programs: Erica Kely
Business Manager: Mary DeRosa

Mission: St. Lukes is a gathering of outstanding musicians whose purpose is to bring the beauty of music and the enlightened communication that is unique to music to as broad an audience as possible.
Founded: 1974
Specialized Field: Orchestra
Status: Professional; Nonprofit
Paid Staff: 15
Income Sources: St. Luke's Chamber Ensemble
Performs At: Merkin Concert Hall; Carnegie Hall
Organization Type: Performing

1437
ORPHEUS CHAMBER ORCHESTRA
490 Riverside Drive, 11th Floor
New York, NY 10027-5788
Phone: 212-896-1700
Fax: 212-896-1717
e-mail: marketing@orpheusnyc.org
Web Site: www.orpheusnyc.com
Officers:
Chairman: Marc O. Mayer
Treasurer: Richard F. Brueckner
Secretary: Paula J. Mueller
Board Member: Douglas Becker
Management:
Executive Director: Krishna Thiagarajan
Personnel Coordinator: Laura Frautschi
Director of Strategic Partnerships: Shruti Adhar
Mark and Patron Services Manager: Serena Robbins
Director of Artistic Administration: Ryun Schienbein
Director of Finance: Kristine Spensieri
General Director: Kristine Pottinger
Director of Artistic Planning and O: Michael Volpert
Special Projects Associate and Boar: Caroline Curatolo
Mission: To provide members an opportunity to work in collaboration on the selection and interpretation of pieces.
Founded: 1972
Specialized Field: Orchestra; Chamber
Status: Professional; Nonprofit
Performs At: Carnegie Hall
Organization Type: Performing; Touring

1438
PEOPLES' SYMPHONY CONCERTS
121 West 27th Street
Suite 703
New York, NY 10001
Phone: 212-586-4680
Fax: 212-581-4029
e-mail: info@pscny.org
Web Site: www.pscny.org
Officers:
Chairperson: Susan Porter
President: Richard R Howe
Treasurer: Richard A. Raffetto
Secretary: Frederick Wertheim
Board Member: Jose Andrade
Management:
Manager: Frank Salomon
Associate Manager: David Himmelheber
Mission: To bring the best music to students and workers at minimum prices.
Specialized Field: Chamber; Ensemble; Symphony

1439
RIVERSIDE SYMPHONY
225 W 99th Street
New York, NY 10025-5014

INSTRUMENTAL MUSIC / New York

Phone: 212-864-4197
Fax: 212-864-9795
e-mail: riverside@riversidesymphony.org
Web Site: www.riversidesymphony.org
Officers:
    Chairman: Michael C. Nardo
    Vice Chairman: Edward L. Schiff
    Treasurer: Jennifer Kosar
    Board Member: Vikrant Bahl
    Board Member: Mary Ekmalian
Management:
    Artistic Director: Anthony Korf
    Conductor/Music Director: George Rothman
    Production Manager: Megan Shumate
    Operations Manager: Angela Sutton
    Operations Assistant: Jonathan Koe
Mission: To present new and less-familiar work; to present emerging artists; to produce American music.
Utilizes: Commissioned Composers; Commissioned Music; Guest Companies; Guest Musical Directors; Multimedia; Original Music Scores; Sign Language Translators; Singers; Soloists; Student Interns
Specialized Field: Symphony; Orchestra
Status: Professional; Nonprofit
Budget: $500,000
Performs At: Alice Tully Hall Lincoln Center
Organization Type: Performing; Resident; Educational

1440
ROULETTE INTERMEDIUM
509 Atlantic Avenue
New York, NY 11217
Phone: 917-267-0363
e-mail: roulette@roulette.org
Web Site: www.roulette.org
Officers:
    President: Jim S. Staley
    Secretary: David Weinstein
    Treasurer: Joseph Walker
    Board Member: Ned Rothenberg
    Board Member: Paul Gertner
Management:
    Artistic Director & Producer: Jim S. Staley
    Technical Director: Ben Manley
    Marketing Director: Ginger Dolden
    Events Director: Loren Mullins
    Director of Post-Production & Roule: Matthew Mehlan
Mission: To be a presenting organization and facility for innovative composers and musicians through its concert series, commissions and recording distribution services; to support a broad range of new music by young established artists.
Specialized Field: Chamber; Ensemble; Ethnic Music; Folk Music; Electronic; Live Electronic; Band
Status: Nonprofit
Performs At: Roul
Organization Type: Presenting

1441
SAINT LUKES CHAMBER ENSEMBLE
450 West 37th Street
Suite 502
New York, NY 10018
Phone: 212-594-6100
Fax: 212-594-3291
e-mail: senelow@oslmusic.org
Web Site: www.oslmusic.org
Officers:
    Chairman: Norman S Benzaquen
    Vice-Chairman: Georgia Frasch
    Board Member: Joseph Anderer
    Board Member: Robert Appel
    Board Member: Katy Clark
Management:
    Administrator, Artistic and Communi: Jose Rincon
    Director of Community & Education: Jennifer Kessler
    Director of Development: Crystal Wei
    Director of Marketing & PR: Bill Rhoads
    Graphic Designer/Media Production M: Irene Lau
    Development Manager, Individual Giv: Sophia Lind
    Development & Executive Assistant: Sarah Dinin
    Business Manager: Mary DeRosa
    Marketing, Finance & Administrative: Caitlin Arias
Mission: Encompasses St. Luke's Chamber Ensemble, Orchestra of St. Luke's, Children's Free Opera and Dance of New York.
Specialized Field: Orchestra; Chamber
Status: Nonprofit
Performs At: Avery Fisher Hall; Merkin Concert Hall; Brooklyn
Organization Type: Performing; Touring; Educational; Sponsoring

1442
SATURDAY BRASS QUINTET
St. Michael's Episcopal Church
225 W 99th Street
New York, NY 10025
Phone: 212-222-2700
Fax: 212-678-5916
Mission: Presenting classics of the brass chamber genre; soliciting and performing new selections for brass.
Specialized Field: Chamber; Brass Ensemble
Status: Professional; Nonprofit
Organization Type: Performing; Touring; Resident; Educational

1443
SHEILA-NA-GIG MUSIC
Hibernian Music
New York, NY 10009-2349
Mailing Address: Po Box 2349
Phone: 212-260-2302
Fax: 212-260-9645
e-mail: hibernian@earthlink.net
Web Site: www.house-of-music.com
Mission: To represent artists from Ireland, Scotland and the US in world and acoustic music.
Founded: 1998
Specialized Field: Ethnic Music

1444
ST. PATRICK'S CATHEDRAL CHAMBER MUSIC SERIES
St. Patrick's Cathedral
460 Madison Avenue
New York, NY 10022-6863
Phone: 212-753-2261
Fax: 212-753-3925
e-mail: RMESPC@aol.com
Web Site: www.saintpatrickscathedral.org
Management:
    Music Adminstrator: Robert Evans
    Director: George Miron
Specialized Field: Chamber; Ensemble
Budget: $10,000

1445
STRING ORCHESTRA OF NEW YORK CITY
100 Overlook Terrace
Suite 86
New York, NY 10040
Phone: 212-543-0475
Fax: 212-543-0885
e-mail: asmira@asmira.net
Web Site: sonyc.org
Officers:
    President: Stephanie Wein
    Vice President: Monica Bauchwitz
    Secretary: Asmira Woodward Page
Management:
    Music Director, Conductor: Robert Spano
Mission: SONYC (String Orchestra of New York City) has established itself as one of the leading young ensembles in New York City; with regular performances at New York's Merkin Concert Hall and Weill Recital Hall at Carnegie Hall. A conductorless chamber ensemble, SONYC members rehearse in a collaborative effort that allows each musician to have an impact on the artistic process.
Utilizes: Arrangers; Artists-in-Residence; Choreographers; Collaborating Artists; Contract Orchestras; Fine Artists; Multimedia; Music; New Productions; Paid Performers; Singers
Founded: 2002
Opened: 2003
Specialized Field: Classical Intrumental
Status: Non-Profit, Professional
Income Sources: Donors
Season: October, January, April
Performs At: St Peter's Church, Guggenheim Museum, Everett Civic Auditorium, Centralia College Corbet Theatre

1446
TAIPEI THEATER OF CHINESE INFORMATION & CULTURE
1230 Avenue of the Americas
New York, NY 10020
Phone: 212-373-1852
Fax: 212-373-1878
e-mail: utheatre@tpts8.seednet.net
Web Site: www.taiwanembassy.org
Specialized Field: Chinese Music

1447
TISCH CENTER FOR THE ARTS
92nd Street Y
1395 Lexington Avenue
New York, NY 10128
Phone: 212-415-5740
Web Site: www.92y.org/Uptown/Tisch-Center-for-the-Arts.aspx
Officers:
    President: Fredic Mack
    Chair of the Board: Michael Goldstein
    Vice President: Len Blavatnik
    Treasurer: Jeffery B Goldenberg
    Secretary: Oliver Stanton
    Co-Chair: Thomas S Kaplan
    Co-Chair: Jonathan P May
Management:
    Director: Hanna Arie-Gaifman
    Director of Music Programming: Catherine Cochran
    Artistic Administrator: Bernard Schwartz
    Managing Director: Ricardo Maldonado
    Artistic Administrator: Clement So

Mission: Promotes individual and family development and participation in civic life within the context of Jewish values and American pluralism.
Utilizes: Singers
Specialized Field: Orchestra; Chamber; Ensemble; Pops; Jazz
Status: Nonprofit
Performs At: Kaufmann Concert Hall
Organization Type: Performing; Educational

1448
PHILHARMONIA VIRTUOSI CORPORATION
PO Box 645
North Salem, NY 10560
Phone: 914-693-5595
Fax: 914-693-7040
Toll-free: 800-973-7729
e-mail: info@pvmusic.org
Officers:
   Chairman: Lucille Werlinich
   President: Stuart Finkelstein
   Vice President: Marion Swett Robinson
   Secretary: Deborah Senft
   Treasurer: Denny P Jacobson
Management:
   Music Director: Richard Kapp
   Executive Director: Barbara Kapp
   Volunteer Coordinator: Barbara Babad
   Concertmaster: Mela Tenenbaum
   Orchestra Librarian: Alexandr Tenenbaum
Mission: To perform an exceptionally broad spectrum of music from the 1600s to the present; to remain a flexible ensemble that performs orchestra concerts with up to 45 players and chamber music programs with as few as three.
Founded: 1968
Specialized Field: Orchestra; Chamber
Status: Professional; Nonprofit
Paid Staff: 5
Volunteer Staff: 60
Paid Artists: 100
Budget: $650,000
Organization Type: Performing; Touring; Educational; Recording

1449
CATSKILL SYMPHONY ORCHESTRA
PO Box 14
Oneonta, NY 13820
Phone: 607-436-2670
Fax: 607-436-2718
Web Site: www.catskillsymphony.net
Officers:
   Chair: Martha Forgiano
   Vice Chair: Karyl Clemens
   President: Cynthia Goertemoeller
   Treasurer: Penny Wightman
   Secretary: Diane Williams
Management:
   General Manager: Deborah Wolfanger
   Personnel Manager: Charles England
   Conductor: Charles Schneider
Mission: Bringing quality music to the immediate and outlying areas of Central New York State.
Founded: 1972
Specialized Field: Symphony; Orchestra
Status: Professional; Nonprofit
Paid Staff: 7
Performs At: Hunt Union; State University of New York-Oneonta
Organization Type: Performing; Educational

1450
ORCHARD PARK SYMPHONY
Your Symphony of the Southtowns
PO Box 332
Orchard Park, NY 14127
Phone: 716-474-5843
e-mail: pegbeyer@gmail.com
Web Site: orchardparksymphony.org
Officers:
   President: Peg Beyer
   President, Womens Committee: Ann Thea Beck
   President Emeritus: Patricia Langmyer
   lst Vice President: Alice Glace
   Recording Secretary: Nancy Cheshire
   Corresponding Secretary: Kay Miller
   Treasurer: Elaine Maloney
Management:
   Conductor/Music Director: Dr David Rudge
   Assistant Conductor: John Maguda
   Personnel Director: Paul Furlong
Mission: The Orchard Park Symphony Orchestra was founded over sixty years ago by eight musicians in the living room of Parl Brooks' home on Clark Street in Orchard Park. With the assistance of the Orchard Park Central School District's adult education program, the embryonic orchestra retained its first conductor, Joseph Wincenc. The first concert actually an open rehearsal featured Betty Smith as its first solo artist performing the 2nd movement of Mozart
Utilizes: Arrangers; Collaborating Artists; Collaborations; Composers; Contract Orchestras; Grant Writers; Multimedia; Music; Paid Performers; Singers
Founded: 1952
Specialized Field: Classical Instrumental
Status: Non-Profit, Professional
Income Sources: Donors, Sponsors
Season: Year Round
Performs At: Orchard Park Pavillion

1451
COLLEGIUM WESTCHESTER
34 South Highland Avenue
Ossining, NY 10562
Phone: 914-282-8611
e-mail: mail@collegiumwestchester.org
Web Site: collegiumwestchester.org
Officers:
   Chairman: Daniel Anker
   Vice Chairman: Gary Betsworth
   Board Member: Thomas Clemmens
   Board Member: Eric Kramer
   Board Member: Carolyn Ramsey
   Board Member: Catherine Ray
   Board Member: Lillian Redl
   Board Member: Gail Watson
Management:
   Music Director, Conductor: Eric Kramer
   Publicity: Mary Peck
   Personnel and Production: Gary Betsworth
   Publicity: Catherine Ray
   Publicity: Ketherine Saenger
   Hospitality Staff: Tom Clemmons
   Hospitality Staff: Lisa Clemmens
   Recording Engineer: Erik Thielking
   Recording Engineer: Eric Paul Nolte
Mission: COLLEGIUM WESTCHESTER Chorus and Orchestra evolved from the choir and guest instrumentalists brought together for a 1996 church concert and became incorporated as an independent entity in 2000. It is modeled on the 17th century Collegium Musicum in that it combines active professional and accomplished avocational musicians into one ensemble. The group performs music from the Baroque era to the present.
Utilizes: Arrangers; Collaborating Artists; Collaborations; Composers; Fine Artists; Local Artists & Directors; Lyricists; Multimedia; Paid Performers; Sign Language Translators; Singers
Founded: 1995
Specialized Field: Modern, Classical, Contemporary Instrumental
Status: Non-Profit, Professional
Income Sources: Donors, Sponsors
Season: November through March
Performs At: First Presbyterian Church, St Bartholomews Church

1452
WAVERLY CONSORT
Patterson, NY 12563
Mailing Address: PO Box 286
Phone: 845-878-3723
Fax: 845-878-3817
e-mail: info@waverlyconsort.org
Web Site: www.waverlyconsort.org
Management:
   Artistic Director: Michael Jaffee
Mission: The presentation of early music to audiences in NY and across the country.
Founded: 1964
Specialized Field: Ensemble
Status: Professional; Nonprofit
Organization Type: Performing; Touring

1453
PENFIELD SMYPHONY ORCHESTRA
1587 Jackson Road
Penfield, NY 14526
Phone: 585-872-0774
e-mail: ps_info@penfieldsymphony.org
Web Site: www.penfieldsymphony.org
Officers:
   President: Carol Lowne
   Vice President Marketing and Develo: Michael Bloch
   Treasurer: David Mear
   Corporate Secretary: John Buhrman, Esq.
   Board Member: Erin Cregan
Management:
   Music Director: David Harman
   Operations Manager: Dianne Stengel
   Personnel Manager: Terry Smith
Mission: Penfield Symphony Orchestra's purpose is to bring enjoyment and appreciation of fine music to the residents of Penfield and the greater Rochester area. An artistic organization with high performance standards, providing an outlet for dedicated and talented musicians and has frequent collaborations with area educational institutions and community groups.
Founded: 1955
Specialized Field: Orchestra

1454
ORCHESTRA OF NORTHERN NEW YORK
PO Box 488
Potsdam, NY 13676
Phone: 315-267-3251
e-mail: info@onny.org
Web Site: www.onny.org
Officers:
   President: Timothy Savage
   Vice President: Alan Wioskowski
   Secretary: Michael G. Draper
   Treasurer: Mary Jane Watson
   Hospitality Coordinator: Suella Young

INSTRUMENTAL MUSIC / New York

Management:
   Music Director, Conductor: Kenneth Andrews
   Business Manager: Jared T Carey
   Personnel Manager: Jill Rubio
Mission: The Orchestra of Northern New York improves the quality of life in Northern New York and Southern Ontario through live performances of orchestral music performed by superb musicians in professional settings.
Utilizes: Arrangers; Collaborating Artists; Collaborations; Composers; Fine Artists; Lyricists; Multimedia; Music; Paid Performers; Singers
Founded: 1988
Specialized Field: Classical And Modern Instrumental
Status: Non-Profit, Professional
Income Sources: Donors, Sponsors, Fundraisers
Season: Year Round
Performs At: Dulles State Office Building, Trinity Episcopal Church, Helen Hosmer Concert Hall

1455
HUDSON VALLEY PHILHARMONIC
35 Market Street
Poughkeepsie, NY 12601
Phone: 845-473-5288
Fax: 845-473-2074
e-mail: SLAMARCA@bardavon.org
Web Site: www.bardavon.org
Officers:
   President: Karen Strain Smythe
   Vice President: Steven Chickery
   Treasurer: Nan Greenwood
   Secretary: Robert A. Kallman
   Board Member: Nancy Belok
Management:
   Music Director: Randall Craig Fleischer
   Executive Director: Chris Silva
   Managing Director: Stephen LaMarca
   Technical/Lighting Director: Jason Adams
   Artistic Coordinator: Kris Konyak
Mission: Dedicated to sponsoring and supporting a professional symphony orchestra which will present performances of the highest artistic quality and further the musical growth of the region.
Founded: 1959
Specialized Field: Symphony; Orchestra; Chamber
Status: Professional
Income Sources: American Symphony Orchestra League; American Society of Composers, Authors and Publishers; Broadcast Music Incorporated
Performs At: Ulster Performing Arts Center; Bardavon 1869 Opera House
Organization Type: Performing; Resident; Sponsoring

1456
LAKE GEORGE CHAMBER ORCHESTRA
9 Snug Harbor Avenue
Queensbury, NY 12804
Phone: 518-798-8962
e-mail: info@lgco.org
Web Site: www.lgco.org
Officers:
   President: Sheldon Hurst
   Treasurer: Milly Koh
   Board Member: Richard Fron
   Board Member: Don Shuler
Management:
   Music Director, Conductor: Vincent Koh
   Publicity Manager: Maggie Stein
   Information Manager: Haw Bin Chai
   Librarian 7: Judy Korot
Mission: The Lake George Chamber Orchestra is a local group of adult and youth Musicians who are committed to the enrichment of personal and community life through the performance of classical music in free concerts that are enhanced by professional guest soloists.
Utilizes: Arrangers; Collaborating Artists; Collaborations; Composers; Fine Artists; Lyricists; Multimedia; Music; Paid Performers; Singers
Specialized Field: Classical Instrumental
Status: Non-Profit, Professional
Income Sources: Donors
Season: November, February, May
Performs At: Helen Froelich Auditorium of the Hyde Collection

1457
CHAMBER MUSIC AT RODEF SHALOM WITH STEPHEN STARKMAN & FRIENDS
51 Ackerthook Road
Rhinebeck, NY 12572
Phone: 845-876-2742
Management:
   Artistic Director: Stephen Starkman
Specialized Field: Chamber
Budget: $10,000-$20,000
Seating Capacity: 500+

1458
RHINEBECK CHAMBER MUSIC SOCIETY
PO Box 465
Rhinebeck, NY 12572
Phone: 845-876-2870
Fax: 845- 87—198
e-mail: info@rhinebeckmusic.org
Web Site: www.rhinebeckmusic.org
Management:
   Artistic Director: Kurt Grishman
Specialized Field: Chamber
Budget: $10,000-$20,000
Performs At: Church of Messiah

1459
EASTMAN PHILHARMONIA
26 Gibbs Street
Eastman School of Music
Rochester, NY 14604
Phone: 585-274-1000
Fax: 716-274-1110
e-mail: scharles@esm.rochester.edu
Web Site: www.esm.rochester.edu
Officers:
   Department Secretary: Sheryle Charles
   Ensemble Coordinator: Katherine Zager
Management:
   Conductor: Neil Varon
   Department Chair: Mark David Scatterday
   Joan and Martin Messinger Dean: Douglas Lowry
Specialized Field: Orchestra; Ensemble

1460
GREECE SYMPHONY ORCHESTRA
950 E Avenue
Rochester, NY 14607
Phone: 716-663-4693
Fax: 716-581-1015
Management:
   Director: David Fetler
Mission: Committed to enhancing the cultural life of Greece and the surrounding area through free concerts and other performances and to sponsoring young artists competitions in local schools.
Founded: 1968
Specialized Field: Orchestra
Status: Semi-Professional; Nonprofit
Paid Staff: 65
Income Sources: Greece (NY) Performing Arts Society
Organization Type: Performing; Sponsoring

1461
CASTLEMAN QUARTET PROGRAMS
1163 E Avenue
#4
Rochester, NY 14607
Phone: 585-274-1592
Fax: 585-442-4282
e-mail: ccastleman@gmail.com
Web Site: www.quartetprogram.com
Officers:
   Chairman: Joesph Cuningham
Management:
   Director: Charles Castleman, ccastleman@gmail.com
Mission: Develop individual and ensemble skills and explore group dynamics for the finest preprofessional musicians.
Founded: 1970
Specialized Field: Ensemble
Status: Professional; Non-Profit
Paid Staff: 15
Paid Artists: 8
Non-paid Artists: 40
Performs At: Grusin Hall in Boulder, CO; Rosch Hall in Fredonia, NY
Seating Capacity: 150
Organization Type: Performing; Resident; Educational; Sponsoring

1462
ROCHESTER CHAMBER ORCHESTRA
Department of Music, University of Rochester
1-315 Dewey Hall, P.O. Box 270052
Rochester, NY 14627-0052
Phone: 585-275-2121
Fax: 716-271-8879
Web Site: www.rochester.edu/College/MUR/index.html
Officers:
   Professor and Chair: John Covach
Management:
   Director: David Fetler
   Director of Orchestral Activities: David Harman
   Manager of Music Performance Progra: Josef Hanson
   Professor of Music: Kim Kowalke
   Director, UR West African Drumming: Kerfala Bangoura
Mission: Offering the Rochester community an outstanding chamber orchestra repertoire from the 17th century to the present; presenting newly commissioned works.
Founded: 1964
Specialized Field: Orchestra; Chamber
Status: Professional; Nonprofit
Performs At: Asbury First Methodist Church
Organization Type: Performing; Sponsoring

1463
SOCIETY FOR CHAMBER MUSIC IN ROCHESTER
PO BOX 20715
Rochester, NY 14602
Phone: 585-377-6770
Fax: 716-359-1132
e-mail: info@chambermusicrochester.org
Web Site: www.chambermusicrochester.org/
Officers:
   Chairman: Donald Hunsberger
   Secretary: Frances Marx
   Treasurer: Dennis Rosenbaum
   President: Linda G. Gillim
   Executive Vice President: Hank Atland

INSTRUMENTAL MUSIC / New York

Management:
    Co-Artistic Director: Juliana Athayde
    Co-Artistic Director: Erik Behr
Specialized Field: Chamber
Budget: $35,000-$60,000
Performs At: Memorial Art Gallery Auditorium; Roberts Wesleyan Auditorium

1464
SARATOGA PERFORMING ARTS CENTER
108 Avenue of the Pines
Saratoga Springs, NY 12866
Phone: 518-587-9330
Fax: 518-584-0809
e-mail: media@spac.org
Web Site: www.spac.org
Officers:
    Chairwoman: Hon. Susan Phillips Read
    Secretary: Frances Marx
    Treasurer: Ronald Riggi
    President: Marcia J. White
    Board Member: Carol Farmer
    Board Member: Susan Law Dake
Management:
    Director of Arts Education: Siobhan Dunham
    Box Office Manager/Group Sales: Deanna Gras
    Director of Youth Arts Programs: Linda Deschenes
    Director of Electronic Marketing: Eric Millington
    Senior Accountant: Cynthia Madcharo
Mission: To host performing arts events.
Utilizes: Singers
Founded: 1966
Specialized Field: Ensemble; Show Tunes; Band; Classical Music; Pops
Status: Professional; Nonprofit
Budget: $11 million
Income Sources: International Association of Auditorium Managers; New York Performing Arts Association; Membership ticket sales
Affiliations: Summer home of New York City Ballet, Philadelphia Orchestra and Saratoga Chamber Music Festival
Annual Attendance: 350,000
Facility Category: Ampitheatre
Type of Stage: Proscenium
Stage Dimensions: 80 W x 60 D
Seating Capacity: 5100
Year Built: 1966
Organization Type: Performing; Educational; Sponsoring

1465
STATEN ISLAND SYMPHONY
1 Campus Road
Staten Island, NY 10301
Phone: 718-390-3426
Fax: 718-420-4145
e-mail: sisymphony@aol.com
Web Site: www.siphilharmonic.org
Officers:
    President: Sandra Sperry
Management:
    Office Manager: Marie Penza
    Executive Director: Elizabeth LaCause
    Music Director: Jose Alejandro
Founded: 1980
Specialized Field: Classical; Symphony
Paid Staff: 3
Volunteer Staff: 20
Paid Artists: 10
Non-paid Artists: 40

1466
ROSEWOOD CHAMBER ENSEMBLE
PO Box 472
Sunnyside, NY 06066
Phone: 718-784-6160
Web Site: www.barbarahopkins.com
Officers:
    Edward J. Lewi:
Mission: Providing the community with quality classical music and offering musical education to young people.
Founded: 1980
Specialized Field: Chamber; Ensemble
Status: Professional; Nonprofit
Organization Type: Performing; Educational

1467
SYRACUSE FRIENDS OF CHAMBER MUSIC
900 South Crouse Ave
Syracuse, NY 13244
Phone: 315-443-1870
Fax: 315-446-0994
Web Site: www.syr.edu/arts/chambermusic/
Management:
    Music Director: Henry Palocz
    Chancellor: Nancy Cantor
Mission: To provide high quality chamber music concerts to Central New York audiences.
Founded: 1950
Specialized Field: Chamber
Volunteer Staff: 10
Budget: $20,000-$35,000
Performs At: High School Auditorium

1468
SYRACUSE SYMPHONY ORCHESTRA
411 Montgomery Street
Syracuse, NY 13202
Phone: 315-424-8222
Fax: 315-424-1131
Toll-free: 800-724-3810
e-mail: webmaster@syracusesymphony.org
Web Site: www.syracusesymphony.org
Officers:
    Chairman: Dr. Arthur Rosenbaum
Management:
    Music Director: Daniel Hege
    Resident Conductor: Grant Cooper
    Conductor Emeritus: Kazuyoshi Akiyama
    Conductor: Kenneth Andrews
    Orchestra Manager: Cornelia Brewster
Mission: To maintain and further develop a resident, professional symphony orchestra; to produce musical performances of the highest artistic quality; to fulfill the cultural, educational and entertainment needs of the Central and Northern New York communities we serve.
Utilizes: Dance Companies; Dancers; Educators; Guest Accompanists; Guest Companies; Guest Directors; Guest Musical Directors; Guest Musicians; Instructors; Local Artists; Multimedia; Original Music Scores; Sign Language Translators; Singers; Soloists; Special Technical Talent
Founded: 1960
Specialized Field: Symphony; Orchestra; Chamber
Status: Professional; Nonprofit
Income Sources: American Symphony Orchestra League; Association of Performing Arts Presenters
Performs At: John H. Mulroy Civic Center
Organization Type: Performing; Touring; Resident; Educational

1469
SYRACUSE SYMPHONY YOUTH ORCHESTRA
411 Montgomery Street
Syracuse, NY 13202
Phone: 315-424-8222
Fax: 315-424-1131
Web Site: www.syracusesymphony.org
Officers:
    Chairman: Dr. Arthur Rosenbaum
Management:
    Conductor: Kenneth Andrews
    Orchestra Manager: Cornelia Brewster
    Education Manager: Cher Leszczewicz
    Youth String/Orchestra Conductor: Muriel Bodley
    Music Director: Daniel Hege
    Resident Conductor: Grant Cooper
Founded: 1961
Specialized Field: Youth Orchestra
Status: Non-Professional; Nonprofit
Paid Staff: 80
Income Sources: American Symphony Orchestra League (Youth Orchestra Division); Syracuse Symphony Orchestra
Performs At: H.W. Smith Elementary School
Organization Type: Performing; Touring; Resident; Educational

1470
FRIENDS OF CHAMBER MUSIC OF TROY
191 University Blvd
Troy, NY 80206
Phone: 518-266-0044
Fax: 518-276-2649
e-mail: herroi@rpi.edu
Web Site: www.friendsofchambermusic.org
Officers:
    President: Lisa Bain
    Vice President: Alix Corboy
    Secretary: Walter Torres
    Treasurer: Allan Rosenbaun
    Board Member: Patsy Aronstein
Management:
    Programming: Susan Blandy
Founded: 1949
Specialized Field: Classical; Chamber
Budget: $10,000-$20,000
Performs At: Kiggins Hall; Emma Willard School

1471
TROY CHROMATICS CONCERTS
P.O. Box 1574
Troy, NY 12181
Phone: 518-273-0038
Fax: 518-273-1564
e-mail: karlmoschner@troychromatics.org
Web Site: www.troychromatics.org
Officers:
    President: Karl Moschner
    Vice President: Mary Ann Willetts
    Membership Chair: Ronald C. Geuther
    Secretary: Jill Nagy
    Treasurer: Elissa R. Prout
Mission: Providing world class artists and programs to New York State's capital region.
Founded: 1895
Specialized Field: Symphony; Chamber; Ensemble; Soloists
Status: Nonprofit
Performs At: Troy Savings Bank Music Hall
Organization Type: Sponsoring

INSTRUMENTAL MUSIC / North Carolina

1472
NASSAU SYMPHONY SOCIETY
859 Willow Road
Uniondale, NY 11010
Phone: 516-565-0646
Fax: 516-481-3382
e-mail: info@npso.org
Web Site: www.npso.org
Management:
  Conductor: Louis Panacciulli
  Executive Director: Sherry Smolev
Mission: The performance of the highest quality symphonic music for residents of all ages on Long Island.
Specialized Field: Symphony
Status: Professional; Nonprofit
Performs At: John Cranford Adams Playhouse; Hofstra University
Organization Type: Performing; Educational

1473
CHAMBER MUSIC SOCIETY OF UTICA
310 Genesee Street
Utica, NY 13502
Phone: 315-822-4392
e-mail: jimit@borg.com
Web Site: www.uticachambermusic.org
Officers:
  President: Marietta von Bernuth
  Vice President: Carmela Brown
  Secretary: Kenneth J. Griffin
  Treasurer: Joan Fiori Blanchfield
  Honorary Trustees: James I. Taylor
Management:
  Tickets: Natalie T. Combar
  Head Music Selection: Dr. Jon Magendanz
Mission: The presentation of an annual series of high-quality chamber music concerts.
Specialized Field: Chamber
Status: Nonprofit
Budget: $10,000-$20,000
Performs At: Munson-Williams-Proctor Museum of Art Auditorium
Annual Attendance: 1,200
Facility Category: Arts Museum
Type of Stage: Open
Stage Dimensions: 15x30
Seating Capacity: 271
Year Remodeled: 1992
Organization Type: Presenting

1474
AMHERST SYMPHONY ORCHESTRA
PO Box 1083
Williamsville, NY 14221-1083
Phone: 716-633-4606
Fax: 716-836-4972
e-mail: asorch46@aolcom
Web Site: www.amherstsymphony.com
Officers:
  President: Nancy E. Wallace
  Vice President: Edward B. Fisher
  Vice President/Contributors: Deborah Bruch Bucki
  Vice President/Promotion: Ronald W. Daniels
  Vice President/Services: Mary Wandling
Management:
  Conductor/Music Director: Steven Thomas
  Personnel Director: Richard Sowinski
  Distribution Librarian: Mary Pouli Sosnowski
  Stage Manager: Mike Sosnowski
Specialized Field: Orchestra
Budget: $35,000-$100,000
Performs At: Amherst Middle School
Seating Capacity: 1475

1475
CHAMBER PLAYERS INTERNATIONAL
PO BOX 9017
Woodbury, NY 11797
Fax: 212-481-7690
Toll-free: 877-444-4488
e-mail: info@chamberplayersinternational.org
Web Site: chamberplayersinternational.org/
Officers:
  President: Steven Leventhal
  Vice President: Joseph F Martorano
Management:
  Executive Director: David Winkler
  Director of Development: Daniel M. Fischer
  Public Relations: Jeffery James
  Volunteer Coordinator: Frances Pierro
Specialized Field: Chamber; Ensemble
Performs At: Poway Center for the Performing Arts
Seating Capacity: 850

1476
MAVERICK CONCERTS
PO Box 9
Woodstock, NY 12498
Phone: 845-679-8217
Web Site: www.maverickconcerts.org
Officers:
  Chairman: David F. Segal
  Vice Chairman: David Gubits
  Treasurer: Lawrence Posner
  Secretary: Dr. Edward Leavit
  Board Member: Marilyn Janow
Management:
  Music Director: Alexander Platt
  House Manager: Reene Samule
  Publicity Director: Mary Fairchild
Mission: To provide Sunday afternoon chamber music concerts in summer.
Specialized Field: Chamber
Status: Professional; Nonprofit
Performs At: Maverick Concert Hall
Organization Type: Performing

North Carolina

1477
ASHEVILLE CHAMBER MUSIC SERIES
34 Wall Street
Suite 407
Arden, NC 28801
Mailing Address: PO Box 1003 Arden, NC 28802
Phone: 828-575-7427
Fax: 828-254-2286
e-mail: support@ashevillechambermusic.org
Web Site: www.ashevillechambermusic.org/
Officers:
  President: Polly Feitzinger
  Vice President: Marilynne Herbert
  Secretary: Jan Van Ess
  Treasurer: Will Baunach
  Trustee: William Clark
Management:
  Program Director: Bill van der Hoeven
Mission: To provide chamber music concerts.
Founded: 1952
Specialized Field: Chamber; Ensemble
Status: Non-Professional; Nonprofit
Budget: $10,000-$20,000
Income Sources: Chamber Music America
Organization Type: Performing

1478
ASHEVILLE SYMPHONY ORCHESTRA
87 Haywood St.
Asheville, NC 28801
Mailing Address: P O Box 2852, Asheville, NC 28802
Phone: 828-254-7046
Fax: 828-254-1716
e-mail: epvarner@ashevillesymphony.org
Web Site: www.ashevillesymphony.org
Officers:
  President: William L. Gettys
  Secretary: Amy S. Kelso
  Treasurer: G. Edward Towson II
  VP - Marketing: Kimberly Cann
  VP - Education: Bonnie Stone
Management:
  Music Director & Conductor: Daniel Meyer
  Executive Director: David N. Whitehill
  Artistic Administrator: Sally J. Keeney
  Marketing and Production Manager: Michael J. Morel
  Education Coordinator: Cara M. Jenkins
  Director of Development: Debora A. Sutton
  Office Administrator: Elisabeth P. Varner
Specialized Field: Orchestra

1479
HOWARD HANGER JAZZ FANTASY
31 Park Avenue N
Asheville, NC 28801
Phone: 828-280-8419
Fax: 828-280-8419
Toll-free: 800-345-1174
e-mail: hangerhall@prodigy.net
Web Site: www.howardhanger.com
Officers:
  Vice Chair: Michell Chapel
  Chair: Jakie Williams
  Treasurer: Paign Hunsan
Management:
  Music Director: Howard Hanger
Mission: Performing new age as well as traditional jazz; introducing children aged 6-12 to jazz.
Founded: 1966
Specialized Field: Ensemble; Electronic; Live Electronic; Jazz
Status: Professional
Paid Artists: 4
Organization Type: Performing; Touring; Educational

1480
MOORE COMMUNITY BAND
Route 1
PO Box 4662
Cameron, NC 28374
Phone: 919-245-7267
e-mail: larry@moorecountyband.com
Web Site: www.moorecountyband.com
  Secretary: Darlene Skinner
  Treasurer: Richard Burke
Management:
  Musical Director, Ex-Officio: David Sieberling
  Transportation (non-board): Hal Reaves
  Public Relations: Sandy Hoy
  Publicity: Tish Hagler
Mission: Offering the opportunity to perform quality band literature; supporting community programs.
Utilizes: Guest Artists; Guest Companies
Founded: 1984
Specialized Field: Band
Status: Nonprofit
Paid Staff: 35
Income Sources: Sandhills Arts Council

INSTRUMENTAL MUSIC / North Carolina

Performs At: Performing Arts Center
Organization Type: Performing; Resident

1481
CHAMBER ORCHESTRA OF THE TRIANGLE
1213 East Franklin Street
Chapel Hill, NC 27514
Phone: 919-360-3382
e-mail: info@chamberorchestraofthetriangle.org
Web Site: www.chamberorchestraofthetriangle.org/
Officers:
  Chairman: David Lindquist
  Vice Chairman: Michael Hamilton
  Treasurer: George Evans
  Recording Secretary: Deborah Finn
  Corresponding Secretary: Kitty Kisslo
  Board Member: Banks Anderson
  Board Member: Nancy Anderson
  Board Member: Lenore Behar
Management:
  Artistic Director, Conductor: Lorenzo Muti
Mission: Dr. Joseph Kitchen organized the Chamber Orchestra of the Triangle originally under the name of St. Stephen's Chamber Orchestra in 1982. Its first conductor was violist George Taylor. In 1988, under the artistic direction of Lorenzo Muti, the ensemble reorganized as a non-profit cultural and educational organization, totally independent of the church where it originated.
Utilizes: Arrangers; Collaborating Artists; Collaborations; Composers; Fine Artists; Lyricists; Multimedia; Music; Paid Performers; Singers
Founded: 1988
Specialized Field: Classical, Contemporary Instrumental
Status: Non-Profit
Income Sources: Donors, Sponsors
Season: Year Round
Affiliations: Concert Singers of Carey, St Joseph's Historic Foundation

1482
CAROLINA PRO MUSICA
PO Box 32022
Charlotte, NC 28232
Phone: 704-334-3468
Fax: 704-333-5239
e-mail: kjacob@vnet.net
Web Site: www.carolinapromusica.org
  Outreach: Rebecca Miller Saunders
Management:
  Artistic Director: Karen Hite Jacob
  Research: Edward Ferrell
  Education Director: Holly Wright Maurer
Mission: The performance of music primarily written before 1800 in an historically-correct style, on period instruments.
Utilizes: Collaborations; Curators; Educators; Guest Accompanists; Guest Directors; Guest Musical Directors; Guest Musicians; Instructors; Lyricists; Multimedia; New Productions; Original Music Scores; Sign Language Translators; Singers; Soloists
Founded: 1977
Specialized Field: Early Music; Medieval; Baroque; Educational
Status: Professional; Nonprofit
Paid Artists: 4
Budget: $15,000-$20,000
Income Sources: Ticket sales; Education grants; Promoters
Performs At: St. Mary's; St. Martin's
Affiliations: Early Music America
Annual Attendance: 750
Facility Category: Churches. St. Mary's; St. Martin's
Seating Capacity: 125/175
Year Built: 1925
Year Remodeled: 1975
Organization Type: Performing; Touring; Educational; Sponsoring
Resident Groups: Belmont Abbey College, Belmont NC

1483
CHAMBER MUSIC OF CHARLOTTE
420 South Tryon Street
Charlotte, NC 28202
Phone: 704-353-9200
Web Site: ticketsupport@bechtler.org
Officers:
  Chair: Carolyn Felton
  Treasurer and Secretary: Karen Walker
Management:
  Executive Director: Elaine Spallone
Mission: To foster the composition, performance and enjoyment of chamber music.
Founded: 1977
Specialized Field: Chamber
Status: Professional; Semi-Professional; Nonprofit
Paid Staff: 15
Organization Type: Performing; Educational

1484
CHARLOTTE PHILHARMONIC ORCHESTRA AND CHORUS
PO Box 470987
Charlotte, NC 28247-0987
Phone: 704-846-2788
Fax: 704-847-6043
e-mail: info@charlottephilharmonic.org
Web Site: www.charlottephilharmonic.org
Officers:
  Chairman: Dr. J Arlen Smith
  President: Albert E Moehring
  Treasurer: C Chandler
Management:
  Maestro: Albert E Moehring
  Orchestra Manager: Patricia Moehring
  Choral Director: Marc Setzer
Mission: Perform a variety of musical entertainment, classical/popular. Provide educational programming for all ages.
Utilizes: Choreographers; Collaborating Artists; Collaborations; Dance Companies; Dancers; Educators; Fine Artists; Five Seasonal Concerts; Guest Accompanists; Guest Artists; Guest Companies; Guest Composers; Guest Directors; Guest Lecturers; Guest Musical Directors; Guest Musicians; Guest Writers; Instructors; Lyricists; Multimedia; Original Music Scores; Resident Professionals; Sign Language Translators; Singers; Soloists
Founded: 1990
Specialized Field: Orchestra
Status: Not-for-profit; Professional Symphonic Orchestra; Amateur Volunteer Chorus
Paid Staff: 4
Volunteer Staff: 100
Paid Artists: 125
Budget: $705,000
Income Sources: Box Office, Private Donations, Grants/Gifts
Affiliations: American Symphony Orchestra League, Association of Symphony Orchestras of North Carolina, Chamber of Commerce, Charlotte Convention Center
Annual Attendance: 15-20,000
Facility Category: Performing Arts Center/Concert Hall
Type of Stage: Proscenium
Stage Dimensions: 60 x 30
Seating Capacity: 2,100
Year Built: 1993

1485
CHARLOTTE SYMPHONY
Two Wachovia Center
301 S Tryon Street
Suite 1700
Charlotte, NC 28202
Phone: 704-972-2003
Fax: 704-972-2012
e-mail: scottb@charlottesymphony.org
Web Site: www.charlottesymphony.org
Officers:
  Chairperson: Emily P. Smith
  Chairperson-Elect: Bbrian S. Cromwell, Esq.
  President & Executive Director: Robert L. Stickler
  Vice Chairperson - Finance: Keith F. Oberkfell, Esq.
  Vice Chairperson-Development: Elizabeth J. McLaughlin
Management:
  Music Director: Christopher Warren-Green
  Director of Digital Media and Commu: Mandy R. Smith, 7
  Director of Education: Chris Stonnell
  Director of Marketing: Scott Belford
  Director of Orchestra Personnel Eng: Celia Jelley
Utilizes: Collaborating Artists; Commissioned Composers; Commissioned Music; Dance Companies; Educators; Five Seasonal Concerts; Grant Writers; Guest Accompanists; Guest Companies; Guest Composers; Guest Directors; Guest Lecturers; Guest Musical Directors; Guest Musicians; Guest Writers; Instructors; Local Unknown Artists; Lyricists; Multimedia; Music; Organization Contracts; Original Music Scores; Resident Artists; Sign Language Translators; Singers
Founded: 1932
Specialized Field: Symphony; Orchestra; Ensemble
Paid Staff: 25
Income Sources: American Symphony Orchestra League; Association of Symphony Orchestras of North Carolina; Arts Advocates of North Carolina
Performs At: North Carolina Blumenthal Performing Arts Center and Various Other Facilities
Facility Category: Multi-purpose performing arts center
Type of Stage: Proscenium
Stage Dimensions: 55 W x 50 D
Seating Capacity: 1970
Year Built: 1992
Cost: $65 Million
Rental Contact: Booking Manager NC Blumenthal

1486
QUEENS UNIVERSITY: QUEENS FRIENDS OF MUSIC CHAMBER SERIES
1900 Selwyn Avenue
Charlotte, NC 28274
Phone: 704-337-2213
Fax: 704-337-2356
e-mail: FOM@queens.edu
Web Site: www.queens.edu/arts-and-culture/performing-arts/friends-of-music.html
Officers:
  President: Fran Mathay
Management:
  Artistic Director: Paul Nitsch
Mission: To present Chamber music concerts and support music education and the Queens Music Department.
Utilizes: Artists-in-Residence; Educators; Guest Musical Directors; Multimedia; Original Music Scores

INSTRUMENTAL MUSIC / North Carolina

Founded: 1983
Specialized Field: Chamber
Paid Staff: 1
Volunteer Staff: 28
Paid Artists: 6
Budget: $10,000-$20,000
Income Sources: Gifts; Ticket Sales
Performs At: Dana Auditorium
Affiliations: Queens University Of Charlotte
Annual Attendance: 1,200
Seating Capacity: 1,000
Year Built: 1962
Year Remodeled: 1995

1487
CHAMBER ARTS SOCIETY
PO Box 90685
Duke University
Durham, NC 27708
Phone: 919-660-3356
Fax: 919-660-3381
e-mail: bryant@math.duke.edu
Web Site: www.chamberartssociety.org
Officers:
  Board Chair: Robert Bryant
Mission: Committed to providing five or six chamber music concerts of the highest possible quality annually, with an emphasis on string quartet.
Founded: 1945
Specialized Field: Chamber
Status: Nonprofit
Paid Staff: 2
Volunteer Staff: 6
Budget: $60,000
Income Sources: Tickets Sales; Contributions Duke Performances
Performs At: Bryan Center
Annual Attendance: 3,000
Seating Capacity: 600
Organization Type: Sponsoring

1488
DURHAM SYMPHONY ORCHESTRA
120 Morris Street
Durham, NC 27702
Mailing Address: PO Box 1993, Durham, NC 27702
Phone: 919-491-6576
e-mail: Office@durhamsymphony.org
Web Site: www.durhamsymphony.org
Officers:
  InterimPresident: Bret E. Chambers
  Vice-President: Marianne Ward
  Treasurer: Dane Byers
  Secretary: Shirley Violand-Jones
  Board Member: Sonny Enslen
Management:
  Marketing/Operations Coordinator: Kelly Kovalesky
  Music Director/Conductor: William Henry Curry
  Executive Director: Eve Snyder
Mission: Foster the appreciation of orchestral music through the production of high-quality music for and by the residents of Durham and the surrounding communities
Specialized Field: Orchestra

1489
MALLARME CHAMBER PLAYERS
Durham Arts Council
120 Morris Street
Durham, NC 27701
Phone: 919-560-2788
Fax: 919-560-2743
e-mail: mallarme@mindspring.com
Web Site: www.mallarmemusic.org
Officers:
  President: Robert Upchurch
  Vice President: Amy Campbell
  Treasurer: Jane Hamborsky
  Secretary: Sarah Woodard
  Board Member: Jennifer Bynum
Management:
  Artistic Director: Suzanne Rousso
  Office Manager: Robin Vail
  Operations Manager: Tony Sprinkle
  Development Consultant: Maggie Clay Love
Mission: To perform concerts that enhance that intamacy of communication that is the special province of chamber music, with professional artists featuring all of the orchestral instruments.
Founded: 1984
Specialized Field: Chamber
Paid Staff: 2
Paid Artists: 30
Budget: $150,000
Income Sources: Earned Revenue; Corporate; Foundations Grants; Individual Donors; Merchandise
Performs At: People Security Insurance Theatre
Affiliations: North Carolina Arts Council
Annual Attendance: 10,000

1490
SYMPHONY FOR UNITED NATIONS
20 Glenmore Drive
Durham, NC 27707
e-mail: eger@symphonyun.org
Web Site: symphonyun.org
Management:
  Music Director, Conductor: Joseph Egar
Mission: SYMPHONY for UNITED NATIONS (SUN) was created to harness the power of music for human concerns. SUN is dedicated to bringing people together: musicians, performing artists and diverse audiences for a shared musical experience in the belief that participation in such events can lead to open-minded dialogue and begin a transforming process toward peaceful resolution of conflict.
Utilizes: Arrangers; Choreographers; Collaborating Artists; Collaborations; Composers; Contract Orchestras; Fine Artists; Grant Writers; Guest Accompanists; Guest Designers; Guest Musicians; Local Unknown Artists; Lyricists; Multimedia; Music; Paid Performers; Sign Language Translators; Singers; Theatre Companies
Founded: 1982
Specialized Field: Classical, Popular, Rock, Folk, Jazz, Instrumental
Status: Non-Profit
Income Sources: Sponsors, Donors, Funraisers
Season: Year Round

1491
CUMBERLAND COUNTY FRIENDS OF THE ORCHESTRA
301 Hay Street
Fayetteville, NC 28302
Phone: 910-323-1776
Fax: 910-323-1727
e-mail: admin@theartscouncil.com
Web Site: www.theartscouncil.com
Officers:
  President: Eric Nobles, Sr.
  Vice President: William M. Brooks, Jr.
  Secretary: Denise M. Wyatt
  Treasurer: Brent Sumner
  Immediate Past President: Anna Hodges Smith
Management:
  Orchestra Coordinator: Janice Swoope
  Artistic Director: Deborah Martin Mintz
  Community Investments Director: Anne Rawson
  Director of Corporate Relations: Tom Lee
  Marketing Director: Mary Kinnery
Mission: To maintain a community support group for the Cumberland County School Orchestra Program, lending volunteer hours and financial aid where needed to maintain excellence in the program.
Utilizes: Guest Companies
Founded: 1980
Specialized Field: Orchestra
Status: Nonprofit
Organization Type: Educational; Sponsoring

1492
HIGHLAND BRITISH BRASS BAND ASSOCIATION
Fayetteville
Fayetteville, NC 28305
Phone: 910-484-0281
Officers:
  Chairman: Robert Downing
Mission: To provide suitable outlet for musically talented adults who are interested in promoting good band music in the British Brass Band format for the instruction and edification of the general public.
Utilizes: Guest Artists
Founded: 1980
Specialized Field: Band; Brass Ensemble
Status: Semi-Professional; Nonprofit
Income Sources: Arts Council of Fayetteville & Cumberland County
Performs At: Methodist College
Organization Type: Performing

1493
GREENSBORO SYMPHONY ORCHESTRA/CAROLINA POPS
200 N Davie Street
Suite 301
Greensboro, NC 27401
Phone: 336-335-5456
Fax: 336-335-5580
e-mail: scordick@greensborosymphony.org
Web Site: www.greensborosymphony.org/
Officers:
  Chairman: Susan Schwartz
  Chairman-Elect & Vice Chair of Deve: Robert Green
  Vice-Chair: Scott Duggan
  President/CEO: Lisa Crawford
  Vice Chair Artistic Advisory: Tim Smyth
Management:
  Music Director/Conductor: Dmitry Sitkovetsky
  Orchestra Personnel Manager: Wendy Rawls
  Director of Marketing & Sales: Sheila Cauthen
  Production Manager: Vito Ciccone
  Box Office Manager: Connie Parrish
Mission: To strive seriously for the highest quality of performance, with the ultimate goal of attaining a truly professional sound, the love of playing orchestral literature remaining the prime factor for participation.
Utilizes: Guest Artists
Founded: 1977
Specialized Field: Orchestra; Pops
Status: Professional
Income Sources: City of Greensboro
Performs At: War Memorial Auditorium
Organization Type: Performing

INSTRUMENTAL MUSIC / North Carolina

1494
PHILHARMONIA OF GREENSBORO
200 N Davie Street, Box 2
The Music Center, City Arts
Greensboro, NC 27401
Phone: 336-373-2549
Fax: 336-373-2659
e-mail: britanygreen@hotmail.com
Web Site: www.philharmoniagreensboro.org
Management:
  Music Director: Robert Gutter
  Executive Director: Lynn H Donovan
Specialized Field: Orchestra

1495
SUMMER STRINGS ON THE MEHERRIN
303 S Elm Street
Greenville, NC 27858
Phone: 919-752-2542
Officers:
  President: John R Kernodle, Jr
  Secretary: Angela Seawell
Management:
  Music Director: Paul Topper
  Chowan College Officer: James Chamblee
Mission: Summer Strings on the Meherrin offers a three-week program for 12 to 18-year-old bowed string players to improve their musicianship and techniques and to present chamber music concerts.
Founded: 1972
Specialized Field: Chamber; String Ensemble
Status: Nonprofit
Income Sources: Chowan College
Performs At: Daniels Hall; Chowan College
Organization Type: Performing; Resident; Educational

1496
HENDERSONVILLE SYMPHONY ORCHESTRA
228 6th Avenue East Hendersonville
PO Box 1811
Hendersonville, NC 28793
Phone: 828-697-5884
Fax: 828-697-5765
e-mail: info@hendersonvillesymphony.net
Web Site: www.hendersonvillesymphony.org
Officers:
  President: Jules Hagymassy
  Vice President: Ken Johnson
  Secretary: Cheryl Hagymassy
  Treasurer: Jack Osterburg
  Board Member: Beth Bell
Management:
  Music Director/Conductor: Dr. Thomas Joiner
  Executive Director: William Humleker
  Orchestra Manager: Eric Scheider
  Office Manager: Turner Rouse
  Stage Manager: Paul Stroebel
Founded: 1971
Specialized Field: Orchestra
Paid Staff: 4
Paid Artists: 65
Budget: $211,000

1497
WESTERN PIEDMONT SYMPHONY
243 3rd Avenue NE
Suite 1-N
Hickory, NC 28601
Phone: 828-324-8603
Fax: 828-324-1301
e-mail: info@wpsymphony.org
Web Site: www.wpsymphony.org
Officers:
  President: D'Ann Grell
  Vice President: Adam Neilly
  Secretary: Barbara Freiman
  Treasurer: Tom Shields
  Board Member: Dan Green
Management:
  Music Director/Conductor: John Gordon Ross
  Executive Director: Reggie Helton
  Business & Box Office Manager: Laura Generous
  Marketing Director: Paulette Miller
  Personnel Manager: Mary Boudreault
Utilizes: Educators
Founded: 1964
Specialized Field: Orchestra
Income Sources: Unifour; Fund-raisers
Performs At: P.E. Monroe Auditorium

1498
SMOKY MOUNTAIN BRITISH BRASS
PO Box 1467
Lake Juanaluska, NC 28745
Phone: 828-253-6842
e-mail: smbrass@asapgroup.com
Web Site: smbrass.com
Management:
  General Manager: Bert Wiley
  Artistic Director: Dr. William Bryant
Mission: Offering quality music for brass band covering all artists and eras.
Utilizes: Guest Artists
Founded: 1981
Specialized Field: Chamber; Band; Brass Ensemble
Status: Semi-Professional
Organization Type: Performing; Touring; Educational

1499
TRINKLE BRASS WORKS
4738 Walteta Way
Lumberton, NC 89119
Phone: 919-671-4556
e-mail: tbw@trinklebrassworks.com
Web Site: www.trinklebrassworks.com
Officers:
  President: Steven Trinkle
  VP: Genie Burkett
  Secretary: Dr. Alan Kalkor
  Treasurer: Joel Gordon
Mission: Established in 1977 to provide art centers, universities and schools with concerts and lecture-recitals in brass and percussion chamber music. Concerts include performances on Renaissance, Baroque and modern instruments.
Utilizes: Singers
Founded: 1977
Specialized Field: Chamber; Brass Ensemble
Status: Professional; Nonprofit
Income Sources: Wisconsin Arts Board
Organization Type: Performing; Touring; Resident; Educational

1500
NORTH CAROLINA SYMPHONY
3700 Glenwood Avenue,
Ste. 130
Raleigh, NC 27612
Phone: 919-733-2750
Fax: 919-733-9920
Toll-free: 877-276-24
e-mail: tickets@ncsymphony.org
Web Site: www.ncsymphony.org
Officers:
  Chair: Jeffrey A. Corbett
  Vice Chair: Mary Susan Fulghum
  Vice Chair: David Strong
  Treasurer: Jeffrey B. Sheehan
  Secretary: Sally C. Johnson
Management:
  Music Director: Grant Llewellyn
  Resident Conductor: William Henry Curry
  Director of Advertising & Promotion: Maria H. Ewing
  Director of Mark, Sales & Service: Emma Wall
  Director of Corporate & Foundation: Ellen Fort
Mission: Presenting live orchestral music for residents of North Carolina; providing music education programs in the schools.
Utilizes: Commissioned Composers; Commissioned Music; Composers-in-Residence; Guest Artists; Guest Musicians; Multimedia; Original Music Scores
Founded: 1932
Specialized Field: Symphony; Orchestra; Chamber; Ensemble
Status: Professional; Nonprofit
Budget: $8.4 million
Income Sources: American Symphony Orchestra League
Organization Type: Performing; Touring; Resident; Educational; Sponsoring

1501
RALEIGH RINGERS
2200 East Millbrook Road
Suite 113
Raleigh, NC 27604
Mailing Address: 8516 Sleepy Creek Drive, Raleigh, N.C. 27613
Phone: 919-847-7574
Fax: 919-847-7574
Toll-free: 866-637-7464
e-mail: rrmgdir@nc.rr.com
Web Site: www.rr.org
Management:
  Music Director: David M Harris
  Managing Director: Nancy Ritter
  Artistic Consultant: Dr. William A Payn
Specialized Field: Handbell Ensemble
Status: Nonprofit

1502
RALEIGH SYMPHONY ORCHESTRA
119 S Pason Street
PO Box 25878
Raleigh, NC 27611-5878
Phone: 919-546-9755
Fax: 919-546-0251
e-mail: manager@raleighsymphony.org
Web Site: www.raleighsymphony.org
Management:
  Music Director: Jim Widdelow
  Executive Director: Irene Burke
Mission: The Raleigh Symphony Orchestra (RSO) is a non-profit organization whose mission is to promote and encourage the understanding and appreciation of music through high quality performances of orchestral and chamber music; to make programs available at a reasonable cost to an increasing and diverse audience from Raleigh and surrounding communities; and to feature and provide opportunities for outstanding musicians of the area.
Founded: 1979
Specialized Field: Symphony; Orchestra; Chamber Music
Status: Non-Profit
Paid Staff: 3
Paid Artists: 70
Non-paid Artists: 40

INSTRUMENTAL MUSIC / North Dakota

1503
TAR RIVER CHORAL & ORCHESTRAL SOCIETY
The Dunn Center 1200
PO Box 8255
Rocky Mount, NC 27804
Phone: 252-985-3055
e-mail: abouttroc@suddenlink.net
Web Site: www.abouttroc.org
Management:
   Conductor: Dr. Alfred E. Sturgis
   General Manager: Beth Kupsco
   Conductor: Dr. Jonathan Wacker
   Conductor: Dr. David McChesney
   Conductor: Michael J. Glasgow
Specialized Field: Orchestra; Band; Swing

1504
SALISBURY SYMPHONY ORCHESTRA
PO Box 4264
Salisbury, NC 28145-4264
Phone: 704-637-4314
Fax: 704-637-4268
e-mail: director@salisburysymphony.org
Web Site: www.salisburysymphony.org
Officers:
   President: Dr. Jerry Cochran
   Vice President: Kathi Hill
   Secretary: Dr. Betty Middleton
   Treasurer: Cynthia A. Thomas, CPA
   Immediate Past President: Robert Clement
Management:
   Music Director/Conductor: David Hagy
   Executive Director: Linda Jones
   Education Director: Susan Trivette
Mission: Performing symphonic music and increasing musical appreciation in the area; offering four full concerts annually, including one free concert for youth.
Utilizes: Collaborations; Guest Accompanists; Guest Musicians; Guest Writers; Multimedia; Singers
Founded: 1966
Specialized Field: Symphony; Orchestra
Status: Professional; Nonprofit
Paid Staff: 3
Paid Artists: 70
Budget: $241,900
Income Sources: Ticket Sales; Program Ads; Sponsorships; Contributions
Performs At: Varick Auditorium; Livingstone College
Seating Capacity: 1,500
Year Built: 1964
Organization Type: Performing; Educational

1505
PADDYWHACK
Route 2
PO Box 60
Tryon, NC 28782
Phone: 704-894-8091
Web Site: www.paddywhack.co.nz
Mission: Playing and promoting 16th-19th century popular music.
Founded: 1978
Specialized Field: Ensemble; Ethnic Music; Folk Music; Band
Status: Semi-Professional
Income Sources: Schiele Museum
Organization Type: Performing; Touring; Educational

1506
WILMINGTON SYMPHONY ORCHESTRA
4608 Cedar Avenue
Suite 105
Wilmington, NC 28403
Phone: 910-791-9262
Fax: 910-791-8970
e-mail: info@wilmingtonsymphony.org
Web Site: www.wilmingtonsymphony.org
Officers:
   President: Marian Hills
   Vice President: Mark Moulin
   Treasurer: Bob Austin
   Secretary: Gaile Zack
   Member-at-large: Robin Robinson
Management:
   Executive Director: Reed M Wallace
   Bookkeeper: Joelle Thomas
   Orchestra Manager/Music Librarian: Shirley Lebo
   Conductor: Steven Errante
   Junior Strings Director: Jane Tierney
Mission: To provide music of the highest integrity and performance quality to the community.
Founded: 1971
Specialized Field: Symphony
Status: Non-Professional; Nonprofit
Paid Staff: 3
Budget: $250,000
Income Sources: Box office; Private donations; Grants
Performs At: Kenan Auditorium
Annual Attendance: 6,000
Seating Capacity: 987
Organization Type: Performing; Educational

1507
NORTH CAROLINA SCHOOL OF THE ARTS SYMPHONY ORCHESTRA
North Carolina School of the Arts
School of Music, 1533 South Main Street
Winston-Salem, NC 27127-2188
Phone: 336-770-3251
Fax: 336-770-3248
e-mail: tclark@ncarts.edu
Web Site: www.uncsa.edu/music/
Management:
   Conductor: Serge Zehnacker
   Dean: Wade Weast
   Administrator Support: Lois Barnes
   Director: Jennifer Alexandra Johnston
   Piano Technician: William Huesman
Founded: 1963
Specialized Field: Orchestra

1508
WAKE FOREST UNIVERSITY SYMPHONY ORCHESTRA
Reynolda Station
Box 7345
Winston-Salem, NC 27109
Phone: 336-758-5364
Fax: 336-758-4935
e-mail: dhagy@wfu.edu
Web Site: www.wfu.edu
Officers:
   President: Nathan O. Hatch
   Provost: Rogan Kersh
   Managing Director: Dr. Edward Abraham
Management:
   Conductor: Dr. David Hagy
   Music Department Chair: Stewart Carter
Specialized Field: Orchestra

1509
WINSTON-SALEM SYMPHONY
201 N Broad Street
Suite 200
Winston-Salem, NC 27101
Phone: 336-725-1035
Fax: 336-725-3924
e-mail: info@wssymphony.org
Web Site: www.wssymphony.org
Officers:
   Board Chair: Joia M. Johnson
   President & CEO: E. Merritt Vale
   Treasurer: Dick Deem
   Secretary: Jerry Silber
   Board Member: Steve Karr
Management:
   Music Director: Robert Moody
   Ticket Sales and Donor Administrati: Latonya Wright
   Communications Manager: Peggy Smith
   Symphony Chorale Director: Carole Ott
   Education and Community Engagement: Jessica Munch-Dittmar
Mission: To present high quality symphonic literature and to provide music education for Winston-Salem children.
Utilizes: Collaborations; Commissioned Composers; Commissioned Music; Educators; Five Seasonal Concerts; Guest Accompanists; Guest Artists; Guest Choreographers; Guest Companies; Guest Composers; Guest Directors; Guest Instructors; Guest Lecturers; Guest Musical Directors; Guest Musicians; Guest Soloists; High School Drama; Local Artists; Lyricists; Multimedia; New Productions; Singers; Visual Arts
Founded: 1947
Specialized Field: Symphony; Orchestra; Chamber; Ensemble
Status: Professional, Nonprofit
Paid Staff: 14
Volunteer Staff: 120
Paid Artists: 75
Non-paid Artists: 80
Budget: $1.4 million
Income Sources: The Arts Council of Winston-Salem/Forsyth County, Wachovia Wealth Management, RJ Reynolds, Partners Medicare Choice, Michael & Mardene Morykwas
Performs At: E. Stevens Center for the Performing Arts
Annual Attendance: 100,000
Seating Capacity: 1,380
Year Remodeled: 1985
Organization Type: Performing; Resident; Educational

North Dakota

1510
BISMARCK-MANDAN SYMPHONY ORCHESTRA
215 N 6th Street
PO Box 2031
Bismarck, ND 58501
Phone: 701-258-8345
Fax: 701-258-8345
e-mail: bmso@bisman.com
Web Site: www.bismarckmandansymphony.org
Officers:
   President: David Schollars
   Vice President: Al Wolf
   Secretary: Carol Russell
   Past President: Margaret Fiechtner
Management:
   Executive Director: Susan Lundberg

INSTRUMENTAL MUSIC / Ohio

Music Director: Beverly Everett
Orchestra Representative: Nora Salveson
Orchestra Representative: Isrea Butler
Members at Large: William Pearce
Mission: To share orchestral music and educational programs of all kinds with the public in many venues.
Utilizes: Guest Musical Directors; Guest Musicians; Local Artists; Multimedia; Original Music Scores; Sign Language Translators
Founded: 1975
Specialized Field: Symphony; Orchestra; Ensemble
Status: Nonprofit
Paid Staff: 3
Volunteer Staff: 200
Paid Artists: 70
Budget: $300,000
Income Sources: Private; Corporate; Grants
Performs At: Belle Mehus City Auditorium
Annual Attendance: 4,000
Facility Category: Auditorium
Type of Stage: Conventional
Stage Dimensions: 40 x 60
Seating Capacity: 836
Year Built: 1914
Year Remodeled: 1997
Cost: 32.5 Million
Organization Type: Performing

1511
GREATER GRAND FORKS SYMPHONY ORCHESTRA
PO Box 5302
Grand Forks, ND 58206-5302
Phone: 701-777-3359
Fax: 701-777-3320
Toll-free: 800-225- 863
e-mail: tamara.mulske@und.nodak.edu
Web Site: www.ggfso.org
Management:
　Music Director: Alexander Platt
　Concertmaster: Alejandro Drago
　Assistant Concertmaster: Joel Alarcon
　Acting Principal: Dr. Gerald Gaul
　Acting Principal: Simona Barbu
Mission: The greater Grand Forks Symphony Association is a regional center for classical music performance and education.
Specialized Field: Orchestra; Ensemble; Chamber
Paid Staff: 3
Paid Artists: 50
Non-paid Artists: 10

1512
MINOT SYMPHONY ASSOCIATION
500 University Avenue W
Minot, ND 58707
Phone: 701-858-4228
Fax: 701-858-3823
Toll-free: 800-777-0750
e-mail: msu@minotstateu.edu
Web Site: www.minotstateu.edu
Officers:
　President: Lou Whitmer
　Treasurer: David Herzig
Management:
　Conductor: Dr. Daniel Hornstein
Mission: To foster and perpetuate the Minot Symphony Orchestra, a college-community orchestra.
Founded: 1965
Specialized Field: Symphony; Orchestra
Status: Professional; Nonprofit
Paid Staff: 70

Income Sources: North Dakota Council of Arts; Minot Area Council of Arts; North Dakota Arts Alliance; American Symphony Orchestra League; National Endowment for the Arts
Performs At: McFarland Auditorium
Organization Type: Performing; Resident

Ohio

1513
AKRON SYMPHONY ORCHESTRA
92 N. Main Street
Akron, OH 44308
Phone: 330-535-8131
Fax: 330-535-7302
e-mail: msnider@akronsymphony.org
Web Site: www.akronsymphony.org
Officers:
　President: Renee Pipitone
　Executive Vice President: Mark Auburn, Ph.D.
　Vice President of Development: Linda McDonald
　Vice President - Finance: Dave Supelak
　Vice President - Marketing & PR: Allan Henderson
Management:
　Music Director& Conductor: Christopher Wilkins
　Director Marketing & Public Relatio: Joanne Green
　Chorus Director: Maria Sensi Sellner
　Director of Artistic Operations: Fran Goldman
　Personnel Manager: Jerome Miskell
Mission: Enhance the quality of life for the greater Akron community through exccellence in music performance and education.
Utilizes: Guest Artists
Founded: 1949
Specialized Field: Ensemble; Symphony
Status: Professional; Nonprofit
Paid Staff: 8
Budget: $1.6 million
Income Sources: American Symphony Orchestra League; Ohio Arts Council; Private/Corporate Donations; Grants; Funding
Performs At: E.J. Thomas Performing Arts Hall
Facility Category: University Performing Arts Hall
Seating Capacity: 3,000
Organization Type: Performing; Educational

1514
AKRON YOUTH SYMPHONY ORCHESTRA
92 N. Main Street
Akron, OH 44308-1946
Phone: 330-535-8131
Fax: 330-535-7302
e-mail: WTurrell@akronsymphony.org
Web Site: www.akronsymphony.org
Officers:
　President: Renee Pipitone
　Executive Vice President: Mark Auburn, Ph.D.
　Vice President of Development: Linda McDonald
　Vice President - Finance: Dave Supelak
　Vice President - Marketing & PR: Allan Henderson
Management:
　Music Director& Conductor: Christopher Wilkins
　Director Marketing & Public Relatio: Joanne Green
　Chorus Director: Maria Sensi Sellner
　Director of Artistic Operations: Fran Goldman
　Personnel Manager: Jerome Miskell
Founded: 1949
Specialized Field: Youth Symphony
Status: Professional; Nonprofit
Paid Staff: 75

Income Sources: Akron Symphony Orchestra; American Symphony Orchestra League (Youth Orchestra Division)
Performs At: E.J. Thomas Performing Arts Hall
Organization Type: Performing; Educational; Sponsoring

1515
ASHLAND SYMPHONY ORCHESTRA
401 College Avenue
Ashland, OH 44805
Phone: 419-289-5115
Fax: 419-289-5329
e-mail: symphony@ashland.edu
Web Site: www.ashlandsymphony.org
Officers:
　President: Dr. John Byron
　Vice-President: Mark Dodson
　Secretary: Theresa Webster
　Treasurer: Charles Ulrich
　Board Member: Dr. Sara Battison
Management:
　Music Director/Conductor: Arie Lipsky
　Personnel Manager: Amanda Bekeny
　Stage Manager: Marty Kral
　House Manager: Nancy Koop
　Assistant Stage Manager: Cameron Dedrick
Mission: Offering symphonic orchestra programs to all residents of Ashland as well as the surrounding area.
Utilizes: Collaborations; Guest Accompanists; Guest Musicians; Original Music Scores; Sign Language Translators
Founded: 1970
Specialized Field: Symphony; Orchestra
Status: Semi-Professional; Nonprofit
Paid Staff: 5
Volunteer Staff: 10
Paid Artists: 7
Budget: $190,000
Income Sources: Box Office; Private Donations; Business Donations
Performs At: Hugo Young Theatre
Affiliations: American Symphony Orchestra League
Annual Attendance: 3,500-6,000
Organization Type: Performing; Educational

1516
ASHTABULA CHAMBER ORCHESTRA
P.O Box 415
Ashtabula, OH 44005
Phone: 440-964-3322
e-mail: Joseph.Tredent@neomin.org
Web Site: www.ashtabulaorchestra.com
Officers:
　President: Joesph Tredent
　Treasurer: Donna Marini
　Acting Secretary: Catherine Schmidt
　Fundraising Chair: Luanne Meinhardt
Management:
　Music Director: Michael Gelfand
　Orchestra Director/Conductor: George Doviak
Mission: To educate the people of the area in all types of stringed music; to provide string ensemble music for public enjoyment; to encourage young people on strings.
Utilizes: Guest Artists; Guest Companies; Singers
Founded: 1982
Specialized Field: Orchestra; Chamber
Status: Non-Professional; Nonprofit
Paid Staff: 35
Income Sources: Kent State University; Ashtabula Campus
Performs At: Kent State University Auditorium; Ashtabula Campus

All listings are in alphabetical order by state, then city, then organization within the city.

INSTRUMENTAL MUSIC / Ohio

Organization Type: Performing; Resident

1517
CLERMONT PHILHARMONIC ORCHESTRA
2400 Clermont Center Dr
Suite 211
Batavia, OH 45103
Phone: 513-735-8337
Fax: 513-735-8370
e-mail: clermontcpo@outlook.com
Web Site: www.clermontphilharmonic.com
Officers:
   President/Chairwoman: Debbie Siegroth
   Treasurer: Ed Brady
   Secretary: Katie Turning
Management:
   Music Director/Conductor: David Smarelli
   General Manager: Angelo Santoro
   Personnel Director: Lisa Momani
   Advisor: Kalley Falene
Specialized Field: Orchestra

1518
CLEVELAND POPS ORCHESTRA
24000 Mercantile Road
Unit 11
Beachwood, OH 44122
Phone: 216-765-7677
Fax: 216-765-7677
e-mail: staff@clevelandpops.com
Web Site: www.clevelandpops.com
Officers:
   Chairman: Dell Duncan
   Vice Chairman: Sondra Boyd
   President and CEO: Shirley Morgenstern
   Treasurer: Mary Andrews
   Secretary: Mary Lou Stricklin
Management:
   Artistic Director & Conductor: Carl Topilow
   Marketing Director: Gordon Petitt
Mission: The Cleveland POPS Orchestra is committed to presenting pops music of the highest artistic quality that is entertaining and exciting to a wide and diverse audience.
Founded: 1994
Specialized Field: Orchestra; Broadway; Jazz; Movie Themes; Patriotic
Paid Staff: 5
Paid Artists: 65
Budget: $800,000
Income Sources: Ticket Sales; Private Contributions; Foundation Grants; Corporate Sponsorships
Performs At: Severance Hall, Playhouse Square Center

1519
OHIO CHAMBER ORCHESTRA
3659 Green Road #118
Beachwood, OH 44122
Phone: 216-464-1755
Fax: 216-464-8628
e-mail: oco@ix.netcom.com
Officers:
   President: Paul R Bunker
   Chairman Executive Committee: William Steffee MD
   Executive Vice Chairman: Robert H Jackson
   Treasurer: James E. Wilcosky
   Secretary: Martha Vail
   President Ohio Chamber Orchestra: Norma Glazer
Management:
   Executive Director: Eugenia L Epperson
Mission: To perform at the highest artistic level possible programs specializing in works written specifically for chamber orchestra in appropriate (intimate) settings, featuring soloists of local and international standing.
Utilizes: Guest Artists
Founded: 1972
Specialized Field: Symphony; Orchestra; Chamber; Ensemble
Status: Professional
Performs At: The Cleveland Play House
Organization Type: Performing; Touring; Resident

1520
SUBURBAN SYMPHONY ORCHESTRA
PO Box 22653
Beachwood, OH 44122
Phone: 440-220-2040
Web Site: www.suburbansymphony.org
Management:
   Music Director: Martin Kessler
   General Manager: Paul Pride
   Concertmaster: Katherine Bormann
   Concertmaster Emeritus: Emilio Llinas
Mission: To offer accomplished professionals and nonprofessionals an opportunity to be part of a symphony orchestra; to present five free concerts each season.
Utilizes: Guest Artists
Founded: 1954
Specialized Field: Symphony; Orchestra
Status: Professional; Semi-Professional; Non-Professional; Nonprofit
Paid Staff: 70
Performs At: Beachwood High School Auditorium
Organization Type: Performing

1521
BALDWIN-WALLACE COLLEGE SYMPHONY ORCHESTRA
275 Eastland Road
Fanny Nast Gamble Auditorium 650
Berea, OH 44017
Phone: 440-826-2900
Fax: 440-826-3239
e-mail: info@bw.edu
Web Site: www.bw.edu
Officers:
   President: Robert C. Helmer, Ph.D., J.D.
   Senior Vice President: Richard L. Fletcher, MBA
   Chair: Paul H. Carleton
   Treasurer: Lee Thomas
   Secretary: Christopher M. Zito
Management:
   Conductor: Dwight Ottman
   Conservatory of Music Director: Peter Landgren
Specialized Field: Orchestra

1522
VENTI DA CAMERA
Bowling Green State University
Bowling Green, OH 43403
Phone: 419-372-2955
Fax: 419-372-2938
Management:
   Oboe/College Musical Arts: John Bentley
   Flute/College Musical Arts: Christina Jennings
   Clarinet; College of Musical Arts: Kevin Schempf
   Bassoon College of Musical Arts: Winston Collier
   Horn; College of Musical Arts: Rosemary Williams
Mission: Presenting works composed for wind quintet as well as other ensembles and offering a wide-ranging repertoire to a broad audience.
Utilizes: Guest Musical Directors; Guest Musicians; Sign Language Translators; Soloists
Founded: 1965
Specialized Field: Chamber; Wind Ensemble
Status: Professional
Income Sources: Bowling Green State University College of Music
Performs At: Bryan Recital Hall
Annual Attendance: 800
Facility Category: Recital Hall
Stage Dimensions: 50'x30'
Seating Capacity: 250
Year Built: 1976
Organization Type: Performing; Touring; Resident; Educational

1523
CANTON SYMPHONY ORCHESTRA
1001 Market Avenue North
Canton, OH 44702-1024
Phone: 330-452-3434
Fax: 330-452-4429
e-mail: lmoorhouse@cantonsymphony.org
Web Site: www.cantonsymphony.org
Officers:
   Chair, Marketing: Jessica Bennet
   Chair, Strategic Planning/Recorder: Linda M. Casey
   Chair, Board of Trustees: Charles H. Hoover
   Chair, Education: Gail L. Martino
   Chair, Investment: Dovid Nolin
Management:
   Music Director: Gerhard Zimmermann
   Assistant Conductor: Rachel L. Waddell
   Executive Director: Michelle Mullaly
   Director of Finance & Admin: Jeanette L. Lee
   Director of Development: Barbara Mucci
Mission: To maintain an orchestra of the highest quality as a cultural and educational resource and to bring the enjoyment and enrichment of great music to increasing numbers of citizens in Northeastern Ohio.
Utilizes: Guest Artists
Founded: 1937
Specialized Field: Symphony; Orchestra; Chamber; Ensemble
Status: Professional; Nonprofit
Paid Staff: 5
Paid Artists: 17
Income Sources: American Symphony Orchestra League
Performs At: William E. Umstattd Performing Arts Hall
Seating Capacity: 1490
Year Built: 1976
Organization Type: Performing

1524
CANTON YOUTH SYMPHONY
1001 Market Avenue North
Canton, OH 44702-1024
Phone: 330-452-3434
Fax: 330-452-4429
e-mail: info@cantonsymphony.org
Web Site: www.cantonsymphony.org
Officers:
   Chair, Marketing: Jessica Bennet
   Chair, Strategic Planning/Recorder: Linda M. Casey
   Chair, Board of Trustees: Charles H. Hoover
   Chair, Education: Gail L. Martino
   Chair, Investment: Dovid Nolin
Management:
   Orchestra Manager: Michae Koscso
   Assistant Conductor: Rachel L. Waddell
   Executive Director: Michelle Mullaly

Director of Finance & Admin: Jeanette L. Lee
Director of Development: Barbara Mucci
Founded: 1962
Specialized Field: Youth Symphony
Status: Non-Professional; Nonprofit
Income Sources: American Symphony Orchestra League (Youth Orchestra Division); Canton Symphony Orchestra
Performs At: Fine and Professional Arts Building
Organization Type: Performing; Educational; Sponsoring

1525
DAYTON CLASSICAL GUITAR SOCIETY
8530 Cherrycreek Drive
Centerville, OH 45458-3215
Phone: 937-435-1858
e-mail: jim@mccutcheonmusic.com
Web Site: mccutcheonmusic.com/dcgs/
Officers:
  President: Jim McCutcheon
Management:
  President: Jim McCutcheon
  Vice President: David Ferrara
  School Representative: Chris Jeffe
  Sales Manager: Rick Shutte
  Purchasing and Merchandise speciali: Haley Kendall
Founded: 1975
Specialized Field: Classical Guitar
Budget: $1,000
Annual Attendance: 500-700
Seating Capacity: 175

1526
CCM PHILHARMONIA & CONCERT ORCHESTRA
College Conservatory of Music
Univ. of Cincinnati
Cincinnati, OH 45221-0003
Phone: 513-556-2696
Fax: 513-556-0201
e-mail: gibsonmi@email.uc.edu
Web Site: musicalworld.com/presenters/ccm-philharmonia-and-concert-orchestra
Officers:
  Conductor: Xian Zhang
  Assistant to the Dean: Carol Brown
Management:
  Dean: Douglas Lowry
  Assistant Dean Performance Manageme: Katherine Mohylsky
  Ignatiou: Alexis
  York: Interim Directo Jody
  Loechle: Supervisor Joe
Specialized Field: Orchestra; Chamber

1527
CINCINNATI CHAMBER ORCHESTRA
105 W Fourth Street
Suite 810
Cincinnati, OH 45202
Phone: 513-723-1182
Fax: 513-723-1057
e-mail: info@ccocinnati.com
Web Site: www.ccocincinnati.org
Officers:
  President: Jennifer Funk
  Vice President: Larry S. Magnesen
  Vice President: Rosemary Schlachter
  Vice President: Michael A. Cioffi
  Treasurer: Ruth Schwallie
Management:
  Business & Development Manager: Ralf Ehrhardt
  Artistic & Orchestra Operations Man: LeAnne Anklan
  Personnel Manager: Manami White
  PR/Communications Manager: Ann Stewart
Mission: To provide high quality classical music in an engaging, innovative, accessible and affordable manner
Utilizes: Guest Composers; Guest Lecturers; Guest Musicians
Founded: 1974
Specialized Field: Chamber; Orchestra
Paid Staff: 5
Volunteer Staff: 40
Paid Artists: 32
Budget: $485,000
Affiliations: American Symphony Orchestra League
Organization Type: Performing; Touring; Educational

1528
CINCINNATI ORCHESTRA
1241 Elm Street
Music Hall
Cincinnati, OH 45202
Phone: 513-621-1919
Fax: 513-744-3535
e-mail: development@cincinnatisymphony.org
Web Site: www.cincinnatisymphony.org
Officers:
  President: Trey Devey
  Vice President and General Manager: Robert McGrath
  Vice President & CFO: Richard Freshwater
  Vice President of Marketing: Sherri Prentiss
  Director of Volunteers & Special Ev: Mary Beth Johnson
Management:
  Music Director: Louis Langr,e
  Director of Orchestra Personnel: Walter Zeschin
  Director of Artistic Administration: Sam Strater
  Director: Kathy Jorgensen-Finley
  Director of Data Systems: Melissa Scott
Mission: Presentation of symphonic concerts, educational activities and pops.
Specialized Field: Orchestra; Ensemble
Paid Staff: 4
Volunteer Staff: 16
Paid Artists: 75

1529
CINCINNATI SYMPHONY YOUTH ORCHESTRA
1241 Elm Street
Music Hall
Cincinnati, OH 45202
Phone: 513-621-1919
Fax: 513-744-3535
e-mail: development@cincinnatisymphony.org
Web Site: www.cincinnatisymphony.org
Officers:
  President: Trey Devey
  Vice President and General Manager: Robert McGrath
  Vice President & CFO: Richard Freshwater
  Vice President of Marketing: Sherri Prentiss
  Director of Volunteers & Special Ev: Mary Beth Johnson
Management:
  Music Director: Louis Langr,e
  Director of Orchestra Personnel: Walter Zeschin
  Director of Artistic Administration: Sam Strater
  Director: Kathy Jorgensen-Finley
  Director of Data Systems: Melissa Scott
Specialized Field: Youth Orchestra

1530
LINTON CHAMBER MUSIC SERIES/ENCORE! LINTON
Music Hall
1241 Elm Street
Cincinnati, OH 45202
Phone: 513-381-6868
e-mail: info@lintonmusic.org
Web Site: www.lintonmusic.org
Management:
  Artistic Director: Sharon Robinson
  Artistic Director: Jaime Laredo
Specialized Field: Chamber
Budget: $20,000-$35,000
Performs At: First Unitarian Church; Cincinnati City Council Chambers

1531
CLEVELAND CHAMBER SYMPHONY
The Music School Settlement
11125 Magnolia Drive
Cleveland, OH 44106
Phone: 216-202-4227
Fax: 216-687-9279
Web Site: www.clevelandchambersymphony.org
Officers:
  President: Richard Rinehart
  Vice President: Heidi Albert
  Secretary: Julie King
  Board Treasurer: Harry Weller
Management:
  Conductor: Steven Smith
  Artistic Director: Steven Smith
  Audio Engineering: David Yost
  Marketing: J. Garlando
Mission: Works to commission, perform, record and promote the dissemination of musical works exclusively by composers of our time.
Utilizes: Guest Composers; Guest Musical Directors; Guest Musicians
Founded: 1980
Specialized Field: Chamber; Symphony
Paid Staff: 3
Paid Artists: 37
Budget: $400,000-$500,000
Income Sources: Individuals; Government & Distinguished Private Foundations; Ohio Arts Council
Performs At: Drinko Recital Hall
Affiliations: National Endowment for the Arts; The Ohio Arts Council; The Ohio Board of Regents; The Cleveland Foundation; The George Gund Foundation
Annual Attendance: 2,700 - 3,300
Facility Category: Recital Hall
Type of Stage: Proscenium
Seating Capacity: 300
Year Built: 1990
Rental Contact: Facilities Coordinator Toni Lovejoy

1532
CLEVELAND INSTITUTE OF MUSIC
11021 E Boulevard
Cleveland, OH 44106
Phone: 216-791-5000
Fax: 216-791-3063
e-mail: cimmktg@po.cwru.edu
Web Site: www.cim.edu
Officers:
  President: Joel Smirnoff
  Vice President, Chief Operating Off: Eric Bower
  Vice President of Institutional Adv: Karin Stone
Management:
  Director Marketing/Communications: Susan M Schwartz

INSTRUMENTAL MUSIC / Ohio

Mission: To provide talented students with a professional, world-class education in the art of music.
Utilizes: Artists-in-Residence; Collaborations; Guest Accompanists; Guest Composers
Founded: 1920
Specialized Field: Educational; Classical Music; World Music
Paid Staff: 65
Paid Artists: 180
Budget: $13,175,000
Affiliations: Cleveland International Piano Competition; Art Song Festival; Western Reserve University
Annual Attendance: 47,000
Facility Category: Music
Seating Capacity: 550
Year Built: 1961
Rental Contact: Lori Wright
Resident Groups: Faculty and Student Performers

1533
CLEVELAND JAZZ ORCHESTRA
713 Lincoln Blvd.
Cleveland, OH 44146
Phone: 440-945-6428
Fax: 216-524-8349
e-mail: colleen@clevelandjazz.org
Web Site: www.clevelandjazz.org
Officers:
  President: Adrienne Stemen
  Executive Vice Presiden: Robert Sikora
  Vice President for Governance: Joel Brotman
  Treasurer: David Gedeon
  Trustee: Dan Leibundgut
Management:
  Executive Director: Colleen Sherman
  Director of Communications & Commun: Mary Glauser
Mission: To establish Cleveland Jazz Orchestra in Northeast Ohio; to enhance availability and quality of jazz; to assist in educating young musicians; to encourage involvement and training of minority musicians.
Founded: 1985
Specialized Field: Jazz Ensemble; Band
Status: Professional; Nonprofit
Paid Staff: 2
Volunteer Staff: 6
Paid Artists: 80
Income Sources: Cuyahoga Community College; Northeast Ohio Jazz Society; Cleveland Playhouse
Annual Attendance: 5,000
Organization Type: Performing; Resident; Educational; Sponsoring

1534
CLEVELAND OCTET
1510 Crest Road
Cleveland, OH 44121
Phone: 216-381-9031
Fax: 216-291-0502
Officers:
  Founder/Director: Erich Eichhorn
Management:
  Columbia Artist Management, NY:
Mission: To present and perform rarely performed masterpieces for ensembles of six to eight players.
Founded: 1977
Specialized Field: Chamber; Ensemble
Status: Professional; Nonprofit
Income Sources: Cleveland Museum of Art; Cleveland Orchestra
Performs At: Cleveland Museum of Art
Organization Type: Performing; Touring

1535
CLEVELAND ORCHESTRA
11001 Euclid Avenue
Severance Hall
Cleveland, OH 44106
Phone: 216-231-1111
Fax: 216-231-0202
e-mail: info@clevelandorchestra.com
Web Site: www.clevelandorch.org
Officers:
  Chairman: Larry Milder
  Chief Marketing Officer: Ross Binnie
  Chief Financial Officer: James E. Menger
  Chief Development Officer: Jon Limbacher
  Managing Director: Bruce Coppock
Management:
  Executive Director: Gary Hanson
  Music Director: Franz Welser-M"st
  General Manager: Jennifer Barlament
  Director of Operations: Julie Kim
  Orchestra Operations Manager: Amy Gill
Utilizes: Guest Artists
Founded: 1918
Specialized Field: Symphony; Orchestra; Ensemble
Status: Professional; Nonprofit; Semi-Volunteer
Paid Staff: 6
Volunteer Staff: 168
Income Sources: American Symphony Orchestra League
Performs At: Severance Hall; Blossom Music Center
Organization Type: Performing; Touring; Resident; Educational; Sponsoring

1536
CLEVELAND ORCHESTRA YOUTH ORCHESTRA
11001 Euclid Avenue
Severance Hall
Cleveland, OH 44106-1796
Phone: 216-231-7352
Fax: 216-231-4077
e-mail: coyo@clevelandorchestra.com
Web Site: www.clevelandorchestrayouthorchestra.com
Management:
  Music Director: Brett Mitchell
  Manager: Ashley Smith
Founded: 1986
Specialized Field: Youth Orchestra
Paid Staff: 2
Paid Artists: 18
Budget: $170,000
Income Sources: Musical Arts Association
Performs At: Concert Hall
Affiliations: The Cleveland Orchestra
Facility Category: Concert Hall
Seating Capacity: 2,000
Year Remodeled: 2000

1537
CLEVELAND PHILHARMONIC ORCHESTRA
8702 Bessemer Avenue
PO Box 16251
Cleveland, OH 44116
Phone: 216-556-1800
e-mail: admin@clevephil.org
Web Site: www.clevephil.org
Officers:
  Director Emeritus: William Slocum
  Music Director: Dr. Victor Liva
  Personnel Manager: Lisa Wilson
  Program Annotator: Brandon Fitch
  Tri-C Metro Stage Manager: Remmie Crawford

Mission: Providing performances of quality at reasonable ticket prices; to train aspiring musicians; to offer musicians a technical education.
Utilizes: Guest Artists
Founded: 1938
Specialized Field: Symphony; Orchestra
Status: Semi-Professional; Nonprofit
Paid Staff: 60
Income Sources: American Symphony Orchestra League; Saint Vincent Quadrangle Association
Performs At: Cuyahoga Community College
Organization Type: Performing; Resident; Sponsoring

1538
NORTHEAST OHIO JAZZ SOCIETY
4614 Prospect Avenue
#533
Cleveland, OH 44103
Phone: 216-426-9900
Fax: 216-426-9906
Officers:
  President: A C Alrey
Specialized Field: Jazz Ensemble
Budget: $60,000-$150,000

1539
SHAKER SYMPHONY ORCHESTRA
Cleveland Institute of Music
11021 East Boulevard
Cleveland, OH 44106
Phone: 216-464-6170
Fax: 216-491-1465
e-mail: hinkleal@adelphia.net
Management:
  Conductor: Allan Hinkle
  Director: David Cerone
Specialized Field: Orchestra

1540
UNIVERSITY CIRCLE CHAMBER ORCHESTRA
Haydn Hall
11118 Bellflower Rd.
Cleveland, OH 44106
Phone: 216-368-2000
Fax: 216-368-6557
e-mail: music@case.edu
Web Site: music.case.edu/ensembles/caseuniversity-circle-symphony-orchestra/
Officers:
  President: Barbara R. Snyder
  Provost and Executive Vice Presiden: W. A. Bud Baeslack III
Management:
  Director: Dr. Kathleen Horvath
Mission: Offering an opportunity to university students as well as interested amateurs, to perform stimulating repertoire in a pleasant but serious atmosphere.
Specialized Field: Symphony; Orchestra; Chamber; Ensemble
Status: Non-Professional; Nonprofit
Paid Staff: 18
Income Sources: Case Western Reserve University
Performs At: Harkness Chapel
Organization Type: Performing; Resident; Educational

1541
APOLLO'S FIRE: THE CLEVELAND BAROQUE ORCHESTRA
3091 Mayfield Road
Suite 217
Cleveland Heights, OH 44118

Phone: 216-320-0012
Fax: 216-320-0129
Toll-free: 800-314-2535
e-mail: info@apollosfire.org
Web Site: apollosfire.org
Officers:
    Chair: Clyde L. Nash, M.D.
    Vice President: Thomas Clark
    Treasurer: Samuel D. Harris
    Secretary: Rebecca Storey
    Chair Emeritus: Norman Harbert
Management:
    Music Director, Conductor: Jeannette Sorrell
    Artistic Operations, Director: Kristen Linfante, klinfante@apollosfire.org
    Marketing Manager & Associate Grant: Sarah Blue, sblue@apollosfire.org
    Finance Director: Christine Meador
    Patron Services: Sarah Kovach
    Operations Coordinator: Tom Dingledein
    Box Office Associate: Margi Haigh
    Production Manager: Tom Frattare
    Production Coordinator: Martins Daukss
Mission: Named for the classical god of music and the sun, Apollo's Fire was founded in 1992 by the award-winning young harpsichordist and conductor Jeannette Sorrell. Sorrell envisioned an ensemble dedicated to the baroque ideal that music should evoke the various Affekts or passions in the listeners. Apollo's Fire is a collection of creative artists who share Sorrell's passion for drama and rhetoric.
Utilizes: Arrangers; Collaborating Artists; Collaborations; Composers; Contract Orchestras; Dancers; Fine Artists; Local Unknown Artists; Lyricists; Multimedia; Music; Paid Performers; Sign Language Translators; Singers; Touring Companies
Founded: 1992
Specialized Field: Classical, Baroque Instrumental, Vocal
Status: Non-Profit, Professional
Income Sources: Donors, Corporate Sponsors
Season: Year Round
Performs At: Trinity Cathedral

1542
CLEVELAND CHAMBER MUSIC SOCIETY
2532 Lafayette Drive
University Heights
Cleveland Heights, OH 44118
Phone: 216-291-2777
Fax: 216-291-9135
e-mail: information@clevelandchambermusic.org
Web Site: www.clevelandchambermusic.org
Officers:
    President: Richard Fried
    1st Vice President: Lois Rose
    2nd Vice President: Anthony Addison
    Recording Secretary: Lenore P. Koppel
    Treasurer: Douglas Rose
Management:
    Executive Secretary: Sharon Muskin
Founded: 1949
Specialized Field: Chamber
Paid Staff: 1
Budget: $60,000-$150,000
Income Sources: Ticket Sales; Endowment
Performs At: Fairmount Temple Auditorium; Church of the Convenant
Annual Attendance: 2,800
Facility Category: Rent
Seating Capacity: 736

1543
HEIGHTS CHAMBER ORCHESTRA
PO Box 18413
Cleveland Heights, OH 44118
Phone: 216-921-4339
Fax: 440-775-8886
e-mail: susanblackwell@hotmail.com
Web Site: http://129.22.153.16/hco/
Officers:
    President: Susan Blackwell
    Vice President: Sue Schieman
    Treasurer: Marlene Englander
    Secretary: Carol Boyd
Management:
    Music Director: Anthony Addison
    Concertmistress: Emily Cornelius
Mission: To provide the community with an orchestra and the schools with music education.
Founded: 1983
Specialized Field: Symphony; Orchestra
Status: Nonprofit
Paid Staff: 52
Income Sources: Cleveland Heights Board of Education; Cleveland Heights Parks & Recreation Department
Performs At: Performing Arts Center; Cleveland Heights High School
Organization Type: Performing

1544
CHAMBER MUSIC COLUMBUS
PO Box 14445
Columbus, OH 43214
Phone: 614-267-2267
e-mail: info@CMColumbus.org
Web Site: www.cmcolumbus.org
Officers:
    President: Daniel L. Jensen
    Vice President: Charles C. Warner
    Secretary: Sally Cleary Griffiths
    Treasurer: Saul Blumenthal
    Immediate Past President: Charles C. Warner
Specialized Field: Chamber
Status: Non Profit
Budget: $150,000
Seating Capacity: 950

1545
COLUMBUS SYMPHONY ORCHESTRA
55 East State Street
Columbus, OH 43215
Phone: 614-228-8600
Fax: 614-224-7273
e-mail: pstetzik@columbussymphony.com
Web Site: www.columbussymphony.com
Officers:
    Chair, Executive Vice President and: Martin Inglis
    Vice Chair, Senior Vice President a: Michael Mahaffey
    Treasurer: Eric N. Sutphin
    Secretary: Derrick Clay
    Trustee: Lisa Barton
Management:
    Music Director: Jean-Marie Zeitouni
    Associate Conductor: Peter Stafford Wilson
    Director of Artistic Planning: Mike Stefiuk
    General Manager: Pavana Stetzik
    Orchestra Personnel Manager: Daren Fuster
Mission: To nurture and further the public's musical knowledge through educational activities and musical performances.
Utilizes: Actors; Dancers; Educators; Grant Writers; Guest Accompanists; Guest Companies; Guest Composers; Guest Designers; Guest Directors; Guest Instructors; Guest Lecturers; Guest Musical Directors; Guest Musicians; Instructors; Local Artists; Multimedia; Music; Original Music Scores; Sign Language Translators; Singers; Soloists
Founded: 1950
Specialized Field: Symphony; Orchestra; Chamber; Ensemble
Status: Professional
Budget: $10.8 million
Income Sources: American Symphony Orchestra League
Performs At: Ohio Theatre; Mershon Auditorium
Annual Attendance: 205,000
Organization Type: Performing; Educational; Sponsoring

1546
COLUMBUS SYMPHONY YOUTH ORCHESTRAS
55 East State Street
Columbus, OH 43215
Phone: 614-228-9600
Fax: 614-224-7273
e-mail: pstetzik@columbussymphony.com
Web Site: www.columbussymphony.com
Officers:
    Chair, Executive Vice President and: Martin Inglis
    Vice Chair, Senior Vice President a: Michael Mahaffey
    Treasurer: Eric N. Sutphin
    Secretary: Derrick Clay
    Trustee: Lisa Barton
Management:
    Music Director: Jean-Marie Zeitouni
    Associate Conductor: Peter Stafford Wilson
    Director of Artistic Planning: Mike Stefiuk
    General Manager: Pavana Stetzik
    Orchestra Personnel Manager: Daren Fuster
Mission: To provide the highest quality educational and performance experiences for Central Ohio's most gifted instrumentalists.
Utilizes: Collaborations; Commissioned Composers; Composers-in-Residence; Educators; Fine Artists; Five Seasonal Concerts; Guest Accompanists; Guest Companies; Guest Composers; Guest Designers; Guest Lecturers; Guest Musical Directors; Multimedia; Music; Organization Contracts; Singers; Soloists
Founded: 1955
Specialized Field: Youth Orchestra; Chamber
Status: Non-Professional; Nonprofit
Paid Staff: 7
Income Sources: American Symphony Orchestra League (Youth Orchestra Division); Columbus Symphony Orchestra; donations; tuiton
Performs At: Mess Hall, Capital University; Capitol Theatre; Verne Ritte Center; Hughes Auditorium; Ohio State University
Organization Type: Performing; Touring; Educational

1547
JAZZ ARTS GROUP OF COLUMBUS
769 E. Long Street
Columbus, OH 43203
Phone: 614-294-5200
Fax: 614-298-6149
e-mail: info@jazzartsgroup.org
Web Site: www.jazzartsgroup.org
Officers:
    President: Vincent Lodico
    President-Elect: Linda J. Siefkas
    Secretary: Jeanetta Darno

INSTRUMENTAL MUSIC / Ohio

Interim Executive Director: Dan Weiss, CPA, JD
1st Vice President: James L. Barnes
Management:
   Orchestra Manager: Karen Atria aupt
   Artistic Director: Bryon Stripling
   Artistic Director Emeritus: Ray Eubanks
   Executive Director: Press Southworth III
   Director Of Jazz In Schools: Judy Shafer
   Director Of Affiliate Musicians: Louis Tsamous
   Business Operations Assistant: Jennifer Pettibone
   Director Marketing/Communications: Scott Vezdos
Mission: To advance the art of jazz through performance and education.
Utilizes: Arrangers; Collaborating Artists; Collaborations; Contract Orchestras; Fine Artists
Founded: 1973
Specialized Field: Performing Arts
Status: Professional; Nonprofit
Paid Staff: 12
Volunteer Staff: 15
Budget: $1.4 million
Income Sources: Ohio Arts Council; Greater Columbus Arts Council; Columbus Foundation; Subscriptions; Sponsorships; Individual Donations; Corporate Donations
Season: September, December, March, April
Performs At: Southern Theatre, Lincoln Theatre
Affiliations: Experience Columbus; Columbus Chamber; CAMA; OAPN; APAP; Jazz Education Network

1548
PRO MUSICA CHAMBER ORCHESTRA OF COLUMBUS
243 N 5th Street
Suite 202
Columbus, OH 43215
Phone: 614-464-0066
Fax: 614-464-4141
e-mail: trussell@promusicacolumbus.org
Web Site: www.promusicacolumbus.org
Officers:
   President: Stephen Keyes
   Co-Vice President: Joan Herbers
   Co-Vice President: Jim Abrams
   Co-Vice President: Ida Copenhaver
   Treasurer: Jacob Gibson
Management:
   Executive Director: Janet Chen
   Music Director: David Danzmayr
   Personnel Manager and Music Librari: Thomas Battenberg
   Finance Manager: Yvette Boyer
   Patron Services Manager: Joseph Calmer
Mission: To establish a partnership with the audience in order to understand and fulfill audience needs for a variety of entertaining and enlightening musical performances as well as educational experiences.
Utilizes: Collaborations; Guest Accompanists; Guest Artists; Guest Composers; Guest Instructors; Guest Musical Directors; Guest Musicians; Instructors; Lyricists; Multi Collaborations; Multimedia; Organization Contracts; Original Music Scores; Selected Students; Sign Language Translators
Founded: 1978
Specialized Field: Symphony; Orchestra; Chamber
Status: Professional; Nonprofit
Paid Staff: 7
Budget: $800,000
Performs At: Southern Theatre
Seating Capacity: 939
Year Built: 1896

Year Remodeled: 1999
Organization Type: Performing; Touring

1549
DAYTON PHILHARMONIC ORCHESTRA ASSOCIATION
126 North Main Street
Suite 210
Dayton, OH 45402
Phone: 937-224-3521
Fax: 937-223-9189
e-mail: info@daytonphilharmonic.com
Web Site: www.daytonphilharmonic.com
Officers:
   Chair: Craig Jennings
   Chair: Rebecca Appenzeller
   President & CEO: Paul Helfrich
   Chief Administrative Officer: Kathy Reed
   Chief Financial Officer: Teri Warwick
Management:
   Artistic Director & Conductor: Neal Gittleman
   Development Director: Laura Fike
   Corporate Gifts & Sponsorship Manag: Laurie Cothran
   Education Director: Gloria Pugh
   Ballet School Administrator: Carol Jean Heller
Mission: Maintaining and nurturing the highest quality professional symphonic orchestra; offering live concerts that promote cultural enhancement.
Utilizes: Guest Artists
Founded: 1933
Specialized Field: Symphony; Orchestra; Chamber
Status: Professional; Nonprofit
Paid Staff: 16
Volunteer Staff: 6
Paid Artists: 88
Non-paid Artists: 120
Income Sources: American Symphony Orchestra League; American Arts Alliance; American Council for the Arts
Performs At: Montgomery County's Memorial Hall; Dayton Convention Center
Organization Type: Performing; Resident; Educational; Sponsoring

1550
DAYTON PHILHARMONIC YOUTH ORCHESTRA
126 North Main Street
Suite 210
Dayton, OH 45402
Phone: 937-224-3521
Fax: 937-223-9189
e-mail: info@daytonphilharmonic.com
Web Site: www.daytonphilharmonic.com
Officers:
   Chair: Craig Jennings
   Chair: Rebecca Appenzeller
   President & CEO: Paul Helfrich
   Chief Administrative Officer: Kathy Reed
   Chief Financial Officer: Teri Warwick
Management:
   Artistic Director & Conductor: Neal Gittleman
   Director Education: Gloria Pugh
   Development Director: Laura Fike
   Corporate Gifts & Sponsorship Manag: Laurie Cothran
   Ballet School Administrator: Carol Jean Heller
Mission: To give aspiring young musicians of the Dayton area an opportunity to work together studying challenging orchestral music; to attempt to strengthen and expand the musical skills, knowledge, talent and experience through the study of the symphonic orchestral literature.
Founded: 1982
Specialized Field: Youth Orchestra
Status: Professional; Nonprofit
Paid Staff: 15
Volunteer Staff: 3
Non-paid Artists: 90
Income Sources: American Symphony Orchestra League (Youth Orchestra Division); Ohio Music Club; Dayton Philharmonic Orchestra
Performs At: Concert Hall; Wright State University
Organization Type: Performing; Educational

1551
SOIREES MUSICALES PIANO SERIES
5300 Philadelphia Drive
Dayton, OH 45407-2433
Phone: 937-228-5802
Fax: 937-228-2380
e-mail: hagpia@interaxs.net
Web Site: www.soireesmusicales.com
Management:
   Series Director: Donald C Hageman
Founded: 1969
Specialized Field: Soloists; Piano
Volunteer Staff: 7
Budget: $10,000-$20,000
Performs At: Shiloh Church

1552
CENTRAL OHIO SYMPHONY ORCHESTRA
24 E. Winter Street
Delaware, OH 43015
Mailing Address: PO Box 619, Delaware, Ohio 43015
Phone: 740-362-1799
Fax: 740-362-1733
Toll-free: 740-417-4517
e-mail: info@centralohiosymphony.org
Web Site: www.centralohiosymphony.org
Officers:
   President: Don Gliebe
   Vice President: David Hejmanowski
   Secretary: Susan Lasley
   Treasurer: Seth Taylor
   Trustee: Eric Batterton
Management:
   Executive Director: Warren W Hyer
   Conductor: Jamie Morales Matos
Founded: 1978
Specialized Field: Orchestra
Paid Staff: 4
Paid Artists: 65
Non-paid Artists: 10
Budget: $120,000
Annual Attendance: 20,000
Facility Category: Concert Hall
Seating Capacity: 1,079
Year Built: 1893
Year Remodeled: 1980

1553
HAMILTON-FAIRFIELD SYMPHONY ORCHESTRA
One High Street
Hamilton, OH 45011
Phone: 513-895-5151
Fax: 513-474-1584
e-mail: info@hfso.org
Web Site: www.hfso.org
Management:

INSTRUMENTAL MUSIC / Ohio

Music Director/Conductor: Paul John Stanbery
Specialized Field: Orchestra

1554
MUSIC FROM THE WESTERN RESERVE
Western Reserve Academy
P.O. Box 998
Hudson, OH 44236
Phone: 330-650-9714
Fax: 330-688-4839
e-mail: info@mftwr.org
Web Site: www.mftwr.org
Officers:
  President: Bruce F Rothmann, MD
  VP: Walter Watson
  Treasurer: Robert L Henke
  Secretary: David Hunter, Esquire
  Recording Secretary: Diana Truyell
Management:
  Concert Manager: Lola Rothmann
  General Manager: Elisabeth Hugh
Mission: Showcasing the abundant musical talent of Northeast Ohio.
Utilizes: Instructors; Multimedia; Original Music Scores; Sign Language Translators; Singers
Founded: 1982
Specialized Field: Chamber
Status: Nonprofit
Volunteer Staff: 6
Budget: $10,000
Performs At: The Chapel, Western Reserve Academy
Annual Attendance: 600-700
Seating Capacity: 450
Year Built: 1836
Organization Type: Sponsoring

1555
LAKELAND CIVIC ORCHESTRA
Lakeland Community College
Lakeland Performing Arts Center 430
Kirtland, OH 44094-5198
Phone: 440-473-9929
Fax: 440-975-4738
Toll-free: 800-589-8520
e-mail: KathyLH22@aol
Web Site: lakelandcc.edu/web/about/music-civic-orchestra
Management:
  Orchestra Director: Kathryn Harsha
  Senior Secretary: Theresa Myllykoski
Specialized Field: Orchestra

1556
LAKESIDE SYMPHONY
236 Walnut Avenue
Lakeside, OH 43440
Phone: 419-798-4461
Fax: 419-798-5033
e-mail: guestinfo@lakeseohio.com
Web Site: www.lakesideohio.com
Officers:
  President & CEO: Kevin Sibbring
  Vice President of Accounting: Sylvia Chappell
  Vice President, Communications: Gretchen Colon
  Chief Financial Officer: Daniel Dudley
  Vice President, Municipal Services: Dave Geyer
Management:
  Executive Director: Bud Cox
  Music Director: Robert L Conquist
  Director of Guest Services: Mary Ann Hirsch
  Property Manager: Steve Koening
  Accounting/IT Assistant: Mandy James

Mission: To maintain a professional resident orchestra for part of the summer season at Lakeside.
Founded: 1925
Specialized Field: Symphony; Orchestra; Chamber
Status: Professional; Nonprofit
Paid Staff: 75
Volunteer Staff: 60
Paid Artists: 10
Performs At: Hoover Auditorium
Organization Type: Performing; Resident; Educational

1557
LIMA SYMPHONY ORCHESTRA
133 N. Elizabeth Street Lima
Lima, OH 45801
Phone: 419-222-5701
Fax: 419-222-6587
e-mail: staff@limasymphony.org
Web Site: www.limasymphony.com
Officers:
  President: Kevin Hawley
  Vice President: U. William Walter
  Secretary: Keith Davis
  Treasurer: Tim Sielschott
  Board Member: Pam Ayers
Management:
  Music Director/Conductor: Crafton Beck
  Executive Director: Elizabeth Brown
  Personnel Manager/Librarian: Anita Sims Skinner
  Development Director: Robert Christian
Mission: Promoting the public's musical appreciation and knowledge through live musical performances, including chamber, opera and symphonic.
Utilizes: Guest Artists; Guest Companies
Founded: 1953
Specialized Field: Symphony; Orchestra; Chamber
Status: Semi-Professional; Nonprofit
Paid Staff: 8
Volunteer Staff: 1
Paid Artists: 85
Budget: $350,000-$400,000
Income Sources: American Symphony Orchestra League
Performs At: Veterans Memorial Civic and Convention Center
Seating Capacity: 1,670
Organization Type: Performing; Educational; Sponsoring

1558
MANSFIELD SYMPHONY ORCHESTRA
The Renaissance
138 Park Ave. West
Mansfield, OH 44902
Phone: 419-522-2726
Fax: 419-524-7005
e-mail: tomc@rparts.org
Web Site: www.mansfieldtickets.com
Officers:
  President: David Daugherty
  Vice President: Rand Smith
  Secretary: Llalan Fowler
  Treasurer: Michael Jefferson
Management:
  Artistic Director: Michael Thomas
  Music Director: Thomas Hong
  Director of Operations, Education,: Chelsie Thompson
  Technical Director: Chad Eaton
  Ddevelopment Director: Colleen Cook
Specialized Field: Orchestra
Facility Category: Theater
Type of Stage: Proscenium
Seating Capacity: 1406

Year Built: 1928
Year Remodeled: 1982

1559
MIDDLETOWN SYMPHONY ORCHESTRA
130 N Verity Parkway
PO Box 411
Middletown, OH 45042
Phone: 513-424-2426
e-mail: mso@middletownsymphony.com
Web Site: www.middletownsymphony.com
Management:
  Music Director: Carmon DeLeone
Founded: 1941
Specialized Field: Orchestra

1560
NEW ALBANY SYMPHONY
PO Box 332
30 West Main Street
New Albany, OH 43054
Phone: 614-323-1237
Fax: 614-245-4701
e-mail: hagrner@newalbanysymphony.com
Web Site: www.newalbanysymphony.com
Officers:
  President: Heather Garner
  EVP: Ann Sproule
  Vice President: Ron Cadieux
  Treasurer: John Garner
  Board Member: Christophe Le Barbier
  Board Member: Sandy Mendoza
  Board Member: Paul Naumoff
  Board Member: Jennifer Spalding
Management:
  Musical Director, Conductor: Luis Biava
  Executive Director: Heather Garner
  Marketing Director: Linda Brill
  Stage Manager: Jason Gay
  Graphic Design: Joel Koehler
  Personnel Manager: Karen Pfeifer
  Opserations Director: Ann Sproule
Mission: To enrich, educate, entertain, and inspire creativity through the arts to peopl of all ages and backgrounds.
Utilizes: Arrangers; Collaborating Artists; Collaborations; Contract Orchestras; Educators; Fine Artists; Lyricists; Multimedia; Music; Paid Performers; Singers
Status: Classical, Contemporary Instrumental
Income Sources: Donors, Corporate Sponsors
Season: October through April
Performs At: Jeanne B McCoy Community Center for the Arts

1561
SOUTHEASTERN OHIO SYMPHONY ORCHESTRA
PO Box 42
Muskingum College
New Concord, OH 43762
Phone: 740-826-8197
Fax: 740-826-8404
e-mail: info@seoso.org
Web Site: www.seoso.org
Management:
  Music Director: Laura E Schumann
  Executive Director: Elizabeth E Broschart
  Symphony Manager: John Kunkel
Specialized Field: Orchestra

INSTRUMENTAL MUSIC / Ohio

1562
TUSCARAWAS PHILHARMONIC
PO Box 406
New Philadelphia, OH 44663
Phone: 330-364-1843
Fax: 330-364-1843
e-mail: ejbisme@gmail.com
Web Site: www.tuscarawasphilharmonic.org
Officers:
  President: Gil Snyder
  VP: Scott Lawrence
  Secretary: Lynn Dischinger
  Treasurer: Robert Bragg
Management:
  Music Director/Conductor: Eric Benjamin
  General Manager: Melanie Winn
  Finance Manager: Robert L Henke
  Personnel Manager/Librarian: Barb Moore
  Webmaster and Tickets Manager: Bud Winn
Mission: To offer musical enjoyment to all ages and enhance the cultural development of the community.
Utilizes: Commissioned Music; Guest Accompanists; Guest Musical Directors; Guest Musicians; Instructors; Local Artists; Original Music Scores; Sign Language Translators; Singers; Soloists
Founded: 1935
Specialized Field: Symphony; Orchestra
Status: Semi-Professional; Nonprofit
Paid Staff: 35
Performs At: Dover High School
Annual Attendance: 4,000 - 6,000
Facility Category: Auditorium
Type of Stage: Proscenium
Seating Capacity: 1,084
Organization Type: Performing

1563
NORTHERN OHIO YOUTH ORCHESTRAS
39 S Main
Suite 244
Oberlin, OH 44074
Phone: 440-775-3059
Fax: 440-774-6160
e-mail: noyo@noyo.org
Web Site: www.noyo.org
Officers:
  President: Nicole McGuire
  Vice-president: Lawrence Ester
  Treasurer: Kay Giardini
  Secretary: Stacey Morris
  Board Member: Robert Cabrera
Management:
  Executive & Artistic Director?? rhy: Michael Roest
  General Manager: Rosalind Soltow
Specialized Field: Youth Orchestra

1564
OBERLIN BAROQUE ENSEMBLE
Conservatory of Music
Oberlin College
Oberlin, OH 44074
Phone: 440-775-8121
Fax: 440-775-8886
e-mail: communications@oberlin.edu
Web Site: new.oberlin.edu/office/summer-programs/baroque-performance-institute
Management:
  Artistic Director: Kenneth Slowik
  Recorder: Michaele Lynn
Mission: The ensemble performs 17th and 18th-century compositions on period instruments.
Founded: 1973
Specialized Field: Chamber; Ensemble; Baroque
Status: Professional
Income Sources: Oberlin College Conservatory of Music
Performs At: Oberlin Conservatory
Organization Type: Performing; Touring; Resident; Educational

1565
MIAMI UNIVERSITY SYMPHONY ORCHESTRA
109 Presser Hall
Miami University
Oxford, OH 45056
Phone: 513-529-3014
Fax: 513-529-3027
e-mail: averbach@muohio.edu
Web Site: www.orgs.muohio.edu/muso/
Officers:
  President: Sarah Blumberg
  Vice-President: Caitlyn Lana
  Treasurer: Laura Feibelman
  Secretary: Molly Jackson
  Social Chair: Abi Marosi
Management:
  Music Director: Jose-Luis Novo
  Orchestra Manager: Kristin Pyles
  Conductor: Ricardo Averbach
  Equipment manager: Scotty McEvoy
Specialized Field: Orchestra

1566
MIAMI WIND QUINTET
Department of Music
Miami University
Oxford, OH 45056
Phone: 513-529-1809
Fax: 513-529-3841
Web Site: arts.muohio.edu/faculty/faculty_r/mwqlpreview_a.html
Management:
  Director Audience Development: Jeanne Conners
Mission: Offering chamber music composed for winds; assisting young wind players.
Founded: 1985
Specialized Field: Chamber; Wind Ensemble
Status: Professional
Income Sources: Miami University
Performs At: Souers Recital Hall; Miami University
Organization Type: Performing; Touring; Resident; Educational

1567
CLEVELAND WOMEN'S ORCHESTRA
2691 Country Club Blvd
Rocky River, OH 44116
Phone: 440-356-1303
e-mail: info@clevelandwomensorchestra.org
Web Site: clevelandwomensorchestra.org
Management:
  Founder: Hymann Schandler
  Music Director, Conductor: Robert Conquist
Mission: During the early part of this century, opportunities for women musicians were few. For the most part, membership in symphonies was open only to men, which led to the formation of numerous women's orchestras in cities across the country. As the last of the many women's orchestras that flourished during the 1920s, 1930s and 1940s, the historic Cleveland Women's Orchestra is the oldest women's orchestra in the country.
Utilizes: Arrangers; Choreographers; Collaborating Artists; Community Members; Composers; Contract Orchestras; High School Drama; Lyricists; Multimedia; Music; Paid Performers; Singers
Founded: 1935
Opened: 1936
Specialized Field: Classical Instrumental
Status: Non-Proit, Professional
Income Sources: Donors, Sponsors, Fundraisers
Season: October through April
Performs At: Severence Hall, Menorah Park, Rocky River Senior Center, National Bohemian Hall, Judson Park

1568
SPRINGFIELD SYMPHONY ORCHESTRA
300 S Fountain Avenue
PO Box 1374
Springfield, OH 45501
Phone: 937-325-8100
Fax: 937-325-2299
e-mail: info@springfieldsym.org
Web Site: www.springfieldsym.org
Officers:
  President: Margaret Roark
  Vice-President: Marlies Hemmann
Management:
  Executive Director: David Dietrick
  Music Director: Peter Stafford Wilson
  Executive Director: David Deitrick
  Director of Operations & Education: Robyn Zimmann
Mission: Providing the best symphonic music for the community; offering music education to youth.
Utilizes: Educators; Guest Accompanists; Guest Artists; Guest Composers; Multimedia
Founded: 1944
Specialized Field: Symphony; Chamber
Status: Professional; Nonprofit
Paid Staff: 60
Paid Artists: 80
Budget: $850,000
Income Sources: American Symphony Orchestra League
Performs At: Kuss Auditorium; Clark State Performing Arts Center
Affiliations: Clark State College
Annual Attendance: 1,200
Seating Capacity: 1,200
Organization Type: Performing; Sponsoring

1569
WITTENBERG UNIVERSITY DEPARTMENT OF MUSIC
Ward Street at Woodlawn Avenue
Box 720
Springfield, OH 45501-0720
Phone: 937-327-7354
Fax: 937-327-7347
Toll-free: 800-677-7558
e-mail: dkazez@wittenberg.edu
Web Site: www4.wittenberg.edu
Management:
  Professor of Music & Music Admissio: Dr. Daniel Kazez
Mission: For over 100 years, Wittenberg has excelled in preparing students for careers in music education, performance, church music, composition, arts administration, and other music fields. Wittenberg's music department has been a member of the National Association of Schools of Music (NASM) for over 75 years.
Specialized Field: Chamber; Folk Music; Jazz; Symphony

INSTRUMENTAL MUSIC / Oklahoma

Performs At: Krieg Hall; Weaver Chapel
Affiliations: National Association of Schools of Music
Seating Capacity: 135

1570
TOLEDO JAZZ SOCIETY
151 Michigan Street
Suite 307
Toledo, OH 43604
Phone: 419-241-5299
Fax: 419-241-4777
Web Site: www.toledojazzsociety.org
Officers:
  President: Jon Richardson
  VP: Jeff Jaffe
  Secretary: Joanne Treuhaft
Management:
  Executive Director: Kim Buehler
  Membership/Marketing Coordinator: Anne Biel
Mission: Promoting the performance of jazz and its preservation as an art form; providing concerts, educational programs and lectures.
Founded: 1980
Specialized Field: Orchestra; Jazz Ensemble; Band
Status: Professional; Nonprofit
Paid Staff: 12
Paid Artists: 100
Income Sources: Association of Performing Arts Presenters; Arts Midwest
Performs At: The Franciscan Theatre And Conference Center In Toledo, Ohio
Organization Type: Performing; Resident; Educational; Sponsoring

1571
TOLEDO SYMPHONY
1838 Parkwood Avenue
Suite 310
Toledo, OH 43624
Mailing Address: PO Box 407, Toledo, OH 43697
Phone: 419-246-8000
Fax: 419-321-6890
Toll-free: 800-348-1253
e-mail: kcarroll@toledosymphony.com
Web Site: www.toledosymphony.com
Officers:
  Chairman: Richard P. Anderson
  Treasurer: William F. Buckley
  Secretary: Frank Jacobs
  President Emeritus/Chief Artistic O: Bob Bell
  President & CEO: Kathleen Carroll
Management:
  Principal Conductor: Stefan Sanderling
  Resident Conductor: Jeffrey Pollock
  Director of Marketing & Public Rela: Ashley Yarnell
  Patron Service Manager: Michelle Keller
  Group Experience Lady: Ellen Critchley Pittman
Mission: To furnish performances of the highest artistic caliber to the widest possible audience; to conduct public service and education functions.
Utilizes: Commissioned Music; Guest Accompanists; Guest Artists; Guest Composers; Guest Lecturers; Original Music Scores; Sign Language Translators; Singers
Founded: 1943
Specialized Field: Symphony; Orchestra; Chamber; Ensemble
Status: Professional; Nonprofit
Performs At: Toledo Museum of Art Peristyle
Organization Type: Performing; Touring; Educational

1572
WESTERVILLE SYMPHONY
167 South State Street, Suite 80
PO Box 478
Westerville, OH 43086-0478
Phone: 614-899-9000
Fax: 614-882-2085
e-mail: info@westervillesymphony.org
Web Site: www.westervillesymphony.org
Officers:
  President: Judy Gilliam
  Secretary: Mary K. Gilbert
  VP Finance/Treasurer: Ron Lykins
  VP Strategic Planning: Jill Schultz
  VP Development: George Pilcher
Management:
  Music Director: Peter Stafford Wilson
  Executive Director: Janelle Myers
Mission: A nonprofit, charitable corporation functioning as an aesthetic, educational and cultural resource, presenting performances primarily of symphonic music; an artistic outlet for amateur and semi-professional musicians.
Founded: 1982
Specialized Field: Symphony; Orchestra; Ensemble
Status: Non-Professional; Nonprofit
Paid Staff: 50
Performs At: Cowan Hall; Otterbein College
Organization Type: Performing; Educational

1573
WOOSTER SYMPHONY ORCHESTRA
Scheide Music Center
525 E. University Street
Wooster, OH 44691
Phone: 330-263-2419
Fax: 330-263-2051
e-mail: stanley@wooster.edu
Web Site: www.wooster.edu/academics/areas/music/ensembles/symphony-orchestra/
Management:
  Director: Prof. Jeffrey Lindberg
Mission: Bringing the community live orchestral repertoire.
Utilizes: Artists-in-Residence; Collaborating Artists; Commissioned Music; Curators; Five Seasonal Concerts; Guest Accompanists; Guest Companies; Guest Composers; Guest Directors; Guest Ensembles; Guest Instructors; Guest Musicians; Guest Soloists; Guest Speakers; Instructors; Local Artists; Multimedia; Music; Organization Contracts; Original Music Scores; Sign Language Translators; Singers; Soloists; Student Interns
Founded: 1915
Specialized Field: Symphony; Orchestra
Status: Non-Professional
Paid Staff: 1
Volunteer Staff: 5
Paid Artists: 18
Non-paid Artists: 55
Budget: $20,000
Income Sources: Women's Committee; ticket sales
Performs At: McGaw Chapel
Affiliations: Colllege of Wooster
Annual Attendance: 6,000 per concert
Organization Type: Performing; Resident

1574
CHAMBER MUSIC YELLOW SPRINGS
Box 448
Yellow Springs, OH 45387
Phone: 937-374-8800
Fax: 937-767-9350
e-mail: info@cmys.org
Web Site: www.cmys.org
Officers:
  President: Mary T White
Mission: Performing professional chamber music of high quality.
Founded: 1983
Specialized Field: Chamber
Status: Professional; Nonprofit
Budget: $25,000-$30,000
Income Sources: Donations: Grants; Tickets
Performs At: First Presbyterian Church
Seating Capacity: 240
Organization Type: Sponsoring

1575
YOUNGSTOWN SYMPHONY ORCHESTRA
260 W Federal Street
Youngstown, OH 44503
Phone: 330-744-4269
Fax: 330-744-1441
e-mail: symphony@youngstownsymphony.com
Web Site: www.youngstownsymphony.com
Officers:
  Chairman of the Board: Gary Balog
  President/CEO: Patricia A Syak
  Vice Chairman: Lewis Kasper
  Secretary: Gloria Detesco
  Treasurer: James Baker
Management:
  Facility Booking Agent: Jane Beckner
  Therater/Facility Manager: Joe Woronka
Utilizes: Guest Composers; Guest Musicians; Singers; Special Technical Talent
Founded: 1931
Specialized Field: Orchestra; Educational
Status: Professional; Nonprofit
Paid Staff: 7
Paid Artists: 500
Budget: $200,000
Income Sources: American Symphony Orchestra League
Performs At: Youngstown Symphony Center; Edward W. Powers Auditorium
Annual Attendance: 131,347
Facility Category: Auditorium
Type of Stage: Proscenium
Stage Dimensions: 60 x 40
Seating Capacity: 2310
Year Built: 1931
Year Remodeled: 1968
Cost: 1.5 Million
Rental Contact: Theatre Coordinator Leslie A. Brown
Organization Type: Performing; Resident; Educational
Resident Groups: Youngstown Symphony Orchestra

Oklahoma

1576
BARTLESVILLE SYMPHONY ORCHESTRA
415 S. Dewey
Suite 215
Bartlesville, OK 74003
Mailing Address: P.O. Box 263, Bartlesville, OK 74005
Phone: 918-336-7177
Fax: 918-333-7989
e-mail: lauren@bartlesvillesymphony.org
Web Site: www.bartlesvillesymphony.org

INSTRUMENTAL MUSIC / Oklahoma

Officers:
- **President:** Bill Riley
- **Vice President:** Mark White
- **Secretary:** John Mallet
- **Treasurer:** Doug Divelbiss
- **Board Member:** Price Connors

Management:
- **Music Director/Conductor:** Lauren Green
- **General Manager:** Lee GrothOlson
- **Director of Development:** Linda Cubbage

Mission: Offering community musicians and audiences an opportunity to experience symphonic professional quality symphonic musical expirences and world-class quest soloists.
Utilizes: Guest Artists; Singers
Founded: 1957
Specialized Field: Symphony; Orchestra
Status: Non-Professional; Nonprofit
Paid Staff: 1
Volunteer Staff: 2
Paid Artists: 20
Non-paid Artists: 45
Budget: $200,000
Income Sources: Tickets; Donations; Fundraising Products
Performs At: Bartlesville Community Center
Annual Attendance: 4,000
Facility Category: Auditoriuam
Type of Stage: Proscenium
Seating Capacity: 1700
Year Built: 1982
Cost: $ 13 Million
Organization Type: Resident

1577
OKLAHOMA MOZART INTERNATIONAL FESTIVAL
415 S Dewey
Suite 100
Bartlesville, OK 74003
Phone: 918-336-9900
Fax: 918-336-9525
e-mail: boxoffice@okmozart.com
Web Site: www.okmozart.com

Officers:
- **Chairman:** Charles Daniels
- **Vice Chair:** Mike Wilt
- **Secretary:** Michel Duncan
- **Treasurer:** Linda K. Jones
- **Board Member:** Thad Kent

Management:
- **Artistic Director:** Constantine Kitsopoulos
- **Artistic Administrator:** Adria Benjamin
- **Executive Director:** Dr. Randy Thompson
- **Development Director:** Jacky Manning
- **Marketing & Public Relations Direct:** Linda Keller

Utilizes: Actors; Artists-in-Residence; Collaborations; Commissioned Music; Dance Companies; Fine Artists; Grant Writers; Guest Accompanists; Guest Companies; Guest Composers; Guest Conductors; Guest Directors; Guest Instructors; Guest Musicians; Multi Collaborations; Multimedia; Original Music Scores; Sign Language Translators; Singers; Touring Companies
Founded: 1985
Specialized Field: Ensemble; Mozart; Chamber; Orchestra
Status: Professional; Nonprofit
Paid Staff: 8
Volunteer Staff: 800
Paid Artists: 150
Non-paid Artists: 300
Budget: $995,000
Income Sources: Oklahoma State Arts Council; National Endowment for the Arts; Individuals; Businesses
Performs At: Bartlesville Community Center
Annual Attendance: 30,000
Facility Category: Concert Hall, Community Center
Seating Capacity: 1700
Year Built: 1982
Organization Type: Sponsoring
Resident Groups: New York Orchestra

1578
ENID-PHILLIPS SYMPHONY ORCHESTRA
301 West Broadway
Enid, OK 73701
Phone: 405-237-9646
Fax: 580-616-2934
e-mail: enidsymphony@att.net
Web Site: www.enidsymphony.org

Officers:
- **President:** Janet Cordell
- **Vice President:** Linda Pickens
- **Secretary:** Rruth Dobbs
- **Treasurer:** David Hume
- **Board Member:** Joan Allen

Management:
- **Music and Executive Director:** Douglas Newell
- **Administrative Associate:** Carolyn Pearson
- **Site Manager:** David Dougherty

Utilizes: Guest Artists
Founded: 1906
Specialized Field: Symphony; Orchestra
Status: Professional; Nonprofit
Income Sources: American Symphony Orchestra League
Performs At: Eugene S. Briggs Auditorium
Organization Type: Performing; Educational

1579
LAWTON PHILHARMONIC ORCHESTRA
6425 NW Cache Road
Suite 115
Lawton, OK 73502
Mailing Address: PO Box 1473, Lawton, OK 73502
Phone: 580-531-5043
e-mail: lawtonphil3647@sbcglobal.net
Web Site: www.lawtonphil.org

Officers:
- **President:** David Jackson
- **First Vice President:** Jason Buschman
- **Second Vice President:** Cindy O'Connor
- **Treasurer:** Bob Zwaan
- **Recording Secretary:** Barbara Moeller

Management:
- **Music Director & Conductor:** Jon Kalbfleisch
- **Executive Director:** Peggy Hightower
- **Musician personnel Manager:** Arthur Busby
- **Production Manager:** Ryan Scott

Mission: To provide high quality cultural experiences to Southwest Oklahoma.
Utilizes: Guest Artists
Founded: 1962
Specialized Field: Symphony; Orchestra
Status: Professional
Paid Staff: 3
Volunteer Staff: 40
Paid Artists: 62
Budget: $260,000
Income Sources: Box office; Grants; Private donations
Performs At: McMahon Memorial Auditorium
Affiliations: American Symphony Orchestra League
Annual Attendance: 10,000
Facility Category: Concert Hall
Seating Capacity: 1,560
Year Built: 1962
Year Remodeled: 2000
Organization Type: Performing; Touring; Resident; Educational; Sponsoring

1580
JAZZ IN JUNE
PO Box 2405
Norman, OK 73070
Phone: 405-325-3388
e-mail: info@jazzinjune.org
Web Site: www.jazzinjune.org

Management:
- **Executive Director:** Phoebe Morales
- **Director of Development:** Norman H. Hammon
- **Webmaster:** Mark Mitchell

Mission: To offer Oklahoma residents a jazz festival.
Utilizes: Singers
Founded: 1985
Specialized Field: Jazz; Ensemble
Status: Professional; Semi-Professional
Income Sources: American Federation of Musicians
Organization Type: Performing

1581
UNIVERSITY OF OKLAHOMA SYMPHONY ORCHESTRA
University of Oklahoma School of Music
500 West Boyd Room 138
Norman, OK 73019-2071
Phone: 405-325-2081
Fax: 405-325-7574
e-mail: chrisdavidwestover@ou.edu
Web Site: ousymphony.ou.edu/

Officers:
- **Assistant Director:** Brian Britt

Management:
- **Director of Orchestra and Opera St:** Jonathan Shames
- **Music School Director:** Dr Steven Curtis
- **Personnel Director:** Shara Long
- **Operations Director:** Timothy Verville

Founded: 1920
Specialized Field: Orchestra; Ensemble
Paid Staff: 6
Performs At: Catlett Music Center

1582
CHAMBER MUSIC IN OKLAHOMA
PO Box 54624
Oklahoma City, OK 73154-1624
Phone: 405-974-3333
Fax: 405-974-3844
Web Site: www.cmok.org

Officers:
- **Vice President & Treasurer:** Brad Ferguson
- **Vice President & Special Projects:** Mary J Rutherford
- **Secretary:** Martha Blaine

Management:
- **Artists & Bookings:** Dr Mark A Everett
- **Publicity & Webmaster:** Dr. H Dean Everett

Founded: 1960
Specialized Field: Chamber
Status: Nonprofit
Budget: $20,000-$35,000
Performs At: Christ the King Church

1583
GO FOR BAROQUE
PO Box 20178
Oklahoma City, OK 73156

INSTRUMENTAL MUSIC / Oregon

Phone: 405-840-0278
e-mail: pgpayne@goforbaroque.org
Web Site: www.goforbaroque.org
Officers:
   Chair: James Pickel
   Vice-Chair: Holbrook Lawson
   Secretary: Jeannette Sias
Management:
   Executive Director: Kim Baker
   Director of Cultural Development: Molly O'Connor
   Deputy Director: Karen Douglas
   Executive Assistant/Office Manager: Margie Stephens
   Grants Director: Meleia Williamson
Mission: To offer formal baroque concerts and young people's concerts.
Founded: 1982
Specialized Field: Chamber; Ensemble; Baroque
Status: Professional
Organization Type: Performing; Touring; Educational

1584
OKLAHOMA CITY PHILHARMONIC ORCHESTRA

428 W California
Suite 210
Oklahoma City, OK 73102
Phone: 405-232-7575
Fax: 405-232-4353
e-mail: info@okcphilharmonic.org
Web Site: www.okcphilharmonic.org
Officers:
   President: Kip Welch
   President Elect: John Higginbotham
   Vice President: Teresa Cooper
   Treasurer: Mike Dickinson
   Secretary: Renate Wiggin
Management:
   Music Director/Conductor: Joel Levine
   Executive Director: Eddie Walker
   General Manager: Kris Markes
   Finance Director: Daniel Hardt
   Stage Manager: J. Leroy Newman
Mission: Performing classical, orchestral, and popular music; entertaining and educating; enhancing the cultural environment of Oklahoma City as well as the state.
Utilizes: Guest Artists; Singers
Founded: 1988
Specialized Field: Symphony; Orchestra
Status: Professional; Nonprofit
Performs At: Rose State Performing Arts Theatre
Affiliations: American Symphony Orchestra League; Allied Arts of Oklahoma City
Organization Type: Performing; Resident

1585
CHAMBER MUSIC TULSA

2210 South Main
Tulsa, OK 74114
Phone: 918-587-3802
Fax: 918-587-0698
e-mail: executivedirector@chambermusictulsa.org
Web Site: www.chambermusictulsa.org
Officers:
   President: Allen Keenan
   Vice President: Ginny Ayling
   Treasurer: Jane Mudgett
   Secretary: Cheryl Cornelius-Ochs
   Past President: Pam Carter
Management:
   Executive Director: Bruce Sorrell
   Manager: Pamela Lucas
   Music Advisor: Marc Gottlieb
Mission: To continue cultivating audiences to enjoy chamber music.
Founded: 1954
Specialized Field: Chamber
Status: Professional; Nonprofit
Income Sources: Chamber Music America
Performs At: John H. Williams Theater; Tulsa Performing Arts Center
Organization Type: Performing; Educational

1586
TULSA YOUTH SYMPHONY

1409 S Elwood Avenue
Tulsa, OK 74119
Phone: 918-592-7725
e-mail: ron.wheeler@tyso.org
Web Site: www.tyso.org
Officers:
   President: Steve Curry
   Treasurer: Martin Howerton
   Secretary: Patricia Davis
Management:
   Co-Conductor: Ronald Wheeler
   Financial Manager: Sue Loomis
   Co-Conductor: Rick Wagner
   Conductor: Pete Peterson
Mission: Tulsa Youth Symphony Orchestra aims to encourage and develop students' musical abilities through rehearsal, concert performance and regular contact with professional musicians, offering training and performance opportunities.
Utilizes: Guest Artists
Founded: 1963
Specialized Field: Youth Symphony; Chamber
Status: Non-Professional; Nonprofit
Paid Staff: 85
Income Sources: American Symphony Orchestra League (Youth Orchestra Division); Tulsa Philharmonic
Performs At: Union High School Performing Arts Center
Seating Capacity: 1,900
Organization Type: Performing; Touring; Educational
Resident Groups: Philharmonic Society; Tulsa Area Youth Association

Oregon

1587
CHAMBER MUSIC CONCERTS

SOSC
1250 Siskiyou Boulevard
Ashland, OR 97520
Phone: 541-552-6154
Fax: 541-552-6380
e-mail: Director@ChamberMusicConcerts.org
Web Site: www.chambermusicconcerts.org/
Officers:
   President: Alexis Packer
   Vice President: Karen Clark
   Secretary: Marilyn Anderson
   Board Member: Ai DeVore
   Board Member: Wayne Thomas
Management:
   Founder/Director: Dr Gregory Fowler
   Assistant: Lesley Pohl
   Executive Director: Jody Schmidt
Mission: To offer Southern Oregon residents the highest possible quality of chamber music.
Founded: 1984
Specialized Field: Chamber
Status: Professional; Nonprofit
Performs At: SOSC Music Building Recital Hall
Organization Type: Performing

1588
ROGUE VALLEY SYMPHONY

SOU Music Hall
1250 Siskiyou Boulevard
Ashland, OR 97520
Phone: 541-552-6354
Fax: 541-552-6353
e-mail: office@rvsymphony.org
Web Site: www.rvsymphony.org
Officers:
   President: Paul Smith
   Secretary: Mary Jo Bergstrom
   Treasurer: Lynn Thompson
   Board Member: Helen Hanson
   Board Member: Sarah Klein
Management:
   Executive Director: Cybele Abbett
   Music Director/Conductor: Martin Majkut
   Patron and Marketing Services Admin: Kristin Kessler
   Personnel Manager: Bruce Dresser
   Publications Manager: Nancy Golden
Utilizes: Choreographers; Commissioned Composers; Dancers; Guest Musicians; Instructors; Sign Language Translators; Singers
Founded: 1966
Specialized Field: Symphony
Paid Staff: 6
Paid Artists: 73
Budget: $500,000
Performs At: SOU Music Recital Hall
Annual Attendance: 20,000
Facility Category: 3 Facilities

1589
CHAMBER MUSIC CORVALLIS

5576 SW Windflower Drive
Corvallis, OR 97333
Phone: 541-752-7222
e-mail: rverhoogen@mac.com
Web Site: www.violins.org
Officers:
   Chairman: Robert Verhoogen
   Vice Chair: Dave Fiske
   Treasurer: Allen Meyer
   Secretary: Sandra Verhoogen
Management:
   Music Director: Chris Rochester, mc_rochester@gmail.com
   Music Director: Carol Fischler, fischler@teleport.com
   Agent Contact: Stefanie Breder-Albright
   Subscriptions/Contributions: Carol Williams
Mission: Present chamber music concerts; outreach to k-12 students
Founded: 1958
Specialized Field: Chamber Music
Status: Non-Profit
Volunteer Staff: 25
Non-paid Artists: 7
Budget: $35,000-$70,000
Income Sources: Ticket Sales; Donations; Grants
Performs At: LaSells Stewart Center; Oregon State University

1590
OSU-CORVALLIS SYMPHONY ORCHESTRA

Corvallis-OSU Symphony
PO Box 1582
Corvallis, OR 97339

INSTRUMENTAL MUSIC / Oregon

Phone: 541-752-2361
Fax: 541-737-4268
e-mail: advertising@cosusymphony.org
Web Site: www.cosusymphony.org
Management:
    Music Director/Conductor: Marian Carlson
Specialized Field: Orchestra

1591
EMERALD CHAMBER PLAYERS
3080 Potter
Eugene, OR 97405
Phone: 541-344-0483
e-mail: ecplayers@comcast.net
Web Site:
home.comcast.net/~tpgettys/ECP_homepage.html
Management:
    Convener: Orval Etter
Mission: To provide amateurs with opportunities to play and perform chamber music.
Founded: 1962
Specialized Field: Orchestra; Chamber; Ensemble
Status: Non-Professional; Nonprofit
Organization Type: Performing

1592
EUGENE SYMPHONY ASSOCIATION
115 W 8th Avenue
Suite 115
Eugene, OR 97401
Phone: 541-687-9487
Fax: 541-687-0527
e-mail: Penny.park@eugenesymphony.org
Web Site: www.eugenesymphony.org
Officers:
    President: Dunny Sorensen
    Vice President: Matthew Shapiro
    Secretary: Jane Eyre McDonald
    Treasurer: Warren Barnes
    Past President: Mary Ann Hanson
Management:
    Music Director/Conductor: Daniel Rachev
    Chorus Director: Sharon Paul
    Executive Director: Scott Frank
    General Manager: Ness Zolan
    Chorus Manager: Amy Adams
Mission: Enriching lives through the power of music.
Utilizes: Commissioned Composers; Composers-in-Residence; Fine Artists; Guest Accompanists; Guest Artists; Guest Directors; Guest Musicians; Guest Writers; Instructors; Original Music Scores; Resident Artists; Sign Language Translators; Singers
Founded: 1966
Specialized Field: Symphony; Orchestra
Status: Professional; Nonprofit
Paid Staff: 9
Volunteer Staff: 160
Paid Artists: 82
Budget: $2.2 million
Income Sources: Ticket Revenues; Contributions
Performs At: Hult Center for the Performing Arts
Facility Category: Hult Center for the Performing Arts
Seating Capacity: 2400
Year Built: 1982
Organization Type: Performing; Resident

1593
OREGON BACH FESTIVAL
1787 Agate
St #V127
Eugene, OR 97403
Mailing Address: 1257 University of Oregon, Eugene, OR 97403-1257
Phone: 541-346-5666
Fax: 541-346-5669
Toll-free: 800-457-1486
e-mail: bachfest@uoregon.edu
Web Site: www.oregonbachfestival.com
Officers:
    Chair: Dave Frosaker
    Vice-Chair: Don Harris
    Secretary: Mary K. Miller
Management:
    Director of Artistic Administration: Michael Anderson
    Artistic Director: Mathew Halls
    Director of Marketing & Communicati: April Libman
    Director Emeritus: Helmuth Rilling
    Chorus Master: Kathy Saltzman Romey
Mission: Further the work, spirit and influence of J.S. Bach.
Utilizes: Singers
Founded: 1970
Specialized Field: Choral-Orchestral, Chamber Music
Paid Staff: 8
Volunteer Staff: 200
Paid Artists: 250
Budget: $2.5 million
Income Sources: Ticket Sales; Sponsorships; Donations
Performs At: Concert Halls
Affiliations: University of Oregon; Chorus America; League of Amer Orchs
Annual Attendance: 42,000
Facility Category: Concert Hall
Type of Stage: Proscenium
Seating Capacity: 2500/550
Organization Type: Performing; Resident; Educational

1594
OREGON MOZART PLAYERS
1590 Williamette Street
Eugene, OR 97440
Mailing Address: P.O. Box 11474, Eugene, OR 97440
Phone: 541-345-6648
Fax: 541-345-7849
e-mail: omp@oregonmozartplayers.org
Web Site: www.oregonmozartplayers.org
Officers:
    President: Charles Wright
    Past President: David Guy
    Secretary: Erin Carey
    Treasurer: Theodore Palmer
    Board Member: Dale Mueller
Management:
    Executive Director: Jeffrey Eaton
Mission: To offer chamber orchestra music; to provide talented, local musicians with opportunities to perform as orchestra members and soloists as well as in chamber ensembles.
Utilizes: Guest Artists; Singers
Founded: 1982
Specialized Field: Orchestra; Chamber; Mozart
Status: Professional; Nonprofit
Performs At: Hult Center For The Performing Arts; Beall Concert
Organization Type: Performing; Touring; Resident; Educational

1595
PACIFIC UNIVERSITY COMMUNITY WIND ENSEMBLE
Pacific University
Music Department
Forest Grove, OR 97116
Phone: 559-453-2267
Fax: 503-359-2910
Web Site: www.fresno.edu/department/music/performance_groups
Management:
    Conductor: Patricia DeBenedetto
Mission: To provide music students with educational training; to offer community members a performing outlet.
Founded: 1849
Specialized Field: Orchestra; Chamber; Wind Ensemble
Status: Non-Professional; Nonprofit
Performs At: University Center
Organization Type: Performing; Resident; Educational

1596
MT HOOD JAZZ FESTIVAL
PO Box 226
Gresham, OR 97030
Phone: 503-669-1937
Fax: 503-667-2848
e-mail: susie.jone52@frontier.com
Web Site: www.mthoodjazz.com
Officers:
    President: Susie Jones
    Vice President: Susie O'Halloran
    Treasurer: KerryAnn O'Halloran
    Secretary: Janine Ross
    Board Member: Bill Whitney
Mission: To provide for the performance of contemporary and classical music and to help promote the fine arts in the Eastern part of Multnoman, Clackamps and Clark counties.
Specialized Field: Pops; Orchestra
Paid Artists: 65
Performs At: Auditorium

1597
GRANDE RONDE SYMPHONY ORCHESTRA
Eastern Oregon University
One University Boulevard
La Grande, OR 97850-2899
Phone: 541-963-9066
Fax: 541-962-3596
e-mail: music@eou.edu
Web Site: www.granderondesymphony.org
Management:
    Music Director and Conductor: Leandro Espinosa
Specialized Field: Orchestra
Performs At: Loso Hall

1598
BRITT FESTIVALS
216 W. Main Street
Medford, OR 97501
Mailing Address: PO Box 1124, Medford, OR 97501
Phone: 541-779-0847
Fax: 541-776-3712
Toll-free: 800-882-7488
e-mail: info@brittfest.org
Web Site: www.brittfest.org
Officers:
    Chairman: Matt Pattern
    Vice-Chairman: Mike Burrill Jr

INSTRUMENTAL MUSIC / Oregon

Treasurer: Dave Bernard
Secretary: Kelsy Ausland
Board Member: Jason Anderson
Management:
  Director of House Operations: Bow Seltzer
  Box Office Manager: Marie Carbone
  Director of Programming: Mike Sturgill
  Marketing Director: Sara King Cole
  Director of Performing Arts: Angela Warren
Mission: To present and sponsor, in Southern Oregon, performing arts of the highest quality for the education, enrichment and enjoyment of all.
Utilizes: Commissioned Music; Dance Companies; Dancers; Guest Musical Directors; Guest Musicians; Multi Collaborations; Multimedia; Original Music Scores; Singers; Special Technical Talent; Theatre Companies
Founded: 1963
Specialized Field: Classical; Jazz; Pops; Country; Folk Music; Bluegrass; World Music; Show Tunes
Paid Staff: 12
Volunteer Staff: 600
Performs At: Outdoor Auditorium
Annual Attendance: 70,000
Facility Category: Outdoor Amphitheatre
Seating Capacity: 2200
Year Built: 1963
Year Remodeled: 1992

1599
OREGON EAST SYMPHONY
345 SW 4th St.
Pendleton, OR 97801
Mailing Address: PO Box 1436, Pendleton, OR 97801
Phone: 541-276-0320
Fax: 541-278-6114
e-mail: oesofficeinfo@gmail.com
Web Site: www.oregoneastsymphony.org
Management:
  Executive Director: Michelle Sitz
  Programs Manager: Cathy Muller
  Publications Director: Tammy Burnett
  Office Support: Phyllis Jerome
  Grants Coordinator: Janet Miller
Utilizes: Dancers; Five Seasonal Concerts; Grant Writers; Guest Accompanists; Guest Composers; Guest Directors; Guest Musical Directors; Guest Musicians; Guest Writers; Local Artists; Music; Original Music Scores; Sign Language Translators; Singers; Soloists
Founded: 1976
Specialized Field: Symphony
Paid Staff: 2
Volunteer Staff: 10
Paid Artists: 70
Non-paid Artists: 30
Budget: $125,000
Income Sources: Sales; Grants; Sponsorship
Performs At: Vert Auditorium
Annual Attendance: 4,000
Facility Category: Hall
Type of Stage: Wooden
Stage Dimensions: 40 x 30
Seating Capacity: 750
Year Built: 1925
Year Remodeled: 1995

1600
CHAMBER MUSIC NORTHWEST
522 SW Fifth Avenue
Suite 920
Portland, OR 97204
Phone: 503-294-6400
Fax: 503-294-1690
e-mail: info@cmnw.org
Web Site: www.cmnw.org
Officers:
  President: Karen Deveney
  Vice-President: Ivan Inger
  Secretary: Jacqueline Bloom
  Treasurer: William Langley
  Immediate Past President: Bill Dameron
Management:
  Executive Director: Peter J. Bilotta, CFRE
  Artistic Director: David Shifrin
  Program and Administrative Assistan: Erica Liebert
  Finance & Administration Director: Katherine King
  Development Director: Noreen Murdock
Mission: To present an annual summer music festival (five weeks/25 concerts) with world renowned performers in residence; to present concerts and educational activities on a year-round basis.
Founded: 1971
Specialized Field: Chamber; Ensemble; Classical Music
Status: Professional; Nonprofit
Paid Staff: 6
Volunteer Staff: 50
Paid Artists: 75
Budget: $1 million
Affiliations: Kaul Auditorium at Reed College; Cabell Theatre at Catlin Gabel School
Annual Attendance: 19,000
Facility Category: Small Concert Hall (private college)
Seating Capacity: 550
Year Built: 1998
Organization Type: Performing

1601
CHAMBER MUSIC SOCIETY OF OREGON
PO Box 2911
Portland, OR 97208-2911
Phone: 503-285-7621
e-mail: info@cmsomus.org
Web Site: www.cmsomus.org
Officers:
  President: Guy Snyder
  Vice-President: John Burkhardt
  Secretary: Joshua Bouchard
  Treasurer: Mary Wawrukiewicz
  Board Member: Larry Greep
Management:
  Music Director and Conductor: Dr. Donald L. Appert
Mission: To promote music in our schools for its value in teaching children how to learn.
Utilizes: Singers
Founded: 1973
Specialized Field: Orchestra; Chamber; Ensemble
Status: Non-Professional; Nonprofit
Performs At: St. Philip Neri Church; Hood River Middle School
Organization Type: Performing; Resident; Educational

1602
FRIENDS OF CHAMBER MUSIC
211 SE Caruthers St
Suite 202
Portland, OR 97214
Phone: 503-224-9842
Fax: 503-228-1407
e-mail: info@focm.org
Web Site: www.focm.org
Officers:
  President: Suzanne Rague
  Immediate Past President: Frank McNamara
  Vice-President: John Strege
  Secretary: Ken Herrick
  Treasurer: William Dolan
Management:
  Executive Director: Pat Zagelow
  Operations Manager: Lori Fitch
Mission: To present a season of five chamber-music concerts annually; to sponsor outreach activities, including workshops and master classes.
Specialized Field: Chamber
Status: Nonprofit
Organization Type: Presenting

1603
FRIENDS OF CHAMBER MUSIC
211 SE Caruthers St
Suite 202
Portland, OR 97214
Phone: 503-224-9842
Fax: 503-228-1407
e-mail: info@focm.org
Web Site: www.focm.org
Officers:
  President: Suzanne Rague
  Immediate Past President: Frank McNamara
  Vice-President: John Strege
  Secretary: Ken Herrick
  Treasurer: William Dolan
Management:
  Executive Director: Pat Zagelow
  Operations Manager: Lori Fitch
Utilizes: Guest Directors; Multimedia; Original Music Scores
Specialized Field: Chamber
Budget: $400,000
Income Sources: Tickets; Contributors
Performs At: Lincoln Performance Hall; Kaul Auditorium
Annual Attendance: 7,000
Type of Stage: Proscenium
Seating Capacity: 476
Year Remodeled: 2010

1604
METROPOLITAN YOUTH SYMPHONY
PO Box 5254
Portland, OR 97208
Phone: 503-239-4566
Toll-free: 888-752-9697
Web Site: www.metroyouthsymphony.org
Management:
  Music Director/Conductor: Lajos Balogh
  Conductor Symphonic Band: Dr. John K Richards
  Conductor Concert Orchestra: Bill Hunt
  Associate Conductor: Mike Ott
  Associate Conductor: Nita Van Pelt
  Conductor Preparatory Band: Larry Wells
  Conductor Overture Orchestra: Kathie Reed
Specialized Field: Youth Symphony; Educational
Performs At: Arlene Schnitzer Concert Hall; Intermediate Theater

1605
OREGON SYMPHONY
921 SW Washington
Suite 200
Portland, OR 97205
Phone: 503-228-4294
Fax: 503-228-4150
e-mail: Symphony@orsymphony.org
Web Site: www.orsymphony.org
Officers:
  Chair: Karl Smith
  Vice Chair: J. Clayton Hering
  Vice Chair: Walter E. Weyler
  Secretary: Gerald R. Hulsman

INSTRUMENTAL MUSIC / Oregon

Treasurer: Ted Austin
Management:
  Operations Manager: Jacob Wade
  Artistic Administrator: Charles Calmer
  Director of Operations: Susan Nielsen
  Program Director: Monica Hayes
  Director of Musician Resources: Bridget Kelly
Founded: 1896
Specialized Field: Symphony Orchestra
Paid Staff: 34
Paid Artists: 79
Budget: $15 million
Income Sources: Ticket Sales; Contributions; Grants

1606
PORTLAND BAROQUE ORCHESTRA
1020 SW Taylor Street
Suite 200
Portland, OR 97205
Phone: 503-222-6000
Fax: 503-226-6635
e-mail: admin@pbo.org
Web Site: www.pbo.org
Officers:
  Chairman: William Willingham
  Secretary: Laura Cunningham
  Treasurer: Todd Hubbell
  Board Member: Jerry Braun
  Board Member: Aron Faegre
Management:
  Artistic Director: Monica Huggett
  Executive Director: Tom Cirillo
  Director of Marketing and Developme: Mark Powell
  Operations Manager: Andrea Hess
  Stage Manager: Robin Greenwood
Utilizes: Guest Accompanists; Guest Musical Directors; Guest Musicians; Local Artists; Multimedia; Original Music Scores
Founded: 1984
Specialized Field: Baroque; Orchestra; Classical on Period Instruments
Status: Tax-exempt

1607
PORTLAND CHAMBER ORCHESTRA ASSOCIATION
PO Box 9024
Portland, OR 97207
Mailing Address: PO Box 9024, Portland OR 97207
Phone: 503-205-0715
Fax: 503-227-7066
e-mail: info@portlandchamberorchestra.org
Web Site: www.portlandchamberorchestra.org
Officers:
  Board President: Cristina Yen
  Vice President: Robert Kingdom
  Secretary: Jerry Hertel
Management:
  Director: Mildred Berthelsdorf, MD
  Conductor: Registered Asso Armore
  Artistic Director: Yaacov Bergman
  Cellist: Katherine Schultz
  Concert Soprano: Bonnie Hensley
Mission: To present free and/or low fee concerts of fine chamber music by outstanding local talent.
Founded: 1946
Specialized Field: Classical; Chamber
Paid Artists: 30
Budget: $44,948
Income Sources: Private; Foundations; Grants; Endowments; Business/corporate donations; Individual donations
Performs At: Scottish Rite Center

Annual Attendance: 255/concert
Facility Category: Performing Arts Center
Type of Stage: Raised
Seating Capacity: 400

1608
PORTLAND COLUMBIA SYMPHONY
PO Box 6559
Portland, OR 97228
Phone: 503-234-4077
Fax: 503-234-4077
e-mail: cso@pacifier.com
Web Site: www.columbiasymphony.org
Officers:
  President: Chalayane Woodke
  Vice President: Ann van Bever
  Secretary: Audrey Julian
  Treasurer: Cindy Bartholomew
  Orchestra Rep: Craig Johnston
Management:
  Executive Director: Betsy Hatton, cso@pacifier.com
  Principal Guest Conductor: Huw Edwards, cso@pacifier.com
  Operations Manager: Kate Rafter
  Production: Danielle McEwan
  Librarian: Sara Pyne
Utilizes: Community Members; Community Talent; Fine Artists; Guest Accompanists; Guest Companies; Guest Composers; Guest Designers; Guest Musical Directors; Guest Musicians; Local Artists; Local Artists & Directors; Organization Contracts; Original Music Scores; Paid Performers; Singers; Soloists; Visual Designers
Founded: 1982
Specialized Field: Orchestra
Paid Staff: 2
Volunteer Staff: 40
Paid Artists: 65
Non-paid Artists: 3
Performs At: Auditorium
Facility Category: Church
Seating Capacity: 600

1609
PORTLAND YOUTH PHILHARMONIC ASSOCIATION
9320 SW Barbur Blvd.
Suite 140
Portland, OR 97219
Phone: 503-223-5939
Fax: 503-223-5003
e-mail: information@portlandyouthphil.org
Web Site: www.portlandyouthphil.org
Officers:
  President: Joseph G. Rakoski
  Vice President: Julie Kim
  Vice President: Sue AuWerter
  Vice President: Gene E. Foley, Jr
  Vice President: Annett Duncan
Management:
  Musical Director: David Hattner
  Finance Manager: Sara Steinman, CPA
  Marketing and Community Relations M: Olivia Kipper
  Office Admin/Mark Assistant: Kathryn Walters
  Operations Manager: Ann Cockerham
Mission: It is the purpose of the Portland Youth Philharmonic to maintain the finest possible resident youth orchestra in order to inspire, train and educate young people in the performance and appreciation of symphonic music and to provide a cultural asset to the community.
Founded: 1924

Specialized Field: Youth Philharmonic; Ensemble
Status: Non-Professional; Nonprofit
Paid Staff: 7
Non-paid Artists: 206
Budget: $500,000
Income Sources: American Symphony Orchestra League (Youth Orchestra Division)
Performs At: Arlene Schnitzer Concert Hall; Civic Auditorium
Organization Type: Performing; Touring; Resident; Educational

1610
ROSE CITY CHAMBER ORCHESTRA
PO Box 6652
Portland, OR 97228-6652
Phone: 503-475-8691
e-mail: mary@rowellmusic.net
Web Site: rosecity.org
Mission: The Rose City Chamber Orchestra was formed in Portland, Oregon by a group of dedicated musicians with the goal to achieve the highest quality musical experience, enjoyed by both performers and the community.
Founded: 1998
Specialized Field: Chamber; Orchestra

1611
SINFONIA CONCERTANTE ORCHESTRA
1640 SE Holly Street
Portland, OR 97214
Phone: 503-231-1421
Fax: 503-236-1655
e-mail: sco@sinfoniapdx.org
Web Site: sinfoniapdx.org
Management:
  Artistic Director & Conductor: Stefan Minde
Mission: To provide the community of the greater metropolitan area with outstanding performances that preserve the classical music tradition. To support mentoring and educational programs for students.
Founded: 1990
Specialized Field: Chamber; Orchestra
Volunteer Staff: 20
Performs At: Lewis & Clark College; Evans Hall; St. Mary's Cathedral

1612
UMPQUA SYMPHONY ASSOCIATION
PO Box 241
Roseburg, OR 97308-2782
Phone: 541-957-1317
e-mail: info@umpquasymphony.org
Web Site: www.umpquasymphony.org
Officers:
  President: Mary Lee Hope
  Vice-president: Sarah Sheeran
  Secretary: Jean Melo
  Treasurer: Rosemary Lint
  Board Member: John Paulson
Management:
  Executive Director: John Granholm
Mission: To offer the local community classical music.
Founded: 1955
Specialized Field: Symphony; Orchestra; Chamber; Ensemble
Status: Nonprofit
Performs At: Umpqua Community College Auditorium
Organization Type: Sponsoring

1613
CAMERATA MUSICA
PO Box 2782
Salem, OR 97302

Phone: 503-364-3929
Fax: 503-362-3290
e-mail: gstruble@willamette.edu
Web Site: cameratamusica.org
Officers:
    President: George Struble
    Vice President: David Gortner
    Secretary: Suzanne Lamon
    Treasurer: Evan Lloyd
Mission: To present free chamber music concerts by local professional musicians. Concerts presented on Sunday afternoons, seven Sundays a year.
Utilizes: Commissioned Composers; Community Talent; Guest Accompanists; Guest Directors; Guest Instructors; Guest Musical Directors; Instructors; Multimedia; Original Music Scores; Singers
Founded: 1976
Specialized Field: Chamber
Status: Professional; Non-Professional; Nonprofit
Volunteer Staff: 3
Paid Artists: 30
Budget: $5,000
Income Sources: Patrons; Grants; Memorial Gifts; Donations at concerts
Performs At: Salem Public Library Lecture Hall
Affiliations: Mid-Valley Arts Council, Salem
Annual Attendance: 1,600
Seating Capacity: 300
Year Built: 1990
Rental Contact: Camerata Musica (free)
Organization Type: Performing; Sponsoring

1614
SALEM CHAMBER ORCHESTRA
388 State Street SE
Suite 475
Salem, OR 97301
Phone: 503-480-1128
Fax: 503-779-2717
e-mail: info@salemchamberorchestra.org
Web Site: www.salemchamberorchestra.org
Officers:
    President: Jenny Gleason
    Vice President: Judith Audley
    Treasurer: Sally Wood
    Secretary: Paul Gehlar
Management:
    Interim Executive Director: Terra Hurdle
    Principal Conductor: Nikolas Caoile
    Orchestra Manager: Kelsey Kinavey
    Artistic Advisory Committee: Kami Hettwer
    Artistic Advisory Committee: Mike Hettwer
Mission: The Salem Chamber Orchestra, through a partnership between Willamette University and the Salem-Keizer community, enriches the Willamette Valley by promoting classical music that entertains, educates, and provides performance opportunities for Willamette students and area musicians.
Founded: 1984
Specialized Field: Classical; Chamber
Paid Staff: 2
Volunteer Staff: 4
Paid Artists: 15
Non-paid Artists: 35
Performs At: Smith Auditorium Willamette university

1615
SUNRIVER MUSIC FESTIVAL
PO Box 4308
Sunriver, OR 97707
Phone: 541-593-1084
Fax: 541-593-6959
e-mail: vicki@sunrivermusic.org
Web Site: www.sunrivermusic.org
Officers:
    President: Jim Putney
Management:
    Executive Director: Pamela Beezley
    Office Manager: Vicki Udlock
    Ticket Office Manager: Robin Burford
Mission: To present quality performances of classical music and support music education programs for the youth of Central Oregon.
Utilizes: Fine Artists; Guest Lecturers; Multimedia; Original Music Scores
Founded: 1971
Specialized Field: Chamber; Orchestra
Paid Staff: 3
Volunteer Staff: 4
Budget: $250,000
Income Sources: Private; Business; Grants
Performs At: Great Hall
Annual Attendance: 3,500

Pennsylvania

1616
ALLENTOWN SYMPHONY ASSOCIATION
Symphony Hall
23 North 6th Street
Allentown, PA 18101
Phone: 610-432-7961
Fax: 610-432-6735
e-mail: sevans@allentownsymphony.org
Web Site: www.allentownsymphony.org
Officers:
    President: John Berseth
Management:
    Music Director/Conductor: Diane M Whittry
    Executive Director: Sheila Evans
    Finance Director/Business Manager: Ed Rice
    Creative Design Manager: Sharon Schenkel
    VP of Marketing & Community Engagem: Lucy Bloise
Mission: To promote cultural values by providing high quality symphonic music and performing arts events, with broad community appeal, and education concerning them, in Allentown's historic Symphony Hall.
Utilizes: Singers
Founded: 1950
Specialized Field: Symphony; Orchestra
Status: Nonprofit
Income Sources: American Symphony Orchestra League; Association of Pennsylvania Orchestras; Lehigh Valley Arts Council; American Society of Composers, Authors and Publishers
Performs At: Symphony Hall
Annual Attendance: 20,000
Seating Capacity: 1246
Year Built: 1899
Year Remodeled: 1998
Rental Contact: John Ebert
Organization Type: Performing; Educational

1617
ALTOONA SYMPHONY ORCHESTRA
1331 12th Avenue, Suite 107
PO Box 483
Altoona, PA 16603
Phone: 814-943-2500
Fax: 814-943-7115
e-mail: aso.jwhite@atlanticbbn.net
Web Site: www.altoonasymphony.org
Officers:
    President: Al Massod
    VP: Karen Shauf
    Second VP: Phil Sukenik
    Secretary: Edith Isacke
    Assistant Secretary: Judy Halbritter
    Treasurer: Heidi Rexford
    Assistant Treasurer: Robert Lamort
Management:
    Music Director and Conductor: Teresa Cheung
    Executive Director: Pamela J. Snyder Etters
    Personnel Manager/Librarian: Sandy Woodward
    Office Manager: Jessica White
Mission: To provide the highest quality fine arts performances to everyone in our community.
Specialized Field: Orchestra

1618
AMBLER SYMPHONY
PO Box 221
Ambler, PA 19002
e-mail: admin@amblersymphony.org
Web Site: amblersymphony.org
Management:
    Artistic Director, Conductor: Jack Moore
    Publicity Director: Marilyn Carlson
Mission: Founded in 1951 under the guidance of Charles Roberts and the direction of Clifford Geary, the Ambler Symphony Orchestra provides cultural enrichment for the community and an opportunity for area musicians to perform. The Orchestra season consists of three subscription concerts performed at area auditoriums, a Children's Concert dedicated to the young and the young at heart, a Menges Scholarship Concert, and a number of public appearances.
Utilizes: Arrangers; Collaborating Artists; Collaborations; Guest Accompanists; Guest Designers; Multimedia; Music; Paid Performers
Founded: 1951
Specialized Field: Classical, Modern, Instrumental, Orchestra
Status: Non-Profit
Income Sources: Donors, Sponsors
Season: October through June
Performs At: Ambler Theater, Dublin Lutheran Church, Wissahickon Hish School

1619
CHAMBER MUSIC SOCIETY OF BETHLEHEM
PO Box 4336
Bethlehem, PA 18018-0336
Phone: 610-435-7611
Fax: 610-967-6569
e-mail: chambermusic@cmsob.org
Web Site: www.cmsob.org
Officers:
    President: Randy Ziegenfuss
    Vice-President: Allen Zinnes
    Treasurer: Christine Roysdan
    Secretary: Martha Reid
    Board Member: Ursala Levy
Mission: To further appreciation of chamber music by presenting concerts to the Lehigh Valley community featuring the highest quality ensembles.
Founded: 1951
Specialized Field: Chamber
Status: Nonprofit
Volunteer Staff: 15
Budget: $50,000
Income Sources: Donations; Subscriptions; Tickets Sales
Annual Attendance: 1,500
Seating Capacity: 425
Organization Type: Performing; Sponsoring

INSTRUMENTAL MUSIC / Pennsylvania

1620
BUTLER COUNTY SYMPHONY
259 South Main Street
Butler, PA 16001
Phone: 724-283-1402
Fax: 724-283-7782
e-mail: info@butlersymphony.org
Web Site: butlersymphony.org
Officers:
  President: Ed Wadding
  Vice President: Joe Kecskemethy
  Secretary: Chuck Davey
  Treasurer: Charlie Stitt
Management:
  Musical Director, Conductor: Matthew Kraemer
  Concertmaster: Elisa Wicks
Mission: The Butler Orchestral Association was established in 1949, with the first board of directors meeting on December 15. The organization was co-sponsored by the Butler Tuesday Musical Club, the Butler Board of Recreation and the Butler Musical Society. I.M. Jaffe was elected the first president. In each season, the Association sponsors six concerts, one of which is a Family Concert geared to all ages.
Utilizes: Arrangers; Collaborating Artists; Collaborations; Composers; Fine Artists; Guest Accompanists; Guest Companies; Lyricists; Multimedia; Music; Paid Performers; Singers
Founded: 1949
Opened: 1950
Specialized Field: Jazz, Orchestra, Classical, Instrumental
Status: Non-Profit
Income Sources: Sponsors, Donors, Advertisers
Season: October through April

1621
ERIE PHILHARMONIC
609 Walnut Street
Erie, PA 16502
Phone: 814-455-1375
Fax: 814-455-1377
e-mail: info@eriephil.org
Web Site: www.eriephil.org
Management:
  Music Director/Conductor: Daniel Meyer
  Executive Director: Jeffery Collier
  Director of Operations, Librarian &: Nathan Barber
  Director of Marketing & PR: Karen Beardsley-Petit
  Patron Services Manager: Rachel Torgesen
Mission: To offer symphonic, youth orchestra and pops concerts; to provide quality music educational experiences; to exhibit leadership in cultural affairs of the tri-state area.
Utilizes: Collaborations; Commissioned Composers; Composers-in-Residence; Dance Companies; Educators; Grant Writers; Guest Accompanists; Guest Artists; Guest Composers; Guest Lecturers; Guest Musical Directors; Guest Musicians; Guest Writers; Instructors; Local Artists; Multimedia; Music; Original Music Scores; Singers
Founded: 1913
Specialized Field: Symphony; Orchestra
Status: Nonprofit; Professional
Paid Staff: 12
Volunteer Staff: 120
Income Sources: Individual; Foundation; Grants
Performs At: Warner Theatre
Seating Capacity: 2500
Organization Type: Performing

1622
SOUTHEASTERN PENNSYLVANIA SYMPHONY ORCHESTRA
PO Box 694
Fansdale, PA 19446
Phone: 215-361-3099
e-mail: info@spso.info
Web Site: northpennsymphony.org
Officers:
  President & Treasurer: Judge Maurino J Rossanese Jr
  Vice President of Marketing: Will Nagle
  Board Member: Karel Wilkins
  Board Member: Andrea V. McCabe
  Board Member: William Bradbury III
  Board Member: Laurie Cipolla
  Board Member: F Lee Mangan
Management:
  Music Director/Conductor: Allan R Scott
  Assistant Conductor: Benjamin Aneff
  Music Conductor Emeritus: Leonard Murphy
  General Manager: Frank Ciccitto
  Personnel Manager: Beth Vilsmeier
  Stage Manager: John Kerney
Mission: The Southeastern Pennsylvania Symphony Orchestra was founded in 1972 and was created to provide performances of the highest artistic caliber to entertain and educate audiences in the region in order to contribute to the well-being of society by enhancing, enriching, and expanding the cultural lives of the residents of Montgomery County and the North Penn region.
Utilizes: Arrangers; Artists-in-Residence; Choreographers; Collaborating Artists; Collaborations; Composers; Contract Orchestras; Fine Artists; Guest Companies; Lyricists; Multimedia; Music; Musical Directors; Paid Performers; Singers
Founded: 1972
Specialized Field: Instrumental Concert Orchestra
Status: Non-Profit, Professional
Income Sources: Donors, Sponsors
Season: November through April
Performs At: Arcadia University

1623
WESTMORELAND SYMPHONY ORCHESTRA
951 Old Salem Road
Greensburg, PA 15601
Phone: 724-837-1850
Fax: 724-837-1342
e-mail: info@westmorelandsymphony.org
Web Site: www.westmorelandsymphony.org
Officers:
  President: Priscilla J. Richardson
  Treasurer: Gunnar Klinga
  Managing Director: Morrie Brand
  Past President: Sande J. Hendricks
  Secretary: Linda Blum
Management:
  Artistic Director: Daniel Meyer
  Executive Director: Morris A Brand
  Marketing Coordinator: Joy Carroll
Mission: Expanding accessibility to the cultural enrichment provided by music; offering enjoyment, inspiration and motivation.
Utilizes: Guest Musicians; Music; Original Music Scores
Founded: 1969
Specialized Field: Symphony; Orchestra; Ensemble
Status: Semi-Professional; Nonprofit
Paid Staff: 4
Budget: $450,000
Performs At: Palace Theatre
Seating Capacity: 1,300
Organization Type: Performing; Educational

1624
GREENVILLE SYMPHONY SOCIETY
PO Box 364
Greenville, PA 16125
Phone: 724-588-6164
e-mail: info@thegreenvillesymphony.org
Web Site: thegreenvillesymphony.org
Management:
  Manager: John H Evans
  Personnel Director: Vicki Poe
  Personnel Director: Jamie Scott
  Conductor: Michael Gelfand
Mission: To provide music education through performances.
Founded: 1927
Specialized Field: Symphony; Orchestra
Status: Nonprofit
Income Sources: Pennsylvania Council on the Arts
Performs At: Passavant Memorial Center; Thiel College
Organization Type: Performing

1625
HANOVER SYMPHONY ORCHESTRA
1150 Carlisle Street, Suite 5
PMB 151
Hanover, PA 17331
Phone: 717-632-8067
e-mail: info@hanoversymphonyorchestra.org
Web Site: hanoversymphonyorchestra.org
Officers:
  President: Clare Klunk
  Vice President: Walter Muast Jr
  Treasurer: Kara Darlington
  Corresponding Secretary: Ima Kay Zimmerman
  Recording Secretary: Linda Zellers
  Orchestra Liason: Jill Slagle
  Board Member: Don Horneff
  Board Member: Debra Markle
Management:
  Music Director: Brian Butterbaugh
  Assistant Conductor and Personnel D: Susan Gross
  Concert Master: Diane Hoffman
  Business Manager: Ima Kay Zimmerman
Mission: Founded in 1995, the Hanover Symphony Orchestra (HSO) is a non-profit, volunteer orchestra dedicated to fostering the love of music through entertainment, encouragement and education. With his tremendous love of music, Maestro Larry Kuntz began with a dream of developing an orchestra for the community - a place where the gifted musicians from the area could give of their talents. This dream became a reality.
Utilizes: Arrangers; Collaborating Artists; Collaborations; Fine Artists; Guest Companies; Multimedia; Music; Paid Performers; Singers; Visual Designers
Founded: 1995
Specialized Field: Classical, Instrumental, Orchestra
Status: Non-Profit, Professional
Income Sources: Donors, Sponsors
Season: March, October, December, January
Performs At: Eichelberger Performing Art's Center

1626
CENTRAL PENNSYLVANIA FRIENDS OF JAZZ
5721 Jonestown Road
Harrisburg, PA 17112

INSTRUMENTAL MUSIC / Pennsylvania

Phone: 717-540-1010
Fax: 717-540-7735
e-mail: friends@friendsofjazz.org
Web Site: www.friendsofjazz.org
Officers:
   President: Gerald Bennett
   First VP: Frank Paul
   2nd Vice President: Keith Thomas
   Third VP: Karen Sheaffer
   Treasurer: Amy Walizer
   Secretary: Tonya Mowry
Management:
   Executive Director: Steven Rudolph
   Executive Director: Andrea Rudolph
Mission: To present, promote and preserve America's unique art form, jazz.
Utilizes: Soloists
Founded: 1980
Specialized Field: Jazz Ensemble
Status: Nonprofit
Paid Staff: 30
Budget: $76,000
Income Sources: Allied Arts Fund; Metro Arts of Central Pennsylvania; Mellon Bank; PA Council on the Arts
Facility Category: Hotel Ballroom
Organization Type: Performing; Educational; Sponsoring

1627
HARRISBURG SYMPHONY ASSOCIATION

800 Corporate Circle
Suite 101
Harrisburg, PA 17110
Phone: 717-545-5527
Fax: 717-545-6501
e-mail: Info@harrisburgsymphony.org
Web Site: www.harrisburgsymphony.org/
Officers:
   Board Chair: William Lehr, Jr.
   Vice-Chair: Phyllis Mooney
   Vice-Chair: Kim S. Phipps, Ph.D.
   Secretary: Stephen C. MacDonald
   Treasurer: James Smeltzer
Management:
   Music Director: Stuart Malina
   Executive Director: Jeff Woodruff
   Director of Development: Ted Reese
   Director of Operations: Susan Klick
   Director of Finance: Michael Murray
Mission: To offer Central Pennsylvania quality symphonic music.
Utilizes: Actors; Collaborations; Dance Companies; Dancers; Grant Writers; Guest Accompanists; Guest Artists; Guest Companies; Guest Directors; Guest Lecturers; Guest Musical Directors; Guest Musicians; Multi Collaborations; Multimedia; Organization Contracts; Original Music Scores; Selected Students; Sign Language Translators; Singers; Touring Companies
Founded: 1930
Specialized Field: Symphony; Orchestra
Status: Professional; Nonprofit
Paid Staff: 15
Volunteer Staff: 300
Income Sources: Grants; Ticket Sales; Fundraising; Corporate and Individual Donations
Performs At: The Forum
Annual Attendance: 140,000
Facility Category: The Forum, State-owned Hall
Seating Capacity: 1,763
Year Built: 1931
Organization Type: Performing

1628
HARRISBURG SYMPHONY ORCHESTRA

800 Corporate Circle
Suite 101
Harrisburg, PA 17101
Phone: 717-545-5527
Fax: 717-545-6501
e-mail: info@HarrisburgSymphony.org
Web Site: www.harrisburgsymphony.org
Officers:
   Board Chair: William Lehr, Jr.
   Vice Chair: Phyllis Mooney
   Vice Chair: Kim S. Phipps, Ph.D
   Secretary: Stephen C. MacDonald
   Treasurer: James Smeltzer
Management:
   Music Director/Conductor: Stuart Malina
   Acting Concertmaster: Peter Sirotin
   Assistant Conductor: Gregory Woodbridge
   Executive Director: Jeff Woodruff
   Director of Development: Ted Reese
Mission: To provide young people with an opportunity to participate in an orchestra.
Specialized Field: Youth Symphony
Status: Non-Professional; Nonprofit
Paid Staff: 70
Income Sources: American Symphony Orchestra League (Youth Orchestra Division)
Performs At: Susquehanna Township Middle School
Organization Type: Performing; Touring; Educational; Sponsoring

1629
HERSHEY SYMPHONY ORCHESTRA

PO Box 93
Hershey, PA 17033
Phone: 717-533-8449
Fax: 717-520-9227
e-mail: management@hersheysymphony.org
Web Site: www.hersheysymphony.org
Officers:
   President: Randy Sibert
   Vice President: Susan Cort
   Vice President: Diane Paul
   Treasurer: Gretchen Cameron
   Secretary: Lee Boltz
Management:
   Music Director: Dr. Sandra Dackow
   Assistant Conductor: Robert Sproul
   Concertmaster: John Gazsi
   Ad Sales: Suzanne Kradel
   Personnel Manager & Librarian: Theresa Swenson
   Archivist: Annette Kilpatrick
Founded: 1969
Specialized Field: Orchestra
Paid Staff: 7
Non-paid Artists: 15

1630
IMMACULATA SYMPHONY

King Road
Immaculata, PA 19345-0703
Phone: 610-408-8342
e-mail: publicity@immacualtasymphony.org
Web Site: www.immaculatasymphony.org
Officers:
   President: Aaron Gould
   Vice President: Kyle Barger
   Secretary: Cynthia White
   Correspondiwng Secretary: Judith Greemayer
   Treasurer: Wendy Wethrill
   Personnel Manager: Marilyn Lutz
   Board Member: Drew Sheinen
Management:
   Music Director, Conductor: Joseph Gehring
   Past Director: Ovidiu Marinescu
   Publicity Officer: Drew Sheinen
Mission: The Immaculata Symphony boasts a long and rich history. It began in the nineteen-twenties as a chamber orchestra, its membership drawn solely from Immaculata students, providing them with a rich performing experience to augment their musical education. In the mid-seventies, the orchestra invited the participation of talented musicians in the local community, and since then has steadily grown into a highly respected ensemble capable of performing.
Utilizes: Arrangers; Collaborating Artists; Collaborations; Composers; Contract Orchestras; Fine Artists; Guest Companies; Lyricists; Multimedia; Music; Musical Directors; Paid Performers; Singers
Specialized Field: Orchestra, Classical, Instrumental
Status: Non-Profit, Professional
Income Sources: Sponsors, Donors, Advertisers
Season: November through April
Performs At: Allumnae Hall

1631
BALTIMORE CONSORT

93 Old York Road
222 Jenkintown Plaza
Jenkintown, PA 19046
Phone: 215-885-6400
Fax: 215-885-9929
e-mail: artists@rilearts.com
Web Site: www.file.com
Management:
   Artist Management: Joanne Rile
Mission: To perform popular music of the fifteen and sixteen hundreds from England, France and Scotland.
Founded: 1980
Specialized Field: Chamber; Ensemble; Folk Music
Status: Professional; Nonprofit
Income Sources: Walters Art Gallery
Organization Type: Performing; Touring; Resident; Educational

1632
JOHNSTOWN SYMPHONY ORCHESTRA

300 Market St.
Suite 300
Johnstown, PA 15901
Phone: 814-535-6738
Fax: 814-535-6739
e-mail: info@johnstownsymphony.org
Web Site: www.johnstownsymphony.org
Officers:
   Chair of the Board: James F. Beener, Esq.
   Vice Chair of the Board: Karen Azer
   President: Dennis McNair, Ph. D.
   Secretary: Rraymond G. Shrift
   Treasurer: Monica M. Graver
Management:
   Music Director and Conductor: Istvan Jaray
   Orchestra Manager: Patricia Hofscher
   Director, Johnstown Symphony Chorus: Samuel Louis Coco
   Assistant Conductor, Johnstown Symp: Maurice Staton
Mission: To provide classical music for greater Johnstown area residents.
Utilizes: Actors; Collaborations; Educators; Fine Artists; Grant Writers; Guest Accompanists; Guest Composers; Guest Lecturers; Guest Musical Directors; Guest Musicians; Guest Writers; Instructors; Local Artists; Multimedia; Original Music Scores; Sign Language Translators; Singers; Soloists

INSTRUMENTAL MUSIC / Pennsylvania

Founded: 1929
Specialized Field: Symphony; Orchestra; Chamber
Status: Professional
Paid Staff: 7
Volunteer Staff: 150
Paid Artists: 80
Non-paid Artists: 80
Budget: $638,000
Income Sources: Individuals; Corporations; Grants; Sponsors
Affiliations: Pasquerilla Performing Arts Center On Campus or University Of Pittsburgh At Johnstown
Annual Attendance: 16,680
Facility Category: Auditorium
Type of Stage: Proscenium with Pit
Stage Dimensions: 40x50
Seating Capacity: 1,000
Year Built: 1990
Cost: $9.6 million
Rental Contact: Bev Walery
Organization Type: Performing

1633
RICHLAND PERFORMING ARTS
One Academic Avenue
Johnstown, PA 15904
Phone: 814-269-0300
Fax: 814-269-2304
e-mail: smiller@richlandpac.com
Web Site: www.richlandpac.com
Officers:
   President: Max Fedore
   1st Vice President: Ann Marley
   2nd Vice President: Annie Rifilato
   Treasurer: Amanda Potasnik
   Secretary: Julius Eckroth
Management:
   Director of Performing Arts Center: Scott D. Miller
   Box Office Manager: Michelle Graham
   Producer / Director of Choirs: Kim Rauch
   Director of Bands / Musical Directo: Jerrod Cannistraci
   Technical Director: Martha Ringler
Mission: To present symphony concerts mainly from symphony repertoire including educational and pops programming.
Utilizes: Guest Artists
Founded: 1930
Specialized Field: Symphony; Orchestra; Ensemble
Status: Professional; Nonprofit
Income Sources: American Symphony Orchestra League; ORACLE; OCCA
Performs At: Renaissance Theatre
Organization Type: Performing; Touring; Educational

1634
KENNETT SYMPHONY
106 W. State St.
PO Box 72
Kennett Square, PA 19438
Phone: 610-444-6363
Fax: 610-925-1599
e-mail: mbuffington@kennettsymphony.org
Web Site: www.kennettsymphony.org
Officers:
   Board President: Paul Merluzzi
   Treasurer: Brad George
   Secretary: Emily Moody
   Board Member: Pam Carter
   Board Member: Sandra P. Yeatman
Management:
   Music Director/Conductor: Mary W Green
   Interim Executive Director: Monica Buffington
   Office Assistant: Julienne Ikegami
   Artistic Director, Kennett Symphony: Eileen Keller
Mission: To support professional symphonic music, to encourage young musicians and to educate young audiences.
Founded: 1940
Specialized Field: Orchestra
Volunteer Staff: 3
Budget: $400,000

1635
RIVERSIDE SYMPHONIA
PO Box 650
Lambertville, New Jersey
Lambertville, PA 08530
Phone: 609-397-7300
e-mail: info@riversidesymphonia.org
Web Site: www.riversidesymphonia.org
Officers:
   Chair: Kathy Hausman
   Young Artists Competition: Candace Phillips
Management:
   Music Director: Mariusz Simolij
   Executive Director: Benita Ryan
Founded: 1990
Specialized Field: Orchestra
Budget: $150,000-$260,000
Performs At: auditorium
Seating Capacity: 450

1636
LEHIGH VALLEY CHAMBER ORCHESTRA
PO Box 20641
Lehigh Valley, PA 18002
Phone: 610-266-8555
Fax: 610-266-8525
e-mail: lvco@fast.net
Web Site: www.lvco.org
Management:
   Executive Director: Llyena Boylan
   Music Director: Donald Spieth
   Office Manager: Holly Stackhouse
Mission: To support and appreciate classical music through performances of the highest standard of excellence; to enhance the quality of life in our community by fostering musical heritage and promoting contemporary American music, providing educational programming and presenting virtuoso performers of international stature; to create and seek opportunities to enhance our reputation.
Founded: 1979
Specialized Field: Orchestra; Chamber
Status: Professional; Nonprofit
Paid Staff: 3
Volunteer Staff: 100
Paid Artists: 100
Income Sources: Individual; Government; Business
Performs At: Dorothy & Dexter Baker Center for the Arts
Annual Attendance: 8,000-10,000
Seating Capacity: 500
Organization Type: Performing; Touring; Educational; Recording

1637
MCKEESPORT SYMPHONY ORCHESTRA
PO Box 354
McKeesport, PA 15134-0354
Phone: 412-664-2854
Fax: 412-460-1415
e-mail: mail@mckeesportsymphony.org
Web Site: www.mckeesportsymphony.org
Officers:
   Composer-in-residence: Todd Goodman
   President: Annette Condeluci
   Vice President: Amy Movic
Management:
   Music Director: Bruce Lauffer
   Concert master: Jason Posnock
   Personel Manager: John Hall
   Orchestra Manager & Librarian: Kevin King
   Youth Orchestra Director: Kevin King
Mission: To present orchestra concerts and other musical events of professional quality for the benefit of the public.
Specialized Field: Orchestra

1638
ALLEGHENY CIVIC SYMPHONY
Music Department
Allegheny College
Meadville, PA 16335
Phone: 814-332-3356
e-mail: rbond@allegro.edu
Management:
   Conductor: Robert Bond
Mission: To provide student artists with an opportunity to perform with experienced musicians; to offer high quality performances.
Founded: 1957
Specialized Field: Symphony
Status: Semi-Professional; Nonprofit
Paid Staff: 60
Income Sources: Allegheny College
Performs At: Raymond P. Shafer Auditorium
Organization Type: Performing; Educational

1639
BACH FESTIVAL OF PHILADELPHIA
P.O. Box 22445
Philadelphia, PA 19110-2445
Phone: 267-240-2586
Fax: 267-597-3811
e-mail: info@choralarts.com
Web Site: www.Bach-Fest.org
Officers:
   President: Lisa Barton, Esq.
   Vice President: Alexis Barron, Esq.
   Second Vice President: Meredith Quirin
   Secretary: Joseph J. Leube, Jr.
   Treasurer: John A. Miller
Management:
   Executive Director: Dr Guido Houden
   Artistic Director: Matthew C. Glandorf
   Press and Media Contact: Inna Lobanova-Heasley
Mission: The Bach Festival of Philadelphia is dedicated to enriching the community through concerts and educational programs presented by some of the best Baroque interpreters in the world.
Utilizes: Collaborations; Guest Composers; Guest Directors; Guest Musical Directors; Guest Musicians; Guest Soloists; Multimedia; Original Music Scores; Sign Language Translators; Singers
Founded: 1976
Specialized Field: Bach; Ensemble; Chamber
Status: Professional; Nonprofit
Paid Staff: 2
Volunteer Staff: 8
Income Sources: Government; Corporate and private foundations; Donations; Ticketsales; Advertising books
Performs At: Churches, Performance halls
Annual Attendance: 2,000-3,000
Organization Type: Educational; Presenting

INSTRUMENTAL MUSIC / Pennsylvania

1640
BIG SPRING SYMPHONY ORCHESTRA
3400 Civic Center Blvd
Philadelphia, PA 12945
Phone: 267-263-5943
Fax: 267-263-0645
e-mail: garaumann@suddenlink.net
Web Site: www.bigspringsymphony.com
Officers:
   President: Eulaine McIntosh
   1st Vice President: Jan Rouille
   1st Vice President/Sales: Dafna Meyer
   2nd Vice President: Fran Emerson
   Secretary: Ellen Austin
   Treasurer: Pauline Nelson
   Advertising Committee Chair: Suzanne Markewell
   Representative: JoBeth Corwin
Management:
   Artistic Director, Conductor: Keith Graumann
   Guest Conductor: John Giordano
   Soprano Soloist: Ava Pine
Mission: Comprised of people of all ages and backgrounds, The Big Spring Symphony works to strengthen community awareness and public appreciation of the Big Spring Symphony and encourages the community to be of support through fundraising, promoting music education, and providing appropriate support services to the symphony.
Utilizes: Arrangers; Artists-in-Residence; Collaborating Artists; Collaborations; Guest Accompanists; Guest Companies; Guest Composers; Multimedia; Music; Paid Performers; Singers
Specialized Field: Intrumental, Classical, Orchestra
Status: Non-Profit, Professional
Income Sources: Donors, Sponsors
Season: Year Round
Performs At: Municipal Auditorium, Philadelphia Civic Center

1641
CHESTNUT BRASS COMPANY
5807 W. 29th Street Road
Philadelphia, PA 80634
Phone: 970-590-4627
e-mail: trompe@aol.com
Web Site: www.chestnutbrass.com/
Officers:
   President: Marian Hesse
Mission: Offering a historical perspective on brass instruments to the public.
Founded: 1977
Specialized Field: Chamber; Brass Ensemble; Jazz
Status: Professional; Nonprofit
Income Sources: Greater Philadelphia Cultural Alliance; Temple University; Esther Boyle School
Organization Type: Performing; Touring; Resident; Educational

1642
CONCERTO SOLOISTS
Walnut Street Theatre Building
9th and Walnut Streets
Philadelphia, PA 19107
Phone: 215-574-3550
Fax: 215-574-3598
Web Site: www.wstonline.org
Management:
   Artistic/Music Director: Marc Mostovoy
   General Manager: Ken Wesler
   Artistic Administrator: Kelli Marshall
Mission: To belong to the Philadelphia community as one of its cultural institutions.
Utilizes: Guest Artists
Founded: 1964
Specialized Field: Orchestra; Chamber; Ensemble; Soloists
Status: Nonprofit
Income Sources: Greater Philadelphia Arts Council; Performing Arts League of Philadelphia; American Symphony Orchestra League
Performs At: Walnut Street Theatre; Church of the Holy Trinity
Organization Type: Performing; Touring; Resident; Educational; Sponsor Produced

1643
MARLBORO SCHOOL OF MUSIC
1528 Walnut Street
Suite 301
Philadelphia, PA 19102
Phone: 215-569-4690
Fax: 215-569-9497
e-mail: info@marlboromusic.org
Web Site: www.marlboromusic.org
Management:
   Administrator: Anthony P Checchia
   Manager: Philip Maneval
   Director Of Admissions: Jennifer Loux
   Director of Dev & Special Projects: Jacob Smith
   Box Office Manager: Brian Potter
Mission: Professional school providing advanced training for chamber musicians.
Founded: 1951
Specialized Field: Chamber; Educational
Status: Professional; Nonprofit
Income Sources: Grants; Ticket Sales; Endowments; Patron Gifts
Performs At: Marlboro College Concert Hall
Annual Attendance: 8,000+
Seating Capacity: 670
Organization Type: Performing; Educational

1644
PETER NERO AND THE PHILLY POPS
260 South Broad Street
16th Floor
Philadelphia, PA 19102
Mailing Address: 1518 Walnut Street, Suite 1706, Philadelphia, PA 19102
Phone: 215-875-8004
Fax: 215-875-8006
e-mail: info@phillypops.org
Web Site: www.phillypops.com
Officers:
   Chairman: Salvatore M. DeBunda, Esq.
   Vice Chairman: Gary A. Frank, J.D.
   President and CEO: Frank Giordano
   Secretary: Charles Keates, Esq.
   Treasurer: Louis K. Habina, Esq
Management:
   Music Director: Michael Krajewski
   Executive Vice President and Chief: Louis Scaglione
   Director of Artistic Administration: George Muller
   Director of Development: Larry Simpson
   Marketing Director: Mark Gissi
   Office Manager: Pat Wells
Mission: POPS concerts run the gamut, from classics to big band, Broadway to rock n' roll. Audiences want an eclectic mix, thats the success of our concerts for we provide quality, variety and a great orchestra that can play anything.
Specialized Field: Orchestra; Pops

1645
PHILADELPHIA CHAMBER MUSIC SOCIETY
1528 Walnut Street
Suite 301
Philadelphia, PA 19102
Phone: 215-569-8587
Fax: 215-569-9497
e-mail: mail@pcmsconcerts.com
Web Site: www.pcmsconcerts.org
Officers:
   Chairman: Jerry G. Rubenstein
   President: Jack R. Bershad, Esq.
   Vice-President: Edward A. Montgomery, Jr.
   Treasurer: Julian A. Brodsky
   Secretary: Susan S. Gould
Management:
   Founding Artistic Director: Anthony Checchia
   Executive Director: Philip Maneval
   Artistic Director: Miles Cohen
   Development and Marketing Director: Jacob Smith
   Education Director: Erik Petersons
Mission: The Philadelphia Chamber Music Society (PCMS) is one of the largest, most accessible music presenting forums in the United States.
Founded: 1986
Specialized Field: Chamber
Performs At: Perelman Theater; Pennsylvania Convention Center

1646
PHILADELPHIA CLASSICAL GUITAR SOCIETY
2038 Sansom Street
Philadelphia, PA 19103
Phone: 215-567-2972
Fax: 215-963-9950
e-mail: artdirector@phillyguitar.com
Web Site: www.phillyguitar.com
Officers:
   President: Fabrizio Franco
   Secretary: Brian Keith
   Treasurer: Dan Spatucci
Management:
   Artistic Director: Joseph Mayes
   Membership Director: Brian Keith
   Fundraising/ Development/Webmaster: Ross Mann
Mission: To present and foster classical guitar-related activities throughout the Greater Philadelphia area; to provide a forum for informal performance, lectures, outreach, and communication between fellow classical guitar enthusiasts.
Specialized Field: Chamber; Classical Guitar
Status: Professional; Nonprofit
Paid Staff: 40
Budget: $10,000-$20,000
Income Sources: Ticket Sales; Patron Gifts; Grants
Performs At: Pennsylvania Convention Auditorium
Seating Capacity: 610

1647
PHILADELPHIA ORCHESTRA
One South Broad Street
14th Floor
Philadelphia, PA 19107
Phone: 215-893-1900
Fax: 215-875-7649
e-mail: philadelphia_orchestra@philadelphiaorchestra.org
Web Site: www.philorch.org
Officers:

All listings are in alphabetical order by state, then city, then organization within the city.

INSTRUMENTAL MUSIC / Pennsylvania

Chairman: Richard B. Worley
President and Chief Executive Offic: Allison Vulgamore
Secretary: Sarah Miller Coulson
Treasurer: Mario Mestichelli
Vice President, Communications and: Katherine E. Blodgett
Vice President, Global Initiatives: Craig Hhamilton
Vice President, Artistic Planning: Jeremy Rothman
Vice President, Development: Marilyn Lucas
Vice President, Marketing: Janice Hay
Management:
   Music Director: Yannick N,zet-S,guin,
   Director of Human Resources: Karen M. Tomlinson
   Director of Touring and Operations: Travis Wells
   Associate Director: Darrin T. Britting
   Concertmaster: David Kim
   Artistic Administrator: Roger Wight
   Manager of Artist Services: Benjamin Spalter
   Gifts Coordinator: Maryann Aguiar
Mission: Maintaining the Philadelphia Orchestra's preeminence as one of the city's outstanding cultural assets.
Utilizes: Guest Artists
Founded: 1900
Specialized Field: Symphony; Orchestra
Status: Professional; Nonprofit
Income Sources: American Symphony Orchestra League
Performs At: Academy of Music
Seating Capacity: 2,897
Organization Type: Performing

1648
PHILADELPHIA STRING QUARTET
PO Box 37127
Philadelphia, PA 98145
Phone: 206-527-8839
Fax: 206-526-8621
Toll-free: 800-335-9521
e-mail: bookings@philadelphiaquartet.com
Web Site: www.philadelphiaquartet.com
Management:
   Executive Director: Alan Iglitzin
   Account Manager: Tom Hallowell
Mission: Performing string quartets; producing the Olympic Music Festival.
Founded: 1960
Specialized Field: Chamber; String Ensemble
Status: Professional; Nonprofit
Organization Type: Performing; Touring; Educational; Sponsoring

1649
PHILADELPHIA YOUTH ORCHESTRA
240 South 20th Street
Philadelphia, PA 19103
Mailing Address: P.O. Box 41810, Philadelphia, PA 19101-1810
Phone: 215-545-0502
Fax: 215-545-7399
e-mail: info@pyos.org
Web Site: www.pyos.org
Officers:
   Chairman: Frank Giordano
   Vice Chairman: W. Matthew Skilton
   President and Music Director: Louis Scaglione
   Treasurer: David R. McShane
   Secretary: Mary Teresa Soltis, Esq.
Management:
   Director of Development: Maria Newman
   Director and Conductor, Bravo Brass: Paul Bryan
   Director and Conductor, PRYSM: Gloria dePasquale
   Director, Tune Up Philly: Delia Raab-Snyder
   Assistant Director and Site Coordin: Paul Smith
Mission: To promote, encourage and foster the study and practice of music by making available to deserving and talented youth opportunities for orchestra instruction and supervision of their work and to provide concerts for promoting musical art and its appreciation.
Founded: 1939
Specialized Field: Youth Orchestra; Chamber; Ensemble
Status: Non-Professional; Nonprofit
Paid Staff: 2
Volunteer Staff: 200
Non-paid Artists: 190
Income Sources: American Symphony Orchestra League (Youth Orchestra Division); Greater Philadelphia Cultural Alliance
Performs At: Academy of Music
Facility Category: Theatres; Schools
Organization Type: Performing; Touring; Educational

1650
PHILADELPHIA CLASSICAL SYMPHONY
419 W. Mt. Pleasant Avenue
Philadelphia, PA 19119
Phone: 215-228-2224
Fax: 610-664-6667
e-mail: info@classicalsymphony.org
Web Site: www.classicalsymphony.org
Management:
   Artistic Director: Karl Middleman
Mission: Believing that music can be a healing, ennobling force in modern life, we present intriguing concerts that aim to make classical music accessible to audiences of all ages. Symphony events are organized around thematic programs and historical practices and frequently offer audience participation.
Founded: 1993
Specialized Field: Orchestra

1651
PIFFARO: THE RENAISSANCE BAND
2258 Fairmount Ave
Philadelphia, PA 19130
Phone: 215-235-8469
Fax: 215-235-8469
e-mail: info@piffaro.com
Web Site: www.piffaro.com
Officers:
   Chairman: William Gross
   Secretary: Susan Karakantas
   Treasurer: Aalan Muirhead
Management:
   Artistic Co-Director: Joan Kimball
   Artistic Co-Director: Robert Wiemken
   Executive Director: Shannon Cline
Mission: Performing early Baroque and Renaissance music using period instruments.
Utilizes: Actors; Collaborations; Dance Companies; Dancers; Guest Musical Directors; Guest Musicians; Multimedia; Original Music Scores; Sign Language Translators; Singers
Founded: 1980
Specialized Field: Chamber; Ensemble; Early Music; Renaissance
Status: Professional; Nonprofit
Paid Staff: 3
Volunteer Staff: 10
Paid Artists: 7
Budget: $170,000
Income Sources: Government; Pennsylvania Council Art Foundation; Ticket sales; Concert fees
Organization Type: Performing; Touring; Educational

1652
PRESIDENTIAL JAZZ WEEKEND
African-American History Museum
701 Arch Street
Philadelphia, PA 19106
Phone: 215-574-0380
Fax: 215-574-3110
Management:
   Jazz Live Director: Rhoda Blount
   Museum Director: Dr. Rowena Stewart
Mission: To celebrate the classical music of African-Americans.
Utilizes: Singers
Founded: 1989
Specialized Field: Jazz Ensemble; Ethnic Music
Status: Professional; Semi-Professional; Nonprofit
Income Sources: Greater Philadelphia Cultural Alliance; American Association of Museums; Coalition of Afro-American Organizations
Organization Type: Performing; Educational; Sponsoring

1653
RELACHE ENSEMBLE
829 North 24th Street
Philadelphia, PA 19130
Phone: 215-574-8248
Fax: 215-574-0253
e-mail: relache@att.net
Web Site: www.relache.org
Officers:
   President: Alexandra Q. Aldridge
   Board Member: Dina Wind
   Board Member: Douglas Schaller
   Board Member: Jean Brody
   Board Member: John Dulik
Management:
   Executive Artistic Director: Joseph Franklin
   Director Planning/Development: Arthur Stidfole
   Director Educational Projects: Laurel Wyckoff
Mission: Developing, producing and presenting the works of living composers.
Specialized Field: Chamber; Ensemble; Electronic; Live Electronic; Contemporary
Status: Professional; Nonprofit
Performs At: Mandell Theater
Organization Type: Performing; Touring; Resident; Educational; Sponsoring

1654
PITTSBURGH CHAMBER MUSIC SOCIETY
315 S. Bellefield Avenue
Suite 305
Pittsburgh, PA 15213
Phone: 412-624-4129
Fax: 412-624-6461
e-mail: info@pittsburghchambermusic.org
Web Site: chambermusicpittsburgh.org
Officers:
   Co-President: William Lafe
   Co-President: Marilyn Larrimer
   Treasurer: Mark Uebele
   Secretary: Kathryn Logan
Management:
   Executive Director: Kristen Linfante
   Marketing & Program Coordinator Acc: Rebecca MacNamee
   Director: Elizabeth Baisley
   Director: Dale Hershey

INSTRUMENTAL MUSIC / Pennsylvania

Mission: To present chamber music of the highest quality performed by internationally and nationally recognized ensembles to tri-state residents; to support and extend the full range of chamber music repertoire through performances and commissions; to support educational activities that encourage more adults and students to appreciate the art form; and to nurture exceptional emerging chamber music ensembles.
Utilizes: Multimedia
Founded: 1961
Specialized Field: Chamber Music
Status: Professional; Nonprofit
Paid Staff: 2
Income Sources: Chamber Music America; PA Presenters
Performs At: Carnegie Music Hall, Oakland
Affiliations: Chamber Music America
Organization Type: Sponsoring

1655
PITTSBURGH NEW MUSIC ENSEMBLE
Duquesne University School of Music
527 Coyne Terrace
Pittsburgh, PA 15233
Mailing Address: PO Box 99476
Phone: 412-889-7231
Fax: 412-682-2955
e-mail: contactpnme@gmail.com
Web Site: www.pnme.org
Officers:
  President: Jeffery Nytch
  Vice President: Thomas Joseph, Esq.
  Secretary/Treasurer: Michael Wagner
  Board Member: Daniel Berczik
  Board Member: Tony Joseph
Management:
  Executive Director: Pamela Murchison
  Artistic Director: Kevin Noe
  Sound Designer: Chris McGlumphy
  Lighting Designer: Andrew Ostrowski
Mission: To encourage the creation, performance, dissemination and appreciation of contemporary music, with special emphasis on American Music and living composers.
Utilizes: Guest Artists
Founded: 1976
Specialized Field: Chamber; Ensemble; Contemporary
Status: Professional; Nonprofit
Paid Staff: 2
Paid Artists: 50
Income Sources: Chamber Music America
Performs At: Levy Hall at The Fulton Theatres
Organization Type: Performing; Touring; Resident; Educational; Sponsoring

1656
PITTSBURGH SYMPHONY ORCHESTRA
Pittsburgh Symphony Heinz Hall
600 Penn Avenue
Pittsburgh, PA 15222-3259
Phone: 412-392-4900
Fax: 412-392-4909
e-mail: customerservice@pittsburghsymphony.org
Web Site: www.pittsburghsymphony.org
Officers:
  President & CEO: James Wilkinson
  Senior Vice President & COO: Michael Bielski
  Vice President of Communications an: Lousie Sciannameo
  Senior Vice President of Artistic P: Bob Moir
  Vice President of Development: Jodi Weisfield
Management:
  Music Director: Manfred Honeck
  Resident Conductor: Fawzi Haimor
  Director of Media Relations: Joyce DeFrancesco
  Director of Events: Shannon Capellupo
  Director of Leadership and Planned: Jan Fleisher
Mission: Striving for and attaining excellence in artistic achievement.
Utilizes: Guest Artists
Founded: 1895
Specialized Field: Symphony; Orchestra; Chamber
Status: Nonprofit
Income Sources: Pittsburgh Symphony Society
Performs At: Heinz Hall for the Performing Arts
Seating Capacity: 2,661
Organization Type: Performing; Touring; Educational; Presenting

1657
PITTSBURGH YOUTH SYMPHONY ORCHESTRA ASSOCIATION
Heinz Hall
600 Penn Avenue
Pittsburgh, PA 15222-3259
Phone: 412-392-4872
e-mail: info@pittsburghyouthsymphony.org
Web Site: www.pittsburghyouthsymphony.org
Officers:
  President: Tammy Ardolino
  Vice President: Cathy Lueers
  Secretary: Beverly Mastalski
  Treasurer: David Ren
  PYSO Board Liaison: Jerry Gindele
Management:
  Music Director: Lawrence Loh
  Executive Director: Craig Johnson
  Program Coordinator, Personnel Mana: Eve Goodman
  Principal Guest Conductor: Leonard Slatkin
  Assistant Conductor: Fawzi Haimor
Mission: To provide the best possible musical training to members of the orchestra and to develop new audiences for symphonic music among youth.
Founded: 1946
Status: Non-Professional; Nonprofit
Income Sources: Grants; Foundations; Corporate/Individual Contribution
Performs At: Pittsburgh Symphony Heinz Hall
Annual Attendance: 5,000
Seating Capacity: 2663
Organization Type: Performing; Touring; Resident; Educational; Sponsoring

1658
RENAISSANCE AND BAROQUE SOCIETY OF PITTSBURGH
5530 Penn Avenue
PO Box 10156
Pittsburgh, PA 15206
Phone: 412-361-2048
Fax: 412-682-5253
e-mail: director@rbsp.org
Web Site: www.rbsp.org
Officers:
  President: Lin Cook
  Vice President: Jeffrey Morrow
  Treasurer: Margaret M. Barth
  Secretary: Paul Heilman
  Board Member: Ray Hricik
Management:
  Managing Director: Gail M. Luley
  Office Assistant: Mia Bonnewell
Mission: Sponsoring national and international touring ensembles who use period instruments to perform early music.
Founded: 1969
Specialized Field: Orchestra; Chamber; Early Music; Baroque
Status: Professional
Performs At: Synod Hall; Sacred Heart Cathedral
Organization Type: Sponsoring
Comments: Special parking/entry for handicap access; Large print programs

1659
RIVER CITY BRASS BAND
500 Grant Street
Suite 2720
Pittsburgh, PA 15219-2502
Phone: 412-322-7222
Fax: 412-235-9015
Toll-free: 800-292-7222
e-mail: info@rcbb.com
Web Site: rivercitybrass.org
Officers:
  Chairman: Paul Furiga
  Vice-Chair: Donald Jacobson
  Vice-Chair: Lisa Valleto
  Vice-Chair: Thomas J. Nist
  Treasurer: Philip G. Petraglia
Management:
  Artistic Director: James Gourlay
  Executive Director: Carolyn Tuminella
  Development & Planning Director: Phil Parr
  Operations & Marketing Director: Cynthia Geib
  Personnel Manager: Bernard Black
Mission: The mision of the River City Brass Band is to propagate and perpetuate musical culture, primarily American musical culture, across a broad spectrum of the public through the presentation of brass band performances, educational programs and the production of recordings. The River City Brass Band has as its central obligation service to the people of Western Pennsylvania.
Utilizes: Commissioned Composers, Dance Companies; Educators; Guest Accompanists; Guest Companies; Guest Musical Directors; Guest Musicians; Local Artists; Organization Contracts; Singers
Founded: 1981
Specialized Field: Band; Brass Ensemble
Status: Professional; Nonprofit
Paid Staff: 8
Paid Artists: 28
Budget: $2 million
Income Sources: Association of Performing Arts Presenters; American Concert Band; National Endowment for the Arts
Performs At: Carnegie Music Hall
Annual Attendance: 140,000
Organization Type: Performing; Touring; Resident; Educational; Recording

1660
TAMBURITZANS FOLK ENSEMBLE
600 Forbes Ave.
Pittsburgh, PA 15282
Phone: 412-396-6000
Fax: 412-396-5583
e-mail: publicsafety@duq.edu
Web Site: www.duq.edu/Tamburitzans
Management:
  Managing Director: Paul G Stafura
Mission: The Duquesne University Tamburitzans is dedicated to preserving and perpetuating the cultural heritages of Eastern Europe and its neighbors through performance, while awarding scholarships to talented and deserving student performers.
Utilizes: Singers
Founded: 1937
Specialized Field: Ensemble; Ethnic Music; Folk Music

INSTRUMENTAL MUSIC / Pennsylvania

Status: Non-Professional; Nonprofit
Paid Staff: 40
Income Sources: Duquesne University
Organization Type: Performing; Touring

1661
READING SYMPHONY ORCHESTRA
147 N 5th Street
Reading, PA 19601-3502
Phone: 610-373-7557
Fax: 610-373-5446
e-mail: readingsym@aol.com
Web Site: www.readingsymphony.com
Officers:
  President: Charles Bock
  First Vice President: Kevin Wagner
  Second Vice-President: Jane Athleen
  Secretary: Dianne Work
  Treasurer: Cynthia Phillips
Management:
  Executive Director: Joseph Tackett
  Music Director: Andrew Constantine
  Concertmaster: Christopher Lee
  Youth Orchestra Music Director: Peter Brye
  Junior String Conductor: Brian Mishler
Mission: Providing the city of Reading and Berks County with high quality orchestral concerts.
Utilizes: Guest Artists
Founded: 1912
Specialized Field: Symphony
Status: Professional; Nonprofit
Paid Staff: 10
Non-paid Artists: 80
Income Sources: Grants; Ticket Sales; Fundraisers
Performs At: Rajah Theatre
Annual Attendance: 10,000+
Seating Capacity: 2,150
Organization Type: Performing; Educational; Sponsoring

1662
николи VALLEY SYMPHONY
270 Walker Dr
#105
State College, PA 16801
Phone: 814-231-8224
Fax: 814-231-0140
e-mail: info@nvs.org
Web Site: www.nvs.org
Management:
  Music Director: Michael Jinbo
  Executive Director: Roberta Strebel
Mission: Pledging to program the best in orchestral music, it presents six concerts a year, including one specially designed for families.
Founded: 1967
Specialized Field: Orchestra
Status: Nonprofit
Income Sources: Ticket Revenue; Grants; Foundation Earnings; Donor Contributions

1663
VILLANOVA UNIVERSITY CHAMBER SERIES
Office of Musical Activities
Villanova University
Villanova, PA 19085-1603
Phone: 610-519-7214
Fax: 610-519-7596
e-mail: john.dunphy@villanova.edu
Management:
  Manager: Peter Marino
Specialized Field: Chamber
Budget: $20,000-$35,000

Performs At: St. Mary's Hall

1664
WARREN CIVIC ORCHESTRA
418 Water Street
Warren, PA 16365
Phone: 614-723-9110
e-mail: info@warrencivicorchestra.org
Web Site: warrencivicorchestra.org
Management:
  Conductor, Cellist: Bryan Eckenrode
  Soprano: Cristen Gregory
  Hornist: Paul Schlossman
Mission: The Warren Civic Orchestra was formed in 1952 by many prominent citizens of the Warren community, with Barbara Baldwin Defrees as the driving force. The purpose of forming the Warren Civic Orchestra was to provide an outlet where qualified adult musicians had the opportunity to rehearse and perform together to foster music performance and appreciation in Warren and the surrounding communities. These purposes remain today.
Utilizes: Arrangers; Collaborating Artists; Collaborations; Composers; Fine Artists; Guest Artists; Lyricists; Multimedia; Musical Directors; Paid Performers; Singers
Founded: 1952
Specialized Field: Intrumental, Classical, Orchestra
Status: Non-Profit, Professional
Income Sources: Sponsors, Donors
Season: November, March
Performs At: Struthers Library Theater

1665
CAMERATA PHILADELPHIA INC
686 Limehouse Road
Wayne, PA 19087
Phone: 215-360-2173
Fax: 215-392-3403
e-mail: info@cameraphiladelphia.org
Web Site: cameraphiladelphia.org
Management:
  Music Director, Conductor: Stephen Framill
  Vocal & Chorus Master: Kyle Engler
  Orchestra Personel Manager: Michelle Bishop
  Booking Representative: Nicholas Klementz
  Booking Representative: Natalia Minibayeva
Mission: CAMERATA PHILADELPHIA is an ensemble without musical boundaries. From symphonies to chamber music to opera to choral, CAMERATA not only brings a fresh and distinct interpretation to the venerated classics, but also seeks to bridge the styles of classical, jazz, folk and world music - each program an eclectic and richly diverse musical offering.Committed to music appreciation for all ages, it is the mission of CAMERATA to make the experience great
Utilizes: Arrangers; Choreographers; Composers; Educators; Fine Artists; Guest Companies; Guest Composers; Lyricists; Multimedia; Music; Paid Performers; Singers
Specialized Field: Classical, Modern, Contemporary, Instrumental, Jazz, Folk
Status: Non-Profit
Income Sources: Sponsors, Donors, Corporate Sponsors
Season: September through November
Performs At: Church of the Holy Trinity

1666
WEST CHESTER UNIVERSITY OF PENNSYLVANIA SCHOOL OF MUSIC
700 South West High Street
West Chester, PA 19383

Phone: 610-436-1000
Fax: 610-436-2673
e-mail: musicinfo@wcupa.edu
Web Site: wcupa.edu
Officers:
  Chairman: Dr Christopher Hanning
  Assistant Chair: Dr Emily Bullock
  Assistant Chair: Dr Patricia Powell
Management:
  Chair, Music Education: J Bryan Burton
  Chair, Theory/Composition: Robert Maggio
  Theory/Composition: Austin Gross
Mission: The mission of the Department of Music Theory, History and Composition is to provide an environment that promotes excellence and diversity in our students' preparation for careers in music theory, music history and composition as scholars, teachers, creative artists and performers.The department is committed to providing the finest instruction in music theory, history and musicianship to students in all degree programs in the School of Music.
Utilizes: Arrangers; Artists-in-Residence; Choreographers; Collaborating Artists; Collaborations; Community Talent; Composers-in-Residence; Fine Artists; Local Artists & Directors; Lyricists; Multimedia; Music; Musical Directors; Paid Performers; Poets; Scenic Designers; Sign Language Translators; Singers; Soloists; Special Technical Talent
Specialized Field: Instrumental Educational
Status: Non-Profit, Non-Professional
Income Sources: Donors, Alumni, Fundraisers, Grants

1667
NORTHEASTERN PENNSYLVANIA PHILHARMONIC
195 Hanover Street
PO Box 4525
Wilkes-Barre, PA 18505
Phone: 570-270-4444
Fax: 570-270-4450
e-mail: info@nepaphil.org
Web Site: nepaphil.org
Management:
  Music Director: Lawrence Loh
  Adminstration, CFO: Pat Arvonio
  Marketing Director: Steve Parulski
  Associate: Sandra Davis
  Corporate/Donor Relations: Lizzy Kuna
  Production Manager: Jerry Miller
  Customer Sales/Services: Mary Orzello
  Personnel Manager & Librarian: Martin Webster
Mission: Today, as the only fully professional symphony in the region, the NEPA Philharmonic regularly performs in two facilities, the Scranton Cultural Center at the Masonic Temple and the F.M. Kirby Center for the Performing Arts in Wilkes-Barre, each with a seating capacity of 1,800. The organization is comprised of a 20 member governing Board of Directors, and five full-time and three part-time employees.
Utilizes: Arrangers; Choreographers; Collaborating Artists; Collaborations; Composers-in-Residence; Fine Artists; Guest Directors; Lyricists; Multimedia; Music; Musical Directors; Paid Performers; Singers; Soloists
Founded: 1969
Opened: 1970
Specialized Field: Instrumental, Archestra, Classical, Modern
Status: Non-Profit, Professional
Income Sources: Donors, Sponsors, Gifting, Galas
Season: October, November, May

INSTRUMENTAL MUSIC / Rhode Island

1668
WILLIAMSPORT SYMPHONY ORCHESTRA
220 West Fourth Street, 3rd Floor
Community Arts Center
Williamsport, PA 17701
Phone: 570-322-0227
Fax: 570-322-7614
e-mail: info@williamsportsymphony.com
Web Site: www.williamsportsymphony.org
Officers:
  President: Michael Vuocolo
  Vice President: Greg Smith
  Treasurer: Nancy Eischeid
  Secretary: Brad Nason
  Past President: Dianne Peeling
Management:
  Music Director: Robin Fountain
  Executive Director: Janet Harris
  Marketing Coordinator: Hind Jabbour
  Orchestra Manager & Librarian: Becky Ciabattari
Mission: To be a cultural asset to the community by providing quality orchestral music, education and performance opportunities for regional talent to an ever-expanding audience.
Specialized Field: Orchestra

1669
YORK SYMPHONY ORCHESTRA
State Capital Building
50 North George Street
York, PA 17401
Phone: 717-812-0717
Fax: 717-650-2308
e-mail: yyso@yorksymphony.org
Web Site: yorksymphony.org
Officers:
  President: Jane Davis
  Vice-President: William Hartman
  Treasurer: Christopher Blumhard
  Secretary: Betsy Keefer
  Orchestra Representative: Richard Konkel
  Chorus Representative: John Stone
  Advisor: Chris Clark
  Advisor: Sally Dixon
  Advisor: David Meckley
Management:
  Executive Director: Ken Wesler
  Development Director: Richard Brown
  Operations Manager: Dale Elkiss
  YSO Office Manager & Admin Coor: Stacey Bear
  Conductor, Artistic Director: Dr Robert Hart Baker
  Concertmaster: John Eaken
  Interim Chorus Director: Randy Day
Mission: The mission of York Symphony Orchestra is to provide live orchestral music to the people of South Central Pennsylvania and Northern Maryland. In 2009, as the leadership of York Symphony begins its planning activities, it has created the following vision of the outcomes of its efforts. We will bring real music to real people. Every year, we reach thousands of people, from all generations, through our concerts and education.
Utilizes: Arrangers; Choreographers; Collaborating Artists; Collaborations; Guest Accompanists; Guest Designers; Lyricists; Multimedia; Music; Original Music Scores; Paid Performers
Founded: 2005
Specialized Field: Orchestra, Classical
Status: Non-Profit, Professional
Income Sources: Donors, Sponsors
Season: Fall
Performs At: Strand Theatre

Rhode Island

1670
RHODE ISLAND CIVIC CHORALE & ORCHESTRA
141 Phenix Ave.
Cranston, RI 02920
Phone: 401-521-5670
Fax: 401-521-5276
e-mail: info@ricco.org
Web Site: www.ricco.org
Management:
  Music Director: Edward Markward
Mission: To enrich the public and performers through artistic concert presentations.
Specialized Field: Orchestra
Status: Non-Profit
Performs At: Veterans Memorial Auditorium

1671
RHODE ISLAND PHILHARMONIC ORCHESTRA AND MUSIC SCHOOL
667 Waterman Avenue
East Providence, RI 02914
Phone: 401-248-7070
Fax: 401-248-7071
e-mail: info@riphil.org
Web Site: www.ri-philharmonic.org
Management:
  Executive Director: David J. Beauchesne
  Director of Education & Music Schoo: Annette Mozzoni
  Director of Finance: Donna Chace-Larson
  Director of Development: Betty Ann Kearney
  Director of Marketing & Communicati: Wayne Wilkins
Utilizes: Actors; Choreographers; Collaborating Artists; Composers-in-Residence; Dance Companies; Dancers; Educators; Fine Artists; Five Seasonal Concerts; Grant Writers; Guest Accompanists; Guest Artists; Guest Choreographers; Guest Companies; Guest Composers; Guest Designers; Guest Directors; Guest Lecturers; Guest Musical Directors; Guest Musicians; Instructors; Local Artists; Multimedia; Music; Original Music Scores; Resident Artists; Sign Language Translators; Singers; Student Interns; Special Technical Talent; Theatre Companies
Founded: 1945
Specialized Field: Symphony; Educational
Status: Professional; Nonprofit
Paid Staff: 10
Paid Artists: 72
Income Sources: Individual; Corporate; Foundation Grants
Performs At: VMA Arts and Cultural Center
Seating Capacity: 2,100
Organization Type: Performing; Resident; Educational

1672
KINGSTON CHAMBER MUSIC FESTIVAL AT THE UNIVERSITY OF RHODE ISLAND
PO Box 1733
Kingston, RI 02881
Phone: 401-874-2060
Fax: 401-874-2380
e-mail: kcmfboxoffice@etal.uri.edu
Web Site: kingstonchambermusic.org
Officers:
  President: Martin Sadd
  Vice President: Michelle Little
  Treasurer: Harold Bibb
  Secretary: Joanne Hall Coombs
  Board Member: Emily Chen
Management:
  Artistic Director: Natalie Zhu
  Managing Director: Brian Mitchell
Mission: To provide outstanding classical music programs in New England. Offers both summer and winter concerts, and also outreach programs at local area schools.
Utilizes: Guest Musical Directors; Multimedia; Original Music Scores
Founded: 1989
Specialized Field: Classical; Chamber
Volunteer Staff: 15
Paid Artists: 1045
Budget: $60,000
Income Sources: Donations; Ticket sales
Affiliations: University of Rhode Island
Annual Attendance: 2800

1673
UNIVERSITY OF RHODE ISLAND SYMPHONY ORCHESTRA
Music Department
105 Upper College Road, Suite E
Kingston, RI 02881
Phone: 401-874-2431
Fax: 401-874-5955
e-mail: abotello@mail.uri.edu
Web Site: http://www.uri.edu/music/Ensembles/Orch.html
Officers:
  Secretary: Jeannette Ruhle
Management:
  Music Department Chair: Ronald Lee
  Director of Orchestral Activities: Ann Danis
Specialized Field: Orchestra
Performs At: Recital Hall, Fine Arts Center

1674
BROWN UNIVERSITY ORCHESTRA
Brown University
1 Young Orchard Avenue
Providence, RI 02912
Mailing Address: PO Box 1924
Phone: 401-863-3234
Fax: 401-863-7552
e-mail: music@brown.edu
Web Site: http://www.brown.edu/Departments/Music/ensembles/orchestra.html
Management:
  Music Director/Conductor: Paul Phillips
Utilizes: Collaborating Artists; Collaborations; Commissioned Composers; Community Members; Composers; Educators; Guest Companies; Guest Composers; Guest Lecturers; Guest Musical Directors; Guest Musicians; Multi Collaborations; Multimedia; Music; Original Music Scores; Singers; Soloists
Founded: 1918
Specialized Field: Orchestra
Performs At: Sayles Hall
Seating Capacity: 400

1675
RHODE ISLAND CHAMBER MUSIC CONCERTS
PO Box 41356
Providence, RI 02940
Phone: 401-863-2416
e-mail: info@ricmc.org
Web Site: www.ricmc.org
Officers:
  President: Joan Lusk
Specialized Field: Chamber

INSTRUMENTAL MUSIC / South Carolina

Budget: $10,000-$20,000
Income Sources: Tickets; Grants; Donations
Facility Category: Church
Type of Stage: Raised Platform
Stage Dimensions: small
Seating Capacity: 400

1676
RHODE ISLAND COLLEGE SYMPHONY ORCHESTRA
600 Mount Pleasant Avenue
Rhode Island College
Providence, RI 02908
Phone: 401-456-8000
Fax: 401-874-2772
e-mail: theweb@ric.edu
Web Site: http://www.ric.edu/mtd/musicProgram_ensemble.php
Management:
   Music Director: Dr. Edward Markward
Specialized Field: Orchestra
Performs At: Roberts Auditorium

South Carolina

1677
ANDERSON SYMPHONY ORCHESTRA
1124 Meridian Plaza
Anderson, SC 46016
Phone: 765-644-2111
e-mail: aso@andersonsymphony.org
Web Site: www.andersonsymphony.org
Officers:
   President: Dr. E. Darlene Miller
   Vice-President: Cindy Lanane
   Secretary: Marissa Skaggs
   Treasurer: Brett Spangler
   Past President: David Shade
Management:
   Music Director: Richard Sowers
   Exeutive Director: Dana E. Stone
Utilizes: Guest Artists
Founded: 1978
Specialized Field: Orchestra
Paid Staff: 74
Budget: $150,000-$260,000
Performs At: Paramount Theatre Centre

1678
CHARLESTON SYMPHONY ORCHESTRA
756 St. Andrews Blvd.
Charleston, SC 29407
Phone: 843-723-7528
Fax: 843-722-3463
e-mail: info@charlestonsymphony.org
Web Site: www.charlestonsymphony.com
Officers:
   President: Cynthia Hartley
   VP Artistic: Edward Hart
   VP Finance: Michael Moody
   VP Marketing: Charlie Cumbaa
   VP Education: James Braunreuther
Management:
   Music Director: Ken Lam
   Exeutive Director: Michael Smith
   Director of Artistic Operations: Kyle Lan
   Director of Patron Services: Cynthia Branch
   Director of Marketing: Tara Scott
Mission: Offering South Carolina residents quality musical performances; educating children through the use of smaller orchestras and ensembles.
Utilizes: Collaborations; Commissioned Composers; Commissioned Music; Fine Artists; Guest Accompanists; Guest Artists; Guest Companies; Guest Directors; Guest Lecturers; Guest Musical Directors; Guest Musicians; Guest Writers; Multimedia; Original Music Scores; Sign Language Translators; Singers
Founded: 1936
Specialized Field: Symphony; Orchestra; Chamber; Ensemble
Status: Professional; Nonprofit
Paid Staff: 11
Volunteer Staff: 1
Budget: $2.5 million
Income Sources: Ticket Sales; Business; Individual Contributions; Grants
Performs At: Gaillard Municipal Auditorium
Facility Category: Multipurpose
Seating Capacity: 2730
Organization Type: Performing; Touring; Resident; Educational

1679
SPOLETO FESTIVAL USA
14 George Street
Charleston, SC 29401-1524
Phone: 843-722-2764
Fax: 843-723-6383
e-mail: info@spoletousa.org
Web Site: www.spoletousa.org
Officers:
   Chairman: Carlos E. Evans
   President: M. Edward Sellers
   Treasurer: Ronald D. Abramson
   General Counsel & Secretary: John B. Hagerty
   Vice President: Jennie L. DeScherer
Management:
   Director of Artistic Planning and O: Nicole Taney
   Development Operations Manager: Neil Benish
   Director of Finance: Tasha Gandy
   Director of Production: Rhys Williams
   Director Of Development: Julia Forster
   Director of Marketing and Public Re: Jennifer Scott
Mission: To present opera, dance, theater, symphonic, choral and chamber music, jazz and visual arts exhibits of the highest quality; to serve as an educational environment for young artists and audiences alike.
Utilizes: Singers
Founded: 1977
Specialized Field: Jazz; Theatrical Dance
Status: Professional; Semi-Professional; Non-Profit
Paid Staff: 18
Budget: $7,000,000
Income Sources: Ticket Revenues; Contributions
Performs At: Gaillard Municipal Auditorium; Dock Street Theater
Annual Attendance: 70,000-80,000
Organization Type: Performing; Educational; Sponsoring

1680
CAROLINA YOUTH SYMPHONY
PO Box 534
Greenville, SC 29602
Phone: 864-232-3963
e-mail: gordon@carolinayouthsymphony.org
Web Site: carolinayouthsymphony.org
Officers:
   President: Skip Gordon
   Vice President: Susan Robbins
   Secretary: Nick DiLeo
   Treasurer: Katie Tuttle
   Immediate Past President: Lisa Cook
Management:
   Music Director: Leslie W Hicken
   Executive Director: Lee Elmore
   Conductor, Concert Orchestra: James F. Kilgus
   Conductor, Repertory Orchestra: Ginger Greer
   Conductor Emeritus: Dr. Robert Chesebro
Specialized Field: Youth Orchestra

1681
GREENVILLE SYMPHONY ORCHESTRA
200 South Main Street
Greenville, SC 29601
Phone: 803-232-0344
Fax: 803-240-3113
e-mail: bill@greenvillesymphony.org
Web Site: www.greenvillesymphony.org
Officers:
   President: Flavia Harton
   1st Vice President: A. Robert Nachman II
   2nd Vice President: Lee S. Dixon
   Secretary: John F. Splike
   Treasurer: Kathleen C. McKinney
Management:
   Music Director/Conductor: Edvard Tchivzhel
   Office Manager: Pam Hunter
   Marketing Director: Todd Weir
   Development Director: Linda Grandy
   Director of Operations & Orchestra: Sherwood Mobley
Mission: Providing our community with the highest quality musical entertainment and education.
Founded: 1948
Specialized Field: Symphony; Chamber; Ensemble; Pops
Status: Professional
Income Sources: American Symphony Orchestra League; American Society of Composers, Authors and Publishers; Broadcast Music Incorporated
Performs At: Peace Center for the Performing Arts
Organization Type: Performing; Resident; Educational

1682
HILTON HEAD SYMPHONY ORCHESTRA
2 Park Lane
Suite 300-301
Hilton Head, SC 29928
Mailing Address: PO Box 5757, Hilton Head, SC 29938
Phone: 843-842-2055
Fax: 843-842-2032
e-mail: mbriggs@hhso.org
Web Site: hhso.org
Officers:
   Chairman: Darle Booher
   Vice-Chair: Jim Collet
   Secretary: Richard Heyman
   Treasurer: Paul Moeri
   Chairman of Marketing/Audience Deve: Winifred A. Baker
   Board Member: Kathleen Corley
   Board Member: Hal Ashworth
   Board Member: Sherman Barker
Management:
   Artistic Director, Conductor: John Morris Russell
   President/CEO: Mary M Briggs
   Director of Mark and PR: Sarah Bergin
   Development Director: Gloria Daly
   Competition Director: Monica Huff
   Project Editor: Gayle Lang
   Administrative Manager: Jim Way
   Chief Accountant: Susan Strange
Mission: Our vision is to be the artistic leader in the presentation of music in the Low Country. The mission of the Hilton Head Symphony Orchestra is to inspire

INSTRUMENTAL MUSIC / South Dakota

and enrich the lives of our citizens and visitors through the performance of outstanding music, educational programs and community partnerships.
Utilizes: Arrangers; Artists-in-Residence; Collaborating Artists; Collaborations; Educators; Fine Artists; Lyricists; Multimedia; Music; Paid Performers; Singers
Founded: 1982
Specialized Field: Intrumental, Orchestra, Classical
Status: Non-Profit, Professional
Income Sources: Donors, Season Subscribers, Sponsors
Season: October through May
Performs At: First Presbyterian Church

1683
LONG BAY SYMPHONY ORCHESTRA
950 48th Avenue North
Suite 202
Myrtle Beach, SC 29577
Phone: 843-448-8379
Fax: 843-946-9897
e-mail: info@longbaysymphony.com
Web Site: longbaysymphony.com
Officers:
  President: Lisa Davis
  1st Vice President, 2nd Vice Presid: Angela Kegler, PhD
  Secretary: Lisa Jennings
  Treasurer: Stan Podkulski
  Participating Director: Kim Alexander
  Participating Director: Jamie Broadhurst
  Participating Director: Lisa Davis
  Participating Director: Llisa Jennings
  Participating Director: Angela Kegler
Management:
  Music Director, Conductor: Dr Charles Jones Evans
  Executive Director: Carolyn Pittman
  Youth Orchestra Manager: Jessica Miller
  Operations Manager: Mike Knight
  Financial Support: Mary Slaby
  Administration and Box Office: Pam Peterson
  Chair Musician: William Terwilliger
Mission: The Long Bay Symphonic Society was founded in 1987 by Dr. Diana Swanner-Scroggins, a local music storeowner. She determined the need for a local symphony orchestra after many customers, both music lovers and musicians, related their interests in such an organization. The first auditions for the Long Bay Symphony produced a core of 36 musicians who performed together for the first time in April of 1988 in Wheelwright Auditorium.
Utilizes: Arrangers; Choreographers; Collaborating Artists; Collaborations; Fine Artists; Guest Accompanists; Guest Speakers; Local Artists & Directors; Lyricists; Multimedia; Music; Paid Performers; Scenic Designers; Singers; Soloists; Special Technical Talent
Founded: 1987
Opened: 1988
Specialized Field: Classical, Instrumental, Orchestra
Status: Non-Profit, Professional
Income Sources: Donors, Sponsors, Grants
Season: October through March
Performs At: Myrtle Beach Highschool Performing Art's Center

1684
CONVERSE SYMPHONY ORCHESTRA
Converse College
580 E Main Street
Spartanburg, SC 29302
Phone: 864-596-9000
Fax: 864-596-9167
Toll-free: 800-766-1125
e-mail: music@converse.edu
Web Site: www.converse.edu
Management:
  Conductor: Paul Davis
  Department Chair: Dr Douglas Weeks
Mission: College student orchestra.
Founded: 1899
Specialized Field: Orchestra
Paid Staff: 2

South Dakota

1685
BROOKINGS CHAMBER MUSIC SOCIETY
Music Department
SDSU, Lincoln Music Hall (SLM) 205
Brookings, SD 57007
Phone: 605-688-5187
Fax: 605-688-4307
e-mail: sdsu_gradschool@sdstate.edu
Web Site: www.sdstate.edu
Officers:
  President: David Reynolds
Management:
  Program Coordinator: John Walker
  Senior Secretary: Teressa Karl
  Secretary: Connie Lemke
  Instructor of Piano: Mary Walker
  Instructor of Music-Voice: Anne Beloncik Schantz
Mission: Offering the South Dakota State University community and the Brookings area the highest quality artists and ensembles.
Utilizes: Collaborations; Fine Artists; Grant Writers; Guest Companies; Guest Directors; Guest Musical Directors; Guest Musicians; Multimedia; Organization Contracts; Original Music Scores; Sign Language Translators; Singers
Founded: 1982
Specialized Field: Orchestra; Chamber; Ensemble
Status: Nonprofit
Volunteer Staff: 16
Paid Artists: 20
Budget: $18,000
Income Sources: Season tickets; Gate; Donations; Endowments; Grants
Performs At: Peterson Recital Hall
Affiliations: SDSU
Annual Attendance: 1,800
Facility Category: Recital Hall
Type of Stage: Open
Stage Dimensions: 40' x 25'
Seating Capacity: 350
Year Built: 1980
Year Remodeled: 1995
Organization Type: Performing; Educational; Sponsoring

1686
SOUTH DAKOTA STATE UNIVERSITY CIVIC SYMPHONY
Music Department
SDSU, Lincoln Music Hall (SLM) 205
Brookings, SD 57007
Phone: 605-688-5187
Fax: 605-688-4307
e-mail: sdsu_gradschool@sdstate.edu
Web Site: www.sdstate.edu
Management:
  Music Director/Conductor: John Browand
  Senior Secretary: Teressa Karl
  Secretary: Connie Lemke
  Instructor of Piano: Mary Walker
  Instructor of Music-Voice: Anne Beloncik Schantz
Mission: Performing symphonic literature from Baroque through contemporary and highlighting outstanding soloists.
Utilizes: Collaborations; Five Seasonal Concerts; Guest Accompanists; Guest Musical Directors; Guest Musicians; Instructors; Local Artists; Multimedia; Original Music Scores; Singers; Soloists; Visual Arts
Founded: 1966
Specialized Field: Symphony; Orchestra
Status: Non-Professional; Nonprofit
Paid Staff: 3
Paid Artists: 10
Non-paid Artists: 40
Budget: $13,000
Income Sources: South Dakota State University; South Dakota Arts Council; Corporate Sponsors; Local Businesses
Performs At: Peterson Recital Hall
Facility Category: Performing Arts Center
Type of Stage: Concert Hall
Stage Dimensions: 96'x63'
Seating Capacity: 1000
Year Built: 2001
Cost: $6.4 million
Organization Type: Performing; Educational

1687
BLACK HILLS SYMPHONY ORCHESTRA
1202 E. St. Francis Street
Rapid City, SD
Mailing Address: PO Box 2246, Rapid City SD 57709
Phone: 605-348-4676
Fax: 605-394-2679
e-mail: contact@bhsymphony.org
Web Site: www.bhsymphony.org
Management:
  Conductor: Jack Knowles
  Concertmaster: Coral White
Mission: To promote music appreciation and knowledge in the area; to offer opportunities for local musicians to grow through performance and education.
Founded: 1931
Specialized Field: Symphony; Orchestra
Status: Nonprofit
Paid Staff: 10
Performs At: Rushmore Plaza Civic Center Theater
Organization Type: Performing; Resident; Educational

1688
SOUTH DAKOTA SYMPHONY
301 South Main Avenue
4th Floor
Sioux Falls, SD 57104
Phone: 605-335-7933
Fax: 605-335-1958
e-mail: sdsymphony@sdsymphony.org
Web Site: www.sdsymphony.org
Officers:
  President: Scott Lawrence
  Vice President: Mary Mastick
  Secretary: Matthew Parker
  Treasurer: Tom Wadsworth
  Past President: James Moore
Management:
  Music Director: Delta David Gier
  Executive Director: Jennifer Boomgaarden
  Director of Marketing and Developme: Anne Lawrence
  Director of Opr and Education: Sarah Burman
  Marketing Assistant: Melysa Rogen

INSTRUMENTAL MUSIC / Tennessee

Mission: Providing the highest quality orchestral music to the people of the Northern Plains, the South Dakota Symphony takes leadership in enhancing the cultural environment of the region, developing an understanding and interest in the people of the state for fine artistic expression.
Utilizes: Commissioned Music; Guest Companies; Guest Composers; Guest Designers; Guest Directors; Guest Lecturers; Guest Musical Directors; Guest Musicians; Local Artists; Multimedia; Original Music Scores; Sign Language Translators; Singers
Founded: 1922
Specialized Field: Symphony; Orchestra; Chamber; Ensemble
Status: Professional; Nonprofit
Paid Staff: 8
Paid Artists: 10
Budget: $1,500,000
Income Sources: Ticket Sales, Donations, grants, fundraising events
Performs At: Washington Pavilion of Arts and Science
Facility Category: Performing arts center
Type of Stage: Multi-purpose
Stage Dimensions: 50'x60'
Seating Capacity: 1,850
Year Remodeled: 1998
Rental Contact: Jeff Venekamp
Organization Type: Performing; Touring; Resident; Educational

Tennessee

1689
CHATTANOOGA SYMPHONY AND OPERA

701 Broad Street
Chattanooga, TN 37402
Phone: 423-267-8583
Fax: 423-265-6520
Web Site: www.chattanoogasymphony.org
Officers:
   President: Spencer McCallie
   Treasurer: Mark A. Smith
   Secretary: Kim Gavin
Management:
   Executive Director: Molly Sasse
   Music Director Emeritus: Robert Bernhardt
   Music Director & Conductor: Kayoko Dan
   Director: Samantha Teter
   Operations Manager: Kathy Allison
Utilizes: Commissioned Composers; Commissioned Music; Educators; Five Seasonal Concerts; Grant Writers; Guest Accompanists; Guest Companies; Guest Composers; Guest Designers; Guest Lecturers; Guest Musical Directors; Guest Musicians; Guest Writers; Instructors; Multimedia; Organization Contracts; Original Music Scores; Playwrights; Sign Language Translators; Singers
Specialized Field: Symphony
Status: Professional; Nonprofit
Paid Staff: 40
Budget: $1.2 million
Income Sources: Tennesseans for the Arts; Opera America; American Symphony Orchestra League
Performs At: Tivoli Theatre
Annual Attendance: 50,000 - 75,000
Facility Category: Theatre and Outdoor
Seating Capacity: 1700
Organization Type: Performing; Touring; Educational

1690
BRYAN SYMPHONY ORCHESTRA

1150 North Dixie Avenue
Cookeville, TN
Mailing Address: 123 W Broad Street, Suite 4,
Cookeville, TN 38501
Phone: 931-525-2633
e-mail: contact@bryansymphony.org
Web Site: bryansymphony.org
Officers:
   President: Sean O'Neil
   Past President: Mike Porten
   President-Elect: Donna Simpson
   Secretary: Teena King
   Treasurer: Lillian Hartgrove
   Advisor: Laura Clemmons
Management:
   Music Director, Conductor: Dan Allcott
   Executive Director: Erin Vickers
Mission: The mission of the Bryan Symphony Orchestra is to provide an orchestra of the highest artistic standards to perform regularly a broad range of repertoire for a wide and diverse audience; to provide quality educational experiences for all ages; and to serve as a leader and a continuing force in the cultural life of the Upper Cumberland Region.
Utilizes: Arrangers; Choreographers; Collaborating Artists; Collaborations; Commissioned Music; Fine Artists; Guest Conductors; Lyricists; Multimedia; Music; Paid Performers; Singers
Founded: 1962
Specialized Field: Clasical, Orchestra
Status: Non-Profit, Professional
Income Sources: Grants, Donors, Sponsors
Season: September through April
Performs At: Wattenbarger Auditorium, Bryan Fine Arts Building

1691
JACKSON SYMPHONY ASSOCIATION

207 E. Lafayette
Jackson, TN 38301
Phone: 901-427-6440
Fax: 901-427-6417
Toll-free: 800-951-6440
e-mail: jso@aeneas.net
Web Site: thejacksonsymphony.org
Officers:
   President: Leonie Hefley
   President-Elect: Nancy McMahon
   Secretary: Jan Boud
   Past-President: Tyler Swindle
Management:
   Music Director and Conductor: Peter Shannon
   Executive Director: Lee Warren
   Marketing and Development Director: Tracy Humphreys
   Operations Manager: Greg Hines
Mission: To support a performing orchestra of increasing quality for Jackson and its surrounding area; to promote the preservation of our musical heritage and audience exposure to the finer aspects of that heritage by providing programs that are attractive and entertaining.
Utilizes: Educators; Grant Writers; Guest Accompanists; Guest Directors; Guest Instructors; Guest Musical Directors; Guest Musicians; Multimedia; Original Music Scores; Sign Language Translators; Singers
Founded: 1961
Specialized Field: Symphony; Orchestra
Status: Semi-Professional
Paid Staff: 6
Volunteer Staff: 1
Budget: $600,000
Performs At: The Jackson Civic Center
Affiliations: American Symphony Orchestra League
Annual Attendance: 30,000
Organization Type: Performing; Touring; Resident; Educational

1692
JOHNSON CITY SYMPHONY ORCHESTRA

3201 Bristol Highway
Suite 2, PO Box 533
Johnson City, TN 37605
Phone: 423-926-8742
Fax: 423-926-8979
e-mail: jcsymphony@earthlink.net
Web Site: www.jcsymphony.com
Officers:
   Past Chair: Nancy Flugrath
   Treasurer: Martha Pointer
   Secretary: Sandy Powell
Management:
   Assistant Conductor: Kellie D. Brown
   Interim General Manager: Lewis Songer
   Music Director/Conductor: Robert J. Seebacher
   Office Manager: Elaine Pectol
Mission: To be a vital regional force providing orchestral music for all ages through education, entertainment, and cultural enrichment.
Founded: 1969
Specialized Field: Orchestra
Paid Staff: 2
Budget: $191,900
Income Sources: Tennessee Arts Commission Grant; Johnson City Area Arts Council Grant; Corporate and Individual Sponsorships and Contributions; Foundation Grants
Performs At: College Chapel; City Auditorium
Affiliations: ASOL; BMI
Annual Attendance: 20,000
Seating Capacity: 1194

1693
SYMPHONY OF THE MOUNTAINS

1200 E Center Street
Suite 311
Kingsport, TN 37660
Phone: 423-392-8423
Fax: 423-392-8428
e-mail: ksorch@aol.com
Web Site: www.kso.bigstep.com
Officers:
   President: Greg McMillan
   First Vice-President: Suzanne Kerney-Quillen
   Second Vice-President: Frank Harrington
   Secretary: Lucy Fleming
   Chief Operating Officer: Cornelia Laemmli Orth
Management:
   Music Director / Conductor: Cornelia Laemmli Orth
   General Manager: Melissa Roberts
   Box Office Manager: Jenny Smith
   Orchestra Manager: Teresa Holland Lundberg
Mission: To offer the public orchestral concerts as well as educational programs.
Utilizes: Collaborations; Guest Artists; Guest Musical Directors; Guest Musicians; Multimedia; Music; Singers
Founded: 1947
Specialized Field: Symphony; Orchestra; Chamber; Ensemble
Status: Semi-Professional; Non-Professional; Nonprofit
Paid Staff: 4
Volunteer Staff: 1

Paid Artists: 75
Budget: $285,000
Income Sources: Tickets sales, TN Arts, Commission grants, private contribution,corp. contributions
Performs At: Tom F Reid Employee Center
Affiliations: ASOL
Facility Category: Auditorium
Seating Capacity: 1,700 +
Organization Type: Performing; Resident; Educational; Sponsoring

1694
KNOXVILLE SYMPHONY ORCHESTRA
100 S. Gay Street
Suite 302
Knoxville, TN 37902
Phone: 865-291-3310
Fax: 865-546-3766
e-mail: abaker@knoxvillesymphony.com
Web Site: www.knoxvillesymphony.com
Officers:
  President: A. Richard Johnson
  President-Elect: Cynthia Moxley
  Past President: Jon R. Lawler
  Vice President - Artistic Affairs: Richard B. Bryan
  Vice President - Development: Russ Watkins
Management:
  Executive Director: Rachel Ford
  Director Development: Mary Sue Greiner
  Director of Communications: Rachel Dellinger
  Director of Education and Community: Jennifer Barnett
  Director of Operations: Stacy Taylor
Mission: To offer the region of East Tennessee a symphony orchestra for its enjoyment and education.
Utilizes: Guest Artists
Founded: 1935
Specialized Field: Symphony; Orchestra
Status: Professional; Nonprofit
Performs At: Tennessee Theater
Organization Type: Performing; Touring; Educational

1695
MEMPHIS SYMPHONY ORCHESTRA AND YOUTH SYMPHONY ORCHESTRA
585 S Mendenhall Road
Suite 501
Memphis, TN 38117
Phone: 901-537-2500
Fax: 901-537-2550
e-mail: information@memphissymphony.org
Web Site: www.memphissymphony.org
Officers:
  Chairman: Gayle S. Rose
  Secretary: Louise Barden
  Treasurer: Lowry Howell
  Immediate Past Chair: Mike Edwards
  Chorus Representative: Lisa Mendel
Management:
  Music Director: Mei-Ann Chen
  Assistant Conductor: Conner Gray Covington
  Director of Artistic Administration: Jenny Compton
  Director of Dev & Corp Relations: Jane Mims
  Director of Marketing: Jessica Batey
Utilizes: Guest Artists
Founded: 1952
Specialized Field: Youth Orchestra; Chamber
Status: Professional; Nonprofit
Paid Artists: 75
Performs At: Eudora Auditorium
Affiliations: American Symphony Orchestra League; Memphis Arts Council
Organization Type: Performing; Educational; Sponsoring

1696
NASHVILLE SYMPHONY
One Symphony Place
Nashville, TN 37201-2031
Phone: 615-687-6500
Fax: 615-687-6505
Web Site: www.nashvillesymphony.org
Officers:
  Board Chair: Edward A. Goodrich
  Secretary: Betsy Wills
  Treasurer: Kevin Crumbo
  President & CEO: Alan D. Valentine
  Board Member: Janet Ayers
  Board Member: Russel Bates
Management:
  Music Director: Giancarlo Guerrero
  Associate Conductor: Byung-Hyun Rhee
  Director of Artistic Administration: Laurence Tucker
  Director of Education: Blair Bodine
  Director of Events: Hays McWhirter,
Mission: Dedicated to enhancing the quality of life in Nashville and the surrounding communities by providing opportunities for all citizens to enjoy live performances of symphonic music in its various forms.
Utilizes: Guest Artists; Singers
Founded: 1946
Specialized Field: Symphony; Orchestra; Chamber
Status: Professional
Income Sources: American Symphony Orchestra League; American Arts Alliance; American Society of Composers, Authors and Publishers; Broadcast Music Incorporated
Performs At: Tennessee Performing Arts Center; War Memorial Auditorium
Organization Type: Performing; Resident; Touring; Educational

1697
OAK RIDGE CIVIC MUSIC ASSOCIATION
205A Badger Road
PO Box 4271
Oak Ridge, TN 03780
Phone: 865-483-5569
e-mail: office@orcma.org
Web Site: www.orcma.org
Officers:
  President: Audrey Stelson
Management:
  Conductor & Music Director: Dan Allcott
  Vice President: David Gurd
  Orchestra Personnel Manager/Librari: Scott Eddlemon
  Chorus Accompanist: Cathy Whitten
  Music Director: Dan Allcott
Mission: Offering the community quality music; providing gifted performers with an outlet.
Utilizes: Guest Artists; Singers
Founded: 1942
Specialized Field: Symphony; Orchestra
Status: Semi-Professional; Nonprofit
Paid Staff: 35
Income Sources: American Symphony Orchestra League; Tennesseans for the Arts
Performs At: Oak Ridge High School Auditorium
Organization Type: Performing; Educational

Texas

1698
ABILENE PHILHARMONIC ASSOCIATION
401 Cypress
Suite 520
Abilene, TX 79601
Phone: 915-677-6710
Fax: 915-676-6343
e-mail: info@abilenephilharmonic.org
Web Site: www.abilenephilharmonic.org
Officers:
  President: Jon Thorne
  President Elect: Jim Pizzorno
  Vice President: Grady Waddell
  Treasurer: Tom Watson
  Secretary: Mandy Gollihar
  Board Member:
Management:
  Music Director and Conductor: David Itkin
  Executive Director: Catherine Lansdowne
  Operations Manager/Education Manage: Dustin Neal
  Development Manager: Molly Longmire
  Office Manager/Box Office Manager: Tiffany Clemons
Mission: Offering the finest in symphonic literature to Abilene area residents.
Utilizes: Guest Artists
Founded: 1950
Specialized Field: Symphony; Orchestra
Status: Professional; Nonprofit
Income Sources: American Symphony Orchestra League
Performs At: Abilene Civic Center
Organization Type: Performing; Educational

1699
ALLEN PHILHARMONIC
102 South Allen Drive
Allen, TX 75013
Mailing Address: PO Box 508, Allen, TX 75013
Phone: 972-359-0656
e-mail: info@allenophilharmonic.org
Web Site: www.aallenphilharmonic.org
Officers:
  President: Kathleen Litinas
  Treasurer: Griff Moore
  Secretary: Connie Rodenbaugh
  Music Society: Judi Altstaff
  Board Member: Charles Beard
  Board Member: Jeremy Stone
Management:
  Conductor, Music Director: Richard C. Giangiullio
  Choral Conductor: Rusty King
Mission: Founded in 1998, the Allen Philharmonic Orchestra & Symphony Chorus is a professional orchestra comprised of 60-70 musicians. With the goal of enhancing its community's rich culture and fostering a community-wide appreciation for the art of music, the Allen Philharmonic presents an annual subscription series of four concerts and a variety of special events, community outreach and youth education programs.
Utilizes: Arrangers; Choreographers; Collaborating Artists; Collaborations; Composers-in-Residence; Fine Artists; Local Artists; Lyricists; Multimedia; Music; Paid Performers; Singers
Founded: 1998
Specialized Field: Orchestra, Classical
Status: Non-Profit, Professional
Income Sources: Sponsors, Donors
Season: September through May
Performs At: Allen High School Performing Arts Center, United Methodist Church

INSTRUMENTAL MUSIC / Texas

1700
AMARILLO SYMPHONY
1000 South Polk Street
Amarillo, TX 79101
Mailing Address: P.O. Box 2586, Amarillo, TX 79105-2586
Phone: 806-376-8782
Fax: 806-376-7127
e-mail: info@amarillosymphony.org
Web Site: www.amarillosymphony.org
Officers:
   President: Alfred J. Smith
   President Elect: Ellen Jones
   Secretary: Charles B. Kitsman
   Treasurer: Victor Glenn
Management:
   Executive Director: Susan White
   Music Director/Conductor: Jacomo Rafael Bairos
   Director of Development and Communi: Trudy Keeling
   Patron Services Coordinator: Ann Marie Rauscher
   Education Coordinator: Ben Smith
Mission: Providing symphonic music to residents of the Texas Panhandle; expanding musical appreciation and knowledge in the area.
Utilizes: Artists-in-Residence; Commissioned Composers; Commissioned Music; Fine Artists; Guest Accompanists; Guest Companies; Guest Composers; Guest Directors; Guest Lecturers; Guest Musical Directors; Guest Musicians; Guest Writers; Instructors; Multimedia
Founded: 1924
Specialized Field: Symphony; Orchestra; Chamber; Ensemble
Status: Professional; Nonprofit
Paid Staff: 6
Budget: $1,300,000
Income Sources: Tickets; Donations
Performs At: Amarillo Civic Center
Affiliations: American Symphony Orchestra League
Annual Attendance: 80,000
Facility Category: Auditorium; Outdoor
Seating Capacity: 2,300
Year Built: 1960
Organization Type: Performing; Educational

1701
AUSTIN CHAMBER MUSIC CENTER
3814 Medical Parkway
Austin, TX 78756
Phone: 512-454-7562
Fax: 512-454-0029
e-mail: info@austinchambermusic.org
Web Site: www.austinchambermusic.org
Officers:
   President: Catherine Wildermuth
   Vice-President: Laura Beussman
   Secretary: Tadd Lanham
   Treasurer: Donald McDaniel
   Board Member: Reed Arnos
Management:
   Artistic Director: Dr. Michelle Schumann
   Business Manager: Ora Shay
   Director of Education: Jenni Gossard
   Manager: Heather Williams
   Director of Operations: Maureen Cross
Mission: To improve the quality of community life by nurturing and expanding the knowledge, understanding, and appreciation of chamber music through education and performance.
Utilizes: Artists-in-Residence; Collaborations; Commissioned Composers; Commissioned Music; Composers-in-Residence; Fine Artists; Guest Accompanists; Guest Directors; Guest Ensembles; Guest Musical Directors; Instructors; Local Artists; Multimedia; Original Music Scores
Founded: 1981
Specialized Field: Chamber
Status: Professional; Nonprofit
Paid Staff: 4
Budget: $350,000
Income Sources: Grants from government; Foundations and corporations; Underwriting; Individuals and corporations; Ticket sales
Annual Attendance: 13,000
Facility Category: Various locations
Organization Type: Performing; Educational; Sponsoring

1702
AUSTIN CLASSICAL GUITAR SOCIETY
PO Box 4072
Austin, TX 78765
Phone: 512-300-2247
Fax: 512-323-9211
e-mail: M@MatthewHinsley.com
Web Site: www.austinclassicalguitar.org
Officers:
   President: Kendal Gladish
   Vice President: John Henry McDonald
   Treasurer: David Lastrapes
   Secretary: Jacqueline Rixen
Management:
   Executive Director: Matthew Hinsley
   Director of Development: April Long
   Director of Community Guitarists: Eric Pearson
   Director of Education & Outreach: Travis Marcum
   Assistant Director of Education & O: Jeremy Osborne
Specialized Field: Classical Guitar
Budget: $10,000

1703
AUSTIN SYMPHONY ORCHESTRA SOCIETY
1101 Red River
Austin, TX 78701
Phone: 512-476-6064
Fax: 512-476-6242
e-mail: tickets@austinsymphony.org
Web Site: www.austinsymphony.org
Officers:
   Chairman: Joe R. Long
   Chair Emeritus: D. J. Sibley, Jr.
   President: Thomas M. Neville
   Executive Vice-President: Charles J. Roesslein
   VP-Budget & Finance: Daniel B. Powell, III
Management:
   Executive Director: Anthony Corroa
   Music Director: Peter Bay
   Director of Education: Susan Mivillie
   Assistant to Executive Director: Shaler Wells
   Director of Operations & Orchestra: Craig Hahn
Mission: To enhance the cultural quality of life for the adults and young people of Austin and Central Texas by providing excellence in music performance and educational programs.
Utilizes: Guest Artists
Founded: 1911
Specialized Field: Symphony; Orchestra; Chamber; Ensemble; Ethnic Music; Folk Music; Band
Status: Professional
Paid Staff: 15
Budget: $3.8 million
Season: September-April
Performs At: University of Texas Theater for the Performing Arts
Affiliations: ASOL
Annual Attendance: 400,000
Organization Type: Performing; Touring; Resident; Educational; Sponsoring

1704
SYMPHONY OF SOUTHEAST TEXAS
4345 Phelan Boulevard
Suite 105
Beaumont, TX 77707
Phone: 409-892-2257
Fax: 409-892-0117
e-mail: sost@sost.org
Web Site: www.sost.org
Officers:
   President: Virginia Bean
   VP-Administration: James Black
   VP-Marketing: Russ Waddill
   VP Education: Virginia Bean
   VP Audience Development: Elaine Allums
Management:
   Executive Director: Douglas J. Fair
   Director of Communications: Melissa Tilley
Mission: Offering residents of Southeast Texas high quality musical performances of all types.
Founded: 1953
Specialized Field: Symphony; Orchestra
Status: Semi-Professional; Nonprofit
Paid Staff: 5
Income Sources: American Symphony Orchestra League; American Society of Composers, Authors and Publishers; Broadcast Music Incorporated
Performs At: Julie Rogers Theatre
Organization Type: Performing; Resident

1705
BRAZOS VALLEY SYMPHONY ORCHESTRA
2501 Earl Rudder Freeway S.
Bryan, TX 77845
Phone: 979-779-6100
Fax: 979-764-2375
e-mail: office@bvso.org
Web Site: www.bvso.org
Officers:
   President: Patricia Burchfield
   1st Vice President: Paul Parrish
   2nd Vice President: Cathy Loving
   Secretary: Doris Watson
   Treasurer: Carol Cantrell
Management:
   Music Director/Conductor: Marcelo Bussiki
   Concermaster: Javier Chaparro
   Executive Director: Dr. Mary Koeninger
   Office & Patron Services: Nika Hancock
Mission: To bring fine orchestral music to the Brazos Valley, home of Bryan/College Station and Texas A&M University. Each year, with generous support from our patrons, the BVSO puts on a full season of performances that delight young and old alike.
Utilizes: Collaborations; Commissioned Composers; Community Members; Guest Accompanists
Founded: 1981
Specialized Field: Symphony; Orchestra; Chamber
Status: Non-Professional
Organization Type: Performing

1706
BRAZOSPORT SYMPHONY ORCHESTRA
400 College Blvd
Clute, TX 77531

Phone: 979-265-7661
Toll-free: 877-265-7661
e-mail: info@bcfas.org
Web Site: bcfas.org
Officers:
   President: JC Mehner
   President Ex-Officio: Barry L. Finley
   Vice-President of Operations: Frances Bitter
   Vice-President of Productions: Mary Meyers
   Treasurer: Tom Fowler
Management:
   Conductor: Bill Atkerson
Mission: In 1981, Dr. Samuel Jones, Director of Rice University's newly formed Shepherd School of Music, contacted Jeralyn Friedli, a former player living in Lake Jackson . Dr. Jones said he had a promising conducting student named Jim Hagberg who wished to become the conductor of a community orchestra after graduation. Since 1984, the Symphony has continued to grow in its quantity of players, audience and budget.
Utilizes: Arrangers; Collaborating Artists; Collaborations; Composers-in-Residence; Lyricists; Multimedia; Music; Paid Performers; Singers
Founded: 1981
Opened: 1983
Specialized Field: Orchestra, Instrumental
Status: Non-Profit, Professional
Income Sources: Donors, Sponsors
Season: September through May
Performs At: Brazosort Center Stages

1707
CONROE SYMPHONY ORCHESTRA
1500 North Frasier Street
Conroe, TX 77301
Phone: 936-760-2144
Toll-free: 888-823-6610
e-mail: symphony@consolidated.net
Web Site: conroesymphony.org
Officers:
   Chairman: Dr Arline Arnold
Management:
   Musical Director, Conductor: Dr Don Hutson
   Executive Director: Dr Arline Arnold
   Youth Orchestra Conductor: Tarvia Bell
   Personnel Manager/Mark Coor: Patricia Duran
   Operations Manager/Conroe Symphony: Stephanie Harris
Mission: The CSO organization includes more than 225 volunteers who provide support for the presentation of five classical concerts, major fundraising events, youth orchestra activities and educational and community outreach programs.The CSO Season includes traditional classical treasures, popular favorites and featured soloists. The major objective is to provide the audience with the best possible musical ex-perience, while showcasing the true talent.
Utilizes: Arrangers; Collaborating Artists; Collaborations; Composers; Educators; Fine Artists; Guest Companies; Multimedia; Music; New Productions; Paid Performers; Scenic Designers; Singers; Soloists
Founded: 1997
Specialized Field: Orchestra, Instrumental, Classical
Status: Non-Profit, Professional
Income Sources: Grants, Donors, Ticket Sales
Season: Year Round
Performs At: Ark Church

1708
CORPUS CHRISTI SYMPHONY ORCHESTRA
555 North Carancachua Street
Tower II, Suite 410
Corpus Christi, TX 78401-0818
Phone: 361-883-6683
Fax: 361-882-4132
Toll-free: 877-286-6683
e-mail: ccso@ccsymphony.org
Web Site: ccsymphony.org
Officers:
   President: Darrell Coleman
   President Elect: Roger TenNapel
   Vice President: Phyllis Roseman
   Vice President: D Scott Ecliff
   Treasurer: Jan Lawrence
   Secretary: Patty Nuss
   Chair: Robert Scott
   Director: John Bell
   Director: Janie Bell
Management:
   Music Director, Conductor: John Giordono
   Executive Director: Robert A. Reed, rreed@ccsymphony.org
   Director of Development & Marketing: Adriana Martinez, vtriplett@ccsymphony.org
   Education & Production Manager: Heather McDonald
Mission: Our season features six stunning classical concerts, an assortment of pops special events and the continuation of our mission to bring music education and entertainment to students. Our classical subscription concerts feature works by your favorite composers in a showcase of talented artists.
Utilizes: Arrangers; Collaborating Artists; Collaborations; Educators; Fine Artists; Guest Companies; Guest Composers; Guest Speakers; Lyricists; Multimedia; Music; Paid Performers; Singers
Founded: 1989
Specialized Field: Classical, Orchestra, Instrumental
Status: Non-Profit, Professional
Income Sources: Advertising, Donors, Sponsors
Season: November through April
Performs At: Texas A&M Performing Art's Center

1709
CORPUS CHRISTI CHAMBER MUSIC SOCIETY
4709 Curtis Clark
Corpus Christi, TX 78411
Mailing Address: PO Box 60124 Corpus Christi, TX 78466-0124
Phone: 361-884-5775
e-mail: jallison3@stx.rr.com
Web Site: www.corpuschristichambermusic.org
Officers:
   President: David Parker
Management:
   Program Director: Joan Allison
Mission: To promote the appreciation and enjoyment of chamber music by bringing the world's finest ensembles together.
Founded: 1982
Specialized Field: Chamber
Volunteer Staff: 25
Paid Artists: 22
Budget: $30,000-$45,000
Income Sources: Private Donors; foundations; ticket sales
Performs At: Wolfe Recital Hall; Art Museum of South Texas
Affiliations: Chamber Music America
Annual Attendance: 2,000
Facility Category: Recital Hall; Auditorium
Seating Capacity: 300; 400

1710
TEXAS JAZZ FESTIVAL SOCIETY
403 N Shoreline Boulevard
Corpus Christi, TX 78403
Phone: 361-688-1296
Fax: 361-883-4500
e-mail: rick.sanchez@att.net
Web Site: www.texasjazz-fest.org/
Officers:
   President: Rick Sanchez
Management:
   Volunteer Information: Betty Torres-Perez
   Membership: Lydia DeeDee Flores
   Sponsorship Information: Gail Sanchez
   Vendor Information: Kathy Reyes
Mission: Producing the Texas Jazz Festival to the public annually, free of charge; promoting and preserving American jazz.
Utilizes: Singers
Founded: 1969
Specialized Field: Jazz Ensemble
Status: Professional; Nonprofit
Performs At: Bayfront Plaza Convention Center
Organization Type: Performing

1711
CHAMBER MUSIC INTERNATIONAL
PO Box 140092
Dallas, TX 75214
Phone: 972-385-7267
Fax: 214-324-1868
e-mail: admin@chambermusicinternational.org
Web Site: www.chambermusicinternational.org
Officers:
   President: Jeffrey Hamilton
   Secretary: Joanna Young
   Treasurer: David Witherspoon
Management:
   Founder and Artistic Director: Phillip Lewis
   General Manager: Sandra Wu
Utilizes: Fine Artists; Guest Accompanists; Guest Musical Directors; Guest Musicians; Instructors; Multimedia; Original Music Scores; Soloists
Founded: 1986
Specialized Field: Chamber
Paid Staff: 1
Paid Artists: 26
Budget: $100,000
Performs At: St. Barnabas Presbyterian Church

1712
DALLAS BACH SOCIETY
PO Box 140201
Dallas, TX 75214-0201
Phone: 214-320-8700
e-mail: DBachSoc@cs.com
Web Site: www.dallasbach.org
Officers:
   President: Stephanie McDonald
   Treasurer: Jack Carney
   Secretary: Kyle Mistrot
   Member at Large: Tracey Deen
   MD, Past President: Ellen Marder
Management:
   Artistic Director: James Richman
   General Manager: Angeline Churchill
Mission: Uniting the finest vocalist and instrumentalists specializing in Baroque and Classical period music, brings lively and informed performances of Handel, Bach, Vivaldi, Mozart and friends to the Dallas-Fort

INSTRUMENTAL MUSIC / Texas

Worth area, featuring outstanding performers from around the Metroplex, New York, the United States and abroad, to assure the highest professional standards of performance practice and technical virtuosity.
Founded: 1982
Specialized Field: Orchestra; Chamber
Status: Professional; Semi-Professional; Nonprofit
Paid Staff: 20
Income Sources: Chorus America; International Bach Society
Performs At: Dallas Museum of Art; Saint Thomas Aquinas Church
Organization Type: Performing; Sponsoring

1713
DALLAS CHAMBER MUSIC SOCIETY
3333 Lee Parkway
Ste. 600
Dallas, TX 75219
Mailing Address: 6611 Hillcrest Avenue, #220, Dallas, Texas 75205
Phone: 972-392-3267
Toll-free: 844-DCM- 844
e-mail: info@dallaschambermusic.org
Web Site: www.dallaschambermusic.org
Officers:
   President: James Scott
   Treasurer: Linda S. Baker
   VP Membership/Accommodations: Arend-Julius Koch
   Secretary: Oneida Cramer
Management:
   Honorary Director: Don Ort
   Artistic Director: Candace Bawcombe
   Executive Director: LaNell E. Armour
   Honorary Director: June Ort
Mission: To offer Dallas audiences low cost chamber music concerts of the highest professional quality.
Founded: 1954
Specialized Field: Chamber
Status: Professional; Nonprofit
Performs At: Caruth Auditorium; Southern Methodist University
Organization Type: Performing; Sponsoring

1714
DALLAS WIND SYMPHONY
P.O. Box 595026
Dallas, TX 75359-5026
Phone: 214-565-9463
Fax: 214-421-2263
Web Site: www.dws.org
Management:
   Artistic Director: Jerry Junkin
   Executive Director/Founder: Kim J Campbell
   Box Office Manager: Sharron Morgan
   Director of Marketing & Comm: April Davis
   Director of Education and Concert O: Gigi Sherrell Norwood
Mission: The Dallas Wind Symphony is the leading professional civilian wind band in the United States today. Comprised of 50 woodwind, brass and percussion players, the band performs an eclectic blend of musical styles ranging from Bach to Bernstein and Sousa to Strauss. They combine the tradition of the British brass band with the musical heritage of the American town band.
Specialized Field: Wind Ensemble; Orchestra

1715
GREATER DALLAS YOUTH ORCHESTRA ASSOCIATION
Sammons Center for the Arts
3630 Harry Hines Boulevard
Dallas, TX 75219
Phone: 214-528-7747
Fax: 214-528-7749
e-mail: info@gdyo.org
Web Site: www.gdyo.org
Officers:
   Chair: Vance Maultsby
   President: C. Dealey Campbell
   Secretary: Louis R. Ainsworth
   Treasurer: Randy A. Gregg
Management:
   Executive Director: Chuck Moore
   Director of Development and Marketi: Amber Oosterwaal
   General Manager/Librarian: Yurie Iwasaki
   Operations Manager: Patrick Herring
   Jazz Institute Manager: Barry Ouosterwaal
Mission: To provide music education and performance opportunities to musically talented youth.
Utilizes: Guest Artists; Guest Companies
Founded: 1972
Specialized Field: Youth Orchestra; Ensemble
Status: Non-Professional; Nonprofit
Budget: $470,000
Income Sources: Tuition; Diversified Grants
Performs At: Morton H Meyerson Symphony Center
Affiliations: League Of American Ochestras
Annual Attendance: 15,000
Organization Type: Performing; Resident; Educational

1716
NEW LIFE SYMPHONY ORCHESTRA
PO Box 12622
Dallas, TX 75225
Phone: 214-686-6874
e-mail: johnny@newlifesymphony.com
Web Site: www.newlifesymphony.com
Officers:
   Chairman, Founder, Music Instructor: Johnny Fuller
   President: Pamela Reynolds
   Vice President: Rob Flickinger
   Secretary: Larry Bailey
   Advisory Committee: Gene Blanton
   Board Member: Janice Bloom
Mission: The New Life Symphony Orchestra [NLSO] is mobilizing Christian instrumentalists to use their God-given gifts and talents to share the Gospel. The orchestra is unique in that it is targeting the symphony halls of the world, reaching a strata of society that would typically never step foot in a church. All of the instrumentalists of the NLSO volunteer their time to prepare and perform free, world-class concerts for the DFW community.
Utilizes: Arrangers; Collaborating Artists; Collaborations; Composers; Composers-in-Residence; Fine Artists; Multimedia; Music; Singers; Soloists
Specialized Field: Gospel, Classical, Orchestra, Instrumental
Status: Non-Profit
Income Sources: Donors, Sponsors
Season: November
Performs At: New Life Church Sanctuary

1717
ORCHESTRA OF NEW SPAIN
10260 North Central Expressway
Suite 276
Dallas, TX 75231
Phone: 214-750-1492
Fax: 214-750-1492
e-mail: info@orchestraofnewspain.org
Web Site: orchestraofnewspain.org
Officers:
   President: Alain Bellet
   Arts Advocate: Barbara Benac
   Partner: Deborah Brown
   Community Volunteer: Mary Ann Caldwell
   Board Member: Barry Green
   Board Member: Joseph R. Jones
   Board Member: Anne Monson
Management:
   Artistic Director, Conductor: Grover Wilkins
Mission: The Orchestra of New Spain was founded in 1989 by conductor Grover Wilkins as a means of enhancing the place of the landmark Cathedral Santuario de Guadalupe in the heart of the aborning Dallas Arts District. Plans for a concert series there led to his 1985 discovery of the neglected, staggeringly beautiful major musical works of the Spanish 17th and 18th centuries.
Utilizes: Arrangers; Choreographers; Collaborating Artists; Collaborations; Composers; Composers-in-Residence; Educators; Fine Artists; Five Seasonal Concerts; Lyricists; Multimedia; Music; Paid Performers; Singers
Founded: 1989
Specialized Field: Spanish Boroque
Status: Non-Profit, Professional
Income Sources: Donors, Corporate Sponsors
Season: September through May
Performs At: Zion Lutheran Church

1718
VOICES OF CHANGE
3630 Harry Hines Blvd.
Dallas, TX 75219
Phone: 214-378-8670
Fax: 214-378-5043
e-mail: info@voicesofchange.org
Web Site: www.voicesofchange.org
Officers:
   President: Harvey Stiegler
   Secretary: Heather Carlile
   Treasurer: Phillip Kappaz
   Vice-President: Francisco Millet
Management:
   Artistic Director: Maria Schleuning
   General Manager: Eileen McKee
   City of Dallas, Office of Cultural: Philip Collins
Mission: To present the works of living composers and classics of the 20th & 21st centuries; to offer a seasonal series, tours, monthly radio broadcasts, recordings, special-event concerts and commissions.
Utilizes: Artists-in-Residence; Collaborations; Commissioned Composers; Commissioned Music; Guest Accompanists; Guest Artists; Guest Companies; Guest Composers; Guest Musical Directors; Guest Musicians; Lyricists; Multimedia; Original Music Scores; Playwrights; Singers
Founded: 1975
Specialized Field: Chamber; Ensemble
Status: Professional; Nonprofit
Paid Staff: 2
Budget: $115,000
Income Sources: Tickets, Gifts, Grants

Performs At: Caruth Auditorium; Southern Methodist University
Affiliations: Chamber Music America; Southern Methodist University; American Music Center; Meet the Composers; Texas Commission on the Arts
Annual Attendance: 5,000
Organization Type: Performing; Touring; Resident; Educational

1719
SOUTH TEXAS SYMPHONY ASSOCIATION
Neuhaus Tower, 200 S. 10th Street
Suite 104
Edinburg, TX 78501
Mailing Address: PO Box 2832 McAllen, TX 78502
Phone: 956-661-1615
Fax: 956-393-2290
e-mail: vivian@valleyorchestra.org
Web Site: www.vsomusic.org
Officers:
  President: Suzanne McDonald
  Vice - President: Carmen Z. Lara
  Secretary: Emily Nielson
  Treasurer: Ernesto Sepulveda
Management:
  Director & Conductor: Dr. Peter Dabrowski
  Director: Vivian V. Vargas
  Director: Dr. David Means
  Orchestra Librarian: Jane Goodman
  Orchestra Personnel Manager: Scott Roeder
Mission: Promoting, nurturing and supporting symphonic music performances in South Texas.
Utilizes: Singers
Founded: 1976
Specialized Field: Symphony; Chamber
Status: Semi-Professional; Nonprofit
Paid Staff: 78
Volunteer Staff: 40
Budget: $529,000
Income Sources: American Symphony Orchestra League; Pan American University
Performs At: Pan American University Fine Arts Auditorium
Annual Attendance: 6,500
Facility Category: Fine Arts Center
Seating Capacity: 1,055
Organization Type: Performing; Resident; Educational

1720
EL PASO PRO-MUSICA
6557 North Mesa
El Paso, TX 79912
Phone: 915-833-9400
Fax: 915-833-9425
e-mail: info@elpasopromusica.org
Web Site: www.elpasopromusica.org
Officers:
  Chairman/President: Charles Dodds III
  President Elect: Teresita Corral
  Secretary: Wendy Sudimack
  Treasurer: James Beale
  VP of Administration: Michael Graham
Management:
  Executive Director: Felipa Solis
  Artistic Director: Zuill Bailey
  Office Manager: Marivi Isaac
Mission: Promoting musical and cultural growth in the El Paso area; presenting chamber music and a chamber music festival.
Utilizes: Guest Artists; Guest Companies
Founded: 1977
Specialized Field: Chamber; Classical Music
Status: Professional; Nonprofit
Organization Type: Performing; Educational; Presenter

1721
EL PASO SYMPHONY ORCHESTRA
Abraham Chavez Theatre
One Civic Center Plaza
El Paso, TX 79901
Mailing Address: P.O. Box 180, El Paso, Texas 79942
Phone: 915-532-3776
Fax: 915-533-8162
e-mail: info@epso.org
Web Site: www.epso.org
Officers:
  Chairman: Kacy Spivack
  Chairman Elect: Arlene Carroll
  Vice President Financial Developmen: Michael Montes
  Vice President Finance and Administ: Bill Holmes
  Vice President Audience Development: Tomas De Leon
Management:
  Executive Manager: Ruth Ellen Jacobson
  Music Director: Bohuslav Rattay
  Business Manager: Linda Fischer
  Resident Conductor: Andy Moran
  Business Manager: Linda Fischer
Mission: Fostering appreciation of symphonic music in the El Paso area.
Utilizes: Collaborations; Commissioned Composers; Commissioned Music; Educators; Grant Writers; Guest Accompanists; Guest Artists; Guest Companies; Guest Composers; Guest Instructors; Guest Lecturers; Guest Musicians; Guest Writers; Guild Activities; Local Artists; Lyricists; Multimedia; Original Music Scores; Singers; Theatre Companies; Touring Companies
Founded: 1930
Specialized Field: Symphony; Orchestra
Status: Professional, Nonprofit
Paid Staff: 100
Budget: $1,000,000
Income Sources: Ticket sales, contributions
Performs At: El Paso Civic Center Theatre
Annual Attendance: 35,000
Facility Category: Theatre
Seating Capacity: 2,400
Organization Type: Performing; Educational; Sponsoring

1722
CLIBURN CONCERTS
Van Cliburn Foundation
2525 Ridgmar Boulevard, Suite 307
Fort Worth, TX 76116
Phone: 817-738-6536
Fax: 817-738-6534
e-mail: cthompson@cliburn.org
Web Site: www.cliburn.org
Officers:
  President and CEO: Jacques Marquis
  Chairman: Carla Kemp Thompson
  Vice chairman: Wesley R. Turner
  Secretary: Kim Darden
  Treasurer: Jeff King
  Chief Financial Officer: Alissa Ford
Management:
  Director of Artistic Planning: Sandra Doan
  Director of Education: Susan Robertson
  Director of Development: Marianne Pohle
  Director of Mark and PR: Maggie Estes
  Office Manager: Marie Giasson
Mission: To produce the Cilburn Piano Series.
Founded: 1962
Specialized Field: Series & Festivals; Instrumental Music; Vocal Music
Status: Non-Profit; Professional
Paid Staff: 13
Paid Artists: 15
Budget: $150,000-$400,000
Performs At: Nancy Lee & Perry R. Bass Performance Hall

1723
FORT WORTH SYMPHONY ORCHESTRA
330 E 4th Street
Suite 200
Fort Worth, TX 76102
Phone: 817-665-6500
Fax: 817-665-6600
e-mail: administration@fwsymphony.org
Web Site: www.fwsymphony.org
Officers:
  Chairman of the Board: Mercedes T. Bass
  Chairman of the Executive Committee: Mark G. Nurdin
  Secretary: Teresa King
  Treasurer: Marvin E. Blum
  President and CEO: Amy Adkins
  Director of Education and Community: Lindsey Stortz Branch
  Production Manager: Jarod Rehkemper
  Orchestra Personnel Manager: Laura Mirahver
  Operations Manager: Lisa Stallings
Mission: To provide the leadership and financial support required to maintain a symphony orchestra of first rank and to build an internationally-recognized chamber orchestra, dedicated to artistic development and performances of superior quality.
Utilizes: Guest Composers; Guest Instructors; Guest Musical Directors; Guest Musicians
Founded: 1925
Specialized Field: Symphony; Orchestra; Chamber
Status: Professional; Nonprofit
Paid Staff: 25
Volunteer Staff: 400
Paid Artists: 80
Budget: $9,900,000
Income Sources: Ticket Sales; Grants; Individual & Corporate Donors
Performs At: Tarrant County Convention Center; Ed Landreth Auditorium
Affiliations: American Symphony Orchestra League
Annual Attendance: 290,000
Rental Contact: Rental Contact Carl Davis
Organization Type: Performing; Touring

1724
YOUTH ORCHESTRA OF GREATER FORT WORTH
4401 Trail Lake Drive
Fort Worth, TX 76109
Phone: 817-923-3121
Fax: 817-924-0007
Web Site: www.yofw.org
Officers:
  President: Kay Goldthwaite
  Ex. Vice President: John Paul Wood, Jr.
  Vice President: June Wolff
  Vice President: Carlos Coscia
  Treasurer: Jerry Daniel
Management:
  Executive Director: Willa Dunleavy
  Orchestra Manager: Linda Moore
  Stage Manager: Michael Bounds
  Office Assistant: Laurielle Warren
  Building Management: Manny Gasea

INSTRUMENTAL MUSIC / Texas

Mission: Educating young musicians from the ages of 3 to 22.
Founded: 1965
Specialized Field: Youth Orchestra
Status: Nonprofit
Paid Staff: 1
Volunteer Staff: 100
Paid Artists: 6
Budget: $200,000
Income Sources: Grants; tuitions; concerts
Performs At: Orchestra Hall
Annual Attendance: 4,000
Type of Stage: Proscenium
Stage Dimensions: 70x40
Seating Capacity: 384
Year Built: 1940
Year Remodeled: 1980
Rental Contact: 817-921-6222 Mike Haley
Organization Type: Performing; Touring; Educational

1725
DALLAS BRASS
4321 Clemson Drive
Garland, TX 75042
Phone: 972-276-7388
e-mail: mail@dallasbrass.com
Web Site: www.dallasbrass.com/
Management:
  Director: Michael Levin
  Booking Coordinator: Wiss Rudd
  Artist Manager, Director of Booking: Kevin Peters
  Concert Coordinator: Barbara Skrebutenas
  Office Manager: Lorraine Levin
Mission: Striving to bridge musical gaps from classical to pop.
Founded: 1982
Specialized Field: Brass Ensemble
Status: Professional; Commercial
Organization Type: Performing; Touring; Resident; Educational

1726
GARLAND SYMPHONY ORCHESTRA
1919 S. Shiloh Rd
Suite 101
Garland, TX 75042
Mailing Address: P.O. Box 461204, Garland, TX 75046
Phone: 972-926-0611
Fax: 972-926-0811
e-mail: info@garlandsymphony.org
Web Site: www.garlandsymphony.org/
Officers:
  Chairman: Jim Moebius
  Vice Chairman: Steve Brezik
  Secretary: Marty Daniel
  Treasurer: Barry Walters
Management:
  Music Director: Robert Carter Austin
  General Manager: Michael Finley
  Education Manager: Alice Allen
  Finance Manager: Gillian Adams
Mission: Presenting the finest possible concerts.
Utilizes: Guest Artists
Founded: 1978
Specialized Field: Symphony; Orchestra
Status: Professional; Nonprofit
Performs At: Garland Performing Arts Center
Organization Type: Performing; Educational

1727
CLEAR LAKE SYMPHONY
PO Box 890582
Houston, TX 77289-0582
Phone: 713-639-0702
e-mail: clsbob@aol.com
Web Site: clearlakesymphony.org/
Officers:
  President/Treasurer: Sherrie Matula
  Vice President: Mike Matula
Management:
  General Manager: Betty Wall
  Music Director & Conductor: Charles A. Johnson
  Assistant Music Director: Bob Wall
Mission: To present classical music for the residents of the Bay area and to provide opportunities to qualified musicians both to perform with a classical orchestra and to participate in the music education of the area.
Founded: 1976
Specialized Field: Symphony; Orchestra
Status: Non-Professional; Nonprofit
Paid Staff: 34
Income Sources: National Symphony Orchestra League
Performs At: Clear Lake Theatre; Gloria Dei Lutheran Church Auditorium
Organization Type: Performing

1728
HOUSTON CIVIC SYMPHONY ORCHESTRA
4378 Harrest Lane
Houston, TX 77004-6606
Mailing Address: P.O. Box 770032, Houston, TX 77215
Phone: 281-586-2100
e-mail: support@civicsymphony.org
Web Site: www.civicsymphony.org
Officers:
  President: Alvin Thomas
  Vice President: Cliff Wright
  Secretary: Amy Kraeger
  Treasurer: Jennifer Isadore
Management:
  Music Director & Conductor: Brian Runnels
  Director: Robert Walp
  Director: Lawrence Rushdi
  Director: Michael Barron
Mission: To provide a playing and performance opportunity for professional and nonprofessional musicians who earn the major portion of their livelihood outside full-time, professional music performances.
Utilizes: Guest Companies
Founded: 1967
Specialized Field: Symphony; Orchestra; Chamber
Status: Semi-Professional; Nonprofit
Paid Staff: 65
Income Sources: University of Houston
Performs At: Cullen Hall; University of Houston
Organization Type: Performing

1729
HOUSTON EARLY MUSIC
PO Box 271193
Houston, TX 77277-1193
Phone: 281-846-4222
e-mail: info@HoustonEarlyMusic.org
Web Site: www.HoustonEarlyMusic.org
Officers:
  President: Ruth Cross
  Secretary: Catherine Whitney
  Treasurer: Terece McGovern
Management:
  Executive Director: Helga Aurisch
  Artistic Director: Nancy Ellis
Mission: Houston Early Music is a chartered, nonprofit, organization whose purpose is to present historically-informed performances of early music from the European traditions and other world cultures in concerts featuring internationally renowned vocal, instrumental and chamber musicians. In addition, we reach out to new and diverse audiences through a cross-disciplinary educational program.
Founded: 1968
Specialized Field: Chamber; Ensemble; Ethnic Music; Folk Music
Status: Professional; Nonprofit
Paid Staff: 8
Organization Type: Educational; Sponsoring

1730
CHAMBER MUSIC HOUSTON
Rice University MS-532
6100 Main Street
Houston, TX 77005-1827
Mailing Address: P. O. Box 1892, Houston, TX 77251-1892
Phone: 713-348-5400
Fax: 713-348-5405
e-mail: cmh@rice.edu
Web Site: chambermusichouston.org
Officers:
  President: Curtis W. Robinson
  Secretary: Jeanne Bauer
  Treasurer: Don Rutledge
Management:
  Administrative Director: Kerryn Barrera
  Audience Development: Ann Fairbanks
  Marketing & Communications: Lucile Agaisse
  Programming: Daniel Musher
  Development: Kirk Weinert
Mission: Presenting chamber ensembles of national and international reputation; developing new audiences.
Founded: 1960
Specialized Field: Chamber; Ensemble
Status: Professional; Nonprofit
Paid Staff: 1
Income Sources: Shepherd School of Music
Performs At: Seude Concert Hall
Organization Type: Performing; Sponsoring

1731
HOUSTON SYMPHONY
615 Louisiana Street
Suite 102
Houston, TX 77002
Phone: 713-224-4240
e-mail: office@houstonsymphony.org
Web Site: www.houstonsymphony.org
Officers:
  Chairman of the Board: Jesse B. Tutor
  President: Robert A. Peiser
  President Elect, VP, Board Governan: Steven P. Mach
  Chief Financial Officer: Rauli Gracia
  Immediate Past Chair: Ed Wulfe
Management:
  Executive Director/CEO: Mark C. Hanson
  General Manager/Chief Operations Of: Steven Brosvik
  Director Human Resources: Meg Philpot
  Director, Human Resources: Meg Philpot
  Director, Popular Programming: Lesley Sabol
  Senior Director, Development: Mark Folkes
  Director, Volunteer Services: Vickie Hamley
  Director, Planned Giving: Patrick Quinn
Mission: The mission of the Houston Symphony is to foster excellence and innovation in the performance and presentation of great music. To enrich the lives of our diverse citizens, to educate current and future

INSTRUMENTAL MUSIC / Texas

audiences and to bring distinciton to our community through the orchestra's international presence and standing.
Specialized Field: Orchestra

1732
RIVER OAKS CHAMBER ORCHESTRA (ROCO)
1973 West Gray
Suite 3
Houston, TX 77019
Phone: 713-665-2700
e-mail: info@rocohouston.org
Web Site: rocohouston.org
Officers:
- **President:** Chris Ross
- **Vice President:** Scott W. Baxter
- **Secretary:** Connie Pfeiffer
- **Treasurer:** Tim Harris
- **Advisor:** Joe Abuso
- **Advisor:** Loretta Cross
- **Advisor:** Kit Gwinn
- **Advisor:** Drew Helmner

Management:
- **Artisitic Director, Founder:** Alecia Lawyer
- **Executive Director:** James Rowland
- **Associate Artistic Director:** Suzanne LeFevre
- **Development Director:** Christine Stevens
- **Marketing and Operations Manager:** Connie Thompson
- **Production Manager:** William von Reichbauer
- **Office Manager:** Anna Harris
- **Bookkeeper:** Teresa Rogers
- **Graphics:** Teresa B. Southwell

Mission: ROCO: an orchestra of all-star musicians, distinguished conductors, and famous composers, who come together from all over the world to present unexpected classics, original compositions, and delightful performances that dissolve the barriers between audience and orchestra.
Utilizes: Arrangers; Collaborating Artists; Collaborations; Community Talent; Designers; Educators; Fine Artists; Local Artists & Directors; Lyricists; Multimedia; Music; Paid Performers; Singers
Founded: 2005
Specialized Field: Instrumental, Classical, Orchestra
Status: Non-Profit, Professional
Income Sources: Donors, Sponsors
Season: Year Round
Performs At: Lawndale Arts Center

1733
SYMPHONY NORTH OF HOUSTON
PO Box 73591
Houston, TX 77273
Phone: 713-867-3465
Web Site: www.symphonynorth.org
Officers:
- **President:** Richard Mintz
- **Secretary:** Marie Rogoff
- **Treasurer:** Carla Marchell
- **Personnel:** Connie Yancey

Management:
- **Conductor:** Dr Reynaldo Ochoa
- **Publicity:** Lynn Coalmer

Mission: A community based orchestra composed of a very special group of classical musicians, which include teachers, homemakers, engineers, lawyers, bankers and many other professionals that enjoy playing classical music.
Founded: 1974
Specialized Field: Orchestra

1734
IRVING SYMPHONY ORCHESTRA ASSOCIATION
225 E. John Carpenter F
Suite 120
Irving, TX 75062
Phone: 972-831-8818
Fax: 972-831-8818
e-mail: irvingsymphony@irvingsymphony.com
Web Site: www.irvingsymphony.com
Officers:
- **Chairman:** Charles Hosler
- **President:** Marguerite Korkmas
- **Secretary:** Nancie Rissing
- **Treasurer:** Carol Little

Management:
- **Music Director/Conductor:** Hector Guzman
- **Administrator:** Daisy Piantini
- **Personnel and Operations:** Jim Gasewicz

Mission: Offering Irving and its surrounding communities outstanding music.
Founded: 1962
Specialized Field: Symphony; Orchestra
Status: Nonprofit
Paid Staff: 1
Volunteer Staff: 220
Paid Artists: 85
Performs At: Carpenter Performance Hall
Affiliations: ASOL; TASO
Organization Type: Performing

1735
LAS COLINAS SYMPHONY ORCHESTRA
Irving Arts Center
3333 North MacArthur
Irving, TX 75014
Mailing Address: PO Box 141446, Irving, TX 75014
Phone: 972-252-4800
Fax: 972-252-4877
Web Site: lascolinassymphony.org
Officers:
- **President:** Dr. David Hawkins
- **Vice President:** Ty Mayes
- **Treasurer:** Gus Tramp
- **Secretary:** Beverly Gray
- **Board Member:** Michael Cate
- **Board Member:** Louise Childs
- **Board Member:** Alan Fleck

Management:
- **Artistic Director, Conductor:** Robert Carter Austin
- **Executive Director:** Deborah Hawkins
- **Education Manager:** Alice Ford
- **Finance Manager:** Gillian Adams

Mission: The Las Colinas Symphony Orchestra is a fully professional ensemble dedicated to excellence in the performance of symphonic music and to the cultural enrichment of the dynamically growing Las Colinas corporate and residential communities, as well as to patrons throughout Irving and adjacent cities.
Utilizes: Arrangers; Collaborating Artists; Collaborations; Educators; Fine Artists; Grant Writers; Guest Composers; Lyricists; Multimedia; Music; Original Music Scores; Paid Performers; Performance Artists; Singers
Founded: 1991
Specialized Field: Classical, Instrumental, Orchestra
Status: Non-Profit, Professional
Income Sources: Donors
Season: Year Round
Performs At: Carpenter Performance Hall

1736
SYMPHONY OF THE HILLS
PO Box 294703
Kerrville, TX 78029-4703
Phone: 830-792-7469
e-mail: info@symphonyofthehills.org
Web Site: symphonyofthehills.org
Officers:
- **President:** Warren Fergusen
- **Vice President:** John Kissek
- **Treasurer & Chief Finantial Officer:** Roger Robertz
- **Recording Secretary:** Dr Tim Summerlin

Management:
- **Conductor & Artistic Director:** Jay B. Dunnahoo
- **Associate Conductor & Associate Con:** Dr. Eugene Dowdy
- **Orchestra Admininistrator:** Margie Schwartz

Mission: The Symphony of the Hills, with a nucleus of seventy-five musicians, performs an extensive repertoire of symphonic music for the enjoyment and enrichment of audiences throughout the beautiful Hill Country of Texas. The orchestra, partnering with Schreiner University, is committed to expanding the appreciation of music and in developing the musical talents of young people throughout the community.
Utilizes: Arrangers; Artists-in-Residence; Collaborating Artists; Collaborations; Composers; Fine Artists; Guest Companies; Lyricists; Multimedia; Music; Paid Performers; Scenic Designers; Singers; Soloists
Founded: 2010
Specialized Field: Instrumental, Classical, Orchestra, Jazz
Status: Non-Profit, Educational
Income Sources: Grants, Donors, Sponsors
Season: Year Round
Performs At: Caillou Theater

1737
KINGSVILLE SYMPHONY ORCHESTRA
Texas A&M Campus
855 North Armstrong
Kingsville, TX 78363
Phone: 361-593-2804
Toll-free: 800-333-5032
e-mail: kingsvillesypmhony@gmail.com
Web Site: kingsvillesymphony.org
Officers:
- **President:** Therese Crocker
- **Vice President:** Abbey Zink
- **Secretary:** Kellie Lignitz-Hahn
- **Corresponding Secretary:** Brenda Lukefahr
- **Treasurer:** Robbie Brown
- **Board Member:** Carol Ann Anderson
- **Baord Member:** Oscar Diaz
- **Advisor:** Mary Tryer
- **Advisor:** Paul Hageman

Management:
- **Violist and Conductor:** Dr. Veronica Salinas
- **Guest Conductor:** Lee Gwozdz
- **Guest Conductor:** Byron Stripling
- **Guest Conductor:** Justin Benavidez

Mission: The presence of a symphony orchestra in a community adds immeasurably to the quality of life for its residents.
Utilizes: Arrangers; Artists-in-Residence; Collaborating Artists; Composers-in-Residence; Educators; Fine Artists; Guest Companies; Guest Composers; Lyricists; Multimedia; Music; Paid Performers; Singers; Soloists
Specialized Field: Instrumental, Orchestra, Classical
Status: Non-Profit
Income Sources: Donors, Sponsors
Season: October, November, April, July

INSTRUMENTAL MUSIC / Texas

Performs At: Edward N Jones Auditorium

1738
LAREDO PHILHARMONIC ORCHESTRA
5201 University Blvd
Laredo, TX 78041
Phone: 956-326-3039
e-mail: townsend.conductor@gmail.com
Web Site: laredophil.com
Officers:
  President: Angela Lutz
  Treasurer: Gloria Flores
  Board Member: Fernando Alderete
  Board Member: Carlos Luna
  Board Member: Tati Friar
Management:
  Music Director: Brendan Townsend
  Personnel Manager: Angeline Townsend
Mission: Contributing to the cultural enrichment of Laredo and the surrounding area.
Founded: 1980
Specialized Field: Symphony; Orchestra; Chamber
Status: Professional; Nonprofit
Performs At: Laredo Civic Center
Organization Type: Performing; Touring; Resident; Educational

1739
LEWISVILLE LAKE SYMPHONY ORCHESTRA
1278 F.M. 407
Suite 109, PMB B30
Lewisville, TX 75077
Phone: 972-874-9087
Toll-free: 800-595-4849
e-mail: info@lewisvillesymphony.org
Web Site: lewisvillesymphony.org
Officers:
  Chairman: R Neil Fergusen
  Chair, Marketing Planning & Audienc: Grace Lawrence
  Treasurer: Martha Whitescarver
  Secretary: Patti McCoy
  Chhair, Nominating Committee: Bill Collins
  Players Representative: Jennifer Griffin
  Chair, Event Coordination & Logisti: Nancy Wright
  Board Member: Sean Kirk
Management:
  Music Director/Conductor: Adron Ming
  Controller: Robert McClellan
Mission: The Lewisville Lake Symphony is dedicated to enhancing the quality of life for people of all ages in North Texas through live and inspiring classical music. The Symphony is committed to educating and supporting rising young talent.
Utilizes: Arrangers; Choreographers; Collaborating Artists; Composers-in-Residence; Educators; Guest Companies; Multimedia; Music; New Productions; Paid Performers; Scenic Designers; Singers; Soloists
Specialized Field: Classical, Instrumental, Orchestra
Status: Non-Profit
Income Sources: Sponsors, Donors, Patron Gifts
Season: September through April
Performs At: MCL Grand Theater

1740
LONGVIEW SYMPHONY ORCHESTRA
Longview Chamber of Commerce
410 N. Center Street
Longview, TX 75601
Phone: 903-237-4000
Fax: 903-237-4049
Web Site: www.longviewtx.com
Officers:
  President: Kelly Hall
  Senior Vice President / Director of: Paul Anderson
  Vice President of Event Operations: Elaine Reynolds
Management:
  Director of Development: Leska Parker
  Membership Services Coordinator: Lisa Null
  Retail Development Coordinator: Diana Northcutt
  Business Development & Special Even: Melissa Saunders
  Convention Meetings and Main Street: Kayla Cantey
Mission: Presenting the highest calibre orchestral music to Texas citizens.
Utilizes: Guest Artists
Founded: 1968
Specialized Field: Symphony; Orchestra
Status: Semi-Professional; Nonprofit
Volunteer Staff: 36
Paid Artists: 75
Budget: $260,000
Income Sources: Ticket sales; Grants; Contributions
Performs At: T.G. Field Auditorium
Annual Attendance: 5,000
Organization Type: Performing; Resident; Educational

1741
LUBBOCK SYMPHONY ORCHESTRA
601 Avenue K
Lubbock, TX 79401
Phone: 806-762-1688
Fax: 806-762-1824
e-mail: msaathoff@lubbocksymphony.org
Web Site: www.lubbocksymphony.org
Officers:
  Chair: Kirk McLaughlin
  President and CEO: Mary Saathoff
  Treasurer: Brian Willcutt
  Secretary: Shannon Taliaferro
  Immediate Past Chair: Pete Daia
Management:
  Music Director: David Cho
  Director of Patron Services: Briana Thompson
  Accounting Services Director: Marilyn Bell
  Director: Alexis Arnold
  Education Director: Alexa Vogelzang
Mission: Offering the Lubbock Area symphonic music and an enhanced quality of life.
Utilizes: Artists-in-Residence; Collaborating Artists; Collaborations; Commissioned Music; Dance Companies; Dancers; Educators; Fine Artists; Grant Writers; Guest Accompanists; Guest Companies; Guest Instructors; Guest Musical Directors; Guest Musicians; Guest Writers; Instructors; Multimedia; Original Music Scores
Founded: 1942
Specialized Field: Symphony; Orchestra; Chamber; Ensemble
Status: Professional; Nonprofit
Paid Staff: 8
Volunteer Staff: 450
Paid Artists: 84
Budget: $900,000
Income Sources: American Symphony Orchestra League; American Society of Composers, Authors and Publishers
Performs At: Lubbock Memorial Civic Center
Annual Attendance: 12,000
Seating Capacity: 1,400
Organization Type: Performing; Educational

1742
MARSHALL SYMPHONY ORCHESTRA
Marshall, TX 75671
Mailing Address: PO Box 421
Phone: 903-935-5266
Fax: 903-938-3531
e-mail: tifn2@yahoo.com
Web Site: www.marshallsymphony.com
Officers:
  President: Milly Johnston Green
  1st Vice-President: Dr. Bruce Tankersley
  2nd Vice-President: Amy Carlile
  Recording Secretary: Dr. Jack Cargill
  Corresponding Secretary: April Spears
Management:
  Artistic Director/Conductor: Leonard Kacenjar
Mission: To provide local musicians with an opportunity to perform along with professional musicians; to provide symphonic music for area audiences.
Utilizes: Guest Artists; Singers
Founded: 1952
Specialized Field: Symphony; Orchestra
Status: Semi-Professional; Nonprofit
Paid Staff: 45
Income Sources: Marshall Regional Arts Council; Texas Association of Symphony Orchestras
Performs At: Marshall Civic Center Theatre
Organization Type: Performing

1743
MIDLAND-ODESSA SYMPHONY AND CHORALE
3100 LaForce Boulevard
PO Box 60658
Midland, TX 79711
Phone: 432-563-0921
Fax: 432-617-0087
e-mail: symphony@mosc.org
Web Site: www.mosc.org
Officers:
  President: Sue Solari
  Executive Vice President: LaDoyce Lambert
  Vice President Finance: Brad Bullock
  Vice President of Fundraising: Maridell Fryar
  Vice President Marketing: Jacqui Gore
Management:
  Marketing Coordinator: Holly Clinton, symphony@mosc.org
  Operations Director: Rino Irwing
  Executive Director: Jeannette Kolokoff
  Choir Director: Emily Baker
  Development Director: Violet Singh
Mission: To offer residents of the Permian Basin symphonic, chamber and choral music.
Utilizes: Collaborations; Commissioned Music; Educators; Grant Writers; Guest Artists; Guest Companies; Guest Directors; Guest Lecturers; Guest Writers; High School Drama; Local Artists; Lyricists; Multi Collaborations; Multimedia; Organization Contracts; Original Music Scores; Singers; Theatre Companies
Founded: 1962
Specialized Field: Symphony; Orchestra; Chamber; Ensemble
Status: Nonprofit
Paid Staff: 6
Volunteer Staff: 100
Paid Artists: 65
Budget: $750,000
Income Sources: Tickets; Grants; Donations
Affiliations: ASOL
Annual Attendance: 10,000
Organization Type: Performing; Educational

INSTRUMENTAL MUSIC / Texas

1744
PLANO SYMPHONY ORCHESTRA
5236 Tennyson Parkway
Suite 200
Plano, TX 75024
Phone: 972-473-7262
Fax: 972-473-4639
e-mail: info@planosymphony.org
Web Site: planosymphony.org
Officers:
  President: Arlene Johnson
  Treasurer: Donald Hair
  Secretary: Matt Howell
  Parliamentarian: Bill Tempest
Management:
  Music Director: Hector Guzman
  Executive Director: Debbie Watson
  Community Relations Director: Nancy Baumgartner
  Finance Director: Kaitlin Ginkauf
  Special Events Coordinator: Christina Forte
  Patron Services Manager: Marc Jennings
  Musician Personnel Manager: Jim Gasewicz
  Creative Services Manager: Kevin Haines
Mission: It is the mission of our orchestra to inspire, educate, entertain and involve the children, youth and adults of our community in the enjoyment of great music. The Plano Symphony has chosen to be a professional orchestra with compensated artistic and management personnel and has sought to attain its high artistic standards through solid institutional planning and faithful adherence to principles of sound non-profit management.
Utilizes: Arrangers; Collaborating Artists; Collaborations; Composers; Composers-in-Residence; Fine Artists; Guest Companies; High School Drama; Multimedia; Music; Original Music Scores; Paid Performers; Singers
Founded: 1983
Specialized Field: Orchestra, Instrumental, Classical
Status: Non-Profit, Professional
Income Sources: Sponsors, Donors
Season: September through April
Performs At: Eisemann Center

1745
THE RICHARD SYMPHONY
2100 North Collins Boulevard
Suite 310
Richardson, TX 70580
Phone: 972-234-4195
Fax: 972-238-7514
Web Site: richardsymphony.org
Officers:
  Chairman: Sally Crawford
  Vice Chairman: John Farrell
  President: George Landis
  Treasurer: Stewart McLauchlan
  Secretary: Lynn McCoy
  Board Member: Arzell Bell
  Board Member: Thelma Ball
  Board Member: Mary Boyter
Management:
  Music Director, Conductor: Clay Couturiaux
  Executive Director: George Landis
  Development Director: Scott Wilkenson
Mission: The new RSO is filled with outstanding musicians motivated by a love of great music and dedicated to sharing the greatest of all art forms with you...our audience. It's a difference you'll hear at each and every concert.
Utilizes: Arrangers; Collaborating Artists; Collaborations; Composers; Composers-in-Residence; Educators; Fine Artists; Guest Companies; Lyricists; Multimedia; Music; Paid Performers; Singers
Specialized Field: Classical, Jazz, Instrumental, Orchestra
Status: Non-Profit, Professiona;
Income Sources: Donors, Corporate Sponsors
Season: October through May
Performs At: Geroge W Eismann Center for the Performing Arts

1746
ROUND ROCK SYMPHONY INC
PO Box 2308
Round Rock, TX 78680
Phone: 512-264-5368
Web Site: roundrocksymphony.org
Officers:
  President: Dr. Debbie Zamora
  Vice President: Vicki Salinas
  Treasurer: Jay Ridgley
  Secretary: Judy McLeod
  Board Member: Dr. Bradley Berg
  Board Member: Beverly Mintz
  Board Member: Robert Butler
  Board Member: Toby Blumenthal Phillips
Management:
  Music Director: Stefan Sanders
  Managing Director: Tim Laughlin
  Artistic Director/Chamber Music: Toby Blumenthal
  Community Engagement Director: Eric Miller
Mission: Mission is to musically enrich the greater Round Rock community by presenting affordable and accessible symphonic concerts of the highest artistic order, promoting the understanding and appreciation of symphonic music by encouraging and educating children and new audiences, providing performance opportunities for professional musicians and promising music students, and facilitating the creation and performance of new American orchestral music.
Utilizes: Arrangers; Collaborations; Composers-in-Residence; Fine Artists; Guest Companies; Guest Composers; Lyricists; Multimedia; Music; Paid Performers; Singers
Specialized Field: Classical, Instrumental, Orchestra
Status: Non-Profit, Professional
Income Sources: Donors, Sponsors
Season: September through June
Performs At: Round Rock ISD Performings Arts Center, Georgetown Public Library

1747
SAN ANGELO SYMPHONY ORCHESTRA AND CHORALE
72 West College
West Mezzanine
San Angelo, TX 76903
Mailing Address: P.O. Box 5922, San Angelo, TX 76902
Phone: 915-658-5877
Fax: 915-653-1045
e-mail: admin@sanangelosymphony.org
Web Site: sanangelosymphony.org
Officers:
  President: Candyce Pfluger
  Vice President: Rev. Bill Proctor
  Secretary: Dr. Karen Cody
  Treasurer: Anna Thomas
  Past President: Bette Allison
Management:
  Music Director/Conductor: Hector Guzman
  Executive Director: Courtney Mahaffey
  Finance Associate: Rhonda Layman
Mission: To further cultural advancement and enjoyment of symphonic music in the San Angelo area.
Utilizes: Singers
Founded: 1948
Specialized Field: Symphony
Status: Professional; Non-Professional; Nonprofit
Paid Staff: 140
Income Sources: Broadcast Music Incorporated; American Society of Composers, Authors and Publishers; American Symphony Orchestra League
Performs At: City Auditorium
Annual Attendance: 50,000
Seating Capacity: 1,590
Organization Type: Performing

1748
SAN ANTONIO CHAMBER MUSIC SOCIETY
PO Box 12702
San Antonio, TX 78212
Phone: 210-408-1558
Fax: 210-408-1558
e-mail: email@sacms.org
Web Site: www.sacms.org
Officers:
  President: Kenneth Bloom
  Vice President: Marcus Henning
  VP Membership: Daavid Shapiro
  Financial Secretary: Mary K Vaughan
  Treasurer: Wayne Beyer
  Secretary: Jan H. Van den Hende
Management:
  Director: Salim Ammar
  Director: Allyson Dawkins
  Director: Jacque Forrest
  Director: Randolph Glickman
  Director: Pauline Glickman
Mission: Chamber music series featuring world chamber music artists.
Founded: 1943
Specialized Field: Chamber; Ensemble
Volunteer Staff: 25
Paid Artists: 5
Budget: $35,000-$60,000
Performs At: Incarnate Word College Auditorium

1749
SAN ANTONIO SYMPHONY
Travis Park Plaza (Jefferson Bank Building),
Suite 235
San Antonio, TX 78205
Mailing Address: P.O. Box 658, San Antonio, TX 78293-0658
Phone: 210-554-1000
Fax: 210-554-1008
e-mail: tickets@sasymphony.org
Web Site: www.sasymphony.org
Officers:
  Chair: Dennert O. Ware
  Vice Chair: James R. Berg
  President: David Gross
  Chief Financial Officer: Richard Roch,
  Vice President of Operations: Janni Toomes
  Exec. Vice President of Development: Cynthia Hamilton
Management:
  Director of Education: Jeremy Brimhall
  Artistic Operations Assistant/Assis: Roxanna Tehrani
  Director of Group and Corporate Sal: Karen Cramer
  Development Associate: Emily Brandesky
  Stage Manager: Robert Mines

INSTRUMENTAL MUSIC / Texas

Mission: Providing an outstanding professional symphony; meeting cultural, entertainment and educational needs of the community.
Utilizes: Choreographers; Dance Companies; Dancers; Educators; Guest Accompanists; Guest Artists; Guest Composers; Guest Conductors; Instructors; Music; Sign Language Translators; Soloists; Student Interns
Founded: 1939
Specialized Field: Symphony; Orchestra
Status: Professional; Nonprofit
Paid Staff: 21
Paid Artists: 77
Budget: $7,500,000
Income Sources: American Symphony Orchestra League
Performs At: Majestic Theatre
Seating Capacity: 2400
Organization Type: Performing; Educational

1750
YOUTH ORCHESTRAS OF SAN ANTONIO
106 Auditorium Circle
Suite 130
San Antonio, TX 78205
Phone: 210-737-0097
Fax: 210-732-7233
e-mail: info@yosa.org
Web Site: www.yosa.org
Officers:
   Chair: Paul Oroian
   Vice Chair, Governance: Thomas Sanders
   Vice Chair, Development: Amy Dameron Phipps
   Vice Chair, Music Programs: Phyllis Malone
   Vice Chair, Marketing: Elizabeth Lorenz
Management:
   Executive Director: Brandon Henson
   Development Director: Martha Bryant
   Development Assistant: Mary Compton
   Operations Coordinator: Stephanie Kocher
   Operations Assistant: Ben Hackett
Specialized Field: Youth Orchestra

1751
MID-TEXAS SYMPHONY ORCHESTRA
Texas Lutheran University
PO Box 3216 TLU
Seguin, TX 78155
Phone: 830-372-8089
Fax: 830-372-8112
e-mail: mts@tlu.edu
Web Site: www.mtsymphony.org
Officers:
   President of Society: Cathy Talcott
   Vice-President of Society: Kathy Nossaman
   Vice-President of Finance and Treas: Chris Bischoff
   Vice-President of Music: Dr. Patt Linden
   Vice-President of Development: Donald Brandeberry
Management:
   Musical Director: David Mairs
   Choral Director: Laurie Jenschke
   Executive Director: Patricia Schofield
   Production & Personnel Coordinator: Melinda Willmann
Mission: The MTS provides a broad array of music from the classics to more modern selections.
Founded: 1978
Specialized Field: Orchestra
Paid Staff: 1
Income Sources: Grants

1752
SHERMAN SYMPHONY ORCHESTRA
900 N Grand Avenue
Suite 61567
Sherman, TX 75090
Mailing Address: P.O. Box 651, Sherman, TX 75091-0651
Phone: 903-813-2251
Fax: 903-813-2273
e-mail: ddominick@austincollege.edu
Web Site: shermansymphony.com
Officers:
   Chair: Amanda Kisselle
   Treasurer: Karen Tooley
   Secretary: Larry Wall
   Board Member: Lesa Hicks
   Board Member: Tracy Murphey
Management:
   Music Director: Daniel Dominick
Mission: To offer concert performances featuring standard orchestral repertoire to area audiences; to provide guest appearances by nationally-known soloists.
Utilizes: Arrangers; Collaborating Artists; Collaborations; Composers; Fine Artists; Guest Choreographers; Guest Companies; Lyricists; Multimedia; Music; Paid Performers; Singers
Founded: 1966
Specialized Field: Symphony; Orchestra
Status: Non-Professional; Nonprofit
Paid Staff: 2
Volunteer Staff: 40
Paid Artists: 30
Budget: $50,000
Season: September Through May
Performs At: Wynne Chapel
Annual Attendance: 3,200
Facility Category: College Chapel; City Concert Hall
Seating Capacity: 300; 1,300
Year Built: 1930
Year Remodeled: 2000

1753
FORT BEND SYMPHONY ORCHESTRA
PO Box 16861
Sugar Land, TX 77496
Phone: 281-276-9642
e-mail: fbso@fbso.org
Web Site: www.fbso.org
Officers:
   President: Katie Truax
   Vice President: Lonny Yu
   Treasurer: Ryan Clift
   Secretary: Serena Landen
Management:
   Director of Fundraising: Donna Fletcher
   Director of Auditions: GloriBelle Kelly
   Director of Personnel: Susan Lynch
   Director of Performance: Erik Quam
   Orchestra Member-at-Large: Katherine Leskin
   Community Member-at-Large: Teresa Reading
   Citizen's Advisory Committee: Julius Baumann
Mission: This full-size orchestra, complete with brass, woodwind, percussion, and strings section, consists of approximately 60 talented and dedicated musicians primarily from the Fort Bend area.
Founded: 1992
Specialized Field: Orchestra

1754
TEMPLE SYMPHONY ORCHESTRA
100 West Adams Avenue
Mailbox 10
Temple, TX 76501
Phone: 254-778-6683
e-mail: templesymphony@gmail.com
Web Site: templesymphony.org
Officers:
   President: Dr. Johnette Frentz
   Treasurer: Andy Montgomery
   Secretary: Maretta Deiterman
Management:
   Music Director, Conductor: Thomas Fairlie
   Personnel Manager: James Flowers
   Director: Don Nelson
   Technical Director: Michael Morris
Mission: The mission of the Temple Symphony Orchestra is to provide music of the highest artistic standard, performing a broad range of repertoire to a wide and diverse audience through live performance; to act as ambassador to the community; to educate students and adults in the rich orchestral traditions of our heritage; and to serve as a leader in the cultural life of Central Texas. The TSO is dedicated to making the orchestral experience accessible.
Utilizes: Arrangers; Collaborating Artists; Collaborations; Composers-in-Residence; Educators; Fine Artists; Guest Composers; High School Drama; Lyricists; Multimedia; Music; Musical Directors; Paid Performers; Singers
Founded: 1993
Specialized Field: Instrumental, Classical, Jazz, Orchestra
Status: Non-Profit, Professional
Income Sources: Donrs, Sponsors, Advertising
Season: Year Round
Performs At: Temple College

1755
EAST TEXAS SYMPHONY ORCHESTRA
107 E. Erwin
Tyler, TX 75702
Mailing Address: P O Box 6323, Tyler, Texas 75711
Phone: 903-526-3876
Fax: 903-592-7649
e-mail: info@etso.org
Web Site: www.etso.org/
Officers:
   Chairman: Steve Wiggs
   Treasurer: Gregory S. Adcock
   Vice Chair, Organization: Deborah Harris
   Vice Chair, Artistic Advisory: Joi Smith
   Vice President, Development: Betty Bower
Management:
   Executive Director: Nancy B. Wrenn
   Director of Finance & Human Resourc: Ris, Jones
   Director of Patron Services: Kathy Housby
   Director of Development: Vel Williamson
   Director: Pam Lisner
Mission: To bring excellent orchestral music to East Texas.
Utilizes: Collaborations; Educators; Fine Artists; Guest Accompanists; Guest Artists; Guest Composers; Guest Writers; Lyricists; Multimedia; Original Music Scores; Singers; Student Interns
Founded: 1936
Specialized Field: Symphony; Orchestra
Status: Professional; Semi-Professional
Paid Staff: 7
Paid Artists: 70
Performs At: Cowan Performing Arts Center; UT-Tyler

INSTRUMENTAL MUSIC / Utah

Affiliations: American Symphony Orchestra League
Seating Capacity: 2,073
Organization Type: Performing

1756
WACO SYMPHONY ORCHESTRA
600 Austin Avenue
Suite 10
Waco, TX 76701
Mailing Address: PO Box 1201 Waco, TX 76703
Phone: 254-754-0851
Fax: 254-752-8611
e-mail: info@wacosymphony.com
Web Site: www.wacosymphony.com
Officers:
  President: John Cullar
  President-Elect, Planning: Brad Holland
  Vice-President: William McGovern
  Vice-President, Artistic Advisory: David A. Smith
  Vice-President, Audience Developmen: Debra Burleson
Management:
  Executive Director: Susan Taylor
  Music Director and Conductor: Stephen Heyde
  Marketing Director: Michael Bracken
  Office Manager: Darlene Spence
Mission: To present live classical music that will enrich the cultural life of the community.
Utilizes: Community Members; Five Seasonal Concerts; Guest Accompanists; Guest Writers; Scenic Designers; Singers; Student Interns; Theatre Companies
Founded: 1962
Specialized Field: Symphonic Orchestral Music
Paid Staff: 7
Paid Artists: 80
Budget: $750,000
Income Sources: Sponsors; Program Ad Sales; Ticket Sales; Donations
Performs At: Waco Hall, Baylor University
Affiliations: League of American Orchestras
Seating Capacity: 2,200

1757
WICHITA FALLS SYMPHONY ORCHESTRA
Kemp Center for the Arts
1300 Lamar
Wichita Falls, TX 76301
Phone: 940-723-6202
Fax: 940-723-6224
e-mail: wfso@sbcglobal.net
Web Site: www.wfso.org
Officers:
  President: Gary Shores
  Vice-President, Secretary: Elizabeth Yeager
  Treasurer: Jim Hoggard
  Board Member: Jesse Rogers
  Board Member: Mary Jane Smith
Management:
  Executive Director: Sherry Ransom
  Music Director and Conductor: Candler Schaffer
Mission: Offering the community the highest quality of symphonic music; educating area youth.
Founded: 1946
Specialized Field: Symphony; Orchestra
Status: Nonprofit
Performs At: Memorial Auditorium
Organization Type: Performing

Utah

1758
CHAMBER MUSIC SOCIETY OF SALT LAKE CITY
807 N Juniperpoint Drive
Salt Lake City, UT 84103
Mailing Address: P. O. Box 58825, Salt Lake City, UT 84158-0825
Phone: 801-561-3999
Fax: 801-581-4148
e-mail: cms@cmsofslc.org
Web Site: www.cmsofslc.org
Officers:
  President: Gene Scoggins
  VP: Henriette Mohebbizadeh
  Treasurer: Paul Griffin
Management:
  Artist Transportation: Bill Wallace
  Artist Transportation: David George
Mission: To entertain and enlighten.
Utilizes: Guest Accompanists; Guest Musical Directors
Founded: 1966
Specialized Field: Chamber
Budget: $40,000-$45,000
Income Sources: Ticket Sales; Contributions
Performs At: Libby Gardner Auditorium - David Gardner Hall
Facility Category: Auditorium
Seating Capacity: 650
Year Remodeled: 1999

1759
EASTERN ARTS INTERNATIONAL DANCE THEATER
PO Box 526362
Salt Lake City, UT 84152
Phone: 801-485-5824
e-mail: kstjohn@burgoyne.com
Web Site: www.easternartists.com
Management:
  Director: Katherine St. John
  Music Director: Lloyd Miller
Mission: To promote time-honored traditions by offering concerts, lectures, and workshops of cultures from Asia and Eastern Europe.
Founded: 1960
Specialized Field: Ethnic Music
Status: Professional; Nonprofit
Paid Staff: 10
Income Sources: Western Alliance of Arts Administrators; Society for Ethno-Musicology; Middle East Studies Association; Society for Dance Ethnology
Organization Type: Performing; Educational; Sponsoring

1760
GINA BACHAUER INTERNATIONAL PIANO FOUNDATION
138 W 300 S
Salt Lake City, UT 84101
Phone: 801-297-4250
Fax: 801-521-9202
e-mail: info@bachauer.com
Web Site: www.bachauer.com
Officers:
  Chairman: Kary Billings
  Vice Chairman: Brad Beagles
  Secretary: Arlo McGinn
  Treasurer: Nathan Morgan
Management:
  Artistic Director: Douglas Humpherys
  Executive Director: Karry Billings
  Accountant: Tonya Roy
  Education Coordinator & Artist Liai: Joanne Rowland
Mission: To further the pianistic art by holding international piano competitions, solo recitals and educational sessions; to enrich the community and build an artistic and educational environment for musicians and nonmusicians alike.
Founded: 1976
Specialized Field: Piano
Status: Nonprofit
Paid Staff: 8
Performs At: Symphony Hall; Salt Lake City Assembly Hall
Organization Type: Performing; Educational; Sponsoring

1761
GRANITE YOUTH SYMPHONY
2500 South State Street
Salt Lake City, UT 84115-3110
Phone: 801-268-8542
Fax: 801-263-6128
Web Site: graniteyouthsymphony.wix.com/site
Officers:
  Conductor and Co-chair: Amber Tuckness
  Conductor and Co-chair: Gary Jenson
Management:
  Conductor: Dr. Jim Thompson
Mission: Dedicated to studying and performing standard symphonic literature.
Utilizes: Guest Artists
Founded: 1957
Specialized Field: Youth Symphony
Status: Nonprofit
Income Sources: Granite School District
Organization Type: Performing; Touring; Educational

1762
ORCHESTRA AT TEMPLE SQUARE
50 North West Temple Street
20th Floor
Salt Lake City, UT 84150
Phone: 801-240-4150
Fax: 801-240-4886
e-mail: Bradfordbd@ldschurch.org
Web Site: www.mormontabernaclechoir.org
Officers:
  Choir President: Ron Jarret
Management:
  Music Director: Mack Wilberg
  Conductor: Igor Gruppman
  Associate Music Director: Ryan Murphy
  Administrative Manager: Barry Anderson
  General Manager: Scott Barrick
Founded: 1999
Specialized Field: Orchestra
Paid Staff: 2
Volunteer Staff: 6
Non-paid Artists: 110
Performs At: Tabernacle on Temple Square
Affiliations: The Church of Jesus Christ of Latter-day Saints
Annual Attendance: 10,000
Facility Category: Church

1763
SALT LAKE SYMPHONY
676 N. East Capitol Blvd.
Salt Lake City, UT 84103
Phone: 801-463-2440
Toll-free: 877-425-1537
e-mail: contact@saltlakesymphony.com
Web Site: saltlakesymphony.org

INSTRUMENTAL MUSIC / Vermont

Officers:
    Chair: Dick Fox
    Treasurer: Loraine Brandt
Management:
    Music Director/Conductor: Robert Baldwin
    Managing Director: Joyce Mahoney
    Graphics and Media Relations: Charlotte Bell
    Stage Manager: Zeph Smith
Founded: 1976
Specialized Field: Orchestra
Income Sources: Individuals; Corporations
Performs At: Abravanel Hall; Jeanne Wagner Concert Hall; Temple Square

1764
UNIVERSITY OF UTAH: SCHOOL OF MUSIC
1375 E Presidents Circle
204 David P. Gardner Hall
Salt Lake City, UT 84112-0030
Phone: 801-581-6762
Fax: 801-581-5683
e-mail: robert.baldwin@music.utah.edu
Web Site: www.music.utah.edu
Management:
    Director School of Music: James Gardner
    Associate Director for Graduate Stu: Robert Baldwin
    Associate Director for Undergraduat: Donn Schaefer
    Administrative Officer: Michelle Coulam Addison
    Director of Development: April Walters Goddard
Specialized Field: Educational
Performs At: David P. Gardner Hall; Libby Gardner Concert Hall; Thompson Chamber Music Hall; Dumke Recital Hall; Mckay Music Library

1765
UTAH CLASSICAL GUITAR SOCIETY
1121 East 200 South
Salt Lake City, UT 84102
Phone: 801-580-9881
e-mail: UtahClassicalGuitarSociety@gmail.com
Web Site: www.ucgs.org
Officers:
    President: Roy Johnson
    Secretary: Stephen Hanka
Management:
    Program Director: David Norton
Mission: Furthering performance and study of classical guitar repertoire in Utah.
Founded: 1984
Specialized Field: Classical Guitar
Status: Nonprofit
Paid Staff: 5
Performs At: First Presbyterian Church; Salt Lake City
Organization Type: Performing

1766
UTAH SYMPHONY
123 West South Temple
Salt Lake City, UT 84101
Phone: 801-533-6683
Fax: 801-869-9048
e-mail: info@usuo.org
Web Site: www.utahsymphony.org
Officers:
    Chair: Patricia A Richards
    President & CEO: Melia P. Tourangeau
    Vice Chair: David A. Petersen
    Vice Chair: William H. Nelson
    Secretary: Annette W. Jarvis
Management:
    Vice President of Symphony Artistic: Anthony Tolokan
    Music Director: Thierry Fischer
    Director of Major Gifts: Shaleane Gee
    Director of Foundation: Hillary Hahn
    Director of Public Relations: Renee Huang
Mission: To maintain a symphony orchestra capable of providing performances of the highest possible quality; to provide performance opportunities for skilled professional musicians; to foster musical education for persons of all ages.
Utilizes: Artists-in-Residence; Collaborating Artists; Commissioned Music; Educators; Fine Artists; Guest Accompanists; Guest Companies; Guest Composers; Guest Directors; Guest Lecturers; Guest Musical Directors; Instructors; Multimedia; Sign Language Translators; Singers; Student Interns; Visual Arts
Founded: 1940
Specialized Field: Symphony
Status: Professional; Nonprofit
Budget: $12,000,000
Income Sources: American Symphony Orchestra League; American Arts Alliance
Performs At: Symphony Hall
Annual Attendance: 200,000
Facility Category: Concert Hall
Seating Capacity: 2,800
Year Built: 1979
Architect: $12,000,000
Organization Type: Performing; Educational

1767
SOUTHWEST SYMPHONY ORCHESTRA
PO Box 423
St George, UT 84771
Phone: 435-879-9130
e-mail: contact@southwestsymphony.org
Web Site: www.southwestsymphony.co/index.html
Officers:
    Chair: J. J. Abernathy
    Chorale President: Jane Anderson
    President, Orchestra Musicians: Craig Beagley
    Trustee and Treasurer: Marge Shakespeare
Management:
    Conductor and Music Director: Gary Caldwell
    Southwest Chorale Director: Dr. Robert Briggs
    Stage Manager: Kameron Mickelson
    Artistic Consultant, Special Projec: NonaMarie Miller
    Associate Concertmaster: Katelyn Wall
    Principal: Debbie Thornton
Mission: The mission of the Southwest Symphony Orchestra and Chorale is to foster excellence and originality in the presentation and performance of great music; to enhance the lives of our citizenry; to educate present and future audiences; to inspire synergistic cultural partnerships; and to bring distinction to the community as a leader in the arts.
Utilizes: Arrangers; Collaborating Artists; Collaborations; Composers-in-Residence; Fine Artists; Guest Accompanists; Guest Composers; Guest Directors; High School Drama; Multimedia; Music; Paid Performers; Singers; Soloists
Founded: 1980
Specialized Field: Classical, Instrumental
Status: Non-Profit, Professional
Income Sources: Donors, Sponsors
Season: October through May
Performs At: O C Tanner Amphitheatre, Cox Performing Arts Center
Affiliations: Orchestra of Southern Utah, Oregon Symphony, San Francisco Symphony

Vermont

1768
BURLINGTON DISCOVER JAZZ FESTIVAL
156 College Street
Suite 202
Burlington, VT 05401
Phone: 802-863-7992
Fax: 802-864-3927
e-mail: info@discoverjazz.com
Web Site: www.discoverjazz.com
Officers:
    Director, Flynn Center: Andrea Rogers
Management:
    Managing Director: Linda Little
    Chief Programming Officer: Arnie Malina
    Associate Director: Geeda Searfoorce
    Artistic Director: Steve MacQueen
    Marketing & Development Manager: Abbie Tykocki
Mission: Offering the widest possible range of jazz and music educational programs; ticketed and free events.
Utilizes: Community Members; Community Talent; Composers; Educators; Guest Directors; Guest Musical Directors; Instructors; Local Artists & Directors; Lyricists; Multimedia; Music; Scenic Designers; Sign Language Translators
Founded: 1984
Specialized Field: Jazz
Status: Non-Profit, Professional
Paid Staff: 2
Volunteer Staff: 350
Budget: $600,000
Income Sources: Burlington City Arts; Flynn Center
Performs At: Multi-disciplinary
Annual Attendance: 45,000
Facility Category: City-wide (Burlington)
Organization Type: Performing; Educational; Sponsoring

1769
VERMONT SYMPHONY ORCHESTRA
2 Church Street
Suite 3B
Burlington, VT 05401-4457
Phone: 802-864-5741
Fax: 802-864-5109
Toll-free: 800-876-9293
e-mail: info@vso.org
Web Site: www.vso.org
Officers:
    Chair: Victoria Young
    Vice-Chair: Andrea Forrest Brock
    Treasurer: Sandy Jacobs
    Secretary: Virginia Roth
Management:
    Executive Director: Jamie Laredo
    Principal Guest Conductor: Anthony Princiotti
    Chorus Director: Robert De Cormier
    New Music Advisor: David Ludwig
    Office Manager: Grace Spain
Founded: 1934
Specialized Field: Symphony; Ensemble
Status: Professional; Nonprofit
Paid Staff: 14
Paid Artists: 54
Budget: $1,400,000
Performs At: Flynn Theatre
Affiliations: American Symphony Orchestra League
Annual Attendance: 65,100
Organization Type: Performing; Touring; Educational

INSTRUMENTAL MUSIC / Virginia

1770
VERMONT YOUTH ORCHESTRA ASSOCIATION
Elley-Long Music Center at St Michael's College
223 Ethan Allen Avenue
Colchester, VT 05446
Phone: 802-655-5030
Fax: 802-655-5034
e-mail: info@vyo.org
Web Site: www.vyo.org
Officers:
  Chair: Mike Noble
  Vice Chair: John Mantegna
  Treasurer: Jeff Nowell
Management:
  Director Of Operations: Art DeQuasie
  Director, Music Day Camp: Tim Buckingham
  Executive Director: Rosina Cannizzaro
  Facilities Manager: Thom Wood
  Operations Assistant & Music Librar: Mia Fritze
Mission: To provide young musicians and singers with superior orchestral and choral performance and educational experiences.
Utilizes: Collaborations; Guest Accompanists; Guest Artists; Guest Companies; Guest Musicians; Instructors; Multimedia; Organization Contracts; Singers; Soloists
Founded: 1964
Specialized Field: Youth Orchestra
Status: Non-Professional; Nonprofit
Paid Staff: 7
Budget: $400,000
Income Sources: American Symphony Orchestra League (Youth Orchestra Division)
Performs At: Private Performance Hall; Rental Available
Seating Capacity: 350
Year Built: 1888
Year Remodeled: 2001
Rental Contact: Kate Graham
Organization Type: Performing; Educational

1771
BANJO DAN AND THE MID-NITE PLOWBOYS
242 Main Street
Montpelier, VT 05602
Phone: 802-223-6965
e-mail: banjodan@pshift.com
Web Site: www.banjodan.com
Management:
  Band Leader/Booking Agent: Dan Lindner
Mission: A professional 5 piece band available to play bluegrass music at concerts, schools and festivals.
Founded: 1972
Specialized Field: Folk Music
Status: Professional
Organization Type: Performing

1772
SKY BLUE BOYS
242 Main Street
Montpelier, VT 05602
Phone: 802-223-6965
e-mail: banjodan@pshift.com
Web Site: www.skyblueboys.com
Management:
  Band Leader/Booking Agent: Dan Lindner
Mission: A professional band available to play acoustic duo at concerts, schools and festivals.
Founded: 1972
Specialized Field: Folk Music
Status: Professional
Organization Type: Performing

Virginia

1773
ALEXANDRIA SYMPHONY ORCHESTRA
2121 Eisenhower Avenue
Suite 608
Alexandria, VA 22314
Phone: 703-548-0885
Fax: 703-548-0985
e-mail: alex@alexsym.org
Web Site: www.alexsym.org
Officers:
  President: Ronal Butler
  Vice President: Linda Bunce
  Vice President, Finance: Anne Rector
  Vice President, Development: Edward J. Stark
  Secretary: Craig S. Miller, Jr.
Management:
  Executive Director: Jessica Goodyear Wisser
  Music Director: Kim Allen Kluge
  General Manager: Ryan Jordan
  Personnel Manager: Susan Kelly
  Stage Manager: Craig B. Teer
Mission: The Alexandria Symphony Orchestra, through its highly respected, innovative, professional programming, is an integral force in the bulding of community in the greater Alexandria area, bringing affordable and accessible music to it families.
Specialized Field: Orchestra

1774
ECLIPSE CHAMBER ORCHESTRA
2308 Mount Vernon Avenue
Suite 721
Alexandria, VA 22301
Phone: 703-635-2770
e-mail: contact@eclipseco.org
Web Site: eclipseco.org
Officers:
  President: Frank M. Hudson
  Vice President: Carole Bean
  Secretary: William Wright
  Board Member: Dr. .William P. Brose
  Board Member: Alice Kogan Weinreb
Management:
  Music Director: David Teie
  Concertmaster: Elisabeth Adkins
Mission: The primary mission of Eclipse Chamber Orchestra is to bring world-class performances of great music to people of every age, ethnic background and economic means. We believe the beauty and richness of live, classical music must be made available to all people, regardless of their station in life.
Utilizes: Arrangers; Collaborating Artists; Collaborations; Composers; Educators; Fine Artists; Guest Accompanists; High School Drama; Local Artists & Directors; Lyricists; Multimedia; Music; Paid Performers; Singers; Soloists
Founded: 1992
Specialized Field: Classical, Instrumental
Status: Non-Profit, Professional
Income Sources: Donors, Sponsors, Grants
Season: Year Round
Performs At: George Washington Masonic Temple

1775
AMERICAN BALALAIKA SYMPHONY
3811 North 14th Street
Arlington, VA 22201
Phone: 703-731-4957
e-mail: talukach@gmail.com
Web Site: www.absorchestra.org
Management:
  Founder/Artistic Director/Conductor: Peter Trofimenko
  Executive Director: Terri Lukach
Specialized Field: Orchestra; Ethnic Music

1776
HESPERUS
3706 N 17th Street
Arlington, VA 22207
Phone: 703-525-7550
Fax: 703-908-9207
e-mail: mail@hesperus.org
Web Site: hesperus.org
Management:
  Artistic Director: Scott Reiss
  Producing Director: Tina Chancey
Mission: To trace, through music, the cultural parallels existing between the Old and New Worlds.
Specialized Field: Chamber; Folk Music; Early Music; Classical Music
Status: Professional; Nonprofit
Performs At: Smithsonian Institute; National Museum of America
Organization Type: Touring; Resident

1777
CHARLOTTESVILLE CLASSICAL GUITAR SOCIETY
1074 Simmons Gap Road
Dyke, VA 22935
Phone: 434-973-0114
Fax: 434-975-3935
e-mail: dave@rediscov.com
Web Site: www.rediscov.com/ccgs
Officers:
  President: David Edwards
  VP: Keith Stevens
Mission: Develop interest in the Classical Guitar, educate and perform community service.
Founded: 1993
Specialized Field: Classical Guitar
Volunteer Staff: 4
Paid Artists: 2
Budget: $2,000
Income Sources: Donations; Ticket Sales
Annual Attendance: 400
Facility Category: Dinner Theater or Church
Type of Stage: Elevated
Seating Capacity: 250
Year Built: 1900

1778
FAIRFAX SYMPHONY ORCHESTRA
3905 Railroad Avenue
Suite 202 N
Fairfax, VA 22030
Phone: 703-563-1990
Fax: 703-563-1992
e-mail: gwixson@fairfaxsymphony.org
Web Site: www.fairfaxsymphony.org
Officers:
  President/CEO: Debra Harrison
  Board Chairman: Tom Brownell
  Vice Chairman: Mark McLeod
  Treasurer: John Lockhart
  Secretary: Brian Lubkeman
Management:
  Communication Director: Steve Zimmerman
  Personnel Manager: Cynthia Crumb
  Stage Manager: Tim Wade
  Accountant: Suzy Dawson
  Education Coordinator: Glen Quadar

INSTRUMENTAL MUSIC / Virginia

Mission: To provide high quality orchestra performances as well as music appreciation and education programs to enhance the quality of life in the metropolitan Washington area.
Utilizes: Guest Musicians; Local Artists
Founded: 1957
Specialized Field: Symphony; Orchestra; Chamber; Ensemble
Status: Professional; Nonprofit
Budget: $1,200,000
Performs At: George Masson University
Affiliations: American Symphony Orchestra League; SOI
Organization Type: Performing; Touring; Resident; Educational

1779
LOUDOUN SYMPHONY
7 Loudoun Street SE, Suite 4
PO Box 4478, Leesburg, VA 20177
Leesburg, VA 20175
Phone: 703-771-8287
Fax: 703-771-8287
e-mail: info@loudounsymphony.org
Web Site: loudounsymphony.org
Officers:
  President: Sandra Kane
  Vice President: Kathleen Greenough
  Treasurer: Mark Snow
  Secretary: Gina Wilcox
  Board Member: Ruth Ahmed
  Board Member: Kelly Blayney
  Board Member: Roger Nakazawa
  Board Member: Rachel Newell
Management:
  General Manager: Karen Knobloch
  Database Administrator: Debbie Cooke
  Stage Manager: Dave Gilstrap
  Stage Manager: Laura Droppa
  Personnel Manager: Maryory Serrano
  Venue Coordinator: Valerie Wride
  Chamber Concerts: David Hughes
  Special Events: Lucky Marks
Mission: The Loudoun Symphony was formed as the Loudoun Community Orchestra (LCO) in the fall of 1990 to provide musicians from Loudoun County and the surrounding area with the opportunity to play and present fine orchestral music to county audiences.
Utilizes: Arrangers; Collaborating Artists; Collaborations; Composers; Composers-in-Residence; Fine Artists; Guest Accompanists; Lyricists; Multimedia; Music; Original Music Scores; Paid Performers; Singers
Founded: 1990
Opened: 1991
Specialized Field: Orchestra, Instrumental, Classical
Status: Non-Profit, Professional
Income Sources: Donors, Sponsors, Galas
Season: Year Round
Performs At: Virginia Academy Community Church, Franklin Park Arts Center

1780
WASHINGTON AND LEE UNIVERSITY CONCERT GUILD
Washington and Lee University
201 DuPont Hall, Department of Music
Lexington, VA 24450-0303
Phone: 540-458-8852
Fax: 540-463-8104
e-mail: gaylardt@wlu.edu
Web Site: music.wlu.edu
Management:
  Music Department Chairman: Timothy Gaylard
  Professor of Music: Barry Kolman

Director of Choral Activities: Shane Lynch
Audio Engineer: Graham Spice
Mission: To bring nationally and internationally recognized classical artists to the campus.
Specialized Field: Chamber; Soloists
Status: Professional; Nonprofit
Paid Artists: 4
Performs At: Lenfest Centre
Organization Type: Educational; Sponsoring

1781
LYNCHBURG SYMPHONY ORCHESTRA
621 Court Street
Lynchburg, VA 24504
Phone: 434-845-6604
Fax: 434-845-0768
e-mail: lso@ntelos.net
Web Site: www.lynchburgsymphony.com
Officers:
  President: Margie Callahan
  Treasurer: Diane Bird
  Secretary: Beth Johnson
  Past President: Linda Edwards
Management:
  Musical Coordinator: Sylvia Noyes, lynsym1@verizon.net
  Office Manager: Laura Kauffman, deserio@ntelos.net
  Development Coordinator: Jennifer Staton
Mission: Enjoy the lovely, lilting sounds of string music with the Ivy Creek String Quartet. The musicians, who also play for the LSO, will perform Dvorak's American Quartet, as well as Queen's Bohemian Rhapsody, Adele's Rolling in the Deep, the Eurythmics' Sweet Dreams are Made of This, and more!
Utilizes: Arrangers; Collaborating Artists; Collaborations; Community Members; Community Talent; Fine Artists; Guest Accompanists; Guest Composers; Guest Directors; Guest Musicians; Multimedia; Music; Paid Performers; Singers
Founded: 1988
Specialized Field: Instrumental, Classical
Status: Non-Profit, Professional
Income Sources: Donors, Sponsors
Season: September through April
Performs At: E C Glass Auditorium, James River Conference Center, Academy Warehouse Theater, At Thomas More Church, Court Street UMC

1782
MCLEAN ORCHESTRA
PO Box 760
McLean, VA 22101
Phone: 703-893-8646
Fax: 703-893-8654
e-mail: info@mclean-orchestra.org
Web Site: mclean-orchestra.org
Officers:
  President: Paul A. Frank
  Immediate Past President: Aileen A. Pisciotta, Esq.
  Vice President, Administration: Christopher Payton
  Vice President/Development: Daren Shumate
  Vice President/Events: Pamela Joyce Wright
  Treasurer: Frank McGovern
  Executive Secretary: Laura Schuldt
  Counsel: David Gische
  Trustee: Michael Cardaci
Management:
  Music Director, Conductor: Miriam Burns
  Executive Director: Mark Francis
  Orchestra Production Manager: Craig Teer
  Personnel Manager/Strings: Stephanie Flack

  Personnel Manager/Winds/Brass: Joanna Dabrowska Huling
  Webmaster: Jennifer Seamster
Mission: McLean Orchestra provides professional-level orchestral concerts in an easily accessible location and at reasonable cost to area residents. A small paid staff and a dedicated board of skilled volunteers support the orchestra's effort to foster the appreciation and enjoyment of live classical music in a growing and enthusiastic audience.
Utilizes: Collaborating Artists; Collaborations; Community Talent; Composers; Composers-in-Residence; Contract Orchestras; Guest Musical Directors; Instructors; Lyricists; Multimedia; Music; Original Music Scores; Paid Performers; Singers
Founded: 1989
Specialized Field: Classical, Contemporary, Instrumental
Status: Non-Profit, Professional
Paid Staff: 5
Income Sources: Sponsor, Donors, Volunteers
Season: October through May
Performs At: Oakcrest School, St Dunstans Episcopal Church, Cooper Middle School, Lyceum

1783
TIDEWATER CLASSICAL GUITAR SOCIETY
Chrysler Hall
201, E Brambleton Avenue
Norfolk, VA 23510
Phone: 757-625-2330
e-mail: tcgs@mac.com
Web Site: www.tidewaterclassicalguitar.org
Officers:
  President: Tony Pezzella
  Grant Applications: W Mead Stith
  Vice President Williamsburg Region: David Wolverton
  Secretary: Patricia Pfeifer
  Treasurer: Chris Basford
Management:
  Artistic Director: Sam Dorsey
  Promotional Materials: Robert Sites
  Marketing Coordinator: Leigh Pinner
Specialized Field: Classical Guitar

1784
VIRGINIA SYMPHONY
150 Boush Street
Suite 201
Norfolk, VA 23510
Phone: 757-466-3060
Fax: 757-466-3046
e-mail: ejohnson@virginiasymphony.org
Web Site: www.virginiasymphony.org
Officers:
  Chair, Virginia Beach: Rony Thomas
  Vice Chair, Virginia Beach: Stephen G. Test
  Treasurer, Norfolk: Elizabeth Foster
  Secretary, Norfolk: Susan Goode
Management:
  President and Executive Director: Eric Borenstein
  Chief Operating Officer: Brad Kirkpatrick
  Executive Assistant and Secretary t: Kelsey Backe
  Director: Justin Ellis
  Operations Manager: Denise Olivieri
  Technical Director: Will Bishop
  Director of Education and Community: Marsha Staples
  Artistic Administrator: Rodney Martell
  Director of Marketing: Tamara Clement

Mission: To present classical, pops, family and educational performances each season and time and time again being recognized for its national caliber of excellence. This acclaimed orchestra includes over seventy professional musicians.
Founded: 1920
Specialized Field: Orchestra

1785
RICHMOND SYMPHONY ORCHESTRA
612 East Grace Street
Suite 401
Richmond, VA 23219
Phone: 804-788-1212
Fax: 804-788-1541
e-mail: patronservices@richmondsymphony.com
Web Site: www.richmondsymphony.com/
Officers:
  Chair: Phil Bennett
  Vice Chair: Rebecca J. Horner
  Immediate Past: John W. Braymer
  Executive Director: David J. L. Fisk
  Secretary: Anne Kenny-Urban
  Treasurer: Mark Wickersham
  Director: Stuart Blain
  Director: Arthur S. Brinkley III
  Director: Cindy Hamner
Management:
  Director of Finance and Administrat: Gail Richmond
  Executive Director: David J.L. Fisk
  Director of Orchestral Operations: Laura Bordner Adams
  Director: Scott Dodson
  Director of Education and Community: Aimee Halbruner
  Asst. Director of Education & Commu: Megan Osborn
  Marketing and PR Manager: Christopher Murphy
  Development Assistant: Kira Hiller
  Business Development Manager: Elyse Jennings
Mission: To perpetuate the orchestral tradition, develop audience enthusiasm, educate future generations of concert goers, and contribute to the enjoyment of the art of symphonic music. We invite you and encourage you to join with us in carrying out the Richmond Symphony's mission.
Utilizes: Singers
Founded: 1908
Specialized Field: Symphony; Orchestra; Chamber; Ensemble
Status: Professional; Nonprofit
Income Sources: American Symphony Orchestra League; Indiana Orchestra Consortium
Performs At: Civic Auditorium
Organization Type: Performing; Resident; Educational

1786
ROANOKE SYMPHONY ORCHESTRA
128 E. Campbell Ave
Roanoke, VA 24011-1406
Phone: 540-343-9127
Fax: 540-343-0065
Toll-free: 866-277-9127
e-mail: tickets@rso.com
Web Site: www.rso.com
Officers:
  Friends of the RSO, President: Marion Vaughn-Howard
  President: Joseph W. Ferguson
  Friends of the RSO, President: Marion Vaughn-Howard
  NRV Friends, President: Rick Furr
  Treasurer: Richard Garbee
  Secretary: Lucas Thornton
Management:
  Music Director/Concuctor: David Stewart Wiley
  Chorus Master: John Hugo
  Director/Public Relations: Joe Cobb
  Executive Director: Beth Pline
  Marketing Director / Designer: Rodney Overstreet
  Development Director: C.W. Markham
  Finance Director: Wendy Warren
  Education Director: Sarah Wardle
  Director of Operations: Grant Ellis
Mission: To enrich lives, educate, and entertain audiences in Western Virginia with the highest quality instrumental and choral concerts, and to enhance traditional performances with innovative programming in a welcoming acoustical environment.
Founded: 1953
Specialized Field: Orchestra
Status: Nonprofit; Education
Paid Staff: 10
Paid Artists: 1
Budget: $1.7 million
Income Sources: Gifts and ticket sales
Facility Category: Civic Center/Auditorium
Seating Capacity: 2,400/848

1787
SYMPHONICITY
291 Independence Blvd.
Ste. 421, Pembroke Four
Virginia Beach, VA 23462
Phone: 757-671-8611
Fax: 757-671-8704
e-mail: wendy.young@symphonicity.org
Web Site: www.symphonicity.org
Officers:
  President: Sheryl Ahern
  VP: Kelton Brandt
  Recording Secretary: Lis‰ Chandler-White
  Treasurer: Alex Rosa
Management:
  Music Director/Conductor: David S Kunkel
  Executive Director: Wendy T Young
  Concertmaster: Megan Van Gomple
  Strings Personnel Manager: Becky Brown
  Winds/Brass Personnel Manager: Alan Brown
Mission: The Virginia Beach Symphony provides a high quality music for everyone, affords an opportunity for players, and young musicians. We perform over 18 concerts a year for the citizens of Virginia Beach and the Hampton Roads area.
Founded: 1981
Specialized Field: Orchestra
Paid Staff: 8
Volunteer Staff: 150
Paid Artists: 2
Non-paid Artists: 100
Performs At: Pavilion Theater, Virginia Beach
Affiliations: ASCAP; BMI; American Symphony Orchestra; Virginians for the Arts; Central Business District; Cultural Alliance of Greater Hampton Roads Chamber
Annual Attendance: 55,000
Facility Category: Theater; Convention
Type of Stage: Proscenium
Seating Capacity: 1000
Year Built: 1981
Rental Contact: Mary Collins

Washington

1788
WHATCOM SYMPHONY ORCHESTRA
PO Box 5892
Bellingham, WA 98227
Phone: 360-756-6752
Fax: 360-756-6455
e-mail: info@whatcomsymphony.com
Web Site: www.whatcomsymphony.com
Officers:
  President: Bruce Cox
  Vice President: Cheryl Maurier, MD
  Secretary: Judy Purcell
  Treasurer: Barbara Curtis
  Past President: Becky Elmendorf
  Board Member: Aliana Coonc
  Board Member: Kathy Diaz
  Board Member: Marty Haines
Management:
  Executive Director: Thom Mayes
  Marketing: Ramona Abbott
  Music Director: Yaniv Attar
  Marketing Director: Noel Evans
Mission: WSO is comprised of over 80 volunteer musicians, including local music teachers, active and retired professional musicians, and talented community members from all backgrounds. The orchestra performs six subscription concerts at the MBT each season, plus maintains an ambitious calendar of community outreach events.
Utilizes: Arrangers; Collaborating Artists; Collaborations; Composers; Composers-in-Residence; Fine Artists; High School Drama; Lyricists; Multimedia; Music; Paid Performers
Founded: 1991
Opened: 1993
Specialized Field: Classical, Instrumental
Status: Non-Profit, Professional
Income Sources: Sponsors, Donors
Season: October through April
Performs At: Mount Baker Theatre

1789
BREMERTON SYMPHONY ORCHESTRA
PO Box 996
535B 5th Street, Suite 16
Bremerton, WA 98337
Phone: 360-373-1722
Fax: 360-405-9665
e-mail: symphony@symphonic.org
Web Site: www.symphonic.org
Officers:
  President: Tom Cameron Ph.D
  First VP: Wendy Clark-Getzin
  Second VP: Holly James
  Secretary: Connie Lord
  Treasurer: Carolyn McClurkan
Management:
  Music Director/Conductor: Alan Futterman
  Executive Director: Gena Wales
  General Manager: Laurie Strange
  Music Director, BSYO: Michael Woods
  Marketing Specialist: Joelle Jensen
Mission: To bring high quality classical instrumental and vocal music to our diverse communities; to serve the skilled amateur musicians of the region by providing performance opportunities; and develop enthusiasm and love of music for the enrichment of the cultural environment of the West Sound.
Utilizes: Singers
Founded: 1942
Specialized Field: Symphony; Orchestra; Ensemble
Status: Non-Professional; Nonprofit

INSTRUMENTAL MUSIC / Washington

Paid Staff: 60
Paid Artists: 10
Budget: $200,000
Income Sources: American Symphony Orchestra League
Performs At: Bremerston High School; Admiral Theatre
Organization Type: Performing; Resident; Educational

1790
CASCADE SYMPHONY ORCHESTRA
8523 215th St. SW
Edmonds, WA 98026
Phone: 425-776-4938
Fax: 425-672-3951
e-mail: executivedirector@cascadesymphony.org
Web Site: www.cascadesymphony.org
Management:
  Conductor: Michael Miropolsky
  Executive Director: Ruby Fusaro
Mission: Performing symphonic literature which ranges from the baroque to the contemporary.
Utilizes: Guest Artists
Founded: 1962
Specialized Field: Symphony; Orchestra; Chamber; Ensemble
Status: Semi-Professional; Non-Professional
Income Sources: American Symphony Orchestra League; Broadcast Music Incorporated; American Society of Composers, Authors and Publishers; American Federation of Musicians
Performs At: Puget Sound Christian College
Organization Type: Performing; Resident; Sponsoring

1791
FEDERAL WAY SYMPHONY
PO Box 4513
Federal Way, WA 98063-4513
Phone: 253-529-9857
e-mail: adminoffice@federalwaysymphony.org
Web Site: www.federalwaysymphony.org
Officers:
  President: David Bruell
  Vice President: Rene' Ewing
  Secretary: Susan White
  Treasurer: John Gibson
Management:
  Executive Director: Anna James Miller
  Marketing Assistant: Alessandra Robatty
  Education Assistant: Ingrid Smith
  Financial Administrator: Jim Englund
Mission: The Federal Way symphony Orchestra remains committed to bringing the finest clasical music to residents of the South Puget Sound region.
Specialized Field: Orchestra

1792
SAMMAMISH SYMPHONY ORCHESTRA ASSOCIATION
PO Box 1173
Issaquah, WA 98027
Phone: 206-517-7777
e-mail: info@sammamishsymphony.org
Web Site: sammamishsymphony.org
Officers:
  President: Armand Binkhuysen
  Vice President: Mark Wiseman
  Treasurer: Donna Mansfield
  Treasurer: Andrea Adee
  Secretary: Cathy Grindle
  Board Member: Dennis Calvin
  Board Member: Dennis Helppie
  Board Member: Andy Hill
Management:
  Music Director/Conductor: R Joseph Scott
  Concert Program/Personnel: Jonathan Feil
  Grants: Armand Binkyuhsen
  Principal Librarian: Loryn Lestz
  Asst Librarian/Violins: Kristin Edlund
  Assistant Librarian/Woodwinds: Shannon Nelson
  Marketing: Renee Kuehn
Mission: Performs on the Sammamish Plateau and various locations in the area. It is committed to offering quality music at affordable prices for Eastside residents. This volunteer ensemble provides the opportunity for talented, dedicated musicians to perform with a full symphony orchestra. In addition, the Orchestra promotes involvement in the arts for young musicians who are given the chance to participate in classical/pops concerts.
Utilizes: Arrangers; Collaborating Artists; Collaborations; Composers; Fine Artists; High School Drama; Lyricists; Multimedia; Music; Organization Contracts; Paid Performers
Founded: 1990
Opened: 1991
Specialized Field: Classical, Pop, Instrumental
Status: Non-Profit, Professional
Income Sources: Donors, Sponsors, Volunteers
Season: October through June
Performs At: Eastlake Performing Arts Center, Maydenbauer Theatre

1793
SKAGIT SYMPHONY
PO Box 1302
Mount Vernon, WA 98273
Phone: 360-848-9336
Fax: 360-424-8715
e-mail: info@SkagitSymphony.com
Web Site: www.skagitsymphony.com
Officers:
  Chairman: Dick Reim
  Treasurer: Heiko Miles
  Secretary/Past Chairman: Dr. Bill Langworthy
Management:
  Artistic Director/Conductor: Roupen Shakarian
  Executive Director: Kathy Ziegler
  Accountant: Teresa Pugh
  Production Manager: Vic Veltkamp
  Graphic Designer/Webmaster: Sue Athmann
  Clarinet Principal: Barry Ulman
  Bassoon Principal: Elizabeth Johnson
Mission: Skagit Symphony's mission is to contribute to the growth and appreciation of classical music in the community by performing a repertoire to a high standard. The mission includes providing the opportunity for skilled musicians in our region to perform with the orchestra, including soloists and local composers.
Utilizes: Arrangers; Collaborating Artists; Collaborations; Composers; Contract Orchestras; Fine Artists; Lyricists; Multimedia; Music; Paid Performers; Sign Language Translators
Founded: 1961
Specialized Field: Instrumental, Classical, Contemporary
Status: Non-Profit, Professional
Income Sources: Volunteers, Corporate Sponsors, Donors
Season: Year Round
Performs At: Mc Intyre Hall

1794
OLYMPIA SYMPHONY ORCHESTRA
3400 Capitol Boulevard S
Suite 203
Olympia, WA 98501-3351
Phone: 360-753-0074
Fax: 360-753-4735
e-mail: oso@olympiasymphony.com
Web Site: www.olympiasymphony.com
Officers:
  President: Mike Ryherd
  Vice President: Keith Playstead
  Vice President: Don Law
  Secretary: Priscilla Lincoln
  Treasurer: Cynthia Cook
  Music Director & Conductor: Haw Edwards
  Bookkeeper: Gerda Wynkoop
  Executive Director: Kate Inglin
Mission: To encourage the growth and development of the symphony orchestra and maintain the orchestra; to promote musical and cultural entertainment in diverse forms; to provide the musicians of Thurston County and its surrounding areas with the opportunity to play in a symphony.
Founded: 1970
Specialized Field: Symphony; Orchestra
Status: Professional; Nonprofit
Paid Staff: 4
Income Sources: American Symphony Orchestra League
Performs At: Washington Center for the Performing Arts
Organization Type: Performing; Educational

1795
PORT ANGELES SYMPHONY
PO Box 2148
Port Angeles, WA 98362
Phone: 360-457-5579
e-mail: pasymphony@olypen.com
Web Site: portangelessymphony.org
Officers:
  President: Bonnie Christianson
  Past President: Bob Coates
  Vice President: Graham Reaves
  Secretary: Paul Crawford
  Treasurer: Barbara Mason
  Assistant Secretary: Marie Meyers
  Assistant Treasurer: John Melcher
  Student Representatives: Reid Henry
  Student Representatives: Selbey Jelle
Management:
  Music Director/Conductor: Adam Stern
  Concertmaster: Kate Southard-Dean
  Assistant Conductor: Ed Grier
  Librarian/Personnel Manager: Sharon Snel
  Adventures in Music Director: Al Harris
  Executive Director: Mark Wendeborn
Mission: The Port Angeles Symphony Orchestra was founded in 1932 and is a 501(c)(3) nonprofit corporation. The Orchestra began with a few fiddlers and horn players performing light opera and Sousa marches in each other's homes and has become today's award-winning orchestra consisting of 80 volunteer musicians.
Utilizes: Arrangers; Collaborations; Composers; Fine Artists; Guest Directors; High School Drama; Multimedia; Music; Paid Performers; Singers; Soloists
Founded: 1932
Specialized Field: Classical, Instrumental
Status: Non-Profit, Professional
Income Sources: Pledges, Donors, Auctions
Season: October through May
Performs At: Holy Trinity Lutheran Church, Port Angeles Highschool Auditorium

INSTRUMENTAL MUSIC / Washington

1796
WASHINGTON IDAHO SYMPHONY
PO Box 9185
Pullman, WA 99163
Mailing Address: 115 NW State Street, Pullman, WA 99163
Phone: 509-332-3408
Fax: 509-335-2220
e-mail: Info@WashingtonIdahoSymphony.org
Web Site: www.washingtonidahosymphony.org
Officers:
 President Pro Tem of the Board: Jane von Frank
 Past President: Dr. Diane Gillespie
 Vice President: Green Baggett
 Finance Officer: William Stanke, CPA
 Secretary: Nancy Lyle
Management:
 Music Director: Jeremy Briggs Roberts
 Executive Asst. and Events Coordina: Sharon Trautwein
 Orchestra Manager: Christopher Wurst
Mission: To offer the enjoyment of music to people of all ages and provide area musicians an opportunity to participate in an orchestra or chorus.
Founded: 1972
Specialized Field: Symphony; Ensemble
Status: Non-Professional; Nonprofit
Paid Staff: 40
Income Sources: American Symphony Orchestra League, Chair Sponsorship Program, Private and Corporate Donations, Ticket Sales
Season: September-April
Performs At: Lewiston High School Auditorium, Clarkston High School Auditorium, Gladish Auditorium
Organization Type: Performing; Resident; Educational

1797
MID-COLUMBIA SYMPHONY
1177 Jadwin Ave
MacHunter Building, Suite 103
Richland, WA 99352
Mailing Address: P.O. Box 606, Richland, WA 99352
Phone: 509-943-6602
Fax: 509-946-7917
e-mail: adm@midcolumbiasymphony.org
Web Site: www.midcolumbiasymphony.org
Officers:
 Board President: Dick Pratt
 Board Secretary: Stephanie Hansen
 Board Treasurer: Christopher Cree
Management:
 Office Manager: Marie Norwood
 Music Director & Conductor: Dr. Nicholas L. Wallin
Mission: The Mid-Columbia Symphony is committed to implementing an inclusive strategy that embraces everyone in the region, creating a cultural entity that is a source of regional pride, creating and implementing a strong educational program.
Founded: 1945
Specialized Field: Symphony; Orchestra
Status: Non-Professional; Nonprofit
Income Sources: American Symphony Orchestra League
Performs At: Richland High School Auditorium
Organization Type: Performing; Resident; Educational

1798
EARLY MUSIC GUILD OF SEATTLE
2366 Eastlake Avenue E
Suite 325
Seattle, WA 98102
Phone: 206-325-7066
Fax: 206-860-9151
e-mail: emg@earlymusicguild.org
Web Site: www.earlymusicguild.org
Officers:
 President: JoLynn Edwards
 Vice President: Peter Seibert
 Secretary: Jamia Hansen-Murray
 Treasurer: Richard Ginnis
Management:
 Early Music Guild Executive Directo: August Denhard
 Seattle Baroque Orchestra Co-Direct: Ingrid Matthews
 Seattle Baroque Orchestra Co-Direct: Byron Schenkman
 Operations Manager: Ann Stickney
 Marketing Director: Hayley Woldseth
Mission: Presenting an annual international six concert series featuring touring ensembles.
Utilizes: Collaborations; Guest Directors; Guest Instructors; Guest Musical Directors; Guest Musicians; High School Drama; Instructors
Founded: 1977
Specialized Field: Chamber; Early Music
Status: Professional; Nonprofit
Budget: $250,000
Organization Type: Educational; Sponsoring

1799
LAKE UNION CIVIC ORCHESTRA
Northgate Station
PO Box 75387
Seattle, WA 98175
Phone: 206-343-5826
e-mail: info@luco.org
Web Site: www.luco.org
Officers:
 Vice President: Al Berg
 President: Terry Cook
 Secretary: Linda Hubert
 Treasurer: Lesley Petty Jones
Management:
 Music Director/Conductor: Christophe Chagnard
 Orchestra Manager: Steven Noffsinger
 Orchestra Representative: Jon Kamrath
 Production Manager: Brant Allen
 Fund Raising: John Dunne
Mission: The Lake Union Civic Orchestra is dedicated to the exploration and performance of symphonic and chamber music with energy and passion, and to sharing that experience with individuals throughout the community.
Founded: 1995
Specialized Field: Orchestra

1800
NORTHWEST SYMPHONY ORCHESTRA
7520 30th Avenue Southwest
Seattle, WA 98126
Phone: 206-242-6321
e-mail: m.balmidiano@yahoo.com
Web Site: www.northwestsymphonyorchestra.org
Officers:
 President: Diane Macewicz
Management:
 Music Director: Anthony Spain
Founded: 1987
Specialized Field: Orchestra
Budget: $35,000
Performs At: Highline Performing Arts Center
Seating Capacity: 900

1801
MUSIC CENTER OF THE NORTHWEST
901 North 96th Street
Seattle, WA 98103
Mailing Address: PO Box 30757, Seattle, WA 98113
Phone: 206-526-8443
Fax: 253-383-1709
e-mail: office@mcnw.org
Web Site: www.mcnw.org/programs/workshops/pscw.htm
Officers:
 Treasurer: Patricia Gillis
 Vice President: Jonathan DeMella
 President: Russell Nickel
 Secretary: Christina Ager
Management:
 Executive Director: Michael Alstad
 Director Emeritus: Janice Gockel
 Program Coordinator: Monica Hernandez
 Administrative Coordinator: Kendal Keyes
Mission: To offer the highest quality chamber music festival.
Specialized Field: Chamber
Status: Nonprofit
Organization Type: Presenting

1802
RAINIER SYMPHONY
PO Box 58182
Seattle, WA 98138
Phone: 206-781-5618
e-mail: questions@rainiersymphony.org
Web Site: rainiersymphony.org
Officers:
 President: Hillary Turtle
 Vice President: Eric Tishkoff
 Treasurer: Nancy Hall
 Corresponding Secretary: Dorothy Smith
 Recording Secretary: Kristine Finch
 Orchestra Representative: Hilary Swanson
 Board Member: Steven Mullet
 Board Member: Michael Zachary
Management:
 Artistic Director/Conductor: David Waltman
 Concertmaster: Ilkka Talvi
 Orchestra Manager: Marisa Hartman
 Volunteer Coordinator: Mike Fowler
 Box Office Manager: Wendy Hilliker
Mission: One of the finest community orchestras on the west coast, Rainier Symphony reaches over 5,000 people a year with a broad range of music from the classical and pops repertoire. Our diverse membership includes teachers, physicians, engineers, business professionals, longshoremen and students who share a love of music and their community.
Utilizes: Arrangers; Collaborating Artists; Collaborations; Composers; Fine Artists; Lyricists; Multimedia; Music; Paid Performers; Volunteer Artists
Founded: 1998
Specialized Field: Classical, Pop, Instrumental
Status: Non-Profit, Professional
Income Sources: Donors, Corporate Sponsors, Advertising
Season: October through May
Performs At: Foster Performing Arts Center, Renton IKEA Performing Arts Center

1803
SEATTLE BAROQUE
2366 Eastlake Avenue E
Suite #335
Seattle, WA 98102-3399

INSTRUMENTAL MUSIC / Washington

Phone: 206-528-1605
Fax: 206-322-3119
e-mail: info@seattleearlydance.org
Web Site: www.seattlebaroque.org/
Management:
   Music Director: Ingrid Matthews
   Artistic Director: Bryon Schenkman
   Executive Director: Joann Mendelsohn
   Marketing/Development Coordinator: Karen Nestvold
Mission: To awaken contemporary audiences to the vitality of 17th and 18th century music through historically informed performance of both familiar and unknown works.
Founded: 1993
Specialized Field: Classical; Baroque
Paid Staff: 6
Volunteer Staff: 6
Paid Artists: 35

1804
SEATTLE PHILHARMONIC ORCHESTRA
PO Box 177
Seattle, WA 98111
Phone: 206-734-4759
e-mail: listenerswelcome@seattlephil.org
Web Site: www.seattlephil.org
Officers:
   President: Michael Moore
   Vice President: Linda Morris
   Secretary: Jonathan Icasas
   Treasurer: Walter Moore
Management:
   Music Director: Adam Stern
   Personnel Manager: Dick Griffith
Founded: 1944
Specialized Field: Orchestra

1805
SEATTLE SYMPHONY ORCHESTRA
200 University Street
Seattle, WA 98111-3906
Mailing Address: P.O. Box 21906, Seattle, WA 98111-3669
Phone: 206-215-4700
Fax: 206-215-4701
e-mail: info@seattlesymphony.org
Web Site: www.seattlesymphony.org
Officers:
   Chair: Leslie Jackson Chihuly
   Vice Chair, Finance: Michael Slonski
   Vice Chair, Governance: Dick Paul
   Vice Chair, Development: Laurel Nesholm
   Vice Chair, Marketing & Communicati: Kjristine Lund
Management:
   Executive Director: Simon Woods
   Executive Assistant and Manager of: Kristen NyQuist
   Legal Counsel: Bernel Goldberg
   Director of Operations and Popular: Kelly Woodhouse Boston
   Personnel Manager: Scott Wilson
Mission: To present symphonic music of the highest quality in a distinctive way for the enjoyment, enrichment and education of the people of the Pacific Northwest.
Utilizes: Commissioned Composers; Commissioned Music; Composers-in-Residence; Curators; Educators; Five Seasonal Concerts; Guest Accompanists; Guest Artists; Guest Companies; Guest Lecturers; Guest Musicians; Guest Soloists; Multimedia; Original Music Scores; Sign Language Translators; Singers; Soloists; Theatre Companies
Founded: 1903
Specialized Field: Symphony; Orchestra; Chamber; Ensemble
Status: Professional; Nonprofit
Paid Staff: 63
Volunteer Staff: 270
Paid Artists: 90
Budget: $20,000,000
Income Sources: Ticket Sales; Donations
Performs At: Benaroya Hall, Seattle
Annual Attendance: 338,000
Facility Category: Symphony Hall
Seating Capacity: 2500; 540
Year Built: 1998
Cost: $11.8 Million
Rental Contact: Troy Skubitz
Organization Type: Performing; Resident; Educational

1806
SEATTLE YOUTH SYMPHONY ORCHESTRA
11065 5th NE
Suite A
Seattle, WA 98125
Phone: 206-362-2300
Fax: 206-361-9254
e-mail: info@syso.org
Web Site: www.syso.org/
Officers:
   President: Dean Willard
   Vice President: John Neeleman
   Secretary: Charles E. Johnson
   Treasurer: Satoru Tashiro
   Board Member: Mary Lou Brown
Management:
   Executive Director: Daniel Petersen
   Box Office Manager: John Empey
   Director of Education, Communicatio: Kathleen Allen
   Orchestra Coordinator: Janice Gatti
   Finance Director: Aimee Tan
Mission: To offer performances that promote music appreciation.
Founded: 1942
Specialized Field: Youth Orchestra
Status: Nonprofit
Paid Staff: 7
Volunteer Staff: 100
Paid Artists: 100
Non-paid Artists: 999
Income Sources: American Society of Composers, Authors and Publishers; Broadcast Music Incorporated
Performs At: Seattle Center Opera House
Organization Type: Performing; Educational

1807
SPOKANE SYMPHONY ORCHESTRA
1001 W. Sprague
Spokane, WA 99201
Mailing Address: P.O. Box 365, Spokane, WA 99210-0365
Phone: 509-624-1200
Fax: 509-252-2637
e-mail: symphonymarketing@spokanesymphony.org
Web Site: www.spokanesymphony.org
Officers:
   President: A. Douglas Belanger
   Executive Vice President: Bassem Bejjani
   Secretary: Mathew Ewers
   Treasurer: Jim Kensok
   Trustee: Ellena Conway
Management:
   Executive Director: Brenda Nienhouse
   Music Director: Eckart Preu
   Director of Marketing and Public Re: Audrey Overstreet
   General Manager: Donald Nelson
   Finance Director: Ellen Weigel
Mission: The Spokane Symphony Society believes that orchestral music nurtures the human spirit and is integral to the presentation and development of our American culture. We are committed to providing performances of the symphonic and chamber orchestra repertoire and to promoting educational and cultural activities which will enhance the knowledge and appreciation of that music for people of all ages.
Utilizes: Guest Artists; Guest Companies; Singers
Founded: 1945
Specialized Field: Symphony; Orchestra; Chamber
Status: Professional; Nonprofit
Paid Staff: 17
Volunteer Staff: 20
Paid Artists: 65
Budget: $3.4 million
Income Sources: Ticket Sales; Contributions; Endorsement
Performs At: Spokane Opera House
Affiliations: ASOL
Annual Attendance: 150,000
Organization Type: Performing; Touring; Resident; Educational; Sponsoring

1808
TACOMA PHILHARMONIC
901 Broadway
Tacoma, WA 98402
Phone: 253-591-5890
Fax: 253-591-2013
e-mail: administration@broadwaycenter.org
Web Site: www.broadwaycenter.org
Officers:
   President: Sara Kendall
   Vice President: Warren Willoughby
   Treasurer: Meng Li Che
   Secretary: Tiffany Harmon
   Immediate Past-President: Scott Shelton
Management:
   Executive Director: David Fischer
   Program Manager: Aaron Stevens
   Box Office Manager: Sean Nash
   Director of Development: Becky Johnson
Founded: 1936
Specialized Field: Classical
Paid Staff: 2
Volunteer Staff: 24
Budget: $150,000-$400,000
Income Sources: Grants; Donations; Ticket Sales
Performs At: Pantages Theater
Annual Attendance: 7,600+
Seating Capacity: 1,186

1809
TACOMA SYMPHONY ORCHESTRA
901 Broadway
Suite 600
Tacoma, WA 98402
Phone: 253-272-7264
Fax: 253-274-8187
e-mail: administration@broadwaycenter.org
Web Site: www.broadwaycenter.org/events/tacoma-symphony-orchestra
Officers:
   President: Sara Kendall
   Vice President: Warren Willoughby
   Treasurer: Meng Li Che
   Secretary: Tiffany Harmon
   Immediate Past-President: Scott Shelton

INSTRUMENTAL MUSIC / Washington

Management:
Executive Director: Mitchell Owens
Music Director: Sarah Ioannides
Program Manager: Aaron Stevens
Director of Development: Becky Johnson
Mission: To offer the community affordable classical music.
Utilizes: Guest Artists
Founded: 1959
Specialized Field: Symphony; Orchestra
Status: Professional; Nonprofit
Paid Staff: 10
Performs At: Pantages Theatre
Organization Type: Performing

1810
TACOMA YOUTH SYMPHONY
901 Broadway Plaza
Suite 500
Tacoma, WA 98402-4415
Phone: 253-627-2792
Fax: 253-627-1682
e-mail: info@tysamusic.org
Web Site: www.tysamusic.org
Management:
Executive Director/Development Offi: Dr. Loma L Cobbs
Music Director and Conductor: Dr. Paul-Elliot Cobbs
Conductor: Elizabeth Ward
Conductor: Dale Johnson
Conductor: Karla Timmerman-Epperson
Mission: Committed to the development of the Tacoma Youth Symphony Association as a quality music education organization that attracts and sustains the highest level of musical excellence for training and performance in the Puget Sound area. The TYSA challenges young musicians to pursue musical excellence, to seek intellectual stimulation, and to experience the love and joy of music making.
Founded: 1963
Specialized Field: Youth Symphony; Chamber; Ensemble
Status: Non-Professional; Nonprofit
Paid Staff: 9
Volunteer Staff: 120
Paid Artists: 8
Non-paid Artists: 15
Income Sources: Tuition/Fees; Ticket Sales; Public & Private Support
Performs At: Rialto Theatre
Organization Type: Performing; Educational

1811
VANCOUVER SYMPHONY ORCHESTRA
1220 Main Street, Suite 410
PO Box 525
Vancouver, WA 98660
Phone: 360-735-7278
Fax: 360-906-0355
e-mail: thevso@vancouversymphony.org
Web Site: www.vancouversymphony.org
Officers:
Chair: Kathy McDonald
Vice Chair: Dr. David Smith
Secretary: LeAnn Gilmore
Treasurer: Matthew Lee
Board Member: Paul Christiansen
Board Member: Jonathan Sauerwein
Board Member: Park Llafet
Management:
Music Director/Conductor: Salvador Brotons
Executive Director: Igor Shakhman
Volunteer Coordinator/Office Manage: Carol Robinson
Concertmaster: Eva Richey
Assistant Concertmaster: Tatiana Kolchanova
Stage Manager: Ron Christopher
Board Liason: Dieter Tazlaf
Mission: To enhance the quality of life in Southwest Washington by providing symphonic music of the highest caliber in live performances, and through music education in the schools, the concert halls, and throughout the community.
Utilizes: Arrangers; Collaborating Artists; Collaborations; Composers-in-Residence; Educators; Fine Artists; Guest Companies; Guest Designers; Lyricists; Multimedia; Music; Paid Performers; Singers
Founded: 1981
Opened: 1982
Specialized Field: Classical, Instrumental
Status: Non-Profit, Professional
Income Sources: Sponsors, Donors
Season: October through May
Performs At: Skyview Concert Hall, Trinity Lutheran Church, Lifepoint Church

1812
WALLA WALLA SYMPHONY
PO Box 92
13 1/2 E. Main, Suite 201
Walla Walla, WA 99362
Phone: 509-529-8020
Fax: 509-529-1353
e-mail: info@wwsymphony.org
Web Site: www.wwsymphony.org
Officers:
President: John Jamison
VP: Edward Foster
Secretary: Andrea Burkhart
Treasurer: Jan Crouter
Board Member: Jack Copperman
Management:
Conductor and Music Director: Yaacov Bergman
Orchestra Manager: Ed Dixon
Bookkeeper: Sheila Fergusson
Operations and Education Coordinato: Elizabeth Tackett
Music Director/Conductor, Youth Orc: Jeremy Mims
Mission: Continuing the tradition of outstanding symphonic music; bringing high-quality performances to the entire community, including children.
Utilizes: Artists-in-Residence; Collaborations; Commissioned Composers; Commissioned Music; Composers-in-Residence; Dancers; Fine Artists; Five Seasonal Concerts; Guest Accompanists; Guest Companies; Guest Composers; Guest Directors; Guest Lecturers; Guest Musical Directors; Guest Musicians; Guest Writers; Multimedia; Organization Contracts; Original Music Scores; Sign Language Translators; Soloists
Founded: 1906
Specialized Field: Symphony; Orchestra
Status: Non-Professional; Nonprofit
Paid Staff: 7
Paid Artists: 80
Budget: $300,000
Performs At: Cordinet Hall
Annual Attendance: 10,000
Seating Capacity: 1,384
Organization Type: Performing

1813
WEATCHEE VALLEY SYMPHONY ORCHESTRA
PO Box 3423
Wenatchee, WA 98807
Phone: 509-667-2640
e-mail: symphony@wenatcheesymphony.org
Web Site: wenatcheesymphony.org
Officers:
President: Teri Snyder
Vice President: Larry McCracken
Secretary: Karen Keleman
Treasurer: Gregory Brault
Board Member: Iris Bolstad
Board Member: Karen Keleman
Board Member: Don Larson
Board Member: Marva Lee McCracken
Management:
Music Director/Conductor: Nikolas Caoile
Concertmaster: Rebekah Poulson
Assistant Concertmaster: Kerry Travers
Musician Coordinator: Cindy Dietz
Mission: Shares witht he world a great passion for music.
Utilizes: Arrangers; Collaborating Artists; Collaborations; Composers; Fine Artists; Guest Companies; High School Drama; Local Artists & Directors; Lyricists; Multimedia; Music; Paid Performers
Specialized Field: Classical, Instrumental
Status: Non-Profit
Income Sources: Sponsors, Donors, Volunteers, Gifts
Season: October, December, February, April
Performs At: Performing Arts Center of Wenatchee

1814
YAKIMA SYMPHONY ORCHESTRA
32 N 3rd Street
Suite 333
Yakima, WA 98901
Phone: 509-248-1414
Fax: 509-457-0980
e-mail: noel@yakimasymphony.org
Web Site: yakimasymphony.org
Officers:
President: Neal Lessenger
Vice-President: Paul Campbell Dempsey
Secretary: Kay Bassett
Treasurer: Abby Sanders
Board Member: Gwen Chaplin
Management:
Conductor: Lawrence Golan
Cover Conductor: Bruce Walker
Development Director: Betsy McCann
Customer Relations Manager: Sue Chirco-Coontz
Operations Manager: Mary Winterfeld
Mission: Performing and promoting symphonic music.
Utilizes: Guest Artists
Founded: 1971
Specialized Field: Symphony; Orchestra
Status: Professional; Nonprofit
Paid Staff: 6
Paid Artists: 65
Income Sources: American Symphony Orchestra League
Performs At: Capitol Theatre
Seating Capacity: 1,500
Year Built: 1971
Organization Type: Performing; Educational

1815
YAKIMA YOUTH ORCHESTRA
PO Box 10613
Yakima, WA 98909

INSTRUMENTAL MUSIC / West Virginia

Phone: 509-248-1414
Fax: 509-457-0980
e-mail: yyso.yes@gmail.com
Web Site: www.yyso.org
Officers:
　Chair: Betsy McCann
　Vice-Chair: Linda Sellers
　Treasurer: Steve Andringa
　Secretary: Julie Conley
Management:
　YYSO Conductor: Bruce Walker
　YES! Conductor: Christy Baisinger
　Assistant to the YES! Conductor: Priscilla Fassett
Specialized Field: Youth Orchestra; Chamber
Status: Non-Professional; Nonprofit
Paid Staff: 20
Income Sources: Yakima Symphony Orchestra
Organization Type: Performing; Educational

West Virginia

1816
CHARLESTON CHAMBER MUSIC SOCIETY
PO Box 641
Charleston, WV 25323
Phone: 304-344-5389
Fax: 304-344-5389
e-mail: ChasChambMusSoc@aol.com
Web Site: www.charlestonchambermusic.org
Management:
　Executive Director: N David Stem
Mission: To bring outstanding chamber-music ensembles to Charleston.
Utilizes: Guest Directors; Multimedia; Original Music Scores
Founded: 1941
Specialized Field: Chamber; Ensemble
Status: Nonprofit
Paid Staff: 1
Volunteer Staff: 7
Budget: $40,000
Income Sources: Association of Performing Arts Presenters; Chamber Music America
Performs At: Christ Church United Methodist
Affiliations: Association od Performing Arts Presenters; Chamber Music America
Annual Attendance: 1500
Facility Category: Church Sanctuary
Type of Stage: 3/4 Round
Seating Capacity: 400+
Organization Type: Performing; Sponsoring

1817
MONTCLAIRE STRING QUARTET
1205 Oakmont Road
Charleston, WV 25314
Mailing Address: PO Box 2292, Charleston, WV 25328
Phone: 304-561-3500
Fax: 304-561-3598
e-mail: info@wvsymphony.org
Web Site: www.wvsymphony.org/meet-the-orchestra/msq
Officers:
　Chairman: John Elliot
　Vice Chairman: Cindy McGhee
　President: Joe Tackett
　Secretary/Treasurer: Charles R. Hageboeck
　Vice President of Development and M: Lisa Lopinsky
Management:
　Executive Director: Paul Helfrich

Advertising Sales Manager: Bethany Kinder
Grants Manager: Rebecca Roth
Marketing and Communications Manage: Tommy Napier
Development Manager: Samuel Settle
Mission: To present the highest quality string quartet repertoire throughout the state of West Virginia; to provide leadership in the West Virginia Symphony Orchestra; to present educational programs in West Virginia schools.
Founded: 1982
Specialized Field: Symphony; Chamber; Ensemble
Status: Professional
Paid Artists: 4
Performs At: Kanawha United Presbyterian Church
Organization Type: Performing; Touring; Resident; Educational; Sponsoring

1818
HUNTINGTON SYMPHONY ORCHESTRA
763 Third Avenue
Huntington, WV 25701
Mailing Address: P.O. Box 2434 Huntington WV 25717
Phone: 304-781-8343
Fax: 304-697-4479
e-mail: levans@huntingtonsymphony.org
Web Site: www.huntingtonsymphony.org
Officers:
　President: Dr. Maurice Mufson
　First Vice President: Pat Bertoia
　Second Vice President: James St Clair
　Secretary: Rebecca Wick
　Treasurer: Barry Burgess
Management:
　Music Director: Kimo Furumoto
　Personnel Manager: Sandy White
Mission: To perform the finest music written for chamber orchestras.
Utilizes: Community Members; Composers; Contract Orchestras; Educators; Five Seasonal Concerts; Guest Composers; Guest Lecturers; Instructors; Local Artists; Multimedia; Organization Contracts; Original Music Scores
Founded: 1970
Specialized Field: Orchestra; Chamber
Status: Professional; Nonprofit
Paid Staff: 3
Volunteer Staff: 50
Income Sources: American Symphony Orchestra League
Performs At: Keith Albee Performing Arts Center
Annual Attendance: 20,000
Organization Type: Performing; Resident

1819
WHEELING SYMPHONY
1025 Main Street
Suite 811
Wheeling, WV 26003
Phone: 304-232-6191
Fax: 304-232-6192
Toll-free: 800-395-9241
e-mail: wso@wheelingsymphony.com
Web Site: www.wheelingsymphony.org
Officers:
　President-elect: Sandra Chapman
　Board Member: Samantha Buch
　Board Member: David Dalzell
　Board Member: Patty Dunlevy
　Board Member: Mary Beth Hughes
Management:
　Executive Director: Bruce Wheeler
　Music Director: Andr, Raphel

Development Director & Orchestra Li: Dr. Gail Looney
Youth Orchestra Manager: Micah Labishak
Design Guru: Paul Smallwood
Mission: To provide balanced and diversified musical programs which broaden audience appreciation and improve the quality of life in our area.
Founded: 1926
Specialized Field: Symphony; Orchestra
Status: Professional; Nonprofit
Paid Staff: 10
Income Sources: Grants; Donations; Ticket Sales
Performs At: Capitol Music Hall
Organization Type: Performing; Touring; Resident; Educational

Wisconsin

1820
FOX VALLEY SYMPHONY
111 West College Ave.
Suite 550
Appleton, WI 54911-5706
Phone: 920-968-0300
Fax: 920-968-0303
e-mail: info@foxvalleysymphony.com
Web Site: www.foxvalleysymphony.com/
Officers:
　President: Beth Flaherty
　Immediate Past President: Phil Snyder
　Treasurer: Jane Chaganos
　Secretary: Priscilla Daniels
　Vice President, Development: Karen Laws
Management:
　Executive Director: Roseanna Cannizzo
　Music Director: Brian Goner
　Concert Orchestra Conductor: Greg Austin
　Director of Marketing & Operations: Jamie LaFreniere
　Youth Orchestra Conductor: Seong-Kyung Graham
Mission: To provide symphonic music for all; to sponsor youth orchestras and to introduce school children to orchestra music.
Utilizes: Commissioned Music; Guest Musical Directors; Guest Musicians; Multimedia; Singers
Founded: 1966
Specialized Field: Symphony
Status: Nonprofit
Paid Staff: 7
Volunteer Staff: 125
Paid Artists: 65
Budget: $424,000
Performs At: Pickard Auditorium; Lawrence University Chapel
Annual Attendance: 6000
Organization Type: Performing; Resident; Educational; Sponsoring

1821
BELOIT JANESVILLE SYMPHONY ORCHESTRA
444 E. Grand Ave.
Suite 100
Beloit, WI 53511
Phone: 608-313-1200
Fax: 608-363-2718
e-mail: service@beloitjanesvillesymphony.org
Web Site: www.beloitjanesvillesymphony.org/
Officers:
　President: Scott Lans
　Vice President: Francisca Amador
　Secretary: Steve Kerchoff

Treasurer: Joanne Acomb
Board Member: Patricia Brock
Management:
　Music Director: Robert Tomaro
　Executive Director: Michael Krueger
　Outreach and Marketing Director: Britney McKay
　Operations Director: Greg Gerard
　Production Coordinator: Jake Hamil
Founded: 1953
Specialized Field: Orchestra
Paid Staff: 5
Volunteer Staff: 130
Paid Artists: 80

1822
FOND DU LAC SYMPHONIC BAND
PO Box 1483
Fond du Lac, WI 54936-1483
Phone: 920-907-7678
e-mail: marthur@fdlsymphonicband.org
Web Site: fdlsymphonicband.org/wordpress2
Management:
　Business Manager: Mary A. Arthur
Mission: To provide quality musical entertainment for our area and beyond; to enhance the image of the concert band as a performing medium; to provide a sophisticated performing opportunity for adult instrumentalists.
Founded: 1898
Specialized Field: Band
Status: Semi-Professional; Nonprofit
Paid Staff: 20
Income Sources: Association of Concert Bands; American Federation of Musicians
Organization Type: Performing; Touring

1823
GREEN BAY SYMPHONY ORCHESTRA
University of Wisconsin - Green Bay
2420 Nicolet Drive
Green Bay, WI 54311-7001
Mailing Address: P.O. Box 13375, Green Bay, WI 54307-3375
Phone: 920-435-3465
Fax: 920-435-1427
e-mail: info@greenbaysymphony.org
Web Site: www.greenbaysymphony.org
Officers:
　President: Bill Guc
　Executive Vice President: Bille Kress
　Treasurer: Patricia McKlosky
　Secretary: Mary Meyer
　Board Member: Mark Radtke
Management:
　Executive Director: Daniel Linssen
　Office Administrator: Melissa Tschamler
　Personnel Administrator: Kate Krueger
　Youth Symphony Conductor: Mike Ross
Mission: To promote orchestras and performances of the highest quality for the enjoyment of ever-widening audiences and pursue educational experiences for youth and adults through musical collaborations.
Founded: 1914
Specialized Field: Symphony; Orchestra; Chamber
Status: Nonprofit
Paid Staff: 7
Volunteer Staff: 135
Paid Artists: 71
Income Sources: American Symphony Orchestra League; Association of Wisconsin Symphony Orchestra
Performs At: Weidner Center for The Performing Arts
Organization Type: Performing; Educational

1824
CARTHAGE CHAMBER MUSIC SERIES
2001 Alford Drive
Carthage College
Kenosha, WI 53140-1994
Phone: 262-551-8500
Fax: 262-551-6208
e-mail: webmaster@carthage.edu
Web Site: www.carthage.edu/music/calendar/chamber-music-series
Officers:
　Chairman Music Department: Dr. RD Sjoerdsma
Management:
　Music Department Chair: James Ripley
Specialized Field: Chamber; Ensemble
Budget: $20,000-$35,000
Performs At: Siebert Chapel

1825
KENOSHA SYMPHONY ASSOCIATION
723 58th Street
#301
Kenosha, WI 53140
Phone: 262-654-9080
Fax: 262-654-8809
e-mail: Admin@KenoshaSymphony.org
Web Site: www.kenoshasymphony.org
Officers:
　President of Board of Directors: Timothy Berlew
　Secretary: Dimitri Shapovalov
　Treasurer: Derek Petersen
Management:
　Musical Director and Conductor: Robert G. Hasty
　Executive Director: Sarah Gorke
　Personnel Manager: Kathryn Krubsack
Mission: To provide a symphony orchestra in a community setting.
Founded: 1941
Specialized Field: Symphony; Orchestra; Chamber
Status: Professional; Semi-Professional; Non-Professional; Nonprofit
Paid Staff: 1
Volunteer Staff: 50
Paid Artists: 70
Income Sources: Kenosha Unified Schools
Performs At: Reuther Auditorium
Organization Type: Performing; Educational

1826
MADISON SYMPHONY ORCHESTRA
222 W. Washington Ave.
Suite 460
Madison, WI 53703
Phone: 608-257-3734
Fax: 608-280-6192
e-mail: info@madisonsymphony.org
Web Site: www.madisonsymphony.org
Officers:
　President: Nicholas Mischler
　Vice President: Edwin O. Sheldon
　Vice President: Mary Lang Sollinger
　Vice President: Anders Yocom
　Secretary: Martha Casey
Management:
　Executive Director: Richard H. Mackie
　General Manager: Ann Bowen
　Director of Development: Casey Oelkers
　Manager of Institutional Giving: Carmel Morgan-Weeisberg
　Director of Marketing: Teri Venker
Utilizes: Sign Language Translators
Founded: 1926
Specialized Field: Symphony
Status: Professional
Paid Staff: 9
Paid Artists: 90
Budget: $2,000,000
Performs At: Oscar Meyer Theatre
Affiliations: Civic Center Box Office
Annual Attendance: 40,000+
Facility Category: Multi Purpose Performance Hall
Seating Capacity: 2,110
Organization Type: Performing; Educational

1827
WISCONSIN CHAMBER ORCHESTRA
321 E. Main Street
PO Box 171
Madison, WI 53701-0171
Mailing Address: PO Box 171
Phone: 608-257-0638
Fax: 608-257-0611
e-mail: wco@wcoconcerts.org
Web Site: www.wcoconcerts.org/
Officers:
　Chair: Gordon Ridley
　Vice Chair: Tom Popp
　Treasurer: Shawn P. Carney
　Secretary: Kate Neitzel
　Board Member: Terry Bolz
Management:
　Executive Director: Robert Sorge
　Music Director: Andrew Sewell
Mission: To perform musical works.
Utilizes: Singers
Founded: 1962
Specialized Field: Orchestra; Chamber
Status: Professional; Nonprofit
Performs At: Capitol Square; First Congregational Church; Wisconsin Union Theater
Seating Capacity: 1,200
Organization Type: Performing

1828
WISCONSIN YOUTH SYMPHONY ORCHESTRAS
455 N. Park Street Room
1625 Humanities Building
Madison, WI 53706
Phone: 608-263-3320
Fax: 608-265-3751
e-mail: wyso@wyso.music.wisc.edu
Web Site: wyso.music.wisc.edu
Officers:
　President: Charlotte Woods
　Treasurer: Graham Fuguitt
　Secretary: Coe Williams
　Vice-President: John Walker
　Vice-President: Eric Baker
Management:
　Music Director: James R Smith
　Executive Director: Bridget Fraser
　Director of Operations & Education: Joe Bernstein
　Percussion Ensemble Director: Vicki Peterson Jenks
　Brass Choirs Director: Daniel J. Brice
　Harp Ensemble Director: Karen Atz
Mission: To meet the symphonic needs of the musically-talented youth of Southern Wisconsin.
Utilizes: Artists-in-Residence; Collaborating Artists; Commissioned Music; Five Seasonal Concerts; Guest Accompanists; Guest Companies; Guest Directors; Organization Contracts; Singers; Soloists
Founded: 1966
Specialized Field: Youth Orchestra

INSTRUMENTAL MUSIC / Wisconsin

Status: Nonprofit
Paid Staff: 25
Volunteer Staff: 50
Performs At: Mills Concert Hall; University of Wisconsin
Annual Attendance: 2,500
Facility Category: music hall
Stage Dimensions: 40x40
Seating Capacity: 750
Organization Type: Performing; Touring; Educational

1829
MARSHFIELD-WOOD COMMUNITY SYMPHONY
2000 W 5th Street
Marshfield, WI 54449
Phone: 715-389-6530
Fax: 715-389-6517
Web Site: www.marshfield.uwc.edu
Officers:
  President: Sarah Hanson
Management:
  Conductor: Timothy McCollum
Mission: To present the best music possible for the least possible cost.
Founded: 1965
Specialized Field: Symphony; Orchestra
Status: Nonprofit
Income Sources: American Symphony Orchestra League
Performs At: Fine Arts Building Theatre
Organization Type: Performing; Educational

1830
MILWAUKEE SYMPHONY ORCHESTRA
1101 North Market Street
Suite 100
Milwaukee, WI 53202
Phone: 414-291-6010
Fax: 414-291-7610
Toll-free: 800-291-7605
e-mail: info@mso.org
Web Site: www.mso.org
Officers:
  VP Marketing & Communications: Susan Loris
  Chairman Of The Board: Douglas M. Hagerman
  Vice-Chair: Michael L. Gonzalez
  Vice-Chair: Eric E. Hobbs
  President & Executive Director: Mark Niehaus
Management:
  Orchestra Personnel Manager: Linda Unkefer
  Music Director: Edo de Waart
  Associate Conductor: Francesco Lecce-Chong
  Chorus Director: Lee Erickson
  Assistant Chorus Director: Timothy J. Benson
Founded: 1959
Specialized Field: Symphony; Orchestra
Status: Professional; Nonprofit
Paid Staff: 5
Budget: $16 million
Income Sources: Ticket Sales; Fees for Services; United Performing Arts Fund; Wisconsin Arts Board; Milwaukee County CAMPAC; Corporate And Individual Giving
Performs At: Marcus Center for the Performing Arts; Uihlein Hall
Annual Attendance: 270,000
Organization Type: Performing; Touring; Educational; Recording

1831
MILWAUKEE YOUTH SYMPHONY ORCHESTRA
325 W Walnut Street
Milwaukee, WI 53212
Phone: 414-267-2906
Fax: 414-267-2960
e-mail: general@myso.org
Web Site: www.myso.org
Officers:
  Chair: Patrick Rath
  Chair Elect: Jennifer Mattes
  Treasurer: Craig Peotter
  Secretary: Patty Hanz
  Vice-President: Michael Van Handel
Management:
  Executive Director: Linda Edelstein
  Artistic Director, Music Director: Carter Simmons
  Senior Symphony Music Director: Margery Deutsch
  Senior Symphony Associate Conductor: Shelby Dixon
  Brass Choir Director: Don Sipe
Mission: Provides training in the finest techniques of orchestral and ensemble musicianship to students ages 8-18 in the greater Milwaukee area, through an extensive schedule of rehearsals, performances and enrichment activities.
Utilizes: Collaborating Artists; Collaborations; Commissioned Composers; Community Members; Composers; Composers-in-Residence; Educators; Grant Writers; Guest Companies; Guest Composers; Guest Musical Directors; Guest Musicians; Guest Soloists; Guest Teachers; High School Drama; Instructors; Lyricists; Multimedia; Music; Original Music Scores; Scenic Designers; Sign Language Translators; Singers; Soloists; Students
Founded: 1956
Specialized Field: Youth Orchestra; Chamber; Ensemble
Status: Non-Professional; Nonprofit; Youth Orchestra
Paid Staff: 40
Budget: $1.5 million
Performs At: Uihlein Hall
Affiliations: LAO; AWSO; YOD
Annual Attendance: 10,000
Seating Capacity: 2,300

1832
PRESENT MUSIC
158 N Broadway
Milwaukee, WI 53202
Phone: 414-271-0711
Fax: 414-271-7998
e-mail: newmusic@presentmusic.org
Web Site: www.presentmusic.org
Officers:
  President: Lois Smith
  Immediate Past President: Catherine Gordon
  VP Fund Development: Sally Duback
  VP Audience Development: Claudia Egan
  Treasure/Secretary/President Elect: David Keen
Management:
  Artistic Director: Kevin Stalheim
  General Manager: Christine Liu
  Audience Development Manager: Erin M. Woehlke
  Events & Outreach: Sarah Warran
Mission: Present music engages artists and audiences in imaginative experiences with new music through ensemble performance education and commissioning.
Utilizes: Artists-in-Residence; Collaborations; Commissioned Music; Guest Companies; Guest Directors; Multimedia; Organization Contracts
Founded: 1982
Specialized Field: Chamber; Ensemble
Status: Professional; Nonprofit
Paid Staff: 35
Paid Artists: 25
Budget: $400,000
Income Sources: Ticket Sales; Philanthropic Support
Annual Attendance: 5,000
Facility Category: Art Museum
Seating Capacity: 750
Year Built: 2001
Organization Type: Performing; Touring; Resident; Educational; Recording

1833
OSHKOSH SYMPHONY ORCHESTRA
290 City Center
Oshkosh, WI 54902
Mailing Address: PO Box 522, Oshkosh, WI 54903
Phone: 920-233-7510
Fax: 920-230-4783
e-mail: symphony@oshkoshsymphony.org
Web Site: www.oshkoshsymphony.org
Officers:
  President: John Bermingham
  Executive VP: Sam Adams
  Secretary: Victoria Beltran
  Treasure: Stuart N. Tribbey
  Marketing Director: Mary Whitlock
Management:
  Conductor: Daniel Black
  Executive Director: James Grine
  Youth Symphony Conductor: Geraldine Grine
Founded: 1940
Specialized Field: Symphony; Orchestra
Status: Semi-Professional
Income Sources: Association of Wisconsin Symphony Orchestra; American Symphony Orchestra League
Performs At: Osh Kosh Civic Auditorium
Organization Type: Performing

1834
RACINE SYMPHONY ORCHESTRA
800 Cedar Street, Suite 120
PO Box 1874
Racine, WI 53403
Phone: 262-636-9285
e-mail: info@racinesymphony.org
Web Site: racinesymphony.org
Officers:
  President: Cory Mason III
  Vice President: Roberta Stark
  Secretary: David Easley
  Treasurer: Steve McLaughlin
  Director: David Beach
  Director: Renee Andronczyk
Management:
  Artistic Director & Conductor: Pasquale Laurino
  Acting Concertmaster: Alexander Mandl
  Principal/Violas: Lynne Fields
  Co-Principal/Cellos: Andrea Nott
  Co-Principal/Cellos: Elizabeth Bender
  Principal/Basses: Charles Grosz
  Executive Director: Bonnie Prochaska
  Patron Services Manager: Susan Ramagli
  Orchestra Personnel Manager: Anna Kojovic
Mission: The vision of the Racine Symphony Orchestra is to provide outstanding music that touches the soul of the community. The mission of the Racine Symphony Orchestra is to enrich, educate, and entertain our communities through the power of music.

Utilizes: Arrangers; Collaborations; Commissioned Music; Composers; Fine Artists; Guest Directors; High School Drama; Lyricists; Multimedia; Music
Founded: 1932
Specialized Field: Classical, Instrumental
Status: Non-Profit, Professional
Income Sources: Donors, Sponsors
Season: October, December, April
Performs At: Racine Festival Hall, First Presbyterian Church

1835
CENTRAL WISCONSIN SYMPHONY ORCHESTRA
1128 Main Street
PO Box 65
Stevens Point, WI 54481
Phone: 715-345-2976
Fax: 715-345-2903
e-mail: info@cwso.org
Web Site: www.cwso.org
Officers:
  President: David Bakken
  Secretary: Tom Stenborg
  Treasurer: Kass Raabe
  Board Member: Lee Ayers
  Board Member: Amy Bakkan
Management:
  Music Director/Conductor: Patrick Miles
  Executive Director: Ann Huntoon
  Operations Manager/Librarian: Megan Lawrence
  Financial Coordinator: Andrea Van Natta
  Program Notes: Linda Schubert
  Graphic Designer: Jenny Harkness
Mission: The Central Wisconsin Symphony Orchestra will enrich the cultural lives of the residents of the Central Wisconsin area by presenting high quality concerts, fostering an appreciation of symphonic music, providing a performance venue for area musicians, and developing an educational opportunity for youth.
Utilizes: Arrangers; Collaborating Artists; Collaborations; Community Talent; Educators; Fine Artists; Guest Companies; Lyricists; Multimedia; Music; Paid Performers; Singers
Founded: 1947
Specialized Field: Instrumental, Classical
Status: Non-Profit, Professional
Income Sources: Donors, Sponsors, Fundraisers
Season: October through April
Performs At: Theater @ 1800

Wyoming

1836
WYOMING SYMPHONY ORCHESTRA
225 South David
Suite B
Casper, WY 82601
Mailing Address: PO Box 667 Casper, WY 82602
Phone: 307-266-1478
Fax: 307-266-4522
e-mail: rachel@wyomingsymphony.org
Web Site: www.wyomingsymphony.org
Officers:
  President: Bobbie Brown
Management:
  Executive Director: Rachel Bailey
  Music Director and Conductor: Matthew Savery
  Director of Development: Lindsey Grant
Mission: To enhance cultural life; to expand childrens' musical horizons; to offer area musicians a performance outlet.
Founded: 1950
Specialized Field: Symphony; Orchestra
Status: Professional; Nonprofit
Paid Staff: 4
Paid Artists: 75
Budget: $300,000
Income Sources: City of Casper; Wyoming Council on the Arts; National Endowment for the Arts; American Symphony Orchestra League; Private Foundations
Performs At: John F. Welsh Auditorium; Natrona County High School
Affiliations: American Symphony Orchestra League
Annual Attendance: 6,400
Facility Category: High School
Organization Type: Performing; Touring; Educational

1837
CHEYENNE SYMPHONY ORCHESTRA
1904 Thomes Avenue
Cheyenne, WY 82001
Phone: 307-778-8561
Fax: 307-634-7512
e-mail: email@cheyennesymphony.org
Web Site: www.cheyennesymphony.org
Officers:
  President: Bob Fecth
  Vice President: Stephen Schmerge
  Secretary: Amy Gruber
  Treasurer: Robert Nelson
  Past President: Patty Benskin
Management:
  Executive Director: Elizabeth McGuire
  Music Director: William Intriligator
  Orchestra Manager: Lindsey Bird Reynolds
Mission: Presenting excellent professionally performed symphonic music to as wide as possible an audience, emphasizing educational outreach.
Utilizes: Guest Artists
Founded: 1954
Specialized Field: Symphony; Orchestra; Chamber
Status: Professional; Nonprofit
Income Sources: American Symphony Orchestra League; Symphony & Choral Society of Cheyenne
Performs At: Cheyenne Civic Center
Organization Type: Performing; Educational

1838
POWDER RIVER SYMPHONY ORCHESTRA
PO Box 3964
Gillette, WY 82717
Phone: 307-670-2856
e-mail: info@prsymphony.org
Web Site: www.prsymphony.org
Officers:
  President: David Dooley
  Vice President: Cheryl Ringer
  Secretary: Melanie Barnes
  Treasurer: Carol Hungerford
  Board Member: Jeff Anderson
  Board Member: Paige Denny
  Board Member: Kris Dickey
Management:
  Artistic Director/Conductor: Norman Gamboa
  Concertmaster: Deb Anderson
  Principal: Sonja Brue
  Principal: Kathie Means
Mission: Music Director of the Powder River Symphony Orchestra, Norman Gamboa is one of the most exciting Latin American conductors of the new generation. His numerous guest conducting appearances include symphony orchestras throughout Texas, Louisiana, Kansas, Missouri, Wyoming, Minnesota, California, Colorado, and Nevada.
Utilizes: Arrangers; Collaborating Artists; Collaborations; Composers; Fine Artists; Lyricists; Multimedia; Music; Paid Performers; Singers
Specialized Field: Classical, Instrumental
Status: Non-Profit, Professional
Income Sources: Donors, Sales, Fundraisers, Advertising
Season: September through May
Performs At: Cam Plex Heritage Center

VOCAL MUSIC / Alabama

Alabama

1839
BIRMINGHAM MUSIC CLUB
PO Box 10486
Birmingham, AL 35202
Phone: 205-903-5007
Fax: 205-322-6206
e-mail: kidconcert@aol.com
Web Site: www.bhammusicclub.org
Officers:
  President: Wyatt R Haskell
  VP: Eloise Williams
  Treasurer: Carolyn Long
  Secretary: Judy H Wiggins
  Senior Advisor: Malcolm Miller
Management:
  Executive Director: Cynthia Harper
Mission: To present talented artists from around the world to the community of Birmingham.
Specialized Field: Ethnic Music; Classical; Contemporary
Status: Non-Profit, Professional
Paid Staff: 4

1840
OPERA BIRMINGHAM
3601 Sixth Avenue South
Birmingham, AL 35222
Phone: 205-322-6737
Fax: 205-322-6206
e-mail: john@bhammusiccoop.org
Web Site: www.operabirmingham.org
Officers:
  General Director: John D Jones
  Guild President: Summer Currier
Management:
  President: Philippe Rathrop
  General Director: John D. Jones
  Principal Conductor: Steven White
  Education and Outreach Manager: Mary K Jackson
  Chorus Master: Daniel Seigel
Mission: Opera Birmingham is committed to creating the finest opera productions, developing local and regional talent through competition and exposure to major artists, and preserving the operatic art form through community-wide education.
Founded: 1955
Specialized Field: Grand Opera; Lyric Opera; Youth Chorus; Classical; Contemporary
Status: Non-Profit, Professional
Paid Staff: 4
Performs At: Alabama Theater

1841
HUNTSVILLE OPERA THEATER
8802 Willow Hills Drive
Huntsville, AL 36660-1633
Phone: 334-476-7377
Fax: 334-476-7153
e-mail: mbeutjer@hiwaay.net
Web Site: www.huntsvilleopera.com/hot.html
Officers:
  President: Steve Russell
  Guild President: Sonja Bruek
Management:
  General Director/Princ Conductor: Jerome Shannoni
  Administrative Director: Merv White-Spunner
  Financial Secretary: Nancy Thomas
  Education Director: Charles Smoke
  Publications Manager: Sarah Wright
  Marketing Director: Larry Wooley
  Development Director: Paul Klotz
Mission: Nurturing the growth of young dancers, singers and technicians.
Founded: 1981
Specialized Field: Grand Opera
Status: Nonprofit
Performs At: Von Braun Civic Center - Playhouse
Organization Type: Performing

1842
MOBILE OPERA
257 Dauthin Street
Mobile, AL 36602
Phone: 251-432-6772
Fax: 251-431-7613
e-mail: info@mobileopera.org
Web Site: www.mobileopera.org
Officers:
  President: Sheryl Bates
  Executive Vice President: Cesar Roca
  Treasurer: Melissa Safin
  VP of Finance: Earl Jackson
  VP Information Technology: John L. Strope
Management:
  President: Sheryl Bates
  General Director: Scott Wright
  Artistic Director: Andy Anderson
  Education Director: Stacey Driskell
  Office Manager: Nicole Harski
Mission: Present professional productions of opera and musical theatre and programs dedicated to in school arts education and community outreach while providing performance opportunities for national and regional artists.
Utilizes: Actors; Artists-in-Residence; Dance Companies; Grant Writers; Guest Accompanists; Guest Artists; Guest Companies; Guest Composers; Guest Conductors; Guest Designers; Guest Writers; Original Music Scores
Founded: 1946
Specialized Field: Grand Opera; Operetta
Status: Non-Profit, Professional
Paid Staff: 4
Volunteer Staff: 10
Paid Artists: 150
Budget: $700,000
Performs At: Mobile Saenger Theatre
Affiliations: Opera America
Annual Attendance: 9,120
Type of Stage: Proscenium
Seating Capacity: 1,900
Year Built: 1927
Year Remodeled: 2004

Alaska

1843
ALASKA CHAMBER SINGERS
P.O. Box 102055
Anchorage, AK 99510
Phone: 907-333-3500
e-mail: info@alaskachambersingers.org
Web Site: alaskachambersingers.org
Officers:
  President: Cindy Bledsoe
  Vice President: Julie Flynn
  Treasurer: Bardon Simons
  Secretary: Carly Horton-Stewart
Management:
  Artistic Director/Conductor: David Hagen
Mission: To expand and invigorate interest in exceptional choral music of varied forms and periods through performances of uncommon style and superlative quality.
Founded: 1986

1844
ANCHORAGE CONCERT CHORUS
165 E 56th Avenue
PO Box 100364
Anchorage, AK 99510-0364
Phone: 907-274-7464
Fax: 907-563-5980
e-mail: concertchorus@gci.net
Web Site: www.anchorageconcertchorus.org
Officers:
  President: Shaun Baines
Management:
  Artistic Director/Conductor: Dr. Grant Cochran, concertchorus@gci.net
  Executive Director: Sandra Adams, concertchorus@gci.net
Mission: To serve Anchorage and surrounding communities by fostering excellence in choral music through world-class vocal performance, community events, and music education.
Utilizes: Guest Artists
Founded: 1947
Specialized Field: Choral
Status: Non-Profit, Non-Professional
Paid Staff: 2
Non-paid Artists: 160
Budget: $240,000
Income Sources: Municipality of Anchorage; Alaska State Council on the Arts, Donations, Dues, Performances
Performs At: Alaska Center for the Performing Arts
Affiliations: Chorus America
Annual Attendance: 12,000-16,000
Organization Type: Performing
Resident Groups: Alaska Center for the Performing Arts

1845
ANCHORAGE OPERA COMPANY
1507 Spar Avenue
Anchorage, AK 99501-1812
Phone: 907-279-2557
Fax: 907-279-7798
e-mail: info@anchorageopera.org
Web Site: www.anchorageopera.org
Officers:
  President: Dr. Donald Endres
  Treasurer: Peter Ricca
  Secretary: Lisa Maurer
  VP: Michael Moore
Management:
  General Director: Torrie Allen
  Production Manager/Technical Dir: Lauren Miller
  Director of Individual Giving: Eva Aigner
  Grants & Education Manager: Lauren Green
  Executive Director: Kevin Patterson
Mission: Provides the finest operatic experiences to residents and visitors while also serving as a professional resource for American artist's, admistrators and technical staff helping them to refine their talent and perfect craft.
Utilizes: Actors; Artists-in-Residence; Collaborations; Community Members; Community Talent; Contract Orchestras; Dancers; Designers; Educators; Five Seasonal Concerts; Grant Writers; Guest Artists; Guest Composers; Guest Lecturers; Guest Musicians; Guest Writers; Instructors; Local Artists & Directors; Lyricists; Multi Collaborations; Multimedia; Music; Original Music

Scores; Poets; Resident Artists; Resident Professionals; Scenic Designers; Sign Language Translators; Singers; Students; Student Interns; Visual Arts
Founded: 1962
Specialized Field: Grand Opera; Light Opera; Lyric Opera; Classical
Status: Non-Profit, Professional
Paid Staff: 6
Volunteer Staff: 90
Paid Artists: 100
Performs At: Alaska Center for the Performing Arts

1846
FAIRBANKS CHORAL SOCIETY
1815 Carr Avenue
PO Box 71336
Fairbanks, AK 99701-1336
Phone: 907-456-1144
e-mail: acontrol@co.fairbanks.ak.us
Web Site: www.fairbankschoralsociety.org
Officers:
  President: Dr. Carol Diehl
  Academic Advisor: Dr. Siri Tuttle
  Secretary: Kathy Vaupel
Management:
  Executive Director: Suzanne Summerville, ssummerville@gmail.com
Mission: Sponsoring the Fairbanks Sing-It-Yourself-Messiah, and concerts for the animals
Utilizes: Guest Artists; Guest Companies; Singers
Founded: 1984
Specialized Field: Classical; Contemporary; Religious
Status: Non-Profit, Non-Professional
Paid Artists: 3
Income Sources: Fairbanks City Bed-Tax And Private Donations
Performs At: University of Alaska; Fairbanks Concert Hall
Organization Type: Performing; Educational; Sponsoring

1847
FAIRBANKS LIGHT OPERA THEATRE
PO Box 72787
Fairbanks, AK 99707
Phone: 907-456-3568
Fax: 907-456-3662
e-mail: flot@flot.org
Web Site: www.flot.org
Officers:
  VP: Amanda Hanson
  Treasurer: Jason Taylor
  Recording Secretary: Lisa Newman
Management:
  President: Kurt Newman
Mission: To offer our community musical theatre and light opera.
Founded: 1969
Specialized Field: Light Opera
Status: Non-Professional; Nonprofit
Performs At: Hering Auditorium; Alaskaland Civic Center
Organization Type: Performing; Touring

1848
OPERA FAIRBANKS
P.O. Box 80305
Fairbanks, AK 99708
Phone: 907-479-7372
e-mail: info@operafairbanks.org
Web Site: operafairbanks.org
Officers:
  President: Thomas Gross
  Vice President: Herta Prechtel
  Treasurer: Jane Sandstrom
  Secretary: Meta Bravos
Management:
  Artistic Director/Conductor: Gregory Buchalter
Founded: 2005
Status: Professional; Nonprofit
Organization Type: Performing

1849
JUNEAU LYRIC OPERA
PO Box 21456
Juneau, AK 99802-1456
Phone: 907-586-2742
e-mail: director@juneauopera.org
Web Site: www.juneauopera.org
Officers:
  President: Susan Auer
  Vice President: John Clough
  Treasurer: Alan Davis
  Secretary: Eve Dillingham
Mission: To present high quality vocal performances and workshops to encourage the growth and education of our musical community. To provide singing, choral and theatrical opportunities for community members.
Founded: 1975
Specialized Field: Opera

1850
JUNEAU ORATORIO CHOIR
PO Box 32760
Juneau, AK 99803-2760
Phone: 907-789-0320
Fax: 907-586-6261
e-mail: jallanmackinnon@gmail.com
Officers:
  President: J Allan MacKinnon
Management:
  Artistic Director: J Allan MacKinnon
Specialized Field: Choral
Status: Non-Profit, Non-Professional

1851
OPERA TO GO
P.O. Box 20684
Juneau, AK 99802
Phone: 907-586-2255
e-mail: info@operatogo.net
Web Site: operatogo.net
Officers:
  President: Anne Weske
  Vice President: Sara Ealy
  Secretary: Rebekah Grimes
Management:
  Artistic Director: William Todd Hunt
Mission: To entertain, to expand the awareness and knowledge of our audiences; to provide opportunity for: community dialogue, and artistic collaboration among multigenerational artists; to create a safe and positive environment for artistic work and development; to bring a fresh new approach to productions of classical music in Juneau; to introduce young people to classical vocal music and include them in performance consistently.
Specialized Field: Opera

Arizona

1852
ARIZONA OPERA
4600 N 12th Street
Phoenix, AZ 85014
Phone: 602-266-7464
Fax: 602-266-5806
e-mail: info@azopera.org
Web Site: www.azopera.com
Officers:
  Chairman: David A. Christensen
  Vice President: Marion Roose Pullin
  Vice President: Judith G. Wolf, Ph.D.
  Treasurer: Jesse B. Simpson
  Secretary: Linda Staubitz
Management:
  Artistic Director: Joel Rezeven
  General Director: Scott Altman
  Principal Conductor: Joel Revzen
  Box Office Manager-Phoenix: Michael Tomaszek
  Box Office Associate: Terri Staats
  Box Office Associate: Paloma Routh
  Administrative Associate: Melanie Booth
  Artistic Administrative Assistant: Shannon Whidden
  Chorus Director: John Massaro
Mission: To offer grand opera to Arizona, in both the Tucson and Phoenix areas.
Utilizes: Guest Artists; Guest Designers; Sign Language Translators
Founded: 1971
Specialized Field: Grand Opera
Status: Professional; Nonprofit
Budget: $5,400,000
Income Sources: Contributed Income; Corporate; Government; Foundations; Individual Donations
Performs At: Tucson Community Center Music Hall; Phoenix Symphony Hall
Annual Attendance: 80,000
Organization Type: Performing

1853
ORPHEUS MALE CHORUS OF PHOENIX
PO Box 217
Phoenix, AZ 85001
Phone: 602-271-9396
e-mail: info@orpheus.org
Web Site: www.orpheus.org
Officers:
  President: Dave Kelly
  Treasurer: Robert L Merer
  President Emeritus: Tom Eccles
  Vice President: Drew Peterson
  Secretary: Dan Tetting
Management:
  Artistic Director: Dr. Brook Larson
  Artistic Director: Dr. Brook Larson
  Assistant Director: Carric Smolnik
Mission: To employ music as a tool to further goodwill as well as to offer an outlet for men who love singing.
Utilizes: Collaborating Artists; Original Music Scores; Singers
Founded: 1929
Specialized Field: Choral; Men's Chorus
Status: Non-Professional, Nonprofit
Paid Artists: 2
Non-paid Artists: 40+
Income Sources: Dues; CD Sales; Contract Concerts; Patron Contributions
Performs At: Trinity Cathedral, Camelback Bible Church, Dupherm Theatre
Organization Type: Performing; Touring

1854
PHOENIX BACH CHOIR
100 W. Roosevelt St
PO Box 16956
Phoenix, AZ 85011-6956

VOCAL MUSIC / Arkansas

Mailing Address: 100 West Roosevelt Street, Phoenix, AZ 85003
Phone: 602-253-2224
Fax: 602-253-5772
e-mail: info@phoenixchorale.org
Web Site: www.bachchoir.org
Officers:
   President: Laura Ladrigan Cobb
   Vice President: Dr. George A. Martinez
   Secretary: Kathay Ladrigan
Management:
   Artistic Director: Charles Bruffy
   Artistic Conductor: Joe Rinsema
   Executive Director & Assistant Cond: Joel Rinsema
   Director of Marketing & Communicati: Jen Rogers
   Marketing & Communications Intern: Lauren Potter
Founded: 1958
Specialized Field: Classical
Status: Non-Profit, Professional
Paid Staff: 5
Paid Artists: 30

1855
PHOENIX BOYS CHOIR
1131 E Missouri Avenue
Phoenix, AZ 85014
Phone: 602-264-5328
Fax: 267-392-3699
e-mail: pat@boyschoir.org
Web Site: www.boyschoir.org
Officers:
   Executive Director: Kathryn Murphy
   Director of Accounting and Finance: Adam Sanders
   Director of Development & Marketing: Cate Hinkle
   Development & Marketing Associate: Jill Christiansen
   Administrative Manager: Patty Midciff
Management:
   Executive Director: Richard Bowers
   Artistic Director: George Stangleberger
   Artistic Assistant: Greg Amerind
Mission: To educate boys in the art of singing.
Founded: 1948
Specialized Field: Youth Chorus
Status: Non-Profit, Non-Professional
Paid Staff: 7
Volunteer Staff: 100
Paid Artists: 8

1856
MUSICANOVA
705 North Pima Rd
Suite 000, PMB 247
Scottsdale, AZ 85255-8388
Phone: 480-955-4485
e-mail: info@musicanova.org
Web Site: www.musicanovaaz.org
Officers:
   President: Barbara Moss
   Vice President: Warren Cohen
   Executive Board: Jill Forsythe Koritala
   Executive Board: Elizabeth McKinnon
   Founding President: William Stanley
Management:
   Music Director: Warren Cohen
   Stage Manager: J T Cole
Mission: We believe in the value of performing great new and neglected musical works of exceptional quality to enhance and enrich the Scottsdale musical experience. Since its founding in 2003, the mission of the MusicaNova Orchestra has been consistent ? to perform great music that is new, suppressed or unfairly neglected. From the start, we understood that the orchestra must be a professional group in order to offer the music a chance to shine.
Utilizes: Arrangers; Collaborating Artists; Collaborations; Composers; Lyricists; Multimedia; Music; Paid Performers
Founded: 2003
Specialized Field: Classical, Symphony Orchestra
Status: Non-Profit, Professional
Income Sources: Donors, Sponsors
Season: January, October, April
Performs At: Scottsdale Center for the Performing Arts

1857
ARIZONA OPERA
1636 N. Central Ave.
Tucson, AZ 85004
Phone: 602-266-7464
Fax: 602-266-5806
e-mail: info@azopera.com
Web Site: www.azopera.com
Officers:
   Chairman: Dr. Judith Wolf
   Vice President: Nancy Spetzler
   Treasurer: Sharon Landis
   Secretary: Linda Staubitz
   Past President: David A. Christensen
Management:
   Artistic Director: Joel Revzen
   Principal Conductor: Joel Revzen
Mission: To offer grand opera to Arizona, in both the Tucson and Phoenix areas.
Utilizes: Guest Composers; Guest Designers; Sign Language Translators
Founded: 1972
Specialized Field: Grand Opera; Light Opera; Lyric Opera; Choral
Status: Non-Profit, Professional
Paid Staff: 30
Budget: $5,400,000
Income Sources: Contributed Income; Corporate; Government; Foundations; Individual Donations
Performs At: Tucson Community Center Music Hall; Phoenix Symphony Hall
Annual Attendance: 80,000
Organization Type: Performing

1858
DESERT VOICES
PO Box 270
Tucson, AZ 85702-0270
Phone: 520-791-9662
Fax: 520-791-3360
e-mail: office@desertvoices.org
Web Site: www.desertvoices.org
Officers:
   President: Carolyn Schurulst
   VP: Sylvia Yeager
   Secretary: Shar Loper Bloch
   Treasurer: Dick Rehse
   Office Manager: Becky Cohen
   General Manager: Jeffrey Scotland
Management:
   Artistic Director: Chris Tackett
Mission: Arizona premiere GLBTS chorus organization is committed to developing talent, fostering artistic integrity, enteraining our audiences and encouraging cooperation across differences supporting diversity.
Founded: 1988
Specialized Field: Alternative
Status: Non-Profit, Non-Professional
Paid Staff: 3
Budget: $60,000
Income Sources: Arizona Commission on the Arts; National Endowment for the Arts; Tucson Pima Arts Council; Amazon Foundation; Southern Arizona Community Foundation
Performs At: Performing Arts Auditorium; Church Sanctuaries
Annual Attendance: 1,000

1859
THE ARIZONA REPERTORY SINGERS
P.O. Box 41601
Tucson, AZ 85717
Phone: 520-792-8141
e-mail: info@arsingers.org
Web Site: arsingers.org
Officers:
   President: John Neve
   Vice President: Julie Patrick
   Treasurer: Jesse Thrall
Management:
   Operations Manager: Jan Sturges

1860
TUCSON ARIZONA BOYS CHORUS
5770 E Pima Street
Tucson, AZ 85712
Phone: 520-296-6277
Fax: 520-296-6751
e-mail: tabc@boyschorus.org
Web Site: www.boyschorus.org
Officers:
   President: Jack Neubeck
   VP: TBA
   Treasurer: William Beard
   Secretary: Steve Perkin
   Past President: Michael Smith
Management:
   Director: Dr Julian Ackerley
   Director of Development: Jennifer Ackerley
   Office Manager: Lisa Slechta
   Project Manager: Wendy Pierce
   Ass. Conductor Director: Mindy L. Martin
Mission: Presents a varied program including traditional boy choir repertoire, songs of the southwest with trick rodeo roping, a choreographed medley of populartunes and stirring patriotic selections.
Founded: 1939
Specialized Field: Youth Chorus
Paid Staff: 4
Paid Artists: 5
Budget: $680,000
Income Sources: Performance Fees; Ticket Sales; Fundraising Programs; Corporate Partners; Foundation Support; Governmental Grants
Affiliations: International SocietyO Children's Choral and Performing Arts; Alliance For Arts and Understanding; American Choral Directors Association

Arkansas

1861
OPERA IN THE OZARKS AT INSPIRATION POINT
16311 Highway 62 W
PO Box 127
Holiday Island, AR 72632
Phone: 479-253-8595
Fax: 501-253-8595
e-mail: info@opera.org
Web Site: www.opera.org
Management:

VOCAL MUSIC / California

Artistic Director: Vern Sutton
Underworld Conductor: Kostis Protopap
Stage Director: Linda Ade Brand
Stage Director: Robert Swedberg
Conductor/Music Director: Adam Kerry Boyles
Specialized Field: Opera; Youth Chorus; Classical for Young Audiences; Educational
Budget: $60,000-$150,000
Season: May - July
Affiliations: South Central of National Federated Music Clubs
Facility Category: Amphitheater
Seating Capacity: 300

1862
DELTA SYMPHONY ORCHESTRA
1605 Garkand Drive
Jonesboro, AR 72401
Phone: 870-761-2747
e-mail: christy.veara@suddenlink.net
Web Site: www.deltasymphony.org
Officers:
  Secretary: Janice Porter
  President: Ronald Foster
  Treasurer: Jessica Foster
Management:
  Conductor: Dr Neale Bartee
Mission: The Delta Symphony Orchestra is the only professional symphony in the Northeast Arkansas Delta region. The Symphony performs three concerts annually in the Fowler Center on Arkansas State University campus. The Delta Symphony has been entertaining, educating, and enriching this community for over thirty years.
Utilizes: Arrangers; Collaborations; Composers; Fine Artists; Local Artists
Specialized Field: Classical Symphony
Status: Non-Profit, Professional
Income Sources: Sponsors
Season: September through November
Performs At: Fowler Center

1863
ARKANSAS CHAMBER SINGERS
P.O. Box 21002
Little Rock, AR 72221
Phone: 501-377-1121
e-mail: info@ar-chambersingers.org
Web Site: ar-chambersingers.org
Officers:
  President: Gary Moore
  Vice President: Elizabeth Minton
  Secretary: T.T. Tyler Thompson
  Treasurer: Walter Walker
Management:
  Artistic Director/Conductor: John Erwin
  Executive Director: Lisette Christensen
Mission: The Arkansas Chamber Singers is an auditioned vocal ensemble dedicated to enriching the lives of the people of Arkansas by performing and promoting the finest of classical and contemporary choral repertoire.
Founded: 1979
Specialized Field: Chamber Music; Choral
Non-paid Artists: 65
Season: October-June

1864
OPERA IN THE ROCK
310 West 17th Street
Little Rock, AR 72206
Phone: 501-244-9944
e-mail: operaintherock@operaintherock.org
Web Site: operaintherock.org
Officers:
  Chairman Of The Board: Steve Bullock
  Vice Chairman Of The Board: Christine Donahue
  Secretary: Alisa Dixon
  Treasurer: Adam Baldwin
Management:
  Executive Director: Ana W. Squire, awsquire@operaintherock.org
  Artistic Director: Arlene Biebesheimer, abiebesheimer@operaintherock.o
Mission: Our purpose is the production of mainstage professional opera, in addition to a continuing opera review series. The mission is to enrich the cultural life of Arkansas through opera by utilizing local, state, and regional artistic talents.
Founded: 2012
Status: Nonprofit; Professional

1865
FOUR SEASONS ORCHESTRA
4972 East Paradise Lane
Scottsdale, AR 85254
Phone: 602-923-0300
e-mail: info@fourseasonorchestra.org
Web Site: www.fourseasonsorchestra.org
Management:
  Conductor/Artistic Director: Dr Carolyn Waters Broe
  Champion Violist: Alexandra Birch
  Senior Violist: Adam Peterson
  Violinist: Bobae Johnson
  Violinist: Linda Han
Mission: The Four Seasons Orchestra is an all professional, twenty-five member ensemble located in Scottsdale, Arizona. This excellent classical orchestra was founded in 1991 by conductor Carolyn Waters Broe and has performed at many public and private events in the Phoenix Metropolitan area.
Utilizes: Arrangers; Collaborating Artists; Collaborations; Composers; Fine Artists; Grant Writers; Guest Directors; Multimedia; Music
Founded: 1991
Specialized Field: Baroque, Classical, Romantic, Standards
Status: Non-Profit
Income Sources: Sponsors, Donors
Season: December, June
Performs At: Scottsdale Center of the Arts, Kerr Cultural Center, Arizona Center

---

California

1866
AUBURN SYMPHONY
985 Lincoln Way
Suite 102
Auburn, CA 95603
Mailing Address: PO Box 74, Auburn, CA 95603
Phone: 530-823-6683
e-mail: AuburnSymphonyOffice@gmail.com
Web Site: www.auburnsymphony.com
Officers:
  President: Joanne Valentine
  1st Vice President: Liz Briggs
  2nd Vice President: Audrey Mueller
  Treasurer: Dee Paull
  Office Manager: Jennifer Sander
Management:
  Artistic Director/Conductor: Maestro Peter Jaffe
  Business Manager: Rob Haswell
  Office Manager: Jennifer Saunders
  Business Manager: Rob Haswell
Mission: The Auburn Symphony season has grown to include three subscription series concerts, one Messiah Sing-Along performance, one KinderKonzert, a free Symphony in the Park concert in Auburn, and a performance at the Mondavi Center for the Performing Arts in Davis. Symphony in the Schools reached 14 schools and 5,000 children this past season and the Young Artist Competition is held annually, and top competitors and winners are invited to play also.
Utilizes: Arrangers; Collaborating Artists; Collaborations; Composers; Fine Artists; Local Unknown Artists; Lyricists; Multimedia; Music
Founded: 1987
Opened: 1990
Specialized Field: Symphony Orchestra
Status: Non-Profit, Professional
Income Sources: Sponsors, Donations
Performs At: Placer High School Auditorium

1867
BERKELEY COMMUNITY CHORUS AND ORCHESTRA
P.O. Box 310
Berkeley, CA 94701
Phone: 510-433-9599
e-mail: manager@bcco.org
Web Site: bcco.org
Officers:
  President: Linda Morris
  Vice President: Jarred Miyamoto-Mills
Mission: to make the joy of choral music available to everyone. As a non-auditioned chorus that performs with an orchestra and professional soloists, we inspire singers at all levels of ability to sing choral masterworks. By presenting free concerts and creating ways to encourage emerging composers and educate young people, we enrich the cultural life of our community.
Specialized Field: Choral
Status: Independent Nonprofit

1868
BERKELEY OPERA
1700 Shattuck Avenue
Suite 312
Berkeley, CA 94709
Phone: 510-841-1903
e-mail: info@westedgeopera.org
Web Site: www.berkeleyopera.org
Officers:
  President: Vincent W. Fogle
  Vice President: Marian Kohlstedt
  Secretary: Cynthia Whitehead
  Treasurer: Steve Holland
Management:
  Artistic Director: Mark Streshinsky
  Audition Secretary: Jane Rateaver
  Orchestra Manager: Bonnie Lockett
  Musical Director: Jonathan Khuner
  Executive Director: Beth Sandefur
Mission: The presentation of opera.
Utilizes: High School Drama
Founded: 1979
Specialized Field: Lyric Opera
Status: Semi-Professional
Paid Staff: 20
Income Sources: Theater Bay Area
Performs At: Julia Morgan Theater; Hillside Club Theater
Organization Type: Performing

VOCAL MUSIC / California

1869
CALIFORNIA CHAMBER ORCHESTRA & CHAMBER OPERA
53 Osage Avenue
Los Altos
Berkeley, CA 94022
Phone: 510-524-3682
Fax: 510-524-3683
e-mail: info@californiachamberopera.com
Officers:
    Musical Director: Roy Firestone
Management:
    Co-Artistic Director: Diane Squires
    Co-Artistic Director: Gretchen McNeil
Specialized Field: Opera
Budget: $260,000-$1,050,000

1870
THE PACIFIC MOZART ENSEMBLE
PO Box 8568
Berkeley, CA 94707-8568
Phone: 510-848-8022
e-mail: pme@pacificmozart.org
Web Site: www.pacificmozart.org
Officers:
    President: Antonia Van Becker
    Vice President: Dale Engle
    Board Member: Alexis Jensen
    Board Member: Larry Moore
    Board Member: Peggy Rock
Management:
    Founder/Artistic Director: Richard Grant
    Music Director: Dr Lynne Morrow
Mission: ounded in 1980 by Artistic Director Richard Grant, the Pacific Mozart Ensemble (PME) delivers passionate, expert and engaging choral performances of music from Brahms to Brubeck to the Beach Boys. During its time, PME has grown to fill an important role in the cultural life of the San Francisco Bay Area, presenting courageous and innovative programs of many works that have never been performed in concert settings.
Utilizes: Arrangers; Artists-in-Residence; Collaborating Artists; Collaborations; Composers; Composers-in-Residence; Guest Companies; Guest Directors; Multimedia; Music; Sign Language Translators; Singers
Founded: 1980
Specialized Field: Choral
Status: Non-Profit
Income Sources: Donors
Season: December, March
Performs At: The Green Room, War Memorial Veterans Building, St Johns Presbyterian Church

1871
LOS ANGELES CONCERT OPERA ASSOCIATION
2250 Gloaming Way
Beverly Hills, CA 90210
Phone: 310-276-2731
Fax: 310-275-8245
Management:
    Acting Director: Nedra Zachary
Mission: To provide young opera singers with performance opportunities of lesser known opera and Viennese operetta.
Founded: 1987
Specialized Field: Operetta; Vocal Music
Status: Nonprofit
Paid Artists: 30
Performs At: Wilshire Ebell Theatre
Organization Type: Performing

1872
CASA ITALIANA OPERA COMPANY
902 N Screenland Drive
Burbank, CA 91505
Phone: 818-559-8696
Fax: 310-411-9349
Web Site: www.casaitalianaopera.org
Officers:
    Founder: Mario Leonetti
Management:
    General Director: Mario E Leonetti
Mission: To reach a growing audience with appreciation for opera, in the classical Italian form as well as expanding the repertoire with lesser known productions.
Founded: 1971
Specialized Field: Opera
Performs At: Casa Italiana Hall and Theater; Wilshire Ebell Theater

1873
HIDDEN VALLEY MUSIC SEMINAR
PO Box 116
Carmel Valley, CA 93924
Phone: 831-659-3115
Fax: 831-659-7442
e-mail: info@hiddenvalleymusic.org
Web Site: www.hiddenvalleymusic.org
Management:
    General Director: Peter Meckel
Mission: Arts training for pre-professional and early professional artists
Founded: 1963
Specialized Field: Choral; Educational
Status: Non-Profit, Professional
Paid Staff: 25
Volunteer Staff: 50
Paid Artists: 30
Non-paid Artists: 30

1874
CORONA SYMPHONEY ORCHESTRA
13111 Rich Springs Way
Corona, CA 92883
Phone: 951-642-0135
Fax: 951-808-3281
e-mail: don@coronasymphonyorchestra.org
Web Site: www.coronasymphonyorchestra.org
Officers:
    Director of Development: Jasmine Broderick
    Conservatory Program Director: Mickey Fruchter
Management:
    Executive Director: Don Kindred
    Music Director/Conductor: Marco Mejia
    Artistic Personnel Director: Noemy Orellana Wheeler, naomiore@hotmail.com
    Personnel Manager: Patricia Maggs
    House Manager: Carolyn Reeve
    Personnel Manager: Patricia Maggs
Mission: The mission of the Corona Symphony Orchestra is to bring the richness of live orchestral music to the people of the Inland Empire and to represent Corona and the region with musical excellence as one of its premier performing ensembles.
Utilizes: Arrangers; Artists-in-Residence; Collaborating Artists; Collaborations; Composers; Contract Orchestras; Lyricists; Multimedia; Music; Organization Contracts
Specialized Field: Classic, Choral Works, Light Opera, Pops, Film and Television Scores, Original Works
Status: Non-Profit, Professional
Income Sources: Donations, Sponsorships, Support
Performs At: North Point Church

1875
ALL AMERICAN BOYS YOUTH CHORUS
1055 Arlington Dr
Costa Mesa, CA 92626
Mailing Address: PO Box 1527, Costa Mesa, California, United States, 92628-15
Phone: 714-708-1670
Fax: 714-557-5447
e-mail: info@taabc.org
Web Site: www.taabc.org
Officers:
    Chairman: William Sanderson
    Chairman Emeritus: Rita M. Pipta
    President: Anthony S Manrique
    Treasurer: Kim Kovacs
Management:
    Executive Director: Anthony S Manrique
    Artistic Director: Wesley Martin
    Music Reading Program Coordinator: Susan Martin
    Voice Coach: Philip Marke
    Transportation Coordinator: Gary March
Mission: To provide each member with the training, motivation, and opportunity to develop and exercise qualities of leadership within an exceptional program of choral music conducted in an environment of high moral standards.
Founded: 1970
Specialized Field: Youth Chorus; Entertainment Chorus
Status: Non-Profit, Non-Professional
Paid Staff: 12

1876
MASTER CHORALE OF ORANGE COUNTY
660 W Baker
Suite 273
Costa Mesa, CA 92626
Mailing Address: PO Box 2156, Costa Mesa, CA. 92628
Phone: 714-997-6504
Fax: 714-556-6341
e-mail: info@whmc.org
Management:
    Music Director: Dr. William D Hall
    Associate Music Director: Dr. Thomas Sheets
    Administrative Director: Sheri Sheperd
Founded: 1956
Specialized Field: Choral
Status: Nonprofit
Paid Staff: 140
Budget: $10,000
Performs At: Orange County Performing Arts Center
Organization Type: Performing

1877
AMERICAN PHILHARMONIC - SONOMA COUNTY
PO Box 7438
Cotati, CA 94931-7438
Phone: 707-206-6775
e-mail: info@apsonoma.org
Web Site: www.apsonoma.org
Officers:
    President: Steven Peterson
    Vice President: Lola Coretti
    Treasurer: Floyd Reinhart
    Secretary: Debra Scheuerman
    Board Member: Eric Anderson
    Board Member: Jim Bray
    Board Member: Mark Kruzas
Management:

VOCAL MUSIC / California

Musical Director: Norman Gamboa
Assistant Conductor: Tristan Arnold
Marketing Director: Linda Welter
New Media: Valerie Richman
Visual Communications: Steven Peterson
Program Notes: Ron Teplitz
Production: Jeff Barnard
Recording Engineer: Jack Kenny
House Manager: Lola Coretti
Mission: A full size symphonic orchestra, the American Philharmonic- Sonoma County (APSC) was conceived from and supported by its resident communities in 1998. Created by a group of musicians dedicated to reinventing the symphony orchestra as we know it, we have grown from our modest beginnings as the Cotati Philharmonic to become the premier professional volunteer orchestra in the North Bay Area.
Utilizes: Arrangers; Collaborating Artists; Fine Artists; High School Drama; Local Artists; Lyricists; Multimedia; Music; Visual Designers
Founded: 1998
Specialized Field: Symphony Orchestra
Status: Non-Profit, Professional
Volunteer Staff: 65
Income Sources: Donations, Sponsors
Season: October, November, May
Performs At: Santa Roa High School Performing Arts Auditorium

1878
CAPITOL OPERA SACRAMENTO
1907 Donner Ave
Unit 3
Davis, CA 95616
Phone: 707-450-8850
e-mail: capitolopera2004@yahoo.com
Web Site: www.capopera.com
Management:
  General Director: Kathleen Torchia
  Acting Artistic Director: Corey Wilkins
  Scene Artist: Roger Smith
Mission: To keep opera alive and provide performing opportunities for developing artists.
Utilizes: Actors; Artists-in-Residence; Choreographers; Dance Companies; Dancers; Designers; Fine Artists; Five Seasonal Concerts; Guest Accompanists; Guest Composers; Guest Writers; Instructors; Local Artists; Multimedia; Music; Resident Professionals; Sign Language Translators; Singers; Soloists; Student Interns
Founded: 1990
Specialized Field: Opera
Volunteer Staff: 10
Income Sources: Tickets; Donations; Seasonal Subscriptions
Affiliations: AACT; Opera America
Annual Attendance: 5,000
Facility Category: Small Theater
Type of Stage: Black Box
Seating Capacity: 50
Year Remodeled: 1993

1879
SACRAMENTO CHORAL SOCIETY AND ORCHESTRA
4025 A Bridge Street
Fair Oaks, CA 95628
Phone: 916-536-9065
Fax: 916-962-0352
e-mail: scso2005@yahoo.com
Web Site: www.sacramentochoral.com
Officers:
  President: James McCormick
  Vice President: Lee Blachowicz
  Second VP/Conductor: Donald Kendrick
  Secretary: Charene Black
  Treasurer: Maria Stefanou
Management:
  Conductor/Artistic Dirctor: Donald Kendrick
  Chorus Operation: Catherine Mesenbrink
  At Large Director: Tery Baldwin
  At Large Director: Scott James
  At Large Director: Kathy Mesic
Mission: To continue the tradition of performing important choral orchestral masterworks for the community; to develop an appreciation of choral music in the community; to encourage choral music education and creativity through workshops, clinics and mentoring; to achieve professional standards of performance; to secure a lasting foundation as a symphonic music organization.
Utilizes: Collaborations; Educators; Five Seasonal Concerts; Guest Accompanists; Guest Composers; Guest Directors; Guest Instructors; Guest Lecturers; Guest Musical Directors; Guest Musicians; Multimedia; Sign Language Translators; Singers; Soloists
Founded: 1996
Specialized Field: Choral
Status: Nonprofit
Paid Staff: 1
Volunteer Staff: 10
Paid Artists: 60
Non-paid Artists: 180
Budget: $500,000
Income Sources: Annual Fund; Program Ads; Fundraising; Corporate Grants; Ticket Sales; CD Sales; Contract Fees
Performs At: Cathedral of the Blessed Sacrament; Sacramento and the Mondavi Center; UC Davis
Type of Stage: Concert Hall
Year Remodeled: 2003
Cost: $34.5 Million

1880
FULLERTON CIVIC LIGHT OPERA
218 W Commonwealth Avenue
Fullerton, CA 92832
Phone: 714-526-3832
Fax: 714-992-1193
e-mail: marilyn@fclo.com
Web Site: www.fclo.com
Officers:
  President: Gordon Haag
Management:
  President: Norma Jones
  Executive Director: Griff Duncan
  Artistic Director: Jan Duncan
Mission: To present live stage musicals and nationwide costume and scenery rentals.
Utilizes: Actors; AEA Actors; Choreographers; Collaborations; Community Talent; Contract Orchestras; Dancers; Designers; Guest Artists; Guest Companies; Guest Conductors; Guest Designers; Guest Lecturers; Guest Writers; Guild Activities; Instructors; Local Artists; Lyricists; Multi Collaborations; Multimedia; Music; Original Music Scores; Resident Professionals; Singers; Students; Special Technical Talent
Founded: 1971
Specialized Field: Light Opera
Status: Non-Profit, Professional
Paid Staff: 34
Volunteer Staff: 40
Paid Artists: 90
Non-paid Artists: 40
Budget: $1.6 million
Income Sources: Ticket Sales; Costume/Scenery Rentals; Contributions
Performs At: Plummer Auditorium
Affiliations: National Alliance of Musical Theatre Producers
Annual Attendance: 50,000
Facility Category: Stage Auditorium
Type of Stage: Proscenium
Stage Dimensions: 36x31
Seating Capacity: 1,314
Year Built: 1934
Year Remodeled: 1993
Cost: $2,700,000
Rental Contact: Fullerton Union High School District
Organization Type: Performing; Resident

1881
ALBERT MCNEIL JUBILEE SINGERS OF LOS ANGELES
Aya World Productions
Management
Hermosa Beach, CA
Phone: 310-379-7897
Fax: 323-375-1783
e-mail: almcneil@aol.com
Web Site: www.amjsla.org
Management:
  Founder/Director: Albert McNeil
  Management: Aaron Nigel Smith
Utilizes: Multimedia; Singers
Founded: 1968
Specialized Field: Gospel Chorus
Paid Staff: 1

1882
LONG BEACH OPERA
PO Box 14895
Long Beach, CA 90803
Phone: 562-439-2580
Web Site: www.lbopera.com/
Management:
  General Director: Michael Milenski
Mission: To offer professional opera to the community of Southern California and to nurture the love for opera and performing arts.
Utilizes: Guest Artists; Guest Companies; Singers
Founded: 1978
Specialized Field: Grand Opera; Lyric Opera
Status: Professional, Nonprofit
Paid Staff: 25
Performs At: Center Theater; Terrace Theater
Organization Type: Performing; Educational

1883
THE LONG BEACH CHORALE AND CHAMBER ORCHESTRA
P.O. Box 14377
Long Beach, CA 90853-4377
Phone: 562-427-1931
e-mail: lbchorale@gmail.com
Web Site: longbeachchorale.org
Management:
  Director: Eliza Rubenstein
Mission: We perform great music at a high level of musicianship, in settings that deliver an unequaled musical experience for the audience and the musicians. Our work fosters a stronger and more peaceful community through those experiences and the relationships they create.
Founded: 1988
Specialized Field: Chamber; Choral
Status: Nonprofit; Volunteer

VOCAL MUSIC / California

1884
LOS ANGELES CHAMBER SINGERS & CAPPELLA
PO Box 64888
Los Angeles, CA 90064-0888
Phone: 310-575-9790
Fax: 310-575-3405
e-mail: voices@lacs.org
Web Site: www.lacs.org
Management:
 Music Director: Peter Rutenberg
Mission: Los Angeles Chamber Singers excels in the art and performance of choral chamber music; preserves and promotes the art form; presents concert programs for the general public and educational programs for elementary, high school and college students; appears on records and radio
Founded: 1990
Specialized Field: Choral
Paid Staff: 1
Volunteer Staff: 5
Paid Artists: 25
Affiliations: Chorus America; Early Music America; RCM Records

1885
LOS ANGELES CHILDREN'S CHORUS
585 East Colorado Blvd
Los Angeles, CA 91101
Phone: 626-793-4231
Fax: 626-793-0173
e-mail: info@lachildrenschorus.org
Web Site: lachildrenschorus.org
Officers:
 Executive Director: Deborah Lewis
 Director of Development: Julie Larson
 Assistant Executive Director: Sue Ll
 Business Manager: Rebecca Smith
 Chorus Manager: Ann Giesler
 Immediate Past Chair: David Scheidemantle
Management:
 Artistic Director: Anne Tomlinson
 Assoc Artyistic Director: Mandy Brigham
 Young Mens Ensemble Director: Steven Kronauer
 Apprentice Choir Director: Diana Landis
 Community Interaction Director: Lissie Quishenberry
 Music Literacy Director: Gail Homan
 Vocal Coach: Wendy Caldwell
 Vocal Coach: Lisa Stidham
 Prinicpal Pianist: Twyla Meyer
Mission: Los Angeles Children's Chorus provides choral music education of the highest quality to young people who represent richly diverse racial, economic, and cultural backgrounds. The program ignites a love of singing and nurtures the full expression of each individual's potential for artistic and personal excellence through the collaborative experience of choral music performance.
Utilizes: Arrangers; Choreographers; Collaborating Artists; Collaborations; Commissioned Composers; Guild Activities; Instructors; Lyricists; Multimedia; Music; Paid Performers; Scenic Designers; Sign Language Translators; Singers; Soloists
Founded: 1985
Specialized Field: Choral
Status: Non-Profit
Income Sources: Donors, Fundraisers
Season: August through December
Performs At: American Ballet Theater, Walt Disney Concert Hall

1886
LOS ANGELES MASTER CHORALE
The Music Center
135 N Grand Avenue
Los Angeles, CA 90012
Phone: 213-972-7282
Fax: 213-972-3136
e-mail: lamc@lamc.org
Web Site: www.lamc.org
Officers:
 Executive Director: Terry Knowles
 Chairman: David Gindler
 Treasurer: Cheryl Petersen
 Vice Chair/Development: Robert M. Hanisee
 Vice Chair/Music Center: Mark Foster
Management:
 Music Director: Grant Gershon
 Associate Conductor: Lesley Leighton
 Music Director Emeritus: Paul Salamunovich
 Composer in Residence: Shawn Kirchner
 Pianist/Musical Assistant: Lisa Edwards
Mission: To educate the public in the art of choral singing and to foster an appreciation of the art form.
Founded: 1963
Specialized Field: Choral
Status: Professional
Paid Staff: 12
Budget: $4mMillion
Income Sources: Ticket Sales; Individual Contributions; Business and Foundation Contributions
Performs At: Walt Disney Concert Hall
Organization Type: Performing; Resident; Educational

1887
LOS ANGELES OPERA
135 N Grand Avenue
Suite 327
Los Angeles, CA 90012
Phone: 213-972-7219
Fax: 213-687-3490
e-mail: laopera@laopera.com
Web Site: www.laopera.com
Officers:
 Chairman: Marc I Stern
 Chairman Executive Committee: Carol F. Henry
 President/CEO: Christopher Koelsch
 Vice President/CFO: Faith Raiguel
 Secretary: Marvin S. Shapiro
 Treasurer: Robert Ronus
Management:
 Executive Director: Placido Domingo
 Artistic Director: Placido Domingo
 Principal Conductor: Grant Gershon
 Artistic Administrator: Susan Langzel
 Costume Director: Jennifer Green
Mission: To present opera at its highest professional standard with international guest artists and a resident company.
Utilizes: Artists-in-Residence; Collaborations; Dancers; Designers; Educators; Grant Writers; Guest Artists; Guest Companies; Guest Conductors; Guest Ensembles; Guest Instructors; Guest Musicians; Guest Soloists; Guest Writers; High School Drama; Instructors; Local Artists; Lyricists; Multimedia; Organization Contracts; Original Music Scores; Poets; Resident Professionals
Founded: 1986
Specialized Field: Opera
Status: Non-Profit, Professional
Income Sources: Ticket Revenue, Contributed Income
Season: July-May
Performs At: Dorothy Chandler Pavilion
Annual Attendance: 160,000
Facility Category: Performing Arts Center
Type of Stage: Proscenium
Seating Capacity: 3,086
Year Built: 1964
Organization Type: Performing; Resident; Educational

1888
OPERA A LA CARTE
556 S. Fair Oaks Avenue
Suite 101-502
Los Angeles, CA 90039
Phone: 626-791-0844
Fax: 626-791-4806
e-mail: info@operaalacarte.org
Web Site: www.operaalacarte.org
Officers:
 President: Katherine Nolan
 VP: June Satton
 Treasurer: John Ledyard
 Secretary: Carol Winston
Management:
 Advisory Board: Steve Hanson
 Advisory Board: Judy Tatum
 Advisory Board: Jane Workman
Founded: 1970
Specialized Field: Musical Theatre; Opera; Gilbert and Sullivan
Status: Non-Profit, Professional
Paid Staff: 1
Paid Artists: 55

1889
UNIVERSITY OF SOUTHERN CALIFORNIA THORNTON OPERA
Booth Hall of Music, Room 112
University Park Campus, 820 W 34th Street
Los Angeles, CA 90089-0851
Phone: 213-740-6935
Fax: 213-740-3217
e-mail: opera@thornton.usc.edu
Web Site: www.usc.edu/music/uscopera
Management:
 Dean: Robert Cutietta
 Conductor/Music Director: Brent McMunn
 Resident Staqe Director: Ken Cazan
 Program Manager: Damien Elwood
Mission: Providing a performance outlet and training for talented young singers in all aspects of performance; presenting two full operas as well as various single scenes.
Founded: 1940
Specialized Field: Grand Opera; Lyric Opera; Light Opera; Operetta
Status: Non-Profit, Non-Professional
Paid Staff: 25
Income Sources: University of Southern California
Performs At: Bing Theater
Organization Type: Performing; Touring; Educational

1890
TOWNSEND OPERA PLAYERS
1214 11th Street
Suite 1
Modesto, CA 95354
Mailing Address: PO Box 4519, Modesto, CA. 95352
Phone: 209-523-6426
Fax: 209-579-0532
e-mail: mbuckman@townsendoperaplayers.com
Web Site: www.townsendoperaplayers.com
Officers:
 President: Steve Collins
 Secretary: Claire Burns
 Treasurer: Norm VanSpronsen
Management:

President: Steve Collins
Executive Director: Matthew Buckman
Operations Manager: Erika Townsend
Production Coordinator: Barbara Wesley
Education Director: Charles Sheaffer
Public Relations/Marketing: Martha Martin
Mission: Performing great opera as well as classics of American Musical Theatre for the enjoyment of San Joaquin Valley and surrounding area residents.
Utilizes: Actors; Choreographers; Collaborations; Dance Companies; Dancers; Designers; Educators; Five Seasonal Concerts; Grant Writers; Guest Accompanists; Guest Artists; Guest Composers; Guest Designers; Guest Directors; Guest Instructors; Guest Musicians; Guest Writers; Guild Activities; Instructors; Local Artists; Lyricists; Multimedia; Music; Resident Professionals; Selected Students; Sign Language Translators; Singers; Soloists; Student Interns; Visual Arts
Founded: 1982
Specialized Field: Grand Opera; Light Opera; Choral; Youth Chorus; Classical
Status: Non-Profit, Professional
Paid Staff: 4
Paid Artists: 100
Non-paid Artists: 150
Budget: $400,000
Income Sources: Membership, Grants, Donation and Ticket Sales
Annual Attendance: 10,000
Facility Category: High School Auditorium
Stage Dimensions: 44'x38'x16'
Seating Capacity: 1,100
Year Built: 1900
Organization Type: Performing; Touring; Educational

1891
CANTABILE YOUTH SINGERS
1901 Old Middlefield Way
Suite 22
Mountain View, CA 94303
Phone: 650-424-1410
Fax: 650-487-6600
e-mail: info@cantabile.org
Web Site: www.cantabile.org
Officers:
　Chairman Of The Board: Lori Mirek
Management:
　Executive Director: Sonja Wohlgemuth
　Artistic Director and Conductor: Elena Sharkova
　Managing Director: Denise Lewis
　Associate Artistic Director: Shane Troll
　Assistant Conductor: Jennah Delp
Founded: 1979
Specialized Field: Vocal Choral
Status: Non-Profit, Non-Professional
Paid Staff: 2
Paid Artists: 4

1892
SCHOLA CANTORUM
2218 Old Middlefield Way
Suite G
Mountain View, CA 94043-2400
Phone: 650-254-1700
Fax: 650-254-1701
e-mail: info@scholacantorum.org
Web Site: www.scholacantorum.org
Officers:
　Chairman: Henry Lesser
Management:
　Music Director: Gregory Wait
　Executive Director: Mary Powell
　Assistant Conductor: Dawn Horst Reyen

Mission: To celebrate the joy of singing with our community: by performing choral music of all styles, including masterpieces and commissioned works; by educating and inspiring our singers and our audiences.
Utilizes: Collaborations; Commissioned Composers; Grant Writers; Guest Directors; Guest Ensembles; Guest Instructors; Guest Musical Directors; Guest Musicians; Guest Soloists; Instructors; Local Artists; Multimedia; New Productions; Original Music Scores; Sign Language Translators; Singers; Soloists
Founded: 1964
Specialized Field: Choral
Status: Non-professional; Nonprofit
Paid Staff: 4
Volunteer Staff: 3
Paid Artists: 2
Budget: $218,000
Income Sources: Ticket Sales; Grants; Donations; Sponsorships;
Annual Attendance: 5,000

1893
MUSICAL AMERICA
North Hollywood High School
5231 Colfax Avenue
North Hollywood, CA 91607
Mailing Address: PO Box 1330, Hightstown, NJ 08520
Phone: 609-448-3346
Fax: 513-677-0690
e-mail: listings@musicalamerica.com
Web Site: www.musicalamerica.com
Management:
　Director: Cornelia Korney
Mission: Educating through the presentation of fine choral music; providing the community with entertainment.
Utilizes: Guest Artists; Singers
Founded: 1969
Specialized Field: Choral
Status: Semi-Professional; Non-Professional
Income Sources: Los Angeles Unified School District
Performs At: North Hollywood High School
Organization Type: Performing; Touring; Educational

1894
KITKA WOMEN'S VOCAL ENSEMBLE
1201 Martin Luther King Jr Way
Suite 103
Oakland, CA 94612
Phone: 510-444-0323
Fax: 510-444-1013
e-mail: staff@kitka.org
Web Site: www.kitka.org
Officers:
　President: Rodney Pasion
　Treasurer: Chitra Arunasalam
　VP: Norman Gelbart
Management:
　Executive Director: Shira Cion, shira@kitka.org
　Interim Music Director: Elizabeth Setzer, elizabeth@kitka.org
　Ensemble Manager: Briget Boyle
Mission: An American women's vocal arts ensemble inspired by traditional songs and vocal techniques from Eastern Europe. Dedicated to developing new audiences for music rooted in Balkan, Slavic, and Caucasian women's vocal traditions, Kitka also strives to expand the boundaries of folk song as a living and evolving expressive art form.
Founded: 1979
Specialized Field: Choral; Ethnic Music; Classical; Contemporary
Status: Non-Profit, Professional
Paid Staff: 9

Volunteer Staff: 26
Paid Artists: 10
Budget: $330,000
Income Sources: National Endowment for the Arts; California Arts Council ARRA Program; City of Oakland Cultural Funding Program; Creative Capital's MAP Fund; William & Flora Hewlett Found
Affiliations: Knudsen Productions; Folk Alliance; Chorus America; Western Arts Alliance; Arts Presenters
Annual Attendance: 12,000-24,000
Facility Category: Concert Halls, Festivals

1895
OAKLAND OPERA THEATER
630 3rd Street Oakland
Oakland, CA 94607
Phone: 510-763-1146
e-mail: info@oaklandopera.org
Web Site: www.oaklandopera.org
Officers:
　President: Jo Vincent Parks
　Treasurer: Steve Snider
Management:
　Artistic Director: Tom Dean
　Director: Brian C Mulhern
　Music Director: Deirdre McClure
　Executive Director: Lori Zook
　Stage Director: Darryl V. Jones
Mission: Produce fully staged productions featuring artists and performers of color, geared to the pace of the 21st century and addressing issues of modern day urban life.
Specialized Field: Opera
Performs At: Oakland Metro

1896
OAKLAND YOUTH CHORUS
685 14th Street
Oakland, CA 94612
Phone: 510-287-9700
Fax: 510-893-7056
e-mail: keri@oaklandyouthchorus.org
Web Site: www.oaklandyouthchorus.org
Officers:
　President: David Bond
　Vice-President: Andrea M. Leal
　Secretary-Treasurer: Rebecca Austin, MD, MBA
Management:
　Executive Director: Keri Butkevich
　Director: Rachelle Rogers Ard
　Interim Managing Director: Jessica Manta Meyer
　Artistic and Education Director: La Nell Martin
　Program and Marketing Director: Angela Dant
Mission: Providing multicultural youth from ages 14-21 with quality professionally-directed training; to advance the choral art form.
Utilizes: Artists-in-Residence; Collaborating Artists; Grant Writers; Guest Accompanists; Guest Artists; Guest Companies; Multimedia; Original Music Scores; Sign Language Translators; Soloists
Founded: 1974
Specialized Field: Opera; Choral; Youth Chorus; Ethnic Music; Classical; Contemporary
Status: Non-Profit, Professional
Paid Staff: 12
Non-paid Artists: 80
Budget: $6,000
Performs At: First Presbyterian Church; Calvin Simmons Theater
Organization Type: Performing; Touring; Sponsoring

VOCAL MUSIC / California

1897
PACIFIC BOYCHOIR ACADEMY
215 Ridgeway Avenue
Oakland, CA 94611
Phone: 510-652-4722
Web Site: pacificboychoiracademy.org
Officers:
   Secretary: Tracy Achorn
   President: Ani Adhikari
   Founder: Kevin Fox
   VP/Chief Financial Officer: Ted Moser
   Chorister Parent: Eric Nelson
   Co-Founder: Marcia Roy
Management:
   Head of Mathematics and Science: Neil Aho
   Choir School Art Teacher: Tracy Atkinson Notzold
   Associate Music Director: Stella Brown
   Founding Artistic Director: Kevin Fox
Mission: Members of the Pacific Boychoir participate in a very old tradition. Boychoirs have been around for hundreds of years, dating back at least to the fourth century. Early modern boychoirs were trained to sing with the collegiate and cathedral choirs of Europe. Today, most American boychoirs are not affiliated with churches, though much of the great music written for boys came out of this tradition.
Utilizes: Arrangers; Collaborating Artists; Collaborations; Educators; Instructors; Local Artists & Directors; Lyricists; Multimedia; Music; Scenic Designers; Sign Language Translators; Singers; Soloists
Founded: 1998
Specialized Field: Choral, Classical
Status: Non-Profit
Income Sources: Donors, Fundraisers
Season: October, December, May
Performs At: Pacific Boychoir Academy

1898
WILLIAM HALL CHORALE
1 University Drive
Orange, CA 92866
Phone: 714-997-6891
Fax: 714-997-6504
e-mail: whall@chapman.edu
Officers:
   Founder: Dr. William D Hall
Management:
   President: Robert Guyett
   VP: David Masone
   Artistic Director: William Hall
Founded: 1956
Specialized Field: Choral Orchestral Literature
Status: Non-Profit, Professional
Paid Staff: 3
Paid Artists: 24

1899
WEST BAY OPERA
221 Lambert Street
Palo Alto, CA 94306
Phone: 650-843-3900
Fax: 650-843-3904
e-mail: GeneralDirector@WBOpera.org
Web Site: www.wbopera.org
Officers:
   President: Michael Sanie
   VP: Jennifer Dahmus
   Secretary: Lee Smith
   Treasurer: Richard Bogart
Management:
   General Director: Jose Luis Moscovich
   Production Manager: Michele Sullivan
   Office Manager: Paul Glew
   Guild President: Pat Markevitch
   Costume Shop Supervisor: Merna Black
Mission: To provide quality opera for the San Francisco Bay Area community and to nurture emerging and established artists.
Utilizes: Guest Artists; Guest Companies
Founded: 1955
Specialized Field: Musical Theatre; Opera; Classical
Status: Non-Profit, Professional
Paid Staff: 3
Performs At: Lucie Stern Theatre
Organization Type: Performing; Educational

1900
LIGHT OPERA THEATRE OF SACRAMENTO
PO Box 188641
Sacramento, CA 95818-8641
Phone: 916-258-5687
e-mail: lightoperasacramento@gmail.com
Web Site: www.lightoperasac.org
Officers:
   Business Manager: Bill Bourne
Management:
   Artistic Director: Mike Baad
   Artistic Director: Debbie Baad
Founded: 1982
Specialized Field: Opera

1901
SACRAMENTO MASTER SINGERS
PO Box 417997
Sacramento, CA 95841
Phone: 916-788-7464
Fax: 916-784-1248
e-mail: smsbusiness@surewest.net
Web Site: www.mastersingers.org
Officers:
   President: Kathy Ossmann
Management:
   Director: Ralph Edward Hughes
   Managing Director: Julie Jenness
   Business Manager: Julie Jenness
Founded: 1983
Specialized Field: Choral
Status: Non-Profit, Professional
Paid Staff: 4

1902
SACRAMENTO MEN'S CHORUS
PO Box 188726
Sacramento, CA 95818
Phone: 916-484-5789
Toll-free: 877-283-1567
e-mail: info@sacmenschorus.org
Web Site: www.sacgaymenschorus.org
Management:
   President: Mark Ebenhoch
   VP: Darryl Strohl
   Chairman Of Board: Daniel Kiermaier
   Artistic Director: Carl Naluai Jr
Founded: 1984
Specialized Field: Men's Chorus
Status: Non-Professional; Nonprofit
Paid Staff: 30
Performs At: First United Methodist
Organization Type: Performing; Touring

1903
SACRAMENTO OPERA COMPANY
PO Box 161027
Sacramento, CA 95816
Mailing Address: PO Box 161027, Sacramento, CA. 95816
Phone: 916-737-1000
Fax: 916-737-1032
e-mail: info@sacopera.org
Web Site: www.sacopera.org
Officers:
   President: Michael E Chase
   Vice President: Joe Hartzog
   Secretary: Sue Miller
   Treasurer: Sue Huscroft
Management:
   Artistic Director: Timm Rolek
   Executive Director: Rod Gideons
   Managing Director: Rod Gideons
   General Director, Patron Services M: Rod Gideons
   Patron Services: Beverly Collard
Mission: To produce outstanding regional opera, to develop & cultivate public interst in opera & its allied arts and to further music education.
Utilizes: Guest Artists; Guest Companies; Singers
Founded: 1947
Specialized Field: Opera
Status: Non-Profit, Professional
Paid Staff: 7
Paid Artists: 150
Budget: $1.6 million
Income Sources: Earned Revenue Donations
Performs At: Theater
Affiliations: Opera America
Annual Attendance: 18,000
Type of Stage: Proscenium
Seating Capacity: 2,380
Organization Type: Performing; Educational

1904
CAMERATAS SINGERS OF MONTEREY COUNTY
P.O. Box 428
Salinas, CA 93902
Phone: 831-642-2701
e-mail: info@camerata-singers.org
Web Site: camerata-singers.org
Officers:
   President: Michael Russell
   Vice President: Jacqueline Henning
   Secretary: Susan Green
   Treasurer: Mary Matthews Hill
Management:
   Artistic Director/Conductor: John Koza
   Administrative Director: Dana GoForth
Mission: The Camerata Singers of Monterey County provides high quality cultural and educational opportunities for a multi-generational audience through the production of choral music recognized for its imaginative programming and performance excellence.
Specialized Field: Contemporary Choral
Status: Charitable Nonprofit

1905
ORCHESTRA NOVA (SAN DIEGO)
11772 Sorrento Valley Road
Suite 212
San Diego, CA 92121
Phone: 858-350-0290
Fax: 858-350-0297
e-mail: stella.karl@orchestranova.org
Web Site: www.orchestranova.org
Officers:
   Advisor: William Corner
   Advisor: Dave Darwin
   Advisor: Albert Hugo Martinez
   Advisor: Frances Hunter

VOCAL MUSIC / California

Advisor: Bill Weber
Management:
  Conductor: Jing-Ho Pak
  Assistant Conductor: Dana Mambourg Zimbric
  Chief Executive Officer: Beverly Lambert
  Concerts Director: Holly Churchill
  Marketing Director: Beck Greefield
  Audience Development: Erin Oleno
  Development Associate: Ericka Ramirez
  Nova Education Ambassador: Ross Moore
Mission: Our mission is to inspire joy through a revolutionary experience for the senses by creating an extraordinary theatrical experience with classical music that attracts people from all ages and backgrounds. Our strategy is to accomplish this through a revolutionary entrepreneurial model for the arts, with a focus on being highly competitive financially and technologically.
Utilizes: Arrangers; Collaborations; Commissioned Composers; Composers; Composers-in-Residence; Educators; Multimedia; Music; Paid Performers
Founded: 1983
Specialized Field: Opera, Orchestra, Classical
Status: Non-Profit, Professional
Income Sources: Donors, Club Nova Members
Affiliations: Hunter Family Music Memory Program, Take 5 for Music

1906
SAN DIEGO CHILDREN'S CHOIR
6635 Flanders Drive
Suite H
San Diego, CA 92121
Phone: 858-587-1087
Fax: 858-587-0071
e-mail: sdcc@sdcchoir.org
Web Site: www.sdcchoir.org
Management:
  Director: Ken Herman
  President: Maureen Lochtefeld
  Chairman: Steve Schroeter
  Executive Director: Donna Icenhower
  Office Manager: Jackie Smith
Utilizes: Collaborations; Composers-in-Residence; Educators; Guest Musical Directors; High School Drama; Instructors; Multimedia; Music; Organization Contracts; Resident Artists; Sign Language Translators; Soloists
Founded: 1990
Specialized Field: Youth Chorus; Choral; Educational
Status: Non-Profit
Budget: $250,000
Affiliations: Chorus America; ACDA;
Annual Attendance: 10,000
Facility Category: Different Venues
Type of Stage: Traditional at all venues
Stage Dimensions: varies
Seating Capacity: 200-2100

1907
SAN DIEGO COMIC OPERA/LYRIC OPERA SAN DIEGO
2891 University Avenue
Suite 1
San Diego, CA 92104
Phone: 619-231-5714
Fax: 619-231-0662
Web Site: www.lyricoperasandiego.com
Officers:
  President: Roberto Cueva
  VP: Richard Brown
  Secretary: Kristin Schuler Hint
  Treasurer: William Mayleas
Management:
  General Director: Leon Natker
  Artistic Director: J Sherwood Montgomery
Mission: To offer quality musical theater and to provide creative employment for area professional artists.
Utilizes: Actors; AEA Actors; Choreographers; Collaborations; Commissioned Composers; Commissioned Music; Dancers; Designers; Grant Writers; Guest Accompanists; Guest Artists; Guest Companies; Guest Composers; Guest Conductors; Guest Writers; Guild Activities; Instructors; Local Artists; Lyricists; Multimedia; Music; Original Music Scores; Resident Professionals; Sign Language Translators; Singers; Soloists; Student Interns; Theatre Companies; Touring Companies
Founded: 1979
Specialized Field: Opera; English Operetta
Status: Non-Profit, Professional
Paid Staff: 6
Paid Artists: 75
Budget: $500,000
Income Sources: Ticket Sales; Membership Dues; Foundations; Grants
Performs At: Indoor Casa del Prado Theater
Affiliations: San Diego Performing Arts League; Opera America; San Diego Arts & Culture Coalition; Downtown Partnership
Annual Attendance: 15,000
Facility Category: Rental
Seating Capacity: 550
Organization Type: Performing; Touring; Resident; Educational

1908
SAN DIEGO MEN'S CHORUS
3749 Park Boulevard
PO Box 33825
San Diego, CA 92163
Phone: 619-296-7664
Fax: 619-296-3471
e-mail: info@sdgmc.org
Web Site: www.sdgmc.org
Officers:
  Treasurer: Homero Escandon
  Secretary: Jacqueline Hanson
Management:
  President: Cheri Curtis
  VP: Marc Mangiantini
  Artistic Director: Gary Holt
  Principal Accompanist: Glenn Ward
  Executive Director: Ben Cartwright
Mission: To foster unity and a love of music through our performances.
Utilizes: Choreographers; Collaborating Artists; Commissioned Composers; Commissioned Music; Composers; Contract Orchestras; Guest Accompanists; Guest Artists; Guest Choreographers; Guest Musical Directors; Guest Musicians; Instructors; Multi Collaborations; Paid Performers; Selected Students; Singers
Founded: 1985
Specialized Field: Men's Chorus
Status: Non-Professional; Nonprofit
Paid Staff: 2
Volunteer Staff: 130
Budget: $150,000
Income Sources: Membership Dues; Ticket Sales; Individual & Business Donations
Performs At: First Unitarian Universalist Church
Affiliations: GALA Choruses
Annual Attendance: 5,000
Seating Capacity: 541
Organization Type: Performing; Touring
Comments: Donates $4,000 annually to local HIV/AIDS organizations

1909
SAN DIEGO OPERA
1200 3rd Avenue
18th Floor, Civic Center Plaza
San Diego, CA 92101-4112
Phone: 619-533-7000
Fax: 619-232-7636
Toll-free: 619-231-6915
e-mail: info@sdopera.com
Web Site: www.sdopera.com
Officers:
  President: William R Stensrud
  Executive VP: Robert B Horsman
  VP Finance: L Renee Comeau
  VP Special Projects: James L. Fitzpatrick
  VP Marketing/Membership: Lisa Briggs
  VP Individual Gifts: Iris Lynn Strauss
  Secretary: James H. Amos Jr.
Management:
  General Director/Artistic Director,: Ian D Campbell
  Director Strategic Planning: Ann S Campbell
  Resident Conductor: Karen Keltner
  Resident Conductor: Karen Keltner
  Director Education/Outreach: Nicolas M Reveles
  Director Marketing/Public Relations: Todd Schultz
  Director Production: Ronald G Allen
  Director Finance: John Sleeper
Founded: 1965
Specialized Field: Opera
Status: For-Profit, Non-Professional
Paid Staff: 35
Performs At: Civic Theatre

1910
STARLIGHT MUSICAL THEATRE
2005 Pan American Plz
PO Box 3519
San Diego, CA 92101
Phone: 619-544-7800
Fax: 619-544-0496
e-mail: info@starlighttheatre.org
Web Site: www.starlighttheatre.org
Management:
  Executive Director: CE Bud Farnks
  Producing Artistic Director: Don Ward
  Producing Artistic Director: Bonnie Ward
Mission: The preservation and promotion of the art form of musical theatre.
Utilizes: Guest Artists; Guest Companies; Singers
Founded: 1946
Specialized Field: Light Opera; Musical Theatre
Status: Professional; Nonprofit
Performs At: Starlight Bowl; Civic Theatre; Spreckles Theatre
Organization Type: Performing; Educational

1911
AMERICAN BACH SOLOIST
44 Page Street
Suite 403
San Francisco, CA 94102-5975
Phone: 415-621-7900
Fax: 415-621-7920
e-mail: info@americanbach.org
Web Site: www.americanbach.org
Officers:
  President: Hugh Davies
  Vice President: Marie Hogan
  Treasurer: Jose Alonso
  Secretary: Angela Hilt
  Advisor: Reverend Marc Andrus

VOCAL MUSIC / California

Advisor: Irving Broido
Advisor: Karen Broido
Advisor: Corty Fengler
Management:
Artistic/Music Director: Jeffrey Thomas
Executive Administrator: Jeff McMillan
Music Adminstrator: Steven Lehning
Production Manager: Philip Daley
Development Consultant: Camille Reed
House Manager: Lisa May
Stage Crew: E J Chavez
Mission: The American Bach Soloists engage and inspire audiences through historically informed performances, recordings, and educational programs that emphasize the music of the Baroque, Classical, and Early Romantic eras.
Utilizes: Arrangers; Collaborating Artists; Collaborations; Composers; Composers-in-Residence; Grant Writers; Guest Companies; Multimedia; Music
Founded: 1989
Specialized Field: Baroque, Classical, Early Romantic
Status: Non-Profit
Income Sources: Donors, Sponsors
Performs At: St Stephen's Church, First Congretional Church, St Mark's Lutheran Church, Davis Community Church, Grace Cathedral

1912
CHANTICLEER
44 Page Street, Suite 604
San Francisco, CA 94102
Phone: 415-252-8589
Fax: 415-252-7941
e-mail: info@chanticleer.org
Web Site: chanticleer.org
Officers:
Board Chair: Kathleen G. Henschel
Vice Chair: Kaatri Griff
Vice Chair: Stephen K. Cassidy
Management:
General Director: Christine Bullin
Interim Music Director: Jace Wittig
Assistant Music Director: Gregory Peebles
Director Of Development: Liv Nilssen
Marketing/Development: Joe Ledbetter
Marketing/Development: Barbara Bock
Mission: To present choral music at the highest level of excellence and to encourage worldwide appreciation for the art of ensemble singing through live performances, education, recording, and the creation of new choral work.
Founded: 1978

1913
GOLDEN GATE MEN'S CHORUS
116 Eureka Street
San Francisco, CA 94114
Phone: 415-668-4462
e-mail: info@ggmc.org
Web Site: ggmc.org
Management:
Music Director: Joseph Piazza
Mission: The Golden Gate Men's Chorus is committed to excellence and joyous music-making; providing a supportive and nurturing atmosphere for our members' artistic and social self-expression; and sharing and expanding the rich and continuing tradition of male choral music.
Founded: 1982
Specialized Field: Chorus
Status: Nonprofit
Season: Spring, Summer, Winter

1914
MEROLA OPERA PROGRAM
301 Van Ness Avenue
San Francisco, CA 94102
Phone: 415-565-6427
Fax: 415-255-6774
e-mail: mop@sfopera.com
Web Site: www.menola.org /merola
Officers:
President: Karl O. Mills
Vice President/Treasurer: Doreen Woo Ho
Mission: Discovering and developing professional opera singers; sponsoring the Merola Opera Program at the San Francisco Opera and the San Francisco Opera Center auditions.
Utilizes: Guest Artists; Guest Companies; Singers
Founded: 1954
Specialized Field: Grand Opera; Lyric Opera
Status: Nonprofit
Income Sources: Central Opera Service
Performs At: War Memorial Opera House
Rental Contact: Bill Bowles
Organization Type: Educational; Sponsoring

1915
POCKET OPERA
469 Bryant Street
San Francisco, CA 94107
Phone: 415-972-8930
Fax: 415-348-0931
e-mail: info@pocketopera.org
Web Site: www.pocketopera.org
Officers:
President: Debra Lambert
1st Vice President: Robert Selinske
2nd Vice President: Yen Bachmeier
Secretary: Patricia Bovan-Campbell
Treasurer: Mel Bachmeier
Management:
Artistic Director: Donald Pippin
Executive Director: Dianna Shuster
Production Manager: Nicolas Aliaga
Marketing Associate: Lainey McKinley
Box Office Associate: Marisa Swain
Mission: To present and promote opera in an accessible, affordable and engaging way by using English settings, minimal props and orchestrations
Utilizes: Choreographers; Guest Designers; Instructors; Organization Contracts; Original Music Scores; Sign Language Translators
Founded: 1978
Specialized Field: Grand Opera; Lyric Opera; Light Opera; Operetta
Status: Professional, Nonprofit
Paid Staff: 5
Volunteer Staff: 2
Paid Artists: 60
Budget: $350,000
Income Sources: Central Opera Service
Performs At: Marines Memorial Theatre In San Francisco; Hillside Club In Berkeley
Organization Type: Performing; Touring; Resident

1916
SAN FRANCISCO BOYS CHORUS
333 Hayes Street
Suite 116
San Francisco, CA 94102
Phone: 415-861-7464
Fax: 415-861-4706
e-mail: info@sfbc.org
Web Site: www.sfbc.org
Officers:
President: Gary Jones
Vice President: Susan E Brown
Secretary/Treasurer: Christine Welcher
Board Member: Lefkos Aftonomos MD
Board Member: Haren Bhatt
Board Member: Jamie Fink
Board Member: Michael Fujimoto
Management:
Artistic Director: Ian Robertson
Assoc Artistic Director/Choral: Margaret Nomura Clark
Junior Apprentice Director: Jennifer Cooper
Assoc Concert Chorus Director: Charles Calhoun
Vocal Director: Jimmy Kansau
Apprentice Chorus Director: Adrian Behrendt
Junior Apprentice Director: Emily Shisko
Intermediate Chorus Director: Betsy Marvit
Preparatory Chorus Director: Tanya Stum
Mission: CONCERT CHORUS is the SFBC's premiere performing ensemble and is comprised of choristers who exhibit vocal excellence, performance flair, and exceptional musicianship skills. Led by Artistic Director, Ian Robertson, the committed Concert Chorus members, ages 10 to 13, presents a full concert series in the San Francisco Bay Area, tour internationally, record and appear annually with renowned artistic partners, such as the San Francisco Opera.
Utilizes: Arrangers; Collaborations; Commissioned Music; Community Members; Community Talent; Composers; Educators; Guest Companies; Guest Composers; Local Artists & Directors; Multimedia; Music; Paid Performers; Scenic Designers; Sign Language Translators; Singers; Soloists
Founded: 1948
Specialized Field: Concert Chorus
Status: Non-Profit
Income Sources: Donors, Corporate Sponsors
Season: November, December
Performs At: War Memorial Opera House, St Dominic's Catholic Church, Cathedral of Christ

1917
SAN FRANCISCO BACH CHOIR
2443 Fillmore
Street #195
San Francisco, CA 94115
Phone: 415-441-4942
Fax: 415-922-2819
Toll-free: 855-732-24
e-mail: westland@sfbach.org
Web Site: www.sfbach.org
Officers:
Treasurer: Sally Neilson
Secretary: Vicki Sung
Management:
Concert Master: Cynthia Roberts
Orchestra Manager: John Thiessen
Managing Director: Martha Westland
Artistic Director: Corey Jamason
President: Judy Stone
Specialized Field: Choral

1918
SAN FRANCISCO CHORAL ARTISTS
PMB 344, 601 Van Ness Avenue
Suite E
San Francisco, CA 94102
Phone: 415-494-8149
e-mail: info@sfca.org
Web Site: www.sfca.org
Officers:
President: John Zorn
Vice President: Carl Boe
Secretary: Pam Matthews

VOCAL MUSIC / California

Management:
    Artistic Director: Magen Solomon, info@sfca.org
    Assistant Conductor: Tina Harrington, info@sfca.org
    Executive Director: Natalie Churchill, info@sfca.org
    Publicity: Wieneke Gorter
    General Manager: Rebecca Scully
Mission: Specializing in the music of living composers, present both contemporary compositions and finest choral works of the last 600 years, delighting audiences, composers, and singers alike.
Utilizes: Arrangers; Collaborating Artists; Collaborations; Commissioned Composers; Commissioned Music; Community Talent; Composers-in-Residence; Guest Accompanists; Guest Companies; Guest Directors; Guest Instructors; Guest Musical Directors; Instructors; Local Artists; Local Artists & Directors; Multimedia; Music; Original Music Scores; Sign Language Translators; Singers; Students
Founded: 1984
Specialized Field: Choral
Status: Professional; Nonprofit
Budget: $2,300,000
Income Sources: Earned and donated revenue sources
Performs At: Primarily acoustically-satisfying church venues such as St. Mark's Lutheran, SF; St. Mark's Episcopal;Marin, CA
Affiliations: Composer's Inc.; Chorus America; American Chorus Director's Association; Various high schools and universities In the San Francisco Bay Area
Organization Type: Performing; Touring; Resident; Educational

1919
SAN FRANCISCO CHORAL ARTISTS
PMB 344, 601 Van Ness Avenue
Suite E
San Francisco, CA 94102
Phone: 415-494-8149
e-mail: info@sfca.org
Web Site: www.sfca.org
Officers:
    President: John Zorn
    Vice President: Carl Boe
    Secretary: Pam Matthews
Management:
    Music Director: Claire Giovannetti
    Associate Conductor: Doug Wyatt
    Development Manager: Teresa Byrne
    Publicity: Audrey Wong
    General Manager: Rebecca Scully
Mission: To develop and maintain an outstanding performing choral ensemble dedicated to the art of modern classical music.
Specialized Field: Choral
Status: Professional; Nonprofit
Performs At: Calvary Presbyterian Church; St. Mark's Episcopal
Organization Type: Performing

1920
SAN FRANCISCO GIRLS CHORUS
44 Page Street
Suite 200
San Francisco, CA 94102-5989
Phone: 415-863-1752
Fax: 415-934-0302
e-mail: info@sfgirlschorus.org
Web Site: www.sfgirlschorus.org
Officers:
    Board President: Natasha Hoehn
Management:
    Artistic Director: Lisa Bielawa
    Executive Director: Melanie Smith
    Communications Manager: Naho Yoshida
Mission: To create outstanding performances featuring the unique and compelling sound of young women's voices through an exemplary music education program.
Founded: 1978
Specialized Field: Choral; Youth Chorus
Status: Non-Profit, Non-Professional
Budget: $2,000,000
Income Sources: Earned Income, Institutional Giving And Individual Giving.

1921
SAN FRANCISCO GIRLS CHORUS AND ASSOCIATION
44 Page Street
Suite 200
San Francisco, CA 94102-5989
Phone: 415-863-1752
Fax: 415-934-0302
e-mail: info@sfgirlschorus.org
Web Site: www.sfgirlschorus.org
Officers:
    Board President: Natasha Hoehn
Management:
    Artistic Director: Lisa Bielawa
    Executive Director: Melanie Smith
    Communications Manager: Naho Yoshida
Utilizes: Collaborating Artists; Commissioned Music; Educators; Five Seasonal Concerts; Grant Writers; Guest Artists; Guest Companies; Guest Instructors; Guest Lecturers; Multimedia; Music; Original Music Scores; Sign Language Translators; Soloists
Specialized Field: Youth Chorus

1922
SAN FRANCISCO OPERA CENTER
San Francisco Opera
301 Van Ness Avenue
San Francisco, CA 94102
Phone: 415-861-4008
Fax: 415-626-1729
e-mail: mop@sfopera.com
Web Site: www.sfopera.com
Officers:
    Chairman: John A. Gunn
    President of the Association: Keith B. Geeslin
    CEO: David M. Gockley
    VP: Lisa Erdberg
    Treasurer: Steven Menzies
    Treasurer: Steven Menzies
    Secretary: Thomas A. Larsen
    Chairman Emeritus: Reid W. Dennis
Management:
    General Director: David Gockley
    Music Director: Nicola Luisotti
    Executive Director: Keithy Cerny
    Production Director: Patrick Markle
    Associate General Director: Matthew Shilvock
Mission: To enhance cultural life; to present masterworks of opera with the San Fransico Opera Orchestra and outstanding casts; to offer training and outreach; to nurture new audiences and talent.
Utilizes: Actors; Artists-in-Residence; Choreographers; Collaborating Artists; Collaborations; Commissioned Composers; Commissioned Music; Composers-in-Residence; Curators; Dance Companies; Dancers; Designers; Educators; Fine Artists; Five Seasonal Concerts; Grant Writers; Guest Accompanists; Guest Artists; Guest Companies; Guest Composers; Guest Conductors; Guest Designers; Guest Ensembles; Guest Instructors; Guest Lecturers; Guest Musical Directors; Guest Musicians; Guest Soloists; Guild Activities; High School Drama; Instructors; Local Artists; Local Unknown Artists; Lyricists; Multi Collaborations; Multimedia; Music; New Productions; Organization Contracts; Original Music Scores; Performance Artists; Poets; Resident Professionals; Selected Students; Sign Language Translators; Singers; Soloists; Student Interns; Theatre Companies; Touring Companies; Visual Arts
Founded: 1932
Specialized Field: Grand Opera; Lyric Opera; Light Opera; Operetta
Status: Professional; Nonprofit
Budget: $51 million
Income Sources: Private and Corporate Donations; Instituional Gifts; Ticket Sales; Government Assistance
Performs At: War Memorial Opera House

1923
SAN FRANCISCO OPERA CENTER
San Francisco Opera
301 Van Ness Avenue
San Francisco, CA 94102
Phone: 415-861-4008
Fax: 415-255-6774
e-mail: mop@sfopera.com
Web Site: www.sfopera.com
Officers:
    Chairman: John A. Gunn
    President of the Association: Keith B. Geeslin
    CEO: David M. Gockley
    VP: Lisa Erdberg
    Treasurer: Steven Menzies
Management:
    General Director: David Gockley
    Music Director: Nicola Luisotti
    Executive Director: Keithy Cerny
    Production Director: Patrick Markle
    Associate General Director: Matthew Shilvock
Mission: To utilize the various affiliate components of the San Francisco Opera Association in a comprehensive and unique professional training program for artists.
Utilizes: Five Seasonal Concerts; Guest Artists; Guest Companies; Singers
Founded: 1982
Specialized Field: Grand Opera; Lyric Opera; Light Opera; Operetta
Status: Professional; Nonprofit
Performs At: Cowell Theater; Herbst Thater; Old First Chruch; Yerba Buena Theater; Stern Grove
Rental Contact: Bill Bowles
Organization Type: Performing; Touring; Resident; Educational; Sponsoring

1924
SAN FRANCISCO RENAISSANCE VOICES
1329 Seventh Avenue
San Francisco, CA 94122
Phone: 415-664-2543
e-mail: sfrvoices@yahoo.com
Web Site: www.sfrv.org
Officers:
    Chairman: Jeff J Badger
    Secretary: John Morales
    Treasurer: Shirley Moore
    General Director: Sara Burke
    General Director: Tamsyn Waterhouse
    Advisor: Todd Jolly
    Advisor: Marsha Genesky
    Advisor: Ian Robertson
Management:
    Music Director: Todd Jolly
    Assistant Music Director: Katherine McKee

VOCAL MUSIC / California

Executive Director: J Jeff Badger
Educational Coordinator: A Cappella Chor Navarro
Choreographer: LeAnna Sharp
Mission: We are a professional mixed-voice ensemble dedicated to performing and exploring the a cappella choral music of the Renaissance particularly lesser-known and rarely-performed works, as well as exploring music from this period outside of the traditional European canon.
Utilizes: Arrangers; Artists-in-Residence; Choreographers; Collaborating Artists; Collaborations; Commissioned Composers; Community Talent; Composers; Composers-in-Residence; Fine Artists; Instructors; Local Artists; Local Artists & Directors; Lyricists; Multimedia; Music; Sign Language Translators; Singers
Founded: 2004
Specialized Field: A Capella Choral
Status: Non-Profit
Income Sources: Donors
Season: October through February
Performs At: 7th Avenue Presbyterian Church, First Lutheran Church

1925
SAN FRANCISCO SYMPHONY CHORUS
San Francisco Symphony
Pouise M. Davies Symphony Hall
San Francisco, CA 94102
Mailing Address: 201 Van Ness Avenue, San Francisco, CA 94102
Phone: 415-864-6000
Fax: 415-554-0108
e-mail: patronservices@sfsymphony.org
Web Site: www.sfsymphony.org
Officers:
  GM: John Kieser
  Production Manager: Tim Carless
  VP: Eff W. Martin
  Secretary: Robert R. Tufts
Management:
  Executive Director: Brent Assink
  Director: John Manghum
  Artistic Administrator: Richard Lonsdorf
  Chorus Manager: Elaine Robertson
Mission: Recognition as a world-class chorus; performance of a wide repertoire of fine music under leading conductors.
Founded: 1973
Specialized Field: Choral
Status: Professional; Nonprofit
Performs At: Louise M. Davies Symphony Hall
Organization Type: Performing

1926
SAN FRANCISCO OPERA
301 Van Ness Avenue
San Francisco, CA 94102
Phone: 415-861-4008
Fax: 415-626-1729
e-mail: webmaster@sfopera.com
Web Site: www.sfopera.com
Officers:
  President: Julia Young
  Vice President: Cathy Homoelle
  Treasurer: Paul Nocero
  Secretary: Kathleen Leones
  Past President: Syndi L. Robertson
Management:
  General Director: David Gockley
  Music Director: Nicola Luisotti
  Production Director: Patrick Markle
  Artistic Administrator: Brad Trexell
  Principal Guest Conductor: Patrick Summers
Founded: 1923
Specialized Field: Opera
Rental Contact: Bill Bowles

1927
THE SAN FRANCISCO CHORAL SOCIETY
263 West Portal
Suite 775
San Francisco, CA 94127
Phone: 415-566-8425
e-mail: inquire@sfchoral.org
Web Site: www.sfchoral.org
Officers:
  President: Julia Young
  Vice President: Cathy Homoelle
  Treasurer: Paul Nocero
  Secretary: Kathleen Leones
  Past President: Syndi L. Robertson
  Board Member: Stacey Giamalis
  Board Member: John Marcom
  Board Member: Frances Varnhagen
Management:
  Artistic Director: Robert Geary
  Assistant Conductor: Bryan Baker
  Executive Director: Alan Kleinschmidt
  Business Manager: Susan Kalman
  Adminstrative Coordinator: Marilyn McDonald
Mission: Inspired by the joy of singing and hearing choral music, the San Francisco Choral Society strives to be a premier symphonic chorus through the outstanding performance of choral masterpieces and new commissioned works. Infused with a commitment to excellence and education, our professional artistic and administrative staff, soloists, and orchestras work collaboratively w/ our all-volunteer auditioned singers to foster a vibrant, diverse community
Utilizes: Arrangers; Collaborating Artists; Collaborations; Commissioned Music; Community Members; Community Talent; Educators; Guest Composers; Local Unknown Artists; Lyricists; Multimedia; Music; Paid Performers; Sign Language Translators; Singers
Founded: 1989
Specialized Field: Choral, Orchestra
Status: Non-Profit, Professional
Income Sources: Donors
Performs At: Calvary Presbyterian, St Paul's Church

1928
WESTERN OPERA THEATER
San Francisco Classical Voice
44 Gough St, Suite 204
San Francisco, CA 94103
Phone: 415-861-4008
Fax: 415-255-6774
e-mail: eric@sfcv.org
Web Site: www.sfcv.org
Officers:
  Chairman: Alisa Won
  Treasurer: John Gambs
  Secretary: Ching Yee Hu
  Executive Director: Don Roth
Management:
  Director: Richard Harrell
  Tour Manager: William Bowles
Utilizes: Artists-in-Residence; Grant Writers; Guest Composers; Guest Designers; Guest Ensembles; Guest Lecturers; Guest Musical Directors; Guest Musicians; Guest Soloists; High School Drama; Instructors; Multimedia; Music; Original Music Scores; Poets; Resident Professionals; Sign Language Translators; Singers; Soloists; Theatre Companies
Specialized Field: Opera; Musical Theatre
Rental Contact: Bill Bowles

1929
OPERA SAN JOSE
2149 Paragon Drive
San Jose, CA 95131
Phone: 408-437-4450
Fax: 408-437-4455
e-mail: info@operasj.org
Web Site: www.operasj.org
Officers:
  President: Frank Veloz
  VP/Chair of Finance: Sharon McCorkle
  Secretary: Jack Schneider
Management:
  Executive Director: Irene Dalis
  Artistic Director: Matt Siek
  Managing Director: Lynda Osborne
  Music Director, Principal Conductor: David Rohrbaugh
  General Manager: Larry Hancock
  Director Communications: Christine Spielberger
  Corporate Relations Manager: Glen Won
Mission: To maintain and enhance a professional opera company of artistic excellence; to provide principally in opera of all periods and secondarily in operetta; to provide opera singers with professional development and performance opportunities; to develop, educate and entertain.
Utilizes: Artists-in-Residence; Commissioned Composers; Commissioned Music; Grant Writers; Guest Artists; Guest Companies; Guest Conductors; Guest Musical Directors; High School Drama; Local Artists; Original Music Scores; Resident Professionals; Sign Language Translators; Singers; Student Interns
Founded: 1984
Specialized Field: Grand Opera; Musical Theatre; Classical
Status: Non-Profit, Professional
Paid Staff: 18
Volunteer Staff: 155
Paid Artists: 224
Budget: $2,765,000
Performs At: Montgomery Theater
Seating Capacity: 519
Organization Type: Performing; Touring; Educational; Sponsoring

1930
PACIFIC CHORALE
3621 S Harbor Boulevard
Suite 220
Santa Ana, CA 92704
Phone: 714-662-2345
Fax: 714-662-2395
e-mail: contactus@pacificchorale.org
Web Site: www.pacificchorale.org
Officers:
  President/CEO: Kelly Ruggirello
Management:
  Artistic Director: John Alexander
  Operations Director: Brian Sullivan
  Marketing Director: Ryan McSweeney
  General Manager & CFO: Dana Ramos
  Director of Development: Alina Mircea-Trotz
Mission: Committed to the highest quality performance and recording of existing choral masterworks and to the creation, performance and recording of future masterworks. We will enrich and educate our current audience as well as singers and audiences of the future.

VOCAL MUSIC / California

Utilizes: Collaborations; Commissioned Composers; Composers-in-Residence; Fine Artists; Guest Accompanists; Guest Choreographers; Guest Musical Directors; Guest Musicians; Guest Writers; Multimedia; Original Music Scores; Sign Language Translators
Founded: 1968
Specialized Field: Choral
Status: Non-Profit, Professional
Paid Staff: 7
Paid Artists: 40
Non-paid Artists: 130
Budget: $1.2 million
Income Sources: Ticket revenue, Contributions
Performs At: Orange County Performing Arts Center
Affiliations: Chorus America, ACDA
Annual Attendance: 10,000+
Organization Type: Performing; Touring; Educational

1931
OPERA SANTA BARBARA
1330 State Street
Suite 209
Santa Barbara, CA 93101
Phone: 805-898-3890
Fax: 805-898-3892
e-mail: info@operasb.com
Web Site: www.operasb.com
Officers:
   President: Joan Rutkowski
   First Vice President: Nancy Golden
   Secretary: Mary Penny
   Treasurer: Eric Oltmann
   Second Vice President: Simon Williams
Management:
   Company Manager: Brian Hotchkin, brian@operasb.com
   Artistic Director: Jose Maria Condemi
   General Director: Steven Sharpe
   Artistic Administrator: Brian Hotchkin
   Marketing & Development Manager: Susan Scott
Mission: Opera Santa Barbara contributes to the cultural enrichment of our audiences by presenting exciting high-quality productions and community programs that celebrate the breadth and beauty of opera. Opera Santa Barbara aspires to be a destination opera company, producing a diverse repertoire of traditional and contemporary operas that engage and excite a broad audience.
Utilizes: Dancers; Grant Writers; Guest Artists; Guest Companies; Guest Composers; Guest Conductors; Guest Designers; Guest Musical Directors; Guest Musicians; High School Drama; Local Artists & Directors; Multimedia; Music; Sign Language Translators; Visual Designers
Founded: 1994
Specialized Field: Opera
Status: Non-Profit, Professional
Paid Staff: 6
Volunteer Staff: 75
Paid Artists: 500
Performs At: Granada; Lobero Theater

1932
MASTERS OF HARMONY
PO Box 3342
Santa Fe Springs, CA 90670
Toll-free: 888-664-8863
e-mail: info@mastersofharmony.org
Web Site: mastersofharmony.org
Officers:
   President: Bill Rosica
Management:
   Chorus Director: Justin Miller
   Production Director: Doug Maddox
   Communications Director: Frank Ortega
   VP/Marketing: Bill Power
   VP/Chapter Development: Ray Johnson
   VP/Music/Performance: Joe D'Amore
   VP/Operations: Tom Christman
   Patron Program Manager: Jim Haggerty
Mission: The Masters of Harmony is a male musical ensemble, performing primarily in the barbershop style and dedicated to musical excellence. Our mission is to preserve the uniquely American art form known as barbershop harmony, promote fellowship among our members, encourage music appreciation in schools and the community, contribute to musical causes, and support other singing organizations.
Utilizes: Arrangers; Collaborating Artists; Collaborations; Composers; Fine Artists; Lyricists; Multimedia; Music; Paid Performers; Sign Language Translators; Singers
Founded: 1985
Specialized Field: Choral
Status: Non-Profit, Professional
Income Sources: Donors
Season: November, February
Performs At: Carpenter Center

1933
MUSICA ANGELICA
1223 Wilshire Blvd
Suite 287
Santa Monica, CA 90403
Phone: 310-458-4504
Web Site: www.musicaangelica.org
Officers:
   President: Laura Carroll
   VP/Marketing: David Watson
   Treasurer: Larry Allen
   Secretary: Merilyn Morgan
   Board Member: Stefanie Becker
Management:
   Music Director/Conductor: Martin Haselbock
   Managing Director: Laura Spino
   Marketing Director: Cynthia Young
   Operation Manager: Chad Miner
   Public Relations: Jenine Baines
   Web/Creative Design: Eduardo Martinez
   Graphic Design: Michael Duckworth
Mission: Musica Angelica is led by Music Director Martin Haselb"ck, the internationally renowned organist, conductor, and composer. Regarded as Southern California's premier Baroque ensemble, Musica Angelica presents wide-ranging programs encompassing music from the early Baroque through the early Classical era.
Utilizes: Arrangers; Collaborating Artists; Commissioned Music; Contract Orchestras; Grant Writers; Guest Accompanists; High School Drama; Instructors; Multimedia; Singers
Founded: 1993
Specialized Field: Baroque Music, Classical, Orchestra
Status: Non-Profit, Professional
Income Sources: Donors, Corporate Sponsors
Performs At: Thayer Hall, Santa Monica 1st Presbyterian, Pasadena Neigborhood Church, AT&T Center Theatre, Walt Disney Concert Hall

1934
GOLDEN GATE OPERA
3030 Bridgeway
(Sausalito)
Sausalito, CA 94965
Phone: 415-339-9546
Fax: 415-339-9547
e-mail: info@goldengateopera.org
Web Site: www.goldengateopera.org
Officers:
   Technical Director: Rod Mortensen
   Development Director: Rachel Ward
   Community Outreach: Maria Chang-Calderon
   President: Roberta Wain-Becker
   Treasurer: Derick Wong, CPA
Management:
   Artistic Director/General Manager: Roberta Becker
   Music Director/Conductor: Geoggrey Gallegos
   Office Organization: Ally Merkeley
   Technical Support: Adly Ayad
   Marketing Manager: Prosser Morrow
Mission: A cooperative of professional musicians, singers and technicians dedicated to producing professional, high-quality and affordable opera.
Founded: 1996
Specialized Field: Opera
Season: September-May
Performs At: Marin Civic Center Showcase Theatre; Marin Center Veteran's Memorail Auditorium; Legion of Honor Florence Gould Theatre

1935
LOS ROBLES MASTER CHORALE
2245 First Street #208
Simi Valley, CA 93065
Phone: 805-526-7464
Web Site: losroblesmasterchorale.org
Officers:
   President: Mike O'Sullivan
Management:
   Executive Director: Lenard Geres, lgeres@losroblesmasterchorale.
   Artistic Producer: Lynn Youngron, lyoungren@losroblesmasterchora
   Artistic Director: Lesley Leighton
Mission: We are a volunteer chorus that presents masterworks and new choral music to our community. We act as stewards of the tradition of choral excellence in our region through performance, collaboration with other arts organizations in our community, education of our audiences and young singers, and encouraging new choral compositions through our Young Artists Choral Composer Competition.

1936
ROGER WAGNER CHORALE
25744 Hood Way
Stevenson Ranch
Stevenson Ranch, CA 91381
Phone: 661-287-3864
Fax: 661-287-3865
e-mail: info@rogerwagnerchorale.com
Web Site: www.therogerwagnerchorale.com
Management:
   Director of Music: Jeannine Wagner
   Founder: Roger Wagner
Specialized Field: Choral

1937
LA MARCA AMERICAN VARIETY CHORUS SINGERS
2655 W 230th Place
Torrance, CA 90505
Phone: 310-325-8708
Fax: 310-325-8708
e-mail: lamarcamusic@earthlink.com
Web Site: www.getlessonsnow.lamarcamusic
Management:

VOCAL MUSIC / California

President: Priscilla Lamarca-Kandel
Mission: To educate and entertain
Utilizes: Musical Directors; Singers
Founded: 1974
Specialized Field: Southern California
Status: Non-Profit, Professional
Paid Staff: 2
Income Sources: International Federation of Festival Organizations
Organization Type: Performing; Touring; Resident; Educational

1938
CANTORI DOMINO
1227 Fourth Street
Valencia, CA 90401
Mailing Address: 1227 Fourth Street, Santa Monica, CA 90401
Phone: 424-272-1460
e-mail: info@cantoridomino.org
Web Site: cantoridomino.org
Officers:
  President: Milton Hinkle
  Teasurer: Judy Elliot
  Secretary: Susan Kasenow
  Board Member: G Brooks Arnold
  Board Member: Nicholas Ash
Management:
  Founder/Artistic Director: Maurita Phillips Thornburgh
  Co-Founder/Admin Coordinator: Mary Gerlitz
  Keyboard Musician: Ray Urwin
Mission: CANTORI DOMINO has, in its more than twenty years of incorporation as a tax exempt California non-profit organization (501(c)(3)), established a remarkable record of growth by several measures, most notably: quality of musical performance, depth of repertoire, fiscal record and audience development.
Utilizes: Arrangers; Collaborations; Commissioned Composers; Composers; Fine Artists; Lyricists; Multimedia; Music; Paid Performers; Sign Language Translators; Singers
Founded: 1990
Specialized Field: Choral
Status: Non-Profit, Professional
Income Sources: Sponsors, Donors
Season: December through May
Performs At: St Augustine by-the-Sea Episcopal Church

1939
DIABLO LIGHT OPERA COMPANY
PO Box 5034
Walnut Creek, CA 94596
Phone: 925-944-1565
Fax: 925-944-1510
e-mail: info@diablotheatre.org
Web Site: www.dloc.org
Officers:
  President: Sherry Caraballo Dorfman
  Operations Vice President: Julie Hahn
  Secretary: Claudia Mauzy Nemir
  Past President: Carole Wynstra
  Marketing Chair: Martha Rosenberg,
Management:
  Artistic Director: Ian Leonard
  Producer: Grete Egan
  Managing Director: Krissy Gray
  Education Coordinator and Performin: Brittany Danielle
  Costume Shop Manager: Carole Edlinger
Mission: Dedicated to enriching our community by producing quality musicals and light opera and by providing educational opportunities in the arts.

Utilizes: Five Seasonal Concerts; Guest Artists; Guest Companies; Singers
Founded: 1960
Specialized Field: Light Opera; Operetta; Musical Theatre
Status: Non-Professional; Nonprofit
Paid Staff: 50
Performs At: Regional Center for the Arts
Organization Type: Performing; Educational

1940
FESTIVAL OPERA
1630 North Main Street
#61
Walnut Creek, CA 94596
Phone: 925-944-9610
Fax: 925-944-1078
e-mail: mimi@festivalopera.org
Web Site: www.festivalopera.com
Officers:
  Board Chair: Susie Hanson
  First Vice Chair: Karin Eames
  Second Vice Chair: Peter Johnson
  Treasurer: David Kingsbury
  Secretary: Katherine Van Hagan
Management:
  Artistic and Music Director: Michael Morgan
  Executive Director: Sara Nealy
  Production Director: Frederic O Boulay
  Assistant Director: Sunshine Deffner
  Marketing Director: Dick Brundage, CBC
Founded: 1991
Specialized Field: Grand Opera
Status: Non-Profit, Professional
Paid Staff: 2
Performs At: Hofmann Theater; Regional Center for the Arts

1941
THE FESTIVAL OPERA ASSOCIATION INC
1630 North Main Street
#61
Walnut Creek, CA 94596
Phone: 925-944-9610
Fax: 925-944-1078
e-mail: mimi@festivalopera.org
Web Site: www.festivalopera.com
Officers:
  Board Chair: Susie Hanson
  First Vice Chair: Karin Eames
  Second Vice Chair: Peter Johnson
  Treasurer: David Kingsbury
  Secretary: Katherine Van Hagan
Management:
  Executive Director: Sara Nealy
  Artistic/Music Director: Michael Morgan
  Production Director: Frederic O Boulay
  Assistant Director: Sunshine Deffner
  Marketing Director: Dick Brundage, CBC
Founded: 1991
Specialized Field: Opera
Status: Non-Profit, Professional
Paid Staff: 3
Paid Artists: 150
Performs At: Redlands Bowl

1942
GAY MEN'S CHORUS OF LOS ANGELES
9056 Santa Monica Blvd
Suite 300
West Hollywood, CA 90069-5545

Phone: 424-239-6514
Toll-free: 800-636-7464
e-mail: mailroom@gmcla.org
Web Site: gmcla.org
Officers:
  Chairman: Hon. John Duran
  Vice Chair: Diana Abbitt
  Secretary: Eric Maryanov
  Treasurer: Steven Mele
  President: Bill Cunningham
Management:
  Artistic Director: E Jason Armstrong
  Executive Director: Chris Verdugo
  Youth Outreach: Lee Stickler
Mission: To create musical experiences that strengthen our role as a leader among lesbian, gay, bisexual, transgender (LGBT) and performing arts organizations, enrich our member-artists, support LGBT youth, challenge homophobia, and expose new communities to our message of equality.
Utilizes: Arrangers; Choreographers; Collaborating Artists; Collaborations; Fine Artists; Lyricists; Multimedia; Music; New Productions; Sign Language Translators; Singers
Founded: 2008
Opened: 2009
Specialized Field: Choral
Status: Non-Profit
Income Sources: Donors, Sponsore, Fundraisers
Season: December, March, June
Performs At: Alex Theater, First Congretional Church of LA, Saban Theater

1943
ANGELES CHORALE
20929 Ventura Boulevard
Suite 47-120
Woodland Hills, CA 91364-2334
Phone: 818-591-1735
Fax: 818-701-7703
Web Site: www.angeleschorale.org
Officers:
  Chair: Sharon Mountford
  President: Gayle Biava
  President-Elect: Steve Green
  Chief Financial Officer: Sue Bell
  Vice-President Chorale Affairs: Christopher Ward
Management:
  Executive Director: Rae MacDonald
  Artistic Director: John Sutton
  Resident Guest Conductor: Donald Neuen
  Accompanist: James Lent
Mission: To reach the community of Los Angeles with high quality choral concerts while developing the talent of the performing musicians.
Utilizes: Collaborations; Guest Musical Directors; Guest Musicians; Instructors; Sign Language Translators
Founded: 1975
Specialized Field: Choral
Status: Non-Profit, Professional
Paid Staff: 1
Paid Artists: 20
Non-paid Artists: 125
Budget: $180,000
Income Sources: Tickets; Donations; Grants
Performs At: Concert hall
Annual Attendance: 7,000
Facility Category: Royce Hall, UCLA + First United Methodist Church-Pasadena
Seating Capacity: 1,800
Year Built: 1924
Cost: $3,000

VOCAL MUSIC / Colorado

Colorado

1944
ASPEN OPERA THEATER CENTER
2 Music School Road
Aspen, CO 81611
Phone: 970-925-3254
Fax: 970-925-3802
e-mail: festival@aspenmusic.org
Web Site: www.aspenmusicfestival.com
Officers:
  President/CEO: Alan Fletcher
  Vice President for Artistic Adminis: Asadour Santourian
  Vice President and Dean of Students: Jennifer Johnston
  Vice President and General Manager: Daniel Song
  Vice President of Development: Alexander Brose
Management:
  Managing Director: James Berdahl
  Music Director: David Zinman
  Manager of Information Services: Fritz Grueter
  Accounting Assistant: Lindsay Pfaffmann
  Assistant Controller: Donna Phelps
Founded: 1949
Specialized Field: Grand Opera; Light Opera; Lyric Opera; Musical Theatre; Choral; Ethnic Music; Classical; Contemporary
Status: Non-Profit, Professional
Paid Staff: 35
Performs At: Wheeler Opera House
Annual Attendance: 5000
Facility Category: Opera House
Type of Stage: Proscenium
Stage Dimensions: 27 x 24
Seating Capacity: 490
Year Built: 1889
Year Remodeled: 1984

1945
WHEELER OPERA HOUSE
320 E Hyman Avenue
Aspen, CO 81611
Phone: 970-920-5770
Fax: 970-920-5780
Toll-free: 866-449-0464
e-mail: heather.larson@ci.aspen.co.us
Web Site: www.wheeleroperahouse.com
Officers:
  Chairperson: Brian O'Neil
  Vice-Chairperson: Bruce Fretz
  Secretary: Richie Cohen
Management:
  Executive Director: Gram Slaton
  Operations Manager: Heather Larson
  Senior Manager For Operations: Amy Kaiser
  Senior Manager for Finance: Rose Bennett
  Marketing Coordinator: Lauren Pierce
Utilizes: Singers
Founded: 1889
Specialized Field: Opera; Folk Music
Status: Non-Profit; Professional
Performs At: Proc Theatre
Facility Category: Theatre
Type of Stage: Procenium
Stage Dimensions: 28'x28'
Seating Capacity: 503
Year Built: 1984
Year Remodeled: 2006
Rental Contact: Operations Manager Heather Larson
Organization Type: Sponsoring

1946
SOUND OF THE ROCKIES
7691 S. University Boulevard
Centennial, CO 80122
Mailing Address: P.O. Box 2242, Denver, CO 80222
Phone: 303-993-3501
e-mail: contact@soundoftherockies.com
Web Site: soundoftherockies.com
Management:
  Director: Darin Drown
Mission: The Sound of the Rockies will be acknowledged as the best in men's a cappella by attracting and developing the best vocal performers, dedicating ourselves to performance excellence, succeeding in barbershop competition, fostering an enjoyable and entertaining experiences for our members and audiences, and engaging in community outreach.
Founded: 2002
Specialized Field: Barbershop; A Cappella
Status: Nonprofit
Organization Type: Performing; Competing

1947
THE CHERRY CREEK CHORALE
Bethany Lutheran Church 4500 E. Hampden Ave.
Cherry Hills Village, CO 80113
Mailing Address: P.O. Box 3272, Greenwood Village, CO 80155
Phone: 303-789-5920
e-mail: info@cherrycreekchorale.org
Web Site: cherrycreekchorale.org
Officers:
  President: Doug Simpson
  Vice President: Leigh Kahn
Management:
  Artistic Director: Brian Patrick Leatherman, director@cherrycreekchorale.or
Mission: Creating choral community, artistry, and excellence.
Founded: 1980
Organization Type: Performing; Touring

1948
CHAMBER SINGERS OF THE COLORADO SPRINGS CHORALE
16 East Platte Avenue
Suite 205
Colorado Springs, CO 80901
Mailing Address: Colorado Springs Choral Society, P.O. Box 2304, Colorado S
Phone: 719-634-3737
Fax: 719-473-0077
e-mail: csc@cschorale.org
Web Site: www.cschorale.org
Officers:
  Chairman: John Underwood
  Vice Chairman: Diane Olivieri
  Secretary: Judy Kramer
  Treasurer: Kipper Fulghum
Management:
  Executive Director: Jim Sena, mark@cschorale.org
  Artistic Director & Conductor: Donald P. Jenkins
  Artistic Director: Deborah J Teske
  Music Director & Conductor: Kimberley Schultz
  Bookeeper & Chefs' Gala Chair: Jackie Foorman
Mission: A representative ensemble of the Colorado Springs Chorale, performing a repertoire of diverse musical styles, performing in schools, service clubs, retirement homes and businesses, and private and public functions.
Founded: 2010
Specialized Field: Lyric Opera; Musical Theatre; Choral; Ethnic Music; Classical; Contemporary; Religious
Status: Non-Profit, Non-Professional
Paid Staff: 2
Volunteer Staff: 14
Paid Artists: 1
Organization Type: Performing; Resident; Educational

1949
COLORADO SPRINGS CHORALE
16 East Platte Avenue
Suite 205
Colorado Springs, CO 80901
Phone: 719-634-3737
Fax: 719-473-0077
e-mail: csc@cschorale.org
Web Site: www.cschorale.org
Officers:
  Chairman: John Underwood
  Vice Chairman: Diane Olivieri
  Secretary: Judy Kramer
  Treasurer: Kipper Fulghum
Management:
  Executive Director: Jim Sena, mark@cschorale.org
  Artistic Director/Conductor: Donald P Jenkins, don@cschorale.org
  Artistic Director: Deborah J Teske, dbrink@coloradocollege.edu
  Music Director & Conductor: Kimberley Schultz
  Bookeeper & Chefs' Gala Chair: Jackie Foorman
Mission: To serve the Pikes Peak region by celebrating the human voice in song and its power to rejoice, console, educate, enrich, unite and inspire
Founded: 1956
Specialized Field: Choral
Status: Non-Profit, Non-Professional
Paid Staff: 4
Non-paid Artists: 150
Budget: $216,000
Income Sources: Grants; Donations; Ticket Sales
Performs At: Pikes Peak Center
Seating Capacity: 1885
Organization Type: Performing; Resident

1950
CENTRAL CITY OPERA
400 S Colorado Boulevard
Suite 530
Denver, CO 80246
Phone: 303-292-6500
Fax: 303-292-4958
Toll-free: 800-851-8175
e-mail: admin@centralcityopera.org
Web Site: www.centralcityopera.org
Management:
  General/Artistic Director: Pelham G Pearce
  Music Director: John Baril
  Artistic Director Emeritus: John Moriarty
Mission: Central City Opera is the nations fifth oldest opera company. The national summer opera festival draws patrons from 48 states, presenting works of artistic excellence from standard and contemporary repertoire.
Utilizes: Sign Language Translators
Founded: 1932
Specialized Field: Opera
Status: Non-Profit, Professional
Paid Staff: 17
Paid Artists: 100
Budget: $4.2 million
Income Sources: Scientifrand Cultural Facilities District

VOCAL MUSIC / Colorado

Season: July - August
Performs At: Central City (Festival Site)
Affiliations: Opera America League of Historic-America Theatres
Annual Attendance: 27,000
Facility Category: Opera House
Type of Stage: Proscenium
Stage Dimensions: 25x34x171/2
Seating Capacity: 552
Year Built: 1878
Cost: $23,000 (built)

1951
COLORADO CHILDREN'S CHORALE
2420 W 26th Avenue
Suite 350 D
Denver, CO 80211-5362
Phone: 303-892-5600
Fax: 303-892-0828
e-mail: mail@childrenschorale.org
Web Site: www.childrenschorale.org
Officers:
   President: Stephen M. Strachan
   Vice President: Frederick K. Trask IV
   Secretary: Rosemary G. Wiedenmayer
   Treasurer: Philip E. Doty
   Immediate Past President: Meg J. Steitz
Management:
   Artistic Director and Conductor: Deborah DeSantis
   Assistant Conductor and Technical C: Travis Branam
   Associate Director and Conductor: Mary Louise Burke
   Costume and Wardrobe Manager: Lynda Fisher
   Development Director: Tina Hansen
Mission: Providing the nation with a performing-arts group that features children and strives for excellence.
Utilizes: Guest Artists
Founded: 1974
Specialized Field: Youth Chorus; Choral; Classical; Folk Music; Ethnic Music; Musical Theatre
Status: Non-Profit, Non-Professional
Paid Staff: 14
Organization Type: Performing; Touring; Educational

1952
COLUMBINE CHORALE
681 Birch Street
Denver, CO 80220
Phone: 415-771-3352
e-mail: info@voltisf.org
Web Site: voltisf.org
Officers:
   President: Mary Ann Shattuck
   Vice President: Emily M De Falla
   Secretary: Richard Collier
   Treasurer: Patricia Casperson
Management:
   Artistic Director: Robert Geary
   Executive Director: Barbara Heroux
   Composer/Advisor: Mark Winges
Mission: Volti's twenty professional singers, under the direction of founder and Artistic Director Robert Geary, are dedicated to the discovery, creation, and performance of new vocal music. The ensemble's mission is to foster and showcase contemporary American music and composers, and to introduce contemporary vocal music from around the world to local audiences.

Utilizes: Arrangers; Choreographers; Collaborating Artists; Collaborations; Community Talent; High School Drama; Local Artists & Directors; Multimedia; Music; Paid Performers; Sign Language Translators; Singers; Soloists
Founded: 1952
Specialized Field: Choral
Status: Non-Profit, Professional
Income Sources: Donors
Season: Year Round

1953
CENTRAL CITY OPERA
400 South Colorado Boulevard, Suite 530
Denver, CO 80246
Phone: 303-292-6500
Fax: 303-292-4958
e-mail: admin@centralcityopera.org
Web Site: centralcityopera.org
Officers:
   Chair: Nancy S. Parker
   President: Maureen K. Barker
   Treasurer: Gregg Kvistad
   Secretary: Michael Huseby
Management:
   General/Artistic Director: Pelham G. Pearce, Jr., ppearce@centralcityopera.org
   Music Director: John Baril, jbaril@centralcityopera.org
   Director Of Marketing: Valerie Hamlin, vhamlin@centralcityopera.org
Founded: 1932
Performs At: The Ellie Caulkins Opera House; The Opera House 124 Eureka Street, Central City, CO

1954
OPERA COLORADO
695 S Colorado Boulevard
Suite 20
Denver, CO 80246
Phone: 303-468-2030
Fax: 303-778-6533
e-mail: info@operacolorado.org
Web Site: www.operacolorado.org
Officers:
   Chairman: Michael Hughes
   President: Marcia Robinson
   Chair Emeritus: Kenneth Barrow
   Lifetime Honorary Chair: Ellie Caulkins
   Secretary: Susan Adams
Management:
   Artistic Director: James Robinson
   General Director: Gregory Carpenter
   Director Marketing: Rex Fuller
   Development Director: Susan Evans
   Director of Artistic Operations: Brad Trexell
Mission: To develope a better appreciation and understanding of opera throughout the community; to produce the highest quality performances of grand operas in their original languages with projected English supertitles translation.
Utilizes: Actors; Artists-in-Residence; Choreographers; Collaborations; Dancers; Designers; Five Seasonal Concerts; Grant Writers; Guest Accompanists; Guest Artists; Guest Composers; Guest Conductors; Guest Designers; Guest Ensembles; Guest Lecturers; Guest Musical Directors; Guest Musicians; Guest Writers; High School Drama; Instructors; Lyricists; Multimedia; Original Music Scores; Resident Professionals; Selected Students; Sign Language Translators; Student Interns; Visual Arts
Founded: 1981
Specialized Field: Grand Opera
Status: Professional; Nonprofit

Paid Staff: 75
Budget: $2-$5 million
Income Sources: Opera America
Rental Contact: Gordon Robertson
Organization Type: Performing; Resident; Educational

1955
ST MARTIN'S CHAMBER CHOIR
2015 Glenarm Place
Denver, CO 80205-3121
Phone: 303-298-1970
Web Site: stmartinschamberchoir.org
Officers:
   President: Michael Smith
   Vice President: Howard Zoufaly
   Secretary: Carol Prescott
   Treasurer: Bob Mosher
   Director: Micaela Larsen Brown
   Director: James East
   Director: Ashley Hoffman
Management:
   Artistic Director: Timothy Krueger
   Executive Director: Steven Grupe
Mission: The mission of St. Martin's Chamber Choir is to perform classical choral music to the highest professional standards, and to inspire appreciation of the choral art by educating audiences and the wider community.
Utilizes: Arrangers; Choreographers; Collaborating Artists; Collaborations; Lyricists; Multi Collaborations; Multimedia; Music; Paid Performers; Sign Language Translators; Singers
Specialized Field: Choral
Status: Non-Profit, Professional
Income Sources: Donors, Sponsors
Season: September through June
Performs At: Bethany Lutheran Church, St Andrews Episcopal Church

1956
DURANGO CHORAL SOCIETY
PO Box 1043
Durango, CO 81302
Mailing Address: PO Box Durango, CO 81302
Phone: 970-759-2206
Fax: 970-382-6910
e-mail: mack_1@fortlewis.edu
Web Site: www.durangochoralsociety.com
Officers:
   President: Margi Coxwell
   Vice President: Kathy Riebau
   Corresponding Secretary: Debra Lehl
   Recording Secretary: Abby Bowen
   Treasurer: Lynn Eustance
   Recording Secretary: Jan Patton
Management:
   President: Jeanne Bandy
   Executive VP: Jacque Hendrick
   Artistic Director: Linda Mack
   Director: Richard Cumming
   Artistic Director: Amy Barrett
Mission: To provide fine choral and orchestral performances for the four-corners area.
Utilizes: Singers
Founded: 1961
Specialized Field: Choral
Status: Non-Profit
Paid Staff: 45
Income Sources: American Choral Directors Association
Organization Type: Performing; Touring; Resident; Educational; Sponsoring

VOCAL MUSIC / Connecticut

1957
LARIMER CHORALE
PO Box 884
Fort Collins, CO 80522
Phone: 970-416-9348
Fax: 970-491-4142
e-mail: lc@fortnet.org
Web Site: www.larimerchorale.org
Officers:
  Executive Director: Vicki Fogel Mykles
  Board President: Clark Mozer
  Treasurer: Andrew Hinds
  Vice-President: Richard Hansen
  Secretary: Angela Bosco-Lauth
Management:
  Artistic Director: Dr Michael T Krueger
  Assistant Conductor: Jean Johnson
  Executive Director: Wendy D. White
Mission: To bring classical choral music to Northern Colorado by singing choral music of the masters.
Utilizes: Actors; Artists-in-Residence; Collaborating Artists; Collaborations; Dance Companies; Dancers; Designers; Educators; Grant Writers; Guest Companies; Guest Composers; Guest Directors; Guest Instructors; Guest Lecturers; Guest Musical Directors; Guest Musicians; Instructors; Local Artists; Lyricists; Multi Collaborations; Multimedia; Organization Contracts; Original Music Scores; Playwrights; Sign Language Translators
Founded: 1977
Specialized Field: Choral
Status: Non-Profit
Paid Staff: 5
Volunteer Staff: 30
Paid Artists: 8
Non-paid Artists: 105
Budget: $80,000
Income Sources: Audionoes, grants, fundraising
Performs At: Lincoln Center
Annual Attendance: 4,000+
Facility Category: Large community auditorium building, 2 stages
Type of Stage: Large for 200 singers/50 symphony
Seating Capacity: 1180, smaller stage 350
Year Built: 1978

1958
OPERA FORT COLLINS
PO Box 503
Fort Collins, CO 80522
Phone: 970-482-0220
e-mail: info@operafortcollins.org
Web Site: www.operafortcollins.com
Officers:
  Vice President: Gerald Holbrook
  President: Christy Bray Ricks
  OFCAA Rep /Secretary: Nathan Hickle
  Treasurer: Terry Shetler
  Past President: John Ostheimer
Management:
  Artistic Director: Brian Clay Luedloff
  Music Director: Wes Kenny
  Chorus Master/Educational Outreach: Gerald W. Holbrook
  Executive Director: Vicki Fogel Mykles
Founded: 1991
Specialized Field: Opera
Status: Non-Profit

1959
LOVLAND OPERA THEATRE
PO Box 7293
Loveland, CO 80537
Phone: 970-593-0085
e-mail: lovelandoperatheatre@gmail.com
Web Site: www.lovelandopera.org
Officers:
  President/Treasurer: Robert Hoch
  Secretary: Patrice Grant
  Vice President: Gordo McQueen
  Board Member: Lynda Beierwaltes
  Board Member: Louise Bercaw
Management:
  Executive Director: Dr Juliana Bishop Hoch
Mission: Loveland Opera Theatre was founded in 2005 by Dr. Juliana Bishop Hoch, for the purpose of bringing opera to the hearts and minds of all. LOT is a 501c3 not-for-profit opera company based in Loveland, Colorado. Dr. Hoch founded LOT to give opportunities to many talented community singers and emerging young artists in Colorado needing a venue in which to perform. LOT has provided a nurturing environment in which these local talents could learn.
Utilizes: Arrangers; Choreographers; Collaborations; Lyricists; Multimedia; Music; Sign Language Translators
Founded: 2005
Specialized Field: Opera, Theater
Status: Non-Profit
Income Sources: Donations, Funraisers, Sponsors
Season: February, June
Performs At: Rialto Theater Center, UNC in Greenley

1960
AURORA SINGERS
Palo Alto Universalist Church
505 E Charleston Road
Palo Alto, CO 94306
Phone: 650-321-4262
e-mail: dawnreyen@yahoo.com
Web Site: www.aurorasingers.net
Officers:
  President: Karen Boyd
Management:
  Director: Dawn Reyen
Mission: To bring quality music to listeners in convalescent homes or senior centers who might otherwise not be able to attend traditional live music concerts.
Utilizes: Guest Companies
Founded: 1988
Specialized Field: Choral
Status: Non-Profit
Paid Staff: 50
Income Sources: City of Aurora
Performs At: Aurora Fox Arts Center
Organization Type: Performing; Resident

Connecticut

1961
NEW ENGLAND LYRIC OPERETTA
PO Box 1007
Darien, CT 06820
Phone: 203-655-0566
Fax: 203-655-8066
Officers:
  Chairman: Stephen Pierson
Management:
  President: William H Edgerton
Mission: Performing the entire range of American and European operetta.
Utilizes: Designers; Guest Musicians; Multimedia; Original Music Scores; Resident Artists; Resident Professionals; Sign Language Translators
Founded: 1986
Specialized Field: Light Opera; Musical Theatre
Status: Non-Profit, Professional
Performs At: Rich Forum; Stauford Center for the Arts
Organization Type: Performing; Resident

1962
FAIRFIELD COUNTY CHORALE
61 Unguowa Road
Fairfield, CT 06824
Phone: 203-254-1333
Fax: 203-319-8273
e-mail: info@fairfieldcountychorale.org
Web Site: www.fairfieldcountychorale.org
Officers:
  Executive Vice President: Wanda Borges
  Treasurer: Larry Erdmann
  Secretary: Whitney Janeway
Management:
  President: Holly Wolff
  Executive Director: John Parkinson
  Artistic Director: Johannes Somary
Mission: To perform classical choral music with professional orchestra and soloists, in the manner in which the composer intended it. To present this to people living in Fairfield County, with the hope of enriching their musical lives.
Utilizes: Collaborations; Guest Accompanists; Guest Musicians; Multimedia; Music; Original Music Scores; Sign Language Translators; Singers
Founded: 1965
Specialized Field: Choral; Classical; Contemporary; Religious
Status: Non-Profit, Non-Professional
Paid Staff: 3
Paid Artists: 120
Budget: $80,000
Income Sources: Tickets; Advertisement Sales; Donations; Fund Raising
Performs At: Norwalk Concert Hall
Annual Attendance: 2,000
Facility Category: Concert Hall
Seating Capacity: 1,064
Rental Contact: City of Norwalk

1963
GREENWICH CHORAL SOCIETY
299 Greenwich Avenue
3rd floor
Greenwich, CT 06830
Mailing Address: P.O. Box 5, Greenwich, CT 06836
Phone: 203-622-5136
Fax: 203-622-8370
Web Site: www.greenwichchoralsociety.org
Officers:
  President:: Bill McCarthy
  Chairman: Roy Pfeil
  Treasurer: Fred Volkwein
  Secretary: Sharon Lemler
  Registrar: Bill Fulton
Management:
  Music Director/Conductor: Paul F Mueller
  Executive Director: Greg Wold
Mission: To offer audiences a wide variety of choral music for their enjoyment and education.
Founded: 1925
Specialized Field: Choral
Status: Nonprofit
Performs At: State University of New York at Purchase
Organization Type: Performing

1964
CONNECTICUT OPERA
226 Farmington Avenue
Hartford, CT 06105

VOCAL MUSIC / Connecticut

Phone: 860-527-0713
Fax: 860-293-1715
e-mail: info@ctopera.org
Web Site: www.ctopera.org
Officers:
  Chairman: John G Ewen
  Vice Chairman: Thomas K Standish
  President: Calvin S Price
Management:
  President: John Kreitler
  Managing Director: Linda Jackson
  Artistic Director: Willie Waters
Mission: To preserve and advance the operatic art form; to make opera accessible to a diverse population; to educate, enlighten and entertain through the medium of opera; to assist young artists, directors, designers and technicians.
Utilizes: Guest Artists; Guest Companies; Singers
Founded: 1942
Specialized Field: Grand Opera; Light Opera
Status: Non-Profit, Professional
Paid Staff: 8
Income Sources: Opera America
Performs At: Horace Bushnell Memorial Hall
Organization Type: Performing; Touring; Resident; Educational; Sponsoring

1965
THE GREATER MIDDLETOWN CHORALE
190 Court Street
Middletown, CT 06457
Phone: 860-316-4854
e-mail: info@gmchorale.org
Web Site: gmchorale.org
Management:
  Artistic Director: Joseph D'Eugenio
  Managing Director: Nancy Kelly
Mission: The Greater Middletown Chorale is committed to excellence in singing while preparing and performing choral masterworks and other outstanding choral music for all generations of listeners.
Founded: 1977

1966
CONNECTICUT CHORAL ARTISTS
90 Main Street
New Britain, CT 06051
Phone: 860-293-0567
Fax: 860-244-0073
e-mail: contact@concora.org
Web Site: www.concora.org
Officers:
  President: Matthew Schreck
  Vice President: Harold Rives
  Marketing Director: Stacy Grimaldi
Management:
  Managing Director: Christine Laird
  Development Director: Cynthia Mellon
  Artistic Director: Richard Coffey
  Executive Director: Ann L. Drinan
  Operations Director: Christine Laird
Mission: To perpetuate and perform with excellence, choral music of the highest quality for the broadest possible audience.
Utilizes: Guest Artists
Founded: 1974
Specialized Field: Choral; Classical; Contemporary; Religious
Status: Non-Profit, Professional
Paid Staff: 4
Paid Artists: 53
Budget: $300,000
Income Sources: Government; Foundations; Individuals
Affiliations: Chorus America
Organization Type: Performing; Touring; Resident; Educational

1967
GREATER NEW BRITAIN OPERA ASSOCIATION
662 E Street
New Britain, CT 06051
Phone: 860-224-2466
Fax: 860-584-9687
Management:
  General Manager: Kenneth A Larson
Mission: To offer a showcase for young artists cast in principal roles; to expose Connecticut youth to opera through work-study programs and classes.
Utilizes: Guest Artists; Guest Companies; Singers
Founded: 1976
Specialized Field: Grand Opera
Status: Professional; Nonprofit
Organization Type: Performing; Resident

1968
YALE OPERA
98 Wall Street
PO Box 208246
New Haven, CT 06520-8246
Phone: 203-432-4155
Fax: 203-432-7448
e-mail: opera.ysm@yale.edu
Web Site: music.yale.edu
Officers:
  Dean of Music/Chairman: Robert Blocker
Management:
  Artistic Director: Doris Yarick Cross
  Voice Coach: Janna Baty
  Opera Coach: Douglas Dickson
  Manager: Erika Niemi
  Song Coach: Kyle Swann
  Acting Coach: Marc Verzatt
Mission: The Yale Opera program at the Yale University School of Music, led by Artistic Director Doris Yarick Cross, has been extraordinarily successful in preparing singers for active professional careers. Graduates of the program appear on the rosters of all of the world's major opera houses, including The Metropolitan Opera, Lyric Opera of Chicago, San Francisco Opera, Santa Fe Opera, Teatro alla Scala (Milan, Italy).
Utilizes: Actors; Arrangers; Artists-in-Residence; Collaborating Artists; Collaborations; Composers-in-Residence; Dance Companies; Dancers; Educators; High School Drama; Local Artists; Local Artists & Directors; Multimedia; Music; Paid Performers; Poets
Founded: 1982
Specialized Field: Opera
Income Sources: Student Funding, Grants
Performs At: Sprague Memorial Hall, Woolsey Hall

1969
YALE RUSSIAN CHORUS
Yale Station
PO Box 202032
New Haven, CT 06520-2032
Phone: 203-432-4776
e-mail: ilyana.sawka@yale.edu
Web Site: www.yalerussianchorus.com
Officers:
  Business Manager: Stephen Bruce
Management:
  President: Ilyana Sawka
  Concert Manager: Helen Deng
  Business Manager: Andrew Schram

Artistic Director: Mark Bailey
Founded: 1953
Specialized Field: Choral

1970
YALE SCHOLA CANTORUM
Yale Institute Of Sacred Music
409 Prospect Street
New Haven, CT 06511
Phone: 203-432-9671
Fax: 203-432-9680
e-mail: dann.coakwell@yale.edu
Web Site: www.yale.edu
Management:
  External Relations Manager: Melissa Maier
  Founder and Conductor: Simon Carrington
  Conductor: Masaaki Suzuki
Mission: The Yale Schola Cantorum, founded in 2003, is a 24-voice chamber choir, specializing in music from before 1750 and from the last 100 years, supported by the Yale Institute of Sacred Music with the School of Music and open by audition to all Yale students. Simon Carrington is the group's founder and conductor. In addition to performing regularly in New Haven, New York and Boston, Schola Cantorum records and tours nationally and internationally.
Utilizes: Sign Language Translators
Founded: 2003
Specialized Field: Vocal Music
Non-paid Artists: 200

1971
CONNECTICUT CHORAL SOCIETY
PO Box 42
Southbury, CT 06488-0042
Phone: 203-206-7186
Toll-free: 888-927-2933
e-mail: info@ctchoralsociety.org
Web Site: ctchoralsociety.org
Management:
  Founder: Christopher Shay
  Conductor: Eric Dale Knapp
  Director: Bonnie Stephens
Mission: The Connecticut Choral Society, Inc. (CCS), established in 1980, is an ensemble of auditioned singers who are joined by their commitment to provide a music resource for Connecticut; to encourage singing and performing choral music of the highest artistic quality; and to stimulate greater appreciation and enjoyment of choral music.
Utilizes: Arrangers; Choreographers; Collaborating Artists; Community Members; Composers; Grant Writers; High School Drama; Multimedia; Music; Paid Performers; Sign Language Translators; Singers
Founded: 1980
Specialized Field: Choral, Concert
Status: Non-Profit, Professional
Income Sources: Donors, Sponsors, Fundraisers
Season: November, December, May
Performs At: Beacon Theater, North Church

1972
CONNECTICUT GRAND OPERA AND ORCHESTRA
307 Atlantic Street
Stamford, CT 06901
Phone: 203-327-2867
Fax: 203-327-1417
e-mail: mail@ctgrandopera.org
Web Site: www.ctgrandopera.org
Officers:
  Chairman: Robert A Wilson
  Secretary: Robert Scrofani
  Treasurer: Philip Giordano

Management:
   General Director: Laurence Gilgore
   Assistant General Manager: Ronald Land
   Comptroller: David Kent
   Director of Patron Services: Kendall Moran
   Conductor: Lawrence Gilgore
Mission: Dedicated to presenting to area residents and visitors world-class operatic and orchestral performances featuring international music talent and innovative productions.
Utilizes: Guest Artists; Guest Companies; Singers
Founded: 1993
Specialized Field: Grand Opera
Status: Non-Profit, Professional
Paid Staff: 6
Volunteer Staff: 40
Income Sources: American Guild of Musical Artists; International Association of Theatrical Stage Employees
Performs At: Palace Theatre of the Arts; Klein Auditorium
Organization Type: Performing; Resident

1973
PRO ARTE CHAMBER SINGERS OF CONNECTICUT
PO Box 4251
Stamford, CT 06905
Phone: 203-322-5970
Management:
   Managing Director: Cynthia King
Mission: Presenting the full depth of choral repertoire, ranging from medieval times to the contemporary.
Utilizes: Singers
Founded: 1974
Specialized Field: Choral
Status: Professional
Performs At: First Presbyterian Church
Organization Type: Performing; Touring

1974
SALT MARSH OPERA
65 Cutler Street
Stonington, CT 06378
Mailing Address: P.O. Box 227, Stonington, CT 06378
Phone: 860-535-3456
Toll-free: 888-788-4188
e-mail: info@saltmarshopera.org
Web Site: saltmarshopera.org
Officers:
   President: Carla M. Stebbins
   Vice President: Michele J. Delmhorst
Management:
   Artistic/General Manager: Simon D. Holt
Mission: Dedicated to producing high-quality, professional opera in Connecticut and Rhode Island and to making its productions available to the entire community. Committed to raising the awareness of opera through educational initiatives and live productions in intimate settings, Salt Marsh Opera enriches the cultural lives of our shoreline communities.
Founded: 2000
Specialized Field: Opera
Status: Professional; Nonprofit
Volunteer Staff: 100

1975
JOYFUL NOISE
Trinity Episcopal Church 220 Prospect Street
Torrington, CT 06790
Mailing Address: P.O. Box 1051, Torrington, CT 06790
Phone: 860-496-8841
e-mail: joyful.noise@snet.net
Web Site: chorusangelicus.com
Officers:
   Chair: Paul Blackman
   Vice Chair: Tom Lang
Management:
   Artistic Director: Gabriel Lofvall
Mission: To develop and nurture in singers of all ages a passion for excellence in choral singing.
Opened: 1991
Specialized Field: Children's Choir

1976
CONNECTICUT CONCERT OPERA
PO Box 370341
West Hartford, CT 06137-0341
Phone: 860-722-2300
Fax: 860-726-1839
e-mail: info@connconcertopera.org
Web Site: www.connconcertopera.org
Management:
   Artistic Director: Doris Lang Kosloff
   President: John Wadhams
   VP: Robert Merritt
Mission: To present less frequently heard operas in original language with supertitles in concert format and to expand opera opportunites in Connecticut and Western Massachusetts.
Founded: 1991
Specialized Field: Opera
Volunteer Staff: 25
Paid Artists: 30

Delaware

1977
DIAMOND STATE CHORUS OF SWEET ADELINES
42 Craig Road
Bear, DE 19701
Phone: 609-358-8995
Fax: 302-378-0935
Web Site: www.diamondstatechorus.org
Officers:
   President: Nikki Gallagher
   VP: Louisa Leipold
   Secretary: Marilyn Ferguson
   Treasurer: Lisa Blozis
Management:
   Chores Manager: Becky Diamond
   Director: Pam Nichols
Mission: Entertaining and educating the public in barber shop harmony as an American art form.
Utilizes: Singers
Founded: 1978
Specialized Field: Women's Chorus
Status: Semi-Professional; Nonprofit
Paid Staff: 50
Organization Type: Performing; Educational

1978
BELLE VOIX
PO Box 7065
Wilmington, DE 19803
Phone: 302-792-9498
Fax: 215-358-5789
Web Site: www.madrigal-singers.org
Officers:
   President: Carol Lind
   Treasurer: Dave Vallee
Management:
   Artistic Director: Jeffrey Anderson
   Accompanist: Kevin Freaney
Mission: To bring audiences great chamber choral music of all periods and genres.
Founded: 1959
Specialized Field: Choral
Status: Non-Profit
Paid Staff: 20
Organization Type: Performing; Touring; Educational

1979
GRAND YOUTH CHORUS
818 Market Street Mall
Wilmington, DE 19801
Phone: 302-658-7897
Fax: 302-652-5346
Toll-free: 800-37 -rand
e-mail: grandopera@grandopera.org
Web Site: www.grandopera.org
Officers:
   Immediate Past Chairman: Francis J. Skip" Pennella
   Chair
   Vice-Chairman: Brian DiSabatino
   Secretary: David Ley Hamilton, Esq.
   Treasurer: Richard Farmer
Management:
   Marketing Director: Cindy Frankey
   Executive Director: Stephen M. Bailey
   Controller: Barbara Kelly
   Director Of Development: Shondell Ayala
   Director Development: Jennifer Mackey
   Controller: Barbara Kelly
   Director Operations: Jamie Bowman
   Media Manager: Paige Wolf
Utilizes: Singers
Founded: 1871
Specialized Field: Classical; Opera; Classical for Young Audiences; Entertainment Chorus
Status: Professional; Nonprofit
Income Sources: 1190; 300
Performs At: 1871
Affiliations: Association of Performing Arts Presenters; League of Historic American Theatres
Annual Attendance: 1973
Year Built: Jenn
Year Remodeled: Uro
Rental Contact: 14-Jul
Organization Type: Performing; Educational; Sponsoring

1980
OPERA DELAWARE
OperaDelaware
4 South Poplar Street
Wilmington, DE 19801
Phone: 302-658-8063
Fax: 302-659-4991
e-mail: opinfo@operade.org
Web Site: www.operade.org
Officers:
   President: John W Rollins III
   Treasurer: John Rollins
   VP: Charles Platznzie
   VP: Linda O'Conner
Management:
   General Director: Brendan Cooke, jkimball@operade.org
   Director Of Development: Carin Brastow
Mission: Mission is to enrich the cultural life of people in the Deleware Valley by producing opera, educational and outreach programs.
Utilizes: Choreographers; Collaborations; Commissioned Composers; Commissioned Music; Composers-in-Residence; Designers; Educators; Grant Writers; Guest Accompanists; Guest Artists; Guest Companies; Guest Composers; Guest Conductors; Guest Designers; Guest Lecturers; Guest Musical Directors; Guest Soloists; Instructors; Local Artists;

VOCAL MUSIC / District of Columbia

Lyricists; Multimedia; Music; New Productions; Organization Contracts; Original Music Scores; Resident Professionals; Selected Students; Sign Language Translators; Singers; Student Interns; Theatre Companies; Visual Arts
Founded: 1948
Specialized Field: Grand Opera
Status: Non-Profit, Professional
Paid Staff: 3
Volunteer Staff: 30
Paid Artists: 100
Budget: $800,000
Income Sources: Delaware Division Of The Arts
Performs At: Grand Opera House
Annual Attendance: 27,000
Type of Stage: Proscenium
Stage Dimensions: 38x30
Seating Capacity: 1,100
Year Built: 1876
Year Remodeled: 1976
Organization Type: Performing; Educational

District of Columbia

1981
UNITED STATES AIR FORCE SINGING SERGEANTS
The United States Air Force Base
201 McChord Street
Bolling AFB, DC 20032-0202
Phone: 202-767-5665
Fax: 202-767-0686
e-mail: bandpublicaffairs@bolling.af.mil
Web Site: www.usafband.com
Management:
  Conductor: Moore Urrutia
  Manager: Patricia Wolfe
  Commander/Music Director: Col Dennis M Layendecker
Utilizes: Fine Artists; Guest Composers; Guest Lecturers; Guest Musical Directors; Organization Contracts; Singers
Founded: 1945
Specialized Field: Choral
Status: Non-Profit, Professional
Paid Staff: 26
Paid Artists: 25
Affiliations: Chorus America; American Choral Directors Association

1982
CATHEDRAL CHORAL SOCIETY
Washington National Cathedral
Massachusetts & Wisconsin Avenues NW
Washington, DC 20016-5098
Phone: 202-537-5527
Fax: 202-537-5648
e-mail: choralsociety@cathedral.org
Web Site: www.cathedralchoralsociety.org
Officers:
  President: Thomas Gallagher
  VP: Diana Dykstra
  Secretary: Teresa Polinski
  Treasurer: Walter Doggett
Management:
  President: Thomas Gallagher
  Interim Executive Director: Margot Young
  Music Director: J Reilly Lewis
Utilizes: Commissioned Composers; Commissioned Music; Educators; Guest Composers; Guest Directors; Guest Instructors; Guest Musical Directors; Guest Musicians; Local Artists; Multimedia; Original Music Scores; Sign Language Translators; Singers
Founded: 1942
Specialized Field: Classical; Contemporary; Religious; Choral
Status: Non-Profit, Professional
Paid Staff: 3
Paid Artists: 3
Non-paid Artists: 130
Budget: $1,044,400
Performs At: Washington National Cathedral
Affiliations: Chorus America; Cultural Alliance of Greater Washington
Annual Attendance: 23,626
Facility Category: Cathedral
Seating Capacity: 1618
Year Built: 1907

1983
THE CHORAL ARTS SOCIETY OF WASHINGTON
5225 Wisconsin Avenue NW
Suite 603
Washington, DC 20015-2024
Phone: 202-244-3669
Fax: 202-244-4244
e-mail: choralarts@choralarts.org
Web Site: www.choralarts.org
Officers:
  Chairman: Diane Schaefer
  Vice Chairman: Nicholas R. Smith
  Secretary: Tiffany Gates
  Special Advisor & Counsel: Laura S. Pruitt
  Immediate Past Chairman: Barbara M. Rossotti
  Immediate Past Chair: Anne Keiser
  Board Member: Tiffany Gates
  Board Member: Anne Hatfield
Management:
  Artistic Director: Scott Tucker
  Executive Director: Debra Kraft
  Artistic Director Emeritus: Norman Scribner
  Development Director: Patricia Kramer
  Marketing Director/Public Relations: Dianna Hosack
Mission: Choral Arts is one of the major choral organizations in the United States. Founded by Norman Scribner in 1965, Choral Arts is pleased to welcome Artistic Director Scott Tucker. Choral Arts presents its symphonic chorus of over 180 professional-caliber volunteer singers in an annual season subscription series at The John F. Kennedy Center for the Performing Arts and other DC-area venues.
Utilizes: Arrangers; Artists-in-Residence; Choreographers; Collaborating Artists; Collaborations; Composers; Composers-in-Residence; Guest Designers; High School Drama; Multimedia; Music; Paid Performers; Sign Language Translators; Singers
Founded: 1965
Specialized Field: Choral, Concert
Status: Non-Profit, Professional
Income Sources: Donors, Sponsors, Fundraisers
Season: October through May
Performs At: Kennedy Center Concert Hall, The George Washington University Lisner Auditorium

1984
CHORAL ARTS SOCIETY OF WASHINGTON
5225 Wisconsin Avenue NW
Suite 603
Washington, DC 20015-2024
Phone: 202-244-3669
Fax: 202-244-4244
e-mail: choralarts@choralarts.org
Web Site: www.choralarts.org
Officers:
  Chairman: Diane Schaefer
  Vice Chairman: Nicholas R. Smith
  Secretary: Tiffany Gates
  Special Advisor & Counsel: Laura S. Pruitt
  Immediate Past Chairman: Barbara M. Rossotti
  Immediate Past Chair: Anne Keiser
  General Counsel: David Brown
  Vice Chair: Cinnie Fehr
Management:
  Artistic Director: Scott Tucker
  Executive Director: Debra Kraft
  Artistic Director Emeritus: Norman Scribner
  Development Director: Patricia Kramer
  Chorus President: Jim McHugh
  Associate Conductor: Joseph Holt
  Director Comm./Education Programs: Alicia Mills
Mission: Committed to the highest standards of excellence in its programming and performance.
Utilizes: Collaborations; Commissioned Music; Guest Artists; Guest Companies; Guest Composers; Guest Directors; Guest Instructors; Guest Lecturers; Guest Musicians; Multi Collaborations; Organization Contracts; Selected Students; Sign Language Translators; Singers; Soloists
Founded: 1965
Specialized Field: Choral
Status: Non-Profit, Professional
Paid Staff: 10
Non-paid Artists: 190
Budget: $2,000,000
Income Sources: Individual Donors; Corporate; Government and Foundation Grants; Gifts
Performs At: John F. Kennedy Center for the Performing Arts
Affiliations: Kennedy Center; Chorus America
Annual Attendance: 17,500
Type of Stage: Concert Hall
Organization Type: Performing; Resident

1985
CHORUS AMERICA
1156 15th Street NW
Suite 310
Washington, DC 20005
Mailing Address: P.O. Box 2646, Arlington, VA 22202-0646
Phone: 202-331-7577
Fax: 202-331-7599
e-mail: webmaster@chorusamerica.org
Web Site: www.chorusamerica.org
Officers:
  Chairman: Gayle M. Ober
  Chairman-Elect: Rollo Dilworth
  Treasurer: Michael McCarthy
  Secretary: Catherine Peterson
Management:
  President & CEO: Ann Meier Baker
  Office Manager: Adam Hall
  Director of Communications: Liza W. Beth
  Director of Operations & Membership: Catherine Davies
  Director of Development: Catherine Dehoney
Mission: To promote the high quality and artistic growth of vocal ensembles; to stimulate further development of remuneration for singers; to encourage greater understanding, appreciation and enjoyment of choral music by all segments of society.
Utilizes: Artists-in-Residence; Collaborating Artists; Collaborations; Commissioned Composers; Commissioned Music; Composers-in-Residence; Educators; Guest Companies; Guest Soloists; Sign Language Translators
Founded: 1977

VOCAL MUSIC / District of Columbia

Specialized Field: Choral
Status: Non-Profit, Non-Professional
Paid Staff: 8
Volunteer Staff: 2

1986
GAY MEN'S CHORUS OF WASHINGTON
2000 P Street NW
Suite 730
Washington, DC 20036
Phone: 202-293-1548
Fax: 202-293-0512
e-mail: info@gmcw.org
Web Site: www.gmcw.org
Officers:
  Chairman: Greg Kubiak
  Vice Chairman: Charlie Beredesco
  Secretary: Rob Hall
  Treasurer: Phillip Carson
  Choral President: Marcus Brown
Management:
  Artistic Director: Jeff Buhrman, artisticdirector@gmcw.org
  Executive Director: David Jobin, executivedirector@gmcw.org
  Associate Music Director: Dr Thea Kano
  Choreographer: Craig Cipollini
  Marketing Director: Taunee Grant
Mission: Now celebrating its 30th Anniversary season, the mission of the Gay Men's Chorus of Washington, DC is to entertain through excellent musical performance, to affirm the place of gay people in society and to educate about the gay experience.
Utilizes: Arrangers; Artists-in-Residence; Choreographers; Collaborating Artists; Collaborations; Dance Companies; Dancers; Fine Artists; Guest Ensembles; High School Drama; Multimedia; Music; Paid Performers; Sign Language Translators; Singers; Special Technical Talent
Founded: 1981
Specialized Field: Chorus
Status: Non-Profit
Income Sources: Fundraisers, Donors, Corporate Sponsors
Season: Year Round

1989
OPERA CAMERATA OF WASHINGTON
1819 Shepherd Street NW
Suite 100
Washington, DC 20011
Phone: 202-386-6008
Fax: 202-291-0877
e-mail: OCW@operacamerata.org
Web Site: www.operacamerata.org
Officers:
  President: Randall Roe
  Secretary: Rafael Prieto
Management:
  Artistic Director/Conductor: Gregory Buchalter
  Chairman/Executive Director: Michael J Reilly
Mission: Production of Opera/Operetta rarities, infrequently produced great works.
Founded: 1990
Specialized Field: Opera; Operetta
Volunteer Staff: 25
Budget: $70,000

1990
OPERA MUSIC THEATER INTERNATIONAL
1201 Pennsylvania Avenue NW
Suite 300
Washington, DC 20004
Phone: 202-683-7874
Fax: 202-661-4699
e-mail: info@omti.org
Web Site: www.omti.org
Officers:
  President: James K McCully
Management:
  General Director: James K McCully
Mission: To showcase multi-cultural opera and music theater performances to draw the diverse DC region together through music.
Specialized Field: Opera; Musical Theatre

1991
SUMMER OPERA THEATRE COMPANY
Music School- CUA
620 Michigan Avenue NE
Washington, DC 20064
Phone: 202-526-1669
Fax: 202-319-5433
Web Site: www.summeropera.org
Officers:
  Chairman: Leilana G Mehler
  Vice Chairman and Dev. Chairman: Elizabeth C Sara
  Secretary: Jaqueline Havener
  Treasurer: Helen Toomey
  Membership Chairman: Mary Frances Lombard
  Board/Staff Liaison: F. Victoria Tresansky
Management:
  General Manager: Deanne Giarraputo
  Artistic Director: Elaine R Walter
Mission: To seek, promote and present young artists ready for work with major opera and musical theatre companies; to offer more established artists the opportunity to prepare and perform new roles.
Utilizes: Guest Artists; Singers
Founded: 1978
Specialized Field: Opera; Musical Theatre
Status: Non-Profit, Professional
Paid Staff: 4
Volunteer Staff: 4
Paid Artists: 200
Budget: $750,000
Income Sources: Private Donations/ Grants/ Box Office
Performs At: The Hartke Theatre
Annual Attendance: 5,900
Facility Category: Theatre
Organization Type: Performing; Resident; Educational

1992
THE CITY CHOIR OF WASHINGTON
PO Box 9673
Washington, DC 20016
Phone: 202-495-1613
e-mail: info@thecitychoirofwashington.org
Web Site: www.thecitychoirofwashington.org
Officers:
  President: Carol Green Edison
  Vice President: Shelley Stewart
  Secretary/Counsel: David Robinson
  Treasurer: Geoffrey Kaiser
  General Manager: Margaret Hemingway
  Board Member: Peter Bonner
  Board Member: Cindy Carlton
  Board Member: Michele Casey
Management:
  Artistic Director: Robert Shafer
  Executive Director: Ann Stahmer
  Assistant Conductor: Brian Bartoldus
  Choral President: Andrea Diggs
  Choral Vice President: William Doepkens
Mission: Critics and audiences alike have praised The City Choir of Washington and its Artistic Director Robert Shafer for consistently beautiful choral tone, clear diction, and exquisite attention to musical detail. The City Choir has performed with The National Symphony and The Washington National Opera Orchestra at The Kennedy Center and at Wolf Trap Park for the Performing Arts under the batons of Stephen Lord, Randall Craig Fleischer and L Wicki.
Utilizes: Arrangers; Choreographers; Collaborating Artists; Collaborations; Community Talent; Guest Companies; Lyricists; Multimedia; Music; Paid Performers; Sign Language Translators; Singers
Specialized Field: Choral
Status: Non-Profit, Professional
Income Sources: Donors, Sponsors
Season: October, December, April
Performs At: Washington National Cathedral

1993
VOCAL ARTS SOCIETY
1818 24th Street NW
Washington, DC 20008
Mailing Address: PO Box 42423 , Washington, DC 20015
Phone: 202-669-1463
Fax: 202-265-7164
e-mail: info@vocalartsdc.org
Web Site: www.vocalartsdc.org
Officers:
  President: Gerald Perman
  Chair Board of Director: Martha Ellison
  Treasurer: Ernest Hamel
  Secretary: Mary Lynne McElroy
Management:
  President: Gerald Perman
  Executive Director: William O Wears
  General Director: Peter Russell
Mission: To promote the classical recital and bring to the Greater Washington area the finest vocals artists in programs of the great and largely underpreformed song literature.
Founded: 1990
Specialized Field: Choral; Classical
Status: Non-Profit, Professional
Paid Staff: 1
Paid Artists: 22
Budget: $170,000
Income Sources: Board/Audience Contributions; Foundation Grants
Performs At: Terrace Theater of the Kennedy Center; French Embassy
Annual Attendance: 3,600
Facility Category: Recital Hall
Seating Capacity: 475; 800

1994
WASHINGTON BACH CONSORT
1010 Vermont Avenue, NW
Suite 202
Washington, DC 20005
Phone: 202-429-2121
Fax: 202-429-2269
e-mail: info@bachconsort.org
Web Site: www.bachconsort.org
Officers:
  Treasurer: Charles Reifel
  Secretary: David Condit
  Bloomberg Government: Sandra Baer
Management:
  President: Charles Kinney
  Executive Director: Marc Eisenberg
  Music Director: J Reilly Lewis
  External Affairs Manager: Janey Moskowitz

VOCAL MUSIC / District of Columbia

Patron Services Manage: Janet Mullany
Mission: Perform to the highest artistic standards the music of JS Bach and his Baroque contemporaries. Expand our audience through concerts, collaborations with other performing ensembles, media appearances, marketable recordings, and tours. Promote current and future appreciation of Bach in our community through compelling music education programs presented by members of the Consort.
Founded: 1977
Specialized Field: Choral; Classical
Status: Non-Profit, Professional
Paid Staff: 6
Paid Artists: 40
Organization Type: Performing; Touring; Educational

1995
WASHINGTON CHORUS
2801 Upton Street, NW
Washington, DC 20008
Phone: 202-342-6221
Fax: 202-342-8208
e-mail: staff@thewashingtonchorus.org
Web Site: www.thewashingtonchorus.org
Officers:
   Chorus/Outreach Administrator: Deborah Paez
   Chairman: Thayer Baine
   Vice Chairman: Donald Borut
   Secretary: Kara Morrissey
   Treasurer: Dennis A. Kernahan
Management:
   Music Director: Julian Wachner
   Executive Director: Dianne Peterson
   Assistant Conductor: John Bradford Bohl
   Manager of Chorus Operations: Amy Lipstein
   Director of Development: Rachel Niehoff
Mission: The Washington Chorus shares, preserves and advances the art of choral singing to help expirence the transforming power od choral music.
Utilizes: Commissioned Music; Guest Accompanists; Guest Musical Directors; Guest Musicians; Multimedia; Original Music Scores; Selected Students; Sign Language Translators; Singers
Founded: 1961
Specialized Field: Choral
Paid Staff: 8
Non-paid Artists: 200
Budget: $807,000
Income Sources: Individual; Foundation; Corporate & Government Support; Ticket Sales
Performs At: Kennedy Center Concert Hall
Annual Attendance: 25,000
Facility Category: Concert Hall

1996
WASHINGTON CONCERT OPERA
1808Connecticut Avenue NW
Suite 101
Washington, DC 20009
Phone: 202-364-5826
Fax: 202-364-5836
e-mail: info@concertopera.org
Web Site: www.concertopera.org
Management:
   Artistic Director/ Conductor: Anthony Walker
   Executive Director: Judy Gruber
   Administrative Manager: Vincent Deschamps
   Production Manager: Peggy Dahlquist
   Orchestra Contractor: Pamela Lassell
Specialized Field: Opera
Performs At: Kennedy Center Concert Hall

1997
WASHINGTON NATIONAL OPERA
2700 F Street, NW
Washington, DC 20566
Phone: 202-467-4600
Fax: 202-295-2479
Toll-free: 800-444-1324
e-mail: info@dc-opera.org
Web Site: www.dc-opera.org
Officers:
   Founding Chairman: Roger L. Stevens
   Board of Trustees, Life Chairperson: Mrs. Eugene B Casey
   Chairperson: David M. Rubenstein
   Chair of the Executive Committee: Mrs. Cristine F Hunter
Management:
   President: Michael M. Kaiser
   Executive Director: Blair Caple
   Artistic Director: Placido Domingo
   Music Director, NSO and Kennedy Cen: Christoph Eschenbach
Mission: To provide highest quality opera; to broaden public awareness and understanding of opera through education and community programming; to support development of young American singers; to encourage work of new composers to maintain opera as a living art form.
Utilizes: Guest Artists; Guest Companies; Singers
Founded: 1956
Specialized Field: Opera
Status: For-Profit, Professional
Paid Staff: 60
Volunteer Staff: 150
Budget: $30,000,000
Income Sources: Box Office; Grants; Private Donations
Performs At: John F. Kennedy Center for the Performing Arts
Affiliations: OPERA America; Washington Opera Guild/Edcuational
Annual Attendance: 135,500
Type of Stage: Open Stage; Proscenium
Seating Capacity: 2,200
Organization Type: Performing; Resident; Educational

1998
WASHINGTON SAVOYARDS
1333 H Street NE
Washington, DC 20002
Phone: 202-399-7993
Fax: 202-399-7993
e-mail: savoyards@savoyards.org
Web Site: www.savoyards.org
Officers:
   President: Ian Grossman
   Vice President: Chris Agan
   Treasurer: Alan Ammerman
   Secretary: Angela Ammerman
   Board Member: James Dean
   Board Member: Christopher Lerbs
   Board Member: Elizabeth Jenkins McFadden
   Advisor: Taylor Wells
Management:
   Artistic Director: N Thomas Pederson
   Associate Artistic Director: Matthew Kacergis
   Staff Associate: John Dellaporta
   Director: Jay D Brock
   Music Director: Jason Solounias
   Choreographer: Christen Svingos
Mission: Founded in 1972, Washington Savoyards spent its early years in Montgomery County, and enjoyed many seasons at the Duke Ellington Theatre in Georgetown performing the works of Gilbert & Sullivan. Now in residence at the Atlas Performing Arts Center, we are dedicated to bringing professional Musical Theatre to the Washington community.
Utilizes: Arrangers; Choreographers; Collaborating Artists; Composers; Designers; Equity Actors; Local Artists & Directors; Multimedia; Music; Paid Performers; Special Technical Talent
Founded: 1972
Specialized Field: Musical Theater
Status: Non-Profit
Income Sources: Donors, Sponsors
Season: Mid-October through November
Performs At: Atlas Performing Arts Center

1999
CRUISERS
617 Warrington Avenue SE
Washington Navy Yard, DC 20374-5054
Phone: 202-433-6090
Fax: 202-433-4108
e-mail: navyband.public.affairs@navy.mil
Web Site: www.navyband.navy.mil
Officers:
   Contracting Officer: Michael A. Curtis
   Recieving Officer: Michael M. Shelburne
   Operations Chief: William P. Gray
   Facilities Engineer: Stephen W. Hassey
   Supply Chief: Trent R. Turner
Management:
   Head Music Librarian: Amy M. Smith
   Head Arranger: Scott A. Silbert
   Staff Arranger: Timothy A. Hill
   Facilities Director: Stephen W. Hassey
Mission: To provide music for such ceremonies, functions and other occasions as may be directed by proper authority in order to best represent the Navy in a musical capacity at the seat of government and elsewhere as directed.
Founded: 1999
Specialized Field: Contemporary
Organization Type: Performing; Touring

2000
SEA CHANTERS
617 Warrington Avenue SE
Washington Navy Yard, DC 20374-5054
Phone: 202-433-3676
Fax: 202-433-4108
e-mail: navyband.public.affairs@navy.mil
Web Site: www.navyband.navy.mil
Officers:
   Contracting Officer: Michael A. Curtis
   Recieving Officer: Michael M. Shelburne
   Operations Chief: William P. Gray
   Facilities Engineer: Stephen W. Hassey
   Supply Chief: Trent R. Turner
Management:
   Head Music Librarian: Amy M. Smith
   Head Arranger: Scott A. Silbert
   Staff Arranger: Timothy A. Hill
   Facilities Director: Stephen W. Hassey
Mission: To provide music for such ceremonies, functions and other occasions as may be directed by proper authority in order to best represent the Navy in a musical capacity at the seat of government and elsewhere as directed.
Founded: 1925
Specialized Field: Traditional Choral Music; Sea Chanteys; Broadway Musicals
Organization Type: Performing; Touring

VOCAL MUSIC / Florida

2001
US NAVY BAND
617 Warrington Avenue SE
Washington Navy Yard, DC 20374-5054
Phone: 202-433-3366
Fax: 202-433-4108
e-mail: navyband.public.affairs@navy.mil
Web Site: www.navyband.navy.mil
Officers:
  Contracting Officer: Michael A. Curtis
  Recieving Officer: Michael M. Shelburne
  Operations Chief: William P. Gray
  Facilities Engineer: Stephen W. Hassey
  Supply Chief: Trent R. Turner
Management:
  Head Music Librarian: Amy M. Smith
  Head Arranger: Scott A. Silbert
  Staff Arranger: Timothy A. Hill
  Facilities Director: Stephen W. Hassey
Mission: To provide music for such ceremonies, functions and other occasions as may be directed by proper authority in order to best represent the Navy in a musical capacity at the seat of government and elsewhere as directed.
Founded: 1925
Specialized Field: Choral
Status: For-Profit, Professional
Paid Staff: 172
Paid Artists: 172
Organization Type: Performing; Touring

Florida

2002
PICCOLO OPERA COMPANY
24 Del Rio Boulevard
Boca Raton, FL 33432-4734
Fax: 561-394-0520
Toll-free: 800-282-3161
e-mail: leejon51@msn.com
Officers:
  Board: Harold Pinales
  Board: Barbara Goldstein
  Secretary: Merry Silber
  Treasurer: M Gordon
Management:
  Executive Director: Marjorie Gordon
Mission: To present opera in English to adults and youngsters with local orchestras, chorus, dancers, or with piano.
Utilizes: Commissioned Music; Music
Founded: 1963
Specialized Field: Opera
Status: Nonprofit, Professional
Budget: $10,000-$50,000
Income Sources: Performances; Grants to Sponsors
Performs At: Varied
Affiliations: Touring Company
Organization Type: Travelling troupe

2003
GOLD COAST OPERA
1420 North Swinton Avenue
Delray Beach, FL 33444
Phone: 561-276-8085
Fax: 561-276-8740
e-mail: sunsetet@aol.com
Web Site: www.goldcoastopera.com
Officers:
  President-Gold Coast Opera, Inc: Joan Readding
  Secretary-Gold Coast Opera, Inc: Salvatore Cordini
Management:
  Operations Director: Dr Joseph Ferrer
  Artistic Director/Conductor: Dr Thomas Cavendish
Mission: To offer the South Florida residents from Ft. Pierce to Ft. Lauderdale fully staged operatic masterpieces using the finest talent from Europe and North America.
Utilizes: Guest Companies; Singers
Founded: 1979
Specialized Field: Opera
Status: Professional; Nonprofit
Paid Staff: 10
Budget: $458,000,000
Income Sources: Tickets Sales, Grants and Contributions
Performs At: theaters in Ft. Pierce, Palm Beach Gardens, Boca Raton, Coral Springs, and Ft. Lauderdale
Organization Type: Performing; Touring; Educational

2004
OPERA GUILD
221 SW 3rd Avenue
Fort Lauderdale, FL 33312-7120
Phone: 954-728-9700
Fax: 954-728-9702
Toll-free: 800-741-1010
e-mail: info@fgo.org
Web Site: www.fgo.org
Officers:
  Chairperson: William K. Hill, Esq.
  Vice Chairperson: Arlene H. Mendelson
  Immediate Past Chairperson: Jane A. Robinson
  Chairperson Elect: Charles E. Porter
  Immediate Past President: Victor H. Mendelson
Management:
  Executive Director: Patrick Flynn
  Artistic Director: Stewart Robinson
  General Director / CEO: Susan T. Danis
  Managing Director: Kevin Mynatt
Mission: Promoting opera and the newer performing arts.
Utilizes: Guest Artists; Guest Companies
Founded: 1944
Specialized Field: Opera
Status: Non-Profit, Professional
Income Sources: Junior Opera Guild/Children's
Performs At: Broward Center for the Performing Arts
Organization Type: Touring

2005
FLORIDA GRAND OPERA
8390 NW 25th Street
Miami, FL 33122
Phone: 305-854-1643
Fax: 305-856-1042
Toll-free: 800-741-1010
e-mail: info@fgo.org
Officers:
  Head of Young Artist Studio: John Keene
Management:
  General Director: Susan Davis
  Managing Director: Kevin Mynatt
  Artistic Administrator: Cassidy Fitzpatrick
  Music Director: Ramon Tebar
Utilizes: Commissioned Composers; Commissioned Music; Composers; Composers-in-Residence; Contract Actors; Contract Orchestras; Educators; Grant Writers; Guest Artists; Guest Composers; Guest Conductors; Guest Designers; Guest Instructors; Guest Soloists; Guest Speakers; Guest Writers; Original Music Scores; Poets; Resident Artists; Resident Companies; Sign Language Translators
Specialized Field: Opera
Budget: 10,000,000

2006
HISPANIC-AMERICAN LYRICAL THEATRE, INC
9130 SW 123 Avenue Court
Miami, FL 33186-7185
Phone: 305-596-5352
e-mail: mattoxg@bellsouth.com
Web Site: www.haltheatre.com
Management:
  Executive Director: George Maddox
Mission: Since it was established in 1987 the Hispanic-American Lyric Theatre has been committed to providing young professional artists in the field of Opera and Ballet, performing opportunities and financial assistance in Miami-Dade. Our performances have also provided cultural awareness of the Zarzuela (Spanish Lyric Theatre) which is very popular in Spain and Latin America.
Utilizes: Arrangers; Artists-in-Residence; Choreographers; Collaborating Artists; Collaborations; Dance Companies; Dancers; Fine Artists; Lyricists; Multimedia; Music; Paid Performers
Founded: 1987
Specialized Field: Opera, Ballet
Status: Non-Profit
Income Sources: Donations, Sponsors, Fundraisers
Performs At: Colony Theater, Mary Alper Jewish Community Center, Manuel Artime Theater

2007
ORLANDO OPERA
1111 N Orange Avenue
Orlando, FL 32804
Phone: 407-426-1717
Fax: 407-426-1705
Toll-free: 800-336-7372
Web Site: www.orlandoopera.org
Officers:
  President/CEO: James D. Ireland, Jr.
  Director Public Relations: Celeste Hart
Management:
  General Director: Robert Swedberg
  Music Director: Robin Stamper
  Production Director: Elizabeth Sutton
Utilizes: Guest Artists; Guest Companies; Sign Language Translators; Singers; Student Interns; Visual Arts
Founded: 1958
Specialized Field: Grand Opera; Light Opera; Youth Chorus; Classical
Status: Non-Profit, Professional
Paid Staff: 18
Paid Artists: 30
Income Sources: Opera America
Performs At: Bob Carr Performing Arts Center
Organization Type: Performing

2008
CHORAL SOCIETY OF PENSACOLA
1000 College Boulevard
Room 803
Pensacola, FL 32504
Phone: 850-484-1806
Fax: 850-484-1835
e-mail: csop1@juno.com
Web Site: www.choralsocietyofpensacola.com
Management:
  President: Ivy Modjeski
  Executive Director: Andy Metzger
  Artistic Director: Xiaolun Chen
  Orchestra Personnel Manager: Dale Riegle

VOCAL MUSIC / Florida

Accompanist: Ila Brown
Mission: The performance of choral literature.
Founded: 1935
Specialized Field: Choral
Status: Non-Profit, Non-Professional
Paid Staff: 4
Paid Artists: 25
Income Sources: Arts Council of North West Florida; Chorus America; Florida Cultural Action Alliance
Performs At: Saenger Theatre; Cokesbury United Methodist Church
Organization Type: Performing; Resident

2009
PENSACOLA OPERA
75 South Tarragona St.
Pensacola, FL 32502
Mailing Address: P.O. Box 1790, Pensacola, FL 32501-1790
Phone: 850-433-6737
Fax: 850-433-1082
e-mail: morgan@pensacolaopera.com
Web Site: www.pensacolaopera.com
Officers:
- **Chairman:** Ruth Orth
- **Vice-Chairman:** Nigel Allen
- **Secretary:** Lois Benson
- **Treasurer:** Perry Palmer

Management:
- **Artistic Director:** Kyle Marrero
- **Business Manager/Dir Of Development:** Erin Sammis
- **Executive Director:** Erin Kelley Sammis
- **Director of Education & Community O:** Chandra Egger McKern
- **Special Events & Marketing Manager:** Morgan Cole

Mission: The mission of Pensacola Opera is to enrich the culture of Northwest Florida by producing professional opera performances, educational programs and other opera related community events for people of all ages, interests and backgrounds.
Utilizes: Artists-in-Residence; Choreographers; Commissioned Composers; Commissioned Music; Dance Companies; Dancers; Designers; Educators; Grant Writers; Guest Accompanists; Guest Artists; Guest Composers; Guest Conductors; Guest Designers; Guest Ensembles; Guest Instructors; Guest Lecturers; Guest Musical Directors; Guest Musicians; Guest Soloists; Guest Writers; High School Drama; Instructors; Multimedia; Music; New Productions; Original Music Scores; Resident Professionals; Sign Language Translators; Singers; Student Interns; Visual Arts
Founded: 1983
Specialized Field: Opera
Status: Non-Profit, Professional
Paid Staff: 5
Volunteer Staff: 15
Paid Artists: 75
Non-paid Artists: 40
Budget: $1,130,000
Income Sources: Ticket Sales; Public and Private Contributions; Other Income
Performs At: Vaudeville Era Theater
Affiliations: OPERA America
Annual Attendance: 12,000
Facility Category: Performing
Type of Stage: Proscenium
Stage Dimensions: 71' X 38'
Seating Capacity: 1,650
Year Built: 1925
Year Remodeled: 2009
Cost: $15 Million

2010
KEY CHORALE
PO Box 20613
Sarasota, FL 34276
Phone: 941-921-4845
e-mail: info@keychorale.org
Web Site: keychorale.org
Officers:
- **President:** Peter Gray
- **Vice President:** Richard Lilley
- **Secretary:** Nancy Yost Olson
- **Treasurer:** Nancy Morris

Management:
- **Artistic Director:** Joseph Caulkins
- **Accompanist:** Nancy Yost Olson
- **Core Singer:** Meagan Schmidt
- **Core Singer:** Glenn Breitzig
- **Core Singer:** Patricia Eastep

Mission: Key Chorale is dedicated to performing and promoting choral music of the highest quality. Located in Sarasota, the Chorale was founded in 1985 by Ann Stephenson-Moe, Organist and Choirmaster of the Church of the Redeemer and Don B. Ryno, Minister of Music at St. Boniface Church. This past season, Reaching Out, took the Chorale as far north as St. Petersburg, south to Venice, and east to Miami.
Utilizes: Arrangers; Artists-in-Residence; Choreographers; Collaborating Artists; Collaborations; Composers; Composers-in-Residence; Grant Writers; Local Unknown Artists; Lyricists; Multimedia; Music; Paid Performers; Sign Language Translators; Singers
Founded: 1985
Specialized Field: Choral
Status: Non-Profit, Professional
Income Sources: Sponsors, Donations
Season: August, January
Performs At: First Congretional Church

2011
SARASOTA OPERA ASSOCIATION
61 N Pineapple Avenue
Sarasota, FL 34236
Phone: 941-366-8450
Fax: 941-955-5571
Toll-free: 888-673-7212
e-mail: info@sarasotaopera.org
Web Site: www.sarasotaopera.org
Officers:
- **Chairman:** Donald Worthington
- **Vice Chairman:** David Chaifetz
- **Treasurer:** Jack Wright
- **Secretary:** Murray Bring

Management:
- **Artistic Administrator:** Greg Trupiano
- **Youth Opera Music Director:** Jesse Martins
- **Technical Director:** Jeff Ellis
- **House Manager:** Chris Burtless
- **Assistant Technical Director:** Joel Cheatham

Mission: To continue to bring quality opera to our community and to showcase it in our own opera house; to educate the general community in an appreciation of opera and send our outreach programs into the schools of both Manatee and Sarasota counties; to offer statewide touring programs.
Utilizes: Guest Artists; Guest Companies; Singers
Founded: 1959
Specialized Field: Grand Opera; Light Opera; Lyric Opera; Musical Theatre; Choral; Youth Chorus; Classical
Status: Non-Profit, Professional
Paid Staff: 25
Paid Artists: 100
Income Sources: Opera America; Central Opera Service; American Guild of Musical Artists
Performs At: Sarasota Opera House
Organization Type: Performing; Educational; Sponsoring

2012
ST.PETERSBURG OPERA COMPANY
P.O. Box 238
St.Petersburg, FL 33731
Phone: 727-823-2040
e-mail: office@stpeteopera.org
Web Site: stpeteopera.org
Officers:
- **Board President:** Tom McCandless
- **Vice President:** Alfred T. May

Mission: The main focus of SPO's mission is to provide stimulating artistic challenges in a professional setting for opera performers in various stages of their development.
Specialized Field: Opera
Status: Professional
Performs At: Palladium Theater, St.Petersburg, Florida
Seating Capacity: 880

2013
FLORIDA STATE OPERA AT FLORIDA STATE UNIVERSITY
School Of Music
002 Hmu
Tallahassee, FL 32306-1180
Phone: 850-645-4903
Fax: 850-644-2566
e-mail: opera@cmr.fsu.edu
Web Site: www.music.fsu.edu
Officers:
- **President, Florida State University:** Eric Barron
- **Dean, College of Music:** Don Gibson

Management:
- **Director Opera Activities:** Douglas Fisher
- **Production Manager:** June Dollar
- **Technical Director:** James Meade
- **Stage Director/Professor Opera:** Matthew Lata

Mission: Providing training for students at Florida State University; serving as a quality cultural resource.
Utilizes: Choreographers; Composers-in-Residence; Designers; Educators; Guest Artists; Guest Companies; Guest Conductors; Guest Designers; Local Artists; Resident Professionals; Singers
Founded: 1963
Specialized Field: Grand Opera; Lyric Opera; Operetta; Musical Theatre
Status: Semi-Professional; Nonprofit
Paid Staff: 10
Volunteer Staff: 200
Performs At: Ruby Diamond Auditorium; Opperman Music Hall
Affiliations: National Opera Association; Central Opera Service; TOG
Organization Type: Performing

2014
MASTER CHORALE OF TAMPA BAY
3755 USF Holly Drive
Suite 102
Tampa, FL 33620
Mailing Address: 30382 USF Holly Drive, Tampa, FL 33620-3038
Phone: 813-974-7726
Fax: 813-258-0988
e-mail: mchorale@tampabay.rr.com
Web Site: www.masterchorale.com
Officers:
- **Chairman:** Robert B Hicks

VOCAL MUSIC / Georgia

Operations Manager: Sandy Ray
Treasurer: David Ezell
Secretary: Elena Richter
Vice Chairman: James B. Heck, Ph.D.
Management:
 Executive Director: Bill Faucett
 Operations Manager: Sandy Ray
 Music and Artistic Director: Dr. James K. Bass
 Project Manager: Jason Burke
 Director of Operations: Kara Dwyer
Mission: To enrich the community by performing and sustaining high quality choral music.
Utilizes: Guest Musical Directors; Organization Contracts
Founded: 1979
Specialized Field: Choral
Status: Non-Profit, Non-Professional
Paid Staff: 4
Paid Artists: 125

2015
SPANISH LYRIC THEATER
2819 Safe Harbor Drive
Tampa, FL 33548
Phone: 813-936-0217
Fax: 813-936-0217
e-mail: jcgonzalez@spanishlyrictheatre.com
Web Site: www.spanishlyrictheatre.com
Officers:
 President/CEO: Thomas P. Keating
Management:
 Founder/Artistic Director: Rene Gonzalez
 Touring Production Manager: Juan Carlos Gonzalez
Founded: 1959
Specialized Field: Light Opera; Lyric Opera; Musical Theatre; Ethnic Music; Classical; Contemporary
Status: Non-Profit, Professional
Paid Staff: 1
Paid Artists: 200
Performs At: Tampa Bay Performing Arts Center

2016
VERO BEACH OPERA INC
PO Box 6912
Vero Beach, FL 32961
Phone: 772-569-5537
e-mail: information@verabeachopera.org
Web Site: verobeachopera.org
Management:
 Artistic Director: Roman Ortega Cowan
 Opera Studies Chair: Wayne Kleinstiver
Mission: Promote, support, professionally produce, present and advance the art of Grand Opera in the community.
Utilizes: Collaborating Artists; Collaborations; Composers; Contract Orchestras; Multimedia; Sign Language Translators; Special Technical Talent
Specialized Field: Opera, Theater
Status: Non-Profit
Income Sources: Donors, Sponsors
Affiliations: Vera Beach Museum of Art

2017
PALM BEACH OPERA
415 S Olive Avenue
West Palm Beach, FL 33401
Phone: 561-833-7888
Fax: 561-833-8294
e-mail: info@pbopera.org
Web Site: www.pbopera.org
Officers:
 Chairman: Dennis Williams
 Vice-Chairman: Sanford H. Fisher
 Vice-Chairman: John J. Raymond
 Vice-President: Helen K. Persson
 Vice-President: Gladys Benenson
Management:
 General Director: Daniel Biaggi
 Managing Director: Greg Hirsch
 Director of Artistic Operations: Scott Guzielek
 Assistant Conductor & Chorus Master: Greg Ritchey
 Company Manager: Katy Reeves
Mission: Dedicated to producing world-class opera and diverse educational programs which play an integral role ni the artistiv and overall enrichment of the communities it serves.
Founded: 1961
Specialized Field: Opera
Status: Non-Profit, Professional
Paid Staff: 25
Volunteer Staff: 5
Paid Artists: 120
Performs At: Kravis Center for the Performing Arts
Organization Type: Performing; Touring; Resident; Educational

---
Georgia

2018
ADRIAN SYMPHONY ORCHESTRA
1280 Peachtree Street NE
Atlanta, GA 30309-3552
Phone: 404-733-4900
Fax: 517-264-3121
e-mail: aso-info@woodruffcenter.org
Web Site: www.aso.org
Officers:
 Co-Chair: Robert Bell
 Co-Chair: Muriel Bell
Management:
 Music Director: Robert Spano
 Executive Director: Susan Hoffman
 Principal Guest Conductor: Donald Runnicles
 Producer: Jimmy Hilburger
 Principal Pops Conductor: Michael Krajewski
Mission: To create grand opera performances for the citizens of Lenawee County, Michigan; to sponsor the Friedrich Schorr Memorial Performance Prize in Voice; to collaborate between the Adrian Symphony and the Croswell Opera House.
Utilizes: Singers
Founded: 1989
Specialized Field: Grand Opera; Lyric Opera; Operetta
Status: Professional; Nonprofit
Income Sources: National Opera Association; Opera America
Performs At: Croswell Opera House
Organization Type: Performing; Resident; Educational

2019
ATLANTA BOY CHOIR
1215 S Ponce De Leon Avenue
Atlanta, GA 30306
Mailing Address: P.O. Box 8583 Atlanta, GA 31106
Phone: 404-378-0064
Fax: 404-378-4722
e-mail: info@atlantaboychoir.org
Web Site: www.atlantaboychoir.org
Officers:
 Founding Director: Fletcher Wolfe
 Visual Arts Director: Roberta Wolfe
 Assistant Director: Lawrence Weaver
 Administrator: Neil Cardwell
Management:
 President: David White
 Administrative/Business Manager: Roberta Kahne
Founded: 1957
Specialized Field: Choral
Status: Non-Profit, Non-Professional
Paid Staff: 3
Paid Artists: 2

2020
ATLANTA OPERA
1575 Northside Drive NW
Building 300, Suite 350
Atlanta, GA 30318
Phone: 404-881-8801
Fax: 404-881-1711
Toll-free: 800-356-7372
e-mail: info@atlantaopera.org
Web Site: www.atlantaopera.org
Officers:
 Chairman: William E. Tucker
 President: Charles R Yates Jr
 Treasurer: Rhys T. Wilson
 Secretary: Michael Keough
Management:
 General Director: Dennis Hanthorn
 Artistic Administration Director: Eric Mitchko
 Company Manager: Elecia Crowley
 Production Manager: Michael Benedict
 Orchestra Manager: Mark McConnell
Mission: To present opera productions of the highest standards possible, while fostering education about the art form and encouraging growth with services and programs designed to fill the needs of the community
Utilizes: Actors; Choreographers; Collaborating Artists; Collaborations; Dancers; Designers; Educators; Five Seasonal Concerts; Grant Writers; Guest Accompanists; Guest Artists; Guest Composers; Guest Conductors; Guest Designers; Guest Ensembles; Guest Instructors; Guest Musical Directors; Guest Musicians; Guest Soloists; Guest Writers; High School Drama; Instructors; Local Artists; Lyricists; Multi Collaborations; Multimedia; New Productions; Original Music Scores; Selected Students; Sign Language Translators; Singers; Soloists; Student Interns; Visual Arts
Founded: 1979
Specialized Field: Grand Opera
Status: Non-Profit, Professional
Paid Staff: 25
Volunteer Staff: 40
Non-paid Artists: 10
Budget: $5.4 million
Income Sources: Ticketing, Foundations, Individuals, Coporate, Government
Performs At: Alliance Theatre; Symphony Hall
Annual Attendance: 50,000+
Seating Capacity: 4514
Year Built: 1920
Organization Type: Performing; Educational

2021
ATLANTA SYMPHONY ORCHESTRA CHORUS
Robert W. Woodruff Arts Center
1280 Peachtree Street NE
Suite 300
Atlanta, GA 30309-3552
Phone: 404-733-4900
Fax: 404-733-4901
e-mail: aso-info@woodruffcenter.org
Web Site: www.atlantasymphony.org
Management:
 President: Allison Vulgamore
 Chief Financial Officer: Donald Fox

VOCAL MUSIC / Hawaii

VP: John Sparrow
Choral Administrator: Jeff Baxter
Music Director: Robert Spano
Founded: 1945
Specialized Field: Grand Opera; Operetta; Arias
Status: Non-Professional; Nonprofit; Volunteer
Performs At: Robert W. Woodruff Arts Center Symphony Hall
Organization Type: Performing; Touring

2022
ATLANTA YOUNG SINGERS OF CALLANWOLDE
1085 Ponce de Leon Avenue
Atlanta, GA 30306
Phone: 404-873-3365
Fax: 404-873-0756
e-mail: info@aysc.org
Web Site: www.aysc.org
Officers:
   President: David Hughes
   VP: Rita Brett
   Secretary: Amanda Freer
   Treasurer: Virginia Ling
Management:
   Executive Director: Virginia M Thompson
   Music Director: Paige Fumbanks Mathis
   Office Coordinator: Michelle Spruell
   Assistant Music Director: Brianne Turgeon
Mission: To provide a program of exceptionally fine training in choral singing for boys and girls, which will develop their appreciation of and talents in choral and musical artistry; to encourage the personal growth of each singer through individual responsibility and group cooperation; to advance the choral art form by presenting traditional and innovative music through the voices of children in live performances to local, national and international com
Utilizes: Guest Accompanists; Guest Musical Directors; Multimedia; Original Music Scores
Founded: 1975
Specialized Field: Youth Chorus
Paid Staff: 4
Volunteer Staff: 400
Paid Artists: 15
Non-paid Artists: 10
Budget: $630,000
Income Sources: Grants; Donations; Performances; Tuition
Annual Attendance: 60,000-90,000

2023
CAPITOL CITY OPERA
1266 West Paces Ferry Road
#451
Atlanta, GA 30327-2306
Phone: 678-301-8013
e-mail: info@ccityopera.com
Web Site: www.ccityopera.com
   President: Bonnie LaForge
   Vice President: Sallie Van Houten
   Secretary: Heather Dittus
   Treasurer: John LaForge
Management:
   Artistic Director: Michael Nutter
   Stage Director: Michael Nutter
   Education Coordinator & Company Adm: Tafee Patterson
   Director Production: Steven Cernek
   Director Marketing: Nichol Julia Jacobs
   New Projects Coordinator: Kathleen Szalay

Mission: To provide Atlanta area classically trained singers the opportunity to learn and perform complete opera roles and continue to develop their vocal and acting skills on a professional level.
Utilizes: Community Talent; Instructors; Local Talent
Founded: 1983
Specialized Field: Opera
Season: October-January; July
Performs At: Falany Performing Arts Center at Reinhardt College; 14th Street Playhouse

2024
CHORAL GUILD OF ATLANTA
PO Box 550772
Atlanta, GA 30355
Phone: 404-223-6362
Fax: 770-641-1385
e-mail: info@cgatl.org
Web Site: www.cgatl.org
Officers:
   Secretary: Marie Juchelka
Management:
   Chairman: Earlene Brasher
   Vice Chairman of Finance: George Taylor
   Artistic Director and Conductor: Clair Maxwell
   Accompanist: Wooyoung Ellie Choi
Mission: Recognition as the foremost large civic chorus in the metro Atlanta area; performance of major works of nonstandard repertoire; increasing financial solvency.
Founded: 1939
Specialized Field: Choral
Status: Semi-Professional; Nonprofit
Organization Type: Performing; Touring

2025
TROIKA BALALAIKES WORLD ARTISTS
World Artists
3126 Bolero Drive
Atlanta, GA 30341
Phone: 678-575-0379
Fax: 770-908-1231
e-mail: LynncMcConnell@gmail.com
Web Site: www.lynnmcconnell.com
Management:
   Director: Lynn Connell
Specialized Field: Russian Folk Music
Affiliations: Cucanandy (Irish), Cowboy Envy, Deluxe Vaudeville Orchestra, Atlanta Brassworks, Hotlanta (Dixieland), Mariachi Vasqukez, Else Witt

2026
AUGUSTA OPERA ASSOCIATION
1301 Greene Street
Suite 100
Augusta, GA 30903
Mailing Address: Post Office Box 240, Augusta, GA 30903
Phone: 706-364-9114
Fax: 706-826-4732
e-mail: theaugustaopera@gmailc.om
Web Site: www.augustaopera.org
   Treasurer: Gordon Bruker
   Secretary: Suzanne Vest
   Executive VP: Gerald Chamber S
   Vice President, Development: Rebbeca Blair
Management:
   President: Dennis Sodomka
   Artistic Director: Mark Flint
   Managing Director: Katherine Deloach
   Marketing Associate: Mary Ann Woodworth
Mission: Strives to present opera music theater productions of the highest standards while encouraging growth of the art form through its programs and outreach services.
Utilizes: Collaborations; Fine Artists; Grant Writers; Guest Artists; Guest Choreographers; Guest Composers; Guest Conductors; Guest Lecturers; Guest Writers; Local Artists; Lyricists; Multi Collaborations; Multimedia; Original Music Scores; Singers; Special Technical Talent
Founded: 1967
Specialized Field: Grand Opera; Light Opera; Lyric Opera; Musical Theatre; Choral
Status: Non-Profit, Professional
Paid Staff: 3
Volunteer Staff: 35
Paid Artists: 3
Non-paid Artists: 128
Budget: $500,000
Income Sources: Subscriptions; Single Ticket Sales; Iundividual Donations; Foundations; Corporations; Government Grants
Performs At: Imperial Theatre
Affiliations: Opera America
Annual Attendance: 9,000
Seating Capacity: 850
Organization Type: Performing; Resident; Educational

2027
GRAND OPERA HOUSE SEASON AT THE GRAND
651 Mulberry Street
Macon, GA 31201
Phone: 478-301-5470
Fax: 912-301-5469
e-mail: tickets@mercer.edu
Web Site: www.thegrandmacon.com
Officers:
   Chair: Mark A. Stevens
Management:
   Managing Director: Karen Lambert
   Artistic Administration Director: Karen Goss
   Executive Director: Betsy Fitzgerald
   Technical Director: Robert Mavity Mavity
Specialized Field: Musical Theatre; Opera
Performs At: Grand Opera House

Hawaii

2028
HAWAII ECUMENICAL CHORALE
3752 Old Pali Road
Honolulu, HI 96817
Phone: 808-595-3447
Fax: 808-521-4595
Management:
   Artistic Director: Eileen Lum
Mission: To provide an opportunity for local singers to participate in more challenging music than average choirs offer; to sponsor a local choral composition contest to encourage indigenous choral work.
Utilizes: Guest Artists; Guest Companies; Singers
Founded: 1979
Specialized Field: Grand Opera; Choral; Ethnic Music; Folk Music
Status: Semi-Professional; Nonprofit
Volunteer Staff: 4
Affiliations: State Foundation on Culture and the Arts
Organization Type: Performing; Resident; Educational

2029
HAWAII OPERA THEATRE
987 Waimanu Street
Honolulu, HI 96814
Mailing Address: 848 S. Beretania St. Suite 301, Honolulu, Hawaii 96813
Phone: 808-596-7858

Fax: 808-596-0379
Toll-free: 800-836-7372
e-mail: hotopera@hawaii.rr.com
Web Site: www.hawaiiopera.org
Management:
    President: Henry G Akina
    Executive Director: Karen Tiller
Mission: To offer opera in Hawaii.
Utilizes: Guest Artists; Guest Companies
Founded: 1962
Specialized Field: Grand Opera
Status: Non-Profit, Professional
Paid Staff: 13
Income Sources: Opera America; Central Opera Service
Performs At: Neal S. Blaisdell Center-Concert Hall
Orchestra Pit: 1
Organization Type: Performing; Touring; Resident; Educational

2030
HONOLULU CHILDREN'S OPERA CHORUS
PO Box 22304
Honolulu, HI 96823
Phone: 808-521-2982
Fax: 808-521-4595
Web Site: www.hyoc.org
Officers:
    President: Daniel Leung
    Vice President: Andrea Hamilton
    Treasurer: Neil Ishida
    Secretary: Mary Wong, Esq
Management:
    Music Director: Nola A Nahulu
    Accompanist: Wendy Chang
    Executive Director: Jean Lilley
    General Manager: Malia Ka'ai Barrett
    Accountant: Carolyn Smith
Mission: Developing and nurturing the performing arts by means of choral music; providing educational and artistic resources for Hawaii.
Founded: 1961
Specialized Field: Grand Opera; Light Opera; Choral; Ethnic Music
Status: Nonprofit
Organization Type: Performing; Educational

2031
OAHU CHORAL SOCIETY
650 Iwilei Road
Suite 202
Honolulu, HI 96817
Phone: 808-524-0815
Fax: 808-524-1507
e-mail: nada@oahuchoral.org
Web Site: www.oahuchoral.com
Officers:
    Secretary: Sally Hattemer
    Treasurer: Elizabeth Conklin
Management:
    President: Nada Marriott
    VP: Alma Grocki
    Artistic Director: Esther S. Yoo
    Executive Director: Valerie Ossipoff
Founded: 1995
Specialized Field: Choral
Status: Nonprofit

Idaho

2032
BIOTZETIK BASQUE CHOIR
PO Box 1011
Boise, ID 83701
Phone: 208-336-8219
e-mail: biotzetik@yahoo.com
Web Site: www.biotzetikbasquechoir.org
Management:
    Business Manager: John Kirtland
    Business Manager: Miren Artiach
    Communicator: Ricardo Yanci
Mission: The promotion and enhancement of our culture through dance, song, language and education.
Utilizes: Guest Companies; Singers
Specialized Field: Ethnic Music; Folk Music
Status: Nonprofit
Paid Staff: 70
Income Sources: Euskaldunak
Performs At: Boise Basque Center
Organization Type: Performing; Touring; Educational

2033
BOISE MASTER CHORALE
519 S. 9th Street
Boise, ID 83702
Phone: 208-344-7901
e-mail: info@boisemasterchorale.org
Web Site: www.boisemasterchorale.org
Officers:
    President: Alana Seacord
    Secretary: Cindy Geile
    Treasurer: Bob Ball
    Membership: Diane Campbell
    Program Director: Leon Collins
    Advertising: Barbara Myhre
Management:
    President: Joanne C Anderson
    Artistic Director: Peter Anastos
    Conductor: Robert Franz
    Guest Composer: Jim Cockey
Mission: Offering the community fine choral music; enabling community members to participate in a high quality choral group.
Founded: 1975
Specialized Field: Choral
Status: Professional; Semi-Professional; Nonprofit
Paid Staff: 125
Performs At: Saint John's Cathedral; Morrison Center for the Arts
Organization Type: Performing

2034
OPERA IDAHO
513 S 8th Street
Boise, ID 83702
Phone: 208-345-3531
Fax: 208-342-7566
e-mail: fernando@operaidaho.org
Web Site: www.operaidaho.org
Officers:
    President: Marshall Garrett
    Vice President: Effie Kaufmann
    Treasurer: Christopher Huntley
    Secretary: Yvonne McCoy
Management:
    General Director: Mark Junkert
    Director of Childrens' Choruses: Linda Berg
    Production Manager: Keith Hazen-Diehm
    Marketing & Development Coordinator: Janessa White
Mission: Opera Idaho's mission for it's professional resident company is to promote opera in general by providing traing and performance opportunities for many talented singers in the Boise area.
Specialized Field: Opera
Performs At: Morrison Center; Esther Simplot Performing Arts Annex

2035
SUN VALLEY OPERA
PO Box 7187
Ketchum, ID 83340
Phone: 208-726-0991
e-mail: maryjohelmeke@cox.net
Web Site: www.sunvalleyopera.com
Officers:
    Chairman: Clif Rippon
    President: Frank Meyer
    EVP: Phebe Thorne
    Secretary: Liz Warrick
    Treasurer: Joe Bauwens
    Honorary Advisor: Phillip Glass
Management:
    Artistic Director/Conductor: Dr Craig Jessop
    Associate Director: Dr Cory Evans
    Executive Director: Mary Jo Helmeke
    Vocal Coach: Melvyn Poll
    Theater Director: Andrew Tsao
    Symphony Conductor: Gerard Schwartz
Mission: Provides a unique opportunity for viewers to learn more about the music and the music-making process, as well as gain exhilarating insights into Dudamel's musical background, his phenomenal relationship with the LA Phil, and his enduring dedication to youth-music education.
Utilizes: Arrangers; Collaborating Artists; Collaborations; Fine Artists; Guest Accompanists; Guest Companies; Guest Musical Directors; Local Unknown Artists; Multimedia; Music; Sign Language Translators; Singers
Specialized Field: Opera, Chorus, Symphony
Status: Non-Profit
Income Sources: Ticket Sales, Advertising
Season: Fall
Performs At: Sun Valley Opera Theater

Illinois

2036
APOLLO CHORUS OF CHICAGO
225 West Washington
Suite 2200
Chicago, IL 60606
Phone: 312-427-5620
e-mail: info@apollochorus.org
Web Site: www.apollochorus.org
Officers:
    President: David Hahn
    Vice President: Barbara Guenther
    Secretary: Joyce Beer
    Treasurer: Melanie Beinlich
    Director/Corporate Relations: Jenna Kaferly
    Director/Development: Melissa Anderson
    Director/Finance: Melanie Beinlich
    Director/Musicianship: David Jolivet
    Director/Marketing: Anne Holton
Management:
    Music Director/Conductor: Stephen Alltop
    General Manager: Greg Kolack
    Ticket Manager: Scott Slein
    Marketing: Anne Holton
    Public Relations: Cameron Heinze
    Information Technology: Volker Kleinschmidt

VOCAL MUSIC / Illinois

Mission: The Apollo Chorus of Chicago is the area's premier volunteer chorus. Its 125-plus auditioned members include men and women of all ages, races, creeds, and occupations brought together by their abiding love of music. The voices of college students blend seamlessly with the voices of retirees who have belonged to Apollo over fifty years. The singers' dedication, artistry, and passion produce performances of unrivalled majesty.
Utilizes: Arrangers; Artists-in-Residence; Choreographers; Collaborating Artists; Collaborations; Composers; Composers-in-Residence; Guest Accompanists; Guest Companies; Guest Composers; Local Unknown Artists; Multimedia; Music; Paid Performers; Sign Language Translators; Singers
Founded: 1872
Opened: 1879
Specialized Field: Orchestra, Classical, Choral, Baroque, Broadway
Status: Non-Profit, Professional
Non-paid Artists: 125
Income Sources: Fundraisers, Donors, Sponsors
Season: November through May
Performs At: First United Church, North Shore Center for the Performing Arts, Harris Theater for Music and Dance

2037
BELLA VOCE
Department of Performing Arts
1040 W Harrison Street
Room L018 MSC 255
Chicago, IL 60607-7130
Phone: 312-479-1096
Toll-free: 877-755-6277
e-mail: mail@bellavoce.org
Web Site: www.bellavoce.org
Officers:
   Board President: Dan Fulweiler
Management:
   Managing Director: Kayleigh Dudevoir, kayleigh@bellavoce.org
   Artistic Director: Andrew Lewis
Mission: Aspires to provide musical experiences that help people transcend their daily lives through the highest quality choral music, locally, nationally, and internationally.
Utilizes: Commissioned Composers; Community Talent; Educators; Five Seasonal Concerts; Guest Musicians; Instructors; Local Artists; Local Artists & Directors; Local Talent; Lyricists; Multimedia; Music; Resident Companies; Sign Language Translators; Singers; Soloists
Founded: 1982
Specialized Field: Choral; Classical; Contemporary; Religious
Status: Non-Profit, Professional
Paid Staff: 2
Volunteer Staff: 30
Paid Artists: 21
Budget: $125,000
Income Sources: Grants; Donations; Concert tickets; CD's
Annual Attendance: 2,500
Organization Type: Performing

2038
CHICAGO A CAPPELLA
2936 N Southport Avenue
2nd Floor
Chicago, IL 60657-4120
Phone: 773-281-7820
Fax: 773-435-6453
Toll-free: 800-746-4969
e-mail: info@chicagoacappella.org
Web Site: www.chicagoacappella.org
Management:
   Executive Director: Matthew Greenberg
   Founder/Artistic Director: Jonathan Miller
   Box Office and Concert Manager: Deb Hoban
   Marketing and Operations Coordinato: Shaina Farwell
Mission: Nine professional vocal soloists committed to furthering the art of singing together without instruments. Chicago a cappella aims to speak directly to the human spirit, through repertoire from the ninth to the twenty-first centuries.
Founded: 1933
Specialized Field: Traditional Choral Music; A Cappella
Status: Professional
Performs At: Civic Center Music Hall

2039
CHICAGO CHILDREN'S CHOIR
78 E Washington
5th Floor
Chicago, IL 60602
Phone: 312-849-8300
Fax: 312-849-8309
e-mail: info@ccchoir.org
Web Site: www.ccchoir.org
Management:
   President and Artistic Director: Josephine Lee
   Director of Advancement: Crystal Bowyer
   Development Director: Eileen Epstein
   Marketing Director: Pat Washington
Utilizes: Artists-in-Residence; Collaborations; Commissioned Music; Educators; Grant Writers; Guest Companies; Guest Composers; Guest Designers; Guest Lecturers; Guest Musical Directors; Guest Musicians; Lyricists; Multimedia; New Productions; Organization Contracts; Sign Language Translators; Singers; Soloists; Special Technical Talent; Theatre Companies; Touring Companies
Founded: 1956
Specialized Field: Grand Opera; Light Opera; Lyric Opera; Musical Theatre; Choral; Youth Chorus; Ethnic Music; Classical; Contemporary; Religious
Status: Non-Profit, Non-Professional
Paid Staff: 31
Volunteer Staff: 100
Budget: $2,500,000
Income Sources: Performance Fees; Corporate; Civic and Private Sponsorships
Performs At: Concert halls, Churches, etc.
Annual Attendance: 1500
Organization Type: Performing; Touring; Educational

2040
CHICAGO CHORALE
1100 East 55th Street
Chicago, IL 60615
Phone: 773-306-6195
e-mail: info@chicagochorale.org
Web Site: chicagochorale.org
Officers:
   President: Angela Grimes
   Treasurer: Mark Schneider
   Secretary: Charis Wuerffel
Management:
   Artistic Director: Bruce Tanmen
   Managing Director: Megan Balderston
Founded: 2001

2041
CHICAGO OPERA THEATER
70-E Lake Street
Suite 815
Chicago, IL 60601-5907
Phone: 312-704-8420
Fax: 312-704-8421
e-mail: info@chicagooperatheater.org
Web Site: www.chicagooperatheater.org
Officers:
   Secretary: Suzanne L. Wagner
Management:
   President: Gregory O'Leary
   General Manager: Jerry Tietz
   General Director: Andreas Mitisek
   Marketing & Public Relations Dir.: Colleen Flanigan
   Artistic Coordinator: Jane Hulburt
Mission: To present Classical, Baroque, and 20th century operas with a strong empasis on education for people young and old.
Founded: 1974
Specialized Field: Classical; Baroque; 20th Century Operas
Status: Professional
Performs At: Harris Theatre
Type of Stage: Athenaeum

2042
CHICAGO SYMPHONY CHORUS
Symphony Center
220 S Michigan Avenue
Chicago, IL 60604
Phone: 312-294-3000
Fax: 312-294-3450
e-mail: chorus@cso.org
Web Site: www.cso.org
Management:
   President: Deborah Card
   Manager: Mark Rulison
   Artistic Director: Duane Wolfe
   Stage Manager: Kelly Kerins
   Stage Technician: David Hartge
Mission: Performance with a leading symphony orchestra.
Founded: 1957
Specialized Field: Choral
Status: Non-Profit, Professional
Paid Artists: 105
Non-paid Artists: 80
Budget: $1,000,000
Performs At: Orchestra Hall; Ravinia Festival
Organization Type: Performing; Touring; Educational

2043
L'OPERA PICCOLA
5239 N. LaCrosse Ave
Chicago, IL 60630
Phone: 312-560-1072
Fax: 847-823-3165
e-mail: sasha@loperapiccola.org
Web Site: www.loperapiccola.org
Officers:
   President: Jerry Lee Brown
   VP: Mark D Holihan
   Treasurer: John Sasser
   Secretary: Lawrence Zimmerman
Management:
   General Manager/Executive Director: Shasha Gerritson
   Music Director: David Richards
   Artistic Director: Shifra Werch
   Executive Producer: Madeline Nelson

VOCAL MUSIC / Illinois

Events Coordinator: Aggie Zarkadas
Mission: To provide a creative outlet for Chicago's aspiring musicians and to reach members of the community with Italian opera production.
Founded: 1996
Specialized Field: Italian Opera
Status: Non-Profit, Professional
Paid Staff: 4
Volunteer Staff: 250
Paid Artists: 200
Budget: $250,000
Income Sources: Grants; Individual Donations; Ticket Sales
Performs At: Athenaeum Theatre
Annual Attendance: 6,000
Seating Capacity: 985

2044
LIRA CHAMBER CHORUS
6525 N Sheridan Road
#CH-LL
Chicago, IL 60626
Phone: 773-508-7040
Fax: 773-508-7043
e-mail: lira@liraensemble.org
Web Site: www.liraensemble.com
Officers:
 President: Maria Ciesla
 Attorney: Donald Grabowski
 Sculptress: Janet Stanton
 Vice President: Frank A. Cizon
 Chairman: Camille Kopielski
Management:
 Artistic Director/General Manager: Lucyna Migala
 Conductor: Mina Zikri
 Choreographer and dance director: Iwona Puc
 Conductor: Malgorzata Borysiewicz
Mission: To bring back Polish Culture into American life.
Specialized Field: Choral; Youth Chorus
Paid Staff: 5
Paid Artists: 50

2045
LIRA SINGERS
6525 N Sheridan Road
#CH-LL
Chicago, IL 60626
Phone: 773-508-7040
Fax: 773-508-7043
e-mail: lira@liraensemble.org
Web Site: www.liraensemble.com
Officers:
 President: Maria Ciesla
 Attorney: Donald Grabowski
 Sculptress: Janet Stanton
 Vice President: Frank A. Cizon
 Chairman: Camille Kopielski
Management:
 Artistic Director/General Manager: Lucyna Migala
 Conductor: Mina Zikri
 Choreographer and Dance Director: Iwona Puc
 Conductor: Malgorzata Borysiewicz
Mission: The Lira Ensemble is the nation's only professional performing arts company specializing in Polish music, song, and dance.
Specialized Field: Choral
Organization Type: Performing

2046
LYRIC OPERA OF CHICAGO
20 N Wacker Drive
Suite 840
Chicago, IL 60606
Phone: 312-332-2244
Fax: 312-419-8345
Web Site: www.lyricopera.org
Management:
 General Director: Anthony Freud
 Music Director: Andrew Davis
 Aristic Director Emeritus: Bruno Bartoletti
 Creative Consultant: Ren,e Fleming
 General Director Emeritus: William Mason
Mission: Offering quality opera to Chicago area residents.
Utilizes: Educators; Guest Artists; Guest Companies; Singers
Founded: 1954
Specialized Field: Grand Opera
Status: Professional, Nonprofit
Income Sources: Lyric Opera Center for American Artists
Performs At: Civic Opera House
Seating Capacity: 3,563
Organization Type: Performing, Sponsoring

2047
MUSIC OF THE BAROQUE CHORUS & ORCHESTRA
111 North Wabash Ave
Suite 810
Chicago, IL 60602
Phone: 312-551-1414
Fax: 312-551-1444
e-mail: baroque@baroque.org
Web Site: www.baroque.org
Officers:
 Chairman: Leland E Hutchinson
 Vice Chairman: James A. White
 Vice Chairman: Thomas O Kuhns
 Secretary: Pamela Baker
 Treasurer: Stanley L. Ferguson
Management:
 Music Director: Jane Glover
 Chorus Director: Edward Zelnis
 Executive Director: Karen Fishman
 House Manager: Janet Benoit
 Artistic Operations Manager: Vincent Carbone
 Special Projects Manager: Jennifer More Glagov
Mission: To perform and increase audience appreciation for choral and orchestral music of the 17th and 18th centuries.
Utilizes: Arrangers; Choreographers; Collaborating Artists; Collaborations; Commissioned Composers; Commissioned Music; Community Members; Composers; Guest Companies; Guest Composers; Multimedia; Music; Original Music Scores; Paid Performers; Sign Language Translators; Singers; Special Technical Talent
Founded: 1972
Specialized Field: Baroque; Choral
Status: Professional
Paid Staff: 6
Paid Artists: 60
Budget: $1,500,000
Season: October through May
Performs At: Church Venues
Annual Attendance: 13,000
Facility Category: Church venues
Type of Stage: Varies
Seating Capacity: 600-2,521

2048
PATRICK G AND SHIRLEY W RYAN OPERA CENTER
20 N Wacker Drive
Suite 700
Chicago, IL 60606
Mailing Address: 20 N Wacker Drive Suite #860
Phone: 312-332-2244
Fax: 312-419-8345
e-mail: atakushi@lyricopera.org
Web Site: www.lyricopera.org/about/ryanoperacenter
Officers:
 Director: Gianna Rolandi
 Administrative/Auditions Coord.: Alicia Takushi
Management:
 Manager: Dan Novak
 Administrative Coordinator: Laura Chambers
 Assistant Controller: Jeff Brown
 Senior Accountant: Cynthia Darling Cynthia Darling
 Audience Education Manager: Jesse Gram
Mission: To administer an apprentice artist program in conjunction with and under the overall direction of the Lyric Opera of Chicago to bridge the gap between a singer's preparation in school and performance on a professional stage.
Utilizes: Guest Companies; Singers
Founded: 1974
Specialized Field: Opera
Status: Vocal Music; Professional Development Program
Paid Staff: 3
Volunteer Staff: 2
Paid Artists: 13
Income Sources: Sponsors; Audition Fees; Lyric Opera of Chicago
Affiliations: Lyric Opera of Chicago
Organization Type: Performing; Educational

2049
THE HAYMARKET OPERA COMPANY
C/O Craig Trompeter
1920 North Seminary Ave, 1F
Chicago, IL 60614
Phone: 312-523-6945
e-mail: info@haymarketopera.org
Web Site: www.haymarketopera.org
Management:
 Genral/Artistic Director: Craig Trompeter
 Stage Director: Ellen Hargis
 Costume Designer: Meriem Bahri
Mission: The Haymarket Opera Company aspires to enrich the musical community of Chicago and the Midwest with performances of 17th and 18th century operas. Chicago does not have an opera company that specializes in the repertoire from the Age of Reason and the Enlightenment. The board of directors, donors, and volunteers of HOC believe that the company will become a cultural gem of the city and region. HOC seeks to engage audiences of all ages with passion
Utilizes: Actors; Arrangers; Collaborating Artists; Collaborations; Contract Orchestras; Fine Artists; Multimedia; Music; Paid Performers
Specialized Field: Opera
Status: Non-Profit, Professional
Income Sources: Donors
Performs At: Theatre Royale

2050
WILLIAM FERRIS CHORALE
Loyola University
1032 W. Sheridan Road
Chicago, IL 60660

VOCAL MUSIC / Illinois

Phone: 773-508-2940
e-mail: requests@williamferrischorale.org
Web Site: www.williamferrischorale.org
Management:
    Music Director: Paul French
    Artistic and Executive Director: John Vorrasi
Utilizes: Collaborating Artists; Composers; Contract Orchestras; Guest Accompanists; Guest Companies; Guest Directors; Guest Musical Directors; Guest Musicians; Guest Soloists; Instructors; Multimedia; Music; Organization Contracts; Original Music Scores; Sign Language Translators; Singers; Students
Founded: 1972
Specialized Field: Choral
Paid Staff: 3
Volunteer Staff: 3
Paid Artists: 35
Budget: $195,000
Annual Attendance: 2,000
Seating Capacity: 400

2051
WINDY CITY PERFORMING ARTS
3023 N Clark Street
Suite 329
Chicago, IL 60657
Mailing Address: Windy City Performing Arts, Inc., 3656 N. Halsted, Chicago,
Phone: 773-661-0928
Fax: 773-404-6815
e-mail: info@windycitysings.org
Web Site: www.windycitysings.org
Officers:
    Chair: Karen Hundrieser
    Vice Chair: Matthew Bahnson
    Treasurer: Curt Eakle
    Secretary: Marquise Neal
Management:
    Interim Music Director: Alan Wellman
    Guest Artistic Director: Jeremiah Selvey
    Accompanist: Madelyn Tan-Cohen
Utilizes: Actors; Artists-in-Residence; Commissioned Composers; Dancers; Guest Companies; Guest Composers; Guest Lecturers; Guest Musical Directors; Guest Musicians; Instructors; Local Artists; Multimedia; Music; Resident Professionals; Sign Language Translators; Singers; Student Interns
Founded: 1979
Specialized Field: Musical Theatre; Choral
Paid Staff: 2
Volunteer Staff: 20
Paid Artists: 6
Non-paid Artists: 100
Budget: $400,000
Annual Attendance: 5,000

2052
MILLIKIN UNIVERSITY OPERA THEATRE
Millikin University
School of Music
1184 West Main
Decatur, IL 62522
Phone: 217-424-6300
Fax: 217-420-6652
Toll-free: 800-373-7733
e-mail: tstone@mail.millikin.edu
Web Site: www.millikin.edu
Officers:
    President: Douglas E. Zemke
    VP University Development: Peggy S. Luy
Management:
    Director: Terry Stone
Mission: To provide professional training and numerous performance opportunities for undergraduates in productions including scenes, chamber operas, fully produced operas and musical theatre.
Utilizes: Artists-in-Residence; Dancers; Designers; Grant Writers; Guest Artists; Guest Composers; Guest Conductors; Guest Designers; Guest Instructors; Guest Lecturers; Guest Musical Directors; Resident Professionals; Soloists; Student Interns
Founded: 1955
Specialized Field: Grand Opera; Light Opera; Lyric Opera; Musical Theatre; Choral; Ethnic Music; Classical; Operetta
Status: Non-Profit, Professional
Paid Staff: 3
Paid Artists: 67
Budget: $15,000
Income Sources: Annual budget; ticket sales
Performs At: Kirkland Fine Arts Center, Albert Taylor Hall, Kaeuper Hall
Affiliations: Opera America, Musical America
Annual Attendance: 2,000
Type of Stage: Proscenium w/hydraulic pit
Organization Type: Educational

2053
DOWNERS GROVE CHORAL SOCIETY
PO Box 655
Downers Grove, IL 60515
Phone: 630-515-0030
Fax: 630-910-8254
e-mail: info@dgcs.org
Web Site: www.dgcs.org
Management:
    Music Director/Conductor: Robert Holst
    Orchestra Manager: Patricia Smith
Specialized Field: Choral

2054
ANIMA SINGERS
799 Roosevelt Road
Building 6, Suite 100
Glen Ellyn, IL 60137-5910
Phone: 630-858-2471
Fax: 630-858-2476
e-mail: info@gechildrenschorus.org
Web Site: www.animasingers.org
Officers:
    President: William Hupp
    Vice-President: Suzanne Armstrong
    Treasurer Investment Officer: Elizabeth Schnell
Management:
    Executive Director: Nondi Orazi
    Artistic Director: Emily Ellsworth
    Principal Accompanist: William Buhr
    Concert Chorus Conductor: Ron Korbitz
Mission: To provide any interested child, regardless of previous musical experience, with an outstanding performance-based music education program offered in a positive and nurturing environment which fosters self-esteem and personal growth.
Utilizes: Guest Companies; Guest Musical Directors; Guest Musicians; Multimedia; Sign Language Translators; Soloists
Founded: 1964
Specialized Field: Youth Chorus; Choral
Status: Non-Profit, Non-Professional
Paid Staff: 12
Organization Type: Performing; Touring; Educational

2055
DUPAGE OPERA THEATER
425 Fawell Blvd.,
Glen Ellyn, IL 60137
Phone: 630-942-2800
Fax: 630-790-9806
e-mail: cebula@cod.edu
Web Site: www.cod.edu
Management:
    Executive Director: Stephen Cummins
    Artistic Director: Kirk Muspratt
    Managing Director: Paula Cebula
Founded: 1977
Specialized Field: Light Opera; Lyric Opera
Status: Non-Profit, Professional
Paid Staff: 5
Paid Artists: 15
Income Sources: Ticket Sales; Individual Donor
Performs At: Arts Center; Mainstage
Seating Capacity: 793
Year Built: 1985

2056
MOLINE BOYS CHOIR
3426 Avenue of City
Moline, IL 61265
Phone: 309-762-5117
e-mail: mobocho@mchsi.com
Web Site: www.molineboyschoir.org
Management:
    President: John Mickiewicz
    Director: Kermit Wells
    Managing Director: Margaret Mangelsdorf
Mission: To perform choral literature of a variety of styles; to provide vocal/choral training to boys of talent, interest and ability.
Founded: 1948
Specialized Field: Light Opera; Musical Theatre; Choral; Youth Chorus; Ethnic Music; Classical; Contemporary; Religious
Status: Non-Profit, Non-Professional
Paid Staff: 2
Volunteer Staff: 1
Organization Type: Performing; Touring; Educational

2057
OPERA ILLINOIS
416 Hamilton Boulevard
Suite 309
Peoria, IL 61602
Phone: 309-673-7253
Fax: 309-673-7211
Web Site: www.operaillinois.com
Officers:
    President: Karl Kuppler
    Vice-President: Camille Gibson
    Treasurer: Mildred Arends
Management:
    President: Joan Janssen
    Executive Director: Margaret Swain
    Artistic Director: Fiora Contino
    General Manager: William Swain
Mission: The mission is to enhance the cultural, educational and economic life of Downstate Illinois by the promotion of opera and the production of professional opera performances.
Utilizes: Actors; Choreographers; Dance Companies; Designers; Educators; Grant Writers; Guest Accompanists; Guest Artists; Guest Composers; Guest Conductors; Guest Designers; Guest Musical Directors; Guest Musicians; Instructors; Local Artists; Multimedia; Music; Original Music Scores; Resident Professionals; Sign Language Translators; Student Interns

VOCAL MUSIC / Illinois

Founded: 1972
Specialized Field: Opera; Classical; Musical Theatre
Paid Staff: 5
Volunteer Staff: 25
Budget: $565,000
Income Sources: Ticket Revenue; Contributed Revenue
Performs At: Peoria Civic Center Theater
Affiliations: Opera America
Annual Attendance: 10,000+
Facility Category: Peorkia, Civic Center, Theatre
Type of Stage: Proscenium
Stage Dimensions: 45'x35'x45'
Seating Capacity: 2131
Year Built: 1981

2058
MUDDY RIVER OPERA COMPANY
200 North 8th Street
Suite 111
Quincy, IL 62301-3930
Phone: 217-214-6762
Fax: 217-222-2869
e-mail: abernzen12@gmail.com
Web Site: www.muddyriveropera.org
Officers:
  President: Jason Stone
Management:
  President/Artistic Director: Avril Marie Bernzen
Mission: To create an opportunity for local performers to work in collaboration with professionals, creating a professional opera experience for the pleasure and education of the local community. To introduce children to the art of Opera.
Utilizes: Actors; Dancers; Designers; Fine Artists; Grant Writers; Guest Accompanists; Guest Artists; Guest Conductors; Guest Designers; Guest Musical Directors; Guest Musicians; Instructors; Local Artists; Lyricists; Multimedia; Music; Original Music Scores; Resident Professionals; Sign Language Translators; Singers; Student Interns; Touring Companies
Founded: 1989
Opened: 1990
Specialized Field: Opera
Status: Non-Profit, Professional
Volunteer Staff: 16
Budget: $49,500
Income Sources: Grants; Memberships; Donations; Ticket Fees
Annual Attendance: 2000
Facility Category: Several theatres
Seating Capacity: 500650
Year Built: 1994

2059
AUGUSTANA CHOIR
Augustana College
639 38th Street
Rock Island, IL 61201
Phone: 309-794-7000
Fax: 309-794-7678
Toll-free: 800-798-8100
e-mail: jonhurty@augustana.edu
Web Site: www.augustana.edu
Officers:
  President: Steven Bahls
  Co-Chair: Dr. Daniel Culver
  Co-Chair: Dr. Jon Hurty
Management:
  Director Choral Activities: Jon Hurty
  Manager Performance/Outreach: Christiana Conner
  Coordinator of Recruiting and Audit: Margaret Ellis
  Manager of Arts Events and Communic: Sam Schlouch
Mission: Augustana Choir brings sacred choral music of the highest caliber to people around the region, nation and the world.
Founded: 1860
Specialized Field: A Cappella; Choral
Status: Non-Profit, Non-Professional
Paid Staff: 6
Paid Artists: 1

2060
ARCH-OPERA HOUSE OF SANDWICH
140 E Railroad Street
Sandwich, IL 60548
Phone: 815-786-2555
Fax: 815-786-7855
e-mail: sandwichoperahouse@hotmail.com
Web Site: www.sandwichoperahouse.org
Officers:
  President: Rich Bryan
  Vice President: Tom Merkel
  Secretary: Ellen Faulk
Mission: To present a variety of high cultural programs to people of all ages in Sandwich and througout our region.
Utilizes: Actors; Dance Companies; Dancers; Educators; Fine Artists; Grant Writers; Guest Accompanists; Guest Directors; Guest Musical Directors; Guest Musicians; Instructors; Multimedia; Original Music Scores; Sign Language Translators; Singers; Soloists; Special Technical Talent; Theatre Companies; Touring Companies
Founded: 1878
Specialized Field: Light Opera; Lyric Opera; Musical Theatre; Choral; Ethnic Music; Classical; Contemporary; Religious
Status: Non-Profit, Non-Professional
Paid Staff: 1
Volunteer Staff: 50
Budget: $110,000
Income Sources: Ticket Sales; Memberships; Donations
Performs At: ARCH-Opera House of Sandwich
Annual Attendance: 20,000
Facility Category: Restored 1878 Opera House
Type of Stage: Proscenium
Stage Dimensions: 20 x 20
Seating Capacity: 310
Year Built: 1878
Year Remodeled: 1986
Cost: $1.75 Million
Rental Contact: Executive Director Sandra Black

2061
ST CHARLES SINGERS
311 North 2nd Street
Suite 201-B
St Charles, IL 60174
Phone: 630-513-5272
e-mail: contact@stcharlessingers.com
Web Site: www.stcharlessingers.com
Officers:
  President: Jay Cunningham
  Vice President: Cathie Ruth
  Treasurer: Jennifer Hunt
  Finance Director: Nanci Tassi
  Board Member: Lynne Nelleman
  Board Member: Steve Wright
  Board Member: Diane Herr
Management:
  Conductor: Jeff Hunt
  President: Jay Cunningham
  Executive Director: Kay Kendall
Mission: We are pleased and proud to be able to present music in what is now our 29th year. We value you, our patrons more than ever. Connecting with you, helping to enrich your lives by presenting great choral music, and being relevant to the community we serve is part of our mission and vision.
Utilizes: Arrangers; Choreographers; Collaborating Artists; Collaborations; Commissioned Music; Composers; Contract Orchestras; Local Artists & Directors; Local Unknown Artists; Lyricists; Multimedia; Music; Paid Performers
Specialized Field: Choral
Status: Non-Profit, Professional
Budget: $150,000.00
Income Sources: Donors, Sponsors
Season: September through March
Performs At: Baker Church, St Vincent DePaul Catholic Church

2062
WAUKEGAN CONCERT CHORUS
2000 Belvidere Street
Waukegan, IL 60085
Phone: 847-360-4700
Fax: 847-622-6621
Web Site: www.waukeganparks.org
Officers:
  President: Terry Duffy
  Vice President: Patricia Foley
  Treasurer: Janet E. Kilkelly
  Commisioner: George Bridges
  Commissioner: William Sarocka
Management:
  Executive Director: Greg Petry
  Superintendent of Park: Mike Tregg
  Superintendent of Recreation: Jay Learner
  Superintendent of Cultural Arts: Claudia Freeman
  Superintendent of Finance: Jim Glogovsky
Utilizes: Guest Lecturers; Guest Writers; Multimedia; Music; Original Music Scores
Founded: 1917
Specialized Field: Choral
Non-paid Artists: 30

2063
WAUKEGAN SYMPHONY ORCHESTRA & CONCERT CHORUS
2000 Belvidere Street
Waukegan, IL 60085
Phone: 847-360-4740
Fax: 847-662-0592
Web Site: www.waukeganparks.org
Officers:
  President: Terry Duffy
  Vice President: Patricia Foley
  Treasurer: Janet E. Kilkelly
  Commisioner: George Bridges
  Commissioner: William Sarocka
Management:
  Executive Director: Greg Petry
  Superintendent of Park: Mike Tregg
  Superintendent of Recreation: Jay Learner
  Superintendent of Cultural Arts: Claudia Freeman
  Superintendent of Finance: Jim Glogovsky
Specialized Field: Choral
Paid Staff: 2
Paid Artists: 6
Non-paid Artists: 60
Facility Category: Auditorium
Type of Stage: Proscenium

VOCAL MUSIC / Indiana

2064
LIGHT OPERA WORKS
516 4th Street
Wilmette, IL 60091-2829
Phone: 847-920-5360
Fax: 847-920-5358
e-mail: info@light-opera-works.org
Web Site: www.light-opera-works.org
Officers:
   President: Dr. Robert Greendale
Management:
   Artistic Director: Rudy Hogenmiller
   General Manager: Briget McDonough
   Business Manager: Mike Kotze
   Production Manager: Paige Keedy
   Director of Audience and Press Serv: Christopher A. Riley
Mission: To produce and present music theater from a variety of world traditions
Utilizes: Guest Artists; Guest Companies
Founded: 1980
Specialized Field: Musical Theatre
Status: Non-Profit, Professional
Paid Staff: 7
Volunteer Staff: 20
Budget: $1.5 million
Income Sources: Tickets, Donations
Performs At: University Theater
Affiliations: National Alliance for Musical Theater, Leagues of Chicago Theaters
Annual Attendance: 25,000
Type of Stage: Proscenium
Stage Dimensions: 45 x 35
Seating Capacity: 1,000
Year Built: 1940
Year Remodeled: 1994
Organization Type: Performing

Indiana

2065
INDIANAPOLIS OPERA
250 E 38th Street
Indianapolis, IN 46205
Phone: 317-283-3470
Fax: 317-923-5611
Toll-free: 800-745-3000
e-mail: info@indyopera.org
Web Site: www.indyopera.org
Officers:
   President: Ruth Vignati
   Vice President: William Garvey
   Vice President: Muffi James
   Vice President: Eric Moy
   Vice President: Judy Woods
Management:
   Executive Director: John Pickett
   Artistic Director: James Caraher
   Marketing and Customer Relations: Mathew Tippel
   Director of Finance & Admin: Michael Jonson
   Director of Marketing: Nicole Brandt
Mission: To produce and present opera in performances of the highest quality and to develop audiences for opera.
Utilizes: Artists-in-Residence; Choreographers; Collaborating Artists; Collaborations; Dance Companies; Dancers; Designers; Educators; Grant Writers; Guest Accompanists; Guest Artists; Guest Composers; Guest Conductors; Guest Designers; Guest Instructors; Guest Musical Directors; Guest Musicians; Guest Soloists; Guest Writers; Instructors; Local Artists; Lyricists; Multimedia; Music; New Productions; Original Music Scores; Resident Professionals; Sign Language Translators; Singers; Soloists; Student Interns
Founded: 1975
Specialized Field: Grand Opera; Light Opera; Lyric Opera; Musical Theatre; Choral; Ethnic Music; Classical; Contemporary; Operetta
Status: Non-Profit, Professional
Paid Staff: 10
Paid Artists: 130
Budget: $2,312,000
Performs At: Clowes Memorial Hall; Butler University
Affiliations: Opera America
Annual Attendance: 16,800
Facility Category: Multiple Use, Concert, Performance Hall
Type of Stage: Proscenium
Stage Dimensions: 52'x 60'
Year Built: 1965
Organization Type: Performing; Touring; Resident; Educational; Sponsoring
Resident Groups: Indianapolis Opera Ensemble

2066
INDIANAPOLIS SYMPHONIC CHOIR
4600 Sunset Avenue
Indianapolis, IN 46208
Phone: 317-940-9057
Fax: 317-940-9058
e-mail: info@indychoir.org
Web Site: www.indychoir.org
Officers:
   Assistant Conductor: Michael Davis
   President: Franklin Whelan
   Voce President: Brian Hostetler
   Treasurer: Kent Shipley
   Secretary: Kathryn Rice
Management:
   Artistic Director: Eric Stark
   Managing Director: Michael Pettry
   Executive Director: Michael Pettry
   General Manager: Andrew Lannerd
   Operations Manager: Stephanie Derybowski
Specialized Field: Choral

2067
VESPER CHORALE
18211 Kern Road
South Bend, IN 46614
Phone: 574-229-2247
e-mail: info@vesperchorale.org
Web Site: vesperchorale.org
Officers:
   Chair: David Jordan
   Chair: Banitha Vinscon
Management:
   Artistic Director: Wishart Bell
   Executive Director: Patricia Doyle
   Administrator: Lisa Bloom
Founded: 1993
Specialized Field: Choral
Status: Nonprofit

2068
VALPARAISO UNIVERSITY CHORALE
Valparaiso University Music Department
1709 Chapel Drive
Valparaiso, IN 46383
Phone: 219-464-5453
Fax: 219-464-5244
Web Site: www.valpo.edu
Management:
   Managing Director: Jeff Hazewinkel
   Choral Director: Christopher M Cock
Mission: To perform works that represent the university's Lutheran heritage and multi-cultural perspectives.
Specialized Field: Choral; Classical; Religious
Status: Non-Profit, Non-Professional
Paid Staff: 30
Non-paid Artists: 50

Iowa

2069
CEDAR RAPIDS OPERA THEATRE
1120 Second Avenue SE
Cedar Rapids, IA 52403
Phone: 319-365-7401
e-mail: vmichalicek@cr-opera.org
Web Site: www.cr-opera.org
Officers:
   President: Mark Zimmerman
   Vice President: Sarah Antin
   Treasurer: John Botkin
   Secretary: Kim Blankenship
Management:
   Executive Director/Conductor: Daniel Kleinknecht
   Development Director: Virginia Michalicek
   Marketing Assistant: Christina Patramanis
Mission: To present two to three operas featuring international and American artists each season, as well as opera outreach performances.
Founded: 1988
Specialized Field: Opera
Status: Nonprofit
Season: January-June

2070
DORIAN MUSIC FESTIVALS
Luther College 700 Drive
Decorah, IA 52101
Phone: 563-387-1389
Fax: 563-387-1076
e-mail: buzzja01@luther.edu
Web Site: www.luther.edu
Officers:
   President: Robert Lillie
   VP: Justine Lionberger
   Secretary/Treasurer: Lynette Wilson
   Director Marketing: Vicki Bjerke
Management:
   Artistic Director: Weston Noble
   Managing Director: Jim Buzza
   Chairman of Music Department: John Strauss
Mission: Offering performance experience to young professionals as well as student artists.
Utilizes: Singers
Founded: 1949
Specialized Field: Multi-Disciplinary; Musical Theatre
Status: Non-Profit, Non-Professional
Paid Staff: 25
Performs At: Luther College Center for Faith and Life
Organization Type: Touring; Resident; Educational

2071
DES MOINES CHORAL SOCIETY
PO Box 93852
Des Moines, IA 50393
Mailing Address: PO Box 31007, Des Moines, IA 50310
Phone: 515-273-5255
e-mail: dmcs@dmchoral.org
Web Site: www.dmchoral.org
Officers:
   President: Sharon Strohmaier

VOCAL MUSIC / Kansas

Vice President, Community Outreach: Barbara Drustrup
Treasurer: Dave Short
Secretary: Gordon Smith
Vice President, Member and Concert: Ashley Maiers
Management:
  Artistic Director: Dr James Rodde
  Office Administrator: Carolyn Petsche
Mission: To inform, educate and stimulate the public toward a better appreciation of choral music.
Specialized Field: Choral; Educational
Paid Staff: 1
Paid Artists: 6
Budget: $85,000
Income Sources: Tickets; Grants; Private Donations
Affiliations: Chorus America; Metro Alliance of Greater Des Moines
Annual Attendance: 2,000

2072
DES MOINES METRO OPERA
106 W Boston Avenue
Indianola, IA 50125-8175
Phone: 515-961-6221
Fax: 515-961-8175
e-mail: dmmo@dmmo.org
Web Site: www.desmoinesmetroopera.org
Officers:
  President: Wendy Carlson
  CEO: Thomas S Smith
Management:
  Artistic Director: Michael Egel
  Executive Director: Thomas S Smith
  Artistic Administrator: Michael Egel
  Development Director: Leslie Garman
  Director of Finance: Elaine Raleigh
Mission: To provide a stage for young american artists, produce high quality performances and educate audiences to opera in the Midwest.
Utilizes: Artists-in-Residence; Choreographers; Dance Companies; Dancers; Designers; Educators; Fine Artists; Guest Writers; High School Drama; Instructors; Local Artists; Multimedia; Organization Contracts; Original Music Scores; Resident Professionals; Sign Language Translators; Soloists; Student Interns
Founded: 1973
Specialized Field: Opera
Status: Non-Profit, Professional
Paid Staff: 9
Paid Artists: 175
Budget: $2.1 million
Income Sources: Revenue and Contributions
Season: June - July
Performs At: Indianola (Festival Site)
Affiliations: Opera America
Annual Attendance: 8,000
Facility Category: Blank Performing Arts Center
Type of Stage: Proscenium with thrust stage
Seating Capacity: 488
Year Built: 1972
Rental Contact: Jim Lile
Organization Type: Performing; Touring; Resident; Educational
Resident Groups: OPERA Iowa - 13 week tour

2073
UNA VOCIS CHORAL ENSEMBLE
P.O. Box 494
Mason City, IA 50402
Phone: 641-430-2959
e-mail: dennis.lee@unavocis.org
Web Site: unavocis.org
Management:
  Artistic Director: Dennis Lee
Mission: Building on the musical heritage of north Iowa, the mission of Una Vocis Choral Ensemble is to cultivate and celebrate the connections among audiences, singers and composers. This diverse community entertains, educates and uplifts through innovative programming and artistic distinction.
Founded: 2005
Status: Nonprofit

2074
PELLA OPERA HOUSE
611 Franklin Street
PO Box 326
Pella, IA 50219
Phone: 641-628-8625
Fax: 641-628-8628
Toll-free: 800-720-6327
e-mail: boxoffice@pellaoperahouse.com
Web Site: www.pellaoperahouse.com
Management:
  General Manager: Barbara Filer
  Assistant Manager: Emily Riley
  Volunteer Coordinator: Vicki Meyers
Mission: Present a variety of performing arts throughout the year for entertainment and educational purposes. To enhance and support the arts community.
Founded: 1900
Specialized Field: Opera; Musical Theatre
Paid Staff: 2
Volunteer Staff: 30
Budget: $260,000
Income Sources: Ticket Sales; Donations; Tours
Annual Attendance: 32,000
Type of Stage: Proscenium
Stage Dimensions: 22x22
Seating Capacity: 324
Year Built: 1900
Year Remodeled: 1990
Cost: $2,000,000
Rental Contact: Emily Riley

Kansas

2075
CENTRAL STANDARD
14704 West 68th Street
Shawnee, KS 66216
Phone: 816-237-0599
e-mail: centralstandardchorus@gmail.com
Web Site: centralstandard.net
Management:
  Director: Robert Mance
Founded: 2007
Specialized Field: Barbershop, A Cappella
Status: Charitable

2076
TOPEKA SYMPHONY CHORUS
PO Box 2206
Topeka, KS 66601-2206
Phone: 785-232-2032
Fax: 785-232-6204
e-mail: tso@topekasymphony.org
Web Site: www.topekasymphony.org
Officers:
  President: Michael Lennen
  President-Elect: Gordon McQuere
  Treasurer: Eric Rea
  Secretary: Jayne Cafer
  Past President: Sarah Bailey
Management:
  Music Director: John Strickler
General Manager: Kathy Mahe
Admin. Assistant: Charles Baker
Founded: 1945
Specialized Field: Choral
Status: Non-Profit, Professional
Paid Artists: 80

2077
WICHITA GRAND OPERA
Concert Hall, Second Floor
225 West Douglas Avenue
Wichita, KS 67202
Phone: 316-262-8054
e-mail: info@wichitagrandopera.org
Web Site: www.wichitagrandopera.org
Officers:
  President: Parvan Bakardiev
  Vice President: Margaret Ann Pent
  Secretary: Chris D'Acosta
  Treasurer: Lisa Klaskin
  Board Member: Joseph Galichia MD
  Board Member: Patrick Gearhart
  Board Member: Richard Guthrie
Management:
  Artistic Director/EVP: Margaret Ann Pent
  Producing Impresario: Parvan Bakardiev
  Conductor: Steven Mercurio
  Conductor: Ken Hakoda
  Conductor/Orchestra Manager: Edward Lada
  Stage Director: Shayna Leahy
  Stage Director: John Stevens
  Choreographer: Diane Gans
Mission: Wichita Grand Opera, Salina's Stiefel Theatre, and the McPherson Opera House announce the formation of the Kansas Performing Arts Consortium. The Consortium's mission will be to develop cultural excellence and accessibility through collaboration among leading performing arts entities in Central Kansas. As three flagship performing arts institutions in the region, we plan to pool resources to enable joint projects, and innovate new ways.
Utilizes: Arrangers; Collaborating Artists; Collaborations; Fine Artists; High School Drama; Multimedia; Music; Paid Performers; Sign Language Translators; Singers
Specialized Field: Opera, Orchestra
Status: Non-Profit, Professional
Income Sources: Donors, Sponsors, Benefits/Galas
Season: Year Round
Performs At: Century II Performing Arts Center

Kentucky

2078
AMERICAN SPIRITUAL ENSEMBLE
333 W. Vine Street, Suite 300
Lexington, KY 40507
Phone: 888-728-8989
Fax: 423-510-0012
e-mail: peggy@globalcreativeconnections.com
Web Site: americanspiritualensemble.com/index.html
Management:
  Music Director: Everett McCorvey
  Company Manager: James E. Lee
Specialized Field: Ensemble
Status: Professional
Organization Type: Performing; Touring

2079
KENTUCKY OPERA
323 West Broadway
Suite 601
Louisville, KY 40202

VOCAL MUSIC / Louisiana

Phone: 502-584-4500
Fax: 502-589-7870
Toll-free: 800-690-9236
e-mail: david_roth@kyopera.org
Web Site: www.kyopera.org
Officers:
- President: Cristy S. Kramer
- Treasurer & Chief: John Sweeney
- Vice Chair: Matthew Hamel
- Secretary: Shannon B. Budnick
- Co-Chair: Ellen B. Finn

Management:
- General Director: Deborah Roth
- Finance Director: Brett Landow
- Development Director: Frances Skolnick
- Director of Education: Deanna Hoying
- Marketing Director: Steve Kelley

Mission: To entertain and educate a broad, diverse audience by producing opera of the highest quality.
Utilizes: Collaborations; Designers; Educators; Grant Writers; Guest Companies; Guest Composers; Guest Conductors; Guest Designers; Guest Writers; Instructors; Lyricists; Multimedia; Original Music Scores; Resident Professionals; Sign Language Translators
Founded: 1952
Specialized Field: Grand Opera; Light Opera; Lyric Opera; Musical Theatre; Choral; Youth Chorus; Ethnic Music; Classical; Contemporary; Religious
Status: Non-Profit, Professional
Paid Staff: 20
Volunteer Staff: 200
Paid Artists: 80
Budget: $2,200,000
Income Sources: Fund for the Arts; Mainstage Performances; Education Programs; Public/Private Philanthropy
Performs At: Kentucky Center for the Arts; Whitney Hall
Annual Attendance: 14,000/25,000 edu
Type of Stage: Proscenium
Stage Dimensions: 59'9"x52'6""x32""
Seating Capacity: 2,406
Year Built: 1983
Year Remodeled: 2002
Organization Type: Performing; Touring; Educational

2080
LOUISVILLE BACH SOCIETY
4607 Hanford Lane
Louisville, KY 40207
Phone: 502-585-2224
Fax: 502-893-7954
e-mail: bach@louisvillebachsociety.org
Web Site: www.louisvillebachsociety.org
Management:
- Founder/Director: Melvin Dickinson
- Founder/Director: Margaret Dickinson

Mission: To perform the choral and orchestral music of Bach, as well as other baroque, modern, classical and romantic composers.
Founded: 1964
Specialized Field: Classical
Status: Non-Profit, Professional
Paid Staff: 4
Income Sources: Kentucky Arts Council; Greater Louisville Fund for the Arts; American Federation of Musicians
Performs At: University of Louisville
Organization Type: Performing; Touring; Resident; Educational

2081
LOUISVILLE CHORUS
6303 Fern Valley Pass
Louisville, KY 40228
Phone: 502-968-6300
e-mail: louisvillechorus@louisvillechorus.org
Web Site: www.louisvillechorus.org
Officers:
- President: Paul Peterson
- VP: Kevin Gilman
- Secretary: Alan Luger
- Treasurer: Vinita Talegaonkar

Management:
- Executive Director: Therese Davis
- Music Director: Daniel Spurlock

Mission: To foster the art of choral music for singers, audiences, students and special constituents by presenting the widest variety of performances and outreach programs.
Utilizes: Guest Artists
Founded: 1939
Specialized Field: Choral
Status: Non-Profit, Professional
Paid Staff: 4
Paid Artists: 45
Income Sources: Individual, Corporate, State Arts Council, Local Metro Government
Performs At: Concert Halls; Churches
Affiliations: Chorus America
Organization Type: Performing; Touring; Educational; Entertaining; Sponsoring

Louisiana

2082
OPERA LOUISIANE
P.O. Box 4908
Baton Rouge, LA 70821
Phone: 225-377-2029
Fax: 225-377-2109
e-mail: info@operalouisiane.com
Web Site: operalouisiane.com
Management:
- General Director: Leanne P. Clement
- Musical Director: Michael Borowitz
- Associate Director: Molly Dahlberg
- Chorusmaster: Jennifer Ellis

Mission: Opera Louisiane presents high quality, professional, operatic performances, showcasing internationally acclaimed talent.
Founded: 2007
Status: Professional

2083
JPAS CHILDREN'S CHORUS/YOUTH CHORALE
Jefferson Performing Arts Society
1118 Clearview Parkway
Metairie, LA 70001
Phone: 504-885-2000
Fax: 504-885-3437
e-mail: info@jpas.org
Web Site: www.jpas.org
Officers:
- Chairman: Hannah Cunningham
- Vice President: Jack Sloan, CFP
- Past President: Daniel Bruza
- Secretary: Sharon Hannahan
- Counselor: Paul Deal

Management:
- President: Deborah R. Rouen
- Co-Founder, Executive/Artistic Dire: Dennis Assaf
- Conductor: Louise Labruyere
- Conductor: Dr. Louise LaBruyere
- Artistic Administrative Assistant,: Lynne L. Bordelon

Mission: To provide a complete music education experience for young people.
Founded: 1984
Specialized Field: Youth Chorus; Opera; Musical Theatre
Status: Non-Profit, Professional
Paid Staff: 4
Volunteer Staff: 20
Paid Artists: 300
Non-paid Artists: 130
Budget: $150,000
Income Sources: JPAS; Tuitions

2084
NEW ORLEANS OPERA ASSOCIATION
616 Girod St.
Suite 200
New Orleans, LA 70130
Phone: 504-529-2278
Fax: 504-529-7668
Toll-free: 800-881-4459
e-mail: robertlyall@neworleansopera.org
Web Site: www.neworleansopera.org
Officers:
- Vice President: Meredith Hathorn Penick
- Treasurer: John Eckholdt
- Secretary: Thomas Davidson
- Secretary: Charles Dupin

Management:
- President: Edward F. Martin
- General and Artistic Director: Robert Lyall
- Administration Director: Rebecca Hildabrant
- Executive Director: Timothy Todd Simmons

Mission: Providing the highest quality grand opera for Louisiana and its surrounding area.
Utilizes: Choreographers; Dancers; Designers; Five Seasonal Concerts; Grant Writers; Guest Accompanists; Guest Composers; Guest Designers; Guest Lecturers; Guest Musicians; Local Artists; Multimedia; Original Music Scores; Resident Professionals; Sign Language Translators
Founded: 1943
Specialized Field: Grand Opera
Status: Non-Profit, Professional
Paid Staff: 8
Paid Artists: 50
Budget: $2.5 million
Income Sources: Individual; Corporate; Foundation; Ticket Sales
Season: October- April
Performs At: Mahalia Jackson Theater of the Performing Arts
Annual Attendance: 18,500
Facility Category: Theater
Year Built: 1975
Organization Type: Performing; Resident; Educational

2085
SYMPHONY CHORUS OF NEW ORLEANS
PO Box 50542
New Orleans, LA 70150
Phone: 504-525-2111
e-mail: info@symphonychorus.org
Web Site: www.symphonychorus.org
Officers:
- Vice President: Michael Baker
- Secretary: Fifi Higgins
- Treasurer: S. Harry Cooper

Management:
- Musical Director: Steven Edwards
- President: Bart Folse
- Administrative Director: Emily Fransen
- Financial Director: Jodee Daroca

Founded: 1981
Specialized Field: Choral; Classical; Religious
Status: Non-Profit, Professional
Paid Staff: 3
Paid Artists: 40

2086
SHREVEPORT OPERA
212 Texas Street
Suite 101
Shreveport, LA 71101
Phone: 318-227-9503
Fax: 318-227-9518
e-mail: edillner@shreveopera.org
Web Site: www.shreveopera.org
Officers:
- President: Mark McCrocklin
- Executive Vice-President: Sybil Patten
- Treasurer: J. Thomas Simms, III
- Secretary: Marcia Moffatt
- Past President: Robert R. Robinson, Dr. P.H.

Management:
- General/Artistic Director: Steve Aiken
- VP Fund Development: Sybil Patten
- Executive Director Marketing: Amanda Joy Bell-Gouthiere,
- Director of Development: Eric Lincoln
- Box Office Manager: Cathey Sholar

Mission: To foster and promote the production of quality performances of opera and music drama; to aid in furthering the development of opera; and to further educational efforts which support the growth, development, and appreciation of opera as a viable art form within the tri-state region.
Utilizes: Collaborations; Dance Companies; Educators; Fine Artists; Guest Composers; Guest Designers; Guest Writers; Original Music Scores; Resident Professionals; Sign Language Translators; Soloists
Founded: 1949
Specialized Field: Opera/Musical Theatre
Status: Non-Profit, Professional
Paid Staff: 7
Volunteer Staff: 450
Paid Artists: 450
Non-paid Artists: 30
Budget: $800,000
Income Sources: Individual; Corporate; Facility; State; Grants
Performs At: Theater
Annual Attendance: 5,500
Facility Category: Civic Theater
Type of Stage: Proscenium
Stage Dimensions: 50' x 40'
Seating Capacity: 2,000
Organization Type: Performing; Touring; Resident; Educational

Maine

2087
MAINE MUSIC SOCIETY
221 Lisbon Street
Lewiston, ME 04240
Phone: 20-778-2722
Fax: 207-782-8192
e-mail: info@mainemusicsociety.org
Web Site: www.mainemusicsociety.org
Officers:
- President: David M. Blocher
- Vice President: Carl Sheline
- Secretary: Susan F. Trask
- Certified Financial Planner: Mindy Davis
- Treasurer: Anne M. Jarvis

Management:
- CPA: Robert C. Grieshaber
- Artistic Director: John Corrie
- Accompanist: Bridget Convey

Mission: The Maine Music Society supports the artistic and educational activities of the professional Maine Chamber Ensemble and the auditioned, mixed-voice Androscoggin Chorale.
Founded: 1991
Specialized Field: Choral; Classical; Religious
Status: Non-Profit, Professional
Paid Staff: 3
Income Sources: Maine Community Foundation; Davis Family Foundation; Helen & George Ladd Charitable Foundation; Maine Arts Commision; Maine Humanities Commission
Performs At: Orchestral; Chamber and Coral Music; Educational Programs
Affiliations: American Symphony Orchestra League; Maine Arts Sponsors Association; Androscoggin County Chamber of Commerce; Maine Association of Non-Profits

2088
PORTLAND SYMPHONIC CHOIR
PO Box 1517
Portland, ME 97207
Phone: 503-223-1217
Fax: 503-223-4840
e-mail: info@pschoir.org
Web Site: www.pschoir.org
Management:
- Artistic Director/Conductor: Dr Steven Zopfi
- General Manager: Mark Petersen
- Assistant Director: Kathryn Lehmann

Founded: 1946
Specialized Field: Choral

2089
PORTOPERA
PO Box 7733
Portland, ME 04112
Phone: 207-879-7678
Fax: 207-879-7681
e-mail: portopera@aol.com
Web Site: www.portopera.org
Officers:
- Immediate Past President: Donald L. Head
- Secretary: Thomas P. Aldrich
- Treasurer: Constance Bingham

Management:
- President: Ann L. Elderkin
- Office Manager: Julia Underwood

Mission: PORTopera is dedicated to equally high standards of artisitc excellence and personal effectiveness. Its mission is to present to the people of Maine great operatic masterpieces in productions that are lively, beautiful and important locally, regionally and nationally. Its objective is to do so within a principled and empowered environment.
Utilizes: Choreographers; Collaborating Artists; Collaborations; Dance Companies; Dancers; Educators; Five Seasonal Concerts; Grant Writers; Guest Accompanists; Guest Artists; Guest Composers; Guest Conductors; Guest Designers; Guest Instructors; Guest Writers; Local Artists; Lyricists; Multimedia; Original Music Scores; Resident Artists; Resident Professionals; Sign Language Translators; Soloists; Student Interns
Founded: 1995
Specialized Field: Grand Opera
Status: Non-Profit, Professional
Paid Staff: 1
Volunteer Staff: 2
Paid Artists: 179
Budget: $500,000
Income Sources: Corporate; Individual Support
Annual Attendance: 6,000
Facility Category: Municipal Theatre
Type of Stage: Proscenium
Stage Dimensions: 52'x40'x35'
Seating Capacity: 1830
Year Built: 1912
Year Remodeled: 1997

2090
BAY CHAMBER CONCERTS
18 Central Street
PO Box 599
Rockport, ME 04856
Mailing Address: P.O. Box 599, Rockport, ME 04856
Phone: 207-236-2823
Fax: 207-230-0454
Toll-free: 888-707-2770
e-mail: info@baychamberconcerts.org
Web Site: www.baychamberconcerts.org
Officers:
- President: Carole Brand
- Treasurer: Laurence Novotney
- Secretary: Warren Schubert
- Vice President Education: Caroline Seamans
- Vice President at Large: Luther Black

Management:
- Artistic Director: Manuel Bagorro
- Executive Director: Monica Kelly
- Development Director: Laura Chaney
- Registrar and Ticketing Coordinator: Joan Kulle
- Marketing Coordinator: Peter Johnson

Mission: To present a variety of music styles and educational programs to reach a diverse audience along the coast of Maine.
Utilizes: Commissioned Music; Dancers; Fine Artists; Grant Writers; Guest Accompanists; Guest Choreographers; Guest Directors; Guest Musical Directors; Guest Musicians; Lyricists; Multimedia; Original Music Scores; Resident Artists; Sign Language Translators; Singers; Special Technical Talent
Founded: 1960
Specialized Field: Music
Status: Non-Profit, Professional
Paid Staff: 9
Budget: $500,000
Performs At: Rockport Opera House
Facility Category: Opera House; Strom Auditorium
Type of Stage: Proscenium; Auditorium
Seating Capacity: 400; 800
Organization Type: Performing

Maryland

2091
ANNAPOLIS OPERA
Maryland Hall for the Creative Arts
801 Chase Street
Room 304
Annapolis, MD 21401
Phone: 410-267-8135
Fax: 410-267-6440
e-mail: admin@annapolisopera.org
Web Site: www.annapolisopera.org
Officers:
- President: Lee Finney

VOCAL MUSIC / Maryland

Management:
  Administration: Jessica Kenney, admin@annapolisopera.org
Mission: To bring affordable opera to the residents of Maryland, educate audiences about opera as an art form, provide opportunities for local artists and technical personnel to involve themselves in all phases of opera production, and discover emerging talent among young Maryland vocal artists through an annual vocal competition.
Utilizes: Collaborating Artists; Collaborations; Community Members; Community Talent; Contract Orchestras; Designers; Educators; Fine Artists; Five Seasonal Concerts; Grant Writers; Guest Accompanists; Guest Artists; Guest Conductors; Guest Ensembles; Guest Instructors; Guest Musical Directors; Guest Musicians; Guest Soloists; Guest Speakers; Instructors; Local Artists; Local Artists & Directors; Local Talent; Lyricists; Multimedia; Music; Original Music Scores; Paid Performers; Resident Artists; Resident Professionals; Sign Language Translators; Singers; Soloists; Student Interns; Touring Companies; Visual Arts; Volunteer Artists
Founded: 1973
Specialized Field: Children's Opera
Status: Professional, Non-Professional, Nonprofit
Paid Staff: 2
Volunteer Staff: 60
Paid Artists: 52
Non-paid Artists: 35
Budget: $300,000
Income Sources: Tickets; Donations; Grants
Performs At: Arts Center Auditorium
Annual Attendance: 5,000
Organization Type: Performing; Educational

2092
BALTIMORE CHORAL ARTS SOCIETY
1316 Park Avenue
Baltimore, MD 21217
Phone: 410-523-7070
Fax: 410-523-7097
Toll-free: 800-750-0875
e-mail: info@baltimorechoralarts.org
Web Site: www.baltimorechoralarts.org
Officers:
  President: Ellen Bernard
  Vice President and Treasurer: Karen Malecki
  Vice President: Richard Dellheim
  Secretary: Polly Behrens
  Chorus Manager: Ellen Clayton
Management:
  Music Director: Tom Hall
  Executive Director: Linda Moxley
  Assistant Conductor: Leo Wanenchak
  Marketing Associate: Jim Smith
  Patron Services Manage: Donna Lashof
Utilizes: Collaborating Artists; Collaborations; Commissioned Composers; Dance Companies; Dancers; Grant Writers; Guest Accompanists; Guest Choreographers; Guest Directors; Guest Instructors; Guest Musical Directors; Guest Musicians; Instructors; Multimedia; Original Music Scores; Sign Language Translators; Singers
Founded: 1966
Specialized Field: Choral
Paid Staff: 4
Volunteer Staff: 1
Paid Artists: 65
Non-paid Artists: 75
Budget: $500,000
Income Sources: Ticket Sales; Contributions; Maryland State Arts Council; Baltimore County Commission on Arts & Science; Mayor's Advisory Committee on Art & Culture; Local Contributors
Performs At: Joseph Meyerhoff Symphony Hall; Krausbaar Auditorium
Affiliations: Member of Chorus America
Annual Attendance: 15,000

2093
BALTIMORE OPERA COMPANY
110 W Mount Royal Avenue
Suite 306
Baltimore, MD 21201
Phone: 410-625-1600
Fax: 410-625-6474
e-mail: info@baltimoreopera.com
Web Site: www.baltimoreopera.com
Management:
  President: Micheal Harrison
  Music Director: James Harp
Utilizes: Dancers; Designers; Grant Writers; Guest Accompanists; Guest Artists; Guest Composers; Guest Conductors; Guest Designers; Guest Instructors; Guest Writers; Resident Professionals; Sign Language Translators
Founded: 1950
Specialized Field: Grand Opera; Light Opera; Lyric Opera; Musical Theatre; Choral; Youth Chorus; Ethnic Music; Classical; Contemporary; Religious
Status: Non-Profit, Professional
Paid Staff: 100
Volunteer Staff: 50
Paid Artists: 20
Budget: $7 million
Annual Attendance: 60,000
Facility Category: Opera House
Type of Stage: Proscenium
Seating Capacity: 2460
Year Built: 1894
Year Remodeled: 1981

2094
BALTIMORE SYMPHONY CHORUS
1212 Cathedral Street
Baltimore, MD 21201-5545
Phone: 410-783-8100
Fax: 410-783-8077
e-mail: jglicker@baltimoresymphony.org
Web Site: www.baltimoresymphony.org
Officers:
  Vice President & Chief Financial Of: Beth Marie Buck
  Vice President of Development: Dale Hedding
  Vice President of Marketing & Commu: Eileen Andrews
  Vice President of Artistic Operatio: Matthew Spivey
  Vice President of Education & Commu: Carol Bogash
Management:
  President & CEO: Paul Meecham
  VP: Karen Swanson
  Director Of Operations: Susan Anderson
  Artistic Coordinator: Carol Oppelaar
  Manager of Facility Sales: Toby Blumenthal
Mission: The choir is the choral arm of the Baltimore Symphony and performs when the Symphony needs singers.
Founded: 1916
Specialized Field: Choral
Status: Nonprofit
Performs At: Joseph Meyerhoff Symphony Hall
Organization Type: Performing

2095
HANDEL CHOIR OF BALTIMORE
3600 Clipper Mill Road
Suite 150
Baltimore, MD 21211
Phone: 410-366-6544
Fax: 410-366-6554
e-mail: info@handelchoir.org
Web Site: www.handelchoir.org
Officers:
  President: Leslie Greenwald
  VP: David Hamburger
  Treasurer: Cynthia Leveriny
Management:
  President: Leslie Greenwald
  Artistic Director: Melinda O'Neal
  Managing Director: Anne Wilson
Utilizes: Collaborations; Commissioned Composers; Community Members; Community Talent; Contract Orchestras; Guest Ensembles; Guest Instructors; Instructors; Original Music Scores
Founded: 1935
Specialized Field: Choral; Youth Chorus; Classical
Status: Non-Profit, Non-Professional
Paid Staff: 2
Paid Artists: 3

2096
OPERA VIVENTE
811 Cathedral Street
Baltimore, MD 21201
Phone: 410-547-7997
Fax: 847-557-2175
e-mail: info@operavivente.org
Management:
  General Director: John Bowen
  Music Director: Aaron Sherber
Utilizes: Collaborations; Grant Writers; Guest Writers; Instructors; Local Artists; Multimedia; Music; Original Music Scores; Resident Professionals; Sign Language Translators
Specialized Field: Opera

2097
WASHINGTON SAVOYARDS
1333 H ST NE
Bethesda, MD 20002
Phone: 202-399-7993
Fax: 202-315-1303
e-mail: Savoyards@Savoyards.org
Web Site: www.savoyards.org
Officers:
  President: Ian M. Grossman
  VP: Chris Agan
  Treasurer: Alan Ammerman
  Secretary: Angela Ammerman
Management:
  Executive Director: Katheleen Mitchell
  Artistic Director: N. Thomas Pedersen
  Associate Artistic Director: Matthew Kacergis
Mission: Provide professional performances of musicals & Gilbert & Sulivans Operettas
Founded: 1973
Specialized Field: Gilbert and Sullivan; Operetta; Light Opera
Status: Non-Profit, Professional
Income Sources: Ticket Sales; Grants
Performs At: Atlas Performing Arts Center

2098
COLUMBIA PRO CANTARE
5404 Iron Pen Place
Columbia, MD 21044

Phone: 410-730-8549
Fax: 410-730-8634
e-mail: chorus@procantare.org
Web Site: www.procantare.org
Officers:
    President: Stephen Mack
    VP: Gregory Stanford
    Secretary: Doris Raytkwich
    Treasurer: Kevin T Howard
Management:
    Executive Director: Elladean Brigham
    Director: Frances Dawson
    Assistant Director: Laura Lee Fischer
    Artistic Director: Frances Motyca Dawson
Mission: A nationally recognized mixed chorus of 130 auditioned volunteer singers based in Howard County which seeks to present the finest choral literature in concerts of high artistic quality to a growing regional audience. It aspires to provide enriching musical experiences for both singers and audience. Its mission is to nourish the human need we all have to participate in something greater than ourselves through the performance of great choral music.
Founded: 1977
Specialized Field: Vocal Music
Status: Non-Profit, Professional
Paid Staff: 5
Volunteer Staff: 1
Paid Artists: 3
Non-paid Artists: 130
Budget: $180,000
Income Sources: Public and Private Grants; Corporations; Individuals
Performs At: Public Theater for performing arts; Also use 2 large churches for smaller concerts.
Affiliations: Maryland State Arts Council; Howard County Arts Council; Chorus America
Annual Attendance: 2,500
Stage Dimensions: 60' x 30'
Seating Capacity: 740
Year Built: 1997

2099
FREDERICK CHORALE
P.O. Box 3009
Frederick, MD 21705-3009
Phone: 301-371-4668
e-mail: info@frederickchorale.org
Web Site: frederickchorale.org
Management:
    Music Director: Douglas D. Cox
Mission: The mission of the Frederick Chorale, an auditioned mixed chorus that values artistic excellence, is to prepare and perform fine choral repertoire of diverse musical styles and to enrich the cultural life of the Frederick County community.
Founded: 1977
Status: Nonprofit

2100
INSTITUTE OF MUSICAL TRADITIONS
PO Box 5930
Takoma Park, MD 20913
Phone: 301-960-3655
Fax: 301-754-3612
e-mail: publicity@imtfolk.org
Web Site: www.imtfolk.org
Officers:
    President: David Richardson
    Vice-President: Kent Murray
    Treasurer: Art Shaw
    Secretary: James Byrne
    Founder, President Emeritus: David Eisner
Management:

Executive Director: Kent Murray
Mission: To present concerts, workshops and educational programs that preserve traditional folk music from around the world and nurtures new styles evolving from these cultural roots.
Utilizes: Arrangers; Collaborating Artists; Collaborations; Community Members; Dance Companies; Educators; Five Seasonal Concerts; Guest Accompanists; Guest Choreographers; Guest Companies; Guest Directors; Guest Ensembles; Guest Musical Directors; Guest Musicians; Guest Speakers; Instructors; Local Talent; Local Unknown Artists; Lyricists; Multi Collaborations; Multimedia; Original Music Scores; Paid Performers; Resident Companies; Sign Language Translators; Student Interns; Theatre Companies; Visual Designers
Founded: 1981
Opened: 1981
Specialized Field: Traditional Folk
Status: Non-Profit
Paid Staff: 3
Volunteer Staff: 20
Paid Artists: 135
Budget: $131,000
Income Sources: Tickets; Public & Private Foundation Grants; Private Donations
Affiliations: Folklore Society Of Greater Washington; International Folk & Dance Alliance; Washington Arts & Music Association
Annual Attendance: 3,500
Facility Category: Church Hall
Type of Stage: Elevated
Stage Dimensions: 16x6
Seating Capacity: 150; 230; 500

2101
CHILDREN'S CHORUS OF MARYLAND & SCHOOL OF MUSIC
100 E Pennsylvania Avenue
Suite 202
Towson, MD 21286
Phone: 410-494-1480
Fax: 410-494-4673
e-mail: ccm@ccmsings.org
Web Site: www.ccmsings.org
Officers:
    Education Director & Associate Cond: Dr Betty Bertaux
    Concert Manager: Andrea Burgoyne
    President: Keith W. May
    Secretary: Anya Grundmann
    Founder & Director: Betty Bertaux
Management:
    General Director: Ramona Galey
    Artistic Director: Mairee Pantzer
    Concert Manager: Andrea Burgoyne
Mission: Children's Chorus of Maryland empowers musical children and promotes the fine art of music. This mission is achieved by providing children with the tool of self-expression, through choral music education and professional performance opportunities, in a program dedicated tio excellence, aesthetic sensitivity, play-based learning, respect, and diversity.
Founded: 1976
Specialized Field: Youth Chorus

Massachusetts

2102
VALLEY LIGHT OPERA
PO Box 2143
Amherst, MA 01004-2143

Phone: 413-549-1098
e-mail: wcvenman@comcast.net
Web Site: www.vlo.org
Management:
    President: Glen Gordon
    Managing Director: Jacqueline Kidwell
    Artistic Director: Joseph Donohue
    General Manager: Bill Venman
Mission: Promotes broad participation and produces fine entertainment.
Founded: 1975
Specialized Field: Light Opera
Status: Non-Profit, Non-Professional
Performs At: Amherst Regional High School Auditorium
Organization Type: Performing

2103
BACK BAY CHORALE
P.O. Box 170051
Boston, MA 02117
Phone: 617-648-3885
e-mail: info@bbcboston.org
Web Site: backbaychorale.org
Management:
    Music Director: Scott Allen Jarrett
Mission: The Back Bay Chorale celebrates the unifying power of music by performing choral masterworks with a passionate commitment to excellence.
Founded: 1973

2104
BOSTON CAMERATA
PO Box 120751
Boston, MA 02466
Phone: 617-262-2092
Fax: 617-262-2091
Toll-free: 866-427-2092
e-mail: manager@bostoncamerata.com
Web Site: www.bostoncamerata.org
Management:
    Artistic Director: Anne Azema
    Music Director Emeritus: Joel Cohen
    General Manager: Andrew Shryock
    Webmaster: Tom Wible
Mission: To reach large audience through teaching, recording and performance by touring.
Founded: 1954
Specialized Field: Lyric Opera; Musical Theatre; Choral; Ethnic Music; Classical
Status: Non-Profit, Professional
Paid Staff: 2
Paid Artists: 30

2105
CANTATA SINGERS
729 Boylston Street
Suite 305
Boston, MA 02116
Phone: 617-868-5885
Fax: 617-868-3772
e-mail: jhughes@cantatasingers.org
Web Site: www.cantatasingers.org
Officers:
    Chair: Mary Beth Stevens
    Treasurer: David J. Cooper
    Chorus President: Kay Patterson-Shaw
    Secretary: Daniel D. Scharfman
Management:
    Executive Director: Jennifer Ritvo Hughes
    Artistic Director: David Hoose
    General Manager: Sara Libenson
    Education Coordinator: Josh Taylor
    Development Director: Robert Pape

VOCAL MUSIC / Massachusetts

Mission: Through vital performances of works old and new, familiar and unfamiliar, Cantata Singers engages and shared with the community the power of music to enrich the human spirit.
Utilizes: Commissioned Composers; Commissioned Music; Educators; Fine Artists; Five Seasonal Concerts; Grant Writers; Guest Directors; Guest Instructors; Guest Musicians; Local Artists; Multimedia; Organization Contracts; Original Music Scores; Sign Language Translators; Singers; Soloists
Founded: 1964
Specialized Field: Choral
Status: Non-Profit, Professional
Paid Staff: 3
Volunteer Staff: 5
Paid Artists: 1
Non-paid Artists: 44
Budget: $400,000
Income Sources: Ticket sales; Contributions; Government Endowments
Performs At: Rented Hall
Affiliations: Chorus America
Annual Attendance: 7,000
Facility Category: Rented Concert Hall at New England Conservatory
Rental Contact: Jon Wulp

2106
HANDEL AND HAYDN SOCIETY
300 Massachusetts Avenue
Boston, MA 02115
Phone: 617-262-1815
Fax: 617-266-4217
e-mail: info@handelandhaydn.org
Web Site: www.handelandhaydn.org
Officers:
  Chairman: Nicholas Gleysteen
  Vice Chair: Julia D. Cox
  Vice Chair: Todd Estabrook
  Vice Chair: Deborah S. First
  Vice Chair: Karen S. Levy
Management:
  Executive Director/CEO: Marie-H,ISne Bernard
  Music Director: Grant Llewellyn
  Artistic Director: Harry Christophers
  Conductor Laureate: Christopher Hogwood
  Associate Conductor and Chorusmaste: John Finney
Mission: Dedicated to promoting the performance, study, composition and appreciation of music.
Utilizes: Commissioned Composers; Guest Composers; Guest Directors; Guest Musical Directors; Guest Musicians; Multimedia; Music; Original Music Scores; Sign Language Translators; Singers
Founded: 1815
Specialized Field: Choral; Classical
Status: Non-Profit, Professional
Paid Staff: 16
Paid Artists: 100
Budget: $2,600,000
Performs At: Symphony Hall; Jordan Hall
Annual Attendance: 40,000
Organization Type: Performing; Touring; Educational; Sponsoring

2107
OPERA BOSTON
25 Kingston Street
3R
Boston, MA 02111-2200
Phone: 617-451-3388
Fax: 617-451-6633
e-mail: info@operaboston.org
Officers:
  Chairman: Winifred Perkin Gray
  President: Randolph Fuller
  Treasurer: Campbell Steward
  Office Administrator: Gillian Morrison
  Secretary: Timothy Gillette
Management:
  General Director: Carole Charnow
  Music Director: Gil Rose
  Director Operations: William Chapman
  Production Manager: Emma Donoghue
  Production Photographer: Clive Grainger
Mission: The company produces staged opera and special events in Boston, as well as presents new productions of rarely-heard works, innovative repertoire, groundbreaking opera education and outreach programs.
Specialized Field: Opera
Status: Professional
Income Sources: Donations
Season: October-April
Performs At: Cutler Majestic Theatre
Year Built: 1903

2108
OPERA NEW ENGLAND
11 Avenue de Lafayette
Boston, MA 02111-1736
Phone: 617-542-4912
Fax: 617-542-4913
e-mail: boxoffice@blo.org
Web Site: www.blo.org
Officers:
  Chair: Steven P Atkin
  Vice Chair: Thomas D Gill Jr
  Treasurer: Frank Wisneski
  Clerk: Catherine E Grein
  President: Horace H Irvine II
Management:
  Marketing Director: Judith McMichael
  General/Artistic Diretor: Esther Nelson
  Production Director: Dan Duro
  Music Director: David Angus
  Marketing & Communications Manager: Amanda Villegas
Mission: To present diverse productions by emerging opera musicians to entertain, educate and inspire audiences.
Founded: 1973
Specialized Field: Lyric Opera; Light Opera
Status: Professional, Nonprofit
Income Sources: Opera Company of Boston
Organization Type: Educational; Sponsoring

2109
BRAINTREE CHORAL SOCIETY
PO Box 850182
Braintree, MA 02184
Mailing Address: P. O. Box 850182, Braintree, MA 02184
Phone: 508-583-5662
e-mail: braintreesings@beld.net
Web Site: www.braintreesings.com
Management:
  President: Kathleen Mullen
  Artistic Director: Justin Smith
  Director: Charles A. Dillingham
Mission: Promoting interest in choral music.
Utilizes: Singers
Founded: 1923
Specialized Field: Classical; Choral
Status: Non-Profit, Non-Professional
Paid Staff: 2
Paid Artists: 2
Organization Type: Performing

2110
KLEZMER CONSERVATORY BAND
83 Inman Street
Cambridge, MA 02139
Phone: 617-354-2884
Fax: 617-776-0955
Web Site: www.klezmerconservatory.com
Management:
  Business Manager Aaron Concert Man: James Guttmann
  Director: Hankus Netsky
  Audio Engineer: Dana Parsons
Mission: To offer Yiddish instrumental and vocal music with many influences (Jazz, Dixieland, Ragtime, Latin and Broadway).
Founded: 1980
Specialized Field: Ethnic Music; Folk Music; Band
Status: Professional
Organization Type: Performing; Touring

2111
MASTERWORKS CHORALE
PO Box 382231
Cambridge, MA 02238
Phone: 617-858-6785
e-mail: info@masterworkschoral.org
Web Site: www.masterworkschorale.org
Management:
  Music Director: Steven Karidoyanes
  Music Director Emeritus: Galen Marshall
Mission: Mission is the performance of manjor choral works
Founded: 1964
Specialized Field: Choral
Status: Non-Profit, Semi-Professional
Paid Staff: 1
Paid Artists: 1
Performs At: Sanders Theatre; Harvard University

2112
RADCLIFFE CHORAL SOCIETY
Harvard University
Holden Chapel
Cambridge, MA 02138
Phone: 617-496-5166
Fax: 617-496-5166
e-mail: manager@radcliffechoralsociety.org
Web Site: www.radcliffechoralsociety.org
Officers:
  President: Amy Lifland
  Vice President: Claire Fitzgerald
  Secretary: Veri Seo
Management:
  Conductor: Michaela Tracy
  Manager: Ananda Martin-Caughey
  Assistant Manager: Katherine Reifler
  Financial Manager: Michelle Chang
Founded: 1899
Specialized Field: Choral; Youth Chorus; Ethnic Music; Classical; Contemporary; Religious
Status: Non-Profit, Non-Professional
Paid Artists: 3

2113
SAVOYARD LIGHT OPERA COMPANY
PO Box 333
Carlisle, MA 01741
Phone: 978-371-7562
Web Site: www.savoyardlightopera.org
Officers:
  Secretary: Laura Gouillart
Management:
  President: Connell Benn

VOCAL MUSIC / Massachusetts

Vice President: Thomas Frates
Secretary: Julie Cornell
Treasurer: Larry Millner
Mission: To associate ourselves for the purpose of encouraging and making generally available performances of the works of W.S. Gilbert and A.S. Sullivan, and other works of similar operatic, musical or theatrical nature in Carlisle and nearby areas.
Founded: 1971
Specialized Field: Light Opera

2114
COLLEGE LIGHT OPERA COMPANY
162 S Cedar Street
Falmouth, MA 02541
Phone: 440-774-8485
Fax: 440-775-8642
e-mail: cloc@oberlin.net
Web Site: www.collegelightopera.com
Officers:
   President: DeWitt C Jones III
   Treasurer: Robert A Haslun
   Secretary: Ursula R Haslun
Management:
   Producer/General Manager: Robert A Haslun
   Producer/Business Manager: Ursula R Haslun
Mission: Musical theatre training ground for undergraduates, singers, musicians, tech & costume staff, business office and production staff.
Utilizes: Actors; Choreographers; Contract Orchestras; Designers; Guest Artists; Guest Companies; Guest Conductors; Guest Designers; Guest Lecturers; Music; Resident Artists; Resident Professionals; Sign Language Translators; Students
Founded: 1969
Specialized Field: Light Opera; Operetta; Musical Theatre
Status: Non-Professional, Nonprofit
Paid Staff: 25
Paid Artists: 18
Non-paid Artists: 32
Budget: $300,000
Income Sources: Box Office; Annual Fund
Performs At: Highfield Theatre
Annual Attendance: 15,200
Type of Stage: Proscenium
Seating Capacity: 300
Year Built: 1947
Year Remodeled: 2007
Cost: $450,000
Organization Type: Performing, Resident, Educational

2115
COMMONWEALTH OPERA
140 Pine Street #12
Florence, MA 01062
Phone: 413-586-5026
Fax: 413-587-0380
Toll-free: 866-733-6737
Web Site: www.commonwealthopera.org
Officers:
   President: Gerry Katz
   VP: Richard Strongren
   Treasurer: Anita Regish
   Guild President: Katherine Willey
Management:
   President: Richard L Stromgren
   Artistic Director: Ron Luchsinger
   Executive Director: Janet Sadler
Mission: Enhancing professional opportunities in and appreciation of grand opera and broadway musicals in the region.

Utilizes: Choreographers; Collaborations; Dance Companies; Dancers; Five Seasonal Concerts; Grant Writers; Guest Accompanists; Guest Companies; Guest Composers; Guest Instructors; Guest Lecturers; Guest Musicians; Guest Writers; Instructors; Multimedia; Original Music Scores; Resident Professionals; Sign Language Translators; Singers
Founded: 1972
Specialized Field: Grand Opera; Lyric Opera
Status: Semi-Professional
Paid Staff: 3
Volunteer Staff: 40
Budget: $250,000
Income Sources: Tickets; Sponsors; Donations
Performs At: Calvin Theatre; Smith College
Organization Type: Performing; Touring

2116
BERKSHIRE OPERA COMPANY
297 N Street
Great Barrington, MA 01201
Phone: 413-442-9955
Fax: 413-442-5995
Web Site: www.berkshireopera.org
Officers:
   Chairman/Treasurer: Norman M Michaels
Management:
   General Director: Ryaniam Taylor
   Artistic Director: Kathleen Kelly
Mission: To produce and present the very finest in professional opera. To provide and enhance educational programming and community activities to people of all ages in Berkshire County.
Utilizes: Guest Companies; Singers
Founded: 1985
Specialized Field: Opera
Status: Non-Profit, Professional
Budget: $1.3 million
Income Sources: Berkshire Hills Visitors Bureau
Performs At: Mahaiwe Theater
Annual Attendance: 3,000
Seating Capacity: 700
Year Built: 1905
Rental Contact: Al Shwartz
Organization Type: Performing; Touring; Resident; Educational

2117
PRISM OPERA
5 Linebrook Road
Ipswich, MA 01938
Phone: 978-356-1787
Toll-free: 888-236-8181
e-mail: prism@prismopera.org
Web Site: www.prismopera.org
Management:
   Executive Director: Arthur Rishi
   Artistic Director: Thomas Stumpf
Mission: Prism Opera is committed to producing effective and moving productions of operatic masterpieces, with a special emphasis on neglected works and on twentieth century repertoire.
Founded: 1995
Specialized Field: Opera

2118
MASTER SINGERS
PO Box 172
Lexington, MA 02173
Phone: 781-862-6459
e-mail: msingers@themastersingers.org
Web Site: www.themastersingers.org
Officers:
   President: Sarah Getty

   Treasurer: Shaylor Lindsay
   Secretary: Virginia Fitzgerald
Management:
   President: Haris Papamichael
   Music Director: Adam Grossman
Mission: To present the chamber chorus repertoire of all eras in an intimate setting aimed at maximum enjoyment for both singers and listeners.
Founded: 1967
Specialized Field: Classical; Contemporary; Grand Opera; Choral; Religious
Status: Non-Profit, Professional
Paid Staff: 30
Income Sources: Massachusetts Cultural Alliance
Performs At: First Parish Church in Lexington
Organization Type: Performing; Touring

2119
LONGWOOD OPERA
1132 Highland Ave.
Needham, MA 02192-3806
Phone: 781-455-0960
Fax: 781-455-0960
e-mail: Encore@LongwoodOpera.org
Web Site: www.longwoodopera.org
Officers:
   Musical Director: Wayne Ward
   Director of Marketing Communication: Harding Ounanian
Management:
   General Director: Scott Brumit
   Musical Director: Jeffrey Brody
Specialized Field: Opera

2120
ZAMIR CHORALE OF BOSTON
1320 Centre Street
Suite 306
Newton Center, MA 02459
Phone: 617-244-6333
Toll-free: 866-926-4720
e-mail: manager@zamir.org
Web Site: www.zamir.org
Officers:
   Chairman: Robert Snyder
   Treasurer: Jeff Rosenberg
   Clerk: Martin A. Oppenheimer
   President: Joshua R. Jacobson
Management:
   Executive Director: Dianne Simmons
   Founder and Artistic Director: Joshua Jacobson
   Accompanist: Edwin Swanborn
   Managing Director: Barbara Gaffin
Mission: To promote, develop and encourage the growth of Jewish choral music through scholarship, performances, recordings and educational programs.
Founded: 1969
Specialized Field: Choral; Ethnic Music
Status: Non-Professional; Nonprofit
Paid Staff: 5
Organization Type: Performing; Touring; Resident; Educational

2121
SMITH COLLEGE GLEE CLUB & CHOIRS
Smith College, Music Department
Northampton, MA 01063
Phone: 413-585-3150
Fax: 413-585-3180
e-mail: gleeclub@smith.edu
Web Site: www.smith.edu/music
Management:
   President: Anna Monas
   Artistic Executive Director: Jonathan Hirsh

All listings are in alphabetical order by state, then city, then organization within the city.

VOCAL MUSIC / Michigan

Founded: 1885
Specialized Field: Grand Opera; Light Opera; Lyric Opera; Musical Theatre; Choral; Youth Chorus; Ethnic Music; Classical; Contemporary; Religious
Status: Non-Profit, Non-Professional
Paid Staff: 2

2122
GLORIAE DEI ARTES FOUNDATION
PO Box 2831
Orleans, MA 02653
Phone: 508-255-3999
Fax: 508-240-1989
e-mail: gda@gdaf.org
Web Site: www.gdaf.org
Officers:
 President: Sarah R Kanaga
Management:
 Choir Director: Elizabeth C Patterson
 Concert Manager: Gail Gibson
 Executive Director: Wendy Saran
Mission: The pursuit of excellence in the performing and visual arts and to the inspiration and education of others. The foundation encompasses twelve arts groups and soloist, including the world renowned choir Gloriae Dei Cantores, Spirit of America band, Stages Theatre Company, Tapestry Dance Company, Archangelus Brass Ensemble, Gloria Dei Ringers, Vox Caeli Sinfonia, Gloriae Dei Chamber Ensemble, Master Schola educational series.
Utilizes: Artists-in-Residence; Choreographers; Collaborating Artists; Composers; Dancers; Designers; Fine Artists; Guest Writers; High School Drama; Multi Collaborations; Multimedia; Music; Paid Performers; Poets; Resident Professionals; Sign Language Translators; Singers; Theatre Companies; Visual Arts; Volunteer Directors & Actors; Writers
Founded: 1995
Specialized Field: Classical; Contemporary; Religious; Choral; Musical Theatre
Status: Non-Profit, Professional

2123
BERKSHIRE LYRIC THEATRE
PO Box 347
Pittsfield, MA 01202
Phone: 413-499-0258
e-mail: info@berkshirelyricinfo.org
Web Site: www.berkshirelyrictheatre.org
Officers:
 President: Jeanne Caluori
 Treasurer: Michael Wessel
 Secretary: Elizabeth Barbour
Management:
 Artistic Director: Jack Brown
 Accompanist, Director of the Berksh: Joe Rose
Mission: To nurture the art of choral singing through diverse concert performances and to educate young musicians.
Utilizes: Singers
Founded: 1963
Specialized Field: Light Opera; Choral
Status: Non-profit
Paid Staff: 40
Organization Type: Performing

2124
PAUL MADORE CHORALE
PO Box 992
Salem, MA 01970-6092
Phone: 781-639-8062
Fax: 781-639-8065
e-mail: info@paulmadorechorale.o
Web Site: www.paulmadorechorale.org
Officers:
 President: Kathleen Snarry
 Vice President: Chris Lemoine
 Treasurer: Marcia Hunkins
 Recording Secretary: Eileen Mackey
 Corresponding Secretary: Elaine Shindle
Management:
 Director: Paul Madore
 Orchestra Manager: Alan Hawryluk
 Chorus Manager: Donna Murphy
 Principal Accompanist: Jeffrey Brody
Mission: Offering choral masterpieces for the enjoyment and cultural advancement of the North Shore/Boston areas.
Utilizes: Guest Musical Directors; Guest Soloists; Multimedia; New Productions; Original Music Scores; Sign Language Translators; Singers
Founded: 1966
Specialized Field: Opera; Choral
Status: Semi-Professional; Nonprofit
Volunteer Staff: 1
Paid Artists: 1
Budget: $50,000
Income Sources: Box Office; Private Donations
Performs At: Churches; Municipal Buildings
Affiliations: Salem Chamber of Commerce; Greater Boston Choral Consortium
Organization Type: Performing

2125
FINE ARTS CHORALE
779 Main Street
South Weymouth, MA 02190
Mailing Address: P.O. Box 32975, Kansas City, MO 64171
Phone: 617-337-3023
Toll-free: 800-230-7555
e-mail: info@FineArtsChoraleKC.org
Web Site: www.fineartschoralekc.org
Officers:
 President: Shirley Fallon
 VP: Olga Gianelis
 Secretary: Vivian Horton
 Treasurer: Philip Brown
Management:
 Music Director/Founder: Peter L Edwards
 Artistic Director & Conductor: Terri Teal
Mission: The presentation of sacred choral masterworks accompanied by a professional orchestra and soloists. There are no dues required.
Founded: 1966
Specialized Field: Choral
Status: Non-Professional; Nonprofit
Paid Staff: 130
Organization Type: Performing

2126
REVELS
80 Mount Auburn Street
Watertown, MA 02472
Phone: 617-972-8300
Fax: 617-972-8400
e-mail: ssmith@revels.org
Web Site: www.revels.org
Officers:
 President: Carl Corey
 VP: Christian W. Hughes
 Treasurer: Richard J. Goettle IV
 Clerk: Maggie B. Tyler
Management:
 Executive Director: Steve Smith
 Artistic Director: Patrick Swanson
 Music Director: George Emlen
 Production: Lynda Johnson
 Marketing and Public Relations: Alan Casso
Mission: To cultivate authentic cultural traditions and celebrate the cycles of the seasons through staged performances of song, dance and drama, education programs, and opportunities for participation by all.
Founded: 1971
Specialized Field: Music; Dance; Theatre
Status: Non-Profit, Professional
Paid Staff: 7
Paid Artists: 20
Performs At: Sanders Theatre; Harvard University
Organization Type: Performing; Educational

2127
SALISBURY SINGERS
370 Main Street
Suite 1200
Worcester, MA 01608
Phone: 508-799-3848
Fax: 508-792-3067
e-mail: info@salisburysingers.org
Web Site: www.salisburysingers.org
Officers:
 Treasurer/Librarian: James Monroe
 Secretary: Margaret Twiss
 Council President: Marie Laverty
Management:
 Music Director: Dr Michelle Graveline
 Chorus Manager: Joyce Messinger
 Assistant Conductor: Joshua Rohde
 Accompanist: Lynne LaComfora
 Program: Carmella Murphy
Mission: To perform classical works for the community of central Massachusetts.
Founded: 1973
Specialized Field: Choral
Status: Non-Profit
Paid Staff: 1
Non-paid Artists: 80
Performs At: Church; Concert Halls

Michigan

2128
BOYCHOIR OF ANN ARBOR
1100 N Main Street
Suite 215
Ann Arbor, MI 48104
Phone: 734-663-5377
e-mail: office@aaboychoir.org
Web Site: www.aaboychoir.org
Officers:
 President: Jeannette Jackson
 Treasurer: Karen Lancaster
 Secretary: Danielle Palincsar
Management:
 Founder & Music Director: Thomas Strode, office@aaboychoir.org
 Assistant Music Director: Alex Sutton
Mission: Through excellence in vocal training and choral performance, the Boychoir of Ann Arbor enriches the life of the community and enhances the social, emotional, and musical development of boys who love to sing.
Utilizes: Community Members; Community Talent; Educators; Grant Writers; Guest Composers; Guest Designers; Guest Directors; Guest Musical Directors; High School Drama; Local Artists & Directors; Lyricists; Multimedia; Music; Original Music Scores; Scenic Designers; Sign Language Translators; Singers; Soloists; Volunteer Artists
Founded: 1986
Specialized Field: Choral; Youth Chorus; Classical

VOCAL MUSIC / Michigan

Status: Non-Profit
Paid Staff: 3
Volunteer Staff: 40
Paid Artists: 2
Non-paid Artists: 2
Budget: $55,000
Income Sources: Performances; Tuition; Donations; Grants
Affiliations: Royal School of Church Music

2129
COMIC OPERA GUILD
PO Box 1922
Ann Arbor, MI 48106
Phone: 734-973-3264
Fax: 734-973-6281
e-mail: constu@comcast.net
Web Site: www.comicoperaguild.org
Officers:
   President: Patrick Johnson
   Secretary: Patricia Petiet
   Treasurer: George Valenta
   Vice President: Bob Seeman
Management:
   Managing Director: Thomas Petiet
Mission: To revive popularity and interest in the medium of comic opera and operetta through performance and recording.
Utilizes: Guest Artists; Guest Companies; Singers
Founded: 1973
Specialized Field: Light Opera; Musical Theatre; Classical
Status: Non-Profit, Non-Professional
Paid Staff: 6
Volunteer Staff: 40
Paid Artists: 25
Non-paid Artists: 50
Performs At: Village Theater
Organization Type: Performing; Touring; Resident

2130
UNIVERSITY MUSICAL SOCIETY CHORAL UNION
881 North University Avenue
Burton Memorial Tower, 881 N University Avenu
Ann Arbor, MI 48109-1011
Phone: 734-764-2538
Fax: 734-647-1171
Toll-free: 800-221-1229
e-mail: umstix@umich.edu
Web Site: www.ums.org
Officers:
   President: Ken Fisher
   Director Administration: John Kennard
   Director Of Development: Margie McKinley
   Interim Director Education: Jim Leja
   Chairperson: Dr. James Stanley
   Vice Chair: David Herzig
   Secretary: Martha Darling
   Treasurer: Robert C. Macek
Management:
   Director Of Programming: Michael Kondziolka
   Director oOf Marketing/Communicatio: Sara Billmann
Mission: To provide professional theatre, dance and music for Southeastern Michigan students and residents.
Utilizes: Guest Artists
Founded: 1879
Specialized Field: Series & Festivals; Musical Performance
Status: Non-Profit; Professional
Paid Staff: 30
Budget: $8,000,000
Income Sources: Ticket Sales; Fundraising
Performs At: Hill Auditorium; University of Michigan
Affiliations: Association of Performing Arts Presenters; International Society of Performing Arts Administrators
Annual Attendance: 150,000
Organization Type: Performing; Touring; Resident; Educational

2131
UNIVERSITY OF MICHIGAN GILBERT AND SULLIVAN
The Michigan League Building
911 N University
Ann Arbor, MI 48109-1265
Phone: 734-647-8436
e-mail: umgassexec@umich.edu
Web Site: www.umgass.org
Officers:
   President: Amanda O'Toole
   VP: Candace Pierce-Winters
   Secretary: Jeremy Williams
   Treasurer: Alexandria Strother
Management:
   Company Promoter: Matthew D Grace
   Programmer: James Allen
Founded: 1947
Specialized Field: Operetta
Status: Non-Professional; Nonprofit
Paid Artists: 30
Performs At: Mendelssohn Theatre; University of Michigan
Organization Type: Performing; Resident; Educational

2132
CHEBOYGAN AREA ARTS COUNCIL/OPERA HOUSE
403 N Huron Street
PO Box 95
Cheboygan, MI 49721
Phone: 231-627-5432
Fax: 231-627-3130
e-mail: pamtheoperahouse.org
Web Site: www.theoperahouse.org
Officers:
   President: Randy Maltby
   Vice-President: Sandra Jeannotte
   Secretary: Jane ROE
   Treasurer: Alice Barron
Management:
   Assistant Director: Vicky Pyrzynski
   Executive Director: Pamela Westover
Mission: To promote and encourage cultural and educational activities within the Straits Area of Northern Michigan and to provide services that stimulate and encourage participation in and appreciation of the arts.
Utilizes: Actors; AEA Actors; Artists-in-Residence; Collaborations; Dance Companies; Dancers; Grant Writers; Guest Accompanists; Guest Choreographers; Guest Lecturers; Guest Musical Directors; Guest Musicians; Guild Activities; Local Artists; Multi Collaborations; Multimedia; Original Music Scores; Resident Artists; Sign Language Translators; Singers; Soloists; Special Technical Talent; Theatre Companies
Founded: 1972
Specialized Field: Multi-Disciplinary
Status: Non-Profit, Professional
Budget: $250,000
Income Sources: Membership; Ticket Sales; Fundraisers; Grants; Other Earned Income
Performs At: Opera House
Affiliations: Association of Performing Arts Presenters; MACAA; LHAT
Annual Attendance: 30,000
Facility Category: Historic Theatre
Type of Stage: Proscenium
Stage Dimensions: 34x20
Seating Capacity: 582
Year Built: 1877
Year Remodeled: 1984
Rental Contact: Pamela Westover
Organization Type: Educational; Sponsoring

2133
TIBBITS OPERA FOUNDATION AND ARTS COUNCIL
14 S Hanchett Street
Coldwater, MI 49036
Phone: 517-278-6029
Fax: 517-279-7594
e-mail: boxoffice@tibbits.org
Web Site: www.tibbits.org
Officers:
   President: Randall Hazelbaker
   Treasurer: Brian Hodson
Management:
   Executive Director: Christine Delaney
   Artisic Director: Charles Burr
Mission: Improve the quality of life by preserving the Tibbits Opera House and promoting arts culture and education.
Founded: 1964
Specialized Field: Live Performance
Status: Non-Profit, Professional
Paid Staff: 8
Volunteer Staff: 300
Budget: $500,000
Income Sources: Membership; Ticket Sales; Annual Auction; Grants - Michigan Council for Arts and Cultural Affairs; Michigan Humanities Council; Branch County Community Foundation; Corporate
Performs At: Tibbits Opera House
Affiliations: League Of Historic American Theatres
Annual Attendance: 30,000
Facility Category: Historic Theatre/Opera House
Type of Stage: Proscenium
Stage Dimensions: 25'x35'
Seating Capacity: 500
Year Built: 1882
Year Remodeled: 1965
Rental Contact: Christine Delaney
Organization Type: Performing; Touring; Resident; Educational; Sponsoring
Resident Groups: Tibbits Summer Theatre - Professional Repertory Company

2134
MICHIGAN OPERA THEATRE
1526 Broadway
Detroit, MI 48226
Phone: 313-237-7464
Fax: 313-237-3412
e-mail: webadministrator@motopera.org
Web Site: www.michiganopera.org
Officers:
   Chairman: R. Jamison Williams
   President: David DiChiera
   Treasurer: Cameron B. Duncan
   Secretary: C. Thomas Toppin
Management:
   General Director: David Dichiera
   Productioin Director: David Osborne
   Director Of Artistic Administration: Roberto Mauro
   Facilities Director: Karen Tjaden
   Administration Director: John Eckstrom
   Marketing Director: Steve Haviaras
   Assistant Marketing Director: Susan Fazzini

VOCAL MUSIC / Minnesota

Mission: To be one of the outstanding opera companies in the United States, serving as a major cultural resource.
Utilizes: Artists-in-Residence; Collaborations; Dance Companies; Educators; Five Seasonal Concerts; Grant Writers; Guest Accompanists; Guest Choreographers; Guest Composers; Guest Conductors; Guest Designers; Guest Instructors; Guest Musical Directors; Guest Musicians; Guest Soloists; Guild Activities; Instructors; Local Artists; Lyricists; Multimedia; Original Music Scores; Playwrights; Resident Artists; Resident Professionals; Selected Students; Sign Language Translators; Singers; Soloists; Student Interns; Theatre Companies
Founded: 1971
Specialized Field: Grand Opera; Operetta; Musical Theatre
Status: Professional; Nonprofit
Paid Staff: 54
Volunteer Staff: 800
Paid Artists: 74
Budget: $12,000,000
Income Sources: Earned and Unearned
Performs At: Stage; Rehearsal Room
Affiliations: International Association of Auditorium Managers
Annual Attendance: 194,608
Facility Category: Performing Arts
Type of Stage: Proscenium
Stage Dimensions: 65x110
Seating Capacity: 2,800
Year Built: 1922
Year Remodeled: 1996
Rental Contact: Facilities Director Karen Tjaden
Organization Type: Performing; Touring

2135
OPERA LITE
27284 Winterset Circle
Farmington Hills, MI 48334
Phone: 248-888-7640
Fax: 248-888-7641
e-mail: dsp96@aol.com
Management:
  President: David Pulice
  Assistant Director: Don Daniels
Founded: 1986
Specialized Field: Grand Opera; Light Opera; Lyric Opera; Musical Theatre; Choral; Youth Chorus; Classical; Religious
Status: Non-Profit, Professional
Paid Staff: 3
Paid Artists: 47
Organization Type: Performing; Touring; Resident

2136
OPERA GRAND RAPIDS
1320 East Fulton
Grand Rapids, MI 49503
Phone: 616-451-2741
Fax: 616-451-4587
Web Site: www.operagr.com
Management:
  Executive Director: Michael Havlicek
  Artistic Director: Robert Lyall
Mission: To enhance the quality of life in the Grand Rapids area and Western Michigan by providing professional-quality operatic/musical theater productions; to raise the level of appreciation and understanding of opera in all residents.
Utilizes: Actors; Dancers; Designers; Five Seasonal Concerts; Grant Writers; Guest Accompanists; Guest Artists; Guest Composers; Guest Conductors; Guest Designers; Guest Instructors; Guest Lecturers; Guest Musical Directors; Guest Musicians; Guest Soloists; Guest Writers; Instructors; Local Artists; Lyricists; Multimedia; Music; Original Music Scores; Resident Professionals; Sign Language Translators; Singers; Soloists; Student Interns
Founded: 1967
Specialized Field: Opera
Status: Non-Profit, Professional
Paid Staff: 5
Budget: $1.2 million
Performs At: DeVos Hall; Van Andel Arena
Annual Attendance: 17,000
Seating Capacity: 2,340
Year Built: 1979
Organization Type: Performing; Educational; Sponsoring

2137
RACKHAM SYMPHONY CHOIR
P.O. Box 36788
Grosse Pointe, MI 48236
Phone: 313-404-0222
Fax: 313-272-5111
e-mail: marg@rackhamchoir.org
Web Site: www.rackhamchoir.org
Officers:
  President: Bud Uhl
  Vice President: James Leyerle
Management:
  Artistic and Music Director: Suzanne Mallare Acton
  Assistant Director And Accompanist: Donald Kukier
  Managing Director: Anne Bak
  Executive Director: Marg Glaza
Mission: To provide choral symphonic performances featuring the works of the classical masters to the Detroit metropolitan area.
Founded: 1949
Specialized Field: Choral
Status: Nonprofit
Paid Staff: 60
Organization Type: Performing; Educational

2138
HOLLAND CHORALE
150 East 8th Street
Holland, MI 49423-3504
Phone: 616-494-0256
Fax: 616-396-6298
e-mail: julia@hollandchorale.org
Web Site: www.hollandchorale.org
Officers:
  President: Karen Bylsma
  Secretary: Robbie Schorle
  Treasurer: Dennis Willaman
Management:
  Operations Manager: Julia Johnson
  Artistic Director: Meredith Bowen
  Accompanist: Emily Bergsma
  Vocal Consultant: Nicholas Loren
  Development Director: Skip Keeter
Founded: 1959
Specialized Field: Choral; Ethnic Music; Classical; Contemporary; Religious
Status: Non-Profit, Non-Professional
Paid Staff: 2
Volunteer Staff: 85

2139
KALAMAZOO SINGERS
P.O. Box 2712
Kalamazoo, MI 49003
Phone: 269-373-1769
e-mail: admin@kalamazoosingers.org
Web Site: kalamazoosingers.org
Officers:
  President: Susan E. Daniels
  Vice President: David Veenhuis
Management:
  Music Director: Richard Phelps
  Composer/Arranger: John C. Griffin
Mission: The Kalamazoo Singers seeks to merge the capabilities of an elite, auditioned chorus with the community need and opportunities for an accomplished vocal ensemble. The prime objective of the Kalamazoo Singers is to perform quality music from opera, operetta, musical theater, and both classic and contemporary choral repertoire.
Founded: 1976
Specialized Field: Choral
Status: Nonprofit

2140
SAGINAW CHORAL SOCIETY
201 N. Washington
Saginaw, MI 48607
Phone: 989-753-1812
Fax: 989-753-1043
e-mail: glenthomas@saginawchoralsociety.com
Web Site: www.saginawchoralsociety.com
Officers:
  Past President: Dave Lyman
  Treasurer: Kristi Krafft-Bellsky
Management:
  President: Karen Stiffler
  Business Manager: Tamara Grafe
  Artistic Director & Conductor: Glen Thomas Rideout
  Executive Director: Tamara Grefe
  Office & Production Manager: Kathleen Scott
Mission: To provide an opportunity for quality singers to join together in singing and performing fine choral music so as to contribute to the enjoyment, musical growth and education of the residents of Saginaw Valley. Regularly performs master works from the classical choral music literature, as a priority in maintaining the firm artistic integrity of the organization.
Founded: 1935
Specialized Field: Choral
Status: Non-Profit, Non-Professional
Paid Staff: 2

Minnesota

2141
THE APOLLO CLUB
2418 West 107th Street
Bloomington, MN 55431
Phone: 612-642-1895
Web Site: theapolloclub.org
Officers:
  President: Darren Jackson
  Vice President: Ray Peterson
  Vice President: Shawn Jones
  Secretary: David Pitt
  Treasurer: Al Buss
Management:
  Artistic Director: Sean Vogt
  General Manager: Tom Peterson
Mission: Apollo Club elevates the consciousness of performance music by creating an authentic stage for amateurs and professionals alike.
Founded: 1985
Specialized Field: Choral
Organization Type: Performing; Touring

VOCAL MUSIC / Minnesota

2142
AUGSBURG CHOIR
Augsburg College
2211 Riverside Avenue South
Minneapolis, MN 55454
Phone: 612-330-1000
Fax: 612-330-1264
e-mail: hendricp@augsburg.edu
Web Site: www.augsburg.edu
Management:
    Choral Activities Director: Dr Peter Hendrickson
Specialized Field: Choral

2143
MINNESOTA CHORALE
528 Hennepin Avenue
Suite 407
Minneapolis, MN 55408
Phone: 612-333-4866
Fax: 612-344-1503
e-mail: we_sing@mnchorale.org
Web Site: www.mnchorale.org
Officers:
    President: Elizabeth Balay
    Vice President: K. Dennis Kim
    Treasurer: Karen M. Touchi-Peters
    Secretary: Ten, Wright
Management:
    General Manager: Bob Peskin
    Operations Director: Melissa Morey
    Executive Director: Bob Peskin
    Director of Grants and Communicatio: Larry Fuchsberg
    Chorus Personnel Manager: Barbara Lundervold
Mission: The Minnesota Chorale is a nationally acclaimed symphonic chorus with a signature flexibility to perform masterfully in ensembles ranging from 20 to 200 voices. Celebrates the human voice in its ability to educate, enrich, and inspire.
Founded: 1972
Specialized Field: Choral; Ethnic Music; Classical
Status: Non-Profit, Professional
Paid Staff: 8
Paid Artists: 40
Non-paid Artists: 230
Income Sources: Chorus America
Performs At: Orchestra Hall; Ordway Music Theatre
Affiliations: Minnesota Orchestra's Principal Chorus
Organization Type: Performing

2144
MINNESOTA OPERA
620 N First Street
Minneapolis, MN 55401
Phone: 612-333-2700
Fax: 612-333-0869
Toll-free: 800-676-6737
e-mail: mnop@mnopera.org
Web Site: www.mnopera.org
Officers:
    Chair: Rachelle D. Chase
    Vice Chair: James Johnson
    Secretary: Robert Lee
    Treasurer: Patricia Johnson
Management:
    President and General Director: Kevin Ramach
    Artistic Director: Dale Johnson
    Music Director: Michael Christie
Mission: To produce opera and opera education programs at the highest artisic level that inspire and entertain our audiences and enrich the cultural life of our community.
Utilizes: Choreographers; Dance Companies; Designers; Educators; Guest Accompanists; Guest Artists; Guest Composers; Guest Conductors; Instructors; Local Artists; Original Music Scores; Resident Professionals; Sign Language Translators
Founded: 1963
Specialized Field: Opera
Status: Non-Profit, Professional
Income Sources: Opera America
Performs At: Ordway Music Theatre
Annual Attendance: 55,000
Facility Category: Rent Ordway Center for the Performing Arts
Seating Capacity: 1764
Year Built: 1985
Organization Type: Performing; Touring; Resident; Educational; Recording

2145
NATIONAL LUTHERAN CHOIR
528 Hennepin Avenue
Suite 302
Minneapolis, MN 55403
Phone: 612-722-2301
Fax: 612-216-4777
Toll-free: 888-747-4589
e-mail: info@nlca.com
Web Site: www.nlca.com
Officers:
    President: Mark B. Uecker
    Vice President: Rebecca Jorgenson Sundquist
    Treasurer: Brenda Bartz
    Secretary: Linda Holmen
Management:
    General Manager: Debby Harrer
    Artistic Director: David Cherwien
    Artistic Director: David Cherwien
    Administrative Director: Randall Davidson
Mission: The National Lutheran Choir seeks to strengthen, renew, and preserve the heritage of sacred choral music through the highest standards of performance and literature.
Founded: 1986
Specialized Field: Choral; Religious
Status: Professional
Paid Staff: 3
Paid Artists: 4
Non-paid Artists: 55
Budget: $250,000
Income Sources: Ticket Sales; General Donations; Corporate Donations
Affiliations: American Council for the Arts; American Lutheran Church Musicians; Chorus America
Annual Attendance: 25,000
Organization Type: Performing

2146
TWIN CITIES GAY MEN'S CHORUS
528 Hennepin Avenue
Suite 307
Minneapolis, MN 55403
Phone: 612-339-7664
Fax: 612-332-8141
e-mail: chorus@tcgmc.org
Web Site: www.tcgmc.org
Management:
    Executive Director: Jeff Heirr
    Artistic Director: Ben Riggs
    Marketing/Development Manager: Christopher Taykalo
Mission: Gay men building community through music.
Utilizes: Choreographers; Commissioned Composers; Commissioned Music; Grant Writers; Guest Accompanists; Guest Artists; Guest Musicians; Selected Students; Sign Language Translators; Singers; Visual Arts
Founded: 1981
Specialized Field: Choral
Status: Non-Profit, Non-Professional
Paid Staff: 5
Volunteer Staff: 20
Non-paid Artists: 150
Budget: $625,000
Income Sources: Ticket Sales; Merchandise; Contributions
Performs At: Ted Menn Concert Hall
Annual Attendance: 9,000
Facility Category: Concert hall
Seating Capacity: 1,100
Organization Type: Performing, Touring, Recording

2147
VOCALESSENCE
1900 Nicollet Avenue
Minneapolis, MN 55403
Phone: 612-547-1451
Fax: 612-547-1484
e-mail: info@vocalessence.org
Web Site: www.vocalessence.org
Officers:
    Vice President: Paul Pribbenow, Ph.D.
    Treasurer: Mike McCarthy
    Secretary: Susan J. Crockett, Ph. D
Management:
    President: David Mona
    Executive Director: Mary Ann Pulk
    Artistic Director: Philip Brunelle
    Associate Conductor: Sigrid Johnson
Mission: Founded as The Plymouth Music Series, explores the interaction of voices and instruments through innovative programming of music, both newly-commissioned and rarely heard.
Founded: 1969
Specialized Field: Musical Theatre; Choral; Classical; Contemporary; Religious
Status: Non-Profit, Professional
Paid Staff: 10
Paid Artists: 32
Non-paid Artists: 80

2148
MINNETONKA CHAMBER CHOIR
Music Association of Minnetonka
18285 Highway 7
Minnetonka, MN 55345
Phone: 952-401-5954
Fax: 952-401-5959
e-mail: mamoffice@musicassociation.org
Web Site: www.musicassociation.org
Officers:
    Office Administrative: Joyce Barnes
    Co-Founder: Donna Hoel
Management:
    Artistic Director/Conductor: Roger S Hoel
    Concert Band Director: Den Geldert
    Civic Orchestra Director: William S Mayson
    Coral Reflections Director: David Halligan
    Concert Choir Director: Andrew Pieper
Mission: Provides enriching classical musical experiences for people of all ages and abilities. Approximately 70 concerts are performed each year.
Founded: 1974
Specialized Field: Choral; Youth Chorus; Ethnic Music; Classical; Contemporary; Religious
Status: Non-Profit, Non-Professional

VOCAL MUSIC / Mississippi

Paid Staff: 3
Paid Artists: 300

2149
MINNETONKA SYMPHONY CHORUS
Music Association of Minnetonka
18285 Highway 7
Minnetonka, MN 55345
Phone: 952-401-5954
Fax: 952-401-5959
e-mail: mamoffice@musicassociation.org
Web Site: www.musicassociation.org
Officers:
   Office Administrator: Joyce Barnes
   Co-Founder: Donna Hoel
Management:
   Artistic Director/Conductor: Roger S Hoel
   Concert Band Director: Den Geldert
   Civic Orchestra Director: William S Mayson
   Coral Reflections Director: David Halligan
   Concert Choir Director: Andrew Pieper
Mission: Provides enriching classical musical experiences for people of all ages and abilities. Approximately 70 concerts are performed each year.
Founded: 1974
Specialized Field: Community Chorus
Status: Non-Profit; Non-Professional
Paid Staff: 3

2150
CONCORD SINGERS OF NEW ULM
PO Box 492
New Ulm, MN 56073
Phone: 507-354-8850
Fax: 507-354-1504
e-mail: concord31@newulmtel.net
Web Site: www.concordsingers.com
Officers:
   President: Joseph Meyer
   VP: Lenny Donahue
Management:
   Manager: John Konz
   Music Director: Robert Beussman
   Secretary: Dick Wilbrecht
Mission: To promote the German language through singing.
Founded: 1931
Specialized Field: Festive German Music
Status: Non-Profit, Non-Professional
Paid Staff: 2
Volunteer Staff: 4
Non-paid Artists: 36
Income Sources: Stipend From The City Plus Performances In Our 5 State Area
Organization Type: Performing; Sponsoring

2151
ST OLAF CHOIR
St Olaf College
1520 St Olaf Avenue
Northfield, MN 55057-1098
Phone: 507-786-3179
Fax: 507-786-3521
Toll-free: 800-363-5487
e-mail: music@stolaf.edu
Web Site: www.stolaf.edu/music
Management:
   Artistic Director: Anton Armstrong
   Managing Director: B J Johnson
   Ensemble Music Coordinator: Mary Davis
Founded: 1912
Specialized Field: Choral; Ethnic Music; Classical; Contemporary; Religious
Status: Non-Profit, Non-Professional

Paid Staff: 6

2152
ROCHESTER SYMPHONY ORCHESTRA & CHORALE
400 S Broadway
Suite 302
Rochester, MN 55904
Phone: 507-286-8742
Fax: 507-280-4136
e-mail: info@rochestersymphony.org
Web Site: www.rochestersymphony.org
Officers:
   President: Randy Chapman
Management:
   Executive Director: Jeffery Amundent
   Artistic Director: Jere Lantz
   Education Coordinator: Amy Lindstrom
   Marketing Coordinator: Laura Gilliland
Mission: Rochester Symphony Orchestra and Chorale seeks to serve our community and region by preserving, nurturing and advancing the art of music through education and high quality performances that seek to touch the soul.
Utilizes: Collaborating Artists; Collaborations; Dancers; Five Seasonal Concerts; Guest Artists; Guest Musical Directors; Guest Musicians; Multimedia; Music; New Productions; Original Music Scores; Sign Language Translators; Singers
Founded: 1919
Specialized Field: Choral; Orchestra
Status: Non-Profit, Professional
Paid Staff: 4
Volunteer Staff: 80
Paid Artists: 75
Non-paid Artists: 80
Budget: $550,000
Income Sources: Ticket Sales; Contributions; Grants
Performs At: Mayo Civic Center
Affiliations: LDA
Annual Attendance: 5,000
Facility Category: Mayo Civic Center

2153
NORTH STAR OPERA
2635 Walnut St.
Saint Paul, MN 80205
Phone: 303-893-0552
Fax: 303-893-0507
e-mail: steve@northstaropera.org
Web Site: www.northstaropera.com
Management:
   Planning Director: Craig Fields
   Artistic Director: Steve Stucki
   Operations Director: Alison Albrecht
   President: Mariellen Jacob
Mission: Developing and showcasing highly-talented, well-qualified professional musicians, singers and related personnel of the local area and upper Midwest; sponsoring college internship programs.
Utilizes: Guest Artists; Guest Companies; Singers
Founded: 1980
Specialized Field: Lyric Opera; Light Opera; Operetta
Status: Professional; Nonprofit
Performs At: O'Shaughnessy Auditorium; Drew Fine Aris Theatre
Organization Type: Performing; Touring; Resident; Educational

2154
MINNESOTA CENTER CHORALE
PO Box 471
St Cloud, MN 56302

Phone: 320-257-0603
e-mail: pwelter@csbsju.edu
Web Site: minnesotacenterchorale.org
Officers:
   President: Mark Braun
   Secretary: Tom Ramsey
   Treasurer: Jonna Thomas
   Vice President: Steve Holste
Management:
   Music Director/Conductor: Jody Martinson
   Operations Coordinator: Michelle Dettmann
   Stage Management: Mark Braun
   Stage Management: Roger McHaney
Mission: The MCC performs a mixture of classical and contemporary music, often with orchesrtal accompaniment.
Utilizes: Guest Companies; Guest Composers; Guest Lecturers; Guest Musical Directors; Guest Musicians; Local Artists; Singers
Specialized Field: Choral
Paid Staff: 1
Budget: $60,000
Annual Attendance: 3,000
Facility Category: Auditorium
Year Built: 1965

Mississippi

2155
GULF COAST OPERA THEATRE
PO Box 118
Biloxi, MS 39533
Phone: 228-436-6514
Fax: 228-374-0152
e-mail: gcmusicaltheatre@hotmail.com
Web Site: www.gulfcoastoperatheatre.net
Management:
   President: Lisa Michell
   General Director: David Daniels
   Artistic Director: Jane Hardin
Mission: Educating Mississippi Gulf Coast residents regarding musical theatre and opera.
Founded: 1973
Specialized Field: Grand Opera; Light Opera; Lyric Opera; Musical Theatre; Choral; Youth Chorus; Classical; Religious
Status: Non-Profit, Professional
Paid Staff: 40
Performs At: Saenger Theatre for the Performing Arts
Organization Type: Performing; Resident

2156
MISSISSIPPI OPERA
PO Box 1551
Jackson, MS 39215-1551
Phone: 601-960-2300
Fax: 601-960-1526
Toll-free: 877-676-7372
e-mail: info@msoperaa.org
Web Site: www.msopera.org
Officers:
   President: Mrs. John Bivins
   Immediate Past President: Don Potts
   Treasurer: Hogan Allen
   Secretary: Ouida Holland
Management:
   Executive Director: Elizabeth Buyan
   Artistic Director: Jay Dean
   Marketing Director: Sherry Harfst
Mission: To enhance Mississippi's cultural and economic development by presenting high quality opera performances in an accessible manner; to identify and

VOCAL MUSIC / Missouri

develop regional operatic artists; and to promote the understanding and appreciation of Opera through education, outreach, and audience development.
Utilizes: Guest Artists; Guest Companies; Singers
Founded: 1945
Specialized Field: Grand Opera; Lyric Opera; Light Opera; Operetta; Musical Theatre
Status: Non-Profit, Professional
Paid Staff: 2
Volunteer Staff: 3
Paid Artists: 1
Non-paid Artists: 1
Budget: $300,000
Performs At: Jackson Municipal Auditorium
Organization Type: Performing; Touring; Educational

Missouri

2157
SAINT LOUIS CHAMBER CHORUS
PO Box 11558
Clayton, MO 63105
Phone: 636-458-4343
Fax: 314-993-6458
e-mail: stchamberchorus@gmail.org
Web Site: www.chamberchorus.org
Officers:
   President: Barbara Uhlemann
   Treasurer: Deane Thompson
   Vice President: Dick Brickson
   Secretary: Suzanne Lagomarcino
Management:
   Executive Director: Linda Ryder
   Artistic Director: Philip Barnes
   Assistant Conductor: Mary Chapman
   Assistant Conductor: Orin Johnson
Mission: Presenting unaccompanied classical choral music, not merely to entertain, but to educate and inspire.
Utilizes: Commissioned Music
Founded: 1956
Specialized Field: A Cappella Choral Music
Status: Not-For-Profit
Paid Staff: 2
Volunteer Staff: 2
Paid Artists: 46
Income Sources: Ticket Sales; Donations; Grants
Affiliations: American Choral Directorss' Association
Annual Attendance: 1,000
Facility Category: Houses of Worship & Concert Halls
Organization Type: Performing; Educational

2158
THE KANSAS CITY CHORALE
5601 Wyandotte, Suite 412
Kansas City, MO 64113
Phone: 816-444-7150
Fax: 816-444-7996
e-mail: info@kcchorale.org
Web Site: kcchorale.org
Management:
   Conductor: Charles Bruffy
   General Manager: Don Loncasty
Founded: 1981
Specialized Field: Choral
Status: Professional

2159
HEARTLAND MEN'S CHORUS
PO Box 32374
Kansas City, MO 64171-5374
Phone: 816-931-3338
Fax: 816-531-1367
e-mail: hmc@hmckc.org
Web Site: www.hmckc.org
Officers:
   Chairman: Matthew Stretz
Management:
   Artistic Director: Joseph Nadeau
   Executive Director: Rick Fisher
Mission: A not-for-profit, volunteer chorus of gay and gay-sensitive people joining together to make a positive cultural contribution to the entire community; advancing men's choral music through excellence in performance.
Founded: 1986
Specialized Field: Choral
Status: Non-Profit, Non-Professional
Paid Staff: 3
Paid Artists: 20
Non-paid Artists: 135
Budget: $695,000
Income Sources: Program Revenues; Donations
Performs At: The Folly Theater
Affiliations: Gay and Lesbian Association Choruses; Chorus America
Annual Attendance: 7,000
Seating Capacity: 1,078
Year Built: 1900
Year Remodeled: 2000
Organization Type: Performing

2160
LYRIC OPERA OF KANSAS CITY
1725 Holmes St.
Kansas City, MO 64108
Phone: 816-471-4933
Fax: 816-471-0602
Web Site: www.kcopera.org
Officers:
   Chief Financial Officer: Gregory A. Hubbard
   President: Richard P. Bruening
   President Elect: Kenneth V. Hager
   Treasurer: J. Michael Sigler
   Vice-President, Development: Lafayette J. Ford, III
Management:
   Artistic Director: Ward Holmquist
   General Director and CEO: Deborah Sandler
   Director of Production: Tracy Davis-Singh
   Director of Development: Michelle LaPointe
   Associate Director of Development: Nancy Steinacker
Mission: The Lyric Opera of Kansas engages people of diverse backgrounds and ages through the region in a broad range of professional operatic experiences to enrich their lives.
Utilizes: Guest Artists; Guest Companies; Singers
Founded: 1958
Specialized Field: Grand Opera; Light Opera; Lyric Opera; Musical Theatre; Choral; Classical; Operetta
Status: Non-Profit, Professional
Paid Staff: 21
Paid Artists: 120
Budget: $5.1 million
Income Sources: Ticket Sales; Contributions
Performs At: Lyric Theatre
Affiliations: Opera America
Annual Attendance: 20,000
Facility Category: Theatre
Type of Stage: Proscenium
Stage Dimensions: 50'x36'
Seating Capacity: 1640
Year Built: 1926
Year Remodeled: 1974
Organization Type: Performing; Touring; Resident

2161
KANSAS CITY SYMPHONY CHORUS
1703 Wyandotte
Suite 200
Liberty, MO 64108
Phone: 816-787-1803
Fax: 816-415-5027
e-mail: tims@kcsymphonychorus.org
Web Site: www.kcsymphonychorus.org
Management:
   Music Department Chair: Mark Schweizer
   Artistic Director: Charles Bruffy
   Executive Director: Timothy Russell
Specialized Field: Choral

2162
BACH SOCIETY OF SAINT LOUIS
3547 Olive
Suite 120
Saint Louis, MO 63103-1024
Phone: 314-652-2224
Fax: 314-289-4029
Web Site: www.bachsociety.org
Officers:
   Chairman: Deane H. Looney
   Vice Chairman: Harley Smith
   Treasurer: Andrew V. Wuellner
   Secretary: Geneen Von Kloha
Management:
   Executive Director: Alayne D Smith
   Music Director and Conductor: Dr A Dennis Sparger
   Composer in Residence: Stephen Mager
Mission: To educate, enrich and entertain the people of the St. Louis region by performing the choral works of Johann Sebastian Bach and other composers.
Founded: 1939
Specialized Field: Choral
Paid Staff: 1
Paid Artists: 25
Non-paid Artists: 35
Budget: $250,000
Income Sources: Individual & Corporate Contributions; Local; Regional & State Grants
Annual Attendance: 5,000

2163
OPERA THEATRE OF SAINT LOUIS
210 Hazel Avenue
PO Box 191910
Saint Louis, MO 63119
Phone: 314-961-0171
Fax: 314-961-7463
e-mail: boxoffice@opera-stl.org
Web Site: www.opera-stl.org
Officers:
   Chairman: Spencer B. Burke
   Vice Chair: Suzanne Engelhardt
   Vice Chair: V. Raymond
   Vice Chair: Stranghoener
   Secretary: Sally S. Levy
Management:
   Artistic Director: James Robinson
   General Director: Timothy O'Leary
   Music Director: Stephen Lord
   Director Finance: Mary Ip
Mission: To offer opera in English; to provide career advancement for young American singers; to offer the direction of renowned conductors and directors.
Utilizes: Guest Companies; Guest Composers; Guest Conductors; Multimedia; Original Music Scores; Sign Language Translators; Singers
Founded: 1976

VOCAL MUSIC / Montana

Specialized Field: Grand Opera; Light Opera; Lyric Opera; Musical Theatre; Choral; Youth Chorus; Ethnic Music; Classical; Contemporary
Status: Non-Profit, Professional
Paid Staff: 25
Budget: $6,500,000
Income Sources: 75% Contributions
Performs At: Loretto-Hilton Center for the Performing Arts
Affiliations: Missouri Arts Council; Regional Arts Commission; National Endowment for the Arts; Arts & Education Council of Greater Saint Louis
Annual Attendance: 29,000
Facility Category: Theater
Type of Stage: Thrust
Seating Capacity: 987
Rental Contact: Stephen Ryan
Organization Type: Performing; Touring; Educational

2164
SAINT LOUIS SYMPHONY CHILDREN'S CHOIR
2842 N Ballas Road
Saint Louis, MO 63131-2311
Phone: 314-993-9626
Fax: 314-993-0264
e-mail: info@slccsing.org
Web Site: www.slccsing.org
Management:
   Executive Director: Sheryl Bennett
   Artistic Director: Barbara Berner
   Choir Manager: Jodi Kratzer
   Ensemble Director: Adrienne Broyles
   Ensemble Director: Whitney Cairns
Mission: To provide young artists the opportunity to experience musical execellence and character development. Performing orchstral works with a chorus.
Specialized Field: Youth Chorus; Classical; Ethnic Music; Choral
Status: Non-Profit, Non-Professional
Paid Staff: 32
Budget: $600,000
Income Sources: Concert Fees; Tuition; Donations; Grants
Performs At: Powell Symphony Hall
Affiliations: Chorus America
Annual Attendance: 38,000

2165
SRO - A LYRIC THEATRE COMPANY
411 N Sherman Parkway
Springfield, MO 65802-3652
Phone: 417-863-1960
Fax: 417-862-7877
e-mail: marketing@srolyrictheatre.org
Web Site: www.srolyrictheatre.org
Officers:
   Chairman: Karen Horny
   President: Jeff Carney
   Vice President: Valia Gardner
   Secretary: Mary Christiano
   Treasurer: Sara Hitesman
Management:
   Managing Director: Tim Caldwell
   Artistic Director/Conductor: Amy Muchnick
Mission: Create lasting memories by presenting, promoting, and developing the art of opera, music, and theatre.
Utilizes: Guest Accompanists; Guest Designers; Local Artists; Multimedia
Founded: 1979
Specialized Field: Grand Opera; Lyric Opera; Light Opera; Operetta
Status: Professional, Nonprofit

Paid Staff: 2
Volunteer Staff: 13
Budget: $189,000
Income Sources: Box Office, Grants, Private Donations
Performs At: Landers Theatre; Hammons Hall
Affiliations: Opera America
Facility Category: Theatre
Type of Stage: Proscenium
Seating Capacity: 600
Year Built: 1920
Year Remodeled: 2005
Organization Type: Performing

Montana

2166
BILLINGS SYMPHONY ORCHESTRA & CHORALE
2721 2nd Avenue North
Suite 350
Billings, MT 59101
Phone: 406-252-3610
Fax: 406-252-3353
e-mail: symphony@billingssymphony.org
Web Site: www.billingssymphony.org
Officers:
   President: Robert Griffin
   VP: Jon Phillips
   Secretary: John Green
   Treasurer: Nicki Larson
Management:
   Music Director/Conductor: Uri Barnea
   Executive Director: Sandra Culhane
   Director of Education: Candy Holzer
   Development Associate: Joanne Copeland
Mission: To encourage artistic excellence and offer symphonic performances and educational programs to the region.
Utilizes: Artists-in-Residence; Collaborations; Composers-in-Residence; Dance Companies; Guest Accompanists; Guest Companies; Guest Composers; Guest Musical Directors; Guest Musicians; Local Artists; Multimedia; Original Music Scores; Sign Language Translators; Touring Companies
Founded: 1950
Specialized Field: Choral
Status: Non-Profit, Professional
Paid Staff: 4
Paid Artists: 85
Budget: $260,000-$1,050,000
Income Sources: Individual; Businesses; Foundations; Government; Ticket Revenue
Performs At: Alberta Bair Theater for the Performing Arts
Annual Attendance: 30,000

2167
INTERMOUNTAIN OPERA BOZEMAN
104 East Main Street
Suite 101
Bozeman, MT 59715
Mailing Address: PO Box 37, Bozeman, MT 59715
Phone: 406-587-2889
e-mail: info@intermountainopera.org
Web Site: www.intermountainopera.org
Officers:
   President: Richard Wolff
   Vice President: Doug Gale
   Secretary: Cindy McCarthy
   Treasurer: Merrilee Glover
   Board Member: Jeff Abelin
   Board Member: Robin Erienbush

Management:
   Artistic Director: Linda Curtis
   Executive Director: Jackie Vick
   Production Coordinator: Margaret Cone
   Chorus Director: Jon Harney
   Office Administrator: Jan Emerson
Mission: Bringing professional opera to Montana since 1979.
Utilizes: Arrangers; Collaborating Artists; Collaborations; Commissioned Music; Grant Writers; Guest Directors; Multimedia; Music; Sign Language Translators; Singers
Founded: 1978
Specialized Field: Opera, Classical
Status: Non-Profit, Professional
Income Sources: Donations, Sponsors, Gifts
Season: Fall
Performs At: Wilson Auditorium

2168
MONTANA CHORALE
214 24th Street SW
Great Falls, MT 59406
Phone: 406-453-0248
Fax: 406-453-7248
Web Site: www.montana-chorale.org
Officers:
   President: Ann Cogswell
   VP: Lorrin Darby
   Treasurer: Sharon Knowles
Management:
   Artistic Director: Kenyard Smith
Mission: To inspire and develop the choral arts in Montana, provide continuing education and employment for professional singers in Montana and develop an artistic climate with international reputation in Montana.
Utilizes: Guest Artists
Founded: 1976
Specialized Field: Choral
Status: Professional; Nonprofit
Income Sources: Chorus America
Performs At: Great Falls Civic Center
Organization Type: Performing; Touring; Sponsoring

Nebraska

2169
OPERA OMAHA
1850 Farnam Street
Omaha, NE 68102
Phone: 402-346-7372
Fax: 402-346-7323
Toll-free: 877-346-7372
e-mail: rweitz@operaomaha.org
Web Site: www.operaomaha.org
Officers:
   Chairman: John Newman
   Treasurer: Stephen Bruckner
   Secretary: Terrence J. Ferguson
   Advisory Board Chair: Jim Winner
Management:
   Executive Director: Joan Desens
   Artistic Director: Hal France
Utilizes: Singers
Founded: 1958
Specialized Field: Grand Opera; Light Opera; Lyric Opera; Musical Theatre; Choral; Youth Chorus; Classical; Contemporary
Status: Non-Profit, Professional
Paid Staff: 13
Budget: $2.4 million

VOCAL MUSIC / Nevada

Income Sources: Individuals; Foundations; Corporations; NEA; Nebraska Arts Council; Douglas County; NE Ticket Income
Performs At: Orpheum Theatre; Witherspoon Concert Hall
Annual Attendance: 9,000
Facility Category: Theater
Type of Stage: Proscenium
Stage Dimensions: 54'w x 30'h x 44'd
Seating Capacity: 2,500
Year Built: 1927
Year Remodeled: 2002
Organization Type: Performing; Touring; Resident; Educational; Sponsoring

2170
RIVER CITY MIXED CHORUS
P.O. Box 3267
Omaha, NE 68103
Phone: 402-341-7464
Web Site: rcmc.org
Management:
    Artistic Director: A. Barron Breland
    Accompanist: Salli Compton
Mission: Building community and enriching the lives of our members and audiences through our passion for music.
Founded: 1984
Specialized Field: Choral
Status: Nonprofit

Nevada

2171
NEVADA OPERA
100 S. Virginia Street
Reno, NV 89501
Mailing Address: PO Box 3256
Phone: 775-786-4046
Fax: 775-786-4063
e-mail: info@nevadaopera.org
Web Site: www.nevadaopera.org
Officers:
    Chair: Patti Mudd
    Vice Chair: Arlen Pritchard
Management:
    Artistic Director: Michael Borowitz
    Artistic Director: Robin Stamper
    Marketing Director: Zoe Rose
Mission: To produce quality professional opera for the broadest possible audience.
Utilizes: Singers
Founded: 1968
Specialized Field: Grand Opera; Light Opera; Lyric Opera; Choral; Classical
Status: Non-Profit, Professional
Paid Staff: 6
Volunteer Staff: 10
Income Sources: Corporate & Donors
Performs At: Pioneer Center for the Performing Arts
Organization Type: Performing; Resident

New Hampshire

2172
CLAREMONT OPERA HOUSE
City Hall on Opera House Square
PO Box 664
Claremont, NH 03743
Phone: 603-542-0064
Fax: 603-542-7014
e-mail: office@claremontoperahouse.org
Web Site: www.claremontoperahouse.com
Management:
    President: John Bennett
    Executive Director: Louanne Lewit
Mission: Multi-use performing arts center.
Utilizes: Guest Accompanists; Guest Musical Directors; Local Artists; Multimedia; Original Music Scores; Soloists; Special Technical Talent; Theatre Companies
Opened: 1977
Specialized Field: Opera; Contemporary
Status: Non-Profit, Professional
Paid Staff: 1
Budget: $150,000
Income Sources: Tickets; Membership; Sponsors
Affiliations: APAP; APNNE
Annual Attendance: 15,000
Facility Category: Theatre
Type of Stage: Proscenium
Seating Capacity: 780
Year Built: 1897
Year Remodeled: 1975

2173
OPERA NORTH
20 W Park Street
Lower Level
Hanover, NH 03766
Phone: 603-448-4141
Fax: 603-448-0999
e-mail: development@operanorth.org
Web Site: www.operanorth.org
Officers:
    President: Virginia Rolett
    President Elect: Caroline Vaillant
    Treasurer: Timothy Wager
    Secretary: Carl Brandon
    Chair: Elizabeth Rattigan
Management:
    Artistic Director: Louis Burkot
    Executive Director: Pamela A. Pantos
    Executive Producer: Florence Klausner
    Director Productions: Ron Luchsinger
    Associate Director of Development a: Sandy Torget
Mission: To produce opera for Northern New England with the highest musical and dramatic standards; to recognize that opera is both entertaining and spiritually enriching, we seek diversified audience through educational and performance programs. Opera North is also committed to the development of young artists through performance opportunities and production experience.
Utilizes: Actors; Artists-in-Residence; Dancers; Designers; Educators; Fine Artists; Five Seasonal Concerts; Grant Writers; Guest Accompanists; Guest Artists; Guest Conductors; Guest Instructors; Guest Musicians; Guest Soloists; Guest Writers; Guild Activities; Local Artists; Multimedia; Original Music Scores; Resident Professionals; Singers; Student Interns
Founded: 1981
Specialized Field: Opera
Paid Staff: 3
Volunteer Staff: 350
Paid Artists: 150
Budget: $540,000
Income Sources: Ticket Sales, Grants, Contributions
Performs At: Lebanon Opera House
Affiliations: Opera America
Annual Attendance: 11,000
Facility Category: Auditorium
Type of Stage: Proscenium
Stage Dimensions: 30 x 30 x 27
Seating Capacity: 800
Year Built: 1920
Year Remodeled: 2001

2174
MANCHESTER CHORAL SOCIETY
88 Hanover Street
Manchester, NH 03101
Phone: 603-472-6627
e-mail: info@mcsnh.org
Web Site: mcsnh.org
Officers:
    President: Sasha Kuftinec
    Vice President: David Betz
    Secretary: Edward Doyle
    Treasurer: Amanda Someone
Management:
    Music Director: Daniel Perkins
    Accompanist: Charles Blood
Mission: The Manchester Choral Society is committed to sharing and promoting the best choral music of a variety of styles and periods through vibrant performances, collaboration, and educational and community outreach.
Founded: 1961
Specialized Field: Choral
Status: Nonprofit

New Jersey

2175
METRO LYRIC OPERA
PO Box 35
Allenhurst, NJ 07711
Phone: 732-531-2378
Fax: 732-531-2752
e-mail: metrolyricopera@yahoo.com
Web Site: www.metrolyricopera.org
Officers:
    President: John Mullins
    VP: John Plunkett
    Secretary: Joan Benoist
Management:
    Founder And Artistic Director: Era Tognoli
    Assistant Artistic Director: Luccio Zachary
    Conductor: Anton Coppola
Mission: To bring opera of a high standard to all people at popular prices; to create a professional outlet for deserving young artists as well as experienced professionals; to bring opera in English to public schools.
Utilizes: Guest Artists; Singers
Founded: 1959
Specialized Field: Grand Opera; Operetta
Status: Professional
Income Sources: Monmouth Opera Guild
Performs At: Paramount Theatre; Strand Theatre
Organization Type: Performing; Educational; Community Service

2176
MUSIC IN THE SOMERSET HILLS
P.O. Box 729
Bernardsville, NJ 07924
Phone: 973-339-7719
e-mail: info@musicsh.org
Web Site: musicsh.org
Management:
    Artistic Director: Stephen Sands

VOCAL MUSIC / New Jersey

Mission: The mission of Music in Somerset Hills is to provide musical experience of the highest quality to those who live and work in the Somerset Hills and the surrounding communities.
Founded: 2010

2177
THE GARDEN STATE OPERA
140 Hadley Avenue
Clifton, NJ 07011
Phone: 973-685-9972
e-mail: gstopera@optonline.net
Web Site: gardenstateopera.homestead.com
Management:
   Artistic/Music Director: Francesco Santelli
   Stage Director: Dan Yates
   Chorus Master: Laura Greenwald
   Accompanist: Susan La Fever
   Marketing: Mary Krous
   Sets Designer: Stephen Sprague
Mission: To offer quality opera productions at low ticket prices in New Jersey.
Founded: 1999
Specialized Field: Opera
Status: Nonprofit

2178
PHILOMUSICA CHOIR
PO Box 6032
East Brunswick, NJ 08816-6032
Phone: 732-545-8434
Toll-free: 888-744-5668
e-mail: info@philomusica.org
Web Site: www.philomusica.org
Officers:
   President: Faith Knabe
   VP: Fred Lawson
   Treasurer: Louise Hyland
   Secretary: Joyce Richardson-Melech
   Member at Large: Miguel Cruz
   Member at Large: Diana Pichardo
Management:
   Music Director / Conductor: Dennis Boyle
Mission: Excellence in choral sound, performance and musicianship.
Utilizes: Collaborations; Community Members; Community Talent; Composers; Contract Orchestras; Five Seasonal Concerts; Guest Directors; Guest Musical Directors; Guest Musicians; Multimedia; Visual Designers
Founded: 1969
Specialized Field: Grand Opera; Light Opera; Lyric Opera; Musical Theatre; Choral; Ethnic Music; Classical; Contemporary; Religious
Status: Non-Profit, Non-Professional
Non-paid Artists: 40+
Affiliations: Middlesex County Cultural/Heritage Commission
Organization Type: Performing; Touring

2179
AMERICAN ATLANTIC CHORALE
1715 7th Street
Ewing, NJ 08638
Phone: 303-807-4512
e-mail: aachorale@gmail.com
Web Site: amchorale.com
Management:
   Director: Randy White
Mission: A choir for singers who are looking for summer performance and travel opportunities. Repertoire varies from contemporary a cappella to sacred.
Founded: 2012

Organization Type: Performing; Touring

2180
BOHEME OPERA
2000 Peenington Road
PO Box 7718
Ewing, NJ 08628-0718
Phone: 609-771-2131
Web Site: www.bohemeopera.com
Officers:
   Chairman: Michael Donahue III Esq
   Chairman Emeritus: Jim Faridy
   Board Member: Bonnie Brenner
   Board Member: Stuart Dembler
   Board Member: Jerry Kalstein
   Life Member: Harvey Milstein
   Honorary Trustee: Richard Billotti
Management:
   Co-Founder/Artistic Director: Joseph Pucciatti
Mission: Boheme Opera was conceived and founded in 1981 as a musicians' guild in an unassuming parking lot of Trenton's St. Joachim's Church (today one of the two churches that comprises Our Lady of the Angels Parish, along with Immaculate Conception Church).
Utilizes: Arrangers; Artists-in-Residence; Collaborating Artists; Collaborations; Commissioned Composers; Composers; Guest Companies; Multimedia; Music; Musical Directors; Paid Performers
Founded: 1981
Opened: 1989
Specialized Field: Opera, Theater
Status: Non-Profit
Income Sources: Sponsors, Advertising
Performs At: The College of New Jersey Auditorium

2181
NEW JERSEY ASSOCIATION OF VERISMO OPERA
PO Box 3024
Fort Lee, NJ 07024-9024
Phone: 201-886-0561
Fax: 201-224-6911
e-mail: comments@njavo.org
Web Site: www.njavo.org
Officers:
   President: Dr. James Garvin
   CFO: Giovanni Simone
   VP: Evelyn Quaife
   VP: Stan Staniloff
   Secretary: Fran Staniloff
   Treasurer: Adora Crager
Management:
   Artistic Director: Lucine Amara
   Music Director/Principal Conductor: Anthony Morss
   Chorus Director: Mara Waldman
   Resident Lightening Director: Adam H. Greeny
Mission: The New Jersey Association of Verismo Opera has been a part of the New Jersey music scene since 1989. It began by sponsoring a vocal competition and an opera workshop.
Founded: 1989
Specialized Field: Grand Opera; Light Opera; Lyric Opera; Musical Theatre; Choral; Youth Chorus; Ethnic Music; Classical; Contemporary; Religious
Status: Non-Profit, Professional

2182
RARITAN VALLEY CHORUS
PO Box 6044
Hillsborough, NJ 08844
Phone: 908-526-8769
e-mail: raritanvalleychorus@gmail.com
Web Site: www.raritanvalleychorus.org

Officers:
   President: Bobbi Agins
Management:
   Artistic Director: Rodney Briscoe
   Accompanist: Christopher Nittoli
Mission: A community based ensemble of varying ages, backgrounds and careers. The choir is open to all residents of the region and offers a range of musical experiences unparalleled in Central New Jersey.
Founded: 1990
Specialized Field: Choral

2183
BROADWAY CENTER STAGE
38 Rutgers Street
Maplewood, NJ 07040
Phone: 973-378-3244
Fax: 973-718-4376
e-mail: manager@broadwaycenterstage.com
Web Site: www.broadwaycenterstage.com
Management:
   Producer: Suzanne Ishee
   Business Manager: Lucy Bowers
   Marketing Director: Jean Kerley
Mission: Presenting the finest, most affordable Broadway programming available, the duo of Broadway stars captures the most memorable moments of Broadway.
Founded: 1995
Specialized Field: Theatrical Dance; Educational
Paid Staff: 2
Volunteer Staff: 1
Paid Artists: 6

2184
NEW JERSEY STATE OPERA
199 Scoles Avenue
Newark, NJ 07102
Phone: 973-928-5650
Fax: 973-623-5761
e-mail: info@njstateopera.org
Web Site: www.njstateopera.org
Officers:
   Chairman: Bernard J. D'Avella, Jr.
   Board President: Kenneth B. Kashkin, MD
   Secretary: Laura Barrett
   Treasurer: Margareth De Jesus
Management:
   Music Director Young Artists Prog: David Maiulloni
   Acting Managing Director: Donna Nichols-Lawrence
   Artistic Director: Jason C. Tramm
Utilizes: Guest Companies; Singers
Founded: 1966
Specialized Field: Opera
Status: Non-Profit, Professional
Paid Staff: 50
Income Sources: Essex County Arts Council; New Jersey State Arts Council
Performs At: New Jersey Performing Arts Center; Prudential Hall
Seating Capacity: 2,750
Organization Type: Performing

2185
ARS MUSICAL CHORALE & ORCHESTRA
PO Box 525
Paramus, NJ 07653-0525
Phone: 973-628-8793
Fax: 973-628-8793
e-mail: info@arsmusica.org
Web Site: www.arsmusica.org
Officers:

VOCAL MUSIC / New Jersey

Vice President: Linda Glasgal
Treasurer: Nicholas Bell
Secretary-Rec.: Liz Blumenthal
Secretary-Corr.: Daniella Ashbahian
Management:
  President: Willis Bott
  Administrative Director: Alexandra Cramer
  Music Director: Robert Long
  Artistic Director: Kelly Crandell
  Admin Manager: Alexandra H. Cramer
Founded: 1965
Specialized Field: Choral
Status: Non-Profit, Non-Professional
Paid Staff: 2

2186
AMERICAN BOYCHOIR
75 Mapleton Road
Princeton, NJ 08540
Phone: 609-924-5858
Fax: 609-924-5812
e-mail: academics@americanboychoir.org
Web Site: www.americanboychoir.org
Officers:
  Chairman: Rob D'Vanzo
  Academic Consultant: Nancy Adair
  Litton-Lodal Music Director: Fernando Malvar'Ruiz
Management:
  Music Director: Fernando Malvar-Ruiz
  Science Teacher: Christine Altomari
  Director of Alumni Chorus: James Litton
  Manager of Donor Records: Ron Hrebik
  Director of Vocal Studies: Fred Meads
Mission: The Boychoir includes choristers from throughout North America, who are students at the internationally-renowned boarding and day choir school (which offers a full academic program).
Utilizes: Commissioned Composers; Commissioned Music; Guest Artists; Theatre Companies
Founded: 1937
Specialized Field: Choral; Youth Chorus
Status: Professional; Nonprofit
Paid Staff: 42
Budget: $3,000,000
Organization Type: Performing; Touring; Educational

2187
PRINCETON PRO MUSICA CHORUS & ORCHESTRA
PO Box 1313
Princeton, NJ 08542
Phone: 609-683-5122
e-mail: info@princetonpromusica.org
Web Site: www.princetopromusic.org
Officers:
  President: Carolyn Landis
  Treasurer: Martin Wheelwright
  Vice President: Fran Perlman
  Secretary: Jan Johnson
Management:
  Executive Director: Mary Trigg
  Music Director: Frances Fowler Slade
  Artistic Director: Ryan James Brandau
  Rehearsal Accompanist: Eric Plutz
  Volunteer Coordinator: Fran Perlman
Mission: To perform masterpieces of the choral repertoire with a professional orchestra and soloists.
Utilizes: Guest Artists
Founded: 1979
Specialized Field: Choral; Classical
Status: Nonprofit
Paid Staff: 4
Volunteer Staff: 25

Income Sources: NJSCA; Individuals
Performs At: Richardson Auditorium; Princeton University
Affiliations: Chorus America; Art Pride
Organization Type: Performing

2188
WESTMINSTER CHOIR COLLEGE
101 Walnut Lane
Princeton, NJ 08540-3899
Phone: 609-921-7100
Fax: 609-921-3012
e-mail: wccinfo@rider.edu
Web Site: www.rider.edu/westminster
Officers:
  Associate Vice President for Planni: Debbie Stasolla
  Executive Assistant to the Presiden: Christine A. Zelenak
Management:
  President: Mordechai Roznski
  Managing Director: Robert Annis
  Director of External Affairs: Anne Sears
  Special Events & Projects Manager: Beverly J. Braddock
Utilizes: Actors; Arrangers; Artists-in-Residence; Collaborations; Commissioned Composers; Community Members; Composers; Guest Accompanists; Guest Designers; Guest Lecturers; Guest Musical Directors; Guest Soloists; High School Drama; Instructors; Multimedia; Music; Original Music Scores; Resident Artists; Resident Companies; Scenic Designers; Sign Language Translators; Singers; Soloists; Students; Special Technical Talent
Founded: 1926
Specialized Field: Grand Opera; Light Opera; Lyric Opera; Musical Theatre; Choral; Youth Chorus; Ethnic Music; Classical; Contemporary; Religious
Status: Non-Profit, Non-Professional
Paid Staff: 25
Paid Artists: 75

2189
PRO ARTE CHORALE
P.O. Box 662
Ridgewood, NJ 07450
Phone: 201-497-8400
Fax: 201-445-1421
e-mail: info@www.proartechorale.org
Web Site: www.proartechorale.org
Officers:
  Vice President: Jane Stein
  Secretary: Jennifer Jones
  Treasurer: Kenneth Benkovic
Management:
  President: Joseph DeFazio
  Music Director: Steven Fox
  Managing Director: Sharon Sauer
  Manager: Patricia Klecanda
  Assistant Conductor and Accompanist: Janet Montgomery
Founded: 1964
Specialized Field: Choral
Status: Non-Profit, Professional
Paid Staff: 3
Paid Artists: 4
Budget: $130,000
Income Sources: State Grant, Corporation Foundation, Private Donations, Ticket Sales, Fund raisers, Membership Dues
Performs At: Concert Hall, Church/Temple
Affiliations: Chorus America

2190
RIDGEWOOD GILBERT AND SULLIVAN OPERA COMPANY
975 E Ridgewood Avenue
Ridgewood, NJ 07450
Mailing Address: P. O. Box 307, Ridgewood, NJ 07451-0307
Phone: 973-423-0300
e-mail: ridgewoodgands@gmail.com
Web Site: www.dancaster.com
Officers:
  President: Timothy Domini
  Treasurer: John Ryle
  Secretary: Carol Ciancia
Management:
  Business Manager: Mike Wiley
  Stage Director: Bill Kaufman
  Music Director: James A. Biddlecome
  Choreographer: Judi Niebuhr
Mission: To present and encourage an appreciation of Gilbert and Sullivan operas.
Founded: 1937
Specialized Field: Light Opera
Status: Non-Professional, Non-profit
Paid Staff: 50
Income Sources: Ticket Sales; Program Ads; Sponsored Performances
Performs At: Local Middle School; Outside Facilities
Affiliations: NJ Council on the Arts
Seating Capacity: 700
Year Built: 1954
Organization Type: Performing; Touring

2191
DIETSCH ARTISTS INTERNATIONAL
143 South Centre Street
South Orange, NJ 07079
Phone: 973-763-8836
Fax: 973-763-8837
e-mail: dietsch@dietschartists.com
Web Site: www.dietschartists.com
Officers:
  President: James Dietsch
  Booking Director: Joseph Flores
  Manager: Samuel De Palma
  Vice President: Manrico Biscotti
Management:
  CEO/Artistic Director: James Dietsch
  Conductor: Ivan Anguelov
  Conductor: Lucy Arner
  Conductor: Michail Jurowski
  Conductor: Ira Levin
  Conductor: Marco Pace
  Stage Director: Andre Barbe
  Stage Director: Giancarlo Del Monaco
  Stage Director: Brigitte Otto
Mission: Dietsch Artists International was founded for the representation of the highest caliber of artist worldwide in every type of venue. We seek to promote artists of the finest technical, stylistic, dramatic and linguistic standards. We represent voices that are called 'signature sounds'. Our roster includes conductors and stage directors who are among the finest in the world.
Utilizes: Arrangers; Collaborating Artists; Collaborations; Commissioned Composers; Commissioned Music; Composers; Composers-in-Residence; Guest Companies; Guest Directors; Multimedia; Music; Paid Performers; Resident Artists
Specialized Field: Opera, Instrumental
Status: Non-Profit, Professional
Income Sources: Ticket Sales, Fundraisers
Affiliations: Mallorca Opera Festival

VOCAL MUSIC / New Mexico

2192
NEW JERSEY STATE REPERTORY OPERA
363 W. South Orange Avenue
South Orange, NJ 07079
Phone: 973-763-7969
e-mail: info@njsro.com
Web Site: njsro.weebly.com
Management:
　Artistic Director: Dita Delman
Mission: State Repertory Opera's primary purpose and mission is to help diverse New Jersey audiences experience excellent opera performances on this side of the Hudson, sung by young New Jersey residents who will be tomorrow's luminaries in the opera world.
Founded: 1975
Specialized Field: Opera
Status: Nonprofit

2193
COMMUNITY OPERA
417 Morris Avenue
22
Summit, NJ 07901
Phone: 908-277-1934
Management:
　President: Edward Q Watts
Mission: Showcasing opera singers as well as modern composers.
Utilizes: Singers
Founded: 1981
Specialized Field: Light Opera; Lyric Opera; Classical; Contemporary; Musical Theatre
Status: Non-Profit, Professional
Income Sources: Orpheus Society
Performs At: Hudson Guild; South Street Seaport-Fulton Center

2194
SUMMIT CHORALE
PO Box 265
Summit, NJ 07902-0265
Phone: 862-926-9605
Fax: 908-464-0959
e-mail: director@summitchorale.org
Web Site: www.summitchorale.org
Officers:
　President: Frank Lampert-Hopkins
　Membership Chair: Ellie Winslow
　Secretary: Kathy Parsons
　Treasurer: Nicole Lash
Management:
　Music Director: Dr. Thomas Juneau
　Accompanist: Douglas Keilitz
　Conductor: Richard Garrin
　Music Director: Richard Garrin
Mission: To promote and cultivate choral music by providing an opportunity for those who enjoy ensemble singing to explore the rich heritage of choral music while studying and singing under the best professional leadership obtainable; to foster public appreciation and enjoyment of choral music through performance as well as educational and community outreach endeavors.
Founded: 1909
Specialized Field: Choral
Status: Non-professional
Volunteer Staff: 12
Budget: $70,000
Income Sources: Private; Public; Box Office; Grants; Fundraising
Performs At: University; Churches; Schools
Organization Type: Performing; Education

2195
CHORAL ARTS SOCIETY OF NEW JERSEY
140 Mountain Ave
Westfield, NJ 07090-3131
Mailing Address: PO BOX 2036, Westfield, NJ 07091
Phone: 908-654-5737
e-mail: Ulf@casofnj.org
Web Site: www.casofnj.org
Officers:
　President/Finance Chair: Ulf Dolling
　VP: Stephen McCarthy
　Treasurer: Denise Gregis
　Secretary: Lois Schmidt
Management:
　Music Director: Martin Sedek
　Accompanist: Mary Beth McFall
　Business Manager: Ralph Jones
　Programs: Ann Hoener
Mission: To study, perform and promote choral works.
Founded: 1962
Specialized Field: Choral
Status: Non-Professional
Organization Type: Performing

New Mexico

2196
OPERA SOUTHWEST
515 15th Street NW
Albuquerque, NM 87104
Mailing Address: P.O. Box 27671, Albuquerque, NM 87125-7671
Phone: 505-242-5837
Fax: 505-242-5837
e-mail: tzanc@operasouthwest.org
Web Site: www.operasouthwest.org
Officers:
　President: Woody Kuehn
　Vice President: Julius Kaplan, Ph.D.
　Treasurer: Sarah Lee
　Secretary: Bernie Holzapfel
Management:
　Artistic Director: David Bartholomew
　Managing Director: Tony Zancanella
　Administrative Advisor: Justine M. Opel
　Production Manager: Mimi Peavy
Mission: To present fully staged, costumed operas with accomplished musicians at the highest artistic level.
Utilizes: Singers
Founded: 1972
Specialized Field: Grand Opera; Lyric Opera; Light Opera; Operetta
Status: Professional; Nonprofit
Paid Staff: 30
Income Sources: Central Opera Service
Performs At: KiMo Theatre
Organization Type: Performing; Educational

2197
SANGRE DE CRISTO CHORALE
PO Box 4462
Santa Fe, NM 87502-4462
Phone: 505-455-3707
Fax: 505-665-4433
e-mail: info@sdcchorale.org
Web Site: www.sdcchorale.org
Officers:
　Treasurer: Don Raish
　Publicity: Andrea Fechter
　Development Chair: Gary Bell
　Performanace Chair: Joan Ellis
Management:
　Director: Doyle Preheim
　Board President: Jerry Nelson
　Business Manager: Ed Van Eeckhout
　Chorale President: Gary Buff
　Artistic Direction: Maxine Th,venot
Mission: Performance of choral music and educational outreach.
Utilizes: Commissioned Composers; Commissioned Music; Guest Composers; Guest Lecturers; Multimedia; Music; Original Music Scores; Sign Language Translators; Soloists
Founded: 1978
Specialized Field: Choral
Volunteer Staff: 10
Paid Artists: 35
Budget: $52,000
Income Sources: Admissions; Contributions; Advertising; Grants
Performs At: Churches, Hotels
Annual Attendance: 1,800
Facility Category: Various venues: churches, hotels
Type of Stage: Choral Risers off Floor

2198
SANTA FE DESERT CHORALE
311 E. Palace Ave
Santa Fe, NM 87501
Phone: 505-988-2282
Fax: 505-988-7522
Toll-free: 800-244-4011
e-mail: jhabermann@desertchorale.org
Web Site: www.desertchorale.org
Officers:
　President: Mary Ann Nelson
Management:
　President: Margaret Wright
　Executive Director: Erich Covollmer
　Artistic Director: Linda Mack
　Music Director: Joshua Habermann, D.M.
　Managing Director: Andreas Tischhauser, D.M.
Mission: To perform music from the choral repertoire within the last five centuries, especially Baroque and Modern.
Founded: 1982
Specialized Field: Choral; Youth Chorus; Classical; Religious
Status: Non-Profit, Professional
Paid Staff: 5
Paid Artists: 20
Income Sources: Chorus America
Performs At: Santuario de Guadalupe; Loretto Chapel
Organization Type: Performing; Educational

2199
SANTA FE SYMPHONY ORCHESTRA AND CHORUS
551 West Cordova Road
Suite D
Santa Fe, NM 87505
Mailing Address: Post Office Box 9692, Santa Fe, NM 87504
Phone: 505-983-3530
Fax: 505-982-3888
Toll-free: 800-480-1319
e-mail: symphony@rt66.com
Web Site: www.sf-symphony.org
Officers:
　President: David Brown
　Vice-President: Ruthe Coleman, Ed.D.
　Vice-President: Penelope Penland, Ed.D.
　Vice-President: Dana Winograd
　Vice President: Michael E. Melody
　Secretary: David Grayson

Treasurer: James R. Atwood
Management:
   Founder/General Director: Gregory W. Heltman
   Operations Manager: Diane Stengle
   Development Director: Jane Barry
   Music Director: Steven Smith
   Choral Director: Linda Raney
Utilizes: Guest Lecturers; Guest Musicians; Lyricists; Multimedia; Sign Language Translators
Founded: 1984
Specialized Field: Choral, Classical
Status: Non-Profit, Professional
Paid Staff: 4
Paid Artists: 80
Budget: $550,000
Income Sources: Contributions; Ticket Sales; Grants
Performs At: Lensic Performing Arts Center
Seating Capacity: 800

2200
THE SANTA FE OPERA
301 Opera Drive
Santa Fe, NM 87506-2823
Mailing Address: P.O. Box 2408, Santa Fe, NM 87504-2408
Phone: 505-986-5900
Toll-free: 800-280-4654
Web Site: santafeopera.org
Officers:
   Chair: Joseph M. Bryan, Jr.
   Vice Chair: Patricia A. McFate
   Vice Chair: James R. Seitz, Jr.
   President: Susan F. Morris
   Vice President: Peter B. Frank
Management:
   Chief Conductor: Harry Bicket
   General Director: Charles MacKay
   Artistic Director: Brad Woolbright
Mission: To advance the operatic art form by presenting ensemble performances of the highest quality in a unique setting with a varied repertoire of new, rarely performed, and standard works; to ensure the excellence of opera's future through apprentice programs for singers, technicians and arts administrators; and to foster and enrich an understanding and appreciation of opera among a diverse public.
Founded: 1957
Specialized Field: Opera
Season: Summer

New York

2201
ALBANY PRO MUSICA
PO Box 3850
Albany, NY 12203-0850
Phone: 518-438-6548
Fax: 518-442-4197
e-mail: info@albanypromusica.org
Web Site: www.albanypromusica.org
Officers:
   Administrative Director: William Tuthill
   Artistic Administrator: Kate Pruzek
   President: Jennifer Amstutz
   Vice President: Karen Hitchcock
   Secretary: Richard Patterson
Management:
   Artistic Director/Conductor: David Griggs-Janower
   Assistant Conductor: Joseph Farrell
   Executive Director: Matthew Kopans
Mission: To be a mixed chorus of selected volunteers who are dedicated to the enhancement of the cultural life in upstate New York and their own musical growth. Albany Pro Musica achieves these objectives through professional quality a cappella performance and accompanies choral repertoire drawn from diverse traditions and styles.
Founded: 1981
Specialized Field: Choral
Performs At: Civic and Community Musical Events
Affiliations: Albany Symphony Orchestra

2202
TRI-CITIES OPERA COMPANY
315 Clinton Street
Binghamton, NY 13905
Phone: 607-729-3444
Fax: 607-797-6344
e-mail: info@tricitiesopera.com
Web Site: www.tricitiesopera.com
Officers:
   Board Chair: Mary Louise Perot
   First VP: Dr. Fran Goldman
   Second First President: Juames Thomas
   Treasurer: Ronald S. Platt
   Secretary: Sharon L. Dyer
Management:
   President: Grant Best
   General Director: Reed Smith
   Artistic Director: Duane Skrabalak
   Associate Artistic Director: Peter Sicilian
   Office/Box Office Manager: David Ramsay
Mission: To produce opera
Utilizes: Artists-in-Residence; Choreographers; Designers; Five Seasonal Concerts; Guest Accompanists; Guest Conductors; Guest Writers; Multimedia; Original Music Scores; Poets; Resident Professionals; Sign Language Translators; Soloists; Student Interns
Founded: 1949
Specialized Field: Grand Opera
Status: Non-Profit, Professional
Paid Staff: 50
Paid Artists: 123
Budget: $1,000,000
Income Sources: American Guild of Musical Artists; American Federation of Musicians; International Association of Theatrical Stage Employees
Performs At: Broome County Forum
Affiliations: Binghamton University
Annual Attendance: 15,000
Seating Capacity: 1500
Year Built: 1920
Year Remodeled: 1975
Organization Type: Performing; Resident; Educational

2203
BERKSHIRE-HUDSON VALLEY FESTIVAL OF OPERA
1400 Benson Street
Suite 5A
Bronx, NY 10461
Phone: 718-877-4211
e-mail: lgalagarza@ramonalsina.org
Web Site: www.ramonalsina.org
Mission: Create and market concerts, recitals and operas to showcase.
Utilizes: Actors; Artists-in-Residence; Choreographers; Collaborating Artists; Collaborations; Commissioned Composers; Commissioned Music; Dance Companies; Dancers; Designers; Educators; Fine Artists; Grant Writers; Guest Accompanists; Guest Artists; Guest Choreographers; Guest Conductors; Guest Designers; Guest Directors; Guest Ensembles; Guest Lecturers; Guest Musical Directors; Guest Musicians; Guest Teachers; High School Drama; Instructors; Local Artists; Lyricists; Multimedia; Music; Organization Contracts; Original Music Scores; Poets; Resident Artists; Resident Professionals; Selected Students; Sign Language Translators; Singers; Soloists; Special Technical Talent; Theatre Companies
Founded: 1971
Specialized Field: Grand Opera; Lyric Opera; Youth Chorus; Classical; Contemporary
Status: Non-Profit, Professional
Volunteer Staff: 5
Paid Artists: 15
Budget: $10,000-$50,000
Income Sources: Tickets; Sponsors; Donations; Grants
Affiliations: Touring Concert Opera Company
Annual Attendance: 5,000 - 10,000
Organization Type: Performing; Touring

2204
THE BRONX OPERA COMPANY
5 Minerva Place
Suite 2-J
Bronx, NY 10468
Phone: 718-365-4209
Web Site: bronxopera.org
Officers:
   President: Peter Heiman
   Treasurer: Maddy Nadelman
Management:
   Artistic Director/Conductor: Michael Spierman
   Associate Artistic Director: Ben Spierman
   Production Manager: Scott Schneider
   Chorus Master: Michael Haigler
   Publicity: Jay Micheals
Mission: The Bronx Opera Company was founded in 1967 by Michael Spierman, the organization's Artistic Director and principal Conductor. Its full productions and community concerts are regularly presented in The Bronx and throughout the region, from Long Island and Westchester to Sullivan and Ulster Counties.
Utilizes: Arrangers; Choreographers; Collaborating Artists; Collaborations; Guest Companies; Local Unknown Artists; Lyricists; Multimedia; Music; Paid Performers; Resident Companies; Sign Language Translators; Singers
Founded: 1967
Specialized Field: Opera
Status: Non-Profit, Professional
Income Sources: Patrons, Donors
Season: January, May
Performs At: Lovinger Theater, Kaye Playhouse

2205
AMERICAN OPERA PROJECTS INC
138 S Oxford Street
Brooklyn, NY 11217
Phone: 718-398-4024
Fax: 718-398-3489
e-mail: info@operaprojects.org
Web Site: www.operaprojects.org
Officers:
   President: Robert E. Lee III
   Vice President: Anna Rabinowitz
   Treasurer: Cassandra Joseph
Management:
   Artistic Director: Steven Osgood
   General Director: Charles Jarden
   Producing Director: Matthew Gray
   Managing Director/President: Robert E. Lee III
   Resident Music Director: Mila Henry
Specialized Field: Opera

VOCAL MUSIC / New York

2206
REGINA OPERA COMPANY
1251 Tabor Court
Brooklyn, NY 11219
Mailing Address: Regina Opera Company, P.O. Box 150253, Brooklyn, New York 11
Phone: 718-259-2772
Fax: 718-232-3555
e-mail: info@reginaopera.org
Web Site: www.reginaopera.org
Officers:
  President/Treasurer: Marie L. Cantoni
  Secretary/Legal Advisor: Linda Cantoni
Management:
  Artistic Director: Alex Alejandro Guzman
  Producer/Chairman/Executive Vice Pr: Francine Garber Cohen
  Principal Stage Director: Linda Lehr
  Principal Conductor: Scott Jackson Wiley
  Associate Stage Director: Linda Cantoni
Mission: Training young professionals and showcasing experienced directors and performers.
Utilizes: Grant Writers; Guest Musicians; Instructors; Local Artists; Sign Language Translators; Singers
Founded: 1970
Specialized Field: Choral; Opera; Musical Theatre
Status: Non-Profit, Non-Professional
Volunteer Staff: 15
Non-paid Artists: 50
Budget: $100,000
Income Sources: Public & Private Funding; Ticket Sales
Performs At: Regina Hall
Annual Attendance: 5,000
Facility Category: School Auditorium
Type of Stage: Proscenium
Stage Dimensions: 30'x18'
Seating Capacity: 325
Year Built: 1950
Organization Type: Performing

2207
BUFFALO PHILHARMONIC CHORUS & CHAMBER SINGERS
PO Box 176
Buffalo, NY 14207-0176
Phone: 716-833-6642
Fax: 716-874-0486
e-mail: BizMgr@BPChorus.org
Web Site: www.bpchorus.org
Officers:
  Accompanist: Bettyalice Riehle
  Vice President: Holly Grant
  Treasurer: Phillip A. Reynolds
  Secretary: Jane Mathias
Management:
  President: Catherine F. Schweitzer
  Music Director: L Brett Scott
Founded: 1936
Specialized Field: Choral
Paid Staff: 3
Volunteer Staff: 15
Paid Artists: 10
Non-paid Artists: 100

2208
CHAUTAUQUA SUMMER SCHOOLS OF FINE AND PERFORMING ARTS
PO Box 1098
Schools Office
Chautauqua, NY 14722
Phone: 716-357-6233
Fax: 716-357-9014
e-mail: smalinoski@ciweb.org
Web Site: www.ciweb.org
Officers:
  President: Thomas Becker
  Vice President/Treasurer: Sebastian Baggiano
  Chief Marketing Officer: George Murphy
Management:
  Student Services Coordinator: Sarah Malinoski
  Housing Coordinator: Jamie Kranak
  Coordinator of Student Services: Sarah Malinoski-Umberger
  Program Coordinator: Wendy Limberg
Mission: To be a center for the arts, education, religion and recreation.
Utilizes: Singers
Founded: 1989
Specialized Field: Theatrical Dance
Status: Pre-Professional
Paid Staff: 120
Paid Artists: 1500
Budget: $15,000,000
Income Sources: Box Office; Grants; Private Donations
Performs At: Amphitheater; Lenna Hall
Affiliations: Opera America; Chamber Music America
Annual Attendance: 150,000
Organization Type: Performing; Religious; Educational; Recreational

2209
GLIMMERGLASS OPERA
PO Box 191
7300 State Highway 80
Cooperstown, NY 13326
Phone: 607-547-0700
Fax: 607-547-6030
e-mail: info@glimmerglass.org
Web Site: www.glimmerglass.org
Officers:
  Chair: Patricia Kavanagh
  President: Sherwin M. Goldman
  Vice-chair: John R. Hupper
  Vice-president: Carole H. Johnson
  Treasurer: James M. Barton
Management:
  Artistic/General Director: Francesca Zambello
  Managing Director: Linda Jackson
  Music Director: David Angus
  Administrative/Operations Director: Andrea Lyons
  Director of Production: Abby Rodd
  Marketing Director: June Dziolo
  Artistic Events/Music Manager: Eric Schnobrick
Mission: A professional non-profit summer opera company dedicated to producing new productions each season. Mission is to produce new, little-known and familiar operas and works of music theater in innovative productions which capitalize on the intimacy and natural setting of the Alice Busch Opera Theater; to promote an artistically-challenging work environment for young Americans; and to engage important directors, designers and conductors
Founded: 1975
Specialized Field: Performing Arts
Status: Non-Profit, Professional
Paid Staff: 25

2210
1891 FREDONIA OPERA HOUSE
9 Church Street
PO Box 384
Fredonia, NY 14063
Phone: 716-679-0891
Fax: 716-679-0899
e-mail: operahouse@fredopera.org
Web Site: www.fredopera.org
Officers:
  Business Manager: Marsha Finley
Management:
  Executive Director: Rick Davis
  Technical Director: Daniel Allen
  Business Manager: Marsha Finley
Mission: Year round performing arts center offering the best in music, theatre and films.
Founded: 1994
Specialized Field: Multidisciplinary
Paid Staff: 3
Volunteer Staff: 60
Performs At: Theatre
Type of Stage: Proscenium
Seating Capacity: 444
Year Built: 1891
Rental Contact: Technical Director Daniel Allen

2211
OPERA OMNIA
3823 9th Street
Long Island City, NY 11101
e-mail: info@operaomnia.org
Web Site: www.operaomnia.org
Management:
  General Manager/Artistic Director: Wesley Chinn
  Artistic Director/Stage Director: Crystal Manich
  Artistic Director/Music Director: Avi Stein
  Mezzo Soprano: Cherry Duke
Mission: Opera Omnia aims to combine a deep knowledge of historical performance practice with a modern theatrical aesthetic to produce performances that are musically and dramatically satisfying to both the veteran classical concertgoer and to those new to the genre. We initially concentrate on musical-dramatic works of the early 17th century, performing them in English translation and modern staging.
Utilizes: Arrangers; Designers; Fine Artists; Lyricists; Multimedia; Music; Sign Language Translators
Founded: 1998
Specialized Field: Opera, Modern Theatrical
Status: Non-Profit, Professional
Income Sources: Donors, Sponsors
Season: Fall

2212
MANHATTAN LYRIC OPERA
5 Old Phillip Hill Road
New City, NY 10956
Phone: 212-879-0144
Fax: 831-305-7228
Web Site: www.manhattanlyric.com
Management:
  Artistic Director/Founder: Anne Tormela
  Baritone: Douglas Jabara
Mission: The Manhattan Lyric Opera is uniquely devoted to presenting concert versions of the classic operas and operettas making them accessible to facilities which otherwise may never have the resources to offer such artistic works in their entirety or part. Our goal is to bring these classic works to life in an elegant, concise concert and staged version so that the audience may enjoy the heart of this great music.
Utilizes: Collaborating Artists; Collaborations; Local Unknown Artists; Multimedia; Music; Paid Performers; Sign Language Translators; Singers
Founded: 1998
Specialized Field: Classic Operas, Operettas, Broadway Works
Status: Profit, Professional

VOCAL MUSIC / New York

Income Sources: Paid Performances
Season: Year Round
Performs At: Varies

2213
NEW ROCHELLE OPERA
PO Box 55
New Rochelle, NY 10804
Phone: 914-576-0365
e-mail: newrochelleopera@aol.com
Web Site: www.nropera.org
Officers:
    Co-Founder/Artistic Director: Camille Coppola
    Co-Founder/Board President: Billie Tucker
    Vice President: Paulette Soffin
    Secretary: Louise Shepherd
    Treasurer: Edward C Flanagan
    Corresponding Secretary: John Fraioli
Management:
    Executive Director: Camille Coppola, camillecoppola@aol.com
    Company Coordinator: Billie Tucker, purepurplelady@yahoo.com
    Conductor: Gregory Ortega
Utilizes: Collaborations; Community Members; Community Talent; Dancers; Designers; Grant Writers; Guest Artists; Guest Composers; Guest Musical Directors; Original Music Scores; Paid Performers; Resident Professionals; Sign Language Translators; Soloists
Founded: 1985
Specialized Field: Grand Opera; Light Opera; Lyric Opera; Musical Theatre; Choral; Youth Chorus; Classical; Religious
Status: Non-Profit, Professional
Volunteer Staff: 15+
Budget: $100,000
Income Sources: Box Office; Grants; Contributions
Performs At: Mainstage: Ursuline Performing Arts Center, New Rochelle, NY; Concerts at Various Locations
Annual Attendance: 3000
Type of Stage: Proscenium
Stage Dimensions: 18 x 30
Seating Capacity: 318

2214
AMERICAN INTERNATIONAL LYRIC THEATRE
322 Duke Ellington Boulevard
New York, NY 10025
Phone: 212-662-3468
Fax: 212-678-0571
Web Site: hometown.aol.com/ppress322/music1/index.htm
Management:
    Managing Director: Paulette Singer
    Artistic Director: Russel Miller
Mission: A traveling company that presents Operettas, Broadway shows, European Operas and dance shows of all kinds using native performers from many different countries.
Utilizes: Theatre Companies
Founded: 1984
Specialized Field: World Music; Theatrical Dance
Status: Non-Profit; Professional
Budget: $500,000
Performs At: Throughout The United States

2215
AMERICAN OPERA MUSIC THEATER
400 W 43rd Street
Suite 19-D
New York, NY 10036
Phone: 212-594-1839
Fax: 212-695-4350
Web Site: www.americanoperacompany.com
Officers:
    Administrator: Christian Miles
Management:
    President: Diana Cortot
    Stage Director: Theodore Mann
Mission: Promote emerging artists with major talent, present new famililar music, with costumed and staged quality productions.
Utilizes: Choreographers; Designers; Fine Artists; Grant Writers; Guest Artists; Guest Composers; Guest Conductors; Guest Designers; Guest Directors; Guest Lecturers; Guest Musical Directors; Guest Musicians; Lyricists; Music; New Productions; Original Music Scores; Sign Language Translators; Singers; Theatre Companies
Founded: 1995
Specialized Field: Lyric Opera; Musical Theatre; Choral; Youth Chorus; Ethnic Music; Classical; Contemporary
Status: Non-Profit, Professional
Paid Staff: 3
Volunteer Staff: 3
Paid Artists: 50
Budget: $350,000-$450,000
Income Sources: Corporate; Donations; Service Revenues
Performs At: Theaters, Concert Halls
Annual Attendance: 30,000
Facility Category: Theaters
Type of Stage: Proscenium, round
Stage Dimensions: 26 x 35 minimum
Seating Capacity: 500 - 3,000

2216
AMERICAN-INTERNATIONAL LYRIC THEATRE
322 Duke Ellington Boulevard
New York, NY 10025-3471
Phone: 212-662-3468
Fax: 212-678-0517
e-mail: ppress322@aol.com
Management:
    Artistic Director: Russell Miller
    Managing Director: Paulette Singer
Founded: 1985
Specialized Field: Lyric Opera; Musical Theatre
Status: Non-Profit, Professional
Paid Staff: 3
Paid Artists: 50
Budget: $500,000
Season: Year round

2217
BACH VESPERS AT HOLY TRINITY
3 W 65th Street
New York, NY 10023
Phone: 212-877-6815
e-mail: office@bachvespersnyc.org
Web Site: www.bachvespersnyc.org
Officers:
    President: Kelly Hall
    Secretary: Robert Crump
    Treasurer: Stephen Hucko
    Office Manager: Tobin Schmuck
Management:
    Cantor: Rick Erickson
    Executive Manager: Donald Meineke
Mission: To bring the cantatas of Bach, and other early music, to the community in context of worship, as was done in 18th century Leipzig.
Utilizes: Guest Soloists; Sign Language Translators; Singers
Founded: 1968
Specialized Field: Baroque; Period Instruments; Choral
Paid Staff: 4
Volunteer Staff: 10
Paid Artists: 24
Income Sources: Donations; Offerings; Endowment
Affiliations: Lutheran (ELCA)
Annual Attendance: 7,500
Facility Category: Church
Seating Capacity: 500
Year Built: 1904
Resident Groups: Bach Choir; Period In

2218
BLEECKER STREET OPERA
115 MacDougal Street
New York, NY 10012
Phone: 917-617-1399
e-mail: bleeckerstreetopera@gmail.com
Web Site: www.bleeckerstreetopera.org
Management:
    Music Director/Conductor: Richard Owen
    Art Director: Richard Ceruillo
    Associate Conductor: Jeff Bradbury
    Project Coordinator: John Kim
    Founding Manager: Irene Frydel Kim
Mission: Our new mission is to continue and enhance the performance work of the Amato Opera Theatre by developing from a chamber ensemble of seven to a full orchestra (yes - we finally have room for strings!). We will continue to offer high-quality productions of beloved operas in intimate surroundings, at a low cost to audiences, and with opportunities for singers to gain experience in all aspects of operatic performance.
Utilizes: Arrangers; Collaborating Artists; Collaborations; Commissioned Composers; Commissioned Music; Fine Artists; Lyricists; Multimedia; Music
Founded: 2008
Specialized Field: Opera, Classical
Status: Non-Profit, Professional
Income Sources: Sponsors, Donors

2219
CANTERBURY CHORAL SOCIETY
2 E 90th Street
Church of the Heavenly Rest
New York, NY 10128
Phone: 212-222-9458
Fax: 212-222-9458
e-mail: dodsley@aol.com
Web Site: www.canterburychoral.org
Officers:
    President: Curtis Strohl
    1st Vice President: Margie McKittrick
    2nd Vice President: Victoria Barker
    Treasurer: Barbara Higgins
Management:
    Conductor: Charles D Walker
Utilizes: Guest Musicians; Original Music Scores; Sign Language Translators; Singers
Founded: 1952
Specialized Field: Religious; Choral
Status: Non-Profit, Professional
Paid Staff: 1
Paid Artists: 12
Non-paid Artists: 100
Performs At: Church
Annual Attendance: 2,000
Facility Category: Church
Seating Capacity: 900

VOCAL MUSIC / New York

Year Built: 1929

2220
CANTICUM NOVUM SINGERS
2576 Broadway
#203
New York, NY 10025
Phone: 914-763-3453
Fax: 914-763-3453
e-mail: haroldrosenbaum@gmail.com
Web Site: www.canticumnovum.org
Officers:
   Chairman: Linda Fusco
   Vice Chair / Secretary: Edith R. Rosenbaum
   Treasurer: Benedetto Fusco
Management:
   Artistic Director/Conductor: Harold Rosenbuam
Founded: 1973
Specialized Field: Choral; Traditional Choral Music
Paid Staff: 1
Non-paid Artists: 24
Budget: $21,000
Income Sources: Individuals; Tickets; Merchandise; Contracted Services; Contributions; Fund Raisers
Performs At: Churches and Concert Halls
Affiliations: In Residence at St. Ignatius of Antioch Episcopal Church, NYC
Annual Attendance: 1,500

2221
CECILIA CHORUS OF NEW YORK
FDR Station
New York, NY 10150-0421
Mailing Address: P.O. Box 421, New York, NY 10150-0421
Phone: 646-638-2535
e-mail: admin@ceciliachorusny.org
Web Site: ceciliachorusny.org
Management:
   Music Director: Mark Shapiro
Founded: 1906
Specialized Field: Classical; Choral
Performs At: Carnegie Hall

2222
CENTER FOR CONTEMPORARY OPERA
PO Box 3169
71 West 47th St, Suite 1605
New York, NY 10036
Phone: 646-481-8110
e-mail: js@conopera.org
Web Site: www.conopera.org
Officers:
   President: Durwood Littlefield
   Secretary: Robert Howard
   Treasurer: Jim Busterud
Management:
   General Director: Jim Schaeffer, js@conopera.org
   Artistic Director: Eric Salzman, es@ericsalzman.com
   Composer-in-Residence: Michael Dellaira
   Founding General Director: Richard Marshall
   Media Relations: Dan Dutcher
   Company Manager: Jami Leonard
Mission: The Center for Contemporary Opera is the leading proponent of new opera in the United States. Based in New York City, the company focuses on producing and developing new opera and music theater works and reviving rarely seen American operas written after the second World War.
Utilizes: Arrangers; Artists-in-Residence; Choreographers; Collaborating Artists; Collaborations; Composers-in-Residence; Educators; Lyricists; Multimedia; Music; Paid Performers; Sign Language Translators; Singers
Founded: 1982
Specialized Field: Opera
Status: Non-Profit, Professional
Income Sources: Donors, Sponsors
Season: Year Round
Performs At: Flea Theatre, The Kaye Playhouse, The National Arts Club, Sharp Theater, Symphony Space

2223
CHELSEA OPERA
PO Box 277
Old Chelsea Station
New York, NY 10113-0277
Phone: 212-260-1796
e-mail: info@chelseaopera.org
Web Site: www.chelseaopera.org
Officers:
   President: Lynne Hayden-Findlay
   Vice President/Secretary: Leonarda Priore
   Vice President: Larry Beers
   Board Member: Courtenay Casey
Management:
   Co-Founder/Co-Producer: Lynne Hayden Findlay
   Co-Founder/Co-Producer: Leonarda Priore
   Ochestracontractor/Violin: Garry Ianco
   Resident Lighting Designer: Michael Megliola
   Production Photographer: Robert Saferstein
   Production Engineer: David Satz
Mission: Chelsea Opera is a professional company presenting fully staged operas with chamber orchestra. Modest in scale yet offering the highest artistic values, Chelsea Opera operates in an intimate performance space in a landmark venue in the Chelsea district of New York City providing opportunities for artists to advance their craft in a professional venue. The company produces standard, modern and new operas, making them engaging and affordable.
Utilizes: Arrangers; Artists-in-Residence; Choreographers; Collaborating Artists; Collaborations; Designers; Lyricists; Multi Collaborations; Multimedia; Music; Paid Performers; Poets; Resident Companies
Founded: 2004
Specialized Field: Performance Opera
Status: Non-Profit, Professional
Income Sources: Donations, Sponsors
Season: November, June

2224
CHILDREN'S AID SOCIETY CHORUS
105 East 22nd Street
New York, NY 10010
Phone: 212-949-4800
Fax: 212-420-9153
e-mail: webmaster@childrensaidsociety.org
Web Site: www.childrensaidsociety.org
Officers:
   President and Chief Executive Offic: Richard R. Buery, Jr.
Management:
   Director of Music: Peter Frost
   Assistant Director: Yi-Ching Lin
   Assistant Program Director: Kelly Campbell
   Associate Conductor: Phyllis Clark
Mission: Strives to provide every child, regardless of socioeconomic situation, the opportunity to study and perform quality choral music with other children from New York City.
Founded: 1997
Specialized Field: Choral; Youth Chorus; Ethnic Music; Classical; Contemporary
Status: Non-Profit, Professional
Paid Staff: 15
Paid Artists: 12
Budget: $142,000

2225
COLLEGIATE CHORALE
115 E 57th Street
Suite 1121
New York, NY 10022
Phone: 646-202-9623
e-mail: info@collegiatechorale.org
Web Site: www.collegiatechorale.org
Officers:
   Co-Chairman: Susan L Baker
   Co-Chairman: George J Grumbach Jr
   Secretary: Christie C Salomon
   Treasurer: Lois Conway
   Vice-Chair: Anna Mann
Management:
   Music Director: James Bagwell
   Executive Director: Jennifer Collins
   General Manager: Julie Morgan
Mission: To enrich the audience through innovative programming and exceptional performances of a broad range of vocal music featuring a premier choral ensemble.
Founded: 1941
Specialized Field: Choral
Status: Non-Profit, Professional

2226
EARLY MUSIC NEW YORK (EM/NY)
10 West 68 Street
New York, NY 10023
Phone: 212-749-6600
Fax: 212-749-2848
e-mail: info@EarlyMusicNY.org
Web Site: www.EarlyMusicNY.org
Officers:
   President: Audrey Boughton
Management:
   Founder/Director: Fredrick Renz, f.renz@EarlyMusicNY.org
   Operations Manager: Aaron Smith, admin@EarlyMusicNY.org
Founded: 1975
Specialized Field: Early Music; Drama & Dance; Medieval; Renassiance; Baroque; Classical
Status: Non-Profit, Professional
Paid Staff: 4
Paid Artists: 100
Budget: $300,000
Income Sources: Ticket Sales; CD Sales; Private Contributions & Grants; Government Awards
Affiliations: Early Music Foundation; New York Early Music Central (NYEMC)

2227
EMPIRE OPERA INC
PO Box 590
Lincolnton Station
New York, NY 10037
e-mail: info@empireopera.org
Web Site: www.empireopera.org
Officers:
   President: Waundell Saavedra
   Treasurer: George Medina
   Secretary: Donna Darden Medina
   Board Member: Candice Donaldson
Management:
   Artistic Director: Waundell Saavedra

VOCAL MUSIC / New York

Guest Conductor: Miran Vaupotich
Music Director: John Rose
Mission: Our mission at Empire Opera is to both promote and advance public interest in opera through the sponsorship and presentation of musical performances, music workshops and lectures, and discussions. We are committed to seeking out and embracing a new audience and make opera lovers of them, especially the youth. Empire Opera (EO) especially wants to support the music of living composers as well as works never and rarely performed.
Utilizes: Arrangers; Collaborating Artists; Collaborations; Composers; Guest Composers; Guest Designers; Guest Directors; Lyricists; Singers; Visual Designers
Specialized Field: Opera, Theater
Status: Non-Profit
Income Sources: Patrons, Sponsors
Season: October
Performs At: National Opera Center America

2228
GOTHAM CHAMBER OPERA
410 West 42nd Street
New York, NY 10036
Phone: 212-868-4460
Fax: 212-868-4462
e-mail: info@gothamchamberopera.org
Web Site: www.gothamchamberopera.org
Officers:
  President Emeritus: Karen Lerner
  Vice President: Ted Trussell Stanton
  Secretary/Treasurer: Ronald Gellert
  Board Member: Robert Bareuther
Management:
  Founding Artistic Director: Neal Goren
  Executive Director: David Bennett
  External Affairs Manager: David Rubeo
  Producing Associate: Naomi Major
  Marketing/Communications Manager: Michelle Tabnick
  Orchestra Contractor: Sato Moughalian
Mission: Gotham Chamber Opera, now on its 11th season, is the nation's leading opera company dedicated to the highest quality productions of chamber operas rarely performed today. Its mission is to produce vibrant, fully-staged productions of works from the Baroque era to the present that are intended for intimate venues. As the only company committed solely to producing chamber opera, Gotham has a unique brand that is recognized nationally.
Utilizes: Arrangers; Collaborating Artists; Collaborations; Commissioned Music; Composers; Educators; Fine Artists; Guest Accompanists; Guest Artists; Guest Choreographers; Guest Companies; Paid Performers; Special Technical Talent; Visual Designers
Founded: 2001
Specialized Field: Opera
Status: Non-Profit
Income Sources: Non-Profit, Sponsors
Season: March

2229
GRACE CHURCH CHORAL SOCIETY
802 Broadway
New York, NY 10003
Phone: 212-254-2000
Fax: 212-673-4938
Web Site: www.thechoralesociety.org
Management:
  Music Director: John Maclay
  Associate Conductor: Tony Bellomy
Mission: A 150-voice ensemble of experienced professional and avocational singers who volunteer their time and talents in the service of the choral art form.
Utilizes: Artists-in-Residence; Commissioned Composers; Commissioned Music; Composers-in-Residence; Guest Companies; Local Artists; Organization Contracts; Original Music Scores; Sign Language Translators; Singers; Soloists
Founded: 1961
Specialized Field: Choral
Paid Staff: 2
Volunteer Staff: 6
Paid Artists: 12
Non-paid Artists: 100
Performs At: Church
Affiliations: Grace Church in New York
Annual Attendance: 2,400

2230
I CANTORI DI NEW YORK
PO Box 1376
New York, NY 10185
Phone: 212-439-4758
e-mail: info@cantorinewyork.com
Web Site: www.cantorinewyork.com
Officers:
  President: Sarah Graham
  VP: Gerald Metz
  Treasurer: Mary Jo Mace
  Secretary: Jonathan Breit
Management:
  Artistic Director: Mark Shapiro
  Assistant Conductor: Jason Wirth
  General Manager: Erol Gurol
Founded: 1984
Specialized Field: Choral
Status: Semi-Professional
Affiliations: Chorus America; Vocal Area Network; Classical Domain
Organization Type: Performing

2231
L'OPERA FRANCAIS DE NEW YORK
PO Box 33
New York, NY 10185
Phone: 212-632-5565
e-mail: info@ofny.org
Web Site: www.ofny.org
Management:
  Co-Artistic/Stage Directors: Jean-Philippe Clarac
  Co-Artistic/Stage Director: Olivier Deloeuil
  Executive Director: Susan Oetgen
  Music Director/Founder: Yves Abel
Mission: The only professional opera company in America devoted exclusively to French operas, a repertory which has been unjustly neglected and under-served by American companies in recent time.
Utilizes: Original Music Scores; Resident Professionals; Sign Language Translators; Singers
Founded: 1988
Specialized Field: Lyric Opera
Status: Professional
Income Sources: French Institute; Alliance Francaise
Performs At: Alice Tull Hall; Kaye Playhouse
Organization Type: Performing

2232
LA GRAN SCENA OPERA COMPANY
211 E 11th Street
Suite 9
New York, NY 10003
Phone: 212-460-9124
Fax: 212-460-9124
e-mail: irasiff@aol.com
Web Site: www.granscena.org
Management:
  President: Ira Siff
  Managing Director: Antonio Tessitore
Utilizes: Five Seasonal Concerts; Grant Writers; Guest Lecturers; Guest Musicians; Sign Language Translators; Singers; Student Interns
Founded: 1981
Specialized Field: Opera
Status: Non-Profit, Professional
Paid Staff: 2
Volunteer Staff: 6
Paid Artists: 15
Budget: $150,000
Income Sources: Funding and Performances
Performs At: Various Auditoriums
Annual Attendance: varies
Facility Category: varies

2233
LONG ISLAND OPERA
P.O. Box 287501
New York, NY 10128
Phone: 631-772-9546
e-mail: info@longislandoperaco.org
Web Site: longislandoperaco.org
Officers:
  Chair: Daniel Hubert
  Treasurer: Genevieve Brown
Management:
  Executive Director: Anne-Julia Audray, anne-julia.audray@longislandop
Mission: Long Island Opera's mission is to provide the highest level of performance true to the vision of the composer, and to enhance the spirit of community through the tradition of opera.
Founded: 1958
Status: Nonprofit

2234
METROPOLITAN OPERA
Lincoln Center
New York, NY 10023
Phone: 212-362-6000
Web Site: www.metopera.org
Officers:
  Chairman: Ann Ziff
  Vice-Chairman: Mercedes T. Bass
  President/CEO: Kevin W. Kennedy
  CEO: William C. Morris
  Honorary Chairman: Christine F. Hunter
  Secretary: Judith-Anne Corrente
Management:
  General Manager: Peter Gelb
  Music Director: James Levine
  Principal Conductor: Fabio Luisi
  Director of Communications: Lee Abrahamian
  Director of Worldwide HD Distributi: Julie Borchard-Young
Mission: A vibrant home for the mose creative and talented artists, including singers, conductors, composers, orchestra musicians, stage directors, designers, visual artists, choreographers, and dancers from around the world.
Founded: 1883
Specialized Field: Grand Opera
Status: Non-Profit, Professional
Season: January-December

VOCAL MUSIC / New York

2235
MUSIC-THEATRE GROUP
20 Jay Street
Suite 740
New York, NY 11201
Phone: 718-797-1145
Fax: 718-408-9575
e-mail: info@musictheatregroup.org
Web Site: www.musictheatregroup.org
Officers:
   Chair: Bill Clark
   President: Diane Wondisford
   Treasurer: Steven L Krueger
   Secretary: Jeff Lee
Management:
   Producing Director/President: Diane Wondisford
   Managing Director: Lisa Phillips
   Producing Associate: George Lam
Mission: Occupies the unique space between music theatre and opera. Generates original work by telling stories driven by music, in experimental forms and interdisciplinary combinations, offering artists the opportunity to carefully and throughfully create new work in a safe, collaborative environment.
Utilizes: Singers
Founded: 1971
Specialized Field: Musical Theatre
Status: Non-Profit, Professional
Paid Staff: 5
Paid Artists: 50
Income Sources: Opera America
Organization Type: Performing; Touring

2236
NEW AMSTERDAM SINGERS
PO Box 373
Cathedral Station
New York, NY 10025
Phone: 212-568-5948
e-mail: info@nasingers.org
Web Site: www.nasingers.org
Management:
   Music Director: Clara Longstreth
Mission: A mid-sized, mixed-voice, avocational chorus dedicated to sharing the love of choral music with each other and with audiences in New York City and abroad. Mission is to educate the listeners and ourselves by performing a diverse and extended repertoire combining traditional choral gems with new and lesser-knows works, many of them a cappella.
Founded: 1972
Specialized Field: Choral
Paid Artists: 3
Budget: $90,000

2237
NEW YORK CHORAL SOCIETY
119 W 57th Street
Suite 1215
New York, NY 10019
Phone: 212-247-3878
Fax: 973-948-4878
e-mail: info@nychoral.org
Web Site: www.nychoral.org
Officers:
   Chair: Michael Colosi
   President: Daniel Stewart
   Executive VP: Joanne W Lawson
   Secretary: Charles Chromow
   Treasurer: Joseph K. Sapora
Management:
   Executive Director: John Lawson
   Music Director: David Hayes
   Assistant Conductor: Malcolm Merriweather
   Accompanist: David Ralph
   Music Director Emeritus: Robert De Cormier
Mission: To share a variety of choral music to enrich the culture of the community, foster community outreach to children and provide challenging experiences for the choir members.
Founded: 1958
Specialized Field: Choral
Status: Non-Professional, Nonprofit
Paid Staff: 280
Volunteer Staff: 50
Paid Artists: 2
Performs At: Carnegie Hall; Lincoln Center
Organization Type: Performing; Touring

2238
NEW YORK CITY OPERA
75 Broad Street
New York, NY 10004
Phone: 646-758-9440
e-mail: webmanager@nycOpera.com
Web Site: www.nycopera.com
Officers:
   Chairman: Charles R. Wall
Management:
   General Manager/Artistic Director: George Steel
   Music Director: George Manahan
   Marketing Director: Tom Trayer
   Managing Director: Andrea Nellis
   Director of Marketing: Bill Updegraff
Mission: Producing grand opera; developing and presenting young American artists; presenting opera as theater.
Utilizes: Singers
Founded: 1943
Specialized Field: Grand Opera
Status: Non-Profit, Professional
Budget: $34 million
Income Sources: Opera America
Performs At: New York State Theatre; Lincoln Center
Annual Attendance: 275,000+
Seating Capacity: 2,763
Organization Type: Performing; Touring; Resident; Educational

2239
NEW YORK GILBERT AND SULLIVAN PLAYERS
302 W 91st Street
New York, NY 10024
Phone: 212-769-1000
Fax: 212-769-1002
e-mail: info@nygasp.org
Web Site: www.nygasp.org
Officers:
   President: Albert Bergeret
   Treasurer: Alan Hill
   Secretary: Christopher P. Nicholas
   Board Chair: Michael Strone
   Board Vice Chair: Judy Hoffstein
Management:
   Artistic Director/General Manager: Albert Bergeret
   Managing Director: David Wannen
   Associate Manager: Joseph Rubin
   Publicity/PR: Peter Cromarty
Mission: Producing and promoting Gilbert and Sullivan's works, along with related works employing orchestras as well as small ensembles.
Utilizes: Sign Language Translators; Singers; Theatre Companies
Founded: 1974
Specialized Field: Operetta; Musical Theatre; Gilbert and Sullivan
Status: Non-Profit, Professional
Paid Staff: 2
Paid Artists: 85
Budget: $1,500,000
Income Sources: Sales; Individual Contributions; Fees for Performance; Government Endowments
Performs At: Symphony Space; City Center; Tour
Affiliations: Actors' Equity Association; American Federation of Musicians of the United States and Canada
Annual Attendance: 20,000
Facility Category: Multiple Locations
Type of Stage: Proscenium
Stage Dimensions: 48 x 30
Seating Capacity: 2500
Year Remodeled: 2001
Cost: $35,000
Rental Contact: Eugene Lowery
Organization Type: Performing; Touring; Resident; Educational

2240
NEW YORK GRAND OPERA COMPANY
250 W 54th Street
Suite 807
New York, NY 10019
Phone: 212-245-8837
Fax: 212-245-8840
e-mail: info@newyorkgrandopera.org
Web Site: www.newyorkgrandopera.org
Management:
   Conductor/Artistic Director: Vincent La Selva
Mission: Unique in the world for presenting professional fully-staged grand opera productions free of charge to the public, giving all people access to opera, regardless of their financial means.
Founded: 1973
Specialized Field: Grand Opera
Season: Summer
Performs At: New York Central Park

2241
NEW YORK OPERA PROJECT
PO Box 0677
New York, NY 10025
Phone: 212-749-6603
Fax: 212-749-6603
e-mail: info@nyop.org
Web Site: www.nyop.org
Officers:
   Board Chairperson: Dorothy Heyl, Esq
   Secretary/Treasurer: Daniel O'Connell Esq
Management:
   Artistic/Executive Director: Fredrick Martell
Mission: To produce the highest possible professional presentation of operatic, concert and chamber vocal music works, to provide educational, performace and professional development opportunities for emerging artists and to provide a high caliber and affordable performing company to the community.
Founded: 1992
Specialized Field: Opera
Paid Staff: 2
Volunteer Staff: 3

2242
NEW YORK TREBLE SINGERS
210 W 89th Street
Suite 4L
New York, NY 10024-1811

VOCAL MUSIC / New York

Phone: 212-496-0094
Fax: 212-496-0094
e-mail: vsdavidson@nytreblesingers.org
Web Site: www.nytreblesingers.org
Officers:
  President: Virginia Davidson
Mission: A professional ensemble of twelve women who specialize in original music, particularly American 20th century, written for treble voices.
Founded: 1985
Specialized Field: Women's Chorus
Status: Non-Profit, Professional
Paid Staff: 1
Volunteer Staff: 3
Paid Artists: 12

2243
THE NEW YORK VIRTUOSO SINGERS
2576 Broadway
#203
New York, NY 10025
Phone: 914-763-3453
Fax: 914-763-3453
e-mail: haroldrosenbaum@gmail.com
Web Site: www.nyvirtuoso.org
Officers:
  Chairman: Linda Fusco
  Vice Chair / Secretary: Edith R. Rosenbaum
  Treasurer: Benedetto Fusco
Management:
  Artistic Director/Conductor: Harold Rosenbaum
Mission: To perform chamber choral works from all periods with a special emphasis on 20th century repertoire; to commission, perform and record premieres.
Utilizes: Commissioned Composers; Grant Writers; Guest Companies; Guest Composers; Guest Musical Directors; Guest Musicians; Multimedia; Original Music Scores; Sign Language Translators; Singers
Founded: 1988
Specialized Field: Choral; Classical; Contemporary; Religious
Status: Non-Profit, Professional
Paid Staff: 1
Paid Artists: 16
Budget: $55,000
Income Sources: Foundations; Corporation; Individuals; Tickets; Merchandise; Contracted Services
Performs At: Churches and Concert Halls
Annual Attendance: 3,000
Organization Type: Performing

2244
OPERA EBONY
2109 Broadway
Suite 1418
New York, NY 10023
Phone: 212-877-2110
Fax: 212-877-2110
e-mail: info@operaebony.org
Web Site: www.operaebony.org
Management:
  Artistic Director: Benjamin Matthews
  Musical Director: Wayne Sanders
  General Director: Gregory Sheppard,
  Associate Music Director: James Davis
  Artistic Consultant: Micheal Philip Davis
Mission: Discovering and promoting singers, composers, directors, choreographers and technicians.
Utilizes: Singers
Founded: 1973
Specialized Field: Grand Opera; Light Opera; Lyric Opera; Musical Theatre; Choral; Ethnic Music; Classical; Contemporary; Religious
Status: Non-Profit, Professional
Paid Staff: 3
Paid Artists: 26
Income Sources: The American Music Center; Opera America
Performs At: Aaron Davis Hall
Organization Type: Performing; Touring; Educational

2245
OPERA NORTHEAST/CHILDREN'S OPERA THEATRE
PO Box 6700
New York, NY 10128
Phone: 212-472-2168
Fax: 212-472-6910
e-mail: donwestwood@earthlink.net
Web Site: www.operamgt.com
Management:
  Artistic Director: Donald Westwood
  Administrative Director: Tracy Throne
Mission: Build a first-class touring organization to produce and present authentic classical lyric theatre.
Utilizes: Collaborations; Grant Writers; Guest Artists; Guest Conductors; Guest Lecturers; Singers
Founded: 1972
Specialized Field: Youth Chorus; Classical for Young Audiences; Opera
Status: Non-Profit, Professional
Paid Staff: 6
Volunteer Staff: 10
Paid Artists: 10
Budget: $250,000
Organization Type: Performing; Touring; Educational

2246
OPERA ORCHESTRA OF NEW YORK
344 3 63rd Street
Suite B-1
New York, NY 10065
Phone: 212-906-9137
Fax: 212-906-9021
e-mail: operaorchestrany@gmail.com
Web Site: www.oony.org
Officers:
  President: Norman Raben
  VP: Sandra Wagenfeld
  Treasurer: Eearle W Kazis
  Secretary: Francine Goldstein
Management:
  Founder/Music Director: Eve Queler
  Executive Director: Deborah Surdi
  Office Manager: Evan Croen
  Business Manager: Tom Weatherly
  Development Manager: Katherine Gulick
Mission: Enriching the musical and cultural vitality of New York City. Gives new life to rarely-heard operas, providing the public with an opportunity to hear these operatic rarities in major concert performances at Carnegie Hall.
Utilizes: Guest Writers; Multimedia; Original Music Scores; Singers
Founded: 1972
Specialized Field: Opera
Status: Non-Profit, Professional
Paid Staff: 4
Volunteer Staff: 6
Paid Artists: 100
Budget: $1.5 million
Income Sources: Ticket sales and donations
Performs At: Carnegie Hall
Organization Type: Performing; Sponsoring

2247
OPERAMISSION
853 Seventh Avenue
Suite 2-A
New York, NY 10019
Phone: 917-520-3063
e-mail: operamission@gmail.com or operajen@yahoo.com
Web Site: www.operamission.org or www.operajen.com
Management:
  Composer/Artistic Director: Jennifer Peterson
  Composer: Clint Borzoni
  Librettist: Edward Ficklin
Mission: The operamission: to bring the art from the composer to the audience.
Utilizes: Arrangers; Collaborations; Composers; Fine Artists; Guest Companies; Lyricists; Multimedia; Music; Organization Contracts
Specialized Field: Opera, Classical Music
Status: Non-Profit
Income Sources: Donors, Sponsors
Season: Fall

2248
ORATORIO SOCIETY OF NEW YORK
1440 Broadway
23rd Floor
New York, NY 10018
Phone: 212-400-7255
e-mail: webmaster@oratoriosocietyofny.org
Web Site: www.oratoriosocietyofny.org
Officers:
  Chairwoman: Ellen L Blair
  President: Richard A Pace
  VP: Mary-Jo P Knight
  VP: Janet Plucknett
  Treasurer: Marie Gangemi
  Secretary: Jay Jacobson
Management:
  Music Director: Kent Tritle
  Associate Conductor: David Rosenmayer
  Accompanist: David Ralph
Mission: Brings together a diverse community of avocational singers who share a passion for choral music. Mission is to contribute to the cultural fabric of New York City through public performance of both classic and contemporary choral works at the highest musical standards. Committed to the musical development of members, audience and artists.
Founded: 1873
Specialized Field: Choral
Status: Non-Profit, Non-Professional
Paid Staff: 2
Paid Artists: 60
Budget: $475,000
Income Sources: Concert Tickets; Contributions; Chorus Dues
Performs At: Carnegie Hall
Seating Capacity: 2,700
Organization Type: Performing; Touring; Resident; Educational

2249
PALA OPERA ASSOCIATION
200 Riverside Boulevard
PH2A
New York, NY 10069-0917
Phone: 212-874-7866
Fax: 212-769-0563
e-mail: elizabethfalk@usa.net
Officers:
  President: Elizabeth Falk
  VP: Martin Piecuch

VOCAL MUSIC / New York

VP: Richard Woitach
Management:
   Producer/Artistic Director: Elizabeth Falk
   Music Director: Martin Piecuch
   Chief Music Consultant: Richard Woitach
Mission: To present high-calibre, ascendant artists with professionalism and elegance, accompanied by a chorus and full orchestra; providing them the opportunity to be heard by discerning, paying audiences as well as critics.
Utilizes: Actors; Collaborating Artists; Dancers; Grant Writers; Guest Artists; Guest Directors; Guest Musical Directors; Guest Musicians; Lyricists; Singers; Student Interns
Founded: 1989
Specialized Field: Grand Opera; Musical Theatre
Status: Professional
Paid Staff: 2
Budget: 75,000-$100,000
Income Sources: Contibutors
Performs At: Town Hall; Players
Organization Type: Performing

2250
THE DICAPO OPERA THEATRE
184 East 76th Street
New York, NY 10021
Phone: 212-288-9438
Fax: 212-868-4444
e-mail: dotproduction@dicapo.com
Web Site: www.dicao.com
Management:
   General/Artistic Director: Michael Capasso
   Childrens Chorus Director: Diane Martindale
   Artistic Development Director: Andrea Delgiudice
Mission: Dicapo Opera Theatre is the only opera company in New York, after the Metropolitan Opera and the City Opera, to present an entire season of opera productions, musical theatre, concerts, family fare, and other events. Co-founded in 1981 by General Director Michael Capasso and Diane Martindale, Dicapo Opera Theatre has annually offered repertoire ranging from the operatic classics by such masters as Mozart, Bellini, Donizetti, and Verdi.
Utilizes: Arrangers; Collaborations; Composers; Composers-in-Residence; Educators; Guest Accompanists; Guest Musicians; Multimedia; Music; Paid Performers
Founded: 1981
Specialized Field: Opera
Status: Donors, Sponsors
Income Sources: Donors, Subscriptions
Season: October through May
Performs At: Dicapo Opera Theatre

2251
THE OPERA ORCHESTRA OF NEW YORK
344 East 63rd Street
Suite B-1
New York, NY 10065
Phone: 212-906-9137
Fax: 212-906-9021
e-mail: operaorchestrany@gmail.com
Web Site: www.operaorchestrany.org
Officers:
   Chairman: Norman Raben
   Treasurer: Earle Kazis
   Secretary: Francine Goldstein
   Board Member: Anna Bulgari
   Board Member: Stuart Greenfield
   Board Member: Marco Gualitieri
Management:
   Executive Director: Deborah Surdi
   Business Manager: Tom Weatherly
   Development: Katherine Gulick
   Music Director: Alberto Veronesi
   Artistic Administrator: Elizabeth Cole
Mission: The mission of The Opera Orchestra of New York is to present high-quality performances of seldom-heard operatic masterpieces in a concert setting featuring internationally acclaimed stars and exceptional young singers; to offer a professional training program to talented emerging artists; and to develop an appreciation of opera among diverse audiences, while cultivating a new generation of supporters.
Utilizes: Arrangers; Collaborations; Designers; Guest Composers; Multimedia; Music; Paid Performers; Singers
Specialized Field: Opera
Status: Non-Profit
Income Sources: Donations, Ticket Sales
Season: January, April
Performs At: Avery Fisher Hall

2252
CHAUTAUQUA OPERA
412 West 42nd Street Suite
Suite 4E4
New York City, NY 10036
Mailing Address: PO Box Q Chautauqua NY 14722
Phone: 212-779-3177
Fax: 212-779-3293
e-mail: admin@chautopera.org
Web Site: opera.ciweb.org
Management:
   Artistic/General Director: Jay Lesenger
   Music Administrator/Chorus Master: Carol Rausch
   Administrative Director: Elizabeth Cheslock
   Company Manager and Media/Publicati: Gabriel Estrin
   Director of Production: Michael Baumgarten
Mission: To produce music of the highest quality in order to extend the appreciation of opera for artists and audiences.
Utilizes: Singers
Founded: 1929
Specialized Field: Grand Opera; Light Opera; Lyric Opera; Musical Theatre; Classical; Contemporary
Status: Non-Profit, Professional
Paid Staff: 3
Income Sources: Opera America
Performs At: Norton Hall
Organization Type: Performing; Resident; Educational

2253
MATAPAT
517 County Highway 27
Richfield Springs, NY 13439
Phone: 315-858-1434
Fax: 315-858-1434
Web Site: www.onqueuartists.com
Management:
   Founder/Agent: Sandra Bernegger
Mission: To perform the traditional music, song and dance of Quebec with contemporary and world music influences.
Founded: 1997
Specialized Field: Folk Music; Ethnic Music
Paid Staff: 3
Paid Artists: 3

2254
LAKE GEORGE OPERA AT SARATOGA
19 Roosevelt Drive
Suite 215
Saratoga Springs, NY 12866
Phone: 518-584-6018
Fax: 518-584-6775
e-mail: info@lakegeorgeopera.org
Web Site: www.lakegeorgeopera.org
Officers:
   Chairman: Robert C Miller
   President: Rosemarie V. Rosen
   Vice President: Robert DeSio
   Treasurer: Norbert Woods
   Secretary: Christine McDonald
Management:
   General Director: Curtis Tucker
   Education Director: Deborah Rocco
   Development Director: Elizabeth Giblin
   Director of Administration & Financ: Patricia Finnerty
   Director of Young Artist Programs: Laurie Rogers
Mission: To produce high quality professional opera and develop the next generation of artists through our Apprentice and school programs.
Utilizes: Artists-in-Residence; Designers; Guest Accompanists; Guest Composers; Guest Designers; Guest Ensembles; Guest Lecturers; Guest Writers; Original Music Scores
Founded: 1962
Specialized Field: Opera
Status: Non-Profit; Professional
Paid Staff: 5
Paid Artists: 95
Budget: $950,000
Income Sources: Endowment; Individual Contributions; Tickets; Private/Public Grants
Performs At: Spac Little Theater; Saratoga Springs State Park
Affiliations: Opera America Professional Company Member
Annual Attendance: 16,000
Type of Stage: Modified Proscenium
Seating Capacity: 500

2255
OPERA SARATOGA
19 Roosevelt Drive
Suite 215
Saratoga Springs, NY 12866
Mailing Address: 21 Roosevelt Drive, Saratoga Springs, NY 12866
Phone: 518-584-6018
Fax: 518-584-6775
e-mail: info@operasaratoga.org
Web Site: www.operasaratoga.org
Officers:
   President: Rosemarie Rosen
   Vice President: Robert DeSio
   Chairman: Robert Miller
   Vice President: Frank Pusateri
   Treasurer: Christine McDonald
   Director: Ron Bentley
   Director: Christopher Cernik
Management:
   General/Artistic Director: Curtis Tucker
   Finance Director: Patricia Finnerty
   Education Director: Deborah Rucco
   Young Artist Director: Laurie Rogers
   Development Manager: Christopher A. Patregnani
Mission: Lake George Opera, now Opera Saratoga, began with a production of Die Fledermaus at the Diamond Point Theatre on July 5, 1962, playing to an

audience of 230. The Company now calls Saratoga Springs home and performs for more than 25,000 people annually. To date, the Company has performed ninety different fully-staged works by fifty-two different composers, including thirty-three works by American composers and ten premiere productions.
Utilizes: Arrangers; Collaborations; Contract Orchestras; Guest Choreographers; Guest Musical Directors; Multimedia; Music; Paid Performers
Founded: 1962
Specialized Field: Opera
Status: Non-Profit
Income Sources: Donations, Sponsors
Season: June-July
Performs At: Sartoga Theater

2256
SCHENECTADY LIGHT OPERA COMPANY
PO Box 1006
Schenectady, NY 12301-1006
Phone: 518-393-5732
Toll-free: 877-350-7378
Web Site: www.sloctheater.com
Officers:
  President: Robert Harrison
  Secretary: Kimberly Reilly
  Treasurer: Paul Franklin
  Vice President: Tom Della Sala
Management:
  Business Manager: Joseph Concra
Mission: To present Broadway Musicals.
Founded: 1926
Specialized Field: Broadway Musicals; Light Opera
Status: Non-Profit
Affiliations: NYSTA
Organization Type: Performing

2257
WESTCHESTER ORATORIO SOCIETY
Box 6
South Salem, NY 10590
Phone: 914-763-9389
Fax: 914-763-8284
e-mail: bobmcdon@optonline.net
Web Site: www.westcheteroratorio.org
Officers:
  Co-President: Irene Muller
  Co-President: Joe Spallina
  Vice-President: Virginia Steinberg
  Treasurer: Marvel Griepp
Management:
  President: Elizabeth McDonald
  Artistic Director: Harold Rosenbaum
  Conductor: Benjamin Niemczyk
Founded: 1997
Specialized Field: Choral; Traditional Choral Music
Status: Non-Profit, Non-Professional
Paid Staff: 2
Paid Artists: 60

2258
SYRACUSE OPERA
PO Box 1223
Syracuse, NY 13201-1223
Phone: 315-475-5915
Fax: 315-475-6319
e-mail: info@syracuseopera.com
Web Site: www.syracuseopera.com
Officers:
  Chairman of the Board: R. Andrew Hagen
  Vice Chairman: Daniel Larson
  Treasurer: James Poole
  Secretary: Amy Van Kirk
  Chairman, Board Development: Sandra Hurd
Management:
  General & Artistic Director: Catherine Wolff
  Director of Music: Douglas Kinney Frost
Mission: To produce for the community professional opera performances of the highest quality promoting young talent from across the country and cultivate a further appreciation of opera within the region, specifically Syracuse and the surrounding six county area by means of outreach and educational programs.
Utilizes: Sign Language Translators; Singers; Student Interns; Theatre Companies
Founded: 1963
Specialized Field: Grand Opera; Lyric Opera; Light Opera; Operetta
Status: Professional; Nonprofit
Paid Staff: 10
Budget: $1 million
Income Sources: New York State Coucil on Arts; County of Onandaga; Natural Heritage Trust; Corporations; Foundations; Individuals
Performs At: Crouse-Hinds Concert Theater
Seating Capacity: 2,042
Organization Type: Performing; Touring; Resident; Educational

2259
TAGHKANIC CHORALE
PO Box 144
Yorktown Heights, NY 10598-0144
Phone: 914-737-6707
e-mail: info@taghkanicchorale.org
Web Site: taghkanicchorale.ontimeonline.com/
Officers:
  President: Peter Hauge
  VP: Pat Miller
  Secretary: Sandra Strubbe
  Treasurer: Dale Sharp
Management:
  President: David Jones
  VP: Pat Miller
  Music Director/Artistic Director: Steven Fox
Mission: Preparation and performance of choral works with emphasis on quality and authenticity.
Utilizes: Singers
Founded: 1967
Specialized Field: Choral
Status: Semi-Professional; Nonprofit
Paid Staff: 100
Income Sources: Chorus America
Organization Type: Performing; Educational

North Carolina

2260
ASHEVILLE LYRIC OPERA
39 S. Market Street
Asheville, NC 28801
Phone: 828-236-0670
e-mail: info@ashevillelyric.org
Web Site: www.ashevillelyric.org
Officers:
  President: Belinda B. Brandon
  Vice President: Clive Possinger
  Treasurer: Allan Morse
  Secretary: Lorrain Marina
Management:
  General/Artistic Director: David Craig Starkey
  Conductor: Delta David Gier
  Principal Guest Conductor: Dr Robert Hart Baker
  Principal Guest Director: Scott Parry
Mission: To build a professional opera company in Asheville and present an educational outreach in the area schools and universities, thereby becoming a part of and enhancing the life of the family of arts and culture in Western North Carolina.
Opened: 1999
Specialized Field: Opera
Income Sources: Sponsors
Season: October-April
Performs At: Diana Wortham Theatre

2261
CAROLINA VOICES
1900 Queens Road
Charlotte, NC 28207
Phone: 704-374-1564
Fax: 704-372-8733
Web Site: www.carolinavoices.org
Officers:
  Chairman: Jim Lozier
  Vice Chairman: Shannon Hoff
  Treasurer: Julia Cook
  Secretary: Sara Brownfiled
  Choral Representative: Vanessa Davis
Management:
  Executive Director: Sue Wheldom
  Associate Executive Director: Beverly Seitz
  Executive Director: Peter Leo
  Music Director: Scott McKenzie
  Director of Festive Season: Donna Hill
Mission: To enrich and educate our community by sharing our passion for quality choral music and uniting the voices of all people in celebration of music, the international language of the soul.
Utilizes: Guest Artists; Guest Companies; Selected Students; Sign Language Translators; Visual Arts
Founded: 1953
Specialized Field: Choral; Ethnic Music; Classical; Contemporary; Religious
Status: Non-Profit, Non-Professional
Paid Staff: 7
Volunteer Staff: 1
Non-paid Artists: 175
Annual Attendance: 30,000

2262
OPERA CAROLINA
Two Wells Fargo Center
301 S Tryon Street Suite 1550
Charlotte, NC 28282
Phone: 704-332-7177
Fax: 704-332-6448
Web Site: www.operacarolina.org
Officers:
  Chair: C. Wells Hall
  Chair Elect: Kay Allison Norris
  Vice Chair: Thomas Hughes
  Vice Chair: Catherine M Connor
  Secretary: Georgette Dixon
  Treasurer: Steven Hershfield
Management:
  General Director/Conductor: James Meena
  Director Production: Michael Baumgarten
  Director of Major Gifts and Externa: Janet Dalton Dickinson
  Head of Music Preparation: Emily Jarrell Urbanek
Mission: To inspire the region's diverse population through the presentation of excellent professional opera, operetta, music, theatre and education and outreach programs that elevate the quality of life in the Carolinas.
Utilizes: Artists-in-Residence; Collaborating Artists; Community Talent; Contract Orchestras; Dancers; Educators; Guest Accompanists; Guest Artists; Guest

VOCAL MUSIC / North Carolina

Companies; Guest Composers; Guest Conductors; Guest Designers; Guest Lecturers; Guest Musical Directors; Guest Musicians; Guest Soloists; Guest Speakers; Guest Teachers; Guest Writers; Instructors; Local Artists; Music; Original Music Scores; Resident Artists; Resident Professionals; Scenic Designers; Sign Language Translators; Singers; Students
Founded: 1948
Specialized Field: Grand Opera
Status: Non-Profit, Professional
Paid Staff: 13
Paid Artists: 150
Budget: $2,500,000
Income Sources: Private Foundations/Grants/Endowments; Business/Coporate Donation; Government Grants; Individual Donations
Performs At: North Carolina Performing Arts Center
Affiliations: Opera America
Annual Attendance: 12,000
Facility Category: Performing Arts Center
Type of Stage: Proscenium
Stage Dimensions: 60'x43'
Year Built: 1970
Year Remodeled: 1992
Rental Contact: NC Performing Arts Center
Organization Type: Performing; Touring; Resident; Educational

2263
DURHAM CIVIC CHORAL SOCIETY
120 Morris Street
Durham, NC 27701
Phone: 919-560-2733
Web Site: www.choral-society.org
  VP: Randy Raasch
  Secretary: Deirdre Callahan
  Treasurer: John Bennett
Management:
  President: Norm Loewenthal
  Director Of Upper School: Michael L Meye
  Artistic Director: Rodney Wynkoop
  Organist And Choir Director: Jane Lynch
  Conductor: Rodney Wynkoop
Mission: Our mission is to bring together persons who share a common interest in high-quality performance of significant choral literature, both sacred and secular.
Founded: 1949
Specialized Field: Choral
Status: Non-Professional; Nonprofit
Paid Staff: 154
Performs At: Duke University Chapel; Baldwin Auditorium
Organization Type: Performing

2264
BEL CANTO COMPANY
200 North Davie Street, Suite 337
Greensboro, NC 27401
Phone: 336-333-2220
e-mail: info@belcantocompany.com
Web Site: belcantocompany.com
Officers:
  President: Constance Kotis
  Chair: Sue Keith
  Secretary: Eddie Bass
  Treasurer: Glenn Strohl
Management:
  Executive Director: Jeffrey Carlson
  Development Manager: Nancy Griffith
  Artistic Director: Welborn Young
Mission: The ensemble's mission is to present exceptional, innovative, and engaging choral performances for diverse audiences in the Triad and beyond.

Opened: 1982
Status: Nonprofit; Professional
Paid Artists: 34

2265
CHORAL SOCIETY OF GREENSBORO
200 N Davie Street
Box 2
Greensboro, NC 27401
Phone: 336-373-2549
Fax: 336-373-2659
Web Site: www.csogso.com
Officers:
  Past President: Laura Worst
  Vice President: Doug Gilbert
  Treasurer/Secretary: Bill Frisch
  Recording Secretary: Mary Alice Squires
Management:
  President: Kelley Griffith
  Managing Director: Lynn H Donovan
  Artistic Director: Welborn Young
  Music Director: Jon Brotherton
Mission: Sharing musical understanding, appreciation, accomplishment and musicianship with the public.
Utilizes: Guest Artists
Founded: 1984
Specialized Field: Choral; Ethnic Music; Classical; Contemporary; Religious
Status: Non-Profit, Non-Professional
Paid Staff: 150
Income Sources: City of Greensboro; The Music Center
Performs At: Dana Auditorium
Organization Type: Performing

2266
GREENSBORO OPERA COMPANY
200 North Davie Street
Box 17
Greensboro, NC 27401
Phone: 336-273-9472
Fax: 336-273-9481
e-mail: info@greensboroopera.org
Web Site: www.greensborooopera.org
Officers:
  President: Bert Davis, Jr.
  Treasurer: Dave Hamilton
  Executive Director: David Barnwell
  Secretary: Matt Bouldin
  Vice President of Education: Anna Clare Allen
Management:
  Artistic Director: Valery Ryvkin
  Company Manager: Elena Deangelis
Mission: Enhancing cultural life in the Greensboro area through developing and promoting a quality program of operas and education.
Utilizes: Singers
Founded: 1981
Specialized Field: Grand Opera; Musical Theatre; Choral; Youth Chorus
Status: Non-Profit, Professional
Income Sources: Opera America; Central Opera Service
Performs At: War Memorial Auditorium; Carolina Theatre
Organization Type: Performing; Educational; Sponsoring

2267
STANLY COUNTY CHORALE
P.O. Box 1038
Norwood, NC 28128

Phone: 704-422-5480
e-mail: info@stanlychorale.org
Web Site: stanlychorale.org
Officers:
  President: Becky Wall
  Vice President: Pam Myers
Management:
  Director: Joseph Judge
Mission: The Stanly County Chorale is the county's longest-running performing arts organization, presenting concerts since its founding in 1968. We present music from a wide range of styles and genres, and we welcome all area singers to join us.
Founded: 1968
Specialized Field: Choral
Season: Fall; Winter; Spring

2268
NORTH CAROLINA OPERA COMPANY
612 Wade Avenue, Suite 100
Raleigh, NC 27605
Phone: 919-792-3850
e-mail: info@ncopera.org
Web Site: ncopera.org
Officers:
  President: C. Thomas Kunz
  Vice President: Ralph Roberson
  Treasurer: John Lunsford
  Secretary: Sterling Perkinson
Management:
  General Director: Eric Mitchko, eric.mitchko@ncopera.org
  Artistic Director: Timothy Myers, timothy.myers@ncopera.org
  Company Manager: Julie Williams, julie.williams@ncopera.org
  Director Of Development: David Walker
Mission: Dedicated to presenting operatic performances at the highest level throughout the Triangle.
Founded: 2010

2269
RALEIGH BOYCHOIR
1329 Ridge Road
Raleigh, NC 27607
Mailing Address: PO Box 12481, Raleigh, NC. 27605
Phone: 919-881-9259
Fax: 919-881-0971
e-mail: raleighboychoir@gmail.com
Web Site: www.raleighboychoir.org
Management:
  Founder/Director: Thomas E Sibley
Mission: To educate and train boys in the art of singing; to perform the finest music in the boychoir tradition; to contribute to musical life in the greater Raleigh area; and to enhance North Carolina's cultural reputation. The Raleigh Boychoir experience develops character, discipline, leadership, and a strong commitment to excellence.
Founded: 1968
Specialized Field: Youth Chorus
Status: Non-Profit, Professional
Paid Staff: 3
Volunteer Staff: 5
Paid Artists: 2

2270
TAR RIVER CHORAL & ORCHESTRAL SOCIETY
The Dunn Center 1200
PO Box 8255
Rocky Mount, NC 27804

Phone: 252-985-3055
Fax: 252-985-3055
e-mail: erdegeist@aol.com
Web Site: www.abouttroc.org
Management:
- Executive Director: Beth Kupsco
- Music Director: Alfred E. Sturgis

Founded: 1986
Specialized Field: Choral; Youth Chorus; Classical
Status: Non-Profit, Professional
Paid Staff: 8

2271
PIEDMONT CHAMBER SINGERS
502 N Broad St.
PO Box 20573
Winston-Salem, NC 27120
Mailing Address: P.O. Box 20573, Winston-Salem, NC 27120
Phone: 336-722-4022
Fax: 336-722-4022
e-mail: manager@piedmontchambersingers.org
Web Site: www.piedmontchambersingers.org
Officers:
- President: Carol Crocker
- VP: Matt Jamison
- Secretary: A. Wayne Ledbetter
- Treasurer: Debbie Robinson
- Secretary: A.Wayne Ledbetter

Management:
- President: Carol Crocker
- Executive Director: Marianne Levigne
- Artistic Director: Wendy Looker
- Accompanist: Norris Norwood

Mission: Over the past two decades, PCS has gained a loyal following of supporters and patrons.
Founded: 1977
Specialized Field: Choral; Classical; Contemporary
Status: Non-Profit, Non-Professional
Paid Staff: 2

2272
PIEDMONT OPERA THEATRE
235 N Cherry Street
Suite 100
Winston-Salem, NC 27101-3929
Phone: 336-725-7101
Fax: 336-725-7131
e-mail: info@piedmontopera.org
Web Site: www.piedmontopera.org/
Officers:
- President: Guy Rudsill
- Treasurer: Gerard R Gunzenhauser
- Secretary: Clyde Fitzgerald
- VP Education: Margaret Kolb

Management:
- Board President: E Gail Phillips
- Artistic Director: James Allbritten
- Executive Director: Frank Dickerson
- Director of Development: Connie Quinn
- Business Manager: Jen Rimes

Mission: To create and support consistently superior opera theatre productions and programs that ensure recognition of the company as an important community asset for entertainment and education, a force in city development, and a magnet attraction for regional and national audiences.
Utilizes: Guest Companies; Singers
Founded: 1978
Specialized Field: Grand Opera; Lyric Opera; Light Opera; Operetta
Status: Professional; Nonprofit

Income Sources: Opera America; Central Opera Service; National Opera Association; Arts Council; Winston-Salem
Performs At: Roger L. Stevens Center for the Performing Arts
Organization Type: Performing; Resident; Educational

2273
WINSTON-SALEM PIEDMONT TRIAD SYMPHONY ASSOCIATION
201 N Broad Street
Suite 200
Winston-Salem, NC 27101
Phone: 336-725-1035
Fax: 336-725-3924
e-mail: mvale@wssymphony.org
Web Site: www.wssymphony.org
Officers:
- Operations/Stage Manager: Beverley Naiditch
- Finance Director: Selina Carter
- Immediate Past President: Roger Bear
- Board Treasurer: Dick Deem

Management:
- President & CEO: Merritt Vale
- Music Director: Robert Moody
- Director Marketing Development: William Cole
- Box Office Manager: Tinay Jeffers
- Artistic Operations Director: Joshua Moyer

Mission: Presenting the finest symphonic as well as choral literature; providing high quality music education for Winston-Salem and Forsythe County children.
Utilizes: Collaborations; Commissioned Composers; Commissioned Music; Educators; Five Seasonal Concerts; Guest Accompanists; Guest Artists; Guest Choreographers; Guest Companies; Guest Composers; Guest Directors; Guest Instructors; Guest Lecturers; Guest Musical Directors; Guest Musicians; Guest Soloists; High School Drama; Local Artists; Lyricists; Multimedia; New Productions; Singers; Visual Arts
Founded: 1947
Specialized Field: Choral
Status: Professional; Nonprofit
Paid Staff: 9
Paid Artists: 80
Budget: $1.4 million
Income Sources: American Symphony Orchestra League; Broadcast Music Incorporated; American Society of Composers, Authors and Publishers; Association of Symphony Orchestras of North Carolina
Performs At: E. Stevens Center for the Performing Arts
Annual Attendance: 100,000
Seating Capacity: 1,380
Year Remodeled: 1985
Organization Type: Performing; Resident; Educational

2274
WINSTON-SALEM SYMPHONY
201 N Broad Street
Suite 200
Winston-Salem, NC 27101
Phone: 336-725-1035
Fax: 336-725-3924
e-mail: boxoffice@wssymphony.org
Web Site: www.wssymphony.org
Officers:
- President/CEO: Merrit Vale
- Immediate Past President: Roger Bear
- Treasurer: Dick Deem
- Secretary: Jerry Silber

Management:
- Music Director: Robert Moody
- Ticket Sales/Donor Administration: Latonya Wright
- Artistic Operations Director: Joshua Moyer

Orchestra Librarian: Michael Di Trolio
Orchestra Personnel Manager and Web: Brian French
Founded: 1947
Specialized Field: Choral
Status: Professional; Nonprofit
Paid Staff: 14
Volunteer Staff: 120
Paid Artists: 75
Non-paid Artists: 80

North Dakota

2275
FARGO-MOORHEAD OPERA COMPANY
114 Broadway
Suite S1
Fargo, ND 58102
Phone: 701-239-4558
Fax: 701-476-1991
Toll-free: 877-687-7469
e-mail: director@fmopera.org
Web Site: www.fmopera.org
Officers:
- President: Dennis Staton
- VP: Thomas Ortmeier
- Treasurer: David Duval
- Secretary: Beth Postema

Management:
- Office Manager: Iris Fogderud
- Executive Director: David Hamilton
- Box Office Manager: Beau Brander
- Marketing Manager: Clark Weyrauch

Mission: To produce professional opera and introduce people to one of the world's oldest art forms.
Utilizes: Selected Students; Singers; Soloists
Founded: 1968
Specialized Field: Opera
Status: Non-Profit, Professional
Paid Staff: 3
Budget: $356,900
Income Sources: National Endowment for the Arts; Alex Stern Family Foundation; Cities of Fargo and Moorhead; Bush Foundation; McKnight Foundation; Minnesota Council on the Arts
Performs At: NDSU Fine Arts Building
Annual Attendance: 3,600
Facility Category: Concert Hall
Organization Type: Performing; Touring; Educational
Resident Groups: Minnesota Association of Community Theatres, Lake Agassiz Arts Council, US Assoc. Community Theatre

Ohio

2276
SAINT SAVA FREE SERBIAN ORTHODOX CHURCH
2151 W Wallings
Broadview Heights, OH 44147
Phone: 440-237-7620
e-mail: webmaster@saintsavachurch.org
Web Site: www.saintsavachurch.org
Management:
- Director: Dragica Zamiska

Mission: To encourage and perpetuate Serbian music, dance, language, culture and heritage.
Founded: 1982
Specialized Field: Ethnic Music; Folk Music; Religious
Status: Non-Professional; Nonprofit

VOCAL MUSIC / Ohio

Income Sources: Saint Sava Free Serbian Orthodox Church; School Congregation; Cleveland Area Arts Council
Organization Type: Performing; Touring; Resident; Educational

2277
CINCINNATI BOYCHOIR
4501 Allison St
Cincinnati, OH 45212
Phone: 513-396-7664
Fax: 513-396-7664
e-mail: christopher.eanes@cincinnatiboychoir.org
Web Site: www.cincinnatiboychoir.org
Management:
  Music Director: Randall Wolfe
  Business Manager: Patty Corfman
  Artistic Director: Christopher Eanes
  Associate Director: Bonnie Spain
  Director of Education & Outreach: KellyAnn Nelson
Mission: To provide high quality music, education, and performance opportunities to boys with unchanged voices and choral music to greater Cincinnati and other regions.
Utilizes: Collaborating Artists; Collaborations; Educators; Guest Artists; Guest Companies; Guest Directors; Guest Musical Directors; Multimedia; Music; Original Music Scores; Sign Language Translators; Soloists
Founded: 1965
Specialized Field: Choral; Youth Chorus; Ethnic Music; Classical; Religious
Status: Non-Profit, Non-Professional
Paid Staff: 2
Volunteer Staff: 10
Paid Artists: 5
Non-paid Artists: 110
Facility Category: Rehearsal Hall
Year Built: 1896
Organization Type: Performing; Touring; Resident; Educational

2278
CINCINNATI OPERA
1243 Elm Street
Cincinnati, OH 45202-7531
Phone: 513-241-2742
Fax: 513-768-5551
Toll-free: 888-533-7149
e-mail: tickets@cincinnatiopera.org
Web Site: www.cincinnatiopera.com
Management:
  Artistic Director: Evans Mirageas
  General Director/CEO: Patricia K Beggs
  Director of Artistic Operations: Marcus Kuchle
  Artistic Coordinator: Lauren Bailey
  Director of Production: Glenn Plott
Mission: To provide opera to the Cincinnati and Tri-State Area.
Utilizes: Guest Artists; Guest Companies; Singers
Founded: 1920
Specialized Field: Grand Opera; Lyric Opera; Operetta
Status: Professional; Nonprofit
Paid Staff: 28
Income Sources: Opera America
Performs At: Music Hall
Organization Type: Performing

2279
CLEVELAND ORCHESTRA CHORUS
11001 Euclid Avenue
Cleveland, OH 44106
Phone: 216-231-1111
Fax: 216-231-0202
Toll-free: 800-686-1141
e-mail: info@clevelandorchestra.com
Web Site: www.clevelandorchestra.com
Officers:
  Chairperson: Margaret B Robinson
Management:
  President: Gary Hansen
  Artistic Director: Franz Mose
  Accompanist/Soloist: Joela Jones
Mission: To assist the Cleveland Orchestra in performing choral-orchestral works.
Utilizes: Guest Artists
Founded: 1952
Opened: cont
Specialized Field: Choral; Opera; Contemporary
Status: Non-Profit, Professional
Paid Staff: 170
Performs At: Severence Hall; Blossom Music Center
Organization Type: Performing; Touring; Resident

2280
LYRIC OPERA OF CLEVELAND
1422 Euclid Avenue
Suite 1052
Cleveland, OH 44115
Phone: 216-575-0903
Web Site: www.clevelandopera.org
Officers:
  President: Don Scippione
  President Guild: Becky Elliot
Management:
  President: Peter Rubin
  Director of Production: Maidie O. Rosenberg
  Director of Development: William Cole
  Director of Marketing/Communication: Catherine Guin
  Director of Finance/Administration: Colleen G. Sherman
  Artistic Advisor: Leon Major
Mission: To utilize talented artists from the North in music theatre productions; to uncover new ideas, fresh concepts and illuminating perspectives in every work it produces; to emphasize training opportunities for professional development.
Utilizes: Actors; AEA Actors; Choreographers; Collaborations; Fine Artists; Grant Writers; Guest Artists; Guest Companies; Guest Composers; Guest Conductors; Guest Designers; Guest Soloists; Guest Writers; High School Drama; Local Artists; Lyricists; Multi Collaborations; New Productions; Resident Professionals; Sign Language Translators; Singers; Student Interns
Founded: 1974
Specialized Field: Opera; Musical Theatre
Status: Non-Profit, Professional
Paid Staff: 4
Paid Artists: 3
Non-paid Artists: 2
Budget: $500,000
Income Sources: Tickets, Cleveland Foundation, Gund & Kyles
Performs At: Cleveland Institute of Music
Annual Attendance: 4,800
Facility Category: Professional Theatre
Type of Stage: Proscenium
Stage Dimensions: 30 X 40
Seating Capacity: 500
Organization Type: Performing; Resident; Educational; Sponsoring

2281
OPERA CIRCLE
6501 Lansing Avenue
Cleveland, OH 44105
Phone: 216-441-2822
Fax: 216-441-2825
e-mail: info@operacircle.org
Web Site: www.operacircle.org
Officers:
  President: Eugene Bak
  EVP: Elliot Schultz
  Treasurer: Eugene Trela
  Secretary: Julian Boryczewski
  Trustee: Shirley Dawson
  Trustee: Kathy Greiser
  Advisor: Piotr Beczala
  Advisor: Halim El Dabh
  Advisor: Andrew Knapp
Management:
  Executive Director: Dorota Sobieska
  Founder/Music Director: Jacek Sobieski
Mission: Opera Circle serves wide public by maintaining a fine balance of two directions, as one feeds the other. The two directions may be summarized as: Opera Circle Classics Series, including traditionally produced opera presented at the Bohemian National Hall, a miniature opera house from Prague. Open Form Opera presented at non-standard locations.
Utilizes: Arrangers; Choreographers; Composers; Composers-in-Residence; Fine Artists; Local Artists & Directors; Lyricists; Multimedia; Music; Poets; Special Technical Talent
Founded: 1995
Specialized Field: Opera, Theater
Status: Non-Profit, Professional
Income Sources: Sponsors
Season: November through April
Performs At: PlayHouse Square Theater
Affiliations: Ohio Arts Council, Art Works, Northern Ohio Opera League

2282
COLUMBUS SYMPHONY CHORUS
55 E State Street
Columbus, OH 43215
Phone: 614-228-9600
Fax: 614-224-7273
e-mail: adimitri@capa.com
Web Site: www.columbussymphony.com
Officers:
  Chair: Martin Inglis
  Vice Chair: Frederick M. Isaac
  Secretary: Michael Mahaffey
  Treasurer: Eric N. Sutphin
Management:
  President: Rosen Stock
  Conductor: Ronald J Jenkins
  Music Director: Jean-Marie Zeitouni
  Managing Director and CEO: William B. Conner, Jr.
Mission: To expose the public to great music.
Utilizes: Commissioned Composers; Commissioned Music; Composers-in-Residence; Dance Companies; Grant Writers; Guest Accompanists; Guest Composers; Guest Lecturers; Guest Musicians; Instructors; Multimedia; Organization Contracts; Original Music Scores; Sign Language Translators; Singers
Founded: 1960
Specialized Field: Light Opera; Lyric Opera; Musical Theatre; Choral; Youth Chorus; Ethnic Music; Classical
Status: Non-Profit, Professional
Paid Staff: 100
Paid Artists: 70

VOCAL MUSIC / Ohio

Income Sources: Columbus Symphony Orchestra
Performs At: Ohio Theatre
Organization Type: Performing; Resident; Educational

2283
OPERA COLUMBUS
55 East State Street
Columbus, OH 43215
Phone: 614-461-8101
Web Site: operacolumbus.org
Officers:
  President: Charles C. Warner
  Development Chair: Johanna DeStefano
  Treasurer: Jack Green
  Secretary: Richard V. Patchen
Management:
  Managing Director: William B. Conner, Jr.
  General Manager: Peggy Kriha Dye, pkrihadye@operacolumbus.org
  Director Of Marketing: Kathy Karnap, kkarnap@columbussymphony.com
  Director Of Development: Diane Cattran
Mission: Opera Columbus enriches Central Ohio, educating, enlightening, and entertaining people of all ages and backgrounds through the live music theatre experience by employing a diverse and far-flung supply of creative talent, ideas, and artistic energies.
Founded: 1981
Performs At: Southern Theatre 21 East Main Street, Columbus, OH

2284
DAYTON OPERA ASSOCIATION
138 N Main Street
Dayton, OH 45402
Phone: 937-228-0662
Fax: 937-228-9612
Toll-free: 800-228-3630
e-mail: info@daytonopera.org
Web Site: www.daytonopera.org
Officers:
  Chair: Greg Robinson
  Vice Chair: Craig Jennings
  Treasurer: Carol Warner
  Secretary: Stanley Herr
Management:
  General/Artistic Director: Thomas Bankston
  Marketing/PR Director: Shannon McClure
  Communications & Media Manager: Chuck Duritsch
  Artistic/Production Administrator &: Pam Eyink
Mission: To increase appreciation for opera through education; to present and promote opera of high quality to the Dayton region in balanced programs; to utilize international artists; to encourage local and regional artistic development.
Founded: 1960
Specialized Field: Grand Opera; Light Opera; Lyric Opera; Musical Theatre; Classical; Contemporary
Status: Non-Profit, Professional
Paid Staff: 30
Budget: $1.3 million
Income Sources: Box Office; Grants; Private Donations
Performs At: Memorial Hall
Affiliations: Opera America; American Arts Alliance; Dayton Performing Arts Fund
Facility Category: War Memorial Theater
Type of Stage: Proscenium
Stage Dimensions: 58 x 36 x 26
Seating Capacity: 2,501
Year Built: 1902
Year Remodeled: 1953
Organization Type: Performing; Resident; Educational

2285
HAMILTON-FAIRFIELD SYMPHONY & CHORALE
One High Street
Hamilton, OH 45011
Phone: 513-895-5151
Fax: 513-844-1584
Web Site: www.hfso.org
Management:
  President: Paul Stanbery
  General Manager: Rita Line
Founded: 1994
Specialized Field: Choral
Status: Non-Profit, Professional
Paid Staff: 5
Paid Artists: 100

2286
LANCASTER CHORALE
109 N. Broad St., Suite 100
PO Box 2450
Lancaster, OH 43130
Phone: 740-687-5855
Fax: 740-653-7074
e-mail: officemanager@lancasterchorale.com
Web Site: www.lancasterchorale.com/
Officers:
  President: Cathy Tolbert
Management:
  Artistic Director: Robert Trocchia
Mission: To perform the finest choral literature, encompassing a wide range of styles, idioms and periods. The Chorale is characterized by its unique versatility, control, precision and blend.
Founded: 1985
Specialized Field: Choral
Status: Non-Profit
Income Sources: Chorus America
Organization Type: Performing; Touring

2287
SORG OPERA COMPANY
65 South Main Street
Middletown, OH 45044
Phone: 513-425-0180
Fax: 513-425-0181
e-mail: gividenn@infinet.com
Web Site: www.sorgopera.com
Officers:
  President: Howard Johnson
  VP: William Hilsmier
  Secretary: Charles Robertson
Management:
  Artistic Director: Charles Combopiano
  Managing Director: Curtis Tucker
Mission: To develop cultural awareness through opera education and to encourage community pride in the Miami Opera Valley through the presentation of high quality opera.
Utilizes: Actors; Artists-in-Residence; Choreographers; Collaborating Artists; Dance Companies; Dancers; Designers; Educators; Fine Artists; Five Seasonal Concerts; Grant Writers; Guest Accompanists; Guest Composers; Guest Designers; Guest Lecturers; Guest Writers; Instructors; Local Artists; Multimedia; Music; Original Music Scores; Sign Language Translators; Singers; Soloists; Visual Arts
Founded: 1990
Specialized Field: Opera
Status: Non-Profit, Professional
Volunteer Staff: 2
Seating Capacity: 700

2288
COLLEGE LIGHT OPERA COMPANY
1625 S Cedar Street
Oberlin, OH 44074
Phone: 440-724-8485
Fax: 440-775-8642
e-mail: bob.haslun@oberlin.edu
Web Site: www.collegelightopera.com
Officers:
  President: DeWitt C Jones III
  Treasurer: Robert A Haslun
  Secretary: Ursula R Haslun
Management:
  Producer/General Manager: Robert A Haslun
  Producer/Business Manager: Ursula R Haslun
Mission: Musical theatre training groud for undergraduates, singers, musicians, tech & costume staff, business office and production staff.
Founded: 1969
Specialized Field: Light Opera; Operetta; Musical Theatre
Status: Non-Professional; Nonprofit
Paid Staff: 25
Paid Artists: 19
Non-paid Artists: 32
Budget: $300,000
Income Sources: Box Office; Annual Fund
Performs At: Highfield Theatre
Annual Attendance: 15,200
Type of Stage: Proscenium
Seating Capacity: 300
Year Built: 1947
Year Remodeled: 1999
Cost: $450,000

2289
TOLEDO OPERA
425 Jefferson Avenue, Suite 601
Toledo, OH 43604-1080
Mailing Address: P.O. Box 2323 Toledo, OH 43603
Phone: 419-255-7464
Fax: 419-255-6344
Toll-free: 866-860-9048
e-mail: info@toledoopera.org
Web Site: toledoopera.org
Officers:
  President: Alex Heard
Management:
  Executive Director: Suzanne Rorick, srorick@toledoopera.org
  Associate Director: Loviah Aldinger, lovialdinger@toledoopera.org
  Assistant Director: Robert Mirakian, rmirakian@toledoopera.org
Mission: The mission of Toledo Opera is to enhance the cultural fabric of the region by creating opera experiences that celebrate, both in the theater and beyond its walls, what is unique to opera: dramatic, passionate stories expressed through glorious music and the powerful voices of classically trained singers.
Founded: 1959
Status: Professional
Performs At: Valentine Theatre
Affiliations: Sound Vision
Seating Capacity: 900

2290
OHIO LIGHT OPERA
College of Wooster
1189 Beall Avenue
Wooster, OH 44691

VOCAL MUSIC / Oklahoma

Phone: 330-263-2345
Fax: 330-263-2272
e-mail: ohiolightopera@wooster.edu
Web Site: www.ohiolightopera.org
Officers:
   President: Grant Cornwell
Management:
   Executive Director: Laura Neill
   Artistic Director: Steven Daigle
   Music Director: Michael Borowitz
Mission: To promote, produce, and preserve the best operettas ever written, and to do them in traditional settings.
Utilizes: Choreographers; Commissioned Composers; Dancers; Designers; Guest Musical Directors; Multimedia; Original Music Scores; Resident Artists; Resident Professionals; Sign Language Translators; Student Interns
Founded: 1979
Specialized Field: Light Opera; Lyric Opera; Musical Theatre; Classical
Status: Non-Profit, Professional
Paid Staff: 120
Paid Artists: 75
Budget: $1,250,000
Income Sources: Private Donations, Ticket Sales
Performs At: Freedlander Theatre
Annual Attendance: 20,000
Seating Capacity: 394

2291
OPERA WESTERN RESERVE
1000 Fifth Avenue
Youngstown, OH 44504-1603
Phone: 330-480-0993
Fax: 330-480-0775
e-mail: info@operawesternreserve.org
Web Site: www.operawesternreserve.org
Officers:
   Chairman: Patricia Fleck Kavic
   Vice Chairman: Elliot Legow
   Secretary: Mary Ann Senediak
   Treasurer: Rodney Lamberson
   Opera Guild President: Carla Infanate
   Board Member: Jacqueline Abrams
   Board Member: Lillie Johnson
   Board Member: Helen Bitonte
   Board Member: Christine Blair Legow
Management:
   Production Director: David Vosburgh
   Musical Director/Conductor: Susan Davenny Wyner
   Chorus Master: Dr Hae Jong Lee
   Youth Chorus Director: Sue Ellen Davis
   Production Stage Manager: Matty Sayre
Mission: To produce and present opera performances of the highest quality to audiences in northeast Ohio and western Pennsylvania. To provide a performance platform for professional artists from northeast Ohio and western Pennsylvania. To take a leadership role in artist training, arts education and audience development, including children and young adults.
Utilizes: Arrangers; Choreographers; Collaborations; Community Talent; Composers; Dancers; Designers; Educators; Guest Speakers; Guest Writers; Guild Activities; Multimedia; Music
Specialized Field: Opera, Youth Chorus, Arts Education
Season: Fall
Affiliations: Western Reserve Theater

Oklahoma

2292
CIMARRON CIRCUIT OPERA COMPANY
555 S University Boulevard
First Presbyterian Church
Norman, OK 73070
Mailing Address: P.O. Box 1085, Norman, OK 73070
Phone: 405-364-8962
Fax: 405-321-5842
e-mail: info@ccocopera.org
Web Site: www.ccocopera.org
Management:
   Director: Erica C Thomas
   Music Director: Kevin W Smith
   Development Manager: Carla Smitherman
   Technical Director: Mark Pooler
   Executive Director: Shari Ransley
Mission: Offering training and experience to young Oklahoma singers; bringing opera to areas in Oklahoma where residents normally wouldn't have access to performances.
Utilizes: Guest Companies
Founded: 1975
Specialized Field: Grand Opera; Light Opera; Lyric Opera; Choral; Youth Chorus; Ethnic Music; Classical; Religious
Status: Non-Profit, Professional
Paid Staff: 5
Income Sources: Central Opera Service; Mid-America Arts Alliance
Performs At: Sooner Theatre; Holmberg Hall
Organization Type: Performing; Touring; Sponsoring

2293
CIMARRON OPERA
555 S University Boulevard
Norman, OK 73069
Mailing Address: P.O. Box 1085, Norman, OK 73070
Phone: 405-364-8962
Web Site: cimarronopera.org
Founded: 1971
Status: Professional

2294
CANTERBURY CHORAL SOCIETY
428 W California
#100
Oklahoma City, OK 73102-2454
Phone: 405-232-7464
Fax: 405-232-7465
e-mail: enquiries@canterburychoral.co.uk
Web Site: www.canterburychoral.co.uk
Management:
   President: James W Bruce Jr
   Executive Director: Kay E Holp
   Artistic Director: Randi Von Ells
Founded: 1969
Specialized Field: Choral
Status: Non-Profit, Non-Professional
Paid Staff: 12
Non-paid Artists: 475

2295
OKLAHOMA OPERA AND MUSIC THEATER COMPANY
Oklahoma City University
2501 N Blackwelder
Oklahoma City, OK 73106-1493
Phone: 405-208-5700
Fax: 405-208-5316
Toll-free: 800-633-7242
e-mail: mparker@okcu.edu
Web Site: www.okcu.edu/music
Officers:
   President: Tom J. McDaniel
Mission: Offering the public high quality performances; providing students with a professional arena in which to develop their talents.
Utilizes: Guest Companies; Singers
Founded: 1904
Specialized Field: Grand Opera; Lyric Opera; Light Opera; Operetta; Choral
Status: Non-Profit, Non-Professional
Paid Staff: 40
Income Sources: Oklahoma City University
Performs At: Kirkpatrick Theater
Organization Type: Performing; Educational

2296
LIGHT OPERA OKLAHOMA - LOOK
Harwelden
2210 S Main
Tulsa, OK 74114
Phone: 918-583-4267
Fax: 918-583-1780
e-mail: eric@lightoperaok.org
Web Site: www.lightoperaok.org
Officers:
   Co VP Finance: Sara Arnold
   VP Human Resources: Polly Bowen
   VP Education: Catherine Cullem
   Co VP Finance: David Emanuel
   VP Special Events: Josie Winter
Management:
   President: Leslie Shelton
   Artistic Director: Eric Gibson, frontoffice@lightoperaok.org
   Founder: John Everitt
   Office Manager: Nancy Gardner
   Marketing Director: Rachel Robb
Mission: To preserve and create awareness of the musical comedy/operetta art form by producing a festival of such every summer in Tulsa, OK.
Founded: 1984
Specialized Field: Light Opera; Musical Theatre
Status: Non-Profit, Professional
Paid Staff: 3
Volunteer Staff: 10
Paid Artists: 100
Non-paid Artists: 10
Budget: $750,000
Income Sources: Foundations; Corporations
Performs At: Tulsa Performing Arts Center - Williams Theatre
Annual Attendance: 6000-7500
Seating Capacity: 425

2297
TULSA OPERA
1610 S Boulder
Tulsa, OK 74119
Phone: 918-582-4035
Fax: 918-592-0380
Toll-free: 866-298-2530
e-mail: kprotopapas@tulsaopera.com
Web Site: www.tulsaopera.com
Officers:
   President: Martin Piplits
   Chairman: Pattie Bowman
   Executive Vice President: Mike Lodes
   VP Board Development: Marilyn Strange
   VP Endowment: Lou Ann Gibson

VOCAL MUSIC / Oregon

Management:
General Director: Carol I Crawford
Director Finance and Planning: Elena Jackson-Forsyth
Director Operations: Amanda Foust
Artistic Director: Kostis Protopapas
Office Manager: Charlotte Curry
Mission: To produce opera of artistic integrity and enrich the regional community through innovative education and outreach programs.
Utilizes: Guest Artists; Guest Companies; Singers
Founded: 1948
Specialized Field: Youth Chorus; Grand Opera
Status: Non-Profit, Professional
Paid Staff: 15
Volunteer Staff: 100
Income Sources: Opera America; American Arts Alliance; Arts & Humanities Council of Tulsa
Performs At: Chapman Music Hall
Organization Type: Performing; Sponsoring

Oregon

2298
EUGENE OPERA
1590 Williamette Street
Eugene, OR 97401
Mailing Address: PO Box 11200, Eugene, OR 97400
Phone: 541-485-3985
Fax: 541-683-3783
e-mail: philip@eugeneopera.com
Web Site: www.eugeneopera.com
Officers:
President: Clay Skurdal
President-Elect: Janice Mackey
Executive Vice President: Philip Piele
Treasurer: Mark Reynolds
Secretary: Reggie Tonry
Management:
General Director: Mark Beudert
Production Manager: Josh Neckels
Chorus Master: John Jantzi
Costume Director: Jonna Hayden
Director of Outreach: Reggie Tonry
Mission: To contribute to the future of opera by increasing the audience, educating the community and utilizing the talents of emerging musicians.
Utilizes: Collaborations; Dancers; Designers; Guest Accompanists; Guest Composers; Guest Designers; Instructors; Multimedia; Original Music Scores; Resident Artists; Resident Professionals; Student Interns
Founded: 1976
Specialized Field: Grand Opera; Lyric Opera; Light Opera; Operetta
Status: Professional, Nonprofit
Paid Staff: 6
Volunteer Staff: 20
Budget: $800,000
Income Sources: Ticket Sales, Grants, Fund Raising
Performs At: Hugh Center for the Performing Arts
Seating Capacity: 2,400
Year Built: 1982
Organization Type: Performing; Educational

2299
CAPPELLA ROMANA
1017 SW Morrison Street, Suite 315
Portland, OR 97205
Phone: 503-236-8202
Web Site: capellaromana.org
Officers:
President: L. Sue Fischer
Vice President: Maria Boyer
Treasurer: Ruud Van Der Salm
Secretary: Martin Nugent
Management:
Artistic Director: Alexander Lingas
Executive Director: Mark Powell
Operations Coordinator: Leslie Simmons
Mission: Cappella Romana is a vocal ensemble dedicated to combining passion with scholarship in its exploration of the musical traditions of the Christian East and West, with emphasis on early and contemporary music.
Founded: 1991
Specialized Field: Choral
Status: Nonprofit; Professional
Organization Type: Performing; Touring

2300
PORTLAND OPERA
211 SE Caruther
Portland, OR 97214
Phone: 503-241-1407
Fax: 503-241-4212
Toll-free: 866-739-6737
e-mail: admin@portlandopera.org
Web Site: www.portlandopera.org
Officers:
President: Jeff Thede
VP: Jeffrey Evershed
VP: Greg Hinckley
Treasurer: Carol Mangan
Secretary: Kathleen Lewis
Management:
Executive Director: Christopher Matpaliano
Associate Director of Marketing & C: Tracy Wenckus
Public Relations Manager: Julia Sheridan
Opera Marketing & Audience Developm: Claudie Fisher
Group & Corporate Sales Manager: Casey McDermott
Utilizes: Collaborations; Grant Writers; Guest Accompanists; Guest Artists; Guest Choreographers; Guest Companies; Guest Composers; Guest Conductors; Guest Designers; Guest Musical Directors; Guest Musicians; Guild Activities; Instructors; Organization Contracts; Original Music Scores; Resident Artists; Resident Professionals; Selected Students; Student Interns; Theatre Companies
Founded: 1964
Specialized Field: Grand Opera; Classical; Contemporary
Status: Non-Profit, Professional
Paid Staff: 50
Budget: $6.7 million
Performs At: Portland Keller Auditorium
Affiliations: Opera America
Annual Attendance: 48,000
Facility Category: Auditorium
Type of Stage: Proscenium
Stage Dimensions: 30 x 60 x 43
Seating Capacity: 3,000
Year Built: 1917
Year Remodeled: 1967
Rental Contact: Lori Leyba Kramer
Organization Type: Performing; Touring; Resident

Pennsylvania

2301
THE ARCADIA CHORALE
102 Shady Lane Road #350
Chinchilla, PA 18410
Phone: 570-871-0350
e-mail: contact@arcadiachorale.org
Web Site: arcadiachorale.org
Officers:
President: Linda Hickernell
Vice President: Llewellyn Miller
Management:
Music Director: Steven Thomas, director@arcadiachorale.org
Mission: Committed to promoting the highest standard of excellence in the performance of choral music for the education and enjoyment of the membership and the community at large.
Founded: 1978
Status: Nonprofit

2302
MARY GREEN SINGERS
990 Old Huntingdon Pike
Huntingdon Valley, PA 19006
Phone: 215-572-5063
Fax: 215-884-5432
Officers:
Music Director/Conductor: Mary Woodmansee Green
Management:
President: Mary Green
Mission: Tax-exempt, non-profit cultural and educational institution.
Founded: 1986
Specialized Field: Choral
Status: Non-Profit, Non-Professional
Paid Staff: 1
Volunteer Staff: 6
Non-paid Artists: 150
Organization Type: Performing; Touring; Educational

2303
FULTON OPERA HOUSE
12 N Prince Street
PO Box 1865
Lancaster, PA 17608-1865
Phone: 717-394-7133
Fax: 717-397-3780
e-mail: info@thefulton.org
Web Site: www.thefulton.org
Officers:
President: Patricia J. Otto
VP: Elliot B. Sterenfeld, MD
Secretary: Michael W. Lambert
Treasurer: Elizabeth H Habecker
Management:
Artistic Director: Marc Robin
Managing Director: Aaron Young
Director Development: Richard Owen
Technical Director: William Mohney
Assistant Technical Director: Mike Meservey
Mission: To produce professional regional theatre of a quality that honors, affirms and extends the Fulton's role in the history of American theatre as a national historic landmark and to provide educational, artistic and cultural benefits that engender community ownership.
Utilizes: Actors; AEA Actors; Artists-in-Residence; Choreographers; Collaborations; Commissioned Music; Dance Companies; Dancers; Designers; Educators; Grant Writers; Guest Accompanists; Guest Artists; Guest Companies; Guest Conductors; Guest Designers; Guest Lecturers; Guest Teachers; Guest Writers; Guild Activities; Instructors; Local Artists; Lyricists; Multimedia; Music; Organization Contracts; Original Music Scores; Performance Artists; Poets; Resident Artists; Resident Professionals; Selected Students; Singers; Soloists; Student Interns
Founded: 1852

VOCAL MUSIC / Pennsylvania

Specialized Field: Opera; Musical Theatre
Status: Non-Profit, Professional
Paid Staff: 30
Paid Artists: 300
Budget: $2,100,000
Income Sources: Earned, Contributed
Performs At: Fulton Opera House
Annual Attendance: 100,000+
Facility Category: Theatre
Type of Stage: Proscenium
Seating Capacity: 684
Year Built: 1852
Year Remodeled: 1995
Architect: $9,500,000
Rental Contact: Managing Director Rod McCullough
Organization Type: Performing, Touring, Educational

2304
LANCASTER OPERA COMPANY
42 N. Prince Street
Ste. M-05
Lancaster, PA 17603
Phone: 717-871-7814
Fax: 717-392-5650
e-mail: info@operalancaster.com
Web Site: www.operalancaster.org
Officers:
  Vice President & Secretary: Cynthia E. Reed, Esq.
  Treasurer: Carolyn K. Moody
Management:
  President: David R. Kohler
  Executive Director: Cheryl Crider
  Artistic Director: Scott Drackley
  Marketing Manager: Dianne Fussaro
  Managing Director: Joshua M. Rinier
Founded: 1952
Specialized Field: Opera
Status: Non-Profit
Paid Staff: 1
Volunteer Staff: 25
Non-paid Artists: 120
Budget: $130,000
Income Sources: Tickets; Grants; Annual Appeal; Corporate Funding
Performs At: Fulton Opera House
Annual Attendance: 5,000+
Facility Category: 150 year-old theater
Type of Stage: Proscenium
Seating Capacity: 684
Year Built: 1852

2305
ACADEMY OF VOCAL ARTS OPERA THEATRE
1920 Spruce Street
Philadelphia, PA 19103
Phone: 215-735-1685
Fax: 215-732-2189
e-mail: info@avaopera.org
Web Site: www.avaopera.org
Officers:
  President and Artistic Director: K. James McDowell
  VP: John A Nyheim
  VP: Laren Pitcairn
  VP: James McKee Ridgway
  VP: Conant Scott Rogers
  Vice Chairman & Secretary: Martha R Hurt
Management:
  Public Relations Officer: Maryann Devine
  Executive Director: K James McDowell
  Music Director: Christofer Macatsoris
  Administrative Associate: John Lane
  Box Office Manager: Bill Buddendorf

Mission: To train young singers for international careers in opera, and present in operas and recitals.
Utilizes: Artists-in-Residence; Guest Conductors; Guest Designers
Founded: 1934
Specialized Field: Lyric Opera; Classical
Status: Non-Profit, Non-Professional
Paid Staff: 33
Non-paid Artists: 25
Performs At: Helen Corning Warden Theater; Academy of Music
Affiliations: N.A.S.M.
Seating Capacity: 180

2306
CENTER CITY OPERA THEATER
PO Box 63848
1412 Chestnut Street
Philadelphia, PA 19147
Phone: 215-238-1555
e-mail: info@operatheater.org
Web Site: www.centercityoperatheater.org
Officers:
  Chairman: Jeffrey Jacobs Esq
  President: Sean Sullivan
  Treasurer: John Durso
  Secretary: Dr Harold Kurtz
  Board Member: Lois Durso
  Board Member: Jack Butler
Management:
  General/Artistic Director: Andrew M Kurtz, akurtz@operatheater.org
  Artistic Director/Creative Dev: Arthur Innaurato, ainnaurato@operatheater.org
  Education Director: Joy Kurtz, jkurtz@operatheater.org
  Marketing Director: Eric Brower
  Artistic Administrator: Jesse Livingston
Mission: The Center City Opera Theater (CCOT) is one of the most innovative opera companies in the United States, praised for its productions of new opera as well as for developing new work, new artists and new audiences. One thing that defines everything CCOT does is an unshakeable belief in the emotional power of telling stories by bringing outstanding theater and live music together.
Utilizes: Actors; Arrangers; Collaborating Artists; Collaborations; Composers; Contract Orchestras; Educators; High School Drama; Multimedia; Sign Language Translators
Founded: 1999
Specialized Field: Opera, Theater
Income Sources: Donations, Sponsors
Season: November through March
Performs At: Prince Music Theater
Affiliations: Opera America

2307
CHORAL ARTS SOCIETY OF PHILADELPHIA
PO Box 22445
Philadelphia, PA 19110
Phone: 215-240-6417
e-mail: info@choralarts.com
Web Site: www.choralarts.com
Officers:
  President: Lisa Barton, Esq.
  Vice President: Alexis Barron, Esq.
  Second Vice President: Meredith Quirin
  Secretary: Joseph J. Leube, Jr.
  Treasurer: John A. Miller
Management:
  Artistic Director: Matthew C. Glandorf

Mission: To present a diverse selection of choral music spanning all musical periods.
Utilizes: Guest Companies; Guest Musical Directors; Guest Musicians; Instructors; Local Artists; Lyricists; Multimedia; Organization Contracts; Original Music Scores; Sign Language Translators; Singers; Theatre Companies
Founded: 1982
Specialized Field: Choral
Status: Professional, Nonprofit
Performs At: Mann Music Center; Academy of Music; Kimmel Center; Churches; Cathedrals
Organization Type: Performing; Touring; Educational

2308
DELAWARE VALLEY OPERA COMPANY
1731 Chandler Street
Philadelphia, PA 19111
Phone: 215-725-4171
e-mail: info@dvopera.org
Web Site: www.dvopera.org
Officers:
  President: Sandra Day
  Secretary: Carol Denenberg
  Treasurer: Alan Edelstein
  Vice-President: Renee Goldman
Mission: To aid aspiring opera musicians with experience, training, education of opera through production and performance.
Utilizes: Singers
Founded: 1988
Specialized Field: Opera
Status: Non-Profit, Professional
Paid Staff: 41
Performs At: Tusten Theatre; Sullivan County Community College
Organization Type: Performing; Educational

2309
LYRIC OPERA THEATRE STREET
1608 S Broad
Philadelphia, PA 19145-1509
Phone: 215-755-1288
Fax: 215-551-1444
e-mail: llotop@aol.com
Web Site: www.surf.2/llotop.com
Officers:
  President: AC Pugliese
  VP/Secretary: Margaret Kastle
Management:
  President: Margaret Kastla
Mission: To provide repertoire experience for deserving amateur, professional and semi-professional singers.
Founded: 1987
Specialized Field: Musical Theatre; Educational
Status: For-Profit, Professional
Paid Staff: 2
Volunteer Staff: 10
Paid Artists: 10
Non-paid Artists: 50
Budget: $35,000-$60,000
Organization Type: Performing; Educational

2310
MENDELSSOHN CLUB OF PHILADELPHIA
1218 Locust Street
Philadelphia, PA 19107
Mailing Address: PO Box 59522, Philadelphia, PA 19102
Phone: 215-735-9922
Fax: 215-573-3786
e-mail: info@mcchorus.org
Web Site: www.libertynet.org

Officers:
- **President:** James B Straw
- **Chairman:** Eleanor M. Elkinton
- **Vice Chairman:** George G. Smith, III
- **Vice Chairman:** Sara A Cerato
- **Vice Chairman:** Laurie Wagman
- **VP:** Benjamin Alexander
- **VP:** Jack R Bershad
- **VP:** Richard A Doran
- **VP/Treasurer:** Albert E Piscopo

Management:
- **Executive Director:** Janelle McCoy
- **Producing Artistic Director:** Robert B Driver
- **Marketing/Communications:** Gary Gansky
- **Production:** Susan Ashbaker
- **Associate Conductor:** John French

Mission: Mendelssohn's Club's mission has been to challenge, enrich, serve and fulfill its singing members, patrons and audiences through the excellence of its performances.
Utilizes: Collaborating Artists; Collaborations; Commissioned Composers; Guest Companies; Guest Composers; Guest Musicians; Sign Language Translators; Singers
Founded: 1874
Specialized Field: Choral; Classical
Paid Staff: 1
Volunteer Staff: 5
Paid Artists: 12
Non-paid Artists: 160
Budget: $222,000
Income Sources: Ticket Sales; Government and Foundation Grants; Individual Contributions
Performs At: Various: Symphony Halls to Churches

2311
OPERA COMPANY OF PHILADELPHIA
1420 Locust Street
Suite 210
Philadelphia, PA 19102
Phone: 215-893-3600
Fax: 215-893-7801
e-mail: marketing@operaphila.org
Web Site: www.operaphila.org
Officers:
- **Chairman:** Daniel K. Meyer, M.D.
- **General Director & President:** David B. Devan
- **Chief Financial Officer & Vice Pres:** Gary Gansky

Management:
- **Artisitc Director:** Robert B Driver
- **Executive Director:** David B Devan
- **CFO:** Gary H Gansky
- **Personnel Manager:** Maurice Marietti

Mission: The city's professional opera company, committed to delivering outstanding productions of traditional repertoire, often presenting these operas in innovative and technologically creative ways, and underwriting and producing new and exciting operatic works that appeal to a socially and culturally diverse audience.
Utilizes: Guest Artists; Guest Companies; Singers
Founded: 1975
Specialized Field: Opera
Status: Professional; Nonprofit
Income Sources: Opera America; Greater Philadelphia Cultural Alliance
Performs At: Academy of Music
Organization Type: Performing

2312
PHILADELPHIA GAY MEN'S CHORUS
P.O. Box 30185
Philadelphia, PA 19103
Phone: 215-731-9230
Toll-free: 877-462-7464
e-mail: info@pgmc.org
Web Site: www.pgmc.org
Officers:
- **President:** Brad Hess
- **VP Membership:** Scott Skip Concilla
- **VP Fundraising:** Edward Stash
- **VP Marketing:** Sandy Smith
- **VP Development:** Mark Vernon
- **VP Production:** Patrick Hagerty
- **Secretary:** J. F. Marino
- **Treasurer:** Terry L. Evans, Jr

Management:
- **Artistic Director:** Joseph J Buches
- **Director, Development:** J. Blaine Bonham, Jr.
- **Director, Marketing:** Paul Fontaine

Mission: The Philadelphia Gay Men's Chorus is a diverse group of gay men presenting a variety of challenging musical experiences, seeking to improve the skills of the members and to reach out to the community.
Founded: 1981
Specialized Field: Alternative; Men's Chorus
Status: Non-profit

2313
PHILADELPHIA SINGERS
1211 Chestnut Street
Suite 610
Philadelphia, PA 19107
Phone: 215-751-9494
Fax: 215-751-9490
e-mail: info@philadelphiasingers.org
Web Site: www.philadelphiasingers.org
Officers:
- **President:** Doralene Davis
- **VP:** Robert E Mortensen
- **VP:** Chef Fritz Blank
- **Secretary:** Michael M. Mills
- **Treasurer:** James K. Abel

Management:
- **President:** Robert E Mortensen
- **VP:** Chef Fritz Blank
- **Music Director:** David Hayes
- **Office Administration:** Matthew Seneca

Mission: To produce high quality choral music and offer opportunities for professional singers.
Utilizes: Commissioned Music; Multimedia; Organization Contracts; Original Music Scores; Sign Language Translators; Singers
Founded: 1972
Specialized Field: Choral
Status: Professional
Paid Staff: 8
Volunteer Staff: 2
Paid Artists: 60
Non-paid Artists: 60
Performs At: Academy of Music; Church of the Holy Trinity
Affiliations: Resident Chorus of the Philadelphia Orchestra
Organization Type: Performing

2314
SINGING CITY
1501 Cherry Street
Philadelphia, PA 19103
Phone: 267-519-5321
Fax: 215-569-9088
e-mail: info@singingcity.org
Web Site: www.singingcity.org
Officers:
- **President:** Cheryl Slipski
- **VP:** Nancy Frandsen
- **Treasurer:** Tim McGarrigan
- **Secretary:** Margaret G. Gregg

Management:
- **Artistic & Music Director:** Jeffrey Brillhart
- **Executive Director:** Lauren Anderson
- **Office Manager and Choir Administra:** Scott Hughes
- **Children's Choir Director:** Steve Fisher

Mission: Present choral music concerts, educational and community outreach programs.
Founded: 1948
Specialized Field: Choral
Paid Staff: 4
Volunteer Staff: 3
Budget: $235,000
Income Sources: Charitable Donations; Contracted Musical Engagements

2315
THE ATLANTIC COAST OPERA FESTIVAL
2028 South 17th Street
Suite 11
Philadelphia, PA 19145-2902
Phone: 215-218-9977
Fax: 215-218-9978
e-mail: beatriceb@atlanticcoastoperafestival.org
Web Site: www.atlanticcoastoperafestival.org
Officers:
- **President:** Anthony Ronzi
- **Vice President:** Mrs Anthony Ronzi
- **Treasurer:** Peter Finnegan
- **Secretary:** Gabrielle Damasco
- **Board Member:** Paul Desanctis
- **Board Member:** Grace Lalitha
- **Advisor:** Carol Neblett
- **Advisor:** Giorgio Tozzi
- **Advisor:** Placido Domingo

Management:
- **Marketing Director:** William Conville
- **Development/Design:** Susan Kelly
- **Development Consultant:** Dr Craig Eisendrath
- **General Manager:** Beatrice Beer

Mission: The Atlantic Coast Opera Festival's mission is to mission is to create a world-class summer opera venue of international stature a la Glyndebourne or Salzburg Festival, featuring unknown, exceptional artists to whom it provides much needed training, stage experience and exposure. The Festival thus endeavors to significantly enrich the cultural landscape of the Philadelphia/Southern New Jersey/Delaware community where Grand Opera is lacking.
Utilizes: Arrangers; Collaborations; Educators; Fine Artists; Guest Composers; Guest Musical Directors; Local Artists; Multimedia; Music
Specialized Field: Opera, Arts Education
Status: Non-Profit, Professional
Income Sources: Donors, Corporation Matched Funds
Season: Summer
Affiliations: Philadelphia Symphony Orchestra

2316
BACH CHOIR OF PITTSBURGH
1108 S Braddock Avenue
Suite A
Pittsburgh, PA 15218
Phone: 412-241-4044
Fax: 412-241-4043
e-mail: info@bachchoirpittsburgh.org
Web Site: www.bachchoirpittsburgh.org
Officers:
- **Chair:** Paul Block, CPA/JD
- **Vice Chair:** Paul Homick

VOCAL MUSIC / Rhode Island

Secretary: Carol Manteris
Treasurer: Kate Sphar
Management:
  Artistic Director: Thomas W Douglas
  Managing Director: Matthew Dooley
  Operations Manager: David A Kotler
  Choir President: Amy Richards
Mission: To perform highly artistic choral music from various musical traditions for the enjoyment of the community and as a discipline to enhance the training of the musicians.
Founded: 1934
Specialized Field: Choral; Classical

2317
MENDELSSOHN CHOIR OF PITTSBURGH
600 Penn Avenue
Pittsburgh, PA 15222
Phone: 412-215-9720
Fax: 412-561-5105
e-mail: mlapinski@themendelssohn.org
Web Site: www.themendelssohn.org
Officers:
  President: Cynthia L. Roth
  Vice President: Marian Block, MD
  Secretary: Terri S. Blanchette
  Treasurer: Mary G. Bachorski
Management:
  Music Director/Conductor: Betsy Burleigh
  Jr Mendelssohn Conductor: Christine Frattare
  Assistant Conductor: Susan Medley
  Managing Director: Elizabeth Andrews
  Choir Manager: Barry Miller
Mission: To perform a versatile repertoire of the highest musical standards to contribute to the choral art and to make an impact on the community.
Founded: 1908
Specialized Field: Choral; Classical

2318
PITTSBURGH CAMERATA
PO Box 81546
Pittsburgh, PA 15217
Phone: 412-421-5884
e-mail: gmluley@pittsburghcamerata.org
Web Site: www.pittsburghcamerata.org
Management:
  Artistic Director: Rebecca Rollett
  Business Manager: Gail Luley
  Managing Director: Gail Luley
Specialized Field: Choral

2319
PITTSBURGH CIVIC LIGHT OPERA
719 Liberty Avenue
Benedum Center
Pittsburgh, PA 15222
Phone: 412-281-3973
Fax: 412-281-5339
e-mail: mail@pittsburghclo.org
Web Site: www.pittsburghclo.org
Officers:
  Honorary Chairman of the Board: Julie Andrews
  Chairman of the Board: Joseph C. Guyaux
  President: William M. Lambert
  Vice Presidents/Audit: Timothy K. Zimmerman
  Vice Presidents/Audit: Todd C. Moules
Management:
  Executive Director: Van Kaplin
  Artistic Director Outreach: Buddy Thompson

Mission: To perpetuate, preserve and create musical, light opera and drama productions for the cultural and educational enrichment of our audiences, primarily in Western Pennsylvania and, secondarily, the United States.
Utilizes: Guest Companies; Singers
Founded: 1946
Specialized Field: Light Opera; Musical Theatre
Status: Non-Profit, Professional
Paid Staff: 25
Income Sources: Musical Theater Works; National Musical Theater Network
Season: June - August
Performs At: Benedum Center for the Performing Arts
Seating Capacity: 2,837
Organization Type: Performing; Educational

2320
PITTSBURGH CONCERT CHORALE
9800 McKnight Road
Suite 210-B
Pittsburgh, PA 15237
Phone: 412-635-7654
Fax: 412-635-9123
e-mail: office@pccsing.org
Web Site: www.pccsing.org
Officers:
  President: Bruce Cooper
  VP: Robb Montgomery
  VP: Charles Morrissey
  VP: Steve Radr
  Treasurer: Alan Crittenden
Management:
  Founder and Music Director Emeritus: Dr. Clark Bedford
  Executive Director: Betty Snyder
  Music Director: Susan Medley
  Assistant Conductor: J. Thomas Taylor
  Featured Artist: David Billings
Mission: To share the joy of fine choral music with exceptional volunteer singers of the community.
Utilizes: Collaborations; Commissioned Composers; Commissioned Music; Grant Writers; Guest Companies; Guest Musicians; Multimedia; Sign Language Translators; Singers
Founded: 1985
Specialized Field: Choral
Status: Volunteer; Not-for-Profit; Tax-Exempt
Paid Staff: 1
Paid Artists: 2
Non-paid Artists: 85
Budget: $18,500
Income Sources: Ticket Sales, Grants, Government, Individuals
Performs At: Orchard Hill Church; Ingomar Methodist Church; Jewish Commuknity Center
Affiliations: Chorus America, Greater Pittsburgh Arts Alliance, Northern Allegheny County Chamber of Commerce
Annual Attendance: 3200

2321
PITTSBURGH OPERA
2425 Liberty Ave.
Pittsburgh, PA 15222
Phone: 412-281-0912
Fax: 412-281-4324
e-mail: info@pittsburghopera.org
Web Site: www.pittsburghopera.org
Officers:
  President: Clyde B. Jones III
  Secretary: Alvin W. Filstrup, Ph.D.
  Treasurer: Robert C. Denove
  Chair: Michele Fabrizi

Management:
  General Director: Christopher Hahn
  Director of Marketing and Communica: Debra Bell
  Music Director: Antony Walker
  General Director and VP: Mark Weinstein
Mission: To culturally enrich Pittsburgh and the tri-state area and to draw national and international attention to the region.
Utilizes: Choreographers; Dancers; Educators; Grant Writers; Guest Artists; Guest Companies; Guest Conductors; Guest Lecturers; Guest Writers; Local Artists; Lyricists; Multimedia; Original Music Scores; Singers; Student Interns
Founded: 1939
Specialized Field: Grand Opera
Status: Professional; Nonprofit
Paid Staff: 30
Volunteer Staff: 300
Paid Artists: 300
Budget: $7.5 million
Income Sources: Ticket Sales; Contributions; Grants
Performs At: Benedum Center for the Performing Arts
Affiliations: Opera America
Annual Attendance: 39,000
Facility Category: Opera House/Multi-purpose Theatre
Type of Stage: Proscenium
Seating Capacity: 2,770
Organization Type: Performing

2322
SUMMER FEST
286 Main Street Third Floor
Pittsburgh, PA 15201
Phone: 412-621-1499
Fax: 412-621-2643
e-mail: info@otsummerfest.org
Web Site: www.operatheaterpittsburgh.org
Officers:
  Chairman: Henry P. Hoffstot, Jr.
  President: Dr. Eugene Myers
  Vice President: Phyllis J. Sidwell
  Secretary: Carol L. Kamin
  Treasurer: Gunnar Klinga
Management:
  Founder: Mildred Posvar
  Artistic & General Director: Jonathan Eaton
  General Manager: Scott Timm
  Artistic Administrator: Dennis Robinson
  Education Coordinator: Christina Farrell
Mission: To offer professional opera to people outside of metropolitan centers; to introduce opera to children; to nurture emerging professionals.
Founded: 1978
Specialized Field: Grand Opera; Youth Chorus; Chamber Opera; Musical Theatre
Status: Professional; Nonprofit
Budget: $35,000-$60,000
Performs At: Byham Theatre; Hazlett Theatre
Affiliations: Carnegie Mellon University
Seating Capacity: 1,200
Organization Type: Performing; Touring; Educational

Rhode Island

2323
RHODE ISLAND CIVIC CHORALE AND ORCHESTRA
141 Phenix Ave
Cranston, RI 02920
Phone: 401-521-5670
e-mail: info@ricco.org
Web Site: www.ricco.org

Officers:
  President: Chester S Labedz, Jr
  First VP: Roberta Padula
  Second VP: Margaret Gidley
  Third VP: Herman Eschentacher
  Secretary: David T. Riedel
  Treasurer: Walter Hope, Jr
  Assistant Treasurer: Joseph A. Goldkamp
Management:
  Director and Conductor: Edward Markward
Mission: To provide artistic enrichment to the public and the singers through presentation of at least three concerts of major choral works per year. These concerts feature the singers of the chorale, along with professional orchestra and soloists.
Utilizes: Guest Artists; Guest Companies
Founded: 1957
Specialized Field: Choral
Status: Nonprofit
Paid Staff: 70
Performs At: Veterans Memorial Auditorium; Grace Church
Organization Type: Performing

2324
THE PROVIDENCE SINGERS INC.
667 Waterman Avenue, Studio 154
East Providence, RI 02914
Phone: 401-751-5700
Fax: 401-751-5722
Web Site: providencesingers.org
Officers:
  Chair: Josh Krugman
  Treasurer: Jim Burress
Management:
  Artistic Director: Christine Noel
  Assistant Director: Michael Galib
  Accompanist: Patrice Newman
  Executive Director: Allison McMillan
  Marketing Director: Jenica Reed
Mission: The Providence Singers presents choral performances of distinction to connect singers, listeners, performers, and composers in creative exploration of the choral art. It performs diverse choral works to preserve the choral tradition and extends that tradition by commissioning and performing new compositions.
Founded: 1971
Status: Nonprofit

2325
OPERA PROVIDENCE
585 Elmgrove Avenue
Providence, RI 02906
Phone: 401-331-6060
e-mail: info@operaprovidence.org
Web Site: www.operaprovidence.org
Officers:
  President: Dr Robert DeRobbio
  Vice President: Anthony Regine DDS
  Treasurer: Nanci DeRobbio
  Secretary: Carolyn DeSpirito
  Chairman/Music/Vocals: Joseph Parillo
  Board Member: Joseph Pisaturo
  Board Member: Dr Joyce Swirka
Management:
  Artistic Director: Rene De La Garza
  Conductor: Christopher McMullen
Mission: Our mission is to engage and inspire audiences through opera as the ultimate theater experience of music. Through increased performance of, education about, and access to the art form of opera, Opera Providence strives to enrich the quality of life for all in our diverse cultural community; educate and inspire children and youth; and engage audiences in thought provoking experiences.
Utilizes: Arrangers; Collaborations; Composers; Contract Orchestras; Multimedia; Music; Sign Language Translators; Singers
Specialized Field: Opera
Status: Professional
Performs At: Cranston's Park Theater
Affiliations: Arte Lyrics, Boston Mid Summer Opera, Intermezzo, Worcester Opera

2326
CHORUS OF WESTERLY
119 High Street
Westerly, RI 02891
Phone: 401-596-8663
Fax: 401-596-1370
e-mail: ryan@chorusofwesterly.org
Web Site: www.chorusofwesterly.org
Officers:
  President: Deborah Dunham
  VP: Ryan Saunders
  Treasurer: Sharon Davis
  Recording Secretary: Aimee Blanchette
Management:
  Music Director: Andrew Howell
  Executive Director: Ryan Saunders
  Operations/Marketing Mannager: Lee Eastbourne
  Director of Development: Jodie Drapal Kluver
Mission: To perform, with artistic intergrity, both the major classic works of the choral literature and new or lesser known pieces of merit. To educate children and adults of diverse backgrounds in the appreciation, understanding and performance of great music. To grow and develop steadily as an organization important to the cultural experiences of the region.
Utilizes: Guest Artists; Guest Designers; Guest Musicians; Sign Language Translators
Founded: 1959
Specialized Field: Choral
Paid Staff: 6
Volunteer Staff: 200
Paid Artists: 16
Non-paid Artists: 200
Budget: $800,000
Income Sources: Tickets; Rental Fees; Gifts; Grants
Performs At: The Chorus of Westerly Performance Hall
Affiliations: Chorus America
Annual Attendance: 30,000
Facility Category: Historic Former Church Building
Seating Capacity: 440
Year Built: 1886
Year Remodeled: 2003
Cost: varies
Rental Contact: Emma Palzere Rae

2327
SALT MARSH OPERA COMPANY
One Canal Street
PO Box 154
Westerly, RI 02891
Phone: 860-535-3456
Fax: 860-535-0753
Toll-free: 888-788-4188
e-mail: info@saltmarshopera.org
Web Site: www.saltmarshopera.org
Officers:
  Chairman: Frederick Nicholas Jr
  President: Carla Stebbins
  VP: Michele J. Delmhorst
  Treasurer: John R. Delmhorst
  Secretary: Michele J, Delmhorst
  Board Member: Nelson Aldrich
  Advisor: Wilma Asch
  Advisor: John Horn
  Advisor: Patricia Hurley
Management:
  Executive/Artistic Director: Simon Holt
  Adminstrator: Liz Hall
  Finance Director: John Delmhorst
  Fundraising: Pamela Cordell Avis
Mission: Founded in 2000, the Salt Marsh Opera Company is dedicated to producing high-quality, professional opera in Connecticut and Rhode Island and to making its productions available to the entire community. Committed to raising the awareness of opera through educational initiatives and live productions in intimate settings, Salt Marsh Opera enriches the cultural lives of our shoreline communities with: Concerts in private and public venues.
Utilizes: Arrangers; Collaborating Artists; Collaborations; Composers; Contract Orchestras; Designers; Fine Artists; Guest Accompanists; Multimedia; Music; Paid Performers; Special Technical Talent
Founded: 2000
Opened: 2001
Specialized Field: Opera
Status: Non-Profit, Professional
Income Sources: Donations, Advertising
Performs At: Old Lighthouse Museum, Old Saybrook Town Green, George Kent Performance Hall, Phoebe Griffin Noyes Library

Tennessee

2328
CHATTANOOGA BOYS CHOIR
700-B Pine Street
Chattanooga, TN 37402
Phone: 423-634-2299
Fax: 423-634-3399
e-mail: voakes@cbchoir.org
Web Site: www.chattanoogaboyschoir.org
Management:
  President: Micheal Brunson
  Artistic / Executive Director: Vincent Oakes
  Managing Director: Kelly Lusk
Mission: To offer comprehensive training that inspires boys to love and appreciate good music.
Founded: 1954
Specialized Field: Youth Chorus
Status: Non-Profit, Professional
Paid Staff: 7
Organization Type: Performing; Touring

2329
CHATTANOOGA SYMPHONY AND OPERA ASSOCIATION
701 Broad Street
Chattanooga, TN 37402
Phone: 423-267-8583
Fax: 423-265-6520
Web Site: www.chattanoogasymphony.org
Officers:
  President: Susan Elliott Rich
  Vice President: Spencer McCallie
  Secretary: Kim Gavin
Management:
  Music Director/Conductor: Kayoko Dan
  Executive Director: Molly Sasse
  Administrative/Production Director: Charlotte Adkins
  Director Of CSO Choruses: Darrin Hassevoort
Utilizes: Guest Artists; Guest Companies; Singers

VOCAL MUSIC / Texas

Specialized Field: Grand Opera; Lyric Opera; Light Opera; Operetta
Status: Professional; Nonprofit
Paid Staff: 40
Budget: $60,000-$150,000
Income Sources: Tennesseans for the Arts; Opera America; American Symphony Orchestra League
Performs At: Tivoli Theatre
Seating Capacity: 1,680
Organization Type: Performing; Touring; Educational

2330
KNOXVILLE OPERA COMPANY
612 E Depot Avenue
Knoxville, TN 37917-0016
Phone: 865-524-0795
Fax: 865-524-7384
e-mail: hello@knoxvilleopera.com
Web Site: www.knoxvilleopera.com
Management:
   Executive Director/Conductor: Brian Salesky, bsalesky@knoxvilleopera.com
   Production Manager and Chorusmaster: Don Townsend, dtownsend@knoxvilleopera.com
   Director, Marketing & Public Rel.: Michael J. Torano, mtorano@knoxvilleopera.com
   Development Manager: Joey DiMenno
   Finance Director and Box Office Man: N. Marie Butler
Mission: To provide the residents of East Tennessee with high quality locally produced operas
Utilizes: Dancers; Guest Writers; High School Drama; Instructors; Local Artists; Lyricists; Multi Collaborations; Music; Paid Performers; Scenic Designers; Sign Language Translators; Singers, Soloists; Touring Companies; Visual Designers
Founded: 1976
Specialized Field: Grand Opera; Light Opera; Lyric Opera; Musical Theatre; Choral; Classical
Status: Non-Profit, Professional
Paid Staff: 8
Paid Artists: 152
Budget: $1.1 million
Income Sources: Opera America
Performs At: Historic Theatre
Annual Attendance: 9,000
Seating Capacity: 1,600
Year Built: 1928
Year Remodeled: 2005
Cost: $25.5 Million
Organization Type: Performing; Sponsoring

2331
LINDENWOOD CONCERTS
2400 Union Avenue
Memphis, TN 38112
Phone: 901-458-8506
Fax: 901-458-0145
e-mail: chris.nemec@lindenwood.net
Web Site: www.lindenwoodcc.com
Officers:
   President: Gary Beard
Management:
   Executive Director: Chris Nemec
   Business Administrator: Alan Dunn
   Media Operations: Alan Wells
   Senior Pastor's Assistant: Cindy Franklin
Mission: To present the musical arts in a setting of a church, as in 17th and 18th century Europe.
Utilizes: Artists-in-Residence; Guest Accompanists; Guest Composers; Guest Musical Directors; Multimedia; Original Music Scores; Sign Language Translators; Singers
Founded: 1979
Specialized Field: Choral; Youth Chorus; Classical; Religious
Status: Non-Profit, Professional
Paid Staff: 2
Volunteer Staff: 25
Non-paid Artists: 85
Income Sources: Box Office and Benefactors
Affiliations: AGO; ACDA; Choristers Guild; Disciples of Christ
Annual Attendance: 1,000
Facility Category: Church Sanctuary
Seating Capacity: 1,000
Year Built: 1966
Year Remodeled: 2010
Rental Contact: Chris Nemec
Resident Groups: Gary Beard Chorale; Lindenwood Chancel Choir

2332
OPERA MEMPHIS
6745 Wolf River Parkawy
Memphis, TN 38120
Phone: 901-257-3100
e-mail: info@operamemphis.org
Web Site: operamemphis.org
Officers:
   Chair: Charles D. Schaffler
   Vice Chair: Paul K. Guibao
   Secretary: Mark McCowan
   Treasurer: Daniel Anglin
Management:
   General Director: Ned Canty, ned@operamemphis.org
   Music Director: Ben Makino, ben@operamemphis.org
   Marketing Coordinator: Tierney Bamrick, tbamrick@operamemphis.org
Mission: To entertain, educate, and inspire the people of Memphis and the Mid-South through the art of opera.
Founded: 1956
Specialized Field: Opera
Performs At: Clark Opera Memphis Center; Germantown Performing Arts Center; The Orpheum; Playhouse On The Square
Organization Type: Performing; Touring

2333
NASHVILLE OPERA ASSOCIATION
3622 Redmon Street
Nashville, TN 37209
Phone: 615-832-5242
Fax: 615-297-6337
e-mail: info@nashvilleopera.org
Web Site: www.nashvilleopera.org
Officers:
   President: Elizabeth Papel
   CEO: Noah E. Spiegel
Management:
   Executive Director: Carol Penterman
   Artistic Director/General Director: John Hoomes
   Artistic Admin Director: Karen Haas
Mission: To present operatic productions to middle Tennesseeans.
Utilizes: AEA Actors; Choreographers; Collaborations; Commissioned Composers; Dancers; Designers; Educators; Five Seasonal Concerts; Grant Writers; Guest Accompanists; Guest Artists; Guest Composers; Guest Conductors; Guest Designers; Guest Directors; Guest Musical Directors; Guest Musicians; Instructors; Multimedia; Original Music Scores; Resident Professionals; Sign Language Translators
Founded: 1981
Specialized Field: Grand Opera; Light Opera; Lyric Opera; Classical; Contemporary
Status: Non-Profit, Non-Professional
Paid Staff: 14
Paid Artists: 60
Budget: $2.4 million
Income Sources: Contributed and Earned Income
Season: September - April
Performs At: Andrew Jackson Hall; Polk Theatre
Affiliations: Opera America
Annual Attendance: 13,000
Organization Type: Performing; Educational

2334
NASHVILLE SYMPHONY CHORUS
One Symphony Place
Nashville, TN 37201-2031
Phone: 615-687-6500
Fax: 615-783-1575
e-mail: info@nashvillesymphony.org
Web Site: www.nashvillesymphony.org
Officers:
   President and CEO: Alan D. Valentine
   Executive Assistant to President: Karen Fairbend
   COO: Mark A. Blakemen
   CFO: Chad Boyd
   Executive Assitant to CEO: Katy Lyles
Management:
   Director of Artistic Administration: Lawrence Tucker
   Manager of Artistic Administration: Ellen Kasperek
   Manager of Artistic Administration: Maiken Knudsen
   Organ Curator: Andrew Risinger
Specialized Field: Choral

Texas

2335
AMARILLO OPERA
2223 S Van Buren Street
Amarillo, TX 79109-2448
Phone: 806-372-7464
e-mail: info@amarilloopera.org
Web Site: amarilloopera.org
Management:
   General Director: David O'Dell, david.odell@amarilloopera.org
   Company Manager: Rebecca Aguilera, rebecca.aguilera@amarilloopera.org
   Director Of Production: Linda Hughes, linda.hughes@amarilloopera.org
Mission: To provide live opera to the Texas Panhandle, nurture local talent and help build community.
Founded: 1988
Status: Professional
Performs At: Globe News Center-Performing Arts 500 S. Buchanan Street, Amarillo, TX
Affiliations: Amarillo College
Annual Attendance: 500,000

2336
AUSTIN LYRIC OPERA
3009 Industrial Terrace
Suite 100
Austin, TX 78758
Phone: 512-472-5927
Fax: 512-472-4143
Toll-free: 800-316-7372
e-mail: jspecter@austinlyricopera.org
Web Site: www.austinlyricopera.org
Officers:
   Chairman: Wendi Kushner
   President: Ernest Auerbach

Secretary: Marilyn Davis Rabkin
Vice President Development: Colleen Cole
Vice President Community Program: Curby Conoley Tableriou
Management:
Chairman: Steve Davis
President: Susan Lubin
Artistic Director: Richard Buckley
Managing Director: Tamara Hale
General Director: Joseph Specter
Mission: To promote and support opera; to foster public awareness of opera as a fine art.
Founded: 1985
Specialized Field: Grand Opera; Light Opera; Lyric Opera; Musical Theatre; Choral; Youth Chorus; Classical
Status: Non-Profit, Professional
Paid Staff: 30
Budget: $5,000,000
Income Sources: Central Opera Service
Performs At: University of Texas Performing Arts Center
Annual Attendance: 48,000
Facility Category: Concert Hall
Type of Stage: Proscenium
Seating Capacity: 2,872

2337
CHORUS AUSTIN
PO Box 204361
Austin, TX 78720
Phone: 512-719-3300
Fax: 512-451-3110
Toll-free: 877-640-8836
e-mail: office@chorusaustin.org
Web Site: www.chorusaustin.org
Officers:
Chair: Angela Fleming
Secretary: Sylvia Cowin
Treasurer: Kara Kirk
Management:
Artistic Director/Conductor: Ryan Heller
Executive Director: David Hayes
Utilizes: Collaborations; Five Seasonal Concerts; Guest Accompanists; Guest Directors; Guest Musical Directors; Guest Musicians; Local Artists; Multimedia; Sign Language Translators; Singers
Specialized Field: Choral

2338
CONSPIRARE, CRAIG HELLA JOHNSON & COMPANY OF VOICES
2702 McCulloum Street
Austin, TX 78703
Phone: 512-476-5775
Fax: 512-481-1676
e-mail: info@conspirare.org
Web Site: www.conspirare.org
Officers:
Board Chairman: Fran Collmann
Management:
Interim Executive Director: Stephanie Sheppard
Founded: 1993
Specialized Field: Series & Festivals; Concerts; Vocal Music
Status: Non-Profit, Professional
Paid Staff: 4
Paid Artists: 35
Affiliations: New Texas Music Works

2339
THE AUSTIN LYRIC OPERA
3009 Industrial Terrace
Suite 100
Austin, TX 78758
Mailing Address: 701 West Riverside Drive, Austin, TX 78759
Phone: 512-472-5927
Fax: 512-472-5992
e-mail: elittle@austinlyricopera.org
Web Site: www.austinlyricopera.org
Officers:
Chairman: Wendi Kushner
President: Ernest Auerbach
Secretary: Marilyn Davis Rabkin
Legal Counsel: Michael Metteauer
VP/Development: Colleen Cole
VP/Community Program: Curby Conoley Taberiou
VP/Trustees: Jerry Gatlin
VP/Special Funding: Jon Nash
VP/Strategic Planning: Kyle Penrose
Management:
General Director: Joseph Specter
Artistic Director: Richard Buckley
Production Coordinator: Elizabeth Cooper
Technical Director: Vincent Herod
Music Administrator: Elden Little
Mission: Founded in May of 1986 as Austin's first professional opera company, Austin Lyric Opera rapidly became a cultural touchstone for the fine arts community in the Central Texas region. Co-founders Joseph McClain and the late Dr. Walter Ducloux envisioned a dynamic company that would enrich, entertain, and educate the community.
Utilizes: Arrangers; Collaborating Artists; Collaborations; Composers; Contract Orchestras; Fine Artists; Grant Writers; Guest Companies; Local Unknown Artists; Multimedia; Music; Sign Language Translators
Founded: 1986
Specialized Field: Opera Music
Status: Non-Profit, Professional
Income Sources: Donations, Corporate Sponsorship
Performs At: Long Center
Affiliations: Austin Lyric Opera, Ballet Austin, Austin Symphony Orchestra

2340
BEAUMONT CIVIC OPERA
4350 Thomas Glen
Beaumont, TX 77706
Phone: 409-892-5408
Management:
Conductor: L Randolph Babin
Business Manager: Delores Black
Mission: Presenting fine musical productions in Southwest Texas and giving young performers opportunities.
Utilizes: Guest Companies; Singers
Founded: 1962
Specialized Field: Grand Opera; Light Opera; Operetta
Status: Nonprofit
Budget: $35,000-$60,000
Income Sources: Opera America
Performs At: Julie Rogers Theatre for the Performing Arts
Seating Capacity: 1,775
Organization Type: Resident

2341
TEXAS A&M UNIVERSITY OPERA & PERFORMING ARTS
MS 1237
Texas A&M University
College Station, TX 77843-1237
Phone: 979-845-1661
Fax: 979-845-8043
Toll-free: 877-672-6727
e-mail: anne-black@tamu.edu
Web Site: www.mscopas.org
Officers:
President: Charley Bankstone
Immediate Past President: Nita Hoelscher
Vice-President/Student Committee Ch: Alex Dunn
President Elect: Tim Jones
OPAS Encore! President: Eric Wylie
Executive Director: Anne T. Black
Business Coordinator: Terri Becker
Marketing & Development Coordinator: Becky Wade
Communications Coordinator: Shanna Wright
Founded: 1972
Specialized Field: Grand Opera; Light Opera; Musical Theatre; Choral; Youth Chorus; Ethnic Music; Classical; Contemporary
Status: Non-Profit, Professional
Paid Staff: 4
Budget: $400,000-$1,000,000

2342
DALLAS OPERA
Winspear Opera House
2403 Flora Street
Suite 500
Dallas, TX 75201
Phone: 214-443-1043
Fax: 214-443-1060
e-mail: suzanne.calvin@dallasopera.org
Web Site: www.dallasopera.org
Officers:
Chairman: T. Peter Townsend
General Director/CEO: William Blaylock
Immediate Past Chair: Kern Wildenthal
Vice Chair: Joy S. Mankoff
VP Development: Holly Mayer
Management:
Artistic Director: Jonathan Pell
Development Director: Gae Whitener
General Director: Keith Cerny
Music Director: Emmanuel Villaume
Technical Director: Drew Field
Mission: The Dallas Opera is an opera company committed to the presentation of opera at the international level. It enriches the community through performances of grand and chamber opera, operatic concerts, recitals and attendant education and community service programs.
Founded: 1957
Specialized Field: Grand Opera; Light Opera; Lyric Opera; Musical Theatre; Choral; Youth Chorus; Ethnic Music; Classical
Status: Non-Profit, Professional
Paid Staff: 35
Paid Artists: 60
Budget: $12,000,000
Performs At: Winspear Opera House Of The AT&T Performing Arts Center
Affiliations: Opera America; American Arts Alliance; Texas Arts Alliance
Annual Attendance: 79,754
Seating Capacity: 2,200

VOCAL MUSIC / Texas

Year Built: 2009
Rental Contact: Director of Production John Gage
Organization Type: Performing; Educational; Sponsoring

2343
DALLAS SYMPHONY CHORUS
Dallas Symphony Association
2301 Flora Street
Dallas, TX 75201
Phone: 214-692-0203
Fax: 214-953-1218
e-mail: customerservice@dalsym.com
Web Site: www.dallassymphony.com
Officers:
   Administrator: Donna Krauss
   President & CEO: Jonathan Martin
   Vice President of People and Facili: Debi Pena
   Vice President of Finance: Randy Leiser
Management:
   President: Fred Bronstein
   Music Director: Jaap van Zweden
   Associate Conductor: Thomas Hong
   Director, Dallas Symphony Chorus: Joshua Habermann
   Executive Assistant to the Presiden: Lisa Anderson
Mission: Supporting the Dallas Symphony Association; performing major choral works in conjunction with the symphony.
Founded: 1900
Specialized Field: Lyric Opera; Light Opera; Operetta; Choral; Ethnic Music; Folk Music
Status: Nonprofit
Paid Staff: 3
Volunteer Staff: 1
Non-paid Artists: 240
Performs At: Meyerson Symphony Center
Organization Type: Performing; Touring; Resident

2344
TURTLE CREEK CHORALE
3630 Harry Hines Boulevard
PO Box 190137
Dallas, TX 75219
Phone: 214-526-3214
Fax: 214-528-0673
Toll-free: 800-746-4412
e-mail: info@turtlecreek.org
Web Site: www.turtlecreek.org
Officers:
   Chorus President: Hank Henley
   Chair: Justin J. Lombardo
Management:
   Executive Director: David Fisher
   Artistic Director: Trey Jacobs
Mission: To perform, unite and educate the audience through the presentation of male choral music and other musical activities.
Utilizes: Singers
Founded: 1980
Specialized Field: Choral
Status: Non-Professional, Nonprofit
Paid Staff: 8
Non-paid Artists: 200
Performs At: Meyerson Symphony Center
Annual Attendance: 30,000
Facility Category: Concert hall
Seating Capacity: 1875
Year Built: 1990
Organization Type: Performing

2345
EL PASO OPERA
310 North Mesa Street
Suite 601
El Paso, TX 79901
Mailing Address: 1 Civic Center Plaza, El Paso, TX 79901
Phone: 915-581-5534
e-mail: david@epopera.org
Web Site: www.opopera.org
Officers:
   President: Robert Gonzalez
   Past President: Michele Levy
   Treasurer: Michael Drapes
   Secretary: Stacey Hunt
   Guild Chair: Wilma Salzman
   Trustee: John Bittrick
   Trustee: Jennifer Cedillo
Management:
   Artistic/Executive Director: David Grabarkewitz
   Music Director: Karl Shymanovitz
   Operations Director: Steven Silver
   Education Director: Jaime Solano
   Young Artists Director: Dr Elisa Fraser Wilson
Mission: To bring professional opera productions that are understandable, accessible, and enjoyable to all the residents of El Paso, Texas and the surrounding communities; and to sponsor educational programs that will introduce both youth and adult populations to the world of great vocal music.
Utilizes: Arrangers; Collaborations; Composers; Contract Orchestras; Lyricists; Multimedia; Music; Sign Language Translators; Singers
Founded: 1992
Specialized Field: Opera
Status: Non-Profit
Income Sources: Contributions, Donations
Season: Fall
Affiliations: National Endowment for the Arts, Texas Commission on the Arts

2346
CHILDREN'S OPERA THEATER
1300 Gendy St.
Fort Worth, TX 76107
Phone: 817-731-0833
Fax: 817-731-0835
e-mail: info@fwopera.org
Web Site: www.fwopera.org
Management:
   Artistic Director: Michael Kaye
Mission: Introducing and involving youth in opera; providing employment for artists as they make the transition to a professional career.
Founded: 1976
Specialized Field: Light Opera; Choral
Status: Professional; Nonprofit
Organization Type: Touring; Educational

2347
FORT WORTH OPERA ASSOCIATION
1300 Gendy Street
Fort Worth, TX 76107
Phone: 817-731-0833
Fax: 817-731-0835
Toll-free: 866-396-7372
e-mail: info@fwopera.org
Web Site: www.fwopera.org
Officers:
   President - Elect, Vice President: John Sutton
   President, Opera Guild of Ft. Worth: Petra Grimes
   Chairperson: Kris Lindsay
   Secretary: Rita O'Farrell
   Treasurer: Kenny Fischer
Management:
   President: Natalie Murray
   Executive Director: Darren Woods
   Managing Director: Keith Wolfe
   General Director: Darren K. Woods
   Music Director: Joe Illick
Mission: Cultivating and promoting the love and understanding of opera.
Utilizes: Actors; Dance Companies; Educators; Grant Writers; Guest Artists; Guest Composers; Guest Designers; Guest Writers; Local Artists; Multimedia; Resident Professionals; Sign Language Translators
Founded: 1946
Specialized Field: Opera
Status: Non-Profit, Professional
Paid Staff: 10
Paid Artists: 55
Budget: $2,700,000
Income Sources: Opera America; Arts Council of Fort Worth & Tarrant County; Private Foundations and Businesses.
Performs At: Bass Performance Hall
Affiliations: Opera America; Arts Council of Forth Worth and Tarrant County
Facility Category: Opera Performance Hall
Stage Dimensions: 57x65
Seating Capacity: 2,000
Year Built: 1999
Rental Contact: Paul Beard
Organization Type: Performing; Resident; Educational

2348
SCHOLA CANTORUM OF TEXAS
2463A Forest Park Boulevard
PO Box 8235
Fort Worth, TX 76124
Mailing Address: PO Box 8235, Fort Worth, TX 76124
Phone: 817-485-2500
Fax: 817-485-0078
e-mail: info@scholatexas.com
Web Site: www.scholatexas.com
Officers:
   President: Susan Seiter
   VP: George Muckleroy
Management:
   Choir Director: Jerry McCoy
   Music Director and Conductor: Dr. Jerry McCoy
   Accompanist: Alan Buratto
Mission: To provide a performance outlet for talented singers, whereby providving outstanding choral music at the Metroplex.
Utilizes: Singers
Founded: 1962
Specialized Field: Choral
Status: Semi-Professional, Nonprofit
Paid Staff: 60
Performs At: Kimbell Art Museum; Irons Recital Hall
Organization Type: Performing

2349
TEXAS BOYS CHOIR
3901 S. Hulen Street
Fort Worth, TX 76109
Phone: 817-924-1482
Fax: 817-926-9932
Web Site: texasboyschoir.org
Management:
   Artistic Director: S. Bryan Priddy
   Executive Director: Clint Riley, clint.riley@texasboyschoir.org
   Marketing Director: Laura Kinkade, laura.kinkade@texasboyschoir.o

VOCAL MUSIC / Texas

Associate Artistic Director: Ellie Lin
Mission: Our mission is to be a world-class boychoir, to develop personal excellence and to inspire a lifelong passion for choral artistry.
Founded: 1946
Specialized Field: Choral
Status: Nonprofit
Organization Type: Touring; Performing

2350
TEXAS GIRLS' CHOIR
4449 Camp Bowie Boulevard
Fort Worth, TX 76107-3834
Phone: 817-732-8161
Fax: 817-732-4774
e-mail: tgc@texasgirlschoir.org
Web Site: www.texasgirlschoir.org
Officers:
   Executive Director: Debi Weir
Management:
   Executive Director: Debi Weir, tgc@texasgirlschoir.org
   Artistic Director: Layne Trent
Mission: To develop little girls' lives through excellence of music.
Utilizes: Commissioned Music; Community Talent; Grant Writers; Guest Accompanists; Guest Companies; Guest Designers; Guest Directors; Guest Lecturers; Guest Musical Directors; Guest Musicians; Guest Soloists; Instructors; Multimedia; Music; Original Music Scores; Sign Language Translators; Singers; Soloists
Founded: 1962
Opened: 1962
Specialized Field: Choral; Youth Chorus; Classical; Contemporary; Religious
Status: Non-Profit, Non-Professional
Paid Staff: 11
Volunteer Staff: 50
Non-paid Artists: 225
Budget: $622,370
Income Sources: Semester Fees; Donations; Concerts; Performances; Fundraisers
Performs At: Concert Hall; Auditorium
Facility Category: Former Church
Type of Stage: Full Width Of Auditorium
Seating Capacity: 600
Year Built: 1949
Rental Contact: Debi Weir
Organization Type: Performing; Touring; Educational

2351
BACH SOCIETY HOUSTON
2353 Rice Boulevard
Houston, TX 77005
Phone: 832-582-1750
e-mail: info@bachsocietyhouston.org
Web Site: bachsocietyhouston.org
Officers:
   President: Douglas D. Koch
   Secretary: Leonard Teich
   Treasurer: Kleta Gerhart
Management:
   Director: Rick Erickson
   Operations Manager: Laurie Hewett
Mission: To present exemplary, historically-informed professional performances of the music of Johann Sebastian Bach and constitute his legacy.
Founded: 1982
Specialized Field: Choral; Classical;
Status: Nonprofit; Professional

2352
HOUSTON CHAMBER CHOIR
1117 Texas
Houston, TX 77002
Mailing Address: P.O. Box 53388, Houston, TX 77052-3388
Phone: 713-224-5566
Fax: 713-222-2412
e-mail: robertsimpson@houstonchamberchoir.org
Web Site: www.houstonchamberchoir.org
Officers:
   President: Francis Kittrell
   Vice President: Roy Nolen
   Secretary: Judy Cronin
   Treasurer: John Catalani
Management:
   Artistic Director: Robert Simpson
   Executive Director: Becky Tobin
Mission: A professional ensemble dedicated to increasing the awareness, appreciation and esteem of choral music and musicians through performance, outreach and education.
Utilizes: Commissioned Composers; Community Members; Guest Accompanists; Guest Companies; Guest Lecturers; Guest Musical Directors; Instructors; Multimedia; Organization Contracts; Original Music Scores; Playwrights; Sign Language Translators; Singers
Founded: 1995
Specialized Field: Choral; Chamber Opera
Status: Non-Profit, Professional
Paid Staff: 4
Volunteer Staff: 15
Paid Artists: 30
Budget: $350,000
Affiliations: Chorus America

2353
HOUSTON GRAND OPERA
510 Preston Street
Suite 500
Houston, TX 77002
Phone: 713-546-0200
Fax: 713-247-0906
Web Site: www.houstongrandopera.org
Officers:
   General Director/CEO: Anthony Freud
   Chief Advancement Officer: Greg Robertson
   Chairman Of The Board: Beth Madison
   Vice Chairman Of The Board: Lynn Wyatt
   Senior Chairman of the Board: Glen A. Rosenbaum
Management:
   Artistic and Music Director: Patrick Summers
   Managing Director: Perryn Leech
   Director of Marketing: Steve Kelley
   Associate Music Director: Eric Melear
   Director of Artistic Administratio: Diane Zola
Mission: To produce opera of consistent excellence offering nontraditional and innovative works; to develop new forms, new artists and new audiences.
Utilizes: Composers; Guest Artists; Guest Companies; Guest Designers; Guest Musicians; Sign Language Translators; Singers
Founded: 1955
Specialized Field: Grand Opera; Lyric Opera; Light Opera; Operetta
Status: Professional; Nonprofit
Volunteer Staff: y
Budget: $20,000,000
Income Sources: Donations
Organization Type: Performing; Touring; Resident; Educational

2354
HOUSTON MASTERWORKS CHORUS
4119 Montrose Boulevard
Suite 260
Houston, TX 77006-4964
Phone: 713-529-8900
e-mail: houstonmasterworks@yahoo.com
Web Site: www.houstonmasterworks.org
Officers:
   President: Rita La Rue
   Secretary: Diane Hackem
   Treasurer: Tom Plapp
Management:
   Interim Managing Director: Martha Knotts
   Assistant Conductor: Paula Acord Blackman
   Artistic Director: Thomas Jaber
   Production Manager: Gary C. Gardner
   Chorus Manager: David L. Hudson
Mission: Dedicated to the presentation of great choral music, and to the continuation of the choral society tradition.
Utilizes: Five Seasonal Concerts; Guest Composers; Guest Musicians
Founded: 1986
Specialized Field: Choral; Classical
Status: Non-Profit, Non-Professional
Paid Staff: 4
Volunteer Staff: 150
Paid Artists: 25
Non-paid Artists: 129
Budget: $344,000
Income Sources: Endowment; Foundations; Individual Contributions

2355
HOUSTON SYMPHONY CHORUS
123 Main Street
Houston, TX 77000
Phone: 713-444-9221
Fax: 713-807-7824
Toll-free: 888-555-5555
e-mail: chorus@sbcglobal.net
Web Site: www.choral.org/grou/hsc/
Management:
   Director: Dr Charles Hausmann
   Chorus Manager: Susan Scarrow
   Assistant Director: Kevin M. Klotz
Utilizes: Guest Artists
Founded: 1946
Specialized Field: Choral
Status: Non-Professional; Nonprofit
Paid Staff: 170
Income Sources: Chorus America
Performs At: Jesse H. Jones Hall for the Performing Arts
Organization Type: Performing; Resident

2356
OPERA IN THE HEIGHTS
Lambert Hall, 1703 Heights Boulevard
Houston, TX 77008
Mailing Address: P.O. Box 7887, Houston, TX 77270
Phone: 713-861-5303
Fax: 888-392-4949
e-mail: info@operaintheheights.org
Web Site: operaintheheights.org
Officers:
   Chair: David W. Douglas
   Vice Chair: Josh Agrons
   Secretary: Corey Powell
   Treasurer: David Cripps
Management:

VOCAL MUSIC / Utah

Artistic Director: Enrique Carreon-Robledo, enrique@operaintheheights.org
Operations Manager: Mariam Khalili, mariam@operaintheheights.org
Director Of Artistic Administration: Keith Chapman
Patron Services Coordinator: Michelle James
Mission: To provide a stage for emerging opera performers and to bring affordable opera to the Greater Houston Area.
Specialized Field: Opera
Status: Professional
Performs At: Lambert Hall
Seating Capacity: 310
Organization Type: Regional; Performing

2357
IRVING CHORALE
3333 N MacArthur Blvd
Suite 300
Irving, TX 75062
Phone: 972-252-2787
Fax: 972-257-1417
e-mail: d.schardt@sbcglobal.net
Web Site: www.irvingchorale.org
Officers:
President: Lita Strubhart
Vice President: Pete Gibbons
Recording Secretary: Annetta Templeton
Treasurer: Robert Boyer
Recording Secretary: Judy Gibson
Management:
Artistic Director: Harry Wooten
President: Donna Schardt
Accompanist: Eunice Tavaglione
Webmaster: Bert Gravley
Grant Writer: Mary Kay Dixon
Specialized Field: Choral

2358
MIDLAND-ODESSA SYMPHONY AND CHORALE
3100 LaForce Boulevard
PO Box 60658
Midland, TX 79711
Phone: 432-563-0921
Fax: 432-617-0087
e-mail: musicdirector@mosc.org
Web Site: www.mosc.org
Management:
CEO: Wade Kelley
General Manager: Ted Hale
Musical Director & Conductor: Gary Lewis
Kids Choir Director: Emily Baker
Operations Director: Rino Irving
Mission: To offer residents of the Permian Basin symphonic, chamber and choral music.
Utilizes: Collaborations; Commissioned Music; Educators; Grant Writers; Guest Artists; Guest Companies; Guest Directors; Guest Lecturers; Guest Writers; High School Drama; Local Artists; Lyricists; Multi Collaborations; Multimedia; Organization Contracts; Original Music Scores; Singers; Theatre Companies
Founded: 1962
Specialized Field: Choral
Status: Non-Profit, Professional
Paid Staff: 5
Volunteer Staff: 100
Budget: $670,000
Income Sources: Tickets; Grants; Donations
Affiliations: ASOL
Annual Attendance: 10,000
Organization Type: Performing; Educational

2359
SAN ANGELO SYMPHONY ORCHESTRA AND CHORALE
PO Box 5922
San Angelo, TX 76902
Phone: 915-658-5877
Fax: 915-653-1045
Web Site: www.sanangelosymphony.org
Officers:
President: Bette Allison
VP: Candyce Pfluger
Secretary: Janet Harvey
Treasurer: Ross Power
Past President: Meredythe McGlothlin
Management:
Music Director/Conductor: Hector Guzman
Executive Director: Courtney Mahaffey
Finance Associate: Rhonda Layman
Music Associate: David Phillips
Mission: To further cultural advancement and enjoyment of symphonic music in the San Angelo area.
Utilizes: Singers
Founded: 1948
Specialized Field: Choral
Status: Professional; Non-Professional; Nonprofit
Paid Staff: 140
Income Sources: Broadcast Music Incorporated; American Society of Composers, Authors and Publishers; American Symphony Orchestra League
Performs At: City Auditorium
Annual Attendance: 50,000
Seating Capacity: 1,590
Organization Type: Performing

2360
TWIN MOUNTAIN TONESMEN
PO Box 2897
San Angelo, TX 76902
Phone: 325-947-8663
e-mail: tonesmen@tonesmen.org
Web Site: www.tonesmen.org
Officers:
President: Don Allison
Vice President of Chapter Developme: Sid Clemmer
Program Vice Presiden: Fred Boston
Music Vice President: Bruce Clark
Secretary: Chris Meadows
Management:
Music Director/Vice President of Ma: Mark E Clark
Uniform Manager: Lyndal Emert
Bulletin Editor: Paul White
Mission: To present Barbershop Singing in our area and compete in contests.
Founded: 1979
Specialized Field: Barbershop Quartet
Status: Non-Professional; Nonprofit; Charitable
Volunteer Staff: 38
Performs At: City Auditorium
Affiliations: Cultural Affairs Council; SOEBSQSA
Organization Type: Performing; Resident

2361
TEXAS BACH CHOIR
PO Box 681058
San Antonio, TX 78268
Phone: 210-872-6743
e-mail: donoughuek@gmail.com
Web Site: www.texasbachchoir.org
Officers:
President: Mary Beth Garay
VP: Katya Thompson-Cantu
President Elect: Steve Matteson
Secretary: Don Peterson
Treasurer: Jim Harnish
Management:
Music Director: Daniel Long
Administrator: Samantha Beer
Mission: The performance of classical sacred choral works of all periods, with emphasis on Baroque.
Utilizes: Singers
Founded: 1976
Specialized Field: Choral; Classical; Traditional Choral Music
Status: Non-Profit, Non-Professional
Paid Staff: 36
Paid Artists: 2
Income Sources: Chorus America
Organization Type: Performing; Touring; Resident

Utah

2362
UTAH FESTIVAL OPERA COMPANY
59 S 100 W
Logan, UT 84321
Phone: 435-750-0300
Fax: 435-753-5856
Toll-free: 800-262-0074
e-mail: opera@ufoc.org
Web Site: www.ufoc.org
Officers:
Chairperson: Melanie Raymond
Vice-Chair: Ralph Binns
Treasurer: Brent Nyman
Management:
General Director: Michael Ballam
Development Director: Lila Geddes
Marketing: Darla Seamons
Ticketing Director: Nansi Blau
Mission: Bringing people together to share ennobling artistic experiences.
Utilizes: AEA Actors; Choreographers; Collaborations; Commissioned Composers; Composers-in-Residence; Dancers; Designers; Grant Writers; Guest Artists; Guest Composers; Guest Conductors; Guest Designers; Guest Directors; Guest Instructors; Guest Lecturers; Guest Musical Directors; Guest Musicians; Guest Soloists; Instructors; Local Artists; Local Unknown Artists; Multimedia; Music; Original Music Scores; Resident Professionals; Sign Language Translators; Singers; Soloists
Founded: 1992
Specialized Field: Grand Opera; Light Opera; Musical Theatre; Operetta
Status: Non-Profit, Professional
Paid Staff: 12
Volunteer Staff: 1
Paid Artists: 200
Budget: $2 million
Income Sources: Box Office; Foundations; Endowment; Government Grants; Private Contributors
Performs At: Ellen Eccles Theatre
Affiliations: Opera America
Annual Attendance: 23,000
Facility Category: Theater
Type of Stage: Proscenium
Stage Dimensions: 36'x 35'x 25'
Seating Capacity: 1,110
Year Built: 1923
Year Remodeled: 1993
Organization Type: Performing; Educational

VOCAL MUSIC / Vermont

2363
MORMON TABERNACLE CHOIR
50 N West Temple Street
Salt Lake City, UT 84150
Phone: 801-240-3221
Fax: 801-240-4886
e-mail: scott.barrick@mormontabernaclechoir.org
Web Site: www.mormontabernaclechoir.org
Officers:
  President: Ron Jarrett
Management:
  Music Director: Mark Wilberg
  General Manager: Scott Barrick
  Organist: Richard Elliott
Founded: 1847
Specialized Field: Choral; Religious
Status: Non-Profit, Non-Professional
Paid Staff: 14

2364
ORATORIO SOCIETY OF UTAH
PO Box 11714
Salt Lake City, UT 84147
Phone: 801-572-7464
Fax: 801-572-9398
Web Site: reality.sgi.com/csp/osutah/
Mission: Performing oratorio music and engaging in cultural exchanges with other countries.
Utilizes: Guest Artists
Founded: 1915
Specialized Field: Choral
Status: Semi-Professional; Nonprofit
Paid Staff: 250
Organization Type: Performing; Touring

2365
SALT LAKE SYMPHONIC CHOIR
3790 S 3145 E
Salt Lake City, UT 84109
Phone: 801-201-5451
Fax: 801-281-0563
e-mail: gbettinson@excite.com
Web Site: www.saltlakesymphonicchoir.org
Officers:
  President: Greg Bettinson
  Executive Secretary: Carolyn Tinsch
  Social Chair: Kathie Trulson
Management:
  Artistic Director: Erin Pike Tall
  VP Public Relations: Vicki I Armitage
  VP Finance: Dennis Gunn
Mission: Presenting choral concerts world-wide.
Founded: 1949
Specialized Field: Choral
Status: Professional; Nonprofit
Non-paid Artists: 100
Organization Type: Performing; Touring

2366
UTAH OPERA COMPANY
Abravanel Hall
123 W South Temple
Salt Lake City, UT 84101
Phone: 801-533-5626
Fax: 801-869-9026
e-mail: info@utahsymphonyopera.org
Web Site: www.utahopera.com
Officers:
  Chairman: William C Bailey
  Senior Vice President & COO: David Green
  Symphony Music Director: Thierry Fischer
  Vice President of Development: Leslie Peterson
Management:
  President & CEO: Melia P. Tourangeau
  Vice President of Finance & CFO: Steve Hogan
  Artistic Director: Christopher McBeth
  General Director: Anne Ewers
  Production Coordinator: Shaun Ricks
  Office Manager: Rhea Bouman
Mission: To offer quality productions featuring standard opera repertoire; to educate the community.
Utilizes: Artists-in-Residence; Choreographers; Guest Composers; Guest Designers; Guest Ensembles; Instructors; Original Music Scores; Resident Professionals; Sign Language Translators
Founded: 1978
Specialized Field: Grand Opera; Light Opera
Status: Professional; Nonprofit
Paid Staff: 30
Budget: $4,500,000
Income Sources: Opera America; American Arts Alliance; Utah Arts Council; Salt Lake City Arts Council
Performs At: Capitol Theatre
Annual Attendance: 9,000
Facility Category: Capitol Theatre
Type of Stage: Proscenium
Seating Capacity: 1,835
Year Built: 1913
Year Remodeled: 1976
Organization Type: Performing; Resident; Educational

2367
UTAH SYMPHONY
123 West South Temple
Salt Lake City, UT 84101
Phone: 801-533-6683
Fax: 801-581-5683
Toll-free: 888-901-7464
e-mail: info@usuo.org
Web Site: www.utahsymphony.org
Officers:
  President/CEO: Melia P Tourangeau
  Vice President of Development: Leslie Peterson
  Vice President of Development and M: Carey Cusimano
Management:
  Artistic Director: Christopher McBeth
  Operations Director: Lindsey Wood
  Marketing Director: Kevin Bentz
  Symphony Music Director: Thierry Fischer
  Principal Pops Conductor: Gerald Steichen
Mission: To give performances which engage, educate and enrich the community.
Utilizes: Guest Composers; Guest Lecturers; Guest Musicians; Multimedia; Sign Language Translators
Founded: 1978
Specialized Field: Choral
Status: Professional
Paid Staff: 5
Volunteer Staff: 10
Budget: 55,000
Income Sources: Performances fees; Fundrasiers
Affiliations: Utah Symphony Orchestra

2368
UTAH CHAMBER ARTISTS
11640 South Littler Road
Sandy, UT 84092
Phone: 801-572-2010
Web Site: utahchamberartists.org
Officers:
  President: John T. Nielsen
  Vice President: David B. Hansen
  Secretary: Joan Clissold
  Treasurer: Karin D. Larson
Management:
  Artistic Director: Barlow Bradford
  Executive Director: Rebecca Durham
Mission: We aspire to create meaningful musical experiences and to provide opportunities for people to gather and enjoy fine music together.
Founded: 1991
Specialized Field: Ensemble; Choral

Vermont

2369
BRATTLEBORO MUSIC CENTER
38 Walnut Street
Brattleboro, VT 05301
Phone: 802-257-4523
e-mail: info@bmcvt.org
Web Site: www.bmcvt.org
Officers:
  President: Tom Cain
  Vice President: William Shakespeare
  Secretary: Veronica Johnson
  Treasurer: Patricia Mangan
  Trustee: Rachel Doty
Management:
  Bookkeeper: Donna Simpson
  Managing Director: Pam Lierle
  Administrative Coordinator: Gay Foster
  Education Programs Director: Carol Compton
  Campaign Director: Eric Russel
Mission: Enriching lives through music. To promote the love and understanding of good music through performance and education, and to make music a vital part of the community.
Founded: 1952
Specialized Field: Classical; Contemporary; Choral
Status: Non-Profit, Professional
Paid Staff: 36
Paid Artists: 30
Performs At: Persons Auditorium; Marlboro College
Organization Type: Performing; Touring; Resident

2370
OPERA COMPANY OF MIDDLEBURY
Town Hall Theater 68 S. Pleasant Street
Middlebury, VT 05753
Mailing Address: P.O. Box 803, Middlebury, VT 05753
Phone: 802-388-7432
Web Site: ocmvermont.org
Officers:
  President: David Clark
  Vice President: Joann Langrock
  Treasurer: Don Devost
  Secretary: Michele Brown
Management:
  Artistic Director: Douglas Anderson
  Music Director: Emmanuel Plasson
  Production Manager: Mary Longey
Mission: The mission of the Opera Company of Middlebury is to bring quality live opera productions and other opera experiences to the Middlebury area.
Performs At: Town Hall Theatre

2371
NORTH COUNTRY CHORUS
PO Box 184
Wells River, VT 05081
Phone: 802-748-5027
e-mail: arowe@stjacademy.org
Web Site: www.northcountrychorus.org
Officers:
  President: Matt Sargent
Management:
  Music Director: Alan Rowe

VOCAL MUSIC / Virginia

Mission: To enrich the musical lives of North Country Area residents; to offer participation to anyone who loves singing.
Utilizes: Guest Companies; Singers
Founded: 1948
Specialized Field: Choral
Status: Semi-Professional; Nonprofit
Season: June - August
Organization Type: Performing; Touring; Resident

Virginia

2372
OPERA THEATRE OF NO VIRGINIA
1916 Wilson Boulevard
Suite 301
Arlington, VA 22201
Mailing Address: PO Box 7027 Arlington, VA 22207
Phone: 703-528-1433
Fax: 703-812-5039
Web Site: www.novaopera.org
Officers:
  President: Jean Shirhall
Management:
  Artistic Director/Conductor: John Edward Niles
Mission: To provide affordable opera in English to the Northern Virginia and Greater Metropolitan Washington Area; to sponsor educational programs and performances geared to young audiences; to provide stage experience.
Utilizes: Guest Companies; Singers
Founded: 1961
Specialized Field: Grand Opera; Light Opera
Status: Professional; Nonprofit
Volunteer Staff: 25
Paid Artists: 50
Budget: $140,000
Income Sources: Ticket Sales; Individuals; Grants; Corporations
Performs At: Thomas Jefferson Community Theatre
Affiliations: Opera America; Cultural Alliance of Greater Washington; ASCAP
Organization Type: Performing; Resident

2373
VIRGINIA CHORAL SOCIETY
PO Box 1742
Newport News, VA 23601
Phone: 757-851-9114
e-mail: marketing@vachoralsociety.org
Web Site: www.vachoralsociety.org
Officers:
  Secretary: Sarah Kressaty
  Treasurer: Al Schweizer II
  VCS Chorus President: Mark Sink
Management:
  Artistic Director: James Powers
  Managing Director: Charles Bump
  Director Of Programming: Lou DeGrace
  Director Of Personnel: James Branstetter
  Artistic Director: Diana Snider
  Artistic Director: James Powers
Mission: The goal of the Virginia Choral Society is to foster a broader awareness of vocal music in the community; cooperate with other groups in support of the arts; and continue our long tradition of presenting only the finest compositions from our rich choral heritage.
Founded: 1931
Specialized Field: Choral
Status: Nonprofit
Paid Staff: 2
Income Sources: Ticket Sales; Grants; Various Fund-Raising Activities
Organization Type: Performing

2374
VIRGINIA OPERA
160 E Virginia Beach Boulevard
Norfolk, VA 23510
Mailing Address: PO Box 2580, Norfolk, VA 23501
Phone: 757-627-9545
Fax: 757-622-0058
Toll-free: 866-673-7282
e-mail: info@vaopera.org
Web Site: www.vaopera.org
Officers:
  President and CEO: Russell P. Allen
Management:
  Artistic Director: Peter Mark
  Associate Artistic Director: Joseph Walsh
  General Director: Paul A Stuhlreyer
  Artistic Advisor: Robin Thompson
Mission: The mission of Virginia Opera is to attract, educate, develop and engage a diverse base of audiences, volunteers and professionals through the promotion and production of quality opera performances in the commonwealth of Virginia.
Utilizes: Guest Artists; Guest Companies; Singers
Founded: 1974
Specialized Field: Grand Opera; Light Opera; Lyric Opera; Choral; Classical
Status: Non-Profit, Professional
Paid Staff: 120
Budget: $4.8 million
Income Sources: Cultural Arts Alliance of Greater Hampton Roads; Opera America; American Arts Alliance; Patrons; Donors; Corporations; Grants
Performs At: Harrison Opera House; Carpenter Center; GMU
Organization Type: Performing; Touring; Educational

2375
VIRGINIA SYMPHONY CHORUS
150 Boush Street
Suite 201
Norfolk, VA 23510
Phone: 757-466-3060
Fax: 757-466-3046
Web Site: www.virginiasymphony.org
Officers:
  Chairman: Rony Thomas
  Chair: Stephen G. Test
  Treasurer: Elizabeth Foster
  Secretary: Susan Goode
  Director: Bert Aaron
Management:
  President and Executive Director: Eric Borenstein
  Music Director: Joanne Fallete
  Resident Conductor: Benjamin Rous
  Director Of Finance: Brad Kirkpatric
  Chorusmaster: Robert Shoup
Mission: To perform symphonic choral repertoire.
Founded: 1920
Specialized Field: Choral

2376
VOCE CHAMBER SINGERS
P.O. Box 8544
Reston, VA 20195-2444
Phone: 703-277-7772
e-mail: info@voce.org
Web Site: voce.org
Officers:
  President: Keyona Taylor
  Treasurer: Gretchen Newman
  Artistic Team Lead: Jane Waldrop
  Production Team Lead: Kathy Brown
  Marketing Team Lead: Jennifer Wells
Management:
  Executive Director: Joan Winter Skerritt, jskeritt@voce.org
  Artistic Director: Richard Giarusso
  Accompanist: CJ Capen
Mission: Voce Chamber Singers is dedicated to presenting the highest caliber of chamber choral music of all musical periods from around the globe and to commissioning new choral works.
Founded: 1989
Specialized Field: Chamber; Choral
Status: Nonprofit; Professional

2377
OPERA ROANOKE
541 Luck Avenue
Suite 209
Roanoke, VA 24065
Phone: 540-982-2742
Fax: 540-982-3601
e-mail: info@operaroanoke.org
Web Site: www.operaroanoke.org
Officers:
  President: Jeffery A. Marks
  VP: Amanda Crotty
  Treasurer: Bruce Johnson
  Secretary: Sally Godsey
Management:
  President: Joseph Logan III
  Executive Director: G Ronald Kastner
  General & Artisic Director: Scott Williamson, D.M.A
  Principal Guest Conductor: Steven White
  Development & Marketing Director: Teresa Carpentieri
Mission: Providing Southwestern Virginia with professional opera.
Utilizes: Guest Companies
Founded: 1977
Specialized Field: Opera
Status: Non-Profit, Professional
Paid Staff: 4
Paid Artists: 250
Budget: $500,000
Income Sources: Box Office; Grants; Individual Donations
Performs At: Shaftman Performance Hall
Facility Category: Performance Hall
Type of Stage: Proscenium
Seating Capacity: 950
Year Remodeled: 2000
Cost: $9.5 Million
Organization Type: Performing; Resident

2378
WOLF TRAP OPERA COMPANY
1645 Trap Road
Vienna, VA 22182-2063
Phone: 703-255-1900
Fax: 703-255-1896
e-mail: wolftrap@wolftrap.org
Web Site: www.wolftrap.org
Officers:
  Chairman: John C. Lee, IV
  President and CEO: Terrence D. Jones
  Vice Chairman and Secretary: Gil Guarino
Management:
  Director: Kim Pensinger Witman
  Program Coordinator: Lee Anne Myslewski

VOCAL MUSIC / Washington

Utilizes: Guest Composers; Guest Designers; Multimedia; Resident Artists; Resident Professionals; Sign Language Translators
Founded: 1971
Specialized Field: Grand Opera; Opera
Status: Non-Profit, Professional
Performs At: Barns of Wolf Trap; Filene Center
Seating Capacity: 350; 7,000

2379
LYRIC OPERA VIRGINIA
2610 Potters Road, Suite 200
Virginia Beach, VA 23452
Phone: 757-446-6666
Fax: 757-961-4283
e-mail: jwalsh@lyricoperavirginia.org
Web Site: lyricoperavirginia.org
Management:
   General/Artistic Director: Joseph Walsh, jwalsh@lyricoperavirginia.org
   Office Manager: Brooke Liss, bliss@lyricoperavirginia.org
   Company Manager: Trentnon Smith, tsmith@lyricoperavirginia.org
Mission: The mission of Lyric Opera Virginia is to present gems of the classical and contemporary opera and musical theatre repertoires in fresh and appealing formats to both new and seasoned opera goers and training talented and promising young artists.
Specialized Field: Opera
Performs At: Oates Theater, Collegiate School; Virginia Museum Of Contemporary Art, Virginia Beach; Modlin Center For The Arts, University

2380
WINTERGREEN PERFORMING ARTS
PO Box 816
Wintergreen, VA 22958
Phone: 434-325-8292
Fax: 888-675-8238
e-mail: info@wintergreenperformingarts.org
Web Site: wintergreenperformingarts.org
Officers:
   President: Thomas W. Steele
   Vice President: Edith Wittig
   Secretary: Janet R. Jones
   Treasurer: Lawrence Luessen
   Board Member: Patricia Turnbull
   Board Member: Lois V Conrad
   Board Member: Lawrence Luessen
   Advisor: Deborah Weigle
Management:
   Artistic/Executive Director: Larry Alan Smith
   Development/Marketing Director: Karen S Quillen
   Academy Director: Joseph Nigro
   Finance Manager: Cindy Michener
   Office Assistant: Lisa Gillmore
Mission: It began on Saturday morning, June 25, 1995, at a meeting of Mountain and Valley music lovers, brought together by Sarah McCracken. At this meeting the group embarked on the writing of a mission statement and the development of a phone survey to assess the degree of community interest in bringing music to Wintergreen.
Utilizes: Arrangers; Collaborating Artists; Collaborations; Community Talent; Guest Accompanists; Guest Choreographers; Guest Companies; Guest Directors; Guest Musical Directors; Multimedia; Music; Paid Performers; Singers; Soloists
Founded: 1995
Specialized Field: Instrumental, Classical, Contemporary
Status: Non-Profit
Income Sources: Donors, Sponsors, Grants

Season: Year Round
Performs At: Lake Monocan Clubhouse, Rockfish Presbyterian Church, Veritas Winery

Washington

2381
KITSAP OPERA
PO Box 1071
Bremerton, WA 98337
Phone: 360-377-8119
e-mail: kitsaopera@gmail.com
Web Site: www.kitsaopera.org
Officers:
   President: Ron Bright
   First Vice President: Fred Karakas
   Second Vice President: Richard Coolen
   Treasurer: Margaret Eddy
   Secretary: Marilyn Mantzke
   Board Member: Rick Ellis
   Board Member: Debbi Hagardt
   Board Member: Lynn Hood
   Board Member: Rebecca Merson
Management:
   Founder/Artistic Director: Leone Cottrell-Adkins
Mission: The Kitsap Opera is an opera group in the European tradition in that we offer an intermediate step for singers between college training and major American opera companies. Mission is to give professional entertainment value to the West Sound region and afford Northwest artists an opportunity to perform major operatic roles.
Utilizes: Arrangers; Collaborations; Composers; Contract Orchestras; Multimedia; Music; Original Music Scores; Sign Language Translators; Singers
Founded: 1992
Specialized Field: Opera, Classical Opera
Status: Non-Profit
Income Sources: Donations, Sponsorships

2382
SKAGIT OPERA
P.O. Box 1756
Mount Vernon, WA 98273
Phone: 360-422-5070
e-mail: info@skagitopera.org
Web Site: skagitopera.org
Mission: Skagit Opera's mission is to produce high-quality, fully staged, professional opera productions in the Pacific Northwest. We are committed to developing a regional audience and nurturing the enjoyment of the classical voice.
Status: Nonprofit; Professional
Performs At: McIntyre Hall

2383
ESOTERICS
1815 24th Ave
Seattle, WA 98122-3014
Phone: 206-935-7779
Fax: 206-344-3327
e-mail: info@TheEsoterics.org
Web Site: www.theesoterics.org
Officers:
   President: Robert Wade
   Vice President: Joe Scott
   Secretary: Natalie Lerch
   Treasurer: Mitchell Baier
Management:
   Founding Director: Eric Banks
   Composer in Residence: Don Skirvin
   Development: Christine Bell
   Artistic Director: Eric Banks

General Manager: Scott Kovacs
Mission: Contemporary a cappella art music.
Founded: 1992
Specialized Field: Choral
Status: Nonprofit
Paid Staff: 1
Volunteer Staff: 1
Paid Artists: 4

2384
NORTHWEST CHOIRS
5031 University Way NE #NB2
Seattle, WA 98105
Phone: 206-524-3234
Fax: 206-651-3408
e-mail: nwc@northwestchoirs.org
Web Site: nwchoirs.org
Officers:
   President: Nathan Torgelson
   Vice President: Susan Stolzfus
   Secretary: Jeanne Acutanza
   Treasurer: Will Wakefield
Management:
   Music Director: Joseph Crnko
   Executive Director: Maria Johnson
Mission: To provide the highest level of music education and vocal performance opportunity to the boys, and young men and women of the Seattle region, and to provide the local community with a unique choral resource.
Founded: 1971
Specialized Field: Choral
Status: Nonprofit

2385
ORCHESTRA SEATTLE & SEATTLE CHAMBER SINGERS
PO Box 15825
Seattle, WA 98115
Phone: 206-682-5208
e-mail: osscs@osscs.org
Web Site: www.osscs.org
Officers:
   Vice-President: Paula Rimmer
   Secretary: Tom Dahlstrom
   Treasurer: Jason Hershey
Management:
   Music Director: George Shangrow
Mission: To perform as a collaborative effort between the orchestra and singers to bring skilled artistry to the Seattle community.
Founded: 1969
Specialized Field: Classical; Choral
Status: Semi-Professional
Paid Staff: 10

2386
SEATTLE CHORAL COMPANY
4759 15th Avenue
Seattle, WA 98105-4404
Phone: 206-363-8714
Fax: 206-365-8714
e-mail: scc@seattlechoralcompany.org
Web Site: seattlechoralcompany.org
Officers:
   President: Phil J. Haas
   Vice President: Joyce Kling, J.D
   Vice President: Anita Whitney
   Treasurer: Kathryn Ong
Management:
   Artistic Director: Freddie Coleman, fred.coleman@seattlechoralcomp

VOCAL MUSIC / West Virginia

Mission: The Seattle Choral Company shares the diverse spectrum of choral music with the widest possible community by presenting accessible, engaging, and informative programs that are respected for their innovation and artistic excellence.
Founded: 1982
Specialized Field: Choral
Status: Nonprofit
Organization Type: Performing; Touring

2387
SEATTLE OPERA
1020 John Street
PO Box 9248
Seattle, WA 98109
Phone: 206-389-7600
Fax: 206-389-7651
e-mail: mary.brazeau@seattleopera.org
Web Site: www.seattleopera.org
Officers:
  Chairman Emeritus: William P. Gerberding
  Vice President: Thomas H. Allen
  Vice President: Dr. Brenda Bruns
  Vice President: Steven A. Clifford
  Vice President: James D. Cullen
Management:
  General Director: Speight Jenkins
  President: William T. Weyerhaeuser
  Executive Vice President: Gerald L. Hanauer
  Treasurer: Gary Houlahan
  Secretary: Ron Hosogi
Mission: Recognized internationally for its theatrically compelling and musically accomplished performances.
Specialized Field: Opera

2388
SEATTLE PRO MUSICA
1770 Northwest 58th Street, Suite 124
Seattle, WA 98107-5218
Phone: 206-781-2766
e-mail: admin@seattlepromusica.org
Web Site: seattlepromusica.org
Management:
  Artistic/Executive Director: Karen P. Thomas
  Managing Director: Katie Skovholt
Mission: To enrich and inspire our audiences, singers, and community through the experience of choral artistry, and to increase access to and appreciation of choral music.
Founded: 1972
Specialized Field: Choral
Performs At: St.James Cathedral; Seattle Town Hall; Chapel At Bastyr University, Phinney Ridge Lutheran Church
Organization Type: Resident; Performing

2389
TACOMA OPERA ASSOCIATION
1119 Pacific Ave.
Suite 405
Tacoma, WA 98402
Phone: 235-627-7789
Fax: 253-627-1620
e-mail: info@tacomaopera.com
Web Site: www.tacomaopera.com
Officers:
  1st Vice President: Jacquelyn Giles
  VP: Wendy Phillips
  VP: Heidi Madson
  Treasurer: Douglas Dorr
  2nd Vice President / Secretary: Cynthia Branson
Management:
  President: Teresa Gutierrez
  Executive Director: Kathryn Smith

Artistic Director: Hans Wolf
Business Manager: Marian Scheele
General Director: Noel Koran
Mission: To offer residents of the South Puget Sound area light opera performed in English.
Utilizes: Grant Writers; Guest Artists; Guest Conductors; Resident Professionals; Sign Language Translators
Founded: 1968
Specialized Field: Opera
Status: Professional
Paid Staff: 4
Volunteer Staff: 4
Paid Artists: 100
Budget: $500,000
Performs At: Pantages Theater; Railto Theater
Affiliations: Opera America
Annual Attendance: 7,200
Facility Category: Renovated Vaudeville House
Type of Stage: Proscenium
Seating Capacity: 1,166
Year Built: 1920
Year Remodeled: 1983
Organization Type: Performing

2390
VASHON OPERA
10407 SW Cowan Road
Vashon, WA 98070
Phone: 206-388-2926
e-mail: info@vashonopera.org
Web Site: www.vashonopera.org
Officers:
  President: Jennifer Krikawa
  Treasurer: Tom Bardeen
  Secretary: Andrew Krikawa
  Board Member: Nancy Bachant
Management:
  Artistic Director/Founder: Jennifer Krikawa
  Baritone Performer: Andrew Krikawa
Mission: Vashon Opera's mission is to enrich our community through the creation of opera in intimate settings. The Vashon Opera was founded in November, 2008 by a small collection of opera lovers who know opera can thrive on Vashon. The process began then to incorporate as a 501(c)(3) non-for-profit organization. La BohŠme was chosen as their first production due to the members' desire to perform the famed Puccini opera.
Utilizes: Arrangers; Choreographers; Collaborating Artists; Collaborations; Composers; Local Unknown Artists; Lyricists; Multimedia; Music; Paid Performers; Sign Language Translators; Singers
Specialized Field: Classical Opera
Status: Non-Profit, Professional
Income Sources: Donors, Ticket Sales
Season: September, May

West Virginia

2391
CHARLESTON CIVIC CHORUS
209 Morris Street
Charleston, WV 25301
Phone: 304-744-5078
e-mail: thedaltons@yahoo.com
Web Site: www.charleston-civic-chorus.com
Officers:
  President: C Conrad Haskell
  Vice President: Jim Merrill
  Treasurer: Evan Buck
Management:
  Artistic Director/Conductor: J Truman Dalton

Accompanist: Randall L. Peters
Mission: To perform high-quality choral classics as well as some lighter fare.
Founded: 1952
Specialized Field: Choral; Classical; Contemporary
Status: Non-Profit, Non-Professional
Paid Staff: 2
Paid Artists: 2
Performs At: The Baptist Temple
Organization Type: Performing; Resident

2392
WEST VIRGINIA SYMPHONY CHORUS
PO Box 2292
Charleston, WV 25328
Phone: 304-561-3500
Fax: 304-561-3598
e-mail: info@wvsymphony.org
Web Site: www.wvsymphony.org
Officers:
  Chairman: John Elliot
  Vice Chairman: Cindy McGhee
  Treasurer/Secretary: Charles R. Hageboeck
Management:
  Director: Joseph Janisch
  Marketing and Communications Manag: Christina Kast
  Donor Relations Manager: Kortney Smith
  Grants Manager: Rebecca Roth
Mission: To assist the West Virginia Symphony Orchestra in performing major choral and orchestral works of high quality artistry.
Specialized Field: Choral
Status: Non-Profit

Wisconsin

2393
NEWVOICES
111 West College Avenue, 4th Floor
Appleton, WI 54912-0221
Mailing Address: P.O. Box 221 Appleton, WV, 54912-0221
Phone: 920-832-9700
e-mail: info@newvoiceschoir.org
Web Site: newvoiceschoir.org
Officers:
  President: Mary Schmidt
  Vice President: Nanci Micke
  Secretary: Jenni Eickelberg
  Treasurer: Liz Sumnicht
Management:
  Executive Director: Jeanie Kurka Reimer
  Artistic Director/Conductor: Phillip A. Swan
  Assistant Conductor: John Stangel
  Assistant Conductor: Dan Van Sickle
  Accompanist: Karen Stangel
Mission: NewVoices presents outstanding choral music and provides significant artistic, educational and entertaining experiences, enriching our performers and our audiences.
Founded: 1978
Specialized Field: Choral
Status: Nonprofit
Non-paid Artists: 75
Organization Type: Regional; Performing

2394
MILWAUKEE OPERA THEATRE
P.O. Box 182
Elm Grove, WI 53122

VOCAL MUSIC / Wisconsin

Phone: 917-684-0512
e-mail: jillanna@milwaukeeoperatheatre.org
Web Site: milwaukeeoperatheatre.org
Officers:
  President: James Zager
  Administrative Vice President: Nathan Wesselowski
  Recording Secretary: Amanda Garry Aliperta
  Treasurer: Kim Zick
Management:
  Producing Artistic Director: Jill Anna Ponasik
  Company Manager: Danny Polaski
Mission: Creating dynamic, singer-centered art; exploring the beauty of the human voice; sparking the imagination of both audiences and artists; and transforming the bountiful landscape of classic and contemporary lyric theatre.
Founded: 1998
Specialized Field: Opera
Status: Professional; Nonprofit

2395
MADISON OPERA
335 W. Mifflin Street
Madison, WI 53703
Phone: 608-238-8085
Fax: 608-233-3431
e-mail: info@madisonopera.org
Web Site: www.madisonopera.org
Officers:
  President: Stephen Hurley
  VP: Phillip Certain
  Secretary: Sally Miley
  Treasurer: Joyce Hirsch
  Immediate Past President: Fran Klos
Management:
  Director Development: Beth Tolles
  Executive Director: Ann Stanke
  General Director: Kathryn Smith
  Artistic Director: John DeMain
  Manager of Marketing and Community: Ronia Holmes
Mission: To bring quality opera, locally produced, to the city of Madison.
Utilizes: Actors; Commissioned Music; Guest Composers; Guest Designers; Guest Lecturers; Guest Musicians; Guest Writers; Original Music Scores; Singers
Founded: 1962
Specialized Field: Grand Opera
Status: Non-Profit, Professional
Paid Staff: 10
Paid Artists: 175
Budget: $900,000
Income Sources: Opera America
Performs At: Oscar Meyer Theatre
Organization Type: Performing; Educational

2396
OPERA FOR THE YOUNG
6441 Enterprise Lane
Suite 207
Madison, WI 53719
Phone: 608-277-9560
Fax: 608-277-9570
e-mail: info@operafortheyoung.org
Web Site: www.operafortheyoung.org
Officers:
  President: Jason Stephens
  Vice President: Barbara Schrank
  Secretary: Selma Van Eyck
  Treasurer: Margaret Bomber
Management:
  Artistic Director: Diane Garton Edie
  Managing Director: Dan Plummer
  General Director: Dan Plummer
  Finance Manager: Sarah Smogoleski
Mission: To engage and educate children about opera with school based performances, to involve students in performance, to provide professional opportunities for emerging artists and to foster the creativity for new opera targeting young audiences.
Utilizes: Sign Language Translators
Founded: 1970
Specialized Field: Classical
Status: Non-Profit, Professional
Paid Staff: 4
Paid Artists: 20
Budget: $235,000
Income Sources: School Fees; Grants
Performs At: Tour To Elementary Schools
Annual Attendance: 80,000
Organization Type: Performing; Touring; Educational

2397
BEL CANTO CHORUS
158 North Broadway Avenue
Milwaukee, WI 53202
Phone: 414-481-8801
Fax: 414-481-8807
e-mail: info@belcanto.org
Web Site: www.belcanto.org
Officers:
  President: Martin Tierney
  Secretary: Marc Cohen
  Treasurer: Jim Hyland
  Director: Joshua Blakely
  Director: Sequoya Borgman
Management:
  Music Director: Richard Haynson
  Assistant Conductor: Michelle Hynson
  Boy Choir Director: Ellen M Shuler
  Executive Director: Nina M. Jones
  Education & Outreach Manager: Rebecca Whitney
Mission: To enrich the lives of its audiences and its singing members through the outstanding live presentation of the finest choral music and to reach out to the community in order to share the benefits and joy of the singing arts.
Utilizes: Sign Language Translators
Founded: 1931
Specialized Field: Choral; Classical; Religious
Status: Non-Profit, Professional
Paid Staff: 3
Volunteer Staff: 10
Paid Artists: 10
Non-paid Artists: 800
Budget: $400,000
Performs At: Churches; Performing Arts Centers
Affiliations: Chorus America, UPAF
Facility Category: Various

2398
FLORENTINE OPERA COMPANY
930 E. Burleigh Street
Lower Level
Milwaukee, WI 53212
Phone: 414-291-5700
Fax: 414-291-5706
Toll-free: 800-326-7372
e-mail: info@florentineopera.org
Web Site: www.florentineopera.org
Officers:
  President: Mark Cameli
  Director Of Finance: Catherine Krekhofer
  Past President: Clay Nesler
  VP/Governance: Adam Wiensch
  VP/Audience Development: Karen Plunkett Muenster
Management:
  General Director: William Florescu
  Marketing Director: Cindy Hosale
  Principal Conductor & Artistic Adv: Joseph Rescigno
  Director of Artistic Administration: Lisa Kay Hanson
  Chorus Master & Associate Conductor: Scott Stewart
Mission: Producing Grand Opera for Wisconsin.
Utilizes: Artists-in-Residence; Collaborations; Dance Companies; Dancers; Designers; Educators; Fine Artists; Grant Writers; Guest Artists; Guest Companies; Guest Composers; Guest Conductors; Guest Instructors; Guest Musical Directors; Guest Musicians; Instructors; Local Artists; Lyricists; Multimedia; New Productions; Organization Contracts; Original Music Scores; Sign Language Translators; Soloists; Students; Touring Companies; Visual Arts
Founded: 1933
Specialized Field: Grand Opera
Status: Professional; Nonprofit
Paid Staff: 15
Paid Artists: 175
Budget: $3.2 million
Income Sources: Private Foundations; Grants; Endowments; Business/Corporate Donations; Government Grants; Individual Donations
Performs At: Marcus Center for the Performing Arts
Affiliations: Opera America; Downtown Theatre District; UPAF
Annual Attendance: 23,000 - 24,000
Seating Capacity: 2,219
Organization Type: Performing; Touring; Educational

THEATRE / Alabama

Alabama

2399
COMMUNITY ACTORS' STUDIO THEATRE INC.
P.O. Box 185
Anniston, AL 36202
Phone: 256-820-2278
e-mail: castalabama@gmail.com
Web Site: castalabama.com
Management:
    Artistic Director: Kimberly Dobbs
Mission: The mission of CAST is to entertain, inform, and educate, thereby enriching the cultural life of North East Alabama. CAST shall provide area residents the opportunity both to attend and to participate in quality presentations of a cross-section of the finest theatrical works available.
Founded: 2003
Status: Volunteer
Performs At: McClellan Auditorium 100 Gamecock Drive, Anniston, AL 36205

2400
AUBURN UNIVERSITY THEATRE
Auburn University
School of Fine Arts, Auburn University
Auburn, AL 36849
Phone: 334-844-4000
Fax: 334-844-4939
e-mail: theatre@auburn.edu
Web Site: www.cla.auburn.edu/theatre
Officers:
    Associate Professor & Chair: Phillips M Scott
Management:
    Chair: John Varner
    Marketing Manager: Bell Linda
    Associate Professor: Jaffe Robin
    Associate Professor: Qualls Chris
Founded: 1856
Specialized Field: Educational; Musical; Comedy; Drama
Budget: $3,000-$5,000
Affiliations: NAST; ATHE
Seating Capacity: 370
Year Built: 1973

2401
BIRMINGHAM CHILDREN'S THEATRE
PO Box 1362
Birmingham, AL 35201
Mailing Address: PO Box 1362
Phone: 205-458-8181
Fax: 205-458-8895
e-mail: jack@bct123.org
Web Site: www.bct123.org
Officers:
    President: Guin Robinson
    First VP: Shannon Lisenby
    Second VP: Glenda E. Nagrodzk
    Third VP: Gaile Pugh Gratton
    Secretary: Marcie Braswell
    Treasurer: Tim Coker
Management:
    Managing Director: Bert Brosowsky
    Administrator: Vivian S Lyle
    House Manager / School Groups Coord: Teresa Shepperd
    Director of Finance: Stephanie Murphy
Mission: The Birmingham Children's Theatre is a professional company providing quality theatre for young people which incorporates literature, art, music and drama into a medium that is both entertaining and educational.
Utilizes: Actors; Artists-in-Residence; Choreographers; Collaborating Artists; Collaborations; Commissioned Composers; Commissioned Music; Composers-in-Residence; Dancers; Designers; Educators; Five Seasonal Concerts; Guest Accompanists; Guest Artists; Guest Choreographers; Guest Companies; Guest Conductors; Guest Designers; Guest Directors; Guest Ensembles; Guest Instructors; Guest Lecturers; Guest Teachers; Instructors; Local Artists; Local Unknown Artists; Lyricists; Multimedia; Music; Organization Contracts; Original Music Scores; Performance Artists; Poets; Resident Professionals; Selected Students; Sign Language Translators; Singers; Student Interns; Special Technical Talent; Theatre Companies
Founded: 1947
Specialized Field: Children's Theater
Status: Non-Profit
Paid Staff: 25
Paid Artists: 50
Budget: $1,425,000
Income Sources: City, County, State, Grants, Corporate, Individuals, Ticket Sales, Tour Revenue
Performs At: Civic Center Theatre; Black Box; Studio Theatre
Annual Attendance: 450,000
Facility Category: Civic Convention Center
Type of Stage: Flex Trust
Stage Dimensions: 140'w x 60'd
Seating Capacity: 250 - 1,100
Year Built: 1974
Year Remodeled: 1997
Organization Type: Performing; Touring; Resident; Educational; Sponsoring

2402
GARDEN VARIETY SHAKESPEARE
Birmingham Botanical Gardens
2126 Lane Park Road
Birmingham, AL 35226
Mailing Address: PO Box 531034, Birnigham, AL. 35253
Phone: 205-879-1227
Specialized Field: Shakespeare; Outdoor Theater

2403
UNIVERSITY OF ALABAMA, BIRMINGHAM: DEPARTMENT OF THEATRE
ASC 255 1200 10th Avenue S
Birmingham, AL 35294-1263
Phone: 205-934-3236
Fax: 205-934-8076
Web Site: www.theatre.hum.uab.edu
Officers:
    Chair: Will York
Founded: 1969
Specialized Field: Educational; Theater Workshops
Status: Non-Profit, Non-Professional
Paid Staff: 23
Seating Capacity: 350
Year Built: 1999

2404
PRINCESS THEATRE CENTER FOR THE PERFORMING ARTS
112 Second Avenue NE
Decatur, AL 25601
Phone: 256-350-1745
e-mail: info@princesstheatre.org
Web Site: princesstheatre.org
Founded: 1887
Status: Nonprofit

2405
SOUTHEAST ALABAMA COMMUNITY THEATRE
PO Box 6065
Dothan, AL 36302
Phone: 334-794-0400
Fax: 334-794-0400
e-mail: seact@seact.com
Web Site: www.seact.com
Officers:
    President: Wayne Patterson
    Vice President: Russell Brooks
    Treasurer: Amy Vinson
    Secretary: David Arnett
Management:
    General Manager: Jennifer Doherty
Mission: To provide Southeast Alabama with performing theatre.
Founded: 1974
Specialized Field: Musical; Comedy; Community Theater; Contemporary
Status: Non-Profit, Non-Professional
Paid Staff: 2
Performs At: Dothan Opera House
Organization Type: Performing

2406
LOONEY'S TAVERN PRODUCTIONS
22400 Highway 278 E
Double Springs, AL 35553
Phone: 205-489-5000
Fax: 205-489-3500
Toll-free: 800-566-6397
e-mail: info@looneystavern.com
Web Site: www.looneystavern.com
Officers:
    President/CEO: Dwain Moody
Mission: To produce live performances of stage plays to include drama, comedy, musical.
Founded: 1989
Specialized Field: Drama; Comedy; Musical
Status: Non-Equity
Paid Staff: 8
Volunteer Staff: 10
Paid Artists: 50
Budget: $500,000
Income Sources: Sales
Season: Year-round
Performs At: Amphitheater; Indoor Theatre
Annual Attendance: 25,000
Type of Stage: Amphitheatre; Theatre
Stage Dimensions: 90'x 40'
Seating Capacity: 1500; 275
Rental Contact: President/CEO Dwain Moody

2407
UNIVERSITY OF NORTH ALABAMA: DEPARTMENT OF MUSIC & THEATRE
UNA Box 5011
Florence, AL 35632-0001
Mailing Address: PO Box 5007, University of North Alabama, Florence, AL 35632
Phone: 256-765-4516
Fax: 256-765-4839
Toll-free: 800-825-5862
e-mail: dmmccullough@una.edu
Web Site: http://www.una.edu/m

Management:
    Chair: David McCullough
Mission: As an accredited institutional member of the National Association of Schools of Music, the UNA Department of Music and Theatre has much to offer—outstanding faculty, exceptional performing ensembles and quality degree programs, including professional degree programs in music education and liberal arts degree programs in music performance and commercial music.
Specialized Field: Music. Theatre
Budget: $2,500-12,000
Seating Capacity: 1700
Year Built: 1969

2408
BROADWAY THEATRE
700 Monroe Street
Huntsville, AL 35801
Phone: 256-518-6155
Fax: 256-551-2990
Web Site: www.broadwaytheatreleague.org
Management:
    Director: Jean S Warren
    Executive Director: Andrew Willmon
    Membership Director: Barry Sublett
    Office Manager: Pennie Wood
    Marketing Director: Amy Jones
Founded: 1959
Specialized Field: Musical; Comedy; Drama
Status: For-Profit, Professional

2409
SAENGER THEATRE
250 Conti Street
Mobile, AL 36602
Phone: 251-208-5600
Fax: 334-433-2087
e-mail: cla.williams@cityofmobile.org
Web Site: www.centrefortheUvingarts.com
Officers:
    Chairman: Mike Rogers
    Treasurer: Meg McGovern
Management:
    General Manager: Mihael D Maxwell
    Executive Director: Robert L. Sain
    Director of Development: Daryn Glassbrook
    Development Coordinator: Elaine Williams
Specialized Field: Drama; Musical

2410
UNIVERSITY OF SOUTH ALABAMA
307 University Boulevard N
Mobile, AL 36688-0002
Phone: 251-460-6101
Fax: 334-461-1511
e-mail: webmaster@usouthal.edu
Officers:
    Department Chair: Dr. Eugene R Jackson
Management:
    President: Gordon Moulton
    Assoc VP: David Stearns
Founded: 1963
Specialized Field: Educational; Theater Workshops
Budget: $17,000-$23,000
Affiliations: ATHE; Alabama Lyric Theatre
Seating Capacity: 180; 800
Year Built: 1999

2411
UNIVERSITY OF MONTEVALLO: DIVISION OF THEATRE
University of Montevallo
Station 6210
Montevallo, AL 35115
Mailing Address: Box 6210, Univ. of Montevallo, Montevallo, AL 35115
Phone: 205-665-6210
Fax: 205-665-6211
e-mail: Callaghand@montevallo.edu
Web Site: www.montevallo.edu/thea
Management:
    Chairman of the Department: Randy Schott
    Director of Theatre: David Callaghan
    Staff Accompanist and Musical Direc: Laurie Middaugh
Specialized Field: Educational; Theater Workshops
Status: Non-Profit, Non-Professional
Paid Staff: 6
Paid Artists: 6
Budget: $4,000-$19,000
Seating Capacity: 1200
Year Built: 1931
Year Remodeled: 1978

2412
AUBURN UNIVERSITY MONTGOMERY THEATRE
Department Communication, Dramatic Arts
Montgomery, AL 36124
Mailing Address: PO Box 244023
Phone: 334-244-3000
Fax: 334-244-3740
Toll-free: 800-227-649
e-mail: martie.mcenerney@aum.edu
Web Site: www.aum.edu
Management:
    Head of Theatre: Bob Gaines
    Department Head: Robert A Gaines
    Vice Chancellor for Advancement: Carolyn C. Golden
    AssVice Chancellor for Advancement: Marilyn Ray
    Senior Development Manager: Martie McEnergy
Founded: 1967
Specialized Field: Comedy; Classic; Contemporary
Status: Non-Profit, Non-Professional
Paid Staff: 600
Budget: $2,000
Affiliations: Alabama Shakespeare Festival
Seating Capacity: 180
Year Built: 1979

2413
VIRGINIA SAMFORD THEATRE
1116 26th Street
South Birmingham, AL 35205
Phone: 205-251-1206
e-mail: info@virginiasamfordtheatre.org
Web Site: virginiasamfordtheatre.org
Mission: The Virginia Stamford Theatre's mission is to further the cultural opportunities for the Greater Birmingham community through arts education and performances of high artistic merit in Theatre, Music, and Dance.
Founded: 1927

2414
THEATRE TUSCALOOSA
9500 Old Greensboro Road #135
Tuscaloosa, AL 35405
Phone: 205-391-2277
e-mail: tickets@theatretusc.com
Web Site: theatretusc.com
Mission: To elevate the consciousness of theater in the greater Tuscaloosa community by providing quality theater opportunities for people interested in participating in live theater and contributing to the cultural education, entertainment, and enrichment of the community through attending live theater.
Founded: 1971

Alaska

2415
ANCHORAGE COMMUNITY THEATRE
1133 E 70th Avenue
Anchorage, AK 99518-2353
Phone: 907-344-4713
Fax: 907-344-6002
e-mail: acthome@gci.net
Web Site: www.actalaska.org
Officers:
    President: Brian Saylor
    Vice President: Paul S. Wilcox
    Treasurer: Len Lambert
    Secretary: Kevin Bennett
Management:
    Executive Director: Bill Cotton
    Assistant Executive Director: Shareen Crosby
    Technical Director: Terence Lindeke
    Volunteer & Education Coordinator: Kate Williams
Mission: Building community through theatre since 1953.
Founded: 1953
Specialized Field: Community Theater
Status: Non-Profit, Non-Professional
Paid Staff: 1
Performs At: Live Theatre
Annual Attendance: 6,000

2416
CYRANO'S THEATRE COMPANY
413 D Street
Anchorage, AK 99501
Phone: 907-274-2599
Fax: 907-277-4698
e-mail: scarlet-cyranos@ak.net
Web Site: www.cyranos.org
Management:
    Producer: Sandy Harper
Founded: 1992
Specialized Field: Drama; Comedy; Musical
Performs At: Cyrano's Off Center Playhouse
Type of Stage: Black Box
Seating Capacity: 86

2417
OUT NORTH - VSA ALASKA
3800 De Barr Road
Anchorage, AK 99508-2011
Phone: 907-279-8099
Fax: 907-279-8100
e-mail: art@outnorth.org
Web Site: www.outnorth.org
Management:
    Executive Artistic Director: Scott Schofield
    Director Of Operations: Eyvette Flynn
Mission: Out North exists to develop and present bold new work that challenges and changes the art, the artist, and the audience. We encourage artistic

THEATRE / Arizona

risk-taking and collaboration, examining today's world through diverse culturel perspectives, and creative community through the arts.
Founded: 1985
Specialized Field: Youth Theater; Ethnic Theater; Community Theater; Contemporary
Status: Non-Profit, Professional
Paid Staff: 5
Volunteer Staff: 50
Paid Artists: 12
Budget: $300,000
Income Sources: Ticket Sales; Government Grants; Private Foundations; Individual Donations
Performs At: Theatre; Film; Fine Arts
Affiliations: National Alliance for Media Arts & Culture; National Performance Network; National Association of Artists Organizations
Annual Attendance: 8,000
Facility Category: Multidisciplinary
Type of Stage: Flexible black box
Seating Capacity: 99
Year Built: 1958
Year Remodeled: 1994
Organization Type: Performing; Educational

2418

UNIVERSITY OF ALASKA, ANCHORAGE: DEPARTMENT OF THEATRE AND DANCE

3211 Providence Drive
Anchorage, AK 99508
Phone: 907-786-1792
Fax: 907-786-1799
Web Site: http://theatre.uaa.alaska.edu/index.html
Officers:
  Assistant Professor, Scenic Design/: Daniel Carlgren
  Professor, Director: David Edgecombe
  Professor, Director, Costume Design: Colleen Metzger
  Professor, Director, Department Cha: Tom T. Skore
Management:
  Assistant Professor: Carlgren Daniel
  Fine Arts Building Manager: Cussin Cedar
  Term Dance Instructor: Kramer Katherine
  Assistant Professor: Metzger Colleen
  Professor: Edgecombe David
Mission: The UAA Theatre program offers a well-rounded liberal arts approach in its curriculum, with courses covering all the basic areas of theatrical endeavor, including acting, directing, stagecraft, scene design, lighting, costuming, makeup, dramatic literature, theatre history, dramatic theory and criticism, and playwriting.
Specialized Field: Educational; Theater Workshops
Budget: $11,000-$26,000
Affiliations: ATHE
Seating Capacity: 171; 99
Year Built: 1986

2419

PERSEVERANCE THEATRE

914 Third Street
Douglas, AK 99824
Phone: 907-364-2421
Fax: 907-364-2603
e-mail: info@perseverancetheatre.org
Web Site: www.perseverancetheatre.org
Officers:
  President: Terry Cramer
  Vice President: Robin Walz Walz
  Treasurer: Kate Bowns

Technology Director: Erik Chadwell
Marketing Director & Artistic Assoc: Bostin Christopher
Asst. Technical Director: Earnest Eckerson
Production Manager: Kathleen Harper
Founded: 1979
Specialized Field: Drama; Comedy; Musical
Status: Non-Profit, Professional
Paid Staff: 10
Paid Artists: 19

2420

UNIVERSITY OF ALASKA, FAIRBANKS: THEATRE DEPARTMENT

311 Tanana Drive
PO Box 755700
Fairbanks, AK 99775-5700
Mailing Address: PO Box 775700, Fairbanks, AK 99775
Phone: 907-474-6590
Fax: 907-474-7048
e-mail: theatre.film@alaska.edu
Web Site: www.uaf.edu/theatre
Officers:
  Theatre Department Chair: Tara Maginnis
  Assistant Professor of Theatre: Brian Cook
  Assistant Professor of Theatre: Bethany Max
  Professor of Theatre & Films: Kade Mendelowitz
  Department Coordinator: Kim Eames
Management:
  Associate Professor of Performance: Carrie Baker
  Technical Director: Kade Mendelowitz
  Director of Film Program: Maya Salganek
  Film Faculty: Miho Aaoki
  Film Faculty: Robert Prince
Founded: 1965
Specialized Field: Educational; Theater Workshops
Status: Non-Profit, Non-Professional
Paid Staff: 7
Paid Artists: 5
Budget: $3,700-$11,000
Affiliations: Fairbanks Drama Associates & Children's Theatre; Fairbanks Shakespeare Theatre; Fairbanks Light Opera Theatre Summer Fine Arts Camp
Seating Capacity: 480; 110;
Year Built: 1968

2421

LYNN CANAL COMMUNITY PLAYERS

PO Box 1030
Haines, AK 99827
Phone: 907-766-2708
Fax: 907-766-2425
Officers:
  Treasurer: Annette Smith
  Secretary: Jane Sebena
  President: Kathy Pashigan
  VP: Tod Sebens
  President: Jerrie Clarke
Management:
  President: Mark Sebens
  Managing Director: Annette Smith
  Secretary: Annette Smith
Mission: Performing in and sponsoring all forms of theatre; hosting the biennial presentation of the Alaska Community Theatre Festival.
Utilizes: Guest Companies; Singers
Founded: 1957
Specialized Field: Musical; Comedy; Youth Theater; Dinner Theater; Community Theater; Contemporary
Status: Non-Profit, Non-Professional
Paid Staff: 1
Volunteer Staff: 1

Income Sources: Arts Southeast
Performs At: Chilkat Center for the Arts
Organization Type: Performing

Arizona

2422

NORTHERN ARIZONA UNIVERSITY: THEATRE DIVISION, SCHOOL OF PERFORMING ARTS

PO Box 6040 Building 37
Room 120
Flagstaff, AZ 86011
Phone: 928-523-3781
Fax: 928-523-5111
e-mail: Theatre@nau.edu
Web Site: www.nau.edu/cal/theatre/
Officers:
  Dean: Michael Vincent
  Associate Dean: Jean Boreen
  Marketing/Coordinator: Elizabeth Hellstern
  Director of Development: Marjorie Kamine
  Department Chair, Theatre Professor: Kathleen M. McGeever
Management:
  Assistant Professor of Practice,Tec: Ben Alexander
  Assistant Professor,Scenic and Prop: Patrick Battles
  Assistant Professor,Costume Design: Kate Ellis
  Assistant Technical Director, Shop: Benjamin W. Grohs
Mission: Offers students the broadest possible understanding of the art and craft of theatre through creative, critical, and applied practice
Specialized Field: Educational; Theater Workshops
Budget: $5,000-$9,650
Affiliations: ATHE
Seating Capacity: 300; 120
Year Built: 1968
Year Remodeled: 1999

2423

HALE CENTRE THEATRE

50 W. Page Avenue
Gilbert, AZ 85233
Phone: 480-497-1181
Fax: 480-497-0277
Web Site: haletheatrearizona.com
Opened: 2003

2424

ARIZONA BROADWAY THEATRE

7701 West Paradise Lane
Peoria, AZ 85382
Phone: 623-776-8400
Fax: 623-776-9974
e-mail: info@azbroadwaytheatre.com
Web Site: azbroadway.org
Mission: Arizona Broadway Theatre enriches lives through the power of the performing arts by producing live theatre and other high quality entertainment.
Status: Nonprofit

2425

THEATER WORKS

8355 West Peoria Avenue
Peoria, AZ 85345
Phone: 623-815-1791
Fax: 623-815-9043
e-mail: dschay@theaterworks.org
Web Site: www.theaterworks.org/

Officers:
- **CEO:** Michael Foulds
- **President:** Robert T Root
- **VP:** David Lunch
- **Treasurer:** Vicky Holly
- **Secretary:** Linda Kidwell
- **Technical Director:** Andrew Nunemacher
- **Director of Sales and Marketing:** Christie King
- **Artistic Director:** Robyn Allen
- **Executive Director:** Dan Schay

Management:
- **Executive Director:** Dan Schay
- **Artistic Director:** Scott Campbell
- **Director of Outreach & Education:** Chris Hambey
- **Marketing & Public Relation:** Skye Fallon
- **Production Manager:** Paris Rhoad

Mission: To provide a diversified, strikingly creative performing arts program of the highest quality, accessible to all in the community.
Utilizes: Actors; Dancers; Resident Professionals; Sign Language Translators; Soloists
Founded: 1986
Specialized Field: Community Theater; Drama; Comedy
Status: Non professional; Nonprofit
Paid Staff: 8
Volunteer Staff: 100
Non-paid Artists: 70
Income Sources: Local Corporations; Arts Commissions; Patrons; Donations
Annual Attendance: 30,000
Seating Capacity: 150

2426
ACTORS THEATRE OF PHOENIX
222 E Monroe
PO Box 1924
Phoenix, AZ 85001
Mailing Address: PO Box 1924, Phoenix, AZ. 85001-1924
Phone: 602-253-6701
Fax: 602-254-9577
e-mail: info@actorstheatrephx.org
Web Site: www.actorstheatrephx.org
Officers:
- **Director Marketing:** Janice Sweeter

Management:
- **Producing Artistic Director:** Matthew Wiener

Mission: Actors Theater of Phoenix is unique in its presentation of contemporary professional theatre that amplifies the cultural conversation of our communities with powerful and innovative programming
Utilizes: Actors; AEA Actors; Choreographers; Guest Companies; Guest Conductors; Guest Designers; Local Artists; Local Artists & Directors; Music; Original Music Scores; Playwrights; Resident Professionals; Selected Students; Student Interns
Founded: 1985
Opened: 1985
Specialized Field: Political Comedy; Thenic Theater; Contemporary
Status: Non-Profit, Professional
Paid Staff: 8
Paid Artists: 40
Budget: $1.1 million
Income Sources: Ticket Sales; Donations; Grants
Performs At: Herberger Theater Center; Stage West
Affiliations: Theatre Communications Group
Type of Stage: Proscenium
Stage Dimensions: 34'x40'
Seating Capacity: 300
Year Built: 1989
Year Remodeled: 2010

Rental Contact: Herberger Theatre Center Shannon O'Hara
Organization Type: Performing

2427
PRESCOTT FINE ARTS
The Corner of Marina and Willis
208 North Marina Street
Prescott, AZ 86301
Phone: 928-445-3286
Fax: 928-778-7888
e-mail: pfaadirector@qwest.net
Web Site: www.pfaa.net
Officers:
- **President:** Sharon Carlin
- **Secretary:** Sandy Moss
- **Treasurer:** Vacant
- **Board Member:** Brad Christensen
- **Board Member:** Lauren Crawford
- **Board Member:** Maryann Dutton

Management:
- **Executive Director:** Jon Meyer, director@pca-az.net
- **Operations Manager:** Jean Maissen, operations@pca-az.net
- **Box Office Manager:** Suzy Campbell, tickets@pfaa.net
- **Technical Director:** Cason Murphy

Mission: To offer cultural and artistic activities.
Utilizes: Actors; Curators; Educators; Fine Artists; High School Drama; Local Artists
Founded: 1969
Specialized Field: Theatre and Music
Status: Nonprofit
Paid Staff: 4
Non-paid Artists: 600
Budget: $225,000
Income Sources: Ticket sales, Grants, Donations
Season: Year Round
Annual Attendance: 20,000
Facility Category: Historic Church
Type of Stage: Proscenium
Seating Capacity: 194
Year Built: 1894
Resident Groups: Yavapai County, North central Arizona

2428
ARIZONA STATE UNIVERSITY THEATRE
Arizona State University
PO Box 872002
Tempe, AZ 85287-2002
Mailing Address: PO Box 872002, Tempe, AZ 85287
Phone: 480-965-5337
Fax: 480-965-5351
e-mail: Jacob.Pinholster@asu.edu
Web Site: www.theatrefilm.asu.edu/
Officers:
- **Interim Chair:** John Saldana
- **Director/Associate Professor:** Jacob Pinholster

Management:
- **Business Manager Sr:** Cindy Noldy

Specialized Field: Educational; Theater Workshops
Budget: $5,500-$10,000
Affiliations: U/RTA; ATHE; Arizona Theatre Company
Seating Capacity: 525; 166; 70
Year Built: 1989

2429
CHILDSPLAY
900 South Mitchell Drive
Tempe, AZ 85281
Phone: 480-921-5700
Fax: 480-921-5777
e-mail: info@childsplayaz.org
Web Site: www.childsplayaz.org
Officers:
- **Artistic Director and Founder:** David P. Saar
- **Managing Director:** Steve Martin

Management:
- **President:** Dana Niell
- **Artistic Director/Managing Director:** David P. Saar
- **Managing Director/Artistic Director:** Steve Martin
- **Production Management:** Anthony Runfola
- **Production Management:** Rachel Solice
- **Associate Managing Director:** Ellen Douthat
- **Finance Assistant:** MaryLisa McKallor

Mission: To create theatre so strikingly original in form, content, or both, that it instills in young people an enduring awe, love and respect for the medium, thus preserving imagination and wonder, the hallmarks of childhood, which are the keys to the future.
Founded: 1977
Specialized Field: Youth Theater; Puppet; Contemporary
Status: Non-Profit, Professional
Paid Staff: 15
Paid Artists: 10
Performs At: Herberger Theater, Scottsdale Center for the Arts, Stage West, Tempe Performing Arts Center
Type of Stage: Proscenium, Black Box
Seating Capacity: 800, 800, 350, 175

2430
ARIZONA THEATRE COMPANY
343 S. Scott Ave.
Tucson, AZ 85701
Mailing Address: Tuscon, AZ
Phone: 520-884-8210
Fax: 520-628-9129
e-mail: dgoldstein@arizonatheatre.org
Web Site: www.arizonatheatre.org
Officers:
- **President:** Aubra Spaulding-Gaston
- **Board Chairman:** Jack Davis
- **Artistic Director:** David Ira Goldstein
- **Managing Director:** Mark Cole

Management:
- **General Manager:** Andrew Holtz
- **Artistic Director:** David Ira Goldstein
- **Managing Director:** Jessica Andrews
- **Marketing Director:** Jennifer Spencer
- **Associate Artistic Director:** Stephen Wrentmore
- **Artistic Associate:** Tim Toothman
- **Company Manager:** Robyn Lambert
- **Assistant Company Manager:** Stephanie Lawson

Mission: Creating outstanding professional theatre for Arizona; having an impact locally and nationally.
Utilizes: Actors; AEA Actors; Artists-in-Residence; Collaborating Artists; Commissioned Composers; Commissioned Music; Curators; Dance Companies; Dancers; Designers; Educators; Fine Artists; Five Seasonal Concerts; Grant Writers; Guest Accompanists; Guest Artists; Guest Companies; Guest Composers; Guest Conductors; Guest Designers; Guest Directors; Guest Instructors; Guest Lecturers; Guest Musical Directors; Guest Soloists; Guest Teachers; Instructors; Local Artists; Multimedia; Music; Original Music Scores; Performance Artists; Poets; Resident Artists; Resident Professionals; Selected Students; Sign Language Translators; Singers; Soloists; Student Interns; Special Technical Talent; Visual Arts
Founded: 1967

THEATRE / Arkansas

Specialized Field: Musical; Comedy; Youth Theater; Ethnic Theater; Community Theater; Classic; Contemporary
Status: Non-Profit, Professional
Paid Staff: 50
Paid Artists: 80
Budget: $6.9 million
Income Sources: Ticket Sales; Donations; Grants; Government
Annual Attendance: 150,000
Facility Category: Temple of Music and Art; Herberger Theatre Center
Type of Stage: Proscenium
Seating Capacity: 622; 800
Year Built: 1927
Year Remodeled: 1990
Organization Type: Resident

2431
SCHOOL OF THEATRE ARTS
University of Arizona
Drama Building, Room 239
Tucson, AZ 85721-0003
Mailing Address: PO Box 210003
Phone: 520-621-7008
Fax: 520-621-2412
e-mail: THEATRE@CFA.ARIZONA.EDU
Web Site: www.tftv.arizona.edu/
Officers:
  President: Robert Shelton
  Director: Bruce Brockman
Management:
  Director: Al Tucci
  Artistic Director: Brent Gibbs
  Assistant to the Director: Justine Collins
  Associate Professor: Yuri Makino
  Business Manager: Stacy J Babler
  Administrative Associate: Enedina G Cervantes
Mission: Provides professional training and education leading to careers in acting, musical theatre, theatre design and technology, theatre education and outreach, and theatre history and dramaturgy. The School is dedicated to educating students through a highly visible production program enriching the university and Tucson communities.
Founded: 1936
Specialized Field: Educational; Theater Workshops
Status: Non-Profit, Professional
Performs At: Theatre
Affiliations: NAST; U/RTA; Arizona Theatre Company
Annual Attendance: 26,000
Facility Category: Theatre
Type of Stage: Proscenium; Black Box
Seating Capacity: 332; 300
Year Built: 1957
Year Remodeled: 1992

Arkansas

2432
LYON COLLEGE THEATRE DEPARTMENT
2300 Highland Road
Batesville, AR 72503
Mailing Address: PO Box 2317, Batesville, AR 72503
Phone: 870-793-1750
Fax: 870-698-4622
Toll-free: 800-423-2542
e-mail: mcounts@lyon.edu
Web Site: www.theatre.lyon.edu
Management:
  Chief Executive Officer: Walter Roettger
  Executive Director: John Peek
  Director of Theatre: Michael L Counts
  Professor of Theatre and Director: Dr. Michael L. Counts
Founded: 1925
Specialized Field: Educational; Theater Workshops; Drama
Status: Non-Profit, Non-Professional
Paid Staff: 2
Budget: $9,800-$12,000
Affiliations: ATHE; KCACTF
Annual Attendance: 600-700
Type of Stage: Black Box
Seating Capacity: 150
Year Built: 1991
Year Remodeled: 1999

2433
ARKANSAS SHAKESPEARE THEATRE
Reynolds Performance Hall
201 Donaghey Ave
Conway, AR 72035
Mailing Address: UCA Box 5136, Conway, AR 72035
Phone: 866-810-0012
e-mail: contact@arkshakes.com
Web Site: arkshakes.com
Management:
  Executive Director: Mary Ruth Marotte
  Producing Artistic Director: Rebekah Scallet
Mission: To entertain, engage and enrich the community by creating professional and accessible productions of Shakespeare and other works that promote educational opportunities, community involvement, and the highest artistic standards.
Founded: 2007
Specialized Field: Shakespeare

2434
UNIVERSITY OF CENTRAL ARKANSAS THEATRE PROGRAM
201 Donaghey Ave
Conway, AR 72035
Mailing Address: PO Box 4942, University of Central AR, Conway, AR 72035
Phone: 501-450-5000
Fax: 501-450-3102
e-mail: gregb@uca.edu
Web Site: www.uca.edu/theatre
Officers:
  President: Alan Meadors
Management:
  Director of Theatre: Gregory Blakey
  Production Manager: Liz Parker
Founded: 1907
Specialized Field: BA/BS in Theatre
Status: Non-Profit, Non-Professional
Paid Staff: 4
Budget: $3,100-$17,500
Affiliations: Home to Arkansas Shakespeare Theatre
Type of Stage: Proscenium/Black Box
Year Built: 1968
Year Remodeled: 1996

2435
UNIVERSITY OF ARKANSAS AT FAYETTEVILLE: DEPARTMENT OF DRAMA
525 Old Main
Fayetteville, AR 72701
Phone: 479-575-4801
Fax: 479-575-7602
e-mail: drama@uark.edu
Web Site: www.drama.uark.edu/
Officers:
  Chair: Dr. Andrew Gibbs
Management:
  President: John White
  Executive Director: Allan Sugg
  Artistic Director: D Andrew Gibbs
Founded: 1871
Specialized Field: Musical; Comedy; Ethnic Theater; Classic; Contemporary
Status: For-Profit, Non-Professional
Seating Capacity: 331; 1205; 75
Year Built: 1950

2436
FORT SMITH LITTLE THEATRE
401 N Sixth Street
PO Box 3752
Fort Smith, AR 72913
Mailing Address: PO Box 3752, Fort Smith, AR 72913
Phone: 479-783-2966
Web Site: www.fslt.org
Officers:
  President: Michael Richardson
  VP: Clara Jane Rubarth
  Treasurer: Mike Tickler
  Secretary: Wendy Quick
  President: Lora Rice
Management:
  President: Carole Rogers
  VP: Dennis Brown
  Secretary: Rosemary Johnson
  Treasurer: Paula Sharum
  Secretary: Rikkee Workman
  Vice-President: Nick Rham Cunningham
  Treasurer: Mike Tickler
Founded: 1948
Specialized Field: Drama; Musical; Comedy
Status: Nonprofit
Income Sources: Ticket Sales
Performs At: Fort Smith Little Theatre
Organization Type: Performing

2437
FOUNDATION OF ARTS
115 E Monroe
Jonesboro, AR 72401
Phone: 870-935-2726
Fax: 870-277-1683
e-mail: info@foajonesboro.org
Web Site: www.foajonesboro.org/
Officers:
  President: Cecelia Woods
  VP: Rham Cunningham
  Secretary: Lora Rice
  Treasurer: Paula Sharum
  Board Member: Suzanne Thomas
  Community Development Director: Kristi Pulliam
  Education Director: Rob Spencer
Management:
  Music Director: Dr. Neale King Bartee
  Executive Director: Margaret Peacock
  Education Director: Lara Shelton
  Marketing/Box Office: Danita Martin-Wilkins
Mission: Education, Community Theatre Workshops, Guest Directors, etc. to conduct workshops. Emphasis on youth, but offered to all ages.
Utilizes: Actors; Choreographers; Educators; Guest Artists; Guest Designers; High School Drama; Instructors; Local Artists; Lyricists; Multimedia; Organization Contracts; Sign Language Translators; Soloists; Student Interns; Touring Companies
Founded: 1978
Specialized Field: Community Theater; Musical; Drama; Comedy
Paid Staff: 5

Budget: $35,000-$100,000
Income Sources: Box Office, Grants, Private Donation, Class Tuition
Annual Attendance: 25,000
Facility Category: Theatre
Type of Stage: Proscenium
Seating Capacity: 670
Year Built: 1940
Year Remodeled: 2000
Rental Contact: Executive Director Sherri Greuel
Resident Groups: Nea Symphony, Theatre on the Ridge, Act Experience, Jonesboro City Ballet

2438
ARKANSAS ARTS CENTER CHILDREN'S THEATER
501 East 9th Street
Little Rock, AR 72202
Mailing Address: P.O. Box 2137 Little Rock, AR 72203
Phone: 501-372-4000
Fax: 501-375-8053
Toll-free: 800-264-2787
e-mail: mpreble@arkarts.com
Web Site: www.arkarts.com
Officers:
  President: Terri Erwin
Management:
  President: Ellen Thummel
  Artistic Director: Bradley D Anderson
Mission: Family theater.
Utilizes: Guest Companies; Singers
Founded: 1979
Specialized Field: Musical; Comedy; Youth Theater; Dinner Theater
Status: Non-Profit, Professional
Performs At: Arkansas Art Center Theater
Annual Attendance: 50,000
Facility Category: Auditorium
Type of Stage: Proscenium
Seating Capacity: 381
Year Built: 1930
Organization Type: Performing; Touring
Resident Groups: Resident Theatre Company

2439
ARKANSAS REPERTORY THEATRE
601 Main Street
PO Box 110
Little Rock, AR 72201
Phone: 501-378-0405
Fax: 501-378-0445
e-mail: tickets@therep.org
Web Site: www.therep.org
Officers:
  Chairman: Wyck Nisbet
  Treasurer: Steve Strickland
  Secretary: Ann Bradford
  Managing Director: Michael McCurdy
  Resident Director & Director of Edu: Nicole Capri
  Producing Artistic Director: Robert Hupp
Management:
  Executive Director: Robert Hupp
  Business Manager: Lynn Frazier
  Development Associate: Wanda Hoover
  General Manager: Michael McCurdy
  Marketing Director: Kelly Ford
  Controller: Lynn Frazier
Mission: To be a professional theatre of excellence that entertains and challenges local, regional, and national audiences. Through educational outreach, and as a creative forum for artists, The Rep strives to provide valuable services to the community and make significant contributions to the national theatre agenda.
Utilizes: Actors; AEA Actors; Choreographers; Collaborations; Dancers; Designers; Grant Writers; Guest Artists; Guest Choreographers; Guest Companies; Guest Composers; Guest Conductors; Guest Designers; Guest Ensembles; Guest Lecturers; Guest Musical Directors; Guild Activities; Instructors; Local Artists; Multimedia; Music; Organization Contracts; Original Music Scores; Resident Professionals; Selected Students; Singers; Theatre Companies; Touring Companies; Visual Arts
Founded: 1976
Specialized Field: Musical; Comedy; Youth Theater; Dinner Theater; Community Theater; Classic; Contemporary
Status: Non-Profit, Professional
Paid Staff: 35
Volunteer Staff: 200
Paid Artists: 160
Non-paid Artists: 10
Income Sources: Corporations; Private; Government; Ticket Sales
Performs At: Arkansas Repertory Theatre
Affiliations: Actors Equity Association and Theatre Communication Group
Annual Attendance: 60,000
Type of Stage: Modified Proscenium
Stage Dimensions: 40' x 30'
Seating Capacity: 350
Year Remodeled: 1988
Rental Contact: Michael McCurdy
Organization Type: Performing; Touring; Resident; Educational; Sponsoring

2440
THE WEEKEND THEATER
1001 W. 7th Street
Little Rock, AR 72201
Mailing Address: P.O. Box 251130 Little Rock, AR 72225-1130
Phone: 501-374-3761
Fax: 501-374-3852
Web Site: weekendtheater.org
Officers:
  President: Kim Labbate
  Vice President: Margaret Parker
Management:
  Artistic Director: Ralph Hyman
  Executive Director: James Norris
Mission: The Weekend Theater is dedicated to personally, interpersonally, and educationally reducing prejudice, cruelty, and indifference through live theater.
Status: Nonprofit

2441
UNIVERSITY OF ARKANSAS AT LITTLE ROCK: DEPARTMENT OF THEATRE AND DANCE
2801 South University
Little Rock, AR 72204
Phone: 501-569-3291
Fax: 501-569-8355
e-mail: kethomas@ualr.edu
Web Site: www.ualr.edu/theatre/
Officers:
  Chair: Dr Jay Raphael
Management:
  Executive Director: Debra Baldwan
  Artistic Chair Person: Robert Hupp
Specialized Field: Musical; Comedy; Ethnic Theater; Classic; Contemporary
Status: Non-Profit, Non-Professional
Paid Staff: 17
Budget: $3,750-$7,800
Affiliations: NAST; ATHE; Arkansas Repertory Theatre; Arkansas Arts Center Children's Theatre; Murray's Dinner Theatre
Seating Capacity: 680; 150

2442
SOUTHERN ARKANSAS UNIVERSITY THEATRE & MASS COMMUNICATIONS DEPARTMENT
100 E University
Magnolia, AR 71753
Mailing Address: Box 9203, Magnolia, AR 71754
Phone: 870-235-4257
e-mail: ddmurphy@saumag.edu
Web Site: www.saumag.edu
Officers:
  Chair: David Murphy
Management:
  President: David Rankin
  Artistic Director: David Murphy
Specialized Field: Comedy; Youth Theater; Ethnic Theater; Community Theater; Classic; Contemporary
Status: Non-Profit, Non-Professional
Paid Staff: 3
Paid Artists: 3
Budget: $550-$2,100
Affiliations: ATHE
Seating Capacity: 475
Year Built: 1975

2443
TWIN LAKES PLAYHOUSE
600 W. 6th Street
Mountain Home, AR 72653
Mailing Address: PO Box 482 Mountain Home, AK
Phone: 870-481-5811
Web Site: www.twinlakesplayhouse.org
Officers:
  Chairman: Cindi Young
  Vice Chairman: Mike Baker
  Secretary: Chrissy Carney
  Treasurer: Chris Dyson
Mission: Providing live theater for the area.
Founded: 1971
Specialized Field: Community Theater
Status: Semi-Professional; Non-Professional; Nonprofit
Paid Staff: 40
Organization Type: Performing

2444
ROGERS LITTLE THEATER
116 S. Second Street
Rogers, AR 72756
Phone: 479-631-8988
e-mail: boxoffice@rogerslittletheater.org
Web Site: rogerslittletheater.org
Mission: Rogers Little Theater provides live theater experiences for audiences, performers, and students, enhancing the Rogers Historic District and creating a regional destination.
Opened: 2001
Status: Nonprofit
Volunteer Staff: 700
Annual Attendance: 20,000

THEATRE / California

California

2445
HUMBOLT STATE UNIVERSITY: DEPARTMENT OF THEATRE, FILM AND DANCE
1 Harpst Street
Arcata, CA 95521
Mailing Address: Arcata, CA
Phone: 707-826-3566
Fax: 707-826-5494
Web Site: http://www.humboldt.edu/theatrefilmanddance/index.shtml
Officers:
- **Chair:** Michael Goodman
- **Technical Director:** Jayson Mohatt

Management:
- **Costume Shop Manager:** Catherine Brown
- **Film and Audio Equipment Technician:** Glen Nagy
- **Film Technician III:** Steve Limonoff
- **Administrative Support Coordinator:** Lorraine Dillon
- **Administrative SupportAssistant II:** Debra Ryerson

Founded: 1913
Specialized Field: Musical; Comedy; Youth Theater; Ethnic Theater; Contemporary
Status: Non-Profit, Professional
Paid Staff: 12
Budget: $6,000-$12,000
Affiliations: NAST; ATHE
Seating Capacity: 810; 140; 125
Year Built: 1959

2446
CALIFORNIA STATE UNIVERSITY, BAKERSFIELD: THEATRE PROGRAM
9001 Stockdale Highway
Bakersfield, CA 93311
Mailing Address: Bakersfield, CA
Phone: 661-664-3093
Fax: 661-665-6901
e-mail: kmendenhall_gregory@csub.edu
Web Site: http://www.csub.edu/theatre/
Officers:
- **Chair:** Mandy Rees
- **Office Coordinator:** Karen Gregory

Management:
- **Theatre History and Literature, Act:** Maria Tania Becerra, PhD
- **Design, Technical Theatre:** Chris Eicher, MFA
- **Acting, Theatre Education:** Mendy McMaster
- **Theatre Education, Youth, Acting:** Kamala Kruszka
- **Acting:** Zoe Saba

Specialized Field: Educational; Theater Workshops
Budget: $6,500
Affiliations: ATHE
Seating Capacity: 500; 100
Year Built: 1980

2447
AURORA THEATRE COMPANY
2081 Addison Street
Berkeley, CA 94704
Mailing Address: PO Box 559, Berkeley, CA. 94701
Phone: 510-843-4042
Fax: 510-843-4826
e-mail: general@auroratheatre.org
Web Site: auroratheatre.org
Officers:
- **Artistic Director:** Tom Ross
- **Managing Director:** Julie Saltzman
- **Development Director:** Deborah Banks
- **Marketing Director:** Rachel Reader

Management:
- **Artistic Director:** Tom Ross
- **Managing Director:** Sandra Wright
- **Secretary:** Gail Oakley
- **Treasurer:** Hilary Perkins
- **Box Office Manager:** Pamela McKinstry
- **Assistant Box Office Manager:** Lori Caldwell
- **Annual Fund Manager:** Deborah Munro
- **Literary Manager:** Josh Costello
- **Costume Coordinator:** Alexae J. Visel

Mission: Produce five professional plays per season.
Founded: 1991
Specialized Field: Drama; Musical; Comedy
Paid Staff: 8
Paid Artists: 50
Performs At: Airpra Theatre
Affiliations: Actor's Equity Theatre Company; Theatre Communications Group; Theatre Bay Area
Type of Stage: Arena
Seating Capacity: 67

2448
BERKELEY COMMUNITY THEATRE
2180 Milvia Street
Berkeley, CA 94704
Phone: 510-644-6001
Fax: 510-845-9674
Management:
- **Theatre Manager:** Judson H Owens
- **Assistant Manager:** Lance C James
- **Facility Reservations:** Yvonne Adams

Mission: To offer the community professional theatre.
Utilizes: Guest Artists; Guest Companies; Singers
Founded: 1950
Specialized Field: Community Theater
Status: Non-Profit, Non-Professional
Paid Staff: 4
Volunteer Staff: 60
Income Sources: Berkeley Unified School District
Performs At: Berkeley Community Theatre
Affiliations: Berkeley Unified School District
Seating Capacity: 3,500
Organization Type: Performing; Touring; Educational

2449
BERKELEY REPERTORY THEATRE
2025 Addison Street
Berkeley, CA 94704
Phone: 510-647-2900
Fax: 510-647-2976
Toll-free: 888-427-8849
e-mail: info@berkeleyrep.org
Web Site: www.berkeleyrep.org
Officers:
- **President:** Nicholas M Graves
- **VP:** Phillip R Trapp
- **Treasurerident:** Kenneth P Avery
- **Secretary:** Jean Strunsky
- **School Administrator:** Kashara Robinson

Management:
- **Executive Director:** Susan Medak
- **Artistic Associate:** Amy Potozkin
- **Litrary Associate:** Julie McCormick
- **Production Manager:** Tom Pearlson
- **Artistic Associate:** Mina Marita

Mission: To set a national standard for ambitious programming, engagement with our audiences, and leadership within the community in which we reside. We endeavor to create a diverse body of work that expresses a rigorous, embracing aesthetic and relects the highest artistic standards, and seek to maintain an environment in which talented artists can do their best work.
Utilizes: Actors; AEA Actors; Choreographers; Collaborations; Designers; Educators; Five Seasonal Concerts; Guest Accompanists; Guest Artists; Guest Designers; Guest Instructors; Guild Activities; High School Drama; Instructors; Local Artists; Lyricists; Multimedia; Original Music Scores; Performance Artists; Resident Professionals; Student Interns; Visual Arts
Founded: 1968
Specialized Field: Drama; Comedy; Musical; Educational
Status: Non-Profit, Professional
Paid Staff: 75
Paid Artists: 50
Budget: $8.9 Million
Income Sources: Tickets; Grants; Donations; Subscriptions
Performs At: Berkeley Repertory Theatre
Affiliations: San Francisco Convention and Visitor Bureau; Berkeley Convention and Visitor Bureau
Annual Attendance: 150,000
Type of Stage: Thrust Stage and Proscenium Stage
Seating Capacity: 400 and 600
Year Built: 1980
Cost: $20 Million
Rental Contact: Alisha Tonsic
Organization Type: Performing; Touring; Resident; Educational

2450
BLACK REPERTORY GROUP
3201 Adeline Street
Berkeley, CA 94703
Phone: 510-652-2120
Fax: 510-652-8030
e-mail: keepersoftheculture@yahoo.com
Web Site: www.blackrepertorygroup.com
Officers:
- **President:** Ella Wiley
- **VP:** Pastor Earl Bill
- **Secretary:** Doreen Zayas
- **Executive/Artistic Director:** Dr. Mona Vaughn Scott

Management:
- **President:** Sean Vaughn Scott
- **Executive Director:** Mona Vaughn Scott
- **Managing Director:** Pamela Spikes

Mission: Building discipline and self-esteem in youth through drama. Showcasing the plays of black playwrights. Providing a folk arts venue for the community.
Utilizes: Guest Companies; Singers
Founded: 1964
Specialized Field: Musical; Comedy; Youth Theater; Dinner Theater; Ethnic Theater; Community Theater; Classic; Contemporary
Status: Non-Profit, Professional
Paid Staff: 4
Paid Artists: 250
Organization Type: Resident

2451
SHOTGUN PLAYERS
1901 Ashby Avenue
Berkeley, CA 94703
Phone: 510-841-6500
e-mail: boxoffice@shotgunplayers.org
Web Site: shotgunplayers.org
Management:
- **Artistic Director:** Patrick Dooley
- **Development Director:** Joanie McBrien
- **Managing Director:** Liz Lisle

Mission: Shotgun Players is a company of artists determined to create bold, relevant, affordable theatre that inspires and challenges audience and artist alike to re-examine our lives, our community, and the ever-changing world around us.
Founded: 1992
Specialized Field: New Works

2452
DELL'ARTE INTERNATIONAL SCHOOL OF PHYSICAL THEATRE
131 H Street
PO Box 816
Blue Lake, CA 95525
Phone: 707-668-5663
Fax: 707-668-5665
e-mail: INFO@DELLARTE.com
Web Site: www.dellarte.com
Officers:
   Chair: Bonnie Neely
   President: Stephanie Thompson
   Producing Artistic Director: Maureen Burke
   CFO: Stephanie Witzel
   Founding Artistic Director: Joan Schirle
   Producing Artistic Director: Michael Fields
   Chief Executive Officer: Stephanie Thompson
Management:
   Producing Artistic Director: Michael Fields
   Director: Calvin Pritner
   School Director: Ronlin Foreman
   Associate School Director: Joe Krienke
   Realtor: Stephany Joy
Mission: International in scope, grounded in the natural living world, inspired by the non-urban setting, explores theatre making, theatre practice and theatre training for ourselves, the world and the future.
Utilizes: Actors; AEA Actors; Choreographers; Collaborating Artists; Collaborations; Dancers; Designers; Educators; Five Seasonal Concerts; Guest Accompanists; Guest Choreographers; Guest Companies; Guest Designers; Guest Ensembles; High School Drama; Local Artists; Original Music Scores; Resident Professionals; Sign Language Translators; Soloists; Theatre Companies
Founded: 1971
Specialized Field: Theatre
Status: Non-Profit, Professional
Paid Staff: 22
Paid Artists: 15
Budget: $1 million
Income Sources: Humboldt Arts Council; Theatre Communications Group, Theatre Bay Area
Performs At: Dell' Arte Theatre
Affiliations: NAST; ATHE
Facility Category: Black Box/Amphitheatre
Type of Stage: Sprung Floor
Seating Capacity: 113; 300
Year Remodeled: 1995
Organization Type: Performing; Touring
Resident Groups: Dell' Arte Company

2453
COLONY THEATRE COMPANY
555 N Third Street
Burbank, CA 91502-1103
Phone: 818-558-7000
Fax: 818-558-7110
e-mail: colonytheatre@colonytheatre.org
Web Site: www.colonytheatre.com
Officers:
   President/Producing Director: Barbara Beckley
   VP: Michael Wadler
   Secretary: Priscilla Davis
   Treasurer: Nonie Lann
   Chairman: Keith Bardellini
   Artistic Director: Barbara Beckley
   Executive Director: Trent Steelman
   Technical Director: Robert Kyle
Management:
   President: Barbara Beckley
   Managing Director: Sean Cutler
Mission: To produce full productions of plays for the public recognized to be of significant artistic, social, and/or historical value.
Utilizes: Actors; AEA Actors; Designers; Guest Conductors; Guest Lecturers; Guest Musical Directors; Instructors; Music; Resident Artists; Resident Professionals; Student Interns
Founded: 1975
Specialized Field: Drama; Comedy; Musical
Status: Non-Profit, Professional
Paid Staff: 7
Volunteer Staff: 10
Budget: $800,000
Income Sources: Subscription & Single Ticket Sales; Individual Donations
Performs At: Burbank Center Stage
Affiliations: Actors Equity Association
Annual Attendance: 20,500
Facility Category: Theater
Type of Stage: Thrust
Stage Dimensions: 37.5 x 22.5
Seating Capacity: 276
Year Built: 2000
Cost: $1,500,000 (built)
Rental Contact: Managing Director Amanda Diamond
Organization Type: Performing; Resident
Resident Groups: Colony Theatre Company

2454
GROVE THEATRE CENTER
1111 B West Clark Avenue
Burbank, CA 91506
Phone: 818-528-6622
Fax: 714-741-9560
Web Site: www.gtc.org/
Management:
   Artistic Director: Kevin Cochran
   Executive Director: Charles Johanson
   Company Manager: Gigi Horowitz
   Casting Coordinator: Hunter Stevenson
   Production Manager: Gabin PanGriff
   Production Stage Manager: Zac Prostein
Utilizes: Actors; AEA Actors; Choreographers; Commissioned Music; Dance Companies; Dancers; Designers; Grant Writers; Guest Accompanists; Guest Artists; Guest Companies; Guest Conductors; Guest Designers; Guest Lecturers; Guest Teachers; Guild Activities; Instructors; Local Artists; Music; Original Music Scores; Performance Artists; Resident Professionals; Selected Students; Student Interns; Theatre Companies
Specialized Field: Musical; Comedy; Drama; Theater Workshops
Status: Nonprofit
Budget: $350,000
Season: Year Round
Annual Attendance: 15,000
Stage Dimensions: 35'x45', 60'x45', 40'x35', 30'x60'
Seating Capacity: 172, 548, 246, 98

2455
PACIFIC REPERTORY THEATRE/CARMEL SHAKESPEARE FESTIVAL
Monte Verde Street
PO Box 222035
Carmel, CA 93922
Phone: 408-622-0700
Fax: 831-622-0703
Toll-free: 866-622-0709
e-mail: contact@pacrep.org
Web Site: www.pacrep.org
Management:
   Eaxecutive Director/Founder: Stephen Moorer
   Business Manager: Julie Hughett
   Developmental Director: Jim Bennett
   Marketing Director: Kathi Kammendiener
Founded: 1982
Specialized Field: Live Professional Theatre
Status: Non-Equity; Nonprofit
Season: February-October
Type of Stage: Proscenium; Thrust; Arena

2456
CALIFORNIA STATE UNIVERSITY, DOMINGUEZ HILLS: DEPARTMENT OF THEATRE
California State University
Carson, CA 90747
Mailing Address: 1000 East Victoria St. LCH A111
Phone: 310-243-3588
Web Site: http://cah.csudh.edu/theatre/
Officers:
   Chairman: Sydell Weiner
Specialized Field: Educational; Theater Workshops
Budget: $8,550-$12,100
Affiliations: NAST
Seating Capacity: 475; 80

2458
CHICO PERFORMANCES
California State University Chico
400 W First Street
Chico, CA 95929-0116
Mailing Address: University Box Office CSU, Chico, Chico, CA 95929-0120
Phone: 530-898-5122
Fax: 530-898-4797
e-mail: upe@csuchico.edu
Web Site: www.chicoperformances.com/
Management:
   President: Paul Zingg
   Executive Director: Richard Jackson
   Artistic Director: Dan Dewayne
Specialized Field: Multi-Media
Status: Non-Profit, Professional
Paid Staff: 9

2459
POMONA COLLEGE DEPARTMENT OF THEATRE AND DANCE
Pomona College
Claremont, CA 91711
Mailing Address: 300 E. Bonita Ave.
Phone: 909-621-8186
Fax: 909-621-8780
e-mail: mtr04747@pomona.edu
Web Site: http://theatre.pomona.edu/
Officers:
   Chair: Sherry Linnell
Management:
   President: David Oxtoby

THEATRE / California

Managing Director: James Taylor
Specialized Field: Musical; Comedy; Ethnic Theater; Classic; Contemporary
Status: For-Profit, Non-Professional
Paid Staff: 15
Paid Artists: 2
Budget: $9,000-$14,000
Affiliations: ATHE
Seating Capacity: 330; 150
Year Built: 1992
Year Remodeled: 1998

2460
LAMB'S PLAYERS THEATRE
1142 Orange Avenue
PO Box 18229
Coronado, CA 92118
Mailing Address: Lamb's Players Theatre P.O. Box 182229
Phone: 619-437-6050
Fax: 619-437-6053
e-mail: ed.hofmeister@lambsplayers.org
Web Site: www.lambsplayers.org/index.html
Officers:
  Chairman: Lisa Ledri-Aguilar
  Art Director: Christian Turner
  Producing Artistic Director: Robert Smyth
Management:
  Producing Artistic Director: W Robert Smyth
  Associate Director: Kerry Meads
  Associate Director: Deborah Smyth
  Art Director: Christian Turner
  Director of Operations: Brian Andrews
  Director of Marketing: Ed Hofmeister
  Associate Artistic Director: Kerry Meads
  Associate Artistic Director: Deborah Gilmour Smyth
  Production Manager: Paul Eggington
Mission: To be a theatre that probes and questions the values and choices of contemporary culture. Celebrates the joys, strengths and diverse traditions of family and community. Explores the spiritual dimension of life.
Utilizes: Guest Companies; Singers
Founded: 1973
Specialized Field: Drama; Comedy
Status: Professional; Nonprofit
Income Sources: Theatre Communications Group; California Theatre Council
Performs At: Harder Stage; Hahn; Lyceum
Type of Stage: Thrust/Proscenium, Flexible
Seating Capacity: 350, 250, 200
Organization Type: Performing; Touring; Resident; Educational

2461
SOUTH COAST REPERTORY
Professional Resident Theatre
655 Town Center Drive
Costa Mesa, CA 92626
Mailing Address: PO Box 2197 Costa Mesa, CA 92628
Phone: 714-708-5500
Fax: 714-708-5522
e-mail: boxoffice@scr.org
Web Site: www.scr.org
Officers:
  Chairman: Damien Jordon
Management:
  Founding Artistic Director: David Emmes
  Artistic Director: Martin Benson
  Managing Director: Paula Tomei
  Associate Artistic Director: John Glore
  Director Development: Susan Reeder
  Director Marketing/Communications: Bil Schroeder
  Production Manager: Josh Marchesi
  Operations Manager: Luis De La Cruz
  Casting Director: Joanne Denaut
Mission: Founded in the belief that theatre is an artform with a unique power to illuminate the human experience. Commit ourselves to exploring the most urgent human and social issues of time, and to merging literature, design and performance in ways that test the bounds of theatre's artistic possibilities.
Utilizes: Actors; AEA Actors; Artists-in-Residence; Choreographers; Collaborating Artists; Commissioned Composers; Commissioned Music; Designers; Five Seasonal Concerts; Grant Writers; Guest Accompanists; Guest Artists; Guest Companies; Guest Conductors; Guest Designers; Guest Lecturers; Guest Musicians; High School Drama; Multimedia; Music; Original Music Scores; Performance Artists; Poets; Resident Artists; Resident Professionals; Selected Students; Soloists; Student Interns; Special Technical Talent; Visual Arts
Founded: 1964
Opened: 1964
Specialized Field: Classical; Contemporary; Multicultural; New York; Student/Youth Programs; Theatre for Young Audiences
Status: Non-Profit, Professional
Paid Staff: 70
Paid Artists: 150
Budget: $9 Million
Income Sources: Ticket Sales; Annual Fund Campaign
Affiliations: American Arts Alliance, the League of Resident Theatres (IORT), Theatre Communications Group (TCG), and Arts Orange County
Annual Attendance: 14,000; 50,000
Facility Category: Folino Theatre Center
Type of Stage: Flexible; Proscenium; End Stage
Seating Capacity: 507; 336; 95
Year Built: 1978
Year Remodeled: 2002
Cost: $29 million
Rental Contact: Nelson Denniston
Organization Type: Performing; Touring; Resident; Educational

2462
THE ACTORS' GANG THEATER
9070 Venice Boulevard
The Ivy Substation
Culver City, CA 90232
Phone: 310-838-4264
Fax: 310-838-4263
e-mail: production@theactorsgang.com
Web Site: www.theactorsgang.com
Management:
  Artistic Director: Tim Robbins
  Managing Director: Gregg Reiner
Founded: 1981
Specialized Field: Drama; Comedy
Status: Non-Profit, Professional
Paid Staff: 4
Paid Artists: 85
Performs At: Actors' Gang Theater, Actors' Gang El Centro
Type of Stage: Flexible Stage
Seating Capacity: 99, 40

2463
KIRK DOUGLAS THEATRE
Center Theatre Group
9820 Washington Boulevard
Culver City, CA 90232
Mailing Address: 601 W Temple St Los Angeles, CA 90012
Phone: 213-628-2772
Fax: 213-972-0746
e-mail: ArtDir@centertheatregroup.org
Web Site: www.centretheatregroup.org
Officers:
  Chairman: Martin Massman
  President: William H Ahmanson
  VP: Ava Fries
  Secretary: Martin C Washton
  Treasurer: Dr Steven Nagelberg
Management:
  Artistic Director: Michael Ritchie
  Managing Director: Charles Dillingham
  Vice President: Ava Fries
Mission: To serve the diverse audiences of Los Angeles by producing and presenting theatre of the highest caliber, by nurturing new artists, by attracting new audiences, and by developing youth outreach and arts education programs. This mission is based on a belief that the art of theatre is a cultural force with the capacity to transform the lives of individuals and society at large.
Utilizes: Actors; AEA Actors; Arrangers; Artists-in-Residence; Choreographers; Collaborating Artists; Collaborations; Community Members; Contract Actors; Dancers; Designers; Educators; Equity Actors; Five Seasonal Concerts; Guest Accompanists; Guest Artists; Guest Companies; Guest Composers; Guest Conductors; Guest Designers; Guest Lecturers; Guest Musical Directors; Guest Teachers; Instructors; Local Artists; Local Artists & Directors; Local Unknown Artists; Lyricists; Multi Collaborations; Multimedia; Music; Organization Contracts; Original Music Scores; Paid Performers; Performance Artists; Poets; Resident Artists; Resident Companies; Resident Professionals; Scenic Designers; Selected Students; Sign Language Translators; Singers; Soloists; Students; Student Interns; Special Technical Talent; Theatre Companies; Touring Companies; Visual Arts; Visual Designers; Volunteer Directors & Actors; Writers
Opened: 2004
Specialized Field: Musical; Comedy; Drama
Status: Non-Profit; Professional
Paid Staff: 350
Performs At: Performing Arts Center of Los Angeles
Affiliations: Ahmanson Theatre; Mark Taper Forum
Annual Attendance: 250,000
Facility Category: Music Center of Los Angeles
Type of Stage: Proscenium
Stage Dimensions: 40Wx28H
Seating Capacity: 317
Year Built: 2004

2464
UNIVERSITY OF CALIFORNIA, DAVIS: DEPARTMENT OF DRAMATIC ART
University of California - Davis
222 Wright Hall, One Shields Avenue
Davis, CA 95616
Mailing Address: 222 Wright Hall, One Shields Avenue
Phone: 530-752-0888
Fax: 530-752-8818
e-mail: theatredancenews@ucdavis.edu
Web Site: http://theatredance.ucdavis.edu/
Officers:
  Department Chair: Melissa Gibson
  Children Theatre/Theatre Education: J Daniel Herring
  African American Theatre: Thomas Witt Ellis
  Scene Design: Jeff Hunter
Management:
  Chair: Barbara Sellers Young

THEATRE / California

Publicity Director: Kathy Morison
Cutter/Draper Tailor: Heather Brown
Costume Shop Director: Roxanne Femling
Master Electrician: Mike Hill
Specialized Field: Educational; Theater Workshops
Budget: $3,600-$11,000
Affiliations: ATHE; Sacramento Theatre Company; Tahoe Shakespeare Festival; Magic Theatre; B Street Theatre
Seating Capacity: 470; 250; 220; 150
Year Built: 1967

2465
CHRISTIAN COMMUNITY THEATER
1545 Pioneer Way
El Cajon, CA 92020
Phone: 619-588-0206
Fax: 619-588-4384
Toll-free: 800-696-1929
e-mail: info@cctcyt.org
Web Site: www.christiancommunitytheater.com/
Management:
 President: Sheryl Russell
 Artistic Director: Paul Russell
 Managing Director: Diane Moses
 Marketing Director: Charles W Patmon, Jr
 Managing Director: Diane Mosce
 Operations Director: Mary Mwanger
 Development Director: Sharon Milligan
Mission: To produce quality wholesome family entertainment and reflect Judeo-Christian values through training in the arts; to provide a children's theatre training program.
Utilizes: Actors
Founded: 1980
Specialized Field: Musical; Youth Theater; Community Theater
Status: Non-Profit, Non-Professional
Paid Staff: 25
Volunteer Staff: 50
Paid Artists: 5
Non-paid Artists: 200
Budget: $2,000,000
Income Sources: Box Office; Tuition; Grants; Private Donations
Performs At: Rented- Outdoor amphitheater and public performance center
Affiliations: American Alliance for Theatre and Education; Christians in Theater Arts
Annual Attendance: 50,000+

2466
WELK RESORT SAN DIEGO THEATRE
8860 Lawrence Walk Drive
Escondido, CA 92026
Phone: 760-749-3448
Fax: 760-749-9592
Toll-free: 888-802-7469
e-mail: box.office@welktheatre.com
Web Site: welkresorts.com/san-diego-theatre/
Management:
 General Manager: Sean Coogan
 Producer/Theatre Manager: Joshua Carr
Utilizes: AEA Actors
Founded: 1981
Specialized Field: Musical
Status: For-Profit, Professional
Paid Staff: 40
Paid Artists: 20
Income Sources: Actors' Equity Association
Performs At: The Welk Resort; San Diego Theatre
Facility Category: Broadway Style Dinner Theatre
Seating Capacity: 339
Organization Type: Performing

2467
FERNDALE REPERTORY THEATRE
447 Main Street
PO Box 892
Ferndale, CA 95536-0096
Phone: 707-786-5483
Fax: 707-786-5480
e-mail: info@ferndale-rep.org
Web Site: www.ferndale-rep.org
Management:
 Director: Marilyn McCormick
 Technical Director: Daniel L Lawrence
Mission: To provide North Coast residents and visitors theatrical performances of the highest quality.
Utilizes: Actors; Designers; Five Seasonal Concerts; Guest Accompanists; Guest Artists; Guest Companies; Guest Conductors; Guest Designers; Guest Ensembles; Guest Instructors; Guest Lecturers; Guest Soloists; High School Drama; Instructors; Local Artists; Multimedia; Resident Professionals; Singers; Soloists; Student Interns
Founded: 1972
Specialized Field: Community Theater
Status: Non-Profit, Non-Professional
Paid Staff: 3
Budget: $160,000
Income Sources: Grants; Ticket sales; Membership
Performs At: Ferndale Repertory Theatre
Facility Category: Live Stage Productions
Type of Stage: Thrust Percenium
Seating Capacity: 265
Year Built: 1922
Year Remodeled: 1972
Organization Type: Performing

2468
CALIFORNIA STATE UNIVERSITY, FRESNO: THEATRE ARTS DEPARTMENT
5241 North Maple
Fresno, CA 93710
Phone: 559-278-2654
Fax: 559-278-7512
e-mail: ckershaw@csufresno.edu
Web Site: www.fresnostate.edu/artshum/theatrearts/
Officers:
 Chair: Kathleen McKinley
Management:
 President: John Wealthy
 Costume Shop Technician: Kelly Pantzlaff Curry
 Scene Shop Supervisor: Michael Hansen
 Promotion Manager: Pamela Dyer
 Costume Shop Supervisor: Stephanie Bradshaw
 Business & Promotions Manager: Pamela Dyer
 Costume Shop Technician: Kelly Pantzlaff Curry
Founded: 1911
Specialized Field: Musical; Comedy; Youth Theater; Ethnic Theater; Community Theater; Classic; Contemporary
Status: For-Profit, Non-Professional
Budget: $2,900-$4,900
Affiliations: NAST; ATHE
Seating Capacity: 360; 200; 100
Year Remodeled: 1991

2469
CALIFORNIA STATE UNIVERSITY, FULLERTON: DEPARTMENT OF THEATRE AND DANCE
800 N State College
Fullerton, CA 92831
Phone: 657-278-3371
Fax: 714-278-7041
Web Site: www.arts.fullerton.edu/events
Officers:
 Chair: Susan Hallman
Management:
 Chairperson: Susan Hallman
Founded: 1957
Specialized Field: Musical; Comedy; Youth Theater; Classic; Contemporary
Status: Non-Profit, Non-Professional
Paid Staff: 47
Budget: $9000-$23,650
Affiliations: NASD; NAST; ATHE; South Coast Repertory; A Noise Within
Seating Capacity: 500; 200; 100
Year Remodeled: 2000

2470
VANGUARD THEATRE ENSEMBLE
120 A W Wilshire Avenue
Fullerton, CA 92832
Phone: 714-526-8007
Fax: 714-451-1372
Web Site: www.vte.org
Management:
 Artistic Director: Wade Williamson
 Managing Director: Paulette Kendall
 Ensemble Director: Jill Cary Martin
Founded: 1992
Specialized Field: Comedy; Youth Theater; Ethnic Theater; Community Theater; Classic; Contemporary
Status: Non-Profit, Professional

2471
GLENDALE CENTRE THEATRE
324 North Orange Street
Glendale, CA 91203
Phone: 818-244-8481
e-mail: boxoffice@glendalecentretheatre.com
Web Site: glendalecentretheatre.com
Founded: 1974

2472
AMERICAN ACADEMY OF DRAMATIC ARTS/HOLLYWOOD
1336 N LaBrea Avenue
Hollywood, CA 90028
Phone: 323-464-2777
Fax: 323-464-1250
Toll-free: 800-222-2867
e-mail: officeassistant@ca.aada.org
Web Site: www.aada.org
Officers:
 Chairman: Michael Gardner
 Vice Chairman: Jolyon F. Stern
 Secretary: E. Robert Goodkind
 Treasurer: Dana Pancrazi
 Chairman Emeritus: Robert E. Wankel
Management:
 Managing Director, Los Angeles: Barbara Hodgen
 Director of Instruction: Theresa Hayes
Mission: To provide students with the tools needed to make acting their profession.
Founded: 1884
Specialized Field: Educational; Acting Course of Study
Status: Non-Profit, Private, Professional
Paid Staff: 23
Paid Artists: 40
Income Sources: Tuition; Donations
Affiliations: NAST; Middle State Commission on Higher Education
Facility Category: Black Box Theater
Type of Stage: Proscenium
Seating Capacity: 150
Year Built: 2000

THEATRE / California

Year Remodeled: 2006

2473
BLANK THEATRE COMPANY
6500 Santa Monica Boulevard
Hollywood, CA 90038
Mailing Address: 1301 Lucile Avenue, Los Angeles, CA. 90026
Phone: 323-662-7734
Fax: 323-661-3903
e-mail: info@theblank.com
Web Site: www.theblank.com
Officers:
  Managing Director: Ed Murphy
  Producing Director: Matthew Graber
  Founding Artistic Director: Daniel Henning
  Artistic Producer: Noah Wyle
  Director of New Play Development: Kirsten Sanderson
Management:
  President: Daniel Henning
  Artistic Producer: Noah Wyle
  Producer: Stacy Reed
Founded: 1990
Specialized Field: Musical; Comedy; Youth Theater; Classic; Contemporary
Status: Non-Profit, Professional
Paid Staff: 3
Paid Artists: 60

2474
HUDSON THEATRE
6539 Santa Monica Boulevard
Hollywood, CA 90038
Phone: 323-856-4249
Fax: 323-856-4829
e-mail: leigh@hudsontheatre.com
Web Site: www.hudsontheatre.com/
Officers:
  Producing Managing Director: Zeke Rettman
  Founding Artistic Director: Elizabeth Reilly
Management:
  Artistic Director: Elizabeth Reilly
  Producing Managing Director: Zeke Rettman
  Technical Director: Christian Smith
  Artistic Director: Leigh McLeod Fortier
  Managing Director: Trevor Ysaguirre
Utilizes: Guest Companies; Singers
Founded: 1991
Specialized Field: Avant-garde; Drama
Status: Professional; Nonprofit
Performs At: Hudson Theatre (Mainstage, Avenue Theatre, Guild Theatre)
Type of Stage: Modified Thrust; Proscenium
Seating Capacity: 99; 99; 43
Organization Type: Producing in House

2475
OPEN FIST THEATRE COMPANY
6209 Santa Monica Boulevard
Hollywood, CA 90038
Mailing Address: 6209 Santa Monica Boulevard, Los Angeles 90038
Phone: 323-882-6912
e-mail: mdemson@openfist.org
Web Site: www.openfist.org
Officers:
  Artistic Director: Martha Demson
Management:
  Director of Development: Samantha Bennett
  Artistic Director: Martha Demson
  Managing Director: David Castellani
  Literary Manager: Laura Flanagan
Mission: The Open Fist Theatre Company is a community of actors, playwrights, designers and directors.
Founded: 1989
Specialized Field: Comedy; Ensembles; Drama
Status: Non-Profit, Professional

2476
STAGES THEATRE CENTER
1540 N McCadden Place
210 S Westgate Avenue
Hollywood, CA 90028
Phone: 323-465-1010
Fax: 323-462-2176
e-mail: e-mail@stagestheatre.org
Web Site: www.stagestheatrecenter.com/
Officers:
  Chairperson: Pompea Smith
  Treasurer: Sonia Lloveras
Management:
  Artistic Director: Paul Verdier
  Managing Director: Sonia Lloveras
Mission: To expose new or unfamiliar works or styles of theater to Los Angeles audiences; to host unique artists-in-residence who utilize distinctive theatrical styles, such as Theater of the Absurd and Commedia del' Arte.
Utilizes: Guest Companies
Founded: 1981
Specialized Field: Experimental
Status: Professional; Nonprofit
Paid Staff: 3
Income Sources: Theatre Communications Group
Performs At: Stages Theatre
Stage Dimensions: 14'x14'
Organization Type: Performing

2477
HUNTINGTON BEACH PLAYHOUSE
7111 Talbert Avenue
Huntington Beach, CA 92648
Phone: 714-375-0696
Fax: 714-375-0698
Web Site: www.hbplayhouse.com/
Officers:
  President: Dawn Conant
  Treasurer: Don Stanton
  Secretary: BJ O'Rourke-Smith
Mission: As a non-profit organization dedicated to community educational and cultural enrichment in dramatic arts, Huntington Beach Playhouse presents dramatic productions, sponsors student scholarships and offers stagecraft workshops.
Utilizes: Guest Companies; Singers
Founded: 1963
Specialized Field: Drama; Comedy; Musical
Status: Non-Profit, Non-Professional
Paid Staff: 4
Volunteer Staff: 100
Non-paid Artists: 75
Income Sources: Ticket Sales
Performs At: Central Library Theatre
Annual Attendance: 27,000
Type of Stage: Proscenium
Seating Capacity: 319
Year Built: 1994
Organization Type: Performing

2478
UNIVERSITY OF CALIFORNIA-IRVINE: DEPARTMENT OF DRAMA
513 Aldrich hall #5
Irvine, CA 92697-2775
Phone: 949-824-5011
Fax: 949-824-3475
e-mail: drama@uci.edu
Web Site: drama.arts.uci.edu
Officers:
  Chair: Eli Simon
Management:
  Information Coordinator: Marcus Beeman
  Professor: Lonnie Alcaraz
  Faculty: Stephen Barker
  Faculty: Richard Brestoff
  Faculty: Robin Buck
Utilizes: Actors; Arrangers; Choreographers; Collaborating Artists; Composers; Dancers; Designers; Educators; Grant Writers; Guest Accompanists; Guest Artists; Guest Companies; Guest Conductors; Guest Designers; Guest Directors; Guest Instructors; Guest Musical Directors; Guest Soloists; Guest Speakers; Guest Teachers; Guest Writers; High School Drama; Instructors; Local Artists & Directors; Lyricists; Multi Collaborations; Multimedia; Music; Organization Contracts; Original Music Scores; Performance Artists; Resident Professionals; Scenic Designers; Soloists; Student Interns; Touring Companies; Visual Arts; Volunteer Directors & Actors; Writers
Founded: 1965
Specialized Field: Drama; Music Theater; Acting; Design (Costume, Lighting, Scene, Sound), Directing, Stage Management, Doctoral (PhD) Studies
Paid Staff: 30
Paid Artists: 20
Budget: $10,050-$49,050
Affiliations: U/RTA;ATHE; South Coast Repertory
Facility Category: 6 Theaters, 2 Studios
Seating Capacity: Variable
Year Built: 1970
Rental Contact: Toby Wwiner

2479
PINE HILLS LODGE AND DINNER THEATRE
2960 La Posada Way
Julian, CA 92036
Phone: 760-765-1100
Fax: 760-765-1121
e-mail: events@pinehillslodge.com
Web Site: www.pinehillslodge.com
Founded: 2003
Specialized Field: Dinner Theater
Status: For-Profit, Professional

2480
KIDS 4 BROADWAY
PO Box 122
Kelseyville, CA 95451
Phone: 707-279-4497
Fax: 707-277-7557
e-mail: kidsplay@pacific.net
Web Site: www.kids4broadway.com/
Mission: Offers a unique opportunity for a school or community to create love, laughter and magic in their childrens lives.
Specialized Field: Children's Theater; Educational

2481
LA JOLLA PLAYHOUSE
2910 La Jolla Villiage Drive
PO Box 12039
La Jolla, CA 92037
Mailing Address: P.O. Box 12039 ,La Jolla CA, 92039
Phone: 858-550-1010
Fax: 858-550-1075
Web Site: www.lajollaplayhouse.com
Management:

THEATRE / California

Executive Director: Terry Dwyer
Artistic Director: Des McAnuff
Literary Manager: Alison Horsley
Mission: Producing bold, innovative, adventurous theater; offering a summer home to America's leading theater artists.
Utilizes: Guest Companies; Singers
Founded: 1947
Specialized Field: Drama; Comedy; Musical
Status: Non-Profit, Professional
Paid Staff: 70
Paid Artists: 100
Income Sources: Actors' Equity Association; League of Resident Theatres; Theatre Communications Group
Season: April - December
Performs At: La Jolla Playhouse; Mandell Weiss Performing Arts
Type of Stage: Proscenium/Thrust
Seating Capacity: 500, 400
Organization Type: Touring; Resident; Educational

2482
UNIVERSITY OF CALIFORNIA-SAN DIEGO: DEPARTMENT OF THEATRE AND DANCE
9500 Gilman Drive
La Jolla, CA 92093
Phone: 858-534-3791
Fax: 858-534-1080
e-mail: theatrefrontdesk@ucsd.edu
Web Site: www.theatre.ucsd.edu
Officers:
 Department Chair: Allison Greene
 MSO: Mark Maltby
 Technical Director: Chris Borreson
 Assistant Technical Director: Michael Schwent
Management:
 Production Manager: Michael Francis
 Network System Administrator: Michael Fullerton
 Financial Manager: Hedi Jafari
 Undergraduate Coordinator: Laura Jimenez
 Chief Administrative Officer: Mark Maltby
Founded: 1973
Specialized Field: Comedy; Youth Theater; Ethnic Theater; Community Theater; Classic; Contemporary
Status: Non-Profit, Non-Professional
Paid Staff: 33
Budget: $3,600-$24,000
Performs At: Mandell Weiss Theater
Affiliations: ATHE; The La Jolla Playhouse
Seating Capacity: 500; 400; 100
Year Built: 1982

2483
UNIVERSITY OF LAVERNE
1950 Third Street
LaVerne, CA 91750
Phone: 909-593-3511
Fax: 909-392-2787
e-mail: tcisneros@ulv.edu
Web Site: www.laverne.edu/
Officers:
 Chair: Elizabeth Pietrzak
Management:
 President: Steve Morgan
 VP: Thil Hawkey
Founded: 1891
Specialized Field: Educational; Theater Workshops
Status: Non-Profit, Non-Professional
Budget: $550-$14,000
Affiliations: U/RTA; ATHE; The Guilford School of Acting (England); The Split International Theatre Festival (Croatia)

Seating Capacity: 175-250; 60; 475
Year Built: 1972

2484
LAGUNA PLAYHOUSE
606 Laguna Canyon Road
PO Box 1747
Laguna Beach, CA 92651
Phone: 949-497-2787
Fax: 949-376-8185
Web Site: www.LagunaPlayhouse.com
Officers:
 Chair: Joe Hanauer
 Treasurer: Cynthia Harriss
 Secretary: Iiona Martin
 Director of Marketing: Greg Renoe
Management:
 Executive Director: Richard Stein
 Artistic Director: Ann E. Wareham
 Managing Director: Kate Hicklin
 Executive Director: Karen Wood
 Production Manager: Jim Ryan
 Business Manager: Kat Hiclklin
 Corporate Development Manager: Elaine Smith
Mission: Committed to excellence in professional theatre.
Founded: 1920
Specialized Field: Musical; Comedy; Youth Theater; Ethnic Theater; Contemporary; Children's Theater
Status: Non-Profit, Professional
Paid Staff: 150
Paid Artists: 20
Income Sources: Inter-theatre Institute; American Association of Theatre Educators
Performs At: Moulton Theater
Organization Type: Performing; Educational

2485
CALIFORNIA REPERTORY COMPANY
1250 Bellflower Boulevard
Long Beach, CA 90840-2701
Phone: 562-985-4500
Fax: 562-985-2263
e-mail: publicrelations@calrep.org
Web Site: http://www.calrep.org/
Officers:
 President: Keith Polakoff, Ph.D.
 Managing Director: Eric Imley
Management:
 Managing Director: Eric Imley
 Artistic Producing Director: Joanne Gordon
 Founder: Howard Burman
 Technical Director: Jeff Hickman
 Designer & Stage Technician: Corey Holst
 Business Manager: Ashley Boehne Ehlers
 Production Manager: Sarah Joynt-Borger
Founded: 1989
Specialized Field: Educational; Theater Workshops
Performs At: UT Theatre, Studio Theatre, Edison Theatre, Players Theatre
Type of Stage: Proscenium, Flexible
Seating Capacity: 400, 225, 99, 90

2486
CALIFORNIA STATE UNIVERSITY, LONG BEACH: DEPARTMENT OF THEATRE
1250 Bellflower Boulevard
Long Beach, CA 90840
Phone: 562-985-5357
Fax: 562-985-2263
Web Site: www.csulb.edu
Officers:
 Chairman: Howard Burman
Management:

 Department Chairman: Joanne Gordon
 Managing Director: Eric Imley
Specialized Field: Educational; Theater Workshops
Status: Non-Profit, Non-Professional
Affiliations: NAST; California Repertory Company
Seating Capacity: 378; 250; 90; 99
Year Built: 1952
Year Remodeled: 1989

2487
FOUND THEATRE
599 Long Beach Blvd. at 6th St.
Long Beach, CA 90813
Phone: 562-433-3363
e-mail: info@foundtheatre.org
Web Site: http://www.foundtheatre.org/
Management:
 Artistic Managing Director: Cynthia Galles
 Literary Director: Virginia DeMoss
 Music Director: Alice Secrist
Mission: To provide professional-quality alternative theatre to the community as inexpensively as possible; to provide a place for actors, directors, and technicians to experiment, refine their craft, and grow as artists.
Founded: 1974
Specialized Field: Drama; Comedy; Musical
Status: Professional; Nonprofit
Performs At: The Found Theatre
Organization Type: Performing

2488
MYART
6285 East Spring Street
Long Beach, CA 90808
Mailing Address: 6285 East Spring Street Long Beach, CA 90808
Phone: 800-400-2985
Toll-free: 800-400-2985
e-mail: info@myart.org
Web Site: http://www.myart.org/
Officers:
 President: Liana Koeppel-Taylor
Management:
 Artistic Director: Dana Hanstein-Hanlan
 Treasurer: Matt Batezel
 Vice President: Vanessa Knowles
Mission: Providing instruction and performance experience in acting, singing, dancing, and stage movement. The program is endorsed as an excellent venue for training in the fine arts by a host of primary and secondary educators and by numerous entertainment professionals and by the Theatre Department at California State University.
Founded: 1989
Specialized Field: Youth Theater; Musical; Educational

2489
BUS BARN STAGE COMPANY
97 Hillview Avenue
PO Box 151
Los Altos, CA 94023-0151
Mailing Address: PO Box 151, Los Altos, CA 94023
Phone: 650-941-0551
Fax: 650-941-0884
e-mail: busbarn@busbarn.org
Web Site: www.busbarn.org
Officers:
 President: Vicki Reeder
 Secretary: Roy Lave
 Treasurer: Jean Mordo
 Managing Director: Gary Landis
Management:
 Executive Dirceton: Gary Landis
 Associate Artistic Director: Daniel P. Wilson

THEATRE / California

Box Office Manager: Lucky Littlewood
Graphic Designer: Shannon Stowe
Photography: Joyce Goldschmid
Box Office Manager: Nada Monaco-Angell
Mission: To engage the community and the artists in a shared experience of intimate, professional-quality theatre. Bus Barn is a professionally managed, community based theatre company serving Los Altos, and the greater South Bay community.
Utilizes: Actors; Guest Artists; Guest Conductors; Guest Lecturers; Original Music Scores; Resident Professionals
Founded: 1995
Specialized Field: Drama; Musical
Status: Nonprofit
Paid Staff: 5
Budget: $260,000
Income Sources: Box Office; Grants; Individual donations
Performs At: Bus Barn Theatre
Affiliations: Theatre Bay Area
Annual Attendance: 7,000
Type of Stage: Proscenium
Seating Capacity: 100
Year Built: 1965
Year Remodeled: 1980

2490
A NOISE WITHIN
234 South Brand Boulevard
Los Angeles, CA 91204
Phone: 818-240-0910
Fax: 818-240-0826
e-mail: pr@anoisewithin.org
Web Site: www.anoisewithin.org
Management:
  Artistic Director/ Founder: Geoff Elliott
  Production Manager: Rebecca Baillie
  Artistic Director/ Founder: Julia Rodriquez
  General Manager: Todd Delliger
  Public Relations: Laura Stegman
Mission: To present the classics of world literature in rotating repertory performed by a classically trained ensemble.
Founded: 1991
Specialized Field: Comedy; Youth Theater
Status: Non-Profit, Professional
Paid Staff: 11
Paid Artists: 35
Type of Stage: Thrust
Seating Capacity: 200 - 300

2491
ACTORS ART THEATRE
6128 Wilshire Boulevard
Los Angeles, CA 90048
Phone: 323-969-4953
Fax: 323-857-5891
e-mail: info@actorsart.com
Web Site: http://www.actorsart.com
Management:
  Artistic Director: Jolene Adams
  Managing Director: Douglas Coler
  Facility Manager: Grady Lee Richmond
Specialized Field: Theater Workshops; Ensembles

2492
ACTORS FOR THEMSELVES
Matrix Theatre
7657 Melrose Avenue
Los Angeles, CA 90048
Phone: 213-852-1445
Management:
  Artistic Director: Joe Stern

Mission: Giving actors a chance to hone their craft and affording them more opportunity to control the production process.
Utilizes: Guest Companies; Singers
Founded: 1974
Specialized Field: Theater Workshops; Drama; Movement Theater
Status: Professional; Nonprofit
Performs At: Matrix Theatre
Organization Type: Performing; Resident; Educational

2493
AHMANSON THEATRE
Center Theatre Group
601 W Temple St
Los Angeles, CA 90012
Mailing Address: 601 W Temple St Los Angeles CA 90012
Phone: 213-628-2772
Fax: 213-972-7431
e-mail: ArtDir@centertheatregroup.org
Web Site: www.centertheatregroup.com
Officers:
  Chairperson: Martin Massman
  President: William A Ahmanson
  VP: Ava Fries
  Secretary: Martin C Washton
Management:
  Artistic Director: Michael Ritchie
  Managing Director: Charles Dillingham
  Vice President: Ava Fries
Mission: To serve the diverse audiences of Los Angeles by producing and presenting theatre of the highest caliber, by nurturing new artists, by attracting new audiences, and by developing youth outreach and arts education programs. This mission is based on a belief that the art of theatre is a cultural force with the capacity to transform the lives of individuals and society at large.
Utilizes: Actors; AEA Actors; Arrangers; Artists-in-Residence; Choreographers; Collaborating Artists; Collaborations; Community Members; Dancers; Designers; Educators; Equity Actors; Five Seasonal Concerts; Guest Accompanists; Guest Artists; Guest Companies; Guest Composers; Guest Conductors; Guest Designers; Guest Lecturers; Guest Musical Directors; Guest Teachers; Instructors; Local Artists; Local Artists & Directors; Local Unknown Artists; Lyricists; Multi Collaborations; Multimedia; Music; Organization Contracts; Original Music Scores; Paid Performers; Performance Artists; Poets; Resident Artists; Resident Companies; Resident Professionals; Scenic Designers; Selected Students; Sign Language Translators; Singers; Soloists; Students; Student Interns; Special Technical Talent; Theatre Companies; Touring Companies; Visual Arts; Visual Designers; Volunteer Directors & Actors; Writers
Founded: 1967
Opened: 1967
Specialized Field: Musical; Drama; Comedy
Status: Non-Profit; Professional
Performs At: Music Center of Los Angeles
Affiliations: Mark Taper Forum. Kirk Douglas Theatre
Facility Category: Music Center of Los Angeles
Type of Stage: Proscenium
Stage Dimensions: 190Wx47Dx67H; 40Wx28H
Seating Capacity: 1,600-2,000
Year Built: 1967
Year Remodeled: 1995
Rental Contact: Gordon Davidson

2494
ATTIC THEATRE CENTRE
5429 W Washington Boulevard
Los Angeles, CA 90016-1112
Phone: 424-209-2284
e-mail: info@attictheatre.org
Web Site: www.attictheatre.org
Management:
  Executive Producer: James Carey
  Artistic Director: August Vivirito
  Managing Producer: T L Kolman
  VP: John Szura
Mission: To provide a small theatre with its own resident company which is also available for rental to outside productions.
Utilizes: Singers
Founded: 1995
Specialized Field: Theater Workshops; Ensembles; Experimental
Status: Professional; Semi-Professional; Commercial
Income Sources: Theatre Los Angeles
Organization Type: Performing; Resident; Sponsoring

2495
BILINGUAL FOUNDATION OF THE ARTS
421 N Avenue 19
Los Angeles, CA 90031
Phone: 323-225-4044
Fax: 323-225-1250
Web Site: www.bfatheatre.org
Officers:
  Chairman: John Echeveste
  Film Festival Director: Froylon Cabuta
  Stage Manager: Cecilia Garcia
Management:
  Artistic Director: Margarita Galban
  Managing Director: Luisa Cariaga
  Associate Professor: Estela Scarlata
  Office Manager: Lina Montalvo
  Marketing Manager: Luis Vela
Mission: Celebrating the richness and diversity of Hispanic Theater by offering theatre produced and directed in English and Spanish.
Utilizes: Guest Companies
Founded: 1973
Specialized Field: Classic; Ensembles; Spanish Language Company
Status: Non-Profit, Professional
Paid Staff: 6
Performs At: The Bilingual Foundation of the Arts Theatre
Affiliations: American Arts Alliance; Theatre Communications Group; California Confederation of the Arts
Annual Attendance: 125,000
Type of Stage: Thrust
Seating Capacity: 99 & 299
Organization Type: Performing; Touring; Educational

2496
BOB BAKER MARIONETTE THEATRE
1345 W First Street
Los Angeles, CA 90026
Phone: 215-250-9995
Fax: 213-250-1120
e-mail: bob@bobbakermarionettes.com
Web Site: http://www.bobbakermarionettes.com/
Mission: Marionette productions available for birthday parties and shop tours.
Utilizes: Soloists; Student Interns
Founded: 1963
Specialized Field: Puppet
Status: Professional

THEATRE / California

Income Sources: Admissions
Performs At: Marionette Theatre
Type of Stage: Proscenium; 3/4 Arena
Seating Capacity: 200
Year Built: 1950
Year Remodeled: 1963
Organization Type: Resident

2497
CALIFORNIA STATE UNIVERSITY-LOS ANGELES - PLAYERS

5151 State University Drive
Los Angeles, CA 90032
Phone: 323-343-4110
e-mail: srothma@exchange.calstatela.edu
Web Site: www.calstatela.edu
Management:
    Chair/Professor Of Theatre Arts: Stephen Rothman
    Assistant Professor Of Theatre Arts: Meredith Greenburg
Founded: 1947
Specialized Field: Educational; Theater Workshops

2498
CORNERSTONE THEATER COMPANY

708 Traction Avenue
Los Angeles, CA 90013
Phone: 213-613-1700
Fax: 213-613-1714
e-mail: info@cornerstonetheater.org
Web Site: www.cornerstonetheater.org
Officers:
    Director of Development: Natalie Conneely
    Director of Engagement: Paula Donnelly
Management:
    Founding Director: Alison Carey
    Program Associate: Teeko Parran
    General Manager: Sara Adelman
    Communications & Development Asst.: James Cheeks III
Founded: 1986
Specialized Field: Multi-Cultural; Ensembles; Contemporary; Drama
Status: Nonprofit
Season: Year Round

2499
EAST WEST PLAYERS

120 N Judge John Aiso Street
Los Angeles, CA 90012
Phone: 213-625-7000
Fax: 213-625-7111
e-mail: info@eastwestplayers.org
Web Site: www.eastwestplayers.org
Officers:
    Chairperson: Lynn Fukuhara Arthurs
    President: Wendy Fujihara Anderson
    Vice President: Chirag Shah
    Chief Financial Officer: David Solin Lee
    President: Robert M. Kawahara
    Arts Education Director: Marilyn Tokuda
    Director of Production: Meg Imamoto
Management:
    PR/Marketing Manager: Jay Africa
    Secretary: Jocelyn R. Wang
    Producing Artistic Director: Tim Dang
    Art Education Director: Marilyn Tokuda
    Marketing Assistant: Krystel Gapasin
Mission: To be a leader in creating engaging, and empowering theatre that gives voice to the Asian Pacific Islander community.

Utilizes: Actors; AEA Actors; Artists-in-Residence; Choreographers; Collaborating Artists; Collaborations; Commissioned Composers; Dancers; Designers; Educators; Five Seasonal Concerts; Grant Writers; Guest Accompanists; Guest Artists; Guest Choreographers; Guest Companies; Guest Composers; Guest Conductors; Guest Designers; Guest Ensembles; Guest Instructors; Guest Lecturers; Guest Musical Directors; Guest Musicians; Guest Soloists; Guest Teachers; High School Drama; Instructors; Local Artists; Local Unknown Artists; Lyricists; Multimedia; Music; Organization Contracts; Original Music Scores; Performance Artists; Playwrights; Poets; Selected Students; Sign Language Translators; Singers; Soloists; Student Interns; Special Technical Talent; Theatre Companies; Visual Arts
Founded: 1965
Specialized Field: Drama; Musical
Status: Professional; Nonprofit
Paid Staff: 10
Volunteer Staff: 300
Paid Artists: 50
Non-paid Artists: 50
Budget: $1,000,000
Annual Attendance: 30,000
Facility Category: Theater
Type of Stage: Open/Modified Proscenium
Seating Capacity: 240
Year Built: 1922
Year Remodeled: 1997
Rental Contact: Meg Imamoto
Organization Type: Performing; Touring; Resident; Educational

2500
ECHO THEATER COMPANY

3269 Casitas Avenue
Los Angeles, CA 90039
Mailing Address: 12400 Ventura Blvd #165 Studio City, CA 91604
Phone: 877-369-9112
e-mail: info@echotheatercompany.com
Web Site: echotheatercompany.com
Management:
    Producing Artistic Director: Chris Fields
    Producing Director: Lauren Bass
    Managing Artistic Director: Drew Dalzell
Status: Nonprofit

2501
FOUNTAIN THEATRE

5060 Fountain Avenue
Los Angeles, CA 90029
Phone: 323-663-1525
Fax: 323-663-1629
e-mail: info@fountaintheatre.com
Web Site: www.fountaintheatre.com
Management:
    Producing Director/Dramaturg: Simon Levy
    Producing Artistic Director: Deborah Lawlor
    Managing Artistic Director: Stephen Sachs
    Media Relations: Lucy Pollak
Mission: A full season of theatre and flamenco.
Founded: 1990
Specialized Field: Theatre; Dance
Status: Non-Profit, Professional
Paid Staff: 5
Paid Artists: 45
Budget: $450,000
Performs At: Fountain Theatre
Affiliations: TCG; Theatre
Type of Stage: Thrust
Seating Capacity: 78

2502
GEFFEN PLAYHOUSE

10886 Le Conte Avenue
Los Angeles, CA 90024
Phone: 310-208-5454
Fax: 310-208-8383
e-mail: boxoffice@geffenplayhouse.com
Web Site: www.geffenplayhouse.com
Officers:
    General Manager: Paul Morer
    Technical Director: Matthew Carleton
    Chief Development Officer: Regine Miller
    Brand Co Chair: Martha Henderson
    Brand Co Chair: Pamela Robinson Hollander
Management:
    President: Gilbert Cates
    Artistic Director: Randall Arney
    Managing Director: Ken Novice
    General Manager: Behnaz Ataee
    Associate Production Manager: Jill Barnes
    Associate Box Office Manager: Janice Bernal
Mission: To produce quality theatre in a broad range of presentations of many moods and characters; to present comedy, drama, musicals, new plays, revivals, classics, experimental children's theatre, special events, multimedia.
Utilizes: Guest Companies; Singers
Founded: 1995
Specialized Field: Drama; Comedy; Musical; Youth Theater; New Plays
Status: Non-Profit
Performs At: Geffen Playhouse
Type of Stage: Proscenium
Seating Capacity: 498
Organization Type: Performing; Resident

2503
GREEK THEATRE

2700 N Vermont Avenue
Los Angeles, CA 90027
Phone: 323-665-5857
Fax: 323-666-8202
e-mail: yourcontact@greektheatrela.com
Web Site: www.greektheatrela.com
Management:
    President: James N Landrella
    General Manager: Susan Rosenbluth
Mission: The Greek Theatre, Los Angeles' premiere outdoor theatre, is nestled in the picturesque tree-enclosed setting of Griffith Park. This award-winning theatre is one of Los Angeles' most historic entertainment venues and has played host to some of the biggest names in entertainment, from pop to classical, reggae to rock. The legendary Greek Theatre offers entertainment to every segment of the population.
Utilizes: Singers
Founded: 1930
Specialized Field: Musical; Ethnic Theater
Status: Commercial
Performs At: Greek Theatre
Organization Type: Performing

2504
GROUNDLING THEATRE

7307 Melrose Avenue
Los Angeles, CA 90046
Phone: 323-934-4747
Fax: 323-934-8143
e-mail: school@groundlings.com
Web Site: www.groundlings.com
Officers:
    Chairman: Ron Hoffman

THEATRE / California

CEO: Guy Greco
Treasurer: Nicholas Antonian
Litigation Attorney: Rick Davis
Management:
    Executive Director: Eric Vennerbeck
    Office Manager &School Coordinator: Carrie LaFerle Gergely
    School Administrator: Tassi Duffner
    Graphic Design &Asst. Box Office Ma: Matthew Buchholtz
Mission: To create new comedy talent and new comedy productions.
Founded: 1974
Specialized Field: Comedy; Improvisation
Status: Nonprofit
Paid Staff: 5
Volunteer Staff: 15
Non-paid Artists: 30
Income Sources: Shows; Donations; School of Improvitional Comedy
Performs At: The Groundling Theatre
Annual Attendance: 20,000
Seating Capacity: 99
Organization Type: Performing; Resident

2505
HOLLYWOOD COMPLEX THEATRE
6476 Santa Monica Boulevard
Los Angeles, CA 90038
Phone: 323-465-0383
Fax: 323-469-5408
e-mail: complexhollywood@hotmail.com
Web Site: www.complexhollywood.com
Management:
    Owner: Matt Chait
    Assistant: Ryan Callahan
    Assistant Manager: David Svengalis
Utilizes: Actors; AEA Actors; Guest Instructors; High School Drama; Resident Artists; Resident Professionals; Student Interns; Special Technical Talent
Founded: 1990
Specialized Field: Drama; Comedy
Status: For-Profit, Non-Professional
Paid Staff: 2
Facility Category: 5 Theaters
Type of Stage: 4 Proscenium, 1 Black Box
Seating Capacity: 42-55
Cost: $150-225 per night
Rental Contact: Matt Ryan
Organization Type: Performing

2507
LOS ANGELES THEATRE CENTER: MOVING ARTS
1822 Hyperion Ave
Los Angeles, CA 90027
Mailing Address: PO BOX 481145 Los Angeles, CA 90048
Phone: 323-666-3259
Fax: 213-622-8946
e-mail: info@movingarts.org
Web Site: www.movingarts.org
Officers:
    Interim Artistic Director: Lee Wochner
    Managing Director: Steve Lozier
Management:
    Artistic Director: Lee Wochner
    Artistic Director: Julie Briggs
    Literary Director: Trey Nichols
    Administrative Director: David Davidson
Mission: We produce new plays that challenge, illuminate, and reveal truths about the human condition in a fresh and startling way.
Utilizes: Actors

Founded: 1992
Specialized Field: Drama; Movement Theater
Paid Staff: 1
Volunteer Staff: 3
Non-paid Artists: 28

2508
LOYOLA MARYMOUNT UNIVERSITY THEATRE ARTS DEPARTMENT
1 LMU Drive, MS 8210
Los Angeles, CA 90045
Phone: 310-338-2837
Web Site: http://cfa.lmu.edu/programs/theatre.htm
Management:
    Chair/Theatre Arts Program: Diane Benedict
    Theatre Arts Staff: Jeanine Conner
Specialized Field: Educational; Theater Workshops
Affiliations: NAST; ATHE
Seating Capacity: 174; 100
Year Built: 1961

2509
MARK TAPER FORUM
Center Theatre Group
601 W Temple Street
Los Angeles, CA 90012
Mailing Address: 601 W Temple St Los Angeles CA 90012
Phone: 213-628-2772
Fax: 213-628-2796
e-mail: ArtDir@centertheatregroup.org
Web Site: www.centretheatregroup.org
Officers:
    Chairman: Martin Massman
    President: William H Ahmanson
    VP: Ava Fries
    Secretary: Martin C Washton
    Treasurer: Dr Steven Nagelberg
Management:
    Artistic Director: Michael Ritchie
    Managing Director: Charles Dillingham
    Vice President: Ava Fries
Mission: To serve the diverse audiences of Los Angeles by producing and presenting theatre of the highest caliber, by nurturing new artists, by attracting new audiences, and by developing youth outreach and arts education programs. This mission is based on a belief that the art of theatre is a cultural force with the capacity to transform the lives of individuals and society at large.
Utilizes: Actors; AEA Actors; Arrangers; Artists-in-Residence; Choreographers; Collaborating Artists; Collaborations; Community Members; Contract Actors; Dancers; Designers; Educators; Equity Actors; Five Seasonal Concerts; Guest Accompanists; Guest Artists; Guest Companies; Guest Composers; Guest Conductors; Guest Designers; Guest Lecturers; Guest Musical Directors; Guest Teachers; Instructors; Local Artists; Local Artists & Directors; Local Unknown Artists; Lyricists; Multi Collaborations; Multimedia; Music; Organization Contracts; Original Music Scores; Paid Performers; Performance Artists; Poets; Resident Artists; Resident Companies; Resident Professionals; Scenic Designers; Selected Students; Sign Language Translators; Singers; Soloists; Students; Student Interns; Special Technical Talent; Theatre Companies; Touring Companies; Visual Arts; Visual Designers; Volunteer Directors & Actors; Writers
Founded: 1967
Opened: 1967
Specialized Field: Musical; Comedy; Drama
Status: Non-Profit; Professional
Paid Staff: 350
Performs At: Performing Arts Center of Los Angeles

Affiliations: Ahmanson Theatre; Kirk Douglas Theatre
Annual Attendance: 250,000
Facility Category: Music Center of Los Angeles
Type of Stage: Thrust
Stage Dimensions: 190Wx47Dx67H; 40Wx28H
Seating Capacity: 739
Year Built: 1967
Year Remodeled: 2008

2511
NINE O'CLOCK PLAYERS
1367 N. St. Andrews Place
Los Angeles, CA 90028-8529
Phone: 323-469-1970
Fax: 323-469-1443
e-mail: gale_jaffe@yahoo.com
Web Site: www.nineoclockplayers.com
Officers:
    Chairman: Sue Leisner
    Chairman/Production: Tricia Schaetzle
Mission: To provide free musical theater for culturally and physically disadvantaged children as well as paid performances for all children of Southern California; to donate proceeds to the services of the Assistance League of Southern California.
Utilizes: Commissioned Composers; Designers; Guest Companies; Music; Organization Contracts; Resident Professionals; Student Interns; Visual Arts
Founded: 1929
Specialized Field: Musical; Ensembles; Children's Theater; Classic Fairy Tales
Status: Semi-Professional; Nonprofit
Paid Staff: 4
Volunteer Staff: 145
Budget: $100,000
Income Sources: Donations; Tickets
Performs At: ALSC Playhouse
Affiliations: Assistance League of Southern California
Annual Attendance: 17,000
Facility Category: Theatre
Seating Capacity: 329
Year Built: 1938
Rental Contact: 323-469-1973 Janet Harrison
Organization Type: Performing; Touring

2512
OCCIDENTAL COLLEGE DEPARTMENT OF THEATRE
1600 Campus Road
Los Angeles, CA 90041
Phone: 323-259-2500
Fax: 213-341-4987
e-mail: beatrice@oxy.edu
Web Site: www.oxy.edu/theater
Officers:
    Chairman: Susan Gratch
Specialized Field: Educational; Theater Workshops
Budget: $4,400-$6,800
Seating Capacity: 400
Year Built: 1988

2513
ODYSSEY THEATRE ENSEMBLE
2055 S Sepulveda Boulevard
Los Angeles, CA 90025
Phone: 310-477-2055
Fax: 310-444-0455
e-mail: boxoffice@odysseytheatre.com
Web Site: www.odysseytheatre.com
Officers:
    President: Sol Rabin
    Secretary: Ben Olan
    VP: David Simon
    Treasurer: Fred Mantner

Management:
  Artistic Director: Ron Sossi
  Associate Artistic Director: Beth Hogan
  Production Manager: Christina Burck
  Associate Artistic Director: Beth Hogan
Mission: The creation of a theatre centre which is experimental and alternative and houses an ensemble company; the development of an international theatre center.
Utilizes: Guest Companies; Singers
Founded: 1969
Specialized Field: Ensembles; Ethnic Theater
Status: Non-Profit, Professional
Paid Staff: 14
Volunteer Staff: 86
Paid Artists: 126
Budget: $700,000
Income Sources: Theatre Consortium (Los Angeles Theatre Pass); League of Producers; Theatres of Los Angeles; Los Angeles Theatre Alliance; Theatre Communications Group
Performs At: Odyssey Theatre
Annual Attendance: 2000
Seating Capacity: 99
Rental Contact: Stephanie Meyer
Organization Type: Performing; Resident; Sponsoring

2514
PLAYWRIGHTS' ARENA
514 S Spring Street
Los Angeles, CA 90013
Phone: 213-627-4459
Fax: 213-473-0620
e-mail: jrivera923@juno.com
Web Site: www.playwrightsarena.org/
Management:
  Artistic Director: Jon Lawrence Rivera
Mission: Dedicated to discovering, nurturing and producing bold new works for the stage written exclusively by Los Angeles playwrights. Develops new materials through several series of readings, workshops and round table discussions. Local playwrights are encouraged to create original, adventurous, daring materials with the intent of challenging the mind, touching the heart and provoking the spirit.
Founded: 1992
Specialized Field: New Plays
Status: Nonprofit
Season: January - December
Type of Stage: Proscenium
Seating Capacity: 35

2515
ROBEY THEATRE COMPANY
514 S Spring Street
Los Angeles, CA 90013
Phone: 213-489-7402
Fax: 213-489-4520
e-mail: robeytc@sbcglobal.net
Web Site: http://www.robeytheatrecompany.com/home.php
Management:
  Artistic Director/ Co-Founder/ Boar: Bennet Guillory
  Co-Founder: Danny Glover
  Development Director: Judith Bowman
  Board Secretary: Diana Smith
  Treasurer: Sarisa Middleton
Founded: 1994
Specialized Field: African American; Multi-Cultural

2516
ROGUE MACHINE THEATRE
504 W. Pico Blvd.
Los Angeles, CA 90019
Mailing Address: 12405 Venice Blvd. #153, Los Angeles, CA 90066
Phone: 855-585-5185
e-mail: roguemachineproductions@gmail.com
Web Site: roguemachinetheatre.com
Management:
  Production Manager: Amanda Mauer
  Artistic Director: John Perrin Flynn
Mission: To serve the greater Los Angeles community in developing and nurturing emerging playwrights, introducing important contemporary works to Southern California, and engaging diverse audiences by presenting vital, invigorating productions.
Founded: 2008
Status: Nonprofit

2517
THEATRE WEST
3333 Cahuenga Boulevard W
Los Angeles, CA 90068
Phone: 323-851-4839
Fax: 323-851-5286
e-mail: theatrewest@theatrewest.org
Web Site: www.theatrewest.org
  Executive Director: John Gallogly
Management:
  Technology Program Manager: Michelle Higgs
  Executive Director: John Gallogly
  Education Director: Heather Keller McCarthy
  Social Media Manager: Corinne Shor
  Public Relations: Philip Sokoloff
Mission: Conducting weekly theater workshops; producing several plays annually; enhancing the cultural life of the community.
Utilizes: Actors; AEA Actors; Collaborations; Five Seasonal Concerts; Guest Companies; Multimedia; Organization Contracts; Original Music Scores; Performance Artists; Resident Professionals; Sign Language Translators; Visual Arts
Founded: 1962
Specialized Field: Musical; Comedy; Youth Theater; Community Theater; Classic; Contemporary
Status: Non-Profit, Professional
Paid Staff: 3
Volunteer Staff: 100
Paid Artists: 20
Income Sources: Dues; fund-raisers; grants; donations, ticket sales
Performs At: Theatre West
Annual Attendance: 19,000
Facility Category: Non-profit
Seating Capacity: 168
Organization Type: Performing; Resident; Educational

2518
UNIVERSITY OF CALIFORNIA-LOS ANGELES: DEPARTMENT OF THEATER
102 E Melnitz
Box 951622
Los Angeles, CA 90095
Phone: 310-206-2738
Fax: 310-825-3383
e-mail: info@tft.ucla.edu
Web Site: www.tft.ucla.edu
Management:
  Chancellor: Albert Carnesale
  Chairman of Theatre Department: William Ward
Founded: 1919
Specialized Field: Educational; Theater Workshops
Status: Non-Profit, Non-Professional
Paid Staff: 3
Paid Artists: 50
Budget: $7,100-$22,500
Affiliations: Geffen Playhouse
Seating Capacity: 589; 200; 100
Year Built: 1963

2519
UNIVERSITY OF SOUTHERN CALIFORNIA: SCHOOL OF THEATRE
1029 Childs Way
Los Angeles, CA 90089-0791
Phone: 213-821-2744
Fax: 213-740-8888
e-mail: info@sda.usc.edu
Web Site: www.theatre.usc.edu
Officers:
  Director of Production: Elsbeth M. Collins
  Technical Director: Duncan Mahoney
  Assistant Dean, Director of Develop: Sara Fousekis
Management:
  Dean: Madeline Puzo
  Theatre Manager: CB Borger
  Assistant Theatre Manager: Fionnegan Justus Murphy
  Assistant Theatre Manager: Christopher Paci
Founded: 1945
Specialized Field: Educational; Theater Workshops
Affiliations: 24th Street Theatre
Seating Capacity: 575; 99; 60
Year Built: 1965

2520
WEST COAST ENSEMBLE
PO Box 868
Los Angeles, CA 91408
Phone: 818-786-1900
Fax: 818-786-1905
e-mail: wcemgmt@aol.com
Web Site: www.westcoastensemble.org/
Officers:
  Managing Director of Marketing: Sara J. Stuckey
  Managing Director of Fund Raising: JJ Jackman
  Managing Director of Membership: Suzanne Doss
  Co-Artistic Director: Richard Israel
  Co-Artistic Director and Founder: Les Hanson
Management:
  Artistic Director and Founder: Les Hanson
  Literary Associate: Don Cummings
  Co Artistic Director: Richard Israel
  Literary Associate: Don Cumming
  Managing Director Of Membership: Suzanne Doss
Founded: 1981
Specialized Field: Musical; Comedy; Drama

2521
WILTERN THEATRE
3790 Wilshire Boulevard
Los Angeles, CA 90010
Phone: 213-388-1400
Fax: 213-388-1400
Management:
  General Manager: Rena Wasserman
Specialized Field: Contemporary; Specialty Acts

2522
ZEPHYR THEATRE
7456 Melrose Avenue
Los Angeles, CA 90046

THEATRE / California

Phone: 323-653-4667
Fax: 323-852-0031
e-mail: thezephyrtheatre@gmail.com.
Web Site: www.zephyrtheatre.com/
Officers:
  Producing Artistic Director: Lee Sankowich
  Production Director: Elizabeth Collins
  Technical Director: Duncan Mahoney
  Development Director: Sara Fousekis
  Managing Director: Linda Toliver
  General Manager: Margie Kment
Mission: Providing a rental venue for independent producers to mount shows.
Utilizes: Guest Companies
Founded: 1977
Specialized Field: Light Theater
Status: For-Profit, Professional
Paid Staff: 2
Income Sources: Los Angeles League of Theaters & Producers
Performs At: Zephyr Theatre
Organization Type: Performing

2523
MENDOCINO THEATRE COMPANY
45200 Little Lake Street
PO Box 800
Mendocino, CA 95460
Phone: 707-937-2718
Fax: 707-937-3625
e-mail: mtc@mcn.org
Web Site: www.mendocinotheatre.org/
Officers:
  President: Douglas Warner
Management:
  Marketing Director: Sara Stuckey
  Membership Director: Suzanne Doss
  House Manager: Cheryl Dupre,
  Producing Director: Felicia Freitas,
  Operations Manager: Jim Gibson
Mission: The mission of the Mendocino Theatre Company is to produce plays of substance and excitement ranging from classics to cutting edge; nurture local talent; and provide meaningful theatrical experiences for both local and visiting audiences.
Founded: 1977
Specialized Field: Comedy; Youth Theater; Community Theater; Contemporary
Status: Non-Profit, Non-Professional
Paid Staff: 12

2524
MENLO PLAYERS GUILD
601 Laurel Street
Menlo Park, CA 90028
Mailing Address: PO Box 301, Menlo Park, CA. 94026
Phone: 213-463-5336
Fax: 213-463-5356
Specialized Field: Community Theater; Drama; Comedy

2525
THEATREWORKS
1100 Hamilton Court, Menlo Park
Menlo Park, CA 94025
Phone: 650-463-7109
Fax: 650-463-1963
Management:
  Casting Director: Leslie Martinson
  Company Manager: Jennifer Brasher
  Artistic Director: Robert Kelley
  Managing Director: Randy Adams
Founded: 1970

Specialized Field: Educational; Theater Workshops; Experimental

2526
MARIN THEATRE COMPANY
397 Miller Avenue
Mill Valley, CA 94941
Phone: 415-388-5208
Fax: 415-388-0768
e-mail: info@marintheatre.org
Web Site: www.marintheatre.org
Officers:
  President: Brian Houghton
  VP: Carl Berry
  Treasurer: Michael Pescatello
  Secretary: Kipp Delbyck
Management:
  Artistic Director: Jasson Minadakis
  Producing Director: Ryan Rilettech
  Development Director: Helen Rigby
  General Manager: Vivienne Dipeolu
  Production Manager: Jennifer Gadda
  Literary Manager/Dramaturg: Margot Melcon
Mission: Presenting a season of performances; developing and producing new plays; providing educational programs to over 6,000 students each year.
Utilizes: Actors; AEA Actors; Artists-in-Residence; Choreographers; Collaborations; Community Members; Composers; Educators; Equity Actors; Five Seasonal Concerts; High School Drama; Multimedia; Performance Artists; Resident Professionals; Students
Founded: 1966
Specialized Field: Live Theatre (Contemporary; Classic; Musicals)
Status: Non-Profit, Professional
Paid Staff: 12
Budget: $2.3 million
Income Sources: Ticket Sales; Grants (Foundation and Government); Individual Donations; Corporate Sponsorship; Special Events
Performs At: Marin Theatre Company
Annual Attendance: 40,000
Seating Capacity: 264
Rental Contact: Production Manager Jennifer Gadda
Organization Type: Performing; Resident; Educational; Sponsoring

2527
SADDLEBACK COLLEGE
28000 Marguerite Parkway
Mission Viejo, CA 92692-3635
Phone: 949-582-4500
Fax: 949-347-8653
e-mail: info@saddleback.cc.ca.us
Web Site: www.saddleback.edu
Management:
  President: Richard McCullough
  Director Performing Arts: Geof English
Specialized Field: Musical; Comedy; Youth Theater; Community Theater; Classic; Contemporary
Status: Non-Profit, Professional
Paid Staff: 10
Performs At: McKinney Theatre; Cabaret Theatre

2528
TEATRO SHALOM
1811 Monarch Drive
Napa, CA 94558
Phone: 707-226-9918
Fax: 707-224-8065
Management:
  Artistic Director: David Gassner
  Managing Director: David Acevedo

Specialized Field: Ethnic Theater; Multi-Cultural; Drama

2529
FOOTHILL THEATRE COMPANY
401 Broad Street
PO Box 1812
Nevada City, CA 95959
Phone: 530-265-9320
Fax: 530-265-9325
Toll-free: 888-730-8587
Web Site: www.foothilltheatre.org
Management:
  President: Alison Jones'Pomatto
  Executive Director: Cheri Slanigan
  Artistic Director: Philip Charles Sneed
Founded: 1977
Specialized Field: Musical; Comedy; Youth Theater; Dinner Theater; Ethnic Theater; Community Theater; Classic; Contemporary
Status: Non-Profit, Professional
Paid Staff: 12
Paid Artists: 100
Performs At: Nevada Theatre
Affiliations: AEA; CAC; TCG
Annual Attendance: 56,000
Facility Category: Historic Structure
Type of Stage: Proscenium
Seating Capacity: 246

2530
ACTORS FORUM THEATRE
10655 Magnolia Boulevard
North Hollywood, CA 91601
Phone: 818-506-0600
Fax: 818-506-0686
e-mail: Actors4mtheatre@aol.com
Web Site: www.actorsforumtheatre.org/
Management:
  Co-Artistic Director: Audrey Marlyn Singer
  Co-Artistic Director: Shawn Michael
Utilizes: Actors; AEA Actors; Artists-in-Residence; Choreographers; Collaborating Artists; Collaborations; Commissioned Composers; Commissioned Music; Composers; Composers-in-Residence; Contract Actors; Contract Orchestras; Curators; Dance Companies; Dancers; Designers; Educators; Filmmakers; Fine Artists; Five Seasonal Concerts; Grant Writers; Guest Accompanists; Guest Artists; Guest Choreographers; Guest Companies; Guest Composers; Guest Conductors; Guest Designers; Guest Directors; Guest Ensembles; Guest Instructors; Guest Lecturers; Guest Musical Directors; Guest Musicians; Guest Soloists; Guest Teachers; High School Drama; Instructors; Local Artists & Directors; Multimedia; Music; Original Music Scores; Paid Performers; Performance Artists; Sign Language Translators; Singers; Soloists
Founded: 1975
Specialized Field: Musical; Comedy; Drama; Theater Workshops
Status: Nonprofit
Income Sources: Patrons; Classes; Rentals; Shows
Facility Category: Theatre
Type of Stage: Floor with curtain
Stage Dimensions: 24' x 20'
Seating Capacity: 49
Year Remodeled: 1994

2531
GROUP REPERTORY THEATRE
10900 Burbank Boulevard
North Hollywood, CA 91601

THEATRE / California

Phone: 818-763-5990
e-mail: info@thegrouprep.com
Web Site: http://thegrouprep.com/index.php/1
Management:
  President: Richard Woody
  Secretary: Melissa Soso
  Treasurer: Lloyd Pedersen
Mission: To stage five to six productions each year emphasizing new works by playwrights and young actors; to work with the Los Angeles Unified School District to produce theatrical presentations for those learning English as a second language.
Founded: 1973
Specialized Field: Ensembles; Theater Workshops; Drama
Status: Professional; Nonprofit
Income Sources: Valley Arts Council
Performs At: Group Repertory Theatre
Organization Type: Performing

2532
SYNTHAXIS THEATRE COMPANY
6310 Whitsett Avenue
North Hollywood, CA 91607
Phone: 213-877-4726
Management:
  Executive Director: Estelle Bush
Mission: Presenting new works as well as lesser-known works of renowned authors; emphasizing works by women; presenting benefit performances and shows for children.
Founded: 1972
Specialized Field: Drama; Experimental; Theater Workshops
Status: Professional; Nonprofit
Income Sources: Los Angeles Theatre Alliance; San Fernando Valley Arts Council
Organization Type: Performing; Touring; Resident; Educational

2533
THE ROAD THEATRE COMPANY
10747 Magnolia Boulevard
North Hollywood, CA 91601
Phone: 818-761-8838
Web Site: roadtheatre.org
Mission: Support world, American and West Coast premieres of theatrical works which introduce new voices and new thoughts to the American stage.
Founded: 1991

2534
CALIFORNIA STATE UNIVERSITY, NORTHRIDGE: DEPARTMENT OF THEATRE
18111 Nordhoff Street
Northridge, CA 91330
Phone: 818-677-3086
Fax: 818-677-2080
e-mail: theatre@csun.edu
Web Site: http://www.csun.edu/theatre/
Officers:
  Dept. Chair: Peter Grego
Management:
  Theatre Manager: William Taylor
  Production Stage Manager: Rick Greaver
  Costume Shop: James DeWitt
Specialized Field: Educational; Theater Workshops
Affiliations: NAST; ATHE; Mark Taper Forum
Seating Capacity: 400; 205; 100
Year Built: 1960

2535
MILLS COLLEGE DEPARTMENT OF DRAMATIC ARTS & COMMUNICATIONS
5000 MacArthur Boulevard
Oakland, CA 94613
Phone: 510-430-2327
Fax: 510-430-3314
Officers:
  Chair: Ken Burke
Specialized Field: Educational; Theater Workshops
Budget: $1,050-$3,200
Seating Capacity: 196; 63
Year Built: 1901
Year Remodeled: 1972

2536
GREAT AMERICAN MELODRAMA AND VAUDEVILLE
1863 Pacific Boulevard, Highway 1
PO Box 1026
Oceano, CA 93445
Phone: 805-489-2499
Fax: 805-489-5539
e-mail: info@americanmelodrama.com
Web Site: www.americanmelodrama.com
Officers:
  President: John Schlenker
Management:
  Artistic Director: Eric Hoit
  Managing Director: Suzanne King
Mission: Produce 7 shows per year.
Founded: 1975
Specialized Field: Musical; Comedy; Drama
Status: For-Profit, Professional
Paid Staff: 8
Paid Artists: 9
Season: Year round
Type of Stage: Proscenium
Stage Dimensions: 20'x 25'
Seating Capacity: 260

2537
SHAKESPEARE ORANGE COUNTY
12762 Main Street
Orange, CA 92840
Mailing Address: PO Box 923, Orange, CA. 92856
Phone: 714-744-7016
Fax: 714-744-7015
Web Site: http://www.shakespeareoc.org/index.php
Management:
  Artistic Director: Thomas F Bradac
Founded: 1990
Specialized Field: Educational; Theater Workshops
Paid Staff: 5

2538
CALIFORNIA SHAKESPEARE THEATER
100 California Shakespeare Theater Way
Orinda, CA 94563
Mailing Address: 701 Heinz Avenue, Berkeley CA 94710
Phone: 510-548-9666
Fax: 510-843-9921
e-mail: info@calshakes.org
Web Site: calshakes.org
Management:
  Artistic Director: Jonathan Moscone
  Managing Director: Susie Falk
Mission: With Shakespeare's depth of humanity as our touchstone, we build character and community through authentic, inclusive, and joyful theater experiences.
Founded: 1974

2539
PALO ALTO CHILDREN'S THEATRE
1305 Middlefield Road
Palo Alto, CA 94301
Phone: 650-463-4930
Fax: 650-324-0291
Web Site: http://www.cityofpaloalto.org/default.asp
Management:
  Director: Patricia Briggs
  Assistant Director: Micheal Litfin
  Technical Director: Henry Loughman
  Costume Supervisor: Alison Williams
  Program Assistant: Sandy Rankin
Mission: To educate young people in all theatre arts including acting, dance, set design and construction, costuming and makeup, the design and use of sound and light systems, and performance direction and production.
Utilizes: Guest Companies; Guest Teachers; Singers
Founded: 1932
Specialized Field: Musical; Youth Theater; Children's Theater
Status: Non-Professional; Nonprofit
Performs At: Palo Alto Children's Theatre
Organization Type: Performing; Educational

2540
PALO ALTO PLAYERS
1305 Middlefield Road
Palo Alto, CA 94301
Phone: 650-329-0891
e-mail: info@paplayers.org
Web Site: paplayers.org
Officers:
  President: Eugenie Watson
  Vice President: Beth Ann Gambardella
Management:
  Artistic Director: Patrick Klein
  Managing Director: Diana Lynn Wiley
Mission: Palo Alto Players is committed to providing a meaningful theatre experience for both audience and production participants.
Founded: 1931
Status: Nonprofit
Performs At: Lucie Stern Theater 1305 Middlefield Road, Palo Alto, CA 94301

2541
THEATREWORKS
8355 West Peoria Avenue
Palo Alto, CA 85345
Mailing Address: 1100 Hamilton Court, Menlo Park, CA 94025
Phone: 650-463-7109
Fax: 650-463-1963
e-mail: boxoffice@theatreworks.org
Web Site: www.theatreworks.org
Officers:
  Chair: Julie Kaufman
  Founder: Nancy Meyer
  MD: Edward T. Anderson
  Director of Sales and Marketing: Christie King
  Managing Director: Phil Santora
  Executive Director: Dan Schay
Management:
  Artistic Director: Robert Kelley
  Managing Director: Phil Santora
  Associate Artistic Director: Leslie Martinson
  Director of New Work: Giovanna Sardelli
  Resident Musical Director: William Liberatore
Utilizes: Guest Companies; Singers
Founded: 1970
Specialized Field: Musical; Ensembles

THEATRE / California

Status: Professional; Semi-Professional; Nonprofit
Income Sources: Theatre Communications Group
Performs At: The Lucy Stern Theatre; The Mountain View Center
Organization Type: Performing

2542
PASADENA PLAYHOUSE
39 S El Molino Avenue
80 S Lake Avenue, Suite 500
Pasadena, CA 91101
Phone: 626-356-7529
Fax: 626-204-7399
e-mail: boxoffice@pasadenaplayhouse.org
Web Site: www.pasadenaplayhouse.org/
Officers:
   First Vice-President: Anne La Rose
   President: Valerie Amidon
   Second Vice-President: Kim O'Rourke
Management:
   Executive Director: Lyla L White
   Artistic Director: Sheldon Epps
   Producing Director: Tom Ware
   General Manager: Tom Ware
   Finance Assistant: Chris Lu
Founded: 1917
Specialized Field: New Plays; Classic; Musical

2543
CINNABAR THEATER
3333 Petaluma Boulevard N
Petaluma, CA 94952
Phone: 707-763-8920
Fax: 707-763-8929
e-mail: info@cinnabartheater.org
Web Site: www.cinnabartheater.org
Officers:
   Executive Director: Elly Lichenstein
Management:
   President: Dick Kapask
   Executive Director: Elly Lichenstein
   Box Office Manager: Madeleine Ashe
Founded: 1974
Specialized Field: Musical; Comedy; Youth Theater; Classic; Contemporary
Status: Non-Profit, Professional
Paid Staff: 11
Paid Artists: 40

2544
THEATRE EL DORADO
El Dorado County Fairgrounds
100 Placerville Drive
Placerville, CA 95667
Phone: 530-626-5193
Specialized Field: Community Theater; Educational

2545
CALIFORNIA STATE POLYTECHNIC UNIVERSITY: DEPARTMENT OF THEATRE AND DANCE
3801 W Temple Avenue
Pomona, CA 91768
Mailing Address: 3801 West Temple Ave. Bldg. 25Pomona, CA 91768
Phone: 909-869-7659
Fax: 909-869-3070
e-mail: mmmaslowski@csupomona.edu
Web Site: www.csupomona.edu
Officers:
   Chair: C. Julian White
Founded: 1963
Specialized Field: Educational; Theater Workshops; Tech Theater
Status: Non-Profit, Non-Professional
Paid Staff: 10
Budget: $5,375-$20,650
Affiliations: Mark Taper Forum; South Coast Repertory
Seating Capacity: 543; 300-500
Year Built: 1965
Year Remodeled: 1998

2546
DRAGON PRODUCTIONS
2120 Broadway Street
Redwood City, CA 94063
Phone: 650-493-2006
e-mail: info@dragonproductions.net
Web Site: dragonproductions.net
Management:
   Executive Artistic Director: Meredith Hagedorn
Mission: Dragon's mission is to produce professional theatre that is uncommon, intimate, and accessible to its audiences, artists, and community.
Opened: 1999

2547
PERFORMANCE RIVERSIDE
4800 Magnolia Avenue
Riverside, CA 92506
Phone: 951-222-8100
Fax: 951-222-8940
Web Site: http://www.performanceriverside.org/
Officers:
   Producing Artistic Director: Matt Neves
Management:
   Executive Director: Steven A Glaudini
   Producing Artistic Director: Rey O'Day
   Production Coordinator: Raymond Couture
   Theatre Box Office Specialist: Jennifer Lawson
   Theatre Scenic Specialist: Jason Graham
Founded: 1983
Specialized Field: Musical; Comedy; Community Theater; Puppet; Ensembles

2548
UNIVERSITY OF CALIFORNIA-RIVERSIDE: DEPARTMENT OF THEATRE
900 University Avenue
Riverside, CA 92521
Phone: 951-827-4602
Fax: 951-827-1255
e-mail: eric.barr@ucr.edu
Web Site: www.theatre.ucr.edu/
Officers:
   Chairman: Eric Barr
Management:
   Chairman: Eric Barr
   Managing Director: Mark Longlois
Founded: 1955
Specialized Field: Comedy; Ethnic Theater; Classic; Contemporary
Status: Non-Profit, Professional
Paid Staff: 4
Paid Artists: 2
Budget: $20,500-$22,500
Affiliations: ATHE; U/RTA
Seating Capacity: 500; 150; 120; 50

2549
SONOMA STATE UNIVERSITY THEATER DEPARTMENT
1801 E Cotati Avenue
Rohnert Park, CA 94928
Phone: 707-664-2474
Fax: 707-664-4332
Web Site: www.sonoma.edu/depts/performingartstheatre
Officers:
   Chair: Jeff Langley
   Chair, Department of Theatre Arts &: Kristen Daley
Management:
   President: Ruben Arminana
   Administrative Coordinator/ Departm: Shelley Martin
Founded: 1968
Specialized Field: Educational; Theater Workshops
Status: Non-Profit, Non-Professional
Paid Staff: 50
Budget: $14,250-$62,000
Affiliations: ATHE
Seating Capacity: 500; 300; 99
Year Built: 1990

2550
MAGIC CIRCLE THEATER
8 El Caminito Road
PO Box 1493
Roseville, CA 93924
Phone: 831-659-7500
Fax: 916-782-1766
e-mail: boxoffice@magiccircletheatre.net
Web Site: www.magiccircletheatre.net
Officers:
   President: Brian Null
Management:
   Artistic Director: Rosemarie Gerould
   Storywriter: James Lee Stantley
   Guitarist: William Kanengiser
Founded: 1987
Specialized Field: Musical; Comedy; Youth Theater; Dinner Theater; Community Theater; Contemporary
Status: Non-Profit, Non-Professional
Paid Staff: 7

2551
MAGIC CIRCLE THEATER
8 El Caminito Road
PO Box 1493
Roseville, CA 93924
Phone: 831-659-7500
Fax: 916-782-1766
e-mail: boxoffice@magiccircletheatre.net
Web Site: www.magiccircletheatre.net
Officers:
   President: Brian Null
Management:
   Artistic Director: Rosemarie Gerould
   Storywriter: James Lee Stantley
   Guitarist: William Kanengiser
Mission: To offer a high quality, full performing arts center for production and performance in the fields of dance, acting, and music. Additionally, we offer superior education and training of new talent in the areas of acting, dancing, technical support, production, and theatre management skills for all age groups. We will continue to invest in the future of our craft, to grow with the communities surrounding us, and to listen to our patrons.
Founded: 1987
Specialized Field: Theater in the Round; Drama
Budget: $500,000
Income Sources: Ads in the Program; Grants; Donations; Ticket Sales; Concessions; Sponsorships; Workshop Fees; Acting Class Fees
Performs At: Community Theatre
Affiliations: Roseville Theatre

THEATRE / California

Facility Category: Community Theatre
Type of Stage: Proscenium
Seating Capacity: 500
Year Built: 1929
Year Remodeled: 2001
Rental Contact: Executive Director Robert Gerould

2552
B STREET THEATER
2711 B Street
Sacramento, CA 95816
Phone: 916-448-9707
Fax: 916-443-0874
Web Site: www.bstreettheatre.org
Officers:
  Treasurer: John Barrett
  Secretary: Lisa Rossie
  Board President: Beth Carlsen
  Vice President: Gene Cheever
Management:
  Producing Artistic Director/CEO: Buck Busfield
  Founder/Owner: Randy Paragary
  Executive Director: Allan Zaremberg
  Board Treasurer: John Barrett
  Board Secretary: Martha Lofgren
Utilizes: Actors; Five Seasonal Concerts; Guest Designers; Instructors; Local Artists; Multimedia; Original Music Scores; Resident Professionals
Founded: 1991
Specialized Field: New American Works
Status: Non-Profit, Professional
Paid Staff: 15
Income Sources: Ticket Sales; Donations; Grants
Performs At: 3/4 Thrust Stage
Facility Category: Small Theatre
Year Built: 1991

2553
CALIFORNIA MUSICAL THEATRE
1419 H Street
Sacramento, CA 95814
Phone: 916-557-1999
Fax: 916-446-1370
e-mail: subscribers@calmt.com
Web Site: www.californiamusicaltheatre.com
Officers:
  President: Richard Lewis
  Chairman: Scott Robertson
  Vice Chair: Lisa Maas
  Secretary: Allan Robin
  Treasurer: Margaret L. Kane
Management:
  President: Richard Lewis
  Artistic Director: Scott Eckern
  Executive Producer: Richard Lewis
  Secretary: Dennis H. Mangers
  Treasurer: Margaret L. Kane
Founded: 1951
Specialized Field: Musical
Status: Non-Profit, Professional
Paid Staff: 25
Season: June-August
Type of Stage: Arena
Seating Capacity: 2500

2554
CALIFORNIA STATE UNIVERSITY, SACRAMENTO: DEPARTMENT OF THEATRE AND DANCE
6000 J Street
Sacramento, CA 95819
Phone: 916-278-6368
Fax: 916-278-5681
e-mail: theatre.dance@csus.edu
Web Site: www.csus.edu/dram
Officers:
  President: Alexander Gonzales
  Chairman of the Department: Linda Goodrich
  Chair: Dr. Melinda Wilson
  Vice Chair, Dance Coordinator: Lorelei Bayne
  Technical Director: Jeff Bercume
Management:
  Administrative Coordinator: Andrea Cool
  Costume Shop Manager: Audrey Walker
Founded: 1948
Specialized Field: Musical; Comedy; Youth Theater; Dinner Theater; Ethnic Theater; Community Theater; Puppet; Classic; Contemporary
Status: Non-Profit, Non-Professional
Paid Staff: 24
Performs At: Theatre (2); Small Outdoor/Indoor Stage; Dance Space (2)
Affiliations: NAST
Seating Capacity: 438;150;70
Year Built: 1957
Year Remodeled: 1970

2555
CAPITAL STAGE COMPANY
2215 J Street
Sacramento, CA 95816
Phone: 916-995-5464
Fax: 916-476-4973
e-mail: info@capstage.org
Web Site: www.capstage.org
Officers:
  Artistic Director: Stephanie Gularte
  Producing Dirctor: Jonathan Williams
  Marketing Director: Peter Mohrmann
Management:
  Artistic Director: Stephanie Gularte
  General Manager: Keith Riedell
  Producing Dirctor: Jonathan Williams
  Marketing Director: Peter Mohrmann
Mission: To provide audiences with quality dinning/live theatre experience with contemporary plays performed by Sacramento top talent.
Founded: 2000
Specialized Field: Dinner Theater
Paid Staff: 3

2556
LAMBDA PLAYERS
1927 L Street
Sacramento, CA 95814
Phone: 916-442-0185
Web Site: www.lambdaplayers.com/
Officers:
  President: Stephen Abate
  Secretary: Gregg Peterson
  Treasurer: Charles Peer
Specialized Field: Alternative; Contemporary
Affiliations: Sacramento Area Regional Theater Alliance and The League of Sacramento Theaters.

2557
SACRAMENTO THEATRE COMPANY
1419 H Street
Sacramento, CA 95814
Phone: 916-443-6722
Fax: 916-446-4066
Toll-free: 888-782-49
e-mail: info@sactheatre.org
Web Site: www.sactheatre.org
Officers:
  President: Carol Wieckowski Dreyer
  Vice President: Denis Davis
  Secretary: Jack Mitchell
  Treasurer: Mary Sue McNamara
Management:
  Producing Director: Michael Laun
  Business Development Director: Martha Lake
  Artistic Director: Matt Miller
  Finance Manager: Natalie Lucas
  Secretary: Jack Mitchell
  Treasurer: Mary Sue McNamara
Mission: To professionally produce contemporary and traditional theatrical works that are engaging to the hearts and minds of a diverse regional audience.
Founded: 1942
Specialized Field: Theater Workshops; Educational
Status: Non-Profit, Professional
Performs At: Mainstage Theatre; Stage 2
Facility Category: Theatre; Conservatory
Seating Capacity: 300/80

2558
WESTERN STAGE
411 Central Avenue Salinas
Salinas, CA 93901
Phone: 831-755-6816
Fax: 831-770-6012
e-mail: education@westernstage.org
Web Site: www.westernstage.org
Officers:
  President: Raul Chavez
  Artistic Director: Jon Selover
  Artistic Program Director: Melissa J. Chin-Parker
Management:
  Artistic Program Director: Melissa J Chin Parker
  Artistic Director: Jon Selover
  Managing/Development Director: John Light
  Marketing & Public Relations Manage: Ron Cacas
Mission: To provide theatre programs that educate and enrich the lives of the people of the Central Coast of California by utilizing professional artists, teachers, students and the community.
Utilizes: Actors; AEA Actors; Choreographers; Collaborations; Dancers; Designers; Educators; Fine Artists; Five Seasonal Concerts; Grant Writers; Guest Accompanists; Guest Artists; Guest Composers; Guest Conductors; Guest Designers; Guest Lecturers; Guest Musical Directors; Guest Teachers; Instructors; Local Artists; Multimedia; Music; Original Music Scores; Performance Artists; Resident Professionals; Sign Language Translators; Soloists; Student Interns; Visual Arts
Founded: 1973
Specialized Field: Drama; Musical
Status: Non-Equity; Nonprofit
Paid Staff: 16
Volunteer Staff: 18
Paid Artists: 41
Non-paid Artists: 11
Budget: $1,100,000
Income Sources: Ticket Sales; Donations; Contract Services
Season: June - August
Performs At: Main Theater; Black Box Studio
Affiliations: NAMT; TCG
Annual Attendance: 35,000
Type of Stage: Proscenium; Black Box
Seating Capacity: 501; 99
Year Built: 1973

THEATRE / California

2559
BROADWAY SAN DIEGO
3666 Fourth Avenue
San Diego, CA 92103
Phone: 619-564-3000
Fax: 619-564-3089
e-mail: info@broadwaysd.com
Web Site: broadwaysd.com
Mission: To bring the best of Broadway to San Diego audiences.
Specialized Field: Broadway Shows

2560
CHRONOS THEATRE GROUP
930 Tenth Avenue
San Diego, CA 92101
Mailing Address: 930 Tenth Avenue, Suite 409, San Diego, CA 92101
Phone: 619-356-1492
e-mail: info@chronostheatre.com
Web Site: chronostheatre.com
Officers:
  President: Goyo Flores
  Vice President: Bryant Hernandez
Management:
  Artistic Director: Celeste Innocenti
Mission: Chronos Theatre Group seeks to connect diverse modern audiences with theater and performing arts from various world cultures and time periods.
Status: Nonprofit
Performs At: The Tenth Avenue Arts Center

2561
CYGNET THEATRE
4040 Twiggs Street
San Diego, CA 92110
Phone: 619-337-1525
Fax: 619-704-2707
e-mail: boxoffice@cygnettheatre.com
Web Site: cygnettheatre.com
Management:
  Artistic Director: Sean Murray
  Executive Director: Bill Schmidt
Mission: Believing in the power of theatre to startle the soul, ignite debate and embrace the diversity of the community in which it serves, Cygnet Theatre Company is fearlessly committed to the dissection, examination and celebration of the human story through the medium of live theatre.
Founded: 2003

2562
HORTON GRAND THEATRE
444 Fourth Avenue
San Diego, CA 92101
Phone: 619-437-6000
Fax: 619-234-3587
Management:
  General Manager: Matt Boden
Utilizes: Guest Companies
Founded: 1985
Specialized Field: Comedy
Paid Staff: 20
Paid Artists: 20
Income Sources: Ticket Sales
Affiliations: San Diego Arts Leauge; San Diego Regional Chamber of Commerce; San Diego Convention & Visitors Bureau
Annual Attendance: 50,000
Facility Category: Rental House
Type of Stage: Proscenium
Stage Dimensions: 29'9x18'x2'6
Organization Type: Performing; Educational; Sponsoring

2563
MARIE HITCHCOCK PUPPET THEATRE IN BALBOA
Balboa Park Management Office
2130 Pan American Plaza
San Diego, CA 92101
Mailing Address: 2130 Pan American Place
Phone: 619-544-9203
Fax: 619-235-1100
e-mail: balboaparkpuppets@yahoo.com
Web Site: http://www.balboaparkpuppets.com/index.html
Officers:
  President: Joe Fitzpatrick
  Vice President: Gastin Morineau
  Treasurer: Millie Patterson
  Secretary: Terri Crook
Specialized Field: Puppet
Affiliations: San Diego Guild of Puppetry
Facility Category: Puppet Theatre
Type of Stage: Proscenium

2564
MYSTERY CAFE
505 Kalmia Street
San Diego, CA 92101
Phone: 619-460-2200
e-mail: info@mysterycafe.net
Web Site: mysterysd.wix.com/mysterycafe
Specialized Field: Interactive Mystery Comedy Theater
Organization Type: Dinner Theatre ; Traveling ; Performing

2565
OLD GLOBE
1363 Old Globe Way
San Diego, CA 92101-1696
Mailing Address: PO Box 122171, San Diego, CA. 92112-2171
Phone: 619-234-1941
Fax: 619-231-5879
e-mail: tickets@TheOldGlobe.org
Web Site: www.theoldglobe.org
Officers:
  Chair: Donald Cohn
  Vice Chair Finance and Treasurer: Anthony Thornley
  Fuson Jr.: Harold W.
Management:
  Executive Director/ CEO: Louis G Spisto
  Artistic Director: Jack O'Brien
  Founding Director: Craig Noel
  General Manager: Michael Murphy
Mission: The mission of The Old Globe is to preserve, strengthen and advance American theatre by: creating theatrical experiences of the highest professional standards; producing and presenting works of exceptional merit, designed to reach current and future audiences; ensuring diversity and balance in programming; providing an environment for the growth and education of theatre professsionals, audiences and the community at large.
Utilizes: Actors; AEA Actors; Choreographers; Commissioned Composers; Commissioned Music; Dancers; Designers; Educators; Five Seasonal Concerts; Guest Accompanists; Guest Artists; Guest Companies; Guest Conductors; Guest Designers; Guest Lecturers; Guest Writers; Guild Activities; High School Drama; Instructors; Local Artists; Multimedia; Music; Original Music Scores; Performance Artists; Poets; Resident Professionals; Selected Students; Singers; Soloists; Special Technical Talent; Visual Arts
Founded: 1935
Opened: 1982
Specialized Field: Drama; Musical; Contemporary
Status: Non-Profit
Paid Staff: 200+
Volunteer Staff: 1555
Non-paid Artists: 150
Budget: $8.5 million
Income Sources: Theatre Communications Group; League of Resident Theatres; American Arts Alliance
Season: January - November
Performs At: Old Globe Theatre; Cassius Carter Centre Stage; Lowell Daives Festival Theatre
Affiliations: Actor's Equity Association; the Society Of Stage Directors and Choreographets; United Scenic Artists Local and International Alliance of Theatric
Annual Attendance: 300,000+
Type of Stage: Proscenium, black box, 3/4 thrust
Seating Capacity: OG Theatre 582; Stage 225; Lowell Theatre 612
Organization Type: Performing; Educational; Sponsoring

2566
PLAYWRIGHTS PROJECT
3675 Ruffin Road,
Ste. #330
San Diego, CA 92123
Phone: 858-384-2970
Fax: 858-384-2974
e-mail: write@playwrightsproject.org
Web Site: www.playwrightsproject.org
Officers:
  Board President: Lisa Kirazian
  Treasurer: David Carr
  Secretary: Judy Leff
  VP: Pat Jacoby
  Executive Director: Cecelia Kouma
Management:
  Executive Director: Cecelia Kouma
  Development Manager: Laurel Withers
  Program Manager, Teaching Programs: Erika Phillips
  Program Manager, Productions & Play: Derek Livingston
  Office Manager: Lizzie Silverman
Mission: To advance literacy, creativity and communication by empowering individuals to voice their stories through playwriting programs and theatre productions.
Utilizes: Artists-in-Residence; Community Talent; Contract Actors; Educators; Five Seasonal Concerts; Guest Accompanists; Guest Conductors; Guest Designers; Guest Speakers; Guest Teachers; High School Drama; Instructors; Local Artists; Local Artists & Directors; Local Talent; Original Music Scores; Paid Performers; Performance Artists; Soloists; Visual Arts; Volunteer Directors & Actors; Writers
Founded: 1985
Specialized Field: Young Playwrights; New Plays
Status: Non-Profit, Professional
Paid Staff: 4

2567
SAN DIEGO JUNIOR THEATRE
1650 El Prado, Balboa Park
#208
San Diego, CA 92101

Phone: 619-239-1311
Fax: 619-239-5048
e-mail: info@juniortheatre.com
Web Site: www.juniortheatre.com
Officers:
   President/Board of Trustees: David Braun
   Artistic Director: Desha Crownover
   Technical Director: Cynthia Bloodgood
   Finance Director: Becky Jonestrask
   Office Manager: Katherine Matlrack
Management:
   Executive Director: Will Neblett
   Box Office Coordinator: Diane Dale
   Production Manager: Tony Cucuzzella
   Music Supervisor: Richard Morrison
   Costume Loft Coordinator: Mallory Devlin
Mission: To offer instruction in theatre arts to youth, aged 8-18.
Utilizes: Guest Companies
Founded: 1948
Specialized Field: Youth Theater; Theater Workshops
Status: Non-Profit, Professional
Paid Staff: 30
Income Sources: SCETA; San Diego Theatre League
Performs At: Casa del Prado Theatre
Organization Type: Performing; Educational

2568
SAN DIEGO REPERTORY THEATRE
79 Horton Plaza
San Diego, CA 92101-6144
Phone: 619-544-1000
Fax: 619-235-0939
e-mail: artistic@sandiegorep.com
Web Site: www.sdrep.com/
Management:
   Artistic Director and Co-Founder: Sam Woodhouse
   Public Relations Manager: Susan Enicoine
Mission: Adventurous theatre.
Founded: 1976
Specialized Field: Educational; Theater Workshops; Contemporary
Paid Staff: 43

2569
SAN DIEGO STATE UNIVERSITY: DEPARTMENT OF THEATRE
5500 Campanile Drive
San Diego, CA 92182-1690
Phone: 619-594-2586
Fax: 619-594-7431
e-mail: alumni@sdsu.edu
Web Site: www.sdsu.edu
Officers:
   Chair: Alicia Annas
   Interim School Director: D.J. Hopkins
Management:
   President: Stephen Weber
   Executive Director: W Nick Reid
   Marketing & Publicity Director: Paula Pearson
   TV/Film Studio Engineer: James B. Ray
Founded: 1935
Specialized Field: Educational; Theater Workshops
Status: For-Profit, Non-Professional
Paid Staff: 25
Budget: $11,347-$12,747
Affiliations: NAST; ATHE
Seating Capacity: 500; 175
Year Built: 1969
Year Remodeled: 1989

2570
SOUTHEAST COMMUNITY THEATRE
5140 Solola Avenue
San Diego, CA 92114
Phone: 619-262-2817
Management:
   Artistic Director: Floyd Gaffney
   Production Manager: Bonnie J Ward
Mission: Promoting African-American playwrights by showcasing non-professional, semi-professional and professional artists.
Utilizes: Guest Companies
Founded: 1976
Specialized Field: Community Theater
Status: Semi-Professional; Nonprofit
Income Sources: American Association of Community Theatres
Performs At: Educational Cultural Complex Performing Arts Theatre
Organization Type: Performing; Resident; Sponsoring

2571
STARLIGHT MUSICAL THEATRE
SAN DIEGO CIVIC LIGHT OPERA ASSOCIATION
2005 Pan American Plaza
San Diego, CA 92101
Mailing Address: P.O Box 3519, San Diego, CA 92163
Phone: 619-232-7827
Fax: 619-232-1882
e-mail: info@starlighttheatre.org
Web Site: http://www.starlighttheatre.org/
Management:
   Executive Director: CE Bud Farnks
   Producing Artistic Director: Don Ward
   Producing Artistic Director: Bonnie Ward
Mission: The preservation and promotion of the art form of musical theatre.
Utilizes: Guest Artists; Guest Companies; Singers
Founded: 1945
Specialized Field: Musical; Classic
Status: Professional; Nonprofit
Performs At: Starlight Bowl; Civic Theatre; Spreckles Theatre
Organization Type: Performing; Educational

2572
AFRICAN AMERICAN DRAMA COMPANY
394 5th Avenue
San Francisco, CA 94118
Phone: 415-378-0064
Fax: 408-216-9877
e-mail: DRAMART@comcast.net
Web Site: http://www.africanamericandramacompany.org/
Management:
   Executive Director: Phillip E Walker
   Co-Executive Director: Ethel Pitts Walker
Mission: To offer American audiences Black history and African plays.
Utilizes: Guest Companies
Founded: 1977
Specialized Field: Drama; African American
Status: Professional
Organization Type: Touring

2573
AMERICAN CONSERVATORY THEATRE
30 Grant Avenue
7th Floor
San Francisco, CA 94108-5800
Mailing Address: 30 Grant Ave, Sixth Floor, San Francisco, CA 94108
Phone: 415-834-3200
Fax: 415-834-3300
e-mail: tickets@act-sf.org
Web Site: www.act-sf.org
Officers:
   Chair: Jack Cortis
   Vice Chair: Nancy Livingston
   Vice Chair: Rusty Rueff
   Vice Chair: Cheryl Sorokin
   Volunteer Coordinator: Barbara Gerber
   Finance Director: Jeffrey P. Malloy
   Marketing Director: Andrew Smith
Management:
   Executive Director: Ellen Richard
   Artistic Director: Carey Perloff
   Young Conservatory Director: Melissa Smith
   Producing Director: James Haire
   Director of Academic Affairs: Jack Sharror
   Producing Director: James Haire
Mission: Performing contemporary and classical plays in conjunction with theatre training.
Utilizes: Guest Companies; Singers
Founded: 1965
Specialized Field: Youth Theater; Classic; Contemporary
Status: Non-Profit, Professional
Paid Artists: 400
Income Sources: League of Resident Theatres; Theatre Communications Group; American Arts Alliance; California Confederation of the Arts; National Corporation Theatre Fund
Performs At: Geary Theatre
Affiliations: American Conservatory Theatre
Type of Stage: Proscenium
Seating Capacity: 1014
Year Built: 1910
Year Remodeled: 1996
Rental Contact: Bob MacDonald (439-2392)
Organization Type: Performing; Resident; Educational

2574
AMERICAN INDIAN DANCE THEATRE
Gary Lindsey Artist Services
2700 15th Avenue
San Francisco, CA 94127
Phone: 415-759-6410
Fax: 415-681-9801
Toll-free: 800-949-2745
e-mail: lindseyart@aol.com
Web Site: www.lindseyartists.com/indian.htm
Management:
   American Indian Dance Theatre Artis: Hanay Geiogamah
Mission: The American Indian Dance Theatre, founded in 1987, is the country's leading native American performing company.
Specialized Field: Traditional Native American Dance

2575
ASIAN AMERICAN THEATER COMPANY
1695 18th Street #101
San Francisco, CA 94107
Phone: 415-378-7521
Fax: 415-440-5597
e-mail: david@asianamericantheater.org
Web Site: www.asianamericantheater.org/
Officers:
   Interim Executive Director: David Tsao
   Interim Managing Director: Pearl Wong
   Executive Director: Darrel D.Chiang
Management:
   Producing Director: Pamela Wu
   Professional Serive Consultant: Conrad Corpus
   Executive Director: Nonoko Sato
   Acting Teacher: Deborah Shaw

THEATRE / California

Fashion Buyer: Annie Wang
Specialized Field: New Plays; Asian American; Asian Pacific Islander; Ethnic Theater

2576
BRAVA! FOR WOMEN IN THE ARTS
2781 24th Street
San Francisco, CA 94110
Phone: 415-641-7657
Fax: 415-641-7684
e-mail: info@brava.org
Web Site: www.brava.org/
Officers:
  Board Co-Chair: Xochitl Carriorn
  Board Vice-President: Brigitte Davila
  Board Co-Chair: Jacquelyn Omotalade
Management:
  Artistic and Executive Director: Ellen Gavin
  Co-Chair: David Mauroff
  Facilities Manager: Darren Hochstedler
  Interim Production Manager: Ari Poppers
  Board Treasurer: Daniel Vasquez
Founded: 1986
Specialized Field: Community Theater; New Plays; Alternative; Ethnic Theater
Performs At: Brava Theatre Center, Barbie Stein Youth Theater
Type of Stage: Thrust, Black Box
Seating Capacity: 375, 100

2577
EL TEATRO DE LA ESPERANZA
PO Box 40578
San Francisco, CA 94140
Phone: 415-255-2320
Management:
  Artistic Director: Rodrigo Durte Clark
  General Manager: Eve Donovan
Mission: To present bi-cultural, bilingual plays that further theatre in the Chicano community.
Specialized Field: Spanish Language Company
Status: Professional; Nonprofit
Performs At: Mission Culture Center
Organization Type: Touring; Resident

2578
EUREKA THEATRE COMPANY
215 Jackson Street
San Francisco, CA 94111
Mailing Address: 555 Howard Street, Suite 201A, San Francisco, CA. 94105
Phone: 415-788-7469
Fax: 415-243-0789
Web Site: www.eurekatheatre.org
Officers:
  Chairman: Frederick Allardyce
  Treasurer: Anne Peskoe
Management:
  Co-Artistic Director: Andrea Gordon
  Co-Artistic Director: Benny Sato Ambush
  General Manager: Victoria Randall
  Executive Director: Torri Randall
Mission: Producing contemporary plays focusing on social and political issues.
Utilizes: Guest Companies; Singers
Founded: 1972
Specialized Field: Drama; Musical
Status: For-Profit, Professional
Income Sources: Actors' Equity Association; Coalition of Bay Area Theatres
Performs At: Eureka Theatre
Type of Stage: Proscenium
Stage Dimensions: 22' x 40'
Seating Capacity: 200

Organization Type: Performing; Resident; Educational

2579
GEORGE COATES PERFORMANCE WORKS
110 McAllister Street
San Francisco, CA 94102
Phone: 415-392-4400
Fax: 415-863-8520
e-mail: info@georgecoates.org
Web Site: www.georgecoates.org
Officers:
  President: Craig Martin
  VP: Richard Cole
  Secretary: Cathy Elienberger-Ubell
  Treasurer: Michael McDonell
Management:
  Artistic Director: George Coates
  Managing Director: Friday Savathphoun
  Production Manager: Chris Read
Mission: To broaden the boundaries of contemporary performances and the creative experience itself; to explore new relationships between performer and audience; to develop new alliances between arts ensembles, individuals and emerging technology industries; emphasis on contemporary vocal expression and multimedia.
Utilizes: Local Talent; Singers
Founded: 1977
Specialized Field: New Plays; Musical
Status: Non-Profit, Professional
Paid Staff: 4
Performs At: Performance Works
Organization Type: Performing; Touring; Resident

2580
ILLUSTRATED STAGE COMPANY
PO Box 640063
San Francisco, CA 94164
Phone: 415-861-6655
Management:
  General Manager: Barbara Malinowski
Utilizes: Guest Companies
Founded: 1979
Specialized Field: Drama; Musical; Contemporary
Status: Professional; Nonprofit
Paid Staff: 1
Performs At: Alcazar Theatre
Organization Type: Performing; Resident

2581
JULIAN THEATRE
777 Valencia
San Francisco, CA 94110
Fax: 415-626-8986
Officers:
  Chairman: George Crowe
Management:
  Artistic/General Director: Richard Reineccius
  Development Director: Veronica Masterson
  Production Manager: Michael Dingle
Mission: To maintain interest in works that have a social or political sense of the times to serve as a multi-cultural theater working with new plays.
Utilizes: Guest Companies; Singers
Founded: 1965
Specialized Field: Ensembles; Drama
Status: Professional; Nonprofit
Income Sources: Actors' Equity Association
Organization Type: Performing; Touring; Resident; Educational; Sponsoring

2582
LORRAINE HANSBERRY THEATRE
450 Post Street,
Suite 305
San Francisco, CA 94102
Phone: 415-345-3980
Fax: 415-288-0353
e-mail: stanley@LHTSF.org
Web Site: www.lhtsf.org/
Officers:
  Artistic Director: Steven Anthony Jones
  Director of Audience Development: Marc Pfquette
  ImaginArts Director: Elizabeth Carter
  President: Albert Dixon
Management:
  Executive Director: Quentin Easter
  Artistic Director: Stanley Williams
  Administrative Director: Tod Green
  Production Associate: Marianella Macchiarini
  Donor Development: Gina Snow
  Theatre Facilities Manager: Jeff Jones
Mission: To produce plays by America's and the world's leading Black writers; to foster the development of new Black writers through the ongoing activities of the playwrights workshop.
Utilizes: Actors; AEA Actors; Artists-in-Residence; Choreographers; Commissioned Music; Dance Companies; Dancers; Designers; Educators; Five Seasonal Concerts; Guest Designers; Guild Activities; High School Drama; Local Artists; Multimedia; Original Music Scores; Resident Professionals; Sign Language Translators; Soloists; Student Interns; Special Technical Talent
Founded: 1981
Specialized Field: Youth Theater; Ethnic Theater; Ensembles; Contemporary
Status: Non-Profit, Professional
Paid Staff: 5
Volunteer Staff: 30
Paid Artists: 5
Performs At: Lorraine Hansberry Theater
Type of Stage: Modified, Proscenium Thrust
Seating Capacity: 300
Organization Type: Performing; Educational

2583
MAGIC THEATRE
Fort Mason Center
Building D
San Francisco, CA 94123
Phone: 415-441-8001
Fax: 415-771-5505
Toll-free: 415-441-8822
Web Site: www.magictheatre.org
Officers:
  President: Corky LaVallee
  VP: Pattie Lawton
  Treasurer: Lynn Goldstein
  Secretary: Patricia Lawton
  Trustee: Bruce Colman
Management:
  Associate Artistic Director: Ryan Purcell
  Production Director: Sara Huddleston
  Managing Director: David Gluck
  Producing Director: Loretta Greco
  Design/Production Intern: Kristine Reyes
Mission: Focused exclusively on developing new plays and playwrights and operating two professional theaters.
Founded: 1967
Specialized Field: Musical; Comedy; Youth Theater; Ethnic Theater; Contemporary; Ensembles

Status: Non-Profit, Professional
Paid Staff: 20
Paid Artists: 30
Budget: $1.1 million
Income Sources: Actors' Equity Association
Season: June - August
Performs At: Northside Theatre; Southside Theatre
Annual Attendance: 20,000
Type of Stage: Proscenium
Stage Dimensions: 18'x 24'
Seating Capacity: 160
Rental Contact: General Manager John Warren
Organization Type: Performing; Resident; Sponsoring

2584
MAKE A CIRCUS: ARCO SPORTS
639 Frederick Street
San Francisco, CA 94117
Phone: 415-665-2276
Fax: 415-566-0102
e-mail: info@acrosports.org
Web Site: www.acrosports.org
Management:
    Executive Director: Dorri Huntington
    Artistic Director: Stephanie Abrams
Mission: To provide opportunities for individuals, families and communities to experience self-empowerment through the magic of particapitory circus theatre.
Utilizes: Actors; Artists-in-Residence; Collaborations; Five Seasonal Concerts; Guest Artists; Guest Companies; Guest Designers; Guild Activities; High School Drama; Local Artists; Original Music Scores; Resident Professionals; Soloists
Founded: 1993
Specialized Field: Youth Theater; Community Theater; Contemporary
Status: Non-Profit, Non-Professional
Paid Staff: 45
Paid Artists: 5
Performs At: Any outdoor 100 x 100 flat, grassy area free of distractions
Annual Attendance: 40,000
Facility Category: Parks
Type of Stage: Outdoor
Stage Dimensions: 100' x 100'
Seating Capacity: 1,000
Organization Type: Performing; Touring; Educational; Participatory

2585
MUSICAL THEATRE WORKS
2340 Jackson Street
San Francisco, CA 94115-1323
Phone: 415-641-5988
e-mail: mtwmzmusic@aol.com
Web Site: www.musicaltheatreworks.org
Management:
    General Director: Carolyn Miller
    Stage Director: Christina Lazo
    Production Manager: Matthew Royce
Mission: Developing and producing new works for American musical theatre.
Utilizes: Singers
Specialized Field: Musical; Ensembles
Status: Professional; Nonprofit
Income Sources: Actors' Equity Association; Theatre Communications Group; Alliance of Resident Theatres/New York
Organization Type: Performing; Resident

2586
NEW CONSERVATORY CENTER THEATRE
25 Van Ness Avenue
Lower Lobby
San Francisco, CA 94102
Phone: 415-861-4914
Fax: 415-861-6988
e-mail: email@nctcsf.org
Web Site: www.nctcsf.org
Officers:
    Chairman: Enrique Monagas
    Vice Chair: Jeff Malloy
    Treasurer: Jim Taul
    Secretary: Brigette Thomas
    Board Chair Emeritus: Curtis Wilhelm
    Chair: Curtis Wilhelm
Management:
    Artistic/Executive Director: Ed Decker
    Operations Manager: Jackie Jordan
    Executive Director: Barbara Hodgen
    Production Coordinator: Lori Fowler
    Conservatory Director: Sylvia Hathaway
Mission: Through our work, we strive to make positive contributions to enrich the cultural and educational well-being of our world.
Utilizes: Actors; Choreographers; Dancers; Designers; Educators; Fine Artists; Five Seasonal Concerts; Grant Writers; Guest Accompanists; Guest Artists; Guest Conductors; Guest Ensembles; Guest Instructors; Guest Lecturers; Guild Activities; High School Drama; Local Artists; Multimedia; Music; Organization Contracts; Original Music Scores; Performance Artists; Resident Professionals; Sign Language Translators; Soloists; Student Interns; Special Technical Talent; Theatre Companies; Touring Companies
Founded: 1981
Specialized Field: Musical; Comedy; Youth Theater; Dinner Theater; Ethnic Theater; Community Theater; Puppet; Classic; Contemporary
Status: Non-Profit, Professional
Paid Staff: 14
Volunteer Staff: 5
Paid Artists: 20
Budget: $950,000
Income Sources: 60% Earned; 40% Contributed
Performs At: The New Conservatory Theatre Center
Annual Attendance: 75,000
Facility Category: Multi-theatre; Art Gallery
Type of Stage: 2 Black Box; 1 Proscenium
Seating Capacity: 50 - 140
Year Built: 1904
Year Remodeled: 1986
Organization Type: Performing; Touring; Educational

2587
PERSONA GRATA PRODUCTIONS
2 Alta Mar
San Francisco, CA 94121
Phone: 415-387-7898
e-mail: paulkwan@personagrataprod.org
Web Site: www.personagrataprod.org
Management:
    Executive Director: Paul Kwan
    Artistic Director: Arnold Iger
Mission: Educational and cross-cultural.
Utilizes: Singers
Founded: 1979
Specialized Field: Ensembles; Puppet
Status: Professional; Nonprofit
Paid Staff: 4
Organization Type: Performing; Educational

2588
PHOENIX ARTS ASSOCIATION THEATRE/WESTCOAST PLAYWRIGHTS ALLIANCE
Phoenix Theatre
414 Mason Street
San Francisco, CA 94117-3930
Mailing Address: 138 Carl Street
Phone: 415-336-1020
e-mail: lbaf23@aol.com
Web Site: www.phoenixtheatresf.org
Management:
    Artistic Director/Managing Director: Linda B Ayres-Frederick
    Technical Director: Ty McKenzie
Mission: To present new and often unperformed scripts and original adaptations of American, British, and European writers by Bay Area Artists as well as premiering the works of the West Coast Playwrights Alliance at their two intimate downtown San Francisco theatres. In recent years to provide performance, rehearsal, and workshop space for the SF Bay area theatre community at reasonable rates.
Founded: 1985
Opened: 1985
Specialized Field: Contemporary & Original New Plays; Classics by the Phoenix & Other Nomadic Theatre Companies; Theatre Workshops in Acting; Scriptwriting; Movement
Paid Staff: 4
Volunteer Staff: 10
Paid Artists: 15
Non-paid Artists: 3
Income Sources: Performances; Contributions; Rentals
Affiliations: Theatre Bay Area
Facility Category: Theatre
Type of Stage: Thrust; Proscenium
Stage Dimensions: 30x20; 28'x20'
Seating Capacity: 49-65; 49
Year Built: 1985
Year Remodeled: 2001
Rental Contact: Artistic & Managing Director Linda Ayres-Frederick

2589
SAN FRANCISCO STATE UNIVERSITY: DEPARTMENT OF THEATRE ARTS
1600 Holloway Avenue
San Francisco, CA 94132
Phone: 415-338-1111
Fax: 415-338-0575
Web Site: www.theatre.sfu.edu/
Officers:
    President: Robert Corrigan
    Scenic Studio Manager: Josh Wickham
    UBA Office Adminitrator: Lauren Synder
    Director of Production Services: Ombra Sandifer
Management:
    Executive Director: Roy Conboy
    Community Engagement Manager: Brad Brock
    Assistant Scene Shop Manager: Colin Campbell
    Sound Designer: Zach Cramer
    Staff Service Associate: Sarah Fernald
Specialized Field: Educational; Theater Workshops
Status: For-Profit, Non-Professional
Budget: $1,000-$5,500
Affiliations: NAST
Seating Capacity: 250; 95

THEATRE / California

2590
SAN FRANCISCO MIME TROUPE
855 Treat Avenue
San Francisco, CA 94110
Phone: 415-285-1717
Fax: 415-285-1290
e-mail: info@sfmt.org
Web Site: www.sfmt.org
Officers:
   Development Director: Season Korchin
Management:
   General Manager: Peggy Rose
   Marketing Director: Miche Hall
   Production Manager: Natalie Saibel
   General Manager: Ellen Callas
   Publicist: Erica Lewis-Finein
   Chief Financial Officer: Michele Rudenko
   Production Manager: Karen Runk
Mission: Creating original, socially-relevant, musical theatre of high professional quality; performing for the broadest audience possible.
Utilizes: Actors; AEA Actors; Artists-in-Residence; Collaborations; Commissioned Composers; Dancers; Designers; Educators; Five Seasonal Concerts; Guest Accompanists; Guest Teachers; Guild Activities; High School Drama; Instructors; Local Artists; Local Unknown Artists; Multimedia; New Productions; Organization Contracts; Original Music Scores; Resident Artists; Resident Professionals; Sign Language Translators; Singers; Soloists; Visual Arts
Founded: 1959
Specialized Field: Musical; Comedy; Youth Theater; Ethnic Theater; Community Theater; Classic; Contemporary
Status: Non-Profit, Professional
Paid Staff: 5
Volunteer Staff: 25
Paid Artists: 10
Budget: $700,000
Income Sources: Free shows in Bay Area Parks; International Touring Engagements; Youth Project for At-risk Communities in San Francisco; Grants; Donations
Performs At: Varies (plays in parks for free in July)
Affiliations: Network of Ensemble Theaters, Theater Bay Area
Annual Attendance: 60,000
Type of Stage: Portable Raked Stage
Organization Type: Performing; Touring; Educational

2591
SHADOWLIGHT PRODUCTIONS
22 Chattanooga Street
San Francisco, CA 94114
Phone: 415-648-4461
Fax: 415-641-9734
e-mail: info@shadowlight.org
Web Site: http://www.shadowlight.org
Officers:
   President: Drew Takahashi
   Treasurer: Gail Silva
   Advisory Board: Ping Chong
   Advisory Board: Peter Coyote
   Advisory Board: Joanna Haigood
Management:
   Artistic/Executive Director: Larry Reed
   Managing Director: Sachiko Willis
   Director of Programs: Leslie Dreyer
   Treasurer: Gail Silva
   Outreach and Education DIR: Andrea Rodriguez

Mission: To nurture indigenous shadow theater traditions and to explore and expand the possibilities of the shadow theatre medium by creating innovative interdisciplinary, multicultural works.
Specialized Field: Storytelling; Shadow Theater; Shadow Theater

2592
STEVE SILVER PRODUCTIONS
678 Green Street
San Francisco, CA 94133
Phone: 415-421-4222
Fax: 415-421-4817
e-mail: bbb@beachblanketbabylon.com
Web Site: www.beachblanketbabylon.com
Management:
   Production Manager: Jo Schuman Silver
Founded: 1974
Specialized Field: Musical; Comedy; Youth Theater
Status: Non-profit, Professional
Paid Staff: 100
Income Sources: San Francisco & California Chambers of Commerce; Theater Bay Area
Performs At: Club Fugazi
Annual Attendance: 150,000
Organization Type: Performing; Resident

2593
THEATER RHINOCEROS
1 Sansome Street #3500
San Francisco, CA 94104
Phone: 415-552-4100
Fax: 415-552-2615
e-mail: jfisher@therhino.org
Web Site: www.therhino.org
Officers:
   President: Catherine Brannigan
   Vice President: James McCunn
   Treasurer: Davd Goodwin
   Operations Chair: John Dunsby
   Facilities Chair: Craig Souza
Management:
   Artistic Director: John Fisher
   Managing Director: John Simpson
   Development Director: Jim Boin
   Marketing Director: Jeffrey Hartgraves
Mission: The presentation of Lesbian and Gay theatre.
Utilizes: Actors; Collaborations; Guest Companies; Local Artists; Original Music Scores; Resident Professionals; Sign Language Translators; Student Interns
Founded: 1977
Specialized Field: Drama; Musical; Contemporary
Status: Professional; Nonprofit
Paid Staff: 4
Budget: $600,000
Income Sources: Non-profit
Performs At: Main Stage; Studio Theater
Annual Attendance: 20,000
Facility Category: Mainstage + Studio
Type of Stage: Proscenium
Seating Capacity: 112/54
Organization Type: Performing; Resident

2594
THEATRE ARTAUD
499 Alabama Street
Studio 445
San Francisco, CA 94110
Phone: 415-626-4370
Fax: 415-621-3764
e-mail: theater@artaud.org
Web Site: www.projectartaud.org
Officers:
   President: Javier Manrique
   Vice President: Laurie Anderson
Management:
   General Manager: Donna Merlino
   President: John Sullivan
   Vice President: Allan Kessler
   Treasurer: David Himmelreich
   Secretary: Sarah Kennedy
Founded: 1972
Specialized Field: Drama; Musical; Contemporary
Paid Staff: 7

2595
THICK DESCRIPTION
1695 18th Street
San Francisco, CA 94107
Mailing Address: P.O. Box 590603, San Francisco, CA 94159
Phone: 415-401-8081
e-mail: info@thickhouse.org
Web Site: www.thickhouse.org
Management:
   Artistic Director: Karen Amano
   Co-Artistic Director: Tony Kelly
   Co-Artistic Director: Rick Martin
Mission: Thick Description is run by a collective of three theater artists who share the duties and responsibilities of traditional artistic director.
Specialized Field: Drama; Classic; Contemporary

2596
TRAVELING JEWISH THEATRE
470 Florida Street
San Francisco, CA 94110
Phone: 415-285-8080
Fax: 415-399-1844
Web Site: www.tjt-sf.org/
Officers:
   Associate Artistic Director: Corey Fisher
   Co-Founder: Corey Fisher
   Executive Director: Sara Schwartz Geller
   Artistic Director and Co-Founder: Naomi Newman
   President: Michael Schrag
Management:
   Marketing Director: Devra Aarons
   Company Manager: Jennifer Hoenigsberg
   Artistic Director: Aaron Davidman
   General Manager: Evan Specter
   Treasurer: Dick Roistacher
   Vice President: Phil Strause
   Secretary: Roberta V. Romberg
Mission: To create and perform original works of theatre, as an ensemble and in collaboration with theatre artists from a variety of cultural and ethnic backgrounds, that contribute to a generous vision of the human condition.
Utilizes: Guest Companies; Singers
Founded: 1978
Specialized Field: Touring Company; Ethnic Theater; Jewish
Status: Professional; Nonprofit
Income Sources: Theatre Communications Group
Organization Type: Performing; Touring; Educational

2597
UN-SCRIPTED THEATER COMPANY
533 Sutter Street
San Francisco, CA 94108
Phone: 415-322-8738
e-mail: info@un-scripted.com
Web Site: un-scripted.com

Mission: The Un-Scripted Theater Company creates smart, innovative, and entertaining improvised theater that delights audiences and advances the craft and art of improvisation.
Founded: 2002
Specialized Field: Improv Theatre
Status: Nonprofit

2598
CHILDREN'S MUSICAL THEATER-SAN JOSE
1401 Parkmoor Avenue
San Jose, CA 95128
Phone: 408-288-5437
Fax: 508-521-8438
e-mail: tickets@cmtsj.org
Web Site: www.cmtsj.org
Officers:
   President: David J Stock
   VP: Rose Froehlich
   Treasurer: G Ron Lester
   Secretary: Kathy Custanza
Management:
   Executive Director: Jennifer Sandretto Hull
   Artistic Director: Kevin R Hauge
   Marketing/PR Director: Micki Sever
   Educational/Outreach Director: Drew Chappell
   Sponsorship Director: Jill Popolizio
   Media Director: Matt Thompson
Mission: Committed to providing excellent, accessible musical theater training for youth, with high-quality performances for families and the entire community.
Founded: 1968
Specialized Field: Children's Theater; Musical
Status: Non-Profit, Non-Professional
Paid Staff: 9
Volunteer Staff: 35
Paid Artists: 86
Rental Contact: Facilities Manager/Rentals: Timme Reinhart

2599
CITY LIGHTS THEATRE COMPANY
529 S 2nd Street
San Jose, CA 95112
Phone: 408-295-4200
Fax: 408-295-8318
e-mail: citylights@cltc.org
Web Site: www.cltc.org
Officers:
   President: Marvin Bamburg
   VP: Virginia Drake
   Secretary: Rick Boyle
   Treasurer: Dave Chandler
Management:
   Artistic Director: Lisa Mallette
   Production Manager: Kit Wilder
   Business Manager: Anne Younan
   Marketing Manager: Johnny Kolasinski
   Production Manager: Ron Gasparinetti
Mission: City Lights is a resident, non-profit company of theater artists dedicated to staging and hosting quality productions year round. This company prides itself on producing works you won't see at any other theater in the area.
Utilizes: Actors; Collaborations; Designers; Educators; Five Seasonal Concerts; Guest Designers; Instructors; Local Artists; Original Music Scores; Resident Professionals; Soloists; Student Interns; Special Technical Talent; Theatre Companies
Founded: 1982
Specialized Field: Musical; Comedy; Community Theater; Contemporary
Status: Non-Profit, Professional

Income Sources: Various
Annual Attendance: 10,000
Facility Category: Transformed Warehouse
Type of Stage: Flexible
Seating Capacity: 110
Rental Contact: Managing Director Lisa Mallette

2600
NORTHSIDE THEATRE COMPANY
848 E William Street
San Jose, CA 95116
Phone: 408-288-7820
e-mail: northside8@hotmail.com
Web Site: www.northsidetheatre.com
Officers:
   Chairperson: Dana Grover
   Vice Chairperson: Valerie Singer
   Treasurer: Matt Singer
   Secretary: Kathy Harwood
   Chairperson: Kathy Glaze
   Vice Chairperson: Rick Bonacoroso
Management:
   Chairperson: Dana Grover
   Artistic Director: Richard T Orlando
   Assistant Director: Darcie Grover
   Communications Manager: Mertedith King
   Treasurer: JeannieRae Orlando
   Secretary: Colleen Maher
Mission: To provide high quality, theatrical opportunities for youth, regardless of economic, educational, cultural or physical limitations. Dedicated to the manifestation of the human spirit.
Utilizes: Singers
Founded: 1978
Specialized Field: Drama; Musical; Contemporary
Status: Non-Profit
Paid Staff: 6
Volunteer Staff: 12
Paid Artists: 25
Non-paid Artists: 50
Budget: $200,000
Income Sources: Community Foundation of Silicon Valley
Annual Attendance: 5,000
Type of Stage: Thurst
Stage Dimensions: 20x20
Year Built: 1965
Year Remodeled: 2000
Organization Type: Performing; Touring; Resident; Educational

2601
SAN JOSE CHILDREN'S MUSICAL THEATER
1401 Parkmoor Avenue
San Jose, CA 95126
Phone: 408-288-5437
Fax: 408-288-6241
e-mail: info@cmtsj.org
Web Site: www.cmtsj.org/
Officers:
   Artistic Director: Kevin R Hauge
   Managing Director: Michael Miller
   Finance Director: Lakshmi Parige
Management:
   Artistic Director: Kevin R Hauge
   Executive Director: Jennifer Sandretto Hull
   Development Director: Rebecca Purdin
   Director Marketing/Programs: Tegan McLane
Mission: Providing excellent, accessible musical theater training and youth theater performances for young audiences, families and the entire Silicon Valley region. Also providing a positive environment in which youth can learn teamwork and communication skills

and experience the pride of accomplishment. Recognizing diversity of racial, ethnic, social and economic backgrounds in our participants and audiences.
Founded: 1968
Specialized Field: Community Theater; Children's Theater; Musical; Puppet; Educational

2602
SAN JOSE REPERTORY THEATRE
101 Paseo De San Antonio
San Jose, CA 95113
Phone: 408-367-7255
Fax: 408-367-7237
e-mail: boxoffice@sjrep.com
Web Site: www.sjrep.com
Officers:
   President: John Michael Sobrato
   Artistic Director: Rick Lombardo
   Managing Director: Nick Nichols
   Director of Outreach/Dramaturg: Karen Altree Piemme
   Associate Artistic Director: Kirsten Brandt
Management:
   Producing Artistic Director: Rick Lombardo
   Managing Director: Alexandra Urbanowski
   Associate Artistic Director: Kirsten Brandt
   Director of Outreach: Karen Altree Piemme
   Outreach Assistant: Tasi Alabastro
Mission: The theatre exists to produce seasons of visually exciting, challenging, entertaining and evocative plays selected from classical and contemporary periods; provide a creative environment for theatre artists and offer opportunities for innovative approaches to existing work and the development of new work; to reflect and enhance the community.
Utilizes: Actors; AEA Actors; Artists-in-Residence; Collaborating Artists; Collaborations; Commissioned Composers; Designers; Five Seasonal Concerts; Grant Writers; Guest Accompanists; Guest Artists; Guest Choreographers; Guest Companies; Guest Conductors; Guest Designers; Guest Ensembles; Guest Lecturers; Guest Musical Directors; Guest Soloists; Guest Teachers; Instructors; Local Artists; Local Unknown Artists; Multimedia; Organization Contracts; Original Music Scores; Performance Artists; Poets; Resident Professionals; Student Interns; Visual Arts
Founded: 1980
Specialized Field: Comedy; Youth Theater; Ensembles; Classic; Contemporary
Status: Non-Profit, Professional
Paid Staff: 70
Volunteer Staff: 100
Budget: $5,900,000
Income Sources: League of Resident Theatres; Theatre Communications Group
Performs At: Performing Arts Complex
Annual Attendance: 110,000
Facility Category: Theater; Performing Arts
Seating Capacity: 533
Year Built: 1997
Cost: $24,000,000
Rental Contact: Drayton Foltz
Organization Type: Performing; Resident; Educational

2603
SAN JOSE STAGE COMPANY
490 S 1st Street
San Jose, CA 95113
Phone: 408-283-7142
Fax: 408-283-7146
e-mail: admin@thestage.org
Web Site: www.thestage.org/
Officers:

THEATRE / California

President: Michael C Froncek
VP: Faye Van Boxtel
Secretary: Les Stevens
Treasurer: Dr. Erik Cohen
Executive Director: Cathleen King
Artistic Director: Randall King
President: Jerry Strangis
Vice President: Charlotte Powers
Management:
   Executive Director: Cathleen King
   Artistic Director: Randall King
   Development Director: Mary Smith
   Production Manager: Scott Tukloff
   Technical Consultant: Scott Baker
   Legal Counsel: Richard T. Hilovsky
   Secretary: Sandra Davidson
   Treasurer: Jason St. Claire
Founded: 1984
Specialized Field: Classic; Contemporary
Status: Non-Profit, Professional
Income Sources: Private Contributions; Ticket/Subscription Revenues
Performs At: Professional Union Playhouse

2604
SAN JOSE STATE UNIVERSITY: DEPARTMENT OF THEATRE ARTS
One Washington Square
San Jose, CA 95192
Phone: 408-924-1000
Web Site: www.info.sjsu.edu
Officers:
   Chairman: Dr. Robert Jeenkins
Specialized Field: Educational; Theater Workshops
Budget: $8,100-$17,000
Affiliations: NAST; ATHE; San Jose Repertory Theatre; Theatreworks; KQED; Paramount Great America; American Musical Theatre; The Barn Theatre
Seating Capacity: 400; 160; 60
Year Built: 1954

2605
TEATRO VISION
1677 Park Avenue
San Jose, CA 95126
Phone: 408-294-6621
Fax: 408-928-5589
e-mail: Teatro@TeatroVision.org
Web Site: www.teatrovision.org
Officers:
   President: Javier Augguire
Management:
   Production Manager: Dianne Vega
   Executive Director: Raul Lozano
   Artistic Director: Elisa Marina Alvarado
Mission: A Chicago theater company that celebrates culture, nurtures community, and inspires vision. Our art serves to move people to feel, think and act to create a better world.
Utilizes: Guest Companies
Founded: 1984
Specialized Field: Comedy; Youth Theater; Ethnic Theater; Community Theater; Contemporary
Status: Non-Profit, Professional
Paid Staff: 12
Paid Artists: 20
Income Sources: Movimiento de Arte y Cultura Latinoamericana; Theatre Bay Area
Organization Type: Performing; Touring

2606
EL TEATRO CAMPESINO
705 Fourth Street
San Juan Bautista, CA 95045
Mailing Address: PO Box 1240
Phone: 831-623-2444
Fax: 408-623-4127
Web Site: http://www.elteatrocampesino.com
Officers:
   Chairman: Luis Valdez
   President: Sandra Jewett
   VP: Virginia Rivera
   Treasurer: Elena Synder
   Secretary: Mary Solice
Management:
   Producing Artistic Director: Kinan Valdez
   Managing Director: Peter Allen
   Programming Manager: Dianne Vega
   Artistic Associate: Rodrigo Gracia
   Artistic Director: Elissa Marina Alvarado
Mission: To be recognized as one of the country's leading Latino/Chicano theaters.
Specialized Field: Ethnic Theater; Spanish Language Company
Status: Professional; Nonprofit
Performs At: El Teatro
Organization Type: Touring; Resident; Educational; Sponsoring

2607
SOUTH ORANGE COUNTY COMMUNITY THEATRE
Camino Real Playhouse
31776 El Camino Real
San Juan Capistrano, CA 92675
Phone: 949-489-8082
Fax: 949-489-8082
Specialized Field: Community Theater

2608
MARIN SHAKESPEARE COMPANY
PO Box 4053
San Rafael, CA 94913
Phone: 415-499-4485
Fax: 415-499-1492
e-mail: management@marinshakespeare.org
Web Site: www.marinshakespeare.org
Management:
   Executive Director: Lesley Schisgall Currier
   Artistic Director: Robert Currier
Mission: Our mission is to acheive excellence in the staging of Shakespearean plays; to celebrate Shakespeare; and to serve as a cultural and educational resource for Marin County, the San Francisco Bay Area and beyond.
Utilizes: Actors; AEA Actors; Choreographers; Collaborating Artists; Collaborations; Commissioned Composers; Commissioned Music; Community Members; Community Talent; Composers; Contract Actors; Designers; Educators; Equity Actors; Guest Accompanists; Guest Artists; Guest Conductors; Guest Designers; Guest Ensembles; Guest Instructors; Guest Musical Directors; Guest Soloists; Guest Speakers; Guest Writers; Guild Activities; High School Drama; Instructors; Local Artists; Local Artists & Directors; Local Talent; Multimedia; Organization Contracts; Original Music Scores; Performance Artists; Playwrights; Poets; Resident Companies; Resident Professionals; Sign Language Translators; Soloists; Students; Student Interns; Special Technical Talent; Theatre Companies; Visual Arts; Visual Designers; Volunteer Artists; Volunteer Directors & Actors; Writers
Founded: 1989
Specialized Field: Shakespeare
Status: Non-Profit, Professional
Paid Staff: 4
Paid Artists: 40
Season: July-September
Affiliations: Shakespeare Theatre Association of America; Theatre Bay Area Chamber of Commerce; Marin Arts Council; San Rafael Chamber of Commerce
Annual Attendance: 10,000
Facility Category: Outdoor Amphitheatre
Type of Stage: Thrust
Seating Capacity: 600
Year Built: 1967

2609
STOP-GAP
1570 Brookhollow Drive, Suite 114
Santa Ana, CA 92626
Phone: 714-979-7061
Fax: 714-979-7065
e-mail: get-info@stopgap.org
Web Site: www.stopgap.org
Officers:
   Executive Director/Founder: Don Laffoon
   Executive Director/Vice President: Kathleen Costello
Management:
   Artistic Director: Fionnuala Kenny
Mission: To use theatre as an educational and therapeutic tool to make a positive difference in individual lives.
Founded: 1978
Specialized Field: Ensembles; Contemporary
Status: Non-Profit, Professional
Paid Staff: 20
Organization Type: Performing; Touring; Educational

2610
ENSEMBLE THEATRE COMPANY OF SANTA BARBARA
914 Santa Barbara Street
Santa Barbara, CA 93101
Mailing Address: PO Box 2307, Santa Barbara, CA. 93120-9946
Phone: 805-865-5400
Fax: 805-568-3806
Web Site: www.ensembletheatre.com/
Officers:
   President: Richard Banks
   Executive Director: Albert Ihde
   Executive Artistic Director: Jonathan Fox
Management:
   Director Of Marketing: James Green
   Director Of Development: Mehgan Tanner
   Artistic Director: Robert Grande-Weiss
   Development Associate: Jennifer Wilson
   Sales Director: Gina Graham
Founded: 1978
Specialized Field: Comedy; Youth Theater; Classic; Contemporary
Status: Non-Profit, Professional

2611
SPEAKING OF STORIES
751 Paseo Nuevo
Santa Barbara, CA 93101
Mailing Address: PO Box 21143, Santa Barbara, CA. 93121
Phone: 805-966-3875
Fax: 805-963-8167
e-mail: speakingof@sbcoxmail.com
Web Site: www.speakingofstories.org
Management:
   President: Carolyn Butcher
   Executive Director: Teri Ball
   Artistic Director: Maggie Mixsell
Mission: Mission is to promote the appreciation of literature through live theatrical readings and community educational programs.

THEATRE / California

Founded: 1994
Specialized Field: Storytelling; Drama; Ensembles
Status: Non-Profit, Professional
Paid Staff: 3
Volunteer Staff: 1
Paid Artists: 50
Budget: $250,000
Income Sources: Volunteers; Contributors; Supporters; Tickets
Facility Category: Theater

2612
UNIVERSITY OF CALIFORNIA-SANTA BARBARA: DEPARTMENT OF DRAMATIC ART
2217 Cheadle Hall
Santa Barbara, CA 93106
Phone: 805-893-3241
Fax: 805-893-2441
e-mail: webmaster@theaterdance.ucsb.edu
Web Site: www.theaterdance.ucsb.edu/
Officers:
  Technical Director: Paul Barnes
  Senior Public Event Manager: Rachel Crandall
  Production Supervisor: Steven Cooper
Management:
  Professor: Irwin Apple
  Associate Professor: Ninotchka Bennahum
  Professor Chair: Risa Brainin
  Lecturer: Ann Bruice
  Senior Lecturer: Nancy Colahan
Specialized Field: Educational; Theater Workshops
Budget: $8,500-$9,000
Affiliations: ATHE; Theatre Artists Group
Seating Capacity: 340; 110; 100
Year Built: 1964

2613
LYRIC THEATRE WAREHOUSE
430 Martin Avenue
Santa Clara, CA 95050-2911
Phone: 408-986-8631
Fax: 408-986-9090
e-mail: lyricmail@yahoo.com
Management:
  Managing Director: Angela Norlander
  Director: Jerald Enos
Mission: Lyric Theatre is a performing group of over 150 dedicated volunteers who have committed themselves to the art of stagecraft.
Founded: 1974
Specialized Field: Community Theater; Musical; Light Theater
Income Sources: Donations
Season: June 6th - August

2614
SANTA CLARA UNIVERSITY THEATRE AND DANCE DEPARTMENT
500 El Camino Real
Santa Clara, CA 95053
Phone: 408-554-4989
Fax: 408-554-5199
Web Site: http://www.scu.edu/theatre/
Management:
  Chairman: Barbara Murray
  Business Manager: Robin Jiguor
Mission: Santa Clara University's Department of Theatre and Dance is a community of artist-scholars, faculty, staff, and students celebrating the creativity of the human spirit through a shared commitment to undergraduate liberal arts education in the Jesuit tradition.
Specialized Field: Educational; Theater Workshops
Budget: $4,650-$10,200
Affiliations: NAST; ATHE; San Jose Repertory Theatre; TheatreWorks; SRI; AMT; PCPA
Seating Capacity: 388; 88-139
Year Built: 1975

2615
KIDS ON BROADWAY
PO Box 3461
Santa Cruz, CA 95063
Phone: 831-425-3455
Web Site: http://www.kidsonbroadway.org/
Officers:
  President: David Lundberg
  Vice President: Miguel Diaz
  Treasurer: John Chin
  Secretary: Nancy Main
  Executive Director: Mary Lundberg
Management:
  Executive Director: Mary Lundberg
Mission: To train students in all areas of theatrical production, including back stage aspects, thus providing through the arts, vital personal growth experiences to promote excellence and confidence.
Founded: 1995
Specialized Field: Children's Theater; Youth Theater

2616
SHAKESPEARE SANTA CRUZ
University of California
1156 High Street
Santa Cruz, CA 95064
Phone: 831-459-2121
Fax: 831-459-3316
e-mail: webmaster@shakespearesantacruz.org
Web Site: www.shakespearesantacruz.org
Officers:
  President: Nancy Austin
  Vice President: Don Rothman
  Vice President: Renee Winter
  Artistic Director: Marco Barricelli
  Managing Director: Kyle Clausen
  SSC Financial Director: Geoff Girard
Management:
  Artistic Director: Marco Barricelli
  Managing Director: Marcus Cato
  Company Manager: Jennifah Chard
  Marketing/PR Director: Kyle Clausen
  Company Manager: Maria Frangos
  Sales Director: Sandy Kurz
Mission: To produce Shakespeare and world drama in translation.
Founded: 1982
Specialized Field: Shakespeare
Paid Staff: 7
Paid Artists: 30
Non-paid Artists: 14
Budget: $1,800,000
Income Sources: Tickets; Grants; Donation
Season: July - August
Performs At: Outdoor, Stanley-Sinsheimer-Glen Theater; Indoor Mainstage
Affiliations: AEA; SSO & C; USA
Annual Attendance: 45,000
Type of Stage: Indoor-Thrust
Seating Capacity: Indoor, 540; Outdoor, 750+

2617
PCPA THEATERFEST
800 S College Drive
Santa Maria, CA 93454
Phone: 805-928-7731
Fax: 805-928-7506
Toll-free: 800-727-2123
e-mail: pcpa@pcpa.org
Web Site: www.pcpa.org
Management:
  Artistic Director: Mark Boher
  Managing Director: Michael Black
  Education Director: Roger DeLaurier
  Casting Director: Erik Stein
Mission: A professional conservatory theatre, committed to reflecting and transforming the diverse community with the art of live theatre. Believe that the theatre has a vital role and responsibility in the community to enrich cultural literacy and improve the quality of life. Committed to serving the current audience, cultivating the future audience and training the next generation of theatre professionals.
Utilizes: Actors; AEA Actors; Artists-in-Residence; Choreographers; Composers-in-Residence; Designers; Educators; Guest Accompanists; Guest Artists; Guest Companies; Guest Conductors; Guest Designers; Guest Lecturers; High School Drama; Instructors; Music; Poets; Resident Artists; Resident Professionals; Soloists; Student Interns
Founded: 1964
Specialized Field: Theatre
Status: Professional; Semi-Professional; Non-Professional; Nonprofit
Paid Staff: 35
Volunteer Staff: 2
Paid Artists: 18
Non-paid Artists: 5
Budget: $4.2 Million
Performs At: Performing Arts Center
Affiliations: U/RTA; AEA; TCG; USA
Annual Attendance: 80,000
Facility Category: Producing Theatre
Type of Stage: 3/4 Thrust
Seating Capacity: 448
Year Built: 1968
Year Remodeled: 2005

2618
ACTORS REPERTORY THEATRE AT SANTA MONICA PLAYHOUSE
1211 4th Street
Santa Monica, CA 90401
Phone: 310-394-9779
Fax: 310-393-5573
e-mail: theatre@santamonicaplayhouse.com
Web Site: www.santamonicaplayhouse.com
Officers:
  Artistic Director: Chris DeCarlo
Management:
  Co-Artistic Director: Evelyn Rudie
  Co-Artistic Director: Chris DeCarlo
  Education Coordinator: Serena Dolinksy
Mission: To educate, enlighten, entertain and enrich the health and well-being of the local and global community through theatre arts, arts education and cultural exchange.
Utilizes: Singers
Founded: 1960
Specialized Field: Theatre and Theatre Arts Education
Status: Non-Profit
Paid Staff: 10
Volunteer Staff: 20
Paid Artists: 50
Income Sources: Theatre Communications Group; Actors' Equity Association; Theatre Los Angeles
Performs At: Santa Monica Playhouse
Facility Category: Theatre Arts Complex
Year Built: 1960

THEATRE / California

Year Remodeled: 1980
Rental Contact: Evelyn Rudie

2619
BROAD STAGE
Madison Project of Santa Monica College
1310 11th Street
Santa Monica, CA 90401
Mailing Address: 1900 Pico Blvd. Santa Monica, CA 90405
Phone: 310-434-3200
Fax: 310-434-3439
e-mail: info@thebroadstage.com
Web Site: www.thebroadstage.com
Officers:
 President: Dr. Chui Tsang
 Director: Dale Franzen
 Chief Operating Officer: Mitchell Heskel
 Director of Marketing: Natasha Shrieves
 Technical Director: David Toledo
Management:
 Director: Dale Franzen
 Deputy Director of Development: Lloyd Tanner
 Producer: Ernest Figueroa
 Operations Manager: David Kessler
 Chief Financial Officer: Majo Nable
Founded: 1999
Specialized Field: Musical; Youth Theater; Ethnic Theater; Community Theater; Classic; Contemporary; Theater Workshops
Status: Non-Profit, Professional
Paid Staff: 4

2620
SUMMER REPERTORY THEATRE
1501 Mendocino Avenue
Santa Rosa, CA 95401
Phone: 707-527-4343
Fax: 707-524-1689
e-mail: jnewman@santarosa.edu
Web Site: www.summerrep.com
Management:
 Artistic Director: James Newman
 Business Manager: Shannon Stevens
Utilizes: Actors; Choreographers; Collaborations; Community Members; Community Talent; Composers; Contract Orchestras; Dancers; Designers; Educators; Grant Writers; Guest Artists; Guest Composers; Guest Conductors; Guest Musical Directors; High School Drama; Local Artists; Local Unknown Artists; Multimedia; Music; Resident Professionals; Scenic Designers; Sign Language Translators; Soloists; Students; Student Interns; Visual Arts
Founded: 1972
Specialized Field: Musical; Comedy; Youth Theater; Classic; Contemporary
Status: Non-Profit, Non-Professional
Paid Staff: 25
Season: May - August
Type of Stage: Proscenium
Stage Dimensions: 36'x 30'

2621
PICKWICK PLAYERS
4579 Cuyamaca Street
Santee, CA 92071
Mailing Address: P.O. Box 711064, Santee, CA, 92072
Phone: 619-448-5673
e-mail: info@pickwickplayers.net
Web Site: pickwickplayers.net
Officers:
 President: Jennie Connard
 Vice President: Kirk Valles
Management:
 Artistic Director: Cameron Williams
Founded: 2008
Status: Nonprofit

2622
ANTENNA THEATER
Fort Cronkhite
Building 1057
Sausalito, CA 94965
Mailing Address: PO Box 939, Sausalito, CA. 94966
Phone: 415-332-8867
Fax: 415-332-8648
Web Site: www.antenna-theatre.org
Management:
 Artistic Director: Chris Hardman
 Managing Director: Sean Horton
 Assistant Director: Erica Wobensmith
Mission: Antenna seeks to invent, discover, and explore ways of involving a variety of artistic disciplines and new technologies in the theatre experience.
Utilizes: Actors; Choreographers; Commissioned Music; Dancers; Designers; Guest Conductors; Guild Activities; Local Artists; Lyricists; Multi Collaborations; Organization Contracts; Original Music Scores; Student Interns
Founded: 1980
Specialized Field: Musical; Comedy; Youth Theater; Dinner Theater; Ethnic Theater; Community Theater; Puppet; Classic; Contemporary
Status: Non-Profit, Professional
Paid Staff: 5
Paid Artists: 5
Budget: $500,000
Income Sources: Theatre Communications Group; California Confederaton of the Arts; Theatre Bay Area
Performs At: Site Specific
Organization Type: Performing; Touring

2623
INDEPENDENT EYE
502 Pleasant Hill
Sebastopol, CA 95472
Phone: 707-824-4307
Fax: 707-824-4307
Toll-free: 800-357-6016
e-mail: eye@independenteye.org
Web Site: www.independenteye.org
Management:
 Artistic Director: Elizabeth Fuller
 Artistic Director: Conrad Fuller
Mission: The Independent Eye is a progressive theatre ensemble, now in its 30th year, devoted to creating new plays and new visions of classics. Based in Northern California, our work reaches a national audience.
Founded: 1974
Specialized Field: Drama; Specialty Acts; Radio Performances
Status: Nonprofit; Non-Equity
Season: Year Round

2624
LA CONNECTION COMEDY THEATRE
13442 Ventura Boulevard
Sherman Oaks, CA 91423
Phone: 818-784-1868
Fax: 818-710-8666
e-mail: madmovies@hotmail.com
Web Site: www.laconnectioncomedy.com
Officers:
 President: Kent Skov
Mission: To produce comedy productions for film, TV, industrial and theatrical shows. Live improvised comedy sketch, movie dubbing, year round. To become a member, performers may audition by appointment.
Founded: 1977
Specialized Field: Comedy; Specialty Acts
Status: For-Profit, Professional
Paid Staff: 6
Volunteer Staff: 1
Season: Year Round
Type of Stage: Thrust
Seating Capacity: 99

2625
NORTH COAST REPERTORY THEATRE
987 Lomas Santa Fe Drive
Ste D
Solana Beach, CA 92075
Phone: 858-481-1055
Fax: 888-776-6278
Toll-free: 858-481-2155
e-mail: boxoffice@northcoastrep.org
Web Site: www.northcoastrep.org
Officers:
 President: Ira Epstein
 VP: Lorraine Stamoulis
 Treasurer: Michael Tedesco
 Secretary: Marvin Read
 Artistic Director: David Ellestein
 Managing Director: Bill Kerlin
 Resident Designer: Marty Burnett
Management:
 Managing Director: Bill Kerlin
 Manager/Director: Veronica Baker
 Development Director: Bill Kerlin
 Group Sales Manager: Leslie Zwail
 Resident Designer: Marty Burnett
Mission: To produce artistically demanding plays of high quality, which include original works, neglected works of literary merit, both contemporary and classical and those which address social issues.
Utilizes: Actors; AEA Actors; Artists-in-Residence; Choreographers; Collaborating Artists; Collaborations; Commissioned Composers; Commissioned Music; Educators; Fine Artists; Grant Writers; Guest Accompanists; Guest Artists; Guest Choreographers; Guest Companies; Guest Conductors; Guest Designers; Guest Ensembles; Guest Instructors; Guest Lecturers; Guest Musical Directors; Guest Soloists; Guild Activities; High School Drama; Instructors; Local Artists; Multimedia; Music; Original Music Scores; Performance Artists; Soloists
Founded: 1982
Specialized Field: Musical; Comedy; Classic; Contemporary; Musical
Status: Non-Profit, Professional
Paid Staff: 10
Volunteer Staff: 300
Paid Artists: 40
Budget: $750,000
Income Sources: San Diego Theatre League; California Arts Council
Performs At: Thomas Santa Fe Plaza
Annual Attendance: 35,000 +
Facility Category: Indoor
Type of Stage: 3/4 Thrust
Seating Capacity: 194
Year Built: 1982
Year Remodeled: 1988
Rental Contact: Sue Schaffner
Organization Type: Performing

2626
SIERRA REPERTORY THEATRE AT EAST SONORA
13891 Mono Way
Sonora, CA 95370

Phone: 209-532-3120
Fax: 209-532-7270
e-mail: tickets@sierrarep.org
Web Site: www.sierrarep.com
Management:
   Producing Director: Dennis Jones
   Managing Director: Sara Jones
   Marketing Director: Jan Mangili
Utilizes: Actors; AEA Actors; Artists-in-Residence; Choreographers; Collaborating Artists; Collaborations; Dancers; Designers; Educators; Guest Accompanists; Guest Artists; Guest Companies; Guest Conductors; Guest Designers; Guest Lecturers; Guild Activities; Instructors; Local Artists; Multimedia; Music; Original Music Scores; Resident Artists; Resident Professionals; Sign Language Translators; Student Interns
Founded: 1980
Specialized Field: Educational; Theater Workshops; Drama; New Plays
Paid Staff: 30
Volunteer Staff: 2
Paid Artists: 140
Budget: $1,000,000
Income Sources: Ticket Sales; National Endowment for the Arts Grants; California Arts Council Grants; Fundraising & Sponsors
Season: Febuary - December
Performs At: Contemporary Live Theatre
Annual Attendance: 54,000
Facility Category: Live Theatre
Type of Stage: Proscenium
Stage Dimensions: 40x30
Seating Capacity: 202; 270
Year Built: 1980
Year Remodeled: 1992

2627
STAGE 3 THEATRE COMPANY
208 S Green Street
Sonora, CA 95370
Phone: 209-536-1778
Fax: 209-536-1778
e-mail: info@stage3.org
Web Site: www.stage3.org
Officers:
   President: Dan Quintom
   Chair: Lary Jones
   Board Member: Sarajo Esch
Management:
   Managing Director: Neil Mill
   Artistic Director: Van Gordon
   Resident Lightening Director: Matthew Leamy
Mission: Stage 3 Theatre Company is dedicated to the development and production of new plays by new playwrights, and contemporary works by established playwrights.
Utilizes: Actors; AEA Actors; Choreographers; Collaborating Artists; Collaborations; Community Talent; Designers; Educators; Guest Accompanists; Guest Artists; Guest Conductors; Guest Designers; Guest Lecturers; Guest Musical Directors; Guest Speakers; Instructors; Local Artists; Multimedia; Music; Original Music Scores; Paid Performers; Performance Artists; Resident Professionals; Scenic Designers; Sign Language Translators; Students; Visual Arts
Founded: 1993
Specialized Field: Comedy; Ensembles; Contemporary
Status: Non-Profit, Non-Professional
Paid Staff: 3
Paid Artists: 40
Budget: $100,000
Income Sources: Ticket Sales; Grants; Contributions; Rentals; Touring; Classes; Advertising Revenue
Annual Attendance: 6,000

Type of Stage: Black Box
Stage Dimensions: 20'x20'
Seating Capacity: 80-100
Year Built: 1996
Rental Contact: Artistic Director Barbara Segal-Mill
Resident Groups: Stage 3 Theatre Company

2628
STOCKTON CIVIC THEATRE
2312 Rose Marie Lane
Stockton, CA 95207
Phone: 209-473-2400
Fax: 209-473-1502
Web Site: www.sctlivetheatre.org
Officers:
   President/Board of Directors: Allison Lafferty
   Vice President/Volunteer Services: Jay Judith Holmes
   Vice President/Fundraising: John Cammack
   Vice President/Finance: Richard Ceresa
   Vice President/Educational Program: Dominee Muller-Kimball, Ed.D
   Secretary: Teresa Hickey
Management:
   Producing Director: Jim Coleman
   Development/Marketing Director: James Treganza
Mission: To provide the community with quality theatre.
Utilizes: Guest Companies
Founded: 1951
Specialized Field: Community Theater; Classic
Status: Non-Profit, Non-Professional
Paid Staff: 4
Volunteer Staff: 300
Non-paid Artists: 200
Income Sources: Patrons
Performs At: Civic Center
Annual Attendance: 25,000
Facility Category: Community Theatre
Type of Stage: Proscenium
Seating Capacity: 275
Year Built: 1980
Rental Contact: Producing Director Paul Bengston
Organization Type: Performing; Resident

2629
TILLIE LEWIS THEATER
Delta College
5151 Pacific Avenue
Stockton, CA 95207
Phone: 209-954-5151
Fax: 209-954-5755
e-mail: pfrancois@deltacollege.edu
Web Site: www.deltacollege.edu
Officers:
   President: Raul Rodriguez
Founded: 1977
Specialized Field: Drama
Status: Non-Profit, Non-Professional
Paid Staff: 4
Facility Category: Theatre
Type of Stage: Proscenium
Seating Capacity: 400
Year Built: 1973
Rental Contact: Dr. Charles Jennings

2630
UNIVERSITY OF THE PACIFIC: DEPARTMENT OF THEATRE ARTS
3601 Pacific Avenue
Stockton, CA 95211

Phone: 209-946-2285
Fax: 209-946-2118
e-mail: cmcclellan@pacific.edu
Web Site: http://web.pacific.edu/x13787.xml
Officers:
   Chairman: Cathie McClellan
Management:
   Director: Gary Armagnac
Specialized Field: Educational; Theater Workshops
Budget: $2,550-$8,600
Affiliations: U/RTA
Seating Capacity: 400; 80-120
Year Built: 1956
Year Remodeled: 1999

2631
ARK THEATRE COMPANY
PO Box 1188
Studio City, CA 91614
Phone: 323-969-1707
e-mail: info@arktheatre.org
Web Site: www.arktheatre.org
Officers:
   President: Denis Shmidt
   Treasurer: Sheri Rhodius
   At Large: Cassandra Hooks
   At Large: Jeffery Kahan
   At Large: Helena Vayna
Management:
   Director: Richard Tatum
   Artistic Director: Derek Medina
   Associate Artistic Director: Richard Tatum
   Treasurer: Sheri Rhodius
Mission: A new Los Angeles theatre company formed to produce and present a repertory season by an ongoing company of actors, writers, directors, and designers.
Specialized Field: Educational; Theater Workshops; Drama; Contemporary

2632
LOS ANGELES DESIGNERS' THEATRE
PO Box 1883
Studio City, CA 91614-0883
Phone: 323-650-9600
Fax: 323-654-3210
Management:
   Artistic Director: Richard Niederberg
Founded: 1970
Specialized Field: Musical; Comedy; Ethnic Theater; Community Theater; Puppet; Classic; Contemporary
Status: Non-Profit, Professional

2633
CALIFORNIA THEATRE CENTER
753 East El Camino Real, Suite B
Sunnyvale, CA 94086
Mailing Address: P.O. Box 2007 Sunnyvale, CA 94087
Phone: 408-245-2978
Fax: 408-940-8252
e-mail: ctc@ctcinc.org
Web Site: www.ctcinc.org
Officers:
   General Director: Gayle Cornelison
   Resident Director: Will Huddleston
   Sales Director: Diana Burnell
   Production Manager: Marley Morris
   Tour Director: Lisa Mallette
   Costume Designer: Jane Lambert
   Stage Manager: Logan Hehn
Mission: Providing children and families with quality theatre.

THEATRE / California

Utilizes: Actors; AEA Actors; Artists-in-Residence; Choreographers; Commissioned Composers; Commissioned Music; Designers; Educators; Guest Accompanists; Guest Artists; Guest Companies; Guest Conductors; Guest Designers; Guest Lecturers; Guest Teachers; Instructors; Local Artists; Multimedia; Music; Original Music Scores; Performance Artists; Poets; Resident Artists; Resident Professionals; Singers; Theatre Companies
Founded: 1976
Specialized Field: Youth Theater
Status: Non-Profit, Professional
Paid Staff: 12
Paid Artists: 20
Budget: $1,750,000
Income Sources: Box Office; Touring; Education; Contributions
Performs At: The Performing Arts Center
Affiliations: Theatre Communications Group
Annual Attendance: 95,000; 150,000
Facility Category: Theatre
Type of Stage: Proscenium
Stage Dimensions: 34x25
Seating Capacity: 200
Year Built: 1974
Year Remodeled: 1991
Organization Type: Performing; Touring

2634
WILL GEER THEATRICUM BOTANICUM
1419 N Topanga Canyon Boulevard
Topanga Canyon, CA 90290
Mailing Address: PO Box 1222 Topanga, CA 90290
Phone: 310-455-2322
Fax: 310-455-3724
e-mail: egtree@theatricum.com
Web Site: www.theatricum.com
Officers:
　President: Mikko Sperber
　Executive Director: Ellen Geer
　Managing Director: Delphine Frost
　Education Director: Susan Angelo
Management:
　Managing Director: Robert Camper
　Artistic Director: Ellen Geer
　MD: Kathy Nixon
　Education Director: Susan Angelo
Mission: To elevate, educate, and entertain audiences of all ages by presenting thought-provoking classics, socially relevant plays, and educaiton programs in a beautiful, natural outdoor sanctuary for the arts. By passing on a sense of history to young people and adults alike, great works of art inform their present and inspire their future. A true renaissance theatre offering a diversity of programming from Shakespeare to poetry to folk music.
Utilizes: Actors; AEA Actors; Designers; Educators; Five Seasonal Concerts; Guild Activities
Founded: 1973
Specialized Field: Theatre
Status: Non-Profit, Professional
Paid Staff: 50
Paid Artists: 28
Budget: $500,000
Income Sources: Tuitions; Ticket Sales; Donations
Season: April - September
Performs At: Outdoor Amphitheatre
Type of Stage: Outdoor
Seating Capacity: 299
Organization Type: Performing; Resident; Educational

2635
CALIFORNIA STATE UNIVERSITY, STANISLAUS
One University Circle
Turlock, CA 95382
Phone: 209-667-3122
Fax: 209-667-3782
e-mail: cevett@csustan.edu
Web Site: www.csustan.edu
Officers:
　Chairman: Clay Everet
　President: Hamid Shirvani
Mission: California State University Stanislaus offers the degree Bachelor of Arts, general acting and technical emphasis.
Founded: 1962
Specialized Field: Educational; Theater Workshops
Status: Non-Profit, Non-Professional
Paid Staff: 12
Budget: $20,000-$25,000
Affiliations: NAST; ATHE
Facility Category: University Theatre
Seating Capacity: 300, 100
Year Built: 1970

2636
UKIAH PLAYERS THEATRE
1041 Low Gap Road
Ukiah, CA 95482
Phone: 707-462-9226
Fax: 707-462-1790
e-mail: adminplayers@pacific.net
Web Site: www.ukiahplayerstheatre.org
Management:
　Executive Director: Kate Magruder
　Artistic Director: Michael Ducharme
　Production Manager: Jonathan Wipple
　Publicity Manager/Director: Dan Hibshman
Mission: Offering the general community a broad range of theatre experience; encouraging and educating theatre artists; providing a cultural venue.
Utilizes: Actors; Artists-in-Residence; Collaborations; Guild Activities; Instructors; Local Artists; Lyricists; Multi Collaborations; Multimedia; Performance Artists; Resident Professionals; Soloists; Touring Companies
Founded: 1977
Specialized Field: Musical; Comedy; Youth Theater; Ethnic Theater; Community Theater; Classic; Contemporary
Status: Non-Profit, Non-Professional
Paid Staff: 4
Volunteer Staff: 200
Paid Artists: 20
Non-paid Artists: 100
Budget: $175,000
Performs At: Community Theatre
Affiliations: AACT, TCS, TBA
Annual Attendance: 10,000
Facility Category: Playhouse
Type of Stage: Proscenium
Stage Dimensions: 24'x38'
Seating Capacity: 120
Year Built: 1981
Year Remodeled: 1985
Rental Contact: Michael Ducharme
Organization Type: Performing; Touring; Resident; Educational; Sponsoring

2637
CALIFORNIA INSTITUTE OF THE ARTS: SCHOOL OF THEATER
24700 McBean Parkway
Valencia, CA 91355
Phone: 661-255-1050
Fax: 661-255-0462
e-mail: theater@calarts.edu
Web Site: www.calarts.edu
Management:
　Executive Director: John Gottlie
Founded: 1976
Specialized Field: Comedy; Youth Theater; Puppet; Classic; Contemporary
Status: For-Profit, Professional
Budget: $6,600-$12,800
Affiliations: NAST; U/RTA
Seating Capacity: 300; 30-100; 30-80
Year Built: 1971
Year Remodeled: 1994

2638
SIX FLAGS MAGIC MOUNTAIN
26101 Magic Mountain Parkway
Valencia, CA 91355
Mailing Address: PO Box 5500, Valencia, CA. 91385
Phone: 661-255-4100
Fax: 661-255-4171
Web Site: www.sixflags.com
Management:
　Entertainment Director: Scott Sterner
Founded: 1971
Specialized Field: Youth Theater; Community Theater
Status: For-Profit, Professional
Type of Stage: Proscenium; Thrust; Flex
Seating Capacity: 200-3000

2639
LOS ANGELES THEATRE WORKS
681 Venice Boulevard
Venice, CA 90291
Phone: 310-827-0808
Fax: 310-827-4949
Toll-free: 310-827-0889
e-mail: latw@latw.org
Web Site: www.latw.org/
Officers:
　President: Doug Jaffe
　Vice President: Aviva Covitz
　Secretary: Doris Blaizely
　Treasurer: Alan Finkel
　Managing Director: Anne Gimbel
　Producing Director: Susan Albert-Loewenberg
　Secretary: Vicki Pearlson
　Treasurer: Alan Finkel
Mission: Los Angeles Theatre Works, a pioneering lab for playwrights, directors and other theatre artists, is committed to the exploration of contemporary work in theatre.
Utilizes: Actors; Artists-in-Residence; Collaborations; Educators; Fine Artists; Five Seasonal Concerts; Grant Writers; Guest Accompanists; Guest Designers; Guest Ensembles; Guest Lecturers; Guest Musical Directors; Guild Activities; High School Drama; Instructors; Local Artists; Multi Collaborations; Music; Original Music Scores; Performance Artists; Sign Language Translators
Founded: 1974
Specialized Field: Radio Performances; Children's Theater
Status: Professional; Nonprofit
Income Sources: California Arts Council
Performs At: Skirball Cultural Center
Facility Category: Auditorium
Seating Capacity: 350
Rental Contact: 310-440-4595 Skirball Cultural Center
Organization Type: Touring; Producing

2640
CELEBRATION THEATRE
7051 Santa Monica Boulevard
Suite 109-1
West Hollywood, CA 90038
Phone: 323-957-1884
Fax: 323-957-1826
e-mail: info@celebrationtheatre.com
Web Site: www.celebrationtheatre.com
Management:
   Artistic Director: Michael Matthews
   Managing Artistic Director: Derek Charles Livingston
   Managing Director: David Tarlow
Mission: To illuminate all aspects of the gay and lesbian experience to the gay community and the community at large, while providing a safe and nurturing environment for gay and lesbian writers, directors, designers, and performers.
Utilizes: Guest Companies; Singers
Founded: 1982
Specialized Field: Drama; Contemporary; Classic
Status: Professional; Nonprofit
Paid Staff: 10
Income Sources: Grants; Ticket Sales; Indunderal Dancers
Performs At: Celebration Theatre
Annual Attendance: 4,000
Type of Stage: Three Quarter Stage
Seating Capacity: 64
Organization Type: Resident; Educational

2641
GROUP AT THE STRASBERG ACTING STUDIO
7936 Santa Monica Boulevard
West Hollywood, CA 90046
Phone: 323-650-7777
Fax: 323-650-7770
e-mail: admissionsla@strasberg.com
Web Site: www.strasberg.com
Management:
   President: Victoria Krane
   Executive Director: Anna Strasberg
   Managing Director: David Strasberg
Founded: 1969
Specialized Field: Comedy; Youth Theater; Community Theater; Classic; Contemporary
Status: For-Profit, Professional
Paid Staff: 50
Paid Artists: 15
Performs At: Marilyn Monroe Theatre, Studio Stras, Stage Lee Strasberg
Type of Stage: Endstage
Seating Capacity: 99, 49, 49

2642
WHITTIER JUNIOR THEATRE
13230 Penn Street
Whittier, CA 90602
Phone: 562-945-8200
Fax: 562-464-3581
e-mail: admin@cityofwhittier.org
Web Site: www.whittierch.org
Officers:
   Treasurer: Katherine Marshall
   Director: Aldo Schindler
   Controller: Rod Hills
   Director: Paymaneh Maghsoudi
Management:
   Director: Steve Helvey
   Managing Director: Dan Walker
   Theatre Manager and Jr Director: Dan Walker
   City Manager: Jeff Collier
   Assistant City Manager: Nancy Mendez
Mission: Offering performance opportunities to children 9 through 18 years old; presenting three productions per year.
Utilizes: Guest Companies
Founded: 1898
Specialized Field: Musical; Comedy; Youth Theater; Community Theater; Classic; Contemporary
Status: For-Profit, Non-Professional
Budget: $18,000
Income Sources: Box Office; Class Registration
Performs At: The Center Theatre
Type of Stage: Proscenium
Seating Capacity: 400
Year Built: 1961
Year Remodeled: 1987
Rental Contact: Michael Eiden
Organization Type: Performing; Touring; Educational

2643
YREKA COMMUNITY THEATRE
810 N Oregon Street
Yreka, CA 96097
Phone: 530-841-2355
Fax: 530-841-2339
Management:
   Business Manager: Jeff Shinn
Mission: To provide a venue for community performances and productions both in-house and private.
Founded: 1976
Specialized Field: Community Theater
Status: Non-Profit, Non-Professional
Paid Staff: 3
Volunteer Staff: 4
Performs At: Yreka Community Theatre
Seating Capacity: 300
Year Built: 1976
Cost: $2 million
Rental Contact: Jeff Shirn

Colorado

2644
AURORA FOX CHILDREN'S THEATRE COMPANY
9900 E Colfax Avenue
Aurora, CO 80010
Mailing Address: PO Box 9 Aurora, CO 80040
Phone: 303-739-1970
Fax: 303-361-2909
Management:
   Children's Theatre Coordinator: Thom Wise
Mission: To provide training and performance opportunities for young people.
Utilizes: Guest Companies; Singers
Founded: 1979
Specialized Field: Community Theater; Children's Theater
Status: Non-Professional
Paid Staff: 8
Non-paid Artists: 60
Budget: $550,000
Income Sources: City of Aurora; SCFO
Performs At: Aurora Fox Arts Center
Annual Attendance: 30,000
Facility Category: Theatre
Type of Stage: Proscenium
Stage Dimensions: 50'w x 40' d x 14'
Seating Capacity: 245
Year Built: 1946
Year Remodeled: 1985
Cost: $1 million
Organization Type: Performing; Resident; Educational

2645
VINTAGE THEATRE PRODUCTIONS
1468 Dayton Street
Aurora, CO 80010
Phone: 303-856-7830
e-mail: info@vintagetheatre.com
Web Site: vintagetheatre.com
Officers:
   President: Deb Persoff
   Vice President: Addison Parker
Management:
   Artistic Director: Craig A. Bond
Mission: Throughout Colorado, from our traditional theatre venues and in private event spaces, Vintage Theatre Productions, Inc. (VTP) proudly presents classics and cutting edge theatre, classes, improv, and staged readings that challenge, entertain, and grow our audience and artistic family alike.
Founded: 2002
Status: Nonprofit

2646
LE CENTRE DU SILENCE MIME SCHOOL
PO Box 1015
Boulder, CO 80306-1015
Phone: 303-661-9271
Fax: 303-604-6046
e-mail: info@bodyspeak.com
Web Site: www.bodyspeak.com
Management:
   Founder/Director: Samuel Avital
Mission: To surpass the normal means of communication offered by the entertainment industry, and society's abuse of the spoken word; to perpetuate and educate in the Art of Silence - MIME.
Founded: 1971
Specialized Field: Musical; Comedy; Youth Theater; Dinner Theater; Ethnic Theater; Community Theater; Puppet; Classic; Contemporary; Mime
Status: For-Profit, Professional
Paid Artists: 1

2647
UNIVERSITY OF COLORADO AT BOULDER: DEPARTMENT OF THEATRE AND DANCE
261 UCP
Boulder, CO 80309
Phone: 303-492-7355
Fax: 303-492-7722
e-mail: thrtdnce@colorado.edu
Web Site: www.theatredance.colorado.edu/
Officers:
   Chair: Bud Coleman
   Associate Chair: Bruce Bergner
   Associate Chair: Onye Ozuzu
Management:
   President: Bruce Benson
   Graduate Theatre Studies Director: Dr Oliver Gerland
   Dance Graduate Studies Director: Michelle Ellsworth
Founded: 1872
Specialized Field: Musical; Youth Theater; Dinner Theater; Ethnic Theater; Community Theater; Classic; Contemporary
Status: Non-Profit, Non-Professional
Paid Staff: 9
Budget: $3,500-$5,500
Affiliations: ATHE; Colorado Shakespeare Festival

THEATRE / Colorado

Seating Capacity: 416; 140; 1004
Year Built: 1902
Year Remodeled: 1989

2648
UPSTART CROW THEATRE COMPANY
2590 Walnut Street
Boulder, CO 80302
Phone: 303-442-1415
e-mail: info@theupstartcrow.org
Web Site: www.theupstartcrow.org
Management:
  President: Richard Bell
Mission: A dedicated core group of actors not only supplies stage talent, but backstage support as well.
Founded: 1980
Specialized Field: Classic
Status: Non-Profit, Professional

2649
BRECKENRIDGE BACKSTAGE THEATRE
121 South Ridge Street
Breckenridge, CO 80424
Phone: 970-453-0199
e-mail: info@backstagetheatre.org
Web Site: backstagetheatre.org
Officers:
  President: Frankie Hood
Management:
  Artistic Director: Christopher Willard
  Executive Director: Mark Lineaweaver
Mission: The Breckenridge Backstage Theatre enriches, educates, and entertains Summit County residents and visitors by letting them participate in and experience the joy of live theatre. Our passion is to inspire the community to embrace the performing arts and to expand their involvement with the theatre.
Status: Nonprofit

2650
CASTLE ROCK PLAYERS
PO Box 1224
Castle Rock, CO 80104
Phone: 866-879-7373
e-mail: info@crplayers.org
Web Site: www.crplayers.org
Management:
  President: Sandy Haworth South
  Vice President: Anne McGhee Stinson
  Artistic Director: Michael A Parker
  Business Manager: Greg Bell
  Director Theatrical Instruction: Jacki Mangan
  Publicity Coordinator: Kimmy Brandon
Mission: Dedicated to providing quality theater experiences for the community.
Utilizes: Actors; Local Artists; Performance Artists
Founded: 1997
Opened: 1997
Specialized Field: Community Theater; Theater Workshops
Affiliations: Castle Rock Chamber of Commerce, Colorado Theatre Guild

2651
CREEDE REPERTORY THEATRE
124 N Main Street
PO Box 269
Creede, CO 81130
Phone: 719-658-2540
Fax: 719-658-2343
Toll-free: 866-658-2540
Web Site: www.creederep.org
Officers:
  President Of The Board: Rpbert Slater
  Vice President: Arvinene VanRy
  Secretary: Charlene Ameel
  Treasurer: Stan Lent
  Executive Director: Maurice La Mee
  Managing Director: Tristan Wilson
  Development Director: Lynnaa Jackson
Mission: To produce a summer repertory season of eight plays; to promote knowledge of performing arts; to raise standards; to increase accessibility.
Utilizes: Guest Companies; Singers
Founded: 1966
Specialized Field: Musical; Comedy; Youth Theater; Puppet; Classic; Contemporary
Status: Non-Profit, Professional
Paid Staff: 5
Paid Artists: 50
Budget: $778,000
Income Sources: Donations; Grants; Box Office
Season: Late May - Early September
Performs At: Creede Repertory Theatre
Annual Attendance: 20,000
Facility Category: Performance Center
Type of Stage: Proscenium
Seating Capacity: 234
Year Remodeled: 1991
Organization Type: Performing; Touring; Educational; Sponsoring

2652
ADAMS MYSTERY PLAYHOUSE
2406 Federal Boulevard
Denver, CO 80211
Phone: 303-455-1848
Fax: 303-477-5900
Web Site: adamsmysteryplayhouse.com
Specialized Field: Dinner Theatre

2653
AND TOTO TOO THEATRE COMPANY
P.O. Box 17163
Denver, CO 80217
Phone: 720-585-3975
e-mail: info@andtototoo.org
Web Site: andtototoo.org
Management:
  Executive Director: Susan Lyles
  Technical Director/Designer: Darren Smith
Mission: And Toto Too Theatre Company promotes women in the arts, with a focus on producing new works by women playwrights. Our goal is to become an incubator for these works, spearheading their productions at venues nationally and internationally.
Founded: 2005
Status: Nonprofit

2654
AVENUE THEATER
417 E 17th Avenue
Denver, CO 80203
Phone: 303-321-5925
e-mail: Avenuetheater@gmail.com
Web Site: http://www.avenuetheater.com/
Management:
  Artistic Director: Bob Wells
  Theatre Director: Dave Johnson
  Administrative Coordinator: Heather Newman
  Treasurer: Ed Chambers
  Secretary: Kay Chambers
Specialized Field: Comedy; Theater Workshops

2655
CHANGING SCENE THEATER
1527 1/2 Champa Street
Denver, CO 80202
Phone: 303-813-1820
e-mail: changingscenenorthwest@hotmail.com
Web Site: www.changingscenenorthwest.org
Management:
  President: Alfred Brooks
  Vice President: Maxine Munt
Mission: To offer experience and performing space to young artists. Specializes in new works.
Utilizes: Guest Companies
Founded: 1968
Specialized Field: Drama; Contemporary; Experimental
Status: Nonprofit
Organization Type: Performing; Resident; Educational; Sponsoring

2656
CURIOUS THEATRE COMPANY
1080 Acoma Street
Denver, CO 80204
Phone: 303-623-0524
e-mail: info@curioustheatre.org
Web Site: curioustheatre.org
Officers:
  President: Jeremy Shamos
  Vice President: Rick Acosta
Management:
  Producing Artistic Director: Chip Walton
  Associate Artistic Director: Kate Marie Folkins
Mission: The mission of Curious Theatre Company is to engage the community in important contemporary issues through provocative modern theatre.
Status: Nonprofit

2657
DENVER CENTER THEATER COMPANY
1101 13th Street
Denver, CO 80204
Phone: 303-893-4100
Fax: 303-893-3206
Toll-free: 800-641-1222
e-mail: agriesmer@dcpa.org
Web Site: www.denvercenter.org
Management:
  Artistic Director: Kent Thompson
  President: Randy Weeks
  Associate Artistic Director: Bruce K Sevy
  General Manager: Charles Varin
  Production Manager: Edward Lapine
  Education Director: Daniel Renner
  Vice President of Mktng & Comm.: Stacy Shaw
Mission: As the flagship theatre of the Rocky Mountain region, The Denver Center for the Performing Arts creates and presents exceptional theatre that engages, excits, provokes and inspires both artists and audience. We emrace the classics while striving to create new plays and musicals that advance the American theatre movement. We are committed to making The Denver Center a center for lifelong learning and civic engagement.
Utilizes: Guest Companies; Singers
Founded: 1979
Specialized Field: Theatre
Status: Non-Profit, Professional
Paid Staff: 78
Income Sources: The Denver Center; Theatre Communications Group; League of Resident Theatres
Performs At: Denver Center Theatre
Affiliations: League of Resident Theatres
Annual Attendance: 170,000
Facility Category: Four-Square Block, 12-Acre Denver Performing Arts Complex
Type of Stage: Thrust, Round, Proscenium, Thrust
Seating Capacity: 750, 650, 250, 200

Organization Type: Performing; Touring; Resident; Educational

2658
DENVER CIVIC THEATRE
721 Sante Fe Drive
Denver, CO 80204
Phone: 303-309-3779
Fax: 303-309-3774
Management:
  President: Richard Bernstein
  Executive Director: James Jay Cardwell
  General Manager: Gary Miller
  Chairman: Mitchell Maxwell
Founded: 1985
Opened: 1991
Specialized Field: Musical; Comedy
Status: Non-Profit

2659
DENVER PUPPET THEATRE
3156 W 38th Avenue
Denver, CO 80211-2004
Phone: 303-458-6446
e-mail: annie@hypermall.net
Web Site: www.denverpuppettheater.com
Management:
  President: Annie Zock
Mission: Top quality puppet performance plus hands on puppet activities year round.
Utilizes: Scenic Designers
Founded: 1989
Specialized Field: Youth Theater; Puppet
Status: For-Profit, Professional
Paid Staff: 24
Paid Artists: 1
Budget: $90,000
Income Sources: Ticket Sales; Puppet Sales; Birthdays
Affiliations: Puppets of America; Theatre of Youth Coalition
Annual Attendance: 20,000
Stage Dimensions: 10'x20'
Seating Capacity: 100
Year Built: 1950
Year Remodeled: 1996
Resident Groups: Denver Puppet Theatre

2660
GERMINAL STAGE INC
2450 W 44th Avenue
PO Box 11139
Denver, CO 80211-0189
Phone: 303-455-7108
e-mail: germinalstage@gmail.com
Web Site: www.germinalstage.com
Management:
  Director/Manager: Ed Baierlein
  Production Assistant: Tad Baierlein
Founded: 1974
Specialized Field: Drama; Contemporary
Status: Professional
Affiliations: Germinal Stage Denver
Stage Dimensions: 20'x15'
Orchestra Pit: 1
Architect: Ron Rinker

2661
IMPULSE THEATER
1634 18th Street
Lower Level
Denver, CO 80202
Phone: 303-297-2111
Fax: 303-297-1378
Toll-free: 877-678-71
e-mail: info@impulsetheater.com
Web Site: www.impulsetheater.com
Management:
  Producer/Director: John Bauers
  Marketing: Noucha Noodele
Mission: Quick-witted cast of talented actors performing a funny mix of comedy, theater, and audience interaction.
Founded: 1987
Opened: 1987
Specialized Field: Musical; Comedy; Youth Theater; Dinner Theater; Ethnic Theater; Community Theater; Puppet; Classic; Contemporary
Status: For-Profit, Professional
Paid Staff: 20
Paid Artists: 15
Seating Capacity: 178

2662
JAFRIKA
3230 Clay Street
Denver, CO 80211
Phone: 303-433-7163
Fax: 303-433-7163
e-mail: tingzen@juno.com
Management:
  Dancer/Choreographer: Ricki Harada
  Musician/Composer: Chris Macor
Mission: Japanese dancer, black poet, white musician.
Utilizes: Soloists
Specialized Field: Drama; Contemporary; New Plays
Paid Artists: 3
Budget: $18,000
Income Sources: Paid by venue
Annual Attendance: 2,000
Facility Category: Schools, Libraries, Festivals

2663
METROPOLITAN STATE COLLEGE OF DENVER: DEPARTMENT OF THEATRE
Campus Box 93
PO Box 173362
Denver, CO 80217
Mailing Address: PO Box 173362
Phone: 303-556-2252
Fax: 303-556-3409
e-mail: eulerm@msudenver.edu ?
Web Site: http://www.mscd.edu/theatre
Management:
  Director of Theatre: Dr. Marilyn Hetzel
  Production Manager: Megan Euler
Specialized Field: Educational; Theater Workshops
Budget: $4,000-$7,000
Affiliations: Denver Civic Theatre; Denver Center for the Performing Arts
Seating Capacity: 99
Year Built: 1967

2664
NATIONAL THEATRE CONSERVATORY
1101 13th Street
Denver, CO 80204
Phone: 303-893-4100
Fax: 303-623-0693
e-mail: agriesmer@dcpa.org
Web Site: www.denvercenter.org
Management:
  Executive Director: Daniel Renner
Founded: 1984
Specialized Field: Educational; Theater Workshops
Status: Non-Profit, Non-Professional
Paid Staff: 28
Budget: $30,000-$46,000
Affiliations: Denver Centre Theatre Company
Seating Capacity: 550; 420; 150
Year Built: 1979

2665
SU TEATRO
721 Santa Fe Drive
Denver, CO 80204
Phone: 303-296-0219
Fax: 303-296-4614
e-mail: elcentro@suteatro.org
Web Site: www.suteatro.org
Officers:
  Board Member: Debra Gallegos
  Tech Director: Arnold King
  Facility Director: Steve Nash
  Executive Artistic Director: Tony Garcia
Management:
  Executive Director: Anthony J Garcia
  Associate Director: Tanya Mote
  Organizational Manager: Mica Garcia de Benavidez
  Office Manager: Valarie Castillo
  Graphic Designer: Archie Villeda
Mission: Speaking to the struggles of the barrios of the Southwest; preserving and perpetuating Chicano culture and language.
Founded: 1971
Specialized Field: Musical; Comedy; Youth Theater; Ethnic Theater; Community Theater
Status: Non-Profit, Professional
Performs At: El Centro Su Teatro
Organization Type: Performing; Touring; Educational; Sponsoring

2666
UNIVERSITY OF COLORADO AT DENVER: DEPARTMENT OF PERFORMING ARTS
1250 14th Street
Denver, CO 80217
Mailing Address: PO Box 173364, Denver, CO 80217
Phone: 303-556-2400
Fax: 303-556-2335
Web Site: www.ucdenver.edu
Management:
  President: James Shore
  Executive Director: Laura Cuepara
  Managing Director: Nathan Thompson
Founded: 1995
Specialized Field: Classic; Contemporary
Status: Non-Profit, Non-Professional
Paid Staff: 15
Budget: $5,000-$7,000
Affiliations: ATHE; Curious Productions; The Denver Center for the Performing Arts
Seating Capacity: 350; 120
Year Built: 2000

2667
UNIVERSITY OF DENVER DEPARTMENT OF THEATRE
1903 East Iliff Avenue
Denver, CO 80208
Phone: 303-871-2518
Fax: 303-871-2505
Web Site: www.du.edu/thea
Management:
  Provost: John Seacoumb
  Chair of Dept: Fredrick Barbaur
  Assistant Professor: Paula Sperry

THEATRE / Colorado

Founded: 1924
Specialized Field: Musical; Comedy; Youth Theater; Dinner Theater; Ethnic Theater; Community Theater; Puppet; Classic; Contemporary
Status: Non-Profit, Non-Professional
Paid Staff: 5
Paid Artists: 11
Budget: $2,700-$4,900
Affiliations: ATHE; KC/ACTF
Seating Capacity: 200-450; 50
Year Built: 1938
Year Remodeled: 1991

2668
DIAMOND CIRCLE MELODRAMA
7th and Main
PO Box 3041
Durango, CO 81302
Phone: 970-247-3400
Fax: 970-375-7136
Web Site: www.diamondcirclemelodrama.com
Management:
    Musical Director: Helen Gregory
Mission: To present quality professional productions. We specialize in Melodrama and Vaudeville.
Founded: 1961
Specialized Field: Drama; Classic
Status: Non-Equity; Commercial
Paid Staff: 25
Paid Artists: 15
Season: June 2 - September 29
Type of Stage: Proscenium
Stage Dimensions: 30'x 20'
Seating Capacity: 250

2669
BAS BLEU THEATRE COMPANY
401 Pine Street
Fort Collins, CO 80524
Phone: 970-498-8949
Web Site: basbleu.org
Officers:
    President: Tom Campbell
    Vice President: Robin Pavel
Management:
    Artistic Director: Wendy Ishii
    General Manager: Jay Benedict Brown
    Production Manager: Tricia Navarre
Mission: Bas Bleu Theatre Company's mission is to present outstanding theater that inspires both audiences and artists alike in an intimate salon setting. Bas Bleu's goal is to enrich the cultural life of the region and, in so doing, add to the common cultural experience that bonds us all to our community and the world around us.
Status: Nonprofit

2670
OPENSTAGE THEATRE AND COMPANY
400 North College Avenue
Fort Collins, CO 80524
Phone: 970-484-5237
Fax: 970-221-6730
Web Site: www.openstagetheatre.org/
Management:
    Managing Director: Jeff Metzger
Mission: To develop and maintain a nationally recognized regional theatre company. Emphasis will be placed on providing the best in quality theatre for the public benefit, on providing educational outreach to the community, and on providing professional opportunities for company members.
Utilizes: Singers
Founded: 1973

Specialized Field: Drama; Contemporary; Experimental
Status: Semi-Professional; Nonprofit
Paid Staff: 25
Income Sources: American Association of Community Theatres; Colorado Theatre Producers Guild; Fort Collins Convention & Visitors Bureau; Fort Collins Chamber of Commerce.
Performs At: Lincoln Center Mini-Theatre
Organization Type: Performing

2671
MESA STATE COLLEGE THEATRE DEPARTMENT
Moss Performing Arts Center
1100 N Avenue
Grand Junction, CO 81501
Phone: 970-248-1020
Fax: 970-248-1159
e-mail: rcowden@mesastate.edu
Web Site: www.coloradomesa.edu/theatre/mainstage.html
Management:
    Department Head: Richard R Cowden
    MSC President: Tim Foster
Specialized Field: Theatre and Dance
Status: Non-Profit, Non-Professional
Paid Staff: 7
Paid Artists: 7
Type of Stage: Proscenium
Stage Dimensions: 50' x 34'
Seating Capacity: 625

2672
LITTLE THEATRE OF THE ROCKIES
Frasier 115
Campus Box 49
Greeley, CO 80639
Phone: 970-351-2991
Fax: 970-351-4897
Web Site: www.arts.unco.edu
Management:
    Theatre Arts Chairman: Dan Guyette
Utilizes: Actors; AEA Actors; Dancers; Educators; Guest Accompanists; Guest Conductors; Guest Musical Directors; Guild Activities; Instructors; Local Artists; Multimedia; Music; Original Music Scores; Resident Artists; Resident Professionals; Sign Language Translators; Soloists; Student Interns
Founded: 1934
Specialized Field: Educational; Theater Workshops
Status: Nonprofit; Non-Equity
Season: Mid June - Early August
Type of Stage: Proscenium
Stage Dimensions: 34' x 32'
Seating Capacity: 600
Rental Contact: Diane Cays

2673
COUNTRY DINNER PLAYHOUSE
6875 S Clinton
Greenwood Village, CO 80112
Phone: 303-799-1410
Fax: 303-790-2615
Toll-free: 888-360-1026
Web Site: www.countrydinnerplayhouse.com
Officers:
    President/Producer/CEO: David M Pritchard
    Executive VP: David Lovinggood
    VP/General Manager: Robert E Buffington
Management:
    President: David Lovinggood
    Artistic Director: Paul Dwyer

    Assistant CEO/Producer/Casting: Patrick Alan Kearns
Utilizes: Singers
Founded: 1970
Specialized Field: Musical; Comedy; Dinner Theater; Contemporary
Status: Professional; AEA
Paid Staff: 85
Paid Artists: 25
Income Sources: Ticket Sales
Affiliations: NDTA; NTA; CTG; Tour Colorado
Annual Attendance: 170,000
Type of Stage: Theater-in-the-round
Seating Capacity: 470
Year Built: 1970
Year Remodeled: 2000
Rental Contact: Technical Director Jacob Weler
Organization Type: Performing

2674
PICKETWIRE PLAYERS
802 San Juan
La Junta, CO 81050
Mailing Address: PO Box 912 La Junta, CO
Phone: 719-384-8320
e-mail: info@picketwireplayers.org
Web Site: www.picketwireplayers.org/
Mission: To provide a showcase for Southeastern Colorado's regional talent.
Utilizes: Guest Artists; Guest Companies
Founded: 1968
Specialized Field: Community Theater
Status: Non-Professional; Nonprofit
Income Sources: La Junta Chamber of Commerce; Colorado Community Theater Coalition
Performs At: Picketwire Center for the Performing and Visual Arts
Organization Type: Performing

2675
LONGMONT THEATRE COMPANY
513 Main Street
PO Box 573
Longmont, CO 80501
Phone: 303-772-5200
Fax: 303-651-0388
e-mail: manager@longmonttheatre.org
Web Site: www.longmonttheatre.org
Officers:
    President: Chris Curtis
    VP: Len Worland
    Treasurer: Mick Finnegan
    Secretary: Brain Curtiss
Management:
    President: Kurt Keilbach
    Executive Director: Cheri E Friedman
Mission: To provide high quality entertainment with a strong educational component for and by the citizens of the Greater Boulder County area and to successfully manage a self-sufficient performing arts center.
Utilizes: Scenic Designers; Soloists
Founded: 1957
Specialized Field: Community Theater
Status: Non-Profit, Non-Professional
Paid Staff: 1
Budget: $160,000
Income Sources: Ticket Sales; Advertising; Concessions; Grants; Donations; In Kind
Annual Attendance: 10,000
Type of Stage: Thurst
Seating Capacity: 294
Year Built: 1939
Year Remodeled: 1991

2676
BROADWAY THEATRE LEAGUE OF PUEBLO
210 N Santa Fe Avenu
Pueblo, CO 81003
Phone: 719-545-4721
Fax: 719-295-7230
e-mail: maggie@sdc-arts.org
Web Site: www.sdc-arts.org
Management:
    President: Ron Dioeosio
    Executive Director: Maggie Divelbiss
Mission: To bring professional theatre to the community.
Utilizes: Original Music Scores; Theatre Companies
Founded: 1960
Specialized Field: Broadway Musical Revivals; Classic
Status: Non-Profit, Professional
Paid Staff: 1
Volunteer Staff: 20
Budget: $200,000
Income Sources: Ticket sales; Donations
Performs At: Pueblo Memorial Hall
Annual Attendance: 5,500
Type of Stage: Proscenium
Seating Capacity: 1,676
Year Built: 1920
Year Remodeled: 1960
Organization Type: Performing; Touring; Sponsoring

2677
IMPOSSIBLE PLAYERS
1201 N Main St
Pueblo, CO 81003
Mailing Address: PO Box 1005
Phone: 719-542-6969
e-mail: impossibleplayers@hotmail.com
Web Site: http://www.impossibleplayers.org/index.html
Officers:
    President: Marlene Schmidt
    Vice President: Bill Mattoon
    Secretary: Carol Martin
    Treasurer: Don Warren
Mission: To promote the enjoyment of the performing arts by the public; to further the education of both members and the public in the skills of those arts; to give people an opportunity to perform for the public.
Founded: 1966
Specialized Field: Community Theater
Status: Non-Professional; Nonprofit
Performs At: Public Community College; The Hoag Theater
Organization Type: Performing; Resident; Educational

Connecticut

2678
BRIDGEPORT THEATRE COMPANY
263 Golden Hill Street
Bridgeport, CT 06604
Phone: 203-416-6446
e-mail: info@bridgeporttheatre.org
Web Site: bridgeporttheatre.org
Officers:
    President: Melinda Zupaniotis
Management:
    Artistic Director: Eli Newsom
Mission: To lead a culturally diverse collective of local artists; to provide a quality, accessible, and affordable theatre arts experience for the community, by the community.
Status: Nonprofit

2679
CHESHIRE COMMUNITY THEATRE
PO Box 149
Cheshire, CT 06410
Phone: 203-272-2787
e-mail: info@CheshireCommTheater.com
Web Site: www.cheshirecommtheater.org/
Officers:
    President: Allison Koppel
    VP: Christopher Jones
    Secretary: Tanya Addio
    Treasurer: Michael Federico
    Business Manager: Michelle Noel
    Business Manager: Kurt Fusaris
    Publicity: Aleta Looker
    Play-Reading: Dorothy Brady
    Technical Director: Richard Conrad
Mission: To develop amateur dramatic talent, to produce plays in which members shall take part as actors, producers, and managers, to encourage the writing of plays by its members, and to encourage dramatic art.
Utilizes: Actors; Choreographers; Dancers; Local Artists; Music; Performance Artists; Sign Language Translators
Founded: 1953
Specialized Field: Musical; Community Theater
Status: Non-Professional; Nonprofit
Budget: $20,000
Income Sources: Ticket Sales; Program Ads; Membership Dues; Donations
Performs At: Cheshire High School
Annual Attendance: 1,800
Seating Capacity: 800
Rental Contact: Cheshire Board of Education
Organization Type: Performing; Resident

2680
EAST-WEST FUSION THEATRE
147 Kent Road
Cornwall Bridge, CT 06754
Phone: 860-672-3938
Fax: 860-672-3938
Officers:
    Technical Director: Jonathan Kendall
    President: Allison Koppel
    Vice President: Paul Byrne
Management:
    Artistic Director: Teviot Fairservis
    Publicity: Jen Berlin
    Business Manager: Michelle Noel
    Treasurer: Tracy Peters
    Membership: Karen Burns
Mission: International and fusion theatre collaborations with artists and scholars from around the world, multicultural arts education.
Utilizes: Actors; Artists-in-Residence; Choreographers; Collaborating Artists; Collaborations; Community Talent; Composers; Contract Actors; Curators; Dancers; Educators; Fellows of Institute; Guest Accompanists; Guest Artists; Guest Choreographers; Guest Conductors; Guest Designers; Guest Speakers; Guest Teachers; High School Drama; Instructors; Local Artists; Lyricists; Multi Collaborations; Original Music Scores; Paid Performers; Performance Artists; Resident Companies; Scenic Designers; Students; Special Technical Talent; Theatre Companies; Visual Arts
Founded: 1975
Specialized Field: Multi-Cultural; International
Paid Staff: 6
Paid Artists: 6
Non-paid Artists: 25
Budget: $50,000
Income Sources: Tour Bookings; Grants; Corporate & Private Donors
Performs At: East-West Arts Retreat
Affiliations: AAP; UCTA
Annual Attendance: 500
Facility Category: Outdoor Spaces; Platforms; Grassy Areas
Stage Dimensions: 20x20 plus
Seating Capacity: 75-350
Year Built: 2001
Rental Contact: Teviot Fairservis

2681
WESTERN CONNECTICUT STATE UNIVERSITY: THEATRE ARTS DEPARTMENT
181 White Street
Danbury, CT 06810
Phone: 203-837-8258
Fax: 203-837-8611
e-mail: trapanis@wcsu.edu
Web Site: http://www.wcsu.edu/theatrearts/
Officers:
    Chairman: William Walton
Management:
    Co-Chair: Sal Trapani
    Co-Chair: Pam McDanial
Specialized Field: Educational; Theater Workshops
Budget: $7,300-$13,500
Affiliations: Circle Repertory; Barrow Group
Seating Capacity: 600; 200
Year Built: 1959
Year Remodeled: 1979

2682
AMERICAN MAGIC-LANTERN THEATER
Box 44
East Haddam, CT 06423
Phone: 860-345-2574
Fax: 860-345-7578
e-mail: tborton@magiclanternshows.com
Web Site: www.magiclanternshows.com/magiclanternshows.htm
    Artistic Director: Terry Borton
Founded: 1650
Specialized Field: Touring Company; Historical; Specialty Acts

2683
GOODSPEED MUSICALS
6 Main Street
Box A
East Haddam, CT 06423
Phone: 860-873-8664
Fax: 860-873-2329
e-mail: info@goodspeed.org
Web Site: www.goodspeed.org
Management:
    Executive Director: Michel Price
    Technical Director: R Glen Grusmark
Mission: Preserving and advancing the American musical as an art form; developing new works to be added to the repertoire.
Founded: 1963
Specialized Field: Musical
Status: Non-Profit, Professional
Performs At: Goodspeed Opera House
Type of Stage: Proscenium
Stage Dimensions: 27'x18'
Orchestra Pit: 1
Architect: William H Goodspeed
Organization Type: Performing; Equity Theater

THEATRE / Connecticut

2684
FAIRFIELD UNIVERSITY: DEPARTMENT OF VISUAL & PERFORMING ARTS
1073 North Benson Rd
Fairfield, CT 06824
Phone: 203-254-4000
e-mail: webmaster@fairfield.edu
Web Site: http://www.fairfield.edu/cas/vpa_index.html
Officers:
   President: Rev Jeffery
Management:
   Director Theatre Program: Dr. Martha LoMonaco
Specialized Field: Educational; Theater Workshops
Budget: $10,250-$20,500
Affiliations: ATHE
Type of Stage: Black Box
Seating Capacity: 150; 750
Year Built: 1989

2685
ARTISTS COLLECTIVE
1200 Albany Avenue
Hartford, CT 06112
Phone: 860-527-3205
e-mail: info@artistscollective.org
Web Site: http://artistscollective.org/
Officers:
   Founding Executive Director: Dollie Mclean
   Co-Founder: Jackie McLean
Management:
   Executive Director: Dollie Mclean
   Creative Director: Jackie McLean
Utilizes: Guest Companies; Singers
Founded: 1970
Specialized Field: Ensembles; Contemporary
Status: Non-Professional; Nonprofit
Organization Type: Resident

2686
HARTFORD STAGE COMPANY
50 Church Street
Hartford, CT 06103
Phone: 860-527-5151
Fax: 860-525-4420
Web Site: www.hartfordstage.org
Officers:
   President: Ann Cooke
   Artistic Director: Darko Tresnjak
   Managing Director: Michael Stotts
   GM: Emily Van Scoy
   Director of Sales: Joe Fedrick
Management:
   Sr. Dramaturg: Elizabeth Williamson
   Artistic Administrator: Harriette Holmes
   Education Director: Jennifer Roberts
   Studio Manager: Emely Larson
   Associate Artistic Director: Maxwell William
Mission: Founded in 1963, the theatre is internationally known for entertaining audiences with a wide range of the best of world drama, from classics to provocative new works and neglected works from the past.
Founded: 1963
Specialized Field: Classic; Contemporary
Status: Non-Profit, Professional
Paid Staff: 50
Affiliations: Hartford Stage Company
Type of Stage: Thrust
Stage Dimensions: 40'x90'x90'
Orchestra Pit: 1
Seating Capacity: 489
Architect: Venturi & Rauch
Rental Contact: Production Manager Candice Chirgotis

2687
NATIONAL THEATRE OF THE DEAF
139 N Main Street
Hartford, CT 06107
Mailing Address: 325 Pequot Ave., New London, CT 06320
Phone: 860-236-4193
Fax: 860-236-4163
Toll-free: 800-300-5179
e-mail: info@ntd.org
Web Site: www.ntd.org
Officers:
   Executive Director/President: Betty Beekman
Management:
   Executive Director/Tour Director: Betty Beekman
   Marketing/Production Consultant: William Martin
Mission: To produce theatrically challenging work at a world class level, drawing from as wide a range of the world's literature as possible; to perform these original works in a style that links American Sign Language with the spoken work; to seek, train, and employ hearing impaired artists; to offer our work to as culturally diverse and inclusive an audience as possible; to provide community outreach activities.
Utilizes: Actors; Artists-in-Residence; Collaborations; Community Members; Community Talent; Educators; Filmmakers; Local Artists; Original Music Scores; Performance Artists; Resident Artists; Resident Companies
Founded: 1967
Specialized Field: Specialty Acts; Alternative
Status: Professional; Nonprofit
Facility Category: Touring Theatre
Organization Type: Performing; Touring; Educational

2688
THEATERWORKS
233 Pearl Street
Hartford, CT 06103
Phone: 860-727-4027
Fax: 860-525-0758
e-mail: info@theaterworkshartford.org
Web Site: http://www.theaterworkshartford.org/
Officers:
   Interim Artistic Director: Rob Ruggiero
   Technical Director: Jon-Paul LaRocco
Management:
   Executive Director: Steve Campo
   Production Manager: Michael Lenaghan
   General Manager: Nicole LaFlair Nieves
   General Manager: Nicole LaFlair Nieves
Mission: To provide unique works, especially recent American plays. We strive to address a diversified range of socially relevant works by important active authors.
Utilizes: Actors; AEA Actors; Original Music Scores; Resident Professionals; Student Interns
Founded: 1985
Specialized Field: Musical; Comedy; Youth Theater; Dinner Theater; Ethnic Theater; Community Theater; Puppet; Classic; Contemporary
Status: Non-Profit, Professional
Season: Year Round
Annual Attendance: 30,000+
Type of Stage: Modified Thrust
Seating Capacity: 197
Year Built: 1927
Year Remodeled: 1996

2689
TRINITY COLLEGE THEATRE AND DANCE DEPARTMENT
300 Summit Street
Hartford, CT 06106
Phone: 860-297-2000
Fax: 860-297-5380
e-mail: pkennedy@trincoll.edu
Web Site: http://www.trincoll.edu/depts/thdn/
Officers:
   Chair: Judy Dworin
   Dean: Katharine Power
   Assistant Professor: Lesley Farlow
Specialized Field: Educational; Theater Workshops
Budget: $12,550-$17,600
Affiliations: La Mama (equity theatre company); National Theater Institute at the Eugene O'Neill Theater Center; Nikitsky-Gates Theater (Moscow)
Seating Capacity: 400; 100; 60
Year Built: 1967

2690
MANCHESTER MUSICAL PLAYERS
Cheney Hall
PO Box 626
Manchester, CT 06045
Phone: 860-649-9065
e-mail: manchestermusicalplayers@gmail.com
Web Site: www.mmplayers.org/
Officers:
   President: David Gorman
   Vice President of Finance: Ann Azevedo
   VP Production: Marge Kelly
   Treasurer: Chris Stone
   Secretary: Dianne Burnham
Mission: 50-year-old community theater organization presenting one major Broadway musical each spring and a cabaret fundraiser in September. Other activities include holiday performances and annual scholarship.
Utilizes: Actors; Choreographers; Community Talent; Contract Orchestras; Dancers; Guest Artists; Guest Companies; Guest Conductors; Guest Designers; Guest Lecturers; Guest Musical Directors; Local Artists; Music; Resident Professionals; Sign Language Translators; Singers
Founded: 1947
Specialized Field: Musical
Status: Semi-Professional; Nonprofit
Non-paid Artists: 60+
Budget: $40,000
Income Sources: Tickets; Grants; Donations; Dues; Annual Fundraiser; Stock Rental; Fundraising Sales
Performs At: Cheney Hall
Annual Attendance: 2,000
Facility Category: Theater
Type of Stage: Theatrical
Seating Capacity: 325
Year Built: 1867
Organization Type: Performing

2691
ODDFELLOWS PLAYHOUSE
128 Washington Street
Middletown, CT 06457
Phone: 860-347-6143
e-mail: info@oddfellows.org
Web Site: www.oddfellows.org/
Officers:
   Chair: Melissa Z Schilke
   Vice Chair: Alain Munkittrick
   Treasurer: Grady L Faulkner Jr
   Secretary: Robert Hoppenstedt
   Chair: Michael Sciola

Vice-Chair: Elizabeth Bobrick
Executive Director: Matthew J. Pugliese
Management:
Artistic Director: Dick Wheeler
Managing Director: Mimi Rich
Technical Director: Charlie McAfee
Development Director: Susan Brown
Associate Artistic Director: Marcella Trowbridge
Mission: Oddfellows Playhouse is a non-profit youth theater and performing arts program that serves over 2,500 central CT young people, ages 6-20, each year through classes, workshops, mini-productions, mainstage shows, neighborhood-based troupes, and special events.
Founded: 1975
Specialized Field: Youth Theater; Theater Workshops
Status: Non-Profit

2692
WESLEYAN UNIVERSITY THEATER DEPARTMENT
275 Washington Terrace
Middletown, CT 06459
Mailing Address: Wesleyan Station
Phone: 860-685-2950
Fax: 860-685-2591
e-mail: kmcqueeney@wesleyan.edu
Web Site: http://www.wesleyan.edu/theater/
Officers:
Chair: Claudia Nascimento
Management:
President: Douglas J Benn
Chair: Alan M Dachs
Vice Chairs: Kofi Appenteng
Founded: 1831
Specialized Field: Educational; Theater Workshops
Budget: $1,500-$9,000
Affiliations: ATHE
Seating Capacity: 400; 150
Year Built: 1973
Year Remodeled: 1994

2693
CENTRAL CONNECTICUT STATE UNIVERSITY: DEPARTMENT OF THEATRE
1615 Stanley Drive
New Britain, CT 06053
Phone: 860-832-3150
Fax: 860-832-3164
e-mail: v.clarkebligh@ccsu.edu
Web Site: www.ccsu.edu
Officers:
Chairman: Lani Beck Johnson
Lecturer: Kenneth Adamson
Professor: Abigail Adams
Management:
Executive Director: Lani Johnson
Managing Director: Sheila Siragusaal, siragusashm@ccsu.edu
Professor: Helen Abadiano
Professor: Fatemeh Abdollahzadeh
Professor: Hazza Abo Rabia
Mission: To provide a concentrated and varied experience in Dance, Performance, Educational Theatre, Directing, Technical Theatre and Costume Design. Students are provided with numerous opportunities to perform on and design for main stage productions, as well as learning about children's theatre and improvisation with touring experience.
Specialized Field: Musical; Comedy; Classic; Contemporary; Educational
Status: Non-Profit, Non-Professional

Paid Staff: 8
Paid Artists: 15
Budget: $38,000
Income Sources: Departmental Funding From State
Performs At: Black Box Theatre; Large and Small Proscenium Spaces
Affiliations: Hartford Stage Company; Goodspeed Opera; Hartford Children's Theatre; Newington Children's Theatre; Bushnell w/Internship Opportunities
Annual Attendance: varies
Type of Stage: Black Box and Proscenium
Seating Capacity: 150; 300; 80
Year Built: 1989

2694
CONNECTICUT THEATRE COMPANY
23 Norden Street
New Britain, CT 06051
Phone: 860-223-3147
e-mail: info@connecticuttheatrecompany.org
Web Site: connecticuttheatrecompany.org
Officers:
President: Sean Taylor
Management:
Executive Director: Duane Campbell
Mission: Our goal is to stimulate, promote, teach, and develop interest in the dramatic arts; to educate the general public in the dramatic arts; to advance the general level of culture in the field of dramatic arts by the production of plays, musicals, readings, dramas, comedies, shows, and dramatic arts in all forms and of the highest standards.
Status: Volunteer ; Nonprofit

2695
HOLE IN THE WALL THEATRE
116 Main Street
New Britain, CT 06051
Phone: 860-229-3049
e-mail: advertise@hitw.org
Web Site: www.hitw.org
Management:
Technical Director: Bill Arnold
Mission: To allow anyone who walks through the door to enjoy theater at whatever level he or she desires.
Utilizes: Actors; Choreographers; Collaborating Artists; Collaborations; Community Talent; Designers; Guest Artists; Guest Conductors; Guest Lecturers; Local Artists; Music; Performance Artists; Resident Artists; Resident Professionals
Founded: 1972
Specialized Field: Musical; Community Theater; Staged Readings
Status: Professional; Nonprofit
Non-paid Artists: all
Budget: $40,000
Income Sources: Box Office; Grants; Individual Audience & Member Donations
Performs At: Black Box Studio Theatre
Affiliations: Greater New Britian Chamber of Commerce
Annual Attendance: 3,500
Facility Category: Thrust or 3/4 stage
Stage Dimensions: 42x30
Seating Capacity: 100
Year Remodeled: 1988
Rental Contact: Board of Directors
Organization Type: Performing; Resident

2696
ELM SHAKESPEARE COMPANY
PO Box 206029
New Haven, CT 06520-6029

Phone: 203-874-0801
Fax: 203-874-0802
e-mail: info@elmshakespeare.org
Web Site: www.elmshakespeare.org
Officers:
President: Cheever Tyler
Vice President: Andrew Boone
Treasurer: John Conte
Management:
Managing Director: Daniel Fitzmaurice
Development Director: Barbara Schaffer
Education Director: Charles McAfee
Artistic Director: James Andreass
Mission: The Elm Shakespeare Company is a professional multicultural non-profit theater company committed to establishing a discourse with the New Haven community through the medium of Shakespeare's plays.
Utilizes: Actors; AEA Actors; Artists-in-Residence; Collaborations; Guest Conductors; High School Drama
Founded: 1995
Specialized Field: Summer Stock
Status: Nonprofit
Paid Staff: 3
Season: August 1 - September 1
Annual Attendance: 30,000
Facility Category: Outdoor
Seating Capacity: 3000

2697
LONG WHARF THEATRE
222 Sargent Drive
New Haven, CT 06511
Phone: 203-787-4284
Fax: 203-776-2287
Toll-free: 800-782-8497
e-mail: info@longwharf.org
Web Site: www.longwharf.org/
Officers:
Artistic Director: Gordon Edelstein
Managing Director: Joshua Borenstein
Management:
Associate Artistic Director: Kim Rubienstien
Artistic Director: Gordan Eledlestein
Managing Director: Michael Stotts
General Manger: Deb Clapp
Associate Artistic Director: Eric Ting
Mission: Offering full production plays.
Utilizes: Actors; Artists-in-Residence; Choreographers; Designers; Educators; Five Seasonal Concerts; Guest Companies; Instructors; Multimedia; Music; Organization Contracts; Performance Artists; Poets; Resident Professionals; Singers
Founded: 1965
Specialized Field: Musical; Drama; Comedy
Status: For-Profit, Professional
Budget: 120,000
Income Sources: League of Resident Theatres; Theatre Communications Group; Connecticut Commission on the Arts; Actors' Equity Association
Performs At: Long Wharf Theatre
Facility Category: 2 stages
Seating Capacity: 487,199
Organization Type: Touring; Resident; Educational; Producing

2698
SOUTHERN CONNECTICUT STATE UNIVERSITY: DEPARTMENT OF THEATRE
501 Crescent Street
New Haven, CT 06515

THEATRE / Connecticut

Phone: 203-392-5200
Fax: 203-392-6105
e-mail: gradinfo@southernct.edu
Web Site: www.southernct.edu/theatre/
Officers:
  Chair: William R Ellwood
Management:
  President: Cheryl Norton
Specialized Field: Musical; Comedy; Ethnic Theater; Puppet; Classic; Contemporary
Status: Non-Profit, Non-Professional
Budget: $29,000-$40,000
Affiliations: ATHE; USITT; NETC; Long Wharf Theatre; Hartford Stage; Shubert Performing Arts Center; Goodspeed Opera; Circle in the Square
Seating Capacity: 1,550; 150; 125
Year Built: 1969
Year Remodeled: 1973

2699
YALE REPERTORY THEATRE
1120 Chapel Street
PO Box 208244
New Haven, CT 6510-8244
Phone: 203-432-1234
Fax: 203-432-6432
e-mail: yalerep@yale.edu
Web Site: www.yalerep.org/
Officers:
  Artistic Associate: Kay Perdue Meadows
  Managing Director: Victoria Nolan
  Production Manager: Jonathan Reed
  Production Manager: Bronislaw J. Sammler
  Properties Stock Manager: Bill Batschelet
Management:
  Artistic Director: James Bundy
  Managing Director: Victoria Nolan
  Associate Artistic Director: Jennifer Kiger
  Resident Costume Designer: Jess Goldstein
  Literary Manager: Amy Boratko
Mission: Producing new American plays, as well as little-known works and classics revisited through contemporary metaphors.
Utilizes: Guest Companies
Founded: 1966
Specialized Field: Comedy; Ethnic Theater; Community Theater; Puppet; Contemporary
Status: Non-Profit, Professional
Income Sources: Actors' Equity Association; Theatre Communications Group; American Arts Alliance; League of Resident Theatres; Connecticut Advocates for the Arts
Performs At: Yale Repertory Theatre; University Theatre
Organization Type: Performing; Resident; Educational

2700
YALE SCHOOL OF DRAMA
PO Box 208325
New Haven, CT 06520
Mailing Address: 149 York Street, New Haven, CT 06511
Phone: 203-432-1507
Fax: 203-432-9668
e-mail: yalerep@yale.edu
Web Site: http://drama.yale.edu/index.html
Management:
  President: Richard Charles Levin
  Dean: James Bundy
  Artistic Director: Jennifer Kiger
  Managing Director: Joshua Borenstein
Founded: 1924
Specialized Field: Educational; Theater Workshops
Budget: $46,200-$77,800
Affiliations: Yale Repertory Theatre
Seating Capacity: 487; 658; 200
Year Built: 1926
Year Remodeled: 2000

2701
CONNECTICUT COLLEGE DEPARTMENT OF THEATRE
270 Mohegan Avenue
New London, CT 06320
Mailing Address: Box 5512
Phone: 860-439-2605
Fax: 860-439-2595
e-mail: dthol@conncoll.edu
Web Site: http://www.conncoll.edu/departments/theater/index.htm
Management:
  Chairmam: Linda Nerr
  Department Chair: Leah Lowe
  Professor Emeritus of Theater: Linda Herr
Specialized Field: Educational; Theater Workshops
Seating Capacity: 1300; 130; 75
Year Built: 1941
Year Remodeled: 2000

2702
CONNECTICUT CONSERVATORY OF THE PERFORMING ARTS
55 W Street
New Milford, CT 06776
Phone: 860-354-3008
Fax: 860-350-0221
Officers:
  President: Jim Wilder
  VP: Sarah Jane Chelminski
  Treasurer: Shirley Waters
  Secretary: Deborah Casey
Management:
  Executive Director: Kristin Marks
  Music Director: John Shackelford
  Dance Department Chair: Robert Maiorano
  Theatre Department Chair: Heather McNeil
Mission: Offers professional training in dance, music, theatre, and voice concurrently with an academic program for grades 7-12.
Utilizes: Artists-in-Residence; Choreographers; Composers; Educators; Guest Accompanists; Guest Artists; Guest Composers; Guest Designers; Guest Musical Directors; Guest Speakers; Guild Activities; High School Drama; Multimedia; Music; Scenic Designers; Students
Founded: 1980
Specialized Field: Educational; Theater Workshops
Paid Staff: 2
Paid Artists: 20
Performs At: Black Box
Facility Category: Small, informal
Seating Capacity: 75
Year Built: 1975
Resident Groups: Conservatory School

2703
CLOCKWORK REPERTORY THEATRE
133 Main Street
Oakville, CT 06779
Phone: 860-274-7247
Fax: 860-274-7247
Web Site: http://www.clockworkrep.com/Home_Page.php
Officers:
  Artistic Director: Susan P. Pantely
  Executive Director: Harold J. Pantely
Management:
  Executive Director: Harold J Pantely
  Artistic Director: Susan P Pantely
  Asst. Artistic Director: William Wilson
Mission: Producing plays, emphasizing new American plays dealing with controversial events.
Utilizes: Guest Companies
Founded: 1977
Specialized Field: Comedy; Community Theater; Contemporary
Status: Non-Profit, Professional
Paid Staff: 5
Paid Artists: 20
Income Sources: New England Theatre Conference
Organization Type: Performing; Resident

2704
TRIARTS SHARON PLAYHOUSE
49 Amenia Road
PO Box 1187
Sharon, CT 06069
Mailing Address: PO Box 1187, Sharon, CT 06069
Phone: 860-364-7469
Fax: 860-364-8043
e-mail: info@triarts.net
Web Site: www.triarts.net
Officers:
  President: David Sims
  VP: Mimi Estes
  Secretary: Emily Soell
  Treasurer: John Stimpson
Management:
  Executive Director: Alice Bemand
  Artistic Director: John Simpkins
  Production Director: Erik Diaz
Mission: To create and administer a dynamic and creative center for the arts, presenting live theatre and other cultural events to the residents of the Tri-State area (Connecticut, New York, and Massachusetts).
Utilizes: Actors; AEA Actors; Choreographers; Community Talent; Educators; Guest Accompanists; Guest Conductors; Guest Designers; Guest Lecturers; Guest Musical Directors; Instructors; Music; Original Music Scores; Resident Professionals; Sign Language Translators; Students
Founded: 1989
Specialized Field: Summer Stock; Contemporary; Drama
Budget: $250,000
Income Sources: Donations; Tickets
Performs At: Theater; Gallery
Annual Attendance: 13,000-15,000
Facility Category: Barn Style Summer Theater; Year-Round Second Stage
Type of Stage: Proscenium
Seating Capacity: 370
Year Built: 1955
Year Remodeled: 1994
Resident Groups: Tri State Center for the Arts

2705
SHERMAN PLAYERS
Junction of Rte. 37 and Rte. 39
Sherman, CT 06784
Phone: 860-354-3622
e-mail: information@theshermanplayhouse.org
Web Site: www.shermanplayers.org
Officers:
  President: Elizabeth Scholze
  VP: Glenn Anderson
  Secretary: Jack Heidt
  Treasurer: Bobbie Tiebout
  Publicity: Jean Buoy
  Membership: Larry Buoy
  Board of Directors: Ellen Burnett

Wardrobe: Alpha Castro
Mission: To provide good theater and related artistic offerings to the CT area.
Utilizes: Actors; Collaborating Artists; Community Talent; Dance Companies; Guest Accompanists; Guest Artists; Guest Companies; Guest Designers; Guest Lecturers; Guest Musical Directors; Guest Soloists; Instructors; Local Artists; Performance Artists; Sign Language Translators; Singers
Founded: 1929
Specialized Field: Musical; Community Theater; Ensembles
Status: Non-Professional; Nonprofit
Paid Staff: n
Paid Artists: y
Budget: $16,000-$32,000
Income Sources: Membership; Playbill Advertising; Contributions; Occasional Fundraisers
Performs At: Sherman Playhouse
Annual Attendance: 3,200
Facility Category: Church, Converted to a Theater
Type of Stage: Proscenium
Stage Dimensions: 15x36
Seating Capacity: 126
Year Built: 1837
Year Remodeled: 1961
Rental Contact: Town of Sherman
Organization Type: Performing; Sponsoring

2706
PALACE THEATRE OF THE ARTS
61 Atlantic Street
307 Atlantic Street
Stamford, CT 06901
Phone: 203-358-2305
Fax: 203-358-2313
Management:
  Facilities Manager: John Hiddlestone
  Marketing Director: Nancy Koffin
  Managing Director: Mike Koffin
Founded: 1983
Specialized Field: Musical; Ensembles
Status: Professional; Commercial
Performs At: Palace Theatre
Affiliations: International Association of Theatrical Stage Employees
Seating Capacity: 1580
Year Built: 1927
Year Remodeled: 1983
Architect: Thomas Lamb
Organization Type: Sponsoring

2707
STAMFORD THEATRE WORKS
200 Strawberry Hill Ave
Stamford, CT 06906
Phone: 203-359-4414
Fax: 203-356-1846
e-mail: stwct@aol.com
Web Site: www.stamfordartstheatreworks.org
Officers:
  President: Steve Karp
  VP: Marietta Morrelli
  Secretary: Charry Boris
Management:
  Producing Director: Steve Karp
  General Manager: Patrick Shea
  Press/Marketing Director: Patricia Blaufuss
  Box Office Manager: Valarie Howard
Mission: To produce plays of cultural and social significance for the benefit of the greater Stamford area; to build a theatre of regional and national prominence, acclaimed for its innovative productions of contemporary and classical plays.
Utilizes: Actors; AEA Actors; Choreographers; Designers; Guest Companies; Guest Designers; Organization Contracts; Original Music Scores; Resident Companies; Resident Professionals; Sign Language Translators; Singers; Soloists; Student Interns
Founded: 1988
Specialized Field: Drama; Musical; Contemporary
Status: Professional; Nonprofit
Paid Staff: 10
Volunteer Staff: 75
Paid Artists: 125
Budget: $800,000
Income Sources: Actors' Equity Association; Society for Stage Directors and Choreographers
Annual Attendance: 16,000
Seating Capacity: 150
Organization Type: Performing

2708
PUPPET HOUSE THEATRE
128 Thimble Island Road
PO Box 3081
Stony Creek, CT 06405
Phone: 203-488-5752
Web Site: http://www.puppethouse.org/index.htm
Management:
  Manager: Christian Pacileo
  Booking Agent, Chief Technician: Andrew Gullans
  Technical Audio Consultant: Gary Bernacki
  Assistant Manager, Booking Agent: Taylor Brown
  Consultant: Adam Phillips
Mission: Presenting theatrical programs of small professional and community groups.
Utilizes: Guest Companies; Singers
Founded: 1972
Specialized Field: Summer Stock; Community Theater; Ethnic Theater; Puppet
Status: Professional; Non-Professional; Nonprofit
Paid Staff: 75
Year Built: 1903
Organization Type: Performing; Touring; Sponsoring

2709
CONNECTICUT REPERTORY THEATRE
802 Bolton Road, Unit 1127
University of Connecticut
Storrs, CT 06269-1127
Phone: 860-486-1629
Fax: 860-486-3110
e-mail: frank.mack@uconn.edu
Web Site: www.crt.uconn.edu
Officers:
  Managing Director: Frank Mack
Management:
  Artistic Director: Gary M English
  Managing Director: Frank Mack
  Business Manager: Cecile Stanzione
  Production Manager: Bob Copley
  Sales Office Manager: Jess Reed
  Company/House Manager: Mary Hurley
Mission: Connecticut Repertory Theatre exists as the primary training mechanism for the Department of Dramatic Arts at the University of Connecticut, and as a nationally recognized professional theatre center for the University.
Founded: 1957
Specialized Field: Educational; Theater Workshops
Status: Nonprofit
Season: June - July
Type of Stage: Proscenium
Stage Dimensions: 30'x 25'
Seating Capacity: 492

2711
UNIVERSITY OF CONNECTICUT: DEPARTMENT OF DRAMATIC ARTS
U-127, University of Connecticut
802 Bolton Road
Storrs, CT 06269
Phone: 860-486-4025
Fax: 860-486-3110
e-mail: dramaoffice@uconn.edu
Web Site: www.drama.uconn.edu
Officers:
  President: Steve Karp
  Vice President: Marietta Morrelli
  Secretary: Cherry Boris
  Business Manager: Stanzione Cecile
  Costume Shop Supervisor: Tolis Susan
Management:
  Artistic Director: Gary English
  Professor - Costume Design: Laura Crow
  Assistant Professor: Lindsay Cummings
  CRT Production Manager: Copley Jr. Robert
  Master Stage Electrician: Demer Michel
Specialized Field: Educational; Theater Workshops
Budget: $8,500-$18,800
Affiliations: NAST; U/RTA; Connecticut Repertory Theatre
Seating Capacity: 500; 100; 90
Year Built: 1960

2712
SQUARE ONE THEATRE COMPANY
2422 Main Street
Stratford, CT 06615
Phone: 203-375-8778
e-mail: tholehan@yahoo.com
Web Site: squareonetheatre.com
Management:
  Artistic Director: Tom Holehan
  General Manager: Richard P. Pheneger
Founded: 1990
Status: Nonprofit

2713
SEVEN ANGELS THEATRE
1 Plank Road, Historic Hamilton Park Pavilion
Waterbury, CT 06705
Mailing Address: PO Box 3358
Phone: 203-757-4676
Fax: 203-757-1807
e-mail: business7angels@yahoo.com
Web Site: http://sevenangelstheatre.org/page/6289-Home
Officers:
  Artistic Director: Semina De Laurentis
  Development Director: Debra Bodnar
  Marketing Director: Paul Roth
Management:
  President of the Board: Allen Cipriano
  Executive Director: Teresa De Laurentis
  Artistic Director: Semina De Laurentis
  Development Director: Debra Bodnar
  Marketing Director: Paul Roth
  Production Stage Manager/Production: Noelle Smith
  Sound Designer & Engineer: Trenton Spears
Founded: 1991
Specialized Field: Musical; Comedy; Youth Theater; Community Theater; Contemporary
Status: Non-Profit, Professional
Paid Staff: 11
Paid Artists: 5

THEATRE / Delaware

2715
NATIONAL THEATER INSTITUTE
EUGENE O'NEILL THEATER CENTER
305 Great Neck Road
Waterford, CT 06385
Phone: 860-443-5378
Fax: 860-443-9653
e-mail: theaterlives@theoneill.org
Web Site: www.theoneill.org
Officers:
   Chairman: Tom Viertel
   Executive Director: Preston Whiteway
   Founder: George C. White
   Secretary: Linda Mariani
Management:
   Executive Director: Preston Whiteway
   Artistic Director: Rachel Jett
   Artistic Director: Paulette Hawpt
   Director: David B Jaffe
Mission: To support the development and education of theatrical artists, students and audiences.
Utilizes: Guest Companies
Founded: 1964
Specialized Field: Educational; Theater Workshops; Drama; Contemporary
Status: Professional; Nonprofit
Performs At: The Rose Barn; The Edith Oliver Theatre; The Amphitheatre
Affiliations: Theatre Communication Group; ATHE; Moscow Art Theater
Seating Capacity: 300; 50
Year Built: 1964
Organization Type: Performing; Educational; Sponsoring

2716
UNIVERSITY OF HARTFORD: DEPARTMENT OF ART HISTORY, CINEMA, DRAMA
200 Bloomfield Avenue
West Hartford, CT 06117
Phone: 860-443-5378
Fax: 860-443-9653
Toll-free: 800-947-4303
e-mail: calafiore@hartford.edu
Management:
   Dean: Power Boothe
   Associate Dean: Thomas Bradley
Founded: 1877
Specialized Field: Educational; Theater Workshops
Status: Non-Profit, Non-Professional
Budget: $6,000-$9,000
Seating Capacity: 200
Year Built: 1960
Year Remodeled: 1996

2717
FAIRFIELD COUNTY STAGE COMPANY
25 Powers Court
Westport, CT 06880
Phone: 203-227-5137
Officers:
   Chairman: Rita Fredricks
   President: Marilyn Hersey
   Secretary: Christopher Cull
   Treasurer: Burry Fredrik
Management:
   Associate Artistic Director: Anne Ueefe
Mission: Professional regional theatre operating under the Letter of Agreement/LORT 'D' Contract with Actors' Equity Association.
Utilizes: Guest Companies
Founded: 1981
Specialized Field: Drama; Musical; Contemporary
Status: Professional
Paid Staff: 40
Paid Artists: 70
Income Sources: Actors' Equity Association; Theatre Communications Group
Organization Type: Performing; Resident

2718
MUSIC THEATRE OF CONNECTICUT
246 Post Road East
Westport, CT 06880
Mailing Address: P.O. Box 344, Westport, CT 06881-0344
Phone: 203-454-3883
Fax: 203-226-6629
e-mail: admin@musictheatreofct.com
Web Site: musictheatreofct.com
Management:
   Artistic Director: Kevin Connors
   Managing Director: Jim Schilling
Founded: 1987
Status: Nonprofit

2719
WESTPORT COMMUNITY THEATRE
Town Hall
110 Myrtle Avenue
Westport, CT 06880
Mailing Address: 110 Myrtle Avenue
Phone: 203-226-1983
e-mail: info@westportcommunitytheatre.com
Web Site: http://www.westportcommunitytheatre.com/index.html
Management:
   Artistic Manager: H Edward Spires
Mission: Offering entertainment and instruction to the community regarding theatre; developing appreciation of theatre.
Utilizes: Guest Artists; Guest Companies
Founded: 1956
Specialized Field: Community Theater
Status: Non-Professional; Nonprofit
Paid Staff: 3
Season: June - September
Organization Type: Performing

2720
WESTPORT COUNTRY PLAYHOUSE
25 Powers Court
PO Box 629
Westport, CT 06880
Phone: 203-227-4177
Fax: 203-221-7482
Web Site: www.westportplayhouse.com
Officers:
   Chair: Michael Klingher
   Vice Chair: Howard J. Aibel
   Treasurer: Kenneth J. Seel,
   Secretary: Ann Sheffer,
   Treasurer: Richard Slavin
Management:
   Executive Director: Alison Harris
   Artistic Advisor: Annie Keefe
   Artistic & Management Coordinator: Kim Furano
   Company Manager: Bruce Miller
Mission: Offering professional theatre to Connecticut.
Utilizes: Guest Companies
Founded: 1930
Specialized Field: Musical; Comedy; Youth Theater; Classic; Contemporary
Status: Non-Profit, Professional
Paid Staff: 16
Paid Artists: 50
Income Sources: Council of Stock Theatres
Season: June-September
Performs At: Westport Summer Country Playhouse
Facility Category: Summer Theatre
Type of Stage: Proscenium
Seating Capacity: 707
Year Built: 1930
Rental Contact: Julie Monahan
Organization Type: Performing; Resident

2721
WILTON PLAYSHOP
The Wilton Playshop
15 Lovers Lane
PO Box 36
Wilton, CT 06897
Mailing Address: PO Box 363, Wilton, Ct. 06897
Phone: 203-762-7629
e-mail: president@wiltonplayshop.org
Web Site: www.wiltonplayshop.org
Officers:
   President: Skip Ploss
   VP: Jon Murray
   Chairman, Trustees: Karen Young
   President: Zelie Pforzheimer
   1st Vice President Production: Janice Dehn
   2nd Vice President Production: Donna Savage
   3rd Vice President, House: Jane Alexander
   4th Vice President, Special Project: Carin Freidag
Management:
   President: Zelie Pforzheimer, president@wiltonplayshop.org
   1st Vice President Production: Janice Dehn, production@wiltonplayshop.org
   2nd Vice President Production: Donna Savage, fundraising@wiltonplayshop.org
   3rd Vice President, House: Jane Alexander
   4th Vice President, Special Project: Carin Freidag
   Recording Secretary/Database Mngr.: Genia Meinhold
   Box Office/Subscriptions: Eva Adaszko
   Publicity: Genia Meinhold
Mission: The presentation of musicals and plays to the general public at an affordable price under high quality conditions.
Founded: 1937
Specialized Field: Ensembles; Drama; Contemporary
Status: Non-Professional
Volunteer Staff: 22
Paid Artists: 75
Non-paid Artists: 75
Budget: $50,000
Income Sources: Ticket Sales & Program Advertising
Performs At: Auditorium; Stage w/Loft;
Annual Attendance: 3,000 - 4,000
Facility Category: Live Theatre; Auditorium
Type of Stage: Proscenium
Stage Dimensions: 18x32
Seating Capacity: 125
Year Built: 1870
Year Remodeled: 2007
Cost: $75,000
Rental Contact: President Zelie Pforzheimer
Organization Type: Performing; Educational
Resident Groups: Community Theatre

Delaware

2722
KENT COUNTY THEATRE GUILD
140 E Roosevelt Avenue
PO Box 783
Dover, DE 19903

Phone: 302-674-3568
e-mail: kctg@kctg.org
Web Site: www.kctg.org/
Officers:
　Vice Chair: Patti Kozerski
　Secretary: Maureen Levine
　Treasurer: Linda Hyler
　Member at large: Terri Thompson
　Member at large: Nancy Mulle
Management:
　Chairman: Mike Polo
　Vice Chair: Pat Musto
　Secretary: Kevin Smith
　Treasurer: Judy Saladino
　Chairperson: John Muller
Mission: Kent County has been providing quality theatre to the central Delaware community since 1953.
Founded: 1953
Specialized Field: Community Theater; Drama; Comedy

2723
POSSUM POINT PLAYERS
441 Old Laurel Road
Georgetown, DE 19947
Mailing Address: P O Box 96, Georgetown DE 19947
Phone: 302-856-3460
Fax: 302-856-4560
e-mail: mail@possumpointplayers.org
Web Site: www.possumpointplayers.org
Officers:
　President: Louise Hartzell
　Vice President: Cluadius Bowden
　Secretary: Pat Erhardt
　Treasurer: Kenny Workman
Management:
　Executive Director: Andre Beaumont
　Executive Administrator: Mary Cahill
Mission: Offering quality theatrical productions to Sussex County, Delaware.
Utilizes: Guest Companies
Founded: 1973
Specialized Field: Musical; Dinner Theater; Community Theater
Status: Non-Professional; Nonprofit
Paid Staff: 50
Income Sources: Delaware Theater Association
Performs At: Possum Hall; Delaware Tech Theater
Organization Type: Performing; Educational

2724
RESIDENT ENSEMBLE PLAYERS
University of Delaware
Roselle Center for the Arts
110 Orchard Road
Newark, DE 19716
Mailing Address: 110 Orchard Road, Newark, DE 19716
Phone: 302-831-2206
Fax: 302-831-8528
e-mail: ud-rep@udel.edu
Web Site: www.rep.udel.edu
Management:
　Producing Artistic Director: Sanford Robbins
　Coordinator of Marketing/PR: Nadine Howatt
Founded: 1743
Specialized Field: Theatre
Performs At: Thompson Theatre/Studio Theatre/Hartshorn Theatre
Affiliations: ATHE, AEA, TCG, TAGP
Facility Category: Proscenium/Black Box/Black Box
Type of Stage: Proscenium; Black Box; Black Box
Seating Capacity: 400; 125; 185
Year Built: 1930
Year Remodeled: 1989

2725
ARTISTS THEATRE ASSOCIATION
PO Box 7258
Wilmington, DE 19803
Phone: 302-798-8775
Web Site: www.dca.net/ata
Officers:
　President: L Jeffrey DiSabatino
　Vice-President: Claire Ennis
　Acting Treasurer: Claire Braun
　Secretary: Tina M. Sheing
　Past President: Tom Marshall
Mission: To further the dramatic arts; to encourage new plays; to present workshops in high schools.
Utilizes: Guest Artists; Guest Companies
Founded: 1968
Specialized Field: Musical; Community Theater
Status: Non-Professional; Nonprofit
Paid Staff: 100
Income Sources: Delaware Theatre Association; Delaware Alliance for Arts Education
Organization Type: Performing

2726
CITY THEATER COMPANY
4 South Poplar Street
Wilmington, DE 19801
Mailing Address: P.O. Box 387, Wilmington, DE 19899-0387
Phone: 302-220-8285
e-mail: info@city-theater.org
Web Site: city-theater.org
Officers:
　President: Michelle Kramer-Fitzgerald
　Vice President: Charles Alfree
Management:
　Producing Artistic Director: Michael Gray
Mission: The mission of City Theater Company is to create a body of work for the stage that is consistently high-quality, provocative and new; a body of work that takes risks and breaks barriers in order to engage new theater audiences in an exciting exchange of ideas, imagse and energies.
Founded: 1993
Status: Nonprofit
Performs At: Opera Delaware Studios

2727
DELAWARE THEATRE COMPANY
200 Water Street
Wilmington, DE 19801-5048
Phone: 302-594-1100
Fax: 302-594-1107
Toll-free: 302-594-1104
Web Site: www.delawaretheatre.com
Officers:
　Vice Chair: Grier Flinn
　Secretary: Brett Jones
　Treasurer: Jared E. Young
　Executive Director: Bud Martin
　Technical Director: Gary Gogal
Management:
　Associate Artistic Director: Michael Mastro
　Business Manager: Jillian Farley
　Audience Service Manager: Jennifer Tinianow
　Education & Community Engagement: Allie Steele
　Chair: Julie Morgan
　Institutional Giving Manager: Joanne Lombardi
　Audience Services Manager: Marielle Eaton
Mission: To create high quality professional theatre in Delaware.
Utilizes: Actors; AEA Actors; Artists-in-Residence; Designers; Educators; Five Seasonal Concerts; Grant Writers; Guest Artists; Guest Companies; Guest Conductors; Guest Designers; Guest Ensembles; Guest Lecturers; Resident Professionals; Student Interns
Founded: 1978
Specialized Field: Musical; Ensembles
Status: Professional; Nonprofit
Paid Staff: 35
Budget: $2.3 million
Performs At: The Delaware Theatre Company
Type of Stage: Semi-Thrust
Seating Capacity: 389
Year Built: 1985
Rental Contact: Tom Kirkpatrick
Organization Type: Performing; Educational

2728
SHOESTRING PRODUCTIONS LIMITED
214 W 18th Street
Wilmington, DE 19802
Phone: 302-655-0299
Management:
　Artistic Director: Deborah Dehart
Mission: Creating, producing and touring original musicals to entertain and educate young audiences.
Utilizes: Multimedia
Founded: 1978
Specialized Field: Musical; Ensembles
Status: Professional
Organization Type: Performing; Touring; Educational

2729
WILMINGTON DRAMA LEAGUE
10 W Lea Boulevard
Wilmington, DE 19802
Phone: 302-764-1172
Web Site: www.wilmingtondramaleague.org/
Management:
　President: Nick D'Argenio
　Treasurer: Dennis Williams
　VP Financial Development: Kate Monaghan
　VP Artistic Development: Alicia Chomo
Mission: To provide low-cost, quality theatre, theatrical activities, and education to the Greater Wilmington Region.
Utilizes: Singers
Founded: 1933
Specialized Field: Community Theater; Ensembles
Status: Non-Professional; Nonprofit
Paid Staff: 1
Volunteer Staff: 300
Budget: $195,000
Income Sources: Ticket Sales; Contribution; State Arts Council
Annual Attendance: 8,000
Facility Category: Theater
Seating Capacity: 256
Year Built: 1940
Year Remodeled: 1999
Organization Type: Performing; Educational

District of Columbia

2730
AFRICAN CONTINUUM THEATRE COMPANY (ACTCO)
3523 12th Street NE
2nd Floor
Washington, DC 20017-2545

THEATRE / District of Columbia

Phone: 202-529-5763
Fax: 202-529-5764
e-mail: questions@africancontinuumtheatre.com
Web Site: www.africancontinuumtheatre.com
Officers:
   President: Ivan Fitzgerald
   Secretary: Arden Phillips
Management:
   Executive Director: JoAnn Williams
   PR and Marketing Consultant: Renee Littleton
Mission: To sustain and grow African-American theater by producing new and traditional art forms that contribute to the understanding and appreciation of the African-American culture.
Founded: 1989
Specialized Field: African American; Ethnic Theater
Paid Staff: 4
Volunteer Staff: 10

2731
AMERICAN UNIVERSITY THEATRE PROGRAM
4400 Massachusetts Avenue
Washington, DC 20016
Phone: 202-885-3414
Fax: 202-885-2429
e-mail: dpa@american.edu
Web Site: http://www.american.edu/cas/performing-arts/theatre.cfm
Officers:
   Chair: Gail Humphries Breeskin
   Co-Chair: Daniel Abraham
Management:
   Associate Professor: Daniel Abraham
   Assistant Professor: Jimi Adams
   Associate Professor: Anthony Ahrens
   Professional Lecturer: Susan Agolini
   Lecturer: A William Avent
Specialized Field: Educational; Theater Workshops
Affiliations: ATHE
Seating Capacity: 175-200; 175

2732
ARENA STAGE
1101 6th Street SW
Washington, DC 20024
Phone: 202-488-3300
Fax: 202-488-4056
e-mail: info@arenastage.org
Web Site: www.arenastage.org
Management:
   President: John M Derrick
   Artistic Director: Molly Smith
   Executive Director: Stephen Richard
   Chair: Wendy Farrow Raines
   Vp: Stephen Richard
   Vp: Riley K Temple
   Secretary: Helga Tarver
   Treasurer: David Shiffin
Mission: To offer huge plays that encompass all that is exuberant, passionate, deep, profound and dangerous in our American spirit. Arena Stage relentlessly pursues excellence and artistic process; flourishes by providing a dynamic and powerful artistic community; champions various diversities throughout our organization and in the community; is recognized as a leader throughout the world.
Utilizes: Guest Companies
Founded: 1950
Specialized Field: Drama; Comedy; Musical; Educational; Theater Workshops
Status: Professional; Nonprofit
Income Sources: Actors' Equity Association; Society for Stage Directors and Choreographers
Performs At: Arena Theatre (Fichandler & Kreeger)
Organization Type: Performing; Educational

2733
CATHOLIC UNIVERSITY OF AMERICA: DRAMA DEPARTMENT
105 Hartke
Washington, DC 20064
Phone: 202-319-5358
Fax: 202-319-5359
e-mail: cua-drama@cua.edu
Web Site: www.cua.edu/as/drama
Officers:
   Chair: Dr. Greta Honegger PhD
Management:
   President: David M O'Conner
Founded: 1881
Specialized Field: Classic; Contemporary; Drama
Status: Non-Profit, Non-Professional
Paid Staff: 12
Budget: $10,100-$15,500
Affiliations: Arena Stage
Seating Capacity: 590; 80; 40
Year Built: 1970
Year Remodeled: 1987

2734
DISCOVERY THEATER
Arts & Industries Building
1100 Jefferson Drive SW
Washington, DC 20560
Mailing Address: P.O. Box 23293 Washington, DC 20026
Phone: 202-633-8700
Fax: 202-343-1073
e-mail: info@DiscoveryTheater.org
Web Site: www.discoverytheater.org
Management:
   Program Manager: Brigitte Blachere
   Artistic Director: Roberta Gasbarre
Mission: The Smithsonian's Discovery Theater, located in the Arts and Industries Building on the National Mall, is dedicated to offering the best in live performing arts for young people.
Founded: 1978
Specialized Field: Children's Theater
Status: Non-Profit, Professional
Paid Staff: 10
Season: September - August
Type of Stage: Thrust
Stage Dimensions: 25' x 10'
Seating Capacity: 175

2735
FLASHPOINT STUDIOS
916 G Street North West
Washington, DC 20001
Phone: 202-315-1305
e-mail: info@onestageproductions.com
Management:
   Founder/Artistic Director: Michael W McCorkle
   Chairperson: Monica S McCorkle
   Vice-Chairperson: Dana Trussell
   Treasurer: Nikisha Long
Mission: Purpose of providing individuals, who would not otherwise have the resources to benefit from the arts with the opportunity to develop and showcase their performing talents and capabilities within a professional environment. Through reading and writing dialogue, memorization, acting and peer mentoring, teens are provided with the academic and social enrichment needed to be successful in education.
Specialized Field: Theater Workshops; Youth Theater

2736
FOLGER SHAKESPEARE LIBRARY
201 E Capitol Street SE
Washington, DC 20003-1094
Phone: 202-544-4600
Fax: 202-544-4623
e-mail: webmaster@folger.edu
Web Site: www.folger.edu
Officers:
   Chair: Louis R. Cohen
   Vice Chairman: Philip J. Deutch
   Ex Officio Member: Michael Witmore
Management:
   Director: Gail Kern Paste
   Executive Director: Janice Delaney
   Artistic Producer: Janet Alexander Griffin
   General Manager For Public Programs: Jane Pisano
   Events and Programming: Folger Consort
Mission: Folger Theatre annually performs a three-play season of innovative productions designed to forge strong connections with modern audiences, continuing the lively legacy of Shakespearean stagecraft. While Shakespeare is central to its mission, the Theatre has produced a variety of other classical works, as well as new plays related to or inspired by Shakespeare.
Utilizes: Actors; AEA Actors; Choreographers; Collaborations; Curators; Dancers; Educators; Five Seasonal Concerts; Guest Choreographers; Guest Conductors; Guest Designers; Guest Directors; Guest Instructors; Guest Musical Directors; Guest Musicians; Guild Activities; Instructors; Local Artists; Local Unknown Artists; Multimedia; Music; Original Music Scores; Performance Artists; Playwrights; Resident Professionals; Selected Students; Sign Language Translators; Singers; Soloists; Student Interns; Special Technical Talent; Theatre Companies
Founded: 1879
Specialized Field: Musical; Shakespeare; Historical; Specialty Acts
Status: Nonprofit
Paid Staff: 25
Volunteer Staff: 35
Paid Artists: 70
Budget: $9,000,000
Income Sources: Grants; Endowments
Performs At: Theater
Annual Attendance: 200,000
Type of Stage: Proscenium
Seating Capacity: 250
Year Built: 1932
Year Remodeled: 1992

2737
FOLGER THEATRE
201 E Capitol Street SE
Washington, DC 20003-1094
Phone: 202-544-4600
Fax: 202-544-4623
e-mail: academic@folger.edu
Web Site: www.folger.edu
Officers:
   Chair: Louis R. Cohen
   Vice Chairman: Philip J. Deutch
   Ex Officio Member: Michael Witmore
Management:
   Executive Director: Kathleen Lynch
   Manager: Jane Pisano
   Production Manager: Jane Pisano
   Events Publicist: Annalisa Rosmarin

Utilizes: Actors; AEA Actors; Guest Conductors; Guest Designers; Local Artists; Original Music Scores; Resident Professionals; Selected Students; Student Interns
Performs At: The Elizabethan Theatre at the Folger
Facility Category: Theatre
Type of Stage: Elizabethan indoor
Seating Capacity: 240
Year Built: 1930

2738
FORD'S THEATRE SOCIETY
511 10th Street NW
Washington, DC 20004
Phone: 202-426-6924
Fax: 202-347-6269
Toll-free: 800-899-2367
e-mail: onstage@fordstheatre.org
Web Site: www.fordstheatre.org
Officers:
    Chairman: Hon. Joseph McDadeny
    Vice Chairman: Gerald M Lowrie
    Secretary: Mrs. Paul Laxalt
    Treasurer: Richard L. Thompson
    Director: Paul R. Tetreault
Management:
    Managing Director: Paul Tetreault
Mission: Presenting live theatre productions to pay tribute to Abraham Lincoln's appreciation for the performing arts.
Founded: 1968
Specialized Field: Musical; Comedy; Youth Theater; Community Theater; Classic
Status: Non-Profit, Professional
Budget: $6,000,000
Performs At: Ford's Theatre
Annual Attendance: 150,000
Facility Category: Theatre House
Type of Stage: Proscenium/Thrust
Seating Capacity: 699
Year Built: 1860
Year Remodeled: 1968
Organization Type: Performing; Educational

2739
GALA HISPANIC THEATRE
3333 14th St NW
Washington, DC 20010
Phone: 202-234-7174
Fax: 202-332-1247
e-mail: info@galatheatre.org
Web Site: www.galatheatre.org
Officers:
    Co-Founder & Executive Director: Rebecca Read Medrano
    Co-Founder & Executive Director: Hugo Medrano
Management:
    Artistic Director: Hugo Medrono
    Associate Producing Director: Abel Lopez
    Development Manager: Emily Goulding
    Production Manager: Anna Bate
    Office Manager: Paulo Andr,s Montenegro
Mission: Expanding and promoting Hispanic culture.
Founded: 1976
Specialized Field: Spanish Language Company; Ethnic Theater
Status: Non-Profit, Professional
Paid Staff: 6
Performs At: GALA Hispanic Theatre
Type of Stage: Proscenium
Seating Capacity: 200
Organization Type: Resident; Educational

2740
GEORGE WASHINGTON UNIVERSITY: DEPARTMENT OF THEATRE AND DANCE
800 21st Street NW Suite 227
Washington, DC 20052
Phone: 202-994-8072
Fax: 202-994-9403
e-mail: onstage@gwu.edu
Web Site: www.gwu.edu/~theatre/
Officers:
    Chair: Leslie B Jacobson
    Deputy Chair, Director MFA: Carl Gudenius
    Chair: Dana Tai Soon Burgess
Management:
    Chair: Dana Tai Soon Burgess
    Executive Coordinator: Marjorie Coleman
    Asst. Professor of Dance: Mary Buckley
    Asst. Professor of Dance: Kate Mattingly
Founded: 1875
Specialized Field: Educational; Theater Workshops
Status: For-Profit, Non-Professional
Budget: $2,900
Affiliations: ATHE
Seating Capacity: 484; 50
Year Built: 1968

2741
HOWARD UNIVERSITY DEPARTMENT OF THEATRE ARTS
Division of Fine Arts
2455 6th Street NW
Washington, DC 20059
Phone: 202-806-7050
Fax: 202-806-9193
e-mail: kbey@howard.edu
Web Site: www.howard.edu/collegefinearts/theatre
Officers:
    Chair: Joe Selmon
Management:
    President: Sidney A. Ribeau
Utilizes: Actors; Artists-in-Residence; Dancers; Educators; Guest Artists; Guest Soloists; High School Drama; Performance Artists; Resident Professionals; Sign Language Translators; Soloists; Theatre Companies
Founded: 1950
Specialized Field: Educational; Theater Workshops
Status: For-Profit, Non-Professional
Paid Staff: 20
Budget: $3,550-$14,000
Affiliations: NAST; ATHE
Type of Stage: Black Box; Proscenium
Seating Capacity: 300; 75
Year Built: 1960
Year Remodeled: 1988
Rental Contact: Professor Denise Saunders Thompson

2742
KENNEDY CENTER AMERICAN COLLEGE THEATRE
John F Kennedy Center for the Performing Arts
Washington, DC 20566-0001
Mailing Address: 2700 F Street
Phone: 202-416-8864
Fax: 202-416-8860
Toll-free: 800-444-1324
e-mail: KCACTF@kennedy-center.org
Web Site: www.kennedy-center.org/education/actf
Officers:
    Program Assistant: Taylor Hitaffer
Management:
    President: Michael Kaiser
    Artistic Director: Ramon Terleckyi
    Artistic Director: Gregg Henry
    Co-Manager: Susan Shaffer
    Artistic Director: Gregg Henry
Utilizes: Actors; Artists-in-Residence; Collaborating Artists; Educators; Guest Accompanists; Guest Conductors; Guest Designers; Guest Soloists; High School Drama; Local Artists; Performance Artists; Resident Professionals; Soloists; Theatre Companies
Founded: 1971
Specialized Field: Educational; Theater Workshops; Classic
Status: Non-Profit, Professional
Paid Staff: 4
Volunteer Staff: 50
Non-paid Artists: 200
Season: April
Performs At: Kennedy Center [Festival Site]
Facility Category: Terrace Theatre; Theatre Lab
Seating Capacity: 513; 388

2743
LIVING STAGE
1101 6th Street SW
Washington, DC 20024
Phone: 202-488-3300
Fax: 202-488-4056
e-mail: info@arenastage.org
Web Site: www.arenastage.org
Management:
    President: Molly Smith
    Executive Director: Stephen Richards
    Operations Manager: Jane Cassanajor
    Managing Director: Guy Berquist
Mission: Change through creative empowerment.
Founded: 1966
Specialized Field: Community Theater
Status: Non-Profit, Professional
Paid Staff: 8
Volunteer Staff: 3
Paid Artists: 6
Non-paid Artists: 1
Performs At: Performance Workshops
Affiliations: A division of Community Engagement at Arena Stage
Type of Stage: Black Box
Stage Dimensions: 45'x 37'
Seating Capacity: varies
Year Built: 1985
Year Remodeled: 1990
Rental Contact: Anne Theisen
Organization Type: Resident

2744
NATIONAL CONSERVATORY OF DRAMATIC ARTS
1556 Wisconsin Avenue Northwest
Washington, DC 20007
Phone: 202-333-2202
Fax: 202-333-1753
e-mail: ncdadrama@aol.com
Web Site: www.theconservatory.org
Officers:
    President: Raymond Ficca
Management:
    Executive Director: Nan Fricca
Utilizes: Actors; AEA Actors; Collaborations; Designers; Educators; Equity Actors; Filmmakers; Grant Writers; Guest Designers; Guest Ensembles; Guest Instructors; Guest Musical Directors; Guest Soloists; Guest Teachers; High School Drama; Instructors; Local

THEATRE / District of Columbia

Artists; Multi Collaborations; Original Music Scores; Performance Artists; Scenic Designers; Soloists; Students; Student Interns; Special Technical Talent
Founded: 1975
Specialized Field: Educational; Theater Workshops
Status: Non-Profit, Non-Professional
Paid Staff: 4
Volunteer Staff: 10
Paid Artists: 22
Budget: $400,000
Income Sources: Tuition; Grants; Federal Funds
Performs At: Theatre; Film
Affiliations: TCG; CAGW; DC Arts & Humanities
Annual Attendance: 8,000
Type of Stage: Black Box
Stage Dimensions: 1,000 square feet
Seating Capacity: 60
Year Built: 1960
Year Remodeled: 2001

2745
NATIONAL THEATRE
1321 Pennsylvania Avenue NW
Washington, DC 20004
Phone: 202-628-6161
Toll-free: 800-447-7400
e-mail: information@nationaltheatre.org
Web Site: www.nationaltheatre.org
Officers:
 President: Donn B. Murphy
 GM: Sarah K. Bartlo
 Accounting Manager: Marc Fitzgerald
 Operation Manager: Bob Lawrence
 Production Manager: Tim Todd
Management:
 General Manager: Harry Teter, Jr
 Theatre Manager: Guy Jordin Heard
 Corporate Administrator: John H. Loomis
 Executive Director: Tom Lee
Mission: The preservation of the historic playhouse; the presentation of top quality touring productions; the showcasing of professional and non-professional groups.
Utilizes: Singers
Founded: 1835
Specialized Field: Musical; Community Theater; Ethnic Theater; Puppet
Status: Professional; Nonprofit; Commercial
Paid Staff: 100
Paid Artists: 3
Income Sources: Actors' Equity Association; International Association of Theatrical Stage Employees; The Shubert Organization
Organization Type: Educational; Sponsoring

2746
POINTLESS THEATRE
P.O. Box 43033
Washington, DC 20010
Phone: 202-733-6321
e-mail: scott@pointlesstheatre.com
Web Site: pointlesstheatre.com
Officers:
 Chair: David Lloyd Olson
Management:
 Production Manager: Mel Bieler
Mission: Pointless Theatre Co. is dedicated to creating bold, visceral, and affordable spectacles that gleefully smash the traditional boundaries between puppetry, theatre, dance, music, and the visual arts.
Founded: 2009
Specialized Field: Puppet Theatre
Status: Sponsored Project Of A Nonprofit Arts Service Organization (Fractured Atlas)
Affiliations: Fractured Atlas

2747
SHAKESPEARE THEATRE COMPANY
516 8th Street SE
Washington, DC 20004
Phone: 202-547-3230
Fax: 202-547-0226
Web Site: www.shakespearetheatre.com
Officers:
 Chairman: Michael R. Klein
 Vice Chairman: Robert E. Falb
 Secretary: Pauline Schneider
 Treasurer: John Hill
 Artistic Director: Michael Kahn
Management:
 Managing Director: Chris Jennings
 Artistic Director: Michael Kahn
 Director Marketing/Communications: Darby I Lunceford
 Chief Development Officer: Ed Zakreski
Mission: The theatre's core mission is to present classic theatre in an accessible, skillful, imaginative, American style that honors playwrights' language and intentions while viewing their plays through a 21st-century lens.
Utilizes: Actors; AEA Actors; Artists-in-Residence; Choreographers; Collaborating Artists; Commissioned Composers; Guest Accompanists; Guest Artists; Guest Companies; Guest Conductors; Guest Designers; Guest Writers; Local Artists; Original Music Scores; Resident Artists; Resident Professionals; Selected Students; Soloists; Student Interns
Founded: 1986
Specialized Field: Shakespeare
Status: Non-Profit, Professional
Paid Staff: 90
Paid Artists: 75
Budget: $13 Million
Income Sources: League of Washington Theatres; Cultural Alliance of Greater Washington
Performs At: Shakespeare Theatre Company at the Lansburgh
Annual Attendance: 145,000
Facility Category: Theatre
Type of Stage: Proscenium
Seating Capacity: 451
Organization Type: Performing; Resident

2748
SOURCE THEATRE COMPANY
1835 14th Street NW
Washington, DC 20009
Phone: 202-204-7800
e-mail: info@sourcedc.org
Web Site: www.sourcetheatre.org
Management:
 Artistic Director: Joe Banno
 Literary Manager: Keith Parker
 Managing Director: Delia Taylor
 Contact: Heather Pagella
Mission: To present innovative and exciting productions of new works and contemporary plays that have relevance to our community; to offer reinterpretations of the classics.
Utilizes: Actors; AEA Actors; Artists-in-Residence; Collaborating Artists; Collaborations; Curators; Dance Companies; Designers; Educators; Fine Artists; Five Seasonal Concerts; Guest Accompanists; Guest Choreographers; Guest Companies; Guest Composers; Guest Designers; Guest Directors; Guest Ensembles; Guest Lecturers; Guest Musical Directors; Guest Musicians; Guest Teachers; Guild Activities; High School Drama; Instructors; Local Artists; Local Unknown Artists; Lyricists; Multi Collaborations; Multimedia; Music; New Productions; Organization Contracts; Original Music Scores; Performance Artists; Poets; Resident Professionals; Selected Students; Sign Language Translators; Singers; Soloists; Student Interns; Special Technical Talent; Theatre Companies; Touring Companies; Visual Arts
Founded: 1977
Specialized Field: Ensembles; Drama; Musical
Status: Professional; Nonprofit
Paid Staff: 4
Volunteer Staff: 40
Paid Artists: 20
Non-paid Artists: 10
Budget: $400,000
Income Sources: Ticket Sales, Grants
Performs At: Theatre
Affiliations: League of Washington Theatres; Theatre Communications Group; Actors' Equity Association
Annual Attendance: 15,000
Type of Stage: Black Box
Year Remodeled: 1998
Rental Contact: Heather Pagella
Organization Type: Performing; Touring; Resident

2749
SPOOKY ACTION THEATRE
1810 16th Street NW
Washington, DC 20009
Phone: 202-248-0301
e-mail: info@spookyaction.org
Web Site: spookyaction.org
Management:
 Artistic Director: Richard Henrich
 Company Manager: Steve Kryzanowski
 Production Manager: Oliver Hinson
Mission: Spooky Action Theater's mission is to recharge our audience's imaginative, intuitive, emotional core and rekindle its shared consciousness, linking artists and audience in this collaborative enterprise.
Founded: 2010
Status: Professional; Nonprofit

2750
STUDIO THEATRE
1501 14th Street Northwest #3
Washington, DC 20005
Phone: 202-232-7267
Fax: 202-332-1187
e-mail: studio@studiotheatre.org
Web Site: www.studiotheatre.org
Officers:
 Chair of the Board of Trustees: Susan L Butler
 Vice Chair of the Board of Trustees: Janet L Dewar
 Chair Emeritus, Board of Trustees: Irene Harriet Blum
 Chair Emeritus, Board of Trustees: Jaylee M Mead
 Artistic Director: David Muse
Management:
 Artistic Director: Joy Zinoman
 Managing Director: Keith Alan Baker
Mission: To produce the best in contemporary theatre and through its Secondstage and Acting Conservatory to provide opportunities for emerging artists and to offer rigorous theatre training. Our commitment to artistic excellence serves the diverse communities of the nation's capital.
Utilizes: Guest Companies
Founded: 1978

THEATRE / Florida

Specialized Field: Comedy; Youth Theater; Dinner Theater; Ethnic Theater; Community Theater; Classic; Contemporary
Status: Non-Profit, Professional
Paid Staff: 32
Budget: $3,000,000
Income Sources: Theatre Communications Group; Cultural Alliance of Greater Washington; League of Washington Theatres
Performs At: The Studio Theatre; The Secondstage
Facility Category: Theatre
Type of Stage: Proscenium
Seating Capacity: 182 Milton/218 Mead/50 Second Stage
Year Remodeled: 1997
Cost: 5.5 million
Rental Contact: Roma Rogers
Organization Type: Performing; Educational; Sponsoring

2751
TAFFETY PUNK THEATRE COMPANY
545 7th Street SE
Washington, DC 20003
Mailing Address: P.O. Box 15392, Washington, Dc 20003
Phone: 202-355-9441
e-mail: info@taffetypunk.com
Web Site: taffetypunk.com
Mission: The mission of the Taffety Punk Theatre is to establish a dynamic ensemble of actors, dancers, and musicians who ignite a public passion for theatre by making the classical and the contemporary exciting, meaningful, and affordable.
Status: Nonprofit

2752
VSA ARTS
1300 Connecticut Avenue
Suite 700
Washington, DC 20036
Phone: 202-628-2800
Fax: 202-737-0725
Toll-free: 800-444-1324
e-mail: KCACTF@kennedy-center.org
Web Site: www.kennedy-center.org
Officers:
  Program Assistant: Taylor Hitaffer
Management:
  President: Michael Kaiser
  Artistic Director: Ramon Terleckyi
  Artistic Director: Gregg Henry
  Co-Manager: Susan Shaffer
  Artistic Director: Gregg Henry
Utilizes: Actors; Artists-in-Residence; Fine Artists; Guest Accompanists; Guest Musical Directors; Guest Musicians; Guild Activities; Instructors; Multimedia; Playwrights; Singers; Touring Companies
Founded: 1974
Specialized Field: Musical; Youth Theater; Ethnic Theater; Community Theater; Puppet; Classic; Contemporary; Alternative; Educational
Status: Non-Profit, Professional
Affiliations: John F Kennedy Center for the Performing Arts

2753
WASHINGTON STAGE GUILD
4018 Argyle Terrace NW
#4
Washington, DC 20011
Phone: 240-582-0050
e-mail: nfo@stageguild.org
Web Site: www.stageguild.org

Officers:
  Producing Artistic Director: Bill Largess
  Executive Director: Ann Norton
Management:
  Producing Artistic Director: Bill Largess
  Executive Director: Ann Norton
Mission: To perform plays that are often overlooked, including lesser-known works of famous playwrights, classics, and new plays of merit.
Utilizes: Singers
Founded: 1986
Specialized Field: Drama; Musical
Status: Professional; Nonprofit
Income Sources: Actors' Equity Association; League of Washington Theatres; Cultural Arts Alliance of DC
Performs At: Carroll Hall
Organization Type: Performing; Resident; Educational

2754
WOOLLY MAMMOTH THEATRE COMPANY
641 D Street NW
Washington, DC 20004
Phone: 202-289-2443
Fax: 202-289-2446
e-mail: info@woollymammoth.net
Web Site: www.woollymammoth.net
Management:
  Artistic Director: Howard Shalwitz
  Managing Director: Jeffrey Herrmann
Mission: To ignite an explosive engagement between theatre artists and the community by developing, producing, and promoting new plays that explore the edges of theatrical style and human experience, and by implementing new ways to use the artistry of theatre to serve the people of Greater Washington, DC.
Utilizes: Guest Companies; Singers
Founded: 1980
Specialized Field: Theater
Status: Non-Profit, Professional
Paid Staff: 65
Budget: $4,085,814
Performs At: Woolly Mammoth Theatre
Type of Stage: Flex-Proscenium
Seating Capacity: 265
Year Built: 2005
Rental Contact: General Manager Brian Smith
Organization Type: Performing; Resident; Educational

Florida

2755
ISLAND PLAYERS
PO Box 20411, St. Simons Island
Anna Maria, FL 31522
Phone: 912-638-0338
e-mail: president@theislandplayers.org
Web Site: www.theislandplayers.com
Management:
  President: Allan Ledingham
  Vice President: Ronald Dempset
  Secretary: Beverly Fetter
  Treasurer: Joyce Ledingham
Mission: To present quality community theatre for the cultural enrichment of the area.
Utilizes: Guest Companies; Singers
Founded: 1948
Specialized Field: Community Theater
Status: Non-Professional; Nonprofit
Performs At: Island Players Theatre
Organization Type: Performing

2756
CALDWELL THEATRE COMPANY
7901 N Federal Highway
Levitz Plaza
Boca Raton, FL 33487
Phone: 561-241-7432
Fax: 561-997-6917
Toll-free: 877-245-7432
e-mail: clive@caldwelltheatre.com
Web Site: www.caldwelltheatre.com
Management:
  Artistic And Marketing Director: Clive Cholerton
  Company Manager: Patricia Burdett
  Production Manager: Thomas Shorrock
Mission: To explore timeless and current human issues through the art of theater, and to provide a creative and caring artistic home for artists, staff, students and audiences of all ages. The Caldwell continues to provide an environment where imaginations soar-and professional theater thrives.
Utilizes: Designers; Guest Companies
Founded: 1975
Specialized Field: Drama; Musical
Status: Professional; Nonprofit
Income Sources: Theatre Communications Group; Florida Professional Theatre Association
Organization Type: Performing; Touring; Resident

2757
FLORIDA ATLANTIC UNIVERSITY: DEPARTMENT OF THEATRE
777 Glade Road
Boca Raton, FL 33431
Phone: 561-297-3810
Fax: 561-297-2180
e-mail: theatre@fau.edu
Web Site: www.fau.edu/theatre
Officers:
  Chair: Gvozden Kopani
Founded: 1967
Specialized Field: Musical; Comedy; Youth Theater; Dinner Theater; Ethnic Theater; Community Theater; Puppet; Educational; Theater Workshops
Status: Non-Profit, Non-Professional
Paid Staff: 15
Paid Artists: 15
Budget: $40,750-$51,000
Affiliations: ATHE
Seating Capacity: 540; 150; 100
Year Built: 1996

2758
SLOW BURN THEATRE CO.
12811 West Glades Road
Boca Raton, FL 33498
Mailing Address: 21218 St. Andres Blvd. #158, Boca Raton, FL 33433
Phone: 866-811-4111
e-mail: slowburntheatre@yahoo.com
Web Site: slowburntheatre.org
Officers:
  President: Mark Traverso
  Treasurer: Beth Schwartz
  Secretary: Deborah Marks
Management:
  Artistic Director: Patrick Fitzwater
  Artistic Director: Matthew Korinko
Mission: To be a locally based professional theatre company providing the South Florida Community the opportunity to see daring, contemporary and intelligent works of musical theatre.
Founded: 2009
Status: Professional; Nonprofit

THEATRE / Florida

2759
MANATEE PLAYERS/RIVERFRONT THEATRE
102 12th Street W
Bradenton, FL 34205
Phone: 941-748-0111
Web Site: www.manateeplayers.com
Officers:
　Artistic Director: Rick Kerby
　Executive Director: Janene Witham
　Technical Director: Bill Booth
Management:
　Artistic Director: Rick Kerby
　Production: Kristin Ribble
　Marketing: Denny Miller
　Costume Shop Manager: Georgina Willmott
Mission: Improving the cultural and educational climate of our community through offering quality live theatre.
Utilizes: Guest Companies; Singers
Founded: 1948
Specialized Field: Community Theater
Status: Nonprofit
Paid Staff: 100
Income Sources: Festival of American Community Theatre; American Association of Community Theatres; Manatee County Cultural Alliance
Performs At: Riverfront Theatre
Organization Type: Performing; Educational

2760
ATLANTIC COAST THEATRE
8297 Champions Gate Boulevard #188
Champions Gate, FL 33896
Phone: 863-242-8656
Fax: 863-424-5130
Toll-free: 877-565-0828
e-mail: shows@atlantic-coast-theatre.com
Web Site: www.atlantic-coast-theatre.com/
Management:
　Education Director: Noel Holland
　Artistic Director: Don Gruel
　Set Designer: Robbin Watts
Mission: Dedicated to bring the art of theatre to children and families. Believe in the amazing imaginations of children. Our mission is to create performances, workshops and educational programs that inspire and encourage discussion
Specialized Field: Children's Theater

2761
CITY PLAYERS
Clearwater Parks And Recreation
Po Box 4748
Clearwater, FL 34618
Phone: 813-462-6035
Management:
　Cultural Arts Supervisor: Margo Walbolt
　Technical Director: Phillip Terry
　Music Director: B.J. Pucci
Mission: To offer the public quality theatre at nominal fees.
Founded: 1971
Specialized Field: Community Theater
Status: Non-Professional; Nonprofit
Paid Staff: 4
Performs At: Ruth Eckerd Hall; Saint Petersburg Junior College
Organization Type: Performing; Educational

2762
SHOWBOAT DINNER THEATRE
3405 Ulmerton Road
Clearwater, FL 34622
Phone: 727-571-1200
Fax: 813-573-2735
Management:
　Owner/President/Producer: Virginia Sherwood
Utilizes: Guest Companies; Singers
Founded: 1967
Specialized Field: Dinner Theater
Status: Professional; Commercial
Organization Type: Performing

2763
SURFSIDE PLAYERS
301 Ramp Road
Cocoa Beach, FL 32932
Phone: 321-783-3127
e-mail: surfside_info@yahoo.com
Web Site: www.surfsideplayers.com/
Officers:
　President: Dave McFarland
　VP: Judy Bate
　Secretary: Kay Grinter
　Treasurer: Marilyn Rigerman
Mission: To produce high quality productions, and educate youth in the performing arts field.
Specialized Field: Children's Theater; Educational

2764
ACTORS' PLAYHOUSE AT THE MIRACLE THEATRE
280 Miracle Mile
Coral Gables, FL 33134
Phone: 305-444-9293
Fax: 305-444-4181
Web Site: www.actorsplayhouse.org
Officers:
　Chairman: Lawrence Stein
　Treasurer: Lawrence Kessler
　Secretary: Leslie Gross
　Chairman: Lawrence E Stein
　Executive Producing Director: Barbara S Stein
　Artistic Director: David Arisco
Management:
　Chairman: Lawrence E Stein
　Executive Producing Director: Barbara S Stein
　Artistic Director: David Arisco
　Development Director: Jerry Brown
　Public Relation Manager: Brooke Nobel
　Assistant Technical Director: Chris Jahn
Mission: Actors' Playhouse at the Miracle Theatre is one of Florida's major, critically acclaimed, non-profit cultural institutions and is dedicated to entertaining and culturally enriching South Florida audiences by producing quality live theatre for adults and children at affordable prices.
Founded: 1988
Specialized Field: Musical
Status: Nonprofit
Season: October - June
Seating Capacity: 600

2765
AREA STAGE COMPANY
1560 S. Dixie Highway
Coral Gables, FL 33146
Phone: 305-666-2078
e-mail: info@areastagecompany.com
Web Site: areastagecompany.com
Management:
　Artistic Director: John Rodaz
　Executive Director: Maria Banda-Rodaz
Mission: To create world-class theatrical productions that help tear down barriers and bridge cultural gaps; to emphasize our similarities and to encourage an appreciation of our differences.
Founded: 1989
Status: Professional; Nonprofit
Performs At: The Riviera Theatre

2766
GABLESTAGE
1200 Anastasia Avenue
Suite 230
Coral Gables, FL 33134
Phone: 305-446-1116
Fax: 305-445-8645
e-mail: contact@gablestage.org
Web Site: www.gablestage.org
Officers:
　Producing Artistic Director: Joseph Adler
Management:
　Chair: Barbara Friedson Garrett
　General Manager: Maria Kronfeld
　Vice Chair: Denise K Ehrich
　Producing Artistic Director: Joseph Adler
　General Manager: Witnie Bresil
Mission: To provide the South Florida community with classical contemporary theatrical productions of artistic excellence. FST hopes to challenge our multi-cultural audience with innovative productions that entertain as well as confront today's issues and ideas.
Utilizes: Singers
Founded: 1979
Specialized Field: Drama; Musical; Specialty Acts
Status: Professional; Nonprofit
Paid Staff: 10
Budget: $1 million
Income Sources: Foundations; Government; Corporations; Individuals; Box Office
Performs At: Biltmore Hotel
Affiliations: Theatre Leader of South Florida
Annual Attendance: 30,000
Type of Stage: Proscenium
Seating Capacity: 150
Year Built: 1995
Organization Type: Performing; Touring; Resident; Educational

2767
TEATRO AVANTE
744 S.W. 8th Street, 2nd Floor
Coral Gables, FL 33130
Phone: 305-445-8877
Fax: 305-445-1301
e-mail: TeAvante@aol.com
Web Site: www.teatroavante.com
Management:
　Producing Artistic Director: Mario Ernesto Sanchez
　Resident Director/Designer: Rolando Moreno
　Technical Coordinator: Manelo Mina
Mission: To further Hispanic theatre.
Utilizes: Guest Companies; Singers
Founded: 1979
Specialized Field: Summer Stock; Multi-Cultural
Status: Professional; Nonprofit
Performs At: El Carruse Theatre
Organization Type: Performing; Touring; Educational

2768
UNIVERSITY OF MIAMI: DEPARTMENT OF THEATRE ARTS
PO Box 248273
Coral Gables, FL 33124
Mailing Address: PO Box 248273, Coral Gables, FL 33124
Phone: 305-284-4474

Fax: 305-284-5702
e-mail: theatredepartment@miami.edu
Web Site: www.as.miami.edu/theatrearts/
Officers:
   Interim Chair: Bruce J Miller
   Chair: Henry Fonte
Specialized Field: Educational; Theater Workshops
Budget: $20,000-$30,000
Affiliations: City Theatre
Seating Capacity: 300-400;45
Year Built: 1951
Year Remodeled: 1996

2769
THE STAGE DOOR THEATRE
8036 W. Sample Road
Coral Springs, FL 33065
Phone: 954-344-7765
e-mail: boxoffice@stagedoorfl.org
Web Site: stagedoortheatre.com
Mission: To bring the best in live performing arts to Broward and other nearby communities and to promote a cultural life that entertains, educates, and invigorates.
Status: Nonprofit

2770
DAYTONA PLAYHOUSE
100 Jessamine Boulevard
Daytona Beach, FL 32118
Phone: 386-255-2431
Fax: 386-255-2432
e-mail: webmaster@daytonaplayhouse.org
Web Site: www.daytonaplayhouse.org/
Management:
   Artistic Director: James F Sturgell
Mission: Since 1946, the Daytona Playhouse has entertained appreciative audiences with wonderful performances in the very best community theater tradition. The Playhouse, a nonprofit organization, is also a source of numerous and varied volunteer opportunities in theater management and production.
Utilizes: Commissioned Music
Specialized Field: Musical; Comedy; Community Theater; Classic; Contemporary
Status: Non-Profit, Non-Professional
Performs At: Daytona Playhouse
Organization Type: Performing; Resident

2771
SEASIDE MUSIC THEATER
901 6th Street
PO Box 2835
Daytona Beach, FL 32120
Phone: 386-252-3394
Fax: 386-252-8991
e-mail: lester.malizia@seasidemusictheater.org
Web Site: www.seasidemusictheater.org
Officers:
   President: William Gillespie
   Vice President: Monya Winzer
Management:
   Artistic Director: Lester Malizia
   Associate Producer/Executive Dir: Julia Trullo
   Production Manager: Bob Fetterman
Mission: To offer the finest examples of opera, operetta and musical theatre in repertory.
Utilizes: Actors; AEA Actors; Artists-in-Residence; Choreographers; Commissioned Composers; Dancers; Designers; Fine Artists; Five Seasonal Concerts; Grant Writers; Guest Accompanists; Guest Artists; Guest Companies; Guest Conductors; Guest Designers; Guest Lecturers; Guest Musical Directors; Music; Original Music Scores; Resident Professionals; Selected Students; Sign Language Translators; Singers; Soloists
Founded: 1977
Specialized Field: Musical
Status: Non-Profit, Professional
Paid Staff: 10
Paid Artists: 250
Budget: $2,800,000
Income Sources: Florida Professional Theatre Association; United States Institute for Theatre Technology; Southeastern Theatre Conference
Season: June - August
Annual Attendance: 40,000
Facility Category: Two Theaters
Type of Stage: Procenium
Stage Dimensions: 6'x30'; 47'x17'
Seating Capacity: 498; 576
Year Remodeled: 1999
Rental Contact: Director of Marketing Kelli Beasley
Organization Type: Performing; Touring; Educational

2772
ATHENS THEATRE
124 North Florida Avenue
DeLand, FL 32720-4208
Phone: 386-736-1500
Web Site: athensdeland.com

2773
DELRAY BEACH PLAYHOUSE
950 NW Ninth Street
Delray Beach, FL 33444
Phone: 561-272-1281
Fax: 561-272-5884
e-mail: delraybeachplayhouse@gmail.com
Web Site: www.delraybeachplayhouse.com
Officers:
   President: George Allenton
Management:
   Executive Director: Susan Easton
   Artistic Director: Randolph DelLago
Mission: To increase community involvement in the performing arts.
Founded: 1948
Specialized Field: Community Theater; Musical; Theater Workshops; Children's Theater
Status: Non-Profit, Non-Professional
Paid Staff: 4
Volunteer Staff: 150
Non-paid Artists: 100
Income Sources: Florida Theatre Conference
Performs At: Delray Beach Playhouse
Facility Category: Non-profit community theatre
Seating Capacity: 238
Organization Type: Performing; Educational

2774
IRISH THEATRE OF FLORIDA
180 NE 1st Street
Delray Beach, FL 33444
Phone: 561-450-6357
Web Site: itofl.com
Officers:
   President: Denis Holmes
   Vice President: Sandra Roberts
   Treasurer: Ernie Kollra
Management:
   Director: Imelda Wellington
   Director: Christopher Harrington
   Director: Jim Doan
Specialized Field: Irish Theatre
Status: Nonprofit

2775
BAY STREET PLAYERS
109 North Bay Street
Eustis, FL 32727
Mailing Address: PO Box 1405, Eustis, FL 32727
Phone: 352-357-7777
Fax: 352-357-7034
e-mail: boxoffice@baystreetplayers.org
Web Site: www.baystreetplayers.org
Officers:
   President: Stephan Toth
   Executive Director: Elizabeth Scholl
Management:
   Director: Deborah Carpenter
   Managing Director: Michael Lake
Mission: To provide practical theater training through hands-on experience.
Utilizes: Guest Companies; Singers
Founded: 1975
Specialized Field: Community Theater
Status: Non-Profit, Non-Professional
Paid Staff: 3
Paid Artists: 6
Performs At: State Theatre
Organization Type: Performing; Touring; Educational

2776
FORT LAUDERDALE CHILDREN'S THEATRE
516 NE 13th Street
Fort Lauderdale, FL 33304
Phone: 954-763-6882
Fax: 954-523-0507
e-mail: info@FLCTStar.org
Web Site: www.flct.org
Officers:
   President: Janet Erlick
Management:
   Managing Director: Sean Cutler
   Education Director r: Patti Kimmel Meyers
   Executive Artistic Director: Janet Erlick
   Producing Director: Sean Cutler
   Education Director: Jennifer Pedraza
Mission: To develop the full potential of students as members of our community; to celebrate the diversity of Broward County's population through the arts; to nurture communication among various performing groups; to advance the highest possible standards of the theatre; to encourage public appreciation of the art form; to develop future audiences and supporters of the cultural arts.
Utilizes: Actors; Collaborating Artists; Collaborations; Commissioned Music; Grant Writers; Guest Accompanists; Guest Artists; Guest Companies; Guest Conductors; Guest Designers; Guest Ensembles; Guest Instructors; Guest Lecturers; Guest Musical Directors; Guild Activities; High School Drama; Instructors; Local Artists; Lyricists; Multimedia; Music; Organization Contracts; Original Music Scores; Resident Professionals; Singers; Soloists
Founded: 1952
Specialized Field: Educational; Children's Theater; Theater Workshops
Status: Non-Profit, Non-Professional
Paid Staff: 12
Volunteer Staff: 50
Budget: $500,000
Income Sources: Classes; Plays; Outreach
Performs At: Dillard Center for the Arts; Hollywood Playhouse
Seating Capacity: 660; 262
Rental Contact: Business Manager Amy Rand
Organization Type: Performing; Touring; Educational

THEATRE / Florida

2777
ONE WAY PUPPETS
PO Box 5346
Fort Lauderdale, FL 33310
Phone: 954-491-4221
Management:
    Director: Bob Dolan
Mission: Entertainment and education through puppetry.
Founded: 1971
Specialized Field: Ensembles; Puppet
Status: Professional
Organization Type: Performing; Educational

2778
BROADWAY PALM DINNER THEATRE
1380 Colonial Boulevard
Fort Myers, FL 33907
Phone: 239-278-4422
Fax: 239-278-5664
Toll-free: 800-475-7256
e-mail: tickets@broadwaypalm.com
Web Site: www.broadwaypalm.com
Officers:
    Executive Produce and Owner: Will Prather
    Artistic Producer: Brian Enzmam
Management:
    President and Owner: Will Prather
    Managing Director: Brian Enzmam
    General Manager: Susan Johnson
    Assistant General Manager: Maryi Lawton
    Box Office Supervisor: Jordan Crouch
Mission: Year-round professional dinner theatre presenting Broadway's brightest musicals and comedies.
Utilizes: Actors; Collaborations; Dancers; Designers; Fine Artists; Guest Artists; Guest Conductors; Guest Designers; Guest Lecturers; Guest Musical Directors; Instructors; Local Artists; Multimedia; Music; Original Music Scores; Resident Professionals; Sign Language Translators; Student Interns; Touring Companies
Founded: 1992
Specialized Field: Musical; Comedy; Youth Theater; Dinner Theater; Ethnic Theater; Community Theater; Contemporary
Status: Professional; Non-Equity
Paid Staff: 100
Paid Artists: 10
Income Sources: Ticket sales; Bar & gift shop revenue
Performs At: Broadway Palm Dinner Theatre
Affiliations: National Dinner Theatre Association
Annual Attendance: 150,000+
Facility Category: Dinner Theatre
Type of Stage: Proscenium
Seating Capacity: 450
Year Remodeled: 1993
Rental Contact: General Manager Susan Johnson

2779
FLORIDA REPERTORY THEATRE
2267 First Street
Fort Myers, FL 33901
Phone: 239-332-4488
Fax: 239-332-1808
Toll-free: 877-787-8053
e-mail: boxoffice@floridarep.org
Web Site: www.floridarep.org
Officers:
    Chairman: Dr Gerald Laboda
    Second Chair: Naomi Bloom
    Secretary: Sonya Lubner
    Treasurer: Arthur Zupko
Management:
    Producing Artistic Director/Pres: Robert Caciopto
    Associate Artistic Director: Chris Clavelli
    Associate Director: Jason Parrish
    Managing Director: John Martin
    General Manager: Sean M. Griffin
Mission: Providing a first class regional theatre for Southwest Florida; creating, nurturing, and developing an ensemble of theatre professionals who will develop long term relationships working on a wide variety of plays; helping improve the quality of life in our community through all arts; and to making the arts-especially theatre-accessible to all.
Founded: 1998
Specialized Field: Educational; Drama; Theater Workshops
Status: Non-Profit, Professional
Paid Staff: 32
Volunteer Staff: 200
Paid Artists: 70
Budget: $1.8 million
Income Sources: Ticket & Subscription Sales/Grants/Corporate & Individual Donations
Performs At: Professional Main Stage & Black Box Theatres; Children's Touring Theatre in the Region's Schools
Annual Attendance: 70,000
Type of Stage: Proscenium; 3/4 Thrust Black Box
Stage Dimensions: 40' x 30'; 15' x 10'
Seating Capacity: 393; 80
Year Built: 1908
Year Remodeled: 1994
Rental Contact: Production Manager Sean Griffin

2780
PENINSULA PLAYERS
1436 Rosada Way
Fort Myers, FL 33901
Phone: 941-476-7305
Officers:
    President: James Zgoda
    VP: Ted Schirm
    Treasurer: Linda Jacobey
    Secretary: Suzanne Beeny
Management:
    Director: Al Richter
    Director: Dan Perry
    Director/Producer: Martha Richter
    General Manager: Tom Birmingham
    Executive Producer: James B McKenzie
Mission: To study, perform and promote choral works.
Founded: 1935
Specialized Field: Dinner Theater; Community Theater
Status: Nonprofit
Income Sources: Lee County Alliance of Arts
Performs At: Peninsula Playhouse
Organization Type: Performing

2781
UNIVERSITY OF FLORIDA: SCHOOL, THEATER AND DANCE
Nadine McGuire Theater and Dance Pavilion
University of Florida
Gainesville, FL 32611
Phone: 352-273-0500
Fax: 352-392-5114
Web Site: www.arts.ufl.edu
Officers:
    Director: Jerry Dicky
Management:
    Chairperson: Kevin Marshall
Founded: 1853
Specialized Field: Musical; Comedy; Ethnic Theater; Classic; Contemporary
Status: Non-Profit, Non-Professional
Paid Staff: 30
Budget: $5,100-$7,200
Affiliations: NAST; U/RTA; ATHE; Hippodrome State Theatre
Seating Capacity: 460; 100; 50
Year Built: 1967
Year Remodeled: 1996

2782
GOLDEN THESPIANS
900 Tyler Street
Hollywood, FL 33019
Phone: 305-920-5492
Officers:
    President: Ellen Bush
    VP: Gloria Williams
    Treasurer: Virginia Godfrey
    Secretary: Madeline Barauskas
Management:
    President/Director Shows: Ellen Bush
Mission: To bring together a senior group of men and women who were professional musicians, singers and dancers in their younger days to perform one-hour vaudeville shows in nursing homes, hospitals and at community affairs.
Founded: 1965
Specialized Field: Musical; Community Theater; Ethnic Theater; Classic
Status: Nonprofit
Paid Staff: 25
Income Sources: President's Council
Performs At: Recreation Center
Organization Type: Performing

2783
HOLLYWOOD PLAYHOUSE
2640 Washington Street
Hollywood, FL 33020
Phone: 954-922-0404
Fax: 954-922-0666
Web Site: http://playhousehollywood.com/
Officers:
    President: Bea Yianilos
    VP: Ivonne Morten
    Secretary/Treasurer: Kothi Glist
Management:
    Executive Artistic Director: Andy Rogow
    Technical Director: David Sherman
Mission: Bringing culture to our community through theatre.
Utilizes: Actors; AEA Actors; Choreographers; Collaborations; Five Seasonal Concerts; Guest Accompanists; Guest Artists; Local Artists; Performance Artists; Resident Professionals; Student Interns
Founded: 1948
Specialized Field: Drama; New Plays; Musical
Status: Professional Regional Theater
Paid Artists: 100
Budget: $750,000
Income Sources: Florida Theatre Conference
Affiliations: Theatre League of South Florida; Hollywood Chamber of Commerce
Facility Category: Proscenium Ttheatre with Ample Fly and Wing Space
Type of Stage: Proscenium
Seating Capacity: 262
Year Built: 1960
Organization Type: Performing

2784
ALHAMBRA DINNER THEATRE
12000 Beach Boulevard
Jacksonville, FL 32216

Phone: 904-641-1212
Fax: 904-642-3505
Toll-free: 800-688-7469
Web Site: www.alhambrajax.com/
Officers:
    President: Tod Booth
Management:
    Executive Producer: Tod Booth
    Marketing Director: Jack Booth
Mission: Producing the finest professional theatrical productions.
Founded: 1880
Specialized Field: Dinner Theater
Status: Professional; Commercial
Paid Staff: 100
Income Sources: Actors' Equity Association; American Dinner Theatre Institute; Society for Stage Directors and Choreographers; American Federation of Musicians
Performs At: Alhambra Dinner Theatre
Annual Attendance: 120,000
Facility Category: Dinner Theatre
Type of Stage: Thrust
Seating Capacity: 400
Year Built: 1967
Rental Contact: Director of Marketing Jack Booth
Organization Type: Performing

2785
RITZ THEATRE AND LA VILLA MUSEUM
829 N Davis Street
Jacksonville, FL 32202
Phone: 904-632-5555
Fax: 904-632-5553
e-mail: ritztheatre@coj.net
Web Site: http://www.ritzjacksonville.com/
Management:
    Executive Director: Carol Alexander
    Production Manager: Teneese Williams
Founded: 1999
Specialized Field: Drama; Musical; Historical; Classic
Status: For-Profit, Professional
Paid Staff: 10

2786
THEATRE JACKSONVILLE
2032 San Marco Blvd.
Jacksonville, FL 32207
Phone: 904-396-4425
e-mail: info@theatrejax.com
Web Site: theatrejax.com
Officers:
    President: Jennifer Mansfield
    Vice President: Mark Wright
Management:
    Executive Director: Sarah Boone
Mission: Theatre Jacksonville is a volunteer based community theatre whose mission is to enrich lives and broaden cultural understanding through community participation in theatre arts.
Founded: 1919

2787
GINSBERG PRODUCTIONS
102050 Overseas Highway- MM 102
Key Largo, FL 33037
Phone: 866-535-7994
e-mail: info@ginsbergproductions.com
Web Site: ginsbergproductions.com
Officers:
    President: Debra Ginsberg
    Vice President: Michael Vadnal
Mission: Dedicated to promoting awareness and appreciation of the performing arts by providing live, quality theatrical performances.
Status: Nonprofit

2788
KEY WEST PLAYERS
310 Wall Street
Key West, FL 33040
Phone: 305-294-5015
Fax: 305-768-0465
e-mail: info@keywestfilm.org
Web Site: www.waterfrontplayhouse.org/
Officers:
    President: Paul Hilson
    VP: Kelly Hedges-Peerman
    Treasurer: Florence Recher
    Artistic Director: Danny x Weathers
    Technical Director: Michael Boyer
Management:
    Vice President/Marketing: Jeff Johnson
Mission: Presenting live professional and amateur entertainment; providing a teaching experience; teaching all of the aspects of theater.
Utilizes: Actors; AEA Actors; Choreographers; Collaborating Artists; Collaborations; Composers; Dancers; Educators; Grant Writers; Guest Accompanists; Guest Artists; Guest Companies; Guest Designers; Guest Ensembles; Guest Instructors; Guest Lecturers; Guest Musical Directors; Guest Musicians; Guest Soloists; Guest Teachers; Guild Activities; High School Drama; Local Artists; Local Unknown Artists; Multimedia; Original Music Scores; Performance Artists; Poets; Resident Companies; Resident Professionals; Scenic Designers; Sign Language Translators; Singers; Soloists; Student Interns; Touring Companies
Founded: 1940
Specialized Field: Drama; Musical; Contemporary
Status: Nonprofit
Paid Staff: 5
Volunteer Staff: 12
Paid Artists: 150
Budget: $270,000
Income Sources: Box Office; Grants; Donations
Performs At: Waterfront Playhouse
Affiliations: FL. Professional Theater Association; League of South FL. Theaters; Theater Communications Group
Annual Attendance: 10,000
Facility Category: Live Performing Arts Theatre
Type of Stage: Proscenium
Stage Dimensions: 25'x35'
Seating Capacity: 180
Year Built: 1853
Year Remodeled: 1960
Rental Contact: George Gugleotti
Organization Type: Performing; Educational

2789
RED BARN THEATRE
319 Duval Street
PO Box 707
Key West, FL 33040
Phone: 305-296-9911
Fax: 305-293-3035
Web Site: www.redbarntheatre.com
Officers:
    President: Kim Works
    Vice President: Michele Grahl
    Secretary: Mimi McDonald
    Treasurer: Lisa Van Gilder
Management:
    President: Steve Russ
    Managing Director: Mimi McDonald
Utilizes: Guest Companies
Founded: 1981
Specialized Field: Drama; Musical; Contemporary
Status: Professional; Nonprofit
Paid Staff: 7
Paid Artists: 90
Income Sources: Theatre Communications Group
Performs At: Red Barn Theatre
Organization Type: Performing; Resident; Educational

2790
FLORIDA SOUTHERN COLLEGE: DEPARTMENT OF THEATRE ARTS
111 Lake Hollingsworth Dr
111 Lake Hollingsworth Drive
Lakeland, FL 33801
Phone: 863-680-4226
Fax: 863-680-4457
Web Site: https://www.flsouthern.edu/academics/theatre/flash/program.html
Officers:
    Chairman: James F Beck
Management:
    Director of Theatre Dept: James Beck
Specialized Field: Educational; Theater Workshops
Budget: $600-$5,000
Seating Capacity: 336; 75
Year Built: 1970

2791
KALEIDOSCOPE THEATRE
207 E 24th Street
Lynn Haven, FL 32444
Phone: 850-265-3226
e-mail: ktplays@kt-online.org
Web Site: http://www.kt-online.org/
Management:
    Board of Directors: Lois Carter
    Board of Directors: David Garcia
    Director/President: Sandy Wilson
Mission: To increase knowledge of theatre and provide cultural enrichment.
Utilizes: Guest Companies; Singers
Founded: 1972
Specialized Field: Musical; Dinner Theater; Community Theater
Status: Non-Professional; Nonprofit
Paid Staff: 300
Performs At: Kaleidoscope Theatre
Organization Type: Performing; Educational

2792
FLORIDA STAGE
262 S Ocean Boulevard
Manalapan, FL 33462
Phone: 561-585-3404
Fax: 561-588-4708
Toll-free: 800-514-3837
Web Site: www.floridastage.org
Officers:
    Chairman of the Board: Dennis Vlassis
    Immediate Past Chairman: Laurie Gildan
Management:
    Managing Director: Nancy Barnett
    President: Louis Tyrrell
    Director Communications: Larry Friedrich
Mission: Dedicated to the production of new American plays by our finest contemporary playwrights.
Founded: 1987
Specialized Field: Musical; Comedy; Drama
Status: Non-Profit, Professional
Paid Staff: 35
Budget: $2.5 million

THEATRE / Florida

Season: October - August
Performs At: Florida Stage
Affiliations: AEA, SSDC, USA
Facility Category: Florida Stage
Type of Stage: Thrust
Seating Capacity: 258

2793
THE PLAZA THEATRE
262 S. Ocean Blvd.
Manalapan, FL 33462
Phone: 561-588-1820
Fax: 786-257-5669
e-mail: mbjacobson@theplazatheatre.net
Web Site: theplazatheatre.net
Management:
    Producing Director: Alan Jacobson
    General Manager: John Lariviere
Specialized Field: Classic And Original Musical Theater
Status: Professional; Nonprofit
Seating Capacity: 250

2794
THEATRE CLUB OF THE PALM BEACHES
262 S Ocean Boulevard
Manalapan, FL 33462
Phone: 407-585-3404
Fax: 407-585-4708
Management:
    Producing Director: Louis Tyrrell
    Company Manager: Nancy Johnson
    Office Manager: Caroline Breder
    Marketing Director: Cheryl Dun
    Development Director: Alison Pruitt
Mission: To present the finest new works of young American playwrights.
Utilizes: Guest Companies
Specialized Field: Drama; Musical; Contemporary; Community Theater
Status: Professional
Paid Artists: Yes
Income Sources: Actors' Equity Association; Society for Stage Directors and Choreographers
Organization Type: Performing

2795
MARATHON COMMUNITY THEATRE
5101 Overseas Highway
Marathon, FL 33050
Mailing Address: PO Box 124
Phone: 305-743-0994
Fax: 305-743-0408
e-mail: gm@marathontheater.org
Web Site: http://www.marathontheater.org/
Management:
    Executive Director: Loretta Geotis
Mission: To offer quality theatre events to adults in our community; to give cultural programs in schools.
Utilizes: Guest Artists; Guest Companies; Singers
Founded: 1957
Specialized Field: Musical; Dinner Theater; Community Theater; Puppet
Status: Nonprofit
Paid Staff: 60
Organization Type: Performing; Sponsoring

2796
MELBOURNE CIVIC THEATRE
817 E Strawbridge Ave
Melbourne, FL 32901
Phone: 321-723-6935
Fax: 321-723-6935
Web Site: www.mymct.org
Officers:
    President: June Borowski
Management:
    President: Bob Sullivan
    Executive Director: Jew Morrow
Mission: Entertaining, educating and enriching the community through the theatre arts.
Utilizes: Guest Writers; Guild Activities; Lyricists; Touring Companies
Founded: 1952
Specialized Field: Community Theater
Status: Non-Profit, Non-Professional
Paid Staff: 1
Volunteer Staff: 60
Non-paid Artists: 30
Budget: $120,000
Income Sources: Ticket Sales, Advertisments, Donations
Annual Attendance: 5,100
Facility Category: Theatre
Type of Stage: variable
Stage Dimensions: variable
Seating Capacity: 97
Rental Contact: Anita Saczeciana
Organization Type: Performing; Educational

2797
FLORIDA INTERNATIONAL UNIVERSITY: DEPARTMENT OF THEATRE AND DANCE
Wertheim Performing Arts Center
11200 SW 8th Street - WPAC 131
Miami, FL 33199
Phone: 305-348-2895
Fax: 305-348-1803
e-mail: carta@fiu.edu
Web Site: theatre.fiu.edu/
Officers:
    Chairman: Dr. Leroy Clark
    Chair, Artistic Director, Costume D: Marilyn R. Skow
    Technical Director: Celso Peruyera
    Interim Marketing Assistant: Natasha Neckles
    Production Assistant: Robert Duncan
Management:
    Executive Director: Leroy Clark
    Managing Director: Abel Cornejo
    Assistant Technical Director: Geordan Gottlieb
    Costume Shop Supervisor, Costume De: Mariana Pareja
Founded: 1972
Specialized Field: Educational; Theater Workshops
Status: Non-Profit, Non-Professional
Paid Staff: 11
Budget: $7,100-$11,900
Affiliations: NAST
Seating Capacity: 240; 150; 150
Year Built: 1996

2798
LAS MASCARAS THEATRE
2833 NW Seventh Street
Miami, FL 33125
Phone: 305-649-5301
Management:
    Artistic Director/Lead Actor: Alfonso Cremata
    Artistic Director/Lead Actor: Salvador Ugarte
Mission: To perform local and international plays in Spanish.
Founded: 1968
Specialized Field: Summer Stock; Musical
Status: Professional; Nonprofit
Performs At: Las Mascaras Theatre #1 & #2
Organization Type: Performing

2799
THE M ENSEMBLE INC.
404 NW 26th Street
Miami, FL 33168
Mailing Address: P.O. Box 1175 Miami, FL 33168
Phone: 305-893-3551
e-mail: info@themensemble.com
Web Site: themensemble.com
Mission: To promote African-American culture through the performing arts.
Founded: 1971
Status: Nonprofit

2800
GOLD COAST THEATRE
345 West 37th Street
Miami Beach, FL 33140-0964
Phone: 305-538-5500
Fax: 305-538-6315
e-mail: judeparry@aol.com
Web Site: www.goldcoasttheatre.org
Management:
    President: Warren Werner
    Executive Director: Jude Parry
Mission: To bring professional theatre to people from all walks of life with multi-media, original shows featuring the art of mime
Utilizes: Singers
Founded: 1982
Specialized Field: Musical; Comedy; Youth Theater; Ethnic Theater; Puppet; Contemporary; Mime
Status: Non-Profit, Professional
Paid Staff: 3
Volunteer Staff: 3
Paid Artists: 32
Budget: $100,000
Performs At: Touring Theatre Specializing in Mime
Annual Attendance: 100,000
Organization Type: Performing; Touring; Educational

2801
MAD CAT THEATRE COMPANY
9816 NE 2nd Avenue
Miami Shores, FL 33138
Mailing Address: P.O. Box 347621, Miami, FL 33234-7621
Phone: 866-811-4111
e-mail: madcattheatre@gmail.com
Web Site: madcattheatre.org
Officers:
    President: Paul Tei
    Chair: Ann Kelly Anthony
Management:
    Artistic Director: Paul Tei
Mission: Mad Cat Theatre Company's mission is to provide theatre that provokes its audience to re-imagine its surrounding world. To promote debate by creating work that illuminates the darker regions of our mental and emotional landscape. To sniff out and ultimately create brazen stories that explore the hypermodernity of society.
Founded: 2000
Status: Nonprofit

2802
BERRY COLLEGE THEATRE COMPANY
Berry College
2277 Martha Berry Hwy NW
Mount Berry, FL 30149

THEATRE / Florida

Phone: 706-232-5374
Fax: 706-802-6739
e-mail: theatre@berry.edu
Web Site: www.berry.edu
Officers:
   Dean of Student Work: Rufus Massey
   Director of Student Work: Mike Burnes
   Coordinator: Robin Holt
   Director of Employment Development: Mark Kozera
   Director, Career Center: Sue Tarpley
Management:
   Technical Director: Christian Boy
   Costume and Make Up Director: Alice Bristow
   Director: John Countryman
Founded: 1952
Specialized Field: Musical; Comedy; Youth Theater; Community Theater; Classic; Contemporary
Status: Non-Profit, Non-Professional
Paid Staff: 30
Affiliations: ATHE; SETC
Seating Capacity: 240; 115
Year Built: 1984

2803
ICEHOUSE THEATRE
1100 North Unser Street 32757
Mount Dora, FL 32756-0759
Mailing Address: PO Box 759
Phone: 352-383-4616
Fax: 352-735-2351
e-mail: jean@icehousetheatre.com
Web Site: www.icehousetheatremd.squarespace.com/
Officers:
   President: JC Bowling
   Vice President: Nanci Darst
   Treausrer: Carolyn Sonnentag
   Secretary: Brneda Aro
   Artistic Director: Darlin Barry
Management:
   Artistic Director: Darlin Barry
Mission: Enhance the cultural life of Central Florida with first-quality theatrical productions and programs designed to inspire and educate patrons and their children. The theatre is also dedicated to providing talented area artists with numerous opportunities to refine their craft.
Utilizes: Actors; Artists-in-Residence; Collaborating Artists; Collaborations; Educators; Fine Artists; Five Seasonal Concerts; Grant Writers; Guest Artists; Guest Conductors; Guest Instructors; Guest Lecturers; Guest Soloists; Guest Writers; Guild Activities; High School Drama; Local Artists; Lyricists; Multimedia; Music; Performance Artists; Resident Professionals; Sign Language Translators; Soloists; Student Interns; Visual Arts
Specialized Field: Musical; Comedy; Drama
Status: Nonprofit
Paid Staff: 5
Paid Artists: 2
Income Sources: Memberships; Corporate Sponsorships
Affiliations: CFTA; AACT
Facility Category: Performing Arts Theatre
Type of Stage: Thrust/Proscenium Combination
Seating Capacity: 274
Year Built: 1947
Year Remodeled: 1953

2804
ORANGE PARK COMMUNITY THEATRE
2900 Moody Avenue
PO Box 391
Orange Park, FL 32067-0391
Phone: 904-276-2599
Fax: 941-472-0055
e-mail: opctweb@yahoo.com
Web Site: www.opct.org
Officers:
   President: Betty Detamore
Management:
   President: Barbara C Wells
   VP Of Production: Michael Ray
Mission: Provides five stage productions annually, including at least one Broadway style musical, to the residents and visitors to the Jacksonville area and Northeast Florida.
Founded: 1969
Specialized Field: Musical; Community Theater
Status: Non-Professional; Nonprofit
Income Sources: Ticket Sales; Program Ads; Grants
Annual Attendance: 7,000
Facility Category: Community
Type of Stage: Proscenium
Stage Dimensions: 26x18
Seating Capacity: 101
Year Built: 1920
Year Remodeled: 1987
Organization Type: Performing; Educational

2805
MAD COW THEATRE
54 West Church Street, Second Floor
Orlando, FL 32801-3201
Mailing Address: P.O. Box 3109, Orlando, FL 32802-3109
Phone: 407-297-8788
Web Site: madcowtheatre.com
Management:
   Executive Director: Mitzi Maxwell
Mission: Mad Cow Theatre is founded on the belief that the Theatre is a dynamic and powerful means of social understanding, as well as a hugely entertaining art form. Through the combination of passionate, skillful acting and compelling, insightful writing, nurtured by an attentive and ever-changing process, Mad Cow presents entertaining works of Theatre to an ever-widening audience- promoting, enhancing, and celebrating the human condition through art.
Founded: 1997
Status: Professional; Nonprofit

2806
ORLANDO BROADWAY DINNER THEATRE
3376 Edgewater Drive
Orlando, FL 32804
Phone: 407-843-6275
Fax: 407-398-0904
Web Site: www.orlando.broadway.com
Management:
   President/CEO: Dori Parker
   Director Of Operations: Scott Reeder
   Production Coordinator: Steve MacKinnon
Mission: Providing Orlando with full scale Broadway musicals and fine dining experience.
Founded: 1986
Specialized Field: Community Theater; Dinner Theater; Musical; Summer Stock; Puppet
Status: For-Profit, Professional
Paid Staff: 40
Paid Artists: 25
Income Sources: Actors' Equity Association; American Dinner Theatre Association
Performs At: Mark Two Dinner Theater
Organization Type: Performing

2807
ORLANDO SHAKESPEARE THEATER
812 E. Rollins Street
Orlando, FL 32803
Phone: 407-447-1700
e-mail: info@orlandoshakes.org
Web Site: orlandoshakes.org
Management:
   Managing Director: PJ Albert
   Artistic Director: Jim Heisinger
Mission: With Shakespeare as our standard and inspiration, the Orlando Shakespeare Theater in Partnership with UCF, produces bold professional theater, develops new plays, and provides innovative educational experiences that enrich our community.
Status: Nonprofit
Affiliations: UCF

2808
SLEUTHS MYSTERY DINNER SHOWS
8267 International Drive
Orlando, FL 32819
Phone: 407-363-1985
Toll-free: 800-393-1958
e-mail: info@sleuths.com
Web Site: www.sleuths.com
Management:
   Production Director: Laurel Clark
Mission: Comedy mystery dinner shows.
Utilizes: Actors
Specialized Field: Comedy; Drama; Theatrical
Status: For Profit
Income Sources: Ticket Sales

2809
THEATRE-IN-THE-WORKS
PO Box 532016
Orlando, FL 32853
Phone: 407-365-7235
Management:
   Producing Director: Edward Dilks
Mission: Developing original musicals, operas and plays primarily written by Floridians.
Founded: 1984
Specialized Field: Drama; New Plays; Contemporary
Status: Professional; Nonprofit

2810
UCF CIVIC THEATRE
1001 E Princeton Street
Orlando, FL 32803
Phone: 407-896-7365
Fax: 407-897-3284
Management:
   Acting Executive Director: Kathryn Seidel
   Youth Program Coordinator: Jeff Revels
Mission: Providing entertainment, information, stimulation, education and an arena for artistic expression.
Utilizes: Guest Artists; Guest Companies; Singers
Founded: 1926
Specialized Field: Community Theater; Youth Theater
Status: Professional; Non-Professional; Nonprofit
Paid Staff: 2
Income Sources: American Association of Community Theatres; Florida Theatre Conference; United Arts
Performs At: Civic Theatre Complex
Organization Type: Performing; Touring; Educational

THEATRE / Florida

2811
UNIVERSITY OF CENTRAL FLORIDA: DEPARTMENT OF THEATRE
12501 Research Parkway
Suite 180
Orlando, FL 32816
Mailing Address: PO Box 162372, Orlando, FL 32816
Phone: 407-823-2862
Fax: 407-823-6446
e-mail: Theatre@ucf.edu
Web Site: www.theatre.ucf.edu
Officers:
   Associate Chair: Joseph Rusnock
Management:
   Department Chairman: Christopher Niess
   Vice Department Chair: Kristina Tollefson
   Director of Production: Bert Scott
Mission: Educational theatre; BA, BFA, MA; MFA degrees
Specialized Field: Educational; Theater Workshops
Status: Non-Profit, Non-Professional
Paid Staff: 45
Paid Artists: 15
Budget: $800,000
Income Sources: State and revenue
Affiliations: ATHE; SEKC; USITT; FTC; TOC
Annual Attendance: 22,000
Type of Stage: Proscenium & Black Box
Seating Capacity: 300; 100
Year Built: 1982

2812
PENSACOLA LITTLE THEATRE
400 S Jefferson Street
Pensacola, FL 32502
Phone: 850-434-0257
Fax: 850-438-2787
Web Site: www.pensacolalittletheatre.com
Officers:
   Operations Manager: Charles Baisden
   Facilities Manager: Mike Tona
   Marketing Director: Mike Dinwiddie
   Interim Box Office Manager: Yasmine Cobbett,
   Security: Colton Cash
Management:
   Technical Director: Jim Culton
   Executive Director: Meg Peltier
   Artistic Director: Jerry Ahillen
   Technical Director: Jim Culton
   Marketing Director: Mike Dinwiddie
Mission: To stimulate interest in performing arts; to provide community members a chance to participate in live theatre.
Founded: 1936
Specialized Field: Community Theater; Children's Theater
Status: Non-Professional; Nonprofit
Paid Staff: 100
Income Sources: Florida Theatre Conference; American Association of Community Theatres; Southeastern Theatre Conference
Performs At: Pensacola Little Theatre
Organization Type: Performing; Educational; Sponsoring

2813
UNIVERSITY OF WEST FLORIDA
Center for Fine and Performing Arts
11000 University Parkway
Pensacola, FL 32514
Phone: 850-474-2000
Fax: 850-474-2714
Toll-free: 800-263-1074
e-mail: admissions@uwf.edu
Web Site: www.uwf.edu
Officers:
   Chair: Lewis Bear Jr.
   Vice Chair: Mort O'Sullivan
   President: Ethan Friedland
   Faculty President: Richard Hough
   Board Member: Robert L. Jones
Management:
   President: Ethan Friedland
   Executive Director: Sandra Flake
   Artistic Director: Suzette Doyan
   Managing Director: Greg Lanier
Founded: 1968
Specialized Field: Educational; Theater Workshops
Status: Non-Profit, Professional
Budget: $13,000-$33,000
Seating Capacity: 426; 120
Year Built: 1991

2814
DOWN IN FRONT THEATER
6501 West Sunrise Blvd.
Plantation, FL 33313
Phone: 954-609-7153
e-mail: downinfronttheater@gmail.com
Web Site: downinfronttheater.com
Management:
   Artistic Director: Gilbert H. Lenchus
Mission: The Down In Front Theater company offers opportunities to actors and new playwrights to present their work. We offer opportunities to the audience to be entertained at prices that they can afford, without mortgaging their house. We are also very proud to work with the special needs community and incorporate talent from every corner of life.

2815
PLANTATION THEATRE COMPANY
1829 N Pineland Road
Plantation, FL 33317
Phone: 954-424-9701
Fax: 954-424-0137
Mission: To afford community members an opportunity to participate in the arts.
Utilizes: Singers
Founded: 1975
Specialized Field: Musical; Community Theater
Status: Semi-Professional; Non-Professional; Nonprofit
Performs At: Diecke Auditorium
Organization Type: Performing; Educational

2816
POMPANO PLAYERS
PO Box 2045
Pompano Beach, FL 33061
Phone: 305-946-4646
Management:
   Director: Penny Manwell
   Technical Director: David Stockton
Mission: To offer live theatre.
Utilizes: Guest Companies; Singers
Founded: 1956
Specialized Field: Musical; Community Theater
Status: Semi-Professional; Nonprofit
Income Sources: Florida Theatre Conference
Performs At: Pompano Players Theatre
Organization Type: Performing; Resident; Educational

2817
CHARLOTTE PLAYERS
1182 Market Circle #1
Port Charlotte, FL 33953
Phone: 941-255-1022
Fax: 941-743-7297
e-mail: charlotteplayers@nut-n-but.net
Web Site: www.charlotteplayers.org
Officers:
   President: Gene Callan
   Executive Director: Sherie M. Moody
Mission: To provide the highest quality theatre arts for our community's diverse culture through performance education and community involvement
Founded: 1960
Specialized Field: Community Theatre
Status: Non-Profit, Non-Professional
Paid Staff: 2
Performs At: Cultural Center Theater
Organization Type: Performing

2818
CORNERSTONE THEATRE COMPANY
115 West 1st Street
Sanford, FL 32771
Mailing Address: 5224 West SR-46, Suite #148, Lake Forest, FL 32771
Phone: 407-312-3361
e-mail: info@cornerstonetheatrecompany.org
Web Site: cornerstonetheatrecompany.org
Management:
   Artistic Director: Nicholas Murphy
   Managing Director: Cheryl Murphy
Mission: Cornerstone's mission is to produce entertaining, inspiring, and innovative professional theatrical productions.
Founded: 2012
Status: Professional; Nonprofit
Performs At: The Princess Theater

2819
PIRATE PLAYHOUSE
975 Rabbit Road
Sanibel, FL 33957
Phone: 239-472-3511
Fax: 941-472-0055
Management:
   Producing Artistic Director: Ralph Elias
   General Manager: Kevin Mooney
Specialized Field: Drama; Comedy

2820
J HOWARD WOOD THEATRE
125 E. Court St.
Suite 1000
Sanibel Island, FL 45202
Phone: 941-472-0006
Fax: 941-472-0055
e-mail: KathyP@theatremanagementcorp.com
Web Site: www.thewoodtheatre.com
Officers:
   President: Winnie Donoghue
   Treasurer: Jim Lavelle
   Secretary: Carla Benninga
Management:
   Managing Director: Cindy Lee Overton
   Artistic Producer: Robert Schelhammer
   Marketing/Public Relations: Honey Larsen
Mission: To present live, professional theatre in Southwest Florida.
Utilizes: Actors; AEA Actors; Artists-in-Residence; Choreographers; Collaborations; Dancers; Designers; Fine Artists; Five Seasonal Concerts; Grant Writers;

THEATRE / Florida

Guest Accompanists; Guest Artists; Guest Designers; Guest Ensembles; Guest Lecturers; Guest Musical Directors; Guest Teachers; Guild Activities; High School Drama; Instructors; Local Artists; Multimedia; Music; Original Music Scores; Performance Artists; Resident Professionals; Sign Language Translators; Soloists; Student Interns; Theatre Companies; Visual Arts
Founded: 1991
Specialized Field: Theater Workshops; Contemporary; Musical; New Plays; Young Playwrights; Children's Theater
Status: Not-for-Profit
Paid Staff: 10
Budget: $750,000
Income Sources: Grants, Donations, Ticket Sales
Performs At: Theatre
Facility Category: Theater
Type of Stage: Thrust Stage
Seating Capacity: 180
Year Built: 1990
Organization Type: Performing; Touring; Resident; Educational; Sponsoring

2821
ASOLO REPERTORY THEATRE
5555 N. Tamiami Trail
Sarasota, FL 34243-2141
Phone: 941-351-8000
Fax: 941-351-5796
Toll-free: 800-361-8388
e-mail: asolorep@asolo.org
Web Site: www.asolorep.org
Officers:
 President: Bob Bartner
 Vice President: Mary Lou Winnick
 Treausrer: DOUGLAS BRADBURY
 Secretary: NANCY MARKLE
 General Counsel: ELIZABETH C. MARSHALL
Management:
 Managing Director: Linda DiGabriele
 Producing Artistic Director: Michael Edwards
 Assistant Managing Director: Corinne Deckard
Mission: Center for theatrical excellence, crafting the highest quality productions of classical, contemporary, and newly commissioned work all performed in the rarest form of rotating repertory. Featuring an accomplished resident company - complimented by distinguished guest artists - Asolo Rep offers audiences a unique and dynamic theatre experience.
Founded: 1960
Specialized Field: Educational; Theater Workshops
Status: Non-Profit
Performs At: Mertz Theatre, Cook Theatre
Affiliations: U/RTA; ATHE
Type of Stage: Proscenium
Seating Capacity: 499, 161

2822
BANYAN THEATER COMPANY
5555 N. Tamiami Trail
Sarasota, FL 34243
Mailing Address: P.O. Box 49483, Sarasota, FL 34230
Phone: 941-358-5330
e-mail: info@banyantheatercompany.com
Web Site: banyantheatercompany.com
Management:
 Executive Director: Jerry M. Finn
Mission: To produce intelligent, significant plays in the summer, showcasing the works of both classic and contemporary playwrights.
Season: Summer
Performs At: The Jane B. Cook Theatre; FSU Center For The Performing Arts

2823
FLORIDA STUDIO THEATRE
1241 N Palm Avenue
Sarasota, FL 34236
Phone: 941-366-9017
Fax: 941-955-4137
e-mail: info@floridastudiotheatre.org
Web Site: www.floridastudiotheatre.org/
Management:
 Associate Director: Kate Alexander
 Artistic Director: Richard Hopkins
 Managing Director: Rebecca Langford
Mission: To produce contemporary theatre with an emphasis on new plays and regional premieres.
Utilizes: Guest Companies; Singers
Founded: 1973
Specialized Field: Ensembles; Theater Workshops; Drama
Status: Professional; Nonprofit
Performs At: Florida Studio Theatre
Affiliations: Small Professional Theatre Assoiacation; Actors' Equity Association
Type of Stage: ThrustBox, Cabaret Space
Stage Dimensions: 30'x35'x25'
Seating Capacity: 173, 100
Rental Contact: John Jacobsen
Organization Type: Performing; Resident; Educational; Touring

2824
PLAYERS THEATRE
838 N Tamiami Trail
Sarasota, FL 34236
Phone: 941-365-2494
Fax: 941-954-0282
e-mail: info@theplayers.org
Web Site: www.theplayers.org
Officers:
 President: Ken Shelin
 Vice President: Barbara Johnson
 Teasurer: Michael G Brown
Management:
 Managing Director: Michelle Bianchi Pingel
Mission: To be the first and only community theatre in Sarasota offering live entertainment, full orchestra, professional direction and children's theatre.
Utilizes: Guest Artists; Guest Companies; Singers
Founded: 1930
Specialized Field: Musical
Status: Non-Profit, Non-Professional
Paid Staff: 7
Volunteer Staff: 700
Budget: $1.2 million
Income Sources: Earned Income & Donations
Performs At: Community Theatre
Annual Attendance: 65,000
Seating Capacity: 497
Year Built: 1970
Organization Type: Performing; Touring; Educational

2825
ECKERD COLLEGE THEATRE DEPARTMENT
4200 54th Avenue South
St Petersburg, FL 33711
Phone: 813-864-8279
Fax: 813-864-7800
Toll-free: 800-569-09
Web Site: http://www.eckerd.edu/academics/theatre/
Officers:
 Chair: Cynthia Totten
Specialized Field: Educational; Theater Workshops
Budget: $2,000-$4,000
Affiliations: ATHE; SETC
Seating Capacity: 350; 60-80
Year Built: 1970

2826
VAUDEVILLE PALACE
7951 9th Street N
St Petersburg, FL 33702
Phone: 813-557-5515
Fax: 813-578-1024
Management:
 Producer/Director: Buddy Graf
 General Manager: Carol Graf
 Box Office Manager: Skip Lewis
Mission: To offer amusing entertainment.
Founded: 1991
Specialized Field: Dinner Theater; Specialty Acts
Status: Professional; Commercial
Performs At: Vaudeville Palace
Organization Type: Performing; Resident

2827
LIMELIGHT THEATRE
11 Old Mission Avenue
PO Box 1196
St. Augustine, FL 32085-1196
Phone: 904-825-1164
Fax: 904-825-4662
e-mail: limeligt@bellsouth.net
Web Site: www.limelight-theatre.com
Officers:
 President: Paul McGuire
 VP: Wayne George
 Treasurer: Wayne Farrell
Management:
 President: Jeanne Krausz
 Artistic Director: Beth Lambert
 Director of Administration: Anne Kraft
 General Manager: Emma Lee Carpenter
Mission: To provide professional entertainment to visitors to the Saint Augustine area.
Utilizes: Actors; Choreographers; Collaborations; Dancers; Designers; Five Seasonal Concerts; Grant Writers; Guest Artists; Guest Conductors; Guest Ensembles; Guest Lecturers; Guest Musical Directors; Guest Musicians; Guest Teachers; Guest Writers; Guild Activities; High School Drama; Instructors; Local Artists; Lyricists; Music; Original Music Scores; Performance Artists; Resident Professionals; Selected Students; Sign Language Translators; Soloists; Student Interns; Theatre Companies; Touring Companies; Visual Arts
Founded: 1992
Specialized Field: Drama; Classic
Status: Non-Profit, Professional
Paid Staff: 4
Volunteer Staff: 80
Paid Artists: 60
Non-paid Artists: 10
Budget: $250,000
Income Sources: Admissions; Subsciptions; Individual and Corporate Donations and Grants
Performs At: Monson Resort
Affiliations: Flager College
Facility Category: Main Stage + Black Box
Type of Stage: Proscenium
Stage Dimensions: 36' x 20'
Seating Capacity: 99
Year Built: 1927
Year Remodeled: 2001
Rental Contact: General Manager Emma Lee Carpenter
Organization Type: Performing

THEATRE / Florida

2828
FLORIDA STATE UNIVERSITY: SCHOOL OF THEATRE
130 Collegiate Loop
Florida State University
Tallahassee, FL 32306-1160
Phone: 850-644-6796
Fax: 850-644-7408
Web Site: theatre.fsu.edu/
Management:
   President: T K Wetherall
   Dean: Steven Wallace
Founded: 1973
Specialized Field: Musical; Educational; Theater Workshops
Status: Non-Profit, Non-Professional
Paid Staff: 40
Budget: $13,750-$37,500
Affiliations: NAST; Asolo State Theatre
Seating Capacity: 500; 191; 200
Year Built: 1969

2829
YOUNG ACTORS THEATRE
609 Glenview Drive
Tallahassee, FL 32303
Phone: 850-386-6602
Fax: 850-422-2084
e-mail: info@youngactorstheatre.com
Web Site: www.youngactorstheatre.com
Officers:
   Executive Director: Cristina F. Williams
   Administrative Director: Valerie W. Smith
   Musical Director: Alison Grimes,
   Dance Director: Vicky Swezey
Management:
   Artristic Director: Robert A. Stuart
   Executive Director: Tina Williams
   Managing Director: Valerie Smith
   Office Manager: Tricia Seale,
   Afternoon Office Assistant: Megan Atkinson
Mission: The education of youth in performance and theatre arts.
Utilizes: Actors; Guest Accompanists; Guest Artists; Guest Companies; Resident Professionals; Sign Language Translators
Founded: 1975
Specialized Field: Musical; Community Theater
Status: Non-Profit, Non-Professional
Paid Staff: 25
Volunteer Staff: 300
Paid Artists: 15
Non-paid Artists: 250
Budget: $550,000
Income Sources: Southeastern Theatre Conference; American Association of Theatre Educators, State of Florida, City of Tallahassee
Performs At: Young Actors Theatre
Affiliations: American Association of Theatre Educators, Southeastern Theatre Conference
Annual Attendance: 10,000
Facility Category: Theatre, Classrooms
Type of Stage: Proscenium
Seating Capacity: 215
Year Built: 1986
Year Remodeled: 1995
Cost: $150,000
Organization Type: Performing; Touring; Educational

2830
BITS 'N PIECES GIANT PUPPET THEATRE
12904 Tom Gallagher Road
Tampa, FL 33527
Phone: 813-659-0659
e-mail: info@PuppetWorld.com
Web Site: www.puppetworld.com
Management:
   President: Jerry Bickel
   Artistic Director: Holli Rubin
   Business Director: Jackie Hiendlmayr
Mission: To offer original, educational musicals featuring unique nine-foot puppets.
Utilizes: Singers
Founded: 1976
Specialized Field: Children's Theater
Status: Non-Profit, Professional
Paid Staff: 4
Paid Artists: 4
Organization Type: Performing; Touring; Resident; Educational

2831
CARROLLWOOD PLAYERS COMMUNITY THEATER
4333 Gunn Highway
Tampa, FL 33618-8729
Phone: 813-265-4000
e-mail: cwptampabay.rr.com
Web Site: carrollwoodplayers.org
Officers:
   President: James Cass
Utilizes: Actors; Choreographers; Community Members; Community Talent; Dancers; Local Artists & Directors; Performance Artists; Sign Language Translators; Student Interns
Founded: 1981
Specialized Field: Community Theater; Classic; Contemporary
Status: Not-for-profit
Volunteer Staff: 30
Non-paid Artists: 100
Facility Category: Theater
Seating Capacity: 96

2832
FLORIDA SUNCOAST PUPPET GUILD
7107 N Howard Avenue
Tampa, FL 33604
Phone: 813-932-9252
Fax: 813-932-9252
e-mail: jodymcat@aol.com
Web Site: www.puppeteers.org/guilds/fla-sunc.htm
Officers:
   Guild President: Jody Wren
   Vice President: Katie Adams
   Secretary/Treasurer: Priscilla Lakus
   Historian: Frank Lakus
Mission: To promote the appreciation of the art of puppetry and all common interests of the membership. This is accomplished through a program of lectures, demonstrations, workshops, TV programs, exhibitions, newsletters, sponsored performances, conferences, etc.
Utilizes: Singers
Founded: 1973
Specialized Field: Puppet
Status: Non-Profit, Professional
Income Sources: Puppeteers of America
Organization Type: Educational; Sponsoring

2833
SPANISH LYRIC THEATRE
2819 Safe Harbor Drive
Tampa, FL 33618
Phone: 813-936-0217
Fax: 813-936-0217
Web Site: www.spanishlyrictheatre.com
Officers:
   Founder: Rene Gonzalez
Management:
   President: Dennis Diera
   Executive Director: Rene J Gonzalez
   Assistant Production Director: Marlyn Wadley
   Touring Production: Juan Carlos Gonzalez
Mission: To promote Spanish musicals, or Zarzuelas; to offer lyric theatre in Spanish and English.
Utilizes: Singers
Founded: 1959
Specialized Field: Musical; Spanish Language Company
Status: Non-Profit, Professional
Paid Staff: 20
Paid Artists: 200
Performs At: Tampa Bay Performing Arts Center
Organization Type: Performing

2834
UNIVERSITY OF SOUTH FLORIDA: SCHOOL OF THEATRE
4202 E Fowler Avenue
TAR 230
Tampa, FL 33620-7450
Mailing Address: School of Theatre & Dance, University of South Florida, 4202
Phone: 813-974-3867
Fax: 813-974-4122
e-mail: mpowers@arts.usf.edu
Web Site: www.theatreanddance.arts.usf.edu/
Management:
   President: Judy Genshaft
   Dean Visual/Performing Arts: Ron Jones
   Dance Director: Marc Powers
Founded: 1956
Specialized Field: Educational; Theater Workshops
Status: Non-Profit, Non-Professional
Performs At: Proscenium Theatre, Black Box Theatre, Studio Theatres
Affiliations: NAST; ATHE
Seating Capacity: 552, 100-200, 80-125
Year Built: 1986
Year Remodeled: 95

2835
VENICE THEATRE
140 W Tampa Avenue
Venice, FL 34285
Phone: 941-488-1115
Fax: 941-484-4033
e-mail: info@venicestage.com
Web Site: www.venicestage.com
Officers:
   Assistant Technical Director: Brian Freeman
   Assistant Costumer: Becky Evans
   Sound Designer: Dorian Boyd
Management:
   Executive/Artistic Director: Murray Chase
   Producing Director: Allan Kollar
   Artistic Advisor: Joe Simmons
   Technical Director: John Andzulis
   Stage Manager: Lisa Million
Mission: To present intellectual and instructive entertainment in the performing arts.
Founded: 1950

Specialized Field: Musical; Comedy; Youth Theater; Ethnic Theater; Community Theater; Classic; Contemporary
Status: Non-Profit, Non-Professional
Paid Staff: 12
Organization Type: Performing

2836
ACTING COMPANY OF RIVERSIDE THEATRE
3250 Riverside Park Drive
Vero Beach, FL 32963
Phone: 772-231-6990
Fax: 561-234-5298
Officers:
  President: Marilyn Chenault
  VP: Pat Trimble
  Treasurer: Rebecca Allen
  Board Secretary: Judy Balph
  Managing Director: Jon R. Moses
Management:
  Artistic Director: Allen D Cornell
  Production Manager: John Moses
  Development Director: Lynn Potter
  Director Education: Linda Downey
Mission: To provide audiences of this region with productions that are relevant either by nature of their importance within a particular genre or as socially vital within the changing environment of our culture.
Utilizes: Guest Companies
Founded: 1995
Specialized Field: Theater Workshops; Drama; Contemporary; Classic
Status: Professional; Nonprofit
Paid Staff: 10
Income Sources: Actors' Equity Association; Theatre Communications Group; Florida Performing Theatre Association
Performs At: Riverside Theatre
Organization Type: Performing

2837
VERO BEACH THEATRE GUILD
2020 San Juan Avenue
Vero Beach, FL 32960
Phone: 772-562-8300
Fax: 772-562-8304
e-mail: verobeachtheatre@gmail.com
Web Site: www.verobeachtheatreguild.com
Officers:
  President: Sara Dessureau
  First VP: Larry Thompson
  Secretary: Pat Kroger
Mission: To enhance appreciation of dramatic and musical pieces through community theater; to offer residents of Florida's Treasure Coast theatrical arts.
Utilizes: Singers
Founded: 1958
Specialized Field: Community Theater
Status: Non-Professional; Nonprofit
Paid Staff: 200
Performs At: Riverside Theatre
Facility Category: Production House
Organization Type: Performing; Educational

2838
PALM BEACH ATLANTIC COLLEGE: DEPARTMENT OF THEATRE
901 S. Flagler Drive
West Palm Beach, FL 33401
Mailing Address: PO Box 24708, West Palm Beach, FL 33416
Phone: 888-468-6722
Fax: 561-803-2424
Web Site: www.pba.edu/theatre
Officers:
  Chair: Dr. Deborah McEniry
Specialized Field: Educational; Theater Workshops
Budget: $8,000-$10,500
Affiliations: Florida Stage
Facility Category: Historical building
Seating Capacity: 220; 80

2839
THEATRE WINTER HAVEN
210 Cypress Gardens Boulevard
PO Drawer 1230
Winter Haven, FL 33880
Mailing Address: PO Box 1230,Winter Haven, FL 33882
Phone: 863-299-2672
Fax: 863-291-3299
e-mail: twh1970@aol.com
Web Site: www.theatrewinterhaven.com
Management:
  Producing Director: Norman Small
  Production Manager: Thom Altman
Mission: Fostering the community's cultural growth by offering quality live theatre.
Utilizes: Actors; AEA Actors; Choreographers; Grant Writers; Guest Artists; Guest Companies; Guest Conductors; Guest Designers; Guest Lecturers; Guest Musical Directors; Instructors; Music; Resident Professionals; Sign Language Translators; Singers
Founded: 1970
Specialized Field: Drama; Musical; Classic
Status: Non-Profit, Non-Professional
Paid Staff: 5
Volunteer Staff: 90
Paid Artists: 6
Non-paid Artists: 140
Budget: $618,000
Income Sources: Various
Affiliations: AACT, FTC
Type of Stage: Proscenium
Stage Dimensions: 30wx16hx28d
Seating Capacity: 332
Year Built: 1977
Rental Contact: Jane Waters
Organization Type: Performing; Educational

2841
BREAKTHROUGH THEATRE
419 W. Fairbanks Avenue
Winter Park, FL 32789
Phone: 407-920-4034
e-mail: wadehair1966@gmail.com
Web Site: breakthroughtheatre.com
Opened: 2009
Status: Non-Equity; Community Theatre

2842
ROLLINS COLLEGE: DEPARTMENT OF THEATRE AND DANCE
1000 Holt Avenue 2735
Winter Park, FL 32789
Phone: 407-646-2000
Fax: 407-646-2257
e-mail: bjohnson@rollins.edu
Web Site: www.rollins.edu/annierussell/
Management:
  Marketing Director: Olivia Horn, ohorn@rollins.edu
  Department Chair: Dr. Jennifer Cavenaugh, jcavenaugh@rollins.edu
Founded: 1885
Specialized Field: Educational; Performance; Tech; Design; Dramaturgy
Status: Non-Profit, Non-Professional
Paid Staff: 4
Paid Artists: 7
Budget: $110,000
Performs At: Historic 377 Seat Broadway-Style Theatre
Annual Attendance: 300
Type of Stage: Proscenium
Seating Capacity: 400; 100
Year Built: 1931
Year Remodeled: 1978
Rental Contact: Kevin Griffin

Georgia

2843
THEATRE ALBANY
514 Pine Avenue
Albany, GA 31701
Mailing Address: PO Box 552 Albany GA 31702
Phone: 229-439-7141
e-mail: mcostello@theatrealbany.com
Web Site: www.theatrealbany.com
Management:
  Artistic Director: Mark Costello
  Technical Director: Steve Felmet
Mission: To expose young people to the art of live performance.
Utilizes: Guest Companies
Founded: 1932
Specialized Field: Musical; Comedy; Youth Theater; Dinner Theater; Ethnic Theater; Community Theater; Puppet; Classic; Contemporary
Status: Non-Profit, Non-Professional
Paid Staff: 2
Income Sources: American Association of Community Theatres; Southeastern Theatre Conference; Georgia Theatre Conference
Performs At: Theatre Albany
Organization Type: Performing; Educational

2844
GABBIES PUPPETS
367 Lexington Heights
Athens, GA 30605
Phone: 706-353-2785
Management:
  Director: Carolyn S Gabb
Mission: Presenting and teaching language communication skills using puppets; storytelling; creative dramatics.
Utilizes: Singers
Founded: 1975
Specialized Field: Puppet
Status: Professional
Organization Type: Performing; Educational

2845
GEORGIA REPERTORY THEATRE
Dept Of Drama, Fine Arts Building
University Of Georgia
Athens, GA 30602-3154
Phone: 706-542-2836
Fax: 706-542-2080
Web Site: www.drama.uga.edu/
Management:
  Producer: Stanley V Longman
  Dramaturg: Allen Partridge
Mission: The production of previously unproduced plays.

THEATRE / Georgia

Founded: 1990
Specialized Field: Educational; Theater Workshops
Paid Staff: 6
Paid Artists: 5
Performs At: Fine Arts Theatre, Cellar Theatre, Seneyu Stovall Theatre
Type of Stage: Arena
Seating Capacity: 250
Year Built: 1941

2846
7 STAGES
1105 Euclid Avenue NE
Atlanta, GA 30307
Phone: 404-522-0911
Fax: 404-522-0913
Web Site: www.7stages.org
Officers:
  Board Chair: Gregory N. Pierce
  Co Vice Chair: Pamela Benson
  President: Andjela Kessler
  Treasurer: Susan Roe
  Board Secretary: Sarah Mauldin
Management:
  Technical Director: Mack Headrick
  Producing Director: Faye Allen
  Artistic Director: Heidi S. Howard
  Managing Director: Mack Hadrick
  Associate Artistic Director: Michael Haverty
Mission: A professional, non-profit theatre company devoted to engaging artists and audiences by focusing on the social, political, and spiritual values of contemporary culture. Give primary emphasis to international work and the support and development of new plays, new playrights and new methods of collaboration.
Founded: 1979
Specialized Field: Comedy; Youth Theater; Ethnic Theater; Contemporary
Status: Non-Profit, Professional
Paid Staff: 6
Volunteer Staff: 12
Paid Artists: 40
Non-paid Artists: 20
Budget: $650,000
Performs At: Renovated Cinema
Type of Stage: Flexible
Stage Dimensions: 45' x 30'
Seating Capacity: 200
Year Built: 1942
Rental Contact: Mark Headrick

2847
ACADEMY THEATRE
119 Center Street Avondale Estates
Atlanta, GA 30002
Phone: 404-474-8332
Fax: 404-525-5659
e-mail: academytheatre@mindspring.com
Web Site: www.academytheatre.org/
Officers:
  Chairman: Jerry Dibble
  President: Frank Wittow
  Artistic Director: Robert Drake
  Director of the Human Service Progr: Brenda Porter Porter
Management:
  Founder/Producing Artistic Director: Frank Wittow
  Managing Director: Lorenne Fey
  Development Director: Nick Rhoton
Mission: Creating and performing orginal plays about critical issues for children and young adults, training teachers in the use of innovative techniques to accelerate learning and retention of knowledge, introducing children to theatre as a measn of self-discovery and self-expression.
Utilizes: Guest Artists; Guest Companies; Singers
Founded: 1956
Specialized Field: Theater Workshops; Children's Theater
Status: Professional; Nonprofit
Paid Staff: 2
Volunteer Staff: 19
Paid Artists: 10
Budget: $370,000
Income Sources: NEA; Georgia Council for the Arts; Fulton County Arts Council; City of Atlanta and Foundations; Individuals
Affiliations: Theatre Communications Group; Atlanta Coalition of Performing Arts; Georgia Shares
Annual Attendance: 70,000
Organization Type: Performing; Touring; Resident; Educational; Sponsoring

2848
ACTOR'S EXPRESS THEATRE
887 W Marietta Street
Suite J-107
Atlanta, GA 30318
Phone: 404-875-1606
Fax: 404-875-2791
Toll-free: 404-607-7469
Web Site: www.actors-express.com
Officers:
  Board Chair: Donna Darroch
  Board Vice-Chair: David Robinson
  Board President: Bruce Cohen
  Community Volunteer: Ronnie Zandman
  Board Secretary: Bruce Griffeth
Management:
  Artistic Director: Freddie Ashley
  Box Office Assistant: Matt Hambrick
  Production Manager: Phillip Male
  Managing Director: Alex Scollon
  Box Office Assistant: Dameka Waller
Mission: We produce a wildly eclectic mix of classic, contemporary, and cutting edge plays.
Utilizes: Actors; AEA Actors; Artists-in-Residence; Choreographers; Collaborations; Commissioned Composers; Commissioned Music; Five Seasonal Concerts; Guest Artists; Guest Companies; Guest Conductors; Guest Designers; Guest Lecturers; Guest Teachers; High School Drama; Instructors; Local Artists; Music; Original Music Scores; Performance Artists; Resident Professionals; Sign Language Translators; Student Interns
Founded: 1988
Specialized Field: Drama; Contemporary; Classic
Status: Non-Profit, Professional
Paid Staff: 714
Affiliations: AEA-GA
Facility Category: Flexible Black Box
Seating Capacity: 120-160
Year Built: 1994

2849
ALLIANCE THEATRE COMPANY
1280 Peachtree Street NE
Atlanta, GA 30309
Phone: 404-733-4650
Fax: 404-733-4625
e-mail: info@alliancetheatre.org
Web Site: www.alliancetheatre.org
Officers:
  Board Chair: Dan Reardon
  First Vice Chair: Vicki Palefsky
Management:
  Artistic Director: Susan V Booth
  Director of Finance/Administration: Brian Shively
  General Manager: Max Leventhal
Mission: Dedicated to celebrating diversity by building bridges that can connect us as human beings through the development and production of exciting, entertaining, and stimulating plays to nurture and enrich the art, the artists, and the audience.
Utilizes: Actors; AEA Actors; Artists-in-Residence; Choreographers; Commissioned Composers; Dancers; Designers; Educators; Guest Companies; High School Drama; Instructors; Local Artists; Multimedia; Music; Original Music Scores; Performance Artists; Resident Professionals; Selected Students; Sign Language Translators; Singers; Soloists
Founded: 1969
Specialized Field: Musical; Comedy; Youth Theater; Ethnic Theater; Classic; Contemporary
Status: Non-Profit, Professional
Paid Staff: 225
Paid Artists: 245
Budget: $10 million
Performs At: Lort Regional Theater
Affiliations: Actors' Equity Association; Society for Stage Directors and Choreographers; League of Resident Theatres; USA
Annual Attendance: 225,000
Type of Stage: Proscenium; Flexible
Stage Dimensions: 40x96; 44x75
Seating Capacity: 800; 200
Year Built: 1968
Year Remodeled: 1996
Organization Type: Performing; Touring; Resident; Educational

2850
CENTER FOR PUPPETRY ARTS
1404 Spring Street
Atlanta, GA 30309
Mailing Address: 1404 Spring Street, NW at 18th, Atlanta, GA 30309-2820
Phone: 404-873-3089
Fax: 404-873-9907
e-mail: info@puppet.org
Web Site: www.puppet.org
Management:
  Executive Director: Vincent Anthony
Mission: To expand public awareness of puppetry.
Utilizes: Actors; Collaborating Artists; Commissioned Composers; Commissioned Music; Designers; Five Seasonal Concerts; Grant Writers; Guest Accompanists; Guest Choreographers; Guest Companies; Guest Conductors; Guest Designers; Guest Ensembles; Guest Instructors; Guest Soloists; High School Drama; Instructors; Local Artists; Multimedia; Original Music Scores; Performance Artists; Poets; Resident Professionals; Singers; Student Interns; Special Technical Talent; Theatre Companies; Visual Arts
Founded: 1978
Specialized Field: Puppet
Status: Non-Profit, Professional
Paid Staff: 59
Volunteer Staff: 30
Performs At: Mainstage Theater; Downstairs Theater
Annual Attendance: 900,000
Type of Stage: Mainstage
Seating Capacity: 345/Downstairs 170
Year Built: 1918
Year Remodeled: 96
Organization Type: Performing; Touring; Resident; Educational; Sponsoring

2851
DAD'S GARAGE THEATRE COMPANY
280 Elizabeth Street Suite C 101
Suite C-101
Atlanta, GA 30307
Phone: 404-523-3141
Fax: 404-688-6644
Web Site: http://www.dadsgarage.com/
Officers:
   President: Andrew Chang
   Vice President: Larry Wexler
   Chairman: Melissa Honbach
   Vice Chair: Scott Wandstrat
   Treasurer: Jeff Silver
Management:
   Artistic Director: Kevin Gillese
   Managing Director: Lena Carstens
   Marketing Director: Linnea Frye
   PGA: Derk Brown
   Financial Advisor: Keith Clemens
Founded: 1995
Specialized Field: Ensembles; Comedy; Improvisation

2852
ESSENTIAL THEATRE
887 W Marietta St. Suite J-107
#6
Atlanta, GA 30318
Phone: 404-212-0815
e-mail: pmhardy@aol.com
Web Site: http://www.essentialtheatre.com/
Management:
   Producing Artistic Director: Peter Hardy
Founded: 1987
Specialized Field: Drama; Contemporary; Improvisation

2853
FABREFACTION THEATRE CONSERVATORY
999 Brady Avenue
Atlanta, GA 30318
Phone: 404-876-9468
e-mail: info@fabrefaction.org
Web Site: fabrefaction.org
Officers:
   Board Chair: Mildred Geckler Dunn
   President: Robert Carter
   Vice President: Rhodes M. Cole
Management:
   Artistic Director: Christina Hoff
   Executive Director: Evelyn Hoff
Mission: Fabrefaction Theatre Company's mission is to produce classic, contemporary, and new works that speak to audiences of all ages, provide educational experiences and training opportunities, and cultivate lifelong theatre artists and patrons.
Founded: 2007
Status: Nonprofit
Organization Type: Educational; Performing

2854
GATEWAY PERFORMANCE PRODUCTIONS
PO Box 8062
Atlanta, GA 31106
Phone: 404-222-9262
Fax: 404-982-9922
e-mail: info@masktheatre.org
Web Site: www.masktheatre.org
Officers:
   President: Sandra Hughes
   Chairperson: Chris Moser
   Treasurer: Michael Hickey
Management:
   Artistic Director: Sandra Hughes
   Company Coordinator: Michael E Hickey
Mission: To create and produce high-quality outreach arts programming for touring theatres, festivals, museums, libraries, colleges, universities, schools, and other community sites. Gateway carries out this mission through touring the following programs and productions- Mask Theatre, Mime, Cultural Arts Programs, Workshops, Classes, Residencies, Demonstrations, and Exhibits.
Utilizes: Singers
Founded: 1974
Specialized Field: Mask Theater
Status: Non-Profit, Professional
Paid Staff: 2
Paid Artists: 2
Organization Type: Performing; Touring; Resident; Educational

2855
GEORGIA SHAKESPEARE
Conant Performing Arts Center
4484 Peachtree Road NE
Atlanta, GA 30319
Phone: 404-504-3400
Fax: 404-504-3414
e-mail: boxoffice@gashakespeare.org
Web Site: www.gashakespeare.org
Officers:
   Producing Artistic Director: Richard Garner
   Managing Director: Lauren Morris
   Education Director: Allen O'Reilly
Management:
   Producing Artistic Director: Richard Garner
   Marketing Director: Stacey Colosa Lucas
   Media & Data Manager: Donna Weber
   Marketing & PR Manager: Marci Tate
Mission: To produce professional plays written by Shakespeare and other enduring authors.
Founded: 1985
Specialized Field: Shakespeare; Classic
Status: Professional; Nonprofit
Paid Staff: 7
Income Sources: Southeastern Theatre Conference; Atlanta Theatre Coalition
Organization Type: Performing; Resident

2856
HORIZON THEATRE COMPANY
1083 Austin Avenue
Corner of Euclid & Austin Avenues
Atlanta, GA 30307
Mailing Address: PO Box 5376 Atlanta, GA 31107
Phone: 404-584-7450
Fax: 404-584-8815
e-mail: boxoffice@horizontheatre.com
Web Site: www.horizontheatre.com
Officers:
   Co-Artistic/Producing Director: Lisa Adler
   Co-Artistic/Technical Director: Jeff Adler
Management:
   President: Lisa Adler
   Public Relationsmarketing Director: Andrea Minadakis
   Coartistic Technical Director: Jeff Adler
   Managing Director: Alison Hayes
   House Manager: Denny Zartman
   Marketing Manager: Kristen Gwock Silton
   Development Manager: Jordan Flowers
Mission: To be a leader in the production and development of contemporary theatre in the Southeast. We present professional area premieres of new and recent plays and develop new artists and audiences for contemporary theatre through education and outreach programs.
Founded: 1983
Specialized Field: Musical; Comedy; Ethnic Theater; Contemporary
Status: Non-Profit, Professional
Paid Staff: 15
Paid Artists: 60
Income Sources: Grants
Performs At: Horizon Theatre
Type of Stage: Flexible
Seating Capacity: 170

2857
JUST US THEATER COMPANY
1665 Havilon Drive Southwest
Atlanta, GA 30311
Phone: 404-753-2399
Fax: 404-758-9200
Officers:
   President: Walter R Huntley
   Treasurer: Pearle Cleage
   Secretary: Zaron W Burnett, Jr
Management:
   Artistic Director: Pearl Cleage
   Producing Director: Zaron Burnett, Jr.
Mission: Just Us Theater Company is a Black professional company dedicated to the development of minority artists and the presentation of quality arts programs that reflect the diversity of our community; focus on sexism and racism.
Utilizes: Guest Companies; Singers
Founded: 1976
Specialized Field: Ensembles; Drama; Contemporary
Status: For-Profit,Non-Professional
Organization Type: Performing; Touring; Resident; Educational

2858
NEW AMERICAN SHAKESPEARE TAVERN
499 Peachtree Street NE
Atlanta, GA 30308
Phone: 404-874-5299
Fax: 404-874-9219
e-mail: becky@shakespearetavern.com
Web Site: www.shakespearetavern.com
Management:
   Artistic Director: Jeffery Watkins
   Managing Director: Kirstein Dunstan
Mission: The New American Shakespeare Tavern is unlike other theaters. It is a place out of time; a place of live music, hand-crafted period costumes, outrageous sword fights with the entire experience centered on the passion and poetry of the spoken word.
Founded: 1984
Specialized Field: Shakespeare
Status: Non-Profit, Professional
Paid Staff: 15
Paid Artists: 20

2859
NEW JOMANDI PRODUCTIONS
675 Ponce De Leon Avenue
City Hall East, 8th Floor
Atlanta, GA 30308
Phone: 404-876-6346
Fax: 404-872-5764
Toll-free: 877-217-4302
e-mail: info@jomandi.com
Web Site: www.jomandi.com
Officers:
   Chairman/State Representative: Bob Holmes

THEATRE / Georgia

Artistic Director: Andrea Frye
Marketing/PR Director: Arnie A. Epps
Management:
   General Manager: Jomal Vailes
   Artistic Director: Carol Michell-Leon
   Communicatons Director: Inda Royall
   Production Manager: Lisa L Watson
   General Manager: Greg Stevens
   Production Manager: Lisa Watson
   Marketing/PR Consultant: Geri Blanchet
Mission: Nurturing new works that reflect the African-American experience; providing theatre artists an opportunity for training and performance.
Utilizes: Guest Companies; Singers
Founded: 1978
Specialized Field: Musical; Comedy; Drama
Status: Non-Profit, Professional
Paid Staff: 10
Paid Artists: 3
Performs At: 14th Street Playhouse
Type of Stage: Proscenium/Thrust
Seating Capacity: 370
Organization Type: Performing; Touring; Resident

2860
OMILAMI PRODUCTIONS/PEOPLE'S SURVIVAL THEATRE
8 E Lake Drive NE
Atlanta, GA 30317
Phone: 404-377-6434
Fax: 404-584-9166
Management:
   Co-Artistic Director: Elizabeth Omilami
   Co-Artistic Director: Afemo Omilami
Mission: To produce, provide and encourage arts programming for impoverished areas that are not serviced by traditional groups; to stimulate and encourage new playwrights and directors to write and direct for the inner city and rural areas.
Utilizes: Guest Companies; Singers
Founded: 1977
Specialized Field: Community Theater
Status: Semi-Professional; Nonprofit
Paid Staff: 8
Organization Type: Performing; Touring; Educational

2861
PINCH N' OUCH THEATRE
1085 Ponce De Leon Ave NE
Atlanta, GA 30306
Phone: 800-838-3006
e-mail: info@pnotheatre.org
Web Site: pnotheatre.org
Management:
   Producing Artistic Director: Grant McGowen
Mission: To advance the vitality and diversity of American theatre by nurturing artists, encouraging repeatable creative relationships, and offering patrons the gift of engaging storytelling that meets them where they are today. Pinch N' Ouch Theatre preserves an ethic of mutual respect for collaborative works that are derived from a sense of truth.
Founded: 2009
Specialized Field: Contemporary
Status: Professional; Nonprofit

2862
SEVEN STAGES THEATRE
1105 Euclid Avenue
Atlanta, GA 30307
Phone: 404-523-7647
Web Site: www.7stages.org
Officers:
   Board Chair: Gregory N. Pierce
   Co Vice Chair: Pamela Benson
   President: Andjela Kessler
   Treasurer: Susan Roe
   Board Secretary: Sarah Mauldin
Management:
   Technical Director: Mack Headrick
   Producing Director: Faye Allen
   Artistic Director: Heidi S. Howard
   Managing Director: Mack Hadrick
   Associate Artistic Director: Michael Haverty
Utilizes: Actors; Artists-in-Residence; Collaborating Artists; Dance Companies; Guest Companies; Local Artists; Multimedia; Original Music Scores; Playwrights
Paid Staff: 7
Volunteer Staff: 2
Paid Artists: 65
Budget: $650,000
Performs At: Renovated Cinema
Affiliations: Theatre Communications Group; Atlanta Coalition for the Performing Arts
Facility Category: 2 Performing Arts Theatres
Type of Stage: Black Boxes
Seating Capacity: 200
Year Built: 1942
Cost: $1.6 million
Rental Contact: Mark Headrick
Organization Type: Performing; Resident
Resident Groups: Seven Stages

2863
SOUTHEASTERN SAVOYARDS
3270 Ivanhoe Drive
Atlanta, GA 30327
Phone: 404-233-7002
Officers:
   President: Jonn H Stevens
   VP: Robert B Langdon
   Treasurer: Fern M Stevens
   Secretary: Marcia Lane
Management:
   Executive Producer: John H Stevens
   Music Director/Artistic: J Lynn Thompson
Mission: Gilbert & Sullivan repertory company.
Utilizes: Guest Companies; Singers
Founded: 1980
Specialized Field: Musical
Status: Professional; Nonprofit
Performs At: Center Stage Theater Atlanta
Organization Type: Theatrical Group

2864
THEATER EMORY
Rich Building, Emory University
Room 230
Atlanta, GA 30322
Phone: 404-727-6462
Fax: 404-727-6253
e-mail: rschult@learnlink.emory.edu
Web Site: www.emory.edu
Management:
   President: Vincent Murphy
   Managing Director: Rosalind Staiv
Founded: 1985
Specialized Field: Comedy; Ethnic Theater; Community Theater; Classic; Contemporary
Status: Non-Profit, Professional
Paid Artists: 50
Performs At: Mary Gray Munroe Theater at Emory University

2865
THEATER OF THE STARS
1100 Spring Street, Suite 830
Atlanta, GA 30309
Mailing Address: P.O. Box 11748, Atlanta, GA 30355
Phone: 404-252-8960
Fax: 404-252-1460
e-mail: theaterofstars@mindspring.com
Web Site: www.theaterofthestars.com
Management:
   President: Christopher B Manos
   Managing Director: Nicholas F Manos
   Artistic Director: Scott Bowker
Utilizes: Singers
Founded: 1953
Specialized Field: Musical
Status: Non-Profit, Professional
Paid Staff: 7
Organization Type: Performing; Touring; Sponsoring

2866
THEATRE GAEL
PO Box 77156
Atlanta, GA 30357
Phone: 404-876-1138
Fax: 404-876-1141
e-mail: theatregael@mindspring.com
Web Site: www.theatregael.com
Management:
   President: Thomas Brennan
   VP: Constance Callahan
   Artistic Director: John Stephens
   Managing Director: Sarah Dasher
Mission: The performance of plays from Scotland, Ireland and Wales.
Utilizes: Guest Companies; Singers
Founded: 1984
Specialized Field: Children's Theater
Status: Professional; Nonprofit
Paid Staff: 3
Volunteer Staff: 10
Paid Artists: 25
Income Sources: American Alliance for Theatre Arts; Alternate Rural Organization of Theaters South
Seating Capacity: 90
Organization Type: Performing

2867
THEATRICAL OUTFIT
84 Luckie Street Northwest
Atlanta, GA 30303
Mailing Address: P.O. Box 1555, Atlanta, GA 30301
Phone: 678-528-1000
Fax: 404-577-5259
Web Site: www.theatricaloutfit.org
Officers:
   President: Bill Bolzer
Management:
   President: Bill Ballver
   Artistic Director: Tom Key
   Marketing/Development Director: Beth Haynes
   General Manager: Rochelle Barker
Mission: Produces contemporary and classical scripts with an emphasis on Southern themes.
Utilizes: Guest Companies; Singers
Founded: 1976
Specialized Field: Drama; Musical; Contemporary
Status: Non-Profit, Professional
Paid Staff: 5
Paid Artists: 50
Budget: $700,000
Income Sources: Ticket Revenue; Private; Corporate; Foundations; Public
Performs At: Rialto Center for the Performing Arts
Organization Type: Performing; Educational

2868
AUGUSTA PLAYERS
PO Box 2352
Augusta, GA 30903-2352
Phone: 706-826-4707
Fax: 706-826-4709
e-mail: info@augustaplayers.org
Web Site: www.augustaplayers.org
Officers:
  President: Patrick Blanchard
Management:
  Executive Director: Debi Ballas
Utilizes: Actors; Community Members; Community Talent; Contract Orchestras; Five Seasonal Concerts; Guild Activities; Local Artists; Local Artists & Directors; Local Talent; Music; Paid Performers; Sign Language Translators; Visual Designers
Founded: 1945
Specialized Field: Musical Theatre
Status: Non-Professional; Nonprofit
Paid Staff: 2
Non-paid Artists: 150
Budget: $300,000
Income Sources: Donations; Grants; Ticket Sales
Affiliations: American Association Of Community Theatres
Organization Type: Performing; Educational

2869
WEST GEORGIA THEATRE COMPANY SUMMER CLASSIC
University Of West Georgia
Theatre Program
1601 Maple Street
Carrollton, GA 30117
Phone: 678-839-4708
Fax: 678-839-4708
e-mail: theatre@westgeorgia.edu
Management:
  Theatre Director: Shelly Elman
  Design Faculty/ Technical Director: Tommy Cox
  Design Faculty/ Costumes: Alan Yoeng
Utilizes: Actors; Collaborating Artists; Collaborations; Designers; Educators; Grant Writers; Guest Accompanists; Guest Artists; Guest Designers; Guest Ensembles; Guest Lecturers; Guest Soloists; High School Drama; Resident Professionals; Sign Language Translators; Soloists; Student Interns; Special Technical Talent; Touring Companies; Volunteer Directors & Actors; Writers
Founded: 1991
Specialized Field: Educational; Theater Workshops
Status: Non-Equity; Nonprofit
Budget: $90,000
Season: June - August
Performs At: Multi-Stage
Affiliations: Georgia Theatre Conference; Southeastern Theatre Conference; Association for the Theatre in Higher Education; USITT
Facility Category: Performing Arts Center
Type of Stage: Proscenium; Balck Box
Seating Capacity: 450; 120

2870
SPRINGER OPERA HOUSE
THE STATE THEATER OF GEORGIA
103 Tenth Street
Columbus, GA 31901
Phone: 706-324-5714
Fax: 706-324-4681
Web Site: www.springeroperahouse.org
Officers:
  Director of Marketing & Sales: Scooter MacMillan
  Associate Artistic Director: Ron Anderson
  Producing Artistic Director: Paul R. Pierce
Management:
  Executive Director: Porrin Trotter
  Artistic Director: Paul R Pierce
  Associate Artistic Director: Ron Anderson
  General Manager: Jamie Fagerstrom
  Box Office Manager: Becky Macy
Mission: Offering the Southeastern United States high quality productions; representing Georgia as its official State Theatre.
Utilizes: Actors; AEA Actors; Choreographers; Designers; Guest Accompanists; Guest Artists; Guest Companies; Guest Conductors; Guest Designers; Guest Instructors; Guest Soloists; High School Drama; Local Artists; Performance Artists; Resident Professionals; Sign Language Translators; Singers
Founded: 1871
Specialized Field: Musical; Light Theater; Classic
Status: Non-Profit, Professional
Paid Staff: 19
Volunteer Staff: 240
Paid Artists: 145
Non-paid Artists: 40
Budget: $1.6 million
Income Sources: Private, Foundation, State, Municipal, Ticket Sales
Performs At: 130 year old National Historic Landmark Theatre
Annual Attendance: 125,000
Facility Category: Theatre
Type of Stage: Proscenium & Studio Theatre
Stage Dimensions: 32 W x 42 Deep
Year Built: 1871
Year Remodeled: 1998
Cost: 12 Million
Rental Contact: Allison Kent
Organization Type: Performing; Touring; Producing

2871
AGNES SCOTT COLLEGE: DEPARTMENT OF THEATRE AND DANCE
141 East College Ave
Decatur, GA 30030
Phone: 404-471-6251
Fax: 404-638-5369
e-mail: admission@agnesscott.edu
Web Site: http://www.agnesscott.edu/academics/undergraduate/theatre
Officers:
  Chair: Dudley Sanders
Management:
  Associate Professor: Dudley W Sanders
Specialized Field: Educational; Theater Workshops
Budget: $2,800-$4,000
Performs At: Winter Theatre
Affiliations: ATHE
Type of Stage: Semi-Thrust
Seating Capacity: 310
Year Built: 1965

2872
PICCADILLY PUPPETS COMPANY
621 Densley Drive
Decatur, GA 30033
Phone: 404-636-0022
Fax: 404-636-0616
Web Site: www.piccadillypuppets.org
Officers:
  President: Jamie Cameron
  Freelance Actress & Puppeteer: Fracena Byrd
  Teaching Artist: Justin Daniel
  Attorney: David Langford
Management:
  President: Pat Temm
  Executive Director: Carol Daniel
  Company Director: Nancy Riggs
Mission: Perform puppet shows for children and families.
Founded: 1969
Specialized Field: Musical; Youth Theater; Community Theater; Puppet; Contemporary; Puppet; Touring Company
Status: Non-Profit, Professional
Paid Staff: 1
Paid Artists: 4
Budget: $75,000
Income Sources: Arts councils; Presenters; Foundation Support
Organization Type: Performing; Touring; Educational

2873
PUSHPUSH THEATER
114 New Street, #D3
Decatur, GA 30030
Phone: 404-377-6332
e-mail: pushpushtheater@gmail.com
Web Site: pushpushtheater.com
Officers:
  Chair: William Chapman
Management:
  Producing Artistic Director: Tim Habeger
  Managing Artistic Director: Shelby Hofer
Mission: To advance cultural progression through the cultivation of distinctive artistic development opportunities for theater and new media artists.
Founded: 1997

2874
AURORA THEATRE
128 East Pike Street
Lawrenceville, GA 30046
Mailing Address: P.O. Box 2014, Lawrenceville, GA 30046
Phone: 678-226-6222
e-mail: boxoffice@auroratheatre.com
Web Site: auroratheatre.com
Management:
  Producing Artistic Director: Anthony Rodriguez
  Associate Producer: Ann-Carol Pence
  Associate Artistic Director: Justin Anderson
  General Manager: D.H. Malcolm, III
Mission: Aurora Theatre is committed to producing quality, professional theatre for the Southeast, North Georgia, and our most ardent supporters, the residents of Gwinnett County. We will serve these communities by offering entertainment that nurtures a love of theatre and develops a new generation of theatergoers.

2875
PARENTHESIS THEATRE CLUB
4336 Highborne Drive
Marietta, GA 30066
Phone: 404-977-8340
Management:
  Artistic Director: Gregory Blum
  Producing Director: Darrell Wofford
Mission: Producing ten minute plays that are socially relevant and original one acts.
Founded: 1991
Specialized Field: Dinner Theater
Status: Semi-Professional
Performs At: Cabaret Space
Organization Type: Performing; Resident

THEATRE / Hawaii

2876
THEATRE IN THE SQUARE
11 Whitlock Avenue
Marietta, GA 30064
Phone: 770-422-8369
Fax: 770-424-2637
Web Site: www.theatreinthesquare.com
Management:
   Producing Director/CoFounder: Palmer Wells
   Managing Director: Raye Varney
   Assistant Artistic Director: Jessica Phelps West
Utilizes: Guest Companies; Singers
Paid Staff: 17
Performs At: Theatre in the Square
Organization Type: Performing; Touring

2877
PERRY PLAYERS
909 Main Street
Perry, GA 31069
Phone: 478-987-5354
e-mail: perryplayers@hotmail.com
Web Site: www.perryplayers.org/
Officers:
   President: Hank Hudson
   Treasurer: Beverly Cooper
   Secretary: Mary Kay Baile
   Vice-President Of Productions: Bill Andrew
Management:
   VP Of Production: Anita Williams
Mission: We offer high-quality entertainment and cultural activities to the citizens of middle Georgia. Individuals who enjoy acting, singing, dancing and producing cultural entertainment share and improve these skills in a welcoming environment of cooperation and enthusiasm.
Utilizes: Singers
Founded: 1982
Specialized Field: Musical; Community Theater
Status: Non-Profit
Paid Staff: 30
Income Sources: Houston County Arts Alliance; Macon Arts Alliance; Perry Chamber of Commerce

2878
GEORGIA ENSEMBLE THEATRE
950 Forrest Street
PO Box 607
Roswell, GA 30077-0607
Mailing Address: P.O. Box 607,Roswell, GA 30077-0607
Phone: 770-641-1260
Fax: 770-641-1360
e-mail: info@get.org
Web Site: www.get.org
Officers:
   President: Andy Ross
   Director Marketing: Tess Kincaias
   Artistic Director: Robert J. Farley
   Managing Director: Anita Allen-Farley
   Resources Director: Tess Malis Kincaid
Management:
   Artistic Director: Robert J. Farley
   Managing Director: Anita Allen-Farley
   General Manager: Gretchen Butler
Founded: 1992
Specialized Field: Ensembles; Drama; Musical
Status: Non-Profit, Professional
Paid Staff: 8
Volunteer Staff: 200
Paid Artists: 25

2879
ART STATION THEATRE
ART Station Contemporary Art Center
5384 Manor Drive
Stone Mountain, GA 30083
Mailing Address: PO Box 1988 Stone Mountain GA 30086
Phone: 770-469-1105
Fax: 770-469-0355
e-mail: info@artstation.org
Web Site: www.artstation.org
Officers:
   President: David Thomas
   Chairman: Rusty McKeller
   Vice Chairperson: Michele Henson
   Secretary: Michael Hidalgo
   Treasurer: Pam Culbersom
   President and Artistic Director: David Thomas
Management:
   President and Artistic Director: David Thomas
   Administrative Manager: Michael Hidalgo
   Program Manager: Jon Goldstein
Mission: Celebration and presentation of southern arts
Founded: 1986
Opened: 1986
Specialized Field: Musical; Comedy; Classic; Contemporary
Status: Non-Profit, Professional
Paid Staff: 5
Volunteer Staff: 2
Budget: $750,000
Income Sources: Government; Corporate; Foundations; Private
Season: September - June
Affiliations: AEA
Annual Attendance: 10,000+
Facility Category: Small Theatre
Type of Stage: Proscenium
Stage Dimensions: 28' x 30'
Seating Capacity: 108
Year Built: 1900
Year Remodeled: 1990
Cost: $1.2 Million
Rental Contact: Jon Goldstein

2880
PEACH STATE SUMMER THEATRE
Department of Communication Arts
Valdosta, GA 31698
Phone: 229-333-5820
Fax: 229-249-2602
e-mail: dguthrie@valdosta.edu
Management:
   Artistic Director: Jacque Wheeler
   Managing Director: Duke Guthrie
Mission: Providing Georgia's Golden Isles residents and visitors with quality musical theatre; offering college interns professional training.
Utilizes: Guest Choreographers; Guest Companies; Singers
Founded: 1990
Specialized Field: Summer Stock; Musical
Status: Professional; Nonprofit
Paid Artists: 65
Income Sources: Valdosta State University
Season: June - August
Performs At: Jekyll Island Amphitheater
Annual Attendance: 10,000
Facility Category: Professional Summer Stock Theatre
Type of Stage: Wooden, uncovered amphitheatre
Seating Capacity: 500
Year Built: 1970
Organization Type: Performing; Touring

2881
SOUTHERN APPALACHIAN STAGES
PO Box 499
Young Harris, GA 30582
Phone: 706-379-1711
Fax: 706-379-1542
Toll-free: 800-262-7664
Web Site: www.reachofsong.org
Management:
   Executive Director: Philip Albert
   Artistic Director: Sharon Albert
Mission: Preservation and presentation of the culture and history of the Southern Appalachian Mountains through the performing arts.
Founded: 1989
Specialized Field: Drama; Musical
Status: Non-Equity; Nonprofit
Paid Staff: 12
Volunteer Staff: 30
Paid Artists: 25
Season: June 20 - August 19
Type of Stage: Proscenium
Seating Capacity: 750

Hawaii

2882
ARMY ENTERTAINMENT PROGRAM
Entertainment Section
Fort Shafter, HI 96858
Phone: 808-438-1980
Fax: 808-438-1980
Management:
   Chief Army Entertainment: Vanita Rae Smith
   Technical Director: Tom Giza
Mission: The goals of the Army Entertainment Program are to provide interested individuals with a constructive outlet for talents, to maintain a high level of morals and to promote good cultural relations with the local civilian community.
Utilizes: Guest Artists; Guest Companies; Singers
Founded: 1949
Specialized Field: Musical; Community Theater
Status: Non-Professional; Nonprofit
Paid Staff: 30
Income Sources: American Association of Community Theatres; Hawaii State Theatre Council
Performs At: Richardson Performing Arts Center
Organization Type: Performing; Resident; Educational

2883
HILO COMMUNITY PLAYERS
PO Box 46
Hilo, HI 96721
Mailing Address: PO Box 46,Hilo HI 96721
Phone: 808-935-9155
e-mail: contact@hilocommunityplayers.org
Web Site: www.hilocommunityplayers.org
Officers:
   President: Gene Gold
   Secretary: Angie Baker
   Treasurer: Glen Swartwout
Management:
   Director: Laura Ward
Mission: Organizing, promoting and conducting an educational amateur drama program on the Island of Hawaii.
Utilizes: Guest Companies
Founded: 1938
Specialized Field: Educational; Community Theater
Status: Non-Profit, Non-Professional
Paid Staff: 100

THEATRE / Hawaii

Paid Artists: 3
Organization Type: Performing; Educational

2884
DIAMOND HEAD THEATRE
520 Makapuu Avenue
Honolulu, HI 96816
Phone: 808-733-0277
Fax: 808-735-1250
e-mail: dht@diamondheadtheatre.com
Web Site: www.diamondheadtheatre.com
Officers:
   Chairman: Chris Kanazawa
Management:
   President: Dennis Francis
   Artistic Director: John Rampage
   Managing Director: Deena Dray
Mission: To present plays and musicals to the community; to hold classes and workshops in acting for all ages; to offer opportunities for all persons interested to participate both on stage and backstage in theatre.
Utilizes: Actors; Choreographers; Dancers; Designers; Guest Accompanists; Guest Artists; Guest Conductors; Guest Designers; Guest Lecturers; Instructors; Local Artists; Music; Resident Professionals; Sign Language Translators; Soloists; Student Interns
Founded: 1915
Specialized Field: Musical; Comedy; Community Theater; Educational
Status: Non-Profit, Non-Professional
Paid Staff: 12
Volunteer Staff: 400
Budget: $1,500,000
Income Sources: Tickets; Donations; State of Hawaii; Foundations
Performs At: Diamond Head Theatre
Annual Attendance: 50,000
Facility Category: Community Theatre
Type of Stage: Proscenium
Seating Capacity: 500
Year Built: 1940
Year Remodeled: 1980
Rental Contact: Managing Director Deena Dray
Organization Type: Performing; Educational

2885
HAWAII THEATRE
1130 Bethel Street
Honolulu, HI 96813-2201
Phone: 808-528-0506
Fax: 808-529-8505
e-mail: burtonwhite@hawaii.rr.com
Web Site: www.hawaiitheatre.com
Officers:
   Chairman of the Board: Robert Midkiff
   Treasurer: Paul Schraff
   Vice Chairman: Mary Foster Weya
   Artistic Director: Burton White
   President: Sarah Richard
Management:
   Theatre Manager: Burton White
   Assistant Theatre Manager: Ryan Sueoka
   Assistant Box Office Manager: Dawn Keeley
   Stage Manager: Jude Lampitelli
   Box Office Senior Clerk: Lisa Lee
Mission: Provide a professional venue for the celebration of cultures and the arts for the people of Hawaii and its visitors.
Founded: 1922
Specialized Field: Drama; Musical; Contemporary
Status: Nonprofit
Paid Staff: 13
Volunteer Staff: 300
Budget: $1,500,000

Annual Attendance: 5,000
Type of Stage: Proscenium
Stage Dimensions: 30x18
Seating Capacity: 325

2886
HONOLULU THEATRE FOR YOUTH
1149 Bethel St.
Suite 700 Honolulu
Honolulu, HI 96813
Phone: 808-839-9885
Fax: 808-839-7018
e-mail: hty@htyweb.org
Web Site: www.htyweb.org/
Officers:
   Artistic Director: Eric Johnson
   Managing Director: Becky Dunning
Management:
   Artistic Director: Mark Lutwak
   Managing Director: Louise Lanzilotti
   Technical Director: Wade Kersey
   Director Of Drama Education: Wade Kersey
Mission: To provide quality drama education and theatre to all children and their families in the state of Hawaii.
Founded: 1955
Specialized Field: Children's Theater; Educational
Status: Non-Profit
Paid Staff: 21
Volunteer Staff: 50
Paid Artists: 35
Budget: $1.4 million
Annual Attendance: 120,000

2887
KUMU KAHUA THEATRE
46 Merchant Street
Honolulu, HI 96813
Phone: 808-536-4222
Fax: 808-536-4226
e-mail: kumukahuatheatre@hawaiiantel.net
Web Site: www.kumukahua.org
Officers:
   President: John Wat
   Managing Director: Donna Blanchard
   Artistic Director: Harry Blanchard
Management:
   Artistic Director: Harry Wong III
   Managing Director: Scott Rogers
Mission: To produce plays by Hawai'i writers writing about Hawaii and plays of interest to Hawai'i's under served communites.
Utilizes: Actors; Collaborating Artists; Collaborations; Community Members; Community Talent; Designers; Educators; Five Seasonal Concerts; Guest Artists; Guest Choreographers; Guest Conductors; Guest Designers; Guest Ensembles; Guest Musical Directors; Guest Speakers; Guest Teachers; High School Drama; Instructors; Local Artists; Local Artists & Directors; Lyricists; Paid Performers; Performance Artists; Scenic Designers; Soloists; Students; Theatre Companies; Volunteer Directors & Actors; Writers
Founded: 1971
Specialized Field: Young Playwrights; Educational
Status: Non-Profit, Non-Professional
Paid Staff: 3
Income Sources: Patrons; Donations; Grants; Sponsors
Performs At: Live Theatre
Annual Attendance: 7,485
Type of Stage: Black Box(Flexible)
Seating Capacity: 1,871
Year Built: 1871
Year Remodeled: 1994

Rental Contact: Managing Director Scott Rogers

2888
WINDWARD THEATRE GUILD
PO Box 624
Kailua, HI 96734
Phone: 808-234-1751
Management:
   Manager: Charles Brockman
Mission: Enhancing and promoting excellence in all aspects of theatrical production.
Utilizes: Guest Companies; Singers
Founded: 1956
Specialized Field: Musical; Dinner Theater; Community Theater
Status: Nonprofit
Paid Staff: 60
Income Sources: Hawaii State Theatre Council; State Foundation for Culture & the Arts; Alliance for Drama Education
Performs At: Boondocker Theatre; Kaneohe Marine Corps Air State
Organization Type: Performing; Educational

2889
WAIMEA COMMUNITY THEATRE
66-1250 Lalamilo Farmlot Road
Kamuela, HI 96743
Phone: 808-885-5818
Web Site: www.waimeacommunitytheatre.org
Officers:
   President: Jack Ross
   VP: Julie Barreto
   Secretary: Jennifer Hussong
   Treasurer: Miguel Bray
   President: Felicity Johnson
Mission: Providing residents of North Hawaii with quality theatrical entertainment; offering community support and educational services in theatrical performance.
Utilizes: Guest Companies; Singers
Founded: 1964
Specialized Field: Musical; Dinner Theater; Community Theater
Status: Non-Profit
Paid Staff: 50
Income Sources: Hawaii State Theatre Council
Performs At: Parker School Auditorium
Organization Type: Performing; Educational

2890
KAUAI INTERNATIONAL THEATRE
Kauai Village
4-831 Kuhio Highway
Kapaa, Kauai, HI 96746
Phone: 808-821-1588
e-mail: thekit@GoKauai.org
Management:
   Executive/Artistic Director: Gabriel Oberman
Specialized Field: New Plays; Dinner Theater
Status: Volunteer

2891
ALOHA PERFORMING ARTS COMPANY
79-7384 Mamalahoa Highway
Kealakekua, HI 96750
Mailing Address: P.O. Box 794, Kealakekua, HI 96750
Phone: 808-322-9924
e-mail: info@apachawaii.org
Web Site: apachawaii.org
Officers:
   President: Miguel Montez
   Vice President: Melissa Atwood
   Secretary: Sara Hagen

THEATRE / Idaho

Treasurer: Joel Gimpel
Management:
  Artistic Director: Jerry Tracy
  Operations Director: Suzanne Murdock
  Technical Director: Gill Pecceu
Mission: APAC's mission is to enrich the lives of Hawaii residents and visitors by presenting quality theatre and providing theatre education. APAC shall also maintain and operate a venue which provides opportunities for APAC and other organizations to present performing arts.
Founded: 1987
Status: Nonprofit

2892
LEEWARD COMMUNITY COLLEGE THEATRE
University of Hawaii Colleges
96-045 Ala Ike
Pearl City, HI 96782
Phone: 808-455-0380
Fax: 808-455-0384
e-mail: lcctheatre@lcc.hawaii.edu
Web Site: www.lcctheatre.hawaii.edu
Officers:
  Technical Director: Sarah Whitehead
  Technical Director: Don Ranney
Management:
  Theatre Manager: Joe Patti
  Assistant Theatre Manager: Lehua Simon
Mission: Our primary goal of LCC Theatre is to promote cultural curiosity. We want our performances to make a connection to the mind, heart or spirit of our audiences; creating and stimulating a hunger for the experiences only achieved through the arts.
Founded: 1974
Opened: 1974
Specialized Field: Comedy; Musical; Educational
Status: Non-Profit, Professional
Paid Staff: 5
Type of Stage: Proscenium
Stage Dimensions: 50 ft x 41 ft
Orchestra Pit: y
Seating Capacity: 580
Year Built: 1974

2893
MAUI ACADEMY OF PERFORMING ARTS
81 N Church Street
Wailuku, HI 96792
Phone: 808-244-8760
Fax: 808-244-6530
e-mail: friendsofmapa@mauiacademy.org
Web Site: www.mauiacademy.org
Officers:
  President: Chris Hart
  Front Office Administrator: Hoku Pavao Jones
  Associate Dance Director: Rebecca Owen
  Director of Programs: Carolyn Wright
  Dance Director: Kathleen Sculz
Management:
  President: Chris Hart
  Executive Director: David Johnston
  Artistic Director: David C Johnston
  Managing Director: Frances A Von Tempsky
  Director of Development: Peggy Harmon
Mission: Offering educational performing arts to youths and adults.
Utilizes: Actors; Artists-in-Residence; Choreographers; Collaborating Artists; Collaborations; Dance Companies; Dancers; Designers; Educators; Five Seasonal Concerts; Grant Writers; Guest Accompanists; Guest Artists; Guest Choreographers; Guest Conductors; Guest Designers; Guest Ensembles; Guest Lecturers; Guild Activities; Multi Collaborations; Music; Organization Contracts; Original Music Scores; Performance Artists; Resident Professionals; Special Technical Talent; Theatre Companies
Founded: 1974
Specialized Field: Comedy; Youth Theater; Ethnic Theater; Classic; Contemporary
Status: Non-Profit, Professional
Paid Staff: 35
Volunteer Staff: 200
Paid Artists: 3
Income Sources: Grants; Fundraising; Earned Revenue
Performs At: Maui Academy of Performing Arts
Annual Attendance: 10,000 +
Facility Category: Performing Arts Classrooms/Theatre
Type of Stage: Multi-forum
Seating Capacity: 150 - 200
Year Built: 2000
Cost: $3.1 million
Rental Contact: David Johnson
Organization Type: Performing; Touring; Educational

Idaho

2894
BOISE CONTEMPORARY THEATER
854 Fulton Street
Boise, ID 83702
Phone: 208-331-9224
e-mail: info@bctheater.org
Web Site: bctheater.org
Officers:
  President: Terri Dillion
  Vice President: Sandra Anderson
  Secretary: Karen Kelley
  Treasurer: Dick Gardner
Management:
  Artistic Director: Matthew Cameron Clark
  Managing Director: Helene Peterson
Mission: Boise Contemporary Theater creates, produces and presents vibrant and dynamic professional theater that illuminates enduring themes while exploring contemporary issues and ideas.
Specialized Field: Contemporary

2895
IDAHO SHAKESPEARE FESTIVAL
PO Box 9365
Boise, ID 83707
Mailing Address: P.O. Box 9365, Boise, ID 83707
Phone: 208-429-9908
Fax: 208-323-0700
Web Site: www.idahoshakespeare.org
Officers:
  President: Cindy Bateman
  Vice President: James Steele
  Secretary: Brandy Stemmler
  Treasurer: Henry Yun
  President: James Steele
  Vice President: Lynn Johnston
Management:
  Artistic Director: Charles Fee
  Managing Director: Mark Hofflund
  Director Of Development: Ann Dehner
  Director Of Finance: Sherrill Livingstone
Mission: The Festival's mission is to produce great theater, entertain and educate.
Founded: 1975
Specialized Field: Shakespeare
Status: Non-Profit, Professional
Paid Staff: 12
Season: May - September
Organization Type: Performing; Touring; Educational

2896
STAGE COACH THEATRE
4802 W. Emerald Street
Boise, ID 83707
Mailing Address: P.O. Box 6523, Boise, ID 83707
Phone: 208-342-2000
e-mail: stagecoachtheatre@gmail.com
Web Site: stagecoachtheatre.com
Officers:
  President: Kevin Kimsey
  Treasurer: Stacey Coleman
  Secretary: Heather Jones
Mission: Stage Coach Theatre is a quality-driven performance organization dedicated to producing live theatre that reflects and celebrates the human spirit.
Status: Nonprofit

2897
COEUR D'ALENE SUMMER THEATRE/CAROUSEL PLAYERS
4951 Building Center Drive
#105
Coeur d'Alene, ID 83815
Mailing Address: PO Box 1119, Coeur d'Alene, ID 83816
Phone: 208-660-2958
Fax: 208-769-7856
Toll-free: 800-423-2849
e-mail: info@cdasummertheatre.com
Web Site: www.cdasummertheatre.com/
Officers:
  Business Manager: Aaron Baldwin
  Marketing & PR Manager: Tyler Kreig
  Box Office Manager: Becca Simms
Management:
  President: Ketty Martus
  Artistic Director: Jadd Davis
  Managing Director: David Hollingshead
  Development Director: Jim Speirs
  Executive Director: Laura Little
Founded: 1968
Specialized Field: Summer Stock
Status: Non-Profit, Professional
Budget: $560,000
Income Sources: Patrons; Donors; Business Advertisers; Grants
Season: July 1 - August 29
Annual Attendance: 30,000
Facility Category: College Auditorium
Type of Stage: Proscenium
Stage Dimensions: 56'x 42'
Seating Capacity: 1100

2898
COMPANY OF FOOLS
110 N. Main St
Hailey, ID 83333
Phone: 208-678-9122
Fax: 208-788-1053
e-mail: info@companyoffools.org
Web Site: www.companyoffools.org
Management:
  President: Benjamin Wood
  Artistic Director: Rusty Wilson
  Managing Director: R I Rowsey
  Associate Artistic Director: Denise Simone
Founded: 1992
Specialized Field: Musical; Classic; Contemporary
Status: Non-Profit, Professional
Paid Staff: 6

Performs At: Liberty Theatre, Mint
Type of Stage: Proscenium, Flexible
Seating Capacity: 240, 30-90

2899
IDAHO FALLS ARTS COUNCIL COLONIAL THEATER
498 A Street
Idaho Falls, ID 83402
Phone: 208-522-0471
Fax: 208-522-0413
e-mail: ifac@idahofallsarts.org
Web Site: www.idahofallsarts.org
Management:
    Executive Director: Carrie Getty
    Artistic Director: Grey Gardner
    Technical Director: Brad Higbee
Mission: To promote and present visual and performing arts in Eastern Idaho.
Founded: 1990
Specialized Field: Drama; Movement Theater; Musical
Status: Non-Profit, Non-Professional
Paid Staff: 10
Paid Artists: 1
Type of Stage: Wood
Seating Capacity: 969
Year Built: 1919
Year Remodeled: 1999
Rental Contact: Linda Evans

2900
IDAHO REPERTORY THEATRE COMPANY
Corner of 6th and Rayburn
Shoup Hall - 2nd Floor
Moscow, ID 83844-3074
Phone: 208-885-6465
Fax: 208-885-2558
e-mail: theatre@uidaho.edu
Web Site: www.uitheatre.com
Officers:
    Lecturer: Carrie Lawrence
    Assistant Professor: David A. Nofsinger
    Clinical Faculty: Robby Valliere
    Professor of Performance: Kelly Quinnett
Management:
    Director: Michael White
    Artistic Director: Robert Caisley
    Producing Director: David Lee Painter
    Professor of Costumer Design: Ann Hoste
    Temporary Faculty Lecturer: Benjamin James
Mission: Providing North Idaho with quality summer theatre.
Utilizes: Guest Companies; Singers
Founded: 1953
Specialized Field: Educational; Theater Workshops
Status: Non-Profit
Paid Staff: 8
Volunteer Staff: 10
Paid Artists: 50
Non-paid Artists: 5
Income Sources: Individual contribution; Business/Corporate Donations; Foundations
Season: May - August
Performs At: Hartung Theatre
Type of Stage: Semi-Thrust/Proscenium
Seating Capacity: 417
Year Built: 1973
Architect: $4,300,000
Organization Type: Performing; Educational

2901
PANIDA THEATRE
300 N 1st Avenue
Sandpoint, ID 83864
Phone: 208-263-9191
Fax: 208-263-1523
e-mail: panida@nidaho.net
Web Site: www.panida.org
Officers:
    Chairman: Erik Daarstad
    Vice-Chairman: Danielle Packard
    Secretary: Steve Garvan
Management:
    President: Debra McShane
    Executive Director: Karen Bowers
    Technical Director: Bill Lewis
Mission: Providing beautiful, versatile space for the presentation of quality performances; continuing to aid in the revitalization of downtown Sandpoint.
Utilizes: Singers
Founded: 1927
Specialized Field: Alternative
Status: Non-Profit, Professional
Paid Staff: 4
Income Sources: Fundraising; grants
Performs At: Panida Theatre
Annual Attendance: 25,000
Seating Capacity: 550
Year Built: 1927
Organization Type: Performing; Resident; Educational; Sponsoring

Illinois

2902
THE ALBRIGHT THEATRE COMPANY
100 N. Island Avenue
Batavia, IL 60510
Mailing Address: P.O. Box 61, Batavia, IL 60510
Phone: 630-406-8838
e-mail: info@albrighttheatre.com
Web Site: albrighttheatre.com
Officers:
    President: Linda Brooks
    Secretary: Veronica Krystal
    Treasurer: Shelly Rolf
Mission: To encourage public interest in, and appreciation of, the dramatic arts, and to provide for interested persons a source of education and practical experience in the dramatic arts, throughout the creation, production and presentation to the public, works of dramatic merit.
Opened: 1974
Status: Nonprofit

2903
ABOUT FACE THEATRE
1222 W Wilson
Suite 2W
Chicago, IL 60640
Phone: 773-784-8565
Fax: 773-784-8557
e-mail: info@aboutfacetheatre.com
Web Site: www.aboutfacetheatre.com
Officers:
    President: William Michel,
    Vice President: Rob Abernathy,
    Treasurer: Ivan Noah Uldall
    Secretary: Drew Kent,
    Marketing Manager: Em Hall
Management:
    Associate Producers: Biz Wells

    Artistic Director: Andrew Volkoff
    MD: Corinne Neal
    Development Director: Benjamin Sprunger
    Education and Outreach Director: Ali Hoefnagel
Founded: 1995
Specialized Field: Musical; Comedy; Youth Theater; Community Theater; Contemporary
Status: Non-Profit, Professional
Paid Staff: 7
Type of Stage: Flexible Thrust Stage
Seating Capacity: 99

2905
AMERICAN THEATER COMPANY
1909 W Byron Street
Chicago, IL 60613
Phone: 773-409-4125
e-mail: info@atcweb.org
Web Site: www.atcweb.org
Officers:
    President: Macie Huwiler
    Vice President: Art Cunningham
    treasurer: David Katz,
    Secretary: Ronald Waetzman
Management:
    Artistic Director: P J Paparelli
    Executive Director: Mary Ruth Coffey
    Artistic Associate: Sandeep Das
    Artistic Fellow: Rebecca Spooner
    Casting Apprentice: Samantha Breske
Mission: American Theatre Company is an ensemble of artists commmitted to producing new and classic American stories that ask the question What does it mean to be an American?. We provide a truly intimate home for the community to experience meaningful stories. We foster a nurturing environment for artists to take risks and create essential work.
Utilizes: AEA Actors; Artists-in-Residence; Choreographers; Collaborating Artists; Collaborations; Community Members; Community Talent; Contract Actors; Designers; Educators; Equity Actors; Five Seasonal Concerts; Grant Writers; Guest Accompanists; Guest Artists; Guest Choreographers; Guest Composers; Guest Conductors; Guest Designers; Guest Directors; Guest Ensembles; Guest Instructors; Guest Lecturers; Guest Musical Directors; Guest Speakers; Multimedia; Original Music Scores; Poets; Resident Companies; Resident Professionals; Students
Founded: 1985
Specialized Field: Musical; Comedy; Classic; Contemporary
Status: Non-Profit, Professional
Paid Staff: 6
Volunteer Staff: 12
Paid Artists: 85
Non-paid Artists: 20
Budget: $800,000
Income Sources: Private Foundations; Grants; Government Grants; Individual Donations
Performs At: American Theater Company
Affiliations: Actors' Equity Association
Annual Attendance: 10,000
Type of Stage: Modified Thrust
Seating Capacity: 107
Year Remodeled: 1993
Rental Contact: Production Manager Emily Ritger

2906
AMERICAN THEATRE
1225 W Belmont
Chicago, IL 60657
Phone: 773-327-5252
Management:

THEATRE / Illinois

Co-Artistic Director: Jim Leaming
Co-Artistic Director: Kate Buddeke
Mission: Developing and producing new plays written by and for Midwesterners.
Founded: 1985
Specialized Field: New American Works; Classic; Historical
Status: Professional; Nonprofit
Paid Staff: 125
Income Sources: League of Chicago Theatres
Organization Type: Performing

2907
AUDITORIUM THEATRE OF ROOSEVELT UNIVERSITY
50 E Congress Parkway
Chicago, IL 60605
Phone: 312-922-2110
Fax: 312-431-2360
e-mail: info@auditoriumtheatre.org
Web Site: www.auditoriumtheatre.org
Officers:
  Chief Marketing/Development Officer: Judie Green
  CFO: Margaret Walsh
  Chief Marketing& Development Office: Judie Moore Green
  Chief Operating Officer& General Ma: Jennifer Turner
Management:
  Executive Director: Brett Batterson
Mission: Restoring the original architectural splendor of the Auditorium Theatre; presenting theatre, dance and music programs.
Utilizes: Singers
Founded: 1960
Specialized Field: Musical; Comedy; Educational
Status: Non-Profit, Professional
Paid Staff: 25
Paid Artists: 100
Performs At: Auditorium Theatre
Facility Category: Performing Arts Center
Type of Stage: Proecenium
Seating Capacity: 3,800
Year Built: 1884
Year Remodeled: 2003
Organization Type: Resident; Educational; Sponsoring

2908
BAILIWICK REPERTORY
6201 North Hermitage Avenue
Chicago, IL 60660
Phone: 773-969-6201
Fax: 773-883-2017
Web Site: https://bailiwickchicago.com/
Officers:
  President: Don Cortelyou
  Treasurer: Elliot Ferdland
  Secretary: Garth Person
  Board of Directors: Gary Skala
Management:
  Artistic Director: David Zak
  Producer: Rusty Hernandez
  General Manager: Jamie Axtell
Mission: To provide contemporary theater with a classical core; to produce vivid productions of the greatest dramatists of all times, alongside great works from our time; to serve as host or co-producer for other productions or attractions with similar artistic aims; to present festivals of one act plays; to showcase new directors and gay and lesbian plays.
Utilizes: Actors; AEA Actors; Artists-in-Residence; Choreographers; Dancers; Designers; Fine Artists; Five Seasonal Concerts; Guest Accompanists; Guest Artists; Guest Companies; Guest Conductors; Guest Designers; Guest Lecturers; Instructors; Local Artists; Local Unknown Artists; Multimedia; Music; Organization Contracts; Original Music Scores; Performance Artists; Playwrights; Poets; Resident Professionals; Selected Students; Sign Language Translators; Soloists; Students; Student Interns; Touring Companies; Visual Arts; Visual Designers
Founded: 1982
Specialized Field: Educational; Theater Workshops
Status: Non-Profit, Professional
Paid Staff: 5
Volunteer Staff: 200
Paid Artists: 195
Budget: $975,000
Income Sources: League of Chicago Theatres; Theatre Communications Group; Illinois Theater Association
Performs At: Bailwell Arts Center
Affiliations: League of Chicago Theatre; Theatre Communications Group
Annual Attendance: 95,000
Facility Category: Performing Arts Center
Year Built: 1995
Organization Type: Performing; Sponsoring

2909
BLACK ENSEMBLE THEATER
4450 North Clark Street
Chicago, IL 60640
Phone: 773-769-4451
Fax: 773-769-4533
e-mail: blackensemble@aol.com
Web Site: www.blackensembletheater.org
Officers:
  Founder, Producer, and Executive Dl: Jackie Taylor
Management:
  Artistic Director/Producer: Jackie Taylor
  Stage Manager: Jackie Taylor
  General Manager: Paul Kartcheske
Mission: Supplying continual employment for the Black artist; adhering to a philosophy of excellence.
Utilizes: Guest Companies
Founded: 1975
Specialized Field: Musical; Ensembles
Status: Non-Profit, Professional
Income Sources: Black Theater Alliance
Performs At: Leo Lerner Theater
Organization Type: Performing; Touring; Resident; Educational

2910
BLAIR THOMAS & CO.
3200 W. Carroll Avenue
Chicago, IL 60624
Phone: 773-722-3248
e-mail: info@blairthomas.org
Web Site: blairthomas.org
Officers:
  President: Kathleen Butera
Management:
  Artistic Director: Blair Thomas
  Development Director: Dana Horst
Mission: Creating innovative puppetry performances incorporating musical, literary and puppetry traditions to create uniquely expressive spectacle theater.
Founded: 2002
Specialized Field: Contemporary Puppet Theatre
Status: Nonprofit

2911
BLIND PARROT PRODUCTIONS
1446 W Berteau
Chicago, IL 60613
Phone: 312-549-3991
Officers:
  President: Fred Hachmeister
  Secretary: Sheri Jones
  Treasurer: Frank Tourangeau
Management:
  Executive Director: Jane Molnar
  Co-Artistic Director: David Perkins
Mission: To produce innovative, intelligent, thought-provoking writing for the stage with a focus on scripts which test the limits of theatrical form; to introduce new concepts; to pursue new relationships between artists and the audience.
Utilizes: Guest Companies
Founded: 1983
Specialized Field: Drama; Musical; Contemporary
Status: Non-Professional
Paid Staff: 20
Income Sources: League of Chicago Theatres
Organization Type: Performing

2912
BODY POLITIC THEATRE
2261 N Lincoln Avenue
Chicago, IL 60614
Phone: 773-549-5788
Fax: 773-549-2777
Officers:
  President: Richard Wier
Management:
  Artistic Director: Albert Pertalion
  Administrative Director: Kim Patrick Bitz
  Business Director: Rick Sheingold
Mission: Provides an intimate forum for the best of classic and contemporary dramatic literature through thought-provoking and entertaining productions.
Utilizes: Guest Companies
Founded: 1966
Specialized Field: New Works of Social Importance; Experimental; Drama
Status: Professional; Nonprofit
Paid Staff: 10
Income Sources: Actors' Equity Association; United Scenic Arts; League of Chicago Theatres; Theatre Communications Group; Producers Association of Chicago Area Theatres
Organization Type: Performing; Touring; Resident; Educational

2913
BROADWAY IN CHICAGO
17 North State Street, Suite 810
Chicago, IL 60602
Phone: 312-977-1700
Fax: 312-977-1740
Web Site: broadwayinchicago.com
Officers:
  President: Lou Raizin
  Vice President: Suzanne Bizer
  Vice President: Eileen LaCario
Founded: 2000
Performs At: Oriental Theatre, Cadillac Palace, Bank Of America Theatre, Broadway Playhouse
Annual Attendance: 1,700,000+
Organization Type: Commercial; Touring

THEATRE / Illinois

2914
CENTER THEATER AND THE TRAINING CENTER
1346 W Devon
Chicago, IL 60660
Phone: 773-508-0200
Fax: 773-508-9584
Management:
  Artistic Director: Dan Lamorte
  General Manager: RJ Coleman
Mission: Educating, inspiring and cultivating theatre audiences; offering actors an ongoing training program.
Utilizes: Guest Companies
Founded: 1985
Specialized Field: Educational; Theater Workshops
Status: Professional; Nonprofit
Paid Staff: 10
Income Sources: Theatre Communications Group; International Association of Theatre for Children and Youth
Performs At: Center Theater
Facility Category: Mainstage Theatre; Studio Theatre
Type of Stage: Thrust, Black Box
Seating Capacity: 60; 30
Organization Type: Performing; Touring; Resident; Educational

2915
CHICAGO ACTORS ENSEMBLE
941 W Lawrence Avenue
5Th Floor
Chicago, IL 60642
Phone: 312-275-4463
Management:
  Artistic Director: Richard Helweg
Utilizes: Guest Companies; Singers
Founded: 1984
Specialized Field: Ensemble
Status: Professional; Nonprofit
Income Sources: League of Chicago Theatres
Organization Type: Performing; Touring; Resident

2916
CHICAGO DRAMATISTS
1105 W Chicago Avenue
Chicago, IL 60622
Phone: 312-633-0630
Fax: 312-633-0840
e-mail: newplays@chicagodramatists.org
Web Site: www.chicagodramatists.org
Officers:
  Artistic Director: Russ Tutterow
  Managing Director: Brian Loevner
  Artistic Director: Russ Tutterow
  Managing Director: Brian Loevner
Mission: Chicago Dramatists is a professional, non-profit theatre, dedicated to the development and advancement of playwrights and new plays.
Utilizes: Actors; AEA Actors; Artists-in-Residence; Choreographers; Designers; Educators; Guest Companies; High School Drama; Instructors; Local Artists; Performance Artists; Poets; Resident Professionals; Student Interns; Special Technical Talent
Founded: 1979
Specialized Field: Young Playwrights; Educational
Status: Non-Profit, Professional
Paid Staff: 5
Volunteer Staff: 150
Paid Artists: 3
Budget: $250,000
Income Sources: Ticket Sales; Grant; Donations; Membership Fees; Class Fees
Performs At: Theatre
Affiliations: League of Chicago Theatre Actors' Equity Association; The Dramatists Guild; TCG
Annual Attendance: 8,000
Facility Category: Theatre
Type of Stage: Proscenium
Stage Dimensions: 24'x24'
Seating Capacity: 77
Year Built: 1884
Year Remodeled: 1998
Organization Type: Performing

2917
CHICAGO SHAKESPEARE THEATER ON NAVY PIER
800 E Grand Avenue
Navy Pier
Chicago, IL 60611
Phone: 312-595-5656
Fax: 312-595-5607
e-mail: customerservice@chicagoshakes.com
Web Site: www.chicagoshakes.com
Officers:
  Chairman: Sheli Z. Rosenberg
  Treasurer: Eric Q. Strickland
  Deputy Chair: Steven J. Solomon
  Partner: Frank D. Ballantine
  Vice Chair: Brit J. Bartter
Management:
  Executive Director: Criss Henderson
  Artistic Director: Barbara Gaines
Mission: Shakespeare offers countless paths of learning to students. Through one of the largest arts-in-education programs in the entire country, Team Shakespeare brings Shakespeare to life for middle school and secondary school students.
Founded: 1986
Specialized Field: Musical; Comedy; Classic; Contemporary
Status: Non-Profit, Professional
Paid Staff: 93
Volunteer Staff: 50
Paid Artists: 42
Performs At: Chicago Shakespeare Theater; Seven Story on Navy Pier
Annual Attendance: 200,000
Facility Category: Courtyard-style Theater
Type of Stage: Modified Thrust; Studio
Seating Capacity: 510; 175
Year Remodeled: 1999
Organization Type: Performing; Touring; Resident; Educational; Sponsoring

2918
CHILD'S PLAY TOURING THEATRE
2518 W Armitage Avenue
Chicago, IL 60647
Phone: 773-235-8911
Fax: 773-235-5478
Toll-free: 800-353-3402
e-mail: cptt@cptt.org
Web Site: www.cptt.org
Officers:
  President: Bernard Garbo
  VP: June Podagrosi
  Secretary: Eve Moran
  Treasurer: Mark Ackerman
Management:
  Executive Director and Producer: Nicole Rohr
  Founder and Executive Director: June Podagrosi
  Marketing: Karen Swatnik
Mission: Performing exclusively original literature authored by children; sharing, encouraging and validating children's creative writing; advancing children's literacy through theatre.
Utilizes: Actors; Collaborating Artists; Collaborations; Commissioned Composers; Educators; Multimedia; Music; Organization Contracts; Original Music Scores; Resident Professionals
Founded: 1978
Specialized Field: Touring Company
Status: Professional; Nonprofit
Paid Staff: 6
Volunteer Staff: 2
Paid Artists: 12
Budget: $800,000
Income Sources: Government; Foundations; Corporations; Individuals; Box Office
Performs At: Seasonal Run at the Goodman Theatre
Affiliations: Illinois Theater Association; Arts and Business Council; League of Chicago Theatres; NAPAMA; Donor's Forum of Chicago
Annual Attendance: 200,000
Facility Category: Off-site
Organization Type: Performing; Touring; Educational

2919
CITY LIT THEATER COMPANY
1020 W Bryn Mawr
Chicago, IL 60660
Phone: 773-293-3682
Fax: 773-293-3684
e-mail: info@citylit.org
Web Site: www.citylit.org
Officers:
  Assitant Marketing Coordinator: Sarah James
Management:
  Artistic Director: Terry McCabe
  Associate Artistic Director: Kristine Thatcher
  Graphic Designer: Lisa Maraldi
  Education Director: Katy Boynton
  Managing Director: Brian Pastor
Mission: City Lit Theater Company's presents both new adaptions of quality literature and extant with a literary bent.
Utilizes: Actors; Commissioned Music; Designers; Five Seasonal Concerts; Guest Accompanists; Guest Companies; Guest Conductors; Guest Designers; Guest Instructors; High School Drama; Instructors; Local Artists; Multimedia; Original Music Scores; Performance Artists; Resident Artists; Resident Professionals; Theatre Companies
Founded: 1979
Specialized Field: Drama; Musical; Historical; Educational
Status: Non-Profit, Professional
Paid Staff: 1
Volunteer Staff: 5
Paid Artists: 35
Type of Stage: Thrust
Stage Dimensions: 16x25
Organization Type: Performing; Touring; Resident; Educational

2920
CLASSICS ON STAGE!
PO Box 25365
Chicago, IL 60625
Phone: 773-989-0532
e-mail: classstage@aol.com
Web Site: www.classicsonstage.com
Management:
  Managing Director: Robert D Boburka
  Artistic Director: Michele L Vacca
Mission: Developing future audiences for legitimate theatre through presentations of live professional theatre.
Utilizes: Singers
Founded: 1976

THEATRE / Illinois

Specialized Field: Musical; Classic
Status: Professional; Commercial
Income Sources: Actors' Equity Association; Association of American Theatre for Youth; League of Chicago Theatres
Organization Type: Performing; Resident; Educational

2921
CONGO SQUARE THEATRE COMPANY
2936 N. Southport Avenue
Chicago, IL 60657
Phone: 773-296-1108
Web Site: congosquaretheatre.org
Management:
    Artistic Director: Samuel Roberson
    Executive Director: TaRon Patton
Mission: Congo Square Theatre Company is an ensemble dedicated to artistic excellence. By producing definitive and transformative theatre, spawned from the African Diaspora as well as other world cultures, Congo Square Theatre Company seeks to establish itself as an institution of multicultural theatre.
Founded: 1999

2922
CORN PRODUCTIONS AT CONSERVATORY
4210 N. Lincoln Avenue
Chicago, IL 60618
Phone: 773-650-1331
e-mail: cornproductions@sbcglobal.net
Web Site: cornservatory.org
Management:
    Artistic Director: Robert Bouwman
Opened: 1992
Specialized Field: Comedy

2923
COURT THEATRE
5535 S Ellis Avenue
Chicago, IL 60637
Phone: 773-702-7005
Fax: 773-834-1897
e-mail: info@courttheatre.org
Web Site: www.courttheater.org
Officers:
    Chairman: Marilyn Fatt Vitale
    Vice Chair: Linda Patton
    Secretary: Joan Coppleson
    Treasurer: Michael McGarry
    Trustee: Mary Anton
Management:
    Executive Director: Stephen Albert
    Artistic Director: Charles Newell
    Resident Artist: Ron OJ Parson
    Resident Dramaturg: Drew Dir
Mission: To celebrate the immutable power and relevance of classic theatre.
Utilizes: Guest Companies; Singers
Founded: 1954
Specialized Field: Classic
Status: Non-Profit, Professional
Paid Staff: 18
Income Sources: Actors' Equity Association; League of Chicago Theatres; Theatre Communications Group; Producers Association of Chicago Area Theatres
Performs At: Court Theatre
Seating Capacity: 250
Organization Type: Performing; Educational

2924
DEPAUL UNIVERSITY MERLE RESKIN THEATRE
60 E Balbo Drive
Chicago, IL 60605
Phone: 312-922-1999
Fax: 773-325-7967
e-mail: jcurns@depaul.edu
Web Site: http://theatreschool.depaul.edu/about_places.php
Management:
    Dean: John Culbert
Utilizes: Soloists
Specialized Field: Educational; Theater Workshops; Children's Theater
Status: Non-Profit, Non-Professional
Facility Category: Proscenium Theatre
Seating Capacity: 1325
Year Built: 1910
Rental Contact: Leslie Shook (773-325-7965)

2925
DREAM THEATRE COMPANY
5026 N. Lincoln Avenue
Chicago, IL 60625
Phone: 773-552-8616
e-mail: annainthedarkness@gmail.com
Web Site: dreamtheatrecompany.com
Officers:
    President: Jeremy Menekseoglu
Management:
    Artistic Director: Jeremy Menekseoglu
    Managing Director: Anna W. Menekseoglu
Mission: Dream Theatre is dedicated to: Produce all original work; shatter the barrier between actor and audience; focus on the development of the actor as an artist; leave no member of the audience to feel as a mere spectator, but to be at the very center of the play; deliver the highest art possible in its most raw, unflinching and entertaining form.
Founded: 1998
Specialized Field: Original Work; Psychological; Thought Provoking
Status: Nonprofit Public Charity Organization

2926
DREISKE PERFORMANCE COMPANY
1517 W Fullerton Avenue
Chicago, IL 60614
Phone: 312-281-9075
Officers:
    Chairman: David Edelberg
    Secretary: Emilye Hunterfields
Management:
    Artistic Director: Nicole Dreiske
    Managing Director: Milos Stehlik
    Literary Manager: Catherine Berkenstein
    General Manager: John Dreiske
Mission: Professional touring ensemble, many of whose productions were developed in historic and on-location projects; The Book of Lear in the Sahara Desert, Macondo in Columbia, South America; currently developing new theater works for performance for international TV and tours.
Utilizes: Guest Companies; Singers
Founded: 1975
Specialized Field: Ensembles; Drama
Status: Professional; Nonprofit
Income Sources: Association for Theatre in Higher Education; International Theatre Institute; League of Chicago Theatres
Performs At: International Performance Studio

Organization Type: Performing; Touring; Resident; Educational

2927
ECLIPSE THEATRE COMPANY
4001 N. Ravenswood Avenue, Suite 602-B
Chicago, IL 60613
Phone: 773-728-2216
e-mail: info@eclipsetheatre.com
Web Site: eclipsetheatre.com
Officers:
    President: Laraine Spector
    Vice President: Bronwyn McDaniel
    Treasurer: Marcus Turnbo
Mission: Eclipse Theatre Company presents the work of one playwright each season. We offer the audience an opportunity, unique in the midwest, to journey with us through the playwright's works. Join us in exploring the breadth and depth of a playwright's artistic worlds. One playwright, one season, one illuminating journey.
Founded: 1992
Performs At: Athenaeum Theatre

2928
ENSEMBLE ESPANOL SPANISH DANCE THEATER
5500 N Saint Louis Avenue
Chicago, IL 60625
Phone: 773-583-4050
Fax: 773-794-5314
e-mail: ensemble-espanol@neiu.edu
Web Site: www.neiu.edu/~eespanol
Officers:
    President: Dr. Angelina Pedroso
    VP: Lou Altman
    Treasurer: Elba Maisonet
    Secretary: Lillian Heminover
Management:
    Director: Libby Komaiko
Mission: The Ensemble Espanol Spanish Dance Theater is chartered to share the rich traditions of Spanish dance, music, art and literature with all of our communities as the Spanish Dance Center in the United States.
Utilizes: Guest Companies
Founded: 1976
Specialized Field: Spanish Language Company; Musical; Educational; Ethnic Theater
Status: Professional; Nonprofit
Paid Staff: 4
Volunteer Staff: 2
Paid Artists: 30
Non-paid Artists: 31
Budget: $400,000
Income Sources: Foundations; Corporations; Government; Private Donations
Annual Attendance: 90,000
Facility Category: Auditorium; Dance Studios
Type of Stage: Proscenium
Stage Dimensions: 25x25
Seating Capacity: 650
Year Built: 1975
Year Remodeled: 2000
Organization Type: Performing; Touring; Resident; Educational; Sponsoring

2929
ETA CREATIVE ARTS FOUNDATION
7558 S Chicago Avenue
Chicago, IL 60619
Phone: 773-752-3955
Fax: 773-752-8727
e-mail: email@etacreativearts.org
Web Site: www.etacreativearts.org

Officers:
- Chairman: Milton Davis
- President: Abena Joan Brown
- Secretary/Treasurer: Velma Wilson
- Finance: Wiley Moore

Management:
- President: Abena Joan P Brown
- Artistic Director: Runako Jahi
- Technical Director: Darryl Goodman

Mission: ETA provides training in the performing and technical aspects of the arts, encouraging the development and employment primarily of Black artists. ETA also works to encourage the development and propagation of the works of Black writers through its productions of original works.
Utilizes: Guest Companies
Founded: 1971
Specialized Field: Multi-Cultural
Status: Non-Profit, Professional
Paid Staff: 6
Volunteer Staff: 50
Paid Artists: 8
Budget: $1.6 million
Income Sources: Earned Funds; Corporate; Individuals
Performs At: ETA Square
Seating Capacity: 200
Organization Type: Performing; Touring; Resident; Educational

2930
FAMOUS DOOR THEATRE
Famous Door Theatre
Box 57029
Chicago, IL 60657
Phone: 773-404-8283
Fax: 773-404-8292
Web Site: www.famousdoortheatre.org

Officers:
- Chair: Dan Rivkin
- Vice-Chair: Don Copper
- Secretary: Leo Aubel
- Treasurer: Jeff Anderle

Management:
- Co-Chairs: Ms Dara Altshu
- General Manager: Hanna Dworkin
- Artistic Director: Marc Grapey
- Managing Director: Dan Rivkin

Founded: 1987
Specialized Field: Drama; Musical; Classic; Contemporary
Paid Staff: 5
Volunteer Staff: 25
Paid Artists: 100
Non-paid Artists: 20
Budget: $500,000
Performs At: Victory Gardens Theatre
Affiliations: AEA; SSDC; TCG
Annual Attendance: 15,000
Type of Stage: Thrust
Seating Capacity: 200

2931
FILAMENT THEATRE
4041 N. Milwaukee Avenue
Chicago, IL 60641
Phone: 773-270-1660
e-mail: info@filamenttheatre.org
Web Site: filamenttheatre.org

Management:
- Artistic Director: Julie Ritchey
- Managing Director: Christian Libonati
- Marketing Director: Peter Oyloe
- Program Director: Jackie Intres

Mission: The Filament Theatre Ensemble creates theatre in a folk tradition, emphasizing community, imagination, and sustainability.
Founded: 2007
Specialized Field: Drama; Comedy
Status: Nonprofit

2932
FREE STREET PROGRAMS
1419 W Blackhawk
Chicago, IL 60622
Phone: 773-772-7248
Fax: 773-772-7248
e-mail: mica@reestreet.org
Web Site: www.freestreet.org

Officers:
- Executive Director: Mica Cole
- President: Jean de St. Aubin
- Secretary: Gina Anselmo
- Treasurer: Deepa Paul
- Press Office: Brooke Collins

Management:
- Associate Artistic Director: Gio Gonzalez
- Artistic Director: Coya Paz
- Managing Director: Rodney Terwilliger
- Creative Director: Anita Evans
- Artistic Associate: Gio Gonzalez

Mission: Free Street Programs is an arts outreach organization that uses the performing arts to enhance the literacy, self-esteem, creativity and employability of populations consistently excluded from mainstream cultural programming.
Founded: 1969
Specialized Field: Youth Theater; Community Theater; Contemporary
Status: Non-Profit, Professional
Paid Staff: 12
Paid Artists: 90
Income Sources: Theatre Communications Group; Illinois Arts Alliance
Performs At: Free Street Teen Street Theater
Organization Type: Performing; Touring

2933
GOODMAN THEATRE
170 N Dearborn Street
Chicago, IL 60601
Phone: 312-443-3800
Fax: 312-443-3800
Web Site: www.goodmantheatre.org/

Management:
- President: Roche Schuler
- Artistic Director: Robert Falls
- Associate Artistic Director: Steve Scott

Mission: To present the classics of our theatre heritage with freshness and new vision; to create an audience that reflects the diversity of the Chicago community; to showcase the finest local, national, and international artists; to provide its staff and artists with the best working conditions possible; to operate with fiscal responsibility.
Utilizes: Guest Companies; Singers
Founded: 1925
Specialized Field: Musical; Comedy; Youth Theater; Ethnic Theater; Puppet; Classic; Contemporary
Status: Non-Profit, Professional
Paid Staff: 100
Budget: $12 million
Income Sources: Foundation; Corporate & Individual Contributions; Ticket Revenue
Performs At: Albert Iva Goodman, Owen Bruner Goodman Theater
Affiliations: TCG, Illinois Arts Alliance, League of Resident Theaters, American Arts Alliance, League of Chicago Theaters, Illinois Theater Association
Annual Attendance: 214,016
Type of Stage: Proscenium, Flexible Courtyard
Seating Capacity: 850 Albert, 345-467 Owen
Year Built: 2000
Organization Type: Performing; Educational; Sponsoring

2934
GRIFFIN THEATRE COMPANY
3711 North Ravenswood Avenue Suite 145
Chicago, IL 60613
Phone: 773-769-2228
e-mail: bill.massolia@rcn.com
Web Site: griffintheatre.com

Officers:
- Chair: Claire Conley

Management:
- Artistic Director: William Massolia
- Artistic Director: Richard Barletta

Mission: The mission of the Griffin Theatre Company is to create extraordinary and meaningful theatrical experiences for both children and adults by building bridges of understanding between generations that instill in its audience an appreciation of the performing arts. Through artistic collaboration the Griffin Theatre Company produces literary adaptations, original work and classic plays that challenge and inspire with wit, style, and compassion.
Founded: 1988
Status: Professional Nonprofit
Organization Type: Performing; Touring

2935
IMAGINATION THEATER
4802 N. Broadway
#201-B
Chicago, IL 60640
Phone: 773-303-0070
Fax: 773-303-0073
e-mail: info@imaginationtheater.org

Management:
- Artistic Director: Warren W Baumgart, Jr

Mission: Committed to the value of creative drama as a tool for learning through two basic programs: participatory theater for children, the elderly, and the disabled; and Child Sexual Abuse Prevention Program, a comprehensive program for teachers, parents and students.
Founded: 1966
Specialized Field: Touring Company; Improvisation
Status: Professional; Nonprofit
Organization Type: Performing; Touring; Educational

2936
JACKALOPE THEATRE COMPANY
5857 N. Kenmore Ave, Suite #3
Chicago, IL 60660
Phone: 773-340-2543
e-mail: jackalope@jackalopetheatre.org
Web Site: jackalopetheatre.org

Management:
- Artistic Director: AJ Ware
- Managing Director: Nate Silver
- Associate Artistic Director: Kaiser Ahmed

Mission: Cultivating theatre that manifests the adventure deeply rooted in the American mythos.
Founded: 2008
Specialized Field: Theatre Americana
Status: Nonprofit

THEATRE / Illinois

2937
LIFELINE THEATRE
6912 N Glenwood
Chicago, IL 60626
Phone: 773-761-4477
Fax: 773-761-4582
e-mail: info@lifelinetheatre.com
Web Site: www.lifelinetheatre.com

Officers:
- **Artistic Director:** Dorothy Milne
- **Managing Director:** Allison Cain
- **Marketing Director & Casting Direct:** Robert Kauzlaric

Management:
- **Artistic Director:** Dorothy Milne
- **Managing Director:** Melissa Bareford

Mission: Lifeline Theatre entertains, educates and empowers our community using an ensemble driven process to bring literature and new works to life.
Utilizes: Actors; Choreographers; Collaborating Artists; Commissioned Composers; Commissioned Music; Educators; Guest Companies; Guest Conductors; Guest Designers; Guest Lecturers; Local Artists; Music; Organization Contracts; Original Music Scores; Resident Professionals; Sign Language Translators; Soloists
Founded: 1982
Specialized Field: Drama; Classic
Status: Non-Profit, Professional
Paid Staff: 7
Volunteer Staff: 1
Budget: $500,000
Income Sources: League of Chicago Theatres, Contributes, Earned
Performs At: Lifeline Theatre
Affiliations: TGG, League of Chicago Theatres, AATE, PACT
Annual Attendance: 20,000
Facility Category: Theatre
Type of Stage: Flexible
Seating Capacity: 100
Year Built: 1930
Year Remodeled: 1992
Rental Contact: John Hildreth
Organization Type: Performing

2938
LIVE BAIT THEATRICAL COMPANY
3914 N Clark Street
Chicago, IL 60613
Phone: 773-871-1212
Fax: 773-871-3191
e-mail: sharon@livebaittheater.org
Web Site: www.livebaittheater.org

Officers:
- **Executive Director:** John Ragir
- **Artistic Director:** Sharon Evans

Management:
- **President:** Donna Benneth
- **Executive Director:** John Ragir
- **Artistic Director:** Sharon Evans

Mission: We produce all new, orginal works by Chicago area playwrights and solo performers.
Founded: 1987
Specialized Field: Musical; Comedy; Puppet; Contemporary; Drama
Status: Non-Profit, Professional
Paid Staff: 4
Performs At: Live Bait Theater
Type of Stage: Black Box
Seating Capacity: 70

2939
LOOKINGGLASS THEATRE COMPANY
821 North Michigan Avenue
Chicago, IL 60611
Phone: 312-337-0655
Fax: 773-477-6932
Web Site: www.lookingglasstheatre.org

Officers:
- **Chairman:** Lisa Green
- **President:** Alex Miller
- **VP/Managing Director:** Joseph Brady
- **Secretary:** Edward Filer
- **Executive Director:** Rachel Kraft
- **Artistic Director:** Andrew White

Management:
- **Executive Director:** Rachel Kraft
- **Artistic Director:** Andrew White
- **General Manager:** Michele Anderson

Founded: 1989
Specialized Field: Youth Theater; Classic; Contemporary
Status: Non-Profit, Professional
Paid Staff: 20
Paid Artists: 10

2940
LOYOLA UNIVERSITY DEPARTMENT OF THEATRE
1032 W. Sheridan Rd.,
Chicago, IL 60626
Phone: 773-274-3000
Fax: 773-508-8748
e-mail: theatre-info@luc.edu
Web Site: www.luc.edu/depts/theatre

Officers:
- **Chairman:** Robert M. Beaver
- **President:** William A. Brandt
- **Executive Vp:** John J. Hartman
- **CEO:** Patrick J. Kelly
- **Architect:** Marvin Herman

Management:
- **Chair Person:** Sarah Gabel
- **Managing Director:** April Browning

Founded: 1960
Specialized Field: Educational; Theater Workshops
Status: Non-Profit, Non-Professional
Paid Staff: 3
Paid Artists: 8
Performs At: Kathleen Mullady Theatre

2941
MAYFAIR THEATRE/SHEAR MADNESS
636 S Michigan Avenue
Chicago, IL 60605
Phone: 312-786-9120

Management:
- **Company Manager:** Roger Gordon
- **Producer:** Marilyn Abrams
- **Managing Director:** Bruce Jordan

Mission: Mayfair Theatre presents 'Shear Madness,' the comedy whodunit that lets the audience play armchair detective. 'Shear Madness' is the longest running play in the history of Chicago theatre.
Founded: 1982
Specialized Field: Drama; Contemporary; Experimental
Status: Professional; Commercial
Income Sources: League of Chicago Theatres
Performs At: Mayfair Theatre
Organization Type: Performing

2942
PEGASUS PLAYERS
Truman College
1145 W Wilson
Chicago, IL 60640
Mailing Address: 1145 West Wilson Ave
Phone: 773-878-9761
Fax: 773-271-8057
e-mail: info@pegasusplayers.org
Web Site: www.pegasusplayers.org

Management:
- **Producing Director:** Ilesa Duncan

Mission: To produce the highest quality artistic work and to provide exemplary theatre, entertainment, and arts education at no charge to people who have little or no access to the arts.
Utilizes: Guest Companies; Singers
Founded: 1979
Specialized Field: Classic; Drama
Status: Professional; Nonprofit
Income Sources: League of Chicago Theatres
Performs At: O'Rourke Center
Organization Type: Performing

2943
PERFORMING ARTS CHICAGO
410 S Michigan Avenue
#911
Chicago, IL 60605
Phone: 312-663-1628
Fax: 312-663-1043
Web Site: www.pachicago.org

Officers:
- **President:** Judys Neisser
- **Executive Director:** Susan Lipman
- **Director:** Christy Uchida

Management:
- **Executive Director:** Susan Lipman
- **Director Marketing/Public Relations:** Heidi Feldman

Mission: To present artists who explore the creative tension between tradition and innovation, to nurture an environment for and bring to performance new works and new performers, and to remain accountable to its community, furthering support for local artists, engagement and education, not only for its direct audience, but for society at large.
Utilizes: Special Technical Talent
Founded: 1960
Specialized Field: New Plays; Experimental; Improvisation; Drama; Musical
Status: Non-Profit, Professional
Paid Staff: 6
Budget: $1,000,000
Performs At: The Civic Theater
Organization Type: Performing; Resident; Educational; Sponsoring

2944
RAVEN THEATRE COMPANY
6157 N Clark
Chicago, IL 60660
Mailing Address: 2549 W Fargo Chicago, IL 60645
Phone: 773-338-2177
Fax: 773-508-9794
e-mail: info@raventheatre.com
Web Site: www.raventheatre.com

Officers:
- **President:** Carol Zsolnay
- **Vice President:** Richard Jamerson
- **Treasurer:** Allan Price
- **Secretary:** Susan Rozendaal
- **Producing Artistic Director:** Michael Menendian

THEATRE / Illinois

Co-Artistic Director: JoAnn Montemurro
Management:
　Producing Artistic Director: Michael Menendian
　Co-Artistic Director: JoAnn Montemurro
　Education Director: Mechelle Moe
　Executive Director: Kelli Strickland
　Publicist: Christa van Baale
Mission: To provide professional theatre affordable and accessible to the broadest cross-section of the people of Chicagoland and to provide the opportunity for local theatre artists to develop a showcase for their talents.
Utilizes: Guest Companies; Singers
Founded: 1983
Specialized Field: Youth Theater; Contemporary
Status: Non-Profit, Non-Professional
Paid Staff: 3
Paid Artists: 10
Income Sources: League of Chicago Theatres
Organization Type: Performing; Resident

2945
REMY BUMPPO THEATRE COMPANY
3717 N. Ravenswood Avenue
Chicago, IL 60614
Phone: 773-404-7336
Fax: 773-296-9243
e-mail: info@remybumppo.org
Web Site: remybumppo.org
Officers:
　President: Genevieve Daniels
　Vice President: Brenda Schnede Grusecki
Management:
　Producing Artistic Director: Nick Sandys
　General Manger: Amy Schultz
Founded: 1996

2946
SAINT SEBASTIAN PLAYERS
St Bonaventure
1625 W Diversey Parkway
Chicago, IL 60614
Mailing Address: 1641 W Diversey Parkway, Chicago IL 60614
Phone: 773-404-7922
Fax: 312-728-0496
e-mail: info@saintsebastianplayers.org
Web Site: www.saintsebastianplayers.org
Officers:
　President: Jonathan Hagloch
　Secretary: Jill Chuckerman
　Treasurer: Jim Masini
Management:
　Public Relations Director: Jill Cluckerman
Mission: To present comedies, dramas, musicals, mysteries and other theatrical events to the Chicago community.
Utilizes: Singers
Founded: 1981
Specialized Field: Classic; Ensembles
Status: Nonprofit
Paid Staff: 7
Income Sources: Ticket Revenue; Concessions Revenue; Playbill Ad Revenue; Donations
Performs At: Saint Bonaventure Parish
Annual Attendance: 1,200-1,500
Type of Stage: Flexible Proscenium
Seating Capacity: 70-100
Organization Type: Performing

2947
SEANACHAI THEATRE COMPANY
4626 North Knox Avenue
Chicago, IL 60630
Phone: 773-878-3727
Fax: 847-729-8274
e-mail: info@seanachai.org
Web Site: www.seanachai.org/
Management:
　Artistic Director: Ira Amyx
　Company Member: Jeff Duhigg
　Company Member: Barbara Figgins
　Company Member: Jeri Frederickson
Specialized Field: Ensembles; Drama; Comedy

2948
SECOND CITY
1616 N Wells Street
Chicago, IL 60614
Phone: 312-664-4032
Fax: 312-664-9837
Toll-free: 877-778-4707
e-mail: aalexander@secondcity.com
Web Site: www.secondcity.com
Officers:
　Executive Producer/CEO: Andrew Alexander
　CEO & Co-Owner: Andrew Alexander
Management:
　President: Andrew Alexander
　Managing Director: Jenna Aotoveoli
　Producer: Kelly Leonard
Mission: Satirical Revue.
Founded: 1959
Specialized Field: Comedy
Status: For-Profit, Professional
Paid Staff: 100
Paid Artists: 50
Performs At: Second City Mainstatge; Second City, Ect.
Type of Stage: Proscenium
Seating Capacity: 350; 180
Organization Type: Performing; Touring; Resident; Educational

2949
SHATTERED GLOBE THEATER
4001 N Ravenswood
Chicago, IL 60613
Phone: 773-770-0333
Fax: 773-404-1237
e-mail: shatteredglobetheater@gmail.com
Web Site: http://www.shatteredglobe.org/index.html
Officers:
　President: Brian Pudil
　VP: Joe Forbrich
　Secretary: Leigh Horsley
　Treasurer: Linda Reiter
Management:
　Artistic Director: Roger Smart
Mission: The foundation of the Shattered Globe is a core of actors, directors, playwrights, designers and teachers working together as the result of having received similar training in the Sanford Meisner technique.
Utilizes: Guest Companies; New Productions; Singers
Founded: 1990
Specialized Field: Contemporary
Status: Semi-Professional; Commercial
Paid Staff: 15
Income Sources: League of Chicago Theatres
Performs At: Chicago Actors Project
Organization Type: Performing; Resident; Educational

2950
STAGE LEFT THEATRE
3408 N Sheffield
Chicago, IL 60657
Phone: 773-883-8830
Fax: 773-472-1336
e-mail: vance@stagelefttheatre.com
Web Site: www.stagelefttheatre.com
Officers:
　President: Jay Tarshis
　Treasurer: Wendy Istvanick
　Secretary: Dr Alice Martin
Management:
　Co-Artistic Director: Jessi D Hill
　Artistic Director: Kevin Heckman
　Development Director: Jacki Singleton
　Company Manager: Leigh Barrett
　business manager: Greg Werstler
　company manager: Kate Black
Mission: Producing plays that raise awareness of social and political issues.
Utilizes: Actors; Artists-in-Residence; Choreographers; Collaborating Artists; Collaborations; Designers; Five Seasonal Concerts; Guest Accompanists; Guest Choreographers; Guest Companies; Guest Conductors; Guest Designers; Guest Musical Directors; Guest Teachers; Instructors; Local Artists; Performance Artists; Poets; Resident Artists; Resident Professionals; Selected Students; Sign Language Translators; Student Interns; Special Technical Talent; Visual Arts
Founded: 1982
Specialized Field: Contemporary
Status: Non-Profit, Professional
Paid Staff: 2
Volunteer Staff: 19
Paid Artists: 20
Income Sources: League of Chicago Theatres
Facility Category: Storefront
Type of Stage: Black Box
Seating Capacity: 50
Organization Type: Performing; Touring; Educational

2951
STEEP THEATRE COMPANY
1115 W. Berwyn Avenue
Chicago, IL 60640
Phone: 866-811-4111
e-mail: steeptheatre@gmail.com
Web Site: steeptheatre.com
Management:
　Artistic Director: Peter Moore
　Business Manager: Katie Piatt-Eckert
　Managing Director: Julia Siple
Mission: We bring out the everyday truth in the stories we tell through ensemble work.
Status: Nonprofit

2952
STEPPENWOLF THEATRE COMPANY
1650 N Halsted Street
Chicago, IL 60614
Phone: 312-335-1650
Fax: 312-335-0440
e-mail: customerservice@steppenwolf.org
Web Site: www.steppenwolf.org
Officers:
　MD: David M. Schmitz
　IT Director: Scott Macoun
　Company Manager: Erin Cook
　Finance Coordinator: Brian Hurst
　Finance Specialist: Jackie Snuttjer
Management:
　Executive Director: David Hawkanson
　Artistic Director: Martha Lavey
　Associate Artistic Director: Erica Daniels
　Director of New Play Development: Aaron Carter
　Producing Assistant: Greta Honold
Mission: Committed to an ensemble approach.

THEATRE / Illinois

Utilizes: Guest Companies; Scenic Designers; Singers; Students
Founded: 1976
Specialized Field: Ensemble
Status: Non-Profit, Professional
Paid Staff: 60
Income Sources: Theatre Communications Group; Actors' Equity Association; Producers Association of Chicago Theatres
Performs At: Steppenwolf Theater
Type of Stage: Removable Thrust
Seating Capacity: 510
Organization Type: Performing; Resident; Educational

2953
STRAWDOG THEATRE COMPANY
3829 N Broadway
Chicago, IL 60613
Phone: 773-528-9696
Fax: 773-528-7238
Web Site: www.strawdog.org
Officers:
  Board Member: Gregory Altman
  Board Member: Meaghan Clayton
  Board Member: Jim Hobart
  Board Member: Jack Rubin
  Board Member: Mark D. Warner
Management:
  Marketing Manager: Juile Stanton
  Press Public Relation: Shanon Hoag
  Artistic Director: Hank Boland
  GM: Mike Mroch
  Board Member: Thomas V. Linguanti
Mission: To inspire and provoke through ensemble based theatrical works.
Founded: 1988
Specialized Field: Staged Readings; Drama
Status: Non-Profit, Professional
Volunteer Staff: 15
Paid Artists: 15
Non-paid Artists: 15

2954
THE RISING STARS THEATRE COMPANY
5900 W. Belmont Avenue
Chicago, IL 60634
Mailing Address: P.O. Box 34197, Chicago, IL 60634
Phone: 773-736-2490
e-mail: info@risingstarschicago.com
Web Site: risingstarschicago.com
Management:
  Director: Staci Singer Kelley
Founded: 1979
Status: Nonprofit
Performs At: The Stahl Family Theatre

2955
THEATRE BUILDING CHICAGO
Performance Community
1225 W Belmont
Chicago, IL 60657
Phone: 773-929-7367
Fax: 312-327-1404
Web Site: www.theatrebuildingchicago.org
Management:
  Executive Director: Joan Mazzonelli
  Artistic Director: John Sparks
  Managing Director: Alan Chambers
Mission: To give exposure to new musicals; to support emerging artists in our Chicago area.
Founded: 1977
Specialized Field: Multi-Media; Musical
Status: Non-Profit, Professional
Paid Staff: 7

Income Sources: League of Chicago Theatres; Theatre Communications Group; National Alliance of Theatre Producers
Performs At: New Tuners Theatre Building
Organization Type: Performing; Resident

2956
THEATRE FIRST
6656 Sioux Avenue
Chicago, IL 60646
Phone: 773-792-2226
Management:
  Executive Producer: Joanne Notz
  Business Manager: William Mages
Utilizes: Guest Artists
Founded: 1952
Specialized Field: Contemporary
Status: Non-Professional
Income Sources: League of Chicago Theatres
Performs At: Athenaeum Theatre
Organization Type: Performing

2957
THEATRE II COMPANY
3700 W 103Rd Street
Chicago, IL 60655
Phone: 773-298-3000
Management:
  Artistic Director: Steve Micotto
  Managing Director: Joanne Fleming
Mission: Providing the Southwest Chicago community with quality live theater.
Utilizes: Singers
Founded: 1978
Specialized Field: Ensembles; Contemporary
Status: Professional; Nonprofit
Income Sources: League of Chicago Theatres; Saint Xavier University
Performs At: McGuire Hall
Organization Type: Performing

2958
TIMELINE THEATRE COMPANY
615 W Wellington Avenue
Chicago, IL 60657
Phone: 773-281-8463
Fax: 773-281-1134
e-mail: info@timelinetheatre.com
Web Site: www.timelinetheatre.com
Officers:
  President: Cindy Giacchetti
  Vice President: Nadim A. Kazi
  Treasurer: Katherine Feucht
  Secretary: Rick Gray
  MD: Elizabeth K. Auman
Management:
  Artistic Director: PJ Powers
  Managing Director: Elizabeth K. Auman
  Associate Artistic Director: Nick Bowling
  Director of Marketing: Lara Goestch
  Development Manager: Lydia P. Swift
Mission: To present plays inspired by history that connect with today's social and political issues.
Founded: 1997
Specialized Field: New Works of Social Importance

2959
VICTORY GARDENS THEATER AT THE BIOGRAPH
2243 N Lincoln Avenue
Chicago, IL 60614
Phone: 773-871-3000
e-mail: information,@victorygardens.org
Web Site: www.victorygardens.org

Officers:
  Artistic Director: Chay Yew
  Executive Director: Jan Kallish
  Director of New Play Development: Geoffrey Jackson Scott
Management:
  Managing Director: Marcelle McVay
  Artistic Director: Dennis Zacek
Mission: Developing Chicago theatre artists, particularly playwrights.
Utilizes: Actors; AEA Actors; Designers; Educators; Five Seasonal Concerts; Guest Companies; Guest Conductors; Guest Designers; High School Drama; Instructors; Local Artists; Multimedia; Original Music Scores; Performance Artists; Poets; Resident Professionals; Selected Students; Singers; Soloists; Student Interns; Special Technical Talent
Founded: 1974
Specialized Field: Musical; Comedy; Ethnic Theater; Contemporary
Status: Non-Profit, Professional
Paid Staff: 14
Paid Artists: 3
Budget: $1.6 million
Performs At: Block Box
Annual Attendance: 60,000+
Type of Stage: Black Box
Seating Capacity: 195
Rental Contact: Elizabeth Auman
Organization Type: Performing; Touring; Resident; Educational

2960
WOMEN'S THEATRE ALLIANCE
2936 N Southport
Suite 1775
Chicago, IL 60657
e-mail: wtachicago@gmail.com
Web Site: http://www.wtachicago.org/1401.html
Officers:
  President: Sara Kelly
  Vice President: Cheri L. McGuire
  Treasurer: Scott Dray
  Members at Large: Brenda E. Kelly
  Members at Large: Katie Carey Louden
Management:
  President: Sara Kelly
  Vice President: Katie Carey
  Treasurer/Secretary: Scott Dray
Specialized Field: Ensembles; Theater Workshops; Specialty Acts

2961
BIG NOISE THEATRE COMPANY
515 E. Thacker Street
Des Plaines, IL 60026
Mailing Address: Marsha Rutenberg, 1895 Clavey Road, Highland Park, IL 60035
Phone: 847-604-0275
e-mail: info@bignoisetheatre.org
Web Site: bignoise.org
Officers:
  President: Jon Cunningham
  Vice President: Michelle Cunningham
Management:
  Artistic Director: Nancy Flaster
Mission: To produce high-quality shows that stretch the creative talents of our actors and staff and surpass the expectations of our audience.
Status: Nonprofit
Performs At: Prairie Lake Community Center Theater

2962
DES PLAINES THEATRE GUILD
620 Lee Street
Des Plaines, IL 60016
Phone: 708-296-1211
Mission: Offering Northwest Suburban Chicago professional level community theatre for the education and entertainment of audiences.
Utilizes: Guest Companies
Founded: 1946
Specialized Field: Community Theater
Status: Non-Professional; Nonprofit
Performs At: Prairie Lake Community Center
Organization Type: Performing

2963
UNIVERSITY THEATRE: SUMMER SHOW BIZ
Southern Illinois University
Campus Box 1777
Katherine Dunham Hall 1031
Edwardsville, IL 62026-1777
Phone: 618-650-2773
Fax: 618-650-3716
Toll-free: 888-328-5168
e-mail: dbrown@siue.edu
Web Site: www.siue.edu/theater
  Dance Director: C Otis Sweezey
  Director Design and Technical: James Dorethy
Founded: 1975
Specialized Field: Musical; Comedy; Youth Theater; Dinner Theater; Ethnic Theater; Community Theater; Puppet; Classic; Contemporary
Status: Non-Profit, Professional
Paid Staff: 1
Paid Artists: 19
Season: June - July
Type of Stage: Proscenium
Stage Dimensions: 50' x 30'
Seating Capacity: 360

2964
NEXT THEATRE COMPANY
927 Noyes Street
Evanston, IL 60201
Phone: 847-475-1875
Fax: 847-475-6767
e-mail: info@nexttheatre.org
Web Site: www.nexttheatre.org
Officers:
  President: Judy Kemp
  Secretary: Ann Zastrow
  Treasurer: Jeff Enrich
Management:
  Artistic Director: Jennifer Avery
  Producing Director: Jim Davis
  Production Manager: Patrick Fries
Mission: We believe theatre promotes awareness and provokes change with more power than any other form of expression, and we are devoted to producing socially provocative artistically challenging entertainment.
Utilizes: Guest Companies; Singers
Founded: 1981
Specialized Field: Comedy; Puppet; Classic; Contemporary
Status: Non-Profit, Professional
Paid Staff: 5
Paid Artists: 50
Budget: $600,000
Income Sources: Actors' Equity Association; Theatre Communications Group; League of Chicago Theatres; Producers Association of Chicago Area Theatres
Performs At: Noyes Cultural Arts Center Theatre

Annual Attendance: 15,000
Type of Stage: Proscenium
Stage Dimensions: 24' x 33'
Seating Capacity: 167
Organization Type: Performing; Resident

2965
NORTHWESTERN UNIVERSITY THEATRE AND INTERPRETATION CENTER
2240 Campus Drive
Evanston, IL 60208
Phone: 847-491-7282
Fax: 847-467-7135
Web Site: www.communication.northwestern.edu/tic/
Officers:
  MD: Diane Claussen
  Financial Assistant: Eunice WoodS
  Program Assistant: Denise McGillicuddy
Management:
  Managing Director: Claudia Kunin
  Artistic Director: David H. Bell
  Music Director: Ryan T. Nelson
Specialized Field: Musical; Comedy; Youth Theater; Ethnic Theater; Community Theater; Puppet; Classic; Contemporary
Status: Non-Profit, Non-Professional
Paid Staff: 20

2966
ORGANIC THEATER COMPANY
1125 W Loyola Avenue
Evanston, IL 60657
Phone: 847-675-5167
Fax: 847-675-2695
Officers:
  President: Holly I Myers
  VP/Secretary: Judith Thomson
  Treasurer: Mark Thomas
Management:
  Producing Artistic Director: Ina Marlowe
  Managing Director: Katie Klemme
Mission: To develop and produce new works of theatre and to nurture the artists involved in that process; interested in adventurous, challenging scripts that truly explore the theatrical medium and its possibilities.
Utilizes: Actors; AEA Actors; Collaborations; Designers; Educators; Five Seasonal Concerts; Guest Companies; Guest Soloists; Guild Activities; High School Drama; Instructors; Lyricists; New Productions; Organization Contracts; Original Music Scores; Performance Artists; Resident Professionals; Student Interns
Founded: 1960
Specialized Field: Educational; Theater Workshops
Status: Professional; Nonprofit
Paid Staff: 5
Volunteer Staff: 15
Paid Artists: 40
Budget: $3,000,000
Income Sources: League of Chicago Theatres; Theatre Communications Group
Affiliations: AEA CAT, TYA
Annual Attendance: 15,000
Facility Category: House
Type of Stage: Proscenium
Seating Capacity: 260
Organization Type: Performing; Educational

2967
PIVEN THEATRE WORKSHOP
927 Noyes Street
Evanston, IL 60201

Phone: 847-866-6597
Fax: 847-866-6614
Web Site: www.piventheatreworkshop.org
Officers:
  President: Marcia Cahn
  Vice President: David Doyle
  Treasurer: Eric Rubenstein
  Secretary: Emily Neuberger
  Co-Founders: Joyce Piven
  Co-Founders: Byrne Piven
  Artistic Director Emeritus: Joyce Piven
  Artistic Director: Jennifer Green
Management:
  Executive Director: Jen Green
  Artistic Director: Joyce Piven
  Managing Director: Jen Sultz
Mission: To provide professional theatre and an actors training center for children and adults.
Utilizes: Actors; AEA Actors; Artists-in-Residence; Choreographers; Collaborations; Commissioned Composers; Commissioned Music; Dancers; Designers; Five Seasonal Concerts; Grant Writers; Guest Accompanists; Guest Artists; Guest Companies; Guest Conductors; Guest Designers; Guest Ensembles; Guest Musical Directors; Guest Teachers; Guild Activities; High School Drama; Instructors; Local Artists; Music; Original Music Scores; Performance Artists; Poets; Resident Professionals; Sign Language Translators; Soloists; Student Interns; Special Technical Talent; Visual Arts
Founded: 1972
Specialized Field: Comedy; Youth Theater; Ethnic Theater; Classic; Contemporary
Status: Non-Profit, Professional
Paid Staff: 20
Paid Artists: 10
Budget: $600,000
Income Sources: Illinois Arts Council; Evanston Arts Council
Performs At: Noyes Cultural Arts Center
Annual Attendance: 7,500
Type of Stage: Black Box
Seating Capacity: 75
Organization Type: Performing; Educational

2968
ORPHEUM THEATRE
57 S Kellogg Street
Galesburg, IL 61401
Phone: 309-342-2299
Fax: 309-342-2515
Web Site: www.theorpheum.org
Management:
  Managing Director: Jennifer Rakestraw
Mission: To promote and preserve the Orpheum Theatre as a premier presentation venue for the community.
Utilizes: Actors; Dance Companies; Educators; Grant Writers; Guest Accompanists; Guest Soloists; Multimedia; Original Music Scores; Sign Language Translators; Soloists; Special Technical Talent; Theatre Companies
Founded: 1916
Specialized Field: Musical; Comedy; Youth Theater; Dinner Theater; Ethnic Theater; Community Theater; Puppet; Classic; Contemporary
Status: Non-Profit, Non-Professional
Paid Staff: 2
Volunteer Staff: 30
Budget: $252,000
Income Sources: City of Galesburg; Illinois
Affiliations: American Society of Composers, Authors and Publishers
Facility Category: Performance Theatre

THEATRE / Illinois

Type of Stage: Proscenium
Stage Dimensions: 59'x 40'
Seating Capacity: 952
Year Built: 1916
Year Remodeled: 1989
Rental Contact: Business Manager Danny Davis
Organization Type: Performing; Touring; Educational
Resident Groups: Prairie Players

2969
PRAIRIE PLAYERS CIVIC THEATRE
160 S Seminary S
Galesburg, IL 61402
Mailing Address: P.O. Box 831 Galesburg, IL 61402-0831
Phone: 309-343-7728
e-mail: info@prairieplayers.com
Web Site: www.prairieplayers.com
Officers:
  President: Dennis Clark
  VP: Kenny Knox
  Secretary: Anita Reese
  Treasurer: Bob Gutermuth
Management:
  President: Judy Diemer
  VP: Jerry Hendel
  Secretary: Don Blaheta
  Treasurer: Vera Fornander
Mission: To sustain live theatre arts in a rural setting.
Utilizes: Guest Companies; Singers
Founded: 1915
Specialized Field: Dinner Theater; Community Theater; Puppet
Status: Non-Profit
Income Sources: Association of Kansas Theatres
Organization Type: Performing; Resident

2970
WRITERS' THEATRE CHICAGO
Books on Vernon
664 Vernon Avenue
Glencoe, IL 60022
Phone: 847-242-6000
Fax: 847-835-5332
Web Site: www.writerstheatre.org
Officers:
  President: Elaine Tinberg
  VP: Joseph G. Dillon
  Civic Leader: Gillian Goodman
  Managing Partner: Beth L. Kronfeld
  Sr. VP: Christopher S. Pfaff
Management:
  Artistic Director: Michael Halberstam
  Executive Director: John W Adams
  Artistic Director: Michael Halberstam
  Executive Director: Kathryn M. Lipuma
  Treasurer: Thomas Hodges
Mission: The Writers Theatre is a professional company dedicated to a theatre of language and passion.
Founded: 1992
Specialized Field: Drama; Young Playwrights
Paid Staff: 9
Performs At: Nichols Pennell Theatre

2971
CONKLIN'S BARN 2 DINNER THEATRE
Conklin Court
PO Box 310
Goodfield, IL 61742
Mailing Address: PO Box 310
Phone: 309-965-2545
Fax: 309-965-2735
Web Site: www.barn2.com
Management:
  President: Mary Simon
  Manager: Chaunce Conklin
Mission: To entertain, to educate and to promote live performance.
Utilizes: Contract Orchestras; Resident Professionals
Founded: 1994
Specialized Field: Dinner Theater
Status: For-Profit, Professional
Organization Type: Performing; Resident

2972
CITADEL THEATRE COMPANY
300 S. Waukegan Road
Lake Forest, IL 60045
Phone: 847-735-8554
e-mail: tickets@citadeltheatre.org
Web Site: citadeltheatre.org
Mission: Citadel Theatre is committed to producing powerful works of insight and complexity that illuminate the challenges and joys of the human experience. Dedicated to maintaining the highest standard of professionalism, Citadel seeks to provide both a creative haven for passionate, visionary directors, writers, actors and designers and a home for an audience that seeks to experience the emotional and intellectual richess that the best theatre inspires.
Status: Professional; Non-Equity; Nonprofit

2973
MARRIOTT'S THEATRE IN LINCOLNSHIRE
10 Marriott Drive
Lincolnshire, IL 60069
Phone: 847-634-0200
Fax: 847-634-7358
Web Site: www.marriottheatre.com
Officers:
  Artistic Director: Aaron Thielen
  Artistic Director: Andy Hite
Management:
  Executive Director: Terry E James
  Artistic Director: Andy Hites
  President of Marriott Corporation: J W Marriott
  Production Manager: Adam Ford
  Artistic Director: Aaron Thielen
Mission: Presenting five productions annually, including classic musicals, rarely-seen musicals, and premieres of new works.
Utilizes: AEA Actors; Choreographers; Dancers; Designers; Local Artists; Music; Resident Professionals; Sign Language Translators
Founded: 1975
Specialized Field: Musical; Comedy; Youth Theater; Dinner Theater
Status: For-Profit, Professional
Income Sources: League of Chicago Theatres; American Dinner Theatre Institute
Performs At: Marriott's Lincolnshire Theatre
Affiliations: NAMT
Annual Attendance: 400,000
Type of Stage: In the Round
Seating Capacity: 882
Year Built: 1978
Organization Type: Performing; Resident

2974
ENCORE PLAYERS
222 E Sargent
Litchfield, IL 62056
Phone: 217-326-4414
Officers:
  President: Keith Purcell
  VP: Joel Schnur
  Treasurer: Dick Butler
  Secretary: Pauline Coughlan
Management:
  Director: Mae Morton
  Director: Dennis Plozizka
  Director: David Lewey
  Director: Tim Price
  Artistic Director: George Dawson
Mission: To promote art and the development of artistic ability as well as related theatrical skills; to encourage public appreciation of theatrical arts.
Utilizes: Guest Companies
Founded: 1968
Specialized Field: Musical; Dinner Theater; Community Theater
Status: Non-Professional; Nonprofit
Performs At: Community Center
Organization Type: Performing

2975
SUMMER MUSIC THEATRE
Western Illinois University Theatre/Dance Dep
Browne Hall 101
Macomb, IL 61455
Phone: 309-298-1543
Fax: 309-298-2695
e-mail: de-patrick@wiu.edu
Web Site: www.wiu.edu/theatre
Management:
  Managing Director: David Patrick
Mission: To offer professional musical theatre to the community; to provide training for students. Western Illinois University offers the BFA in musical theatre, BA and MFA degrees in acting, directing, and design.
Utilizes: Guest Companies; Singers
Founded: 1972
Specialized Field: Musical; Summer Stock
Status: Non-Profit, Non-Professional
Paid Staff: 10
Season: June - August
Performs At: Hainline Theatre and Horrabin Theatre
Type of Stage: Proscenium/Thrust
Seating Capacity: 387/150
Year Built: 1972
Organization Type: Performing; Resident; Educational

2976
COLEMAN PUPPET THEATRE
1516 S Second Avenue
Maywood, IL 60153
Phone: 708-344-2920
Management:
  Director: FR Coleman
  Director: Barbara Coleman
Mission: To preserve and perpetuate stories, both classic and modern through dramatization with puppets.
Founded: 1947
Specialized Field: Puppet
Status: Professional
Income Sources: Puppeteers of America; Chicagoland Puppetry Guild; Puppeteers of America
Organization Type: Performing; Touring

2977
TIMBER LAKE PLAYHOUSE
8215 Black Oak Road
Mt. Carroll, IL 61053
Mailing Address: P.O. Box 29, Mt. Carroll, Illinois 61053
Phone: 815-244-2035
Fax: 815-244-2035
e-mail: info@timberlakeplayhouse.org
Web Site: www.timberlakeplayhouse.org
Officers:

President: Diane Olds
Artistic Director: James Beaudry
Management:
　Artistic Director: Brad Lyons
Mission: Dedicated to providing a center for cultural opportunity for developing artists and a showcase of quality theatre for the residents of the Midwest, particularly in Northwestern Illinois and Eastern Iowa.
Founded: 1961
Specialized Field: Musical; Comedy; Youth Theater; Contemporary; Summer Stock
Status: Non-Profit, Professional
Paid Staff: 2
Season: June - September
Type of Stage: Semi-Thrust
Seating Capacity: 375

2978
HEARTLAND THEATRE COMPANY
1110 Douglas Street
Normal, IL 61761
Mailing Address: P.O. Box 1833, Bloomington, IL 61702-1833
Phone: 309-452-8709
e-mail: boxoffice@heartlandtheatre.org
Web Site: heartlandtheatre.org
Management:
　Interim Artistic Director: Julie Kistler
Mission: To provide the citizens of Central Illinois with quality theatre utilizing first-rate talent, and to provide a lasting and meaningful theatre experience for our patrons.
Status: Professional-Quality; Nonprofit

2979
ILLINOIS SHAKESPEARE FESTIVAL
Illinois State University
Box 5700
Normal, IL 61790-5700
Phone: 309-438-8974
Fax: 309-438-5806
Toll-free: 866-457-4253
e-mail: shake@ilstu.edu
Web Site: thefestival.org
Management:
　Managing Director: Dick Folse
　Artistic Director: Kevin Rich
Utilizes: Actors; AEA Actors; Designers; Guest Conductors; Guest Designers; Guest Writers; Guild Activities; Original Music Scores; Resident Artists; Resident Professionals; Soloists; Student Interns
Founded: 1978
Specialized Field: Outdoor Theater; Classic; Shakespeare
Status: Non-Profit, Professional
Paid Staff: 80
Paid Artists: 40
Budget: $1.2 Million
Income Sources: Box Office, Fund Raising
Season: June - August
Performs At: Ewing Manor
Affiliations: U/RTA; Actors' Equity Association; SSDC
Annual Attendance: 14,000
Facility Category: Outdoor
Type of Stage: Thrust
Seating Capacity: 438
Year Built: 2000
Cost: $1.65 million
Organization Type: Performing; Educational

2980
OAK PARK FESTIVAL THEATRE
PO Box 4114
Oak Park, IL 60303
Phone: 708-445-4440
Fax: 708-524-4950
e-mail: ArtisticDirector@oakparkfestival.com
Web Site: http://oakparkfestival.com/
Officers:
　President: Brat Bartels
　Vice President: Paul Engelhardt
　Secrtary: Molly Surowitz
　Treasurer: Robert Behr
　Artistic Director: Jack Hickey
　Casting Director: Lucy Carr
Management:
　Artistic Director: Jack Hickey
　Managing Director: Lisa Gordon
Utilizes: Actors; AEA Actors; Collaborations; Designers; Guest Companies; Guest Instructors; Instructors; Local Artists; Resident Professionals; Selected Students; Singers; Soloists; Student Interns
Founded: 1975
Specialized Field: Summer Stock
Status: Professional; Nonprofit
Paid Staff: 20
Volunteer Staff: 14
Budget: $160,000
Income Sources: Illinois Arts Council; Oak Park Area Arts Council; Foundations; Membership
Season: July - August
Performs At: Outside
Affiliations: Actors Equity Association; League of Chicago Theatres; Producers Association of Chicago
Facility Category: Outdoor
Type of Stage: Platform
Seating Capacity: 350
Organization Type: Performing

2981
VILLAGE PLAYERS THEATER
1010 W Madison Street
Oak Park, IL 60302
Phone: 708-921-0645
Fax: 708-383-9829
e-mail: tickets@village-players.org
Web Site: www.village-players.org
　Treasurer: Robby Robinson
Management:
　Artistic Director: Dan Taube
　Production Manager: Rick Julien
Mission: Promoting community involvement in cultural arts; developing theatrical ability through public performances and education.
Utilizes: Actors; AEA Actors; Choreographers; Dancers; Designers; Educators; Five Seasonal Concerts; Grant Writers; Guest Accompanists; Guest Artists; Guest Companies; Guest Conductors; Guest Directors; Guest Lecturers; Guest Musical Directors; High School Drama; Instructors; Local Artists; Multimedia; Music; New Productions; Original Music Scores; Performance Artists; Resident Professionals; Sign Language Translators; Soloists; Student Interns; Special Technical Talent
Founded: 1961
Specialized Field: Musical; Comedy; Youth Theater; Ethnic Theater; Community Theater; Classic; Contemporary
Status: Non-Profit, Professional
Paid Staff: 90
Paid Artists: 10
Budget: $280,000
Income Sources: Tickets; Tuition; Grants
Performs At: Persidium
Affiliations: Village Players Theater School
Annual Attendance: 20,000
Facility Category: Mainstage/Blackbox
Type of Stage: Proscenium
Seating Capacity: 222
Organization Type: Performing Resident; Educational

2982
DRURY LANE OAKBROOK TERRACE
100 Drury Lane
Oakbrook Terrace, IL 60181
Phone: 708-530-8300
Fax: 630-530-0436
Web Site: www.drurylaneoakbrook.com
Management:
　Executive Director: Kyle DeSantis
　General Manager: John Tapia
　Artistic Director: Bill Osetek
　Production Manager: Juli Walker
Mission: To present large-scale musicals and comedies that feature leading theatre artists.
Utilizes: Actors; AEA Actors; Choreographers; Music; Resident Professionals
Founded: 1984
Specialized Field: Musical; Dinner Theater
Status: Professional; Non-Professional; Commercial
Income Sources: American Dinner Theatre Association
Performs At: Drury Lane Theater
Facility Category: Theatre/Conference House
Type of Stage: Proscenium
Seating Capacity: 959
Year Built: 1984
Organization Type: Performing; Touring

2983
PEORIA PLAYERS THEATRE
14300 N University
Peoria, IL 61614
Fax: 309-688-4474
e-mail: players@mtco.com
Web Site: www.peoriaplayers.org
Officers:
　President: Stan Ellwood
　Business Administrator: Nicki Haschke
Mission: Enhances and promotes a tradition of excellence in community theatre by providing theatrical entertainment and by giving everyone an opportunity to participate in the theatre experience.
Founded: 1919
Specialized Field: Musical; Comedy; Youth Theater; Community Theater; Puppet; Classic; Contemporary
Status: Non-Profit, Non-Professional
Paid Staff: 2
Volunteer Staff: 50
Non-paid Artists: 100
Budget: $150,000
Income Sources: American Association of Community Theatres; Illinois Theatre Association
Performs At: Peoria Players Theatre
Annual Attendance: 13,000
Facility Category: Handicap-Accessible
Type of Stage: Proscenium
Stage Dimensions: 20x36
Seating Capacity: 350
Year Built: 1957
Year Remodeled: 2000
Rental Contact: Nicki Haschke
Organization Type: Performing; Resident; Educational

2984
CIRCA '21 DINNER PLAYHOUSE
1828 3rd Avenue
Rock Island, IL 61201
Phone: 309-786-7733
Fax: 309-786-4119
e-mail: dpjh@circa21.com
Web Site: www.circa21.com

THEATRE / Illinois

Management:
Producer: Dennis Hitchcock
Mission: To offer professional musicals and plays year-round along with the finest in dining.
Utilizes: Dancers; Grant Writers; Guest Artists; Guest Lecturers
Founded: 1921
Specialized Field: Dinner Theater
Status: Professional; Commercial
Paid Staff: 65
Affiliations: Vaudeville House Converted
Annual Attendance: 65,000
Type of Stage: Proscenium with Thrust
Seating Capacity: 336
Year Built: 1920
Year Remodeled: 1977
Cost: $500,000
Organization Type: Performing; Touring; Resident

2985
FOX VALLEY REPERTORY
4051 E. Main Street
Saint Charles, IL 60174
Phone: 630-584-6342
Fax: 630-443-0520
e-mail: info@foxvalleyrep.org
Web Site: foxvalleyrep.org
Management:
Artistic Director: John Gawlik
Managing Director: Colleen Tovar
Production Manager: Laura Eilers
Mission: Dedicated to entertaining, enriching, and educating lives in the Fox Valley Area. As the largest, professional arts organization in the area, FVR strives to present outstanding productions and provide exceptional education programs through the FVR Performing Arts Academy.
Founded: 1964
Status: Professional; Nonprofit
Seating Capacity: 320
Organization Type: Educational; Performing

2986
NORTHLIGHT THEATRE
9501 Skokie Boulevard
Skokie, IL 60077
Phone: 847-673-6300
Fax: 847-679-1879
e-mail: bjjones@northlight.org
Web Site: www.northlight.org/
Officers:
Artistic Director: BJ Jones
Executive Director: Timothy J. Evans
Management:
Artistic Director: BJ Jones
Managing Director: Philip Santora
General Manager: Janet Mullet
Mission: The theatre's objective is to challenge, as well as entertain its audiences with a focus to produce compelling new interpretations of contemporary plays drawn from an international repertoire and to create stage adaptions inspired by the full spectrum of artistic disciplines.
Founded: 1974
Specialized Field: Drama; Comedy; Educational
Status: Professional; Nonprofit
Income Sources: Theatre Communications Group; League of Resident Theatres; American Arts Alliance
Performs At: North Shore Center for the Performing Arts
Organization Type: Resident; Producing

2987
PHEASANT RUN THEATRE
4051 E Main
PO Box 64
St Charles, IL 60174
Phone: 630-584-6300
Toll-free: 800-474-3272
e-mail: info@pheasantrun.com
Web Site: http://www.pheasantrun.com/activities/theater.php
Management:
Producer/Director: Diana Martinez
Utilizes: Guest Companies
Founded: 1964
Specialized Field: Dinner Theater
Status: Professional; Commercial
Organization Type: Performing

2988
LITTLE THEATRE ON THE SQUARE
16 E Harrison Street
PO Box 288
Sullivan, IL 61951-0288
Mailing Address: P.O. Box 288, Sullivan, 61951-0288
Phone: 217-728-2065
Fax: 217-728-7525
Toll-free: 888-261-9675
e-mail: theshow@thelittletheatre.org
Web Site: www.thelittletheatre.org
Officers:
Executive Director: John Stephens
Creative Director: Joshua Zecher-Ross
Education Director: Lauren Patton
Management:
President: Leonard A Anderson
Artistic Director: M Seth Reines
Founded: 1957
Specialized Field: Musical; Comedy; Youth Theater; Community Theater; Contemporary
Status: Non-Profit, Professional
Paid Staff: 10
Paid Artists: 30
Season: June - August
Type of Stage: Proscenium
Stage Dimensions: 28' x 27'
Seating Capacity: 450
Year Built: 1928
Year Remodeled: 1958

2989
CHAMPAIGN URBANA THEATRE COMPANY
608 N. Cunningham, Ave.
Urbana, IL 61802
Phone: 217-344-3884
e-mail: manager@cutc.org
Web Site: cutc.org
Officers:
President: Sandra Jones
Vice President: Brice Hutchcraft
Secretary: Dennis Donaldson
Treasurer: Shawna Barbee
Management:
Executive Director: Ella Van Wyk
Mission: Committed to providing the people of East Central Illinois with experience in all aspects of the performing arts through volunteer opportunities in the theater trades, on stage and off stage, in the course of presenting high-quality theatrical productions, and through education and leadership in the promotion of theater arts to the community.
Founded: 1991
Status: Nonprofit; Community Theater
Performs At: Parkland College, 2400 W. Bradley Ave., Champaign, IL 61821

2990
BOWEN PARK THEATRE & OPERA
2000 Belvidere Street
Waukegan, IL 60085
Phone: 847-360-4700
Fax: 847-662-0592
Web Site: www.waukeganparks.org
Management:
Executive Director: Claudia Patrauski
Founded: 1982
Specialized Field: Light Theater; Classic
Status: For-Profit, Professional
Paid Staff: 4
Paid Artists: 40

2991
CLOCKWISE THEATRE
221 North Genesee
Waukegan, IL 60031
Mailing Address: P.O. Box 223, Gurnee, IL 60031
Phone: 847-775-1500
e-mail: info@clockwisetheatre.org
Web Site: clockwisetheatre.org
Management:
Artistic Director: Madelyn Sergel
Managing Director: Patrick Kerr
Status: Professional; Non-Equity; Nonprofit

2992
THEATRE OF WESTERN SPRINGS
4384 Hampton Avenue
Western Springs, IL 60558
Phone: 708-246-4043
Fax: 708-246-4015
e-mail: ad@theatrewesternsprings.com
Web Site: www.theatrewesternsprings.com
Management:
Business Manager: Allison Burkharht
Artistic Director: Jack Phillips
Children's Theatre Director: Scott Illingwarth
Mission: Promoting, developing and maintaining a community theatre that produces interesting, significant plays; providing a forum for artists.
Utilizes: Actors; Collaborations; Designers; Five Seasonal Concerts; Guest Artists; Guest Designers; Guest Lecturers; Guest Soloists; Guest Teachers; Guild Activities; High School Drama; Instructors; Local Artists; Multimedia; Music; Organization Contracts; Original Music Scores; Performance Artists; Resident Artists; Soloists; Student Interns; Special Technical Talent
Founded: 1928
Specialized Field: Community Theater; Children's Theater
Status: Non-Profit, Non-Professional
Paid Staff: 17
Volunteer Staff: 400
Paid Artists: 3
Budget: $750,000
Facility Category: Two theatres
Type of Stage: One open proscenium, one black box
Seating Capacity: 410; 120
Year Built: 1962
Rental Contact: Jeff Arena
Organization Type: Performing; Educational; Sponsoring

2993
INVENTIONS
1047 Gage Street
Winnetka, IL 60093

THEATRE / Indiana

Phone: 847-446-0183
Fax: 847-446-0183
Web Site: http://home.earthlink.net/~inventions4
Management:
- Co-Founder: T Daniel
- Co-Founder: Laurie Willets
- Co-Founder: John Bruce Yeh
- Co-Founder: Teresa Reilly

Mission: An innovative foursome that strikes out in a new direction! A visual slant to cleverly interpret Classical Music and Mime for the new Century.
Founded: 2000
Specialized Field: Musical; Ensembles
Status: Professional
Paid Staff: 2
Volunteer Staff: 2
Organization Type: Performing; Touring

2994
T DANIEL PRODUCTIONS
6619 N Campbell Street
Winnetka, IL 60645
Phone: 773-743-0277
Fax: 773-743-0276
e-mail: info@tdanielcreations.com
Web Site: www.tdanielcreations.com
Management:
- Artistic Co-Director/Co-Founder: T Daniel
- Artistic Co-Director/Co-Founder: Laurie Willets

Mission: To create, educate and tour theatrical productions, shows and concert programs dynamically based upon the Art of Mime for audiences of all ages.
Utilizes: Collaborations; Multi Collaborations
Founded: 1971
Specialized Field: Movement Theater
Status: Non-Profit, Professional
Paid Staff: 2
Paid Artists: 2

2995
WOODSTOCK OPERA HOUSE
121 Van Buren Street
PO Box 190
Woodstock, IL 60098
Phone: 815-338-4212
Fax: 815-334-2287
e-mail: jscharres@woodstockil.gov
Web Site: www.woodstockoperahouse.com
Officers:
- Production Assistant: Scott Creighton

Management:
- Managing Director: John H Scharres
- Building Manager: Mark Greenleaf
- Box Office Manager: Daniel Campbell
- Office Manager: Lorraine Steinkamp

Founded: 1890
Specialized Field: Musical; Comedy; Youth Theater; Ethnic Theater; Community Theater; Puppet; Classic; Contemporary
Status: Non-Profit, Non-Professional
Paid Staff: 11
Paid Artists: 4

2996
ZION PASSION PLAY
2500 Dowie Memorial Drive
Zion, IL 60099
Phone: 847-746-2221
Fax: 847-746-1452
e-mail: klangley@ccczion.org
Web Site: www.ccczion.org
Management:
- Artistic Director: Ron Arden

Mission: Biblical production about the life of Jesus Christ.
Utilizes: Singers
Founded: 1935
Specialized Field: Community Theater
Status: Non-Profit, Non-Professional
Paid Staff: 1
Paid Artists: 3
Income Sources: Christ Community Church
Performs At: Christian Arts Auditorium
Seating Capacity: 522
Organization Type: Performing; Resident; Educational

Indiana

2997
LITTLE THEATRE OF BEDFORD
1704 Brian Lane Way
PO Box 142
Bedford, IN 47421
Phone: 812-279-3009
e-mail: boxoffice@ltb.org
Web Site: www.ltb.org
Officers:
- Treasurer: Denny Underwood
- VP: Tom Taylor
- Secretary: Rachel Fishback
- President: Roger Manning
- President: Nina Peterson
- Vice-President: Joe Voris
- Secretary: Laura Henley
- Tresurer: Cheri Barnes
- Tresurer: Joe Voris

Management:
- President: Todd Taylor
- VP: Nathan Walden

Mission: To offer an opportunity for amateur directors and performers to entertain our community.
Founded: 1960
Specialized Field: Musical; Community Theater
Status: Nonprofit
Paid Staff: 150
Performs At: Little Theatre
Organization Type: Performing

2998
SHAWNEE THEATRE OF GREENE COUNTY
PO Box 22
Bloomfield, IN 47424
Phone: 812-384-3559
Fax: 812-384-8773
e-mail: shawneetheatre@hotmail.com
Web Site: http://www.shawneetheatre.org/
Officers:
- President: Mary Aiken

Management:
- Producing Director: Matthew Graber

Founded: 1960
Specialized Field: Summer Stock
Status: Non-Equity; Nonprofit
Paid Staff: 6
Volunteer Staff: 26
Paid Artists: 20
Season: June - July
Annual Attendance: 4,900
Type of Stage: Proscenium
Stage Dimensions: 36' x 20'
Seating Capacity: 360
Year Built: 1979

2999
BLOOMINGTON COUNTY PLAYHOUSE
Indiana University
Bloomington, IN 47405
Phone: 812-855-0074
e-mail: hkibbey@indiana.edu
Specialized Field: Educational; Theater Workshops

3000
COMMUNITY THEATRE OF CLAY COUNTY
8 E National
Brazil, IN 47834
Phone: 812-442-1059
Fax: 973-455-1607
Officers:
- President: Susan M Bradbury
- VP: John Berry
- Secretary/Treasurer: Lois Myers

Mission: To provide opportunities for involvement in the arts in Clay County for all ages, by presenting dinner theatre, musicals, children's workshops, senior citizens programs, and sponsoring drama scholarships.
Utilizes: Guest Artists; Guest Companies; Singers
Founded: 1983
Specialized Field: Musical; Dinner Theater; Community Theater
Status: Non-Professional; Nonprofit
Paid Staff: 200
Income Sources: Arts Indiana; Indiana Theatre Association
Organization Type: Performing; Educational

3001
ELKHART CIVIC THEATRE
Bristol Opera House
210 E Vistula, PO Box 252
Bristol, IN 46507-0252
Phone: 574-848-4116
e-mail: webmaster@elkartcivictheatre.org
Web Site: www.elkartcivictheatre.org
Officers:
- President: Cynthia Antonelli
- VP: Stephanie Yoder
- Treasurer: Timothy Yoder
- Secretary: Connie Deuschle

Management:
- Artistic Director: Leslie Torok
- Technical Director: John Shoup

Mission: To produce and present a high-quality and award-winning community theater.
Utilizes: Actors; Choreographers; Collaborations; Dancers; Grant Writers; Guest Artists; Guest Companies; Guest Conductors; Guest Lecturers; Guild Activities; High School Drama; Local Artists; Organization Contracts; Sign Language Translators; Soloists
Founded: 1946
Specialized Field: Community Theater
Status: Non-Professional; Nonprofit
Paid Staff: 2
Paid Artists: 2
Non-paid Artists: 200
Budget: $125,000
Income Sources: Indiana Arts Commission; Local & Regional Government & Foundation Sources; Business Community; Private & Individual Sources
Performs At: Bristol Opera House
Affiliations: American Association of Community Theatres; ICTL; Performing Arts & Cultural Entertainment of Elkhart County
Annual Attendance: 13,000

THEATRE / Indiana

Facility Category: Intimate Vaudeville Style Wood Frame/Historic
Type of Stage: Proscenium/Thrust
Stage Dimensions: 17Wx25D
Seating Capacity: 192
Year Built: 1897
Year Remodeled: 1992
Organization Type: Performing; Resident; Educational

3002
JACKSON COUNTY COMMUNITY THEATRE

121 West Walnut Street
Brownstown, IN 47220
Mailing Address: PO Box 65,Brownstown, IN 47220
Phone: 812-358-5228
e-mail: mail@jcct.org
Web Site: www.jcct.org
Officers:
   President: Joe Bradley
Management:
   President: Dot Goodwin
Mission: Producing live plays; bringing cultural programs to our community.
Utilizes: Guest Companies
Founded: 1971
Specialized Field: Dinner Theater; Community Theater
Status: Non-Professional; Nonprofit
Income Sources: Indiana Theatre Association
Performs At: Royal Office Square Theatre
Organization Type: Performing; Educational

3003
4TH STREET THEATER

125 N. Fourth Street
Chesterton, IN 46304
Mailing Address: P.O. Box 2281, Chesterton, IN 46304
Phone: 219-926-7875
e-mail: ncca4thstreet@comcast.net
Web Site: 4thstreetncca.org
Officers:
   President: Linda Pauli
   President Elect: David Pifko
Founded: 1990

3004
DERBY DINNER PLAYHOUSE

525 Marriott Drive
Clarksville, IN 47129
Phone: 812-288-8281
Fax: 812-288-2636
Toll-free: 877-898-8577
e-mail: tickets@derbydinner.com
Web Site: www.derbydinner.com
Management:
   Executive Director: Cindy Knopp
   Artistic Director: Lee Buckholz
   Owner: Bekki Jo Schneider
Mission: Professional dinner theatre.
Utilizes: Actors; Commissioned Composers; Commissioned Music; Designers; Educators; Guest Artists; Guest Companies; Guest Conductors; Guest Designers; Guild Activities; Organization Contracts; Original Music Scores; Performance Artists; Resident Artists; Singers; Soloists; Student Interns
Founded: 1974
Specialized Field: Musical; Comedy; Youth Theater; Dinner Theater
Status: For-Profit, Professional
Paid Staff: 80
Volunteer Staff: 10
Paid Artists: 30
Budget: $4 million
Income Sources: Ticket Sales; Gift Shop, Food, Drink
Performs At: Derby Dinner Playhouse
Affiliations: NAMT, NDTA, ABA, NTA
Annual Attendance: 200,000
Facility Category: Dinner Theatre
Type of Stage: Theatre-in-the-round
Stage Dimensions: 20'x20'
Seating Capacity: 520
Year Remodeled: 1998
Rental Contact: Group Sales Cindy Nevitt
Organization Type: Performing

3005
CROWN POINT COMMUNITY THEATRE

1125 Merrillville Road
Crown Point, IN 46307
Mailing Address: P.O. Box 238, Crown Point, IN 46308
Phone: 219-805-4255
e-mail: info@cpct.biz
Web Site: cpct.biz
Officers:
   President: Joe Culley
   Vice President: Kerry Fitch
Mission: The mission of Crown Point Community Theatre is to foster an appreciation of the theatre arts by providing learning opportunities and creative outlets for community members, and to produce outstanding theatrical presentations for the community at large.
Founded: 2004
Status: Nonprofit

3006
REPERTORY PEOPLE OF EVANSVILLE

Old Courthouse Building
Room 200
Evansville, IN 47708
Mailing Address: PO Box 3555, Evansville, IN 47734
Phone: 812-423-2060
Web Site: www.repertorypeople.net
Officers:
   Founder: Tom Angermeier
Management:
   Director: Jim Jackson
   Executive Producer: Tom Angermeier
Mission: To present serious American dramas and occasionally comedies.
Founded: 1973
Specialized Field: Community Theater; Educational
Status: Non-Professional; Nonprofit
Organization Type: Performing; Resident

3007
ARENA DINNER THEATRE

719 Rockhill Street
Fort Wayne, IN 46802
Mailing Address: PO Box 11992
Phone: 260-424-5622
Web Site: http://www.arenadinnertheatre.org/
Officers:
   President: Terry McCaffrey
   Vice-President: Fred Krauskopf
   Treasurer: Dave Thompson
   Secretary: Suzan Moriarty
Management:
   President: Dave Frey
   Vice President: Fred Karuskopf
   Secretary: David Siples
   Treasurer: Brian Schilb
Mission: To provide an additional option for actors and theatre-goers in the community.
Founded: 1974
Specialized Field: Dinner Theater; Community Theater
Status: Non-Professional
Paid Staff: 50
Income Sources: Fine Arts Foundation; Indiana Theatre Association
Organization Type: Performing

3008
FIRST PRESBYTERIAN THEATER

300 W Wayne Street
Fort Wayne, IN 46802
Phone: 260-422-6329
Fax: 260-422-5111
e-mail: thofrichter@firstpres-fw.org
Web Site: www.firstpres-fw.org/the_arts/theater/
Officers:
   Managing Artistic Director: Thom Hofrichter
Management:
   Managing Artistic Director: Thom Hofrichter
   Box Office Manager: Beth Robison
   Technical Director: Bob Sutton
Mission: To produce provocative contemporary and classical drama in a supportive atmosphere.
Utilizes: Guest Companies
Founded: 1968
Specialized Field: Community Theater
Status: Nonprofit
Paid Staff: 2
Volunteer Staff: 14
Non-paid Artists: 75
Income Sources: Fort Wayne Community Arts Council
Annual Attendance: 8000
Facility Category: 300 Seat Proscenium
Type of Stage: Proscenium
Stage Dimensions: 50 x 22
Seating Capacity: 300
Year Built: 1968
Year Remodeled: 2001
Organization Type: Performing; Educational

3009
FORT WAYNE CIVIC THEATRE

303 E Main Street
Fort Wayne, IN 46802
Phone: 260-422-8641
Fax: 260-422-6699
e-mail: pcolglazier@fwcivic.org
Web Site: www.fwcivic.org
Officers:
   President: Randall Steiner
   1st Vice President: John Burns
   Treasurer: Mark Rupp
   Secretary: Edward Kos
   2nd Vice President: Ken Menefee
Management:
   President: Phillip Colglazier
   Business Director: Mahlon Houlihan
   Marketing Director: Carolyn Hasty
Mission: Dedicated to strengthening itself as a significant cultural force in the Fort Wayne area through excellence in programming, theatre education and development of talent in the disciplines of theatre and the related performing arts.
Utilizes: Actors; Choreographers; Collaborating Artists; Collaborations; Commissioned Music; Dancers; Designers; Educators; Fine Artists; Five Seasonal Concerts; Grant Writers; Guest Accompanists; Guest Artists; Guest Designers; Guest Musical Directors; Guest Writers; Guild Activities; Instructors; Lyricists; Multimedia; Music; New Productions; Organization Contracts; Resident Professionals; Sign Language Translators; Soloists; Student Interns; Touring Companies; Visual Arts
Founded: 1928
Specialized Field: Musical; Comedy; Youth Theater; Community Theater
Status: Non-Profit, Non-Professional

THEATRE / Indiana

Paid Staff: 11
Performs At: The Performing Arts Center
Annual Attendance: 50,000
Facility Category: Community Theatre
Type of Stage: Proscenium
Stage Dimensions: 60x30
Seating Capacity: 669
Year Built: 1973
Rental Contact: Shellie Englehart
Organization Type: Resident

3010
BEEF AND BOARDS DINNER THEATRE
9301 N Michigan Road
Indianapolis, IN 46268
Phone: 317-872-9664
Fax: 317-876-0510
e-mail: boxoffice@beefandboards.com
Web Site: www.beefandboards.com
Management:
  Managing Director: Robert Zehr
  Artistic Director: Douglas Stark
  Associate Producer: Eddie Curry
  Media Relations: JoEllen Miller
Utilizes: Actors; AEA Actors; Choreographers; Dancers
Founded: 1971
Specialized Field: Dinner Theater
Status: For-Profit, Professional
Paid Staff: 100
Income Sources: National Dinner Theatre Association; American Dinner Theatre Institute
Performs At: Beef and Boards Dinner Theatre
Facility Category: Dinner Theatre
Type of Stage: 3/4 Thrust
Seating Capacity: 480
Rental Contact: Pat Minneman
Organization Type: Performing

3011
CABARET AT THE COLUMBIA CLUB
The Cabaret at the Columbia Club
121 Monument Circle
Indianapolis, IN 46204
Phone: 317-275-1169
Fax: 317-686-5443
e-mail: info@thecabaret.org
Web Site: www.thecabaret.org
Officers:
  Managing & Artistic Director: Shannon Forsell
  Director of Marketing and Audience: Anne Miller
  Chair: Doris Anne Sadler
  Vice Chair: Roger Schmelzer
Management:
  Marketing & PR Manager: Ann Miller, anne@thecabaret.org
  Managing & Artistic Director: Shannon Forsell, shannon@thecabaret.org
Mission: To elevate the cabaret art form; attract, develop and retain high quality local performance talent; and to provide a unique and important contribution to the city's artistic and cultural life.
Utilizes: Actors; Choreographers; Dancers; Designers; Educators; Five Seasonal Concerts; Grant Writers; Guest Accompanists; Guest Artists; Guest Companies; Guest Conductors; Guest Soloists; Instructors; Multi Collaborations; Multimedia; Music; Organization Contracts; Original Music Scores; Performance Artists; Resident Professionals; Sign Language Translators; Student Interns
Founded: 1989
Specialized Field: Cabaret Theatre
Status: Non-Profit, Professional
Annual Attendance: 60,000
Facility Category: Theatre

Type of Stage: Proscenium
Seating Capacity: 125
Year Remodeled: 2010
Rental Contact: Shannon Forsell

3012
EDYVEAN REPERTORY THEATRE
University of Indianapolis
PO Box 47509
Indianapolis, IN 46227-7509
Phone: 317-788-2072
Fax: 317-788-2079
Toll-free: 800-807-7732
Web Site: www.edyvean.org
Management:
  Artistic Director: Rose Kleiman
  Managing Director: Bill Simmons
  Administrative Director: Frederick Marshall
  Market/Public Relations Director: Anne Penny
  Tech Director/Production Manager: Michael Moffatt
Mission: Illuminates the human journey by exploring its many dimensions and celebrating its possibilities.
Founded: 1967
Specialized Field: Educational; Theater Workshops
Status: Professional
Performs At: Ransburg Auditorium, University of Indianapolis
Annual Attendance: 12,000
Type of Stage: Proscenium
Seating Capacity: 750

3013
INDIANA REPERTORY THEATRE
140 W Washington Street
Indianapolis, IN 46204-3465
Phone: 317-635-5252
Fax: 317-236-0767
e-mail: ticketoffice@irtlive.com
Web Site: www.irtlive.com/
Officers:
  President: William E Smith
  Vice President: David Klapper
  VP: Jane Schlegel
  Secretary: Marjorie Herald
  Treasurer: David L. Morgan
Management:
  Artistic Director: Janet Allen
  Managing Director: Daniel Baker
  Marketing Director: Richard Ferguson
  Development Director: Meg Gamage Tucker
Mission: Through innovative productions of classic and contemporary plays, the Indiana Repertory Theatre creates high quality, professional theatre of consistent artistic and cultural significance; the theatre also offers student programs.
Utilizes: Actors; AEA Actors; Artists-in-Residence; Choreographers; Collaborating Artists; Collaborations; Commissioned Composers; Commissioned Music; Designers; Educators; Fine Artists; Five Seasonal Concerts; Grant Writers; Guest Accompanists; Guest Artists; Guest Companies; Guest Composers; Guest Conductors; Guest Designers; Guest Ensembles; Guest Lecturers; Guest Musical Directors; Guest Musicians; Guest Soloists; Guest Teachers; High School Drama; Instructors; Local Artists; Lyricists; Multimedia; Music; Original Music Scores; Performance Artists; Playwrights; Poets; Resident Professionals; Selected Students; Sign Language Translators; Singers; Soloists; Visual Arts
Founded: 1972
Specialized Field: Musical; Comedy; Youth Theater; Classic; Contemporary
Status: Non-Profit, Professional

Paid Staff: 35
Paid Artists: 100
Budget: $4,900,000
Income Sources: League of Resident Theatres; Grants from the National Endowment for the Arts; Lila Wallace-Reader's Digest Fund; Schubert Foundation; Ticket Sales
Performs At: Indiana Theatre
Annual Attendance: 124,000
Facility Category: Historic Theatre; Ballroom
Type of Stage: Mainstage; Upperstage; Cabaret
Year Built: 1927
Year Remodeled: 2001
Rental Contact: Erika Keller
Organization Type: Performing; Resident; Educational

3014
PHOENIX THEATRE
749 N Park Avenue
Indianapolis, IN 46202
Phone: 317-635-7529
Fax: 317-635-0010
e-mail: info@phoenixtheatre.org
Web Site: www.phoenixtheatre.org/
Officers:
  Development Director: Russell Bennett
  Marketing and Media Relations Direc: Lori Raffel
  Producing Director: Bryan Fonseca
  Finance Director: Lara Schmutte
  Technical Director: Nolan Brokamp
Management:
  President: Frank M Basile
  VP: John Fischer
  Producing Director: Bryan Fonseca
  Managing Director: Sharon Gamble
Founded: 1982
Specialized Field: Drama; Comedy; Theater Workshops
Status: Nonprofit
Budget: $400,000

3015
THEATRE ON THE SQUARE
627 Massachusetts Avenue
Indianapolis, IN 46204-1606
Phone: 317-685-8687
Fax: 317-637-0302
e-mail: lbaltz@tots.org
Web Site: www.tots.org
Management:
  Executive Artistic Director: Ron Spencer
  Development Director: Lori Raffel
  Business & Marketing Director: Laura Baltz
Mission: To explore contemporary, classic plays and musicals in an intimate environment.
Founded: 1988
Specialized Field: Drama; Comedy

3016
STAR PLAZA THEATRE
I-65 & US 30
8001 Deleware Place
Merrillville, IN 46410
Phone: 219-769-6311
Fax: 219-756-0604
Web Site: www.starplazatheatre.com
Officers:
  President: Charles Blum
Management:
  President: Charles Blum
  General Manager: Mark Bishop
Founded: 1979
Specialized Field: Musical
Status: For-Profit, Professional

THEATRE / Indiana

Facility Category: Theatre
Seating Capacity: 3400
Year Built: 1979

3017
FOOTLIGHT PLAYERS, INC.
1705 Franklin Street
PO Box 46
Michigan City, IN 46360
Phone: 219-874-4035
Fax: 866-612-3436
e-mail: info@footlightplayers.org
Web Site: www.footlightplayers.org
Officers:
  Secretary: Marsha Markle
  Vice President: Diana Hirsch
  President: Janice Rice
  Treasurer: William Wild
Management:
  General Manager: Kit Lyons
  Designer and Technical Director: Richard Heffner
  Artistic Director: Dorothy D'Anna
  Director: Jacqueline Verdeyen
  Treasure/Publicity/Chair: William Wild
Mission: To offer community members an opportunity for self-expression through amateur theatre; to provide education in drama and related subjects.
Utilizes: Guest Companies
Founded: 1950
Specialized Field: Community Theater; Drama
Status: Non-Professional; Nonprofit
Income Sources: Individual donors; business sponsors
Performs At: Footlight Players Theatre
Organization Type: Performing; Resident

3018
RIDGEWOOD ARTS FOUNDATION: THEATRE AT THE CENTER
1040 Ridge Road
Munster, IN 46321-1876
Phone: 219-836-3255
Fax: 219-836-0159
Toll-free: 800-511-1552
Management:
  Artistic Director: Michael Weber
Utilizes: Actors; AEA Actors; Choreographers; Dancers; Designers; Five Seasonal Concerts; Grant Writers; Guest Artists; Guest Companies; Guest Composers; Guest Conductors; Guest Designers; Guest Lecturers; Guest Musical Directors; Local Unknown Artists; Multimedia; Music; Original Music Scores; Performance Artists; Resident Professionals; Sign Language Translators; Soloists
Founded: 1991
Specialized Field: Musical
Status: Nonprofit
Season: January - December
Type of Stage: Thrust; Flexible
Stage Dimensions: 12' x 8'
Seating Capacity: 454

3019
THE ROUND BARN THEATRE AT AMISH ACRES
Amish Acres, LLC
1600 W Market Street
Nappanee, IN 46550
Phone: 574-773-4188
Fax: 219-773-4180
Toll-free: 800-800-4942
e-mail: amishacres@amishacres.com
Web Site: www.amishacres.com
Management:
  Artistic Director: Laurie Schotz
  Producer: Richard Pletcher
Founded: 1986
Specialized Field: Musical; Comedy; Youth Theater; Dinner Theater; Ethnic Theater; Classic; Contemporary
Status: Professional
Income Sources: Ticket Sales
Season: April - December
Performs At: Relocated Historical Round Barn
Type of Stage: Proscenium
Stage Dimensions: 25' x 35'
Seating Capacity: 360
Year Built: 1911
Year Remodeled: 1999
Cost: $1,000,000

3020
BROWN COUNTY PLAYHOUSE
48 South Van Buren Street,
Nashville, IN 47448
Mailing Address: PO Box 1187 Nashville, IN 47448
Phone: 812-988-2123
Fax: 812-856-0698
e-mail: jkinzer@indiana.edu
Web Site: www.browncountyplayhouse.org/
Officers:
  President: Suzannah Levett Zody
Management:
  President: R Keith Michael
  Executive Director: Jonathan Michaelson
  Artistic Director: Dale McFadden
  Managing Director: Marilyn Norris
Mission: The Brown County Playhouse, a professional theatre operated in conjunction with the Indiana University Department of Theatre and Drama, is located in the center of scenic Nashville.
Founded: 1949
Specialized Field: Comedy; Contemporary
Status: Non-Profit, Professional
Paid Staff: 20
Paid Artists: 30

3021
UNIVERSITY OF NOTRE DAME DEPARTMENT OF FILM, TELEVISION & THEATRE
230 DeBartolo Performing Arts Cente
Notre Dame, IN 46556
Phone: 574-631-7054
Fax: 219-631-3566
Web Site: www.ftt.nd.edu/
Officers:
  Television Concentration: Christine Becker
  Emeriti Faculty: Reginald Bain
  Concurrent Faculty: Ted Barron
  Concurrent Faculty: Scott Jackson
  Staff: Geoffrey Carter
Management:
  Manager-Washington Hall: Tom Barkes
  Film Concentration: Jim Collins
  Film Concentration: Donald Crafton
  Theatre Concentration: C. Kenneth Cole
  Theatre Concentration: Richard E. Donnelly
Specialized Field: Educational; Theater Workshops

3022
BROADWAY THEATRE LEAGUE OF SOUTH BEND
209 N. Main Street
Suite 201B
South Bend, IN 46601
Phone: 574-234-4044
Fax: 219-288-0290
Toll-free: 877-315-1234
Web Site: www.broadwaytheatreleague.com
Management:
  President: Micheal Harding
  Executive Director: Andrew Hoffmann
Founded: 1959
Specialized Field: Youth Theater; Classic; Contemporary; Broadway Musical Revivals
Status: Non-Profit, Professional
Paid Staff: 4
Performs At: Morris Performing Arts Center

3023
CROSSROADS REPERTORY THEATRE
540 N. 7th Street
Terre Haute, IN 47809
Phone: 812-237-3333
Web Site: crossroadsrep.com
Management:
  Artistic Director: Arthur Feinsod
  Associate Artistic Director: Chris Berchild
  Production Manager: David G. Del Colletti
  Company Manager: Toni Roloff

3024
INDIANA STATE UNIVERSITY SUMMER STAGE
Indiana State University
540 N 7th Street
Terre Haute, IN 47809
Phone: 812-237-3336
Fax: 812-237-3954
Management:
  Chairman/Artistic Director: Arthur Feinsod
  Production/Business Manager: David Del Colletti
Founded: 1965
Specialized Field: Educational; Theater Workshops
Status: Non-Equity; Nonprofit
Paid Staff: 20
Paid Artists: 20
Season: June 15 - July 28
Type of Stage: Thrust; Arena
Seating Capacity: 250

3025
VALPARAISO THEATRICAL COMPANY
3401 Valparaiso Street
Valparaiso, IN 46383
Phone: 219-309-6794
e-mail: colleenzana@gmail.com
Web Site: valparaisotheatricalcompany.org
Officers:
  President: Colleen Zana
  Vice President: Steve Zana
  Artistic Chair: Vickie Cash
Mission: The mission of Valparaiso Theatrical Company is to offer professional style theater at an affordable price while giving to charitable causes.
Status: Nonprofit

3026
VINCENNES UNIVERSITY SUMMER THEATRE
1002 N First
Vincennes, IN 47591
Phone: 812-885-4256
Fax: 812-885-5868
Management:
  Managing/Artistic Director: James J Spurrier, PhD

THEATRE / Iowa

Mission: Offering quality theatrical entertainment to Vincennes and surrounding areas in the summer months.
Utilizes: Singers
Founded: 1968
Specialized Field: Summer Stock; Musical
Status: Semi-Professional; Nonprofit
Performs At: Shircliff Theatre
Organization Type: Performing; Resident; Educational

3027
WAGON WHEEL THEATRE
2517 E Center Street
PO Box 804
Warsaw, IN 46580
Phone: 219-267-8041
Fax: 219-269-7996
Toll-free: 866-823-2618
Web Site: http://www.wagonwheeltheatre.com/theatre
Officers:
　Business Maneger: Carol Craig
　Director Marketing: Carla Robinson
　Director of Operations: Will Dawson
　Artistic Director: Scott Michaels
Management:
　Artistic Director: Roy Hine
　Director Marketing: Dan Rhodes
　Production Manager: Mike Higgins
Utilizes: Actors; AEA Actors; Choreographers; Dancers; Designers; Guest Conductors
Founded: 1956
Specialized Field: Theater in the Round
Status: Non-Equity; Commercial
Season: June - September
Type of Stage: Arena
Stage Dimensions: 32' x 35'
Seating Capacity: 835

3028
PURDUE PROFESSIONAL SUMMER THEATRE
1376 Stewart Center
Room 85
West Lafayette, IN 47907
Phone: 317-494-3082
Fax: 317-494-3660
Management:
　Division Theater: Jim O'Connor
　Associate Professor of Theatre: Russ Jones
　Scenic Construction Supervisor: Ron Clark
　Marketing/Public Relations Director: Lori Sparger
Mission: To present more recent American plays both dramatic and comedic.
Utilizes: Guest Companies; Singers
Founded: 1958
Specialized Field: Educational; Theater Workshops
Status: Professional; Nonprofit
Income Sources: Purdue University
Performs At: Experimental Theater
Organization Type: Performing

Iowa

3029
OLD CREAMERY THEATRE COMPANY
3023 220th Trail
Amana, IA 52203
Phone: 319-622-6034
Fax: 319-622-6262
Toll-free: 800-352-6262
e-mail: octc@southslope.net
Web Site: www.oldcreamery.com
Officers:

President: Peter R. Teahen
VP: Debra Brooks
Secretary: Paulette Milewski
Treasurer: Brandon Yuska
Director: Ericka Bennett
Vice President: Darryl Tower
President: Steve Arnold
Treasurer: Brandon Yuska
Management:
　Marketing Manager: Lily Allen
　Associate Artistic Director: Meg Merckens
　Artistic Director: Sean McCall
　GM: Pat Wagner
　Director of Education: Jackie McCall
Mission: To bring live theater to as many people as possible in rural Iowa.
Utilizes: Actors; AEA Actors; Choreographers; Five Seasonal Concerts; Guest Accompanists; Guest Companies; Guest Conductors; Guest Designers; Multi Collaborations; Resident Professionals
Founded: 1971
Specialized Field: Musical; Comedy; Youth Theater; Community Theater; Contemporary
Status: Non-Profit, Professional
Paid Staff: 25
Paid Artists: 20
Season: March - December
Performs At: Main Stage; Courtyard Stage; The Old Creamery Theatre-Amana
Affiliations: Actors' Equity Association
Annual Attendance: 30,000
Type of Stage: Proscenium; Courtyard Stage
Seating Capacity: 300
Year Built: 1988
Organization Type: Performing; Touring; Resident; Educational

3030
CLINTON AREA SHOWBOAT THEATRE
303 Riverview Drive
Clinton, IA 52732
Phone: 563-242-6760
Fax: 563-242-9247
e-mail: Tommy@summer-stock.org
Web Site: www.clintonshowboat.org/
Officers:
　Artistic Director: Tommy Iafrate
Specialized Field: Summer Stock; Musical; Drama; Comedy
Season: May - August

3031
BROADWAY THEATRE LEAGUE OF THE QUAD-CITIES
PO Box 130
Davenport, IA 52805
Phone: 319-326-1916
Mission: Supporting New York tours featuring Broadway theatre productions.
Founded: 1960
Specialized Field: Broadway Musical Revivals
Status: Nonprofit
Performs At: Adler Theatre
Organization Type: Sponsoring

3032
JUNIOR THEATRE
2822 Eastern Avenue
Davenport, IA 52803
Phone: 563-326-7862
Fax: 563-888-2216
Web Site: http://www.davenportjuniortheatre.com/
Officers:
　Artistic Director: Daniel DP Sheridan

Management:
　President: Rebecca Gulling
　Executive Director: Bonnie Guenther
　Artistic Director: Daniel Sheridan
　Front Desk Clerk: Kristin Meyer
　Dance Coordinator: Rachel Shipley
　Facility Coordinator: Tyson Danner
Mission: To offer classes in dance play production and creative drama to students in kindergarten through high school; To present five major productions and twenty eight touring productions.
Utilizes: Artists-in-Residence; Collaborations; Dancers; Grant Writers; Guest Artists; Guest Lecturers; Guild Activities; Instructors; Local Artists; Multimedia; Soloists; Theatre Companies
Founded: 1951
Specialized Field: Musical; Youth Theater; Community Theater; Children's Theater
Status: Non-Profit, Non-Professional
Paid Staff: 15
Volunteer Staff: 12
Paid Artists: 5
Income Sources: Local grants/class fees
Performs At: Mary Fluhrer Nighswander Junior Theatre
Affiliations: AATE
Annual Attendance: Classrooms
Facility Category: Theatre, Dance Studio
Type of Stage: Proscenium
Stage Dimensions: 46 W x 30 D with thrust
Seating Capacity: 440
Year Remodeled: 1981
Organization Type: Performing; Touring; Educational
Resident Groups: Professional Modern Dance Company

3033
THE CURTAINBOX THEATRE COMPANY
1035 W. Kimberly Road
Davenport, IA
Phone: 563-650-8121
e-mail: reservations@thecurtainbox.com
Web Site: thecurtainbox.com
Mission: The mission of The Curtainbox Theatre Company and Conservatory is to produce professional theatre of the highest quality to enrich the theatre community of the Quad Cities and provide employment opportunities to local and non-local artists
Founded: 2001
Status: Professional

3034
STAGEWEST THEATER COMPANY
221 Walnut Street
Des Moines, IA 50309
Mailing Address: P.O. Box 12127, Des Moines, IA 50312
Phone: 515-309-0251
e-mail: ublong@stagewestiowa.com
Web Site: stagewestiowa.com
Officers:
　President: Ashlea Lantz
　Vice President: Alex Hart
　Treasurer: Sue Dittmer
　Secretary: Jennifer Nostrala
Management:
　Producing Artistic Director: Todd Buchacker
　Production Manager: Shelby Burgus
　Business Manager: Bryan Doty
Mission: StageWest, by cultivating new opportunities for theatre artists and audiences, seeks to increase the understanding and enjoyment of life, society and the world through the presentation of progressive, contemporary theater.

THEATRE / Iowa

Founded: 1995
Status: Nonprofit

3035
GRAND OPERA HOUSE
135 8th Street
PO Box 632
Dubuque, IA 52001
Phone: 563-588-4356
Fax: 563-588-3497
e-mail: director@thegrandoperahouse.com
Web Site: www.thegrandoperahouse.com
Officers:
   President: Paul Hemmer
Management:
   President: Peter Soraparu
   Executive Director: Paul Hemmer, director@thegrandoperahouse.co
   Office & Box Office Manager: Jell Keck
   Technical Director: Tracey Richardson
   Box Office Assistant: Chris Scmitz
Mission: To offer quality entertainment and contribute to the community's cultural growth.
Utilizes: Guest Companies
Founded: 1889
Specialized Field: Musical; Community Theater
Status: Non-Profit, Non-Professional
Paid Staff: 3
Volunteer Staff: 100
Paid Artists: 45
Budget: $450,000
Income Sources: Iowa Community Theatre Association; Dubuque, Galena & Dyersville Area Chambers of Commerce
Performs At: Community Theater
Annual Attendance: 10,000
Facility Category: Non union shop, utilizing volunteers as operating personnel.
Type of Stage: Procenium arch 30' high x 35' wide
Stage Dimensions: 34' x 34', main curtain 4' back
Seating Capacity: 640
Year Built: 1989
Year Remodeled: 2010
Cost: $3.5 million
Rental Contact: Paul Hemmer
Organization Type: Performing; Educational

3036
IOWA SUMMER REPERTORY
107 Theatre Building
Iowa City, IA 52242
Phone: 319-335-2700
Fax: 319-335-3568
Toll-free: 800-426-2437
e-mail: eric-forsythe@uiowa.edu
Web Site: theatre.uiowa.edu/production/iowa-summer-rep
Officers:
   Assistant Professor: Paul Kalina
   Assistant Professor: Anne Marie Test
   Assistant Professor: Tlaloc Rivas
   Adjunct Instructor: Fannie Hungerford
Management:
   President: Eric Forsythe
   Production Manager: Rick Loula
   Professor: John Cameron
   Acting: Susan Chambers
   Professor: Eric Forsythe
Mission: Retrospective of plays by a single contemporary playwright each season and the development of new scripts.
Utilizes: Actors; AEA Actors; Artists-in-Residence; Commissioned Music; Composers-in-Residence; Designers; Grant Writers; Guest Accompanists; Guest Conductors; Guest Designers; Guest Lecturers; Instructors; Local Artists; Multimedia; Music; Original Music Scores; Performance Artists; Poets; Resident Artists; Resident Professionals; Selected Students; Student Interns; Visual Arts
Founded: 1920
Specialized Field: Comedy; Dinner Theater; Contemporary
Status: Non-Profit, Professional
Paid Staff: 30
Paid Artists: 20
Budget: $170,000
Income Sources: Box Office, Grants
Season: May - July
Affiliations: AEA; URTA
Type of Stage: Proscenium; Flexible; Black Box
Seating Capacity: 477, 165, 135
Year Remodeled: 1986

3037
SIOUX CITY COMMUNITY THEATRE
1401 Riverside Boulevard
Sioux City, IA 51109
Mailing Address: PO Box 512
Phone: 712-233-2719
Fax: 712-233-1611
e-mail: scct@cableone.net
Web Site: www.scctheatre.org
Officers:
   President: Greg Gregerson
   Vice President: Mike Mattison
   Secretary: Jackie Kelly
   Treasurer: Heather Marreel
   Education Director: Christine Wolf
Mission: SCCT enhances quality of life by providing opportunities for accessible and lifelong education, volunteerism and entertainment in the performing arts for people of all ages.
Founded: 1948
Specialized Field: Musical; Comedy; Drama
Status: Non-Profit, Non-Professional
Paid Staff: 3
Volunteer Staff: 500
Non-paid Artists: 100
Income Sources: Iowa Community Theatre Association
Performs At: Shore Acres
Seating Capacity: 314
Organization Type: Performing

3038
RIVERSIDE THEATRE
3250 Riverside Park Drive
Vero Beach, IA 32963
Phone: 772-231-6990
Fax: 772-234-5298
Toll-free: 800-445-6745
e-mail: info@riversidetheatre.org
Web Site: www.riversidetheatre.org
Officers:
   President: E Bradley Jones
   VP: Marty Gibson
   Treasurer: Richard Stark
   Secretary: Thomas Slaughter
Management:
   Executive Director: Chuck Still
   Artistic Director: Jody Hovland
   Education Director: Linda Downey
   Production Manager: Ron Clark
   Development Director: Jennifer Holan
Mission: To provide an artistic home for theatre professionals from Iowa and beyond, and to entertain audiences with intimate, engaging productions from the classics to world premieres.
Utilizes: Actors; AEA Actors; Choreographers; Commissioned Composers; Dancers; Designers; Educators; Guest Conductors; Guest Designers; Guild Activities; Instructors; Local Artists; Music; Performance Artists; Resident Professionals; Soloists; Student Interns
Founded: 1973
Specialized Field: Drama; Musical
Status: Nonprofit, Professional
Paid Staff: 35
Volunteer Staff: 150
Budget: $3 million
Income Sources: Ticket Sales; Annual Giving; Rentals; Special Events
Affiliations: Actors' Equity Association; Florida Professional Theatre Association; LORT
Annual Attendance: 110,000
Facility Category: Theatre
Type of Stage: Proscenium; Black Box
Stage Dimensions: 40x30
Seating Capacity: 610; 300
Year Built: 1973
Year Remodeled: 1990
Rental Contact: Jon Moses
Organization Type: Performing; Touring; Resident; Educational; Sponsoring

3039
WATERLOO COMMUNITY PLAYHOUSE & BLACK HAWK CHILDRENS THEATRE
225 Commercial Street
Waterloo, IA 50701
Phone: 319-235-0367
Fax: 319-235-7489
e-mail: info@wcpbhct.org
Web Site: www.wcpbhct.org
Management:
   President of the Board: David Hildahl
   Artistic Managing Director: Charles Stilwill
   Marketing/Development Director: Danny Katz
   Administrative Director: Ethan Fischer
   Designer/Production Manager: Katrina Sandvik
Mission: Providing quality theatre productions; enhancing the cultural growth of Northeast Iowa.
Founded: 1916
Specialized Field: Musical; Comedy; Youth Theater; Community Theater; Classic; Contemporary
Status: Non-Profit, Non-Professional
Paid Staff: 9
Paid Artists: 6
Non-paid Artists: 400
Budget: $552,450
Income Sources: American Association of Community Theatres; Association of American Theatre for Youth; Waterloo, Cedar Falls & Waverly Chambers of Commerce; Iowa Community Theatre Association
Performs At: American Association of Community Theatres; Association of American Theatre for Youth; Waterloo/Cedar Falls/Waverly Chambers
Annual Attendance: 31,640
Facility Category: Arts Center
Type of Stage: Proscenium
Seating Capacity: 367
Year Built: 1965
Year Remodeled: 1977
Organization Type: Performing; Educational; Sponsoring

3040
TALLGRASS THEATRE COMPANY
1401 Vine Street
West Des Moines, IA 50265

Mailing Address: P.O. Box 65932, West Des Moines, IA 50265
Phone: 515-505-3504
e-mail: info@tallgrasstheatre.org
Web Site: tallgrasstheatre.org
Management:
   Executive Director: Jessie Phillips
Mission: Tallgrass Theatre Company strives to enrich the greater Des Moines community by providing a venue for new and unique performance work that is both entertaining and evocative.
Founded: 2002
Performs At: Rex Mathes Auditorium

Kansas

3041
AUGUSTA ARTS COUNCIL/AUGUSTA HISTORIC THEATRE
523 State Street
Augusta, KS 67010
Phone: 316-775-2900
Fax: 316-775-7475
e-mail: augustaarts@sbcglobal.net
Web Site: www.augustahistorictheatre.com
Officers:
   President: William Morris
   Executive Director: DeAnn Triboulet
Founded: 1975
Specialized Field: Musical; Comedy; Youth Theater; Dinner Theater; Ethnic Theater; Community Theater; Puppet; Historical; Classic
Status: Non-Profit, Professional
Paid Staff: 1
Performs At: Auditorium
Seating Capacity: 500
Year Built: 1935

3042
CHANUTE COMMUNITY THEATRE
101 S. Lincoln
P.O. Box 907
Chanute, KS 66720
Phone: 620-431-5200
Fax: 620-431-5209
e-mail: city@chanute.org
Web Site: www.chanute.org
Mission: To offer the community wide-ranging theatrical entertainment.
Founded: 1978
Specialized Field: Musical; Dinner Theater; Community Theater
Status: Non-Professional; Nonprofit
Income Sources: Association of Kansas Theatres
Performs At: Memorial Auditorium; Chanute Country Club
Organization Type: Performing; Resident; Educational

3043
COFFEYVILLE COMMUNITY THEATRE
400 West 11th
Coffeyville, KS 67337
Mailing Address: PO Box 317
Phone: 620-251-7700
e-mail: markf@coffeyville.edu
Web Site: http://www.coffeyville.edu/activities/theatre/index.htm
Management:
   Director: Mark Frank
Mission: Providing live theatre for the community.
Founded: 1945
Specialized Field: Musical; Dinner Theater; Community Theater
Status: Non-Professional; Nonprofit
Paid Staff: 35
Income Sources: Association of Kansas Theatres; Kansas Arts Council
Performs At: Floral Hall
Organization Type: Performing

3044
BROWN GRAND THEATRE
310 W 6th Street
Concordia, KS 66901
Phone: 785-243-2553
e-mail: browngrand@nckcn.com
Web Site: www.browngrand.org
Officers:
   President: Everett Miller
   VP: Paul Rimovsky
   Secretary/Treasurer: Wonda Phillips
Management:
   Executive Director: Susan Maxson, browngrand@nckcn.com
Mission: Maintaining the historic Brown Grand Theatre; enhancing the cultural life of the area by providing quality theatre.
Utilizes: Guest Artists; Guest Companies; Singers
Founded: 1907
Specialized Field: Musical; Community Theater; Ethnic Theater; Puppet
Status: Professional; Nonprofit
Income Sources: Mid-America Arts Alliance
Organization Type: Performing; Educational; Sponsoring

3045
KANSAS UNIVERSITY THEATRE
317 Murphy Hall, 1530 Naismith Drive
Lawrence, KS 66045
Phone: 785-864-3982
Web Site: kutheatre.com
Officers:
   Department Chair: Mechele Leon
Management:
   Artistic Director: Dennis Christilles
Organization Type: Educational

3046
THE MARTIN CITY MELODRAMA & VAUDEVILLE COMPANY LTD.
9601 Metcalf
Overland Park, KS 66212
Phone: 913-642-7576
e-mail: martincitymelo@yahoo.com
Web Site: martincitymelodrama.org
Management:
   Artistic Director: Jeanne M. Beechwood
Founded: 1985
Status: Nonprofit

3047
SALINA COMMUNITY THEATRE
303 E Iron
PO Box 2305
Salina, KS 67401
Phone: 785-827-6126
Fax: 785-827-6319
Toll-free: 877-414-2367
e-mail: sctstaff@salinatheatre.com
Web Site: www.salinatheatre.com
Officers:
   Executive Director: Michael Spicer
   Scenic Designer/Technical Director: J.R. Lidgett
   Education Director: Jordan Martens
Management:
   President: Shirley Braxton
   Executive Director: Mike Spicer
   VP Director: John Quinley
Mission: To offer entertainment to the community; to provide recreation for those who would like to participate in theatrical productions.
Utilizes: Guest Companies
Founded: 1960
Specialized Field: Musical; Community Theater
Status: Non-Professional; Nonprofit
Paid Staff: 50
Organization Type: Performing; Sponsoring

3048
BARN PLAYERS THEATRE
6219 Martway
Shawnee Mission, KS 66202
Mailing Address: PO Box 12767
Phone: 913-432-9100
e-mail: admin@thebarnplayers.org
Web Site: http://www.thebarnplayers.org/
Officers:
   President: Margaret Godfrey
   VP: Shirley Wagner
   Secretary: Martha Coulter
   Secretary: Cecelia Baty
   Artistic Director: Eric Magnus
   Vice-President: Eric Van Horn
   President: Vida Bikales
   Acting Treasurer: Maneesh Jhunjhunwala
Management:
   Managing Director: Margaret Godfrey
   Artistic Director: Max Beatty
   Webmaster/Director: Richard Buswellk
   Marketing Director/House Manager: Tricia Kyler
   Developer/Technical Director: Scott Bowling
Mission: To promote artistic excellence through theatre; to produce community theatre productions; to encourage participation by interested persons; to promote theatre interest in the community.
Utilizes: Singers
Founded: 1956
Specialized Field: Community Theater
Status: Nonprofit
Income Sources: Association of Kansas Theatres; American Association of Community Theatres
Performs At: Overland Theatre
Organization Type: Performing

3049
TOPEKA CIVIC THEATRE & ACADEMY
3028 SW 8th Street
Topeka, KS 66606
Phone: 785-357-5211
Fax: 913-357-0719
Web Site: www.topekacivichteatre.com
Officers:
   President & CEO: Vickie Brokke
Management:
   Producing Artistic Director: Michael Wainstein
   Business Director: Brett Landow
Mission: Stimulating, entertaining, educating and serving our community; providing opportunities for performing and developing theatrical skills.
Utilizes: Guest Artists; Guest Companies
Founded: 1936
Specialized Field: Musical; Dinner Theater; Community Theater
Status: Non-Professional; Nonprofit
Paid Staff: 100
Income Sources: American Association of Community Theatres; Association of Kansas Theatres; Kansas Community Theatre Conference
Performs At: Topeka Civic Theatre
Type of Stage: Proscenium

THEATRE / Kentucky

Seating Capacity: 286
Organization Type: Performing

3050
COLUMBIAN THEATRE: MUSEUM & ART CENTER
521 Lincoln Avenue
PO Box 72
Wamego, KS 66547
Phone: 785-456-2029
Fax: 785-456-9498
Toll-free: 800-899-1893
e-mail: boxoffice@columbiantheatre.com
Web Site: www.columbiantheatre.com
Officers:
   President: Lance White
Management:
   Executive Director: Vivian Orndorff
   Artistic Director: Ariane Chapman
   Marketing/Events Director: Kayla Oney
Founded: 1989
Specialized Field: Specialty Acts; Historical; Drama
Status: Non-Profit, Non-Professional
Paid Staff: 4
Performs At: Peddicord Playhouse
Rental Contact: Marketing/Events Director Kayla Oney

3051
MUSIC THEATRE OF WICHITA
225 West Douglas
Suite 202
Wichita, KS 67202
Phone: 316-265-3253
Fax: 316-265-8708
Toll-free: 800-899-1893
e-mail: wayne@mtwichita.org
Web Site: www.mtwichita.org
Management:
   Producing Artistic Director: Wayne Bryan, wayne@mtwichita.org
   Producing Associate: Nancy Reeves, nancy@mtwichita.org
   Executive Director: Clint Stueve
   Administrative Coordinator: Brooke Rindt
Mission: Dedicated to stimulating and nurturing interest in musical theatre by producing and or presenting Broadway quality productions, while entertaining and educating patrons, the community, and the theatrical artists.
Founded: 1972
Specialized Field: Musical
Status: Non-Profit, Professional
Paid Staff: 8
Volunteer Staff: 200
Paid Artists: 250
Budget: $3,000,000
Income Sources: Ticket Sales; Fundraisers; Set Rentals; State Funding; Grants
Season: June - August
Performs At: Century II Concert Hall
Affiliations: National Alliance for Musical Theatre
Annual Attendance: 60,000
Facility Category: Civic Arts Center
Type of Stage: Proscenium
Stage Dimensions: 44'Wx45'Dx22'H
Seating Capacity: 2,100
Year Built: 1969
Organization Type: Performing; Educational

3052
WICHITA COMMUNITY THEATRE
258 N Fountain
Wichita, KS 67208
Phone: 620-686-1282
e-mail: president@wichitact.org
Web Site: www.wichitact.org
Officers:
   President: Blankley Ben
   VP: Eubank Casey
   Secretary: Green Mary Tosh
   Treasurer: Pearce Cherly
   Technical Directors: Tanner Jane
Management:
   Chief Executive Officer: Mary Tush Green
Mission: Providing the community with a wide range of theatrical entertainment; offering opportunities to amateur performers and technicians.
Founded: 1946
Specialized Field: Community Theater
Status: Non-Professional; Nonprofit
Income Sources: Association of Kansas Theatres
Performs At: Century II Civic Center; Workshop
Organization Type: Performing

3053
HORSEFEATHERS & APPLESAUCE SUMMER DINNER THEATRE
Southwestern College
100 College Street
Winfield, KS 67156-2499
Phone: 620-229-6328
Fax: 620-229-6335
e-mail: amoon@sckans.edu
Management:
   Manager/Director: Nulson Moon
Founded: 1973
Specialized Field: Educational; Theater Workshops; Summer Stock
Status: Non-Equity; Nonprofit
Paid Staff: 35
Volunteer Staff: 10
Season: June 1 - July 31
Type of Stage: Proscenium
Seating Capacity: 240

Kentucky

3054
STEPHEN FOSTER-MUSICAL
411 East Stephen Foster Avenue
PO Box 546
Bardstown, KY 40004
Phone: 502-348-5971
Fax: 502-349-0574
Toll-free: 800-626-1563
e-mail: info@stephenfoster.com
Web Site: www.stephenfoster.com
Officers:
   Chairman: Nicky Rapier
   Vice Chairman: Louis Ballard
Management:
   Artistic Director: Rick Dildine
   General Manager: Betty Kelley
Mission: Fostering area cultural activities.
Utilizes: Actors; Choreographers; Commissioned Music; Educators; Fine Artists; Multimedia; Original Music Scores; Sign Language Translators; Singers
Founded: 1959
Specialized Field: Musical; Comedy; Youth Theater; Classic; Contemporary
Status: Non-Profit, Professional
Paid Staff: 70
Paid Artists: 50
Budget: $900,000
Performs At: J. Dan Talbott Amphitheatre
Annual Attendance: 60,000+
Facility Category: Outdoor Amphitheatre
Seating Capacity: 1,500
Year Built: 1958
Year Remodeled: 1997
Organization Type: Amphitheatre

3055
FOUNTAIN SQUARE PLAYERS
313 State Street
Bowling Green, KY 42101
Phone: 270-782-3119
e-mail: info@fountainsquareplayers.org
Web Site: http://www.fountainsquareplayers.org/
Officers:
   Secretary: Lynn Gilcrease
   Social Co-chair: Linda Hill
   President: Jeff Moore
   Treasurer: Bill Russell
Management:
   Secretary: Lynn Gilcrease
   Social Co-chair: Linda Hill
   President: Jeff Moore
   Treasurer: Bill Russell
   House Manager: Jerry Wallace
Mission: To promote appreciation and enjoyment of theatre.
Founded: 1978
Specialized Field: Community Theater
Status: Non-Professional; Nonprofit
Paid Staff: 150
Income Sources: American Arts Alliance
Performs At: Capitol Arts Center
Organization Type: Performing

3056
PINE KNOB THEATRE
2250 Pine Knob Road
Caneyville, KY 42721
Phone: 270-879-8190
e-mail: pineknob@windstream.net
Web Site: pineknob.com

3057
PIONEER PLAYHOUSE OF KENTUCKY
840 Stanford Road
Danville, KY 40422
Phone: 859-236-2747
Fax: 859-236-4321
e-mail: pioneer@mis.net
Web Site: www.pioneerplayhouse.com
Management:
   Artistic Director: Holly Henson
   Producer: Charlotte Henson
Mission: Maintaining an arts vocational training center with professionals as performers and teachers.
Founded: 1950
Specialized Field: Summer Stock; Musical; Dinner Theater
Status: Professional; Nonprofit
Paid Staff: 30
Income Sources: Southeastern Theatre Conference; Kentucky Theatre Association
Season: June - August
Performs At: Colonel Eben Henson Amphitheatre
Organization Type: Performing; Resident; Educational

3058
HARDIN COUNTY PLAYHOUSE
209 West Dixie Ave.
Elizabethtown, KY 42701
Phone: 270-351-0577
e-mail: playhouse@hardincountyplayhouse.com
Web Site: www.hardincountyplayhouse.com
Officers:

President: Claire Allen
VP: Andy Frueh
Treasurer: Mitzi Lynch
Secretary: Caroline Cline
Management:
President: Danny Darnall
Managing Director: Dee Corkran
Mission: To provide performing arts for the community.
Utilizes: Guest Companies; Singers
Founded: 1969
Specialized Field: Musical; Comedy; Dinner Theater; Ethnic Theater; Community Theater; Contemporary
Status: Non-Profit, Non-Professional
Paid Staff: 1
Income Sources: Grants
Performs At: Hardin County Playhouse
Annual Attendance: varies
Organization Type: Performing

3059
KINCAID REGIONAL THEATRE
400 Main Street
Falmouth, KY 41040
Phone: 859-654-2117
Fax: 859-654-2117
Toll-free: 800-647-7469
e-mail: krtshows@fuse.net
Web Site: http://www.krtshow.com/page/page/244016.htm
Officers:
President: Gene Kearns
VP: Myron Doan
Secretary: Barbara Browning
Management:
General Manager: Shirley Merrill
Mission: Employing talented actors and offering quality entertainment to the region.
Utilizes: Guest Artists; Guest Companies; Singers
Founded: 1983
Specialized Field: Musical; Ensembles
Status: Professional; Nonprofit
Income Sources: Southeastern Theatre Conference
Performs At: Falmouth Auditorium
Organization Type: Performing; Resident; Educational; Sponsoring

3060
FAR-OFF BROADWAY PLAYERS
115 East Main St
Glasgow, KY 42141
Phone: 270-651-8612
e-mail: president@faroffbroadwayplayers.org
Web Site: http://www.faroffbroadwayplayers.org/
Officers:
President: Peggy Goodman
VP: Denise Johnson
Secretary: Zona Cetera
Treasurer: Diane Beeckler
Secretary: Wendy Salsbery
Vice President: Dane Bowles
President: Denise Williams
Mission: To study and perform amateur drama.
Founded: 1980
Specialized Field: Community Theater
Status: Non-Professional; Nonprofit
Paid Staff: 40
Organization Type: Performing; Resident

3061
MUHLENBERG COMMUNITY THEATRE
119 N Main Street
Greenville, KY 42345-7165
Phone: 270-338-7165
e-mail: mctikynews@gmail.com
Web Site: www.mctiky.org
Officers:
President: Jeff Dickinson
VP: John Stewart
Secretary: Leslie England
Treasurer: Daven Edmonds
Treasurer: Sherry Lorenzen
Assistant Treasurer: Daven Edmonds
President: Jeff Dicikinson
Treasurer: Daven Edmonds
Secretary: Leslie England
Management:
President: Jeff Dicikinson
Mission: Promoting the theatrical arts.
Utilizes: Guest Artists; Guest Companies; Singers
Founded: 1980
Specialized Field: Musical; Dinner Theater; Community Theater
Status: Professional; Semi-Professional; Nonprofit
Paid Staff: 20
Income Sources: American Association of Community Theatres
Performs At: Palace Theatre
Year Remodeled: 1999
Organization Type: Performing; Touring; Resident; Educational

3062
LEGEND OF DANIEL BOONE/JAMES HARROD AMPHITHEATRE
Box 365
Harrodsburg, KY 40330
Phone: 606-734-3346
Fax: 602-734-3348
Management:
General Manager: Maureen Daly
Founded: 1963
Specialized Field: Summer Stock
Status: Non-Equity; Nonprofit
Season: Mid June - Late August
Type of Stage: Amphitheatre
Stage Dimensions: 60'x 40'
Seating Capacity: 600

3063
HORSE CAVE THEATRE
101 E Main Street
PO Box 215
Horse Cave, KY 42749
Phone: 270-786-1200
Fax: 270-786-5298
Toll-free: 800-342-2177
Web Site: www.horsecavetheatre.org
Officers:
President: Carla Wertzer
Management:
Artistic Director: Robert Brock
Education Associate: Lynn Gilcrease
Marketing Director: Melissa McGoire
Development Director: Kim Harrison
Mission: To be the only resident professional theater outside of metropolitan Louisville that provides a forum for Kentucky writers to produce their works; to present an annual Shakespeare production that assists in meeting the needs of students.
Utilizes: Actors; AEA Actors; Educators; Guest Artists; Guest Conductors; Guest Designers; Local Artists; Performance Artists; Poets; Resident Professionals; Soloists
Founded: 1977
Specialized Field: Comedy; Youth Theater; Classic; Contemporary
Status: Non-Profit, Professional
Paid Staff: 30
Paid Artists: 7
Budget: $625,000
Income Sources: Kentucky Arts Council; KY Tourism Cabinet; Corporations; Foundations; Businesses & Individuals
Season: June - December
Performs At: Horse Cave Theatre
Annual Attendance: 30,000
Facility Category: Theatre
Type of Stage: Thrust
Seating Capacity: 346
Year Built: 1977
Year Remodeled: 1993
Architect: Tate Jacobs
Cost: $1,500,000
Organization Type: Performing; Touring; Resident; Educational

3064
ACTORS' GUILD OF LEXINGTON
P.O Box 964
Lexington, KY 40588
Phone: 859-309-1909
Fax: 859-233-3773
e-mail: info@actors-guild.org
Web Site: www.actorsguildoflexington.org
Officers:
President: Peggy Goodman
Management:
Director: Richard Saintpeter
Managing Director: Steven Koehler
Artistic Director: Eric Seal
Assistant to the Artistic Director: Chrisena Ricci
Production Manager: Tommy Gatton
Mission: To produce compelling contemporary theatre for the region.
Founded: 1984
Specialized Field: Musical; Comedy; Ethnic Theater; Community Theater; Contemporary
Status: Non-Profit, Professional
Paid Staff: 4
Paid Artists: 40

3065
BROADWAY LIVE AT THE OPERA HOUSE
430 W Vine
Lexington, KY 40507
Phone: 859-233-4567
Fax: 859-253-2718
e-mail: webmaster@lexingtoncenter.com
Web Site: www.lexingtonoperahouse.com
Officers:
President: Jeff Dickson
Vice President: Onallee Kidd
Management:
Managing Director: Tom Habermann
Utilizes: Actors; AEA Actors; Choreographers; Collaborations; Dance Companies; Dancers; Educators; Fine Artists; Guild Activities; Local Artists; Local Artists & Directors; Multimedia; Original Music Scores; Singers; Special Technical Talent; Theatre Companies
Founded: 1976
Specialized Field: Musical; Comedy; Youth Theater; Ethnic Theater; Classic; Light Theater
Status: Non-Profit, Non-Professional
Performs At: Broadway Live Series; Variety Series; Local Artist Groups
Affiliations: APAP; WTAT
Facility Category: Theatre
Type of Stage: Proscenium

THEATRE / Kentucky

Stage Dimensions: 37'3x21'""
Seating Capacity: 1,000
Year Built: 1886
Year Remodeled: 1976
Rental Contact: Program Director Luanne Franklin

3066
LEXINGTON CHILDREN'S THEATRE
418 W Short Street
Lexington, KY 40507
Phone: 859-254-4546
Fax: 859-254-9512
Toll-free: 800-928-4545
e-mail: info@lctonstage.org
Web Site: www.lctonstage.org
Officers:
　Development Director: Rachel Ray
　Marketing & Sales: Tiffany Dupont
　Associate Education Director: Amie Kisling
　Technical Director: Jeremy Villines
　Lightening Director: Justine Barke
Management:
　President: Wander Faircloth
　Producing Director: Larry Snipes
　Artistic Director: Vivian R.Snipes
　Associate Artistic Director: Jeremy Kisling
　Managing Director: Lesley Farmer
　Production Stage Manager: Dawn Crabtree
　Resident Designer: Eric Morris
　Technical Director: Thomas Taylor
Founded: 1938
Specialized Field: Youth Theater; Children's Theater
Status: Non-Profit, Professional
Paid Staff: 10
Paid Artists: 30

3067
STUDIO PLAYERS
154 West Bell Court
Lexington, KY 40508
Mailing Address: PO Box 23252, Lexington, KY. 40523
Phone: 859-253-2512
e-mail: bsingleton99@yahoo.com
Web Site: http://www.studioplayers.org/index.htm
Officers:
　President: Scott Turner
　Past President: David Bratcher
　President Elect: Debbie Sharp
　Secretary: Ellen Hellard
　Treasurer: Bob Kinstle
Mission: Studio Players has presented plays since 1953.
Founded: 1953
Specialized Field: Drama; Comedy
Status: Nonprofit

3068
ACTORS THEATRE OF LOUISVILLE
316-320 W Main Street
Louisville, KY 40202-4218
Phone: 502-584-1205
Fax: 502-561-3300
Toll-free: 800-422-5849
e-mail: mail@actorstheatre.org
Web Site: www.actorstheatre.org
Officers:
　President: Bruce C Merrick
　VP Finance: Frederic H Davis
　Treasurer: Bruce K Dudley
　Secretary: Sarah D. Fuller
Management:
　Executive Director: Sandy Speer
　Artistic Director: Marc Masterson
　Managing Director: Fraizer Mash
Mission: To offer the finest in professional entertainment to a wide audience at reasonable prices; to maintain fiscal responsibility.
Utilizes: Actors; AEA Actors; Artists-in-Residence; Choreographers; Collaborations; Commissioned Composers; Commissioned Music; Dancers; Designers; Educators; Grant Writers; Guest Accompanists; Guest Artists; Guest Choreographers; Guest Companies; Guest Conductors; Guest Directors; Guest Ensembles; Guest Instructors; Guest Lecturers; Guest Musicians; Guest Teachers; Guest Writers; Guild Activities; Instructors; Local Artists; Multimedia; Music; Organization Contracts; Original Music Scores; Performance Artists; Playwrights; Poets; Resident Professionals; Selected Students; Sign Language Translators; Singers; Special Technical Talent; Touring Companies; Visual Arts
Founded: 1964
Specialized Field: Touring Company
Status: Non-Profit, Professional
Paid Staff: 152
Paid Artists: 150
Budget: $8 million
Income Sources: Ticket sales; grants; contributions
Affiliations: League of Resident Theatres
Annual Attendance: 240,000
Facility Category: 3 theatre complex
Type of Stage: 2 thrust stages and an arena
Seating Capacity: 637; 318; 159
Year Built: 1972
Year Remodeled: 1994
Rental Contact: Mike Brooks
Organization Type: Performing; Resident

3069
KENTUCKY SHAKESPEARE FESTIVAL
323 W. Broadway Suite 401
Louisville, KY 40208
Phone: 502-574-9900
Fax: 592-566-9200
e-mail: tofter@aol.com
Web Site: www.kyshakespeare.com/
Officers:
　Vice President: Elizabeth W. Davis
　Treasurer: Elizabeth Rounsavall
　Secretary: Philip C. Eschels
　Secretary: Philip C. Eschels
Management:
　President: Charles Keaton
　Artistic Director: Curt Toftelund
　Managing Director: Steven Renner
Mission: To provide accessible, professional, classical theatre and quality education touring programs.
Utilizes: Actors; Artists-in-Residence; Collaborating Artists; Collaborations; Designers; Educators; Five Seasonal Concerts; Guest Accompanists; Guest Conductors; Guest Ensembles; Guild Activities; High School Drama; Local Artists; Original Music Scores; Resident Artists; Resident Professionals; Selected Students; Soloists; Student Interns; Theatre Companies
Founded: 1960
Specialized Field: Shakespeare
Status: Non-Profit, Professional
Paid Staff: 7
Paid Artists: 20
Budget: $600,000
Income Sources: Corporate, Foundation, Individuals, Government, Fund, Earned
Season: May - August
Performs At: C. Douglas Ramey Amphitheater
Annual Attendance: 10,000
Facility Category: Outdoor Ampitheatre
Type of Stage: Thrust
Seating Capacity: 1000
Year Built: 1963
Year Remodeled: 1993
Organization Type: Performing; Resident; Touring; Educational

3070
MUSIC THEATRE LOUISVILLE
323 West Broadway, Suite 600
Louisville, KY 40202
Phone: 502-589-4060
Fax: 502-589-4344
e-mail: info@musictheatrelouisville.com
Web Site: www.musictheaterlouisville.com
Officers:
　President: Peter Holloway
Management:
　Director: Norma O'Berst
　Artistic Director: Steven Jones
　Education Director: Lucas Adams
　Director Marketing: Kara Brown
　Director Education: Sharon Kinnison
　Operations Director: Bill Beauchamp
Founded: 1981
Specialized Field: Musical; Comedy; Community Theater
Status: Non-Profit, Non-Professional
Paid Staff: 100
Paid Artists: 100
Season: May - August
Type of Stage: Proscenium
Stage Dimensions: 60' x 50'
Seating Capacity: 1600

3071
STAGE ONE: THE LOUISVILLE CHILDREN'S THEATRE
323 West Broadway, Suite 600
Louisville, KY 40202
Phone: 502-589-4060
Fax: 502-588-5910
Toll-free: 800-989-5946
e-mail: stageone@stageone.org
Web Site: www.stageone.org
Officers:
　Producing Artistic Director: Peter Holloway
　Chair: Carl M.Thomas
　Ex-Officio: Leslie Broecker
　Honorary Members: Mike Berry
Management:
　Artistic Director: J Daniel Herring
　Education: Lucas Adams
　Executive: Peter Holloway
　Finance: Mike Brooks
　Group Sales: Susan Duffy
Mission: To provide high-quality, professional, live theatre for young audiences that develops the whole child, supports the learning environment and builds strong family bonds.
Utilizes: Actors; AEA Actors; Collaborations; Designers; Educators; Guest Companies; Guest Conductors; Guest Lecturers; Multimedia; Original Music Scores; Performance Artists; Resident Artists; Resident Professionals; Singers
Founded: 1946
Specialized Field: Musical; Comedy; Youth Theater; Contemporary
Status: Non-Profit, Professional
Paid Staff: 25
Paid Artists: 15
Budget: $1.8 million
Income Sources: Ticket sales; Grants; Donations
Performs At: Kentucky Center for the Arts; Brown Theatre

Affiliations: The Kentucky Center for the Arts
Annual Attendance: 150,000
Organization Type: Performing; Touring; Educational

3072
TWILIGHT CABARET PRODUCTIONS
600 Driftwood Drive
Murray, KY 42071
Phone: 270-436-2399
e-mail: twilight@vci.net
Web Site: twilightcabaretproductions.org
Mission: To provide a complete spectrum of professional entertainment for an undeserved area; to create an atmosphere in which both audience and performing members receive a lifelong understanding of the Arts for the benefit of the community and the world around them; to bring original work to Kentucky, for Kentucky, and about Kentucky.
Status: Professional; Nonprofit
Season: Summer

3073
THEATRE WORKSHOP OF OWENSBORO
407 W 5th Street
PO Box 644
Owensboro, KY 42302
Phone: 270-683-5003
Fax: 270-683-5003
e-mail: tickets@theatreworkshop.org
Web Site: www.theatreworkshop.org
Management:
  President: Teresa Wills
  Executive Director: Johnmike Filbin
  Education Director: Sean Dysinger
Mission: To offer quality amateur theatre to the Owensboro area; to provide area performers and technicians with opportunities to practice their crafts.
Utilizes: Actors
Founded: 1955
Specialized Field: Musical; Comedy; Youth Theater; Ethnic Theater; Theater Workshops
Status: Non-Profit, Non-Professional
Paid Staff: 4
Non-paid Artists: 350
Budget: $140,000
Income Sources: Corporate; Indivdual; Grants
Performs At: Old Trinity Centre; River Park Center
Annual Attendance: 4000
Facility Category: Church
Stage Dimensions: 20' x 22'
Seating Capacity: 100
Year Remodeled: 1999
Organization Type: Performing; Resident

3074
MARKET HOUSE THEATRE
141 Kentucky Avenue
Paducah, KY 42003
Mailing Address: 132 Market House Square, Paducah, KY 42001-0778
Phone: 270-444-6829
Fax: 270-575-9321
Toll-free: 888-648-7529
e-mail: info@mhtplay.com
Web Site: www.mhtplay.com
Officers:
  President: Kristin Williams
  VP: Kent Price
  Treasurer: Pam Benzing
  Secretary: Denise Bristol
Management:
  Artistic/Executive Director: Michael Cochran
  Business Manager: Marsha Cash
Mission: To enrich the cultural and artistic life of the community through the presentation of a diverse season; touring; providing educational programs.
Utilizes: Guest Companies; Singers
Founded: 1963
Specialized Field: Community Theater
Status: Non-Professional; Nonprofit
Paid Staff: 7
Paid Artists: 10
Non-paid Artists: 200
Budget: $462,000
Income Sources: 70% Earned; 30% Contributed
Type of Stage: Proscenium
Stage Dimensions: 22' x 35'
Seating Capacity: 230
Year Remodeled: 1980
Organization Type: Performing; Touring; Educational

3075
JENNY WILEY THEATRE
121 Theatre Court
PO Box 22
Prestonburg, KY 41653
Mailing Address: PO Box 22
Phone: 606-886-9274
Fax: 606-886-8875
Toll-free: 877-225-5598
e-mail: marty@jwtheatre.com
Web Site: www.jwtheatre.com
Management:
  Executive Director: Martin Childers, marty@jwtheatre.com
  Marketing Director: Carolyn Glodfelter
  Technical Director: DARRYL WILLARD
Mission: Our mission is to enhance the quqality of life in eastern Kentucky by providing professional theatre and exceptional educational opportunities in the performing arts.
Utilizes: Actors; Choreographers; Collaborating Artists; Commissioned Composers; Community Talent; Contract Actors; Dancers; Designers; Educators; Filmmakers; Five Seasonal Concerts; Guest Artists; Guest Ensembles; Local Artists & Directors; Multimedia; Organization Contracts; Original Music Scores; Performance Artists; Resident Professionals; Selected Students; Sign Language Translators; Student Interns; Theatre Companies
Founded: 1965
Specialized Field: Musical
Status: Nonprofit; Non-Equity
Paid Staff: 4
Volunteer Staff: 30
Paid Artists: 30
Non-paid Artists: 20
Budget: $800,000
Income Sources: Grant; Ticket Sales; Donations; Corporate Support
Season: May 30 - August 24
Performs At: Amphitheatre; Convention Center; and Arts Center
Affiliations: Kentucky Theatre Association; TCG; IOD; SETC
Annual Attendance: 32,000
Type of Stage: Proscenium
Stage Dimensions: 44' x 28'
Seating Capacity: 580
Year Built: 1962
Year Remodeled: 1992

3076
RICHMOND CHILDREN'S THEATRE
114 West Broad St
Richmond, KY 23220
Phone: 804-783-1688
Fax: 859-254-9512
Web Site: http://www.theatreivrichmond.org/
Management:
  Artistic Director: Bruce Miller
  Managing Director: Phil Whiteway
Mission: To provide young people, ages 8-18, an opportunity to become involved in theatre arts through participation in performances, workhops, stagecraft and crew.
Utilizes: Guest Companies; Singers
Founded: 1978
Specialized Field: Musical; Community Theater
Status: Non-Professional; Nonprofit
Income Sources: Richmond Parks & Recreation Department
Performs At: Eastern Kentucky University Campus Theatre
Organization Type: Performing; Touring; Educational

Louisiana

3077
BATON ROUGE LITTLE THEATER
7155 Florida Boulevard
PO Box 64967
Baton Rouge, LA 70806
Phone: 225-924-6496
Fax: 225-924-9972
e-mail: boxoffice@brlt.org
Web Site: www.brlt.org
Officers:
  President: Sara Downing
  Vice President Administration: David Kiesel
  VP Publicity: Diane Mayer
  VP Production: Lynn Noland
  Treasurer: Louis LoBue
  Secretary: Gary Schaefer
  President: Stephen Toups
Management:
  President: John Gum Jr
  Managing Director: Keith Dixon
  Theatre Manager: Jody Banta
Mission: Entertaining, educating and providing an artistic outlet.
Utilizes: Guest Artists; Guest Companies
Founded: 1946
Specialized Field: Community Theater
Status: Non-Profit, Non-Professional
Paid Staff: 7
Volunteer Staff: 100
Non-paid Artists: 200
Organization Type: Performing; Educational

3078
SWINE PALACE PRODUCTIONS
105 Music and Dramatic Arts Building Dalrymp
Baton Rouge, LA 70803
Phone: 225-578-3527
Fax: 504-388-4135
Management:
  Founding Artistic Director: Barry Kyle
  Executive Director: Marilyn Hersey
  Executive Producing Director: Michael Tick
Founded: 1992
Specialized Field: Educational; Theater Workshops; Touring Company
Status: Nonprofit
Performs At: Claude L. Shaver Theatre
Type of Stage: Traverse
Stage Dimensions: 111' x 47'
Seating Capacity: 488

THEATRE / Louisiana

3079
COLUMBIA THEATRE/FANFARE
220 E Thomas Street
SLU 10797
Hammond, LA 70402
Phone: 985-543-4366
Fax: 985-543-4369
e-mail: kcouret@selu.edu
Web Site: www.selu.edu
Management:
   Director: Donna Gay Anderson
   Associate Director/Marketing: Tonya Lowentritt
Mission: The mission and purpose of the Columbia Theatre for the Performing arts is to enhance and support Southeastern Louisiana University which serves the educational, economic and cultural needs of Southeastern Louisiana.
Founded: 1986
Specialized Field: Drama; Musical; Classic
Status: Non-Profit, Professional
Paid Staff: 8
Volunteer Staff: 55
Paid Artists: 25
Non-paid Artists: 10
Budget: $305,811
Income Sources: Ticket Renue; Rental Income; Sorporate Sponsorships; Business and Individual Donations; Poster Sales; Merchandise Commissions
Affiliations: Association of Performing Arts Presenters
Annual Attendance: 51,000
Stage Dimensions: 31'x6'x22'
Seating Capacity: 889
Year Built: 1928
Year Remodeled: 2001
Rental Contact: Pete Pfeil

3080
ARTISTS' CIVIC THEATRE AND STUDIO
One Reid Street
PO Box 278
Lake Charles, LA 70602
Phone: 337-433-2287
Fax: 337-436-5908
e-mail: mail@actstheatre.com
Web Site: www.actstheatre.com
Management:
   President: Anita Fields-Gold
   Executive Director: Marc Pettaway
Mission: To give local talent a place to work under the direction of a trained professional director where production values are maintained at a high level; to offer formal classes in various aspects of theatre.
Utilizes: Singers
Founded: 1966
Specialized Field: Community Theater; Youth Theater
Status: Non-Profit, Non-Professional
Paid Staff: 1
Volunteer Staff: 70+
Non-paid Artists: -50
Income Sources: Ticket sales; Grants
Performs At: ACTS' One Reid Street Theatre
Facility Category: Community Theatre
Seating Capacity: 125
Organization Type: Performing; Touring; Resident; Educational

3081
SOUTHERN REP THEATRE
333 Canal Street
PO Box 34
Lake Charles, LA 70130
Phone: 504-522-6545
Fax: 504-523-9859
e-mail: info@southernrep.com
Web Site: www.southernrep.com
Officers:
   President: Richard Lee Mathis
   Secretary: Holly Wiseman
   Treasurer: J. Kerry Clayton
   Immediate Past President: Susan Krinksy
Management:
   Managing Director: Marieke Gaboury
   Artistic Director: Aimee Hayes
   Marketing & Development Director: Rachel Gorman
   Arts Coordinator: Elizabeth Harwood
   Education Director: Laura Friedmann
Mission: Recognizing a need for professional theater in New Orleans, Dr. Rosary Hartel O'Neill, Dick O'Neill, Nancy Mendard and Clydia Davenport founded Southern Rep Theatre in 1986 with the goal of creating a leading center for Southern playwrights and plays.
Utilizes: Actors; AEA Actors; Collaborating Artists; Collaborations; Community Talent; Contract Actors; Designers; Educators; Equity Actors; Instructors; Local Artists; Local Artists & Directors; Original Music Scores; Performance Artists; Students
Founded: 1986
Specialized Field: Theatreys
Status: Non-Profit, Professional
Paid Staff: 8
Volunteer Staff: 40
Paid Artists: 100
Affiliations: NNPN; TCG
Facility Category: Indoor Theatre
Type of Stage: Modified Thrust
Seating Capacity: 144
Organization Type: Performing

3082
JUNEBUG PRODUCTIONS
PO Box 2331
New Orleans, LA 70176
Phone: 504-524-8257
Officers:
   Chairman: Wallace Young
   President: John O'Neal
   Treasurer: Theresa Holden
   Secretary: John T. Scott
Management:
   Artistic Director: John O'Neal
   Managing Director: Theresa Holden
Mission: To produce, present and support the development of high-quality theater, dance, music, storytelling and other artistic work that represents, supports and encourages African Americans in the Black Belt South.
Utilizes: Actors; AEA Actors; Artists-in-Residence; Choreographers; Collaborating Artists; Collaborations; Commissioned Composers; Commissioned Music; Composers-in-Residence; Dancers; Designers; Educators; Five Seasonal Concerts; Grant Writers; Guest Accompanists; Guest Choreographers; Guest Designers; Guest Ensembles; Guest Musical Directors; Guest Teachers; Guild Activities; High School Drama; Instructors; Local Artists; Lyricists; Multimedia; Organization Contracts; Original Music Scores; Performance Artists; Playwrights; Selected Students; Sign Language Translators; Singers; Soloists; Student Interns; Touring Companies
Founded: 1980
Specialized Field: Musical; Storytelling; African American
Status: Professional; Nonprofit
Budget: $300,000
Affiliations: Alternate ROOTS, National Performance Network
Facility Category: Touring theater
Organization Type: Performing; Touring; Educational; Sponsoring

3083
LE PETIT THEATRE DU VIEUX CARRE
616 Saint Peter Street
New Orleans, LA 70116
Phone: 504-522-2081
e-mail: info@lepetittheatre.com
Web Site: lepetittheatre.com
Officers:
   Chair: Bruce R. Hoefer Jr.
   Vice Chair: Jackie Clarkson
   Vice Chair: Mike Mitchell
   Secretary: Kathlee Favrot Van Horn
   Treasurer: Leon Contavesprie
Management:
   Executive Director: Cassie Steck Worley
Mission: Le Petit Theatre du Vieux Carre is dedicated to presenting high quality theatrical performances to entertain, inform, and educate the diverse population of the region and enhance vitality of the greater New Orleans area.
Founded: 1916
Status: Nonprofit

3084
NEW ORLEANS RECREATION DEPARTMENT THEATRE
545 St. Charles Avenue, PO Box 791344
Lafayette Street Entrance
New Orleans, LA 70179
Phone: 504-565-7860
Fax: 504-565-6084
Mission: To present musical comedy productions three times yearly and to involve children, teenagers, and adults.
Utilizes: Sign Language Translators; Students
Founded: 1960
Specialized Field: Educational; Theater Workshops
Paid Staff: 4
Non-paid Artists: Var
Budget: $10,000-$50,000
Performs At: NORD Theatre
Annual Attendance: 5,000
Facility Category: Recreation Center
Type of Stage: Proscenium
Seating Capacity: 99

3085
SAENGER THEATRE
143 N Rampart Street
New Orleans, LA 70112
Phone: 504-524-2490
Fax: 504-569-1533
Web Site: www.saengertheatre.com
Management:
   General Manager: Cynthia Argo
   Booking and Special Sevents Manager: Patricia Baham
   Head of Production: Scott Stewart
   Marketing Director: Mason Wood
Founded: 1929
Specialized Field: Broadway Musical Revivals
Status: For-Profit, Professional
Paid Staff: 200

3086
SHAKESPEARE FESTIVAL AT TULANE
215 McWilliams Hall
Tulane University
New Orleans, LA 70118
Phone: 504-865-5105
Fax: 504-865-5205
e-mail: box@tulane.edu
Web Site: www.neworleansshakespeare.com
Officers:
   Artistic Director: Marty Sach
   Managing Director: Clare Moncrief
Management:
   Artistic Director: Ron Gural
   Managing Director: Clare Moncrief
   Operations Director: Brad Robbert
Mission: To provide professional Shakespeare productions to the Greater New Orleans and surrounding Gulf South area along with educational programs to the schools.
Utilizes: Actors; AEA Actors; Artists-in-Residence; Choreographers; Collaborating Artists; Collaborations; Commissioned Composers; Commissioned Music; Composers; Educators; Five Seasonal Concerts; Guest Artists; Guest Companies; Guest Instructors; Guest Musical Directors; Guest Soloists; Guest Teachers; High School Drama; Local Artists; Multimedia; Organization Contracts; Original Music Scores; Performance Artists; Resident Artists; Resident Professionals; Soloists; Students; Special Technical Talent
Founded: 1993
Specialized Field: Classic; Shakespeare; New Plays; Classic; Contemporary
Status: Professional; Nonprofit
Paid Staff: 6
Paid Artists: 60
Budget: $250,000
Income Sources: Public; Private; Corporate; Foundation; Box Office; Tuition
Facility Category: Equity Small Professional Theatre
Type of Stage: Black Box; Laboratory
Seating Capacity: 150; 60

3087
SOUTHERN REP
365 Canal Street
Box 34
New Orleans, LA 70130
Phone: 504-566-9212
Fax: 504-566-9214
e-mail: info@southernrep.com
Web Site: www.southernrep.com
Officers:
   Producing Artistic Director: Aim,e Hayes
Management:
   Managing Director: Marieke Gaboury
   Artistic Director: Aimee Hayes
Mission: Professional theatre created for the audience by paying the actors, stage manager, and designers for their art, as contrasted to community and educational theatres which create for educational and social experiences with volunteers. Selections for each season strive to include one masterpiece adapted to a Southern setting; a classic Southern play; and a play which addresses a Southern issue.
Utilizes: Actors; AEA Actors; Collaborating Artists; Collaborations; Community Talent; Contract Actors; Designers; Educators; Equity Actors; Instructors; Local Artists; Local Artists & Directors; Original Music Scores; Performance Artists; Students
Founded: 1986
Specialized Field: Theatre

Organization Type: Performing; Educational

3088
ST. JOHN THEATRE
115 W 4th Street
Reserve, LA 70084
Mailing Address: PO Box 188
Phone: 985-536-6630
e-mail: info@stjohntheatre.com
Web Site: www.stjohntheatre.org
Officers:
   President: Sterling Snowdy
   VP: Suzette Hullette
   Treasurer: Donna Conran
   Members at Large: Mike Brooks
   Members at Large: Robert Beadle
Management:
   President: Sterling Snowdy
   VP: Suzette Hullette
   Treasurer: Donna Conran
   Managing Director: Beverly Beard
   Secretary: Debbie Stricks
Mission: Providing live theatre for the community, with particular emphasis on schools and students.
Utilizes: Guest Companies; Guest Speakers; Singers
Founded: 1981
Specialized Field: Musical; Community Theater
Status: Non-Professional; Nonprofit; Corporation
Paid Staff: 50
Performs At: St. John Theatre Stage
Organization Type: Performing; Educational

3089
RIVER CITY REPERTORY THEATRE
2829 Youree Drive Suite 4
Shreveport, LA 71104
Phone: 318-868-5888
e-mail: therep@rivercityrep.org
Web Site: rivercityrep.org
Management:
   Artistic Director: Patric McWilliams
Founded: 2006
Status: Professional Nonprofit
Performs At: The Rep At East Bank Theatre- 630 Barksdale Blvd., Bossier City, LA 71111

3090
SHREVEPORT LITTLE THEATRE
812 Margaret Place
Shreveport, LA 71101
Mailing Address: PO Box 4853
Phone: 318-424-4439
Fax: 318-424-4440
e-mail: boxoffice@shreveportlittletheatre.com
Web Site: www.shreveportlittletheatre.org
Officers:
   President: Dr. David Pov
   VP: Jan Pov
   Treasurer: Janice Nelson
   Secretary: Marcia Cassanova
Management:
   President: Gene Bozeman
   Artistic Director: Robert K Darrow
Mission: Committed to producing a variety of quality live theatre with predominantly volunteer participation from the community, with the guidance of trained artistic and managerial leadership, for entertainment, enlightenment and growth of audience awareness and pride.
Utilizes: Guest Companies
Founded: 1921
Specialized Field: Community Theater
Status: Non-Profit, Non-Professional
Paid Staff: 2

Budget: $165,000
Income Sources: Memberships; Ticket Sales; Contributions; Annual Fund; Grants
Affiliations: American Association of Community Theatres
Annual Attendance: 10,000+
Facility Category: Theater
Seating Capacity: 140
Year Built: 1925
Year Remodeled: 2002
Cost: $125,000
Organization Type: Performing; Touring

Maine

3091
ARUNDEL BARN PLAYHOUSE
53 Old Post Road
Arundel, ME 04046
Phone: 207-985-5552
Web Site: www.arundelbarnplayhouse.com
Management:
   Executive Director: Adrienne Wilson Grant
Founded: 1998
Specialized Field: Drama; Musical
Status: For-Profit, Professional
Season: June - September
Type of Stage: Proscenium
Stage Dimensions: 25' x 22'
Seating Capacity: 225

3092
PENOBSCOT THEATRE COMPANY
131 Main Street
Bangor, ME 04401
Phone: 207-942-3333
Fax: 207-947-6678
e-mail: info@penobscottheatre.org
Web Site: www.penobscottheatre.org/
Officers:
   VP: Fritz Oldenburg
   Secretary: John Gregory
   Treasurer: Maria Mason
   Artistic Director: Bari Newport
   Board Director: Shaun Dowd
Management:
   President: Cheryl Olson
   Artistic Director: Mark Torres
   Producing and Artistic Director: Mark Torres
   Marketing Director: Mark Torres
Mission: To offer high quality, professional theatre experiences staged throughout the year; to provide educational outreach programs, and to develop and enrich new and existing audiences and artists.
Utilizes: Guest Companies; Singers
Founded: 1974
Specialized Field: Musical; Drama; Comedy; Youth Theater; Theater Workshops
Status: Professional; Nonprofit
Paid Staff: 8
Type of Stage: Proscenium
Seating Capacity: 132
Organization Type: Performing; Touring; Resident; Sponsoring

3093
HACKMATACK PLAYHOUSE
538 Route 9
Beaver Dam
Berwick, ME 03901

THEATRE / Maine

Phone: 207-698-1807
Fax: 207-698-1162
e-mail: HackPlayhouse@aol.com
Web Site: http://www.hackmatack.org/hackmatack/
Officers:
  Artistic Director: Sharon Hilton
  Director: Jerard-James Craven
Management:
  Artistic/Production Director: Sharon Hilton
Founded: 1971
Specialized Field: Summer Stock; Drama; Theater Workshops
Status: Non-Equity; Nonprofit
Season: June 27 - September 2
Seating Capacity: 200

3094
CAROUSEL MUSIC THEATRE
196 Townsend Avenue
Boothbay Harbor, ME 04538
Mailing Address: PO Box 665
Phone: 207-633-5297
Fax: 207-663-5297
Toll-free: 800-757-5297
e-mail: info@carouselmusictheatre.com
Web Site: www.carouselmusictheatre.com
Management:
  Owner/Producer: Theresa Falco
  Director/Choreograper: Rosie North
  Music Director: Rob Spring
Founded: 1978
Specialized Field: Cabaret; Musical
Status: For-Profit, Professional
Paid Staff: 10
Paid Artists: 6
Season: May - October
Type of Stage: Proscenium; Thrust

3095
MAINE STATE MUSIC THEATRE
22 Elm Street
Brunswick, ME 04011
Phone: 207-725-8760
Fax: 207-725-1199
Toll-free: 866-854-1200
e-mail: jobs@msmt.org
Web Site: www.msmt.org
Officers:
  President: Kathy Greason
  Vice President: Doug Niven
  Secretary: Susan Sharpan
  Treasurer: Thomas Pierle
Management:
  Company Manager: Kathi Kacinski
  Executive Director: Steven C Peterson
Mission: Live professional performances and outreach opportunities that entertain, educate, and enrich lives with power and passion.
Utilizes: Guest Companies; Selected Students; Sign Language Translators; Singers; Soloists; Student Interns
Founded: 1959
Specialized Field: Summer Stock; Musical
Status: Professional; Nonprofit
Paid Staff: 6
Volunteer Staff: 100
Budget: $4 Million
Income Sources: Ticket Sales; Sponsorships; Donations; Advertising; Fundraising
Season: May - August
Performs At: AEA summer musical theatre
Annual Attendance: 60,000+
Type of Stage: Proscenium
Stage Dimensions: 36 x 32, 5'5 R 5'5 L

Seating Capacity: 600
Organization Type: Performing; Resident; Educational

3096
FIGURES OF SPEECH THEATRE
77 Durham Road
Freeport, ME 04032
Phone: 207-865-6355
Fax: 207-865-6355
e-mail: info@figures.org
Web Site: www.figures.org
Management:
  Managing Director: Carol Farrell
  Artistic Director: John Farrell
Mission: Tours nationally and internationally. Award winning adult productions as well as family shows. Presenters include Kennedy Center, New Victory Theatre, Jim Henson festival.
Utilizes: Actors; Collaborating Artists; Collaborations; Commissioned Composers; Commissioned Music; Composers; Guest Companies; Guest Conductors; Guest Designers; Guest Lecturers; Guest Musical Directors; Local Artists; Original Music Scores; Resident Professionals; Sign Language Translators; Visual Arts
Founded: 1982
Specialized Field: Staged Readings; Contemporary
Status: Non-Profit, Professional
Paid Staff: 2
Volunteer Staff: 3
Paid Artists: 8
Non-paid Artists: 1
Income Sources: Earned & contributed
Annual Attendance: 25,000

3097
PUBLIC THEATRE
31 Maple Street
Lewiston, ME 04240
Phone: 207-782-3200
e-mail: info@thepublictheatre.org
Web Site: www.thepublictheatre.org
Officers:
  President: Sheri Olstein
  Vice President: Kathy Gleason
  Treasurer: Thomas H Platz
  Secretary: Candace Walworth
  Board Member: Martin Andrucki
Management:
  Artistic Director: Christopher Schario
  Administrative Director: Carol Ham
  Co- Artistic Director: Janet Mitchko
  Technical Director: Jim Alexander
  Office Manager: Carol Ham
Mission: Founded to bring a high quality professional theatre to the people of Maine, at an affordable price. In choosing the season, we look for plays that speak from the ehart; that are life-affirming and uplifting even when the subject matter is dark or painful; that use our languageinpowerful and provocative ways; that invite the audience to see their worls in a new way.
Utilizes: Actors; AEA Actors; Collaborating Artists; Collaborations; Composers; Contract Actors; Designers; Equity Actors; Five Seasonal Concerts; Guest Accompanists; Guest Artists; Guest Designers; Guest Ensembles; Guest Speakers; Local Artists & Directors; Organization Contracts; Original Music Scores; Resident Professionals; Scenic Designers; Soloists; Students
Founded: 1991
Specialized Field: Mostly Contemporary Plays; Youth Theater
Status: Non-Profit, Professional
Paid Staff: 7
Volunteer Staff: 65

Budget: $500,000
Income Sources: Ticket Sales; Grants; Corporate Support; Donations
Affiliations: AEA
Annual Attendance: 17,000
Type of Stage: Proscenium
Stage Dimensions: 36' x 33'
Seating Capacity: 307

3098
DOWNRIVER THEATRE COMPANY
9 O'Brien Avenue
Machias, ME 04654-1397
Mailing Address: P.O. Box 75,Machias, ME 04654
Phone: 207-255-1200
Fax: 207-255-4864
Toll-free: 888-468-6866
e-mail: downrivertheatrecompany@yahoo.com
Web Site: www.downrivertheatrecompany.com
Officers:
  President: Skip Cole
  President: Nicole S. Ball
  Vice President: John Shaw
  Treasurer: Marjorie Ahlin
Management:
  President: Sue Huseman
  VP: Cynthia Huggins
Mission: The Downriver Theatre Company will present its 2003 bill of fare in the spacious and well-appointed Performing Arts Center at the University of Maine and Machias.
Founded: 1990
Specialized Field: Educational; Theater Workshops
Status: Non-Equity; Nonprofit
Season: June 15 - August 15

3099
THEATRE AT MONMOUTH
PO Box 385
Monmouth, ME 04259-0385
Phone: 207-933-9999
Fax: 207-933-2952
e-mail: boxoffice@theateratmonmouth.org
Web Site: www.theatreatmonmouth.org
Officers:
  President: Ricky D. Dosedlo
  First VP: Ryan Dumais
  Treasurer: Dave Heckman
  Secretary: Ellen O'Brien
  Executive Producer: Robin M. Struck
Management:
  Artistic Director: Sally Wood
  Producing Director: David Greenham
  Producing Artistic Director: Dawn McAndrews
  Associate Artistic Director: Bill Van Horn
Founded: 1970
Specialized Field: Comedy; Youth Theater; Dinner Theater; Classic
Status: Non-Profit, Professional
Paid Staff: 50
Paid Artists: 20

3100
ACADIA REPERTORY THEATRE
1154 Main Street
Mount Desert, ME 04660
Phone: 207-244-7260
Toll-free: 888-362-7480
e-mail: arep@acadia.net
Web Site: www.acadiarep.com/
Management:
  Artistic Director: Ken Stack

Mission: In our quaint performance space which seats 148, we have presented an impressive mix of comedies, dramas, mysteries, and children's theatre for over a quarter of a century.
Founded: 1973
Specialized Field: Summer Stock
Status: Non-Equity; Commercial
Season: July - September
Type of Stage: Flexible; Thrust
Stage Dimensions: 20'x 25'
Seating Capacity: 148

3101
ACADIA REPERTORY THEATRE
1154 Main Street
Mt. Desert, ME 04660
Mailing Address: P.O. Box 106, Mt.Desert, ME 04660
Phone: 207-244-7260
e-mail: art@acadiarep.ocom
Web Site: acadiarep.com
Management:
  Producing Director: C. Andrew Mayer
  Artistic Director: Cheryl Willis
  Executive Director: Ken Stack
Founded: 1973
Season: Late June-Labor Day
Seating Capacity: 148

3102
MARITIME PRODUCTIONS
PO Box 2400
Ogunquit, ME 03907
Phone: 207-641-2313
Fax: 207-641-2314
Management:
  Artistic Director: Rene Risher
Founded: 1993
Specialized Field: Theater Cruise; Historical
Status: Non-Equity; Commercial
Season: June - October

3103
OGUNQUIT PLAYHOUSE
PO Box 915
Ogunquit, ME 03907
Phone: 207-646-5511
Fax: 207-646-4732
e-mail: boxoffice@ogunquitplayhouse.org
Web Site: www.ogunquitplayhouse.org
Officers:
  President: Larry Smith
Management:
  Producer: Roy Rogosin
  Marketing Director: Christina Williams
  Assistant Producer: Jean Benda
  Director Operations: Kimberly Starling
Founded: 1933
Specialized Field: Summer Stock
Status: Professional; Commercial
Paid Staff: 29
Volunteer Staff: 10
Paid Artists: 50
Season: June - September
Performs At: Ogunquit Playhouse
Annual Attendance: 40,000
Facility Category: Summer Theatre
Type of Stage: Proscenium
Seating Capacity: 750
Rental Contact: Kemberly Starling
Organization Type: Sponsoring

3104
GOOD THEATER
76 Congress Street
Portland, ME 04112
Mailing Address: P.O. Box 347, Portland, ME 04112
Phone: 207-885-5883
e-mail: info@goodtheater.com
Web Site: goodtheater.com
Management:
  Executive/Artistic Director: Brian P. Allen
  Production Manager: Stephen Underwood
Mission: Good Theater is dedicated to presenting quality theatrical productions that are entertaining, uplifting, and inspiring, using the best artists available.
Founded: 2001
Status: Professional; Nonprofit
Performs At: The St.Lawrence Arts Center

3105
PORTLAND STAGE COMPANY
25A Forest Avenue
Portland, ME 04101
Mailing Address: PO Box 1458 Portland ME 04104
Phone: 207-774-0465
Fax: 207-774-0576
e-mail: info@portlandstage.org
Web Site: www.portlandstage.org
Officers:
  President: Allison Paine
  Advisory Board: Jonathon Aldrich
  Advisory Board: Daniel Amory
  Advisory Board: Nancy Berrang
  Advisory Board: Norm Brackett
Management:
  President: Valerie Gallin
  Artistic Director: Anita Stewart
  Managing Director: Camilla Barrantes
  Company Manager: Ella Wrenn
  Sound Supervisor: Emily Kenny
Mission: The leading professional theater in Northern New England, Portland Stage Company entertains, educates and engages its audiences by producing a wide range of artistic works and programs that explore basic human issues and concerns relevant to the communities served by the theater. The guiding principle is to promote creativity and dialogue among artists, staff, board and audience.
Utilizes: Actors; AEA Actors; Artists-in-Residence; Choreographers; Commissioned Composers; Dancers; Designers; Educators; Five Seasonal Concerts; Grant Writers; Guest Accompanists; Guest Artists; Guest Companies; Guest Conductors; Guest Designers; Guest Instructors; Guest Lecturers; Guest Musicians; Guest Soloists; Guild Activities; Local Artists; Local Unknown Artists; Multimedia; Music; Original Music Scores; Performance Artists; Selected Students; Soloists; Visual Arts
Founded: 1974
Specialized Field: Contemporary
Status: Non-Profit, Professional
Budget: $1,200,000
Income Sources: Ticket Sales; Donations
Performs At: Portland Performing Arts Center
Affiliations: LORT; SDC; USA; TCG
Annual Attendance: 50,000
Facility Category: Theater
Seating Capacity: 286
Year Built: 1920
Year Remodeled: 1979
Rental Contact: Camilla Barrantes
Organization Type: Performing; Resident; Educational

3106
THE EVERYMAN REPERTORY THEATRE
86 Pascal Avenue
Rockport, ME 04856
Mailing Address: P.O. Box 938, Rockport, ME 04856
Phone: 207-236-0173
e-mail: phodgson@everymanrep.org
Web Site: everymanrep.org
Officers:
  President: Seth Silverton
  Treasurer: Lisa Breheny
Management:
  Artistic Director: Paul Hodgson
  Producing Director: Jen Hodgson
  Production Stage Manager: David Troup
Mission: To present high quality, creative and engaging theatre for people from all age groups living in midcoast Maine through the efforts of a corps of professional actors, designers, and directors.
Status: Professional; Nonprofit

3107
LAKEWOOD THEATER
PO Box 331
Skowhegan, ME 04976
Phone: 207-474-7176
e-mail: generalinfo@lakewoodtheater.org
Web Site: http://www.lakewoodtheater.org/
Management:
  Treasurer: Jeffrey Quinn
Mission: Standing in a high grove of stately white birch, Lakewood Theater, the State Theater of Maine, presents high quality entertainment and stage education at a unique and beautiful site that is particularly Maine.
Founded: 1901
Specialized Field: Summer Stock; Drama; Comedy; Youth Theater
Status: Non-Equity; Nonprofit
Season: May - September
Type of Stage: Proscenium
Seating Capacity: 300

3108
MAD HORSE THEATRE COMPANY
24 Mosher Street
South Portland, ME 04106
Phone: 207-747-4148
e-mail: madhorsetheatre@gmail.com
Web Site: madhorse.com
Officers:
  President: David Jacobs
  Vice President: Laurie Hasty
Mission: To produce plays which compassionately examine and illuminate the enduring aspects of the human experience.
Status: Professional
Organization Type: Resident

3109
SANFORD MAINE STAGE COMPANY
PO Box 486
Springvale, ME 04086
Phone: 207-324-9691
Officers:
  President: Leo Lunser
  Secretary: Melanie Emmons
Management:
  Buisness Manager: Mary Stair
Mission: We are a community theater located on Beaver Hill in Springvale, Maine. We offer quality, affordable entertainment for Southern Maine.
Founded: 1984

THEATRE / Maryland

Specialized Field: Musical; Drama; Comedy
Status: Non-Equity; Nonprofit
Season: April - December
Type of Stage: Proscenium
Stage Dimensions: 30' x 30'
Seating Capacity: 160

Maryland

3110
ANNAPOLIS SUMMER GARDEN THEATRE
143 Compromise Street
Annapolis, MD 21401
Phone: 410-268-0809
e-mail: info@summergarden.com
Web Site: www.summergarden.com/
Officers:
  President: Carolyn Kirby
  Vice President: Sharon Cimaglia
  Secretary: Lori Tietz
Founded: 1966
Specialized Field: Outdoor Theater; Musical; Theater Workshops; Youth Theater

3111
ARENA PLAYERS
801 McCulloh Street
Baltimore, MD 21201
Phone: 410-728-6500
Fax: 410-728-6503
Web Site: www.arenaplayersinc.com/
Officers:
  Chairman: Edward Smith
  Board Member: Jeffery Pope
  Board Member: Catherine Orange
  Board Member: Daisy Brown
  Board Member: Kweisi Mfume
Management:
  Artistic Director: Ed Terry
  Artistic Director: Donald Owen
  Managing Director: Rodney Orange Jr
  President: Edward Smith
Mission: Discovering, fostering and showcasing community talent.
Utilizes: Guest Companies
Founded: 1953
Specialized Field: Community Theater
Status: Non-Profit, Professional
Paid Staff: 1
Volunteer Staff: 20
Non-paid Artists: all
Income Sources: National Endowment for the Arts; Maryland State Arts Council; Mayor's Committee
Annual Attendance: 12,000
Facility Category: Community Theatre
Type of Stage: Thrust
Stage Dimensions: 22x14
Seating Capacity: 300
Year Remodeled: 1975
Organization Type: Performing; Touring; Educational

3112
BALTIMORE ACTORS' THEATRE
The Dumbarton House
300 Dumbarton Road
Baltimore, MD 21212
Phone: 410-337-8519
Fax: 410-337-8582
e-mail: batpro@baltimoreactorstheatre.org
Web Site: www.baltimoreactorstheatre.org
Officers:
  President: Helen M. Grigal

Executive Director: Walter Anderson
Mission: Teaching and performing at a professional level.
Founded: 1959
Specialized Field: Musical; Educational
Status: Non-Profit, Professional
Paid Staff: 10
Paid Artists: 8
Performs At: Oregon Ridge Dinner Theatre
Organization Type: Performing; Touring; Educational

3113
CENTER STAGE
700 N Calvert Street
Baltimore, MD 21202-3686
Phone: 410-332-0033
Fax: 410-725-2522
e-mail: info@centerstage.org
Web Site: www.centerstage.org
Officers:
  Associate Managing Director: Del W. Risberg
  Management Fellow: Kevin Maroney
  Managmnet Intern: Katie Macdonald
Management:
  Director: Lynn Deering
  Artistic Director: Irene Lewis
  Managing Director: Michael Ross
  Director of Audience Development: Barbara Watson
  Media Relations Director: Steve Lickteig
Mission: To serve as Maryland's official theatrical company.
Utilizes: Guest Companies
Founded: 1963
Specialized Field: Musical; Comedy; Youth Theater; Ethnic Theater; Classic; Contemporary
Status: Non-Profit, Professional
Paid Staff: 100
Volunteer Staff: 800
Paid Artists: 150
Performs At: Pearlstone Theater, Head Theater
Affiliations: BACVA; Baltimore Tourism Association; Baltimore Theatre Alliance; TCG; AEA
Annual Attendance: 106,462
Type of Stage: Thrust, Flexible
Stage Dimensions: 40' x 36'; 67' x 118'
Seating Capacity: 541, 100-400
Organization Type: Performing; Resident; Educational

3114
COCKPIT IN COURT SUMMER THEATRE
CCBC, Essex Campus
7201 Rossville Boulevard
Baltimore, MD 21237-3899
Phone: 443-840-2787
Fax: 443-840-1615
e-mail: cockpitincourt@ccbcmd.edu
Web Site: www.ccbc.edu
Officers:
  President: William Pheil
  Vice President: H Ray Lawson
  Recording Secretary: Ellen Moats
  Corresponding Secretary: Jennifer Otero
Management:
  Artistic Director: James Hunnicutt, jhunnicutt@ccbcmd.edu
  Administrative Manager: Lisa L Boeren, lboeren@ccbcmd.edu
Mission: Community-based performing arts organization dedicated to providing a variety of quality live theatre opportunities to our performers and audiences including musicals, Shakespeare, drama and children's theatre.
Founded: 1972

Specialized Field: Community Theater
Status: Non-Profit, Non-Professional
Paid Staff: 5
Volunteer Staff: 50
Paid Artists: 20
Non-paid Artists: 75
Season: June - August
Type of Stage: Proscenium

3115
DUNDALK COMMUNITY THEATRE
7200 Soillers Point Road
Baltimore, MD 21222
Phone: 410-285-9667
Fax: 443-840-1615
e-mail: lboeren@ccbcmd.edu
Officers:
  President: Kevin Ecker
  Vice President: John Amato
  Secretary: Cheryl Vourvoulas
Management:
  Artistic & Technical Director: Marc Smith
  Managing Director: Tom Colonna
Mission: Community-based performing arts organization of a professional quality at a reasonable ticket price and to be a resource for expanding the cultural experiences of the community
Utilizes: Actors; Choreographers; Community Talent; Educators; Instructors; Local Artists; Music; Resident Professionals
Founded: 1974
Specialized Field: Musical; Comedy; Community Theater; Contemporary
Status: Non-Profit, Non-Professional
Paid Staff: 3
Non-paid Artists: 104
Budget: $90,000
Income Sources: Ticket Sales; Subscription Sales; Private Donations; Grants
Performs At: Dundalk Community Theatre
Annual Attendance: 6,800
Seating Capacity: 388
Year Built: 1981
Rental Contact: Mary Huffman

3116
EVERYMAN THEATRE
315 West Fayette Street
Baltimore, MD 21201
Phone: 410-752-2208
Web Site: everymantheatre.org
Management:
  Artistic Director: Vincent M. Lancisi
  Managing Director: Ian Tresselt
  Production Director: Kyle Prue
  Technical Director: Bill Jamieson
Mission: The theatre is dedicated to engaging the audience through a shared experience between actor and audience seeking connection and emotional truth in performance.
Founded: 1990
Status: Professional

3117
THEATRE HOPKINS
3400N Charles Street
The Johns Hopkins University
Baltimore, MD 21218
Phone: 410-516-8000
Fax: 410-261-1217
e-mail: thehop@jhu.edu
Web Site: www.jhu.edu/~theatre
Officers:
  Director: John Astin

Management:
Artistic Director: Suzanne Straughn Pratt
Managing Director: Graham Yearley
Mission: Theatre Hopkins presents a four-play season.
Founded: 1921
Specialized Field: Classic
Status: Non-Profit, Non-Professional
Paid Staff: 2

3118
THEATRE PROJECT

45 W Preston Street
Baltimore, MD 21201
Phone: 410-752-8558
e-mail: office@theatreproject.org
Web Site: www.theatreproject.org
Officers:
President: Gary Pasternack
VP: John C. Wilson
Secretary: Anne Cantler Fulwiler
Treasurer: Pat Dzierwinski
, **Treasurer:** Pat Dzierwinski
Management:
Producing Director: Chris Pfingsten, anne@theatreproject.org
Gallery Curator: Sidney Pink,
Mission: Through the presentation of a diverse array of original and experimental theatre, music, and dance, Theatre Project connects the artists and audiences of Baltimore with a global community of performers. We seek to nurture those artists who are actively experimenting with new forms of expression and support both performers of international reputation and emerging local companies creating new work.
Utilizes: Collaborating Artists; Collaborations; Community Members; Community Talent; Grant Writers; Guest Accompanists; Guest Artists; Guest Choreographers; Guest Companies; Guest Composers; Guest Conductors; Guest Designers; Guest Directors; Guest Ensembles; Guest Lecturers; Guest Musical Directors; Guest Musicians; Guest Speakers; Guest Teachers; Instructors; Local Artists & Directors; Local Talent; Lyricists; Multi Collaborations; Multimedia; Original Music Scores; Paid Performers; Soloists; Students
Founded: 1971
Opened: 1971
Specialized Field: Performing Arts; Theatre; Dance; Opera; Music
Status: Non-Profit, Professional; 501(3)k
Paid Staff: 3
Volunteer Staff: 10
Budget: $250,000
Income Sources: Ticket Sales; Individual & Corporate Donors; William G Baker Memorial Fund; Baltimore County; Baltimore City; Maryland State Arts Council
Performs At: Theatre Project
Affiliations: Theatre Communications Group
Annual Attendance: 11,000
Type of Stage: Modified Black Box
Stage Dimensions: 35' x 35'
Seating Capacity: 150
Year Built: 1887
Year Remodeled: 1985
Cost: $1,000/day; $3,000/week
Rental Contact: Anne Fulwiler
Organization Type: Sponsoring

3119
AMERICAN ENSEMBLE COMPANY

P.O. Box 34420
Bethesda, MD 20827
Phone: 301-897-8411
Fax: 212-684-7857
e-mail: americanensemble@gmail.com
Web Site: www.americanensemble.com
Management:
Artistic Director: Martin Blank
General Manager: Robert Dominguez
Managing Director: Ali Miller
Literary Manager: Cynthia Burns Coogan
Associate Artistic Director: Anthony van Eyck
Mission: Production of plays and musicals of literary merit and development of a working ensemble of actors, directors, designers, and writers.
Utilizes: Singers
Founded: 1967
Specialized Field: Musical; Ensembles
Status: Professional; Nonprofit
Organization Type: Performing; Touring; Resident; Educational

3120
IMAGINATION STAGE

4908 Auburn Avenue
Bethesda, MD 20814
Phone: 301-961-6060
e-mail: boxoffice@imaginationstage.org
Web Site: www.imaginationstage.org/
Officers:
Founder: Bonnie Fogel
President: Jane Fairweather
Secretary: Evonne Courtney Connolly
Treasurer: Fredric T. Walls, II,
Management:
Founder/Executive Director: Janet Stanford
Artistic Director: Jerry Morenoff
Managing Director: Richard Bradbury
Coordinating Producer: Judi Canter
Director Instructional Advancement: Kathryn Chase Bryer
Associate Artistic Director: Patricia Kratzer
Director Financial Services: Laurie Levy-Page
Director Marketing/Public Relations: David Markey
Director Theatre Education: Charlotte Sommers
Mission: Nuture the creative spirit in all children and to cultivate skills that will serve them throughout their lives. In offering diverse and inclusive theatre education programs,aim to develop the whole child by encouraging self-expression, instilling respect for others and providing opportunities and accomplishment. Respect all talent, value all artistry and welcome all children.
Specialized Field: Children's Theater; Theater Workshops

3121
ROUND HOUSE THEATRE

4545 East-West Highway
Bethesda, MD 20824
Mailing Address: PO Box 30688 Bethesda, MD 20824-0688
Phone: 240-644-1099
Fax: 301-565-1601
e-mail: roundhouse@roundhousetheatre.org
Web Site: www.roundhousetheatre.org
Officers:
President: Mitchell S. Dupler
VP: Susan Gilbert
Treasurer: Brian M. Madden
Secretary: Bruce S. Lane
Board Member: Michael Beriss
Management:
President of Board of Trustees: Donald Boardman
Artistic Director: Jerry B. Whiddon
Producing Artistic Director: Ryan Rilette
Business Manager: Tim Conley
Development Director: Sarah Sexton
Mission: To vitalize an ever increasing circle of individuals and communities with a multitude of compelling theatre expirences through performance and education.
Utilizes: Guest Companies; Singers
Founded: 1978
Specialized Field: Musical; Comedy; Youth Theater; Contemporary
Status: Non-Profit, Professional
Paid Staff: 30
Income Sources: Actors' Equity Association
Performs At: Professional LORT-D Theatre
Organization Type: Performing; Touring; Resident Educational

3122
REP STAGE

10901 Little Patuxent Parkway
Columbia, MD 21044
Phone: 443-518-1510
Fax: 410-772-4040
e-mail: mstebbins@howardcc.edu
Web Site: www.repstage.org
Officers:
Production Manager: Dana Whipkey
Co Producing Artistic Director: Joseph Ritsch
Management:
Artistic Director: Michael Stebbins
Production Manager: Brett Ashley Crawford
Co Producing Artistic Director: Suzanne Beal
MD: Nancy Tarr Hart
Mission: Red Stage' mission is to provide Howard Country residents professional theatre, including classics, recently released plays from Broadway and off-Broadway plus new works.
Utilizes: Actors; AEA Actors; Choreographers; Designers; Guest Conductors; High School Drama; Instructors; Local Artists; Music; Performance Artists; Resident Professionals; Selected Students; Visual Arts
Founded: 1993
Specialized Field: Drama; Classic
Status: Non-Profit, Professional
Paid Staff: 5
Volunteer Staff: 100
Paid Artists: 75
Season: September - March
Affiliations: LOW7, BTA
Annual Attendance: 10,000
Facility Category: Two theatres
Type of Stage: Proscenium; Flexible
Stage Dimensions: 60' x 40'
Seating Capacity: 250; 200
Rental Contact: Janelle Broderick

3123
CUMBERLAND THEATRE

101 North Johnson Street
Cumberland, MD 21502
Phone: 301-759-4990
Fax: 301-777-7189
e-mail: boxoffice@cumberlandtheatre.com
Web Site: www.cumberlandtheatre.com
Management:
Artistic Director: Don Whisted
Utilizes: Community Members; Equity Actors
Founded: 1987
Specialized Field: Musical; Comedy; Youth Theater; Classic; Contemporary
Status: Non-Profit, Professional
Paid Staff: 30

THEATRE / Maryland

Paid Artists: 30
Season: June - December
Type of Stage: Proscenium; Thrust
Stage Dimensions: 40' x 28'
Seating Capacity: 197

3124
ADVENTURE THEATRE: GLEN ECHO PARK
7300 MacArthur Boulevard
Glen Echo, MD 20812
Phone: 301-634-2270
Fax: 301-320-3108
e-mail: info@adventuretheatre-mtc.org
Web Site: www.adventuretheatre.org
Officers:
   President: Carol Leahy
   Producing Artistic Director: Michael J. Bobbitt
   Managing Director: Joseph A. Rossi
   Technical Director: Andrew Berry
Management:
   Marketing Manager: Tyler Whitmore
Founded: 1951
Specialized Field: Children's Theater
Status: Non-Profit, Professional
Paid Staff: 50
Paid Artists: 100

3125
PETRUCCI'S DINNER THEATRE
312 Main Street
Laurel, MD 20707
Phone: 301-490-1993
Management:
   Producer: C David Petrucci
   Producer: Angela Jo Leonard
Founded: 1977
Specialized Field: Dinner Theater
Status: Commercial
Income Sources: National Dinner Theatre Association
Organization Type: Performing

3126
YOUNG ARTISTS THEATRE
Route 29 & 216 Cherry Tree Center
Laurel, MD 20723
Mailing Address: 11200 Scaggsville Road #127,
Laurel, MD 20723
Phone: 301-604-2844
Fax: 301-604-2845
e-mail: contactus@yatheatre.com
Web Site: www.yatheatre.com
Officers:
   Chairman: William P Furr
   Vice Chairman: Henry Mitchell
   Secretary: Carolyn Turner
   Treasurer: Wade Reece
Management:
   Director: Kathryn MacDonald, contactus@yatheatre.com
Mission: Providing performing arts instruction, educational workshops, original musical comedies, field trips and artists in residence
Founded: 1994
Specialized Field: Children's Theater; Educational; Musical Theatre
Status: Non-Profit, Non-Professional
Affiliations: Howard County Arts Council; Girl Scouts of the Nation's Capital & Central Maryland
Facility Category: Theatre and Dance Studio
Type of Stage: Thrust
Stage Dimensions: 32'x15
Seating Capacity: 140
Year Built: 1996

Rental Contact: Director Kathy MacDonald

3127
SMALLBEER THEATRE COMPANY
4107 33rd Street
Mt. Rainier, MD 20712-1947
Phone: 301-277-8117
Fax: 703-993-2191
Management:
   Artistic Director: Lynnie Raybuck
Founded: 1987
Specialized Field: Musical; Comedy; Ethnic Theater; Puppet; Contemporary
Status: Non-Profit, Professional
Paid Artists: 8
Season: September - June

3128
OLNEY THEATRE CENTER
NATIONAL PLAYERS
2001 Olney-Sandy Spring Road
Olney, MD 20832
Phone: 301-924-3400
Fax: 301-924-2654
e-mail: wbrown@olneytheatre.org
Web Site: www.olneytheatre.org
Officers:
   President: Jennifer L. Kneeland
   Chair: Susan Finkelstein
   VP: Megan Davey Limarzi
   Treasurer: Pat Woodbury
   Secretary: Robert Mitchell
Management:
   Artistic Director: Michael Bobbitt
   Managing Director: Joseph Rossi
   Technical Director: Andrew Berry
Mission: Mission is to create professional theater productions and other programs to nurture the artist, student, technician, administrator and audience member; to develop each of these individual's potenial and skills using comprehensive possibilities of theater and the performing arts.
Utilizes: Actors; AEA Actors; Choreographers; Dancers; Five Seasonal Concerts; Grant Writers; Guest Accompanists; Guest Artists; Guest Composers; Guest Conductors; Guest Designers; Guest Lecturers; Guest Musical Directors; Guest Teachers; Instructors; Local Artists; Multimedia; Music; Original Music Scores; Performance Artists; Resident Professionals; Sign Language Translators; Soloists; Student Interns; Visual Arts
Founded: 1938
Specialized Field: Drama; Musical; Community Theater
Status: Professional; Nonprofit
Paid Staff: 25
Volunteer Staff: 300
Paid Artists: 200
Budget: $2.5 million
Income Sources: Actors' Equity Association; Society for Stage Directors and Choreographers
Season: March - Decembers
Performs At: Mainstage; Theatre Lab; Amphitheater
Annual Attendance: 70,000+
Seating Capacity: 450
Year Built: 1938
Year Remodeled: 1992
Rental Contact: Bill Synder
Organization Type: Performing; Touring; Educational

3129
PUMPKIN THEATRE
2905 Walnut Avenue
Owings Mills, MD 21117
Phone: 410-902-1814
Fax: 410-902-1954
e-mail: pumpkintheatre@verizon.net
Web Site: pumpkintheatre.com
Officers:
   President: Ana Goldseker
   Vice President: Mike Schleifer
Management:
   Producing Artistic Director: Jimi Kinstle
Mission: Pumpkin Theatre's mission is to entertain, educate and empower young children through theatrical productions and education.
Founded: 1967
Status: Nonprofit
Organization Type: Educational; Family Friendly

3130
INTERACT STORY THEATRE
32 Pennydog Cour
Silver Spring, MD 20902
Phone: 301-879-9305
Fax: 240-491-9884
Toll-free: 888-501-7986
e-mail: info@interactstory.com
Web Site: www.interactstory.com/
Officers:
   Associate Artist(: Anna Jackson
   Technology Advisor: Aisha Jorda
   Performing Artist(Drama & Story): Marian Licha
   Performing & Teaching Artist: Diane Macklin
Management:
   Director: Lenore Blank Kelner
   Performing & Teachinh Artist: Kwame Ansah Brew
   Teaching Artist(Drama & Music): Valerie Bayne Carroll
   Teaching Artist(Theatre): Gwendolyn Briley Strand
   Teaching Artist(Music): Cecilia Esquivel
Mission: Our professional actors are also experienced educators helping students, parents and teachers unlock and maximize their creative potential.
Specialized Field: Youth Theater; Theater Workshops

3131
SILVER SPRING STAGE
10145 Colesville Road
Silver Spring, MD 20901
Mailing Address: PO Box 3086 Silver Spring, MD 20918-3086
Phone: 301-593-6036
Web Site: www.ssstage.org/
Officers:
   Chairperson: Seth Ghitelman
   Vice-Chairperson: Pam Burks
   Secretary: Lennie Magida
   Treasurer: Ted Culler
   Members-at-large: Jacy D'Aiutolo
   Chair: Pauline GrillerMitchell
   Vice-Chairperson: Andrea Spitz Greenleaf
   Facilities Coordinator/Director: Bill Strein
   External/Community Affairs: Norm Seltzer
   Grants/Fund Raising: Judie Chaimson
   Membership Director: Neil Edgell
   Volunteer Development: Leon Levenson
Specialized Field: Community Theater; Drama; Comedy

THEATRE / Massachusetts

Massachusetts

3132
PILGRAM THEATER RESEARCH & PERFORMANCE COLLABORATION
1948 Conway Road
Ashfield, MA 01330
Phone: 413-628-0112
Fax: 413-628-0112
e-mail: pilgrim@mit.edu
Web Site: www.pilgrimtheatre.org
Management:
  President: Kim Mancuso
  Executive Director: Kermit Dumkelberg
Founded: 1986
Specialized Field: Contemporary; Experimental
Status: Non-Profit, Professional
Paid Staff: 8
Paid Artists: 8

3133
BELMONT DRAMATIC CLUB
123 D Sycamore Street
Apartment 1
Belmont, MA 02478
Phone: 617-484-2529
e-mail: info@belmontdramaticclub.org
Web Site: www.belmontdramaticclub.org
Officers:
  President: Vern Gerig
  Vice President: Clifford Grubb
  Secretary: Roy Johnson
  Treasurer: Carter Lehmann
Management:
  President: Carolyn Binghan
Mission: Providing quality drama for the community.
Utilizes: Guest Companies
Founded: 1903
Specialized Field: Drama; New Plays
Status: Non-Profit, Non-Professional
Paid Staff: 3
Volunteer Staff: 10
Paid Artists: var
Non-paid Artists: var
Income Sources: Ticket Sales
Performs At: Payson Park Church
Organization Type: Performing

3134
NORTH SHORE MUSIC THEATRE
62 Dunham Road
Beverly, MA 01915
Phone: 978-232-7200
Fax: 978-921-9999
Toll-free: 800-926-9220
e-mail: NorthShoreMusicTheatre@nsmt.org
Web Site: www.nsmt.org
Officers:
  President: John P Drislane
  Vice President: Donald J Short
  Treasurer: Wendell P Wood
  Owner / Producer: Bill Hanney
  Artistic Director: Arianna Knapp
  Director of Patron Services: Suzanne Kendall
  Director of Marketing & Communicati: Mike Ceceri
Management:
  President: John Kimbell
  Executive Director: James K Polese
  Executive Producer: Jon Kimbell
  Marketing Director: Joesph Amaral
  Chairman: Kevin Bottomley
  Vice Chairman: Thomas S Barenboim
  Vice Chairman: David Fellows
  Secretary/Clerk: Marcia Ruderman
  Director Marketing: Joseph Amaral
Mission: To emphasize the development of new musical works and the expansion of educational programming to capture the interest of all age groups in the creative process.
Utilizes: Guest Companies
Founded: 1955
Specialized Field: Comedy; Youth Theater; Dinner Theater; Puppet; Contemporary
Status: Non-Profit, Professional
Paid Staff: 220
Volunteer Staff: 500
Paid Artists: 400
Budget: $11,000,000
Income Sources: Ticket Sales; Contributions
Season: April - December
Performs At: North Shore Music Theatre
Annual Attendance: 350,000
Type of Stage: In-the-Round
Seating Capacity: 1800
Year Built: 1955
Year Remodeled: 1990
Organization Type: Performing; Touring; Educational

3135
BOSTON CHILDREN'S THEATRE
316 Huntington Avenue
Boston, MA 02115
Phone: 617-424-6634
Fax: 617-424-7108
e-mail: info@bostonchildrenstheatre.org
Web Site: www.bostonchildrenstheatre.org
Officers:
  Board President: Henry J. Lukas
  Clerk: Peggy Barresi
  Treasurer: Michael Travaglini
Mission: To promote live theatre for children, by children; Enchanted Forest. Hosted at the Franklin Park Zoo in October.
Utilizes: Guest Companies; Singers
Founded: 1951
Specialized Field: Musical; Comedy; Youth Theater; Classic; Contemporary
Status: Non-Profit, Non-Professional
Paid Staff: 20
Income Sources: New England Theatre Conference; Association of American Theatre for Youth; Massachusetts Cultural Alliance
Performs At: New England Life Hall
Organization Type: Performing

3136
COMPANY ONE
539 Tremont Street
Boston, MA 02116
Phone: 617-292-7110
Fax: 617-307-4475
e-mail: info@companyone.org
Web Site: companyone.org
Management:
  Artistic Director: Shawn LaCount
  Managing Director: Sarah Shampnois
  Production Manager: Karthik Subramanian
  Director Of Marketing: Natalie VanLandingham
Mission: To change the face of Boston theatre by uniting the city's diverse communities through innovative, socially provocative performance and developing civically engaged artists.
Founded: 1998

3137
HUNTINGTON THEATRE COMPANY
Boston University
264 Huntington Avenue
Boston, MA 02115
Phone: 617-266-0800
Fax: 617-421-9674
e-mail: tickets@huntingtontheatre.org
Web Site: www.huntingtontheatre.org
Management:
  Development Director: Howard L Breslau
  Marketing: Temple Gill
Utilizes: Actors; AEA Actors; Choreographers; Designers; Guest Designers; Resident Professionals; Selected Students
Founded: 1982
Status: Non-Profit, Professional
Budget: $8 milliom
Income Sources: Ticket Sales; Donations
Season: September - June
Performs At: Boston University Theatre
Annual Attendance: 175,000
Facility Category: Theatre
Type of Stage: Proscenium
Seating Capacity: 890
Rental Contact: Roger Meeker
Organization Type: Performing; Resident

3138
LYRIC STAGE COMPANY OF BOSTON
140 Clarendon Street
Boston, MA 02116
Phone: 617-585-5678
Fax: 617-536-2830
Web Site: www.lyricstage.com
Officers:
  President: Steven Wasser
  VP: Joseph Richard
  Clerk: Richard Daynard
  Immediate Past President: Christopher Hills
Management:
  Director: Ellen Carno
  Managing Director: Sara Gildden
  Producing Artistic Director: Spiro Veloudos
  Director of Marketing & PR: Henry Luisser
  Production Manager: Matt Whiton
Mission: Offering high-quality, professional theatre to audiences at low prices, so that they can appreciate their theatrical heritage.
Utilizes: Actors; AEA Actors; Choreographers; Dancers; Designers; Guest Artists; Guest Companies; Guest Designers; Guest Musical Directors; Guild Activities; Local Artists; Multimedia; Music; New Productions; Organization Contracts; Resident Professionals; Sign Language Translators; Soloists; Student Interns
Founded: 1974
Specialized Field: Drama; Classic
Status: Professional; Nonprofit
Paid Staff: 5
Volunteer Staff: 50
Paid Artists: 55
Budget: $750,000
Income Sources: Actors' Equity Association; New England Area Theatres
Season: September - May
Affiliations: AEA, SSOC
Type of Stage: 3/4 Thrust
Seating Capacity: 236
Organization Type: Performing

THEATRE / Massachusetts

3139
NORTHEASTERN THEATRE
180 Ryder Hall, Northeastern University
360 Huntington Avenue
Boston, MA 02115
Phone: 617-373-2244
Fax: 617-373-4149
e-mail: c.najarian@neu.edu
Web Site: www.northeastern.edu
Management:
    Producer: Alicia Grega-Pikul
Founded: 1992
Specialized Field: Drama; Comedy; Theater Workshops

3140
PUBLICK THEATRE
398 Columbus Avenue #248
Boston, MA 02116
Phone: 617-782-5425
e-mail: info@publicktheatre.com
Web Site: www.publicktheatre.com/
Officers:
    President: Michael McDermott
    Treasurer: Randall Filer
    Artistic Director: Diego Arciniegas
    Producing Director: Susanne Nitter
Management:
    Artistic Director: Diego Arciniegas
    Producing Director: Susanne Nitter
    Artistic Director: Diego Arciniegas
    Artistic Associate: Susanne Nitter
    Production Manager: Maureen Heakey
Mission: To discover, develop and showcase Boston-area theatrical talent in programs of professional quality that are accessible to a diverse audience.
Utilizes: Guest Companies
Founded: 1970
Specialized Field: Musical; Ensembles
Status: Professional; Nonprofit
Season: June - September
Performs At: The Publick Theatre
Organization Type: Performing; Touring; Resident; Sponsoring

3141
SCIENCE FICTION THEATRE COMPANY
791 Tremont Street
Boston, MA 02118
Phone: 781-780-3016
e-mail: thecollective@sciencefictiontheatrecompany.com
Web Site: sciencefictiontheatrecompany.com
Mission: To create high quality theatre using science fiction stories and concepts to frame a thought provoking narrative. To cast new light on important cultural and philosophical ideas. To create an inclusive environment, showcasing the work of diverse members of our artistic community.

3142
SPEAKEASY STAGE COMPANY
538 Tremont Street
Boston, MA 02116
Phone: 617-482-3279
Fax: 617-933-8600
e-mail: info@speakeasystage.com
Web Site: speakeasystage.com
Management:
    Producing Artistic Director: Paul Daigneault
    Production/General Manager: Paul Melone
    Director Of Marketing: Jim Torres
Mission: SpeakEasy Stage Company's mission is to connect, inspire, and challenge our audiences with the most socially relevant theatrical premieres featuring the most talented artists in Boston.
Status: Nonprofit

3143
WHEELOCK FAMILY THEATRE
200 The Riverway
Boston, MA 02215
Phone: 617-879-2147
Fax: 617-879-2021
e-mail: tickets@wheelock.edu
Web Site: www.wheelockfamilytheatre.org
Officers:
    VP: Carola Cadley
    President: Carole Charnow
    MD: Jeff Coburn
    Teacher: Priscilla Fales
    Executive Director: Andi Genser
Management:
    Producer: Susan Kosoff
    Artistic Director: Jane Staab
    Marketing & PR Director: Charles Baldwin
    Education Director: John Bay
    Administrative Manager: Kay Arden Elliott
Mission: To improve the lives of children and families through the shared experience of live performance.
Founded: 1981
Specialized Field: Performance And Education For Youth
Status: Non-Profit, Professional
Paid Staff: 7
Volunteer Staff: 100
Paid Artists: 50
Season: October - November
Affiliations: AEA; TCG; StageSource; TAMA; CBACT; Colleges of the Fenway; Fenway Alliance
Annual Attendance: 30,000
Type of Stage: Proscenium
Seating Capacity: 650

3144
PUPPET SHOWPLACE THEATRE
32 Station Street
Brookline, MA 02445
Phone: 617-731-6400
Fax: 617-731-0526
e-mail: info@puppetshowplace.org
Web Site: www.puppetshowplace.org
Officers:
    Board Chairperson: Alice Schaefer
    Artistic Director: Roxanna Myhrum
    Executive Director: Isabel Fine
    Communications Director: Brenda Huggins
Management:
    Executive Director: Kris Higgins
    Artistic Director: Roxie Myhrum
    Artist-In-Residence: Brad Shurs
    Box Office Manager: Kate Ott
    Marketing Director: Ben Henry
Mission: A non-profit performing arts organization committed to excellence in puppetry for all audiences.
Utilizes: Artists-in-Residence
Founded: 1974
Specialized Field: Puppet; Children's Theater
Status: Non-Profit, Professional
Paid Staff: 7
Income Sources: Puppeteers of America; United International Marionette Association
Seating Capacity: 100
Organization Type: Performing; Touring; Resident; Sponsoring

3146
AMERICAN REPERTORY THEATRE
Loeb Drama Center, Harvard University
64 Brattle Street
Cambridge, MA 02138
Phone: 617-495-2000
Fax: 617-495-1705
e-mail: info@amrep.org
Web Site: www.amrep.org
Officers:
    Artistic Director/CEO: Diane Paulus
    Producer/Intern Managing Director: Diane Borger
    Director of Special Projects: Ariane Barbanell
Management:
    Executive Director: Robert J Orchard
    Artistic Director: Robert Woodruff
    General Manager: Jonathan Seth Miller
    Associate Director: Francois Rochaix
Mission: The American Repertory Theatre is a separately incorporated, not-for-profit organization chartered to provide a service to the widest possible public in the Boston/Cambridge community and to the theatre world in general.
Utilizes: Guest Companies
Founded: 1966
Specialized Field: Educational; Theater Workshops
Status: Professional; Nonprofit
Paid Staff: 7
Income Sources: Major Grants, Andrew W. Mellon Foundation; The Harold and Mimi Steir Charitable Trust; National Endowment for the Arts; Shubert Foundation; Massachusetts Cultural Council
Affiliations: Andrew W. Mellon Foundation; Harold and Mimi Steinberg Charitable Trust; National Endowment for the Arts; Shubert Foundation; PaineWebber Group
Seating Capacity: 556; 353
Organization Type: Performing; Touring; Resident; Educational

3147
CHARLESTOWN WORKING THEATER
442 Bunker Hill Street
Charlestown, MA 02129
Phone: 617-242-3285
Fax: 617-242-3285
e-mail: info@workingtheater.org
Web Site: http://www.charlestownworkingtheater.org/
Management:
    Managing Director: Kristen Johnson
Mission: To enhance the quality of life through the artistic process.
Utilizes: Guest Companies; Singers
Founded: 1972
Specialized Field: Summer Stock; Community Theater; Puppet
Status: Professional; Semi-Professional; Non-Professional; Nonprofit
Income Sources: Massachusetts Council on the Arts & Humanities
Organization Type: Performing; Touring; Resident; Educational; Sponsoring

3148
APOLLINAIRE THEATRE COMPANY
189 Winnisimmet Street
Chelsea, MA 02150
Phone: 617-887-2336
Web Site: apollinairetheatre.com
Specialized Field: Provocative Contemporary Theatre
Performs At: Chelsea Theatre Works

3149
CHESTER THEATRE COMPANY
PO Box 722
Chester, MA 01011
Phone: 413-354-7770
Fax: 413-354-7825
e-mail: byam@chestertheatre.org
Web Site: www.chestertheatre.org
Officers:
   Chair: Cipora Feiner
   Vice Chair: Harley Erdman
   Treasurer: Ron Belfiglio
Management:
   Artistic Director: Byam Stevens
   Business Manager: Victoria Braim
   Associate Artistic Director: Daniel Elihu Kramer
   Marketing & Development Dir: Todd Trebour
   Development Coordinator: Alexandra Tasak
Utilizes: Actors; AEA Actors; Artists-in-Residence; Collaborations; Commissioned Composers; Commissioned Music; Designers; Fine Artists; Five Seasonal Concerts; Guest Accompanists; Guest Companies; Guest Designers; Guest Lecturers; Guest Musical Directors; Guest Teachers; Instructors; Local Artists; Multimedia; Original Music Scores; Performance Artists; Playwrights; Poets; Resident Artists; Resident Professionals; Selected Students; Soloists; Student Interns; Special Technical Talent; Theatre Companies; Touring Companies; Visual Arts
Founded: 1990
Specialized Field: Summer Stock
Status: Nonprofit
Budget: $175,000
Season: July - September
Performs At: Theatre
Annual Attendance: 5,500
Facility Category: Town Hall
Type of Stage: Proscenium
Stage Dimensions: 25' x 15'
Seating Capacity: 150

3150
STRAWBERRY PRODUCTIONS
34-40 Front St.
Chicopee, MA 01021
Phone: 413-304-2112
Fax: 413-594-7758
e-mail: info@milestoneevents.org
Web Site: www.milestoneevents.org
Officers:
   President: Jack Desroches
Management:
   Producer: Jack Desroches
   Division Manager: Nancy J Floyd
   Technical Director: Gary Bessett
Founded: 1976
Specialized Field: Drama; Classic
Status: Commercial; Non-Equity
Season: Year Round

3151
YARD
Middle Road
Chilmark, MA 02535
Mailing Address: PO Box 405
Phone: 508-645-9662
Fax: 508-645-3176
e-mail: admin@dancetheyard.org
Web Site: www.dancetheyard.org
Officers:
   Executive and Artistic Director: David R. White
   Associate Director and General Mana: Alison Manning
   Founder: Patricia N. Nanon
Management:
   Artistic Director: David R White
   MD: Allison Manning
   Technical Director: Scott Nelson
   Staff Photographer: Sally Cohn
   Artistic Associate: Linda Tarnay
Mission: Stives to promote growth and experimentation in theatre arts with its mission to give professional artists the time and space to create and perform dance, music, theatre pieces in a concentrated and supported environment.
Founded: 1973
Specialized Field: Youth Theater; Community Theater; Contemporary
Status: Non-Profit, Professional
Paid Staff: 3
Paid Artists: 50
Season: Summer
Type of Stage: Black Box
Stage Dimensions: 34'x 28'
Seating Capacity: 100

3152
BAY COLONY PRODUCTIONS
2 School Street
Foxboro, MA 02035
Mailing Address: P.O. Box 266, Foxboro, MA 02035
Phone: 508-543-2787
e-mail: info@orpheum.org
Web Site: baycolonyproductions.com
Officers:
   President: Gail Gilman
Management:
   Executive Director: Bill Cunningham
   Resident Director: Dori Bryan-Ployer
Mission: To present quality performing arts for the entertainment of the community, to provide a facility and an environment in which residents of the region can learn and practice their crafts.
Founded: 1992
Performs At: The Orpheum Theatre
Seating Capacity: 427
Organization Type: Community Theatre

3153
GLOUCESTER STAGE COMPANY
267 E Main Street
Gloucester, MA 01930
Phone: 987-281-4433
Fax: 508-283-5150
Web Site: www.gloucesterstage.com/
Officers:
   Artistic Director: Eric Engel
   Managing Director/General Manager: Andrew Burgreen
   Development/Marketing Director: John E. North
   Managing Director: Costin Manu
   Artistic Director: Eric Angle
Management:
   Artistic Director: Israel Horovitz
   Publicity Director: Heidi J Dallin
   Production Stage Manager: Janet Howes
   Technical Director: Rob Duggan
   Production Coordinator: Keri Ellis Cahill
   Assistant Artistic Director: Robbie Chasitz
   Media & Education: Heidi J Dallin
Mission: To support contemporary playwrights through staged readings and productions of important new plays.
Utilizes: Guest Companies; Singers
Founded: 1979
Specialized Field: Ensemble
Status: Professional; Nonprofit
Organization Type: Performing; Resident; Educational; Sponsoring; Producing

3154
ARENA CIVIC THEATRE
PO Box 744
Greenfield, MA 01302
Phone: 413-863-2281
e-mail: info@arenacivictheatre.org
Web Site: www.arenacivictheatre.org
Officers:
   President: Jerry Marcanio
   VP (External): Phyllis Roy
   VP (Internal): Steve Woodard
   Secretary: Elisa Martin
   Treasurer: Sondra Radosh
Management:
   President: Jerry Marcanio
   VP: Robert Freedman
Mission: To recognize the unique ability of theatre to provide spiritual fulfillment and personal growth for its participants.
Utilizes: Guest Companies; Singers
Founded: 1970
Specialized Field: Community Theater
Status: Non-Profit
Paid Staff: 70
Income Sources: National Association of Local Arts Agencies; Mohawk Trail Association
Performs At: Shea Theater; Turner Falls, MA
Organization Type: Performing

3155
HINGHAM HIGH SCHOOL AUDITORIUM
17 Union Street
Hingham, MA 02043
Phone: 781-741-1500
Fax: 781-741-1515
Officers:
   Chair: Christine Smith
Utilizes: Guest Artists; Guest Companies; Singers
Status: Non-Profit, Non-Professional
Performs At: Hingham High School Auditorium
Organization Type: Performing; Resident; Educational

3156
CAPE COD MELODY TENT
21 W Main Street
Hyannis, MA 02601
Phone: 508-775-5630
Fax: 508-778-0899
e-mail: info@themusiccircus.org
Web Site: www.melodytent.com
Officers:
   Director of Marketing and Public Re: Howard Turkenkopf
Management:
   Director: Vince Longo
   Director of Marketing: Paula Gates
   Marketing Associate: Jaime Saine, jsaine@themusiccircus.org
Founded: 1950
Specialized Field: Musical; Comedy; Community Theater; Classic; Summer Stock
Status: Non-Profit, Professional
Paid Staff: 70
Paid Artists: 600
Season: June 1 - September
Seating Capacity: 2300

3157
VILLAGE PLAYERS
PO Box 81
Hyannis, MA 69350

THEATRE / Massachusetts

Phone: 308-458-2701
Management:
    Artistic Director: Al Davis
Mission: To present and sponsor theatre.
Utilizes: Singers
Founded: 1980
Specialized Field: Summer Stock; Musical; Dinner Theater
Status: Professional; Semi-Professional; Nonprofit; Commercial
Organization Type: Performing; Touring; Sponsoring

3158
FOOTLIGHT CLUB
Eliot Hall
7A Eliot Street
Jamaica Plain, MA 02130
Phone: 617-524-3200
Fax: 617-524-6506
e-mail: boxoffice@footlight.org
Web Site: www.footlight.org
Officers:
    President: Maria Wardwell
    VP: Kristin MacDougall
    Secretary: Carol Pyper
    Treasurer: Jason Sheehan
    Facility Director: Jesse Martin
    VP: Kristin MacDougall
    Secretary: Carol Pyper
    Treasurer: Jason Sheehan
Management:
    President: Maria Wardwell
    Front-of House Director: Jason Dawson
    Membership Director: Rebecca Glucklich
    Promotion Director: Susanna M. Crampton
    VolunteersDirector: Elizabeth Bean
Mission: To provide quality theatre as an integral component of a vital arts community and to offer involvement to anyone interested in theatre.
Founded: 1877
Specialized Field: Community Theater
Status: Non-Professional
Paid Staff: 200
Performs At: Eliot Hall
Organization Type: Performing; Resident

3159
SHAKESPEARE & COMPANY
70 Kemble Street
Lenox, MA 01240-2813
Phone: 413-637-3353
Fax: 413-637-4274
e-mail: general@shakespeare.org
Web Site: www.shakespeare.org
Officers:
    President: Tony Simotes
    Board Chairman: Richard Mescon
Management:
    Managing Director: Nicholas J. Puma, Jr., npuma@shakespeare.org
    Artistic Director: Tony Simotes, tsimotes@shakespeare.org
    Founding Artisitic Director: Tina Packer, tina@shakespeare.org
    General Manager: Steve Ball
    Artistic Associate: Elizabeth Aspenlieder
Mission: To create a theatre of unprecedented excellence in the Elizabethan ideals of inquiry, balance and harmony. To establish a theatre company which, by its commitment to the creative impulse, is a revolutionary force in society, which connects the truths of the past to the challenges and possibilities of today, which finds its source in the performance of Shakespeare's plays and reaches the widest possible audience through trainig and education.
Founded: 1978
Specialized Field: Shakespeare; Contemporary; New Plays
Status: Non-Profit, Professional
Paid Staff: 34
Volunteer Staff: 250
Paid Artists: 180
Budget: $4.3 million
Income Sources: Earned Income; Contributions
Season: May - January
Performs At: Founders' Theatre, SpringLawn Theatre and Outdoor Space at 70 Kemble Street.
Affiliations: AEA
Annual Attendance: 52,000

3160
MERRIMACK REPERTORY THEATRE
50 Warren St Lowell
Lowell, MA 01852
Phone: 987-654-4678
Fax: 978-934-0166
e-mail: info@merrimackrep.org
Web Site: www.merrimackrep.org
Officers:
    Executive Director: Elizabeth Kegley
    Production Director: Justin ROWLAND
    Finance Director: Ed Cyrus
    Stage Manager: Bree Sherry
    Marketing Director: Kate Brandt
Management:
    Artistic Director: Charles Towers
    Managing Director: Lisa B Merrill-Buttzak
    General Manager: Edgar Cyrus
    Marketing Manager: Paul Marsh
    Production Manager: Justin Rowland
    Stage Manager: Emily McMullen
Mission: To present engaging, vital theatre that communicates to the audience.
Utilizes: Actors; AEA Actors; Artists-in-Residence; Choreographers; Collaborating Artists; Collaborations; Commissioned Music; Composers; Contract Actors; Dancers; Designers; Educators; Fine Artists; Guest Accompanists; Guest Artists; Guest Companies; Guest Composers; Guest Conductors; Guest Designers; Guest Directors; Guest Instructors; Guest Lecturers; Guest Musical Directors; Guest Speakers; Guest Teachers; High School Drama; Instructors; Local Artists; Local Unknown Artists; Multimedia; Music; Original Music Scores; Paid Performers; Performance Artists; Resident Professionals; Scenic Designers; Sign Language Translators; Singers; Students; Visual Arts
Founded: 1979
Specialized Field: Contemporary; Drama
Status: Non-Profit, Professional
Paid Staff: 20
Paid Artists: 50
Budget: $1.8 million
Season: September - June
Performs At: Liberty Hall
Affiliations: Society for Stage Directors and Choreographers; Actors' Equity Association; USA; Dramatists Guild
Annual Attendance: 60,000
Type of Stage: 3/4 Thrust
Stage Dimensions: 34x30
Seating Capacity: 384
Year Built: 1900
Year Remodeled: 1984
Organization Type: Performing; Resident

3161
WOODLAND THEATRE COMPANY
88R South Street
Medfield, MA 02052
Mailing Address: P.O. Box 538, Sherborn, MA 01770
Phone: 508-655-0687
e-mail: tickets@woodlandtheatre.com
Web Site: woodland-theatr.com
Management:
    Producing Artistic Director: Doug Hodge
    Executive Producer: Sam Carioti
    Director Of Operations: Kelly Hodge
    Director Of Finance: Patricia Weller
Mission: Our goal is to create a place where family and friends can come together and experience an evening of wonderful, imaginative, and meaningful entertainment not far from home.
Opened: 2010
Specialized Field: Broadway Shows
Status: Nonprofit

3162
ACTORS THEATRE OF NANTUCKET
PO Box 1297
Nantucket, MA 02554-1297
Phone: 508-228-4305
Web Site: www.nantuckettheatre.com
Management:
    Associate Director: Richard Cary
    Artistic Director and Founder: Richard Cary
Mission: To offer professional theatre to Nantucket Island.
Utilizes: Guest Companies; Playwrights; Singers
Founded: 1992
Specialized Field: Musical; Children's Theater
Status: Professional; Nonprofit; Non-Equity
Organization Type: Performing; Resident; Educational; Sponsoring

3163
THEATRE WORKSHOP OF NANTUCKET
PO Box 1297
Nantucket, MA 02554
Phone: 508-228-4305
e-mail: productionmgr.twn@gmail.com
Web Site: www.theatreworkshop.com
Officers:
    President: Joe Hills
    VP: Ellen Ross
    Clerk: Susan Lucier
    Treasurer: Jim Bennet
Management:
    Business Manager: Edgar A Anderson
    Artistic Director: S. Warren Krebs
Mission: To bring theatrical stage entertainment to the community using local talent; to offer year-round productions.
Utilizes: Guest Companies
Founded: 1956
Specialized Field: Community Theater
Status: Non-Professional; Nonprofit
Paid Staff: 25
Performs At: Bennett Hall
Organization Type: Performing; Educational

3164
NEW REPERTORY THEATRE
200 Dexter Avenue
Newton, MA 02472
Phone: 617-923-7060
Fax: 617-527-5217
e-mail: info@newrep.org
Web Site: www.newrep.org

Management:
Director: Laura M Crary
Managing Director: Harriet Sheets
Producing Artistic Director: Rick Lombardo
Artistic Associate: Cory Elizabeth Nelson
Mission: Producing 5 professional theatre productions each year with an emphasis on area premieres and the classics.
Founded: 1984
Specialized Field: Musical; Comedy; Classic; Contemporary
Status: Non-Profit, Professional
Paid Staff: 7
Volunteer Staff: 100
Paid Artists: 200
Season: September - June
Affiliations: TCG; NEAT; NETC; MASSK
Type of Stage: Thrust
Stage Dimensions: 20' x 30'
Seating Capacity: 160

3165
JEWISH THEATRE OF NEW ENGLAND
Leventhal-Sidman Jewish Community Center
333 Nahanton Street
Newton Center, MA 02459-3213
Phone: 617-558-6480
Fax: 617-244-8290
Management:
Performance Artistic Director: Barrie Keller
Founded: 1984
Specialized Field: Jewish; Ethnic Theater
Status: Nonprofit
Season: Fall & Spring
Type of Stage: Thrust
Stage Dimensions: 48' x 30'
Seating Capacity: 250-450

3166
NEW CENTURY THEATRE
1 Green Street
Northampton, MA 01060
Mailing Address: PO Box 186, Northampton, MA 01061
Phone: 413-587-3933
Fax: 413-585-3354
e-mail: info@newcenturytheatre.org
Web Site: www.newcenturytheatre.org
Officers:
Producing Director: Sam Rush
Management:
Producing Director: Sam Rush
Mission: Produces four productions from June-August and is beginning to produce productions in the fall and spring.
Founded: 1991
Specialized Field: Comedy; Youth Theater; Ethnic Theater; Contemporary
Status: Non-Profit, Professional
Paid Staff: 5
Paid Artists: 30
Budget: $200,000
Season: June - August
Affiliations: AEA
Annual Attendance: 11,000
Type of Stage: Proscenuim
Seating Capacity: 450

3167
FIDDLEHEAD THEATRE COMPANY
109 Central Street
Norwood, MA 02062
Phone: 617-888-5365
e-mail: contactus@fiddleheadtheatre.com

Management:
President: Meg Fofonoff
Associate Producer: Stacie Moye
Business Manager: Darrell Moye
Mission: The Fiddlehead Theatre Company in Norwood, MA is a non-profit orginazation which draws its strength from the rich talents of local amateurs and volunteers as well as gifted professionals, and has already brought pleasures to thousands of Boston area residents.
Specialized Field: Community Theater; Musical
Status: Non-Profit

3168
ACADEMY OF PERFORMING ARTS
120 Main Street
PO Box 1843
Orleans, MA 02653
Phone: 508-255-3075
Fax: 508-255-3075
Web Site: www.apacape.org/
Officers:
President: Edward Lewis
Vice President, Production: Dick Hatch
Treasurer: C Page McMahan
Management:
Managing Director: Peter Earle
Director: Marcia Galazzi
Executive Administrator: Ralph Bassett
Mission: To provide an educational opportunity for students and people of all ages and backgrounds to further their abilities, understanding and appreciation for jazz. To increase public awareness and appreciation for jazz as an American art form. To preserve the history and foster the development of this unique music. To bring world class performers and educators to greater Cleveland audiences.
Utilizes: Actors; Choreographers; Collaborating Artists; Collaborations; Community Talent; Composers; Educators; Guest Accompanists; Guest Artists; Guest Companies; Guest Designers; Guest Lecturers; Guest Musical Directors; Guest Musicians; Guest Speakers; Guest Teachers; Guild Activities; High School Drama; Instructors; Local Artists; Multimedia; Music; Organization Contracts; Original Music Scores; Paid Performers; Performance Artists; Playwrights; Resident Professionals; Scenic Designers; Sign Language Translators; Singers; Special Technical Talent; Visual Arts
Founded: 1975
Specialized Field: Musical; Comedy; Youth Theater; Ethnic Theater; Classic; Contemporary
Status: Non-Profit, Non-Professional
Paid Staff: 6
Income Sources: Productions; Memberships; Fundraising & Events; Private Donation
Performs At: Academy Playhouse
Affiliations: Orleans Chamber of Commerce
Annual Attendance: 21,000
Facility Category: Playhouse
Type of Stage: Arena
Seating Capacity: 162
Rental Contact: Artistic Director Peter Bartle
Organization Type: Performing; Touring; Educational; Sponsoring

3169
BARRINGTON STAGE COMPANY
30 Union Street
Pittsfield, MA 01201
Phone: 413-236-8888
Fax: 413-499-5447
e-mail: info@barringtonstageco.org
Web Site: www.barringtonstageco.org

Officers:
Chair: Mary Ann Quinson
President: Marita O' Dea Glodt
VP: Rosita Sarnoff
Secretary: Heather Nolin
Treasurer: Ira Yohalem
Management:
Artistic Director: Julianne Boyd
Interim Managing Director: Tristan Wilson
Director Education: Hester Kamin
Lauraal Manager: Marketing Manager
Utilizes: Actors; Community Members; Community Talent; Dancers; Designers; Instructors; Local Artists & Directors; Original Music Scores; Resident Professionals; Sign Language Translators; Students
Founded: 1995
Specialized Field: Summer Stock
Orchestra Pit: 5
Seating Capacity: 520
Year Built: 1911

3170
PROVINCETOWN REPERTORY THEATRE
238 Bradford St
Provincetown, MA 02657
Mailing Address: PO Box 812
Phone: 508-487-9793
e-mail: operations@provincetowntheater.com
Web Site: http://www.provincetowntheater.com
Officers:
Chairman: Brian O'Malley
President: Tim McCarthy
Vice President: Joy McNulty
Management:
Director: Dave Fortuna
General Director: Ted Vitale
Administrative Director: Margie Mahrdt
Specialized Field: Summer Stock
Performs At: Pilgrim Monument

3171
ROBBINS-ZUST FAMILY MARIONETTES
20 Reservoir Road
Richmond, MA 01254
Phone: 413-698-2591
Fax: 413-698-2080
e-mail: dionrz@gmail.com
Web Site: www.berkshireweb.com/zust
Management:
Director: Genie Zust
Mission: To pass on to the next generations the ancient stories and the art and craft of puppetry and to delight all ages.
Founded: 1971
Specialized Field: Puppet
Status: For-Profit, Professional
Paid Staff: 5
Paid Artists: 5
Budget: $30,000
Income Sources: Performances
Performs At: Theatres; Homes; Stores; Schools throughout New England/New York
Annual Attendance: 10,000+
Type of Stage: Marionette
Stage Dimensions: 14'x8'x10'
Organization Type: Performing; Touring

3172
SALEM THEATRE
90 Lafayette Street
Salem, MA 01970

THEATRE / Massachusetts

Mailing Address: P.O. Box 306, Salem, MA 01970
Phone: 978-790-8546
e-mail: info@salemtheatre.com
Web Site: salemtheatre.com
Officers:
   President: Norene Gachignard
   Vice President: Peg Voss Howard
Management:
   Artistic Director: Matt Gray
   Managing Director: Gary LaPart
Mission: Our mission is to enrich the artistic, cultural, and economic life of the greater Salem region through the performance of classic, contemporary, and new works of exceptional theater; to move and inspire our audiences; and to build connections with new diverse audiences and theater artists through arts education outreach.
Founded: 2002
Status: Nonprofit

3173
SHARON COMMUNITY THEATRE
53 High Street
Sharon, MA 02067
Phone: 617-784-3721
Management:
   Business Manager: Tina Koppel
   Publicity Director: Dick Leemon
Mission: To present family-oriented, high quality, local entertainment consisting mainly of play productions to the South Shore area at reasonable prices.
Utilizes: Guest Companies; Singers
Founded: 1975
Specialized Field: Community Theater
Status: Nonprofit
Paid Staff: 60
Income Sources: New England Theatre Conference
Performs At: Sharon Recreation Department Mini-Theatre
Organization Type: Performing; Educational

3174
THE DINNER DETECTIVE
30 Washington Street
Somerville, MA 02143
Phone: 617-628-1000
e-mail: boston.info@thedinnerdetective.com
Web Site: thedinnerdetective.com/sites/boston
Status: Professional
Performs At: Holiday Inn Boston Bunker Hill

3175
SUMMER THEATRE AT MT. HOLYOKE COLLEGE
Alice Withington Rooke Theatre
50 College Street
South Hadley, MA 01075
Phone: 413-538-2000
Fax: 413-538-3838
e-mail: theatre@mtholyoke.edu
Web Site: www.mtholyoke.edu/acad/theat
Officers:
   President: Debra Guston
   VP: Jennifer Symington
   Treasurer: Roger Allard
Management:
   Director: Roger Babb
Mission: To provide Western Massachusetts with the highest quality summerstock entertainment while educating and nurturing a new genetration of theatre artists.
Utilizes: Students; Special Technical Talent
Founded: 1970
Specialized Field: Summer Stock
Status: For-Profit, Non-Professional
Budget: $425,000
Income Sources: Ticket Sales; Sponsors; Donors; Businesses; Grants
Season: June - August
Annual Attendance: 15,000
Facility Category: Mainstage
Type of Stage: Thrust
Stage Dimensions: 36'x36'
Seating Capacity: 400
Year Remodeled: 2000

3176
BERKSHIRE THEATRE FESTIVAL
6 East Street
Stockbridge, MA 01262
Phone: 413-298-5576
Fax: 413-298-3368
Toll-free: 866-811-4111
e-mail: info@berkshiretheatre.org
Web Site: www.berkshiretheatre.org
Officers:
   CO-President: Lee Perlman
   CO-President: David Lloyd
   Secretary: Randolph Hawthorne
   Treasurer: Neil Ellenoff
   Vice President: B Carger White
   Artistic Director/CEO: Kate Maguire
   Director of Productions and Facilit: Peter Durgin
   Director Finance: Linda Ludwig
Management:
   Artistic Director/CEO: Kate Maguire
   Assistant Artistic Director: E Gray Simons III
   General Manager: Peter Durgin
   Director Finance/Administration: Linda Ludwig
   Director Development: Craig Smith
   Director Marketing/Public Relations: Jamie Davidson
Mission: To produce and promote thought-provoking theatre for its community throughout the summer through performance and educational activities.
Utilizes: Singers
Founded: 1928
Specialized Field: Drama; Classic; Contemporary; Musical
Status: Professional; Nonprofit
Paid Staff: 12
Income Sources: Actors' Equity Association; Council of Resident Summer Theatres
Season: June - September
Performs At: Playhouse, Unicorn Theatre
Type of Stage: Proscenium, Thrust
Seating Capacity: 415, 122
Organization Type: Performing; Resident; Educational; Sponsoring

3177
VINEYARD PLAYHOUSE
24 Church Street
Box 2452
Vineyard Haven, MA 02568
Phone: 508-696-6300
Fax: 508-696-9299
e-mail: info@vineyardplayhouse.org
Web Site: www.vineyardplayhouse.org
Officers:
   Chairperson: George L Cohn
   Clerk: Gerald Yukevich
   Treasurer: Ted E Desrosiers
   Artistic Director: Mj Bruder Munafo
Management:
   Artistic Director: Mj Bruder Munafo
   Artistic Associate: Jon Lipsky
Mission: Community based professional theater dedicated to developing, producing and presenting exceptional live theater for adults and children; to providing educational programs; and to encourage and supporting the work of theater artists of all ages, abilities and ethnic and social background.
Founded: 1983
Specialized Field: Summer Stock; Ensembles; Drama
Status: Nonprofit
Paid Staff: 6
Paid Artists: 100
Budget: $450,000
Season: June - October
Type of Stage: Black Box
Seating Capacity: 120

3178
SPINGOLD THEATER CENTER
Brandeis University
415 S Street
Waltham, MA 02454
Phone: 781-736-2000
Fax: 781-736-3408
e-mail: theater@brandeis.edu
Web Site: www.brandeis.edu
Officers:
   President: Jehuda Reinharz
   Chair: Susan Dibble
Management:
   Artistic Director: Eric Hill
   Director: David Colfer
   Manager: Irene Vienneau
Income Sources: New England Theatre Conference; Massachusetts Cultural Alliance
Performs At: Spingold Theater Center
Organization Type: Performing; Educational

3179
BLUE SPRUCE THEATRE
321 Arsenal Street
Watertown, MA 02472
Phone: 978-667-0512
e-mail: info@bluesprucetheatre.org
Web Site: bluesprucetheatre.org
Management:
   Producing Artistic Director: Jesse Strachman
   Co-Producer: PJ Strachman
Mission: Our mission is to produce works that connect us to each other as people, and hopefully provide us with better understanding of who we are, where we came from, and where we are headed.
Founded: 2006

3180
HISTORY MAKING PRODUCTIONS
100 Summer
Suite 3-6
Watertown, MA 02172
Phone: 617-924-4430
Officers:
   Chairperson: Lisa Gregory
   Secretary Clerk: Judith Einach
   Treasurer: Richard Freedberg
Management:
   Director: Linda Myer
Mission: To tour live, professional plays which dramatize historical events and people; to bring literature to life; to spark critical thinking and thoughtful discussion on gender, race, social diversity and social change.
Utilizes: Guest Companies; Singers
Founded: 1976
Specialized Field: Historical; Contemporary; Drama
Status: Professional; Nonprofit

Income Sources: Massachusetts Advocates for Arts; Sciences & Humanities; Stage Source
Organization Type: Performing; Touring; Educational

3181
WELLFLEET HARBOR ACTORS THEATER
PO Box 797
Wellfleet, MA 02667
Phone: 508-349-9428
Toll-free: 866-282-9428
e-mail: info@what.org
Web Site: www.what.org/
Officers:
  President: John Dubinsky
  Honorary Chair Person: Julie Harris
  Interim Director of Marketing: Linda Thomas
  Executive Director: Jeffry George
  Artistic Director: Dan Lombardo
  President and CEO: Bruce Bierhans
Management:
  Artistic Director: Jeff Zinn, jz@what.org
Mission: To present a most adventurous professional theater company.
Founded: 1985
Specialized Field: Drama; Comedy
Status: Nonprofit; Equity
Paid Staff: 25
Volunteer Staff: 125
Paid Artists: 50
Budget: $1.3 million
Season: May - October
Affiliations: TCG
Type of Stage: Proscenium
Seating Capacity: 220; 90
Year Built: 2007
Cost: $5 Million
Rental Contact: Artistic Director Jeff Zinn

3182
HARWICH JUNIOR THEATRE
105 Division Street
PO Box 168
West Harwich, MA 02671
Phone: 508-432-2002
Fax: 508-432-0726
Web Site: www.hjtcapecod.org
Management:
  President: Richard Rust
  Artistic Director: Nina Schuessler
  Managing Director: Tamara Harper
Mission: To provide young people with the opportunity to explore and expand their creative talents and aspirations; to entertain, develop, and foster a love and full appreciation of theatre and the enrich lives through the theatrical experience.
Founded: 1951
Specialized Field: Musical; Comedy; Ethnic Theater; Community Theater; Classic; Contemporary
Status: Non-Profit, Non-Professional
Paid Staff: 3
Paid Artists: 50
Season: June - August
Type of Stage: Thrust
Stage Dimensions: 20' x 30'
Seating Capacity: 210

3183
NEW PHOENIX
42 Cold Spring Road
Williamstown, MA 01267
Phone: 413-458-2411
Officers:
  President: Ralph Hamman
  Vice President: Dana Swanson
Management:
  Artistic Director/Producer: Ralph Hammann
  Associate Director: Douglas Bradburd
Mission: To produce a diversity of small-cast, transportable theatre pieces; special interest in Samuel Beckett, mono dramas, psychological thrillers and black comedies.
Utilizes: Guest Companies
Founded: 1975
Specialized Field: Drama; Touring Company; Ensembles
Status: Professional; Semi-Professional; Nonprofit
Organization Type: Performing; Touring; Educational; Sponsoring

3184
WILLIAMSTOWN THEATRE FESTIVAL
PO Box 517
Williamstown, MA 01267-0517
Phone: 413-597-3400
Fax: 413-458-3147
e-mail: wtfinfo@wtfestival.org
Web Site: www.wtfestival.org
Officers:
  President: Dr. Ira Lapidus
  Vice President: Brian D Cabral
  Secretary: Fred A Windover
  Treasurer: Jid Sprague
  Archivist: Juliet Flynt,
Management:
  Producer: Stephen Kaus
  Artistic Associate: John Baker,
  Producing Associate: Sally Cade Holmes
  Workshop Artistic Producer: Laura Savia
  Business Manager: Amy Russell
  Development Director: Bart Reidy
  Production Manager: Christopher Atkins
  Workshop Director: Amanda Charlton
  Company Manager: Michael Coglan
Mission: To present outstanding productions of modern classics on our main stage; to develop new acting, writing and musical talent.
Utilizes: Actors; AEA Actors; Artists-in-Residence; Choreographers; Commissioned Composers; Commissioned Music; Designers; Educators; Guest Accompanists; Guest Artists; Guest Companies; Guest Conductors; Guest Designers; Guest Ensembles; Guest Lecturers; Guest Musical Directors; High School Drama; Music; Original Music Scores; Performance Artists; Poets; Resident Artists; Resident Professionals; Singers; Soloists; Student Interns
Founded: 1954
Specialized Field: Drama; Classic; Contemporary; Musical
Status: Non-Profit, Professional
Paid Staff: 75
Volunteer Staff: 150
Paid Artists: 100
Non-paid Artists: 40
Budget: $2,500,000
Performs At: Adams Memorial Theater; Nikos Stage
Annual Attendance: 50,000
Seating Capacity: 520
Organization Type: Performing
Comments: September-May in NYC 212-395-9090

3185
KIDSTOCK CREATIVE THEATER EDUCATION CENTER
50 Cross Street
Winchester, MA 01890
Phone: 781-729-5543
e-mail: postmaster@kidstocktheater.com
Web Site: www.kidstocktheater.com/
Management:
  Creative Director: Brian Milauskas
Mission: To empower young artists and actors to express themselves by providing them with quality resources and instruction; promoting creative problem solving, cooperative planning and public speaking skills through dramatic play.
Utilizes: Soloists
Founded: 1991
Specialized Field: Children's Theater; Educational

3186
BOOTH PRODUCTIONS
144 Granite Street
Worcester, MA 01604
Phone: 508-797-9277
Management:
  Artistic Director: Richard A Booth, Senior
  Technical Director: Jeff Boutiette
  Chief Stage Technician: James Gagaglio
  Sound Technician: Rob Steere
  Music Director: Daniel Zabinski
  Music Director: Robert Rucinski
  Prime Theatre Director: Christine Seger
Mission: Providing the opportunity for all to learn and develop theater skills by participating in the many aspects of theater, both on stage and behind the scenes. Strengthening the value of friendship, team effort, and a sense of community. Enabling all participants to achieve their fullest potential. Also providing the community with quality theater.
Specialized Field: Summer Stock
Performs At: Holy Name Theater

3187
FOOTHILLS THEATRE COMPANY
100 Front Street
Suite 100
Worcester, MA 01608
Phone: 508-754-3314
Fax: 508-767-0676
Web Site: www.foothillstheatre.com
Officers:
  President: Guy Jones
  Treasurer: James F Goulet
  Clerk: Hon Mel Greenberg
Management:
  Artistic Director: Brad Kenney
  Business Manager: Lisa Ayotte
Mission: To provide professional regional theatre for Worcester and the Central New England Region and serve the region by providing many ancillary services including a theatre conservatory, intern/apprentice programs, youth services, services for the communicatively and physically disabled and more.
Utilizes: Guest Companies; Singers
Founded: 1974
Specialized Field: Musical; Comedy; Classic; Contemporary
Status: Non-Profit, Professional
Income Sources: Actors' Equity Association
Season: October - May
Performs At: Foothills Theatre Company
Type of Stage: Proscenium
Seating Capacity: 349
Organization Type: Performing

3188
WORCESTER CHILDREN'S THEATRE
6 Chatman Street
Worcester, MA 01609

THEATRE / Michigan

Phone: 404-315-0235
Management:
- Director Programs/Development: Mary Pantano
- Managing Director: Liz Humphreys
- Artistic Director: Steven Braddock

Mission: Providing performances and educational programming that educates children about theatre.
Utilizes: Guest Companies
Founded: 1968
Specialized Field: Children's Theater
Status: Professional; Semi-Professional; Nonprofit
Performs At: Worcester State College; Administration Building
Organization Type: Performing; Touring; Educational

Michigan

3189
THUNDER BAY THEATRE
400 N Second Avenue
Alpena, MI 49707
Phone: 989-354-2267
e-mail: TBT@ThunderBayTheatre.com
Web Site: www.thunderbaytheatre.com
Officers:
- Treasurer: Barb Bourdelais
- Vice President: Peggy Tomaszewski
- President: Paulette Bremer
- Secretary: Gordon Snow

Management:
- President: Kathryn Kunze
- VP: Maggie Lamb
- Artistic Director: Hal Adams
- Treasurer: Barb Bourdelais

Mission: To enhance the cultural life of Northeast Michigan.
Utilizes: Guest Companies; Singers
Founded: 1967
Specialized Field: Summer Stock; Musical; Ensembles
Status: Professional; Nonprofit; Non-Equity
Season: May - September
Performs At: Thunder Bay Theatre
Type of Stage: Proscenium
Stage Dimensions: 33' x 15'
Seating Capacity: 180
Year Built: 1930
Organization Type: Performing; Resident; Educational

3190
PERFORMANCE NETWORK OF ANN ARBOR
Performance Network Theatre
120 E Huron
Ann Arbor, MI 48104-1437
Phone: 734-663-0681
Fax: 734-663-7367
e-mail: info@performancenetwork.org
Web Site: www.performancenetwork.org
Officers:
- Board President: Ron Maurer
- Associate Artistic Director: Carla Milarch
- Associate Development Director: Logan Ricket
- Technical Director: Joshua Parker
- Children's Theatre Director: Becky Fox

Management:
- Artistic Director: David Wolber
- Executive Director: Carla Milarch
- Marketing Director: Chelsea Sadler
- MD: Erin Sabo
- Artistic Director: David Wolber

Mission: To provide uncompromising artistic leadership in the region and produce works that engage, challenge and inspire audiences and artists.
Utilizes: Actors; AEA Actors; Choreographers; Contract Actors; Designers; Equity Actors; Local Artists; Local Artists & Directors; Original Music Scores; Performance Artists
Founded: 1981
Specialized Field: Drama, Comedy; Youth Theater; Classic; Contemporary
Status: Non-Profit, Professional
Paid Staff: 8
Volunteer Staff: 300
Paid Artists: 50
Budget: $750,000
Affiliations: AEA
Seating Capacity: 139
Year Built: 2000

3191
UNIVERSITY PRODUCTIONS: UNIVERSITY OF MICHIGAN
1100 Baits Dr.
Ann Arbor, MI 48109-1265
Phone: 734-764-0583
Fax: 734-763-5097
e-mail: theatre.info@umich.edu
Web Site: www.music.umich.edu/departments/theatre/
Management:
- Director: Erik Fredricksen
- Managing Director: Jeffrey Kuras
- Dean School of Music: Karen Wolff

Mission: To create 10 productions annually through the departments of Musical Theatre, Opera and Theatre and Dance.
Utilizes: Guest Choreographers; Guest Companies
Founded: 1973
Specialized Field: Drama; Educational; Theater Workshops
Status: Non-Profit, Non-Professional
Paid Staff: 22
Performs At: Power Center for the Performing Arts; Trueblood Theatre
Type of Stage: Flexible; Proscenium; Arena
Seating Capacity: 1414; 650; 200
Organization Type: Performing; Educational

3192
BARN THEATRE
13351 W Michigan 96
Augusta, MI 49012
Phone: 616-731-4545
Fax: 616-731-2306
e-mail: mibarntheatre@aol.com
Web Site: www.barntheatre.com
Management:
- Founder/Producer: Jack P Ragotzy
- Assistant Producer: Brendan Ragotzy
- General Manager: Howard McBride
- Resident Manager: James B Knox

Mission: To offer high-quality professional summer theatre to Southwestern Michigan.
Utilizes: Designers
Founded: 1946
Specialized Field: Summer Stock; Musical
Status: Professional; Commercial
Paid Staff: 14
Paid Artists: 40
Income Sources: Actors' Equity Association
Organization Type: Performing; Resident

3193
BAY CITY PLAYERS
1214 Columbus Avenue
Bay City, MI 48708
Phone: 989-893-5555
e-mail: info@baycityplayers.com
Web Site: www.baycityplayers.com
Officers:
- Secretary: Cathie Stewart
- 2nd Vice-President: John Tanner
- 1st Vice-President: Trevor Keyes
- President: Greg Burke
- Treasurer: Tracy Teich

Mission: To provide quality theatrical productions for our area.
Founded: 1917
Specialized Field: Musical; Community Theater
Status: Nonprofit
Income Sources: Community Theatre Association of Michigan
Facility Category: Theatre
Organization Type: Performing

3194
CALUMET THEATRE COMPANY
340 Sixth Street
PO Box 167
Calumet, MI 49913
Phone: 906-337-2166
Fax: 906-337-3763
e-mail: boxoffice@calumettheatre.com
Web Site: www.calumettheatre.com
Officers:
- Board Director: Johnnie De Bernard
- Board Director: Andrew Gryuruch
- Executive Director: Laura Miller
- Artistic/Technical Director: Davey Holmbo

Management:
- Executive Director: Jim Lowell
- Managing Director: Christine Fanning
- Artistic/Technical Director: Davey Holmbo

Mission: Hosting and sponsoring performing events.
Founded: 1900
Specialized Field: Musical; Comedy; Community Theater; Classic; Contemporary; Musical; Ethnic Theater
Status: Non-Profit, Non-Professional
Paid Staff: 5
Income Sources: Michigan Association of Community Arts Agencies
Organization Type: Educational; Sponsoring

3195
PURPLE ROSE THEATRE COMPANY
137 Park Street
Chelsea, MI 48118
Phone: 734-433-7673
Fax: 734-475-0802
e-mail: info@purplerosetheatre.org
Web Site: www.purplerosetheatre.org
Officers:
- Executive Director: Jeff Daniels

Management:
- Artistic Director: Guy Sanville
- Managing Director: Alan Ribant

Founded: 1991
Specialized Field: Musical; Comedy; Classic; Contemporary
Status: Non-Profit, Professional
Paid Staff: 17
Paid Artists: 75
Season: September - August
Type of Stage: Thrust
Seating Capacity: 160

THEATRE / Michigan

3196
ATTIC / NEW CENTER THEATRE
2990 W Grand Boulevard
Suite 308
Detroit, MI 48202
Phone: 313-875-8285
Officers:
   Chairman: Andy Soffel
   President: Lavinia Moyer
   Treasurer: Peter C Gray
   Secretary: Paul R. Retenbach
Management:
   Artistic Director: Lavinia Moyer
   Managing Director: Jim Moran
Mission: Attic/New Center Theatre is a resident, professional theatre company committed to the development of actors, directors, playwrights, and technicians as craftsmen in the art of theatre. It exists to create new works and to present new and challenging plays by contemporary playwrights.
Utilizes: Guest Companies; Singers
Founded: 1975
Specialized Field: Musical; Ensembles
Status: Professional; Nonprofit
Income Sources: Theatre Communications Group; Foundation for the Extension and Development of American Professional Theatre
Performs At: The New Center Theatre
Organization Type: Performing; Touring; Resident; Educational

3197
DETROIT REPERTORY THEATRE
13103 Woodrow Wilson
Detroit, MI 48238
Phone: 313-868-1347
Fax: 313-868-1705
e-mail: detrepth@aol.com
Web Site: www.detroitreptheatre.com
Officers:
   Board Chair: Shyvonne Davis
Management:
   Artistic Director: Bruce Millan
Mission: The Detroit Repertory Theatre has demonstrated that racial harmony and non-traditional casting (casting without racial distinction) can produce an artistic vitality and quality second to none and win over an audience in sufficient numbers to prove viability.
Utilizes: AEA Actors; Contract Actors; Designers; Equity Actors; High School Drama; Original Music Scores; Playwrights; Resident Companies; Resident Professionals; Touring Companies
Founded: 1956
Specialized Field: Theater; Classic; Contemporary
Status: Non-Profit, Professional
Paid Staff: 7
Volunteer Staff: 6
Paid Artists: 22
Budget: $800,000
Income Sources: Box Office; Grants; Contributors
Season: November - June
Performs At: Theatre
Affiliations: TCG, AFA, DMCVB
Annual Attendance: 30,000+
Type of Stage: Proscenium
Stage Dimensions: 28' x 26'
Seating Capacity: 194
Year Remodeled: 1990
Organization Type: Performing
Resident Groups: Hire only indigenous professional artists.

3198
HILBERRY THEATRE, WAYNE STATE UNIVERSITY
4743 Cass Avenue
Detroit, MI 48202
Phone: 313-577-2972
Fax: 313-577-0935
e-mail: ac8806@wayne.edu
Web Site: www.hilberry.com
Officers:
   Interim Chair: James Thomas
Founded: 1963
Specialized Field: Educational; Theater Workshops
Status: Non-Professional; Nonprofit
Paid Staff: 60
Volunteer Staff: 100
Budget: $2.5 million
Income Sources: Box Office; Fundraising; Grants; University
Performs At: Hilberry Theatre
Affiliations: Association for Theatre in Higher Education; U/RTA; National Association of Schools of Theatre
Annual Attendance: 50,000
Facility Category: Theatre
Type of Stage: Thrust
Seating Capacity: 530
Year Remodeled: 1963
Organization Type: Performing; Touring; Resident; Educational; Sponsoring
Resident Groups: Repertory Company

3200
MATRIX THEATRE COMPANY
2730 Bagley Street
Detroit, MI 48216
Phone: 313-967-0999
Fax: 313-961-1016
e-mail: info@matrixtheatre.org
Web Site: matrixtheatre.org
Officers:
   President: Suzanne Sattler
   Vice President: Joseph Heaphy
Management:
   Artistic Director: Megan Buckley-Ball
   Director Of Operations: Jane Hooker
Mission: Matrix Theatre Company uses the transformative power of theatre to change lives, build community, and foster social justice.
Founded: 1991
Status: Professional

3201
THEATER GROTTESCO
PO Box 32658
Detroit, MI 48232
Phone: 313-961-5880
Management:
   Co-Artistic Director: John Flax
   Co-Artistic Director: Elizabeth Wiseman
Mission: To create modern original plays; to conduct master classes and training workshops.
Founded: 1983
Specialized Field: Contemporary; New Plays; Theater Workshops
Status: Professional; Nonprofit
Income Sources: Association of Performing Arts Presenters; Theatre Communications Group; Arts Midwest; National Association for Campus Activities
Organization Type: Performing; Touring; Educational

3202
CIRCLE THEATRE
1607 Robinson Road SE
Grand Rapids, MI 49506
Phone: 616-632-1980
Fax: 616-456-8540
Web Site: www.circletheatre.org
Officers:
   President: R. Scott Keller
   VP: Brian Bakkila
   Secretary: Will Guyeskey
   Treasurer: Gary Malburg
   Past President: Patricia Dutkiewicz
Management:
   Managing Director: Lynn B. Temper
   Technical Director: Don Wilson
   Costume Shop Manager: Brandon Bacon
   Box Office Manager: Rob Karel
   Marketing &Finance Director: Virginia Juresich
Founded: 1953
Specialized Field: Musical; Comedy; Community Theater; Puppet; Classic; Contemporary
Status: Non-Profit, Non-Professional

3203
CIVIC THEATRE & SCHOOL OF THEATRE
30 N Division Avenue
Grand Rapids, MI 49503
Phone: 616-222-6650
Fax: 616-222-6660
Web Site: www.grct.org/
Officers:
   President: William P. Scarbrough
   President Elect: Chuck Burpee
   VP: Chuck Smeester
   Treasurer: Peggy Murphy
   Secretary: Matt Vicari
Management:
   Executive Director: Bruce Tinker
   Associate Director: Penelope Notter
   Director of Operations: Marry J. Denolf
   Dev & Community Relations Director: Nancy Brozek
   Graphic Designer: Jenna Ritsema
Utilizes: Student Interns
Founded: 1925
Specialized Field: Community Theater; Theater Workshops; Educational

3204
URBAN INSTITUTE FOR CONTEMPORARY ARTS
2 West Fulton
Grand Rapids, MI 49503
Phone: 616-454-7000
Fax: 616-454-7013
e-mail: info@uica.org
Web Site: www.uica.org
Officers:
   President: Tom Clinton
   Vice President: Daryl Fischer
   Second VP/Secretary: Heidi Holst Leeestma
   Treasurer: David J. Everett
   Board President: Kathryn Chaplow
Management:
   Director: Jeff Meeuwsen
   Executive Director: Jill Donabauer
   Program Manager: Gail Philbin
   Facilities Manager: Aaron Smith
   Special Events Coordinator: Carole Walters
   Marketing/Communications/Director: Karen Spelling

THEATRE / Michigan

Mission: To foster cultural dialogue and creative activity through innovative and diverse events and services.
Utilizes: Touring Companies
Founded: 1977
Specialized Field: Comedy; Youth Theater; Ethnic Theater; Community Theater; Classic; Contemporary
Status: Non-Profit, Professional
Seating Capacity: 170

3205
ACTING UP THEATRE COMPANY
PO Box 1070
Grayling, MI 49738
Phone: 989-348-3587
e-mail: actingup03@yahoo.com
Web Site: www.actingup.biz/
Management:
 Artistic Director: Kurt Thoma
 Creative Director: Chad Patterson
Mission: Providing schools, institutions and libraries with unique brand of educational theatre. Striving to teach students about theatre by providing them with the opportunity to write, produce and act in their own plays. Involve, Inform and Entertain. 'Anything is Possible.'
Founded: 1996
Specialized Field: Children's Theater; Summer Stock; Touring Company

3206
HOPE SUMMER REPERTORY THEATRE
Hope College
141 E. 12th Street
Holland, MI 49423
Phone: 616-395-7600
Fax: 616-395-7130
Toll-free: 800-968-7850
e-mail: robins@hope.edu
Web Site: www.hope.edu
Management:
 Producing Director: Mary Schafer
 Artistic Director: David Colacci
Founded: 1851
Specialized Field: Educational; Theater Workshops; Summer Stock
Status: Non-Equity; Nonprofit
Season: June - August
Type of Stage: Thrust
Seating Capacity: 500

3207
IRONWOOD THEATRE
113 E Aurora Street
Ironwood, MI 49938
Phone: 906-932-0618
Fax: 906-932-0457
Web Site: www.ironwoodtheatre.net/
Officers:
 President: Tom Williams
 VP: Betsy Wesselhoft
 Secretary: Sam Filipo
 Treasurer: Lee Ann Garske
 MD: Bruce Greenhill
Management:
 Chairman: Tom Brown
 Board Member: Molly Chabalowski
 Board Member: Larry Gabka
 Board Member: Karen Hagemann
 Board Member: Nicole Holmes
Mission: To provide cultural entertainment of the highest possible quality to the greatest number of people in the Western Upper Peninsula of Michigan and Northern Wisconsin.

Utilizes: Dance Companies; Dancers; Guest Writers; Guild Activities; Multi Collaborations; Multimedia; New Productions; Original Music Scores; Sign Language Translators; Special Technical Talent; Theatre Companies
Founded: 1928
Specialized Field: Drama; Musical
Status: Non-Profit, Non-Professional
Paid Staff: 3
Budget: $125,000
Income Sources: Grants; State of Michigan; Fund Raisers
Performs At: Auditorium
Affiliations: Michigan Council for Arts-Cultural Affairs
Annual Attendance: 20,000
Facility Category: Performing Arts Center
Type of Stage: Proscenium
Stage Dimensions: 28'6w x 23'l''''
Seating Capacity: 732
Year Built: 1928
Year Remodeled: 1983
Cost: $160,000
Rental Contact: Managing Director Kaye Johnson

3208
ACTORS & PLAYWRIGHTS' INITIATIVE
359 S Burdick Street
Suite 205, Epic Center
Kalamazoo, MI 49007
Phone: 616-343-8090
Fax: 616-343-8450
Management:
 Artistic Director: Robert C Walker
 Marketing Director: Jeremy M Morris
Founded: 1989
Specialized Field: Young Playwrights; Theater Workshops; New Plays
Paid Staff: 6
Volunteer Staff: 12
Paid Artists: 20
Non-paid Artists: 12
Performs At: Epic Center
Facility Category: Theatre
Type of Stage: Black Box
Seating Capacity: 120

3209
KALAMAZOO CIVIC PLAYERS
329 S Park Street
Kalamazoo, MI 49007
Phone: 269-343-1313
Fax: 269-343-0532
Web Site: www.kazoocivic.com
Officers:
 President: Tim Kilmartin
 VP: Rob Kerschbaum
 Secretary: Pam Sackett
 Treasurer: Cory Wietfeldt
Management:
 Box Office Manager: LYN ALBERT
 Box Office Associate: KIM CHANDLER
 Scenic Carpenter: Sarah Davidson
 Graphic Designer: Tamara Diamond
 Custodian: Evan Jones
Mission: Offering the finest possible dramatic experience to the area.
Utilizes: Guest Companies
Founded: 1929
Specialized Field: Musical; Comedy; Community Theater; Classic; Contemporary
Status: Non-Profit, Non-Professional
Paid Staff: 30
Income Sources: American Association of Community Theatres; Community Theatre Association of Michigan

Performs At: Civic Auditorium; Carver Center
Organization Type: Performing

3211
PORT HURON CIVIC THEATRE
701 Me Morran Boulevard
PO Box 821
Port Huron, MI 48060
Phone: 810-984-4014
Fax: 810-985-3358
e-mail: info@phct.com
Web Site: www.phct.com/
Officers:
 President: Ernest Werth
 1st Vice President: Bryan Shelby
 Second VP: Denise Selby
 Secretary: Chris Hendrickson
 Treasurer: Jennifer Dent
Management:
 Marketing Director: Sarah McCollum
 Sales Director: Karen Pennewell
Mission: To offer a theatre season each year; to train and educate; to promote theatre arts.
Utilizes: Guest Companies
Founded: 1957
Specialized Field: Community Theater
Status: Semi-Professional; Nonprofit
Paid Staff: 200
Income Sources: Saint Clair County Community College
Performs At: McMorran Place Theatre
Organization Type: Performing; Educational

3212
SHELDON THEATRE
443 W 3rd Street
PO Box 34
Red Wing, MI 55066
Phone: 651-388-8700
Fax: 651-385-3663
e-mail: buytickets@sheldontheatre.org
Web Site: www.sheldontheatre.org
Officers:
 Board President: William Foot
 Executive Director: Sean Dowse
Management:
 Costume Shop Rental: Russel Johnson
Founded: 1904
Specialized Field: Drama; Musical; Classic
Status: Non-Profit, Professional
Paid Staff: 16

3213
MEADOW BROOK THEATRE
Oakland University
Rochester, MI 48309-4401
Phone: 248-377-3300
Fax: 248-370-3344
e-mail: kgentile@mbtheatre.com
Web Site: www.mbtheatre.com
Management:
 Artistic Director: David Regal
 Managing Director: Gregg Bloomfield
 Director Marketing: Rob Gold
Mission: To present a broad variety of top-quality live theatre, ranging from classic to contemporary works; to offer seven plays each season.
Utilizes: Actors; Designers; Guest Artists; Guest Companies; Guest Conductors; Guest Designers; Guest Lecturers; Guest Writers; Local Artists; Local Unknown Artists; Multimedia; Music; Original Music Scores; Performance Artists; Poets; Resident Professionals; Selected Students; Sign Language Translators; Singers; Student Interns; Visual Arts

Founded: 1967
Specialized Field: Musical; Classic; Contemporary
Status: Non-Profit, Professional
Paid Staff: 40
Income Sources: Oakland University; Concerned Citizens for the Arts in Michigan
Season: September - May
Affiliations: LORT
Annual Attendance: 100,000+
Facility Category: Theatre
Type of Stage: Proscenium
Seating Capacity: 584
Year Built: 1963
Organization Type: Performing; Touring

3214
RED BARN PLAYHOUSE
3657 63rd Street
Saugatuck, MI 49453
Mailing Address: PO Box 512, Saugatuck, MI 49453
Phone: 269-857-5300
Fax: 616-857-7803
e-mail: lakeshorearts@comcast.net
Web Site: www.redbarnsaugatuck.com/
Specialized Field: Summer Stock; Musical; Drama; Comedy
Season: June - September

3215
YOUTHEATRE
Michigan Performing Arts
15600 JL Hudson Drive
Box B
Southfield, MI 48075
Phone: 248-557-7529
Fax: 248-557-4415
Web Site: www.youtheatre.org
Management:
 President: Lou Longo
 Executive Director: Paul Berg
Mission: Youtheatre is a program of Michigan Performing Arts, organization dedicated to providing the best in professional, family entertainment to its audience.
Founded: 1964
Specialized Field: Children's Theater; Youth Theater
Status: Non-Profit, Professional
Paid Staff: 5
Paid Artists: 120
Income Sources: Michigan Council of Arts & Cultural Affairs; City of Detroit Cultural Affairs Department; National Endowment for the Arts; McGregor Fund
Seating Capacity: 1,100
Cost: $900,000 (message)

3216
OLD TOWN PLAYHOUSE
148 E 8th Street
PO Box 262
Traverse City, MI 49684
Phone: 231-947-2210
Fax: 231-947-4955
e-mail: office@oldtownplayhouse.com
Web Site: www.oldtownplayhouse.com
Officers:
 President: Larry Avery
 VP: Craig Rosenberg
 Treasurer: Dennis Lauterbach
 Secretary: Loren Gardner
Management:
 Executive Director: Phil Murphy
 Development Director: Betsy Willis,
 Education Director: Mychelle Hopkins,
 Business Manager: Linda , Enger
Mission: Assisting, encouraging, promoting and improving the cultural development of our community through education and entertainment.
Utilizes: Actors; Choreographers; Collaborations; Five Seasonal Concerts; Instructors; Local Artists; Music; Performance Artists; Resident Professionals; Sign Language Translators; Soloists; Student Interns
Founded: 1960
Specialized Field: Musical; Comedy; Community Theater; Classic; Contemporary
Status: Non-Profit, Non-Professional
Paid Staff: 5
Volunteer Staff: 150
Budget: $300,000
Income Sources: Ticket Sales; Season Subscribers; Donors, Fund Devlopment and Grants
Affiliations: CTAM; AACT; MACAA
Annual Attendance: 18,000
Facility Category: Community Theatre
Type of Stage: Mainstage; Black Box
Stage Dimensions: 358; 80
Seating Capacity: 358; 80
Year Built: 1903
Year Remodeled: 1997
Cost: $400,000
Organization Type: Performing; Educational
Resident Groups: Traverse City Civic Players

3217
BLUE LAKE REPERTORY THEATRE
Route #2
300 E
Twin Lake, MI 49457
Phone: 616-894-2540
Fax: 231-893-5123
Management:
 President: Fritz Stansell
 Treasurer: Reverend Walter Marek
Mission: To present summer-stock theatre of quality for our community.
Founded: 1966
Specialized Field: Summer Stock; Musical
Status: Semi-Professional
Income Sources: Blue Lake Fine Arts Camp
Performs At: Howmet Playhouse
Organization Type: Performing; Resident; Educational

3218
JET THEATRE
6600 W Maple Road
West Bloomfield, MI 48322-3002
Phone: 248-788-2900
Fax: 248-788-5160
e-mail: c.bremer@jettheatre.org
Web Site: www.jettheatre.org
Management:
 Director: Jonathan Frank
 Artistic Director: Evelyn Orbach
 Managing Director: Christopher Bremer
 Literary Manager: Pearl Orbach
Founded: 1989
Specialized Field: Jewish; Ethnic Theater; New Works of Social Importance
Status: Non-Profit, Professional
Paid Staff: 7
Paid Artists: 25

3219
JEWISH ENSEMBLE THEATRE
6600 W Maple Road
West Bloomfield, MI 48322-3002
Phone: 248-788-2900
Fax: 248-788-5160
e-mail: c.bremer@jettheatre.org
Web Site: www.jettheatre.org
Management:
 Director: Jonathan Frank
 Artistic Director: Evelyn Orbach
 Managing Director: Christopher Bremer
 Literary Manager: Pearl Orbach
Founded: 1989
Specialized Field: Comedy; Jewish; Classic; Contemporary
Status: Non-Profit, Professional
Paid Staff: 5
Performs At: Aaron DeRoy Theatre
Type of Stage: Thrust
Seating Capacity: 193

Minnesota

3220
THEATRE L'HOMME DIEU
1875 County Road 120 Northeast
Alexandria, MN 56308
Phone: 320-846-3150
Fax: 320-308-2902
e-mail: tlhd@tlhd.org
Web Site: www.tlhd.org
Officers:
 President: Linda Roles
 Board Member: Jeanne Batesole
 Executive Director: Joanna Hoch
 Board Member: Donna Jensen
 Board Member: Lisa Gustafson
Management:
 President: Elizabeth Mohror-Hill
 Artistic Director: Bruce Hyde
 Marketing Director: Laveda Holtberg
 Executive Director: Sara Schwabe
 Board Member: Linda Akenson
Founded: 1960
Specialized Field: Musical; Comedy; Ethnic Theater; Community Theater; Contemporary
Status: Non-Profit, Professional
Paid Staff: 15
Volunteer Staff: 15
Budget: $125,000
Income Sources: Grants; Box Office; University Subsidy
Season: June-August
Affiliations: St. Claude State University
Annual Attendance: 8,000
Facility Category: Theatre
Type of Stage: Proscenium
Stage Dimensions: 40' x 18'
Seating Capacity: 265
Year Built: 1961
Year Remodeled: 2000
Cost: $50,000

3221
MATCHBOX CHILDREN'S THEATRE
328 N Main Street
PO Box 576
Austin, MN 55912
Phone: 507-437-9078
e-mail: info@matchboxchildrenstheatre.org
Web Site: www.matchboxchildrenstheatre.org/
Officers:
 President: Carrie Parker
 VP: Barb Kasel
 Treasurer: Linda Sistek
 Secretary: Cindy Bellrichard

THEATRE / Minnesota

Mission: To produce creative, professional quality children's theatre on a consistent basis. Strive to produce well-rounded shows excelling in all aspects; script choice, direction, technical design and execution, costuming, make-up and the use of music. Primary focus is theatre for children, rather than by children. When appropriate roles are available children are casted.
Utilizes: Guest Companies; Singers
Founded: 1975
Specialized Field: Musical; Community Theater
Status: Non-Profit,Non-Professional
Performs At: Austin Community College Theatre
Organization Type: Performing; Resident

3222
PAUL BUNYAN PLAYHOUSE
1831 Anne Street
Suite 210
Bemidji, MN 56601
Phone: 218-444-1234
Fax: 218-444-1121
Toll-free: 800-276-8015
e-mail: info@paulbunyan.net
Web Site: www.paulbunyan.net
Officers:
   President: Becky Lueben
   VP: Kristine Cannon
   Treasurer: Karen Moe
   Secretary: Sandy Johnson
Management:
   Artistic Director: Curtiss Grittner
Mission: To produce the best possible theatre utilizing local and regional talent as well as interns from Bemidji State University.
Utilizes: Guest Companies; Singers
Founded: 1951
Specialized Field: Summer Stock; Musical
Status: Professional; Nonprofit
Paid Staff: 15
Performs At: Paul Bunyan Playhouse; Old Chief Theatre
Organization Type: Performing; Educational

3223
CHANHASSEN DINNER THEATRE
501 W 78th
PO Box 100
Chanhassen, MN 55317
Phone: 952-934-1525
Fax: 612-952-1511
Toll-free: 800-362-3515
e-mail: information@chanhassentheatres.com
Web Site: www.chanassentheatres.com
Officers:
   VP: Michael Brindisi
Management:
   President: Thomas K Scallen
   Artistic Director: Michael Brindisi
   General Manager: Solveig Huseth
   Director Public Relations: Kris Howland
Mission: To present fine theatre and dining.
Utilizes: Guest Companies; Singers
Founded: 1968
Specialized Field: Musical; Comedy; Dinner Theater
Status: For-Profit, Professional
Paid Staff: 250
Paid Artists: 50
Performs At: Chanhassen Dinner Theatres
Annual Attendance: 250,000
Facility Category: Professional Dinner Theater
Seating Capacity: 600
Organization Type: Performing

3224
COLDER BY THE LAKE COMEDY THEATRE
PO Box 3473
Duluth, MN 55803-3473
Phone: 218-722-8867
e-mail: info@colderbythelake.com
Web Site: www.colderbythelake.com
Officers:
   President: Mary Anderson
   VP: Dr Scott Wolf
   Secretary/Treasurer: Mary Treuer
Mission: Colder by the Lake presents all original theater, specifically: satire, comedy and the offbeat.
Utilizes: Guest Companies
Founded: 1983
Specialized Field: Comedy
Status: Nonprofit
Organization Type: Performing; Touring

3225
THE DULUTH PLAYHOUSE
506 W. Michigan Street
Duluth, MN 55802
Phone: 218-733-7555
Web Site: duluthplayhouse.org
Management:
   Executive/Artistic Director: Christine Gradl Seitz
   Production Manager: Jeff Brown
Mission: The mission of the Duluth Playhouse is to offer exceptional entertainment, training, and performance opportunities in theater arts that may inspire, challenge, and engage the region we serve.
Founded: 1914
Seating Capacity: 282
Organization Type: Educational; Performing

3226
UNIVERSITY OF MINNESOTA DULUTH: DEPARTMENT OF THEATRE
University of Minnesota at Duluth
141 Mpac
Duluth, MN 55812
Phone: 218-726-8562
Fax: 218-726-6798
e-mail: th@d.umn.edu
Web Site: www.d.umn.edu/theatre
Officers:
   Chancellor: Chan. Lendley Black
   Associate Dean: Arden Weaver
   Professor: Tom Isbell
   Practicum Instructor: Kendra Carlson
Management:
   Chancellor: Katherine A Matine
   Department Head: Patricia Dennis
   Associate Professor: Patricia Dennis
   Directing the Dance: Ann A Bergeron
   Associate Professor: Mark Harvey
Specialized Field: Musical; Tech Theater; Educational
Status: Non-Profit, Non-Professional
Paid Staff: 17

3227
UNIVERSITY OF MINNESOTA DULUTH: DEPARTMENT OF THEATRE
University of Minnesota at Duluth
141 MPAC
Duluth, MN 55812
Phone: 218-726-8562
Fax: 218-726-6798
e-mail: th@d.umn.edu
Web Site: www.d.umn.edu/theatre
Officers:
   Chancellor: Chan. Lendley Black
   Associate Dean: Arden Weaver
   Professor: Tom Isbell
   Practicum Instructor: Kendra Carlson
Management:
   Chancellor: Katherine A Matine
   Department Head: Patricia Dennis
   Associate Professor: Patricia Dennis
   Directing the Dance: Ann A Bergeron
   Associate Professor: Mark Harvey
Specialized Field: Educational; Theater Workshops
Performs At: Marshall Performing Arts Center

3228
OLD LOG THEATER
5175 Meadville Street
PO Box 250
Excelsior, MN 55331
Phone: 952-474-5951
Fax: 952-474-1290
Toll-free: 866-653-5641
e-mail: info@oldlog.com
Web Site: www.oldlog.com
   President: Don Stolz
Mission: To offer entertainment to the public.
Utilizes: Actors; AEA Actors; Choreographers; Dancers; Designers; Grant Writers; Guest Artists; Guest Lecturers; Guest Musical Directors; Multimedia; Music; Original Music Scores; Performance Artists; Resident Artists; Resident Professionals; Selected Students; Sign Language Translators; Student Interns
Founded: 1940
Specialized Field: Dinner Theater
Status: Professional
Paid Staff: 30
Paid Artists: 12
Income Sources: Ticket sales
Performs At: Old Log Theatre
Affiliations: Actors' Equity
Type of Stage: Proscenium
Stage Dimensions: 70x80x24
Seating Capacity: 655
Year Built: 1960
Rental Contact: Don Stocz
Organization Type: Performing; Touring; Resident

3229
STAGES THEATRE COMPANY
1111 Main Street
Hopkins, MN 55343
Phone: 952-979-1123
Fax: 952-979-1124
e-mail: info@stagestheatre.org
Web Site: www.stagestheatre.org
Officers:
   Chair: Kristin Parrish,
   Chair-Elect: Susan W. Allen,
   Treasurer: Lisa Kline,
   Secretary: Dawn Pruitt,
Management:
   Director: G Bryan Fleming
   Artistic Director: Steve Barberio
   Managing Director: John Montilino
Mission: To provide entertainment and theatre education for families and young people.
Utilizes: Guest Companies; Singers
Founded: 1984
Specialized Field: Musical
Status: Semi-Professional; Nonprofit
Paid Staff: 30
Performs At: Eisenhower Community Center; Hopkins
Organization Type: Performing; Resident; Educational

3230
LONG LAKE THEATER
12183 Beacon Road
Hubbard, MN 56470
Phone: 218-732-0099
e-mail: longlaketheater@gmail.com
Web Site: longlaketheater.com
Management:
   Artistic/Managing Director: Bruce Bolton
Founded: 2002
Seating Capacity: 100

3231
CLIMB THEATRE
6415 Carmen Avenue E
Inner Grove Heights, MN 55076
Phone: 651-453-9275
Fax: 651-453-9274
Toll-free: 800-767-9660
e-mail: mail@climb.org
Web Site: www.climb.org
Officers:
   President: Peg Wetli
   Chair: Jim Gambone
   President: Bonnie C. Matson
Management:
   Outreach Department: Jessica Hassler
   Gaming Department: Laurie Gluesing
   Teaching Company: Lauren Diesch
   Performing Company: Buffy Sedlachek
Founded: 1975
Specialized Field: New Works of Social Importance
Status: Non-Profit, Professional
Paid Artists: 24
Season: July - May

3232
COMMONWEAL THEATRE COMPANY
208 Parkway Avenue N
Lanesboro, MN 55949
Mailing Address: PO Box 15
Phone: 507-467-2525
Fax: 507-467-2587
Toll-free: 800-657-7025
e-mail: info@commonwealtheatre.org
Web Site: www.commonwealtheatre.org
Officers:
   Board President: David Ruen
   Executive Director: Hal Cropp
   Director of Development/Managing Di: Stef Dickens
Management:
   Executive Director: Hal Cropp
   Marketing Director: Jill Underwood
   Special Events Director: Adrienne Sweeney
   Development Director: David Hennessey
Mission: The Commonwealth is a nonprofit professional thatre company dedicated to delighting and challenging the audiences of our region and beyond.
Utilizes: Actors; Artists-in-Residence; Commissioned Music; Designers; Educators; Fine Artists; Grant Writers; Guest Conductors; Guest Designers; High School Drama; Instructors; Multimedia; Music; Original Music Scores; Performance Artists; Resident Artists; Resident Professionals; Selected Students; Soloists
Founded: 1989
Specialized Field: Musical; Comedy; Classic; Contemporary
Status: Non-Profit, Professional
Paid Staff: 9
Paid Artists: 35
Budget: $600,000
Income Sources: 64% Contributed Income
Season: February - December
Performs At: Brand New 186-Seat Thrust Theatre Due To Be Completed In July, 2007
Annual Attendance: 18,000
Facility Category: Until July, 2007; Converted Silent Movie House
Type of Stage: Proscenium
Stage Dimensions: 23' x 30'
Seating Capacity: 126
Year Built: 1896

3233
GREEN EARTH PLAYERS
216 W Main Street
Luverne, MN 56156
Phone: 507-283-9891
Mission: To bring live theatre to the area.
Utilizes: Guest Companies
Founded: 1978
Specialized Field: Musical; Community Theater
Status: Nonprofit
Income Sources: Minnesota Arts Council; Southern Minnesota Arts & Humanities Council
Performs At: Palace Theatre
Organization Type: Performing

3234
HIGHLAND SUMMER THEATRE
Minnesota State University
201 Performing Arts Center
Mankato, MN 56001
Phone: 507-389-2118
Fax: 507-389-2922
Toll-free: 800-722-0544
e-mail: paul.hustoles@mnsu.edu
Web Site: www.msutheatre.com
Officers:
   President: Richard Davenport
   Dance Director: Julie Kerr-Berry
   Dance Technique: Daniel Stark,
   Music Director: Nick Wayne
Management:
   Artistic Director: Paul J Hustoles
   Technical Director: George E.Grubb
   Scenic Design: John D. Paul
   Acting & Directing: Heather E. Hamilton
   Lighting Design: Steven Smith
Mission: Summer stock theatre in its 45th season
Founded: 1967
Specialized Field: Musical; Comedy; Summer Stock
Status: Non-Profit, Professional
Paid Staff: 30
Volunteer Staff: 4
Paid Artists: 15
Non-paid Artists: 20
Income Sources: Ticket Revenue; State Support
Season: May - July
Affiliations: Minnesota State University Mankato
Annual Attendance: 40,000
Facility Category: Performing Arts Center
Type of Stage: Proscenium; Black Box
Stage Dimensions: 38' x 38'; 60' x 70'
Seating Capacity: 529; 250

3235
ARTS MIDWEST
2908 Hennepin Avenue
Suite 200
Minneapolis, MN 55408-1954
Phone: 612-341-0755
Fax: 612-341-0902
e-mail: yumiko.inomata@artsmidwest.org
Web Site: www.artsmidwest.org
Officers:
   Treasurer: Bruce Bernberg
   Vice Chair: Peter Capell
   Chair: Dennis Holub
   Secretary: Sylvia C. Kaufman
Management:
   Executive Director: David Fraher
   Assistant Director: Susan T Chandler
   Program Director: Ken Carlson Carlson
   Development Assistant: Julia Barlow
   Assistant Director: Susan T. Chandler
Founded: 1985
Specialized Field: Educational; Community Theater
Status: Non-Profit

3236
BRAVE NEW WORKSHOP
2605 Hennepin Ave St
Minneapolis, MN 55408
Phone: 612-332-6620
Fax: 612-647-5637
e-mail: theatre@bravenewworkshop.com
Web Site: www.theatre.bravenewworkshop.com
Management:
   Producing Director: Dudley Riggs
   Co-Director of Student: Joe Bozic
   Managing Director: Erin Farmer
   Co-Director of Student: Mike Fotis
   Director of Theatre Mgt.: Greg Hersman
Founded: 1954
Specialized Field: Drama; Musical; Contemporary
Performs At: Dudley Riggs Theatre
Type of Stage: Modified Thrust
Seating Capacity: 260

3237
CHILDREN'S THEATER COMPANY
2400 3rd Avenue S
Minneapolis, MN 55404-3597
Phone: 612-874-0500
Fax: 612-874-8119
e-mail: info@childrenstheatre.org
Web Site: www.childrenstheatre.org
Officers:
   Chairman: Fran Davis
   Vice Chiar: Lili Hall
   Vice Chair: Geoff Jue
   Treasurer: George E. Tyson,II
   Secretary: Betsy Russomanno
Management:
   Artistic Director: Peter C Brosius
   Managing Director: Tim Jennings
Mission: To produce significant theatre experiences for young people and their families through nuturing a creative ensemble of the highest professional quality.
Utilizes: Guest Companies; Singers
Founded: 1965
Specialized Field: Youth Theater; Children's Theater
Status: Non-Profit, Professional
Paid Staff: 75
Paid Artists: 75
Budget: $9 million
Income Sources: Theatre Communications Group; International Association of Theatre for Children and Youth; Actors' Equity Association
Performs At: Children's Theatre Company
Annual Attendance: 350,000
Facility Category: Theater
Type of Stage: Proscenium
Seating Capacity: 745
Organization Type: Performing; Touring; Educational

THEATRE / Minnesota

3238
COMMEDIA THEATER COMPANY
3040 10Th Avenue S
Minneapolis, MN 55407
Phone: 612-788-2157
Management:
  General Manager: Linda Bruning
  Chief Financial Officer: Rudd Rayfield
Mission: To bring improvisational comedy with direct audience contact, into communities unfamiliar with live theater.
Founded: 1975
Specialized Field: Comedy; Improvisation
Status: Professional
Organization Type: Performing; Touring; Educational

3239
GUTHRIE THEATER
818 South 2nd Street
Minneapolis, MN 55415
Phone: 612-377-2224
Fax: 612-347-1188
Toll-free: 877-447-8243
e-mail: webmaster@guthrietheater.org
Web Site: www.guthrietheater.org
Officers:
  Chair: Lee B. Skold
  Past Chair: Wendy Chair
  Director: Joe Dawling
  Treasurer: Steven C. Webster
  Secretary: Martha Goldberg Aronson
Management:
  Director: Joe Dowling
  Production Director: Frank Butler
  CAO: Adam W. Cox
  Development Director: Danielle St.Germain
  Sr. Producer: Trish Santini
Mission: To serve as a vital artistic resource for the people of Minnesota and the region; to celebrate, through theatrical performances, the common humanity binding us all together; devoted to the traditional classical repertoire.
Utilizes: Actors; Artists-in-Residence; Choreographers; Collaborating Artists; Collaborations; Commissioned Music; Designers; Educators; Five Seasonal Concerts; Guest Accompanists; Guest Artists; Guest Choreographers; Guest Companies; Guest Conductors; Guest Designers; Guest Directors; Guest Ensembles; Guest Instructors; Guest Soloists; Guest Teachers; High School Drama; Instructors; Local Artists; Multimedia; Original Music Scores; Performance Artists; Playwrights; Resident Professionals; Selected Students; Soloists; Student Interns; Theatre Companies; Visual Arts
Founded: 1963
Specialized Field: Musical; Comedy; Classic; Contemporary
Status: Non-Profit, Professional
Season: June - February/March
Performs At: The Guthrie Theater
Affiliations: League of Resident Theatres
Type of Stage: Modified Thrust
Seating Capacity: 1300
Year Built: 1963
Year Remodeled: 1993
Cost: 3.5 Million
Organization Type: Performing; Touring; Resident

3240
HIDDEN THEATRE
4600 Oakland Avenue
Minneapolis, MN 55407-3536
Phone: 612-822-6060
Fax: 612-332-6037
e-mail: hiddentheatreyork@gmail.com
Web Site: www.sites.google.com/site/hiddentheatreyork
  Founder, Artistic Director: Laura Elizabeth Rice
Founded: 1994
Specialized Field: Drama

3241
ILLUSION THEATER
528 Hennepin Avenue
Suite 704
Minneapolis, MN 55403
Phone: 612-339-4944
Fax: 612-337-8042
e-mail: info@illusiontheater.org
Web Site: www.illusiontheater.org
Officers:
  Communication Director: Raina Linnerson
  Producing Director: Bonnie Morris
  Development Coordinator: Tiffany Robins
Management:
  Director: Michael Robins
  Managing Director: Mike Halls
  Education Director: Karen Gundlach
  Producing Director: Bonnie Morris
  Audience Service Manager: Shandai Kurylo
Utilizes: Actors; AEA Actors; Artists-in-Residence; Collaborations; Dance Companies; Dancers; Designers; Educators; Filmmakers; Five Seasonal Concerts; Grant Writers; Guest Artists; Guest Companies; Guest Conductors; Guest Lecturers; Guest Musical Directors; Guest Teachers; Local Artists; Local Unknown Artists; Multi Collaborations; Multimedia; Organization Contracts; Original Music Scores; Performance Artists; Poets; Resident Professionals; Selected Students; Sign Language Translators; Soloists; Student Interns; Visual Arts
Founded: 1974
Specialized Field: Musical; Comedy; Youth Theater; Contemporary
Status: Non-Profit, Professional
Paid Staff: 10
Paid Artists: 100
Budget: $1,500,000
Income Sources: Actors' Equity Association; Small Professional Theatre Association; Grants; Box Office
Season: September - August
Performs At: Hennepin Center for the Arts
Annual Attendance: 15,000
Facility Category: Theater
Type of Stage: Proscenium
Seating Capacity: 225
Year Remodeled: 1999
Organization Type: Performing; Touring; Resident; Educational; Sponsoring

3242
IN THE HEART OF THE BEAST PUPPET AND MASK THEATRE
1500 E Lake Street
Minneapolis, MN 55407
Phone: 612-721-2535
Fax: 612-721-7174
e-mail: info@hobt.org
Web Site: www.hobt.org
Officers:
  Chairman: Sue Melrose
  Vice Chairman: Kirstin Wiegmann
  Executive Director: Loren Niemi
  Secretary: Dan Herber
  Treasurer: Dan Newman
Management:
  Artistic Director: Sandy Spieler
  Executive Director: Loren Niemi
  Technical Director: Steve Ackerman
  Development/Marketing Director: Rick Bernardo
  Education Director: Bart Buch
Utilizes: Actors; Artists-in-Residence; Commissioned Composers; Guest Companies; Guest Conductors; Student Interns; Special Technical Talent
Founded: 1973
Specialized Field: Puppet; Mask Theater
Status: Non-Profit, Professional
Paid Staff: 13
Volunteer Staff: 350
Non-paid Artists: 20
Income Sources: Grants from Private and Public Sectors; Ticket Revenue and Earned Fees
Performs At: Restored Movie Theater
Annual Attendance: 100,000
Facility Category: Theatre
Type of Stage: Proscenium
Seating Capacity: 300
Year Built: 1937
Year Remodeled: 1997
Rental Contact: Paul Robinson
Organization Type: Performing; Touring; Resident; Educational; Sponsoring

3243
JACKSON MARIONETTE PRODUCTIONS
1500 E Lake Street
Minneapolis, MN 55407
Phone: 612-721-2535
Management:
  Manager: Sara Jackson
Utilizes: Singers
Specialized Field: Puppet
Status: Professional
Income Sources: Puppeteers of America; United International Marionette Association; Twin City Puppeteers
Organization Type: Performing; Touring

3244
JUNGLE THEATER
2951 S Lyndale Avenue
Minneapolis, MN 55408
Phone: 612-822-7063
Fax: 612-822-9408
e-mail: info@jungletheater.com
Web Site: www.jungletheater.com
Officers:
  Marketing Director: Sonja Wahlberg
  Vice Chair: Carol Lansing
  Chair: Barbara Bencini
  Treasurer: Ed Foppe
  Secretary: Tyler Treat
Management:
  Artistic Director: Bain Boehlke
  Managing Director: Margo Sagisselman
  Development Director: Don Sommer
  Community Programs Manager: Charles Bethel
  Finance Manager: Susan Sutton
Mission: To produce high quality theatre in an intimate setting.
Founded: 1991
Specialized Field: Contemporary
Status: Non-Profit, Professional
Paid Staff: 15
Volunteer Staff: 80
Paid Artists: 200
Budget: $1.1 million
Income Sources: Earned; Contributions
Performs At: Theater
Affiliations: Theatre Communications Group

Annual Attendance: 26,000
Facility Category: Theater
Type of Stage: Proscenium
Seating Capacity: 135
Year Built: 1911
Year Remodeled: 1999
Rental Contact: Charlie Bethel

3245
MARGOLIS BROWN THEATRE COMPANY
3112 17th Avenue S
Minneapolis, MN 55407
Phone: 612-722-2333
e-mail: margolisbrown@aol.com
Web Site: www.margolisbrown.org
   Artistic and Executive Director: Tony Brown
   Artistic and Executive Director: Karl Margolis
Mission: To create original multimedia productions of movement theatre; to share our facilities with other artists.
Utilizes: Singers
Founded: 1983
Specialized Field: Multi-Media; Movement Theater
Status: Professional; Nonprofit
Income Sources: National Movement Theatre Association
Organization Type: Performing; Touring; Resident; Educational; Sponsoring; Dramatic Movement School

3246
MEDORA MUSICAL
528 Hennepin Avenue
Suite 206
Minneapolis, MN 55403
Phone: 612-333-3302
Fax: 612-333-4337
Toll-free: 800-633-0721
e-mail: cw@troopamerica.com
Web Site: www.troupeamerica.com
Management:
   President: Curtis N Wollan
   Managing Director: John Tsafoyanni
   Executive Director: Cort Wollen
Utilizes: Actors; AEA Actors; Choreographers; Collaborations; Commissioned Composers; Commissioned Music; Dancers; Designers; Guest Artists; Instructors; Music; Organization Contracts; Original Music Scores; Resident Professionals; Sign Language Translators; Student Interns
Founded: 1992
Specialized Field: Musical; Comedy; Contemporary
Status: For-Profit, Professional
Paid Staff: 18
Paid Artists: 15
Budget: $500,000
Income Sources: Ticket Sales; Grants; Donations
Season: June - September
Annual Attendance: 115,000
Facility Category: Ampitheatre
Type of Stage: Outdoor
Stage Dimensions: 90' x 60'
Seating Capacity: 3000
Year Built: 1992
Cost: $4 Million

3247
MIXED BLOOD THEATRE COMPANY
1501 S 4th Street
Minneapolis, MN 55454
Phone: 612-338-0937
Fax: 612-338-1851
e-mail: boxoffice@mixedblood.com
Web Site: www.mixedblood.com

Officers:
   President: Ronald McKinley
   Vice President: Tabitha Montgomery
   Treasurer: Molly Bott
   Secretary: Eric Hyde
   President Emerita: Susan P. Mackay
Management:
   Artistic Director: Jack Reuler
   Production Manager: Caitlin Milligan Sheaffer
   General Manager: Charlie Moore
Mission: A multiracial, professional theatre ensemble employing colorblind casting, and dedicated to fostering the spirit of Dr. Martin Luther King's dream.
Utilizes: Actors; AEA Actors; Designers; Educators; Fine Artists; Five Seasonal Concerts; Guest Companies; Instructors; Local Artists; Organization Contracts; Original Music Scores; Performance Artists; Resident Professionals; Selected Students; Soloists; Student Interns; Theatre Companies
Founded: 1976
Specialized Field: Ethnic Theater; Community Theater; Contemporary
Status: Non-Profit, Professional
Paid Staff: 8
Paid Artists: 75
Budget: $1 million
Income Sources: Society for Stage Directors and Choreographers
Season: September - May
Annual Attendance: varies
Type of Stage: Flexible
Seating Capacity: 200
Organization Type: Performing; Touring; Educational

3248
MU PERFORMING ARTS
2700 NE Winter Street
Suite 1A
Minneapolis, MN 55413
Phone: 612-824-4804
Fax: 612-824-3396
e-mail: info@muperformingarts.org
Web Site: www.muperformingarts.org
Officers:
   Marketing Intern: Bri Heu
Management:
   Artistic Director: Randy Reyes
   Managing Director: Don Eitel
   Artistic Director: Iris Shiraishi
   Development Director: Sara Ochs
   Marketing Coordinator: Eric Sharp
Founded: 1992
Specialized Field: Musical; Comedy; Ethnic Theater; Puppet; Contemporary
Status: Non-Profit, Professional
Paid Staff: 6
Paid Artists: 50

3249
OPEN EYE FIGURE THEATRE
506 East 24th Street
Minneapolis, MN 55404
Phone: 612-874-6338
e-mail: info@openeyetheatre.org
Web Site: openeyetheatre.org
Officers:
   President: Michelle Pett
   Vice President: Craig Harris
Management:
   Artistic Producing Director: Susan Haas
Mission: Open Eye Figure Theatre creates original figure theatre, animating the inanimate on an intimate scale; trains the next generation of figure theatre artists; and advances adventurous, artist-driven programming.
Specialized Field: Puppetry

3250
PANGEA WORLD THEATER
711 Westlake Street
Suite 101
Minneapolis, MN 55408
Phone: 612-203-1088
Fax: 612-821-1070
e-mail: pangea@pangeaworldtheater.org
Web Site: www.pangeaworldtheater.org
Officers:
   Board Chair: June LaValleur
Management:
   Artistic Director: Dipankar Mukherjee
   Executive/Literary Director: Meena Natrajan
   Office Manager: Katie Herron Robb
Founded: 1996
Specialized Field: Comedy; Ethnic Theater; Classic; Contemporary
Status: Non-Profit, Professional
Paid Staff: 3

3251
PILLSBURY HOUSE THEATRE
3501 Chicago Avenue S
Minneapolis, MN 55407
Phone: 612-825-0459
Fax: 612-827-5818
e-mail: info@pillsburyhousetheatre.org
Web Site: www.pillsburyhousetheatre.org
Officers:
   Development Manager: Corrie Zoll
   Production Manager: Elizabeth R.MacNalley
   Artistic Program Associate: Kurt Kwan
   Community Liaison: Mike Hoyt
Management:
   Director: Tony Wagner
   Managing Director: Noel Raymond
   Co-Artistic Director: Faye Price
   Co-Artistic Director: No%ol Raymond
   Director of Communications: Alan Berks
Founded: 1992
Specialized Field: Youth Theater; Ethnic Theater; Contemporary
Status: Non-Profit, Professional
Paid Staff: 8

3252
PLAYWRIGHTS' CENTER
2301 Franklin Avenue E
Minneapolis, MN 55406-1099
Phone: 612-332-7481
Fax: 612-332-6037
e-mail: info@pwcenter.org
Web Site: www.pwcenter.org
Officers:
   Board President: Elizabeth Grant,
   Board Vice President: John Geelan
   Treasurer: Charlie Quimby
   Secretary: Barbara Davis
   Artistic Director: Carlyle Brown
Management:
   Producing Artistic Director: Jeremy Cohen,
jeremyc@pwcenter.org
   MD: Keri Kellerman
   Office Assistant: Julia Brown
   Development Manager: Sarah Blain Chaplin
   Associate Artistic Director: Hayley Finn
Mission: The Playwrights' Center champions playwrights and plays to build upon a living theater that demands new and innovative works.

THEATRE / Minnesota

Utilizes: AEA Actors; Artists-in-Residence; Collaborating Artists; Collaborations; Community Members; Community Talent; Educators; Equity Actors; Five Seasonal Concerts; Guest Accompanists; Guest Choreographers; Guest Conductors; Guest Designers; Guest Ensembles; Guest Musical Directors; Guest Soloists; High School Drama; Instructors; Local Artists & Directors; Local Talent; Multi Collaborations; Multimedia; Original Music Scores; Performance Artists; Students; Student Interns; Special Technical Talent; Volunteer Directors & Actors; Writers
Founded: 1971
Specialized Field: Musical; Comedy; Young Playwrights; Ensembles; Classic; Contemporary
Status: Non-Profit, Professional
Paid Staff: 13
Paid Artists: 100
Income Sources: Actors' Equity Association; Theatre Communications Group
Season: July - August
Year Built: 1900
Year Remodeled: 2000
Cost: $1,100,000
Organization Type: Touring; Educational; Sponsoring; Developmental Workshops; Reading

3253
RED EYE
15 W 14th Street
Minneapolis, MN 55403
Phone: 612-870-7531
e-mail: staff@theredeye.org
Web Site: www.redeyetheater.org
Management:
  Managing Director: Miriam Must
  Artistic Director: Steve Busa
  Production and Facility Manager: Tim Heins
Mission: To provide experimental theatre; to develop multimedia theater productions.
Utilizes: Guest Companies; Singers
Founded: 1983
Specialized Field: Experimental; Multi-Media
Status: Professional; Nonprofit
Income Sources: National Endowment for the Arts; Dayton Hudson Foundation; Jerome Foundation; McKnight Foundation; United Artists; Metropolitan Regional Arts Council
Performs At: Red Eye's 14th Street Theatre
Organization Type: Performing; Touring; Resident; Educational

3254
THEATER LATTE DA
1170 15th Avenue SE, Suite 203
Minneapolis, MN 55414
Phone: 612-339-3003
e-mail: info@latteda.org
Web Site: theaterlatteda.com
Management:
  Artistic Director: Peter Rothstein
  Resident Music Director: Denise Prosek
  Office Manager: Matt Cerar
  Director Of External Relations: Seena Hodges
Mission: Theater Latte Da seeks to create new connections between story, music, artist, and audience by exploring and expanding the art of musical theater.
Founded: 1998
Specialized Field: Musical Theatre

3255
THEATRE DE LA JEUNE LUNE
105 N 1st Street
Minneapolis, MN 55401
Phone: 612-460-1051
Fax: 612-332-0048
e-mail: info@ariamps.com
Web Site: www.jeunelune.org
Management:
  Executive Director: Steve Richardson
  Artistic Director: Robert Rosen
  Artistic Director: Dominique Serrand
  Artistic Director: Vincent Gracieux
  Business Director: Kit Waickman
  Development Director: Jennifer Halcrow
  Marketing Director: Steve Richardson
Mission: The production of immediate, energetic, dynamic, theatre through company creations and scripted material.
Founded: 1978
Specialized Field: Musical; Comedy; Community Theater; Puppet; Contemporary
Status: Non-Profit, Professional
Paid Staff: 10
Paid Artists: 10
Income Sources: Foundation for the Extension and Development of American Professional Theatre
Season: September - June
Type of Stage: Mobile
Stage Dimensions: 60' x 100'; 47' x 30'
Seating Capacity: 500;100-150
Organization Type: Performing; Touring

3256
THEATRE IN THE ROUND
245 Cedar Avenue
Minneapolis, MN 55454-1054
Phone: 612-333-3010
e-mail: editorial@theatremania.com
Web Site: www.theatreintheround.org
Officers:
  President: Lauren May
  Vice President: Francine Corcoran
  Treasurer: Chris Styring
  Secretary: Stephanie Long
Management:
  President: Melanie Ulrich
  Managing Director: Steve Antenucci
  Assistant Administrator: Greg Johnson
  Technical Volunteer Coordinator: Benjamin Kutschied
  Executive Director: Steven Antenucci
Mission: To bridge the gap between professional and amateur theatre with quality drama; to entertain the community; to educate.
Utilizes: Guest Companies; Singers
Founded: 1952
Specialized Field: Drama; Educational
Status: Non-Profit, Non-Professional
Paid Staff: 3
Paid Artists: 9
Income Sources: American Association of Community Theatres; Minnesota Association of Community Theatres
Performs At: Theatre-in-the-Round
Organization Type: Performing; Resident; Educational

3257
TROUPE AMERICA
3313 Republic Avenue
Minneapolis, MN 55426
Phone: 612-333-3302
Fax: 952-345-3309
e-mail: johnt@troupeamerica.com
Web Site: www.troupeamerica.com
Officers:
  President: Curtis N Wollan
  Secretary/Treasurer: Jane Wollan
Management:
  President: Curtis N Wollan
  Managing Director: John Tsafoyanni
  Executive Director: Cort Wollen
Mission: To provide top quality theatrical experiences for our audiences, on the road and in the Twin Cities.
Utilizes: Actors; Artists-in-Residence; Choreographers; Collaborating Artists; Collaborations; Community Talent; Composers; Contract Actors; Dancers; Designers; Equity Actors; Guest Designers; Guest Lecturers; Local Unknown Artists; Multimedia; Music; Organization Contracts; Original Music Scores; Performance Artists; Resident Professionals; Selected Students; Theatre Companies
Founded: 1987
Specialized Field: Musical; Comedy; Contemporary
Status: For-Profit, Professional
Paid Staff: 23
Paid Artists: 35
Budget: $1,750,000
Income Sources: Ticket Sales; Concessions; Touring Fees
Season: September - August
Affiliations: Southeastern Theatre Conference; United Professional Theatre Association
Annual Attendance: 100,000
Facility Category: Plymouth Playhouse; and Touring Venues
Type of Stage: Semi Thrust
Stage Dimensions: 30x24
Seating Capacity: 211
Year Built: 1974
Year Remodeled: 1998
Cost: $150,000
Rental Contact: Production Manager Scott Herbst
Organization Type: Performing; Touring; Resident; Sponsoring

3258
WALKER ART CENTER
1750 Hennepin Avenue
Minneapolis, MN 55403
Phone: 612-375-7600
Fax: 612-375-7618
e-mail: leigha.horton@walkerart.org
Web Site: www.walkerart.org
Management:
  Director: Kathy Halbreich
  Curator Performing Arts: Philip Bither
Mission: To serve as a catalyst regionally and internationally for emerging forms of expression; to engage the audience in contemporary arts issues.
Utilizes: Artists-in-Residence; Choreographers; Collaborating Artists; Collaborations; Commissioned Composers; Commissioned Music; Composers-in-Residence; Curators; Dance Companies; Educators; Fine Artists; Guest Soloists; Instructors; Original Music Scores; Poets; Selected Students; Student Interns; Touring Companies
Founded: 1887
Specialized Field: Drama; Contemporary; Multi-Media
Status: Non-Profit, Professional
Paid Staff: 150
Income Sources: Endowment; Grants; Ticket Revenue; Donations
Performs At: Walker Art Center Auditorium
Facility Category: Multidisciplinary Arts Center
Seating Capacity: 350
Organization Type: Performing; Touring; Resident; Educational; Sponsoring; Exhibition

THEATRE / Minnesota

3259
WORLD TREE PUPPET THEATER
3305 E Calhoun Parkway
Minneapolis, MN 55408
Phone: 612-824-3112
Management:
  Director: Joan Mickelson
Mission: To use the traditions of puppetry and adaptations of folklore to entertain families and children; to employ experimental uses of puppets, dolls and masks for adult theater.
Founded: 1982
Specialized Field: Puppet
Status: Professional
Organization Type: Performing; Touring; Resident

3260
GOOSEBERRY PARK PLAYERS
PO Box 362
Moorhead, MN 56561
Phone: 218-299-3728
e-mail: info@gooseberryparkplayers.org
Web Site: www.gooseberryparkplayers.org
Officers:
  President: Ann Vandermaten
Management:
  Artistic Director: Jim Cermack
Mission: Provide a summer outdoor theatre for and by children for family entertainment providing a fun, educational experience for young people.
Utilizes: Singers
Founded: 1984
Specialized Field: Summer Stock; Children's Theater
Status: Nonprofit
Income Sources: Moorhead Parks & Recreational Department
Organization Type: Performing

3261
STRAW HAT PLAYERS
Minnesota State University Moorhead
1104 7th Avenue South
Moorhead, MN 56563
Phone: 218-477-2271
Fax: 218-477-4612
e-mail: craig.ellingson@mnstate.edu
Web Site: www.mnstate.edu/strawhat
Management:
  Executive Director: Craig A Ellingson
Founded: 1963
Specialized Field: Classic; Musical
Status: Non-Profit, Professional
Paid Staff: 10
Paid Artists: 35
Season: May - July
Type of Stage: Thrust
Seating Capacity: 800

3262
OFF-BROADWAY MUSICAL THEATRE
4401 Xylon Avenue N
New Hope, MN 55428
Phone: 612-544-3810
Fax: 612-545-3622
Web Site: www.obmt.org
Management:
  Director: Shawn McWhorter
  Stage Manager: Tara Neilson
  Vocal and Orchestra Director: David Lamprecht
  Set Design: Molly Kern
  Choreographer: Angela Cain
Mission: To offer major musicals employing local talent of all ages and degrees of proficiency.
Utilizes: Guest Artists; Guest Companies; Singers
Founded: 1979
Specialized Field: Community Theater; Musical
Status: Nonprofit
Income Sources: Minnesota State Arts Council
Performs At: New Hope Outdoor Theatre; Brooklyn Center Civic
Organization Type: Performing

3263
LITTLE THEATRE OF OWATONNA
Dunell Drive
Owatonna, MN 55060
Mailing Address: PO Box 64, Owatonna, MN 55060
Phone: 507-451-0764
e-mail: info@littletheatreofowatonna.org
Web Site: www.littletheatreofowatonna.org
Officers:
  President: Vidette Ostermeir
  Vice President: Sandee Hagan
  Secertary: Lori Beadell
Management:
  Executive Secretary: Sharon Stark
Mission: To bring performing arts, particularly theatre, to the community.
Utilizes: Guest Companies
Founded: 1966
Specialized Field: Drama; Community Theater
Status: Non-Professional; Nonprofit
Organization Type: Performing

3264
ROCHESTER CIVIC THEATRE
20 Civic Drive
Rochester, MN 55904
Phone: 507-282-8481
Fax: 507-282-0608
e-mail: info@rochestercivictheatre.org
Web Site: www.rochestercivictheatre.org/
Management:
  Technical Associate: Todd Schroeder
  Executive Director: Gregory Stavrou
  Artistic Director: Greg Miller
  Education Director: Denise Ruemping
  Box Office Associate: Sunny Hartert
Mission: Promoting interest in and appreciation of dramatic arts through programs and productions.
Utilizes: Guest Companies; Singers
Founded: 1951
Specialized Field: Musical; Comedy; Community Theater; Puppet; Classic; Contemporary
Status: Non-Profit, Non-Professional
Paid Staff: 6
Income Sources: Minnesota Association of Community Theatres
Organization Type: Performing; Touring; Educational

3265
CLIMB THEATRE - CREATIVE LEARNING IDEAS
6415 Carmen Ave E
Suite 220
Saint Paul, MN 55076
Phone: 651-453-9275
Fax: 651-453-9274
Toll-free: 800-767-9660
e-mail: mail@climb.org
Web Site: www.climb.org/contactus.aspx
Officers:
  Chair: Jim Gambone
Management:
  Executive Director, Founder: Peg Wetli
  Residency Company Manager: Peg Endres
Mission: To harness and direct the creative power and artistic talents of its writers, directors, actors and educators to create and perform plays, classes and other creative works which communicate matters of social or educational significance to all citizens.
Utilizes: Singers
Founded: 1975
Specialized Field: New Works of Social Importance; Educational
Status: Professional; Nonprofit
Organization Type: Performing; Touring; Educational

3266
GREAT AMERICAN HISTORY THEATRE
30 E 10th Street
Saint Paul, MN 55101
Phone: 651-292-4323
Fax: 651-292-4322
e-mail: boxofc@historytheatre.com
Web Site: www.historytheatre.com/about/
Officers:
  President: Jeff Perterson
  VP: Connie Braziel
  Treasurer: Tyler Zehring
  Secretrary: Roger Brooks
Management:
  Artistic Director: Ron Peluso
  Managing Director: Karen Mueller
  Production Manager: Janet L. Hall
  Technical Director: Gunther Gullickson
Mission: To create new plays about Minnesota the Midwest and the diverse American experience.
Founded: 1978
Specialized Field: Musical; Historical
Status: Professional; Nonprofit
Paid Artists: 40
Income Sources: 70% Earned; 30% Contributed
Annual Attendance: 54,000

3268
NAUTILUS MUSIC-THEATER
308 Prince Street
#250
Saint Paul, MN 55101
Phone: 651-298-9913
Fax: 651-298-9924
e-mail: ben@nautilusmusictheater.org
Web Site: www.nautilusmusictheater.org
Management:
  Artistic Director: Ben Krywosz
  Managing Director: Bethany Gladhill
Mission: To develop and produce new musical theater works; to nurture the creative artist.
Founded: 1986
Specialized Field: Musical; Classic; Contemporary
Status: Non-Profit, Professional
Paid Staff: 2
Paid Artists: 200
Budget: $250,000
Organization Type: Performing; Educational

3269
PARK SQUARE THEATRE COMPANY
20 W. 7th Place
Saint Paul, MN 55102-1130
Phone: 651-291-7005
Fax: 651-291-9180
Toll-free: 877-291-7001
e-mail: parksquare@parksquaretheatre.org
Web Site: www.parksquaretheatre.org
Officers:
  President: Jeff Johnson
  VP of Finance: Judy Mcnamara
  Immediate Past President: Elizabeth Cobb

THEATRE / Mississippi

Vice President: Sara I. Beckstrand
Secretary: Julie Cox
Management:
　Develoment Director: Michael Pease
　Executive Director: C. Michael-jon Pease, CFRE
　Audience Services Director: Eric M Herr
　Education Director: Mary Finnerty
　Technical Director: Rob Jensen
Mission: Entertaining and enriching area audiences with quality productions of the classics.
Utilizes: Actors; AEA Actors; Choreographers; Commissioned Music; Designers; Guest Accompanists; Guest Artists; Guest Companies; Guest Conductors; Guest Lecturers; Local Artists; Original Music Scores; Resident Professionals; Selected Students; Student Interns
Founded: 1975
Specialized Field: Comedy; Classic; Contemporary
Status: Non-Profit, Professional
Paid Staff: 10
Paid Artists: 100
Budget: $1.2 million
Income Sources: Sales; Contributions
Season: January - August
Annual Attendance: 54,000
Facility Category: Rental
Type of Stage: Proscenium
Stage Dimensions: 34' x 30'
Seating Capacity: 340
Organization Type: Performing

3270
PENUMBRA THEATRE COMPANY
270 N Kent Street
Saint Paul, MN 55102
Phone: 651-224-3180
Fax: 612-224-7074
e-mail: info@penumbratheatre.org
Web Site: http://penumbratheatre.org
Officers:
　Secretary: Mark A. McLellan
　Treasurer: Chris Roberts
　Second Vice Chair: Jeffrey N. Saunders
　Chair: Bill Stevens
　First Vice Chair: Scott K. Cabalka
Management:
　Founder & Artistic Director: Lou Bellamy
　General Manager: Jayne Khalifa
　Associate Artistic Director - Educa: Sarah Bellamy
Mission: To present high quality theatre from the Pan African/American viewpoint.
Utilizes: Guest Companies
Founded: 1976
Specialized Field: Musical; Ethnic Theater
Status: Professional; Nonprofit
Income Sources: Actors' Equity Association
Season: August - June
Type of Stage: Proscenium/Thrust
Stage Dimensions: 27' x 41'
Seating Capacity: 260
Organization Type: Performing; Touring; Educational

3271
RAINBO CHILDREN'S THEATRE COMPANY
688 Selby Avenue
Saint Paul, MN 55104
Phone: 651-293-9043
Management:
　Founder/Managing Artistic Director: Merline Batiste Doty
Mission: To bring children together for cultural exchange through participation in the performing arts.
Utilizes: Guest Companies; Singers
Founded: 1979
Specialized Field: Community Theater; Ethnic Theater
Status: Professional; Nonprofit
Paid Staff: 10
Organization Type: Performing; Touring; Resident; Educational; Sponsoring

3272
LAKESHORE PLAYERS
4820 Stewart Avenue
White Bear Lake, MN 55110
Phone: 651-429-5674
e-mail: info@lakeshoreplayers.com
Web Site: www.lakeshoreplayers.com
Management:
　Business Manager: Sherrie Tarble
Mission: To provide entertainment for the community.
Utilizes: Guest Companies; Singers
Founded: 1953
Specialized Field: Musical
Status: Nonprofit
Paid Staff: 25
Income Sources: Minnesota Association of Community Theatres
Performs At: Lakeshore Playhouse
Organization Type: Performing; Educational

3273
SHAKESPEARE & COMPANY
Century College, W Campus
3300 Century Avenue N
White Bear Lake, MN 55110
Phone: 651-779-5818
Fax: 651-779-5802
e-mail: info@shakespeareandcompany.org
Web Site: www.shakespeare-company.org
Management:
　Director: Larry Litecky
　Artistic Director: George M Roesler
Mission: To provide an environment where families can come and enjoy an informal picnic atmosphere and see performances of Shakespeare and other classical plays.
Founded: 1976
Specialized Field: Educational; Shakespeare
Status: Professional
Performs At: Outdoor Theatre Complex, West Campus of Century College

Mississippi

3274
CORINTH THEATRE-ARTS
303 Fulton Drive
Corinth, MS 38834
Mailing Address: PO Box 127 Corinth, MS. 38835
Phone: 662-287-2995
Fax: 662-287-6272
e-mail: corinth.theatre.arts@gmail.com
Web Site: www.corinththeatrearts.com
Officers:
　Chairman: John Treadway
　Vice Chairman: Paul Schumacher
　Secretary: Gentry Parker
　Treasurer: Becky Williams
　VP Of Operations: Tonya Freeman
　Artistic Director: Cristina Skinner
　Technical Director: David Maxedon
　Managing Director: Tommy Ledbetter
Mission: To offer theatrical performances, arts education, economic stimulation and quality arts entertainment.
Founded: 1968
Specialized Field: Community Theater
Status: Non-Profit, Professional
Paid Staff: 2
Volunteer Staff: 2
Paid Artists: 10
Non-paid Artists: 500
Budget: $105,000
Income Sources: Theatre Patrons; Box Office; Grants
Performs At: Crossroads Playhouse; Coliseum Civic Center
Annual Attendance: 8500
Type of Stage: Proscenium
Stage Dimensions: 19 x 30
Seating Capacity: 204
Organization Type: Resident

3275
DELTA CENTER STAGE
323 S. Main Street
Greenville, MS 38701
Mailing Address: P.O. Box 14, Greenville, MS 38702
Phone: 662-378-9849
e-mail: info@deltastage.com
Web Site: deltastage.com
Founded: 1979

3276
NEW STAGE THEATRE
1100 Carlisle Street
Jackson, MS 39202
Mailing Address: PO Box 4792 Jackson MS 39296
Phone: 601-948-3533
Fax: 601-948-3538
e-mail: mail@newstagetheatre.com
Web Site: www.newstagetheatre.com
Management:
　Artistic Director: Francine Thomas Reynolds
　General Manager: Bill McCarty III
　Managing Director: Dawn Buck
　Marketing Director: Melissa Tillman
　Education Director: Chris Roebuck
Utilizes: Actors; AEA Actors; Choreographers; Collaborations; Contract Actors; Designers; Educators; Equity Actors; Five Seasonal Concerts; Grant Writers; Guest Accompanists; Guest Artists; Guest Conductors; Guest Designers; Guest Ensembles; Guest Lecturers; Guest Musical Directors; Guest Speakers; Guest Teachers; High School Drama; Instructors; Local Artists; Local Artists & Directors; Multimedia; Music; Original Music Scores; Poets; Resident Companies; Resident Professionals; Scenic Designers; Soloists; Students; Theatre Companies; Visual Designers; Volunteer Directors & Actors; Writers
Founded: 1965
Opened: 1965
Specialized Field: Musical; Comedy; Ethnic Theater; Classic; Contemporary
Status: Non-Profit, Professional
Paid Staff: 13
Paid Artists: 5
Budget: $900,000
Season: September - June
Affiliations: Actors' Equity Association
Facility Category: New Stage Theatre
Type of Stage: Proscenium
Seating Capacity: 364
Organization Type: Resident; Educational; Producing

3277
PUPPET ARTS THEATRE
1927 Springridge Drive
Jackson, MS 39211

THEATRE / Missouri

Phone: 601-956-3414
Fax: 601-956-3414
e-mail: puppetartssacramento@gmail.com
Web Site: www.puppetarts.com
Management:
   Managing Director: Peter Zapletal
   Business Manager: Jarmila Zapletal
   Artistic Director: Art Grueneberger
Mission: To offer entertainment and education in the Southeast through programs featuring puppets and classical music.
Founded: 1968
Specialized Field: Puppet; Children's Theater
Status: For-Profit, Professional
Paid Staff: 10
Paid Artists: 10
Organization Type: Performing; Touring

Missouri

3278
ARROW ROCK LYCEUM THEATRE
114 High Street
P.O. Box 14
Arrow Rock, MO 65320
Phone: 660-837-3311
Fax: 660-837-3112
e-mail: lyceumtheatre@lyceumtheatre.org
Web Site: www.lyceumtheatre.org
Officers:
   President: Dick Malon
   Vice President: Robert Lamm
   Treasurer: John Fletcher
   Secretary: Bea Smith, Ph.D.
   Past President: Dave Criggs
Management:
   Artistic Director: Quinn Gresham
   Managing Director: Steve Bertani
   Marketing Director: Jackie Buckley
   Group Sales: Lisa Boudreau
Mission: To touch, enrich and entertain human beings with live professional theatre.
Utilizes: Actors; AEA Actors; Artists-in-Residence; Choreographers; Designers; Guest Artists; Guest Companies; Guest Musical Directors; Instructors; Music; Original Music Scores; Resident Artists; Resident Professionals; Sign Language Translators; Singers; Soloists
Founded: 1960
Specialized Field: Drama; Musical
Status: Professional; Nonprofit
Paid Staff: 25
Volunteer Staff: 80
Paid Artists: 35
Non-paid Artists: 80
Budget: $750,000
Income Sources: Actors' Equity Association
Season: June - August
Performs At: Lyceum Theatre
Annual Attendance: 35,000
Facility Category: Indoor A/C Theatre
Type of Stage: Proscenium w/thrust
Seating Capacity: 408
Year Remodeled: 1993
Rental Contact: Business Manager Elizabeth Ostrin
Organization Type: Performing; Touring; Resident

3279
SHEPHERD OF THE HILLS
5586 W. Hwy 76
Branson, MO 65616-0000
Phone: 417-334-4191
Fax: 417-334-4617
Toll-free: 800-653-6288
e-mail: groups@tablerock.net
Web Site: www.oldmatt.com
Management:
   Director: Keith Thurman
   General Manager: Richard Bittle
   Operations Manager: Jim O'Donnell
Mission: In 1907, a novel was published that forever changed the way of life for Branson area residents. That novel, The Shepherd of the Hills, sold millions of copies and attracts many people to the Ozark hills around which its story is centered.
Founded: 1907
Specialized Field: Summer Stock; Historical
Status: For-Profit, Professional
Season: April - October
Type of Stage: Outdoor
Seating Capacity: 1100

3280
TRILAKES COMMUNITY THEATRE
PO Box 1301
Branson, MO 65616
Phone: 417-335-4241
e-mail: board@tlctheatre.org
Web Site: www.tlctheatre.org
Officers:
   President: John Spencer
   VP Business: Gail Wehr
   VP Production: Kim Hale
   Secretary: Morgan Harp
   Treasurer: Glenda Justus
Mission: To foster the Performing Arts; to entertain the community.
Utilizes: Singers
Founded: 1983
Specialized Field: Musical; Community Theater
Status: Nonprofit
Paid Staff: 30
Income Sources: Missouri Arts Council
Organization Type: Performing

3281
STAGES ST. LOUIS
444 Chesterfield Center
Suite 215
Chesterfield, MO 63017
Phone: 314-821-2412
Fax: 314-821-2191
e-mail: mailbox@stagesslouis.com
Web Site: www.stagesstlouis.com
Officers:
   Chairman: Betty Von Hoffmann
   Treasurer: Kara A. Meister
   VP: Susan M. Hale
   Secretary: Philip S. Roush
Management:
   President: Merry L. Mosbacher
   Artistic Director: Michael Hamilton
   Executive Producer: Jack Lane
   Production Stage Manager: Judith Grothe Cullen
   Production Manager: John Cattanach
Mission: To produce the indigenous American art form of musical theatre which artfully combines the three disciplines of music, dance and drama. Through vital and unique interpretations of classic musicals, Stages strives to keep this threatened art form alive.
Utilizes: Actors; AEA Actors; Contract Actors; Dancers; Guest Conductors; Instructors; Local Artists; Music; Original Music Scores; Resident Professionals; Selected Students; Sign Language Translators; Soloists; Student Interns
Founded: 1987
Specialized Field: Musical; Comedy; Youth Theater; Dinner Theater; Ethnic Theater; Community Theater; Puppet
Status: Non-Profit, Professional
Paid Staff: 19
Paid Artists: 100
Budget: $1,200,000
Income Sources: Ticket Revenue; Private Donors; Corporations and Foundations
Performs At: Reim Theatre
Annual Attendance: 46,000
Facility Category: Theatre
Type of Stage: Proscenium
Stage Dimensions: 24'Dx34'W
Seating Capacity: 380
Year Built: 1960
Rental Contact: Kirkwood Civic Center

3282
NEW JEWISH THEATRE
2 Millstone Campus Drive
Creve Coeur, MO 63146
Phone: 314-432-5700
e-mail: housemgr@jccstl.org
Web Site: newjewishtheatre.org
Management:
   Artistic Director: Kathleen Sitzer
   Production Manager: Tara Santiago
Founded: 1997

3283
FLORISSANT CIVIC CENTER THEATER
955 Rue St. Francois
Florissant, MO 63031
Phone: 314-921-5700
Fax: 314-921-7111
e-mail: citymail@florissantmo.com
Web Site: www.florissantmo.com
Management:
   General Manager: Gary Gaydos
   Economic Director: Bob Russell
   Chief Financial Officer: Randy McDaniel
Founded: 1972
Opened: 1972
Specialized Field: Musical; Comedy; Community Theater; Puppet; Classic; Contemporary
Status: Non-Profit, Professional
Paid Staff: 8
Type of Stage: Proscenium; Moderate Thrust
Stage Dimensions: 40'x40'
Year Built: 1972
Year Remodeled: 2004
Cost: $1.5 Million
Rental Contact: Manager Gary Gaydos

3284
CITY THEATRE OF INDEPENDENCE
Roger T Sermon Center
201 N Dodgion Street
Independence, MO 64050
Phone: 816-325-7376
e-mail: sharonpropst@comcast.net
Web Site: www.citytheatreofindependence.org
Officers:
   President: Jamie Close
   VP of Production: Michael Masterson
   VP of Operations: Jackie Coombs
   Treasurer: Steve Kennedy
   Secretary: Joyce Stone
Management:
   Advertising Chair: Norita Taylor
   Hospitality Chair: Erin Brown
   Seasonal Production Manager: RJ Parish

THEATRE / Missouri

Founded: 1980
Specialized Field: Community Theater

3285
ACTORS STUDIO
1010 W. 39th Street
Suite 102
Kansas City, MO 64111
Phone: 816-531-5454
Fax: 212-302-1926
Toll-free: 800-884-2772
e-mail: brian@actorsstudio.com
Web Site: www.actorsstudio.com
Officers:
  Founder/CEO: Alan S Nusbaum
Management:
  Artistic Director: Estelle Parsons
  Administrator: Rebecca L Scott
Mission: To provide actors with a center where they can focus on the business of their careers in addition to learning the the necessary skills to compete as an actor.
Founded: 1986
Specialized Field: Theater Workshops; Educational
Status: Non-Profit; Professional
Organization Type: Resident

3286
COTERIE THEATRE
2450 Grand Avenue
Suite 144
Kansas City, MO 64108-2520
Phone: 816-474-6552
Fax: 816-474-2225
e-mail: jchurch@coterietheatre.org
Web Site: www.thecoterie.com
Officers:
  President: Susan Johnson
  VP: Mike Enos
  VP: Lisa Shadid
  Treasurer: Tom Kientz
  Secretary: Jennifer Fuller
Management:
  President: Bruce Allen
  Executive Director: Jolette M Pelster
  Producing Artistic Director: Jeff Church
  Marketing Manager: Karen Vanasdale
  Business & Box Office Manager: Jolie Spatz
Mission: To provide professional classic and contemporary theater which challenges the audience as well as the artist; to provide educational dramatic outreach programs in the community.
Utilizes: Guest Companies
Founded: 1979
Specialized Field: Youth Theater
Status: Non-Profit, Professional
Paid Staff: 8
Paid Artists: 30
Income Sources: Theatre Communications Group; International Association of Theatre for Children and Youth
Performs At: Coterie Theatre
Type of Stage: Flexible
Seating Capacity: 240
Organization Type: Performing; Touring; Resident; Educational

3287
FOLLY THEATER
1020 Central
Suite 200
Kansas City, MO 64105
Mailing Address: PO Box 26505, Kansas City, MO 64105
Phone: 816-842-5500
Fax: 816-842-8709
e-mail: gale@follytheater.org
Web Site: www.follytheater.org
Officers:
  President: Pete Browne
  V.P., Development: Stewart S. Koesten
Management:
  Executive Director: Gale Tallis
  Events Manager: Stephanie Spatz-Ornburn
Utilizes: Lyricists; Multimedia; Original Music Scores; Special Technical Talent; Theatre Companies
Founded: 1900
Specialized Field: Musical
Status: Non-Profit, Professional
Paid Staff: 4
Volunteer Staff: 1
Budget: $60,000-$150,000
Performs At: Performing Arts
Annual Attendance: 55,000
Type of Stage: Proscenium
Stage Dimensions: 34'x31'
Seating Capacity: 1,078
Year Built: 1900
Year Remodeled: 2000
Cost: $2,500,000
Rental Contact: Events Manager Kate Egan

3288
MID-AMERICA ARTS ALLIANCE
2018 Baltimore Avenue
Kansas City, MO 64108
Phone: 816-421-1388
Fax: 816-421-3918
Toll-free: 800-473-3872
e-mail: info@maaa.org
Web Site: www.maaa.org
Officers:
  Chief Executive Officer: Mary Kennedy
  President: Ed Clifford
  Chair: Miltrerd Franco
  Owner: Garbo Hearno
  Chairman: Don Munro
Management:
  Program Manager: Jenny Tritt
  Director of Programs: Dana M. Knapp
  Executive Director: Joy Pennington
Founded: 1974
Specialized Field: Drama; Musical
Status: Non-Profit, Professional

3289
MISSOURI REPERTORY THEATRE
4949 Cherry Street
Kansas City, MO 64110-2499
Mailing Address: 4949 Cherry Street, Kansas City, Missouri 64110
Phone: 816-235-2700
Fax: 816-233-5550
Toll-free: 888-502-2700
e-mail: info@kcrep.org
Web Site: www.kcrep.org
Officers:
  Chairman: William C. Nelson
  Vice Chairman: John H. Johntz, Jr.
  President: George Shadid
  Vice President: Bunni Copaken
Management:
  Executive Director: Peter Altman
  Managing Director: Cynthia Rider
  Production Director: Jerry Genochio
  Artistic Director: Eric Rosen
  Advisory Director: Donald J. Hall
Utilizes: Guest Companies; Singers
Founded: 1964
Specialized Field: Educational; Contemporary
Status: Non-Profit, Professional
Paid Staff: 25
Volunteer Staff: 10
Paid Artists: 30
Budget: $5,000,000
Season: August - May
Performs At: Helen F. Spencer Theatre
Type of Stage: Proscenium
Seating Capacity: 700
Organization Type: Performing; Resident; Educational

3290
QUALITY HILL PLAYHOUSE
303 W Tenth Street
Kansas City, MO 64105-1615
Phone: 816-421-1700
Fax: 816-221-6556
e-mail: info@qualityhillplayhouse.com
Web Site: www.qualityhillplayhouse.com
Officers:
  President: Dale Wassergord
  VP: Jack Rosenfield
  Secretary: Debbie MacLaughlin
  Treasurer: Kent Maughan
  Executive Director: J Kent Barnhart
  Managing Director: Rick Truman
  Assistant Executive Director: Nancy Nail
Utilizes: Actors; AEA Actors; Choreographers; Collaborations; Dancers; Designers; Five Seasonal Concerts; Grant Writers; Guest Artists; Guest Musical Directors; Guest Musicians; Instructors; Local Artists; Local Unknown Artists; Multimedia; Music; Organization Contracts; Original Music Scores; Resident Professionals; Selected Students; Sign Language Translators; Singers; Soloists; Student Interns; Special Technical Talent
Founded: 1995
Specialized Field: Cabaret; Musical
Status: Non-Profit, Professional
Paid Staff: 8
Volunteer Staff: 98
Paid Artists: 30
Budget: $650,000
Income Sources: Ticket Sales; Contributions
Performs At: Quality Hill Playhouse
Annual Attendance: 30,000
Facility Category: Theatre
Type of Stage: Thrust
Stage Dimensions: 12' x 28'
Seating Capacity: 153
Year Built: 1989
Rental Contact: Nancy Nail
Comments: Handicapped Accessible

3291
STARLIGHT THEATRE
4600 Starlight Road
Kansas City, MO 64132-2032
Phone: 816-363-7827
Fax: 816-361-6398
Toll-free: 800-776-1730
e-mail: starlight@kcstarlight.com
Web Site: www.kcstarlight.com
Officers:
  Chairman of the Board: John W Kennedy
  Treasurer: Howard Cohen
  Secretary: Adele Hall
Management:
  President & Executive Producer: Denton Yockey

VP Marketing/Sales & Development: Cindy Jeffries
VP Finance: Brenda Mortensen
Mission: To present first quality professional entertainment and arts education to diverse audiences, while building an appreciation for the performing arts and preserving and enhancing the Starlight venue for future generations. As it carries out this mission, Starlight will remain committed to family-oriented entertainment at affordable prices, with a focus on musical theatre.
Founded: 1951
Specialized Field: Musical
Status: Non-Profit, Professional
Volunteer Staff: 193
Budget: $12 million
Income Sources: Ticket Sales; Fundraising
Season: May-September
Performs At: Live Theatrical Performance Including Plays And Concerts
Annual Attendance: 250,000
Facility Category: Outdoor Ampitheater
Type of Stage: Proscenium
Stage Dimensions: 68'x 48'
Seating Capacity: 8,000
Year Built: 1950
Year Remodeled: 2000

3292
UNICORN THEATRE
3828 Main Street
Kansas City, MO 64111
Phone: 816-531-7529
Fax: 816-531-0421
e-mail: unicornnews@unicorntheatre.org
Web Site: www.unicorntheatre.org
Officers:
  President: John Escalada
  VP: Dan Woodall
  Secretary: Roberta Brown
  Treasurer: Sally Selby
  Co-Vice President: Tim Degnan
Management:
  Producing Artistic Director: Cynthia Levin
  Managing Director: Jason Kralicek
  Marketing Director: Chris Hernandez
  Development Department: Celeste Lupercio
  Technical Supervisor: Glenn Lewis
Mission: To enhance the cultural life of Kansas City by producing professional contemporary, thought-provoking theater which inspires emotional response and stimulates discussion.
Utilizes: Guest Companies; Singers
Founded: 1974
Specialized Field: Musical; Comedy; Contemporary
Status: Non-Profit, Professional
Paid Staff: 7
Income Sources: Actors' Equity Association; Theatre Communications Group
Season: September - June
Performs At: Unicorn Theatre
Affiliations: Actors' Equity Association; National New Play Network; Arts Council of Metropolitan Kansas City; Realtors For the Arts
Annual Attendance: 20,000
Type of Stage: Thrust
Seating Capacity: 175
Organization Type: Performing
Comments: Discounts for students, seniors and working artists

3293
MEMPHIS COMMUNITY PLAYERS
106 East Madison Street
Memphis, MO 63555
Phone: 660-465-2277
Mission: To offer summer musical theatre to our area.
Founded: 1974
Specialized Field: Musical; Community Theater
Status: Non-Professional; Nonprofit
Performs At: Memphis Cinema
Organization Type: Performing; Resident; Educational

3294
MOBERLY COMMUNITY THEATRE
212 Crest Drive
Moberly, MO 65270
Phone: 660-263-3345
e-mail: carolee@mcmsys.com
Management:
  President: Carolee Hazlet
  VP: Bob Wright
Mission: Working together as a community to promote the performing arts.
Utilizes: Guest Companies; Singers
Founded: 1979
Specialized Field: Community Theater
Status: Non-Profit, Non-Professional
Paid Staff: 50
Performs At: Moberly Municipal Auditorium; Peppermint Loft
Organization Type: Performing; Sponsoring

3295
MARK TWAIN OUTDOOR THEATRE
12665 Fox Run Place
New London, MO 63459
Phone: 573-221-5204
Management:
  Managing Director: Sharon Donegan
Founded: 1979
Specialized Field: Summer Stock
Status: Non-Equity; Commercial
Season: May - September
Type of Stage: Outdoor
Stage Dimensions: 150' x 20'
Seating Capacity: 500+

3296
OZARK ACTORS THEATRE
701 N Cedar St
PO Box K Rolla
Rolla, MO 65402
Mailing Address: PO Box K, Rolla, MO 65402
Phone: 573-364-9523
Fax: 573-364-9523
e-mail: oat@ozarkactorstheatre.org
Web Site: www.ozarkactorstheatre.org
Management:
  Artistic Director: F Reed Brown
  Director: Jasson Cannon
  Assistant Director/Company Manager: Jim Welch
  Musical Director: Susan Holmes
Mission: Ozark Actors Theatre is a professional, summer stock theatre. Professional actors, directors, technicians, and designers are employed by OAT on a seasonal basis.
Founded: 1988
Specialized Field: Musical; Summer Stock;
Status: Non-Profit
Season: July - August
Type of Stage: Proscenium
Stage Dimensions: 36' x 24'
Seating Capacity: 188

3297
EDISON THEATRE
Mallinckrodt Cente
6445 Forsyth Blvd, Room 203
Saint Louis, MO 63130-4899
Phone: 314-935-6543
Fax: 314-935-7362
e-mail: edison@wustl.edu
Web Site: www.artsci.wustl.edu/edison
Management:
  Executive Director: Charles E Robin
  Operations Manager: Bill Larson
  Marketing Manager: Jennifer Killion
  Technical Director/Facility Manager: Michael Hensley
  Technical Director/Master Electrici: Jason Irons
Founded: 1973
Specialized Field: Musical; Community Theater
Status: Professional; Nonprofit
Paid Staff: 12
Budget: $150,000-$400,000
Performs At: Edison Theatre; Mallinckrodt Drama Studio
Facility Category: Concert Hall; Performance Theatre
Type of Stage: Proscenium
Seating Capacity: 656
Rental Contact: Melinda Compton
Organization Type: Performing; Touring; Educational; Sponsoring; Presenting

3298
HOT CITY THEATRE
3547 Olive Street
Suite #203
Saint Louis, MO 63103
Phone: 314-289-4060
Web Site: www.hotcitytheatre.org/contact.html
Officers:
  President: Joseph Potter
  Vice President: Opal Andrews
  Treasurer: Thomas Schroedeer
  Secretary: Chris Peimann
  Webmaster: Michael B. B. Perkins
Management:
  Managing Director: Bess Moynihan
  Artistic Director: Marty Stanberry
  Marketing Director: Allyson Ditchey
  Associate Director: Chuck Harper
  Associate Director: Annamaria Pileggi
Mission: HotHouse's mission is to produce thought-provoking theatre dedicated to cultural enhancement.
Founded: 1997
Specialized Field: Drama; Comedy
Status: Nonprofit
Season: October - May
Type of Stage: Flexible Black Box
Seating Capacity: 90

3299
METRO THEATER COMPANY
3311 Washington Avenue
Saint Louis, MO 63103
Phone: 314-932-7414
Fax: 314-997-1811
e-mail: community@metrotheatercompany.org
Web Site: www.metrotheatercompany.org
  VP: Margaret RaschMcDonald
  CFO/Treasurer: John Weil
  Secretary: Sam H Hausfather, Ph.D.
  CFO & Treasurer: John D. Weil
Management:
  President: Suzan Z. Gamble

THEATRE / Missouri

Artistic Director: Carol North
Booking Director: Rita Mocek
Mission: Metro Theater Company is a professional touring ensemble that develops and produces original theater pieces that respect the intelligence and emotional wisdom of young people, blend drama, movement, music, and design, and challenge both the artists who develop the work and the audience who receive it.
Utilizes: Actors; Artists-in-Residence; Collaborating Artists; Collaborations; Commissioned Composers; Composers; Contract Actors; Curators; Educators; Guest Artists; Guest Conductors; Guest Lecturers; Guest Speakers; Organization Contracts; Original Music Scores; Performance Artists; Resident Professionals; Soloists
Founded: 1973
Specialized Field: Comedy; Youth Theater; Contemporary
Status: Non-Profit, Professional
Paid Staff: 7
Paid Artists: 7
Budget: $535,000
Income Sources: Contributions; NEA; Missouri Arts Council; Regional Arts Commission of St. Louis; Arts & Education Council of Greater St. Louis
Season: August - May
Affiliations: American Alliance for Theatre & Education; International Association of Theatre for Children and Youth/USA; Theatre Communications Group, Inc.
Annual Attendance: 60,000+
Type of Stage: Proscenium
Stage Dimensions: 30x25x15
Rental Contact: Managing Director Joan T. Briccetti
Organization Type: Performing; Touring; Resident; Educational

3300
MUNICIPAL THEATER ASSOCIATION OF SAINT LOUIS

1 Theater Drive
Saint Louis, MO 63112
Phone: 314-361-1900
Fax: 314-361-0009
e-mail: munyinfo@muny.org
Web Site: www.muny.com
Management:
 President & CEO: Dennis M Reagan
 Executive Producer: Mike Isaacson
 Company Manager: Sue Greenberg
 Director of Marketing and Publicity: Laura Peters
Mission: To perform and produce musical theater shows 7 nights a week, during the summer only.
Utilizes: Selected Students; Sign Language Translators; Singers; Student Interns; Theatre Companies
Founded: 1919
Specialized Field: Summer Stock; Community Theater
Status: Non-Profit, Professional
Paid Staff: 500
Paid Artists: 200
Income Sources: NAMTP; Arts & Education Council of Greater Saint Louis
Performs At: The MUNY; Forest Park
Organization Type: Performing; Educational

3301
NEW THEATRE

634 N Grand Boulevard
Suite 10-C
Saint Louis, MO 63103
Phone: 314-531-8330
Fax: 314-533-3345
Officers:
 President: DeLancey Smith
 VP: Suzanne Couch
 Treasurer: James F O'Donnell
 Secretary: Agnes Wilcox
Management:
 Artistic Director: Agnes Wilcox
 Production Manager: Amy Allen
 Director Public Relations: Dean Minderman
Mission: To provide innovative professional theatre in accessible locations for Saint Louis audiences.
Utilizes: Guest Companies; Singers
Founded: 1985
Specialized Field: New Plays; Contemporary
Status: Professional; Nonprofit
Income Sources: Theatre Communications Group: League of Saint Louis Theatres
Organization Type: Performing

3302
REPERTORY THEATRE OF SAINT LOUIS

130 Edgar Road
Box 191730
Saint Louis, MO 63119
Phone: 314-968-7340
Fax: 314-968-9638
e-mail: mail@repstl.org
Web Site: www.repstl.org
Officers:
 President: James E. Dillon
 Public Relations: Brad Graham
 Vice President: Mary Atkin
 Vice President: Michael Oberlander
 Vice President, Volunteers: Laura Greenberg
Management:
 Box Office Manager: Kathleen Belt
 Managing Director: Mark Bernstein
 Accounting Assistant: Suzanne Bodenstein
 Director of Marketing: Lory Bowman
 Associate Director of Education & P: Sarah Brandt
Mission: Dedicated to producing live theatre of superior quality. In celebrating the joy of live performance, this theatre is committed to building and sustaining a vital connection among all its stakeholders.
Utilizes: Guest Companies; Singers
Founded: 1966
Specialized Field: Theater Workshops; Drama; Contemporary
Status: Professional
Income Sources: Actors' Equity Association; Society for Stage Directors and Choreographers; American Federation of Musicians; International Association of Theatrical Stage Employees
Season: September - April
Performs At: Loretto-Hilton Center for the Performing Arts
Type of Stage: Thrust; Flexible
Seating Capacity: 734; 125
Organization Type: Performing

3303
SAINT LOUIS BLACK REPERTORY COMPANY

1717 Olive Street
Fourth Floor
Saint Louis, MO 63103
Phone: 314-534-3807
Fax: 314-534-8456
e-mail: info@theblackrep.org
Web Site: www.theblackrep.org
Officers:
 Vice President: James E. Butler
 Chair, Finance: Barbara Feiner
 Secretary: M. Denise Thomas
 Chair, Nominating: Joyce Price
Management:
 President: Wyndel E. Hill
 Producing Director: Ron Himes
 Business Manager: Susan Hayden
Mission: To provide platforms for theatre, dance and other creative expressions from the African-American perspective that heighten the social and cultural awareness of its audiences.
Utilizes: Actors; AEA Actors; Guest Artists; Guest Designers; Guest Writers; Performance Artists; Resident Professionals; Theatre Companies
Founded: 1976
Specialized Field: Musical; African American; Community Theater; Classic; Contemporary
Status: Non-Profit, Professional
Paid Staff: 12
Volunteer Staff: 50
Performs At: Grandel Square Theatre
Affiliations: Theatre Communications Group; Actors' Equity Association
Annual Attendance: 75,000
Seating Capacity: 467
Organization Type: Performing; Touring; Educational; Sponsoring

3304
THEATER FACTORY SAINT LOUIS

4265 Shaw Avenue
Saint Louis, MO 63110
Phone: 314-771-0780
Web Site: www.abouttheartists.com
Management:
 Artistic Director: Hope Wurdack
 Managing Director: Earl D Weaver
Utilizes: Guest Artists; Guest Companies; Lyricists; Singers
Founded: 1982
Specialized Field: Summer Stock
Status: Professional
Income Sources: League of St. Louis Theatres
Organization Type: Performing; Educational

3305
WEST END PLAYERS GUILD

Union Avenue Christian Church
733 Union Boulevard
Saint Louis, MO 63108
Mailing Address: 733 Union Boulevard
Phone: 314-367-0025
Web Site: http://www.westendplayers.org
Officers:
 President: Robert Ashton
 Vice President: Renee Sevier-Monsey
 Secretary: Sean Ruprecht-Belt
 Treasurer: Mark Abels
 Director Emeritus: Fay McKenna,
Management:
 Artistic Director: Fay McKenna
Mission: Compromises two groups, the Players Guild and the West End Players, both of which originated and prospered in the city's Central West End.
Founded: 1911
Specialized Field: Drama
Status: Non-professional

3306
LIBERTY CENTER

111 W 5Th
Sedalia, MO 65301

Phone: 660-827-3228
Fax: 816-827-3103
e-mail: webmaster@.art-graphicinnovations.com
Web Site: www.art-graphicinnovations.com
Management:
    Administrator: Patti McFatrich
Mission: Promoting the Arts and cultural activities in the community.
Utilizes: Singers
Founded: 1981
Specialized Field: Musical; Community Theater; Puppet
Status: Professional; Non-Professional; Nonprofit
Paid Staff: 100
Performs At: Liberty Center
Organization Type: Performing; Touring; Educational; Sponsoring

3307
SIKESTON LITTLE THEATRE
506 South Kingshighway
Sikeston, MO 63801
Phone: 573-681-9400
Web Site: www.sikestonlittletheater.com
Management:
    Administrator: Lynn A Colley
Mission: To nurture theatrical arts in the Sikeston area; to provide theatre experience for students.
Founded: 1959
Specialized Field: Musical; Community Theater
Status: Non-Professional; Nonprofit
Paid Staff: 150
Income Sources: Missouri Community Theatre Association
Performs At: Chaney-Harris Cultural Center
Organization Type: Performing; Resident

3308
GOLDENROD SHOWBOAT DINNER THEATRE
1000 Riverside Drive
St. Charles, MO 63301
Phone: 636-946-2020
Fax: 636-946-0946
Specialized Field: Specialty Acts; Mystery; Dinner Theater

3309
MULE BARN THEATRE OF TARKIO COLLEGE
PO Box 114
224 Main Street
Tarkio, MO 64491
Phone: 816-736-4185
Mission: To provide cultural and educational enrichment for the area featuring the American musical and children's theatre, theatre for area residents and training for young professionals in theatre.
Utilizes: Singers
Founded: 1967
Specialized Field: Educational; Theater Workshops
Status: Professional; Nonprofit
Paid Staff: 15
Performs At: Mule Barn Theatre
Organization Type: Performing

3310
ROYAL ARTS COUNCIL
PO Box 273
107 S Monroe
Versailles, MO 65084
Phone: 573-378-6226
e-mail: royalart@advertisnet.com
Web Site: www.theroyaltheatre.com
Officers:
    President: Richard Williott
    VP: Kevin Schehr
    Secretary: Michelle Gerlt
    Treasurer: Cindy Davenport
Management:
    Executive Director: Pam Voth
    Director: Steve Bannon
    Director: Mary Jo Jackson
    Director: Lana James
    Director: Lois Viebrock
Mission: Promote the appreciation of various art disciplines through education, presentation, organization and the provision of an appropriate facility.
Utilizes: Community Talent; Guest Companies; Guild Activities; Instructors; Local Artists; Multimedia; Paid Performers; Sign Language Translators; Singers; Theatre Companies
Founded: 1984
Specialized Field: Musical; Community Theater
Status: Non-Professional; Nonprofit
Paid Staff: 1
Budget: $60,000
Income Sources: Ticket Sales; MAC Funding; Corporate Funding; Concessions; Program Advertising; Donations
Performs At: Royal Theatre
Annual Attendance: 4,000
Facility Category: Converted movie theatre with enlarged stage
Stage Dimensions: 34'x5 1/2'x22'
Seating Capacity: 294
Year Built: 1931
Year Remodeled: 2000
Rental Contact: Executive Director Pam Voth
Organization Type: Performing; Educational; Sponsoring

3311
INSIGHT THEATRE COMPANY
530 East Lockwood Avenue
Webster Groves, MO 63119
Phone: 314-556-1293
e-mail: info@insighttheatrecompany.com
Web Site: insighttheatrecompany.com
Mission: To produce the highest quality of plays and musicals in order to entertain, inspire, and reveal the complexity of the human spirit.
Status: Professional
Performs At: Heagney Theatre At Nerinx Hall

Montana

3312
BIGFORK SUMMER PLAYHOUSE
PO Box 456
Bigfork, MT 59911
Phone: 406-837-4886
e-mail: dthomson@bigforksummerplayhouse.com
Web Site: www.bigforksummerplayhouse.com
Management:
    Producer: Don Thomson
    Associate Producer: Jude Thomson
    Associate Producer/Company Manager/: Brach Thomson
Founded: 1960
Specialized Field: Musical; Summer Stock
Status: For-Profit, Professional
Paid Staff: 55
Paid Artists: 25
Season: May - August

3313
ALBERTA BAIR THEATER
2801 3rd Avenue
Billings, MT 59101
Mailing Address: PO Box 1556, Billings, MO. 59103
Phone: 406-256-6052
Fax: 406-256-5060
Toll-free: 877-321-2074
e-mail: woody@albertabairtheater.org
Web Site: www.albertabairtheater.org
Officers:
    President Elect: Doug James
    Immediate Past-President: Wayne Hirsch
    Treasurer: Leslie Pitman
    Secretary: Jackie Zawada
Management:
    President: Alice Gordon
    Executive Director: William R. Wood
    Artistic Director: Corby Skinner
Utilizes: Actors; Collaborations; Dance Companies; Dancers; Educators; Guest Accompanists; Guest Artists; Guest Choreographers; Guest Composers; Guest Directors; Guest Ensembles; Guest Instructors; Guest Musical Directors; Guest Soloists; Guest Teachers; High School Drama; Instructors; Local Artists; Lyricists; Multimedia; Original Music Scores; Playwrights; Resident Artists; Selected Students; Sign Language Translators; Singers; Special Technical Talent; Theatre Companies
Founded: 1984
Specialized Field: Drama; Musical; Contemporary
Status: Non-Profit, Professional
Paid Staff: 15
Volunteer Staff: 200
Budget: $1.2 million
Income Sources: Ticket income
Annual Attendance: 123,000

3314
MONTANA SHAKESPEARE IN THE PARKS
Black Box Theater
11th and Grant, MSU Campus
Bozeman, MT 59717-4120
Phone: 406-994-3901
Fax: 406-994-4591
e-mail: info@shakespeareintheparks.org
Web Site: www.shakespeareintheparks.org
Management:
    Artistic Director: Joel Jahnke
    Development/Marketing Director: Moira Keshishian
Founded: 1973
Specialized Field: Musical; Comedy; Classic
Status: Non-Profit, Professional
Paid Staff: 4
Volunteer Staff: 82
Paid Artists: 30
Budget: $400,000
Income Sources: Grants; Corporate Sponsorship; Montana State University; Inidvdual Donations; Earned Income
Season: June - September
Affiliations: Montana State University
Annual Attendance: 26,000
Facility Category: Portable Elizabethan-style wood stage

3315
VERGE THEATER
2304 North 7th Avenue, Suite C-1
Bozeman, MT 59715

THEATRE / Nebraska

Phone: 406-587-0737
e-mail: info@vergetheater.com
Web Site: vergetheater.com
Mission: To create offbeat, thought provoking, heart-inspiring theater that is masterful in execution, empowering to children, teens and adults, and evocative of our vibrant local community.

3316
VIGILANTE THEATRE COMPANY
111 S Grand
Suite 201
Bozeman, MT 59715
Phone: 406-586-3897
e-mail: office@vigilantetheatrecompany.com
Web Site: www.vigilantetheatrecompany.com
Officers:
   President: Eileen Hosking
   Community Representative: Jim Banks
   Community Member: Charles Broughton
   Board Member: Marjorie Smith
Management:
   Artistic Director: John Hosking
   Marketing Director: Cathy Kohler
Mission: To stimulate, cultivate and promote interest in theatre; to tour original, professional-level theatre in the Northwest.
Utilizes: Choreographers; Collaborations; Guest Companies; Guest Conductors; Guest Designers; Guest Lecturers; Guest Teachers; Multimedia; Music; Organization Contracts; Performance Artists; Resident Professionals; Student Interns; Theatre Companies; Visual Arts; Volunteer Directors & Actors; Writers
Founded: 1981
Specialized Field: Musical; Comedy; Puppet; Contemporary
Status: Non-Profit, Professional
Paid Staff: 6
Paid Artists: 4
Income Sources: Bookings; Ticket Sales; Grants; Membership; Contributors
Season: January - December
Annual Attendance: 14,000
Organization Type: Performing; Touring; Educational

3317
ALEPH MOVEMENT THEATRE
822 E 6Th Avenue
Helena, MT 59601
Phone: 406-443-1274
Mission: To perform movement theatre; to provide an opportunity for education; to foster cultural exchange.
Utilizes: Guest Companies; Singers
Founded: 1985
Specialized Field: Movement Theater
Status: Professional; Nonprofit
Income Sources: National Mime Association
Organization Type: Performing; Touring; Educational

3318
MISSOULA CHILDREN'S THEATRE
200 N Adams Street
Missoula, MT 59802-4718
Phone: 406-728-1911
Fax: 406-721-0637
e-mail: mmcgill@mctinc.org
Web Site: www.mctinc.org
Officers:
   President: Alane Harkin
   Vice-President: Bill Silverman
   Chief Executive Officer: Jim Caron
   Secretary/Treasurer: Barb Callaghan
Management:
   Executive Director: Michael McGill

Artistic Director: Joseph Martinez
Project Development Director: Greg Boris
Mission: The development of lifeskills through participation in the performing arts
Founded: 1971
Specialized Field: Musical; Youth Theater; Children's Theater

3319
MONTANA REPERTORY THEATRE
Performing Arts Center
University of Montana
Missoula, MT 59812-8136
Phone: 406-243-6809
Fax: 406-243-5726
e-mail: salina.chatlain@umontana.edu
Web Site: www.montanarep.org
Management:
   Artistic Director: Salina Chatlain
   Production Manager: Steve Wing
   Assistant Artistc Director: Mary Ann Riddle
Mission: To tell the great stories of our world to an ever expanding community.
Utilizes: Actors; AEA Actors; Choreographers; Collaborating Artists; Commissioned Composers; Contract Actors; Designers; Educators; Guest Accompanists; Guest Companies; Guest Conductors; Guest Designers; Guest Teachers; Instructors; Local Artists; Original Music Scores; Performance Artists; Resident Professionals; Soloists; Students; Student Interns
Founded: 1976
Specialized Field: Drama; Historical
Status: Professional; Nonprofit
Paid Staff: 4
Budget: $900,000
Income Sources: Box Office; Grants; State Aid
Season: November - April
Performs At: Montana Theatre; University of Montana
Affiliations: Society for Stage Directors and Choreographers; Actors' Equity Association; International Alliance of Theatrical Stage Employees
Annual Attendance: varies
Facility Category: Educational
Type of Stage: Proscenium
Seating Capacity: 499
Year Built: 1985
Organization Type: Performing; Touring; Resident; Educational

3320
WHITEFISH THEATRE COMPANY
One Central Avenue
Whitefish, MT 59937
Phone: 406-862-5371
Fax: 406-863-9200
e-mail: info@whitefishtheatreco.org
Web Site: www.whitefishtheatreco.org
Officers:
   President: Rebecca Blickenstaff
   Technical Advisor: Scotty McLaren
Management:
   Executive Director: Carolyn Pitman
   Artistic Director: Jesse DeVine
   MD: Gayle McLaren
   Development Director: Jen Asebrook
   Facilities Supervisor: Fred Warf
Mission: To nurture the creative and artistic passions of our community by bringing the arts to life.
Founded: 1978
Specialized Field: Performing Arts; Theatre; Dance Series; Music; Film
Paid Staff: 8
Budget: $450,000

Annual Attendance: 13,000
Facility Category: 326 Multiuse-Thrust Stage
Type of Stage: Thrust
Seating Capacity: 326
Year Built: 1998

Nebraska

3321
BELLEVUE LITTLE THEATRE
203 Mission Ave.
Bellevue, NE 68005
Phone: 402-291-1554
Fax: 402-291-3809
e-mail: cyberma609@aol.com
Web Site: www.bellevuelittletheatre.com
Officers:
   Vice President: Robin Klushmire
   Recording Secretary: Terry Schmidt
   Corresponding Secretary: Clara Sue Arnsdorff
   Former President: Dr.Edward (Ted) Roche
Management:
   President: Curtis Leach, ebroche@cox.net
Mission: To create a superior environment for the promotion of the performing arts through the presentation of comedy, drama, and musical theatre productions; and to stimulate educational and recreational programs in the technical and artistic venues of the performing arts for the citizens of the city of Bellevue, Sarpy County, and the Greater Omaha Metropolitan Area.
Utilizes: Guest Companies; Singers
Founded: 1968
Specialized Field: Musical; Comedy; Ethnic Theater; Community Theater; Contemporary
Status: Non-Profit, Non-Professional
Seating Capacity: 244
Year Built: 1942
Organization Type: Performing; Educational

3322
POST PLAYHOUSE INCORPORATED
PO Box 365
Crawford, NE 69339
Phone: 308-665-1976
Fax: 308-432-6396
e-mail: tickets@postplayhouse.com
Web Site: www.postplayhouse.com
Management:
   Executive Director: Roger Mays
   Artistic Director: Tom Ossowski
Mission: A Summer Repertory Theatre for tourists and residents.
Utilizes: Actors; Guest Artists; Guest Designers; Guest Lecturers; Resident Artists; Student Interns
Founded: 1966
Specialized Field: Summer Stock
Status: Non-Equity; Nonprofit
Paid Staff: 15
Budget: $80,000
Income Sources: Ticket Sales; Nebraska Arts Council; Chadron stage College
Season: May - August
Performs At: Proscenium Theater
Annual Attendance: 9-12,000
Type of Stage: Proscenium
Stage Dimensions: 24' x 30'
Seating Capacity: 182
Year Remodeled: 1991

THEATRE / Nebraska

3323
GOTHENBURG COMMUNITY PLAYHOUSE
10th and D Street
PO Box 15
Gothenburg, NE 69138
Mailing Address: PO Box 15
Phone: 308-537-7596
e-mail: sbooth@nebnet.net
Web Site: www.users.connections.net/NACT/Default.htm
Management:
   President: Ryan Lovell
   Vice President: Jamie Ulmer
Mission: To offer cultural, literary and educational opportunities to residents of the community and region.
Utilizes: Guest Companies; Singers
Founded: 1967
Specialized Field: Community Theater
Status: Non-Profit, Non-Professional
Paid Staff: 3
Performs At: Sun Theatre
Organization Type: Performing; Resident; Sponsoring

3324
CRANE RIVER THEATER COMPANY
2202 Central Avenue, Suite 8
Kearney, NE 68847
Phone: 308-627-5796
e-mail: info@cranerivertheater.org
Web Site: cranerivertheater.org
Mission: Crane River Theater was created to serve Central Nebraska as a professional theater production company providing a home for the presentation, education and promotion of the arts.
Founded: 2009
Status: Professional; Nonprofit

3325
KEARNEY COMMUNITY THEATRE
83 Plaza Boulevard
Kearney, NE 68845
Phone: 308-234-1529
e-mail: boxoffice@kctonline.com
Web Site: www.kctonline.com
Officers:
   President: David Rozema
   VP: Brette Ensz
   Treasurer: Stan Dart
   Secretary: Phyllis Haverkamp
   Past Officer: Mary Haeberle
Management:
   Executive Director: Rick Marlatt, marlattr@kctonline.com
Mission: To present five shows annually, as well as a summer children's workshop.
Utilizes: Music; Paid Performers; Sign Language Translators; Soloists; Student Interns; Visual Designers; Volunteer Artists
Founded: 1977
Specialized Field: Musical; Community Theater
Status: Non-Profit, Non-Professional
Paid Staff: 2
Volunteer Staff: 4
Income Sources: Nebraska Arts Council; Nebraska Association of Community Theatres; American Association of Community Theatres
Performs At: Kearney Community Theatre
Organization Type: Performing; Educational; Sponsoring

3326
LINCOLN COMMUNITY PLAYHOUSE
2500 S 56th Street
Lincoln, NE 68506
Mailing Address: P.O. Box 6426, Lincoln, NE 68506
Phone: 402-489-7529
Fax: 402-489-1035
Web Site: www.lincolnplayhouse.com
Officers:
   President: Bob Everitt
   Secretary: Katie Taddeucci
   Treasurer: Kyle Cech
   President Elect: Andy Wilcox
Management:
   Executive Director: Morrie Enders
   Office Manager: Bryan Johnson
   Development Director: Stephanie Geery-Zink
   Education Director: Andy Dillehay
   Technical Director: Nick Turner
Mission: To offer quality theatrical experiences to the community.
Utilizes: Guest Companies
Founded: 1946
Specialized Field: Musical; Comedy; Community Theater; Puppet; Classic; Contemporary
Status: Non-Profit, Non-Professional
Paid Staff: 10
Volunteer Staff: 400
Income Sources: NE Arts Council
Performs At: Oliver T. Joy Mainstage; L.L. Coryell & Sons
Affiliations: American Association of Community Theatres; Nebraska Association of Community Theatres
Organization Type: Performing

3327
NEBRASKA REPERTORY THEATRE
215 Temple Building
12th and R Streets
Lincoln, NE 68588-0201
Phone: 402-472-2072
Fax: 402-472-9055
Toll-free: 800-432-3231
e-mail: jhagemeier1@unl.edu
Web Site: www.unl.edu/rep
Officers:
   President: Larry Frederick
   Past President: Joyce Cartmill
   GM: Julie Hagemeier
   Production Stage Manager: Brad Buffum
Management:
   Director: Larry Frederick
   General Manager: Julie Hagemeier
   Production Stage Manager: Brad Buffum
   Executive Director: Paul Stagger
   Artistic Director: Virginia Smith
Utilizes: Actors; AEA Actors; Designers; Educators; Guest Accompanists; Guest Conductors; Guest Designers; High School Drama; Instructors; Original Music Scores; Resident Professionals; Singers; Soloists; Student Interns
Founded: 1968
Specialized Field: Contemporary; Ensembles
Status: Non-Profit, Professional
Paid Staff: 6
Volunteer Staff: 30
Paid Artists: 24
Budget: $176,000
Income Sources: Ticket Sales; University; Contributions
Season: June - August
Performs At: Howell Theatre; Studio Theatre; Carson Theatre
Affiliations: TCG, ATHE, KC/ACTF, NAST, UIRTA
Annual Attendance: 6,000
Type of Stage: Proscenium; Black Box
Seating Capacity: 320; 240
Year Built: 1908
Year Remodeled: 1980
Rental Contact: Brad Buffum
Organization Type: Performing; Resident

3328
THE HAYMARKET THEATRE
803 Q Street
Lincoln, NE 68508
Phone: 402-477-2600
e-mail: info@haymarkettheatre.org
Web Site: haymarkettheatre.org
Officers:
   President: Jan Tuckerman
   Vice President: Michelle Diamant
   Secretary: Heather Kadavy
Management:
   Executive Director: Amy Ossian
   Artistic Director: Jordan Deffenbaugh
Mission: The Haymarket Theatre's mission is to enrich, educate, entertain, and empower our community through live theatre and youth performing arts education programs for all.
Founded: 2002
Status: Nonprofit
Seating Capacity: 145
Organization Type: Youth Theatre

3329
BRIGIT SAINT BRIGIT THEATRE COMPANY
2854 Redick Avenue
Omaha, NE 68112
Phone: 402-502-4910
e-mail: info@bsbtheatre.com
Web Site: bsbtheatre.com
Management:
   Artistic Director: Cathy Kurz
Mission: To enrich Omaha and its surrounding areas with the highest quality, professional theatre, meant to engage, educate and entertain, stimulating both feeling and thought.
Founded: 1993
Status: Professional
Season: September-May

3330
CENTER STAGE
3010 R Street
Omaha, NE 68107
Phone: 402-444-6230
Management:
   Executive Director: Linda Runice
Mission: The presentation of ethnic performances.
Utilizes: Guest Companies; Singers
Founded: 1980
Specialized Field: Community Theater
Status: Non-Professional; Nonprofit
Performs At: LaFerne Williams Center
Organization Type: Performing

3331
CIRCLE THEATRE
726 South 55th Street
Omaha, NE 68106

All listings are in alphabetical order by state, then city, then organization within the city.

THEATRE / Nevada

Phone: 402-553-4715
Fax: 402-553-4715
e-mail: ldmarr@cox.net
Web Site: www.circletheatreomaha.org
Officers:
  President: Ward Peters
  VP: Robert Bradley
  Treasurer: Karen Dowell
  Secretary: Nancy Ross
Management:
  Chief Executive Officer: Nancy Bradley
  Executive Director: Laura Marr
  Artistic Director: Doug Marr
Mission: Developing and producing new plays by Nebraska playwrights, employing Nebraska artists.
Founded: 1983
Specialized Field: Comedy; Community Theater; Contemporary
Status: Non-Profit, Professional
Paid Staff: 10
Paid Artists: 10
Budget: $120,000
Income Sources: Nebraska Arts Council; Local Foundation; Private Support
Annual Attendance: 10,000
Type of Stage: Black Box
Seating Capacity: 100
Year Built: 1945
Organization Type: Performing; Touring; Resident

3332
GRANDE OLDE PLAYERS THEATRE COMPANY
8831 Harney Street
Omaha, NE 68114
Phone: 402-399-1714
Fax: 402-573-7532
e-mail: contactGOPT@goptheatre.org
Web Site: www.goptheatre.org
Officers:
  President: David Kistler
  VP: Kieth Homan
  Treasurer: Jack Kincaid
  Secretary: Riza Breen
Management:
  President: Ranita Lilyhorn
  Executive Director: Mark Manhart
Mission: Provide live community theatre experience with and for senior citizens.
Utilizes: Actors; Choreographers; Community Talent; Dancers; Guest Artists; Guest Companies; Guest Conductors; Guest Designers; Guest Lecturers; Guest Musical Directors; Guest Speakers; Local Artists; Performance Artists; Resident Professionals; Sign Language Translators
Founded: 1984
Specialized Field: Drama; Specialty Acts
Status: Non-Profit, Non-Professional
Non-paid Artists: 125
Budget: $59,000
Income Sources: Ticket Sales
Annual Attendance: 5,000
Facility Category: Live Theatre
Type of Stage: Proscenium
Stage Dimensions: 43'x17'
Seating Capacity: 141
Year Remodeled: 1993
Rental Contact: Executive Director Warren H. Johnson
Organization Type: Performing; Touring; Educational

3333
OMAHA COMMUNITY PLAYHOUSE
6915 Cass Street
Omaha, NE 68132-2696
Phone: 402-553-0800
Fax: 402-553-6288
Toll-free: 888-782-4338
e-mail: info@omahaplayhouse.com
Web Site: www.OmahaPlayhouse.com
Officers:
  President: Tim Schmad
  Finance Director: Catherine Demes Maydew
  Accounting Manager: Michelle Garrity
  Director of Finance: Catherine Demes Maydew
  Accounting Manager: Michelle Garrity
  Artistic Director: Carl Beck
  Associate Artistic Director: Susan Baer Collins
Mission: To offer the finest possible theatre to our audiences; to provide a performance outlet for amateur actors.
Utilizes: Actors; Artists-in-Residence; Choreographers; Collaborating Artists; Collaborations; Commissioned Composers; Commissioned Music; Dancers; Educators; Fine Artists; Grant Writers; Guest Accompanists; Guest Designers; Guest Ensembles; Guest Instructors; Guest Musical Directors; Guest Soloists; Guest Teachers; Guest Writers; Guild Activities; High School Drama; Instructors; Local Artists; Lyricists; Multi Collaborations; Multimedia; Music; New Productions; Organization Contracts; Original Music Scores; Poets; Resident Artists; Resident Professionals; Selected Students; Sign Language Translators; Singers; Soloists; Student Interns; Theatre Companies; Touring Companies; Visual Arts
Founded: 1924
Specialized Field: Community Theater
Status: Non-Profit, Non-Professional
Paid Staff: 40
Paid Artists: 120
Budget: $4,000,000
Income Sources: Donations; Subscribers; Single Ticket Revenue
Season: September - June
Performs At: Omaha Community Playhouse
Annual Attendance: 110,000
Facility Category: Theatre
Type of Stage: Traditional Proscenium & Black Box
Seating Capacity: 600; 235
Year Built: 1959
Year Remodeled: 1986
Organization Type: Performing; Touring

3334
OMAHA THEATRE COMPANY FOR YOUNG PEOPLE
2001 Farnam Street
Omaha, NE 68102
Phone: 402-345-4852
Fax: 402-344-7255
e-mail: boxoffice@otcmail.org
Web Site: www.otcyp.org
Officers:
  President: Richard Heyman
  VP Marketing: Stephen Zubrod
  Past President: Tracy Stanko
  Foundation Representative: Susie Buffett
Management:
  Executive Director: Roberta Wilhelm
  Artistic Director: James Larson
Mission: Providing quality theater for Omaha children and their families.
Utilizes: Guest Companies; Singers
Specialized Field: Youth Theater; Young Playwrights
Status: Professional; Nonprofit
Paid Staff: 32
Volunteer Staff: 15
Paid Artists: 10
Budget: $2.4 million
Income Sources: Theatre Communications Group; Nebraska Arts Council; Douglas County; National Endowment for the Arts; Corporations; Private Donations
Facility Category: Live Theatre for Children and Their Families
Type of Stage: Proscenium; Black Box
Stage Dimensions: 48'& 31' deep. Pit 11'x6'/11'X 6'
Year Built: 1927
Year Remodeled: 1994
Cost: $5.9 million
Rental Contact: Stan Kiepke
Organization Type: Performing; Touring; Resident; Educational

3335
SHAKESPEARE ON THE GREEN
Department of Fine Arts
Creighton University
Omaha, NE 68178
Phone: 402-280-2391
Fax: 402-280-2320
e-mail: mbamber@nebraskashakespeare.com
Web Site: www.nebraskashakespeare.com
Management:
  Chancelor: Nancy Belck
  Co-Founder and Artistic Director: Alan Klem
  Managing Director: Micheal Markey
  Marketing Director: Nellie Sudavicius MacCallum
  Director of Production: Wesley A. Houston
Founded: 1986
Specialized Field: Educational; Theater Workshops
Status: Non-Equity
Season: May - July
Type of Stage: Outdoor
Stage Dimensions: 100' x 300'
Seating Capacity: 5000

Nevada

3336
BREWERY ARTS CENTER
449 W King Street
Carson City, NV 89703
Phone: 775-883-1976
Fax: 775-883-1922
e-mail: info@breweryarts.org
Web Site: www.breweryarts.org
Officers:
  President: Chris Bayer
Management:
  Development Director: Bill Cowee
  Sr. Staff: John Shelton
  Program Director: Tami Castillo
  Lighting Technician: Tabitha Keeling
  Volunteer: Jonni Moon
Mission: To provide and promote the arts and culture in Carson City.
Founded: 1976
Specialized Field: Musical; Drama
Status: Non-Profit, Professional
Paid Staff: 2
Volunteer Staff: 100
Performs At: Carson City Community Center; Brewery Arts Center
Organization Type: Performing; Sponsoring

3337
WESTERN NEVADA MUSICAL THEATRE COMPANY
2201 West College Parkway, Cedar Building 113
Carson City, NV 89703

Phone: 775-445-4249
Fax: 775-445-3154
Web Site: wnmtc.com
Management:
  Producer/Director: Stephanie Arrigotti
Season: May, November
Seating Capacity: 800

3338
ACTORS REPERTORY THEATRE
1824 Palo Alto Circle
Las Vegas, NV 89108
Mailing Address: 1515 SW Morrison St. Portland, Oregon 97205
Phone: 503-241-1278
Fax: 503-241-8268
e-mail: boxoffice@artistsrep.org
Web Site: www.artistsrep.org
Officers:
  President: Michael Levy
  Chair: Kris Olson
  Vice Chair: Anna Helton
  Treasurer: Denise Carty
  Secretary: Cody Hoesly
Management:
  Artistic Director: Georgia Neu
  Managing Director: Sarah Horton
  Literary Manager: Stephanie Mulligan
Mission: Dedicated to training for, and the performance of, the classics, and the best in modern and musical theatre, with special emphasis given to new works of exceptional merit.
Specialized Field: Educational; Theater Workshops
Performs At: Summerlin Performing Arts Center
Comments: Summerlin Theatre is accessible to the mobility impaired and listening assistance devices are available.

3339
LAS VEGAS LITTLE THEATRE
3920 Schiff Drive
Las Vegas, NV 89103
Phone: 702-362-7996
e-mail: info@lvlt.org
Web Site: www.lvlt.org
Management:
  President: Walter Niejadli
  VP: TJ Larsen
  Treasurer: Frank Mengwasser
  Secretary: Katie Affentranger
Mission: To educate and entertain the community; to provide hands-on training for interested artists.
Utilizes: Singers
Founded: 1978
Specialized Field: Musical; Community Theater
Status: Non-Profit
Income Sources: Nevada Community Theatre Association; Allied Arts Council of Southern Nevada; American Association of Community Theatres
Organization Type: Performing; Educational

3340
THEATER COALITION/THE LEAR THEATER
300 E. 2nd Street
Reno, NV 89501
Phone: 775-332-1538
Fax: 775-786-4350
e-mail: office@renoisartown.com
Web Site: www.leartheater.org
Management:
  Executive Director: Susan Mayes-Smith
Founded: 1994
Specialized Field: Drama; Comedy; Musical; Classic

Paid Staff: 5
Volunteer Staff: 50

New Hampshire

3341
MAINSTAGE CENTER FOR THE ARTS
Camden County College
PO Box 200
Blackwood, NH 08012
Phone: 856-232-1012
Fax: 856-401-1776
e-mail: stage3091@snip.net
Web Site: www.mainstage.org
Management:
  President: Edward P Fiscella
  Artistic Director: Susan Waldi
  Managing Director: Bret Schneider
Founded: 1987
Specialized Field: Youth Theater; Classic; Drama
Status: Non-Profit, Professional
Paid Staff: 1
Paid Artists: 53

3342
THE HAMPSTEAD STAGE COMPANY
1053 North Barnstead Road
Center Barnstead, NH 03225
Phone: 800-619-5302
Fax: 603-776-6151
e-mail: info@hampsteadstage.org
Web Site: hampsteadstage.org
Management:
  Executive Director: Michael Phillips
Mission: The Hampstead Stage Company's mission is to save theatre by educating audiences throughout the country by bringing classic literature to life through live theatre, thus sparking an interest in reading the classics, instilling a love and appreciation of the arts, and preserving theatre for future generations.

3343
COMMUNITY PLAYERS OF CONCORD
PO Box 681
Concord, NH 03302-0681
Phone: 603-668-5466
e-mail: wtarrytown@aol.com
Web Site: www.communityplayersofconcord.org
Officers:
  President: Kevin Belvel
  VP: Wally Pineault,
  Secretary: EJ Cohen,
  Treasurer: Marlin Kaufman,
Management:
  President: Kevin Belvel
  VP: Wally Pineault,
Mission: To nurture interest in all aspects of community theater.
Founded: 1927
Specialized Field: Community Theater
Status: Nonprofit
Income Sources: New Hampshire Community Theater Association
Performs At: Concord City Auditorium
Organization Type: Performing

3344
RB PRODUCTIONS
P.O. Box 67
Concord, NH 03302
Phone: 603-568-5099
e-mail: rbproductions@comcast.net
Web Site: rb-productions.com

Mission: RB Productions aims to provide high quality educational and recreational theatre arts training activities (workshops) and productions to individuals of all ages and abilities. RB productions promotes all elements of theatre production and the importance of integrating those elements to tap creative artistic syngergy.
Founded: 2003
Organization Type: Youth Theatre; Professional Level Community Theatre

3345
HAMPTON PLAYHOUSE
2 Academy Avenue
Hampton, NH 03842
Phone: 603-926-3368
e-mail: trustees@hampton.lib.nh.us
Web Site: www.hampton.lib.nh.us
Officers:
  Chair: Linda Sadlock
  Vice chair: Richard Laskey
  Treasurer: Mary Lou Heran
  Secretary: Robert Bob Lamothe
Management:
  Producing/Artistic Director: Alfred Christie
  Producer: John Vari
Utilizes: Guest Companies; Singers
Founded: 1948
Specialized Field: Summer Stock; Musical
Status: Professional; Commercial
Income Sources: Actors' Equity Association; Society for Stage Directors and Choreographers; Council of Resident Summer Theatres
Season: June - September
Performs At: Hampton Playhouse Theatre Arts Workshop
Organization Type: Performing; Resident; Educational

3346
PAPERMILL THEATRE/NORTH COUNTY CENTER FOR THE ARTS
34 Papermill Drive
PO Box 1060
Lincoln, NH 03251
Phone: 603-745-2141
Fax: 603-745-6032
e-mail: info@jeansplayhouse.com
Web Site: www.papermilltheatre.org
Officers:
  Vice President: David Yager
  Treasurer: Tom Bringola
  Secretary: Martha Mcleod
Management:
  Technical Director: Kyle Trumble
  Director: Vicki Etchings
  Artistic Director: Kim Barber
  Production Director: Scott H. Severance
  Business Manager: Christa Hollingsworth
Founded: 1986
Specialized Field: Summer Stock
Status: Non-Profit, Professional
Paid Staff: 50
Paid Artists: 55
Season: June - August
Type of Stage: Proscenium
Stage Dimensions: 36' x 40'
Seating Capacity: 250

3347
STAGEONE PRODUCTIONS
201 Hanover Street
Manchester, NH 03101

THEATRE / New Hampshire

Mailing Address: 124 Bridge Street, Manchester, NH 03104
Phone: 603-669-5511
e-mail: boxoffice@stageoneproductions.net
Web Site: stageoneproductions.net
Management:
    Producing Director: George F. Piehl
Season: November; January-April
Performs At: The Chateau Restaurant
Organization Type: Dinner Theatre

3348
LAKES REGION SUMMER THEATRE
Route 25
Meredith, NH 03253
Phone: 603-279-9933
Fax: 603-279-4525
e-mail: meredith@lr.net
Specialized Field: Summer Stock
Season: June - September

3349
THE WINNIPESAUKEE PLAYHOUSE
50 Reservoir Road
Meredith, NH 03253
Phone: 603-279-0333
e-mail: info@winniplayhouse.org
Web Site: winnipesaukeeplayhouse.org
Management:
    Executive Director: Bryan Halperin
    Artistic Director: Neil Pankhurst
Mission: To develop and stage professional and community-based theatrical productions and to provide opportunities in theatre and the performing arts for the community.
Founded: 2004
Status: Nonprofit
Seating Capacity: 194

3350
MOUNT WASHINGTON VALLEY THEATRE COMPANY
PO Box 265, Main Street
North Conway, NH 03860
Phone: 603-356-5776
Fax: 603-356-8357
e-mail: boxoffice@mwvtheatre.org
Web Site: www.mwvtheatre.org
Management:
    Director: Linda Pinkham
    Stage Director: Nathaniel Shaw
    Technical Director: Carl L. Sage
    Musical Director: Michael Hopewell
Founded: 1971
Specialized Field: Summer Stock; Musical
Status: Nonprofit
Season: June - August
Type of Stage: Proscenium
Seating Capacity: 183

3351
PETERBOROUGH PLAYERS
PO Box 118
Peterborough, NH 03458
Phone: 603-924-9344
Fax: 603-924-6359
e-mail: info@peterboroughplayers.org
Web Site: www.peterboroughplayers.org
Officers:
    President: Jim Borsari
    Artistic Director: Gus Kaikkonen
    Managing Director: Keith Stevens
Utilizes: Guest Companies; Singers
Founded: 1933
Specialized Field: Drama; Ensembles
Status: Non-Profit, Professional
Paid Staff: 60
Paid Artists: 70
Income Sources: Actors' Equity Association; Council of Resident Summer Theatres
Season: June - September
Organization Type: Performing; Resident; Educational

3352
PONTINE THEATRE
959 Islington Street
Portsmouth, NH 03801
Phone: 603-436-6660
Fax: 603-436-1577
e-mail: info@pontine.org
Web Site: www.pontine.org
Officers:
    President: Gary Bashline
    Vice President: Kay Scott
    Secretary/Treasurer: Ellen Breed
Management:
    Co-Director: Greg Gather
    Co-Director: M. Marguerite Mathews
Mission: Dedicated to the cultural enhancements of its various publics, its performances and educational programs are offered to inform the public in the art of corporeal mime and to the preservation and development of this exciting theatrical form.
Utilizes: Dance Companies; Dancers; Guest Directors; Original Music Scores; Resident Artists; Student Interns; Special Technical Talent; Theatre Companies
Founded: 1977
Specialized Field: Youth Theater; Puppet; Contemporary
Status: For-Profit, Professional
Paid Staff: 5
Paid Artists: 2
Budget: $101,000
Performs At: McDonough Street Theater
Affiliations: New Hampshire State Council on the Arts
Annual Attendance: 1,200
Facility Category: Studio/theatre
Type of Stage: Black Box
Stage Dimensions: 20'x20'
Seating Capacity: 48
Year Built: 1900
Year Remodeled: 1987
Rental Contact: Greg Gathers
Organization Type: Performing; Touring; Resident; Educational; Sponsoring
Resident Groups: Pontine Movement Theatre

3353
SEACOAST REPERTORY THEATRE
125 Bow Street
Portsmouth, NH 03801
Phone: 603-433-4793
Fax: 603-431-7818
Toll-free: 800-639-7650
e-mail: info@seacoastrep.org
Web Site: www.seacoastrep.org
Officers:
    President: Alan E. Gold
    VP: Sarah Serling
    Treasurer: Wayne Lehna
    Treasurer: Kate Belavitch
Management:
    Producing Artistic Director: Craig J. Faulkner
    Associate Director/Producer: Eileen Rogosin
    Assistant Artistic Director: Jean Benda
    Director Marketing/Publicity: Stacy Baker
    General Manager: Chase Bailey
Mission: To provide a safe haven for performers and audiences.
Utilizes: Actors; AEA Actors; Artists-in-Residence; Choreographers; Collaborating Artists; Commissioned Music; Five Seasonal Concerts; Grant Writers; Guest Accompanists; Guest Artists; Guest Choreographers; Guest Companies; Guest Conductors; Guest Designers; Guest Ensembles; Guest Musical Directors; Instructors; Local Artists; Multimedia; Music; Original Music Scores; Resident Professionals; Sign Language Translators; Soloists; Student Interns; Visual Arts
Founded: 1986
Specialized Field: Drama; Musical; Comedy
Status: Non-Profit, Professional
Paid Staff: 15
Volunteer Staff: 6
Budget: $1,100,000
Income Sources: Ticket Sales; Sponsorships; Fundraising Events
Season: Summer and All - Year
Annual Attendance: 50,000
Facility Category: Live Theatre
Type of Stage: 3/4 Thrust
Seating Capacity: 235
Year Built: 1890
Year Remodeled: 1970
Rental Contact: Sandi Clark
Organization Type: Performing; Resident; Educational

3354
BARNSTORMERS
PO Box 434
104 Main Street
Tamworth, NH 03886
Phone: 603-323-8500
Fax: 603-323-3351
e-mail: tickets@barnstormerstheatre.org
Web Site: www.barnstormerstheatre.org
Officers:
    Secretary: Anne Batchelder
    Treasurer: Parker Roberts
    Vice Chair: Lou DeMaio
    Chair: H. Parker Roberts
Management:
    Producing Artistic Director: Clayton Phillips
    Asst. Producing Artistic Director: Claire Van Cott
Mission: To provide a theatre program featuring old—and some new—plays.
Founded: 1931
Specialized Field: New Plays; Classic
Status: Professional; Nonprofit
Income Sources: Actors' Equity Association
Season: June - August
Performs At: The Barnstormers Theatre
Affiliations: AEA
Facility Category: Theatre-Proscenium
Type of Stage: Wood
Stage Dimensions: 30'x40'
Seating Capacity: 282
Year Built: 1931
Year Remodeled: 1997
Rental Contact: Clayton Phillips
Organization Type: Performing; Resident

3355
WEATHERVANE THEATRE
389 Lancaster Road
Whitefield, NH 03598
Mailing Address: P.O. Box 127, Whitefield, NH 03598
Phone: 603-837-9010
Fax: 603-837-3333
e-mail: wvtheatre@aol.com
Web Site: www.weathervanetheatre.org
Officers:

President: Richard Portner
Vice-president: John Wissler
Treasurer: David Kenney
Secretary: Mary Jane Chase
Management:
  COO: Dan Salomon
  Managing Director: Lyn Osborne Winter
  Artistic Director: Jacques Stewart
  Producing Director: Gibbs Murray
Mission: To present 7-8 shows each season, including musicals.
Utilizes: Actors; AEA Actors; Collaborations; Guest Artists; Guest Designers; Local Artists; Multimedia; Music; Original Music Scores; Resident Artists; Soloists; Student Interns
Founded: 1965
Specialized Field: Musical; Comedy; Youth Theater; Contemporary
Status: Non-Profit, Professional
Paid Staff: 5
Paid Artists: 50
Non-paid Artists: 15
Budget: $300,000
Income Sources: Box Office; Grants; Donor Appeal
Season: July - August
Performs At: Barn Theatre
Affiliations: Actors' Equity Association
Annual Attendance: 10,000
Type of Stage: Open Thrust
Seating Capacity: 250
Year Built: 2002
Organization Type: Performing

3356
ANDY'S SUMMER PLAYHOUSE
Issac Frye Highway
PO Box 601
Wilton, NH 03086
Phone: 603-654-2613
e-mail: info@andyssummerplayhouse.org
Web Site: www.andyssummerplayhouse.org
Officers:
  President: Rose Lowry
  Vice President: Linda Tanner
  Secretary: Tom Bascom
  Treasurer: Dave Smith
Management:
  Artistic Director: DJ Potter
  Managing Director: Lizzie Harris
  Executive Director: Alexandra Urbanowski
  Technical Director: Mark Haley, M. Ed.
Mission: Andy's Summer Playhouse is innovative theater by children for people of all ages. We serve all of Southern New Hampshire from Nashua to Keene, and from Concord to Massachusetts.
Founded: 1970
Specialized Field: Children's Theater; Summer Stock; Educational
Season: June - August
Type of Stage: Flexible
Stage Dimensions: 40' x 50'
Seating Capacity: 152

New Jersey

3357
REVISION THEATRE
707 Bangs Street
Asbury Park, NJ 07712-0973
Mailing Address: P.O. Box 973, Asbury Park, NJ 07712-0973
Phone: 732-455-3059
e-mail: info@revisiontheatre.org
Web Site: revisiontheatre.org
Officers:
  President: Jeanne Montano Gianetta
  Vice President: Jules L. Plangere, III
Mission: ReVision Theatre is a professional regional theatre company dedicated to producing invigorating theatre with a fresh new perspective reaching the diverse community of Asbury Park, Monmouth County, and beyond.
Founded: 2008
Status: Professional; Nonprofit

3358
OCEAN PROFESSIONAL THEATRE COMPANY
180 Bengal Boulevard
Barnegat, NJ 08005
Mailing Address: P.O. Box 35, Manahawkin, NJ
Phone: 609-312-8306
e-mail: info@oceantheatre.org
Web Site: oceantheatre.org
Management:
  Artistic Director: Steve Steiner
  Managing Director: Ruth Blankemeyer
  Production Manager: Gail Anderson
Founded: 2011

3359
SURFLIGHT THEATRE
201 Engleside Ave.
PO Box 1155
Beach Haven, NJ 08008
Phone: 609-492-9477
Fax: 609-492-4469
e-mail: surflight@comcast.net
Web Site: www.surflight.org
Officers:
  Chair: Arthur Abramowitz
  Vice President: Barbara K Pruittg
  Secretary: Sandy Martin
  Treasurer: Ellen Dondero Meyer
Management:
  Press Director: Charlie Siedenburg
  Development Director: Bill Lawton
  Education Director: Jessica O'Brien
  General Manager: William C. Martin
  Finance Manager: Jennifer Moch
  Chief Financial Officer: Tim Laczynski
Utilizes: Actors; AEA Actors; Artists-in-Residence; Choreographers; Collaborations; Dancers; Designers; Five Seasonal Concerts; Guest Accompanists; Guest Artists; Guest Companies; Guest Conductors; Guest Designers; Guest Ensembles; Guest Lecturers; Guest Musical Directors; Guest Writers; High School Drama; Instructors; Local Artists; Multimedia; Music; Original Music Scores; Performance Artists; Poets; Resident Artists; Resident Professionals; Sign Language Translators; Soloists; Student Interns; Special Technical Talent
Founded: 1950
Specialized Field: Theatrical Productions, Musicals, Comedies, Dramas, Children's Theatre, Concerts, Special Events, Holiday Shows
Status: Non-Profit, Professional
Paid Staff: 25
Volunteer Staff: 25
Paid Artists: 60
Non-paid Artists: 20
Budget: $1,500,000
Income Sources: Box Office; NJSCA; Donations
Performs At: Theatre
Affiliations: New Jersey Theatre Alliance
Annual Attendance: 60,000
Facility Category: Theatre House
Type of Stage: Proscenium
Stage Dimensions: 24x35
Seating Capacity: 450
Year Built: 1987
Rental Contact: Gail Anderson Steiner
Organization Type: Performing; Resident

3360
SOUTH CAMDEN THEATRE COMPANY
400 Jasper Street
Camden, NJ 08104
Phone: 856-409-0365
e-mail: info@southcamdentheatre.org
Web Site: southcamdentheatre.org
Officers:
  President: Robert A. Bingaman
  Vice President: Lisa Delduke
Management:
  Producing Artistic Director: Joseph M. Paprzycki
  Acting Managing Director: Brad Reiter
  Production Manager: Ashley Reiter
Mission: The South Camden Theatre Co. produces quality professional theater, encouraging residents from throughout the region to return for a positive experience in Camden, N.J., aiding its rebirth.
Status: Professional
Performs At: Waterfront South Theatre

3361
CAPE MAY STAGE
31 Perry Street
Cape May, NJ 08204
Phone: 609-884-1341
Fax: 609-884-4224
e-mail: roy@capemaystage.com
Web Site: www.capemaystage.com
Officers:
  President: Mary T Trella
  1st Vice President: Stephen Miller
  2nd Vice President: Leslie Martel
  Treasurer: Catherine Rein
  Secretary: Heather Turner
Management:
  Artistic Director: Roy Steinberg
  Managing Director: Joe Pannullo
  Associate Producer: John Alvarez
  Marketing Director: Alicia Grasso
  Production Stage Manager: Benjamin Loverin
Mission: To be a professional theatre company with a spirit of community. Places emphasis on acting, directing and playwriting excellence.
Specialized Field: Drama; Comedy; Educational
Season: May - December
Performs At: Theater at Bank & Lafayette Streets

3362
CRANFORD DRAMATIC CLUB
78 Winans Avenue
PO Box 511
Cranford, NJ 07016
Phone: 908-276-7611
e-mail: info@cdctheatre.org
Web Site: http://www.cdctheatre.org/contact.html
Mission: To stimulate interest in theatre.
Founded: 1919
Specialized Field: Community Theater
Status: Non-Professional; Nonprofit
Performs At: Cranford Dramatic Club
Organization Type: Performing

THEATRE / New Jersey

3363
PLAYS-IN-THE-PARK
Middlesex County Department of Parks and Recreation
1 Pine Drive/Roosevelt Park
Edison, NJ 08837
Phone: 732-548-2884
Fax: 732-548-1484
e-mail: pipoffice@playsinthepark.com
Web Site: www.playsinthepark.com
Management:
   Producer/Director: Gary Cohen
   Choreographer: Michelle Massa
   Scenic Designer: Mike D'Arcy
   Lighting Designer: Roman Klima
   Props Mistress: Gabrielle Komlesk
Utilizes: Actors; Artists-in-Residence; Choreographers; Dance Companies; Dancers; Designers; Educators; Fine Artists; Five Seasonal Concerts; Guest Choreographers; High School Drama; Local Artists; Multimedia; Music; Resident Artists; Resident Professionals; Selected Students; Sign Language Translators; Singers; Soloists; Student Interns; Special Technical Talent
Founded: 1963
Specialized Field: Musical; Community Theater; Contemporary
Status: Non-Profit, Non-Professional
Paid Staff: 30
Volunteer Staff: 75
Non-paid Artists: 100
Budget: $405,000
Income Sources: Middlesex County Department of Parks and Recreation; Middlesex County Taxpayers; Patrons
Season: June - August
Performs At: Indoor/Outdoor Amphitheater
Annual Attendance: 60,000
Type of Stage: Proscenium
Stage Dimensions: 40'x20'
Year Built: 1963
Year Remodeled: 1975

3364
SKYLINE THEATRE COMPANY
10-10 20th Street
Fair Lawn, NJ 07410
Phone: 800-474-1299
e-mail: info@skylinetheatrecompany.org
Web Site: skylinetheatrecompany.org
Officers:
   President: Michele McConnell
   Vice President: Joshua D. Levine
Management:
   Artistic Director: Sam Scalamoni
   Managing Director: Victoria Sollecito
Mission: To bring together professional artists to create quality theatre that entertains and inspires an audience.
Founded: 1995
Status: Professional; Nonprofit
Performs At: Fair Lawn Community Center, George Frey Center For Arts And Recreation

3365
CENTENARY STAGE COMPANY
715 Grand Avenue
Hackettstown, NJ 07840
Mailing Address: 400 Jefferson Street, Hackettstown, NJ 07840
Phone: 908-979-0900
e-mail: info@centenarystageco.org
Web Site: centenarystageco.org
Management:
   Artistic Director: Carl Wallnau
   General Manager/Program Director: Catherine Rust
Mission: Our mission as a theatre has always been to entertain, to enlighten, and to inspire, and each year we venture forth on a journey we hope will have an impact on the lives of our diverse audience.

3366
MILE SQUARE THEATRE
720 Monroe Street #E209
Hoboken, NJ 07030
Phone: 201-683-7014
e-mail: info@milesquaretheatre.org
Web Site: milesquaretheatre.org
Officers:
   President: Zabrina Stoffel
Management:
   Artistic Director: Chris O'Connor
Mission: To produce contemporary and classical works, while advancing theatre arts education for adults and children.
Status: Professional

3367
HOLMDEL THEATRE COMPANY
36 Crawfords Corner Rd
Musical Theater; Drama;
Holmdel, NJ 07733
Mailing Address: PO Box 182
Phone: 732-946-0427
e-mail: info@holmdeltheatrecompany.org
Web Site: http://www.holmdeltheatrecompany.org/abouthc_people.html
Officers:
   President: Rebecca Zaccagnino
   Vice President: Kelly Bird
   Treasurer: Michael Serluco
Management:
   Creative Director: Geoff Shields
   Executive Producer: Kelly Bird
   Educational Director: Cody Dalton
   Building Director: Greg Santopadre
   Marketing Director: Rebecca Harris Flynn
Mission: To provide artistic/theatrical opportunities for community residents to perform and create in a professional environment.
Founded: 1985
Specialized Field: Musical; Comedy; Drama
Status: Semi-Professional
Performs At: Duncan Smith Theatre

3368
ATTIC ENSEMBLE
83 Wayne Street
Jersey City, NJ 07302
Phone: 201-413-9200
Fax: 201-434-0568
e-mail: info@atticensemble.org
Web Site: www.atticensemble.org
Founded: 1970
Specialized Field: Ensemble
Income Sources: Donors; New Jersey Stage Council on the Arts; Hudson County Department of Cultural & Heritage Affairs

3369
NEW JERSEY REPERTORY COMPANY
179 Broadway
Long Branch, NJ 07740
Phone: 732-229-3166
Fax: 732-229-3167
e-mail: njrep@njrep.org
Web Site: www.njrep.org
Officers:
   Director Marketing: Debbie Mura
   Chairperson: Marilyn Pearlman
   Vice-Chairperson: Carl Hoffman
   Treasurer: Nate Gorham
   Secretary: Marianne Pedersen
Management:
   Artistic Director: Suzanne Barabas, suzanne@njrep.org
   Executive Producer: Gabor Barabas, gabor@njrep.org
   Managing Director: Jane E. Huber, janey@njrep.org
   Group Sales: Doris Dunigan
   Stage Manager: Jennifer Tardibuono
Mission: The primary mission of the theater is to develop and produce new plays with diverse themes. It is also devoted to creating an atmosphere where classics can take on a fresh look and forgotten plays can find a home.
Utilizes: Actors; AEA Actors; Choreographers; Collaborations; Community Talent; Composers; Contract Actors; Designers; Equity Actors; Five Seasonal Concerts; Grant Writers; Guest Accompanists; Guest Artists; Guest Companies; Guest Conductors; Guest Designers; Guest Lecturers; Guest Musical Directors; Guest Soloists; Guest Teachers; Guest Writers; Instructors; Local Artists & Directors; Local Unknown Artists; Lyricists; Multi Collaborations; Multimedia; Music; Organization Contracts; Original Music Scores; Paid Performers; Performance Artists; Playwrights; Resident Artists; Resident Companies; Resident Professionals; Scenic Designers; Sign Language Translators; Students; Student Interns; Special Technical Talent; Visual Arts
Founded: 1997
Specialized Field: New Plays; Classic
Status: Non-Profit, Professional
Paid Staff: 6
Income Sources: Donations, Grants
Facility Category: Theater
Type of Stage: Black Box
Year Remodeled: 1998

3370
PLAYWRIGHTS THEATRE OF NEW JERSEY
28 Walnut Street
Madison, NJ 07940
Mailing Address: PO Box 1295, Madison, NJ 07940
Phone: 973-514-1787
Fax: 973-514-2060
e-mail: info@ptnj.org
Web Site: www.ptnj.org
Officers:
   Board President: John Bodnar
   Chair: Leanna Brown
   Arts Eductaion Consultant: Anthony Buscetti
   Treasurer: Richard Dalba
   Secretary: Edward K. DeHope
Management:
   Board President: Gene V. Ciccone
   Artistic Director: John Pietrowski
   Managing Director: Elizabeth Murphy
   Resident Stage Manager: Danielle Constance
   Associate Artistic Director: James Glossman
Mission: Provides opportunities for writers to develop their work in a nurturing environment and connect with new audiences. Four step process through which playwrights, theatre artists and audiences collaborate to bring selected texts from rough draft to finished production. Education programs for students of all ages and backgrounds.

Utilizes: Actors; AEA Actors; Artists-in-Residence; Collaborations; Designers; Educators; Guest Conductors; Guest Designers; Instructors; Local Artists; Original Music Scores; Performance Artists; Playwrights; Resident Professionals; Selected Students
Founded: 1986
Specialized Field: Young Playwrights; New Plays
Status: Non-Profit, Professional
Paid Staff: 10
Volunteer Staff: 30
Paid Artists: 150
Budget: $900,000
Income Sources: Earned; Government; Corporate Foundation; Individuals
Season: September - June
Affiliations: AEA; SSDC; USA
Annual Attendance: 6,000
Type of Stage: Black Blox
Stage Dimensions: 30' x 18'
Seating Capacity: 125
Year Built: 1985

3371
SIMULATIONS
PO Box 399
Martinsville, NJ 08836
Phone: 732-356-7800
Fax: 732-601-1911
Web Site: www.simulationsinc.com
Officers:
  President: Margaret McGovern
  Program Director: Annie McGovern
  Project Manager: Ellen McGovern-Stevens
Founded: 1979
Specialized Field: Educational
Status: For-Profit, Professional

3372
FORUM THEATRE
314 Main Street
Metuchen, NJ 08840
Phone: 732-548-4670
Fax: 732-548-4230
e-mail: forumtheatre@yahoo.com
Web Site: www.forumtheatrecompany.com
Officers:
  President: Peter Loewy
Management:
  Artistic Director: Ellen Beattie
Founded: 983
Specialized Field: Musical; Comedy; Classic; Contemporary
Status: Non-Profit, Professional
Paid Staff: 16
Paid Artists: 44
Season: October - June
Type of Stage: Proscenium/Thrust

3373
PAPER MILL PLAYHOUSE
22 Brookside Drive
Millburn, NJ 07041
Phone: 973-379-3636
Fax: 973-376-0825
e-mail: info@papermill.org
Web Site: www.papermill.org
Officers:
  Chairman of the Board: Kenneth Wegner
  Vice Chair: Jane E. Higgins
  Vice President: Deborah Kennedy
  Secretary: John F. Nietzel
  Treasurer: Margy Coll
Management:
  Managing Director: Todd Schmidt
  Producing Artistic Director: Mark S Hoebee
  Director of Press/Public Relations: Shayne Miller
  Associate Director of Marketing: Deborah Walkoczy
  Marketing Associate: Bridget Bross
Mission: To enrich the cultural lives of a wide and diverse audience. A nationally recognized professional arts center committed to excellence and to preserving the rich heritage of plays and musicals through productions of the highest quality; to develop new works; collaborating with established and emerging artists, providing arts education for all ages; and to maintaining a leadership role in the community.
Utilizes: Guest Artists; Guest Companies; Singers
Founded: 1934
Specialized Field: Musical Theatre; Arts Education
Status: Non-Profit, Professional
Paid Staff: 45
Volunteer Staff: 30
Paid Artists: 500
Budget: $15 million
Income Sources: Earned & Contributed
Season: September - June
Annual Attendance: 200,000
Facility Category: Theatre
Type of Stage: Proscenium
Seating Capacity: 1200
Year Built: 1938
Year Remodeled: 1982
Organization Type: Performing; Touring; Resident; Educational; Sponsoring

3374
ARTSPOWER NATIONAL TOURING THEATRE
39 S Fullerton Avenue
Montclair, NJ 07042-3354
Phone: 973-239-0100
Fax: 973-239-0165
Toll-free: 888-278-7769
e-mail: info@artspower.org
Web Site: www.artspower.org
  Board President: Stuart D. Liebman
Management:
  Artistic Director: Greg Gunning
  Executive Producer: Gary Blackman
Utilizes: AEA Actors; Designers; Five Seasonal Concerts; Guest Designers; Music; Organization Contracts; Performance Artists; Resident Professionals; Selected Students; Soloists; Special Technical Talent; Theatre Companies
Founded: 1985
Specialized Field: Youth Theater; Touring Company
Status: Non-Profit, Professional
Paid Staff: 9
Paid Artists: 32
Budget: $1.7 million
Income Sources: Ticket Sales; Presenting Fees; Grants
Season: October - June
Performs At: Performs in 40 states across US
Affiliations: AEA
Facility Category: Touring Theatre
Organization Type: Varies

3375
YASS HAKOSHIMA MIME THEATRE
239 Midland Avenue
Montclair, NJ 07042
Phone: 973-783-9845
Fax: 973-783-0001
e-mail: yasshakoshima@verizon.net
Web Site: www.yasshakoshima.com
Management:
  Artistic Director: Yass Hakoshima
  Director: Anne Benbow
  Assistant Director: Renate A Boue
Mission: To present the highest form of the art of mime through performances, master classes, lecture demonstrations and workshops worldwide.
Utilizes: Student Interns
Founded: 1976
Specialized Field: Mime
Status: Professional; Nonprofit
Paid Staff: 4
Organization Type: Performing; Touring; Resident; Educational

3376
GROWING STAGE THEATRE COMPANY
Route 183
7 Ledgewood Avenue
Netcong, NJ 07857
Mailing Address: PO Box 36
Phone: 973-347-4946
Fax: 973-691-7069
e-mail: exdir@growingstage.com
Web Site: www.growingstage.com/who-home/who-board/
Officers:
  Chair: Dominick V. Romano
  President: William H. Byrnes Jr
  Vice President: Theresa Scarpone
  Secretary: Manny Fernandes
  Treasurer: Michael Kochan
Mission: Bringing families together through theatre, giving children the attention they deserve and helping adults to see the importance of imagination in their lives.
Founded: 1995
Specialized Field: Children's Theater
Performs At: Historic Palace Theatre

3377
CROSSROADS THEATRE COMPANY
7 Livingston Avenue
PO Box 238
New Brunswick, NJ 08901
Phone: 732-545-8100
Fax: 732-907-1864
e-mail: membership@crossroadstheatrecompany.org
Web Site: www.crossroadstheatrecompany.org
Officers:
  President: Ted Bennett
  Vice President: Debra Napier
  Treasurer: Griffin Haviken
  Secretary: John A. Hinds
Management:
  Co-Founder and Creative Advisor: Ricardo Khan
  Director: Sagine Valla
  Producing Artistic Director: Marshall Jones, III
  Director of Audience Development: Susan Settles
  Group Sales Director: Eloise Robinson
Mission: To provide a professional environment to encourage public interest of all backgrounds; to present honest portrayals and uphold the highest standard of artistic excellence of professional Black Theatre.
Utilizes: Guest Artists; Guest Companies; Singers
Founded: 1978
Specialized Field: African American; Ethnic Theater
Status: Professional; Nonprofit
Income Sources: Private Foundations/Grants; Business/Corporate Donations; Box Office; Government Grants; Individual Donations
Season: September - May
Performs At: Crossroads Theatre

THEATRE / New Jersey

Affiliations: NJ Performing Arts Center, Newark; New Victory Theatre, NYC
Type of Stage: Modified Thrust
Seating Capacity: 300
Organization Type: Touring; Resident; Educational

3378
GEORGE STREET PLAYHOUSE
9 Livingston Avenue
New Brunswick, NJ 08901
Phone: 732-846-2895
Fax: 732-247-9151
e-mail: gryan@georgestplayhouse.org
Web Site: www.georgestplayhouse.org
Officers:
  MD: Kelly Ryman
  Business Manager: Karen Price
  Technological Director: Mark Kieran
  Volunteer Coordinator: Joel Schwartz
Management:
  Artistic Director: David Saint
  Education Director: Jim Jack
  Producing Associate: Scott Goldman
  Development Director: Lisa Giannascol
  Development Associate: Patrick Albanesius
Mission: To produce new musicals and world premieres; to revitalize contemporary classics.
Utilizes: Guest Companies; Singers
Founded: 1974
Specialized Field: Musical; Contemporary
Status: Professional; Nonprofit
Income Sources: Theatre Communications Group
Season: September - May
Performs At: George Street Playhouse
Type of Stage: Proscenium/Thrust
Seating Capacity: 367
Organization Type: Performing; Touring; Resident; Producing

3379
NEWARK PERFORMING ARTS CORPORATION/NEWARK SYMPHONY HALL
1030 Broad Street
Newark, NJ 07102
Phone: 973-643-4550
Fax: 973-643-6722
e-mail: ticketservices@newarksymphonyhall.org
Web Site: www.newarksymphonyhall.org
Officers:
  Chairman: Robert Provost
  Vice Chairperson: Alfred Bundy
  Secretary: Claudia Granados
Management:
  President: Marc Berson
  Executive Director: Gwen Moten
  Artistic Director: Catherine Lenix-Hooker
Mission: To enhance the cultural and community life of the citizens of the greater Newark area by presenting a program of the highest quality and artistic integrity and to complement that activity by providing first class facilities for classical, ethnic, popular and community arts groups, for arts education, and civic/social organizations.
Utilizes: Actors; Collaborating Artists; Collaborations; Dance Companies; Dancers; Designers; Five Seasonal Concerts; Grant Writers; Guest Accompanists; Guild Activities; Lyricists; Multi Collaborations; Multimedia; Original Music Scores; Resident Artists; Resident Professionals; Special Technical Talent; Theatre Companies
Founded: 1925
Specialized Field: Musical; Community Theater
Status: Non-Profit, Professional
Paid Staff: 16
Paid Artists: 96
Budget: $2,178,000
Income Sources: Box Office Receipts; State & City Government Grants; Space Rental Fees; Concessions; Foundation & Corporation Grants
Performs At: Newark Symphony Hall
Affiliations: American Society of Composers, Authors, & Publishers; Garden State Theatrical Organ Society; Broadcast Music, Inc.
Annual Attendance: 250,000+
Facility Category: Performing Arts Center
Type of Stage: Proscenium
Stage Dimensions: 63'x40'
Seating Capacity: 2,800
Year Built: 1925
Rental Contact: General Manager Oscar N. James
Organization Type: Performing; Presenting
Resident Groups: African Globe Theatre Works Company; Kabu Okai-Davies

3380
THEATRE AT RARITAN VALLEY COMMUNITY COLLEGE
Route 28 & Lamington Road
North Branch, NJ 08876
Phone: 908-725-3420
e-mail: theatre@rvccArts.org
Web Site: www.rvccArts.org
Officers:
  President: Casey Crabill
Management:
  Director: Alan Liddel
Founded: 1985
Specialized Field: Educational; Theater Workshops
Status: For-Profit, Professional
Paid Staff: 4

3381
CREATIVE THEATRE
102 Witherspoon Street
Princeton, NJ 08540
Phone: 609-924-8777
Fax: 609-921-0008
e-mail: carmstrong@artscouncilofprinceton.org
Web Site: www.artscouncilofprinceton.org
Officers:
  President: Cindi Venizelos
  Vice President: Kathleen Bagley
  Vice President: Debbie Schaeffer
  Treasurer: Anne VanLent
  Secretary: Marlyn Zucosky
Management:
  Executive Director: Carly Tilton
  Artistic Director: Maria Evans
  Education Director: Liz Murray
  Production Assistant: Dave Haggerty
  Director of Operations: Mark Germond
Mission: To provide theatre and creative drama for children.
Founded: 1969
Specialized Field: Children's Theater
Status: Professional; Nonprofit
Organization Type: Performing; Touring; Resident; Educational

3382
MCCARTER THEATRE
91 University Place
Princeton, NJ 08540
Phone: 609-258-6500
Fax: 609-497-0369
Toll-free: 888-278-7932
e-mail: admin@mccarter.org
Web Site: www.mccarter.org
Officers:
  President: Brian J. McDonald
  Vice President: Sharon D'Agostino
  Vice President: James J. Marino
  Vice President: Kathleen Nolan
  Treasurer: Robert T. Keck
Management:
  Artistic Director: Emily Mann
  Managing Director: Timothy Shields
  Special Programming Director: William W Lockwood
  Producing Associate: Chelsea Adams
  Literary Director: Emilia LaPenta
Mission: The Theatre is one of the most active cultural centers in the nation, offering 200 performances of theatre, dance, music and special events each year.
Utilizes: Actors; AEA Actors; Artists-in-Residence; Choreographers; Dance Companies; Dancers; Designers; Educators; Fine Artists; Five Seasonal Concerts; Guest Artists; Guest Choreographers; Guest Companies; Guest Conductors; Guest Designers; Guest Directors; Guest Lecturers; Guest Musical Directors; Guest Musicians; Guild Activities; Local Unknown Artists; Multimedia; Music; Original Music Scores; Performance Artists; Poets; Resident Professionals; Sign Language Translators; Soloists; Student Interns; Theatre Companies; Visual Arts
Founded: 1930
Specialized Field: Drama; Musical
Status: Non-Profit, Professional
Paid Staff: 80
Season: September - May
Affiliations: McCarter Theatre Company
Annual Attendance: 200,000+
Facility Category: Performing Arts Center
Type of Stage: Proscenium
Stage Dimensions: 42' x 36'
Orchestra Pit: 1
Seating Capacity: 1078
Year Built: 1930
Architect: DK Este Fisher
Rental Contact: General Manager Tom Nuzan

3383
PRINCETON REP COMPANY/PRINCETON REP SHAKESPEARE FESTIVAL
1 Palmer Square
Suite 541
Princeton, NJ 08542
Phone: 609-921-3682
Fax: 609-921-3962
e-mail: prcreprap@aol.com
Web Site: www.princetonrep.org
Management:
  President: Victoria Liberatori
  Executive Director: Janice Orlandi
Mission: Princeton Repertory Company was founded in 1984 and is a professional theatre company operating under a Small Professional Theatre Contract with Actors' Equity Association.
Founded: 1984
Specialized Field: Comedy; Youth Theater; Classic; Contemporary
Status: Non-Profit, Professional
Season: June - August

3384
TWO RIVER THEATER COMPANY
21 Bridge Avenue
Red Bank, NJ 07701
Phone: 732-345-1400
Fax: 732-345-1414
e-mail: info@trtc.org
Web Site: www.trtc.org
Officers:
  President: Todd Herman
  1st Vice President: Marilyn Broege
  2nd Vice President: Jim Hickey
  Secretary: Kathryne Singleton
  Treasurer: William J. Marraccini
Management:
  Founder/Executive Producer: Robert M. Rechnitz
  Artistic Director: John Dias
  Managing Director: Michael Hurst
  Associate Artistic Director: Stephanie Coen
  General Manager: Seth Shepsle
Mission: Dedicated to presenting works, which most richly direct our gaze to the life of the human spirit. Our mission is to produce works, from the classical and contemporary canons, which are literary and intelligent. Two River's programs include not only mainstage productions, but special performances including a student matinee series (for high school classes), singles nights and sign-interpretation and audio-described performances.
Utilizes: Actors; AEA Actors; Guest Conductors; Guest Designers
Founded: 1993
Specialized Field: Classic; Contemporary; Educational
Status: Nonprofit
Season: September - May
Affiliations: AEA
Annual Attendance: 25,000
Type of Stage: Proscenium
Stage Dimensions: 35' x 35'
Seating Capacity: 300
Year Built: 2005
Rental Contact: Sales Director Sydney Mehrlander

3385
THEATRE AT RARITAN VALLEY COMMUNITY COLLEGE
Route 28 & Lamingdon Road
PO Box 3300
Somerville, NJ 08876-1265
Phone: 908-725-3420
Fax: 908-526-7890
e-mail: alan@rvccArts.org
Web Site: www.rvccarts.org
Officers:
  President: G Jeremiah Ryan
  Senior VP: Marie Gnage
  VP: Thomas Carroll
Management:
  Director Of Theatre: Alan Liddell
  Communications Director: Alan Liddell
  Theatre Manager: Cindy Alexander
  Production Director: John Wiedermann
  Theatre Associate: Cristina Lankay
Utilizes: Artists-in-Residence; Dance Companies; Fine Artists; Special Technical Talent; Theatre Companies
Founded: 1985
Specialized Field: Educational; Theater Workshops
Status: Nonprofit
Paid Staff: 7
Volunteer Staff: 60
Paid Artists: 100
Budget: $600,000
Income Sources: Ticket Sales, Facility Rental; Contributions; Concessions
Performs At: Edward Nash Theatre; Welpe Theatre
Affiliations: APAP; IPAY; IAAM
Annual Attendance: 30,000
Stage Dimensions: 46'x40'
Seating Capacity: 984
Year Built: 1985

3386
ALLIANCE REPERTORY THEATRE COMPANY
426 Springfield Avenue
Summit, NJ 07901
Phone: 908-276-0276
e-mail: latenightmike_2000@yahoo.com
Web Site: alliancerep.org
Management:
  Artistic Director: Michael Driscoll
  Managing Director: Leslie Williams Reagoso
Founded: 1999
Status: Nonprofit

3387
DREAMCATCHER REPERTORY THEATRE
120 Morris Avenue
Summit, NJ 07901
Phone: 908-514-9654
e-mail: info@dreamcatcherrep.org
Web Site: dreamcatcherrep.org
Management:
  Artistic Director: Laura Ekstrand
  Managing Director: Steve McIntyre
  Business Manager: Roberta Palant
Mission: Dreamcatcher Repertory Theatre is a professional ensemble of actors who build community with the audience by sharing life-affirming storise in an intimate environment.
Opened: 1995
Status: Professional; Nonprofit

3388
TEANECK NEW THEATRE
PO Box 71
Teaneck, NJ 07666-0071
Phone: 201-692-0200
e-mail: tnthattie@aol.com
Web Site: www.njtheater.com
Management:
  Director/President: Bruce Cascor
Mission: We try to introduce our audience to new playwrights while continuing to present classics along with current well known plays.
Founded: 1990
Specialized Field: Community Theater
Status: Non-Profit, Non-Professional
Volunteer Staff: 20
Non-paid Artists: var
Budget: $10,000
Income Sources: Tickets; Local Support
Performs At: Bogart Memorial Church
Annual Attendance: 900
Facility Category: Auditorium
Type of Stage: Raised Proscenium
Seating Capacity: 100

3389
PASSAGE THEATRE COMPANY
219 East Hanover St
Trenton, NJ 08608
Mailing Address: PO Box 967 Trenton NJ 08605-0967
Phone: 609-392-0766
Fax: 609-392-0318
e-mail: info@passagetheatre.org
Web Site: www.passagetheatre.org
Management:
  Executive Artistic Director: June Ballinger
  Producer: Kacy O'Brien
  Director of Marketing: Marisa Taliferro
Mission: Committed to staging dynamic works that celebrate the human experience across cultural lines.
Founded: 1985
Specialized Field: New Plays
Status: Non-Profit, Professional
Paid Staff: 3
Season: September - June
Stage Dimensions: 30' x 22'
Seating Capacity: 125

3390
PATRIOTS THEATER AT THE WAR MEMORIAL
PO Box 232
Trenton, NJ 08625
Phone: 609-984-8484
Fax: 609-777-0581
Toll-free: 800-955-5566
e-mail: thewarmemorial@sos.state.nj.us
Web Site: www.thewarmemorial.com
Management:
  Executive Director: Molly S McDonough
  Production Coordinator: Bill Nutter
  Ticketing/Sales Director: Andrew Burkett
  Ticketing/Sales Director: Rebecca Jensen
Mission: Proudly hosts a diverse and exciting array of theatrical and concert events — from comedy to ballet, from opera to gospel, from international to jazz, from classical to country to rock, pop, and folk.
Founded: 1932
Specialized Field: Drama; Historical
Status: Non-Profit, Professional
Paid Staff: 20
Volunteer Staff: 100
Income Sources: State of New Jersey
Affiliations: State of New Jersey, Department of State Division of War Memorial
Facility Category: Theater
Type of Stage: Proscenium
Stage Dimensions: 50 x 30
Seating Capacity: 1800; 12,000 sq ft
Year Built: 1932
Year Remodeled: 1998
Cost: $ 34.5 Million
Rental Contact: Executive Director Molly S. McDonough
Resident Groups: New Jersey Symphony, Greater Trenton Sympony, Boheme Opera, American Repertory Ball

3391
MONTCLAIR STATE UNIVERSITY
1 Normal Ave
Upper Montclair, NJ 07043-9987
Phone: 973-655-5112
Fax: 973-655-5335
Web Site: www.montclair.edu
Officers:
  President: Susan A. Cole
  Chief of Staff: Keith D. Barrack
  Executive Assistant to President: Phyllis L. Wooster
  Program Assistant: Brian McArdle
Management:
  Stage/Production Management: Michael Allen

THEATRE / New Mexico

Mission: Evolving theatre featuring new works and American standards.
Specialized Field: Educational; Theater Workshops
Status: Nonprofit
Paid Staff: 50
Volunteer Staff: 15
Paid Artists: 40
Budget: $550,000
Income Sources: Grants; Ticket Revenue; Individuals
Season: June - August
Performs At: Alexander Kasser Theater
Affiliations: LOA; SPT
Annual Attendance: 15,000
Facility Category: Equity Theater
Type of Stage: 2 Prosceniums and Flexible
Stage Dimensions: 40' x 36'
Seating Capacity: 950 + 99
Year Remodeled: 2002
Rental Contact: John Wooten

3392
PUSHCART PLAYERS
261 Bloomfield Avenue
Verona, NJ 07044
Phone: 973-857-1115
Fax: 973-857-4366
e-mail: information@pushcartplayers.org
Web Site: www.pushcartplayers.org
Management:
  Executive Artistic Director: Ruth Fost
  Production Director: Goffrey Morris
  Managing Director: Stephanie Carr
  Arts-In-Education Director: Harry Patrick Christian
Mission: Pushcart Players is an award-winning professional theatre and arts-in-education company for young audiences. Pushcart programs offer the finest artists and arts educators available in the field, bringing the best of theatre arts to young viewers in schools and local theatres.
Founded: 1974
Specialized Field: Musical; Youth Theater; Touring Company; Educational
Status: Non-Profit, Professional
Paid Staff: 25
Paid Artists: 25
Season: September - June

3393
CUMBERLAND PLAYERS
Community Theatre
Sherman Avenue & SE Boulevard
PO Box 494
Vineland, NJ 08362-0494
Mailing Address: Cumberland Players Post Office Box 494, Vineland, NJ 08362-0
Phone: 856-692-5626
e-mail: theatre@cumberlandplayers.com
Web Site: www.cumberlandplayers.com
Officers:
  President: Michael Blandino
  VP Production: Bill Barnin
  VP Finance: Sue Ryan
  VP Public Relation: Heidi Dugan
  Secretary: Megan Kleefeld
Management:
  VP Production: D. Michael Farley
Mission: Promoting opportunities for grassroots participation amoung young and old theatre lovers. Dedicated to enriching the culture life, spirit of volunteerism, community service and love for the theatre.

Utilizes: Actors; Choreographers; Community Members; Community Talent; Local Artists; Local Artists & Directors; Local Talent; Music; Performance Artists; Visual Designers
Founded: 1946
Specialized Field: Community Theater; Musical; Drama; Comedy
Status: Non-Profit
Income Sources: Grants; Donations; Ticket Sales
Seating Capacity: 143

3394
SHADOW LAWN SUMMER STAGE
Monmouth University
Woods Theatre, Cedar Ave
West Long Branch, NJ 07764
Phone: 732-571-3442
Fax: 732-263-5330
e-mail: jburke@monmouth.edu
Web Site: www.monmouth.edu
Management:
  Chair Music/Theatre Arts: John J Burke
  Technical Director/Set Designer: Fernando Del Guercio
Utilizes: Actors; Dancers; Designers; Five Seasonal Concerts; Grant Writers; Guest Conductors; Guest Ensembles; High School Drama; Multimedia; New Productions; Original Music Scores; Resident Professionals; Soloists; Touring Companies; Visual Arts
Founded: 1979
Specialized Field: Musical; Summer Stock
Status: For-Profit, Non-Professional
Season: June - August
Performs At: Lauren K Woods Theatre
Type of Stage: Thrust
Stage Dimensions: 35' x 20'
Seating Capacity: 148

3395
LUNA STAGE
555 Valley Road
West Orange, NJ 07052
Phone: 973-395-5551
e-mail: info@lunastage.org
Web Site: lunastage.org
Management:
  Artistic Director: Cheryl Katz
  Managing Director: John Penn Lewis
  Production Manager: Liz Cesario
Mission: The mission of Luna Stage is to produce thought-provoking theatre that gives voice to emerging American playwrights and re-examines contemporary and classic plays that speak to our times.
Founded: 1992
Status: Nonprofit

3396
MAURICE LEVIN THEATER SEASON
760 Northfield Avenue
West Orange, NJ 07052
Phone: 973-530-3400
Fax: 973-736-6871
e-mail: afeldman@jccmetrowest.org
Web Site: www.jccmetrowest.org
Officers:
  Chief Executive Officer: Alan Feldman
  Chief Financial Officer: Stephen Lasser
Management:
  President: Sharon Seiden
  Executive Director: Michael Hopkins
  Director: Julie Rossi
  Manager, Center for the Arts: Carol Berman
Founded: 1877

Specialized Field: Drama; Specialty Acts; Summer Stock
Status: Non-Profit
Paid Staff: 100
Budget: $500,000-$600,000
Performs At: Maurice Levin Theater

New Mexico

3397
ADOBE THEATER
9813 4th Street NW
Albuquerque, NM 87114
Mailing Address: PO Box 276, Corrales, NM. 87048
Phone: 505-898-9222
Fax: 505-892-9761
e-mail: info@adobetheater.org
Web Site: www.adobetheater.org
Officers:
  Secretary: Taunya Crilly
  Treasurer: Fred Schwab
Management:
  President: Phil Boehler
  VP: Cy Hoffman
  Treasurer: Fred Schwab
  Secretary: Gail Spidle
Mission: To provide an educational vehicle to produce plays, musicals and other entertainments, primarily for the Westside and Greater Albuquerque Communities, including Bernalillo, Sandoval, Valencia and Cibola Counties. To furnish an opportunity for learning experiences for theater enthusiasts of all ages with any degree of experience.
Founded: 1957
Specialized Field: Community Theater; Drama; Comedy
Budget: $40 million
Income Sources: Box Office; Individual Donations
Season: Year-round
Performs At: Adobe Theatre
Annual Attendance: 9,000
Type of Stage: Thrust
Stage Dimensions: 24 x 24
Seating Capacity: 90
Year Built: 1960

3398
ADOBE THEATRE COMPANY
9813 4th St. NW
Albuquerque, NM 87114
Phone: 505-898-9222
Fax: 212-352-0441
e-mail: info@adobetheater.org
Web Site: www.adobetheater.org
Officers:
  President: Michelle Boehler
  Vice President: Cy Hoffman
  Secretary: Taunya Crilly
  Treasurer: Fred Schwab
Management:
  President: Phil Boehler
  VP: Cy Hoffman
  Treasurer: Fred Schwab
  Secretary: Gail Spidle
Founded: 1991
Specialized Field: New Plays; Theater Workshops
Performs At: Ohio Theatre
Type of Stage: Flexible Stage
Seating Capacity: 75

THEATRE / New York

3399
ALBUQUERQUE LITTLE THEATRE
224 San Pasquale SW
Albuquerque, NM 87104
Phone: 505-242-4750
e-mail: dehron@abqlt.org
Web Site: www.albuquerquelittletheatre.org
Officers:
  President: Jane Dixon
  VP: Art Tedesco
  Secretary: Carolyn Hogan
  Treasurer: Jason Lambros
Management:
  Executive Director: Henry Avery
  Technical Director: Colby Landers
Founded: 1930
Specialized Field: Community Theater; Theater Workshops
Status: Not-for-profit
Affiliations: Albuquerque Children's Theatre

3400
CITY OF ALBUQUERQUE KIMO THEATRE
423 Central NW
Albuquerque, NM 87102
Phone: 505-768-3522
Fax: 505-768-3542
e-mail: crivera@cabq.gov
Web Site: www.cabq.gov/kimo
Management:
  Managing Director: Craig Rivera
  Technical Manager: Dennis Potter
Founded: 1927
Specialized Field: Drama; Classic; Contemporary
Status: For-Profit, Professional
Paid Staff: 4
Budget: $55,000
Type of Stage: Proscenium
Seating Capacity: 650
Year Built: 1927
Year Remodeled: 2000

3401
LA COMPANIA DE TEATRO DE ALBUQUERQUE
La Compania North Albuquerque
PO Box 884
Albuquerque, NM 87103-0884
Phone: 505-242-7929
e-mail: support@jstor.org
Web Site: www.about.jstor.org
Management:
  Artistic Director: Ramon A Flores
Mission: To reflect, preserve and empower the New Mexican society and culture through professional production; Southwest bilingual theatre.
Utilizes: Singers
Founded: 1977
Specialized Field: Multi-Cultural; Ethnic Theater; Spanish Language Company
Status: Semi-Professional; Nonprofit
Budget: $95,000
Performs At: KiMo Theatre; South Broadway Cutural Center
Annual Attendance: 10,000
Seating Capacity: 700; 309
Organization Type: Performing; Touring; Resident; Educational

3402
MUSICAL THEATRE SOUTHWEST
6320 Domingo Road NE Ste B
Albuquerque, NM 87108
Mailing Address: P.O. Box 81502, Albuquerque, NM 87108
Phone: 505-265-9119
e-mail: info@musicaltheatresw.com
Web Site: musicaltheatresw.com
Officers:
  President: Laura Nuzum
  Vice President: Vicki Marie Singer
Mission: MTS is a leader in New Mexico theatre that supports and educates the community through artistic collaboration
Founded: 1960
Specialized Field: Broadway Style Musicals

3403
SANDSTONE PRODUCTIONS
901 Fairgrounds Road
Farmington, NM 87401
Phone: 505-599-1140
Management:
  Producer: Shawn F Lyle
Founded: 1993
Specialized Field: Summer Stock; Musical
Status: Non-Equity; Nonprofit
Season: June - August
Type of Stage: Outdoor
Stage Dimensions: 150' x 100'
Seating Capacity: 600

3404
LAS CRUCES COMMUNITY THEATRE
313 N Downtown Mall
Las Cruces, NM 88001
Phone: 505-523-1200
e-mail: president@lcctnm.org
Web Site: www.lcctnm.org
Officers:
  Chairman: Naomi Rupp
Management:
  Acting President: Joe Pfeiffer
  Treasurer: Heather Pfeiffer
  Secretary: Janet Mazdra
Mission: Las Cruces Community Theatre is an all volunteer non-profit organization with many opportunities for involvement.
Utilizes: Singers
Founded: 1963
Specialized Field: Community Theater
Status: Non-Professional; Nonprofit
Organization Type: Performing

3405
THEATERWORK
1060 Cerrillos Road
Santa Fe, NM 87504-0842
Mailing Address: P.O. Box 842, Santa Fe, NM 87504-0842
Phone: 505-471-1799
e-mail: mail@theaterwork.org
Web Site: twnm.org
Management:
  Artistic Director: David Olson
  Managing Director: Paula Olson
  Technical Director: Jack Sherman
Performs At: James A. Little Theater, New Mexico School For The Deaf

3406
WORKING CLASS THEATRE
1335 Gusdorf Road, Suite L
Taos, NM 87571
Phone: 575-613-2069
e-mail: info@workingclasstheatrenm.org
Web Site: workingclasstheatrenm.org
Management:
  Artistic Director: Ron Usherwood
  Business Manager/Producer: Dancer Dearing
Mission: To produce provocative and socially relevant theatre, create new theatrical works, develop emotionally authentic ensemble acting and foster a nurturing environment where theatre artists at any stage in their development may train and assist in the production of a professional theatre.
Founded: 2007
Status: Professional; Nonprofit

New York

3407
BLACK EXPERIENCE ENSEMBLE
5 Homestead Avenue
Albany, NY 12203
Phone: 518-482-6683
Officers:
  President/Founder: Mars Hill
Mission: To provide cultural exposure and enrichment to the minority community through the performing arts.
Utilizes: Singers
Founded: 1968
Specialized Field: Community Theater; African American
Status: Professional; Nonprofit
Paid Staff: 5
Income Sources: Albany League of Arts
Organization Type: Performing; Touring; Sponsoring

3408
PARK PLAYHOUSE INCORPORATED
PO Box 525
Albany, NY 12201
Phone: 518-434-2035
Fax: 518-434-1048
e-mail: info@parkplayhouse.com
Web Site: www.parkplayhouse.com
Officers:
  Chairman: Kathleen Lasch McNamee
  President: Allen S. Goodman
  Vice President: Christine Bell
  Treasurer: Nicholas Alesandro
  Secretary: Gene Tarler
Management:
  Assistant Producer: Shirley W Aren
  Park Supervisor: Lee T Griffin
  Producer: Venustiano Borromeo
  Producing Artistic Director: Owen M. Smith
  Director of Education: Shirley Arensberg
Founded: 1989
Specialized Field: Summer Stock
Status: Nonprofit
Season: July - August
Type of Stage: Proscenium
Stage Dimensions: 56' x 36'
Seating Capacity: 900

3409
AUBURN PLAYERS COMMUNITY THEATRE
PO Box 543
Auburn, NY 13021

All listings are in alphabetical order by state, then city, then organization within the city.

THEATRE / New York

Phone: 315-702-7832
e-mail: mgmword@twcny.rr.com
Web Site: www.auburnplayers.net
Officers:
   President: Stephen Gamba
   Secretary: Lorraine Fraher
   Administrative Treasurer: Joel Weirick
   Production Treasurer: Elisa Carabajal Hunt
Management:
   Administrative VP: Lindsay Day
   Production VP: Seth Kennedy
Mission: To be a non-profit, educational and cultural organization; to present dramatic productions; to increase appreciation for the theatre.
Founded: 1961
Specialized Field: Community Theater
Status: Nonprofit
Paid Staff: 100
Organization Type: Performing

3410
MERRY-GO-ROUND PLAYHOUSE
17 William Street
2nd Floor
Auburn, NY 13021
Phone: 315-255-1305
Fax: 315-252-3815
e-mail: info@merry-go-round.com
Web Site: www.merry-go-round.com
Officers:
   President: Robert Simmons
   1st Vice President: Jan Smolak
   2nd Vice President: Connie Bouck
   Treasurer: Carl Bartolotta
   Secretary: Judy Foresman
Management:
   Director: Anthony D. Franceschelli
   Director Of Marketing: Nancy Calocerinos
   Producing Director: Ed Sayles
   Business Manager: Lynnette Lee
   Youth Theatre Production Manager: Mark Goodloe
Mission: The Merry-Go-Round Playhouse is a professional theatre providing a Summer Season of Broadway quality musicals.
Founded: 1975
Specialized Field: Musical
Status: Non-Profit, Professional
Paid Staff: 20
Season: June - August
Annual Attendance: 17,000
Seating Capacity: 325

3411
MOHAWK PLAYERS
PO Box 382
Babylon, NY 11702
Phone: 516-669-7605
Mission: To present live theatre to diverse groups at libraries.
Founded: 1954
Specialized Field: Community Theater; Touring Company
Status: Nonprofit
Paid Staff: 10
Income Sources: New York State Coucil on Arts
Organization Type: Performing; Touring

3412
RIVER ARTS REPERTORY
Route 212
Bearsville, NY 12409
Phone: 914-679-7693
Fax: 845-679-9239
Management:
   Managing Director: Albert Idhe
   Co-Artistic Director: Michael Cristofer
   Managing Director: Albert Idhe
Mission: To offer new interpretations of the classics; to create innovative new works.
Utilizes: Singers
Founded: 1979
Specialized Field: Summer Stock; Puppet
Status: Professional; Nonprofit
Income Sources: Actors' Equity Association; Theatre Communications Group
Performs At: Bearsville Theatre
Organization Type: Performing; Sponsoring

3413
GATEWAY PLAYHOUSE
215 S Country Road
Box 5
Bellport, NY 11713
Phone: 631-286-1133
Fax: 631-286-5806
Toll-free: 888-484-9669
e-mail: boxoffice@gatewayplayhouse.com
Web Site: www.gatewayplayhouse.com
Management:
   Producer: Paul Allan
   Associate Producer: Jeff Bellante
   General Manager: Dom Ruggiero
Founded: 1950
Specialized Field: Musical; Children's Theater; Theater Workshops
Status: Commercial
Season: May - December
Type of Stage: Proscenium
Stage Dimensions: 30' x 8'
Seating Capacity: 500

3414
BELMONT PLAYHOUSE
2385 Arthur Avenue
Bronx, NY 10458
Phone: 718-364-4700
Fax: 718-563-5053
e-mail: thebelmont@hotmail.com
Management:
   Artistic Director: Dante Albertie
Founded: 1991
Specialized Field: Ethnic Theater; Classic; New Plays
Performs At: Belmont Playhouse
Type of Stage: Black Box, Platform
Seating Capacity: 75, 25-100

3415
PREGONES THEATER
571-575 Walton Avenue
Bronx, NY 10451
Phone: 718-585-1202
Fax: 718-585-1608
e-mail: info@pregones.org
Web Site: www.pregones.org
Management:
   Artistic Director: Rosalba Rolon
   Managing Director: Maggie Gonzales
   Associate Artistic Director: Alvan Colon Lespier
   Associate Director: Jorge Merced
Mission: To offer bilingual theatre mainly for Latino audiences; to present a broad range of professional performers.
Founded: 1979
Specialized Field: Musical; Comedy; Community Theater; Classic; Contemporary
Status: Non-Profit, Professional
Organization Type: Performing; Touring

3416
AAI PRODUCTIONS
528 5th Street
Suite 4R
Brooklyn, NY 11215
e-mail: 7sinsin60@gmail.com
Web Site: www.7sinsin60.com
Officers:
   Playwright: Chisa Hutchinson
   Lighting Designer: Joyce Liao
   Dance Choreographer: Kendra Ross
   Director: Melanie Sutherland
   Producer: Lanie Zipoy
Management:
   Artistic Director: Melanie Sutherland
   Producer: Lanie Zipoy
   Event producer: Julie Carpenter Sylvester
   Associate Artistic Director: Linda Chapman
   Producer/general manager/labor lead: Dorothy Olim
Mission: To offer classical and contemporary plays developed by theatre artists of a resident company.
Utilizes: Singers
Founded: 1976
Specialized Field: Comedy; Puppet; Classic; Contemporary
Status: Non-Profit, Professional
Paid Staff: 1
Organization Type: Performing; Touring; Resident

3417
ADELPHIAN PLAYERS
8515 Ridge Boulevard
Brooklyn, NY 11209
Phone: 718-238-3308
Fax: 718-238-2894
Management:
   Artistic Director: Russell E Bonanno
   Business Manager: Philip Stone
   Director Advancement: Albert C Corham
Mission: To provide quality theatre for the residents of Brooklyn.
Founded: 1964
Specialized Field: Summer Stock
Status: Non-Professional
Paid Staff: 25
Volunteer Staff: 10
Performs At: Adelphi Academy
Organization Type: Performing; Educational

3418
BILLIE HOLIDAY THEATRE
1368 Fulton Street
Brooklyn, NY 11216
Mailing Address: PO Box 470131, Brooklyn, NY 11247-0131
Phone: 718-636-0919
Fax: 718-636-2165
e-mail: billieholidaytheatre@yahoo.com
Web Site: www.thebillieholiday.org
Management:
   President: Marjorie Moon
Mission: To offer trained Black artists a professional environment; to provide theatre that enlightens and educates the community.
Utilizes: Singers
Founded: 1972
Specialized Field: African American
Status: Non-Profit, Professional
Paid Staff: 4
Stage Dimensions: Proscenium
Seating Capacity: 200
Organization Type: Performing; Resident

THEATRE / New York

3419
CONEY ISLAND USA
1208 Surf Avenue
Brooklyn, NY 11224-2816
Phone: 718-372-5159
Fax: 718-372-5101
e-mail: info@coneyisland.com
Web Site: www.coneyisland.com
Management:
　Artistic Director: Dick Zigun
　Managing Director: Jennifer Upchurch
Mission: To present America's popular art forms in innovative sideshow parades, performances and exhibitions.
Utilizes: Singers
Founded: 1980
Specialized Field: Specialty Acts; Musical
Status: Non-Profit, Professional
Paid Staff: 12
Volunteer Staff: 4
Paid Artists: 8
Budget: 250,000
Income Sources: Alliance of Resident Theatres/New York
Performs At: Sideshows by the Seashore, Coney Island Museum
Annual Attendance: 75,000+
Facility Category: Sideshows by the seashore, Coney Island Museum
Type of Stage: Arena, Cabaret
Seating Capacity: 99; 74
Organization Type: Performing; Educational; Sponsoring

3420
IRONDALE ENSEMBLE PROJECT
85 S. Oxford Street
Brooklyn, NY 11217
Phone: 718-488-9233
e-mail: jim@irondale.org
Web Site: irondale.org
Officers:
　President: Hollis Headrick
　Vice President: Ken Rothchild
Management:
　Artistic Director: Jim Niesen
　Executive Director: Terry Greiss
　Managing Director: Maria Knapp
Mission: Through the power of the ensemble process, Irondale creates and presents alive, compelling theater, performance, and education programs that challenge traditional assumptions about art, and help us to better interpret contemporary culture.

3421
MODERN-DAY GRIOT THEATRE COMPANY
138 South Oxford Street
Brooklyn, NY 11217
Phone: 718-247-9417
Fax: 718-398-2794
e-mail: contactus@moderndaygriot.org
Web Site: moderndaygriot.org
Management:
　Artistic Director: Pharah Jean-Philippe
　Associate Artistic Director: Liza Bulos
　Managing Director: Zenobia Connor
　Associate Artistic Director: Jamila Sockwell
Founded: 2010
Status: Nonprofit
Volunteer Staff: 4

3422
RYAN REPERTORY COMPANY AT HARRY WARREN THEATRE
2445 Bath Avenue
Brooklyn, NY 11214
Phone: 718-996-4800
Fax: 718-996-4800
e-mail: ryanrep@juno.com
Management:
　Executive Director: Barbara Parisi
　Technical Director: Michael Pasterneck
　Artistic Director: John Sannuto
Mission: Developing new musicals and working on new plays.
Utilizes: Actors; AEA Actors; Artists-in-Residence; Choreographers; Collaborating Artists; Composers-in-Residence; Designers; Educators; Five Seasonal Concerts; Guest Designers; Music; Organization Contracts; Performance Artists; Poets; Resident Professionals; Sign Language Translators; Soloists; Special Technical Talent
Founded: 1972
Specialized Field: Musical; New Plays
Status: Professional; Nonprofit
Volunteer Staff: 18
Non-paid Artists: 200
Budget: $60,000
Performs At: Harry Warren Theatre
Annual Attendance: 2000
Stage Dimensions: 12 x 12
Seating Capacity: 40
Year Built: 1990
Organization Type: Performing; Resident

3423
AFRICAN AMERICAN CULTURAL CENTRE
350 Masten Avenue
Buffalo, NY 14209
Phone: 716-884-2013
Fax: 716-885-2590
e-mail: africancultural350@gmail.com
Web Site: www.africancultural.org
Officers:
　Chairperson: Hary Stokes
　Vice Chairperson: Emma Bassett
　Secretary: Gwendolyn Neal
　Treasurer: Paulette S. Counts
Management:
　Artistic Dir Paul Robeson Theatre: Paulette Harris
　Artistic Dir Dance/Drum Department: Linda Barr
　Artistic Dir Dance/Drum Department: Theresa Mingo
　Assistant Director: Alicia M. Banner
Mission: To develop and nurture an appreciation for Black Theatre in the Black community, especially among Black youth.
Utilizes: Singers
Founded: 1958
Specialized Field: African American; Ethnic Theater; Community Theater; Youth Theater; Multi-Cultural
Status: Non-Profit, Non-Professional
Paid Staff: 50
Performs At: Paul Robeson Theatre
Organization Type: Performing; Educational

3424
ALLEYWAY THEATRE
One Curtain Up Alley
Buffalo, NY 14202-1911
Phone: 716-852-2600
Fax: 716-852-2266
e-mail: email@alleyway.com
Web Site: www.alleway.com
Management:
　Executive Director: Neal Radice
　Director Public Relations/Literary: Joyce Stilson
　Resident Designer/Associate Directo: Todd Warfield
　Associate Director: Kim Piazza
　House Manager: Jessica Werner
Mission: To develop and produce new theatre.
Utilizes: Actors; AEA Actors; Artists-in-Residence; Choreographers; Collaborations; Designers; Educators; Five Seasonal Concerts; Guest Accompanists; Guest Companies; Guest Conductors; Guest Designers; Guest Soloists; Guest Teachers; High School Drama; Instructors; Local Artists; Original Music Scores; Performance Artists; Poets; Resident Professionals; Sign Language Translators; Student Interns; Visual Arts
Founded: 1980
Specialized Field: New Plays
Annual Attendance: 17,000
Type of Stage: Black Box
Seating Capacity: 100

3425
IRISH CLASSICAL THEATRE COMPANY
625 Main Street
Buffalo, NY 14203
Phone: 716-853-4282
Fax: 716-853-0592
e-mail: iclassical@aol.com
Web Site: www.irishclassicaltheatre.com
Management:
　President: Vincent O'Neill
　Business Manager: Nancy Dohry
Mission: To present the greatest works of dramatic literture, international classics, modern plays of exceptional merit, and Irish plays, both traditional and contemporary; to produce them at the highest level of artistic excellence; to offer them to the public of Buffalo, Western New York and Southern Ontario, and subsequently, for national and international audiences.
Founded: 1990
Specialized Field: Ethnic Theater; Classic
Status: Non-Profit, Professional
Paid Staff: 12
Paid Artists: 12
Annual Attendance: 25,000+
Type of Stage: In The Round
Seating Capacity: 200
Year Built: 1998

3426
KAVINOKY THEATRE
320 Porter Avenue
Buffalo, NY 14201
Phone: 716-829-7668
Fax: 716-829-7790
e-mail: kavinokytheatre@dyc.edu
Web Site: www.kavinokytheatre.com
Management:
　Artistic Director: David Lamb
　Executive and Managing Director: Steve Cooper
Founded: 1980
Specialized Field: Musical; Classic; New Plays
Status: Non-Profit, Professional
Paid Staff: 4
Volunteer Staff: 300
Paid Artists: 40
Performs At: D'Youville College campus
Type of Stage: Proscenium/Thrust
Seating Capacity: 260

THEATRE / New York

3427
PANDORA'S BOX THEATRE COMPANY
One Curtain Up Alley
Buffalo, NY 14202
Phone: 716-852-2600
Fax: 716-852-2266
e-mail: jkittsley@alleyway.com
Web Site: www.alleyway.com/pandorasbox
Management:
    President of the Board: Leonard London
    Executive Director: Neal Radice
    Artistic Director: Julie Kittsley
Mission: To produce plays about women and their experiences.
Utilizes: Actors; AEA Actors; Choreographers; Collaborations; Designers; Five Seasonal Concerts; Guest Conductors; Guest Designers; Instructors; Performance Artists; Playwrights; Resident Professionals; Singers; Theatre Companies; Visual Arts
Founded: 1995
Specialized Field: Women's Theater
Status: Non-Profit, Professional
Paid Staff: 2
Paid Artists: 40

3428
SHAKESPEARE IN DELAWARE PARK
PO Box 716
Buffalo, NY 14205
Phone: 716-515-3960
e-mail: saulelkin@shakespeareindelawarepark.org
Web Site: www.shakespeareindelawarepark.org
Officers:
    President: Anne K. Kyzmir
    Vice President: Christopher Less
    Treasurer: Larry Nowak
    Secretary: Susan Marriott
Management:
    Artistic Director: Saul Elkin
    Program Director: Roger Keicher
    Managing Director: Lisa Ludwig
    Office Manager: Tracy Snyder
    Development Coordinator: Kristen Pope
Mission: Shakespeare in Delaware Park is a not-for-profit, professional theatre company dedicated to providing free, high-quality public theatre to the widest possible audience by performing Shakespearean plays outdoors.
Utilizes: Scenic Designers; Soloists
Founded: 1976
Specialized Field: Classic; Shakespeare
Status: Professional; Nonprofit
Season: June - August

3429
STUDIO ARENA THEATRE
710 Main Street
Buffalo, NY 14202-1990
Phone: 716-856-8025
Fax: 716-856-3415
Toll-free: 800-777-8243
Officers:
    President: James Anderson
Management:
    Artistic Director: Gavin Cameron-Webb
    Executive Director: Ken Neufeld
    Director Development: Carol Halter
    Director Marketing: Bil Schroeder
Mission: To provide Western New York with a varied theatre season of the finest quality.
Utilizes: Actors; AEA Actors; Artists-in-Residence; Collaborations; Designers; Educators; Fine Artists; Five Seasonal Concerts; Guest Companies; Guest Conductors; Guest Designers; High School Drama; Instructors; Local Artists; Lyricists; Original Music Scores; Performance Artists; Resident Professionals; Scenic Designers; Singers; Soloists; Students
Founded: 1927
Specialized Field: Musical; Drama; Comedy
Status: Non-Profit
Budget: $4.5 million
Income Sources: League of Resident Theatres; Theatre Communications Group; Actors' Equity Association
Season: September - May
Affiliations: Theatre Communications Group; League of Resident Theatres
Annual Attendance: 100,000
Type of Stage: Semi-Thrust
Seating Capacity: 637
Year Remodeled: 2001
Organization Type: Performing; Educational

3430
THEATRE OF YOUTH COMPANY
203 Allen Street
Allendale Theatre
Buffalo, NY 14201
Phone: 716-884-4400
Fax: 716-819-9653
e-mail: info@theatreofyouth.org
Web Site: www.theatreofyouth.org
Officers:
    President: Allegra Jaros, MBA
    VP: Bonnie A. Redder, Esq.,
    Secretary: Deborah Burns Houck
    Treasurer: Chris Ware
Management:
    Artistic Director: Meg Quinn
    Managing Director: Robert Brunschmid
Utilizes: Singers
Founded: 1972
Specialized Field: Children's Theater
Status: Non-Profit
Annual Attendance: 53,000
Facility Category: Theatre
Type of Stage: Proscenium
Year Built: 1913
Year Remodeled: 1999
Organization Type: Performing; Touring; Educational

3431
ARENA PLAYERS REPERTORY THEATRE COMPANY OF LONG ISLAND
269 West 18th Street
Centerport, NY 11729
Phone: 516-293-0674
e-mail: arena109@aol.com
Web Site: www.arenaplayers.org
Officers:
    President/Director/Producer: Frederic De Feis
Management:
    Director of Operations/Creative: Carolyn De Melo
Mission: To develop and encourage a love of arena theatre; to assist new playwrights as they develop original scripts.
Utilizes: Actors; Artists-in-Residence; Collaborating Artists; Commissioned Music; Organization Contracts; Original Music Scores; Performance Artists; Resident Artists
Founded: 1955
Specialized Field: Youth Theater; Ethnic Theater; Community Theater; Classic; Contemporary
Status: Non-Profit, Professional
Paid Staff: 3
Volunteer Staff: 5
Paid Artists: 10
Non-paid Artists: 5
Budget: $450,000
Income Sources: Theatre Communications Group
Season: Year-Round
Performs At: Arena Players Repertory Theater
Annual Attendance: 30,000
Facility Category: 2 stages
Type of Stage: Arena
Seating Capacity: 240; 100
Year Remodeled: 1970
Organization Type: Performing; Touring

3432
MAC-HAYDN THEATRE
1925 New York
PO Box 203
Chatham, NY 12037
Mailing Address: PO Box 204
Phone: 518-392-9292
Fax: 518-392-4547
Web Site: www.machaydntheatre.org
Officers:
    President: Lynne Hayden
    Artistic Producing Director: Linda MacNish
Founded: 1969
Specialized Field: Musical; Summer Stock
Status: Non-Profit, Professional
Season: May - September
Annual Attendance: 40,000+
Facility Category: Theatre
Type of Stage: In the Round
Seating Capacity: 350

3433
HUDSON VALLEY SHAKESPEARE FESTIVAL
140 Main Street
Cold Spring, NY 10516
Phone: 845-265-9575
Fax: 845-265-1037
e-mail: boxoffice@hvshakespeare.org
Web Site: www.hvshakespeare.org
Officers:
    President: Robin Shelby Arditi
    Vice President: Patricia King
    Secretary: Suzanne B. Baker
    Treasurer: Betsy Swanson
Management:
    Artistic Director: Terrence O'Brien
    Executive Director: Maggie Whitum
    Director Marketing: Abigail Adams
Mission: Dedicated to producing and performing the plays of Shakespeare with clarity, energy and invention.
Founded: 1987
Specialized Field: Shakespeare; Classic
Status: Non-Profit, Professional
Paid Staff: 25
Paid Artists: 34
Performs At: Boscabel Restoration

3434
LEATHERSTOCKING THEATRE COMPANY
Box 711
Cooperstown, NY 13775
Phone: 607-547-1363
Fax: 607-547-6144
Management:
    Artistic Director: Mercedes Gotwald
Founded: 1991
Specialized Field: Summer Stock; Drama; Comedy
Status: Nonprofit
Season: July - September

Type of Stage: Proscenium
Seating Capacity: 150

3435
CORTLAND REPERTORY THEATRE
PO Box 783
Cortland, NY 13045
Phone: 607-753-6161
Fax: 607-753-0047
Toll-free: 800-427-6160
e-mail: cortlandrep@hotmail.com
Web Site: www.cortlandrep.org
Officers:
   President: John Folmer
   VP: Tom Knobel
   Treasurer: Garrison Marsted
   Secretary: Dorothea Fowler
Management:
   Producing Artistic Director: Kerby Thompson
Mission: To offer residents of Central New York an opportunity to experience, at an accessible price, the range and scope of excellent professional theatre.
Utilizes: Actors; AEA Actors; Choreographers; Dancers; Designers; Guest Accompanists; Guest Artists; Guest Conductors; Guest Designers; Guest Lecturers; Guest Musical Directors; Guest Writers; Instructors; Local Artists; Multimedia; Music; Original Music Scores; Resident Professionals; Selected Students; Sign Language Translators; Soloists; Student Interns; Visual Arts
Founded: 1972
Opened: 1972
Specialized Field: Summer Stock Theatre; Musicals; Non Musicals
Status: Non-Profit, Professional
Paid Staff: 2
Volunteer Staff: 150
Paid Artists: 100
Budget: $480,000
Income Sources: NYSCA; Grants; Corporate Sponsors; Individual Donations
Season: June - August
Performs At: Summer Stock Theatre
Annual Attendance: 17,000
Facility Category: Converted National Historic Dance Pavilion
Type of Stage: 3/4 Thrust, Wood Floor
Seating Capacity: 250
Year Built: 1906
Year Remodeled: 1972
Organization Type: Performing

3436
AURORA PLAYERS
Roycroft Pavillion
East Aurora, NY 14052
Mailing Address: P.O. Box 206, East Aurora, NY 14052
Phone: 716-687-6727
e-mail: info@auroraplayers.org
Web Site: auroraplayers.org
Officers:
   President: Liz Cassidy
   Vice President: Catherine Burkhart
Mission: To create interest in, and to foster enthusiasm for, the study of the dramatic arts; to provide a medium of expression for those who have a natural love for the theatre in any of its phases; and to be the means of bringing together in organized activities all those of kindred spirit whose interest centers about the drama.

3437
JOHN DREW THEATER AT GUILD HALL
158 Main Street
East Hampton, NY 11937
Phone: 631-324-0806
Fax: 631-324-2722
e-mail: info@guildhall.org
Web Site: www.guildhall.org
Officers:
   Chairman: Melville Starrus
   1st Vice Chair: Mike Clifford
   2nd Vice Chair: Michael Lynne
   Treasurer: Muriel Siebert
   Secretary: Thomas A. Twomey, Jr.
   Executive Director: Ruth Appelhof
   Artistic Director: Josh Gladstone
   Managing Director: Jeannine Dyner
   Marketing Assistant: Lauren Baker
Mission: The John Drew Theater of Guild Hall operates under an educational/arts charter; dedicated to the presentation of the finest in the performing arts.
Founded: 1931
Specialized Field: AEA LOA Prodctions; Musical; Comedy; Community Theater; Puppet; Classic; Contemporary
Status: Non-Profit, Professional
Paid Staff: 30
Volunteer Staff: 50
Paid Artists: 200
Non-paid Artists: 200
Budget: $2.3 million
Income Sources: Actors' Equity Association
Season: May-September
Performs At: John Drew Theater
Affiliations: Film Society Lincoln Center; Hamptons International Film Festival; Playwrights Theatre of the Hampton
Annual Attendance: 20,000
Type of Stage: Proscenium
Stage Dimensions: 25'x34'
Seating Capacity: 360
Year Built: 1931
Year Remodeled: 2008
Cost: $14 Million
Rental Contact: Josh Gladstone
Organization Type: Performing; Educational

3438
SHADOWLAND ARTISTS
157 Canal Street
Ellenville, NY 12428
Phone: 845-647-5511
Fax: 845-647-3510
e-mail: mail@shadowlandstheatre.org
Web Site: www.shadowlandtheatre.org
Officers:
   Vice President: John Eckert
   Secretary: Denise Moore
Management:
   Director: William H. Collier III
   Executive Director: William Morris
   Producing Artistic Director: Brendan Burke
Founded: 1985
Specialized Field: Drama; Musical; New Plays
Status: Non-Profit, Professional
Season: May - September
Type of Stage: Thrust
Stage Dimensions: 36' x 24'
Seating Capacity: 148

3439
ROCKAWAY THEATRE COMPANY
P.O. Box 950398
Far Rockaway, NY 11695-0398
Phone: 718-374-6400
e-mail: info@rockawaytheatrecompany.org
Web Site: rockawaytheatrecompany.org
Opened: 1997
Status: Nonprofit; Charity

3440
QUEENS COLLEGE SUMMER THEATRE
Rathaus Hall 213
65-30 Kissena Boulevard
Flushing, NY 11367
Phone: 718-997-5000
Fax: 718-997-3095
Web Site: www.qc.cuny.edu
Management:
   Production Manager: Ralph Carhart
Mission: Educational setting presenting diverse productions and programs in the arts. Three theatre complex with seating for 100 to 500.
Founded: 1970
Specialized Field: Drama; Summer Stock
Status: Non-Equity; Nonprofit
Season: July - August
Performs At: Two Black Boxes; One Fly Space
Affiliations: CUNY
Type of Stage: Proscenium; Thrust
Stage Dimensions: 45' x 45'; 30' x 25'
Seating Capacity: 476

3441
FORESTBURGH PLAYHOUSE
39 Forestburgh Road
Forestburgh, NY 12777
Phone: 845-794-2005
Fax: 845-794-9347
e-mail: WebEnquiry@fbplayhouse.org
Web Site: www.fbplayhouse.org
Management:
   Producer: Franklin Trapp
   Artistic Supervisor: Ron Nash
   Consulting Managing Director: Norman Duttweiler
   Director/Choreographer: Dann Dunn
   Director: Larry Smiglewski
Founded: 1947
Specialized Field: Summer Stock; Cabaret; Children's Theater
Status: Equity; Commercial
Season: June - September
Type of Stage: Proscenium
Seating Capacity: 150

3442
ADIRONDACK THEATRE FESTIVAL
207 Glen Street
Glens Falls, NY 12801
Mailing Address: PO Box 3203, Glens Falls, NY 12801
Phone: 518-798-7479
Fax: 518-793-1334
e-mail: atf@atfestival.org
Web Site: www.atfestival.org
Officers:
   President: Kristine K. Flower
   VP: Sean Magee
   Treasurer: Robert J. Joy
   Secretary: Jane Gibbs
   Broadway Stage Manager: Kate Broderick
Management:
   Producing Artistic Director: Mark Fleischer

THEATRE / New York

General Manager: Tracy Long
Technical Director: Scott Wolfson
Mission: A professional not-for-profit summer theatre located in Glens Falls, NY. Strives to challenge, entertain and nourish its audience through the development and production of new and contemporary musicals and plays. This relationship engages the commnuity as audience members and participants in workshops, discussions and educational programming.
Utilizes: Actors; AEA Actors; Choreographers; Commissioned Composers; Designers; Local Unknown Artists; Music; Organization Contracts; Original Music Scores; Performance Artists; Resident Professionals; Student Interns
Founded: 1994
Specialized Field: Theater
Status: Nonprofit
Paid Staff: 11
Volunteer Staff: 10
Paid Artists: 36
Budget: $400,000
Income Sources: Ticket Sales; Donations; Grants
Season: June - July
Performs At: Charles R Wood Theater
Affiliations: AEA
Annual Attendance: 6,100
Facility Category: Theater
Type of Stage: Proscenium
Seating Capacity: 294
Year Built: 2004

3443
YOUTHEATRE
10 Windy Hill Road
Glens Falls, NY 12801
Phone: 518-793-3521
e-mail: lgyoutheatre@aol.com
Web Site: www.lgyoutheatre.com
Management:
  Director/Producer: Michael Luce
  Music Director: Laura Lee Conti
  Asst. Director: Lanni Luce West
  Scenic Artist Director: Amity Luce-Aurilio
  Asst. to the Director: Dan Slavin

3444
STAGEWORKS
41-A Cross Street
Hudson, NY 12534
Phone: 518-828-7843
Fax: 518-828-4026
e-mail: contact@stageworkstheater.org
Web Site: www.stageworkshudson.org
Officers:
  President: Barry M. Herbold
  Vice President & Treasurer: Eric Semel
  Secretary: Nancy Laribee
  Dramaturg: James Farrell
  Staff Photographer: Rob Shannon
Management:
  Production Artistic Director: Laura Margolis
  Administrative Director: Phil Gliman
  Executive Artistic Director: Laura Margolis
  General Manager: Phillip Elman
  Producing Associate: Jennifer Schilansky
Utilizes: Actors; AEA Actors; Choreographers; Collaborations; Commissioned Composers; Designers; Educators; Five Seasonal Concerts; Guest Accompanists; Guest Artists; Guest Choreographers; Guest Companies; Guest Conductors; Guest Designers; Guest Ensembles; Guest Lecturers; Guest Teachers; High School Drama; Instructors; Music; Original Music Scores; Performance Artists; Resident Professionals; Soloists; Student Interns; Visual Arts
Founded: 1993
Specialized Field: Drama; Comedy
Status: Nonprofit
Budget: $190,000
Income Sources: Earned and Unearned
Season: April - November
Affiliations: Theater Communications; Hudson Valley East Consortium of Professional Theaters
Facility Category: North Point in Kinderhook, NY
Type of Stage: Thrust
Stage Dimensions: 40' x 20'
Seating Capacity: 100-125

3445
CORNELL UNIVERSITY THEATRE, FILM & DANCE DEPARTMENT
Cornell University
Ithaca, NY 14853-6902
Phone: 607-254-2733
Fax: 607-254-2700
e-mail: av45@cornell.edu
Web Site: www.theatrefilmdance.cornell.edu
Officers:
  Acting Department Chair: Sabine Haenni
Management:
  Manager: Kristina Baier
  Director: Mary Fessenden
Specialized Field: Educational; Theater Workshops
Affiliations: Cornell Concert Series
Facility Category: Dance Hall
Resident Groups: Cornell Savoyards

3446
HANGAR THEATRE
171 East State Street
Suite 230
Ithaca, NY 14851
Mailing Address: PO Box 205 Ithaca NY, 14851
Phone: 607-273-8588
Fax: 607-273-4516
e-mail: rhoan@hangartheatre.org
Web Site: www.hangartheatre.org
Officers:
  President: Shelley S. Semmler
  VP: Magaret Shackell
  Secretary: Judith Pastel
  Past President: Ann Costello
  Honorary: Marty Allee
Management:
  Director: Lisa Bushlow
  Acting Artistic Director: Stephanie Yankwitt
  Business Director: Jennifer D. Anderson
  Director of Marketing & Communicati: Sharon Marmora
  Executive Director: Lisa Bushlow
Mission: As a professional theatre the Hangar hires Equity and nonequity actors, designers and directors for each play the theatre produces during the summer.
Utilizes: Selected Students; Singers; Student Interns
Founded: 1974
Specialized Field: Musical; Comedy; Community Theater; Puppet; Classic; Contemporary
Status: Non-Profit, Non-Professional
Paid Staff: 20
Paid Artists: 20
Budget: $900,000
Income Sources: Foundation; Individual; Grant; Earned
Season: May - August
Performs At: Hangar Theatre; Cass Park
Affiliations: Actors Equity Association; United Scenic Artists; Society of Stage Directors and Choreography; Drama League
Annual Attendance: 20,000
Type of Stage: Thrust
Seating Capacity: 349
Organization Type: Performing; Educational

3447
KITCHEN THEATRE COMPANY
417 W. State / W. MLK, Jr. Street
Ithaca, NY 14850
Mailing Address: P.O. Box 429, Ithaca NY 14851
Phone: 607-272-0403
Fax: 607-273-4816
e-mail: kitchenithaca@aol.com
Web Site: www.kitchentheatre.org
Officers:
  Vice President: Karen Brown
  Treasurer: Thomas Evans
  Secretay: Jim Bouderau
Management:
  President: Roger Sibley
  Artistic Director: Rachel Lampert
  Managing Director: Stephen Nunley
  Associate Producing Director: Lesley Greene
  Production Stage Manager: LaShawn Keyser
Utilizes: Actors; AEA Actors; Collaborating Artists; Commissioned Composers; Dancers; Designers; Five Seasonal Concerts; Grant Writers; Guest Accompanists; Guest Choreographers; Guest Companies; Guest Conductors; Guest Designers; Guest Directors; Guest Lecturers; Guild Activities; Instructors; Local Artists; Local Unknown Artists; Multimedia; Music; Original Music Scores; Performance Artists; Playwrights; Resident Professionals; Selected Students; Soloists; Student Interns; Special Technical Talent
Founded: 1992
Specialized Field: Community Theater; New Plays
Status: Non-Profit, Professional
Paid Staff: 5
Volunteer Staff: 50
Paid Artists: 15
Season: August - May
Annual Attendance: 10,000
Type of Stage: 3/4 Thrust
Seating Capacity: 73

3448
YUEH LUNG SHADOW THEATRE
34-41 74Th Street
Jackson Heights, NY 11372
Phone: 718-457-1627
Fax: 718-457-1627
Management:
  Executive/Artistic Director: Joe Humphrey
  Assistant Director: Sarah Jonker-Burke
Mission: To preserve and perpetuate the art of shadow theatre, which began in China 2000 years ago.
Founded: 1976
Specialized Field: Ethnic Theater; Puppet; Multi-Cultural
Status: Professional; Nonprofit
Income Sources: Alliance of Resident Theatres/New York; United International Marionette Association; Queens Council on Arts; Puppeteers of America; UNIMA
Organization Type: Performing; Touring; Educational

3449
AFRIKAN POETRY THEATRE
176-03 Jamaica Avenue
Jamaica, NY 11432-5503
Phone: 718-523-3312
Fax: 718-523-1054
e-mail: jwatusi@aol.com
Web Site: www.afrikanpoetrytheatre.org

Management:
    Chairman: Ann Cheatham
    Executive Director: John Watusi Branch
    Program Coordinator: Sekou Branch
Mission: To offer performances, classes, workshops, cultural reference sources and exhibits to the community.
Founded: 1976
Specialized Field: Music; Poetry; Dance; Children's Crafts
Status: Non-Profit, Professional
Paid Staff: 3
Volunteer Staff: 10
Budget: $450,000
Income Sources: Public Funds, Foundation's Sales
Performs At: Afrikan Poetry Theatre
Annual Attendance: 10,000
Type of Stage: Platform
Stage Dimensions: 18 x 20
Seating Capacity: 100
Year Built: 1930
Year Remodeled: 1979
Rental Contact: Executive Director John Watusi Branch
Organization Type: Performing; Touring; Educational; Sponsoring

3450
NEW YORK STREET THEATRE CARAVAN
8705 Chelsea Street
Jamaica Estates, NY 11432
Phone: 718-657-8070
Management:
    Artistic Director: Marketa Kimbrell
Founded: 1968
Specialized Field: Community Theater; Touring Company; Outdoor Theater
Status: Professional
Organization Type: Performing

3451
COACH HOUSE PLAYERS
12 Augusta Street
Kingston, NY 12402
Mailing Address: PO Box 3481, Kingston, NY 12402
Phone: 845-331-2476
e-mail: mbennett@hvc.rr.com
Web Site: http://www.coachhouseplayers.org/
Mission: To offer the finest possible productions in every aspect of theatre.
Founded: 1950
Specialized Field: Musical; Community Theater
Status: Nonprofit
Performs At: J. Watson Bailey School
Facility Category: Caoch House Building
Organization Type: Performing; Educational

3452
LAKE GEORGE DINNER THEATRE
2223 Canada Street, Rte.9
Lake George, NY 12845
Mailing Address: PO Box 4623, Queensbury, NY. 12804
Phone: 518-306-4404
Fax: 518-798-0735
e-mail: lgot@nycap.com
Web Site: www.lakegeorgedinnertheatre.com
Management:
    Producer: Vicky Eastwood
Founded: 1968
Specialized Field: Summer Stock; Dinner Theater
Status: Professional Equity
Paid Staff: 8
Season: June - October
Organization Type: Performing

3453
CHINESE THEATRE WORKS
37-18 Northern Blvd
Suite 105
Long Island City, NY 11101
Phone: 718-392-3493
Fax: 718-392-3493
e-mail: chinese.theatre.works@gmail.com
Web Site: www.chinesetheatreworks.org
Management:
    Founder, Executive Director, Co-Art: Kuang Yu Fong
    Founder, Co-Artistic Director, Arts: Stephen Katlin
Founded: 1975
Specialized Field: Musical; Ethnic Theater; Community Theater; Puppet; Multi-Cultural
Status: Non-Profit, Professional
Paid Staff: 5
Season: Year-Round

3454
OPEN EYE THEATER
Box 959
960 Main Street
Margaretville, NY 12455
Phone: 845-586-1660
Fax: 845-586-1660
e-mail: openeye@catskill.net
Web Site: www.theopeneye.org
Officers:
    President: Amie Brockway
    Vice President: Linda Kundell,
    Treasurer: Laura Battelani,
    Secretary: Elizabeth Sherr,
    Trustee: Michael Cioffi,
Management:
    Producing Artistic Director: Amie Brockway
    Literary Associate: Sharone Stacey
    Teaching Artists: Elizabeth Sherr
Mission: To create, develop and produce plays for a diverse audience. To provide children, youth, and adults with quality hands-on theatre arts education and performance experiences.
Utilizes: Actors; Artists-in-Residence; Choreographers; Collaborating Artists; Collaborations; Commissioned Composers; Commissioned Music; Composers-in-Residence; Dancers; Designers; Educators; Five Seasonal Concerts; Grant Writers; Guest Accompanists; Guest Artists; Guest Companies; Guest Conductors; Guest Designers; Guest Ensembles; Guest Lecturers; Guest Teachers; Guild Activities; Instructors; Local Artists; Local Artists & Directors; Music; Original Music Scores; Performance Artists; Resident Professionals; Selected Students; Soloists; Student Interns
Founded: 1972
Specialized Field: Educational; Drama; Youth Theater
Status: Non-Profit, Professional
Paid Staff: 5
Volunteer Staff: 30
Paid Artists: 30
Budget: $90,000
Affiliations: TCG; ART/NY; ASS/TEJ/USA; AATE
Annual Attendance: 1,000
Facility Category: Church and Community Hall
Type of Stage: Flexible
Stage Dimensions: 12x16
Seating Capacity: 75
Year Built: 1943

3455
BRISTOL VALLEY THEATER
151 S Main Street
Naples, NY 14512
Mailing Address: PO Box 218, Naples, NY 14512
Phone: 585-374-9032
Fax: 585-374-8520
e-mail: bvt@bvtnaples.org
Web Site: www.bvtnaples.org
Officers:
    President: Susanne G. Kennedy
    Vice President: Richard Booth
    Treasurer: Tim Stone
    Secretary: Laura Harkness
Management:
    Managing Director: Barbara Allen
    Artistic Director: Karin Bowersock
    Associate Artistic Director: David Shane
Mission: Professional summer stock theater.
Founded: 1986
Specialized Field: Musical; Comedy; Contemporary; New Plays
Status: Non-Profit, Professional
Paid Staff: 60
Paid Artists: 30
Season: June - September
Annual Attendance: 10,000
Type of Stage: Proscenium
Seating Capacity: 200

3456
THEATER BARN
654 Route 20
New Lebanon, NY 12125
Phone: 518-794-8989
Web Site: www.theaterbarn.com
Management:
    President: Teresa Brewer
    Vice President: Susan Cobb
    Treasurer: Rosie Interrante
Founded: 1984
Specialized Field: Musical; Comedy; Contemporary
Status: Non-Profit, Professional
Season: June - October
Type of Stage: Proscenium
Stage Dimensions: 30' x 16'
Seating Capacity: 134

3457
NEW PALTZ SUMMER REPERTORY THEATRE
Department of Theatre, Ct 102
SUNY New Paltz, 1 Hawk Drive
New Paltz, NY 12561-2443
Phone: 845-257-3880
Fax: 845-257-3859
e-mail: trezzaf@newpaltz.edu
Web Site: www.newpaltz.edu/summerrep/contact.html
Management:
    Producer: Frank Trezza
    Director of Art Services: David Cavallaro
Founded: 1973
Specialized Field: Educational; Theater Workshops; Summer Stock
Status: Non-Equity; Nonprofit
Season: June - August
Type of Stage: Thrust
Stage Dimensions: 20' x 24'
Seating Capacity: 212

THEATRE / New York

3458
FLEETWOOD STAGE
44 Wildcliff Drive
New Rochelle, NY 10805
Phone: 914-654-8533
Fax: 914-235-4459
e-mail: mailbox@fleetwoodstage.org
Web Site: www.fleetwoodstage.org
Management:
    Producing Director: Lewis Arlt
Founded: 1993
Specialized Field: Musical; Comedy; Youth Theater
Status: Non-Profit, Professional
Performs At: Playhouse at Wildcliff
Type of Stage: Proscenium
Seating Capacity: 100

3459
52ND STREET PROJECT
789 Tenth Avenue
New York, NY 10019
Phone: 212-333-5252
Fax: 212-333-5598
e-mail: info@52project.org
Web Site: www.52project.org
Officers:
    Chairperson: Cathy Dantchik
    President: Robert Goldberg
    MD: Valerie Kay
    Boss: Frances McDormand
Management:
    Director: Steven Graham
    Executive Director: Carol Ochs
    Artistic Director: Gus Rogerson
    Director of Development: John Sheehy
    Arts Administrator: Rachel Chanoff
Founded: 1981
Specialized Field: Experimental; Classic; Contemporary; Ensembles
Status: Non-Profit, Professional
Paid Staff: 7

3460
ABINGDON THEATRE COMPANY
312 W. 36th Street
Sixth floor
New York, NY 10018-7570
Phone: 212-868-2055
Fax: 212-868-2056
e-mail: atcnyc@aol.com
Web Site: www.abingdontheatre.org
Officers:
    Chairman: Timothy P. Speiss
    Vice Chairman: Judy Gluckstern
    Secretary: Susan M. Brown
    Treasurer: Heather Henderson
Management:
    Artistic Director: Jan Buttram
    Managing Director: Samuel J Bellinger
    Associate Artistic Director & Liter: Kim T. Sharp
    Development Director: Heather Henderson
    General Manager: Amanda Kate Joshi
Specialized Field: Staged Readings; Studio Productions

3461
ACTING COMPANY
630 Ninth Avenue
Suite 214
New York, NY 10036
Mailing Address: PO Box 898 New York, NY 10108-0898
Phone: 212-258-3111
Fax: 212-258-3299
e-mail: mail@theactingcompany.org
Web Site: www.theactingcompany.org
Officers:
    Chairman: Edgar Lansbury
    President: Joan M Warburg
    Vice Chairman: Earl D Weiner
    VP: Robert T Goldman
    VP: John C McDonald
    VP: Elinor A Seevak
    Treasurer: Mark Levenfus
    Secretary: Wade Nichols
Management:
    Chairman of the Board: Earl Weiner
    Producing Artistic Director: Margot Harley
    Artistic Director: Ian Belknap
    Director of Development and Communi: Gerry Cornez
    General Manager: Nancy Cook
Mission: Dedicated to the development of classical repertory actors and a national audience for the theatre.
Utilizes: Actors; AEA Actors; Commissioned Music; Five Seasonal Concerts; Guest Companies; Guest Conductors; Guest Designers; Resident Professionals; Singers; Student Interns
Founded: 1972
Specialized Field: Comedy; Youth Theater; Classic; Contemporary
Status: Non-Profit, Professional
Paid Staff: 17
Volunteer Staff: 2
Paid Artists: 20
Budget: $2,500,000
Income Sources: Foundations; Corporations; Individuals
Season: September - May
Affiliations: Actor's Equity; USA; SSDC
Annual Attendance: 65,000
Organization Type: Performing; Touring; Resident; Educational

3462
ACTING STUDIO
CHELSEA REPERTORY COMPANY
Shetler Studio & Theatre
244 W 54th Street, 12th Floor
New York, NY 10019
Phone: 212-580-6600
e-mail: actingstudioinc@yahoo.com
Web Site: www.actingstudio.com
Management:
    Executive Director: James Price
    Associate Director: John Grabowski
Mission: To serve as a training institution; to develop new scripts; to provide a resident theatre company.
Founded: 1983
Specialized Field: Meisner Technique; Theater Workshops
Status: For-Profit, Professional
Paid Staff: 10
Organization Type: Performing; Resident; Educational

3464
AMAS MUSICAL THEATRE
115 MacDougal Street
New York, NY 10012
Phone: 212-563-2565
Fax: 212-239-8332
e-mail: amas@amasmusical.org
Web Site: www.amasmusical.org
Officers:
    Chairman: Marvin Kahan
    President/Secretary: Kermitt Brooks
    Treasurer: Michael Rubenstein
    Vice Chair: Karen Pickerill
Management:
    Founder: Rosetta LeNoire
    Producing Director: Donna Trinkoff
    Teaching Artist/Director: Stephen Nachamie
Mission: To provide a starting place for new American theatrical pieces in a multi-racial environment which instills creative professionalism.
Utilizes: Singers
Founded: 1968
Specialized Field: Musical; Dinner Theater; Classic; Contemporary; Ethnic Theater
Status: Non-Profit, Non-Professional
Paid Staff: 5
Volunteer Staff: 4
Paid Artists: 40
Budget: $200,000-$300,000
Organization Type: Performing; Touring; Resident; Educational; Sponsoring

3465
AMERICAN CENTER FOR STANISLAVSKI THEATRE ART
485 Park Avenue
New York, NY 10022
Phone: 212-308-5458
Management:
    Artistic Director: Sonia Moore
Mission: Bringing Stanislavski's ultimate acting technique and solution to spontaneity, the method of Physical Actions, to American theatre.
Utilizes: Singers
Founded: 1964
Specialized Field: Theater Workshops; Stanislavski Technique; Drama
Status: Professional; Nonprofit
Paid Staff: 15
Income Sources: Alliance of Resident Theatres/New York
Performs At: Trinity Presbyterian Church
Organization Type: Performing; Touring; Educational

3466
AMERICAN PLACE THEATRE
One East 53rd Street
8th Floor
New York, NY 10022
Phone: 212-594-4482
Fax: 212-594-4208
e-mail: contact@americanplacetheatre.org
Web Site: www.americanplacetheatre.org
Officers:
    Chairman: Louis L. Gonda
    Director Theatre/Film: Peter Askin
    Chair: Pamela Fielder
    DBF Associate: David B. Ford
Management:
    Executive Director: David Kener
    Artistic Director: Wynn Handman
    Managing Director/Acting Executive: Jennifer Barnette
    Director of National Education: Gwen Brownson
    Associate Director of Literature to: Rob Bradshaw
Mission: Committed to producing high quality new work by diverse American writers and ti pursuing pluralism and diversity in all endeavors.
Utilizes: Actors; AEA Actors; Artists-in-Residence; Collaborating Artists; Designers; Educators; Guest Accompanists; Guest Conductors; Guest Designers; Guest Teachers; Instructors; Local Artists; Original Music Scores; Performance Artists; Resident Professionals; Soloists; Student Interns
Founded: 1963

THEATRE / New York

Specialized Field: Arts & Literacy
Status: Professional; Nonprofit
Paid Staff: 20
Paid Artists: 25
Budget: $1,200,000
Season: Year-Round
Performs At: Main Stage; Subplot Theatre; First Floor Theatre
Affiliations: AEA; IATSE
Annual Attendance: 10,000
Type of Stage: Proscenium; Black Box
Stage Dimensions: 55' x 35'; 40'x 30'
Seating Capacity: 199-349; 74
Year Built: 1970
Rental Contact: Genral Manager Zafra Whitcomb
Organization Type: Performing

3467
AMERICAN THEATRE OF ACTORS
314 W 54th Street
New York, NY 10019
Phone: 212-581-3044
Fax: 212-956-5761
Web Site: www.americantheatreofactors.org
Management:
   President: James Jennings
   Vice President: Jane Culley
   Secretary: James Bernet
   Treasurer: Jacqueline Pace
Mission: To help to develop new actors, playwrights and directors; to produce new plays.
Founded: 1977
Specialized Field: New Plays
Status: Non-Profit, Professional
Paid Staff: 5
Paid Artists: 120
Organization Type: Performing

3468
ATLANTIC THEATER COMPANY
76 Ninth Avenue
Suite 537
New York, NY 10011
Phone: 212-691-5919
Fax: 212-691-6280
e-mail: admissions@atlantictheater.org
Web Site: www.atlantictheater.org
Officers:
   Chairman: Olaf Olafsson
   Chair, Executive Committee: Carol B. Auerbach
   Chair, Finance Committee: Dan Gross
   Chair, Nominating Committee: Roger E. Kass
   Chair, Education Committee: Michael Slosberg
Management:
   Artistic Director: Neil Pepe
   Managing Director: Jeffory Lawson
   Literary Manager: Abigail Katz
   Director Admissions: Heather Baird
   Director of Development: Cynthia Flowers
Founded: 1985
Specialized Field: Comedy; Youth Theater; Contemporary
Status: Non-Profit, Professional
Performs At: Atlantic Theater Mainstage, Black Box
Type of Stage: Proscenium
Seating Capacity: 160, 70

3469
AXIS COMPANY
1 Sheridan Square
New York, NY 10014
Phone: 212-807-9300
Fax: 212-807-9039
e-mail: info@axiscompany.org
Web Site: axiscompany.org
Management:
   Artistic Director: Randy Sharp
   Executive Producer: Jeff Resnick
Mission: Axis Company was formed with a mission to present aggressive surrealism, classic vaudeville turns and vanguard adaptation.
Founded: 1997

3470
BARROW GROUP
312 W 36th Street
3rd Floor
New York, NY 10018
Phone: 212-760-2615
Fax: 212-760-2962
e-mail: school@barrowgroup.org
Web Site: www.barrowgroup.org
Management:
   Artistic Director: Seth Barish
   Artistic Director: Lee Brock
   Producing Director: Porter Pickard
   School Director: Christel Ferguson
   Director of Education: Robert Serrell
Founded: 1986
Specialized Field: Musical; Comedy; Ethnic Theater; Classic; Contemporary
Status: Non-Profit, Professional
Paid Staff: 5

3471
BAT THEATRE COMPANY
Flea Theater
41 White Street
New York, NY 10013
Phone: 212-226-0051
Fax: 212-965-1808
e-mail: theflea@thebat.com
Web Site: www.theflea.org
Officers:
   Company Manager: Erin Daley
   Audience Development Associate: Ellen Joffred,
Management:
   Artistic Director: Jim Simpson
   Managing Director: Beth Dembrow
   Literary Manager: Gary Winter
   Technical Director: Ben Rush
   Development Associate: Alek Deva
   General Manager: Todd Rosen
   Office Manager: Jen McKenna
   Stage Manager: Rebecca Gura
Founded: 1996
Specialized Field: Comedy; Puppet; Contemporary
Status: Non-Profit, Professional
Paid Staff: 5

3472
BEST OF BROADWAY
729 7th Avenue, 7th Floor
New York, NY 10019
Phone: 212-398-8383
Fax: 916-974-6281
e-mail: gsbo@broadway.com
Web Site: www.broadway.com
Management:
   President: George Royston
   Executive Director: Nina Johnson
   Artistic Director: David L MacDonald
Mission: Dedicated to bringing a live theatrical experience to the community of Sacramento. Through music, song and dance its goals are to educate, entertain and inspire local children, youth and adults.
Utilizes: Selected Students; Sign Language Translators; Soloists; Student Interns
Founded: 1973
Specialized Field: Musical
Status: Non-Profit, Non-Professional
Paid Staff: 2
Volunteer Staff: 100
Paid Artists: 1
Non-paid Artists: 250
Budget: $250,000
Income Sources: Grants; Ticket sales; Concessions
Annual Attendance: 12,000
Facility Category: High School Auditorium
Type of Stage: Proscenium
Seating Capacity: 1,400 per performance
Year Built: 1950
Year Remodeled: 1990

3473
BIG LEAGUE THEATRICALS, INC.
630 Ninth Avenue
Suite 900
New York, NY 10036
Phone: 212-575-1601
Fax: 212-575-9817
e-mail: generalinfo@bigleague.org
Web Site: www.bigleague.org
Officers:
   President/Executive Producer: Daniel Sher
   Vice President/Director of Booking: John Starr
Management:
   General Manager: Mark Johnson
   Associate General Manager: Michael Coglan
   Director/Sales: John Starr
Specialized Field: Specialty Acts

3474
BLACK SPECTRUM
177 Street & Baisley Blvd. Entrance
New York, NY 11434
Mailing Address: 119-07 Merrick Boulevard, Jamaica, NY 11434-2204
Phone: 718-723-1800
Fax: 718-723-1806
Web Site: www.blackspectrum.com
Management:
   Chairperson: Bob Law
   1St Vice Chairman Treasurer: Timothy James
   2Nd Vice Chairman: Arthur French
   Executive Producer & CEO: Carl Clay
Mission: To present socially significant Black classical as well as contemporary works.
Utilizes: Singers
Founded: 1970
Specialized Field: Musical; Dinner Theater; African American
Status: Non-Profit,Professional
Organization Type: Performing; Touring; Educational

3475
BOND STREET THEATRE COALITION
2 Bond Street
New York, NY 10012
Phone: 212-254-4614
Fax: 212-460-9378
e-mail: info@bondst.org
Web Site: www.bondst.org
Officers:
   President: Frank Juliano
   VP: Joanna Sherman

THEATRE / New York

President Emeritus: Patrick Sciarratta
Secretary: Ruth Wikler-Luker
Management:
   Artistic Director: Joanna Sherman
   Managing Director: Michael McGuigan
   Music Director: Sean Nowell
   Communications Director: Olivia Harris
   Project Director: Anna Zastrow
Mission: To develop new works of theatre employing an imagistic and physical vocabulary; to explore politically relevant themes for diverse audiences.
Utilizes: Singers; Soloists; Student Interns
Founded: 1978
Specialized Field: Comedy; Youth Theater; Puppet; Contemporary; Community Theater
Status: Non-Profit, Professional
Paid Staff: 3
Volunteer Staff: 4
Paid Artists: 12
Budget: $150,000
Income Sources: Trust for Mutual Understanding; Art Link; Arts International
Affiliations: ART/NY; NPCC
Organization Type: Performing; Touring; Sponsoring; Artists' Colony

3476
BROADWAY TOMORROW
191 Claremont Avenue
Suite 53
New York, NY 10027
Phone: 212-531-2447
Fax: 212-531-2447
e-mail: solight@aorldnet.att.net
Web Site: www.home.att.~solight
Officers:
   President: Elyse Curtis PhD
   VP: Mitchell Robinson
   Secretary/Treasurer: Norman Curtis
Management:
   Artistic Director: Elyse Curtis
   Music Director: Norman Curtis
Mission: To foster new musicals.
Utilizes: Singers
Founded: 1983
Specialized Field: Musical; New Plays
Status: Professional; Nonprofit
Budget: $25,000
Income Sources: Donations
Organization Type: Performing

3477
CASTILLO THEATRE
543 W 42nd Street
New York, NY 10036
Phone: 212-941-5800
Fax: 212-941-8340
e-mail: castilloth@aol.com
Web Site: www.castillo.org
Management:
   Artistic Director: Dan Friedman
   VP: Diane Stiles
   Dramaturg: Dan Friedman
Founded: 1983
Specialized Field: Musical; Comedy; Community Theater; Puppet; Classic; Contemporary
Status: Non-Profit, Professional
Paid Staff: 2
Volunteer Staff: 70
Non-paid Artists: 18
Performs At: Castillo Theatre
Affiliations: TCG; ART; NY
Type of Stage: Thrust
Seating Capacity: 71
Year Built: 1989

3478
CHICAGO CITY LIMITS
318 W 53rd Street
New York, NY 10019
Phone: 212-888-5233
Fax: 212-888-0810
e-mail: info@chicagocitylimits.com
Web Site: www.chicagocitylimits.com
Officers:
   Director/Executive Producer: Paul Zuckerman
Management:
   Producer: Linda Gelman, info@chicagocitylimits.com
Mission: To offer satirical comedy revues that incorporate audience suggestions for an evening of improvisation, comedy and song. Chicago City Limits also teaches corporate workshops, improv classes, and performs at private events.
Utilizes: Actors; Artists-in-Residence; Composers; Dancers; Filmmakers; Multimedia; Original Music Scores; Resident Artists; Sign Language Translators; Theatre Companies; Volunteer Directors & Actors; Writers
Founded: 1977
Specialized Field: Improvisation
Status: For-Profit, Professional
Paid Staff: 3
Paid Artists: 15
Season: Year-Round
Performs At: Chicago City Limits Theater
Type of Stage: Proscenium
Seating Capacity: 75
Year Built: 1971
Rental Contact: Producer Linda Gelman
Organization Type: Performing; Touring; Resident; Educational
Resident Groups: Chicago City Limits

3479
CLASSIC STAGE COMPANY
136 E 13th Street
New York, NY 10003
Phone: 212-677-4210
Fax: 212-477-7504
Toll-free: 866-811-4111
e-mail: info@classicstage.org
Web Site: www.classicstage.org
Officers:
   Chair: Lynn Angelson
   Vice Chair: Kenneth G. Bartels
   Chair Emeritus: Donald Francis Donovan
Management:
   Executive Director: Greg Reiner
   Artistic Director: Brian Kulick
   General Manager: Jeff Griffin
   Company Manager: John C. Hume
   Marketing & Communications Manager: Meghan Balcom
Mission: Award-winning Off-Broadway theatre committed to re-imagining the classical repertory for a contemporary American audience
Utilizes: Actors; AEA Actors; Choreographers; Collaborating Artists; Collaborations; Commissioned Composers; Commissioned Music; Dance Companies; Educators; Five Seasonal Concerts; Guest Conductors; Guest Designers; Guest Instructors; Guest Musicians; Guest Teachers; Performance Artists; Resident Professionals; Sign Language Translators; Singers; Soloists; Student Interns; Special Technical Talent
Founded: 1967
Specialized Field: Classic
Status: Non-Profit, Professional
Paid Staff: 9
Paid Artists: 100
Budget: $2,000,000
Income Sources: Various
Season: September - May
Performs At: Theater
Affiliations: Actors Equity; USA; American Guild of Musical Artists
Annual Attendance: 17,000
Facility Category: Theater
Type of Stage: 3/4 Thrust
Stage Dimensions: 25'x30'
Seating Capacity: 199
Year Built: 1800
Year Remodeled: 2000
Rental Contact: General Manager Jeff Griffin
Organization Type: Performing; Resident

3480
CREATION PRODUCTION COMPANY
127 Greene Street
New York, NY 10012
Phone: 212-674-5593
Fax: 212-974-5593
e-mail: mosakowski@creationproduction.org
Web Site: www.creationproduction.org/who.htm
Management:
   Executive Director: Jerald Clark
   Director: Anne Hemenway
   Co-Artistic Director: Matthew Maguire
   Co-Artistic Director: Susan Mosakowski
Mission: To create experimental theatre.
Founded: 1977
Specialized Field: Contemporary; Experimental
Status: Non-Profit, Professional
Season: Year-Round
Organization Type: Performing; Touring; Educational

3481
CREATIVE ARTS TEAM
101 W. 31st Street
6th Floor
New York, NY 10001
Phone: 212-652-2800
Fax: 212-995-4151
e-mail: info@creativeartsteam.org
Web Site: www.creativeartsteam.org
Management:
   Executive Director: Lynda Zimmerman
   Artistic and Education Advisor: Chris Vine
   Managing Director: Leslie White
   Playwright-In-Residence: Jim Mirrione
   Artistic & Education Director: Gwendolen Hardwick
Founded: 1974
Specialized Field: Musical; Comedy; Community Theater; Puppet; Classic; Contemporary
Status: Non-Profit, Professional
Paid Staff: 60
Paid Artists: 40
Income Sources: New York State Council on Arts; Theatre Communications Group; New York University
Organization Type: Performing; Touring; Resident; Educational

3482
DISNEY THEATRICAL PRODUCTIONS
214 W. 42nd Street
#300
New York, NY 10036
Phone: 212-827-5400
Fax: 212-703-1048
e-mail: michele.gold@disney.com
Web Site: www.disneyonbroadway.com

Management:
- **Director:** Michele Gold
- **Director/Booking:** Jim Lanahan

Specialized Field: Disney Theater; Touring Company

3483
DIXON PLACE
161A Chrystie St
New York, NY 10002
Phone: 212-219-0736
Fax: 212-219-0761
e-mail: contact@dixonplace.org
Web Site: www.dixonplace.org
Officers:
- **Founder:** Ellie Covan
- **General Contractor:** Michael Howett
- **Port Authorit of NY:** Eric Jensen
- **National Association of Insurance:** Gary Mescher

Management:
- **Founder & Executive Director:** Ellie Covan
- **Managing Director:** Emily Morgan
- **Business & Finance Director:** Benjamin Soencksen
- **Development Director:** Catherine Porter
- **Marketing Director:** Tim Ranney

Founded: 1986
Specialized Field: Ensembles; Contemporary
Performs At: Dixon Place
Type of Stage: Thrust
Seating Capacity: 70

3484
DO GOODER PRODUCTIONS
233 East 86th Street
Suite 2A
New York, NY 10028
Phone: 212-581-8852
e-mail: dgp@dogooder.org
Web Site: www.dogooder.org
Management:
- **Founding/Artistic Executive Directo:** Mark Robert Gordon

Mission: Not for profit, off Broadway theatre company that works in partnership with designated charities.
Founded: 1994
Specialized Field: Theatre
Paid Staff: 2

3485
DON QUIXOTE CHILDREN'S THEATRE
250 W 65th Street
New York, NY 10023
Phone: 212-579-2358
Management:
- **Artistic Director:** Oswaldo Pradere
- **Resident Director:** Stefanie Scott
- **Administrator:** Jim Finn

Mission: To inspire, entertain and educate children through theatre.
Founded: 1972
Specialized Field: Musical; Children's Theater; Puppet
Status: Professional; Nonprofit
Organization Type: Performing; Touring; Resident; Educational

3486
DOWNTOWN ART COMPANY
64 E 4Th Street
New York, NY 10003
Phone: 212-479-0085
e-mail: info@downtownart.org
Web Site: www.downtownart.org
Management:
- **Artistic Director:** Ryan Gilliam

Producing Director: Cliff Scott
Mission: To support the development of contemporary performance works.
Utilizes: Singers
Founded: 1987
Specialized Field: Contemporary
Status: Professional; Nonprofit
Income Sources: National Association of Artists; Alliance of Resident Theatres/New York
Organization Type: Performing; Touring; Sponsoring

3487
DRAMA DEPARTMENT
451 Greenwich Street
7th Floor
New York, NY 10013
Phone: 212-633-9108
Fax: 212-633-9578
e-mail: info@dramadept.org
Web Site: www.dramadept.org
Officers:
- **Development Director:** Clinton Cargill
- **Ticketing Director:** Cheryl French

Management:
- **Artistic Director:** Douglas Carter Beane
- **Managing Director:** Michael S Rosenberg
- **Head Production:** Ilene Rosen
- **Director Operations:** Alexis Rehrmann
- **Director Development:** Clinton Cargill

Mission: A collective of actors, directors, designers, writers and stage managers who collaborate to create new works and revive neglected classics.
Utilizes: AEA Actors; Choreographers; Designers; Filmmakers; Five Seasonal Concerts; Instructors; Local Unknown Artists; Multimedia; Music; Original Music Scores; Performance Artists; Poets; Resident Artists; Resident Professionals; Sign Language Translators; Visual Arts
Founded: 1995
Specialized Field: New Plays; Classic
Status: Non-Profit, Professional
Paid Staff: 2
Volunteer Staff: 2
Budget: $1,000,000
Income Sources: Ticket sales; Grants; Private contributions
Season: July - June
Annual Attendance: 10,000+
Facility Category: Great theatre in old settlement house
Type of Stage: Proscenium
Stage Dimensions: 35'x20'
Seating Capacity: 99
Year Built: 1916
Year Remodeled: 2001
Cost: $3,000,000+
Rental Contact: Alexis Rehrmann

3488
EMERGING ARTISTS THEATRE COMPANY
15 West 28th Street
3rd Floor
New York, NY 10001
Phone: 212-247-2429
e-mail: EatTheatre@gmail.com
Web Site: www.emergingartiststheatre.org
Officers:
- **President:** Roland Dib
- **Senior VP:** Brad Punty
- **VP:** Leigh Giroux
- **Treasurer:** Roger Cooper
- **Chairperson:** Barbara Grecki

Management:
- **Artistic Director:** Paul Adams
- **Manager For Directors:** Blake Lawrence
- **Manager For Playwrights:** Johnathan Reuing
- **Managing Director:** Brad Punty
- **Sales And Marketing:** Ilona Lima

Mission: Emerging Artists Theatre Company exists to provide a safe and secure home for new playwrights to develop their work from an idea to fully realized production and where the playwright remains the key component in the creation and birth of that work.
Founded: 1993
Specialized Field: New Plays; Young Playwrights

3489
EN GARDE ARTS
225 Rector Place
Suite 3A
New York, NY 10280
Phone: 212-941-9793
Fax: 212-274-8123
Management:
- **Managing Director:** Ron Aja
- **Director Development:** Mary McBride

Mission: To commission artists for the purpose of creating theatrical productions that are inspired by socially, historically or architecturally significant sites.
Specialized Field: Experimental; Touring Company
Status: Professional; Nonprofit
Organization Type: Performing

3490
ENSEMBLE STUDIO THEATRE
549 W 52nd Street
2nd Floor
New York, NY 10019
Phone: 212-247-4982
Fax: 212-664-0041
e-mail: info@ensemblestudiotheatre.org
Web Site: www.ensemblestudiotheatre.org
Officers:
- **Treasurer, Chair Emeritus:** G. H. Denniston, Jr.
- **Members Council Co-Chair:** Abigail Gampel
- **Chairman:** Bob Jaffe
- **Vice Chair:** Ann Sachs
- **Secretary:** Susan Vitucci

Management:
- **Artistic Director:** William Carden
- **Managing Director:** John McCormick
- **Executive Director:** Paul A. Slee
- **Finance Director:** Randee Smith
- **Marketing and Box Office Manager:** Ryan Hugh McWilliams

Mission: To nurture and develop the American theatre artist.
Utilizes: Actors; AEA Actors; Choreographers; Dance Companies; Designers; Educators; Guest Designers; Guest Teachers; High School Drama; Instructors; Local Artists; Original Music Scores; Performance Artists; Resident Artists; Resident Professionals; Soloists
Founded: 1972
Specialized Field: Ensembles; New Plays
Status: Non-Profit, Professional
Paid Staff: 14
Volunteer Staff: 25
Paid Artists: 500
Budget: $1.3 million
Season: October - June
Performs At: The Ensemble Studio Theatre
Type of Stage: Black Box; Proscenium
Seating Capacity: 99; 60
Organization Type: Performing

THEATRE / New York

3491
ERGO THEATRE COMPANY
Times Square Station
PO Box 290
New York, NY 10108
Phone: 212-501-2710
e-mail: info@ergotheatre.org
Management:
   Artistic Director: Robert Jay Cronin
   Managing Director: Johanna Pinzler
   Business Manager: Katherine Clark Helzer
Mission: Ergo Theatre Company is making a new home for bright rising talent in the New York theatre community.
Founded: 1997
Specialized Field: Theater Workshops; Staged Readings
Status: Non-Profit

3492
FIJI COMPANY
47 Great Jones Street
New York, NY 10012
Phone: 212-254-7228
Management:
   Artistic Director: Ping Chong
   Managing Director: Joe Jeffcoat
Mission: Created out of a desire to incorporate the visual arts (dance, film, video and theater) into a multimedia show questioning the syntax of global theater.
Utilizes: Singers
Founded: 1972
Specialized Field: Multi-Cultural
Status: Professional; Nonprofit
Income Sources: Theatre Communications Group; Alliance of Resident Theatres/New York
Organization Type: Performing; Touring; Resident; Educational

3493
FOLKSBIENE YIDDISH THEATRE
90 John Street, Suite 410
New York, NY 10038
Phone: 212-213-2120
Fax: 212-213-2186
Web Site: folksbiene.org
Officers:
   Chairman: Jeffrey S. Wiesenfeld
   Vice Chairman: Feliks Frenkel
   President: Mark Mlotek
   Executive Vice President: Charlie Rose
   Vice President: Barnett Zumoff
   Treasurer: Stuart Rosen
   Secretary: Fay Rosenfeld
Management:
   Executive Director: Bryna Wasserman
   Artistic Director: Zalmen Mlotek
Mission: The National Yiddish Theatre- Folksbiene's mission is to celebrate the Yiddish experience through the performing arts and to transmit a rich cultural legacy in exciting new ways that bridge social and cultural divide.
Founded: 1915
Specialized Field: Yiddish Theatre

3494
GLINES
240 W 44th Street
New York, NY 10036
Phone: 212-354-8899
e-mail: Info@DJMProductions.net
Web Site: www.theglines.com
Officers:
   President/Treasurer: John Glines
   VP: Steve Carpenter
   Secretary: Malcolm Wexchler
   Board of Director: Mark Hostetter
Management:
   Artistic Director: John Glines
Mission: To promote positive gay images and dispel negative stereotyping.
Founded: 1976
Specialized Field: Alternative
Status: Nonprofit
Organization Type: Performing

3495
HARBOR THEATRE
90 Main Street
New York, NY 11963
Phone: 631-725-0010
e-mail: harbortheatrenyc@gmail.com
Web Site: www.harbortheatre.org
Management:
   Artistic Director: Stuart Warmflash
   Webmaster: Mark E Lang
   Artistic Associate: Marc Gellar
Mission: In 1994 a group of writers, under that artistic leadership of Stuart Warmflash, began a theatre workshop that would focus on the written word. Its purpose was to provide a safe haven for a few dedicated playwrights to express and refine their personal vision.
Founded: 1994
Specialized Field: Contemporary; Drama
Status: Non-Profit, Professional

3496
HARLEM ARTISTS DEVELOPMENT LEAGUE
207 W 133rd Street
New York, NY 10030
Phone: 212-368-9314
Fax: 212-368-9314
e-mail: harlemplayer@yahoo.com
Web Site: www.harlemplayer.org
Officers:
   Chairwoman of the Board: Delores Dixon
   CEO: Gertrude Jeanette
Management:
   Founder: Gerturde Jeanette
   Artistic Director: Janice Jenkins
   Managing Director: Eric Coleman
Mission: To offer professional theatre to residents of the Harlem community at modest prices; to train artists in speech, acting and dance.
Utilizes: Singers
Founded: 1975
Specialized Field: New Plays; African American; Theater Workshops
Status: Non-Profit, Professional
Paid Staff: 4
Volunteer Staff: 20
Non-paid Artists: 50
Income Sources: NY State Council on the Arise-NYC Cultural Affairs
Performs At: Saint Philips Church
Organization Type: Performing; Resident; Educational

3498
HERE ARTS CENTER
145 6th Avenue Front 1
New York, NY 10013
Phone: 212-647-0202
Fax: 212-647-0257
e-mail: info@here.org
Web Site: www.here.org
Officers:
   Artistic Director: Kristen Marting
   Producing Director: Kim Whitener
   Director: Basil Twist
Management:
   Executive Director: Kristen Marting
   Producer: Barbara Busackijno
   General Manager: Toni Marie Davis
   Founder: Randy Rollison
   General Manager: Amanda Cooper
   Marketing Associate: Trevor Martin
Mission: To support emerging and mid-career artist in all disciplines.
Founded: 1993
Specialized Field: Multi-Media
Status: Nonprofit
Paid Staff: 21
Volunteer Staff: 6
Budget: $1.2 million
Income Sources: Earned; Contributions
Affiliations: Art NY Member
Annual Attendance: 75,000
Facility Category: Multi-Arts Center
Type of Stage: Flexible
Seating Capacity: 99
Year Built: 1993

3499
HISPANIC ORGANIZATION OF LATIN ACTORS
107 Suffolk Street
Suite 302
New York, NY 10002
Phone: 212-253-1015
Fax: 212-253-9651
e-mail: holagram@hellohola.org
Web Site: www.hellohola.org
Officers:
   Chairman HOLA Board: Gonzalo Armendariz
   Executive Director: Manny Alfaro
   President: Manolo Garcja Oliva
   Treasurer: Juan Carlos
   Board Member: Edwin Pag n
Mission: To offer workshops, advocacy-training and referrals.
Utilizes: Singers
Founded: 1975
Specialized Field: Spanish Language Company
Status: Non-Profit, Professional
Paid Staff: 4
Paid Artists: 4
Organization Type: Arts Service Organization

3500
HUDSON GUILD THEATRE
441 W 26th Street
New York, NY 10001
Phone: 212-760-9800
Fax: 212-268-9983
e-mail: info@hudsonguild.org
Web Site: www.hudsonguild.org
Officers:
   President: Arthur Aufses
   Chairman: Paul Balser
   Executive Director: Ken Jockers
   Deputy Executive Director: Miguel Pedraza-Cumba
   Director of Development and Externa: Theresa McKenna

Director of Children and Youth Serv: LeeAnn Scaduto
Management:
   Theatre Director: Jim Furlong
Utilizes: Actors; Commissioned Composers; Commissioned Music; Composers-in-Residence; Five Seasonal Concerts; Guest Accompanists; Guest Choreographers; Guest Conductors; Guest Designers; Local Artists; Performance Artists; Resident Professionals; Singers; Special Technical Talent
Founded: 1895
Specialized Field: Community Theater
Status: Non-Profit
Paid Staff: 1
Budget: $35,000
Facility Category: Theatre
Stage Dimensions: 28'x29'
Seating Capacity: 104
Rental Contact: Jim Furlong
Organization Type: Performing

3501
IGLOO, THE THEATRICAL GROUP
225 E 4th Street
Apartment 6
New York, NY 10009
Phone: 212-460-9055
Web Site: www.iglooigloo.org/
Management:
   Artistic Director: Maria Taribassi
   Artistic Director: Chris Peditto
   Artistic Director: Paul Peditto
Mission: Dedicated to ensemble production of new and rarely seen works.
Founded: 1985
Specialized Field: Musical; New Plays
Status: Professional; Nonprofit
Paid Staff: 10
Organization Type: Performing; Resident

3502
INTAR THEATRE
500 W 52nd Street, 4th Floor
PO Box 756
New York, NY 10108
Mailing Address: PO Box 756, New York, NY, 10108
Phone: 212-695-6134
Fax: 212-268-0102
e-mail: intar@intartheatre.org
Web Site: www.intartheatre.org
Management:
   Executive Director: Editha Rosario
   Artistic Director: Eduardo Machado
   Founder: Max Ferra
Mission: INTAR brings to the public the vital and energetic voices of both promising & accomplished Latin theatre professionals.
Utilizes: Actors; AEA Actors; Curators; Designers; Fine Artists; Local Artists; Performance Artists; Resident Professionals; Singers; Visual Arts
Founded: 1966
Specialized Field: New Plays; Spanish Language Company
Status: Non-Profit, Professional
Paid Staff: 5
Income Sources: Non-profit funding
Season: October - June
Affiliations: Theatre Communications Group, Alliance of Resident Theatres (NY)
Facility Category: Off-Broadway Theater
Organization Type: Performing

3503
INTERBOROUGH REPERTORY THEATER
154 Christopher Street
Suite 3B
New York, NY 10014
Phone: 212-206-6875
Fax: 212-206-7037
e-mail: info@irttheater.org
Web Site: http://irttheater.org
Officers:
   President: Mimi Craig
   Secretary: Pamala L La Bonne
   Associate Producer: Chad Kessler
   Artistic Consultant: Dorit Avganim
Management:
   Artistic Director: Kori Rushton
   Executive Director: Jonathan Fluck
   Development Director: Stacy Donovan
   Artistic Consultant: Ben Vershbow
   Technical Director: Matthew Vieira
Mission: To offer adaptations of literature and history as well as issues of interest to disenfranchized audiences; to provide standard repertory for general audiences.
Utilizes: Singers
Founded: 1986
Specialized Field: Musical; Historical
Status: Semi-Professional; Nonprofit
Income Sources: Brooklyn Arts & Cultural Association; Actors' Equity Association; Encore; Saturday Theater for Children; Division of American Theater Wing
Organization Type: Performing; Touring; Educational

3504
IRISH ARTS CENTRE THEATRE
553 W 51st Street
New York, NY 10019
Phone: 212-757-3318
Fax: 212-247-0930
e-mail: info@irishartscenter.org
Web Site: http://irishartscenter.org/
Management:
   Artistic Director: Neal Jones
Mission: Preserving, celebrating and developing Irish culture in America through producing New Irish, Classic Irish, and Irish-American plays.
Founded: 1972
Specialized Field: Children's Theater; Theater Workshops
Status: Professional; Nonprofit
Paid Staff: 50
Volunteer Staff: 30
Season: Year-Round
Performs At: Irish Arts Center Theatre
Stage Dimensions: 23x15x1000
Seating Capacity: 99
Year Built: 1972
Year Remodeled: 1995
Organization Type: Performing; Resident

3505
IRONDALE ENSEMBLE PROJECT
PO Box 150604
New York, NY 11215
Mailing Address: 85 South Oxford Street, Brooklyn, NY 11217
Phone: 718-488-9233
Fax: 718-488-9185
e-mail: press@irondale.org
Web Site: www.irondale.org
Officers:
   Managing Director: Maria Knapp
   Artistic Director: Jim Niesen
   Executive Director: Terry Greiss
   Education Director: Amanda Hinkle
Management:
   Facilities Manager: Michaelangelo DeSerio
Founded: 1983
Specialized Field: Comedy; Youth Theater; Classic; Contemporary
Status: Non-Profit, Professional
Paid Staff: 4
Paid Artists: 8

3506
JAM AND COMPANY
331 W 38th Street
#5
New York, NY 10018
Phone: 212-714-2263
Fax: 212-594-1245
Management:
   Artistic Director: John Amudd
Founded: 1985
Specialized Field: Drama; Contemporary
Status: Semi-Professional
Organization Type: Performing

3507
JEAN COCTEAU REPERTORY
330 Bowery
New York, NY 10012
Phone: 212-677-0060
Fax: 212-777-6151
e-mail: cocteau@jeancocteaurep.org
Web Site: www.jeancocteaurep.org
Officers:
   President: David Jiranek
   VP: John Horn
   Secretary: Carmen Anthony
Management:
   President: Mark Gamell
   Artistic Director: David Fuller
   Managing Director: Merediph Zolty
   Director Development: Deborah Aaronson
Mission: Committed to presenting innovative productions of the world's classics; dedicated to sustaining a resident company presenting rotating repertory.
Utilizes: Actors; Artists-in-Residence; Choreographers; Collaborating Artists; Commissioned Music; Designers; Guest Artists; Guest Companies; Guest Conductors; Guest Designers; Guest Lecturers; Music; Original Music Scores; Performance Artists; Resident Artists; Resident Professionals; Soloists; Student Interns; Theatre Companies
Founded: 1971
Specialized Field: Musical; Comedy; Classic; Contemporary
Status: Non-Profit, Professional
Paid Staff: 10
Volunteer Staff: 5
Paid Artists: 20
Budget: $850,000
Income Sources: Box Office; Individuals; Corporations; Foundation
Performs At: Bouwerie Lane Theatre
Affiliations: Theatre Communications Group; Alliance of Resident Theatres/New York
Annual Attendance: 22,000
Facility Category: Theatre
Type of Stage: Proscenium
Stage Dimensions: 17'x22'x13'
Seating Capacity: 140
Year Built: 1960
Year Remodeled: 1996
Rental Contact: Ernest Johns

THEATRE / New York

Organization Type: Performing; Resident; Educational
Resident Groups: Jean Cocteau Repertory

3509
KOHAV THEATRE FOUNDATION
118 Riverside Drive
New York, NY 10024
Phone: 212-877-1667
Fax: 212-799-3589
Management:
   President: Hava Beller
   Production Assistant: Kathleen Greene
   Counsel: Herbert C Kantor
Utilizes: Singers
Founded: 1979
Specialized Field: Contemporary
Status: Non-Profit, Professional
Organization Type: Performing

3510
LA MAMA EXPERIMENTAL THEATRE
74A E 4th Street
New York, NY 10003
Phone: 212-475-7710
Fax: 212-254-7597
e-mail: lamama@lamama.org
Web Site: www.lamama.org
Management:
   President: Frank Carucci
   Founder/Director: Ellen Stewart
   Associate Director: Beverly Petty
   Business Manager: Gretchen Green
Utilizes: Student Interns; Touring Companies; Visual Arts
Founded: 1961
Specialized Field: Experimental
Status: Non-Profit, Professional
Budget: $1,500,000
Income Sources: Foundations; Government; Ticket Revenue; Playwright Royalties
Performs At: Experimantal Theatre; Dance; Opera
Annual Attendance: 30,000
Facility Category: Theatre (3 venues) 1 Gallery
Seating Capacity: 100; 400
Organization Type: Performing; Producing

3511
LABYRINTH THEATER COMPANY
155 Bank Street
New York, NY 10014
Phone: 212-513-1080
e-mail: lab@labtheater.org
Web Site: labtheater.org
Officers:
   Chairman: Jeffrey A. Horwitz
Management:
   Artistic Director: Mimi O'Donnell
   Managing Director: Danny Feldman
   General Manager: Robert A. Sherrill
Founded: 1992
Performs At: Bank Street Theater

3512
LAMB'S THEATRE COMPANY
130 W 44th Street
New York, NY 10036
Phone: 212-575-0300
Fax: 212-302-7847
e-mail: office@lambstheatre.org
Web Site: http://www.lambsthreatre.org/
Officers:
   Chairman: Kendyl K Monroe
   Secretary: Patricia McCorkle
Management:
   Producing Director: Carolyn Rossi-Copeland
   Production Manager: Clark Cameron
   Producer: Carolyn Rossi-Copeland
   Assistant to the Producer: Chris Cragin Day
   House Manager/ Assistant to the Pro: Mary Kickel
Mission: To develop and present the work of new American theatre artists hoping to offer positive solutions to modern ethical problems.
Founded: 1980
Specialized Field: New American Works
Status: Professional; Nonprofit
Income Sources: Theatre Communications Group; Alliance of Resident Theatres/New York
Performs At: Lamb's Theatre; Lamb's Little Theatre
Organization Type: Performing; Touring; Educational

3513
LATIN AMERICAN THEATRE EXPERIMENT & ASSOCIATES
107 Suffolk Street
New York, NY 10002
Phone: 212-529-1948
Management:
   Executive Director: Margarita Toirac
   Founder: Mario Pena
Mission: Our purpose is to expand the theatre movement to the Spanish and English communities.
Founded: 1970
Specialized Field: Spanish Language Company; Experimental
Status: Professional; Nonprofit
Type of Stage: Proscenium
Stage Dimensions: 25'x20'x14'
Seating Capacity: 150
Organization Type: Performing; Touring; Resident; Educational

3514
LIGHTNING STRIKES THEATRE COMPANY
PO Box 1545
New York, NY 10028
Phone: 212-713-5335
Management:
   Artistic Director: John Mcdermott
   Managing Director: Lori Funk
Specialized Field: Experimental; New Plays

3515
LIVING THEATRE
21 Clinton Street
New York, NY 10002
Phone: 212-982-2335
Fax: 212-865-3234
Web Site: www.livingtheatre.org/
Officers:
   President: Hanon Reznikov
Management:
   Executive Director: Hanon Reznikov
   Artistic Director: Judith Malina
   Managing Director: Joanie Fritz
Mission: To create socially relevant theatre to be performed by an artistic ensemble of the highest calibre.
Founded: 1947
Specialized Field: New Works of Social Importance
Status: Nonprofit
Income Sources: Alliance of Resident Theatres/New York; Theatre Communications Group
Organization Type: Performing; Touring; Resident; Educational

3516
MABOU MINES
Peter Stuyvesant Station
PO Box 4910
New York, NY 10009
Phone: 212-473-0559
Fax: 212-473-2410
e-mail: info@maboumines.org
Web Site: www.maboumines.org
Officers:
   President: Sharon Fogarty
   Artistic Director: Ruth Maleczech
   Artistic Director: Julie Archer
   Artistic Director: Lee Breuer
   Artistic Director: Sharon Fogarty
   Artistic Director: Frederick Neumann
Management:
   President: Joe Stalkell
   Artistic Director: Ruth Maleczech
Mission: To look at theater in fresh ways by re-exploring existing theatrical works and creating new ones.
Utilizes: Singers
Founded: 1970
Specialized Field: Classic; Contemporary
Status: Non-Profit, Professional
Affiliations: Theatre Communications Group; Alliance of Resident Theatres/New York
Type of Stage: Block Box
Organization Type: Performing; Touring; Educational

3517
MANHATTAN THEATRE CLUB
311 W 43rd Street
8th Floor
New York, NY 10036
Phone: 212-399-3040
Fax: 212-399-3066
e-mail: patron@mtc-nyc.org
Web Site: www.manhattantheatreclub.com
Officers:
   Chairman: David C. Hodgson
   President: Bethany Millard
   Treasurer: W. Gregg Slager
   Secretary: Barbara J. Fife
Management:
   Artistic Director: Lynne Meadow
   Executive Producer: Barry Grove
   General Manager: Florie Seery
Mission: Encouraging, developing, and presenting important new American and international work that provides insight into culture, life and conflict.
Founded: 1970
Specialized Field: Musical; Comedy; Ethnic Theater; Contemporary
Status: Non-Profit, Professional
Paid Staff: 60
Volunteer Staff: 25
Income Sources: Theatre Communications Group; Alliance of Resident Theatres/New York; Foundation for the Extension and Development of American Professional Theatre
Organization Type: Performing

3518
MARCEL MARCEAU MIME THEATER
253 W 73rd Street
Suite 8G
New York, NY 10023
Phone: 212-874-2030
Fax: 212-874-1175
e-mail: staff@marceau.org
Specialized Field: Mime

3519
MCC THEATER
311 W 43rd Street
New York, NY 10036
Phone: 212-727-7722
Fax: 212-727-7780
e-mail: mcc@mcctheater.org
Web Site: www.mcctheater.org
Management:
    Executive Director: John Schultz
    Artistic Director: Robert Lupone
    Literary Manager: Stephen Willems
Founded: 1986
Specialized Field: Drama; Musical
Status: Non-Profit, Professional
Paid Staff: 9
Paid Artists: 6

3520
METROPOLITAN PLAYHOUSE
220 E 4th Street
New York, NY 10009
Phone: 212-995-8410
e-mail: connect@metropolitanplayhouse.org
Web Site: www.metropolitianplayhouse.org
Management:
    President: Alex Roe
    Comapany Manager: Ed Chemaly
    Literary Manager: Kim Wadsworth
Founded: 1992
Specialized Field: Drama; Comedy; Musical
Status: Non-Profit, Professional
Paid Artists: 4

3521
MINT THEATER COMPANY
311 West 43rd Street, 3rd Floor
New York, NY 10036
Phone: 212-315-9434
Fax: 212-977-5211
e-mail: mint@minttheater.org
Web Site: minttheater.org
Management:
    Producing Artistic Director: Jonathan Bank
Mission: Mint Theater Company commits to bringing new vitality to worthy but neglected plays. We excavate buried theatrical treasures; reclaiming them for our time through research, dramaturgy, production, publication, and a variety of enrichment programs; and we advocate for their ongoing life in theaters across the world.
Founded: 1992
Status: Nonprofit

3522
MIRROR REPERTORY COMPANY
PO Box 478,
217 E. 70th Street
New York, NY 10021
Phone: 646-688-4365
Fax: 646-688-4365
Toll-free: 866-647-7371
e-mail: mirrorrep@gmail.com
Web Site: www.mirrorrepertory.com
Management:
    Board Chairman: Donna Ward
    Managing Director: Marilyn Miller
    Artistic Director: Sabra Jones
Mission: The Mirror Repertory Company, aka Mirror Theatre Ltd., was founded in 1983. It was a daring return to the European theatre style of alternating repertory theatre—a different play each night as in the ballet and the opera.
Founded: 1982
Specialized Field: Musical; Comedy; Youth Theater; Ethnic Theater; Classic; Contemporary
Status: Non-Profit, Professional
Paid Staff: 6
Income Sources: Actors' Equity Association
Performs At: Mirror Repertory Theater
Organization Type: Performing; Resident; Educational

3523
MUSIC THEATRE ASSOCIATES
1841 Broadway
Suite 914
New York, NY 10023
Phone: 212-841-9690
Fax: 212-841-9542
e-mail: jsimpson@cami.com
Web Site: www.camitheatricals.com
Management:
    President: Gary McKvay
    COO: Aldo Scrofani
Founded: 1981
Specialized Field: Musical; Contemporary; New Plays
Paid Staff: 100
Paid Artists: 100

3524
MUSIC THEATRE GROUP AT LENOX ARTS CENTER
30 W 26th Street #1001
New York, NY 10010
Phone: 212-366-5260
Fax: 212-366-5265
Officers:
    Co- Chairman: Katheryn Walker
    Co- Chairman: Charles Hollerith
    President: Lyn Austin
    VP: Lynda Sthrner Traum
Management:
    Producing Director: Lyn Austin
    General Director: Diane Wondisford
    Associate Producer: Charlotte Kreutz
    Development: Peter Krasny
Mission: Exclusively engaged in and dedicated to the creation of new musical theatre works with distinctive focus on developing new forms and artists through unique combinations of music, theatre, dance and visual arts.
Utilizes: Singers
Founded: 1970
Specialized Field: Musical; New Plays
Status: Professional; Nonprofit
Budget: $80,000
Income Sources: Box Office, Grants, Private Donations
Organization Type: Performing; Touring

3525
NATIONAL BLACK THEATRE
2031 5th Avenue
New York, NY 10035
Phone: 212-722-3800
Fax: 212-926-1571
e-mail: info@nationalblacktheatre.org
Web Site: http://www.nationalblacktheatre.org/
Officers:
    Founder/CEO: Barbara Ann Teer
Management:
    Executive Director: Shirley Faison
    Performing Program Director: Tunde Samuel
    Action Arts Director: Ade Faison
Mission: To enhance human dignity by increasing the unity, appreciation and availability of Black Theatre.
Founded: 1968
Specialized Field: African American
Status: Professional; Nonprofit
Affiliations: Harlem Strategic Cultural Collaborative, Coalition of Theatres of Color and Harlem Arts Alliance

3526
NATIONAL BLACK TOURING CIRCUIT
790 Riverside Drive
Suite 3E
New York, NY 10032
Phone: 212-283-0974
Fax: 212-353-1176
e-mail: NATBLKTC@AOL.COM
Web Site: www.nationalblacktouringcircuit.org
Officers:
    Co-Chairman: Shaunielle Perry
Management:
    Producer/Director: Woodie King Jr
    Associate Producer: Ashia Dervisa
Mission: To tour plays to colleges, festivals, and black cultural institutions across the USA, Europe, and Africa.
Utilizes: Singers; Special Technical Talent; Theatre Companies
Founded: 1976
Specialized Field: African American; Touring Company
Status: Professional; Nonprofit
Paid Staff: 3
Paid Artists: 25
Non-paid Artists: 2
Budget: $240,000
Income Sources: Contracted Services
Organization Type: Performing; Touring; Resident; Educational

3527
NATIONAL IMPROVISATIONAL THEATRE
223 8th Avenue
New York, NY 10011
Phone: 212-243-7224
Fax: 212-366-4312
Management:
    Executive Director: Christopher Smith
    Artistic Director: Tamara Wilcox-Smith
    VP Public Relations: Robert Martin
    VP Operations: Eva Mahoney
Mission: To bring art improvisation to the highest possible level.
Founded: 1984
Specialized Field: Improvisation
Status: Professional; Nonprofit
Paid Staff: 30
Organization Type: Performing; Educational

3528
NATIONAL SHAKESPEARE COMPANY
353 W 48th Street
3Rd Floor
New York, NY 10036
Phone: 212-265-1340
Fax: 212-265-1258
e-mail: nsc62@aol.com
Management:
    Producing Director: Deborah Teller
    Tour Director: Val Sherman
    Education Director: Heather Drastal
Mission: Nurturing and developing performing arts through touring professional, live theatre to American communities.
Founded: 1963
Specialized Field: Touring Company; Shakespeare
Status: Professional
Season: September - May
Organization Type: Performing; Touring

THEATRE / New York

3529
NEGRO ENSEMBLE COMPANY
303 W 42nd St, Ste 501
New York, NY 10036
Phone: 212-582-5860
Fax: 212-582-9639
e-mail: newgroup1@earthlink.net
Web Site: www.necinc.org/
Management:
    Artistic Director: Scott Elliot
    Executive Director: Geoffrey Rich
    Literary Manager: Ian Morgan
    Associate Executive Director: Josh Boggioni
Mission: To offer plays about the Black experience.
Utilizes: Singers
Founded: 1967
Specialized Field: African American; Multi-Cultural
Status: Professional; Nonprofit
Performs At: Theatre Four
Organization Type: Performing; Touring

3530
NEW DRAMATISTS
424 W 44th Street
New York, NY 10036
Phone: 212-757-6960
Fax: 212-265-4738
e-mail: newdramatists@newdramatists.org
Web Site: www.newdramatists.org
Officers:
    Chairman: Seth Gelblum
    President: Isobel Robins Koneccy
Management:
    Executive Director: Joel K Rukark
    Artistic Director: Todd London
Mission: To develop plays and playwrights.
Founded: 1949
Specialized Field: New Plays; Young Playwrights
Status: Non-Profit, Professional
Paid Staff: 7
Volunteer Staff: 50
Non-paid Artists: 55
Income Sources: National Endowment for the Arts
Performs At: New Dramatists Theater
Organization Type: Resident; Educational

3531
NEW FEDERAL THEATRE
292 Henry Street
New York, NY 10002
Phone: 212-353-1176
Fax: 212-353-1088
e-mail: info@newfederaltheatre.org
Web Site: www.newfederaltheatre.org
Management:
    Producing Director: Woodie King Jr
    Company Director: Pat White
    Marketing Director: Shea Douglas
Mission: To present both new and unknown works; to allow unknown and known directors and actors the opportunity to work together.
Utilizes: Actors; AEA Actors; Performance Artists; Resident Professionals
Founded: 1970
Specialized Field: Musical; Comedy; Community Theater; Classic; Contemporary
Status: Non-Profit, Professional
Income Sources: Actors' Equity Association; Alliance of Resident Theatres/New York; Theatre Communications Group; Foundations; Corporate and Private Individuals
Season: September 30 - June 30
Performs At: Henry Street Settlement; New Federal Theater
Organization Type: Performing; Resident

3532
NEW GEORGES
109 W 27th Street
Suite 9A
New York, NY 10001
Phone: 646-336-8077
Fax: 646-336-8077
e-mail: info@newgeorges.org
Web Site: www.newgeorges.org
Management:
    Artistic Director: Susan Bernfield
    Associate Director: Sarah C Sunde
Founded: 1992
Specialized Field: Women's Theater
Status: Non-Profit, Professional
Paid Staff: 2
Paid Artists: 30

3533
NEW PERSPECTIVES THEATRE COMPANY
456 West 37th Street
New York, NY 10018
Phone: 212-630-9945
Fax: 212-594-2553
e-mail: contact@newperspectivestheatre.org
Web Site: newperspectivestheatre.org
Officers:
    Executive Director: Ellen Richard
    Chair: Stephen Foreht
Management:
    Artistic Director: Melody Brooks
    General Manager: Catharine Guiher
Mission: To develop and present new plays and playwrights, particularly women and people of color; present classic plays in a style that sheds new light on our lives and work and; present theatre to under-served audiences-especially young people- to build life skills and promote participation in our society.
Status: Nonprofit

3534
NEW RAFT THEATER COMPANY
450 W 42nd Street
Suite 2J
New York, NY 10036
Phone: 212-268-5501
Fax: 212-967-1458
Management:
    Executive Director: Eric Krebs
    Artistic Director: Avi Ber Hoffman
    Executive Director: Eric Krebs
Mission: To find and develop original plays and musicals.
Founded: 1976
Specialized Field: Musical; New Plays
Status: Professional; Nonprofit
Performs At: Houseman Theatre Complex
Organization Type: Performing

3535
NEW YORK STAGE & FILM
109 West 27th Street
Suite 9A
New York, NY 10001
Phone: 646-336-8077
Fax: 646-336-8077
e-mail: info@newyorkstageandfilm.org
Web Site: http://www.newyorkstageandfilm.org/
Officers:
    President: Marc Segan
Management:
    Producing Director: Woodie King Jr
    Company Director: Pat White
    Marketing Director: Shea Douglas
Founded: 1984
Specialized Field: New Plays

3536
NEW YORK THEATRE WORKSHOP
79 E 4th Street
New York, NY 10003
Phone: 212-780-9037
Fax: 212-460-8996
e-mail: TellJim@nytw.org
Web Site: www.nytw.org
Officers:
    Education Director: Bryn Thorsson
    Marketing Director: Rebekah Paine
    Ticket Service Manager: Danielle Doherty
    Director of Finance & Administratn: Rachel McBeth
Management:
    Artistic Director: James C. Nicola
    Managing Director: Jeremy Blocker
    Associate Artistic Director: Linda S. Chapman
    Casting Director: Jack Doulin CSA
    Artistic Intern: Madie Oldfield
Mission: To offer inventive new plays; to showcase new directors.
Founded: 1980
Specialized Field: Theater Workshops; Educational
Status: Non-Profit, Professional
Paid Staff: 25
Volunteer Staff: 25
Paid Artists: 150
Non-paid Artists: 300
Income Sources: Actors' Equity Association; Theatre Communications Group; Alliance of Resident Theatres/New York
Performs At: New York Theatre Workshop
Type of Stage: Proscenium
Seating Capacity: 189
Organization Type: Performing

3537
OHIO THEATRE
66 Wooster
New York, NY 10012
Phone: 212-966-4844
Management:
    Artistic Director: Robert Lyons
Mission: To offer experimental theatre.
Founded: 1977
Specialized Field: Experimental
Status: Professional
Income Sources: Downtown Theatre Coalition
Performs At: Ohio Theatre
Organization Type: Performing; Sponsoring

3538
ONTOLOGICAL-HYSTERIC THEATER
260 West Broadway
New York, NY 10013
Phone: 212-941-8911
Fax: 212-334-5149
e-mail: ontological@mindspring.com
Web Site: www.ontological.com
Officers:
    Artistic Director: Richard Foreman
    Administrator Director: Mimi Johnson
Management:
    Artistic Director: Richard Foreman
    Administrator: Mimi Johnson

Mission: Producing and presenting the works of playwright, director and designer Richard Foreman.
Founded: 1968
Specialized Field: New Plays; Contemporary
Status: Non-Profit
Paid Staff: 1
Paid Artists: 8
Performs At: Ontological at St. Mark's Theater
Type of Stage: Black box
Seating Capacity: 85
Organization Type: Performing

3539
OPEN BOOK
525 W End Avenue
12E
New York, NY 10024-3207
Phone: 212-362-0329
e-mail: info@openbooktheatre.org
Web Site: www.theopenbook.net
Officers:
    Board: Mary Higgins Clark
    Board: Mario Fratti
    Board: Rev Kathleen L Camera
    Board: Marc Lewis
    Board: Beverly Penberthy
Management:
    Artistic Director: Marvin Kaye
    Public Relations Director: Nancy Temple
    Educational Division Director: Kathleen C Szaj
Mission: Producing new and little-known literature of quality in readers theatre format.
Founded: 1975
Specialized Field: Reading Theatre
Status: Professional; Nonprofit
Volunteer Staff: 3
Income Sources: Various
Performs At: Various
Annual Attendance: 300 - 500
Type of Stage: Modified Platform
Stage Dimensions: Varies
Seating Capacity: 70 - 100
Organization Type: Performing; Touring; Resident

3540
OPEN EYE: NEW STAGINGS
270 W 89th Street
New York, NY 10024
Fax: 212-769-4141
Officers:
    Chairman: Stephen Graham
    VP: Joan Stein
    Secretary: Elliot Brown
Management:
    Founding Director: Jean Erdman
    Artistic Director: Amie Brockway
    Production Manager/Business Manager: Adrienne Brockway
Mission: Presents productions of new and rare plays, plays geared for family audiences and provides playwrights the opportunity to develop new works through the New Stagings Lab.
Utilizes: Singers
Founded: 1972
Specialized Field: New Plays
Status: Professional; Nonprofit
Income Sources: Theatre Communications Group; Alliance of Resident Theatres/New York; International Association of Theatre for Children and Youth
Performs At: The Open Eye; New Stagings
Organization Type: Performing; Touring; Educational

3541
PAN ASIAN REPERTORY THEATRE
520 8th Avenue
3rd Floor, Room 314
New York, NY 10018
Mailing Address: 47 Great Jones Street, New York, NY, 10012
Phone: 212-868-4030
Fax: 212-868-4033
e-mail: info@panasianrep.org
Web Site: www.panasianrep.org
Officers:
    Chairman: Sybil Nadel
    Vice Chairman: Muzaffar Chishti
    Artistic Producing Director: Tisa Chang
    Chair: Dale Leach
Management:
    Chairman: Sybel Nadel
    Artistic Producing Director: Tisa Chang
    Communications Director: Sylvie H Fan
Mission: To offer new Asian-American plays of the highest artistic standards, as well as adaptations of classics from around the world; to premiere Asian masterworks in America.
Founded: 1983
Specialized Field: Asian American; Multi-Cultural
Status: Professional; Nonprofit
Paid Staff: 4
Volunteer Staff: 10
Paid Artists: 50
Income Sources: Theatre Communications Group: Alliance of Resident Theatres/New York
Performs At: West End Theatre
Type of Stage: Proscenium
Organization Type: Performing; Touring; Resident; Educational

3542
PAPER BAG PLAYERS
185 East Broadway
New York, NY 10002
Phone: 212-353-2332
Fax: 212-362-0431
Toll-free: 800-777-2247
e-mail: pbagp@verizon.net
Web Site: http://www.thepaperbagplayers.org
Officers:
    President: Alison Harmelin
    Treasurer: Judi Blitzer
    Secretary: Patricia Langer
Management:
    Managing Director: Michael Oakes
    Artistic Director: Ted Brackett
    Education Director: Audrey Reilly
Mission: To create a contemporary theatre for children with shows based on a child's everyday experiences and perceptions of the world.
Utilizes: Actors; Choreographers; Collaborating Artists; Collaborations; Contract Actors; Dancers; Designers; Equity Actors
Founded: 1958
Specialized Field: Children's Theater
Status: Professional; Nonprofit
Paid Staff: 9
Paid Artists: 10
Budget: $90,000
Organization Type: Performing; Touring; Resident; Educational

3543
PARK AVENUE THEATRICAL GROUP
404 Park Avenue S
10th Floor
New York, NY 10016
Phone: 212-213-5270
Fax: 212-689-9140
e-mail: jkravat@parny.com
Management:
    Director Sales: Carol Bresner
Specialized Field: Drama; Contemporary

3544
PARTIAL COMFORT PRODUCTIONS
520 8th Avenue Suite 331
New York, NY 10018
Phone: 212-502-7985
e-mail: chad@partialcomfort.org
Web Site: partialcomfort.org
Management:
    Artistic Director: Chad Beckim
    Artistic Director: Molly Pearson
    Associate Producer: John Baker
Mission: Devoted to development and production of innovative theatrical events. Our plays are written by our member writers and brought to life on stage by our actors, directors, and designers. We strive to produce theater that is both inspiring and challenging to the first time theatergoer and the seasonal aficionado alike.
Founded: 2002
Status: Nonprofit
Performs At: The Wild Project 195 East 3rd Street, New York, NY 10009

3545
PEARL THEATRE COMPANY
307 West 38th Street #1805
New York, NY 10003
Phone: 212-505-3401
Fax: 212-505-3404
e-mail: info@pearltheatre.org
Web Site: www.pearltheatre.org
Officers:
    Chairperson: Brian Heidtke
    President: Ellen Hirsch
    Treasurer: Jean Cheever
    Secretary: Ellen Jakobson
    Artistic Director: Hal Brook
    Managing Director: David Roberts
    Marketing Director: Jess Burkle
Management:
    Executive Director: Shepard Sobel
    Director Development: Margaret Benson
    Marketing Director: Jess Burkle
    Dramaturg: Kate Farrington
    GM: Corey Pearlstein
    Production Manager: Dale Smallwood
    Dramaturg and Artistic Associate: Kate Farrington
Mission: To present a full-range repertory strongly rooted in the classics with a resident acting company, guest artists and theatre staff.
Founded: 1982
Specialized Field: Classic; Ensembles
Status: Non-Profit, Professional
Paid Staff: 8
Volunteer Staff: 50
Paid Artists: 35
Budget: $1.5 million
Income Sources: Foundations; Individual Giving; Earned Income
Performs At: Theatre
Annual Attendance: 27,000

THEATRE / New York

Facility Category: Theatre with Lobby, Box Office and Dressing Rooms
Type of Stage: Proscenium
Stage Dimensions: 22' x 44'
Seating Capacity: 160
Rental Contact: Production Manager Dale Smallwood
Organization Type: Performing; Resident; Educational

3546
PECULIAR WORKS PROJECT
595 Broadway
2nd Floor
New York, NY 10012-3222
Phone: 212-529-3626
Fax: 212-529-3626
e-mail: info@peculiarworks.org
Web Site: www.peculiarworks.org
Management:
    President: Ralph Lewis
    Artistic Director: Catherine Porter
    Managing Director: Barry Rowell
Mission: Peculiar Works Project generates original, multi-disciplinary performance that is accessible and fun for diverse audiences.
Founded: 1993
Specialized Field: Multi-Media; Touring Company; New Plays
Status: Non-Profit, Professional
Paid Artists: 20

3547
PING CHONG & COMPANY
47 Great Jones Street
New York, NY 10012
Phone: 212-529-1557
Fax: 212-529-1703
e-mail: info@PINGCHONG.ORG
Web Site: http://www.pingchong.org/info.html
Management:
    Artistic Director: Ping Chong
    Managing Director: Bruce Allardice
Specialized Field: Touring Company; Contemporary; Multi-Cultural

3548
PLAYWRIGHTS HORIZONS
416 W 42nd Street
New York, NY 10036
Phone: 212-564-1235
Fax: 212-594-0296
e-mail: marketing@playwrightshorizons.org
Web Site: www.playwrightshorizons.org
Officers:
    Chair: Judith Rubin
    Vice Chair: Lawrence Buttenwieser
    Secretary: Amy McIntosh
    Treasurer: Herbert Morey
    Artistic Director: Tim Sanford
Management:
    Artistic Director: Tim Sanford
    Managing Director: Leslie Marcus
    General Manager: Carol Fishman
    Associate General Manager: Casey York
Mission: Developing American composers, lyricists and playwrights; offering internships and training programs.
Utilizes: Singers
Founded: 1971
Specialized Field: Musical; Comedy; Contemporary
Status: Non-Profit, Professional
Paid Staff: 25
Income Sources: Actors' Equity Association; Alliance of Resident Theatres/New York; New York University
Performs At: Mainstage Theatre; Studio Theatre
Facility Category: Theater
Type of Stage: Proscenium
Seating Capacity: 141
Organization Type: Performing; Educational

3549
PRIMARY STAGES COMPANY
307 W 38th St
Ste 1510
New York, NY 10018
Phone: 212-840-9705
Fax: 212-840-9725
e-mail: info@primarystages.org
Web Site: www.primarystages.org
Officers:
    President: Barbara S. Thomas
    First VP: Jeremy Smith
    Second VP: Doug Nevin
    Treasurer: Gregory M. Macosko
    Secretary: Arlene L. Goldman
Management:
    Artistic Director: Andrew Leynse
    Managing Director: Elliot Fox
    Associate Artistic Director: Michelle Bossy
Mission: Discovering and producing the finest new American plays.
Utilizes: Singers
Founded: 1984
Specialized Field: Theatre
Facility Category: 199 Seats; 59 Theatres
Organization Type: Performing

3550
PROCESS STUDIO THEATRE
257 Church Street
New York, NY 10007
Phone: 212-271-0410
Management:
    Artistic Director: Bonnie Loren
    Technical Director: Anthony Sandkamp
Mission: Promoting new artists and works; offering a home to professional artists.
Utilizes: Singers
Founded: 1977
Specialized Field: Musical; New Plays
Status: Professional; Nonprofit
Organization Type: Performing; Touring; Resident; Educational; Sponsoring; Outreach

3552
PUBLIC THEATRE
425 Lafayette Street
New York, NY 10003
Phone: 212-539-8500
Fax: 212-539-8705
e-mail: press@thepublictheatre.org
Web Site: www.publictheather.org
Officers:
    President: Kathy Gleason
    VP: Kathy Stuchiner
    Treasurer: Thomas H Platz
    Secretary: Carol Murrell
Management:
    Artistic Director: Oskar Eustis
    Executive Director: Andrew D. Harrington
Mission: The Public Theater produces new plays, musicals, productions of Shakespeare, as well as other classics. In addition to its theatrical programming, The Public Theater trains the next generation of classical performers through The Shakespeare Lab, an annual summer acting intensive.
Founded: 1954
Opened: 1967
Specialized Field: Shakespeare; Classic; Summer Stock
Status: Non-Profit, Professional
Paid Staff: 7
Volunteer Staff: 65
Paid Artists: 8
Budget: $450,000
Income Sources: Ticket Sales; Grants; Corporate Support; Donations
Annual Attendance: 250,000
Facility Category: Theatre
Type of Stage: Proscenium
Stage Dimensions: 36' x 33'
Seating Capacity: 307

3553
PUERTO RICAN TRAVELING THEATRE COMPANY
304 West 47th Street
New York, NY 10036
Phone: 212-354-1293
Fax: 212-307-2769
e-mail: prtt@prtt.org
Web Site: www.prtt.org/
Officers:
    Artistic Director: Miriam Colon Valle
    Director: Allen Davis III
    Director: Ricardo Puente
    Controller: Alexandra Minchala
    Plant Manager: Luis Arias
Management:
    President: Miriam Colon Valle
    Director: Allen Davis
    Director: Ricardo Puente
    Controller: Alexandra Minchala
    Assistant Bookepper: Ana Santos
Mission: Presenting bilingual plays; conducting workshops for underprivileged youth; providing training for playwrights.
Utilizes: Singers
Founded: 1967
Specialized Field: Musical; Touring Company; Spanish Language Company; Multi-Cultural
Status: Non-Profit, Professional
Performs At: Puerto Rican Travelling Theatre
Organization Type: Performing; Touring; Educational

3554
RAJECKAS AND INTRAUB MOVEMENT THEATRE
AKA Theatremoves
275 E 7th Street #4
New York, NY 10009
Mailing Address: PO Box 1333
Phone: 212-529-8068
Fax: 212-529-8068
e-mail: info@theatremoves.com
Web Site: www.theatremoves.com
Management:
    Co-Director: Paul Rajeckas
    Co Director: Neil Intraub
Founded: 1988
Specialized Field: Movement Theater
Status: Non-Profit, Professional
Paid Staff: 5
Paid Artists: 5

3555
RATTLESTICK THEATRE
224 Waverly Place
New York, NY 10014
Phone: 212-627-2556
Fax: 630-839-8352
Web Site: www.wegothere.org/
Management:

THEATRE / New York

Artistic Director: Albert Harris
Mission: The production of new works; the presentation of neglected works by established writers.
Utilizes: Singers
Founded: 1994
Specialized Field: Musical; Ensembles; New Plays
Status: Non-Profit, Professional
Income Sources: Actors' Equity Association; Alliance of Resident Theatres/New York
Performs At: Theatre Off Park
Organization Type: Educational

3556
REPERTORIO ESPANOL
138 E 27th Street
New York, NY 10016
Phone: 212-225-9999
Fax: 212-686-3732
Web Site: www.repertorio.org/
Officers:
   Chair: Andrew Thomas
   Vice Chair: Marianna Sabater
   Advisory Board: Norberto Bogard
   Advisory Board: Myriam Castillo
   Advisory Board: Joel Epstein
Management:
   Artistic Director: Rene Buch
   Associate Artistic Producer: Robert Federico
   Producer: Gilberto Zaldivar
Specialized Field: Spanish Language Company; Multi-Cultural

3557
RIDGE THEATER
125 West 12th Street #1c
New York, NY 10011
Phone: 646-279-3206
Fax: 212-674-5485
e-mail: ridgetheater@earthlink.net
Web Site: www.ridgetheater.org
Officers:
   Director: Bob McGrath
Management:
   President: Laurie Olinder
   Director: Bob McGrath
   Visual Design: Laurie Olinder
   Film: Bill Morrison
Mission: Exploring the boundaries of theatre and opera.
Founded: 1987
Specialized Field: Contemporary; Experimental
Status: Non-Profit, Professional
Paid Staff: 5
Paid Artists: 5
Facility Category: Theatre
Organization Type: Performing

3558
RIVER REP THEATRE COMPANY
100 E 4 Street
New York, NY 10003
Phone: 212-674-8181
Management:
   Artistic Director: Warren Kelley
   Managing Director: Joan Shepard
Mission: To bring 11 weeks a year of fulfilling theatre to the shoreline of Eastern Connecticut.
Founded: 1987
Specialized Field: Drama; Musical; Comedy; Classic
Status: Non-Profit
Paid Staff: 15
Volunteer Staff: 10
Paid Artists: 18
Non-paid Artists: 5
Season: June - September
Performs At: Chester Meeting House, Chester CT
Type of Stage: Proscenium
Stage Dimensions: 18' x 30'

3559
RIVERSIDE SHAKESPEARE COMPANY
Shakespeare Center
165 W 86th Street
New York, NY 10024
Phone: 212-505-2021
Fax: 212-505-2054
Management:
   Executive Director: Ann Harvey
   Artistic Director: Gus Kaikkonen
   Academy Director: Robert Mooney
Mission: Bringing classic works to life and making them more accessible.
Utilizes: Singers
Founded: 1976
Specialized Field: Shakespeare
Status: Professional
Organization Type: Performing; Touring; Resident; Educational

3560
ROGER FURMAN THEATRE
60 E 42nd Street
Suite 1336
New York, NY 10017
Phone: 212-599-1922
Fax: 212-599-2414
Management:
   Executive Director: Voza Rivers
Mission: Encouraging cultural pluralism in New York City through the presentation of high-quality, professional Black theatre.
Utilizes: Singers
Founded: 1964
Specialized Field: African American; Multi-Cultural
Status: Professional; Nonprofit
Paid Staff: 5
Income Sources: National Endowment for the Arts; Department of Cultural Affairs
Performs At: Roger Furman Theater; B Smiths Rooftop Cafe
Organization Type: Performing; Touring; Resident; Educational

3561
ROUNDABOUT THEATRE COMPANY
231 W 39th Street
Suite 1200
New York, NY 10018
Phone: 212-719-1300
Fax: 212-869-8817
e-mail: info@roundabouttheatre.org
Web Site: www.roundabouttheatre.org
Management:
   President: Todd Haimes
   Managing Director: Harold Wolpert
Mission: To produce the classics, both ancient and modern.
Utilizes: Singers
Founded: 1965
Specialized Field: Musical; Comedy; Classic; Contemporary; Renaissance
Status: Non-Profit, Professional
Affiliations: Actors' Equity Association; League of Resident Theatres; Society for Stage Directors and Choreographers
Facility Category: Theatre
Type of Stage: Proscenium
Seating Capacity: 700
Rental Contact: Christine Vall
Organization Type: Performing; Resident

3562
SAINT BART'S PLAYERS
325 Park Avenue
51ST Street
New York, NY 10022
Mailing Address: 325 Park Avenue,?New York, NY 10022
Phone: 212-378-0248
Fax: 212-378-0281
e-mail: CENTRAL@STBARTS.ORG
Web Site: www.stbarts.org
Officers:
   Co-Chair: Maryjane Baer
   Co-Chair: Merrill Vaughn
Management:
   Director St. Bart's Central: Veronica Shea
Utilizes: Singers
Founded: 1927
Specialized Field: Musical; Educational; Theater Workshops
Status: Non-Profit, Non-Professional
Paid Staff: 75
Income Sources: Theatre Communications Group
Performs At: Saint Bartholomew's Community House
Organization Type: Performing; Resident; Educational

3563
SALT AND PEPPER MIME COMPANY
320 E 90th
#1B
New York, NY 10128
Phone: 212-262-4989
Fax: 212-262-4989
Management:
   Artistic Manager/Producer: Scottie Davis
   Director: Chuck Wise
   Resident Playwright: Mark Pearce
Mission: Preserving the art forms of vaudeville and mime through performances, exhibitions and workshops.
Utilizes: Singers
Founded: 1978
Specialized Field: Musical; Mime; Drama; Children's Theater
Status: Professional; Nonprofit
Income Sources: Alliance of Resident Theatres/New York; Westside Arts Coalition
Performs At: Lincoln Square Theatre; Studio Theatre
Organization Type: Performing; Touring; Educational

3564
SARATOGA INTERNATIONAL THEATER INSTITUTE
SITI Company
520 8th Avenue
Suite 310
New York, NY 10018
Phone: 212-868-0860
Fax: 212-868-0837
e-mail: inbox@siti.org
Web Site: www.siti.org
Officers:
   Executive Director: Megan Wanlass Szalla
   Deputy Director: Micelle Preston
   Chair: Ruth Nightengale
   Treasurer: Christopher Healy
   Secretary: Kim Ima
Management:
   Artistic Director: Anneeen Bogart
   Managing Director: Megan Wanlass Szalla
   General Manager: Vanessa Sparling

THEATRE / New York

Interim Executive Director: Michelle Preston
Special Project Producer: Megan Wanlass
Mission: SITI exemplifies the disciplines it practices and the artistic values it develops in its work; to create new works for the theater; to perform and tour these productions nationally and internationally; to provide ongoing training for young theater professionals in an approach to acting that forges unique and highly disciplined artists for the theater; to foster opportunities for cultural exchange.
Founded: 1992
Specialized Field: New Plays; Touring Company
Status: Nonprofit
Paid Staff: 5
Volunteer Staff: 3
Paid Artists: 16

3565
SECOND STAGE THEATRE
305 W 43rd Street
New York, NY 10036
Phone: 212-246-4422
Fax: 212-397-7066
Web Site: www.2st.com/
Officers:
  Executive Director: Ellen Richard
  Artistic Director: Carole Rothman
  Executive Director: Casey Reitz
Management:
  Artistic Director: Carole Rothman
  General Manager: Dean Carpenter
Mission: To produce plays of the recent past which we feel deserve a second production; to produce world and New York premieres by emerging authors, with emphasis on women authors and authors of color.
Utilizes: Actors; AEA Actors; Artists-in-Residence; Choreographers; Commissioned Composers; Commissioned Music; Designers; Educators; Five Seasonal Concerts; Guest Accompanists; Guest Artists; Guest Conductors; Guest Designers; Guest Lecturers; Instructors; Local Unknown Artists; Multimedia; Music; New Productions; Original Music Scores; Performance Artists; Resident Professionals; Selected Students; Soloists; Visual Arts
Founded: 1979
Specialized Field: Musical; Comedy; Contemporary
Status: Non-Profit, Professional
Paid Staff: 20
Paid Artists: 25
Annual Attendance: 67,000
Facility Category: Theatre
Seating Capacity: 296
Year Built: 1999
Rental Contact: Producing Manager Peter Davis
Organization Type: Performing

3566
SHADOW BOX THEATRE
325 W End Avenue
New York, NY 10023
Phone: 212-724-0677
Fax: 212-724-0767
e-mail: sbt@shadowboxtheatre.org
Web Site: www.shadowboxtheatre.org
Officers:
  Executive/Artistic Director: Sandra Robbins
  Managing/Arts Education Director: Carol Prud'homme Davis
Management:
  Artistic Director: Sandra Robbins
  Managing/Education Director: Carol Prud'homm Davis
  Booking & Operations Manager: Raymond Todd
  Technical Director: Pope Jackson

Music Director: Greg Alexander
Mission: To serve inner city disadvantaged children with a high quality art-in-education program.
Founded: 1967
Specialized Field: Musical; Ethnic Theater; Puppet; Shadow Theater
Status: Non-Profit, Professional
Paid Staff: 5
Paid Artists: 10
Affiliations: NYC Board of Education Vendor
Organization Type: Performing; Touring; Resident; Educational; Sponsoring

3567
SIGNATURE THEATRE COMPANY
480 West 42nd St
New York, NY 10036
Phone: 212-967-1913
Fax: 212-967-2957
Web Site: www.signaturetheatre.org
Officers:
  Chairman: Peter Norton
  President: Michael Rauch
  VP: Christine M Millen
  VP: Marian Succoso
  Executive Director: Erika Mallin
  Artistic Director: James Houghton
Management:
  Executive Director: Erika Mallin
  Artistic Director: James Houghton
  Director Development: Katherine Thomas
  Production Manager: Paul Ziemer
  General Manager: Adam Bernstein
Founded: 1991
Specialized Field: Drama; Musical; Comedy
Status: Non-Profit, Professional
Paid Staff: 13
Volunteer Staff: 1
Paid Artists: 150
Affiliations: Alliance of Resident Theatres, NY; Theatre Communications Group
Type of Stage: Proscenium
Seating Capacity: 160

3568
SOHO REPERTORY THEATRE
401 Broadway,
Suite 300
New York, NY 10013
Phone: 212-941-8632
Fax: 212-941-7148
e-mail: sohorep@sohorep.org
Web Site: www.sohorep.org
Officers:
  Artistic Director: Sarah Benson
Management:
  Executive Director: Cynthia Flowers
  Artistic Director: Sarah Benson
  Playwright in Residence: David Adjmi
  Development Manager: Talia Corren
  Theatre & Office Manager: Chip Rodgers
Founded: 1975
Specialized Field: Comedy; Community Theater; Contemporary; New Plays
Status: Non-Profit, Professional
Paid Staff: 3
Seating Capacity: 70

3569
SOUPSTONE PROJECT
309 E 5th Street
Suite 19
New York, NY 10003
Phone: 212-473-7584

Management:
  Director/Literary Manager: Neile Weissman
Mission: To expand the theatergoing audience through free, trilingually-accessible presentations of new American plays.
Founded: 1985
Specialized Field: New Plays; Multi-Cultural; Contemporary
Status: Professional
Performs At: Henry Street Settlement; Louis Abrons Art Center
Organization Type: Performing

3570
SPANISH THEATRE REPERTORY COMPANY
138 E 27th Street
New York, NY 10016
Phone: 212-225-9999
Fax: 212-225-9085
Web Site: http://www.repertorio.org/
Officers:
  Chair: Andrew Thomas
  Vice-Chair: Marianna Sabater
  Advisory Board: Norberto Bogard
  Advisory Board: Myriam Castillo
  Advisory Board: Joel Epstein
Management:
  Producer: Gilbert Zaldivar
  Associate Producer: Robert Federico
  Press Agent: Ellen Jacobs
Mission: To offer Spanish-language professional theatre; to promote Hispanic culture.
Founded: 1969
Specialized Field: Musical; Community Theater; Spanish Language Company
Status: Professional
Income Sources: Theatre Communications Group; American Arts Alliance; Alliance of Resident Theatres/New York
Performs At: Gramercy Arts Theatre; Equitable Tower Auditorium
Organization Type: Performing

3571
STAGEWRIGHTS
PO Box 4745
Rockefeller Center Station
New York, NY 10185
Phone: 212-768-8964
Mission: To develop scripts.
Founded: 1983
Specialized Field: New Plays; Young Playwrights
Status: Semi-Professional; Nonprofit
Paid Staff: 100
Organization Type: Writer's Theatre

3572
TADA!
15 W 28th Street
3rd Floor
New York, NY 10001
Phone: 212-252-1619
Fax: 212-252-8763
e-mail: info@tadatheater.com
Web Site: www.tadtheater.com
Management:
  President: Stephen T Rodd
  Executive Director: Janine Nina Trevens
Founded: 1984
Specialized Field: Youth; Musical Theatre
Paid Staff: 10
Performs At: Theater; Rehearsal; Studio
Facility Category: Theater

THEATRE / New York

Type of Stage: Procenium
Stage Dimensions: 20 x 30 x 11
Seating Capacity: 99
Rental Contact: Andrew Bryant

3573
TALKING BAND
PO Box 293
Prince Street Station
New York, NY 10012
Phone: 212-295-0371
Web Site: http://talkingband.org/panic/about.html
Management:
    Artistic Director: Paul Zinet
Mission: The creation and performance of new theatre works.
Specialized Field: New Plays
Status: Professional; Nonprofit
Organization Type: Performing; Touring

3574
TARGET MARGIN THEATER
138 South Oxford Street #5A
New York, NY 11217
Phone: 718-398-3095
Fax: 212-725-4627
Web Site: www.targetmargin.org/
Management:
    Artistic Director: David Herskovits
    Managing Director: Meredith Palin
    Development Director: Tonya Canada
Specialized Field: Specialty Acts; Hellenic Drama

3575
THE CLASSICAL THEATRE OF HARLEM
566 West 159th Street, Suite 44
New York, NY 10032
Phone: 347-688-6304
e-mail: info@cthnyc.org
Web Site: cthnyc.org
Management:
    Producing Artistic Director: Ty Jones
    Managing Director: David Roberts
Mission: To maintain a professional theatre company dedicated to presenting the classics in Harlem; to create employment and educational outreach opportunities in the theatre arts community; to create and nurture a new, young, and culturally diverse audience for the classics; and to heighten the awareness of theatre and of great art in Harlem.
Founded: 1999
Specialized Field: Adaptations Of World Literature Classics
Status: Nonprofit; Professional

3576
THE NEW GROUP
The Pershing Square Signature Center
480 West 42nd Street
New York, NY 10036
Phone: 212-244-3380
e-mail: info@thenewgroup.org
Web Site: thenewgroup.org
Officers:
    Chairman: Serge Nivelle
    President: Robert J. Rosenberg
    Treasurer: John Greenwood
Management:
    Artistic Director: Scott Elliott
    Executive Director: Adam Bernstein
Mission: The New Group has a commitment to developing and producing powerful, contemporary theater.
Founded: 1995

Status: Nonprofit

3577
THEATER BY THE BLIND
306 W 18th Street
New York, NY 10011
Phone: 212-243-4337
Fax: 212-243-4337
e-mail: ischambelan@nyc.rr.com
Web Site: www.tbtb.org
Officers:
    Chairperson: Beth Blickers
    Secretary/Treasurer: Josie Lawrence
    Arts Administrator: Joan Duddy
    Manager of Institutional Giving: Susan Ferziger
    Artistic Director: Ike Schambelan
Management:
    Artistic Director: Ike Schambelan
Mission: To change the image of the blind from one of dependence to independence.
Founded: 1979
Specialized Field: Alternative
Status: Non-Profit, Professional
Paid Staff: 4
Paid Artists: 17

3578
THEATER FOR THE NEW CITY
155 1st Avenue
New York, NY 10003
Phone: 212-245-1109
Fax: 212-979-6570
e-mail: info@theaterforthenewcity.net
Web Site: www.theaterforthenewcity.net
Management:
    Executive Director: Crystal Field
    Production Manager: Mark Marcante
    Administrator: Jerry Jaffe
    Development Director: Victoria Linchon
Mission: To embody the vision of a center for new and innovative theater arts that would be truly accessible to the community and its experimental theater artists; to discover relevant new writing and to nurture new playwrights; to be a bridge between playwright, experimental theater artist, and the ever growing audiences in the community; to create spaces where a new vision can breathe and be nourished by a working process.
Utilizes: Singers
Founded: 1970
Specialized Field: Experimental; Young Playwrights
Status: Professional; Nonprofit
Paid Staff: 5
Volunteer Staff: 20
Performs At: Four Theatre Complex
Affiliations: Alliance of Resident Theatres/New York; Theatre Communications Group; American Arts Alliance
Annual Attendance: 30,000
Facility Category: Multi-theater complex
Type of Stage: Black Box; Cabaret; Flexible Stage
Seating Capacity: 270; 99; 74; 104
Organization Type: Performing; Touring

3579
THEATRE DU GRAND-GUIGNOL DE PARIS
310 E 70th Street
New York, NY 10021
Phone: 212-861-1813
Fax: 212-861-1813
Management:
    Embassy of Montmartre: Barry Alan Richmond

Mission: Specializing in grotesquerie, shock, terror, the macabre and earthy laughter.
Utilizes: Singers
Founded: 1896
Specialized Field: Multi-Cultural; Drama; Comedy; Alternative
Status: Professional; National Theatre of Montmartre
Income Sources: State Theatre of the Republic of Montmartre
Organization Type: Performing; Touring; Resident

3580
THEATRE FOR A NEW AUDIENCE
154 Christopher Street
Suite 3D
New York, NY 10014
Phone: 212-229-2819
Fax: 212-229-2911
Toll-free: 866-811-4111
e-mail: info@tfana.org
Web Site: www.tfana.org
Officers:
    Founding Artistic Director: Jeffrey Horowitz
    Managing Director: Dorothy Ryan
    Director of Development: James J. Lynes
    Education Director: Katie Miller
Management:
    Managing Director: Dorothy Ryan
    General Manager: Theresa Von Klug
Mission: Producing works of poetic imagination; building a diverse audience.
Founded: 1979
Specialized Field: New Plays
Status: Professional; Nonprofit
Income Sources: Theatre Communications Group
Performs At: Lucille Lortel Theatre
Organization Type: Performing; Educational

3581
RAJECKAS AND INTRAUB - MOVEMENT THEATRE
PO Box 1333
New York, NY 10009
Phone: 212-529-8068
Fax: 212-529-8068
e-mail: nintraub@aol.com
Management:
    Co-Artistic Director: Neil Intraub
    Co-Artistic Director: Paul Rajeckas
Mission: Increasing public exposure to the art form of movement theatre.
Specialized Field: Community Theater; Movement Theater
Status: Professional; Nonprofit
Organization Type: Performing; Touring; Educational

3582
THEATREWORKS USA
151 W 26th Street
New York, NY 10001
Phone: 212-647-1100
Fax: 212-924-5377
e-mail: info@theatreworksusa.org
Web Site: www.theatreworksusa.org
Officers:
    Chairman: Judith Prince
    President: Ken Arthur
    Secretary: Charles Hull
    VP/Treasurer: Joseph Scudese
    Founder: Jay Harnick
Management:
    Artistic Director: Barbara Pasternack
    Producing Director: Ken Arthur
    Business Manager: Claudia Stuart

THEATRE / New York

Associate Business Manager: Adra Greenstein
Co Marketing Director: Steve Cochran
Mission: Theatreworks/USA, a nonprofit organization and America's largest theatre creating, producing, and touring plays for young audiences, has presented more than 27,000 performances to well over 22 million young people in schools, art centers, museums and theatres, in 49 states.
Utilizes: Actors; AEA Actors; Artists-in-Residence; Choreographers; Collaborating Artists; Collaborations; Commissioned Composers; Commissioned Music; Dancers; Designers; Educators; Five Seasonal Concerts; Guest Accompanists; Guest Artists; Guest Choreographers; Guest Companies; Guest Composers; Guest Conductors; Guest Designers; Guest Ensembles; Guest Lecturers; Guest Teachers; Guild Activities; High School Drama; Local Unknown Artists; Lyricists; Music; New Productions; Original Music Scores; Performance Artists; Resident Professionals; Sign Language Translators; Singers; Soloists; Special Technical Talent; Theatre Companies; Visual Arts
Founded: 1961
Specialized Field: Musical; Comedy; Youth Theater; Community Theater; Contemporary
Status: Non-Profit, Professional
Paid Staff: 21
Budget: $10 million
Performs At: Town Hall; Promenade Theatre; Variety Arts Theatre
Affiliations: AEA, SSDC, USA, AGG, IAPAYP, APAP
Annual Attendance: 4.6 million
Organization Type: Performing; Touring; Resident; Educational; Sponsoring

3583
THERESA LANG THEATRE
Marymount Manhattan College
221 E 71 Street
New York, NY 10021
Phone: 212-774-0760
Fax: 212-774-0770
Web Site: www.mmm.edu
Management:
  President: Judson Shaver
  Executive Director: Mary Fleischer
Specialized Field: Musical; Comedy; Classic; Contemporary
Status: For-Profit, Non-Professional

3584
THUNDER BAY ENSEMBLE
17 N. Court Street
New York, NY P7A 4T4
Phone: 80-734-5055
Fax: 807-345-0173
Toll-free: 866-831-1144
e-mail: info@thunderbayus.org
Web Site: www.thunderbayus.org
Management:
  President: Beth Skinner
  Artistic Director: Edward Herbst
Founded: 1987
Specialized Field: Ensembles; Contemporary
Status: Non-Profit, Professional
Paid Staff: 4
Paid Artists: 8

3585
TVI ACTORS STUDIO
165 W 46th Street
Suite 509
New York, NY 10036
Phone: 212-302-1900
Fax: 212-302-1926
Toll-free: 800-884-2772
Web Site: www.tvistudios.com
Officers:
  Founder/CEO: Alan S Nusbaum
Management:
  President: Alan Nusbaum
  Executive Director: Deborah Kossler
  Managing Director: Susan Sleeper
Mission: Provide actors with a center where they can focus on the business of their careers in addition to learning the necessary skills to compete as an actor.
Founded: 1986
Specialized Field: Musical; Youth Theater
Status: For-Profit, Professional
Paid Staff: 12
Performs At: Actors Studio
Organization Type: Resident

3587
VINEYARD THEATRE
108 E 15th Street
New York, NY 10003
Phone: 212-353-3366
Fax: 212-353-3803
e-mail: boxoffice@vineyardtheatre.org
Web Site: www.vineyardtheatre.org
Officers:
  Chairman: Jill S. Gabb
  VC: Ken Greiner
  President: Annette Stoven
  Secretary: Judy Kuhn
  Treasurer: Richard Mccune
Management:
  Artistic Director: Douglas Aibel
  Executive Director: Jennifer Garvey-Blackewell
  Co Artistic Director: Sarah Stern
  Business Affair Director: Dennis Hruska
  Marketing Director: Eric Pargac
Mission: Developing musical theatre and new plays.
Utilizes: Actors; AEA Actors; Artists-in-Residence; Choreographers; Collaborating Artists; Collaborations; Commissioned Composers; Commissioned Music; Designers; Five Seasonal Concerts; Grant Writers; Guest Accompanists; Guest Artists; Guest Companies; Guest Composers; Guest Conductors; Guest Designers; Guest Lecturers; Guest Musical Directors; Guild Activities; Instructors; Local Artists; Local Unknown Artists; Multimedia; Music; Original Music Scores; Performance Artists; Playwrights; Poets; Resident Professionals; Sign Language Translators; Soloists
Founded: 1981
Specialized Field: Musical; New Plays
Status: Non-Profit
Paid Staff: 8
Budget: $1.6 million
Income Sources: Theatre Communications Group; Opera America
Season: Late-Fall - Spring
Affiliations: AEA, AFM, SSDC
Type of Stage: Flexible; Thrust
Seating Capacity: 129
Rental Contact: General Manager Jodi Schoenbrun
Organization Type: Performing

3588
VIVIAN BEAUMONT THEATER
150 W 65th Street
New York, NY 10023
Phone: 212-362-7600
Fax: 212-873-0761
e-mail: info@lct.org
Web Site: www.lct.org
Officers:
  Assistant Treasurer: Robert A Belkin
  Box Office Treasurer: Fred Bonis
  Artistic Director: Andre Bishop
  Managing Director: Adam seigel
Management:
  Artistic Director: Andre Bishop
  Director Development: Hattie K Jutagir
  Production Manager: Jeff Hamlin
  Assistant Production Manager: Paul Smithyman
  Associate General Manager: Mala Yee Mosher
  Management Assistant: Melanie Weiner
  Company Manager: Adam Siegal
  Assistant Company Manager: Anthony LaTorella
Utilizes: Singers
Founded: 1985
Specialized Field: Musical; Drama
Status: Non-Profit, Professional
Performs At: Vivian Beaumont Theater; Mitzi E Newhouse Theater
Facility Category: Theater
Organization Type: Performing

3589
WEISSBERGER THEATER GROUP
909 3rd Avenue
27th Floor
New York, NY 10022
Phone: 212-339-5529
Fax: 212-486-8996
Management:
  Producer: Jay Harris
Founded: 1992
Specialized Field: New Plays

3590
WHITE HORSE THEATRE COMPANY
205 Third Avenue, 6N
New York, NY 10003
Phone: 212-592-3706
e-mail: cymarion@whitehorsetheater.com
Web Site: whitehorsetheater.com
Management:
  Producing Artistic Director: Cyndy A. Marion
  Managing Director: Vanessa R. Bombardieri
  Director Of Marketing: Loretta Hunt Marion
  Founding Artistic Director: Rod Sweitzer
Mission: White Horse is committed to making high-quality theater we are truly passionate about with the goal of sharing our passion for American plays and playwrights with our fellow artists and audiences.
Founded: 2003
Specialized Field: American Plays
Status: Nonprofit

3591
WINGS THEATRE COMPANY
611 W. 137th St. #5
New York, NY 10031
Phone: 212-627-2960
Fax: 212-462-0024
e-mail: jcorrick@wingstheatre.com
Web Site: www.wingstheatre.com
Management:
  Literary Manager: Laura Kleeman
  President: Jeffery Corrick
  Managing Director: Robert Mooney
  Rentals Manager: Robert Mooney

Mission: To engourage artists and arts organizations other than our own-theatre and dance companies, comedy troupes, film-makers-by producing and by making our space available for productions and rentals. We receive scripts and choose 5 for each year for Equity Tier II Showcase Productions (5 week runs). We have a gay plays series as well as a new musicals series.
Founded: 1986
Specialized Field: New Plays
Status: Non-Profit, Professional
Paid Staff: 3
Volunteer Staff: 3
Paid Artists: 30
Non-paid Artists: 20
Income Sources: Box Office; Grants; Rentals
Facility Category: Fully Equipped Theatre
Type of Stage: Proscenium
Stage Dimensions: 20 x 20, 2 side stages
Seating Capacity: 74-95
Year Built: 1990
Rental Contact: Rmooney@Verizon.Net Robert Mooney

3592
WOMEN'S INTERART CENTER
549 W 52nd Street
New York, NY 10019
Phone: 212-246-1050
Management:
  Artistic Director: Margot Lewitin
  Dramaturge: Jean Rowan
  Development Director: Susan Waring Morris
Mission: To explore all avenues of theatrical expression; to emphasize the work of new playwrights.
Utilizes: Singers
Founded: 1971
Specialized Field: Women's Theater; New Plays
Status: Professional; Nonprofit
Income Sources: Actors' Equity Association
Performs At: Interart Theater
Organization Type: Performing

3593
WOMEN'S PROJECT & PRODUCTIONS
55 W End Avenue
New York, NY 10023
Phone: 212-765-1706
Fax: 212-765-2024
e-mail: info@womensproject.org
Web Site: www.womensproject.org
Officers:
  Producing Artistic Director: Julie Crosby
  Managing Director: Lisa Fane
  Director of Marketing: Deane Brosnan
Management:
  Producing Artistic Director: Loretta Greco
  Associate Artistic Director: Lisa McNulty
  Managing Director: Jane Ann Crum
  Literary Manager: Karen Keagle
  Associate Artistic Director: Megan E Carter
Mission: Promoting and developing women directors and playwrights in the theatre.
Utilizes: Singers
Founded: 1978
Specialized Field: Women's Theater; New Plays
Status: Non-Profit, Professional
Paid Staff: 10
Income Sources: Theatre Communications Group; Alliance of Resident Theatres/New York
Organization Type: Performing; Resident; Educational; Sponsoring

3594
WOOSTER GROUP
Canal Street Station
PO Box 654
New York, NY 10013
Phone: 212-966-9796
Fax: 212-226-6576
e-mail: mail@thewoostergroup.org
Web Site: www.thewoostergroup.org
Officers:
  President: Kate Valk
  Marketing Manager: Mike Farry
  Development Manager: Leanne Mella
  Art Education Coordinator: Kaneza Schaal
Management:
  Artistic Director: Elizabeth Lecompte
  Managing Director: Joel Bassin
  General Manager: Sandra Garner
  Archivist: Clay Hapaz
  Producer: Cynthia Hedstrom
Mission: An artists collective working together on live performances.
Founded: 1967
Specialized Field: Ensembles; New Plays
Status: Non-Profit, Professional
Paid Staff: 17
Budget: $1 million
Income Sources: Ticket Sales; Touring; Grants & Contributions
Performs At: The Performing Garage
Annual Attendance: 15,000
Facility Category: Flexible black box
Type of Stage: Flexible floor
Seating Capacity: 100
Year Built: 1950
Organization Type: Performing; Touring; Resident; Sponsoring

3595
WORKING THEATRE COMPANY
520 Eighth Avenue, Suite 303
New York, NY 10018
Phone: 212-244-3300
Fax: 212-244-3302
e-mail: info@theworkingtheater.org
Web Site: www.theworkingtheater.org/
Officers:
  Chairman: Larry Beers
  Producing Artistic Director: Mark Plesent
  Managing Director: Laura Carbonell Smith
Management:
  Artistic Director: Bill Mitchelson
  Development Director: Honour Molloy
Mission: America's only professional theatre company dedicated to producing new plays of cultural diversities that reflect the issues and concerns that working people face in the modern world.
Specialized Field: Young Playwrights; Drama; Comedy
Status: Professional; Nonprofit
Organization Type: Performing; Educational

3596
WPA THEATRE
159 W 23rd Street
Suite 301
New York, NY 10001
Phone: 212-206-0523
Fax: 212-637-7154
Management:
  Artistic Director: Kyle Renick
  Managing Director: Donna Lieberman
Mission: Committed to fostering realistic writing, acting and design in American repertory.
Founded: 1977
Specialized Field: New Works
Status: Professional; Nonprofit
Income Sources: Alliance of Resident Theatres/New York; Theatre Communications Group
Season: September - June
Performs At: Chelsea Playhouse
Type of Stage: Proscenium
Seating Capacity: 160
Organization Type: Performing

3597
YORK THEATRE COMPANY
619 Lexington Avenue @ 54th Street
New York, NY 10022-4610
Phone: 212-935-5820
Fax: 212-832-0037
e-mail: jmorgan@yorktheatre.org
Web Site: www.yorktheatre.org
Officers:
  President: James Morgan
Management:
  Director: David McCoy
  Artistic Director: Jim Morgan
  President: Sarah Tod Smith
Mission: A professional equity off-Broadway company dedicated to presenting great classical works as well as revivals and/or premieres of unusual, avant-garde musicals.
Utilizes: Singers
Founded: 1969
Specialized Field: Musical; Youth Theater; Contemporary
Status: Non-Profit, Professional
Paid Staff: 6
Paid Artists: 300
Affiliations: Actors' Equity Association
Organization Type: Performing

3598
YOUNG PLAYWRIGHTS
321 W 44th Street
Suite 906
New York, NY 10036
Phone: 212-307-1140
Fax: 212-307-1454
Management:
  Artistic Director: Sheri Goldhirsch
  Managing Director: Brett Reynolds
  Project Administrator: Rebecca Sheir
  Literary Associate: Ruth McKee
Specialized Field: Young Playwrights; Theater Workshops

3599
PUPPET THEATRE: DANCE AND MUSIC FROM INDONESIA
P.O. Box 691
Northport, NY 11768
Phone: 631-754-5035
Fax: 631-754-2341
e-mail: javapuppets@aol.com
Web Site: www.indonesianshadowplay.com
Management:
  President: Tamara Fielding
Founded: 1975
Specialized Field: Multi-Cultural; Puppet; Ethnic Theater
Status: For-Profit, Professional
Paid Staff: 2
Paid Artists: 6

THEATRE / New York

3600
TAMARA AND THE SHADOW THEATRE OF JAVA
P.O. Box 691
Northport, NY 11768
Phone: 631-754-5035
Fax: 631-754-2341
e-mail: javapuppets@aol.com
Web Site: www.indonesianshadowplay.com
Management:
    Artistic Director: Tamara Fielding
Founded: 1975
Specialized Field: Multi-Cultural; Shadow Theater; Ethnic Theater; Musical
Status: For-Profit, Professional
Paid Staff: 2
Volunteer Staff: 1
Paid Artists: 20

3601
ELMWOOD PLAYHOUSE
10 Park Street
Nyack, NY 10960
Mailing Address: 249 South Blvd, Nyack, NY 10960
Phone: 845-353-1313
Fax: 845-348-9397
e-mail: elmwoodplayhouse@aol.com
Web Site: www.elmwoodplayhouse.com
Officers:
    President: Larry Beckerle
    VP: Alison Costello
    VP: Peter Garruba
    Treasurer: Derek Tarson
    Board Member: Jim Lugo
    Board Member: Phil Hannah
Management:
    Operations Manager: Evelyn Russo
Founded: 1964
Specialized Field: Musical; Comedy; Community Theater
Status: Non-Profit, Non-Professional
Paid Staff: 4
Volunteer Staff: 200
Income Sources: Art Council of Rockland County
Performs At: Elmwood Playhouse
Affiliations: ACOR, AACT
Facility Category: Community Theatre
Seating Capacity: 99
Organization Type: Performing; Educational

3602
OGDENSBURG COMMAND PERFORMANCES
1100 State Street
Ogdensburg, NY 13669
Phone: 315-393-2625
Fax: 315-393-3745
e-mail: ocp@ogdensburgk12.org
Web Site: www.ilovetheatre.org/
Management:
    Administrative Coordinator: Sally Palao
Mission: To offer theatrical productions, drama and music for the enjoyment and inspiration of the residents of Ogdensburg and the North Country.
Founded: 1963
Specialized Field: Drama; Classic
Status: Professional; Nonprofit
Paid Staff: 2
Performs At: George Hall Auditorium; Ogdensburg Free Academy
Organization Type: Sponsoring

3603
ORPHEUS THEATRE
31 Maple Street
PO Box 1014
Oneonta, NY 13820
Phone: 607-432-1800
Fax: 607-436-9682
e-mail: orpheus@orpheustheatre.org
Web Site: www.orpheustheatre.org/
Officers:
    President: Kathy Tobiassen
    VP: Brooke Tallman
    Treasurer: Casey Thomas
    Secretary: Adrienne Wise
    Treasurer: Rosalie Benson
    CEO: Sammy Dallas Bayes
    President: Kathy Tobiassen
    VP: John Chamard
Management:
    Co-Producers: Peter Macris
    Business Manager: Michelle Gardener
Founded: 1983
Specialized Field: Musical; Theater Workshops
Status: Nonprofit; Non-Equity
Season: September - August
Type of Stage: Proscenium
Stage Dimensions: 49' x 35'
Seating Capacity: 497

3604
IMAGO, THE THEATRE MASK ENSEMBLE
163 Amsterdam Avenue #121
Pawling, NY 10023
Phone: 212-799-4814
Fax: 212-874-3613
Management:
    Artistic Director: Carol Trifle
    Artistic Director: Jerry Mouwad
Mission: To present our unique art form.
Utilizes: Singers
Founded: 1981
Specialized Field: Summer Stock; Community Theater; Mask Theater
Status: Professional
Income Sources: Westaff Touring Program; North Carolina Touring Program; Arts Midwest; Performing Arts Touring Program of Oregon
Organization Type: Performing; Touring; Resident; Educational

3605
THEATRE THREE PRODUCTIONS
412 Main Street
PO Box 512
Port Jefferson, NY 11777
Phone: 631-928-9100
Fax: 631-928-9120
e-mail: maureen@theatrethree.org
Web Site: www.theatrethree.org
Officers:
    President: Andrew Markowitz
Management:
    Executive Artistic Director: Jeffrey Sanzel
    Managing Director: Vivian Koutrakos
Mission: Dedicated to developing an appreciation for the art of live theatre among the residents of Long Island by involving as large a constituency as possible in a rich variety of programming which includes Mainstage, Second Stage, Cabaret and Children's Theatre productions.
Utilizes: Singers
Founded: 1969
Specialized Field: Live Theatre
Status: Non-Profit, Non-Professional
Paid Staff: 15
Volunteer Staff: 15
Paid Artists: 75
Non-paid Artists: 20
Budget: $1.1 million
Income Sources: Port Jefferson Arts Council
Season: July - June
Type of Stage: Thrust
Seating Capacity: 247
Organization Type: Performing; Touring; Resident; Educational

3606
NEW DAY REPERTORY COMPANY
29 N Hamilton Street
PO Box 269
Poughkeepsie, NY 12602
Phone: 845-485-7399
Fax: 845-485-6544
e-mail: newdayrep@netzero.com
Officers:
    Chairman: Al Coley
    Treasurer: Dr. Tansukh Dorawala
    Secretary: Dorothy Paulin
Management:
    President: Rodney K Douglas
    Managing Director: Jerry Naple
Mission: Make quality life theatre accessible to culturally/socially diverse, economically disadvantaged, and underserved audiences of all ages
Utilizes: Student Interns
Founded: 1963
Specialized Field: Classic; Contemporary
Status: Non-Profit, Professional
Paid Staff: 2
Budget: $160,000
Performs At: Vassar Institute Theatre
Facility Category: Schools; Colleges; Community Centers; Churches
Type of Stage: Proscenium
Seating Capacity: 1,100
Year Remodeled: 1997
Organization Type: Performing; Touring; Resident; Educational

3607
POWERHOUSE THEATER AT VASSAR
Vassar College
124 Raymond Avenue
Poughkeepsie, NY 12604-0225
Phone: 845-437-7000
Fax: 845-437-7209
e-mail: powerhouse@vassar.edu
Web Site: www.powerhouse.vassar.edu
Officers:
    President: Marc Segan
Management:
    Artistic Director: Johanna Pfaelzer
    General Manager: Nathan Baynard
Status: Non-Profit, Professional
Season: June - August
Type of Stage: Black Box
Seating Capacity: 130

3608
BLACKFRIARS THEATRE
795 E. Main Street
Rochester, NY 14605
Phone: 585-454-1260
e-mail: mail@blackfriars.org
Web Site: www.bftix.org
Management:

President: Katharine Fischer
Artistic Director: John Halboupis
Mission: A professional oriented community theater.
Founded: 1950
Specialized Field: Community Theater; Musical; Comedy; Classic; Contemporary
Status: Non-Profit, Professional
Paid Staff: 4
Paid Artists: 15
Facility Category: Theatre
Type of Stage: Thrust Stage; Flexible
Stage Dimensions: 20'x40'
Seating Capacity: 99-165
Year Remodeled: 1997

3609
GEVA THEATRE
75 Woodbury Boulevard
Rochester, NY 14607-1717
Phone: 716-232-1366
Fax: 716-232-4031
e-mail: gevatalk@gevatheatre.org
Web Site: www.gevatheatre.org
Officers:
   Chairman: Peter Messner
   VP: Sergio Esteban
   Secretary: Helen Zamboni
   Treasurer: Terry Hartmann
   Artistic Director: Mark Cuddy
   Executive Director: Tom Parrish
   Director of Education/ Artist in Re: Skip Greer
Management:
   Artistic Director: Mark Cuddy
   Production Manager: Matt Reinert
   Associate Director of Education: Lara Rhyner
Mission: To produce work that celebrates the human spirit.
Utilizes: Singers
Founded: 1972
Specialized Field: Drama; Musicals; New Plays; World Classics
Status: Not-For-Profit, Professional
Paid Staff: 85
Volunteer Staff: 120
Paid Artists: 125
Income Sources: Theatre Communications Group; American Arts Alliance; League of Resident Theatres
Season: September - June
Performs At: Elaine Wilson Theatre, Ronald and Donna Fielding Nextstage
Annual Attendance: 160,000
Type of Stage: Thrust, Proscenium
Stage Dimensions: 50' x 40'
Seating Capacity: 552, 180
Organization Type: Performing; Resident; Educational

3610
ROCHESTER BROADWAY THEATRE LEAGUE
885 E Main Street
Rochester, NY 14605
Phone: 585-325-7760
e-mail: info@rbtl.org
Web Site: www.rbtl.org
Officers:
   Chairman: Arnie Rothschild
   VC Finance: Richard Kaplan
   VC Education: Philip J. Puchalski
   VC Development: Bill Sullivan
   Secretary: Lydia Boddie

Mission: The Rochester Broadway Theatre League was founded in 1957 by a small group of volunteers to stimulate, promote and develop interest in the dramatic and musical arts for the cultural benefit of the community.
Founded: 1957
Specialized Field: Broadway Musical Revivals; Summer Stock; Touring Company
Status: Non-Profit
Seating Capacity: 2,458

3611
THEATRE ON THE RIDGE
200 Ridge Road W
Building 28
Rochester, NY 14652
Phone: 716-722-9449
Fax: 716-477-8041
Management:
   Manager: David R Dunn
Mission: To provide entertainment for Eastman Kodak Company as well as the local community.
Specialized Field: Musical; Dinner Theater; Community Theater
Status: Professional; Commercial
Organization Type: Performing; Resident; Sponsoring

3612
UNIVERSITY OF ROCHESTER THEATRE PROGRAM
107 Todd Union
Rochester, NY 14627
Phone: 716-275-4088
Fax: 716-461-4547
Web Site: www.rochester.edu/college/eng/theatre/
Officers:
   Artistic Director: Nigel Maister
Management:
   Artistic Director: Mervyn Willis
   Administrator: Katherine Mcgill
   Associate Director/ Art Director: Nigel Maister
   Technical Director: John Gilfus
   Administrator: Katie Farrell
   Production Manager: Gordon Rice
Mission: To offer modern, contemporary and classical plays; to provide professional training.
Utilizes: Singers
Founded: 1968
Specialized Field: Educational; Theater Workshops
Status: Semi-Professional; Nonprofit
Paid Staff: 4
Paid Artists: 10
Performs At: Black Box Theatre
Organization Type: Performing; Resident; Educational

3613
CAPITOL THEATRE SUMMERSTAGE
220 W Dominick Street
Rome, NY 13440
Phone: 315-337-6277
Fax: 315-337-6277
Web Site: www.theatreorgans.com/ny/rome
Officers:
   President: Peter Ehrnstrum
Management:
   Director: Eileen Trnobis
   Executive Director: Art Pierce
Mission: Offering the community an opportuniity for participation in quality music performances.
Founded: 1928
Specialized Field: Musical; Summer Stock
Status: Non-Profit, Professional
Paid Staff: 5
Paid Artists: 50

Season: July - August
Type of Stage: Proscenium
Stage Dimensions: 40' x 25'
Seating Capacity: 1700

3614
BROADHOLLOW PLAYERS LIMITED
80 13th Avenue
Building 5, Unit 6
Ronkonkoma, NY 11779
Phone: 631-471-0064
Fax: 631-471-8276
e-mail: broadhollowweb@aol.com
Management:
   Executive Producer: Jerry Zaback
Founded: 1973
Specialized Field: Community Theater; Children's Theater; Educational
Status: Nonprofit
Season: Year-Round
Seating Capacity: 175; 288; 250;

3615
BAY STREET THEATRE
1 Bay Street
PO Box 810
Sag Harbor, NY 11963
Phone: 631-725-9500
Fax: 631-725-0906
e-mail: boxoffice@baystreet.org
Web Site: www.baystreet.org
Management:
   Executive Director: Tracy Mitchell
   Artistic Director: Scott Schwartz
   Producer: Gary Hygom
   Director of Marketing & PR: Tim Kofahl
   Director Development: Diana Aceti
Founded: 1991
Specialized Field: Drama; Musical
Status: Non-Profit, Professional
Facility Category: Theater
Type of Stage: Thrust Stage
Seating Capacity: 299

3616
FORT SALEM THEATRE
Box 10
Salem, NY 12865
Phone: 518-854-9200
Fax: 518-854-9200
e-mail: fortsalem@gmail.com
Web Site: www.fortsalemtheater.com/
Management:
   President: Kim Shernan
   Artistic Director: Kathy Beaver
Mission: Bring professional theatre to the Washington county and Saratoga springs area.
Founded: 1972
Specialized Field: Musical; Comedy; Youth Theater
Status: Non-Profit, Professional
Paid Staff: 10
Volunteer Staff: 10
Paid Artists: 15
Non-paid Artists: 10
Season: June - September
Type of Stage: Proscenium
Stage Dimensions: 41' x 25'
Seating Capacity: 200

3617
METTAWEE THEATRE COMPANY
209 Dunnigan Road
Salem, NY 12865

THEATRE / New York

Phone: 518-854-9357
Fax: 518-854-9321
e-mail: info@mettawee.org
Web Site: www.mettawee.org
Officers:
   President: Stephanie Gallas
Management:
   Artistic Director: Ralph Lee
   Managing Director: Casey Compton
Mission: To offer original theatre works incorporating masks, live music and figures that are larger than life to illustrate the myths and legends of different cultures.
Founded: 1975
Specialized Field: New Plays; Storytelling; Ethnic Theater
Status: Professional; Nonprofit
Organization Type: Performing; Touring

3618
PENDRAGON THEATRE
15 Brandy Brook
Saranac Lake, NY 12983
Phone: 518-891-1854
Fax: 518-891-7012
e-mail: pdragon@northnet.org
Web Site: www.pendragontheatre.org
Officers:
   Vice President: Cyndee McGuire
   Secretary: Margaret Sorensen
   President: Charles Carroll
   Treasurer: Penny Dieffenbach
Management:
   Artistic Director: Karen Kirkham
   Managing Director: David Zwierankin
Mission: Pendragon is an ensemble of artists based in the Adirondacks dedicated to preserving the vitality and enhancing the quality of professional theatre through year round performance and education programs.
Founded: 1980
Specialized Field: Theatre
Status: Non-Profit, Professional
Paid Staff: 1
Volunteer Staff: 20
Paid Artists: 20
Budget: $280,000-$300,000
Season: June - September
Facility Category: Black Box
Type of Stage: Proscenium
Stage Dimensions: 30' x 24'
Seating Capacity: 130

3619
SARATOGA PERFORMING ARTS CENTER
108 Avenue of the Pines
Saratoga Springs, NY 12866
Phone: 518-584-9330
Fax: 518-584-0809
e-mail: general@spac.org
Web Site: www.spac.org
Officers:
   Honorary Chairman: Cornelius Whitney
   Chairman: Charles V Wait
   President: Herbert A Chesbrough
   Secretary: Walter M. Jeffords, Jr
   Treasurer: Harold N. Langlitz
Mission: To host performing arts events.
Utilizes: Singers
Founded: 1966
Specialized Field: Drama; Musical; Comedy; Classic
Status: Professional; Nonprofit
Budget: $11 million
Income Sources: International Association of Auditorium Managers; New York Performing Arts Association; membership ticket sales
Affiliations: Summer home of New York City Ballet, Philadelphia Orchestra and Saratoga Chamber Music Festival
Annual Attendance: 350,000
Facility Category: Ampitheatre
Type of Stage: Proscenium
Stage Dimensions: 80 W x 60 D
Seating Capacity: 5100
Year Built: 1966
Organization Type: Performing; Educational; Sponsoring

3620
PROCTOR'S THEATRE
432 State Street
Schenectady, NY 12305
Phone: 518-346-6204
Fax: 518-346-2468
e-mail: boxoffice@proctors.org
Web Site: www.proctors.org
Officers:
   President, XAR Corporation: Ronald Backer
   Executive VP: Jeffery A. Lawrence
   President: Anthony J. Mashuta
   Chairman of Power Technologies: Lionel Barthold
   Assistant to President: Anthony J. Bifaro
Management:
   CEO: Philip Morris
Mission: Presenting Broadway, opera, popular music, dance and classical
Founded: 1926
Specialized Field: Musical; Classic; Contemporary
Status: Non-Profit, Professional
Paid Staff: 40
Volunteer Staff: 900
Paid Artists: 35

3621
SCHENECTADY CIVIC PLAYERS
12 S Church Street
Schenectady, NY 12305
Phone: 518-382-2081
e-mail: postmaster@civicplayers.org
Web Site: www.civicplayers.org
Officers:
   President: Charles Hepburn
   VP: Laura Houlihan
   Secretary: Gail Kitchen
   Treasurer: Melissa Brown
   President: Duncan Morrison
   VP: Debbie May
Management:
   President: Melissa Brown
Mission: Continuation of long tradition of providing non-profit community theatre.
Founded: 1928
Specialized Field: Community Theater
Status: Non-Professional; Nonprofit
Income Sources: New York State Community Theatre Association; New York State Theater Festival Association
Organization Type: Performing; Resident

3622
STERLING RENAISSANCE FESTIVAL
15385 Farden Road
Sterling, NY 13156
Phone: 315-947-5783
Fax: 315-947-6905
Toll-free: 800-879-4446
e-mail: office@sterlingfestival.com
Web Site: www.sterlingfestival.com
Officers:
   President: Alisa Cook
   VP: John Kissler
   Secretary: Phil Holding
   Treasurer: Marylee Pangman
Management:
   President: Virginia Young
   Executive Director: Gerald Young
   Artistic Director: Gary Izzo
   Sales Director: Marilyn Goldthwait
Mission: To present interactive and staged performances.
Founded: 1977
Specialized Field: Musical; Comedy; Community Theater; Renaissance; Classic
Status: Non-Profit, Professional
Paid Staff: 10
Paid Artists: 80
Season: June - August
Annual Attendance: 100,000
Facility Category: Outdoor
Type of Stage: 8 Stages
Year Built: 1977

3623
PENGUIN REPERTORY COMPANY
Crickettown Road
Box 91
Stony Point, NY 10980
Phone: 845-786-2873
Fax: 914-786-3638
e-mail: info@penguinrep.org
Web Site: www.penguinrep.org
Officers:
   President: Angelo Parra
   VP: Patty Maloney
   Treasurer: Gray Pratt
   Secretary: Susanne Pepis
Management:
   Executive Director: Andrew Horn
   Artistic Director: Joe Brancato
Mission: To give new playwrights opportunities through mounting new plays; to stage works that are tried and true.
Founded: 1977
Specialized Field: New Plays; Classic
Status: Non-Profit, Professional
Paid Staff: 25
Paid Artists: 20
Income Sources: Actors' Equity Association; Society for Stage Directors and Choreographers
Season: May - October
Annual Attendance: 7,000-10,000
Type of Stage: Proscenium
Stage Dimensions: 23' x 25'
Seating Capacity: 108
Year Built: 1830
Year Remodeled: 1986
Organization Type: Performing

3624
THALIA SPANISH THEATRE
41-17 Greenpoint Avenue
PO Box 4368
Sunnyside, NY 11104
Phone: 718-729-3880
Fax: 718-729-3388
e-mail: info@thaliatheatre.org
Web Site: www.thaliatheatre.org

THEATRE / New York

Officers:
Chairperson/Treasurer: Walter Bracero
President: Angel Gil Orrios
VP: Mitchell Draizin
Secretary: Ada Suarez
Management:
Artistic/Executive Director: Angel Gil Orrios, agil@thaliatheatre.org
Administrative Director: Kathryn A Giaimo
Managing Director: Soledad Lopez, slopez@thaliatheatre.org
Technical Director: Fabricio Saquicela
Mission: To celebrate the vibrancy and diversity of Spanish and Latin American culture and heritage with unique productions of theatre, music and dance. Every month is Hispanic Heritage Month.
Utilizes: Actors; AEA Actors; Choreographers; Collaborations; Commissioned Composers; Dance Companies; Dancers; Designers; Grant Writers; Guest Accompanists; Guest Artists; Guest Choreographers; Guest Companies; Guest Conductors; Guest Designers; Guest Directors; Guest Lecturers; Guest Musical Directors; High School Drama; Instructors; Local Artists; Multimedia; Music; Organization Contracts; Resident Professionals; Sign Language Translators; Singers; Soloists; Student Interns; Special Technical Talent; Visual Arts
Founded: 1969
Specialized Field: Musical; Community Theater; Bilingual Theatre
Status: Professional; Nonprofit
Paid Staff: 4
Volunteer Staff: 6
Paid Artists: 90
Budget: $586,000
Income Sources: National Endowment for the Arts; New York State Coucil on Arts; New York City-Department of Cultural Affairs; NY Community Trust; JP Morgan Chase Foundation; Con Edison
Annual Attendance: 7,000
Facility Category: Theatre
Type of Stage: Proscenium
Seating Capacity: 72
Year Remodeled: 1992
Organization Type: Performing; Touring; Resident

3625
OPEN HAND THEATER
518 Prospect Avenue
Syracuse, NY 13205
Phone: 315-476-0466
Fax: 315-472-2578
e-mail: info@openhandtheater.org
Web Site: www.openhandtheater.org
Officers:
President: Samuel Gordon
Artistic Director: Geoffrey Navias
Management:
Artistic Director: Geoffrey Navias
Producer: Leslie Archer
Founded: 1980
Specialized Field: Puppet
Status: Non-Profit, Professional
Paid Staff: 5
Volunteer Staff: 85
Paid Artists: 4
Non-paid Artists: 4

3626
REDHOUSE ARTS CENTER
201 South West Street
PO Box 11506
Syracuse, NY 13202
Phone: 315-425-0405
Fax: 315-425-0561
e-mail: info@theredhouse.org
Web Site: www.theredhouse.org
Officers:
President: Timothy Mulver, Esq
Executive Director: Terrance Demas
Management:
Artistic Associate: Laura Austin
Mission: To offer contemporary drama; to encourage works-in-progress through stage readings; to provide programs in schools.
Founded: 1978
Specialized Field: Musical; Comedy; Classic; Contemporary
Status: Non-Profit, Professional
Paid Staff: 15
Paid Artists: 80
Organization Type: Performing

3627
SYRACUSE STAGE
820 E Genesee Street
Syracuse, NY 13210-1508
Phone: 315-443-4008
Fax: 315-443-9846
e-mail: syrstage@syr.edu
Web Site: www.syracusestage.org
Officers:
Chair: Robert Pomfrey
President: Lou Marcoccia
VP: Janet Audunson
Treasurer: Brian Sischo
Secretary: Rod McDonald
Management:
Administrative Director: Diana Coles
HR Adminintrator: Kathy Zappala
Producing Artistic Director: Timothy Bond
Artistic Assistant: Chris Botek
Managing Director: Jeffery Woodward
Dir Communications/Special Event: Heidi Holtz
Chris:
Kyle: Botek Artistic Assistant
Mission: To enrich, empower and entertain our community through the creation of professional theatre and to be an essential element in affecting the lives of thoughts in our community.
Utilizes: Actors; AEA Actors; Choreographers; Collaborations; Designers; Guest Designers; Guest Writers; Lyricists; Music; Original Music Scores; Resident Professionals; Selected Students; Soloists; Touring Companies
Founded: 1974
Specialized Field: Drama; Musical; New Works of Social Importance
Status: Non-Profit, Professional
Paid Staff: 90
Paid Artists: 30
Budget: $3.3 million
Income Sources: Theatre Communications Group; League of Resident Theatres; Actors' Equity Association
Season: September - May
Performs At: The John D Archbold Theatre
Annual Attendance: 90,000
Type of Stage: Proscenium
Seating Capacity: 499
Organization Type: Performing; Touring; Educational

3628
NEW YORK STATE THEATRE INSTITUTE
37 1st Street
Troy, NY 12180
Phone: 518-274-3200
Fax: 518-274-3815
e-mail: nysti@capital.net
Web Site: www.nysti.org
Officers:
Chairman: David Morris
Management:
Producing Artistic Director: Patricia D Benedette Snyder
Mission: To provide production of a high quality professional theatre; extensive arts in education programs; new play development; international cultural exchange.
Utilizes: Selected Students; Soloists; Students; Theatre Companies
Founded: 1976
Specialized Field: Drama; Multi-Cultural
Status: Non-Profit, Professional
Paid Staff: 33
Volunteer Staff: 250
Annual Attendance: 50,000
Facility Category: Theatre
Type of Stage: Proscenium
Stage Dimensions: 48'x30'
Seating Capacity: 850

3629
NEW YORK RENAISSANCE FAIRE
600 Route 17A
Tuxedo, NY 10987
Phone: 845-351-5171
Fax: 845-351-2073
e-mail: chrisdetroy@rec.com
Web Site: www.renfair.com
Management:
President: Stanley Gilbert
Executive Director: Bob Corsett
Artistic Director: Christopher Detroy
Finance Manager: Douglas DeTroy
Office Manager: Melissa McKeever
Founded: 1977
Specialized Field: Renaissance
Status: For-Profit, Professional
Paid Staff: 200
Paid Artists: 150
Season: July - September

3630
BROADWAY THEATRE LEAGUE OF UTICA
258 Genesee Street
Utica, NY 13502
Phone: 315-724-7196
Fax: 315-724-1227
e-mail: btlutica@dreamscape.com
Web Site: www.broadwayutica.com
Management:
Director: Marolyn Wilson
Executive Director: Robert A Lewis
Founded: 1957
Specialized Field: Touring Company; Broadway Musical Revivals; Classic
Status: Non-Profit,Professional
Paid Staff: 3

3631
PLAYERS OF UTICA
1108 State Street
Utica, NY 13502
Mailing Address: P.O. Box 29, New Hartford, NY 13413
Phone: 315-724-7624
e-mail: info@playersofutica.org
Web Site: playersofutica.org

THEATRE / North Carolina

Opened: 1913
Status: Nonprofit; Amateur

3632
WATERTOWN LYRIC THEATER PRODUCTIONS
317 Washington Street
Watertown, NY 13601
Phone: 315-785-9742
Fax: 315-779-8002
e-mail: info@watertownlyrictheater.org
Web Site: watertownlyrictheater.org/
Officers:
  President: James S Williams Jr
  Treasurer: Steve Hunt
  President: John Michael
  Vice President: Jeff Comet
  Secretary: Kate Wehrle
Management:
  Director: John Michael
  Managing Director: Joan Jones
Mission: To offer the community live theatre employing local talent; to provide young people with training in musical theatre.
Utilizes: Singers
Founded: 1959
Specialized Field: Musical; Community Theater
Status: Non-Profit, Non-Professional
Volunteer Staff: 360
Non-paid Artists: 150
Performs At: State Office Building Auditorium
Organization Type: Performing; Educational

3633
DAS PUPPENSPIEL PUPPET THEATER
1 1/2 E Main Street
Westfield, NY 14787
Phone: 716-326-2611
Fax: 716-326-2601
Toll-free: 877-326-2611
e-mail: sadpupp@puppets.org
Web Site: www.puppets.org
Management:
  Artistic Director: Myriam Mayshark
  Managing Director: Kevin Kuhlman
Founded: 1974
Specialized Field: Children's Theater; Touring Company; Puppet
Status: Non-Profit, Professional
Paid Staff: 5
Paid Artists: 4
Income Sources: United International Marionette Association; Puppeteers of America; Children's Theatre Association of America
Organization Type: Performing; Touring; Educational

3634
STREET THEATER
228 Fisher Avenue
White Plains, NY 10606
Phone: 914-761-3307
Fax: 914-422-2340
e-mail: thestreettheater@aollll.com
Management:
  Artistic Director: Gray Smith
Mission: Committed to educational programs. Mission: to insure success in school for disadvantaged students through early literacy programs. Program components: weekly performance-based instruction by professional actors, teacher training, curriculum materials, parent participation, professional touring company.
Utilizes: Singers
Founded: 1970
Specialized Field: Educational; Theater Workshops; Youth Theater
Status: Professional; Semi-Professional; Nonprofit
Income Sources: Actors' Equity Association
Organization Type: Performing; Touring; Educational

3635
COMMON STAGE THEATRE COMPANY
PO Box 1028
Woodstock, NY 12498
Phone: 845-679-9256
Mission: Developing and producing plays by women.
Utilizes: Singers
Founded: 1989
Specialized Field: Women's Theater
Status: Semi-Professional; Nonprofit
Paid Staff: 10

North Carolina

3636
ASHEVILLE COMMUNITY THEATRE
35 East Walnut Street
Asheville, NC 28801
Phone: 828-254-2939
Fax: 828-252-4723
Web Site: ashevilletheatre.org
Officers:
  President: Craig Justus
  Vice President: Susan Maley
Management:
  Managing Director: Susan Harper
  Business Manager: Tamara Sparacino
  Program Director: Chanda Calentine
  Marketing Director: Jenny Bunn
Mission: To provide entertainment, enrichment, and education through the practice and celebration of the theatre arts.
Founded: 1946

3637
BLACK SWAN THEATER
109 Roberts Street
#318
Asheville, NC 28801
Phone: 828-254-6057
Fax: 828-251-6603
e-mail: swantheatre@aol.com
Web Site: blackswan.org
Management:
  Director: David B Hopes
Mission: To produce original contemporary scripts and reinterpret the classics.
Utilizes: Actors; Choreographers; Collaborating Artists; Collaborations; Commissioned Composers; Commissioned Music; Community Talent; Composers; Dance Companies; Dancers; Designers; Guest Accompanists; Guest Artists; Guest Choreographers; Guest Companies; Guest Conductors; Guest Designers; Guest Lecturers; Guest Musical Directors; Guest Musicians; Guest Writers; Instructors; Local Artists; Multi Collaborations; Organization Contracts; Original Music Scores; Paid Performers; Performance Artists; Playwrights; Resident Professionals; Sign Language Translators; Singers; Special Technical Talent; Theatre Companies; Visual Arts
Founded: 1988
Specialized Field: Contemporary; Classic; New Plays
Status: Non-Professional; Nonprofit
Paid Staff: 70
Income Sources: University of North Carolina at Asheville Creative Writing Department; Ticket Sales
Organization Type: Performing; Touring; Sponsoring

3638
DIANA WORTHAM THEATRE AT PACK PLACE
2 S Pack Square
Asheville, NC 28801
Phone: 828-257-4530
Fax: 828-251-5652
e-mail: jellis@dwtheatre.com
Web Site: www.dwtheatre.com
Officers:
  Managing Director: John Ellis
  Marketing Director: Elly Wels
Management:
  Managing Director: John Ellis
  Associate Director: Rae Geoffery
  Operations Manager: Tiffany Santiago
  Production Coordinator: Erik McDaniel
  Box Office Manager: Coco Palmer
Founded: 1993
Specialized Field: Youth Theater; Puppet; Classic; Contemporary
Status: Non-Profit, Professional
Paid Staff: 3
Volunteer Staff: 30
Budget: $400,000
Annual Attendance: 40,000
Facility Category: Performing Arts Center
Type of Stage: Proscenium
Stage Dimensions: 40x40
Seating Capacity: 500
Year Built: 1992

3639
SMOKY MOUNTAIN REPERTORY THEATRE
26 S Lexington Street
Asheville, NC 28801
Phone: 704-252-9661
Management:
  Managing Director: H Byron Ballard
  Business Manager: Joe Fioccola
  Technical Director: M Michael Hyatt
  Youth Director: Vivienne Conjura
Mission: Producing new works and adaptations with particular emphasis on plays of regional significance.
Utilizes: Singers
Founded: 1981
Specialized Field: Ethnic Theater; Ensembles
Status: Professional; Semi-Professional; Nonprofit
Paid Staff: 10
Performs At: First Artists Studio Theater
Organization Type: Performing; Touring; Resident; Educational

3640
LEES-MCRAE COLLEGE
Performing Arts Department
191 Main Street
Banner Elk, NC 28604
Mailing Address: PO Box 128
Phone: 828-898-8721
Fax: 828-989-3467
e-mail: joslinp@lmc.edu
Web Site: www.lmc.edu
Management:
  President: Dr. Barry M Buxton
  Summer Theatre, Artistic Director: Dr. Janet Barton Speer
  Chair, Div of Creative & Fine Arts: Dr. Tessa Carr
  Operations Manager: Pamela Wilder Joslin
Mission: LMST is a professional company that shows three musicals each summer.
Founded: 1900

Opened: 1984
Specialized Field: Musical Summer Stock
Status: Non-Profit, Non-Professional
Paid Staff: 13
Paid Artists: 15
Season: June - August

3641
BLOWING ROCK STAGE COMPANY
152 Jamie Fort Rd
Blowing Rock, NC 28605
Phone: 828-295-9168
Fax: 828-295-9104
e-mail: theatre@blowingrock.com
Web Site: www.blowingrockstage.com
Officers:
  President: Connie Baird
  VP: Rebecca Wright
  Treasurer: Jerry Burns
  Secretary: Yvonne Myers
Management:
  President: Freda Smith
  Artistic Director: Kenneth Kay
  General Manager: Robert Miller
Founded: 1986
Specialized Field: Musical; Comedy; Summer Stock
Status: Non-Profit, Professional
Paid Staff: 2
Paid Artists: 40
Season: June - September
Type of Stage: Proscenium
Stage Dimensions: 28'x 36'
Seating Capacity: 240

3642
ARTSCENTER
300-G E Main Street
Carrboro, NC 27510
Phone: 919-929-2787
Fax: 919-969-8574
e-mail: info@artscenterlive.org
Web Site: www.artscenterlive.org
Officers:
  Chairman: Steve Benezra
Management:
  Executive Director: Jon Wilner
  Booking Manager: Tess O'Cana
Mission: To inspire a love of the arts through presentation of a broad range of artists and educational programs, and by supporting the development of young artists; to create an environment for exploring and appreciating artistic expression.
Utilizes: Guest Companies; Singers
Founded: 1973
Specialized Field: Young Playwrights; Youth Theater; Community Theater; Puppet
Status: Non-Profit, Professional
Paid Staff: 6
Volunteer Staff: 30
Paid Artists: 250
Income Sources: Grants; Ticket Sales; Class Tuitions; Donars; Foundations
Performs At: Earl Wynn Theatre
Annual Attendance: 83,750
Seating Capacity: 350
Year Built: 1972
Year Remodeled: 1986
Organization Type: Performing; Touting; Resident; Educational; Sponsoring

3643
DEEP DISH THEATER COMPANY
201 South Estes Drive
Chapel Hill, NC 27514
Phone: 919-968-1515
e-mail: info@deepdishtheater.org
Web Site: deepdishtheater.org
Officers:
  Chair: Kenneth Broun
  Vice Chair: Karen Curtin
Management:
  Artistic Director: Paul Frellick
Opened: 2001
Status: Nonprofit

3644
INSTITUTE OF OUTDOOR DRAMA
CB 3240, 1700 Airport Road
UNC
Chapel Hill, NC 27599-3240
Phone: 252-328-5363
Fax: 252-328-0968
e-mail: outdoor@unc.edu
Web Site: www.outdoordrama.org
Management:
  President: Scott J Parker
Mission: Sponsors regional auditions for performers and technicians in outdoor dramas; hosts management conference annually; conducts feasibility studies.
Utilizes: Singers
Founded: 1963
Specialized Field: Outdoor Theater; Drama
Status: Non-Profit, Professional
Paid Staff: 3
Organization Type: Educational; Sponsoring

3645
PLAYMAKERS REPERTORY COMPANY
Centers for Dramatic Art
CB #3235
Chapel Hill, NC 27599-3235
Phone: 919-962-7529
Fax: 919-962-5791
e-mail: prcboxoffice@unc.edu
Web Site: www.playmakersrep.org
Officers:
  Carpenter: Justin Carnes
  Scenic Arltist: Cassie Handzo
  Prop Master: Aline Johnson
  Technical Director: Adam Maxfield
  Stage Manager: Sarah Smiley
Management:
  Managing Director: Hannah Grannemann
  Producing Artistic Director: Joseph Haj
  General Manager: Heidi Reklis, hreklis@email.unc.edu
  Costume Director: Judy Adamson
  Stage Manager: Chuck Bayank
Mission: To engage our community in an ongoing exploration of and significance of theatre in contemporary life; to investigate the theatrical events and the methods used for its realization in performance.
Utilizes: Dancers; Guest Lecturers; Instructors; Paid Performers; Scenic Designers; Soloists
Founded: 1976
Specialized Field: Contemporary Works; Classics; New Works of Social Importance
Status: Professional
Paid Staff: 15
Budget: $2.4 million
Income Sources: Private Foundations; Grants; Endowments; Business; Ccorporte Donations; Box Office; Government Grant; Individual Donors
Performs At: Paul Green Theatre; Elizabeth Price Kenan Theatre
Affiliations: League of Resident Theatres; Actors' Equity Association; Society for Stage Directors and Choreographers
Type of Stage: Thrust
Seating Capacity: 499;285
Year Built: 1976
Year Remodeled: 2010
Organization Type: Performing; Educational

3646
ACTOR'S THEATRE OF CHARLOTTE
650 E Stonewall Street
Charlotte, NC 28202
Phone: 704-342-2251
Fax: 704-342-1229
e-mail: actorstheatre@bellsouth.net
Web Site: www.actorstheatrecharlotte.org
Officers:
  Executive Director: Dan Shoemaker
  Artistic Director: Chip Decker
  Marketing/Development Director: Robert Touchstone
Management:
  President: Dan Shoemaker
  Managing Director: Chip Decker
Mission: The mission of Actor's Theatre of Charlotte is to produce bold and innovative new works by contemporary playwrights.
Founded: 1989
Specialized Field: Drama; Contemporary
Status: Non-Profit, Professional
Paid Staff: 3
Volunteer Staff: 6
Paid Artists: 37
Budget: $197,000
Type of Stage: Proscenium

3647
CENTRAL PIEDMONT COMMUNITY THEATRE
1201 Elizabeth Avenue
Charlotte, NC 28204
Mailing Address: P.O. Box 35009, Charlotte, NC 28235-5009
Phone: 704-330-6534
Fax: 704-330-6290
Web Site: www.cpcc.edu
Management:
  Producer and Director: Tom Vance
  Director: Tom Hollis
Mission: To offer quality entertainment to the community; to provide training for students aspiring to careers in professional theatre.
Utilizes: Guest Companies; Singers
Founded: 1974
Specialized Field: Musical; Community Theater
Status: Non-Profit, Professional
Paid Staff: 40
Income Sources: North Carolina Theatre Conference; Southeastern Theatre Conference
Performs At: Pease Auditorium
Organization Type: Performing; Educational

3648
CHILDREN'S THEATRE OF CHARLOTTE
300 East 7th Street
Charlotte, NC 28202
Phone: 704-973-2828
Fax: 703-973-2800
e-mail: info@ctcharlotte.org
Web Site: www.ctcharlotte.org
Officers:
  Executive Director: Bruce LaRowe
Management:
  Artistic Director: Alan Poindexter
  Education Director: Valerie Rhymer
  Interim executive Director: Linda Reynolds

THEATRE / North Carolina

Artistic Director: Adam Burke
Eduction Director: Michelle Long
Mission: To enrich the lives of young people, ages 3-18, of all cultures, through theatre and education experiences of the highest quality.
Founded: 1948
Specialized Field: Children's Theater, Youth Education
Status: Non-Profit, Professional
Paid Staff: 30
Paid Artists: 80
Income Sources: Arts and Science Council; Cultural Education Collaborative; North Carolina Arts Council; National Endowment for the Arts

3649
THEATRE CHARLOTTE
501 Queens Road
Charlotte, NC 28207
Phone: 704-334-9128
Fax: 704-347-5216
e-mail: ron@theatrecharlotte.org
Web Site: www.theatrecharlotte.org
Officers:
  Executive Director: Ron Law
  Director of Development: Jackie Timmons
  Director of Business and Audience S: Nancy Scala Wilson
Mission: To offer community members an opportunity to participate in or attend amateur theatre productions.
Utilizes: Actors; Collaborations; Commissioned Music; Educators; Fine Artists; Grant Writers; Guest Artists; Guest Companies; Guest Conductors; Guest Lecturers; Guild Activities; Local Artists; Multi Collaborations; Organization Contracts; Singers; Touring Companies
Founded: 1927
Specialized Field: Community Theater
Status: Nonprofit
Paid Staff: 6
Income Sources: First Nighters
Facility Category: Community Theatre
Type of Stage: Proscenium
Seating Capacity: 221
Year Built: 1941
Year Remodeled: 1998
Cost: $100,000
Organization Type: Performing; Educational

3650
CAROLINA THEATRE OF DURHAM
309 W Morgan Street
Durham, NC 27701-2119
Phone: 919-560-3030
Fax: 919-560-3065
e-mail: connie@carolinatheatre.org
Web Site: www.carolinatheatre.org
Officers:
  Chair: Tim Alwar
  Vice Chair: Scott Harmon
  Secretary: Cecily Durrett
  Treasurer: Ronie Eubank
Management:
  President: Ed Rose
  Executive Director: Connie Campanero
  Programming Rentals Director: Jim Carl
Mission: To manage, operate and program the creative theater for the city of Durham.
Utilizes: Dance Companies; Filmmakers; Local Artists; Original Music Scores; Theatre Companies
Founded: 1992
Specialized Field: Community Theater; Musical
Status: Non-Profit, Professional
Paid Staff: 60
Volunteer Staff: 200
Paid Artists: 30
Budget: $1,000,000
Performs At: Fletcher Hall
Annual Attendance: 150,000
Facility Category: Performance Center/Cinemas
Type of Stage: Proscenium
Stage Dimensions: 30'x 60'
Seating Capacity: 1,015
Year Built: 1926
Year Remodeled: 1994
Rental Contact: Jim Carl

3651
MANBITES DOG THEATER
703 Foster Street
Durham, NC 27702
Mailing Address: P.O. Box 402, Durham, NC 27702
Phone: 919-682-4974
e-mail: manbitesdogtheater@gmail.com
Web Site: manbitesdogtheater.org
Officers:
  President: Michael Hayes
  Vice President: Jeff Storer
Management:
  Artistic Director: Jeff Storer
  Managing Director: Edward Hunt
  Associate Artistic Director: Jay O'Berski
Founded: 1987
Status: Professional; Nonprofit

3652
THEATRE PREVIEWS AT DUKE
109 Page
Durham, NC 27708-0680
Phone: 919-660-3343
Fax: 919-684-8906
e-mail: mmsauls@duke.edu
Web Site: www.theaterstudies.duke.edu
Management:
  Director of Theater: Miriam Sauls
Mission: Theatre Previews is the professional prodcing arm of the Duke University Department of Theater Studies and a laboratory for the professional development and production of new plays on Duke's campus.
Founded: 1986
Specialized Field: Musical; Comedy; Classic; Contemporary; Educational
Status: Non-Profit, Professional
Paid Staff: 1
Facility Category: Theater
Seating Capacity: 600

3653
CHILDREN'S THEATRE OF EDEN
PO Box 547
Eden, NC 27288
Phone: 336-725-4531
Fax: 336-725-4531
Mission: To provide professional plays for all children in Eden City schools at no cost.
Founded: 1971
Specialized Field: Musical; Ethnic Theater; Puppet; Children's Theater
Status: Professional; Nonprofit
Performs At: High School Auditorium
Organization Type: Sponsoring

3654
ANAM CARA THEATRE COMPANY
P.O. Box 1995
Enka, NC 28728
Phone: 828-633-1773
e-mail: info@anamcaratheatre.org
Web Site: anamcaratheatre.org
Management:
  Artistic Director: Erinn Hartley
  Marketing Coordinator: Kristen Aldrich
Mission: Anam Cara Theatre Company aims to produce progressive work that provides audiences and company members alike, with an experience that makes evident the eternal connection of all humanity, in turn promoting social change, and striving for the equality of all people.
Status: Charitable Organization
Performs At: Toy Boat Community Arts Space 101 Fairview Rd., Asheville, Nc 28803

3655
CAPE FEAR REGIONAL THEATRE
1209 Hay Street
Fayetteville, NC 28305
Mailing Address: PO Box 53723, Fayetteville, NC 28305
Phone: 919-323-4233
Fax: 919-323-0898
e-mail: bothorp@cfrt.org
Web Site: www.cfrt.org
Management:
  Artistic Director: Tom Quaintance
  MD: Frank Moorman
  Production Coordinator: Ken Blinn
  Technical Director: James Roger
  Marketing Director: Leslie Flom
Mission: To offer a diverse program of plays to the Cape Fear Region.
Utilizes: AEA Actors; Curators; Guest Artists; Guest Companies; Singers
Founded: 1962
Specialized Field: Musical; Community Theater; Puppet; Drama
Status: For-Profit,Professional
Income Sources: North Carolina Theatre Conference; Southeastern Theatre Conference; Arts Council
Seating Capacity: 327
Organization Type: Performing

3656
GILBERT THEATER
116 Green Street
Fayetteville, NC 28301
Phone: 910-678-7186
e-mail: gilberttheater@aol.com
Web Site: www.gilberttheater.com/
Officers:
  Founding Artistic Director: Lynn Pryer
  Artistic Director, Co-Director, Edu: Robyne Parrish
  Managing Director and Co-Director,: Jeremy Fiebig
Management:
  Executive Director: Gerald Ellison
  Artistic Director: Lynn Pryer
  Managing Director: Andrew Morfesis
Mission: Our purpose is to use our creativity and enthusiasm to support and inspire others as we all freely express our talents in joyfulness, harmony and love.
Founded: 1994
Specialized Field: Contemporary; Classic
Status: Non-Profit, Professional

3657
FLAT ROCK PLAYHOUSE
2661 Greenville Highway
Flat Rock, NC 28731

Phone: 828-693-0731
Fax: 828-693-6795
e-mail: frp@flatrockplayhouse.org
Web Site: www.flatrockplayhouse.org
Management:
   Producing Artistic Director: Vincent Marini
   Managing Director: Paige Posey
   Associate Artistic Director: Scott Treadway
Mission: To produce the highest quality professional theatre while teaching theatre arts through a multifaceted educational program.
Founded: 1937
Specialized Field: Musical; Comedy; Youth Theater; Contemporary; Theater Workshops
Status: Non-Profit, Professional
Paid Staff: 30
Volunteer Staff: 10
Paid Artists: 100
Budget: $2.6 million
Income Sources: Ticket Sales; Grants; Donations
Season: May - October
Performs At: Flat Rock Playhouse
Affiliations: Actor's Equity Association; South Eastern Theatre Conference; North Carolina Theatre Conference
Annual Attendance: 100,000
Type of Stage: Proscenium
Stage Dimensions: 30'x40'
Seating Capacity: 500
Year Built: 1956
Organization Type: Performing; Touring; Resident; Educational; Sponsoring

3658
LITTLE THEATER OF GASTONIA
238 Clay Street
PO Box 302
Gastonia, NC 28053
Mailing Address: P O Box 302, Gastonia, NC 28053
Phone: 704-865-0160
e-mail: ewixson@prodigy.net
Web Site: www.littletheatergastonia.com
Management:
   President: Susan Lisle
Mission: To offer entertainment as well as education in the theatre arts.
Utilizes: Singers
Founded: 1950
Specialized Field: Musical; Comedy; Community Theater; Classic; Contemporary
Status: Non-Profit, Non-Professional
Paid Staff: 50
Volunteer Staff: 6
Income Sources: Ticket Sales; Season Memberships
Performs At: The Little Theatre of Gastonia
Organization Type: Performing; Educational

3659
CITY ARTS DRAMA CENTER
200 N Davie Street
Box 2
Greensboro, NC 27401
Phone: 336-335-6426
Fax: 336-373-2659
e-mail: stephen.hyers@greensboro-nc.gov
Web Site: www.TheDramaCenter.com
Management:
   Managing Director: Stephen D. Hyers
Mission: To present six musicals annually. The programs presented are: Livestock Players, Greensboro Children's Theatre, Greensboro Playwrights' Forum, 3rd Stage Theatre Company, Greene Pictures.
Utilizes: Guest Artists; Guest Companies

Founded: 1971
Specialized Field: Musical; Drama; Ensembles; Children's Theater
Status: Non-Profit, Non-Professional
Paid Staff: 2
Paid Artists: 10
Income Sources: Southeastern Theatre Conference
Performs At: Carolina Theatre
Organization Type: Performing

3660
COMMUNITY THEATRE OF GREENSBORO
200 N Davie Street
Suite 9
Greensboro, NC 27401
Phone: 336-333-7470
Fax: 336-333-2607
e-mail: ctgemail@aol.com
Web Site: www.ctgso.com
Officers:
   President: Pam Murphy
   VP Admin: Paul Le Houillier
   VP Education: Cindy Bower
   VP Production: Maria Warner
   Secretary: Walter Laney
   Director of Education: Rozalynn Fulton
   Director of Operations: Rich Gilliland
Management:
   President: Chris Lamey
   Executive Director: Mitchel Sommers
   Director Marketing/Development: Robert Ankrom
   Director Education: Pauline Cobrda
Mission: To provide an outlet in the community whereby persons may participate avocationally in a live theatrical experience of high calibre, both as talent and audience under professional guidance.
Utilizes: Actors; Choreographers; Dancers; Grant Writers; Guest Artists; Guest Composers; Guest Lecturers; Music; Resident Professionals; Student Interns
Founded: 1954
Specialized Field: Musical; Community Theater
Status: Non-Profit, Non-Professional
Paid Staff: 5
Budget: $552,000
Income Sources: United Arts Council of Greensboro; Fundraising
Performs At: Carolina Theatre; GSO Cultural Center
Annual Attendance: 35,000
Organization Type: Performing; Resident; Educational

3661
GREENSBORO CHILDREN'S THEATRE
200 N Davie Street
Greensboro, NC 27401
Phone: 336-373-2728
Fax: 336-373-2659
e-mail: barbara.britton@ci.greensboro.nc.us
Web Site: www.ci.greensboro.nc.us/leisure/drama/gct.htm
Management:
   Director: Barbara Britton
Mission: To offer a series of drama classes and three quality plays annually by and for children and families as part of a recreation program.
Utilizes: Guest Companies
Founded: 1971
Specialized Field: Musical; Community Theater; Children's Theater
Status: Non-Professional; Nonprofit
Paid Staff: 2
Volunteer Staff: 10
Paid Artists: 50

Income Sources: City of Greensboro NC Parks and Recreation Depertment; Ticket Sales
Performs At: Weaver Education Center Theatre
Affiliations: Southeastern Theatre Conference; City Arts Drama; NC Theatre Conference
Annual Attendance: 2,500-3,000
Facility Category: Rented
Type of Stage: Proscenium Stage
Organization Type: Performing

3662
HICKORY COMMUNITY THEATRE
30 3rd Street NW
Hickory, NC 28601
Phone: 828-328-2283
Fax: 828-328-2284
e-mail: pam@hct.org
Web Site: www.hickorytheatre.org
Officers:
   President: Lee Pugh
Management:
   Artistic Director: Pamela Livingstone
   MD: John Rambo
   Administrative Director: Christine Stinstone
   Technical Director: Tony Chamber
Mission: To offer quality theatre to the community; to provide a performance outlet for talented local performers.
Utilizes: Actors; Grant Writers; Guest Artists; Guest Companies; Guest Designers; Guest Directors; Guest Lecturers; High School Drama; Local Artists; Multimedia; Music; Performance Artists; Resident Professionals; Singers; Soloists
Founded: 1949
Specialized Field: Musical; Comedy; Community Theater; Classic; Contemporary
Status: Non-Profit, Non-Professional
Paid Staff: 5
Budget: $412,000
Income Sources: Catawba County Council for the Arts; Box Office; Grants; Donatios
Performs At: Old City Hall
Affiliations: AACT; NCTC; SETA
Facility Category: Community Theatre
Type of Stage: Proscenium/Cabaret
Seating Capacity: 382; 72
Organization Type: Performing; Touring; Resident; Educational

3663
YOUTHEATRE
810 8th Street NE
Hickory, NC 28601
Phone: 828-324-5354
Management:
   Owner/Executive Director: Sylvia B Hoffmire
Mission: To provide an arena for the creative expression of young people through performance and study.
Utilizes: Guest Companies; Singers
Founded: 1976
Specialized Field: Community Theater; Youth Theater
Status: Professional; Semi-Professional; Commercial
Income Sources: Catawba County Council for the Arts
Organization Type: Performing; Touring; Educational; Sponsoring

3664
HIGH POINT COMMUNITY THEATRE
921 Eastchester Dr
PO Box 1152
High Point, NC 27261

THEATRE / North Carolina

Mailing Address: PO Box 1152, High Point, NC 27261
Phone: 336-882-2542
Fax: 336-882-4178
e-mail: jblevins@hpcommunitytheater.org
Web Site: www.hpct.net/
Management:
   Director: Ed Cornwell
   Executive Director: Jennifer Blevins
Mission: To promote community involvement in performing arts; to provide high quality entertainment for citizens in our area.
Utilizes: Guest Artists; Guest Companies; Singers
Founded: 1976
Specialized Field: Community Theater
Status: Non-Profit, Non-Professional
Paid Staff: 1
Paid Artists: 25
Income Sources: High Point Arts Council
Performs At: High Point Theatre
Affiliations: High Point Area Arts Council
Organization Type: Performing

3665
NORTH CAROLINA SHAKESPEARE FESTIVAL
807 West Ward Avenue
High Point, NC 27260
Mailing Address: PO Box 6066, High Point, NC 27262
Phone: 336-841-2273
Fax: 336-841-8627
e-mail: wil.elder@ncshakes.org
Web Site: www.ncshakes.org
Officers:
   Chairman: Ashley Hedgecock
   Ex officio: Joane Lawrence
   Ex officio: Tim Mabe
   Resident Director: Steve Umberger
   Outreach & Education Director: Michael Huie
   Technical Director: Tim Kottyan
Management:
   Managing Director: Pedro Silva
Mission: Seeks to serve the cultural and educational needs of North Carolina audiences through traditional and nontraditional staging of the plays of Shakespeare and other classic playwrights.
Founded: 1977
Specialized Field: Youth Theater; Classic
Status: Non-Profit, Professional
Paid Staff: 7
Paid Artists: 55
Budget: $1,400,000
Income Sources: Ticket Sales; Touring Fees; Contributors
Season: Late August - December
Performs At: High Point Theatre
Organization Type: Performing; Touring; Resident; Educational

3666
LOST COLONY
1409 National Park Drive
Manteo, NC 27954
Phone: 252-473-2127
Fax: 252-473-6000
Toll-free: 866-468-7630
Utilizes: Actors; Dancers; Grant Writers; Multimedia; Music; Selected Students; Sign Language Translators; Soloists; Student Interns
Founded: 1937
Specialized Field: Summer Stock
Status: Non-Equity; Nonprofit
Season: June - August
Type of Stage: Amphitheatre
Stage Dimensions: 80' x 40'
Seating Capacity: 1650
Year Built: 1937
Year Remodeled: 1998

3667
FOOTHILLS COMMUNITY THEATRE
24 S Main Street
PO Box 1417
Marion, NC 28752
Phone: 828-659-7529
e-mail: info@fctplays.org
Web Site: www.fctplays.org
Management:
   Artistic Director: Sandra Epperson
Mission: To offer opportunities for participation in the performing arts; to enhance cultural life and provide entertainment.
Utilizes: Guest Artists; Guest Companies; Singers
Founded: 1972
Specialized Field: Community Theater
Status: Non-Professional; Nonprofit
Income Sources: McDowell Arts & Craft Association
Performs At: McDowell East Junior High; McDowell Technical Company
Organization Type: Performing

3668
SOUTHERN APPALACHIAN REPERTORY THEATRE
Mars Hill College
PO Box 1720
Mars Hill, NC 28754
Phone: 828-689-1384
Fax: 828-689-1272
e-mail: sart@mhc.edu
Web Site: sartplays.org/
Officers:
   Artistic Director: Bill Gregg
Management:
   President: Richard Morgan
   Artistic Director: William Gregg
   Managing Director: Rob Miller
   Production Manager: Neil St Clair
Mission: From the beginning, SART's purpose has been to produce quality theatre by a professional non-profit company in an area considered economically and culturally deprived, to present plays concerning Applachia that portray the rich culture and heritage of its people.
Utilizes: Guest Companies; Singers
Founded: 1975
Specialized Field: Comedy; Ensembles; Contemporary
Status: Non-Profit, Professional
Paid Staff: 4
Volunteer Staff: 3
Paid Artists: 60
Non-paid Artists: 4
Income Sources: Mars Hill College; Ticket Sales
Performs At: Owen Theatre
Year Built: 1887
Organization Type: Performing; Touring; Resident

3669
MATTHEWS PLAYHOUSE
100 McDowell Street
Matthews, NC 28105
Phone: 704-846-8343
Web Site: www.matthewsplayhouse.com/
Management:
   President: Howie Labiner
   Vice President: Patty Jones
   Treasurer: Tom Gooley
   Secretary: Tiffany Dunagan
   Artistic Director: June Bayless
   Resident Director: Jamey Varnadore
Mission: To provide the good people of our community with theatrical experience, educational opportunities, and quality entertainment.
Founded: 1995
Specialized Field: Children's Theater; Educational; Musical

3670
MOORESVILLE COMMUNITY THEATRE
PO Box 194
Mooresville, NC 28115
Phone: 704-664-3783
Fax: 704-662-3344
Web Site: www.main.nc.us
Officers:
   President: Larry Gambill
   VP: Julian D'Amico
   Secretary/Treasurer: Clayton Miller
Management:
   President: Julian D'Amico
Mission: To provide live theatre for the Mooresville area.
Utilizes: Actors; Choreographers; Guest Designers; Instructors; Local Artists; Multimedia; Resident Professionals; Sign Language Translators
Founded: 1973
Specialized Field: Musical; Comedy; Community Theater; Contemporary; New Plays
Status: Non-Profit, Non-Professional
Paid Staff: 4
Volunteer Staff: 10
Paid Artists: 4
Income Sources: Box; Office Receipts
Performs At: Joe V Knox Auditorium
Organization Type: Performing

3671
JUDSON THEATRE
3395 Airport Road
Pinehurst, NC 28374
Phone: 800-514-3849
e-mail: judsontheatre@gmail.com
Web Site: judsontheatre.com
Management:
   Executive Producer: Morgan Sills
   Artistic Director: Daniel Haley
Performs At: Owens Auditorium At Sandhills Community College

3672
UNTO THESE HILLS
PO Box 398
Pittsboro, NC 28719
Phone: 828-497-2111
Fax: 828-497-6987
Toll-free: 866-554-4557
e-mail: cheratt@dnet.net
Web Site: www.untothesehills.com/
Management:
   Artistic Director: Peter Hardy
   General Manager: Barry Hipps
Mission: America's most popular outdoor drama, Unto These Hills, is the tragic and triumphant story of the Cherokee.
Founded: 1950
Specialized Field: Drama; Multi-Cultural; Historical
Status: Non-Profit, Professional
Paid Staff: 290
Paid Artists: 70
Season: May - August

THEATRE / North Carolina

3673
ACTORS COMEDY LAB
1610 Midtown Place
Raleigh, NC 27609
Phone: 919-873-1333
Fax: 919-875-0703
e-mail: info@actorscomedylab.com
Web Site: www.actorscomedylab.com
Officers:
  Board Member: Nancy Rich
Specialized Field: Comedy
Status: Nonprofit

3674
BURNING COAL THEATRE COMPANY
224 Polk Street
PO BOX 90904
Raleigh, NC 27675-0904
Mailing Address: P.O. Box 90904, Raleigh NC 27675-0904
Phone: 919-834-4001
Fax: 919-834-4002
e-mail: coalartisticdir@ncrrbiz.com
Web Site: www.burningcoal.org
Officers:
  Board of Directors: Kate Day
  Board of Directors: William Lightfoot
  Board of Directors: Marvin Swirsky
  Board of Advisors: Wiliam Peeples
Management:
  Artistic Director: Jerome Davis
  Managing Director: Simmie Kastner
Mission: To produce, literate, visceral, affecting theatre that is experienced, not simply seen.
Specialized Field: Musical; Drama; Comedy
Status: Incorporated; Nonprofit
Income Sources: City of Raleigh Arts Commission; United Arts
Facility Category: Flexible Black Box

3675
NORTH CAROLINA THEATRE
One E S Street
Raleigh, NC 27601
Phone: 919-831-6941
Fax: 919-831-6951
e-mail: nct@nctheatre.com
Web Site: www.nctheatre.com
Officers:
  President: Duke Fentress
  Technical Director: Bill Yates
  Development Director: Melanie Doerner
  President & CEO: Lisa Grele Barrie
  Founder: De Ann S. Jones
Management:
  Director: Robert Monroe
  Executive Director: William Jones
  Founder: De Ann S Jones
Mission: To provide Broadway-quality professional theatre at an affordable price as well as provide available employment to theatre artists and craftsmen.
Utilizes: Actors; AEA Actors; Choreographers; Dancers; Designers; Educators; Guest Accompanists; Guest Artists; Guest Conductors; Guest Designers; Guest Directors; Guest Ensembles; High School Drama; Instructors; Local Artists; Multimedia; Music; Original Music Scores; Resident Professionals; Selected Students; Sign Language Translators; Student Interns; Theatre Companies
Founded: 1983
Specialized Field: Broadway Musical Revivals
Status: Non-Profit, Professional
Paid Staff: 10
Budget: $678,000
Income Sources: Grants; Sponsors; Donations; Ticket Sales; Kids' Programs
Facility Category: Auditorium
Seating Capacity: 2000-2500
Year Remodeled: 2002
Organization Type: Performing

3676
SIDE BY SIDE
150 Fayetteville Street
PO Box 19416
Raleigh, NC 27601
Phone: 919-833-1141
Management:
  Director: Paul B Conway
Mission: To provide entertainment.
Founded: 1981
Specialized Field: Musical; Dinner Theater; Community Theater; Ethnic Theater
Status: Semi-Professional; Nonprofit
Organization Type: Performing

3677
THEATRE IN THE PARK
107 Pullen Road
Raleigh, NC 27607-7367
Phone: 919-831-6936
Fax: 919-831-9475
e-mail: info@theatreinthepark.com
Web Site: www.theatreinthepark.com
Officers:
  President: Bill Parmelee
  VP: G Troy Page
  Secretary: Camille Patterson
  Treasurer: Johy Taylor
Management:
  Director: Van Eure
  Executive Director: Ira David Wood
  Financial Director: Sue R Hill
  Director Of Managing: Dolly R Sickle
Mission: North Carolina's largest community theatre. Each year, theatre in the park produces humorous productions, Shakepeare and original plays.
Utilizes: Guest Companies
Founded: 1973
Specialized Field: Musical; Community Theater
Status: Non-Professional; Nonprofit
Paid Staff: 6
Volunteer Staff: 10
Non-paid Artists: 120
Income Sources: American Alliance for Theatre Arts; North Carolina Community Theatre
Performs At: Theatre In The Park
Organization Type: Performing; Touring; Resident; Educational; Sponsoring

3678
PIEDMONT PLAYERS THEATRE
213 S Main Street
PO Box 762
Salisbury, NC 28144
Mailing Address: PO Box 762, Salisbury, NC 28145
Phone: 704-633-5471
Fax: 704-633-4653
e-mail: bm@piedmontplayers.com
Web Site: www.piedmontplayers.com
Officers:
  President: David Crook
  VP: John Sofley
  Treasurer: John Brincefield
Management:
  Director: Monica Bigsbi
  Resident Director: Reid Leonard
  Sales Director: Laura Sandridge
Mission: To entertain and educate the community.
Utilizes: Educators; Guest Artists; Multi Collaborations; Multimedia; Organization Contracts; Singers
Founded: 1961
Specialized Field: Musical; Comedy; Youth Theater; Ethnic Theater; Community Theater; Classic; Contemporary
Status: Non-Profit, Non-Professional
Paid Staff: 2
Volunteer Staff: 100
Budget: $255,700
Income Sources: Season Memberships; Ticket Sales; Donations
Performs At: The Meroney Theatre
Affiliations: NC Center for Non-Profits
Annual Attendance: 16,000
Facility Category: Performing Arts Center
Type of Stage: Proscenium
Stage Dimensions: 24'x32'x30' deep, 12' wings
Seating Capacity: 361
Year Built: 1906
Year Remodeled: 1995
Architect: Newman & Jones
Cost: $1,800,000
Rental Contact: Faculty Manager Diana Moghrabi
Organization Type: Performing

3679
TEMPLE THEATRE COMPANY
120 Carthage Street
Sanford, NC 27330
Mailing Address: PO Box 1391, Sanford, NC 27331
Phone: 919-774-4512
Fax: 919-774-7531
Web Site: www.templeshows.com
Officers:
  President: Lee West
  VP: Robert Jasany
  Treasurer: Ted Havens
  Secretary: Pete Johnson
  BM: Sheila Brewer
Management:
  President: Cinny Beggs
  Artistic Director: Peggy Taphorn
  Technical Director: Steven Harrington
  Box Office Manager: Maryanna McDonald
  Director of Marketing & BD: Chris deLambart
Mission: To entertain, enlighten, educate, and enrich lives through the performing arts.
Utilizes: Actors; AEA Actors; Choreographers; Collaborations; Commissioned Composers; Commissioned Music; Grant Writers; Guest Artists; Guest Choreographers; Guest Companies; Guest Conductors; Guest Designers; Guest Lecturers; Guest Musical Directors; Music; Original Music Scores; Resident Professionals; Sign Language Translators; Student Interns; Theatre Companies
Founded: 1925
Specialized Field: Drama; Musical; Comedy; Classic
Status: Non-Profit, Professional
Paid Staff: 5
Volunteer Staff: 30
Paid Artists: 60
Budget: $330,000
Income Sources: State; Local Government; Corporate; Individuala Theatre Conference
Performs At: Temple Theatre
Affiliations: SETC, NCTC
Annual Attendance: 21,000
Facility Category: Theatre
Type of Stage: Proscenium
Seating Capacity: 339
Year Built: 1925

THEATRE / North Carolina

Year Remodeled: 1984
Cost: $500,000
Rental Contact: Jerry Sipp
Organization Type: Performing; Educational; Sponsoring

3680
SNOW CAMP HISTORICAL DRAMA SOCIETY
301 Drama Road
Snow Camp, NC 27349
Phone: 336-376-6948
Toll-free: 800-726-5115
e-mail: snowcampot@aol.com
Web Site: www.snowcampdrama.com
Officers:
    President: Carol Guthrie
    Secretary/General Manager: James Wilson
Founded: 1974
Specialized Field: Outdoor Theater; Drama; Classic
Status: Non-Profit, Professional
Paid Staff: 40
Paid Artists: 20
Season: Year Round
Type of Stage: Amphitheater
Stage Dimensions: 100' x 400'
Seating Capacity: 500

3681
OLD COLONY PLAYERS
PO Box 112
Valdese, NC 28690
Phone: 828-879-2120
Fax: 828-874-0176
e-mail: bhefner@ci.valdese.nc.us
Web Site: www.oldcolonyplayers.com
Officers:
    President: Marvin Folger
    VP: Chuck Moseley
    Treasurer: Mark Rostan
    Secretary: Nancy McFadden
Management:
    Executive Director: Knolan Benfield
    Business Manager: Knolan Benfield
Mission: To produce the historical outdoor drama from this day forward annually; to produce Dickens' A Christmas Carol annually; to produce other dramas, engage in outreach activities, and sponser workshops and cultural events.
Utilizes: Guest Artists; Guest Companies; Singers
Founded: 1936
Specialized Field: Outdoor Theater; Historical; Theater Workshops
Status: Non-Profit, Non-Professional
Paid Staff: 2
Paid Artists: 30
Income Sources: Southeastern Theatre Conference; North Carolina Theatre Conference; North Carolina Association of Professional Theatres; Burke County Chamber of Commerce; Burke Arts Council
Season: July - August
Performs At: Old Colony Players Amphitheater; Old Rock School
Organization Type: Performing; Touring; Resident; Educational

3682
HAYWOOD ARTS REGIONAL THEATRE
250 Pigeon Street
Waynesville, NC 28786
Mailing Address: P.O. Box 1024, Waynesville, NC 28786
Phone: 828-456-6322
Fax: 828-456-6501
e-mail: hearttheater@gmail.com
Web Site: harttheatre.com
Management:
    Executive Director: Steven Lloyd
Founded: 1985
Opened: 1997
Performs At: The Performing Arts Center At The Shelton House
Organization Type: Volunteer Based Community Theatre

3683
MARTIN COMMUNITY PLAYERS
300 North Watts Street
Williamston, NC 27892-2099
Phone: 252-792-1521
Fax: 252-792-0826
Management:
    Artistic Director: Allan Osborne
Mission: To offer theatre to all citizens in our county, primarily through the schools, providing one selected offering annually.
Founded: 1974
Specialized Field: Musical; Community Theater
Status: Non-Professional; Nonprofit
Performs At: Martin County Auditorium
Organization Type: Performing; Resident

3684
OPERA HOUSE THEATRE COMPANY
2011 Carolina Beach Road
Wilmington, NC 28401
Phone: 910-762-4234
Fax: 910-251-9800
e-mail: operahousetheatre@yahoo.com
Web Site: www.operahousetheatrecompany.net/
Management:
    Executive Director/Founder: Lou Criscuolo
Mission: To produce and promote high quality, accessible, professional theatre; to train and develop the talents of musicians, actors and technicians.
Utilizes: Actors; Choreographers; Dancers; Designers; Grant Writers; Guest Artists; Guest Companies; Guest Conductors; Guest Designers; Instructors; Local Artists; Multimedia; Music; Resident Professionals; Sign Language Translators; Singers; Student Interns
Founded: 1985
Specialized Field: Summer Stock; Musical
Status: Professional
Paid Staff: 20
Performs At: Thalian Hall Center for the Performing Arts
Organization Type: Performing; Educational

3685
CHILDREN'S THEATRE BOARD
2400 3rd Avenue South
Winston-Salem, NC 55404
Phone: 612-874-0400
Fax: 612-874-0500
e-mail: tickets@childrenstheatre.org
Web Site: www.childrenstheatre.org
Officers:
    President: Mary Harper
    President Elect: Libby Noah
    Treasurer: Leslie Madigan
    Treasurer-Elect: Ernestine Worley
    Immediate Past President: Janet Bondurant
    Artistic/Education Director: Bobby Bodford
    Technical Director: Vincent Whitt
Management:
    President: Keith Gardner
    Executive Director: Pat Land
    Director Marketing/ Development: Jennifer Lewis
    General Manager: Karen McHugh
Mission: To provide opportunities for students, educators and families to experience and participate in the performing arts; to offer multidisciplinary, culturally diverse programs to foster sensitivity and acceptance of others. Our programs are accessible and entertaining, our vision is to reach young people through experimental learning.
Utilizes: Singers
Founded: 1940
Specialized Field: Musical; Comedy; Youth Theater; Puppet; Classic
Status: Non-Profit, Professional
Paid Staff: 2
Performs At: The Arts Council Theatre; W-S/FC Schools
Organization Type: Performing; Educational; Sponsoring

3686
LITTLE THEATRE OF WINSTON-SALEM
610 Coliseum Drive
Winston-Salem, NC 27106
Phone: 336-748-0857
Fax: 336-727-4841
e-mail: theatre@littletheatreonline.com
Web Site: www.littletheatreonline.com
Officers:
    President: Eva Wu
Management:
    President: Christine Gorelick
    Executive Director: Mark Pirolo
    Operations Director: Cheri Vanloon
    Box Office Manager: Janice Dearth
    Education Director: Angela Chance
Mission: To provide for all within the community an avenue for education and development in all aspects of theatrical arts and to provide entertainment for the community by offering a series of well-staged performances of live theatre.
Utilizes: Guest Companies; Singers
Founded: 1935
Specialized Field: Musical; Comedy; Community Theater; Contemporary
Status: Non-Profit, Non-Professional
Paid Staff: 11
Income Sources: Winston-Salem Arts Council
Performs At: Hanes Community Center; Arts Council Theatre
Organization Type: Performing; Educational

3687
NORTH CAROLINA BLACK REPERTORY COMPANY
610 Coliseum Drive
PO Box 2793
Winston-Salem, NC 27106
Phone: 336-723-2266
Fax: 336-723-2223
e-mail: info@ncblackrep.org
Web Site: www.ncblackrep.org/
Management:
    Artistic Director: Larry Leon Hamlin
Mission: To offer professional productions of musicals and plays including original and renowned works with universal as well as ethnic (African-American) themes.
Utilizes: Guest Companies; Singers
Founded: 1979
Specialized Field: Musical; African American
Status: Professional; Nonprofit
Season: September - June
Performs At: Winston-Salem Arts Council Theatre
Type of Stage: Proscenium

Seating Capacity: 541
Organization Type: Performing; Touring; Resident; Educational; Sponsoring

3688
YADKIN PLAYERS
PO Box 667
226 E. Main Street
Yadkinville, NC 27055
Phone: 336-679-2941
Fax: 336-677-3962
e-mail: yadkinarts@yadtel.net
Web Site: www.yadkinarts.org
Officers:
  President: John Willingham
  VP/Treasurer: Mark Brandon
  Board Member: Ann Ashman
  Board Member: Cindy Austin
  Board Member: Jeanette Brown
Management:
  Director: Camara Collins
  Executive Director: Michael Orsillo
Utilizes: Guest Companies
Founded: 1975
Specialized Field: Community Theater
Status: Non-Profit, Non-Professional
Paid Staff: 1
Paid Artists: 12
Organization Type: Performing; Touring; Educational

North Dakota

3689
FARGO-MOORHEAD COMMUNITY THEATRE
333 S 4th Street
Fargo, ND 58103
Phone: 701-235-1901
Fax: 701-235-2685
Toll-free: 877-687-7469
e-mail: boxoffice@fmct.org
Web Site: www.fmct.org
Officers:
  President: Dawn Duncan
  VP: Robin Hoffer
  Treasurer: Dave Stende
  Secretary: Kim Horab
Management:
  Director: Michael Lowchow
  Artistic Director: Charlene Hudgins
  Business Director: Shannyn Jacobson
  Development Director: Sherry Shadley
Mission: To provide quality avocational theatre opportunities to the cities of Fargo and Moorhead, as well as the region.
Utilizes: Actors; Choreographers; Collaborating Artists; Collaborations; Commissioned Music; Designers; Educators; Five Seasonal Concerts; Grant Writers; Guest Accompanists; Guest Artists; Guest Companies; Guest Composers; Guest Conductors; Guest Designers; Guest Ensembles; Guest Lecturers; Guest Musical Directors; Guest Soloists; Guest Writers; High School Drama; Local Artists; Multimedia; Resident Professionals; Selected Students; Singers; Soloists; Student Interns; Touring Companies
Founded: 1946
Specialized Field: Musical; Comedy; Community Theater; Classic; Contemporary
Status: Non-Profit, Professional
Paid Staff: 12
Volunteer Staff: 500
Paid Artists: 50
Income Sources: American Association of Community Theater; Lake Agassiz Arts Council; North Dakota Community Theatre Association; Minnesota Association of Community Theaters
Performs At: Emma K. Herbst Playhouse
Annual Attendance: 28,000
Facility Category: Theatre
Type of Stage: Thrust
Seating Capacity: 302-380
Year Built: 1965
Year Remodeled: 1994
Organization Type: Resident

3690
LITTLE COUNTRY THEATRE
PO Box 5691
Fargo, ND 58102-5691
Phone: 701-231-9442
Web Site: www.ndsu.edu/finearts/theatre_arts/lct.shtml
Management:
  Artistic Director: Donald Larew
  Managing Director: M Joy Erickson
Mission: To produce theatrical productions reflecting a high degree of professionalism; to develop artists in the theatre as well as responsive audiences.
Utilizes: Singers
Founded: 1914
Specialized Field: Drama; Musical
Status: Nonprofit
Paid Staff: 50
Income Sources: American College Theatre Festival; United States Institute for Theatre Technology
Performs At: Askanase Auditorium; Walsh Studio Theatre
Organization Type: Educational

3691
THE TIN ROOF THEATRE COMPANY
333 4th Street
Fargo, ND 58103
Phone: 701-235-6778
e-mail: tinroof05@gmail.com
Web Site: tinroofttheatre.org
Officers:
  President: Michael Lochow
  Vice President: Karla Underdahl
Mission: To produce high-quality, challenging, theatrical productions focusing primarily on American classics that entertain, enrich, and educate the community.
Status: Nonprofit

3692
THEATRE B
716 Main Avenue
Fargo, ND 58103
Phone: 701-729-8880
e-mail: info@theatreb.org
Web Site: theatreb.org
Management:
  Executive Director: Carrie Wintersteen
Mission: To engage regional audiences through innovative theatrical productions that are culturally and artistically invigorating.
Founded: 2003
Status: Professional; Nonprofit
Season: Fall-Spring

3693
FORT TOTTEN LITTLE THEATRE
PO Box 97
Fort Totten, ND 58335
Phone: 701-766-4473
Web Site: www2.stellarnet.com
Officers:
  President: Carol Leevers
  VP: Jane Traynor
  Treasurer/Secretary: Dean Petska
  Artistic Director: Judy Ryan
Management:
  Community Relation Director: Carol Leevers
Mission: Provide an opportunity for talented people to have theatre experience; attract tourists to a state historic site; entertainment for the citizens of rural areas.
Utilizes: Singers
Founded: 1962
Specialized Field: Musical; Community Theater
Status: Semi-Professional; Non-Professional; Nonprofit
Paid Staff: 20
Income Sources: North Dakota Council of Arts; Council of Lake Region
Season: June - August
Performs At: Cavalry Square; Historic Site
Organization Type: Performing; Resident

3694
EMPIRE THEATRE COMPANY
415 Demers Avenue
Grand Forks, ND 58201
Phone: 701-746-5500
e-mail: etc@empireartscenter.com
Web Site: empireartscenter.com
Management:
  Artistic Director: Chris Berg
Mission: ETC's mission is to stimulate and fill empty theatre seats with a generation of new audiences and keep them coming back for more by producing contemporary, thought-provoking live plays and musicals that are well-crafted and bold.

Ohio

3695
CAROUSEL DINNER THEATRE
3750 South Mason Street
Akron, OH 80525
Phone: 970-225-2555
Fax: 330-724-2232
Toll-free: 800-362-4100
e-mail: carousel@carouseldinnertheatre.com
Web Site: www.adinnertheatre.com/
Officers:
  President/Owner/Executive Producer: Prescott F Griffith
Management:
  Director Sales/Marketing: Jeffrey Lynch
Mission: Elegant Dinner Theatre featuring live Broadway musical productions withprofessional New York talent.
Utilizes: Actors; AEA Actors; Choreographers; Commissioned Music; Community Talent; Contract Orchestras; Dancers; Designers; Guest Artists; Guest Conductors; Guest Designers; Guest Lecturers; Multi Collaborations; Multimedia; Music; Original Music Scores; Resident Professionals; Selected Students; Sign Language Translators; Singers; Soloists; Students; Student Interns; Visual Arts
Founded: 1973
Specialized Field: Dinner Theater
Status: For-Profit, Professional
Paid Staff: 175
Income Sources: Box Office; Ticket Sales
Affiliations: National Dinner Theatre Association; Actors' Equity Association
Annual Attendance: 200,000
Facility Category: Dinner Theatre

THEATRE / Ohio

Type of Stage: Proscenium
Stage Dimensions: 60'x40'x18'
Seating Capacity: 1,130
Year Built: 1988
Year Remodeled: 1988
Rental Contact: Producer Marc A Resnik
Resident Groups: Sheila A Fetterman

3696
MAGICAL THEATRE COMPANY
565 W Tuscarawas Avenue
PO Box 386
Barberton, OH 44203
Phone: 330-848-3708
Fax: 330-848-5768
e-mail: magicaltheatre@aol.com
Web Site: www.magicaltheatre.org
Officers:
   President: Tim Papp
   Co-Producing Director: Holly Barkdoll
   Co-Producing Director: Dennis O'Connell
   Lighting Designer: John Ebert
Management:
   Co-Producing Director: Holly Barkdoll
Mission: Resident and touring, educational and entertainment resource for young audiences. In partnership with schools and other organizations, we are leaders in providing a positive cultural service as a strong and energetic professional theatre serving Northeast Ohio. We enhance learning, growth and civic improvement through live theatre.
Utilizes: Actors; Choreographers; Collaborations; Community Talent; Contract Actors; Local Artists; Original Music Scores; Resident Companies; Scenic Designers; Selected Students; Soloists; Student Interns; Special Technical Talent; Theatre Companies
Founded: 1972
Specialized Field: Musical; Comedy; Ensembles; Classic; Contemporary
Status: Non-Profit, Professional
Paid Staff: 4
Volunteer Staff: 1
Paid Artists: 55
Budget: $415,000
Income Sources: Foundations; Corporate Donors; Ticket Sales
Affiliations: Akron Area Arts Alliance; Cleveland Theatre Collective Ticket Sales; Fees; Foundations; Individual & Corporate Donors
Annual Attendance: 50,000
Facility Category: Former Movie Theatre
Type of Stage: Proscenium; Thrust
Seating Capacity: 285
Year Built: 1919
Year Remodeled: 2000
Cost: $500,000
Rental Contact: Co-Producing Director Dennis O'Connell
Organization Type: Performing; Touring; Resident; Educational

3697
HUNTINGTON THEATRE
28601 Lake Road
Bay Village, OH 44140
Mailing Address: P.O. Box 770056 Lakewood, OH 44107
Phone: 216-871-8333
Fax: 216-221-9495
e-mail: huntingtonplayhouse@huntingtonplayhouse.com
Web Site: www.huntingtonplayhouse.com/
Mission: To maintain a community theatre.
Utilizes: Guest Companies; Singers
Founded: 1958
Specialized Field: Musical; Community Theater
Status: Non-Professional; Nonprofit
Paid Staff: 100
Performs At: Huntington Playhouse
Organization Type: Performing; Educational

3698
BRECKSVILLE LITTLE THEATRE
Box 41131
Brecksville, OH 44141
Phone: 440-526-4477
e-mail: mail@brecksvillelittletheatre.org
Web Site: www.brecksvillelittletheatre.org/
Mission: To offer good theatre; to provide performance opportunities.
Utilizes: Guest Artists; Guest Companies; Singers
Founded: 1941
Specialized Field: Musical; Community Theater
Status: Non-Professional; Nonprofit
Paid Staff: 100
Performs At: Old Towne Hall; Brecksville Square
Organization Type: Performing; Resident; Educational

3699
THEATRE ON THE SQUARE
PO Box 41002
Brecksville, OH 44141
Phone: 440-526-6436
Fax: 440-526-6591
Toll-free: 800-895-4708
e-mail: theatre@btots.org
Web Site: www.btots.org
Officers:
   President: Scott McPherson
Management:
   Director: Lynda Demko
   Education Director: Michele Cotner
   Business Director: Steve Demko
   Managing Director: Jean Marincic
Mission: Presenting touring and original plays.
Utilizes: Guest Companies
Founded: 1975
Specialized Field: Musical; Drama; New Plays
Status: Professional; Commercial
Performs At: Theatre on the Square
Stage Dimensions: 40x32
Seating Capacity: 750
Year Built: 1924
Organization Type: Performing; Touring

3700
PLAYERS GUILD OF CANTON
1001 Market Avenue N
Canton, OH 44702
Phone: 330-453-7619
Fax: 330-453-8368
e-mail: info@playersguildtheatre.com
Web Site: www.playersguildtheatre.com
Officers:
   Chairman: Denny Carrol
   Vice Chairman: Ryan Kuchmaner
   Treasurer: Kim Conley
   Director: Justin Luntz
   Director: Mary Merkt
Management:
   Artistic Manager: Tricia Ostertag
   Administrative Director: Jean Reahm
   Technical Director: Craig M Betz
Mission: A charitable and educational institution which produces and exhibits plays and provides instruction of the theatre arts for the purpose of fostering and advancing education in and appreciation of the theatre by and among the people of the Greater Canton Area.
Utilizes: Actors; Artists-in-Residence; Choreographers; Commissioned Music; Guest Companies
Founded: 1932
Specialized Field: Musical; Comedy; Community Theater; Classic; Contemporary
Status: Non-Profit, Non-Professional
Paid Staff: 5
Volunteer Staff: 500
Paid Artists: 6
Non-paid Artists: 150
Budget: $700,000
Facility Category: Community Theatre
Type of Stage: Proscenium; Thrust
Stage Dimensions: 60'x40'; 30'x20'
Seating Capacity: 478; 139
Year Built: 1970
Rental Contact: Bil Pfuderer
Organization Type: Performing

3701
CHAGRIN VALLEY LITTLE THEATRE
40 River Street
Chagrin Falls, OH 44022
Phone: 440-247-8955
e-mail: cvlt@cvlt.org
Web Site: www.cvlt.org
Management:
   Business Manager: Rollin DeVere
Mission: To provide community theater.
Founded: 1929
Specialized Field: Community Theater
Status: Non-Professional; Nonprofit
Seating Capacity: 262
Organization Type: Performing

3702
TECUMSEH!
PO Box 73
Chillicothe, OH 45601
Phone: 740-775-4100
Fax: 740-775-4349
Toll-free: 866-775-0700
e-mail: tecumseh@bright.net
Web Site: www.tecumsehdrama.com
Officers:
   President: Beth Beatty
Utilizes: Actors; AEA Actors; Guest Designers; Original Music Scores; Soloists; Student Interns
Founded: 1973
Specialized Field: Outdoor Theater; Drama; Historical
Status: Non-Profit, Professional
Paid Staff: 100
Paid Artists: 60
Season: June - September
Annual Attendance: 44,000
Facility Category: Outdoors
Type of Stage: Amphitheater
Stage Dimensions: 150'x50'
Seating Capacity: 1,700
Year Built: 1971
Year Remodeled: 1998
Cost: $ 1.4 million

3703
ARTREACH: A DIVISION OF THE CHILDREN'S THEATRE OF CINCINNATI
5020 Oaklawn Drive
Cincinnati, OH 45227
Phone: 513-569-8080
Fax: 513-569-8084
e-mail: computertotskentco@comcast.net
Web Site: www.thechildrenstheatre.com
Officers:

Director of Marketing & Public Rela: Krista Katona Pille
Management:
  Artistic Director: Kelly Germain
  Business Manager: Chris Casazza
Mission: The Children's Theatre of Cincinnati and Theatre IV merged to provide fully produced Broadway-syle productions and theatrical experiences for school aged children throughout the region.
Utilizes: Actors; Educators; Guest Companies; Local Artists; Multimedia; Original Music Scores; Resident Professionals; Singers; Theatre Companies
Founded: 1976
Specialized Field: Musical; Comedy; Youth Theater; Classic; Contemporary
Status: Non-Profit, Professional
Paid Staff: 3
Paid Artists: 14
Income Sources: Theatre Communications Group; Association of Performing Arts Presenters; American Association of Theatre Educators; Arts Midwest
Season: September - May
Performs At: Touring

3704
CINCINNATI PLAYHOUSE IN THE PARK
962 Mt Adams Circle
PO Box 6537
Cincinnati, OH 45202
Phone: 513-345-2242
Fax: 513-345-2254
Toll-free: 800-823-08
e-mail: administration@cincyplay.com
Web Site: www.cincyplay.com
Officers:
  Board of Trustees President: Jack D Osborn
  Boarf of Trustees VP: Richard Curry
Management:
  Director: Ed Stern
  Executive Director: Buzz Ward
  Public Relations Director: Christa Skiles
Mission: Produced on stage in a fiscally responsible manner, and through stimulating educational and outreach programs.
Utilizes: Guest Companies; Singers
Founded: 1960
Specialized Field: Musical; Comedy; Community Theater; Classic; Contemporary
Status: Non-Profit, Professional
Paid Staff: 74
Budget: $9 million
Performs At: Robert S Marx Theatre; Thompson Shelterhouse Theatre
Affiliations: League of Cincinnati Theatres
Annual Attendance: 250,000
Facility Category: Robert S Marx Theatre; Thomson Shelterhouse Theat
Type of Stage: Thrust
Seating Capacity: 626; 225
Rental Contact: 513-345-2242 Norma Nilnemets
Organization Type: Performing; Resident

3705
ENSEMBLE THEATRE OF CINCINNATI
1127 Vine Street
Cincinnati, OH 45202
Phone: 513-421-3555
Fax: 513-562-4104
e-mail: director@cincyetc.com
Web Site: www.ensemblecincinnati.org/
Officers:
  Producing Artistic Director: D Lynn Meyers
  Managing Director: Richard Diehl
  Director of Communications & Develo: Jocelyn Meyer
  Director of Education: Amy King Ruggaber
  Director of Patron Services & Devel: Jared Doren
Management:
  Director Of Operations: Trent Kotch
  Producing Artistic Director: D Lynn Meyers
  Director Of Marketing and Public Re: Sue Cohen
Mission: Professional equity theatre dedicated to the production and development of new works and works new to the region.
Founded: 1986
Specialized Field: Ensembles; New Plays
Paid Staff: 15
Volunteer Staff: 50
Performs At: Ensemble Theatre
Type of Stage: Thrust
Seating Capacity: 202

3706
MADCAP PRODUCTIONS PUPPET THEATRE
3316 Glenmore Avenue
Cincinnati, OH 45211
Phone: 513-921-5965
Fax: 513-921-3845
Toll-free: 866-215-65
e-mail: info@madcappuppets.com
Web Site: www.madcappuppets.com
Officers:
  President: Greg Schaiper
  VP: Conrad Thiede
  Secretary: Darci Guriel
  Treasurer: Amy Cheney
  Sr. VP: Lisa Clark
Management:
  President: Betsy Meyer
  Artistic Director: Jerry Handorf
  Managing Director: Vickie Francis
Mission: To present educational theatre experiences and further the art of puppet theatre.
Utilizes: Actors; Collaborations; Five Seasonal Concerts; Guest Artists; Guest Conductors; Guest Designers; Guest Musical Directors; Local Artists; Lyricists; Multimedia; Original Music Scores; Selected Students; Singers
Founded: 1981
Specialized Field: Youth Theater; Classic; Puppet
Status: Non-Profit, Professional
Paid Staff: 9
Paid Artists: 9
Performs At: Touring Company; Resident Theatre at Cincinnati Art Museum
Affiliations: Puppeteers of America; Ohio Theatre Alliance; League of Cincinnati Theatres
Annual Attendance: 450,000
Organization Type: Performing; Touring; Educational

3707
MARIEMONT PLAYERS
4101 Walton Creek Road
Cincinnati, OH 45227
Phone: 513-271-1661
e-mail: ArtK@fuse.net
Web Site: www.mariemontplayers.com/
Mission: To produce plays for the enrichment and enjoyment of area audiences.
Founded: 1936
Specialized Field: Community Theater
Status: Non-Professional; Nonprofit
Income Sources: American Association of Community Theatres-Cincinnati; Ohio Community Theatre Alliance
Performs At: Walton Creek Theater
Organization Type: Performing

3708
SHARK EAT MUFFIN THEATRE COMPANY
219 Loraine Avenue #2
Cincinnati, OH 45220
Phone: 513-399-7179
e-mail: info@sharkeatmuffin.com
Web Site: sharkeatmuffin.com
Management:
  Artistic Director: Catie O'Keefe
Mission: Through a cross-cultural lens, Shark Eat Muffin Theatre Company professionally explores new works of theatre as well as modern and classic plays with fresh and innovative initiatives.
Organization Type: Touring; Performing

3709
SHOWBOAT MAJESTIC
PO Box 5255
Cincinnati, OH 45205-0255
Phone: 513-241-6550
e-mail: info.crc@rcc.org
Specialized Field: Summer Stock; Musical; Comedy
Season: April - October

3710
STAGECRAFTERS
7325 Brookcrest Drive
Cincinnati, OH 45237
Phone: 513-893-6237
Fax: 513-761-0084
e-mail: info@StagecraftersInc.org
Web Site: www.stagecraftersinc.org/
Mission: To provide a performance outlet and entertainment for the community.
Utilizes: Guest Companies; Singers
Founded: 1952
Specialized Field: Community Theater
Status: Non-Professional
Paid Staff: 25
Income Sources: American Association of Community Theatres; Ohio Community Theatre Alliance
Performs At: Jewish Community Center
Organization Type: Performing; Resident

3711
CLEVELAND PLAY HOUSE
1407 Euclid Avenue
Cleveland, OH 44115
Phone: 216-241-6000
Fax: 216-400-7096
Toll-free: 800-278-1274
e-mail: mbloom@clevelandplayhouse.com
Web Site: www.clevelandplayhouse.com
Officers:
  Chairman: Alan Rauss
  Secretary: Raymond M Malone
Management:
  Artistic Director: Michael Bloom
Mission: To provide the experience of a complete performing arts environment through its varied repertoire of classical and contemporary theatre, facilities and the continuance of young people's theatre training.
Utilizes: Artists-in-Residence; Collaborations; Commissioned Music; Dancers; Designers; Educators; Guest Artists; Guest Companies; Guest Composers; Guest Conductors; Guest Designers; Guest Ensembles; Guest Lecturers; Guest Writers; Guild Activities; Instructors; Local Artists; Lyricists; Music; Organization Contracts; Performance Artists; Resident Professionals; Selected Students; Sign Language Translators; Singers; Soloists; Touring Companies

THEATRE / Ohio

Founded: 1915
Specialized Field: Musical; Comedy; Classic; Contemporary
Status: Non-Profit, Professional
Paid Staff: 150
Volunteer Staff: 300
Paid Artists: 50
Budget: $6.5 million
Income Sources: Ticket Sales; Grants; Donations
Performs At: Bolton Theatre; Drury Theatre; Brooks Theatre
Affiliations: League of Resident Theatres; Theatre Communications Group; Ohio Arts Council
Annual Attendance: 300,000
Facility Category: Regional Theatre
Type of Stage: Proscenium;
Seating Capacity: 504; 500; 120
Year Built: 1916
Year Remodeled: 1991
Rental Contact: Managing Director Dean R Gladden
Organization Type: Performing; Educational

3712
CLEVELAND PUBLIC THEATRE
6415 Detroit Avenue
Cleveland, OH 44102-3011
Phone: 216-631-2727
Fax: 216-631-2575
e-mail: info@cptonline.org
Web Site: www.cptonline.org
Officers:
   President: George H Carr
   VP: Jillian Davis
Management:
   President: James Levin
   Artistic Director: Randy Rollison
   Managing Director: Dennis Griesmer
   Director Marketing and Public Relat: Dan Kilpane
   General Manager: Dennis Griesmer
   Box Office Manager: James Kosmatka
Mission: To inspire, nurture, challenge, amaze, educate and empower artists and audiences in order to make the Cleveland public a more conscious and compassionate community.
Utilizes: Guest Companies; Singers
Founded: 1983
Specialized Field: Community Theater
Status: Non-Profit, Professional
Paid Staff: 15
Volunteer Staff: 40
Paid Artists: 170
Budget: $1.2 million
Income Sources: Foundations; Government; Individual; Corporate
Affiliations: Ohio Theatre Association; Theatre Communications Group; Ohio Arts Council; National Endowment for the Arts
Annual Attendance: 20,000
Facility Category: Multi Theatre
Type of Stage: Proscenium; Black Box
Year Built: 1920
Year Remodeled: 2000
Rental Contact: James Levin
Organization Type: Performing; Touring; Resident; Educational; Sponsoring

3713
CLEVELAND SIGNSTAGE THEATRE
8500 Euclid Avenue
Cleveland, OH 44106
Phone: 216-229-2838
Fax: 216-229-2769
e-mail: deaftheatre@signstage.org
Web Site: www.signstage.org

Management:
   President: Richard Slozar
   Artistic Director: William Morgan
Mission: FTD accepts the unique responsibility for providing theatrical and educational performances and workshops for deaf, hearing impaired and hearing people.
Utilizes: Actors; AEA Actors; Commissioned Music; Designers; Educators; Five Seasonal Concerts; Guest Accompanists; Guest Artists; Guest Companies; Guest Conductors; Guest Teachers; Local Artists; Lyricists; Original Music Scores; Performance Artists; Resident Artists; Resident Professionals; Selected Students; Singers; Theatre Companies
Founded: 1975
Specialized Field: Theatre for Deaf; Alternative
Status: Non-Profit, Professional
Paid Staff: 2
Volunteer Staff: 2
Paid Artists: 6
Budget: $800,000
Performs At: Cleveland Play House
Facility Category: Resident Theatre
Stage Dimensions: 25'x25'
Seating Capacity: 139
Organization Type: Performing; Touring; Resident; Educational

3714
KARAMU HOUSE
2355 E 89th Street
Cleveland, OH 44106-3403
Phone: 216-795-7070
Fax: 216-795-7073
e-mail: info@karamu.com
Web Site: www.karamu.com
Officers:
   Board Chairman: Stanley Jackson Jr
Management:
   Marketing Manager: Vivian C Wilson
   Executive Director: Gregory J Ashe
Mission: To support and encourage the preservation, celebration and evaluation of African American culture and provide a vehicle for social, eccnomic and educational development.
Utilizes: Actors; Choreographers; Collaborations; Educators; Fine Artists; Guest Accompanists; Guest Artists; Guest Conductors; Guest Designers; Guest Lecturers; Guest Teachers; Guild Activities; High School Drama; Instructors; Local Artists; Multimedia; Music; Performance Artists; Resident Professionals; Sign Language Translators; Singers; Soloists; Student Interns; Touring Companies
Founded: 1915
Opened: 1915
Specialized Field: Multi-Cultural; Drama; Musical; African American
Status: Semi-Professional; Nonprofit
Paid Staff: 38
Volunteer Staff: 20
Paid Artists: 5
Non-paid Artists: 170
Budget: $1,795,000
Income Sources: Foundations; Corporations; Fees
Affiliations: American Alliance for Theatre Arts
Annual Attendance: 20,000
Facility Category: Multi-Cultural Arts Center
Type of Stage: Arena; Proscenium
Seating Capacity: 100/225
Year Built: 1948
Organization Type: Performing; Educational

3715
NEAR WEST THEATRE
3606 Bridge Avenue
Cleveland, OH 44113
Phone: 216-621-1919
Fax: 216-621-3202
e-mail: info@nearwesttheatre.org
Web Site: www.nearwesttheatre.org/
Management:
   Executive Director: Stephanie Morrison-Hrbek
   Artistic Director: Bob Navis, Jr
   Technical Director: Michael Larochelle
   Development Director: Laura R Hammel
   Business Operations Director: Carole Leiblinger-Hedderson
Mission: Delivers an inclusive, self-esteem building process that results in high-quality theatre productions and programming that help build Cleveland's west side and surrounding neighborhoods. Educates and raises awareness around issues of social justice discrimination and stigma and it provides people of all ages with the the ability to nurture their sense of identity and strengthen their purposes as individuals and as a community.
Specialized Field: Community Theater; Musical

3716
PLAYHOUSE SQUARE FOUNDATION
1501 Euclid Avenue
Suite 200
Cleveland, OH 44115
Phone: 216-771-4444
Fax: 216-771-0217
Toll-free: 800-492-6048
Web Site: www.playhousesquare.com
Officers:
   President: Art Falco
   Chairman: Thomas Stevens
   Treasurer: Thomas Wagner
   Vice Chair: Chris Conner
   Vice Chair: James Ratner
Management:
   Executive Director/CEO: Art Falco
   Director: Patricia Gaul
   Technical Director: Bob Rody
   Director of Marketing: Autum Tiser
Mission: The renovation and operation of five theatres in the Playhouse Square Center.
Founded: 1970
Specialized Field: Drama; Musical; Comedy; Classic; Touring Company
Status: Non-Profit, Non-Professional
Paid Staff: 250
Budget: $34 million
Income Sources: Ticket Sales; Contributions
Performs At: Five historic theatres ranging in size from 750 to 3100.
Annual Attendance: 1,200,000
Facility Category: Performing Arts Center
Type of Stage: Proscenium
Rental Contact: Hallie Yavitch 216-348-5257
Organization Type: Performing; Touring; Resident; Educational

3717
CAIN PARK THEATRE
Lee and Superior Road
Cleveland Heights, OH 44118
Mailing Address: 40 Severance Circle
Phone: 216-371-3000
Fax: 216-371-6995
e-mail: cainpark@clvhts.com
Web Site: http://www.cainpark.com/contact.asp

Management:
General Manager: Erin Cameron
Specialized Field: Outdoor Theater; Summer Stock
Season: June - August
Facility Category: Amphitheater

3718
DOBAMA THEATRE
2340 Lee Boulevard
Suite 325
Cleveland Heights, OH 44118
Phone: 216-932-6838
Fax: 216-932-3259
e-mail: dobama@dobama.org
Web Site: www.dobama.org
Officers:
President: Jennifer Stapleton
VP: Donna Korn
Secretary: Margi Herwald Zitelli
Treasurer: Jimmy Forbes
Immediate Past President: Laura Anderson
Management:
Artistic/Managing Director: Joyce Casey
Mission: Produce five plays not yet available to Cleveland Heights audiences; encourage new American playwrights by offering staged readings and full world premiere productions of their work; encourage creative expression in children through annual Marilyn Biarchi Kids Playwriting Festival.
Founded: 1959
Specialized Field: New Plays; Young Playwrights; Drama; Contemporary
Status: Non-Profit, Professional
Paid Staff: 2
Paid Artists: 68
Income Sources: Ohio Theatre Association
Performs At: Dobama Theatre
Type of Stage: Thrust
Seating Capacity: 200
Organization Type: Performing; Resident; Educational

3719
ACTORS' THEATRE COMPANY
1000 City Park
Columbus, OH 43206
Phone: 614-444-6888
e-mail: jdoklovic@vscat.com
Web Site: www.theactorstheatre.org
Officers:
President: Joel M Winston
1st VP: Debbie Matan
2nd VP: Noel C Shepard
Treasurer: Eric A Carlson
Secretary: Kara L Miller
Management:
Director: Geoffery Martin
Executive Director: Frank Barnhart
Artistic Director: John Kuhn
Managing Director: Jeanne Earhart
Mission: To make quality theatre accessible by providing free outdoor plays, particularly entertaining Shakespeare productions.
Utilizes: Guest Artists; Guest Companies; Singers
Founded: 1982
Specialized Field: Shakespeare
Status: Semi-Professional; Nonprofit
Paid Staff: 100
Performs At: Schiller Park Amphitheatre
Organization Type: Performing; Touring; Resident; Educational

3720
CATCO (CONTEMPORARY AMERICAN THEATRE COMPANY)
77 S High Street
2Nd Floor
Columbus, OH 43215
Phone: 614-461-1382
Fax: 614-461-8241
e-mail: webmaster@catco.org
Web Site: www.catco.org
Management:
Artistic Director: Geoffrey Nelson
Development Director: Patrick Roehrenbeck
Executive Director: David Edelman
Mission: Entertaining theatre company, dramatically different.
Founded: 1984
Specialized Field: Contemporary
Status: Nonprofit
Paid Staff: 25
Volunteer Staff: 4
Paid Artists: 7
Income Sources: Organizations; Individuals; Foundations

3721
COLUMBUS CHILDREN'S THEATRE
177 E. Naghten St.
Columbus, OH 43215
Phone: 614-224-6672
e-mail: cctboxoffice@sbcglobal.net
Web Site: www.colschildrenstheatre.org
Officers:
President: Susan Levin
VP: Dr. John Weiss
Treasurer: Allison Finkelstein
Secretary: Marilyn Magin
Managing Director: Elizabeth Williamson
Artistic Director: William Goldsmith
Executive Director: Laurie Lathan
Management:
Managing Director: Steven Bridgeland
Executive and Artistic Director: William Goldsmith
Education Director: Mark Mann
Mission: CCT is committed to the proposition that the best way for young people to understand and appreciate the theatre arts is through direct participation. Our focus is on professionally directed, interactive, hands-on programs that celebrate young people's spirit, creativity and fresh perspective... to provide creative outlets, structure and discipline for young people to progress in the theatre arts.
Founded: 1963
Specialized Field: Children's Theater
Status: Non-Profit, Non-Professional
Paid Staff: 5
Paid Artists: 100
Annual Attendance: 100,000

3722
MADLAB
227 North 3rd Street
Columbus, OH 43215
Phone: 614-221-5418
e-mail: publicity@madlab.net
Web Site: madlab.net
Status: Nonprofit

3723
OHIO STATE UNIVERSITY-DEPARTMENT OF THEATRE
1089 Drake Center
1849 Cannon Drive
Columbus, OH 43210-5821
Phone: 614-292-5821
Fax: 614-292-3222
e-mail: theatre@osu.edu
Web Site: www.the.ohio-state.edu
Officers:
Chairperson: Dan Gray
Utilizes: Actors; Artists-in-Residence; Collaborating Artists; Collaborations; Community Talent; Curators; Dancers; Designers; Educators; Equity Actors; Filmmakers; Guest Designers; Guest Ensembles; Guest Instructors; Guest Soloists; High School Drama; Instructors; Local Talent; Lyricists; Multi Collaborations; New Productions; Performance Artists; Poets; Resident Professionals; Soloists; Theatre Companies; Volunteer Directors & Actors; Writers
Founded: 1870
Specialized Field: Educational; Theater Workshops
Status: Non-Profit, Professional
Paid Staff: 8
Performs At: Thuber Theatre; Bowen Theatre
Type of Stage: Proscenium; Thrust
Seating Capacity: 600; 250

3724
PHOENIX THEATRE FOR CHILDREN
39 E State Street
PO Box 06238
Columbus, OH 43206
Phone: 614-464-9400
Fax: 614-464-9402
e-mail: mail@thephoenixonline.org
Web Site: www.thephoenixonline.org
Management:
Artistic Director: Steven C Anderson
Education Director: Vanessa Becker
General Manager: Lonelle Yoder
Business Manager: Thom O'Reilly
Mission: A non-profit theatre for young audiences dedicated to providing quality arts opportunities and arts education programs for Central Ohio.
Utilizes: Actors; Community Talent; Educators; Guest Accompanists; Guest Conductors; Guest Designers; Local Artists; Original Music Scores; Resident Artists
Founded: 1993
Specialized Field: Children's Theater
Status: Professional; Nonprofit
Paid Staff: 8
Paid Artists: 10
Performs At: Vern Riffg Center for Government and the Arts
Facility Category: Government Run Facility
Type of Stage: 3/4 Thrust and Proscenium
Seating Capacity: 180 and 240
Organization Type: Performing; Educational

3725
REALITY THEATRE
Axis Nightclub
775 N High St
Columbus, OH 43215
Phone: 614-265-7337
e-mail: info@realitytheatre.com
Web Site: www.realitytheatre.com
Management:
President: Jeffrey Smith
VP: Randee Estep
Executive Director: Mollie Levin

THEATRE / Ohio

Mission: Primarily dedicated to the development of experimental plays and also the presentation of original scripts written by Ohio playwrights.
Utilizes: Guest Companies
Founded: 1985
Specialized Field: Experimental; New Plays
Status: Semi-Professional; Nonprofit
Organization Type: Performing; Resident

3726
RED HERRING THEATRE ENSEMBLE
Vern Riffe Center Theater Complex
77 South High Street, Second Floor
Columbus, OH 43215
Phone: 614-469-0939
Fax: 614-291-8654
e-mail: info@redherring.org
Management:
    President: Mo Ryan
    Managing Director: Nancy Fox
Mission: To provide unique theatre experience for audiences of central Ohio.
Specialized Field: Musical; Ensembles

3727
ROSEBRIAR SHAKESPEARE COMPANY
549 Franklin Avenue
Columbus, OH 43202
Phone: 614-470-1616
e-mail: sdvavies@ohiohistory.org
Management:
    Managing Director: Sandra Davies
    Artistic Director: John Heisel
Founded: 1990
Specialized Field: Community Theater; Shakespeare; Classic; Drama; Comedy
Income Sources: Grants from the Ohio Arts Council; Jefferson Center for Learning and the Arts
Performs At: Davis Discovery Center's Van Fleet Theatre

3728
SCARLET MASK SOCIETY
1739 N High Street
211 Ohio Union, Rm 307
Columbus, OH 43210
Phone: 614-292-6614
e-mail: colleary.1@osu.edu
Web Site: www.theatre.org.ohio-state.edu/about.html
Officers:
    Executive Artistic Director: Kelly Hartman
    Artistic Director: Eric Colleary
Management:
    Artistic Director: Eric Colleary
    Producer: Liz Botros
    Press/Publicity: Betsy Pandora
Mission: Offering Ohio State University students and community members an opportunity for participation in all areas of performing arts and affordable quality theatre productions.
Founded: 1892
Specialized Field: Musical; Community Theater
Status: Non-Professional; Nonprofit
Organization Type: Performing

3729
SHADOWBOX CABARET
503 South Front Street #260
Columbus, OH 43215
Phone: 614-416-7625
Fax: 614-416-7630
Toll-free: 888-887-4230
e-mail: info@shadowboxcabaret.com
Web Site: www.shadowboxlive.org
Management:
    Director: Steven Guyer
    Artistic Director: Rebecca Gentile
    Managing Director: Julie Klein
Mission: To change the face of live entertainment so that it meets our standards and to create a self-perpetuating organization that acts as a virus by breeding change and dynamism.
Founded: 1992
Specialized Field: Comedy; Cabaret
Status: Non-Profit, Professional
Paid Staff: 97
Volunteer Staff: 3
Paid Artists: 97
Budget: $2.5 million
Income Sources: Tickets Sales
Annual Attendance: 100,000
Facility Category: Multi-stage Theaters

3730
SRO THEATRE COMPANY
1393 E Broad Street
Suite 103
Columbus, OH 43205
Phone: 614-258-9495
Fax: 614-258-9499
e-mail: gplt@glt-theatre.org
Web Site: www.sro-theatre.org
Officers:
    President: Karen Clark-Carpenter
    Secretary: Ruth Fullen
    Treasurer: Tom Giusti
    Vice President: E Joel Wesp
Management:
    Executive/Artistic Director: Nancy S Nocks
    SRO Touring Director: Ronald E. Nocks
    Consultant: Scott Phillips,
    Advisory board: Billie Hazelbaker
Mission: Five original shows and a home season emphatically shatters myths about aging and celebrates life experience. Create theatre that joyously takes risks, is sometimes provacative, but always truthful and unafraid.
Founded: 1985
Specialized Field: Musical; Comedy; New Plays; Contemporary
Status: Non-Profit, Semi-Professional
Paid Staff: 2
Volunteer Staff: 80
Paid Artists: 22
Non-paid Artists: 47
Budget: $94,000
Income Sources: Private Foundations; Grants; Business & Corporate Donations; Box Office; Government Grants; Individual Donations
Affiliations: Senior Theatre League Of America; Ohio Arts Presenters Network; Greater Columbs Convention and Visitors Bureau; Central Ohio Theatre Roundtable

3731
STAR PLAYERS THEATRE
1701 Eastgate Parkway
Columbus, OH 43230
Phone: 614-501-7827
e-mail: info@starplayerstheatre.org
Web Site: starplayerstheatre.org
Management:
    Executive Director: Tanya Shtein
    Artistic Director: Andi Malinger

3732
DAYTON PLAYHOUSE
1301 E Siebenthaler Avenue
Dayton, OH 45415
Phone: 937-424-8477
Fax: 930-333-2827
e-mail: dave@daytonplayhouse.com
Web Site: www.daytonplayhouse.com
Officers:
    Chairman: Betty Gould
    Treasurer: Gwen Eberly
Management:
    Director: Debra Strauss
    Executive Director: Dave Seyer
Utilizes: Guest Companies; Singers
Founded: 1959
Specialized Field: Musical; Community Theater
Status: Non-Professional; Nonprofit
Paid Staff: 2
Volunteer Staff: 600
Income Sources: Membership; MCACD, Culture Works
Performs At: Dayton Playhouse
Affiliations: OCTA; Culture Works
Annual Attendance: 3,000
Seating Capacity: 200
Year Built: 1987
Organization Type: Performing

3733
THE HUMAN RACE THEATRE COMPANY
126 N Main Street
Suite 300
Dayton, OH 45402-1710
Phone: 937-461-3823
Fax: 937-461-7223
e-mail: contact@humanracetheatre.org
Web Site: www.humanracetheatre.org
Management:
    President of the Board: Robert Compson
    Producing Artistic Director: Kevin Moore
Mission: Works to affect the conscience of our community, to see our audience as our partner in the creative experience, to provide a platform for our artists to evolve and explore and to be an educational resource for our community. As our name suggests, we present universal themes that explore the human condition and startle us all into a reward awareness of ourselves.
Founded: 1986
Specialized Field: New works of social importance; Contemporary and classic plays and musicals
Status: Non-Profit, Professional
Paid Staff: 9
Paid Artists: 200
Budget: $1.2 million
Season: September - June
Performs At: The Loft Theatre; Victoria Theatre
Affiliations: AEA
Annual Attendance: 30,000
Type of Stage: Thrust, Proscenium
Seating Capacity: 219/1139

3734
THE ZOOT THEATRE COMPANY INC.
456 Belmonte Park North
Dayton, OH 45402
Phone: 937-512-0140
e-mail: zoot@zoottheatrecompany.org
Web Site: zoottheatrecompany.org
Management:
    Artistic Director: D. Tristan Cupp
    Executive Producer: Michael S. Sticka
Mission: The Zoot Theatre Company Inc. aims to stimulate the creative spirit through the collaboration of all forms of the visual and performing arts, including;

professional acting, masks, and puppetry by bringing the theatrical and visual arts to a variety of peoples in educational and regional venues.
Founded: 2006
Specialized Field: Puppet Theatre
Status: Nonprofit
Organization Type: Touring, Performing, Educational

3735
SUMMER STOCK AT THE UNIVERSITY OF FINDLAY
1000 N Main Street
Findlay, OH 45840
Phone: 419-434-4562
Fax: 419-424-4822
Toll-free: 800-472-9502
e-mail: hayes@findlay.edu
Web Site: www.findlay.edu
Management:
   Program Director: Scott Hayes
   Curtain Raiser Advisory Chair: Anne Hermiller
Mission: Provide professional theatre opportunities for pre professional thatre students, and produce quality. affordable thatre for northwest Ohio.
Utilizes: Actors; AEA Actors; Artists-in-Residence; Choreographers; Collaborations; Dancers; Grant Writers; Guest Accompanists; Guest Artists; Guest Conductors; Guest Designers; Guest Ensembles; Guest Lecturers; Guild Activities; High School Drama; Instructors; Local Artists; Multimedia; Music; Original Music Scores; Resident Professionals; Sign Language Translators; Soloists
Founded: 1977
Specialized Field: Summer Stock
Status: Non-Profit, Professional
Paid Staff: 8
Volunteer Staff: 10
Paid Artists: 8
Non-paid Artists: 15
Season: June - August
Type of Stage: Proscenium
Stage Dimensions: 28' x 30'
Seating Capacity: 222
Year Built: 1964
Year Remodeled: 2001

3736
FOSTORIA FOOTLIGHTERS
225 S Poplar Street
PO Box 542
Fostoria, OH 44830
Phone: 419-435-7501
Utilizes: Guest Companies
Founded: 1959
Specialized Field: Musical; Community Theater
Status: Non-Professional; Nonprofit
Paid Staff: 100
Income Sources: Ohio Community Theatre Alliance
Performs At: Fostoria Footlighters
Organization Type: Performing; Resident; Educational

3737
CURTAIN PLAYERS
5691 Harlem Road
Galena, OH 43021
Mailing Address: PO Box 1143 Westerville, OH 43086
Phone: 740-965-4690
e-mail: info@curtainplayers.com
Web Site: www.curtainplayers.org
Officers:
   President: Michael Fusco
   Vice President: Kate Charlesworth-Miller
   Secretary: Leia Bame
   Treasurer: Charlie Sloin
   Trustee: Drew Washburn
Management:
   President: Jim Petsche, president@curtainplayers.com
   Production Manager: Michael Day, production@curtainplayers.com
   Business Manager: Lisa Billing, business@curtainplayers.com
Founded: 1963
Specialized Field: Community Theater
Seating Capacity: 76

3738
PORTHOUSE THEATRE COMPANY
PO Box 5190
1325 Theatre Drive
Kent, OH 44242-0001
Mailing Address: Kent State
Phone: 330-672-3884
Fax: 330-672-2889
Toll-free: 800-304-2363
e-mail: porthouse@kent.edu
Web Site: www.porthousetheatre.com
Officers:
   Producing Director: Cynthia Stilings
   Artistic Director: Terri Kent
   Managing Director: Rebecca Gates
   Production Manager/ Associate Artis: Karl Erdmann
Management:
   Executive Director: Cynthia Stilings
   Artistic Director: Terri Kent
   Managing Director: Rebeccath Gates
   Producing Manager: Karl Erdmann
   Managing Director: Jeff Cruszewski
Utilizes: Guest Artists; Guest Companies; Singers
Founded: 1968
Specialized Field: Summer Stock
Status: Non-Profit, Professional
Paid Staff: 100
Paid Artists: 50
Income Sources: Kent State University
Season: June - August
Performs At: Porthouse Theatre of Blossom Music Center
Affiliations: Kent State University
Type of Stage: Outdoor, Covered Pavilion Theatre
Seating Capacity: 450
Organization Type: Performing; Educational

3739
BECK CENTER FOR THE CULTURAL ARTS
17801 Detroit Avenue
Lakewood, OH 44107
Phone: 216-521-2540
Fax: 216-228-6050
Web Site: www.beckcenter.org/
Officers:
   President: Rosemary Corcoran
   VP: Brian King
   Treasurer: Marjorie Wiess
Management:
   Artistic Director: Scott Spence
   Managing Director: Andrea Krist
   Executive Director: Bill Beckenbach
   Director Education: Linda Sackett
   Production/Design: Don McBride
Mission: To be a comprehensive community arts center focusing on theater, arts education, and gallery exhibitions.
Utilizes: Guest Artists; Guest Companies; Singers
Founded: 1930
Specialized Field: Multi-Cultural; Drama; Musical
Status: Non-Professional
Paid Staff: 200
Annual Attendance: 12,000
Organization Type: Performing; Touring; Resident; Educational

3740
LOVELAND STAGE COMPANY
111 South 2nd Street (Rt.48)
Loveland, OH 45140-3026
Phone: 513-443-4572
Web Site: lovelandstagecompany.org
Officers:
   President: Tom Cavano
   Vice President: Kay Hasty
Founded: 1979
Status: Nonprofit

3741
MANSFIELD PLAYHOUSE
95 E Third Street
Mansfield, OH 44902
Phone: 419-522-2883
Fax: 419-522-8446
Web Site: www.mansfieldplayhouse.com
Officers:
   President: Steve Zigmund
   First VP: John Moser
   Second VP: Lynda Smith
   Secretary: Millie Leverton
   BM: Cliff Mears
Management:
   Business Manager: Dave Rinehart
   Theatre Manager: Susie Schaus
Mission: Providing entertainment and encouraging all branches of theatre arts.
Utilizes: Guest Artists; Guest Companies; Guest Ensembles; Singers
Founded: 1929
Specialized Field: Musical; Community Theater
Status: Non-Professional
Paid Staff: 2
Volunteer Staff: 200
Income Sources: Ohio Theatre Association; Ohio Arts Council; Ohio Community Theatre Alliance
Organization Type: Performing; Touring; Resident; Educational

3742
RENAISSANCE THEATRE
138 Park Avenue W
PO Box 789
Mansfield, OH 44901-0789
Phone: 419-522-2726
Fax: 419-524-7098
e-mail: rpaa@rparts.org
Web Site: www.mansfieldtickets.com/
Officers:
   President/CEO: Dr. Thomas J Carto
Management:
   President: Thomas Carto
   Artistic Director: Robert Frans
   Managing Director: Darlene Taylor
   Development Director: Shelley A Mauk
   CEO: Tom Cardo
Mission: To operate a community and regional entertainment, cultural, educational and civic center; to preserve and restore the Renaissance Theatre.
Utilizes: Actors; Collaborations; Dancers; Five Seasonal Concerts; Guest Accompanists; Guest Artists; Guest Choreographers; Guest Companies; Guest Designers; Guest Directors; Guest Musical Directors; Guest Musicians; Instructors; Local Artists; Original

THEATRE / Ohio

Music Scores; Resident Professionals; Selected Students; Singers; Student Interns; Special Technical Talent; Theatre Companies
Founded: 1979
Specialized Field: Renaissance; Community Theater; Classic
Status: Non-Profit, Professional
Paid Staff: 15
Volunteer Staff: 300
Budget: $1.4 million
Income Sources: Association of Performing Arts Presenters; ORACLE; Ohio Theatre Association
Performs At: Renaissance Theatre
Affiliations: American Symphony Orchestra league; Association of Performing Arts Presenters
Annual Attendance: 65,000
Facility Category: Performing arts theatre
Type of Stage: proscenium
Stage Dimensions: 47 x 26
Seating Capacity: 1,406
Year Built: 1928
Year Remodeled: 1982
Cost: $2.5 Million
Rental Contact: Operations Manager Darlene Taylor
Organization Type: Performing; Educational; Sponsoring

3743
SHOWBOAT BECKY THATCHER
237 Front Street
PO Box 572
Marietta, OH 45750
Phone: 740-373-6033
Fax: 740-373-6084
Toll-free: 877-746-2628
e-mail: beckythatcher@sbc.yahoo.com
Web Site: www.marietta-ohio.com/becky thatcher
Management:
  President: Craig Hartline
  Executive Director: Jena L Blair
Founded: 1975
Specialized Field: Comedy; Musical; Historical
Status: Non-Profit, Professional
Paid Staff: 6
Volunteer Staff: 25
Paid Artists: 30
Non-paid Artists: 10
Season: June - August
Type of Stage: Proscenium
Stage Dimensions: 26' x 14'
Seating Capacity: 200
Year Built: 1926

3744
PALACE THEATRE
276 W Center Street
Marion, OH 43302
Phone: 740-383-2101
Fax: 740-387-3425
Web Site: www.marionpalace.org
Officers:
  Board President: Sue Jacob
  Board VP: Mike Greeley
  Executive Director: Bev Ford
  Director of Finance: Veronica Bodine
  Technical Director: Steve Beltz
Management:
  Executive Director: Elaine Merchant
  Operations Director: Suzanne Walke
  Business Manager: Veronica Bodine
  Stage Manager: Steve Beltz
Mission: To stimulate, promote and develop interest in the dramatic arts by operation of a permanent theatre.
Founded: 1928

Specialized Field: Musical; Comedy; Classic; Contemporary
Status: Non-Profit, Professional
Paid Staff: 8
Income Sources: Ohio Arts Council; Private Foundations; Donations
Performs At: Palace Theatre
Affiliations: League of Historic American Theatres
Annual Attendance: 77,650
Seating Capacity: 1420
Year Built: 1928
Year Remodeled: 1976
Organization Type: Performing; Educational

3745
TRUMPET IN THE LAND
Schoenbrunn Amphitheatre
PO Box 450
New Philadelphia, OH 44663
Phone: 330-364-5111
Fax: 330-339-1132
e-mail: trumpet@tusco.net
Web Site: www.trumpetintheland.com
Officers:
  President: Linda M. Eaton
Management:
  General Manager: Margaret M. Bonamico
Founded: 1965
Specialized Field: Comedy; Contemporary
Status: Non-Profit, Professional
Paid Staff: 60
Paid Artists: 40
Season: June - August
Type of Stage: Proscenium
Stage Dimensions: 40' x 30'
Seating Capacity: 1400

3746
LICKING COUNTY PLAYERS
131 W Main Street
Newark, OH 43055
Phone: 740-345-2287
e-mail: lcplayers@midohio.twcbc.com
Web Site: www.lickingcountyplayers.org/
Officers:
  President: Helen Lawrence
  Vice Pesident: Charles Hupp
  Secretary: Tiffani Lawrence
  Treasurer: Opha Lawson
Management:
  President: John Roberts
  Vice Pesident: Christina Barth
  Secretary: Baird Krueger
  Treasurer: Tim Gardner
Mission: To preserve, promote, and perform all types of living theater in the community.
Specialized Field: Community Theater; Musical; Drama; Comedy
Status: Non-Profit

3747
WEATHERVANE PLAYHOUSE
1301 Weathervane Lane
PO Box 607
Newark, OH 44313
Phone: 330-836-2626
Fax: 330-344-3185
e-mail: info@weathervaneplayhouse.com
Web Site: www.weathervaneplayhouse.com/
Officers:
  President: Michael Gaffney
  1st VP: Lucy J. Randles
  2ND VP: Ian S. Haberman
  Secretary: Debbie Shama

  Treasurer: Jim Horvath
Management:
  Executive Director: John Hedges
  Director of Advancement: Jenis Harcar
  Education Director: Melanie Y.C. Pepe
  Eductaion Outreach Coordinator: Sarah Bailey
  Eductaion Outreach Coordinator: Lisa Manfield
Founded: 1935
Specialized Field: Community Theater; Drama; Comedy; Musical; Children's Theater; Educational
Status: Non-Equity; Nonprofit
Season: June - August
Type of Stage: Thrust
Stage Dimensions: 30' x 30'
Seating Capacity: 333

3748
TOWNE AND COUNTRY PLAYERS
PO Box 117
Norwalk, OH 45380
Phone: 937-526-5566
e-mail: info@tcplayers.com
Web Site: www.tcplayers.com
Management:
  Executive Director: Ronn Koerper
Mission: Providing family entertainment.
Utilizes: Singers
Founded: 1973
Specialized Field: Musical; Dinner Theater; Community Theater
Status: Semi-Professional; Nonprofit
Paid Staff: 2
Performs At: Historic Shrine Theatre
Annual Attendance: 40,000
Year Remodeled: 1941
Organization Type: Performing

3749
CEDAR POINT LIVE ENTERTAINMENT
One Cedar Point Drive
Sandusky, OH 44870-5259
Phone: 419-627-2390
Fax: 419-627-2389
e-mail: liveshows@cedarpoint.com
Web Site: www.cedarpoint.com
Management:
  Vice President Live Entertainment: Marje Rody
  Manager: Herbe Donald
Utilizes: Actors; Choreographers; Dancers; Designers; Guest Artists; Guest Companies; Guest Conductors; Guest Designers; Guest Directors; Guest Ensembles; Guest Musical Directors; Guest Musicians; Guest Soloists; High School Drama; Multimedia; Music; Original Music Scores; Resident Professionals; Singers; Student Interns; Visual Arts
Founded: 1870
Specialized Field: Musical; Contemporary
Paid Staff: 100
Paid Artists: 100
Season: May - October
Annual Attendance: 3 million
Facility Category: Theme Park

3750
SANDUSKY STATE THEATRE
107 Columbus Avenue
Sandusky, OH 44870
Phone: 419-626-1950
Fax: 419-626-2994
Toll-free: 877-378-2150
e-mail: tkazmierczak@sanduskystate.com
Web Site: www.sanduskystate.com/
Officers:
  Executive Director: Thomas T. Kazmierczak

President: Paul Koch
VP: Kitty Smith
Management:
    Executive Director: Terri Bergman
    Managing Director: Steve Ernst
Mission: Performing Arts Center.
Founded: 1988
Specialized Field: Musical; Comedy; Classic; Contemporary
Status: Non-Profit, Non-Professional
Paid Staff: 9
Volunteer Staff: 150
Budget: $150,000-$400,000
Income Sources: Ticket Sales; Sponsorship; Grants
Type of Stage: Proscenium
Seating Capacity: 1,600

3751
RITZ THEATRE
30 S Washington Street
PO Box 289
Tiffin, OH 44883
Phone: 419-448-8544
Fax: 419-448-7410
e-mail: michael@ritztheatre.org
Web Site: www.ritztheatre.org
Officers:
    President: Dominic Fabrizio
    Executive Director: Michael Strong
    Development Director: Jessica Dickney
Management:
    Executive Director: Michael Strong
    Production Manager: John Spahr
    Development Director: Jessica Dickney
Founded: 1983
Specialized Field: Musical; Community Theater; Classic; Contemporary
Status: Non-Profit, Professional
Paid Staff: 8
Volunteer Staff: 250
Budget: $1 million
Facility Category: Restored Movie Theatre
Type of Stage: Proscenium
Stage Dimensions: 29 x 29
Seating Capacity: 1,260
Year Built: 1928
Year Remodeled: 1998
Rental Contact: Michael Strong

3752
TOLEDO REPERTOIRE THEATRE
16 10th Street
Toledo, OH 43606
Phone: 419-243-9277
Fax: 419-321-1930
e-mail: gmoulopoulos@toledorep.org
Web Site: www.toledorep.org
Officers:
    Chairman: Jori Jex
    Business Manager: Kathleen McGovern
Management:
    Artistic Director: Gloria Moulopoulos
Mission: To entertain, educate, and provide services to Toledo and the surrounding region through the disciplines of theatre.
Utilizes: Guest Artists; Guest Companies; Singers
Founded: 1933
Specialized Field: Drama; Musical
Status: Semi-Professional; Nonprofit
Income Sources: Ohio Concerned Citizens for the Arts
Organization Type: Performing; Educational

3753
MAD RIVER THEATER WORKS
PO Box 248
West Liberty, OH 43357
Mailing Address: PO Box 156, Zanesfield, OH 43360
Phone: 937-465-6751
e-mail: bob@madrivertheater.org
Web Site: www.madrivertheater.org
Officers:
    Producing Director, Composer, Music: Bob Lucas
Management:
    Administrative Director: Laurie Collins
    Producing Director: Bob Lucas
    Youth Works Director: Michelle F. Cornell
    Producing Director: Jeff Hooper
    MD: Christopher Westhoff
Mission: Our purpose is to create and produce plays that explore the concerns of rural people and to perform these works for multi-generational, primarily rural audiences.
Utilizes: Guest Companies; Singers
Founded: 1978
Specialized Field: Musical
Status: Professional; Nonprofit
Income Sources: Theatre Communications Group
Organization Type: Performing; Touring; Resident; Educational

3754
BLUE JACKET, FIRST FRONTIER
PO Box C
Xenia, OH 45385
Phone: 937-376-4358
Fax: 937-376-5364
Toll-free: 877-465-2583
e-mail: tracy@bluejacketdrama.com
Web Site: bluejacketdrama.com
Officers:
    Board President: Tim Hancy
    Chief of Operations/Education: Tracy Leake
    CFO: Michael Stricka
    Business Development Manager: Joanna Stevens
Mission: Produces the Epic Outdoor Drama, Blue Jacket, along with other education works and events. First Frontier strives to preserve and promote the history of the Ohio Territory through educational programs and artistic preservations. Through our efforts, we strive to support historic preservation, provide valuable educational opportunities and provide diverse cultural enrichment.
Utilizes: Actors; AEA Actors; Commissioned Composers; Commissioned Music; Designers; Guest Conductors; Guest Designers; Multimedia; Organization Contracts; Original Music Scores; Performance Artists; Resident Artists; Resident Professionals; Selected Students; Sign Language Translators; Soloists
Founded: 1982
Specialized Field: Outdoor Theater
Status: Non-Profit, Professional
Paid Staff: 100
Paid Artists: 60
Budget: $100,000,000
Income Sources: Ticket Sales; Fundraising; Special Events
Season: June - August
Annual Attendance: 40,000
Facility Category: Outdoor Amphitheatre
Type of Stage: Amphitheater
Stage Dimensions: 3 acres
Seating Capacity: 1,400 (stadium seats)
Year Built: 1978

Oklahoma

3755
BULLSHED THEATRE PROJECT
5505 E Mountain View Road
Edmond, OK 73034
Phone: 405-341-0928
e-mail: bullshedtheatre@aol.com
Web Site: www.geocities.com/bullshedtheatre
Management:
    Artistic Director: Don Shirey
    Producing Director: Anne Lower-Shirey
Mission: Using a minimalist approach without sacrificing the artistic intent. From Shakespeare to Shepard, we produce gypsy/guerilla theatre fare. Minimal design, minimal cast equals maximum overdrive.
Founded: 1999
Specialized Field: New Plays; Contemporary; Drama
Status: For-Profit, Professional

3756
POLLARD THEATRE
120 W Harrison
PO Box 38
Guthrie, OK 73044
Phone: 405-282-2800
Fax: 405-282-0061
Web Site: www.thepollard.org/
Management:
    President: Don Coffin
    Artistic Director: W Jerome Stevenson
    Managing Director: Donna Dickson
Founded: 1987
Specialized Field: Musical; Comedy; Classic; Contemporary
Status: Non-Profit, Professional
Paid Staff: 11
Paid Artists: 11
Season: July - June
Type of Stage: Proscenium
Stage Dimensions: 50' x 50'
Seating Capacity: 277

3757
THE POLLARD THEATRE
120 West Harrison Avenue
Guthrie, OK 73044
Mailing Address: P.O. Box 38, Guthrie, OK 73044
Phone: 405-282-2800
Web Site: thepollard.org
Management:
    Artistic Director: W. Jerome Stevenson
    Managing Director: Van French
Mission: The mission of the Guthrie Arts & Humanities Council is to nurture endeavors in the arts and humanities that enrich the diverse culture of the Guthrie community, and encourage neighbors from near and far to share in that culture.
Opened: 1987

3758
CAMERON UNIVERSITY: THEATRE ARTS DEPARTMENT
2800 W Gore Boulevard
Lawton, OK 73505
Phone: 580-581-2378
e-mail: thescoop@cameron.edu
Web Site: www.cameron.edu/theatre_arts
Officers:
    Chair: Scott Richard Klein
    Assistant Professor: Eric Abbot
    Assistant Professor: Deidre Onishi

THEATRE / Oklahoma

Assistant Professor: Judd Vermillion
Specialized Field: Educational; Theater Workshops
Facility Category: Auditorium; Studio Performance; Theatre House
Type of Stage: Flexible; Proscenium
Rental Contact: Scott Hofmann

3759
LAWTON ARTS & HUMANITIES THEATER
801 NW Ferris
Lawton, OK 73507
Phone: 580-581-3470
Fax: 580-581-3473
e-mail: scheatwood@cityos.lawton.ok.us
Web Site: www.cityos.lawton.ok.us
Management:
    Executive Director: Bobby Matchett
    Artistic Director: Sharon Cheatwood
Specialized Field: Community Theatre
Status: Non-Profit, Professional
Paid Staff: 7

3760
SOONER THEATRE OF NORMAN
101 E Main Street
Norman, OK 73069
Phone: 405-321-9600
Fax: 405-364-0543
e-mail: tickets@soonertheatre.com
Web Site: www.soonertheatre.com
Officers:
    President: Amy Pepper
    VP: Meg Newville
    Executive Director: Jennifer Heavner Baker
    Associate Artistic Director: Brandon Adams
    Development and Marketing Director: Nancy Coggins, APR
Management:
    Executive Director: Jennifer Heavner Baker
    Production Manager: Brandon Adams
    Marketing Director: Jessica George
Mission: To present live entertainment and theatrical productions including music concerts, movies and other special events.
Founded: 1979
Specialized Field: Musical; Comedy; Community Theater; Classic; Contemporary
Status: Non-Profit, Non-Professional
Paid Staff: 4

3761
LYRIC THEATRE OF OKLAHOMA
1727 NW 16th Street
Civic Center Music Hall-Performance Venue
Oklahoma City, OK 73106
Phone: 405-524-9310
Fax: 405-524-9316
e-mail: amy@lyrictheatreokc.com
Web Site: www.lyrictheatreokc.com
Officers:
    President: David J. Flesher
    VP Eductaion: Robin Lister
    VP Development: Lori Mathena
    VP Marketing: Nancy J. Forenger
    VP Facilities: Scott McLaws
Management:
    Executive Director: Paula Stover
    Artistic Director: Michael Baron
    Associate Artistic Director: Ashley Well
    Education Director: Stephen Hilton
    Marketing Director: Daniel Siler
Mission: Oklahoma's only professional Musical Theatre for 44 years.
Utilizes: Actors; AEA Actors; Choreographers; Collaborations; Dancers; Designers; Five Seasonal Concerts; Grant Writers; Guest Accompanists; Guest Companies; Guest Composers; Guest Conductors; Guest Designers; Guest Lecturers; Guest Writers; Instructors; Local Artists; Lyricists; Music; New Productions; Organization Contracts; Original Music Scores; Poets; Resident Artists; Resident Professionals; Selected Students; Sign Language Translators; Singers; Soloists; Student Interns; Visual Arts
Founded: 1763
Specialized Field: Musical
Status: Professional; Nonprofit
Paid Staff: 10
Budget: $2 million
Income Sources: Ticket Sales; Donations from Foundations; Corporations; Individuals
Performs At: The Civic Center Music Hall
Affiliations: AEA; SSDC; IATSE
Annual Attendance: 50,000
Facility Category: Theatre
Type of Stage: Proscenium
Seating Capacity: 1,396
Year Built: 1932
Year Remodeled: 1999
Rental Contact: Bart Wells
Organization Type: Performing; Resident

3762
OKLAHOMA CHILDREN'S THEATRE
Fair Park
3000 General Pershing Boulevard
Oklahoma City, OK 73107-6202
Phone: 405-951-0000
Fax: 405-951-0003
e-mail: cacoct@swbell.net
Web Site: www.cityartscenter.org
Officers:
    Executive Director: Mary Ann Prior
    Development Director: Margaret Creighton
    Director of Finance & Administratio: Gloria Dale
    Deputy Director & Director of Prog: Robin Huston
Management:
    City Arts President: James Piskel
    Executive Director: Mary Ann Prior
Mission: To provide entertaining, educational and accessible experiences through theatrical productions, creative programming and events.
Founded: 1986
Specialized Field: Musical; Community Theater; Contemporary; Touring Company; Children's Theater
Status: Non-Profit, Professional
Paid Staff: 6
Volunteer Staff: 3
Paid Artists: 40
Performs At: City Arts Center

3763
OKLAHOMA OPERA & MUSICAL THEATER COMPANY
2501 N Blackwelder
Oklahoma City University
Oklahoma City, OK 73106
Phone: 405-521-5000
Fax: 405-521-5971
e-mail: mparker@okcu.edu
Web Site: www.okcu.edu
Management:
    Dean: Mark Edward Parker
Specialized Field: Educational; Musical
Budget: $10,000-$20,000
Performs At: Kirkpatrick Fine Arts Auditorium; Burg Theater; Wymberly

3764
OKLAHOMA SHAKESPEARE IN THE PARK
301 West Reno Avenue
PO Box 1437
Oklahoma City, OK 73102
Phone: 405-235-3700
Fax: 405-235-3700
e-mail: okshakespr@aol.com
Web Site: www.oklahomashakespeare.com
Officers:
    President: Rob Gallavan
    Secretary: Deanna Gallavan
    Treasurer: Bridget Jaime
Management:
    Managing Director: Sue Ellen Reiman
    Execitive/Artistic Director: Kathryn McGill
Mission: To produce works of Shakespeare; to teach Shakespeare in school.
Founded: 1985
Specialized Field: Comedy; Classic; Shakespeare
Status: Non-Profit, Professional
Paid Staff: 10
Volunteer Staff: 20
Paid Artists: 40
Non-paid Artists: 12
Budget: $120,000
Income Sources: Ticket Sales; Donations
Season: June - September
Affiliations: Oklahoma City University
Annual Attendance: 10,000
Facility Category: Ampitheatre
Type of Stage: Amphitheatre
Stage Dimensions: 50' x 25'
Seating Capacity: 750
Year Built: 1990
Year Remodeled: 2002
Cost: $50,000

3765
REDUXION THEATRE COMPANY
914 North Broadway Avenue Ste 120
Oklahoma City, OK 73102
Mailing Address: P.O. Box 61128, Oklahoma City, Ok 73146-1128
Phone: 405-651-3191
e-mail: info@reduxiontheatre.com
Web Site: reduxiontheatre.com
Officers:
    Chair: Paul James
    Vice Chair: Tim Berg
Management:
    Artistic Director: Tyler Woods
    Managing Director: Erin Woods
Mission: To professionally produce both classical and contemporary theatre, enriching Oklahoma's cultural, educational and economic climate, attracting artists and audiences from around the world.
Founded: 2007
Specialized Field: Shakespeare; Interactive Theatre
Status: Nonprofit

3766
PONCA PLAYHOUSE
301 South 1st Street
Ponca City, OK 74601
Mailing Address: PO Box 1414 Ponca City, OK 74602
Phone: 580-765-5360
e-mail: PoncaPlayhouse@gmail.com
Web Site: www.poncaplayhouse.com/
Officers:
    Vice President: Ruslyn Hermanson
    Secretary: Paula Coppock

Treasurer: Ardeth Mason
Management:
President: Dave Guinn
Mission: To offer interested area amateurs opportunities to participate in producing live theatre for the benefit of a discriminating audience.
Utilizes: Guest Companies; Singers
Founded: 1959
Specialized Field: Musical; Comedy; Community Theater
Status: Non-Profit, Non-Professional
Paid Staff: 1
Income Sources: American Association of Community Theatres; Oklahoma Community Theatre Association; Southwest Theatre Association
Organization Type: Performing; Touring; Resident

3767
CHEROKEE NATIONAL HISTORICAL SOCIETY

21192 S. Keeler Drive
Tahlequah, OK 74451
Mailing Address: PO Box 515, Tahlequah, OK 74465-0515
Phone: 918-456-6007
Fax: 918-456-6165
Toll-free: 888-999-6007
e-mail: tourism@cherokeeheritage.org
Web Site: www.cherokeeheritage.org
Officers:
President: Charles/Chief Boyd
VP: Mary Ellen Meredith
Management:
President: Richard Fields
Drama Producer: Patrick Whelan
Marketing Director: Marilyn Craig
Mission: Seeks to preserve the history and traditions of the Cherokee Indian tribe and to educate the public concerning the Cherokee story through the presentation of the Trail of Tears drama and other cultural presentations.
Utilizes: Actors; Dance Companies; Dancers; Designers; Filmmakers; Fine Artists; Five Seasonal Concerts; Guest Ensembles; Guest Instructors; Guest Musical Directors; Instructors; Local Artists; Sign Language Translators; Soloists; Student Interns; Special Technical Talent; Theatre Companies; Touring Companies
Founded: 1967
Specialized Field: Outdoor Theater; Historical
Status: Non-Profit, Professional
Paid Staff: 23
Volunteer Staff: 25
Income Sources: Tourism and Recreation Department, State of Oklahoma
Performs At: Cherokee Heritage Center Tsa La Gi Amphitheater
Annual Attendance: 16,000
Facility Category: Amphitheater
Stage Dimensions: 80'x40'
Seating Capacity: 1,800
Year Built: 1969
Cost: 500,000
Rental Contact: Seth Hecht
Organization Type: Resident; Educational

3768
NORTHEASTERN STATE UNIVERSITY SIZZLIN' SUMMER SHOWCASE

Northeastern State University
College of Arts & Letters
600 N Grand Avenue
Tahlequah, OK 74464
Phone: 918-456-5511
Fax: 918-458-2337
Toll-free: 800-229-14
e-mail: nsuinfo@nsuok.edu
Web Site: www.nsuok.edu
Officers:
President: Dr. Steve Turner, Ph.D.
Vice President: Dr. Laura Boren
Representative of the Operations Di: Patti Buhl
Executive Director: Mr. Ben Hardcastle
Vice President: Mr. David Koehn
Acting Vice President: Dr. Pamela Fly
Management:
Director: Dr. Martha Albin
Director: Gayle Anderson
Director: Patti D Buhl
Assistant Vice President: Sue S Catron
Director: Dr. Teri Cochran
Director: Kimberly Dawson
Director: Todd Enlow
Director: Dr. Phyllis Fife
Assistant Vice President: Dr. Pamela Fly
Founded: 1983
Specialized Field: Summer Stock
Status: Non-Profit, Non-Professional
Paid Staff: 50
Volunteer Staff: 1
Paid Artists: 35
Season: June - August
Type of Stage: Proscenium
Stage Dimensions: 35' x 40'
Seating Capacity: 200

3769
THEATRE TULSA

412 North Boston Avenue
Tulsa, OK 74103
Mailing Address: PO Box 995 Tulsa, OK 74101
Phone: 918-587-8402
Fax: 918-592-0848
e-mail: info@theatretulsa.org
Web Site: www.theatretulsa.org
Officers:
VP Marketing: Jarrod Kopp
VP Treasurer: J.P. Szafranski
VP Development: Teresa Nowlin
Advertising Director: Hunter Cates
Secretary: Kristin Harding
Programming: Rebecca Miller
Member-at-Large: Lisa Marie Horton
Member-at-Large: Mollie Rogers
Member-at-Large: Adam Strange
Management:
Director, Music Director: Samuel Jeremy Stevens
President/Artistic Director: Sara Phoenix
Assistant Choreographer and Dance C: Brooke Gibson
Director of Education, Stage Manger: Laura Dossett
Mission: To provide enrichment, entertainment and education to all sectors of the community by facilitating participation in the theatre arts.
Utilizes: Guest Artists; Guest Companies; Singers
Founded: 1922
Specialized Field: Community Theater
Status: Non-Profit, Non-Professional
Paid Staff: 1
Income Sources: Oklahoma Community Theatre Association; State Arts Council of Oklahoma
Performs At: Tulsa Performing Arts Center
Organization Type: Performing; Touring; Resident; Educational; Sponsoring

3770
WOODWARD ARTS AND THEATRE COUNCIL

818 Main
PO Box 1523
Woodward, OK 73801
Phone: 580-256-7120
Fax: 580-256-7121
e-mail: watc@att.net
Web Site: www.woodwardartstheatre.com/
Officers:
Vice President: Carol Bradley
Treasurer: Jim Treadaway
Secretary: Genie Koen
Member: Melinda Kinney
Member: Kenton Baird
Member: Justin Eilers
Member: Viktor Desai
Member: Bret Brewe
Custodial: Linda Cline
Management:
President: Judith White
Executive Director: Charlie Burns
Mission: To foster and promote cultural arts activities in Woodward and surrounding areas; to own and operate Woodward Arts Theatre.
Utilizes: Singers
Founded: 1981
Specialized Field: Community Theater
Status: Non-Profit, Professional
Paid Staff: 1
Income Sources: State Arts Council of Oklahoma
Organization Type: Performing; Sponsoring

Oregon

3771
OREGON SHAKESPEAREAN FESTIVAL ASSOCIATION

15 S Pioneer Street
PO Box 158
Ashland, OR 97520
Phone: 541-482-2111
Fax: 541-482-0446
Toll-free: 800-219-8161
e-mail: BoxOffice@orshakes.org
Web Site: www.osfashland.org
Officers:
Vice President: Kathryn Ma
Secretary: Gail Lopes
Treasurer: Susan Cain
Member: Joel Axelrod
Member: Rick Bleiweiss
Member: Lynne Carmichael
Member: Yogen Dalal
Member: Julie Strasser Dixon
Member: Mary Driver
Management:
President: Sid DeBoer
Artistic Director: Libby Appel
Artistic Director: Bill Rauch
Executive Director: Cynthia Rider
Associate Artistic Director: Christopher Acebo
Mission: To create bold new interpretations of contemporary and classic plays in repertory, influenced by American diversity and inspired by the high standard of Shakespeare.
Utilizes: Guest Companies; Singers
Founded: 1935
Specialized Field: Shakespeare; Classic; Contemporary
Status: Non-Profit, Professional

THEATRE / Oregon

Paid Staff: 450
Volunteer Staff: 750
Budget: $23 million
Income Sources: Earned; Contributed
Season: June - August
Performs At: Angus Bowmer Theatre; New Theatre; Elizabethan Theatre
Affiliations: Actors' Equity Association; ATA; University/Resident Theatre Association; Theatre Communications Group
Annual Attendance: 375,000
Type of Stage: Thrust Stage; Black Box; Outdoors
Seating Capacity: 601; 270; 360
Organization Type: Performing; Touring; Resident; Educational

3772
QUARTZ THEATRE
392 Taylor
Ashland, OR 97520
Phone: 513-482-8119
Management:
  Artistic Director: Robert Spira
Mission: The development of playwrights.
Founded: 1976
Specialized Field: Young Playwrights; New Plays
Status: Nonprofit
Organization Type: Performing

3773
CASCADES THEATRICAL COMPANY
148 NW Greenwood Avenue
Bend, OR 97701
Phone: 541-389-0803
Fax: 541-383-2879
e-mail: ctcinfo@cascadestheatrical.org
Web Site: www.cascadestheatrical.org
Officers:
  Vice President: Gloria Anderson
  Treasurer: Robert Goold
  Secretary: Lisa Haney
  Secretary: Lilly Ann Foreman
Management:
  President: Rena Bennett-Dellwo
  Marketing Director: Lana Shane
Mission: To offer quality live theatre to the community and Central Oregon
Utilizes: Singers
Founded: 1978
Specialized Field: Comminity Theater
Status: Non-Profit, Non-Professional
Paid Staff: 2
Volunteer Staff: 100
Budget: $150,000
Income Sources: Oregon Theatre Association
Performs At: Theatre
Affiliations: AACT
Annual Attendance: 18,000
Facility Category: Simi Thrust
Type of Stage: Flat Floor-No
Stage Dimensions: 43' WideX20' Deep
Seating Capacity: 131
Year Built: 1920
Year Remodeled: 1978
Rental Contact: Lana Shane
Organization Type: Performing

3774
ACTORS CABARET/MAINSTAGE THEATRE COMPANY
996 Willamette Street
PO Box 11732
Eugene, OR 97401
Phone: 541-683-4368
Fax: 541-485-5503
e-mail: admin@eugenechamber.com
Web Site: www.eugenechamber.com
Officers:
  President: David Hauser, CCE
Management:
  Executive Director: Jim Roberts
  Business Manager: Barb Brunton
  Director of Business Advocacy: Brittany Quick-Warner
  Director of Publications & Informat: Susan Miller
  Entrepreneurial Resources: Carrie Russo
Mission: To offer a broad range of experiences to participants and audiences in both a professional theater and community theatre atmosphere.
Founded: 1979
Specialized Field: Musical; Comedy; Cabaret; Dinner Theater; Classic; Contemporary
Status: Non-Profit, Non-Professional
Paid Staff: 10
Performs At: Downtown Cabaret; Eugene Downtown Mall
Organization Type: Performing

3775
OREGON CONTEMPORARY THEATRE
194 West Broadway
Eugene, OR 97401
Phone: 541-684-6988
Web Site: octheatre.org
Management:
  Artistic Director: Craig Willis
  Marketing/PR/Production Manager: Tara Wibrew
Mission: Oregon Contemporary Theatre creates bold entertainment, challenges expectation, inspires curiosity, encourages dialogue, and supports positive change.
Founded: 1992

3776
OREGON FANTASY THEATRE
Celeste Rose
820 E 36Th Avenue
Eugene, OR 97405
Phone: 541-686-1574
Management:
  Director: Celeste Rose
Mission: Producing and performing puppet shows which combine live actors with hand puppets, marionettes, shadows and masks.
Utilizes: Singers
Founded: 1978
Specialized Field: Puppet; Musical; Community Theater
Status: Professional; Non-Professional; Commercial
Paid Staff: 3
Income Sources: Puppeteers of America
Performs At: Hult Center for the Performing Arts
Organization Type: Performing; Touring; Educational

3777
ROGUE MUSIC THEATRE
PO Box 862
980 SW 6th Street
Grants Pass, OR 97528
Phone: 541-659-0602
Fax: 541-471-0919
e-mail: info@roguemusictheatre.org
Web Site: www.roguemusictheatre.org
Officers:
  President: Sal Blydenburgh
  Vice President: Molly Means
  Treasurer: Cathy Cardoza
  Secretary: Jim Thorpe
Management:
  Director: Bruce Walden-Dixson
  Music Director: David Hegdahl
  choreographer: Tianna Eddy
  Stage Manager: Jacqueline Sundin
Mission: To provide the highest quality musical theatre to the home region and beyond.
Founded: 1982
Specialized Field: Musical; Educational
Status: Non-profit; Professional
Paid Staff: 4
Volunteer Staff: 100
Paid Artists: 110
Non-paid Artists: 10
Budget: $150,000-$400,000
Annual Attendance: 11,000
Facility Category: Outdoor ampitheatre
Type of Stage: Proscenium
Stage Dimensions: 35'x70'
Seating Capacity: 1,385
Year Built: 1915
Year Remodeled: 1978

3778
LAKEWOOD CENTER FOR THE ARTS
368 S State Street
PO Box 274
Lake Oswego, OR 97034
Phone: 503-635-3901
Fax: 503-635-2002
e-mail: center.info@lakewood-center.org
Web Site: www.lakewood-center.org
Officers:
  President: Michelle Dorman
  Treasurer: Don Irving
Management:
  Executive Producer: Kay Vega
  Executive Director: Andrew Edwards
  Education Coordinator/Production As: Steve Knox
  Development Director: Peter Jurney
Mission: Establishment and maintenance of a permanent multi-arts and theatre facility; the sponsorship and coordination of education and cultural programming in visual arts, theatre and community events.
Founded: 1952
Specialized Field: Musical; Drama; Multi-Media; Community Theater
Status: Non-Profit, Professional
Paid Staff: 14
Volunteer Staff: 150
Paid Artists: 150
Non-paid Artists: 100
Budget: $1,300,000
Income Sources: Oregon Theatre Association; Oregon Advocates for the Arts; Portland Area Theatre Alliance
Season: June - September
Annual Attendance: 30,000
Facility Category: Arts Facility
Type of Stage: Thrust
Stage Dimensions: 30'x30'
Seating Capacity: 196
Year Built: 1980
Cost: $80,000
Organization Type: Performing; Resident; Educational; Sponsoring

3779
GALLERY THEATRE OF OREGON
210 N Ford Street
PO Box 245
McMinnville, OR 97128

THEATRE / Oregon

Phone: 503-472-2227
Fax: 503-434-1394
e-mail: execdirector@gallerytheatre.org
Web Site: www.gallerytheatre.org
Officers:
  President: Ken Moore
  VP: Lea New
  Secretary: Meridith Symons
  Treasurer: Paula Terry
Management:
  President: Carolyn McCloskey
  Managing Director: Ginger Williams
Mission: To provide a performing arts center in Yamhill County.
Utilizes: Guest Companies; Singers
Founded: 1968
Specialized Field: Drama; Musical; Comedy; Contemporary
Status: Non-Profit, Non-Professional
Paid Staff: 2
Type of Stage: Black Box; Mainstage
Stage Dimensions: 20'x40'
Seating Capacity: 240-100
Year Built: 1968
Year Remodeled: 1992
Organization Type: Performing; Educational

3780
BRITT FESTIVALS
PO Box 1124
Medford, OR 97501
Phone: 541-779-0847
Fax: 541-776-3712
Toll-free: 800-882-7488
e-mail: info@brittfest.org
Web Site: www.brittfest.org
Officers:
  Executive Director: Donna Briggs
  Finance Director: Kevin Forde
  Director of Education and Community: Rachel Jones
  Marketing Director: Sara King Cole
Management:
  President & CEO: Donna Briggs
  Director of Education and Community: Rachel Jones
  Director of House Operations: Bow Seltzer
  Director of Programming: Mike Sturgill
  Development Associate: Mark Knippel
  Development Associate: Sky Loos
  Office Manager: Vicki Rosette
  Marketing Director: Sara King Cole
  Development & Sales Associate: Bobby Abernathy
Mission: To present and sponsor, in Southern Oregon, performing arts of the highest quality for the education, enrichment and enjoyment of all.
Utilizes: Guest Artists; Guest Companies
Founded: 1963
Specialized Field: Classic; Contemporary; Ethnic Theater; Comedy; Drama
Status: Non-Profit, Professional
Paid Staff: 12
Volunteer Staff: 600
Performs At: The Britt Gardens
Annual Attendance: 70,000
Facility Category: Outdoor Amphitheatre
Seating Capacity: 2200
Year Built: 1963
Year Remodeled: 1992
Organization Type: Performing; Touring; Resident; Educational; Sponsoring

3781
RED OCTOPUS THEATRE COMPANY
777 West Olive Street
Newport, OR 97365
Phone: 541-265-2787
e-mail: redoctopustheatre@gmail.com
Web Site: redoctopustheatre.org
Founded: 1978
Performs At: The Newport Performing Arts Center

3782
DOLPHIN PLAYERS
2540 Union
North Bend, OR 97459
Phone: 503-756-7088
Mission: Presenting quality theater in a comfortable intimate setting.
Founded: 1980
Specialized Field: Musical; Dinner Theater; Community Theater
Status: Non-Professional; Nonprofit
Paid Staff: 50
Organization Type: Performing; Resident; Educational; Sponsoring

3783
ARTISTS REPERTORY THEATRE
1515 SW Morrson St.
Portland, OR 97205
Phone: 503-241-1278
Fax: 503-241-8268
e-mail: boxoffice@artistsrep.org
Web Site: www.artistsrep.org
Management:
  President: Allen Nause
  Artistic Director: D maso Rodriguez
  Managing Director: Sarah Horton
  Director of Finance & Administratio: Jim Neuner
  Finance & Administrative Assistant: Carol Ann Wohlmut
  Marketing & PR Director: Nicole Lane
  Marketing & PR Manager: Jessica Gleason
  Audience Services Manager: Karen Rathje
  Box Office Manager: Devin McCarthy
Founded: 1981
Specialized Field: Musical; Comedy; Classic; Contemporary
Status: Non-Profit, Professional
Paid Staff: 20
Paid Artists: 20
Performs At: Reiersgaard Theatre
Type of Stage: Flexible Black Box
Seating Capacity: 170

3784
BRODY THEATER
16 NW Broadway
97210
Portland, OR
Mailing Address: 5032242227
Toll-free: www-bro-ythe
Web Site: info@brodytheater.com
Mission: The Brody's double focus on entertainment and experiment, marks it as a showcase for both audience-pleasing performances and cutting edge theatrical presentation.
Founded: 1996
Specialized Field: Experimental

3785
MIRACLE THEATRE GROUP
525 SE Start St.
Portland, OR 97214
Phone: 503-236-7253
Fax: 503-236-4174
e-mail: info@brodytheater.com
Web Site: www.milagro.org
Officers:
  Chair Board of Directors: Ann Marcus
  Treasurer: Anthony Tomashek
  President: John Rodarte
  Secretary: Judi Ranton
  Director of Marketing Strategy: Maria E. Gonzalez
Management:
  President: John Rodarte
  Artistic Director: Olda Sanchez
  Artistic Director and Founder: Danielle Malan
  Director Dance Education: Catherine Evleshin
  Executive Director & Founder: Jos, Eduardo Gonz lez
Mission: Provides programming that includes public performances as well as specialized touring and education projects that currently encompass all of the Western states and the countries of Mexico and Canada. Incorporated as a nonprofit organization in 1985. The Miracle Theatre Group oversees three professional performance companies: Miracle Mainstate, Teatro Milagro, and the Milagro Bailadores.
Founded: 1985
Specialized Field: Musical; Comedy; Classic; Contemporary
Status: Non-Profit, Professional
Paid Staff: 15
Paid Artists: 10
Performs At: Miracle Theatre; 525 SE Stark
Rental Contact: Alice Snyder

3786
OREGON CHILDREN'S THEATRE
1939 NE Sandy Blvd.
Portland, OR 97232
Phone: 503-228-9571
Fax: 503-228-3545
e-mail: info@octc.org
Web Site: www.octc.org
Officers:
  President: Kregg Arntson
  Senior Vice President: Mark Friel
  Treasurer: Dann Wheeler
  Secretary: Vatea Herman
  ETP Artistic Director: Marcella Crowson
Management:
  Founder: Sondra Pearlman
  Director Marketing: Natasha Kautsky
  Artistic Director: Stan Foote
  Director, Education & Children's Te: Kelliann Garcia
  Managing Director: Ross McKeen
Mission: To present professional live theatre for youth at a price affordable to schools and families; to educate young people to the wonders of live theatre.
Utilizes: Actors; High School Drama; Original Music Scores
Specialized Field: Contemporary; Children's Theater
Performs At: Keller Auditorium
Annual Attendance: 100,000

3787
PORTLAND ACTORS ENSEMBLE
PO Box 8671
Portland, OR 97207
Phone: 503-467-6573
e-mail: info@portlandactors.com
Web Site: www.portlandactors.com
Officers:
  Board Chair: Margaret Darling Lillie
  Board Member: Dennis Fitzpatrick

THEATRE / Pennsylvania

Board Member: Samuel Kuzma
Administrative Board Member: KJ McElrath
Administrative Board Member: Athena McElrath
Mission: To bring financially accessible classical theatre to Portland communities in a non-traditional environment.
Founded: 1970
Specialized Field: Shakespeare; Outdoor Theater

3788
PORTLAND CENTER STAGE
Gerding Theater at the Armory
128 NW Eleventh Avenue
Portland, OR 97209
Phone: 503-445-3700
Fax: 503-445-3701
e-mail: boxoffice@pcs.org
Web Site: www.pcs.org
Management:
  General Manager: Creon Thorne
  HR & Capital Campaign Director: Lisa Sanman
  Finance Director: Lisa Comer
  Accounting Manager: Jerome Faulkner
  Accountant: Alan King
  Database Administrator: Bob Thomas
  IT Administrator: Christian Kisanga
  Associate Artistic Director: Rose Riordan
  Producing Associate: Brandon Woolley
Founded: 1988
Specialized Field: Drama; Comedy; Musical; Classic
Status: Non-Profit, Professional
Season: October - April
Type of Stage: Partial Thrust
Seating Capacity: 590

3789
PENTACLE THEATRE
145 Liberty Street
Suite 102
Salem, OR 97301
Phone: 503-485-4300
Fax: 503-485-4301
e-mail: tickets@pentacletheatre.org
Web Site: www.pentacletheatre.org
Officers:
  Founder: Robert Putnam
Management:
  President: Robert Sarberg
  Executive Director: Randy Boyd
  VP: Jay Howe
  Production Director: Tony Zandol
Mission: Pentacle's History begin in the early 1950's when a small group of theatre enthusiasts rented a barn (that subsequently became known as The Old Barn) and mounted a four production summer season.
Utilizes: Actors; Choreographers; Community Members; Community Talent; Educators; Equity Actors; Guest Writers; Instructors; Paid Performers; Volunteer Artists
Founded: 1954
Opened: 1954
Specialized Field: Year Round Community Theater
Status: Non-Profit, Non-Professional
Paid Staff: 5
Volunteer Staff: 800
Non-paid Artists: 200
Budget: $450,000
Income Sources: Ticket Sales, Grants, Membership, Donations
Affiliations: AACI
Year Built: 1963
Cost: $1,000,000

3790
CAMELOT THEATRE COMPANY
101 Talent Avenue
Talent, OR 97540
Mailing Address: P.O. Box 780, Talent, OR 97540
Phone: 541-535-5250
e-mail: info@camelottheatre.org
Web Site: camelottheatre.org
Management:
  Artistic Director: Livia Genise
  Production Manager: Roy Von Rains Jr
  Office Manager: Marlena Gray
Founded: 1982
Status: Charitable Organization
Performs At: James M. Collier Theatre
Seating Capacity: 164
Organization Type: Semi-Professional

3791
BROADWAY ROSE THEATRE COMPANY
12850 SW Grant Avenue
Tigard, OR 97223
Mailing Address: P.O. Box 231004 Tigard, OR 97281
Phone: 503-620-5262
Fax: 503-670-8512
e-mail: info@broadwayrose.com
Web Site: www.broadwayrose.org/
Officers:
  President: Scott Schiefelbein
  Vice President: Chuck Carpenter
  Treasurer: Jennifer Dale
  Secretary: Barbara Amling
Management:
  Producing Artistic Director: Sharon Maroney
  General Manager: Dan Murphy
  Marketing Director: Alan Anderson
  Development Manager: Brisa Peters
  Executive Director: Brenda MacRoberts
  Communications Manager: Emily Dew
  Grants Manager: Quimby Lombardozzi
  Patron Services Manager: Beth Moore
  Assistant Patron Services Manager: Steven Patton
Mission: Broadway Rose has been producing live, fun, professional summer stock theater since 1992. As the only professional theater company in Washington County, we provide accessible, quality entertainment.
Founded: 1992
Specialized Field: Summer Stock
Status: Professional; Nonprofit
Season: June - August
Performs At: Deb Fennell Auditorium

3792
ENCHANTED FOREST SUMMER THEATRE
8462 Enchanted Way SE
Turner, OR 97392
Phone: 503-371-4242
Fax: 503-364-1134
e-mail: info@enchantedforest.com
Web Site: www.enchantedforest.com
Officers:
  President: Roger Tofte
Management:
  Executive Director: Susan Vasley
Mission: To make people of all ages laugh and leave our theatre with wonderful memories.
Utilizes: Actors; Choreographers; Composers; Composers-in-Residence; Contract Actors; Dancers; Designers; Local Unknown Artists; Multimedia; Organization Contracts; Original Music Scores; Performance Artists; Sign Language Translators
Founded: 1972
Specialized Field: Musical; Comedy; Contemporary; Summer Stock
Status: For-Profit, Non-Professional
Paid Staff: 10
Paid Artists: 12
Income Sources: Paid Admission
Season: May - September
Performs At: 200 Seat Outdoor, Stage Covered
Annual Attendance: 100,000
Facility Category: Theme Park
Type of Stage: Proscenium
Stage Dimensions: 22' x 25'
Seating Capacity: 200
Year Built: 1972

Pennsylvania

3793
ACT II PLAYHOUSE
56 E Butler Ave.
Ambler, PA 19002
Phone: 215-654-0200
Fax: 215-654-9050
e-mail: info@act2.org
Web Site: www.act2.org/
Officers:
  President: Berne Siergiej
  Board Vice President: Leslie Mayer
  Board Treasurer: Frank 'Bud' Martin
  Secretary: Debra Friedman
  Chairman: Phil Albright
Management:
  Artistic Director: Tony Braithwaite
  Managing Director: Howie Brown
  Business Manager: Beth Dietzler
  Production and Company Manager: Andy Shaw
  Communications and Education Direct: Bill D'Agostino
  Stage Manager: Pat Sabato
  Audience Services Manager: Carolina Millard
  Box Office Associate/House Manager: Rebecca May Flowers
  Box Office Associate/House Manager: Melissa Murray
Founded: 1999
Specialized Field: Drama; Musical; Comedy
Status: Non-Profit, Professional
Paid Staff: 6
Paid Artists: 19

3794
SOUTH PARK THEATRE
P.O. Box 133
Bethel Park, PA 15129
Phone: 412-831-8552
Fax: 412-831-1647
e-mail: sopktheat@aol.com
Web Site: southparktheatre.com/
Officers:
  President: Joyce Hegedus
Management:
  Executive Director: Kathleen Caliendo
  Managing Director: Lorraine Mszanski
  Associate Director: Amber Kocher
  Children's Theatre Director: Kathy Hawk
  Technical Director: Kevin Kocher
Mission: To provide highest quality opera; to broaden public awareness and understanding of opera through education and community programming; to support development of young American singers; to encourage work of new composers to maintain oper as a living arts form.

Founded: 1995
Specialized Field: Musical; Drama; Comedy
Status: Non-Equity; Nonprofit
Season: May - September
Type of Stage: Proscenium
Stage Dimensions: 24' x 36'
Seating Capacity: 136

3795
TOUCHSTONE THEATRE
321 East 4th Street
Bethlehem, PA 18015
Phone: 610-867-1689
Fax: 610-867-0561
e-mail: touchstone@touchstone.org
Web Site: www.touchstone.org
Officers:
  President: Alex Shade
  Vice President: Jeanne B. Shook
  Treasurer: John Fallock
  Secretary: Alexis Leon
Management:
  Producing Director/Ensemble Member: Lisa Jordan
  Production Manager/Ensemble Member: James P. Jordan
  Touring Manager/Ensemble Member: Bill George
  Education Director/Ensemble Assoc.: Cathleen O'Malley
  Director Of Development: Amy Meleck
Mission: Dedicated to being an active force in the renewal of theatre as a vital art form. At our center is a resident professional acting ensemble rooted both in the local community of Bethlehem, Pennsylvania and the international community of the actor-creater.
Utilizes: Actors; Collaborating Artists; Collaborations; Community Members; Community Talent; Composers; Contract Actors; Curators; Designers; Educators; Five Seasonal Concerts; Guest Accompanists; Guest Choreographers; Guest Companies; Guest Conductors; Guest Designers; Guest Directors; Guest Ensembles; Guest Lecturers; Guest Musical Directors; Guest Speakers; Guest Teachers; High School Drama; Instructors; Local Artists; Local Artists & Directors; Local Talent; Lyricists; Multi Collaborations; Music; Organization Contracts; Original Music Scores; Paid Performers; Performance Artists; Poets; Resident Artists; Resident Companies; Soloists; Student Interns; Visual Designers
Founded: 1981
Specialized Field: Comedy; Classic; Contemporary; Ensembles
Status: Non-Profit, Professional
Paid Staff: 8
Volunteer Staff: 50
Paid Artists: 5
Income Sources: Theatre Communications Group; Theatre Association of Pennsylvania; National Mime Association
Performs At: Touchstone Theatre
Seating Capacity: 72
Year Built: 1981
Organization Type: Performing; Touring; Resident; Educational; Sponsoring

3796
BLOOMSBURG THEATRE ENSEMBLE
226 Center Street
PO Box 66
Bloomsburg, PA 17815
Phone: 570-784-8181
Fax: 570-784-4912
Toll-free: 800-282-0283
e-mail: feedback@bte.org
Web Site: www.bte.org
Officers:
  President: Christina Francis PhD
  Vice President: Karl A Meyer
  Secretary: Geeta Krishnan MD
  Treasurer: Mark Gardner
Management:
  Administrative Director: J S Atherton
  Technical Director: Earl Martz
  Director Development: Beth Larson
  Managing Director: Jon White-Spunner
  Communications Director: Syreeta CombsCannaday
Utilizes: Actors; Collaborations; Community Members; Community Talent; Designers; Educators; Five Seasonal Concerts; Guest Accompanists; Guest Conductors; Guest Instructors; Guest Lecturers; Guest Musical Directors; Guest Soloists; Guest Speakers; Instructors; Original Music Scores; Resident Professionals; Selected Students; Soloists; Students; Theatre Companies; Visual Arts
Founded: 1978
Specialized Field: Ensembles; Drama
Status: Nonprofit
Paid Staff: 25
Volunteer Staff: 4
Paid Artists: 7
Budget: $650,000
Performs At: Alvina Krause Theatre
Type of Stage: Proscenium
Seating Capacity: 350
Rental Contact: J S Atherton
Organization Type: Performing; Touring; Resident; Educational; Sponsoring

3797
ALLENBERRY RESORT INN AND PLAYHOUSE
1559 Boiling Springs Road
Boiling Springs, PA 17007
Phone: 717-258-3211
Fax: 717-960-5280
Toll-free: 800-430-5468
e-mail: aberry@allenberry.com
Web Site: www.allenberry.com
Management:
  Producer: John J Heinze
  Artistic Director: Ed Aldridge
Mission: A repertory equity theatre with a season running from March-November.
Utilizes: Actors; AEA Actors; Artists-in-Residence; Choreographers; Commissioned Music; Dancers; Designers; Educators; Fine Artists; Grant Writers; Guest Accompanists; Guest Artists; Guest Conductors; Guest Designers; Guest Lecturers; Guest Teachers; Instructors; Local Artists; Music; Performance Artists; Poets; Resident Artists; Resident Professionals; Sign Language Translators; Soloists; Student Interns
Founded: 1949
Specialized Field: Musical; Comedy; Classic
Status: For-Profit, Professional
Paid Staff: 15
Paid Artists: 30
Income Sources: Actors' Equity Association; Society for Stage Directors and Choreographers
Season: April - November
Performs At: Allenberry Playhouse
Affiliations: AEA, SSDC, USSA
Annual Attendance: 60,000
Type of Stage: Proscenium
Stage Dimensions: 28'x60'x28'
Seating Capacity: 400
Year Built: 1949
Year Remodeled: 1988
Organization Type: Performing; Resident

3798
BRISTOL RIVERSIDE THEATRE
120 Radcliffe Street
PO Box 1250
Bristol, PA 19007
Phone: 215-785-6664
Fax: 215-785-2762
e-mail: info@brtstage.org
Web Site: www.brtstage.org
Officers:
  President: Brian McPeak
  Founding Director: Susan Atkinson
Management:
  Artistic Director: Keith Baker
  Founding Director: Susan Atkinson
  Managing Director: Amy Kaissar
  Artistic Administrator: David Abers
  Marketing Director: Rayna Adams
  Audience Development Coordinator: Greg Hartley
  Institutional Giving Coordinator: Sara Accardi
  Company Manager: Kevin Drogalis
  Production Manager: Andrew Deppen
Founded: 1983
Specialized Field: Drama; Comedy; Musical
Status: Non-Profit, Professional
Paid Staff: 10
Budget: $35,000-$60,000
Performs At: Bristol Riverside Theatre
Type of Stage: Flexible
Seating Capacity: 302

3799
PENNSYLVANIA SHAKESPEARE FESTIVAL
DeSales University
2755 Station Avenue
Center Valley, PA 18034
Phone: 610-282-9455
Fax: 610-282-2084
e-mail: psf@pashakespeare.org
Web Site: www.pashakespeare.org
Officers:
  President: John Russo
  Vice President: Jo-Ann S. Kelly
  Secretary: Kathleen Kund Nolan
Management:
  Producing/Artistic Director: Patrick Mulcahy
  General Manager: Casey William Gallagher
  Director of Development: Debra Walter
  Education Director/Assistant Genera: Jill Arington
  Director of Marketing & Public Rela: Lisa Higgins Pechter
  Box Office Manager: Dael Jackson
  Business Manager: Janice S. Hein
  Production Manager: Matthew Given
  Associate Box Office Mgr.: Nicole Moyer
Mission: A professional theatre compnay and the Official shakespeare festival of the Commonwealth of Pennsylvania. Our mission is to enrich, inspire, engage and entertain the widest possible audience through first-rate professional productions of classical and contemporary plays, with a core commitment to the works of Shalespeare and other master dramatists and through an array of educational outreach and mentorship programs.
Founded: 1991

THEATRE / Pennsylvania

Specialized Field: Shakespeare; Classic
Status: Non-Profit, Professional
Paid Staff: 8
Volunteer Staff: 200
Season: May - August
Type of Stage: Thrust
Stage Dimensions: 38' x 40'
Seating Capacity: 473

3800
UPPER DARBY SUMMER STAGE
601 N Lansdowne Avenue
Drexel Hill, PA 19026
Phone: 610-394-1570
Fax: 610-622-6960
e-mail: hdietzler@rcn.com
Web Site: www.udpac.org
Management:
   Executive/Artistic Director: Harry Dietzler
Mission: One of the nations most sucessfully youth theater programs, producing six children's musicals and a mainstage Broadway show. We involve more than 600 youth ages 11 through 25 and employ more than 70 professionals and staff.
Founded: 1976
Specialized Field: Musical; Summer Stock
Status: Non-Profit, Non-Professional
Paid Staff: 80
Paid Artists: 25
Budget: $300,000
Income Sources: Government; Fundraising; Ticket Sales
Season: July - August
Facility Category: Performing Arts Center
Type of Stage: Thrust
Stage Dimensions: 50' x 40'
Year Built: 1960
Year Remodeled: 1974

3801
STATE THEATRE CENTER FOR THE ARTS
453 Northampton Street
Easton, PA 18042
Phone: 610-258-7766
Fax: 610-258-2570
Toll-free: 800-999-7828
e-mail: info@statetheatre.org
Web Site: www.statetheatre.org
Officers:
   President/CEO: Shelley Brown
Management:
   Operations: Mark Rafinski
   Marketing: Jamie Balliet
Specialized Field: Children's Theater; Broadway Musical Revivals
Status: Non-Profit, Non-Professional
Paid Staff: 12
Annual Attendance: 100,000
Seating Capacity: 1,500
Year Built: 1922
Year Remodeled: 2000

3802
CRESSON LAKE PLAYHOUSE
107 South Center Street
Ebensburg, PA 15931
Phone: 814-472-4333
Fax: 814-472-4419
e-mail: cressonlakeplayhouse@verizon.net
Web Site: www.cressonlake.com/
Officers:
   President: Sr Linda Karas
   Treasurer: Gary Bradley
   Vice President: Jim Pollino
Management:
   Executive Director: Elaine Mastalski
Mission: Cresson Lake Playhouse is governed by a Board of Directors. It is a not-for-profit organization. It is sponsored in part by Pennsylvania Council on the Arts. The theatre's mission since its founding in 1974 is to bring quality to live entertainment to the underserved rural areas of the Appalachian Mountains at affordable family prices.
Utilizes: Actors; Artists-in-Residence; Choreographers; Collaborations; Composers-in-Residence; Dancers; Designers; Educators; Five Seasonal Concerts; Grant Writers; Guest Artists; Guest Conductors; Guest Designers; Guest Directors; Guest Ensembles; Guest Lecturers; Guest Musical Directors; Guest Musicians; Guild Activities; High School Drama; Instructors; Local Artists; Multi Collaborations; Multimedia; Music; New Productions; Organization Contracts; Performance Artists; Resident Professionals; Sign Language Translators; Singers; Soloists; Student Interns; Touring Companies; Visual Arts
Founded: 1974
Specialized Field: Community Theater
Status: Non-Profit, Non-Professional
Paid Staff: 2
Volunteer Staff: 30
Paid Artists: 75
Non-paid Artists: 125
Season: May-December
Performs At: Historic Theatre Built In 1854, Equipped With State-Of-The-Art Sound System; Air-Conditioned And Heated; Ample Parking
Annual Attendance: 15,000-17,000
Facility Category: Indoor Theatre-Air Conditioned And Heated
Type of Stage: Alley/Black Box Theatre
Stage Dimensions: 20x17
Seating Capacity: 199
Year Built: 1850
Year Remodeled: 1974
Rental Contact: Elaine Mastalski

3803
TOTEM POLE PLAYHOUSE
9555 Golf Course Road
PO Box 603
Fayetteville, PA 17222
Phone: 717-352-2164
Fax: 717-352-8870
Toll-free: 888-805-7056
e-mail: boxoffice@totempoleplayhouse.org
Web Site: www.totempoleplayhouse.org
Officers:
   President: Dana Witt
   Treasurer: Jake Kaufman
Management:
   Marketing and Public Relations: Sue McMurtray
   Artistic Director: Ray Ficca
   Production Manager: Michael Domme
   Associate Producer: Chris Russo
   General Manager: Daphne Blair
   Box Office Manager: Renee Rankin
   House Manager: Wes Jackson
   Hospitality Manager: Beverly McNew
Mission: To provide professional theatre to the Cumberland Valley.
Utilizes: Actors; AEA Actors; Artists-in-Residence; Choreographers; Designers; Grant Writers; Guest Artists; Guest Composers; Guest Conductors; Guest Designers; Guest Lecturers; Guest Musical Directors; Instructors; Resident Artists; Resident Professionals
Founded: 1950
Specialized Field: Professional Theatre
Status: Professional; Commercial
Paid Staff: 4
Volunteer Staff: 30
Paid Artists: 50
Budget: $1,100,000
Income Sources: Ticket Sales; Tax Deductible Gifts; Corporate Sponsors
Season: June - August
Performs At: Totem Pole Playhouse
Affiliations: Actors Equity Association
Annual Attendance: 29,000
Facility Category: Air-Conditioned Enclosure
Type of Stage: Proscenium
Seating Capacity: 389
Year Built: 1970
Organization Type: Performing; Resident

3804
BARROW-CIVIC THEATRE
1223 Liberty Street
PO Box 1089
Franklin, PA 16323
Phone: 814-437-3440
Fax: 814-432-6608
Toll-free: 800-537-7769
e-mail: john@barrowtheatre.com
Web Site: www.barrowtheatre.com
Officers:
   Chairman: Stephen Teig
   1st Vice Chair, Programming Chair: Jennifer Fox
   2nd Vice Chair: Carol Brown
   Finance Chair: Dawn Caiarelli
   Secretary: Jodi Hoover
   Warehouse Chair, Marketing Chair: Davin Cutchall
   Youth Chair: Martha Heise
   Facilities Chair: Chuck Gibbons
   Fundraising Chair: Mary Ann Richardson
Management:
   Director: Mary Ann Richardson
   Managing Director: John McConnell
   General Manager: Penny B Gustavson
   Technical Director: Bruce Warner
Mission: Committed to providing leadership and education in cultural development and performing arts to the region, striving to create a legacy of quality entertainment by tapping the resources of all age group and encouraging the pursuit of artistic talents.
Founded: 1992
Specialized Field: Drama; Musical
Status: Non-Profit, Non-Professional
Paid Staff: 3
Seating Capacity: 497

3805
OPEN STAGE OF HARRISBURG
223 Walnut Street
Harrisburg, PA 17101
Phone: 717-232-6736
Fax: 717-232-1505
e-mail: info@openstagehbg.com
Web Site: www.openstagehbg.com
Officers:
   President: Hon Ben Allatt
   Vice President: Abby Tierney
   Secretary: Karen H Lehman
   Treasurer: Nicholas D Hughes
Management:
   Director: Susan Kadel
   Executive Artistic Director: Donald L Alsedek
   Managing Director: Terry Sneed
   Educational Director: Anne L Alsedek
   Executive Artistic Director: Donald Alsedek
   Resident Costume Designer: Gwen Alsedek

Marketing & Sales Manager: Stuart Landon
Mission: To develop and support an ensemble of theatre artists for the purpose of presenting modern, contemporary and original dramatic literature in close relationship with its audiences; to provide educational opportunites through a school and outreach program.
Utilizes: Actors; AEA Actors; Artists-in-Residence; Collaborating Artists; Guest Companies; Guest Conductors; Guest Directors; Guest Instructors; Guest Soloists; Guild Activities; High School Drama; Local Artists; Lyricists; New Productions; Original Music Scores; Student Interns; Touring Companies
Founded: 1983
Specialized Field: New Plays; Contemporary
Status: Non-Profit, Professional
Paid Staff: 5
Paid Artists: 40
Budget: $406,315
Income Sources: Theatre Communications Group; Citizens for the Arts in Pennsylvania; Theatre Association of Pennsylvania; Box Office; Student Tuition; Individual, Public and Private Fundings.
Performs At: Citizens for the Arts in PA
Affiliations: Theatre Communications Group
Annual Attendance: 9000
Facility Category: Theatre
Type of Stage: Black Box
Stage Dimensions: 18x24
Seating Capacity: 99
Year Remodeled: 1991
Rental Contact: Donald L Alscolk
Organization Type: Performing; Touring; Resident; Educational; Sponsoring

3806
THEATRE HARRISBURG
513 Hurlock Street
Harrisburg, PA 17110-1489
Phone: 717-232-5501
Fax: 717-232-5912
e-mail: email@theatreharrisburg.com
Web Site: www.theatreharrisburg.com
Officers:
  President: Joe Rebarchak
  Executive Director: Samuel Kuba
  Technical Director: Nels Martin
Management:
  Executive Director: Samuel Kuba
  Costume Designer: Paul Foltz
  Office Administrator: Myrna Fink
  Technical Director: Nels Martin
  Artistic Administrator: Diedra Adamiak
Mission: To provide quality theatrical experiences, opportunities and education to the Capital Region.
Utilizes: Guest Companies
Founded: 1926
Specialized Field: Musical; Community Theater
Status: Non-Profit, Non-Professional
Paid Staff: 5
Income Sources: Grants
Performs At: Whitaker Center and Krevsky Production Center
Annual Attendance: 21,000
Organization Type: Performing; Educational

3807
HERSHEY THEATRE
15 E Caracas Avenue
PO Box 395
Hershey, PA 17033
Phone: 717-534-3405
Fax: 717-533-2882
e-mail: htheatre@hersheytheatre.com
Web Site: www.hersheytheatre.com
Officers:
  Executive Director: Susan R. Fowler
Mission: Premiere performing arts center presenting the finest in touring Broadway shows, classical music and dance attractions, and world-renowned entertainers.
Utilizes: Original Music Scores; Selected Students; Theatre Companies
Founded: 1933
Specialized Field: Drama; Musical; Light Theater; Classic; Children's Theater
Status: Non-Profit, Non-Professional
Paid Staff: 5
Volunteer Staff: 400
Performs At: Hershey Theatre
Annual Attendance: 75,000
Facility Category: Theatre
Type of Stage: Proscenium
Seating Capacity: 1,904
Year Built: 1933
Year Remodeled: 2002
Cost: $3,000,000
Rental Contact: Executive Director Susan Fowler
Organization Type: Touring; Sponsoring

3808
HERSHEYPARK ENTERTAINMENT
100 W Hersheypark Drive
Hershey, PA 17033
Phone: 717-534-3349
Fax: 717-534-3336
e-mail: audition@hersheypa.com
Web Site: www.hersheypark.com/shows/resident_shows.php
Management:
  Executive Director: Cherie Vanzant
Founded: 1976
Specialized Field: Community Theater; Musical
Status: For-Profit, Professional
Season: May - September

3809
KEYSTONE REPERTORY THEATER
104 Waller Hall
Indiana, PA 15705
Mailing Address: 401 S 11th Street Indiana, PA 15705
Phone: 724-357-2965
Fax: 724-357-3885
e-mail: theater-info@iup.edu
Web Site: www.arts.iup.edu/krt
Officers:
  President: George Fender
Management:
  Artistic Director: Barbara Blackledge
  Associate Artistic Director: Brain Jones
Mission: Professional summer theater bringing theater to rural western PA.
Founded: 1997
Specialized Field: Summer Stock
Status: Nonprofit
Paid Staff: 22
Volunteer Staff: 5
Paid Artists: 80
Budget: $45,000-$60,000
Income Sources: Grants; Tickets; Subscriptions; Advertising; Donations
Season: June - July
Affiliations: AEA Special Appearence Contracts
Annual Attendance: 2000-2500
Type of Stage: Black Box
Seating Capacity: 199
Year Built: 1915
Year Remodeled: 1989
Cost: $2 Million

3810
MOUNTAIN PLAYHOUSE
PO Box 205
Jennerstown, PA 15547
Phone: 814-629-9201
Fax: 814-629-9201
e-mail: info@greengablesrestaurant.com
Web Site: www.mountainplayhouse.com
Management:
  Director: Danny Gidron
  Deputy Director: Chan Harris
  Associate Director: Guy Stroman
  Mountain Playhouse Producer: Teresa Stoughton Marafino
  Marketing Director: Mary Louise Stoughton
Utilizes: Guest Companies
Founded: 1939
Specialized Field: Dinner Theater; Comedy; Musical; Drama; Classic
Status: Non-Profit, Professional
Paid Staff: 40
Season: May - October
Performs At: Mountain Playhouse
Facility Category: Resident; Educational
Organization Type: Resident; Educational

3811
FULTON OPERA HOUSE/ACTOR'S COMPANY OF PENNSYLVANIA
12 North Prince Street
PO Box 1865
Lancaster, PA 17608
Phone: 717-397-7425
Fax: 717-397-3780
e-mail: info@thefulton.org
Web Site: www.fultontheatre.org
Officers:
  President: Elliot Sterenfeld, MD
  Vice President: Dave Taylor
  Treasurer: Curtis J. Myers
  Secretary: Michael Lambert
Management:
  Artistic Director: Marc Robin
  Managing Director: Aaron A. Young
Founded: 1963
Specialized Field: Musical; Light Theater
Performs At: Fulton Opera House; Studio Theatre
Type of Stage: Proscenium, Black Box
Seating Capacity: 630, 100

3812
SESAME PLACE
100 Sesame Road
Langhome, PA 19047
Phone: 215-752-7070
Fax: 215-741-5307
Toll-free: 866-464-3566
e-mail: michael.joyce@anheuser-busch.com
Web Site: www.sesameplace.com
Officers:
  Chairman: Jan Cavanaugh
  Vice-Chairman: Ann Marie Boweyer
  Treasurer: Michael Eiser
  Secretary: Joanne Bujnoski
Management:
  EVP: Robert Caruso
  Director Entertainment: Michael Joyce
Founded: 1980
Specialized Field: Specialty Acts; Children's Theater
Status: For-Profit, Non-Professional
Season: May - October
Stage Dimensions: 30' x 32'
Seating Capacity: 1000

THEATRE / Pennsylvania

3813
SAINT VINCENT SUMMER THEATRE
Saint Vincent College
300 Fraser Purchase Road
Latrobe, PA 15650
Phone: 724-537-8900
Fax: 724-537-4554
Web Site: www.svst.org
Officers:
   Acting President: Bonaventure Curtis
Management:
   Artistic Director: Colleen Reilly
Mission: To continue to bring quality opera to out community and to showcase it in out own opera house; to educate the general community in an appreciation of opera and send our outreach programs into the schools of both Manatee and Sarasota counties; to offer statewide touring programs.
Founded: 1969
Specialized Field: Touring Company; Drama; Musical
Status: Non-Profit, Professional
Paid Staff: 2
Paid Artists: 7
Season: May - August
Type of Stage: Half-Round
Stage Dimensions: 32' x 20'
Seating Capacity: 280

3814
PEOPLE'S LIGHT AND THEATRE COMPANY
39 Conestoga Road
Malvern, PA 19355
Phone: 610-647-1900
Fax: 610-640-9521
Web Site: www.peopleslight.org
Officers:
   President: L Frederick Sutherland
   Vice President: Kenneth Mumma
   Treasurer: Brian Doerner
   Secretary: Hal Real
Management:
   Managing Director: Grace Grillet
   Director: Ellen Anderson
   Communications Director: Mary Bashaw
   Artistic Director: Abigail Adams
   Marketing Director: Wendy E Worthington
Mission: To help unify a culturally diverse society by giving the community barrier-free access to drama that celebrates our joys, terrors and dreams as we struggle to live together in difficult times.
Utilizes: Actors; AEA Actors; Artists-in-Residence; Choreographers; Collaborating Artists; Collaborations; Commissioned Composers; Commissioned Music; Designers; Grant Writers; Guest Accompanists; Guest Artists; Guest Companies; Guest Conductors; Guest Designers; Guild Activities; Instructors; Local Artists; Lyricists; Multi Collaborations; Multimedia; Music; Original Music Scores; Performance Artists; Poets; Resident Artists; Resident Professionals; Selected Students; Soloists
Founded: 1974
Specialized Field: Light Theater; Multi-Cultural
Status: Professional; Nonprofit
Income Sources: Actors' Equity Association; League of Resident Theatres
Season: Year-round
Performs At: The People's Light Theater
Organization Type: Performing; Resident; Educational

3815
HEDGEROW THEATRE
146 West Rose Valley Rd.
Media, PA 19086
Mailing Address: The Hedgerow Theatre, 64 Rose Valley Road, Media, PA 19063
Phone: 610-565-4211
Fax: 610-565-1672
e-mail: company@hedgerowtheatre.org
Web Site: www.hedgerowtheatre.org
Officers:
   President: Shiela Kutner
Management:
   Producing Artistic Director: Penelope Reed
   Managing Director: Darlene McClellan
   Operations Manager: Zoran Kovcic
   Group Sales and School Tours: Art Hunter
   Associate Artistic Director: Jared Reed
Mission: Seeks to connect and enrich the lives of actors and audiences through the shared intimate experiences of excellence. We have a wide variety of year-round ofering between our Premier Series, Horizon Series, and Children's Theatre, as well as classes for both children and adults through our Theatre School.
Utilizes: Guest Companies; Singers
Founded: 1923
Specialized Field: Drama; Musical; Classic
Status: Non-Profit, Professional
Paid Staff: 30
Volunteer Staff: 5
Paid Artists: 70
Performs At: Theatre
Facility Category: Theatre
Type of Stage: Proscenium
Stage Dimensions: 19'x27'
Seating Capacity: 144
Year Built: 1840
Year Remodeled: 1985
Organization Type: Performing; Touring; Resident; Educational

3816
MEDIA THEATRE FOR THE PERFORMING ARTS
104 E State Street
Media, PA 19063
Phone: 610-891-0100
e-mail: info@mediatheatre.org
Web Site: www.mediatheatre.org
Officers:
   President: Jack Holefelder
   Chairperson: Tom Hibberd
   Executive Director: Patrick Ward
   Artistic Director: Jesse Cline
   Development Director: Austin Connors
   Music Director: Scott Anthony
   Technical Director: Robert A. White
Mission: Promote and nurture the imagination, diversity and joy unique to music theatre by the production of new and classic works.
Utilizes: Actors; AEA Actors; Artists-in-Residence; Choreographers; Five Seasonal Concerts; Grant Writers; Guest Artists; Guest Conductors; Guest Designers; Guest Lecturers; Guild Activities; High School Drama; Music; Sign Language Translators; Soloists; Student Interns
Founded: 2002
Specialized Field: Musical
Status: Non-Profit, Professional
Paid Staff: 10
Paid Artists: 30
Budget: $2,000,000
Income Sources: Grants; Membership; Ticket Sales
Performs At: Proscenium
Affiliations: AEA
Annual Attendance: 80,000
Facility Category: Theatre
Type of Stage: Proscenium
Seating Capacity: 632
Year Built: 1927
Year Remodeled: 1993
Cost: $1,500,000
Rental Contact: Artistic Director Jesse Cline

3817
ROBERT MORRIS UNIVERSITY COLONIAL THEATRE
6001 University Blvd
Moon Township, PA 15108
Phone: 412-397-5407
Fax: 412-262-8606
Toll-free: 800-762-0097
e-mail: locke@rmu.edu
Web Site: www.rmu.edu/theatre
Management:
   Theatre Program Communications: Robert J Locke
   Events Manager/Operations: Rebecca M Diana
   Events Manager/Facilities: Webley J Yeardie
Mission: Professional quality, student-focused, theatrical productions for the university and surrounding community.
Utilizes: Guest Companies; Singers
Founded: 1967
Specialized Field: Community Theater
Status: Non-Professional; Nonprofit
Paid Staff: 1
Income Sources: Fundraising
Performs At: Massey Theatre
Annual Attendance: 1,200
Organization Type: Performing; Educational

3818
VAGABOND ACTING TROUPE
PO Box 355
Morgantown, PA 19543-0355
Phone: 610-286-5567
Fax: 610-286-5567
e-mail: vagabondactingtroupe@gmail.com
Web Site: www.vagabondactingtroupe.org
Officers:
   President: Ty Furman
   Secretary, Board of Directors/Core: Clare Goilden Drake
   Treasurer: Gavin McCulloch
Management:
   Executive Director: Aileen McCullogh
   Bookkeeper: Gavin McCullogh
   Resident Music Director: Jeff Beideman
   Resident Music Director: Dave Morrison
   Assistant Director Classical Studie: Kait Skrocki
   Board of Directors: ELLEN JOFFRED
   Board of Directors: JENNIFER WILKIN
Mission: Family and adult theatre utilizing an intense physical style.
Utilizes: Students; Special Technical Talent; Theatre Companies
Founded: 1993
Specialized Field: Children's Theater; Educational; Experimental; New Plays
Status: Non-Profit, Educational
Paid Staff: 2
Paid Artists: 100
Budget: $50,000

Income Sources: Ticket Sales; Educational Tuition; Advertising; Individual Donors; Foundation, Government and Corporate Sponsorships
Affiliations: Theatre Alliance of Greater Philadelphia
Annual Attendance: 5,000
Type of Stage: Black Box
Stage Dimensions: Changeable
Seating Capacity: 200; 399
Year Built: 1970
Rental Contact: Aileen McCulloch

3819
GRETNA PRODUCTIONS
107 N. Main st,
PO Box 578
Mount Gretna, PA 24557
Phone: 434-656-3377
Fax: 717-964-2189
e-mail: info@gretnatheatre.com
Web Site: www.gretnatheatre.com
Officers:
  President: J. Thomas Dunlevy
  Vice President: Barclay Fitzpatrick
  Treasurer: James G. Cassel
  Secretary: Fred Horowitz
Management:
  Artistic Director: Will Stutts
  Associate Artistic Director: Renee T Krizan
  Managing Director: Larry Frenock
  Musical Director: Nathan Perry
  Producing Artistic Director: Larry Frenock
Mission: Nonprofit professional theatre dedicated to producing and presenting work that appeals to a diverse audience and community.
Utilizes: Guest Companies; Singers
Founded: 1927
Specialized Field: Musical; Classic
Status: Non-Profit, Professional
Paid Staff: 3
Paid Artists: 100
Income Sources: League of Resident Theatres; Actors' Equity Association; Theatre Association of Pennsylvania; Metro Arts of Harrisburg
Performs At: Mt. Gretna Playhouse
Organization Type: Performing; Touring

3820
TIMBERS DINNER THEATRE
350 Timber Road
PO Box 10
Mount Gretna, PA 17064
Phone: 717-964-3601
Web Site: www.gretnatimbers.com
Management:
  President: John Briody
  Artistic Director: Andy Robert
  Production Manager: Katheleen Briody
Mission: Family entertainment, affordable price.
Founded: 1975
Specialized Field: Dinner Theater; Musical
Status: For-Profit, Professional
Paid Staff: 25
Paid Artists: 10
Season: June - September
Performs At: Timbers Summer Dinner Theatre
Facility Category: Outdoor/Under Roof (semi-enclosed)
Type of Stage: Proscenium
Seating Capacity: 450
Year Built: 1950
Year Remodeled: 1976
Organization Type: Performing

3821
POCONO PLAYHOUSE
Playhouse Lane
Mountainhome, PA 18342
Phone: 570-595-7456
Fax: 570-595-7465
Management:
  Owner/Producer: Hubert Fryman
  General Manager: Donna McMicken
Utilizes: Guest Companies
Founded: 1947
Specialized Field: Musical; Ensembles
Status: Professional; Commercial
Season: June - October
Performs At: Pocono Playhouse
Organization Type: Performing; Educational

3822
BUCKS COUNTY PLAYHOUSE
70 South Main Street
PO Box 313
New Hope, PA 18938
Phone: 215-862-2121
Fax: 215-862-0220
e-mail: mail@buckscountyplayhouse.com
Web Site: www.buckscountyplayhouse.com
Officers:
  President: Ralph Miller
Management:
  Artistic Director: Stephen Casey
Utilizes: Guest Companies
Founded: 1939
Specialized Field: Musical
Status: Professional; Commercial
Performs At: Bucks County Playhouse
Organization Type: Performing; Educational; Partial-Equity Season

3823
1812 PRODUCTIONS
2329 South 3rd Street
Philadelphia, PA 19148
Phone: 215-592-9560
Web Site: 1812productions.org
Management:
  Artistic Director: Jennifer Childs
  Managing Director: Kate Tejada
  Marketing And Public Relations: Tyler Melchior
Mission: 1812 Productions is dedicated to creating theatrical works of comedy and comedic works of theater that explore and celebrate our sense of community, our history and our humanity.
Founded: 1997
Specialized Field: Comedy
Status: Nonprofit
Budget: 900,000 annual
Income Sources: National Theatre Company Grant From The American Theatre Wing
Performs At: Arcadia Stage At Arden Theatre Company 40 N. 2nd Street, Philadelphia, PA 19106

3824
AMERICAN FAMILY THEATER
1429 Walnut Street
4th Floor
Philadelphia, PA 19102
Phone: 215-563-3501
Fax: 215-563-1588
Toll-free: 800-523-4540
e-mail: atafyinfo@atafy.org
Web Site: www.atafy.org
Management:
  President: Bob Steck
  Artistic Director: Don Kersy
  Account Executive: Amy Wozniak
Founded: 1971
Specialized Field: Youth Theater; Classic; Contemporary
Status: Non-Profit, Professional
Paid Staff: 35

3825
AMERICAN MUSIC THEATER FESTIVAL/PRINCE MUSIC THEATER
1412 Chestnut Street
Philadelphia, PA 19102
Phone: 215-569-9700
Fax: 215-972-1000
e-mail: info@princemusictheater.org
Web Site: www.princemusictheater.org
Officers:
  President: Robert A. Fox
  Vice-President: Howard Morgan
  Secretary-Treasurer: Lee Tolbert
  CEO: David C. Bernstein
Management:
  Executive Director: James E. Hines
  Controller: Louis J. Coppola
  Finance Consultant: Hallie Bressler
  Finance Consultant: Bart Isdaner
  Director of Development: Heather S. Giampapa
  Artistic Administrator: Nancy Lee Kathan
  Volunteer / President: Ed Kasses
  Volunteer / President and CEO: Lawrence J. Wilker
Founded: 1984
Specialized Field: Musical; Classic
Status: Non-Profit, Professional
Paid Staff: 35
Performs At: Prince Music Theater
Facility Category: Theater
Type of Stage: Proscenium
Seating Capacity: 450

3826
AMERICAN THEATER ARTS FOR YOUTH
1429 Walnut Street
Philadelphia, PA 19102
Phone: 800-822-8487
Fax: 215-563-3501
Toll-free: 800-523-4540
e-mail: atafyinfo@atafy.org
Web Site: www.atafy.org
Management:
  Artistic Director: Don Kersey
Founded: 1971
Specialized Field: Touring Company; Children's Theater
Status: Nonprofit; Non-Equity
Season: October - May

3827
ARDEN THEATRE COMPANY
40 N 2nd Street
Philadelphia, PA 19106
Phone: 215-922-1122
Fax: 215-922-7011
e-mail: info@ardentheatre.org
Web Site: www.ardentheatre.org
Officers:
  President: Brian Abernathy
  Vice President: Nancy Burd
  Vice President: Holly Kinser
  Treasurer: Michael A. Donato
  Secretary: Nancy Hirsig
Management:
  Managing Director: Amy L Murphy

THEATRE / Pennsylvania

Producing Artistic Director: Terrence J Nolen
Associate Artistic Director: Edward Sobel
Associate Artistic Director: Matthew Decker
Artistic Assistant: Bryan Kerr
Mission: Dedicated to bringing to life the greatest stories by the greatest storytellers of all times.
Founded: 1988
Specialized Field: Musical; Comedy; Classic; Contemporary
Status: Non-Profit, Professional
Paid Staff: 30
Budget: $3,000,000
Performs At: Hass Stage/Mainstage; Arcadia Stage/Studio Theatre
Affiliations: LORT; AEA
Annual Attendance: 90,000
Type of Stage: Flexible Stage
Seating Capacity: 400-175
Rental Contact: General Manager Jenn Peck

3828
BIG MESS THEATRE
1112 Manning Street
Philadelphia, PA 19107
Phone: 215-829-8333
e-mail: bigmessthr@aol.com
Management:
  Artistic Director: Greg Giovanni
Mission: Big Mess Theatre dedicates itself to visionary forms of theatre and theatrical experience.
Founded: 1988
Specialized Field: New Plays; Experimental; Classic

3829
BUSHFIRE THEATRE OF PERFORMING ARTS
224 South 52nd Street
Philadelphia, PA 19139
Phone: 215-747-9230
Fax: 215-747-9236
e-mail: TheBushfire@verizon.net
Web Site: www.bushfiretheatre.org
Officers:
  Secretary: Gwen Braxton
  Secretary: Ruth Sharpe
Management:
  Artistic Director: Al Simpkins
  Executive Director: Verlina Dawson
  Consultant: Kya Simpkins
  Communications: Dawn Sheppard
  Office Manager: Jean Austin
Mission: Is to offer greater opportunity for black professional and non-professional actors, playwrights and other theatre personnel to develop their skills and careers.
Utilizes: Guest Companies; Singers
Founded: 1977
Specialized Field: Musical
Status: Professional; Nonprofit
Income Sources: Actors' Equity Association
Performs At: Bushfire Theatre of Performing Arts; Writers Works
Organization Type: Performing; Educational

3830
FREEDOM REPERTORY THEATRE
1346 N Broad Street
Philadelphia, PA 19121
Phone: 267-687-1764
Fax: 215-765-4191
Web Site: www.freedomtheatre.org
Officers:
  Chair: D. Keith Hargreaves
Management:
Executive Director: Sandra Haughton
Managing Director of Training: Patricia Scott Hobbs
Associate Managing Director of Trai: Diane Leslie
Admissions Representative: Thom Page
Director of Finance: Quinton Joyner
Accounting Manager: Tamara Brown
Receptionist: Larry Andrews
Founded: 1966
Specialized Field: Drama; Musical; Educational
Performs At: John E Allen Theatre, Freedom Cabaret Theatre
Type of Stage: Proscenium; Flexible
Seating Capacity: 299-120

3831
GERMANTOWN THEATRE GUILD
4801 Courthouse Street
Suite 220
Philadelphia, PA 23188
Phone: 215-621-7759
Fax: 215-991-0419
e-mail: gtcstage@lycos.com
Web Site: www.gtcstage.com
Officers:
  President and CEO: Jacob Harold
  Chair: Mari Kuraishi
  Secretary: Charles Best
  Treasurer: Tom Tinsley
Management:
  Artistic Director: Mark Hallen
  Managing Director: Darla Max
  Technical Director: GA Carafelli
Mission: Germantown Theatre Center is a place for arts education in the northwest neighborhood of Philadelphia, providing classes, residencies and performances which excite and inspire a diverse economic, ethnic and racial population and enhance cultural and community revitalization.
Utilizes: Guest Companies
Founded: 1933
Specialized Field: Community Theater; Theater Workshops
Status: Professional; Nonprofit
Income Sources: Theatre Alliance of Pennsylvania; Greater Philadelphia Cultural Alliance; Citizens for the Performing Arts in Pennsylvania; Performing Arts League of Philadelphia
Organization Type: Performing; Touring; Educational; Sponsoring

3832
INDIAN RIVER THEATRE OF THE PERFORMING ARTS
32735-B County Rte. 29
Philadelphia, PA 13673
Phone: 315-642-3441
Fax: 315-642-3738
e-mail: pdixon@mail.ircsd.org
Web Site: www.ircsd.org
Management:
  Theatre Secretary: Pamela Dixon
  Assistant Principal: John Davis
  Technical Director: Phillip Dyke
  Theater Manager: Kristi Fuller
Mission: Community Theatre arts education theatre.
Utilizes: Actors; AEA Actors; Arrangers; Artists-in-Residence; Choreographers; Collaborating Artists; Collaborations; Commissioned Composers; Commissioned Music; Community Members; Community Talent; Composers; Composers-in-Residence; Contract Actors; Contract Orchestras; Curators; Dance Companies; Dancers; Designers; Educators; Equity Actors; Fellows of Institute; Filmmakers; Fine Artists; Five Seasonal Concerts; Grant Writers; Guest Accompanists; Guest Artists; Guest Choreographers; Guest Companies; Guest Composers; Guest Conductors; Guest Designers; Guest Directors; Guest Ensembles; Guest Instructors; Guest Lecturers; Guest Musical Directors; Guest Musicians; Guest Soloists; Guest Speakers; Guest Teachers; Guest Writers; Guild Activities; High School Drama; Instructors; Local Artists; Local Artists & Directors; Local Talent; Local Unknown Artists; Lyricists; Multi Collaborations; Multimedia; Music; Musical Directors; New Productions; Organization Contracts; Original Music Scores; Paid Performers; Performance Artists; Playwrights; Poets; Resident Artists; Resident Companies; Resident Professionals; Scenic Designers; Selected Students; Sign Language Translators; Singers; Soloists; Students; Student Interns; Special Technical Talent; Theatre Companies; Touring Companies; Visual Arts; Visual Designers; Volunteer Artists; Volunteer Directors & Actors;
Founded: 1995
Specialized Field: Musical; Classic; Contemporary
Status: Non-Profit, Non-Professional
Paid Staff: 3
Facility Category: Community School Theatre
Type of Stage: Proscenium
Stage Dimensions: 60'x24'
Seating Capacity: 1400
Year Built: 1995
Rental Contact: Theatre Secretary Pamela Dixon

3833
INTERACT THEATRE COMPANY
2030 Sansom Street
Philadelphia, PA 19103
Phone: 215-568-8077
Fax: 215-568-8095
e-mail: interact@interacttheatre.org
Web Site: www.interacttheatre.org
Officers:
  President: Tom Tirney
  Chair: Wendy White
  Vice Chair: Barry S. Brownstein
  Treasurer: Michael F. Sutter
  Secretary: Robin Bender Stevens
  CEO: Victoria Yancey
Management:
  Producing Artistic Director: Seth Rozin
  General Manager: Daniel X. Guy
  Managing Director: Anneliese Van Arsdale
  Education Director: Dwight Wilkins
  Artistic Associate: Kittson O'Neill
Mission: Believes in developing and producing important new plays that represent our time and place, and introducing new writers to local audiences.
Founded: 1988
Specialized Field: New Plays; New Works of Social Importance
Paid Staff: 8
Paid Artists: 75
Performs At: Adrienne
Type of Stage: Proscenium
Seating Capacity: 106

3834
LANTERN THEATER COMPANY
923 Ludlow Street
Philadelphia, PA 19107
Mailing Address: P.O. Box 53428, Philadelphia, PA 19105-3428
Phone: 215-829-9002

Fax: 215-829-1161
e-mail: email@lanterntheater.org
Web Site: lanterntheater.org
Management:
   Artistic Director: Charles McMahon
   Production Manager: Meghan Jones
   Managing Director: Anne Shuff
   Marketing & Development Director: Jennifer Pratt Johnson
Mission: Lantern Theater Company is committed to an authentic and intimate exploration of the human spirit in our choice of classics, modern, and original works.
Status: Nonprofit
Performs At: St.Stephen's Theater

3835
NEW CITY STAGE COMPANY
2008 Chesnut Street
Philadelphia, PA 19103
Phone: 215-563-7500
e-mail: info@newcitystage.org
Web Site: newcitystage.org
Management:
   Producing Artistic Director: Russ Widdall
   Marketing & Public Relations: Sarah Scholl
Mission: New City Stage Company is dedicated to presenting high quality professional theatre that engages audiences on a variety of levels; not only entertaining them but also encouraging awareness of issues relevant to the community.
Founded: 2006
Status: Nonprofit; Professional
Performs At: The Adrienne Theatre 2030 Sansom Street, Philadelphia, PA 19103

3836
PHILADELPHIA THEATRE COMPANY
215 S. Broad Street
10th Floor
Philadelphia, PA 19107
Phone: 215-985-1400
Fax: 215-985-5800
e-mail: info@phillytheatreco.com
Web Site: www.philadelphiatheatrecompany.org
Officers:
   President: Priscilla M. Luce
   VP: David L. Colman, AIA
   VP: Julia Ericksen, Ph.D.
   VP: Glenn Gundersen
   VP: Harriet Weiss
   Treasurer: Neal Cupersmith
   Secretary: Brigitte F. Daniel
Management:
   Executive Producing Director: Sara Garonzik
   General Manager: Ada Coppock
   Managing Director: Shira Beckerman
   Literary Manager and Dramaturg: Carrie Chapter
   Director of Education: Maureen Sweeney
   Assistant Director of Education: Will Dennis
   Marketing Manager: Rose Schnall
   Director of Production: Roy W. Backes
   Company Manager: Bridget A Cook
Mission: Dedicated to producing the Philadelphia and world premieres of major works by contemporary American playwrights.
Utilizes: Actors; AEA Actors; Artists-in-Residence; Collaborations; Designers; Five Seasonal Concerts; Guest Accompanists; Guest Conductors; Guest Designers; Guest Ensembles; Guest Instructors; Guest Soloists; Guest Teachers; Guild Activities; Instructors; Local Artists; Original Music Scores; Performance Artists; Poets; Resident Professionals; Selected Students; Soloists; Visual Arts
Founded: 1975

Specialized Field: Musical; Comedy; Classic; Contemporary
Status: Non-Profit, Professional
Paid Staff: 14
Volunteer Staff: 200
Budget: $1.7 million
Income Sources: Foundations; Corporations; Individuals
Performs At: Plays and Players Theater
Affiliations: AEA; LORT; TCG; PCVB; TAGP; GPCA; Philadelphia Chamber of Commerce
Annual Attendance: 40,000
Facility Category: Historic
Type of Stage: Proscenium
Stage Dimensions: 25'x25'
Seating Capacity: 324
Year Built: 1919
Organization Type: Performing; Resident

3837
PRINCE MUSIC THEATER
1412 Chestnut Street
Philadelphia, PA 19102
Phone: 215-972-1000
Fax: 215-972-1020
e-mail: info@princemusictheater.org
Web Site: www.princemusictheater.org
Officers:
   President: Robert A. Fox
   Vice-President: Howard Morgan
   Chairman: Herbert Lotman
   Secretary-Treasurer: Lee Tolbert
Management:
   Producing Artistic Director: Marjorie Samoff
   Development: Amy Singer
   Marketing Director: Jennifer Donnelly
   Production: Jim Griffith
   Executive Director: James E. Hines
   Controller: Louis J. Coppola
   Finance Consultant: Hallie Bressler
   Finance Consultant: Bart Isdaner
   Finance Consultant: Heather S. Giampapa
Mission: Dedicated to developing music theatre in its various forms.
Utilizes: Actors; AEA Actors; Choreographers; Collaborating Artists; Collaborations; Commissioned Composers; Dancers; Designers; Fine Artists; Five Seasonal Concerts; Grant Writers; Guest Accompanists; Guest Artists; Guest Companies; Guest Composers; Guest Conductors; Guest Designers; Guest Ensembles; Guest Lecturers; Guest Musical Directors; Guest Musicians; Guest Soloists; Guest Teachers; Guild Activities; Instructors; Local Artists; Local Unknown Artists; Multi Collaborations; Multimedia; Music; Organization Contracts; Original Music Scores; Performance Artists; Poets; Resident Professionals; Sign Language Translators; Singers; Soloists; Student Interns; Visual Arts
Founded: 1984
Specialized Field: Musical
Status: Nonprofit
Annual Attendance: 100,000
Seating Capacity: 450
Year Built: 1999
Rental Contact: Managing Director Joe Farina
Organization Type: Sponsoring

3838
SOCIETY HILL PLAYHOUSE
507 South 8th Street
Philadelphia, PA 19147

Phone: 215-923-0210
Fax: 215-923-1789
e-mail: shp@erols.com
Web Site: www.societyhillplayhouse.org
Management:
   Director: Deen Kogan
Mission: To present works of the finest contemporary American and European writers.
Founded: 1959
Specialized Field: New American Works; Classic; International
Status: Professional; Nonprofit
Performs At: Society Hill Playhouse
Affiliations: Theatre Communications Group; American Arts Alliance; Theatre Alliance
Annual Attendance: 100,000
Facility Category: Historic Building
Type of Stage: Proscenium; Cabaret
Seating Capacity: 250; 99
Year Built: 1900
Year Remodeled: 1979
Rental Contact: Lee Vaughn
Organization Type: Performing; Touring; Educational

3839
WALNUT STREET THEATRE
825 Walnut Street
Philadelphia, PA 19107
Phone: 215-574-3550
Fax: 215-574-3598
Web Site: www.walnutstreettheatre.org
Officers:
   President: Louis Fryman
   Chair: Denise Daher Hodgson
   Immediate Past Chairman: Richard E. Woosnam
   Vice Chairman: Robert L. B. Harman
   Vice Chairman: Francis J. Mirabello, Esq.
   Vice Chairman: David S. Blum
   Secretary: Lauren A. Harrington
   Treasurer: R. Todd Ireland
Management:
   President and Producing Artistic Di: Bernard Harvard
   Managing Director: Mark D. Sylvester
   Director Development: Rebekah Sassi
   Director of Marketing and Public Re: Ralph Weeks
   Director of Education: Thomas P. Quinn
   Production Manager: Joel Markus
   Company Manager/ Assistant to the M: Kathryn McCumber
Mission: The mission of the Walnut Street Theatre Company is to sustain the tradition of professional theatre and contribute to its future viability and vitality. It does so through: the production and presentation of professional theatre; the encouragement, training and development of artists; the development of diverse audiences; the preservation and chronicling of its theatre building, a National Historic Landmark.
Utilizes: Actors; AEA Actors; Choreographers; Collaborations; Commissioned Composers; Dancers; Designers; Educators; Filmmakers; Five Seasonal Concerts; Grant Writers; Guest Accompanists; Guest Artists; Guest Choreographers; Guest Companies; Guest Composers; Guest Conductors; Guest Designers; Guest Ensembles; Guest Lecturers; Guild Activities; High School Drama; Instructors; Local Artists; Local Unknown Artists; Multimedia; Music; Organization Contracts; Original Music Scores; Performance Artists; Poets; Resident Professionals; Sign Language Translators; Soloists; Student Interns; Special Technical Talent; Theatre Companies
Founded: 1809

THEATRE / Pennsylvania

Specialized Field: Drama; Comedy; Musical; Classic; Contemporary
Status: Nonprofit
Paid Staff: 100
Budget: $10 million
Income Sources: Tickets; Grants; Funders
Affiliations: Greater Philadelphia Cultural Alliance; National Alliance of Musical Theaters; Theatre Community Group; League of Historic American Theatres
Annual Attendance: 300,000
Facility Category: Mainstage; Studio
Type of Stage: Proscenium; Black Box
Seating Capacity: 1,075; 80
Year Built: 1809
Year Remodeled: 1969
Rental Contact: D Jadico

3840
WILMA THEATER
265 S Broad Street
Philadelphia, PA 19107
Phone: 215-893-9456
Fax: 215-893-0895
e-mail: info@wilmatheater.org
Web Site: www.wilmatheater.org
Officers:
   Chair: David U'Prichard, PhD
   Vice Chair: David E. Loder
   Secretary: Clare D'Agostino, Esq.
   Treasurer: Thomas Mahoney
Management:
   Artistic Director: Blanka Zizka
   Marketing Director: Aaron Immediato
   Managing Director: James Haskins
   Production Manager: Clayton Tejada
   Technical Director: Ethan M Mimm
   Director Development: Iain Campbell
   Director Marketing: Liz Walsh
   General Manager: Maggie Arbogast
   Office Manager: Andrea Sotzing
Mission: To produce innovative theatre of the highest artistic quality from international and contemporary American repertoires.
Utilizes: Actors; Choreographers; Collaborations; Commissioned Composers; Composers-in-Residence; Dance Companies; Dancers; Designers; Educators; Filmmakers; Fine Artists; Five Seasonal Concerts; Grant Writers; Guest Accompanists; Guest Artists; Guest Choreographers; Guest Companies; Guest Composers; Guest Conductors; Guest Designers; Guest Directors; Guest Ensembles; Guest Instructors; Guest Lecturers; Guest Musical Directors; Guest Musicians; Guest Soloists; Guest Speakers; Guest Teachers; Guest Writers; Guild Activities; High School Drama; Instructors; Local Artists; Local Artists & Directors; Local Unknown Artists; Lyricists; Multi Collaborations; Multimedia; Music; New Productions; Organization Contracts; Original Music Scores; Paid Performers; Performance Artists; Playwrights; Poets; Resident Artists; Resident Companies; Resident Professionals; Selected Students; Sign Language Translators; Singers; Soloists; Student Interns; Special Technical Talent; Theatre Companies; Touring Companies; Visual Arts
Founded: 1973
Specialized Field: Drama; Comedy; Theater Workshops
Status: Professional; Nonprofit
Paid Staff: 21
Budget: $1.5 million
Income Sources: Theatre Communications Group
Facility Category: 1 Stage Studio
Type of Stage: Proscenium

Stage Dimensions: 44'x46'
Seating Capacity: 296
Year Built: 1996
Architect: Hugh Hardy
Rental Contact: Neal Racioppo
Organization Type: Performing

3841
CITY THEATRE COMPANY
1300 Bingham Street
Pittsburgh, PA 15203
Phone: 412-431-2489
Fax: 412-431-5535
e-mail: caquiline@citytheatrecompany.org
Web Site: www.citytheatrecompany.org
Management:
   President: Ed Saler
   Artistic Director: Tracy Brigben
   Managing Director: Mark R. Power
   Director of Finance: Jan Ripper
   Director of Development: Maggie Schmidt
Mission: To provide an artistic home for the development and production of contemporary plays of substance and ideas that engage and challenge diverse audiences.
Utilizes: Guest Companies; Singers
Founded: 1974
Specialized Field: Drama; Comedy; Contemporary
Status: Non-Profit, Professional
Paid Staff: 50
Volunteer Staff: 5
Paid Artists: 15
Income Sources: Theatre Communications Group
Performs At: City Theatre
Type of Stage: Flexible; Black Box
Seating Capacity: 272; 99
Organization Type: Performing; Resident; Educational

3842
DANCE ALLOY THEATER
5530 Penn Avenue
Pittsburgh, PA 15206
Phone: 412-363-4321
Fax: 412-363-4320
e-mail: caitlin@dancealloy.org
Web Site: www.dancealloy.org
Officers:
   President: Thomas K Whitford
   VP: J Nicole Wilson
Management:
   Artistic Director: Beth Corning
   Managing Director: Susan Sparks
Mission: We are a performing professsional company, a studio open for dance and movement classes as well as a provider of dance education in the Pittsburgh Public Schools.
Utilizes: Choreographers; Commissioned Music; Curators; Dance Companies; Dancers; Educators; Five Seasonal Concerts; Grant Writers; Guest Artists; Guest Companies; Guest Conductors; High School Drama; Original Music Scores; Poets; Soloists
Founded: 1976
Specialized Field: Modern
Status: Professional, Nonprofit
Paid Staff: 6
Paid Artists: 5
Budget: $700,000
Income Sources: Foundations; Corporations; Government
Performs At: Kelly Strayhorn Theatre
Annual Attendance: 4,500
Organization Type: Performing; Touring; Educational

3843
PITTSBURGH INTERNATIONAL CHILDREN'S THEATER
803 Liberty Avenue
Pittsburgh, PA 15222
Phone: 412-321-5520
Fax: 412-321-5212
e-mail: boxoffice@pghkids.org
Web Site: www.pghkids.org
Officers:
   Board Chair/President: Karen Flam
Management:
   Executive Director: Pam Leberman
   Founding Artistic Director: Maranne Purcell Welch
Mission: Presents a professional theater series and International Children's Festival.
Founded: 1969
Specialized Field: International; Children's Theater; Musical
Status: Non-Profit, Professional
Paid Staff: 3
Paid Artists: 40
Budget: $615,000
Income Sources: Ticket Sales; Contributions; Concession; Special Events; Program Ads
Performs At: Byham Theatre; Area Schools
Affiliations: IPAY (International Performing Arts for Youth)
Annual Attendance: 56,000

3844
PITTSBURGH IRISH & CLASSICAL THEATRE
PO Box 7964
Pittsburgh, PA 15216
Phone: 412-561-6000
Fax: 412-561-6686
e-mail: pictassistant@picttheatre.org
Web Site: www.picttheatre.org
Officers:
   President: Charles Moellenberg
   Vice President: Erin Shannon-Auel
   2nd Vice President: David Kremen
   Treasurer: Michael Burns
   Secretary: Dina Fulmer
Management:
   Producing Artistic Director: Andrew S Paul
   General Manager: Stephanie Riso
   Marketing Director: Michelle Belan
   Office Administrato: Carolyn Ludwig
   Development Director: Gale McGloin
   Artistic and Executive Director: Alan Stanford
   Managing Director: Stephanie Riso
   Production Manager & IT Lead: George DeShetler
   Development Associate: Jennifer Trehar
Mission: To challenge, educate and entertain Pittsburgh audiences by providing quality, professional, text-driven theatre at a reasonable price, while respectfully utilizing and compensating local talent, and by encouraging collaborative efforts with other successful theatres and individuals, particularly focusing on theatre of an Irish, English and Classical nature.
Founded: 1996
Specialized Field: Classic
Status: Professional

3845
PITTSBURGH MUSICAL THEATER
327 South Main Street
Pittsburgh, PA 15220

THEATRE / Pennsylvania

Phone: 412-539-0900
Fax: 412-539-0998
Web Site: pittsburghmusicals.com
Officers:
  President: Cheryl Begandy
  Vice President: Wendy Maletta
Management:
  Founding Director: Ken V. Gargaro
  General Manager: Colleen Petrucci
  Development And Marketing: Patti Knapp
Mission: Committed to quality productions of the best of Pittsburgh's own professional talent at a price affordable to all residents, especially children and families.
Founded: 1990
Status: Professional; Nonprofit
Organization Type: Performing; Educational

3846
PITTSBURGH PUBLIC THEATER
621 Penn Avenue
Pittsburgh, PA 15222
Phone: 412-316-8200
Fax: 412-316-8216
e-mail: info@ppt.org
Web Site: www.ppt.org
Officers:
  Secretary: Ted Bobby
  Treasurer: John P. Friel
  Counsel: Thomas M. Thompson
Management:
  President: Michael Ginsberg
  Executive Director: Ted Pappas
  Producing Artistic Director: Ted Pappas
  General Manager: Cynthia J. Tutera
  Payroll & Benefits Manager: Sherri Houston
  Director of Finance & Administratio: Catherine Bogats
  Executive Assistant to the Producin: Susan Hall
  Director of Development: Gerri Weiss
  Company Manager: Jenn Sharon
Mission: To provide artistically diverse experiences of the highest quality, thereby holding a preeminent position among American theaters. We strive to serve, challenge, stimulate, and entertain an expanding audience while operating in a fiscally responsible manner.
Utilizes: Actors; AEA Actors; Choreographers; Collaborations; Commissioned Composers; Commissioned Music; Designers; Educators; Guest Artists; Guest Companies; Guest Composers; Guest Conductors; Guest Designers; Guest Ensembles; Guest Lecturers; Guest Soloists; Guild Activities; High School Drama; Instructors; Local Artists; Music; Organization Contracts; Original Music Scores; Performance Artists; Selected Students; Sign Language Translators; Singers; Soloists; Student Interns
Founded: 1974
Specialized Field: Musical; Comedy; Classic; Contemporary
Status: Non-Profit, Professional
Paid Staff: 44
Volunteer Staff: 400
Paid Artists: 30
Budget: $6.3 million
Income Sources: Actors' Equity Association; League of Resident Theatres
Performs At: O'Reilly Theater
Affiliations: AEA, SSDC, USA, IATSE
Annual Attendance: 110,000
Type of Stage: Thrust
Seating Capacity: 650
Year Built: 1999
Cost: 25 Million

Rental Contact: Jason Hassell
Organization Type: Performing; Educational

3847
POINT PARK UNIVERSITY'S PITTSBURGH PLAYHOUSE
222 Craft Avenue
Pittsburgh, PA 15213
Phone: 412-392-8000
Fax: 412-621-4762
e-mail: rlindblom@pointpark.edu
Web Site: www.pittsburghplayhouse.com
Management:
  Artistic Director: Ronald Allan-Lindblom
  Producing Director: Earl Hughes
  Managing Director: David Vinski
  Director of Finance: Beverly D. Weber
  Production Manager: Kim Martin
  Dean: Fedrick Johnson
  Director of Marketing and Public Re: Ramesh Santanam
  Associate Director, Artistic Recrui: Bonnie Sampson
  Production Manager, Dance: Jonathan Surmacz
Mission: The performing arts cetner of the Point Park University and the Conservatory of Performing Arts. The three-theater performing arts center is home to The REP, the professional theatre company and three student companies-Conservatory Theatre Company, Conservatory Dance Company and Playhouse Jr. Maintains a rigorous performance calendar with eighteen major productions and 235 performances entertaining more than 30,000 patrons annually.
Specialized Field: Educational; Theater Workshops

3848
PRIME STAGE
PO Box 99446
Pittsburgh, PA 15233
Phone: 724-773-0700
Fax: 412-771-8585
e-mail: studentmat@primestage.com
Web Site: www.primestage.com
Officers:
  Chairman: Thomas Wettach Esquire
  VP: Martha Trombold
  President: Jim Karcher
  Secretary/Treasurer: Connie Brinda
Management:
  Co-Founder/Artistic Director: Wayne Brinda
  Assistant Producer: Lynn DeBree
  Managing Director: Susan Blackman
  Co-Founder/Finance Director/Secreta: Connie Brinda
  Education Box Office Manager: Mary Windstein
  Operations Director: Connie Brinda
  Education Director: Monica Stephenson
  Administrator: Dan Styche
  Production Manager: George DeShelter
Mission: We are commited to exposing and engaging young people and families in the discovery of live theatre. We accomplish this by producing new plays and other works, which celebrate the achievements of young people and adults.
Founded: 1996
Specialized Field: Youth Theater; Young Playwrights
Status: Non-Profit, Professional
Affiliations: American Alliance for Theatre and Education.
Annual Attendance: 9,000

3849
QUANTUM THEATRE
218 North Highland Avenue, Suite SW
Pittsburgh, PA 15206
Phone: 412-362-1713
Web Site: quantumtheatre.com
Officers:
  President: Mary Murrin
Management:
  Artistic Director: Karla Boos
  Director Of Community Relations: Stevie Herendeen
  Director Of Production: R.J. Romeo
  Director Of Operations: Teresa Trich
Founded: 1990

3850
SALTWORKS THEATRE COMPANY
569 N. Neville St.
Pittsburgh, PA 15213-2812
Phone: 412-621-6150
Fax: 412-621-6010
e-mail: nalrutz@saltworks.org
Web Site: www.saltworks.org
Officers:
  Chair: Kathy Woll
  Vice Chair: Laura Penrod Kronk
  President, Executive Director: Norma Alrutz
Management:
  Director of Marketing: Barbara Baun
  Bookkeeper and Webmaster: Kay Burkot
  Educational Assistant and Technical: Taylor Couch
  Graphic Design and Database Adminis: Davida van Mook
  Marketing/Teaching Artist: Michelina Pollini
Mission: To perform plays for youth and families that address social issues.
Utilizes: Actors; Choreographers; Educators; Guest Artists; Guest Lecturers; High School Drama; Local Artists; Music; Original Music Scores; Soloists; Student Interns
Founded: 1981
Specialized Field: Educational; Youth Theater; New Works of Social Importance
Status: Non-Profit, Professional
Paid Staff: 12
Paid Artists: 7
Budget: $450,000
Affiliations: ARAD; Tix for Teachers
Annual Attendance: 7,000
Seating Capacity: 150-250
Year Built: 1986
Organization Type: Performing; Touring; Educational

3851
VERONICA'S VEIL PLAYERS
44 Puis Street
Pittsburgh, PA 15203
Phone: 412-431-5550
Fax: 412-431-3463
e-mail: vvplayers@aol.com
Web Site: www.trfn.clpgh.org/vvp
Management:
  Managing Director: Dennis M Thompston
Mission: We are dedicated to continuing the tradition of presenting the Lenten drama Veronica's Veil as well as presenting other quality theatrical productions at affordable prices.
Utilizes: Actors; Choreographers; Collaborations; Dancers; Guest Designers; Local Artists; Multimedia; Music
Founded: 1910

THEATRE / Rhode Island

Specialized Field: Classic; Historical
Status: Nonprofit
Volunteer Staff: 5
Non-paid Artists: 200
Performs At: Theater
Seating Capacity: 833
Year Built: 1900
Year Remodeled: 1925

3852
READING COMMUNITY PLAYERS
403 N 11th Street
Reading, PA 19604
Mailing Address: PO Box 1032 Reading, PA 19603-1032
Phone: 610-375-9106
e-mail: rcptheatre@gmail.com
Web Site: www.rcptheatre.org
Officers:
   President: Ruth Martelli
   VP: Tracy Bukowski
Management:
   Production Manager: Lisa Uliasz
   Publicity: Julia Parsons
Mission: To develop the community's interest in theatrical arts; provide true live community theatre; and provide artistic opportunities for local talent.
Founded: 1920
Specialized Field: Musical; Community Theater
Status: Non-Profit, Non-Professional
Paid Staff: 114
Affiliations: American Association of Community Theatre; Berks Arts Council
Organization Type: Performing; Educational

3853
SHAWNEE PLAYHOUSE
552 River Road
Shawnee-on-Delaware, PA 18356
Mailing Address: P.O. Box 159, Shawnee on Delaware, Pennsylvania 18356
Phone: 570-421-5093
Fax: 570-421-4914
Toll-free: 800-742-9633
e-mail: request@theshawneeplayhouse.com
Web Site: www.theshawneepl
Management:
   Executive Director: Midge McClosky
   Box Office Manager: Mary Horn
   Sales and Marketing: Becky Haskell
   Group Sales: Mary Horn
   Intern Program: Midge McClosky
Mission: To provide professional quality live theatre to the residents and visitors of Shawnee.
Founded: 1978
Specialized Field: Staged Readings; Musical; Children's Theater
Status: Non-Equity; Commercial
Season: June - December
Performs At: Historic Theatre
Type of Stage: Proscenium
Seating Capacity: 200

3854
MONTGOMERY THEATER
124 Main Street
Souderton, PA 18964
Mailing Address: P.O. Box 64033, Souderton, PA 18964
Phone: 215-723-9984
e-mail: play@montgomerytheater.org
Web Site: montgomerytheater.org
Officers:
   Chair: Christian Moffitt
   Vice Chair: Laura Heckler
Management:
   Artistic Director: Thomas Quinn
   Managing Director: Allegra Ketchum
Mission: Dedicated to bringing new life to old tales, and giving age and wisdom to new ones.
Opened: 1993
Status: Nonprofit

3855
STRUTHERS LIBRARY THEATRE
302 West Third Avenue
PO Box 6
Warren, PA 16365
Phone: 814-723-7231
Fax: 814-723-3856
e-mail: librarytheatre@westpa.net
Web Site: www.strutherslibrarytheatre.com
Officers:
   President: The Honorable M Phillips
   Vice President: Ellen Putnam Paquette
   Secretary/Treasurer: Robert Crowley
Management:
   Executive Director: Marcy O'Brien
   Administrative Manager: Jeremy Jeziorski
   Artistic Director: Sue Spencer
   Facility Manager: Robert Priest
   Educational Director: Jennifer Koebley
   Technical Director: Barb Crowley
Founded: 1883
Specialized Field: Community Theater; Classic
Status: Non-Profit, Professional
Paid Staff: 3
Season: June - August
Type of Stage: Proscenium
Stage Dimensions: 35' x 26'
Seating Capacity: 989

3856
MARY L WELCH THEATRE
700 College Place
Lycoming College, Theatre Department
Williamsport, PA 17701
Phone: 570-321-4000
Fax: 570-321-4090
e-mail: stanley@lycoming.edu
Web Site: www.lycoming.edu
Management:
   President: James Douthat
   Department Chair: J Stanley, stanley@lycoming.edu
   Production Director: Robert Graham
Founded: 1964
Specialized Field: Drama; Musical; Comedy
Status: Non-Profit, Non-Professional
Paid Staff: 3
Paid Artists: 2
Non-paid Artists: 5
Budget: $45,000
Income Sources: Ticket Sales
Season: June - July
Affiliations: Actor Equity Association; TCG
Type of Stage: Thrust
Seating Capacity: 204
Year Built: 1964

3857
MOVEMENT THEATRE INTERNATIONAL
50 Bernard Drive
Yardley, PA 19067
Phone: 800-908-4490
Fax: 215-337-9100
e-mail: MAPedretti@aol.com
Mission: Provide space for area troupes and general services to mime field.
Founded: 1979
Specialized Field: Movement Theater
Paid Staff: 1
Volunteer Staff: 3
Budget: $20,000-$35,000
Income Sources: Retails, Box Office, Gifts
Type of Stage: Proscenuim
Seating Capacity: 299
Year Built: 1890
Year Remodeled: 1986
Cost: 1,000,000

Rhode Island

3858
ASTORS BEECHWOOD MANSION
580 Bellevue Avenue
Newport, RI 02840
Phone: 401-846-3772
Fax: 401-849-6998
e-mail: casting@astors-beechwood.com
Management:
   Executive Director: Charlotte C Lee
   Marketing Director: Karen Leepman
Mission: Victorian Living History
Founded: 1881
Specialized Field: Multi-Media; Drama; Historical
Paid Staff: 10
Paid Artists: 18
Season: year round
Year Built: 1851

3859
SANDRA FEINSTEIN-GAMM THEATRE
172 Exchange Street
Pawtucket, RI 02860
Phone: 401-723-4266
e-mail: info@gammtheatre.org
Web Site: www.gammtheatre.org
Officers:
   President: Leon C. Boghossian III
   Vice President: Coline Covington
   Treasurer: Bob Andrade
   Secretary: Eliza Green Chace Collins
   Vice President: Luz Bravo-Gleicher
Management:
   Box Office Manager: Shannon Carroll
   Artistic Director: Tony Estrella
   Production Manager: Jessica Hill
   Communications & Marketing Director: Gail Hulbert
   Education Director: Steve Kidd
   Managing Director: David M. Wax
   Sales Manager: Tracy Morreo
   Marketing & Design Associate: Courtney A. Martin
   House Managers: Jessica Bradley
Mission: To create intimate, professional, actor-centered theater which delights and inspires through the communal experience of the telling of great stories.
Utilizes: Guest Companies
Founded: 1984
Specialized Field: Storytelling
Status: Professional; Semi-Professional; Nonprofit
Paid Staff: 5
Volunteer Staff: 10
Paid Artists: 15
Organization Type: Performing

THEATRE / Rhode Island

3860
BROWN SUMMER THEATRE
77 Waterman Street
Box 1897
Providence, RI 02912
Phone: 401-863-3283
Fax: 401-862-7529
e-mail: taps@brown.edu
Web Site: www.brown.edu
Management:
    Artistic Director: Lowry Marshal
Utilizes: Actors; Soloists
Founded: 1969
Specialized Field: Contemporary; New Plays; Summer Stock
Status: Non-Profit, Non-Professional
Season: June - August
Type of Stage: Arena
Stage Dimensions: 22' x 16'
Seating Capacity: 200

3861
BROWN UNIVERSITY THEATRE
83 Waterman Street
Box 1897
Providence, RI 02912
Phone: 401-863-3283
Fax: 401-863-7529
e-mail: taps@brown.edu
Web Site: www.brown.edu/tickets
Officers:
    Chairman: Spencer Golub
Management:
    Director: Ruth Simmon
    Sales Director: Brian Gaston
    Production Manager: Brian Gaston
Mission: To offer a balanced theatrical season during the academic year and in the summer for the university community and Providence area; to train students.
Utilizes: Guest Companies
Founded: 1901
Specialized Field: Educational; Theater Workshops
Status: Non-Profit, Non-Professional
Paid Staff: 20
Performs At: Stuart Theatre; Leeds Theatre
Organization Type: Performing; Resident; Educational; Sponsoring

3862
LOOKING GLASS THEATRE
312 Wickenden Street
Providence, RI 02093
Phone: 401-331-9080
Fax: 401-351-2051
Toll-free: 866-742-9080
e-mail: lgtinc@msn.com
Web Site: www.lookingglasstouringtheatre.org
Management:
    Executive Director: Fred Sailer
    Artistic Director: Diane Postoian
    Managing Director: Pat McDougal
Mission: To enlighten and educate children and their families through audience participation, theater and follow-up workshops; to present new productions annually focusing on the classics and topical issues.
Founded: 1965
Specialized Field: Touring Company; Children's Theater
Status: Non-Profit, Professional
Paid Staff: 7
Paid Artists: 10
Income Sources: Theatre Communications Group
Performs At: Looking Glass Theatre
Facility Category: Touring Theatre
Organization Type: Touring; Educational; Sponsoring

3863
RITES AND REASON
Brown University
Box 1904
Providence, RI 02912
Phone: 401-863-3137
Fax: 401-863-3559
Web Site: www.brown.edu/Departments/Africana_Studies/rites_reason/
Management:
    Executive Director: Anthony Bogues
    Artistic Director: Elmo Terry-Morgan
    Managing Director: Karen Allen Baxter
    Research Director: Rhett S Jones
    Technical Director: Alonzo T. Jones
Mission: Developmental research theatre committed to offering new plays celebrating and exploring Africana culture and history.
Utilizes: Actors; AEA Actors; Artists-in-Residence; Choreographers; Collaborating Artists; Commissioned Composers; Commissioned Music; Curators; Designers; Educators; Filmmakers; Five Seasonal Concerts; Guest Artists; Guest Companies; Guest Conductors; Guest Designers; Guest Ensembles; Guest Instructors; Guest Lecturers; Guest Musical Directors; Guest Soloists; Guest Teachers; High School Drama; Instructors; Local Artists; Local Unknown Artists; Multimedia; Music; Original Music Scores; Performance Artists; Playwrights; Poets; Resident Professionals; Sign Language Translators; Soloists; Student Interns; Visual Arts
Founded: 1970
Specialized Field: African American; Historical
Status: Non-Profit, Non-Professional
Paid Staff: 5
Income Sources: University/Resident Theatre
Affiliations: Black Theatre Network; National Alliance for Music Theatre
Annual Attendance: 2,000
Type of Stage: Black Box
Seating Capacity: 125
Organization Type: Performing; Touring; Resident; Educational

3864
TRINITY REPERTORY COMPANY
201 Washington Street
Providence, RI 02903
Phone: 401-351-4242
Fax: 401-751-5577
e-mail: info@trinityrep.com
Web Site: www.trinityrep.com
Officers:
    Chairman: Heidi Keller Moon
    Vice-Chair: Marc Perlman
    Vice-Chair: Donald R. Quattrucci
    Treasurer: Kathryn Sabatini
    Secretary: Allison Vareika
Management:
    Artistic Director: Curt Columbus
    Managing Director: Michael Gennaro
    Executive Director: Michael Gennaro
    General Manager: Katie Byrnes
    Production Director: Laura E. Smith
    Associate Production Director: Mark Turek
    Asst. Production Director: Anne L. Harrigan
    Technical Director: Karl Orrall
Mission: Providing theatrical performances as well as educational services for Rhode Island and surrounding New England audiences.
Utilizes: Actors; AEA Actors; Artists-in-Residence; Choreographers; Collaborating Artists; Collaborations; Dance Companies; Dancers; Designers; Educators; Fine Artists; Grant Writers; Guest Accompanists; Guest Artists; Guest Choreographers; Guest Companies; Guest Designers; Guest Directors; Guest Ensembles; Guest Instructors; Guest Lecturers; Guest Musical Directors; Guest Soloists; Guest Teachers; High School Drama; Instructors; Local Artists; Multimedia; Music; New Productions; Original Music Scores; Performance Artists; Resident Artists; Resident Professionals; Selected Students; Sign Language Translators; Soloists; Student Interns; Special Technical Talent; Theatre Companies; Visual Arts
Founded: 1964
Specialized Field: Drama; Theater Workshops
Status: Non-Profit, Professional
Paid Staff: 130
Budget: $7.2 million
Income Sources: League of Resident Theatres
Performs At: Trinity Repertory Company
Affiliations: AEA, LORT, TEG, SSD&C
Annual Attendance: 145,000
Facility Category: Theater
Type of Stage: Two
Stage Dimensions: Flexible
Seating Capacity: 300;600
Year Built: 1917
Year Remodeled: 1973
Rental Contact: Bob Whitney
Organization Type: Performing; Touring; Educational

3865
2ND STORY THEATRE
28 Market Street
Warren, RI 02885
Phone: 401-247-4200
e-mail: boxoffice@2ndstorytheatre.com
Web Site: 2ndstorytheatre.com
Management:
    Artistic Director: Ed Shea
    Executive Director: Lynne Collinson
    General Manager: Charles Lafond
    Operations Manager: Max Ponticelli
    Productions Manager: Rachel Nadeau
Status: Nonprofit Charitable Organization

3866
OCEAN STATE THEATRE
1245 Jefferson Boulevard
Warwick, RI 02886
Phone: 401-921-1777
Fax: 401-921-8262
Web Site: oceanstatetheatre.org
Officers:
    Chair: Anthony F. Miccolis Jr.
    Secretary: Christine McLacken
    Treasurer: Andrew Cohen
Management:
    Producing Artistic Director: Aimee Turner
    Director Of Marketing: Karen Gail Kessler
    Managing Producer: Joel Kipper
Mission: The purpose set forth by Ocean State Theatre Company, Inc. is to preserve and pass on the tradition of live, professional theatre- including the American musical- and to pursue avenues of enrichment and education for the benefit of the state of Rhode Island and the surrounding region through the theatre arts.
Founded: 2007

THEATRE / South Carolina

South Carolina

3867
AIKEN COMMUNITY PLAYHOUSE
126 Newberry Street
Aiken, SC 29801
Phone: 803-648-1438
e-mail: info@aikencommunityplayhouse.com
Web Site: www.aikencommunityplayhouse.com/
Officers:
  Treasurer: Lisa Kirschner
  Secretary: Margaret Tribert
Management:
  Publicity Director: Elizabeth Mouser
  Executive Director: Mike Gibbons
  Artistic Director: Marcia Harris
  Facilities Manager: Thurmond Whatley
  Marketing Director: Lisa Tharp-Bernard
Mission: To offer community members an opportunity to participate in legitimate theatre; to encourage the public's appreciation of theatre arts.
Founded: 1953
Specialized Field: Community Theater
Status: Nonprofit
Income Sources: South Carolina Theatre Association
Performs At: Aiken Community Playhouse
Organization Type: Performing

3868
PURE THEATRE
477 King Street
Charleston, SC 29403
Phone: 843-723-4444
Toll-free: 866-811-4111
e-mail: info@puretheatre.org
Web Site: puretheatre.org
Management:
  Artistic Director: Sharon Graci
  Managing Director: Laurens Wilson
  Producing Director: Rodney Lee Rogers
  Associate Artistic Director: David Mandel
  Technical Director: Carly Ridgeway
Specialized Field: Contemporary
Status: Professional

3869
SPOLETO FESTIVAL USA
14 George Street
Charleston, SC 29401-1524
Phone: 843-722-2764
Fax: 843-723-6383
e-mail: info@spoletousa.org
Web Site: www.spoletousa.org
Officers:
  Chairman: Carlos E. Evans
  President: M. Edward Sellers
  Treasurer: Ronald D. Abramson
  General Counsel & Secretary: John B. Hagerty
  Vice President: Jennie L. DeScherer
  Vice President: Richard J. Almeida
  Vice President: Lou Rena Hammond
  Vice President: Marie Land
  Vice President: William G. Medich
Management:
  Artistic Director-Choral Activities: Joseph Flummerfelt
  Director, Chamber Music: Geoff Nuttall
  General Director: Nigel Redden
  Producer: Nunally Kersh
  Director Of Development: Julia Forster
  Director Marketing/Public Relations: Jennifer Scott
  Company Manager: Aimee Sullivan
  Producing Assistant: Sara Bennett
  Technology Manager: David Robinson
Mission: To present opera, dance, theater, symphonic, choral and chamber music, jazz and visual arts exhibits of the higest quality; to serve as an educational environment for young artists and audiences alike.
Utilizes: Singers
Founded: 1977
Specialized Field: Jazz; Theatrical Dance
Status: Professional; Semi-Professional; Non-Profit
Paid Staff: 18
Budget: $7,000,000
Income Sources: Ticket Revenues; Contributions
Performs At: Gaillard Municipal Auditorium; Dock Street Theater
Annual Attendance: 70,000-80,000
Organization Type: Performing; Educational; Sponsoring

3870
THE FOOTLIGHT PLAYERS
20 Queen Street
Charleston, SC 29403
Phone: 843-722-7521
e-mail: info@footlightplayers.net
Web Site: footlightplayers.net
Officers:
  Chair: Jane Broadwater
  Vice Chair: Mike Clouse
  Treasurer: Ginna Waddell
  Secretary: Kerry Spencer
Management:
  Executive Director: Don Bradenburg
  Director Of Development: Melonea Marek
Mission: The mission of the Footlight Players is to provide professional quality, affordable, community theatre for the citizens of Charleston and the South Carolina lowcountry tri-counties.
Founded: 1932

3871
THRESHOLD REPERTORY THEATRE
84 1/2 Society Street
Charleston, SC 29401
Phone: 843-277-2172
e-mail: thresholdrep@gmail.com
Web Site: charlestontheater.com
Management:
  Executive Director: Courtney Daniel
  Artistic Director: Pamela Galle
Founded: 2010
Status: Nonprofit; Professional
Seating Capacity: 99

3872
VILLAGE REPERTORY COMPANY
34 Woolfe Street
Charleston, SC 29401
Phone: 843-856-1579
e-mail: info@woolfestreetplayhouse.com
Web Site: woolfestreetplayhouse.com
Management:
  Producing Artistic Director: Keely Enright
  Managing Director: David Reinwald
  Associate Artistic Director: Robbie Thomas
  Marketing Coordinator: Eileen Easler
Opened: 2001
Status: Nonprofit; Professional
Performs At: Woolfe Street Playhouse

3873
COLUMBIA STAGE SOCIETY AT TOWN THEATRE
1012 Sumter Street
Columbia, SC 29201
Phone: 803-799-2510
Fax: 803-799-6463
e-mail: town@towntheatre.com
Web Site: www.towntheatre.com
Mission: To encourage and develop musical, vocal, and dramatic talent of those in the city and surrounding areas and to provide theatrical entertainment.
Utilizes: Guest Artists
Founded: 1919
Specialized Field: Community Theater
Status: Non-Professional; Nonprofit
Income Sources: South Carolina Theatre Association
Performs At: The Town Theatre
Annual Attendance: 20,000
Year Built: 1924
Year Remodeled: 1993
Cost: $1,200,000
Organization Type: Performing; Educational

3874
TRUSTUS
520 Lady Street
Columbia, SC 29201
Phone: 803-254-9732
Fax: 803-771-9153
e-mail: trustus@trustus.org
Web Site: www.trustus.org
Management:
  Artistic Director: Dewey Scott-Wiley
  Producing Director: Kay Thigpen
  Managing Director: Larry Hembree
  Technical Director: Brandon McIver
  Production Manager: Chad Henderson
  Education Director: Vicky Saya Henderson
  Operations Director: Frank Kiraly
  Assistant Technical Director: Joe Morales
  Director of Marketing: Chad Henderson
Mission: To bring to the area a professional theatre dedicated to new works, plays of literary and artistic merit, and quality mainstream theatre in an environment that allows us to reach a broad spectrum of patrons.
Utilizes: Guest Companies; Singers
Founded: 1985
Specialized Field: Drama; Comedy
Status: Professional; Nonprofit
Paid Staff: 5
Income Sources: Theatre Communications Group; South Carolina Theatre Association
Organization Type: Performing; Resident; Educational

3875
SWAMP FOX PLAYERS
710 Front Street
Georgetown, SC 29442
Mailing Address: P.O. Box 911, Georgetown, SC 29442
Phone: 843-527-2924
Fax: 843-546-6193
e-mail: swampfoxplayers@frontier.com
Web Site: www.swampfoxplayers.com
Officers:
  President: Jo Camlin
  Secretary: Stacy Rabon
  Treasurer: Betty Haring
Management:
  Theater Manager: Foy Ford
Mission: To offer a cultural center to the area; to provide dramatic presentations for area citizens.

Founded: 1971
Specialized Field: Musical; Comedy; Classic; Contemporary
Status: Non-Profit, Non-Professional
Paid Staff: 1
Performs At: Strand Theatre
Year Built: 1937
Organization Type: Performing; Resident

3876
BOB JONES UNIVERSITY CONCERT, OPERA & DRAMA SERIES
1700 Wade Hampton Blvd
Greenville, SC 29614
Phone: 864-242-5100
Fax: 864-770-1375
e-mail: finearts@bju.edu
Web Site: www.bju.edu
Officers:
   President: Dr Stephen D. Pettit Sr.
Management:
   Dean Fine Arts/Communication: Dr Darren Lawson
Founded: 1927
Specialized Field: Educational; Drama; Theater Workshops
Status: For-Profit, Professional
Budget: $35,000-$60,000
Performs At: Founder's Memorial Auditorium
Seating Capacity: 7,000

3877
CENTRE STAGE-SOUTH CAROLINA
Morgan Stanley Smith Barney Building
501 River Street
Greenville, SC 29601
Mailing Address: Post Office Box 8451, Greenville, SC 29604
Phone: 864-233-6733
Fax: 864-233-3901
Toll-free: 877-377-1339
e-mail: information@centrestage.org
Web Site: www.centrestage.org
Officers:
   Board Co-President: Jack Ashton
   Board Vice President: Robyn Zimmerman
   Treasurer: Josh Capps
   Secretary: Stacy Walker
Management:
   Executive & Artistic Director: Glenda ManWaring
   Marketing Director: Allen Evans
   Director of Creative Education Prog: Ellen Jones
   Box Office Manager: Beau Phillips
   Technical Director: Thom Seymour, Jr.
   Director of Development: Kirsten D. Floyd
   Production Manager/New Play Festiva: Melanie Ann Wiliford
   Business Manager: Bruce Meahl
Mission: To be a cornerstone of the performing arts by providing captivating entertainment, intellectual stimulation, and adding to the quality of life in Upstate South Carolina.
Founded: 1983
Specialized Field: Drama; Musical
Paid Staff: 5
Volunteer Staff: 200
Type of Stage: Thrust
Seating Capacity: 285

3878
WAREHOUSE THEATRE
37 Augusta Street
Greenville, SC 29601
Phone: 864-235-6948
e-mail: info@warehousetheatre.com
Web Site: www.warehousetheatre.com
   President: Tom Strange
   Vice President: Linda Archer
   Secretary: Ingrid Erwin
   Treasurer: Susan Bichel
Management:
   IT Director: Justin Ames
   Producing Artistic Director: John Fagan
   Resident Dramaturg: Elisa Golden
   Box Office Manager/Production Manag: Jaime Keegstra
   Technical Director: John Keenan
   Operations Manager: Charles Brewer
   Director: Roy Fluhrer
Mission: To excite the imagination; to examine the signposts/symbols of our time; to test the old, explore the new; to allow our audience to test-drive parts of the human experience.
Founded: 1974
Specialized Field: Drama; Musical; Classic
Status: Nonprofit
Paid Staff: 4
Volunteer Staff: 50
Paid Artists: 20
Non-paid Artists: 50
Budget: $260,000
Season: September - June
Type of Stage: Flexible; Proscenium
Seating Capacity: 170; 349

3879
CRABPOT PLAYERS
1137 Johnnie Dodds Boulevard
Mt.Pleasant, SC 29464
Phone: 888-303-0763
e-mail: info@crabpotplayers.com
Web Site: crabpotplayers.com
Management:
   Artistic Director: Jimmy Ward
   Operations Manager: Daniel Prentice
Mission: To encourage and promote live theatre through the medium of acting and to provide educational opportunities for emerging performing artists of all ages throughout the Charleston area.
Founded: 1993
Status: Nonprofit

3880
ATLANTIC STAGE
900 79th Avenue North
Myrtle Beach, SC 29572
Mailing Address: P.O. Box 7402, Myrtle Beach, SC 29572
Phone: 877-287-8587
e-mail: info@atlanticstage.com
Web Site: atlanticstage.com
Officers:
   President: Steve Earnest
   Vice President: Beth McVeigh
   Secretary: Kelly Graham
   Treasurer: Richard Castrodale
Management:
   Artistic Director: Thom Penn
Mission: The purpose of Atlantic Stage is to enhance the cultural landscape of the Myrtle Beach area by providing quality theatrical productions of classical, contemporary, and new works that are entertaining and enlightening.
Founded: 2008
Status: Professional
Performs At: 79th Avenue Theater
Organization Type: Resident Performing

3881
NEWBERRY COLLEGE THEATRE
Newberry College
2100 College Street
Newberry, SC 29108
Phone: 803-276-5010
Fax: 803-321-5627
Toll-free: 800-845-4955
e-mail: info@newberry.edu
Web Site: www.newberry.edu
Officers:
   Director Theatre/Dept. Chair: Patrick Gagliano
   Treasurer: L. Wayne Pearson
   Secretary: Fred B. Johnson
   Vice Chairman: Joel M. Carter
Mission: To provide a performing arts program of quality in the environment of a liberal arts college.
Utilizes: Collaborations; Fine Artists; Grant Writers; Guest Artists; Guest Companies; Guest Musical Directors; High School Drama; Instructors; Sign Language Translators; Singers; Soloists
Founded: 1856
Specialized Field: Theater Workshops; Drama; Musical
Status: College
Paid Staff: 3
Type of Stage: Proscenium; Thrust; Flexible
Seating Capacity: 100-200
Organization Type: Performing; Educational

3882
SOUTH OF BROADWAY THEATRE COMPANY
1080 E. Montague Avenue
North Charleston, SC 29405
Phone: 843-745-0317
e-mail: mgould@southofbroadway.com
Web Site: southofbroadway.com
Management:
   Producer: Mary Gould
   Artistic Director: Mark Gorman
   Assistant Producer: Kristen Kos
Mission: South of Broadway Theatre Company (SOBTC) produces theatre of the highest professional standards, ensuring diversity in programming to further an enduring educational and culturally enriched environment.
Status: Professional; Nonprofit

South Dakota

3883
ABERDEEN COMMUNITY THEATRE
415 S Main
PO Box 813
Aberdeen, SD 57401
Phone: 605-225-2228
Fax: 605-226-5494
e-mail: act@nvc.com
Web Site: www.aberdeencommunitytheatre.com
Officers:
   President: Dr. Warren Redmond
   Vice-President: Barb Evans
   Secretary: Linda Bartholomew
   Treasurer: Kathy Stuck
Management:
   Director: Ann Rassussman
   Executive Director: Jim Walker
   Artistic/Managing Director: James L. Walker
   Education/Technical Director: Brian T. Schultz
Mission: To educate, entertain and further performing arts through community involvement.

THEATRE / South Dakota

Utilizes: Guest Companies
Founded: 1979
Specialized Field: Musical; Comedy; Community Theater
Status: Non-Profit, Non-Professional
Paid Staff: 3
Volunteer Staff: 300
Paid Artists: 2
Income Sources: American Association of Community Theatres; South Dakota Theatre Association
Performs At: Capitol Theatre
Seating Capacity: 450
Organization Type: Performing; Educational; Sponsoring

3884
PRAIRIE REPERTORY
P.O. Box 2218
Brookings, SD 57007-1197
Phone: 605-688-6045
e-mail: john.ackman@sdstate.edu
Web Site: prairierep.org
Mission: Prairie Repertory is proud of their ongoing mission to provide outstanding training for their student company members and the best possible entertainment for their patrons.
Founded: 1971
Season: Summer
Performs At: Donner Auditorium, Brandon Valley Performing Arts Center
Organization Type: Performing; Educational

3885
BLACK HILLS COMMUNITY THEATRE
713 7th Street
Rapid City, SD 57701
Mailing Address: P.O. Box 4007, Rapid City, SD 57709-4007
Phone: 605-394-1786
Fax: 605-394-2679
e-mail: info@bhct.org
Web Site: www.bhct.org
Officers:
   President: Mary Stein
   Vice President: Marnie Gould
   Treasurer: Kelly Foreman
   Secretary: Chris Coleman
Management:
   General Manager: Merritt Olsen
   Managing Artistic Director: Michael Kraklio
   Executive Director: Nicolas Johnson
   Interim Artistic Director: Justin Speck
Mission: To offer quality theatre employing community talent.
Founded: 1968
Specialized Field: Community Theater
Status: Nonprofit
Paid Staff: 150
Income Sources: South Dakota Arts Council; Allied Arts Fund
Organization Type: Performing

3886
BLACK HILLS PLAYHOUSE
PO Box 2513
Rapid City, SD 57709
Phone: 605-255-4141
Fax: 605-255-4242
e-mail: contact@blackhillsplayhouse.com
Web Site: www.blackhillsplayhouse.com
Officers:
   President: Eric Hagen
   Vice President: Lia Green
   Secretary: Todd Brink
   Treasurer: Eileen Rossow
Founder: Doc Lee
Management:
   Director: Micheal Fellner
   Executive Director: Linda Kern Anderson
   Artistic Director: Dan Workman
   Operations Manager: Jason Reuter
   Business Manager: Ingrid K. Reuter
Mission: To offer high quality performances to audiences; to provide theatre students with intensive professional training.
Utilizes: Guest Companies; Selected Students; Singers
Founded: 1946
Specialized Field: Musical; Comedy; Theater Workshops; Summer Stock
Status: Non-Profit, Non-Professional
Paid Staff: 2
Paid Artists: 70
Budget: $400,000
Income Sources: Box Office; Grants; Donations
Season: May - August
Performs At: Black Hills Playhouse (Custer State Park)
Affiliations: University of South Dakota
Annual Attendance: 16,000
Facility Category: Theatre
Type of Stage: Modified Thrust
Seating Capacity: 360
Year Built: 1955
Organization Type: Performing; Resident; Educational

3887
SIOUX FALLS COMMUNITY PLAYHOUSE
315 N Phillips Avenue
PO Box 767
Sioux Falls, SD 57101
Phone: 605-336-7418
Fax: 605-336-0926
e-mail: sfcp@sfcp.org
Web Site: www.sfcp.org
Officers:
   President: Darren Lee
   Vice President: Chris Weigandt
   Treasurer: Brenda Odle-Scott
   Secretary: Dick Koch
Management:
   Executive Director: Patrick Pope
   Technical Director: Dion Denevan
   Artistic Assoc/Education Director: Lee Shackelford
Mission: To offer the community and the area opportunities for experiencing live theatre through participation on a variety of levels.
Founded: 1930
Specialized Field: Community Theater
Status: Nonprofit
Paid Staff: 8
Non-paid Artists: 200
Budget: $250,000
Income Sources: American Association of Community Theatres; South Dakota Arts Council
Performs At: Sioux Falls Community Playhouse
Annual Attendance: 10,000
Seating Capacity: 262
Year Remodeled: 1999
Cost: $1,200,000
Organization Type: Performing; Touring; Resident; Educational; Sponsoring

3888
BLACK HILLS PASSION PLAY
PO Box 2513
Spearfish, SD 57709
Phone: 605-255-4141
Fax: 605-642-7993
Toll-free: 800-457-0160
e-mail: bhpp@blackhills.com
Web Site: www.blackhills.com/bhpp
Officers:
   President: Eric Hagen
   Vice President: Lia Green
   Secretary: Todd Brink
   Treasurer: Eileen Rossow
Management:
   Director: Johanna Meier
   Executive Director: Linda Kern Anderson
   Artistic Director: Dan Workman
   Operations Manager: Jason Reuter
   Business Manager: Ingrid K. J. Reuter
Founded: 1932
Specialized Field: Drama; Historical; Classic
Status: For-Profit, Professional
Paid Staff: 76
Volunteer Staff: 150
Paid Artists: 24
Season: June - August
Type of Stage: Amphitheatre
Seating Capacity: 5600

3889
MATTHEWS OPERA HOUSE SOCIETY
612 N. Main St.
Spearfish, SD 57783
Phone: 605-642-7973
Fax: 605-642-3477
e-mail: scah@rushmore.com
Web Site: www.matthewsoperahousetheater.com
Management:
   Director: Ardis Golay
   Managing Artistic Director: R David Whitlock
   Executive Director: Sian Young
   Marketing Manager: Jayne Rose
   Gallery & Events Manager: Ava Sauter
Mission: To offer opportunities for talented people interested in theatre; to continue restoration of the Opera House.
Utilizes: Actors; Educators; Fine Artists; Instructors; Local Artists; Music; Soloists; Touring Companies
Founded: 1906
Specialized Field: Musical; Light Theater
Status: Non-Professional; Nonprofit
Paid Staff: 2
Volunteer Staff: 12
Budget: $300,000
Income Sources: Show Fees; Festival Fees; Grants
Performs At: Senior High Theatre; Matthews Opera House
Annual Attendance: 12,000 - 15,000
Seating Capacity: 230
Year Built: 1906
Year Remodeled: 1997
Rental Contact: Ardis Golay
Organization Type: Performing; Educational

3890
SPEARFISH CENTER FOR THE ARTS
Spearfish Arts Center and Matthews Opera Hous
612 N Main St
Spearfish, SD 57783
Phone: 605-642-7973
Fax: 605-642-3477
e-mail: director@spearfishartscenter.org
Web Site: www.spearfishartscenter.org
Officers:
   President: Joe Barany
   Vice President: Jon Steven Wiley
   Secretary: Holly Downing

Treasurer: Kim Larson
Management:
Executive Director: Sian Young
Performing Arts Manager: Dwight Myers
Administrative Manager: Shelly Brito
Mission: To provide quality programming while preserving the Matthews Opera House.
Utilizes: Actors; Educators; Fine Artists; Instructors; Local Artists; Music; Soloists; Touring Companies
Founded: 1906
Specialized Field: Contemporary
Status: Non-Profit, Non-Professional
Paid Staff: 3
Volunteer Staff: 20
Paid Artists: 15
Budget: $300,000
Income Sources: Show Fees; Festival Fees; Grants; Memberships Fees
Performs At: Senior High Theatre; Matthews Opera House
Annual Attendance: 12,000 - 15,000
Seating Capacity: 230
Year Built: 1906
Year Remodeled: 1997
Rental Contact: Ardis Golay
Organization Type: Performing; Educational

3891
TOWN PLAYERS
5 South Broadway
Watertown, SD 57201
Phone: 605-882-2076
Fax: 605-882-2076
e-mail: townplayers@townplayers.net
Web Site: www.townplayers.net
General Manager: Nancy Johnson
Mission: To promote appreciation of dramatic arts.
Utilizes: Guest Artists; Guest Companies; Singers
Founded: 1940
Specialized Field: Community Theater; Drama
Status: Non-Profit, Non-Professional
Paid Staff: 45
Paid Artists: 1
Organization Type: Performing; Touting; Resident

3892
LEWIS & CLARK THEATRE COMPANY
328 Walnut Street
PO Box 836
Yankton, SD 57078-4345
Phone: 605-665-4711
e-mail: LCTCyankton@yahoo.com
Web Site: www.lctcyankton.com
Management:
President: Barbara Christenson
Executive Director: Joel Vermuele
Artistic Director: Allison Spak
Founded: 1961
Specialized Field: Musical; Comedy; Classic; Contemporary
Status: Non-Profit, Non-Professional
Paid Staff: 5
Paid Artists: 20
Season: June - August
Type of Stage: Proscenium
Stage Dimensions: 60' x 36'
Seating Capacity: 640

Tennessee

3893
THEATRE BRISTOL
512 State Street
Bristol, TN 37620
Phone: 423-383-5979
Fax: 423-968-4978
e-mail: info@theatrebristol.org
Web Site: www.theatrebristol.org
Officers:
Board President: Mike Musick
Vice President: Steve Baskett
Treasurer: Samantha Gray
Secretary: Suzanne Eleas
Management:
Artistic Director: Robert Dean
General Manager: Emily Anne Thompson
Technical Director: Jim Quensenberry
Director Education: Amy Bussey
Mission: Theatre Bristol is a regional theatre that uses the arts to inspire educate and entertain.
Utilizes: Actors; Artists-in-Residence; Choreographers; Collaborations; Dancers; Designers; Educators; Guest Accompanists; Guest Artists; Guest Companies; Guest Conductors; Guest Designers; Guest Lecturers; Guest Musical Directors; Guest Writers; Guild Activities; High School Drama; Instructors; Local Artists; Lyricists; Multimedia; Music; Performance Artists; Resident Professionals; Sign Language Translators; Soloists; Student Interns; Touring Companies; Visual Arts
Founded: 1965
Specialized Field: Musical; Community Theater
Status: Non-Profit, Non-Professional
Paid Staff: 3
Volunteer Staff: 20
Performs At: Paramount Center for the Arts; Theatre Bristol Artspace
Seating Capacity: 756; 95
Organization Type: Performing; Resident; Educational; Sponsoring

3894
ROXY THEATER
100 Franklin Street
Clarksville, TN 37040
Phone: 931-645-7699
e-mail: roxytheatre@bellsouth.net
Web Site: www.roxyregionaltheatre.org
Management:
Executive Director: Tom Thayer
Artistic Director: John McDonald
Mission: To promote and produce the performing and visual arts.
Utilizes: Guest Companies
Founded: 1983
Specialized Field: Musical; Community Theater
Status: Professional; Nonprofit
Paid Staff: 2
Organization Type: Performing; Educational

3895
CUMBERLAND COUNTY PLAYHOUSE
221 Tennessee Avenue
PO Box 484
Crossville, TN 38555
Mailing Address: PO Box 484 Crossville, TN 38557
Phone: 931-484-5000
Fax: 931-484-6299
Toll-free: 877-868-8710
e-mail: info@ccplayhouse.com
Web Site: www.ccplayhouse.com
Officers:
President: Tom Weesley
Executive Director: Jim Crabtree
Business Manager: Janet Kluender
Mission: To provide cultural enrichment for the area and beyond.
Utilizes: Actors; Choreographers; Collaborating Artists; Collaborations; Dancers; Designers; Educators; Fine Artists; Five Seasonal Concerts; Guest Accompanists; Guest Artists; Guest Composers; Guest Conductors; Guest Designers; Guest Ensembles; Guest Lecturers; Guest Musical Directors; Guest Musicians; Guild Activities; Instructors; Local Artists; Local Unknown Artists; Multimedia; Music; Organization Contracts; Original Music Scores; Performance Artists; Poets; Resident Artists; Resident Professionals; Sign Language Translators; Singers; Soloists; Student Interns
Founded: 1965
Specialized Field: Musical; Comedy; Contemporary
Status: Non-Profit, Professional
Paid Staff: 20
Paid Artists: 35
Budget: $2.1 million
Income Sources: 80% Earned Income; Grants; Donations
Season: Year-round
Performs At: Cumberland County Playhouse
Annual Attendance: 145,000
Type of Stage: 2 indoor; 1 outdoor
Year Built: 1965
Year Remodeled: 1992
Rental Contact: Producing Director Jim Crabtree
Organization Type: Performing; Touring; Resident; Educational; Sponsoring

3896
PULL-TIGHT PLAYERS
112 2nd Avenue South
Franklin, TN 37064
Mailing Address: P.O. Box 105, Franklin, TN 37065-0105
Phone: 615-791-5007
e-mail: thespian@pull-tight.com
Web Site: www.pull-tight.com
Officers:
President: Justin McIntosh
Vice President: Heather Bottoms
Secretary: Beth Woodruff
Tresurer: Iain MacPhearson
Founder: Vance Ormes
Management:
Director: Mark Hyssong
Executive Producer: Jeremy Hargis
Technical Director: Jim Anderson
Box Office Manager: Heather Bottoms
Mission: To provide quality community theatre for Williamson County and the surrounding area.
Utilizes: Guest Companies
Founded: 1968
Specialized Field: Community Theater
Status: Non-Professional; Nonprofit
Paid Staff: 60
Organization Type: Performing; Resident

3897
SWEET FANNY ADAMS THEATRE & MUSIC HALL
461 Parkway
Gatlinburg, TN 37738
Phone: 865-436-4039
Fax: 865-436-4038
Toll-free: 877-388-5784
e-mail: BoxOffice@SweetFannyAdams.com
Web Site: www.sweetfannyadams.com

THEATRE / Tennessee

Management:
  Executive Director: Jennifer MacPherson-Evans
  Director: Chris MacPherson
  Technical Director/Operations Manag: Laurence Evans
Utilizes: Actors; Commissioned Composers; Guest Companies; Original Music Scores; Visual Arts
Founded: 1977
Specialized Field: Musical; Drama
Status: Professional
Paid Staff: 6
Paid Artists: 8
Season: May - October
Annual Attendance: 20,000
Facility Category: Theatre
Type of Stage: Thrust
Stage Dimensions: 12'x13'
Seating Capacity: 184
Year Built: 1877
Year Remodeled: 1996
Rental Contact: Don MacPherson

3898
GERMANTOWN COMMUNITY THEATRE
3037 Forest Hill-Irene Road
Germantown, TN 38138
Phone: 901-754-2680
Fax: 901-755-1185
e-mail: officemgr@germantowncommunitytheatre.org
Web Site: www.germantowncommunitytheatre.org
Officers:
  Guild President: Joyce Burti
  President: Hal Beckham
  1st Vice President: Jackie Flaum
  2nd Vice President: Jennifer Watson
  Treasurer: Jeff McCune
  Secretary: Shirley Gee
Management:
  Executive Director/Producer: Dr. Michael D. Miles
  Artistic Director: Leigh Eck
  Production Coordinator: Kerry Strahm
  Director: Renee Davis Brame
Founded: 1972
Specialized Field: Community Theater
Status: Non-Profit, Non-Professional
Paid Staff: 5
Volunteer Staff: 20
Income Sources: Memphis Arts Council; Germantown Arts Alliance
Seating Capacity: 112

3899
POPLAR PIKE PLAYHOUSE
7653 Old Poplar Pike
Germantown, TN 38138
Phone: 901-755-7775
Fax: 901-755-6951
e-mail: PoplarPikePlayhouse@gmail.com
Web Site: www.ppp.org
Officers:
  Director: E. Frank Bluestein
Mission: To present educational theatre at Germantown High School.
Utilizes: Arrangers; Guest Accompanists; Guest Conductors; Guest Designers; Guest Ensembles; Guest Soloists; Guild Activities; High School Drama; Instructors; Local Artists; Music; Performance Artists; Poets
Founded: 1976
Specialized Field: Theater
Status: Nonprofit
Paid Staff: 10
Volunteer Staff: 5
Paid Artists: 3
Budget: $50,000
Income Sources: Shelby County Schools; Germaston Arts Alliance
Annual Attendance: 5,000
Facility Category: Theatre
Type of Stage: Proscenium
Stage Dimensions: 55'x40'
Seating Capacity: 285
Year Built: 1975
Year Remodeled: 1998
Rental Contact: Director E Frank Bluestein
Organization Type: Performing; Educational

3900
JACKSON THEATRE GUILD
314 E Main Street
Jackson, TN 38301
Mailing Address: PO Box 7041 Jackson, TN 38301
Phone: 731-427-3200
Fax: 731-425-8674
e-mail: contact@jtgonline.com
Web Site: www.jtgonline.com
Officers:
  President: Billy Worboys
  VP: Brenda Poteet
  Secretary: Ann Bailey
  Treasurer: Sue Barnes
  Board President: Jeff Howell
Management:
  Office Manager: Susan Kriaski
  Dir. of Marketing and Development: Christina Torres
Mission: To promote public education appreciation and enjoyment of dramatic literature, current stage craft, and theatre by the presentation of quality productions. Also, by conducting other related activities, we reflect our diverse community.
Utilizes: Guest Companies; Singers
Founded: 1966
Specialized Field: Comedy; Youth Theater; Community Theater; Contemporary
Status: Non-Profit, Non-Professional
Paid Staff: 1
Income Sources: Tickets; Grants
Annual Attendance: 6,900
Seating Capacity: 400
Organization Type: Performing; Resident; Educational

3901
ACTORS CO-OP
1760 North Gower St.
Knoxville, TN 90028
Phone: 323-462-8460
Fax: 323-462-3199
e-mail: actorscoopinc@bellsouth.net
Web Site: www.actorsco-op.org/
Officers:
  President: John Winemiller
Management:
  Artistic Director: Amy Hubbard
  Production Manager: Rory Patterson
  Producer: Catherine Gray
  Producer: Rhonda Kohl
  Producer: David Scales
  Producer: Selah Victor
Specialized Field: Drama; Comedy; Theater Workshops

3902
ARTS & CULTURE ALLIANCE OF GREATER KNOXVILLE
Emporium Center, 100 S. Gay Street
Suite 201
Knoxville, TN 37902
Mailing Address: P.O. Box 2506, Knoxville, TN 37901
Phone: 865-523-7543
Fax: 865-523-7312
e-mail: info@knoxalliance.com
Web Site: www.knoxalliance.com
Officers:
  President: Patrick Roddy
  Treasurer: Kathy Hamilton
  VP: Jefferson Hcapma
  VP: Lila Plfleger
Management:
  Executive Director: Liza Zenni
  Deputy Director: Suzanne Cada
Mission: To unite, strenghen, and promote arts and culture activities in East Tennessee.
Founded: 1976
Specialized Field: Musical; Community Theater
Status: Nonprofit
Organization Type: Educational

3903
CARPETBAG THEATRE
1323 North Broadway
#106
Knoxville, TN 37917
Phone: 865-544-0447
Fax: 423-524-6631
e-mail: info@carpetbagtheatre.org
Web Site: www.carpetbagtheatre.org
Officers:
  Chair: Ronald A. Loving
  Secretary: Dorothy Bennett
  Treasurer: Maxine Thompson
Management:
  Executive/Artistic Director: Linda Parris-Bailey
  Managing/Technical Director: Jeff Cody
  Office Coordinator: Linda Upton Hill
Mission: To give artistic voice to the underserved. We address the issues and dreams of people who have historically been silenced by racism, classism, sexism and ageism; tell stories of empowerment; celebrate our culture; and reveal hidden stories.
Utilizes: Guest Companies; Singers
Founded: 1970
Specialized Field: Ensembles; Multi-Cultural; Ethnic Theater
Status: Professional; Nonprofit
Income Sources: National Endowment for the Arts; Tennessee Arts Commision; East Tennessee Community Foundation
Organization Type: Touring

3904
CLARENCE BROWN THEATRE COMPANY
206 McClung Tower
Knoxville, TN 37996-0420
Phone: 865-974-6011
Fax: 865-974-4867
e-mail: cbt@utk.edu
Web Site: www.clarencebrowntheatre.org
Officers:
  Chairperson: Andrew White
  Chair: Georgiana Vines
  Secretary: Susan Sgarlat
  Treasurer: Bob Parrott
Management:
  Producing Artistic Director: Cal MacLean
  Managing Director: David B. Byrd
  Interim Managing Director: David Brian Alley
  Company Manager: Betty Tipton
  Business Manager: Sharon Ward
  Production Manager Technical Direct: Andrew Karlin

Utilizes: Actors; AEA Actors; Artists-in-Residence; Collaborations; Educators; Guest Accompanists; Guest Companies; Guest Conductors; Guest Designers; Guild Activities; Local Artists
Founded: 1974
Specialized Field: Musical; Comedy; Ethnic Theater; Classic; Contemporary
Status: Non-Profit, Professional
Budget: $1.5 million
Income Sources: League of Resident Theatres; Theatre Communications Group; Knoxville Arts Council; University of Tennessee
Performs At: Clarence Brown Theatre, Carousel Theatre
Affiliations: Actors' Equity Association; League of Resident Theatres; SSOC
Annual Attendance: 34,000
Facility Category: Theatre
Type of Stage: Proscenium; Arena
Stage Dimensions: 60'x32'
Seating Capacity: 600; 250
Year Built: 1970
Rental Contact: Product Manager Laura Sims
Organization Type: Performing; Touring; Resident

3905
TENNESSEE STAGE COMPANY
PO Box 1186
Knoxville, TN 37901
Phone: 865-546-4280
Fax: 865-546-9677
e-mail: tennesseestage@comcast.net
Web Site: www.tennesseestage.com
Officers:
  Chair: Jennifer Bolt
  Vice-chair: Julianna Sanderson
  Secretary: Eileen Conway
  Production Committee Chair: Eileen Conway
  Education & Outreach Chair: Rachel Dellinger
  Treasurer: Steve Dupree
Management:
  Artistic Director: Tom Parkhill
Mission: To serve the Knoxville and East Tennessee area by producing exciting, high quality, productions of primarily American plays, both classical and current, while providing professional opportunities for regional artists.
Founded: 1989
Specialized Field: Shakespeare; Classic
Status: Non-Profit, Professional
Paid Staff: 1
Paid Artists: 30
Income Sources: Arts Council of Greater Knoxville; Community Televison of Knoxville; Comcast
Season: August
Stage Dimensions: 24' x 24'
Seating Capacity: 1,300

3906
THEATER KNOXVILLE
Bijou Theater
803 South Gay Street
Knoxville, TN 37902
Mailing Address: PO Box 1746 Knoxville, TN 37901
Phone: 865-522-0832
Fax: 865-522-5182
e-mail: info@KnoxBijou.com
Web Site: www.knoxbijou.com
Officers:
  President: David Arning
  Vice President: Julie Gause
  Treasurer: Greg Marret
  Secretary: Becky Hancock
Management:
  General Manager: Tom Bugg
  Assistant Manager: Jeanine Fowler
  Technical/Director: Lee Hamby
  Development Manager: Amanda Womac
Mission: To provide quality productions employing community members as actors and technicians.
Utilizes: Singers
Founded: 1976
Specialized Field: Community Theater
Status: Non-Professional; Nonprofit
Performs At: The Bijou Theater
Organization Type: Performing; Touring; Educational

3907
TENNESSEE PLAYERS
304 West Due West Avenue
Madison, TN 37115
Phone: 615-868-3738
Fax: 615-868-3738
e-mail: DearWorld@bellsouth.net
Web Site: www.tennesseeplayers.org
Management:
  Executive Director: Thurston Moore
Mission: To create something beautiful for somebody else.
Founded: 1986
Specialized Field: Multi-Media; Classic
Status: Non-Profit, Professional
Paid Staff: 1
Volunteer Staff: 3
Annual Attendance: 15,000
Organization Type: Performing; Touring; Educational

3908
CIRCUIT PLAYHOUSE
51 S Cooper
Memphis, TN 38104
Phone: 901-725-0776
Fax: 901-272-7530
e-mail: circuit@playhouseonthesquare.org
Web Site: www.playhouseonthesquare.org
Officers:
  President: PJ Smoot
  VP: Leigh McLean
Management:
  Managing Director: Whitney Jo
  Executive Producer: Jackie Nichols
  Associate Producer/Development: Michael Detroit
  Associate Director: Dave Landis
  Director of Marketing: Lisa Lynch
Founded: 1969
Specialized Field: New Plays; Musical; Drama; Comedy; Community Theater
Income Sources: Southeastern Theatre Conference; Theatre Communications Group; Tennessee Theatre Association; Playhouse on the Square
Performs At: Circuit Playhouse; Playhouse on the Square

3909
EWING CHILDREN'S THEATRE
2635 Avery Avenue
Memphis, TN 38112
Phone: 901-452-3968
Fax: 901-452-3805
Officers:
  President: June Scudder
  Secretary/Treasurer: Pat Barnes
Management:
  Theatre Director: Kay Lighfoot
Mission: Memphis Children's Theatre uses children, ages 5-17, and involves them in all aspects of theatre.

Utilizes: Actors; Choreographers; Collaborations; Dancers; Guest Accompanists; Guest Choreographers; Guest Companies; Guest Conductors; Guest Designers; Guest Ensembles; Guild Activities; Local Artists; Multimedia; Music; Organization Contracts; Performance Artists; Resident Professionals; Sign Language Translators; Singers; Soloists; Student Interns; Theatre Companies
Founded: 1949
Specialized Field: Community Theater
Status: Nonprofit
Paid Staff: 6
Income Sources: Memphis Park Services; American Children's Theatre Association; Tennessee Theatre Association; Southeastern Theatre Conference
Annual Attendance: 10,000
Facility Category: Theatre
Seating Capacity: 200
Year Remodeled: 1979
Organization Type: Performing; Educational

3910
PLAYHOUSE ON THE SQUARE
66 South Cooper St.
Memphis, TN 38104
Phone: 901-725-0776
Fax: 901-272-2309
e-mail: info@playhouseonthesquare.org
Web Site: www.playhouseonthesquare.org
Management:
  Founder And Executive Producer: Jackie Nichols
  Development Director: Donna Sue Shannon
  Associate Producer/Development: Michael Detroit
  Associate Director: Dave Landis
  Director of Marketing: Lisa Lynch
Mission: Producing live theatrical productions including new plays, Broadway and off-Broadway shows.
Utilizes: Guest Companies; Singers
Founded: 1969
Specialized Field: Drama; Broadway Musical Revivals
Status: Professional; Nonprofit
Paid Staff: 10
Income Sources: Theatre Communications Group; Circuit Playhouse
Season: Year round
Performs At: Playhouse on the Square
Organization Type: Performing; Touring; Resident; Educational

3911
MORRISTOWN THEATRE GUILD
314 S Hill Street
PO Box 1502
Morristown, TN 37816
Phone: 423-586-9260
Web Site: http://www.theatreguildinc.org/
Officers:
  Chairman: Jean Carter
  Vice-Chairman: Kay Flockhart
  Secretary: Kathy Hodge
  Treasurer: Larry McGowan
Management:
  Artistic Director: David Horton
Mission: To provide exposure to live theatre; to offer school-age children educational training.
Founded: 1934
Specialized Field: Musical; Dinner Theater; Community Theater
Status: Non-Professional; Nonprofit
Paid Staff: 50
Income Sources: Tennessee Theatre Association
Performs At: Theatre Guild
Organization Type: Performing; Educational

THEATRE / Tennessee

3912
CHAFFIN'S BARN DINNER THEATRE
8204 Highway 100
Nashville, TN 37221
Phone: 615-646-9977
Fax: 615-662-5439
Toll-free: 800-282-2276
e-mail: chaffinsboxoffice@yahoo.com
Web Site: www.dinnertheatre.com
Officers:
   Co-Owner: John Chaffin
   Co-Owner: Janie Chaffin
Management:
   Artistic Director: Martha Wilkinson
   Sales Director: Vanessa Wynn
   Stage Manager: Liz Fletcher
Mission: To produce top quality mysteries, comedies, and musicals.
Founded: 1967
Specialized Field: Musical; Dinner Theater
Status: Non-Profit, Professional
Facility Category: Dinner Theatre
Type of Stage: In the Round
Stage Dimensions: 16'x16'
Seating Capacity: 300
Year Built: 1967
Rental Contact: Regina Brock

3913
DARKHORSE THEATER
4610 Charlotte Avenue
Nashville, TN 37209
Phone: 615-297-7113
Fax: 615-665-3336
e-mail: info@darkhorsetheater.com
Web Site: www.darkhorsetheater.com
Management:
   Managing Director: Shannon Wood
Mission: To provide home to the Nashville creative performance community. Darkhouse theater presents an eclectic mix of original, classic, alternative, collorative, controversial and relevant theater and dance.
Founded: 1990
Specialized Field: Musical; Classic; Alternative; Contemporary

3914
DAVID LIPSCOMB UNIVERSITY THEATER
3901 Granny White Pike
Nashville, TN 37204-3951
Phone: 615-279-5715
Fax: 615-279-6516
e-mail: larry.brown@lipscomb.edu
Web Site: www.theatre.lipscomb.edu
Officers:
   President: Steven Flatt
   Theater Director: Larry Brown
Founded: 1891
Specialized Field: Educational
Status: Non-Profit, Non-Professional
Paid Staff: 1
Type of Stage: Black Box
Seating Capacity: 140

3915
MOCKINGBIRD PUBLIC THEATRE
PO Box 24002
Nashville, TN 37202
Phone: 615-242-6704
Fax: 615-242-7201
e-mail: mockingbirdpublictheatre@comcast.net
Officers:
   Chairman: Chris Chamberlin
   Treasurer: Rueben Buck
   Secretary: Pamela Crosby
Management:
   Artistic Director: David Alford
   Associate Artistic Director: Rene Copeland
   General Manager: Kara V Kindall
Mission: To produce theatre that is relevant to the life of our community, maintain artistic integrity and pursue a standard of excellence; to promote, develop and support the culture and artists of our region.
Utilizes: Actors; AEA Actors; Collaborating Artists; Collaborations
Founded: 1994
Specialized Field: Community Theater
Status: Professional; Nonprofit
Paid Artists: 40
Budget: $250,000-$300,000
Income Sources: Foundation; Private; Government
Performs At: Tennesee Performing Arts Center
Annual Attendance: 9,000-10,000

3916
NASHVILLE CHILDREN'S THEATRE
25 Middleton St.
Nashville, TN 37210
Phone: 615-252-4675
Fax: 615-810-8534
e-mail: info@nashvillechildrenstheatre.org
Web Site: www.nashvillechildrenstheatre.org
Officers:
   Chair: Winston N. Harless
   Vice Chair: Leslie Trayte Peters
   Secretary: Curtis L. Fisher
   Treasurer: Rich Lockwood
   Vice Chair: Leslie Trayte Peters
Management:
   Producing Director: Scot Copeland
   Producing Director: Jean Johnson
   Managing Director: Kathryn Colegrove
   Marketing/PR Director: Brenda Green
   Education Director: Alicia Fuss
   Box Office Manager: Jennifer Fernandez
   Business Manager: Michelle Taylor
   Development Director: Aimee Vance
   Technical Assistant: Bo Bogaev
Mission: An ensemble of professional artists who bring unique vision and compelling voice to the creation of meaningful theatre for young audiences at NCT. We strive to make live theatre a vital part of the childhood experience for all young people in Nashville and Middle Tennessee.
Utilizes: Guest Companies; Singers
Founded: 1931
Specialized Field: Children's Theater
Status: Non-Profit, Professional
Paid Staff: 12
Paid Artists: 60
Income Sources: Box Office; Government Grants & Individual; Corporate & Foundation Support
Performs At: Hill Theatre, Cooney Playhouse
Affiliations: ASSITEJ/USA; AEA:TYA
Type of Stage: Main Stage; Black Box
Seating Capacity: 690; 300
Year Built: 1960
Organization Type: Performing; Resident; Educational

3917
NASHVILLE SHAKESPEARE FESTIVAL
161 Raine Avenue
Nashville, TN 37203
Phone: 615-255-2273
Fax: 615-248-2273
e-mail: denice@nashvilleshakes.org
Web Site: www.nashvilleshakes.org
Officers:
   Chair: Donald Capparella
   Secretary: Ann Marie Deer-Owens
   Treasurer: Chad Milom
Management:
   Artistic Director: Denice Hickes
   Managing Director: Robert Marigza
   Development Director: Nicole Sibilski
   Operations Manager: Robert Marigza
   Education Director: Nettie Kraft
Mission: To educate and entertain the mid-south community through professional Shakespearean experiences.
Founded: 1988
Specialized Field: Shakespeare; Outdoor Theater
Status: Professional
Paid Staff: 4
Volunteer Staff: 40
Paid Artists: 25
Non-paid Artists: 15
Budget: $330,000
Season: August
Performs At: Centennial Park Bandshell
Affiliations: Shakespeare Theatre Association of America
Annual Attendance: 18,000
Organization Type: Performing; Resident; Touring; Educational

3918
STREET THEATRE COMPANY
1933 Elm Hill Pike
Nashville, TN 37216
Mailing Address: P.O. Box 160979, Nashville, TN 37216
Phone: 615-554-7414
e-mail: info@streettheatrecompany.org
Web Site: streettheatrecompany.org
Management:
   Executive Artistic Director: Cathy Street
Mission: Dedicated to fostering professional, affordable and accessible theatre, music and arts education in Nashville by producing the highest quality performances and educational workshops, and providing artistic opportunities for young people. STC strives to provide excellence with heart.
Status: Professional; Nonprofit
Organization Type: Performing; Educational

3919
TENNESSEE REPERTORY THEATRE
161 Rains Avenue
Nashville, TN 37203
Phone: 615-244-4878
Fax: 615-349-3222
e-mail: david@tennesseerep.org
Web Site: www.tennesseerep.org
Management:
   Executive Artistic Director: David Alford
   Producing Director: Rene Copeland
   General Manager: David Wilkerson
   Director of Finance and Administrat: Kay Adams
   Development Director: Jill Moore
   Marketing Director: Pat Patrick
   Technical Director: Tyler Axt
Mission: The presentation of quality, professional theatre and a complete season of plays.
Utilizes: Actors; AEA Actors; Choreographers; Collaborations; Grant Writers; Guest Artists; Guest Companies; Guest Conductors; Guest Designers;

Guest Lecturers; Guest Writers; Guild Activities; Instructors; Local Artists; Music; Original Music Scores; Performance Artists; Resident Professionals; Selected Students; Soloists
Founded: 1985
Specialized Field: Drama; Musical; Classic
Status: Professional
Paid Staff: 18
Volunteer Staff: 20
Paid Artists: 40
Income Sources: Ticket Sales; Fund-raising
Performs At: James K. Polk Theater; Tennessee Performing Arts Center
Affiliations: League of Resident Theatres; Actors' Equity Association; SSD&C
Annual Attendance: 70,000
Facility Category: Performing Arts Center
Type of Stage: Proscenium
Seating Capacity: 1,000
Year Built: 1980
Organization Type: Performing; Resident

3920
TENNESSEE THEATRE COMPANY
9 Music Square South #117
Nashville, TN 37203
Phone: 615-264-8999
e-mail: tntheatrecompany@aol.com
Web Site: tennesseetheatrecompany.com
Mission: The mission of the Tennessee Theatre Company is to produce quality theatre and student productions that are relevant to the life of our community, to pursue a standard of excellence and to promote, develop and support arts education and artists of our region.
Founded: 1998
Status: Professional Nonprofit
Organization Type: Touring; Performing; Educational

3921
OAK RIDGE PLAYHOUSE
27 E Tennessee Avenue at Jackson Square
Oak Ridge, TN 37831
Mailing Address: P.O. Box 5705, Oak Ridge, TN 37831-5705
Phone: 865-482-9999
Fax: 865-482-0945
e-mail: playhouse@orplayhouse.com
Web Site: www.orplayhouse.com
Officers:
  President: Steve Belding
  Vice President: Kathy Tallent
  Secretary: Michael Higdon
  Treasurer: Gene Spejewski
  Junior Playhouse Chair: Missy Blackwell
Management:
  Managing Artistic Director / Scenic: Reggie Law
  Technical Director: David Zannucci
  Public Relations Director: Karen Brunner
Mission: To provide quality theatre for the community while maintaining volunteer status.
Utilizes: Actors; AEA Actors; Choreographers; Collaborations; Dance Companies; Dancers; Designers; Educators; Grant Writers; Guest Accompanists; Guest Artists; Guest Choreographers; Guest Companies; Guest Conductors; Guest Designers; Guest Ensembles; Guest Lecturers; Guild Activities; High School Drama; Instructors; Local Artists; Lyricists; Multimedia; Music; Original Music Scores; Resident Professionals; Sign Language Translators; Soloists; Student Interns
Founded: 1943
Specialized Field: Drama
Status: Nonprofit
Paid Staff: 3
Volunteer Staff: 100
Paid Artists: 15
Non-paid Artists: 10
Budget: $250,000
Income Sources: Box Office; Grants; Private Donations; Corporate Donations & Sponsors; Subscription
Performs At: Oak Ridge Playhouse in Jackson Square
Affiliations: SE Theatre Conference; Knoxville Area Theatre Coalition; Arts Council of Oak Ridge; American Assoc of Community Theatres; Knoxville Arts Council
Annual Attendance: 25,000
Facility Category: Community Theatre; Children's Theatre
Type of Stage: Proscenium
Stage Dimensions: 40'x25'
Seating Capacity: 344
Year Built: 1943
Year Remodeled: 1988
Rental Contact: Reggie Law
Organization Type: Performing

3922
DIXIE STAMPEDE
3849 Parkway
PO Box 58
Pigeon Forge, TN 37868
Phone: 865-453-9473
Fax: 865-908-7061
Toll-free: 800-356-1676
e-mail: justiny@dixiestampede.com
Web Site: www.dixiestampede.com
Management:
  General Manager: John Shaver
Founded: 1988
Specialized Field: Dinner Theater
Status: Non-Equity; Commercial
Season: March - December
Type of Stage: Arena
Stage Dimensions: 75' x 150'
Seating Capacity: 1000

Texas

3923
WATERTOWER THEATRE
15650 Addison Road
Addison, TX 75001
Phone: 972-450-6230
Fax: 972-450-6244
e-mail: info@watertowertheatre.org
Web Site: www.watertowertheatre.org
Officers:
  President: Derek Blount
  Vice President: Ben Cunningham
  Secretary: Katie Myatt
  Treasurer: Jimmy Niemann
Management:
  Producing Artistic Director: Terry Martin
  Director/Education: Landrie Bock
Founded: 1977
Specialized Field: Musical; Comedy; Classic; Contemporary
Status: Non-Profit, Professional
Paid Staff: 7
Paid Artists: 50
Annual Attendance: 20,800

3924
FORT GRIFFIN FANDANGLE ASSOCIATION
2 Railroad Street
PO Box 155
Albany, TX 76430
Mailing Address: PO Box 2017 Albany, TX 76430
Phone: 325-762-3838
Fax: 325-762-3125
e-mail: fandangle@bitstreet.com
Web Site: http://www.fortgriffinfandangle.org/
Officers:
  President: John Matthews
  VP: Harold Law
  VP/Treasurer: Winifred Waller
  Executive Secretary: Debbie Hudman
Mission: To present historical narration with song and dance.
Utilizes: Singers
Founded: 1937
Specialized Field: Staged Readings; Historical
Status: Non-Professional; Nonprofit
Paid Staff: 250
Season: June
Performs At: Fort Griffin Fandangle Outdoor Theatre
Facility Category: Outdoor Ampitheater
Type of Stage: Grass
Seating Capacity: 1,800
Year Built: 1951
Organization Type: Performing

3925
AMARILLO LITTLE THEATRE
2019 Civic Circle
Amarillo, TX 79109
Phone: 806-355-9991
e-mail: info@amarillolittletheatre.com
Web Site: amarillolittletheatre.com
Management:
  Artistic Director: Allen Shankles
Mission: Amarillo Little Theatre is dedicated to the promotion and furtherance of live, nonprofit community theatre as an art form, stressing local and area participation in every facet of theatre production.
Founded: 1927
Status: Nonprofit
Organization Type: Performing

3926
CREATIVE ARTS THEATRE AND SCHOOL
602 E., South St.
Arlington, TX 76010
Phone: 817-861-2287
Fax: 817-274-0793
e-mail: cats@creativearts.org
Web Site: www.creativearts.org
Management:
  Executive Director: Heather Simmons
  Producing Director: Merry Brewe
  Technical Director: Richard Blake
  Bookkeeper: Michael Magnus
Mission: To develop the potential of young people from diverse backgrounds through performing arts training and performance opportunities. Devoted to professionally training, enriching and inspiring all youth by igniting within them an enduring passion for the arts. A theatre....by youth for youth.
Utilizes: High School Drama; Soloists
Founded: 1977
Specialized Field: Children's Theater; Theater Workshops
Status: Non-Profit

THEATRE / Texas

Income Sources: Tuition; Ticket Sales; Donations; Grants
Seating Capacity: 350

3927
THEATRE ARLINGTON
305 W Main St.
Arlington, TX 76010
Phone: 817-275-7661
Fax: 817-275-3370
e-mail: info@theatrearlington.org
Web Site: www.theatrearlington.org
Management:
  Executive Producer: Norman Ussery
  Director of Development: Kim Lawson
  Marketing Director: Emmy Klein
  Education Director: Cindy Honeycutt
  Outreach Manager: Jacque Campbell Disher
  Marketing Manager/Volunteer Coordin: Gary Payne
  Box Office/Office Manager: Troy Stidham
  Technical Director: Brian Scheffer
  Facility Manager: Julia Broussard
Mission: Dedicated to the cultural enrichment, education and entertainment of the citizenry of Arlington and the North Texas Community.
Utilizes: Guest Companies; Singers
Founded: 1973
Specialized Field: Musical; Comedy; Classic; Contemporary
Status: Non-Profit, Professional
Paid Staff: 6
Volunteer Staff: 100
Paid Artists: 3
Income Sources: Texas Nonprofit Theatre
Performs At: Theatre Arlington
Organization Type: Performing; Resident; Educational

3928
AUSTIN MUSICAL THEATRE
2011 E Riverside Drive
Suite C
Austin, TX 78741
Phone: 512-428-9696
Fax: 512-428-9699
e-mail: jhammond@amtpresents.org
Web Site: www.amtpresents.com
Management:
  Producing Artistic Director: Scott Thompson
  Managing Artistic Director: Richard Byron
  Production Manager: Jeanine Lisa
  Executive Director: Jared Hammond
  Academy Coordinator: Ginger Morris
  Academy Assistant: Kevin Archambeault
  Marketing Director: Suzie Harriamn
Utilizes: Actors; Dancers; Designers; Five Seasonal Concerts; Grant Writers; Guest Ensembles; Guest Lecturers; Guest Musical Directors; High School Drama; Instructors; Local Artists; Multimedia; Music; Original Music Scores; Resident Professionals; Selected Students; Sign Language Translators; Soloists; Student Interns
Founded: 1996
Specialized Field: Musical; Theater Workshops
Paid Staff: 10
Paid Artists: 100
Budget: $3,500,000
Income Sources: Donations; Grants; Academy Revenue; Ticket Sales
Performs At: The Paramount Theatre
Affiliations: Actors' Equity Association; International Alliance of Theatrical Stage Employees
Annual Attendance: 50,000
Type of Stage: Proscenium

Seating Capacity: 1,200
Year Built: 1915
Year Remodeled: 1975

3929
AUSTIN THEATRE FOR YOUTH
713 Congress Avenue
Austin, TX 78701
Phone: 512-472-5470
Fax: 512-472-5824
e-mail: info@austintheatre.org
Web Site: www.austintheatre.org
Officers:
  President: Duff M. Stewart
  Secretary: Grace F. Renbarger
  Treasurer: Sharon Francia
  Immediate Past President: Frances H. Bennett
Management:
  Executive/Artistic Director: Rick Schiller
  Associate Artistic Director: Rod Caspers
  Director Community Outreach/PR: Regina Rosenthal
  Director Marketing/Development: Elena Coates
  Events Manager: Stefanie Crock
  CEO/Executive Director: Jim Ritts
  Executive Director of Programming: Lietza Brass
  Executive Marketing Director: Stacey Fellers
  Executive Director of Development: Maica Jordan
Mission: To create relevant, enriching and entertaining theatre experiences for Central Texas families and youth.
Specialized Field: Children's Theater

3930
FRONTERA
511 W 43rd Street
Austin, TX 78751
Phone: 512-479-7530
Fax: 512-479-7531
e-mail: ken@hydeparktheatre.org
Web Site: www.fronterafest.org
Officers:
  President: Jon Hockenyos
  Secretary: Mical Trejo
Management:
  Artistic Director: Ken Webster
  Business Manager: Tammy Whitehead
  Publicity Director: Katherine Catmull
Founded: 1992
Specialized Field: Drama; Musical
Performs At: Hyde Park Theatre
Type of Stage: Flexible
Seating Capacity: 90

3931
PENFOLD THEATRE
P.O. Box 81044
Austin, TX 78708
Phone: 512-850-4849
e-mail: info@penfoldtheatre.org
Web Site: penfoldtheatre.org
Management:
  Producing Artistic Director: Ryan Crowder
  Associate Artistic Director: Nathan Jerkins
  Managing Director: Zena Vaughn
Mission: To empower artists to create work of the highest caliber and to engage diverse audiences through stories that inspire and impact our community.
Founded: 2008
Status: Professional; Nonprofit

3932
RUDE MECHANICALS
2211-A Hidalgo Street
Suite 220
Austin, TX 78702
Phone: 512-476-7833
Fax: 512-477-3157
e-mail: info@rudemech.com
Web Site: www.rudemechs.com
Officers:
  President: Dave Hime
  VP: Bonnie Reese
  Treasurer: Matt Bennison
  Secretary: Sarah Sloan
Management:
  Director: Thomas Graves
  Development Director: Erin Harrell
  Business Manager/Marketing Director: Lana Lesley
  Grrl Action Director: Madge Darlington
Specialized Field: Ensembles

3933
STATE THEATER COMPANY
PO Box 8252
Austin, TX 05000
Phone: 884-155-333
Fax: 882-316-310
e-mail: info@austintheatre.org
Web Site: www.statetheatercompany.com
Officers:
  CEO: Dan Fallon
  President: Duff M. Stewart
  Secretary: Grace F. Renbarger
  Treasurer: Sharon Francia
  Immediate Past President: Frances H. Bennett
  Board Chair: John Irving
Management:
  Producing Artistic Director: Scott Kanoff
  Associate Artistic Director: Michelle Polgar
  Technical Director: Mark Porter
  Production Manager: Jeanine Lisa
  Executive Director of Development: Maica Jordan
  Chief Executive Officer/Producer: Rob Brookman
  Artistic Director: Geordie Brookman
  Marketing Manager: Kristy Rebbeck
  Marmeting Coodrinator: Madeleine Smith
Founded: 1982
Specialized Field: Theater Workshops; Drama; Musical
Status: For-Profit, Professional
Paid Staff: 5
Paid Artists: 75
Income Sources: Corporations; Foundations; Individual Gifts
Season: March - August

3934
VORTEX REPERTORY COMPANY
2307 Manor Road
PO Box 33125
Austin, TX 78722
Phone: 512-478-5282
e-mail: ponty@jollylox.com
Web Site: www.vortexrep.org
Management:
  Managing Director: Steve Bacher
  Producing Artistic Director: Bonnie Cullum
Mission: To create new, innovative performances, including original works, new plays, revitalized classics, and to present nationally-recognized, cutting edge touring artists.

Utilizes: Guest Companies; Singers
Founded: 1988
Specialized Field: New Plays; Classic; Contemporary
Status: Professional; Nonprofit
Paid Staff: 200
Performs At: Vortex Performance Care
Organization Type: Performing; Touring; Resident; Educational; Sponsoring

3935
ZACHARY SCOTT THEATRE CENTER
1510 Toomey Road
Austin, TX 78704
Phone: 512-476-0541
Fax: 512-476-0314
e-mail: info@zachscott.com
Web Site: www.zachscott.com
Officers:
   President: Joy H. Selak
   Immediate Past President: Bruce McCann
   Vice President: Dr. Gary Goldstein
   Secretary: Larry Connelly
   Treasurer: Hiten Patel
Management:
   Producing Artistic Director: Dave Steakley
   Managing Director: Elisbeth Challener
   Business Manager: Linda Wilson
   Director of Education: Nat Miller
Mission: To offer the finest contemporary and classical scripts and original works for young people; to maintain a multicultural company.
Utilizes: Singers
Founded: 1977
Specialized Field: Musical; Comedy; Classic; Contemporary
Status: Non-Profit, Professional
Paid Staff: 35
Paid Artists: 40
Income Sources: Theatre Communications Group; American Association of Theatre Educators; Theatre in Disability; Austin Circle of Theatres
Performs At: ZSTC Arena; ZSTC Kleberg
Organization Type: Performing; Touring; Educational

3936
BASTROP OPERA HOUSE
711 Spring Street
PO Box 691
Bastrop, TX 78602
Phone: 512-321-6283
e-mail: chester@bastropoperahouse.com
Web Site: www.bastropoperahouse.com
Management:
   Executive Director: Chester Eitze
Mission: To present dance, music and theatre in a performing arts center at the restored Old Bastrop Opera House.
Utilizes: Guest Companies; Singers
Founded: 1889
Specialized Field: Summer Stock; Musical; Dinner Theater
Status: Semi-Professional; Non-Professional; Nonprofit
Performs At: Old Bastrop Opera House
Organization Type: Performing; Sponsoring

3937
BAYTOWN LITTLE THEATER
4328 Hugh Echolds Boulevard
Baytown, TX 77521
Mailing Address: P.O. Box 2022, Baytown, TX 77522
Phone: 281-424-7617
e-mail: info@baytownlittletheater.org
Web Site: baytownlittletheater.org
Officers:
   President: Patti Meiners
   Vice President: Sam Estrada
   Secretary: Mark Fleming
   Treasurer: Dawn Daily
Management:
   Production Manager: Maegan Carnew-Megginson
   Theater Manager: Kathryn Saenger
Mission: Offer the play-going public the very best in comedy, dramatic, and musical productions.
Founded: 1961
Status: Nonprofit; Volunteer
Organization Type: Performing

3938
ONSTAGE IN BEDFORD
2801 Forest Ridge Drive
Bedford, TX 76021
Mailing Address: P.O. Box 211234, Bedford, TX 76095-8234
Phone: 817-354-6444
Web Site: onstageinbedford.com
Officers:
   President: Gayle Ormsby Hargis
   Treasurer: Laura Bray
Management:
   Artistic Director: Michael Winters
Founded: 1982
Status: Nonprofit

3939
CAMILLE PLAYERS
1 Dean Porter Park
Brownsville, TX 78520
Phone: 956-542-8900
Fax: 956-542-0567
e-mail: PatCranick@aol.com
Web Site: www.freewebs.com/camilleplayhouse/
Officers:
   President: Stephen Shull
   Vice President: Lecia Chaney
   Second VP: Fidencio Zavala
   Treasurer: Jaime Lucio
   Secretary: Ana Rodriguez
Management:
   Executive Director: Ben Agresti
   Executive Artistic Director: Eric A. Vera
Mission: To stimulate interest in drama through presenting plays.
Utilizes: Actors; Choreographers; Dancers; Multimedia; Music; Resident Professionals; Sign Language Translators; Soloists
Founded: 1964
Specialized Field: Musical; Classic; Contemporary
Status: Non-Profit, Non-Professional
Paid Staff: 2
Volunteer Staff: 3
Budget: $9,000
Performs At: Camille Lightner Playhouse
Annual Attendance: 5,000
Facility Category: Theatre
Type of Stage: Proscenium
Stage Dimensions: 30'x25'
Seating Capacity: 301
Year Built: 1964
Year Remodeled: 1995
Organization Type: Performing

3940
TEXAS PANHANDLE HERITAGE FOUNDATION
1514 5th Avenu
Canyon, TX 79015
Phone: 806-655-2181
Fax: 806-655-7778
e-mail: info@tphf.com
Web Site: www.texas-show.com
Officers:
   Chairman of the Board: Jayne Brainard
   Vice Chairman: Martha Chow
   Secretary: Gene Morrison
Management:
   Artistic Director: David Yinak
   Executive Director: Kris Miller
   General Manager: Staci Wyatt
Mission: To preserve and present Texas history and culture through education and entertainment.
Utilizes: Actors; Choreographers; Dancers; Multimedia; Original Music Scores; Sign Language Translators; Singers
Founded: 1961
Specialized Field: Musical; Historical
Status: Non-Profit, Non-Professional
Paid Staff: 11
Paid Artists: 60
Income Sources: Texas Panhandle Heritage Foundation
Performs At: Pioneer Amphitheatre
Annual Attendance: 85,000
Facility Category: Outdoor Theatre
Seating Capacity: 1723
Year Built: 1965
Rental Contact: Blaine Bertrand
Organization Type: Performing; Educational

3941
PLAZA THEATRE COMPANY
111 South Main Street
Cleburne, TX 76033
Phone: 817-202-0600
e-mail: jace@plaza-theatre.com
Web Site: plaza-theatre.com
Founded: 2007
Specialized Field: Musical Theatre And Plays
Status: Nonprofit
Organization Type: Performing; Educational

3942
STAGECENTER
201-B W 26th St
College Station, TX 77803-3215
Mailing Address: PO Box 6166, Bryan, TX 77805-6166
Phone: 979-823-4297
e-mail: stage.center@hotmail.com
Web Site: http://www.stagecenter.net
Officers:
   President: Reid Self
   Secretary: Kristie Hanle
   Treasurer: Evelyn Callaway
Mission: To offer community members an opportunity for participation in theatre.
Utilizes: Guest Companies; Singers
Founded: 1966
Specialized Field: Community Theater
Status: Nonprofit
Paid Staff: 50
Income Sources: Arts Council of Brazos Valley
Organization Type: Performing; Educational

3943
CORSICANA COMMUNITY PLAYHOUSE
119 W 6th Avenue
Corsicana, TX 75110
Phone: 903-872-5421
Management:
   Director: H M Dabnpork

THEATRE / Texas

Executive Director: Sandra McCluremahood
Mission: To provide quality theatrical performances for Corsicana and the north and east Texas regions.
Founded: 1971
Specialized Field: Community Theater
Status: Non-Profit, Non-Professional
Paid Staff: 3
Income Sources: Texas Nonprofit Theatre
Performs At: Warehouse Living Arts Center
Organization Type: Performing; Touring

3944
CABBAGES AND KINGS
7436 Kenshine Lane
Dallas, TX 75230
Phone: 214-363-7292
Fax: 214-867-7615
Management:
   Founder/Artistic Director: Linda Comess
   General Manager: Tricia Avery
Mission: To entertain and enlighten families and children; to present original plays which are based on mythology and stories and are relevant to modern life.
Utilizes: Guest Companies; Singers
Founded: 1984
Specialized Field: Children's Theater; Historical
Status: Professional; Nonprofit
Income Sources: Actors' Equity Association
Performs At: Addison Centre Theatre
Organization Type: Performing; Touring

3945
DALLAS CHILDREN'S THEATER
5938 Skillmans Street
Dallas, TX 75231
Phone: 214-978-0110
Fax: 214-978-0118
e-mail: family@dct.org
Web Site: www.dct.org
Officers:
   Marketing Director: Trish Long
   Accounting Assistant: Donna Keeler
   Development Associate: Reg Platt
   Development Assistant: Wanda Roberson
   Director of Ticketing and Patron Se: Steve Jones
   Public Relations Manager: Sherry Ward
Management:
   President: Kandace Winslow
   Executive Artistic Director: Robyn Flatt
   Education Director: Nancy Schaeffer
   Tour Director: Sally Fiorello
   Artist-In-Residence: Kathy Burks
   Associate Artistic Director: Artie Olaisen
   Director of Finance & Human Resourc: Janet L. Massey
   Finance Manager: Jim Amrhein
Mission: To enrich children's lives through theater arts.
Utilizes: Actors; AEA Actors; Artists-in-Residence; Choreographers; Collaborating Artists; Commissioned Composers; Commissioned Music; Designers; Educators; Five Seasonal Concerts; Guest Accompanists; Guest Artists; Guest Companies; Guest Conductors; Guest Designers; Guest Directors; Guest Lecturers; Instructors; Local Artists; Lyricists; Multimedia; Music; Organization Contracts; Original Music Scores; Performance Artists; Poets; Resident Professionals; Selected Students; Sign Language Translators; Soloists; Student Interns; Special Technical Talent; Theatre Companies; Visual Arts
Founded: 1984
Specialized Field: Musical; Comedy; Youth Theater; Puppet; Educational
Status: Non-Profit, Professional
Paid Staff: 22
Volunteer Staff: 100
Paid Artists: 175
Budget: $2,500,000
Income Sources: International Association of Theatre for Children and Youth; Corporate; Foundation; Individuals; Grants; Ticket Purchases
Performs At: El Centre College Theatre; Crescent Theatre
Affiliations: TGG; AEA; AATE; TNT; ASSITEJ
Annual Attendance: 245,000
Organization Type: Performing; Touring; Educational

3946
DALLAS PUPPET THEATER
3905 Main Street
Dallas, TX 75226
Phone: 214-515-0004
Web Site: www.puppetry.org
Management:
   Executive Director: Pix Smith
   Artistic Director: Michael Robinson
   Founding Artistic Director: James Smith
Mission: Dedicated to promoting and advancing the performing, visual, and creative art of puppetry.
Utilizes: Guest Companies; Singers
Founded: 1982
Specialized Field: Puppet
Status: Non-Profit, Professional
Paid Staff: 20
Paid Artists: 20
Organization Type: Performing; Touring; Resident; Educational; Sponsoring

3947
DALLAS THEATER CENTER
2400 Flora Street
Dallas, TX 75201
Phone: 214-526-8210
Fax: 214-521-7666
e-mail: info@dallastheatercenter.org
Web Site: www.dallastheatercenter.org
Officers:
   Chair: Rebecca Fletcher
   President: Tina Barry
   Executive Vice President: Tina Barry
   Secretary: James Waters
   Treasurer: Curt FitzGerald
Management:
   General Manager: Hillary J Hart
   Managing Director: Heather M. Kitchen
   Artistic Director: Kevin Moriarty
Mission: To offer excellent professional theatre that produces classic, contemporary and new plays of the highest artistic quality.
Utilizes: Guest Companies; Singers
Founded: 1920
Specialized Field: Classic; Contemporary
Status: Professional; Nonprofit
Income Sources: Theatre Communications Group; League of Resident Theatres; American Arts Alliance
Performs At: Kalita Humphreys Theater; Arts District Theater
Type of Stage: Flexible; Thrust
Seating Capacity: 530; 466
Organization Type: Performing; Resident; Educational

3948
DRAMA CIRCLE THEATRE
2929 Mayhew
Dallas, TX 75228
Phone: 972-270-9255
Management:
   Managing Director: Linda Boatman
   Founder: Bill Green
Co-Founder: Nan Truax
Mission: To promote the theatre arts.
Founded: 1971
Specialized Field: Drama
Status: Semi-Professional; Nonprofit
Paid Staff: 30
Organization Type: Performing; Touring; Educational

3949
ECHO THEATRE
PO Box 820698
Dallas, TX 75328
Phone: 214-904-0500
e-mail: mail@echotheatre.org
Web Site: www.echotheatre.org
Officers:
   Co-Founder: Linda Marie Ford
   Co-Founder: Pam Myers-Morgan
   Co-Founder: Suzy Blaylock
Mission: For years, theatre seasons at all levels of production have been programmed mainly wiht works by male playwrights, often resulting in an absence of the female voice.
Founded: 1997
Specialized Field: Women's Theater
Status: Non-Profit

3950
JUNIOR PLAYERS
4054 McKinney Avenue
Suite 104
Dallas, TX 75204
Phone: 214-526-4076
Fax: 214-526-0114
e-mail: info@juniorplayers.org
Web Site: www.juniorplayers.org
Officers:
   President: John Cravens
   Vice President: Lueretha Slack
   Treasurer: Bill Rolley
   Secretary: Diann L'Roy
Management:
   Executive Director: Kirsten Brandt James
   Program Director: Rosaura Cruz
Mission: Junior Players uses the arts to provide role models, increase literacy, self-esteem and communication skills for the Dallas youth.
Specialized Field: Children's Theater; Educational; Summer Stock
Status: Nonprofit

3951
KATHY BURKS THEATRE OF PUPPETRY ARTS
5938 Skillman
Dallas, TX 75231
Phone: 214-587-7543
e-mail: kburkstx@yahoo.com
Web Site: http://www.kathyburkspuppets.com
Management:
   Artistic Director: Kathy Burks
Mission: To perform using all styles of puppetry and perpetuate the art of puppetry. Material for the shows range from classic stories and fairytales to original work.
Founded: 1973
Specialized Field: Puppet
Status: Professional; Nonprofit
Income Sources: Puppeteers of America; Lone Star Puppet Guild
Performs At: The Loft Puppet Theatre at Fairview Farms
Organization Type: Performing; Resident; Educational

3952
KITCHEN DOG THEATER
3120 McKinney Avenue
Ste. 100
Dallas, TX 75204
Phone: 214-953-1055
Fax: 214-953-1873
e-mail: admin@kitchendogtheater.org
Web Site: www.kitchendogtheater.org
Officers:
- **Co-President/Board Director:** Jason Ankele
- **Co-President/Board Director:** Susan Albritton

Management:
- **President:** Jayson Ankele
- **Artistic Director:** Dan Day
- **Co-artistic Director:** Tina Parker

Mission: It is the mission of Kitchen Dog Theater to provide a place where questions of justice, morality, and human freedom can be explored. We choose plays that challenge our moral and social consciences, and invite our audiences to be provoked, challenged, and amazed. We believe that the theater is a site of individual discovery as well as a force against conventional views of the self and experience.
Founded: 1990
Specialized Field: Comedy; Classic; Contemporary
Status: Non-Profit, Professional
Paid Staff: 4
Performs At: McKinney Avenue Contemporary
Affiliations: National New Play Network; Dallas Theatre League; Theater Communications Group
Type of Stage: Thrust; Black Box
Seating Capacity: 150; 75-100
Year Built: 1994

3953
PEGASUS THEATRE
Magdalen Road
Suite 147 PMB 773
Dallas, TX 75214
Phone: 186-581-2160
Fax: 186-581-2170
e-mail: comedy@pegasustheatre.com
Web Site: www.pegasustheatre.com
Management:
- **Artistic Director:** Kurt Kleinmann
- **Producer:** Barbara Weinberger, barb@pegasustheatre.com

Mission: A professional live stage theatre specializing in new and original comedies. They offer one main stage production each season and one black box prodution.
Utilizes: AEA Actors; Designers; Equity Actors; Guest Designers; Instructors; Local Artists; Original Music Scores; Performance Artists; Resident Professionals
Founded: 1985
Specialized Field: Musical; Classic
Status: Professional; Nonprofit
Paid Staff: 1
Budget: $150,000
Income Sources: Stage
Performs At: Eisemann Cetner
Type of Stage: Proscenium
Organization Type: Performing; Touring

3954
POCKET SANDWICH THEATRE
5400 East Mockingbird Ln
Suite 119
Dallas, TX 75206
Phone: 214-821-1860
Fax: 214-821-4742
e-mail: pst@dallas.net
Web Site: www.pocketsandwich.com
Management:
- **President:** Joe Dickinson
- **Owner and Technical Director:** Rodney Dobbs

Mission: To offer variety in live theatre performances.
Utilizes: Guest Companies; Singers
Founded: 1980
Specialized Field: Comedy; Dinner Theater
Status: For-Profit, Professional
Paid Staff: 20
Performs At: Pocket Sandwich Theatre
Organization Type: Performing

3955
SHAKESPEARE DALLAS
3630 Harry Hines Boulevard, 3rd Floor
Dallas, TX 75219
Phone: 214-559-2778
Fax: 214-559-2782
e-mail: info@shakespearedallas.org
Web Site: shakespearedallas.org
Officers:
- **Chair:** Adam Reed
- **Vice Chair:** Darren Dittrich

Management:
- **Executive/Artistic Director:** Raphael Parry

Mission: The mission of the Shakespeare Dallas is to create exemplary cultural programs for North Texas that are affordable and accessible to the community inspired by the quality and standards found in the works of William Shakespeare.
Specialized Field: Shakespeare
Status: Nonprofit
Performs At: Samuell Grand Amphitheatre At Addison Circle Park
Organization Type: Performing; Touring

3956
TEATRO HISPANO DE DALLAS
1331 Record Crossing Road
Dallas, TX 75235
Phone: 214-689-6492
e-mail: info@teatrodallas.org
Web Site: www.teatrodallas.org
Officers:
- **President:** John Fulliwider
- **Vice President:** Miguel Marrero
- **Treasurer & Co-Founder:** Jeff Hurst

Management:
- **Artistic/Managing Director:** Cora Cardona
- **Administrator:** Marti Etheridge

Utilizes: Actors; AEA Actors; Artists-in-Residence; Collaborating Artists; Community Members; Dance Companies; Designers; Educators; Five Seasonal Concerts; Guest Accompanists; Guest Choreographers; Guest Companies; Guest Conductors; Guest Designers; Guest Directors; Guest Ensembles; Guest Instructors; Guest Musical Directors; Guest Teachers; Lyricists; Multimedia; Original Music Scores; Performance Artists; Resident Professionals; Singers; Soloists; Student Interns; Theatre Companies
Founded: 1985
Specialized Field: Community Theater
Status: Professional; Semi-Professional; Nonprofit
Paid Staff: 2
Budget: $250,000
Performs At: Teatro Dallas
Annual Attendance: 15,000
Facility Category: Leases various venues
Organization Type: Performing

3957
TEXAS INTERNATIONAL THEATRICAL ARTS SOCIETY
2100 Ross Avenue
Suite 650
Dallas, TX 75201
Phone: 214-528-6112
Fax: 214-528-2617
e-mail: csantos@titas.org
Web Site: www.titas.org
Officers:
- **President:** Steven Gendler
- **Treasurer:** Michael Titens
- **Secretary:** Saundra Steinberg
- **Vice President of Strategic Plannin:** Gayle Ziaks Halperin
- **Vice President of Marketing/Communi:** Jacques Vroom III

Management:
- **Executive Director/Artistic Directo:** Charles Santos
- **Marketing/Public Relations:** Scott Rozsa
- **Special Events Director:** John Frazier
- **Director of Finance:** Tamara Elkins

Mission: To create opportunities otherwise unavailable in Dallas and North Texas for the community to experience an abundant mixture of the best American and international dance, performance art, and music through performances and cultural and educational outreach activities.
Founded: 1982
Specialized Field: Drama; Musical
Status: Non-Profit, Professional
Paid Staff: 8
Volunteer Staff: 70
Budget: $2,100,000
Income Sources: Private; Corporate; Foundation; Individual; Box Office
Performs At: McFarlin Auditorium; Southern Methodist University
Affiliations: Association of Performing Arts Presenters; International Society of Performing Arts
Annual Attendance: 52,000
Facility Category: Auditorium
Seating Capacity: 2,383
Rental Contact: Director Melissa Berry
Organization Type: Presenting; Educational

3958
THEATRE GEMINI
PO Box 191225
Dallas, TX 75219
Phone: 214-521-6331
Management:
- **General Manager:** Craig Hess

Founded: 1984
Specialized Field: Community Theater
Status: Non-Professional; Nonprofit
Paid Staff: 60
Organization Type: Performing; Educational

3959
THEATRE THREE
2800 Routh Street 168
Dallas, TX 75201
Phone: 214-871-3300
Fax: 214-871-3139
e-mail: admin@theatre3dallas.com
Web Site: www.theatre3dallas.com
Officers:
- **Chairman:** Marion L. Brockette, Jr.

Management:
- **President:** Jack Alder

THEATRE / Texas

Managing Director: Tarry Dobson
Executive Producer-Director: Jac Alder
Company Manager: Terry Dobson
Director of Business Affairs: Joan Sleight
Mission: To offer professional theatre as well as related activities to the Dallas-Ft. Worth area and to further the artistic careers of theatre artists who reside in North Texas.
Utilizes: Actors; AEA Actors; Choreographers; Dancers; Designers; Guest Artists; Guest Designers; Guest Musical Directors; Guest Teachers; Instructors; Local Artists; Music; Original Music Scores; Performance Artists; Poets; Resident Professionals; Sign Language Translators; Soloists; Student Interns
Founded: 1961
Specialized Field: Musical; Comedy; Classic
Status: Non-Profit, Professional
Paid Staff: 30
Budget: $1.4 million
Income Sources: Admission Earnings; Miscellaneous Earnings; Government; Corporate; Foundation; Individual Grants/Donations
Performs At: Theatre in the round
Affiliations: AEA; Southwest Theatre Association; Texas Non Profit Theatres
Facility Category: Theatre
Seating Capacity: 242; 70
Year Built: 1969
Year Remodeled: 1986
Organization Type: Performing; Touring; Resident; Educational; Sponsoring

3960
UNDERMAIN THEATRE
3200 Main Street
PO Box 144466
Dallas, TX 75226
Mailing Address: 3100 Main St. #16, Dallas, TX 75226
Phone: 214-747-5515
Fax: 214-747-1863
e-mail: mail@undermain.org
Web Site: www.undermain.com
Management:
    Founder/Artistic Director: Katherine Owens
    Operations Manager: Samantha Eberle
    Events Coordinator: Liz Acklin
    Development Director: Maryam Baig
    Technical Director: Kenneth Bernstein
    Founder and Executive Producer: Bruce DuBose
    Associate Producer: Suzanne Thomas
    Development Consultant: JoLynne Jensen
    Press Director: Dana Cobb
Mission: To focus on regionally and nationally premiering work that is challenging intellectually, emotionally and philosphically.
Utilizes: Guest Companies; Singers; Touring Companies
Founded: 1984
Specialized Field: Experimental; New Plays
Status: Professional; Nonprofit
Performs At: Undermain Theatre Basement
Affiliations: Actors' Equity Association; TCG; National Endowment for the Arts
Facility Category: Basement Theatre
Type of Stage: Flexible
Seating Capacity: 90
Year Built: 1900
Organization Type: Performing

3961
UPTOWN PLAYERS
3636 Turtle Creek Boulevard
Dallas, TX 75219
Mailing Address: P.O. Box 192264, Dallas, TX 75219
Phone: 214-219-2718
e-mail: info@uptownplayers.org
Web Site: uptownplayers.org
Mission: The mission of Uptown Players is to present professional theatre that meets a rising demand in the community for audiences to see their life experiences.
Founded: 2001
Status: Nonprofit; Professional
Performs At: Kalita Humphreys Theater
Annual Attendance: 10,000

3962
BREAD AND CIRCUS THEATRE
1009 Bull Run
Denton, TX 76201
Phone: 614-464-6809
e-mail: bctco1@gmail.com!
Web Site: www.bctco.org
Management:
    Managing Director: Connie Whitt-Lambert
Mission: To offer fun theatrical experiences to children and adults through audience participation.
Utilizes: Singers
Founded: 1982
Specialized Field: Summer Stock; Community Theater; Musical
Status: Professional; Semi-Professional
Organization Type: Performing; Touring

3963
DENTON COMMUNITY CAMPUS THEATRE
214 W Hickory
PO Box 1931
Denton, TX 76201
Phone: 940-382-1915
Fax: 940-891-1691
Toll-free: 800-733-7014
e-mail: thedctteam@campustheatre.com
Web Site: www.campustheatre.com
Officers:
    President: Steve Plunkett
Management:
    Executive Director: Scott Wilkinson
Mission: To offer artistic, educational experiences to participants; to provide quality theatre for audiences.
Utilizes: Actors; Choreographers; Collaborations; Dance Companies; Designers; Guest Artists; Guest Companies; Guest Conductors; Guest Lecturers; Local Artists; Original Music Scores; Resident Professionals; Singers; Special Technical Talent
Founded: 1949
Specialized Field: Community Theater
Status: Non-Professional; Nonprofit
Paid Staff: 5
Volunteer Staff: 50
Paid Artists: 300
Non-paid Artists: 300
Budget: $450,000
Income Sources: City of Denton
Performs At: Campus Theatre
Affiliations: ACT; SWTC; TNT
Annual Attendance: 30,000
Type of Stage: Proscenium
Stage Dimensions: 40'x40'
Seating Capacity: 299
Year Built: 1949
Year Remodeled: 1985
Cost: $2 million
Organization Type: Performing; Educational

3964
BAY AREA HARBOUR PLAYHOUSE
3803 Highway 3
Dickinson, TX 77539
Phone: 281-337-7569
Web Site: harbourplayhouse.com
Mission: To provide quality arts education and entertainment to the surrounding communities.
Status: Nonprofit
Organization Type: Educational; Performing

3965
EL PASO ASSOCIATION FOR THE PERFORMING ARTS/VIVA EL PASO!
PO Box 31340
El Paso, TX 79931-0340
Phone: 915-231-1165
Fax: 915-565-6999
e-mail: VivaEP@Yahoo.com
Web Site: www.viva-ep.org
Management:
    Managing Director: David Mills
    Director of Marketing: Mario A Duron
Founded: 1978
Specialized Field: Outdoor Theater; Musical; Educational
Status: Non-Equity; Nonprofit
Season: June - August
Type of Stage: Amphitheatre
Stage Dimensions: 80' x 40'
Seating Capacity: 1500

3966
SOUTHWEST REPERTORY ORGANIZATION
1301 Texas Avenue
El Paso, TX 79901
Phone: 915-534-7653
Management:
    Interim Executive/Artistic Director: Ed Hamilton
    Technical Director: Glen O Brooks
    General Manager: Glenda Nevarez
Mission: To provide a main season including musicals, comedies and contemporary dramas; to offer a summer repertory featuring contemporary plays as well as classes in directing, acting and the technical aspects of theatre.
Utilizes: Guest Companies
Founded: 1978
Specialized Field: Musical; Community Theater
Status: Non-Professional; Nonprofit
Organization Type: Performing; Touring

3967
ALLIED THEATRE GROUP/STAGE WEST
821/823 W. Vickery Blvd.
Fort Worth, TX 76104
Phone: 817-784-9378
Fax: 817-735-4065
e-mail: stagewest@gbronline.com
Web Site: www.stagewest.org
Officers:
    President: Bronson Davis
    Secretary: Maggie Knapp
    Treasurer: Nelson Claytor
    Immediate Past President: Guy Manning
    Vice-President: Larry Anfin
Management:
    Director:
    Executive Director: Jerry Russell
    Co-Producing Director: Jim Covault
    Technical Director and Facilities M: Jason Domm
    Co-Producing Director: Dana Schultes

THEATRE / Texas

Founded: 1979
Specialized Field: Musical; Comedy; Classic; Contemporary
Status: Non-Profit, Professional
Paid Staff: 10
Paid Artists: 35

3968
ALLIED THEATRE GROUP/STAGE WEST
821/823 W. Vickery Blvd.
Fort Worth, TX 76104
Phone: 817-924-9454
Fax: 817-926-8650
e-mail: stagewest@gbronline.com
Web Site: www.stagewest.org
Officers:
  President: Guy Manning
Management:
  Producing Artistic Director: Jim Covault
  Administrative Director: Jenae Yerger
  Literary Associate: Natalie Gaupp
  Technical Director and Facilities M: Jason Domm
  Co-Producing Director: Dana Schultes
Mission: To produce a minimum of six major productions annually, including some musicals; to offer a broad range of works from classical to new and contemporary.
Utilizes: Guest Companies; Singers
Founded: 1979
Specialized Field: Drama; Musical
Status: Professional; Nonprofit
Paid Staff: 10
Volunteer Staff: 100
Non-paid Artists: 20
Income Sources: Actors' Equity Association; Theatre Communications Group; Texas Nonprofit Theatre; Live Theatre League of Tarrant County; Arts Council of Fort Worth & Tarrant County
Performs At: Stage West
Facility Category: Theatre-in-the-Round
Seating Capacity: 200
Year Remodeled: 1993
Organization Type: Performing

3969
CASA MANANA MUSICALS
3101 West Lancaster Avenue
Fort Worth, TX 76107
Phone: 817-332-2272
Fax: 817-332-5711
Web Site: www.casamanana.org
Officers:
  Immediate Past Chairman: Taylor Gandy
  Past-Chairman: Colby Siratt
  Secretary: Daniel Washburn
  Treasurer: Connie Fagg
  Vice Chair, Production Committee: Denise Mullins
  Vice Chair, Board Cultivation Commi: Ramsay Slugg
  Vice Chair, Development Committee: Karen Denney
  Vice Chair, Education & Outreach: Andrea Pavell
  Vice Chair, Strategic Planning Comm: Colby Don Siratt
Management:
  Producer: Denton Yockey
  Associate Producer: Scott Galbraith
Utilizes: Actors; AEA Actors; Choreographers; Dancers; Designers; Educators; Five Seasonal Concerts; Guest Artists; Guest Companies; Guest Conductors; Guest Designers; Instructors; Local Artists; Multimedia; Original Music Scores; Resident Professionals; Sign Language Translators; Singers; Soloists; Student Interns; Special Technical Talent; Theatre Companies
Founded: 1958
Specialized Field: Musical; Comedy; Youth Theater; Contemporary
Status: Non-Profit, Professional
Paid Staff: 20
Paid Artists: 100
Performs At: Casa Manana Theatre; Bass Performance Hall
Affiliations: National Alliance for Musical Theatre; Live Theatre League of Tarrant County; Texas Nonprofit Theatre Association
Organization Type: Performing; Touring; Resident; Educational

3970
CASA MANANA PLAYHOUSE
3101 West Lancaster Avenue
Fort Worth, TX 76107
Phone: 817-332-2272
Fax: 817-332-5711
Web Site: www.casamanana.org
Officers:
  Chairman: Taylor Gandy
  Past-Chairman: Colby Siratt
  Secretary: Glen Hahn
  Treasurer: Henry Borbolla, III
  Vice Chair, Production Committee: Michael Sharpe
Management:
  Executive Producer: Wally Jones
  Business Manager: Leslie Bradford
  Director of Development: Victor Mashburn
Mission: To present plays for children Fridays and Saturday with special weekday performances for local schools; to present Casa Kids, 15 children who provide free performances for area civic and nonprofit organizations.
Utilizes: Guest Companies
Founded: 1962
Specialized Field: Musical; Children's Theater
Status: Professional; Nonprofit
Income Sources: International Association of Theatre for Children and Youth; Actors' Equity Association; American Federation of Musicians
Performs At: Casa Manana Theatre
Organization Type: Performing; Resident; Educational

3971
CIRCLE THEATRE
230 West Fourth Street
PO Box 470456
Fort Worth, TX 76147-0456
Mailing Address: P.O. Box 470456, Fort Worth, TX 76147
Phone: 817-921-3040
Fax: 817-877-3536
e-mail: plays@circletheatre.com
Web Site: www.circletheatre.com
Officers:
  President: Joan Kline
  VP: Robert I Fenandez
  VP: Tom Gaffney
  Corresponding Secretary: Kim Kirk
  Recording Secretary: Sherry Jackson
  Treasurer: Marilyn Austin
Management:
  Executive Director: Rose Pearson
  Managing Director: Bill Newberry
  Director Public Relations/Marketing: Carlo Cuesta
  Associate Producer: Tim Long
Mission: Our mission is the advocacy of contemporary plays rarely seen in this community. We are commited to presenting professional, innovative theatre in an intimate setting.
Utilizes: Singers
Founded: 1981
Specialized Field: Drama; Classic
Status: Semi-Professional; Nonprofit
Organization Type: Performing; Resident

3972
FORT WORTH THEATRE
4401 Trail, Ake Drive
Fort Worth, TX 76109
Phone: 817-921-5300
Web Site: fwtheatre.homestead.com
Management:
  Artistic Director: William Garber
  Administrative Director: Brynn Bristol
Mission: To offer quality theatre to Fort Worth; to provide an outlet for talented amateurs.
Utilizes: Guest Companies
Founded: 1955
Specialized Field: Community Theater
Status: Non-Professional; Nonprofit
Performs At: William Edrington Scott Theatre
Organization Type: Performing; Resident

3973
HIP POCKET THEATRE
1950 Silver Creek Road
Fort Worth, TX 76108
Mailing Address: P.O. Box 136758 Fort Worth, TX 76136
Phone: 817-246-9775
Fax: 817-246-5651
e-mail: hpt@hippocket.org
Web Site: www.hippocket.org
Officers:
  President: Judy Clark
  President Elect: Ralph Watterson
  Secretary: Judy Golden
  Treasurer: Jessica Weaver
Management:
  Executive Director: Diana Simons
  Artistic Director: Johnny Simons
Mission: Showcasing the original work of regional composers and playwrights, as well as works rarely seen in this area.
Utilizes: Guest Companies; Singers
Founded: 1977
Specialized Field: Musical; Comedy; Puppet; Classic; Contemporary
Status: Non-Profit, Non-Professional
Paid Staff: 4
Volunteer Staff: 2
Paid Artists: 2
Non-paid Artists: 30
Budget: $165,000
Income Sources: Texas Commission on the Arts; National Endowment
Performs At: Oak Acres Amphitheatre
Affiliations: Live Theatre League Arts Council at Fort Worth
Facility Category: Outdoor Amphitheatre
Type of Stage: Multi-leveled tree house
Seating Capacity: 175
Year Built: 1978
Rental Contact: Diene Simons
Organization Type: Performing; Touring; Resident; Educational

THEATRE / Texas

3974
JUBILEE THEATRE
506 Main Street
Fort Worth, TX 76102
Phone: 817-338-4204
Fax: 817-338-4604
Web Site: jubileetheatre.org
Officers:
   President: Barbara Cager
   Vice President: Monroe Howard
   Treasurer: Michael Cinati
   Secretary: Kimberly Johnson
Management:
   Managing Director: Glenda Thompson
   Artistic Director: Tre Garrett
   Marketing And Operations Manager: David Hadlock
Mission: To create and present theatrical works which reflect the African-American experience.
Founded: 1981
Status: Nonprofit

3975
STAGE WEST
821/823 W. Vickery Blvd.
Fort Worth, TX 76104
Phone: 817-735-9995
Fax: 817-735-4065
e-mail: stgwest@ix.netcom.com
Web Site: www.stagewest.org
Officers:
   VP: Bronson Davis
   Treasurer: Nelson Claytor
   Immediate Past President: Al Celaya
   Secretary: Maggie Knapp
   Executive Director: Jerry Russel
   Artistic Director: Jim Covault
   Technical Director and Facilities M: Jason Domm
   Co-Producing Director: Dana Schultes
Mission: To provide Shakespeare-in-the-Park for Fort Worth residents at no cost.
Utilizes: Actors; AEA Actors; Five Seasonal Concerts; Guest Accompanists; Guest Designers; Guest Instructors; Guest Lecturers; Guest Musical Directors; Student Interns
Founded: 1979
Specialized Field: Drama; Musical
Status: Non-Profit, Professional
Paid Staff: 12
Paid Artists: 35
Income Sources: Texas Christian University; City of Fort Worth
Performs At: Indoor venue; Outdoor venue
Annual Attendance: 125,000
Facility Category: Park Site Fort Worth's Trinity Park, Stagewest
Rental Contact: Managing Director Mark Waltz
Organization Type: Performing; Touring

3976
GALVESTON OUTDOOR MUSICALS
PO Box 5253
Galveston, TX 77554
Phone: 409-737-1744
Fax: 409-737-2033
Founded: 1977
Specialized Field: Musical; Outdoor Theater
Status: Nonprofit
Season: June - August
Type of Stage: Amphitheatre
Stage Dimensions: 150' x 150'
Seating Capacity: 1766

3977
GARLAND CIVIC THEATRE
108 N 6th Street
Garland, TX 75040
Phone: 972-485-8884
Fax: 214-553-0081
Web Site: http://www.garlandcivictheatre.org/index.php
Management:
   Producing Director: James Weir
   Administrative Director: Linda White
   Technical Director: Dwight Swanson
Mission: To offer quality entertainment to our audiences; to provide space for community performers; to advance theatre.
Founded: 1967
Specialized Field: Musical; Community Theater
Status: Semi-Professional; Nonprofit
Income Sources: Texas Nonprofit Theatre; Theatre Communications Group
Performs At: Garland Center for the Performing Arts
Organization Type: Performing; Resident

3978
SOMERVELL COUNTY EXPO CENTER
202 Bo Gibbs Boulevard
PO Box 8
Glen Rose, TX 76043
Phone: 254-897-4509
Fax: 254-897-7713
e-mail: elaine.mcpeek@co.somervell.tx.us
Web Site: www.glenroseexpo.org
Management:
   Public Events Director: Frank Abbott
   Business Office Manager: Elaine Bell
   Operations Manager: Mike Summers
   Office Clerk III: Cheri Buccino
   Crew Supervisor: Francisco Tovar
Founded: 1989
Specialized Field: Musical; Outdoor Theater
Status: For-Profit, Non-Professional
Paid Staff: 12
Paid Artists: 3
Season: June - October
Type of Stage: Amphitheatre
Stage Dimensions: 130' x 64'
Seating Capacity: 3200

3979
GRANBURY OPERA HOUSE THEATRE
133 East Pearl St.
Granbury, TX 76048
Phone: 817-579-0952
Fax: 817-579-5529
Toll-free: 866-572-0881
e-mail: granburytheatrecompany@gmail.com
Web Site: www.granburyoperahouse.org
Management:
   Managing Director And Producer: Marty Van Kleeck
   Technical Director: Adam Puglielli
   Executive Director: Kent Whites
   General Manager: Jake Jacobs
Founded: 1975
Specialized Field: Musical; Classic
Status: Nonprofit
Income Sources: Box Office; Texas Commission for the Arts Grant; Individual Donors
Season: Year round
Performs At: Granbury Opera House
Annual Attendance: 63,000
Organization Type: Performing; Educational

3980
A.D. PLAYERS
2710 W Alabama Street
Houston, TX 77098
Phone: 713-526-2721
Fax: 713-439-0905
e-mail: boxoffice@adplayers.org
Web Site: www.adplayers.org
Officers:
   Chairman: Howard C. Lee
Management:
   Founder/Artistic Director: Jeannette Clift George
   Managing Director: Ric Hodgin, ric@adplayers.org
   Technical Director: Mark A Lewis, makr@adplayers.org
   Director of Development: Irby Bair
   Children's Theater Director: Kevin Dean
   Production Stage Manager: Hannah Smith
   Business Manager: Kevin Fisher
   Scheduling Coordinator: Chip Simmons
   Operations Manager: Craig Griffin
Mission: A professional theatre ministry communicating through various mediums under the creative signature of God.
Utilizes: Actors; AEA Actors; Designers; Five Seasonal Concerts; Grant Writers; Guest Accompanists; Guest Lecturers; High School Drama; Resident Artists; Resident Companies; Resident Professionals; Sign Language Translators; Soloists; Theatre Companies
Founded: 1967
Specialized Field: Musical; Comedy; Classic; Contemporary
Status: Non-Profit, Professional
Paid Staff: 45
Paid Artists: 40
Income Sources: Texas Nonprofit Theatre; Theatre Communications Group; Houston Theatre Association; Cultural Arts Council of Houston
Season: September - August
Performs At: Grave Theatre; Rotunda Theater
Type of Stage: Proscenium; Arena; Round
Seating Capacity: 220; 149
Organization Type: Performing; Touring; Resident; Educational

3981
ACTORS THEATRE OF HOUSTON
2506 South Blvd
Houston, TX 77098
Phone: 713-529-6606
e-mail: kgeorgeb@flash.net
Web Site: www.houstontheatre.com
Management:
   Producing Director: Chris Wilson
Founded: 1986
Specialized Field: Drama; Comedy; Theater Workshops

3982
ALLEY THEATRE
615 Texas Avenue
Houston, TX 77002
Phone: 713-220-5700
Fax: 713-222-6542
e-mail: webmaster@alleytheatre.org
Web Site: www.alleytheatre.org
Management:
   Artistic Director: Gregory Boyd
   Managing Director: Dean R. Gladden
   Associate Director: James Black
   Associate Director/Design: Kevin Rigdon
   Associate Literary Manager & Dramat: Jacey Little

Artistic Coordinator/Production Sta: Christa Bean
General Manager: Ten Eyck Swackhamer
Associate General Manager: Kate Morrow
Controller: Kay Ross
Mission: The chief aims of the Alley, under the direction of Artistic Director Gregory Boyd and Managing Director Dean Gladden are to present a wide range of plays, embracing classic, new and neglected plays, and to produce these plays to the highest standards and to serve the widest audience.
Utilizes: Guest Companies; Singers
Founded: 1947
Specialized Field: Comedy; Contemporary
Status: Non-Profit, Professional
Paid Staff: 80
Income Sources: Sponsors; Corporations
Performs At: Alley Theatre
Affiliations: League of Resident Theatres; Actors' Equity Association; USA; Society for Stage Directors and Choreographers
Seating Capacity: 824; 310
Organization Type: Performing; Touring; Resident; Educational; Sponsoring

3983
CHANNING PLAYERS
PO Box 631363
Houston, TX 77263
Phone: 713-785-9492
Management:
  Artistic Director: Janis Halliday
  Technical Director: Donald Williams
Mission: Producing quality plays.
Utilizes: Singers
Founded: 1955
Specialized Field: Community Theater
Status: Nonprofit
Paid Staff: 50
Income Sources: Cultural Arts Council of Houston; Texas Nonprofit Theatre
Organization Type: Performing; Educational

3984
ENSEMBLE THEATRE
3535 Main Street
Houston, TX 77002
Phone: 713-520-0055
Fax: 713-520-1269
e-mail: jcosley@ensemblehouston.com
Web Site: www.ensemblehouston.org
Officers:
  Chair: Argentina M. James
  VP Operations: Vernon Landers
  Secretary: Alaina R. Benford
  Treasurer: Mary D. Simon
  Assistant Treasurer: Tony Black
Management:
  President: Jackie Phillips
  Executive Director: Jeanette Cosley
  Artistic Director: Eileen J. Morris
  Audience Development / Public Relat: Robert J. Ross
  Events Coordinator: Willda S. Jackson
  Development Director: Kathy Kelley
  Artistic Associate & Director: Teresa White
  Technical Director: Ray Walker
Mission: The Ensemble Theatre is the Southwest's largest African American theatre presenting a season of classic and contemporary works featuring local and national artists.
Utilizes: Guest Companies; Singers
Founded: 1976
Specialized Field: Ethnic Theater
Status: Non-Profit, Professional
Paid Staff: 10
Paid Artists: 115
Performs At: The Ensemble Theatre
Organization Type: Performing; Touring; Resident; Educational

3985
HOUSTON SHAKESPEARE FESTIVAL
University of Houston
School of Theatre and Dancem, 133 CWM
Houston, TX 77204-4016
Phone: 713-743-3003
Fax: 713-749-1420
Web Site: www.houstonfestivalscompany.com
Officers:
  President: Annabella Sahakian
  Vice President: Bob Bourdeaux
Management:
  Producing Director: Sidney L Berger
  Adminstrative Director: Jerry Aven
Mission: To provide classical theater at no cost to citizens of Houston and surrounding areas.
Founded: 1975
Specialized Field: Shakespeare; Classic
Status: Professional; Nonprofit
Income Sources: University of Houston
Performs At: Miller Outdoor Theatre
Organization Type: Performing

3986
MAIN STREET THEATER
2540 Times Boulevard
Houston, TX 77005
Phone: 713-524-3622
Fax: 713-524-3977
e-mail: nstinfo@mainstreettheatre.com
Web Site: www.mainstreettheater.com
Officers:
  President: Kevin Dubose
  Vice President: John M. Cornwell
  Secretary: Victoria Benson Schutter
Management:
  Executive Artistic Director: Rebecca Greene Udden
  Production Manager: Andrew Ruthven
  Managing Director: Robbye Floyd-Archibald
  Marketing Associate: Misty Johnson
  Director Education: Jonathan Gonzalez
  Technical Director: Mark Roberts
  Capital Campaign Director: Joe Kirkendall
  Business Manager: Angela Harris-Cannizzo
  Assistant Director of Education: Lauren Evans
Mission: To offer a lively year-round repertory of classic and contemporary plays for audiences of all ages; to provide a much-needed showcase for Houston theatre professionals. Main Street Theatre is a member of Theatre Communications Group, the national organization of professional not-for-profit theatres and produces under an agreement with Actors' Equity Association, the union of professional actors.
Founded: 1975
Specialized Field: Classic; Contemporary
Status: Professional; Semi-Professional; Non-Professional
Organization Type: Performing; Touring; Resident

3987
STAGES REPERTORY THEATRE
3201 Allen Parkway
Suite 101
Houston, TX 77019
Phone: 713-527-0220
Fax: 713-527-8669
e-mail: kmclaughlin@stagestheatre.com
Web Site: www.stagestheatre.com
Management:
  Producing Artistic Director: Kenn McLaughlin
  Properties Master: Jodi Bobrovsky
  Master Carpenter: Joseph Blanchard
  Marketing Director: Lise Bohn
  Associate Artistic Director: Josh Morrison
  Artistic Associate: Mitchell Greco
  Administrative Director: Todd Molesky
  Marketing Director: Lise Bohn
  Controller: Bob Canino
Mission: To present plays that are challenging to a developing company and are of social value and that set a standard of excellence.
Utilizes: Guest Companies; Singers; Students
Founded: 1978
Specialized Field: Drama; New Plays
Status: Professional; Nonprofit
Paid Staff: 27
Volunteer Staff: 2
Paid Artists: 128
Budget: $1.5 million
Income Sources: Ticket Sales; Private Foundations; Corparations; Local and State Funding
Season: Year round
Performs At: Arena Theatre; Thrust Theatre
Affiliations: Actors' Equity Association; TCG; ASSITJ
Annual Attendance: 60,000
Facility Category: Dual Stages
Stage Dimensions: 19'x 20'; 23'x 30'
Seating Capacity: 229;171
Year Built: 1933
Year Remodeled: 1983
Rental Contact: Managing Director Thomas M. Smith
Organization Type: Performing; Touring; Resident; Educational; Sponsoring

3988
TALENTO BILINGUE DE HOUSTON
333 S Jenson
Houston, TX 77003
Phone: 713-222-1213
Fax: 713-222-1426
e-mail: info@tbhcenter.org
Web Site: www.tbhcenter.org
Officers:
  Past Chair: Rogelio Marroquin
  Chair: Saul Valentin
  Secretary: Shelia Briones
  Finance Chair: Ricardo Fernandez
  Governance Chair: Alejandro Colom
  Chair-Elect: Dan Arguijo
Management:
  Director: Joeseph Cooper
  Artistic Director: Jorge Pina
  Technical Director: Corey Forehand
  Publicity: Jim Bratton
  Special Events: Rick Camargo
  Program Manager: Fernando Perez
  Administrative Assistant : Viri Maldonado
  Director of Operations : Javier Perez
  Facilities Manager : Alex Hernandez
Mission: A non-profit cultural and educational organization.
Utilizes: Guest Companies
Founded: 1977
Specialized Field: Spanish Language Company; Multi-Cultural; Ethnic Theater
Status: Non-Profit, Professional
Paid Staff: 3
Paid Artists: 40

THEATRE / Texas

Organization Type: Performing; Touring; Educational; Sponsoring

3989
THEATRE SUBURBIA
4106 Way Out West Dr
Suite N
Houston, TX 77092
Mailing Address: PO Box 920518, Houston, TX 77292-0518
Phone: 713-682-3525
e-mail: info@theatresuburbia.org
Web Site: www.theatresuburbia.com
Officers:
　President: Elvin Moriarty
　Secretary: Judith Mallernee
　Treasurer: Marilyn Faulkner
Management:
　General Manager: Doris Merten
　Technical Director: Darrell Krause
Mission: To provide the public with quality entertainment consisting of light comedy through heavy drama; to achieve recognition as a producer of the finest quality original scripts.
Utilizes: Guest Companies
Founded: 1960
Specialized Field: Light Theater; Drama
Status: Non-Professional; Nonprofit
Performs At: Theatre Suburbia
Organization Type: Performing

3990
THEATRE UNDER THE STARS
800 Bagby
Suite 200
Houston, TX 77002-2525
Phone: 713-558-2600
Fax: 713-558-2650
e-mail: tuts@tuts.com
Web Site: www.tuts.com
Officers:
　Chairperson: C. Gregory Harper
　Chairperson- Elect: Amy G. Pierce
　President/CEO: John C. Breckenridge
　Vice Chairperson: Robert G. Gwin
　Vice Chairperson: Bart McAndrews
　Vice Chairperson: Jeffrey T. Stadler
　Vice Chairperson: Randall D. Stilley
　Secretary: Franklin D. R. Jones, Jr.
　Treasurer: Sigmund L. Cornelius
Management:
　Executive Director and Founder: Frank M Young
　Producing Director: John Holly
　Managing Director: Cissy Segall
　General Manager: Vivian Flynn
　Artistic Director: Bruce Lumpkin
　Director, Administration and Educat: Bob Lawson
　Director, Finance : Joel Szulc
　Manager, Administration: Patrick Plunk
　Executive Assistant to the Presiden: Journey Bova
Mission: To present light opera regionally as well as on tour; to operate a school for aspiring artists; to foster the development of new musical theatre works.
Specialized Field: Musical
Status: Professional; Nonprofit
Performs At: The Music Hall
Organization Type: Performing; Touring; Educational

3991
HILL COUNTRY ARTS FOUNDATION/POINT THEATRE
120 Point Theatre Road South
Ingram, TX 78025
Mailing Address: PO Box 1169 Ingram, TX 78025
Phone: 830-367-5121
Fax: 830-367-4332
Toll-free: 800-459-4223
e-mail: davidc@hcaf.com
Web Site: www.hcaf.com
Officers:
　President: Mark Jackson
　Vice President - Visual Arts: Mary Kathryn Collins
　Vice President - Theatre: Ann Galland
　Secretary: Kari Short
　Treasurer: Barbara von Brandt-Siemers
Management:
　Executive Director: Katharine Schaafs
　Business Manager: Leddy Gonzalez
　Administrative Assistant/Developmen: Rosanne Thrall
　Artistic Director: Lorenzo Nichols
　Technical Director: Bobby Dale Sands
　Visual Arts Director/ Development D: Rosanne Thrall
　Visual Arts Coordinator: Phyllis Garey
　President: David Howard
　Vice Presiden: Julie Sentell
Mission: To sustain a center for the visual and performing arts that promotes education and a public interest in the arts.
Utilizes: Guest Artists; Guest Companies
Founded: 1958
Specialized Field: Drama; Musical
Status: Non-Profit, Non-Professional
Paid Staff: 6
Volunteer Staff: 400
Income Sources: Texas Nonprofit Theatre; Texas Educators Theatre Association
Performs At: Smith-Ritch Point Theater
Affiliations: Hill Country Arts Foundation
Type of Stage: Outside Amphitheater; Pavilion
Seating Capacity: 722; 140
Organization Type: Performing; Touring; Educational

3992
IRVING COMMUNITY THEATER
2333 W Rochelle Rd
Irving, TX 75062
Phone: 972-594-6104
e-mail: info@irvingtheatre.org
Web Site: www.irvingtheatre.org
Mission: To promote the cultural, educational, and literary advancement of the residents of Irving and surrounding areas.
Utilizes: Guest Companies
Founded: 1971
Specialized Field: Musical; Comedy; Community Theater
Status: Non-Profit, Non-Professional
Paid Staff: 1
Income Sources: Cultural Affairs Council
Performs At: Irving Center for Cultural Arts
Organization Type: Performing; Resident

3993
TEXAS SHAKESPEARE FESTIVAL
1100 Broadway
Kilgore, TX 75662
Mailing Address: PO Box 2788, Kilgore, TX 75663
Phone: 903-983-8117
Fax: 903-983-8124
e-mail: info@texasshakespeare.com
Web Site: www.texasshakespeare.com
Officers:
　Founder: Raymond Caldwell
Management:
　Artistic Director: Raymond Caldwell
　Managing Director: John Dodd
Mission: To provide quality professional productions for East Texas of dramatic masterpieces, employing professional theatre artists from throughout the nation.
Founded: 1986
Specialized Field: Musical; Classic; Contemporary
Status: Non-Profit, Professional
Paid Staff: 2
Paid Artists: 75
Budget: $560,000
Income Sources: Kilgore College; TSF Foundation; City Of Kilgore; Grants; Donations; Ticket Sales
Season: June - July
Performs At: Indoor
Affiliations: S.T.A.A.
Annual Attendance: 8,000
Facility Category: Indoor Facility
Type of Stage: Proscenium
Stage Dimensions: 30' x 40'
Seating Capacity: 200
Year Built: 1966
Year Remodeled: 2008

3994
VIVE LES ARTS THEATRE
3401 South WS Young Drive
PO Box 10657
Killeen, TX 76547
Phone: 254-526-9090
Fax: 254-526-6906
e-mail: vh@desklink.com
Web Site: www.vlakilleen.org
Officers:
　Chairman: Cyd West
　1st Vice Chairman: Leslie Gilmore
　1st Vice Chairman: John Gilmore
　2nd Vice Chairman: David Bryan
　2nd Vice Chairman: Nancy Bryan
　Secretary: Donna Connell
　Secretary: Mitch Connell
　Treasurer: Summer Heidtbrink
　Treasurer: Barry Heidtbrink
Management:
　Director: Eric Shephard
　Administrative Director: Tami Young
　Technical Director: John Arceneaux
　Children's Theatre Director: Amy Ball
　Executive Director: Jenny Davis
　Administrative Assistants: Samantha Udeagha
Mission: To provide artistic and cultural activities in the areas of Killeen, Fort Hood, Copperas Cove and Harker Heights.
Utilizes: Guest Artists; Singers
Founded: 1976
Specialized Field: Musical; Community Theater; Children's Theater
Status: Professional; Non-Professional; Nonprofit
Paid Staff: 4
Income Sources: City of Killeen Hotel Motel Occupancy Tax; Meadows Foundation
Performs At: Vive Les Arts Center for the Arts
Type of Stage: Thrust
Seating Capacity: 400
Year Built: 1991
Rental Contact: Tam Young

Organization Type: Performing; Touring; Sponsoring

3995
GASLIGHT BAKER THEATRE
216 South Main Street
Lockhart, TX 78644
Mailing Address: P.O. Box 1152, Lockhart, TX 78644
Phone: 512-376-5653
e-mail: info@gaslightbakertheatre.org
Web Site: gaslightbakertheatre.org
Officers:
   President: John Lairsen
   Vice President: Tysha Calhoun
Management:
   Artistic Director: David Schneider
Status: Nonprofit

3996
MESQUITE COMMUNITY THEATRE
1527 N Galleway Ave.
Mesquite, TX 75149
Mailing Address: PO Box 870431 Mesquite, TX 75187-0431
Phone: 972-216-8126
e-mail: info@mesquitecommunitytheatre.com
Web Site: www.mctweb.org
Officers:
   Chairman: Scott Croy
   Vice-Chairman: Linda Iwanski
   Secretary: Jan Summar
   Treasurer: Doug Luke
Mission: To offer quality live theatre to the Mesquite Community.
Utilizes: Guest Companies; Singers
Founded: 1983
Specialized Field: Community Theater
Status: Professional; Semi-Professional; Nonprofit
Performs At: East Ridge Park Christian Church
Type of Stage: Black Box
Seating Capacity: 492
Year Built: 1995
Organization Type: Performing

3997
LAMP-LITE THEATER
4128 Old Tyler Road
Nacogdoches, TX 75964
Mailing Address: P O Box 630446, Nacogdoches, TX 75963-0446
Phone: 936-564-8300
e-mail: info@lamplitetheatre.org
Web Site: www.lamplitetheatre.org
Management:
   Director: Sarah McMullan
Mission: To provide quality live theatre for the East Texas region; to offer a dynamic creative experience for actors and related artists.
Founded: 1971
Specialized Field: Musical; Community Theater
Status: Non-Professional; Nonprofit
Volunteer Staff: 120
Income Sources: Ticket sales
Performs At: Lamp-Lite Theater
Annual Attendance: 1,500
Seating Capacity: 237
Year Built: 1979
Organization Type: Performing; Touring; Educational

3998
GLOBE OF THE GREAT SOUTHWEST THEATRE
2308 Shakespeare Road
Odessa, TX 79761
Phone: 915-332-1586
Fax: 915-332-1587
e-mail: hamlet@globesw.org
Web Site: www.globesw.org
Officers:
   President: G William Fowler
   Treasurer: La Doyce Lambert
   Secretary: Jerri Nickel
Management:
   Artistic Director: Anthony Ridley
   General Manager: Ann Wilson
Mission: To provide Shakespearean and classical plays that are educational; to present contemporary and religious plays and musicals; to present an annual Shakespeare Festival; to advance the enjoyment, appreciation and study of great literature; to make available the Globe Building and grounds to the community for all the arts.
Utilizes: Actors; Artists-in-Residence; Commissioned Music; Guest Companies; Local Artists; Multimedia; Original Music Scores; Singers
Founded: 1958
Specialized Field: Community Theater; Shakespeare
Status: Professional; Nonprofit
Paid Staff: 4
Volunteer Staff: 100
Paid Artists: 6
Non-paid Artists: 150
Income Sources: Grants; Patron Membership Ffees; Ssponsorships
Performs At: An authentic replica of an Elizabethan Theatre
Affiliations: Shakespeare Theatre Association of America; Texas Nonprofit Theatres
Annual Attendance: 15,000
Facility Category: Elizabethan Theatre
Type of Stage: Thrust
Seating Capacity: 400
Year Built: 1968
Rental Contact: Anthony Ridley
Organization Type: Performing; Educational

3999
PERMIAN PLAYHOUSE OF ODESSA
310 W 42nd Street
PO Box 13374
Odessa, TX 79764
Phone: 432-550-5456
Fax: 915-362-2678
e-mail: permianplay@yahoo.com
Web Site: www.permianplayhouse.com
Officers:
   Board President: Vicki Gomez
   First VP: Melissa Hirsch
   Second VP: Vonnie Downey
Management:
   Director: Brenda Denton
   Educational Director: Laura Bond
Mission: To provide high quality, culturally diverse theatrical experiences and educational programs to enrich the lives of the people in the Permian Basin.
Utilizes: Guest Artists; Guest Companies; Singers
Founded: 1939
Specialized Field: Community Theater
Status: Non-Profit
Paid Staff: 5
Volunteer Staff: 25
Income Sources: American Association of Community Theatres; Southwest Theatre Association; Texas Nonprofit Theater; Season Membership; Ticket Sales
Performs At: Permian Playhouse of Odessa
Facility Category: Community Theatre
Seating Capacity: 400
Year Built: 1966
Organization Type: Performing; Touring; Educational

4000
GUADALUPE CULTURAL ARTS CENTER
1300 Guadalupe Street
San Antonio, TX 78207
Phone: 210-271-3151
Fax: 210-271-3480
e-mail: mariat@guadalupeculturalarts.org
Web Site: www.guadalupeculturalarts.org
Officers:
   Chairman: Hector Fransto
Management:
   Managing Director: Leroy Martinez
Mission: To present and promote Mexican-American arts; to facilitate a deeper knowledge and appreciation of Native American and Latino cultures as well as their artistic expressions.
Utilizes: Actors; Artists-in-Residence; Collaborating Artists; Commissioned Music; Curators; Dancers; Filmmakers; Fine Artists; Five Seasonal Concerts; Guest Artists; Guest Companies; Guest Conductors; Guest Designers; Guest Lecturers; Guest Soloists; Guest Teachers; High School Drama; Local Artists; Multimedia; Organization Contracts; Original Music Scores; Performance Artists; Playwrights; Touring Companies
Founded: 1979
Specialized Field: Multi-Media
Status: Non-Profit, Professional
Paid Staff: 18
Paid Artists: 25
Budget: $1,500,000
Income Sources: Corporations; Foundations; City & Federal funding
Performs At: Guadalupe Theater
Annual Attendance: 190,000
Facility Category: Theater; Gallery
Seating Capacity: 372
Year Built: 1940
Year Remodeled: 1984
Organization Type: Performing; Touring; Resident; Educational; Sponsoring; Presenting
Resident Groups: Grupo Animo Youth Theatre; Folk Flamenco Dance Company

4001
JUMP-START PERFORMANCE COMPANY
710 Fredericksburg Road
San Antonio, TX 78201
Phone: 210-227-5867
Fax: 210-322-2231
e-mail: info@jump-start.org
Web Site: www.jump-start.org
Officers:
   President: Michele Brinkley
   Treasurer: Billy Mu¤oz
   Secretary: Sandy Dunn
   Vice President: Roland Mazuca
Management:
   Education Director: S T Shimi
   Financial Manager: Maria Ayala
   Marketing Director: Erik Bosse
   Office Manager: Chayo Zaldjvar
   Technical Director: Felice Garcia
Mission: Committed to the creation of art that is a lasting voice of many diverse cultures.
Utilizes: Guest Companies
Founded: 1985
Specialized Field: Contemporary
Status: Non-Profit, Professional
Paid Staff: 9
Paid Artists: 20

THEATRE / Utah

Income Sources: American Association of Community Theatres; Rural Organization of Theaters South
Performs At: Jump-Start Theater
Organization Type: Performing; Touring; Resident; Educational; Sponsoring; Commissioning

4002
MAGIK THEATRE
420 S Alamo St.
San Antonio, TX 78205
Phone: 210-227-2751
Fax: 210-227-2753
e-mail: aimee@magiktheatre.org
Web Site: www.magiktheatre.org
  President: Alan Petlin
  Vice President: John Heard
Management:
  Director: Alan Petlin
  Music Director: Ricky Hernandez
  Operations Manager: David Ankrom
  Grants Manager: Jon Blanks
  Academy Director: Dave Cortez
  Academy Director: Angela Hoeffler
  Costume Manager: Greg Hinojosa
Mission: To promote literacy and learning, strengthen family life; to offer quality and affordable live theatrical presentations for the entire community and create tomorrow's live theater audience.
Utilizes: Actors; Artists-in-Residence; Collaborations; Dancers; Guest Artists; Guest Conductors; Guild Activities; Local Artists; Multi Collaborations; Multimedia; Original Music Scores; Performance Artists; Resident Artists; Resident Professionals; Sign Language Translators; Touring Companies; Visual Arts
Founded: 1984
Specialized Field: Children's Theater
Status: Non-Profit, Professional
Paid Staff: 15
Paid Artists: 11
Budget: $900,000
Income Sources: Box Office; Classes; Tours; Contributed Income
Performs At: Theatre
Affiliations: ASSITES/USA; SATCO; TNT, ATHE
Annual Attendance: 155,000
Facility Category: Theatre
Type of Stage: Thrust
Stage Dimensions: 30'x42'
Seating Capacity: 600
Year Built: 1899
Year Remodeled: 1939
Rental Contact: Operations Manager David Ankrom
Resident Groups: Magik Theatre Company

4003
SAN PEDRO PLAYHOUSE
800 West Ashby Place
PO Box 12356
San Antonio, TX 78212
Mailing Address: PO Box 12356, San Antonio, TX 78212
Phone: 210-733-7258
Fax: 210-734-2651
e-mail: info@theplayhousesa.org
Web Site: www.sanpedroplayhouse.com
Officers:
  President: Janet Nevenschwander
  1st VP: Joe Medina
  Second VP: Rickard Archer
  Secretary: Thomas W. Nyman
  Treasurer: Natalie Luna, CPA, CFE
Management:
  President & CEO: Asia Ciaravino
  Executive Director: Diann Sneed
  Artistic Director: Frank Latson
  Education Director: Alicia Tafoya
  Technical Director: Alfy Valdez
Mission: Literary and educational community theatre.
Utilizes: Actors; Choreographers; Collaborating Artists; Dancers; Designers; Educators; Five Seasonal Concerts; Grant Writers; Guest Accompanists; Guest Artists; Guest Companies; Guest Conductors; Guest Designers; Guest Directors; Guest Ensembles; Guest Instructors; Guest Lecturers; Guest Musical Directors; Guest Musicians; Guest Soloists; Guest Speakers; Guest Teachers; High School Drama; Instructors; Local Artists; Local Unknown Artists; Multimedia; Music; Original Music Scores; Performance Artists; Resident Professionals; Selected Students; Sign Language Translators; Singers; Soloists; Student Interns
Founded: 1912
Specialized Field: Musical; Comedy
Status: Non-Profit, Professional
Paid Staff: 8
Budget: $450,000
Income Sources: Private Donations; Business Donations
Annual Attendance: 35,000
Type of Stage: Proscenium; Thrust
Seating Capacity: 400; 60
Year Built: 1929
Year Remodeled: 2000
Rental Contact: Yvette Oakes
Organization Type: Performing; Educational

4004
TEMPLE CIVIC THEATRE
2413 South 13th Street
Temple, TX 76504
Phone: 254-778-4751
Fax: 254-778-4980
e-mail: tct@artstemple.com
Web Site: www.artstemple.com
Officers:
  President: Jody Donaldson
  Vice-President, Production: Jacob Duncan
  Vice-President, House & Grounds: Craig Connolly
  Vice-President, Front of House: Chris Ling
  Secretary: Natasha Tolleson
  Treasurer: Al Dobos
Management:
  Managing & Artistic Director: Tim Campbell
  Technical Director: Dustin Ozment
  General Manager: Aileen Snyder
Mission: To promote community involvement in theatre arts; to offer an outlet for talent in the community.
Utilizes: Guest Companies
Founded: 1965
Specialized Field: Community Theater
Status: Non-Profit, Non-Professional
Paid Staff: 3
Affiliations: Texas Non-Profit Theatre's; Southwest Teatre Association
Organization Type: Performing; Educational

4005
WICHITA FALLS BACKDOOR PLAYERS
501 Indiana Ave.
PO Box 896
Wichita Falls, TX 76307
Mailing Address: P.O. Box 896 Wichita Falls, Texas 76307
Phone: 940-322-5000
Fax: 940-322-8167
e-mail: backdoor1@wf.net
Web Site: www.backdoortheatre.org
Management:
  General Manager: Weldon Fraker
  Managing Artistic Director: Linda Bates
  Executive Director: Gail Smith
Mission: To offer participation in all areas of theatre to anyone interested regardless of experience.
Utilizes: Actors; Choreographers; Collaborating Artists; Designers; Grant Writers; Guest Artists; Guest Companies; Guest Designers; Guild Activities; High School Drama; Local Artists; Performance Artists; Singers
Founded: 1971
Specialized Field: Community Theater
Status: Non-Profit, Professional
Paid Staff: 3
Volunteer Staff: 200
Paid Artists: 3
Non-paid Artists: 20
Organization Type: Performing

Utah

4006
UTAH SHAKESPEAREAN FESTIVAL
351 W Center Street
Cedar City, UT 84720
Phone: 435-586-7880
Fax: 435-865-8003
Toll-free: 800-pla-ytix
e-mail: guestservices@bard.org
Web Site: www.bard.org
Officers:
  Development Director: Jyl L. Shuler
Management:
  Founder and Executive Producer Emer: Fred C. Adams
  Production Manager: Ray Inkel
  Art Director: Philip W. Hermansen
  Associate Artistic Director: JR Sullivan
  Marketing Director: Kami Terry Paul
  Production Manager: Ran Inkel
  Director Plays-in-Progress: George Judy
  Education Director: Michael Don Bahr
  Publications Director: Bruce Lee
Mission: To present six classic and Shakespearean works in repertory each summer and fall.
Utilizes: Actors; Guest Conductors; Guest Designers; Guest Writers; Guild Activities; Performance Artists; Resident Professionals; Student Interns
Founded: 1961
Specialized Field: Shakespeare
Status: Professional; Nonprofit
Paid Staff: 25
Volunteer Staff: 250
Paid Artists: 200
Budget: $5 million
Income Sources: Box Office Sales; Contributed Income; Endowment Income; Merchandise Sales
Season: June - August
Performs At: Adams Memorial Stage; Randall L. Jones Theatre; University Stage
Affiliations: USA; SSD&C; Actors' Equity Association; LORT; TCG
Annual Attendance: 155,000
Facility Category: Outdoor/Indoor
Type of Stage: Thrust; Proscenium
Stage Dimensions: 50Wx30D; 22Hx42Wx25D; 18Hx44Wx39D
Seating Capacity: 887; 769; 981
Year Remodeled: 1989
Rental Contact: Production Manager Ray Inkel
Organization Type: Performing; Resident; Educational

THEATRE / Utah

4007
OLD LYRIC REPERTORY COMPANY
4035 Old Main Hill
Logan, UT 84322-4030
Phone: 435-797-8022
Fax: 435-797-0107
e-mail: craig.jessop@usu.edu
Web Site: arts.usu.edu/lyric/
Management:
   Office Manager: LuAnn Baker
   Marketing Director: Denise Albiston
   Executive Producer: Craig Jessop
   Producer: Kenneth Risch
   Co-Artistic Director: Dennis Hassan
Mission: A professional theater group that produces four repertory shows through the summer months. It also serves as a training ground for advanced theatre students from Utah State University.
Utilizes: Actors; AEA Actors; Designers; Guest Accompanists; Guest Conductors; Guest Designers; Original Music Scores; Resident Professionals; Soloists; Student Interns
Founded: 1967
Specialized Field: Musical; Comedy; Classic; Contemporary; Educational
Status: Non-Profit, Professional
Paid Staff: 35
Paid Artists: 40
Season: May - August
Performs At: Legitimate Theatre
Type of Stage: Proscenium
Stage Dimensions: 22' x 18'
Seating Capacity: 380

4008
OFF BROADWAY THEATRE
272 South Main Street
Salt Lake City, UT 84101
Phone: 801-355-4628
Fax: 801-355-4641
e-mail: sandy@theobt.com
Web Site: www.theobt.com
Management:
   President: Sandy Jensen
   Artistic Director: Eric Jensen
   Owner: Ben Poter
   Owner: Sandy Jensen
Founded: 1994
Specialized Field: Musical; Comedy
Status: For-Profit, Professional
Paid Staff: 3
Volunteer Staff: 8
Paid Artists: 26

4009
PIONEER THEATRE COMPANY
University of Utah
300 South 1400 East
Salt Lake City, UT 84112-0660
Phone: 801-581-6961
Fax: 801-581-5472
e-mail: karen.azenberg@ptc.utah.edu
Web Site: www.pioneertheatre.org
Officers:
   Chairman: Paul M. Durham
   President: Jack A. Buttars
   Vice President for Institutional Ad: Fred Esplin
   Chief Operating Officer: Devon M. Glenn
Management:
   Artistic Director: Karen Azenberg
   Managing Director: Chris Lino
   Business Manager: Jack Mark
   Development Director: Diane Parisi
   Marketing Director: Kwin Peterson
Mission: Dedicated to offering high quality professional theater to Utah as well as the Northwestern United States.
Utilizes: Actors; AEA Actors; Choreographers; Composers-in-Residence; Designers; Fine Artists; Guest Companies; Guest Conductors; Guest Designers; Guest Writers; Instructors; Multimedia; Resident Artists; Resident Professionals; Singers
Founded: 1962
Specialized Field: Musical; Classic; Contemporary
Status: Non-Profit, Professional
Budget: $3.5 million
Income Sources: Ticket Sales; Donations; Grants
Performs At: Pioneer Memorial Theater
Affiliations: Theatre Communications Group
Annual Attendance: 94,000
Type of Stage: Proscenium
Seating Capacity: 932
Year Built: 1962
Year Remodeled: 2000
Organization Type: Performing; Educational

4010
PLAN - B THEATRE COMPANY
138 W 300 S
Salt Lake City, UT 84101
Phone: 801-297-4200
Fax: 801-466-3840
Web Site: www.planbtheatre.org
Officers:
   President: Brian Johnson
   Vice President: Tami Marquardt
   Secretary: Kay Sheen
   Treasurer: Brian Doughty
Management:
   Managing Director: Cheryl Ann Cluff
   Producing Director: Jerry Rapier
   Stage Manager: Jennifer Freed
   Technical Director: Randy Rasmussen
Specialized Field: Comedy; Radio Performances; Puppet

4011
PLAN-B THEATRE COMPANY
138 W 300 S
Salt Lake City, UT 84101
Phone: 801-297-4200
Web Site: planbtheatre.org
Officers:
   President: Brian Johnson
   Vice President: Tami Marquardt
   Secretary: Kay Shean
Management:
   Producing Director: Jerry Rapier
   Managing Director: Cheryln Ann Cluff
Founded: 1991
Specialized Field: Socially Conscious Theatre
Budget: 200,000 annual
Performs At: The Rose Wagner Performing Arts Center

4012
SALT LAKE ACTING COMPANY
168 W 500 N
Salt Lake City, UT 84103
Phone: 801-363-7522
Fax: 801-532-8513
e-mail: info@saltlakeactingcompany.org
Web Site: www.saltlakeactingcompany.org
Officers:
   President: Don Sorensen
   Vice President: Marian Jacobsen
   Secretary: Colleen Sorensen
   Treasurer: Byron Barkley
   Past President: Brett Johnson
Management:
   Executive Producer: Keven Myhre
   Executive Producer: Cynthia Fleming
   Director of Communication: Polly Nevins
   Director of Development: Jennie Nicholls-Smith
   Grants Coordinator: Sasha Solomonov
Mission: Produces seasons of thoughtful, provocative, regional and world premiers; nurtures, supports and develops a community of professional artists; produces and supports emerging playwrights, and makes a significant contribution to the community and to the American theatre field by commissioning, developing and producing new plays.
Utilizes: Guest Companies
Founded: 1970
Specialized Field: Musical; Comedy; Classic; Contemporary
Status: Non-Profit, Professional
Paid Staff: 15
Income Sources: Theatre Communications Group
Performs At: The Salt Lake Acting Company Theater
Organization Type: Performing

4013
SUNDANCE INSTITUTE
PO Box 3630
Salt Lake City, UT 84110
Phone: 801-328-3456
Fax: 801-575-5175
e-mail: institute@sundance.org
Web Site: www.sundance.org
Officers:
   President & Founder: Robert Redford
   Chairman: Walter L. Weisman
   Vice Chairman of the Board: Pat Mitchell
Management:
   Executive Director: Keri Putnam
   Director, Film Music Program: Peter Golub
   Artistic Director: Phillip Himberg
   Managing Director: Jill Miller
   Press Contact: Patrick Hubley
   Co-Managing Director: Sarah Pearce
   Director: John Cooper
   Director: Jennifer Arceneaux
Mission: Dedicated to the development of artists of independent vision and the exhibition of their new work.
Utilizes: Actors; Artists-in-Residence; Choreographers; Collaborating Artists; Collaborations; Composers-in-Residence; Dancers; Designers; Educators; Filmmakers; Guest Accompanists; Guest Companies; Guest Conductors; Guest Designers; Guest Directors; Guest Ensembles; Guest Instructors; Guest Lecturers; Guest Musicians; Guest Teachers; Instructors; Local Artists; Music; Organization Contracts; Original Music Scores; Performance Artists; Poets; Resident Professionals; Selected Students; Sign Language Translators; Soloists; Student Interns
Founded: 1981
Specialized Field: Musical; Comedy; Drama; Young Playwrights; New Plays; Contemporary; Experimental
Status: Non-Profit, Non-Professional
Paid Staff: 30
Budget: $10,600,000
Income Sources: 35% Earned; 65% Contributed Income
Type of Stage: Outdoor; Indoor
Organization Type: Educational

4014
UTAH REPERTORY THEATER COMPANY
130 S 800 W
Salt Lake City, UT 84104

THEATRE / Vermont

Phone: 435-612-0037
e-mail: admin@utahrep.org
Web Site: utahrep.org
Management:
  Artistic Director: Johnny Hebda
  Business Manager: JC Carter
  Marketing Director: Blair Howell
Mission: Independent theater group dedicated to producing dramas and musicals with strong messages that are thought-provoking.
Founded: 2012
Status: Semi-Professional; Nonprofit

4015
SUNDANCE CHILDREN'S THEATRE
Rural Route 3
PO Box 624-D
Sundance, UT 84604
Phone: 801-328-3456
Fax: 801-225-3096
e-mail: institute@sundance.org
Web Site: www.sundance.org
Officers:
  President & Founder: Robert Redford
  Chairman: Walter L. Weisman
  Vice Chairman of the Board: Pat Mitchell
Management:
  Chairman: Walter Weisman
  Executive Director: Keri Putnam
  Artistic Director: Jerry Parch
  Managing Director: Jill Miller
  Director, Film Music Program: Peter Golub
  Co-Managing Director: Sarah Pearce
  Director: John Cooper
  Director: Jennifer Arceneaux
Mission: To develop and produce new plays for young audiences.
Utilizes: Guest Companies
Founded: 1990
Specialized Field: Children's Theater
Status: Non-Profit, Non-Professional
Paid Staff: 65
Organization Type: Performing; Touring

4016
HALE CENTRE THEATRE AT HARMAN HALL
3333 South Decker Lake Drive
2200 W
West Valley City, UT 84119
Phone: 801-984-9000
Fax: 801-984-9009
e-mail: info@halecentretheatre.org
Web Site: www.halecentretheatre.org
Officers:
  Vice President & Chief Administrati: Brent Lange
  Associate Vice President of Develop: Clint Rice
  Associate Vice President of Develop: Quinn Dietlein
  Associate Vice President of Develop: Sara Staheli
Management:
  President, CEO & Executive Producer: Mark Dietlein
  Vice President & Executive Producer: Sally Dietlein
  Education Director: Tracy Evans
  Technical Director: Andrew Barrus
  Costumer Rentals: Amy Glaser
  Office Manager: Tammy Morgan
  Marketing Director/Building Rentals: JaceSon Barrus
Founded: 1985

Specialized Field: Musical; Comedy; Community Theater
Status: Non-Profit, Non-Professional
Paid Staff: 70
Paid Artists: 250
Performs At: Comedies; Musicals
Rental Contact: Marketing Director JaceSon Barrus

Vermont

4017
OLDCASTLE THEATRE COMPANY
Bennington Center for the Arts
331 Main Street
PO Box 1555
Bennington, VT 05201
Phone: 802-447-0564
Fax: 802-442-3704
e-mail: theatre-info@oldcastletheatre.org
Web Site: www.oldcastle.org
Officers:
  President: Charles Putney
  Vice President: Cinda Morse
  Treasurer: Edward Connelly
  Secretary: Melissa Hepler
Management:
  President: Lisa Catapano-Friedman
  Producing Artistic Director: Eric Peterson
  Associate Artistic Director: Richard Howe
  Director Production: Kenneth Mooney
  Director of Marketing and Developme: Elizabeth Stott
  House/Box Office Manager: Jana Lillie
Mission: Resident professional theatre company.
Utilizes: Actors; AEA Actors; Choreographers; Community Talent; Contract Actors; Dancers; Designers; Guest Artists; Guest Companies; Guest Conductors; Guest Designers; Guest Lecturers; Guest Musical Directors; Guild Activities; Local Artists; Music; Original Music Scores; Performance Artists; Resident Artists; Resident Companies; Resident Professionals
Founded: 1972
Specialized Field: New Plays
Status: Non-Profit, Professional
Paid Staff: 3
Paid Artists: 35
Budget: $400,000
Income Sources: Ticket Revenue; Donations; Special Events; Corporate Underwriting; Grants
Season: March - October
Performs At: Bennington Center for the Arts
Affiliations: Actors' Equity Association; Society for Stage Directors and Choreographers
Annual Attendance: 10,000
Facility Category: Auditorium & Art Gallery
Type of Stage: Proscenium
Seating Capacity: 313
Year Built: 1994
Rental Contact: Oldcastle Theatre Company Eric Peterson
Organization Type: Performing; Touring; Resident; Educational; Sponsoring

4018
NATIONAL MARIONETTE THEATRE
350 Putney Road
Brattleboro, VT 05301
Mailing Address: PO Box 1311 Brattleboro, VT 05302-1311
Phone: 802-579-1032
Fax: 802-257-4079
e-mail: nmtshow@comcast.net
Web Site: www.nmtshow.com

Management:
  Artistic Director: David A. Syrotiak
  Production Manager: Peter Syrotiak
  Managing Director: David J. Syrotiak
  Production Manager: Peter Syrotiak
  Director of Education and Outreach: Mariana Palade Syrotiak
Utilizes: Singers
Founded: 1968
Specialized Field: Puppet
Status: Professional; Nonprofit
Income Sources: Association of Performing Arts Presenters; NECA; New England Arts Foundation
Organization Type: Performing; Touring

4019
VERMONT STAGE COMPANY
110 Main Street
Burlington, VT 05401
Phone: 802-862-1497
Fax: 802-862-1257
e-mail: vsc@vtstage.org
Web Site: www.vtstage.org
Officers:
  Chair: Darrilyn Peters
  Chair: Allie Stickney
  Secretary: John Shullenberger
  Treasurer: Christopher Kaufman Ilstrup
Management:
  Producing Artistic Director: Cristina Alicea
  Business Manager: Emily Rozanski
  General Manager: Molly K. Kurent
Mission: Works to make theatre that matters. By creating professional theatre that is emotionally, intellectually, and physically engaging, committing to the belief that theatre can make a positive difference in the community and in the world.
Founded: 1994
Specialized Field: Drama; Contemporary
Status: Non-Profit, Professional
Paid Staff: 2
Volunteer Staff: 50
Budget: $275,000
Income Sources: Ticket Sales; Corporate Sponsorships; Program Advertising; Private Contributions
Season: September - May
Affiliations: Flynn Center for the Performing Arts
Annual Attendance: 6,000-7,000
Type of Stage: Flexible; Black Box
Seating Capacity: 150

4020
AMERICAN THEATRE WORKS
PO Box 510
P.O. Box 50458 Palo Alto, CA 94303-0458
Dorset, VT 05251
Phone: 650-463-1950
Fax: 650-463-1963
e-mail: boxoffice@theatreworks.org
Web Site: www.theatredirectories.com
Officers:
  President: Robert G Bushell Jr
  VP: Jean Miller
  Treasurer: Ben Weil
Management:
  Producing and Artistic Director: John Nassivera
  General Manager: Scott DeVine
  Managing Director: Phil Santora
  Associate Artistic Director: Leslie Martinson
Mission: To offer a season of five plays each summer, as well as a writers' colony.

Utilizes: Actors; AEA Actors; Artists-in-Residence; Designers; Guest Designers; Instructors; Music; Performance Artists; Resident Professionals; Soloists
Founded: 1976
Specialized Field: Summer Stock
Status: Non-Profit
Income Sources: Theatre Communications Group
Performs At: Dorset Playhouse
Seating Capacity: 290
Year Remodeled: 2001
Organization Type: Performing; Resident; Educational; Publishing

4021
POTOMAC THEATRE PROJECT
330 West 16th Street
Middlebury, VT 05753
Phone: 802-388-3318
e-mail: faraone@middlebury.edu
Web Site: www.potomactheatreproject.org
Management:
 Producing Director: Cheryl Faraone
 Director: James Petosa
 Director: Richard Romagnoli
 Co-Artistic Director: Jim Petosa
 Co-Artistic Director: Cheryl Faraone
 Co-Artistic Director, Co-Founder: Richard Romagnoli
Mission: Producing highly theatrical new works; Providing professional theatre training.
Founded: 1977
Specialized Field: New Plays; Theater Workshops
Status: Professional; Nonprofit
Paid Staff: 15
Income Sources: Alliance of Resident Theatres/New York; Vermont Council on the Arts
Performs At: Hall of Nations
Organization Type: Performing; Resident; Educational

4022
LOST NATION THEATER
39 Main Street
Montpelier, VT 05602
Phone: 802-229-0492
Fax: 802-223-9608
e-mail: info@lostnationtheater.org
Web Site: www.lostnationtheater.org
Management:
 President: Kim Bent
 Artistic Director: Kathleen Jeenan
Founded: 1977
Specialized Field: Drama; Historical
Status: Non-Profit, Professional
Paid Staff: 7
Season: June - October
Type of Stage: Flexible Thrust
Stage Dimensions: 32' x 28'
Seating Capacity: 124

4023
VERMONT SHAKESPEARE COMPANY
P.O. Box 24
North Hero, VT 05474
Phone: 877-874-1911
e-mail: info@vermontshakespeare.org
Web Site: vermontshakespeare.org
Officers:
 President: John Nagle
 Treasurer: Adam Necrason
 Secretary: Marianne Dimascio
Management:
 Artistic Director: Jena Necrason
 Executive Director: John Nagle
 Associate Producer: Tracy Liz Miller
Mission: Vermont Shakespeare Company is dedicated to presenting wildly innovative productions of Shakespeare and to finding an exhilarating way to connect the beauty of our natural world to the magic of live theatre.
Founded: 2005
Status: Professional; Nonprofit
Season: Summer
Performs At: Knight Point State Park, Shelburne Museum, The Royall Tyler Theatre At The University Of Vermont

4024
GREEN MOUNTAIN GUILD
PO Box 659
Pittsfield, VT 05762
Phone: 802-746-8320
Management:
 Program Coordinator/Managing Dir: Marjorie O'Neill-Butler
 Artistic Director: Robert O'Neill-Butler
 Associate Artistic Director: Jay Berkow
Mission: Developing and promoting excellence in Northern New England's performing arts.
Utilizes: Guest Companies
Founded: 1971
Specialized Field: Summer Stock; Musical; Youth Theater
Status: Professional
Paid Staff: 3
Income Sources: New England Theatre Conference; Vermont Council on the Arts; New England Touring Foundation
Season: July - August
Performs At: Killington Playhouse
Organization Type: Performing; Touring; Resident

4025
CATAMOUNT FILM AND ARTS COMPANY
115 Eastern Avenue
Saint Johnsbury, VT 05819
Mailing Address: P.O. Box 324, St. Johnsbury, VT 05819
Phone: 802-748-2600
Fax: 802-748-0852
Toll-free: 888-757-5559
e-mail: info@catamountarts.org
Web Site: www.catamountarts.com
Officers:
 President: Linda Wacholder
 Vice President: Greg MacDonald
 Treasurer: Elizabeth Wilson
 Secretary: Bob Amos
 Co-Chair: Bob Bishop
 Co-Chair: Bob Swartz
Management:
 President: Bob Amos
 Executive Director: Jody Fried
 Artistic Director: Jerry Aldredge
 Development Director: Amy Stetson Rebollo
 Membership Coordinator: Martin Bryan
Mission: To perform community-based multidisciplinary presentations.
Founded: 1975
Specialized Field: Musical; Contemporary; Mime
Status: Non-Profit, Professional
Paid Staff: 3
Volunteer Staff: 15
Paid Artists: 40
Organization Type: Performing; Educational

4026
WESTON PLAYHOUSE
703 Main Street
Weston, VT 05161
Phone: 802-824-8167
Fax: 802-419-3151
e-mail: mail@westplay.com
Web Site: www.westonplayhouse.org
Officers:
 Chair: Anthony C. Wood
 Vice Chair: Janet Warren
 2nd Vice Chair: Steve Stettler
 Secretary: Ludy Biddle
 Treasurer: Evandro Braz
Management:
 Producing Director: Malcolm Ewen
 General Manager: Stuart Duke
 Producing Director: Tim Fort
 Producing Director: Steve Stettler
 Company Manager: Aidan O'Reilly
 Office Manager: Debora Harry-Spencer
 Director of Development: Lindsey Carlson
 Operations Manager: Bridget Sullivan
 Interim Managing Director: Leseley Kenig
Founded: 1937
Specialized Field: Musical; Drama; Comedy
Status: Nonprofit
Season: June - September
Type of Stage: Proscenium
Seating Capacity: 285

4027
WICHITA FALLS BACKDOOR PLAYERS
501 Indiana Ave.
PO Box 896
White River Junction, VT 76307
Mailing Address: P.O. Box 896 Wichita Falls, Texas 76307
Phone: 940-322-5000
Fax: 940-322-8167
e-mail: backdoor1@wf.net
Web Site: www.backdoortheatre.org
Management:
 General Manager: Weldon Fraker
 Managing Artistic Director: Linda Bates
 Executive Director: Gail Smith
Mission: Dedicated to presenting new interpretations of classics, regional premieres of recent and new works, and professioanl theater education.
Utilizes: Actors; AEA Actors; Artists-in-Residence; Choreographers; Collaborating Artists; Collaborations; Commissioned Composers; Designers; Educators; Filmmakers; Fine Artists; Grant Writers; Guest Accompanists; Guest Artists; Guest Companies; Guest Conductors; Guest Designers; Guest Ensembles; Guest Instructors; Guest Lecturers; Guest Musical Directors; Guild Activities; High School Drama; Instructors; Local Artists; Multimedia; Music; Original Music Scores; Performance Artists; Resident Artists; Resident Professionals; Sign Language Translators; Soloists; Student Interns; Theatre Companies; Visual Arts
Founded: 1992
Specialized Field: Musical; Comedy; Classic; Contemporary
Status: Non-Profit, Professional
Paid Staff: 25
Volunteer Staff: 60
Paid Artists: 8
Season: September - December
Affiliations: TCG
Facility Category: Theater
Type of Stage: 3/4 Thrust

THEATRE / Virginia

Stage Dimensions: 50' x 24'

Virginia

4028
BARTER THEATRE - STATE THEATRE OF VIRGINIA
127 West Main Street
PO Box 867
Abingdon, VA 24210
Phone: 276-628-3991
Fax: 276-619-5466
e-mail: barterinfo@bartertheatre.com
Web Site: www.bartertheatre.com
Management:
    Artistic Director/Producer: Rex Partington
    Artistic Director: Richard Rose
    Business Manager: Joan Ballou
    Development Director: Lisa Alderman
    Marketing Director: Debbie Addison
    Associate Artistic Director: John Hardy
    Group Sales Reservationist: Linda Pruner
    Media Specialist/Web/Graphics: Stacy Fine
Mission: Performing the finest in contemporary and classical theatre for residents as well as visitors to our region.
Utilizes: Guest Companies
Founded: 1933
Specialized Field: Musical; Comedy; Classic; Contemporary
Status: Non-Profit, Professional
Paid Staff: 125
Income Sources: Actors' Equity Association; League of Resident Theatres; Theatre Communications Group
Performs At: Barter Playhouse; Barter Theatre House
Type of Stage: Proscenium, Flexible Stage
Seating Capacity: 508, 140
Organization Type: Performing; Touring; Resident; Educational

4029
KATHY HARTY GRAY DANCE THEATRE
PO Box 3291
Alexandria, VA 22302
Phone: 703-413-3811
Fax: 703-413-4198
e-mail: info@khgdt.org
Web Site: www.khgdt.org
Officers:
    Chair: Jim Rubin
    Vice Chair: Cathy Malin
    Sec.: Linda Botsford
    Treas.: Marilyn Barner
Management:
    Artistic Director: Kathy Harty Gray
    Designer & Editor: Brenn Huckstep
    Staff reporter: Meghan Welsh
    Webmaster: Dale Parker
Mission: Mondern dance company providing concerts, school shows, residencies and master classes.
Founded: 1978
Specialized Field: Musical; Movement Theater
Status: Professional
Paid Staff: 1
Volunteer Staff: 1
Paid Artists: 10

4030
METROSTAGE
1201 N Royal St.
Alexandria, VA 22314
Phone: 703-548-9044
Fax: 703-548-9089
e-mail: info@metrostage.org
Web Site: www.metrostage.org
Officers:
    President of Board: Mark Feldheim
Management:
    Producing Artistic Director: Carolyn Griffin
Mission: Offers comtemporary plays and musicals in an intimate theatre setting, including many new plays and musicals
Utilizes: Actors; AEA Actors; Designers; Guest Companies; Music
Founded: 1984
Specialized Field: Musical; Comedy; Contemporary
Status: Non-Profit, Professional
Paid Staff: 2
Volunteer Staff: 2
Paid Artists: 50
Budget: $500,000
Income Sources: Box Office; Contributions
Performs At: Theatre
Affiliations: League of Washington Theatres; Alexandria Convention and Visitors Association
Annual Attendance: 4,000
Facility Category: Theatre
Type of Stage: Modified Thrust
Stage Dimensions: 26'x 20'
Seating Capacity: 130
Year Remodeled: 2001
Cost: $450,000
Organization Type: Performing; Touring; Educational

4031
MOUNT VERNON COMMUNITY CHILDREN'S THEATRE
1900 Elkin Street
Suite 225
Alexandria, VA 22308
Phone: 703-360-0686
Fax: 703-360-9722
e-mail: admin@mvcct.org
Web Site: www.mvcct.org
Officers:
    President: Laura Marshall
    Vice President Programs: Pam Peckar
    Vice President, Administration: Sharon Roberts
    Treasurer: Kyle Roberts
Management:
    Programs Coordinator: Pam Peckar
    Director of Education and Outreach: Rachel Witt-Callahan
    Education Coordinator: Crystal Mills
    Marketing Director: Robin Havens-Parker
Mission: Committed to providing opportunities of creative expression to children of all ages through drama education and live theatrical production.
Founded: 1980
Specialized Field: Children's Theater; Theater Workshops

4032
HORIZONS THEATRE
1083 Austin Avenue NE
Suite 127
Arlington, VA 30307
Phone: 404-523-1477
Fax: 404-584-8815
e-mail: info@horizonstheatre.org
Web Site: www.horizonstheatre.org
Management:
    Artistic Director: Leslie B Jacobson
    Managing Director: Cameron Kelley
    Co-Artistic Director: Lisa Adler
    Co-Artistic Director: Jeff Adler
    Artistic & Education Assistant: Kelly Criss
Founded: 1976
Specialized Field: Women's Theater
Status: Non-Equity; Nonprofit

4033
SIGNATURE THEATRE
4200 Campbell Ave
Arlington, VA 22206
Phone: 703-820-9771
Fax: 703-845-0236
Web Site: www.sig-online.org
Officers:
    Chair: Bonnie Feld
    Vice Chair/Secretary: Dottie Bennett
    Secretary: Bonnie Feld
    Vice Chair/Treasurer: Peter Tanous
    Vice Chair: Kathleen T. Ross
Management:
    Artistic Director: Eric Schaeffer
    Managing Director: Maggie Boland
    Associate Artistic Director: Matthew Gardiner
    Director of Production: Michael D. Curry
    Associate Production Manager/Rental: Jennifer Moss Kincaid
    Assistant Production Manager: Ian Frazier
    Technical Director: Andrew Fox
    Assistant Technical Director: Natalie Bell
    Director of Development: Christine Stanley
Mission: To reinvent musical classics and premiere groundbreaking new work by today's best writers
Founded: 1990
Specialized Field: Classic; New Plays
Status: Nonprofit

4034
OFFSTAGE THEATRE
PO Box 131
Charlottesville, VA 22902
Phone: 804-295-7249
Management:
    Co-Artistic Director: Tom Coash
    Co-Artistic Director: Doug Grissom
    Resident Director: John Quinn
    Public Relations Director: Amy Lowenstein
Mission: Producing new plays of high quality in nontraditional, low-cost theatre environments.
Utilizes: Guest Companies
Founded: 1989
Specialized Field: New Plays; Contemporary
Status: Professional; Semi-Professional; Nonprofit
Organization Type: Performing; Touring; Resident; Educational

4035
SWIFT CREEK MILL PLAYHOUSE
17401 Jefferson Davis Hwy
Colonial Heights, VA 23834
Mailing Address: P.O. Box 41, Colonial Heights, VA 23834
Phone: 804-748-5203
Fax: 804-748-4411
e-mail: groupsales@swiftcreekmill.com
Web Site: www.swiftcreekmill.com
Officers:
    Secretary: Pam Martin Comstock
    Past President: Patricia A. Harvey
    Vice President: Lu H. Henderson
    President: Julian Porter
    Treasurer: William A. Young, Jr., CPA (Bil
Management:
    Artistic Director: Tom Width

THEATRE / Virginia

Director of Development and Marketi: Jennifer Procise
Group Sales Manager: Robert Albertia
Foodservice and Office Manager: Darlene Arrington
Director of Sales: Megan Davis
Founded: 1965
Specialized Field: Musical; Comedy; Contemporary
Status: Non-Profit, Professional
Paid Staff: 3
Paid Artists: 25

4036
RIVERSIDE CENTER DINNER THEATER
95 Riverside Parkway
Fredericksburg, VA 22406
Phone: 540-370-4300
Fax: 540-370-4304
Toll-free: 888-999-8527
e-mail: riversided@aol.com
Web Site: www.riversidedt.com
Management:
  Music Director: Rollin Wehman
  Producer Assistant: Stephen R Hayes
  Artistic Director and General Manag: Rollin E Wehman
Mission: Presentation of Broadway musicals, children's theatre musicals, and education of youth and adults in all aspects of the performing arts, while providing an outlet for the diverse talents of area actors, musicians, and dancers.
Founded: 1998
Specialized Field: Musical; Children's Theater
Paid Staff: 12
Volunteer Staff: 8
Paid Artists: 35
Non-paid Artists: 6
Budget: $2.4 million
Income Sources: Group Sales; General Public; Bus-Tour Companies; Season Subscribers
Annual Attendance: 50,000
Type of Stage: Proscenium
Stage Dimensions: 35' x 30'
Year Built: 1998
Cost: $30 million

4037
NEXTSTOP THEATRE COMPANY
269 Sunset Park Drive
Herndon, VA 20170
Mailing Address: P.O. Box 5006, Herndon, VA 20172
Phone: 703-481-5930
e-mail: info@nextstoptheatre.org
Web Site: nextstoptheatre.org
Management:
  Producing Artistic Director: Evan Hoffmann
Status: Professional; Nonprofit

4038
LIME KILN THEATER
607 Borden Rd
Lexington, VA 24450
Mailing Address: P.O. Box 1244, Lexington, VA 24450
Phone: 540-463-7088
Fax: 540-463-1082
e-mail: limekiln@cfw.com
Web Site: www.limekilntheater.org
Officers:
  President: Paul Belo
  Chairman: Amy Gianniny
  Treasurer: George Huger
  Secretary: Dennis Cropper
Management:
  Executive Director: Tony Russell
  Box Office Manager: Alice Williams
  Office Manager & Box Office Manager: LauraJane Baur
  Technical Director: John Lindberg
  Front of House Manager: Mark Bowman
Mission: Promoting and preserving the traditions of the Southern Appalachian Mountains and exploring their myths as well as their potential.
Utilizes: Actors; AEA Actors; Artists-in-Residence; Choreographers; Designers; Guest Accompanists; Guest Designers; Guest Ensembles; Guest Instructors; Guest Lecturers; Guest Musical Directors; Guest Soloists; Guild Activities; Instructors; Local Artists; Multimedia; Music; Original Music Scores; Resident Artists; Resident Professionals; Sign Language Translators; Soloists; Student Interns
Founded: 1982
Specialized Field: Summer Stock; Musical; Ethnic Theater
Status: Professional; Nonprofit
Paid Staff: 6
Volunteer Staff: 100
Paid Artists: 50
Budget: $500,000
Income Sources: Private; earned; government
Season: May - September
Performs At: Lime Kiln Theater-Outdoor
Annual Attendance: 17,000
Facility Category: Theatre and Concert Venue
Type of Stage: Outdoor
Seating Capacity: 388; 700
Rental Contact: Jennifer D. Anderson
Organization Type: Performing; Touring; Resident; Educational; Sponsoring
Resident Groups: Artists-in-Residence

4039
LIME KILN THEATER
607 Borden Rd
Lexington, VA 24450
Mailing Address: P.O. Box 1244, Lexington, VA 24450
Phone: 540-463-7088
Fax: 540-463-1082
e-mail: limekiln@ntelos.net
Web Site: www.limekilntheater.org
Officers:
  Chairman: Amy Gianniny
  Treasurer: George Huger
  Secretary: Dennis Cropper
Management:
  Box Office Manager: Alice Williams
  Executive Director: Tony Russell
  Office Manager & Box Office Manager: LauraJane Baur
  Technical Director: John Lindberg
  Front of House Manager: Mark Bowman
Mission: To promote entertainment and education in the arts while exploring Appalachian traditions and culture.
Founded: 1983
Specialized Field: Summer Stock; Touring Company; Musical; Ethnic Theater
Status: AEA-LOA/Outdoor Drama; Professional; Nonprofit
Paid Staff: 5
Volunteer Staff: 100
Paid Artists: 50
Non-paid Artists: 4
Budget: $629,000
Income Sources: Private; Earned; Foundation; Government
Performs At: Lime Kiln Theater
Affiliations: AEA; Institute of Outdoor Drama
Annual Attendance: 17,000
Facility Category: Outdoor Theater and Concert Venue
Seating Capacity: 388; 700
Year Built: 1983
Rental Contact: Jennifer D Anderson

4040
SPENCERS: THEATER OF ILLUSION
PO Box 10396
Lynchburg, VA 24506
Mailing Address: PO Box 10396, Lynchburg, VA 24506
Phone: 434-384-4740
Fax: 434-384-8032
e-mail: booking@theatreofillusion.com
Web Site: www.theatreofillusion.com
Officers:
  President: Kevin Spencer
Management:
  Executive Director: Cindy Spencer
  Artistic Director: Joanie Spina
Founded: 1982
Specialized Field: Youth Theater; Drama; Classic
Status: For-Profit, Professional
Paid Staff: 4
Paid Artists: 2

4041
ALDEN THEATRE SERIES
1234 Ingleside Avenue
McLean, VA 22101
Mailing Address: 234 Ingleside Ave. McLean, VA 22101
Phone: 703-790-0123
Fax: 703-506-6832
e-mail: clare.kiley@fairfaxcounty.gov
Web Site: www.mcleancenter.org
Officers:
  Chairman: Kevin Dent
  Vice Chair: Chad Quinn
  Treasurer/Chairman, Finance: Sean Dunn
  Chairman, Program Committee: Jay Howell
  Chairman, Communications Committee: Robin Walker
Management:
  Executive Director: George Sachs
  Information Officer: Sabrina Anwah
  Graphic Artist: Hussain Mohammed
  Facilities Manager: Joe McGovern
  Office Manager: Lindsey Forbush
  Comptroller: Ashok Karra
  Director of Communications & Market: Sabrina Anwah
Utilizes: Actors; Choreographers; Dance Companies; Dancers; Designers; Grant Writers; Guest Accompanists; Guest Artists; Guest Conductors; Guest Designers; Guest Directors; Guest Ensembles; Guest Instructors; Guest Musical Directors; Guest Soloists; Instructors; Local Artists; Multimedia; Music; Original Music Scores; Resident Professionals; Sign Language Translators; Soloists; Student Interns; Special Technical Talent; Theatre Companies
Founded: 1975
Specialized Field: Musical; Comedy; Classic; Contemporary
Status: Non-Profit, Professional
Paid Staff: 20
Volunteer Staff: 30
Paid Artists: 35
Budget: $400,000
Type of Stage: Proscenium
Stage Dimensions: 28 x 35
Seating Capacity: 424
Year Built: 1975

THEATRE / Virginia

Year Remodeled: 1988
Rental Contact: Performing Arts Director Clare Kiley

4042
WAYSIDE THEATRE
7853 Main Street
PO Box 260
Middletown, VA 22645
Mailing Address: P.O. Box 260, 7853 Main Street, Middletown, VA 22645
Phone: 540-869-1776
Fax: 540-869-1746
e-mail: info@waysidetheatre.org
Web Site: www.waysidetheatre.org
Officers:
   President: Dr. Byron Brill
   Vice President: Mary Ruth Alred Follett
   Secretary: Tara Shostek
   Treasurer: Adele Skolits
Management:
   Artistic Director: Warner Crocker
   Costume Shop Manager: Caleb Blackwell
   Resident Lighting Designer: Wes Calkin
   Technical Director: Will Gautney
   Production Stage Manager: Kendra Watkins
   Artistic Associate: Leslie Putnam
Mission: Community based professional theatre which strives to enrich the lives of the people of our community through a broad spectrum of live professional theatre and performance opportunities that are entertaining, challenging, educational and accessible, and which effectively transmits that wonder to future generations.
Utilizes: Actors; AEA Actors; Choreographers; Collaborations; Grant Writers; Guest Artists; Guest Companies; Guest Designers; Guest Lecturers; Guild Activities; Local Artists; Music; Resident Professionals; Singers; Student Interns
Founded: 1961
Specialized Field: Musical; Comedy
Status: Non-Profit, Professional
Paid Staff: 5
Paid Artists: 26
Budget: $500,000
Income Sources: Ticket Sales; Corporate/Foundation Grants; Government Grants; Program Advertising; Concession Sales
Season: May - December
Affiliations: AEA
Annual Attendance: 15,000
Facility Category: Historic Proscenium
Type of Stage: Proscenium
Stage Dimensions: 24'x22'
Seating Capacity: 173
Year Built: 1942
Year Remodeled: 1962
Rental Contact: Artistic Director Warner Crocker
Organization Type: Performing; Touring; Resident

4043
2ND STORY THEATRE COMPANY
28 Market Street
Suite 210
Norfolk, VA 02885
Phone: 401-247-4200
Fax: 757-623-1777
e-mail: 2ndstory@brucehartmandesign.com
Web Site: www.brucehartmandesign.com
Officers:
   President/Director: Ed Shea
   Treasurer/Director: Lynne Collinson
   Secretary/Director: Rae Mancini
Management:
   Co-Owner/Producer: Ethan Marten
   Co-Owner/Producer: Richard Marten
   Webmaster/Advertising Design: Bruce Hartman
   Lighting Design: Yoni Charry
   Stage Manager: Sheri Beyrau
   Graphic/Web/Print Designer: Bruce Hartman
   Artistic Director: Ed Shea
   Executive Director: Lynne Collinson
   General Manager: Charles Lafond
Mission: 2nd Story Theatre has functioned as a community resource encouraging the development and employment of local and regional talent, and activly fostering the performance of sister arts in Tidewater, Virginia. Committed to the concept of training and developing the talents of aspiring theatre professionals.
Specialized Field: Comedy

4044
GENERIC THEATER
Generic Theater
215 St. Paul's Blvd.
Norfolk, VA 23501
Mailing Address: Generic Theater, PO Box 566, Norfolk, VA 23501
Phone: 757-441-2160
Fax: 757-441-2729
e-mail: contact@generictheater.org
Web Site: www.generictheater.org
Officers:
   President: Patti Wray
Management:
   Managing Director: Denise Dillard
   Production Manager: Betty Xander
   Artistic Team: Matt Friedman
   Artistic Team: Jeannette Rainey
Mission: To produce innovative productions of contemporary works, new plays, and reinterpretations of the classics.
Utilizes: Actors; Community Talent; Designers; Guest Accompanists; Guest Conductors; Guest Designers; High School Drama; Local Artists; Original Music Scores; Performance Artists; Resident Professionals; Soloists; Student Interns
Founded: 1981
Specialized Field: Contemporary; Drama; Comedy
Paid Staff: 2
Paid Artists: 50
Non-paid Artists: 50
Budget: $100,000
Income Sources: Ticket Sales; State and Local Grant Organizations; Contributions
Performs At: Theater
Affiliations: Generic Theatre
Annual Attendance: 4,000 - 5,000
Facility Category: Black Box
Type of Stage: Proscenium
Stage Dimensions: 28'x56'
Seating Capacity: 80
Rental Contact: Artistic Director (757-441-2729) Steven Harders

4045
LITTLE THEATRE OF NORFOLK
801 Claremont Avenue
Norfolk, VA 23507
Mailing Address: 801 Claremont Ave, Norfolk, VA 23507
Phone: 757-627-8551
e-mail: info@ltnonline.org
Web Site: www.ltnonline.org
Officers:
   President: Jeff Corriveau, MA, MFA
   Chairman: Melissa Sullivan, M.Ed
Management:
   Technical Director: Shawn Crawford
Mission: To offer excellent amateur theatre and give non-professionals an opportunity to utilize their talents.
Founded: 1926
Specialized Field: Community Theater
Status: Nonprofit
Performs At: Little Theatre of Norfolk
Organization Type: Performing

4046
VIRGINIA STAGE COMPANY
108 E. Tazewell St
PO Box 3770
Norfolk, VA 23514
Mailing Address: 108 E. Tazewell St., P.O. Box 3770, Norfolk, VA 23514
Phone: 757-627-1234
Fax: 757-628-5958
e-mail: boxoffice@vastage.com
Web Site: www.vastage.com
Officers:
   President: Tyler Leinbach
   VP Strategic Planning - Secretary: Anthony Vittone
   Executive Director: Keith Stava
   VP Finance - Treasurer: Mike Askew
   VP Development: Sarah B. Clarkson, MD
   Vice-President: Barry Pollara
Management:
   Marketing Director: Marilyn Johnson, mjohnson@vastage.com
   Managinng Director: Keith Stava
   Box Office Manager: Sabrina Clark, boxoffice@vastage.com
   Director of Marketing: Janelle Burchfield
   Sales Director: Janelle Burchfield
   Production & Facilities Manager: Terry Flint
   Production Management Aapprentice: Gretchen Schaefer
   Company Manager: Kerry Jahn
   Production Manager: Randy Foster
Mission: To develop and sustain a fully professional theatre serving Southeastern Virginia which enriches the region and the field through the production of theatrical art of the highest quality.
Utilizes: Artists-in-Residence; Community Talent; Guild Activities; Resident Companies; Singers; Students
Founded: 1980
Specialized Field: Musical; Comedy; Classic; Contemporary
Status: Non-Profit, Professional
Paid Staff: 22
Volunteer Staff: 50
Paid Artists: 22
Budget: $2 million
Income Sources: Ticket Sales; Grants; Personal and Business Giving
Performs At: Wells Theatre
Affiliations: League Of Resident Theatres; Theatre Communication Group
Annual Attendance: 55,000
Facility Category: Theatre
Type of Stage: Proscenium; Hemp House
Stage Dimensions: 36'x36'
Seating Capacity: 677
Year Built: 1913
Year Remodeled: 1986
Rental Contact: Beth Spangler
Organization Type: Performing; Resident; Educational; Sponsoring

4047
ROADSIDE THEATER
PO Box 771
Norton, VA 24273

Mailing Address: P.O. Box 771 Norton, VA 24273
Phone: 276-679-3116
Fax: 276-679-3116
e-mail: contact@roadside.org
Web Site: www.roadside.org
Management:
 Director: Jan Cohen-Cruz
 Managing Director: Donna Porterfield
 Director: Dudley Cocke
 Composer: Michael Keck
 Artistic Director: Bill Rauch
Specialized Field: Drama; Theater;

4048
LONG WAY HOME
PO Box 711
Radford, VA 24141
Phone: 540-639-0679
Fax: 540-731-8306
Management:
 Technical Director: Al Shumate
Founded: 1971
Specialized Field: Historical; Outdoor Theater; Drama; Summer Stock; Storytelling
Status: Nonprofit
Season: June - August
Type of Stage: Amphitheatre, Open Stage
Seating Capacity: 500

4049
BARKSDALE THEATRE
1601 Willow Lawn Drive
Suite 301-E
Richmond, VA 23230
Mailing Address: 1601 Willow Lawn Drive Richmond, VA 23230
Phone: 804-282-9440
Fax: 804-288-6470
e-mail: development@barksdalerichmond.org
Web Site: www.barksdalerichmond.org
Officers:
 President: Donald B. Garber
 Vice President: Monroe E. Harris
 Secretary: Carolyn Paulette
 Treasurer: George W. Riegel Jr.
Management:
 Managing Director: Phil Whiteway
 Artistic Director: Bruce Miller
 Director Development: Victoria McClure Mautinko
 Box Office Manager: Pam Northrup
 Technical Director: Bruce Rennie
Mission: To produce diverse and outstanding contemporary plays to a growing regional audience.
Utilizes: Actors; AEA Actors; Choreographers; Collaborations; Dancers; Designers; Educators; Grant Writers; Guest Artists; Guest Companies; Guest Composers; Guest Conductors; Guest Designers; Guest Directors; Guest Ensembles; Guest Instructors; Guest Lecturers; Guest Musical Directors; Guest Soloists; Guest Teachers; Guild Activities; Instructors; Local Artists; Lyricists; Multimedia; Music; Organization Contracts; Original Music Scores; Performance Artists; Playwrights; Resident Professionals; Selected Students; Sign Language Translators; Singers; Soloists; Touring Companies; Visual Arts
Founded: 1953
Specialized Field: Musical
Status: Professional; Nonprofit
Paid Staff: 7
Volunteer Staff: 50
Budget: $750,000
Income Sources: Ticket Sales; Program Advertising; Charitable Contributions
Performs At: 214 Theatre-in-the-Round

Affiliations: TCG; Richmond Alliance of Professional Theatres
Annual Attendance: 30-40,000
Type of Stage: 3/4 Thrust
Seating Capacity: 190
Organization Type: Performing; Touring

4050
CADENCE THEATRE COMPANY
P.O. Box 7119
Richmond, VA 23221
Phone: 804-233-4894
e-mail: info@cadencetheatre.org
Web Site: cadencetheatre.org
Officers:
 President: Denis Riva
Management:
 Artistic/Managing Director: Anna Johnson
Mission: The mission of Cadence Theatre Company is to inspire and transform our community by presenting contemporary, award-winning plays, and musicals that uplift the spirit, challenge the mind, and honor both our individuality and our shared humanity.
Founded: 2009
Specialized Field: Contemporary Theatre
Status: Nonprofit
Performs At: The Sara Belle And Neil November Theatre, Marjorie And Arenstein Stage, Theatre Gym-114 West Broad Street, Richmond, VA

4051
HENLEY STREET THEATRE
4305 Sulgrave Road
Richmond, VA 23221
Mailing Address: P.O. Box 7265, Richmond, VA 23221
Phone: 804-340-0115
e-mail: info@henleystreettheatre.org
Web Site: henleystreettheatre.org
Management:
 Artistic Director: Jan Powell
 Managing Director: Jacquie O'Connor
Mission: We stage classical and contemporary works that are relevant, affordable and alive. Our artistic standards are guided by three core values: a reverence for language, a commitment to diversity, and a spirit of adventure.
Specialized Field: Shakespeare

4052
MYSTERY DINNER PLAYHOUSE
5351 Richmond Road
Suite 206
Richmond, VA 23188
Mailing Address: 6531 W. Broad Street, Richmond, VA 23230
Phone: 804-649-2583
Fax: 804-649-7419
Toll-free: 888-471-4802
e-mail: info@mysterydinner.com
Web Site: www.mysterydinner.com
Management:
 President: James Daab
Utilizes: Actors; Contract Actors; Local Artists; Local Artists & Directors; Organization Contracts; Original Music Scores; Performance Artists; Special Technical Talent
Founded: 1993
Specialized Field: Comedy; Dinner Theater
Status: For-Profit, Professional
Paid Staff: 7
Paid Artists: 24
Budget: $800,000
Income Sources: Ticket Sales

Performs At: Double Tree, Sheraton, Crowne Plaza, Clarrion Inn
Affiliations: RMA, WHMA, GWCTA, ACVA
Annual Attendance: 24,000
Facility Category: Hotel
Type of Stage: Promenade
Seating Capacity: 100; 150; 150
Organization Type: Commercial

4053
THEATRE IV
114 W Broad St.
Richmond, VA 23220
Mailing Address: 114 West Broad St., Richmond VA 23220
Phone: 804-783-1688
Fax: 804-775-2325
Toll-free: 800-235-8687
e-mail: vareptheatre@gmail.com
Web Site: www.theatreiv.org
Officers:
 President: Donald B. Garber
 Vice President: Dr. Monroe E. Harris Jr.
 Secretary: Carolyn Paulette
 Treasurer: George W. Riegel Jr.
Management:
 Director of Tour Operations: Eric Williams
 Arts in Education Manager: Ronnie Brown
 Company Manager: Ford Flannagan
 Tour Manager: Gordon Bass
 Arts in Education Assistant: Jessica Malicki
Mission: To create exciting and innovative professional theatrical productions of high quality.
Utilizes: Guest Companies; Singers
Founded: 1975
Specialized Field: Youth Theater
Status: Non-Profit, Professional
Paid Staff: 40
Paid Artists: 100
Income Sources: Theatre Communications Group
Performs At: The Empire Theatre; The Little Theatre
Type of Stage: Proscenium; Flexible
Seating Capacity: 604; 84
Organization Type: Performing; Touring; Resident; Educational

4054
VIRGINIA REPERTORY THEATRE
114 West Broad Street
Richmond, VA 23230
Phone: 804-282-2620
e-mail: vareptheatre@gmail.com
Web Site: virginiarep.org
Officers:
 President: Donald B. Garber
 Vice President: Monroe E. Harris Jr.
Management:
 Artistic Director: Bruce Miller
 Managing Director: Phil Whiteway
Mission: Virginia Rep presents national caliber productions of the great dramas, comedies, and musicals- past, present, and future. With equal enthusiasm we explore the classics, contemporary works and world premieres, always seeking to demonstrate the unique power of theatre to engage, enthrall, educate, and inspire.
Founded: 2012

4055
MILL MOUNTAIN THEATRE
1 Market Square
Roanoke, VA 24011

THEATRE / Washington

Mailing Address: 1 Market Square SE, Roanoke, VA 24011-1437
Phone: 540-342-5749
Fax: 540-342-5745
Toll-free: 800-317-6455
e-mail: mmtmail@millmountain.org
Web Site: www.millmountain.org
Officers:
 President: Jack Avis
 VP: John Jessee
 Treasurer: John Light
 Secretary: Ted Feinour
Management:
 Managing Director/Education Directo: Ginger Poole
 Production Manager: Shelby Taylor Love
 Director Development: John Levin
 Director of Music: Susan Braden
 Teaching Director: Karen Gierchak
 Director Finance: Jim Ayers
 Director Audience Services: Dick Vipperman
 Group Sales Coordinator: John Whitney
 Production Manager: Doug Flinchum
Mission: Professional production of musicals, dramas and comedies with particular emphasis on the production and development of original works.
Utilizes: Actors; AEA Actors; Artists-in-Residence; Choreographers; Collaborating Artists; Collaborations; Commissioned Composers; Dancers; Designers; Grant Writers; Guest Accompanists; Guest Artists; Guest Companies; Guest Composers; Guest Conductors; Guest Designers; Guest Instructors; Guest Lecturers; Guest Soloists; Guild Activities; High School Drama; Local Artists; Multimedia; Organization Contracts; Original Music Scores; Performance Artists; Poets; Resident Professionals; Sign Language Translators; Soloists; Student Interns
Founded: 1964
Specialized Field: Musical
Status: Professional; Nonprofit
Paid Staff: 35
Volunteer Staff: 300
Budget: $2,000,000
Income Sources: Box Office Sales; Private & Public Support
Season: October - August
Performs At: Mill Mountain Theatre; Trinkle Main Stage; Waldron Stage
Affiliations: Theatre Communications Group; Southeastern Theatre Conference; Society for Stage Directors and Choreographers; Actors Equity
Annual Attendance: 60,000
Facility Category: Performing; Touring
Type of Stage: Proscenium; Black Box
Stage Dimensions: 44'x34'; 15'x20'
Seating Capacity: 400; 110
Year Built: 1983
Rental Contact: Doug Flinchum
Organization Type: Performing; Resident; Educational

4056
SHENANDOAH SHAKESPEARE
20 S. New Street
Fourth Floor
Staunton, VA 24401
Mailing Address: 13 W Beverley Street 4th Floor, Staunton, VA 24401
Phone: 540-885-5588
Fax: 540-885-4886
Toll-free: 877-682-4236
e-mail: shsh@shenandoahshakespeare
Web Site: www.americanshakespearec
Management:
 Director of Mission: Ralph Alan Cohen
 Artistic Director: Jim Warren
 Managing Director: Amy Wratchford
 Business Manager: Mary Knapp
 Education Director: Sarah Enloe
 Director Community Relations: Susan Hawthorne
 Managing Director: Sandie Nelson
 Artistic Director: Jim Warren
 Associate Artistic Director/Casting: Jay McClure
Mission: Shenandoah shakespeare through its performances, its theatres, its exhibitions, and its educational programs, seeks to make Shakespeare, the joys of theatre and language, and the communal experience of the Renaissance stage accessible to all.
Utilizes: Actors
Founded: 1988
Specialized Field: Shakespeare
Status: Non-Profit,Professional
Income Sources: Sponsors; Donor

4057
BABCOCK SEASON
134 Chapel Road
Sweet Briar College
Sweet Briar, VA 24595
Mailing Address: 134 Chapel Road, Sweet Briar, VA 24595
Phone: 804-381-6100
Fax: 804-381-6263
Toll-free: 800-381-6001
e-mail: info@sbc.edu
Web Site: www.theatre.sbc.edu
Officers:
 Chairman: Virginia Warrenton
 Vice-Chairman: Elizabeth H.S. Wyatt
Management:
 Babcock Theatre Manager: Loretta Wittman
Utilizes: Actors; Artists-in-Residence; Choreographers; Collaborating Artists; Collaborations; Dance Companies; Dancers; Educators; Fine Artists; Grant Writers; Guest Accompanists; Guest Artists; Guest Choreographers; Guest Instructors; Guest Musical Directors; Guest Soloists; Guild Activities; High School Drama; Local Artists; Multimedia; Music; Organization Contracts; Original Music Scores; Performance Artists; Poets; Resident Professionals; Sign Language Translators; Soloists; Special Technical Talent; Theatre Companies
Specialized Field: Educational; Theater Workshops
Budget: $39,000
Income Sources: College Budget, Grants
Performs At: Babcock Auditorium
Affiliations: Association of Performing Arts Presenters; Virginia Arts Presenters
Annual Attendance: 5,000
Facility Category: General Purpose Theatre
Type of Stage: Proscenium
Seating Capacity: 652
Year Built: 1962

4058
VIRGINIA MUSICAL THEATRE
265 Kings Grant Rd
Suite 100
Virginia Beach, VA 23452
Mailing Address: 265 Kings Grant Rd, Suite 100, Virginia Beach, VA 23452
Phone: 757-340-5446
Fax: 757-962-1490
e-mail: mark.vmt@vacoxmail.com
Web Site: www.vmtheatre.org
Officers:
 President: Mark Batzel
 First Vice President: Barbara Lewis
 Second Vice President: Nancy Creech
 Treasurer: Robin Harvey
 Secretary: Joan Bryan
 Past President: Margaret Eure
Management:
 Managing Director: Mark Hudgins
 Founder: Jeff Meredith
 Media Specialist: John Langlois
 Office Assistants: Mary Blair
 Project Angel Coordinator: Ed Hart
Mission: Preservation of musical theatre as a uniquely american art form
Founded: 1991
Specialized Field: Musical
Status: Non-Profit, Professional
Paid Staff: 4
Volunteer Staff: 10
Paid Artists: 300
Budget: $1 million
Income Sources: Ticket Sales; Fundraising
Season: October - July
Performs At: Performing Arts Center
Affiliations: AEA; SSD&C
Annual Attendance: 40,000
Type of Stage: Proscenium
Stage Dimensions: 50' x 35'
Seating Capacity: 1,300
Year Built: 2006
Cost: $53 Million

4059
VIRGINIA SHAKESPEARE FESTIVAL
College of William and Mary
PO Box 8795
Williamsburg, VA 23187-879
Mailing Address: P.O. Box 8795, Williamsburg, VA 23187-8795
Phone: 757-221-2683
Fax: 757-221-2636
e-mail: clowen@wm.edu
Web Site: www.wm.edu
Management:
 Producing Artistic Director: Christopher Owens
Mission: To produce professional classic theatre for Tidewater region of Virginia and provide educational opportunities for young people to learn more about the works of William Shakespeare and his contemporaries.
Utilizes: Singers
Founded: 1978
Specialized Field: Shakespeare
Status: Professional; Nonprofit
Paid Staff: 6
Volunteer Staff: 2
Paid Artists: 40
Budget: $300,000
Income Sources: 65% Earned; 35% Contributions
Season: July - August
Affiliations: AEA Guest Artist
Annual Attendance: 9,000
Type of Stage: Proscenium, Sprung, Traps
Stage Dimensions: 36' x 36'
Seating Capacity: 600
Year Built: 1957
Organization Type: Performing; Educational

Washington

4060
BAINBRIDGE PERFORMING ARTS
200 Madison Avenue North
Bainbridge Island, WA 98110
Mailing Address: 200 Madison Avenue North, Bainbridge Island, WA 98110
Phone: 206-842-4560

THEATRE / Washington

Fax: 206-842-0195
e-mail: dcantwell@bainbridgeperformingarts.org
Web Site: http://www.bainbridgeperformingarts.org
Officers:
    President: Debbie MacLeod
    Vice President & Secretary: Peter Denis
    Treasurer: Neil Marck
Management:
    Executive Director: Domonique Cantwell
    Artistic Director: Steven Fogell
    Operations Manager: Shannon Dowling
    Graphic Design: Don Flora
    Director of Education: Victoria Whitlow
    Production Manager: Deirdre Hadlock
    Technical Director: Alex King
    Front of House Manager: Siobhan Maguire
    Music Director: Wesley Schulz
Specialized Field: Musical; Drama; Comedy

4061
IDIOM THEATER
1418 Cornwall Avenue
Bellingham, WA 98225
Phone: 360-305-3524
e-mail: info@idiomtheater.com
Web Site: idiomtheater.com
Management:
    Artistic Director: Glenn Hergenhahn-Zhao
    Managing Director: Chris Coombs
    Technical Director: Jaz Okura-Youtsey
    Marketing Director: Ron Warner
    Marketing Director: Wes Davis
Founded: 2001
Status: Nonprofit
Organization Type: Performing

4062
MBT STUDIO THEATRE
104 North Commercial Street
Bellingham, WA 98225
Mailing Address: 104 North Commercial Street
Bellingham, WA 98225
Phone: 360-733-5793
Fax: 360-671-0114
e-mail: tickets@mountbakertheatre.com
Web Site: www.mountbakertheatre.com
Officers:
    Past President: Daniel Larner
    President: John Pedlow
    Vice-President: Edwin H. Williams
    Secretary: Jane Carten
    Treasurer: Mark Thoma
Management:
    Executive Director: Brad Burdick
    Technical Director: John Zoehrer
    Deputy Director: Kim Laskey
    Finance Director: Sharon Cassidy
    Development Director: Larry Feder
    Marketing Manager: Beth McPeek
Mission: Dedicated to showcasing some of the best live performing artists on both the professional and community levels for audiences in the North Puget Sound area and the Lower Mainland of British Columbia.
Founded: 1983
Specialized Field: Jazz, Cabaret, Small Theatre Acts, Chamber Ensembles
Status: Non-Profit, Professional
Paid Staff: 20
Type of Stage: Black Box
Seating Capacity: 140-200

4063
MOUNT BAKER THEATRE
104 North Commercial Street
Bellingham, WA 98225
Mailing Address: 104 North Commercial Street
Bellingham, WA 98225
Phone: 360-733-5793
Fax: 360-671-0114
e-mail: tickets@mountbakertheatre.com
Web Site: www.mountbakertheatre.com
Officers:
    Past President: Daniel Larner
    President: John Pedlow
    Vice-President: Edwin H. Williams
    Secretary: Jane Carten
    Treasurer: Mark Thoma
Management:
    Executive Director: Brad Burdick
    Technical Director: John Bauer
    Exec Asst/Volunteer Coordinator: Cindi Pree
    Deputy Director: Kim Laskey
    Finance Director: Sharon Cassidy
    Development Director: Larry Feder
    Marketing Manager: Beth McPeek
Mission: To provide arts, entertainment, and social interaction which through a wide variety of programs, results in personal enrichment, enjoyment and a sense of community for diverse audiences in the region; and to preserve the restored historic Mount Baker Theatre as a home for local performing arts organizations, film, a venue for touring performers and community events.
Founded: 1983
Specialized Field: Musical; Comedy
Status: Non-Profit, Professional
Paid Staff: 19
Volunteer Staff: 275
Facility Category: Performing Arts
Type of Stage: Proscenium
Stage Dimensions: 45'x26'
Orchestra Pit: y
Seating Capacity: 1,509
Year Built: 1927
Year Remodeled: 1995
Cost: $1.6 million

4064
WWU SUMMER STOCK
VU 513
Bellingham, WA 98225
Mailing Address: VU 513, Bellingham, WA 98225
Phone: 360-650-6112
Fax: 360-650-3028
e-mail: theatre@cc.wwu.edu
Web Site: www.as.wwu.edu
Management:
    Productions Director: Daley Smith
    Films Coordinator: Cody Olsen
    Special Events Coordinator: Jordan Renshaw
    VU Gallery Director: Hannah Fenske
    Review Editor-in-Chief: Megan Thompson
Specialized Field: Musical; Comedy; Classic; Contemporary
Status: For-Profit, Non-Professional
Paid Staff: 20
Paid Artists: 10
Season: Jule - August

4065
ADMIRAL THEATRE FOUNDATION
515 Pacific Avenue
Bremerton, WA 98337
Mailing Address: 515 Pacific Avenue, Bremerton, WA 98337
Phone: 360-373-6810
Fax: 360-405-0673
e-mail: admiraltheatre@admiraltheatre.org
Web Site: www.admiraltheatre.org
Officers:
    Chairman: Joanne Haselwood
    President: Brian Buskirk
    Vice President: Liz Gross
    Treasurer: Greg Meyer
    Secretary: Earle Smith
    Vice President: Carol Sue Rogers
Management:
    Technical Director: Tim Hoffman
    Executive Director: Brian Johnson
    Finance Director: Terry Hoffman
    Production Stage Manager: Trisha Galla
    Development Director: Nita Hartley
    Director of Operations: Tim Lavin
    Marketing Director: Tami Browning
    Box Office Manager: Ted Ness
Specialized Field: Drama; Musical
Paid Staff: 5

4066
BERMERTON COMMUNITY THEATRE
599 Lebo Boulevard
Bremerton, WA 98310
Mailing Address: 599 Lebo Boulevard, Bremerton, WA 98310
Phone: 360-373-5152
Fax: 360-373-6754
Toll-free: 800-863-1706
e-mail: frontofhouse@bctshows.com
Web Site: www.bremertoncommunitytheatre.org/
Officers:
    President: David Tucker
    Vice President: Trina Williamson
    Treasurer: Gary Fetterplace
    Secretary: Raymond Deuel
Management:
    At Large, Technical Director: Eric Spencer
    At Large, Building & Grounds: Bill Buhl
    Production Coordinator: Rana Tan
    Volunteer Coordinator: Linda Jensen
    At Large, Front of House: Mitch Ycaza
Mission: Production of amateur dramas, comedies, mysteries and musicals for the local community.
Utilizes: Guest Artists; Guest Companies; Singers
Founded: 1945
Specialized Field: Musical; Community Theater
Status: Non-Professional; Nonprofit
Volunteer Staff: 12
Non-paid Artists: 100
Organization Type: Performing

4067
EVERETT THEATRE
2911 Colby
Everett, WA 98201
Mailing Address: 2911 Colby Avenue, Everett, WA 98201
Phone: 425-258-6766
Fax: 425-257-0620
e-mail: boxoffice@everetttheatre.org
Web Site: www.everetttheatre.org
Officers:
    President: Michael Hebner
    Vice President: Ralph Homan
    Secretary: L. Sam Samano
    Treasurer: Kathleen Sweek
Management:

THEATRE / Washington

Box Office and Contracts Manager: Kathee Sweek
Technical/Artistic Director: Michael Olson
Founded: 1901
Specialized Field: Musical; Comedy; Classic; Contemporary
Status: Non-Profit, Professional
Paid Staff: 3

4068
VILLAGE THEATRE
303 Front Street North
Everett, WA 98027
Mailing Address: 2710 Wetmore Avenue, Everett, WA 98201
Phone: 425-392-1942
Fax: 425-391-3242
e-mail: feedback@villagetheatre.org
Web Site: www.villagetheatre.org
Officers:
 Past President: Heather Ullberg
 President: Bruce Wanta
 Treasurer: Leigh Kraft
 Secretary: Daryl Orts
Management:
 Executive Producer: Robert Hunt
 Artistic Director: Steve Tomkins
 General Manager: Keith Daahgren
 Production Manager: Jay Markham
 Technical Director: Brad Bixler
 Associate Production Manager: Ciera Iveson
 Director of Youth Education and Out: Kati Nickerson
 Director of Finance: Diana Wright
Mission: The mission of Village Theatre is to be a regionally recognized and nationally influenced center of excelent in family theatre.
Founded: 1979
Specialized Field: Musical; Educational
Status: Non-Profit, Professional
Paid Staff: 50
Paid Artists: 150
Budget: $6.1 million
Performs At: Francis J Gaudette Theatre; Everett Performing Arts Center

4069
KNUTZEN FAMILY THEATRE - CITY OF FEDERAL WAY
3200 SW Dash Point Rd.
Federal Way, WA 98023
Mailing Address: 3200 SW Dash Point Road, Federal Way, WA 98003
Phone: 253-661-1444
Fax: 253-835-2010
e-mail: johng@fedway.org
Web Site: www.knutzenfamilytheatre.com
Officers:
 President: Stephen Smith
 Vice President: Cindy Ducich
 Secretary: Alicia Talley
 Treasurer: Stephen Percival
Management:
 Managing Artistic Director: Alan Bryce
 Office and Marketing Manager: Laura Campbell
 Business Manager: Judy Kent
 Box Office: Jackie Freet
 Technical Director: Amy Silveria
Founded: 1998
Specialized Field: Youth Theater; Drama; Classic
Status: Non-Profit, Non-Professional
Paid Staff: 2

4070
SAN JUAN COMMUNITY THEATRE AND ARTS CENTER
100 2nd Street
PO Box 1063
Friday Harbor, WA 98250
Mailing Address: 100 2nd Street, PO Box 1063, Friday Harbor, Washington 98250
Phone: 360-378-3210
Fax: 360-378-2398
e-mail: sjarts@rockisland.com
Web Site: www.sanjuanarts.org
Officers:
 President: Susan Mazzarella
 Treasurer: Ken Blaker
 Past President: Patricia Nieman
 Secretary: Ralph Hahn
 President Elect: Madelyn Busse
Management:
 Chief Administrative Officer: Mary Blevins
 Executive Director: Merritt Olsen
 Artistic Director: Susan Williams
 Production Manager: John Shaller
 Promotion Director: Jan Bollwinkel-Smith
 Development Director: Tanja Williamson
 House and Administrative Manager: Amanda Lee Smith
Mission: To maintain a center for visual and performing arts for the residents of the island.
Founded: 1989
Specialized Field: Community Theater
Status: Non-Professional; Nonprofit
Paid Staff: 6
Volunteer Staff: 350
Organization Type: Performing; Educational; Sponsoring

4071
PARADISE THEATRE
9911 Burnham Dr NW
PO Box 4
Gig Harbor, WA 98335
Mailing Address: PO BOX 4, Gig Harbor, WA 98335
Phone: 253-851-7529
Fax: 253-851-7503
e-mail: vrichards@paradisetheatre.org
Web Site: www.paradisetheatre.org
Officers:
 President: Noelle Brambila
 Secretary / Treasurer: Kerry Scarvie
 Treasurer: Lynn Bromley
 Secretary: Gus Berry
Management:
 Executive Artistic Director: Vicki Richards
 Managing Director: Jeff Richards
Mission: To promote theatre arts and cultural enrichment through performances as well as educational workshops and classes.
Utilizes: Singers
Founded: 2000
Specialized Field: Musical
Status: Semi-Professional; Nonprofit
Paid Staff: 4
Volunteer Staff: 15
Paid Artists: 16
Non-paid Artists: 15
Income Sources: Grants; Individual Donations; Ticket Sales
Performs At: Paradise Theatre
Type of Stage: Proscenium
Seating Capacity: 50 indoor; 800 outdoor
Year Built: 1900
Year Remodeled: 2000
Organization Type: Performing; Touring; Educational

4072
VILLAGE THEATRE
303 Front Street North
Issaquah, WA 98027
Mailing Address: 303 Front Street North, Issaquah, WA 98027
Phone: 425-392-2202
Fax: 425-391-3242
e-mail: boxoffice@villagetheatre.org
Web Site: www.villagetheatre.org
Officers:
 Past President: Heather Ullberg
 President: Bruce Wanta
 Treasurer: Leigh Kraft
 Secretary: Daryl Orts
 Vice President, Development: Derek Watanabe
Management:
 Executive Producer: Robb Hunt
 Artistic Director: Steve Tomkins
 Production Manager: Jay Markham
 Production Manager: Ciera Iveson
 Technical Director - Issaquah: Brad Bixler
 Asst Technical Director, Scenery: Scott Fyfe
 Director of Finance: Diane Wright
 House/Facilities Manager - Issaquah: Robert Russell
 General Manager - Everett: Sherrill Dryden
Mission: The mission of Village Theatre is to be a regionally recognized and nationally influenced center of excelent in family theatre.
Founded: 1979
Specialized Field: Musical
Budget: $6.1 million
Performs At: Francis J Gaudette Theatre; Everett Performing Arts Center
Facility Category: Theatre

4073
COLUMBIA THEATRE FOR THE PERFORMING ARTS
1231 Vandercook Way
Longview, WA 98632
Mailing Address: PO Box 1026, Longview, WA 98632
Phone: 360-575-8499
Fax: 360-423-8626
Toll-free: 888-575-8499
e-mail: info@columbiatheatre.com
Web Site: www.columbiatheatre.com
Officers:
 President: David Nelson
 Treasurer: Ted Davis
 Secretary: Rosemary Siipola
Management:
 House Manager: Deborah Wornick
 Executive Director: Gian Paul Morelli
 Technical Director: Kelly Ragsdale
 Stage Manager: Rick Rothwell
 Development Director: Michellel Musso
Mission: To provide engaging theatre experience of the highest quality that we always strive to uplift and entertain; to instill in audience and theatre members the value of our integrity as a source of inspiration and hope.
Founded: 1981
Specialized Field: Musical; Community Theater
Status: Non-Profit, Professional
Paid Staff: 10
Annual Attendance: 60,000
Facility Category: Performing Arts Center
Type of Stage: Proscenium
Seating Capacity: 1,000
Year Built: 1925

THEATRE / Washington

Organization Type: Performing; Sponsoring

4074
CUTTER THEATRE
PO Box 133
302 Park Street
Metaline Falls, WA 99153
Mailing Address: 302 Park Street, PO Box 133, Metaline Falls, WA 99153
Phone: 509-446-4108
Fax: 509-446-3037
e-mail: cutter@potc.net
Web Site: www.cuttertheatre.com
Officers:
  President: Liz Ellsworth
  Executive Director: Jennifer Snead
Management:
  ArtScape Creative Director: Linda Bataller
  Facility & Project Manager: Van Whysong
Founded: 1982
Specialized Field: Musical; Comedy; Classic; Contemporary
Status: Non-Profit, Non-Professional
Paid Staff: 2
Budget: $93,000
Seating Capacity: 156

4075
HARLEQUIN PRODUCTIONS
State Theater
202 4th Avenue East
Olympia, WA 98501
Mailing Address: 202 Fourth Avenue East, Olympia, Washington 98501
Phone: 360-786-0151
Fax: 360-534-9659
e-mail: linda@harlequinproductions.org
Web Site: www.harlequinproductions.org
Management:
  Managing Artistic Director: Scot Whitney
  Artistic Director: Linda Whitney
  Production Manager: Derron Peterson
  General Manager: Aleena Schneider
  Technical Director: Mark Bujeaud
  Development Manager: Mark Alford
  Assistant Technical Director: Toby Batcheldor
  Production Coordinator: Gina Salerno
  Box Office Manager: Korja Giles
Mission: A nonprofit theater founded with the goal of producing a more challenging style of theater than what was already available in the community.
Founded: 1991
Specialized Field: Musical; Comedy; Contemporary
Status: Non-Profit, Professional
Paid Staff: 8
Season: May - December
Type of Stage: Thrust
Stage Dimensions: 48'6 x 32'""
Seating Capacity: 218

4076
BEASLEY PERFORMING ARTS COLISEUM
PO Box 641710
Pullman, WA 99146-1710
Mailing Address: PO Box 641710, Washington State University, Pullman WA 99164
Phone: 509-335-3525
Fax: 509-335-3853
e-mail: udy@wsu.edu
Web Site: www.beasley.wsu.edu
Management:
  Staff Technician: Chris VanHarn
  Director: Leo A. Udy
  Assistant Director: Russ Driver
  Tech Service Manager: Patrick Starr
Founded: 1972
Specialized Field: Musical; Comedy; Classic; Contemporary
Status: Non-Profit, Professional
Paid Staff: 6

4077
PULLMAN SUMMER PALACE
Theatre Program
Washington State University
Pullman, WA 99164-5300
Mailing Address: Washington State University, PO Box 645300, Pullman, WA 9916
Phone: 509-335-3898
Fax: 509-335-4245
e-mail: music@wsu.edu
Web Site: libarts.wsu.edu/musicandtheatre
Management:
  Managing Director: George Caldwell
  Administrative Manager: Rosanne Chandler
  Stage Manager: James Harris
  Website Administrator: Joe Sartori
  Performing Arts Facilities Coordina: Sandra Lea Albers
Founded: 1977
Specialized Field: Educational; Theater Workshops
Status: Non-Equity; Nonprofit
Season: July - August
Type of Stage: Proscenium
Stage Dimensions: 45' x 45'
Seating Capacity: 460

4078
ACT THEATRE
Kreielsheimer Place
700 Union Street
Seattle, WA 98101-4037
Mailing Address: Kreielsheimer Place, 700 Union St., Seattle WA 98101-4037
Phone: 206-292-7660
Fax: 206-292-7670
e-mail: service@acttheatre.org
Web Site: www.acttheatre.org
Officers:
  Chairman: Charles Sitkin
  President: Colin Chapman
  Vice President: Richard Hesik
  Treasurer: Lisa Simonson
  Secretary: Bill Kuhn
Management:
  Executive Director: Gian-Carlo Scandiuzzi
  Producing Director: Joan Toggenburger
  Artistic Director: Kurt Beattie
  Volunteer Coordinator: Lyam White
  Executive and Artistic Manager: Robert Hankins
  Associate Executive Director: Nicole Boyer Cochran
  Central Heating Lab Production: Alyssa Byer
  Casting Director & Artistic Associa: Margaret Layne
  Operations Manager: Adam Moomey
Mission: To offer the best in contemporary theater.
Utilizes: Guest Companies; Singers
Founded: 1965
Specialized Field: Contemporary
Status: Professional; Nonprofit
Paid Staff: 75
Paid Artists: 170
Budget: $5,500,000
Income Sources: Actors' Equity Association; League of Resident Theatres; American Arts Alliance; Washington State Arts Alliance
Season: March - December
Performs At: A Contemporary Theatre
Annual Attendance: 125,000
Facility Category: 4 Venue Performance Facility
Type of Stage: 3/4 Thrust; Arena; Caberat
Year Built: 1925
Year Remodeled: 1996
Rental Contact: Kristina Wicke
Organization Type: Resident

4079
BATHHOUSE THEATRE
7312 West Green Lake Dr. N-
Seattle, WA 98103
Mailing Address: 7312 West Green Lake Dr. N. Seattle, WA 98103
Phone: 206-524-1300
Fax: 206-527-1942
e-mail: boxoffice@seattlepublictheater.org
Web Site: http://www.seattlepublictheater.org
Officers:
  President: Neill Warfield
  Vice President: Wendy Woolery
  Treasurer: Greg Piantanida
  Secretary: Rebekah Hewitt
Management:
  Artistic Director and Education Dir: Shana Bestock
  Managing Director: Zo‰ Alexis Scott
  Front of House Manager: Emily Purington
  Technical Director/Production Manag: Kyna Shilling
  Communications/PR: Cole Hornaday
Mission: To develop our full potential as a resident theatre company; to put excellent theatre within reach of the widest possible audience.
Utilizes: Guest Companies
Founded: 1970
Specialized Field: Contemporary
Status: Professional; Nonprofit
Income Sources: Theatre Communications Group; Actors' Equity Association; Small Professional Theatre Association
Performs At: Bathhouse Theatre
Organization Type: Performing; Touring; Resident

4080
BOOK-IT REPERTORY THEATRE
158 Thomas Street
Seattle, WA 98109
Phone: 206-216-0877
Fax: 206-428-6263
e-mail: info@book-it.org
Web Site: book-it.org
Officers:
  President: Joann Byrd
  Vice President: Thomas Oliver
  Treasurer: Kristine Villiot
  Secretary: Shirley Robinson
Management:
  Artistic Director: Jane Jones
  Artistic Director: Myra Platt
  Managing Director: Charlotte M. Tiencken
Mission: Dedicated to transforming great literature into great theatre through simple and sensitive production and to inspiring its audiences to read.
Founded: 1990
Specialized Field: Literature To Theatre
Status: Nonprofit
Performs At: The Center Theatre 305 Harrison Street, Seattle, WA 98109
Organization Type: Performing; Touring

THEATRE / Washington

4081
EMPTY SPACE THEATRE
901 12th Avenue
PO Box 222000
Seattle, WA 98122-1090
Mailing Address: 901 12th Avenue, P.O. Box 222000, Seattle, WA 98122
Phone: 206-547-7500
Fax: 206-547-7635
e-mail: emptyspace@emptyspace.org
Web Site: www.emptyspace.org
Officers:
  Chair: Erik Blachford
  President: Ann Rickett
  Treasurer: Kathy Clark
  Secretary: Christer Hellstrand
Management:
  Managing Director: Melanie Mathews
  Artistic Director: Allison Narver
  Artisitc Associate: Shiela Daniels
  Marketing/Development Director: Christine Kolodge
  Production Manager: Amy Poisson
  Volunteer Coordinator: Jo Addison
Mission: Strives to make theater an event - bold, provocative, celebratory - bringing audiences and artists to a common ground through an uncommon experience.
Utilizes: Actors; AEA Actors; Artists-in-Residence; Designers; Five Seasonal Concerts; Guest Accompanists; Guest Conductors; Guest Designers; Guest Lecturers; Instructors; Local Artists; Original Music Scores; Performance Artists; Poets; Resident Professionals
Founded: 1971
Specialized Field: Musical
Status: Non-Profit
Paid Staff: 6
Volunteer Staff: 80
Paid Artists: 30
Non-paid Artists: 3
Budget: $600,000
Income Sources: Ticket Sales; Donations; Grants
Affiliations: TCG, TPS, AEA
Annual Attendance: 10,000
Facility Category: Theater
Type of Stage: Flexible Black Box
Seating Capacity: 150
Year Built: 1940
Year Remodeled: 2006
Cost: $7 million
Rental Contact: 206-296-5360 Steve Galato
Organization Type: Performing; Resident; Educational

4082
INTIMAN THEATRE COMPANY
201 Mercer Street, Seattle Center
PO Box 19537
Seattle, WA 98109
Mailing Address: PO Box 19537, Seattle, WA 98109
Phone: 206-441-7178
Fax: 206-269-1928
e-mail: info@intiman.org
Web Site: www.intiman.org
Officers:
  Immediate Past President: Terry Jones
  Treasurer: Joel Bodansky
  Secretary: Mary Ann Midori Goto
  President: Cynthia Huffman
Management:
  Technical Director: Dana Perreault
  Artistic Director: Andrew Russell
  Managing Director: Keri Kellerman
  Production Director: Evan Tucker
  Office Manager: Molly Benson
  General Manager: Art Bridenstine
  Associate Managing Director: Rebecca Sherr
  Assistant/Managing Director: Precious Butiu
  Production Manager: David A Mulligan
Mission: To produce engaging dramatic work that celebrates the intimate relationship among audience and language and, through the exploration of enduring themes, illuminates the shared human experience of our diverse community.
Founded: 1972
Specialized Field: Drama; New Works of Social Importance
Season: May - December
Performs At: Intiman Playhouse
Type of Stage: Modified Thrust
Seating Capacity: 480
Year Remodeled: 1987
Cost: $1,200,000

4083
NEW CITY THEATER
1404 18th Avenue
Seattle, WA 98122
Mailing Address: 1404 18th Avenue, Seattle, WA 98122
Phone: 206-271-4430
Fax: 206-328-4683
e-mail: newcitytheater@comcast.net
Web Site: www.newcitytheater.org
Management:
  Artistic Director: John Kazanjian
  Theater Manager: Alan Horton
Mission: Dedicated to research and development in the contemporary arts.
Utilizes: Guest Companies
Founded: 1982
Specialized Field: Contemporary
Status: Professional; Nonprofit
Income Sources: Theatre Communications Group
Performs At: The New City Theatre
Organization Type: Performing; Resident

4084
NORTHWEST PUPPET
9123 15th Avenue NE
Seattle, WA 98115
Mailing Address: 9123 15th Ave. NE, Seattle, WA 98115
Phone: 206-523-2579
Fax: 206-523-8078
e-mail: info@nwpuppet.org
Web Site: www.nwpuppet.org
Management:
  Executive Co-Director: Stephen Carter
  Executive Co-Director: Chris Carter
Mission: To create professional puppet theater; to present top quality puppet theater; to teach puppet skills and cultural knowledge; to serve children and adults by providing entertainment and education.
Founded: 1985
Specialized Field: Puppet
Status: Professional; Nonprofit
Paid Staff: 2
Income Sources: Puppeteers of America; United International Marionette Association
Organization Type: Performing; Touring; Resident; Educational; Sponsoring

4085
SEATTLE CHILDREN'S THEATRE
201 Thomas Street
Seattle, WA 98109
Mailing Address: 201 Thomas Street, Seattle, WA 98109
Phone: 206-443-0807
Fax: 206-443-0442
e-mail: sctpr@sct.org
Web Site: www.sct.org
Officers:
  President: Terrence I. Danysh
  First Vice President: Bob Evans
  Second Vice President: Stacie Foster
  Secretary: Robert Grant
  Treasurer: Laura Smith
  Immediate Past President: Mark Sherman
Management:
  Artistic Director: Linda Hartzell
  Managing Director: Mary Ann Ehlshlager
  Director of Finance: Dean Barney
  Special Events Manager: Barrie Cohen
  Marketing & PR Coordinator: Chris Allen
  Properties Shop Manager: Elizabeth Friedrich
  Company Manager: Alexis Garrigues
  Technical Director: Michael K. Hase
  Production Manager: Michael Wellborn
Mission: To produce professional theater for the young with appeal to people of all ages; to provide theater education and theater arts training; to develop scripts and musical scores for new theater works.
Founded: 1975
Specialized Field: Children's Theater; Drama
Status: Non-Profit, Professional
Budget: $5,300,000
Performs At: Charlotte Martin Theatre; Eve Alvovd Theatre
Affiliations: ASSITES/USA; Actors' Equity Association/TYA; American Association of Theatre Educators; International Alliance of Theatrical Stage Employees; TCG
Annual Attendance: 250,000
Seating Capacity: 480; 285
Year Built: 1993
Rental Contact: General Manager Shelley Sanders
Organization Type: Performing; Touring; Resident; Educational

4086
SEATTLE MIME THEATRE
915 E Pine Street
Suite 419
Seattle, WA 98122
Mailing Address: 915 East Pine Street, #419 Seattle WA 98122
Phone: 206-324-8788
Fax: 206-322-5569
e-mail: admin@seattlemime.org
Web Site: www.seattlemime.org
Management:
  President: Richard Davidson
  Managing Director: Hal Ryder
  Artistic Director: Bruce Wylie
Mission: Dedicated to enlivening the imaginations of minds and bodies of people of all ages with its unique form of physical theater through the interlaced processes of creation, teaching and performances.
Utilizes: Actors; Artists-in-Residence; Choreographers; Collaborating Artists; Collaborations; Community Talent; Contract Actors; Dance Companies; Dancers; Educators; Guest Artists; Guest Companies; Guest Designers; Instructors; Local Artists; Lyricists; Multi Collaborations; Performance Artists; Selected Students; Soloists; Theatre Companies
Founded: 1977
Specialized Field: Comedy; Contemporary
Status: Non-Profit, Professional
Paid Staff: 3

Paid Artists: 3
Facility Category: Offices and Theater
Type of Stage: Black Box
Stage Dimensions: 55'x40'
Seating Capacity: 49
Rental Contact: Richard Davidson
Organization Type: Performing; Touring; Educational

4087
SEATTLE REPERTORY THEATRE
155 Mercer Street
PO Box 900923
Seattle, WA 98109
Mailing Address: 155 Mercer Street, PO Box 900923, Seattle, WA 98109
Phone: 206-443-2222
Fax: 206-443-2379
Toll-free: 877-900-9285
e-mail: info@seattlerep.org
Web Site: www.seattlerep.org
Officers:
  Chair: Shauna Woods
  President: Becky Lenaburg
  Vice President/Treasurer: Jean-Pierre Green
  Secretary: Earle J. Hereford
  President-Elect: Tamara Chandler
Management:
  Acting Artistic Director: Braden Abraham
  Managing Director: Benjamin Moore
  Technical Director: Brian Fauska
  Associate Production Manager: Matt Giles
  Production Management: Katie O'Kelly
  Associate Artistic Director: Braden Abraham
  Company Manager: Sarah Schezer
  Director of Board Relations: Sarah Newell
  Production Coordinator: Sann Hall
Mission: To offer professional live theatre and education for residents of the Pacific Northwest.
Utilizes: Actors; AEA Actors; Choreographers; Commissioned Composers; Commissioned Music; Designers; Five Seasonal Concerts; Guest Accompanists; Guest Artists; Guest Companies; Guest Conductors; Guest Designers; Guest Lecturers; Guest Musical Directors; Guest Soloists; Guest Teachers; High School Drama; Local Artists; Multimedia; Music; Original Music Scores; Performance Artists; Resident Professionals; Selected Students; Singers; Student Interns
Founded: 1963
Specialized Field: Musical; Comedy; Classic; Contemporary
Status: Non-Profit, Professional
Paid Staff: 150
Income Sources: Actors' Equity Association; League of Resident Theatres
Performs At: Bagley Wright Theatre
Facility Category: Theatre
Type of Stage: Proscenium
Seating Capacity: 856 and 286
Year Built: 1983
Year Remodeled: 1996
Rental Contact: Ten Eyck Swackharner
Organization Type: Performing; Resident

4088
TAPROOT THEATRE COMPANY
204 N 85th Street
PO Box 30946
Seattle, WA 98103
Mailing Address: PO Box 30946, Seattle, WA 98113
Phone: 206-781-9705
Fax: 206-297-6882
e-mail: info@taproottheatre.org
Web Site: www.taproottheatre.org
Officers:
  President: Scott Nolte
  Treasurer: Peter Morrill
  Board Chair: Larry Bjork
  Vice Chairman: Dale Smith
  Secretary: Rob Zawoysky
  Secretary: Carolyn Hanson
  Immediate Past Chair: George Myers
Management:
  Producing Artistic Director, Presid: Scott Nolte
  Associate Artistic Director: Karen Lund
  Design Director: Mark Lund
  Production Stage Manager: Micah Trapp
  Costume Shop Manager: Sarah Burch Gordon
  Marketing Director: Nikki Visel
  Finance and Operations Director: Rick Rodenbeck
  Communications Manager: Elizabeth Griffin
  Marketing Associate: Sonja Lowe
Mission: Taproot Theatre exists to create theatre that explores the beauty and questions of life while providing hope to our search for meaning.
Utilizes: Actors; AEA Actors; Designers; Guest Accompanists; Guest Artists; Guest Companies; Guest Conductors; High School Drama; Local Artists; Multimedia; Organization Contracts; Original Music Scores; Resident Artists; Resident Professionals; Sign Language Translators
Founded: 1976
Specialized Field: Classic
Status: Non-Profit, Professional
Paid Staff: 24
Volunteer Staff: 285
Paid Artists: 98
Affiliations: TCG; CITA; Greenwood Chamber of Commerce
Annual Attendance: 85,000
Facility Category: Renovated historic cinema
Type of Stage: Thrust
Stage Dimensions: 15'x22'
Seating Capacity: 226
Year Built: 1915
Year Remodeled: 1996
Rental Contact: Anne Hitt
Organization Type: Performing; Touring; Resident

4089
THEATER SCHMEATER
2125 3rd Ave.
Seattle, WA 98121
Mailing Address: 1500 Summit Ave., Seattle, WA 98122
Phone: 206-324-5801
e-mail: md@schmeater.org
Web Site: http://www.schmeater.org/index.php
Officers:
  President: Andrew Bishop
  Vice President: Katherine Woolverton
  Secretary: Jill Snyder Marr
  Treasurer: Amy Wallace
Management:
  Artistic Associate: J.D. Lloyd
  Managing Director: Teri Lazzara
  Managing Director: Roger Huston
  Resident Lighting Designer: Steve Cooper
  Artistic Associate/Casting Director: Julia Griffin
  Artistic Director: Doug Staley
  Assistant Managing Director: Jaime Shure
  Production Manager: Carrisa Meisner Smit
  Resident Stage Manager: Lisa A. Stahler
Specialized Field: Classic; Contemporary

4090
INTERPLAYERS ENSEMBLE THEATRE
174 S Howard Street
Spokane, WA 99201
Mailing Address: 174 S. Howard Street, Spokane, WA 99201
Phone: 509-455-7529
e-mail: info@interplayers.com
Web Site: www.Interplayers.com
Officers:
  President: Lucretia Pladera
  Vice President: George Lathrop
  Business Manager: Esta Rosevear
  Secretary: Patricia Dicker
Management:
  Executive Director: Pamela Brown
  Artistic Director: Reed McColm
Mission: Serving Spokane with challenging, diverse and inspiring productions, Interplayers is a major contributor to the Inland Northwest cultural quality of life. A professional theatre listed on the National Register of Historic Places and the Washington State Historic Register, Interplayers is pivotal to the economic revitalization of downtown Spokane.
Founded: 1980
Specialized Field: Ensembles
Paid Staff: 8

4091
SPOKANE CIVIC THEATRE
1020 N. Howard Street
PO Box 5222
Spokane, WA 99201
Mailing Address: 1020 N. Howard Street, Spokane, WA 99201
Phone: 509-325-2507
Fax: 509-325-9287
Toll-free: 800-446-9576
e-mail: civictheatre@mindspring.com
Web Site: www.spokanecivictheatre.com
Officers:
  President: Larry Wooley
  Vice President: Jason Coleman-Heppler
  Treasurer: Bob Francis
  Member-at-Large: Barry Jones
Management:
  Technical Director: David Baker
  Artistic Director: Keith Dixon
  Managing Director: James Humes
  Education Director: Christopher Taylor
  Assistant Technical Director: Matthew Egan
Mission: To offer opportunities for participation in the art of theatre; to promote new plays.
Utilizes: Actors; Artists-in-Residence; Choreographers; Collaborations; Dancers; Designers; Fine Artists; Five Seasonal Concerts; Grant Writers; Guest Accompanists; Guest Artists; Guest Designers; Guest Ensembles; Guest Lecturers; Guest Teachers; Guild Activities; Local Artists; Multimedia; Music; Organization Contracts; Original Music Scores; Performance Artists; Selected Students; Sign Language Translators; Singers; Student Interns; Touring Companies
Founded: 1947
Specialized Field: Community Theater
Status: Non-Profit, Non-Professional
Paid Staff: 7
Budget: $625,000
Income Sources: Washington State Arts Commission; Allen Foundation; Box Office
Performs At: Spokane Civic Theatres
Affiliations: American Association of Community Theatres; WA Arts Alliance; TCG
Annual Attendance: 35,000

THEATRE / West Virginia

Facility Category: Theatre
Type of Stage: Proscenium; Black Box
Seating Capacity: 339; 100
Year Built: 1966
Year Remodeled: 1999
Rental Contact: Jack Phillips
Organization Type: Performing; Educational

4092
SPOKANE INTERPLAYERS ENSEMBLE
174 S Howard Street
Spokane, WA 99204
Mailing Address: 174 S. Howard Street, Spokane, WA 99201
Phone: 509-455-7529
Fax: 509-624-9348
e-mail: info@interplayers.com
Web Site: www.interplayers.com
Officers:
   President: Lucretia Pladera
   Vice President: George Lathrop
   Secretary: Patricia Dicker
   Business Manager: Esta Rosevear
Management:
   Executive Director: Pamela Brown
   Artistic Director: Reed McColm
   Marketing and Development: Grant Smith
   Production Manager: Jason Lewis
   Box Office Manager: Kyrstin Vens
   Box Office Assistant: Denise Olson
   Communications Manager: Andrew Mitchell
   Manager: Toni Plastino
   Volunteer Coordinator: Jamie Sciarrio
Mission: To maintain a resident non-profit, professional theatre company offering an annual season ranging from contemporary and classic to original works.
Utilizes: Actors; Collaborations; Designers; Fine Artists; Guest Companies; Guest Conductors; Guest Designers; High School Drama; Instructors; Local Artists; Original Music Scores; Performance Artists; Resident Professionals; Student Interns
Founded: 1980
Specialized Field: Musical; Comedy; Contemporary; Ensembles
Status: Non-Profit, Professional
Paid Staff: 14
Volunteer Staff: 150
Paid Artists: 100
Budget: $485,000
Income Sources: Ticket Sales; Grants
Performs At: Spokane Interplayers Ensemble Theatre
Affiliations: Theatre Communications Group
Annual Attendance: 25,000
Type of Stage: Thrust
Seating Capacity: 253
Year Built: 1926
Year Remodeled: 1980
Organization Type: Performing; Resident; Educational

4093
TACOMA ACTORS GUILD
901 Broadway
Suite 600
Tacoma, WA 98402
Phone: 253-272-3107
Fax: 253-272-3358
Management:
   General Manager: Chris Shelton
   Artistic Director: Pat Petttan
Mission: To offer quality theatre and to entertain and enrich the South Puget Sound area.

Utilizes: Actors; AEA Actors; Choreographers; Educators; Guest Companies; Guest Designers; Guest Lecturers; Guest Musical Directors; Multimedia; Music; Original Music Scores; Resident Professionals; Student Interns; Visual Arts
Founded: 1978
Specialized Field: Drama; Theater Workshops
Status: Professional; Nonprofit
Income Sources: Theatre Communications Group
Performs At: Tacoma Actors Guild
Annual Attendance: 35,000
Seating Capacity: 302
Year Built: 1998
Cost: $8,000,000
Organization Type: Performing; Resident

4094
SLOCUM HOUSE THEATRE COMPANY
3909 Main st
Vancouver, WA 98663
Mailing Address: 3909 Main st, Vancouver, WA 98663
Phone: 360-696-2427
e-mail: info@slocumhouse.com
Web Site: www.slocumhouse.com
Officers:
   Vice President: Rebecca Kramer
   President: Jim Fully
   Treasurer: Steve Herron
   Secretary: Beth Duvall
Mission: The restoration of the Slocum House Theatre and the production of 19th-century plays.
Founded: 1966
Specialized Field: Musical; Community Theater
Status: Non-Profit
Organization Type: Resident

4095
COLUMBIA GORGE REPERTORY THEATRE
9215 NE 316th Street
White Salmon, WA 98629
Mailing Address: 1381 Snowden Road, White Salmon, WA 98672
Phone: 503-367-2538
Fax: 360-666-4936
Toll-free: 800-405-3450
e-mail: BlueMoon91@aol.com
Web Site: www.cgrep.com
Management:
   Artistic Director: Jesse Merz
   Executive Director: Jan James
   Dance Director: Jennifer Seigle
   Camp Director: Laurel Merz
   Camp Director: Karisa Chappell
Founded: 1996
Specialized Field: Summer Stock; New Plays
Status: Non-Equity; Commercial
Season: June - September
Type of Stage: Proscenium
Stage Dimensions: 30' x 40'
Seating Capacity: 150

West Virginia

4096
THEATRE WEST VIRGINIA
PO Box 1205
Beckley, WV 25802
Mailing Address: PO Box 1205, Beckley, WV 25802
Phone: 304-256-6800
Fax: 304-256-6807

Toll-free: 800-666-9142
e-mail: theatrewv@suddenlinkmail.com
Web Site: www.theatrewestvirginia.com
Officers:
   President: John Rist
   VP: Mike Cavendish
   Secretary: Cindy Worley
   Treasurer: Brad Wartella
   Marketing Director: Lola Rizer
Management:
   General Manager: Gayle Bowling
   Executive Director: Marina Hunley
   Office Manager/Touring Sales Direct: Lou Ann Grose
   Facilities Manager: Acie Toler
   Receptionist: Lisa Mills
Mission: To provide theatre of the highest quality to community and state residents as well as tourists.
Utilizes: Actors; Choreographers; Dancers; Designers; Local Artists; Music; Original Music Scores; Resident Professionals; Sign Language Translators; Soloists; Student Interns
Founded: 1961
Specialized Field: Touring Company; Marionettes; Educational
Status: Non-Profit, Professional
Paid Staff: 60
Paid Artists: 70
Season: June - August
Annual Attendance: 120,000
Facility Category: Amphitheatre; Touring
Stage Dimensions: 60'x60'
Seating Capacity: 1,259
Year Built: 1960
Year Remodeled: 1991
Organization Type: Performing; Touring; Educational; Sponsoring

4097
KANAWHA PLAYERS
Kanawha Players Theatre
309 Beauregard St.
Charleston, WV 25301
Mailing Address: 309 Beauregard St., Charleston, WV 25301
Phone: 304-343-7529
e-mail: info@kanawhaplayers.org
Web Site: www.kanawhaplayers.org
Officers:
   President: Katonya Hart
   President: Ginger Workman
   Treasurer: Mary Nichols
   Secretary: Christopher Weddle
   Vice President: Stephen Baier
Management:
   Artistic Director: Jeff Haught
   Historian: Jimmy Stann
Utilizes: Singers
Founded: 1922
Specialized Field: Community Theater
Status: Non-Profit, Non-Professional
Paid Staff: 2
Income Sources: Arts Advocacy of West Virginia
Performs At: Charleston Civic Center-Little Theatre
Organization Type: Performing; Touring; Educational

4098
SEVEN STORIES THEATRE COMPANY
146 Michael Development Road
Fairmont, WV 26554
Phone: 304-212-8038
e-mail: joey@sevenstoriestheatre.org
Web Site: sevenstoriestheatre.org
Management:

Artistic Director: Joey Madia
Mission: To use the performing arts, literary, and visual arts as a means of engaging young people, faculty, families, and communities in explorations of cultural and social issues affecting our lives.
Founded: 2005
Status: Nonprofit
Organization Type: Performing; Educational

4099
APPLE ALLEY PLAYERS
PO Box 144
Keyser, WV 26726
Phone: 304-788-1105
Fax: 304-788-5883
e-mail: applealleyplayers@yahoo.com
Web Site: applealleyplayers.com/
Officers:
 President: Annette Favara
 VP: Bob Shadier
 Secretary: Alexa Fazenbaker
 Treasurer: Sandy Shadler
Management:
 Manager: Vinnie Favara
Mission: To provide quality theatre for the surrounding area.
Utilizes: Singers
Founded: 1980
Specialized Field: Community Theater
Status: Nonprofit
Performs At: McKee Art Center; Potomac State College
Organization Type: Resident; Sponsoring

4100
GREENBRIER VALLEY THEATRE
113 E Washington Street
PO Box 494
Lewisburg, WV 24901
Mailing Address: 113 East Washington Street, P.O. Box 494, Lewisburg, WV 2490
Phone: 304-645-3838
Fax: 304-645-3818
Toll-free: 866-888-1411
e-mail: info@gvtheatre.org
Web Site: www.gvtheatre.org
Officers:
 President: Claire LaRocco
 Secretary: Carolyn Rudley
 Treasurer: Stephen P King
Management:
 Artistic Director: Cathey Crowell Sawyer
 General Manager: Pamela Paul
 Publicity/Marketing Director: Michelle James
 House Manager/Volunteer Director: Jane Matheny
 Technical Director: Josh Robinson
 Volunteer Director: Jane Matheny
Mission: To provide a vehicle for bringing live, professional-quality theatre experiences to our community; to explore all practical means of encouraging the performing arts and artists in our area.
Utilizes: Actors; AEA Actors; Choreographers; Collaborations; Dancers; Educators; Five Seasonal Concerts; Grant Writers; Guest Accompanists; Guest Artists; Guest Choreographers; Guest Conductors; Guest Designers; Guest Ensembles; Guest Instructors; Guest Lecturers; Guest Musical Directors; Guest Teachers; Guild Activities; Instructors; Local Unknown Artists; Multimedia; Music; Original Music Scores; Performance Artists; Playwrights; Resident Artists; Resident Professionals; Soloists; Student Interns
Founded: 1966

Specialized Field: Contemporary; Classic; Musical; Children's Theater; Educational
Status: Non-Profit, Professional
Paid Staff: 18
Budget: $400,000
Income Sources: Private Donations; Foundation
Performs At: Hollowell Theatre; Black Box Flexible Seating
Annual Attendance: 10,000
Facility Category: Black Box
Type of Stage: Flexable-Sprung Floor
Stage Dimensions: Fexible
Seating Capacity: 150; 200
Year Built: 1953
Year Remodeled: 2000
Cost: $1,700,000
Rental Contact: Cathy Sawyer
Organization Type: Performing; Touring; Educational

4101
ARACOMA STORY
214 Main Street
PO Box 2016
Logan, WV 25601
Mailing Address: 214 Main Street, PO Box 2016, Logan, West Virginia 25601
Phone: 304-752-0253
Fax: 304-752-0253
e-mail: thearacomastoryinc@gmail.com
Web Site: www.thearacomastory.com
Officers:
 Board Chairman: Liz Spurlock
 President: Diana O'Briant
 Vice President: Gary Hylton
 Secretary: Carol Cole
Management:
 President: Lez Spurlock
 Executive Director: Jeannie Gore
 Stage Manager: Emma Squire
 Assistant Technical Director: Seth Dempsey
 Technical Director: Hayes O'Brien
Founded: 1976
Specialized Field: Musical; Puppet
Status: Non-Profit, Non-Professional
Paid Staff: 4
Volunteer Staff: 5
Paid Artists: 5
Non-paid Artists: 50
Season: June - August
Annual Attendance: 3,000
Facility Category: Amphitheatre
Type of Stage: Proscenium-Wood Walls
Stage Dimensions: 60' x 40'
Seating Capacity: 650
Year Built: 1982
Year Remodeled: 2002

4102
COLLEGE OF CREATIVE ARTS
West Virginia University
PO Box 6111
Morgantown, WV 26506-6111
Mailing Address: PO Box 6111, Morgantown, West Virginia 26506-6111
Phone: 304-293-4841
Fax: 304-293-6896
e-mail: mark.oreskovich@mail.wvu.edu
Web Site: www.ccarts.wvu.edu
Management:
 Director Of Recruitment: Amy Burgess
 Administrative Secretary: Catherine Roberto
 Chief Business Officer: Vicki Grim
 Office Administrator: Scott Morrison

 Director of Student Records & Advis: Jeanne Frieben
 Public Relations Specialist: Charlene Lattea
 Director of Development: Glenn Rosswurm
 Assistant Director of Creative Arts: Mark Oreskovich
 Accounting Assistant II: Natalie Buckley
Mission: Educational facility
Utilizes: Actors; AEA Actors; Artists-in-Residence; Choreographers; Collaborating Artists; Commissioned Music; Community Talent; Composers; Curators; Dance Companies; Dancers; Designers; Educators; Guest Accompanists; Guest Artists; Guest Companies; Guest Composers; Guest Designers; Guest Directors; Guest Instructors; Guest Lecturers; Guest Speakers; High School Drama; Instructors; Multimedia; Music; Original Music Scores; Paid Performers; Performance Artists; Sign Language Translators; Singers; Students; Special Technical Talent; Theatre Companies; Visual Arts
Specialized Field: Musical
Income Sources: Stage; Private
Performs At: Lyell B. Clay Concert Theatre, Gladys G. Davis Theatre, Antoinette A. Falbo Theatre, Vivian Davis Michael Laboratory Theatre
Affiliations: NASM - National Association of Schools of Theatre; NASAD - National Association of Schools of Art and Design
Annual Attendance: 1,000
Facility Category: Educational
Type of Stage: Proscenium
Stage Dimensions: 16'x32'
Seating Capacity: 75
Year Built: 1968
Year Remodeled: 1998
Cost: $50,000

4103
WEST VIRGINIA PUBLIC THEATRE
111 High Street
Morgantown, WV 26505
Mailing Address: 111 High Street, Morgantown, WV 26505
Phone: 304-291-4117
Fax: 304-291-4125
Toll-free: 877-999-WVPT
e-mail: info@wvpublictheatre.org
Web Site: www.wvpublictheatre.org
Management:
 President: Ron Iannone
 Managing Director: Mary Beth Sickles
Utilizes: Actors; Contract Actors; Contract Orchestras; Five Seasonal Concerts; Guest Accompanists; Guest Choreographers; Performance Artists
Founded: 1985
Specialized Field: Drama; Musical
Status: Non-Profit, Professional
Paid Staff: 3
Paid Artists: 200
Season: June - August
Seating Capacity: 650

4104
CONTEMPORARY AMERICAN THEATER FESTIVAL
Sheperd University
PO Box 429
Shepherdstown, WV 25443
Mailing Address: PO Box 429, Shepherdstown, WV 25443
Phone: 304-876-3473
Fax: 304-876-5443
e-mail: info@catf.org
Web Site: www.catf.org
Officers:

THEATRE / Wisconsin

President: Jenny Ewing Allen
VP Operations: Skip Adkins
Secretary: Michael Proffitt
Treasurer: Karen Rice
Vice President: Ann Harkins
Management:
Technical Director: Patrick Wallace
Managing Director: James McNeel
Producing Director/ Founder: Ed Herendeen
Associate Producing Director: Peggy McKowen
Production Coordinator: Christina Smith
Director of Production: Patrick H. Wallace
Founded: 1991
Specialized Field: Contemporary
Status: Non-Profit
Performs At: Main Stage; Studio Theater
Type of Stage: Proscenium, Black Box
Seating Capacity: 350; 99

4105
BROOKE HILLS PLAYHOUSE
140 Gist Drive
PO Box 186
Wellsburg, WV 26070
Mailing Address: PO Box 186, Wellsburg, WV 26070
Phone: 304-737-3344
Fax: 304-737-4247
e-mail: juliabarnhart@aol.com
Web Site: http://brookehillsplayhouse.com
Officers:
President: Julia Barnhart
Vice President: Charles Calabrese
Secretary: Amy Balog
Treasurer: Diana Mendel
Founded: 1972
Specialized Field: Musical; Contemporary
Status: Non-Profit, Non-Professional
Paid Staff: 4
Volunteer Staff: 6
Income Sources: Ticket Sales
Season: June - August
Annual Attendance: 4,000
Facility Category: Barn
Type of Stage: Proscenium
Stage Dimensions: 26' x 22'
Seating Capacity: 195

Wisconsin

4106
AL RINGLING THEATRE LIVELY ARTS SERIES
136 Fourth Avenue
PO Box 381
Baraboo, WI 53913
Mailing Address: 136 Fourth Avenue, P.O. Box 381, Baraboo, WI 53913
Phone: 608-356-8864
Fax: 608-356-0976
e-mail: info@alringling.com
Web Site: www.alringling.com
Officers:
President: Charlene Flygt
Vice President: Carol Kratochwill
Treasurer: Stephanie Potter
Secretary: Rebecca Oettinger
Management:
Executive Director: Brian Heller
Director: Brian Heller
Assistant Director: Beth Rozman
Founded: 1989
Specialized Field: Musical; Comedy; Puppet
Status: Non-Profit, Non-Professional
Paid Staff: 4
Volunteer Staff: 80
Budget: $20,000-$35,000
Facility Category: Vandeville/Movie Palace
Type of Stage: Proscenium
Stage Dimensions: 37' x 27'
Seating Capacity: 750
Year Built: 1915

4107
CHIPPEWA VALLEY THEATRE GUILD
102 W Grand Avenue
Eau Claire, WI 54703
Mailing Address: 102 West Grand Avenue, Eau Claire, WI 54703
Phone: 715-832-7529
Fax: 715-832-7528
e-mail: cvtgact@aol.com
Web Site: www.cvtg.org
Officers:
President: Jim Matteson
Vice President: Karen Welch
Executive Director: Ann Sessions
Management:
Executive Director: Ann Sessions
Volunteer Coordinator: Sandy Barsamian
Mission: To bring quality theatre productions to our area, as well as allowing community members to perform in a theatrical production.
Utilizes: Singers
Founded: 1982
Specialized Field: Musical; Comedy
Status: Non-Profit, Non-Professional
Paid Staff: 2
Volunteer Staff: 300
Income Sources: Eau Claire Parks & Recreation
Performs At: The State Regional Arts Center
Annual Attendance: 10,500
Seating Capacity: 1,117
Organization Type: Performing; Educational

4108
EAU CLAIRE CHILDREN'S THEATRE
1814 N Oxford Avenue
Eau Claire, WI 54703
Mailing Address: 1814 N Oxford Avenue, Eau Claire, WI 54703
Phone: 715-839-8877
e-mail: info@ecct.org
Web Site: www.ecct.org
Management:
Executive Director: Wayne Marek
Marketing/Outreach Director: Lee Heike
Costume Designer: Ann Behrens
Promotions Director: Shelly Grokowsky
Scenic Coordinator: Mike Kolstad
Costume Assistant: Kate DiSalle
Special Events Coordinator: Shelly Grokowsky
Mission: Providing quality theatrical and educational experiences for western Wisconsin residents of all ages.
Specialized Field: Community Theater; Theater Workshops

4109
SUNSET PLAYHOUSE
800 Elm Grove Road
Elm Grove, WI 53122
Mailing Address: P.O. Box 2, Elm Grove, WI 53122
Phone: 262-782-4430
Fax: 262-782-3150
e-mail: mtucker@sunsetplayhouse.com
Web Site: www.sunsetplayhouse.com
Officers:
President: Marla Eichmann
Vice President: Richard Katschke
Treasurer: Paul Armstrong
Secretary: Tamara Martinsek
Management:
Artistic Director: Nancy Visintainer-Armstron
Technical Director: Michael Desper
Managing Director: Jonathan West
Education Director: Erika Navin
Association Director: Karen Owecki
Production Volunteer Coordinator: Kristen Kraklow
Box Office Manager: Stephanie Rejman-Staufenbeil
Operations Manager: Michelle Tucker
Mission: To introduce as many new people as possible to live entertainment.
Founded: 1954
Specialized Field: Drama; Summer Stock
Status: Non-Profit, Non-Professional
Paid Staff: 7
Performs At: Sunset Playhouse
Organization Type: Performing; Open Auditions

4110
AMERICAN FOLKLORE THEATRE
PO Box 273
Fish Creek, WI 54212
Mailing Address: P.O. Box 273, Fish Creek, WI 54212
Phone: 920-854-6117
Fax: 920-854-9106
e-mail: gen@folkloretheatre.com
Web Site: www.folkloretheatre.com
Officers:
Chairperson: Mary Seeberg
Vice Chairperson: Cynthia Stiehl
Treasurer: Thomas A. Moore
Secretary: Barbara Gould
Management:
Managing Director: Dave Maier
Artistic Director: Jeffrey Herbst
Technical Director: David Alley
Production Stage Manager: Neen Rock
Company Manager: Pete Evans
Office Manager: Carey Hale
Box Office Manager: Natalie Gorchynsky
Mission: To develop and present professional dramatic productions of a cultural and/or educational nature which will futher the knowledge and appreciation of the heritage of the United States.
Founded: 1990
Specialized Field: Musical; Ethnic Theater
Status: Non-Profit, Professional
Budget: 850,000
Income Sources: Box Office; Donations; Sponsorships; Grants
Season: May - September
Affiliations: TCG; NAMT; Theatre Wisconsin
Annual Attendance: 50,000
Facility Category: Indoor and Outdoor
Type of Stage: Proscenium
Stage Dimensions: 35' x 15'
Seating Capacity: 750
Year Built: 1962
Year Remodeled: 2003

4111
PENINSULA PLAYERS
W 4351 Peninsula Players Road
Fish Creek, WI 54212
Mailing Address: W4351 Peninsula Players Road, Fish Creek, WI 54212
Phone: 920-868-3287

THEATRE / Wisconsin

Fax: 920-868-2295
e-mail: ticket@peninsulaplayers.com
Web Site: www.peninsulaplayers.com
Management:
   Production Manager: Michelle Raymonde
   Stage Manager: Alden Vasquez
   Executive Producer: Todd Schmidt
   Sound Design: Nick Keenan
   Lighting Design: Stephen Roy White
Mission: As America's oldest professional resident summer theatre, our purpose is to present the latest of Broadway fare.
Founded: 1935
Specialized Field: Musical; Comedy; Summer Stock
Status: Non-Profit, Professional
Income Sources: Council of Resident Summer Theatres; Actors' Equity Association
Season: June - October
Performs At: Theatre in a Garden; Open Air Pavilion
Organization Type: Performing; Resident; Educational

4112
NORTHERN LIGHTS PLAYHOUSE
5611 US Highway 51
Hazelhurst, WI 54531
Mailing Address: PO Box 395, Hazelhurst, WI 54531
Phone: 715-356-0003
Fax: 715-356-1851
e-mail: nlplays@newnorth.net
Web Site: www.northernlightsplayhouse.com
Officers:
   President: Micheal Cupp
Management:
   Technical Director: Eric J. Rautmann
Founded: 1976
Specialized Field: Drama; Musical
Status: Non-Profit, Non-Professional
Season: May - October
Type of Stage: Proscenium
Seating Capacity: 299

4113
BROOM STREET THEATER
1119 Williamson Street
Madison, WI 53703
Mailing Address: 1119 Williamson St., Madison, WI 53703
Phone: 608-244-8338
e-mail: board@bstonline.org
Web Site: http://www.bstonline.org
Officers:
   Chairperson: Rod Clark
   Acting Chairperson/Vice Chairperson: Kurt Meyer
   Treasurer: Joseph Lutz
   President: Scott Feiner
Management:
   Artistic Director: Heather Renken
   Technical Director: Matt Kenyon
   Development Director: Odari McWhorter
Mission: Produces eight original plays by Madison playwrights per year. The shows are directed or supervised by the play-wrights. Our work is highly visual and physical. We are one of the oldest experimental theaters in the United States, and occasionally tour.
Founded: 1968
Specialized Field: Drama; Contemporary
Status: Professional; Nonprofit
Paid Staff: 150
Organization Type: Performing

4114
FOUR SEASONS THEATRE
P.O. Box 8765
Madison, WI 53708
Phone: 608-616-5721
e-mail: smarty@fourseasonstheatre.com
Web Site: fourseasonstheatre.com
Management:
   Producing Artistic Director: Sarah Marty
Mission: Using musical theatre as a means of engagement, Four Seasons Theatre strives to create a strong organization which provides a consistent, high quality experience for everyone involved onstage, backstage, in the audience, and in the community.
Founded: 2005
Status: Public Charity
Organization Type: Performing; Educational

4115
MADISON REPERTORY THEATRE
1 South Pinckney Street
Suite 340
Madison, WI 53703
Mailing Address: 1 South Pinckney Street, Madison, WI 53703
Phone: 608-256-0029
Fax: 608-256-7433
e-mail: postmaster@madisonrep.org
Web Site: www.madisonrep.org
Officers:
   President: Tim Christen
   President Elect: Robert Birkhauser
Management:
   President: Lee Eisenberg
   VP: Jennifer Kraemer
   Artistic Director: Richard Corley
Mission: Mission is to produce, in an intimate setting, both new and classical work for a diverse audience.
Utilizes: Selected Students; Student Interns
Founded: 1969
Specialized Field: Drama; Comedy; Youth Theater
Status: Professional
Paid Staff: 20
Volunteer Staff: 350
Paid Artists: 18
Budget: $1,300,000
Income Sources: 60% Earned; 40% Conutributed
Affiliations: Actors' Equity Association; TCG
Annual Attendance: 35,000
Type of Stage: Thrust Stage
Stage Dimensions: 24'x30'
Seating Capacity: 335
Year Built: 1978
Year Remodeled: 2004
Rental Contact: Madison Civic Center
Organization Type: Performing; Resident

4116
MADISON THEATRE GUILD
2410 Monroe Street
Madison, WI 53711
Mailing Address: 2410 Monroe Street, Madison, WI 53711
Phone: 608-238-9322
e-mail: info@madisontheatreguild.org
Web Site: www.madisontheatreguild.org
Officers:
   President: Jim Chiolino
   Treasurer: Ilona Pinzke
   Vice President: Betty Diamond
   Secretary: Emily Ranney
Management:
   Costume Shop Manager: Robby Sonzogi
Mission: To provide education and recreation through theatrical production.
Utilizes: Singers
Founded: 1946
Specialized Field: Community Theater
Status: Nonprofit
Paid Staff: 150
Income Sources: Wisconsin Theatre Association
Performs At: McDaniels Auditorium
Organization Type: Performing; Educational

4117
WISCONSIN UNION THEATER
800 Langdon Street
Madison, WI 53706
Mailing Address: 800 Langdon St., Madison, WI 53706
Phone: 608-262-2202
Fax: 608-265-5084
e-mail: cvweisse@wisc.edu
Web Site: www.union.wisc.edu/theater
Officers:
   Vice Chairs: Miguel Guevara
   Executive Secretary: Mark Guthier
   Treasurer: Theodore Crabb
   Assistant Treasurer: Hank Walter
Management:
   Artistic Director: Ralph Risco
   Operations Manager: Bruce Ehlinger
   Assistant Director for Facilities M: Paul Broadhead
   Director: Mark Guthier
   Assistant Director for Dining Servi: Carl Korz
   Associate Director: Hank Walter
   Information Technology Director: Kevin Breese
Mission: Cultural, entertainment and educational programming for university and community audiences.
Utilizes: Singers
Founded: 1939
Specialized Field: Classic
Status: Non-Profit, Professional
Paid Staff: 30
Volunteer Staff: 80
Budget: $900,000
Income Sources: Ticket Reserves
Performs At: Wisconsin Union Theater
Annual Attendance: 120,000
Type of Stage: Proscenium
Stage Dimensions: 36x24
Seating Capacity: 1,300
Year Built: 1934
Organization Type: Sponsoring

4118
MABEL TAINTER MEMORIAL THEATER
205 Main Street East
PO Box 250
Menomonie, WI 54751
Mailing Address: 205 Main Street East, Menomonie, WI 54751
Phone: 715-235-9726
Fax: 715-235-9736
e-mail: info@mabeltainter.org
Web Site: www.mabeltainter.org
Officers:
   President: Cindy Quilling
   Vice President: John Zbornjk
   Treasurer: Bill Butsic
   Secretary: Lucy Weidner
Management:
   Executive Director: Amy Reise
   Facility Manager and Technical Dire: Jeff Torgerson
   Technical Manager: Christopher Carpenter

THEATRE / Wisconsin

Box Office Manager: Abbey Goers
Facilities Manager and Maintenance: Dave Halama
Mission: Historic 1890's theater with a performing arts season.. Our mission is dedicated to promoting and enhancing the region's cultural life.
Utilizes: Actors; Artists-in-Residence; Collaborations; Dance Companies; Dancers; Designers; Educators; Fine Artists; Five Seasonal Concerts; Guest Accompanists; Guest Choreographers; Guest Directors; Guest Instructors; Guest Soloists; Instructors; Local Artists; Lyricists; Multi Collaborations; Multimedia; Original Music Scores; Playwrights; Sign Language Translators; Singers; Soloists; Student Interns; Special Technical Talent; Theatre Companies
Founded: 1890
Specialized Field: Musical; Classic
Status: Professional; Nonprofit
Paid Staff: 12
Volunteer Staff: 51
Paid Artists: 30
Budget: $330,000
Income Sources: Tickets; Tours; Rentals; Donations; City and County
Performs At: Mabel Tainter Memorial Theater
Facility Category: Theater and Gift Shop
Type of Stage: Opera House w/orchestra pit
Stage Dimensions: 26'6"x20'
Seating Capacity: 313
Year Built: 1889
Cost: $106,000
Rental Contact: Jeff Torgorson
Organization Type: Sponsoring

4119
ACACIA THEATRE

3195 S Superior
St #414
Milwaukee, WI 53207
Mailing Address: 3195 S. Superior St. #414, Milwaukee, WI 53207
Phone: 414-744-5995
Fax: 414-744-5996
e-mail: acacia@acaciatheatre.com
Web Site: http://www.acaciatheatre.com/contact.php
Officers:
  President: Randy Peterson
Management:
  Artistic Director: Janet Peterson
  Business Manager: Ben Parman
  Touring Coordinator: Dawn Purpura
  Sales and Marketing Manager: Abbey Sours
Mission: To produce plays with a Christian viewpoint.
Utilizes: Singers
Founded: 1980
Specialized Field: Contemporary
Status: Semi-Professional; Nonprofit
Paid Staff: 10
Organization Type: Touring; Resident; Educational

4120
FIRST STAGE CHILDREN'S THEATER

325 W. Walnut St.
Milwaukee, WI 53212
Mailing Address: 929 North Water Street, Milwaukee
Phone: 414-267-2929
Fax: 414-273-5595
e-mail: rgoodman@firststage.org
Web Site: www.firststage.org
Officers:
  President: Carol Gehl
  Treasurer: Joel Nettesheim
  Secretary: Sheila Reynolds
  VP of Governance: Bob Arzbaecher

VP of Marketing: Lauren Pagenkopf
Management:
  Managing Director: Betsy Corry
  Artistic Director: Jeff Frank
  Technical Director: Robb Bessey
  Properties Director: Mark Hare
  Production Manager: Jared Clarkin
Founded: 1987
Specialized Field: Musical; Children's Theater
Status: Non-Profit, Professional
Paid Staff: 32
Paid Artists: 50
Performs At: Marcus Center for the Performing Arts's Todd Wehr Theater
Type of Stage: Thrust
Seating Capacity: 500

4121
GREAT AMERICAN CHILDREN'S THEATRE COMPANY

2400 3rd Av. S
Milwaukee, WI 55404
Phone: 612-874-0500
Fax: 414-276-2214
e-mail: info@childrenstheatre.org
Officers:
  President: Paul Medved
  VP Development: Danita Medved
  Secretary/Treasurer: Thomas Balgeman
  Chair: Fran Davis
  Vice Chair: Lili Hall
  Treasurer: George E. Tyson, II
  Secretary: Betsy Russomanno
Management:
  Managing Director: Tim Jennings
  Contact: Teri Solomon Mitze
  Artistic Director: Peter C. Brosius
Mission: To provide quality theatre for young audiences.
Utilizes: Singers
Founded: 1975
Specialized Field: Children's Theater
Status: Professional; Nonprofit
Performs At: Pabst Theatre
Organization Type: Performing; Touring; Educational; Sponsoring

4122
MILWAUKEE CHAMBER THEATRE

158 N Broadway
5th Floor
Milwaukee, WI 53202
Mailing Address: 158 N. Broadway, 5th Floor, Milwaukee, WI 53202
Phone: 414-276-8842
Fax: 414-277-4474
e-mail: mail@chamber-theatre.com
Web Site: www.chamber-theatre.com
Officers:
  President: Keith Anderson
  Chairman: David A. Paris
  Special Events Chairman: Cathy Costantini
  Secretary: Donald A. Cress
  Treasurer: Patrick Fennelly
Management:
  Artistic Director: Davis Montgomery
  Managing Director: Kirsten Mulvey
  Subscription Manager: Sharon Middleton
  Development Director: Linnea Koeppel
  Production Manager/Company Manager: Brand Kline
  Marketing Director: Cara McMullin
  Producing Artistic Director: C. Michael Wright

Mission: To produce the only annual Shaw festival in the nation and is committed to employing primarily Wisconsin actors and artists. Each season Chamber Theatre offers a wide variety of plays with strong literary and philosophical merit and produces World and regional premieres.
Founded: 1975
Specialized Field: Comedy; Classic; Contemporary
Status: Non-Profit, Professional
Paid Staff: 6
Volunteer Staff: var
Paid Artists: 30
Non-paid Artists: var
Income Sources: Individual Ticket Revenue; Foundation; Corporation; Goverment Grants
Performs At: Broadway Theatre Center
Annual Attendance: 12,500
Facility Category: 2 Theatres (Cabot; Studio)
Stage Dimensions: 358; 96
Organization Type: Performing; Touring; Resident

4123
MILWAUKEE PUBLIC THEATRE

626 East Kilbourn
Suite 802
Milwaukee, WI 53202
Mailing Address: 626 East Kilbourn, Suite 802, Milwaukee, WI 53202
Phone: 414-347-1685
Fax: 414-347-1690
e-mail: mpt@milwaukeepublictheatre.org
Web Site: www.milwaukeepublictheatre.org
Officers:
  President: Theresa Anne Kenney
  Vice President: Willie Johnson Jr.
  Secretary: James Madlom
  Treasurer: Katy Sommer
  Executive Director: Gary Tuma
Management:
  CoFounder/Artistic/Producing Dir: Barbara Leigh
  Marketing Communications Manager: Linda Beckstrom
  Bookkeeper, Administrative Coordina: Katharina Hren
  Outreach Coordinator: Carolyn Mello
  Producer/Special Projects Director: Kathleen Stacy
  Healing Arts Director: Karen Stobbe
Mission: To create and present of visual, theatrical, and performing arts productions and related activites through the developement and maintenance of a professional company.
Utilizes: Singers
Founded: 1973
Specialized Field: Musical; Puppet
Status: Non-Profit, Professional
Paid Staff: 5
Paid Artists: 30
Income Sources: Theatre Communications Group; WTA
Season: June - August
Organization Type: Performing; Touring; Resident; Educational; Sponsoring

4124
MILWAUKEE REPERTORY THEATER

108 East Wells Street
Milwaukee, WI 53202
Mailing Address: 108 East Wells Street, Milwaukee, WI 53202
Phone: 414-224-1761
Fax: 414-224-9097
e-mail: tickets@milwaukeerep.com
Web Site: www.milwaukeerep.com

THEATRE / Wisconsin

Officers:
- **President:** Judy Hansen
- **President-Elect:** James E. Braza
- **Vice President:** John Greene
- **Secretary:** Matt Bartel
- **Treasurer & Grant Signer:** Kathleen A. Gray

Management:
- **Artistic Director:** Mark Clements
- **Managing Director:** Chad Bauman
- **General Manager:** Claude Binder
- **Company Manager:** Dawn Marie Ross
- **Education Director:** Jenny Kostreva
- **Education Director:** Jenny Toutant
- **Production Manager:** Melissa Nvari Vartanian
- **Technical Director:** Tyler Smith
- **Production Stage Manager:** Sarah Hoffmann

Mission: To play a vital role in the cultural life of our region through: creating theatrical productions of the highest standard which explore and illuminate the human condition; providing an artistic home for a diverse company of theater professionals; and providing a variety of educational programs for all ages.
Utilizes: Selected Students; Sign Language Translators; Singers; Soloists; Student Interns; Special Technical Talent; Theatre Companies; Visual Arts
Founded: 1954
Specialized Field: Drama
Status: Non-Profit, Professional
Paid Staff: 120
Volunteer Staff: 8
Paid Artists: 170
Non-paid Artists: 30
Budget: $8,800,000
Income Sources: Ticket Sales; Foundations; Corporations; Individuals; Merchandise
Performs At: Milwaukee Repertory Theater
Affiliations: Actors' Equity Association; Lort; TCG
Annual Attendance: 225,000
Type of Stage: Thrust; Black Box; Cabaret
Stage Dimensions: 3 theater complex and full support
Year Built: 1900
Year Remodeled: 1987
Rental Contact: Associate Manager Rebecca Stibbe
Organization Type: Performing; Resident; Educational

4125
MILWAUKEE THEATRE
500 W Kilbourn Avenue
Milwaukee, WI 53203
Mailing Address: 400 W. Wisconsin Avenue, Milwaukee, WI 53203
Phone: 414-908-6000
Fax: 414-908-6010
Toll-free: 800-745-3000
e-mail: GroupSales@wcd.org
Web Site: www.milwaukeetheatre.org

Officers:
- **President:** Richard A Geyer

Management:
- **Director of Sports & Entertainment:** Tony Dynicki
- **Group Sales Manager:** Chris Kroening
- **Director of Public Safety:** Jeremie Ott
- **Special Projects & Purchasing Manag:** George Walls
- **Sales Manager:** David Schneider

Mission: The Milwaukee Theatre, the newst jewel in Milwaukee's flourishing downtown, opened in November, 2003 with seating for 4,100 and the flexibility to create a full house of as few as 2,500 patrons. The Milwaukee Theatre offers regional audiences a breathtaking and elegant seating for a wide variety of entertainment.
Opened: 1998
Specialized Field: Drama
Seating Capacity: 4,087

4126
NEXT ACT THEATRE
255 S. Water St.
PO Box 394
Milwaukee, WI 53201
Mailing Address: PO Box 394, Milwaukee, WI 53201-0394
Phone: 414-278-7780
Fax: 414-278-5930
e-mail: info@nextact.org
Web Site: www.nextact.org

Officers:
- **President:** Michael Burzynski
- **Vice President:** Annie Jansen Jurczyk
- **Secretary:** Joyce Mielke
- **Treasurer:** Sean Rierdon
- **Immediate Past President:** Steve Marcus

Management:
- **Resident Technical Director:** Mike Van Dreser
- **Producing Artistic Director:** David Cecsarini
- **Managing Director:** Charles Kakuk
- **Development Marketing Director:** Susan Zellner
- **Development Director:** Heidi Boyd

Mission: To produce engaging and thought-provoking up close and personal theatre, highlighting the Milwaukee area's finest talent.
Founded: 1990
Specialized Field: Musical; Comedy
Status: Non-Profit, Professional
Paid Staff: 16
Paid Artists: 25
Income Sources: Wisconsin Professional Community Theatre Association
Performs At: Off Broadway Theatre; Stiemke Theater
Affiliations: Corporate member of the United Performing Arts Fund; Wisconsin Arts Board
Organization Type: Performing

4127
REED MARIONETTES
3216 S Quincy Avenue
Milwaukee, WI 53207
Toll-free: 877-803-6575
e-mail: tim@reedmarionettes.com
Web Site: www.reedmarionettes.com

Management:
- **Managing Director/President:** Tim Reed

Mission: A professional touring company presenting colorful, entertaining and faithful versions of children's classics, combining the best of the arts of puppetry and theatre.
Utilizes: Singers
Founded: 1950
Specialized Field: Puppet
Status: Professional
Income Sources: Puppeteers of America; Wisconsin Puppetry Guild
Organization Type: Performing; Touring

4128
RENAISSANCE THEATERWORKS
158 N Broadway
Milwaukee, WI 53202
Mailing Address: 158 N. Broadway, Milwaukee, WI 53202
Phone: 414-273-0800
Fax: 414-273-0801
e-mail: info@r-t-w.com
Web Site: www.r-t-w.com

Officers:
- **President:** Gabrielle Davidson
- **Vice President:** Tracey Carson
- **Treasurer:** Laura Arnow
- **Secretary:** Joyce Rubenstein

Management:
- **Producing Director:** Julie Swenson Petras
- **Development Director:** Lisa Rasmussen
- **Marketing & PR Director:** Mallory Metoxen
- **Artistic Directors:** Suzan Fete

Mission: To produce classical and contemporary theater of the highest artistic quality, rooted in the humanist tradition and with particular interest in the feminine voice.
Founded: 1993
Specialized Field: Dinner Theater; Contemporary
Status: Non-Profit, Professional
Paid Staff: 2
Volunteer Staff: 35
Paid Artists: 30

4129
SKYLIGHT OPERA THEATRE
158 N Broadway
Milwaukee, WI 53202
Mailing Address: 158 N. Broadway, Milwaukee, WI 53202
Phone: 414-291-7811
Fax: 414-271-7815
e-mail: skylight@skylightopera.com
Web Site: www.skylightopera.com

Officers:
- **President:** John Flanagan
- **Secretary:** John Flanagan
- **Treasurer:** Michael Lueder

Management:
- **Artistic Director:** Viswa Subbaraman
- **Managing Director:** Amy S. Jensen
- **Education Administrator:** Robin Dennis
- **Marketing Manager:** Rose Hebein
- **Finance Director:** Cindy Haas
- **Education Manager:** Amanda Eaton
- **Development Director:** Becca Kitelinger
- **Associate Artistic Director:** Ray Jivoff
- **Production and Facilities Director:** Mark Turner

Mission: To bring the full spectrum of music theatre works to a wide and diverse audience in a celebration of the musical and theatrical arts and their reflection of the human condition.
Founded: 1959
Specialized Field: Musical
Status: Non-Profit, Professional
Paid Staff: 35
Budget: $2.2 million
Income Sources: Box Office; Rentals; Private Foundations/Grants/Endowments; Business/Corporate Donations; Government Grants; Individual Donations
Performs At: Cabot Theatre
Affiliations: Skylight Opera Theatre
Facility Category: Theatre House; Opera House; Room
Type of Stage: Flexible; Platform
Stage Dimensions: 12'x24' Expandable
Orchestra Pit: 1
Architect: Wenzler & Associates
Rental Contact: Artistic Administrator John VandeWalle

4130
THEATRE X
158 N Broadway
Milwaukee, WI 53202
Phone: 414-278-0555
Fax: 414-278-8233
e-mail: theatrex@sbcglobal.net

Management:
- **President:** David Garnham
- **Executive Director:** John Loscuito

THEATRE / Wyoming

Artistic Director: John Schneider
Founded: 1969
Specialized Field: Summer Stock
Status: Non-Profit, Professional
Paid Staff: 3
Paid Artists: 65
Season: September - May
Type of Stage: Black Box
Stage Dimensions: 27' x 70'
Seating Capacity: 99

4131
PLAYTIME PRODUCTIONS

1277 County Highway Z
Mount Horeb, WI 53572
Mailing Address: 1277 County Hwy Z, Mt. Horeb, WI 53572
Phone: 608-437-4217
e-mail: playtime@mhtc.net
Web Site: www.playtimeproductions.org
Management:
  Founding Director: Teddy Studt
  Managing/Artistic Director: Renaye Leach
  Stage Manager/Costume Designer: Hannah Zoromski
  Graphic Artist: Joanne McKenzie
  Musical Director: Bev Pizzingrilli
  Choreographer: Deb Rabin
Mission: Delighting audiences with its creative and spirited renditions of classic tales. Brings the magic of theater to thousands of people through out Dane County, Wisconsin.
Specialized Field: Children's Theater

4132
PORTAGE AREA COMMUNITY THEATRE

PO Box 263
Portage, WI 53901
Mailing Address: P.O. Box 263, Portage, WI 53901
Phone: 608-742-6942
Web Site: www.portageareacommunitytheatre.org
Officers:
  President: Pat Madoni
  VP: Lisa Piekarski
  Secretary/Registered Agent: Fran Malone
  Treasurer: Hans Jensen
Management:
  Director: Sheril Lannoye
Mission: To promote, encourage and increase the public's knowledge and appreciation of the arts, especially theatre, and to provide an outlet for the above.
Founded: 1971
Specialized Field: Community Theater
Status: Non-Professional; Nonprofit
Paid Staff: 300
Income Sources: Wisconsin Theatre Association; Wisconsin Council on the Arts
Organization Type: Performing

4133
SHAWANO COUNTY ARTS COUNCIL

N5649 N. Airport Road
Shawano, WI 54166
Mailing Address: N5649 N. Airport Road, Shawano, WI 54166
Phone: 715-526-2525
e-mail: lindabl@netnet.net
Web Site: www.shawanoarts.com
Officers:
  President: Rusty Mitchell
  VP: Deb Lonick
  Treasurer: Jaquee Salzman
Management:

Events & General Information: Mary Beth Kuester
Art & Crafts Fair: Cheryl Folkerts
Folk Music Festival: Dori Jerger
Founded: 1967
Specialized Field: Musical; Community Theater
Status: Nonprofit
Performs At: Mielke Theatre
Organization Type: Resident; Sponsoring

4134
SHEBOYGAN THEATRE COMPANY

607 South Water Street
Sheboygan, WI 53081
Phone: 920-459-3779
Fax: 920-459-4021
e-mail: mbestul@sheboygan.k12.wi.us
Web Site: www.sheboygantheatercomapny.com
Officers:
  President: Eric Johnson
  Vice President: Joe Feustel
  Secretary: Sheri Ruehl
  Treasurer: Philip Zimmermann
Management:
  Production Manager: Dustin Uhl
  Admin Marketing Coordinator: Michelle Bestul, mbestul@sheboygan.k12.wi.us
  Business Manager: Steve Scharrer
  Managing Director: Dennis Gleason
Mission: STC exists to provide quality performances for its audiences and quality opportunities to participate and learn to all who might be interested.
Utilizes: Actors; Choreographers; Dancers; Guest Artists; Guest Lecturers; Guest Musical Directors; Music; Performance Artists; Sign Language Translators
Founded: 1934
Specialized Field: Musical; Comedy; Community Theater
Status: Non-Profit
Paid Staff: 2
Volunteer Staff: 250
Paid Artists: 5
Budget: $250,000
Income Sources: Tickets; Donations; Concessions; Program Advertisements; Rentals
Performs At: Leslie W Johnson Theatre; Horace Mann Middle School
Affiliations: Sheboygan Area School District
Annual Attendance: 18,000-20,000
Facility Category: Standard Theatre
Type of Stage: Thrust; Proscenium
Seating Capacity: 750
Year Built: 1970
Organization Type: Performing; Resident; Educational

4135
AMERICAN PLAYERS THEATRE

PO Box 819
Spring Green, WI 53588
Mailing Address: PO Box 819, Spring Green, WI 53588
Phone: 608-588-2361
Fax: 608-588-7085
e-mail: ebeck@americanplayers.org
Web Site: www.americanplayers.org
Officers:
  President: Barbara Swan
  Vice President: Stephen D. Brown
  Treasurer: Paul J. Hartung
  Vice President: W. David Romoser
  Vice President: John Frautschi
Management:
  Box Office Manager: Emily Beck
  Artistic Director: David Frank
  Director of Development: Aleta Barmore

Facilities Assistant: Cassandra Berg
Production Assistant: Christopher Baker
Utilizes: Singers; Theatre Companies
Founded: 1980
Specialized Field: Classical Repertory Theatre
Status: Non-Profit, Professional
Paid Staff: 22
Volunteer Staff: 120
Budget: $4.5 million
Income Sources: Ticket Sales; Concessions; Giftshop; Individual Giving; Corporate Giving; Grants
Season: June - October
Performs At: Classical Outdoor Repertory
Affiliations: Actors' Equity Association; Theatre Communications Group, Shakespeare Theatres Assoc. Of America; Theatre Wisconsin
Annual Attendance: 100,000
Facility Category: Outdoor Amphitheatre
Type of Stage: Thrust
Seating Capacity: 1,148
Year Built: 1980
Rental Contact: Production Manager Michael Broh
Organization Type: Performing; Touring; Resident; Educational
Resident Groups: Lort C Special

4136
WAUKESHA CIVIC THEATRE

Margaret Brate Bryant Civic Theatre
264 West Main Street
PO Box 221
Waukesha, WI 53186
Mailing Address: 264 West Main Street, Waukesha, WI 53186
Phone: 262-547-4911
Fax: 262-547-8454
e-mail: jcramer@waukeshacivictheatre.org
Web Site: www.waukeshacivictheatre.org
Officers:
  President: Gary Ebert
  Vice President: Angela Penzkover
  Secretary: Susan Herro
  Treasurer: Mary Dembinski
  Past President: Kurt Magoon
Management:
  Managing Artistic Director: John Cramer
  Office Manager: Heidi Tufte
  Education & Outreach Administrator: Doug Jarecki
  House Manager: Denise Meagher
  Box Office Supervisor and Marketing: Katie Danner
Mission: Mission is to enrich, challenge and entertain participants through the performance of live theatre.
Utilizes: Actors; Educators; Fine Artists; Five Seasonal Concerts; Grant Writers; Guest Accompanists; Guest Artists; Guest Conductors; Guest Designers; Guest Directors; Guest Ensembles; Guest Instructors; Guest Lecturers; Guest Soloists; Instructors; Local Artists; Multimedia; Music; Original Music Scores; Resident Professionals; Selected Students; Sign Language Translators; Soloists; Student Interns; Visual Arts
Founded: 1957
Specialized Field: Musical; Drama; Comedy
Organization Type: Performing; Educational

Wyoming

4137
CHEYENNE LITTLE THEATRE PLAYERS

2706 E Pershing Boulevard
Cheyenne, WY 82001

THEATRE / Wyoming

Mailing Address: PO Box 20087 Cheyenne, WY 82003
Phone: 307-638-6543
Fax: 307-638-6430
e-mail: cltpinfo@cheyennelittletheatre.org
Web Site: www.cheyennelittletheatre.org
Officers:
   President: John Lyttle
   VP of Programming: Rory Mack
   VP of Finance: Don Threewitt
   VP of Fund Development: Pat Lauber
   VP of Administration: George O'Hare
Management:
   Managing and Artistic Director: Randy Bernhard
   Communications Coordinator: Justin Batson
   Bookkeeper: Sandy Colvin
   Office/Tech Coordinator: Maria Thompson
Mission: To entertain and educate through theatre; to promote creativity among volunteers.
Utilizes: Guest Companies
Founded: 1930
Specialized Field: Musical; Dinner Theater; Community Theater
Status: Non-Profit, Non-Professional
Paid Staff: 4
Volunteer Staff: 2
Non-paid Artists: 150
Budget: $350,00
Income Sources: American Association of Community Theatres
Performs At: Mary Godfrey Playhouse; Atlas Theatre
Organization Type: Performing; Educational

4138
OFF SQUARE THEATRE COMPANY

240 South Glenwood
Jackson, WY 83001
Mailing Address: P.O. Box 2920, Jackson, WY 83001
Phone: 307-733-3021
e-mail: info@offsquare.org
Web Site: offsquare.org
Officers:
   President: Erika Pearsall
   President: Patty Cook
   Vice President: Ed Smail
   Secretary: Susan Brooks
   Treasurer: Scott Williams
Management:
   Executive Director: Clare Payne Symmons
   Artistic Director: Natalia Duncan
Mission: Our Mission is to produce and present theater of the highest professional standards that inspires, stimulates, and entertains our diversity audiences, to conduct training and educational programs that enhance the quality of life for those we serve, and to help ensure the future of theater.
Founded: 1998

4139
SHERIDAN CIVIC THEATRE GUILD

419 Delphi Avenue
Sheridan, WY 82801
Mailing Address: PO Box 1, Sheridan, Wyoming 82801
Phone: 307-672-9886
Web Site: http://www.civictheaterguild.org/
Officers:
   President: Leon Schatz
   VP: Matt Davis
   Secretary: Dimitra Dugal
   Treasurer: Kim Detmer
Management:
   Manager: Judi O'Neal

Mission: To foster community theatre in our area; to involve community members in all areas of theatre; to entertain.
Utilizes: Guest Artists; Singers
Founded: 1953
Specialized Field: Musical; Community Theater
Status: Nonprofit
Performs At: Carriage House Theatre
Organization Type: Performing; Resident

SERIES & FESTIVALS / Alabama

Alabama

4140
BIRMINGHAM INTERNATIONAL CENTER
1500 First Avenue N
Suite #M133
Birmingham, AL 35203
Phone: 205-252-7652
Fax: 205-252-7656
e-mail: igross@bic-al.org
Web Site: bic-al.org
Officers:
   President: Mark A. Forehilich
   President Elect: Martin J. Conors Jr
   Vice President: T Atkins Roberts Jr
   Vice President: Tanveer Patel
   Treasurer: Cecil Bostany
   Executive Director: Iris Gross
Management:
   Executive Director: Iris Gross
   Director's Assistant: Jason Novak
   Fundraising: Julie Ann Fleming
   Education Director: Jonnie Griffin
   IT Director: Hank Grossq
   Assistant to Executive Director: Jason Novak
Mission: The Birmingham International Center is the nation's oldest cultural-education organization. We serve as a clearinghouse for international economic development and intercultural education across the state of Alabama. Founded in 1951, the Birmingham International Center has grown into the premier resource for international business-education needs, including intercultural training, heritage and arts programming, and foreign trade.
Utilizes: Collaborations; Curators; Dancers; Educators; Filmmakers; Five Seasonal Concerts; Guest Composers; Guest Lecturers; Guest Musical Directors; Guest Musicians; Instructors; Lyricists; Multimedia; Original Music Scores; Selected Students; Singers; Soloists; Touring Companies
Founded: 1951
Specialized Field: Series & Festivals: Cultural Diversity
Status: Non-Profit, Professional
Paid Staff: 3
Volunteer Staff: 1k+
Income Sources: Donor, Sponsors, Partners
Season: April 4 - 20
Performs At: Various venues throughout Alabama
Affiliations: Russian American Chamber of Commerce; The Japan Society of Alabama; Alabama Germany Partnership; Non-Profit Resource Center of Alabama
Annual Attendance: 50,000
Facility Category: Public park
Seating Capacity: 1,200

4141
INDEPENDENT PRESBYTERIAN CHURCH-NOVEMBER ORGAN RECITAL SERIES
3100 Highland Avenue South
Birmingham, AL 35205
Phone: 205-933-1830
Fax: 205-933-1836
e-mail: jwooten@ipc-usa.org
Web Site: www.ipc-usa.org
Officers:
   Moderator: Burch Barger
   Vice-Moderator: Buddy Parsons
   Secretary: Rowena Macnab
   Usher Captain: Robert Hill
Management:
   Executive Director: Jim Wooten, jwooten@ipc-usa.org
   Associate Pastor/Director: Reverend Bobbie Epting, bepting@ipc-usa.org
Mission: More than 150 artists representing the finest talent from the United States and Europe performed on IPC's previous Aeolian-Skinner organ over the past 48 years. All programs are offered as a gift to the community and are open to the public.
Utilizes: Grant Writers; Guest Accompanists; Guest Artists; Guest Companies; Guest Designers; Guest Musicians; Guest Soloists
Specialized Field: Instrumental Organ
Status: Non-Profit, Religious
Income Sources: Donor, Partial Sponsors
Season: November
Performs At: Independent Presbyterian Church

4142
PRINCESS THEATRE PROFESSIONAL SERIES
112 Second Avenue NE
Decatur, AL 35601
Phone: 256-350-1745
Fax: 256-350-1712
e-mail: lindy@princesstheatre.org
Web Site: www.princesstheatre.org
Management:
   Executive Director: Lindy Ashwander, lindy@princesstheatre.org
   Technical Director: Penny Linville, penny@princesstheatre.org
   Rental Event Planner: Gail Williams, emily@princesstheatre.org
   Office Manager: Debbie Nieberlein
Mission: Local performing groups make their home on the Princess stage, presenting children's theater, choral concerts, musicals and theater. Located in downtown Decatur's New Decatur/Albany Historic District, the Princess Theatre Center for the Performing Arts serves the community as a 677-seat theatre that presents a variety of arts events, provides a multipurpose rental facility, serves as an arts in education resource.
Utilizes: Collaborations; Dance Companies; Educators; Fine Artists; Guest Accompanists; Guest Companies; Guest Directors; Guest Musical Directors; Guest Musicians; Instructors; Local Unknown Artists; Lyricists; Multimedia; Music; Paid Performers; Soloists; Student Interns; Special Technical Talent; Theatre Companies; Visual Arts
Founded: 1983
Specialized Field: Dance; Vocal Music; Instrumental Music; Theater
Status: Nonprofit
Paid Staff: 5
Volunteer Staff: 250
Budget: $570,000
Income Sources: Tickets, Rentals, Sponsors, Donors, Special Events
Performs At: Princess Theatre
Annual Attendance: 50,000
Facility Category: Performing Arts Center
Type of Stage: Proscenium
Stage Dimensions: 40'x35'x18'.6"
Seating Capacity: 700
Year Built: 1919
Year Remodeled: 2000
Cost: $6 million
Rental Contact: Penny Linville
Organization Type: Performing; Educational

4143
COFFEE COUNTY ARTS ALLIANCE
PO Box 310447
Enterprise, AL 36331
Phone: 334-406-1617
e-mail: coffeecaa@aol.com
Web Site: www.coffeecountyartsalliance.com
Officers:
   President: Suzanne Sawyer
   Treasurer: Charles Canon
Management:
   Musical Director: Mac Frampton
   Assistant Director: Cecil Welch
Mission: Coffee County Arts Alliance contributes to the betterment of the community by offering our citizens an opportunity to attend cultural activities near home at an affordable price. CCAA is the only continuing source in the community for visual arts and crafts, and a variety of music, dance and drama. Featuring professional artists, our programs include Alabama artists, children's entertainment, symphonies, choirs, and other types of entertainment
Utilizes: Collaborations; Composers; Dance Companies; Dancers; Fine Artists; Guest Accompanists; Guest Artists; Guest Choreographers; Guest Companies; Guest Composers; Guest Designers; Guest Musical Directors; High School Drama; Local Artists & Directors; Local Talent; Local Unknown Artists; Lyricists; Multi Collaborations; Multimedia; Music; Original Music Scores; Paid Performers
Founded: 1974
Specialized Field: Series & Festivals: Broadbased Entertainment In Arts and Crafts Festival
Status: Non-Profit, Non-Professional
Income Sources: Donors, Corporate Sponsors
Season: October through April
Performs At: Enterprise Performing Arts Center, Enterprise State Community College, Elba Highschool
Affiliations: All About Art, Sudden Broadway

4144
WC HANDY MUSIC FESTIVAL
Music Preservation Society
PO Box 1827
217 E. Tuscaloosa St.
Florence, AL 35631
Phone: 256-766-7642
Fax: 256-776-7549
e-mail: WChandymusicfest@aol.com
Web Site: www.wchandymusicfestival.org
Officers:
   Festival Chairman: Tori Bailey
Management:
   Executive Director: Nancy C Gonce
   Public Relations Coordinator: Melanie Orseske, WChandymusicfest@aol.com
Mission: Music Preservation Society, a non-profit organization, was established in 1982 to preserve, present and promote the musical heritage of Northwest Alabama. MPS has a strong educational mission, and educational programs are a big part of the schedule during the W.C. Handy Music Festival. MPS provides scholarships for students to learn from professionals who provide musical expertise to those who would othwise have no access to that level skill.
Utilizes: Arrangers; Collaborating Artists; Collaborations; Educators; Fine Artists; Guest Accompanists; Guest Choreographers; Guest Companies; Guest Directors; Guest Ensembles; Guest Musical Directors; Multimedia; Music; Paid Performers; Theatre Companies
Founded: 1982

SERIES & FESTIVALS / Alabama

Specialized Field: Series & Festivals; Instrumental Music; Vocal Music; Theatre; Youth; Ethnic Performances
Status: Non-Profit, Professional
Paid Staff: 1
Income Sources: Corporate Sponsors
Performs At: Norton Auditorium
Affiliations: Alabama Music Hall of Fame, Belle Mont Mansion, Indian Mound Museum, Pope's Tavern Museum, Kennedy Douglas Center for the Arts

4145
CITY OF GULF SHORES ENTERTAINMENT SERIES
1905 W. 1st St.
PO Box 299
Gulf Shores, AL 36547
Phone: 251-968-2425
e-mail: info@ci.gulf-shores.al.us
Web Site: www.ci.gulf-shores.al.us
Management:
  City Administrator: Steve Griffin
  Special Events Coordinator: Blake Phelps, bphelps@gulfshoreal.gov
  Special Events Director: Brigette Reynolds
Mission: The City of Gulf Shores has officially announced its lineup for the Entertainment Series. The Entertainment Series, now in its 26th year at the Erie Meyer Civic Center, has become an annual tradition for residents and visitors alike. The series will feature 11 shows from six different acts. Whether you like comedy and jazz, or choreography and big bands, theis series is for you.
Utilizes: Collaborations; Grant Writers; Guest Accompanists; Guest Choreographers; Guest Companies; Guest Composers; Guest Designers; Guest Ensembles; Guest Musicians; Multimedia; Music; Original Music Scores; Paid Performers
Income Sources: Tickets Sales, Sponsors
Performs At: Erie Meyer Civic Center
Rental Contact: Kathy Van Cor

4146
OAKWOOD COLLEGE ARTS & LECTURES
Oakwood College Music Department
7000 Adventist Boulevard
Huntsville, AL 35896
Phone: 256-726-7278
Fax: 256-726-7481
e-mail: lmoncur@oakwood.edu
Web Site: www.oakwood.edu
Management:
  President: Dr. Leslie Pollard
  Executive Director: John Anderson
  Artistic Director: Audley Chembers
Mission: Music education & performances.
Founded: 1896
Specialized Field: Series and Festivals; Instrumental Music; Vocal Music; Music Education; Music Performance
Status: Non-Profit, Non-Professional
Paid Staff: 11
Paid Artists: 1
Budget: $8,500
Income Sources: Tuition
Performs At: Seventh-Day Adventist Church
Annual Attendance: 12,000
Facility Category: Auditorium
Seating Capacity: 400
Year Built: 1899
Year Remodeled: 1998

4147
PANOPLY ARTS FESTIVAL
The Arts Council
700 Monroe Street, Suite 2
Huntsville, AL 35801-5579
Phone: 256-519-2787
Fax: 256-533-3811
e-mail: info@artshuntsville.org
Web Site: www.artshuntsville.org
Officers:
  Co-Chairman: Jan Dorning
  Co-Chairman: Cathy Callaway
  President: Chuck Allen
  Vice President: Steve Johnson
  Treasurer: Jim Link
  Secretary: Drew Battle
  Past President: Gaylen Pugh
Management:
  Executive Director: Allison Dillon Jauken
  Sponsorship and Promotions Manager: Joanna Broad White
  Events Manager: Amy Mayfield
Mission: The Panoply Arts Festival celebrates the arts with a wide array of performances, exhibits, demonstrations, and hands-on activities. Panoply showcases the best in local and touring performances. Each year, three stages, located throughout the park, offer a variety of performances from jazz bands, bluegrass, gospel and more. You're likely to see puppet performances, educational groups that teach different musical styles, as well as local theatres.
Utilizes: Guest Accompanists; Guest Artists; Guest Choreographers; Guest Companies; Guest Composers; Guest Conductors; Guest Designers; Guest Directors; Guest Ensembles; Guest Instructors; Guest Lecturers; Guest Musical Directors; Guest Musicians; Guest Soloists; Original Music Scores; Paid Performers
Founded: 1962
Specialized Field: Series and Festivals: Music
Status: Non-Profit, Professional
Paid Staff: 8
Paid Artists: 20
Income Sources: Ticket Sales, Volunteers, Sponsors
Season: Annually in April
Performs At: Big Spring International Park
Annual Attendance: 90,000
Facility Category: Three outdoor tents with stages; Concert Hall

4148
ALABAMA SHAKESPEARE FESTIVAL
1 Festival Drive
Montgomery, AL 36117
Phone: 334-271-5300
Fax: 334-271-5348
Toll-free: 800-841-4273
Web Site: www.asf.net
Officers:
  Chairman: Dr Laurie Jean Weil
  Vice Chairman: Gordon G. Martin
  Secretary: Gene C. Crane
  Treasurer: Dr Eugene Stanaland
  Board Member: Owen Aronov
  Board Member: Beverly Poole Baker
  Board Member: Carol Ballard
Management:
  Producing Artistic Director: Geoffrey Sherman, kstewart@asf.net
  Chief Operating Officer: Michael Vigilant
  Associate Director: Nancy Rominger
  Development Director: Eve Loeb
  Marketing Director: Meg Lewis
  Properties Master: Charles Kilian
Mission: The Alabama Shakespeare Festival, located in Montgomery - Alabama's state capital - is a fully professional regional theatre that produces around ten productions each season in association with Actors' Equity Association, The Stage Directors and Choreographers Society and United Scenic Artists union. Productions of Shakespeare are at the artistic core of the company. Broadway musicals, children's productions, American classics and world premieres
Utilizes: Guest Accompanists; Guest Choreographers; Guest Companies; Guest Conductors; Guest Designers; Guest Directors; Guest Ensembles; Guest Instructors; Guest Lecturers; Guest Musical Directors; Guest Musicians; Guest Soloists; Paid Performers; Singers
Founded: 1972
Specialized Field: Series and Festivals: Performing Arts and Theatre
Status: Non-Profit, Professional
Income Sources: Donors, Sponsors
Performs At: Alabama Shakespeare Festival
Organization Type: Performing; Touring; Resident; Educational; Sponsoring

4149
ART ASSOCIATION OF EAST ALABAMA
1032 South Railroad Avenue
Opelika, AL 36801
Phone: 334-749-8105
Fax: 334-749-8105
e-mail: info@eastalabamaarts.org
Web Site: www.eastalabamaarts.org
Mission: The mission of The Arts Association of East Alabama is to provide rewarding and exciting experiences for the citizens of this area by developing innovative programming that will stimulate interest in the arts, eagerness to learn through the arts, and broader participation in and support of the arts. Founded in 1965 as the Opelika Arts Association, renamed The Arts Association of East Alabama in 2007 to reflect its larger service area.
Founded: 1965
Specialized Field: Series & Festivals; Instrumental music; Vocal music; Theater; Youth; Dance; Ethnic performances
Status: Non-Profit, Non-Professional
Paid Staff: 2
Income Sources: Donors, Sponsors, Ticket Sales
Season: Year Round
Performs At: Opelika Center for the Performing Arts

4150
SELMA COMMUNITY CONCERT ASSOCIATION
1034 Dawson Avenue
PO Box 310
Selma, AL 36701
Phone: 334-872-3527
Fax: 334-872-3504
e-mail: hollandschool@bellsouth.net
Web Site: www.selmaalabama.com
Management:
  President/Executive Director: Doris Holland
Mission: Dedicated to providing classical and popular performances.
Utilizes: Guest Lecturers; Guest Musical Directors; Multimedia; Music; Original Music Scores
Founded: 1940
Specialized Field: Concerts; Classical; Jazz
Status: Non-Profit, Professional
Paid Staff: 2
Income Sources: Ticket Sales
Season: October
Performs At: Pickard Auditorium

SERIES & FESTIVALS / Alaska

4152
ARTS COUNCIL OF TUSCALOOSA FANFARE
PO Box 1117
600 Greensboro Avenue
Tuscaloosa, AL 35403-1117
Mailing Address: PO Box 1117 Tuscaloosa, AL 35403
Phone: 205-758-5195
Fax: 205-345-2787
e-mail: education@tuscarts.org
Web Site: www.tuscarts.org
Officers:
   President: Ann Bourne
   Vice President: Brenda Randall
   Secretary: Amy Ahmed
   Treasurer: Debbie Watson
   Member Organization Rep: Katie McAllister
   Past President: Rebecca Rothman
   Member at Large: Bill Buchanan
   Member at Large: Valery Minges
   Member at Large: Marcelyn Morrow
Management:
   Executive Director: Sandra Wolfe, director@tuscarts.org
   Education Director: Sharon Rudowski, education@tuscarts.org
   Publicity: Kevin Ledgewood, pr@tuscarts.org
   Bama Theatre Manager: David Allgood
   Marketing Coordinator: Meghan Truhett
Mission: The Mission of The Arts Council is to promote and encourage the arts and humanities in Tuscaloosa County. The Arts Council serves as the umbrella organization for 50 Member Organizations, offers educational programs and manages the historic Bama Theatre.
Utilizes: Artists-In-Residence; Instructors; Local Artists; Special Technical Talent; Touring Companies
Founded: 1970
Specialized Field: Series & Festivals; Instrumental Music; Vocal Music; Theatre; Youth; Dance
Status: Non-Profit, Professional
Paid Staff: 4
Budget: $20,000-35,000
Income Sources: Donors, Sponsors
Performs At: Bama Theatre
Annual Attendance: 7,500-10,000
Facility Category: Presentation House
Seating Capacity: 1000
Year Built: 1938
Year Remodeled: 1976

4155
UNIVERSITY OF ALABAMA SCHOOL OF MUSIC CELEBRITY SERIES
PO Box 870366
810 Second Avenue
Tuscaloosa, AL 35487
Mailing Address: PO Box 870366 Tuscaloosa, AL 35487
Phone: 205-348-7110
Fax: 205-348-1473
e-mail: ssnead@music.ua.edu
Web Site: www.music.ua.edu
Management:
   Director, School of Music: Charles Snead
   Director/Choral Music Education: Marvin Lattimer
   Director/Community Music School: Jane Weigel
   Associate Director/Bands: Randall Coleman
   Professor/Conducting: Kenneth Ozello
   Office Associate Senior: Cathie Daniels
   Head/Audio/Visual: Arthur Diaz
   Arts Events Coordinator: Tiffany Schwartz
Mission: Our School of Music is more than a collection of curricular and facilities; it is a community with a unique culture that has evolved over the past century.
Founded: 1987
Budget: $60,000-150,000
Performs At: Concert Hall, Moody Music Building
Seating Capacity: 934

Alaska

4156
ANCHORAGE CONCERT ASSOCIATION
430 W. 7th Avenue
Suite 200
Anchorage, AK 99501
Phone: 907-272-1471
Fax: 907-272-2519
e-mail: info@anchorageconcerts.org
Web Site: www.anchorageconcerts.org
Officers:
   Board President: Linda Winters
   President Elect: Kristen Lindsey
   Board Treasurer: Pam Bruno
   Secretary: Anna Haylock
   Director: Bij Agarwal
   Director: Thomas Buskirk
Management:
   Executive Director: Jason Hodges, jhodges@anchorageconcerts.org
   Business Manager: Willow Zamos, wzamos@anchorageconcerts.org
   Marketing Director: Jason Gren, jgrenn@anchorageconcerts.org
   Event Manager: Kathryn Easley
   Communications Specialist: Kim Marek
   Operations Specialist: James Frederick
Mission: The Anchorage Concert Association, (501(c)3) non-profit corporation) was founded in 1950 by a group of classical music enthusiasts. They were committed to bringing the finest classical musicians to perform for the people of Anchorage. Today, our purpose includes presenting internationally acclaimed artists from the entire spectrum of the performing arts in Alaska. Our public performances and outreach activities entertain, uplift, and educate.
Utilizes: Grant Writers; Guest Accompanists; Guest Artists; Guest Choreographers; Guest Companies; Guest Composers; Guest Conductors; Guest Designers; Guest Directors; Guest Ensembles; Guest Instructors; Guest Lecturers; Guest Musical Directors; Guest Musicians; Local Artists & Directors; Local Unknown Artists; Lyricists; Multi Collaborations; Multimedia; Music; Original Music Scores; Performance Artists
Founded: 1950
Specialized Field: Performing Arts Presenter
Status: Non-Profit, Professional
Paid Staff: 9
Volunteer Staff: 82
Income Sources: Donors, Sponsors
Season: Year Round
Performs At: Atwood Concert Hall, Discovery Theatre, Sydney Laurence Theatre

4157
ANCHORAGE FESTIVAL OF MUSIC
PO Box 100272
Anchorage, AK 99510
Phone: 907-276-2465
Fax: 907-276-2540
e-mail: info@anchoragefestivalmusic.com
Web Site: www.anchoragefestivalmusic.com
Officers:
   President: Jim Rooney
   Treasurer: Mary Ann Molitor
   Secretary: Flo Rooney
   Board Member: Janet Emerman
   Board Member: Yvette Galbraith
   Board Member: Gunnar Knapp
Management:
   Executive Director: Steven Alvarez
   Artistic Director: Dr Laura Koenig
Mission: Music is essential to the aesthetic, intellectual and spiritual development of individuals and their community, and should be made available to people of diverse ages, abilities and means. Therefore, the Anchorage Festival of Music is dedicated to uniting the talents of local and guest artists to create and share the rich beauty of classical and contemporary music through a program of music education and performances.
Utilizes: Guest Artists
Founded: 1976
Specialized Field: Instrumental; Choral; Educational
Status: Professional; Nonprofit
Paid Staff: 30
Income Sources: Donors, Volunteers
Season: June
Performs At: Anchorage (Festival Site)
Affiliations: Alaska Center for the Performing Arts
Seating Capacity: 300; 800; 2,200
Organization Type: Performing

4158
FAIRBANKS CONCERT ASSOCIATION MASTER SERIES
PO Box 80547
Fairbanks, AK 99708
Phone: 907-474-8081
Fax: 907-474-0266
e-mail: info@fairbanksconcert.org
Web Site: www.fairbanksconcert.org
Officers:
   President: Cori Anthony
Management:
   Executive Director: Anne Biberman
Mission: The mission of the Fairbanks Concert Association is to present, promote, and sponsor artistically and culturally diverse performing arts events and educational opportunities of the highest quality from stages around the world.
Utilizes: Actors; Artists-in-Residence; Collaborations; Dance Companies; Dancers; Educators; Guest Accompanists; Guest Choreographers; Guest Composers; Guest Designers; Guest Ensembles; Guest Musical Directors; Guest Musicians; Guild Activities; Multimedia; Original Music Scores; Sign Language Translators; Singers; Theatre Companies
Founded: 1947
Specialized Field: Music; Dance; Speakers
Status: Non-Profit, Professional
Paid Staff: 2
Budget: $60,000-150,000
Performs At: Hering Auditorium; Charles W Davis Concert Hall
Annual Attendance: 13,000
Facility Category: Proscenium Auditorium
Type of Stage: Proscenium
Stage Dimensions: 47'10x22'x36'6"
Seating Capacity: 1305; 967

4159
FAIRBANKS SUMMER ARTS FESTIVAL
PO Box 82510
Fairbanks, AK 99708

SERIES & FESTIVALS / Alaska

Phone: 907-474-8869
Fax: 907-474-8617
e-mail: festival@alaska.net
Web Site: www.fsaf.org
Officers:
  President: Glenn Brady
  Vice President: Mike Brose
  Secretary: Don Gray
  Treasurer: Lloyd Huskey
  Past President: Patty Kastelic
Management:
  Director: Terese Kaptur, director@fsaf.org
  Communications/Operations Manager: Emilie L. S. Wright, emilie@fsaf.org
  Technical Artistic Coordinator: James Wardlaw Bailey, james@fsaf.org
  Production Manager: Jeffrey Lee
  Operations Office Manager: Kathryn Kiefhaber
  Communications: Emily Anderson
  Denali Outreach Coordinator: Kris Capps
  Outreach Coordinator: Emily Anderson
  Sound and Lighting Designer: Josh Bennett
Mission: The Festival's mission is to provide highly qualified guest artists who offer multidisciplinary study and performance opportunities that increase both personal growth and arts appreciation to all participants. Our philosophy is to enrich the lives of all with whom we associate-through study and performances-by engaging their spirit, intellect and energy in an empowering way.
Utilizes: Actors; Artists-in-Residence; Choreographers; Collaborations; Dancers; Educators; Fine Artists; Grant Writers; Guest Accompanists; Guest Artists; Guest Companies; Guest Composers; Guest Designers; Guest Ensembles; Guest Lecturers; Guest Musical Directors; Guest Musicians; High School Drama; Instructors; Local Artists; Multimedia; Music; Original Music Scores; Sign Language Translators; Singers; Soloists; Touring Companies
Founded: 1980
Specialized Field: Study Performance Festivals
Status: Non-Profit
Paid Staff: 3
Volunteer Staff: 60
Paid Artists: 100
Budget: $500,000
Income Sources: Registration Fees; Corporate/Private Donations; Grants
Season: July - August
Affiliations: University of Alaska Fairbanks
Annual Attendance: 1,000
Facility Category: University of Alaska Fairbanks
Seating Capacity: 1,000
Year Built: 1917
Organization Type: Performing; Educational

4160
CROSSSOUND
1109 C Street
Juneau, AK 99801
Phone: 907-586-9601
e-mail: directors@crosssound.com
Web Site: www.crosssound.com
Management:
  Composer/Stage Director/Production: Cecelia Heejeong Kim
  Composer: Yuriko Hase Kojima
  Composer: Karola Obermueller
  Founder/Director: Jocelyn Clark
  Publicity Manager: Rada Khajinova
  Project Manager: Liz Dodd
Mission: CrossSound is dedicated to the pursuit of three artistic priorities: to serve a rising generation of Alaskan, American, and international creative and interpretive artists in the field of musical arts, to engage musicians and audiences from across the state, meeting them at the earliest stages of their artistic development, to commission and present new works by local and international composers that take into account Alaska's uniqueness.
Utilizes: Arrangers; Choreographers; Grant Writers; Guest Accompanists; Guest Artists; Guest Choreographers; Guest Companies; Guest Composers; Guest Conductors; Guest Designers; Guest Directors; Guest Ensembles; Guest Instructors; Guest Lecturers; Guest Musical Directors; Guest Musicians
Founded: 1999
Specialized Field: Sereise & Festivals; New Music; Chamber Music; Multi Media
Status: Non-Profit, Professional
Paid Staff: 2
Volunteer Staff: 10
Paid Artists: 30
Income Sources: Donors, Corporate Sponsors
Season: June, July
Performs At: Church of the Holy Trinity, VSA Arts Alaska, Sitka Community Performing Arts Center

4161
JUNEAU ARTS & HUMANITIES COUNCIL
Performing Arts & Culture Concert Series
350 Whittier St.
Suite 101
Juneau, AK 99801
Phone: 907-586-2787
Fax: 907-586-2148
e-mail: info@jahc.org
Web Site: www.jahc.org
Officers:
  President: Teri Rasmussen
  Secretary: Dan Hopson
Management:
  Executive Director: Nancy DeCherney
  Program Coordinator: Mary Wood
Mission: The Juneau Arts & Humanities Council was established in 1973 as the official arts agency of the City & Borough of Juneau.
Utilizes: Guest Choreographers; Guest Musical Directors; Guest Musicians; Local Artists; Original Music Scores; Touring Companies
Founded: 1973
Specialized Field: Series and Festivals; Instrumental Music; Vocal Music; Youth; Dance; Ethnic Performances; Performing Arts; Visual Arts
Status: Non-Profit, Professional
Paid Staff: 2
Volunteer Staff: 40
Paid Artists: 20
Budget: For concert series $56,000
Performs At: Juneau-Douglas H.S. Auditorium; ANB Community Hall
Facility Category: High School Auditorium
Type of Stage: Proscenium
Stage Dimensions: 40 x 50
Seating Capacity: 1,000

4162
KODIAK ARTS COUNCIL
Kodiak Baranof Productions
PO Box 1792
Kodiak, AK 99615
Phone: 907-486-5291
Fax: 907-486-5591
e-mail: kodiak-arts-council@gci.net
Web Site: www.kodiakartscouncil.org
Officers:
  President: Mike Wall
  Vice President: Darcy Stielstra
  Secretary: Wes Hanna
  Treasurer: Elke Carros
  Board Member: Skip Bolton
  Board Member: Ce Ce Esparza
  Board Member: Wes Hanna
Management:
  Executive Director: Katie Oliver
  Program Coordinator: Katie Helligso
Mission: The Kodiak Arts Council serves the Kodiak Area Community as a leader and representative in matters that affect the arts. Provide and support quality programs in diverse art forms. Increase revenues and maintain financial stability while keeping programs affordable. Encourage individual involvement in the arts.
Utilizes: Arrangers; Artists-in-Residence; Choreographers; Community Talent; Grant Writers; Guest Accompanists; Guest Artists; Guest Choreographers; Guest Companies; Guest Composers; Guest Conductors; Guest Directors; Guest Musical Directors; Lyricists; Multimedia; Music; Paid Performers
Founded: 1963
Status: Non-Profit, Professional
Paid Staff: 1
Volunteer Staff: 1
Paid Artists: 100
Budget: $200,000
Income Sources: Grants; Membership; Ticket Sales
Performs At: Gerald C Wilson Auditorium
Affiliations: Kenney Center
Type of Stage: Proscenium
Stage Dimensions: 40' x 35'
Seating Capacity: 750
Year Built: 1986
Cost: $10 Million

4163
SITKA SUMMER MUSIC FESTIVAL
104 Jeff Davis Street
PO Box 3333
Sitka, AK 99520
Phone: 907-747-6774
Fax: 907-277-4842
e-mail: director@sitkamusicfestival.org
Web Site: www.sitkamusicfestival.org
Officers:
  President: Jim Steffen
  Vice President: Kari Lundgren
  Treasurer: Cynthia Gibson
  Secretary: Joyce Hughes
  Board Member: Jeff Budd
  Board Member: Cynthia Gibson
  Board Member: Kari Lundgren
  Board Member: Cynthia Westergaard
Management:
  Executive Director: Kayla Boettcher
  Artistic Director: Zuill Bailey
Mission: Festival now holds three annual chamber music series - the Sitka Summer Music Festival in June in Sitka, the Autumn and Winter Alaska Airlines Classics in Anchorage, Fairbanks, and Sitka. In collaboration with the National Endowment for the Arts, Festival musicians present touring concerts in more remote and underserved areas of the state in conjunction with the summer and winter series.
Utilizes: Guest Musicians
Founded: 1972
Specialized Field: Classical
Status: Professional
Volunteer Staff: 80
Paid Artists: 15
Non-paid Artists: 30
Budget: $250,000
Season: June
Performs At: Harrigan Centennial Hall

SERIES & FESTIVALS / Arizona

Annual Attendance: 8,000
Facility Category: Performance Hall
Seating Capacity: 500
Year Built: 1970
Year Remodeled: 1998
Organization Type: Performing; Touring

Arizona

4164
DESERT FOOTHILLS MUSICFEST
7518 E. Elbow Bend
Suite A-3
Carefree, AZ 85377
Mailing Address: PO Box 5254 Carefree, AZ 85377
Phone: 480-488-0806
Fax: 480-488-1401
e-mail: azmusicfest@azmusicfest.org
Web Site: www.azmusicfest.org
Officers:
   Chairman: Chuck Goldthwaite
   Vice-Chairman: Ann Wallenmeyer-Krahman
   Treasurer: Richard Gunderson
   Treasurer: Robert Goulstone
   Board Member: Susan Black
   Board Member: Mary Carey
   Board Member: Jon Caotes
   Board Member: Mary Goldwaite
Management:
   Administration Director: Jo Ellen McCall, jo@azmusicfest.org
   Operations Director: Jay Good, jay@azmusicfest.org
   Artistic Director: Robert Moody, donna@azmusicfest.org
   Executive Director: Allan Naplan
Mission: We are a community-based organization, conceived 19 years ago to bring great music to our neighborhoods. We are citizen-volunteers who cherish our way of life here in Arizona and are driven to enhance it. We hold firm to our core of quality Classical music, and are proud of our multi-faceted Festival and Musicale traditions of Broadway, Jazz, and myriad other expressions of musical excellence.
Utilizes: Five Seasonal Concerts; Guest Accompanists; Guest Musical Directors; Guest Soloists; Guest Teachers; Multimedia; Music; Original Music Scores; Sign Language Translators; Singers; Soloists
Founded: 1992
Specialized Field: Series & Festivals; Instrumental Music; Vocal Music; Youth
Status: Non-Profit, Professional
Paid Staff: 3
Paid Artists: 30
Budget: $400,000
Income Sources: Individual Contributions; Corporate Sponsors; Grants; Ticket Revenue
Season: February
Performs At: Carefree; Cave Creek; North Scottsdale
Annual Attendance: 4,500
Seating Capacity: 250 - 700
Organization Type: Performing; Educational

4165
PINAL COUNTY FINE ARTS COUNCIL: ARTS IN THE DESERT
8470 North Overfield Road
Central Arizona College
Coolidge, AZ 85128-9779
Phone: 520-494-5444
Fax: 520-426-4224
Toll-free: 1 8-0 2-7 98
e-mail: centralhelpdesk@centralaz.edu
Web Site: www.centralaz.edu
Management:
   President: Terry Callaway
   Executive Director: Jim Lamb
   Cultural Events Coordinator: Cheryl R Sanborn
Utilizes: Artists-in-Residence; Dance Companies; Dancers; Fine Artists; Guest Accompanists; Instructors; Multimedia; Original Music Scores; Sign Language Translators; Singers; Soloists
Founded: 1975
Specialized Field: Series & Festivals; Instrumental Music; Vocal Music; Theatre; Youth; Dance; Ethnic Performances
Status: Non-Profit, Professional
Paid Staff: 1
Volunteer Staff: 15
Paid Artists: 135
Budget: $44,000
Income Sources: Series Subscribers
Performs At: Pence Auditorium, Centeral Arizona College
Annual Attendance: 6,000-7,500
Facility Category: Auditorium
Type of Stage: Proscenium
Stage Dimensions: 45'x20'
Seating Capacity: 735
Year Built: 1969
Rental Contact: Cheryl Ragsdale

4166
VERDE VALLEY CONCERT ASSOCIATION
14 S Main Street
PO Box 26
Cottonwood, AZ 86326
Phone: 928-639-0636
Fax: 928-639-2185
e-mail: vvca@wildapache.net
Web Site: www.verdevalleyconcerts.com
Officers:
   President: Harve Grady
   Vice President: Cynthia Fox
   Treasurer: Abbie Denton
   Secretary: Julie Grady
   Board Member: Arleen Wright
   Board Member: Val Petrosky
   Board Member: Maxine Cockrell
   Board Member: Matthew Heble
Management:
   President: Arleen Wright
   Office Manager: Leah Kolb
   Director of the Restorative Justice: Dee Zenk
Mission: The VVCA mission is to: present a balanced variety of professional performing arts accessible to residents of the Verde Valley; promote the knowledge and appreciation of performing arts by contributing educational opportunities to students; and provide performance opportunities for talented Arizona artists.
Utilizes: Artists-in-Residence; Dance Companies; Fine Artists; Grant Writers; Guest Lecturers; Original Music Scores; Singers; Theatre Companies
Founded: 1952
Specialized Field: Series & Festivals; Chamber music; Instrumental Music; Vocal Music
Status: Non-Profit, Professional
Paid Staff: 1
Income Sources: Donors, Sponsors, Scholarships
Season: Year Round
Performs At: Mingus Union High School Auditorium
Seating Capacity: 852

4167
FLAGSTAFF FESTIVAL OF THE ARTS
PO Box 1607
211 W. Aspen
Flagstaff, AZ 86001
Phone: 928-774-9541
Fax: 928-556-1308
Web Site: www.flagstaffguide.com/festival
Management:
   Managing Director: Larry Reid
   Orchestra Conductor: Irwin Hoffman
   Theatre Artistic Director: Tal Russell
Mission: This major performing and visual arts festival of Arizona is held in Flagstaff on the campus of Northern Arizona University. The affair began in the early 1960s as a music camp and became a full-fledged festival in 1966. It ran one week that year, and today is a four-week festival with more than 48 events: symphonic and chamber music concerts, ballet, theater, film showings, and art exhibits.
Utilizes: Guest Artists; Guest Companies; Singers
Founded: 1966
Specialized Field: Dance; Vocal Music; Instrumental Music; Theater; Festivals
Status: Professional; Semi-Professional; Nonprofit
Income Sources: Northern Arizona University
Performs At: Ardrey Auditorium; Creative Arts Theatre
Organization Type: Performing; Educational

4168
NORTHERN ARIZONA UNIVERSITY JAZZ MADRIGAL FESTIVAL
CAL, School of Music
PO Box 6040, Bldg 37, Rm 120
Flagstaff, AZ 86011-6040
Phone: 928-523-3731
Fax: 928-523-5111
e-mail: music@nau.edu
Web Site: www.cal.nau.edu/music
Management:
   Director: Todd Sullivan, Todd.Sullivan@nau.edu
   Associate Director/Undergraduates: Rick Stamer, Rick.Stamer@nau.edu
   Associate Director/Graduate Studies: John Masserini, John.Masserini@nau.edu
Mission: The annual Northern Arizona University Vocal Jazz Madrigal Festival, one of the largest festivals of its kind in the Southwestern United States, features special guest clinicians and over 140 high school ensembles from Arizona and nearby states. The two-day festival includes a host concert in which choirs from NAU and professional groups of national and international stature appear.
Utilizes: Arrangers; Collaborations; Community Members; Composers-in-Residence; Educators; Guest Accompanists; Guest Choreographers; Guest Companies; Guest Composers; Guest Designers; Guest Directors; Guest Musical Directors; High School Drama; Multimedia; Music; Paid Performers; Scenic Designers; Singers; Soloists
Specialized Field: Jazz, Choral, Orchestra, Classical, Contemporary
Status: Non-Profit, Educational
Budget: $60,000-150,000
Income Sources: Grants, Donors, Sponsors
Season: February
Performs At: Ardrey Auditorium
Seating Capacity: 1500

4169
GRAND CANYON MUSIC FESTIVAL
PO Box 1332
Grand Canyon, AZ 86023

SERIES & FESTIVALS / Arizona

Phone: 928-638-9215
Fax: 520-638-3373
Toll-free: 800-997-8285
e-mail: gcmf@infomagic.net
Web Site: www.grandcanyonmusicfest.org
Officers:
   President: Claire West
   Vice-president/Treasurer: Helen Schaefer
   Secretary: Robert Bonfiglio
Management:
   Founding Director: Robert Bonfiglio
   Artistic Director: Clare Hoffman
Mission: To present a series of concerts in Grand Canyon National Park each September, maintaining high musical standards and diversity of programming; to commission new chamber music from American composers; to give a public service tour to schools in Northern Arizona.
Founded: 1984
Specialized Field: Instrumental; Jazz
Status: Nonprofit
Budget: $20,000-$35,000
Season: August-September
Performs At: Grand Canyon National Park (Festival Site)
Affiliations: Shrine of the Ages
Seating Capacity: 310
Organization Type: Presenting

4170
PARADISE VALLEY JAZZ PARTY
6014 N Nauni Valley Drive
Paradise Valley, AZ 85253
Phone: 480-948-7993
Fax: 480-991-5732
e-mail: dzmiller@cox.net
Web Site: www.paradisevalleyjazz.com
Management:
   President/Founder: Don Z Miller
Mission: The Paradise Valley Jazz Party, one of the longest-running jazz events in the United States, joins forces with MIM for Year 35! Featuring more than twenty top artists sharing the stage over two days, this jam session extravaganza is the hottest ticket in town.
Utilizes: Arrangers; Collaborating Artists; Guest Accompanists; Guest Choreographers; Guest Companies; Guest Directors; Guest Musical Directors; High School Drama; Lyricists; Multimedia; Music; Paid Performers
Founded: 1978
Specialized Field: Series & Festivals: Instrumental Music & Concerts
Status: For-Profit, Professional
Paid Staff: 1
Volunteer Staff: 5
Income Sources: Ticket Sales
Season: April
Performs At: MIM Theater

4171
ARIZONA EXPOSITION & STATE FAIR
1826 W. Mcdowell Rd
Phoenix, AZ 85007
Phone: 602-252-6771
Fax: 602-495-1302
e-mail: info@azstatefair.com
Web Site: www.azstatefair.com
Management:
   Event Coordinator: Stephen King
   Executive Director: Don West
   Deputy Director: Wanell Costello
   Assist. Executive Director/ Enterta: Jen Yee
   Entrie Director: Dionna Dallas
   Marketing Director: Kristi Walsh
   Operations Supervisor: Alex Ramirez
   Sponsorship Director: Jen Yee
   Sponsorship Coordinator: Mary Evanson
Mission: Annual State Fair.
Income Sources: Sponsors, Ticket Sales, Vendors
Season: October-November

4172
GILA VALLEY ARTS COUNCIL
PO Box 1022
980 South 14th Avenue
Safford, AZ 85546
Phone: 928-428-0081
Fax: 520-428-2772
e-mail: kokopeli@zekes.com
Web Site: www.gila.org
Officers:
   President: Tom Green
   Treasurer: Lori Rhinehart
   Residency Co-Chair: Leslie Campos
   Recording Secretary: Mary Ann Ripplinger
   Residencies Chair: Ali Harris
Management:
   Artistic Director: Jack Kukuk
   Executive Director: Shelly Williams
Mission: Gila Valley Arts Council's mission is to facilitate the visual and performing arts in this Arizona region through a jam-packed season featuring the finest talent around-locally, nationally and internationally. The organization has brought a variety of talent to the Gila Valley, including performances from the Kremlin Orchestra, the International Children's Choir, the Arizona Opera, jazz greats and dance companies.
Utilizes: Arrangers; Artists-in-Residence; Choreographers; Collaborating Artists; Collaborations; Community Talent; Dancers; Guest Accompanists; Guest Choreographers; Guest Companies; Guest Musical Directors; Local Artists; Local Artists & Directors; Lyricists; Multimedia; Paid Performers; Singers; Soloists; Students
Founded: 1985
Specialized Field: Dance, Opera, Children'S Chorus, Jazz
Budget: $35,000-60,000
Performs At: Eastern Arizona College, Fine Arts Auditorium
Seating Capacity: 941+; 300

4173
SCOTTSDALE ARTS FESTIVAL
Scottsdale Center for the Arts
7380 East Second Street
Scottsdale, AZ 85251
Phone: 480-994-2787
Fax: 480-874-4699
e-mail: janiceb@sccarts.org
Web Site: www.scottsdalearts.org
Officers:
   Chairman: Mike Miller
   Vice Chairman: Ellen Andres-Schneider
   Treasurer: Ken Olson
   Secretary: John Morrell
   Trustee: Carolyn Allen
   Trustee: Jennifer Anderson
   Trustee: Dave Barber
   Trustee: Keith Baum
   Trustee: Don Cogmann
Management:
   President/CEO: William H Banchs
   Vice President/CFO: Jeff Nichols
   Vice President and Director: Cory Baker
   Operations Director: Larry Edmonds
   Operations Assistant: Karen Cardoza
   Event Manager: Jamie Prins
   Programming Adminstrator: Abbey Messmer
   Programming Coordinator: Leanne Cardwell
   Development Director: Eileen Wilson
Mission: In 1971, a group of Scottsdale citizens created the first-ever Scottsdale Arts Festival — then a month-long celebration, held at various locations, that included performances by local dance and music groups, exhibitions by Arizona craftsmen and of Native American Arts, a juried show by the Scottsdale Artists League, and tours of fine artists' and crafts artists' studios.
Founded: 1975
Specialized Field: Performing Arts
Status: Non-Profit, Professional
Income Sources: Sponsors, Ticket Sales
Season: March
Performs At: Scottsdale Center for the Performing Arts

4174
CHAMBER MUSIC SEDONA
1487 W SR 89A
Ste 9
Sedona, AZ 86336
Phone: 928-204-2415
Fax: 928-282-0893
e-mail: info@chambermusicsedona.org
Web Site: www.chambermusicsedona.org
Officers:
   President: John Steinbrunner
   Vice President: Pamela Fazzini
   Treasurer: Dwight Kadar
   Secretary: Mary Lee Warner
   Board Member: Daren Burns
   Board Member: Thomas Cleman
   Advisory Chairman: James Pease
   Advisory Vice Chairman: Edward Ingraham
   Past Chair: Al Wolfe
Management:
   Executive Director: Bert Harclerode
   General Manager: Anna Cates
   Marketing Coordinator: Kristine Follett
   Administration: Marisol Molina
   Artistic Advisor: Nicholas Canellakis
   Artistic Advisor: Alexander Fiterstein
   Artistic Advisor: Marian Hahn
   Artistic Advisor: Benjamin Jacobson
Mission: The mission of Chamber Music Sedona is to enrich the lives of Northern Arizona residents and visitors by presenting the finest international, national, and regional performing artists and to promote a love of the performing arts through arts education programs.
Utilizes: Artists-in-Residence; Collaborating Artists; Commissioned Music; Five Seasonal Concerts; Grant Writers; Guest Companies; Guest Directors; Guest Lecturers; Guest Musical Directors; Local Artists; Multimedia
Specialized Field: Chamber; Jazz
Paid Staff: 2
Paid Artists: 52
Budget: $200,000
Income Sources: Ticket Sales, Sponsor, Donors
Performs At: St. John Vianney Church; Museum of Northern Arizona
Affiliations: CMA, ACA
Annual Attendance: 4000
Seating Capacity: 250; 200

4175
SEDONA JAZZ ON THE ROCKS
2020 Contractors Road
Suite 5
Sedona, AZ 86336

SERIES & FESTIVALS / Arizona

Phone: 928-282-1985
Fax: 928-282-0590
e-mail: office@sedonajazz.com
Web Site: www.sedonajazz.com
Officers:
President: Bettye Wilson
Management:
Executive Director: Carol Golden
Mission: To celebrate jazz as a living art form through education and performance programs
Utilizes: Guest Accompanists; Instructors; Original Music Scores; Sign Language Translators; Soloists
Specialized Field: Jazz
Status: Non-Profit, Non-Professional
Paid Staff: 3
Volunteer Staff: 200
Non-paid Artists: 4
Budget: $400,000
Income Sources: Box Office; Corporate Sponsors; Grants
Season: September
Performs At: Sedona Cultural Park (Festival Site)
Annual Attendance: 6,000
Facility Category: Various Venues
Seating Capacity: 200-4,500
Organization Type: Performing; Sponsoring

4176
WEST VALLEY ARTS COUNCIL
PO Box 754
13243 N Founders Park Blvd
Surprise, AZ 85395
Phone: 623-935-6384
Fax: 623-935-4327
e-mail: admin@westvalleyarts.com
Web Site: www.westvalleyarts.com
Officers:
Chariman of the Board: Bill Sheldon
Vice Chair: Jennifer McSweeney
Secretary: David Robey
Treasurer: Rob Bohr
Past Chair: Hal DeKeyser
Financial Consultant: Mary Estrada
Board Member: Patricia Lewis
Board Member: David Robey
Management:
Executive Director: Bernadette Mills
Director of Operations: Desiree van de Christopher, dchristopher@westvalleyart.org
Director of Programs and Education: Janene Van Leeuwen, jvanleeuwen@westvalleyart.org
Administration: Linda Silva
Mission: WVAC was incorporated as the Cultural Arts Society West in 1969, and changed its name to the West Valley Fine Arts Council in 1989 to reflect a broader, more inclusive vision. It became the West Valley Arts Council in 2004. WVAC has been central to creating what is recognized as a high quality of life for West Valley residents, and is the only multi-disciplinary arts organization of its type and scope in the Valley.
Utilizes: Arrangers; Artists-in-Residence; Collaborations; Composers; Dance Companies; Dancers; Fine Artists; Grant Writers; Guest Accompanists; Guest Choreographers; Guest Companies; Local Artists & Directors; Lyricists; Multimedia; Music; Paid Performers
Founded: 1969
Specialized Field: Series & Festivals; Visual arts; Music festivals; Dance; Theatre
Status: Non-Profit, Professional
Paid Staff: 12
Income Sources: Donors, Sponsors, Ticket Sales, Advertising
Season: August-April
Performs At: Marley Park Community

4177
ARIZONA STATE UNIVERSITY PUBLIC EVENTS
Arizona State University
PO Box 870205
Tempe, AZ 85287-0205
Phone: 480-965-5062
Fax: 480-965-7663
e-mail: mreed@asu.edu
Web Site: www.asugammage.com
Management:
President: Micheal Crow
Executive Director: Colleen Jennings-Roggensack, cjr@asu.edu
Business Services Director: Neva Bochenek, neva@asu.edu
Operations Director: Terri Cranmer
Marketing Director: Victor Hamburger
Audience Services Director: Karie Lurie
Development Director: Peter Means
Programs Director: Michael Reed
Public Relations Manager: Dana McGuiness
Mission: ASU Gammage is among the largest university-based presenters of performing arts in the world. ASU Gammage is the home theater of the PROGRESSIVE Broadway Across America - Arizona series and the ASU Gammage Beyond series. Its mission is to connect communities through artistic excellence and educational outreach. ASU Gammage is an historic hall designed by internationally renowned architect, Frank Lloyd Wright.
Utilizes: AEA Actors; Artists-in-Residence; Choreographers; Collaborating Artists; Collaborations; Commissioned Composers; Commissioned Music; Composers-in-Residence; Curators; Dance Companies; Dancers; Educators; Grant Writers; Guest Artists; Guest Companies; Guest Conductors; Guest Directors; Guest Instructors; Guest Lecturers; Guest Soloists; Instructors; Multimedia; Organization Contracts; Original Music Scores; Playwrights; Selected Students; Singers; Soloists; Special Technical Talent; Theatre Companies; Touring Companies
Founded: 1967
Specialized Field: Performing Arts
Status: Non-Profit, Non-Professional
Paid Staff: 54
Volunteer Staff: 400
Budget: $1,000,000+
Income Sources: Corporate Sponsors, Ticket Sales, Donors
Performs At: Grady Gammage Memorial Auditorium; Sundome Center
Affiliations: Arts Presenters, ISPAA, WAA
Annual Attendance: 500,000
Facility Category: Auditorium
Type of Stage: Prosenium Sprungwood
Seating Capacity: 3011
Year Built: 1967
Rental Contact: Terri Cranmer

4178
PIMA COMMUNITY COLLEGE FOR THE ARTS
2202 W. Anklam Rd.
Tucson, AZ 85709-0225
Phone: 520-206-4500
Fax: 520-206-6670
e-mail: centerforthearts@pima.edu
Web Site: www.pima.edu
Officers:
Chairperson: Wendy Turner
Co-Chairperson: Mykle Zoback
Secretary: Donna Cohn
Historian: Jorge Cabllero
Roll Keeper: Shani Stewart
Program Director: Leighann Langel
Technical Director: Warren Loomis
Utilizes: Scenic Designers; Soloists; Students
Founded: 1994
Specialized Field: Series and Festivals; Plays; Dances; Shows; Theatre
Status: Non-Profit, Professional
Budget: $20,000-35,000
Performs At: Proscenium Theatre; Black Box Theatre; Recital Hall
Seating Capacity: 425;170;120

4179
SOUTHERN ARIZONA ARTS AND CULTURAL ALLIANCE
7225 N Oracle Road
Suite 112
Tucson, AZ 85704
Phone: 520-797-3959
Fax: 520-531-9225
e-mail: info@saaca.org
Web Site: www.saaca.org
Officers:
President: Gregg Forszt
Vice President: Al Cook
Secretary: Maya Dillard Lidell
Treasurer: Tom Binder
Board Member: Donald Luria
Board Member: Melanie Larson
Board Member: Thomas Alex Benavidez
Board Member: Jennifer McMahon
Management:
Executive Director: Kate Marquez, kate@saaca.org
Programs Coordinator: Pat Deely, pat@saaca.org
Special Events Director: Jonas Hunter, jonas@saaca.org
Communications Specialist: Chelsey Killebrew
Development Manager: Liz Stern
Office Manager: Chris Kochmann
Program Event Specialist: Mitch Turbenson
Mission: The Southern Arizona Arts and Cultural Alliance (SAACA) is a not-for-profit organization dedicated to the preservation, expansion and creation of Arts and Culture in Southern Arizona. SAACA exists to ensure that, through engagement in arts and culture, our communities produce strong, inspired citizens. SAACA enlists artists, businesses, governments, and individuals to expand artistic and cultural opportunities in their respective communities.
Founded: 1997
Specialized Field: Culinary Arts, Visual Arts, Art Education, Youth Art, Festivals, Cultural Arts, Films
Status: Non-Profit
Income Sources: Tickets Sales, Spqonsors, Donors

4180
ST. PHILIP'S IN THE HILLS FRIENDS OF MUSIC
4440 N Campbell Avenue
Tucson, AZ 85718
Mailing Address: PO Box 65840 Tucson, Arizona 85728
Phone: 520-299-6421
Fax: 520-299-0712
e-mail: office@stphilipstucson.org
Web Site: www.stphilipstucson.org
Management:
Music Director: Woosung Kang

Associate Music Director: Jeffery Campbell
Facilities Use Coordinator: Jeffri Sanders
Communications Director: Sue Agnew
Children and Families Director: Bruce Phillips
Youth Ministries Apprentice: Sara Talley
Outreach: Nancy Atherton
Outreach: Pat Kinsman
Stewardship: John Waszczak
Mission: To present concert series within the ministry.
Utilizes: Arrangers; Community Talent; Educators; Multimedia; Music
Founded: 1989
Specialized Field: Series and Festivals; Instrumental Music; Vocal Music; Youth; Ethnic Performances; Classical Ensembles
Status: Non-Profit, Professional
Paid Staff: 2
Paid Artists: 25
Budget: $10,000-20,000
Income Sources: Donors, Fundraisers
Performs At: St. Philip's in the Hills Episcopal Church
Seating Capacity: 500

4181
TUCSON WINTER CHAMBER MUSIC FESTIVAL
PO Box 40845
Tucson, AZ 85717
Phone: 520-577-3769
e-mail: office@arizonachambermusic.org
Web Site: www.arizonachambermusic.org
Officers:
  President: Jean-Paul Bierny
  Vice President: Bryan Daum
  Treasurer: Wes Addison
  Corresponding Secretary: Joseph Tolliver
  Recording Secretary: Helmut Abt
  Board Member: Walter Swap
  Board Member: Thomas Aceto
  Board Member: Nancy Bissell
Management:
  Artistic Director: Peter Rejto
  Program Notes: Nancy Monsman
  Fundraising: Cathy Anderson
Mission: Our mission is to present the world's great chamber music, performed by the world's finest chamber musicians in a friendly and inviting atmosphere. Through two concert series, the acclaimed Tucson Winter Chamber Music Festival, a dynamic program to commission new works, our extensive outreach to schools, and our affordable ticket prices, we aim to bring the joy of this great music to as wide an audience as possible.
Utilizes: Arrangers; Collaborating Artists; Collaborations; Community Talent; Composers; Educators; Fine Artists; Local Artists & Directors; Lyricists; Multimedia; Music; Paid Performers
Specialized Field: Chamber
Status: Non-Profit
Budget: $60,000-$150,000
Income Sources: Fundraisers, Donors
Season: February - March
Affiliations: Leo Rich Theatre; Tucson Convention Center
Seating Capacity: 550

4182
UA PRESENTS
1020 E University Blvd.
PO Box 210158
Tucson, AZ 85721-0029
Phone: 520-621-3341
Fax: 520-621-8991
e-mail: uapresents@arizona.edu
Web Site: www.uapresents.org
Officers:
  Chairman: Lori Banzhaf
  Advisory Board: Terry Coleman
  Advisory Board: George Davis
  Advisory Board: Dr Ellis Friedman
  Advisory Board: Kate Garner
  Advisory Board: Norma Gentry
Management:
  Interim Executive Director: Charles Tennes
  Development Director: Jennifer Camano
  Programming Coordinator: Staci Santa
  Outreach Coordinator: Sarah Smith
  Marketing Director: Jo Alenson
  Publicity Manager: Darsen Campbell
  Patron Relations Director: Ana Maria Acuria
  Group Sales Coordinator: Sandra Garcia
  Ticketing Supervisor: Petra Garcia
Mission: The mission of UApresents is to educate, enlighten and inspire by bringing performing arts and artists together with the diverse communities of Southern Arizona. UApresents is a nationally recognized host of world-class performances and programs for the communities of Southern Arizona, which provides the opportunity to experience a broad range of activities with the goal of developing a lifelong love and respect for the performing arts.
Utilizes: Arrangers; Artists-in-Residence; Choreographers; Collaborating Artists; Collaborations; Dancers; Educators; High School Drama; Instructors; Local Artists; Local Artists & Directors; Lyricists; Multimedia; Music; Paid Performers
Founded: 1891
Opened: 1892
Specialized Field: Performing Arts
Status: Non-Profit
Income Sources: Ticket Sales, Donors, Sponsors
Season: Year Round
Performs At: Centennial Hall

Arkansas

4183
OUACHITA BAPTIST UNIVERSITY: ARTISTS SERIES
410 Ouachita St.
Arkadelphia, AR 71998
Phone: 870-246-5129
Fax: 870-245-5274
e-mail: gerberg@obu.edu
Web Site: www.obu.edu/music
Management:
  President: Dr Rex M Horne Jr
  Communications Director: Tiffany Burich
  Development Officer: Clayton Chapuis
  Development Officer: John Cloud
  Dean/School of Fine Arts: Scott Holsclaw
Mission: Students are provided a wide range of performance opportunities through the artists series in the spring and other events.
Utilizes: Scenic Designers; Soloists; Students; Touring Companies
Income Sources: Donors, Grants, Sponsors
Season: Year Round
Performs At: Jones Performing Arts Center; W Francis McBeth Recital Hall
Seating Capacity: 1500; 267

4184
WALTON ARTS AND IDEAS
University of the Ozarks
415 North College Avenue
Clarksville, AR 72830
Phone: 479-979-1346
Fax: 501-979-1349
e-mail: gemyers@ozarks.edu
Web Site: www.ozarks.edu
Management:
  President: Dr Rick Niece
  Executive Director: Ginny Myers
  Assistant Director of Admission: Mr. Joey Hughes
  Admission Counselor: Ms. Samantha Hoing
  Director of National & JLC Recruitm: Mr. Hunter Jackson
  Admission Counselor: Mr. Shaun Wiseman
  Office Manager & Campus Visit Coord: Ms. Emma Lee Morrow
  Enrollment Data Manager: Ms. Patti Schuh
Mission: True to our Christian heritage, we prepare those who seek to live life fully, those who seek the richness of life provided by study of the liberal arts and the quality of life provided by professional preparation. We provide a uniquely supportive, academically sophisticated and challenging environment. Our first priority is the education of students who come to us from diverse religious, cultural, educational, and economic backgrounds.
Specialized Field: Series and Festivals: Different Events
Status: Non-Profit, Professional
Paid Staff: 3
Performs At: Seay Theatre
Seating Capacity: 699

4185
UNIVERSITY OF CENTRAL ARKANSAS PUBLIC APPEARANCES
201 Donaghey Avenue
Conway, AR 72035-0001
Phone: 501-450-5000
Fax: 501-450-3296
e-mail: admissions@uca.edu
Web Site: www.uca.edu/cfac
Management:
  President: Tom Courtway
  President Elect: Richard Dunsworth
  Vice President: Jeff Pitchford
  Administration: Susan Lilly
Mission: The Walton Arts and Ideas Series will be offering something different and, we hope, appropriate for the occasion: a season of reflection. Instead of bringing the richness of the world beyond to our campus, we intend to celebrate the richness among us. A panel of four students were asked to select a person who made them think or feel more deeply.
Founded: 1909
Specialized Field: Higher Education
Status: Non-Profit, Professional
Paid Staff: 900
Income Sources: Grants, Donors
Season: September-November
Performs At: Ida Waldran Auditorium; Conway Public Schools Auditorium
Seating Capacity: 1100-1500

SERIES & FESTIVALS / Arkansas

4186
INSPIRATION POINT FINE ARTS COLONY
Opera in the Ozarks
16311 Highway 62 W
PO Box 127
Eureka Springs, AR 72632
Phone: 479-253-8595
e-mail: info@opera.org
Web Site: www.opera.org
Officers:
   President: Carole Langley
   Vice-President: Sue Breuer
   Treasurer: Duane D. Langley
   Corresponding Secretary: Lavonna Whitesell
   Recording Secretary: Jean Moffat
   Newsletter Editor: Don F. Dagenais
Management:
   Artistic Director/Conductor: Thomas Cockrell
   Conductor: Adam Kerry Boyles
   Director: Linda Ade Brand
   Director: Robert Swedberg
   principal coach: Michael Dauphinais
   costume designer: Miriam Patterson
Mission: Opera in the Ozarks is a summer program that trains opera singers and stages performances at Inspiration Point, overlooking the White River seven miles west of Eureka Springs (Carroll County). The company has always performed in repertory style, with each student learning several roles over the season. Generally, three operas make up the summer season, with at least one being performed in the original language.
Utilizes: Guest Artists; Guest Companies; Singers
Founded: 1950
Specialized Field: Instrumental Music; Lyric Opera; Grand Opera
Status: Non-Professional; Nonprofit
Paid Staff: 7
Income Sources: National Federation of Music Clubs; donations
Performs At: Inspiration Point Fine Arts Colony
Organization Type: Performing; Educational; Sponsoring

4187
SEASON OF ENTERTAINMENT
University of Arkansas-Fort Smith
5210 Grand Avenue
PO Box 3649
Fort Smith, AR 72913-3649
Phone: 479-788-7000
Toll-free: 888-512-5466
e-mail: boxoffice@uafortsmith.edu
Web Site: www.uafortsmith.edu/season/
Officers:
   Vice Chancellor Campus Events: Stacey Jones
Management:
   Chancellor: Paul B. Beran
   Exectuive Director: Stacey Jones
   Vice Chancellor for University Rela: Mark Horn
   Vice Chancellor for Finance and Adm: Darrell Morrison
   Vice Chancellor for Student Affairs: Lee E. Krehbiel
Mission: Annual concert series that combines national touring productions with UA Fort Smith productions.
Specialized Field: Theater, Choral Ensembles, Jazz Band, Symphonic
Income Sources: Sponsors
Season: Year Round
Performs At: Breedlove Fine Arts Auditorium; Fort Smith Civic Center
Seating Capacity: 440; 1,300

4188
WARFIELD CONCERTS
123 Stonebrooke
PO Box 81
Helena, AR 72342
Phone: 870-338-8327
e-mail: info@warfieldconcerts.com
Web Site: www.warfieldconcerts.com
Management:
   Committee Member: Maureen Jones
   Committee Member: Don Etherly
   Committee Member: Susan Carter
Mission: Musical events made available free of charge through the generosity of the late Samuel Drake Warfield.
Founded: 1968
Specialized Field: Instrumental; Multi-Media; Opera; Choral; Jazz; Dance; Theatre; Childrens'; Educational
Paid Staff: 1
Volunteer Staff: 3
Paid Artists: 160
Budget: $20,000-$35,000
Season: Late April - Early May
Performs At: Philips Colliseum Fine Arts Center (Festival Site)
Affiliations: Lily Peter Auditorium
Seating Capacity: 1,250

4189
HOT SPRINGS MUSIC FESTIVAL CHAMBER ORCHESTRA
468 Prospect Avenue
Hot Springs, AR 71901
Phone: 501-623-4763
Fax: 501-624-6440
e-mail: festival@hotmusic.org
Web Site: www.hotmusic.org
Management:
   General Director: Todd Cranson
   Music Advisor/Conductor: Peter Bay
   Festival Chorus Director: Lynn Payette
   Executive Director: Marcy Mermel
Mission: The Hot Springs Music Festival's mission is twofold: (1) to provide performance experience and mentorship opportunities to especially talented international pre-professional musicians, and (2) to provide high-quality music performances and performing arts-related activities at reasonable cost to residents of and visitors to Arkansas and the Hot Springs community.
Utilizes: Arrangers; Artists-in-Residence; Choreographers; Collaborating Artists; Community Members; Grant Writers; Guest Directors; Local Artists & Directors; Local Unknown Artists; Lyricists; Multimedia; Music; Paid Performers
Founded: 1996
Specialized Field: Series and Festivals; Instrumental Music; Vocal Music
Status: Non-Profit, Non-Professional
Paid Staff: 3
Paid Artists: 30
Income Sources: Tickets Sales, Sponsors

4190
FOWLER CENTER AT ARKANSAS STATE UNIVERSITY
201 Olympic Drive
PO Box 2339
Jonesboro, AR 72467
Mailing Address: PO Box 2339 State University, AR 72467
Phone: 870-972-3471
Fax: 870-972-3748
e-mail: fowlercenter@astate.edu
Web Site: www.fowlercenter.astate.edu
Management:
   Director: Wendy Hymes
   Director: Lee Christensen
   Technical Director: Jeff McLaughlin
   Assistant Technical Director: Evan Palumbo
Mission: The mission is to present to the students, faculty and staff of Arkansas State University and the citizens of Northeast Arkansas an opportunity to exprience visual and performing arts events of national and international stature.
Utilizes: Dance Companies; Multimedia; Original Music Scores
Founded: 2001
Specialized Field: Music; Theatre; Visual Art
Status: Nonprofit
Paid Staff: 5
Budget: $400,000
Income Sources: Arkansas State University; Endowments; Ticket Sales
Performs At: Fine Arts Recital Hall; Wilson Auditorium
Facility Category: Concert Hall, Drama Theatre
Type of Stage: Proscenium
Seating Capacity: 975; 342
Year Built: 2000
Rental Contact: Manager Jerry Biebesheimer

4191
ARTSPREE
University of Arkansas at Little Rock
164 Fine Arts Building
2801 S University
Little Rock, AR 72204
Phone: 501-569-3288
Fax: 501-569-8775
e-mail: fwmartin@ualr.edu
Web Site: ualr.edu
Management:
   President: Donald Bobbitt
   Chancellor: Joel Anderson
   Chancellor Advisor: Mary Good
   Vice Chancellor: Stacey Robertson
   Vice Chancellor/Student Services: Charles Donaldson
   Vice Chancellor/Finance: Bob Adams
   Vice Chancellor/Advancement: Bill Walker
   Chief of Staff: Priscilla McChristian
   Executive Director: Judy Williams
Mission: Celebrating Milestones through Music.
Founded: 1993
Specialized Field: Series & Festivals: Music & Dance
Status: Non-Profit, Professional
Income Sources: Ticket Sales, Donors, Sponsors
Season: September, November, February, April
Performs At: University Theatre; Stella Boyle Smith Concert Hall
Seating Capacity: 679; 312

4192
HARDING UNIVERSITY CONCERT & LYCEUM SERIES
Harding University
PO Box 10877
915 E. Market Street
Searcy, AR 72143
Phone: 501-279-4000
Fax: 501-279-4086
e-mail: music@harding.edu
Web Site: www.harding.edu

Management:
University President: David Burks
Mission: Four events per season, mostly classical, for a college community.
Utilizes: Guest Accompanists; Multimedia; Theatre Companies
Founded: 1924
Specialized Field: University With Performing Series
Status: Non-Profit, Non-Professional
Budget: $11,000
Performs At: Auditorium
Annual Attendance: 1,200
Type of Stage: Proscenium
Seating Capacity: 900
Rental Contact: David Briggs

4193
JOHN BROWN UNIVERSITY LYCEUM CONCERT SERIES
2000 West University Street
Siloam Springs, AR 72761
Phone: 479-524-7358
e-mail: jbuinfo@jbu.edu
Web Site: www.jbu.edu
Officers:
Chair Communications/Fine Arts Dept: Terri Wubbena
Vice President for University Advan: Dr. Jim Krall
Management:
Director Music Theatre: Donna Rollene
Media Relations Coordinator: Lindsey Dikes-Larsen
Director of Advancement Services: Steve Onnen
Assistant Director of Advancement D: Sonya Price
Administrative Assistant/Receptioni: Joyce Fiet
Graphic Designer: Kelly Saunders
Creative Director: Matt Snyder
Mission: Concert series highlighting the works of various artists throughout the year and usually free to the public.
Paid Staff: 1
Volunteer Staff: 3
Budget: $9,000
Income Sources: Fees (student); grants
Performs At: Jones Recital Hall; Cathedral of the Ozarks
Annual Attendance: 500-600
Facility Category: Small recital hall; large sanctuary with platform
Seating Capacity: 159; 1000
Year Built: 1991

4194
GRAND PRAIRIE FESTIVAL OF THE ARTS
PO Box 65
Stuttgart, AR 72160
Phone: 870-673-1781
Fax: 870-673-1781
Management:
Director: Wanda Loudermilk
Mission: To provide a diverse program of performing arts for the Grand Prairie community.
Utilizes: Guest Companies
Founded: 1956
Specialized Field: Vocal Music; Instrumental Music; Theater
Status: Professional; Non-Professional
Income Sources: Grand Prairie Arts Council
Performs At: Grand Prairie War Memorial Auditorium
Organization Type: Educational; Sponsoring

California

4195
KELSONARTS PERFORMANCES
315 Crest Avenue
Alamo, CA 94507
Phone: 925-934-4566
Fax: 925-934-4536
e-mail: info@kelsonarts.com
Web Site: www.kelsonarts.com
Management:
Managing Director: Linus Eukel
Performs At: Various Sites
Seating Capacity: 200-750

4196
ALHAMBRA PERFORMING ARTS
150 E St
Alhambra, CA 94553
Phone: 626-570-5044
Fax: 626-282-9419
e-mail: webmaster@cityof alhambra.org
Web Site: www.cityofalhambra.org
Management:
Artistic Director: Cynthia Jarvis
Managing Director: Coludine Meeker
Director of Community Programs: Mike Macias
Mission: To administer, manage and implement leisure service programs accommodating a variety of interests, ages, cultures, and abilities
Founded: 1804
Specialized Field: Series & Festivals; Instrumental Music; Vocal Music; Youth; Dance; Ethnic Performances
Status: Non-Profit, Professional
Paid Staff: 100
Season: Summer festival; free admission and parking
Performs At: Outdoor Bandshell
Seating Capacity: 750-1000

4197
OLD PASADENA JAZZ FESTIVAL - JAZZFEST WEST
27101 Aliso Creek Road
Suite 154
Aliso Viejo, CA 92656
Phone: 949-362-3366
Fax: 949-362-5366
e-mail: info@omegaevents.com
Web Site: www.omegaevents.com
Management:
President: Rich Sherman
Founded: 1995
Specialized Field: Producing Concerts
Status: For-Profit, Non-Professional
Income Sources: Ticket Sales; Commercial sponsorship,
Season: Two-day festival; July;
Performs At: Outdoors; Bonelli Park , San Dimas, CA;

4198
NORTH ORANGE COUNTY COMMUNITY CONCERTS ASSOCIATION
623 S Clara Street
Anaheim, CA 92804
Phone: 714-535-8925
e-mail: membership@northocconcerts.org
Web Site: www.northocconcerts.org
Officers:
VP Memberships: John Jackson
Management:
President: Frank Knouse
Founded: 1945
Specialized Field: Series & Festivals; Instrumental Music; Vocal Music; Ethnic Performances
Status: Non-Profit, Professional
Income Sources: Season subscription sales; donations, advertisements
Performs At: Fullerton First United Methodist Church
Seating Capacity: 700

4199
SHASTA COMMUNITY CONCERT ASSOCIATION
6396 Vista Del Sierra Drive
P.O. Box 493979, Redding
Anderson, CA 96049-3979
Phone: 530-247-7355
Fax: 530-365-2664
Web Site: www.shastacommunityconcerts.com
Officers:
President: Jane G Wittmann
Management:
President: Jane Wippmann
Founded: 1938
Specialized Field: Series and Festivals; Instrumental Music; Vocal Music; Youth; Dance
Status: Non-Profit, Professional
Income Sources: Season Memberships, Patron Donors
Performs At: Redding Convention Center

4200
PACIFIC UNION COLLEGE FINE ARTS SERIES
Pacific Union College
One Angwin Avenue
Angwin, CA 94508
Phone: 707-965-6201
Fax: 707—96-5-67
Web Site: www.puc.edu/academics/departments/music/home
Management:
Manager: Del Case
Mission: University Department of Music Performance Series
Performs At: Paulin Hall
Seating Capacity: 465

4201
BEAR VALLEY MUSIC FESTIVAL
PO Box 5068
Bear Valley, CA 95223
Phone: 209-753-2574
Fax: 209-753-2576
Toll-free: 800-458-1618
e-mail: music@bearvalleymusic.org
Web Site: www.bearvalleymusic.org
Officers:
Executive Director: Caroline Schirato
Offfice Manager: Pati Hendersot
Production Manager: Myke Kunkel
Controller: Kathleen Lowe
Management:
Music Director: Carter Nice
President: Randy Hanvelt
VP: Ann Hicks
Director: Robert Bess
Founded: 1968
Specialized Field: Instrumental;Symphonic concerts; Opera; Jazz; Childrens'
Budget: $20,000-$35,000
Income Sources: Subscription and Individual Ticket Sales;Corporate Sponsors; Individual Donors; 501C3 non-profit organization
Season: July - August

SERIES & FESTIVALS / California

Performs At: Bear Valley (Festival Site)
Facility Category: Festival Tent
Seating Capacity: 1,200

4202
NOTRE DAME DE NAMUR RALSTON CONCERT SERIES
NDNU Music Department
1500 Ralston Avenue
Belmont, CA 94002
Phone: 650-508-3597
Fax: 650-508-3736
e-mail: mschmitz@ndnu.edu
Web Site: www.music.ndnu.edu
Officers:
   President: Judith Maxwell Greig, Ph.D.
   Vice President for Enrollment Manag: Jason Murray
   Vice President for Finance and Admi: Henry Roth
Management:
   President: John B O'Blak
   Chairman Music Department: Debra Lambert
   Stage Director: Greg Fritsch
Mission: University Department of Music Performance Series
Founded: 1851
Specialized Field: Series & Festivals; Instrumental Music; Vocal Music; Theatre; Dance
Status: Non-Profit, Professional
Paid Staff: 20
Performs At: Ralston Ballroom
Seating Capacity: 200

4203
BERKELEY FESTIVAL & EXHIBITION
UC Berkeley, Cal Performances
101 Zellerbach Hall, #4800
Berkeley, CA 94720-4800
Mailing Address: P.O. Box 10151 Berkeley, CA 94709
Phone: 510-642-0212
Fax: 510-643-6707
e-mail: rcole@calperfs.berkeley.edu
Web Site: www.bfx.berkeley.edu
Management:
   General Director: Robert W Cole
Mission: Produced by Cal Performances in association with University Department of Music. San Francisco Early Music Society; Early Music America
Specialized Field: Instrumental
Budget: $150,000-$400,000
Season: June
Performs At: Berkeley; University of California (Festival Site)
Affiliations: Various Bay Locations
Seating Capacity: 400 - 2,000

4204
CALIFORNIA SHAKESPEARE THEATER
701 Heinz Avenue
Berkeley, CA
Berkeley, CA 94710
Phone: 510-548-3422
Fax: 510-843-9921
e-mail: info@calshakes.org
Web Site: www.calshakes.org
Officers:
   Director of Finance: Noralee Rockwell
   President: Buddy Warner
   Development Director: Jim Huntley
   Marketing & Public Relations Dir.: Marilyn Langbehn
   First Vice President: Jean Simpson
   Vice President: Marshall Kido
   Vice President: Alan Schnur
   Secretary: Ellen Dale
   Treasurer: Jay Yamada
Management:
   Artistic Director: Jonathan Moscone
   Managing Director: Susie Folk
   Associate Artistic Director: Jessica Richards
   Production Manager: Jean Paul Grassieux
Mission: To make boldly imagined and deeply entertaining interpretations of Shakespeare's plays and other works of classic theater.
Utilizes: Actors; AEA Actors; Artists-in-Residence; Choreographers; Collaborations; Commissioned Music; Designers; Educators; Five Seasonal Concerts; Guest Instructors; Guest Soloists; Instructors; Local Artists; Multimedia; Organization Contracts; Original Music Scores; Performance Artists; Poets; Resident Professionals
Founded: 1973
Specialized Field: Theatre: Classics
Status: Non-Profit, Professional
Paid Staff: 25
Paid Artists: 50
Budget: $3,400,000
Income Sources: Ticket Sales; Government; Individuals; Corporations; Foundations
Season: June - October
Performs At: Bruns Memorial Amphitheater
Annual Attendance: 46,000
Facility Category: Outdoor Amphitheater
Seating Capacity: 545
Year Built: 1990
Year Remodeled: 2010
Organization Type: Performing; Touring; Educational

4205
EARLY MUSIC IN MARIN
PO Box 10151
Berkeley, CA 94709-1516
Phone: 510-528-1725
Fax: 510-843-9921
e-mail: sfems@sfems.org
Web Site: www.sfems.org
Officers:
   President: John Phillips
   Vice President: Yuko Tanaka
   Vice President: Robert Cole
   Treasurer: Marilyn Marquis
   Secretary: Sally Blaker
Management:
   Coordinator: Alisa Gould Sugden
   Executive Director: Harvey Malloy
   Operations Manager: Dorothy Manly
   Festival and Workshop Administrator: Katie Hagen
   Publications Editor: Jonathan Harris
   IT Manager: Jody Ames
Mission: To create an appreciative and supportive environment for the study and performance of medieval, Renaissance, and baroque music.
Founded: 1975
Specialized Field: Instrumental
Budget: $10,000
Season: June - July
Performs At: Dominican Colliseum; San Rafael (Festival Site)
Affiliations: Angelico Hall; Meadowlands Assembly Hall
Seating Capacity: 500; 100

4206
FOUR SEASONS CONCERTS
2930 Domingo Avenue
#190
Berkeley, CA 94705
Phone: 510-845-4444
Fax: 510-549-3504
e-mail: fsa@fsarts.org
Web Site: www.fourseasonsconcerts.com
Officers:
   President: Kay Adams
   Secretary: Sylvester Brooks
   Treasurer: Anthony Taplin
Management:
   Anthony: Jesse W Anthony
   Assistant: Barbara A. Bauer
   Cultural Attach,: Sylvester Brooks
   Box Office Services and Development: Carol L. Carpenter
   Development Director: Mary Jo Hudgel
   Technical Assistant: William S. Kruse
   Concert Administrator: Janet Warzyn
   Tour and Transportation Coordinator: Jan Wire
Founded: 1958
Performs At: Berkeley Piano Club, Berkeley; Herbst Theatre, San Francisco; Regents' Theatre at Valley Center, Holy Names University, Oakla
Seating Capacity: 1497; 915; 3176

4207
UNIVERSITY OF CALIFORNIA-BERKELEY CALIFORNIA
101 Zellerbach Hall
#4800
Berkeley, CA 94720-4800
Phone: 510-642-0212
Fax: 510-643-6707
e-mail: rcole@calperfs.berkeley.edu
Web Site: www.calperfs.berkeley.edu
Officers:
   CEO: Lori Cripps
   Chair: Gail Rubinfeld
   Vice Chair: Markus Trice
   Vice Chair & Treasurer: Susan Graham Harrison
   Secretary: Deborah Van Nest
   Board of Trustee: Eric Allman
   Board of Trustee: Nancy Axelrod
   Board of Trustee: Janaki Bakhle
   Board of Trustee: Annette Campbell-White
Management:
   Executive Director: Robert Cole
   Assistant Director: Robin Tomeromce
   Associate Director: Rob Bailis
   General Manager: Douglas Warrick
   Director/Marketing/Sales: Mary Dixon
   Executive and Artistic Director: Matjas Tarnopolsky
   Executive Assistant to the Director: Eve Gordon
   Artistic Administrator: Robin Pomerance
   Office Manager: Loretta Hill
Mission: To offer professional performances in the performing arts to students.
Founded: 1904
Specialized Field: Performing Arts
Status: Non-Profit, Professional
Paid Staff: 60
Income Sources: Association of Performing Arts Presenters; International Society of Performing Arts Administrators; Western Alliance of Arts Administrators
Performs At: Zellerbach Auditorium; University of California
Organization Type: Educational; Sponsoring

4208
INTERNATIONAL CONCERTS EXCHANGE
1124 Summit Drive
Beverly Hills, CA 90210

SERIES & FESTIVALS / California

Phone: 213-272-5539
Fax: 213-272-5539
Management:
   Producer/Managing Director: Dr. Irwin Paones
Utilizes: Singers
Founded: 1942
Specialized Field: Festivals
Status: Professional; Semi-Professional; Non-Professional; Nonprofit
Organization Type: Performing; Educational

4209
PLAYBOY JAZZ FESTIVAL
9242 Beverly Boulevard
Beverly Hills, CA 90210
Phone: 310-449-4070
Fax: 310-786-7440
Web Site: www.playboy.com/arts-entertainment/features/jazzfest2008
Officers:
   President: Richard Rosenzweig
   Public Relations: Nina Gordon
   Communications Director: Bill Farley
Management:
   Producer: Hugh Hefner
   Producer: George Wein
   Associate Producer: Darlene Chan
   Festival Manager: Jonne-Marie Switzler
Mission: Providing a community service; enabling the residents of Los Angeles to enjoy jazz.
Founded: 1979
Specialized Field: Jazz
Status: Professional
Budget: $1.5-2 Million
Season: June Weekend
Performs At: Hollywood Bowl (Festival Site)
Annual Attendance: 35,000
Seating Capacity: 18,000
Year Built: 1922
Year Remodeled: 2003
Organization Type: Sponsoring

4210
MUSIC AT KOHL MANSION
2750 Adeline Drive
Burlingame, CA 94010
Phone: 650-762-1130
Fax: 650-343-8464
e-mail: info@musicatkohl.org
Web Site: www.musicatkohl.org
Officers:
   Chairman: Ernest L. Littauer
   Vice Chairman: Ernest Littaur
   Treasurer: Lorentz E. Wigby
   Secretary: Anita Galeana
   President: Judy Thompson
   Vice-President: Nancy Jalonen
Management:
   Executive Director: Patricia Kristof Moy
   Musicologist: Kai Christiansen
   Finance and Accounting Services: Paula Wong
   Education Chair: Anneke Gaenslen
   Program Administrator: Yvonne Wun
   Recording Engineer: Richard Links
   Production Stage Manager: Sarah Vardigans
   Summer Intern: Kathryn Dragun
Mission: To offer chamber music performance and music education for adults and children.
Utilizes: Guest Directors; Multimedia
Performs At: Great Hall; Kohl Mansion
Seating Capacity: 200

4211
CARMEL BACH FESTIVAL
NW Corner of 10th & Mission
Cottage 16
Carmel, CA 93921
Mailing Address: PO Box 575 Carmel, CA 93921
Phone: 831-624-1521
Fax: 831-624-2788
e-mail: info@bachfestival.org
Web Site: www.bachfestival.org
Officers:
   President: Betsey Pearson
   1st Vice President: Alan Carlson
   2nd vice president: Lyn Evans
   CFO/Treasurer: Howard Fisher
   Secretary: Fran Lozano
Management:
   Artistic Director: Bruno Weill
   Executive Director: Debbie Chinn
   General Manager: Elizabeth Pasquinelli
   Marketing Director: Erin Sullivan
   Director of Development and Marketi: Nicola Reilly
   Community Engagement Manager: Julia Robertson
   General Management Fellow: Miranda Olivares
   Administrative Coordinator: Liz Schrey
Mission: Performing the works of Johann Sebastian Bach, as well as other classical compositions.
Founded: 1935
Specialized Field: Series & Festivals; Instrumental; Opera; Choral; Childrens'; Educational
Status: Non-Profit, Professional
Paid Staff: 4
Paid Artists: 100
Non-paid Artists: 30
Budget: $2,300,000
Income Sources: Private Donations
Season: July - August
Performs At: Carmel (Festival Site)
Affiliations: Various Sites in the vicinity of Carmel-by-the-Sea
Annual Attendance: 17,000
Facility Category: Community Auditorium
Type of Stage: Proscenium
Seating Capacity: 733; 400; 250; 200
Year Built: 1928
Organization Type: Performing; Educational

4212
CARMEL MUSIC SOCIETY
PO Box 22783
Carmel, CA 93922
Phone: 831-625-9938
Fax: 831-625-6823
e-mail: carmelmusic@sbcglobal.net
Web Site: www.carmelmusic.org
Officers:
   Co-President: Anne Thorp
   1st Vice President: Victoria Davis
   2nd vice president: Rudolf Schroeter
   Third Vice President: Larry Davidson
   Secretary: Beverly Dekker Davidson
   Treasurer: Tim Brown
Management:
   Director of Marketing: Ginna Gordon
   Office Administrator: Lucy Faridany
Mission: To present classical music performances and foster the appreciation of classical music across the community.
Utilizes: Fine Artists; Guest Accompanists; Guest Directors; Guest Musical Directors; Multimedia; Original Music Scores; Theatre Companies

Founded: 1927
Specialized Field: Classical Music Presentation
Status: Non-Profit, Professional
Paid Staff: 2
Volunteer Staff: 10
Paid Artists: 30
Budget: $60,000-150,000
Income Sources: Ticket Sales; Grants; Donations
Performs At: Concert Hall or Church
Seating Capacity: 300-1,200

4213
FUJITSU-CONCORD JAZZ FESTIVAL
PO Box 845
Concord, CA 94522
Phone: 925-682-6770
Fax: 925-682-3508
e-mail: info@concordrecords.com

4214
ORANGE COAST COLLEGE COMMUNITY EDUCATION
2701 Fairview Road
PO Box 5005
Costa Mesa, CA 92626-0120
Phone: 714-432-5880
Fax: 714-432-5902
Toll-free: 888-622-5376
e-mail: jwood@occ.cccd.edu
Web Site: occtickets.com
Management:
   Administative Dean: George Blanc
   Lead Technician: Brock Cilley
   Administrative Secretary: Helen McGinley
Mission: To offer an enriching and affordable quality performing arts season for adults and school children.
Utilizes: Dancers; Guest Accompanists; Guest Instructors; Guest Soloists; Instructors; Local Artists; Original Music Scores; Special Technical Talent; Theatre Companies
Founded: 1947
Specialized Field: Band
Status: Semi-Professional
Paid Staff: 3
Budget: $350,000 Artist Fees
Income Sources: Orange Coast College
Performs At: Robert B Moore Theatre; Fine Arts Recital Hall; Drama Lab
Affiliations: WAA
Annual Attendance: 55,000
Facility Category: Concert Hall
Stage Dimensions: 40'x 50'
Seating Capacity: 916
Year Built: 1950
Year Remodeled: 1996
Rental Contact: Brock Cilley
Organization Type: Performing; Touring; Educational

4215
DEL NORTE ASSOCIATION FOR CULTURAL AWARENESS
Performance Series
501 H St
Crescent City, CA 95531 - 37
Mailing Address: PO Box 1480
Phone: 707-464-1336
Fax: 707-464-4842
e-mail: dnaca@harborside.com
Web Site: www.dnaca.net
Management:
   Executive Director: Holly O Austin

SERIES & FESTIVALS / California

Mission: The Del Norte Association for Cultural Awareness provides support and excitement for all the creative arts, to inspire community vitality and harmony.
Founded: 1981
Opened: 1983
Specialized Field: Mulit-disciplinary local arts agency
Paid Staff: 1
Volunteer Staff: 4
Performs At: Crescent Elk Auditorium; Procenium arch
Seating Capacity: 530
Year Built: 1930
Rental Contact: Del Norte County USD

4216
UC DAVIS PRESENTS
200 B Street
Suite A
Davis, CA 95616-8561
Phone: 530-757-3488
Fax: 530-757-6815
Web Site: www.ucdavispresents.ucdavis.edu
Performs At: Freeborn Hall
Seating Capacity: 1280

4217
REDWOOD COAST DIXIELAND JAZZ FESTIVAL
523 5th Street
P.O. Box 314
Eureka, CA 95502
Phone: 707-445-3378
Fax: 707-445-1240
e-mail: info@redwoodjazz.org
Web Site: www.redwoodjazz.org
Management:
  President: Russ Harris
  Executive Director: Brenda Steinberg
Founded: 1991
Specialized Field: Series & Festivals; Instrumental Music; Vocal Music
Status: Non-Profit, Professional
Paid Staff: 2
Paid Artists: 20
Income Sources: Ticket Sales, Sponsors
Performs At: Six local venues, including The Adorni Center, The Arkely Center, Municipal Auditorium, Red Lion, Francheschi Hall and Vicker

4218
FAIRFIELD CITY ARTS
Cityarts Fairfield
411 Wessel Drive
Fairfield, CA 45014
Phone: 513-867-5348
Fax: 513-867-6070
e-mail: parks@fairfield-city.org
Web Site: www.ci.fairfield.ca.us/cs-artscenter.htm
Management:
  President: Robert Reich
  Executive Director: John De Lorenzo
Founded: 1990
Specialized Field: Series & Festivals; Music and Performing Arts; Recitals; Concerts
Status: Non-Profit, Non-Professional
Paid Staff: 10
Performs At: Fairfield Center for Creative Arts
Seating Capacity: 368

4219
LIVELY ARTS FOUNDATION
1379 Crown Drive, Alameda CA
Fresno, CA 94501
Toll-free: 877-608-5883
e-mail: Livelyarts2@aol.com
Web Site: www.livelyarts.org
Management:
  Artistic Director: Diane K Mosler
  Technical Director: Tom Wolfgang
  Associate Artistic Director: Yukari Thiesen
Mission: A non-profit presenting and support organization to help establish the Fresno metropolitan area as a major cultural force by providing a variety of wold-class music, dance, and drama and dance outreach.
Founded: 1989
Performs At: William Saroyan Theatre
Seating Capacity: 2300

4220
FULLERTON FRIENDS OF MUSIC
1417 Kensington Drive
Fullerton, CA 92631
Phone: 714-525-5836
Fax: 714-529-1512
e-mail: fullerton-friends-of-music@webpanache.com
Web Site: www.webpan.com/fullerton-friends-of-music
Officers:
  Past President: Dave Mears
  Treasurer: Claude Coppel
  Recording Secretary: Ruth Rogers
  Corresponding Secretary: Phyllis Pivar
  Graphic Arts: Allen Strickler
Management:
  President: Lynn Rogers
  President Elect/Webmaster: Tony Dycks
  Artistic Director: Valerie Bernstein
  Membership: Laurel Stevens
  Founder/Historian/Archivist: Beulah Strickler
  Stage Manager: Ubaldo Ponce
  Receptions Coordinator: Ann-Marie Ross
Mission: Dedicated to providing live music concerts featuring professional Classical Chamber Music and Early Period ensembles and artists, free of charge to the public.
Founded: 1958
Performs At: Sunny Hills High School Performing Arts Center
Seating Capacity: 350

4221
CITRUS COLLEGE HAUGH PERFORMING ARTS CENTER
1000 West Foothill Boulevard
Glendora, CA 91741-1899
Phone: 626-852-8046
Fax: 626-335-4715
e-mail: ghinrichsen@citruscollege.edu
Web Site: www.haughpac.com
Management:
  Performing Arts Center Director: John Vaughan
  Marketing Director: Linda Graves
  Technical Director: Dan Vilter
  Stage Manager/Haugh Rental Coordina: Karen Taulbee
  Administrative Secretary: Sharol Carter
Utilizes: Artists-in-Residence; Fine Artists; Guest Instructors; High School Drama; Resident Professionals; Soloists; Special Technical Talent; Theatre Companies
Founded: 1971
Specialized Field: Music, Theatre, Education, Dance
Status: Non-Profit, Professional
Paid Staff: 25
Non-paid Artists: 300
Budget: $1 Million
Income Sources: College Support & Ticket Sales; Donations; Rentals
Performs At: Proscenium Venue
Annual Attendance: 125,000
Facility Category: Proscenium Theatre
Type of Stage: Sprung Wooden
Stage Dimensions: 54' opening
Seating Capacity: 1400
Year Built: 1971
Year Remodeled: 2005
Rental Contact: Greg Hinrichsen

4222
RUSSIAN RIVER BLUES FESTIVAL
Omega Events
10 Rancho Circle
Suite 135
Guerneville, CA 92630
Phone: 949-360-7800
Fax: 949-362-5366
e-mail: info@omegaevents.com
Web Site: www.omegaevents.com
Officers:
  President/CEO: Rich Sherman
  VP of Operations: Ryan Cueva
Management:
  Operations: Ryan Hardin
  Manager: Pamela Forney
Utilizes: Singers
Status: For-Profit
Income Sources: Fundraisers, Private and Corporate Donations, Ticket Sales
Season: September
Performs At: Johnson's Beach; Guerneville
Organization Type: Performing

4223
CALIFORNIA STATE UNIVERSITY EAST BAY
CSUEB Theatre And Dance Department
25800 Carlos Bee Boulevard
Hayward, CA 94542
Phone: 510-885-3000
Fax: 510-885-4748
e-mail: thomas.hird@csueastbay.edu
Web Site: www.class.csueastbay.edu/theatre
Officers:
  President: Mohammad Qayoumi
  Program Chair: Thomas Hird
  Production Manager: Richard Olmstead
Mission: University education in the performing arts, community service (performance), occassional privately funded guest artists, and community use facility.
Founded: 1964
Specialized Field: Theatre; Dance; Music
Status: Non-Profit, Non-Professional
Paid Staff: 2
Paid Artists: 10
Budget: $100,000
Income Sources: State Institutional Funds; Activity Board; Ticket Sales
Performs At: Educational Theatre
Annual Attendance: 12,000
Facility Category: University Theatre; Studio Theatre
Type of Stage: Proscenium
Stage Dimensions: 36'x 40' x 22'
Seating Capacity: 480
Year Built: 1975
Rental Contact: Facility Reservations Cecilia Grima-Torres

SERIES & FESTIVALS / California

4224
HEALDSBURG JAZZ FESTIVAL
PO Box 266
Healdsburg, CA 95448
Phone: 707-433-4633
Fax: 707-431-8371
e-mail: info@healdsburgjazzfestival.org
Web Site: www.healdsburgjazzfestival.com
Officers:
  Chair: Rollie Atkinson
  Vice Chair: Jessica Felix
  Treasurer: Dennis Abbe
  Secretary: Edward Flesch
Management:
  Artistic Director: Jessica Felix
  President Healdsburg Arts Counsil: Janet Norton
  Community Services Director: Marla Young
  VP Of Marketing: Dan Wildermuth
Founded: 1998

4225
RAMONA BOWL AMPHITHEATRE
27400 Ramona Bowl Road
Hemet, CA 92544
Phone: 951-658-3111
Fax: 951-658-2695
Toll-free: 800-645-4465
e-mail: ramona@ramonabowl.com
Web Site: www.ramonabowl.com
Officers:
  President of the Board: Jim Pomeroy
  Board Member: Don Meak
Management:
  Artistic Director: Dennis Anderson
  General Manager: Janine Reitenbach
  Marketing & Development: Judy Zulfiqar
Mission: To bring California history to life through performances highlighting the region's Indian and Spanish cultures.
Utilizes: Actors; Collaborations; Curators; Dance Companies; Dancers; Designers; Educators; Filmmakers; Guest Companies; Guest Designers; Guest Directors; Guest Musical Directors; Guild Activities; High School Drama; Instructors; Local Artists; Multimedia; Music; Original Music Scores; Poets; Resident Professionals; Selected Students; Sign Language Translators; Singers; Soloists; Student Interns; Special Technical Talent
Founded: 1923
Specialized Field: Outdoor Drama
Status: Non-Profit, Non-Professional
Paid Staff: 5
Paid Artists: 2
Non-paid Artists: 600
Income Sources: Box Office; Private Donations; Grants
Performs At: Ramona Bowl Outdoor Amphitheatre
Affiliations: NTA; INTIX; Institute of Outdoor Drama; California Arts Council
Rental Contact: Events Coordinator Linda Hoogestraat
Organization Type: Performing; Resident; Educational

4226
RAMONA HILLSIDE PLAYERS
27402 Ramona Bowl Road
Hemet, CA 92544
Phone: 951-658-5300
e-mail: info@hillsideplayers.org
Web Site: www.ramonahillsideplayers.org
Officers:
  President: Crist P. Thomas
  Vice President: Thomas W. Berry II
  Treasurer: Crist P. Thomas
  Secretary: Cheryl Howerton
  Technical Supervisor: Kim Negrete
Mission: To offer professional education in theatre performance and a series of performances.
Utilizes: Guest Companies
Founded: 1941
Specialized Field: Vocal Music; Instrumental Music; Theater
Status: Non-Professional; Nonprofit
Performs At: Ramona Hillside Playhouse
Organization Type: Performing; Resident; Educational

4227
HOLLYWOOD BOWL SUMMER FESTIVAL
Los Angeles Philharmonic Association
2301 North Highland Avenue
Hollywood, CA 90068
Phone: 323-850-2000
Fax: 323-850-5376
Web Site: www.hollywoodbowl.org
Officers:
  Chairman: Diane B. Paul
  President/CEO: Deborah Borda
  Secretary: Alan Wayte
Management:
  VP/General Manager Presentations: Arvind Manocha
  Orchestra Director: John Mauceri
  Program Director World Music: Tom Schnabel
  Philharmonic Music Director: Esa-Pekka Salonen
Mission: The summer home to the Los Angeles Philharmonic, which offers pop, classical and jazz performances. Offers a variety of free or low cost summer series events for children ages 3-11, and other performances.
Founded: 1922
Specialized Field: Instrumental; Multi-Media; Opera; Choral; Jazz; Folk; Dance; Theatre; Ethnic; Educational
Status: Professional; Nonprofit
Budget: $1,000,000
Income Sources: Los Angeles Philharmonic
Season: June - September
Performs At: Hollywood (Festival Site)
Facility Category: Hollywood Bowl
Seating Capacity: 17,400
Organization Type: Performing; Touring; Resident; Educational; Sponsoring

4228
IDYLLWILD ARTS-ACADEMY & SUMMER PROGRAM
52500 Temecula Drive
PO Box 38
Idyllwild, CA 92549
Phone: 951-659-2171
Fax: 951-659-4383
e-mail: admission@idyllwildarts.org
Web Site: www.idyllwildarts.org
Management:
  Director Summer Program: Steven Fraider
  Director Of Marketing: Darren Schilling
Mission: To provide pre-professional training in the arts and a comprehensive college preparatory curriculum in an environment conducive to positive personal development for gifted young artists from all over the world.
Founded: 1950
Specialized Field: Arts and Academics
Status: Non-Profit, Non-Professional
Performs At: Idyllwild Arts Foundation Theatre; Holmes Amphitheater
Seating Capacity: 300
Organization Type: Performing; Educational

4229
ECLECTIC ORANGE FESTIVAL
2082 Business Center Drive
Suite 100
Irvine, CA 92612
Phone: 949-553-2422
Fax: 949-553-2421
e-mail: contactus@philharmonicsociety.org
Web Site: www.eclecticorange.org
Management:
  Executive Director: Dean Corey
  Media: Chantel Chen
Mission: As a project of the Philharmonic Society of Orange County, to foster, promote and increase the knowledge and appreciation of music and the arts through the presentation of performances of national and international stature; to development and implementation of a wide variety of education outreach programs.
Founded: 1999
Specialized Field: Classical
Paid Staff: 25
Volunteer Staff: 999
Paid Artists: 45

4230
UNIVERSITY OF CALIFORNIA IRVINE CULTURAL EVENTS
University Of California Irvine
103 Gateway
University Of California
Irvine, CA 92602-5075
Phone: 949-824-7215
Fax: 949-824-3056
Management:
  Manager Cultural Events: Desiree Mallory
Mission: To provide professional performances for students and residents of the surrounding area.
Founded: 1965
Specialized Field: Dance; Instrumental Music; Theater
Status: Professional; Nonprofit
Performs At: Irvine Barclay Theatre; Bren Events Center
Organization Type: Educational; Sponsoring; Presenting

4231
TAHOE JAZZ FESTIVAL
PO Box 2390
Kings Beach, CA 96143
e-mail: info@tahoejazz.org
Web Site: www.tahoejazz.org

4232
CELEBRITY PRESENTATIONS
PO Box 457
La Canada, CA 91012
Phone: 818-790-3944
Fax: 818-790-2544
Management:
  President: Sunny Charla Asch
Utilizes: Dance Companies; Guest Musicians; Multimedia; Original Music Scores; Special Technical Talent
Specialized Field: Series and Festivals; Instrumental Music; Vocal Music; Theatre; Dance; Ethnic Performances
Status: Non-Profit, Non-Professional
Paid Staff: 2
Budget: $60,000-150,000
Type of Stage: Proscenium

SERIES & FESTIVALS / California

4233
LA JOLLA MUSIC SOCIETY SUMMERFEST
7946 Ivanhoe Avenue
Suite 309
La Jolla, CA 92037
Phone: 858-459-3724
Fax: 858-459-3727
e-mail: info@LJMS.org
Web Site: www.ljms.org
Officers:
  Development Director: Ferdinand Gasand
  Business Manager: Chris Benavides
  Promotions manager: Anne Heinlein
  Chair: Martha Dennis, Ph.D.
  Treasurer: Theresa Jarvis
  Secretary: Jean Shekhter
  Past Chair: Clifford Schireson
  Member at Large: Christopher Beach
  Member at Large: Karen Brailean
Management:
  President/Artistic Director: Christopher Beach
  SummerFest Music Director: Cho-Liang Lin
  Director of Artistic Planning & Edu: Leah Z Rosenthal
  Marketing Director: Kristen Sakamoto
  Artist Services Coordinator: Jazmin N. Morales
  Education Coordinator: Jonathan Piper Ph.D.
  Development Director: Ferdinand Gasang
  Development Coordinator: Benjamin Guercio
  Finance Director: Chris Benavides
Mission: Presents a variety of presentations year-round including jazz, classical, and contemporary music and dance.
Founded: 1941
Specialized Field: Series & Festival; Classical Music
Status: Non-Profit, Professional
Paid Staff: 16
Volunteer Staff: 50
Budget: $3.5 Million
Income Sources: Tickets, Contributions, Grants

4234
UNIVERSITY EVENTS OFFICE
9500 Gilman Drive
UCSD Campus
La Jolla, CA 92093-0077
Phone: 858-534-4090
Fax: 858-534-7665
e-mail: knlee@ucsd.edu
Web Site: ueo.ucsd.edu
Management:
  Director: Martin Wollesen
  Assistant Director: Brian Ross
  Business Manager: Beverly Ward
  Marketing Manager: Amy Thomas
Mission: University Events Office, a department of Student Affairs at UC San Diego, is dedicated to presenting entertaining performing artists and film to expose the campus and community of the various art forms and diverse cultures of the world.
Utilizes: Actors; Choreographers; Dance Companies; Dancers; Filmmakers; Fine Artists; Guest Artists; Guest Instructors; Guest Lecturers; Guest Musical Directors; Guest Soloists; Multimedia; Special Technical Talent
Founded: 1965
Paid Staff: 8
Volunteer Staff: 25
Paid Artists: 30
Budget: $120,000 presenting only
Income Sources: Student Registration Fees; Ticket Sales; Patrons
Performs At: Mandeville Center

Affiliations: California Presenters
Annual Attendance: 20,000-30,000
Facility Category: Concert
Type of Stage: Proscenium
Stage Dimensions: 100'x40'
Seating Capacity: 788
Year Built: 1968
Rental Contact: Russell King

4235
DEL VALLE FINE ARTS CONCERT SERIES
PO Box 2335
Livermore, CA 94551-2335
Phone: 925-447-3564
e-mail: info@delvallefinearts.org
Web Site: www.delvallefinearts.org
Officers:
  Jr President: Ervin C Woodward
  President: Jeffrey B Garberson
Mission: To present outstanding classical chamber music groups along with a bit of non-traditional music.
Founded: 1980
Performs At: First Presbyterian Church
Seating Capacity: 450

4236
CITY OF LOS ANGELES CULTURAL AFFAIRS DEPARTMENT
201 North Figueroa St
Suite 1400
Los Angeles, CA 90012
Phone: 213-202-5500
Fax: 213-202-5517
Web Site: www.culturela.org
Management:
  Executive Director: Olga Garay
  Assistant General Manager: Matthew Rudnick
  Marketing & Development: Will Caperton y Montoya
  Public Art Division Director: Felicia Filer
  Grants Administration Division Dire: Joe Smoke
  Community Arts Division Director: Leslie Thomas
Mission: To promote varied performing arts performances in the Los Angeles community.
Utilizes: Guest Artists; Guest Companies; Singers
Founded: 1980
Specialized Field: Dance; Vocal Music; Instrumental Music; Theater; Festivals
Status: Nonprofit
Organization Type: Performing

4237
GRAND PERFORMANCES
350 S Grand Avenue
Suite A-4
Los Angeles, CA 90071
Phone: 213-687-2190
Fax: 213-687-2191
e-mail: Comments@grandperformances.org
Web Site: www.grandperformances.org
Officers:
  Office Administrator: Zindy Landeros Valle
  Production Manager: Fred Stites
  Chair: Janice W. Geringer Fogelman
  Treasurer: John Perfitt
  Secretary: Anahita Ferasat
  Immediate Pasr Chair: Karen Molleson
Management:
  Executive & Artistic Director: Michael Alexander
  Marketing Director: Amanda Wah
  Director of Programming: Leigh Ann Hahn
  Business Manager: Lee Lawlor

  Development Associate: Karlee Decima
  Office Adminstrator: Zindy Landeros Valle
  Production Manager: Fred Stites
  Technical Director: Mark Baker
  Director of Development: Christie Lesinski
Founded: 1987
Specialized Field: Series & Festivals; Instrumental Music; Vocal Music; Theatre; Dance; Ethnic Performances; Multi Disciplinary Performing Arts Presenter
Status: Non-Profit, Professional
Paid Staff: 10
Volunteer Staff: 2
Paid Artists: 504
Budget: $1.3 million
Income Sources: Contracts; Grants
Affiliations: APAP; WAA; California Presenters; California Arts Advocates
Annual Attendance: 65,000
Facility Category: Outdoor Plaza
Type of Stage: Thrust
Seating Capacity: 2,000; 6,500
Year Built: 1992

4238
JAZZ AT DREW LEGACY MUSIC & CULTURAL MARKETPLACE
1730 E 120th Street
Charles Drew University of Medicine & Science
Los Angeles, CA 90059
Phone: 323-563-5850
Fax: 323-563-4919
e-mail: robetts@cdrewu.edu
Web Site: www.cdrew.edu
Management:
  Executive Producer/Founder: Roland H Betts
  Producer Assistant: Toni Abdul-Hanson
Mission: To offer jazz performances as public relation events and fundraisers.
Founded: 1991
Specialized Field: Instrumental Music (Jazz)
Paid Staff: 2
Volunteer Staff: 125
Paid Artists: 11

4239
LMU GUITAR CONCERT & MASTERCLASS SERIES
Loyola Marymount University Music Department
One LUM Drive
Los Angeles, CA 90045-8347
Phone: 310-338-5142
Fax: 310-338-5046
e-mail: mmiranda@lmumail.lmu.edu
Web Site: www.lmu.edu/guitarseries
  Department Chair: Mary Breden
  Administrative Assistant & Producti: Tashi Cardinali
Management:
  President: Michael Miranda
Founded: 1999
Specialized Field: Series & Festivals: Instrumental Music
Status: Non-Profit, Professional
Paid Staff: 1
Paid Artists: 4
Performs At: Murphy Recital Hall

4240
LOS ANGELES BACH FESTIVAL
First Congregational Church
540 South Commonwealth Avenue
Los Angeles, CA 90020

SERIES & FESTIVALS / California

Phone: 213-385-1345
Fax: 213-487-0461
e-mail: musicinfo@fccla.org
Web Site: www.fccla.org
Officers:
   Events Manager: June Flowers
Management:
   Music Director: Dr. Jonathan Talberg
   Organist-in-Residence: Christoph Bull
   Chief Administrative Officer: Susan Leary
   Accounting Manager: Darice Bailey
   Office Manager: Jade lin Hornbaker
   Manager: Julianne James
   Director of Technology: Jose Reyes
   Director of Communications: Curtis Rhodes
Mission: To provide this city with a unique opportunity to celebrate the musical genius of Johann Sebastian Bach in the neo-gothic beauty of the sanctuary and chapel of First Church.
Founded: 1934
Specialized Field: Instrumental; Choral; Folk
Budget: $20,000-$35,000
Affiliations: First Congregational Church of Los Angeles
Seating Capacity: 150
Year Built: 1867

4241
LACMA MONDAY EVENING CONCERTS
3710 S. Robertson Blvd.
Suite 200
Los Angeles, CA 90232
Phone: 213-260-1632
Fax: 323-857-6214
e-mail: dstalvey@lacma.org
Web Site: www.lacma.org
Management:
   President: Andrea Rich
   Artistic Director: Dorrance Stalvey
Founded: 1939
Specialized Field: New Music
Status: Non-Profit, Professional
Paid Staff: 3
Volunteer Staff: 5
Paid Artists: 60
Performs At: Leo S. Bing Theatre
Seating Capacity: 600

4242
MOUNT SAINT MARY'S COLLEGE - THE DA CAMERA SOCIETY
10 Chester Place
Los Angeles, CA 90007s
Phone: 213-477-2929
Fax: 213-477-2959
e-mail: mbonino@msmc.la.edu
Web Site: www.dacamera.org
Officers:
   Client Services Manager: Patrick Schirato
   Membership & Development: Wendy Gragg
   Publications & Marketing: Ed Murray
Management:
   Founder/Artistic Director: Dr. MaryAnn Bonino
   General Director: Kelly Garrison
   Associate Director of Administratio: Sherrill Bennet Herring
   Production & Music Education Manage: Sean Bradley
   Production Assistant: Terence Huntoon
   Membership & Development Coordinato: Brittany Gash
Mission: Presenting chamber music in historic sites that include the Doheny Mansion, walking and driving tours in Boyle Heights, San Pedro, Camarillo, and San Fernando.
Founded: 1973
Specialized Field: Series & Festivals: Music Chamber Concert Series
Status: Non-Profit, Professional
Performs At: Doheny Mansion; Los Angeles' Union Station; The Queen Mary; The former Bullocks Wilshire
Seating Capacity: 50-2000

4243
MUSIC CENTER OF LOS ANGELES COUNTY
135 N Grand Avenue
Los Angeles, CA 90012
Phone: 213-972-7211
e-mail: general@musiccenter.org
Web Site: www.musiccenter.org
Officers:
   Music Director/Philharmonic: Esa-Pekka Salonen
   Music Director/Chorale: Grant Gershon
   Chair: Lisa Specht
   Vice Chair: Robert J. Abernethy
   Vice Chair: Michael J. Pagano
   Treasurer: Thomas R. Weinberger
   Assistant Treasurer and Chief Finan: Lisa Whitney
   Board Member: Wallis Annenberg
   Board Member: Colleen Bell
Management:
   Chairman, Board of Directors: John B Emerson
   President and CEO: Stephen D Roundtree
   Artistic Director/Theatre Group: Michael Ritchie
   Music Director/Opera: James Conlon
   Executive Vice President & Chief Op: Howard Sherman
   Senior Vice President & Chief Finan: Lisa Whitney
   Senior Vice President of Advancemen: Elizabeth Kennedy
   Vice President of Programming: Renae Williams Niles
   Director of School Programs: Leonardo Bravo
Founded: 1964
Specialized Field: Series and Festivals; Instrumental Music; Dance; Ethnic Performances
Status: Non-Profit, Professional
Paid Staff: 225

4244
MUSIC GUILD
PO Box 307
Suite 203
Los Angeles, CA 61266-0307
Phone: 309-762-6610
Fax: 323-954-0303
e-mail: themusicguild@aol.com; tickets@themusicguild.org
Web Site: www.themusicguild.org
Officers:
   President: Anne Mor
   Secretary: Eugene Golden
Management:
   Executive/Artistic Director: Eugene Golden
   Executive Administrator: Pam Pantell
Mission: To present classical music in an intimate setting; to introduce children at an early age; to provide free intruments ; to encourage them to study music.
Founded: 1944
Specialized Field: Series & Festivals: Chamber Music Concerts
Status: Non-Profit, Professional
Paid Staff: 3
Volunteer Staff: 4
Budget: $250,000-$300,000
Income Sources: Ticket Sales; Private Donations
Performs At: Chamber Music Groups Presenter
Affiliations: Cal State Northridge & Long Beach; UCLA; University Synagogue
Annual Attendance: 1,500-2,000
Seating Capacity: 1294

4245
OCCIDENTAL COLLEGE ARTIST SERIES
1600 Campus Road
Los Angeles, CA 90041
Phone: 323-259-2500
Fax: 323-259-2958
e-mail: music@oxy.edu
Web Site: www.oxy.edu/Arts
Management:
   Department Chair: Irene Girton
   Director of Instrumental Music: Allen Gross
Specialized Field: Dance; Vocal Music; Instrumental Music; Theater; World Music
Status: Nonprofit
Performs At: Thorne Hall; Keck Theater
Organization Type: Sponsoring

4246
FAMILY CAREGIVER ALLIANCE
785 Market St
Suite 750
Los Angeles, CA 94103
Phone: 323-857-6115
Fax: 323-857-6214
e-mail: dstalvey@lacma.org
Web Site: www.lacma.org
Officers:
   President: Ping Hao
   Vice President: Jacquelyn Kung
   Treasurer: Jeff Kumataka
Management:
   Music Director: Dorrance Stalvey
   Executive Director: Kathleen Kelly
   Education Coordinator: A. J. Dugay
   Director of Operations and Planning: Leah Eskenazi
Founded: 1996
Specialized Field: Chamber Music
Performs At: Leo S Bing Thaetre; LA County Museum of Art
Seating Capacity: 600

4247
SWEET & HOT SUMMER MUSIC FESTIVAL
PO Box 642269
Los Angeles, CA 90064-2269
e-mail: sweethot@sweethot.org
Web Site: www.sweethot.org
Management:
   Executive Director: Wally Holmes
   Director: John Kennebeck
   Chief Financial Officer: Gilles Mongeau
   Associate Director: Laurie Whitlock
Mission: The Sweet and Hot Music Foundation is a California 501c3 non-profit corporation dedicated to American's Golden Age of Popular Music.
Founded: 1996

4248
MASS ENSEMBLE
3815 Grand View BLVD
Malibu, CA 90066

All listings are in alphabetical order by state, then city, then organization within the city.

SERIES & FESTIVALS / California

Phone: 310-390-3313
Fax: 310-313-8586
e-mail: ac@arthouse-live.com
Web Site: www.massensemble.com
Management:
   Production Manager: Ron Doroba
   Artistic Director: William Close
   Business Manager: Andrew Cohen
   Associate Director: Andrea Brook

4249
MAMMOTH LAKES JAZZ JUBILEE
PO Box 909
Mammoth Lakes, CA 93546-0909
Phone: 760-709-5299
Fax: 760-934-2478
e-mail: info@mammothjazz.org
Web Site: www.mammothjazz.org
Management:
   Director: Ken Coulter
   Director: Flossie Coulter
Mission: To bring to a small town-big time entertainment. To keep America's true art form alive.
Founded: 1989
Specialized Field: Series & Festivals: Jazz
Status: Non-Profit, Professional
Paid Staff: 2
Volunteer Staff: 500
Paid Artists: 140
Facility Category: 10 Venues in Tents

4250
YUBA COUNTY-SUTTER COUNTY REGIONAL ARTS COUNCIL TOURING/PRESENTING PROGRAM
624 & 630 E Street
PO Box 468
Marysville, CA 95901
Phone: 530-742-2787
Fax: 530-742-1171
e-mail: email@yubasutterarts.org
Web Site: www.yubasutterarts.org
Officers:
   President: Cynthia Fontayne
   Vice President: David Read
   Secretary: Craig Starkey
   Treasurer: Kelly Rickcreek
Management:
   Executive Director: Marika Garcia
   Business Manager: Jim Jenkins
   Arts Coordinator: Lily Noonan
Performs At: Marysville Auditorium
Seating Capacity: 1,083

4251
MENDOCINO MUSIC FESTIVAL
PO Box 1808
Mendocino, CA 95460
Phone: 707-937-2044
Fax: 707-937-1045
e-mail: music@mendocinomusic.com
Web Site: www.mendocinomusic.com
Officers:
   President: Barbara Faulkner
   VP: Roger Schwartz
   Treasurer: Jim Havlena
   Secretary: Marcia Lotter
Management:
   Artistic Director: Allan Pollack
   Festival Manager: Nancy Harris
Mission: To enrich, educate and entertain all ages of residents and visitors by presenting world class musicians and music on the Mendocino Coast.
Utilizes: Guest Accompanists; Guest Instructors; Multimedia; Original Music Scores; Singers
Founded: 1986
Specialized Field: Series & Festivals; Youth; Dance; Ethnic Performances; Classical Music Festival
Status: Non-Profit, Professional
Paid Staff: 5
Volunteer Staff: 250
Paid Artists: 130
Budget: $480,000
Income Sources: Ticket Revenues, Donations, Sponsorhips, Program Ads, Events
Season: July
Performs At: Mendocino Headlands State Park (Festival Site)
Annual Attendance: 10,000
Facility Category: Tent/Concert Hall
Seating Capacity: 808
Organization Type: Performing

4252
SADDLEBACK COLLEGE GUEST ARTISTS SERIES
Division of Fine Arts Media Technology
28000 Marguerite Parkway
Mission Viejo, CA 92692-3635
Phone: 949-582-4413
Fax: 949-347-8315
e-mail: nwelch@saddleback.edu
Web Site: www.saddleback.edu
Officers:
   Public Information Officer: Nina Welch
   President: Dr. Tod A. Burnett
   Manager, Office of the President: Sophie Miller
   Vice President for Instruction: Dr. Kathy Werle
   Director of Public Information and: Jennie McCue
Management:
   Dean of Fine Arts: Bart McHenry
   Performing Arts Director: Kate Realista
   Fine Arts Public Information: Nina Welch
Utilizes: Actors; Artists-in-Residence; Choreographers; Collaborations; Community Members; Composers; Contract Orchestras; Dancers; Filmmakers; Fine Artists; Five Seasonal Concerts; Grant Writers; Guest Accompanists; Guest Companies; Guest Designers; Guest Musical Directors; Instructors; Local Artists & Directors; Multimedia; Music; Paid Performers; Resident Professionals; Scenic Designers; Sign Language Translators; Student Interns; Theatre Companies; Visual Arts
Founded: 1977
Specialized Field: Series & Festivals; Instrumental Music; Vocal Music; Theatre; Youth; Dance; Ethnic Performances
Status: Non-Profit, Professional
Paid Staff: 7
Performs At: McKinney Theatre
Seating Capacity: 405

4253
STARLITE PATIO THEATER SUMMER SERIES
2064 Magnolia Ave.
Benito And Fremont
Montclair, CA 91762-6033
Phone: 909-986-4321
Fax: 909-399-9751
Management:
   Manager/Program Director: Harve Edwards
   Facility Supervisor: Shirley Wofford
Mission: Offering summer cultural entertainment (eight programs) at no charge on Tuesdays.
Founded: 1963
Specialized Field: Dance; Theater
Status: Nonprofit
Paid Staff: 3
Paid Artists: 16
Budget: $2,400
Season: July and August
Performs At: The Starlite Patio Theater, 5111 Benito Street
Facility Category: Outdoor Patio
Type of Stage: Small Outdoor; Covered
Seating Capacity: 200
Organization Type: Performing

4254
DIXIELAND MONTEREY
177 Webster Street
#206
Monterey, CA 93940
Phone: 831-675-0298
Toll-free: 888-349-6879
e-mail: email@dixieland-monterey.com
Web Site: www.dixieland-monterey.com
Management:
   President: April DeShields
   Vice President: Steve Carlisle
   Special Events Director: Donna DaVigo
   Marketing Director: Richard Hughett
Founded: 1980

4255
MONTEREY JAZZ FESTIVAL
9699 Blue Larkspur Lane
Suite 204
Monterey, CA 93940
Mailing Address: PO Box Jazz Monterey, CA 93942
Phone: 831-373-3366
Fax: 831-373-0244
e-mail: jazzinfo@montereyjazzfestival.org
Web Site: www.montereyjazzfestival.org
Officers:
   Development Director: Paul Mondestin
   Education Director: Dr. Rob Klevan
   Marketing Director: Paul S Fingerote
   Stage Manager: Mike Wilmot
Management:
   Artistic Director: Tim Jackson
   Artist Liaison: David Murray
   Managing Director: Chris Doss
   Administrative Coordinator: Jan Stotzer
   Production Manager: Bill Wagner
   Production Stage Manager: Mike Wilmot
   Education Stage: Paul Contos
   Development Director: Andrew T. Sudol
Mission: To perpetuate jazz and further jazz education.
Founded: 1958
Specialized Field: Entertainment and Music Presentation
Status: Non-Profit, Professional
Paid Staff: 7
Paid Artists: 500

4256
MUSIC IN THE VINEYARDS
Napa Valley Cahmber Music Festival
1020 Clinton Street
Suite 201
Mt. Helena, CA 94559
Mailing Address: P.O. Box 6297 Napa, CA 94581
Phone: 707-258-5559
Fax: 707-258-5566
e-mail: info@musicinthevineyards.org
Web Site: www.musicinthevineyards.org
Officers:
   President: Anne Golden

SERIES & FESTIVALS / California

Vice President: Lona Hardy
Secretary: Paul Cantey
Treasurer: Rick Boland
Management:
  Co-Artistic Director: Daria Adams
  Co-Artistic Director: Michael Adams
  Executive Director: Evie Ayers
  Marketing Manager: Christy Bors
  PR Manager: Natasha Biasell
  Office Manager: Susanne Deiss-Costanzo
  Community Outreach: Kathleen de Vries
  Systems Manager: Jed Coffin
  Finance Manager: Nancy Sellers
Mission: Dedicated to bringing together outstanding artists to perform in the unique vineyard settings of the Napa Valley so that both the performers and the audience can experience the intimacy of chamber music as it was intended to be performed.
Utilizes: Multimedia; Original Music Scores
Founded: 1995
Specialized Field: Chamber Music Festival
Paid Staff: 3
Volunteer Staff: 120
Paid Artists: 45
Budget: $140,000
Season: August
Performs At: Napa Valley (Festival Site)
Affiliations: Various vineyards and related venues
Seating Capacity: 150 - 250

4257
MUSIC IN THE MOUNTAINS
530 Searls Avenue, Suite A
PO Box 1451
Nevada City, CA 95959
Phone: 530-265-6173
Fax: 530-265-6810
Toll-free: 800-218-2188
e-mail: mim@musicinthemountains.org
Web Site: www.musicinthemountains.org
Officers:
  President: Dan Halloran
  Vice President: John Fuller
  Vice President: Barbara Hampton
  Vice President: Ginny Riffey
  Treasurer: Terry Brown
  Secretary: Judith Ciphers
Management:
  Artistic Director: Paul Perry
  Executive Director: Christine Kelly
  Artistic Coordinator: Neil Tatman
  Marketing Director: Jeanne Duerst
  Patron Services Manager: Nancy Donahue
  Events and Production Coordinator: Kay Drake
  Education Coordinator: Mark Vance
  Resident Conductor: Ryan Murray
  Artistic Advisor: Pete Nowlen
Mission: To present high-quality classical, jazz and Broadway music at affordable prices.
Utilizes: Artists-in-Residence; Collaborating Artists; Commissioned Music; Grant Writers; Guest Companies; Guest Directors; Guest Musical Directors; Guest Musicians; Instructors; Multi Collaborations; Multimedia; Organization Contracts; Original Music Scores; Sign Language Translators; Singers; Student Interns
Founded: 1982
Specialized Field: Series & Festivals; Instrumental Music; Vocal Music; Instrumental; Choral ; Jazz; Educational; Childrens'
Status: Professional; Nonprofit
Paid Staff: 6
Volunteer Staff: 300
Paid Artists: 175
Budget: $700,000-$1,000,000
Income Sources: Donation; Grants; Ticket Sales; Benefit Events; Advertising; Sponsoring
Season: November; December; April; June; July
Performs At: Festival sites around Nevada City & Grass Valley
Affiliations: Chamber Music America; American Symphony Orchestra League; Association of California Symphony Orchestras; BMI; ASCAP
Annual Attendance: 17,000
Facility Category: Renovated Concert Hall; Outdoor Tent
Stage Dimensions: 48'x56'
Seating Capacity: 550 inside; 4,000 outside
Year Remodeled: 2001
Organization Type: Performing; Resident; Educational; Sponsoring

4258
CENTER FOR THE VISUAL AND PERFORMING ARTS
California State University, Northbridge
18111 Nordhoff Street
Northridge, CA 91330
Phone: 818-677-1200
Fax: 818-677-5472
e-mail: info@ArtsNorthridge.csun.com
Web Site: www.cvpa.csun.com
Officers:
  Dean: William Toultant
  Associate Dean: Cynthia Raywrtch
Management:
  General Director: Karen Kearns
  Concert Production: Guy Fabre
  Administrative Coordinator: Jill Price
  Director of Public Relations: Mary Reale
Mission: To provide cultural, educational and artistic experiences that enrich lives and promote lifelong learning in and through the arts to the community we serve.
Founded: 1996
Specialized Field: Jazz Series; Dance Series; Celebrity Shows Series
Paid Staff: 10
Volunteer Staff: 75
Budget: $300,000
Income Sources: University Subsidy; Tickets Sales; Contributions
Performs At: USU, Northridge Performing Arts Center; Plaza del Sol Performance Hall
Annual Attendance: 50,000
Type of Stage: Proscenium
Seating Capacity: 500/150
Year Built: 1994
Rental Contact: Kathy Anthony

4259
MULTI-CULTURAL MUSIC AND ART FOUNDATION OF NORTHRIDGE (MCMAFN)
9015 Wilbur Ave.
Northridge, CA 91324
Mailing Address: P.O. Box 280101 Northridge, CA 91328
Phone: 818-349-3400
Fax: 818-349-0716
e-mail: info@mcmafn.org
Web Site: www.mcmafn.org
Officers:
  President: W M Paulin
  Vice President/Histortial: Paul A. Dentzel
Management:
  Program Coordinator/Creative Dir: Elisabeth Waldo-Dentzel
  Secretary: Paul Dentzel
  Chief Financial Officer: William Paulin
Mission: Supporting a wide range of performing and visual arts, particularly music and dance.
Utilizes: Actors; Curators; Dancers; Educators; Filmmakers; Five Seasonal Concerts; Grant Writers; Guest Accompanists; Guest Instructors; Guest Lecturers; Guest Musical Directors; Guest Musicians; Multi Collaborations; Multimedia; Organization Contracts; Original Music Scores; Resident Professionals; Sign Language Translators; Singers; Soloists; Touring Companies; Visual Arts
Founded: 1998
Specialized Field: Dance; Vocal Music; Instrumental Music; Festivals
Status: Non-Profit,Non-Professional
Paid Staff: 2
Budget: $100,000
Income Sources: Memberships, Grants, Admissions to Theatre
Performs At: New Mission Theatre
Affiliations: All Los Angeles Museums, ASCAP, Local 47 AIF
Type of Stage: Expandable
Seating Capacity: 150, outdoors; 300 seats
Year Remodeled: 1995
Rental Contact: Booking Calendar Hengamett
Organization Type: Performing; Educational

4260
MILLS COLLEGE MUSIC DEPARTMENT
5000 Macarthur Boulevard
Oakland, CA 94613
Phone: 510-430-2255
Fax: 510-430-3228
e-mail: music@mills.edu
Web Site: www.mills.edu/music
Officers:
  President: Janet L. Holmgren
  Vice President Finance: Elizabeth Burwell
Management:
  Concert Coordinator: Steed Cowart
  Technical Director: Les Stuck
Founded: 1852

4261
REDWOOD ART COUNCIL
PO Box 449
Occidental, CA 95465
Phone: 707-874-1124
Fax: 707-583-7810
e-mail: racmusic@sonic.net
Web Site: www.redwoodarts.org
Officers:
  President/Director: Kathryn Neustadter
Management:
  Director: Candace Rossman
Mission: To present exceptional chamber music.
Utilizes: Guest Musical Directors; Multimedia; Original Music Scores; Sign Language Translators; Singers; Soloists
Founded: 1980
Specialized Field: Series & Festivals: Chamber Music Concerts
Status: Non-Profit, Professional
Paid Staff: 15
Volunteer Staff: 15
Paid Artists: 30
Budget: $50,000
Income Sources: Tickets, Donations, Grants
Performs At: Occidental Community Church
Annual Attendance: 1,500-2,000

SERIES & FESTIVALS / California

Facility Category: Mostly Churches
Type of Stage: Platform
Stage Dimensions: 8' x 20'
Seating Capacity: 150
Year Built: 1876

4262
OJAI MUSIC FESTIVAL
201 South Signal Street
PO Box 185
Ojai, CA 93024
Mailing Address: PO Box 185 Ojai CA 93024
Phone: 805-646-2094
Fax: 805-646-6037
e-mail: info@ojaifestival.org
Web Site: www.ojaifestival.org
Officers:
  President: Stuart Meikkejohn
  Vice President: Barbara Hirsch
  Secretary: Cathryn Krause
  Treasurer: Jon Hogen
Management:
  Executive Director: Janneke Straub
  Artistic Director: Thomas W. Morris
  Festival Producer: Elaine Martone
  Director of Marketing: Gina Gutierrez
  Festival Producer: Elaine Martone
  Director of Development: Anna Cho Wagner
  Development Associate: Frances Muenzer
Mission: To foster a healthy spirit of eclecticism in adventurous programs, attracting artists who are given artistic freedom to perform exceptional pieces of classical music.
Utilizes: Choreographers; Collaborations; Commissioned Composers; Community Members; Composers; Dance Companies; Instructors; Multimedia; Original Music Scores
Founded: 1947
Specialized Field: Series & Festivals: Classical Music
Status: Non-Profit, Professional
Paid Staff: 8
Volunteer Staff: 150
Paid Artists: 60
Season: June
Performs At: Libby Bowl

4263
OJAI SHAKESPEARE FESTIVAL
PO Box 575
Ojai, CA 93024-0575
Phone: 805-646-9455
Fax: 805-646-9455
e-mail: info@ojaishakespeare.org
Web Site: www.ojaishakespeare.org
Officers:
  VP: Bruce Wallace
  Treasurer: Wayne Francis
  Secretary: Marilyn Wallace
  Madrigali Representative: Dave Farber
Management:
  Producer: Peter Fox
  Producer: Kathy Zotnowski
  Co-Producer: Julie Fox
  Director: Paul Amadio
  Marketing/Public Relations: Dina Pielaet
Founded: 1991
Status: Non-Profit,Non-Professional
Season: August
Type of Stage: Amphitheatre
Stage Dimensions: 38'x32'
Seating Capacity: 650

4264
OROVILLE CONCERT ASSOCIATION
P.O. Box 2530
Oroville, CA 95965
Phone: 530-589-0836
e-mail: swedin@cncnet.com
Web Site: orovilleconcertassociation.org/
Officers:
  President: Sharon Wedin
  1st Vice President: Ginger Ewalt
  2nd Vice President: Rhonda Williams
  3rd Vice President: Janet Jensen
  Secretary: Linda Dewey
  Treasurer: Pat Doering
  Membership Secretary: Joan Briggs
  Concert Chairs: Duane Zanon
Mission: To offer every man, woman and child in the community the opportunity to experience the magic of affordable, live, quality performances.
Founded: 1952
Specialized Field: Series and Festivals: Community Concerts
Status: Non-Profit, Professional
Income Sources: Supported by theater ticket sales, and patron and corporate sponsorships
Performs At: State Theater, in downtown Oroville
Seating Capacity: 612

4265
CANYON INDUSTRIES
PO Box 256
Palm Springs, CA 92263
Phone: 760-778-7966
Fax: 760-778-4890
e-mail: simone@angelshq.com
Web Site: www.canyonentertainment.com
Management:
  President: Simone Sheffield
Utilizes: Actors; AEA Actors; Artists-in-Residence; Choreographers; Collaborating Artists; Commissioned Composers; Commissioned Music; Dance Companies; Dancers; Designers; Filmmakers; Grant Writers; Guest Companies; Guest Designers; Guest Musical Directors; Guest Soloists; Local Unknown Artists; Multimedia; Music; Original Music Scores; Performance Artists; Poets; Selected Students; Sign Language Translators; Soloists; Special Technical Talent; Theatre Companies
Founded: 1981
Paid Staff: 30
Volunteer Staff: 100
Paid Artists: 10
Non-paid Artists: 10
Budget: $400,000-1,000,000

4266
CATALINA ISLAND JAZZTRAX FESTIVAL
611 S Palm Canyon Drive
Suite 7-458
Palm Springs, CA 92264-7402
Phone: 760-323-1171
Fax: 760-323-5770
Toll-free: 888-330-5252
e-mail: info@jazztrax.com
Web Site: www.jazztrax.com/jazz/catalina.html
Management:
  Founder: Art Good
  Festival Director: Gregg Hudson
Mission: Jazz festival held for three weekends at the beautiful Avalon Harbor on Catalina Island.
Founded: 1987
Season: October

4267
CALTECH PUBLIC EVENTS SERIES
Caltech Public Events
Mail Code 332-92
Pasadena, CA 91125
Phone: 626-395-4638
Fax: 626-395-5890
e-mail: events@caltech.edu
Web Site: www.events.caltech.edu
Management:
  Assistant VP for Community Relation: Denise Nelson Nash
  Manager: Cara Stemen
  Outreach Associate: Mary Herrera
  Stage Technician: Erick Ferguson
Budget: $60,000-150,000
Performs At: Beckman Auditorium; Ramo Auditorium; Dabney Lounge
Seating Capacity: 1165; 423; 200

4268
COLEMAN CHAMBER CONCERTS
225 S Lake Avenue
Ste. 300
Pasadena, CA 91101
Phone: 626-793-4191
Fax: 818-787-1294
e-mail: info@colemanchambermusic.org
Web Site: www.coleman.caltech.edu
Officers:
  President: Jerome Hamburger, M.D.
  Vice President & Treasurer: Susan Grether
  Secretary: Phyllis Hudson
Management:
  Executive Director: Kathy Freedland
Mission: To present international chamber ensembles, both established and emerging.
Utilizes: Guest Directors
Founded: 1904
Specialized Field: Chamber
Status: Nonprofit
Paid Staff: 1
Volunteer Staff: 50
Income Sources: Western Alliance of Arts Administrators; Chamber Music America; California Presenters; Ticket Sales, Membership Dues, Endowment Income and Gifts from Organizations
Season: October-April
Performs At: Caltech Beckman Auditorium
Stage Dimensions: 24x43x16
Seating Capacity: 1,150
Year Built: 1904
Organization Type: Sponsoring

4269
SONGFEST
6369 Euclid Road
Pasadena, CA 45236
Phone: 310-384-3706
Fax: 626-405-0151
e-mail: songfest@earthlink.net
Web Site: www.songfest.us
Management:
  Executive/Artistic Director: Rosemary Ritter
  Dean School Of Music: Elaine Chow
  Associate Artistic Directors: Matthew Morris
  Associate Artistic Directors: Liza Stepanova
  Publications and Graphic Design: Rosalinda Monroy
  Bookkeeper: Julia Kyser
Mission: To advance the art of song by cultivating its musical literary traditions and promoting its contemporary development, with both artists and

audiences. To provide both professional and pre-professional artists with unique opportunity of close working association with some of the world's most distinguished artists.
Founded: 1996
Specialized Field: Series & Festivals: Classical Voice and Piano
Status: Non-Profit, Non-Professional
Paid Staff: 1
Volunteer Staff: 7
Paid Artists: 10
Budget: $110,000
Income Sources: Private Donors, Tuitions, and grants for the Aaron Copland Fund for Music, The Marc and Eva Stern Foundation, and The Ann and Gordon Getty Foundation
Affiliations: Chapman University
Facility Category: Music School

4270
GOLDEN GATE INTERNATIONAL CHILDREN'S CHORAL FESTIVAL
3629 Grand Avenue
Piedmont, CA 94610
Phone: 510-547-4441
Fax: 510-451-2947
e-mail: info@goldengatefestival.org
Web Site: www.piedmontchoirs.org
Officers:
  President: Annette Clear
  Vice President: Alene Kemper
  Vice President: Susan Kelley
  Vice President: Jukka Valkonen
  Treasurer: Leon Tuan
  Secretary: David Baraff
Management:
  Artistic Director: Robert Geary
  Executive Director: Julia Richter
  Program Manager: Christa Tumlinson
  Marketing: Cynthia Doll
Mission: The GGF, the first international children's choral festival in the western U.S., promotes international understanding through music, and musical excellence in choral singing, through competition and performance.
Founded: 1991
Season: July

4271
IAI PRESENTATIONS
Peking Acrobats
PO Box 4
Pismo Beach, CA 93448
Phone: 805-476-8422
Fax: 805-476-8426
Toll-free: 800-424-3454
e-mail: don@iaipresentations.com
Web Site: www.iaipresentations.com
Officers:
  President: Don Hughes
Management:
  Producer: Don Hughes
  Artistic Director: Ken Hai
  Production Associate: Melinda Hai
  Production Associate: Steven Hai
  International Productions Tour Mana: Helen Hai
  Group Leader: Jiang Fu Jun
  Tour Manager: Shao Kun Wan
  Tour Manager: Mei Ying Hai
  Technical Director: Mark Mallory

4272
CALIFORNIA INSTITUTE OF MUSIC
PO Box 9401
Rancho Santa Fe, CA 92067
Phone: 858-259-2503
Fax: 858-259-5508
e-mail: office@cimwebsite.org
Web Site: www.cimwebsite.org
Officers:
  President CEO and Producer: Michael Tseitlin
  Vice President, COO and Producer: Cynthia A. Dike-Hughes
  Physical Plant and Shipping and Rec: Macario Cabaong
Management:
  Artistic Director: Irina Tseitlin
  President: Michael Tseitli
Founded: 1990
Specialized Field: Recitals: Southern California Youth Symphony and Sinfonietta
Income Sources: Tuition and individual patrons, donors, and Sponsors
Performs At: California Center for the Arts; Horizon Auditorium
Seating Capacity: 1600; 650

4273
CARMEL VALLEY LIBRARY CONCERT SERIES
3919 Townsgate Dr.
Rancho Santa Fe, CA 92130-2584
Phone: 858-552-1668
Fax: 858-259-5508
Management:
  Artistic Director: Michael Tseitlin
Budget: $35,000-60,000
Performs At: Concert Hall
Seating Capacity: 300

4274
INTERNATIONAL INSTITUTE OF MUSIC FESTIVAL
150 West 85 St.
Rancho Santa Fe, CA 10024
Phone: 212-580-0210
Fax: 212-580-1738
e-mail: info@ikif.org
Web Site: www.ikif.org
Management:
  Executive Director: Michael Tseitlin
  Administrative Director: Paul Lindenauer
  Artistic Advisor: Giuseppe Nova
Specialized Field: Instrumental; Educational
Budget: $35,000-$60,000
Season: July
Performs At: Bayerische Musikakademie; Marktoberdorf (Festival Site)
Seating Capacity: 400 - 800

4275
RIVERCITY JAZZ FESTIVAL
4055 Oro Street
Redding, CA 96001-2937
Phone: 530-244-6033
e-mail: rhuff@c-zone.net
Web Site: www.rivercityjazz.com
Management:
  President: Roger Tompkins
  Festival Director: Maurice Huff
  Membership: Lorna Burke
Mission: The Redding Jazz Festival, offered in April, is one of the performance events offered by the Rivercity Jazz Society. Other performances from March through December include the Annual Youth Jazz Concert, Ken Brock & Friends, Jasscity, Delta Flyers, Jelly Roll jazz Band and Straight Ahead Big Band. These performances are held in Redding, Stockton, Sacramento, Vacaville, Emeryville, Wallace, and Fairfield
Founded: 1986
Season: April
Performs At: Mt. Shasta Mall in Redding

4276
REDLANDS BOWL SUMMER MUSIC FESTIVAL
168 South Eureka Street
Redlands, CA 92373-4620
Phone: 909-793-7316
Fax: 909-793-5086
e-mail: info@redlandsbowl.org
Web Site: www.redlandsbowl.org
Officers:
  Executive Director: Beverly Noerr
  President: Robert Dawes
  Vice President: Jan Hudson
  Treasurer: Joan Benson
  Corporate Secretary: Susan Sequeira
  Member at Large: Bryan C. Hartnell
  Chairman of the Board: Jeffrey L. Waldron
  Member of the Board: Paul T. Barich
  Member of the Board: Beatrice H. Brown
Management:
  President: Robert Dawes
  Executive Director: Beverly Noerr
  Program Director: Tracy Massimiano
  Office Manager: Kristi Marnell
  Publications: Jerri Graham
  Program Associate: Valerie Peister
  Technical Director: Tim Mahoney
  Stage Manager: Nathan Prince
Mission: Providing a range of performing arts to residents of Redlands at no admission charge.
Utilizes: Dance Companies; Dancers; Grant Writers; Guest Accompanists; Guest Musical Directors; Guest Musicians; Multimedia; Music; Original Music Scores; Singers; Special Technical Talent
Founded: 1923
Specialized Field: Series & Festivals; Instrumental; Opera; Choral; Traditional Jazz; Dance; Childrens'
Status: Non-Profit, Non-Professional
Paid Staff: 2
Volunteer Staff: 100
Budget: $150,000-$400,000
Income Sources: Freewill Donations; Underwriting; Grants
Season: Late June - Late August
Performs At: Redlands Open-air Amphitheatre (Festival Site)
Affiliations: Redlands Bowl
Annual Attendance: 80,000 to 100,000
Seating Capacity: 3,750
Organization Type: Performing; Sponsoring

4277
JAZZ ON THE LAKE: PEOPLE PRODUCTIONS
663 W. 100 South
B#-17
Redway, CA 84104
Phone: 801-400-8826
Fax: 707-923-4509
e-mail: people@humboldt.net
Web Site: www.peopleproductions.net
Management:
  Executive Director: Carol Bruno

SERIES & FESTIVALS / California

Artistic Director: Michelle Patrick
Education Director: William Ferrer
Artistic Advisor: Richard Scharine
Founded: 1985
Specialized Field: Series & Festivals: Music Productions and Promotions
Status: For-Profit, Non-Professional
Paid Staff: 8
Paid Artists: 30
Performs At: 1976

4278
SUMMER ARTS & MUSIC FESTIVAL
59 Rusk Ln.
PO Box 1910
Redway, CA 95560
Phone: 707-923-3368
Fax: 707-923-3370
e-mail: office@mateel.org
Web Site: www.mateel.org
Officers:
  President: Garth Epling
  Vice President: Andrew Burnett
  Treasurer: Casandra Taliaferro
  Secretary: Jackie Pantaleo
Management:
  General Manager / Talent Coordinato: Justin Crellin
  Office Administrator: Katz Boose
  Sponsorship and Ad Sales: Cathy Miller
  Special Projects: Casandra Taliaferro
  Hall Rentals / Office Manager: Charity Green
  Hall Manager: John Jennings
Mission: To involve segments of the community in the creative actualization of a cultural vision embracing diversity, vitality, justice, and sustainability. Our programs and events serve changing community needs, emphasizing the performing and visual arts.
Founded: 1976
Specialized Field: 100 diverse performances on 5 stages, over 150 handmade craft and food booths, fine arts showcase.
Status: Non-Profit, Professional
Paid Artists: 20
Non-paid Artists: 40
Season: Late June
Performs At: Benbow Lake State Recreation Area in Humboldt County
Facility Category: Outdoor venue
Seating Capacity: 6,000

4279
WINTER ARTS FAIRE
59 Rusk Ln.
PO Box 1910
Redway, CA 95560
Phone: 707-923-3368
Fax: 707-923-3370
e-mail: office@mateel.org
Web Site: www.mateel.org
Officers:
  President: Garth Epling
  Vice President: Andrew Burnett
  Treasurer: Casandra Taliaferro
  Secretary: Jackie Pantaleo
Management:
  General Manager / Talent Coordinato: Justin Crellin
  Office Administrator: Katz Boose
  Sponsorship and Ad Sales: Cathy Miller
  Special Projects: Casandra Taliaferro
  Hall Rentals / Office Manager: Charity Green
  Hall Manager: John Jennings
Mission: To involve segments of the community in the creative actualization of a cultural vision embracing diversity, vitality, justice, and sustainability. Our programs and events serve changing community needs, emphasizing the performing and visual arts.
Founded: 1976
Specialized Field: Series & Festivals; Instrumental Music; Vocal Music; Youth; Dance; Ethnic Performances; Instrumental; Jazz
Status: Non-Profit, Professional
Paid Artists: 1
Season: December, second weekend
Affiliations: Mateel Community Center; Redway
Annual Attendance: 1,500 per day
Facility Category: Community Center/Performance Hall

4280
INDIAN WELLS VALLEY CONCERT ASSOCIATION
PO Box 1802
Ridgecrest, CA 93556-1802
Phone: 760-375-5600
Fax: 760-375-3330
e-mail: iwvca@hotmail.com
Web Site: www.iwvca.com
Officers:
  President: Gregory V. Morrow, Jr.
  Vice President: John Edge-O'Bergfell
  Secretary: Robert B. McDiarmid
  Treasurer: Robert A. Covington
Management:
  Business Manager: Carl N Helmick Jr
  Lighting Director: Jim Bego
  Sound Director: Clarence Dent
  Artist Selection Coordinator: Philip Mieseala
Mission: To present leading performing artists in the fields of music, dance & stage to the residents of Western Mojave Desert, since 1947
Founded: 1947
Specialized Field: Performing Artists; Primarily Music (Classical & Non-Classical); Some Dance & One Person Stage
Volunteer Staff: 11
Paid Artists: 6
Budget: $47,000
Income Sources: Season Subscriptions; Contributions
Performs At: China Lake Auditorium
Affiliations: Western Arts Alliance
Annual Attendance: 3,000
Facility Category: Parker Performing Arts Center
Type of Stage: Proscenium
Seating Capacity: 608
Year Built: 1968
Year Remodeled: 2000

4281
PERFORMING ARTS PRESENTATIONS
University of California Music Department
900 University Ave.
Riverside, CA 92521
Phone: 951-827-1012
Fax: 952-827-4651
e-mail: traceys@ucr.ed
Web Site: www.performingarts.ucr.edu
Management:
  Management Services Officer: Tracey J Scholtemeyer
  Department Chair: Walter Clark
  Financial Analyst: Cynthia Redfield
  Publicity/Publications: Kathleen DeAtley
  Financial & Administrative Officer: Reasey Heang
  Financial Assistant: Shellee Kreuter
  Academic Advisor: Viviane Baerenklau
  Program Promotions Manager: Kathleen DeAtley
Mission: Providing educational and cultural resources for students and area residents.
Founded: 1973
Specialized Field: Dance; Vocal Music; Instrumental Music; Theater
Status: Professional; Nonprofit
Income Sources: Western Alliance of Arts Administrators; Association of Performing Arts Presenters; California Presenters
Performs At: University Theatre
Organization Type: Sponsoring

4282
CALIFORNIA STATE SUMMER SCHOOL FOR THE ARTS
4825 J Street
Suite 120
Sacramento, CA 95819-3747
Mailing Address: PO Box 1077 Sacramento, CA 98512-1077
Phone: 916-227-5160
Fax: 916-227-5170
e-mail: application@innerspark.us
Web Site: www.csssa.org/
Officers:
  Chair: Susan Dolgen
  VP: Megan Chernin
  VP Finance: Lewis Sharpstone
  Secretary: Donna Miller Casey
Management:
  Director: Robert M Jaffe
  Deputy Director: Joseph Alameida
  Program Analyst: Katrina Dolenga
  Office Assistant: Cynthia Glenn
  Development Director: Joan Newberg
Mission: The California State Summer School for the Arts is a rigorous, month long training program in the visual and performing arts, creative writing, animation and film for talented artists of high school age.
Founded: 1987
Budget: $1.9 million
Performs At: Various Auditoriums
Facility Category: Rented College Campus

4283
FESTIVAL OF NEW AMERICAN MUSIC
Music Department, CSU
6000 J Street
Sacramento, CA 95819-6015
Phone: 916-278-5191
Fax: 916-278-7217
e-mail: fenam@csus.edu
Web Site: www.csus.edu/music
Management:
  Department Chair: Ernie Hills
  Information Secretary: Shea Grimm
  Events Manager: Glenn Disney
  Secretary: Karen Sorenson
Mission: To showcase the works of contemporary American composers. All Festival events are free.
Founded: 1964
Specialized Field: Contemporary American Music
Status: Non-Profit, Professional
Paid Artists: 60
Budget: $60,000-$150,000
Season: Early-mid November, 12 days
Performs At: Sacremento (Festival Site)
Facility Category: Music Recital Hall
Seating Capacity: 350
Organization Type: Performing; Educational; Sponsoring

SERIES & FESTIVALS / California

4284
FINEST ASIAN PERFORMING ARTS
PO Box 162163
Sacramento, CA 95816
Phone: 916-924-1212
Fax: 916-924-7212
Officers:
  Founder and President: Martha Liao
  Vice-President: Celeste Fleming
  Secretary: Woon Ki Lau
  Tresurer: Jan Steinhauser
Management:
  Executive Director: Anna Y Mayo
  Secretary: Lucy Nemac
  Music Director/Advisor: Yan Zhang
Mission: To expose the Western community to Eastern culture works.
Utilizes: Singers
Founded: 1988
Specialized Field: Dance; Vocal Music; Instrumental Music; Festivals
Status: Non-Profit,Professional
Paid Staff: 12
Income Sources: Finest Asian Music Festival
Organization Type: Performing; Sponsoring

4285
HUGHES STADIUM
3835 Freeport Boulevard
Sacramento, CA 95822
Phone: 916-558-2111
Fax: 916-558-2030
Web Site: www.scc.losrios.edu
Management:
  President: Robert Harris
  Executive Director: Mary Leland
  Facility Manager: Vicki Byers
Founded: 1916
Specialized Field: Sub-venue of Sacramento City College
Status: Non-Profit, Professional

4286
CHAMBER MUSIC IN NAPA VALLEY
4375 Atlas Peak Road
Saint Helens, CA 94558
Phone: 707-226-6785
Fax: 707-963-4512
e-mail: cmnv@napanet.net
Web Site: www.chambermusicnapa.org
Management:
  Director: John Kongsgaard
  Director: Maggy Kongsgaard
Mission: Presenters of world-renowned artists including Emanuel Ax, Garrick Ohlsson, St Petersburg String Quartet, et cetera in an intimate concert setting.
Founded: 1979
Status: Nonprofit
Income Sources: Private and Corporate Donations, Ticket Sales, Grants
Season: October-May
Performs At: United Methodist Church, Napa Valley Opera House
Seating Capacity: 320

4287
LIPINSKY FAMILY SAN DIEGO JEWISH ARTS FESTIVAL
2165 San Diego Avenue
Suite 201
San Diego, CA 92110
Phone: 619-232-0222
Fax: 619-235-0939
e-mail: artistic@sandiegorep.com
Web Site: www.sandiegorep.com
Management:
  Artistic Director: Sam Woodhouse
Founded: 1976
Status: Professional
Paid Artists: 800

4288
MAINLY MOZART FESTIVAL
444 W Beech
St #220
San Diego, CA 92101
Mailing Address: PO Box 124705 San Diego, CA 92112-4705
Phone: 619-239-0100
Fax: 619-233-4292
e-mail: admin@mainlymozart.org
Web Site: www.mainlymozart.org
Officers:
  Chair: Alexander Pearson
  President: Christopher Wier
  Secretary/Treasurer: Linda Satz
Management:
  Executive Director: Nancy Laturno Bojanic
  Artistic Director: David Atherton
  Development Director: Veronica Baker
  Director Administration: Robert Fishman
Utilizes: Educators; Guest Accompanists; Guest Musical Directors; Guest Musicians; Multimedia
Founded: 1988
Specialized Field: Series & Festivals; Instrumental Music; Classical Music; Jazz; Education
Status: Non-Profit, Professional
Paid Staff: 7
Paid Artists: 80
Budget: $700,000 - 800,000
Income Sources: Box Office Receipts; Grants; Donations; Memberships; Special Events; Retail
Season: June
Performs At: Balboa Theatre downtown
Affiliations: Spreckels Theatre; Neurosciences Institution; St Pauls Cathedral; US Grant Hotel; East County Performing Arts Center; Lambs Theatre
Annual Attendance: 26,000
Seating Capacity: 1,500

4289
POINT LOMA NAZARENE UNIVERSITY CULTURAL EVENTS SERIES
3900 Lomaland Drive
San Diego, CA 92106-2810
Phone: 619-849-2200
Fax: 619-849-2668
e-mail: music@pointloma.edu
Web Site: www.ptloma.edu
Officers:
  President: Robert Brower
  Chairman: Steve Scott
  Vice Chair: Craig Furusho
  Secretary: Jan Stone
Management:
  Cultural Events Coordinator: Betsy Northam, BetsyNortham@pointloma.edu
  Building Coordinator: Laurie Oliver, LaurieOliver@pointloma.edu
Utilizes: Fine Artists; Guest Companies; Guest Directors; Guest Instructors; Guest Soloists; Multimedia; Sign Language Translators; Singers
Founded: 1902
Specialized Field: Series & Festivals; Instrumental Music; Vocal Music
Status: Non-Profit, Professional
Paid Staff: 3
Paid Artists: 9
Performs At: Performance Hall; Chapel
Seating Capacity: 380; 1800
Year Built: 1995
Cost: $6,000,000

4290
SAN DIEGO EARLY MUSIC SOCIETY
PO Box 82008
San Diego, CA 92138
Phone: 619-291-8246
e-mail: sdems@sdems.org
Web Site: www.sdems.org
Officers:
  President: Mark Lester
  Vice President: Laurent Planchon
  Treasurer: Martha Altus-Buller
  Secretary: Angela Quinn
  Grants Coordinator: Duane Gruber
Management:
  International Series Director: Laurent Planchon
  Museum Series Director: Diemet Rose
  Conductor: Elizabeth Zuehlke
  Choral Conductor: Stephen Sturk
  Program Director: Geoffrey Brooks
  Grants Coordinator: Duane Gruber
Mission: To encourage the appreciation of medieval, renaissance, and baroque music; to present two series of six concerts each, outreach programs, and annual workshop for instrumentalists and vocalists.
Utilizes: Guest Musical Directors; Instructors; Multimedia; Original Music Scores; Sign Language Translators
Founded: 1981
Specialized Field: Early Music (Classical)
Status: Nonprofit
Paid Staff: 1
Budget: $65,000
Income Sources: Box Office; Members; Ads; Grants
Season: October-April
Performs At: St. James-by-the-Sea; Sherwood Auditorium At S.D. Museum of Contemporary Art, La Jolla; S.D. Museum of Art
Affiliations: Early Music America; San Diego Performing Arts League
Annual Attendance: 2,500
Seating Capacity: 400; 500; 100

4291
SAN DIEGO STATE UNIVERSITY-SCHOOL OF MUSIC AND DANCE
San Diego State University
5500 Campanile Drive
San Diego, CA 92182-7902
Phone: 619-594-6031
Fax: 619-594-1692
e-mail: music.dance@mail.sdsu.edu
Web Site: www.musicdance.sdsu.edu
Management:
  Director: Donna Conaty
  Administrative Support Coordinator: Debbie Willis
  Student Coordinator: Sandra Konar
  Public Affairs/Communications: Rhoda Nevins
Mission: To deliver specialized educational instruction, experiences and career development for students by creating an artistic environment based on the unique strengths and knowledge ofour accomplished facility.

SERIES & FESTIVALS / California

Programs emphasize experiential development through high quality performances, professional engagement and applied practical training in music and dance.
Founded: 1897
Specialized Field: Music; Dance

4292
SAN DIEGO THANKSGIVING, DIXIELAND JAZZ FESTIVAL
PO Box 880387
San Diego, CA 92168-0387
Phone: 619-297-5277
Fax: 619-297-5281
e-mail: jazzinfo@dixielandjazzfestival.org
Web Site: www.dixielandjazzfestival.org
Officers:
  President: Bill Adams
  Vice President: Bill Adams
Management:
  Executive Director: Paul Daspit
  Artistic Director: Hal Smith
  Treasurer: Gretchen Haugen
  Secretaty: Myrna Goodwin
Mission: A non-profit organization composed of more than 1,000 members dedicated to the preservation and perpetuation of our country's only original art form - Traditional Jazz.
Founded: 1979
Season: November Jazz Festival and monthly concerts July through Jan

4293
CHAMBER MUSIC MASTERS
San Francisco Conservatory of Music
50 Oak Street
San Francisco, CA 94102-6011
Phone: 415-864-7326
Fax: 415-503-6299
e-mail: mcocco@sfcm.edu
Web Site: www.sfcm.edu
Management:
  President: Colin Murdoch
  Assistant to the President: Laura Reynolds
  Manager, Concert Operations: Seth Ducey
  Special Events Coordinator: Trista Cunningham
  Director: Joan Gordon
  Vice President of Advancement: Stacy Cullison
Mission: Offering advanced students and faculty the opportunity to perform with outstanding guest artists and providing Bay Area audiences with concerts featuring highly imaginative programming.
Specialized Field: Chamber Master Classes and Performances
Status: Professional; Nonprofit
Organization Type: Performing; Educational

4294
CORPUS ACROBATIC THEATRE
Gary Lindsey Artist Services
2700 15th Avenue
San Francisco, CA 94127
Phone: 415-759-6410
Fax: 415-681-9801
e-mail: lindseyart@aol.com

4295
GRACE CATHEDRAL CONCERTS
Grace Cathedral
1100 California Street
San Francisco, CA 94108
Phone: 415-749-6300
Fax: 415-749-6301
e-mail: concerts@gracecathedral.org
Web Site: www.gracecathedral.org
Management:
  President: Alan Jones
  Concerts Manager: Rebecca Nestle
Utilizes: Multimedia; Original Music Scores; Sign Language Translators; Singers
Founded: 1965
Specialized Field: Series & Festivals; Instrumental Music; Vocal Music; Youth; Dance; Ethnic Performances
Status: For-Profit, Professional
Paid Staff: 1
Paid Artists: 30
Performs At: Grace Cathedral
Facility Category: Church
Seating Capacity: 1309
Year Built: 1934

4296
IRINA DVOROVENKO
Gary Lindsey Artist Services
2700 15th Avenue
San Francisco, CA 94127
Phone: 415-759-6410
Fax: 415-681-9801
Toll-free: 800-949-2745
e-mail: LindseyArt@aol.com

4297
MASSENKOFF RUSSIAN FOLK FESTIVAL
Sandra Calvin, Artist Representative
2700 15th Ave
San Francisco, CA 94127
Phone: 415-759-6410
Fax: 415-564-4602
e-mail: russianfok@aol.com
Web Site: www.nikolaimassenkoff.us
Management:
  Singer/Director: Nikolai Massenkoff
  Artist Representative: Sandra Calvin, sandracalvin@att.net
Mission: To provide entertainment and expand knowledge of Russian culture and people.
Founded: 1975
Specialized Field: Russian Music; Song; Dance
Facility Category: Flexible
Type of Stage: Flexible
Seating Capacity: 500-50,000

4298
MAXIM BELOTSERKOVSKY
Gary Lindsey Artist Services
2700 15th Avenue
San Francisco, CA 94127
Phone: 415-759-6410
Fax: 415-681-9801
Toll-free: 800-949-2745
e-mail: LindseyArt@aol.com

4299
MIDSUMMER MOZART FESTIVAL
PO Box 882754
#749
San Francisco, CA 94188
Phone: 415-596-5712
Fax: 415-627-9142
e-mail: mozartinjuly@gmail.com
Web Site: www.midsummermozart.org
Officers:
  Chair: George Cleve
  Treasurer: Meina Xu
  Secretary: Tom Bria
Management:
  Executive Director: Lori Noack
  Music Director and Conductor: George Cleve
  Production Coordinator: Sue Edwards
  Concert Master: Robin Hansen
  General Manager: Kelly Good-Morgan
  Production Director: Deward Hastings
Mission: To present the music of Wolfgang Amadeus Mozart to expanding Bay Area audiences through performances of unparalleled excellence.
Founded: 1975
Specialized Field: Instrumental
Status: Professional; Nonprofit
Budget: $10,000
Income Sources: American Symphony Orchestra League; California Confederation of the Arts; Association of California Symphony Orchestras
Season: July
Affiliations: Various venues throughout California
Seating Capacity: 928; 700; 315; 600; 300
Organization Type: Performing

4300
MORRISON ARTIST SERIES
San Francisco State University Music Departme
1600 Holloway Avenue
San Francisco, CA 94123
Phone: 415-338-1111
Fax: 415-338-6159
e-mail: sgropman@sfsu.edu
Web Site: www.musicdance.sfsu.edu/morrison
Management:
  Artistic Director: Saul Gropman
Mission: Bringing Bay Area audiences the world's finest chamber music. The Morrison Artists Series concert program presents six free Sunday afternoon performances each year by acclaimed chamber music ensembles.
Founded: 1955
Specialized Field: Series & Festivals: Chamber Music Concerts
Status: Non-Profit, Professional
Paid Staff: 2
Performs At: McKenna Theatre
Seating Capacity: 700

4301
NATIONAL SONG AND DANCE COMPANY OF MOZAMBIQUE
Gary Lindsey Artist Services
2700 15th Avenue
San Francisco, CA 94127
Phone: 415-759-6410
Fax: 415-681-9801
Toll-free: 800-949-2745
e-mail: LindseyArt@aol.com
Management:
  Artistic Director: David Abillio

4302
NOONTIME CONCERTS-SAN FRANCISCO'S MUSICAL LUNCH BREAK
660 California Street
San Francisco, CA 94108
Phone: 415-777-3211
Fax: 415-777-3244
e-mail: info@noontimeconcerts.org
Web Site: www.noontimeconcerts.org
Officers:
  Board Member: Robin Wirthlin
  Board Member: Michael Abrahams
  Board Member: David Rickey
  Board Member: Carol Verburg
Management:
  Executive Director: James Rittell

SERIES & FESTIVALS / California

Program Coordinator: Duc Joie Tran
Production Coordinator: Kervin McGlynn
Mission: To enrich the cultural life of Sand Francisco and the Bay Area. Performed by professional local and international touring artists. The concerts are not ticketed, but free-will donations are solicited. Performances are offered at a time convenient for downtown workers, visitors, students, shoppers, and music lovers.
Founded: 1988
Season: Weekly on Tuesdays
Performs At: Old St. Mary's Cathedral
Seating Capacity: 900

4303
OLD FIRST CONCERTS
1751 Sacramento Street
San Francisco, CA 94109
Phone: 415-474-1608
Fax: 415-474-6533
e-mail: staff@oldfirstconcerts.org
Web Site: www.oldfirstconcerts.org
Officers:
  President: Thomas Culp
  Secretary: Randal P. Wong
  Treasurer: Darren Presher
Management:
  Director: Kathy Barr
  Program Associate: Rick Bahto
  House Manager: Chris Andersen
  Director of Marketing: Leslie Stafford
Mission: To contribute to and enhance the artistic life of the Bay Area by offering the public a wide variety of musical forms and expressions that ranges from classical recital and chamber performances to blues, folk, avant-garde, and jazz, as well as multicultural concerts and world music.
Founded: 1970
Specialized Field: Theatre: Chamber Music
Status: Non-Profit, Professional
Paid Artists: 200
Performs At: Old First Church
Facility Category: Presbyterian Church
Type of Stage: Raised; Wooden
Seating Capacity: 450

4304
OMNI FOUNDATION FOR THE PERFORMING ARTS
236 West Portal Ave.
#1
San Francisco, CA 94127
Phone: 415-242-4500
Toll-free: 888-400-6664
e-mail: info@omniconcerts.com
Web Site: www.omniconcerts.com
Management:
  Director: Richard Patterson
Mission: To bring the world's finest acoustic guitarists to the San Francisco Bay Area. Although our series present acoustic guitarists of all genres, such as flamenco, jazz, and fingerstyle, the primary focus is on the classical guitar. Omni presents over 20 exceptional guitarists each season.
Founded: 1981
Specialized Field: Series and Festivals: Guitar Concert Series
Status: Non-Profit, Professional
Paid Staff: 2
Paid Artists: 12
Budget: $165,000
Season: September through April

Performs At: Herbst Theatre, the Green Room in the Veterans Building, the San Francisco Conservatory of Music, and The Palace of Fine Arts
Annual Attendance: 6,000
Seating Capacity: 915

4305
OTHER MINDS MUSIC FESTIVAL
333 Valencia Street
Suite 303
San Francisco, CA 94103
Phone: 415-934-8134
Fax: 415-934-8136
e-mail: otherminds@otherminds.org
Web Site: www.otherminds.org
Officers:
  President: Curtis Smith
  President Emeritus, Treasurer: Jim Newman
  Vice President: Andrew Gold
  Secretary: Mitchell Yawitz
Management:
  Executive and Artistic Director: Charles Amirkhanian
  Business Manager: Carole Goerger
  Associate Director: Adam Fong
  Development Director: Emma Moon
Mission: To support and present the works of composers of new music.
Founded: 1993
Specialized Field: Series and Festivals; Instrumental Music; Vocal Music; Ethnic Performances
Status: Non-Profit, Professional
Paid Staff: 5
Paid Artists: 25
Budget: $35,000-$60,000
Season: Late March
Annual Attendance: 2,000
Seating Capacity: 500

4306
SAN FRANCISCO BLUES FESTIVAL
PO Box 460608
San Francisco, CA 94146-0608
Phone: 415-979-5588
Fax: 415-826-6958
e-mail: SFblues@earthlink.net
Web Site: www.sfblues.com
Management:
  Director: Tom Mazzolini
  Stage Manager: Mike Dingle
  Director Of Logistics: Scott Redmond
Founded: 1973
Specialized Field: Blues
Annual Attendance: 18,000-20,000
Facility Category: Outdoors Lawns

4307
SAN FRANCISCO ETHNIC DANCE FESTIVAL
World Arts West, Fort Mason Center 2 Marina B
#230
San Francisco, CA 94123-1282
Phone: 415-474-3914
Fax: 415-474-3922
Toll-free: 888-756-0888
e-mail: info@worldartswest.org
Web Site: www.worldartswest.org
Officers:
  President: Esther Li
  Vice President: Amanda Almonte
  Vice President: Sheree Chambers
  Secreaty: Elaine Connell
Management:
  Executive Director: Julie Mushet

Festival Arts Director: Carlos Carvajal
Festival Arts Director: CK Ladzekpo
Production Manager: Jack Carpenter
Office Manager: Robert Taylor
Marketing: Joann Driscoll
Mission: To present and to promote ethnic and cultural diversity through the performance and teaching of world dance traditions.
Founded: 1978
Specialized Field: Dance; Ethnic
Status: Professional; Non-Profit
Volunteer Staff: 15
Budget: $60,000-$150,000
Income Sources: Sponsors; Donations
Season: June
Affiliations: Palace of Fine Arts
Annual Attendance: 7,600
Seating Capacity: 1,000

4308
SAN FRANCISCO FRINGE FESTIVAL
156 Eddy Street
San Francisco, CA 94102
Phone: 415-931-1094
Fax: 415-931-2699
e-mail: mail@sffringe.org
Web Site: www.sffringe.org
Officers:
  President: Geoffrey Link
  Board Member: Chris Barnett
  Board Member: Frank Aflague
  Board Member: Carmen White
Management:
  Artistic Director: Christina Augello
  Managing Director: Richard Livingston
  Production Manager: Amanda Ortmayer
Founded: 1992
Specialized Field: Series and Festivals: Theatre
Status: Non-Profit, Professional
Paid Staff: 4
Volunteer Staff: 100
Paid Artists: 50
Season: September
Performs At: Exit Theatre
Annual Attendance: 10000

4309
SAN FRANCISCO JAZZ SPRING SEASON
SF Jazz
201 Franklin St.
San Francisco, CA 94102
Phone: 415-398-5655
Fax: 415-398-5569
Toll-free: 800-850-7353
e-mail: info@sfjazz.org
Web Site: www.wsfjazz.org
Officers:
  Chair: Bannus Hudson
  Vice Chair: Mark Edmunds
  President: Randal Kline
  Treasurer: Brian E. Hollins
  Controller: Jennifer Schwartz
  Director Development: Donna Blakemore
  Director Marketing/PR: Jennifer Joyce
  Operations Manager: Eric Allen
  Director Production: David Coffman
Management:
  Executive Director, Artistic Direct: Randall Kline
  Artist Administrator: Laura Evans
  Director Education: Cory Combs
  Director of Operations and Finance: David Miller
  Chief Executive Officer: Donald Derheim
  Marketing Director: Patty Gessner
  Director of Development: Barrett Shaver

SERIES & FESTIVALS / California

Mission: Offering the finest Bay Area and national jazz performers in San Francisco venues.
Utilizes: Poets
Founded: 1983
Specialized Field: Dance; Vocal Music; Instrumental Music; Festivals; Jazz; World Class Music
Status: Professional; Nonprofit
Paid Staff: 22
Volunteer Staff: 300
Paid Artists: 40
Non-paid Artists: 25
Budget: 4.6 million
Income Sources: Private and Corporate Donations, Organizations
Season: June-March
Performs At: Various Venues
Annual Attendance: 100,000
Organization Type: Performing; Resident; Educational; Presenter

4310
SAN FRANCISCO PERFORMANCES
500 Sutter Street
Suite 710
San Francisco, CA 94102
Phone: 415-398-6449
Fax: 415-398-6439
e-mail: info@performances.org
Web Site: www.performances.org
Officers:
  Chair: Patrick R. McCabe
  Vice Chair: Thomas G Beischer
  Vice Chair: Martin Quinn
  Secretary: Camilla Smith
  Treasurer: Berit S. Muh
  President: Ruth A. Felt
Management:
  President: Ruth A Felt
  Director Public Relations: Karen Hershenson
  Director Development: Michele Casau
  Director of Finance and Administrat: Christian A Jessen
  Director Education Programs: Melanie Smith
  Director Marketing: Thea Stein Skafft
Mission: To present outstanding national, international and emerging artists; to introduce innovative programs; to build new and diversified audiences for the arts.
Utilizes: Artists-in-Residence; Collaborations; Commissioned Composers; Commissioned Music; Dance Companies; Guest Accompanists; Guest Choreographers; Lyricists; Multimedia; Original Music Scores; Sign Language Translators; Singers
Founded: 1979
Specialized Field: Series & Festivals; Instrumental Music; Vocal Music; Youth; Dance; Ethnic Performances
Status: Non-Profit, Professional
Paid Staff: 13
Budget: $2 million
Income Sources: Ticket Sales; Grants & Contributions
Season: September - May
Performs At: Herbst Theatre; St. John's Presbyterian Church, Novellus Theater, Hotel Rex
Affiliations: Association of Performing Arts Presenters; International Society of Performing Arts Administrators; Western Arts Alliance
Annual Attendance: 48,000
Organization Type: Sponsoring
Resident Groups: Alexander String Quartet; Guitarist, Manuel Barrueco; Jazz Violin, Regina Clark

4311
SAN FRANCISCO SHAKESPEARE FESTIVAL
PO Box 460937
San Francisco, CA 94146-0937
Phone: 415-558-0888
Fax: 415-865-4433
e-mail: sfshakes@sfshakes.org
Web Site: www.sfshakes.org
Officers:
  Chair: Pamela Sogge
  Vice-Chair: Eleanor Jacobs
  Executive Director: Toby Leavitt
  CFO: Robert J. Chansler
  Secretary: Michael Li-Ming Wong
  Past Chair: Raymond Kutz
Management:
  Resident Director: Kenneth Kellenher
  Artistic Associate: Rebecca Ennals
  Executive Director: Toby Leavitt
  Marketing Director: John Western
  Education Director: Carl Holvick-Thomas
  Technical Director / Resident Desig: Steve Mannshardt
Mission: Mission of the Festival is to make the words and themes of Shakespeare accessible to everyone regardless of age, ethnicity, financial status, or level of education.
Founded: 1983
Specialized Field: Series & Festivals; Music; Theatre
Status: Non-Profit, Professional
Paid Staff: 6
Volunteer Staff: 5
Paid Artists: 200
Budget: $825,000
Income Sources: Camp Fees; Tour Fees; Individual; Government; Institutional Gifts
Season: July - October
Seating Capacity: 1100

4312
SFJAZZ
201 Franklin St.
Lower Lobby
San Francisco, CA 94102
Phone: 415-398-5655
Fax: 415-398-5569
Toll-free: 800-850-7353
e-mail: info@sfjazz.org
Web Site: www.sfjazz.org
Officers:
  Chair: Bannus Hudson
  Vice Chair: Mark Edmunds
  President: Randal Kline
  Treasurer: Brian E. Hollins
  Secretary: Charles Charnas
Management:
  Executive and Artistic Director: Randall Kline
  Artistic Administrator: Laura Evans
  Director of Education: Cory Combs
  Director of Operations and Finance: David Miller
  Chief Executive Officer: Donald Derheim
  Marketing Director: Patty Gessner
  Director of Development: Barrett Shaver
Founded: 1983
Specialized Field: Series & Festivals; Instrumental Music; Vocal Music; Theatre; Youth; Dance; Ethnic Performances
Status: Non-Profit, Professional
Paid Staff: 22
Season: Year Round Programs

4313
STERN GROVE FESTIVAL ASSOCIATION
832 Folsom Street
Suite 1000
San Francisco, CA 94107
Phone: 415-252-6252
Fax: 415-252-6250
e-mail: info@sterngrove.org
Web Site: www.sterngrove.org
Officers:
  Chairman: Douglas E. Goldman
  Vice Chairman: Robin W. Michel
  Treasurer: Deborah E Gallegos
  Secretary: Gregory L Lippetz
  Governance Chair: Karla L Martin
  Development Chair: Elizabeth Goldstein
Management:
  Executive Director: Steven P Haines
  Director of Development: Pamela Sullivan
  Operations/Administration: Robb Huddleston
  Director of Programming: Judy Tsang
  Community Affairs Manager: Joey Babbitt
Mission: An independent, non-profit arts presenting organization, founded by civic activist and arts patron Rosalie M. Stern, committed to providing the people of the Bay Area with admission-free access to diverse performing arts.
Utilizes: Dance Companies; Dancers; Instructors; Lyricists; Multimedia; Original Music Scores; Sign Language Translators
Founded: 1938
Specialized Field: Intsrumental Music; Vocal Music; Dance
Status: Non-Profit
Paid Staff: 8
Volunteer Staff: 300
Paid Artists: 300
Budget: $1.1 million
Income Sources: Foundations; Individuals; Government; Corporate
Season: June - August
Performs At: Sigmund Stern Grove Amphitheater (Festival Site)
Annual Attendance: 95,000
Facility Category: Ampitheatre
Seating Capacity: 8,000 - 10,000
Year Built: 1932
Organization Type: Sponsoring

4314
SWINGDANCE AMERICA
Gary Lindsey Artist Services
P.O. BOX 3220
San Francisco, CA 60011
Phone: 847-382-0285
Fax: 415-681-9801
e-mail: miller3220@aol.com
Management:
  Event Director: Glen Miller
  General Manager: Alfred Dahma

4315
WORLD ARTS ETHNIC FESTIVAL: WEST
Fort Mason Center
2 Marina Blvd., Bldg. D, #230
San Francisco, CA 94123-1284
Phone: 415-474-3914
Fax: 415-474-3922
e-mail: info@worldartswest.org
Web Site: www.worldartswest.org
Officers:
  President: Esther Li
  Vice President: Amanda Almonte

SERIES & FESTIVALS / California

Vice President: Sheree Chambers
Secreatry: Elaine Connell
Management:
　Executive Director: Julie Mushet
　Artistic Director: Carlos Carvajal
　Artistic Director: CK Ladzekipo
　Artistic Director Liaison: Tyese Wortham
Mission: The San Francisco Ethnic Dance Festival celebrates and fosters appreciation for the diverse ethnic communities in the Bay Area through an annual performance season.
Founded: 1978
Specialized Field: Series & Festivals; Dance; Ethnic Performances
Status: Non-Profit, Professional
Paid Staff: 8
Paid Artists: 300
Budget: $60,000-$150,000
Season: June
Affiliations: Palace of Fine Arts
Seating Capacity: 1,000

4316
WORLD ARTS WEST
Fort Mason Center
2 Marina Blvd., Bldg. D, #230
San Francisco, CA 94123-1284
Phone: 415-474-3914
Fax: 415-474-3922
Toll-free: 888-756-0888
e-mail: info@worldartswest.org
Web Site: www.worldartswest.org
Officers:
　President: Ester Li
　Vice President: Amanda Almonte
　Vice President: Sheree Chambers
　Secreatry: Elaine Connell
Management:
　Executive Director: Julie Mushet
　Artistic Director: Carlos Carvajal
　Artistic Director: CK Ladzekipo
　Production Manager: Jack Carpenter
Mission: To honor and celebrate culturally diverse dance forms through presentation, education, and support of artists and their traditions.
Utilizes: Dance Companies; Dancers
Founded: 1978
Specialized Field: Series & Festivals: Dance
Status: Non-Profit, Professional
Paid Staff: 8
Paid Artists: 150
Performs At: Palace of Fine Arts
Seating Capacity: 1000

4317
CAL POLY ARTS PRESENTS & GREAT PERFORMANCES
One Grand Avenue
San Luis Obispo, CA 93407-0334
Phone: 805-756-6556
Fax: 805-756-6558
e-mail: cparts@polymail.calpoly.edu
Web Site: www.calpolyarts.org
Officers:
　President: Harry Heilenbrond
Management:
　Director: Steve Lerian
　Chair, Theatre & Dance Dept: Tim Dugan
　Chair, Music Department: W. Terrance Spiller
　Office Administrator: Valerie Bluett
　Development: Terri Cook
　Program Mgr./Development: Denise Leader Stoeber
　Public Relations: Lisa Woske

Mission: To provide a broad program of high quality, professional touring performances, exhibitions, and readings for the Central Coast community while also assisting with the educational needs of university students through various artist-in-residency and outreach activities.
Founded: 1985
Specialized Field: Series and Festivals; Instrumental Music; Vocal Music; Theater; Youth; Dance; Ethnic Performances; Presentation of Tour and Performing Arts
Status: Non-Profit, Non-Professional
Paid Staff: 5
Volunteer Staff: 175
Budget: $1 million
Income Sources: Box Office; Grants; Private Donations; Corporate Donations
Performs At: Cushman Auditorium, Harman hall, Spanos Theatre
Affiliations: California Presenters; Association of Performing Arts Presenters; Western Arts Alliance
Annual Attendance: 75,000
Facility Category: Performing Arts Center; SLO
Type of Stage: Proscenium
Stage Dimensions: 49'x23'
Seating Capacity: 1,300; 497
Year Built: 1996
Cost: $34 million
Rental Contact: Ron Regier

4318
CUESTA COLLEGE PERFORMING ARTS
PO Box 8106
San Luis Obispo, CA 93403-8106
Phone: 805-546-3132
Fax: 805-546-3968
e-mail: gstone@cuesta.edu
Web Site: www.academic.cuesta.edu/performingarts
Management:
　Dean of Students, Performing Arts: Pamela Ralston
　Chair: Jennifer Martin
　Music Director: George Stone
　Drama Director: Bree Valle
Founded: 1929
Specialized Field: Education
Status: Non-Profit, Professional
Performs At: College Auditorium; Cuesta Interact Theatre
Seating Capacity: 810; 150

4319
FESTIVAL MOZAIC
PO Box 311
2050 Broad Street
San Luis Obispo, CA 93406
Phone: 805-781-3009
Fax: 805-781-3011
Toll-free: 877-818-99
e-mail: operations@festivalmozaic.com
Web Site: www.mozartfestival.com
Officers:
　President: Steve Bland
　Vice President: Charles Myers
　Secretary: Peter Zaleski
　Treasurer: John Doyle
Management:
　Music Director: Scott Yoo
　Executive Director: Bettina Swigger
　Volunteer Coordinator: Nan Hamilton
　Office manager: Kathy East
　Operations Manager: Janet Hillson
　Technician Director: Zachary Hubbard

Mission: To present a classical music festival highlighting Mozart and other classical and contemporary composers.
Founded: 1971
Status: Non-Profit, Professional
Paid Staff: 3
Paid Artists: 100
Budget: $150,000-$400,000
Season: July - August
Performs At: Throughout San Luis Obispo County (Festival Sites)

4320
SAN LUIS OBISPO MOZART FESTIVAL
PO Box 311
2050 Broad Street
San Luis Obispo, CA 93406
Phone: 805-781-3008
Fax: 805-781-3011
e-mail: info@mozartfestival.com
Web Site: www.mozartfestival.com
Officers:
　President: Steve Bland
　Vice President: Charles Myers
　Secretary: Peter Zaleski
　Treasurer: John Doyle
Management:
　Music Director: Scott Yoo
　Executive Director: Bettina Swigger
　Volunteer Coordinator: Nan Hamilton
　Office manager: Kathy East
　Operations Manager: Janet Hillson
　Technician Director: Zachary Hubbard
Mission: To present a classical music festival highlighting Mozart and other classical and contemporary composers.
Utilizes: Commissioned Composers; Commissioned Music; Guest Composers; Guest Lecturers; Guest Musical Directors; Multimedia; Original Music Scores; Singers
Founded: 1970
Status: Professional; Nonprofit
Budget: $150,000-$400,000
Season: July - August
Performs At: Throughout San Luis Obispo County (Festival Sites)
Affiliations: San Luis Performing Arts Center; Wineries; Chapels
Seating Capacity: 1,300
Organization Type: Performing; Educational

4321
CENTERSTAGE, OSHER MARIN JEWISH COMMUNITY CENTER
Osher Marin Jewish Community Center
200 N San Pedro Road
San Rafael, CA 94903
Phone: 415-444-8000
Fax: 415-491-1235
e-mail: centerstage1@marinjcc.org
Web Site: www.marinjcc.org
Officers:
　President: Deborah Stadtner
　Vice President: Susan Lachtman
　Treasurer: Eric Toizer
　Secretary: Nicole Blacksburg
Management:
　Managing Director, Performing Arts: Linda Bolt
　Events Manager: Pam Day
　Operations Coordinator: Kathy Langrock
　Production Coordinator: Josh Korbel
　Executive Director: Judy Wolff-Bolton
　Director of Development: Masha Shifs
　Controller: Tim Egan

All listings are in alphabetical order by state, then city, then organization within the city.

SERIES & FESTIVALS / California

Human Resources Director: Lee Ann Guerrero Buckley
Information Technology Manager: Brian Buckley
Utilizes: Dance Companies; Dancers; Guest Directors; Guest Instructors; Instructors; Local Unknown Artists; Multimedia; Original Music Scores; Sign Language Translators; Singers
Founded: 1990
Specialized Field: Series & Festivals; Classical; Dance; Lectures; Jazz; Broadway music; World music; One Man shows; Literary Arts and Conversation; Comedy
Status: Non-Profit, Professional
Paid Staff: 10
Performs At: Auditorium
Seating Capacity: 500

4322
COMMUNITY ARTS AND MUSIC ASSOCIATION OF SANTA BARBARA-CAMA
2060 Alameda Padre Serra
Suite 201
Santa Barbara, CA 93103
Phone: 805-966-4324
Fax: 805-962-2014
e-mail: info@camasb.org
Web Site: www.camasb.org
Officers:
President: Dolores M Hsu
First Vice-President: Andre Saltoun
Second vice president: Nancy L Wood
Treasurer: John Lundegard
Management:
Executive Director: Mark Trueblood
Concert and Publicity Manager: Justin Weaver
Director of Development: Nancy R Lynn
Office Manager/Subscriber Services: Linda Proud
Mission: To bring the world's greatest orchestras and soloists to Santa Barbara and enrich the cultural aspect of our community.
Utilizes: Guest Artists
Founded: 1919
Specialized Field: Series & Festivals; Classical Instrumental Music; Vocal Music
Status: Non-Profit, Professional
Paid Staff: 4
Budget: $1,200,000
Income Sources: Grants; Foundations; Individual Donations; Investment Income
Season: October-April
Performs At: Arlington Theatre; Lobero Theatre
Annual Attendance: 18,000
Facility Category: Historic Movie House and Concert Hall; Historic Opera House
Type of Stage: Theatre Stage; Opera Stage
Seating Capacity: 2,018
Year Built: 1923
Year Remodeled: 1976
Rental Contact: Karen Killingworth
Organization Type: Sponsoring

4323
MUSIC ACADEMY OF THE WEST FESTIVAL
1070 Fairway Road
Santa Barbara, CA 93108-2899
Phone: 805-969-4726
Fax: 805-969-0686
e-mail: festival@musicacademy.org
Web Site: www.musicacademy.org
Officers:
Chair: Robert Toledo
First Vice Chairman: Margaret Cafarelli
Treasurer: Thomas Orlando
Second Vice Chairman: Judith P. Getto
Secretary: Regina Roney
Management:
President: NancyBell Coe
VP Artistic Programs: Richard Feit
VP Marketing Communications: Susan Gwynne
VP Finance: Barbara J Robertson
Mission: To maintain a pre-professional instrumental company with vocal instruction.
Utilizes: Artists-in-Residence; Collaborating Artists; Educators; Grant Writers; Guest Artists; Guest Companies; Guest Composers; Guest Directors; Guest Instructors; Resident Professionals
Founded: 1947
Specialized Field: Instrumental; Opera; Educational
Status: Non-Profit, Non-Professional
Paid Staff: 30
Volunteer Staff: 90
Paid Artists: 40
Budget: $1,050,000 - 3,600,000
Income Sources: Individual Contributions; Foundations; Corporations
Season: June - August
Performs At: Santa Barbara (Festival Site)
Affiliations: Lobero Theatre
Annual Attendance: 17,000
Seating Capacity: 680
Year Built: 1909
Organization Type: Performing; Educational; Sponsoring
Resident Groups: The Canadian Brass

4324
SANTA BARBARA FESTIVAL BALLET
1019 Chapala Street
Santa Barbara, CA 93101 - 93
Phone: 805-966-0711
Fax: 805-966-9521
e-mail: sbballetcenter@gmail.com
Web Site: www.santabarbaraballetcenter.com
Management:
Artistic Director: Michele Rinaldi
Co-Artistic Director: Denise Rinaldi
Co-Artistic Director: Michele Anderson

4325
SUMMERDANCE SANTA BARBARA
1008 De La Vina
Santa Barbara, CA 93101
Phone: 805-563-2844
Fax: 805-568-0637
e-mail: festival@summerdance.com
Web Site: www.sbdanceworks.com
Officers:
President: Megan Matthieson
Treasurer: Daniel Vapnek
Secretary: Randy Franks
Management:
Executive Director: Dianne Vapnek
Managing Director: Laurie Burnaby
Executive Director: David Asbell
Mission: A multi-week festival of contemporary dance, is to build audiences for dance, to provide a place for emerging and established choreographers to create work, and to share the inspiration of great dance through performances, educational evetns and community outreach.
Founded: 1997
Specialized Field: Contemporary Dance
Status: Non-Profit; Professional
Paid Staff: 3
Volunteer Staff: 1
Income Sources: Foundations; Ticket Sales; Grants; Donations
Performs At: Center Stage Theatre; Libaro Theatre

4326
UCSB ARTS & LECTURES
University of California
Building 402
Santa Barbara, CA 93106-5030
Phone: 805-893-3535
Fax: 805-893-8637
e-mail: aandl-info@sa.ucsb.edu
Web Site: www.artsandlectures.ucsb.edu
Management:
Director: Celesta Billeci
Performing Arts Manager: Cathy Oliverson
Director Operations: Laureen Lewis
Programming Associate: Heather Silva
Mission: To present a wide variety of professional touring artists and ensembles in dance, theater, classical music, ethnic and traditional arts, film and literature for campus and community audiences.
Utilizes: Actors; Artists-in-Residence; Collaborations; Dance Companies; Dancers; Guest Soloists; Multimedia; Special Technical Talent; Theatre Companies
Founded: 1959
Specialized Field: Dance; Vocal Music; Instrumental Music; Theater
Status: Professional; Non-Profit
Paid Staff: 14
Income Sources: Western Alliance of Arts Administrators; Arts Presenters; California Presenters
Performs At: Campbell Hall
Seating Capacity: 860
Organization Type: Performing; Educational; Presenting

4327
CABRILLO FESTIVAL OF CONTEMPORARY MUSIC
147 South River Street
Suite 232
Santa Cruz, CA 95060
Phone: 831-426-6966
Fax: 831-426-6968
e-mail: info@cabrillomusic.org
Web Site: www.cabrillomusic.org
Officers:
President: Jim Petersen
Vice President: Michel Protti
Vice President: Birgit Weskamp
CFO: Fran Fisher
Secretary: Liza Culick
Management:
Executive Director: Ellen M Primack
Director of Development: Tom Fredericks
Associate Director: Jessica Frye
Music Director/Conductor: Marin Alsop
Technical Director: Mike Johnson
Founded: 1963
Specialized Field: Contemporary instrumental music
Budget: $480,000
Season: July
Performs At: S. Cruz Civic Auditorium; Mission San Juan Bautista
Seating Capacity: 1,000

4328
SANTA CRUZ BAROQUE FESTIVAL
PO Box 482
Santa Cruz, CA 95061

SERIES & FESTIVALS / California

Phone: 197-4 -
e-mail: info@scbaroque.org
Web Site: www.scbaroque.com
Management:
   Artistic Director: Linda Burman-Hall
   President: Kathryn Tobisch
   Treasurer: David Wilson
   Ad Coordinator: Gertrude Fator
Mission: Offering a series of early music concerts each spring.
Founded: 1974
Specialized Field: Instrumental
Status: Professional; Nonprofit
Budget: $10,000-$20,000
Season: February - May
Facility Category: Various auditoriums
Seating Capacity: 400
Organization Type: Performing; Sponsoring

4329
UC SANTA CRUZ ARTS & LECTURES

University of California at Santa Cruz
D106 Porter
1156 High Street
Santa Cruz, CA 95064
Phone: 831-459-3861
Fax: 831-459-4521
e-mail: artslecs@ucsc.edu
Web Site: www.artslectures.ucsc.edu
Management:
   Arts and Lectures Director: Jeanette Pilak
   Production Manager: Greg Arrufat
Mission: UC Santa Cruz Arts & Lectures is the largest interdisciplinary presenting organization in the Monterey Bay region, with a mission to transform lives through excellence, innovation, and diversity in the performing arts.
Utilizes: Actors; Dance Companies; Dancers; Instructors; Multimedia; Original Music Scores; Playwrights; Selected Students; Singers; Special Technical Talent; Theatre Companies
Specialized Field: Dance; Theater; Spoken Word/Lectures; World Music; Classical; Jazz
Performs At: Performing Arts Theater
Seating Capacity: 528

4330
CONCERTS WEST

630 San Vicente Boulevard
Unit T
Santa Monica, CA 90402
Phone: 310-393-1155
Fax: 310-393-1155
e-mail: mpreston@ix.netcom.com
Management:
   Artistic Director: Howard Colf
Performs At: Unitarian Universalist Community Church of Santa Monica
Seating Capacity: 225

4331
OAKMONT CONCERT SERIES

444 Crestridge Place
#13
Santa Rosa, CA 95409
Phone: 707-539-7066
Fax: 707-539-0894
e-mail: bartok2@sonic.net
Web Site: www.oakmontconcertseries.org
Officers:
   Secretary/Treasurer: Maurine Christ
Management:
   Artistic Director: Robert Hayden
   Associate Director: Rosemarie Waller
   Programs: Judy Burness
Founded: 1990
Specialized Field: Performing Series
Status: Non-Profit, Professional
Volunteer Staff: 4
Paid Artists: 24
Budget: $24,000
Income Sources: Entrance Fees
Season: One concert per month throughout the year, usually on the s
Performs At: Auditorium
Affiliations: Oakmont Village Association
Annual Attendance: 3,000
Facility Category: Auditorium
Type of Stage: Raised & Curtained
Seating Capacity: 400
Year Built: 1990
Year Remodeled: 2002

4332
SANTA ROSA CONCERT ASSOCIATION

50 Santa Rosa Avenue
Suite 410
Santa Rosa, CA 95404
Phone: 707-546-7097
Fax: 707-546-0460
e-mail: info@santarosasymphony.com
Web Site: www.srconcert.org
Officers:
   President: James Hinton
   Vice-President: Sara Woodfield
   Treasurer: Harry Rubins
   Secretary: Judith Gappa
Management:
   Music Director & Conductor: Bruno Ferrandis
   Executive Director: Alan Silow
   Director of Artistic Operations: Timothy L. Beswick
   Director of Marketing & Public Rela: Sara Mitchell
   Director of Development: Kathleen Morgan
Mission: All-volunteer organization bringing noted musicians to Santa Rosa audiences since 1948, introducing a viariety of musical experiences to audiences at great prices.
Founded: 1948
Performs At: Wells Fargo Theater
Seating Capacity: 1500

4333
SANTA ROSA JUNIOR COLLEGE CHAMBER MUSIC SERIES

1501 Mendocino Avenue
Santa Rosa, CA 95401-4395
Phone: 707-527-4249
Fax: 707-521-7988
e-mail: erussell@santarosa.edu
Web Site: www.santarosa.edu/music/chamber
Officers:
   Department Chair: Dr. Mark Anderman
Management:
   Department Chair: Dr. Mark Anderman
   Director of Vocal Music: Jody Benecke
   Office Manager: Elona Russell
Specialized Field: Classical; Chamber
Income Sources: Private and Corporate Donations, Ticket Sales
Season: October-December
Performs At: Burbank Auditorium, Randolph Newman Auditorium
Annual Attendance: 1,200
Seating Capacity: 700, 350

4334
MOUNTAIN WINERY

14831 Pierce Road
Saratoga, CA 95070
Phone: 408-741-2822
Fax: 408-741-2818
e-mail: events@mountainwinery.com
Web Site: www.mountainwinery.com
Management:
   President: Stuart Ferguson
   General Manager: Don Riccardi
   Director of Finance: Rick Eldridge
   Executive Chef: David Sidoti
   Director of Marketing: Katelvn Studebaker
   Event Coordinator: Kirsten Spitzer
Mission: To enhance the cultural atmosphere of the San Francisco Bay Area
Utilizes: Filmmakers; Instructors; Local Unknown Artists; Multimedia; Original Music Scores; Sign Language Translators; Theatre Companies
Founded: 1957
Specialized Field: Summer Concerts
Status: For-Profit, Non-Professional
Paid Staff: 70
Performs At: Mountain Winery
Annual Attendance: 100,000
Facility Category: Winerey
Type of Stage: Open Air
Stage Dimensions: 27'x24'
Seating Capacity: 1,700
Year Built: 1902
Rental Contact: Mark Karakas
Organization Type: Performing; Sponsoring

4335
TAHOE ARTS PROJECT

PO Box 14281
South Lake Tahoe, CA 96151
Phone: 530-542-3632
Fax: 530-542-4792
e-mail: tahoearts@aol.com
Web Site: www.tahoeartsproject.org
Officers:
   President: Nancy Muller
   Vice President: Pam Singer
   Secretary/Treasurer: Marianne Poohachoff
   Treasurer: Kerri Montgomery
Management:
   Executive Director: Peggy Thompson
Mission: To provide cultural enrichment and diversity for the community through the arts and education, with particular focus on our youth.
Utilizes: Artists-in-Residence; Dance Companies; Fine Artists; Instructors; Multimedia; Original Music Scores; Sign Language Translators; Special Technical Talent; Theatre Companies
Founded: 1987
Status: Nonprofit
Paid Staff: 2
Paid Artists: 5
Budget: $100,000
Income Sources: Grants; Donations; Fundraising Events
Facility Category: Schools
Seating Capacity: 200-1,200

4336
STANFORD JAZZ FESTIVAL & WORKSHOP

PO Box 20454
Stanford, CA 94309

SERIES & FESTIVALS / California

Phone: 650-736-0324
Fax: 650-856-4155
e-mail: info@stanfordjazz.org
Web Site: www.stanfordjazz.org
Management:
　Artistic & Executive Director: Jim Nadel
　Managing Director: Jeffrey Babcock
　Marketing Director: Ernie Rideout
　Education Program coordinator: Ivor Holloway
　Director of Program Operations: Janel Thysen
Mission: Each year the festival presents more than 30 performances by jazz masters, acclaimed contemporary standouts, and emerging stars. Renowned for presenting straight-ahead jazz, flavored with innovative modern stylings, traditional, blues, salsa, Brazilian, and other cross-cultural approaches to musical improvisation.
Specialized Field: Jazz
Season: June - August

4337
STANFORD LIVELY ARTS
365 Lasuen Street
Second Floor
Stanford, CA 94305
Phone: 650-723-2551
Fax: 650-725-6230
e-mail: stanfordlive@stanford.edu
Web Site: www.livelyarts.stanford.edu
Management:
　Artistic and Executive Director: Jenny Bilfield
　Special Events Coordinator: Mary Ancell
　Financial Coordinator: Precy Cabanatan
　Public Relations Manager: Bob Cable
　Communications Manager: Robert Cable
　Technical Manager: Drew Farley
　Director of Development: Kyle J. Polite
　Production Manager: Kimberly Pross
　General Manager: Jan Sillery
Mission: To create unique experiences for diverse communities and artists to share passion, knowledge, creative inspiration, and cultural traditions through live performance and arts education.
Utilizes: Artists-in-Residence; Collaborating Artists; Collaborations; Commissioned Music; Dance Companies; Dancers; Grant Writers; Guest Choreographers; Guest Musical Directors; Guest Musicians; Lyricists; Multimedia; Singers; Special Technical Talent; Theatre Companies
Founded: 1969
Specialized Field: Series & Festivals: Chamber Music and Dance
Status: Non-Profit, Professional
Performs At: Memorial Auditorium and other campus venues
Annual Attendance: 55,000
Facility Category: Theater
Type of Stage: Proscenium
Stage Dimensions: 40'x50'
Seating Capacity: 1710

4338
UNIVERSITY OF THE PACIFIC CONSERVATORY OF MUSIC - RESIDENT ARTIST SERIES
3601 Pacific Avenue
Stockton, CA 95211
Phone: 209-946-2417
Fax: 209-946-2770
e-mail: gongaro@pacific.edu
Web Site: www.pacific.edu/conservatory
Officers:
　President: Pamela Eibeck
Management:
　Dean, Conservatory of Music: Giulio M. Ongaro
　Assistant Dean: Robyn Cheshire
　Director of Development: Holly Stanko
　Stage & Technical Director: James Gonzales
　Operations Manager: Stephen Perdicaris
Mission: A major resource for the region with more than 120 musical performances each year featuring students, faculty, guest artists, and alumni.
Founded: 1924
Specialized Field: Conservatory
Status: Non-Profit, Professional
Performs At: Faye Spanos Concert Hall, Recital hall
Seating Capacity: FSCH-946; RH-119

4339
ARTS FOR THE SCHOOLS
10046 Church Street
Tahoe Vista, CA 96148
Mailing Address: P. O. Box 866 Truckee, CA 96160
Phone: 530-582-8278
Fax: 530-582-8228
e-mail: program@artsfortheschools.org
Web Site: www.aftstahoe.org
Management:
　President: Terry Yagura
　Executive Director: Joanne Snarr
Mission: To provide artistic, educational and cultural opportunities for students, residents, and guests in Lake Tahoe.
Founded: 1984
Specialized Field: Series & Festivals; Instrumental Music; Vocal Music; Theater; Youth; Dance; Ethnic Performances
Status: Non-Profit, Professional
Paid Staff: 2
Paid Artists: 50
Performs At: School Auditorium; Cal-Neva
Seating Capacity: 300; 350

4340
CALIFORNIA LUTHERAN UNIVERSITY MUSIC SERIES
60 West Olsen Road
Thousand Oaks, CA 91360-2787
Phone: 805-492-2411
e-mail: morton@clunet.edu
Web Site: www.clunet.edu
Officers:
　President: John Sladek
Management:
　Director: Daniel M Greeting
　Music Department Chair: Wyant Morton
　Professor of Music: Dorothy Elliott Schechter
　Assistant Professor of Music: Mark Spraggins
Founded: 1959
Specialized Field: Performances by University Symphony, CLU Choir, Wind Ensemble, Women's Chorale, and Jazz Ensemble
Status: Non-Profit, Professional
Paid Staff: 23

4341
CALIFORNIA LUTHERAN UNIVERSITY MUSIC SERIES
60 West Olsen Road
Thousand Oaks, CA 91360-2787
Phone: 805-492-2411
Fax: 805-493-3479
e-mail: morton@clunet.edu
Web Site: www.clunet.edu
Management:
　Orchestra Conductor: Daniel Geeting
　Chair Music Department: Wyant Morton
Budget: $10,000
Performs At: Samuelson Chapel; Forum
Seating Capacity: 650; 250

4342
CONEJO RECREATION & PARK DISTRICT SUMMER CONCERT SERIES
403 W Hill Crest Drive
Thousand Oaks, CA 91360
Phone: 805-495-6471
Fax: 805-497-3199
e-mail: recadmin@crpd.org
Web Site: www.crpd.org
Officers:
　Chair: Joe Gibson
　Vice Chair: Ed Jones
　Director: George M. Lange
　Director: Susan L. Holt
　Director: Chuck Huffer
Management:
　General Manager: Jim Friedl
　Recreation Services Manager: Brenda Coleman
　Recreation Supervisor; Cultural: Scott Buchanan
　Administrator: Sheryl Lewanda
Mission: To present cultural programs including The Young Artists Ensembles, Teen Summer Musical, classes and workshops in visual and performing arts, community theater, music and dance, special performances, and gallery showings.
Founded: 1964
Status: For-Profit, Professional
Performs At: Outdoors
Annual Attendance: 12,000-15,000
Type of Stage: Stage
Seating Capacity: 4600

4343
SPRING MUSIC FESTIVAL: CALIFORNIA UNIVERSITY OF ARTS
California Institute of The Arts
24700 Mcbean Parkway
Valencia, CA 91355
Phone: 661-222-2778
Fax: 661-255-0938
e-mail: music.calarts.edu
Web Site: music.calarts.edu
Management:
　President: Steven D Lavin
　Dean School Of Music: David Rosenboom
　Chair in Music: Richard Seaver
Founded: 1961
Status: Professional; Nonprofit
Organization Type: Performing; Educational

4344
VENTURA MUSIC FESTIVAL
472 E Santa Clara St.
Ventura, CA 93001
Phone: 805-648-3146
Fax: 805-648-4103
Toll-free: 888-882-8263
e-mail: contact@venturamusicfestival.org
Web Site: www.venturamusicfestival.org
Officers:
　President: Ivor Davis
　President-Elect: Eric Oltmann
　Secretary: Virginia Norris
　Treasurer: Patricia Maki
Management:
　Artistic Director: Nuvi Mehta
　Executive Director: Cheryl Heitmann
　Operations Manager: Ann Willard-Bevans

SERIES & FESTIVALS / Colorado

Mission: Annual music festival
Utilizes: Artists-in-Residence; Collaborating Artists; Commissioned Composers; Commissioned Music; Composers-in-Residence; Curators; Dance Companies; Educators; Fine Artists; Grant Writers; Guest Accompanists; Guest Companies; Guest Soloists; Local Artists; Multimedia; Original Music Scores; Playwrights; Singers; Student Interns
Founded: 1994
Specialized Field: Series & Festivals; Instrumental Music; Vocal Music; Ethnic Performances
Status: Non-Profit, Professional
Paid Staff: 4
Volunteer Staff: 300
Budget: $60,000-$400,000
Season: May
Affiliations: American Symphony League; Chamber Music America
Annual Attendance: 4,000
Facility Category: Historic buildings in downtown Ventura
Seating Capacity: 100 - 1,100

4345
VISALIA CULTURAL PROGRAMS-ON STAGE VISALIA
400 N. Church St.
Visalia, CA 93291
Phone: 559-713-4000
Fax: 559-738-3579
Toll-free: 800-225-2277
e-mail: vcc@ci.visalia.ca.us
Web Site: www.visalia.org
Management:
 General Manager: Wally Roeben

4346
MOUNT SAN ANTONIO COLLEGE PERFORMING ARTS CENTER
1100 N Grand Avenue
Walnut, CA 91789
Phone: 909-594-5611
e-mail: slong@mtsac.edu
Web Site: www.performingarts.mtsac.edu
Officers:
 President: Dr. Christopher O'Hearn
Management:
 Chair, Music Department: Katherine Charl Calkins
 Director of Instrumental Jazz: Jeffrey Ellwood
 Director of Choral Activities: Bruce Rogers
 Department Secretary: Jeannie DeVito
Founded: 1946
Specialized Field: Series & Festivals; Music; Dance; Theatre; Radio; Education (Community College)
Status: Non-Profit, Professional
Paid Staff: 2

4347
COLLEGE OF THE SISKIYOUS PERFORMING ARTS SERIES
800 College Avenue Weed
Weed, CA 96094
Phone: 530-938-5555
Fax: 530-938-5570
Toll-free: 888-397-4339
e-mail: cozzalio@siskiyous.edu
Web Site: www.siskiyous.edu
Management:
 Academic Senate President: Michael Graves
 Vice President of Instruction: Barry A Russell
Mission: The Performing Arts Series is carefully planned to present the residents of Siskiyou County with the highest quality performances, at the most reasonable prices, within Northern California and southern Oregon. The series provides local residents an opportunity to see internationally renowned performing groups at prices set especially for families.
Specialized Field: Family Programming
Status: Non-Profit, Professional
Paid Staff: 2
Performs At: Kenneth W. Ford Theatre
Seating Capacity: 584

4348
SACRAMENTO JAZZ JUBILEE
106 K Street
Suite #1
West Sacramento, CA 95814
Phone: 916-444-2004
Fax: 916-372-3479
e-mail: info@sacjazz.com
Web Site: www.sacjazz.com
Officers:
 President: Tom Duff
 Vice President: Ron Jones
 Treasurer: Lisa Negri
 Secretary: Judy Hendricks
Management:
 Executive Director: Greg Willett
Mission: Sacramento Traditional jazz Society, sponsors of the Sac. Jazz Jubilee- is a non-profit organization dedicated to the preservation and promotion of traditional jazz, Dixieland, and classic jazz music.
Founded: 1974
Specialized Field: Music
Status: Nonprofit
Paid Staff: 5
Volunteer Staff: 4000
Budget: $1.8 million
Income Sources: Admissions, Sponsorships, Grants, Food Concession Sales, Souvenir Sales, Private and Corporate Donations, Memberships, Ticket Sales
Season: May
Performs At: Old Sacramento and Midtown
Affiliations: 40 Sacramento Area Venues (Indoor & Outdoor)
Annual Attendance: 102,000
Seating Capacity: 250-2,500

4349
WHITTIER COLLEGE BACH FESTIVAL
13406 E Philadelphia Street
PO Box 634
Whittier, CA 90608
Phone: 562-907-4238
Fax: 562-907-4870
e-mail: dlozano@whittier.edu
Web Site: www.web.whittier.edu
Management:
 Music Department Chair: David J. Muller
 Associate Professor of Music: Stephen Cook
 Associate Professor of Music: Danilo Lozano
 Associate Professor of Music: Teresa LeVelle
Founded: 1936
Specialized Field: Featuring rock, classical, jazz, R&B, Latino pop, country, cowboy, Dixieland, and folk music.
Paid Artists: 20
Budget: $10,000
Season: March
Performs At: Whittier College Campus (Festival Site)
Facility Category: Whittier College Memorial Chapel & other venues
Seating Capacity: 300

4350
VALLEY CULTURAL CENTER CONCERTS IN THE PARK
21550 Oxnard Street
Suite 470
Woodland Hills, CA 91367
Phone: 818-704-1358
Fax: 818-704-1604
e-mail: info@valleycultural.org
Web Site: www.valleycultural.org
Officers:
 Chairman: Roshan Ghaznavi
 CFO/Executive Vice Chair: Gwyn W. Petrick
 Vice Chair - Board Development: I. Allan Oberman
 Vice Chair - Community Outreach: Leslie DeBeauvais
 Secretary: Glenda Patton
Management:
 CEO/President: James W Kinsey III
 Director of Operations: Don Sweeney
 Stage Manager: Jonathan Herndon
Mission: The Valley Cultural Center serves the greater San Fernando Valley as the prominent resource in promoting the performing and visual arts, offering free concerts in the park.
Founded: 1975
Status: Non-Profit, Professional
Paid Staff: 6
Paid Artists: 300
Season: June - August
Performs At: Lou Bredlow Pavillion; Warner Park

Colorado

4351
ASPEN MUSIC FESTIVAL AND SCHOOL
225 Music School Road
Aspen, CO 81611
Phone: 970-925-3254
Fax: 970-920-1643
e-mail: festival@aspenmusic.org
Web Site: www.aspenmusicfestival.com
Officers:
 President/CEO: Don Roth
Management:
 President: Don Roth
 General Manager: James Berdahl
 Artistic Director: Asadour Santourian
 Music Director: David Zinman
Founded: 1949
Specialized Field: Vocal Music: Classical
Status: Non-Profit, Professional
Paid Staff: 100
Paid Artists: 250
Budget: $11,000,000
Performs At: Joan & Irving Harris Concert Hall; Benedict Music Tent
Seating Capacity: 500; 2,050
Year Built: 2000

4352
JAZZ ASPEN SNOWMASS
110 E Hallam Street
Suite 104
Aspen, CO 81611
Phone: 970-920-4996
Fax: 970-920-9135
e-mail: jazzaspen@jazzaspen.org
Web Site: www.jazzaspen.org
Officers:
 President & CEO: James Honowitz

SERIES & FESTIVALS / Colorado

Executive VP/Sales/Marketing: Marc Breslin
Chairman: Marianne Elmasri Buchholz
Vice Chairman: Richard Goodman
Development Chair: David Chazen
Management:
  Founder/President/CEO: James Horowitz
  Finance & HR Director: Mindi VanMoorsel
  Marketing, PR & Sponsorship Directo: Andrea Beard
  Development Manager: Holly Upper
Mission: To create world-class programing of jazz, American and world music, to educate and entertain audiences of diverse tastes and backgrounds, to preserve America's musical heritage.
Founded: 1991
Specialized Field: Series & Festivals; Instrumental Music; Vocal Music; Theatre; Youth; Dance; Ethnic Performances; Music; Jazz
Status: Non-Profit, Professional
Paid Staff: 6
Paid Artists: 60
Income Sources: Ticket Sales; Grants; Donations

4353
BOULDER BACH FESTIVAL
PO Box 1896
Boulder, CO 80306
Phone: 303-776-9666
Fax: 303-652-9101
e-mail: info@boulderbachfest.org
Web Site: www.boulderbachfest.org
Officers:
  President: Dan Seger
  Vice President: Edward McCue
  Secretary: Molly Hardman
  Treasurer: Jim Topping
Management:
  President: Dan Seger
  Executive Director: Marcia Schirmer
  Artistic Director: Robert Spillman
  Music Director: Zachary Carrettin
  Concert Manager: Glenn Ross
  Education Manager: Alexandra Eddy
  Marketing: Holly Hickman
Founded: 1981
Specialized Field: Music of Bach
Status: Non-Profit, Professional
Paid Staff: 1
Paid Artists: 40

4354
BOULDER INTERNATIONAL MUSIC FESTIVAL FOR YOUNG PERFORMERS
801 Vinial Street
Suite 300
Boulder, CO 15212
Phone: 412-642-2778
Fax: 412-642-2779
e-mail: info@earlymusic.org
Officers:
  President: Christopher Bone
  Vice President: Thomas Forrest Kelly
  Vice President: Angela Mariani
  Vice President: Debra Nagy
  Secretary: Charlotte Newman
  Assistant Secretary: Kathleen Moretto Spencer
  Treasurer: Marie-H,ISne Bernard
Management:
  President: Christopher Bone
  Artistic Director: Ann Felter
  Membership Director: Dina Scarpino
  Special Projects Coordinator: Jessica Hohman
Founded: 1998

Specialized Field: Series & Festivals: Instrumental Music
Status: Non-Profit, Non-Professional
Season: June
Facility Category: Saint Paul United Methodist Church

4355
COLORADO MAHLERFEST
PO Box 1314
Boulder, CO 80306-1314
Phone: 303-492-8970
e-mail: barry.knapp@msn.com
Web Site: www.mahlerfest.org
Officers:
  President: Barry Knapp
  Vice-President: Keith Bobo
  Treasurer: Eric Hall
  Secretary & Orchestra Liaison: Rowanna Bobo
Management:
  President: Barry Knapp
  Artistic Director: Robert Olson
Mission: To perform all the music of Gustav Mahler.
Utilizes: Guest Instructors; Guest Soloists; Instructors
Founded: 1988
Specialized Field: Music of Gustav Mahler
Status: Non-Profit, Professional
Budget: $45,000
Income Sources: Box Office; Grants; Donations
Season: July
Performs At: University of Colorado; Boulder (Festival Site)
Facility Category: University Auditorium
Seating Capacity: 2,000
Year Built: 1896
Year Remodeled: 1982

4356
COLORADO MUSIC FESTIVAL & ROCKY MOUNTAIN CENTER FOR MUSICAL ARTS
900 Baseline Road
Cottage 100
Boulder, CO 80302
Phone: 303-449-1397
Fax: 303-449-0071
e-mail: info@comusic.org
Web Site: www.comusic.org
Officers:
  President: Jan Burton
  Executive Director: Catherine Underhill
  VP for Education/Outreach | Communi: Kitty Dawson
  Administrator: Norma Ekstrand
  Treasurer: David Brunel
  Director of Oncology Services: Connie Holden
  VP for Human Resources: Madeleine Holland
  Music Educator (retired): Caryl F. Kassoy
  Professor: Christopher Mueller
Management:
  Music Director: Michael Christie
  Development Director: Ethan Hecht
  Marketing & Development Assistant: Brandi Numedahl
  Registrar & Operations Coordinator: Nancy Brace
  Ticketing Manager: Margaret Romero
  Data Manager: Ken Thorne
  Administration & Marketing Coordina: Kim Brody
  Bookkeeper: Kari Bartkus
Mission: To inspire and connect community members of all ages by providing access to the best of the world's music through education and performance

Utilizes: Guest Accompanists; Guest Composers; Guest Directors; Guest Musical Directors; Guest Musicians; Instructors; Multimedia; Original Music Scores; Singers
Founded: 1977
Specialized Field: Music performance and education
Status: Non-Profit, Professional
Paid Staff: 12
Volunteer Staff: 75
Paid Artists: 100
Budget: $1.9 Million
Income Sources: Ticket Sales, Tuition, Grants and Donations
Season: June - August
Performs At: Historic landmark auditorium
Annual Attendance: 25,000
Facility Category: Chautauqua Auditorium, Boulder
Seating Capacity: 1,200
Year Built: 1898
Organization Type: Performing

4357
COLORADO SHAKESPEARE FESTIVAL
University of Colorado
1301 Grandview Avenue
277 UCB
Boulder, CO 80309-0277
Phone: 303-492-1527
Fax: 303-735-5140
e-mail: shakes@colorado.edu
Web Site: www.coloradoshakes.org
Management:
  Business Manager: Ray Kemble
  Producing Artistic Director: Timothy Orr
  General Manager: Lynn Nichols
  Business Director: Carrie Howard
  Development: Lissy Garrison
  Marketing: Laima Haley
Mission: To produce an aesthetically challenging mix of both traditional and innovative productions of Shakespeare's plays, as well as other classic and contemporary plays.
Utilizes: Actors; AEA Actors; Commissioned Music; Designers; Guest Accompanists; Guest Designers; Guest Writers; Instructors; Original Music Scores; Resident Professionals; Selected Students; Soloists
Founded: 1958
Specialized Field: Theater
Status: Professional; Nonprofit
Paid Staff: 10
Volunteer Staff: 500
Paid Artists: 150
Budget: $1 Million
Income Sources: Blue Mountain Arts
Season: June 27th - August 17th
Performs At: Mary Rippon Outdoor Theatre, University Mainstage Theatre
Annual Attendance: 41,000
Facility Category: Outdoor Theatre, Indoor Theatre
Type of Stage: Greco-Roman, Proscenium
Seating Capacity: 1,004, 406
Year Built: 1936
Organization Type: Performing

4358
CU COORS EVENTS
Conference Center
University of Colorado
60 West North Temple
Boulder, CO 84150
Phone: 801-240-0075
Fax: 303-492-4801
e-mail: eggertk@spot.colorado.edu
Web Site: www.colorado.edu

SERIES & FESTIVALS / Colorado

Management:
President: Steve Wells
Founded: 1979
Specialized Field: Events Setups; Event Facility
Status: Non-Profit, Non-Professional
Paid Staff: 7

4359
EARLY MUSIC COLORADO FALL FESTIVAL OF EARLY MUSIC
PO Box 19078
Boulder, CO 80308-2078
Phone: 720-304-6255
e-mail: info@earlymusiccolorado.org
Web Site: www.earlymusiccolorado.org
Officers:
President: Heather G. Irons
Ex-Officio: Rebecca Beshore
Vice President: Dan Seger
Management:
President: Heather G Irons
Vice President: Dan Seger
Artistic Director: Frank Nowell
Founded: 1992
Specialized Field: Instrumental; Choral
Status: Nonprofit; Tax-Exempt
Paid Artists: 50
Non-paid Artists: 50
Budget: $10,000
Season: February, May, July, October
Affiliations: Denver Aqmerican Recorder Society
Facility Category: Boulder Public Library
Seating Capacity: 500-700

4360
UNIVERSITY OF COLORADO CONCERTS
302 UCB
University of Colorado
Boulder, CO 80309-0302
Phone: 303-492-8008
Fax: 303-492-5619
e-mail: musictix@colorado.edu
Web Site: www.cuconcerts.org
Officers:
President: Daryl James
Management:
Executive Director: Joan McLean Braun
Marketing Director: Laima Haley
Operations Manager: Nicholas Vocatura
Director of Development: Lissy Garrison
Scheduling and Programs Manager: Myra Jackson
Assistant Director of Development: Mary Jarchow
Box Office Manager: Andrew Metzroth
Graphic Designer: Karen Schuster
Mission: The Artsist Series offers the highest quality emerging and internationally acclaimed soloists and ensembles with related educational programs and residency activities.
Utilizes: Dance Companies; Multimedia; Singers
Founded: 1937
Specialized Field: Series & Festivals; Instrumental Music; Vocal Music; Theatre; Youth; Dance; Ethnic Performances
Status: Non-Profit, Professional
Paid Staff: 5
Performs At: Macky Auditorium

4361
BRECKENRIDGE MUSIC FESTIVAL ORCHESTRA
PO Box 1254
217 S. Ridge Street
Breckenridge, CO 80424
Phone: 970-453-9142
Fax: 970-453-9143
e-mail: bmi@breckenridgemusicfestival.com
Web Site: www.breckenridgemusicfestival.com
Officers:
President: Laura Dziedzic
Treasurer: Wally Ducayet
Secretary: Sue Carver
Management:
Music Director/Conductor: Gerhardt Zimmermann
Executive Director: Marcia Kaufmann
Concertmaster: Nathan Olson
Production Manager: Vito Ciccone
Dir. Of Marketing and Administratio: Olivia Grover
Development Director: Tamara Nuzzaci Park
Stage Manager: Julia Lochra
Mission: The Breckenridge Music Festival's mission is to provide performing arts programs and arts education to the communities of Summit, Park and Lake Counties.
Utilizes: Guest Artists
Founded: 1980
Specialized Field: Jazz, Folk Music; Educational
Status: Professional, Nonprofit
Performs At: Breckenridge Event Tent
Organization Type: Performing; Educational

4362
NATIONAL REPERTORY ORCHESTRA
PO Box 6336
111 S Main Street
Breckenridge, CO 80424
Phone: 970-453-5825
Fax: 970-453-5833
e-mail: info@nromusic.com
Web Site: www.nromusic.com
Officers:
Past President: Kate Taucher
President: Barbara Vonderheid
Vice President: Michael Bruggeman
Secretary: Nancy French
Treasurer: Kyle Richardson
Management:
Music Director: Carl Topilow
Director of Marketing & Development: Julie Chandler
Artistic & Operations Director: Cecile L. Forsberg
Patron Relations Manager: Kathleen Clabby
Office Manager: Tara Sieber
Mission: Education and performance.
Specialized Field: Orchestra
Paid Staff: 16
Volunteer Staff: 35
Budget: $260,000-1,050,000
Performs At: Riverwalk Center at Breckenridge
Facility Category: Amphitheater
Seating Capacity: 750

4363
COLORADO COLLEGE DANCE FESTIVAL
261 UCB
Colorado Springs, CO 80309-0261
Phone: 303-492-7355
Fax: 303-492-7722
Toll-free: 877-894-8727
e-mail: summerdance@coloradocollege.edu
Web Site: www.ArtsFestival.ColoradoCollege.edu/dancefestival
Officers:
Department Chair: Bud Coleman
Associate Chair / Director, Dance: Michelle Ellsworth
Management:
Festival Director: Patrizia Herminjard
PR Director: Clay Evans
Marketing Director: Laima Haley
Marketing and PR Coordinator: Daniel Leonard
Mission: To support dance education and performance by fostering a creative environment where all dancers, including students and members of the community, can come together to cultivate and discover the intrinsic value of the many facets of dance. We do this by providing a variety of training in diverse forms across the discipline of dance.
Utilizes: Guest Composers; Guest Musical Directors; Multimedia; Original Music Scores
Founded: 2001
Specialized Field: Dance
Status: Non-Profit, Professional
Paid Staff: 3
Volunteer Staff: 5
Paid Artists: 16
Budget: $50,000
Income Sources: Internal and Private Funding
Season: June 25-July 16
Performs At: Large Theater
Affiliations: Colorado Dance Alliance
Annual Attendance: 60class/1200perfor
Facility Category: Dance Studio
Type of Stage: Marley
Seating Capacity: 750
Year Built: 1975

4364
COLORADO SPRINGS FINE ARTS CENTER PERFORMING ARTS SERIES
30 West Dale Street
Colorado Springs, CO 80903
Phone: 719-643-5583
Fax: 719-634-0570
e-mail: rgeers@aol.com
Officers:
Chair: Jim Raughton
Vice Chair: Ann Winslow
Treasurer: Kimberley Sherwood
Secretary: Kate Faricy
Management:
Executive Director: Fran Holden
Executive Director: Fran Holden
Deputy Director: Nancy Sullivan
Performs At: Theatre
Seating Capacity: 450

4365
CRESTED BUTTE CHAMBER MUSIC FESTIVAL
PO Box 2117
Crested Butte, CO 81224
Phone: 970-349-0619
Fax: 970-349-0620
e-mail: alexander@mycbmf.com
Web Site: crestedbuttemusicfestival.com
Officers:
President: Paul Witt
Vice-President: Stephanie Seymour
Treasurer: Clyde Wyant
Assistant Treasurer: Anne Ronai
Secretary: Danek Bienkowski

SERIES & FESTIVALS / Colorado

Management:
   Festival Director: Alexander Scheirle
   Director of Development: Kim Carroll Bosler
   Director of Marketing and Comm: Susan Gellert
   Director of Operations: Crista Ryan
   Director of Artistic Admin-Opera: Mark Moorman
Specialized Field: Instrumental; Choral; Folk; Ethnic

4366
CHERRY CREEK ARTS FESTIVAL
2 Steele Street
Suite B-100
Denver, CO 80206
Phone: 303-355-2787
Fax: 303-355-2788
e-mail: management@cherryarts.org
Web Site: www.cherryarts.org
Officers:
   President/CEO: Terry Adams
   Chair: Dave Dixon
   Chair Elect: Stacia Freimuth
   Secretary / Treasurer: Michael Smith
Management:
   Executive Director: Terry Adams
   Associate Director: Tara Brickell
   Marketing & Operations Director: Tony Smith
Utilizes: Dance Companies; Dancers; Fine Artists; Instructors; Multimedia; Original Music Scores; Sign Language Translators; Singers; Theatre Companies; Touring Companies
Founded: 1990
Specialized Field: Instrumental; Folk; Dance; Theatre
Status: Non-Profit
Paid Staff: 8
Volunteer Staff: 800
Non-paid Artists: 200
Budget: $60,000-$150,000
Season: July
Performs At: Cherry Creek North Business District (Festival Site)
Annual Attendance: 350,000
Facility Category: Outdoor
Stage Dimensions: 24'x 32'; 20'x16'; 20'x16'
Seating Capacity: 3,000; 1,000; 450

4367
COLORADO COUNCIL ON THE ARTS
1625 Broadway
Suite 2700
Denver, CO 80202
Phone: 303-892-3870
Fax: 303-894-2615
e-mail: coloarts@state.co.us
Web Site: www.coloarts.state.co.us
Officers:
   Chairman: Donald K Bain
Management:
   Program Administrator: Barbara Schaffer
   Executive Director: Elaine Mariner
   Associate Director: Maryo Ewell
   Animating Democracy Co-director: Pam Korza
Mission: To stimulate arts development in the state, to assist and encourage artists and arts organizations, and to help make the arts more accessible statewide.
Founded: 1967
Specialized Field: Visual; Performing; Literary Arts.
Status: Professional; Nonprofit; State Agency
Paid Staff: 7
Budget: $1,900,000
Income Sources: Annual State Appropriation; Federal Grants; Foundation Grants
Affiliations: National Endowment for the Arts; Western States Arts Federation; National Association of Local Arts Agencies

Organization Type: Sponsoring; Grant Making

4368
MUSIC IN THE MOUNTAINS CLASSICAL MUSIC FESTIVAL
1063 Main Avenue
Durango, CO 81301
Phone: 970-385-6820
Fax: 970-382-0982
e-mail: info@musicinthemountains.com
Web Site: www.musicinthemountains.com
Officers:
   President: John Anderson
   President Elect: Mary Barter
   Past President: Terry Bacon
   Treasurer: Steve Short
   Secretary & Education Committee Cha: Gordon Thomas
Management:
   President: John Anderson
   Festival Artistic Director: Greg Hustis
   Music Director And Condutor: Guillermo Figueroa
   Conservatory Artistic Director: Arkady Fomin
   Executive Director: Angela Beach
   Operations Manager: Julie Brown
   Program & Education Manager: Amber Neumann
   Accounting Manager: Cory Jameson
Mission: To produce an exceptional summer music festival with musicians of the highest caliber, entertain, educate and delight audiences with the richness of classical music, and complement concerts with educational programs.
Utilizes: Community Talent; Contract Orchestras; Educators; Guest Accompanists; Guest Companies; Guest Composers; Guest Musical Directors; Guest Musicians; High School Drama; Multimedia; Music; Original Music Scores; Soloists; Students
Founded: 1987
Specialized Field: Series and Festivals: Classical Music and Conservatory for Children
Status: Non-Profit, Professional
Paid Staff: 3
Volunteer Staff: 100
Paid Artists: 200
Non-paid Artists: 100
Budget: $700,000
Income Sources: Individual Donations, Foundations, Corporate Sponsors, Ticket Sales
Season: July - August
Performs At: Durango Mountain Resort (Festival Tent Site), Community Concert Hall, and more than 6 other venues throughout Durango & SW CO
Facility Category: Tent
Seating Capacity: 50-640

4369
ROCKY RIDGE MUSIC CENTER
465 Longs Peak Road
Estes Park, CO 80517-1790
Phone: 970-586-4031
Fax: 970-586-6685
e-mail: info@rockyridge.org
Web Site: www.rockyridge.org
Officers:
   Founder: Beth Miller Harrod
   President: Madison Casey
   VP: Miriam Reitz Baer
Management:
   President: Norman Taulu
   Music Director: Carina Voly
   Assistant Music Director: Connie G Cook
Mission: To offer summer programs of conservatory-level music training for young people, with emphasis on Youth Orchestra, young pianists, chamber music and composition; to offer this program simultaneously with the summer concert series, Music in the Mountains.
Utilizes: Artists-in-Residence; Guest Artists; Multimedia
Founded: 1942
Specialized Field: Series & Festivals: Instrumental Music
Status: Non-Profit, Professional
Paid Staff: 4
Annual Attendance: 300
Facility Category: Log cabins - historical
Seating Capacity: 150
Year Built: 1900
Year Remodeled: 1990
Organization Type: Performing; Educational

4370
SUMMIT JAZZ SWINGING JAZZ CONCERTS
PO Box 1150
Evergreen, CO 80437-1150
Phone: 303-670-8471
Fax: 360-379-8811
e-mail: info@summitjazz.org
Web Site: www.summitjazz.org
Officers:
   President: Alan P Frederickson
   Secretary/Treasurer: Juanita P Greenwood
Management:
   President: Alan P Frederic
   Secretary and Treasurer: Juanita P Green
Mission: to foster awareness and appreciation of traditional jazz through public concert performances by internationally recognized artists who have earned their reputation as dedicated exponents of this musical genre.

4371
MESA COUNTY COMMUNITY CONCERT ASSOCIATION
P.O. Box 4615
#801
Grand Junction, CO 81502
Phone: 970-243-1979
e-mail: mcca@acsol.net
Web Site: mesacountyconcertassociation.org
Officers:
   Secretary: Jackie Porter
Management:
   President: Jerry A M Brosier
   Stage Manager: Jonathan Jones
Founded: 1944
Specialized Field: Series and Festivals: National and International Concerts
Status: Non-Profit, Professional
Paid Artists: 6
Performs At: Grand Junction High School Auditorium

4372
LOVELAND FRIENDS OF CHAMBER MUSIC
1000 King Drive
Loveland, CO 80537
Phone: 970-663-7928
e-mail: frhale@msn.com
Management:
   President: Ruth J Hale
Founded: 1995
Specialized Field: Series & Festivals; Instrumental Music; Vocal Music; Youth; Chamber Music
Status: Non-Profit, Professional
Paid Artists: 25
Performs At: Private Homes

SERIES & FESTIVALS / Connecticut

4373
MUSIC IN OURAY
PO Box 145
Ouray, CO 81427
Phone: 970-626-5506
Fax: 970-626-4341
e-mail: ouray@ouraycolorado.com
Web Site: www.musicinouray.com
Management:
  Director: Soozie Arnold
Specialized Field: Instrumental
Budget: $35,000 - 60,000
Season: Early June
Performs At: [Festival Site]
Facility Category: Wright Opera House, Ouray
Seating Capacity: 200

4374
SANGRE DE CRISTO ARTS AND CONFERENCE CENTER
210 N Santa Fe Avenue
Pueblo, CO 81003
Phone: 719-295-7200
Fax: 719-295-7222
e-mail: mail@sdc-arts.org
Web Site: www.sdc-arts.org
Officers:
  Chair: Carol Spradley
  Treasurer: Roxy Pignanelli
  Secretary: Erin Hergert
  Vice Chair/ Chair-Elect: Rob Redwine
Management:
  Intirim Executive Director: Jim Richerson
  Associate Director: Jennifer Cook
  Technical Director: Timothy F Gately
  Controller: Rochelle Spoone
  Artistic Director of Dance: Stephen Wynne
Founded: 1972
Specialized Field: Dance; Vocal Music; Instrumental Music; Theater; Festivals; Lyric Opera
Status: Professional; Nonprofit
Paid Staff: 40

4375
TELLURIDE CHAMBER MUSIC FESTIVAL
324 W. Colorado Avenue
Telluride, CO 81435
Phone: 877-358-7122
Fax: 866-366-2329
Toll-free: 800-525-3455
e-mail: chambermusictelluride@yahoo.com
Web Site: www.telluride.com/chamber.html
Officers:
  President: Kay Langstraff
Management:
  Founder/Co-Director: Roy Malan
  Co-Director: Robin Sutherland
Mission: Talented musicians visit our area each year and enrich us with their musical mastery.
Founded: 1973
Specialized Field: Instrumental
Status: Professional
Budget: $10,000
Income Sources: Individual Donations, Grants, Telluride Foundation
Season: August
Performs At: Telluride; Festival Site
Facility Category: Sheridan Opera House
Seating Capacity: 240

4376
TELLURIDE JAZZ CELEBRATION
Telluride Society for Jazz
PO Box 2132
Telluride, CO 81435
Phone: 970-728-7009
Fax: 970-728-5834
e-mail: info@telluridejazz.org
Web Site: www.telluridejazz.com
Officers:
  Treasurer: Fred Williams
  Secretary: Chris Vann
Management:
  President: John Burchmore
  Executive Producer: Paul Machado
  Director of Sales & Marketing: Adam Smith
Mission: Jazz music
Founded: 1977
Specialized Field: Series & Festivals: Music festival.
Status: Non-Profit, Professional
Paid Staff: 1
Volunteer Staff: 125
Paid Artists: 40
Non-paid Artists: 60
Budget: $300,000
Seating Capacity: 3,000

4377
ACADEMY CONCERTS
USAFA/34TRW/SDAE
2302 Cadet Drive, Suite 12
USAF Academy, CO 80840-6099
Phone: 719-333-4497
Fax: 719-333-4597
Management:
  Cultural Arts/Entertainment Directo: Candyce Thomas
Mission: To offer the Cadet Wing cultural enhancements, entertaining rock concerts, and comedians; to offer our military personnel and community cultural events.
Founded: 1959
Specialized Field: Series & Festivals: Instrumental Music
Status: Non-Profit, Professional
Paid Staff: 4
Performs At: Arnold Hall Theater
Annual Attendance: 28,000
Facility Category: Theater; Concert Hall
Type of Stage: Proscenium
Seating Capacity: 2,809
Year Built: 1957
Year Remodeled: 1999

4378
BRAVO! VAIL VALLEY MUSIC FESTIVAL
PO Box 2270
Vail, CO 81658
Phone: 970-827-5700
Fax: 970-827-5707
Toll-free: 877-827-5700
e-mail: bravo@vail.net
Web Site: www.vailmusicfestival.org
Officers:
  Chair: Russell Molina
  Treasurer: Dan Godec
  Secretary: Betsy Wiegers
Management:
  Executive Director: James Palermo
  Artistic Director: Anne-Marie McDermott
Utilizes: Artists-in-Residence; Commissioned Music; Guest Companies; Guest Composers; Guest Directors; Guest Musicians; Guest Writers; Soloists
Founded: 1987
Specialized Field: Vocal Music: Classical
Status: Non-Profit, Professional
Paid Staff: 25
Budget: $2,000,000
Season: June - August
Performs At: Venues throughout Vail, Beaver Creek (Festival Site)
Annual Attendance: 48,000
Seating Capacity: 2,500; 250

4379
VAIL JAZZ FESTIVAL
953 S. Frontage Road West
Suite 106
Vail, CO 81657
Mailing Address: PO Box 3035 Vail, CO 81658
Phone: 970-479-6146
Fax: 970-477-0866
Toll-free: 800-824-5526
e-mail: operations@vailjazz.org
Web Site: www.vailjazz.org
Officers:
  Chairman: Howard L Stone
Management:
  Executive Director: Robin Litt
  Education Director: John Clayton Jr
  Development Manager: Owen Hutchinson
  Operations Coordinator: Christin Fergus-Jean
Mission: Dedicated to the perpetuation of jazz through the presentation of jazz performances and jazz education, with special emphasis on young musicians and young audiences.
Founded: 1995
Status: Non-Profit,Professional

4380
JAZZ IN THE SANGRES
PO Box 327
Westcliffe, CO 81252
Phone: 303-794-4170
e-mail: design@creativeminds.com
Web Site: www.custerguide.com/jazz

4381
WESTMINSTER COMMUNITY ARTIST SERIES
4476 W 68th Ave
Westminster, CO 80030
Phone: 303-429-1999
Fax: 303-469-4599
e-mail: http://www.nmarts.net
Management:
  President: Patrick Payne
  Executive Director: Dona Waddell
Mission: To bring world class visual and performing artists to audiences in the Westminster Area.
Utilizes: Singers
Founded: 1983
Specialized Field: Performing Arts
Status: Non-Profit, Non-Professional
Organization Type: Performing

Connecticut

4382
GREAT CONNECTICUT JAZZ FEST
3 Colony St.
Suite 301
Branford, CT 06450

SERIES & FESTIVALS / Connecticut

Phone: 203-235-7901
Fax: 203-481-2603
Toll-free: 800-468-3836
e-mail: ct.traditional.jazz@snet.net
Web Site: www.ctjazz.org
Officers:
   Chamber President: S,an W. Moore
   Vice President: Rosanne P. Ford
   Office Assistant: Darlene Belanger
Founded: 1985
Specialized Field: Dixieland Jazz; Swing Jazz
Volunteer Staff: 375
Paid Artists: 138
Non-paid Artists: 46
Annual Attendance: 10,000
Facility Category: Tent

4383
ASTON MAGNA FOUNDATION
P.O. Box 28
Danbury, CT 01230
Phone: 413-528-3595
Fax: 203-744-7244
Toll-free: 800-875-7156
e-mail: astonmagna@optonline.net
Web Site: www.astonmagna.org
Officers:
   Chair: Catherine Liddell
   Treasurer: Robert S. Strassler
   Secretary: Stephen Pearlman
Management:
   Artistic Director: Daniel Stepner
   Acadmey Director: Raymond Erickson
   Executive Director: Susan B. Obel
   Artistic Administrator: Joseph Orchard
   Artistic Director: John Hsu
Mission: The mission of the Aston Magna Foundation is to enrich the appreciation of music of the past and the understanding of the cultural, political and social contexts in which it was composed and experienced.
Utilizes: Educators
Founded: 1972
Specialized Field: Chamber; Early Music
Status: Professional, Nonprofit
Paid Staff: 4
Volunteer Staff: 6
Income Sources: Massachusetts Cultural Council; Grants
Season: July-August
Performs At: St James Church Festival in Great Barrington, Daniel Arts Center at Simon's Rock College
Organization Type: Performing; Touring; Educational; Sponsoring

4384
GOODSPEED OPERA HOUSE
6 Main Street
PO Box A
East Haddam, CT 06423
Mailing Address: PO Box A, East Haddam, CT 06423-0281
Phone: 860-873-8664
Fax: 860-873-2329
e-mail: info@goodspeed.org
Web Site: www.goodspeed.org
Officers:
   Chairman: Francis G. Adams Jr.
   President: John Wolter
   Vice President: Jeffrey S. Hoffman
   First Vice President: Robert Landino
   Treasurer: Mark Masselli
Management:
   President: John Wolter
   General Manager: Hattie Guin Kittner
   Associate Producer: Sue Frost
Founded: 1963
Specialized Field: Series and Festivals: Musicals
Status: Non-Profit, Professional
Performs At: Goodspeed Opera House; Goodspeed-at-Chester
Type of Stage: Proscenium; Adaptable Proscenium
Seating Capacity: 400; 200

4385
ENFIELD CULTURAL ARTS COMMISSION
19 North Main Street
Enfield, CT 06422
Phone: 860-253-6421
Fax: 860-253-5147
Officers:
   Chairman: Priscilla D McManus
Management:
   President: Theresa Jedyniak
Specialized Field: Series and Festivals Instrumental Music; Vocal Music; Theatre; Youth; Dance; Ethnic Performances
Status: Non-Profit, Non-Professional

4386
HOT STEAMED JAZZ FESTIVAL
Valley Railroad
PO Box 293
Essex, CT 06426
Phone: 860-767-3968
Fax: 860-767-3968
Toll-free: 800-348-0003
e-mail: info@hotsteamedjazz.com
Web Site: www.hotsteamedjazz.com
Officers:
   President: Shirley Bombaci
   Tresurer: Nina Sulinski
   Secretary: Beth Fitzsimmons
   Vice President: Bob Brummett
Management:
   President: Shirley Bombaci
   Artistic Director: Richard Moore
   Band Contact: Dick Moore
Mission: Providing good jazz for the Whole in the Wall Camp.
Founded: 1992
Specialized Field: Series & Festivals; Instrumental Music; Vocal Music; Youth; Dance; Ethnic Performances; Traditional jazz
Status: Non-Profit, Non-Professional
Volunteer Staff: 30
Paid Artists: 50
Budget: $35,000
Income Sources: Ticket Sales; Donations
Annual Attendance: 22,000

4387
CHESTNUT HILL CONCERTS
PO Box 183
Guilford, CT 06437
Phone: 203-245-5736
e-mail: ads@chestnuthillconcerts.org
Web Site: www.shorelinearts.org
Officers:
   President: David A. Rackey
Management:
   Owner: William Donald
   Artistic Director: Ronald Thomas
   Managing Director: Vincent P. Oneppo
   Bookkeeper: Paula Raggio
Mission: Brings world-class chamber music to the shoreline at the Katharine Hepburn Cultural Arts Center in Old Saybrook on the first four Fridays of August
Founded: 1969
Specialized Field: Instrumental
Paid Staff: 1
Budget: $10,000
Season: August
Performs At: Madison, CT (Festival Site)
Facility Category: First Congregational Church of Madison
Seating Capacity: 500

4388
SHORELINE ARTS ALLIANCE
725 Boston Post Road
Guilford, CT 06437
Phone: 203-453-3890
Fax: 203-453-0611
e-mail: info@shorelinearts.org
Web Site: www.shorelinearts.org
Officers:
   President: Julie McClenan
   VP: Deborah Abildsoe
   Treasurer: Armand Rossi
Management:
   Program Coordinator: Donita Aruny
   Administrative Coordinator: Jennifer Zeliff Kearney
Mission: A performance and service organization offering juried competitions for artists, photographers and writers; student scholarships within the local region; and a performance series.
Utilizes: Touring Companies
Status: Nonprofit
Budget: $100,000
Income Sources: Grants; Foundations; Memberships
Resident Groups: Connecticut Commission on the Arts

4389
FIRST NIGHT HARTFORD
1028 Boulevard
#323
Hartford, CT 06119
Phone: 860-727-0050
Fax: 860-722-9627
e-mail: info@firstnighthartford.org
Web Site: www.firstnighthartford.com
Management:
   President: James Gordon
   Executive Director: Pamela Amodio
Mission: Offering downtown Hartford an alcohol-free New Year's Eve celebration.
Utilizes: Singers
Founded: 1988
Specialized Field: Series & Festivals: Produce Arts Festival
Status: Non-Profit, Professional
Paid Staff: 1
Volunteer Staff: 200
Paid Artists: 30
Budget: $250,000
Income Sources: Corporate Sponsorships; Foundation Grants; Admissions
Season: December - January
Performs At: Downtown Hartford (Festival Site)
Annual Attendance: 30,000
Organization Type: Performing

4390
TALCOTT MOUNTAIN MUSIC FESTIVAL, SUMMER SERIES
Hartford Symphony
100 Pearl Street 2nd Floor, East Tower
Hartford, CT 06103

SERIES & FESTIVALS / Connecticut

Phone: 860-246-8742
Fax: 860-247-1720
e-mail: info@hartfordsymphony.org
Web Site: www.hartfordsymphony.org
Officers:
   President: Carrie Hammond
   VP Finance: Thomas R Wildman, Esquire
   VP Marketing: Robinson A Grover
   VP Administration: John H Beers
   Chairman: James S. Remis
   Vice Chairman: Mark Mandell
Management:
   President & CEO: David Fay
   Executive Director: Charles Owens
   Artistic Director: Edward Cumming
Utilizes: Actors; Collaborating Artists; Collaborations; Commissioned Composers; Commissioned Music; Composers-in-Residence; Dancers; Five Seasonal Concerts; Grant Writers; Guest Accompanists; Guest Companies; Guest Composers; Guest Lecturers; Guest Musical Directors; Guest Musicians; Instructors; Lyricists; Multi Collaborations; Multimedia; Original Music Scores; Sign Language Translators; Singers; Theatre Companies
Founded: 1944
Specialized Field: Instrumental
Status: Non-Profit, Professional
Paid Staff: 178
Paid Artists: 178
Season: July
Performs At: Simsbury (Festival Site); Iron Horse Boulevard; Simsbury
Annual Attendance: 21,300

4391
WOODLAND CONCERT SERIES
10 Woodland Street
Hartford, CT 06105
Phone: 860-527-8121
Fax: 860-293-1404
e-mail: immanvel@iccucc.org
Web Site: www.woodlandconcertseries.org
Management:
   Artistic Director: Edward Tyler
   Managing Director: Deborah Flower
   Director of Music: Mark Singleton
Utilizes: Collaborating Artists; Commissioned Music; Guest Accompanists; Guest Companies; Guest Directors; Guest Instructors; Guest Musicians; Guest Soloists; Instructors; Local Artists; Multimedia; Music; Organization Contracts; Original Music Scores; Playwrights; Singers; Soloists
Performs At: Immanuel Congregational Church
Seating Capacity: 700

4392
MUSIC MOUNTAIN
PO Box 738
Lakeville, CT 06039
Phone: 860-824-7126
Fax: 860-364-2090
e-mail: boxoffice@musicmountain.org
Web Site: www.musicmountain.org
Officers:
   President: Nicholas Gordon
Mission: To provide professional chamber music to western Connecticut through a Summer Chamber Music Festival, as well as broadcasts to over 200 radio stations and 220 foriegn countries.
Utilizes: Guest Musical Directors; Multimedia; Original Music Scores
Founded: 1930
Specialized Field: Series and Festivals: Chamber Music
Status: Non-Profit, Professional
Paid Staff: 1
Volunteer Staff: 30
Paid Artists: 150
Income Sources: Ticket Sales; Donations; Bequests; Foundations; Government Grants
Season: June - September
Performs At: Gordon Hall; Falls Village
Annual Attendance: 10,000
Facility Category: Colonial Concert Hall
Stage Dimensions: 18'x36'
Seating Capacity: 344
Year Built: 1930
Rental Contact: President Nicholas Gordon
Organization Type: Performing; Educational; Sponsoring

4393
LITCHFIELD JAZZ FESTIVAL
174 W Street
PO Box 69
Litchfield, CT 06759
Phone: 860-361-6285
Fax: 860-361-6288
Management:
   Executive Director: Vita West Muir
   PR & Marketing Director ?: Lindsey Turner
   Assistant Director / Project Manage: Karen Simpson
   Beliveau: Matthew

4394
LITCHFIELD PERFORMING ARTS SERIES
40 W Street
PO Box 69
Litchfield, CT 06759
Phone: 860-361-6285
Fax: 860-361-6288
e-mail: lpai@ct1.nai.net
Management:
   Executive Director: Vita West Muir
   PR & Marketing Director ?: Lindsey Turner
   Assistant Director / Project Manage: Karen Simpson
   Beliveau: Matthew
Performs At: Church

4395
SILVERMINE GUILD ART CENTER SERIES
1037 Silvermine Road
New Canaan, CT 06840
Phone: 203-966-9700
Fax: 203-966-2763
e-mail: sgac@silvermineart.org
Web Site: www.silvermineart.org
Officers:
   Chair: Roger Mudre
   Co-Vice-Chairs: Leslie Giuliani
   Secretary: Marcia Harris
   Treasurer: LaVern Burton
Management:
   Executive Director: Leslee Asch
   Program Director: Carol Nordgren
Mission: Arts, education and appreciation.
Utilizes: Collaborations; Curators; Educators; Fine Artists; Guest Accompanists; Guest Ensembles; Guest Instructors; Guest Musical Directors; Guest Musicians; Guest Soloists; Guest Teachers; Guest Writers; Instructors; Local Artists; Lyricists; Multi Collaborations; Multimedia; Original Music Scores; Playwrights; Singers; Soloists; Touring Companies
Founded: 1922
Specialized Field: Visual Art; Concerts
Status: Non-Profit, Professional
Paid Staff: 15
Volunteer Staff: 15
Budget: $1.6 Million
Income Sources: Tuition; Private Donations; Art Sales
Performs At: Multi-Purpose
Facility Category: Galleries; Auditorium
Seating Capacity: 125
Year Remodeled: 2000

4396
INTERNATIONAL FESTIVAL OF ARTS & IDEAS
195 Church Street
12th Floor
New Haven, CT 06510
Phone: 203-498-1212
Fax: 203-498-2106
Toll-free: 888-278-4332
e-mail: chedstrom@artidea.org
Web Site: www.artidea.org
Management:
   Program Director: Cynthia Hedstrom
Specialized Field: Instrumental; Dance; Theatre; Childrens'; Ethnic
Season: June - July

4397
NEW HAVEN JAZZ FESTIVAL
New Haven Festivals
165 Church Street
New Haven, CT 06510
Mailing Address: P.O. Box 2964, New Haven, CT 06515
Phone: 203-946-7821
Fax: 203-946-5750
e-mail: info@newhavenjazz.com
Web Site: www.newhavenjazz.com
Officers:
   President and Director: Craig O'Connell
   Vice President and Director: Dave Johnson
   Treasurer and Director: Rick Mayer
   Secretary and Director: Cynthia Morrill
Management:
   Director: Barbara Lamb
Founded: 1982
Specialized Field: Music

4398
CONNECTICUT COLLEGE: ON STAGE
270 Mohegan Avenue
PO Box 5216
New London, CT 06320-4196
Phone: 860-439-2787
Fax: 860-439-2695
e-mail: onstage@conncoll.edu
Web Site: www.onstage.conncoll.edu
Management:
   Director: Robert A Richter
Mission: To present a varied annual series of the world's great performing artists thereby enriching and enhancing the cultural life of our community.
Founded: 1939
Specialized Field: Series and Festivals Instrumental Music; Theatre; Dance; Vocal Music
Status: Professional; Non-Profit
Paid Staff: 2
Budget: $139,000
Performs At: Palmer Auditorium; Evans Hall
Organization Type: Performing; Presenting

SERIES & FESTIVALS / Connecticut

4399
CONNECTICUT EARLY MUSIC FESTIVAL
PO Box 329
New London, CT 06320
Phone: 860-444-2419
Web Site: www.ctearlymusic.org
Officers:
  President: John P. Anthony
  Vice President: Wendy W. Schnur
  Secretary: Priscilla Bollard Wilder
  Treasurer: Archie C. Swindell
Management:
  Artistic Director: Eric Rice
  Executive Director: Patrica Ann Neely
Mission: To provide performances of music from the 16th-19th centuries on period instruments.
Utilizes: Guest Artists
Founded: 1983
Specialized Field: Instrumental
Status: Professional; Nonprofit
Season: Mid June
Performs At: New London; Noank; Niantic; Waterford
Seating Capacity: 125; 500
Organization Type: Performing

4400
SUMMER MUSIC
6300 College Station
Suite 400
New London, CT 04011-8463
Phone: 207-373-1400
Fax: 207-373-1441
Toll-free: 855-832-3393
e-mail: info@bowdoinfestival.org
Web Site: www.summer-music.org
Officers:
  Chairman: James T. Morgan
  Vice Chairman: Beatrice Francais
  Treasurer: Peter Griffin
  Secretary: William Rogers, Jr.,
Management:
  Executive Director: Peter Simmons
  Chairman: Raymond Johnson
  Director: Lewis Kaplan
  Director of Development: Kippy Rudy
  Director of Admissions: Jennifer G. Means
  Financial Officer: Brittan Pistole
  Admissions Assistant: Leah Paris
Founded: 1983
Specialized Field: Music festivals
Status: Non-Profit, Professional
Paid Staff: 2

4401
NEWTOWN FRIENDS OF MUSIC
PO Box 295
Newtown, CT 06470-0295
Phone: 203-426-6470
Fax: 203-426-4587
e-mail: comments@newtownfriendsofmusic.org
Web Site: www.newtownfriendsofmusic.org
Officers:
  President: Ellen K Parrella
  Vice-President: Robert L Shohet
  Secretary: William C Timmel
  Treasurer: Dorothea S LaBelle
Mission: To present exquisite-superbly performed
Utilizes: Artists-in-Residence; Multimedia; Original Music Scores
Founded: 1978
Specialized Field: Series & Festivals; Instrumental Music; Chamber Music; Recitals; Chamber Orchestra
Status: Non-Profit, Professional

Volunteer Staff: 16
Paid Artists: 22
Performs At: Edmond Town Hall
Annual Attendance: 2,500
Seating Capacity: 450

4402
NORFOLK CHAMBER MUSIC FESTIVAL/YALE SUMMER SCHOOL OF MUSIC
Ellen Battell Stoeckel Estate
Route 44 & 272
Norfolk, CT 06058
Mailing Address: P.O. Box 545, Norfolk, CT 06058-0545
Phone: 860-542-3000
Fax: 860-542-3004
e-mail: norfolk@yale.edu
Web Site: www.yale.edu/norfolk
Management:
  Director: Paul Hawkhaw
  General Manager: James Nelson
  Associate Manager: Deanne Chin
  Operations and Administrative Assoc: Donna Yoo
Founded: 1941
Specialized Field: Series and Festivals: Chamber Music
Status: Non-Profit, Professional
Paid Staff: 12
Paid Artists: 40

4403
PROJECT TROUBADOR
374 Taconic Road
Salisbury, CT 06068
Phone: 860-435-0561
Fax: 860-435-0561
e-mail: louise@projecttroubador.org
Web Site: www.projecttroubador.org
Management:
  Executive Director: Louise Lindenmeyr
  Artistic Director: Eliot Osborn
Mission: Music, theatre and humor are powerful universal vehicles of communication yet there is little opportunity for cross-cultural sharing to take place on a person-to-person level around the world. Project Troubador is unique in its fulfillment of this need-offering a way for both performing artists and audiences to meet on common ground in celebration.
Founded: 1978
Specialized Field: National Development/Performance
Status: Non-Profit, Professional
Paid Staff: 2
Paid Artists: 75

4404
FALCON RIDGE FOLK FESTIVAL
POB 144
Sharon, CT 06069
Phone: 860-364-2138
Fax: 860-364-4678
e-mail: anne@falconridgefolk.com
Web Site: www.falconridgefolk.com
Officers:
  Executive Director: Howard Randall
Management:
  Artistic Director: Anne Saunders
  Executive Director: Howard Randall
  Vendor Coordinator: Leslie Sullivan Sachs
Utilizes: High School Drama; Multimedia; Original Music Scores; Playwrights; Selected Students; Sign Language Translators; Students

Founded: 1988
Specialized Field: Folk Music; Dance
Paid Staff: 5/6/
Paid Artists: 50
Income Sources: Ticket Sales
Performs At: Long Hill Farm
Affiliations: National Folk Alliance; International Bluegrass; Americana Music Association
Annual Attendance: 10-15,000
Facility Category: Corporation

4405
NORTHWEST CORNER YOUNG ARTISTS SERIES
18 Old Sharon Road
#3
Sharon, CT 06069
Phone: 860-364-0253
Management:
  Artistic Director: DeeAnne Hunstien
Performs At: Private Homes

4406
CENTENNIAL THEATER FESTIVAL
2300 Lonsdale Avenue
Simsbury, CT 06070
Phone: 604-983-6450
Fax: 604-983-6463
e-mail: ctcboxoffice@northvanrec.com
Management:
  Artistic Director: Dean Adams
  Theatre Operations and Publicity: Kristin Fraser
  Technical Supervisor: Matt Frankish
  Technical Supervisor: Stuart McArthur
  Front of House Supervisor: Agnes Mendoza
  Box Office Operations: Arianna McGregor
Utilizes: Actors; AEA Actors; Dance Companies; Dancers; Designers; Grant Writers; Guest Accompanists; Guest Artists; Guest Conductors; Guest Designers; Guest Lecturers; Multimedia; Music; Original Music Scores; Resident Professionals; Student Interns; Theatre Companies
Founded: 1990
Specialized Field: Festival
Status: Nonprofit
Season: June 11 - August 1
Annual Attendance: 8,000
Facility Category: Theater; Air Conditioned, Handicap Access
Type of Stage: Proscenium
Stage Dimensions: 29' x 35'
Seating Capacity: 400
Year Built: 1989

4407
CONNECTICUT THEATER FESTIVAL
700 North Salem Road
Simsbury, CT 06877
Phone: 860-651-6329
Fax: 860-408-5301
e-mail: ctfestival@hotmail.com
Web Site: www.ctfestival.com
Officers:
  President: Bill Prenetta
  Vice President: Sherry Cox
  Secretary: Ethan Warner
  Treasurer: Lenore Grunko
Management:
  Producing Artistic Director: Dean Adams
Utilizes: Actors; AEA Actors; Dance Companies; Dancers; Designers; Grant Writers; Guest Accompanists; Guest Artists; Guest Conductors; Guest

Designers; Guest Lecturers; Multimedia; Music; Original Music Scores; Resident Professionals; Student Interns; Theatre Companies
Founded: 1990
Status: Nonprofit
Season: June 11 - August 1
Annual Attendance: 8,000
Facility Category: Theater; Air Conditioned; Handicap Access
Type of Stage: Proscenium
Stage Dimensions: 29' x 35'
Seating Capacity: 400
Year Built: 1989

4408
STRATFORD FESTIVAL THEATER
1850 Elm Street
P.O. Box 520
Stratford, CT 06615
Phone: 203-378-1200
Fax: 203-378-9777
Management:
    Dramaturg: J Wishnia
Founded: 1996

4409
ARMSTRONG CHAMBER CONCERTS
29 Hemlock Hill Road
PO Box 367
Washington Depot, CT 06759
Phone: 860-868-0522
Fax: 860-868-0522
e-mail: accnct@aol.com
Web Site: www.accnct.org
Officers:
    President/Treasurer: Helen Armstrong
    VP: Ajit Hutheesing
    Secretary: Greta Pofcher
    Secretary: Ann Wade
    Secretary: Suzanne Geiss-Robbins
Management:
    President: Helen Armstrong
    Operations Manager: Kathie Plaskiewicz
    Grant Writer: Carol Mallquist
Mission: To provide concerts of professional chamber music to diverse audiences.
Utilizes: Artists-in-Residence; Collaborations; Guest Accompanists; Guest Musical Directors; Guest Musicians; Multimedia; Original Music Scores; Singers
Founded: 1983
Specialized Field: Series & Festivals; Instrumental Music; Chamber Music
Status: Non-Profit; Professional
Paid Staff: 2
Paid Artists: 15
Income Sources: Grants; Donations; Box Office
Performs At: Litchfield
Affiliations: Chamber Music America; Ulenfield Hills Visitors Bureau; American Symphony League
Annual Attendance: 5-6,000
Organization Type: Performing; Touring; Resident; Educational

4410
HARTT SCHOOL CONCERT SERIES
200 Bloomfield Avenue
West Hartford, CT 06117
Phone: 860-768-4454
Fax: 860-768-4441
e-mail: jessilevi@hartford.edu
Web Site: www.hartford.edu/hartt
Management:
    Dean: Aaron A. Flagg
    Executive Director: Michael Yaffe
    Executive Assistant to the Dean: Philip Grover
    Director of Admissions: Megan Abernathy
    Public Relations Manager: Sheri A. Ziccardi
    Hartt Facilities Manager: Leonard Bretton
Founded: 1920
Specialized Field: Music; Dance; Theatre
Performs At: Millard Auditorium; Lincoln Theater
Rental Contact: DaVid Bell

4411
SOUTH SHORE MUSIC
13 Washington Street
Westport, CT 02188
Phone: 781-331-3333
Fax: 203-454-3682
e-mail: southshoremusic@bigplanet.com
Web Site: www.southshoremusic.com
Officers:
    President/Program Chairman: Marianne Liberatore
Mission: To present chamber music concerts
Utilizes: Guest Musical Directors; Multimedia
Founded: 1933
Specialized Field: Classical Chamber Music
Volunteer Staff: 6
Budget: $100,000
Income Sources: Tickets; Ads; Contributions
Season: June-September
Performs At: Saugatuck Congregational Church

4412
TEMPLE ISRAEL
2324 Emerson Avenue South
Westport, CT 55405
Phone: 612-377-8680
Fax: 612-377-6630
e-mail: information@templeisrael.com
Web Site: www.tiwestport.org
Management:
    Executive Director: Miriam Seidenfeld
    Development Director: Jeri Glick-Anderson
    Associate Executive Director: Liz Mack
    Finance Director: Anne Rasmussen
Status: Non-Profit; Professional
Performs At: Temple Israel

Delaware

4413
UNIVERSITY OF DELAWARE PERFORMING ARTS SERIES
413 Academy Street
Second Floor
Newark, DE 19716
Phone: 302-831-2201
Fax: 302-831-3673
e-mail: dpugh@udel.edu
Web Site: www.vdel.edu
Management:
    Assistant Director: Robert Snyder
Mission: A public service for local community.
Founded: 1979
Paid Staff: 3
Volunteer Staff: 20
Paid Artists: 20
Performs At: Mitchell Hall

4414
DELAWARE CHAMBER MUSIC FESTIVAL
PO Box 3537
Wilmington, DE 19807-3537
Phone: 302-442-0572
Fax: 302-636-9400
e-mail: info@dcmf.org
Web Site: www.dcmf.org
Officers:
    President: Ruth Govatos
    VP: Tamara Lyn Smith
    Treasurer: Mark Sharnoff
    Secretary: Jane Dilley
Management:
    Music Director: Barbara Govatos
    Co-Administrator: Cher Astolfi
    Co-Administrator: Tracy Ann Smith
    Founder: Geraldine Barbaras
    Administrator: Angie Edwards
Paid Staff: 3
Volunteer Staff: 20
Paid Artists: 25

District of Columbia

4415
AMERICAN COLLEGE THEATER FESTIVAL
John F Kennedy Center
2700 F Street, NW
Washington, DC 20566
Phone: 202-416-8864
Fax: 202-416-8802
e-mail: ghenry@kennedy-center.org
Management:
    Director: Gregg Henry

4416
AMERICAN MUSIC FESTIVAL
National Gallery of Art
2000B South Club Drive
Washington, DC 20785
Phone: 202-737-4215
Fax: 202-789-3246
e-mail: der-info@nga.gov
Web Site: www.nga.gov
Officers:
    Chairman?: Sharon Percy Rockefeller
    President?: Victoria P. Sant
    Treasurer: William W. McClure
    Secretary and General Counsel: Elizabeth A. Croog
Management:
    Music Director: George Manos
    Music Program Specialist: Stephen Ackert
    Director: Earl A. Powell III
    Deputy Director: Franklin Kelly
    Administrator: Darrell Willson
Specialized Field: Instrumental; Choral; Jazz; Educational
Season: May, Sundays only
Performs At: Washington, DC (Festival Site)
Seating Capacity: 500

4417
ARTS IN THE ACADEMY, NATIONAL ACADEMY OF SCIENCES
500 Fifth St.
Washington, DC 20001
Phone: 202-334-2000
Fax: 202-334-1687
e-mail: jtomlins@nas.edu
Web Site: www.national-acadamies.org/arts
Management:
    Director: Janis Tomlinson
    Executive Director: Robert M. Hauser

SERIES & FESTIVALS / District of Columbia

Director: Miron L. Straf
Director: Ann G. Polvinale
Associate Executive Director: Patricia L. Morison
Performs At: Auditorium
Seating Capacity: 670

4418
CHILDREN'S NATIONAL MEDICAL CENTER, NEW HORIZONS PROGRAM
111 Michigan Avenue NW
Washington, DC 20010
Phone: 202-476-5000
Fax: 202-884-3489
e-mail: tlassite@cnmc.org
Management:
  Manager: Tina S Lassiter
  Performance Coordinator: Arabella Johnson
Mission: To provide multi-disciplined high quality arts programming to patients at bedside, in playrooms and, in the Atrium space in order to expedite the healing process.
Founded: 1978

4419
DC SPORTS & ENTERTAINMENT COMMISSION
2400 E Capitol Street
SE RFK, 4th Floor
Washington, DC 20003
Phone: 202-547-0977
Fax: 202-547-7460
e-mail: newwa@aol.com
Web Site: www.dcsec.dcgov.org
Management:
  Executive Director: James Dalrymple
  Marketing Director: Neville Waters
  Stadium Manager: Anthony Burnett
  Event Manager: Chenier Adelle
  Director of Communications and Publ: Hubbard Chinyere
  Chief Executive Officer: Moses Erik A
  Director of Public Affairs: Washington Teri
Mission: To promote Washington, DC as a location for holding sporting events to enhavne the city's economic development and welfare, and expand the city's national and international exposure. The Commission also creates opportunities for community outreach and local recreation for all residents of the district, particularly youths.
Seating Capacity: 56; 692

4420
DISTRICT CURATORS
PO Box 14197
Washington, DC 20044
Phone: 202-783-0360
Fax: 202-783-4185
Management:
  Executive Director: Bill Warrell
  Producer: Katea Stitt
Mission: Presenting the finest new performing arts to Washington DC and mid-Atlantic audiences; advancing cultural opportunities world-wide for artists and audiences.
Specialized Field: Ethnic
Status: Nonprofit
Organization Type: Presenting

4421
DUMBARTON CONCERT
3133 Dumbarton Street NW
Washington, DC 20007
Phone: 202-965-2000
Fax: 202-965-2004
e-mail: dumbartonc@aol.com
Web Site: www.dumbartonconcerts.org
Officers:
  Vice-Chairman: Ian K. Portnoy
  Chairman Emeritus: Angelo Cicolani
  Treasurer: Joan duB. Burroughs
  Founding Director: Constance S. Zimmer
Management:
  Chairman: Charles A. Miller
  Executive Director: Catherine Payling
  Managing Director: Mimi Newcastle
  House Manager: Megan Holeva
Mission: To provide a venue for the world's finest young musicians in the US capital.
Founded: 1978
Specialized Field: Chamber Music
Status: Non-Profit, Professional
Paid Staff: 4
Paid Artists: 25
Income Sources: Box Office; Grants; Private Donations
Performs At: Dumbarton Church
Facility Category: Historic Church
Seating Capacity: 375
Organization Type: Presenting

4422
EMBASSY SERIES
PO Box 9871
Washington, DC 20016
Phone: 202-625-2361
Fax: 301-588-6445
e-mail: concerts@embassyseries.org
Web Site: www.embassyseries.com
Officers:
  President: Jim Langley
  Chairman of the Board: Ian K. Portnoy, Esq.
  Chief Operating Officer: Daniella Y. Taveau
  Treasurer: Michael Sorrells
  Secretary: David J. Umansky
Management:
  Founder and Director: Jerome Barry
Mission: Presents programs at embassies with local international artists and musicians.
Founded: 1981
Specialized Field: Chamber; Vocal Music

4423
GEORGE WASHINGTON'S SERIES AT MOUNT VERNON COLLEGE
2121 Eye Street, NW
Washington, DC 20052
Phone: 202-994-1000
Fax: 202-338-1089
e-mail: mvcfw@gwu.edu
Web Site: www.gwu.edu
Management:
  Artistic Director: Carla Hubner
Performs At: Hand Chapel

4424
IMAGINATION CELEBRATION - KENNEDY CENTER PERFORMANCES FOR YOUNG PEOPLE
John F Kennedy Center for the Performing Arts
2700 F Street NW
Washington, DC 20566
Phone: 202-416-8000
Fax: 202-416-8802
Web Site: www.kennedy-center.org
Officers:
  VP Education: Derek Gordon
  Chairman: David M. Rubenstein
  President: Michael M. Kaiser
Management:
  Music Director: Christoph Eschenbach

4425
KENNEDY CENTER ANNUAL OPEN HOUSE ARTS FESTIVAL
Kennedy Center for the Performing Arts
2700 F Street NW
Washington, DC 20566
Phone: 202-467-4600
Fax: 202-416-8205
Toll-free: 800-444-1324
Web Site: www.kennedy-center.org
Officers:
  Chairman: James A Johnson
  President: Laurence J Wilker
  Founding Chairman: Roger L Stevens
Management:
  President: Michael Kaiser
  Music Director/Orchestra: Leonard Slatkin
Specialized Field: Series and Festivals; Instrumental Music; Vocal Music; Theatre; Youth; Dance; Ethnic Performances
Status: Non-Profit, Professional
Season: September
Performs At: Kennedy Center (Festival Site)

4426
KENNEDY CENTER/MARY LOU WILLIAMS WOMEN IN JAZZ FESTIVAL
2700 F Street NW
Washington, DC 20566
Phone: 202-416-8824
Fax: 202-416-8876
Toll-free: 800-444-1324
e-mail: kastruthers@kennedy-center.org
Web Site: www.kennedy-center.org/womeninjazz
Officers:
  President: Michael M. Kaiser
  Executive Director: Claudette Donlon
Management:
  Jazz Programming Director: Kevin A. Struthers
  Music Director/Orchestra: Leonard Slatkin
Founded: 1971
Specialized Field: Series and Festivals; Instrumental Music; Vocal Music; Theatre; Youth; Dance; Ethnic performances; Education; Jazz
Status: Non-Profit, Professional

4427
LIBRARY OF CONGRESS CHAMBER MUSIC CONCERT SERIES
Library of Congress Music Division
101 Independence Avenue SE
Washington, DC 20540-4710
Phone: 202-707-5503
Fax: 202-707-0621
Web Site: www.lcweb.loc.gov/concert
Management:
  Chief Music Division: Jon Newsom
  Producer: Anne McLean
Mission: To present free concerts of the highest artistic caliber, with a special emphasis on american music and musicians.
Founded: 1925
Specialized Field: Chamber Music; Jazz; America Music Theatre; Dance
Status: Non-Profit, Non-Professional
Paid Staff: 6
Volunteer Staff: 6

SERIES & FESTIVALS / Florida

Paid Artists: 120

4428
NATIONAL ACADEMY OF SCIENCES CONCERTS
2100 C St NW
Washington, DC 20048
Phone: 202-334-2436
Fax: 202-334-1690
e-mail: arts@nas.edu
Web Site: www.nationalacademies.org/arts
Officers:
   Chair: David Kapp
   President: Bruce Fowle
   Treasurer: Deven Parekh
Management:
   Director: J D Talasek
Specialized Field: Series & Festivals: Instrumental Music
Status: Non-Profit, Professional
Paid Staff: 1000
Seating Capacity: 670

4429
NATIONAL GALLERY OF ART/CONCERT SERIES
2000B South Club Drive
Washington, DC 20785
Phone: 202-737-4215
Fax: 202-842-2407
e-mail: der-info@nga.gov
Web Site: www.nga.gov
Officers:
   Chairman?: Sharon Percy Rockefeller
   President?: Victoria P. Sant
   Treasurer: William W. McClure
   Secretary and General Counsel: Elizabeth A. Croog
Management:
   Music Director: George Manos
   Music Program Specialist: Stephen Ackert
   Director: Earl A. Powell III
   Deputy Director: Franklin Kelly
   Administrator: Darrell Willson
Mission: To provide the public with free concerts at the National Gallery of Art.
Founded: 1941
Specialized Field: Symphony; Orchestra; Chamber; Ensemble
Status: Nonprofit
Paid Staff: 8
Performs At: Museum Garden Courts; National Gallery
Annual Attendance: 14,000
Seating Capacity: 500
Organization Type: Performing

4430
OPERA LAFAYETTE
10 Fourth Street NE
Washington, DC 20002
Phone: 202-546-9332
e-mail: operalafayette@operalafayette.org
Web Site: www.operalafayette.org
Officers:
   President and Chair: J. Cari Elliott
   First Vice Chair: Chris W. O'Flinn
   Vice Chair, Operations: Dorsey C. Dunn
   Treasurer: Walter R. Arnheim
   Secretary: Susan A. Lynner
Management:
   General Manager: Henry Valoris, henryvaloris@operalafayette.or
   Artistic Director: Ryan Brown, ryanbrown@operalafayette.org
   Marketing & Development Director: Charles Rohlfs
   Orchestra Personnel Manager: Nancy Jo Snider
   Graphic Art Director: Suzan Reed Weaver
Mission: An American period instrument ensemble focused on the French 18th century opera repertoire and its precursers, influences, and artistic legacy.
Utilizes: Actors; Dancers; Educators; Five Seasonal Concerts; Guest Accompanists; Multimedia; Original Music Scores; Singers; Soloists; Students
Specialized Field: Opera
Status: Nonprofit
Paid Staff: 2
Volunteer Staff: 5
Paid Artists: 70
Budget: $725,000
Income Sources: Ticket and CD Sales; Government and Private Grants; Corporations; Individual Donors
Season: August
Annual Attendance: 3,000
Facility Category: Concert Halls (Kennedy Center, Lincoln Center)
Type of Stage: Proscenium
Seating Capacity: 3,000

4431
PHILLIPS COLLECTION SUNDAY CONCERTS
1600 21st Street NW
Washington, DC 20009
Phone: 202-387-2151
Fax: 202-387-2436
e-mail: concerts@phillipscollection.org
Web Site: www.phillipscollection.org/music
Management:
   Artistic Director: Caroline Mousset
   Director of The Museum: Doroth Kosinski
Founded: 1921
Specialized Field: Modern Art Museum
Status: Non-Profit, Professional

4432
SMITHSONIAN INSTITUTION: THE SMITHSONIAN ASSOCIATES
The Smithsonian Associates
PO Box 23293
Washington, DC 20026-3293
Phone: 202-357-3030
Fax: 202-786-2034
e-mail: customerservice@residentassociates.org
Web Site: www.smithsonianassociates.org
Management:
   Director: Mara Mayor
   Deputy Director: Barbara Tuceling
   Assoc Dir Marketing And Membership: Robert Anastasi
   Educational And Cultural Programs: Carol Bogash
   Associate Director: Carol Bogash
   Associate Director/Marketing: Robert Anastasio
   Webmaster: Dennis R Smoot
Mission: Encouraging and supporting the participation of the Washington DC community in Smithsonian Institution performing arts events.
Founded: 1964
Specialized Field: Dance; Vocal Music; Instrumental Music; Theater
Status: Professional; Nonprofit
Paid Staff: 100
Volunteer Staff: 200
Performs At: Hirshhorn Museum Auditorium; Baird Auditorium
Organization Type: Educational; Sponsoring
Resident Groups: Smithsonian Chamber Music Society

4433
SOCIETY OF THE CINCINNATI CONCERTS AT ANDERSON HOUSE
2118 Massachusetts Avenue NW
Washington, DC 20008-2810
Phone: 202-785-2040
Fax: 202-293-3350
Management:
   Museum Director: Kathleen Betts
   Executive Director: Jack Duane Warren, Jr.
   Assistant to the Executive Director: Katherine Neill Ridgley
   Director of Education: Eleesha Tucker
   Director of Finance: Susan M. Benjamin
Performs At: Ballroom

4434
WASHINGTON PERFORMING ARTS SOCIETY
2000 L Street NW
Suite 510
Washington, DC 20036
Phone: 202-833-9800
Fax: 202-331-7678
e-mail: wpas@wpas.org
Web Site: www.wpas.org
Officers:
   Chair: Reginald Van Lee
   Vice Chairman: James F Sandman
   Vice Chairman: AW Smith Jr
   Vice Chairman: Paul Martin Wolff
   CFO/Operations Director: Teri McDonald
   Treasurer: Steven Kaplan
   Secretary: Christina Co Mather
Management:
   President and CEO: Jenny Bilfield
   Chief Administrative Officer: Allen Lassinger
   Director of Development: Mitchell Bassion
Mission: To present the world's finest artists in the nation's capital; to present over 100 concerts annually on the major stages, as well as over 800 concerts each year in the schools of the metropolitan Washington area using resident artists.
Utilizes: Guest Artists; Guest Companies
Founded: 1966
Specialized Field: Performing Arts
Status: Non-Profit, Professional
Paid Staff: 50
Performs At: WPAS Is A Presenter That Presents At A Variety Of Venues In DC, VA, And MD
Organization Type: Educational; Sponsoring

Florida

4435
MIAMI INTERNATIONAL PIANO FESTIVAL
20191 E Country Club Drive
Suite 709
Aventura, FL 33180
Phone: 305-935-5115
Fax: 305-935-9087
e-mail: info@miamipianofest.com
Web Site: www.miamipianofest.com
Officers:
   President: Jack Brodsky

All listings are in alphabetical order by state, then city, then organization within the city.

SERIES & FESTIVALS / Florida

Treasurer: Steven Grant
Management:
President: Jack Brodsky
Executive Director: Barbara Muze
Managing Director: Gisela Brodsky
Founded: 1997
Specialized Field: Series & Festivals; Piano; Education; Promotion
Status: Non-Profit, Non-Professional
Paid Staff: 2
Volunteer Staff: 10
Paid Artists: 2

4436
PERFORMING ARTS SOCIETY OF SOUTH FLORIDA
2851 Leonard Drive
Suite J403
Aventura, FL 33160
Phone: 305-682-4999
e-mail: passouth@earthlink.net
Web Site: www.cdg.org
Management:
Managing Director: Darrell Calvin
Mission: To bring the best entertainment to a diverse community.
Founded: 1984
Specialized Field: Dance; Music; Theatre; Pop
Status: Nonprofit
Paid Staff: 2
Volunteer Staff: 6
Budget: $200,000
Income Sources: Box Office; Grants; Gifts; In Kind Services
Affiliations: APAP; IEG
Annual Attendance: 5,500

4437
SOUTH FLORIDA COMMUNITY COLLEGE CULTURAL SERIES
600 West College Drive
Avon Park, FL 33825
Phone: 863-453-6661
Fax: 863-784-7190
e-mail: andrewst@southflorida.edu
Web Site: www.sfcc.cc.fl.us
Officers:
Chairman Cultural Affairs: Douglas Andrews
Management:
President: Norman Steven
Artistic Director: Doug Andrews
Founded: 1965
Specialized Field: Series and Festivals; Instrumental Music; Theatre; Youth; Dance; Ethnic Performances
Status: Non-Profit, Professional
Paid Staff: 250
Paid Artists: 32
Performs At: College Auditorium

4438
CLEARWATER JAZZ HOLIDAY
600 Cleveland Street
Ste 200
Clearwater, FL 33755
Mailing Address: PO Box 7278 Clearwater, FL 33758-7287
Phone: 727-461-5200
Fax: 727-461-1292
e-mail: evelyn@clearwaterjazz.com
Web Site: www.clearwaterjazz.com
Management:
President: Larry Gerwig
VP: David Ruppel

4439
FESTIVAL MIAMI
University of Miami, Frost School of Music
PO Box 248165
Coral Gables, FL 33124-2975
Mailing Address: 5807 Ponce de Leon Boulevard, Suite 202
Phone: 305-284-4940
Fax: 305-284-3901
e-mail: festivalmiami.music@miami.edu
Web Site: www.festivalmiami.com
Management:
Marketing/Communications Director: Julia Berg
Ticket Office Coordinator: Kimberly Engelhardt
Events Director: Marianne Mijares
Asst Coordinator: Ron Wideman
Dean: Shelton Berg
Mission: To provide a high quality music education and training for its undergraduate and graduate majors as well as to expose the community to a diverse range of cultures through music. Intends to foster advancements in music performance, creativity, scholarship, and teaching among its faculty and staff.
Utilizes: Artists-in-Residence; Collaborating Artists; Collaborations; Commissioned Composers; Commissioned Music; Composers-in-Residence; Educators; Grant Writers; Guest Companies; Guest Composers; Guest Musical Directors; Guest Musicians; Local Artists; Multimedia; Organization Contracts; Original Music Scores; Resident Artists; Sign Language Translators; Special Technical Talent; Theatre Companies
Founded: 1983
Specialized Field: Series & Festivals: Concerts
Status: Non-Profit, Professional
Paid Staff: 8
Volunteer Staff: 21
Paid Artists: 20
Budget: $300,000
Income Sources: Ticket Sales; Sponsorships; Donations; Grants
Season: Mid September - Mid October
Performs At: UM Maurice Gusman Concert Hall
Affiliations: Association of Performing Arts Presenters, Arts & Business Council of Miami, Florida Festivals & Events Association
Annual Attendance: 12,000-14,000
Facility Category: Indoor/Concert Hall
Seating Capacity: 600

4440
MIAMI BACH SOCIETY/TROPICAL BAROQUE MUSIC FESTIVAL
PO Box 4034
Coral Gables, FL 33114
Phone: 305-669-1376
Fax: 305-669-1376
e-mail: info@miamibachsociety.org
Web Site: www.miamibachsociety.org
Officers:
President: Mark Hart
VP: George Berberian
Secretary: Claire Veater
Treasurer: Kingsley Bewley
Vice-Chairman: Thomas Abbott
Chairman: Volker Anding
Management:
President: Michael Berke
Executive Director: Kathryn B. Gaubatz
Artistic Director: Donald Oglesby
Co-Artistic Director: Miles Morgan
Co-Artistic Director: Jay Bernfeld
Technical Director: Jancy Ball
Mission: To perform and present the music of Johann Sebastian Bach and his baroque composer contemporaries to the people and visitors of the sociable Florida community.
Utilizes: Guest Directors; Guest Musical Directors; Guest Musicians; Multimedia; Original Music Scores
Founded: 1984
Specialized Field: Series & Festivals: Performing Music Before 1800
Status: Non-Profit, Professional
Paid Staff: 4
Paid Artists: 2
Budget: $300,000
Income Sources: Corporations; Government; Indivdual Donations; Ticket Sales
Annual Attendance: 5,000
Organization Type: Performing and Presenting Musical Organization
Resident Groups: MBS Chorus and Orchestra

4441
CENTRAL FLORIDA CULTURAL ENDEAVORS
PO Box 1310
Daytona Beach
Daytona Beach, FL 32114
Mailing Address: PO Box 1310 Daytona Beach, FL 32115-1310
Phone: 386-872-2324
Fax: 386-238-1663
e-mail: fifcfce@n-jcenter.com
Web Site: www.fif-lso.org
Officers:
President: Jacob Harold
Treasurer: Tom Tinsley
Chair: Mari Kuraishi
Secretary: Charles Best
Management:
Executive Director: Eric Lariviere
Operations Manager: Erin Bailey
Mission: To provide world class chamber music and orchestra concerts for Daytona Beach audiences.
Utilizes: Educators; Fine Artists; Guest Artists; Guest Writers; Multimedia; Original Music Scores; Sign Language Translators
Founded: 1982
Specialized Field: Series and Festivals: Instrumental Music
Status: Non-Profit, Professional
Paid Staff: 8
Budget: $240,000
Income Sources: Individuals; Corporations; City; County; State; Grants
Performs At: Peabody Auditorium
Affiliations: Association of Performing Arts Presenters; FL Arts Presenters; INTIX
Facility Category: Churches
Seating Capacity: 600-1,200
Organization Type: Sponsoring

4442
DAYTONA BEACH INTERNATIONAL FESTIVAL
212 S Beach Street
Daytona Beach, FL 32114
Phone: 386-872-2323
Fax: 386-238-1663
Toll-free: 866-849-0731
e-mail: info@dbif.com
Web Site: www.dbif.com
Management:
Founder/Director: Tippen Davidson
President: Eric Larivivere

SERIES & FESTIVALS / Florida

Director of Operations: Robert Cox
Marketing/Communications: Manuel Bornia
Mission: To provide the citizens of Volusia County and its visitors with a high quality, broadly based performing arts series built around the biennial residency of the London Symphony Orchestra, thereby promoting Daytona Beach as a culturally diverse and informed area.
Utilizes: Artists-in-Residence; Dance Companies; Dancers; Educators; Fine Artists; Guest Accompanists; Guest Artists; Guest Companies; Guest Composers; Guest Directors; Guest Instructors; Guest Lecturers; Guest Musicians; Guest Soloists; Guest Writers; High School Drama; Instructors; Lyricists; Multimedia; Organization Contracts; Original Music Scores; Sign Language Translators; Singers; Soloists
Founded: 1974
Specialized Field: Series and Festivals; Instrumental Music; Dance; Ethnic Performances
Status: Non-Profit, Non-Professional
Paid Staff: 8
Paid Artists: 200
Budget: $2,400,700
Income Sources: Local Individuals, Corporations; City, County, State & other Grants
Performs At: Peabody Auditorium; Ocean Center; Ormond Beach, PA
Affiliations: Association of Performing Arts Presenters; FL Arts Presenters; INTIX
Seating Capacity: 200-9,000
Organization Type: Performing; Educational; Sponsoring

4443
FLORIDA INTERNATIONAL FESTIVAL FEATURING THE LONDON SYMPHONY ORCHESTRA
126 East Orange Ave.
Daytona Beach, FL 32114
Mailing Address: PO Box 1310 Daytona Beach, FL 32115-1310
Phone: 386-255-0981
Fax: 386-258-5104
e-mail: info@daytonachamber.com
Web Site: www.fif-lso.org
Management:
  General Manager: Dewey Anderson
  President/CEO: Larry McKinney
Utilizes: Artists-in-Residence; Dance Companies; Guest Choreographers; Guest Composers; Guest Instructors; Guest Musicians; Multimedia; Original Music Scores; Singers; Theatre Companies
Founded: 1974
Specialized Field: Music
Paid Staff: 6
Volunteer Staff: 100
Paid Artists: 200
Budget: $400,000 - 1,000,000
Income Sources: Ticket Sales; Contributions; Grants
Season: July
Performs At: Daytona Beach area [Festival Site]; Various
Annual Attendance: 2,000-40,000
Facility Category: Peabody Aud; Ocean Cntr; Ormond Beach Cntr; etc.
Seating Capacity: 250 - 8,000

4444
BEETHOVEN BY THE BEACH
Florida Philharmonic Orchestra
244 2nd Avenue North, Suite 420
Fort Lauderdale, FL 33701
Phone: 727-892-3331
Fax: 727-892-3338
Toll-free: 800-662-7286
e-mail: admin@floridaorchestra.org
Web Site: www.floridaphilharmonic.org
Officers:
  President and CEO: Michael Pastreich
Management:
  Music Director: James Judd
Specialized Field: Instrumental; Childrens'
Budget: $60,000 - 150,000
Season: July
Performs At: Fort Lauderdale [Festival Site]

4445
BROADWAY IN FORT LAUDERDALE
201 SW Fifth Avenue
Fort Lauderdale, FL 33312
Phone: 954-522-5334
Fax: 954-764-0708
Toll-free: 800-764-0700
e-mail: fortlauerdalebroadwayseries@clearchannel.com
Web Site: www.broadwayacrossamerica.com
Management:
  President: Bryan Becker
  Executive Director: Fusie Krajsa
  Managing Director: John Poland
Specialized Field: Touring Broadway
Status: Non-Profit, Professional
Paid Staff: 60

4446
CORAL RIDGE PRESBYTARIAN CHURCH CONCERT SERIES
5555 N Federal Highway
Fort Lauderdale, FL 33308
Phone: 954-491-1103
Fax: 954-491-7374
Toll-free: 800-987-9818
e-mail: cboatright@crpc.org
Web Site: www.crpc.org
Management:
  Executive Director: Charlie Boatright
Utilizes: Artists-in-Residence; Grant Writers; Guest Artists; Guest Lecturers; Multimedia; Music; Organization Contracts; Original Music Scores; Sign Language Translators; Singers; Soloists
Founded: 1971
Specialized Field: Series and Festivals; Instrumental Music; Vocal Music; Theatre; Dance; Ethnic Performances
Status: Non-Profit, Professional
Paid Staff: 3
Volunteer Staff: 2
Performs At: Coral Ridge Presbyterian Church
Annual Attendance: 50,000
Facility Category: Church
Type of Stage: Chancel
Seating Capacity: 2000
Year Built: 1971

4447
FLORIDA ARTS CONCERT SERIES
1226 N. Tamiami Trail
Suite 300
Fort Myers, FL 34236
Phone: 941-306-1200
Fax: 941-923-0754
e-mail: jimflarts@earthlink.net
Officers:
  Board Chair: Mary Elizabeth Carey
  Secretary: Ray Broth
  Treasurer: Jim Norris
Management:
  Executive Director/Chairman: John Alan Fischer
  Artistic Director: Lee Dougherty Ross

4448
FORT MYERS COMMUNITY CONCERT ASSOCIATION SERIES
PO Box 606
PO Box 606
Fort Myers, FL 33902
Phone: 239-693-4849
Officers:
  President: Mary Lee Mann
  Vice President: Kay Holloway
  Secretary: Kathy Dean
  Treasurer: David C. Hall
Performs At: Barbara B Mann Performing Arts Hall

4449
FIRST ARTS SERIES
103 First Street SE
Fort Walton Beach
Fort Walton, FL 32548
Phone: 850-863-2436
Fax: 850-243-0905
e-mail: director@firstartsconcerts.org
Web Site: ww.firstartsconcerts.org
Management:
  Director: Karen Tindall
  Concert Hospitality: Karen Tindall
  Treasurer: Joan Moody
Founded: 1989
Volunteer Staff: 12
Budget: $25,000
Income Sources: Tickets; Donations
Facility Category: Church Sanctuary

4450
NYK PRODUCTIONS
1747 Van Buren Street
Suite 700
Hollywood, FL 33028
Phone: 954-929-6010
Fax: 954-929-6399
Management:
  Chief Officer: Arie Kaduri
Performs At: Various Auditoriums

4451
DELIUS FESTIVAL
PO Box 5621
Jacksonville, FL 32247-5621
Phone: 904-384-3956
Management:
  Director: Jeff Driggers
  Director: Michael Blachly
  Assistant Director: Kay Holcomb
  Operations Manager: Matt Koropeckyj-Cox
  Assistant Director: Deborah C. Rossi
  Technical Director: Steve Schell
Specialized Field: Instrumental; Choral
Budget: $10,000
Season: April
Performs At: Jacksonville (Festival Site)
Facility Category: Terry Concert Hall; Friday Musicale Auditorium
Seating Capacity: 450; 250

SERIES & FESTIVALS / Florida

4452
FLORIDA THEATRE PERFORMING ARTS SERIES
128 E Forsyth Street
Suite 300
Jacksonville, FL 32202
Phone: 904-355-5661
Fax: 904-358-1874
e-mail: stillcool@flordiatheatre.com
Web Site: www.floridatheatre.com
Officers:
   President: Numa Saisselin
Management:
   Executive Director: J Erik Hart
   Director of Marketing: Vincent Iaropoli
   Director of Rental Operations: Toni Alison Chadwell
   Director of Development: Holly E. Hammond
   House Manager: Jennifer Dobrowolski
   Ticket Office Manager: Anne Lawson
   Ticket Office Manager: Lynda Lee
   Technical Director: Saul Lucio
   Finance Director: Cynthia de Vinna
Founded: 1985
Specialized Field: Series & Festivals; Instrumental Music; Vocal Music; Theater; Youth; Dance; Ethnic Performances
Status: Non-Profit, Non-Professional
Performs At: Flordia Theatre

4453
JACKSONVILLE UNIVERSITY MASTER-CLASS & ARTISTS SERIES
College of Fine Arts, Jacksonville University
2800 University Blvd N
Jacksonville, FL 32211
Phone: 904-256-7371
Fax: 904-256-7375
Toll-free: 800-225-2027
e-mail: tnetter@ju.edu
Web Site: www.ju.edu
Management:
   President: Kerry Ronberg
   Dean College Fine Arts: D Terence Netter
   Dean College of Fine Arts: Patty Aniole
Mission: Cultural enrichment of the university community and the community at large.
Founded: 1958
Specialized Field: Series & Festivals; Art; Dance; Music; Theatre
Status: Non-Profit, Non-Professional
Paid Staff: 12
Paid Artists: 20
Performs At: Terry Concert Hall

4454
KUUMBA FEST
PO Box 12001
Jacksonville, FL 92101
Phone: 904-353-2270
Fax: 904-355-0567
e-mail: kuumbafest@gmail.com
Web Site: kuumbafestival.tripod.com

4455
WJCT JACKSONVILLE JAZZ FESTIVAL
117 W. Duval St.
Suite 280
Jacksonville, FL 32202
Phone: 904-630-3690
Fax: 904-630-4744
e-mail: events@coj.net
Web Site: www.jaxjazzfest.com
Management:
   Executive Producer: Vic DiGenti
   Event Specialist: Emily Armusik
   Media Support Specialist: Tanisha Brown

4456
BEACHES FINE ARTS SERIES
416 12th Avenue North
Jacksonville Beach, FL 32250
Phone: 904-270-1771
Fax: 904-270-2074
e-mail: beachesfinearts@aol.com
Management:
   Executive Director: Kathryn Wallis
Founded: 1973
Specialized Field: Present Concerts for Community
Status: Non-Profit, Non-Professional
Paid Staff: 2
Performs At: St. Pauls By-the-Sea Episcopal Church

4457
KEY WEST COUNCIL ON THE ARTS SERIES
1100 Simonton St.
Key West, FL 33040
Phone: 305-295-4369
Officers:
   chair: Theresa Axford
   vice-chair: Lucy Elyse Carleton
   secretary: Michael Marrero
   Treasurer: Gayle Hewlett
Management:
   Artistic Director: RJ Weiss

4458
BACH FESTIVAL OF CENTRAL FLORIDA
PO Box 2764
Lakeland, FL 33806-2764
Phone: 863-299-2555
Fax: 863-439-0759
e-mail: info@bachfestivalofcentralflorida.org
Web Site: www.bachfestivalofcentralflorida.org
Officers:
   Chairman: Dr John Thomason
   Past Chairman: Marie Hasse
   Treasurer: Paul Benner
   Corresponding Secretary: Tom Oldt
   Recording Secretary: Dr. Linwood Bond
Management:
   Correspondence Secretary: Thomas Oldt, tom@troldt.com
Mission: To make the music of J.S. Bach and contemporaries a powerful and relevant force on society through performance and education.
Utilizes: Collaborating Artists; Community Members; Community Talent; Grant Writers; Guest Designers; Guest Musical Directors; Instructors; Scenic Designers; Singers
Founded: 1974
Specialized Field: Baroque Music
Status: Non-Profit, Professional
Budget: $25,000
Income Sources: Donations, Tickets, Sponsorships
Performs At: None
Affiliations: Early Music America, Polk Arts Alliance, Red Cross Alliance
Annual Attendance: 1,000

4459
FLORIDA SOUTHERN COLLEGE
111 Lake Hollingsworth Drive
Lakeland, FL 33801
Phone: 863-680-4111
Fax: 863-680-3758
Toll-free: 800-274-4131
e-mail: fla@flsouthern.edu
Web Site: www.flsouthern.edu
Management:
   President: Nanne Kerr
   Executive Director: Robert Macdonald
Founded: 1961
Specialized Field: Series & Festivals; Classical Music; Theatre and Art
Status: Non-Profit, Professional
Paid Staff: 6
Paid Artists: 12

4460
LAKELAND CENTER
701 W Lime Street
Lakeland, FL 33815
Phone: 863-834-8100
Fax: 863-834-8101
Web Site: www.thelakelandcenter.com
Management:
   Executive Director: Mike LaPan
   Assistant Manager: Scott Sloman
Utilizes: Collaborations; Dance Companies; Guest Accompanists; Guest Choreographers; Multimedia; Original Music Scores; Theatre Companies
Founded: 1974
Paid Staff: 33
Volunteer Staff: 100
Performs At: The Lakeland Center/The Youkey Theater
Facility Category: Event, Sports & Convention complex
Stage Dimensions: 78'x47'
Seating Capacity: 2,246 w/pit seats 2,296
Year Built: 1974
Year Remodeled: 1996
Rental Contact: Scott Sloman

4461
SUNCOAST DIXIELAND JAZZ CLASSIC
PO Box 8707
Largo, FL 33758
Phone: 727-248-9441
Fax: 727-536-0064
e-mail: jazzclassic@aol.com
Web Site: www.jazzclassic.net
Officers:
   Secretary: Jim Sullivan
   Treasurer: Danni Sullivan
Management:
   Festival Director: Joan Dragon
Mission: To keep traditional jazz and the traditions of jazz alive and provide financial assistance to youth for musical study
Founded: 1990
Specialized Field: Series and Festivals; Dixieland Jazz; Instrumental; Traditional
Status: Non-Profit, Professional
Paid Staff: 90
Volunteer Staff: 200
Performs At: Hotels; Indoor Venues
Affiliations: Suncoast Dixieland Jazz Society
Annual Attendance: 4,500

4462
NORTH FLORIDA COMMUNITY COLLEGE
325 NW Turner Davis Drive
Madison, FL 32340

SERIES & FESTIVALS / Florida

Phone: 850-973-2288
Fax: 850-973-1685
Toll-free: 866-937-6322
e-mail: artistseries@nfcc.edu
Web Site: www.nfcc.edu
Officers:
  Artists Series Chairman: Kim Scarboro
Management:
  President: John Gross Kopf
  Performance Coordinator: Kim Scarboro
Mission: To provide cultural enrichment through live performances for audiences of all ages residing in the North Florida area.
Utilizes: Collaborations; Dance Companies; Dancers; Fine Artists; Grant Writers; Guest Directors; Guest Instructors; Guest Soloists; Guild Activities; High School Drama; Local Artists; Multimedia; Original Music Scores; Playwrights; Selected Students; Sign Language Translators; Singers; Soloists; Student Interns; Special Technical Talent; Theatre Companies
Founded: 1980
Specialized Field: Series & Festivals: Performing Artists series - Live Performances
Status: Non-Profit, Professional
Paid Staff: 3
Volunteer Staff: 5
Paid Artists: 7
Non-paid Artists: 11
Budget: $40,000
Income Sources: Ticket Sales; Private & Corporate Donations; Grants
Performs At: Van H. Priest Auditorium
Annual Attendance: 6,000
Facility Category: Auditorium
Type of Stage: Resilient Wood
Stage Dimensions: 29'x40'
Seating Capacity: 580
Year Built: 1992

4463
CHIPOLA COLLEGE ARTIST SERIES
3094 Indian Circle
Marianna, FL 32446-2206
Phone: 850-526-2761
Fax: 850-718-2206
e-mail: stadsklevj@chipola.edu
Web Site: www.chipola.edu
Officers:
  President: Dr. Gene Prough
  Executive Director: Joan Stadsklev
Founded: 1947
Specialized Field: Series & Festivals; Instrumental Music; Vocal Music; Theatre; Ethnic Performances; Fine & Performing Arts
Status: Non-Profit, Professional
Paid Staff: 8
Budget: $15,000
Performs At: Chipola Junior College Auditorium
Facility Category: Theatre
Type of Stage: Proscenium
Seating Capacity: 355

4464
KEY WEST MUSIC FESTIVAL
1057 NE 210 Terrace
Miami, FL 33179
Phone: 305-651-5525
Fax: 305-651-0885
e-mail: kwmfestival@aol.com
Web Site: www.keywestmusicfestival.com/
Budget: $10,000 - 20,000
Season: May
Performs At: Key West (Festival Site)
Facility Category: San Carlos Institute

Seating Capacity: 400

4465
MIAMI CIVIC MUSIC ASSOCIATION SERIES
P.O. Box 565607
Miami, FL 33256-5607
Phone: 786-565-8530
Fax: 305-595-9597
e-mail: info@miamicivicmusic.org
Officers:
  President: Rosalina G. Sackstein
  Executive Vice President: Dr. Jay B. Hess
  Vice President: Dr. Armen Shaomian
  Secretary: Vivian Waddell
  Treasurer: Alan Caves
Management:
  Artistic Director: Rosalina G. Sackstein
Founded: 1932
Specialized Field: Series & Festivals; Instrumental Music; Vocal Music; Theatre; Ethnic Performances
Status: Non-Profit, Professional
Performs At: Gusman Hall, University of Miami

4466
MIAMI DADE COMMUNITY COLLEGE
300 NE 2nd Avenue
Suite 1423
Miami, FL 33132
Phone: 305-237-3010
Fax: 305-237-7559
e-mail: caffairs@mdc.edu
Web Site: www.culture.mdc.edu
Management:
  President: Eduardo Padron
  Executive Director: Michelle H Hayes
  Artistic Director: Gregory Jackson
Utilizes: Artists-In-Residence; Choreographers; Collaborations; Commissioned Music; Dance Companies; Dancers; Guest Accompanists; Guest Choreographers; Guest Ensembles; Guest Musical Directors; Instructors; Multi Collaborations; Organization Contracts; Playwrights; Selected Students; Sign Language Translators; Soloists; Special Technical Talent; Theatre Companies
Founded: 1990
Specialized Field: Series & Festivals; Instrumental Music; Vocal Music; Theater; Youth; Dance; Ethnic Performances
Status: Non-Profit, Professional
Paid Staff: 5
Paid Artists: 75
Budget: $1,000,000
Income Sources: Miami-Dade Community College; Miami-Dade County; State of Florida
Performs At: Auditorium
Annual Attendance: 10,000
Facility Category: Various

4467
TEMPLE BETH AM SERIES
60 East Madison Avenue
P.O. Box 1200
Miami, FL 10965
Phone: 845-735-5858
Fax: 845-735-9858
Officers:
  President: Michael Bittel
  Executive VP: Bea Citron
  Corresponding Secretary: Randy Fisher
  Recording Secretary: Debbie Rosenthal
  Treasurer/Financial Secretary: Irwin Katz
Management:
  Executive Director: Irene Warner

  Finance Director: Hellene Strul
  Operations: Lori Solomon
  Commmunications Director: Helene Layne
  Administration Secretary: Rita Diaz
  Administration Assistant: Marylin Harrison
  Donations: Barbara Hoffman
  Receptionist: Sandy Morrison
Performs At: Temple Sanctuary

4468
CONCERT ASSOCIATION OF FLORIDA
PO Box 522636
Miami Beach, FL 33052-2636
Phone: 305-808-7446
Fax: 305-808-7463
e-mail: info@concertfla.org
Web Site: www.concertfla.org
Officers:
  Director Public Relations/Marketing: Craig Hall
  President: John Cooper
  Second Vice President: Joyce Packman
  Secretary: Claudia Hamrick
  Treasurer: Arnie Steinmetz
Founded: 1967
Performs At: Dade County Auditorium

4469
ORLANDO-UCF SHAKESPEARE FESTIVAL
812 E Rollins St.
Suite 100
Orlando, FL 32803
Phone: 407-447-1700
Fax: 407-447-1701
e-mail: info@shakespearefest.org
Web Site: www.shakespearefest.org
Officers:
  Chair: Rita Lowndes
  President: Suzanne Gilbert
  Vice President: Shirley Bias
  Vice President: John S. Lord
  Treasurer: John Quigley
  Secretary: R. Dean Bosco
  Immediate Past President: Keith Hesse
Management:
  Executive Director: Mary Ann
  Artistic Director: Jim Helsinger
  Managing Director: PJ Albert
  Technical Director: James Erwin
  Production Manager: George Hamrah
  Director of Finance & Operations: Barbara Muzeni
  House Manager: Colin Worley
Mission: Will serve as a cultural resource to the community by presenting the plays of Shakespeare and other theatrical works, as well as the artistic and educational activities inspired by them. Festival presentations will reflect the highest possible artistic, educational and ethical values. We will strive fore artistic and educational excellence and innovation.

4470
SOCIETY OF THE FOUR ARTS
2 Four Arts Plaza
Palm Beach, FL 33480
Phone: 561-655-7227
Fax: 561-655-7233
e-mail: contactus@fourarts.org
Web Site: www.fourarts.org
Officers:
  President: Ervin S. Duggan
  Executive VP: Nancy Mato
  Vice Chairman: W. Dale Brougher
  Secretary: William S. Gubelmann

SERIES & FESTIVALS / Florida

Management:
: Marketing/Corporate Development Dir: Katie Edwards

Mission: A cultural center which features international traveling art exhibitions, a lecture series of world renowned personages, a distinguished concert series, two film series, and a young peoples series for children. Also maintains two libraries-the main Four Arts Library and a children's library, as well as a botanical garden and The Philip Hulitar Sculpture Garden.
Founded: 1936
Specialized Field: Series & Festivals: Art exhibitions.
Status: Non-Profit, Professional
Paid Staff: 30
Volunteer Staff: 6
Budget: $4.6 Million
Income Sources: Donations; Ticket Sales; Membership; Endowment Income
Annual Attendance: 111,563
Facility Category: Cultural Institution
Type of Stage: Proscenium
Stage Dimensions: 25' x 30'
Seating Capacity: 700
Year Built: 1948
Year Remodeled: 1994

4471
TREASURE COAST CONCERT ASSOCIATION
2394 SW Foxpoint Way
Palm City, FL 34990
Phone: 772-220-8400
Fax: 772-220-8401
e-mail: ehberlin@adelphia.net
Web Site: www.ovationconcerts.org
Officers:
: President: Ernest Berlin

Management:
: President: Ernest Berlin

Utilizes: Guest Directors; Guest Musical Directors; Guest Musicians; Multimedia; Original Music Scores; Singers; Theatre Companies
Founded: 1984
Specialized Field: Series & Festivals: Instrumental Music
Status: Non-Profit, Professional
Performs At: Lyric Theatre

4472
BAY ARTS ALLIANCE
8 Harrison Avenue
Panama City, FL 32401
Phone: 850-769-1217
Fax: 850-785-5165
e-mail: info@bayarts.org
Web Site: www.bayarts.org
Officers:
: Executive Director: Jennifer Jones
  President: Robert Wilkos
  Secretary: Tanya Deal
  Development PR Chair: Jim Hayden
  President Elect: Jody Walls
  Programming Co-Chair: Bryan Taylor
  Finance Chair: Frank Martin
  Member at Large: Doug Moore
  Member at Large: Frank Hall

Management:
: Facility Manager: Donald Schwartz
  Executive Director: Jennifer Jones
  Technical Director: John Sharp
  Membership/Box Office Manager: Mary DeCarmo

Specialized Field: Series & Festivals; Instrumental Music; Vocal Music; Theatre; Youth; Dance; Ethnic Performances
Status: Non-Profit, Non-Professional
Performs At: Marina Civic Theatre

4473
PANAMA CITY MUSIC ASSOCIATION SERIES
8 Harrison Avenue
Panama City, FL 32401
Phone: 850-236-1260
Fax: 850-913-0498
e-mail: PCMAevents@knology.net
Web Site: www.panamacitymusicassoc.org
Officers:
: President: Dr. Carolyn Wilson
  First Vice President: Dr Greg Grantham
  Talent Chairman: Bob Borich
  Second Vice President: Jim Green
  Secretary: Gigi Zimmerman
  Immediate Past President: Dr. Mimi Bozarth
  Membership Consultant: Joyce Harrison

Founded: 1941
Specialized Field: Series & Festivals; Classical Music; Opera; Ballet Dance; Orchestras
Status: Non-Profit, Non-Professional
Volunteer Staff: 40
Paid Artists: 5
Budget: $120,000
Income Sources: Ticket Sales(Season)
Performs At: Municipal Auditorium

4474
CLASSICFEST: PENSACOLA SUMMER MUSIC FESTIVAL
18 West Wright Street
P.O. Box 12683 Pensacola, FL 32591
Pensacola, FL 32501
Phone: 850-432-5115
Fax: 850-434-8700
e-mail: ccpns@aol.com
Web Site: www.christ-church.net
Management:
: Rector: Rev Russell Jones Levenson
  Associate Rector: Rev D Wallace Adams Riley

Founded: 1764

4475
MUSIC HALL ARTIST SERIES
University of West Florida
11000 University Parkway
Bldg. 82
Pensacola, FL 32514
Phone: 850-474-2541
Fax: 850-474-3247
e-mail: cfpa@uwf.edu
Web Site: www.uwf.edu/cfpa
Management:
: Chairman: Richard Glaze
  Director: Brendan Kelly
  Assistant Director: Jerre Brisky
  Program Director: John Markowitz
  Chair of Theatre: Charles Houghton
  Chair of Music: Joseph Spaniola

Mission: To provide the Pensacola community with world-class performances of chamber music.
Utilizes: Actors; Choreographers; Collaborating Artists; Collaborations; Community Talent; Composers; Contract Orchestras; Curators; Dance Companies; Dancers; Designers; Educators; Fine Artists; Five Seasonal Concerts; Grant Writers; Guest Accompanists; Guest Artists; Guest Choreographers; Guest Companies; Guest Composers; Guest Conductors; Guest Designers; Guest Directors; Guest Instructors; Guest Lecturers; Guest Musical Directors; Guest Musicians; Guest Soloists; Guest Speakers; Guest Teachers; Guest Writers; Guild Activities; High School Drama; Instructors; Local Artists; Local Unknown Artists; Lyricists; Multi Collaborations; Multimedia; Music; New Productions; Original Music Scores; Paid Performers; Performance Artists; Playwrights; Resident Professionals; Scenic Designers; Selected Students; Sign Language Translators; Singers; Soloists; Students; Student Interns; Special Technical Talent; Theatre Companies; Touring Companies; Visual Arts
Founded: 1970
Specialized Field: Vocal Music: Classical
Status: Non-Profit, Professional
Paid Staff: 1
Paid Artists: 6
Budget: $10,000
Income Sources: SGA; University President; Private Funding
Performs At: Music Hall
Annual Attendance: 1,000
Facility Category: Education
Type of Stage: Proscenium; Arena; Concert Hall
Seating Capacity: 426; 120; 307
Year Built: 1992
Rental Contact: Linda May
Organization Type: Sponsoring

4476
SOUTH FLORIDA JAZZ
10460 Kestrel St.
Plantation, FL 33324
Phone: 754-816-6101
Fax: 954-424-4417
e-mail: rw@southfloridajazz.org
Web Site: www.southfloridajazz.org
Management:
: President: Ronald B Weber

Founded: 1992
Specialized Field: Series and Festivals; Jazz Performance; Jazz Education
Status: Non-Profit, Professional
Paid Artists: 50

4477
FRIENDS OF MUSIC OF CHARLOTTE COUNTY CONCERT SERIES
22959 Bayshore Road
Port Charlotte, FL 33980
Phone: 941-629-7278
e-mail: HistoricalCenter@CharlotteFL.com
Web Site: ccflhistory.contentdm.oclc.org/
Management:
: Concert Series Director: Mauriel Van Patten

Utilizes: Artists-in-Residence; Collaborations; Fine Artists; Guest Accompanists; Guest Choreographers; Guest Musical Directors; Guest Musicians; Guild Activities; Lyricists; Multimedia; Original Music Scores; Sign Language Translators; Singers; Theatre Companies
Performs At: Port Charlotte Cultural Center Theatre
Facility Category: Concert Hall
Seating Capacity: 418

4478
BIG ARTS: GREAT PERFORMERS SERIES
900 Dunlop Road
Sanibel, FL 33957
Phone: 239-395-0900
Fax: 239-395-0330
e-mail: info@BIGARTS.org
Web Site: www.bigarts.org

Management:
- **Executive Director:** Lee Ellen Harder
- **Associate Executive Director:** Jessica Baxter
- **Development Director:** Howard Wheeldon
- **Office Manager:** Marina Dowling
- **Director of Marketing & Sales:** Betsy Bender
- **Stage & Company Manager:** P. J. McCready
- **House Manager:** Debi Neri

Utilizes: Artists-in-Residence; Dance Companies; Dancers; Fine Artists; Guest Accompanists; Guest Choreographers; Guest Directors; Guest Instructors; Guest Soloists; High School Drama; Multimedia; Singers; Soloists; Theatre Companies
Founded: 1979
Specialized Field: Series and Festivals; Instrumental Music; Vocal Music; Theatre; Dance; Ethnic Performances
Status: Non-Profit, Professional
Paid Staff: 8
Volunteer Staff: 40
Budget: $700,000
Facility Category: Cultural Center
Seating Capacity: 414
Year Built: 1979
Year Remodeled: 1997

4479
SANIBEL MUSIC FESTIVAL
PO Box 1623
Sanibel, FL 33957-1623
Phone: 239-344-7025
Fax: 941-395-1375
Web Site: www.sanibelmusicfestival.org
Management:
- **Artistic Director:** Jim Griffith

Founded: 1980
Season: March
Performs At: Sanibel Island (Festival Site)
Facility Category: Sanibel Congregational Church
Seating Capacity: 350

4480
ASOLO THEATRE FESTIVAL
5555 N Tamiami Trail
Sarasota, FL 34243
Phone: 941-351-9010
Fax: 941-351-5796
Toll-free: 800-361-8388
e-mail: asolo@asolo.org
Web Site: www.asolo.org
Officers:
- **President:** Bob Bartner

Management:
- **Producing Artistic Director:** Michael Donald Edwards
- **Managing Director:** Linda M Digabriele
- **Assistant Managing Director:** Corinne Gabrielson Deckard
- **Managing Director:** Linda M Digabriele

Mission: To produce and present the highest quality professional theatre in a fiscally responsible manner for its community. The Asolo performs primarily in rotating repertory with a resident company.
Utilizes: Guest Companies; Singers
Founded: 1960
Specialized Field: Professional Theatre
Status: Non-Profit, Professional
Paid Staff: 100
Volunteer Staff: 300
Paid Artists: 15
Non-paid Artists: 60
Budget: $5 million
Income Sources: Theatre Communications Group; American Arts Alliance; Actors' Equity Association; League of Resident Theatres
Performs At: Harold E and Esther M Mertz Theatre; Jane B Cook Theatre
Affiliations: Florida State University
Annual Attendance: 92,000
Organization Type: Performing; Educational

4481
BONK FESTIVAL OF NEW MUSIC
New College of USF, Humanities Division
5700 N Tamiami Trail
Sarasota, FL 34243-2197
Phone: 813-930-8440
Fax: 941-359-4479
e-mail: info@bonkfest.org
Web Site: www.bonkfest.org
Specialized Field: Instrumental; Multi-Media; Dance; Educational
Budget: $10,000
Season: February - March
Performs At: Tampa, Sarasota, St. Petersburg (Festival Site)
Facility Category: Theatres; Auditoriums; Museums

4482
FLORIDA WEST COAST SYMPHONY SERIES
709 North Tamiami Trail
Sarasota, FL 34236
Phone: 941-953-4252
Fax: 941-953-3059
Toll-free: 800-287-9634
e-mail: symphony@fwcs.org
Web Site: www.fwcs.org
Officers:
- **President:** Jack Jost
- **Vice President:** Beatrice Friedman
- **VP:** Susan Weinkle
- **Secretary:** Lois Stuberg
- **Treasurer:** Willian J. Sedgeman

Management:
- **Executive Director:** Joseph McKenna
- **Artistic Director:** Leis Vjailand
- **Finance:** Trevor Cramer
- **Educational Director Programminfg:** Rosanne McCabe
- **Music Director:** Anu Tali
- **President & CEO:** Joseph McKenna
- **Executive Assistant & Board Liaison:** Mary Persico

Mission: To present Florida symphonies, festivals, orchestras and youth orchestra.
Utilizes: Artists-in-Residence; Collaborating Artists; Collaborations; Commissioned Composers; Commissioned Music; Educators; Fine Artists; Five Seasonal Concerts; Grant Writers; Guest Accompanists; Guest Artists; Guest Companies; Guest Composers; Guest Directors; Guest Instructors; Guest Musical Directors; Guest Musicians; High School Drama; Instructors; Local Artists; Multimedia; New Productions; Original Music Scores; Resident Artists; Singers; Soloists
Founded: 1949
Specialized Field: Series & Festivals; Instrumental Music; Festivals
Status: Non-Profit, Professional
Paid Staff: 28
Paid Artists: 100
Budget: $3,800,000
Income Sources: Ticket Sales; Donations
Performs At: Holley Hall; Van Wezel Performing Arts Hall
Annual Attendance: 100,000
Facility Category: Concert Hall
Type of Stage: Raised Open
Stage Dimensions: 16'x32'
Seating Capacity: 500
Year Remodeled: 1985
Architect: Garry Hoyt
Cost: $800,000
Organization Type: Performing; Resident; Educational; Sponsoring

4483
LA MUSICA FESTIVAL
Sarasota, FL
Mailing Address: PO Box 5442 Sarasota, FL 34277
Phone: 941-366-8450
Fax: 941-346-2414
e-mail: info@lamusicafestival.org
Web Site: www.lamusicafestival.org
Officers:
- **President:** Frederick Derr
- **Vice President:** Charlotte Isaacs
- **Chief Financial Officer:** David Hess
- **Recording Secretary:** Sally Faron

Management:
- **Executive Director:** Sally R Faron
- **Artistic Director:** Bruno Giuranna
- **Associate Artistic Director:** Derek Han

Mission: Bring European & American Artists together to present 5 concerts of outstanding chamber music. Daily rehearsals are open to the public.
Utilizes: Commissioned Composers; Commissioned Music; Guest Musical Directors; Multimedia
Founded: 1987
Specialized Field: Chamber Music Festival
Paid Staff: 6
Volunteer Staff: 10
Paid Artists: 15
Budget: $270,000
Income Sources: Tickets; Sponsorships; Gifts
Season: April
Performs At: University of South Florida, Sainer Center (Festival Site); Rehearsal Hall
Annual Attendance: 4,500
Facility Category: St. Thomas More Church
Seating Capacity: 770

4484
SARASOTA CONCERT
777 N. Tamiami Trail
Sarasota, FL 34236
Phone: 941-955-7676
Fax: 941-951-1449
Toll-free: 800-269-03
e-mail: streetleit@aol.com
Officers:
- **President:** Martha Leiter

Management:
- **Artistic Selection Chairman:** Martha Leiter

Founded: 1940
Specialized Field: Series & Festivals; Instrumental Music; Vocal Music; Dance; Ethnic Performances; Orchestra
Status: Non-Profit, Professional
Paid Staff: 26
Paid Artists: 5
Performs At: Van Wezel Performing Arts Hall

4485
SARASOTA JAZZ FESTIVAL
330 South Pineapple Ave
Suite 111
Sarasota, FL 34236

SERIES & FESTIVALS / Florida

Phone: 941-366-1552
Fax: 941-366-1553
e-mail: admin@jazzclubsarasota.com
Web Site: www.jazzclubsarasota.com
Officers:
　President: Bobby Prince
Management:
　Vice President: Wesley Bearden
Founded: 1980
Specialized Field: Series & Festivals; Instrumental Music; Vocal Music
Status: Non-Profit, Professional
Paid Staff: 1
Paid Artists: 300

4486
SARASOTA MUSIC FESTIVAL
709 North Tamiami Trail
Sarasota, FL 34236
Phone: 941-953-4252
Fax: 941-953-3059
e-mail: rmccabe@sarasotaorchestra.org
Web Site: www.sarasotaorchestra.org
Officers:
　President: Joseph McKenna
　CFO: Douglas Shanley
　CMO: Gordon Greenfield
　Stuberg: Lois
　Sedgeman: Secretary Willian J.
Management:
　Artistic Director: Robert Levin
　Education Director: RoseAnne McCabe
　Music Director: Anu Tali
　President & CEO: Joseph McKenna
　Executive Assistant & Board Liaison: Mary Persico
Mission: To present chamber music, master classes and concerts by artists and students from around the world in a three week event on Florida's West Coast.
Founded: 1964
Specialized Field: Chamber; Orchestra
Status: Non-Profit, Professional, Student
Income Sources: Chamber Music America
Performs At: Holley Hall; Sarasota Opera House
Facility Category: Chamber Music; Music Education
Organization Type: Performing; Educational

4487
SEASIDE INSTITUTE SERIES
30 Smolian Circle, 2nd Floor
PO Box 4875
Seaside, FL 32459
Phone: 850-231-2421
Fax: 850-231-1884
e-mail: institute@seasidefl.org
Web Site: www.theseasideinstitute.org
Management:
　Executive Director: Diane Dorney
　Director Of Programme: Leslie W Picke
　Manager: Casey Johnston
　Assistant: Leslie Kennedy
Performs At: Seaside Meeting Hall

4488
MAHAFFEY THEATER
400 First St. S
St Petersburg, FL 33701
Phone: 727-892-5767
Fax: 727-892-5897
Toll-free: 800-874-9015
e-mail: info@themahaffey.com
Web Site: www.themahaffey.com
Management:
　Marketing/Booking Manager: Lauren Kleinfeld
Specialized Field: Festival
Performs At: Mahaffey Theatre for the Performing Arts

4489
MUSEUM OF FINE ARTS SERIES
255 Beach Drive NE
St Petersburg, FL 33701-3498
Phone: 727-896-2667
Fax: 727-894-4638
e-mail: webmonkey@fine-arts.org
Web Site: www.fine-arts.org
Management:
　Director: Dr. Kent Lydecker
　Assistant to Director: Vicki Sofranko
Mission: To present classical concerts.
Founded: 1896
Specialized Field: Tampa Bay
Paid Staff: 4
Volunteer Staff: 6
Paid Artists: 12

4490
ST PETERSBURG COLLEGE
6605 Fifth Avenue North
St Petersburg, FL 33710
Mailing Address: PO Box 13489 St Petersburg, FL 33733
Phone: 727-341-4360
Fax: 727-341-4744
e-mail: steelej@spcollege.edu
Web Site: www.spcollege.du/spg/music
Management:
　Program Director: Jonathan E Steele
　Coordinator Human Resources: Cathy Ladewig
Mission: Education
Founded: 1927
Specialized Field: Music; Choral; Instrumental; Piano; Vocal; Guitar
Paid Staff: 60

4491
TALLAHASSEE MUSEUM
3945 Museum Drive
Tallahassee, FL 32310-6325
Phone: 850-575-8684
Fax: 850-574-8243
e-mail: karen@tallahasseemuseum.org
Web Site: www.tallahasseemuseum.org
Management:
　Executive Director/CEO: Russell S. Daws
　Artistic Director: Jennifer Golden
　Managing Director: Sherri Hall
　Director of Finance: Rebekka K. Wade
　Finance Assistance: Frank Watson
　Facilities Manager: Mike Sullivan
Founded: 1957
Specialized Field: Education
Status: Non-Profit, Non-Professional
Paid Staff: 50
Paid Artists: 20

4492
ATLANTIC SHAKESPEARE FESTIVAL
1435 22nd Avenue
Vero Beach, FL 32960
Phone: 772-569-0132
e-mail: atlanticshakes@yahoo.com
Web Site: www.geocities.com
Management:
　President: Jon A Putzke
Mission: Was founded to provide classical theatrical works, with an emphasis on the works of William Shakespeare, to the residents and visitors to St. Augustine, Florida.
Founded: 1997
Specialized Field: Series & Festivals; Theatre; Youth
Status: Non-Profit, Professional
Income Sources: Program Ad Sales; Production Sponsors; Grants; Private Donations
Facility Category: Outdoor Amphitheatre
Type of Stage: Proscenium
Stage Dimensions: 60;x30'
Seating Capacity: 2200
Year Built: 1995

4493
REGIONAL ARTS MUSIC AT THE KRAVIS CENTER FOR THE PERFORMING ARTS
701 Okeechobee Boulevard
West Palm Beach, FL 33401
Phone: 561-835-4141
Fax: 561-835-0738
Toll-free: 800-572-8471
e-mail: mcdaniel@kravis.org
Web Site: www.kravis.org
Officers:
　Chief Executive Officer: Judith A. Mitchell
　Regional Arts Programming Assoc.: Sharon McDaniel
　Chair: Jane M. Mitchell
　Vice-Chair: Michael J. Bracci
　Treasurer: William A. Meyer
　Secretary: Stephen L. Brown
Utilizes: Guest Musical Directors; Guest Musicians; Multimedia
Founded: 1974
Specialized Field: Vocal Music; Classical
Status: Non-Profit, Professional
Paid Staff: 2
Performs At: Kravis Center for the Arts

4494
SUNFEST OF PALM BEACH COUNTY
525 Clematis Street
West Palm Beach, FL 33401
Phone: 561-659-5980
Fax: 561-659-3567
e-mail: customerservice@sunfest.com
Web Site: www.sunfest.org
Officers:
　President: Carrie Bradburn
　President Elect: Wil White
　Treasurer: Wilson Enriquez
　Secretary: Michelle McGovern
　Legal Counsel: Steve Mayans
Management:
　President: Carrie Bradburn
　Event Manager: Stewart Auville
　Marketing Manager: Terri Neil
Mission: To support a variety of quality visual and performing arts festivals and entertainment events meeting the highest degree of excellence.
Utilizes: Student Interns
Founded: 1982
Specialized Field: Festivals
Status: Nonprofit
Paid Staff: 10
Paid Artists: 210
Income Sources: International Festival Association
Performs At: Along the Intracoastal Waterway; Flagler Drive
Organization Type: Resident

SERIES & FESTIVALS / Georgia

4495
POLK COMMUNITY COLLEGE SPECIAL PERFORMANCE SERIES
999 Avenue H NE
Winter Haven, FL 33881
Phone: 863-297-1050
Fax: 863-297-1053
e-mail: sbevis@polk.edu
Web Site: www.polk.edu
Management:
  President: Larry Durrence
  Executive Director: William N Ryan
Founded: 1960
Specialized Field: Education
Status: Non-Profit, Non-Professional
Paid Staff: 2
Volunteer Staff: 4
Paid Artists: 6

4496
BACHS FESTIVAL SOCIETY OF WINTER PARK
1000 Holt Avenue - 2763
Winter Park, FL 32789
Phone: 407-646-2182
Fax: 407-646-2692
e-mail: info@bachfestivalflorida.org
Web Site: www.bachfestivalflorida.org
Officers:
  President: Eric Ravndal III
  Vice President and Secretary: Robert A. White
  Treasurer: Michael Kakos
Management:
  President: Eric Ravndal III
  Artistic Director: John V Sinclair
  Executive Director: Elizabeth Gwinn
  Patron Engagement Manager: Zac Alfson
Founded: 1937
Specialized Field: Vocal Music: Classical
Status: Non-Profit, Professional
Paid Staff: 4
Paid Artists: 20
Season: February
Performs At: Rollins Colliseum, Winter Park (Festival Site)
Facility Category: Knowles Memorial Chapel
Seating Capacity: 500

4497
FESTIVAL OF ORCHESTRAS
1353 Palmetto Avenue
Suite 100
Winter Park, FL 32789
Phone: 407-539-0245
Fax: 407-539-1525
Toll-free: 800-738-8188
e-mail: greatorchs@cfl.rr.com
Web Site: www.festivaloforchestras.com
Officers:
  CEO: Joseph J Rizzo
Management:
  President: Ellen Thompson
Mission: The mission of the Festival of Orchestras (FOI) is to present premier live performances to the world's great symphony orchestras to the Central Florida public, and at a reasonable price for all. Introducing young children and their teachers, from local schools to world-class orchestral concerts. We also encourage support from the local business community, by providing introductions to international business leaders.
Founded: 1984
Specialized Field: Series and Festivals: Vocal Music
Status: Non-Profit, Professional
Paid Staff: 3
Volunteer Staff: 3
Performs At: Bob Carr Performing Arts Center
Affiliations: OCCA

Georgia

4498
PORTERFIELD MEMORIAL UNITED METHODIST CHURCH - DISTINGUISHED ARTIST SERIES
2200 Dawson Road
Albany, GA 31707
Phone: 229-436-6336
Fax: 229-439-9141
e-mail: stevenjones@porterfieldchurch.org
Web Site: www.porterfieldchurch.org
Management:
  Sr Pastor: Mason Gadly
  Music Ministries Director: Steven Jones
Founded: 1956
Specialized Field: Series & Festivals; Instrumental Music; Vocal Music; Theatre; Youth; Dance; Ethnic Performances
Status: Non-Profit, Non-Professional
Paid Staff: 25
Seating Capacity: 850

4499
GEORGIA SOUTHWESTERN STATE UNIVERSITY CHAMBER CONCERT SERIES
800 Wheatley Street
Americus, GA 31709-4693
Phone: 229-931-2204
Fax: 229-931-2927
e-mail: jem@canes.gsw.edu
Officers:
  Fine Arts Department Chairman: Julie Megginson
Specialized Field: Music
Performs At: Fine Arts Theatre
Seating Capacity: 250

4500
FORTE: THE UNIVERSITY UNION PERFORMING ARTS SERIES
600 Park Street
Fort Hays State University
Athens, GA 67601
Phone: 706-542-6396
Fax: 706-542-5584
e-mail: tigerinfo@fhsu.edu
Web Site: www.uga.edu/stuart
Management:
  President: Erin Bohan
  Student Coordinator: Nathan Copeland
Mission: To deliver a culturally and artistically diverse programming schedule to the University community.
Utilizes: Artists-in-Residence; Guest Soloists; Multimedia; Original Music Scores; Resident Artists; Singers; Theatre Companies
Specialized Field: Series & Festivals; Programming For Concerts; Shows
Status: For-Profit, Non-Professional
Paid Staff: 2
Volunteer Staff: 15
Paid Artists: 6
Budget: $143,850
Income Sources: Student Activity Fees; Ticket Sales

4501
ATLANTA DOWNTOWN FESTIVAL AND TOUR
Atlanta Downtown Neighborhood Association
PO Box 57021
Atlanta, GA 30343
e-mail: downtownatl@hotmail.com
Web Site: www.atlantadna.org/festival.htm
Management:
  Co-Chairman: Chris Raffield
  Vice President Of Special Events: Mary Elizabeth Harmon
Season: June
Performs At: Centennial Olympic Park (Festival Site)
Seating Capacity: 1,000

4502
ATLANTA JAZZ FESTIVAL
City of Atlanta Office of Cultural Affairs
233 Peachtree Street, NE
Suite 1700
Atlanta, GA 30303
Phone: 404-546-6815
Fax: 404-658-6945
Web Site: www.atlantafestivals.com
Management:
  Manager: Alonzo Craig
  Supervisor: Selena Harper
  Festivals Manager: Melissa R. Laurenceau
  Coordinator: Nnena U Nchege
Mission: To offer a showcase for talented local and national performers; to provide Atlanta citizens with jazz music.
Founded: 1978
Specialized Field: Series & Festivals; Instrumental Music; Vocal Music; Theatre; Youth; Ethnic Performances
Status: Non-Profit, Professional
Paid Staff: 12
Performs At: Grant Park
Organization Type: Performing; Educational

4503
CHASTIAN PARK AMPHITHEATRE ATLANTA SYMPHONY ORCHESTRA FESTIVAL POPS
4469 Stella Drive
Suite 300
Atlanta, GA 30327
Phone: 404-733-4900
Fax: 404-733-4901
e-mail: aso-info@woodruffcenter.org
Web Site: www.classicchastian.org
Officers:
  Executive Director: Allison Vulgamore
  Director Public Relations: Minde Herbert
Management:
  Music Director: Robert Spano
  Conductor: Jere Flint
  Conductor: Michael Krajewski
  Principal Guest Conductor: Donald Runnicles
Mission: Provides young instrumentalists an opportunity to perform orchestral masterworks under the city's finest conductors.
Founded: 1945
Specialized Field: Orchestral
Status: Nonprofit
Paid Staff: 40
Volunteer Staff: 200
Budget: $6 million
Income Sources: Donations and Sponsors.
Season: June - August

SERIES & FESTIVALS / Georgia

Performs At: Atlanta Symphony Hall; Woodruff Arts Center
Affiliations: Atlanta Symphony Orchestra
Annual Attendance: 160,000
Facility Category: Chastian Park Amphitheatre
Type of Stage: Plywood/ Shell
Seating Capacity: 6,291
Year Built: 1933
Year Remodeled: 1989
Resident Groups: Atlanta Symphony Orchestra

4504
GEORGIA SHAKESPEARE FESTIVAL
Conant Performing Arts Center
4484 Peachtree Road NE
Atlanta, GA 30319
Phone: 404-504-1473
Fax: 404-504-3414
e-mail: boxoffice@gashakespeare.org
Web Site: www.gashakespeare.org
Officers:
  Chair: Daniel Norris
  Treasurer: Paul Thodeson
  General Counsel: Peter Coffman
  Secretary: Soyia Ellison
Management:
  Managing Director: Jennifer Bauer-Lyons
  Producing Artistic Director: Richard Garner
  Education Director: Allen O'Reilly
  Associate Production Manager: Dusty Brown
  Production Manager: Mike Post
  Development Director: Jordan Flowers
  Business Manager: Hazel Douglas
  Graphic Designer: Daryl Fazio
  Costume Coordinator: Katy Munroe
Mission: To produce professional plays written by Shakespeare and other enduring authors.
Founded: 1985
Specialized Field: Series & Festivals; Theatre; Festivals
Status: Non-Profit, Professional
Paid Staff: 7
Income Sources: Southeastern Theatre Conference; Atlanta Theatre Coalition
Organization Type: Performing; Resident

4505
NATIONAL BLACK ARTS FESTIVAL
NABF
504 Fair Street
Suite 500
Atlanta, GA 30313
Phone: 404-730-7315
Fax: 404-730-7104
e-mail: info@nbaf.org
Web Site: www.nbaf.org
Officers:
  President/CEO: Neil A. Barclay
  Chair: Sonya M. Halpern
  Vice Chair: Charmaine Ward
  Secretary: Stephanie M. Russell
  Treasurer: John W. Brewer
Management:
  Director, Artistic Programming: Leatrice Ellzy
  Deputy Director: Muriel Hepburn
Mission: To engage, cultivate and educate diverse audiences about the arts and culture of the African Diaspora and provide opportunities for artistic and creative expression.
Utilizes: Actors; AEA Actors; Artists-in-Residence; Choreographers; Collaborating Artists; Collaborations; Commissioned Composers; Composers-in-Residence; Curators; Dance Companies; Dancers; Designers; Educators; Filmmakers; Fine Artists; Five Seasonal Concerts; Guest Accompanists; Guest Artists; Guest Choreographers; Guest Companies; Guest Composers; Guest Conductors; Guest Designers; Guest Directors; Guest Ensembles; Guest Instructors; Guest Musical Directors; Guest Musicians; Guest Soloists; Guest Teachers; High School Drama; Instructors; Local Artists; Local Unknown Artists; Lyricists; Multimedia; Music; Original Music Scores; Performance Artists; Playwrights; Poets; Resident Professionals; Sign Language Translators; Singers; Soloists; Special Technical Talent; Theatre Companies; Touring Companies; Visual Arts
Founded: 1987
Specialized Field: Multi-Disciplinary
Status: Non-Profit, Professional
Paid Staff: 10
Volunteer Staff: 200
Paid Artists: 800
Budget: $2 Million
Income Sources: Fulton County Arts Council; Ticket Sales; Corporate Sponsors; Foundations
Organization Type: Presenting

4506
OGLETHORPE UNIVERSITY-ARTS AND IDEAS AT OGLETHORPE
4484 Peachtree Road NE
Atlanta, GA 30319
Phone: 404-261-1441
Fax: 404-364-8442
Toll-free: 800-428-4484
e-mail: iray@oglethorpe.edu
Web Site: www.oglethorpe.edu
Officers:
  President: Lawrence Schall
Management:
  President: Lawrence Schall
  Music Director: W Irwin Ray
Mission: To support the programming of the university.
Founded: 1835
Specialized Field: Instrumental Music; Vocal Music; Choral; Theatre; Ethnic Performances
Status: Non-Profit; Educational; Professional
Paid Staff: 1
Volunteer Staff: 4
Performs At: Conant Center for the Performing Arts

4507
SCHWARTZ CENTER FOR PERFORMING ARTS AT EMORY
1700 North Decatur Road
Suite 251
Atlanta, GA 30322
Phone: 404-727-5050
Fax: 404-712-2296
e-mail: boxoffice@emory.edu
Web Site: www.emory.edu/arts/
Management:
  Managing Director: Robert McKay
  Assistant Marketing and PR Director: Sally Corbett
  Assistant Director Programming: Debbie Joyal
  Box Office Manager: Piper Phillips
Utilizes: Actors; AEA Actors; Choreographers; Collaborating Artists; Collaborations; Curators; Dance Companies; Dancers; Designers; Educators; Filmmakers; Fine Artists; Five Seasonal Concerts; Grant Writers; Guest Accompanists; Guest Artists; Guest Choreographers; Guest Composers; Guest Designers; Guest Directors; Guest Ensembles; Guest Instructors; Guest Lecturers; Guest Musical Directors; Guest Musicians; Guest Soloists; Guest Teachers; Guest Writers; Guild Activities; High School Drama; Instructors; Local Artists; Local Unknown Artists; Multi Collaborations; Multimedia; Music; Original Music Scores; Performance Artists; Playwrights; Poets; Resident Artists; Resident Professionals; Sign Language Translators; Singers; Soloists; Student Interns; Special Technical Talent; Theatre Companies; Touring Companies; Visual Arts
Specialized Field: Music; Dance; Theatre
Paid Staff: 9
Performs At: Glenn Memorial Auditorium; Munroe Theater; Dance Studio; Music; Dance; Theater; Schwartz Center for Performing Arts
Annual Attendance: 30,000
Facility Category: Multiple Facilities

4508
SIX FLAGS OVER GEORGIA
275 Riverside Parkway, SW
Atlanta, GA 30168
Phone: 770-739-3400
Fax: 770-739-3457
Web Site: www.sixflags.com
Management:
  Production Coordinator: Daniel Barr
Founded: 1967
Specialized Field: Entertainment; Teen-Park
Status: Non-Profit, Non-Professional
Season: March - November
Type of Stage: Semi-Thrust
Stage Dimensions: 45' x 30'
Seating Capacity: 750

4509
SPELMAN COLLEGE FRESH IMAGES CHAMBER MUSIC SERIES
Spelman College Department of Music
350 Spelman Lane, SW
Atlanta, GA 30314
Phone: 404-270-5476
Fax: 404-215-7771
e-mail: kjohns10@spelman.edu
Web Site: www.spelman.edu
Officers:
  Chairman Music Department: Kevin Johnson
Management:
  President: Dr Beverly Daniel Tatum
  Associate Director: Monica Rodgers
Mission: To fully empower black women to fully use their talents to succees and to better the world.
Founded: 1881
Specialized Field: Music
Budget: $58 Million
Performs At: Sisters Chapel

4510
GREATER AUGUSTA ARTS COUNCIL
1301 Greene Street
PO Box 1776
Augusta, GA 30903
Phone: 706-826-4702
Fax: 706-826-4723
e-mail: arts@augustaarts.com
Web Site: www.augustaarts.com
Officers:
  President: Lisa Taylor
  1st Vice President: Crystal Eskola
  2nd Vice President: Robert Bennett
  3rd Vice President: Daphne Jones
  Secretary: Evett Davis
  Treasurer: Dennis Sodomka
  Past President: Mike Sleeper
  Member at Large: Cheri Tutt
Management:
  Executive Director: Brenda Durant

Outreach Director: Sallie West
Intern: Jamie Lowe

4511
GEORGIA PERIMETER COLLEGE GUEST ARTIST SERIES
555 N Indian Creek Drive
Clarkston, GA 30021
Phone: 404-299-4150
Fax: 404-299-4271
e-mail: ssigmon@gpc.edu
Web Site: www.gpc.edu
Management:
President: David Kauffman
Executive Director: Susan Sigmon
Managing Director: Richards Rogers
Founded: 1970
Specialized Field: Series and Festivals: Classical Music
Status: Non-Profit, Professional
Paid Staff: 13
Paid Artists: 13
Performs At: Marvin Cole Auditorium

4512
ARTS ASSOCIATION IN NEWTON COUNTY
1106 Washington Street
Covington, GA 30014
Phone: 770-786-8188
Fax: 770-784-1692
e-mail: info@newtoncountyarts.org
Web Site: www.newtoncountyarts.org
Management:
Executive Director: Buncie Hay Lanners
Artistic Director: Ric Chiapetta
Business Manager: Katie Vaughn
Young Artists Program Director: Abigail Morgan Coggin
Marketing Director: Michelle Bryant Johnson
Founded: 1989
Specialized Field: Series and Festivals; Instrumental Music; Vocal Music; Theatre; Youth; Dance; Ethnic Performances
Status: Non-Profit, Professional
Paid Staff: 4
Paid Artists: 90
Performs At: Olive Swann Porter Hall

4513
NORTH GEORGIA COLLEGE & STATE UNIVERSITY MUSIC SERIES
One Park Place South
Suite 823
Dahlonega, GA 30303
Mailing Address: P.O. Box 3984 30302-3984
Phone: 706-864-1643
Fax: 706-864-1647
e-mail: wthomas@ngcsu.edu
Web Site: www.ngc.peachnet.edu
Management:
Student Activities Director: Wesley Thomas
Professor Music/Keyboarding: Joe Chapman
Director Choral Activities: John Broman
Director Bands/Music Education: Andy David
Founded: 1970
Specialized Field: Series & Festivals; Instrumental Music; Vocal Music; Theater; Dance; Ethnic Performances; Performing Arts
Status: Non-Profit
Performs At: Student Center Auditorium

4514
GILMER ARTS & HERITAGE ASSOCIATION SERIES
207 Dalton Street
Suite 103-B
Ellijay, GA 30540
Phone: 706-635-5605
Fax: 706-636-5606
e-mail: gaha@ellijay.com
Web Site: www.gilmercounty.com/gaha
Management:
President: Jane Layman
Executive Director: Mary Sparks
Utilizes: Educators; Fine Artists; Guest Instructors; Guest Soloists; Guild Activities; Instructors; Local Artists; Multimedia; Original Music Scores; Playwrights; Special Technical Talent; Theatre Companies; Touring Companies
Founded: 1979
Specialized Field: Series & Festivals; Instrumental Music; Vocal Music; Theatre; Youth; Dance; Ethnic Performances
Status: Non-Profit, Professional
Paid Staff: 1
Volunteer Staff: 30
Non-paid Artists: 35
Performs At: Ellijay Elementary School Theatre
Seating Capacity: 600

4515
ARTS COUNCIL
201 Green Street
Gainesville, GA 30501
Mailing Address: PO Box 1632 Gainesville, GA 30503-1632
Phone: 770-534-2787
Fax: 770-534-2973
e-mail: info@theartscouncil.net
Web Site: www.theartscouncil.net
Management:
Executive Director/CEO: Gladys Wyant
Mission: To enhance, educate and expand public interest in the arts.
Founded: 1970
Opened: 1972
Specialized Field: Series & Festivals; Music; Dance; Visual Arts
Status: Non-Profit, Professional
Paid Staff: 4
Volunteer Staff: 300
Paid Artists: 200
Non-paid Artists: 20
Budget: $420,000
Income Sources: Memberships; Corporate Sponsors; Foundations; Ticket Revenue; GA Council for the Arts; South Arts; Rentals; Endowment
Performs At: Pearce Auditorium; Arts Council Smithgall Arts Center; GA Mtns Center Arena & Theatre
Affiliations: Brenau University; Crawford W Lang Museum; Elachee Nature Science Center; Gainesville Ballet Company; Gainesville Chorale; Gainesville Theatre
Seating Capacity: 720
Rental Contact: Gladys Wyant

4516
MACON CONCERT ASSOCIATION
P.O. Box 5694
Macon, GA 31208
Phone: 478-743-6940
Officers:
VP: Edward Eikner
Management:
Executive Director: Lynn Cass
President: Stella Tsai
Founded: 1927
Specialized Field: Instrumental Music; Vocal Music; Classical Music
Status: Non-Profit, Professional
Paid Staff: 1
Performs At: Porter Auditorium

4517
MUSIC MERCER SERIES
Mercer University
1400 Coleman Avenue
Music Department
Macon, GA 31207
Phone: 478-301-2748
Fax: 478-301-5633
Toll-free: 800-342-0841
e-mail: roberts_jn@mercer.edu
Web Site: www.mercer.edu
Officers:
Music Department Chairman: Dr. John Roberts
Management:
President: William D. Underwood
Executive Director: Kirby Godsey
Artistic Director: Patty Crocker
Managing Director: John Roberts
Founded: 1833
Specialized Field: Vocal Music: Classical Music
Status: Non-Profit, Professional
Paid Staff: 27
Paid Artists: 18
Performs At: McCorkle Music Building; Recital Hall
Affiliations: NASM
Seating Capacity: 190
Year Built: 2001
Cost: 7,000,000

4518
BREWTON-PARKER COLLEGE FINE ARTS COUNCIL
US 280
P. O. Box 197
Mount Vernon, GA 30445
Phone: 912-583-3133
Fax: 912-583-3136
Toll-free: 800-342-1087
e-mail: pdickens@bpc.edu
Web Site: www.bpc.edu
Officers:
Chairman: Pierce Dickens
Management:
President: David R Smith
Founded: 1903
Specialized Field: Education
Status: Non-Profit, Professional
Paid Staff: 200
Paid Artists: 7
Performs At: Gilder Recital Hall

4519
ARMSTRONG ATLANTIC STATE UNIVERSITY
11935 Abercorn Street
Savannah, GA 31419
Phone: 912-344-2556
Fax: 912-344-3419
Toll-free: 800-633-2349
e-mail: finearts@mail.armstrong.edu
Web Site: www.finearts.armstrong.edu
Management:
President: Tom Jones
Founded: 1935

SERIES & FESTIVALS / Hawaii

Specialized Field: Series & Festivals; Instrumental Music; Vocal Music; Theater; Youth
Status: Non-Profit, Non-Professional
Performs At: AASU Fine Arts Auditorium
Seating Capacity: 960
Year Built: 1975

4520
SAVANNAH CONCERT ASSOCIATION
P.O. Box 1088
Savannah, GA 31402-1088
Phone: 912-236-9511
e-mail: calendar@savannahnow.com
Web Site: http://events.savannahnow.com/
Officers:
   President: Martin Greenburg
Management:
   President: Byron Boyd
   Publisher: Michael C. Traynor
   Vice President of Audience: Steve Yelvington
   Executive Editor: Susan Catron
   Marketing Director: Stacy Jennings
   HR Director: Frankie Fort
   Production Director: Sean Ruth
Founded: 2003
Specialized Field: Instrumental Music; Classical Music
Status: Non-Profit

4521
SAVANNAH MUSIC FESTIVAL
200 East St. Julian Street
Suite 601
Savannah, GA 31401
Mailing Address: PO Box 8105 Savannah, GA 31412-8105
Phone: 912-234-3378
Fax: 912-236-1989
Toll-free: 800-868-3378
e-mail: info@savannahmusicfestival.org
Web Site: www.savannahmusicfestival.org
Management:
   President: Rob Gibson
   Managing Director: Melissa Paulsen
Mission: Music festival in historic Savannah, Georgia.
Founded: 1988
Specialized Field: Series & Festivals; Instrumental Music; Vocal Music; jazz; Youth; Dance; Ethnic Performances
Status: Non-Profit, Professional
Paid Staff: 6
Volunteer Staff: 260
Paid Artists: 75
Non-paid Artists: 78
Budget: $866,000
Income Sources: Box Office; Grants; Corporate; Foundation; Individuals; Government
Season: March
Performs At: Historic District of Savannah (Festival Site)
Annual Attendance: 20,000
Facility Category: Historic Churches; Synagogues; Recital Halls
Seating Capacity: 400 - 1,200 (indoors); 3,000 (outdoors)

4522
THOMASTON-UPSON ARTS COUNCIL PERFORMING SERIES
118 South Church Street
PO Box 211
Thomaston, GA 30286
Phone: 706-647-1605
Fax: 706-647-2187
e-mail: tuarts@alltel.net
Web Site: www.tuac.com
Management:
   President: Jaye Eubanks
   Executive Director: Carmen Ellerbee
   Vice President: Lauri Irvin
Founded: 1986
Specialized Field: Series and Festivals; Instrumental Music; Vocal Music; Theatre; Youth; Dance; Ethnic Performances
Status: Non-Profit, Professional
Paid Staff: 2
Organization Type: Performing; Educational; Sponsoring

4523
THOMASVILLE ENTERTAINMENT FOUNDATION
600 East Washington Street
Thomasville, GA 31792
Mailing Address: PO Box 1976 Thomasville, GA 31799
Phone: 229-226-7404
Fax: 229-226-0599
e-mail: tef@rose.net
Web Site: www.tefconcerts.com
Officers:
   President: Kenneth J Rebman
Management:
   Executive Director: Janice Faircloth
   Music Director: Clayton J. Poole
Founded: 1937
Specialized Field: Series and Festivals; Instrumental Music; Vocal Music; Theatre; Youth; Dance; Ethnic Performances
Status: Non-Profit, Professional
Paid Staff: 1
Volunteer Staff: 12
Income Sources: Ticket Sales; Private Contributions
Performs At: Thomasville Cultural Center
Seating Capacity: 500

4524
JEKYLL ISLAND MUSICAL THEATRE FESTIVAL
204 W. Brookwood Dr.
1500 N. Patterson St.
Valdosta, GA 31698
Phone: 229-259-7770
Fax: 229-249-2602
e-mail: dguthrie@valdosta.edu
Management:
   Managing Director: H. Duke Guthrie
   Dean School of the Arts: Dr. Lanny Milbrandt
   Artistic Director: Jacque Wheeler
Mission: Providing Georgia's Golden Isles residents and visitors with quality musical theatre; offering college interns professional training.
Utilizes: Guest Choreographers; Guest Companies; Singers
Founded: 1990
Specialized Field: Summer Stock; Musical
Status: Professional; Nonprofit
Paid Artists: 65
Income Sources: Valdosta State University
Season: June - August
Performs At: Jekyll Island Amphitheater
Annual Attendance: 10,000
Facility Category: Professional Summer Stock Theatre
Type of Stage: Wooden, uncovered amphitheatre
Seating Capacity: 500
Year Built: 1970
Organization Type: Performing; Touring

4525
LOWNDES/VALDOSTA ARTS COMMISSION
527 N Patterson St.
Valdosta, GA 31601
Phone: 229-247-2787
Fax: 229-247-8978
e-mail: l/vac@surfsouth.com
Web Site: www.turnercentre.com
Officers:
   Board Chair: Archie Waldron
   Vice Chair: Gail Hobgood
   Treasurer: Bob Goddard
   Secretary: Paula Fricker
Management:
   President: Paula Brown
   Executive Director: Cheryl Oliver
   Creative Administrator: Bill Shenton
   Communications Administrator: Rebecca Brosemer
Specialized Field: Series & Festivals: Theatre
Status: Non-Profit, Professional
Performs At: Mathis Municipal Auditorium

Hawaii

4526
HAWAII CONCERT SOCIETY
UH Hilo Performing Arts Center
200 W. Kawili St.
Hilo, HI 96720-4091
Phone: 808-932-7490
Fax: 808-932-7494
e-mail: jwakely@packagehomes.com
Web Site: http://artscenter.uhh.hawaii.edu/
Officers:
   VP: Judith Wakely
Management:
   President: Tom Geballe
   Manager: Lee Dombroski
   Technical Director: Rob Abe
   Associate Manager: Dori Yamada
Founded: 1956
Specialized Field: Series & Festivals; Instrumental Music; Vocal Music; Dance; Ethnic Performances
Status: Non-Profit, Non-Professional
Performs At: University of Hawaii at Hilo Theatre
Seating Capacity: 600

4527
HONOLULU CHAMBER MUSIC SERIES
P.O. Box 2233
Honolulu, HI 96804-2233
Phone: 808-528-8226
Fax: 808-956-9422
e-mail: info@honoluluchambermusic.org
Web Site: honoluluchambermusicseries.org
Officers:
   President: Jonathan Korth
   Vice President: John Love
   Treasurer: Luise Braun
   Assistant Treasurer: Pamela Simon
   Secretary: Joan Canfield
Performs At: Orvis Auditorium

4528
UNIVERSITY OF HAWAII SERIES
Sinclair Library 301
2425 Campus Road
Honolulu, HI 96822

SERIES & FESTIVALS / Idaho

Phone: 808-956-7221
Fax: 808-956-9422
e-mail: ochelp@hawaii.edu
Web Site: www.outreach.hawaii.edu
Management:
    President: David McClain
    Executive Director: Peter Tanaka
Mission: Presenting organization
Founded: 1907
Specialized Field: Series and Festivals: Ethnic Performances
Status: For-Profit, Professional
Paid Staff: 4
Performs At: Various Auditoriums

4529
MAUI COMMUNITY COLLEGE SERIES
310 Kaahumanu Avenue
Kahului, HI 96732
Phone: 808-984-3500
Fax: 808-244-9632
e-mail: rwehrman@hawaii.edu
Web Site: www.maui.hawaii.edu
Management:
    Assistant Music Professor: Robert Wehrman
Performs At: Maui Arts & Cultural Center

4530
HALAU HULA KA NO'EAU
Hawai'i Arts Ensemble
600 Queen Street
Suite 2403
Kamuela, HI 96813
Mailing Address: PO Box 1907
Phone: 808-285-4035
Fax: 808-885-9018
e-mail: HuliauDanceCo@aol.com
Web Site: www.artofhula.com
Management:
    Artistic Director: Kuma Hula
    Director: Michael Pili Pang
    Technical: Barbara Thompson
Mission: To promote and sustain the inherent cultural and artistic values of Hawaiian Dance.
Founded: 1986
Specialized Field: Hula; Hawaiian Chant and Music

4531
BRIGHAM YOUNG UNIVERSITY: HAWAII PERFORMANCE SERIES
55-220 Kulanui Street
Laie, HI 96762-1294
Phone: 808-675-3211
Fax: 808-293-3374
e-mail: lucerod@byuh.edu
Web Site: www.byuh.edu
Management:
    Managing Director: David Lucero
Founded: 1955
Specialized Field: Series & Festivals; Instrumental Music; Vocal Music; Dance; Ethnic Performances
Status: Non-Profit, Non-Professional
Paid Staff: 1
Performs At: David O. McKay Auditorium
Seating Capacity: 649

Idaho

4532
BOISE CHAMBER MUSIC SERIES
1910 University Drive
Boise, ID 83725-1560
Phone: 208-426-1216
Fax: 208-426-1771
e-mail: jbelfy@boisestate.edu
Web Site: www.boisechambermusicseries.org
Management:
    Artistic Director: Jeanne Belfy
Founded: 1984
Specialized Field: Chamber Music Presenting
Status: Non-Profit, Professional
Paid Staff: 1
Performs At: Morrison Center Recital Hall

4533
SHAKESPEARE FESTIVAL
PO Box 9635
Boise, ID 83707
Phone: 208-429-9908
Fax: 208-429-8798
e-mail: info@idahoshakespeare.org
Web Site: www.idahoshakespeare.org
Officers:
    President: John Sims
    Vice President: Karen Meyer
    Secretary: J. Walter Sinclair
    Treasurer: Robert P. Aravich, Jr.
    Past President: Lynn Johnston
    Executive Director: Charles Fee
    Managing Director: Mark Hosslund
    Educational Director: Carole Whiteleather
Mission: To provide live, professional theater for the cultural enrichment and theater-arts education of children, young adults and their families at a cost which makes the programs easily accessible to all.
Utilizes: Guest Companies; Singers
Founded: 1981
Specialized Field: Theatre; Classical; Theatrical Group
Status: Non-Profit, Professional
Paid Staff: 5
Non-paid Artists: 15
Performs At: Morrison Center for the Performing Arts, Fulton St. Theatre
Annual Attendance: 25,000 - 30,000
Seating Capacity: 200; 200
Organization Type: Performing; Touring; Educational

4534
CALDWELL FINE ARTS SERIES
2112 Cleveland Blvd.
Caldwell, ID 83605
Phone: 208-459-5783
Fax: 208-459-5885
e-mail: info@caldwellfinearts.org
Web Site: www.caldwellfinearts.org
Officers:
    President: Dr Lisa Derry
Management:
    Executive Director: Sylvia Hunt
Mission: To offer professional performances in the performing arts; to provide local industry groups and schools with training and support.
Founded: 1961
Specialized Field: Series & Festivals: Classical
Status: Non-Profit, Professional
Paid Staff: 1
Income Sources: Pacific Northwest Presenters
Performs At: Jewett Auditorium
Organization Type: Educational; Sponsoring

4535
AUDITORIUM CHAMBER MUSIC SERIES
University of Idaho
PO Box 444015
Moscow, ID 83844-4015
Phone: 208-885-7557
Fax: 208-885-7254
e-mail: chmusic@uidaho.edu
Web Site: www.class.uidaho.edu/concerts
Management:
    Director: Mary DuPree
Mission: Offers a yearly concert series and we also sponsor activities throughout the Palouse bringing visiting artists into direct contact with school children, university students and community members.
Status: Nonprofit
Paid Staff: 2
Paid Artists: 20
Income Sources: National Endowment for the Arts, Idaho Commission on the Arts
Season: September-April
Performs At: University of Idaho Auditorium

4536
LIONEL HAMPTON JAZZ FESTIVAL
University of Idaho
875 Perimeter Dr.
Moscow, ID 83844-4257
Phone: 208-885-5900
Fax: 208-885-6513
Toll-free: 800-639-4160
e-mail: jazzinfo@uidaho.edu
Web Site: www.jazz.uidaho.edu
Management:
    President: Tim White
    Executive Director: Steven Remington
    Student Performance Evaluations: Tia Christiansen
    Artist Relations: Travis Labbe
    Marketing and Development: Steven Remington
    Administrative Coordinator: Jeanine Berglund
    Volunteer Programs: Erin Turner
Mission: Through four days of student competitions, artist workshops and world class concerts, the Lionel Hampton Jazz Festival keeps the magic, music and spirit of jazz alive for generations to come by inspiring students, teachers and artists of all ages and abilities to support music education in schools and colleges throughout the US and Canada and very directly at the University of Idaho.
Founded: 1967
Specialized Field: Education
Status: Non-Profit, Professional
Paid Staff: 5
Volunteer Staff: 400
Paid Artists: 60
Budget: $ 1 Million
Income Sources: Ticket Sales; Sponsorships; Registration Fees
Affiliations: University of Idaho
Annual Attendance: 25,000-30,000
Facility Category: University
Stage Dimensions: 50x100
Seating Capacity: 10,000

4537
MOUNTAIN HOME ARTS COUNCIL
P.O. Box 974
Mountain Home, ID 83647
Phone: 208-587-3706
e-mail: mh-arts@qwestoffice.net
Web Site: www.mharts.org
Officers:
    President: Denise Barresi
    Vice-President: Linda Kirkendall
    Treasurer: Chris DeVore
    Secretary: Frank Monasterio
Management:
    Executive Director: Sally J. Cruser

SERIES & FESTIVALS / Illinois

Mission: To offer diverse professional, performing arts presentations to the Mountain Home community.
Specialized Field: Dance; Vocal Music; Instrumental Music; Theater
Status: Non-Professional
Organization Type: Performing; Educational

4538
BRIGHAM YOUNG UNIVERSITY
Brigham Young University
525 South Center St.
Rexburg, ID 83460
Phone: 208-496-1411
Fax: 208-496-1884
e-mail: ask@byui.edu
Web Site: www.byui.edu
Management:
    Executive Director: Don Sparhawk
Mission: Our year round series of more than 20 performance offers a variety of music, dance and theater that is intended to entertain, uplift and enlighten both our students and the surrounding community.
Utilizes: Guest Musical Directors; Guest Musicians; Multimedia; Singers
Founded: 1888
Specialized Field: Classical and Contemporary Music
Status: Non-Profit, Professional
Paid Staff: 1
Performs At: Hart Auditorium; Barrus Concert Hall; Kirkham Auditorium

4539
SALMON ARTS COUNCIL
200 Main Street
Salmon, ID 83467
Phone: 208-756-2987
Fax: 208-756-4840
e-mail: caroline.stivers@salmonarts.org
Web Site: www.salmonidaho.com
Officers:
    President: Bradley Barrios
    Vice-President: Don Ward
    Secretary: Dr. David Wood
    Treasurer: Stephanie Smith
Management:
    Executive Director: Caroline Stivers
    Office Administrator: Tammy Dahle
Founded: 1978
Specialized Field: Series & Festivals; Instrumental Music; Vocal Music; Theatre; Youth; Dance; Ethnic Performances
Status: Non-Profit, Professional
Paid Staff: 1
Performs At: Salmon High School Gymnasium

4540
FESTIVAL AT SANDPOINT
525 Pine St.
Suite 207
Sandpoint, ID 83864
Mailing Address: PO Box 695 Sandpoint, ID 83864
Phone: 208-265-4554
Fax: 208-263-6858
Toll-free: 888-265-4554
e-mail: festival@sandpoint.net
Web Site: www.festivalatsandpoint.com
Officers:
    Board President: Bob Witte
    Vice President: Grant Nixon
    Treasurer: Mark Berryhill
    Secretary: Barbara Buchanan
Management:
    Executive Director: Diana Wahl
    Office Manager: Carol Winget

    Production Manager: Dave Nygren
    Stage/Site Manager: Paul Gunter
    Transportation Manager: Mary Vail
Founded: 1983
Specialized Field: Series & Festivals: Music
Status: Non-Profit, Professional
Paid Staff: 3
Performs At: Memorial Field; Schweitzer Mountain Resort (Festival Site)
Facility Category: Memorial Field
Seating Capacity: 2,500

4541
PEND OREILLE ARTS COUNCIL
302 N. 1st Avenue
Sandpoint, ID 83864
Mailing Address: PO Box 1694 Sandpoint, Idaho 83864
Phone: 208-263-6139
Fax: 208-255-1869
e-mail: poac@artinsandpoint.net
Web Site: www.artinsandpoint.org
Management:
    President: Carol Deaner
    Director: Kim Brown
    Executive Director: Debbie Love
    Assistant: Kaori Parkinson
Mission: Exists to facilitate and present the finest quality experiences in the arts for the people of the Sandpoint area.
Performs At: Panida Theatre

4542
SUN VALLEY SUMMER SYMPHONY
120 North 2nd Avenue
Suite 103
Sun Valley, ID 83353
Mailing Address: PO Box 1914 Sun Valley, Idaho 83353
Phone: 208-622-5607
Fax: 208-622-9149
e-mail: info@svsummersymphony.org
Web Site: svsummersymphony.org
Officers:
    President: Maggie Sturdevant
    Vice-President: Mary Jane Armacost
    VP: Preston Strazza
    Treasurer: Deb Mello
    Secretary: Wilson McElhinny
Management:
    Music Director: Alasdair Neale
    Founder: Carl Eberl
    Executive Director: Jennifer Teisinger
    Administrative/Finance Manager: Vicki Abrams
    Operations Director: Deanna Immel
    Development Director: Carol O'Loughlin
    Education Director: Kim Gasenica
    Stage Manager: Jack Beuttler
Mission: To provide quality free, classical music performances that have cultural, educational, and artistic relevance.
Utilizes: Collaborations; Guest Musicians; Music; Original Music Scores
Founded: 1985
Paid Staff: 1.5
Paid Artists: 90
Budget: $860,000
Income Sources: Individual; Business; Private Donations
Season: Late July - Mid August
Performs At: Sun Valley (Festival Site)
Facility Category: Sun Valley Esplanade Tent
Stage Dimensions: 60'x 40'
Seating Capacity: 1,000

4543
ARTS ON TOUR SERIES
PO Box 456
Twin Falls, ID 83303
Phone: 208-732-6288
Fax: 296-991-66
e-mail: cbarigar@csi.edu
Web Site: artsontour.csi.edu
Officers:
    Chair: Rob Hurcum
Performs At: Auditorium

Illinois

4544
ARTS AT ARGONNE MUSIC SERIES
Argonne National Laboratory
9700 S Cass Avenue, Building 221
Argonne, IL 60439
Phone: 630-252-2000
Fax: 630-252-6104
e-mail: arts@anl.gov
Web Site: www.anl.gov/arts
Officers:
    Chairman/President: Dr. Branko Ruscic
Management:
    Director: Peter B. Littlewood
    Deputy Laboratory Director for Prog: Alfred P. Sattelberger
    Deputy Laboratory Director for Oper: Paul Kearns
    Associate Laboratory Director: Mark Peters
    Associate Laboratory Director: Rick Stevens
Mission: Supporting world class cultural presentations for employees of Argonne National laboratory and their families and for residents of neighboring communities.
Utilizes: Fine Artists; Multimedia; Original Music Scores; Singers
Founded: 1988
Specialized Field: Series & Fetivals: Instrumental Music
Status: Non-Profit, Professional
Volunteer Staff: 15
Budget: $20,000-$35,000
Income Sources: Ticket Sales; Illinois Arts Council
Performs At: Auditorium
Affiliations: Chicago Music Alliance
Facility Category: Auditorium
Seating Capacity: 400
Organization Type: Sponsoring

4545
PARAMOUNT ARTS CENTRE PERFORMING ARTS SERIES
1300 Winchester Avenue
Suite 230
Aurora, IL 41101
Phone: 606-324-3175
Fax: 630-892-1084
e-mail: info@paramountarts.com
Web Site: www.paramountarts.com
Officers:
    Chairman: MW Meyer
    Vice Chairman: Richard Hawks
    Treasurer: Donna Williams
    Secretary: Gyda Stoner
Management:
    Executive Director: Bruce Marquis
    Theatre Services Coordinator: Jeff Wells
    Box Office Manager: Jill Martin
    Box Office Manager: Jonnell Crawford
    Executive Director: Janet R Bean

SERIES & FESTIVALS / Illinois

Mission: To present a variety of quality performances at moderate prices in a convenient location, plus educational opportunities and activities; supports other not-for-profit performing arts organizations.
Founded: 1931
Specialized Field: Series & Festivals; Theatre; Youth; Dance; Ethnic Performances
Status: Non-Profit, Professional
Budget: $3.0 million
Income Sources: Ticket Sales; Theatre Rentals; Grants; Donations; Sponsors; Program Ads; Fundraisers
Annual Attendance: 100,000
Facility Category: Performance Center
Type of Stage: Proscenium
Stage Dimensions: 48'x2" x 38'
Seating Capacity: 1888
Year Built: 1931
Year Remodeled: 1975
Rental Contact: Theatre Center Coordinator Jeff Wells (630-264-7202)

4546
FERMILAB ARTS SERIES
PO Box 500
Kirk Road & Pine Street
Batavia, IL 60510-0500
Phone: 630-840-2787
Fax: 630-840-5501
e-mail: audweb@fnal.gov
Web Site: www.fnal.gov/culture
Management:
 Arts Coordinator: Janet MacKay-Galbraith
 Box Office Manager: Colleen Choy
 Cultural Arts Supervisor: Denise M Adducci
Mission: To provide professional performing arts for the Batavia community.
Specialized Field: Dance; Instrumental Music; Theater; Comedy; Jazz
Status: Nonprofit
Paid Staff: 3
Budget: $35,000-$60,000
Income Sources: Fermi National Accel Laboratories
Performs At: Ramsey Auditorium
Organization Type: Sponsoring

4547
UNIVERSITY OF ILLINOIS: ASSEMBLY HALL
1800 S First Street
Champaign, IL 61820
Phone: 217-333-2923
Fax: 217-244-8888
e-mail: webcomment@ahmail.assembly.uiuc.edu
Web Site: www.uofiassemblyhall.com
Management:
 Director: Kevin Ullestad
Specialized Field: Series & Festivals: Arena

4548
ANNUAL CHICAGO JAZZ FESTIVAL
78 E. Washington St.
4th Floor
Chicago, IL 60602
Phone: 312-744-3315
Fax: 312-744-0613
e-mail: specialevents@cityofchicago.org
Web Site: www.cityofchicago.org/specialevents
Management:
 Coordinator: Jennifer J Washington
Mission: To present a festival, free to the public featuring jazz in all of its forms.
Founded: 1979
Specialized Field: Vocal Music; Instrumental Music; Jazz
Status: Professional
Season: September
Performs At: Symphony Music Shell; Petrillo Music Shell
Organization Type: Performing

4549
CHICAGO COLLEGE OF PERFORMING ARTS MUSIC CONSERVATORY SERIES
430 S Michigan Avenue
Chicago, IL 60605
Phone: 312-341-2500
Fax: 312-341-6358
e-mail: lberna@roosevelt.edu
Web Site: www.ccpa.roosevelt.edu
Management:
 President: Charles Middleton
 Director: Linda Berna
 Dean: Henry Fogel
 Associate Dean: Rudy Marcozzi
 Assistant to Dean: Bonnie Wedington
 Admission Counselor: Amanda Horvath
 Administrative Clerk: Sean Archer
 Administrative Clerk: Ora Ross
 Assistant to the Director: Mariama Torruella
Founded: 1997
Specialized Field: Series & Festivals; Instrumental Music; Vocal Music; Theatre
Status: Non-Profit, Professional
Paid Staff: 80
Paid Artists: 20

4550
CHICAGO STUDIO OF PROFESSIONAL SINGING PERFORMANCE SERIES
1040 W Granville Avenue
STE 103
Chicago, IL 60660
Phone: 773-764-5022
Fax: 773-764-5022
e-mail: info@sitesabreeze.com
Web Site: www.professionalsinging.com
Management:
 Director and Master Voice Teacher: Janice Pantazelos
 Assistant Marketing Director: Joyce Chacko
 Voice Teacher: Monique Robertson
 Voice Teacher: Grace Sanchez
Mission: CSPS performance series showcase top professional singers from the Chicagoland area.
Specialized Field: Edgewater
Paid Staff: 3
Income Sources: Tickets; Advertising
Affiliations: NATS

4551
CRYSTAL BALLROOM CONCERT ASSOCIATION SERIES
1332 W. Burnside
#521
Chicago, IL 97209
Phone: 503-225-0047
e-mail: crystal@mcmenamins.com
Web Site: www.crystalballroompdx.com
Management:
 Executive Secretary/Program Dir: Beverly DeFries-D'Albert
Mission: To provide performances of local and international artists for the Chicago community.
Founded: 1984
Specialized Field: Dance; Vocal Music; Instrumental Music; Festivals
Status: Professional; Nonprofit
Paid Staff: 50
Income Sources: Zoltan Kodaly Academy & Institute
Performs At: Crystal Ballroom
Organization Type: Performing; Educational; Sponsoring

4552
DAME MYRA HESS MEMORIAL CONCERT SERIES
30 East Adams Street
Suite 1206
Chicago, IL 60603
Phone: 312-670-6888
Fax: 312-670-9166
e-mail: info@imfchicago.org
Web Site: www.imfchicago.org
Officers:
 President: Emil Zbella
 Vice President: Will McGrath
 Secretary: Desiree Grode
 Treasurer: Michael Rose
Management:
 Program Coordinator: John Lee
 Executive Director: Ann Murray
 Program Coordinator: Maria Valdes-Vargas
 Program Coordinator: John Lee
Founded: 1978
Specialized Field: Classical Music
Paid Staff: 3
Volunteer Staff: 4
Paid Artists: 79
Annual Attendance: 25,000

4553
FRIDAY NOON CONCERT SERIES
Fourth Presbyterian Church
126 E. Chestnut Street
Chicago, IL 60611-2014
Phone: 312-787-4570
Fax: 312-787-4584
e-mail: music@fourthchurch.org
Web Site: www.fourthchurch.org
Management:
 Music Director/Organist: John W W Sherer
 Associate Organist: Thomas Gouwens

4554
GRANT PARK MUSIC FESTIVAL
205 E Randolph Street
Chicago, IL 60601
Phone: 312-742-7638
Fax: 312-742-7662
e-mail: info@grantparkmusicfestival.com
Web Site: www.grantparkmusicfestival.com
Management:
 Executive Director: James W Palermo
 Managing Director: Leigh Levine
 Artistic Director: Carlos Kalmar
Mission: To offer symphonic concerts at no cost to Chicago residents.
Utilizes: Guest Artists
Founded: 1934
Specialized Field: Series and Festivals; Instrumental Music; Vocal Music
Status: Non-Profit, Professional
Paid Staff: 100
Paid Artists: 100
Season: June - August
Performs At: Grant Park, Chicago
Organization Type: Performing; Resident; Educational

SERIES & FESTIVALS / Illinois

4555
ILLINOIS INSTITUTE OF TECHNOLOGY, UNION BOARD CONCERTS
3201 S State Street
Chicago, IL 60616
Phone: 312-567-3080
Fax: 312-567-8917
e-mail: ub@iit.edu
Web Site: www.ub.iit.edu
Management:
   Student Activities Director: Daniel DiCesare
Specialized Field: Series & Festivals: Cultural Events
Status: Non-Profit, Professional
Paid Artists: 150

4556
JAZZ INSTITUTE OF CHICAGO
410 S Michigan Avenue
#500
Chicago, IL 60605
Phone: 312-427-1676
Fax: 312-427-1684
e-mail: laurend@flash.net
Web Site: www.jazzinchicago.org
Officers:
   President: Rik Geiersbach
   Executive Director: Lauren Deutsch
   Vice Chairman: Timuel Black
   Secretary: Jim DeJong
   Treasurer: Darryl Wilson
Management:
   Executive Director: Lauren Deutsch
   Education Program Director: Diana Chandler-Marshall
   Communications & Marketing Director: Mekeda Johnson-Brooks
   Operatons Manager: Alex Betzel
   Event Production Manager and Book k: Lawrence Rocks
   Education Associate: Zakiya Powell
   Education Associate: Katie Ernst
Founded: 1969
Specialized Field: Series & Festivals; Instrumental Music; Vocal Music; Theatre; Youth; Dance; Ethnic Performances; Jazz
Status: Non-Profit, Professional
Paid Staff: 3
Season: Labor Day Weekend
Performs At: Grant Park, Chicago (Festival Site)
Facility Category: Perillo Band Shell & Jazz on Jackson Stage
Seating Capacity: 5,000 seats, 100,000 lawn seating

4557
LOYOLA UNIVERSITY OF CHICAGO SEASON SUBSCRIPTION SERIES
1032 W. Sheridan Road
Chicago, IL 60660
Phone: 773-508-7510
Fax: 773-508-7515
e-mail: abrowni@luc.edu
Web Site: www.bogs.luc.edu
Management:
   Chairperson: Sarah Gabel
   Technical Director: Joseph Gluecker
   Managing Director: April Browning

4558
NEWBERRY CONSORT
60 W Walton
Chicago, IL 60610
Phone: 312-255-3610
Fax: 312-255-3680
e-mail: info@newberryconsort.org
Web Site: www.newberryconsort.org
Management:
   Director: David Douglass
   Director: Ellen Hargis
   General Manager: Ken Perlow
Founded: 1987
Specialized Field: Series &Festivals; Instrumental Music; Vocal Music
Status: Non-Profit; Professional
Seating Capacity: 310

4559
PERFORMING ARTS ASSOCIATION
630 9th Avenue
Suite 213
Chicago, IL 10036-4752
Phone: 212-206-8490
Fax: 212-206-8603
Officers:
   President: Hosang Ahn
   Executive Director: Susan Lipman
   Director: Christy Uchida
   Operations Manager: Laurell Zahrobsky
   Development Assistant: Brigid Flynn
   Treasurer: Jeff Daniel
   Secretary: Claudia Toni
   Chair: Anthony Sargent
   Chair-Elect: Mary Lou Aleskie
Management:
   President: Frederic W Schwartz
   Chief Executive Officer: David Baile
   Manager of Membership and Events: Ann Norris Pattan
   Program and Development Associate: Nicole Merritt
   Communications and Events Coordinat: Minji Kim
   Bookkeeper: Melanie Hopkins
Mission: To present artists who explore the creative tension between tradition and innovation, to nurture an environment for and bring to performance new works and new performers, and to remain accountable to its community, furthering support for local artists, engagement and education, not only for its direct audience, but for society at large.
Utilizes: Special Technical Talent
Founded: 1954
Specialized Field: Series & Festivals: Individual Concerts
Status: Non-Profit, Professional
Budget: $1,000,000
Performs At: The Civic Theater
Organization Type: Performing; Resident; Educational; Sponsoring

4560
UNIVERSITY OF CHICAGO PROFESSIONAL INSTRUMENTAL MUSIC SERIES
University Of Chicago Music Department
1010 East 59th Street
Chicago, IL 60637
Phone: 630-655-9538
Fax: 630-655-8807
e-mail: philharmonia@yahoo.com
Management:
   Executive Director: Mark Epstein
   Artistic Director: Farobaghomi Cooper
Founded: 1985
Specialized Field: Series and Festivals: Instrumental Music
Status: Non-Profit, Professional
Paid Staff: 7
Paid Artists: 75

4561
UNIVERSITY OF CHICAGO PROFESSIONAL INSTRUMENTAL MUSIC SERIES
University Of Chicago Music Department
1010 East 59th Street
Chicago, IL 60637
Phone: 773-702-8484
Fax: 773-753-0558
e-mail: jmaxwell@uchicago.edu
Web Site: www.music.uchicago.edu
Management:
   Director Of Public Relations: Jennifer Maxwell
Performs At: Mandel Hall

4562
UNIVERSITY OF ILLINOIS AT CHICAGO FINE ARTS SERIES
340 Student Center East
750 South Halsted St.
Chicago, IL 60607
Phone: 312-413-5070
Fax: 312-413-5074
Management:
   Executive Director: Jill Rothamer
   Artistic Director: Melissa Cfoke
   Associate Director: Joey Hampton
   Director: Joy Vergara
   Associate Director: Carrie Grogan
   Front Office Manager: Valerie Gordon
Specialized Field: Higher Education
Status: Non-Profit, Professional
Paid Staff: 20

4563
URBAN GATEWAYS SERIES: CENTER FOR ARTS EDUCATION
205 W Randolph St.
Suite #1700
Chicago, IL 60606
Phone: 312-922-0440
Fax: 312-922-2740
e-mail: info@urbangateways.org
Web Site: www.urbangateways.org
Officers:
   Chairman: Thomas D. Abrahamson
   President: RuthAnn Green
   Vice-President: Anton J. Britton
   Secretary: Jane R. Bilger
   Treasurer: Joseph Kye
Management:
   Executive Director: Eric Delli Bovi
   Producing Director: Tim Sauers
   Director of Finance and Operations: John W. Adams
   Program Associate: Kelly Christiel
   Director of Development: Sherre Jennings Cullen
   Director of Marketing & Sales: Brian Foster
   Marketing & Sales Associate: Anna Joranger
Mission: To provide comprehensive arts education programs, to serve locally as a resource, and nationally as a model for incorporating the arts in all levels of education for aesthetic, academic, cultural and personal development.
Founded: 1961

SERIES & FESTIVALS / Illinois

Specialized Field: Series & Festivals; Arts Education; Instrumental Music; Vocal Music; Theatre; Youth; Ethnic Performances
Status: Non-Profit, Professional
Paid Staff: 20
Paid Artists: 160
Budget: $2.3 million
Income Sources: Ticket Sales; Fees for Service; Grants; Corporation; Government; Contributions

4564
WILBUR COLLEGE CULTURAL EVENTS SERIES
4300 N Narragansett Ave.
Chicago, IL 60634
Phone: 773-481-8144
Fax: 773-481-8147
e-mail: bgilbert@ccc.edu
Seating Capacity: 200
Year Built: 1993
Rental Contact: Director Student Affairs Betty Gilbert

4565
NORTHERN ILLINOIS UNIVERSITY FINE ARTS SERIES
NIU, University Programming
Campus Life Building 160
De Kalb, IL 60115
Phone: 815-753-1580
Fax: 815-753-2905
e-mail: cab@niu.edu
Web Site: www.niu.edu/cab
Officers:
   President: Scott Friedman
   Vice-President of Operations: Rainn Darring
   Office Manager: Sumiko Keay
Management:
   Assistant Director: Mary Tosch
Utilizes: Dance Companies; Dancers; Fine Artists; Instructors; Local Artists; Multimedia; Sign Language Translators; Soloists; Special Technical Talent; Theatre Companies; Touring Companies
Founded: 1895
Specialized Field: Series & Festivals; Instrumental Music; Vocal Music; Theatre; Dance; Ethnic Performances
Status: Non-Profit, Professional
Performs At: Carl Sandburg Auditorium; Duke Ellington Ballroom

4566
PERFORMING ARTS SERIES FOR STUDENTS
600 East Fourth Street
PO Box 1607
Decatur, IL 56267
Phone: 217-423-3189
Fax: 217-423-3194
e-mail: arts4all@decaturarts.org
Web Site: www.decaturarts.org
Management:
   President: Mike Gibson
Founded: 1967
Specialized Field: Facilitator for Arts
Status: Non-Profit, Non-Professional
Paid Staff: 5

4567
PERFORMING ARTS SERIES FOR STUDENTS
600 East Fourth Street
PO Box 1607
Decatur, IL 56267
Phone: 217-423-3189
Fax: 217-423-3194
e-mail: arts4all1@aol.com
Management:
   Executive Director: Susan Smith
Performs At: Kirkland Fine Arts Center

4568
TRINITY COLLEGE SCHOOL OF MUSIC
2065 Half Day Road
Deerfield, IL 60015
Phone: 847-945-8800
Fax: 847-317-4786
e-mail: music@tiu.edu
Web Site: www.tiu.edu
Management:
   Department Of Music Coordinator: Melody Velkuer
   Department Of Music: Don Hedges
Mission: The TIU Department of Music exists to foster the understanding, teaching and performance of music as an arts & discipline, profession and a calling, and as a means to worship God and serve others.
Specialized Field: Series & Festivals; Instrumental Music; Vocal Music; Youth
Status: Non-Profit, Professional
Performs At: Arnold T. Olson Chapel

4569
MAINE TOWNSHIP COMMUNITY CONCERT ASSOCIATION
4801 Courthouse Street
Suite 220
Des Plaines, IL 23188
Phone: 847-824-2591
Officers:
   President: Anne Evans
   Chair: Mari Kuraishi
   Secretary: Charles Best
   Treasurer: Tom Tinsley
Management:
   President: Ann Evans
Founded: 1947
Specialized Field: Series & Festivals: Classical Music
Status: Non-Profit, Non-Professional
Performs At: High School Auditorium

4570
ARTISTS SHOWCASE WEST
Downers Grove Concert Association
4422 Douglas Road
Downers Grove, IL 60515
Phone: 630-252-7160
Fax: 630-252-5986
Web Site: www.dgconcerts.org
Management:
   President: Audra Hamernik
Founded: 1945
Specialized Field: Series & Festivals; Instrumental Music; Vocal Music
Status: Non-Profit, Professional

4571
DOWNERS GROVE CONCERT ASSOCIATION SERIES
4422 Douglas Road
Downers Grove, IL 60515
Phone: 630-963-9093
Fax: 630-252-5986
Web Site: www.dgconcerts.org
Officers:
   President: Tom Hamernik
Management:
   Artistic Director: Robert Johnson
Mission: To increase public support for performing arts in Downers Grove through the presentation of professional dancers and musicians.
Founded: 1976
Specialized Field: Dance; Instrumental Music
Status: Non-Profit
Volunteer Staff: 20
Budget: $20,000-$35,000
Income Sources: Ticket Sales; Village of Downers Grove; Illinois Art Council
Performs At: Downers Grove North High School Auditorium
Affiliations: Chicago Music Alliance
Facility Category: Auditorium
Seating Capacity: 1,000
Organization Type: Sponsoring

4572
ILLINOIS CENTRAL COLLEGE SUBSCRIPTION SERIES
Illinois Central College
Performing Arts Center
East Peoria, IL 61635
Mailing Address: 1 College Dr., East Peoria
Phone: 309-694-5136
Fax: 309-694-5268
e-mail: drademaker@icc.edu
Web Site: www.icc.edu
Management:
   President: John Erwin
   Executive Director: Jeffery Hoover
   Managing Director: Dana Rademaker
Founded: 1967
Specialized Field: Series & Festivals; Traditional Jazz and Broadway Music; General Popular Entertainment
Status: Non-Profit, Professional
Paid Staff: 20
Volunteer Staff: 20
Budget: $35,000
Income Sources: Funded by the School
Performs At: Performing Arts Center
Affiliations: Illinois Presenters Network
Annual Attendance: 25,000
Type of Stage: Prosceium; Thurst
Stage Dimensions: 40'x36'
Seating Capacity: 500
Year Built: 1979
Cost: $4,000,000

4573
SOUTHERN ILLINOIS UNIVERSITY EDWARDSVILLE SERIES
Campus Box 1608
Edwardsville, IL 62026
Phone: 618-650-2626
Fax: 618-650-5050
e-mail: gandree@siue.edu
Web Site: www.artsandissues.com
Management:
   Director Artist Issues: Grant Andree
Mission: Performing arts/speaker series
Founded: 1985
Status: Non-Profit, Professional
Paid Staff: 3
Paid Artists: 30
Income Sources: Association of Performing Arts Presenters
Performs At: University Center and Communications Theater
Organization Type: Educational; Sponsoring

SERIES & FESTIVALS / Illinois

4574
ELMHURST COLLEGE JAZZ FESTIVAL
190 Prospect Avenue
Elmhurst, IL 60126-3296
Phone: 630-617-3500
Fax: 630-617-3738
e-mail: barbv@elmhurst.edu
Web Site: www.elmhurst.edu
Officers:
  Chair: Barbara J. Lucks
  Vice Chair: Edward J. Momkus
Management:
  President: S. Alan Ray
  Executive Director: Doug Beach
Mission: To offer both jazz performances and the opportunity for artists to give constructive critiques, advice, demonstration of skills and guest band appearances.
Founded: 1967
Specialized Field: Series & Festivals; Instrumental Music; Vocal Music; Jazz
Status: Non-Profit;Collegiate/Professional
Paid Staff: 2
Volunteer Staff: 150
Affiliations: UCC, Community
Annual Attendance: 3,000
Facility Category: Chapel-Multi Purpose
Type of Stage: Indoor Elevated
Seating Capacity: 850
Year Remodeled: 1994

4575
PRINCIPIA COLLEGE CONCERT SERIES
Principia College
13201 Clayton Road
Elsah, IL 63131-1002
Phone: 314-434-2100
Fax: 618-374-5911
e-mail: rer@prin.edu
Web Site: www.principia.edu
Management:
  Concert Coordinator: John Near
Founded: 1898
Specialized Field: Series & Festivals; Instrumental Music; Vocal Music; Theatre
Status: Non-Profit, Professional
Performs At: Cox Auditorium

4576
BACH WEEK FESTIVAL IN EVANSTON
PO Box 1832
Evanston, IL 60204-1832
Phone: 847-868-6015
Fax: 847-945-1106
e-mail: info@bachweek.org
Web Site: www.bachweek.org
Management:
  Music Director: Richard R Webster
  Festival Manager: Michael Cansfield
Founded: 1974
Season: May
Facility Category: Saint Luke's Episcopal Church, Evanston
Seating Capacity: 450

4577
NORTHWESTERN UNIVERSITY SUMMER DRAMA FESTIVAL
Theatre Department
2240 Campus Drive
Evanston, IL 60208
Phone: 847-491-7282
Fax: 847-467-7135
e-mail: n-barnett@northwestern.edu
Web Site: www.northwestern.edu
Officers:
  Department of Theatre Chair: Joseph Appelt
Management:
  Chairman: Rives Collins
  Managing Director: Diane Claussen
  Box Office Manager: Jamie Mayhew
  Artistic Director: David H. Bell
Founded: 1954
Specialized Field: Series & Festivals: Acting and Musical Theatre
Status: Non-Profit, Non-Professional
Paid Staff: 20
Paid Artists: 28
Season: June - August
Type of Stage: Thrust
Stage Dimensions: 21' x 30'
Seating Capacity: 450

4578
KNOX-ROOTABAGA JAMM JAZZ FESTIVAL
Knox College
2 East South Street
Galesburg, IL 61401
Phone: 309-341-7265
Fax: 309-289-2823
e-mail: rootabaga@knox.edu
Web Site: www.knox.edu/knoxjazzrootabaga
Management:
  President: Nicole Whittaker
Mission: Entertainment and education.
Founded: 1989
Specialized Field: Series & Festivals; Instrumental Music; Vocal Music; Youth
Status: Non-Profit, Professional
Paid Staff: 1
Volunteer Staff: 50
Paid Artists: 20
Non-paid Artists: 40

4579
COLLEGE OF LAKE COUNTY - PERFORMING ARTS BUILDING
19351 W Washington Street
Graylake, IL 60030-1198
Phone: 847-543-2000
Fax: 847-543-2629
e-mail: gbronner@clc.cc.il.us
Web Site: www.clc.cc.il.us
Management:
  President: Gretchen Naff
  Executive Director: Gwethalyn Bronner
  Technical Coordinator: Jeremy Eiden
  Media Coordinator: Lyla Maclean
Founded: 1997
Specialized Field: Perfoming arts
Status: Non-Profit, Professional
Paid Staff: 20
Performs At: Mainstage

4580
GREENVILLE COLLEGE GUEST ARTIST SERIES
315 East College Avenue
P.O. Box 159
Greenville, IL 62246-0159
Phone: 618-664-2800
Fax: 618-664-6580
e-mail: achaussee@greenville.edu
Management:
  Manager: Andrea Chaussee
Mission: Acts enrichment in a small community
Performs At: LaDue Auditorium

4581
RAVINIA FESTIVAL
PO Box 896
Highland Park, IL 60035
Phone: 847-266-5100
Fax: 847-266-0641
e-mail: ravinia@ravinia.org
Web Site: www.ravinia.org
Officers:
  President/CEO: Welz Kauffman
  Chairman: John L. Anderson
  Treasurer: Jennifer W. Steans
  Secretary: Kelly Grier
Management:
  President: Welz Kauffman
  Artistic Director: Erik Soderstrom
  Music Director: James Conlon
  General Manager: Patricia Patricia
  Director: Nick Pullia
Mission: To present, at low cost, quality classical, jazz, folk, and pop music to the public.
Utilizes: AEA Actors; Artists-in-Residence; Choreographers; Collaborating Artists; Commissioned Composers; Commissioned Music; Dance Companies; Dancers; Designers; Five Seasonal Concerts; Guest Artists; Guest Choreographers; Guest Companies; Guest Composers; Guest Conductors; Guest Designers; Guest Directors; Guest Ensembles; Guest Instructors; Guest Lecturers; Guest Musical Directors; Guest Musicians; Guest Soloists; High School Drama; Local Artists; Multimedia; Music; Original Music Scores; Resident Professionals; Sign Language Translators; Singers; Soloists; Student Interns; Theatre Companies
Founded: 1935
Status: Professional; Nonprofit
Paid Staff: 50
Volunteer Staff: 50
Non-paid Artists: 100
Season: June - September
Performs At: Ravinia Park, Highland Park (Festival Site)
Annual Attendance: 500,000
Facility Category: Ravinia Pavilion; Martin Theatre; Bennet-Gordon Hall
Seating Capacity: 3,200; 850; 450
Year Built: 1955
Year Remodeled: 1995
Organization Type: Performing; Educational

4582
STARRY NIGHTS SUMMER CONCERT SERIES
3301 Flossmoor Road
Homewood, IL 60422
Phone: 708-957-0300
Fax: 708-957-0267
e-mail: hfinfo@hfparks.com
Web Site: www.hfparks.com/
Management:
  President: Patrick Nevins
  Director: Greg Meyer
  VP: Melissa Barrett
  Commissioner: Pete Camin
Season: June - July
Performs At: Homewood (Festival Site)
Facility Category: Marie Irwin Community Center Bandshell, Homewood
Seating Capacity: 4,000

SERIES & FESTIVALS / Illinois

4583
MYSTERY CAFE SERIES
P.O. Box 1024
Indianapolis, IL 55025-1024
Phone: 763-566-2583
e-mail: info@themysterycafeindy.com
Web Site: www.mysterycafeonline.com
Founded: 1990

4584
BARAT COLLEGE PERFORMING ARTS CENTER SEASON
1501 N. Oakley Blvd.
Lake Forest, IL 60622
Phone: 847-574-2465
Fax: 847-604-6342
e-mail: drakethe@barat.edu
Web Site: www.barat.edu
Officers:
   CEO/Chair: Sheila A. Smith
   Vice Chair: Kathleen Gillespie
   Treasurer: Michael Dimengo
   Secretary: Sarah Highstone
Management:
   Theatre Department Chair: Steve Carmichael
   Assistant Producer: Jeannie Petkewicz
Budget: $10,000-$20,000
Performs At: Drake Theatre
Facility Category: College
Type of Stage: Proscenium
Seating Capacity: 625

4585
MCKENDREE COLLEGE FINE ARTS SERIES
Mckendree College
701 College Road
Lebanon, IL 62254
Phone: 618-537-4481
Fax: 618-537-6259
Toll-free: 800-232-7228
e-mail: inquiry@mckendree.edu
Web Site: www.mckendree.edu
Officers:
   Chairperson Music Department: Dr. Nancy Ypma
   Chair: Daniel C. Dobbins
   Vice Chair: Daniel J. Lett
   Secretary: John L. Bailey
   Treasurer: Philip R. Schwab
Mission: For education of students and community.
Paid Staff: 2
Paid Artists: 5
Performs At: Bothwell Chapel; Pearsons Hall

4586
WESTERN ILLINOIS UNIVERSITY BCA PERFORMING ARTIST SERIES
Bureau of Cultural Affairs
114 Browne Hall, 1 University Circle
Macomb, IL 61455
Phone: 309-298-3571
Fax: 309-298-2879
e-mail: bca@wiu.edu
Web Site: www.bca.wiu.edu
Management:
   Director Performing Arts: Dan Maxwell
   Performing Arts Assistant Director: Christi Steelman
Founded: 1968
Specialized Field: Series & Festivals; Instrumental Music; Vocal Music; Theatre; Youth; Dance; Ethnic Performances
Status: Non-Profit, Professional
Paid Staff: 10
Performs At: Western Hall

4587
QUAD-CITIES JAZZ FESTIVAL
1601 River Drive
Suite 110
Moline, IL 61265
Phone: 309-277-0937
Toll-free: 800-477-00
e-mail: cvb@visitquadcities.com
Officers:
   Chairman: Carmen Darland
   First Vice Chair: Al Higley
   Second Vice Chair: Laura Duran
   Treasurer: Rick Palmer
   Past Chair: Myron Scheibe
Management:
   Director: Nathaniel Lawrence
Founded: 1994
Paid Staff: 1

4588
NAPERVILLE-NORTH CENTRAL COLLEGE PERFORMING ARTS SERIES
30 N. Brainard Street
Naperville, IL 60540
Phone: 630-637-5100
Fax: 630-637-5121
Management:
   Director Fine Arts: Brian Lynch
Founded: 1974
Specialized Field: Dance; Vocal Music; Instrumental Music; Theater
Status: Non-Professional; Nonprofit
Income Sources: North Central College
Performs At: Pfeiffer Hall
Organization Type: Sponsoring

4589
ILLINOIS SHAKESPEARE FESTIVAL
Illinois State University
Box 5700
Normal, IL 61790-5700
Phone: 309-438-8974
Fax: 309-438-5806
e-mail: shake@ilstu.edu
Web Site: www.thefestival.org
Management:
   Managing Director: Dick Folse
   Artistic Director: Kevin Rich
   Producer: Janet Wilson
   Dean: James E. Major
   Production Manager: Adam Fox
Utilizes: Actors; AEA Actors; Designers; Guest Conductors; Guest Designers; Guest Writers; Guild Activities; Original Music Scores; Resident Artists; Resident Professionals; Soloists; Student Interns
Founded: 1978
Specialized Field: Festivals
Status: Non-Profit
Paid Staff: 80
Paid Artists: 40
Budget: $1.2 Million
Income Sources: Box Office, Fund Raising
Season: June - August
Performs At: Ewing Manor
Affiliations: UARTA; Actors' Equity Association; SSOC
Annual Attendance: 15,000
Facility Category: Outdoor
Type of Stage: Thrust
Seating Capacity: 438
Year Built: 2000
Cost: $1.65 million
Organization Type: Performing; Educational

4590
BRADEN AUDITORIUM
100 N University St.
Campus Box 2640
Normal, IL 61761-4441
Phone: 309-438-4636
Fax: 309-438-3544
e-mail: InfoCentre@IllinoisState.edu
Web Site: www.bsc.ilstu.edu/bsc
Management:
   Coordinator: Jennifer Booher
   Box Office Manager: Amy Johnson
   Director: Michelle S. Paul
   Associate Director: Barb Dallinger
   Assistant Director: Melody Palm
   Office Manager: Shirley McCauley
   Manager: Rick Holmes
Founded: 1973
Specialized Field: Education
Status: For-Profit, Professional
Paid Staff: 100
Volunteer Staff: 20
Non-paid Artists: 200
Performs At: Auditorium
Affiliations: Illinois State University
Facility Category: Auditorium
Seating Capacity: 3,457
Rental Contact: Coordinator Jennifer Booher

4591
FIRST FOLIO SHAKESPEARE FESTIVAL
1717 W 31st St
Oak Brook, IL 60523
Mailing Address: 146 Juliet Center Claredon Hill, IL 06514
Phone: 630-986-8067
Fax: 630-455-0071
e-mail: firstfolio@firstfolio.org
Web Site: www.firstfolio.org
Management:
   President: Alison C Vesely
   Managing Director: David Rice
   Artistic Director: Alison Vesely
Mission: Bring attention to the historic and environmental site here. Mission emphasizes a training intiative for young theatre artists, including a college intern program.
Founded: 1996
Specialized Field: Series & Festivals: Classical Theatre
Status: Non-Profit, Professional
Paid Staff: 2
Volunteer Staff: 60
Paid Artists: 30
Season: July - September
Type of Stage: Thrust
Stage Dimensions: 40' x 30'

4592
COMMUNITY CHILDREN'S THEATRE OF PEORIA PARK DISTRICT
1125 W Lake Ave
Peoria, IL 61614
Phone: 309-682-1200
Fax: 309-686-3352
e-mail: lhuff@peoriaparks.org
Web Site: www.peoriaparks.org
Officers:
   President: Timothy J. Cassidy
   Treasurer: Kris Griffith
   Vice President: Kelly A. Cummings
   Secretary: Sally Robertson

SERIES & FESTIVALS / Illinois

Trustee: James T. Hancock
Trustee: Robert L. Johnson Sr.
Management:
  Fine Arts Coordinator: Linda Elegant Huff
Mission: To foster participation among the young people in the community in children's theatre activity; to present educational programs, with the purpose of raising awareness and standards of such programs.
Utilizes: Choreographers; Dancers; Educators; Grant Writers; Guest Artists; Guest Designers; Guest Lecturers; Guild Activities; High School Drama; Instructors; Local Artists; Multimedia; Music; Sign Language Translators; Soloists; Student Interns
Founded: 1957
Specialized Field: Theatre: Children's Theatre
Status: Non-Profit, Non-Professional
Paid Staff: 1
Volunteer Staff: 200
Paid Artists: 4
Non-paid Artists: 65
Budget: $20,000
Income Sources: Tickets Sales and Concessions; Donations; Grants
Performs At: Theatre; Schools
Affiliations: Illinois Theatre Association
Annual Attendance: 5,000
Facility Category: Theatre
Type of Stage: Proscenium
Seating Capacity: 360

4593
MIDWEST JAZZ HERITAGE FESTIVAL
PO Box 754
Peoria, IL 61652-0754
Phone: 309-672-2004
e-mail: bduffy@bigplanet.com
Web Site: www.midil.com/jazzpeoria.html
Management:
  Prducer and Promoter: B Duffy

4594
PEORIA CIVIC CENTER
201 SW Jefferson Ave.
Peoria, IL 61602
Phone: 309-673-8900
Fax: 309-673-3200
e-mail: dritschel@peoriaciviccenter.com
Web Site: www.peoriaciviccenter.com
Management:
  Director Marketing: Marc Burnett
  General Manager: Jim Wetherington
  Director Operations: Will Kenney
  Event Manager: Beth Anderson
  Box Office Manager: Stephen Hefler
Founded: 1982
Specialized Field: Series and Festivals; Instrumental Music; Vocal Music; Theatre; Youth; Dance; Ethnic Performances
Status: For-Profit, Professional
Paid Staff: 500

4595
QUINCY CIVIC MUSIC ASSOCIATION
PO Box 1165
Quincy, IL 62306-1165
Phone: 217-224-5499
e-mail: qcma@att.net
Web Site: www.cma.home.insightbb.com
Management:
  Second Vice President: Merle Crossland
  First Vice President: Mary Anne Klein
  President: Mowbray Allan
Founded: 1928
Specialized Field: Series & Festivals; Instrumental Music; Vocal Music; Dance; Ethnic Performances
Status: Non-Profit, Professional

4596
DOMINICAN UNIVERSITY PERFORMING ARTS CENTER
7900 West Division Street
River Forest, IL 60305
Phone: 708-366-2490
Fax: 708-524-5990
e-mail: lrodriguez@dom.edu
Web Site: www.dom.edu
Officers:
  Chair: Kevin M. Killips
  Vice Chair: Daniel C. Hill
  President: Donna M. Carroll
  Vice President: Claire Noonan
  Vice President: Jill Albin-Hill
  Secretary: Alexandra Garcia
Management:
  Operations/Marketing Manager: Leslie Rodriguez
  Technical Director: Bill Jenkins
  Administrativ Associate: Julianna Mendelson
Utilizes: Actors; Artists-in-Residence; Choreographers; Collaborating Artists; Commissioned Music; Dance Companies; Dancers; Designers; Educators; Filmmakers; Fine Artists; Five Seasonal Concerts; Grant Writers; Guest Accompanists; Guest Artists; Guest Choreographers; Guest Companies; Guest Conductors; Guest Designers; Guest Ensembles; Guest Instructors; Guest Lecturers; Guest Musical Directors; Guest Musicians; Guest Soloists; Guest Teachers; High School Drama; Instructors; Local Artists; Multi Collaborations; Multimedia; Music; Original Music Scores; Performance Artists; Playwrights; Poets; Resident Professionals; Sign Language Translators; Singers; Soloists; Theatre Companies; Touring Companies; Visual Arts
Founded: 1901
Specialized Field: Theatre/Music
Paid Staff: 4
Performs At: Lund Auditorium; Martin Hall
Affiliations: Dominican University
Annual Attendance: 45,000
Facility Category: Fine Arts Building
Type of Stage: Proscenium
Seating Capacity: 1,000; 180
Year Built: 1952
Year Remodeled: 1992
Rental Contact: Bill Jenkins

4597
QUAD CITY ARTS
1715 Second Avenue
Rock Island, IL 61201
Phone: 309-793-1213
Fax: 309-793-1265
e-mail: info@quadcityarts.com
Web Site: www.quadcityarts.com
Officers:
  Executive Director: Carmen Darland
Management:
  Performing Arts Director: Susan Wohlman
  Executive Director: Carmen Darland
  Visual Arts Director: Dawn Wohlford-Metallo
  Community Arts Director: Jessi Black
Mission: To offer professional concerts by area performing artists.
Utilizes: Actors; Artists-in-Residence; Collaborations; Dance Companies; Dancers; Educators; Fine Artists; Five Seasonal Concerts; Grant Writers; Guest Accompanists; Guest Choreographers; Guest Designers; Guest Ensembles; Guest Instructors; Guest Musical Directors; Guest Musicians; Guest Soloists; Guest Teachers; Guild Activities; High School Drama; Instructors; Local Artists; Local Unknown Artists; Lyricists; Multi Collaborations; Multimedia; Music; New Productions; Original Music Scores; Performance Artists; Playwrights; Sign Language Translators; Soloists; Special Technical Talent; Theatre Companies; Touring Companies
Founded: 1973
Specialized Field: Series and Festivals; Instrumental Music; Vocal Music; Theatre; Youth; Dance; Ethnic Performances; Regional arts council
Status: Non-Profit, Non-Professional
Paid Staff: 6
Budget: $130,000
Income Sources: Grants; Foundations; Fund Drive
Performs At: Deere and Company; St. Ambrose University; Augustana College
Affiliations: Association of Performing Arts Presenters; Music America; American For The Arts
Facility Category: Arts Center
Year Remodeled: 1988
Organization Type: Performing; Educational

4598
ROCK VALLEY COLLEGE LECTURE/CONCERT SERIES
3301 North Mulford Road
Rockford, IL 61114
Phone: 815-921-7821
Fax: 815-654-4402
e-mail: m.sink@rvc.cc.il.us
Management:
  Program Director: Monique Aduddell
Performs At: Performing Arts Room

4599
UNIVERSITY OF ILLINOIS AT SPRINGFIELD SANGAMON PERFORMING ARTS SERIES
Sangamon Auditorium
One University Plaza, MS PAC 397
Springfield, IL 62703-5407
Phone: 217-206-6150
Fax: 217-206-6391
Toll-free: 800-207-6960
e-mail: sangamonauditorium@uis.edu
Web Site: www.sangamonauditorium.org
Management:
  Director: Bob Vaughn
  Event Manager: Elise Robertson
  Business Administrative Associate: Briana Fugnitti
  Administrative Aide: Alice Bettis
  Ticket Office Manager: Shannon Smith
Mission: To present a varied professional performing arts program to audiences in central illinois.
Founded: 1981
Specialized Field: Series & Festivals; Instrumental Music; Vocal Music; Theatre; Dance; Ethnic Performances
Status: Non-Profit, Professional
Paid Staff: 10
Volunteer Staff: 250
Budget: $2 Million
Annual Attendance: 100,000
Facility Category: Proscenium; Black Box
Stage Dimensions: 62' x 55'
Seating Capacity: 2018
Rental Contact: Elise Robertson

SERIES & FESTIVALS / Indiana

4600
ST CHARLES ART & MUSIC FESTIVAL
1040 Dunham Road
The Dellora A Norris Cultural Arts Center
St Charles, IL 60174
Mailing Address: PO Box 3340 St. Charles, IL 60174
Phone: 630-584-7200
e-mail: jgranquist@norrisculturalarts.com
Web Site: www.norrisculturalarts.com
Officers:
  President: James L. Collins
  Secretary: Jo Anne de Simone
  Treasurer: Mark D. Smith
Management:
  Director Of Operations: Jo Anne Granquist
  Technical Director: John Mizanin
Performs At: St. Charles & Tri-City Area (Festival Site)
Facility Category: Norris Cultural Arts Center
Seating Capacity: 980

4601
KRANNERT CENTER MARQUEE SERIES, UNIVERSITY OF ILLINOIS
500 S Goodwin Ave.
Urbana, IL 61801-3788
Phone: 217-333-6700
Fax: 217-244-0810
e-mail: kran-tix@uiuc.edu
Web Site: www.krannertcenter.com
Management:
  Director: Mike Ross
  Assistant Director: Gary Bernstein
  Accounting Staff: Lynn Bierman
  Art Director: Vanessa Burgett
Founded: 1969
Specialized Field: Series and Festivals; Instrumental Music; Vocal Music; Theatre; Youth; Dance; Ethnic Performances
Status: Non-Profit, Non-Professional
Paid Staff: 80
Performs At: Foellinger Great Hall

4602
UNIVERSITY OF ILLINOIS: SUMMERFEST
4-122 Krannert Center for Performing Arts
500 S Goodwin Avenue
Urbana, IL 61801
Phone: 217-333-2371
Fax: 217-244-1861
e-mail: theater@uiuc.edu
Web Site: www.theatre.uiuc.edu
Officers:
  Head: Robert Graves
Management:
  Chairman of University: Robert Graves
  Chancellor of Unversity: Richard Herman
  Production Director: J B Harris
Utilizes: Actors; Designers; Guest Conductors; Guest Designers; Local Artists; Multimedia; Original Music Scores; Resident Professionals
Founded: 1991
Specialized Field: Theatre; Musical; Comedy; Dinner; Ethnic Theater; Theatrical Group; Classical; Contemporary; Theatre Education
Status: Non-Profit, Professional
Paid Staff: 34
Volunteer Staff: 9
Paid Artists: 8
Season: June - August
Performs At: Performing Arts Center
Facility Category: Studio Theatre
Type of Stage: Flexible
Seating Capacity: 200

4603
ARTIST SERIES AT WHEATON COLLEGE
Wheaton Conservatory of Music
501 College Avenue
Wheaton, IL 60187-5593
Phone: 630-752-5000
Fax: 630-752-5341
Toll-free: 800-325-8718
e-mail: artistseries@wheaton.edu
Web Site: www.wheaton.edu
Officers:
  Chairman: Dr. David K. Gieser
  Vice Chairman: Mr. Philip G. Hubbard
  Secretary : Mr. Steven C. Preston
Management:
  President: Duane Litfin
  Artistic Director: Tony Payne
  Managing Director: Rhaondas Sission
Founded: 1950
Specialized Field: Series and Festivals; Instrumental Music; Vocal Music; Theatre; Youth
Status: Non-Profit, Non-Professional
Paid Staff: 4
Volunteer Staff: 10
Paid Artists: 6
Budget: $300,000
Income Sources: Box Office; Private Donationas; Corporate Donations
Performs At: Edman Memorial Chapel
Affiliations: Wheaton College
Annual Attendance: 12,500
Facility Category: Auditorium/Hall
Type of Stage: Proscenium
Stage Dimensions: 35'x 60'
Seating Capacity: 2,350
Year Built: 1960

4604
MUSIC INSTITUTE OF CHICAGO SERIES
1702 Sherman Avenue
Winnetka, IL 60201
Phone: 847-905-1500
Fax: 847-446-3876
e-mail: info@musicinst.com
Web Site: www.musicinst.com
Officers:
  Chairman: William J Eichar
  President: Mark George
  Executive Vice President: Edward W. Horner, Jr.
  Vice President of Administration: Sue Polutnik
Management:
  President and CEO: Mark George
  Executive Director: Richard Rohrer
Mission: To provide the foundation for a lifelong enjoyment of music.
Utilizes: Collaborations; Educators; Guest Instructors; Soloists
Founded: 1931
Specialized Field: Series & Festivals; Instrumental Music; Vocal Music; Theatre; Youth & Adults
Status: Non-Profit, Professional
Paid Staff: 150
Budget: 4 million
Income Sources: Tuition; Donations
Performs At: Recital Hall
Annual Attendance: 1,000+
Facility Category: Recital Hall
Seating Capacity: 150
Year Built: 1956
Rental Contact: Jim Brown

4605
WOODSTOCK FINE ARTS ASSOCIATION - MUSIC FOR A SUNDAY AFTERNOON SERIES
PO Box 225
Woodstock, IL 60098
Phone: 815-338-0175
e-mail: info@woodstockfinearts.org
Management:
  Contact: Mary Sircar
Performs At: Auditorium

4606
WOODSTOCK MOZART FESTIVAL
121 W Van Buren St
Woodstock, IL 60098
Phone: 815-338-4212
Fax: 815-334-2287
e-mail: mozartfest@aol.com
Web Site: www.mozartfest.org
Officers:
  President: Maija Mizens, Ph. D.
  Vice President: Judysharon Buck, Ph. D.
  M.D., Secretary: Mark Schiffer
  Treasurer: Amy Ottens
Management:
  President: Louise Le Coque
  General Director: Anita Whelan
  Artistic Advisor: Mark Peskanov
Utilizes: Guest Accompanists; Guest Composers; Guest Musicians; Multimedia; Original Music Scores
Founded: 1987
Specialized Field: Series & Festivals: Instrumental Music
Status: Non-Profit, Professional
Paid Staff: 3
Paid Artists: 40
Budget: $130,000
Income Sources: Individuals, Corporations, Foundations
Facility Category: Woodstock Opera House
Seating Capacity: 412
Year Built: 1889
Year Remodeled: 1977

Indiana

4607
FOUNTAIN/WARREN MUSICAL ARTS SERIES
PO Box 6
Attica, IN 47918
Phone: 765-762-9014
Fax: 765-762-2487
e-mail: wrghthsm@hscast.com
Officers:
  Secretary: Mike Wrighthouse
Management:
  President: Wade C Harrison
  Artistic Director: Mike Wrighthouse
Utilizes: Guild Activities; Multimedia; Sign Language Translators; Singers; Soloists
Founded: 1985
Specialized Field: Series & Festivals; Chamber Music; Solo
Status: Non-Profit, Professional
Budget: $11,000
Performs At: Harrison Hills Country Club

SERIES & FESTIVALS / Indiana

4608
DEARBORN HIGHLANDS ARTS COUNCIL SERIES
331 Walnut Street
PO Box 193
Aurora, IN 47025
Phone: 812-926-1778
Fax: 812-926-4700
Toll-free: 866-818-2787
e-mail: dearbornarts@comcast.net
Web Site: www.all4art.org
Management:
    Executive Director: Marilyn Bower
Mission: To serve, expand and enrich the lives of residents of Dearborn County and adjacent areas through education, exposure, diversity, enjoyment and participation in the performing and visual arts.
Founded: 1982
Specialized Field: Series and Festivals; Instrumental Music; Vocal Music; Theatre; Youth; Dance; Ethnic Performances; Education Programmes
Status: Non-Profit, Non-Professional
Paid Staff: 1
Volunteer Staff: 215
Budget: $100,000
Income Sources: Grants; Memberships; Ticket Sales; Corporate; Private Support
Performs At: Lawrenceburg HS Auditorium; South Dearborn HS Auditorium; Public Libraries
Annual Attendance: 4800
Facility Category: Auditorium, city park

4609
BLOOMINGTON EARLY MUSIC FESTIVAL
PO Box 734
Bloomington, IN 47402
Phone: 812-219-3377
Fax: 812-331-1263
e-mail: info@blemf.org
Web Site: www.blemf.org
Officers:
    President: Mary Tilton
    Chair, Program Commitee: Gesa Kordes
Management:
    President: Mary Tilton
    Interim Executive Director: Martha Perry
Utilizes: Choreographers; Collaborating Artists; Collaborations; Dancers; Designers; Guest Accompanists; Guest Artists; Guest Designers; Guest Directors; Guest Instructors; Guest Musical Directors; Guest Musicians; Guest Soloists; Instructors; Local Artists; Lyricists; Multi Collaborations; Multimedia; Music; Original Music Scores; Resident Professionals; Sign Language Translators; Soloists
Founded: 1992
Specialized Field: Series & Festivals: Presenting In Early Music Festival
Status: Non-Profit, Professional
Paid Staff: 2
Volunteer Staff: 25
Paid Artists: 100
Non-paid Artists: 50
Season: May
Performs At: Bloomington (Festival Site)
Facility Category: Concert Halls, Opera Theatre
Seating Capacity: 230; 450

4610
INDIANA UNIVERSITY SUMMER MUSIC FESTIVAL
Indiana University Jacobs School of Music
1201 East Third Street
Bloomington, IN 47405
Phone: 812-855-9846
Fax: 812-855-9847
e-mail: musicpub@indiana.edu
Web Site: www.music.indiana.edu
Officers:
    President: Adam Herbert
Management:
    Director, Marketing and Publicity: Alain Barker
    Director, Design: Neil Robinson
Mission: To provide a program of professional performing arts events for students and community members.
Specialized Field: Ballet theatre; Music; Instrument ensemble
Status: Non-Profit, Non-Professional
Income Sources: International Association of Auditorium Managers; Association of Performing Arts Presenters
Performs At: Indiana University Auditorium
Organization Type: Educational; Sponsoring

4612
BROADWAY SERIES: INDIANAPOLIS
100 Marott Center
342 Massachusetts Avenue
Carmel, IN 46204
Phone: 317-632-7469
Fax: 317-917-0456
Toll-free: 800-793-7469
Web Site: www.broadwayseries.com

4613
COLUMBUS AREA ARTS COUNCIL
300 Washington Street
Columbus, IN 47201
Phone: 812-376-2539
Fax: 812-376-2589
e-mail: caac@artsincolumbus.org
Web Site: www.artsincolumbus.org
Officers:
    President: Erin Hawkins
    Vice President: Sarah Cannon
    Treasurer: Scott Poling
    Secretary: Jan Banister
Management:
    President: Warren Ward
    Executive Director: G. Karen Shrode
    Marketing & Media Director: Arthur Smith
    Program Director: Tami Sharp
    Technical Director: Chris Crawl
Performs At: The Commons

4614
CONNERSVILLE AREA ARTISTS SERIES
500 N. Central Avenue
Connersville, IN 47331
Phone: 765-825-4211
Fax: 765-825-0858
e-mail: info@connersvillein.gov
Management:
    Manager: David Caldwell
Performs At: Robert Wise Auditorium

4615
CULVER MILITARY ACADEMY CONCERT SERIES
Culver Academies
1300 ACADEMY RD.
Culver, IN 46511
Phone: 574-842-7000
Fax: 219-842-7994
Management:
    Theatre Director: Richard Coven
Performs At: Eppley Auditorium

4616
FORT WAYNE PARKS & RECREATION FESTIVAL
705 E State Street
Fort Wayne, IN 46805
Phone: 260-427-6000
Fax: 260-427-6020
Officers:
    President: Richard Samek
    Vice President: Pamela Kelly, M.D.
Management:
    Manager: Michael Thompson
    Executive Director: Al Moll
    Deputy Director-Finance & Administr: Garry Morr
    Public Information Officer: Natalie Eggeman
    Office Supervisor: Rhonda Berg
    Marketing Manager: Kathy Pargmann
    Manager of Information & Developmen: Sarah Nichter
Utilizes: Guest Speakers; Local Artists; Multimedia; Original Music Scores
Paid Staff: 7
Income Sources: Budget, Grants, Donations
Affiliations: Fort Wayne Parts and Recreation
Annual Attendance: 52,000
Facility Category: Outdoor Theatre
Seating Capacity: 2,500
Year Built: 1949
Year Remodeled: 1976
Rental Contact: Mike Thompson

4617
DEPAUW UNIVERSITY PERFORMING ARTS SERIES
DePauw University
P.O. Box 37
Greencastle, IN 46135-0037
Phone: 765-658-4800
Fax: 765-658-4356
e-mail: rdye@depauw.edu
Management:
    Coordinator: Ron Dye
Performs At: Auditoriums

4618
HANOVER COLLEGE COMMUNITY ARTIST SERIES
Hanover College
484 Ball Drive
Hanover, IN 47243
Mailing Address: PO Box 108 Hanover, IN, 47243
Phone: 812-866-7264
Fax: 812-866-7229
e-mail: hildebrand@hanover.edu
Web Site: www.hanover.edu/arts
Officers:
    President of Hanover College: Sue DeWine
Management:
    Producer: Mark Fearnow

SERIES & FESTIVALS / Indiana

Mission: Presents a subscription series of 4-5 public events from September through April
Utilizes: Dance Companies; Multimedia; Original Music Scores; Sign Language Translators; Special Technical Talent
Founded: 1951
Specialized Field: Series & Festivals; Music; Theatre; Performing Arts and Dance
Status: Non-Profit, Professional
Budget: $60,000
Income Sources: Ticket Sales; Donations & Sponsorships; Grants
Performs At: Recital Hall
Annual Attendance: 3,000
Type of Stage: Proscenium
Seating Capacity: 700; 350

4619
CONCESCO FIELDHOUSE
One Conseco Court
125 S Pennsylvania Street
Indianapolis, IN 46204
Phone: 317-917-2500
Fax: 317-917-2599
Web Site: www.consecofieldhouse.com
Management:
  President/CEO: Donnie Walsh
  Owner: Melvin Simon
  Owner: Herbert Simon
  VP Facilities Administration: Harry James
Specialized Field: Home of the Indiana Pacers and downtown home of the Indianapolis Ice (IHL)
Seating Capacity: 18,000
Year Built: 1999

4620
ENSEMBLE MUSIC SOCIETY OF INDIANAPOLIS SERIES
PO Box 40188
Indianapolis, IN 46240
Phone: 317-818-1288
Fax: 317-818-8425
e-mail: info@ensemblemusic.org
Web Site: www.ensemblemusic.org
Management:
  President: Pamela Steele
Founded: 1944
Specialized Field: Series & Festivals: Chamber Music Concerts
Status: Non-Profit, Professional
Paid Artists: 15

4621
FESTIVAL MUSIC SOCIETY OF INDIANA
6471 Central Avenue
Indianapolis, IN 46220
Phone: 317-251-5190
Fax: 317-251-8027
e-mail: merfms@msn.com
Web Site: www.emimdy.org
Officers:
  President: David A Garrett
  VP: Gail Bowler
  Treasurer: Neal Rothman
Management:
  Director: Frank Cooper
  Executive Secretary: Mary Ellen Roberts
Mission: To present early music including educational programs to diverse audiences at affordable prices.
Founded: 1969
Specialized Field: Early Music; Baroque; Renaissance
Paid Staff: 2
Volunteer Staff: 27
Budget: $100,000
Income Sources: Contributions; Grants; Ticket Sales
Season: June - July
Performs At: Inside Auditorium, Indianapolis (Fesitval Site)
Annual Attendance: 1,200
Facility Category: Indiana Historical Society
Stage Dimensions: 16'x32'
Seating Capacity: 300
Year Built: 1940
Year Remodeled: 1996

4622
INDY JAZZ FESTIVAL
55 Monument Circle
Ste 1115
Indianapolis, IN 46204
Phone: 317-966-7854
Fax: 317-635-2010
Toll-free: 800-983-4639
e-mail: info@indyjazzfest.org
Web Site: www.indyjazzfest.org

4623
NATIONAL WOMEN'S MUSIC FESTIVAL
PO Box 1427
Indianapolis, IN 46206
Phone: 317-395-3809
e-mail: nwmfpro@yahoo.com
Web Site: www.wiaonline.org
Management:
  Producer: Jane Weldon
  Administration: Ann Arvidson
Season: June
Performs At: Muncie (Festival Site)
Facility Category: Emens Auditorium
Seating Capacity: 2,500

4624
JASPER COMMUNITY ARTS
951 College Ave
Jasper, IN 47546
Phone: 812-482-3070
Fax: 812-634-6997
e-mail: jasperarts@psci.net
Web Site: www.jasperarts.org
Officers:
  President: Michael Jones
  Vice President: Gary Moeller
  Secretary: Linda Kahle
Management:
  Director: Kit Miracle
  Technical Director / Building Manag: Doreen Lechner
  Administrative Assistant / Box Offi: Karen Grewe
  Education Coordinator: Donna Schepers
  Visual Arts Coordinator: Erin Stenftenagel
Mission: The mission of the Jasper Community Arts Commission is to stimulate and encourage an appreciation of and participation in the arts.
Founded: 1975
Specialized Field: Music; Theatre; Mono-Acting
Status: Non-Profit, Professional
Paid Staff: 8
Paid Artists: 12
Budget: $650,000
Performs At: Multi-Discipline Performing; Visual; Dance; Education
Affiliations: APAP; INPN; IAC
Annual Attendance: 35,000-40,000
Facility Category: Performing Arts Center; Visual; Dance
Type of Stage: Proscenium
Stage Dimensions: 30X40
Seating Capacity: 675
Year Built: 1975
Year Remodeled: 2006
Rental Contact: Doreen Lechner

4625
CANTERBURY SUMMER THEATRE/THE FESTIVAL PLAYERS GUILD
PO Box 157
807 Franklin
Michigan City, IN 46360
Phone: 219-874-4269
Fax: 219-879-6377
e-mail: info@festivalplayersguild.org
Management:
  Productions Administrator: Gerald E Peters
  Office Manager: Sue Vail
  Artistic Director: Ray Scott
  Associate Artistic Director: David Graham
Founded: 1969
Specialized Field: Summer Theater
Status: Non-Equity; Nonprofit
Season: June - August
Type of Stage: Proscenium
Stage Dimensions: 26'x 26'

4626
BETHEL COLLEGE FINE ARTS SERIES
1001 W Mckinley Avenue
Mishawaka, IN 46545
Phone: 574-259-3331
Fax: 574-257-3513
Toll-free: 800-422-4101
e-mail: jacobss@bethelcollege.edu
Web Site: www.bethel-in.edu
Management:
  Director: Erin Wagler
  Assistant Director: Becky Schaut
  Assistant Director: Sheila Jacobsen
Performs At: Everest-Rohrer Auditorium

4627
EMENS AUDITORIUM
Ball State University
Muncie, IN 47306
Phone: 765-285-1539
Fax: 765-285-3719
Toll-free: 877-993-6367
Web Site: www.bsu.edu/emens
Management:
  Manager: Robert Myers
  Assistant Manager: Darcy Wood
Founded: 1964
Specialized Field: Series & Festivals; Vocal Music; Theatre; Youth; Dance; Ethnic Performances
Status: Non-Profit, Professional
Paid Staff: 15
Annual Attendance: 10,000+
Facility Category: Performing Arts Center
Seating Capacity: 3309
Year Built: 1964
Rental Contact: Bob Myers

4628
SAINT MARY'S COLLEGE CULTURAL ARTS SEASON
Saint Mary's College
Moreau Center for the Arts
Notre Dame, IN 46556-5001
Phone: 574-284-4000
Fax: 219-284-4784
e-mail: webmaster@saintmarys.edu
Web Site: www.saintmarys.edu
Management:

SERIES & FESTIVALS / Indiana

President: Carol Ann Mooney
Performs At: O'Laughlin Auditorium

4629
ARTS PLACE, INC.
PO Box 804
131 East Walnut Street
Portland, IN 47371
Phone: 260-726-4809
Fax: 260-726-2081
Toll-free: 866-539-9911
e-mail: artsland@artsland.org
Web Site: www.artsland.org
Officers:
   President: Kyle Teeter
   Second Vice President: Paula Sibery
   Corporate Secretary: Carol Trimmer
   First Vice President: Martha Weaver
   Treasurer: William Hess
Management:
   Executive Director: Eric R. Rogers
   Director of Administration: Heidi Bouse
   Marketing Associate: Tavia Boolman
   Director of Devel and Volunteerism: Sue Burk
   Collective Center Director: Mary Hone
Mission: To nurture the creative spirit by making arts,experiences, education, and services accessible to the regions residents, artists, and cultural organizations.
Founded: 1967
Specialized Field: Arts Council
Paid Staff: 10
Budget: $700,000
Income Sources: Private Contributions; Endowments; Grants; Tickets And Instructional Fees
Performs At: Hall Memorial Theatre
Facility Category: Arts Center
Type of Stage: Proscenium
Seating Capacity: 283
Year Built: 1985
Year Remodeled: 2000

4630
EARLHAM COLLEGE GUEST ARTIST SERIES
801 National Road West
Richmond, IN 47374-4095
Phone: 765-983-1373
Fax: 765-983-1291
Web Site: www.earlham.edu
Officers:
   Chair: Deborah Miller Hull
   Vice Chair: John G. Young
   Secretary: Raymond Ontko
Management:
   President: David Dawson
   VP: James McKey
   Chairman of the Board: Deborah Miller Hull
Founded: 1847
Status: Non-Profit, Non-Professional
Performs At: Goddard Auditorium

4631
FIREFLY FESTIVAL FOR THE PERFORMING ARTS
112 W Jefferson Boulevard
Suite 511
South Bend, IN 46601
Phone: 574-288-3472
Fax: 574-288-3478
e-mail: firefly@fireflyfestival.com
Web Site: www.fireflyfestival.com
Management:
   President: Candace Butler

Promotion Director: Wendy Little
Office Assistant: Judy West
Mission: To promote and present to the general public artistic performanaces which have as their general theme music, dance, drama, and other arts.
Utilizes: Actors; Dance Companies; Guest Accompanists; Guest Artists; Guest Companies; Guest Musical Directors; Guild Activities; Local Artists; Multimedia; Original Music Scores; Selected Students; Singers; Special Technical Talent; Theatre Companies
Founded: 1981
Specialized Field: Series and Festivals; Music; Theatre; Dance
Status: Non-Profit, Professional
Paid Staff: 3
Volunteer Staff: 140
Budget: $330,000
Income Sources: Grants; Sponsors; Advertisers; Ticket Sales; In-kind Donations; Private Donations; Business Donations
Season: June - August
Performs At: St. Patrick's County Park, South Bend (Festival Site)
Annual Attendance: 18,000
Facility Category: Robert J Fischgrund Center for the Performing Arts
Type of Stage: Proscenium
Stage Dimensions: 30x60
Seating Capacity: 6,000
Year Built: 1986
Rental Contact: St. Patrick's County Park
Organization Type: Performing; Educational

4632
PERFORMING ARTS SERIES OF INDIANA STATE UNIVERSITY
200 N. Eighth Street
Terre Haute, IN 47809
Phone: 812-237-3770
Toll-free: 877-478-8497
e-mail: david.dekolletti@indstate.edu
Web Site: www.indstate.edu
Management:
   Program Coordinator: David Dekolletti
Founded: 1865
Specialized Field: Series & Festivals; Music; Device; Theatre
Status: Non-Profit, Professional
Paid Staff: 1
Performs At: Tilson Auditorium
Seating Capacity: 1,684

4633
VALPARAISO UNIVERSITY GUEST ARTISTS SERIES
VU Center for the Arts
Valparaiso, IN 46383-6493
Phone: 219-464-5000
Fax: 219-464-5381
e-mail: sarah.rothaar@valpo.edu
Web Site: www.valpo.edu
Management:
   President: Dr. Mark Heckler
   VP Academic Affair: Roy A Austensen
   VP Admin And Finance: Charley Gillispie
Performs At: Chapel of the Resurrection

4634
VINCENNES UNIVERSITY COMMUNITY SERIES
1002 North First Street
DC-38
Vincennes, IN 47591

Phone: 812-888-4354
Fax: 812-888-5942
Toll-free: 800-945-ALUM
e-mail: bprimus@vinu.edu
Web Site: http://alumni.vinu.edu/communityseries
Management:
   President: Richard Helton
   Executive Director: Donna Clinkenbeard
Utilizes: Special Technical Talent; Theatre Companies
Founded: 1950
Specialized Field: Series & Festivals; Vocal Music; Ethnic Performances
Status: Non-Profit, Professional
Performs At: Auditorium
Facility Category: High School Auditorium
Seating Capacity: 900

4635
PURDUE UNIVERSITY CONVOCATIONS & LECTURES
128 Memorial Mall
STEW 194
West Lafayette, IN 47907-2016
Phone: 765-494-9712
Fax: 765-494-0540
Toll-free: 800-914-SHOW
e-mail: convos@purdue.edu
Web Site: www.purdue.edu/convos
Management:
   Director: Todd E Wetzel
   Assistant Director: Laura Clavio
   Director of Marketing: Abby Eddy
   Director of Development: Amanda Dunkle
   Manager of Production: Kathy Dietz
   Business Manager: Debbie Siciliano
Specialized Field: Theatre: Musical
Status: Professional
Paid Staff: 13
Performs At: Edward C. Elliot Hall of Music

4636
MASTERWORKS FESTIVAL
1001 College Ave?
Winona Lake, IN 46590
Mailing Address: PO Box 700 Winona Lake, IN 46590
Phone: 574-267-5973
Fax: 574-267-8315
Toll-free: 888-836-2723
e-mail: cpaf@christianperformingart.org
Web Site: www.masterworksfestival.org
Management:
   Artistic Director: Dr Patrick Kavanaugh
   Music Director: Dr James Kraft
   Administrator: Arturo Osorio
   Office Manager: Cyd Kumi
   Publicity Coordinator: Erin Richard
Mission: To train the next generation of Christian performing artists.
Utilizes: Actors; Arrangers; Choreographers; Collaborating Artists; Community Members; Composers; Dancers; Designers; Educators; Filmmakers; Grant Writers; Guest Accompanists; Guest Composers; Guest Designers; Guest Ensembles; Guest Instructors; Guest Lecturers; Guest Musical Directors; Guest Musicians; Guest Speakers; High School Drama; Multimedia; Paid Performers; Sign Language Translators; Soloists; Students; Student Interns
Founded: 1997
Specialized Field: Classical
Status: Professional; Nonprofit; Educational; Religious
Budget: $300,000 - $500,000
Income Sources: Donations, Tuition, Foundations
Performs At: Grace College

SERIES & FESTIVALS / Iowa

Annual Attendance: 3,500 - 4,500
Facility Category: 4 Stages: 2 Concert, 1 Recital Hall, 1 Outdoor Ampitheater
Seating Capacity: 300, 500, 150, 300
Year Built: 1999

Iowa

4637
IOWA STATE UNIVERSITY PERFORMING ARTS COUNCIL SERIES
Iowa State Center, ISU Scheman Building
Suite 102
Ames, IA 50011-1113
Phone: 515-294-3347
Fax: 515-294-3349
Toll-free: 877-843-2368
e-mail: iscinfo@iastate.edu
Web Site: www.center.iastate.edu
Officers:
  SMG Regional Vice President: Joseph Romano
Management:
  General Manager: Mark North
  Development & Sponsorship Manager: Patti Cotter
  Business Manager: Linda Wilcox
  Director of Marketing: Angela Ossian
  Payroll & Personnel Administrator: Susan Lund
  Director of Event & Conference Serv: Pat Dennis
  Guest & Client Services Manager: Tim Hinderks
  Theaters - Technical Director: Steve Harder
Founded: 1969
Specialized Field: Multi
Paid Staff: 30

4638
CASS COUNTY ARTS COUNCIL
Box 902
Atlantic, IA 75551
Phone: 903-756-7062
Fax: 712-243-4182
e-mail: info@cassarts.org
Web Site: cassarts.org/

4639
BURLINGTON CIVIC MUSIC ASSOCIATION
PO Box 812
Burlington, IA 52601
Phone: 319-752-0336
Fax: 319-754-6824
Toll-free: 800-397-1708
e-mail: bwilson@thehawkeye.com
Web Site: burlcivicmusic.com/
Officers:
  Program Chairman: Bobby Wilson
  President: Barbara McRoberts
Performs At: Memorial Auditorium

4640
UNIVERSITY OF NORTHERN IOWA ARTISTS SERIES
University of Northern Iowa
Gallagher Bluedorn Performing Arts Center
8201 Dakota Street
Cedar Falls, IA 50613
Phone: 319-273-3660
Fax: 319-273-7470
Toll-free: 877-549-7469
e-mail: gbpac@uni.edu
Web Site: www.gbpac.com
Officers:
  President: Benjamin Allen
  Assistant VP Events Management: Steve Carignan
Management:
  Director of Education: Amy Hunzelman
  Event Management Director: Chris Kremer
  Executive Director: Steve Carignan
  Development Director: Dianne Campbell
  Director of Finance: Jocelyn Moeller
  Technical Services Director: Sandy Nordahl
  Volunteer Coordinator: Vee Shaffer
  Assistant Technical Director/Lighti: William Tuzicka
  Assistant Director: Molly Hackenmiller
Utilizes: Artists-in-Residence; Choreographers; Collaborations; Dance Companies; Dancers; Educators; Guest Accompanists; Guest Choreographers; Guest Conductors; Guest Instructors; Guest Musical Directors; Guest Musicians; Local Artists; Lyricists; Multimedia; Original Music Scores; Selected Students; Sign Language Translators; Soloists; Special Technical Talent; Theatre Companies
Founded: 2000
Specialized Field: Performing Art
Status: Non-Profit, Non-Professional
Paid Staff: 13
Volunteer Staff: 350
Budget: 1.8 Million
Income Sources: Tickets; Grants; Fundraising; State Support
Performs At: Theatre/Concert Hall
Affiliations: APAP
Annual Attendance: 120,000
Facility Category: Multi-Venue, Performing Arts Center
Type of Stage: Proscenium/Thrust
Stage Dimensions: 30'x 40'
Seating Capacity: 1,700
Year Built: 2000
Cost: $27,000
Rental Contact: Director Steve Carignan

4641
CEDAR RAPIDS COMMUNITY CONCERTS ASSOCIATION
123 Third Avenue SE
Cedar Rapids, IA 52401
Phone: 319-398-5226
e-mail: info@crcommunityconcerts.org
Web Site: http://www.crcommunityconcerts.org/
Management:
  President: Robert Massey
  Bruce: Ellen Pelzer 1st Vice President
  Treasurer: Ivan Chester
  Secretary: Mary Ann Wetherbee
  General Manager: Jason Anderson
  Interim Executive Director: Sharon Cummins
  Director of Events/Production: Scott Piquard
  Chief Marketing Officer: Alexis Kenleigh
Founded: 1930
Specialized Field: Series & Festivals; Instrumental Music; Theatre; Youth; Dance; Ethnic Performances
Status: Non-Profit, Professional
Performs At: Paramount Theatre for the Performing Arts

4642
COE COLLEGE JAZZ SUMMIT
1220 First Avenue NE
Marquis 104
Cedar Rapids, IA 52402
Phone: 319-399-8500
Fax: 319-399-8209
Toll-free: 877-CAL- COE
e-mail: btiede@coe.edu
Web Site: www.coe.edu
Management:
  Director Of Marketing: Rod Pritchard
  Associate Director Of Marketing and: Lonnie Zingula
  Director Of Production: Carole Butz
Mission: To offer student musicians the opportunity to work with renowned professional players/teachers.
Founded: 1851
Specialized Field: Jazz
Status: Nonprofit
Paid Staff: 5
Volunteer Staff: 40
Paid Artists: 6
Non-paid Artists: 20
Annual Attendance: 1,500

4643
COE COLLEGE MARQUIS SERIES
1220 1st Avenue NW
Cedar Rapids, IA 52402
Phone: 319-366-6237
e-mail: ggriffin@coe.edu
Web Site: www.coe.edu
Management:
  President: Greg Griffins
Specialized Field: Performance Arts Community
Status: Non-Profit, Professional
Paid Staff: 6

4644
LEGION ARTS
1103 Third St SE
Cedar Rapids, IA 52401-2305
Phone: 319-364-1580
Fax: 319-362-9156
e-mail: info@legionarts.org
Web Site: www.legionarts.org
Management:
  Executive Director: F John Herbert
  Producing Director: Mel Andringa, mel@legionarts.org
Mission: Promotes new and innovative expression in the visual, performing, literary and electronic arts; fosters creative interaction between artists, their communities and society; and encourages the imaginative exploration of contemporary ideas and experience.
Utilizes: Artists-in-Residence; Choreographers; Collaborating Artists; Dance Companies; Dancers; Fine Artists; Guest Accompanists; Guest Choreographers; Guest Designers; Guest Directors; Guest Ensembles; Guest Musical Directors; Guest Musicians; Multimedia; Original Music Scores; Playwrights; Resident Artists; Sign Language Translators; Student Interns; Special Technical Talent; Theatre Companies
Founded: 1981
Specialized Field: Visual Arts; Theatre; Music; Dance; Film; Spoken Word
Status: Non-Profit, Professional
Paid Staff: 4
Budget: $300,000
Income Sources: Public and Private Grants; Earned Income
Performs At: Proscenium; Black Box; Concert Halls; Cabaret
Affiliations: NPN; NAAO; APAP
Annual Attendance: 20,000
Facility Category: Contemporary Arts Center
Type of Stage: Black Box; Proscenium

SERIES & FESTIVALS / Iowa

Seating Capacity: 75/175
Year Built: 1893
Year Remodeled: 2010
Rental Contact: Mel Andrinca
Organization Type: Performing; Touring; Sponsoring

4645
GLENN MILLER FESTIVAL
122 West Clark Street
PO Box 61
Clarinda, IA 51632
Phone: 712-542-2461
Fax: 712-542-2868
e-mail: gmbs@glennmiller.org
Web Site: www.glennmiller.org
Officers:
    President: Marvin Negley
Management:
    President: Marvin Negley
    Office Manager: Jodi Eberly
    Secertary of Board: Arlene Leonard
Founded: 1978
Specialized Field: Series and Festivals; Instrumental Music; Vocal Music; Youth; Dance; Life and Memory of Glenn Miller
Status: Non-Profit, Non-Professional
Paid Staff: 1
Volunteer Staff: 15

4646
BIX BIEDERBECKE MEMORIAL JAZZ FESTIVAL
311 N Ripley Street
PO Box 3688
Davenport, IA 52808
Phone: 563-324-7170
Fax: 563-326-1732
Toll-free: 888-249-5487
e-mail: info@bixsociety.org
Web Site: www.bixsociety.org
Officers:
    President: Mike Boyler
    Vice President: Joe Hesse
    Secretary: Leo Schubert
    Treasurer: Todd Whitlow
Management:
    President: Mike Boyler
    Executive Director: Rich Johnson
    Festival Director: Ray Voss
    Music Director: Josh Duffee
Mission: To honor the memory and perpetuate the music of Leon Bix Beiderbecke, a Davenport native son, who was a world-renowned jazz cornetist, pianist and composer.
Founded: 1972
Specialized Field: Series & Festivals; Instrumental Music; Youth
Status: Non-Profit, Professional
Volunteer Staff: 450
Paid Artists: 100
Season: July
Annual Attendance: 10,000

4647
MISSISSIPPI VALLEY BLUES FESTIVAL
102 South Harrison Street
Suite 300
Davenport, IA 52801
Phone: 563-322-5837
Fax: 563-322-5832
e-mail: mvbs@mvbs.org
Web Site: www.mvbs.org
Officers:
    President: Kevin Nolan
    Vice President: Julie Reyes
    Treasurer: Joe Griffen
    Secretary: Kristy Bennett
Management:
    President: Kevin Nolan
    Vice President: Julie Reyes
    Treasurer: Joe Griffen
    Secretary: Kristy Bennett
Founded: 1984
Specialized Field: Education of Blues with Residency
Status: Non-Profit, Non-Professional
Paid Staff: 1

4648
LUTHER COLLEGE CENTER STAGE SERIES
Luther College
700 College Drive
Decorah, IA 52101
Phone: 563-387-1536
Fax: 563-387-1765
Toll-free: 800-458-8437
e-mail: gertta01@luther.edu
Web Site: www.programming.luther.edu
Management:
    Director Campus Programming: Tanya M B Gertz
    Campus Programming Office Coordinat: Susan Peterson
    Campus Programming Assistant/Box Of: Bradley Phillips
    Head Technician, Campus Programming: Kendall Thompson
    Campus Programming Technician: Paul Atkins
    Coordinator: Mike Anderson
Founded: 1861
Specialized Field: Performing Arts
Paid Staff: 6
Volunteer Staff: 40
Performs At: Center for Faith & Life
Annual Attendance: 9,300
Facility Category: Performing Arts Facility
Type of Stage: Thrust & Perscenium
Stage Dimensions: 48'x 32'
Seating Capacity: Thrust - 1,400; Perscenium - 950
Year Built: 1977

4649
CIVIC MUSIC ASSOCIATION OF DES MOINES
900 Mulberry Street
Suite 203
Des Moines, IA 50309
Phone: 515-280-4020
Fax: 515-286-4080
e-mail: debbie@civicmusic.org
Web Site: www.civicmusic.org
Officers:
    President: Kent Fieldsend
    1st Vice President: Jeff Kane
    2nd Vice President: Karen Jackson
    Treasurer: Bill Bartine
    Secretary: DeeAnn Drew
Management:
    Executive Director: Carrie Clogg
    Marketing & Patron Services Manager: Debbie Martin
Founded: 1925
Specialized Field: Classical and Jazz Music
Status: Non-Profit, Professional
Paid Staff: 1
Paid Artists: 15
Seating Capacity: 770

4650
GRAND VIEW COLLEGE-NIELSEN CONCERT SERIES
1200 Grand View Avenue
Des Moines, IA 50316
Phone: 515-263-2800
Fax: 515-263-6192
Toll-free: 800-444-6083
e-mail: kduffy@gvc.edu
Web Site: www.gvc.edu
Management:
    Chairperson of the Committee: Katherine P Duffy
Founded: 1981
Specialized Field: Series & Festivals; Instrumental Music; Vocal Music
Status: Non-Profit, Professional

4651
GRAND VIEW COLLEGE-NIELSEN CONCERT SERIES
1200 Grand View Avenue
Des Moines, IA 50316
Phone: 515-263-2800
Fax: 515-263-6192
Toll-free: 800-444-6083
e-mail: kduffy@gvc.edu
Web Site: www.gvc.edu
Management:
    Director: Dr. Katherine Pohlmann Duffy
Performs At: College Center Theatre

4652
CLARKE COLLEGE CULTURAL EVENTS SERIES
1550 Clark Drive
Dubuque, IA 52001
Phone: 563-588-6316
Fax: 319-588-6789
Toll-free: 800-383-2345
Web Site: www.clarke.edu
Officers:
    Chairman of the Board: Carolyn Sanders Haupert
    Vice Chair: John P. Beaver
    President: Joanne M. Burrows, SC, Ph.D.
    Vice President: Timothy J. Conlon
Management:
    President: Joanne M. Burrows, SC, Ph.D.

4654
LORAS COLLEGE ARTS & LECTURE SERIES
1450 Alta Vista
Dubuque, IA 52004-0178
Phone: 319-588-7153
Fax: 319-557-4086
e-mail: bhughes@loras.edu
Web Site: www.loras.edu
Officers:
    Chairman: Brian Hughes
Management:
    Chairman: Brain Hughes
Mission: To bring high quality cultural activity to the college and community.
Founded: 1985
Specialized Field: Insturmental Music; Vocal Music; Dance; Multi-Cultural; Theatre; Lecture
Volunteer Staff: 10
Performs At: St. Joseph Auditorium

SERIES & FESTIVALS / Iowa

4655
WALDORF COMMUNITY ARTISTS SERIES
Waldorf College
106 S 6Th Street
Forest City, IA 50436
Phone: 641-585-2450
Fax: 641-582-8194
Toll-free: 877-267-2157
e-mail: onlineadmissions@waldorf.edu
Web Site: www.waldorf.edu
Management:
  President: Richard A Hanson PhD
  Assistant To President: Cindy Carter
Mission: To offer the finest in performing arts events to the Forest City and Waldorf communities.
Founded: 1988
Specialized Field: Dance; Vocal Music; Instrumental Music; Theater; Lyric Opera; Grand Opera
Status: Nonprofit
Income Sources: Waldorf College
Organization Type: Sponsoring

4656
GRINNELL COLLEGE MUSIC DEPARTMENT CONCERT SERIES
Music Department
1115 Eighth Ave
Grinnell, IA 50112
Phone: 641-269-3064
Fax: 641-269-4420
Web Site: www.grinnell.edu/music/
Officers:
  Music Department Chairman: Jonathan Chenette
Management:
  Chair: John Rommereim
  Music Technical Assistant: Paul E. Nelson
  Academic Support Assistant II: Ivy Van Ersvelde
  Coordinator of Peace Studies Progra: Valerie M Vetter
Performs At: Sebring-Lewis Hall

4657
FRIDAY NIGHT CONCERT SERIES
PO Box 3128
Iowa City, IA 52244-3128
Phone: 319-337-7944
Fax: 319-358-9094
e-mail: info@summerofthearts.org
Web Site: www.summerofthearts.org
Officers:
  Past President: Steve Parrott
  President: Diana Lundell
  Vice President: Mark Zaiger
  Treasurer: Jason Weeks
  Secretary: Brent Hawkins
Management:
  Executive Director: Lisa Barnes
  Associate Executive Director: Shane Schemmel
  Development Director: Emily McMahon
  Volunteer & Community Relations Man: Alex Stanton
Founded: 1991

4658
IOWA ARTS FESTIVAL
PO Box 3128
Iowa City, IA 52244-3128
Phone: 319-337-7944
Fax: 319-358-9094
e-mail: info@summerofthearts.org
Web Site: www.summerofthearts.org
Officers:
  Past President: Steve Parrott
  President: Diana Lundell
  Vice President: Mark Zaiger
  Treasurer: Jason Weeks
  Secretary: Brent Hawkins
Management:
  Executive Director: Lisa Barnes
  Associate Executive Director: Shane Schemmel
  Development Director: Emily McMahon
  Volunteer & Community Relations Man: Alex Stanton
Founded: 1982
Paid Artists: 20

4659
IOWA CITY JAZZ FESTIVAL
PO Box 3128
Iowa City, IA 52244-3128
Phone: 319-337-7944
Fax: 319-358-9094
e-mail: info@summerofthearts.org
Web Site: www.summerofthearts.org
Officers:
  Past President: Steve Parrott
  President: Diana Lundell
  Vice President: Mark Zaiger
  Treasurer: Jason Weeks
  Secretary: Brent Hawkins
Management:
  Executive Director: Lisa Barnes
  Associate Executive Director: Shane Schemmel
  Development Director: Emily McMahon
  Volunteer & Community Relations Man: Alex Stanton
Founded: 1982

4660
IOWA PICTURE SHOW
PO Box 3128
Iowa City, IA 52244-3128
Phone: 319-337-7944
Fax: 319-358-9094
e-mail: info@summerofthearts.org
Web Site: www.summerofthearts.org
Officers:
  Past President: Steve Parrott
  President: Diana Lundell
  Vice President: Mark Zaiger
  Treasurer: Jason Weeks
  Secretary: Brent Hawkins
Management:
  Executive Director: Lisa Barnes
  Associate Executive Director: Shane Schemmel
  Development Director: Emily McMahon
  Volunteer & Community Relations Man: Alex Stanton
Founded: 1991

4661
SAND IN THE CITY
PO Box 3128
Iowa City, IA 52244-3128
Phone: 319-337-7944
Fax: 319-358-9094
e-mail: info@summerofthearts.org
Web Site: www.summerofthearts.org
Officers:
  Past President: Steve Parrott
  President: Diana Lundell
  Vice President: Mark Zaiger
  Treasurer: Jason Weeks
  Secretary: Brent Hawkins
Management:
  Executive Director: Lisa Barnes
  Associate Executive Director: Shane Schemmel
  Development Director: Emily McMahon
  Volunteer & Community Relations Man: Alex Stanton
Founded: 1982
Paid Artists: 20

4662
JACKSON CONCERT SERIES
Elm Road
Wesley United Methodist Church
Muscatine, IA 52761
Phone: 563-263-1596
Fax: 563-263-1631
e-mail: wesleymethodist@machlink.com
Web Site: www.wesleymethodist.org/jackson.htm
Management:
  Choir Director: Dr Richard Smith
  Sr Pastor Of Worship/Administration: Dr Hal Green
  Youth Director: Julie MacLachlan
  Exec. Director of Operations: Jeff Slemp
  Director of Music and Worship: Rochelle Collette
  Director of Facilities: Fred Luper
  Financial Administrator: Sheryl Miller
  Director of Media and Communication: Brian Mattson
  Financial Secretary: Carol Parker
Performs At: Wesely United Methodist Church

4663
ORANGE CITY ARTS COUNCIL
PO Box 202
125 Central Ave SE
Orange City, IA 51041
Phone: 712-707-4885
Fax: 712-707-4351
e-mail: ocarts@juno.com
Web Site: orangecityarts.net/
Officers:
  President: Phyllis Van Gelder
  Vice President: Mark Volkers
  Secretary: Angela Kroeze-Visser
  Treasurer: Sandie Vant Hof
Management:
  Program Director: Joyce Bloemendaal
Utilizes: Actors; Artists-in-Residence; Dance Companies; Fine Artists; Guest Accompanists; Instructors; Local Artists; Multimedia; Original Music Scores; Special Technical Talent; Theatre Companies
Founded: 1977
Specialized Field: Series and Festivals; Present Arts for Variety Music; Dance; Theatre
Status: Non-Profit, Non-Professional
Paid Staff: 1
Performs At: Christ Chapel

4664
BUENA VISTA UNIVERSITY ACADEMIC & CULTURAL EVENTS SERIES
Buena Vista University
610 W 4th Street
Storm Lake, IA 50588
Phone: 800-383-9600
Fax: 712-749-2037
Toll-free: 800-383-2821
e-mail: wagnerl@bvu.edu
Web Site: www.bvu.edu/students
Management:
  President: Fred Moore
  Managing Director: Lisa Wagner
Founded: 1988

SERIES & FESTIVALS / Kansas

Specialized Field: Series & Festivals; Instrumental Music; Vocal Music; Theatre; Dance; Ethnic Performances
Status: Non-Profit, Non-Professional
Paid Staff: 1
Budget: $140,000
Performs At: Anderson Auditorium
Affiliations: APAP
Annual Attendance: 3,500-4,000
Facility Category: Multi Use
Type of Stage: Proscenium
Seating Capacity: 822
Year Built: 1999
Rental Contact: Katie Schwint

4666
ALLIANCE WORLD FESTIVAL OF WOMEN SINGING
34 Fox Creek Drive
Waukee, IA 50263
Phone: 515-987-1405
Fax: 515-987-5480
e-mail: allianceforartsu@qwest.net
Web Site: www.allianceforartsandunderstanding.com
Officers:
  Founder, CEO: Yonatan Stern
Management:
  President: Rich Carpenter
  Executive Director: Donald Morse
  Artistic Director: Carol Stewart
  Managing Director: Steve Ricci
  Founder, CEO & Chief Scientist: Yonatan Stern
  Chief Financial Officer: Paul Boulanger
  Vice President of Engineering: Eugenia Gillan
  Vice President of Sales: Mark Ruthfield
  Vice President of Marketing: Hila Nir
Founded: 1993
Specialized Field: Series and Festivals: Festivals of Choral Singing
Status: Non-Profit, Professional
Paid Staff: 6
Season: October
Performs At: St. John's University [Festival Site]
Facility Category: Abbey Cathedral
Seating Capacity: 2,000

4667
WARTBURG COLLEGE ARTISTS SERIES
100 Wartburg Boulevard
Waverly, IA 50677-1003
Mailing Address: PO Box 1003
Phone: 319-352-8409
Fax: 319-352-8685
Toll-free: 800-772-2085
e-mail: artistseries@wartburg.edu
Web Site: www.wartburg.edu
Officers:
  President: Darrel Colson
Management:
  Artistic Director: Myrna Culbertson
Mission: To provide diverse performing artists with community service and educational venues.
Founded: 1920
Specialized Field: Series & Festivals; Instrumental Music; Vocal Music; Theater; Dance; Ethnic Performances
Status: Non-Profit, Professional
Paid Staff: 1
Performs At: Neumann Auditorium
Organization Type: Sponsoring

Kansas

4668
GREAT PLAINS THEATRE FESTIVAL
PO Box 476
300 N. Mulberry Street
Abilene, KS 67410
Phone: 785-263-4574
Fax: 785-263-9960
Toll-free: 888-222-4574
e-mail: marc@greatplainstheatre.com
Web Site: www.greatplainstheatre.com
Management:
  Executive Artistic Director: Richard Esvang
  Associate Artistic Director: Michelle Meade
Utilizes: Actors; AEA Actors; Choreographers; Five Seasonal Concerts; Guest Designers; Guest Lecturers; Guild Activities; Instructors; Local Artists; Multi Collaborations; Multimedia; New Productions; Organization Contracts; Original Music Scores; Performance Artists; Resident Artists; Sign Language Translators; Soloists; Touring Companies
Founded: 1994
Status: Nonprofit
Performs At: Remodeled Stone Church; State of the Art Theatre.
Affiliations: Equity
Facility Category: Theatre
Type of Stage: Proscenium
Stage Dimensions: 45' x 26'
Seating Capacity: 199
Year Built: 1880
Year Remodeled: 1994

4669
COFFEYVILLE CULTURAL ARTS COUNCIL INC
102 W. 7th St.
P.O. Box 1629
Coffeyville, KS 67337
Phone: 620-252-6100
Fax: 620-252-6175
Web Site: http://www.coffeyville.com/Culture.htm#Center_For_the_Arts
Management:
  Executive Director: Kenneth H Burchinal
  President: John Isaacs
  Treasurer: Robert Erickson
  Secretary: Nedra Troxel
Specialized Field: Series; Youth Choir
Paid Staff: 1
Performs At: JH Benefiel Auditorium

4670
EMPORIA ARTS COUNCIL PERFORMING ARTS/CONCERT/CHILDREN'S SERIES
618 Mechanic St
Emporia, KS 66801
Phone: 620-340-6473
Web Site: emporiaksarts.org
Officers:
  President: Jan Laurent
  President-Elect: Teresa Maley
  Treasurer: Roberta Swanson
  Secretary: Robbie Hill
  Immediate Past President: Dan Robertson
Management:
  Executive Director: Melissa Windsor
  Marketing Manager & Development Coo: Jennifer Sweetman-LeClair
Specialized Field: Choral, Dance, Theater, Instrumental Music, Series, Youth

Status: Non-Profit, Professional
Performs At: Albert Taylor Hall

4671
GOODLAND ARTS COUNCIL
120 W 12th
PO Box 526
Goodland, KS 67735
Phone: 785-890-6442
Fax: 785-890-6335
e-mail: gidarts@st/tel.net
Web Site: www.goodlandnet.com/artcenter
Officers:
  President: Jacque Schields
  Executive Director: Kay Younger
Management:
  Executive Director: Kay Younger
Founded: 1979
Specialized Field: Visual Arts
Status: Non-Profit, Non-Professional
Paid Staff: 2
Paid Artists: 5
Performs At: Auditorium

4672
FORT HAYS STATE UNIVERSITY ENCORE SERIES
600 Park Street
Hays, KS 67601
Phone: 785-628-4000
Fax: 785-628-4007
Web Site: www.fhsu.edu
Management:
  Executive Director: Carol Brock
Founded: 1981
Specialized Field: Series & Festivals: Multidisciplinary
Status: Non-Profit, Professional
Paid Staff: 2
Performs At: Felton-Start Theatre

4673
HESSTON/BETHEL PERFORMING ARTS SERIES
325 S. College Dr.
Box 3000
Hesston, KS 67062
Phone: 620-327-4221
Fax: 620-327-8300
Web Site: www.hesston.edu/hbpa/
Officers:
  Chairman: Jacob Rittenhouse
  Executive Secretary: David W Rhodes
Mission: To provide high quality cultural programming for the Hesston College/Bethel College student bodies and the immediate Hesston and Newton communities
Utilizes: Contract Orchestras; Educators; Guest Directors; Guest Instructors; Guest Musical Directors; Guest Musicians; Multimedia; Paid Performers; Sign Language Translators
Founded: 1982
Specialized Field: Vocal Music; Instrumental Music
Status: Nonprofit
Budget: $45,000
Income Sources: Season Tickets; Single Ticket Sales; Patrons; City Support
Performs At: Yost Center, Hesston College; Memorial Hall, Bethel College
Annual Attendance: 500
Facility Category: Gymnasium/Field House
Seating Capacity: 1,000
Year Built: 1983
Organization Type: Sponsoring

SERIES & FESTIVALS / Kansas

4674
MESSIAH FESTIVAL OF MUSIC
Bethany College
421 N 1st Street
Lindsborg, KS 67456
Phone: 913-227-3311
Fax: 913-721-2110
Management:
  Conductor: Gregory Aune
  Public Relations/Ticket Information: Jud Barclay
  Music Director: Daniel Mahraun
Founded: 1882
Specialized Field: Vocal Music; Instrumental Music
Status: Nonprofit
Income Sources: Bethany College
Performs At: Presser Hall Auditorium
Organization Type: Performing; Sponsoring

4675
BOWLUS CULTURAL ATTRACTIONS SERIES
PO Box 705
205 E Madison Ave.
Lola, KS 66749
Phone: 620-365-4765
Fax: 316-365-4767
e-mail: mary.bowlus@iolaks.com
Web Site: www.bowluscenter.com
Officers:
  President: Tony Leavitt
  Vice President: Don Snavely
Management:
  Director: Mary Martin
  Executive Director: Susan Raines
  Facility Manager/Technical Director: Jeff Jordan
  Assistant Technical Director: John Higginbotham
  Marketing and Volunteer Coordinator: Judy Cochran
  Book keeper: Traci Plumlee
  Maintenance: Dan Stotler
Seating Capacity: 752

4676
KANSAS STATE UNIVERSITY MCCAIN PERFORMANCE SERIES
Kansas State University
211 McCain Auditorium
Manhattan, KS 66506-4711
Phone: 785-532-6428
Fax: 785-532-5870
e-mail: mccain@k-state.edu
Web Site: www.ksu.edu/mccain
Management:
  President: Wes Sald
  Artistic Director: Richard Martin
  Associate Director: Terri Lee
  Executive Director: Todd Holmberg
  Technical Director: Kyle McGuffin
  Ticket Services Manager: Stefani Schrader
Founded: 1971
Specialized Field: Series & Festivals: Theatre
Status: Non-Profit, Professional
Paid Staff: 7
Seating Capacity: 1800

4677
OTTAWA MUNICIPAL AUDITORIUM ENTERTAINMENT SERIES
301 S Hickory St.
PO Box 462
Ottawa, KS 66067
Phone: 785-242-8810
Fax: 785-229-3760
e-mail: omalive@grapevine.net
Web Site: www.grapevine.net/~omalive
Management:
  Administrative Manager: Shonda Stitt
  Operations Manager: Sam Parkins
Founded: 1978
Specialized Field: Series and Festivals: Vocal Music
Status: Non-Profit, Professional
Paid Staff: 9

4678
OVERLAND PARK ARTS COMMISSION
8500 Santa Fe Drive
Overland Park, KS 66212
Phone: 913-895-6000
Fax: 913-895-6365
e-mail: city@opkansas.org
Web Site: www.opkansas.org
Management:
  Executive Director: Julie K Bilyea
Founded: 1962
Specialized Field: Series and Festivals: Performance and Visual Arts
Status: For-Profit, Non-Professional
Paid Staff: 1

4679
PITTSBURG STATE UNIVERSITY SOLO & CHAMBER MUSIC SERIES
PSU Department of Music
1701 S Broadway
Pittsburg, KS 66762
Phone: 620-235-4466
Fax: 620-235-4468
e-mail: music@pittstate.edu
Web Site: www.pittstate.edu/music
Management:
  President: Tom Bryant
  Chaiman of the Music Department: Dr. Russell Jones
  Series Director: Susan Marchant
Specialized Field: Series and Festivals; Instrumental Music; Vocal Music; Ethnic Performances
Status: Non-Profit, Professional
Paid Staff: 20
Paid Artists: 19

4680
SALINA ARTS & HUMANITIES COMMISSION
PO Box 2181
Salina, KS 67402-2181
Phone: 785-309-5770
Fax: 785-826-7444
e-mail: sahc@salina.org
Web Site: salinaarts.com/
Officers:
  Executive Director: Brad Anderson
Management:
  Executive Director: Brad Anderson
  Arts Education Coordinator: Sharon Benson
  Marketing & Development Coordinator: Kay Quinn
  Office Manager: Karla Prickett
  Program Assistant: Amanda Morris
  Account Technician: Glenda Johnson

4681
STERLING COLLEGE ARTIST SERIES
Sterling College
125 W. Cooper
Sterling, KS 67579
Phone: 316-278-2173
Web Site: www.sterling.edu
Management:
  Chair, Music Department: Dr. Brad Nix
Specialized Field: Instrumental Music
Performs At: Culbertson Auditorium

4682
TOPEKA PERFORMING ARTS CENTER
214 SE 8th Avenue
Topeka, KS 66603
Phone: 785-234-2787
Fax: 785-234-2307
Web Site: www.tpactix.org
Officers:
  Board President: John Bardsley
  Board Vice-President: Sue Buckley
  Board Treasurer: Susan Lacey
  Board Past President: Curtis Sneden
Management:
  Executive Director: Barbara Wiggins
  Marketing Manager: Abby Howard
  Event & Sales Manager: Tonya Frost
  Business Manager: Linda Nedved
  Technical & Operations Coordinator: Brent Venis
  Office Assistant/Volunteer Coordina: Erin Grieve
Mission: To promote and preserve jazz.
Founded: 1991
Specialized Field: Performing Arts Center
Status: Non-Profit, Professional
Paid Staff: 6
Volunteer Staff: 60
Performs At: Theater
Seating Capacity: 2,461

4683
FRIENDS UNIVERSITY MILLER FINE ARTS SERIES
2100 W. University Ave.
Wichita, KS 67213
Phone: 316-295-5849
Fax: 316-295-5593
e-mail: riney@friends.edu
Web Site: www.friends.edu
Officers:
  Fine Arts Division Chairman: Cecil J Riney
  Chair: Dr. John Lewis
  Vice Chair: Kelly Linnens
  Secretary: Duane Hansen
  Treasurer: Dr. Cliffton Loesch
Management:
  Chair: Dr. John Lewis
  Assistant Chair: Toni Liphart
Specialized Field: Series & Festivals; Instrumental Music; Vocal Music; Theatre; Dance
Status: Non-Profit, Professional
Paid Staff: 15
Paid Artists: 20
Performs At: Alexander Auditorium

4684
WICHITA STATE UNIVERSITY CONNOISSEUR SERIES
College of Fine Arts, 415 Jardine Hall
1845 Fairmount
Wichita, KS 67260

SERIES & FESTIVALS / Kentucky

Phone: 316-978-3456
Fax: 316-978-3951
e-mail: webmaster@wichita.edu
Web Site: webs.wichita.edu/

Kentucky

4685
ARTISTS IN CONCERT SERIES
1226 N. Tamiami Trail
Suite 300
Ashland, KY 34236
Phone: 941-306-1200
Fax: 941-923-0754
e-mail: aic@artistsinconcert.com
Web Site: www.artistsinconcert.com
Officers:
　Board Chair: Mary Elizabeth Carey
　Secretary　: Ray Broth
　Treasurer: Jim Norris
Management:
　President: John Barker
　Artistic Director: Lee Dougherty
　Executive Director: John Alan Fischer
Founded: 1983
Specialized Field: Sereis & Festivals: Classical Music
Status: Non-Profit, Non-Professional
Performs At: Ashland Community College Auditorium

4686
BEREA COLLEGE CONVOCATION SERIES
Frost Room 107 CPO 2160
Berea College
Berea, KY 40404-2160
Phone: 859-985-3359
Fax: 859-985-3642
e-mail: randall_roberts@berea.edu
Web Site: www.berea.edu/convocations/default.asp
Management:
　Instructor In General Studies: Randall Roberts
Performs At: Phelps - Stokes Auditorium

4687
CAPITOL ARTS ALLIANCE
416 East Main Street
Bowling Green, KY 04101
Mailing Address: P.O. Box 748 Bowling Green, KY 42102
Phone: 270-904-5000
Fax: 270-904-0842
Toll-free: 877-694-2787
e-mail: mike.thomas@capitolarts.com
Web Site: www.capitolarts.com
Management:
　President/Executive Director: Mike Thomas
　Managing Director: Dawn Wesley
　Gallery Director: Lynn Robertson
　Operations Manager: Jeff Smith
Founded: 1981
Specialized Field: Series & Festivals; Instrumental Music; Vocal Music; Theatre; Youth; Dance; Ethnic Performances; Gallery
Status: Non-Profit, Professional
Paid Staff: 12
Paid Artists: 200
Seating Capacity: 840

4688
CENTRAL KENTUCKY ARTS SERIES
PO Box 383
Campbellsville, KY 42719
Phone: 207-789-5340
Fax: 270-789-5524
e-mail: aocunha@campbellsville.edu
Web Site: www.centralkentuckyarts.org
Officers:
　President: Tony Cunha
Mission: To provide professional programs in all the arts.
Founded: 1967
Specialized Field: Series & Festivals; Instrumental Music; Vocal Music; Theatre; Youth; Dance; Ethnic Performances
Status: Non-Profit, Professional
Volunteer Staff: 10
Income Sources: Individual and Corporate Donations
Facility Category: Recital Hall; Auditoriums

4689
GREAT AMERICAN BRASS BAND FESTIVAL
PO Box 429
Danville, KY 40423
Phone: 859-319-8426
Fax: 859-236-9610
e-mail: info@gabbf.org
Web Site: www.gabbf.org/
Officers:
　President: Martha King
　Vice President: Terry Crowley
　Treasurer: John Albright
　Secretary: Jennifer Kirchner
Management:
　Director: George Foreman
　Executive Director: Niki Kinkade
　Assistant Director: Leigh Jefferson

4690
FOUST ARTIST SERIES
Georgetown College
400 East College Street
Georgetown, KY 40324
Phone: 502-863-8000
e-mail: sburnett@georgetowncollege.edu
Web Site: www.georgetowncollege.edu/foust/
Management:
　President: M. Dwaine Greene
　Foust Artistic Series Director: Sonny Burnette
　Provost/Dean of the College: Rosemary A. Allen
　Director of Athletics: Brian Evans
　Vice President/Chief Financial Offi: James A. Moak, Jr.
Founded: 1987
Specialized Field: Series & Festivals; Instrumental Music; Vocal Music; Theatre; Dance; Ethnic Performances; Music
Status: Non-Profit, Professional
Paid Staff: 1
Performs At: John L. Hill Chapel

4691
GREATER HAZARD AREA PERFORMING ARTS SERIES
One Community College Drive
Hazard, KY 41701
Phone: 606-436-5721
Fax: 606-439-2988
Toll-free: 800-246-7521
e-mail: tammy.duff@kctcs.edu
Web Site: www.hazardperformingarts.com
Officers:
　Chair, Executive Council: Jan Maygard
　Chair, Advisory Committee: Terry Thies
Management:
　Performing Arts Director: Tammy Duff
Mission: Assist in the development of the arts and arts education in the Southeast Kentucky region
Founded: 1974
Specialized Field: Southeast Kentucky
Status: Non-Profit, Professional
Paid Staff: 2
Budget: $100,000+
Income Sources: Ticket Sales; Corporate/Private Support; Grants
Performs At: First Federal Center
Affiliations: Hazard Community & Technical College, Hazard Independent College Foundation
Facility Category: Conference Center, Convention Hall & Theatre
Type of Stage: Proscenium/Portable
Seating Capacity: 800
Year Built: 1992

4692
PENNYROYAL ARTS COUNCIL SERIES
PO Box 1038
Hopkinsville, KY 42241
Phone: 270-887-4295
Fax: 270-887-4027
e-mail: paci@bellsouth.net
Web Site: www.pennyroyalarts.org
Officers:
　President: Marla White
　President-Elect: Beth Frerichs
　Secretary/Treasurer: Robbie Haggard
　Public Relations Chair: Becky Williamson
　Past President: Ann Nichols
Management:
　Executive Director: Margaret Prim
　Office Administrator: Doris Ann Russell
　Arts Education Coordinator: Wayne Eastham
Mission: To encourage, develop and promote the appreciation of the arts through: education, support, service and presentation.
Founded: 1977
Specialized Field: Art Performances for Children and Adults
Status: Non-Profit, Non-Professional
Paid Staff: 4
Income Sources: Grants & Fund Drive
Performs At: Alhambra Theatre
Facility Category: Theatre
Type of Stage: Proscenium
Stage Dimensions: 32'x 26'
Seating Capacity: 760
Year Built: 1928
Rental Contact: Carol Barta

4693
UNIVERSITY OF KENTUCKY SINGLETARY CENTER FOR THE ARTS
405 Rose Street
Lexington, KY 40508
Phone: 859-257-1706
Fax: 859-323-9991
e-mail: michael.grice@uky.edu
Web Site: www.uky.edu/scfa
Management:
　Executive Director: Michael Grice
　Marketing Director: Summer Gossett
　Production Director: Tanya Harper
　Office Manager: Elizabeth Navarra
　Fiscal Affairs Director: Melinda Hautala
　Patron Services Coordinator: Hong Shao
　Assistant Production Director & Lig: Danny Bowling
　Technical Services Assistant & Soun: Seth Murphy

SERIES & FESTIVALS / Louisiana

Utilizes: Collaborations; Composers; Grant Writers; Guest Accompanists; Guest Companies; Guest Composers; Guest Directors; Guest Instructors; Guest Musical Directors; Guest Musicians; Guest Soloists; Instructors; Lyricists; Multimedia; Original Music Scores; Paid Performers; Sign Language Translators; Singers; Students; Student Interns; Theatre Companies
Founded: 1979
Opened: 1979
Specialized Field: Sereis & Festivals: Music Shows
Status: Non-Profit, Non-Professional
Paid Staff: 7
Volunteer Staff: 71
Income Sources: Rentals; Ticket Revenue
Annual Attendance: 100,000
Facility Category: Concert Hall & Recital Hall
Seating Capacity: 1,467; 381
Year Built: 1979
Year Remodeled: 2003
Rental Contact: Tanya Harper

4694
UNIVERSITY OF KENTUCKY ARTISTS SERIES

405 Rose Street
Singletary Center for the Arts
Lexington, KY 40508
Phone: 859-257-1706
Fax: 859-323-9991
e-mail: hbsali00@pop.uky.edu
Web Site: www.uky.edu/SCFA/
Management:
  Executive Director: Michael Grice
  Marketing Director: Summer Gossett
  Production Director: Tanya Harper
  Office Manager: Elizabeth Navarra
  Fiscal Affairs Director: Melinda Hautala
  Patron Services Coordinator: Hong Shao
  Assistant Production Director & Lig: Danny Bowling
  Technical Services Assistant & Soun: Seth Murphy
Performs At: Otis A. Singletary Center for the Arts Concert Hall

4695
SUE BENNETT COLLEGE, APPALACHIAN FOLK FESTIVAL

Box 7014
London, KY 24142
Phone: 540- 83-1536
Fax: 606-539-4404
Web Site: www.radford.edu/
Management:
  Chairperson: Madge Chestnut
Mission: To offer arts, performances and events showcasing Appalachian heritage.
Founded: 1973
Specialized Field: Vocal Music; Festivals
Status: Nonprofit
Performs At: Sue Bennett College Auditorium
Organization Type: Performing; Educational

4696
KENTUCKY SHAKESPEARE FESTIVAL

323 W. Broadway
Suite 401
Louisville, KY 40202
Phone: 502-574-9900
Fax: 502-566-9200
Toll-free: 877-655-2273
e-mail: info@kyshakes.org
Web Site: www.kyshakes.org

Officers:
  President: Karen H. Taylor-Richardson
  Interim Treasurer: Allen Harris
  Secretary: Amanda Gregory
Management:
  Executive Director: Steven Renner
  Producing Artistic Director: Matt Wallace
  Director Education: Doug Sumey
  Director of Operations and Marketin: Rob Silverthorn III
  Education Programs Manager: Hannah Pruitt
Mission: To provide accessible, professional, classical theatre and quality education touring programs.
Utilizes: Actors; Artists-in-Residence; Collaborating Artists; Collaborations; Designers; Educators; Five Seasonal Concerts; Guest Accompanists; Guest Conductors; Guest Ensembles; Guild Activities; High School Drama; Local Artists; Original Music Scores; Resident Artists; Resident Professionals; Selected Students; Soloists; Student Interns; Theatre Companies
Founded: 1960
Specialized Field: Free Shakespeare Performances; Educational Outreach Programming
Status: Non-Profit, Professional
Budget: $750,000
Income Sources: Corporate; Foundation; Individuals; Government; Fund; Earned
Season: May - August
Performs At: C Douglas Ramey Amphitheater
Annual Attendance: 67,500
Facility Category: Outdoor Amphitheatre
Type of Stage: Thrust
Seating Capacity: 1,000
Year Built: 1963
Year Remodeled: 1993
Cost: $1,000,000
Organization Type: Performing; Resident; Touring; Educational

4698
MURRAY CIVIC MUSIC ASSOCIATION SERIES

Murray State University, Music Department
504 Fine Arts Center
Murray, KY 42071
Phone: 270-809-4288
Fax: 270-762-3965
e-mail: msu.music@murraystate.edu
Web Site: www.murraystate.edu/music
Officers:
  VP Programming: Robert Murray
Mission: To provide Murray with the finest in performing arts events.
Founded: 1959
Specialized Field: Dance; Vocal Music; Instrumental Music; Theater; Lyric Opera; Grand Opera
Status: Nonprofit
Performs At: Lovett Auditorium; Murray State University
Organization Type: Sponsoring

4699
PIKEVILLE CONCERT ASSOCIATION SERIES

291 Summer St
Pikeville, KY 41501
Phone: 606-218-5250
Fax: 606-218-5269
e-mail: webmaster@pc.edu
Web Site: www.pa.pc.edu/pca/index.htm
Management:
  President: Robert Eugene Schindeler

  Vice President/Administration: Jeanette Anderson
Founded: 1952
Specialized Field: Series & Festivals; Instrumental Music; Vocal Music; Dance; Orchestra
Status: Non-Profit, Non-Professional
Performs At: Auditorium

4700
ALICE LLOYD COLLEGE CANEY CONVOCATION SERIES

100 Purpose Road
Pippa Passes, KY 41844
Phone: 606-368-6000
Fax: 606-368-6217
Toll-free: 888-804-52
Web Site: www.alc.edu/
Performs At: Estelle Campbell Center for the Arts

4701
ASBURY COLLEGE ARTIST SERIES

Asbury College
One Macklem Drive
Wilmore, KY 40390
Phone: 859-858-3511
Fax: 859-858-3921
Toll-free: 800-888-1818
e-mail: mstratford@asbury.edu
Web Site: www.asbury.edu
Officers:
  Chairman: Kevin Sparks
Management:
  President: Paul Rader
Founded: 1890
Performs At: Hughes Memorial Auditorium

4702
WINCHESTER COUNCIL FOR THE ARTS SERIES

37 North Main Street
Winchester, KY 40391
Phone: 859-744-4275
Fax: 859-744-8211
Toll-free: 888-772-6985
e-mail: contact@leedscenter.org
Web Site: www.leedscenter.com
Management:
  President: Fara Tyree
  Executive Director: Peggy Case
Founded: 1986
Specialized Field: Series & Festivals; Instrumental Music; Vocal Music; Theatre; Youth
Status: Non-Profit, Non-Professional
Paid Staff: 1
Paid Artists: 10
Performs At: Leeds Theatre & Performing Arts Center

Louisiana

4703
LSU UNION GREAT PERFORMANCES THEATER SERIES

LSU Box 25123
101 LSU Student Union Building
Baton Rouge, LA 70803
Phone: 225-578-5782
Fax: 225-578-0612
e-mail: mderr@lsu.edu
Web Site: www.unionweb.lsu.edu
Management:
  Associate Director: Michael Derr
  Assistant Director Event Developmen: Terry Sirio

All listings are in alphabetical order by state, then city, then organization within the city.

SERIES & FESTIVALS / Louisiana

Customer Service Coordinator:: Ashley Marshall

Union Box Office Manager:: Jennifer Doerfler
Technical Operations Manager: Deanna Gaharan
Union Theater Lighting Technician: James Queen
Union Theater Audio Technician: Ricky Berlin
Founded: 1963
Specialized Field: Series and Festivals; Instrumental Music; Vocal Music; Theatre; Youth; Dance; Performances of LSU Union Theatre
Status: For-Profit, Professional

4704
FANFARE FESTIVAL
200 E. Thomas Street
Hammond, LA 70401
Mailing Address: SLU 10797
Phone: 985-543-4366
Fax: 985-543-4374
e-mail: fanfare_ctpa@selu.edu
Web Site: www.selu.edu/fanfare
Management:
- Associate Director For Programming: Keiron Couret
- Director: C. Roy Blackwood
- Business Manager: Carol Knott
- Associate Director and Programming: Keiron Covrest
- Associate Director For Operation: Peter Pfeil
- Operations And Production Technical: David Avelae II
- Administrative Cordinator: Beanie Stansbury

Founded: 1986
Paid Staff: 8
Volunteer Staff: 22
Paid Artists: 25
Non-paid Artists: 10

4705
SOUTHEASTERN LOUISIANA UNIVERSITY ARTS & LECTURES SERIES
Slu 346
Hammond, LA 70402
Phone: 985-549-2000
Fax: 504-549-5647
e-mail: jmchodgkins@selu.edu
Web Site: www.southeastern.edu/
Officers:
- Assistant Vice President for Studen: Jim McHodgkins
- Director of Recreational Sports & W: Dollie Crouch
- Director for Student Engagement: Cherie Thriffiley
- Director of Student Union: Jonathan Ambrose
- Director for Shuttle Services: Gary Prescott
- Coordinator of Campus Activities Bo: Todd McElroy

4706
JEFF DAVIS ARTS COUNCIL
PO Box 1068
Jennings, LA 70546
Phone: 337-824-5060
Fax: 337-824-1070

4707
FESTIVAL INTERNATIONAL DE LOUISIANE
444 Jefferson Street
Lafayette, LA 70501
Phone: 337-232-8086
Fax: 337-233-7536
e-mail: info@festivalinternational.com
Web Site: www.festivalinternational.com
Officers:
- Executive Director: Missy Paschke-Wood
- President: Craig Minnick
- VP Development: Sarah Moss
- Secretary: Randy Guidry
- Treasurer: Eric Gammons
- VP Marketing: Tucker Sappington
- VP Production: Scott Feehan
- VP Programming: Sami Parbhoo
- Member-at-Large: Jason Fontenot

Management:
- Marketing Coordinator: Apiyo Obala
- Programming Coordinator: Lisa Stafford
- Executive Director: Missy Paschke-Wood
- Production Director: Diane Harris
- Development Director: Michelle Minyard
- Technical Director: Greg Robertson
- Bookkeeper: Micki McCord

Mission: Free family event celebrating the French cultural heritage of southern Louisiana - a combination of French, African, Caribbean and Hispanic influences.
Founded: 1986
Specialized Field: Series & Festivals; Instrumental Music; Vocal Music; Theatre; Youth; Dance; Ethnic Performances; Visual; Performing And Culinary Arts
Status: Non-Profit, Professional
Paid Staff: 3
Volunteer Staff: 1500
Paid Artists: 250
Season: April
Performs At: Kimmel Center for the Performing Arts

4708
LAFAYETTE COMMUNITY CONCERTS SERIES
3600 West Congress Street
Lafayette, LA 70506
Phone: 337-233-1035
Web Site: www.lcband.org/
Officers:
- President: George E Arceneaux
- Secretary/Treasurer: Susan Ellis

Management:
- Business Manager: Diane Robin
- Property Manager: Greg Guidroz
- Publicity Coordinator: Kent Hanes
- Conductor/Music Director: Gerald Guibeaux
- Assistant Conductor: Alex Hilliard
- Personnel Manager: Cindy Sabo

4709
PERFORMING ARTS SOCIETY OF ACADIANA SERIES
109 E. Vermilion St.
Suite 101
Lafayette, LA 70501
Mailing Address: PO Box 52979 Lafayette, LA 70505
Phone: 337-237-2787
Fax: 337-237-3974
e-mail: pasajll@aol.com
Web Site: www.pasa-online.org
Officers:
- President: Dan Hare
- President-Elect: Michael Castille
- Secretary: Christy Harson
- Treasurer: Matt Dugas
- Immediate Past President: Dr. Ronnie Daigle

Management:
- President: Dan Hare
- Managing Director: Mary Coleman
- Executive Director: Vicki Chrisman
- Operations Manager: Denise Duhon
- Development Director: Sarah Brown
- Marketing Associate: Colin Miller

Founded: 1989
Specialized Field: Series and Festivals; Instrumental Music; Vocal Music; Theatre; Youth; Dance; Ethnic Performances
Status: Non-Profit, Professional
Paid Staff: 7

4710
UNIVERSITY OF LOUISIANA AT LAFAYETTE CONCERT SERIES
104 E. University Circle
Lafayette, LA 70503
Phone: 337-482-1000
Fax: 337-482-5017
e-mail: pdm0677@louisiana.edu
Web Site: www.louisiana.edu/
Officers:
- University Concert Committee Chair: Dr. Paul Morton

4711
UNIVERSITY OF SOUTHWESTERN LOUISIANA CONCERT SERIES
104 E. University Circle
Lafayette, LA 70503
Phone: 337-482-1000
Fax: 337-482-5017
Web Site: www.louisiana.edu/
Management:
- Assistant Professor: Paul Morton

4712
MAMOU CAJUN MUSIC FESTIVAL
420 E Street
Apartment 1
Mamou, LA 70554
Phone: 337-468-2258
Web Site: www.mamoucajunmusicfestival.com
Mission: To offer traditional Cajun music, as well as related events.
Utilizes: Singers
Founded: 1972
Specialized Field: Vocal Music; Festivals
Status: Nonprofit
Organization Type: Performing; Resident; Educational

4713
JEFFERSON PERFORMING ARTS SOCIETY
1118 Clearview Parkway
Metairie, LA 70001
Phone: 504-885-2000
Fax: 504-885-3437
e-mail: info@jpas.org
Web Site: www.jpas.org
Officers:
- Chairman: Hannah Cunningham
- President: Deborah B. Rouen
- Past President: Daniel Bruza
- Secretary: Subhash Kulkarni
- Vice President: Jack Sloan
- Treasurer: Dawn Laborie
- Member of the Board: Kellie M. Barnes
- Member of the Board: Howard Bennett
- Member of the Board: Darrel Beerbohm

Management:
- Business Manager: Donna Barber
- Executive/Artistic Director: Dennis G Assaf

SERIES & FESTIVALS / Louisiana

Chairman: Hannah J Cunningham
Company/Production Manager: Nicholas Frederick
Artistic Administrative Assistant: Lynne L. Bordelon
Business Manager: Donna Barber
Box Office Manager: Phillip Benson
Director of Development: Velerie Hart
Director of Cultural Crossroads: Karel Sloane-Boekbinder
Mission: Supporting performance and education in the performing arts.
Utilizes: Actors; Artists-in-Residence; Choreographers; Collaborating Artists; Collaborations; Dance Companies; Dancers; Five Seasonal Concerts; Grant Writers; Guest Accompanists; Guest Artists; Guest Choreographers; Guest Companies; Guest Composers; Guest Designers; Guest Directors; Guest Lecturers; Guest Musical Directors; Guest Musicians; Instructors; Local Artists; Multi Collaborations; Multimedia; Music; Organization Contracts; Original Music Scores; Playwrights; Sign Language Translators; Singers; Soloists; Student Interns; Special Technical Talent; Theatre Companies
Founded: 1978
Specialized Field: Series & Festivals; Instrumental Music; Vocal Music; Theatre; Youth; Dance; Ethnic Performances
Status: Non-Profit, Professional
Paid Staff: 14
Volunteer Staff: 100
Paid Artists: 100
Budget: 1.2 million
Income Sources: Box Office; Ads; Sponsorships; Grants
Affiliations: APAP; ACDA; ASOL; Conductor's Guild
Annual Attendance: 30,000
Facility Category: Theater
Type of Stage: Proscenium Arch
Stage Dimensions: 42'x 35'
Seating Capacity: 1,350
Year Built: 1952
Year Remodeled: 1999
Organization Type: Performing; Educational

4714
UNIVERSITY OF LOUISIANA AT MONROE PERFORMING ARTS SERIES

700 University Avenue
Monroe, LA 71209-0385
Phone: 318-342-3811
Fax: 318-342-1599
e-mail: long@ulm.edu
Web Site: www.ulm.edu/vapa
Management:
  Director: L Keith White
Paid Staff: 1
Paid Artists: 50

4715
NORTHWESTERN STATE UNIVERSITY CONCERT SERIES

715 University Parkway
Northwestern State University of Louisiana
Natchitoches, LA 71497
Phone: 318-357-4522
Fax: 318-357-5906
e-mail: bandcamps@nsula.edu
Web Site: www.nsula.edu
Officers:
  Chairman: Bill Brent
Management:
  Artistic Director: Roger Chaenler

Chairman: Bill Brant
Founded: 1886
Specialized Field: Series and Festivals: Music
Status: Non-Profit, Professional
Paid Staff: 60
Paid Artists: 3
Performs At: Fine Arts Auditorium

4716
NEW ORLEANS FRIENDS OF MUSIC SERIES

5500 Prytania Street, PMB #402
New Orleans, LA 70115
Phone: 504-895-0690
Fax: 504-282-4008
e-mail: neworleansfom@aol.com
Web Site: www.friendsofmusic.org
Officers:
  President: Margaret Shields
  Vice President: Jonathan McCall
  Secretary: Courtney Courtney
  Treasurer: Alison Mehr
  Immediate Past-President: Ranney Mize

4717
NEW ORLEANS INTERNATIONAL PIANO COMPETITION & KEYBOARD FESTIVAL

1930 General Pershing St.
New Orleans, LA 70115
Mailing Address: P.O. Box 750698 New Orleans, La 70175-0698
Phone: 504-899-4826
Fax: 504-899-4826
e-mail: director@masno.org
Web Site: www.masno.org
Management:
  Artistic Director: Danial Weilbaecher
  Co-Director: Dr. Allan Chow
Founded: 1980
Specialized Field: Classical Piano Music
Budget: $200,000

4718
THE NEW ORLEANS JAZZ & HERITAGE FESTIVAL AND FOUNDATION, INC.

1205 N Rampart Street
New Orleans, LA 70116
Phone: 504-558-6100
Fax: 504-558-6122
Toll-free: 888-652-8751
e-mail: dmarshall@jazzandheritage.org
Web Site: www.nojhf.org
Officers:
  Chief Administrative Officer: Marsha A. Boudy
  Chief Financial Officer: Sheri LaBranche
  President: Anthony J. Ruda
  First Vice President: Demetric Mercadel
  Second Vice President: Donna Santiago
  Secretary: Kathleen Turner
  Treasurer: Jeffrey Goldring
Management:
  Programs, Markg & Comm Coordinator: Kia Robinson
  Executive Director: Don Marshall
  Director of Programs: Scott Aiges
  Development Associate: Shanna E. Hudson-Stowe
  Archivist: Rachel Lyons
Mission: The presentation and preservation of Louisiana's culture and music.
Founded: 1970
Specialized Field: Band; Jazz; Historical Music
Status: Nonprofit

Paid Staff: 12
Organization Type: Performing

4719
SHAKESPEARE FESTIVAL AT TULANE

6823 St. Charles Ave.
215 McWilliams Hall
New Orleans, LA 70118
Phone: 504-865-5105
Fax: 504-865-5205
e-mail: ctullos@tulane.edu
Web Site: www.neworleansshakespeare.com
Officers:
  Chair: Edward F. Martin
  Vice Chair: Mark Adams
  Secretary: Barbara Motley
Management:
  Artistic Director: Aimee K Michel
  Managing Director: Clare Moncrief
  Operations Director: Chaney Tullos
  Artistic Director: Martin Sachs
  Business Manager: Ardice Cotter
Mission: To provide professional Shakespeare productions to the Greater New Orleans and surrounding Gulf South area along with educational programs to the schools.
Utilizes: Actors; AEA Actors; Artists-in-Residence; Choreographers; Collaborating Artists; Collaborations; Commissioned Composers; Commissioned Music; Composers; Educators; Five Seasonal Concerts; Guest Artists; Guest Companies; Guest Instructors; Guest Musical Directors; Guest Soloists; Guest Teachers; High School Drama; Local Artists; Multimedia; Organization Contracts; Original Music Scores; Performance Artists; Resident Artists; Resident Professionals; Soloists; Students; Special Technical Talent
Founded: 1993
Specialized Field: Classical Theatre; Shakespeare; New Works; Modern Classics
Status: Professional; Nonprofit
Paid Staff: 6
Paid Artists: 60
Budget: $250,000
Income Sources: Public; Private; Corporate; Foundation; Box Office; Tuition
Facility Category: Equity Small Professional Theatre
Type of Stage: Black Box; Laboratory
Seating Capacity: 150; 60

4720
LOUISIANA TECH CONCERT ASSOCIATION SERIES

Tech Station
PO Box 8608
Ruston, LA 71272
Phone: 318-257-2711
Fax: 318-257-4571
e-mail: krobbins@latech.edu
Web Site: www.performingarts.latech.edu
Management:
  President: Dan Reneau
  Executive Director: Kenneth Robbins
  Theatre Director: Cherrie Sciro
  Co-Director: Alan Goldspiel
Founded: 1944
Specialized Field: Music; Theatre; Dance
Status: Non-Profit, Non-Professional
Paid Staff: 8
Paid Artists: 1
Budget: $133,000
Income Sources: Ticket Sales
Performs At: Howard Center for the Performing Arts
Annual Attendance: 6,000

All listings are in alphabetical order by state, then city, then organization within the city.

SERIES & FESTIVALS / Maine

Facility Category: Conference Hall
Type of Stage: Proscenium
Seating Capacity: 1,051

4721
FRIENDS OF MUSIC SERIES
Hurley School of Music, Centenary College
2911 Centenary Boulevard
Shreveport, LA 71104
Phone: 318-869-5235
Fax: 318-869-5248
e-mail: music@centenary.edu
Web Site: www.centenary.edu/music
Management:
   Manager: Dr. Gale Odom
Performs At: Hurley Recital Hall

4722
RED RIVER REVEL ARTS FESTIVAL
101 Crockett Street
Suite C
Shreveport, LA 71101
Phone: 318-424-4000
Fax: 318-226-9559
e-mail: rrr@redriverrevel.com
Web Site: www.redriverrevel.com
Officers:
   President: John T Hubbard
Management:
   Executive Director: Kevin Stone
Mission: Eight day celebration of the Arts.
Founded: 1976
Specialized Field: Series and Festivals; Instrumental Music; Vocal Music; Theatre; Youth; Dance; Ethnic Performances
Status: Non-Profit, Professional
Paid Staff: 4
Volunteer Staff: 6
Income Sources: Corporate Sponsors; Underwriters; State; Local Grants
Annual Attendance: 180,000-200,000
Facility Category: Outdoor Festival

4723
SLIDELL DEPARTMENT OF CULTURAL AFFAIRS
444 Erlanger Street
PO Box 828
Slidell, LA 70459
Phone: 504-646-4375
Fax: 504-646-4231
Web Site: www.slidell.la.us
Management:
   Director: Kelli Gustafson
Utilizes: Dancers; Guest Musical Directors; Instructors; Special Technical Talent; Touring Companies
Performs At: Auditorium

4724
IMPRESARIO'S CHOICE-THE BROADWAY SERIES AT THE MONROE CIVIC THEATRE
267 Verhagen Road
PO Box 828
Tallulah, LA 71284-0828
Phone: 318-574-0440
Fax: 318-574-0440
Toll-free: 888-822-0440
e-mail: impresariosmail@aol.com
Web Site: www.impresarioschoice.com
Officers:
   President: Douglas Leporati
   Vice-President: Greg Speed
   Secretary: Betty Lemmer
   Trasurer: Mark Henderson
   Public Realtions: Ruby James
   Education Outreach Director: Mark Henderson
Management:
   President: Douglas Leoreti
   Executive Director: Ezekial J Moore
   Artistic Director: Raymond Poliquit
Mission: It is our mission to bring high quality national touring Broadway musicals to Northeast Louisiana, and to expand the theatregoing audience, both in number and diversity.
Founded: 1988
Specialized Field: Series & Festivals: Theatre
Status: Non-Profit, Professional
Paid Staff: 1
Volunteer Staff: 1
Budget: $275,000
Income Sources: Corporate Sponsorship
Affiliations: Impresario's Friends
Annual Attendance: 6,200
Facility Category: Civic Center
Type of Stage: Procenium
Seating Capacity: 2,100

4725
NICHOLLS STATE UNIVERSITY ARTISTS & LECTURE SERIES
P.O. Box 2023
Thibodaux, LA 70310
Phone: 985-448-4453
Fax: 985-449-7110
e-mail: angela.hammerli@nicholls.edu
Web Site: www.nicholls.edu
Management:
   Director: Angela Hammerli
Specialized Field: Series & Festivals; Instrumental Music; Vocal Music; Theatre; Youth; Dance; Ethnic Performances
Status: Non-Profit
Paid Staff: 2
Performs At: Auditorium

Maine

4726
NEW MUSIK DIRECTIONS SERIES
67 Green Street
Augusta, ME 04330
Phone: 207-623-1941
Fax: 207-623-1941
Management:
   Director: Joseph Baltar
Mission: To provide a network for artists in film, video and new music.
Founded: 1981
Specialized Field: Festivals
Status: Professional; Commercial
Organization Type: Performing; Educational; Sponsoring

4727
BAR HARBOR MUSIC FESTIVAL
59 Cottage St
59 Cottage Street
Bar Harbor, ME 04609-1800
Phone: 207-288-5744
Fax: 207-288-5886
e-mail: info@barharbormusicfestival.org
Web Site: www.barharbormusicfestival.org
Management:
   Artistic Director: Francis Fortier
Founded: 1967
Specialized Field: Vocal Music; Festivals, Opera, Instrumental Music
Paid Staff: 2

4728
CHOCOLATE CHURCH ARTS CENTER FESTIVAL
804 Washington Street
Bath, ME 04530-2617
Mailing Address: POBox 252 Bath, Me 04530
Phone: 207-442-8455
Fax: 207-442-8637
e-mail: info@chocolatechurcharts.org
Web Site: www.chocolatechurcharts.com
Officers:
   President: Joseph Byrnes
   Secretary: Ken Safford
Management:
   Executive Director: Jennifer DeChant
   Front Office Manager: Lisa Schinhofen
Founded: 1975
Specialized Field: Series and Festivals; Instrumental Music; Vocal Music; Theatre; Youth; Dance; Ethnic Performances
Status: Non-Profit, Professional
Paid Staff: 2
Paid Artists: 30
Seating Capacity: 294

4729
KNEISEL HALL CHAMBER MUSIC FESTIVAL
54 Main Street
Blue Hill, ME 04614
Mailing Address: PO Box 648 Blue Hill, ME 04614
Phone: 207-374-2811
Fax: 207-374-2811
e-mail: festival@kneisel.org
Web Site: www.kneisel.org
Management:
   President: Saul Cohen
   Executive Director: Ellen Werner
   Artistic Director: Seymour Lipkin
   Office Manager: Danielle Harriman
   Financial Officer: Brittan Pistole
Mission: To foster the art of chamber music through teaching and performance.
Founded: 1902
Specialized Field: Music and Education
Status: Non-Profit, Professional
Paid Staff: 5
Paid Artists: 14
Budget: $485,000
Income Sources: Donations; Grants; Ticket Sales
Annual Attendance: 2,500
Facility Category: Historic Hall
Seating Capacity: 175
Year Built: 1922
Rental Contact: Ellen Werner

4730
BOWDOIN COLLEGE CONCERT SERIES
Music Department, Gibson Hall
6300 College Station
Brunswick, ME 04011-8463
Phone: 207-373-1400
Fax: 207-373-1441
Toll-free: 855-832-3393
e-mail: info@bowdoinfestival.org
Web Site: www.bowdoinfestival.org/
Officers:
   Chairman: James T. Morgan
   Vice Chairman: Beatrice Francais

SERIES & FESTIVALS / Maine

Treasurer: Peter Griffin
Secretary: William Rogers, Jr., Esq.
Management:
Director: Lewis Kaplan
Executive Director: Peter Simmons
Director of Development: Kippy Rudy
Director of Admissions: Jennifer G. Means
Financial Officer: Brittan Pistole
Admissions Assistant: Leah Paris
Development Assistant: Mitchell Frizzell
Housing Coordinator (rentals): Deb Zorach
Specialized Field: College Music Department
Performs At: Kresge Auditorium, Pickard Theater and Chapel

4731
BOWDOIN INTERNATIONAL MUSIC FESTIVAL
6300 College Station
Bowdoin College
Brunswick, ME 04011
Phone: 207-373-1400
Fax: 207-373-1441
Toll-free: 855-832-3393
e-mail: info@bowdoinfestival.org
Web Site: www.bowdoinfestival.org
Officers:
Chairman of the Board: James T. Morgan
Vice Chairman: Beatrice Francais
Treasurer: Peter Griffin
Secretary: William Rogers, Jr., Esq.
Management:
Director: Lewis Kaplan
Executive Director: Peter Simmons
Director of Development: Kippy Rudy
Director of Admissions: Jennifer G. Means
Financial Officer: Brittan Pistole
Admissions Assistant: Leah Paris
Development Assistant: Mitchell Frizzell
Housing Coordinator (rentals): Deb Zorach
Mission: To provide the most promising music students from around the world with opportunities to further their musical development, and to present chamber music performed to the highest standards by distinguished professional musicians.
Utilizes: Composers; Composers-in-Residence; Guest Ensembles; High School Drama; Scenic Designers
Founded: 1964
Specialized Field: Chamber
Status: Nonprofit
Budget: $1,100,000
Income Sources: Contributions; Ticket Sales; Tution
Performs At: Crooker Theater, Brunswick High School; Studzinski Recital Hall, Bowdoin College
Affiliations: Chamber Music America; Major Conservatories; Maine Performing Arts Network
Annual Attendance: 10,000
Seating Capacity: 600;200
Year Built: 1995
Organization Type: Educational; Presenting

4732
BOWDOIN SUMMER MUSIC FESTIVAL
6300 College Station
Bowdoin College
Brunswick, ME 04011
Phone: 207-373-1400
Fax: 207-373-1441
Toll-free: 855-832-3393
e-mail: info@bowdoinfestival.org
Web Site: www.bowdoinfestival.org
Officers:
Chairman of the Board: James T. Morgan
Vice Chairman: Beatrice Francais
Treasurer: Peter Griffin
Secretary: William Rogers, Jr., Esq.
Management:
Director: Lewis Kaplan
Executive Director: Peter Simmons
Director of Development: Kippy Rudy
Director of Admissions: Jennifer G. Means
Financial Officer: Brittan Pistole
Admissions Assistant: Leah Paris
Development Assistant: Mitchell Frizzell
Housing Coordinator (rentals): Deb Zorach
Mission: To provide the most promising music students from around the world with opportunities to further their musical development, and to present chamber music performed to the highest standards by distinguished professional musicians.
Utilizes: Commissioned Music; Composers-in-Residence; Grant Writers; Guest Companies; Guest Musical Directors; Multimedia
Founded: 1964
Specialized Field: Vocal Music: Chamber Music
Status: Non-Profit, Professional
Paid Staff: 3
Paid Artists: 50
Budget: $1,100,000
Income Sources: Contributions; Ticket Sales; Tution
Performs At: Crooker Theater, Brunswick High School
Affiliations: Chamber Music America; Major Conservatories; Maine Performing Arts Network
Annual Attendance: 10,000
Seating Capacity: 600
Year Built: 1995
Organization Type: Educational; Presenting

4733
GAMPER FESTIVAL OF CONTEMPORARY MUSIC
Bowdoin Internatinal Music Festival
6300 College Station
Brunswick, ME 04011-8463
Phone: 207-373-1400
Fax: 207-373-1441
e-mail: info@bowdoinfestival.org
Web Site: www.bowdoinfestival.org
Officers:
President: William Rogers
Executive Director: Peter Simmons
Chairman: James T. Morgan
Vice Chairman: Beatrice Francais
Treasurer: Peter Griffin
Secretary: William Rogers, Jr., Esq.
Management:
Director: Lewis Kaplin
Executive Director: Peter Simmons
Director of Development: Kippy Rudy
Director of Admissions: Jennifer G. Means
Financial Officer: Brittan Pistole
Admissions Assistant: Leah Paris
Development Assistant: Mitchell Frizzell
Housing Coordinator (rentals): Deb Zorach
Founded: 1964
Specialized Field: Series and Festivals: Chamber Music
Status: Non-Profit, Professional
Paid Staff: 100
Paid Artists: 50

4734
UNIVERSITY OF MAINE AT FORT KENT, INTERNATIONAL PERFORMERS SERIES
University of Maine at Fort Kent
23 University Dr.
Fort Kent, ME 04743
Phone: 207-834-7500
Fax: 207-834-7503
Toll-free: 888-879-8635
e-mail: rphinney@maine.edu
Web Site: www.umfkmaine.edu
Management:
Assoc. Director Student Activities: Raymond Phinney
Paid Staff: 4
Facility Category: University
Type of Stage: Proscenium
Stage Dimensions: 30 X 24
Seating Capacity: 450
Year Built: 1965
Rental Contact: Fran Picard

4735
BATES DANCE FESTIVAL
305 College St.
Lewiston, ME 04240-6016
Phone: 207-786-6381
Fax: 207-786-8332
e-mail: dancefest@bates.edu
Web Site: www.bates.edu/dancefest
Officers:
Director: Laura Faure
Associate Director/Registrar: Nancy Salmon
Mission: The Bates Dance Festival brings an artistically and ethnically diverse group of the best contemporary dance artists to Maine during the summer season to teach, perform, and create new work; encourages and inspires established and emerging artists by providing them with a creative, supportive environment in which to work; and actively engages people from the community and region in a full range of dance activities.
Utilizes: Singers
Founded: 1982
Specialized Field: Series and Festivals; Youth; Dance; Ethnic Performances
Status: Non-Profit, Professional
Paid Staff: 8
Volunteer Staff: 14
Paid Artists: 35
Budget: $800,000
Income Sources: Public; Private; and Earned Income
Performs At: Schaeffer Theatre
Affiliations: Bates College
Annual Attendance: 4,000
Type of Stage: Proscenium
Stage Dimensions: 28'x35'
Seating Capacity: 300
Year Built: 1952
Organization Type: Resident; Educational; Sponsoring

4736
L/A ARTS
221 Lisbon Street
Lewiston, ME 04240
Phone: 207-782-7228
Fax: 207-782-8192
Toll-free: 800-639-2919
e-mail: mail@laarts.org
Web Site: www.laarts.org
Management:
Executive Director: Richard Willing
Mission: To offer diverse performing arts to Central Maine communities.
Founded: 1973
Specialized Field: Series and Festivals; Vocal Music; Theatre; Youth; Dance; Instrumental Music; Theatre; Festivals
Status: Non-Profit, Professional
Paid Staff: 3

SERIES & FESTIVALS / Maine

Income Sources: Association of Performing Arts Presenters; Maine Arts Sponsor Association
Organization Type: Performing; Educational; Sponsoring

4737
MT DESERT FESTIVAL OF CHAMBER MUSIC
PO Box 862
Northeast Harbor, ME 04662
Phone: 207-276-3988
e-mail: info@mtdesertfestival.org
Web Site: www.mtdesertfestival.org
Management:
   Founder: Matthew Raimondi
   Executive Director: Natalie Raimondi
   Music Director: Todd Crow
   Associate Executive Director: Margo Bailey
Founded: 1963
Specialized Field: Vocal Music: Chamber Music
Status: Non-Profit, Professional

4738
SACO RIVER FESTIVAL
PO Box 610
Parsonsfield, ME 04047
Phone: 207-625-7116
e-mail: srfa@psouth.net
Web Site: www.sacoriverfestival.org/
Management:
   President: Judy Ingram
   Executive Director: James O'Neil
   Artistic Director: Scott Woolwever
Founded: 1974
Specialized Field: Series and Festivals: Music
Status: Non-Profit, Professional
Paid Staff: 1

4739
LARK SOCIETY FOR CHAMBER MUSIC
PO Box 11
Portland, ME 04112
Phone: 207-761-1522
Fax: 207-780-6554
e-mail: lark@larksociety.org
Web Site: www.larksociety.org/
Officers:
   President: Jana Magnuson
   Vice President: George Burns
   Secretary: Dean Stein
   Treasurer: Tracey Richardson-Newton
Management:
   President: Jana Magnuson
   Executive Director: Jeanie J. Wester
   Artistic Directors: Julia Adams
   Artistic Directors: Ronald Lantz
   Artistic Directors: Paul Ross
   Artistic Directors: Dean Stein
Mission: Committed to supporting and presenting a Portland concert series and educational presentations by the Portland String Quartet. Presenters of the Portland Concert Series, and supporters of the PSQ's outreach activities, we promote chamber music and music education in the state of Maine.
Founded: 1980
Specialized Field: Series & Festivals; Chamber Music; Education; Performance
Status: Non-Profit, Professional
Paid Staff: 1
Income Sources: Chamber Music America
Organization Type: Performing; Touring; Resident; Educational

4740
MAINE ARTS SERIES
193 State Street
Suite 3
Portland, ME 04333-0025
Phone: 207-287-2724
Fax: 207-287-2725
e-mail: MaineArts.info@maine.gov
Web Site: www.mainearts.org
Management:
   Executive Director: Julie A. Richard
   Artistic Director: Dona McNeil
   Media Arts and Performing Arts Dire: Kerstin Gilg
   Visual Arts Director: Julie Horn
   Director of Arts Education: Argy Nestor
   Office Manager: Christine Norris
   Office Assistant: Priscilla Kelley
   Senior Grants Director: Kathy Ann Shaw
   Communications Director: Marc Spruiell
Mission: To provide artistic opportunities and to encourage the advancement of the performing and the visual arts in Maine through the presentation of a public program of services to artists.
Founded: 1977
Specialized Field: Series and Festivals: Ethnic Performances
Status: Non-Profit, Professional
Paid Staff: 9
Performs At: Downtown Portland; Thomas Point Beach
Organization Type: Sponsoring

4741
MAINE FESTIVAL
193 State Street
Portland, ME 04333-0025
Phone: 207-772-9012
Fax: 207-287-2725
e-mail: nbloom@mainearts.org
Web Site: www.mainearts.org
Management:
   Director: Nicolaus Bloom
   Executive Director: Julie A. Richard
   Artistic Director: Dona McNeil
   Media Arts and Performing Arts Dire: Kerstin Gilg
   Visual Arts Director: Julie Horn
   Director of Arts Education: Argy Nestor
   Office Manager: Christine Norris
   Office Assistant: Priscilla Kelley
   Senior Grants Director: Kathy Ann Shaw

4742
PCA GREAT PERFORMANCES
Portland Concert Association
50 Monument Square
2nd Floor
Portland, ME 04101
Phone: 207-773-3150
Fax: 207-774-1018
e-mail: info@portlandovations.org
Web Site: www.pcagreatperformances.org
Management:
   Executive Director: Judith Adams
   Director of Ovations Offstage: Gretchen Berg
   Director of Development: Mary C. Campbell
   Director of Marketing and Audience: Charles Kibort
   Cross Media Marketing Associate: Bethany Roberge
   Ovations Offstage Assistant: Vanessa Romanoff
   Programming and Development Adminis: Laura A. Stauffer
Founded: 1931
Specialized Field: Series & Festivals; Instrumental Music; Vocal Music; Theatre; Youth; Dance; Ethnic Performances
Status: Non-Profit, Professional
Paid Staff: 6
Volunteer Staff: 200
Annual Attendance: 35,000-50,000
Seating Capacity: 1,908
Year Remodeled: 1997

4743
PORTLAND CHAMBER MUSIC FESTIVAL
50 Market Street
Suite 137
Portland, ME 04106
Toll-free: 800-320-0257
e-mail: jenny@maine.rr.com
Web Site: www.pcmf.org
Officers:
   President ?: Hugh Judge
   Vice President: Frank Douglass
   Treasurer: Douglas Chene
   Secretary: Sean Sinclair
Management:
   Executive/Artistic Director: Jennifer Elowitch
   Co-Artistic Director: Dena Levine
   Operations Manager: Maria Wagner
Mission: Annual summer chamber music festival presenting concerts by nationally renowned performers and composers.
Utilizes: Artists-in-Residence; Collaborations; Commissioned Music; Composers-in-Residence; Multimedia; Original Music Scores; Poets
Founded: 1994
Specialized Field: Performing Arts; Classical Music; Summer Festival
Paid Staff: 2
Paid Artists: 20
Budget: $100,000
Income Sources: Individual; Corporate; Grants
Performs At: Concert Hall; Hannaford Hall; Abromson Center
Annual Attendance: 1,000
Seating Capacity: 250

4744
PORTLAND STRING QUARTET CONCERT SERIES/WORKSHOP
60 Candlewyck Terrace
Portland, ME 04102
Phone: 207-774-5144
Fax: 207-780-6554
e-mail: arpeggio@worldnet.att.net
Web Site: www.portlandstringquartet.org
Officers:
   President: Jana Magnuson
   Vice President: George Burns
   Secretary: Dean Stein
   Treasurer: Tracey Richardson-Newton
Management:
   LARK Society Executive Director: Jeanie J. Wester
   Artistic Directors: Julia Adams
   Artistic Directors: Ronald Lantz
   Artistic Directors: Paul Ross
   Artistic Directors: Dean Stein
Founded: 1969

4745
FORUM SERIES
84 Mechanic Street
PO Box 784
Presque Isle, ME 04769

SERIES & FESTIVALS / Maryland

Phone: 207-764-0491
Fax: 207-764-2525
e-mail: theforum@mfx.net
Web Site: www.presqueisleforum.com
Management:
    Director Forum: James F Kaiser
Founded: 1978
Specialized Field: Auditorium and Arena
Status: For-Profit, Non-Professional
Paid Staff: 18

4746
BAY CHAMBER CONCERTS
18 Central Street
PO Box 599
Rockport, ME 04856
Phone: 207-236-2823
Fax: 207-230-0454
Toll-free: 888-707-2770
e-mail: info@baychamberconcerts.org
Web Site: www.baychamberconcerts.org
Officers:
    President: Edes Gilbert
    Vice President at Large: Luther Black
    Treasurer: Harris J. Bixler
    Secretary: Warren Schubert
    Chair of Overseers: Alexandra Wolf Fogel
    Vice President Education: Eleanor Barlow
    Vice President for Marketing: Paul Cavalli
Management:
    Executive Director: Monica Kelly
    Artistic Director: Manuel Bagorro
    Development Director: Laura Chaney
    Registrar and Ticketing Coordinator: Joan Kulle
Mission: To present a variety of music styles and educational programs to reach a diverse audience along the coast of Maine.
Utilizes: Commissioned Music; Dancers; Fine Artists; Grant Writers; Guest Accompanists; Guest Choreographers; Guest Directors; Guest Musical Directors; Guest Musicians; Lyricists; Multimedia; Original Music Scores; Resident Artists; Sign Language Translators; Singers; Special Technical Talent
Founded: 1960
Specialized Field: Music
Status: Non-Profit, Professional
Paid Staff: 9
Budget: $500,000
Performs At: Rockport Opera House
Facility Category: Opera House; Strom Auditorium
Type of Stage: Proscenium; Auditorium
Seating Capacity: 400; 800
Organization Type: Performing

4747
COLBY MUSIC SERIES
Colby College
4000 Mayflower Hill
Waterville, ME 04901-8840
Phone: 207-859-4000
Fax: 207-859-4055
e-mail: dlkadyk@colby.edu
Web Site: www.colby.edu/music
Management:
    President: William Adams
    Music Department Chairman: Steve Saunders
Founded: 1987
Specialized Field: Series and Festivals; Instrumental Music; Vocal Music; Ethnic Performances
Status: Non-Profit, Professional
Paid Staff: 10
Performs At: Given Auditorium; Lorimer Chapel

Maryland

4748
ST. JOHN'S COLLEGE CONCERT SERIES
St John'S College
60 College Avenue
Annapolis, MD 21401
Phone: 410-263-2371
Fax: 410-626-2886
Web Site: www.sjc.edu/
Performs At: Francis Scott Key Auditorium

4749
ARTSCAPE-BALTIMORE'S FESTIVAL OF THE ARTS
7 E Redwood Street
Suite 500
Baltimore, MD 21202
Phone: 410-752-8632
Fax: 410-385-0361
e-mail: kajanku@promotionandarts.com
Web Site: www.artscape.org
    Arts Education Coordinator: Kibibi Ajanku
    School 33 Art Center Director: Jody Albright
Specialized Field: Three day regional festival of the literary; visual; and performing arts.
Status: Non-Profit

4750
BALTIMORE SYMPHONY ORCHESTRA SUMMER MUSIC FEST: OREGON RIDGE CONCERT SERIES
1212 Cathedral Street
Baltimore, MD 21201
Phone: 410-783-8100
Fax: 410-783-8004
Toll-free: 877-DSO-1444
e-mail: tickets@baltimoresymphony.com
Web Site: www.bsomusic.org/
Officers:
    President: John Gidwitz
Management:
    President: James Glicker
    Artistic Director: Mario Venzago
    Music Director: Yuri Temirkanov
Founded: 1906
Specialized Field: Series & Festivals; Instrumental Music; Theatre; Youth; Classical Music
Status: Non-Profit, Professional
Paid Staff: 75
Paid Artists: 100

4751
CONCERT ARTISTS OF BALTIMORE
1114 St Paul Street
Baltimore, MD 21202-2615
Phone: 410-625-3525
Fax: 410-625-9343
e-mail: info@cabalto.org
Web Site: www.cabalto.org
Officers:
    President Of The Board: Barry F. Williams
    Board Vice-President: Barbara J. Cox
    Board Secretary: Mitchell Nelson
Management:
    Artistic Director: Edward Polochick
    General Manager: Sean McDonnell, cheryl@cabalto.org
    President Of The Board: Barry F. Williams, bfw53@aol.com
    Development Director: Nan Rosenthal
    Artistic Administrator: Felice Homann
    Box Office | Administrative Assista: Kathy Walsh

    Art Director | Public Relations: Wesley Stuckey
    Production Manager & Librarian: Drew Rieger
Mission: To present chamber orchestra and vocal ensemble works in the classical music genre.
Founded: 1987
Specialized Field: Chamber; Orchestra; Vocal Ensemble
Status: Non-Profit, Professional
Paid Staff: 4
Volunteer Staff: 10
Paid Artists: 70
Budget: $300,000
Income Sources: Grants; Ticket Sales; Corporate Foundations; Individual Giving
Annual Attendance: 7,500-10,000
Type of Stage: Proscenium

4752
MARYLAND INTERNATIONAL CHAMBER MUSIC FESTIVAL
PO Box 28060
Baltimore, MD 21239
Phone: 410-830-2838
Fax: 410-426-6062
e-mail: intermuse@email.com
Web Site: www.internmusearts.org
Management:
    Coordinator: Barry Goldstein
    Director: Cathy Jones
Mission: To promote classical music in Maryland.
Founded: 1985
Specialized Field: Classical

4753
NOTRE DAME OF MARYLAND UNIVERSITY
Music at CND Concerts
4701 North Charles Street
Baltimore, MD 21210
Phone: 410-435-0100
Fax: 410-435-5937
e-mail: eragogini@ndm.edu
Web Site: www.ndm.edu
Officers:
    Professor of Music: Dr. Ernest Ragogini
Management:
    College President: Dr James Seurkamp
    Founder/Artistic Director: Ernest Ragogini
Mission: Outreach to community by presenting free professional concerts
Utilizes: Collaborating Artists; Collaborations; Commissioned Composers; Composers; Grant Writers; Guest Companies; Guest Directors; Guest Lecturers; Guest Musical Directors; Guest Musicians; Local Artists & Directors; Lyricists; Multimedia; Organization Contracts; Original Music Scores; Paid Performers; Sign Language Translators; Singers
Founded: 1969
Specialized Field: Series & Festivals; Instrumental Music; Vocal Music; Ethnic Performances; Jazz; Classical
Status: Non-Profit, Professional
Volunteer Staff: 1
Paid Artists: 10
Budget: $10,000-$12,000
Income Sources: Donations; College Support
Performs At: LeClerc Auditorium
Annual Attendance: 1,200
Type of Stage: Proscenium; Thrust
Stage Dimensions: 55w xc 30d
Seating Capacity: 995
Year Built: 1895
Year Remodeled: 1970

All listings are in alphabetical order by state, then city, then organization within the city.

SERIES & FESTIVALS / Maryland

Rental Contact: Kara Yendell

4754
RES MUSICAMERICA SERIES
211 Goodwood Gardens
Baltimore, MD 21210
Phone: 410-889-3939
Management:
    President: Vivian A Rudow
Founded: 1980
Specialized Field: Series & Festivals: American Music
Status: Non-Profit, Professional

4755
SHRIVER HALL CONCERT SERIES
Shriver Hall/Suite 105
3400 N. Charles Street
Baltimore, MD 21218-2698
Phone: 410-516-7164
Fax: 410-516-7165
e-mail: info@shriverconcerts.org
Web Site: www.shriverconcerts.org
Officers:
    President: Stephen Jacobsohn
    VP: Harriet Panitz
    Chair: Geoffrey L. Greif
    Vice Chair: Edward F. McCarthy
    Secretary: Heidi Hutton
    Treasurer: Julie A. Schwait
Management:
    Executive Director: David J Baldwin
    Office Manager: Devon Maloney
    Marketing and Community Engagement: Elizabeth Amrhein
Mission: Present solo and chamber music concerts.
Utilizes: Educators; Guest Musical Directors; Guest Musicians; Lyricists
Founded: 1965
Specialized Field: Series & Festivals; Chamber Music; Solo Recitals
Status: Non-Profit, Professional
Paid Staff: 3
Paid Artists: 9
Budget: $650,000
Income Sources: Ticket sales, contributions, ads, grants
Annual Attendance: 8,000+
Facility Category: Auditorium
Type of Stage: Proscenium
Stage Dimensions: 40x80
Seating Capacity: 1,100
Year Built: 1953
Rental Contact: 410-516-2224 Pat Forrester

4756
YOUNG AUDIENCES OF MARYLAND
2601 North Howard Street
Suite 1300
Baltimore, MD 21218
Phone: 410-837-7577
Fax: 410-837-7579
e-mail: info@yamd.org
Web Site: www.yamd.org
Officers:
    President: Bill Buckner
    Vice President: E. Scott Johnson
    Treasurer: Gregory Blake
    Secretary: Sheelagh M. Allston
Management:
    Executive Director: Stacie Sanders Evans
    Director Administration: Donna Sherman
    Education Director: Pat Cruz
    Director of Development: Jennifer Andiorio
    Marketing/PR Manager: Michelle Clesse
    Communications Manager: Meaghan Farno
    Development Assistant: Kevin Adekoya
    Education Associate: Emily Norris
    Artist Associate: Kevin Martin
Mission: Transforms the lives and education of our youth through the arts by connecting educators, professional artists, and communities. Provides artistically excellent programs, expertise and resources to ensure opportunities for all students across the state of Maryland.
Utilizes: Actors; Artists-in-Residence; Collaborating Artists; Collaborations; Dance Companies; Dancers; Educators; Fine Artists; Grant Writers; Guest Artists; Guest Companies; Guest Directors; Guest Ensembles; Guest Instructors; Guest Musical Directors; Guild Activities; Local Artists; Lyricists; Multi Collaborations; Multimedia; Original Music Scores; Playwrights; Poets; Selected Students; Sign Language Translators; Singers; Special Technical Talent; Theatre Companies; Touring Companies
Founded: 1950
Specialized Field: Series & Festivals; Vocal Music; Instrumental Music; Theatre Arts; Education
Status: Non-Profit, Professional
Paid Staff: 11
Volunteer Staff: 3
Paid Artists: 100
Budget: $1 Million
Income Sources: Programs; Special Events; Corporate; Foundations; Individual Contributions
Performs At: Maryland Schools; Libraries; Festivals
Affiliations: National Young Audiences
Annual Attendance: 200,000
Facility Category: School
Organization Type: Performing; Educational; Sponsoring

4757
MUSIC IN THE GREAT HALL SERIES
1922 Portobago Lane
Catonsville, MD 21076
Phone: 410-989-1973
e-mail: greathall@verizon.net
Web Site: www.migh.org
Officers:
    President: Diana Sayler
    Vice President: Sheila Haghighat
    Treasurer: Dan Nicolaisen
    Secretary: Ina Allen
Management:
    President: Diana Sayler
    Artistic Director: Michael Dabroski
    Managing Director: Mike Repper
Founded: 1973
Specialized Field: Series and Festivals: Present Chamber Music Concerts
Status: Non-Profit, Professional

4758
WASHINGTON COLLEGE CONCERT SERIES
300 Washington Avenue
Chestertown, MD 21620
Phone: 410-778-2800
Toll-free: 800-221-82
Web Site: http://news.washcoll.edu/concertandfilmseries.php
Officers:
    Chairman: Edward P. Nordberg
    Vice Chairman: H. Lawrence Culp, Jr.
    Secretary: Nina Rodale Houghton
    Treasurer: Geoffrey M. Rogers
Management:
    Director: Kate Bennett
Founded: 1951
Specialized Field: Instrumental Music
Performs At: Tawes Theater

4759
UNIVERSITY OF MARYLAND INTERNATIONAL WILLIAM KAPELL PIANO COMPETITION & FESTIVAL
3800 The Clarice Smith Performing Arts Center
University of Maryland
College Park, MD 20742-1625
Phone: 301-405-7794
Fax: 301-405-5977
e-mail: sfarr@umd.edu
Web Site: www.claricesmithcenter.umd.edu
Management:
    Executive Director: Martin Wollesen
    Director, Artist Partner Program: Paul Brohan
    Director of Development: Edward J. Lewis
    Technical Director: Mark Rapach
    Production Coordinator: Kate Gibson
Founded: 1971
Specialized Field: Series and Festivals; Instrumental Music; Vocal Music; Theatre; Youth; Dance; Ethnic Performances
Status: Non-Profit, Professional
Paid Staff: 50
Paid Artists: 100

4760
BALTIMORE-WASHINGTON JAZZFEST
5430 Vantage Point Road Columbia
Columbia, MD 21044
Phone: 410-730-7106
Fax: 410-715-7105
e-mail: africanartmuseum@erols.com
Web Site: www.baltowashjazzfest.org
Officers:
    Chairman: Claude M Ligon
Specialized Field: Jazz

4761
COLUMBIA FESTIVAL OF THE ARTS
5575 Sterrett Place
Suite 300
Columbia, MD 21044
Phone: 410-715-3044
Fax: 410-715-3056
e-mail: info@columbiafestival.com
Web Site: www.columbiafestival.com
Officers:
    Executive Director: Nichole J. Hickey
Mission: To present a variety of art forms and to make these accessible to the public.
Utilizes: Dancers; Singers; Touring Companies
Founded: 1987
Specialized Field: Dance; Vocal Music; Instrumental Music; Theater; Festivals
Status: Non-Profit
Volunteer Staff: 350
Paid Artists: 250
Budget: $750,000
Income Sources: Major business sponsors; individual & corporate support
Performs At: Merriweather Post Pavilion
Affiliations: The Baltimore Sun; Columbia Association; Columbia Flier
Organization Type: Presenting

SERIES & FESTIVALS / Massachusetts

4762
EASTERN SHORE CHAMBER MUSIC FESTIVAL
114 N Washington St
Ste 20
Easton, MD 21601
Phone: 410-819-0380
Fax: 410-819-0038
e-mail: managingdirector@musicontheshore.org
Web Site: www.musicontheshore.org
Management:
  President: James Campbell
  Artistic Director: J Lawrie Bloom
  Artistic Director: Marcy Rosen
  Managing Director: Donald C Buxton
Founded: 1985
Specialized Field: Series and Festivals: Instrumental Music
Status: Non-Profit, Professional
Paid Staff: 2

4763
FREDERICK COMMUNITY COLLEGE ARTS SERIES
7932 Opossumtown Pike
Frederick Community College
Frederick, MD 21702
Phone: 301-846-2513
Fax: 301-624-2878
e-mail: wpoindexter@frederick.edu
Web Site: www.frederick.edu
Officers:
  Chair: Debra S. Borden
  Vice Chair: David F. Bufter
Management:
  President: Douglas D. Browning
  Director: Wendell Poindexter
Founded: 1989
Specialized Field: Series & Festivals; Plays; Music; Lecture Series
Status: Non-Profit, Professional
Paid Staff: 12
Paid Artists: 20
Performs At: Jack B. Kussmaul Theatre
Seating Capacity: 409

4764
FROSTBURG STATE UNIVERSITY CULTURAL EVENTS SERIES
Lane Center 203
Frostburg State University
Frostburg, MD 21532
Phone: 301-687-4151
Fax: 301-687-7049
e-mail: ces@frostburg.edu
Web Site: ces.frostburg.edu/
Officers:
  Chairman: Bill Mandicott
Management:
  Executive Director: Bill Manvicott
  Director: Mary Jane Plummer
  Assistant Director: Melanie Moore
  Artistic Development: William Mandicott
  Box Office Manager: Donna Briner
  Educational Outreach Coordinator: Hannah Byler
  Grants Associate: Susan Manger
Specialized Field: Series & Festivals; Instrumental Music; Vocal Music; Theatre; Youth; Dance; Ethnic Performances
Status: For-Profit, Non-Professional
Paid Staff: 11
Performs At: Physical Education Center

4765
CITY OF GAITHERSBURG CULTURAL ARTS DIVISION
31 S Summit Ave
Gaithersburg, MD 20877
Phone: 301-258-6310
Fax: 301-948-6149
e-mail: cityhall@gaithersburgmd.gov
Web Site: www.gaithersburgmd.gov/
Management:
  Cultural Arts Director: Denise Kayser
  Arts Barn Director: Marty Willey
Mission: To promote, present, and support rge arts and hummanities.
Founded: 1989
Specialized Field: All Areas
Performs At: Various Auditoriums

4766
OPEN SKY
PO Box 10356
Rockville, MD 20849

Management:
  Principal: Suzan Jenkins
  Principal: Willard Jenkins
Mission: Open Sky has amassed over thirty years as industry leader in various facets of the jazz, arts, the recording business and jazz media. Provides multifaceted consulting services that tap into its unrivaled acumen in the profit and nonprofit music business and recording industry arenas.
Specialized Field: Jazz

4767
CAPITAL JAZZ FESTIVAL
PO Box 2129
Upper Marlboro, MD 20773
Phone: 301-780-9300
Toll-free: 877-192-29
Web Site: www.capitaljazz.com
Management:
  Producer: Cliff Hunte
Specialized Field: Jazz festival (contemporary jazz and soul); jazz cruises
Status: Professional

Massachusetts

4769
MUSIC AT AMHERST SERIES
Music Department at Amherst College
P.O. Box 5000
Amherst, MA 01002-5000
Phone: 413-542-2195
Fax: 413-542-2678
e-mail: mhbaumgarten@amherst.edu
Web Site: www.amherst.edu/~concerts
Management:
  Concert Manager: Michael Baumgarten
Specialized Field: Series & Festivals; Instrumental Music; Vocal Music; Ethnic Performances
Status: Non-Profit, Professional
Performs At: Buckley Recital Hall

4770
ANN ARBOR SUMMER FESTIVAL
400 Fourth Street
#150
Ann Arbor, MA 48103
Phone: 734-647-2278
Fax: 734-936-3393
e-mail: rwoulfe@umich.edu
Web Site: www.mlive.com/aasf/
Officers:
  President: Peter F. Schork
  Chair: John C. Clark
  Secretary: Sadie B. Garner
  Treasurer: Connie M. Kinnear
Management:
  Executive Director: Evy Warshawski
  Accountant: Jennifer Fike
  Development Director: Astrid Giese
  Marketing Manager: Amy K. MIlligan
  Development Manager: Heidi Grix

4771
ELECTRIC SYMPHONY FESTIVAL
PO Box 1316
Arlington, MA 02474
Phone: 877-646-1304
Fax: 877-646-1304
e-mail: mail@wildflowerpublishers.com
Web Site: www.electricsymphony.com
Management:
  Director: James Forte
  Co-Founder / Strategy: David Hassard
  Co-Founder / Operations: Aaron Shapiro
  Co-Founder / Sales: Pat Carroll
Mission: Exploring the spirit in music since 1988

4772
JACOB'S PILLOW DANCE FESTIVAL
358 George Carter Road
Becket, MA 01223
Phone: 413-243-9919
Fax: 413-243-4744
e-mail: info@jacobspillow.org
Web Site: www.jacobspillow.org
Management:
  Jazz/Musical Dance Director: Chet Walker
  Marketing Director: Mariclare Hulbert
Mission: The mission of Jacob's Pillow is to support dance creation, presentation, education, and preservation and to engage and deepen public appreciation and support for dance.
Utilizes: Artists-in-Residence; Choreographers; Dance Companies; Dancers; Educators; Guest Accompanists; Guest Artists; Guest Choreographers; Guest Ensembles; Guest Instructors; Guest Soloists; Guest Speakers; Instructors; Multi Collaborations; Paid Performers; Resident Companies; Soloists; Students
Founded: 1933
Specialized Field: Dance
Status: Professional, Nonprofit
Income Sources: Corporate; Endowment; Foundations; Governments; Membership; Planned Giving
Season: June-August
Performs At: Doris Duke Theatre; Marcia & Seymour Simon Performance Space; Ted Shawn Theatre
Annual Attendance: 70,000
Type of Stage: Flexible
Seating Capacity: 620, 220

4773
BOSTON CONSERVATORY
8 The Fenway
Boston, MA 02215
Phone: 617-536-6340
Fax: 617-912-9101
e-mail: admissions@bostonconservatory.edu
Web Site: www.bostonconservatory.edu
Officers:

SERIES & FESTIVALS / Massachusetts

President: Richard Ortner
Management:
   President: Richard Ortner
Founded: 1867
Specialized Field: Series & Festivals; Music; Dance; Theater
Status: For-Profit, Professional

4774
CHARLES RIVER CONCERT SERIES
262 Beacon Street
3rd Floor
Boston, MA 02116
Phone: 617-262-0650
Fax: 617-267-6539
Management:
   Manager: Kathleen Fay

4775
EMMANUEL MUSIC BACH CANTATA SERIES
15 Newbury Street
Boston, MA 02116
Mailing Address: PO Box 171184 Boston, MA 02117
Phone: 617-536-3356
Fax: 617-536-3315
e-mail: music@emmanuelmusic.org
Web Site: www.emmanuelmusic.org
Management:
   Executive Director: Patricia Krol
   Artistic Director: Michael Beattie
   Director of Development: Jude Epsztein Bedel
   Artistic Director: Ryan Turner
   Orchestra Personnel Manager: Joan Ellersick

4776
FIRST NIGHT BOSTON
31 Snake James Avenue
Suite 949
Boston, MA 02116
Phone: 617-542-1399
Fax: 617-426-9531
e-mail: info@firstnight.org
Web Site: www.firstnight.org
Officers:
   Co-Chairman: Eric Schwarz
   Co-Chairman: Edwin P Tiffany
   Clerk: Royal Dunham Jr
   Treasurer: Charles A Ansbacher
Management:
   Executive Director: Geri Guardino
   Production Director: Amy Havwood
   Marketing Manager: Barbara Wojslawowicz
   Marketing Assistant: Barbara Wojslawowicz
Mission: To use a street fair venue to broaden and deepen the public's appreciation for the visual and performing arts.
Utilizes: Actors; Artists-in-Residence; Choreographers; Collaborations; Dance Companies; Dancers; Fine Artists; Guest Artists; Guest Companies; Guest Musical Directors; Guest Musicians; Instructors; Local Artists; Lyricists; Multi Collaborations; Multimedia; New Productions; Original Music Scores; Playwrights; Selected Students; Sign Language Translators; Soloists; Touring Companies; Visual Arts
Founded: 1976
Specialized Field: Series & Festivals; Instrumental Music; Vocal Music; Theatre; Dance
Status: Non-Profit, Professional
Paid Staff: 12
Volunteer Staff: 400
Paid Artists: 1000
Budget: $1,600,000
Annual Attendance: 2,000,000
Organization Type: Art Presenter

4777
FLEETBOSTON CELEBRITY SERIES
20 Park Plaza
Suite 1032
Boston, MA 02116
Phone: 617-482-2595
Fax: 617-482-3208
e-mail: info@celebrityseries.org
Web Site: www.celebrityseries.org
Officers:
   President: Gary Dunning
   Chair: Joshua Boger, Ph.D.
   Treasurer: Mary Elisabeth Swerz
   Clerk: Ilene B. Jacobs
Management:
   President and Executive Director: Gary Dunning
   Director, Performance Operations: Karen Brown
   Director, Performance Operations: Karen Brown
   Manager of Individual Giving: Erin Coffey
   Development Coordinator: Melody Pao
   Associate Director of Marketing: Gillian Morrison
   Director of Development: Sara Robinson
   Chief Financial Officer: Edwin Derecho
   Director of Marketing and Communica: Jack Wright
Mission: To bring Boston the world's greatest performing artists.
Utilizes: Actors; Artists-in-Residence; Collaborating Artists; Collaborations; Commissioned Composers; Commissioned Music; Composers-in-Residence; Dance Companies; Dancers; Designers; Educators; Five Seasonal Concerts; Guest Accompanists; Guest Choreographers; Guest Companies; Guest Conductors; Guest Directors; Guest Instructors; Guest Musical Directors; Guest Musicians; Instructors; Local Artists; Lyricists; Multi Collaborations; Multimedia; New Productions; Organization Contracts; Original Music Scores; Resident Professionals; Sign Language Translators; Singers; Special Technical Talent; Theatre Companies
Founded: 1938
Specialized Field: Dance; Vocal Music; Instrumental Music; Theater
Status: Non-Profit
Paid Staff: 22
Budget: 6.3 Million
Income Sources: Ticket Sales; Sponsorship; Fundraising
Season: October - January
Performs At: Symphony Hall; Wang Center; Jordan Hall; Shubert Theatre
Affiliations: Association of Performing Arts Presenters; International Society of Performing Arts Dance USA
Annual Attendance: 100,000+
Organization Type: Presenting

4778
HARVARD MUSICAL ASSOCIATION IN BOSTON
57A Chesnut Street
Boston, MA 02108
Phone: 617-523-2897
Fax: 617-523-2897
Web Site: hmaboston.org/
Management:
   President: Stephen Friedlaender
   Program Director: F Lee Eiseman
Founded: 1837
Specialized Field: Series & Festivals: Chamber Music
Status: Non-Profit, Professional
Paid Staff: 3

4779
KING'S CHAPEL CONCERT SERIES
64 Beacon St.
Boston, MA 02108
Phone: 617-227-2155
Fax: 617-227-4101
e-mail: frontdesk@kings-chapel.org
Web Site: www.kings-chapel.org
Management:
   Music Director: Heinrich Christensen
   Parish Administrator: Julina Rundberg
   Lead Guide: Theresa Cooney O'Hara
Mission: To offer chamber music, particularly Baroque and contemporary works.
Utilizes: Singers
Founded: 1958
Specialized Field: Series & Festivals; Instrumental Music; Vocal Music; Youth
Status: Non-Profit, Professional
Performs At: King's Chapel
Organization Type: Performing

4780
MUSEUM OF FINE ARTS CONCERTS & PERFORMANCES
465 Huntington Avenue
Boston, MA 02115
Phone: 617-267-9300
Fax: 617-267-9328
e-mail: webmaster@mfa.org
Web Site: www.mfa.org
Management:
   Concert Co-ordinator: Laurie Thomas

4781
BRIDGEWATER STATE COLLEGE PROGRAM COMMITTEE
American College Personnel Association
One Dupont Circle Suite 300
Bridgewater, MA 20036
Phone: 202-835-2272
Fax: 202-296-3286
Toll-free: 800-531-2292
e-mail: info@acpa.nche.edu
Web Site: www.bridgew.edu/tepte
Management:
   President: Thrish Realduto
   Executive Director: Mac Miller
Specialized Field: Series & Festivals; Instrumental Music; Vocal Music; Ethnic Performances; Comedy; Concert In Spring
Status: Non-Profit, Professional
Paid Artists: 100

4782
MASSASOIT COMMUNITY COLLEGE BUCKLEY ARTS CENTER PERFORMANCE SERIES
One Massasoit Blvd.
Brockton, MA 02302
Phone: 508-588-9100
Fax: 508-427-1267
Web Site: www.massasoit.mass.edu/buckley/about.cfm
Management:
   Director: Michael Pevzner
Founded: 1983
Paid Staff: 3

SERIES & FESTIVALS / Massachusetts

4783
BOSTON EARLY MUSIC FESTIVAL
43 Thorndike Street
Suite 302
Cambridge, MA 02141
Phone: 617-661-1812
Fax: 617-661-1816
e-mail: bemf@bemf.org
Web Site: www.bemf.org
Officers:
  Chairman: Bernice K. Chen
  President: David Halstead
  Vice President: Constance Goldstein
  Treasurer: David Cook
  Clerk: Peter L. Faber
Management:
  Executive Director: Kathleen Fay
  Director of Marketing: Brian R. Stuart, brian@bemf.org
  Artistic Director: Stephen Stubbs
  Artistic Director: Paul O'Dette
  General Manager: Carla Chrisfield
  Director of Artist Relations: Maria van Kalken
  Exhibition Manager & Orchestra Mana: Peter Charig
  Director of Operations & Box Office: David Cronin
  Director of Education: David Coffin
Mission: To discover and reproduce how early music originally sounded to a composer and his audience; to produce a biennial international festival in Boston; to educate youth.
Utilizes: Guest Artists; Guest Companies; Singers
Founded: 1980
Specialized Field: Series & Festivals; Instrumental Music; Vocal Music; Youth; Dance; Vocal Music; Instrumental Music
Status: Non-Profit, Professional
Paid Staff: 7
Paid Artists: 100
Seating Capacity: 557
Organization Type: Performing; Touring; Educational; Sponsoring

4784
BOSTON GLOBE JAZZ & BLUES FESTIVAL
135 Morrissey Boulevard
Cambridge, MA 02107-2378
Phone: 617-929-3460
Web Site: www.boston.com/jazzfest
Management:
  VP: Lisa Desisto
  Director Of Product Development: Michael Manning

4785
CAMBRIDGE SOCIETY FOR EARLY MUSIC: CHAMBER MUSIC SERIES
PO box 380-336
Cambridge, MA 02238-0336
Phone: 617-489-2062
Fax: 617-489-0686
e-mail: info@csem.org
Web Site: www.csem.org
Officers:
  President: James Nicolson
  Vice-president: Clifford Boehmer
  Secretary: Kenneth Thomson
  Treasurer: Eric Darling
Management:
  Music Director: Bernard Brauchli
Mission: To entertain, enlighten, educate, and in general promote the rich musical culture of five centuries of Western music occuring up to the early nineteenth century.
Performs At: Fogg Art Museum

4786
MIT GUEST ARTISTS SERIES
77 Massachusetts Avenue
Rm. 4-246
Cambridge, MA 02139-4307
Phone: 617-253-3210
Fax: 617-253-4523
e-mail: mta-request@mit.edu
Web Site: www.mit.edu/activities/mta/music/events.html
Management:
  Director: Clarise Snyder
  Artistic Director: David Deveau
  Event Manager: Vanessa Gardner
  Piano Technician: Victor Belanger
Utilizes: Artists-in-Residence; Composers; Educators; Guest Directors; Guest Musical Directors; Instructors
Performs At: Kresge Auditorium

4787
REGATTABAR JAZZ FESTIVAL AT THE CHARLES HOTEL
Charles Hotel
One Bennett Street
Cambridge, MA 02138
Phone: 617-864-1200
Fax: 617-864-5715
Toll-free: 800-882-1818
e-mail: generalmail@charleshotel.com
Web Site: www.charleshotel.com
Management:
  Lounge Manager: Jeffrey Keyes

4788
WORLD MUSIC FESTIVAL
720 Massachusetts Ave
Cambridge, MA 02139
Phone: 617-876-4275
Fax: 617-876-9170
e-mail: info@WorldMusic.org
Web Site: www.worldmusic.org
Management:
  President: Maure Aronson
  Associate Director: Susan Weiler
Founded: 1990
Specialized Field: Series & Festivals: Concert Promoter
Status: Non-Profit, Non-Professional
Paid Staff: 7

4789
KING RICHARD'S FAIRE
PO Box 419
Carver, MA 02330
Phone: 508-866-5391
Fax: 508-866-8600
e-mail: info@kingrichardsfaire.net
Web Site: kingrichardsfaire.net/
Management:
  Producer: Bonnie Shapiro
  General Manager: Aimee Sedley
Founded: 1982
Specialized Field: Festival
Status: Non-Equity; Commercial
Season: September - October
Performs At: Outdoor with 10 stages and a Tourney Field
Annual Attendance: 200,000

4790
FRIENDS OF THE PERFORMING ARTS
51 Walden Street
PO Box 251
Concord, MA 01742
Phone: 978-369-7911
e-mail: fopac@tiac.net
Web Site: www.tiac.net/users/fopac
Officers:
  President: Becky Gladstone
  Treasurer: Josephine Starr
  Secretary: Marijane Benner Browne
Management:
  Manager: Kathleen Chick
  Drama Director: Joseph Catalfano
  Musical Drama Director: Scott Walker
  Band Director: Robert Martel
  Choral Director: Ida Pappas
  A Cappella Advisor: Josh Bridger
Performs At: Auditorium

4791
ASTON MAGNA FESTIVAL
323 Main Street
PO Box 28
Great Barrington, MA 01230
Phone: 413-528-3595
Fax: 732-572-5119
Toll-free: 800-875-7156
e-mail: astonmagna@optonline.net
Web Site: www.astonmagna.org
Officers:
  Chair: Catherine Liddell
  Treasurer: Robert S. Strassler
  Secretary: Stephen Pearlman
Management:
  Artistic Director: Daniel Stepner
  Executive Director: Susan B. Obel
  Artistic Director Emeritus: John Hsu
  Marketing Consultant: Laureen Bubniak
  Artist Administrator: Joseph Orchard
Founded: 1978
Specialized Field: Classical; Baroque

4792
CLOSE ENCOUNTERS WITH MUSIC SERIES
PO Box 34
Great Barrington, MA 01230
Phone: 413-392-6677
Fax: 413-392-9782
Toll-free: 800-843-0778
e-mail: cewmusic@aol.com
Web Site: www.cewm.org/
Officers:
  President: Marcie Setlow
  Vice President and Secretary: Hannah Hanani,
  Treasurer: Reid White
Management:
  Artistic Director: Yehunda Hanani
  Marketing Associate: Lauren Sottile
  Coordinator: Joseph E. McCarthy
  Production: Vanessa Leikvoll
  Director of Marketing and Public Re: Pamela Dreyfus Smith
Performs At: St. James Church, Great Barrington

4793
HUDSON COMMUNITY ARTS SERIES
155 Apsley Street
Hudson, MA 01749-1697

SERIES & FESTIVALS / Massachusetts

Phone: 978-562-1646
Fax: 978-567-9659
e-mail: info@upwitharts.org
Web Site: www.upwitharts.org
Management:
- **President:** Alison Doherty
- **Executive Director:** Lynne Johnson
- **Marketing & Development Coordinator:** Denise Reid
- **Contracted Graphic Designer:** Diane Ferris

Specialized Field: Series & Festivals; Vocal Music; Theatre; Youth; Dance; Ethnic Performances
Status: Non-Profit, Professional
Performs At: Hudson High School Auditorium

4794
ENSEMBLE MUSIC SOCIETY OF INDIANAPOLIS SERIES
PO Box 40188
Ipswich, MA 46240
Phone: 317-818-1288
Fax: 317-818-8425
e-mail: info@ensemblemusic.org
Web Site: www.ensemblemusic.org
Management:
- **President:** Pamela Steele

Mission: To offer a range of performing arts events at the historic R.T. Crane Estate.
Utilizes: Guest Artists; Original Music Scores; Singers
Founded: 1951
Specialized Field: Vocal Music; Instrumental Music; Limited Small Scale Performances With Local Artists
Status: Professional; Nonprofit
Organization Type: Performing; Educational; Sponsoring

4795
TANGLEWOOD FESTIVAL
Tanglewood Music Center
301 Massachusetts Ave.
Lenox, MA 02115
Phone: 617-638-9230
Fax: 617-638-9342
e-mail: tmc@bso.org
Web Site: www.bso.org
Officers:
- **Chairman:** James Levine

Management:
- **Managing Director:** Mark Volpe
- **Guest Conductor:** Thomas Ades
- **Guest Conductor:** Stephane Deneve
- **Guest Conductor:** Christoph Eschenbach

Utilizes: Guest Artists; Singers
Founded: 1940
Income Sources: Ticket sales, contributions
Season: Summer
Performs At: Tanglewood
Organization Type: Performing; Educational
Comments: Information at Tanglewood for the disabled is available at the Access Services Center at the Main Gate. The Service Center has alternate format materials, medical equipment, and trained staff available to assist patrons on an as-needed b

4796
CAPE & ISLANDS CHAMBER MUSIC FESTIVAL
Main Street Mercantile Unit 6
3 Main Street
North Chatham, MA 02651
Mailing Address: PO Box 1934 North Eastham, MA 02651
Phone: 508-247-9400
Fax: 508-945-8059
Toll-free: 800-818-0608
e-mail: info@capecodchambermusic.org
Web Site: www.capecodchambermusic.org
Officers:
- **President:** David B. Farer
- **Vice President:** Susan Hamilton
- **Secretary:** Lawrence M. Handley
- **Treasurer:** Inez D'Arcangelo

Management:
- **President:** David B. Farer
- **Executive Director:** Pamela Patrick
- **Artistic Director:** Jon Manasse
- **VP:** George Dillon

Mission: To present the finest classical and contemporary chamber music by both world-class ensembles and exceptional young emerging artists to Cape Cod audiences; to develop new and younger audiences for chamber music.
Founded: 1980
Specialized Field: Chamber Music
Paid Staff: 2
Volunteer Staff: 30

4797
CAPE COD CHAMBER MUSIC FESTIVAL
Main Street Mercantile Unit 6
3 Main Street
North Chatham, MA 02651
Mailing Address: PO Box 1934 North Eastham, MA 02651
Phone: 508-247-9400
Fax: 508-945-8059
Toll-free: 800-818-0608
e-mail: contact@capecodchambermusic.org
Web Site: www.capecodchambermusic.org
Officers:
- **President:** David B. Farer
- **Vice President:** Susan Hamilton
- **Treasurer:** Inez D'Arcangelo
- **Secretary:** Lawrence M. Handley

Management:
- **President:** David B. Farer
- **Executive Director:** Nora Hayes
- **Artistic Director:** Jon Manasse
- **Managing Director:** Susan Chalmers

Mission: To present the finest classical and contemporary chamber music by both world-class ensembles and exceptional young emerging artists to Cape Cod audiences; to develop new and younger audiences for chamber music; to commission new chamber works whenever possible; and to provide educational activities and programs which encourage, broaden and deepen appreciation of the chamber music art form.
Founded: 1979
Specialized Field: Series & Festivals; Instrumental Music; Vocal Music; Youth; Dance; Chamber Music
Status: Non-Profit, Professional
Paid Staff: 3
Paid Artists: 30
Facility Category: Usually churches
Seating Capacity: 250 - 300
Organization Type: Performing; Educational

4798
MASSACHUSETTS INTERNATIONAL FESTIVAL OF THE ARTS
56 Suffolk Street
Suite 300
Northampton, MA 01040
Phone: 413-540-0200
Fax: 413-540-0225
Toll-free: 800-224-6432
e-mail: info@mifafestival.org
Web Site: www.mifafestival.org
Management:
- **Managing Director:** Marta Ostapiuk
- **Artistic/Executive Director:** Donald T Sanders

Mission: To present the finest contemporary practice in opera, theatre, dance, music, film and the visual arts in three counties of the Pioneer Valley of Western Massachusetts.
Founded: 1993
Specialized Field: Series & Festivals; Theatre; Dance; Opera; Music; Visual arts
Status: Non-Profit, Professional
Paid Staff: 4
Volunteer Staff: 5
Paid Artists: 150

4799
SOUTH MOUNTAIN CONCERTS
PO Box 23
Pittsfield, MA 01202
Phone: 413-442-2106
Web Site: www.southmountainconcert.org
Management:
- **Director:** Lou R Steigler

Founded: 1918
Specialized Field: Series & Festivals: Chamber Music Concerts
Status: Non-Profit, Professional
Paid Staff: 2
Paid Artists: 5

4800
ROCKPORT CHAMBER MUSIC FESTIVAL
PO Box 312
Rockport, MA 01966
Phone: 978-546-7391
Fax: 978-546-7391
e-mail: rcmf.info@verizon.net
Web Site: www.rcmf.org
Officers:
- **President:** Phillip D Cutter MD
- **VP:** Dianne Anderson
- **VP:** Barbara Sparks
- **Treasurer:** William Hausman
- **Clerk/Secretary:** Mollie Byrnes

Management:
- **President:** Cameron Smith
- **Executive Director:** Elizabeth Redmond
- **Artistic Director:** David Deveau

Mission: The presentation of a 16-concert series in June, featuring chamber ensembles performing alone and in collaboration.
Founded: 1982
Specialized Field: Series and Festivals: Chamber Music Concerts
Status: Non-Profit, Professional
Paid Staff: 2
Paid Artists: 30
Performs At: Rockport Art Association
Organization Type: Presenting

4801
BERKSHIRE CHORAL FESTIVAL
245 North Undermountain Road
Sheffield, MA 01257
Phone: 413-229-8526
Fax: 413-229-0109
e-mail: bcf@choralfest.org
Web Site: www.choralfest.org
Officers:

SERIES & FESTIVALS / Massachusetts

President/CEO: Debralee L. Kennedy
Chair: Laurie Martin
Vice Chair: Richard Aldrich
Treasurer: Bonnie English
Secretary: Joseph Kolodziej
Management:
  Music Director: Frank Nemhauser
  Marketing & Development Director: Lusha Martin
  Finance Director: Andrea Shackford
Mission: A not-for-profit educational institution dedicated to enhancing the skkills of choral singers while extending the knowledge & appreciation of choral singing and its tradition to singers and audiences.
Founded: 1982
Specialized Field: Classical Choral; Orchestral Works
Status: Non-Profit

4802
MOHAWK TRAIL CONCERTS/MUSIC IN DEERFIELD

75 Bridge Street
PO Box 75
Shelburne, MA 01370
Phone: 413-625-9511
Fax: 413-625-0221
Toll-free: 888-682-6873
e-mail: info@mohawktrailconcerts.org
Web Site: www.mohawktrailconcerts.org/tickets.html
Management:
  Artistic Director-Deerfield: John Montanari
  Artistic Director-Mohawk Trail: Ruth Black
  Artistic Director-Deerfield: John Montanari
Mission: To offer professional chamber music in the fall and summer; to provide educational music programs.
Utilizes: Collaborations; Five Seasonal Concerts; Guest Accompanists; Guest Companies; Guest Composers; Guest Designers; Guest Directors; Guest Lecturers; Guest Musical Directors; Guest Musicians; Instructors; Local Unknown Artists; Multimedia; Music; New Productions; Organization Contracts; Original Music Scores; Selected Students; Sign Language Translators; Singers
Founded: 1969
Specialized Field: Vocal Music; Instrumental Music; Festivals
Status: Professional; Nonprofit
Paid Staff: 3
Budget: $200,000
Performs At: Federated Church
Annual Attendance: 5,500
Seating Capacity: 225-500
Organization Type: Performing; Touring; Resident; Educational; Sponsoring

4803
MUSICORDA SUMMER FESTIVAL

PO Box 557
38 Morgan St.
South Hadley, MA 01075
Phone: 413-493-1465
Fax: 413-493-1944
e-mail: musicorda@aol.com
Web Site: www.musicorda.org
Management:
  Executive Director: Janet Sadler
  Artistic Director: Rachel B Pine
Founded: 1987
Specialized Field: Series & Festivals; Violin; Viola; Cello; Piano; Chamber Music
Status: Non-Profit, Professional
Paid Staff: 3
Paid Artists: 20

4804
AMERICAN INTERNATIONAL COLLEGE SERIES

Sprague/Griswold Cultural Arts Center
1000 State Street
Springfield, MA 01109
Phone: 413-747-6393
Fax: 413-737-2803
Web Site: www.aic.edu/
Management:
  Visual/Performing Arts Director: Alvin Paige
Performs At: Auditorium

4805
SPRINGFIELD PERFORMING ARTS DEVELOPMENT CORPORATION

One Columbus Center
150 Bridge Street
Springfield, MA 01103
Phone: 413-788-7646
Fax: 413-737-9991
e-mail: tdagostino@citystage.symphonyhall.com
Web Site: www.citystage.symphonyhall.com
Management:
  President: Tina D'Agostino
  Marketing Director: Ken Scally
  Technical Director: Chad Labombard
  Box Office Manager: Brian Askin
  Group Sales: Sue Prairie
  House Manager: Amanda Spear
  Director of Development: Heather White
Mission: Professional presenting theatres.
Founded: 1998
Specialized Field: Series & Festivals; Theater; Youth; Dance; Ethnic Performances
Status: Non-Profit, Professional
Paid Staff: 8
Volunteer Staff: 50

4806
BERKSHIRE THEATRE FESTIVAL

6 East Street
Stockbridge, MA 01262
Phone: 413-298-5536
Fax: 413-298-3368
Toll-free: 866-811-4111
e-mail: info@berkshiretheatre.org
Web Site: www.berkshiretheatre.org
Officers:
  President: Ruth Blodgett
  Vice President: David L. Lloyd, Jr.
  Secretary: Robert M. Berzok
  Treasurer: Lee Perlman
Management:
  Artistic Director: Kate Maguire
  Artistic Director: E Gray Simons III
  Production Manager: Corey Cavenaugh
  Director Finance/Administration: Richard Czelusniak
  Director Development: Nina Garlington
  Director Marketing/Public Relations: Christina Riley
  Box Office/Subscriptions Manager: Ronald Nantell
  Director Of Education: Allison Rachele Bayles
  Finance Manager: Brandon Belote
Mission: To produce and promote thought-provoking theatre for its community throughout the summer through performance and educational activities.
Utilizes: Singers
Founded: 1928
Specialized Field: Theater; Festivals
Status: Professional; Nonprofit
Paid Staff: 12
Income Sources: Actors' Equity Association; Council of Resident Summer Theatres
Season: June - September
Performs At: Playhouse, Unicorn Theatre
Type of Stage: Proscenium, Thrust
Seating Capacity: 415, 122
Organization Type: Performing; Resident; Educational; Sponsoring

4807
BENTLEY COLLEGE BOWLES PERFORMANCE SERIES

STU 330, 175 Forest Street
Waltham, MA 02452-4705
Phone: 781-891-2000
Fax: 781-891-2839
e-mail: aluminfo@bentley.edu
Web Site: www.bentley.edu
Management:
  Performing Arts Coordinator: Jim Morris
Specialized Field: Series & Festivals; Instrumental Music; Vocal Music; Theatre; Dance; Ethnic Performances
Status: Non-Profit, Professional
Performs At: Lindsay Auditorium

4808
BRANDEIS UNIVERSITY SPINGOLD THEATER CENTER SERIES

Spingold Theater Center, Brandeis University
MS072, PO Box 549110 415 South Street
Waltham, MA 02453-2728
Phone: 781-736-3340
Fax: 781-736-3389
e-mail: theater@brandeis.edu
Web Site: www.brandeis.edu/theater
Management:
  Head of Department: Eric Hill
  General Manager: David Colfer
  Management Assistant, House Manager: Alyssa Avis
  Costume Director: Miranda Giurleo
  Director of Production: Leslie Chiu
  Technical Director: Chris Tedford
Founded: 1948
Specialized Field: Student Theatre Productions Featuring Brandies Graduates; Undergraduate Actors; Guest Artists
Status: Non-Profit, Professional
Seating Capacity: 744

4809
WALTHAM COMMUNITY CONCERT SERIES

119 School Street
Suite 2
Waltham, MA 02451
Phone: 781-893-2787
Fax: 781-891-3740
e-mail: sbkilgore@mediaone.net
Web Site: www.walthamarts.org/
Management:
  Director: Stephen Kilgore
Performs At: Waltham Public Library

4810
ALL NEWTON MUSIC SCHOOL, THE ANDREW WOLF CONCERT SERIES

321 Chesnut Street
West Newton, MA 02465

SERIES & FESTIVALS / Michigan

Phone: 617-527-4553
Fax: 617-527-7710
e-mail: info@allnewtonmusicschool.com
Web Site: www.allnewtonmusicschool.com
Officers:
   President: Steve Logowitz
   Executive Director: Paulette Brown
   Vice President: Chris Markiewicz
   Treasurer: Rachel Grant
Management:
   Director: Paulette Bowes
   Director of Development: Michael Ibrahim
   Director of Communications: Michelle Shoemaker
   School Administrator: Matthew Williams
Utilizes: Collaborations; Guest Companies; Guest Instructors; Guest Musical Directors; Guest Musicians; Guest Writers; Multimedia
Founded: 1911
Specialized Field: Music Instruction
Status: Non-Profit, Professional
Paid Staff: 4
Paid Artists: 65
Budget: $1,500,000
Income Sources: Tuition; Grants; Donations
Performs At: Salon
Annual Attendance: 800
Facility Category: Mansion
Type of Stage: Salon in the Round
Seating Capacity: 175
Year Built: 1900

4811
WESTFIELD STATE COLLEGE MUSIC & MORE PERFORMING ARTS SERIES
Western Avenue
Westfield, MA 01086
Phone: 413-572-5438

4812
CONCERTS-AT-THE-COMMON
Harvard Unitarian Church
POBox 217; 9 Ayer Rd.
32 Coburn Road
Weston, MA 01451
Phone: 978-779-2876
Fax: 978-456-9021
Web Site: http://www.uuharvard.org/CongregationalLife/SpecialEvents/Concerts.aspx
Officers:
   Concert Series Director: Bernard J Fine
Management:
   Planning Committee: Pat White
   Planning Committee: Eleanor Toth
   Director of Religious Education: Melinda Green
   Organist and Choir Master: Ted Johnson
   Clerk: Sharlotte Eiland
Mission: To present community concerts.
Founded: 1979
Specialized Field: Vocal Music; Instrumental Music
Status: Nonprofit
Organization Type: Sponsoring

4813
WILLIAMS COLLEGE SERIES
Bernhard Music Center
54 Chapin Hill Drive
Williamstown, MA 01267-2687
Phone: 413-597-2127
Fax: 413-597-3100
e-mail: eclark@williams.edu
Web Site: www.williams.edu/music
Officers:
   Chair Dept. of Music: W. Anthony Sheppard
Management:
   President: Morton Schupiro
   Executive Director: David Kechley
   Artistic Director: Ronald Feltman
   Managing Director: Ernest Clark
Founded: 1700
Specialized Field: Series & Festivals; Instrumental Music; Vocal Music; Ethnic Performances
Status: Non-Profit, Professional
Paid Staff: 1
Paid Artists: 50

4814
WILLIAMSTOWN THEATRE FESTIVAL
PO Box 517
Williamstown, MA 01267-0517
Phone: 413-458-3200
Fax: 413-458-3147
e-mail: wtfinfo@wtfestival.org
Web Site: www.wtfestival.org
Officers:
   President: Dr. Ira Lapidus
   Vice President: Brian D Cabral
   Secretary: Jeffrey Johnson
   Treasurer: Donald B. Elitzer
   Chairman: Matthew C. Harris
   Vice Chair: Joe Finnegan
   Vice Chair: Barbara McLucas
   Past Chair: Ira Lapidus
Management:
   Producer: Michael Ritchie
   General Manager: Deborah Fehr
   Associate Producer: Jenny Gersten
   Business Manager: Amy Russell
   Development Director: Jen Crowell
   Production Manager: Christopher Atkins
   Workshop Director: Amanda Charlton
   Company Manager: Liz Mahan
Mission: To present outstanding productions of modern classics on our main stage; to develop new acting, writing and musical talent.
Utilizes: Actors; AEA Actors; Artists-in-Residence; Choreographers; Commissioned Composers; Commissioned Music; Designers; Educators; Guest Accompanists; Guest Artists; Guest Companies; Guest Conductors; Guest Designers; Guest Ensembles; Guest Lecturers; Guest Musical Directors; High School Drama; Music; Original Music Scores; Performance Artists; Poets; Resident Artists; Resident Professionals; Singers; Soloists; Student Interns
Founded: 1954
Specialized Field: Series & Festivals: Theatre
Status: Non-Profit, Professional
Paid Staff: 75
Volunteer Staff: 150
Paid Artists: 100
Non-paid Artists: 40
Budget: $2,500,000
Performs At: Adams Memorial Theater; Nikos Stage
Annual Attendance: 50,000
Seating Capacity: 520
Organization Type: Performing
Comments: September-May in NYC 212-395-9090

4815
WORCESTER MUSIC FESTIVAL
323 Main Street
Worcester, MA 01608
Phone: 508-754-3231
Fax: 508-754-8698
e-mail: music@musicworcester.org
Web Site: www.musicworcester.org
Officers:
   President: W. Peter Metz, M.D.
   Vice President: Kirk A. Carter, Esq.
   Treasurer: David Mayotte
   Clerk: Cynthia Pitcher
Management:
   Executive Director: Adrien C. Finlay
   Marketing Assistant: Avril K Waye
   Marketing Coordinator: Cynthia Wood
   Director of Development: Lisa Dutton-Swain
   Director of Marketing: Margaret Blue Hamilton
   Business Manager: Carol Jones
Mission: To present performances of the highest quality through Worcester Music Festival, International Artist Series, Mass Jazz Festival and Music for Children; to educate all ages about music composers, history, etc.
Utilizes: Collaborations; Dance Companies; Guest Choreographers; Guest Directors; Guest Instructors; Guest Musical Directors; Guest Musicians; Multimedia; Original Music Scores; Sign Language Translators; Singers; Student Interns; Theatre Companies
Founded: 1858
Specialized Field: Classical Orchestras; Soloist; Chamber Ensembles; Jazz Groups; Dance Ensembles
Status: Nonprofit; Cultural Organization
Paid Staff: 5
Performs At: Mechanics Hall; Tuckerman Hall
Annual Attendance: 26,000
Facility Category: Concert Halls
Seating Capacity: 1,550 & 550 (2 stages)

Michigan

4816
ADRIAN COLLEGE EVENTS SERIES
Pellowe Hall
110 S Madison Street
Adrian, MI 49221
Phone: 517-265-5161
Fax: 517-264-3156
e-mail: mmoran@adrian.edu
Web Site: www.adrian.edu
Management:
   President: Stanley Paine
   Artistic Director: Thomas Hodzman
Founded: 1859
Specialized Field: Liberal Arts College
Status: Non-Profit, Non-Professional
Performs At: Dawson Auditorium

4817
ALBION PERFORMING ARTIST & LECTURE SERIES
Albion College
611 E Porter Street
Albion, MI 49224
Phone: 517-629-1000
Fax: 517-629-0566
Web Site: www.albion.edu
Management:
   President: Robert D. Musser III
   Executive Director: Joseph S. Calvaruso
   Executive Director: Faith E. Fowler
Founded: 1835
Performs At: Goodrich Chapel

4818
GRAND VALLEY STATE UNIVERSITY ARTS AT NOON SERIES
Grand Valley State University
1300 Performing Arts Center
Allendale, MI 49401

Phone: 616-895-3484
Fax: 616-895-3100
e-mail: worthemc@gvsu.edu
Web Site: www.gvsu.edu/music/arts-at-noon-197.htm
Management:
  Arts At Noon Coordinator: Julianne Vanden Wyngaard
Performs At: Louis Armstrong Theatre

4819
ALMA COLLEGE PERFORMING ARTS SERIES
Heritage Center
614 W Superior St.
Alma, MI 48801
Phone: 989-463-7111
Fax: 517-463-7277
e-mail: boxoffice@alma.edu
Web Site: www.alma.edu
Management:
  President: Dave Blanford
  Managing Director: Dave Young
Founded: 1993
Specialized Field: Musician; Lecture; Dance Groups; Theatre
Status: Non-Profit, Professional
Paid Staff: 12
Performs At: Heritage Center for the Performing Arts

4820
THUNDER BAY ARTS COUNCIL
127 W. Chisholm St.
Alpena, MI 49707
Phone: 989-356-6678
e-mail: tbartscouncil@frontier.com
Web Site: www.alpenatbarts.org
Officers:
  President: Tim Kuehnlein
  1st Vice-President: Roger Baumgardner
  2nd Vice-President: Clint Kendziorsk
  Secretary: Ruth LeBarre
  Treasurer: Marsette Dubie
Mission: The promotion of cultural arts through the coordination of events and the sponsoring of various performances.
Utilizes: Guest Artists; Guest Companies; Singers
Founded: 1971
Specialized Field: Dance; Vocal Music; Instrumental Music; Theatre; Lyric Opera
Status: Professional; Nonprofit
Organization Type: Educational; Sponsoring

4821
ANN ARBOR BLUES & JAZZ FESTIVAL
PO Box 7456
Ann Arbor, MI 48107
Phone: 734-747-9955
e-mail: info@jazzfest.org
Web Site: www.a2.blues.jazzfest.org

4822
ANN ARBOR SUMMER FESTIVAL
310 Depot Street
Suite 3
Ann Arbor, MI 48104
Phone: 734-994-5999
Fax: 734-994-5885
e-mail: info@a2sf.org
Web Site: www.annarborsummerfestival.org
Officers:
  Business Manager: Jeanne Rowlette
  Marketing Director: Colleen Murdock
  President: John C Clark
  Chairman: Anne K. Rubin
Management:
  President: Ingrid Sheldon
  Production Manager: Evy Warshawski
  Executive Director: Amy Nesbitt
  Operations Manager: Mike Michelon
  Development Director: Leslie Keeton
  Programs Assistant: Kari Dion
Mission: To offer both ticketed and free of charge performing arts events to Ann Arbor area residents.
Utilizes: Artists-in-Residence; Collaborating Artists; Dance Companies; Dancers; Guest Choreographers; Guest Directors; Guest Instructors; Guest Musicians; Lyricists; Multimedia; Original Music Scores; Sign Language Translators; Singers; Special Technical Talent; Theatre Companies
Founded: 1978
Specialized Field: Series and Festivals; Instrumental Music; Vocal Music; Theatre; Dance; Ethnic Performances; Festivals
Status: Non-Profit, Professional
Paid Staff: 5
Volunteer Staff: 100
Paid Artists: 75
Budget: $1,000,000
Income Sources: Donations from Businesses & Individuals; Grants
Performs At: Power Center; Lydia Mendelssohn; Top of the Park
Affiliations: University of Michigan; City of Ann Arbor
Annual Attendance: 50,000
Type of Stage: Thrust, Proscenium
Stage Dimensions: 40x60
Seating Capacity: 1,300
Organization Type: Performing; Sponsoring

4823
MICHIGAN ASSOCIATION OF COMMUNITY ARTS AGENCIES
107 Miller Avenue
Ann Arbor, MI 48099
Phone: 734-996-2500
Fax: 734-996-3317
Toll-free: 800-649-3777
e-mail: macaa@macaa.com
Web Site: www.macaa.com
Officers:
  President: Oliver Ragsdale, Jr.
Management:
  Executive Director: Deborah E Mikula
Mission: Exists to support, strengthen, and unite community arts and organizations in Michigan.
Founded: 1977
Specialized Field: Arts Service Organization
Status: Non-Profit
Paid Staff: 7

4824
MPULSE ANN ARBOR
1100 Baits Drive
1281 Moore Bldg
Ann Arbor, MI 48109-2085
Phone: 734-936-2660
Fax: 734-647-0140
Toll-free: 866-936-2660
e-mail: mpulse@umich.edu
Web Site: www.music.umich.edu/mpulse
Management:
  Program Manager: Sarah J. Rau
  Program Coordinator: Sigal Hemy
  Program Coordinator: Robin Myrick
Mission: MPulse Ann Arbor is a summer phenomenon on the University of Michigan xcampus carrying high school students to exciting new levels of excellence in usic performance, music technology, musical theatre, theatre and dance.

4825
MUSICAL SOCIETY OF THE UNIVERSITY SERIES
Burton Memorial Tower
881 N University
Ann Arbor, MI 48109-1011
Phone: 734-764-2538
Fax: 734-647-1171
Toll-free: 800-221-1239
e-mail: umstix@umich.edu
Web Site: www.ums.org
Officers:
  Chairperson: Beverley Geltner
  Vice Chair: Lester Monts
  Secretary: Pruuueu Rosentnal
  Treasurer: David Featherman
  President: Kenneth C. Fischer
Management:
  President: Ken Fisher
  Director Programming: Michael Kondziolka
  Director Administration: John Kennard
  Director Development: Christina Thoburn
  Director Education: Ben Johnson
Mission: To provide professional theatre, dance and music for Southeastern Michigan students and residents.
Utilizes: Singers; Special Technical Talent; Theatre Companies
Founded: 1879
Specialized Field: Series & Festivals: Musical Performance
Status: Non-Profit, Professional
Paid Staff: 30
Budget: $6,000,000
Income Sources: Ticket Sales; Fundraising
Performs At: Hill Auditorium; Power Center; Rackham Auditorium
Annual Attendance: 150,000
Organization Type: Performing; Educational

4826
BAY ARTS COUNCIL
901 N. Water St.
Bay City, MI 48708
Phone: 989-893-0343
Fax: 989-893-6443
e-mail: director@bayartscouncil.org
Web Site: www.bayartscouncil.org
Management:
  President: Cynthia Gracey
  Managing Director: Tom Niemann
Founded: 1978
Specialized Field: Series & Festivals; Vocal Music; Theatre; Youth; Dance
Status: Non-Profit, Professional
Paid Staff: 2
Volunteer Staff: 50
Paid Artists: 25
Non-paid Artists: 10

4827
BAY VIEW MUSIC FESTIVAL
PO Box 583
Bay View, MI 49770
Mailing Address: PO Box 1596, Bay View, MI 49770
Phone: 231-225-8877
e-mail: cludwa@gmail.com
Web Site: www.bayviewfestival.org

SERIES & FESTIVALS / Michigan

Management:
- **Artistic Director:** Chris Ludwa

Specialized Field: Vocal Music; Instrumental Music; Opera; Chamber Music; Chamber Orchestra; Theater

4828
FERRIS STATE UNIVERSITY-ARTS & LECTURES SERIES
1201 S State Street
CSS 208A
Big Rapids, MI 49307
Phone: 231-591-2340
Fax: 231-591-3067
Toll-free: 800-562-9130
e-mail: hadley-p@ferris.edu
Web Site: www.ferris.edu
Officers:
- **Chairman:** Daniel Cronk
- **Chairman:** J Randall Groves

Management:
- **President:** Davis Eisler
- **Executive Director:** Dan Cronk
- **Auditorium Manager:** Michael Terry

Utilizes: Dance Companies; Dancers; Fine Artists; Guest Musicians; Guest Soloists; Local Artists; Multimedia; Original Music Scores; Selected Students; Singers; Theatre Companies
Specialized Field: Series & Festivals; Instrumental Music; Vocal Music; Theatre; Youth; Dance; Ethnic Performances
Status: Non-Profit, Professional
Paid Staff: 2
Budget: $40,000
Income Sources: Ticket Sales; Donations; Grants
Performs At: Williams Auditorium
Affiliations: Michigan Nonprofit Presenters Network
Type of Stage: Proscenium
Seating Capacity: 1,800

4829
AMERICAN ARTISTS SERIES
435 Goodhue Road
Bloomfield Hills, MI 48304
Phone: 313-547-2230
Fax: 313-547-1525
Toll-free: 800-806-7206
Web Site: www.americanartistsseries.com
Management:
- **Executive Director:** Leonard Mazern
- **Artistic Director:** Joann Freeman
- **Business Manager:** Morton Malitz

Mission: Sponsoring diverse performing arts programs, which include guest artists and native musicians.
Utilizes: Dance Companies
Founded: 1970
Specialized Field: Instrumental Music; Theatre; Chamber Music
Status: Professional; Nonprofit
Performs At: Kingswood Auditorium
Organization Type: Performing; Touring; Sponsoring

4830
CRANBROOK MUSIC GUILD CONCERT SERIES
Cranbrook Music Guild
PO Box 402
Bloomfield Hills, MI 48303
Phone: 248-645-0256
e-mail: mail@cranbrookmusicguild.org
Web Site: www.cranbrookmusicguild.org
Officers:
- **Program Chairman:** Anita Demarco Goor
- **President:** William R Brashear

Management:
- **Contact:** Anita Goor

Specialized Field: Chamber Music
Performs At: Cranbrook House Library

4831
GOPHERWOOD CONCERT SERIES
4320 E. 46 Rd.
Cadillac, MI 49601
Phone: 231-846-8383
e-mail: pbrown@michweb.net
Web Site: www.users.michweb.net/~pbrown/gopherwood.htm
Performs At: Auditorium

4832
VILLAGE BACH FESTIVAL
P.O. Box 15126
Cass City, MI 92659
Phone: 949-548-8198
Fax: 517-872-2301
e-mail: info@luthertours.com
Web Site: www.luthertours.com/tours/item/122-music-art-and-culture.html
Mission: Promoting professional musical events in Michigan's Thumb Area.
Founded: 1979
Specialized Field: Vocal Music; Instrumental Music; Festivals
Status: Professional; Nonprofit
Organization Type: Performing

4833
CHEBOYGAN AREA ARTS COUNCIL/OPERA HOUSE
403 N Huron Street
Cheboygan, MI 49721
Phone: 231-627-5432
Fax: 231-627-3130
e-mail: pam@theoperahouse.org
Web Site: www.theoperahouse.org
Officers:
- **President:** Randy Maltby
- **Vice-President:** Sandra Jeannotte
- **Secretary:** Jane Roe
- **Treasurer:** Alice Barron

Management:
- **Executive Director:** Pam Westover
- **Manager:** Dolores Kozlowski
- **Box Office Manager:** Patty Corkwell

Founded: 1877
Status: Non-Profit, Professional

4834
CASA DE UNIDAS SERIES
P.O. Box 40115
Detroit, MI 55104
Phone: 651-646-.555
Fax: 313-843-7307
e-mail: info@casadeesperanza.org
Web Site: www.casadeunidad.org
Officers:
- **Executive Director:** Veronica A. Paiz

Management:
- **Program Coordinator:** Marta Lagos

Mission: Providing community-based, performing arts presentations for Detroit's Hispanic communities.
Utilizes: Guest Companies; Singers
Founded: 1981
Specialized Field: Series & Festivals; Dance; Vocal Music; Instrumental Music; Theatre; Youth
Status: Non-Profit, Non-Professional
Paid Staff: 10
Performs At: Clark Park Theatre
Organization Type: Performing; Touring; Educational; Sponsoring

4835
DETROIT FESTIVAL OF THE ARTS
4735 Cass Avenue
Detroit, MI 48202
Phone: 313-577-5088
Fax: 313-577-3332
e-mail: maureen.riley@wayne.edu
Web Site: www.detroitfestival.com
Officers:
- **President:** Susan Mosey

Management:
- **President:** Sue Mosey
- **Executive Director:** Moreen Riley
- **Artistic Director:** Njia Kai

Mission: To encourage use of the University Cultural Center of Detroit, and introduce the resources of the area to the metropoliton community.
Founded: 1976
Specialized Field: Series & Festivals: Music
Status: Non-Profit, Professional
Paid Staff: 7
Volunteer Staff: 400
Paid Artists: 60
Non-paid Artists: 150
Budget: 1,300,000
Income Sources: Corporate; Private; State
Performs At: Outdoors; 20 Blocks
Affiliations: Wayne State University and University Cultural Center Association
Annual Attendance: 300,000
Facility Category: Various Outdoor Venues
Type of Stage: 3 Main, 1 Childrens, 2 Coffeehouses

4836
FORD DETROIT INTERNATIONAL JAZZ FESTIVAL
660 Woodward Ave.
Ste. 13
Detroit, MI 48226
Phone: 313-447-1144
Fax: 313-447-1145
Web Site: www.detroitjazzfest.com
Management:
- **President:** Cameron Duncan
- **Artistic Director:** Frank Malfitano
- **Managing Director:** Jeff Wilson
- **Director Media Relations:** Michael Vigilant

Mission: Preserving, promoting and maintaining the understanding and appreciation of jazz music.
Founded: 1980
Specialized Field: Series & Festivals: Jazz
Status: Non-Profit, Professional
Annual Attendance: 770,000
Facility Category: Outdoor Festival
Organization Type: Performing; Sponsoring

4837
SYRACUSE JAZZ FESTIVAL
#2815
Detroit, MI 48226
Phone: 313-961-2166
Fax: 313-961-2177
e-mail: info@syracusejazzfest.com
Web Site: www.syracusejazzfest.com

4838
UNITED BLACK ARTISTS: USA SERIES
7661 Lasalle Boulevard
Detroit, MI 48206

SERIES & FESTIVALS / Michigan

Phone: 313-898-5574
Fax: 313-898-5574
Management:
  President: Robert Warren
  Volunteer Artistic Director: Ann Marshall
Mission: Encouraging cultural opportunities and education among Detroit's black communities.
Founded: 1987
Specialized Field: Promotions Of Potential Black Artists
Status: Non-Profit, Non-Professional
Paid Staff: 20
Income Sources: Harmony Park Playhouse
Organization Type: Educational; Sponsoring

4839
FLINT INSTITUTE OF MUSIC
1025 E Kearsley Street
Flint, MI 48503
Phone: 810-238-1350
Fax: 810-238-6385
Toll-free: 800-395-4849
e-mail: fim@thefim.com
Web Site: www.flintinstituteofmusic.com
Officers:
  President: Paul Torre
Management:
  President: Paul Torre
  Marketing Director: Andrew Ward
  Director Flint School Performing: Davin Piersontorre
  Manager Flint Symphony: Tom Glasscok
  Director Ticket: Linda Tomlinson
  Director Development: Carol Hartley
  Director: Wendy Bloom
Mission: Providing a lifelong continuum of music and dance.
Utilizes: Guest Artists; Singers
Founded: 1917
Specialized Field: Music
Status: Non-Profit, Professional
Paid Artists: 75
Performs At: Whiting Auditorium
Annual Attendance: 3,500

4840
MUSIC IN THE PARKS
1784 W. Schuylkill Road
Flint, MI 19518
Fax: 610-327-4786
Toll-free: 800-323-0974
e-mail: info@edprog.com
Web Site: www.educationalprograms.com/frame_mitp.html
Management:
  President: Dr James R Wells
  Program Coordinator: Kathy Bird

4841
GAYLORD AREA COUNCIL FOR THE ARTS
319 W Main
Gaylord, MI 49735
Phone: 989-732-4000
Toll-free: 800-345-8621
e-mail: nordeen@avci.net
Web Site: www.gaylordchamber.com/
Officers:
  Chairman: Jenni A. Caverson
  Vice-Chair: Paul Gunderson
  Treasurer: Kevin Reynolds
  Immidiate Past-Chairman: Justin Kowatch
Management:
  Manager: Kate Nordeen
  Executive Director: Paul Beachnau
  Special Events Coordinator: Tiffany Larson
  Administrative Receptionist: Stephanie Lesage
  Membership Services Coordinator: Gayla FitzGerald
  Information Center Coordinator: Pam Anthony
  Information Specialist: Jean Morris
Performs At: Auditorium

4842
FESTIVAL OF THE ARTS
650 Laguna Canyon Road
161 Ottawa NW #300
Grand Rapids, MI 92651
Phone: 949-494-1145
Fax: 616-459-7160
Web Site: www.foapom.com/
Management:
  Executive Director: Tammy Ramaker
Mission: To support the arts and artists of the Greater Grand Rapids Community; to promote and support the arts financially and through technical assistance to organizations or individuals; to promote experiences for participants and observers from within the general public.
Utilizes: Instructors
Founded: 1970
Specialized Field: Dance; Vocal Music; Instrumental Music; Theater; Festivals
Status: Professional; Nonprofit
Paid Staff: 3000
Budget: $300,000
Performs At: Calder Plaza
Annual Attendance: 300,000
Organization Type: Sponsoring
Resident Groups: Regional artists only

4843
REIF ARTS CENTER
720 Conifer Drive
Grand Rapids, MI 55744
Phone: 218-327-5780
Fax: 218-327-5798
e-mail: dmarty@reifcenter.org
Web Site: www.reifcenter.org
Officers:
  Board Chair: Scott Larson
  President: David Marty
  Vice Chair: Dan Margo
  Secretary: Cathy Shields
  Treasurer: Gene Baker
  At-Large: Barb McDonald
  Past Chair: Kirk Adams
Management:
  President: David Marty, dmarty@reifcenter.org
  Marketing: Katie Benes
  Development: Jeremy Dewey
  Box Office Manager: Patti Hadersbeck
  Bookkeeper: Pat Hoff
  Technical Director: John Miller
Mission: Stimulating arts in Northern Minnesota.
Founded: 1981
Opened: 1981
Specialized Field: Series and Festivals; Instrumental Music; Vocal Music; Theatre; Youth; Dance; Ethnic Performances; Multi-Disciplinary
Status: Non-Profit, Professional
Paid Staff: 8
Paid Artists: 150
Budget: $980,000
Income Sources: Sales; Grants; Tuition
Annual Attendance: 24,000
Type of Stage: Proscenium; Modified Thrust
Stage Dimensions: 50' x 38'
Seating Capacity: 642
Year Built: 1981
Year Remodeled: 2005
Rental Contact: John Miller

4844
GROSSE POINTE WAR MEMORIAL
32 Lake Shore Drive
Grosse Pointe Farms, MI 48236
Phone: 313-881-7511
Fax: 313-884-6638
e-mail: mweber@warmemorial.org
Web Site: www.warmemorial.org
Management:
  President: Mark R Weber
  Community Relations and Development: Teri L Carroll
  Finance Director: Elizabeth A Berry
  Director Lifelong Learning: Lou Anne Wattrick
Mission: To offer outdoor performances in the summer via Summer Music Festival and other events during the year.
Utilizes: Guest Artists; Singers
Founded: 1949
Specialized Field: Vocal Music; Instrumental Music; Theater; Festivals; Lyric Opera
Status: Professional; Nonprofit
Performs At: Terrace of Alger House
Organization Type: Performing; Touring; Resident

4845
PINE MOUNTAIN MUSIC FESTIVAL
PO Box 406
Hancock, MI 49930
Phone: 906-482-1542
Toll-free: 888-309-7861
e-mail: festival@pmmf.org
Web Site: www.pmmf.org
Officers:
  President: Candace E. Koski Janners
  Vice President: Dr. Sigurds Janners
  Secretary: Michael Neuman
  Treasurer: David Geisler
Management:
  Executive Director: Peter Van Pelt
  Artistic Director: Joshua Major
  Bookkeeper: Karen Fredrickson
  Manager of Festival Services: Eric Eckerberg
Mission: Serve upper Midwest with opera, symphony, and chamber music during June and July.
Founded: 1991
Specialized Field: Series & Festivals; Instrumental Music; Vocal Music; Youth; Classical Music; Opera Symphony Chamber
Status: Non-Profit, Professional
Paid Staff: 4
Volunteer Staff: 200
Paid Artists: 100
Budget: $500,000
Income Sources: Grants; Box Office; Donations; Foundations
Performs At: Rented Theaters
Affiliations: Opera America
Annual Attendance: 8,000
Facility Category: Various

4846
HOLLAND AREA ARTS COUNCIL
150 East 8th Street
Holland, MI 49423
Phone: 616-396-3278
Fax: 616-396-6298
Web Site: www.hollandarts.org/
Officers:

SERIES & FESTIVALS / Michigan

President: Patricia Flynn
Vice President: Dennis Foley
Vice President: Mike Dunlap
Treasurer: Kenneth Breese
Secretary: Anne Gaskin Nemschoff
Management:
    Executive Director: Lorma Williams Freestone
    Program Director: Mary Sundstrom
    Communications & Volunteer Coordina: Margaret Foreman
    Business Manager: Carol Vredeveld
    Membership Care: Tennina Miozza
    Regranting Administrator Events Coo: Lori Gramer

4847
HOPE COLLEGE GREAT PERFORMANCE SERIES
Hope College
PO Box 9000
Holland, MI 49422-9000
Phone: 616-395-7893
Fax: 616-395-7191
e-mail: emerson@hope.edu
Web Site: www.hope.edu/arts
Management:
    President: Jim Boltman
    Executive Director: Derek Emerson
Utilizes: Actors; Artists-in-Residence; Dance Companies; Dancers; Multimedia; Playwrights; Special Technical Talent
Founded: 1975
Specialized Field: Series & Festivals; Chamber Music; Dance; Theatre
Status: Non-Profit, Professional
Paid Staff: 1
Paid Artists: 6
Performs At: DeWitt Center
Annual Attendance: 4000
Facility Category: 3 different venues

4848
MICHIGAN RENAISSANCE FESTIVAL
12600 Dixie Highway
Holly, MI 48442
Phone: 248-634-5552
Fax: 248-634-7590
Toll-free: 800-601-4848
e-mail: renaissancegraphics@comcast.net
Web Site: www.michrenfest.com
Management:
    General Manager: Kathy Parker
    Site Operations/Special Events: Jason Parker
    Marketing Coordinator: Anna Peterson
    Marketing Coordinator: Kim Heidger
    Sales Manager: Kim Petit
    Entertainment Director: Maria Christian
    Craft Coordinator: April Corey
    Graphic Designer & Webmaster: Sarah Kladzyk
Mission: Promoting Renaissance traditions in the area of Southeastern Michigan.
Founded: 1980
Specialized Field: Dance; Vocal Music; Instrumental Music; Theater; Festivals
Status: Professional; Commercial
Paid Staff: 30
Volunteer Staff: 200
Paid Artists: 100
Non-paid Artists: 100
Performs At: Hollygrove; Holly
Organization Type: Performing

4849
MTU/GREAT EVENTS SERIES
1400 Townsend Drive
Center Room 106
Houghton, MI 49931
Phone: 906-487-2067
Fax: 906-487-1841
e-mail: vpa@mtu.edu
Web Site: www.greatevents.mtu.edu
Management:
    Director Great Events: Valerie Pegg
Utilizes: Actors; Artists-in-Residence; Collaborations; Commissioned Music; Dance Companies; Dancers; Fine Artists; Grant Writers; Guest Accompanists; Guest Choreographers; Guest Composers; Guest Designers; Guest Instructors; Guest Lecturers; Guest Musical Directors; Guest Musicians; Guest Soloists; Instructors; Local Artists; Local Unknown Artists; Multimedia; Music; Organization Contracts; Original Music Scores; Playwrights; Resident Artists; Resident Professionals; Selected Students; Sign Language Translators; Singers; Soloists; Student Interns; Special Technical Talent; Theatre Companies; Visual Arts
Specialized Field: Performing; Educational
Paid Staff: 7
Volunteer Staff: 60
Budget: $130,000
Income Sources: Box Office; Grants; Private Donations
Performs At: Performing Arts Theatre; Concert Hall
Facility Category: Performing Arts Center
Seating Capacity: 1,101
Year Built: 2000
Rental Contact: Kelly Thomas

4850
INTERLOCHEN CENTER FOR ARTS
4000 Highway M-137
Interlochen, MI 49643
Mailing Address: PO Box 199 Interlochen, MI 49643-0199
Phone: 231-276-7200
Fax: 231-276-7442
e-mail: woodwr@interlochen.org
Web Site: www.interlochen.org
Management:
    President: Jeffrey Kimpton
    Executive Director: William Wood
    Artistic Director: Tim Wade
    Managing Director: Jennifer Weising
Founded: 1928
Specialized Field: All Kinds of Arts; Summercamp
Status: Non-Profit, Non-Professional
Paid Staff: 198
Paid Artists: 50

4851
MICHIGAN SHAKESPEARE FESTIVAL
2111 Emmons Road
Jackson, MI 49203
Phone: 517-788-5032
Fax: 517-788-5254
Toll-free: 866-705-2636
e-mail: thebard@michshakefest.org
Web Site: www.michshakefest.org
Officers:
    President: Ann Green
    VP: Tom Mitchell
    Secretary: Rick Davies
    Treasurer: Margaret Musser
Management:
    Artistic Director: Janice L Blixt
    President: Rick Davies
    VP: Jennifer Brunk
    Managing Director: Julie Dougherty Brunzell
Mission: Quality outdoor Shakespeare.
Founded: 1995
Status: For-Profit, Professional
Paid Staff: 8
Volunteer Staff: 6
Paid Artists: 60
Season: July - August
Type of Stage: Thrust
Stage Dimensions: 40' x 30'
Seating Capacity: 350

4852
BACH FESTIVAL SOCIETY OF KALAMAZOO
Kalamazoo College
1200 Academy Street
Kalamazoo, MI 49006-3295
Phone: 269-337-7407
Fax: 269-337-7407
e-mail: bach@kzoo.edu
Web Site: www.kalamazoobachfestival.org/
Officers:
    President: Fred Sang
    Vice President: Gordon Bolar
    Secretary: Victor Garcia
    Treasurer: Nijole Botyrius
Management:
    Music Director: James Turner

4853
FONTANA FESTIVAL OF MUSIC & ART
Fontana Concert Society
821 W South Street
Kalamazoo, MI 49007
Phone: 616-382-0826
Fax: 616-382-0812
e-mail: fontana@iserv.net
Web Site: www.fontanafestival.org
Officers:
    Chairman: Thomas C. Bailey
    Vice Chairman: Thomas Seiler
    Treasurer: Dave Rozelle
    Secretary: Lee Kirk
Management:
    Executive Director: David Baldwin
    General Manager: Jill Perney
    Artistic Administrator: Betsy Bogner Wong
    Operations Coordinator: Charlie Tomlinson
    Accounting Assistant: Terri Hunter

4854
IRVING S GILMORE INTERNATIONAL KEYBOARD FESTIVAL
359 S Kalamazoo Mall
Suite 101
Kalamazoo, MI 49007
Phone: 269-342-1166
Fax: 269-342-0968
Toll-free: 855-845-1768
e-mail: gilmore@gilmore.org
Web Site: www.gilmore.org
Officers:
    President: Frank J. Sardone
    Vice President: Donald Parfet
    Secretary: Janice M. Brown
    Treasurer: Michael L. Mueller
Management:
    Director Of Development: Alice Kemerling
    Director: Dan Gustin
    Operations Director: Dan Gustin

Director Public Relations and Marke: Mary McCormick
Box Office Manager/Secretary: Diane Gill
Director of Finance: Cindy VanDenBerg
Director of Operations: Maria Schneider
Director of Education: Adam Schumaker
Development and Finance Assistant: Terri Hunter
Mission: Identifying and supporting concert pianists; producing a biennial festival.
Utilizes: Collaborations; Commissioned Composers; Guest Directors; Guest Musical Directors; Guest Musicians; Guest Soloists; Multimedia; Organization Contracts; Original Music Scores; Singers
Founded: 1989
Specialized Field: Festivals
Status: Nonprofit
Paid Staff: 10
Income Sources: Association of Performing Arts Presenters
Performs At: Miller Auditorium; Dalton Center Recital Hall; others
Annual Attendance: Biennial Festival
Resident Groups: Gilmore Artist; Gilmore Young Artists

4855
NEW YEAR'S FEST
141 E. Michigan Ave.
Suite 100
Kalamazoo, MI 49007
Phone: 269-388-2830
Fax: 616-388-2830
e-mail: deb@eventkalamazoo.com
Web Site: www.newyearsfest.com/
Officers:
  President: Larry Potter
  Vice President/Entertainment Chair: David Overton
  Recording Secretary: Steve Ellis
  Treasurer: Brenda Keelan
Mission: To offer an alcohol-free celebration of New Year's Eve featuring performing arts to Kalamazoo.
Founded: 1986
Specialized Field: Dance; Vocal Music; Instrumental Music; Theatre; Festivals; Lyric Opera
Status: Nonprofit
Organization Type: Festival

4856
MATRIX: MIDLAND FESTIVAL-CELEBRATION OF THE ARTS, SCIENCES & HUMANITIES
1801 W. Saint Andrews Road
Midland, MI 48640
Phone: 989-631-5930
Fax: 989-631-7890
Toll-free: 800-523-7649
e-mail: sabin@mcfta.org
Web Site: www.mcfta.org
Officers:
  Chair: Lee Rouse
  Immediate Past Chair: David Ramaker
  Vice-Chair: Bill Collins
  Treasurer: Brian Rodgers
  Secretary: Melissa Barnard
Management:
  President: Michael Hayes
  Executive Director: Dick Jellum
  Managing Director: Phyllis B Sabin
  IT Manager: Penny Tabor
  House Manager: Katy Gaertner
  Special Events & Marketing Coordina: Mara Simanskey
  Communications Manager: Julie Dukes
  Facilities Director: Larry Salva
Mission: To encourage creativity of the highest level in the arts, sciences, humanities and all aspects of their interelationships.
Founded: 1978
Specialized Field: Series & Festivals; Arts; Theatre; Museum
Paid Staff: 40
Budget: $250,000
Income Sources: Corporate Sponsorships
Annual Attendance: 12,000

4857
CROOKED TREE ARTS COUNCIL
461 E Mitchell Street
Petoskey, MI 49770
Phone: 231-347-4337
Fax: 231-347-5414
e-mail: liz@crookedtree.org
Web Site: www.crookedtree.org
Officers:
  President: Phoebea Wietzke
  VP: Stephen Palmer
  Treasurer: Richard Lent
  Secretary: Jane Miller
Management:
  President: Steve Palmer
  Executive Director: Liz Ahrens
  Artistic Director: Gail DeMeyere
  Marketing Director: Elizabeth Ahrens
Mission: To sponsor and encourage cultural and educational activities in the fine arts for Charlevoix and Emmet Counties.
Founded: 1972
Specialized Field: Visual and Performing Arts
Status: Non-Profit, Professional
Paid Staff: 10
Paid Artists: 4
Income Sources: National Guild of Community Schools of the Arts; Michigan Association of Community Arts Agencies; Michigan Council on the Arts
Performs At: Crooked Tree Arts Center
Annual Attendance: 50,000
Year Remodeled: 2002
Organization Type: Performing; Educational; Sponsoring

4858
TEMPLE THEATRE ORGAN CLUB
315 Court Street
Saginaw, MI 48602
Phone: 517-754-2575
Fax: 517-793-7225
Management:
  General Manager: Ken Wuepper
Mission: Restoring the Temple Theatre and reestablishing it as a prominent performing arts center.
Founded: 1960
Status: Nonprofit
Organization Type: Educational; Sponsoring; Historic Preservation

4859
LAKE SUPERIOR STATE UNIVERSITY CULTURAL EVENTS SERIES
Lake Superior State Univesity
650 W. Easterday Ave
Sault Sainte Marie, MI 49783
Phone: 906-635-2665
Fax: 906-635-2856
e-mail: foundation@lssu.edu
Web Site: www.lssu.edu/
Officers:
  Cultural Events Chairman: John Wilkinson
Management:
  Executive Director: Tom Coates
  Director of Constituent Relations: Sharon Dorrity
  Director of Alumni Relations: Susan Fitzpatrick
  Director of Development: Virginia Zinser
Performs At: Auditoriums

4860
WEST SHORE COMMUNITY COLLEGE CULTURAL SERIES
3000 N Stiles Road
Scottville, MI 49454
Phone: 231-845-6211
Fax: 231-843-2680
Toll-free: 800-848-9722
e-mail: contactus@westshore.edu
Web Site: www.westshore.edu
Officers:
  Chair: James Jensen
  Vice Chair: Michael Ennis
  Treasurer: Bruce C. Smith
  Secretary: Richard M. Wilson, Jr.
Management:
  President: Charles Dillon
  VP: Virginia Fox
  Managing Director: Tom Davis
  Cultural Arts Director: Rick Plummer
Specialized Field: Education
Status: Non-Profit, Professional
Paid Staff: 150
Volunteer Staff: 2
Paid Artists: 19
Non-paid Artists: 35
Performs At: Media Center Auditorium
Annual Attendance: 12,000+
Type of Stage: Thrust
Seating Capacity: 279
Year Built: 1971
Year Remodeled: 1999

4861
GREAT LAKES CHAMBER MUSIC FESTIVAL
20300 Civic Center Drive
Suite 100
Southfield, MI 48076
Phone: 248-559-2097
Fax: 248-559-2098
e-mail: info@greatlakeschambermusic.com
Web Site: www.greatlakeschambermusic.com
Management:
  Executive Director: Maury Okun
  Artistic Director: James Tocco
Founded: 1994
Specialized Field: Series & Festivals; Instrumental Music; Vocal Music; Youth
Status: Non-Profit, Professional
Paid Staff: 4

4862
DOWNRIVER COUNCIL FOR THE ARTS
Downriver Council for the Arts
81 Chestnut
Taylor, MI 48192
Phone: 734-720-0671
Fax: 734-720-0672
e-mail: dc4arts@downriverarts.org
Web Site: www.downriverarts.org
Management:
  Executive Director: Tammy Trudelle
  Gallery Director: Martine MacDonald
  Office Manager: Lynn Campbell

SERIES & FESTIVALS / Minnesota

Mission: Promoting a range of the fine and performing arts in Downriver communities.
Utilizes: Collaborations; Guest Artists; Guest Writers; New Productions; Singers; Touring Companies
Founded: 1978
Specialized Field: Dance; Vocal Music; Instrumental Music; Theater; Festivals
Status: Professional; Nonprofit
Paid Staff: 35
Income Sources: Grants, Donations, Membership
Organization Type: Educational; Sponsoring

4863
SAGINAW VALLEY STATE UNIVERSITY CONCERT: LECTURE SERIES

Campus Life
7400 Bay Road
University Center, MI 48710
Phone: 989-964-4000
Fax: 517-249-1695
e-mail: ebusch@tardis.svsu.edu
Web Site: www.svsu.edu/fallfocus/
Management:
   Director: Eric Buschlen
Seating Capacity: 400

4864
WATERFORD CULTURAL COUNCIL

5860 Andersonville Road
Waterford, MI 48329-1510
Phone: 248-623-9389
Fax: 248-623-7907
e-mail: waterfordcc@earthlink.net
Web Site: www.waterford.wb.mi.us/win/ncc
Management:
   President: Marleen Rudolph
   Program Director: Debra Berry
Mission: To strenthen, enrich and unite the community through the arts.
Founded: 1994
Specialized Field: Series & Festivals; Instrumental Music; Performing; Visual
Status: Non-Profit, Professional
Paid Staff: 4
Volunteer Staff: 120
Paid Artists: 4
Budget: $260,000
Income Sources: United Way; Waterford Township; Waterford Schools
Performs At: Waterford Mott High School Auditorium
Annual Attendance: 16,000
Facility Category: Performance Arena
Seating Capacity: 650

Minnesota

4865
ALEXANDRIA FESTIVAL OF THE LAKES

610 Fillmore Street
Suite 6
Alexandria, MN 56308
Phone: 320-762-5666
Fax: 320-762-8246
e-mail: tickets@rea-alp.com
Web Site: www.AlexFest.org
Management:
   Artistic Director: Nina Tobias
Founded: 1993
Specialized Field: Chamber Music

4866
HOBSON UNION PROGRAMING BOARD PERFORMING ARTISTS SERIES

Bemidji State University
1500 Birchmont Avenue NE
Bemidji, MN 56601-2699
Phone: 218-755-2001
Fax: 218-755-4048
Toll-free: 800-475-2001
e-mail: hupb@hotmail.com
Web Site: www.bemidjistate.edu
Management:
   President: Sara Lewanbowski
   Executive Director: Lauralynn Keuchle
Specialized Field: Series & Festivals; Instrumental Music; Vocal Music
Status: Non-Profit, Non-Professional
Paid Staff: 1
Paid Artists: 1
Performs At: Various Auditoriums

4867
COLLEGE OF ST. SCHOLASTICA MITCHELL AUDITORIUM

1200 Kenwood Avenue
Duluth, MN 55811-4199
Phone: 218-723-6000
Fax: 218-723-6290
Toll-free: 800-447-5444
e-mail: ngawinsk@css.edu
Web Site: www.css.edu
Management:
   President: Larry Goodwin
   Office Assistant: LeAnn Jopke
Utilizes: Actors; Artists-in-Residence; Collaborations; Commissioned Composers; Commissioned Music; Dance Companies; Dancers; Educators; Fine Artists; Guest Accompanists; Guest Instructors; Guest Musical Directors; Guest Musicians; Guest Soloists; Guild Activities; Instructors; Local Artists; Multi Collaborations; Multimedia; Organization Contracts; Original Music Scores; Playwrights; Selected Students; Sign Language Translators; Singers; Soloists; Special Technical Talent; Theatre Companies; Touring Companies
Founded: 1912
Paid Staff: 12
Performs At: Mitchell Auditorium
Annual Attendance: 38,000
Facility Category: Orchestra Hall/Arts Center
Type of Stage: Sprung Wood Maple Dance Floor
Stage Dimensions: 30 deep X 60 wide
Seating Capacity: 585
Year Built: 1993
Cost: $4.6 million
Rental Contact: Director Neil A. Gawinski

4868
REIF GREENWAY SERIES

720 NW Conifer Drive
Grand Rapids, MN 55744
Phone: 218-327-5780
Fax: 218-327-5798
e-mail: dmarty@reifcenter.org
Web Site: www.reifcenter.org
Officers:
   Board Chair: Scott Larson
   Vice Chair: Dan Margo
   Secretary: Cathy Shields
   Treasurer: Gene Baker
   At-Large: Barb McDonald
   Past Chair: Kirk Adams
Management:
   President: David Marty

   Executive Director: David Marty
   Marketing: Katie Benes
   Development: Jeremy Dewey
   Box Office Manager: Patti Hadersbeck
   Bookkeeper: Pat Hoff
   Technical Director: John Miller
Mission: Stimulating arts in Northern Minnesota.
Founded: 1980
Specialized Field: Musical Theatre
Status: Non-Profit, Non-Professional
Paid Staff: 10
Budget: $520,000
Income Sources: Box Office; Grants; Foundations
Annual Attendance: 12,500
Facility Category: Auditorium
Type of Stage: Modified Thrust
Stage Dimensions: 45 x 46 (curtain lines)
Seating Capacity: 645
Year Built: 1980
Year Remodeled: 1999
Rental Contact: John Miller
Organization Type: Presenting

4869
BETHANY LUTHERAN COLLEGE CONCERTS & LECTURES

700 Luther Drive
Mankato, MN 56001-6163
Phone: 507-344-7000
Fax: 507-344-7380
Toll-free: 800-944-3066
e-mail: ljaeger@blc.edu
Web Site: www.blc.edu
Officers:
   President: Dan R. Bruss, Ph.D.
Management:
   Fine Arts Director: Lois Jaeger
   Admissions Counselor: Tom Flunker
   Admissions Counselor: Dan Gerdts
   Admissions Counselor: Dan Gerdts
   Director of Admissions: Dan Tomhave
Founded: 1927
Specialized Field: Series & Festivals: Chamber Performances and Theatre Performances
Status: Non-Profit, Non-Professional
Paid Staff: 10
Paid Artists: 10
Performs At: Theatre

4870
INTERMEDIA ARTS

2822 Lyndale Avenue South
Minneapolis, MN 55408-2108
Phone: 612-871-4444
Fax: 612-871-6927
e-mail: info@IntermediaArts.org
Web Site: www.intermediaarts.org
Officers:
   Board Chair: Andrea Jenkins
   Vice Chair: Mark Waller
   Secretary: Beth Daniels
   Treasurer: Jeff Gatesmith
Management:
   Executive Director: Theresa Sweetland
   Artistic Director: Sandy Agustin
   Associate Director: Julie Bates
   Director of Youth Development: Michael Hay
   Production Manger: Jake Davis
   Programs & Communications Coordinat: Jessie Roelofs
   Community Engagement Coordinator: Nicole M. Smith
Mission: Intermedia Arts is a catalyst that builds understanding among people through art.

SERIES & FESTIVALS / Minnesota

Founded: 1973

4871
MINNEAPOLIS PARK & RECREATION BOARD-SUMMER MUSIC IN THE PARKS
2117 West River Road
Minneapolis, MN 55411-1400
Phone: 612-230-6400
Fax: 612-230-6500
e-mail: concerts@minneapolisparks.org
Web Site: www.minneapolisparks.org
Officers:
   Board President: Jon Olson
Management:
   Concert Coordinator: Goeff Walsh
   Concert/Events Coordinator: Jessica Berg
Founded: 1883
Specialized Field: Parks Center Recreation
Status: Non-Profit, Non-Professional
Paid Staff: 20

4872
UNIVERSITY OF MINNESOTA AT MINNEAPOLIS SERIES
84 Church Street SE
Suite 90
Minneapolis, MN 55455
Phone: 612-625-6600
Fax: 612-626-1750
e-mail: northrop@umn.edu
Web Site: www.northrop.umn.edu
Management:
   President: Dale Schatzlein
   Operations Manager: Sally Dischinger
Specialized Field: Series & Festivals: Dance & Jazz
Status: Non-Profit, Professional
Paid Staff: 13
Performs At: Northrop Memorial Auditorium

4873
VOCALESSENCE
1900 Nicollet Avenue
Minneapolis, MN 55403
Phone: 612-547-1451
Fax: 612-547-1484
e-mail: info@vocalessence.org
Web Site: www.vocalessence.org
Officers:
   President: Paul Pribbenow, Ph.D.
   Vice President: Kathryn Roberts
   Treasurer: Mike McCarthy
   Secretary: Susan J. Crockett, Ph. D
Management:
   Artistic Director: Philip Brunelle
   Managing Director: Mary Ann Pulk
   Executive Director: Mary Ann Aufderheido
   Education Manager and Music Librari: Robert Graham
   Development and Marketing Associate: Laura Holst
   Operations Manager and Executive As: Joel Swearingen
   Director of Development and Communi: Katrina Wallmyer
   Grants & Special Events Manager: Elissa Weller
Mission: The presentation of newly commissioned choral and orchestral works.
Founded: 1969
Specialized Field: Vocal Music: Choral Music
Status: Non-Profit, Professional
Paid Staff: 9
Paid Artists: 32
Non-paid Artists: 75
Budget: 1.2 million
Affiliations: Chorus America; IFCM
Organization Type: Performing; Educational; Sponsoring
Resident Groups: Ensamble Singers

4874
ALLIED CONCERT SERVICES
3535 Plymouth Boulevard
Suite 212
Minnetonka, MN 55447
Phone: 763-559-8019
Fax: 763-559-8030
Web Site: www.alliedconcertservices.com/
Officers:
   President: Paul Folin
Management:
   President: Paul Folin
Founded: 1947
Specialized Field: Series & Festivals; Instrumental Music; Vocal Music; Theatre; Youth; Dance; Ethnic Performances
Status: For-Profit, Professional
Paid Staff: 4

4875
CONCORDIA COLLEGE CULTURAL EVENTS SERIES
901 8th St S
Moorhead, MN 56562
Phone: 218-299-4000
Fax: 218-299-3191
e-mail: info@cord.edu
Web Site: www.cord.edu
Management:
   President of the University: Pamela Jolicouer
   Director of Cultural Events Series: Lowell Larson
Founded: 1985
Specialized Field: Series & Festivals; Instrumental Music; Vocal Music; Youth; Dance; Ethnic Performances; Performing Skits
Status: Non-Profit, Professional
Paid Staff: 2
Paid Artists: 8

4876
MINNESOTA STATE UNIVERSITY MOOREHEAD SERIES
250D Bridges Hall
1104 7th Ave South
Moorhead, MN 56563
Phone: 218-477-2271
Fax: 218-287-5037
e-mail: wigtil@mnstate.edu
Web Site: www.mnstate.edu/perform
Management:
   President: Roland Barden
   Executive Director: Craig Ellingson
Mission: To provide cultural programming of the highest calibre to the community and campus audiences.
Utilizes: Collaborations; Dance Companies; Dancers; Multi Collaborations; Multimedia; Original Music Scores; Singers; Special Technical Talent; Theatre Companies
Founded: 1930
Specialized Field: Series and Festivals; Dance; Theatre; Music
Status: Non-profit, Professional
Paid Staff: 5
Budget: $80,000
Performs At: Center for the Arts
Annual Attendance: 5,000
Facility Category: Center for the Arts
Type of Stage: Proscenium
Stage Dimensions: 41'x22'x33'
Seating Capacity: 850
Year Built: 1963
Organization Type: Performing; Educational; Sponsoring

4877
UNIVERSITY OF MINNESOTA MORRIS CAC PERFORMING ARTS SERIES
Office of Student Activities, UMM
600 East Fourth Street
Morris, MN 56267-2134
Phone: 320-589-6050
Fax: 320-589-6084
e-mail: urel@morris.umn.edu
Web Site: www.morris.umn.edu
Management:
   Graphic Designer: Kari Adams
   Project Manager: Megan Welle
   Editor/Writer: Jenna Ray
   Director: Mellissa Weber
Performs At: Edson Auditorium

4878
CARLETON COLLEGE CONCERT SERIES
One North College Street
Northfield, MN 55057
Phone: 507-222-4000
Fax: 507-633-4347
e-mail: admissions@carleton.edu
Web Site: www.carleton.edu/
Management:
   Concert Manager: Harry Nordstrom
Mission: Providing excellently performed music; offering an educational program.
Founded: 1945
Specialized Field: Vocal Music; Instrumental Music
Status: Professional; Nonprofit
Performs At: Carleton Concert Hall; Skinner Chapel
Organization Type: Educational; Sponsoring

4879
ST. OLAF COLLEGE ARTIST SERIES
1520 St. Olaf Avenue
St Olaf College
Northfield, MN 55057-1098
Phone: 507-786-2222
Fax: 507-646-3527
Toll-free: 800-363-5487
e-mail: music@stloaf.edu
Web Site: www.stolaf.edu
Management:
   President: Christopher Thomforde
   Music Organizations Manager: Bj Johnson
Founded: 1912
Specialized Field: Series & Festivals; Music; Band Choir
Status: Non-Profit, Non-Professional
Paid Staff: 60
Performs At: Skoglund Auditorium

4880
ROCHESTER CIVIC MUSIC
201 4th Street SE
Suite 170
Rochester, MN 55904
Phone: 507-328-2000
Fax: 507-328-2202
Toll-free: 800-657-3980
e-mail: info@riversideconcerts.com
Web Site: www.riversideconcerts.com
Officers:
   Band & Choir Director: Charles E. Blattner

SERIES & FESTIVALS / Mississippi

Management:
  General Manager: Steven J Schmidt
  Assistant General Manager: Chris Alcott
  Operations-Production: Deana Carr
Utilizes: Artists-in-Residence; Collaborations; Commissioned Composers; Commissioned Music; Composers-in-Residence; Guest Accompanists; Guest Composers; Guest Directors; Guest Lecturers; Guest Musical Directors; Guest Musicians; Instructors; Local Artists; Multi Collaborations; Multimedia; Music; Organization Contracts; Original Music Scores; Selected Students; Sign Language Translators; Singers
Specialized Field: Series & Festivals; Riverside Live; Down by the Riverside; Concerts
Status: Non-Profit, Professional
Paid Staff: 5
Performs At: Mayo Civic Center

4881
ST CLOUD STATE UNIVERSITY PROGRAM BOARD PERFORMING ARTS SERIES
Atwood Memorial Center 139
720 4th Avenue South
Saint Cloud, MN 56301
Phone: 320-308-2205
Fax: 320-308-1669
e-mail: upb@stcloudstate.edu
Web Site: www.stcloudstate.edu/upb
Officers:
  President: Chris Trankel
  VP of Marketing: Chelsea VanLoon
Management:
  President: Chris Trankel
  Artistic Director: Janice Courtney
  Office Manager: Anita Binnie
  Associate Director: Tommy Balicky
Founded: 1978
Specialized Field: Series & Festivals; Vocal Music; Theatre; Youth; Dance; Ethnic Performances
Status: Non-Profit, Professional
Paid Staff: 10
Paid Artists: 10
Performs At: Atwood Center Ballroom

4882
PACIFIC COMPOSERS FORUM
522 Landmark Center
75 West 5th Street
Saint Paul, MN 55102-1439
Phone: 651-228-1407
Fax: 651-291-7978
e-mail: info@composersforum.com
Web Site: www.composersforum.com
Officers:
  Chair: David O'Fallon
  Vice Chair: Dan Thomas
  Vice Chair: Nancy Uscher
  Treasurer: Sam Hsu
  Secretary: Kathleen van Bergen
  Past Chair: Carol Heen, Ph.D.
Management:
  Senior Program Director: Philip Blackbur
  Innova Assistant: Chris Campbell
  Finance Manager: Paul Hanson
Founded: 1973

4883
SCHUBERT CLUB INTERNATIONAL ARTIST SERIES
302 Landmark Center
75 W 5th Street
Saint Paul, MN 55102
Phone: 651-292-3267
Fax: 651-292-4317
e-mail: schubert@schubert.org
Web Site: www.schubert.org
Officers:
  President: Nina Archabal
  Vice President: Mark Anema
Management:
  President: Nina Archabal
  Executive Director: Barry Kempton
  Museum and Education Manager: Kate Cooper
  Program Associate: Max Carlson
  Artistic Director: Julie Himmelstrup
  Director of Development: Paul D. Olson
  Marketing & Audience Development Ma: Tessa Retterath Jones
Mission: To promote the art of music, particularly recital music through education, performance and museum programs and to maintain a high standard of artistic excellence
Founded: 1882
Specialized Field: Series and Festivals; Instrumental Music; Vocal Music; Youth; Ethnic Performances
Status: Non-Profit, Professional
Paid Staff: 10

4884
SCHUBERT CLUB INTERNATIONAL ARTIST SERIES
302 Landmark Center
75 W 5th Street
Saint Paul, MN 55102
Phone: 651-292-3267
Fax: 651-292-4317
e-mail: schubert@schubert.org
Web Site: www.schubert.org
Officers:
  President: Nina Archabal
  Vice President: Mark Anema
Management:
  Executive Director: Barry Kempton
  Museum and Education Manager: Kate Cooper
  Program Associate: Max Carlson
  Artistic Director: Julie Himmelstrup
  Director of Development: Paul D. Olson
  Marketing & Audience Development Ma: Tessa Retterath Jones
Mission: To promote the art of music, particularly recital music through education, performance, and museum programs and to maintain a high standard of artistic excellence.
Founded: 1982
Specialized Field: Performing Music Series and Museum.
Paid Staff: 10
Performs At: Ordway Music Theatre

4885
GUSTAVUS ADOLPHUS COLLEGE ARTIST SERIES
Gustavus Adolphus College
800 West College Avenue
Saint Peter, MN 56082
Phone: 507-933-8000
Fax: 507-933-6253
e-mail: web@gustavus.edu
Web Site: www.gustavus.edu
Management:
  President: James Peterson
  Executive Director: Alan Behrends
Founded: 1862
Specialized Field: Fine Arts
Status: Non-Profit, Professional
Paid Staff: 600
Performs At: Bjorling Concert Hall

Mississippi

4886
JAZZ IN THE GROVE
1840 Wollombi Road
Bay Springs, MS 02325
Phone: 249-981-576
Fax: 601-764-6866
Toll-free: 800-898-2782
e-mail: wines@stonehurst.com.au
Web Site: www.stonehurst.com.au
Management:
  President: Joseph Fail
  Director: Emily Mixon
Founded: 1996
Specialized Field: Performing Series - Jazz Festival
Status: Non-Profit, Non-Professional

4887
UNIVERSITY OF SOUTHERN MISSISSIPPI SCHOOL OF MUSIC
118 College Drive
#5081
Hattiesburg, MS 39406-0001
Phone: 601-266-5543
Fax: 601-266-6427
e-mail: music@usm.edu
Web Site: www.usm.edu/music
Officers:
  President: Rodney D. Bennett
  Vice President: Dr. Douglas Vinzant
Management:
  Director: Dr Michael Miles, michael.a.miles@usm.edu
  Associate Director: Dr Jennifer Shank, jennifer.shank@usm.edu
Mission: Recognized for its eminence in musical artistry, education and community service. Provides a wealth of valuable opportunities for the professional and artistic growth of the students.
Utilizes: Actors; Artists-in-Residence; Choreographers; Commissioned Music; Composers-in-Residence; Dance Companies; Dancers; Educators; Grant Writers; Guest Accompanists; Guest Artists; Guest Choreographers; Guest Companies; Guest Composers; Guest Conductors; Guest Designers; Guest Directors; Guest Ensembles; Guest Instructors; Guest Lecturers; Guest Musical Directors; Guest Musicians; Instructors; Multimedia; Music; Original Music Scores; Resident Artists; Resident Professionals; Sign Language Translators; Singers; Soloists; Student Interns; Special Technical Talent; Theatre Companies; Touring Companies; Visual Arts
Founded: 1910
Specialized Field: Orchestra; Chamber; Ensemble; Choral; Band
Status: Non-Profit, Non-Professional
Budget: $35,000-60,000
Income Sources: State Funded
Seating Capacity: 1,000

4888
BELHAVEN COLLEGE PRESTON MEMORIAL SERIES
Belhaven College
1500 Peachtree Street
Jackson, MS 39202-1789

SERIES & FESTIVALS / Missouri

Phone: 601-968-5940
Fax: 601-968-9998
Toll-free: 800-960-5940
e-mail: admission@belhaven.edu
Web Site: www.belhaven.edu
Officers:
Music Department Chairman: Christopher Shelt
Performs At: Girault Auditorium

4889
MISSISSIPPI ARTS COMMISSION
501 North West Street
Suite 1101A Woolfolk Building
Jackson, MS 39201
Phone: 601-359-6030
Fax: 601-359-6008
e-mail: lpowell@arts.state.ms.us
Web Site: www.arts.state.ms.us
Officers:
Chair: Nan Sanders
First Vice Chair: Rachel Shemper Schwartz
Second Vice Chair: Peggy Sprabery
Management:
Executive Director: Dr. Tom Pearson
Deputy Director: Larry Morrisey
Fiscal Officer: Christopher Brooks
Public Relations Director: Susan Liles
Systems Administrator: Shirley Smith
Director of Grants: Diane Williams
Arts Industry Director: Turry M. Flucker
Arts Education Director: Charlotte Smelser
Founded: 1968
Specialized Field: Grant and Technical Assistance
Status: For-Profit, Professional
Paid Staff: 12

4890
WORLD PERFORMANCE SERIES: THALIA MARA FOUNDATION
1305 Poplar Blvd.
Jackson, MS 39202
Phone: 601-354-3172
Fax: 601-354-2781
e-mail: mail@thaliamara.org
Web Site: www.imaginarycompany.com/
Management:
Executive Director: Leanne Mahoney
Creative Director: Vidal Blankenstein
Budget: $400,000-1,000,000

4891
MISSISSIPPI STATE UNIVERSITY LYCEUM SERIES
Colvard Student Union
PO Box 5368
Mississippi State, MS 39762
Phone: 662-325-2930
Fax: 662-325-3323
e-mail: lyceum@msstate.edu
Web Site: www.msstate.edu/dept/lyceum
Management:
Series Coordinator: Brenda Neubauer
Assistant Director: Amelia Treptow
Director of Student Activities: Jackie Mullen
Founded: 1961
Specialized Field: Series and Festivals; Instrumental Music; Vocal Music; Theatre; Dance; Ethnic Performances; Orchestra
Status: Non-Profit, Professional
Paid Staff: 1
Budget: $20,000-35,000
Performs At: Humphery Coliseum

4892
NATCHEZ FESTIVAL OF MUSIC
Alcorn State University
Box Office, P.O. Box 2207
Natchez, MS 39121
Phone: 601-446-6631
Fax: 601-442-9686
Toll-free: 800-647-6742
e-mail: info@natchezpilgrimage.com
Web Site: www.natchezfestivalofmusic.com
Officers:
Interim President: Malvin Williams
Chairman of the Board: Robert Gage
Executive Vice President: Rudolph Walters
Management:
Artistic Director: Jay Dean
Mission: Teach variety of research activities that focus on biotechnology, energy, meat, ecology, farming and alternative crops.
Founded: 1989
Specialized Field: Series & Festivals; Opera; Jazz; Musical Theatre; Broadways; Concerts
Status: Non-Profit, Professional
Paid Staff: 6
Paid Artists: 40
Performs At: Margaret Martin Performing Arts Center

4893
UNIVERSITY OF MISSISSIPPI ARTIST SERIES
University of Mississippi Artists Series
PO Box 1848
University, MS 38677
Phone: 662-915-7193
Fax: 662-915-5013
e-mail: art@olemiss.edu
Web Site: www.olemiss.edu/depts/music/artist.html
Officers:
Chairman: Dr. Robert Riggs
Budget: $35,000-60,000
Performs At: Fulton Chapel

Missouri

4894
FRIENDS OF HISTORIC BOONVILLE PERFORMING ARTS
614 E Morgan Street
PO Box 1776
Boonville, MO 65233
Phone: 660-882-7977
Fax: 660-882-9194
Toll-free: 888-588-1477
e-mail: fohboonville@gmail.com
Web Site: www.friendsofhistoricboonville.org/
Officers:
President: Ron Lenz
Second VP: Barbara Holtzclaw
First VP: Gary Campbell
Secretary: Debby Koerner
Management:
President: Camt Bell
Executive Director: Marry Mcvicker
Artistic Director: Dave Para
Mission: To provide a community arts program in our historic theatre, Thespian Hall.
Utilizes: Actors; Artists-in-Residence; Collaborations; Dance Companies; Guild Activities; Instructors; Local Artists; Multimedia; Original Music Scores; Sign Language Translators; Soloists; Touring Companies
Founded: 1971
Specialized Field: Community Arts
Status: Non-Profit, Professional
Paid Staff: 1
Budget: $60,000-150,000
Income Sources: Donations; earned income
Performs At: Thespian Hall
Annual Attendance: 7,500
Facility Category: Theatre; Performing Arts Center
Type of Stage: Proscenium
Stage Dimensions: 80x100
Seating Capacity: 600
Year Built: 1857
Year Remodeled: 1980
Organization Type: Performing; Educational; Sponsoring

4895
MISSOURI RIVER FESTIVAL OF THE ARTS
PO Box 1776
614 E Morgan
Boonville, MO 65233
Phone: 660-882-7977
Fax: 660-882-9194
Toll-free: 888-588-1477
e-mail: friendsart@mid-mo.net
Web Site: www.mid-mo/friendsart
Management:
Administrator: Maryellen H McVicker
Founded: 1975
Seating Capacity: 600
Year Built: 1855
Year Remodeled: 2002

4896
SOUTHEAST MISSOURI STATE UNIVERSITY: CULTURAL SERIES
Southeast Missouri State University
One University Plaza
Cape Girardeau, MO 63701
Phone: 573-651-2000
Fax: 573-651-2893
e-mail: contact@semo.edu
Web Site: www.semo.edu/
Management:
Dean College of Humanities: Dr. Martin Jones
Chairperson/Speech Communications: Dr. Ray G Ewing
Mission: To attract professional quality performing arts to the Southeast Missouri area; to offer professional workshops.
Founded: 1873
Specialized Field: Dance; Vocal Music; Instrumental Music; Theatre
Status: Nonprofit
Income Sources: Missouri Council on the Arts
Performs At: Academic Hall Auditorium
Organization Type: Educational; Sponsoring

4897
UNIVERSITY OF MISSOURI: COLUMBIA CONCERT SERIES
409 Jesse Hall
Columbia, MO 65211
Phone: 573-882-3875
Fax: 573-882-2636
Toll-free: 800-292-9136
e-mail: dunnm@missouri.edu
Web Site: www.concertseries.org
Officers:
Executive Director: Michael Dunn
Management:
Assistant Director: Kimberly Mouser

SERIES & FESTIVALS / Missouri

Utilizes: Actors; Artists-in-Residence; Collaborations; Dance Companies; Dancers; Grant Writers; Guest Composers; Guest Musicians; Multi Collaborations; Original Music Scores; Selected Students; Sign Language Translators; Theatre Companies
Specialized Field: Choral; Dance; Opera; Instrumental Music; Theatre
Status: Non-Profit, Professional
Paid Staff: 20
Volunteer Staff: 50
Paid Artists: 42
Budget: $400,000-1,000,000
Income Sources: Ticket Sales; Private Donations; Corporate Support; Grants
Performs At: Performing Arts Center
Affiliations: University Of Missouri
Annual Attendance: 65,000
Seating Capacity: 1,784

4898
CENTRAL METHODIST COLLEGE CONVOCATIONS
Central Methodist University
411 Central Methodist Square
Fayette, MO 65248
Phone: 660-248-3391
Fax: 660-248-2622
Toll-free: 877-268-1854
e-mail: mkelty@centralmethodist.edu
Web Site: www.centralmethodist.edu
Officers:
   Chairman: Dr Mary Kelty
Founded: 1854
Budget: $20,000-35,000
Performs At: Little Theater; Lynn Memorial Chapel; Field House

4899
WILLIAM WOODS UNIVERSITY CONCERT & LECTURE SERIES
William Woods University
One University Avenue
Fulton, MO 65251
Phone: 573-642-2251
Fax: 573-592-1146
Toll-free: 800-995-3159
e-mail: Admissions@WilliamWoods.edu
Web Site: www.williamwoods.edu
Management:
   President: Jahnae Barnett
   Artistic Director of Theatre: Joe Potter
Utilizes: Artists-in-Residence; Choreographers; Collaborations; Dance Companies; Dancers; Educators; Fine Artists; Grant Writers; Guest Artists; Guest Companies; Guest Conductors; Guest Designers; Guest Instructors; Guest Lecturers; Guest Soloists; Guild Activities; High School Drama; Instructors; Local Artists; Music; Original Music Scores; Playwrights; Poets; Resident Professionals; Selected Students; Sign Language Translators; Soloists; Student Interns; Special Technical Talent; Theatre Companies; Touring Companies; Visual Arts
Founded: 1870
Specialized Field: Series & Festivals; Vocal Music; Theatre; Youth; Dance; Ethnic Performances
Status: For-Profit, Non-Professional
Budget: $10,000
Performs At: Cutlip Auditorium; Dulany Auditorium

4900
HANNIBAL CONCERT ASSOCIATION
WLIQ AM 1530
404 N. 24th St.
Hannibal, MO 62301
Phone: 217-223-5292
Fax: 573-221-4091
e-mail: sanorth@adams.net
Web Site: wliqlite1530.com/
Management:
   President: Rita Cornelius
   Program Director: Jeff Dorsey
   General Manager: Dave Greene
   Director of Sales: Jeff Asmussen
Founded: 1944
Specialized Field: Series and Festivals; Instrumental Music; Vocal Music; Youth; Dance; Ethnic Performances; Presenting Performances
Status: Non-Profit, Professional
Budget: $10,000-20,000

4901
CAPITAL CITY COUNCIL ON THE ARTS
1203 Missouri Blvd.
Jefferson City, MO 65109
Phone: 573-635-8355
Fax: 573-634-3805
e-mail: artsadmin@capitalarts.org
Web Site: www.capitalarts.org
Officers:
   Treasurer: Vicki Myers
   Vice President: Janis Burgin
   Secretary: Shelly Hittner
Management:
   President: Tony Lutz
   Executive Director: Joyce Neuenswander
Founded: 1957
Specialized Field: Programs for Children; Support Community Art
Status: Non-Profit, Professional
Paid Staff: 1
Paid Artists: 15
Budget: $10,000

4902
PRO MUSICA
211 S. Main Street
Suite 312
Joplin, MO 64801
Phone: 417-625-1822
Fax: 417-625-1822
e-mail: info@promusicajoplin.org
Web Site: www.promusicajoplin.org
Officers:
   President: Joe L. Kirk
   Vice President: Virginia J. Laas
   Secretary: Gina Atteberry
   Treasurer: Alexander B. Curchin
Management:
   Artistic Director: Brian Fronzaglia
Founded: 1986
Specialized Field: Chamber Music
Status: Non-Profit, Professional
Paid Staff: 2
Volunteer Staff: 1
Budget: $35,000-60,000

4903
HEART OF AMERICA SHAKESPEARE FESTIVAL
3619 Broadway
Suite 2
Kansas City, MO 64111
Phone: 816-531-7728
Fax: 816-531-1911
e-mail: info@kcshakes.org
Web Site: www.kcshakes.org
Officers:
   Founder and Co-Chairman: Marilyn Strauss
   Co-Chairman: Shirley Bush Helzberg
   President: Dan Bukovac
   Executive Vice-President / Presiden: Linda Word
   Vice President, Education: Patricia Davison
   Vice-President, Special Events: Cindy Pratt-Stokes
   Treasurer: Chuck McCann
   Secretary: Scott Ashcraft, M.D.
   Immediate Past President: Steve Chick
Management:
   Executive Director: Lisa Cordes
   Executive Artistic Director: Sidonie Garrett
   Cooper: Elizabeth
   Rapport: Director of Ope Matt
Mission: To make Shakespeare's works accessible to a diverse audience through free professional theater and educational programs. Vision is to use the power and presence of live professional performance to enhance the meaning of life and to illustrate the indomitability of the human spirit through the works of William shakespeare.
Utilizes: Actors; AEA Actors; Choreographers; Collaborations; Dancers; Designers; Educators; Guest Designers; Guest Soloists; Local Artists; Multimedia; Resident Professionals; Selected Students; Student Interns
Founded: 1991
Specialized Field: Series & Festivals: Shakespeare Theatre in the Park
Status: Professional; Non-Profit
Paid Staff: 4
Volunteer Staff: 400
Paid Artists: 55
Budget: $650,000
Income Sources: Foundations; Individuals; Corporations
Season: June - July
Performs At: Outdoor Theatre, Southmoreland Park 47th and Oak Street
Annual Attendance: 18,000-26,000
Facility Category: Outdoor Park Setting
Stage Dimensions: 45'x 30'
Seating Capacity: 2,500

4904
KANSAS CITY BLUES & JAZZ FESTIVAL
1616 East 18th Street
Suite 230
Kansas City, MO 64108
Phone: 816-474-8463
Fax: 816-474-0074
Toll-free: 800-530-5266
e-mail: kcbluesjazz@kcbluesjazz.org
Web Site: www.americanjazzmuseum.org
Officers:
   Chairman of the Board: C. S. Runnion III
   Vice Chair: Michael Gerken
   Vice Chair: Anita Maltbia
   Secretary: John Readey
   Treasurer: Courtney Jones
Management:
   Director: Greg Patterson
   Assistant Director: Connie Hemiston
   Chief, Executive Officer: Gregory A. Carroll
   Executive Administrative Assistant: Karen Anderson
   Receptionist/Membership Coordinator: Arlene Walker

SERIES & FESTIVALS / Missouri

General Manager: Gerald Dunn
Director of Finance: Joyce Johnson
Marketing Manager: Chris Burnett
Founded: 1991
Specialized Field: Music Festival
Paid Staff: 2
Volunteer Staff: 500
Paid Artists: 50

4905
KANSAS CITY RENAISSANCE FESTIVAL
628 N. 126th Street
Suite 206
Kansas City, MO 66012
Phone: 913-721-2110
Fax: 816-561-6493
Toll-free: 800-373-0357
e-mail: renfest@kcrenfest.com
Web Site: www.kcrenfest.com
Management:
　Executive Director: Carrie Shoptaw
　Director of Entertainment: Jim Stamberger
　Marketing and Sales Manager: Roger Clements
　Marketing and Sales Director: Will Peterson
　Marketing and Donation Coordinator: Alex Harmon
　Fundraising Opportunities: Kaye Cummings
Mission: To entertain and educate using a Renaissance theme.
Founded: 1977
Specialized Field: Performing Arts
Status: Professional
Paid Staff: 15
Volunteer Staff: 2
Income Sources: Ticket sales; sponsorships
Annual Attendance: 180,000
Facility Category: 12 Outdoor Stages
Type of Stage: 4 Proscenium; 1 Jousting Field
Year Built: 1977

4906
KANSAS CITY YOUNG AUDIENCES SERIES
5601 Wind Art
Kansas City, MO 64113
Phone: 816-531-4022
Fax: 816-960-1519
e-mail: dwindham@crn.org
Web Site: www.kcya.org
Officers:
　Chair: Chris Mounts
　Vice-Chair Elect: Brian Williams
　Co-Vice Chair: Cynthia L. Williams
　Co-Vice Chair: Qiana Thomason
　Treasurer: Michael Cline
　Secretary: LaDonna Gooden
Management:
　President/CEO: Daniel Windham
　Executive Director: Martin English
　Project Coordinator: Shawna Downing
　Development Associate: Lisa Smith
　Director of Arts Education: Kara Armstrong
　Arts Partners Coordinator: Shannon Fowler
　Director of Development: Mary Needham
　Director of Finance: Tim Valverde
Founded: 1962
Specialized Field: Series & Festivals: Instrumental Music
Status: Non-Profit, Professional

4907
SUMMERFEST CONCERTS
PO Box 22697
Kansas City, MO 64113-0697
Phone: 816-510-0978
e-mail: info@summerfestkc.org
Web Site: www.summerfestconcertsinc.com
Officers:
　Treasurer: Stephanie Smith
　Secretary: Mary Redmon
Management:
　President: Mary Zimmerman
　Vice President: Don Dagenais
　Artistic Advisor: Alexander East
　Artistic Advisor: Shannon Finney
　Artistic Advisor: Jane Carl
　Business Manager: Shirley Quastler
Founded: 1991
Specialized Field: Chamber Music

4908
UNIVERSITY OF MISSOURI-KANSAS CITY CONSERVATORY SERIES
4949 Cherry Street
Kansas City, MO 64110-2229
Phone: 816-235-2900
Fax: 816-235-5265
e-mail: urbana@umkc.edu
Web Site: www.umkc.edu/conservatory
Management:
　Dean of Conservatory: Randall Pembrook
　Marketing Director: Al Urban
Founded: 1906
Specialized Field: Series & Festivals; Instrumental Music; Vocal Music; Dance
Status: Non-Profit, Professional
Paid Staff: 105
Paid Artists: 5
Budget: $35,000-60,000
Performs At: White Recital Hall; Center for the Performing Arts

4909
TRUMAN STATE UNIVERSITY LYCEUM SERIES
McClain 101
100 E Normal Street
Kirksville, MO 63501
Phone: 600-785-4016
Fax: 660-785-4019
e-mail: heidi@truman.edu
Web Site: www.lyceum.truman.edu
Officers:
　Lyceum Committee Co-Chairman: Winston Vanderhoof
　Lyceum Committee Co-Chair: Zach Burden
Management:
　Director of Public Relations: Heidi Templeton
Budget: $60,000-150,000
Performs At: Baldwin Hall Auditorium

4910
HARRIMAN-JEWELL COLLEGE
William Jewell College
500 College Hill, Campus Box 1015
Liberty, MO 64068-1896
Phone: 816-415-5025
Fax: 816-415-5035
Toll-free: 888-528-5521
e-mail: info@hjseries.org
Web Site: www.hjseries.org
Officers:
　President: Dave Sallee
Management:
　Executive & Artisitic Director: Clark Morris
　Associate Executive Director: Tim Ackerman
　Development and Finance Manager: Austin Baragary
　Director of Development: Eryn Bates
　Communications Manager: DeEtta Bohling
　Executive and Artistic Director: Clark Morris
　Ticketing Services Manager: Ann Reed
Mission: To bring the best of the performing arts to Kansas City.
Founded: 1965
Specialized Field: Series & Festivals: Classical music
Status: Non-Profit, Professional
Paid Staff: 6

4911
NORTHWEST MISSOURI STATE UNIVERSITY PERFORMING ARTS SERIES
800 University Drive
Maryville, MO 64468
Phone: 660-562-1562
Fax: 660-562-1121
Toll-free: 800-633-1175
e-mail: admissions@nwmissouri.edu
Web Site: www.nwmissouri.edu
Officers:
　Board Chair: Dr. Mark H. Hargens
　Board Vice Chair: Joseph B. Bosse
Management:
　President: Eric Hubbard
　Managing Director: Bart Pitchford
Mission: Providing a range of lectures and performing arts for the University and area residents.
Founded: 1992
Specialized Field: Series & Festivals; Theatre; Dance; Ethnic Performances
Status: For-Profit, Non-Professional
Paid Staff: 1
Budget: $60,000-150,000
Income Sources: Missouri Arts Council
Performs At: Charles Johnson Theatre; Mary Linn Performing Arts
Organization Type: Educational; Sponsoring

4912
MOBERLY AREA COUNCIL ON THE ARTS
Moberly Area Community College
101 College Ave. H37 Komar Hall
Moberly, MO 65270
Phone: 660-263-4110
Fax: 660-263-6448
e-mail: scottm@macc.edu
Web Site: moberlyarts.org/
Officers:
　President: Deb McDonough
　Vice President: Jordan Perry
　Secretary: Mike Thornton
　Treasurer: Dennis Berding
Budget: $20,000-35,000

4913
COTTEY LECTURERS & ARTISTS SUPER SERIES
Cottey College
1000 W. Austin
Nevada, MO 64772
Phone: 417-667-8181
Fax: 417-667-8103
e-mail: kkorb@cottey.edu
Web Site: www.cottey.edu
Officers:
　President: Judy Robinson Rogers, Ph.

All listings are in alphabetical order by state, then city, then organization within the city.

SERIES & FESTIVALS / Missouri

Vice President for Academic Affairs: Cathryn G. Pridal, Ph.D.
Interim Vice President for Administ: Amy Ruetten
Vice President for Student Life: Mari Anne Phillips, Ed.D
Vice President for Institutional Ad: Judyth Wier
Chair: Janet Brown
Vice Chair: Greg Hoffman
Secretary: Mathilda Hatfield
Management:
    Coord. Campus Activities: Kristi Korbrs
Founded: 1990
Specialized Field: Series & Festivals; Instrumental music; Vocal music; Theatre; Youth; Dance; Ethnic Performances
Status: Non-Profit, Professional
Paid Staff: 1
Paid Artists: 5
Budget: $20,000-35,000
Performs At: Center for the Arts
Type of Stage: Auditorium
Stage Dimensions: 40X40
Seating Capacity: 495
Year Built: 1990

4914
THERON C BENNET RAGTIME & EARLY JAZZ FESTIVAL
21554 Lawrence 1032
Pierce City, MO 65723
Phone: 417-476-5408
Web Site: www.sound.net/~gary/theron/theron.htm
Management:
    Festival Organizer: Murray Bishoff

4915
PERFORMING ARTS ASSOCIATION OF SAINT JOSEPH
719 Edmond Street
Saint Joseph, MO 64501
Phone: 816-279-1225
Fax: 816-233-6704
e-mail: info@paastjo.org
Web Site: www.saintjosephperformingarts.org
Management:
    Executive Director: Teresa Fankhauser
    Director: Beth Sharp
Founded: 1962
Specialized Field: Jazz; Theater; Instrumental Music; Dance
Status: Non-Profit, Non-Professional
Paid Staff: 3
Budget: $60,000-150,000
Performs At: Missouri Theatre

4916
CITICORP SUMMERFEST
Powell Symphony Hall
718 N Grand Boulevard
Saint Louis, MO 63103
Phone: 314-533-2500
Fax: 314-286-4188
Toll-free: 800-232-1880
Web Site: www.slso.org
Management:
    President: Randy Adams
    Artistic Director: Kathleen Vanberger
    Music Director/Conductor: David Robertson
Utilizes: Guest Artists
Founded: 1880
Specialized Field: Series & Festivals: Classical music
Status: Non-Profit, Professional
Paid Staff: 150
Paid Artists: 60
Performs At: Powell Symphony Hall At Grand Center
Affiliations: Saint Louis Symphony Orchestra
Organization Type: Performing

4917
FOX ASSOCIATES
539 N Grand Boulevard
Suite 300
Saint Louis, MO 63103
Phone: 314-534-1678
Fax: 314-534-8702
Toll-free: 800-293-5949
e-mail: foxtheatre.stl@gmail.com
Web Site: www.fabouousfox.com
Officers:
    Executive Director: Richard Baker
Mission: Present live entertainment.
Founded: 1929
Specialized Field: Series & Festivals: Broadway Shows and Concerts
Status: For-Profit, Professional
Paid Staff: 100
Budget: $1,000,000+

4918
JUNETEENTH HERITAGE & JAZZ FESTIVAL
625 N Euclid
Suite 225
Saint Louis, MO 63108
Phone: 314-367-0100
Fax: 314-367-0200
Toll-free: 877-586-8684
e-mail: juntnthjaz@aol.com
Web Site: www.juneteenthjazz.com
Officers:
    Chair: Manty Ellis
    Vice-Chairman: John Thompson
Management:
    Executive Producer: Curtis Faulkner

4919
NEW MUSIC CIRCLE SERIES
PO Box 9337
Saint Louis, MO 63117
Phone: 314-995-4963
Fax: 314-567-5384
e-mail: info@newmusiccircle.org
Web Site: www.newmusiccircle.org
Officers:
    President: John Newman
    Vice-President: Fred Tompkins
    Treasurer: Sherri Lyss
    Secretary: Gary Gronau
Management:
    Music Department: Rich O'Donnell
Utilizes: Guest Musical Directors
Founded: 1959
Paid Staff: 2
Volunteer Staff: 5
Paid Artists: 30
Budget: $34,000
Income Sources: St. Louis Regional Arts Commission, Missouri Arts Council
Annual Attendance: 1,000
Facility Category: Venues

4920
SAINT LOUIS CATHEDRAL CONCERTS
4431 Lindell Boulevard
Saint Louis, MO 63108
Phone: 314-533-7662
Fax: 314-373-8292
e-mail: concerts@cathedralstl.org
Web Site: www.stlcathedralconcerts.org
Officers:
    President: Paul Mittelstadt
    Vice President: Dennis Flatness
    Vice-President: Elizabeth Robb
    Treasurer: Jim Smith
    Secretary: Anthony Fathman, M.D.
Management:
    Executive Director: Scott Kennebeck
    Development Director: Nicole Heerlein
    Group Sales Director: Ruth Ferris
    Artistic Director: Dr. Horst Buchholz
    House Manager: Monica Vogel
    Hospitality Manager: Peggy Grotpeter
    Bookkeeper: Jonathan Klimpel
Mission: Cathedral Concerts mission is to present affordable live concerts in the Cathedral Basilica of St. Louis featuring world-class musicians and the finest repertoire of sacred and classical music for the cultural enrichment, education, and enjoyment of the entire region.
Founded: 1992
Opened: 1993
Specialized Field: Music
Status: Non-Profit, Professional
Paid Staff: 3
Volunteer Staff: 70
Paid Artists: 300
Budget: $350,000-400,000
Income Sources: Ticket Sales; Donations
Annual Attendance: 10,000
Seating Capacity: 1,500

4921
SAINT LOUIS SYMPHONY: CLASSICS IN THE LOOP FESTIVAL
Saint Louis Symphony Orchestra
718 North Grand Boulevard
Saint Louis, MO 63103
Phone: 314-533-2500
Fax: 314-286-4111
Toll-free: 800-232-1880
e-mail: symph@admiral.umsl.edu
Web Site: www.slso.org
Officers:
    Chair: Barry H. Beracha
    Vice Chairman: Kimberley Ann Eberlein
    Vice Chairman: Jo Ann Taylor Kindle
    Vice Chairman: David Steward
    Secretary: Donna Wilkinson
    General Counsel: Lawrence P. Katzenstein
    Treasurer: Rick A. Short
    Assistant Treasurer: Donald Suggs
Management:
    President: Randy Adams
    Chief Financial Officer: James Garrone
    Artistic Director: Kathleen Van Bergen
    Orchestra Manager: Susan Lim
    VP for Artistic Administration: Bret Dorhout
    VP for Marketing: Jonna Robertson
    VP for Development: John Easley
    VP for Orchestra Operations & Facil: Anna Kuwabara

4922
SAINT LOUIS HILLS ARTS COUNCIL
332 Emmanuel Court
Saint Louis, MO 63088-2312

SERIES & FESTIVALS / Montana

Phone: 314-352-1838
Fax: 314-352-3049
Toll-free: 866-840-1838
e-mail: johnpwalsh@aol.com
Web Site: www.JohnPowelWalsh.com
Officers:
    President: John Powel Walsh
Budget: $10,000-20,000
Performs At: Powell Symphony Hall

4923
UNIVERSITY OF MISSOURI: SAINT LOUIS PREMIER PERFORMANCES
1 University Blvd.
Saint Louis, MO 63121-4400
Phone: 314-516-5818
Fax: 314-516-5881
e-mail: klbmezzo@umsl.edu
Web Site: www.umsl.edu/~premier
Management:
    Director: Katharine Lawton Brown
    Production Associate: Gloria Kohn
Founded: 1986
Specialized Field: Series & Festivals; Instrumental Music; Vocal Music; Chamber Music
Status: Non-Profit, Professional
Paid Staff: 2
Volunteer Staff: 2
Non-paid Artists: 50
Budget: $35,000-60,000
Income Sources: Public, Private and Grants
Performs At: Sheldon Concert Hall; Ethical Society Auditorium
Seating Capacity: 700/419

4924
SCOTT JOPLIN RAGTIME FESTIVAL
507 S. Ohio
P.O. Box 1244
Sedalia, MO 65302
Phone: 660-826-2271
Fax: 660-826-5054
Toll-free: 866-218-6258
e-mail: ragtimer@scottjoplin.org
Web Site: www.scottjoplin.org
Management:
    President: Jody Boswell
    Managing Director: Kim Phillip
Mission: To expose a greater variety of people to the historical and aesthetic value of Scott Joplin and ragtime music; to enrich our understanding.
Utilizes: Singers
Founded: 1974
Specialized Field: Series & Festivals; Instrumental Music; Vocal Music; Youth; Dance; Ethnic Performances; Orchestra; Ensemble; Instrumental Group; Electronic & Live
Status: Non-Profit, Professional
Paid Staff: 1
Paid Artists: 50
Organization Type: Performing; Educational

4925
EVANGEL UNIVERSITY ARTISTS & LECTURESHIP SERIES
1111 N Glenstone Ave.
Springfield, MO 65802
Phone: 417-865-2815
Fax: 417-865-9599
Toll-free: 800-382-6435
e-mail: bernetg@evangel.edu
Web Site: www.evangel.edu
Management:
    President: Dr. Carol Taylor
    Executive Director: John S Shows
    Dean: Glenn Bernet
Founded: 1955
Specialized Field: Education
Status: Non-Profit, Non-Professional
Paid Staff: 100
Budget: $10,000-20,000

4926
LINDENWOOD COLLEGE MAINSTAGE SEASON
J. Scheidegger Center for the Arts
2300 West Clay Street
St. Charles, MO 63301
Phone: 636-949-4433
e-mail: Scheidegger@lindenwood.edu
Web Site: www.lindenwood.edu
Management:
    President: Dennis Stellmann
    Executive Director: Marsha Parker
    Manager: Ted Gregory
Founded: 1827
Specialized Field: Series & Festivals; Instrumental Music; Vocal Music; Theatre; Youth; Dance; Ethnic Performances
Status: Non-Profit, Non-Professional
Paid Staff: 8
Paid Artists: 5

4927
ROYAL ARTS COUNCIL
107 S Monroe St
Versailles, MO 65084
Phone: 573-378-6226
Fax: 573-378-6928
e-mail: theroyaltheatre@sbcglobal.net
Web Site: www.theroyaltheatre.com
Management:
    President: Richard Leass
    Executive Director: Cindy Davenport
Founded: 1981
Specialized Field: Series & Festivals; Instrumental Music; Vocal Music; Theatre; Youth; Dance
Status: Non-Profit, Non-Professional
Paid Staff: 1
Budget: $10,000-20,000

4928
UNIVERSITY OF CENTRAL MISSOURI
Performing Arts Series, Administration Buildi
Suite 196
Warrensburg, MO 64093
Phone: 660-543-4263
Fax: 660-543-8998
Toll-free: 877-729-8266
e-mail: pas@ucmo.edu
Web Site: www.cmsu.edu/pas
Officers:
    Associate VP: Dale Carder
Management:
    Manager: Michelle Schubert
Founded: 1988
Specialized Field: Series and Festivals; Instrumental Music; Theatre; Youth; Dance
Status: Non-Profit, Professional
Paid Staff: 2
Budget: $60,000-150,000
Performs At: Hendricks Hall
Seating Capacity: 1300

Montana

4929
RED LODGE MUSIC FESTIVAL
3501 Briarwood Blvd.
Billings, MT 59101
Phone: 406-256-5210
e-mail: enrollment@rlmf.org
Web Site: www.redlodgemusicfestival.org
Officers:
    President: Kenneth Gilstrap
Management:
    President: Kennith Gilstrap
    Artistic Director: Mike Peterson
Founded: 1963
Specialized Field: Series and Festivals; Instrumental Music; Youth
Status: Non-Profit, Non-Professional
Paid Artists: 30

4930
ASSOCIATED STUDENTS OF MONTANA STATE UNIVERSITY
Strand Union Building
221 Strand Union
Bozeman, MT 59717
Phone: 406-994-2933
Fax: 406-994-6911
e-mail: asmsu@montana.edu
Web Site: www.montana.edu/asmsu/
Officers:
    President: Lindsay Murdock
    Vice President: Lukas Smith
Utilizes: Collaborations; Dancers; Filmmakers; Guest Instructors; Guest Soloists; Instructors; Lyricists; Multimedia; Theatre Companies
Budget: $20,000-35,000
Performs At: Wilson Auditorium; Reynolds Recital Hall; Northwest Lounge

4931
DILLON COMMUNITY CONCERT ASSOCIATION
P.O. Box 627
25 W. Granite
Dillon, MT 59701
Phone: 406-683-2285
Web Site: mtstandard.com
Officers:
    Drive Chairman: Ingrid Joy Kaushagen
Specialized Field: Vocal Music; Instrumental Music
Status: Non-Profit
Budget: $10,000-20,000

4932
MONTANA TRADITIONAL JAZZ FESTIVAL
PO Box 956
Great Falls, MT 59403
Phone: 406-771-1642
Fax: 406-453-6625
e-mail: jazzfeset@montana.com
Web Site: www.montanatradjazz.com
Management:
    Director: Don West

4933
HAVRE COMMUNITY CONCERT ASSOCIATION
1150A SUB Drive
P.O. Box 7751
Havre, MT 59501-7751

SERIES & FESTIVALS / Nebraska

Phone: 406-265-5254
e-mail: brewer@msun.edu
Web Site:
https://www.msun.edu/stuactivities/showcase.aspx
Officers:
　President: Dan Heltne
Budget: $10,000-20,000

4934
NORTHERN SHOWCASE CONCERT ASSOCIATION
MSU-Northern
PO Box 7751
Havre, MT 59501
Phone: 406-265-3700
Fax: 406-265-3785
Toll-free: 800-662-6132
e-mail: brewer@msun.edu
Web Site: www.msun.edu
Officers:
　Chair: Denise Brewer
Management:
　Executive Director: Debbie Ritz
Mission: To provide fine arts/culture to the Havre community and MSU Northern students.
Utilizes: Community Members; Community Talent; Five Seasonal Concerts; Original Music Scores
Founded: 1932
Specialized Field: Havre and the Hiline community
Status: Non-Profit, Professional
Volunteer Staff: 15
Paid Artists: 6
Budget: $10,000-20,000

4935
FLATHEAD VALLEY FESTIVAL
15 Depot Park
Kalispell, MT 59901
Phone: 406-758-2800
Fax: 406-257-1065
Toll-free: 888-888-2308
e-mail: festival@cyberport.net
Web Site: www.cyberport.net/festival
Officers:
　VP: Bob Kieser
　Treasurer: Kris Fuehrer

4936
UNIVERSITY OF MONTANA PERFORMING ARTS SERIES
University Of Montana
32 Campus Drive
Missoula, MT 59812
Phone: 406-243-4970
Fax: 406-243-4905
e-mail: cvpadean@umontana.edu
Web Site: www.umproductions.org
Management:
　Executive Director: Dave Van
　Concert Coordinator: Elizabeth Wilhelm
　Advisor: Marlene Hendckson
Founded: 1918
Specialized Field: Series & Festivals; Instrumental Music; Vocal Music; Theatre; Dance; Ethnic Performances
Status: Non-Profit, Non-Professional
Paid Staff: 9
Income Sources: Student Funded
Performs At: Fieldhouse; Wilma Theatre; University Theater; UC Ballroom; Arena; Theaters
Facility Category: Theater
Type of Stage: Built In
Seating Capacity: 1,000

Year Remodeled: 1998
Rental Contact: Tom Webster

4938
OLD TIMERS CONCERT SERIES
Sheridan High School
4588 Morgan View Road
Sheridan, MT 14454
Phone: 585-243-6000
Fax: 585-243-0286
Web Site:
https://www.facebook.com/events/223619694453273/
Management:
　Manager: Sue Nottingham
　Administrator: Tim Anderson
　Assistant Administrator: Sally Smith R.N.
Mission: To encourage community talent; to raise money for scholarships and school music programs.
Utilizes: Guest Artists; Guest Companies; Singers
Founded: 1974
Specialized Field: Dance; Vocal Music; Instrumental Music; Theatre; Festivals
Status: Semi-Professional; Non-Professional
Paid Staff: 50
Performs At: Sheridan School Gym
Organization Type: Performing; Resident

4939
FLATHEAD FESTIVAL OF THE ARTS
PO Box 1780
Whitefish, MT 59937/WHIT
Phone: 406-862-1780
Management:
　Executive Director: Charles Buchwalter
　Artistic Director: Gordon Johnson
　Administrative Director: Rebecca Grouse
Founded: 1986
Specialized Field: Vocal Music Instrumental Music; Festivals; Lyric Opera
Status: Nonprofit
Organization Type: Performing; Touring; Educational; Sponsoring

Nebraska

4940
HARLAN COUNTY ARTS COUNCIL
PO Box 166
311 Main Street
Alma, NE 68920
Phone: 308-928-9989
Web Site: www.manta.com
Officers:
　President: Cindy Kauk
Budget: $10,000-20,000

4941
BASSETT ARTS COUNCIL
PO Box 383
Bassett, NE 68714
Phone: 402-684-3319
Fax: 402-684-2546
e-mail: bassettcda@bassettnebr.com
Web Site: bassettnebr.com/arts.asp
Officers:
　President: Linda May
　VP: Kathy Jorgensen
　Treasurer: Betty Hall
　Secretary: Mary M. Schelkopf
Management:
　Secretary/ Contact Person: Mary M Schelkopf

Utilizes: Actors; Artists-in-Residence; Choreographers; Collaborations; Commissioned Music; Curators; Dance Companies; Dancers; Educators; Fine Artists; Guest Accompanists; Guest Choreographers; Guest Instructors; Guest Soloists; Guild Activities; Instructors; Local Artists; Lyricists; Multimedia; New Productions; Original Music Scores; Playwrights; Sign Language Translators; Soloists; Special Technical Talent; Theatre Companies; Touring Companies
Paid Staff: 50
Budget: $20,000-35,000

4942
COLUMBUS FRIENDS OF MUSIC ASSOCIATION
1619 9th Street
Columbus, NE 68601
Phone: 402-563-1247
e-mail: rtjjhawk@frontiernet.net
Web Site: www.concertassociation.net/columbusne/
Officers:
　President: Willie Piitz
　Vice President: Sharon Brown
　Secretary: Carol Cook
　Treasurer: David Scharff
　Executive Director: Tracy Augustine

4943
MIDLAND LUTHERAN COLLEGE CONCERT: LECTURE SERIES
900 North Clarkson
Fremont, NE 68025
Phone: 402-721-5480
e-mail: info@midlandu.edu
Web Site: www.midlandu.edu/
Officers:
　VP Institutional Advancement: Fred Pyle

4944
ABENDMUSIK SERIES
2000 D Street
Lincoln, NE 68502-1698
Phone: 402-476-9933
Fax: 402-476-8402
e-mail: info@abendmusik.org
Web Site: www.abendmusik.org
Management:
　Executive Director: Jeremy Bankson
　Artistic Director: Tom Trenney
　Administrative Director: Rebecca Shane
Mission: Gathering to experience excellence in the performing arts
Founded: 1972
Specialized Field: Series & Festivals; Instrumental Music; Vocal Music; Concert Series
Status: Non-Profit, Professional
Paid Staff: 3
Budget: $60,000-150,000
Performs At: First-Plymouth Church
Facility Category: Church
Seating Capacity: 670-750
Rental Contact: Louise Bremers

4945
LIED CENTER FOR PERFORMING ARTS
Lied Center for Performing Arts
12th and R Streets, PO Box 880151
Lincoln, NE 68588-0151
Phone: 402-472-4747
Fax: 402-472-4730
Toll-free: 800-432-3231
e-mail: info@liedcenter.org
Web Site: www.liedcenter.org

Officers:
- **President:** Richard Vierk
- **President Elect.:** Chuck Harris

Management:
- **Executive Director:** Bill Stephan
- **Artistic Director:** Ann Chang
- **Managing Director:** Charles Henry Bethea
- **Marketing & Sales Manager:** Matthew Boring
- **Communications Coordinator:** Carrie Christensen
- **Graphics Specialist:** Kira Geiger
- **Administrative Technician/Developme:** Donna Seefeld
- **Director of Business Services:** Natalie Stroud
- **Business Office Supervisor:** Connie Mendoza

Founded: 1989
Specialized Field: Series and Festivals; Instrumental Music; Vocal Music; Theatre; Youth; Dance; Ethnic Performances
Status: Non-Profit, Professional
Paid Staff: 30
Volunteer Staff: 300

4946
HERITAGE DAYS FESTIVAL
PO Box 984
McCook, NE 21501-0984
Phone: 301-722-0037
Fax: 301-722-8344
e-mail: info@heritagedaysfestival.com
Web Site: www.heritagedaysfestival.com/

Management:
- **Director:** Moris Owen
- **Assistant Director:** Joan Parsons

Founded: 1969
Specialized Field: Dance; Vocal Music; Instrumental Music; Arts and Crafts
Status: Non-Professional; Nonprofit
Organization Type: Sponsoring

4947
BROWNVILLE CONCERT SERIES
740 S 75th Street
P.O. Box 4
Omaha, NE 68321
Phone: 402-825-3331
Fax: 402-346-1355
Web Site: brownvilleconcertseries.com/2014-concert-season

Officers:
- **Program Chairman:** James H. Keene III
- **Development Chairman:** John Lauber
- **Public Relations Chairman:** Jan Chism Wright
- **Treasurer:** Jennifer James

Management:
- **Technical Director:** Luther MacNaughton
- **Asst. Technical Director:** Haney Milstead

Budget: $20,000-35,000

4948
CATHEDRAL ARTS PROJECT SERIES
100 North 62nd Street
Omaha, NE 68132
Phone: 402-558-3100
Fax: 402-558-3026
e-mail: dorthy@tuma.net
Web Site: www.cathedralartsproject.org

Officers:
- **President:** Michael McCabe
- **Vice-President:** Jon A. Jacobsen
- **Secretary:** Betty J. Davis
- **Treasurer:** Carol Ebdon

Management:
- **Executive Director:** William Woeger
- **Adminstrative Assistant:** Dorothy Tuma

Founded: 1985
Specialized Field: Visual/Performing
Paid Staff: 2
Volunteer Staff: 50
Budget: $10,000-20,000
Performs At: St. Cecelia Cathedral

4949
NEBRASKA SHAKESPEARE FESTIVAL
Department of Fine Arts, Creighton University
2500 California Plaza
Omaha, NE 68178
Phone: 402-280-2700
e-mail: info@creighton.edu
Web Site: www.nebraskashakespeare.com

Officers:
- **Co-Chairmen:** Fred Simon
- **Co-Chairmen:** Eve Simon
- **Chairman Emeritus:** Harold W. Andersen

Management:
- **Executive Director:** Mary Ann Bamber
- **Director of Production/Education:** Sarah Carlson-Brown
- **Marketing Director:** Nellie Sudavicius MacCallum
- **Co-Founder and Interim Artistic Dir:** Alan Klem
- **Interim Artistic Director:** Vincent Carlson-Brown
- **Director of Production:** Wesley A. Houston

Specialized Field: Theater

4950
TUESDAY MUSICAL CONCERT SERIES
8543 Hickory Street
P.O. Box 6132
Omaha, NE 68106-0132
Phone: 402-551-2234
Fax: 402-397-9510
e-mail: tuesmus@aol.com
Web Site: www.tuesdaymusicomaha.org

Management:
- **President:** Frederica Perhulste
- **Program Chairman:** Barbara Taxman

Mission: Offering an annual professional concert series.
Utilizes: Guest Accompanists; Multimedia
Founded: 1892
Specialized Field: Series & Festivals: Recitals Series
Status: Non-Profit, Professional
Volunteer Staff: 30
Budget: $35,000-60,000
Income Sources: Ticket sales; Donations; Grants
Performs At: Joslyn Art Museum
Annual Attendance: 600
Facility Category: Art Museum/Concert Hall
Seating Capacity: 1,000
Organization Type: Sponsoring

4951
UNIVERSITY OF NEBRASKA AT OMAHA MUSIC SERIES
Music Department
60 and Dodge Street
Omaha, NE 68182
Phone: 402-554-3427
Fax: 402-554-2252
e-mail: gperdue@mail.unomaha.edu
Web Site: www.music.unomaha.edu

Officers:
- **Chairman Department of Music:** Melissa Berke

Management:
- **Event Coordinator/Performace Series:** Greg Perdue

Utilizes: Artists-in-Residence; Commissioned Music; Guest Accompanists; Guest Companies; Guest Directors; Guest Instructors; Guest Lecturers; Guest Musical Directors; Guest Musicians; High School Drama; Local Artists; Multimedia; Music; Organization Contracts; Singers
Founded: 1918
Specialized Field: Series & Festivals: Chamber Music
Status: Non-Profit, Professional
Paid Staff: 10
Paid Artists: 20
Non-paid Artists: 50
Budget: $25,000
Income Sources: University Funds, Foundation Support, Grants, Ticket Sales
Performs At: Strauss Performing Arts Center
Annual Attendance: 50,000+
Facility Category: Concert Hall
Type of Stage: Concert Only
Stage Dimensions: 36'8"-37'7" x 40'
Seating Capacity: 474
Year Built: 1975
Cost: $23 million
Rental Contact: Events Coordinator T. Heil

4952
CONCORDIA UNIVERSITY CONCERT SERIES
800 N Columbia Avenue
Seward, NE 68434
Phone: 402-643-7411
Fax: 402-643-4073
Budget: $10,000

4953
WAYNE STATE COLLEGE SPECIAL PROGRAMS BLACK & GOLD SERIES
Wayne State College
1111 Main St.
Wayne, NE 68787
Phone: 402-375-7359
Fax: 402-375-7204
Web Site: www.wsc.edu/schools/ahu/events/

Management:
- **Dean:** James O'Donnell

Utilizes: Actors; Artists-in-Residence; Dance Companies; Dancers; Fine Artists; Guest Accompanists; Guest Directors; Guest Instructors; Guest Musical Directors; Guest Musicians; Guest Soloists; Multimedia; Original Music Scores; Playwrights; Sign Language Translators; Singers; Touring Companies
Budget: $35,000-60,000
Performs At: Ramsey Theatre; Ley Theatre

Nevada

4954
BOULDER CITY ARTS COUNCIL
PO Box 61314
Boulder City, NV 89006
Phone: 702-294-1499
Fax: 702-293-7743
Budget: $10,000

4955
NEVADA ARTS COUNCIL
716 N Carson Street
Suite A
Carson City, NV 89701
Phone: 775-687-6680
Fax: 775-687-6688
Toll-free: 800-326-6888
e-mail: rhodgkins@nevadaculture.org
Web Site: nac.nevadaculture.org

SERIES & FESTIVALS / New Hampshire

Management:
    Community Development: Robin Hodgkins
    Executive Director: Susan Boskoff
    Administrative Services Officer: Linda Ficklin
    Accountant Technician: Bandi Huckabay
Founded: 1967

4956
CHURCHILL ARTS COUNCIL
PO Box 2204
Fallon, NV 89407
Phone: 775-423-1440
Fax: 775-423-0779
e-mail: charts@phonewave.net
Web Site: www.churchillarts.org
Management:
    President: Ted Balash
    Executive Director: Valerie J Serpa
    Program Director: Kirk Robertson
Founded: 1986
Specialized Field: Multidisplinary Organisation.
Status: Non-Profit, Professional
Paid Staff: 2
Volunteer Staff: 20
Paid Artists: 35

4957
REED WHIPPLE CULTURAL ARTS CENTER
821 Las Vegas Boulevard N
Las Vegas, NV 89101
Phone: 702-229-6211
Fax: 702-382-5199
Web Site: www.lasvegasnevada.gov
Management:
    Manager: Nancy Deaner
    Executive Director: Bob Jackson
    Artistic Director: Patricia Harris
Mission: Developing the arts community via programming, community involvement and education.
Utilizes: Singers
Founded: 1961
Specialized Field: Series and Festival; Instrumental music; Vocal music; Theatre; Youth; Dance; Ethnic Performances; Visual Arts
Status: Non-Profit, Professional
Paid Staff: 50
Paid Artists: 100
Income Sources: American Council for the Arts; Nevada Recreation & Parks Society; Nevada Presenters Network
Affiliations: Las Vegas Civic Center; Las Vegas Woodwing Quintet
Type of Stage: Proscenium
Stage Dimensions: 18'x45'x24'
Seating Capacity: 300
Rental Contact: Patricia Harris
Organization Type: Performing; Touring; Educational; Sponsoring
Resident Groups: Rainbow Theatre Company

4958
UNIVERSITY OF NEVADA PERFORMING ARTS CENTER
4505 Maryland Parkway
Box 455005
Las Vegas, NV 089154-500
Phone: 702-895-3535
Fax: 702-895-4714
Web Site: www.pac.unlv.edu
Management:
    Dir Artistic Programming/Production: Larry Henley
    Technical Director: Trent Downing
    Director Of Marketing: Shaun Franklin-Sewell
    Director of Finance and Guest Relat: Lori James
    Director of Development: Anne Mulloy
    Stage Manager / Theatre Technician: David Gruzin
    Dean: Jeffrey Koep, Ph.D.
Founded: 1976
Specialized Field: Dance; Music; Theatre
Paid Staff: 8
Non-paid Artists: 20
Performs At: Performing Arts Center Consisting Of Three Theatres
Affiliations: University Government
Annual Attendance: 132,000
Type of Stage: Concert Hall, Theatre, Blackbox
Seating Capacity: 1830; 550; 175
Rental Contact: Dir Artistic Programming/Production Larry Henley

4959
NEVADA SHAKESPEARE FESTIVAL
1670-200 North Virginia Street
P.O. Box 8029
Reno, NV 89507-8029
Phone: 775-784-6587
Fax: 775-784-6527
Toll-free: 800-382-5023
e-mail: information@nevada-shakespeare.org
Web Site: www.nevada-shakespeare.org
Officers:
    Chair: John Patrick Rice
    Vice Chair: Kelly Mays
Management:
    President: Joan Walker
    Executive Director: Christina Barr
    Artistic Director: Jeanmarie Simpson
    Communications Director: Lindsey Stedsand
    Program Coordinator: Rachel Hopkin
    Program Coordinator: Bobbie Ann Howell
    Fiscal Officer: Christine Myers
    Managing Editor: Karen Wikander
Mission: Presents language-rich works that mine the core as archaeologist to soul, making a case, in these tenuous times, for the preservation of humankind and the world that we inhabit. NSC is driven to create a new action-based stagings that are theatrical rather than cinematic or realistic. Embracing principles of Universal Access, the company serves more than 100,000 children, youth and adults each year with theatre outreach.
Founded: 1989
Specialized Field: Series and Festivals; Theatre; Youth; Ethnic Performances
Status: Non-Profit, Professional
Paid Staff: 3
Paid Artists: 12

4960
UNIVERSITY OF NEVADA: RENO PERFORMING ARTS SERIES
UNR School Of The Arts/048
Reno, NV 89557-0048
Phone: 775-784-4278
Fax: 775-784-3566
e-mail: cmoney@unr.edu
Web Site: www.unr.edu/pas
Officers:
    President: Chris Baum
    Vice President: Joe Kelley
    Vice President: John Leinen
Management:
    Assistant Director Of Programs: Chris Money
    Executive Director: Jennifer Cunningham
    Director of Finance: Brian Rivers
Utilizes: Collaborations; Multimedia
Founded: 1960
Specialized Field: Performing Arts
Paid Staff: 2
Paid Artists: 20
Budget: $62,000-80,000
Income Sources: University Administration, Students, State And Local Grants, Ticket Income, Other Sources
Annual Attendance: 3000
Facility Category: Concert Hall
Type of Stage: Proscenium
Seating Capacity: 618
Year Built: 1988

New Hampshire

4961
KEISER CONCERT SERIES
Saint Paul's School
325 Pleasant Street
Concord, NH 03301-2591
Phone: 603-229-4600
Fax: 603-229-5695
e-mail: dseaton@sps.edu
Web Site: www.sps.edu
Management:
    Music Director: David D Seaton
    Director: Scott P. Bohan
    Executive Director: Robert H. Rettew, Jr.
    Director: Scott E. Heitmiller
Mission: To bring professional solo and chamber music concerts to St. Paul's school.
Founded: 1974
Specialized Field: Series and Festivals; Instrumental Music; Vocal Music
Status: Non-Profit, Professional
Paid Staff: 5
Paid Artists: 5
Budget: $30,000
Income Sources: Funding
Performs At: Intimate Chamber Music Hall
Seating Capacity: 150
Year Built: 1979

4962
WILLIAM H GILE TRUST FUND CONCERT SERIES
17 Pleasant View Avenue
Concord, NH 03301-2555
Phone: 603-224-1217
Fax: 603-228-3901
e-mail: info@sulloway.com.
Web Site: www.sulloway.com/index.php?...william-h-gile-trust-fund
Officers:
    Committee Chairman: Dr. Robert C Rainie
    Advisor: MT Mennino
Management:
    President: M T Menino
    Firm Administrator: Thomas W. Brightman
    Human Resource Administrator: Jennifer L. Iacopino
    Information Technology Manager: Christopher Descoteau
    Facilities Manager: Ronald W. Higgins
    Marketing Coordinator: Nicole M. Manteau
    Research Coordinator: Amy W. Bline
Specialized Field: Series & Festivals; Instrumental Music; Vocal Music; Theatre; Youth; Dance; Ethnic Performances
Status: Non-Profit, Professional
Paid Staff: 3

Budget: $85,000
Income Sources: Trust Fund
Performs At: Chubb Theatre; Capitol Center for the Arts
Annual Attendance: 1,400/performance
Facility Category: Capiyol Center for the Arts
Stage Dimensions: 40' wide/24 1/2' deep/4 1/2' apron
Seating Capacity: 1,425
Rental Contact: CEO M.T. Mennino

4963
NEW HAMPSHIRE SHAKESPEARE FESTIVAL
PO Box 191
Deerfield, NH 03037
Phone: 603-666-9088
e-mail: nhsf@nhsf.org
Web Site: www.nhsf.org
Management:
    Executive Director: Gail Mills
Founded: 1993
Status: Non-Equity; Nonprofit
Season: July - August

4964
UNIVERSITY OF NEW HAMPSHIRE CELEBRITY SERIES
Paul Creative Arts Center, M202
30 Academic Way
Durham, NH 03824
Phone: 603-862-7222
Fax: 603-862-3155
e-mail: arts.tickets@unh.edu
Web Site: www.unh.edu/celebrity
Management:
    Manager: Mary Deturk
Utilizes: Dancers; Guest Directors; Multimedia; Special Technical Talent; Theatre Companies
Specialized Field: Series & Festivals; Instrumental Music; Vocal Music; Theatre; Dance
Status: Non-Profit, Non-Professional
Paid Staff: 1
Budget: $60,000-150,000
Performs At: Johnson Theatre
Type of Stage: proscenium
Stage Dimensions: 20x40
Seating Capacity: 688a
Year Built: 1960
Rental Contact: Theatre & Dance Dept. Michael Woood

4965
DARTMOUTH COLLEGE HOPKINS CENTER PERFORMING SERIES
Hopkins Center
6041 Lower Level Wilson Hall
Hanover, NH 03755-3543
Phone: 603-646-2422
Fax: 603-646-3911
e-mail: hopprogramming@dartmouth.edu
Web Site: www.hop.dartmouth.edu
Management:
    Executive Director: Lewis Crickard
    Artistic Director: Margaret Lawrence
Founded: 1962
Specialized Field: Series & Festivals; Instrumental Music; Vocal Music; Theatre; Youth; Dance; Ethnic Performances
Status: Non-Profit, Professional
Paid Staff: 43
Paid Artists: 175
Budget: $400,000-1,000,000
Performs At: The Moore Theatre; Rollins Chapel

4966
NEW ENGLAND COLLEGE CULTURAL EVENTS SERIES
98 Bridge Street
Henniker, NH 03242-0793
Phone: 603-428-2303
Web Site: www.nec.edu/
Budget: $10,000

4967
BELKNAP MILL SOCIETY
The Mill Plaza
25 Beacon Street East
Laconia, NH 03246
Phone: 603-524-8813
Fax: 603-528-1228
Web Site: www.belknapmill.org
Officers:
    President: Chris Santaniello
    Vice-President: Allison Ambrose
    Treasurer: David Stamps
Management:
    President: Peter Ellis
    Executive Director: Denise Sharlow
    Program Director: Beth San Soucie
    Bookkeeping: Lisa Magerer
    Publicity: Thomas Caldwell
    Office Assistant: Nancy Paquette
Founded: 1971
Specialized Field: Multidisciplinary Art Center
Status: Non-Profit, Professional
Paid Staff: 7
Budget: $10,000

4968
NORTH COUNTRY CHAMBER PLAYERS SUMMER FESTIVAL: MUSIC IN THE WHITE MOUNTAINS
115 Eastern Avenue
Littleton, NH 05819
Mailing Address: P.O. Box 324, St. Johnsbury, VT 05819
Phone: 802-748-2600
Fax: 802-748-0852
Toll-free: 888-757-5559
e-mail: info@catamountarts.org
Web Site: www.newww.com/org/nccp
Officers:
    President, Board of Directors: Linda Wacholder
    Vice President: Greg MacDonald
    Secretary: Bob Amos
    Treasurer: Elizabeth Wilson
Management:
    Executive Director: Jody Fried
    Artistic Director: Jerry Aldredge
    Development Director: Amy Stetson Rebollo
    Membership Coordinator: Martin Bryan
    Box Office Manager & Head Projectio: Patrick Black
Mission: Culturally enrich New Hamphire through chamber music performance and music education
Founded: 1978
Status: Nonprofit
Paid Staff: 1
Paid Artists: 12
Budget: $400,000-500,000
Income Sources: Earned Revenues by Government; Foundation; Corporate and Individual Donors

4969
SAINT ANSELM COLLEGE PERFORMING ARTS SERIES
Dana Humanities Center
100 Saint Anselm Drive
Manchester, NH 03102-1310
Phone: 603-641-7710
Fax: 603-641-7332
e-mail: dana@anselm.edu
Web Site: www.anselm.edu
Management:
    President: Fr Jonathan Defelice
    VP Of Student Affairs: Joseph M Horto
    Director: Bob Shea
    Production Manager and Technical Di: Joe Deleault
Founded: 1889
Budget: $150,000-400,000
Performs At: Koonz Theatre

4970
AMERICAN STAGE FESTIVAL PEACOCK PLAYERS
14 Court Street
Nashua, NH 03060
Phone: 603-889-2330
Fax: 603-889-2336
e-mail: keithw@peacockplayers.org
Web Site: www.peacockplayers.org
Officers:
    President: Brad Jamieson
    Vice President: Brad Galinson
    Treasurer: Lisa Bingham
    Interim Secretary: Gail Chazanovitz
    Director: Maggie Mahony
    Wing Chairperson: Shannon Galinson
Management:
    Production Artistic Director: Robert Walsh
    Artistic Director: Keith Weirich
    General Manager: Emerson Kelly
    Summer Theatre Camp Manager: Sarah Evans
Founded: 2002
Specialized Field: Series & Festivals; Theatre; Youth
Status: Non-Profit, Non-Professional
Season: June - August
Type of Stage: Proscenium
Stage Dimensions: 40' x 38'
Seating Capacity: 497

4971
NASHUA COMMUNITY CONCERT ASSOCIATION
PO Box 1563
Nashua, NH 03061-1563
Phone: 603-318-1792
e-mail: Membership@NashuaCommunityConcerts.org
Web Site: www.nashuacommunityconcerts.org
Officers:
    President: Carol P. Marshall
Management:
    President: Carol P. Marshall
    Membership Secretary: Mary E. Sayre
    Vice-President: Calvin Knickerbocker
    Corresponding Secretary: Betty Williams
    Treasurer: William Doll
    Assistant Treasurer: Jean Lyons
    Campaign Chairman: Jeanne Klink
Founded: 1931
Specialized Field: Series & Festivals; Vocal Music; Choral; Theatre; Dance; Ethnic Performances; Orchestra
Status: Non-Profit, Professional
Budget: $35,000-60,000

SERIES & FESTIVALS / New Hampshire

4972
COLBY-SAWYER COLLEGE
Ware Campus Center
541 Maint Street
New London, NH 03257
Phone: 603-526-3759
Fax: 603-526-2135
e-mail: sazodi@colby-sawyer.edu
Web Site: www.colby-sawyer.edu
Management:
 President: Ann Ponder
 Campus Activities Director: Sharon Williamson
Founded: 1857
Specialized Field: Series & Festivals: Theatre
Status: Non-Profit, Non-Professional
Budget: $10,000-20,000

4973
SUMMER MUSIC ASSOCIATES SERIES
PO Box 603
New London, NH 03257
Phone: 603-526-8234
e-mail: info@summermusicassociates.com
Web Site: www.nl-nh.com
Management:
 Program Committee Chairman: Robert Fraley
Mission: Presenter of four summer concerts.
Founded: 1974
Specialized Field: Vocal Music; Instrumental Music
Status: Nonprofit
Budget: $45,000
Income Sources: Contributions; ticket sales
Performs At: College/high schoool/church/town hall facilities
Annual Attendance: 1500
Seating Capacity: 700
Organization Type: Sponsoring

4974
MONADNOCK MUSIC
2A Concord Street
Peterborough, NH 03458
Phone: 603-924-7610
Fax: 603-924-9403
Toll-free: 800-868-9613
e-mail: mm@monadnockmusic.mv.com
Web Site: www.monadnockmusic.org
Officers:
 President: Amy Knight - Jaffrey
 Treasurer: Kevin McElhinney
 Secretary: Therry Neilsen-Steinhardt
 Vice President: Michael Petrovick
Management:
 Artistic Director: Gil Rose
 Artistic Director: Laura Gilbert
 Managing Director: Christopher Sink
Mission: To make exceptional music accessible to all in intimate and informal settings through a commitment to varied and imaginative performances to keep a sense of musical daring and discovery alive.
Utilizes: Guest Directors; Guest Musicians; Multimedia; Original Music Scores; Sign Language Translators; Singers
Founded: 1966
Specialized Field: Vocal Music; Instrumental Music; Festivals; Lyric Opera
Status: Professional; Nonprofit
Paid Staff: 5
Paid Artists: 50
Budget: $350,000
Income Sources: Grants; Private Donations
Performs At: Churches; Meetinghousese
Seating Capacity: 200
Organization Type: Performing; Educational

4975
FRIENDS OF THE ARTS REGIONAL ART COUNCIL
PO Box 386
Plymouth, NH 03264-0386
Phone: 603-536-1182
Fax: 603-536-1182
e-mail: friends@friends-of-the-arts.org
Web Site: www.friends-of-the-arts.org
Management:
 President: Margaret Turner
 Executive Director: Jane Hamor
 Artistic Director: Cynthia Robinson
Founded: 1973
Specialized Field: Series and Festivals: Ethnic Performances
Status: Non-Profit, Professional
Paid Staff: 3
Budget: $20,000-35,000
Performs At: Silver Hall

4976
PLYMOUTH STATE UNIVERSITY
Silver Center For The Arts
Plymouth State University
Plymouth, NH 03264
Mailing Address: MSC 36-17 High Street
Phone: 603-535-2801
Fax: 603-535-2917
e-mail: djeffery@plymouth.edu
Web Site: silver.plymouth.edu
Management:
 Director: Diane Jeffery
 House Manager: Ginny Fisher
 Technical Operations Manager: Stuart Crowell
 Technical Operations Supervisor: Bob Bruemmer
 Technical Production Assistant: Heather Manfredi
 Box Office Manager: Trudy Pelletier
 Events Coordinator: Melissa Furbish
 Business Coordinator: Sureya Ennabe
 Assistant House Manager: Susanne Hastings
Utilizes: Artists-in-Residence; Collaborating Artists; Collaborations; Dance Companies; Dancers; Educators; Guest Accompanists; Guest Choreographers; Guest Musical Directors; Guest Musicians; Guest Soloists; Lyricists; Multi Collaborations; Multimedia; Original Music Scores; Playwrights; Selected Students; Soloists; Special Technical Talent; Theatre Companies
Specialized Field: Central NH
Paid Staff: 20
Paid Artists: 14
Budget: $35,000-60,000
Income Sources: Ticket Revenue, Sponsorships, Grants, and Donations.
Performs At: Hanaway Theatre; Smith Recital Hall; Studio Theatre
Facility Category: Performing Arts Center
Type of Stage: Proscenium
Stage Dimensions: 90' x 36'
Seating Capacity: 650
Year Built: 1992
Year Remodeled: 1992
Rental Contact: Director Diane Jeffery

4977
FRIENDS OF THE MUSIC HALL CONCERT SERIES
104 Congress Street
Suite 203
Portsmouth, NH 03801
Phone: 603-433-3100
Fax: 603-431-4103
e-mail: tlagamma@themusichall.org
Web Site: www.themusichall.org
Officers:
 President: Robert W. Hickey
 Vice-President: Jo Lamprey
 Secretary: Barbara Henry
 Treasurer: Edwin Garside
Management:
 President: Patricia Lynch
 Artistic Director: Theresa La Gamma
 Executive Director: Patricia Lynch
 Executive Administrative Assistant: Todd Hunter
 Chief Financial Officer: Kriston Briggs
 Director of Marketing: Monte Bohanan
 Director of Operations: Michael Tucker
 Box Office Manager: Mark Pruett
 Production Manager: Zhana Morris
Founded: 1986
Specialized Field: Series & Festivals; Music; Theatre; Dance; Films
Status: Non-Profit, Professional
Paid Staff: 20
Budget: $150,000-400,000

4978
HARBOR ARTS JAZZ NIGHT: PORTSMOUTH JAZZ FESTIVAL
93 High Street
PO Box 4585
Portsmouth, NH 03802-4585
Phone: 603-436-8596
Fax: 603-433-2787
e-mail: richard@cuzinrichard.com
Web Site: www.jazznite.org
Officers:
 President: John Hauschildt
Management:
 Managing Director: Richard Smith
Mission: Raise funds for Harbor Arts Museum and for school music art departments/music schools, other non profits.
Utilizes: Collaborating Artists; Composers-in-Residence; Guest Accompanists; Instructors; Local Artists & Directors; Music; Original Music Scores; Paid Performers; Playwrights; Scenic Designers; Students; Visual Arts; Visual Designers
Founded: 1991
Specialized Field: Series & Festivals: Museum and jazz music
Status: Non-Profit, Professional
Volunteer Staff: 25
Paid Artists: 10

4979
PRESCOTT PARK ARTS FESTIVAL
PO Box 4370
105 Marcy Street
Portsmouth, NH 03802-4370
Phone: 603-436-2848
Fax: 603-436-1034
e-mail: info@prescottpark.org
Web Site: www.prescottpark.org
Officers:
 President: Claudette Barker
 Vice President: Bill Duncan

Secretary: Aileen Dugan
Treasurer: Matt Williams
Management:
Executive Director: Ben Anderson
Festival Coordinator: Ellen Foord
Music Director: Catherine York
Stage Manager/Production Manager: David D'Agostino
Managing Director: John Moynihan
Mission: To provide a professional wide-ranging arts festival for a diverse audience combining ticketed and free access.
Utilizes: Singers
Founded: 1974
Specialized Field: Dance; Vocal Music; Theatre; Festivals
Status: Nonprofit
Season: July - August
Performs At: Prescott Park
Organization Type: Performing; Touring; Resident; Educational; Sponsoring

4980
FRANKLIN PIERCE COLLEGE CRIMSON-GREY CULTURAL SERIES
Franklin Pierce College
PO BOX 60
Rindge, NH 03461
Mailing Address: PO BOX 60 RINDGE, NH 03461
Phone: 603-899-4152
Fax: 603-899-6448
Web Site: www.creativeground.org/
Budget: $10,000-20,000
Performs At: Fieldhouse; Ravencroft Theater

4981
WATERVILLE VALLEY FOUNDATION SUMMER FESTIVAL
1 Ski Area Road
PO Box 540
Waterville Valley, NH 03215
Phone: 603-236-8311
Fax: 603-236-4344
Toll-free: 800-468-2553
e-mail: info@waterville.com
Web Site: www.waterville.com
Management:
Town Square Manager: April Smith
Mission: To present a summer festival of the arts.
Utilizes: Singers
Founded: 1985
Specialized Field: Vocal Music; Instrumental Music; Festivals; Concerts
Status: Nonprofit
Performs At: Town Square Concert Pavillion
Organization Type: Performing; Educational

4982
GREAT WATERS MUSIC FESTIVAL
15 Varney Road
PO Box 488
Wolfeboro, NH 03894
Phone: 603-569-7710
Fax: 603-569-7715
e-mail: info@greatwaters.org
Web Site: www.greatwaters.org
Officers:
Chairperson: Barbara Lobdell
Vice Chair: Sue Ayers
Treasurer: Paul Olzerowicz
Secretary: Madge Nickerson
Management:
Executive Director: Ben Anderson

Mission: To present a diversified summer concert series.
Founded: 1995
Status: Non-Profit
Facility Category: Acoustic Tent

New Jersey

4983
ASBURY PARK JAZZ FESTIVAL
1 Municipal Plaza
Asbury Park, NJ 07712
Phone: 732-502-5728
Fax: 732-502-5738
Web Site: www.jerseyshorefestival.org/

4984
GREAT GORGE FESTIVAL
575 Ash Street
Belleville, NJ 81212
Phone: 719-275-1578
e-mail: dquinn711@aol.com
Web Site: www.eventticketscenter.com/
Management:
Producer: Daniel P Quinn

4985
SCANDINAVIAN FEST
NJ Vasa Park
1 Wolfe Road
Budd Lake, NJ 07872
Phone: 610-417-1483
e-mail: info@ScanFest.org
Web Site: www.ScanFest.org
Officers:
President: Palmer Hval
General Chair/Entertainment Coord: Kathy Hval
Publicity/Promotion: Carl Anderson
Vendor Chair: Lisbet Price
Utilizes: Actors; Dance Companies; Dancers; Fine Artists; Five Seasonal Concerts; Grant Writers; Guest Accompanists; Guest Directors; Guest Instructors; Guest Musical Directors; Guest Musicians; Guest Soloists; High School Drama; Instructors; Multimedia; Original Music Scores; Sign Language Translators; Singers; Soloists; Student Interns; Special Technical Talent; Theatre Companies
Founded: 1985
Volunteer Staff: 30
Paid Artists: 20
Budget: $40,000-$50,000
Income Sources: Admission Fees, Donations, Sponsorhsip, Vendor Fees
Performs At: Outdoor park with covered/roofed performance areas
Annual Attendance: 5,000
Facility Category: Outdoor park with covered stages, 1 Indoor stage
Type of Stage: Covered Outdoors, One Indoor
Stage Dimensions: varies to 40x80
Seating Capacity: 200-500

4986
CAPE MAY JAZZ FESTIVAL
PO Box 2065
Cape May, NJ 08204
Phone: 609-884-7277
Fax: 609-884-7248
e-mail: jodi@capemayjazz.com
Web Site: www.exit0jazzfest.com
Officers:
President: Carol Stone
Management:

President: Woody Woodland
Executive Director: Lelah Ettenbazh
Artistic Director: Carol Stone
Mission: To hold 2 jazz festivals per year, education programs and promote jazz to region
Founded: 1994
Specialized Field: Series & Festivals; Instrumental Music; Vocal Music
Status: Non-Profit, Professional
Paid Staff: 3
Volunteer Staff: 200
Annual Attendance: 15,000

4987
CAPE MAY MUSIC FESTIVAL
1048 Washington St.
PO Box 340
Cape May, NJ 08204
Phone: 609-884-5404
Fax: 609-884-5064
Toll-free: 800-275-4278
e-mail: info@capemaymac.org
Web Site: www.capemaymac.org
Management:
Chief Outreach Officer: Mary E Stewart, mstewart@capemaymac.org
Mission: Preservation, interpretation and cultural enrichment
Utilizes: Commissioned Music; Community Talent; Curators; Five Seasonal Concerts; Guest Directors
Founded: 1970
Opened: 1990
Specialized Field: Music; Instrumental
Status: Non-Profit
Paid Staff: 20
Volunteer Staff: 50
Paid Artists: 100
Budget: $250,000
Income Sources: Grants, Donationa, Admissions
Type of Stage: Altar Area
Seating Capacity: 200-400
Year Built: 1800

4988
EDISON ARTS SOCIETY
390 Mac Lane
Edison, NJ 08832
Mailing Address: 15 Midland Road Edison. NJ 08820
Phone: 732-548-9134
Fax: 732-225-1703
e-mail: edisonarts@edisonarts.org
Web Site: www.edisonnarts.org
Officers:
President: Gloria S. Dittman
Vice President: Nicole Visceglia Rodgers
Secretary/Treasurer: Elaine Kaufman
Secretary: Karen McNamara
Management:
President: Gloria S. Dittman
Executive Director: Hand Nina
Founded: 1998
Specialized Field: Series & Festivals; Symphonic Orchestra
Status: Non-Profit, Professional
Paid Staff: 2
Paid Artists: 3

4989
APPEL FARM ARTS AND MUSIC CENTER
PO Box 888
457 Shirley Road
Elmer, NJ 08318

SERIES & FESTIVALS / New Jersey

Phone: 856-358-2472
Fax: 856-358-6513
Toll-free: 800-394-1211
e-mail: info@appelfarm.org
Web Site: www.appelfarm.org
Officers:
- President: Denise Hayman-Loa
- Vice President: Ronnie Cimprich
- Secretary: Franklin Moore
- Treasurer: Anita Zippert

Management:
- Executive Director: Cori Solomon
- Artistic Director: Sean Timmons
- Director Special Projects: Judy Henson
- Director of Arts Education and Outr: Kerri Sullivan
- Conference Center Director: Wesley Bogan
- Director of Development: Lawrence Schmidt
- Director of Marketing: Heather Yelle
- Office Manager: Matina Lagakos
- IT Support Coordinator: Domarino Greco

Utilizes: Artists-in-Residence; Multimedia; Original Music Scores
Founded: 1960
Specialized Field: Series & Festivals; Dance; Vocal Music; Instrumental Music; Theatre; Festivals
Status: Non-Profit, Professional
Paid Staff: 18
Volunteer Staff: 500
Paid Artists: 21
Budget: $2.3 million
Affiliations: ArtPRIDE, NJSCA, SJCA, ABP
Facility Category: Regional Performing Arts Center
Type of Stage: Indoor/Outdoor
Stage Dimensions: 40'x50'
Seating Capacity: 250/12,000
Year Built: 1965
Rental Contact: Conference Center Director Walt Sibley
Organization Type: Performing; Resident; Educational

4990
JOHN HARMS CENTER FOR THE ARTS

30 N Van Brunt Street
Englewood, NJ 07631
Phone: 201-567-5797
Fax: 201-567-7357
Web Site: www.johnharms.org
Management:
- Executive Director: Jessica Finkelberg
- Business Manager: Steve Nemiroff
- Director Education: Cathy Roy
- Communications/Marketing: Ed Kirchdoerffer

Founded: 1976
Status: Nonprofit
Paid Staff: 14
Volunteer Staff: 150
Paid Artists: 250
Budget: $3,000,000
Income Sources: Foundations, Grants, Corporate Support, Individuals, Earned
Annual Attendance: 300,000
Facility Category: Theater
Type of Stage: Proscenium
Stage Dimensions: 33 x 30
Seating Capacity: 1322
Year Built: 1926

4991
COLLEGE OF NEW JERSEY CENTER FOR THE ARTS

PO Box 7718
Ewing, NJ 08628-0718
Phone: 609-771-2563
Fax: 609-637-5134
e-mail: centered@tcnj.edu
Web Site: www.tcnj.edu/cfa
Officers:
- Dean: John C Laughton

Management:
- Director of Arts Facilities: Richard Kroth
- Coordinator of Audience Services: Susan O'Connor
- Director of Operations: Richard A. Kroth
- Director: Emily Croll
- Coordinator of Communications & Com: Deanna Biase
- Oversees Kendall Theater Facilities: Dale Simon
- Manager: Kevin Potucek

Mission: Serves as a focal point for the Arts at the College and will function to promote arts activities, both on and off campus, collaborate with arts organization in New Jersey and beyond, advocate for arts education in schools and communities, and serve as a link to the curricular needs of all of the schools in the College of New Jersey.
Founded: 1855

4992
FAIR LAWN SUMMER FESTIVAL

Federated Arts Council
185 Prospect Avenue, Apartment 12M
Hackensack, NJ 07601
Phone: 201-646-1061
Fax: 201-796-5667
Web Site: musicalworld.com/presenters/fair-lawn-summer-festival
Management:
- Director: Isadore Freeman

Founded: 1960
Specialized Field: Series & Festivals; Instrumental Music; Vocal Music; Theatre; Youth; Dance; Ethnic Performances
Status: Non-Profit, Professional
Paid Staff: 2
Budget: $10,000
Annual Attendance: 1,000
Facility Category: Band Shell
Year Built: 1992

4993
SOUNDFEST CHAMBER MUSIC FESTIVAL, COLORADO QUARTET

10 Hillside Circle
Suite B
Hackensack, NJ 06268
Phone: 508-548-2290
Fax: 201-498-0019
e-mail: cq@coloradoquartet.com
Web Site: www.coloradoquartet.com
Management:
- Director: Diane Chaplin
- Festival Manager: Lydia Redding

4994
CENTENARY STAGE COMPANY AND PERFORMING ARTS GUILD

400 Jefferson Street
Hackettstown, NJ 07840
Phone: 908-979-0900
Fax: 908-979-4297
e-mail: boxoffice@centenarystageco.com
Web Site: www.centenarystageco.org
Management:
- Artistic Director: Carl Wallnau
- General Manager: Catherine Rust
- Development Associate: Lea Antonlini
- Theatre Office Manager: Pat Lanciano
- Program Assistant: Rita Medina
- Assistant Program Director: Lea Antolini
- Director of YPW: Michael Blevins
- Costume Designer: Julia Sharp
- Marketing Assistant: Nick Ardito-Martelli

Mission: A not-for-profit professional Equity Theatre dedicated to bringin the performing arts to the Warren, Sussex, Morris and Hunterdon County areas. OUr actors are a part of the Actors Equity Association, the professional union for actors. We are an associate member of the New Jersey Theatre Alliance.
Founded: 1987
Specialized Field: Theatre; Music; Dance
Status: Non-Profit, Professional
Paid Staff: 4
Volunteer Staff: 5

4995
COMMUNITY ARTS PARTNERSHIP SERIES WITH PEDDIE SCHOOL

The Peddie School
201 South Main Street
Hightstown, NJ 08520-3349
Phone: 609-490-7500
Fax: 609-944-7901
e-mail: sjames@peddie.org
Web Site: www.peddie.org
Officers:
- Chair: Christopher J. Acito

Management:
- Head Of School: Peter Quinn
- Director Of Athletics: Jim Domoracki
- Dean Of Students: Melaine A. Clements
- Dean Of Faculty: Timothy Garcia
- Director of Marketing: Deanna K.G. Ferrante
- Director of Admission: Raymond Cabot
- Director of College Counseling: Jason Honsel
- Assistant Head for Finance & Operat: Michael McKitish
- Director of Security: Paul Miller

Mission: Performing and Visual Arts Presenter and Producer
Utilizes: Actors; Collaborations; Dance Companies; Guest Ensembles; Guest Instructors; Guest Musical Directors; Guild Activities; Instructors; Multi Collaborations; Original Music Scores; Sign Language Translators; Special Technical Talent; Touring Companies
Founded: 1864
Budget: $250,000
Performs At: William Mount-Burke Theatre; Masland Room
Type of Stage: Proscenium
Seating Capacity: 535

4996
AM PRODUCTIONS SERIES

2 Woodland Road
Holmdel, NJ 07733
Phone: 732-264-2111
Fax: 732-264-0081
Toll-free: 800-995-8085
e-mail: amprod@aol.com
Officers:
- President: Stanley Andrucyk

Management:
- President: Stanley Andrucyk
- Marketing: Terry Y McDermott

Founded: 1979
Specialized Field: Series & Festivals: Concerts
Status: For-Profit, Professional
Paid Staff: 28

Volunteer Staff: 30

4997
NEW JERSEY REPERTORY COMPANY
179 Broadway
Long Branch, NJ 07740
Phone: 732-229-3166
Fax: 732-229-3167
e-mail: njrep@njrep.org
Web Site: www.njrep.org
Officers:
 Director Marketing: Adele Sammarco
 Chairperson: Marilyn Pearlman
 Vice-Chairperson: Carl Hoffman
 Treasurer: Gabor Barabas
 Secretary: Marianne Pedersen
Management:
 President: David Lumia
 Executive Producer: Gabor Barabas
 Artistic Director: Suzanne Barabas
 Literary Manager: Sarah Congress
 Stage Manager: Jennifer Tardibuono
 Director of Marketing and Communic: Adele Sammarco
 Technical Director: Michael Carroll
Mission: The primary mission of the theater is to develop and produce new plays with diverse themes. It is also devoted to creating an atmosphere where classics can take on a fresh look and forgotten plays can find a home.
Founded: 1997
Specialized Field: Series & Festivals: Theatre
Status: Non-Profit, Professional
Paid Staff: 12
Paid Artists: 12
Income Sources: Donation, Grants
Facility Category: Theater
Type of Stage: Black Box
Year Remodeled: 1998

4998
SHAKESPEARE THEATER OF NEW JERSEY
36 Madison Avenue (at Lancaster Road)
Madison, NJ 07940
Phone: 973-408-5600
Fax: 973-408-3361
e-mail: info@shakespearenj.org
Web Site: www.shakespearenj.org
Officers:
 Board President: John Rathgeber
 Honorary Chairman: Thomas H. Kean
Management:
 Artistic Director: Bonnie J Monte
 Managing Director: Jeanne Barrett
 Chairman of the Board: Martin Prentice
 Director of Development: Heidi Speckhart
 Director of Education: Brian B. Crowe
 Business Manager: Duane Dietz
 Company Manager: Amanda Lenti
 Director of Marketing: Rick Engler
 Director of Production and Faciliti: Steven L. Beckel
Mission: The Festival strives to illuminate the universal and lasting relevance of the classics for contemporary audiences, and its mission places an equal emphasis on education, for young artists and audiences alike.
Utilizes: Guest Companies; Singers
Founded: 1962
Specialized Field: Series and Festivals: Theatre
Status: Non-Profit, Professional
Paid Staff: 35
Paid Artists: 150
Budget: 2.6 million
Income Sources: Actors' Equity Association; Society for Stage Directors and Choreographers; New Jersey State Council on the Arts; Corporations; Foundations, Businesses; Individuals
Season: May - December
Performs At: F.M. Kirby Shakespeare Theatre
Affiliations: New Jersey Theatre Group; Theatre Communications Group; Shakespeare Association of America; ArtPride; Artsweb NJ/NY
Annual Attendance: 100,000
Stage Dimensions: 28' wide x 33' deep
Seating Capacity: 308
Year Built: 1998
Organization Type: Performing; Educational; Sponsoring; Touring

4999
ALGONQUIN ARTS
173 Main Street
Manasquan, NJ 08736
Phone: 732-528-9211
Fax: 732-528-3881
e-mail: boxoffice@algonquinarts.org
Web Site: www.algonquinarts.com
Officers:
 Board Chair: Raymond Brunt
 Director Development: Patrick O'Hagan
 Director Communications: Dana Roberts
 Director Operations: Jane E. Huber
 Vice Chair: Joseph Higgins
 Treasurer: Robert Allison
 Secretary: Stephanie Ferrier
Management:
 Executive Director: William Whitefield
 Director of Operations: David Weber
 Director of Education: Julie Nagy
 Director of Finance: Lori Belasco
 Technical Director: Jan Topoleski
 House Manager: Nicole Blake
 Box Office Manager: Janice Coogan
 Box Office Associate: Connor Sheridan
 Graphic Designer: Tracy Furr
Founded: 1992
Specialized Field: Series and Festivals; Instrumental Music; Vocal Music; Theatre; Dance; Ethnic Performances
Status: Non-Profit, Professional
Paid Staff: 4
Volunteer Staff: 2
Paid Artists: 120
Non-paid Artists: 25

5000
ACADEMY OF SAINT ELIZABETH PERFORMING ARTS SERIES
Saint Elizabeth
2 Convent Road
Morristown, NJ 07960-6989
Phone: 973-290-4000
Web Site: www.cse.edu/
Management:
 Artist in Residence: Dr. Teresa Walters
Budget: $10,000
Performs At: Founders Hall; McGuire Lounge

5001
ARTS COUNCIL OF THE MORRIS AREA
14 Maple Avenue
Suite 301
Morristown, NJ 07960
Phone: 973-285-5115
Fax: 973-285-1199
e-mail: info@morrisarts.org
Web Site: www.morrisarts.org
Officers:
 Executive Director: Tom Werder
 Board President: Thomas N. McMillian
 Vice President: Susan Donnell Budd
 Vice President: Kerry Mowry
 Secretary: Cheryl Ellis
 Treasurer: Richard J. Mahler
Management:
 Executive Director: Tom Werder
 Director of Arts in Community: Kadie Dempsey
 Director of Development: Gina Moran
 Director of Arts Participation & Co: Dr. Lynn L. Siebert
 Director of Finance: Anne Dodd
 Director of Arts in Education: Barbara Reuther
 Administrative Program Assistant: Kaity De Laura
Mission: Engaging and building community throught the arts.
Founded: 1973
Specialized Field: Series and Festivals; Instrumental Music; Vocal Music; Theatre; Dance; Ethnic Performances
Status: Non-Profit, Professional
Paid Staff: 7
Budget: $900,000-950,000

5002
RUTGERS UNIVERSITY CONCERT SERIES
33 Livingston Avenue
New Brunswick, NJ 08901
Phone: 848-932-5210
Fax: 732-932-2217
e-mail: visualarts@masongross.rutgers.edu
Web Site: www.masongross.rutgers.edu
Management:
 President: George Stauffer
 Assistant Dean Arts Programming: Meg Frantz
 Publicity Director: Ellen Saxon
 Operations Manager: Kevin Coleman
 Box Office Manager: Jeanne Salzman
Mission: To offer performances by contemporary musicians.
Founded: 1976
Specialized Field: Series & Festivals; Instrumental Music; Vocal Music; Theatre; Youth; Dance; Ethnic Performances; Instrumental Music; Visual Arts
Status: Non-Profit, Non-Professional
Paid Staff: 50
Paid Artists: 10
Performs At: Rutgers Arts Center
Organization Type: Presenting

5003
STATE THEATRE REGIONAL ARTS CENTER AT NEW BRUNSWICK
11 Livingston Avenue
New Brunswick, NJ 08901-1903
Phone: 732-247-7200
Fax: 732-247-4005
Toll-free: 877-782-8311
e-mail: info@statetheatrenj.org
Web Site: www.statetheatrenj.org
Officers:
 President: Mark W. Jones
 Chairman: Warren R. Zimmerman
 Vice Chairman: Douglas M. Garback
 Treasurer: John S. Fitzgerald
 Secretary: Peter Stavrianidis
Management:
 President: Mark W. Jones
 Vice President for Education: Lian Farer

SERIES & FESTIVALS / New Jersey

General Manager: David Hartkern
Director of Operations: Dave Hartkern
Chief Financial Officer: Jerry Campagna
Director of Major Gifts: Linda Van Derveer
Art Director: Tracy Furr
Vice President for Education: Lian Farrer
Vice President of Development: Anna Marie Gewirtz
Mission: To present the finest of the performing arts.
Founded: 1988
Specialized Field: Series & Festivals; Instrumental Music; Vocal Music; Theatre; Dance; Ethnic Performances; Presenting Theatre Opera; Ballet
Status: Non-Profit, Professional
Paid Staff: 35
Budget: $2,000,000
Performs At: State Theatre
Seating Capacity: 1800
Year Built: 1921
Year Remodeled: 1987
Organization Type: Performing; Educational; Sponsoring

5004
CATHEDRAL BASILICA OF THE SACRED HEART CONCERT SERIES

89 Ridge Street
Newark, NJ 07104
Phone: 973-484-2400
Fax: 973-497-9336
e-mail: jmiller@cathedralbasilica.org
Web Site: www.cathedralbasilica.org/concert/
Management:
    Director Music Ministry: John J Miller
Mission: Offerring quality musical programs to Newark area residents.
Founded: 1983
Specialized Field: Symphony; Orchestra; Chamber; Ensemble

5005
NEW JERSEY SYMPHONY ORCHESTRA AMADEUS FESTIVAL

60 Park Place
9th Floor
Newark, NJ 07102
Phone: 973-624-3713
Fax: 973-624-2115
Toll-free: 800-255-3476
e-mail: kswanson@njsymphony.org
Web Site: www.njsymphony.org
Officers:
    Chairman Emeritus: Dr. Victor Parsonnet
    Vice Chair: Albert D. Angel
    Treasurer: David R. Huber
    Secretary: Alan L. Danzis
Management:
    President: James Roe
    Music Director: Neeme Jarvi
    Chief Operating Officer: Susan Stucker
    Office Manager: Karen Duda
    Controller: Denise Jaffe
    Chief Financial Officer: Roxanne Kam
    Stage Technician: Brian Donnelly
    Art Director: Requel Bonassisa
    Director of Marketing & External Af: Amy Brondyke
Specialized Field: Symphony Orchestra Tickets
Status: Non-Profit, Professional

5006
NEWARK MUSEUM ASSOCIATION

49 Washington Street
PO Box 540
Newark, NJ 07102-3176
Phone: 973-596-6550
Fax: 973-596-6613
Toll-free: 800-768-7386
e-mail: pubblicrelations@newarkmusium.org
Web Site: www.newarkmuseum.org
Mission: The americas and the Pacific, Ancient Egypt, Greece and Rome, Decorative Arts, Science, Planetarium, Mini Zoo, Natural Sciences, Newark Black Film Festival, Jazz in the Garden, Family, Adult and children's programing
Founded: 1909
Specialized Field: American; Fold; Tibetan; Asian; Africa
Status: Non-Profit
Budget: $20,000-35,000
Performs At: Billy Johnson Auditorium

5007
ANNUAL OCEAN GROVE CHOIR FESTIVAL

54 Pitman Avenue
PO Box 248
Ocean Grove, NJ 07756
Phone: 732-775-0035
Fax: 732-775-5689
Toll-free: 800-773-0097
e-mail: information@oceangrove.org
Web Site: www.oceangrove.org
Management:
    Music Director: Lewis A Daniels
    Executive Director: J.P. Gradone
    Director of Operations: Bill Bailey
    Administrative Coordinator: Lisa Schultheis
    Receptionist: Vicki Bacolo
    Development Coordinator: Sharyn Krzyzanowski
    Program Director: Shelley Belusar
    Manager: Robin Brown
    Controller: Bobbie Kehoe
Founded: 1954
Status: Non-Profit

5008
RARITAN RIVER MUSIC

PO Box 454
Oldwick, NJ 08858
Phone: 908-213-1100
Fax: 908-213-1100
e-mail: info@raritanrivermusic.org
Web Site: www.raritanrivermusic.org
Officers:
    President: Rosanna Hunt
    Treasurer: Lucinda Chou
Management:
    Music Co-Director: Michael Newman
Mission: Offers the Raritan River Music Festival May, the Artists-in-the-Community Residency Program, and a New Music Commissioning Program
Founded: 1989
Specialized Field: Instrumental Music; Vocal Music; Chamber Music
Status: Nonprofit
Budget: $10,000

5009
RARITAN RIVER MUSIC

PO Box 454
Oldwick, NJ 08858
Phone: 908-213-1100
Fax: 908-213-1100
e-mail: info@raritanrivermusic.org
Web Site: www.raritanrivermusic.org
Officers:
    President: Rosanna Hunt
    Treasurer: Lucinda Chou
Management:
    Co-Music Director: Thomas Gallant
Founded: 1989
Specialized Field: Instrumental Music; Vocal Music; Chamber Music
Status: Nonprofit

5010
JULIUS FORSTMANN LIBRARY SECOND SUNDAY SERIES

195 Gregory Avenue
Passaic, NJ 07055
Phone: 973-779-0474
Fax: 973-779-0889
Web Site: www.bccls.org/passaic
Management:
    Music Director: Laurie Sansone
Status: Non-Profit, Professional

5011
PASSAIC COUNTY COMMUNITY COLLEGE SERIES

1 College Boulevard
Paterson, NJ 07505-1179
Phone: 973-684-6555
Fax: 973-523-6085
Web Site: www.pccc.edu/culturalaffairs
Officers:
    President: Steven Rose
Management:
    Cultural Affairs Director: Maria M Gillan
Mission: To serve poets and poetry, bring performing arts to elementary schools and enjoy the arts as a community.
Utilizes: Actors; Curators; Dance Companies; Fine Artists; Original Music Scores; Playwrights; Selected Students; Special Technical Talent; Touring Companies
Founded: 1968
Specialized Field: Poetry Center; Art Gallery; Theatre & Poetry Project; Passaic County Cultural & Heritage Council
Status: Non-Profit, Non-Professional
Paid Staff: 7
Paid Artists: 45
Budget: $35,000-60,000
Income Sources: Nassaic County College; NJ State Council of the Arts; Geraldine K. Dodge Foundation
Performs At: Theater; Reading Rooms
Type of Stage: Proscenium
Seating Capacity: 300
Year Built: 1968
Year Remodeled: 1999
Rental Contact: Edna Ortiz

5012
CRESCENT CONCERTS

716 Watchung Avenue
Plainfield, NJ 07060
Phone: 908-756-2468
Fax: 908-756-3158
Web Site: www.crescentonline.org
Officers:
    President: Alan Ganun
Management:
    Executive Director: Allan Ganun
    Director: Ronald Thayer

SERIES & FESTIVALS / New Jersey

Director of Music Ministries: F Allen Artz,III
Director of Children's Ministry: Stephanie DeGeneste
Office Administrator: Ruth Mikalonis
Mission: Classical concert series, one per month from October to May, all performances at Crescent Avenue Presbyterian Chruch.
Founded: 1981
Specialized Field: Series & Fesivals: Vocal and Instrumental Music
Status: Non-Profit, Professional
Paid Staff: 1
Volunteer Staff: 12
Paid Artists: 50
Non-paid Artists: 125

5013
PRINCETON SHAKESPEARE FESTIVAL
1 Palmer Square
Suite 541
Princeton, NJ 08542
Phone: 609-921-3682
Fax: 609-921-3962
e-mail: prcreprap@aol.com
Web Site: www.princetonrep.org
Management:
   Artistic Director: Rachel Wilson
   Executive Producer: Anne Reiss
   Press Contact: Carol Fineman
   Production Manager: Malena de la Fuente
   Publicity Director: Emily Fockler
   Technical Director: Douglas Ashley
   Community Liason: Arianna Lanz
   Historian/Archivist: Sam Gelman
   Graphic Designer: Julia Peiperl
Founded: 1995
Status: Professional; Not-for-Profit

5014
PRINCETON UNIVERSITY CONCERTS
Woolworth Center
Room 301
Princeton, NJ 08544
Phone: 609-258-4239
Fax: 609-258-1179
Web Site: www.princetonuniversityconcerts.org
Management:
   Concert Manager: Nathan A Randall
Budget: $60,000-150,000
Performs At: Richardson Auditorium

5015
YOUNG AUDIENCES OF NEW JERSEY
200 Forrestal Road
Suite B102
Princeton, NJ 08540
Phone: 609-243-9000
Fax: 609-243-5999
Toll-free: 866-500-9265
e-mail: info@yanj.org
Web Site: www.yanj.org
Officers:
   Chair: Richard Goldman
   Vice Chairs: Tanuja M. Dehne
   Treasurer: Gil Blitz
   Recording Secretary: Pamela Parsons
Management:
   Executive Director: Kris Bolden Wenger
   Artistic Director: Steve Mosel
   President & CEO: Laurrence Capo
   Director of Arts and Education: Maureen Heffernn
   Development Director: Ann Betterton
   Finance Director: Debra Mindlin
   Director of Marketing & PR: Denyce Mylson

Technology Coordinator: Chris Schondel
Programming Director: Donnajean Reckelhoff
Mission: To provide arts in education programs and services to schools and other community settings.
Founded: 1973
Specialized Field: Arts Education
Status: Non-Profit, Professional
Budget: $400,000-1,000,000

5016
RINGWOOD FRIENDS OF MUSIC SERIES
PO Box 427/145 Carletondale Rd
Ringwood, NJ 07456
Phone: 973-962-9356
Budget: $10,000
Performs At: Ringwood Community Church

5017
WILLIAMS CENTER FOR THE ARTS
One Williams Plaza
Rutherford, NJ 07070
Phone: 201-939-6969
Fax: 201-939-0843
Web Site: www.williamscenter.org
Officers:
   President: Richard Theryoung
   Vice President: Carolyn Spann-Swallwood
   Secretary: Dr. Joseph DeFazi
   Treasurer: Evelyn Spath-Mercado
Management:
   Executive Director: Gw McLuckey
Mission: To provide programs of artistic excellence at affordable prices.
Utilizes: Actors; AEA Actors; Dance Companies; Local Artists; Multimedia; Original Music Scores; Student Interns; Theatre Companies
Founded: 1978
Paid Staff: 22
Budget: $650,000
Income Sources: Ticket Sales; grants; sponsorships; rentals
Performs At: Newman Theatre
Annual Attendance: 50,000
Facility Category: Performing Arts Center
Type of Stage: Black Box; Proscenium Arch
Seating Capacity: 200; 642
Year Built: 1922
Year Remodeled: 1992
Rental Contact: G.W. McLuckey

5018
WATERLOO FOUNDATION FOR THE ARTS SERIES
525 Waterloo Road
Stanhope, NJ 07874
Phone: 973-347-0900
Fax: 973-347-3573
e-mail: info@waterloovillage.org
Web Site: www.waterloovillage.org
Officers:
   Controller: Cule Jorden
Management:
   Executive Director: Gregory Gaertner
   Director Museum Operations: John Kraft
Mission: To combine history, music, art and architecture; to educate all persons in the state of New Jersey in appreciation of these arts forms.
Utilizes: Collaborations; Curators; Educators; Five Seasonal Concerts; Guest Artists; Guest Companies; Guest Directors; Guest Instructors; Guest Lecturers; Guest Musical Directors; Guest Soloists; Instructors; Multimedia; Original Music Scores; Playwrights
Founded: 1967

Specialized Field: Educational Programs for School Children
Status: Non-Profit
Paid Staff: 10
Volunteer Staff: 40
Budget: $ 2.5 Million
Income Sources: Gate Admissions; New Jersey State Council of the Arts; New Jersey Tourism Council; Business/Corporate Donations
Season: April - November
Performs At: Waterloo Music Festival Tent; Waterloo Concert Field
Affiliations: New Jersey Tourism Council
Annual Attendance: 150,000
Facility Category: Seasonal
Seating Capacity: 2,200-15,000
Year Built: 1964
Year Remodeled: 1997
Organization Type: Performing; Sponsoring

5019
CENTRAL PRESBYTERIAN CHURCH
Sanctuary Arts Series
70 Maple Street
Summit, NJ 07901
Phone: 908-273-0441
Fax: 908-273-0444
e-mail: jdaurio@centralpres.org
Web Site: www.centralpres.org
Management:
   Contact: Joyce Brandt
Mission: Friday Music (Mid-day concerts on Fridays during Advent and Lent), Special music and concerts announced through website.
Specialized Field: Series & Festivals; Instrumental Music; Vocal Music; Youth; Ethnic Performances
Status: Non-Profit,Professional

5020
OCEAN COUNTY COLLEGE FINE & PERFORMING ARTS SELECT-A-SERIES
Ocean County College
College Drive
Toms River, NJ 08754
Phone: 732-255-0500
Fax: 732-864-3853
e-mail: rkrantz@ocean.edu
Web Site: ocean.edu
Officers:
   Chair: Carl V. Thulin, Jr.
   Vice Chair: Linda L. Novak
   Treasurer: Jerry Dasti
   Secretary: Stephan R. Leone
Management:
   Fine Arts Center Director: Roberta F Krantz
Mission: Tol provide quality production at an amenable price for the Ocean County Community.
Utilizes: Actors; Dance Companies; Dancers; Designers; Fine Artists; Five Seasonal Concerts; Guest Accompanists; High School Drama; Instructors; Multimedia; Music; Original Music Scores; Resident Professionals; Sign Language Translators; Singers; Soloists; Special Technical Talent; Theatre Companies; Visual Arts
Paid Staff: 3
Budget: $35,000-60,000
Income Sources: Ticket Sales
Facility Category: Fine Arts Center
Type of Stage: Proscenium
Seating Capacity: 564
Year Built: 1972

SERIES & FESTIVALS / New Mexico

5021
JETTE PERFORMANCE COMPANY
10 Raymond Terrace
Vauxhall, NJ 07008
Phone: 908-397-1714
Fax: 212-840-0344
e-mail: jettejazz@excite.com
Web Site: www.jettejazz.org
Mission: Creates a fusion of classical and commersials styles of dance and brings them to the concert stage.
Founded: 1996
Specialized Field: Dance

5022
JAZZ IT UP FESTIVAL
William Paterson University
300 Pompton Road
Wayne, NJ 07470
Phone: 973-720-3641
Fax: 973-720-2035
e-mail: graduate@wpunj.edu,
Web Site: www.wpunj.edu

5023
WILLIAM PATERSON COLLEGE: THE JAZZ ROOM SERIES
300 Pompton Road
Wayne, NJ 07470
Phone: 973-720-3641
Fax: 973-720-2035
e-mail: graduate@wpunj.edu
Web Site: www.ww2.wpunj.edu
Officers:
  President: Arnold Speert
  Secretary: Vincent Mazzola
  Chair: Robert Taylor
  Vice-Chair: Carla Temple
Mission: Presenting a complete range of jazz music.
Founded: 1978
Specialized Field: Series & Festivals; Instrumental Music; Vocal Music; Theatre; Youth; Ethnic Performances
Status: For-Profit, Professional
Performs At: Shea Center for the Performing Arts
Organization Type: Performing

5024
WILLOWBROOK JAZZ FESTIVAL
William Paterson College
300 Pompton Road
Wayne, NJ 07470
Phone: 201-595-2268
Fax: 201-595-2460
Management:
  Special Projects Assistant: Dr. Martin Krivin
  Director Jazz Program at William: Rufus Reid
Mission: Making jazz accessible by offering free concerts at convenient times and places.
Specialized Field: Jazz
Status: Professional; Nonprofit
Performs At: Willowbrook Mall
Organization Type: Performing

5025
YM-YWHA OF NORTH JERSEY CULTURAL ARTS SERIES
1 Pike Drive
Wayne, NJ 07470-2497
Phone: 973-595-0100
Fax: 973-595-5234
Management:
  Executive Director: Josh Samborn
  Cultural Arts Director: Sheila Hellman
Specialized Field: Series and Festivals; Instrumental Music; Theatre; Youth; Fitness
Status: Non-Profit, Professional
Paid Staff: 75
Paid Artists: 75
Budget: $60,000-150,000
Performs At: Rosen Auditorium

New Mexico

5026
CHAMBER MUSIC ALBUQUERQUE PRESENTS THE JUNE MUSIC FESTIVAL
1209 Mountain Road Place
Suite D Ne
Albuquerque, NM 87110
Mailing Address: P.O. Box 3343 Albuquerque, NM 87190
Phone: 505-268-1990
Fax: 505-268-6288
e-mail: cma@cma-abq.org
Web Site: www.cma-abq.org
Officers:
  President: Jonathon Gerson
  VP: Calla Ann Pepmueller
  Secretary: Betsy Ebert Schmidt-Nowara
  Treasurer: Devon Day
Management:
  Administrative Director: Judith O Smith
  General Manager: Staci Robbins
  Financial Consultant: Michael Tamasi
  Stage Manager: Curtis Mark
  Technical Support: TJ Bowlin
Mission: To present the world's finest chamber musicians in live performance, sharing the power of great music with the community.
Founded: 1942
Affiliations: June Music Festival; Chamber Music at the Simms

5027
NEW MEXICO JAZZ WORKSHOP
5500 Lomas Boulevard NE
Albuquerque, NM 87110
Phone: 505-255-9798
Fax: 505-232-8420
e-mail: nmjw@flash.net
Web Site: www.nmjazz.org
Officers:
  Board President: Chris Cordova
  Executive Director: Charles W. Lowery II, BS, MA
  Vice President: Sandra Liakus-Pilcher
  Treasurer: Jacob Sena
  Secretary: Marcus Ray, Jr.
  Immediate Past President: Jose Ponce
Management:
  Executive Director: Maud Beenhouwer
  Assistant Director: Vicki Dugger
  Empowerment Through Music Coordinat: Debo Orlofsky
  Education Coordinator: Nicole Larsen
Mission: To present major jazz artists January-May for performing and educational activities.
Utilizes: Educators; Fine Artists; Grant Writers; Guest Directors; Guest Instructors; Guest Musical Directors; High School Drama; Local Artists; Multimedia; Original Music Scores
Founded: 1978
Specialized Field: Series & Festivals; Instrumental Music; Youth; Ethnic Performances; Jazz
Status: Non-Profit, Professional
Paid Staff: 2
Volunteer Staff: 50
Paid Artists: 30
Performs At: Hiland Theater; Kimo Theater
Facility Category: Various local venues
Organization Type: Performing; Touring

5028
CARLSBAD COMMUNITY CONCERT ASSOCIATION
611 N 4th Street
Carlsbad, NM 88220
Phone: 505-885-8255
e-mail: jedhoward@leaco.net
Management:
  President: Jared Howard
Founded: 1946
Specialized Field: Series & Festivals; Instrumental Music; Vocal Music; Dance; Ethnic Performances; Classical Music
Status: Non-Profit, Professional
Budget: $20,000-35,000

5029
DONA ANA ARTS COUNCIL
PO Box 1721
Las Cruces, NM 88004
Phone: 575-523-6403
Fax: 575-523-4760
Web Site: www.las-cruces-arts.org
Officers:
  President: Scott Breckner
  Vice President: Philip Lewis
  Secretary: Kathe Stark
  Treasurer: Kelly Sweetser
  Past President: Lanova Sheets
  Member-At-Large: Jan Harrison
Management:
  President: Scott Breckner
  Past-President: Kathleen Squires
  Vice President: Philip Lewis
  Interim Executive Director and Prog: Kathleen Albers
  Rio Grande Theatre Manager: David Salcido
  Finance Director: Victoria Frederick
  Development / Volunteer Coordinator: Katy Milligan
  Events Coordinator: Patricia Black
Founded: 1974
Specialized Field: Series & Festivals; Instrumental Music; Vocal Music; Theatre; Youth; Ethnic Performances
Status: Non-Profit, Professional
Budget: $20,000-35,000

5030
PAN AMERICAN CENTER
MSC 35E
1810 E. University Ave.
PO Box 30001
Las Cruces, NM 88003
Phone: 505-646-4413
Fax: 505-646-3605
e-mail: panam@nmsu.edu
Web Site: www.panam.nmsu.edu
Management:
  President: Will Lofdahl
Mission: Special events facilities, 13,000 seat arena, 500 seat Performing Arts Center
Specialized Field: Series & Festivals: Concerts and Basketball Games
Status: Non-Profit, Professional
Paid Staff: 14

SERIES & FESTIVALS / New Mexico

5031
LOS ALAMOS CONCERT ASSOCIATION
P.O. Box 572
Los Alamos, NM 87544
Phone: 505-662-9000
e-mail: rheller88@cybermesa.com
Web Site: www.losalamosconcert.org
Officers:
  President: Carolyn Mangeng
  1st Vice Pres.: David Watkins
  2nd Vice Pres.: Marilyn Smith
  Secretary: Terry Izraelevitz
  Treasurer: Greg McIntosh
Management:
  Artistic Director: Ann McLaughlin
  Artistic Director emeritus: Rosalie Heller
Founded: 1946
Volunteer Staff: 20
Paid Artists: 5
Budget: $35,000-60,000
Performs At: Duane Smith Auditorium

5032
PLACITAS ARTISTS SERIES
PO Box 944
Placitas, NM 87043
Phone: 505-867-8080
e-mail: info@placitasartistsseries.org
Web Site: www.placitasarts.org
Officers:
  President: Diana Shomaker
  Vice President: Jean Reid
  Treasurer: Jackie Ericksen
  Secretary: Lois Gonzalez
Mission: Providing music of a consistently high quality, at extremely modest cost in a tranquil rural setting. The organization promotes interest in the musical and visual arts, encourages musicians and artists, and brings music, arts and theater to children in schools throughout the country.
Founded: 1986
Specialized Field: Series and Festivals: Chamber Music
Status: Non-Profit, Professional
Paid Staff: 1
Paid Artists: 90
Budget: $25,000-35,000
Seating Capacity: 185

5033
EASTERN NEW MEXICO UNIVERSITY
Station 17
1500 S Ave K
Portales, NM 88130
Phone: 575-562-1011
Fax: 505-562-2822
Toll-free: 800-367-3668
e-mail: webmaster@enmu.edu
Web Site: www.enmu.edu/athletics.html
Management:
  President: Steven Gamble
  VP Business Affiars: Scott Smart
  Vp: Paul Jones
  Athletic Director: Michael Mcguire
Founded: 1934
Specialized Field: Degrees and all College Eduation
Status: Non-Profit, Professional

5034
SANTA FE CHAMBER MUSIC FESTIVAL
208 Griffin Street
Santa Fe, NM 87501
Mailing Address: PO Box 2227, Santa Fe, NM 87504-2227
Phone: 505-983-2075
Fax: 505-986-0251
Toll-free: 888-221-9836
e-mail: info@sfcmf.org
Web Site: www.santafechambermusic.org
Officers:
  President: Kenneth R. Marvel
  Vice President: Arnold Tenenbaum
  Secretary: David Frank
Management:
  Artistic Director: Marc Neikrug
  Executive Director: Steven Ovitsky
  Production Director: Linda Klosky
  Volunteer Coordinator: Toni Wilkinson
  Artistic Services Manager: Julie Rodriguez
  Director of Development: Shelley Winship
  Marketing Manager: Derek DeVelder
  Ticket Office Manager: Toni Pittman
  Event & Donor Relations Manager: Allison Hooper
Mission: To produce innovative chamber music concerts and related educational programs of exceptional artistic quality; to serve as a chamber music center attracting American musicians, composers and audiences whose combined influence, stimulation and energy will benefit American culture.
Utilizes: Sign Language Translators
Founded: 1973
Specialized Field: Chamber Music; Jazz; World Music
Status: Professional; Nonprofit
Paid Staff: 12
Budget: 1.6 k
Performs At: Saint Francis Auditorium; Museum of Fine Arts
Annual Attendance: 11,000
Organization Type: Performing; Touring; Resident; Educational

5035
SANTA FE CONCERT ASSOCIATION
324 Paseo de Peralta
Suite A
Santa Fe, NM 87501
Mailing Address: PO Box 4626, Santa Fe, NM. 87502
Phone: 505-984-8759
Fax: 505-820-0588
e-mail: info@performancesantafe.org
Web Site: www.musicone.org
Officers:
  President: Clifford Vernick
Management:
  Managing Director: William Mullen
Founded: 1937
Specialized Field: Vocal Music: Classical Music
Status: Non-Profit, Professional
Paid Staff: 1
Paid Artists: 300
Budget: $60,000-150,000
Performs At: St. Francis Auditorium; James A. Little Theatre

5036
TWENTIETH CENTURY UNLIMITED SERIES
PO Box 2631
Santa Fe, NM 87504-2631
Phone: 505-820-6401
Fax: 505-995-0941
Management:
  Director: Eleanor C Eisenmenger

5037
TAOS ART ASSOCIATION
133 Paseo del Pueblo Norte
Taos, NM 87571
Phone: 505-758-2052
Fax: 505-751-3305
e-mail: info@tcataos.org
Web Site: www.taoscenterforthearts.org
Officers:
  Treasurer: James Day
  Secretary: Kandace Nachtrab
  President: Alford Johnson
  Vice President: John Hamilton
  Office Manager: Holly White
Management:
  Executive Director: Deborah McLean
  General Manager: Holly White
  Co- Theater Manager: Juniper Purinton
  Co- Theater Manager: Damon Klassen
  House Manager and Voluteer Coordina: Carlene Christie
  Projectionist and Film Programmer: Peter Halter
Mission: Inspires creative expression throughout this diverse community by providing facilities and programming in the visual, performing and media arts.
Founded: 1952

5038
TAOS SCHOOL OF MUSIC
PO Box 2630
Taos, NM 87571
Phone: 575-776-2388
Fax: 575-776-2388
e-mail: tsofm@newmex.com
Web Site: www.taosschoolofmusic.com
Officers:
  Chair: R Jameson Burns
  Vice-chair: Lou Sturbois
  Secretary: Robert Burke
  Treasurer: Judith Anderson
Management:
  Executive Director: Kahleen Anderson Knox, tsofm@newmex.com
  Elise: McDonald Artistic Director
  Chilton: Olonia Administrative Assis
Mission: Study and performance of chamber music.
Utilizes: Artists-in-Residence; Composers; Educators; Five Seasonal Concerts; Guest Directors; Guest Musical Directors; High School Drama; Multimedia; Poets; Singers; Soloists
Founded: 1963
Opened: 1963
Specialized Field: Series & Festivals: Instrumental Music
Status: Non-Profit, Professional
Paid Staff: 2
Volunteer Staff: 10
Paid Artists: 15
Budget: $100,000
Income Sources: Contributions; Grants; Tuition
Performs At: Taos Community Auditorium; Hotel St. Bernard; Taos Ski Valley
Affiliations: Chamber Music America
Annual Attendance: varies
Facility Category: Auditorium
Type of Stage: Platform
Seating Capacity: 290; 150
Organization Type: Performing; Educational
Resident Groups: Chicago String Quartet

SERIES & FESTIVALS / New York

New York

5039
ALBANY SYMPHONY ORCHESTRA
AMERICAN FESITVAL
19 Clinton Avenue
Albany, NY 12207
Phone: 518-465-4755
Fax: 518-465-3711
e-mail: info@albanysymphony.com
Web Site: www.albanysymphony.com
Officers:
  Chair: Marisa Eisemann, MD
  Vice Chair: Jerel Golub
  Vice Chair: Marc H. Paquin
  Secretary: Spencer B. Jones
  Treasurer: David Rubin
  Immediate Past Chair: Steven Lobel
Management:
  Chairman: Allan Goldberg
  Artistic Director: David Alan Miller
  General Manager: Alison Bolton
  Executive Director: Lawrence J. Fried
  Box Office Manager: Ella Golding
  Finance Director: Scott Allen
  Finance Assistant: Erica Sparrow
  Personnel Manager: Susan Libby
Founded: 1931
Specialized Field: Series & Festivals; Instrumental Music; Youth; Classical Music
Status: Non-Profit, Professional
Paid Staff: 7
Paid Artists: 30

5040
L'ENSEMBLE CHAMBER MUSIC
PO Box 38024
Albany, NY 12203-8024
Phone: 518-436-5321
Fax: 518-436-5322
Management:
  Executive/Artistic Director: Ida Faiella

5041
ALFRED UNIVERSITY PERFORMING ARTS
1 Saxon Drive
Alfred, NY 14802
Mailing Address: PO Box 781
Phone: 607-871-2115
Fax: 607-871-2587
e-mail: performs@alfred.edu
Web Site: www.alfred.edu
Officers:
  President: Charles Edmondson
  Performing Arts Head: S Crosby
Management:
  Admissions Director: Earl Pierce
  Tech Theater: Zachary Hamm
  Theater Designs: Marketa Fantova
Mission: To provide professional performing artists for the area.
Founded: 1836
Specialized Field: Series and Festivals; Dance; Instrumental Music; Theatre; Education
Status: Non-Profit, Non-Professional
Paid Staff: 3
Non-paid Artists: 4
Facility Category: Proscenium Theater, Black Box Theater
Seating Capacity: 450; 180
Organization Type: Performing; Educational; Sponsoring

5042
MUSIC FESTIVAL OF THE HAMPTONS
PO Box 1525
Amagansett, NY 11930
Toll-free: 800-644-4418
Web Site: http://www.musicfestivalofthehamptons.com/
Management:
  Artistic Director: Lukas Foss

5043
AMSTERDAM AREA COMMUNITY CONCERT ASSOCIATION
31 Young Avenue
Amsterdam, NY 12010
Phone: 518-843-3247
Fax: 518-842-4072
e-mail: apboschi@verizon.net
Web Site: musicalworld.com/
Management:
  Stage Manager: Robert Swenson
Specialized Field: Series & Festivals; Instrumental Music; Vocal Music; Dance; Ethnic Performances; Symphony; Classical; Choral Group
Status: Non-Profit, Non-Professional
Budget: $10,000-20,000

5044
BARD MUSIC FESTIVAL
Bard College
Annandale-on-Hudson, NY 12504
Phone: 845-758-7410
Fax: 845-758-7043
e-mail: bmf@bard.edu
Web Site: www.bard.edu/bmf
Officers:
  Executive Director: Irene Zedlacher
Management:
  Artistic Director: Leon Botstein
  Artistic Director: Christopher Gibbs
  Artistic Director: Robert Martin
Founded: 1991
Specialized Field: Series & Festivals: Classical Music Festival
Status: Non-Profit, Professional

5045
LORRAINE PRODUCTIONS: EAST/WEST
28-04 33Th Street
Suite 8
Astoria, NY 11102
Phone: 718-721-9785
Management:
  Executive Director: Scott Douglas Morrow
Budget: $150,000-400,000

5046
GENESEE COMMUNITY COLLEGE
Genesee College for the Arts
One College Road
Batavia, NY 14020-9704
Phone: 585-343-0055
Fax: 585-345-6815
e-mail: boxoffice@genesee.edu
Web Site: www.genesee.edu
Management:
  Director of Fine/Performing Arts: Maryanne Arena
  Technical Director: Vincent Elliott
  Audience Services Manager: Christopher M Montpetit
Mission: Commits to providing educational experiences which promote intellectual and social growth, workforce and economic development and global citizenship.
Utilizes: Actors; Collaborations; Dance Companies; Dancers; Educators; Fine Artists; Guest Instructors; Guest Soloists; Guild Activities; High School Drama; Instructors; Local Artists; Multimedia; Soloists; Student Interns; Touring Companies
Income Sources: Ticket Sales; College Funding; Grants
Performs At: Theatre, Rehearsal Space, Lobby Art Exhibits
Facility Category: Theatre
Type of Stage: Proscenium
Stage Dimensions: 40' x 35'
Seating Capacity: 3400
Year Built: 1992
Rental Contact: Mary Anne Arena

5047
PROFESSIONAL PERFORMING ARTS SERIES
Queensborough Community College/Cuny
222-05 56 th Avenue
Bayside, NY 11364-1497
Phone: 718-631-6311
Fax: 718-631-6033
e-mail: agin@qcc.cuny.edu
Web Site: www.qcc.cuny.edu/boxoffice
Management:
  President: Marti Agin
  Executive and Artistic Director: Susan Agin
Utilizes: Actors; Artists-in-Residence; Dance Companies; Dancers; Multimedia; Original Music Scores; Theatre Companies
Founded: 1965
Specialized Field: Performing Arts
Status: Non-Profit, Professional
Paid Staff: 5
Budget: $60,000-150,000
Annual Attendance: 12,000-15,000
Facility Category: Conventional Theatre
Type of Stage: Proscenium
Stage Dimensions: 40x40
Seating Capacity: 875
Year Built: 1970
Rental Contact: Terry Doria

5048
BINGHAMTON SUMMER MUSIC FESTIVAL
P.O. Box 6000
Binghamton, NY 13902-6000
Phone: 607-777-2792
Fax: 607-777-6661
e-mail: cice@binghamton.edu
Web Site: www.summermusic.binghamtom.edu
Officers:
  President: Jim Reyer
  VP: Karl Hirshman
  Secretary: Jim Gacioch
  Treasurer: Larry Deminster
Management:
  Executive Director: Thomas F. Kowalik
  Advisor: Roni O'Geen
  Online Program Manager: Debbie Collett-O'Brien
Mission: To provide an annual summer performing arts program for audiences in New York's Southern Tier.
Founded: 1985
Specialized Field: Dance; Vocal Music; Instrumental Music; Festivals
Status: Nonprofit
Paid Staff: 1
Volunteer Staff: 24
Paid Artists: 9
Performs At: Anderson Center for Performing Arts

SERIES & FESTIVALS / New York

Organization Type: Performing; Educational

5049
STATE UNIVERSITY OF NEW YORK AT BINGHAMTON PERFORMING ARTS SERIES
Binghamton University
Anderson Center for the Arts, PO Box 6000
Binghamton, NY 13902-6000
Phone: 607-777-6802
Fax: 607-777-6771
Web Site: www.anderson.binghamton.edu
Management:
   President: Llis B Befleur
   Executive Director: Gary Pedro
   Assistant to the Executive Director: Patricia J. Benjamin
   Operations Director: Annette M. Burnett
   Marketing Director: Rosanne Norris
   Technical Director: Steven D. Machlin
   Assistant Technical Director: Daniel W. Sonnen
   House Operations Director: Casey Korchynsky
   Box Office Manager: June Christensen
Founded: 1985
Specialized Field: Series & Festivals; Instrumental Music; Vocal Music; Theatre; Youth; Dance; Ethnic Performances
Status: Non-Profit, Professional
Paid Staff: 10
Budget: $60,000-150,000
Performs At: Cmaber Hall; Watters Theater

5050
BAY SHORE-BRIGHTWATERS LIBRARY PERFORMING ARTS SERIES
1 S. Country Road
Brightwaters, NY 11718
Phone: 631-665-4350
Fax: 631-665-4958
e-mail: staff@bsbwlibrary.org
Web Site: www.bsbwlibrary.org/events/category/friends_performing-arts-series/
Management:
   Executive Director: Eileen Kavanagh
   Library Director: Michael Squillante
   Reference and Adult Services: Adele Fitzgerald
   Facilities Staff: James Persson
   Facilities Staff: Robert Tuthill
Founded: 1968
Specialized Field: Series and Festivals; Dance; Theatre
Status: Non-Profit, Professional
Volunteer Staff: 6
Paid Artists: 7
Budget: $35,000-60,000
Performs At: Suffolk Community College
Facility Category: Auditorium
Seating Capacity: 75-100

5051
651 ARTS
651 Fulton Street
Brooklyn, NY 11217
Phone: 718-636-4181
Fax: 718-636-4166
e-mail: info@651arts.org
Web Site: www.651arts.org
Officers:
   Chair: Valencia Yearwood
   Vice Chair: Scafford Simmonds, Jr.
   Treasurer: Margaret Anadu
Management:
   Executive Director: Shay Wafer
   Special Projects: Candace Feldman
   Production Manager: Robert W. Henson, Jr.
   Development Manager: Jessica Lynne
   Producing Associate: Aaron Mckinney
   Media Intern: Omari Miller
Founded: 1988
Specialized Field: Performing Arts

5052
ARTS AT ST. ANN'S
55 Washington Street
Suite 458
Brooklyn, NY 11201
Phone: 718-834-8794
Fax: 718-522-2470
e-mail: info@stannswarehouse.org
Web Site: www.artsatstanns.org
Officers:
   Chairman: Joseph S. Steinberg
   President-/Artistic Director: Susan Feldman
   Vice President: Steven B. Rissman
   Treasurer: Kay Ellen Consolver
   Secretary: Thomas H. French
Management:
   Artistic Director: Susan Feldman
   Co Producer: Kim Whitener
   Executive Director: Andrew D. Hamingson
   Director of External Affairs: Marilynn Donini
   General Manager: Erik Wallin
   Director of Finance: Abby Marcus
   Production Manager: Owen Hughes
   Director of Marketing: Emily Kent
   Box Office Manager: Karl C. Sturk
Founded: 1979
Specialized Field: Series and Festivals; Instrumental Music; Vocal Music; Theatre; Youth; Ethnic Performances; Performing Arts
Status: Non-Profit, Professional
Paid Staff: 11
Volunteer Staff: 10
Paid Artists: 200
Budget: $1,500,000
Income Sources: Foundation; Corporate; Government; Individual; Earned Income

5053
BROOKLYN ACADEMY OF MUSIC
30 Lafayette Avenue
Brooklyn, NY 11217
Phone: 718-636-4100
Fax: 718-857-2021
e-mail: info@bam.org
Web Site: www.bam.org
Officers:
   Board Chair: Alan H. Fishman
   Board Vice Chair: William I. Campbell
   Board Vice Chair: Adam E. Max
   Vice Chairman: I. Stanley Kriegel
   VP: David Kleiser
   Executive VP: Judith E. Daykin
   Treasurer: James I. McLaren
   President: Karen Brooks Hopkins
Management:
   President: Karen Brooks Hopkins
   Executive Director: Joseph V. Melilo
   Finance: Richard Balzano
   Promotion/Marketing: Doug Allan
Mission: Programming policy involves a commitment to provide our audiences with quality performing arts, new and innovative theatre, and dance and music, both foreign and domestic, as well as diversified choices in all areas at affordable and accessible prices.
Utilizes: Singers
Founded: 1861
Specialized Field: Series & Festivals; Instrumental Music; Vocal Music; Theatre; Youth; Dance; Ethnic Performances
Status: Non-Profit, Professional
Paid Staff: 150
Income Sources: New York Department of Cultural Affairs
Performs At: Brooklyn Academy of Music
Organization Type: Performing; Touring; Educational; Sponsoring

5054
CELEBRATE BROOKLYN FESTIVAL
95 Prospect Park West
Brooklyn, NY 11215
Phone: 718-965-8951
Fax: 718-802-9095
e-mail: info@prospectpark.org
Web Site: www.briconline.org
Officers:
   President: Nanette Rainone
Management:
   Director/Producer: Jack Walsh
Mission: Supporting Brooklyn's international community through the presentation of original and professional performing arts.
Founded: 1979
Specialized Field: Series & Festivals; Instrumental Music; Vocal Music; Theatre; Dance; Ethnic Performances
Status: Non-Profit, Professional
Paid Staff: 100
Performs At: Prospect Park Bandshell and Picnic House
Annual Attendance: 200,000
Facility Category: Ampitheatre
Type of Stage: Sprung Wood
Stage Dimensions: 70x40
Seating Capacity: 10,000
Year Built: 1939
Year Remodeled: 1999
Cost: $3.4 million
Rental Contact: Director Jack Walsh
Organization Type: Performing

5055
CW POST CHAMBER MUSIC FESTIVAL
Long Island University, CW Post Campus
720 Northern Boulevard
Brookville, NY 11548-1300
Phone: 516-299-2103
Fax: 516-299-2884
Web Site: www.liu.edu/cwpost/svpa/music/festival
Management:
   Festival Director: Susan Deaver
   Assistant Director: Dale Stuckenbruck
   Faculty Ensemble-In-Residence: Pierrot Consort
Mission: To study and perform standard chamber music repertoire
Founded: 1981
Paid Staff: 2
Volunteer Staff: 2
Paid Artists: 15
Performs At: Tilles Center; Hillwood Recital Hall

5056
AFRICAN-AMERICAN CULTURAL CENTER
350 Masten Avenue
Buffalo, NY 14209

SERIES & FESTIVALS / New York

Phone: 716-884-2013
Fax: 716-885-2590
e-mail: aacc@pcom.net
Web Site: www.aaccbuffalo.org
Officers:
  Chairman: Darlene Badgett
  Vice Chairman: Emma Bassett
  Secretary: Gwendolyn Neal
  Treasurer: Paulett S. Counts
Management:
  Executive Director: Agnes M Bain
  Artistic Director: Paulette D Harris
Mission: Developing appreciation for African traditions through cultural events and the arts.
Founded: 1958
Specialized Field: Dance; Theater
Status: Nonprofit
Paid Staff: 35
Performs At: Paul Robeson Theatre
Type of Stage: proscenium
Stage Dimensions: 40x18
Seating Capacity: 130
Organization Type: Performing; Sponsoring

5057
JUNE IN BUFFALO
220 Baird Hall
Buffalo, NY 14260-4700
Phone: 716-645-2765
Fax: 716-645-3824
e-mail: mus-info@buffalo.edu
Web Site: www.music.buffalo.edu/jib
Officers:
  Secretary: Katherine Phillips
  Concert Manager: Philip Rehard
  Assistant to the Chair: Dusti Dean
Management:
  Director of Student Programs: Karen Sausner
  Financial Officer: Dusti Dean
  Director Music Technology: Chris Jacob
  Artistic Director: David Felder
  Managing Director: J. T. Rinker
  Grant Writer: Eileen Felder
  Technology, Sound Reinforcement, an: Chris Jacobs
  Website Manager: Ethan Hayden
Mission: To sponsor festival and conference dedicated to emerging composers, and the opportunity to work with outstanding professional musicians and distinguished composition faculty.
Founded: 1975
Specialized Field: Series & Festivals; Instrumental Music; Vocal Music
Status: Non-Profit, Professional
Paid Staff: 15
Paid Artists: 50

5058
VIVA VIVALDI FESTIVAL XXIII
Ars Nova Musicians Chamber Orchestra
136 Goethe Street
Buffalo, NY 14206
Phone: 716-896-2515
Fax: 716-894-2456
e-mail: arsnovamusicians@aol.com
Web Site: arsnovamusicians.com
Management:
  President: Dorothy Smith
  Executive/Managing Director: Marylouise Nanna
  Business Manager: Susan Willet
Mission: ARS Nova Musicians is dedicated to performing a varied repertoire that extends from early Baroque through contemporary music, including frequent premiers. Constantly aspire through creative and innovative means to attract new audiences to this wonderful medium of the musical art, called Chamber Music.
Founded: 1974
Specialized Field: Series & Festivals; Instrumental Music; Vocal Music; Chamber Music
Status: Non-Profit, Professional
Paid Staff: 2

5059
CHAUTAUQUA INSTITUTION
1 Ames Avenue
Chautauqua, NY 14722
Mailing Address: Po Box 28
Phone: 716-357-6200
Fax: 716-357-9014
Toll-free: 800-836-2787
e-mail: slundine@ciweb.org
Web Site: www.ciweb.org
Officers:
  President: Thomas M Becker
  Chair: James A. Pardo, Jr.
Mission: Combining the arts, religion, recreation and education in a Victorian community.
Utilizes: Singers
Founded: 1874
Specialized Field: Series & Festivals; Dance; Vocal Music; Instrumental Music; Theatre; Grand Opera
Status: Professional; Semi-Professional; Non-Professional; Nonprofit
Paid Staff: 300
Income Sources: Opera America; American Symphony Orchestra League; Association for Performing Arts Presenters; Music Educators National Conference; American Arts Alliance
Performs At: Amphitheater; Norton Hall
Organization Type: Performing; Resident; Educational; Sponsoring

5060
PERFORMING ARTS AT HAMILTON
198 College Hill Road
Hamilton College
Clinton, NY 13323
Phone: 315-859-4011
Fax: 315-859-4457
Toll-free: 866-729-0314
e-mail: performingarts@hamilton.edu
Web Site: www.hamilton.edu
Management:
  President: Michelle Reiser-Memmer
Founded: 1985
Specialized Field: Vocal Music: Classical Music
Status: Non-Profit, Professional
Paid Staff: 2
Paid Artists: 30
Budget: $60,000-150,000
Performs At: Wellin Hall; Schambach Center

5061
HUDSON VALLEY SHAKESPEARE FESTIVAL
140 Main Street
Cold Spring, NY 10516
Phone: 845-265-9575
Fax: 845-265-1037
e-mail: boxoffice@hvshakespeare.org
Web Site: www.hvshakespeare.org
Officers:
  President: Robin Shelby Arditi
  Vice President: Patricia King
  Secretary: Suzanne Baker
  Treasurer: Betsy Swanson
Management:
  Executive Director: Susan Landstreet
  Artistic Director: Terrence O'Brien
  Director Marketing: Abigail Adams
Mission: Dedicated to producing and performing the plays of Shakespeare with energy and invention, challenging the audience to take a fresh look at what is essential in the presentations.
Utilizes: Actors; AEA Actors; Artists-in-Residence; Choreographers; Commissioned Composers; Educators; Five Seasonal Concerts; Guest Artists; Guest Companies; Guest Conductors; Guest Designers; Guest Soloists; Original Music Scores; Soloists; Student Interns; Theatre Companies
Founded: 1987
Specialized Field: Summer Theater
Status: Nonprofit
Volunteer Staff: 250
Paid Artists: 24
Non-paid Artists: 11
Budget: $735,000
Income Sources: Ticket Sales and Fundraising
Season: June, July, August
Performs At: Boscabel Restoration
Annual Attendance: 24,000
Type of Stage: Thrust
Seating Capacity: 450

5062
COOPERSTOWN CONCERT SERIES
PO Box 624
Cooperstown, NY 13326
Phone: 607-547-1812
Fax: 607-293-6124
Web Site: www.chamberorganizer.com/cooperstown/mem_coopconcert
Officers:
  Co-Director: Jane Johngren
  Co-Director: Donna Thomson
  Treasurer: Lois Hopper
  Secretary: Dottie Leslie
Management:
  Co-Director: Richard Brown
  Co-Director: Pamela Huntsman
Mission: To promote the cultural growth of our community by presenting live performances of high quality.
Founded: 1970
Specialized Field: Dance; Vocal Music; Instrumental Music; Theatre
Status: Nonprofit
Budget: $10,000-20,000
Performs At: Sterling Auditorium
Organization Type: Sponsoring

5063
COOPERSTOWN THEATRE & MUSIC FESTIVAL
PO Box 851
Cooperstown, NY 13326
Phone: 607-547-2335
e-mail: info@cooperstowntheatrefestival.org
Web Site: http://www.CooperstownTheatreFestival.org
Management:
  Producer: Margarita Malinova

5064
CLARION CONCERTS IN COLUMBIA COUNTY
PO Box 43
Copake, NY 12516

SERIES & FESTIVALS / New York

Phone: 518-329-5613
e-mail: LeafPeepers@fairpoint.net
Web Site: www.leafpeeperconcerts.org/
Management:
  Music Director: Sanford Allen
  Founder: Newell Jenkins
  Founder: Jack Hurley

5065
A FESTIVAL OF ART
79 West Market Street
Suite 8, Market Street
Corning, NY 14830
Phone: 607-962-1332
Fax: 607-962-4128
e-mail: thearts@stny.lrun.com
Web Site: www.eARTS.org
Officers:
  President: Kamala Keeley
  Vice President: Steve Kettelle
  Secretary: Vishoka Balasubramanian
  Treasurer: Jane Garnett
  Immediate Past President: Brad Turner
Management:
  Executive Director: Ginnie Lupi
  Community Folk Arts Coordinator: Constance R. Sullivan-Blum, Ph.D.
  Special Projects Coordinator: Tamar Samuel-Siegel
  Community Arts Manager: Chris Walters
  Development Assistant: Laura Charles

5066
CORNING-PAINTED POST CIVIC MUSIC ASSOCIATION
PO Box 1402
Corning, NY 14830
Phone: 607-936-9493
Fax: 607-974-7522
Toll-free: 800-531-3679
Web Site: www.corningcivicmusic.org/
Mission: To provide professional performers at the lowest possible cost.
Founded: 1928
Specialized Field: Dance; Vocal Music; Instrumental Music; Jazz; Classical Presentation
Status: Professional
Budget: $60,000-150,000
Performs At: Corning Glass Center Auditorium
Organization Type: Performing

5067
STATE UNIVERSITY OF NEW YORK AT CORTLAND: CAMPUS ARTIST & LECTURE SERIES
Corey Union
Room 406
Cortland, NY 13045
Phone: 607-753-2321
Fax: 607-753-2808
Web Site: www2.cortland.edu/events/cals/index.dot
Officers:
  President: Joanne Barry
  Vice President: Gradin Avery
  Assistant Treasurer: Joshua Fugura
  Secretary: Ben Patrick
Management:
  President: Joanne Barry
  Asst Director, Campus Activities: Sandra Wohlleber
Mission: To enhance the cultural awareness of the Cortland College and general community.
Founded: 1984
Specialized Field: Series & Festivals; Instrumental Music; Vocal Music; Theatre; Dance; Ethnic Performances; Dance
Status: Non-Profit, Professional
Paid Staff: 6
Budget: $45,000
Income Sources: Grant Funded
Performs At: Varied
Organization Type: Presenting

5068
GREAT PERFORMERS IN WESTCHESTER SERIES
5 Joseph Wallace Drive
Croton-on-Hudson, NY 10520
Mailing Address: PO Box 321979, New York, NY 10032
Phone: 914-271-2595
e-mail: info@performersofwestchester.org
Web Site: performersofwestchester.org/
Officers:
  President: George Rehl
  Vice President: Julianne Kelly
  Treasurer: Boyce Bennett
  Secretary: Sandra Zinman
Management:
  Executive Director: Beth Jennings Eggar
Budget: $10,000

5069
ROYCROFT CHAMBER MUSIC FESTIVAL
PO Box 281
East Aurora, NY 14052
Phone: 716-457-3565
Fax: 716-457-4119
e-mail: martha@marthabuyer.com
Web Site: www.roycroftchambermusic.org/
Officers:
  Chair: Bill Pictor
Management:
  Artistic Directors: Nancy Gaub
  Artistic Directors: Eugene Gaub

5070
PIANOFEST
1701 E12th Street, 21 Tower
East Hampton, NY 44114
Mailing Address: P.O. Box 639 Hudson, OH 44236
Phone: 718-544-5891
Fax: 631-329-9115
e-mail: pschenly@aol.com
Web Site: www.pianofest.org
Management:
  Director: Paul Schenly
  Manager: Hyperion Knight

5071
ISLIP ARTS COUNCIL CHAMBER MUSIC SERIES
50 Irish Lane
East Islip, NY 11730
Phone: 631-224-5420
Fax: 631-224-5440
e-mail: iacouncil@aol.com
Web Site: www.islipartscouncil.org
Officers:
  President: Helene Katz
  VP: Nicholas Wartella
  Secretary: Jean Lipshie
  Treasurer: Edward E. Wankel
Management:
  President: Steve Bard
  Executive Director: Lynda A. Moran
  Artistic Director: Dorothy Kalson
  Clerk Typist: Angela Wallace
  Program Assistant: Victoria Berger
  Finance Assistant: Rosa Ramos
  Adminstrative Assistant: Catherine Dale
  Museum Exhibition Director: Beth Giacummo
Mission: To present a variety of disciplines ranging from fine classical music to young persons' programs to avant garde performance art; to enable and emerging art organizations to gain information and assistance from the Arts Council library and staff in applying for not-for-profit status, funding, computer services, publicity, mailing lists, etc.
Utilizes: Singers
Founded: 1974
Specialized Field: Series & Festivals: Music Concerts
Status: Non-Profit, Professional
Paid Staff: 3
Budget: $250,000
Income Sources: Town of Islip; Suffolk County
Performs At: Sayville Schools; Dowling College
Type of Stage: Semi-Thurst
Organization Type: Performing

5072
COLDEN CENTER PERFORMANCES
Colden Center for the Performing Arts
Queens College
Flushing, NY 11367-1597
Phone: 718-544-2996
Fax: 718-261-7063
e-mail: v.charlop@coldcenter.org
Web Site: www.coldencenter.org
Management:
  Tecnical Director: Tony Fitsch
  Executive Director: Vivian Charlop
  Office Manager: Gail Marcus
  Operation Manager: Michael Kelleher
Founded: 1961
Budget: $150,000-400,000
Performs At: Irving & Susan Wallack Goldstein Theatre

5073
FLUSHING COUNCIL ON CULTURE & THE ARTS
Flushing Town Hall
137-35 Northern Boulevard
Flushing, NY 11354
Phone: 718-463-7700
Fax: 718-445-1920
e-mail: info@flushingtownhall.org
Web Site: www.flushingtownhall.org
Officers:
  President: Howard Graf
Management:
  Executive & Artistic Director: Ellen Kodadek
  Deputy Director: Sami Abu Shumays
  Jazz Producer: Clyde Bullard
  Director of Education & Public Prog: Gabrielle M. Hamilton
  Education Coordinator: Jiyoung Kim
  Finance Manager: Rocio Garcia
  Director of Production: Mike Riggs
  Director of Facilities and Operatio: Kevin Meegan
Mission: Founded to be a revitalizing force for its community, a catalyst for developing and promoting the arts throughout Queens, and a bridge to promote intercultural understanding through the arts in the most culturally diverse county in the country.
Founded: 1979
Specialized Field: Music and the Arts
Status: Non-Profit, Professional
Paid Staff: 16
Volunteer Staff: 900

SERIES & FESTIVALS / New York

Seating Capacity: 340
Rental Contact: Susan Agin

5075
SUFFOLK Y JCC INTERNATIONAL JEWISH ARTS FESTIVAL & THE CELEBRATION SERIES
5 Yorktown Place
Fort Salonga, NY 11768
Phone: 516-261-1576
Toll-free: 516-754-4616
Web Site: www.jewishartsfest.com
Officers:
  President: Matthew Kreinces
  First Vice President: Saul Goodhart
  Recording Secretary: Marilyn Monter
  Financial Secretary: Tina Indenbaum
  Treasurer: Howard Baker
Management:
  Specialist to the Arts: Rea Jacobs
  Executive Director: Adam Bendeson

5076
NASSAU COMMUNITY COLLEGE CULTURAL PROGRAM
Nassau Community College
One Education Drive
Garden City, NY 11530-6793
Phone: 516-572-7501
Fax: 516-222-2962
e-mail: informationservices@ncc.edu
Web Site: www.ncc.edu
Officers:
  Chair: Jorge Gardyn
  Vice Chair: Kathy Weiss
  Chair Emerita: Mary A. Adams
  Member: Anthony Cornachio
  Member: John DeGrace
  Member: Arnold W. Drucker
  Member: Wanda Jackson
  Member: Edward W. Powers
  Student Trustee: Patrick Deegan
Management:
  Student Activities Counselor: Phyllis Kurland
Mission: On campus presentations for student body.
Founded: 1970
Budget: $10,000-20,000
Performs At: College Center-Multipurpose Room
Type of Stage: Resess
Stage Dimensions: 16 x 24
Seating Capacity: 300

5077
HUDSON HIGHLANDS MUSIC FESTIVAL
PO Box 1702
507 Chestnut Street
Garrison, NY 28741
Phone: 828-526-9060
Fax: 828-526-4893
e-mail: hccmf@frontier.com
Web Site: www.highlands.com/MusicFestival
Officers:
  President: Kathy Whitehead
Management:
  Artistic Director: Heidi Stubner

5078
SUNY COLLEGE AT GENESEO LIMELIGHT ARTIST SERIES
College Union, SUNY College at Geneseo
1 College Circle
Geneseo, NY 14454
Phone: 585-245-5876
Fax: 585-245-5400
e-mail: limelight@geneseo.edu
Web Site: www.geneseo.edu/limelightandaccents/
Management:
  Campus Activities Director: Thomas Rodgers
Budget: $60,000-150,000
Income Sources: Student Feed; Ticket Revenue
Performs At: Wadsworth Auditorium
Affiliations: Arts Presenters National Association for Campus Activities
Facility Category: Auditorium
Type of Stage: Proscenium

5079
GENEVA CONCERTS
PO Box 709
Geneva, NY 14456
Phone: 315-568-8767
Fax: 315-781-3660
e-mail: horvath_susan@hotmail.com
Web Site: www.genevaconcerts.org
Officers:
  President: Ford Weiskittel
  Vice-President for Education and Ou: Tom McClure
  Secretary: Hilda Collins
  Treasurer: Joanna Whelan
Management:
  President: Susan Horvath
  Artistic Director & CEO: Bengt Jorgen
  Business Operations Coordinator: Cody Neville
  Development Community Coordinator: Melissa Forstner
  Director of Touring: Cameron Smillie
  Dance Coordinator: Kia Kotsanis
  Atlantic Coordinator: Peggy Walt
  Education Manager: Clea Iveson
  Production Manager: Cindy Smith
Mission: To promote the arts in Geneva and the surrounding Finger Lakes community by presenting music, dance and vocal performances.
Utilizes: Artists-in-Residence; Dance Companies; Dancers; Multimedia; Original Music Scores; Theatre Companies
Founded: 1938
Specialized Field: Series & Festivals: Music and Dance Performance
Status: Non-Profit, Non-Professional
Volunteer Staff: 22
Paid Artists: 290
Budget: $60,000-150,000
Performs At: Smith Opera House
Annual Attendance: 3,000
Facility Category: Opera House
Type of Stage: Proscenium Arts; Thrust Stage
Seating Capacity: 1,500
Year Built: 1894
Year Remodeled: 2000
Rental Contact: Kevin Mitchell
Organization Type: Educational; Sponsoring

5080
ADIRONDACK THEATRE FESTIVAL
PO Box 3203
Glens Falls, NY 12801
Phone: 518-798-7479
Fax: 518-793-1334
e-mail: atf@atfestival.org
Web Site: www.atfestival.org
Officers:
  President: Kristine K. Flower
  Vice President: Sean Magee
  Treasurer: Robert J. Joy
  Secretary: Jane Gibbs
Management:
  Producing Artistic Director: Mark Fleischer
  General Manager: Landrie Bock
  Technical Director: David Pierce
  Technical Associate: Wynne Dawson
Mission: A professional not-for-profit summer theatre located in Glens Falls, NY, strives to challenge, entertain, and nourish its audience through the development and production of new and contemporary musicals and plays. This relationship engages the community as audience members and participants in workshops, discussions and educational programming.
Utilizes: Actors; AEA Actors; Choreographers; Commissioned Composers; Designers; Local Unknown Artists; Music; Organization Contracts; Original Music Scores; Performance Artists; Resident Professionals; Student Interns
Founded: 1994
Specialized Field: Theater
Status: Nonprofit
Paid Staff: 11
Volunteer Staff: 10
Paid Artists: 36
Budget: $400,000
Income Sources: Ticket Sales; Donations; Grants
Season: June - July
Performs At: Charles R Wood Theater
Affiliations: AEA
Annual Attendance: 6,100
Facility Category: Theater
Type of Stage: Proscenium
Seating Capacity: 294
Year Built: 2004

5081
LOWER ADIRONDACK REGIONAL ARTS COUNCIL
7 Lapham Place
Glens Falls, NY 12801
Phone: 518-798-1144
Fax: 518-798-9122
e-mail: gallery@larac.org
Web Site: www.laracarts.org
Officers:
  Chair: Sharon Conrick
  Vice Chair: Rene Clements
  Vice Chair: Tim Reed
  Secretary: Nancy Quillinan
  Treasurer: Michael Laney
Management:
  President: Patricia Joyce
  Executive Director: Ellen Butz
  Marketing & Festivals: Stacy Bissell
  Gallery, Shop & Programs Coordinato: Jenny Hutchinson
  Community Outreach Coordinator: Candice Frye
Mission: To lead in the improvement of the quality of life for the people of the lower Adirondack region by supporting the arts and culture.
Founded: 1972
Specialized Field: Series and Festivals
Status: Non-Profit, Non-Professional
Paid Staff: 3
Affiliations: New York State Council on the Arts

5082
GLYDE RECITALS: NEW YORK VIOLA SOCIETY
26 Green Hill Road
Golden's Bridge, NY 10526

SERIES & FESTIVALS / New York

Mailing Address: New York Viola Society, PO Box 61, New York, NY 10019
Phone: 914-232-8159
Fax: 914-232-0521
e-mail: wsalchow@computer.net
Web Site: www.viola.com/nyvs
Management:
  President: William Salchow
  Director: Chris Ims
Budget: $10,000

5083
FESTIVAL OF BAROQUE MUSIC
Foundation for Baroque Music
165 Wilton Road
Greenfield Center, NY 12833
Phone: 518-893-7527
Fax: 518-893-2351
e-mail: rconant@baroquefestival.org
Web Site: www.baroquefestival.org
Management:
  President: Robert Conant
Founded: 1959
Specialized Field: Series & Festivals; Instrumental Music; Vocal Music; Youth; Dance
Status: Non-Profit, Professional
Paid Staff: 1
Paid Artists: 18

5084
LONG ISLAND UNIVERSITY/TILLES CENTER
Route 25A
Greenvale, NY 11548-0570
Phone: 516-299-2752
Fax: 516-299-2520
e-mail: elliott.stroka@liu.edu
Web Site: www.tillescenter.org
Officers:
  Executive Director: Elliot Sroka
Management:
  General Manager: George N. Lindsay Jr.
  Executive Director: Elliott Sroka
  Business Manager: Marc Courtade
  Artistic Director: Caroline Stoessinger
  Executive Producer: Jack Globenfelt
  Director of Ticket Services: Daniel Coners
  Director of Arts Education: Stephanie Turner
  Campus Arts Liaison: Clara Zahler
  Director of Development: Marc Cincone
Mission: Long Island's premiere concert venue and presenter of world class live performances.
Founded: 1981
Specialized Field: Series & Festivals; Instrumental Music; Vocal Music; Theatre; Youth; Dance; Ethnic Performances
Status: Non-Profit, Professional
Paid Staff: 80
Volunteer Staff: 20
Budget: $6,000,000
Income Sources: Ticket Sales; Private Donations; NYSCA
Performs At: Concert Hall; Recital Hall
Affiliations: Ticketmaster
Annual Attendance: 200,000
Facility Category: Theatre
Type of Stage: Wood
Stage Dimensions: 70 X 35
Seating Capacity: 2,242
Year Built: 1981
Rental Contact: General Manager George Lindsay

5085
COLGATE UNIVERSITY CONCERT SERIES
Colgate University, Music Department
13 Oak Drive
Hamilton, NY 13346-1398
Phone: 315-228-7642
Fax: 315-228-7557
e-mail: shealey@mail.colgate.edu
Web Site: www.colgate.edu
Officers:
  Chairperson: Mariette Cheng
  Director, Chenango Summer Mus. Fest: Laura Klugherz
Management:
  President: Rebeca Chopp
  Managing Director: Roberta Healey
Mission: To provide music concerts for Colgate students and the surrounding community.
Utilizes: Guest Companies; Guest Directors; Guest Musical Directors; Guest Musicians
Founded: 1836
Specialized Field: Series and Festivals; Instrumental Music; Vocal Music; Theatre; Ethnic Performances
Status: Non-Profit, Professional
Paid Staff: 2
Paid Artists: 40
Budget: $20,000-35,000
Income Sources: Private
Performs At: Colgate Memorial Chapel
Facility Category: chapel
Type of Stage: wooden
Seating Capacity: 750
Organization Type: Educational; Sponsoring
Resident Groups: University Orchestra, Chamber Players, Chorus, Jazz Ensemble

5086
BELLEAYRE MUSIC FESTIVAL
PO Box 198
Highmount, NY 12441
Mailing Address: PO Box 198
Phone: 845-254-5600
Fax: 845-254-5608
Toll-free: 800-942-6904
e-mail: festival@catskill.net
Web Site: www.belleayremusic.org
Management:
  Executive/Artistic Director: Mel Litoff
  Administrative Manager: Don L Myers
Mission: To bring the arts and culture to this Catskill highpeaks area
Founded: 1992
Specialized Field: All Types Of Music From Opera To Orchestra, Folk To Pop
Status: Non-Profit, Professional
Paid Staff: 4
Volunteer Staff: 30
Paid Artists: 250
Non-paid Artists: 50
Budget: $800,000
Income Sources: Ticket Sales; Contributions
Performs At: Tent & Lawn Summer Music Festival
Affiliations: Festival Is Held On The Grounds & Belleayre Ski Center
Annual Attendance: 10,000
Facility Category: Performance Tent
Type of Stage: Wood Platform
Stage Dimensions: 30'x40'
Seating Capacity: 650
Year Built: 2003

5087
HORNELL AREA ARTS COUNCIL
PO Box 627
82 Main St.
Hornell, NY 14843
Phone: 607-324-3822
Fax: 607-324-3822
Web Site: www.cityofhornell.com/hornell_arts_center.php
Management:
  Executive Director: Rene, Coombs
Budget: $10,000-20,000

5088
HOUGHTON COLLEGE ARTIST SERIES
Houghton College
One Willard Avenue
Houghton, NY 14744
Phone: 585-567-9468
Fax: 585-567-9517
e-mail: music@houghton.edu
Web Site: www.houghton.edu/music/
Management:
  Director: Dr. Bruce Brown
Mission: To offer the finest music concerts.
Utilizes: Artists-in-Residence; Dance Companies; Guest Accompanists; Guest Choreographers; Guest Composers; Guest Directors; Guest Lecturers; Multimedia; Original Music Scores; Sign Language Translators; Special Technical Talent; Theatre Companies
Founded: 1930
Specialized Field: Vocal Music; Instrumental Music; Theatre; Grand Opera
Status: Nonprofit
Budget: $20,000-35,000
Income Sources: Association of Performing Arts Presenters
Performs At: Wesley Chapel
Organization Type: Performing; Educational; Sponsoring

5089
HUNTINGTON ARTS COUNCIL
213 Main Street
Huntington, NY 11743
Phone: 631-271-8423
Fax: 631-271-8428
e-mail: info@huntingtonarts.org
Web Site: www.huntingtonarts.org
Officers:
  President: Debbi Honorof
  Vice President: Susan Miller
  Vice President: William F. Bonesso
  Treasurer: Gerald F. Moss
  Secretary: Lisa Arden
Management:
  President: Debbi Honorof
  Executive Director: Diana Cherryholmes
  Vice President: Susan Miller
  Program Director: Dan Forte
Mission: The Huntington Arts Council supports and fosters the arts to enhance the lives of the citizens of Huntington Township and their visitors.
Founded: 1963
Specialized Field: Presenting; Education; Re-grants; Technical Assistance
Paid Staff: 8
Volunteer Staff: 27
Paid Artists: 57
Income Sources: Grants; Sponsorchip; Town and County Funding; Membership Dues
Annual Attendance: 90,000

SERIES & FESTIVALS / New York

Seating Capacity: 5,500
Year Built: 1979
Rental Contact: Dan Forte

5090
HUNTINGTON SUMMER ARTS FESTIVAL
Huntington Arts Council
213 Main Street
Huntington, NY 11743
Phone: 631-271-8423
Fax: 631-271-8428
e-mail: hsaf@huntingtonarts.org
Web Site: www.huntingtonarts.org
Officers:
   President: Debbi Honorof
   Vice President: Susan Miller
   Vice President: William F. Bonesso
   Treasurer: Gerald F. Moss
   Secretary: Lisa Arden
Management:
   President: Debbi Honorof
   Executive Director: Diana J Cherryholmes
Founded: 1962
Status: Non-Profit, Professional
Paid Staff: 7

5091
CORNELL CONCERT SERIES
Cornell University
147 Goldwin Smith Hall
Ithaca, NY 14853 -320
Phone: 607-255-4833
Fax: 607-254-2877
Web Site: www.arts.cornell.edu/ccs
Management:
   Managing Director: Kiko Nobusawa
   Harold Tanner Dean: Gretchen Ritter
   Director: Kathleen Gemmell
Mission: Concert events per academic year, from solo recitals to orchestras presents; musicians of international renown.
Founded: 1903
Specialized Field: Series & Festivals; Instrumental Music; Vocal Music; Dance; Ethnic Performances; Classical Music; Jazz; World Music
Status: Non-Profit, Professional
Paid Staff: 2
Volunteer Staff: 80
Paid Artists: 10

5092
ITHACA COLLEGE CONCERTS
Ithaca College School of Music
953 Danby Road
Ithaca, NY 14850-7240
Phone: 607-274-3011
Fax: 607-274-3201
e-mail: ekibelsbeck.ithaca.edu
Web Site: www.ithaca.edu/music
Management:
   Concert Manager: Erik Kibelsheck
Founded: 1892
Specialized Field: Series & Festivals: Classical Music
Status: Non-Profit, Non-Professional
Budget: $20,000-35,000
Income Sources: Ticket Revenue
Performs At: Ford Hall
Facility Category: Concert Hall
Type of Stage: Proscenium
Seating Capacity: 737
Year Built: 1960

5093
NEW DIRECTIONS CELLO FESTIVAL
501 Linn Street
Ithaca, NY 14850
Phone: 607-277-1686
Fax: 607-277-1686
Toll-free: 877-665-5815
e-mail: info@newdirectionscello.com
Web Site: www.newdirectionscello.com
Management:
   Director: Joel Cohen
   General Director: Chris White
   Assistant Director: Sera Surslen
   Artistic Advisors: David N. Baker
Mission: To bring together cellists and others interested in nonclassical uses of cello (jazz, blues, folk, rock, etc.). Workshops, jams, concerts.
Utilizes: Artists-in-Residence; Collaborations; Guest Accompanists; Guest Directors; Guest Musical Directors; Guest Musicians; Multimedia; Organization Contracts; Original Music Scores; Soloists
Founded: 1995
Specialized Field: Series & Festivals; Instrumental Music; Youth; Ethnic Performances; Promotion of Non Classical Usage of Cello
Status: For-Profit, Professional
Paid Staff: 3
Volunteer Staff: 10
Paid Artists: 12
Budget: Under $10,000
Income Sources: Sponsors, Participants, Donations
Season: July 11 - 13, 1999
Performs At: University of Connecticut, Storrs [Festival Site]
Annual Attendance: 100
Facility Category: Mehden Auditorium/Recital Hall
Stage Dimensions: 50x25
Seating Capacity: 500
Year Built: 1985
Cost: $150 - 3 day

5094
ARTS COUNCIL FOR CHAUTAUGUA COUNTY
116 E Third Street
Jamestown, NY 14701
Phone: 716-664-2465
Fax: 716-661-3829
e-mail: heather@artscouncil.com
Web Site: www.artscouncil.com
Management:
   Executive Director: David Schein
Founded: 1970
Status: Non-Profit, Non-Professional
Budget: $60,000-150,000
Performs At: Reg Lenna Civic Center

5095
JAMESTOWN CONCERT ASSOCIATION
315 North Main St.
Suite 200
Jamestown, NY 14701
Phone: 716-487-1522
Fax: 716-483-5051
e-mail: jcamusic@excite.com
Web Site: www.jamestownconcertassociation.org
Officers:
   President: R Richard Corbin
   VP: Sally Ulrich
   Treasurer: F John Fuchs
   Secretary: Mary Weeden
Management:
   President: Richard Corbin
   Executive Director: Sally Ulrich
   Managing Director: Jack Hemink
Mission: Purpose of presenting live classical performances in the Jamestown area.
Founded: 1934
Specialized Field: Series and Festivals; Instrumental Music; Vocal Music; Youth; Ethnic Performances
Status: Non-Profit, Professional
Volunteer Staff: 16
Paid Artists: 200
Budget: $20,000-35,000
Income Sources: NYSCA; Local Foundations; PENNPAT

5096
CARAMOOR CENTER FOR MUSIC AND THE ARTS
149 Girdle Ridge Rd
PO Box 816
Katonah, NY 10536
Phone: 914-232-5035
Fax: 914-232-5521
e-mail: info@caramoor.org
Web Site: www.caramoor.org
Officers:
   President/CEO: Erich Vollmer
   Chairman: James A. Attwood, Jr.
   Vice Chairman: Peter Kend
   Treasurer: Paul S. Bird
   Secretary: Angela Haines
Management:
   Executive Director: Howard Herring
   Managing Director: Paul Rosenblum
   Director Development: Susan Shine
   Director Operations: Melissa Montera
   Box Office Manager: Sal Vaccaro
   Artistic Coordinator: Ellie Gisler
   Chief Executive Officer: Jeffrey Haydon
   National Press: Lois Cohn
Mission: To offer a performing arts venue in Bedford and New York State.
Founded: 1945
Specialized Field: Vocal Music; Instrumental Music; Festivals
Status: Professional; Nonprofit
Performs At: Museum Music Room Venetian Theatre
Organization Type: Performing; Educational; Sponsoring

5097
CARAMOOR INTERNATIONAL MUSIC FESTIVAL
PO Box 816
149 Girdle Ridge Rd
Katonah, NY 10536
Phone: 914-232-1252
Fax: 914-232-5521
e-mail: info@caramoor.org
Web Site: www.caramoor.com
   Chairman: James A. Attwood, Jr.
   Vice Chairman: Peter Kend
   Treasurer: Paul S. Bird
   Secretary: Angela Haines
Management:
   Chief Executive And Generaldirector: Michael Barrett
   Artistic Director: Joe Lovano
   Managing Director: Paul Rosenblum
   Vice President & Chief Financial Of: Tammy Belanger
   Vice President & Chief Marketing Of: Tahra Millan
   Artistic Coordinator: Ellie Gisler
   Chief Executive Officer: Jeffrey Haydon

National Press: Lois Cohn

5098
LAKE GEORGE JAZZ WEEKEND
Lake George Arts Project
1 Amherst Street
Lake George, NY 12845
Phone: 518-668-2616
Fax: 518-668-3050
e-mail: mail@lakegeorgearts.org
Web Site: www.lakegeorgearts.org/
Officers:
  President: Ed Ostberg
Management:
  Executive Director: John Strong
  Music Director: Paul Pines
Mission: Sponsoring a two-day jazz festival every September featuring nationally acclaimed as well as emerging jazz artists.
Founded: 1980
Specialized Field: General Arts Organisation
Status: Non-Profit, Professional
Paid Staff: 1
Paid Artists: 5
Performs At: Shepard Park Bandstand
Organization Type: Performing; Touring

5099
LUZERNE CHAMBER MUSIC FESTIVAL
PO Box 39
203 Lake Tour Rd.
Lake Luzerne, NY 12846
Phone: 518-696-2771
Fax: 518-696-4903
Toll-free: 800-874-3202
e-mail: info@luzernemusic.org
Web Site: www.luzernemusic.org
Officers:
  Vice Chairman: Michael K. Conway
  President, CEO and Artistic Directo: Elizabeth Pitcairn
  Treasurer: Kenneth McPartlin
  Governance Chair: Darrin C. Milling
Management:
  President, CEO and Artistic Directo: Elizabeth Pitcairn
  Registrar and Camp Director: Elliot Downey
  Assistant Camp Director: Audrey Williams
Founded: 1980
Specialized Field: Series & Festivals; Chamber Music; Summer Music Camp
Status: Non-Profit, Professional
Paid Staff: 20
Paid Artists: 20

5100
ARTPARK
450 S 4th Street
Lewiston, NY 14092
Phone: 716-754-9000
Fax: 716-754-2741
e-mail: gosborne@artpark.net
Web Site: www.artpark.net
Officers:
  President: George D Osborn
  Director Finance: Jean Stopa
  Productions Manager: Susan Stimson
Management:
  President: George Osborne
Mission: To provide arts education and programming to nuture and develop the talents of visual and performing artists; to provide quality volunteer experiences in the arts; to produce and present a series of theatre productions and concert events that will entertain and enrich the residents of Western New York, southeastern Canada, and area tourists.
Utilizes: Actors; AEA Actors; Artists-in-Residence; Choreographers; Dance Companies; Dancers; Designers; Fine Artists; Local Artists; Multimedia; Music; Original Music Scores; Resident Professionals; Sign Language Translators; Soloists; Touring Companies; Visual Arts
Founded: 1974
Specialized Field: Series & Festivals; Dance; Vocal Music; Instrumental Music; Festivals
Status: Non-Profit, Professional
Paid Staff: 100
Volunteer Staff: 300
Paid Artists: 200
Budget: $4 Million
Income Sources: Tickets; Grants; Sponsors
Season: June - September
Affiliations: Actors' Equity Association; International Association of Theatrical Stage Employees; American Guild of Musical Artists
Annual Attendance: 300,000
Facility Category: Theater & Ampi-Theater
Type of Stage: Sprung
Seating Capacity: 2,324
Year Built: 1974
Cost: $7,200,000
Rental Contact: Productions Manager Susan Stimson
Organization Type: Performing; Resident; Sponsoring

5101
BEETHOVEN FESTIVAL
Friends of the Arts
PO Box 702
Locust Valley, NY 11560
Phone: 516-922-0061
Fax: 516-922-0770
e-mail: info@fotapresents.org
Web Site: www.fotapresents.org
Management:
  Executive Director: Maryann Beaumant
Mission: Presenting Beethoven's lifetime body of work during one spectacular weekend.
Founded: 1972
Specialized Field: Series & Festivals; Concerts And Presenters; Educational Programs Jazz; Classical And Pop
Status: Non-Profit, Professional
Paid Staff: 8
Performs At: Planting Fields Arboretum
Organization Type: Performing

5102
BASKETBALL CITY
3100 47th Avenue
2nd Floor
Long Island City, NY 11103
Phone: 718-786-4242
Fax: 718-786-4252
e-mail: bruce@basketballcity.com
Web Site: www.basketballcity.com
Management:
  Director: Bruce D. Radler
Founded: 1997
Specialized Field: Basketball
Status: For-Profit, Professional

5103
EMELIN THEATRE FOR THE PERFORMING ARTS
153 Library Lane
P.O. Box 736
Mamaroneck, NY 10543-0736
Phone: 914-698-3045
Fax: 914-698-1404
e-mail: info@emelin.org
Web Site: www.emelin.org
Officers:
  President: Mark D. Ettenger
  1st Vice President: Karen Isaac
  2nd Vice President: Paul Cantwell
  Treasurer: Robert Nathan
  Secretary: Emily Grant
Management:
  Managing Director: John Raymond
  Company Manager: Charles Zavelle
  Executive Director: Lisa Reilly
  Marketing Director: Ashley Prymas
  Production Manager: Bryan McPartlan
  Development Director: Soledad Fernandez
Founded: 1973
Status: Non-Profit, Professional
Budget: $150,000-400,000
Performs At: Emelin Theatre
Type of Stage: Proscenium
Seating Capacity: 280

5104
OYSTER BAY ARTS COUNCIL
977 Hicksville Road
Massapequa, NY 01757
Phone: 516-797-7926
Fax: 516-797-7919
e-mail: sbetz@oysterbay-ny.gov
Web Site: www.tobac.org
Management:
  Executive Director: Joanne Reeves
Mission: The Art Council's mission is to promote, encourage, publicize and stimulate performing & visual arts in our community.
Founded: 1973
Status: Non-Profit, Non-Professional
Volunteer Staff: 19
Budget: $10,000
Income Sources: Membership; Fundraising

5105
DOROTHY TAUBMAN SEMINAR AT LINCOLN CENTER
The Taubman Institute
245 Route 351
Medusa, NY 12120
Phone: 518-966-5558
Fax: 518-966-5998
Toll-free: 800-826-3720
e-mail: es@taubman-institute.com
Web Site: www.taubman-institute.com
Management:
  Director: Enid Stettner
Mission: June 21, 22, 23, (2007)
Founded: 1977
Paid Artists: 13

5106
CHAMBER MUSIC FESTIVAL OF THE EAST
Chamber Music Conference
900 W. 190th St. #11-O
Melville, NY 10040
Phone: 201-242-1277
e-mail: chmusic@tiac.net
Web Site: cmceast.org/
Management:
  Chairman of Board: Stephen Reid
  Music Director: Shem Guibbory
Founded: 1945

SERIES & FESTIVALS / New York

Specialized Field: Chamber Music; Study Organization
Status: Non-Profit, Professional
Paid Staff: 60

5107
MOUNT KISCO CONCERT ASSOCIATION
34 Lakeside Road
P.O. Box 198
Mount Kisco, NY 10549
Phone: 914-666-9181
Fax: 914-241-0034
e-mail: djnmrili@aol.com
Web Site: www.escherquartet.com/
Officers:
   Artist Selection Chairperson: Michael G Rothenberg
Management:
   President: Eedee Rothenberg
   Artistic Director: Micheal Rothenberg
Founded: 1967
Specialized Field: Series & Festivals: Chamber Music
Status: Non-Profit, Professional
Paid Artists: 3
Budget: $20,000-35,000

5108
PIANO SUMMER AT NEW PALTZ
SUNY at New Paltz, Music Department
1 Hawk Drive
New Paltz, NY 12561-2443
Phone: 845-257-2700
Fax: 845-257-3121
Web Site: www.newpaltz.edu/piano
Management:
   Artistic Director: Vladimir Feltsman

5109
92ND STREET Y
92nd Street Y
1395 Lexington Avenue
New York, NY 10128
Phone: 212-415-5500
Fax: 212-415-5788
e-mail: webmaster@92ndsty.org
Web Site: www.92ndsty.org
Officers:
   President: Stuart J. Ellman
   Chairman: Thomas S. Kaplan
   Vice Presidents: Laurence D. Belfer
   VP: Lini Lipton
   Treasurer: Paul Levy
   Secretary: Marcia Eppler Colvin
Management:
   President: Michael Goldstein
   Executive Director: Henry Timms
   Director: Tamar C Podell
   Production Manager: Zoe Markwalter
   Associate Executive Director: Eric J. Lange
   Associate Executive Director: Alyse Myers
   Director of Tradition and Innovatio: Rabbi Dan Ain
   Director, IT: Cornelius Cadigan
Mission: Serves over 400,000 people annually and offers 200 programs daily. The center holds lectures and oanel discussion, concerts of classical, jazz and popular music, dance performances, literary readings, film screenings and more.
Founded: 1874
Status: Nonprofit

5110
AMERICAN FESTIVAL OF MICROTONAL MUSIC
318 East 70th Street
Suite 5FW
New York, NY 10021
Phone: 212-517-3550
Fax: 212-517-3550
e-mail: afmmjr@aol.com
Web Site: www.afmm.org
Officers:
   President: Edgar E Coons
Management:
   Director: Johnny Reinhard
Founded: 1981
Specialized Field: Series & Festivals; Instrumental Music; Vocal Music; Theatre; Youth; Dance; Ethnic Performances
Status: Non-Profit, Professional
Paid Artists: 30

5111
AMERICAN INDIAN COMMUNITY HOUSE SERIES
254 West 29th Street
2nd Floor
New York, NY 10003
Phone: 212-598-0100
Fax: 212-598-4909
e-mail: akwesasne@aol.com
Web Site: www.aich.org
Management:
   Executive Director: Rosemary Richmond
   Performing Arts Director: Jim Cyrus
Founded: 1969
Status: Non-Profit, Professional
Paid Staff: 40
Budget: $10,000-20,000
Season: September - June

5112
AMERICAN LANDMARK FESTIVALS
26 Wall Street
New York, NY 10005
Phone: 212-866-2086
Fax: 212-866-2086
e-mail: AmLandmarKFstvls@gmail.com
Web Site: www.americanlandmarkfestivals.org
Officers:
   Founding Director: Francis L Heilbut
   President: Gena Rangel
   Treasurer: Joe Pearce
Management:
   Director: Gena Rangel
   Director Of Technology: John F. Rangel
   Artistic Director: Tanja Dorn
   Financial Officer: Joseph R. Pearce
Mission: To present cultural and performing arts events in landmarks of sign, science, and to promote better understanding of landmarks and the performing arts.
Utilizes: Singers
Founded: 1973
Specialized Field: Performing Arts
Status: Professional
Paid Staff: 2
Volunteer Staff: 3
Paid Artists: 20
Non-paid Artists: 20
Organization Type: Performing

5113
ARTS INTERNATIONAL
526 W 26th Street
Suite 516
New York, NY 10001
Phone: 212-924-0771
Fax: 212-924-0773
e-mail: info@artsinternational.org
Web Site: www.artsinternational.org
Officers:
   President: Noreen Tomassi
Management:
   President: Noreen Tomassi
   Director Of Development: Esther McGowan
   Director: Renata Petroni Petroni
Founded: 1981

5114
ASIA SOCIETY
725 Park Avenue
New York, NY 10021-5025
Phone: 212-288-6400
Fax: 212-517-8315
e-mail: info@asiasociety.org
Web Site: www.asiasociety.org
Management:
   President: Vishakha N Desai
   VP External Affairs: Carol P Herring
   VP Marketing/Communications: Karen Karp
   VP Finance/Administration: Shin R Miyoshi
Founded: 1956

5115
BANG ON A CAN
80 Hanson Place
New York, NY 11217
Phone: 718-852-7755
Fax: 718-852-7732
e-mail: info@bangonacan.org
Web Site: www.bangonacan.org
Management:
   President: Adam Wolfensohn
   Executive Director: Kenny Savelson
   Artistic Director: Michael Gordon
   Artistic Director: Julia Wolfe
   Artistic Director: David Lang
   Development Director: Tim Thomas
   Program Manager: Phillippa Thompson
   Production Manager: Sruly Lazaros
Mission: To present contemporary musical works by emerging and young composers.
Utilizes: Choreographers; Commissioned Composers; Commissioned Music; Designers; Five Seasonal Concerts; Grant Writers; Guest Accompanists; Guest Artists; Guest Choreographers; Guest Companies; Guest Composers; Guest Conductors; Guest Designers; Guest Directors; Guest Ensembles; Guest Musical Directors; High School Drama; Instructors; Multimedia; Original Music Scores; Resident Professionals; Sign Language Translators; Singers; Student Interns; Special Technical Talent; Visual Arts
Founded: 1987
Specialized Field: Series and Festivals; Instrumental Music; Vocal Music; Presenting New Music
Status: Non-Profit, Professional
Paid Staff: 6
Income Sources: Public; Private Funding; Earned Income
Organization Type: Performing

SERIES & FESTIVALS / New York

5116
BELL ATLANTIC JAZZ FESTIVAL
74 Leonard Street
New York, NY 10013
Phone: 212-219-3006
Fax: 212-219-3401
Web Site: www.jazfest.com

5117
BLOOMINGDALE SCHOOL OF MUSIC CONCERT SERIES
323 West 108th Street
New York, NY 10025
Phone: 212-663-6021
Fax: 212-932-9429
e-mail: info@bsmny.org
Web Site: www.bsmny.org
Officers:
   President: Kenneth Michaels
   Vice President: Paul Ness
   Secretary: Susan Lanter Blank
   Treasurer: Brian Upbin
Management:
   Executive Director: Lawrence Davis
   Interim Director: Barbara Adler
   Educational Project Manager: Jeremy Blanden
   Project Manager: Margalit Cantor
   Business Manager: Chen Chu
Founded: 1964
Specialized Field: Series & Festivals: Music
Status: Non-Profit, Professional
Budget: $10,000
Performs At: David Greer Recital Hall

5118
BOPI'S BLACK SHEEP/DANCE BY KRAIG PATTERSON
Jaf Station
PO Box 372
New York, NY 10116
Phone: 212-262-9499
Fax: 212-399-1349
e-mail: dancebopi@aol.com
Web Site: www.bopi.org
Management:
   Artistic Director: Kraig Patterson
   Booking Agent: Micocci Productions
Mission: Performance, touring and creation of works.
Specialized Field: Modern Dance
Paid Staff: 2
Paid Artists: 12

5119
BRIDGEHAMPTON CHAMBER MUSIC FESTIVAL
850 Seventh Avenue
Suite 700
New York, NY 10019
Phone: 212-741-9073
Fax: 212-741-9403
e-mail: info@bcmf.org
Web Site: www.bcmf.org
Officers:
   Chairman: Kenneth S. Davidson
Management:
   Executive Director: Michael Lawrence
   Artistic Director: Marya Martin
Founded: 1984
Specialized Field: Series & Festivals; Classical Music; Instumental Music
Status: Non-Profit, Professional
Paid Staff: 1
Paid Artists: 40

5120
CATHEDRAL ARTS
1047 Amsterdam Avenue
PO Box 6000
New York, NY 13902-6000
Phone: 607-777-6802
Fax: 607-777-6771
Web Site: www.anderson.binghamton.edu
Management:
   President: James A Kowski
   Director: Canon Tom Miller
   Executive Director: Gary Pedro
   Assistant to the Executive Director: Patricia J. Benjamin
   Operations Director: Annette M. Burnett
   Marketing Director: Rosanne Norris
   Technical Director: Steven D. Machlin
   Assistant Technical Director: Daniel W. Sonnen
   House Operations Director: Casey Korchynsky
Founded: 1892
Specialized Field: Series & Festivals; Instrumental Music; Vocal Music; Youth; Ethnic Performances; Concerts
Status: Non-Profit, Professional
Budget: $10,000-20,000

5121
CENTRAL PARK SUMMERSTAGE
5th Avenue and 72nd Street
New York, NY 10021
Phone: 212-360-2756
Fax: 212-360-2754
e-mail: info@summerstage.org
Web Site: www.summerstage.org
Management:
   Director Of Marketing And Public Re: Debbie Ferraro
   Executive Director: David Rivel
   Director Of Operations: Josy Dussek
   Production Director: John McDonald
Founded: 1986
Specialized Field: Music; Dance; Spokin Word; Opera
Status: Nonprofit
Paid Staff: 76
Volunteer Staff: 300
Paid Artists: 90
Budget: $800,000
Income Sources: Ticket Sales; State Local Grants; Memberships; Endowment Funds
Performs At: Rumsey Playfield
Annual Attendance: 350,000
Stage Dimensions: 36'x42'
Seating Capacity: 4,000-6,000
Year Built: 1986
Year Remodeled: 2000

5122
CLARION MUSIC SOCIETY
Kaye Playhouse
695 Park Avenue
New York, NY 10065
Phone: 212-772-4448
Fax: 212-650-3661
e-mail: kayeinfo@hunter.cuny.edu
Web Site: www.kayeplayhouse.org
Management:
   Executive Director: Sandra Davis
Budget: $35,000-60,000
Performs At: Kaye Playhouse

5123
CONCERT ARTISTS GUILD NEW YORK RECITAL SERIES
850 Seventh Avenue PH-A
Suite 1205
New York, NY 10019
Phone: 212-333-5200
Fax: 212-977-7149
e-mail: caguild@concertartists.org
Web Site: www.concertartists.org
Officers:
   President: Richard Weinert
   Executive VP: Amy Roberts Frawley
   Senior VP: Brian D Bumby
Management:
   President: Richard Weinert
   Executive VP: Amy Roberts Frawley
   Senior VP Artist: Steven D Shaiman
   Comptroller: Christine Sperry
   Programs Assistant: Susan Mandel
   Director of Artistic Programs: Jessica Hadler
   Seior Associate: Cindy S. Hwang
Founded: 1951
Specialized Field: Classical
Performs At: Weill Recital Hall at Carnegie Hall

5124
CONCERT SOCIALS
110 W 96th Street
Suite 9D
New York, NY 10025
Phone: 212-749-5464
Web Site: musicalworld.com/presenters/concert-socials-inc/
Management:
   Executive Director/President: Rae Metzgar
Performs At: Weill Recital Hall at Carnegie Hall

5125
CONCERTS AT THE CLOISTERS
The Cloisters
99 Margaret Corbin Drive, Fort Tryon Park
New York, NY 10040
Phone: 212-923-3700
Fax: 212-795-3640
Web Site: www.metmuseum.org
Management:
   Concert Manager: Nancy Wu
Budget: $50,000-100,000
Performs At: Fuentiduena Chapel; Metropolitan Museum of Art

5126
CREATIVE TIME SERIES
59 East 4th Street
6th Floor
New York, NY 10003
Phone: 212-206-6674
Fax: 212-255-8467
e-mail: staff@creativetime.org
Web Site: www.creativetime.org
Management:
   President and Artistic Director: Anne Pasternak
   Producer And Curator: Alexa Coyne
   Director Of Development: Alyssa Nitchun
   Chairman Of Executive Committee: Philip Aarons
   Project Manager: Marcus Mitchell
   Deputy Director: Katie Hollander
Founded: 1973
Budget: $10,000-20,000

SERIES & FESTIVALS / New York

5128
EARLY MUSIC NEW YORK (EM/NY)
10 West 68 Street
New York, NY 10023
Phone: 212-749-6600
Fax: 212-749-2848
e-mail: info@earlymusicny.org
Web Site: www.EarlyMusicNY.org
Officers:
  President: Audrey Boughton
Management:
  Founder/Director: Frederick Renz, f.renz@EarlyMusicNY.org
  Operations Manager: Aaron Smith, admin@EarlyMusicNY.org
Mission: To foster historically informed performances
Founded: 1974
Specialized Field: Early Music; Dance & Music Drama; Medieval; Renaissance; Baroque; Classical
Status: Non-Profit; Professional
Paid Staff: 4
Budget: $300,000
Income Sources: Ticket Sales; CD Sales; Private Contributions & Grants; Government Awards
Performs At: Cathedral of Saint John the Divine
Affiliations: Early Music Foundation; New York Early Music Central (NYEMC)

5129
ELAINE KAUFMAN CULTURAL CENTER PRESENTATIONS
129 West 67th St.
New York, NY 10023
Phone: 212-501-3300
Fax: 212-874-7865
e-mail: info@kaufmanmusiccenter.org
Web Site: www.kaufman-center.org
Officers:
  Chairman: Rosalind Devon
  President: Andrea Brown
  Honorary Chair: Leonard Goodman
  Vice President: Charles Dimston
  Vice President: Phyllis Feder
  Treasurer: Christina M. Mason
  Secretary: Cathy White O'Rourke
Management:
  Executive Director: Lydia Kontos
  Merkin Concert Hall Director: Karen Chester
  Communications Director: Lizanne Hart
  Director of Administration: Kathy Hubbard
  Executive Assistant to Lydia Kontos: Kathy Karpinski
  Director of Operations: Toby Rappaport
  Human Resources Administrator: Stacey Lancaster
  Information Technology Manager: Revanth Anne
  Production Manager: Collin Costa
Founded: 1952
Specialized Field: Performing Arts; Presentation; Education
Status: Non-Profit, Professional
Budget: $60,000-150,000
Performs At: Ann Goodman Recital Hall

5130
FESTIVAL OF NEW MUSIC
Sacramento State Department Of Music
6000 J Street
New York, NY 95819-6015
Phone: 646-489-0367
Fax: 212-544-0738
e-mail: info@threetwo.org
Web Site: www.threetwo.org

Management:
  Co-Director: Taimur Sullivan
  Chair: Ernie Hills
  Secretary: Karen Sorenson
  Budget Off.: Teresa Gomez
  Events/Facility: Glenn Disney
  Instrument Tech.: Baldwin Wong
Founded: 1994

5131
FOOLS COMPANY
356 W 44th Street
PO Box 413
New York, NY 10108-0413
Phone: 212-307-6000
Fax: 212-307-6003
e-mail: foolsco@att.net
Web Site: www.foolsco.org
Officers:
  President: James Wertheim
  VP: Marcus Bicknell
  Secretary/Treasurer: Joseph Benitez
Management:
  Executive Director: Jill Russell
  Artistic Director: Martin Russell
  Executive Administrator: Susan Cline
Mission: To produce a theatre arts festival and other works and workshops in the performing arts.
Founded: 1970
Specialized Field: Theater; Festivals
Status: Professional; Nonprofit
Budget: $10,000
Performs At: John Houseman Theatre Studio
Organization Type: Performing; Educational

5132
FRENCH INSTITUTE ALLIANCE FRANCAISE
22 East 60th Street
New York, NY 10022
Phone: 212-355-6100
Fax: 212-935-4119
e-mail: reception@fiaf.org
Web Site: www.fiaf.org
Officers:
  Chairman: Robert G. Wilmers
Management:
  President: Marie Steckel-Monique
  Client Relations Manager: Kin Hernandez
  Artistic Director: Jacqueline Chambord
  Managing Director: John Franco
Founded: 1898
Specialized Field: French Classes; French Library; French Programs; French Films
Status: Non-Profit, Professional
Paid Staff: 100
Budget: $150,000-400,000
Performs At: Theater, Dance, Music, Lecture and Film
Facility Category: Cultural Organization
Type of Stage: Proscenium
Stage Dimensions: 35'x22'
Seating Capacity: 400
Year Built: 1989
Rental Contact: Client Relations Manager Kin Hernandez

5133
FRICK COLLECTION CONCERT SERIES
1 East 70th Street
New York, NY 10021
Phone: 212-288-0700
Fax: 212-628-4417
e-mail: info@frick.org
Web Site: www.frick.org

Officers:
  Chairman: Margot Bogert
  Vice Chair: Aso O. Tavitian
  Treasurer: Franklin W. Hobbs
  Secretary: Michael J. Horvitz
Management:
  Concerts Coordinator: Joyce Bodig
  Director: Ian Wardropper
  Deputy Director: Robert Goldsmith
  General Counsel and Assistant Secre: Alison Lonshein
  Chief Financial Officer and Assista: Michael Paccione
  Head of Retail and Visitor Services: Kate Gerlough
  Head of Operations: Dennis Sweeney
  Head of Education: Rika Burnham
Founded: 1935
Specialized Field: Chamber; Vocal; Early; Instumental music
Status: Non-Profit, Professional
Budget: $60,000-150,000

5134
GOTHAM EARLY MUSIC SCENE
340 Riverside Drive
Suite 1-A
New York, NY 10025
Phone: 212-866-0468
Fax: 212-866-0477
e-mail: info@gemsny.org
Web Site: www.gemsny.org
Officers:
  President: John Austin, M.D.
  Secretary: Laurence Sutter
Management:
  Executive Director: Gene Murrow
  Operations: Paul Ross
  Office Manager & Newsletters Editor: Naomi Morse
  Development Director: Amanda Keil
  GEMS Live! Senior Artist Representa: Wendy Redlinger
  Midtown Concerts Manager: Francesca Galesi
Budget: $150,000-400,000
Performs At: Weill Recital Hall at Carnegie Hall; Ethical Culture Society

5135
GREENWICH HOUSE ARTS: NORTH RIVER MUSIC
224 West 30th Street
Suite 302
New York, NY 10001
Phone: 212-991-0003
Fax: 646-365-5730
e-mail: gharts@greenwichhouse.org
Web Site: www.gharts.org
Officers:
  Chairman: Samir Hussein
  Vice Chairman: Edward A.K. Adler
  Vice-Chair: George Davidson
  Vice-Chair: Elissa Kramer
  Secretary: Jan-Willem van den Dorpel
  Treasurer: Myrna Chao
Management:
  Chairman: Samir Hussein
  Vice Chairman: Edward A.K. Adler
  Executive Director and CEO: Roy Leavitt
  Director of Barrow Street Nursery S: Nancy Glauberman
  Director of Development, Public Rel: Andrea Newman
  Facilities Manager: Tedd Havlicek

SERIES & FESTIVALS / New York

Founded: 1902
Specialized Field: Music; Theatre
Budget: $10,000-20,000
Performs At: Renee Weiler Concert Hall

5136
HELICON FOUNDATION
2067 Broadway
Studio 50
New York, NY 10023
Phone: 212-874-6438
Fax: 212-874-6438
e-mail: helicon@dti.net
Web Site: www.helicon.org
Officers:
  President: Lisa Welch
  Vice-President: Pamela Drexel
  Treasurer: William A. Simon
  Secretary: Karen McLaughlin
Management:
  Executive Director: James Roe
  Artistic Director: Avi Stein
Budget: $10,000-20,000

5137
HENSON INTERNATIONAL FESTIVAL OF PUPPET THEATRE
584 Broadway
Suite 1007
New York, NY 10021
Phone: 212-680-1400
Fax: 212-439-6036
e-mail: info@hensonfestival.org
Web Site: www.hensonfestival.org
Management:
  Executive Producer: Cherly Henson
  General Manager: Heidi Wilenius
  Development Officer: Meg Daniel
Mission: To provide some of the finest international puppetry performers for American audiences; to present the finest international puppet artists to American audiences.
Specialized Field: Theatre: Puppet Theatre
Status: For-Profit, Professional
Paid Staff: 20
Performs At: Joseph Papp Public Theater
Organization Type: Sponsoring

5138
HISTORIC BRASS SOCIETY - EARLY BRASS FESTIVAL
148 West 23rd Street
Suite #5F
New York, NY 10011
Phone: 212-627-3820
Fax: 212-627-3820
e-mail: president@historicbrass.org
Web Site: www.historicbrass.org
Management:
  President: Jeff Nussbaum
  Executive Editor: Stewart Carter
  Advertising Manager: John Benoit
  Webmaster: Steven Lundahl
Mission: To promote the study and performance of brass music.
Founded: 1988
Specialized Field: Study and History of Brass Instruments and Brass Music
Status: Non-Profit, Professional
Volunteer Staff: 20

5139
HUDSON RIVER FESTIVAL
250 Vesey Street
15th Floor
New York, NY 10281-1021
Phone: 212-417-7000
Fax: 212-945-3392
e-mail: arts@brookfield.com
Web Site: www.worldfinancialcenter.com
Management:
  Director: Melissa Coley
Founded: 1988

5140
INTERNATIONAL OFFESTIVAL
Fools Company
PO Box 413
New York, NY 10108
Phone: 212-307-6000
Fax: 212-307-6003
e-mail: foolsco@att.net
Web Site: www.foolsco.org
Management:
  Executive Director: Jill Russell
  Artistic Director: Martin Russell

5141
JAPAN SOCIETY PERFORMING ARTS SERIES
333 E 47th Street
New York, NY 10017
Phone: 212-832-1155
Fax: 212-715-1262
e-mail: yshioya@japansociety.org
Web Site: www.japansociety.org
Officers:
  Vice President, External Relations: Shane Williams-Ness
  Vice President, Finance & Administr: Lisa Bermudez
Management:
  President: Motoatsu Sakurai
  Artistic Director: Yoko Shioya
  Director of Policy Projects: Betty Borden
  Director of Human Resources: Jane Fenton
  Director, Education and Family Prog: Jeffrey Miller
  Deputy Director, Education & Family: Kazuko Minamoto
  Program Officer: Aiko Masubuchi
  Director of Gallery: Miwako Tezuka
Founded: 1907
Specialized Field: Series & Festivals; Arts & Culture; Education; Global Affairs programming; Instrumental Music; Vocal Music; Theatre; Youth; Dance; Ethnic Performanc
Status: Non-Profit, Professional
Paid Staff: 50
Budget: $60,000-150,000
Performs At: Lila Acheson Wallace Auditorium
Annual Attendance: 6,000
Seating Capacity: 278
Year Built: 1971

5142
JAZZ AT LINCOLN CENTER: ESSENTIALLY ELLINGTON JAZZ FESTIVAL
3 Columbus Circle
12th Floor
New York, NY 10019
Phone: 212-258-9800
Fax: 212-258-9900
e-mail: subscriptions@jalc.org
Web Site: www.jalc.org/EssentiallyEllington
Officers:
  Chairman: Robert J. Appel
  Vice Chair: Shahara Ahmad-Llewellyn
  Treasurer: John Arnhold
Management:
  President: Robert J. Appel
  Artistic Director: Wynton Marsalis
  Executive Director: Adrian Ellis
Specialized Field: Series & Festivals; Instrumental Music; Youth
Status: Non-Profit, Professional

5143
JAZZ IN JULY
92nd Street Y
1395 Lexington Avenue
New York, NY 10128
Phone: 212-415-5500
Fax: 212-415-5738
Web Site: www.92ndsty.org
Management:
  Artistic Director: Dick Hyman

5144
JVC JAZZ FESTIVAL NEW YORK
311 W 74th Street
PO Box 1169, Ansonia Station
New York, NY 10023
Phone: 212-501-1390
Fax: 212-877-9916
e-mail: info@fpiny.com
Web Site: www.festivalproductions.net
Management:
  CEO: George Wein
  President: John Phillip
Founded: 1954
Specialized Field: Concert Productions
Status: For-Profit, Non-Professional

5145
LEAGUE OF COMPOSERS-ISCM NEW YORK SEASON
PO Box 250281
New York, NY 10025
Phone: 718-442-5225
e-mail: lqc5590@is9.nyu.edu
Web Site: www.unix.temple.edu/~mrimple/iscm.html
Officers:
  President: Dan Wanner
Management:
  Executive Director: Louis Conti
Budget: $10,000-20,000

5146
LOTUS FINE ARTS PRODUCTIONS
336 West 37th Street
Suite 315
New York, NY 10018
Phone: 212-627-1076
Fax: 212-675-7191
e-mail: info@lotusmusicanddance.org
Web Site: www.lotusarts.com
Officers:
  Chair/Secretary: Malabika Biswas
Management:
  Executive Director: Edward Schoelwer
  Artistic Director: Kamala Cesar
Founded: 1989
Specialized Field: Series & Festivals; Instrumental Music; Dance; Singing

SERIES & FESTIVALS / New York

Status: Non-Profit, Professional
Paid Staff: 4
Paid Artists: 12

5147
MANNES COLLEGE OF MUSIC INTERNATIONAL KEYBOARD INSTITUTE AND FESTIVAL
150 West 85th Street
New York, NY 10024
Phone: 212-580-0210
Fax: 212-580-1738
e-mail: info@ikif.org
Web Site: www.mannes.edu/iki
Officers:
  President: Joel Lester
Management:
  Director: Jerome Rose
Specialized Field: Series & Festivals: Music
Status: Non-Profit, Non-Professional

5148
MELLON JAZZ IN PHILADELPHIA
PO Box 1169
New York, NY 10023
Phone: 212-496-9000
Fax: 212-877-9916
e-mail: dan.melnick@fpiny.com
Web Site: www.festivalproductions.net
Management:
  Senior Producer: Dan Melnick

5149
METROPOLITAN MUSEUM CONCERTS AND LECTURES
1000 Fifth Avenue
New York, NY 10028-0198
Phone: 212-535-7710
Fax: 212-650-2253
e-mail: communications@metmuseum.org
Web Site: www.metmuseum.org
Management:
  President: Dave McKinney
  Executive Director: Philippe D'Montebello
  General Manager: Hilde Annik Limondjian
Mission: As one of the major presenting organizations in New York City to reflect the museum's charter in promoting education and cultural events which reflect the museum's holdings.
Founded: 1954
Specialized Field: Musical Concerts; Art; Music Lectures
Status: Non-Profit, Professional
Paid Staff: 2000
Income Sources: American Association of Museums
Performs At: Grace Rainey Rogers Auditorium
Seating Capacity: 705
Organization Type: Sponsoring

5150
MIDAMERICA PRODUCTIONS
132 West 36th Street
Fourth Floor
New York, NY 10018
Phone: 212-239-0205
Fax: 212-563-5587
Toll-free: 800-842-6747
e-mail: tiboris@midamerica-music.com
Web Site: www.midamerica-music.com
Management:
  General Director/Artistic Director: Petern Tiboris
  Executive Director: Norman Dunfee
  Artistic Administrator: Eilana Lappalainen
  General Director and Music Director: Peter Tiboris
  Vice President, Director of Adminis: Joseph J. Bill
  Vice President, Director of Program: Sara Bong
Budget: $1,000,000+
Performs At: Avery Fisher Hall; Lincoln Center; Lakka Open Theatre

5151
MOSTLY MOZART FESTIVAL
70 Lincoln Center Plaza
New York, NY 10023
Phone: 212-875-5135
Fax: 212-875-5145
Web Site: www.lincolncenter.org
Officers:
  Chair: Katherine Farley
  President: Jed Bernstein
  Vice Chairs: Adrienne Arsht
  Treasurer: Blair W. Effron
Management:
  President: Jed Bernstein
  Artistic Director: Jane Moss
  Managing Director: Honnako Yamaguchi
  Music Director: Louis Longrey
Founded: 1966
Specialized Field: Instrumental; Dance; Opera
Status: Non-Profit, Professional
Paid Staff: 500

5152
MUSIC BEFORE 1800
Music Before 1800, Inc.
Corpus Christi Church
529 West 121st Street
New York, NY 10027
Phone: 212-666-9350
Fax: 212-531-2487
e-mail: mb1800@aol.com
Web Site: www.mb1800.org
Management:
  Executive Director: Msgr. Kevin Sullivan, mb1800@aol.com
  Director of Music & Organist: Louise Basbas
Mission: Offering performances of vocal and instrumental chamber music from before 1800 on historic instruments.
Founded: 1975
Opened: 1975
Specialized Field: Chamber; Early Music
Status: Professional
Paid Staff: 2
Volunteer Staff: 20
Paid Artists: 60
Budget: $150,000
Performs At: Corpus Christi Church
Annual Attendance: 2,600
Seating Capacity: 500
Year Built: 1935
Year Remodeled: 2007

5153
MUSIC FROM JAPAN
7 E 20th Street
Suite 6F
New York, NY 10003-1106
Phone: 212-529-1888
Fax: 212-529-7855
e-mail: mfjrc@aol.com
Web Site: www.musicfromjapan.org
Management:
  Artistic Director: Naoyuki Miura
Utilizes: Guest Companies; Guest Musical Directors; Organization Contracts
Founded: 1975
Specialized Field: Music
Status: Non-Profit, Professional
Paid Staff: 2
Volunteer Staff: 2
Budget: $270,000
Income Sources: NYSCA; Japanese Government; Corporations; Foundations
Performs At: Merkin Concert Hall
Facility Category: Baruch Performing Arts Center/Freer Gallery of Art

5154
MUSIC IN THE PARK: THIRD STREET MUSIC SCHOOL SETTLEMENT
235 East 11th Street
New York, NY 10003-7398
Phone: 212-777-3240
Fax: 212-477-1808
e-mail: info@thirdstreetmusicschool.org
Web Site: www.thirdstreetmusicschool.org
Officers:
  Chairman: Vincent C. Perro
  Vice President: Erik D. Lindauer
  Vice President: Jeannie Park
  Treasurer: W. Curtis Livingston
  Secretary: Peter Flint, Jr.
Management:
  Executive Director: Valerie Lewis
  Director of Programs: Shalisa Kline Ugaz
  Assistant Director of Programs: Ivan Antonov
  Program Coordinator: James Hall
Founded: 1894
Specialized Field: Quality Instruction in Music; Dance; Visual Arts
Status: Non-Profit, Professional
Paid Staff: 120
Paid Artists: 100
Budget: $10,000
Performs At: Abe Lebewohl Park
Facility Category: Outdoor

5155
NOONDAY CONCERTS AT ONE
The Interchurch Center
475 Riverside Drive
New York, NY 10115
Phone: 212-870-2200
Fax: 212-870-2440
e-mail: admin@interchurch-center.org
Web Site: www.trinitywallstreet.org
Management:
  President/Executive Director: Paula M. Mayo
  Tenant Relations Manager: Rachel Rivera
  Director of Capital Projects and PI: Michele Fox
  Curator: Frank DeGregorie
  Receptionist: Peola Romano
  Assistant to the President/Executiv: Donna Niemann
  Director of Chapel Music: Christopher Johnson
  Medical Director: Dr. Carlton Boxhil
Founded: 1697
Specialized Field: All Manner In Music
Status: Non-Profit, Professional
Paid Staff: 135
Paid Artists: 100
Budget: $35,000-60,000
Performs At: St. Paul's Chapel & Trinity Church

5156
PEOPLES' SYMPHONY CONCERTS
201 West 54th Street
Suite 703
New York, NY 10001
Phone: 212-586-4680
Fax: 212-581-4029
e-mail: info@pscny.org
Web Site: www.pscny.org
Officers:
   Chairperson: Susan Porter
   President: Richard R Howe
   Treasurer: Richard A. Raffetto
   Secretary: Frederick Wertheim
Management:
   Manager: Frank Salomon
   Production Manager: Amanda James
   Associate Manager: David Himmelheber

5157
PLURAL ARTS INTERNATIONAL
22 E 67th Street
New York, NY 10021
Phone: 212-439-9800
e-mail: info@pluralarts.org
Web Site: www.pluralarts.org
Management:
   Executive Director: Todd J Fletcher

5158
PRO PIANO NEW YORK RECITAL SERIES
Pro Piano
1225 Park Avenue
New York, NY 10128
Phone: 212-206-8794
Fax: 917-525-2704
Toll-free: 800-367-0777
e-mail: ricard@propiano.com
Web Site: www.propiano.com
Management:
   Founder/Executive Director: Ricard de La Rosa
   Artistic Director: Chitose Okashiro
Mission: Present pianists to perform at Weill Hall NYC annually.
Budget: $60,000-150,000
Performs At: Weill Recital Hall at Carnegie Hall

5159
SCHNEIDER CONCERTS AT THE NEW SCHOOL
55 West 13th Street
Room 929
New York, NY 10011
Phone: 212-229-5873
Fax: 212-229-5306
e-mail: nsc@newschool.edu
Web Site: www.schneiderconcert.org
Management:
   President: Bob Carry
   Managing Director: Rohana Keninll
   Administrator: Rohana Keninll
   Dean: Richard Kessler
Mission: To offer young profesional classical musicians performance opportunities and exposure at a vital stage of career development and to present chamber music concerts of the highest quality at modest ticket prices.
Utilizes: Multimedia
Founded: 1957
Specialized Field: Series and Festivals: Instrumental Music
Status: Non-Profit, Professional
Paid Staff: 2
Volunteer Staff: 2
Non-paid Artists: 4
Budget: $30,000-45,000
Income Sources: Box Office; NYSCA; Private Donors; Foundations
Annual Attendance: 4,000
Facility Category: Auditorium
Type of Stage: Proscenium
Seating Capacity: 510

5160
SEVENARS CONCERTS MUSIC FESTIVAL
30 East End Avenue
Ste. 3A
New York, NY 10028
Phone: 413-238-5854
Fax: 212-288-4261
e-mail: sevenars@aol.com
Web Site: www.sevenars.org/id2.html
Officers:
   President/Artistic Director: Robert W Schrade
   VP/Executive Director: Rolande Y Schrade
   Director: David F James
   Director: Robelyn Schrade-James
   Director: Randolph RA Schrade
   Director: Rorianne C Schrade
   Executive Director: Rolande Young Schrade
Management:
   Executive Director: Rolande Young Schrade
   Artistic Director: Robert W Schrade
Mission: To present music of the highest quality to the widest possible audience in an atmosphere of family warmth, acoustical perfection and serene beauty.
Utilizes: Collaborating Artists; Guest Accompanists; Guest Musical Directors; Multimedia; Original Music Scores
Founded: 1968
Specialized Field: Instrumental Music
Status: Professional; Nonprofit
Budget: $70,000-$80,000
Income Sources: Individual contributions; foundations; corporations & local cultural councils
Season: May to October in Worthington, Massachusetts
Performs At: Historic Academy/Concert Hall
Affiliations: Conservatories, universities, independent schools
Annual Attendance: 250+ at 7-8 events
Facility Category: Historic Academy
Type of Stage: Raised; Acoustic
Seating Capacity: 250 - 350
Year Built: 1800
Year Remodeled: 1976
Organization Type: Performing; Educational
Resident Groups: Schrade and James family pianists
Comments: May-October: c/o Schrade, Worthington, Massachusetts, 01098, phone (413-338-5854)

5161
SHANDELEE MUSIC FESTIVAL
36 East 74th Street
New York, NY 10021
Mailing Address: P. O. Box 1264 Livingston Manor, NY 12758
Phone: 212-288-4152
Fax: 212-879-2462
e-mail: danieldstroup@gmail.com
Web Site: www.shandelee.org
Officers:
   Co-Chair / Founding President: Daniel Stroup
   VP: Stephen Johnson
   Co-Chair: Marjorie Feuerstein
   Treasurer: Harvey Susswein
   Secretary: Jane Susswein
Management:
   Co-Chair / Founding President: Daniel Stroup
   Artistic Director: Lana Ivanov
   Technical Operations: Christopher Kennedy
   Youth & Outreach Program Director: Ann Krupski
   Kitchen Staff: Jennifer Bull
   Office Manager: Roberta Michel
   Chef: Rosa Ruiz
Founded: 1993
Specialized Field: Classical
Performs At: Concert Hall; Sunset Concert Pavilion
Seating Capacity: 200
Year Built: 2001

5162
ST. PATRICK'S CATHEDRAL CHAMBER MUSIC SERIES
Saint Patrick's Cathedral
14 East 51st Street
New York, NY 10022
Phone: 212-753-2261
Fax: 212-755-4128
e-mail: spctrojas@saintpatrickscathedral.org
Web Site: www.saintpatrickscathedral.org
Officers:
   Chairman & Chief Executive Officer: John K. Castle
   Vice Chairman: Samuel A. Di Piazza Jr.
   Executive Vice President: Carl D. Folta
Management:
   Director of Building Operations: Kevin T. Donohue
   Campaign Director: Helen Lowe
   Director of Development: Loual Puliafito
   Development Officer: Sylvia Rivas
   Director of Music and Organist: Jennifer Pascual, DMA
Founded: 1879
Specialized Field: Church
Status: Non-Profit, Professional
Paid Staff: 16
Paid Artists: 3
Budget: $10,000

5163
SUMMERGARDEN
The Museum of Modern Art
11 W 53rd Street
New York, NY 10019
Phone: 212-708-9400
Fax: 212-708-9889
e-mail: info@moma.org
Web Site: www.moma.org
Management:
   President: Robert Menschel
   Director: Glenn Lowry
Founded: 1929
Specialized Field: Museum; Art institution
Status: Non-Profit, Professional
Paid Staff: 600

5164
SYMPHONY SPACE
2537 Broadway
New York, NY 10025-6990
Phone: 212-864-1414
Fax: 212-932-3228
e-mail: info@symphonyspace.org
Web Site: www.symphonyspace.org
Officers:
   Executive VP: Joanne Cossa
   Past Chair: Steven M. Alden
   Chair: Steven Aresty

SERIES & FESTIVALS / New York

Vice Chair: Christopher P. Dixon
Vice Chair: Amy Wilson
President & CEO: Cynthia Elliott
Secretary: Louis B. Bernstein
Treasurer: Claire Aidem
Management:
  President & CEO: Cynthia Elliott
  Executive Director: Cynthia Elliott
  Director Marketing: Johanna H. Thomsen
  Managing Director: Peggy Wreen
  Producer Music/Dance Program: Maren Bethelsen
  Senior VP for Administration: Peg Wreen
  Director of Development: DJ Brumfield
  Director of Information Technology: Charles Blanchard
  Office Manager: Robert Leeper
Founded: 1978
Specialized Field: Series and Festivals; Instrumental Music; Vocal Music; Theatre; Youth; Dance
Status: Non-Profit, Professional
Paid Staff: 32
Facility Category: Theater
Rental Contact: Patricia Sinnott

5165
THIRD STREET MUSIC SCHOOL SETTLEMENT FACULTY ARTISTS SERIES
235 East 11th Street
New York, NY 10003
Phone: 212-777-3240
Fax: 212-477-1808
e-mail: info@thirdstreetmusicschool.org
Web Site: www.thirdstreetmusicschool.org/alumni.htm
Management:
  Community Affairs/Concerts Director: Beth Flusser
Budget: $10,000
Performs At: Mark's Park

5166
TRIBECA PERFORMING ARTS CENTER
199 Chambers Street
#S110SC
New York, NY 10007
Phone: 212-220-1460
Fax: 212-732-2482
e-mail: boxoffice@tribecapac.org
Web Site: www.tribecapac.org
Management:
  Marketing Director: John Malatesta
  Executive Director: Linda Herring
  Operations Director: Carol Cleveland
  Program Director: Jeff Mousseau
Utilizes: Artists-in-Residence; Dance Companies; Soloists; Special Technical Talent; Theatre Companies
Founded: 1983
Budget: $60,000-150,000

5167
USDAN CENTER FOR THE CREATIVE & PERFORMING ARTS: FESTIVAL CONCERTS
420 East 79th Street
New York, NY 10075
Phone: 631-643-7900
Fax: 631-643-6309
Web Site: www.usdan.com
Officers:
  Past President: Dr. Jerrold Ross
  President: John Usdan
  Treasurer: Lillian Z. Cohen
  Secretary: Michele Lowe
  Founding Trustee: Suzanne Usdan
  Executive Director: Dale Lewis
Management:
  President: Mrs James A Block
  Executive Director: Dale Lewis
  Artistic Director: Dennis Nahat
  Assistant Director: Allison Bitz
  Associate Executive Director: Andrew Copper

5168
WASHINGTON SQUARE MUSIC FESTIVAL
Friends of Washington Square Park
7-13 Washington Square North
New York, NY 10003
Phone: 212-677-6783
e-mail: pacrasia@aol.com
Web Site: www.washingtonsquaremusicfestival.org
Officers:
  Chairman: Douglas H. Evans
  President: Anne-Marie W. Sumner
  Vice President: Emily Kies Folpe
  Secretary: Richard E. Richard E.
Management:
  Executive Director: Peggy Friedman
  Music Director: Lutz Rath
  Festival Manager: Jean Lyman Geotz
Mission: To present free classical and classical jazz and salsa concerts in Washington Square Park in the summer, for the largest possible audiences. Outreach activities announce the series to as large and diverse asegment of the metropolitan population as possible.
Founded: 1953
Specialized Field: Series & Festivals; Classical Chamber; Orchestra music
Status: Non-Profit, Professional
Paid Staff: 3
Volunteer Staff: 15
Paid Artists: 50
Budget: $55,000
Income Sources: Public and Private Funds; NYSCA; NYC Cultural Affairs; Trust Fund through 802
Affiliations: Whashington Square Association
Annual Attendance: 6,000
Facility Category: Park

5169
WASHINGTON SQUARE CONTEMPORARY MUSIC SOCIETY
NYU Music Department Fas
24 Waverly Place Room 268
New York, NY 10003
Phone: 212-998-8300
Fax: 212-995-4147
e-mail: fas.music@nyu.edu
Web Site: www.washingtonsquaremusic.org
Management:
  Co-Director: Brian Fennelly
Budget: $10,000-20,000
Performs At: Merkin Hall

5170
WORLD FINANCIAL CENTER ARTS & EVENTS PROGRAM
250 Vesey Street
15th Floor
New York, NY 10281-1021
Phone: 212-417-7000
Fax: 212-945-3392
e-mail: arts@brookfield.com
Web Site: www.worldfinancialcenter.com
Management:
  Artistic Director and VP: Melissa Coley
Founded: 1988
Budget: $150,000-400,000
Performs At: World Financial Center Winter Garden & Plaza

5171
WORLD MUSIC INSTITUTE
101 Lafayette Street
#801
New York, NY 10013
Phone: 212-545-7536
Fax: 212-889-2771
e-mail: wmi@heartheworld.org
Web Site: www.worldmusicinstitute.org/
Officers:
  Chairman: Paul Palmer
  Secretary: Zette Emmons
Management:
  Artistic & Executive Director: Karen Sander
  Senior Director, Marketing & Progra: Alexa Burneikis
  Director of Finance and Administrat: Pearl Chin
  Development: Jude-Laure Denis
  Production Manager: Chris McIntyre
Founded: 1985
Specialized Field: Series & Festivals: Ethnic Performances
Status: Non-Profit, Professional
Paid Staff: 10
Budget: $150,000-400,000
Performs At: Washington Square Church; Sylvia & Danny Kaye Playhouse

5172
YOUNG CONCERT ARTISTS SERIES
250 West 57th Street
Suite 1222
New York, NY 10107
Phone: 212-307-6655
Fax: 212-581-8894
e-mail: yca@yca.org
Web Site: www.yca.org
Officers:
  Chairman: Michael Nash Ambler
  Chairman of the Executive Committee: Sheldon Soffer
  Vice Chairmen: Esther B. Ferguson
  Vice Chairmen: Esther B. Ferguson
  Vice Chairmen: Sahra T. Lese
  Vice Chairmen: Ellen Marcus
  Treasurer: John W. Thorne, III
  Secretary: Annaliese Soros
Management:
  Director: Susan Wadsworth
  Public Relations: Karen Karush
  Associate Director: Mark Hayman
  Director of Development: Sarah Graham
  Artist Manager: Vicki Margulies
  Operations Manager: Brian D. Bumby
  Program Manager: Jennifer DeCinque
  Information Systems Manager: Tim McCarthy
  Auditions/Media Assistant: Justin LaDeau
Budget: $60,000-150,000
Performs At: Kaufmann Concert Hall; Terrace Theatre; Kennedy Center

5173
GREECE PERFORMING ARTS SOCIETY SERIES
P.O. Box 26643
North Greece, NY 14626
Phone: 585-234-5636
Web Site: www.greeceperformingarts.org/

SERIES & FESTIVALS / New York

Officers:
President: Rick Stein
Treasurer: William Coons
Secretary: Carol Coons
Management:
Program Coordinator: William Coons
Mission: To foster the development, in the community of Greece, of an appreciation for artistic and cultural activities, GPAS sponsors the Greece Symphony Orchestra, Greece Community Orchestra and Greece Choral Society & GPAS Summer Theatre.
Founded: 1972
Specialized Field: Vocal Music; Instrumental Music; Theatre
Status: Nonprofit
Organization Type: Sponsoring

5174
CHENANGO COUNTY COUNCIL FOR THE ARTS
27 West Main Street
Norwich, NY 13815
Phone: 607-336-2787
Fax: 607-336-1893
e-mail: info@chenangoarts.org
Web Site: www.chenangoarts.org
Officers:
President: Lisa A. Natoli, Esq.
Vice President: V. Peter V.R. Mason
Secretary: Jeff Genung
Treasurer: Joseph Skundrich
Management:
Executive Director: Victoria Calvert Kappel
Program Director/Development Associ: Michelle Connelly
Operations & Program Director: Joyce C. Zummo
Specialized Field: Series & Festivals; Vocal Music; Theatre; Youth; Dance; Ethnic Performances
Status: Non-Profit, Professional
Paid Staff: 7
Budget: $10,000-20,000

5175
NYACK COLLEGE PROGRAM OF CULTURAL EVENTS
Nyack College
1 South Boulevard
Nyack, NY 10960
Phone: 845-358-1710
Fax: 845-358-1718
Web Site: www.nyack.edu/
Provost and Vice President for Acad: Dr. David F. Turk
Vice President for Enrollment and M: Dr. Andrea M. Hennessy
Dean: Dr. Ronald Walborn
Budget: $10,000
Performs At: Pardington Hall; Olson Auditorium

5176
OGDENSBURG COMMAND PERFORMANCES
1100 State Street
Ogdensburg, NY 13669
Phone: 315-393-2625
Fax: 315-393-2625
e-mail: ocp@ogdensburgk12.org
Web Site: www.ilovetheatre.org/
Officers:
President: Linda Griffin
Vice President: Becky Bailey
Secretary: Cheryl Ladouceur
Treasurer: Brenda Trivilino
Management:
Administrative Coordinator: Sally Palao

5177
ARTS CENTER/OLD FORGE
3273 State Route 28
PO Box 1144
Old Forge, NY 13420
Phone: 315-369-6411
Fax: 315-369-2431
e-mail: info@viewarts.org
Web Site: www.viewarts.org
Officers:
President: Helene McAleese
Vice President: Deborah Carhart
Treasurer: Frances Parent
Secretary: Gary Lee
Immediate Past President: John Munyan
Management:
Exhibitions Manager: Cory Card
Executive Director: Jennifer Potter Hayes
Artistic Director: Julie Tabbitas
Operations Manager: Linda Bamberger
Education & Artistic Programs Manag: Barbara Getty
Exhibitions Manager: Cory Card
Events Manager: Stephen Wick
Performing Arts Program Manager: Alan Saban
Marketing Manager: John Brennan
Utilizes: Actors; Educators; Fine Artists; Guest Accompanists; Guest Instructors; Instructors; Multimedia; Selected Students; Special Technical Talent; Touring Companies
Founded: 1952
Specialized Field: Series & Festivals: Exhibition
Status: Non-Profit, Professional
Paid Staff: 6
Volunteer Staff: 6
Paid Artists: 8
Budget: $250,000-300,000
Income Sources: Private Donations; Membership; State & Local Government
Annual Attendance: 30,000
Facility Category: Community Arts Center
Stage Dimensions: varies
Seating Capacity: 150

5178
FRIENDS OF GOOD MUSIC
PO Box 222
Olean, NY 14760
Phone: 716-373-1776
Fax: 716-373-2662
e-mail: fogm@friendsofgoodmusic.com
Web Site: www.friendsofgoodmusic.com/
Budget: $35,000-60,000

5179
FESTIVAL OF THE ARTS
11 Ford Ave.
Upper Catskill Community Council of the Arts
Oneonta, NY 13820
Phone: 607-432-2070
Fax: 607-431-9319
e-mail: admin@CANOneonta.org
Web Site: canoneonta.org/
Management:
Director: Pamela Cooley
Founded: 1969
Specialized Field: Dance; Vocal Music; Instrumental Music; Theatre; Festivals
Status: Professional; Nonprofit
Income Sources: State University of New York-Oneonta
Performs At: Slade Auditorium; Anderson Theater
Organization Type: Educational; Sponsoring

5180
HARTWICK COLLEGE FOREMAN CREATIVE & PERFORMING ARTS SERIES
Office of Events Planning
Shineman Chapel
Oneonta, NY 13820
Phone: 607-431-4034
Fax: 607-431-4043
e-mail: markusonc@hartwick.edu
Web Site: www.hartwick.edu
Management:
Event Planning/Stewardship Director: Cira P Markuson
Budget: $20,000-35,000
Performs At: Slade Theatre

5181
UPPER CATSKILL COMMUNITY COUNCIL OF THE ARTS
11 Ford Avenue
Oneonta, NY 13820
Phone: 607-432-2070
Fax: 607-431-9319
e-mail: admin@CANOneonta.org
Web Site: canoneonta.org/
Officers:
President: Stan Rabbiner
Management:
Executive Director: Kathleen Frascatore
Mission: Sponsoring community performances and coordinating secondary and elementary school performances.
Founded: 1970
Specialized Field: Non-Profit Arts
Status: Non-Profit, Professional
Paid Staff: 4
Paid Artists: 100
Organization Type: Educational; Sponsoring

5182
OSWEGO HARBOR FESTIVALS
41 Lake Street
Oswego, NY 13126
Phone: 315-343-6858
Fax: 315-343-7390
e-mail: info@oswegoharborfest.com
Web Site: www.oswegoharborfest.com
Management:
Executive Director: Steve Fulton
Business Manager: Barb Manwaring
Mission: To promote and increased public awareness of, and civic pride in, the unique history and geography as well as the varied cultural and recreational to be found in the City of Oswego and its waterfront, the County of Oswego, the Oswego River and the southeastern shore of Lake Ontario. This will include, but not be limited to, providing a series of events or activities that highlight the quality in this area.
Founded: 1988
Specialized Field: Series & Festivals; Instrumental Music; Vocal Music; Theatre; Youth; Dance; Ethnic Performances
Status: Non-Profit, Professional
Paid Staff: 4
Budget: $800,000
Income Sources: Sponsorships; Memberships; Grants
Affiliations: IFEA, New York Festival & Events Association
Annual Attendance: 200,000

SERIES & FESTIVALS / New York

Facility Category: Outdoor Lawn

5183
PAWLING CONCERT SERIES
700 Route 22
PO Box 163, Pawling NY 12564
Pawling, NY 12564
Phone: 845-855-3100
Fax: 845-855-3816
e-mail: ned@pawlingconcertseries.org
Web Site: www.pawlingconcertseries.org
Officers:
President: Ned Reade
Management:
Artistic Director: Keir Donaldson
Mission: To bring excellent live jazz, classical, folk and ethnic music to the Eastern Dutchess, Putnam and Westchester counties in New York.
Utilizes: Multimedia; Original Music Scores
Founded: 1973
Specialized Field: Series & Festivals; Instrumental Music; Vocal Music
Status: Non-Profit, Professional
Paid Staff: 1
Volunteer Staff: 13
Non-paid Artists: 24
Budget: $53,000
Income Sources: Subscriptions; Private & Corporate Grants
Performs At: Gardner Theatre, All Saints Chapel, McGraw Pavillion
Affiliations: Trinity Pawling School
Annual Attendance: 1,200
Facility Category: Theatre
Type of Stage: Procenium
Stage Dimensions: 26X26
Seating Capacity: 200; 250; 35
Year Built: 2004
Cost: $1.3 Million
Organization Type: Sponsoring; Presenting

5184
CLASSICAL FRONTIERS
446 Pelhamdale Avenue
Pelham, NY 10803
Phone: 914-738-6537
Web Site: www.yelp.com/biz/classical-frontiers-pelham
Budget: $10,000

5185
YATES PERFORMING ARTS SERIES
PO Box 503
Penn Yan, NY 14527
Phone: 315-536-2095
Web Site: www.nonprofitfacts.com New York
Management:
President: Sylvia Eisenhart
Mission: To provide entertainment for Yates County residents.
Founded: 1972
Specialized Field: Series & Festivals: Vocal Music & Instrumental Music concerts
Status: Non-Profit, Non-Professional
Performs At: Penn Yan Academy
Organization Type: Performing; Touring

5186
MUSICAL CONCERTS AT THE BURLINGHAM INN
29 Vinegar Hill Road
Pine Bush, NY 12566
Phone: 845-744-8499
Fax: 845-744-8936
e-mail: BIConcerts@aol.com
Web Site: www.burlinghaminn.com/concerts
Management:
Director: Jonathan Bley
Budget: $10,000
Performs At: Burlingham Inn Hall

5187
MUSIC AT PORT MILFORD
288 Washington Avenue
Pleasantville, NY 10570
Phone: 914-439-5039
Fax: 914-729-3489
e-mail: director@mpmcamp.org
Web Site: www.mpmcamp.org
Management:
Artistic Director: Meg Hill
Business Manager, Webmaster: David Hill
Founded: 1987
Specialized Field: Series & Festivals; Instrumental Music; Vocal Music; Youth
Status: Non-Profit, Professional
Paid Staff: 9
Paid Artists: 30

5188
SUMMIT MUSIC FESTIVAL
270 Washington Avenue
Pleasantville, NY 10570
Phone: 914-747-2020
Fax: 917-261-4684
e-mail: info@summitmusicfestival.org
Web Site: www.summitmusicfestival.org/
Officers:
Chairman: Tania Ahuja
Vice Chairman: Jeffrey Shah
Management:
Executive Director/Founder: David Krieger
Artistic Director/Founder: Efrem Breskin
Administrator: Miriam Derivan
Business Manager: Richard Lindner
Recording Engineer: Michael Briskin
Assistant Program Director: Yoni Krieger
Program Director: Massimiliano Mainolfi
Director of the Aaron Rosand Progra: Christina Khimm
Mission: To provide an enriching musical experience for area students and exposure to the finest in solo, chamber, and orchestra performances.
Founded: 1991
Specialized Field: Classical Instrumental Music Instruction and Performance for Pre - Professional High School and College Age Students
Paid Staff: 7
Paid Artists: 20

5189
COMMUNITY PERFORMANCE SERIES
Snell Music Theatre
Bishop Hall, SUNY
Potsdam, NY 13676
Phone: 315-267-2277
Fax: 315-267-2869
e-mail: olsenka@potsdam.edu
Web Site: www.potsdam.edu/cps
Management:
Executive Director: Amy Flack
Managing Director: Amy Slack
Box Office Manager: Jason L. Dominie
Graphic Design & Webmaster: Jill Falcone Vedric
Production Coordinator: Jared T. Carey
Utilizes: Actors; Artists-in-Residence; Collaborating Artists; Collaborations; Dance Companies; Dancers; Guest Accompanists; Guest Artists; Guest Choreographers; Guest Directors; Guest Instructors; Guest Musical Directors; Guest Musicians; Lyricists; Multimedia; Original Music Scores; Singers; Theatre Companies
Founded: 1986
Specialized Field: Series & Festivals: Instrumental Music
Status: Non-Profit, Professional
Paid Staff: 4
Paid Artists: 50
Non-paid Artists: 20
Budget: $300,000
Performs At: Hosmer Concert Hall; Snell Music Theater; MaxcyHall
Annual Attendance: 7,000
Facility Category: Concert Hall
Stage Dimensions: 40 x 40
Seating Capacity: 1,200
Year Built: 1971
Year Remodeled: 2000

5190
CRANE SCHOOL OF MUSIC ANNUAL SPRING FESTIVAL OF THE ARTS
State University of NY at Potsdam
389 VHE, SUNY Potsdam
Potsdam, NY 13676
Phone: 315-267-2167
Fax: 315-267-3350
e-mail: clear@potsdam.edu
Web Site: www.potsdam.edu/crane
Management:
Executive Director: Kathleen Olsen
Founded: 1986
Specialized Field: Series & Festivals: Arts Presentation
Status: Non-Profit, Professional
Paid Staff: 4
Paid Artists: 12

5191
CLEARWATER'S GREAT HUDSON RIVER REVIVAL
724 Wolcott Ave
Poughkeepsie, NY 12508
Phone: 845-265-8080
Fax: 845-831-2821
e-mail: office@clearwater.org
Web Site: www.clearwater.org
Officers:
President: Anne Todd Osborn
Vice President: Ross Gould, Esq.
Treasurer: Scott Berwick
Secretary: Roberta Goldberg
Management:
Executive Director: Peter A. Gross
Director: Manna Jo Greene
Office Manager: Amy Bonder
Financial Director: Roger D'Aquino
Festival Director: Steve Lurie
Assistant Festival Director: Will Solomon
Development Associate: Ann Mellor
Communications Manager: Julia Church

5192
SUFFOLK THEATER
118 East Main Street y
Riverhead, NY 11901

Phone: 631-727-4343
Fax: 631-727-4345
e-mail: info@suffolktheater.com
Web Site: www.suffolktheater.com
Management:
   Executive Producer: Bob Spiotto, bobspiotto@optonline.net
Utilizes: Actors; Collaborations; Educators; Guest Conductors; Guest Directors; Guest Instructors; Guest Lecturers; Guest Soloists; Local Artists; Lyricists; Multimedia; Organization Contracts; Original Music Scores; Performance Artists; Resident Professionals; Sign Language Translators; Soloists; Student Interns; Special Technical Talent
Specialized Field: Series & Festivals; Instrumental Music; Theatre; Ethnic Performances; One Man Shows; Theater for Young Audiences
Status: Non-Profit, Professional
Performs At: Monroe Lecture Center Theater

5193
EASTMAN SCHOOL OF MUSIC
26 Gibbs Street
Rochester, NY 14604
Phone: 585-274-1110
Fax: 585-274-1073
e-mail: agreen@esm.rochester.edu
Web Site: rochester.edu/eastman/
Management:
   Director of Concert Operations: Andrew Green
Budget: $60,000-150,000
Performs At: Kilbourn Hall; Eastman Theatre

5194
NAZARETH COLLEGE ARTS CENTER SERIES
4245 East Avenue
Rochester, NY 14618-3090
Phone: 585-389-2180
Fax: 716-389-2182
e-mail: nlpeet@naz.edu
Web Site: artscenter.naz.edu/
Officers:
   Chairman: Fred E Strauss
   President of the College: Dr. Rose Marie Beston
Management:
   School Program Coordinator: Nancy Peet
   Director: Susan Chekow Lusignan
   Assistant Director: Terry Meyer
   Marketing & Publicity Manager: Mare Millow
   Box Office Manager: Deborah Foster
   Budget and Facilities Manager: Lindsay Chasse
   Director of Technical Operations: Bets Quackenbush
   Assistant Director of Technical Ope: Kevin DeHollander
Mission: To present a subscription series of professional performing artists and organizations for the benefit of Nazareth students and the community of Rochester.
Founded: 1967
Specialized Field: Dance; Vocal Music; Instrumental Music; Theatre
Status: Professional; Nonprofit
Budget: $150,000-400,000
Income Sources: Association of Performing Arts Presenters
Performs At: Nazareth College Arts Center
Organization Type: Performing; Sponsoring

5195
ROBERTS WESLEYAN COLLEGE
Roberts Cultural Life Center
2301 Westside Drive
Rochester, NY 14624
Phone: 585-594-6000
Fax: 585-594-6059
Toll-free: 800-777-4792
e-mail: dunndr@roberts.edu
Web Site: www.rwc.edu
Management:
   President: John Martin
   Managing Director: Jim Cughbert
Founded: 1866
Specialized Field: Series and Festivals; Instrumental Music; Vocal Music; Theatre; Youth
Status: Non-Profit, Professional
Paid Staff: 6
Volunteer Staff: 45
Non-paid Artists: 155
Budget: $35,000-60,000
Income Sources: Ticket Sales
Performs At: Hale Auditorium
Annual Attendance: 45,000
Facility Category: Performing Arts
Type of Stage: Proscenium
Stage Dimensions: 50'x30'x25'
Seating Capacity: 1000
Year Built: 1996
Cost: $8 Million
Rental Contact: David Dunn

5196
ROCHESTER PHILHARMONIC ORCHESTRA
108 East Avenue
Rochester, NY 14604
Phone: 585-454-7311
Fax: 585-423-2256
e-mail: rpyo@rpyo.org
Web Site: www.rpyo.org
Officers:
   President/CEO: Charles Owens
   President Emeritus: Josephine Whang
   Secretary: Jeanne Gray
   Chairman: David Ackroyd
   Board Member: Randall Curren
   Advisor: Vicky Feathers
   Treasurer: Darrell Haynes,
Management:
   Music Director, Conductor: Dr. David Harmon
   General Staff Manager: Susan Basu
   Music Director, Conductor: Dr. David Harmon
Mission: Providing enriching musical and educational experiences to highly capable and committed young musicians. The Rochester Philharmonic Youth Orchestra (RPYO) is a symphony orchestra comprised of young musicians in grades eight through twelve from schools throughout the greater Rochester area.
Utilizes: Arrangers; Collaborating Artists; Collaborations; Educators; Fine Artists; Instructors; Lyricists; Multimedia; New Productions; Paid Performers; Scenic Designers; Singers; Soloists
Founded: 1970
Specialized Field: Series and Festivals; Instrumental Music; Vocal Music; Youth
Status: Non-profit, Professional
Income Sources: Ticket Sales, Fundraisers, Donors
Season: September through May
Performs At: Hochstein Performance Hall, Carnegie Hall, Kodak Hall at Eastman Theater, Hale Auditorium

5197
MUSIC FROM SALEM
HUBBARD HALL
25 E. Main Street
Salem, NY 12816
Phone: 518-677-2495
e-mail: info@musicfromsalem.org
Web Site: www.musicfromsalem.org
Management:
   Artistic Director: Lila Brown
   Administrator: Susan Alancraig
   Consulting Directors: Judith Gordon
   President: Rob Bauer
Mission: To provide a summer home to international chamber musicians.
Founded: 1985
Specialized Field: Vocal Music; Instrumental Music
Status: Professional
Performs At: Hubbard Hall
Organization Type: Performing; Resident

5198
HILL & HOLLOW MUSIC
Weatherwatch Farm
550 Number 37 Road
Saranac, NY 12981
Phone: 518-293-7613
Fax: 518-293-7634
e-mail: hillholl@hughes.net
Web Site: www.hillandhollowmusic.com
Management:
   President: J Kellum Smith Jr
   Executive Director: Angela Brown
   Co-Director: Angela Brown
Mission: To promote and present classical chamber music in a rural area.
Utilizes: Artists-in-Residence; Grant Writers; Guest Directors; Guest Instructors; Multimedia; Singers
Founded: 1995
Specialized Field: Series & Festivals; Instrumental Music; Vocal Music; Chamber Music
Status: Non-Profit, Professional
Volunteer Staff: 2
Paid Artists: 20
Budget: $100,000
Income Sources: Box office, Grants, Private contributions
Performs At: Church in the Hollow; Highschool Auditorium
Affiliations: Chamber Music America; Country Dance & Song Society
Facility Category: Rural Venues
Seating Capacity: 220
Year Built: 1862

5199
ADIRONDACK FESTIVAL OF AMERICAN MUSIC
Gregg Smith Singers
42 Custer Avenue
Saranac Lake, NY 10701
Phone: 914-376-8899
Fax: 518-891-1057
e-mail: greggroz1@aol.com
Web Site: www.greggsmithsingers.com/about.php
Management:
   Artistic Director: Gregg Smith
   Director Vocal Workshop: Linda Ferriera
Mission: To offer a program including American music of the present and past, and some traditional repertoire.
Specialized Field: Vocal Music; Instrumental Music; Choral
Status: Professional; Nonprofit

SERIES & FESTIVALS / New York

Performs At: Town Hall
Organization Type: Performing; Educational

5200
SARATOGA PERFORMING ARTS FESTIVAL SERIES
Saratoga Performing Arts Center
Saratoga Springs, NY 12866
Phone: 518-584-9330
Fax: 518-584-0809
e-mail: info@spac.org
Web Site: www.spac.org
Officers:
  Honorary Chairwoman: Marylou Whitney
  President: Marcia J. White
  Vice Chairman: E. Stewart Jones
  Secretary: Edward J. Lewi
  Treasurer: Ronald Riggi
Management:
  President & Executive Director: Marcia White
  Supervisor of Maintenance & Operati: Kevin Appler
  Assistant Box Office Manager: Eric Brower
  Director of Youth Arts Programs: Linda Deschenes
  Director of Arts Education: Siobhan Dunham
  Box Office Manager: Deanna Gras
  Public Relations/Development: Lisa Hill
  Director of Artistic Administration: Sharon Walsh
Mission: To cultivate, promote, forster, sponsor and develop among its menbers and the community at large, appreciation, understanding and love of the performing arts.
Founded: 1966
Specialized Field: Series & Festivals: Classical Music
Status: Non-Profit, Non-Professional
Paid Staff: 13

5201
SKIDMORE MUSIC DEPARTMENT
Skidmore College
815 North Broadway
Saratoga Springs, NY 12866
Phone: 518-580-5000
Fax: 518-580-5340
e-mail: info@skidmore.edu
Web Site: www.skidmore.edu
Officers:
  Chair: Joel Brown
  President: Philip A. Glotzbach
  Vice Chair of the Board: Susan Gottlieb Beckerman
Management:
  Chair, Department of Music: Joel Brown, jbrown@skidmore.edu
  Concerts and Events Manager: Shelley Curran, mcurran@skidmore.edu
Founded: 1922
Specialized Field: Series & Festivals; Instrumental Music; Vocal Music; Dance; Ethnic Performances
Status: Non-Profit, Professional
Paid Staff: 25
Budget: $35,000-60,000
Performs At: Filene Recital Hall

5202
SCHENECTADY MUSEUM: UNION COLLEGE CONCERT SERIES
857 Northumberland Drive
Schenectady, NY 12309
Phone: 518-372-3651
Officers:
  Chairman: Dr. Daniel Berkenblit
Budget: $35,000-60,000
Performs At: Union College Memorial Chapel

5203
SKANEATELES FESTIVAL
97 E Genesee Street
Skaneateles, NY 13152
Phone: 315-685-7418
Fax: 315-685-4802
e-mail: music@scanfest.org
Web Site: www.skanfest.org
Officers:
  President: Dave Birchenough
  Vice President: Doug Sutherland
  Treasurer: George Bain
Management:
  President: Dave Birchenough
  Executive Director: Susan Mark
  Artistic Director: Diane Walsh
  Vice President: Doug Sutherland
Mission: Bringing world-class musicians to this lakeside community for five weeks of chamber music, chamber orchestra and children's concerts in the late summer.
Founded: 1980
Specialized Field: Festivals
Status: Professional; Nonprofit
Organization Type: Performing; Educational

5204
SPENCERTOWN ACADEMY PERFORMING SERIES
790 Route 203
PO Box 80
Spencertown, NY 12165
Phone: 518-392-3693
Fax: 518-392-8694
e-mail: info@spencertownacademy.org
Web Site: www.spencertown.org
Officers:
  President: Roberta Reynes
  Vice President: Ben Puccio
  Secretary: Claire Verenezi
  Treasurer: Jan Steinbrenner
Management:
  President: Kate Cohen
  Executive Director: Judy Staber
  Associate Director: Susan Davis
Mission: To preserve the historic building and provide a welcoming space for all the arts.
Founded: 1972
Specialized Field: Series & Festivals; Classical; Traditional; Spoken Word; Film; Chamber Theatre Production Music series
Status: Non-Profit, Professional
Paid Staff: 3
Volunteer Staff: 10+
Paid Artists: 40
Non-paid Artists: 5
Budget: $100,000
Income Sources: Private Funds; Ticket Sales; Art Sales
Annual Attendance: 5,000
Facility Category: Performance & Visual Arts Center
Type of Stage: Proscenium
Seating Capacity: 130
Year Built: 1867
Year Remodeled: 1999

5205
STERLING RENAISSANCE FESTIVAL
15385 Farden Road
Sterling, NY 13156
Phone: 315-947-5782
Fax: 315-947-6905
Toll-free: 800-879-4446
e-mail: ad@sterlingfestival.com
Web Site: www.sterlingfestival.com
Officers:
  President: Alisa Cook
  VP: John Kissler
  Secretary: Phil Holding
  Treasurer: Marylee Pangman
Management:
  Office Manager and Sales Director: Kelli Raymond
Mission: To present interactive and staged performances.
Paid Staff: 10
Paid Artists: 80
Season: June - August
Annual Attendance: 100,000
Facility Category: Outdoor
Type of Stage: 8 Stages
Year Built: 1977

5206
STATE UNIVERSITY OF NEW YORK AT STONY BROOK CONCERT SERIES
Stony Brook
Staller Center For the Arts, room 2030A
Stony Brook, NY 11794
Phone: 631-632-7235
Fax: 631-632-7354
e-mail: AInkles@stallercenter.com
Web Site: www.stallercenter.com
Management:
  Director: Alan Inkles
Budget: $150,000-400,000
Performs At: Staller Center for the Arts; Three Black Box Theatres

5207
CIVIC MORNING MUSICALS
124 Victoria Place
Syracuse, NY 13210
Phone: 315-254-7136
Web Site: www.civicmorningmusicals.org/
Officers:
  President: Norma Tippett
  Treasurer: Sally Gould
  Recording Secretary: Mary Schwarz
  Corresponding Secretary: Josy McGinn
Management:
  Public Relations Coordinator: Irene Boheme
Budget: $10,000
Performs At: Hosmer Auditorium; Everson Museum of Art

5208
CULTURAL RESOURCES COUNCIL OF SYRACUSE
411 Montgomery Street
Syracuse, NY 13202
Phone: 315-435-2155
Fax: 315-435-2160
Web Site: www.cspot.org
Management:
  Executive Director: Leo Crandall
Mission: Promote cultural development in Central NY; identify, coordinate, promote, and present performing arts for a 10-county area in Cedntral New York. Education and trainging; technical assistance.
Utilizes: Singers
Founded: 1968

SERIES & FESTIVALS / New York

Specialized Field: Series & Festivals; Theatre; Youth; Ethnic Performances; Dance; Theatre; Festivals; Music; Visual Advocacy; Training; Education
Status: Non-Profit, Non-Professional
Paid Staff: 8
Paid Artists: 150
Income Sources: International Society of Performing Arts Administrators
Performs At: Civic Center of Onondaga County
Organization Type: Performing

5209
SYRACUSE SOCIETY FOR NEW MUSIC
438 Brookford Road
Syracuse, NY 13224
Phone: 315-446-5733
e-mail: npilgrim@aol.com
Web Site: www.societyfornewmusic.org
Management:
   President: Rob Bridge
   Program Advisor: Neva Pilgrim
Utilizes: Commissioned Composers; Composers; Guest Artists; Guest Companies; Guest Composers; Instructors; Multi Collaborations; Multimedia; Original Music Scores; Playwrights
Founded: 1971
Specialized Field: Series & Festivals: Contemproray & Classical Music
Status: Non-Profit, Professional
Paid Artists: 25
Budget: $20,000-35,000
Performs At: Everson Museum; Carrier Theatre
Annual Attendance: 13,000

5210
TICONDEROGA FESTIVAL GUILD
124 Montclaim Street
PO Box 125
Ticonderoga, NY 12883
Phone: 518-585-7015
Fax: 518-543-6654
e-mail: cburdick5@nycap.rr.com
Web Site: tfguild.wordpress.com/
Management:
   Executive Director: Cathie Burdick
Mission: To provide cultural events for a rural area.
Founded: 1980
Specialized Field: Festivals
Status: Nonprofit
Budget: $40,000
Income Sources: Grants; Donations; Tickets
Annual Attendance: 3500
Type of Stage: Wood
Stage Dimensions: 20'x30'
Seating Capacity: 200
Organization Type: Performing

5211
HUDSON VALLEY COMMUNITY COLLEGE CULTURAL AFFAIRS PROGRAM
80 Vandenburgh Avenue
Troy, NY 12180
Phone: 518-629-4822
Toll-free: 877-325-4822
e-mail: boggesar@hvcc.edu
Web Site: https://www.hvcc.edu/culture/
Officers:
   Chairman: Conrad H. Lang, Jr.
   Vice Chairman: Neil J. Kelleher
   Secretary to the Board: George J. Raneri
Management:
   Community Relations Director: Sarah Boggess
Budget: $10,000
Performs At: Maureen Stapleton Theatre

5212
A GOOD OLD SUMMER TIME'S GENESEE STREET FESTIVAL
520 Seneca Street
Utica, NY 13502
Phone: 315-733-6976
Fax: 315-724-3177
Web Site: www.goodoldsummertime.org
Officers:
   President: Mark Minasi

5213
MOHAWK VALLEY COMMUNITY COLLEGE CULTURAL SERIES
1101 Sherman Drive
Utica, NY 13501
Phone: 315-731-5722
Fax: 315-792-5678
e-mail: wdustin@mvcc.edu
Web Site: www.mvcc.edu/culture
Officers:
   Chair: David Mathis
   Vice Chairman: William S. Calli, Jr.
Management:
   Events Administrator: Bill Dustin, wdustin@mvcc.edu
Founded: 2000
Specialized Field: Series & Festivals; Plays; Lectures; Music; Instrumental; Vocal; Theatre; Youth; Events; Dance; Films
Status: Non-Profit, Non-Professional
Paid Staff: 5
Paid Artists: 1
Budget: $10,000

5214
MUNSON-WILLIAMS-PROCTOR ARTS INSTITUTE
310 Genesee Street
Utica, NY 13502-4799
Phone: 315-797-0000
Fax: 315-797-5608
Toll-free: 800-754-8920
e-mail: gtrudeau@mwpi.edu
Web Site: www.mwpai.edu
Management:
   President: Milton Bloch
   Artistic Director: Paul Schwizer
   Director Performing Arts: Robert Mortis
Mission: To provide exemplary programs and educational opportunites in the performing and cinematic arts, setting a national standard for artistic achievement.
Utilizes: Artists-in-Residence; Choreographers; Curators; Dance Companies; Dancers; Filmmakers; Fine Artists; Guest Accompanists; Guest Artists; Guest Choreographers; Guest Directors; Guest Musical Directors; Guest Musicians; Guest Soloists; High School Drama; Instructors; Multimedia; Original Music Scores; Selected Students; Sign Language Translators; Singers; Theatre Companies; Touring Companies
Founded: 1932
Specialized Field: Series & Festivals: Exhibitions of Paintings & Sculptures
Status: Non-Profit, Professional
Paid Staff: 300
Volunteer Staff: 30
Paid Artists: 270
Budget: $919,000 (performing arts)
Income Sources: Ticket sales; grants; sponsorships; program advertising; endowment
Performs At: Stanley Performing Arts Center
Affiliations: International Society of Performing Arts Administrators, INTIX, American Symphony Orchestra League, Wellinhall/Hamilton Colletge
Annual Attendance: 45,550
Facility Category: Arts center
Type of Stage: Proscenium, thrust, museum courtyad
Seating Capacity: 2,960, 271, 500
Year Built: 1960
Cost: 10 Million
Organization Type: Performing; Educational; Sponsoring

5215
WESTBURY MUSIC FAIR
960 Brush Hollow Road
Westbury, NY 11590
Phone: 516-334-0800
Fax: 516-333-7991
e-mail: westburyreplies@clearchannel.com
Web Site: www.musicfair.com
Management:
   Executive VP: Jason Stone
   Theatre Manager: John Blenn
   Marketing Director: Dan Kellachan
   Publicist: Laura Nuzzolo
   Group Sales Manager: Ed Denning
Mission: To offer the best entertainment of all kinds to metropolitan New York.
Utilizes: Singers
Founded: 1956
Specialized Field: Dance; Vocal Music; Instrumental Music; Theater
Status: Professional; Commercial
Season: year-round
Facility Category: Year-round Indoor
Type of Stage: In the round
Seating Capacity: 2,742
Year Built: 1956
Year Remodeled: 1998
Rental Contact: 516-333-2101 Ed Denning
Organization Type: Performing

5216
ARTS COUNCIL FOR THE NORTHERN ADIRONDACKS
PO Box 187
6 Champlain Ave
Westport, NY 12993
Phone: 518-962-8778
Fax: 518-962-8797
Toll-free: 800-661-4704
e-mail: artsco@westelcom.com
Web Site: www.artsnorth.org
Officers:
   President: Peter Seward
   Secretary: Heather Olsen
   Treasurer: Joe Provonca
Management:
   Executive Director: Caroline Rubino
   Outreach Coordinator: Karin Keene
   Outreach Coordinator: Karin Keene
Founded: 1984
Specialized Field: Art Services
Status: Non-Profit, Non-Professional
Paid Staff: 2
Budget: $10,000-20,000

SERIES & FESTIVALS / North Carolina

5217
MAVERICK CONCERTS
Maverick Concerts
120 Maverick Rd.
Woodstock, NY 12498-2503
Mailing Address: P.O. Box 9 Woodstock, NY 12498
Phone: 914-338-3074
Fax: 914-338-3074
e-mail: musicmavrk@aol.com
Web Site: www.beekman.net/maverickconcerts
Officers:
  Chairman: David F. Segal
  Vice Chairman: David Gubits
  Treasurer: Lawrence Posner
  Secretary: Dr. Edward Leavitt
Management:
  Music Director: Alexander Platt
  Publicity Director: Mary Fairchild
Mission: To provide Sunday afternoon chamber music concerts in summer.
Budget: $60,000-150,000

North Carolina

5218
ASHEVILLE CHAMBER MUSIC SERIES
P.O. Box 1003
Arden, NC 28802
Phone: 828-575-7427
e-mail: support@ashevillechambermusic.org
Web Site: www.main.nc.us/ashevillechambermusic/
Officers:
  President: Dr. Harold Rotman
  VP: Philip Walker
  Secretary: Perien Gray
  Treasurer: J. H. Wynn
Management:
  Program Director: Bill van der Hoeven
Mission: To provide chamber music concerts.
Founded: 1952
Specialized Field: Instrumental Music
Status: Non-Professional; Nonprofit
Budget: $10,000-20,000
Income Sources: Chamber Music America
Organization Type: Performing

5219
UNIVERSITY OF NORTH CAROLINA AT ASHEVILLE CULTURAL & SPECIAL EVENTS
Highsmith Center
1 University Heights CPO2150
Asheville, NC 28804
Phone: 828-251-6600
Fax: 828-251-6614
e-mail: bhalton@unca.edu
Web Site: www.unca.edu/culturalarts
Management:
  Director Office Of Cultural Events: Barbara Halton-Subkis
Utilizes: Artists-in-Residence; Choreographers; Collaborations; Dance Companies; Dancers; Guest Accompanists; Guest Choreographers; Guest Ensembles; Guest Musical Directors; Guest Musicians; Guest Teachers; Instructors; Lyricists; Multi Collaborations; Multimedia; Original Music Scores; Playwrights; Sign Language Translators; Singers; Soloists; Special Technical Talent; Theatre Companies
Founded: 1982
Status: Non-Profit, Professional
Paid Staff: 2
Budget: $60,000-150,000
Performs At: Lipinsky Auditorium; Thomas Wolfe Auditorium; Diana Wortham Theatre
Annual Attendance: 7,000+
Facility Category: Campus Auditorium
Type of Stage: Proscenium
Seating Capacity: 600

5220
BEAUFORT COUNTY COMMUNITY CONCERTS ASSOCIATION
1117 Whealton Point Road
Aurora, NC 27806
Mailing Address: PO Box 1024 Washington, NC 27889-1024
Phone: 252-322-5259
Web Site: www.gobcca.org/
Officers:
  President: Larry Ahlman
  Vice President: Jack Piland
  Treasurer: Ed Mann
  Secretary: Pat Wheelock
Management:
  Stage Managers: Travis Carter
Budget: $20,000-35,000

5221
LEES-MCRAE COLLEGE FORUM
PO Box 649
191 Main Street
Banner Elk, NC 28604
Phone: 828-898-8748
Fax: 828-898-8814
Toll-free: 800-280-4562
e-mail: admissions@lmc.edu
Web Site: www.lmc.edu
Officers:
  President: Barry M. Buxton
  Vice President: Dick Collins
  Treasurer: Paul Weber
Management:
  President of Forum: Barry M. Buxton
  President of College: Earl Robinson
  Special Events Coordinator: Sandy M Ramsey
Mission: To bring a stimulating series of cultural events to the area.
Utilizes: Artists-in-Residence; Dance Companies; Dancers; Instructors; Multimedia; Original Music Scores; Sign Language Translators; Singers
Founded: 1979
Specialized Field: Series & Festivals: Performing Arts
Status: Non-Profit, Professional
Paid Staff: 2
Volunteer Staff: 4
Paid Artists: 7
Budget: $40,000-45,000
Income Sources: Donations
Performs At: Hayes Auditorium
Annual Attendance: 6500
Facility Category: Concert hall/performance center
Seating Capacity: 750

5222
GARDNER-WEBB UNIVERSITY DISTINGUISHED ARTIST SERIES
P.O. Box 997
110 S. Main Street
Boiling Springs, NC 28017
Phone: 704-406-4000
Fax: 704-406-3920
e-mail: psparti@gardner-webb.edu
Web Site: gardner-webb.edu/
Officers:
  Fine Arts Department Chairman: Dr. Patricia Sparti
Budget: $10,000-20,000
Performs At: Hamrick Hall Auditorium; Dover theatre

5223
AN APPALACHIAN SUMMER FESTIVAL
Appalachian State University
Office of Arts & Cultural Programs
733 Rivers St.
Boone, NC 28608
Mailing Address: PO Box 32045 Boone, NC 28607
Phone: 828-262-6084
Fax: 828-262-2848
Toll-free: 800-841-2787
e-mail: boxoffice@appstate.edu
Web Site: ww.appsummer.org
Officers:
  Chair: Nancy Schaffel
  Vice Chair: Mary Friedman
Management:
  Director: Denise Ringler
  Director of Development: LaTanya Afolayan
  Dean: William L. Pelto
  Vice Chancellor: Susan Pettyjohn
  Associate Vice Chancellor: Hank Foreman
Mission: To enrich, expand and enhance the cultural climate of Appalachian State University and the Regional Community through the ongoing presentation of intellecutally and aesthetically challenging programs which may not otherwise be available.
Founded: 1983
Specialized Field: Multi-Disciplinary;(Music; Dance; Theatre; Visual Arts)
Paid Staff: 11
Paid Artists: 30
Annual Attendance: 26,000
Facility Category: Auditorium
Seating Capacity: 1700

5224
APPALACHIAN STATE UNIVERSITY PERFORMING ARTS & FORUM SERIES
Appalachian State University
PO Box 32045
Boone, NC 28608-2045
Phone: 828-262-6084
Fax: 828-262-2848
e-mail: weissbergdr@appstate.edu
Web Site: www.oca.appstate.edu/
Management:
  Director: Denise Ringler
Budget: $150,000-400,000
Performs At: Farthing Auditorium; Rosen Concert Hall; Valborg Theatre

5225
HORN IN THE WEST
PO Box 295
Brevard
Boone, NC 28607
Phone: 828-264-2120
Fax: 828-264-4529
e-mail: smalling@boone.net
Web Site: www.boonenc.org/saha
Management:
  General Manager/Museum Director: Curtis Smalling
  Assistant General Manager: Debbie Grant
Mission: To bring the past to life, with emphasis on the Revolutionary War and the struggle between settlers and Native Americans.
Founded: 1952

SERIES & FESTIVALS / North Carolina

Specialized Field: Dance; Vocal Music; Theater; Festivals
Status: Professional; Nonprofit
Income Sources: Southern Appalachian Historical Association
Season: June - Ausust
Performs At: Horn In The West
Organization Type: Performing; Educational

5226
BREVARD MUSIC FESTIVAL
1000 Probart Street
PO Box 312
Brevard, NC 28712
Phone: 828-862-2100
Fax: 828-884-2036
e-mail: brevardmusic@citcom.net
Web Site: www.brevardmusic.org
Officers:
  Chair: Falls Harris
Management:
  President: Mark Weinstein
  Artistic Director: Keith Lockhart
  Director of Artistic Planning & Edu: Jason Posnock
Founded: 1936
Specialized Field: Series & Festivals; Instrumental Music; Vocal Music; Theatre; Youth; Dance; Ethnic Performances; Music
Status: Non-Profit, Non-Professional
Paid Staff: 14
Paid Artists: 25
Income Sources: Ticket Sales; Tuition; Donation
Performs At: Concert Hall
Annual Attendance: 70,000
Facility Category: Covered, Open-Sided Auditorium
Seating Capacity: 1,800
Year Built: 1965
Year Remodeled: 1998

5227
CAMPBELL UNIVERSITY COMMUNITY CONCERT SERIES
Music Department
PO Box 70, Campbell University
Buies Creek, NC 27506
Phone: 910-931-4996
Fax: 910-893-1515
Toll-free: 800-334-4111
e-mail: wilson@mailcenter.cambell.edu
Web Site: www.campbell.edu/
Management:
  Director: Charles D Wilson
Budget: $10,000-20,000
Performs At: Scott Concert Hall

5228
CAROLINA UNION PERFORMING ARTS SERIES
Carolina Union
201 Student Union Building
Chapel Hill, NC 27599-5210
Phone: 919-966-3120
Fax: 919-962-3719
e-mail: lused@email.unc.edu
Web Site: carolinaunion.unc.edu
Management:
  Director: Don Luse
  Production Services Ass't Director: Michael Johnson
Budget: $150,000-400,000
Performs At: Memorial Hall university of North Carolina
Annual Attendance: 10,000

5229
CAROLINAS CONCERT ASSOCIATION
PO Box 11356
Charlotte, NC 28220
Phone: 704-527-6680
Fax: 704-527-1846
e-mail: bratton@carolinasconcert.com
Web Site: www.carolinasconcert.com
Management:
  President: Richard Grove
  Executive Director: Ron Law
  Booking Director: John Whitaker
Utilizes: Dance Companies; Fine Artists; Multimedia; Original Music Scores
Founded: 1930
Specialized Field: Series & Festivals; Instrumental Music; Orchestra
Status: Non-Profit, Professional
Paid Staff: 3
Budget: $150,000-400,000
Performs At: North Carolina Blumenthal Performing Arts Center

5230
CHARLOTTE CENTER CITY PARTNERS
200 S. Tryon Street
Suite 1600
Charlotte, NC 28202
Phone: 704-332-2227
Fax: 704-342-1233
e-mail: rkrumbine@charlottecentercity.org
Web Site: www.charlottecentercity.org
Officers:
  Chairman: Ernie Reigel
Management:
  President & CEO: Michael Smith
  VP Events: Rovbert Krumbine
  Chief Operating Officer: Moira Quinn
  Senior Vice President of Planning &: Cheryl Myers
  Vice President of Marketing: David Snapp
  Vice President of Finance: Eleni Saunders
  Director of Business Recruitment: Chris Hemans
Founded: 1979
Specialized Field: Downtown Development
Status: Non-Profit, Non-Professional
Paid Staff: 12

5231
QUEENS UNIVERSITY: QUEENS FRIENDS OF MUSIC CHAMBER SERIES
1900 Selwyn Avenue
Charlotte, NC 28274
Phone: 704-337-2204
Fax: 704-337-2356
e-mail: deanjm@queens.edu
Web Site: www.queens.edu/alumni/friends/music.asp
Management:
  Artistic Director: Paul Nitsch
Utilizes: Artists-in-Residence; Educators; Guest Musical Directors; Multimedia; Original Music Scores
Founded: 1983
Specialized Field: Chamber Music
Paid Staff: 1
Volunteer Staff: 28
Paid Artists: 6
Budget: $10,000-20,000
Income Sources: Donations; Ticket Sales
Performs At: Dana Auditorium
Annual Attendance: 1,200
Year Built: 1961
Year Remodeled: 1995

5232
WESTERN CAROLINA UNIVERSITY LECTURES, CONCERTS & EXHIBITIONS
Western Carolina University
University Center
Cullowhee, NC 28723
Phone: 828-227-7234
Fax: 828-227-7250
Web Site: www.wcu.edu News & Events
Management:
  LCE Series: Beth Johnson
Utilizes: Dance Companies; Dancers; Multimedia; Original Music Scores; Playwrights; Sign Language Translators; Special Technical Talent
Paid Staff: 1
Budget: $35,000-60,000
Performs At: Ramsey Activities Center; Hoey Auditorium

5233
AMERICAN DANCE FESTIVAL
Box 90772
Durham, NC 27708-0772
Phone: 919-684-6402
Fax: 919-684-5459
e-mail: adf@americandancefestival.org
Web Site: www.americandancefestival.org
Officers:
  President: Charles L Reinhart
  Chairman: Allen D. Roses, MD
Management:
  Director: Charles L Reinhart
  Director: Jodee Nimerichter
  Dean: Gerri Houlihan
  Director of Finance and Administrat: Cynthia Wyse
  Director of Archives and Preservati: Dean Jeffrey
  Director of Communications & Market: Sarah Tondu
  Marketing & Audience Services Assoc: Katie Peeler
  Director of Development: Diane M. Robertson
Mission: Committed to serving the needs of dance, dancers, choreographers and professionals in dance-related fields.
Founded: 1934
Specialized Field: Series & Festivals: Modern Dance
Status: For-Profit, Professional
Budget: $2,000,000
Performs At: Page Auditorium; Reynolds Industries Theatre; others
Annual Attendance: 25,000
Stage Dimensions: 30'x 37',48'x 35'
Seating Capacity: 1232; 589
Organization Type: Educational; Sponsoring

5234
BULL DURHAM BLUES FESTIVAL
Hayti Historic Center
804 Fayetteville Street
Durham, NC 27701
Phone: 919-683-1709
Fax: 919-682-5869
e-mail: info@hayti.org
Web Site: www.hayti.org
Management:
  President: Dianna Pledger
Specialized Field: Series & Festivals: Cultural Arts
Status: Non-Profit, Non-Professional
Paid Staff: 8

SERIES & FESTIVALS / North Carolina

5235
DUKE UNIVERSITY UNION BROADWAY COMMITTEE / ON STAGE COMMITTEE
Box 90193, 411 Chapel Drive
Duke University
Durham, NC 27708
Phone: 919-660-5880
Fax: 919-660-5923
e-mail: pcoyle@acpub.duke.edu
Web Site: library.duke.edu/rubenstein/findingaids/uaduuref/
Management:
    Associate Dean: Peter Coyle
Budget: $35,000-60,000
Performs At: Page Auditorium
Seating Capacity: 1232

5236
SUMMER FESTIVAL OF CHAMBER MUSIC AT DUKE UNIVERSITY
Box 90665, 105 Mary Duke Biddle Music Bldg.
Duke University
Durham, NC 27708-0665
Phone: 919-660-3300
Fax: 919-660-3301
e-mail: duke-music@duke.edu
Web Site: https://music.duke.edu/
Management:
    Office of University Life Dean: Susan Coon

5237
TRIANGLE THEATRE FESTIVAL
100 Timber Ridge Drive
Durham, NC 27713-9330
Phone: 919-490-8603
Fax: 919-401-3565
e-mail: info@theatrefestival.org
Web Site: www.theatrefestival.org
Management:
    Director: Anthony C Caporale

5238
COA COMMUNITY CENTER AUDITORIUM
Box 90193
Elizabeth City, NC 27906-2327
Phone: 252-335-9050
Fax: 252-337-6622
Toll-free: 800-335-9050
e-mail: lmanning@albemarle.edu
Web Site: www.albemarle.cc.nc.us/acadaff/finearts
Management:
    Facility Supervisor: Dave Griffie
    Events Coordinator/Box Office Mgr: Leslie Manning
Paid Staff: 4
Volunteer Staff: 20
Budget: $30,000-50,000
Performs At: Proscenium House Auditorium
Seating Capacity: 1,000
Rental Contact: Dave Griffie

5239
ELIZABETH CITY STATE UNIVERSITY LYCEUM SERIES
1704 Weeksville Road
Campus Box 831
Elizabeth City, NC 27909
Phone: 252-335-3359
Fax: 252-335-3779
e-mail: gjknight@mail.ecsu.edu
Web Site: www.ecsu.edu/academics/music
Management:
    Chairperson: Gloria Knight
    Assistant Professor: Mary Hellmann
    Academic Counselor: Ellard Forrester
Specialized Field: Series & Festivals; Instrumental Music; Vocal Music; Theatre; Youth; Dance; Ethnic Performances
Status: Non-Profit, Non-Professional

5240
ELON UNIVERSITY LYCEUM COMMITTEE
2800 Campus Box
Elon, NC 27244-2010
Phone: 336-278-5607
Fax: 336-278-5609
e-mail: troxlerg@elon.edu
Web Site: www.elon.edu/e-net/cultural
Management:
    President: Leo Lambert
    Dean of Cultural and Special Progra: George Troxler
Specialized Field: Series & Festivals; Instrumental Music; Vocal Music; Dance; Theatre of Illusion
Status: For-Profit, Non-Professional
Paid Staff: 4
Budget: $35,000-60,000
Income Sources: University Funds
Performs At: McCrary Theatre; Whitley Auditorium
Seating Capacity: 572/370

5241
FARMVILLE COMMUNITY ARTS COUNCIL
PO Box 305
3723 N. Main Street
Farmville, NC 27828
Phone: 252-753-3832
Fax: 252-753-6910
e-mail: info@farmvillearts.org
Web Site: www.farmvillearts.org
Management:
    Executive Director: Eraina Oakley
Founded: 1977
Specialized Field: Theatre; Community; Theatre
Status: For-Profit, Non-Professional
Paid Staff: 2
Budget: $10,000
Performs At: Stage-Theater-Arts Center

5242
ARTS COUNCIL OF FAYETTEVILLE/CUMBERLAND COUNTY
301 Hay Street
Fayetteville, NC 28301
Mailing Address: PO Box 318, Fayetteville, NC 28302
Phone: 910-323-1776
Fax: 910-323-1727
e-mail: admin@theartscouncil.com
Web Site: www.theartscouncil.com
Officers:
    President: Eric Nobles, Sr.
    Vice President: William M. Brooks, Jr.
    Secretary: Denise M. Wyatt
    Treasurer: Brent Sumner
    Immediate Past President: Anna Hodges Smith
    At-Large: Jerome T. Scott
    At-Large: Bobbi Mattocks
    Past President and advisory committ: Dr. J. Wayne Riggins
Management:
    Executive Director: Deborah Martin Mintz
    General Manager: Nancy Silver
    Marketing Director: Mary Kinney
    Operations Director: Robert Pinson
    Operations Assistant: Gretchen Anderson
    Community Investments Director: Anne Rawson
    Community Investments Associate: Adrienne Trego
    Director of Corporate Relations: Tom Lee
    Receptionist: Barbara Hayes
Founded: 1973
Specialized Field: Rotating Art Exhibit; Funding agency for artists in organization
Status: Non-Profit, Professional
Paid Staff: 9
Budget: $10,000

5243
ARTS COUNCIL OF MACON COUNTY
PO Box 726
Franklin, NC 28744-0726
Phone: 828-524-7683
Fax: 828-524-7683
Web Site: www.artscouncilofmacon.org/
Management:
    Executive Director: Bobbie Contino
Budget: $10,000
Performs At: Franklin Fine Arts Center; Highlands Civic Center

5244
EASTERN MUSIC FESTIVAL & SCHOOL
200 North Davie St.
Suite 303
Greensboro, NC 27401
Mailing Address: PO Box 22026, Greensboro, NC 27420
Phone: 336-333-7450
Fax: 336-333-7454
Toll-free: 877-833-6753
e-mail: info@easternmusicfestival.org
Web Site: www.easternmusicfestival.org
Officers:
    Chair: Frederick B. Starr
    Immediare Pasr Chair: Barbara R. Morgenstein
    Executive Director: Stephanie Cordick
    Chair Elect: Mary Bernard Magrinat
    Treasurer: Dr. Samuel M. Lebauer
    Secretary: Donald C. McMillion
Management:
    Music Director: Gerard Schwarz
    Director Of Marketing: Courtney Shaw
    Executive Director: Stephanie B. Cordick
    Director Of Finance: Gary Core
    Director Of Admissions: Melissa M. Edwards
    Director of Operations: Beverly Naiditch
    Marketing Assistant: Magena Morris
Mission: The EMF mission is to promote musical enrichment, excellence, professional collaboration, innovation and diversity through a nationally recognized teching program, music festival, concerts and other programs which will enchance the quality of life, health and vitality of our region.
Utilizes: Guest Artists
Founded: 1961
Specialized Field: Festival and Summer Music Academy; Orchestral; Chamber and Piano Performance Program; Special Attractions Ranging From Americana To Jazz; Blues; Etc
Status: Non-Profit, Professional
Paid Staff: 100
Paid Artists: 200
Non-paid Artists: 200
Budget: $2.5 million
Income Sources: Tickets; Tuition; Fees; Grants; Sponsorship; Private Contributions
Annual Attendance: 60,000
Organization Type: Performing; Educational

SERIES & FESTIVALS / North Carolina

5245
GUILFORD COLLEGE ARTS
5800 West Friendly Avenue
Greensboro, NC 27410
Phone: 336-316-2000
Fax: 336-316-2949
e-mail: scrisp@guilford.edu
Web Site: www.guilford.edu
Management:
   President: Kent John Chabotar
   Executive Associate to the Presiden: Joyce Eaton
Founded: 1837
Budget: $35,000-60,000
Performs At: Dana Auditorium; Sternberger Auditorium

5246
NORTH CAROLINA A&T STATE UNIVERSITY LYCEUM SERIES
North Carolina A&T State University
Greensboro, NC 27411
Phone: 336-334-7500
Fax: 336-256-2145
Toll-free: 800-443-8964
e-mail: jhgarner@ncat.edu
Web Site: www.ncat.edu/news/2013/03/lyceum-series-april.html
Officers:
   Chairman: Peter D. Hans
   Student Affairs Vice-Chancellor: Dr. Sullivan Wellbourne, Jr
   Vice Chairman: H. Frank Grainger
   Secretary: Ann B. Goodnight
Status: Nonprofit
Budget: $35,000-60,000

5247
UNITED ARTS COUNCIL OF GREENSBORO
200 N Davie Street
Greensboro, NC 27401
Mailing Address: PO Box 877 Greensboro, NC 27402
Phone: 336-373-7523
Fax: 336-373-7553
Web Site: www.uncarts.org
Management:
   President: Jeanie Duncan
   Marketing Director: Liz Summers
Founded: 1962
Specialized Field: Fund raising and Advocacy
Status: Non-Profit, Professional
Paid Staff: 5

5248
UNIVERSITY OF NORTH CAROLINA AT GREENSBORO CONCERT/LECTURE SERIES
Aycock Auditorium, Spring Garden at Tate Stre
PO Box 26170
Greensboro, NC 27402-6170
Phone: 336-334-5789
Fax: 336-334-5497
e-mail: ucls@uncg.edu
Web Site: www.ucls.uncg.edu
Management:
   President: Bruce Michael
   Associate Director: Checkle Leinwell
Utilizes: Actors; Dance Companies; Dancers; Fine Artists; Guest Composers; Guest Musical Directors; Guest Musicians; Singers; Special Technical Talent; Theatre Companies
Founded: 1891
Specialized Field: Arts and Humanities
Status: Non-Profit, Professional
Paid Staff: 16
Budget: $150,000-400,000
Income Sources: Ticket Revenue
Performs At: Aycock Auditorium
Affiliations: NCPC; APAP
Type of Stage: Black Pine
Stage Dimensions: 39'8"
Seating Capacity: 2300
Year Built: 1926
Year Remodeled: 1970
Rental Contact: 336-334-5118 Jan Hullihan

5249
EAST CAROLINA UNIVERSITY RUDOLPH ALEXANDER PERFORMING ART SERIES
East Fifth Street
East Carolina University
Greenville, NC 27858-4353
Phone: 252-328-6131
Fax: 252-328-2336
Toll-free: 800-328-2787
e-mail: clutterw@mail.ecu.edu
Web Site: www.ecuarts.com
Management:
   Asst VC for Student Experiences: William B Clutter
   Managing Director: Carol Woodruff
Utilizes: Dance Companies; Fine Artists; Multimedia; Original Music Scores; Selected Students; Student Interns; Theatre Companies
Founded: 1907
Specialized Field: Series and Festivals: Youth
Status: Non-Profit, Professional
Paid Staff: 2
Budget: $150,000-400,000
Performs At: Wright Auditorium
Annual Attendance: 14,000
Type of Stage: Proscenium
Seating Capacity: 1,500
Year Remodeled: 1985

5250
PITT COUNTY ARTS COUNCIL
PO Box 8191
404 S. Evans St.
Greenville, NC 27858
Phone: 252-551-6947
e-mail: info@pittcountyarts.org
Web Site: www.pittcountyarts.org/
Officers:
   President: Barbour Strickland
   Vice-President: Harvey Sharp Wooten
   Treasurer: Jeffrey Johnson
   Secretary: Andy Bates
   President-Elect: Jennifer Tripp
   Past-President: Jane Austen Behan
Management:
   Executive Director: Holly Garriott
   Programs & Finance Director: Cathy Hardison
   Marketing Director: Heather Dail
   Education & Outreach Coordinator: Paula Rountree
Budget: $35,000-60,000

5251
NORTH CAROLINA SHAKESPEARE FESTIVAL
807 West Ward Avenue
High Point, NC 27260
Mailing Address: PO Box 6066 High Point, NC 27262-6066
Phone: 336-841-2273
Fax: 336-841-8627
e-mail: pedro@ncshakes.org
Web Site: www.ncshakes.org
Officers:
   Chairman: Ms. Ashley Hedgecock
Management:
   Sales Director: Casey Schmidt
   Artistic Director: Pedro Silva
   Production Manager: Joel Radatz
Mission: Seeks to serve the cultural and educational needs of North Carolina audiences through traditional and nontraditional staging of the plays of Shakespeare and other classic playwrights.
Founded: 1977
Specialized Field: Theater
Status: Professional; Nonprofit
Paid Staff: 10
Paid Artists: 55
Budget: $1,400,000
Income Sources: Ticket sales; Touring fees; Contributors
Season: Late August - December
Performs At: High Point Theatre
Organization Type: Performing; Touring; Resident; Educational

5252
HIGHLANDS CASHIERS CHAMBER MUSIC FESTIVAL
PO Box 1702
507 Chestnut Street
Highlands, NC 28741
Phone: 828-526-9060
Fax: 828-526-4893
e-mail: hcomf@frontier.com
Web Site: www.h-cmusicfestival.org
Officers:
   President: Kathy Whitehead
   Treasurer: Julian Franklin
   Executive Director: Nancy Gould-Aaron
Management:
   Artistic Director: William Ransom
Mission: To promote the performance and appreciation of chamber music.
Utilizes: Original Music Scores
Founded: 1982
Specialized Field: Series and Festivals; Instrumental Music; Vocal Music; Chamber Music
Status: Non-Profit, Professional
Paid Staff: 2
Volunteer Staff: 15
Paid Artists: 24
Budget: $250,000
Income Sources: Contributions; Ticket Sales; Fund Raising
Performs At: Highlands Performong Arts Center
Affiliations: Chamber Music America
Annual Attendance: 3500
Facility Category: Performing Arts Center
Seating Capacity: 200;100
Year Remodeled: 2001
Organization Type: Performing; Touring; Resident; Educational; Sponsoring

5253
COASTAL CAROLINA COMMUNITY COLLEGE
444 Western Boulevard
Jacksonville, NC 28546-6877

SERIES & FESTIVALS / North Carolina

Phone: 910-455-1221
Fax: 910-455-7027
Web Site: www.coastal.cc.nc.us
Management:
    President: Ronald Lingle
    Music Instructor: Michael Daughtey
Founded: 1963
Specialized Field: Education
Status: Non-Profit, Professional
Paid Staff: 200
Budget: $10,000-20,000
Performs At: CCCC Fine Arts Auditorium
Seating Capacity: 182

5254
LINCOLN ART COUNCIL
PO Box 45
1701 South 17th Street, Suite 1A
Lincolnton, NC 68502
Phone: 402-434-2787
Fax: 704-732-9057
e-mail: merrylac@bellsouth.net
Web Site: www.lincolnartcouncil.org
Officers:
    President: Jeffre Chadwick
    First VP: Kenneth Brown
    Second VP: Beverly McAdams
    Secretary: John Badami
Management:
    President: Jeffre Chadwick
    Executive Director: Aryaane Howare
Mission: To develop, promote and foster all forms of creative and performing arts by arranging and offering exhibits, lectures, demonstrations, classes and performances, etc.
Founded: 1973
Specialized Field: Presentation of Art Circle
Status: Non-Profit, Professional
Paid Staff: 1
Paid Artists: 4
Income Sources: North Carolina Association of Arts Councils; North Carolina Arts Council
Performs At: Lincoln Citizens Center; Lincoln Cultural Center
Organization Type: Performing; Educational; Sponsoring

5255
LOUISBURG COLLEGE CONCERT SERIES
Louisburg College
501 N Main Street, Box 3125
Louisburg, NC 27549
Phone: 919-497-3251
Fax: 919-496-7141
Toll-free: 866-773-6354
e-mail: rpoole@louisburg.edu
Web Site: www.louisburg.edu
Officers:
    President: Dr Mark LaBranche
Management:
    Executive Director: Robert Poole
    VP Development: Kurt Carlson
    Box Office Manager: Anna Stallings
Mission: To provide cultural arts education and entertainment to the people of Franklin County and surrounding areas through music, dance, drama & visual arts.
Utilizes: Actors; Dance Companies; Dancers; Guest Instructors; Guest Musical Directors; Guest Soloists; Guild Activities; Instructors; Local Artists; Multimedia; Original Music Scores; Playwrights; Sign Language Translators; Singers; Soloists; Special Technical Talent; Theatre Companies; Touring Companies

Founded: 1957
Specialized Field: All
Status: Non-Profit, Professional
Paid Staff: 3
Volunteer Staff: 15
Paid Artists: 10
Income Sources: Ticket Sales; Patron Gifts
Performs At: Louisburg College Auditorium
Annual Attendance: 6,000
Facility Category: PAC
Type of Stage: Proscenium
Stage Dimensions: 40' x 30'
Seating Capacity: 1,180
Year Built: 1989
Rental Contact: Robert Poole

5256
ROANOKE ISLAND HISTORICAL ASSOCIATION
1409 National Park Road
Manteo, NC 27954
Phone: 252-473-2127
Fax: 252-473-6000
e-mail: info@thecolony.org
Web Site: www.thecolony.org
Officers:
    Chairman: Rick Gray
    Vice-Chairman: Norma Mills
    Secretary: Julie Daniels Nowells
    Treasurer: Stuart Bell
Management:
    Executive Production Coordinator: Rhoda Dresken
    Marketing/PR Associate: Joshua M Gilliam
    Membership/Development Associate: Bette Self
    Office Manager: Terry Fowler
Mission: To celebrate the history of the first English colonies on Roanoke Island NC; to honor the founders of The Last Colony, to promote awareness of the historical value of this event; to educate through drama and literature.
Founded: 1937
Specialized Field: Dance; Theater
Status: Non-Equity; Nonprofit
Paid Staff: 30
Paid Artists: 145
Budget: $1.5 million
Income Sources: Ticket Sales; Grants; Donations
Performs At: Waterside Theatre
Affiliations: Professional Theatre Workshop (in-house)
Annual Attendance: 60,000-70,000
Facility Category: Outdoor
Type of Stage: Amphitheatre
Stage Dimensions: 80' x 40'
Seating Capacity: 1534
Year Built: 1937
Year Remodeled: 1998
Organization Type: Performing

5257
PFEIFFER UNIVERSITY ARTIST SERIES
Pfeiffer University
Misenheimer, NC 28109
Phone: 704-463-1360
Fax: 704-463-1363
e-mail: sharrill@pfeiffer.edu
Web Site: www.pfeiffer.edu
Management:
    President: Charles Amerons
    Artistic Director: Doug Staeter
    Manager: Stephen Harrill
Founded: 1885
Specialized Field: Series & Festivals: Theatre
Status: Non-Profit, Professional

Paid Staff: 10
Paid Artists: 5
Budget: $10,000
Performs At: Henry Pfeiffer Chapel

5258
SURRY ARTS COUNCIL
PO Box 141
218 Rockford Street
Mount Airy, NC 27030
Phone: 336-786-7998
Fax: 336-786-9822
e-mail: arts@surryarts.org
Web Site: www.surryarts.org/
Management:
    Executive Director: Tanya Rees
Mission: To give direction and encouragement in the arts via performances, workshops and classroom instruction to residents of all ages in Surry County.
Utilizes: Guest Artists; Guest Companies
Founded: 1968
Specialized Field: Musical
Status: Nonprofit
Budget: $60,000-150,000
Performs At: Andy Griffith Playhouse; Mount Airy Fine Arts Center
Organization Type: Educational; Sponsoring

5259
ARTS NCSTATE
North Carolina State University
Campus Box 7306
Raleigh, NC 27695
Phone: 919-513-1820
e-mail: artsncstate@ncsu.edu
Web Site: www.fis.ncsu.edu/arts
Management:
    Museum Tech/Righteous Sister: Claire Ashby
    Director: Christina Menges
    Director: Jill Powell
    Coordinator: Amy Sawyers
    Director: Katherine Fuller
    Director: Sharon Moore

5260
ARTSPLOSURE: 2003 SPRING JAZZ & ART FESTIVAL
313 S. Blount Street
Suite 200B
Raleigh, NC 27601
Mailing Address: PO Box 391 Raleigh, NC 27602-0391
Phone: 919-832-8699
Fax: 919-832-0890
e-mail: info@artsplosure.org
Web Site: www.atsplosure.org
Officers:
    President: Tom Hester
    Vice President: Lori Vitale
    Secretary: Caroline Russell
    Treasurer: Linda Lillis
    Immediate Past President: Woody Dicus
Management:
    Executive Director: Michael Lowder
    Entry Coordinator: Christa Misenheiner
    Program Director: Terri Dollar
    Bookkeeper and Volunteer Coordinato: Glynda Westerbeek
Founded: 1979
Specialized Field: Visual Arts; Music
Status: Nonprofit
Income Sources: Sposors; Grnats; Donations
Annual Attendance: 75,000
Facility Category: Outdoor Stages

SERIES & FESTIVALS / North Carolina

5261
FIRST NIGHT RALEIGH
PO Box 391
Raleigh, NC 27602
Phone: 919-832-8699
Fax: 919-832-0890
e-mail: info@artsplosure.org
Web Site: www.artsplosure.org
Officers:
  President: Tom Hester
  Vice President: Lori Vitale
  Secretary: Caroline Russell
  Treasurer: Linda Lillis
  Immediate Past President: Woody Dicus
Management:
  Executive Director: Michael Louder
  Program Director: Terri Dollar
  Operations Manager: Dylan Morris
  Bookkeeper and Volunteer Coordinato: Glynda Westerbeek
Mission: To offer annual arts festivals to enhance cultural life in the communities of Raleigh and Walce.
Utilizes: Actors; Artists-in-Residence; Collaborating Artists; Collaborations; Dance Companies; Dancers; Educators; Fine Artists; Five Seasonal Concerts; Guest Conductors; Guest Directors; Guild Activities; Instructors; Local Artists; Lyricists; Multi Collaborations; Multimedia; New Productions; Original Music Scores; Playwrights; Resident Artists; Selected Students; Sign Language Translators; Singers; Soloists; Student Interns; Special Technical Talent; Theatre Companies; Touring Companies
Founded: 1979
Specialized Field: Series & Festivals; Instrumental Music; Vocal Music; Theatre; Youth; Dance; Ethnic Performances
Status: Non-Profit, Professional
Paid Staff: 4
Annual Attendance: 50,000
Organization Type: Performing; Festivals

5262
GALLERY OF ART & DESIGN
North Carolina State University
Campus Box 7102
1005 Capability Drive, Room 240
Raleigh, NC 27695
Phone: 919-515-2872
Fax: 919-515-2873
e-mail: claire_ashby@ncsu.edu
Web Site: www.gad.ncsu.edu
Management:
  Museum Tech/Righteous Sister: Claire Ashby

5263
NORTH CAROLINA ARTS COUNCIL
MSC #4632
109 East Jones Street
Raleigh, NC 27699-4632
Phone: 919-807-6500
Fax: 919-807-6532
e-mail: ncarts@ncdcr.gov
Web Site: www.ncarts.org
Officers:
  Chair: Robin Rogers Branstrom
Management:
  Executive Director: Wayrle Martin
  Deputy Director: Nancy Trovillion
  Senior Program Director: Michelle Lanier
Founded: 1967
Specialized Field: Series & Festivals; Instrumental Music; Vocal Music; Theatre; Youth; Dance; Ethnic Performances; State Arts Agency for North Carolina
Status: For-Profit, Non-Professional
Paid Staff: 25

5264
PINE CONE-PIEDMONT COUNCIL OF TRADITIONAL MUSIC
PO Box 28534
227 W. Martin St.
Raleigh, NC 27601
Phone: 919-664-8333
Fax: 919-664-8301
e-mail: pinecone1@mindspring.com
Web Site: www.pinecone.org
Management:
  Executive Director: Susan Newberry
  Program Associate: William Lewis
Mission: Pine Cone is dedicated to preserving, promoting, and presenting traditonal forms of music and dance and other folk performing arts in North Carolina.
Founded: 1984
Specialized Field: Series & Festivals: Concerts In Traditional Music
Status: Non-Profit, Non-Professional
Paid Staff: 2

5265
UNITED ARTS COUNCIL OF RALEIGH AND WAKE COUNTY
410 Glenwood Avenue
Suite 170
Raleigh, NC 27603
Phone: 919-839-1498
Fax: 919-839-6002
e-mail: follow@unitedarts.org
Web Site: www.unitedarts.org
Officers:
  Chair: Slee Arnold
  Chair-Elect: Bruce Sharpe
  President/CEO: Eleonor H Oakley
  Secretary: Dena Silver
  Treasurer: Helen Ballentine
  Vice Chair - Administration: V R Ramanan
  Vice Chair Development: Jack Alphin
  Vice Chair Grants: Elizabeth Grime Droessler
Management:
  Program Co-ordinator: Ragen Carlile
  Accounting Manager: Cindy Botts
  Special Events Co-ordiantor: Grahan Satisky
  Director of Development: Sarah Gardner
Mission: Builds better communities through support and advocacy of true arts.
Utilizes: Artists-in-Residence; Guest Artists; Touring Companies
Founded: 1962
Status: Nonprofit
Volunteer Staff: 1
Budget: 1.5 million
Organization Type: Educational; Sponsoring

5266
JOHNSTON COMMUNITY COLLEGE ON STAGE CONCERT SERIES
245 College Road
PO Box 2350
Smithfield, NC 27577
Phone: 919-934-3051
Fax: 919-209-2133
e-mail: dnjohnson@johnstoncc.edu
Web Site: www.johnstoncc.edu
Officers:
  Chair: Lyn T. Austin
  Vice Chair: Robert W. Bryant, Jr.
  President: David Johnson
  Performing Arts Manager: Zilphia Adcock
  Director of Economic Development: Rosa Andrews
Founded: 1989
Specialized Field: Series and Festivals: National and International Events
Status: Non-Profit, Non-Professional
Paid Staff: 3
Budget: $40 million
Performs At: Paul A. Johnston Auditorium
Type of Stage: Proscenium
Seating Capacity: 1,000
Rental Contact: Ken Mitchell

5267
ARTS COUNCIL OF MOORE COUNTY
PO Box 405
Southern Pines, NC 28388
Phone: 910-692-2787
Fax: 910-693-1217
e-mail: acmc@pinehurst.net
Web Site: www.artscouncil-moore.org
Management:
  Assistant Director: Katherine MacRae
  Executive Director: Chris Dunn
  Financial Manager: Paula Montgomery
  Youth Program Director: Kim Sobat
  Office Assistant: Jeanne Zimmerman
Founded: 1976
Specialized Field: Series & Festivals; Arts Council; Childrens Program
Status: Non-Profit, Non-Professional
Paid Staff: 4
Budget: $20,000-35,000

5268
SWANNANOA CHAMBER MUSIC FESTIVAL
WWC 6062
701 Warren Wilson Road
Swannanoa, NC 28778
Phone: 828-771-3050
Fax: 828-254-1733
e-mail: chamber@warren-wilson.edu
Web Site: www.swannanoachambermusic.com/
Management:
  Director: Frank Ell
  Administrator: Margaret Gormley-Chapman
Mission: Five weeks of chamber music featuring compositions of traditional and contempory composers.
Founded: 1969
Specialized Field: Asheville; Hendersonville; Waynesville; North Carolina
Paid Staff: 1
Volunteer Staff: 15
Paid Artists: 9

5269
EDGECOMBE COUNTY ARTS COUNCIL
130 Bridgers Street
Tarboro
Tarboro, NC 27886
Phone: 252-823-4159
Fax: 252-823-6190
e-mail: edgecombearts@embarqmail.com
Web Site: www.edgecombearts.org
Officers:
  Board President: Barbara Campbell Davis
  Board Vice President: Ashley Myers
  Treasurer: Calvin Anderson
  Board Secretary: Lucinda Plasencio
Management:
  Executive Director: Joyce Turner
  Assisstant Director: Carol Banks

SERIES & FESTIVALS / North Carolina

Mission: Promote and preserve cultural heritage of the county.
Founded: 1985
Specialized Field: Visual Arts In School; Festival
Paid Staff: 4
Volunteer Staff: 12
Paid Artists: 1
Budget: $10,000
Income Sources: Private Donations; State and Local Government
Facility Category: Outdoor Stage; Intimate Gallery

5270
MESSIAH 2000
PO Box 502
Troy, NC 27371
Phone: 910-576-8742
e-mail: tmusic@mc-online.net
Officers:
   President: Dr. Paul Chandley

5271
TRYON CONCERT ASSOCIATION SUBSCRIPTION SERIES
PO Box 32
34 Melrose Avenue
Tryon, NC 28782
Phone: 828-859-8322
Fax: 828-859-0271
e-mail: tfac@alltel.net
Web Site: www.tryonconcerts.com
Officers:
   President: Philip Cooper
Budget: $20,000-35,000
Performs At: Tryon Fine Arts Center

5272
SOUTHEASTERN COMMUNITY COLLEGE PERFORMING ARTS SERIES
4564 Chadbourn Highway
PO Box 151
Whiteville, NC 28472
Phone: 910-642-7141
Fax: 910-642-5658
e-mail: webmaster@sccu.edu
Web Site: www.sccnc.edu
Officers:
   President: Kathy S Matlock, Ph.D.
   VP Workforce & Community: Beverlee Nance
   VP Operations & Finance: Betty Jo Ramsey
   VP Academic & Student Affairs: Dr. Morgan Phillips
Management:
   President: Brantley Briley
Founded: 1964
Specialized Field: Education
Status: Non-Profit, Non-Professional
Paid Staff: 250
Budget: $20,000-35,000
Performs At: College Auditorium; Bowers Auditorium

5274
UNIVERSITY OF NORTH CAROLINA AT WILMINGTON
Kenan Auditorium
601 South College Road
Wilmington, NC 28403-5966
Phone: 910-962-3500
Fax: 910-962-7008
Toll-free: 800-732-3643
e-mail: bemelmansn@uncw.edu
Web Site: www.uncw.edu/arts
Management:
   Director Cultural Arts: Norman Bemelmans, bemelmansn@uncw.edu
   Assisstant Director of Cultural Art: Courtney Reilly
   Office Manager: Jeannie Leary
   Production Manager: Tara Noland
   House Manager: Gina Gambony
Utilizes: Dance Companies; Dancers; Educators; Filmmakers; Fine Artists; Guest Accompanists; Guest Directors; Guest Instructors; Guest Musical Directors; Guest Musicians; Guest Soloists; Guild Activities; High School Drama; Local Artists; Multimedia; Original Music Scores; Sign Language Translators; Singers; Soloists; Special Technical Talent; Theatre Companies
Founded: 1970
Specialized Field: Series and Festivals; Instrumental Music; Vocal Music; Theatre; Youth; Dance; Ethnic Performances
Status: Non-Profit, Professional
Paid Staff: 12
Volunteer Staff: 15
Budget: $60,000-150,000
Income Sources: University Support, Ticket Sales
Performs At: Kenan Auditorium
Affiliations: Kennedy Center Arts In Education Partner
Facility Category: Auditorium/Concert Hall
Seating Capacity: 1,000
Year Built: 1970
Year Remodeled: 2005
Rental Contact: Operations Manager Jeremy Summers

5275
BARTON INTERNATIONAL
Six Warren Street
Glen Falls
Wilson, NC 12801
Phone: 518-798-5462
Fax: 518-798-5728
e-mail: lhutchinson@barton.edu
Web Site: www.barton.com
Management:
   President: Norval Kaneten
   Chaplain: Loura Hutchinson
Specialized Field: Series & Festivals; Instrumental Music; Vocal Music; Theatre; Youth; Dance; Ethnic Performances
Status: Non-Profit, Professional
Paid Staff: 1
Budget: $10,000
Performs At: Howard Chapel

5276
WINGATE UNIVERSITY
220 N Camden Street
Wingate University
Wingate, NC 28174
Phone: 704-233-8000
Fax: 704-233-8309
Toll-free: 800-755-5550
e-mail: admit@wingate.edu
Web Site: www.wingate.edu
Officers:
   President: Dr. Jerry E McGee
   Executive Assisstant to president: Dr. Heather Campbell
   Executive Secretary to president: Dr. Betty Manus
   VP for Business & CFO: William H Durham
Management:
   Director of International studies: Jennifer Armentrout
   Director PA Program: Rosalind V Becker
   Registrar: Nicci Brown
Mission: Educational
Founded: 1896
Performs At: Hannah Covington McGee Theatre; Recital Hall; Helms Art Gallery; Austin Auditorium
Affiliations: NC Baptist Convention
Facility Category: Performing Arts
Type of Stage: Full Staging
Seating Capacity: 554
Year Built: 1896

5277
NORTH CAROLINA SCHOOL OF THE ARTS: SCHOOL OF MUSIC PERFORMANCE SERIES
1533 S Main Street
Winston-Salem
Winston-Salem, NC 27127-2738
Mailing Address: PO Box 12189
Phone: 336-770-3333
Fax: 336-631-1229
e-mail: admissions@uncsa.edu
Web Site: www.uncsa.edu
Officers:
   Chair: Dolores Watson
   Chair Elect: Patsy Seiler
   President: Susan Mann
   Vice President: Chris Chapman
   Secretary: Bill A Davis
Management:
   Director: Sheeler Lawson
Budget: $10,000
Performs At: Crawford Hall; Stevens Center

5278
SALEM COLLEGE
601 South Church
Winston-Salem
Winston-Salem, NC 27101
Phone: 336-721-2600
Fax: 336-721-2683
e-mail: barbara.lister-sink@salem.edu
Web Site: www.salem.edu
Officers:
   Chair: Charles A Blixt
   Vice Chair: Leigh Flippin Krause
   President: Susan E Pauly
Management:
   President, Salem College: Susan Pauly
   Acting Director, School Of Music: Barbara Lister-Sink
   Treasurer: D. Wayne Burkette
   Secretary: Anna McCoy Smith
   Actuary: D. Joeff Williams
Founded: 1772
Specialized Field: Series & Festivals; Instrumental Music; Vocal Music; Theatre; Dance; Ethnic Performances
Status: Non-Profit, Professional
Budget: $10,000
Performs At: Hanes Auditorium; Shirley Recital Hall

5279
WAKE FOREST UNIVERSITY
1834 Wake Forest Road
Winston-Salem, NC 27106
Phone: 336-758-5000
Fax: 336-758-4935
e-mail: sheltolb@wfu.edu
Web Site: www.wfu.edu/secrestartists
Management:
   Executive Director: Lillian Shelton
Founded: 1930
Specialized Field: Series & Festivals: Classical Music

SERIES & FESTIVALS / North Dakota

Status: Non-Profit, Professional
Paid Staff: 1
Budget: $60,000-150,000
Performs At: Wait Chapel; Brendle Hall

5280
CASWELL COUNCIL FOR THE ARTS
536 Main Street E
PO Box 609
Yanceyville, NC 27379-0609
Phone: 336-694-4591
Fax: 336-694-5675
e-mail: ccarts@caswell.k12.nc.us
Web Site: ccfta.org
Officers:
  President: Barbara Berger
  Vice President: Cliff Matkins
  Secretary: Patricia Price Lea
  Treasurer: Steve Davis
Management:
  Executive Director: H. Lee Fowlkes
  Box Office Mngr, Bookkeeper & Sec: Foye S. Lockhart
  Technical Director: Lynn Grose
Utilizes: Actors; Artists-in-Residence; Dance Companies; Dancers; Educators; Fine Artists; Instructors; Multimedia; Original Music Scores; Playwrights; Sign Language Translators; Soloists; Student Interns; Special Technical Talent; Theatre Companies; Touring Companies
Founded: 1979
Specialized Field: Series & Festivals; Instrumental Music; Vocal Music; Theatre; Youth; Dance; Ethnic Performances
Status: Non-Profit, Professional
Paid Staff: 4
Volunteer Staff: 30
Budget: $150,000
Annual Attendance: 7,000
Facility Category: civic center
Type of Stage: proscenium
Stage Dimensions: 45 x 30
Seating Capacity: 912
Year Built: 1979
Rental Contact: Hilce Fowlfes

North Dakota

5281
NORTH DAKOTA STATE UNIVERSITY LIVELY ARTS SERIES
North Dakota State University
1340 Administrative Avenue
Fargo
Fargo, ND 58102
Mailing Address: PO Box 6050
Phone: 701-231-8011
Fax: 701-231-8043
e-mail: gerard.e.beaubrun@ndsu.edu
Web Site: www.ndsu.nodak.edu
Officers:
  President: L Bresciani
  VP for Finance & Administratation: Bruce Bollinger
  VP for Agricultural Affairs: Ken Grafton
  VP for Student Affairs: Prakash C Mathew
  Vice President for Equity: Evies Myers
Management:
  Coordinator: Gerard Beaubrun
  Interim Executibe Director: Chuck Hoge
  Manager: Wendy McCrory

Mission: To provide a quality performing arts program for all members of the university community including students, faculty, staff, alumni, guests, parents and Fargo-Moorhead community members. Performing arts provided by the Lively Arts Series must challenge and stimulate creativity and positive regard for a multicultural perspective and provide students with opportunities for experiential learning and involvement related to performing arts.
Founded: 1910
Specialized Field: Series & Festivals; Instrumental Music; Vocal Music; Theatre; Dance; Ethnic Performances
Status: Non-Profit, Professional
Paid Staff: 2
Paid Artists: 50
Budget: $30,000-50,000
Income Sources: Grants; Community Support
Affiliations: Lake Agassiz Arts Council
Annual Attendance: 2,000-3,000
Facility Category: Fully Functional Concert Hall
Seating Capacity: 1,000

5282
NORTH DAKOTA MUSEUM OF ART
261 Centennial Drive Stop
7305 Grand Forks
Grand Forks, ND 58202
Phone: 701-777-4195
Fax: 701-777-4425
e-mail: ndmoa@ndmoa.com
Web Site: www.ndmoa.com
Officers:
  Chairman: Darrell Larson
  President: Mary Matson
  Vice President: Julie Blehm
  CEO: Bruce Gjovig
Management:
  Director: Laurel Reuter
  Secretary: Sally Miskavige
Founded: 1972
Paid Staff: 15
Volunteer Staff: 70
Budget: $20,000-30,000
Performs At: museum gallery
Facility Category: Art Museum
Seating Capacity: 300

5283
MAYVILLE STATE UNIVERSITY (ND) FINE ARTS SERIES
330 Third Street NE
Mayville
Mayville, ND 58257
Mailing Address: 400 Groveland Avenue Minneapolis MN, 55403
Phone: 612-874-9238
Fax: 701-786-4748
Toll-free: 800-437-4104
e-mail: apthien@msn.com
Web Site: www.mayvillestate.edu
Officers:
  President: Dr. Gary Hagen
Management:
  Series Director: Dr. Anthony Thein
Income Sources: Student Activity Fee, Concert Tickets, Contributions
Annual Attendance: 15-200
Facility Category: Fieldhouse
Type of Stage: Concrete
Seating Capacity: 400
Year Built: 1969

Ohio

5284
OHIO NORTHERN UNIVERSITY ARTIST SERIES
525 S Main Street
Ada
Ada, OH 45810
Phone: 419-772-2000
Fax: 419-772-1932
e-mail: k-baker@onu.edu
Web Site: www.onu.edu
Officers:
  Chairman Music Department: Dr. Edwin Williams
Management:
  President: Kendall Baker
  VP: Anne Lippert
Utilizes: Actors; Artists-in-Residence; Collaborating Artists; Collaborations; Commissioned Music; Dance Companies; Dancers; Designers; Educators; Five Seasonal Concerts; Grant Writers; Guest Accompanists; Guest Artists; Guest Choreographers; Guest Companies; Guest Composers; Guest Conductors; Guest Designers; Guest Directors; Guest Ensembles; Guest Instructors; Guest Lecturers; Guest Musical Directors; Guest Musicians; Guest Soloists; High School Drama; Local Artists; Multi Collaborations; Multimedia; Music; Organization Contracts; Original Music Scores; Performance Artists; Playwrights; Poets; Resident Artists; Resident Professionals; Sign Language Translators; Singers; Soloists; Touring Companies
Founded: 1871
Specialized Field: Music; Dance; Theater
Paid Staff: 10
Budget: $35,000-60,000
Performs At: Freed Center for the Performing Arts
Facility Category: Concert Hall
Type of Stage: Moveable Proscenium/Black Box
Seating Capacity: 550/136
Year Built: 1990
Cost: $7,000,000
Rental Contact: Andrea Lawson

5285
CHILDREN'S CONCERT SOCIETY OF AKRON
Edwin J Thomas Performing Arts Hall
198 Hill Street
Akron, OH 44325-0501
Phone: 330-972-2504
Fax: 330-972-6571
e-mail: ccs@uakron.edu
Web Site: www.childrensconcertsociety.org
Officers:
  President: Cheryl Boigegrain
  Vice President: Karin Jackoboice-Lesneski
  Treasurer: Renee Pinsky
  Secretary: Karen Myers
  Past President: Diane Lazzerini
Management:
  Administrative Director: Elizabeth Butler
Budget: $60,000-150,000
Seating Capacity: 2800

5286
GREATER AKRON MUSICAL ASSOCIATION
92 N. Main Street
Akron
Akron, OH 44308

SERIES & FESTIVALS / Ohio

Phone: 330-535-8131
Fax: 330-535-7302
e-mail: generalinformation@akronsymphony.org
Web Site: www.akronsymphony.org
Officers:
   Chair: Jerry Irby
   President: Renne Pipitone
   Executive Vice President: Mark Auburn
   VP Development: Linda McDonald
   VP Finance: Dave Supelak
Management:
   Executive Director: Paul Jarrett
   Director of Artistic Operations: Fran Goldman
   Director of Marketing: Joanne Green
   Ticket Service Mnaager: Sharon Smith
   Development Co-ordinator: Nikole Dack
Mission: To provide the Greater Akron Area with the finest quality symphonic and choral music and related fine arts; to educate the local public with respect to classical and contemporary music.
Utilizes: Guest Artists
Founded: 1950
Specialized Field: Orchestra of Music
Status: Non-Profit, Professional
Paid Staff: 10
Paid Artists: 80
Performs At: E.J. Thomas Hall
Organization Type: Performing; Educational

5287
MUSIC FROM STAN HYWET

714 N Portage Path
Akron
Akron, OH 44303
Phone: 330-836-5533
Fax: 330-688-4839
Toll-free: 888-836-5533
e-mail: Info@StanHywet.org
Web Site: www.stanhywet.org
Officers:
   Concert Chairman: Lola Rothmann
Budget: $10,000
Seating Capacity: 160

5288
TUESDAY MUSICAL ASSOCIATION

One South Main Street
Suite 301
Akron, OH 44325-0501
Phone: 330-761-3460
Fax: 330-761-3454
e-mail: info@tuesdaymusical.org
Web Site: www.tuesdaymusical.org
Officers:
   Executive Director: Barbara Feld
Management:
   Executive Director: Jarrod Hartzler
   Director of Development & Marketing: Jenne Garlando
   Artistic Administrator: Karla Jenkins
Budget: $60,000-150,000
Performs At: Edwin J. Thomas Performing Arts Hall

5289
UNIVERSITY OF AKRON: EJ THOMAS HALL SERIES

198 Hill Street
Akron, OH 44325-0501
Phone: 330-972-7595
Fax: 330-972-6571
e-mail: cfelder@uakron.edu
Web Site: www.uaevents.com/site/page.php?id=132
Management:
   Executive Director: Dan Dahl
   Managing Director: Cynthia A. Hollis
   Assistant Managing Director: Carrie Felder
   Marketing Manager: Nancy Logan Barton
   Press/Promotions Coordinator: Beth Fazio Lynch
Budget: $400,000-1,000,000
Seating Capacity: 2,956

5290
OHIO UNIVERSITY PERFORMING ARTS SERIES

Templeton-Blackburn Alumni Memorial Auditoriu
second floor east
Athens, OH 45701-2979
Phone: 740-593-1780
Fax: 740-593-1763
e-mail: performingarts@ohio.edu
Web Site: www.ohio.edu/performingarts
Management:
   President: Rodney McDavis
   Public Occassions Director: Grethen L Stephens
Specialized Field: Series & Festivals; Instrumental Music; Vocal Music; Theatre; Youth; Dance; Ethnic Performances
Status: Non-Profit, Professional
Paid Staff: 4
Budget: $60,000-150,000
Seating Capacity: 2,000

5291
LOGAN COUNTY COMMUNITY CONCERTS

PO Box 442
1200 Milligan Road
Bellefontaine, OH 43311
Phone: 937-592-5863
e-mail: barnwell@loganrec.com
Officers:
   Treasurer: Robert J Barnell
Budget: $20,000-35,000

5292
BALDWIN-WALLACE UNIVERSITY

275 Eastland Road
Berea
Berea, OH 44017-2088
Phone: 440-826-2900
Fax: 440-826-8138
e-mail: info@bw.edu
Web Site: www.bw.edu/academics/libraries/bach
Officers:
   Chair: Paul H Carleton
   President: Robert C Helmer
   Senior VP: Richard L Fletcher
   VP for Finace & Administration: William M Reniff
   VP for Enrollment Manager: Susan Dileno
Management:
   President: Mark Collier
   Executive Director: Catherine Jarjisian
   Coordinator: Mary Tuck
   Secretary: Christopher M Zito
   Treasurer: Lee Thomas
Founded: 1930
Specialized Field: Series & Festivals; Instrumental Music; Vocal Music
Status: Non-Profit, Professional
Paid Staff: 4

5293
BALDWIN-WALLACE COLLEGE ACADEMIC & CULTURAL EVENTS SERIES

275 Eastland Road
Berea, OH 44017
Phone: 440-826-2157
Fax: 440-826-3020
e-mail: jhairsto@bw.edu
Management:
   Program Director: Jay Hairston
Specialized Field: Series & Festivals; Instrumental Music; Vocal Music; Dance; Ethnic Performances
Status: Non-Profit, Professional
Budget: $10,000
Performs At: John Patrick Theatre; Kulas Musical Arts Building

5294
BLUFFTON UNIVERSITY ARTIST SERIES

1 University Drive
Bluffton
Bluffton, OH 45817-2104
Phone: 419-358-3000
Fax: 419-358-3323
Toll-free: 800-488-3257
e-mail: schatta@bluffton.edu
Web Site: www.bluffton.edu
Officers:
   President: James H Harder
   Artists Series Director: Dr. Adam J Schattschneider
Management:
   President: Lee Snyder
   Executive Director: Adam Schattschneider
   Artist Series Coordinator: Anna Stembler-Smith
Founded: 1899
Specialized Field: Series & Festivals; Instrumental Music; Vocal Music; Theatre; Youth; Dance; Ethnic Performances
Status: Non-Profit, Professional
Paid Staff: 2
Paid Artists: 6
Budget: $10,000-20,000
Performs At: Yoder Recital Hall; Founders Hall; Mosiman Hall

5295
BOWLING GREEN STATE UNIVERSITY: NEW MUSIC & ART FESTIVAL

Bowling Green
Bowling Green, OH 43403-0001
Phone: 419-372-2521
Fax: 419-372-2938
e-mail: bbeerma@bgnet.bgsu.edu
Web Site: www.bgsu.edu/colleges/music/maccm
Officers:
   President: Mary Ellen Mazey
Management:
   Director: Burton Beerman

5296
BOWLING GREEN STATE UNIVERSITY FESTIVAL SERIES

Bowling Green
Bowling Green, OH 43403-0001
Phone: 419-372-2521
Fax: 419-372-2938
e-mail: dfleitz@bgnet.bgsu.edu
Web Site: www.bgsu.edu/colleges/music
Officers:
   President: Mary Ellen Mazey
Management:
   President: Sidney Ribeau
   Public Events Director: Deborah L Fleitz
Founded: 1910
Specialized Field: Educational; Public University
Status: Non-Profit, Non-Professional
Budget: $60,000-150,000

SERIES & FESTIVALS / Ohio

Performs At: Kobacker Hall; Bryan Hall

5297
CRAWFORD COUNTY COMMUNITY CONCERT ASSOCIATION
PO Box 469
Bucyrus, OH 44820
Phone: 419-562-3719
Fax: 416-562-9098
e-mail: slater@cybrtown.com
Web Site: www.slatertours.com
Officers:
   President: Robert A Slater
Budget: $35,000-60,000
Performs At: Bucyrus Middle School Auditorium

5298
LITHOPOLIS PERFORMING ARTISTS SERIES
3825 Cedar Hill Road
Canal Winchester, OH 43110-8929
Phone: 614-837-8925
Fax: 614-837-4765
Management:
   President: Leland Smith
   Series Director: Virginia E Heffner
Founded: 1972
Specialized Field: Series & Festivals; Concert Series; School Residency
Status: Non-Profit, Professional
Paid Artists: 20
Budget: $10,000-20,000
Performs At: Wagnalss Memorial Auditorium

5299
CEDARVILLE UNIVERSITY ARTIST SERIES
251 N Main Street
Box 601
Cedarville, OH 45314
Phone: 937-766-7700
Fax: 937-766-7581
Toll-free: 800-233-2784
Web Site: www.cedarville.edu
Management:
   Ass't Campus Activities Director: Jeff Beste
   Director: Scott Van Loo
Budget: $20,000-35,000
Performs At: James T. Jeremiah Chapel

5300
COLLEGE-COMMUNITY ARTS COUNCIL
7600 State Route 703E
Celina, OH 45822
Phone: 419-678-2950
Fax: 419-678-2950
e-mail: eeweber@bright.net
Officers:
   President: Eugene Weber
Budget: $10,000-20,000
Seating Capacity: 150-470

5301
CINCINNATI ARTS ASSOCIATION: ARONOFF CENTER FOR THE ARTS
650 Walnut Street
Cincinnati, OH 45202
Phone: 513-977-4123
Fax: 513-977-4150
Web Site: www.cincinnatiarts.org
Officers:
   President/Executive Director: Stephen A Loftin
   VP/General Manager: Janet L Taylor
Founded: 1992
Specialized Field: Series & Festivals; Music; Theatre; Dance; Education
Status: Non-Profit, Professional
Paid Staff: 100
Budget: $10,000,000
Performs At: Proctor & Gamble Hall; Jarson-Kaplin Theater; Fifth Third Bank Trust
Annual Attendance: 1,100,000
Seating Capacity: 2,719; 437; 150

5302
CINCINNATI FOLK LIFE SERIES
PO Box 9008
Cincinnati, OH 45209
Phone: 513-533-4822
Fax: 513-533-4828
e-mail: cfl@zoomtown.com
Web Site: www.cincinnaticalticfestival.com
Management:
   Managing Director: Joann Buck
Founded: 1981
Specialized Field: Series and Festivals: Folk Music
Status: Non-Profit, Professional
Paid Staff: 1
Budget: $20,000-35,000
Seating Capacity: 150-500

5303
CINCINNATI GARDENS
2250 Seymour Avenue
Cincinnati, OH 45212
Phone: 513-631-7793
Fax: 513-631-2666
Web Site: www.cincygardens.com
Officers:
   Owner/Chairman: Gerry Robinson
   President/CEO: Pete Robinson
   CFO/VP Business Operations: Renne Jose
Management:
   Director: Joseph F Jagoditz
   General Manager: Joe Jagoditz
   Director of PR: Greg Waddell
   Operations Manager: Jerry Henderson
   Ticket Office Manager: Carol Ladwig

5304
CINCINNATI MAY FESTIVAL
1241 Elm Street
Cincinnati
Cincinnati, OH 45202
Phone: 513-621-1919
Fax: 513-744-3535
e-mail: information@mayfestival.com
Web Site: www.mayfestival.com
Officers:
   Chairman: J Shane Starkey
   Vice Chairman: J Mark Holcomb
   Secretary: Ruthy Korelitz
Management:
   Music Director: James Conlon
   Executive Director: Steven Sunderman
   Chorus Director: Robert Porco
   Director Marketing/Development: Vera Menner
   Youth Chorous Director: James Bagwell
Mission: Cincinnati May Festival presents an exciting repertoire of choral and orchestral music featuring the May Festival Chorus, world-renowned guest soloists and conductors and the Cincinnati Symphony Orchestra.
Utilizes: Guest Artists
Founded: 1873
Specialized Field: Series & Festivals; Vocal Music; Instrumental Music; Festivals
Status: Non-Profit, Professional
Paid Staff: 200
Income Sources: Cincinnati Symphony Orchestra
Performs At: Music Hall; Cathedral Basillica of the Assumption
Organization Type: Performing; Resident; Sponsoring

5305
CINCINNATI OPERA ASSOCIATION SUMMER FESTIVAL
1243 Elm Street
Cincinnati
Cincinnati, OH 45202-7531
Phone: 513-768-5500
Fax: 513-768-5552
Toll-free: 888-533-7149
e-mail: info@cincinnatiopera.com
Web Site: www.cincinnatiopera.com
Officers:
   Co-Chairman: Cathy Crain
   Co-Chairman: Robert W Olson
   President: Murray Sinclaire
   Vice President: Harry Fath
   Vice President: Charlin Briggs
Management:
   Managing Director: Patricia Beggs
Founded: 1920
Specialized Field: Vocal Music: Opera
Status: Non-Profit, Professional
Paid Staff: 26
Paid Artists: 300

5306
CINCINNATI SHAKESPEARE FESTIVAL
719 Race Street
Cincinnati
Cincinnati, OH 45202-4304
Phone: 513-381-2273
Fax: 513-334-2244
e-mail: info@cincyshakes.com
Web Site: www.cincyshakes.com
Officers:
   President: Don Tecklenburg
Management:
   Producing Artistic Director: Bryan I Phillips
   Managing Director: Lettie Van Hermert
   Education Director: Jenna Vellaon
   Executive Director: Joy Wallington
Founded: 1994
Specialized Field: Series & Festivals; Theatre; Youth
Status: Non-Profit, Professional
Paid Staff: 15
Volunteer Staff: 20
Paid Artists: 15
Season: August - June
Type of Stage: Proscenium
Stage Dimensions: 24' x 32'
Seating Capacity: 163

5307
CLASSICAL GUITAR SERIES
Xavier University
3800 Victoria Parkway
Cincinnati, OH 45207-2717
Phone: 513-745-3000
Fax: 513-745-3232
Toll-free: 800-344-4698
e-mail: webmaster@xavier.edu
Web Site: www.xu.edu
Officers:
   Chairman: Robert J Kohlhepp
   President: Micahel J Graham
   Senior VP & CFO: Maribeth Amyot
   VP for University Relations: Gary Massa

All listings are in alphabetical order by state, then city, then organization within the city.

SERIES & FESTIVALS / Ohio

VP for Facilities: Robert Sheeran
Management:
   Executive Director: John P Heim S J
   Director: Jack Heim
   Dean college of arts & Science: Dr. Janice Walker
Founded: 1976
Specialized Field: Series & Festival; Classical Piano; Classical Guitar; Swing/Jazz
Status: Non-Profit, Professional
Paid Staff: 2
Paid Artists: 20
Budget: $20,000-35,000
Performs At: University Center Theatre
Seating Capacity: 395

5308
CLASSICAL PIANO SERIES
Xavier University
3800 Victoria Parkway
Cincinnati, OH 45207-2717
Phone: 513-745-3000
Fax: 513-745-4223
e-mail: webmaster@xavier.edu
Web Site: www.xu.edu
Officers:
   Chairman: Robert J Kohlhepp
   President: Micahel J Graham
   Senior VP & CFO: Maribeth Amyot
   VP for University Relations: Gary Massa
   VP for Facilities: Robert Sheeran
Management:
   President: Michael Graham
   Director of Performing Arts: Catherine Springfield
   Director of Music Series: Jack Heim
   Dean college of arts & Science: Dr. Janice Walker
Founded: 1831
Status: Non-Profit, Professional
Paid Staff: 2
Budget: $20,000-35,000
Performs At: University Center Theatre
Seating Capacity: 395

5309
FALL ARTS FESTIVAL/JEWISH FOLK FESTIVAL
2615 Clifton Avenue
Cincinnati, OH 45220
Phone: 513-221-6728
Fax: 513-221-7134
e-mail: email@hillelcincinnati.orgf
Management:
   Executive Director: Rabbi Abie Ingber
Mission: Folkmusic, Theatre and World Music especially Jewish artists.
Founded: 1977
Specialized Field: Music; Theatre; (Small Production; One Person Show)
Paid Staff: 6
Volunteer Staff: 35
Paid Artists: 3
Non-paid Artists: 3

5310
JAZZ GUITAR SERIES
Xavier University
3800 Victoria Parkway
Cincinnati, OH 45207-2717
Phone: 513-745-3000
Fax: 513-745-2083
e-mail: webmaster@xavier.edu
Web Site: www.xu.edu
Officers:
   Chairman: Robert J Kohlhepp
   President: Micahel J Graham
   Senior VP & CFO: Maribeth Amyot
   VP for University Relations: Gary Massa
   VP for Facilities: Robert Sheeran
Management:
   Director: Father Jack Heim
   Dean college of arts & Science: Dr. Janice Walker

5311
JAZZ PIANO SERIES
Xavier University
3800 Victoria Parkway
Cincinnati, OH 45207
Phone: 513-745-3000
Fax: 513-745-2083
Toll-free: 800-344-4698
e-mail: webmaster@xavier.edu
Web Site: www.xu.edu
Officers:
   Chairman: Robert J Kohlhepp
   President: Micahel J Graham
   Senior VP & CFO: Maribeth Amyot
   VP for University Relations: Gary Massa
   VP for Facilities: Robert Sheeran
Management:
   Vice Chairperson: Robert J Kohlhepp
   President: Michael J Graham
   Dean college of arts & Science: Dr. Janice Walker

5312
LINTON CHAMBER MUSIC SERIES/ENCORE
1241 Elm Street
Cincinnati, OH 45202
Phone: 513-381-6868
Fax: 513-232-0949
e-mail: info@lintonmusic.org
Web Site: www.lintonmusic.org
Officers:
   Chairman: Chad Wick
   Vice President: Lee Oberlag
Management:
   Executive Director: Julie Montgomery
   Artistic Director: Jaime Laredo
   Artistic Director: Sharon Robinson
   Education Director: Donna Doran
   Founding Director: Richard Waller
Founded: 1977
Specialized Field: Series and Festivals: Chamber Music
Status: Non-Profit, Professional
Paid Staff: 1
Paid Artists: 20
Budget: $20,000-35,000
Performs At: First Unitarian Church; Cinicinnati City Council Chambers

5313
LINTON'S PEANUT BUTTER & JAM SESSIONS
1241 Elm Street
Cincinnati, OH 45202
Phone: 513-381-6868
Fax: 513-381-6888
e-mail: lintoninc@aol.com
Web Site: lintonmusic.org/
Officers:
   Chairman: Chad Wick
   Vice President: Lee Oberlag
   Treasurer: John G. Earls
Management:
   Artistic Director: Jaime Laredo
   Artistic Director: Sharon Robinson
   Associate Artistic Director: Michael Chertock
   Executive Director: Julie Montgomery
   Education Director: Donna Doran
Budget: $20,000-35,000
Performs At: First Unitarian Church; Cincinnati City Council Chambers

5314
ART SONG FESTIVAL
11021 East Boulevard
Cleveland
Cleveland, OH 44106
Phone: 216-791-5000
Fax: 216-791-3063
e-mail: cimweb@cwru.edu
Web Site: www.cim.edu
Officers:
   Chairman: A. Malachi Mixon
   Vice Chairman: Brent M Buckley
   Prsident & CEO: Joel Smirnoff
   Vice President & COO: Eric W Bower
   VP for Institutional Advancement: Karin Stone
Management:
   Dean: Dr. Adrian Daly
   Executive Coordinator: Dr Joanne Uniatowski
Founded: 1985

5315
CHINA MUSIC PROJECT
334 Claymore Boulevard
Cleveland, OH 44143-1730
Phone: 216-531-2188
Management:
   Director: Marjorie Ann Ciarlillo

5316
CLEVELAND MUSEUM OF ART PERFORMING ARTS SERIES
11150 East Blvd.
Cleveland, OH 44106
Phone: 216-421-7350
Fax: 216-707-6867
e-mail: perform@clevelandart.org
Web Site: www.clevelandart.org
Officers:
   Chairman: R. Steven Kestner
   Vice Chair & Secretary: Sarah S Cutler
   Vice Chairman: Scott C Mueller
   Vice Chairman: James A Ratner
   Vice President: Sharon Reaves
Management:
   Director/Performing Arts,Music,Film: Massoud Saidpour
   Associate Director, Music: Thomas Welsh
   Interim Director: Frederick E Bidwell
   Deputy Director: August A Napoli
Founded: 1916
Specialized Field: Art Collection
Status: Non-Profit, Professional
Paid Staff: 3
Budget: $35,000-60,000
Performs At: Gartner Auditorium
Organization Type: Educational; Sponsoring

5317
CLEVELAND MUSIC SCHOOL SETTLEMENT ARTISTS CONCERT SERIES
11125 Magnolia Drive
Cleveland, OH 44106
Phone: 216-421-5806
Fax: 216-231-5005
e-mail: cmsselee@aol.com
Web Site: www.thecmss.org

SERIES & FESTIVALS / Ohio

Officers:
- **Chair:** Geralyn M. Presti
- **First Vice Chair:** Maura L. Hughes
- **Second Vice Chair:** Craig M. Brown
- **Treasurer:** Steven P. Muir
- **Secretary:** Elisabeth R. Stahl

Management:
- **Executive Director:** Daniel Windham

Founded: 1911
Specialized Field: Series and Festivals; Instrumental Music; Vocal Music; Youth
Status: Non-Profit, Professional
Budget: $10,000
Seating Capacity: 200

5318
CLEVELAND SHAKESPEARE FESTIVAL

2843 Washington Blvd
Cleveland
Cleveland, OH 44118
Phone: 216-732-3311
e-mail: info@cleveshakes.org
Web Site: www.cleveshakes.org

Officers:
- **Chair:** Rodger M Govea
- **Vice Chairman:** Larry Nehring

Management:
- **Artistic Director:** Tyson Douglas Rand
- **Operations Director:** Brian Pedaci
- **Board Secretary:** Kristina Hewis
- **Theatre Artist:** Christine McBurney

Mission: To produce exceptional, accessible theater free of charge. Celebrate the talents of local artists in all aspects of production and excite contemporary audiences with the timeless themes of Shakespearean theater. Dedicated to bringing plays of professional quality to the greater Cleveland area as a way of encouraging community through theater.
Founded: 1998
Specialized Field: Free Outdoor Summer Festival

5319
DARIUS MILHAUD SOCIETY

15715 Chadbourne Road
Cleveland, OH 44120
Phone: 216-921-4548
Fax: 216-921-4548

Officers:
- **President:** Katherine M Warne

Budget: $10,000-20,000
Seating Capacity: 500

5320
GREAT LAKES THEATER

1501 Euclid Avenue
Suite 300
Cleveland, OH 44115
Phone: 216-241-5490
Fax: 216-241-6315
e-mail: mail@greatlakestheater.org
Web Site: www.greatlakestheater.org

Officers:
- **Chair:** Thomas G Stafford
- **President:** Samuel Hartwell
- **Co-Chairman:** John Katzenmeyer
- **Co-Chairman:** Joseph Lopresti

Management:
- **Public Relations Director:** Todd Krispinsky, tkrispinsky@greatlakestheatre
- **Producing Artistic Director:** Charles Fee
- **Executive Director:** Bob Taylor
- **Director of Development:** Don Bernardo
- **Artistic Associate:** Sara Bruner

Mission: To bring pleasure, power, and relevance of classic theatre to the widest possible audience through its main stage productions and education programs.
Utilizes: Actors; Choreographers; Designers; Educators; Guest Artists; Guest Conductors; Guest Designers; Guest Lecturers; Music; Resident Professionals
Founded: 1962
Specialized Field: Classical Theatre, Youth
Status: Non-Profit, Professional
Paid Staff: 14
Budget: $3.6 million
Income Sources: League of Resident Theatres; American Arts Alliance
Performs At: Hanna Theatre, Playhouse Square
Affiliations: LORT
Seating Capacity: 550
Year Built: 1921
Year Remodeled: 2008
Organization Type: Performing; Educational

5321
TRI-C JAZZFEST

2900 Community College Avenue
Theatre 11
Cleveland, OH 44115
Phone: 216-987-4400
Fax: 216-987-4422
Toll-free: 800-954-8742
e-mail: jay.albert@tri-c.edu
Web Site: www.tri-c.edu/

Management:
- **Executive Director:** Lawrence Simpson
- **Artistic Director:** Willard Jenkins
- **Managing Director:** Jay Albert
- **Education Events Coordinator:** Susan Stone

Mission: To provide an educational opportunity for students and people of all ages and backgrounds to further their abilities, understanding and appreciation for jazz. To increase public awareness and appreciation for jazz as an American art form. To preserve the history and foster the development of this unique music. To bring world class performers and educators to greater Cleveland audiences.
Utilizes: Artists-in-Residence; Collaborating Artists; Commissioned Music; Educators; Grant Writers; Guest Accompanists; Guest Companies; Guest Composers; Guest Directors; Guest Ensembles; Guest Lecturers; Guest Musical Directors; Guest Musicians; Local Artists; Multimedia; Music; Original Music Scores; Sign Language Translators; Singers; Soloists; Student Interns
Founded: 1980
Specialized Field: Series and Festivals: Jazz Music
Status: Non-Profit, Professional
Paid Staff: 4
Volunteer Staff: 20
Paid Artists: 100
Budget: 500,000
Income Sources: Foundations; Corporate; Government; Private
Performs At: College Campus Auditorium; Severance Hall; Metro Campus
Affiliations: Cuyahoga Community College; International Association of Jazz Educators
Annual Attendance: 30,000-40,000
Type of Stage: Proscenium
Seating Capacity: 360-3,000
Organization Type: Performing; Educational
Resident Groups: Swing City; Tri-C Jazz Fest; High School All-Stars

5322
SHALHAVET FESTIVAL

2140 Lee Road
Suite 218
Cleveland Heights, OH 44118
Phone: 216-932-3455
Management:
- **Executive Director:** Clara Amster

5323
COLUMBIANA SUMMER CONCERT ASSOCIATION

2905 Middleton Road
Columbiana, OH 44408-9550
Phone: 330-482-2978
Officers:
- **Chairman:** Fred A Lynn

Budget: $10,000-20,000
Performs At: Firestone Park Gazebo Entertainment Center

5324
COLUMBUS ARTS FESTIVAL

100 E Broad Street
Suite 2250
Columbus, OH 43215
Phone: 614-224-2606
Fax: 614-224-7461
e-mail: festival@gcac.org
Web Site: www.gcac.org

Officers:
- **Chair:** Karen Bell
- **Vice Chair:** David Clifton
- **Immediate Past Chair:** Robert Falcone
- **Treasurer:** Cheryle Russo
- **Secretary:** Lori Barreras

Management:
- **President of Arts Council:** Ray Hanley
- **Director of Arts Festival:** Katie Lucas
- **Director of Finance & Admin:** Kayla Green
- **Executive Assisstant:** Sue Jones
- **Grants Co-ordinator:** Sean Kessler

Mission: To offer an annual festival of the arts.
Founded: 1961
Specialized Field: Dance; Vocal Music; Instrumental Music; Festivals; Fine Art; Fine Craft
Status: Non-Profit, Professional
Paid Staff: 2
Volunteer Staff: 300
Income Sources: Greater Columbus Arts Council
Annual Attendance: 550,000
Facility Category: Outdoor Stage
Organization Type: Performing; Festival

5325
COLUMBUS ASSOCIATION FOR THE PERFORMING ARTS: SIGNATURE SERIES

55 E State Street
Columbus
Columbus, OH 43215-4264
Phone: 614-469-1045
Fax: 614-461-0429
e-mail: meilley@capa.com
Web Site: www.capa.com

Officers:
- **Chair:** Michael Petrecca
- **Vice Chair:** Lawrence L Fisher
- **Secretary:** Barabara B Lach
- **VP:** Michael Rilley
- **President & CEO:** William B Conner

Management:
- **Executive Director:** Douglas F Kridler

SERIES & FESTIVALS / Ohio

Director of Ticketing: John Sherwood
Ticket Donation Requests: Stewart Bender
Facility Rental: Elena Perantoni
Programming: Rich Corsi

Mission: To utilize entertainment to enliven and enrich metropolitan life through its work in all its venues, enhance a continuing downtown renaissance and install appreciation for diverse forms of entertainment.
Utilizes: Actors; Artists-in-Residence; Choreographers; Collaborating Artists; Collaborations; Commissioned Composers; Commissioned Music; Dance Companies; Dancers; Educators; Filmmakers; Fine Artists; Grant Writers; Guest Accompanists; Guest Artists; Guest Choreographers; Guest Companies; Guest Composers; Guest Designers; Guest Musical Directors; Guest Musicians; High School Drama; Instructors; Local Artists; Multimedia; Music; Original Music Scores; Poets; Selected Students; Sign Language Translators; Singers; Soloists; Special Technical Talent; Theatre Companies
Founded: 1969
Budget: $15,000,000+
Income Sources: 90 per cent Ticket Sales; Rentals; Grants;Contributions
Performs At: Ohio Theatre; Palace Theatre; Southern Theatre; Riffe Center Theatre; Chicago Theatre; Shubert Theater
Annual Attendance: 1,000,000+

5326
COLUMBUS SYMPHONY ORCHESTRA: PICNIC WITH THE POPS
55 E State Street
Columbus, OH 43215
Phone: 614-228-8600
Fax: 614-228-9600
Web Site: www.columbussymphony.com
Officers:
Chair: Martin Inglis
Vice Chair: Michael Mahaffey
Treasurer: Eric N Sutphin
Secretary: Derrick Clay
Executive VP: Lisa Barton
Management:
Executive Director/President: Daniel Hart
Music Director: Jean - Marie Zeitouni
Paid Staff: 35
Volunteer Staff: 750
Paid Artists: 8

5327
COOPER STADIUM
330 Huntilngton Park Lane
Columbus
Columbus, OH 43215
Phone: 614-462-5250
Fax: 614-462-3271
e-mail: info@clippersbaseball.com
Web Site: www.clippersbaseball.com
Management:
General Manager: Ken Schnake
Seating Capacity: 15,000

5328
EARLY MUSIC IN COLUMBUS
1 college and Main
Columbus, OH 43209-2394
Phone: 614-236-6011
Fax: 614-861-4569
e-mail: mkwole@insight.rr.com
Web Site: www.capital.edu/acad/cons/erly/earlymusic.htm
Officers:
President & CEO: Denvy A Bowman

Management:
Program Director: Katherine Wolfe
Dean of the College: Cedric Adderley
Paid Staff: 1
Volunteer Staff: 20
Paid Artists: 30
Budget: $20,000-35,000
Performs At: Mees Hall; Capital University; Huntington Recital Hall

5329
JEFFERSON ACADEMY OF MUSIC
OSU School of Music
1866 College Road
Columbus, OH 43210
Phone: 614-292-2693
Fax: 614-292-1102
e-mail: jeffacad@osu.edu
Web Site: music.osu.edu
Management:
Executive Director: Ruth Triplett Haddock
Founded: 1979
Specialized Field: Series & Festivals; Instrumental Music; Vocal Music; Youth; Dance
Status: Non-Profit, Professional
Paid Staff: 18
Paid Artists: 18
Budget: $10,000-20,000
Performs At: Battle Fine Arts Center; Children's Hospital Auditorium

5330
MUSIC IN THE AIR
549 Franklin Avenue
Columbus, OH 43215
Phone: 614-645-7995
Fax: 614-645-6278
e-mail: mita@columbus.gov
Web Site: www.musicintheair.org
Management:
Executive Director: Wayne A Roberts
Managing Director: Karen Wiser
Mission: Presents a variety of musicians and performers with four summer music series and Festival Latino. All performances are free.
Founded: 1973
Specialized Field: Present Festivals and Performances in Columbus
Status: Non-Profit, Professional
Paid Staff: 5
Paid Artists: 150
Budget: 450,000
Performs At: Outdoor Amphitheater; Mobile Stage Van
Annual Attendance: 200,000
Seating Capacity: 5,000
Rental Contact: Karen Wiser

5331
SHORT NORTH PERFORMING ARTS ASSOCIATION
1187 Noth High Sl
Columbus
Columbus, OH 43201
Phone: 614-291-5854
Fax: 614-291-5854
e-mail: stageleft@shortnorthstage.org
Web Site: www.shortnorthstage.org
Officers:
President: Peter Yockel
Secretary: Cathy Huston
Treasurer: Anita St. John
Management:
Artistic Director: Steve Rosenberg

Mission: To present the finest chamber and folk music and to provide after school programs in music to inner city children.
Utilizes: Guest Directors; Instructors; Multimedia; Original Music Scores
Founded: 1983
Specialized Field: Instrumental Music
Status: Nonprofit
Paid Staff: 2
Volunteer Staff: 1
Budget: $50,000-70,000
Income Sources: Ticket sales, grants, sponsorships, contributions
Performs At: Short North Tavern; Little Brothers; Greek Orthodox Church

5332
TRIUNE CONCERT SERIES
St John'S Evangelical Church
59 E Mound Street
Columbus, OH 43215
Phone: 614-224-8634
Fax: 614-224-6375
Web Site: www.stjohnschurchcolumbus.org
Management:
Minister of Music: Mary Schwarz
Budget: $10,000
Seating Capacity: 1,000

5333
WOMEN IN MUSIC: COLUMBUS
PO Box 14722
Columbus
Columbus, OH 43214
Phone: 614-263-1263
Fax: 614-263-1263
e-mail: info@womeninmusiccolumbus.com
Web Site: womeninmusiccolumbus.com
Officers:
President: Jan Ryan
Vice President: Kim Kramer
Secretary: Mary Anne Christman
Treasurer: Meredith Wolfe
Performs At: Mees Hall; Huntington Recital Hall

5334
DAYTON'S JAZZ AT THE BEND FESTIVAL
City of Dayton
216 N Main Street
Dayton, OH 45402
Phone: 937-223-2489
Fax: 937-223-0795
e-mail: ccultural2@aol.com
Management:
President: Carol Sampson
Executive Director: Cathy Shanklin
Artistic And Festival Director: Walter Williams
Founded: 1996
Specialized Field: Series & Festivals; Cultural Events; Vocal Music; Theatre; Youth; Dance; Ethnic Performances
Status: Non-Profit, Professional
Paid Staff: 5

5335
THE WRIGHT STATE UNIVERSITY NUTTER CENTER
3640 Colonel Glenn Highway
Suite 430
Dayton, OH 45435-0001

Phone: 937-775-3498
Fax: 937-775-2060
e-mail: nutterguest@wright.edu
Web Site: www.nuttercenter.com
Management:
  Executive Director: Jim Brown
  Assistant Director: John Cox
  Marketing Manager: Misty Cox
  Business Manager: Becky Sparks
  General Manager: John McDufford
Founded: 1990
Specialized Field: Series & Festivals; Music Concerts; Sports (Hockey & Basketball)
Status: Professional
Paid Staff: 24
Performs At: Arena
Facility Category: Arena
Type of Stage: Stage Right
Seating Capacity: 11500
Year Built: 1990

5336
SOIREES MUSICALES PIANO SERIES
834 Riverview Terrace
Dayton, OH 45407-2433
Phone: 937-228-5802
Fax: 937-228-2380
e-mail: hagpia@riva.net
Web Site: www.soireesmusicales.com
Management:
  Founder and Director: Donald C Hageman
Founded: 1969
Specialized Field: Series & Festivals: Piano Recitals
Status: Non-Profit, Professional
Paid Artists: 5
Budget: $10,000-20,000
Performs At: Shiloh Church

5337
UNIVERSITY OF DAYTON ARTS SERIES
University of Dayton
300 College Park
Dayton, OH 45469-1494
Phone: 937-229-2787
Fax: 937-229-4638
e-mail: info@udayton.edu
Web Site: www.udayton.edu/artssciences/artsseries/
Officers:
  President: Dr. Daniel J. Curran
Management:
  Director, Arts Series: Eileen Carr
Mission: To present an annual performing arts series to campus and community.
Utilizes: Collaborations; Dance Companies; Dancers; Educators; Five Seasonal Concerts; Guest Accompanists; Guest Musical Directors; Guest Musicians; Guest Soloists; Instructors; Local Artists; Multimedia; Original Music Scores; Playwrights; Sign Language Translators; Singers; Soloists; Special Technical Talent; Theatre Companies; Touring Companies
Founded: 1961
Specialized Field: Series and Festivals; Instrumental Music; Vocal Music; Theatre; Dance; Ethnic Performances
Status: Non-Profit, Professional
Paid Staff: 1
Budget: $60,000
Income Sources: Ohio Arts Council; Box Office; Montgomery County; University Subsidy
Performs At: Boll Theatre
Annual Attendance: 2,000
Facility Category: Theater
Seating Capacity: 378

Organization Type: Performing; Sponsoring

5338
VANGUARD CONCERTS
5335 Far Hills Avenue
Suite 304
Dayton, OH 45429
Phone: 937-434-6902
Fax: 937-434-6903
e-mail: vanguard@woh.rr.com
Management:
  Director: Elana Bolling
Utilizes: Guest Musical Directors; Guest Musicians; Multimedia
Founded: 1961
Specialized Field: Series & Festivals: Chamber Music Series
Status: Non-Profit, Professional
Paid Staff: 3
Budget: $20,000-35,000
Performs At: Dayton Art Institute

5339
WRIGHT STATE UNIVERSITY ARTIST SERIES
3640 Colonel Glenn Highway
Dayton
Dayton, OH 45435
Phone: 937-775-2346
Fax: 937-775-3786
e-mail: music@wright.edu
Web Site: www.wright.edu/academics/music
Management:
  Manager: Alison Y Schray
Specialized Field: Series &Festivals; Classical Music; Concerts
Status: Non-Profit; Professional
Budget: $20,000-35,000
Performs At: Creative Arts Center Concert Hall

5340
MIDAMERICA CHAMBER MUSIC FESTIVAL
Marblecliffchambertplayers
c/o Dept Of Music Ohio Wesleyan University
Delaware, OH 43015
Phone: 614-261-7903
Fax: 740-368-3723
e-mail: mccp@marblecliffchamberplayers.org
Web Site: www.owu.edu/~machmi
Management:
  Artistic Director: Charles Wetherbee
  Director: Charles Wetherber
Founded: 1995
Specialized Field: Music
Paid Staff: 2
Paid Artists: 8

5341
OHIO WESLEYAN UNIVERSITY PERFORMING ARTS SERIES
Sanborn Hall
23 Elizabeth Street
Delaware, OH 43015
Phone: 740-368-3629
Fax: 740-368-3723
e-mail: paseries@owu.edu
Web Site: pas.owu.edu/
Officers:
  President: Mark Huddleston
Management:
  Concert Chairman: Nancy Gamso
Founded: 1856

Specialized Field: Liberal Arts
Status: For-Profit, Professional
Paid Staff: 7
Budget: $20,000-35,000
Performs At: Gray Chapel

5342
LORAIN COUNTY COMMUNITY COLLEGE: STOCKER ARTS CENTER PROGRAMMING
1005 N Abbe Road
Elyria, OH 44035
Phone: 440-366-4140
Fax: 440-366-4101
Toll-free: 800-995-LCCC
e-mail: kcrooker@lorainccc.edu
Web Site: www.lorainccc.edu
Officers:
  Chairman: Lawrence Goodman
  Vice Chairman: Benjamin Flinger
Management:
  President: Janet H Barlow
Founded: 1980
Specialized Field: Series & Festivals; Instrumental Music; Vocal Music; Theatre; Youth; Dance; Ethnic Performances
Status: Non-Profit, Non-Professional
Budget: $150,000-400,000
Performs At: Stocker Arts Center

5343
ARTS PARTNERSHIP OF GREATER HANCOCK COUNTY
618 South Main Street
Findlay
Findlay, OH 45840
Phone: 419-422-4624
Fax: 419-424-9103
Toll-free: 800-750-0750
e-mail: boxoffice@artspartnership.com
Web Site: www.artspartnership.com
Officers:
  President: Steve Bihn
  President Elect: Donna Ridenour
  Secretary: Heather Granger
  Treasurer: Nikki Clement
Management:
  Executive Director: Peggy Grandbois
  Operations Director: Desiree Ciraldo
  Event Director: Sarah Foltz
  Education Director: Craig Vanrenterghem
Mission: To offer a variety arts and education programs for all ages.
Utilizes: Artists-in-Residence; Collaborations; Dancers; Educators; Five Seasonal Concerts; Guest Accompanists; Guest Ensembles; Guest Musical Directors; Guest Soloists; Guild Activities; High School Drama; Multimedia; Original Music Scores; Selected Students; Soloists; Special Technical Talent; Theatre Companies
Founded: 1979
Specialized Field: Performing; Educational
Paid Staff: 45
Volunteer Staff: 500
Paid Artists: 20
Budget: $500,000
Income Sources: Box office, grants, private and corporate donations
Performs At: Several Facilities but primarily Auditorium
Annual Attendance: 5,000
Facility Category: Auditorium
Type of Stage: Proscenium
Stage Dimensions: 56x23

SERIES & FESTIVALS / Ohio

Seating Capacity: 1418
Year Built: 1940
Year Remodeled: 1987
Cost: @$1000 per day
Rental Contact: 419-425-8257 Kelly Fletcher

5344
DENISON UNIVERSITY VAIL SERIES
100 West College Street
Granville
Granville, OH 43023
Phone: 614-587-0525
Fax: 614-587-6602
e-mail: wales@denison.edu
Web Site: vailseries.org
Management:
    Director: Lorraine Wales

5345
MIAMI UNIVERSITY: HAMILTON ARTIST SERIES
1601 University Boulevard
Hamilton, OH 45011
Phone: 513-785-3264
Fax: 513-785-3145
e-mail: epsteihr@muohio.edu
Web Site: www.regionals.miamioh.edu
Management:
    Artistic Director: Howard Epsteis
Founded: 1968
Specialized Field: Music
Status: Non-Profit, Professional
Paid Staff: 1
Paid Artists: 9
Budget: $20,000-35,000
Performs At: Parrish Auditorium

5346
HIRAM COLLEGE CONCERT & ARTIST SERIES
11715 Garfield Road
PO Box 67
Hiram, OH 44234
Phone: 330-569-3211
Fax: 330-569-5479
e-mail: willsoneb@hiram.edu
Web Site: www.hiram.edu
Officers:
    President: Thomas V Chema
Management:
    President: Tom Chema
Specialized Field: Community
Status: Non-Profit, Non-Professional
Paid Staff: 2
Budget: $10,000-20,000
Performs At: Hayden Auditorium

5347
FOOTHILLS ART FESTIVAL, SOUTHERN HILLS ARTS COUNCIL
Box 149
Jackson, OH 45640
Phone: 740-286-6355
Fax: 740-286-6355
e-mail: shac@zoomnet.net
Management:
    President: Maxine Plummer
    Executive Director: Barbara Summers
    Artistic Director: Barbara Summers
    Managing Director: Barbara Summers
Mission: Southern Hius Arts Council is Renovating a 1930 Art Deco movie house for live performances until it is ready we have 3 musical presentation per year during the festival-3rd weekend in October.
Specialized Field: Visual Performance and Musical arts
Status: Non-Profit, Non-Professional
Paid Staff: 2

5348
KENT/BLOSSOM MUSIC, KENT STATE UNIVERSITY
E101 M&S,
PO Box 5190
Kent, OH 44242
Phone: 330-672-2613
Fax: 330-672-7837
e-mail: kbm@kent.edu
Web Site: dept.kent.edu/blossom
Management:
    Director: Jerome Lacorte
Mission: Six-week summer program for young musicians embarking on professional careers for the intensive study and performance of chamber music with principles/members of The Cleveland Orchestra and other visiting artists Scholarship.
Founded: 1968
Specialized Field: Education-Chamber Music Summer (Advanced Training Institute)
Status: Non-Profit, Professional
Paid Staff: 2
Paid Artists: 30
Affiliations: The Cleveland Orchestra; Blossom Music Center

5349
KENTFEST
PO Box 248
Kent, OH 44240-0237
Phone: 330-673-1599
Officers:
    Chairman: Mary Drongowski

5350
LAKESIDE CHATAUQUA
236 Walnut Avenue
Lakeside, OH 43440
Phone: 419-798-4461
Fax: 419-798-5033
e-mail: schedule@lakesideohio.com
Web Site: www.lakesideohio.com
Officers:
    President/CEO: Kevin Sibbring
    Vice President of Accounting: Sylvia Chappell
    Chief Financial Officer: Daniel Dudley
    Vice President of Programming: Shirley Stary
    Vice President of Facilities: Dave Geyer
Management:
    Director of Guest Services: Mary Ann Hirsch
    Director of Hospitality: Steve Koenig
    Director of Conference: Amber LeSage
    Director of Marketing: Alexandrea Stelzer
    Director of Educational Programming: Jeanne Mauriocourt
Mission: To establish and maintain schools, conferences, institutes, lecture courses and other means of aesthetic culture.
Utilizes: Guest Artists
Founded: 1873
Specialized Field: Dance; Vocal Music; Instrumental Music; Theater
Status: Professional; Nonprofit; Commercial
Performs At: Auditorium
Type of Stage: Proscenium
Seating Capacity: 2,900
Year Built: 1929
Organization Type: Sponsoring

5351
CLEVELAND SHAKESPEARE FESTIVAL
2843 Washington Blvd
Cleveland
Lakewood, OH 44118
Phone: 216-732-3311
Toll-free: 877-280-1646
e-mail: info@cleveshakes.org
Web Site: www.cleveshakes.com
Officers:
    Chair: Rodger M Govea
    Vice Chairman: Larry Nehring
Management:
    Operations Director: Brian Pedaci
    Board Secretary: Kristina Hewis
    Theatre Artist: Christine McBurney
Mission: Committed to producing the plays of Shakespeare in the way that the author intened—fun, at the speed of thought, and in the midst of a vibrant community. To that end, they are committed to free admission, a festive atmosphere, and an earned attention to the work of the play.
Specialized Field: Free Outdoor Summer Festival

5352
LANCASTER FESTIVAL
127 West Wheeling Street
Lancaster, OH 43130
Phone: 740-687-4808
Fax: 740-687-1980
Toll-free: 800-LAN-FEST
e-mail: lanfest@lanfest.org
Web Site: www.lanfest.org
Officers:
    President: Mina Ubbing
    Vice President: Benjy Uhl
    Treasurer: Jennifer Walters
    Secretary: Jennifer D'Onofrio
Management:
    Artistic Director: Gary Sheldon
    Executive Director: Lou Ross
    Office Administration: Carol Shofner
    Finance and Funding: Jennifer Walters
    Orchestra Manager: Steve Rosenberg
Utilizes: Actors; Artists-in-Residence; Choreographers; Collaborating Artists; Collaborations; Commissioned Composers; Commissioned Music; Curators; Dance Companies; Dancers; Fine Artists; Grant Writers; Guest Accompanists; Guest Artists; Guest Choreographers; Guest Companies; Guest Directors; Guest Instructors; Guest Musical Directors; Guest Musicians; Instructors; Local Artists; Lyricists; Multimedia; Organization Contracts; Original Music Scores; Playwrights; Poets; Sign Language Translators; Singers; Soloists; Student Interns; Special Technical Talent; Theatre Companies; Touring Companies
Founded: 1985
Specialized Field: Orchestra; Pops; Chamber; Various
Status: Non-Profit, Professional
Paid Staff: 1
Volunteer Staff: 300
Paid Artists: 65
Budget: $800,000
Income Sources: Grants; Individual & Corporate Donations; Ticket Sales
Affiliations: Ohio Citizens For The Arts
Annual Attendance: 50,000
Facility Category: Indoor/Outdoor Festival
Stage Dimensions: 40'x60'

SERIES & FESTIVALS / Ohio

5353
COUNCIL FOR THE ARTS OF GREATER LIMA
130 W Elm Street
PO Box 1124
Lima, OH 45801
Phone: 419-222-1096
Fax: 419-222-3871
Web Site: www.limaartscouncil.org
Officers:
  President: Greg Phipps
  VP: Mike Hoffman
  Financial Officer: Terry Webb
  Secretary: Brenda Ellis
Management:
  Executive Director: Bart Mills
  Education Director: Sally Windle
  Operations Manager: Chris Craft
Mission: To enrich the quality of life in the Greater Lima community, the Council for the Arts will promote and encourage appreciation, respect and understanding of the arts through advocacy, education and programming.
Utilizes: Artists-in-Residence; Choreographers; Collaborations; Curators; Dance Companies; Dancers; Educators; Fine Artists; Five Seasonal Concerts; Guest Accompanists; Guest Designers; Guest Directors; Guest Ensembles; Guest Instructors; Guest Musical Directors; Guild Activities; Local Artists; Lyricists; Multi Collaborations; Multimedia; Performance Artists; Playwrights; Poets; Resident Artists; Sign Language Translators; Singers; Soloists; Special Technical Talent; Theatre Companies
Founded: 1966
Specialized Field: Dance; Vocal Music; Instrumental Music; Theater; Festivals; Lyric Opera
Status: Nonprofit
Performs At: Civic Center
Organization Type: Educational; Sponsoring

5354
LIVELY ARTS SERIES: PALACE CULTURAL ARTS ASSOCIATION
276 W Center Street
Marion, OH 43302
Phone: 740-383-2101
Fax: 740-387-3425
Web Site: www.marion.net/palace
Management:
  President: Diane Glassmeyer
  Managing Director: Elaine Merchant
Specialized Field: Performing Arts
Status: Non-Profit, Professional
Paid Staff: 8

5355
DRAKE COUNTY CENTER FOR THE ARTS
Medina County Performing Arts Foundation
520 Sycamore Street
Box 718
Medina, OH 45331-0718
Phone: 937-547-0908
e-mail: DCCA@CenterForArts.net
Web Site: www.centerforarts.net
Officers:
  Chairman: Gary Brown
  Vice Chair: Antonia Baker
  Secretary: Kathy Warner
  Treasurer: Becky Luce
Management:
  Executive Director: Andrea Jordan
  Artistic Director: Keith Rawlins
  Marketing Director: Karen Herndon
  Sound Technician: Doug Cole
  Anna Bier Gallery Director: Marcia Weidner
Utilizes: Dance Companies; Fine Artists; Multimedia; Original Music Scores; Selected Students; Theatre Companies
Founded: 1978
Specialized Field: Series and Festivals: Instrumental Music
Status: Non-Profit, Professional
Paid Staff: 3
Paid Artists: 12
Budget: $60,000-150,000
Performs At: Henry St. Clair Memorial Hall
Annual Attendance: 15,000
Type of Stage: Proscenium
Stage Dimensions: 30'x24'x28'
Seating Capacity: 632
Year Built: 1912

5356
MENTOR PERFORMING ARTISTS CONCERT SERIES
6477 Center Street
Mentor, OH 44060
Phone: 440-205-3333
Fax: 440-974-5216
Web Site: www.mentorconcertseries.com
Management:
  Director: Theodore Hieronymus
Budget: $150,000-400,000
Performs At: Mentor Schools Fine Arts Center

5357
MOUNT VERNON NAZARENE COLLEGE: LECTURE ARTIST SERIES
Mount Vernon Nazarene University
800 Martinsburg Road
Mount Vernon, OH 43050
Phone: 740-397-6868
Fax: 740-392-1689
e-mail: bcochran@mvnu.edu
Web Site: www.mvnc.edu
Management:
  Dean Of School Of Arts And Humaniti: Dr David Wilke
Utilizes: Actors; Fine Artists; Guest Accompanists; Guest Directors; Guest Instructors; Guest Musical Directors; Guest Musicians; Guest Soloists; Instructors; Multimedia; Sign Language Translators; Special Technical Talent
Founded: 1970
Volunteer Staff: 10
Budget: $10,000-20,000
Income Sources: Institutional budget
Performs At: R.R. Hodges Chapel-Auditorium; Recital Hall-Theater
Annual Attendance: 3,225
Facility Category: 2 Theatres
Seating Capacity: 2,000; 300
Year Built: 1990

5358
OHIO OUTDOOR HISTORICAL DRAMA ASSOCIATION
Trumpet In The Land Outdoor Drama
1600 Trumpet Drive NE
New Philadelphia, OH 44633
Mailing Address: PO Box 450, New Philadelphia, Ohio 44663
Phone: 330-339-1132
Fax: 330-339-8140
e-mail: trumpet@frontier.com
Web Site: www.trumpetintheland.com
Management:
  General Manager: Margaret M Bonamico
  Director: Joseph Bonamico
Mission: To preserve the rich history of the Tuscarawas Valley through the production of an outdoor, symphonic drama and other cultural programs. And to increase opportunities for employment in cultural programs in Mideast Ohio as well as to assist in the development of the economy through the expansion of travel and tourism in Ohio.
Utilizes: Guest Companies; Singers
Founded: 1967
Specialized Field: Musical
Status: Nonprofit
Income Sources: Actors' Equity Association
Performs At: Schoenbrunn Amphitheatre
Facility Category: Outdoor amphitheatre
Seating Capacity: 1200
Organization Type: Educational; Sponsoring

5359
CENTRAL OHIO TECHNICAL COLLEGE
1179 University Drive
Newark, OH 43055-1767
Phone: 740-366-9494
Fax: 740-364-9646
e-mail: webmaster@cotc.edu
Web Site: www.cotc.edu
Officers:
  Chair: Cheryl Snyder
  Vice Chair: John Hinderer
Management:
  Executive Director: Amy Greenland
  Assistant Director: Krista Irmscher
Specialized Field: Series and Festivals; Theatre; Ethnic Performances; Programming for Students
Status: Non-Profit, Non-Professional
Paid Staff: 1
Budget: $10,000-20,000
Performs At: Founders Hall

5360
OBERLIN BAROQUE PERFORMANCE INSTITUTE & FESTIVAL
77 W College Street
Oberlin
Oberlin, OH 44074-1588
Phone: 440-775-8044
Fax: 440-775-6840
e-mail: anna.hoffmann@oberlin.edu
Web Site: www.oberlin.edu/con/summer/bpi
Management:
  Artistic Director: Kenneth Slowik
Founded: 1971
Specialized Field: Series & Festivals; Instrumental Music; Vocal Music; Dance
Status: Non-Profit, Professional
Paid Staff: 25
Paid Artists: 25

5361
OBERLIN COLLEGE CONSERVATORY OF MUSIC ARTIST: RECITAL SERIES
39 W College Street
Oberlin
Oberlin, OH 44074
Phone: 440-775-8474
Fax: 440-775-8942
e-mail: communications@oberlin.edu
Web Site: www.oberlin.edu
Management:
  Assistant Dean: Marci Alegant

SERIES & FESTIVALS / Ohio

Utilizes: Guest Directors; Guest Musical Directors; Multimedia; Singers
Budget: $60,000-150,000
Performs At: Finney Memorial Chapel

5362
MIAMI UNIVERSITY PERFORMING ARTS SERIES
102 Hall Auditorium
Oxford
Oxford, OH 45056
Phone: 513-529-6333
Fax: 513-529-5482
e-mail: performingartsseries@miamioh.edu
Web Site: www.muohio.edu/performingartsseries
Management:
 Executive Director: Patti Hannan Swofford
 Director: Patti Liberatore
 Administrative Assisstant: Pate Rudolph
 Assisstant Director: Lindsay Sheridan
Budget: $150,000-400,000
Performs At: Millett Hall; Gates-Abegglen Theater; Art Museum; Hall Auditorium
Seating Capacity: 730

5363
VALLEY ARTISTS SERIES
University Of Rio Grande
Fine & Performing Arts Center
Rio Grande, OH 45674
Phone: 740-245-7360
Fax: 740-245-7101
Toll-free: 800-282-7201
e-mail: www.gmiler@rio.edu
Management:
 President: Gary Stewart
 Fine and Performing Arts Coordinato: Greg Miller
Founded: 1981
Specialized Field: Series & Festivals; Instrumental Music; Vocal Music; Theatre; Dance; Ethnic Performances; Concerts
Status: Non-Profit, Professional
Paid Staff: 50
Paid Artists: 30
Budget: $20,000-35,000
Performs At: Fine Arts Theater

5364
LANGE TRUST
1402 Columbus Avenue
Sandusky, OH 44870
Phone: 419-625-8312
Fax: 419-625-8380
e-mail: ernst@bex.net
Officers:
 Chairman: Diane Ernst
Mission: To bring events of good quality and variety to the people of our county at no charge.
Utilizes: Collaborations; Dance Companies; Multimedia; Original Music Scores; Theatre Companies
Founded: 1973
Paid Staff: 1
Budget: $50,000
Income Sources: Interest income from the Lange Trust
Performs At: State Theatre
Affiliations: Ohio Arts Presenter Network, Association of Performing Arts Presenters
Facility Category: Renovated Vaudovillle House
Type of Stage: Proscenium
Stage Dimensions: 25x40
Seating Capacity: 1,570
Year Built: 1924

5365
SANDUSKY CONCERT ASSOCIATION
PO Box 1537
Sandusky, OH 44871-1537
Phone: 419-433-2399
e-mail: pedajd@aol.com
Web Site: www.sanduskyconcert.com
Management:
 Talent Coordinator: Paul Dahnke
Founded: 1928
Specialized Field: Series & Festivals; Instrumental Music; Vocal Music; Youth; Dance; Ethnic Performances
Status: Non-Profit, Non-Professional
Budget: $30,000
Income Sources: Tickets sales, local support
Performs At: Sandusky State Theatre & Local Churches
Affiliations: AOR Hearthland

5366
SPRINGFIELD ARTS COUNCIL
117 South Fountain Avenue
P O Box 745
Springfield, OH 45501
Phone: 937-324-2712
Fax: 937-324-3170
Toll-free: 866-324-2712
e-mail: saconline@springfieldartscouncil.org
Web Site: www.springfieldartscouncil.org
Officers:
 President: Debbie LeMelle
 President - Elect: Lisa Dickerson Watson
 Past President: Tim Shepherd
 Treasurer: Thomas T Taylor
 Secretary: Susan Sheridan Smith
Management:
 Director Of Development: William Schwartz
 Executive Director: Chris Moore
 Director Of Finance: Margaret Schief
 Director Of Marketing And Design: Tim Rowe
 Business Manager: Sarah V Michelson
Budget: $60,000-150,000
Performs At: Kuss Auditorium; Clark State Performing Arts Center

5367
SPRINGFIELD ARTS COUNCIL
117 South Fountain Avenue
P O Box 745
Springfield, OH 45501
Phone: 937-324-2712
Fax: 937-324-3170
Toll-free: 866-324-2712
e-mail: saconline@springfieldartscouncil.org
Web Site: www.springfieldartscouncil.org
Officers:
 President: Debbie LeMelle
 President - Elect: Lisa Dickerson Watson
 Past President: Tim Shepherd
 Treasurer: Thomas T Taylor
 Secretary: Susan Sheridan Smith
Management:
 Executive Director: J Chris Moore
 Director Of Marketing And Design: Tim Rowe
 Business Manager: Sarah V Michelson
 Development Manager: Monica M Miller
 Production Manager: Jordan Taylor
Founded: 1967
Specialized Field: Series & Festivals; Instrumental Music; Vocal Music; Theatre; Youth; Dance; Ethnic Performances
Status: Non-Profit, Professional
Paid Staff: 7

5368
ARTS COUNCIL LAKE ERIE WEST
1700 N Reynolds Road
Toledo, OH 43615
Phone: 419-531-2046
Fax: 419-531-5049
Toll-free: 888-297-6645
e-mail: martinnagy@aol.com
Web Site: www.aclew.org
Management:
 President: Hugh Gaylord
 Executive Director: Martin W Nagy
Mission: To support, nourish, and provide for a quality environment for the arts to flourish in our region.
Founded: 1983
Specialized Field: Programs for Children; Paintings; Music
Status: Non-Profit, Professional
Paid Staff: 4
Paid Artists: 4
Budget: $10,000-20,000
Income Sources: Admission; grants; donations; sales
Affiliations: Americans for the Arts
Facility Category: Auditorium
Type of Stage: Proscenium
Stage Dimensions: 16 x 44
Seating Capacity: 800
Year Built: 1920
Year Remodeled: 2001

5369
UPPER ARLINGTON CULTURAL ARTS COMMISSION
3600 Tremont Road
Upper Arlington, OH 43221
Phone: 614-583-5310
Fax: 614-442-3208
Toll-free: 888-722-5845
Web Site: www.ua.ohio.net
Management:
 Arts Manager: Diane Deane
 Arts Coordinator: Lynette Santoro-Au
Mission: Encouraging, promoting and providing cultural opportunities for community enrichment.
Founded: 1972
Specialized Field: Dance; Vocal Music; Instrumental Music; Facility; Theater; Festivals
Status: Nonprofit
Paid Staff: 2
Volunteer Staff: 78
Budget: $82,000
Income Sources: OAC; Ohio Humanities Donations; In Kind
Performs At: Upper Arlington Municipal Center
Annual Attendance: 200-30,000
Facility Category: Schools; City Buildings
Organization Type: Sponsoring

5370
FINE ARTS COUNCIL OF TRUMBULL COUNTY
170 North Park Ave.
PO Box 48
Warren, OH 44482
Phone: 330-719-1199
Fax: 330-399-7710
e-mail: info@TrumbullArts.Org
Web Site: www.trumbullarts.org
Management:
 Executive Director: Bobbie Brown

SERIES & FESTIVALS / Oklahoma

Utilizes: Artists-in-Residence; Multimedia; Selected Students
Founded: 1971
Specialized Field: Arts Council
Status: Non-Profit, Non-Professional
Paid Staff: 1
Budget: $80,000

5371
WARREN CIVIC MUSIC ASSOCIATION
1703 Mahoning Ave
Warren, OH 44483
Phone: 330-399-4885
Fax: 330-393-5348
Web Site: www.warrencivicmusic.com
Officers:
   Talet Chairperson: Jeannine Morris
   President: Jeffrey E Dreves
   Secretary: Roz Jackson
   Treasurer: William J Long
   Assistant Treasurer: Richard A Polko
Management:
   President: Kenneth Matheny
   Artistic Director: Karl Morrs
Mission: Building and maintaining a permanent audience for concerts in Warren and the surrounding areas; cultivating interest in music; encouraging performance by skilled artists.
Founded: 1937
Specialized Field: Series & Festivals; Instrumental Music; Vocal Music; Theatre; Youth; Dance; Ethnic Performances
Status: Non-Profit, Professional
Budget: $60,000-150,000
Income Sources: Ohio Arts Council
Performs At: W.D. Packard Music Hall and Convention Center
Organization Type: Performing; Educational; Sponsoring

5372
OTTERBEIN UNIVERSITY
1 South Grove Street
Westerville
Westerville, OH 43081
Phone: 614-890-3000
Fax: 614-823-1360
e-mail: pkessler@otterbein.edu
Web Site: www.otterbein.edu
Officers:
   Chairman: Mark R Thresher
   Vice Chairman: Peggy M Ruhlin
   Vice Chairman: William E Harrell
   President: Kathy A Krendl
   Secretary: Alec Wightman
Management:
   Executive Director: Patricia Kessler
Budget: $35,000-60,000
Performs At: Cowan Hall

5373
CHAMBER MUSIC CONNECTION
242 Sinsbury Drive North
Worthington, OH 43085-3563
Phone: 614-848-3312
e-mail: artsdir@cmconnection.org
Web Site: www.cmconnection.org
Officers:
   President: Hector Garcia
   Treasurer: Hyacinth Macintosh
   Secretary: Lorrie Hernandez
Management:
   Artistic Director: Deborah Price
Founded: 1992
Specialized Field: Chamber Music
Paid Staff: 3
Volunteer Staff: 5
Paid Artists: 40

5374
WORTHINGTON ARTS COUNCIL
777 Evening Street
Worthington
Worthington, OH 43085
Phone: 614-431-0329
Fax: 614-431-2491
e-mail: arts@mcconnellarts.org
Web Site: www.mcconnellarts.org
Management:
   Executive Director: Jon Cooper
   Director of Operations: Andy Herron
   Director of Programming & outreach: Kendra Roberts
   Operations Assisstant: Brad Grunwell
   Marketing: Jon Boley
Mission: To encourage arts appreciation, awareness and participation in Worthington.
Utilizes: Dance Companies; Dancers; Fine Artists; Guest Accompanists; Instructors; Multi Collaborations; Multimedia; Original Music Scores; Sign Language Translators; Theatre Companies; Touring Companies
Founded: 1977
Specialized Field: Community
Paid Staff: 4
Volunteer Staff: 15
Paid Artists: 4
Budget: $200,000
Income Sources: Grants; Sponserships; Ticket Sales
Performs At: Theaters
Annual Attendance: 4,000
Seating Capacity: 1,174

5375
MONDAY MUSICAL CLUB OF YOUNGSTOWN, OHIO
1000 5th Avenue
Suite 3
Youngstown, OH 44504-1603
Phone: 330-743-2717
Fax: 330-743-3745
e-mail: tickets@mondaymusical.com
Web Site: www.mondaymusical.com
Management:
   President: Jane Evans
   Executive Director: Kathy Doyle
   Artistic Director: Gloria Mosur
Founded: 1896
Specialized Field: Series & Festivals: Concerts
Status: For-Profit, Professional
Paid Staff: 2
Volunteer Staff: 30
Paid Artists: 5
Budget: $60,000-150,000
Performs At: Stambaugh Auditorium
Seating Capacity: 2,535
Year Built: 1926

5376
YOUNGSTOWN STATE UNIVERSITY: DANA CONCERT SERIES
Youngstown University
1 University Plaza
Youngstown, OH 44555
Phone: 330-941-3625
Fax: 330-941-1490
e-mail: mrcrist@ysu.edu
Web Site: web.ysu.edu
Management:
   Coordinator: Michael D Gelfand

5377
ZANESVILLE CONCERT ASSOCIATION
320 Main Street
Zanesville, OH 43701
Phone: 740-452-4325
Fax: 740-453-3103
Web Site: www.zanesvilleconcertassociation.com
Officers:
   President: Michael Abood
   Vice President: Janet Slack
   Secretary: Anna Marie Katt
   Treasurer: Rick Aichele
Management:
   Booking Agent: Carol Boyse
Seating Capacity: 35,000-60,000

Oklahoma

5378
COMMUNITY CONCERTS OF BARTLESVILLE
PO Box 651
Bartlesville, OK 74005
Phone: 918-333-4599
e-mail: Cjswango@aol.com
Officers:
   President: Carol Swango
Budget: $20,000-35,000

5379
OKLAHOMA MOZART INTERNATIONAL FESTIVAL
415 S Dewey
Suite 100
Bartlesville, OK 74003
Phone: 918-333-9900
Fax: 918-336-9525
e-mail: bwilliams@okmozart.com
Web Site: www.okmozart.com
Officers:
   Chairman: Tawny Saddoris
   Vice Chairman: Michel Duncan
Management:
   Executive Director: Ginger Griffen
   Artistic Director: Constantine Kitsopoulos
   Development Director: Amy Livington
Utilizes: Actors; Artists-in-Residence; Collaborations; Commissioned Music; Dance Companies; Fine Artists; Grant Writers; Guest Accompanists; Guest Companies; Guest Composers; Guest Conductors; Guest Directors; Guest Instructors; Guest Musicians; Multi Collaborations; Multimedia; Original Music Scores; Sign Language Translators; Singers; Touring Companies
Founded: 1985
Specialized Field: Dance; Vocal Music; Instrumental Music; Festivals; Grand Opera
Status: Professional; Nonprofit
Paid Staff: 8
Volunteer Staff: 800
Paid Artists: 50
Budget: $890,000
Income Sources: Oklahoma State Arts Council; National Endowment for the Arts; Individuals; Businesses
Performs At: Bartlesville Community Center
Annual Attendance: 30,000
Facility Category: Concert Hall, Community Center
Seating Capacity: 1700
Year Built: 1982

SERIES & FESTIVALS / Oklahoma

Organization Type: Sponsoring
Resident Groups: New York Orchestra

5380
CHISHOLM TRAIL ARTS COUNCIL
810 W. Walnut
Duncan
Duncan, OK 73533-4951
Phone: 580-252-4160
Fax: 580-252-1631
e-mail: ctac@texhoma.net
Web Site: www.chisholmtrailarts.com
Officers:
   President: Loisdawn Jones
   President Elect: Me Lissa Lansford
   Treasurer: Tim Garrett
   Secretary: Lois Wilson
Management:
   President: Gina Flesher
   Executive Director: Darcy Reeves
Mission: To promote the arts in all discipline in the community.
Utilizes: Actors; Artists-in-Residence; Collaborating Artists; Dance Companies; Dancers; Educators; Filmmakers; Fine Artists; Guest Instructors; Guest Soloists; Guild Activities; High School Drama; Instructors; Local Artists; Lyricists; Multimedia; Performance Artists; Playwrights; Poets; Selected Students; Singers; Special Technical Talent; Theatre Companies; Touring Companies
Founded: 1976
Specialized Field: Series & Festivals; Instrumental Music; Vocal Music; Youth; Ethnic Performances
Status: Non-Profit, Professional
Paid Staff: 1
Volunteer Staff: 50
Budget: $60,000-150,000
Income Sources: Public and private support
Performs At: Jack A. Mauer Convention Center
Seating Capacity: 750
Year Built: 1990

5381
CENTRAL OKLAHOMA CONCERT SERIES
PO Box 5272
Edmond, OK 73083
Phone: 405-340-3500
Fax: 405-844-8795
e-mail: janstan@swbell.net
Web Site: www.chopinsociety.com
Management:
   Executive Director: Jan Steele
Founded: 1986
Specialized Field: Series & Festivals: Concert
Status: Non-Profit, Professional
Budget: $20,000-35,000
Performs At: Mitchell Hall UCO Campus

5382
PHILADELPHIA FOUNDATION
1234 Market Street
Suite 1800
Edmond, OK 19107
Phone: 215-563-6417
Fax: 215-563-6882
e-mail: info@pfconcerts.org
Web Site: www.philafound.org
Officers:
   Chair: Lawrence J Beaser
   CEO: Kathleen S Allison
   Treasurer: William C Bullitt
   President: R. Andrew Swinney
Management:
   Concert Series Director: Ryan Malone
   Executive Assisstant: Andrea Congo
   Interactive design Co-ordinator: Danielle Cerceo
   Controller: Mark Froehlick
   Staff Accountant: Mary Feingold
Founded: 1998
Status: Nonprofit
Stage Dimensions: 21x56
Seating Capacity: 900
Year Built: 2001

5383
TRI-STATE MUSIC FESTIVAL
2402 E Maine
P O Box 5908
Enid, OK 73702
Phone: 580-237-4964
Fax: 580-237-1767
e-mail: enidtristate@yahoo.com
Web Site: www.tristatemusicfestival.com
Management:
   President: Jerry Allen
   Executive Director: C W Simmons Jr
   Managing Director: Russell L Wiley
Founded: 1932
Specialized Field: All Kinds of Music
Status: Non-Profit, Non-Professional
Paid Staff: 2

5384
CAMERON UNIVERSITY: LECTURE & CONCERT SERIES
2800 W Gore Boulevard
Lawton Olhahoma
Lawton, OK 73505-6377
Phone: 580-581-2200
Fax: 580-581-2867
e-mail: thescoop@cameron.edu
Web Site: www.cameron.edu
Officers:
   VP for Academic Affairs: Dr Ronna Vanderslice
Management:
   President: Cindy Ross
Founded: 1908
Specialized Field: General University
Status: For-Profit, Professional
Budget: $10,000
Seating Capacity: 500

5385
JAZZ IN JUNE
PO Box 2405
Norman, OK 73070
Phone: 405-325-2222
Fax: 405-325-7129
e-mail: info@jazzinjune.org
Web Site: www.jazzinjune.org
Management:
   Managing Director: Karen Holp
   Director of Development: Norman H Hammon
Mission: To offer Oklahoma residents a jazz festival.
Utilizes: Singers
Founded: 1985
Specialized Field: Series & Festivals; Instrumental Music; Vocal Music; Jazz Concerts
Status: Non-Profit, Professional
Income Sources: American Federation of Musicians
Organization Type: Performing

5386
ARTS COUNCIL OF OKLAHOMA CITY
400 W California
Oklahoma City, OK 73102
Phone: 405-270-4848
Fax: 405-270-4888
e-mail: info@artscouncilokc.com
Web Site: www.artscouncilokc.com
Officers:
   President: Michael Palmer
   First VP: Daniel Adams
   Secretary: Eric Joiner
   Manager of Financial Reporting: Tony LoPresto
   Senior VP: Kati Christ
Management:
   Executive Director: Peter Dolese
   Development Coordinator: Liz Blood
   Operations Manager: Don Busk
   Finance Director: Marie Smith
   Office Manager: Becki Warner
Utilizes: Actors; Collaborations; Dance Companies; Educators; Fine Artists; Guest Artists; Guest Conductors; Guest Lecturers; Instructors; Local Artists; Multimedia; Original Music Scores; Special Technical Talent; Theatre Companies
Founded: 1967
Status: Non-Profit, Non-Professional
Paid Staff: 17
Paid Artists: 144
Income Sources: Grants; Corporate Sponsors; Ticket Sales
Performs At: Stage Center; 400 West Sheridan
Annual Attendance: 44,700
Facility Category: Theatre
Type of Stage: 3/4 Round; Full Round
Seating Capacity: 580; 210
Year Built: 1970
Year Remodeled: 1987
Rental Contact: Kevin Lesley

5387
CHARLIE CHRISTIAN INTERNATIONAL JAZZ FESTIVAL
PO Box 11014
Oklahoma City, OK 73136
Phone: 405-524-3800
Fax: 405-524-3800
Web Site: charliechristianmusicfestival.com
Management:
   President: Fe Burroughs
   Executive Director: Anita G Arnold
Founded: 1971
Specialized Field: Series & Festivals; Instrumental Music; Vocal Music; Theatre; Youth; Dance; Ethnic Performances
Status: Non-Profit, Professional
Paid Staff: 1
Volunteer Staff: 3
Paid Artists: 15

5388
DUSK TILL DAWN BLUES FESTIVAL
701 DC Minner Street
Rentiesville, OK 74459
Phone: 918-473-2411
Fax: 918-473-0033
e-mail: dcminner@windstream.net
Web Site: www.dcminnerblues.com
Management:
   President: Selby Minner
   Executive Director: D C Minner
   Vice President: Pam Sharp
Mission: To showcase the Oklahoma blues tradition, music strong on electric guitars and full bands.
Founded: 1988
Specialized Field: Series & Festivals; Vocal Music; Youth; Dance; Ethnic Performances; Band Music
Status: Non-Profit, Professional

SERIES & FESTIVALS / Oregon

Volunteer Staff: 60
Paid Artists: 200

5389
OKLAHOMA BAPTIST UNIVERSITY ARTIST SERIES
500 West University
Shawnee
Shawnee, OK 74804
Phone: 405-275-2850
Fax: 405-878-2328
Toll-free: 800-654-3285
e-mail: paul.hammond@okbu.edu
Web Site: www.okbu.edu
Management:
  President: David Whitlock
  Dean: Paul Hammond
  Executive Secretary: Nancy Deichman
  Director of Executive Offfices: Tonia Kellogg
Utilizes: Guest Directors; Guest Musicians; Multimedia; Singers
Founded: 1910
Specialized Field: Series & Festivals; Instrumental Music; Vocal Music; Chamber Music; Solo Recitals
Status: Non-Profit, Non-Professional
Paid Staff: 2
Budget: 20,000
Performs At: Yarborough Auditorium
Facility Category: Recital Hall
Seating Capacity: 2,000/400
Year Built: 1963
Year Remodeled: 2000

5390
OKLAHOMA STATE UNIVERSITY ALLIED ARTS
Oklahoma State University
058 Student Union
Stillwater, OK 74078
Phone: 405-744-7509
Fax: 405-744-2680
e-mail: allied.arts@okstate.edu
Web Site: alliedarts.okstate.edu
Management:
  Special Events Coordinator: Brandon Mitts
  Ticketing/Marketing Manager: Meghann O'Harrah
  Coordinator: Brandon Mitts
  Administrative Assisstant: Meghann O Harrah
Mission: Cultural and educational programming presentation.
Utilizes: Actors; Dance Companies; Dancers; Guest Directors; Guest Musical Directors; Guest Musicians; Multimedia; Original Music Scores; Sign Language Translators; Singers; Special Technical Talent; Theatre Companies
Founded: 1922
Specialized Field: Series and Festivals; Instrumental Music; Vocal Music; Dance; Ethnic Performances
Status: Non-Profit; Educational
Paid Staff: 2
Volunteer Staff: 2
Budget: $60,000-82,000
Income Sources: Student Fees; Ticket Sales; Grants
Performs At: MB Seretean Center Concert Hall
Affiliations: APAP; SWPAP
Facility Category: Concert Hall
Type of Stage: Proscenium
Stage Dimensions: 38x44
Seating Capacity: 801

5391
NORTHEASTERN OKLAHOMA STATE UNIVERSITY ALLIED ARTS SERIES
College of Liberal Arts
Tahlequah, OK 74464
Phone: 918-456-5511
Fax: 918-458-2348
Toll-free: 800-722-9614
e-mail: nsuinfo@nsuok.edu
Web Site: www.nsuok.edu
Officers:
  Series Chairperson: Dr. Kathryn Robinson
  President: Dr Steve Turner
  VP Student Affairs: Dr Laura Boren
  VP Business & Finance: David Koehn
  Assisstant VP: Sue Catron
Management:
  Dean: Paul Westbrooke
  Director Human Resource: Dr Matha Albin
  Director Career Service: Gayle Anderson
  Director Public Safety: Patti D Buhl
  Director Athetics: Tony Duckworth
Specialized Field: Series and Festivals; Instrumental Music; Vocal Music; Theatre; Ethnic Performances
Status: Non-Profit, Non-Professional
Paid Staff: 100
Budget: $10,000-20,000

5392
CONCERTIME
11317 E 4th Street
Tulsa, OK 74128-2006
Phone: 918-438-2582
Fax: 918-437-1848
e-mail: organist@mciworld.com
Web Site: www.webtek.com/concertime
Management:
  Manager: Alta Selvey
Budget: $20,000-35,000
Performs At: Patti Johnson Wilson Hall; Philbrook Museum

5393
LIGHT OPERA OKLAHOMA - LOOK
2210 South Main
Tulsa, OK 74114
Phone: 918-583-4267
Fax: 918-583-1780
e-mail: eric@lightoperaok.org
Web Site: looktheatre.org
Officers:
  President: Susan Young
  VP Finance: Sara Arnold
  VP Human Resource: Polly Bowen
  VP Finance: David Emanuel
  VP Special Events: Calvin Moniz
Management:
  President: Jason McIntoch
  Artistic Director: Eric Gibson
  Artistic Director Emeritus/Founder: John Everitt
  Attorney: Caroline Abbott
Mission: To preserve and create awareness of the musical comedy/operetta art form by producing a festival of such every summer in Tulsa, OK.
Founded: 1983
Specialized Field: Series & Festival; Musical Theatre; Opera
Status: Non-Profit, Professional
Paid Staff: 3
Volunteer Staff: 10
Paid Artists: 100
Non-paid Artists: 10
Budget: $300,000-350,000
Income Sources: Foundations; Corporations
Performs At: University of Tulsa School of Theatre
Annual Attendance: 6000-7500
Seating Capacity: 375

5394
TULSA PERFORMING ARTS CENTER TRUST
110 E 2nd Street
Tulsa, OK 74103-3212
Phone: 918-596-7122
Fax: 918-596-7144
Toll-free: 800-364-7111
e-mail: shirleyelliott@ci.tulsa.ok.us
Web Site: www.tulsapac.com
Management:
  Executive Director: John E Scott
  PAC Assisstant Director: Janet Rockefeller
Founded: 1977
Specialized Field: Entertainment; Performing Arts
Status: Non-Profit, Professional
Paid Staff: 33

5395
TULSA PERFORMING ARTS CENTER TRUST
110 E 2nd Street
Tulsa, OK 74103-3212
Phone: 918-596-7122
Fax: 918-596-7144
Toll-free: 800-364-7111
e-mail: tgrufik@ci.tulsa.ok.us
Web Site: www.tulsapac.com
Management:
  Program Director: Terry Grufik
  PAC Assisstant Director: Janet Rockefeller
Budget: $150,000-400,000
Performs At: Chapman Music Hall; Williams Theatre; Doenges Theatre

Oregon

5396
CHILDREN'S PERFORMING ARTS SERIES
Albany Parks & Recreation
333 Broadalbin Street SW
Albany, OR 97321-2247
Phone: 541-917-7500
Fax: 541-917-7776
Toll-free: 800-735-2900
Web Site: www.cityofalbany.net/parks
Management:
  Director Of Parks & Recreation: Ed Hodney
Founded: 1978
Specialized Field: Childrens Performance
Status: Non-Profit, Professional
Paid Staff: 8
Paid Artists: 6
Budget: $10,000
Performs At: Linn Benton Community College Forum

5397
CITY OF ALBANY PARKS AND RECREATION DEPARTMENT
433 SW 4th Avenue
Albany, OR 97321
Phone: 541-917-7777
Fax: 514-917-7776
Management:
  Director: Dave Clark
  Program Coordinator: Sherry Halligan

SERIES & FESTIVALS / Oregon

Mission: To offer an outdoor concert series in summer at no cost, as well as a concert series for children.
Utilizes: Singers
Founded: 1983
Specialized Field: Vocal Music; Instrumental Music; Festivals
Status: For-Profit, Non-Professional
Organization Type: Sponsoring

5398
RIVER RHYTHMS
Albany Parks & Recreation
333 Broadalbin Street SW
Albany, OR 97321-2247
Phone: 541-917-7500
Fax: 541-917-7776
Toll-free: 800-735-2900
e-mail: jan.taylor@cityofalbany.net
Web Site: www.cityofalbany.net
Management:
   President: Ed Hodney
   Artistic Director: Jan Taylor
   Managing Director: Katie Noofhazar
Mission: To build community.
Founded: 1983
Specialized Field: Series & Festivals: Performance & Concerts
Status: Non-Profit, Professional
Paid Staff: 16
Volunteer Staff: 12
Paid Artists: 7

5399
ASHLAND FOLK MUSIC CLUB
PO Box 63
Ashland, OR 97520-0003
Phone: 541-488-0679
Fax: 541-552-6693
e-mail: ashlandfolk@iname.com
Web Site: socontra.org
Officers:
   President: Jay Michalson
   VP: Gordon Enns
Mission: Supporting traditional music and dance.
Founded: 1984
Specialized Field: Dance; Vocal Music; Instrumental Music
Status: Nonprofit
Volunteer Staff: 8
Performs At: Carpenter Hall
Organization Type: Performing; Sponsoring

5400
OREGON SHAKESPEAREAN FESTIVAL ASSOCIATION
15 S Pioneer Street
PO Box 158
Ashland, OR 97520
Phone: 541-482-2111
Fax: 541-482-0446
Toll-free: 800-219-8161
Web Site: www.osfashland.org
Management:
   President: Chuck Butler
   VP: Nancy Tait
   Artistic Director: Libby Appel
   Treasurer: Dan Thorndike
Mission: To create bold new interpretations of contemporary and classic plays in repertory, influenced by American diversity and inspired by the high standard of Shakespeare.
Utilizes: Guest Companies; Singers
Founded: 1935
Status: Professional; Nonprofit
Paid Staff: 450
Volunteer Staff: 750
Budget: $17.1 million
Season: June - August
Performs At: Angus Bowmer Theatre; Black Swan; Elizabethan Theatre
Affiliations: Actors' Equity Association; ATA; University/Resident Theatre Association; Theatre Communications Group
Annual Attendance: 375,000+
Type of Stage: Thrust Stage; Black Box; Outdoors
Seating Capacity: 601; 250; 1188
Organization Type: Performing; Touring; Resident; Educational

5401
CASCADE FESTIVAL OF MUSIC
505 NW Franklin Avenue
Bend, OR 97701
Phone: 541-382-8381
Fax: 541-388-2814
Toll-free: 888-545-7435
e-mail: musicinfo@cascademusic.org
Web Site: www.cascademusic.org
Management:
   President: Kay Lucas
   Executive Director: Sally Russenberger
   Artistic Director: Murry Sidlan
   Business Manager: Cindy Sundquist
Mission: Classical music event in Central Oregon as an eight day festival in late August
Founded: 1981
Specialized Field: Classical
Status: Non-Profit, Professional
Paid Staff: 4
Volunteer Staff: 200
Paid Artists: 90
Performs At: Tent
Annual Attendance: 7,000 - 8,000

5402
OREGON COAST MUSIC FESTIVAL
235 Anderson Avenue
Coos Bay
Coos Bay, OR 97420
Phone: 541-267-0938
Fax: 541-267-0938
Toll-free: 877-897-9350
e-mail: info@oregoncoastmusic.com
Web Site: www.oregoncoastmusic.com
Officers:
   Co-President: Linnae Beechly
   Co-President: Kathy Metzger
   Co-President: Sally Harrold
   Co-President: Gail Virgili
   Treasurer: Deryl Beebe
Management:
   President: Jane Hooper
   Music Director: James Paul
   Director: Deb Wright
   Director: Sue Cameron
   Director: Tricia Miller
Mission: To present an annual Classical Music festival of the highest professional caliber and to support a wide range of year-round musical performances and educational activities.
Founded: 1979
Specialized Field: Series & Festivals; Instrumental Music; Vocal Music; Youth; Ethnic Performances; Live Music
Status: Non-Profit, Professional
Paid Artists: 100

5403
COQUILLE PERFORMING ARTS
PO Box 53
Coquille, OR 97423
Phone: 541-396-5131
e-mail: rwiese@ucinet.com
Officers:
   President: Rochelle Wiese
Budget: $10,000
Performs At: Sawdust Theatre

5404
CORVALLIS-OREGON STATE UNIVERSITY MUSIC ASSOCIATION
3328 NW Firwood Drive
Corvallis, OR 97330
Phone: 541-737-1879
Fax: 541-346-5764
e-mail: mcclintt@ucs.orst.edu
Web Site: oregonstate.edu
Officers:
   Chairman Program Committee: Thomas C McClintock
   President: Larry Blus
   Treasurer: Len Webber
   Secretary: Midge Mueller
Utilizes: Dancers; Guest Musical Directors; Guest Musicians; Multimedia; Original Music Scores; Sign Language Translators; Singers; Theatre Companies
Founded: 1948
Specialized Field: Classical; Orchestra
Volunteer Staff: 15
Budget: $20,000-35,000
Income Sources: Ticket Sales, Member and Corporate Donations, Foundation Grants
Performs At: Austin Auditorium; LaSells Stewart Center
Annual Attendance: 20,000
Facility Category: Auditorium in Conference Center
Type of Stage: Proscenium
Seating Capacity: 1,200
Year Built: 1981

5405
OREGON BACH FESTIVAL
1257 University of Oregon
Eugene, OR 97403-1257
Phone: 541-346-5666
Fax: 541-346-5669
Toll-free: 800-457-1486
e-mail: bachfest@uoregon.edu
Web Site: oregonbachfestival.com
Officers:
   President & General Director: John Evans
Management:
   Executive Director: H Royce Saltzman
   Artistic Director: Matthew Halls
   Marketing Director: George Evano
   Director Emeritus: Helmuth Rilling
   Director Emeritus: Royce Saltzman
Mission: To offer high quality performances that elevate the spirits of both performers and audiences.
Utilizes: Singers
Founded: 1970
Specialized Field: Choral-Orchestra
Status: Non-Profit, Professional
Paid Staff: 10
Budget: 1.3 Million
Income Sources: Box office; Grants; Private Donations
Performs At: University of Oregon School of Music; Beall Concert
Affiliations: University of Oregon School of Music
Annual Attendance: 33,000

SERIES & FESTIVALS / Oregon

Facility Category: Concert Hall
Type of Stage: Proscenium
Seating Capacity: 2500/550
Organization Type: Performing; Resident; Educational

5406
OREGON FESTIVAL OF AMERICAN MUSIC
The Shedd
868 High Street
Eugene
Eugene, OR 97401
Mailing Address: PO Box 1497, Eugene, OR. 97440
Phone: 541-687-6526
Fax: 541-687-1589
Toll-free: 800-248-1615
e-mail: info@theshedd.net
Web Site: www.theshedd.org
Management:
  President: Jim Ralph
  Executive Director: James Ralph
Mission: Year-round production and presenting of American music genres.
Founded: 1991
Specialized Field: Series & Festivals; Instrumental Music; Vocal Music; Youth; Dance
Status: Non-Profit, Professional
Paid Staff: 16

5407
UNIVERSITY OF OREGON CHAMBER MUSIC SERIES
US School of Music and Dance
1225 University of Oregon
Eugene, OR 97403-1225
Phone: 541-346-3761
Fax: 541-346-5669
e-mail: chambermusic@beall/ jjs@oregon.uoregon.edu
Web Site: music.uoregon.edu/cmb
Officers:
  President: Larry Blus
  Treasurer: Len Webber
  Secretary: Midge Mueller
Management:
  Director: Janet J. Stewart
  Chairman Program Committee: Thomas McClintock
Mission: To present the highest quality of chamber music possible in the Eugene-Springfield area with attention to a wide range of repertoire and genres that will enhance the educational missions of the University of Oregon School of Music and Dance and the Oregon Bach Festival.
Founded: 1974
Specialized Field: Chamber Music
Status: Non-Profit, Professional
Paid Staff: 8
Budget: $75,000
Income Sources: Ticket Revenues; Sponsorships; Private Philanthropy; University Support
Performs At: Concert Hall
Affiliations: University Of Oregon; School Of Music And Dance; Oregon Bach Festival
Annual Attendance: 3,000
Seating Capacity: 540
Year Built: 1921

5408
MT. HOOD COMMUNITY COLLEGE
26000 SE Stark Street
Gresham
Gresham, OR 97030
Phone: 503-491-6422
Fax: 503-491-6077
Web Site: www.mhcc.edu
Management:
  President: Robert Silverman
Founded: 1968
Specialized Field: Junior College
Status: Non-Profit, Non-Professional
Budget: $10,000

5409
KLAMATH COMMUNITY CONCERTS
PO Box 1214
Klamath Falls, OR 97601
Phone: 541-850-1290
Fax: 541-273-0497
e-mail: kccaklamathfalls@aol.com
Web Site: www.kcca.us
Officers:
  President: Susan Fortune
Management:
  President: Lynne D Dalla
Founded: 1936
Specialized Field: Series and Festivals; Instrumental Music; Vocal Music; Theatre; Dance
Status: Non-Profit, Professional
Budget: $20,000-35,000
Performs At: Ross Ragland Theater

5410
EASTERN OREGON STATE COLLEGE PERFORMING ARTS PROGRAM
Student Activities Office
1 University Boulevard, Hoke Center, Suite 32
La Grande, OR 97850-2899
Phone: 541-962-3704
Fax: 541-962-1849
e-mail: ese@eou.edu
Management:
  ESE Director: Shean Lattin
  Student Activities Director: Jeff Dunbar
Specialized Field: Series & Festivals; Instrumental Music; Vocal Music; Theater; Dance
Status: Non-Profit, Professional
Paid Staff: 7
Paid Artists: 9
Budget: $10,000
Performs At: Inlow Hall; Loso Hall

5411
LAKE OSWEGO FESTIVAL OF THE ARTS
368 S State Street
PO Box 385
Lake Oswego, OR 97034
Phone: 503-635-3901
Fax: 503-635-2002
Web Site: www.lakewood-center.org
Officers:
  President: Michelle Dorman
  Treasurer: Don Irving
Management:
  Director: Dean Denton
  Director: Andrew Edwards
Founded: 1962
Specialized Field: Art
Status: Non-Profit
Paid Staff: 1
Volunteer Staff: 22
Budget: $150,000
Income Sources: Gifts; Grants; Commisions
Annual Attendance: 22,000
Facility Category: Arts Center and Park
Type of Stage: Outdoor
Seating Capacity: 500-1,000

5412
CASCADE HEAD MUSIC FESTIVAL
PO Box 752
1226 SW 13Th
Lincoln City, OR 97367
Phone: 541-994-9994
Toll-free: 877-994-5333
Web Site: www.cascadeheadmusic.org
Management:
  Music Director: Sergiu Luca
  Manager: Mark Imscher
Founded: 1986
Paid Staff: 1

5413
MARYLHURST UNIVERSITY MUSIC DEPARTMENT
17600 Pacific Highway
PO Box 261
Marylhurst, OR 97036-0261
Phone: 503-636-8141
Fax: 503-636-9982
Toll-free: 800-634-9982
e-mail: admissions@marylhurst.edu
Web Site: www.marylhurst.edu
Officers:
  Chair: Andrew MacRitchie
  President: Dr. Jerry Hudson
  Secretary-Treasurer: Xandra McKeown
Management:
  President: Nancy Wilgendusch
  Department Head of Music: George Paul
Utilizes: Collaborations; Guest Accompanists; Guest Companies; Guest Ensembles; Guest Musical Directors; Guest Musicians; Guest Soloists; Guest Teachers; Instructors; Local Artists; Multimedia; Original Music Scores; Playwrights; Sign Language Translators; Singers; Soloists
Specialized Field: Series and Festivals; Instrumental Music; Vocal Music; Youth; Music Therapy
Status: Non-Profit, Non-Professional
Paid Staff: 3
Performs At: St. Anne's Chapel; Wiegand Recital Hall
Annual Attendance: 1,000
Facility Category: Chapel
Seating Capacity: 325
Cost: $690/day

5414
BRITT FESTIVALS
216 W.Main Street
Medford, OR 97501
Mailing Address: PO Box 1124, Medford, OR 97501
Phone: 541-779-0847
Fax: 541-776-3712
Toll-free: 800-882-7488
e-mail: info@brittfest.org
Web Site: www.brittfest.org
Officers:
  President & CEO: Donna Briggs
Management:
  Development & Sales Associate: Bobby Abernathy
  Box Office Manager: Marie Carbone
  Marketing Director: Sara King Cole
  Director of House Operations: Bow Seltzer
  Development Associate: Mark Knipple
  Director of Performing Arts: Angela Warren
Mission: To present and sponsor, in Southern Oregon, performing arts of the highest quality for the education, enrichment and enjoyment of all.
Utilizes: Guest Artists; Guest Companies
Founded: 1963

SERIES & FESTIVALS / Oregon

Specialized Field: Series & Festival; Live Music; Country Music
Status: Non-Profit, Professional
Paid Staff: 12
Volunteer Staff: 600
Performs At: The Britt Gardens
Annual Attendance: 70,000
Facility Category: Outdoor Amphitheatre
Seating Capacity: 2200
Year Built: 1963
Year Remodeled: 1992
Organization Type: Performing; Touring; Resident; Educational; Sponsoring

5415
WESTERN OREGON UNIVERSITY EDGAR H SMITH FINE ARTS SERIES
345 N Monmouth Avenue
Monmouth, OR 97361
Phone: 503-838-8000
Fax: 503-838-8880
Toll-free: 877-877-1593
e-mail: las@wou.edu
Web Site: www.wou.edu/las
Management:
 President: Dr John P Minahan
 Chair-Division Of Creative Arts: Diane Tarter
Utilizes: Artists-in-Residence; Dance Companies; Dancers; Guest Choreographers; Guest Musical Directors; Multimedia; Original Music Scores; Special Technical Talent
Founded: 1976
Paid Staff: 1
Volunteer Staff: 16
Paid Artists: 4
Budget: $35,000-60,000
Performs At: Rice Auditorium
Facility Category: College Auditorium
Type of Stage: Proscenium
Stage Dimensions: 30 X 55
Seating Capacity: 617

5416
ERNEST BLOCH MUSIC FESTIVAL AT NEWPORT
PO Box 1617
Newport, OR 97365
Phone: 541-574-0614
Fax: 541-265-5008
e-mail: baymusic@newportnet.com
Web Site: www.baymusic.org
Management:
 President: Ken Combs
 Director: Mary Lee Scoville
Founded: 1994

5417
CHAMBER MUSIC NORTHWEST
522 SW 5th Avenue
Suite 920
Portland, OR 97204-2126
Phone: 503-223-3202
Fax: 503-294-1690
e-mail: info@cmnw.org
Web Site: www.cmnw.org
Officers:
 President: Karen Deveney
 Vice President: Ivan Inger
 Secretary: Jacqueline Bloom
 Treasurer: William Langley
 Immediate Past President: Bill Dameron
Management:
 Executive Director: Peter Bilotta

 Artistic Director: David Shifrin
 Finance Director: Katherine King
 Marketing Manager: Garen Horgend
 Box Office Manager: David Tallman
Mission: To present an annual summer music festival (five weeks/25 concerts) with world renowned performers in residence; to present concerts and educational activities on a year-round basis.
Founded: 1971
Specialized Field: Series and Festivals: Chamber Music
Status: Non-Profit, Professional
Paid Staff: 6
Budget: One Million
Performs At: Reed College
Affiliations: Kaul Auditorium at Reed College; Cabell Theatre at Catlin Gabel Schhool
Annual Attendance: 19,000
Facility Category: Concert Hall (private college)
Seating Capacity: 550
Year Built: 1998
Organization Type: Performing

5418
MOUNT HOOD FESTIVAL OF JAZZ: THE GOVERNOR BUILDING
15 NE 3rd
Gresham
Portland, OR 97030
Phone: 503-621-6316
Fax: 503-232-2336
Web Site: www.mthoodjazz.com
Officers:
 President: Susie Jones
 Vice President: Sue O'Halloran
 Secretary: Janine Ross
 Treasurer: KerryAnn O'Halloran
Management:
 Artistic Director: Kyle O Brien

5419
PORTLAND UNIVERSITY PORTLAND INTERNATIONAL: PERFORMANCE FESTIVAL
133 SW Second Avenue
Suite 420
Portland, OR 97204
Phone: 503-228-5299
Fax: 503-725-4840
e-mail: info@pdxjazz.com
Web Site: portlandjazzfestival.org
Management:
 Artistic Director: Michael Griggs
 Managing Director: Don Lucoff
 Operations Manager: Franny Kane
 Production Manager: Alex Donovan
 Ticketing and Membership: Keith Imper

5420
PORTLAND STATE UNIVERSITY PIANO RECITAL SERIES
1620 SW Park Avenue
Lincoln Hall
Portland, OR 97201
Mailing Address: PO Box 751, Portland, OR 97207-0751
Phone: 503-725-3105
Fax: 503-725-3351
Toll-free: 800-547-8887
e-mail: the-arts@pdx.edu
Web Site: www.pdx.edu
Management:
 Executive Director: Pat Zagelow

 Dean: Robert Bucker
Mission: The piano recital series is dedicated to presenting the finest pianists in the world in recital settings and outreach for the purpose of enriching and educating our community.
Utilizes: Guest Directors; Multimedia; Singers
Budget: $200,000
Income Sources: Tickets; Contributions
Performs At: Lincoln Hall Auditorium
Annual Attendance: 6,000
Type of Stage: Proscenium
Seating Capacity: 476

5421
TRIANGLE PRODUCTIONS
8420 SW Canyon Lane #13
Portland, OR 97225
Phone: 503-239-5919
Fax: 503-239-5928
e-mail: trianglepro@juno.com
Web Site: www.tripro.org/general.html
Officers:
 Triangle Productions Board: Lennky Borer
 Board: Dennis Dohtery
 Board: Larry Esau
 Board: Sherman Tam
 Board: Edd Scott
 Board: Donald I Horn
Management:
 Managing Director and Founder: Donald I Horn
Founded: 1989
Opened: 1989
Status: Not-for-profit
Paid Staff: 1
Volunteer Staff: 50
Paid Artists: 40
Performs At: Various
Affiliations: Dramatists Guild

5422
UNIVERSITY OF PORTLAND MUSIC AT MIDWEEK
5000 N Williamette Boulevard
Portland, OR 97203
Phone: 503-943-7228
Fax: 503-943-7399
Toll-free: 800-BAP-ILOT
e-mail: pfa@up.edu
Web Site: college.up.edu
Management:
 Manager: Roger Doyle
Founded: 1901
Specialized Field: Series & Festivals; Instrumental Music; Vocal Music; Theatre; Dance; Ethnic Performances
Status: Non-Profit, Non-Professional

5423
ABBEY BACH FESTIVAL
One Abbey Drive
Saint Benedict, OR 97373
Phone: 503-845-3030
Fax: 503-845-3594
e-mail: info@mountangelabbey.org
Web Site: www.mountangelabbey.org
Officers:
 President: Abbot Gregory Duerr OSB
Management:
 Executive Director: Rev Paschal Cheline OFB
Utilizes: Multimedia; Original Music Scores; Singers
Founded: 1972
Specialized Field: Series & Festivals: Instrumental Music
Status: Non-Profit, Professional

SERIES & FESTIVALS / Pennsylvania

Performs At: Damian Center
Annual Attendance: 1500
Type of Stage: Proscenium
Seating Capacity: 500
Year Built: 1936
Year Remodeled: 1983
Organization Type: Performing

5424
SUNRIVER MUSIC FESTIVAL
PO Box 4308
Sunriver, OR 97707
Phone: 541-593-1084
Fax: 541-593-6959
e-mail: tickets@sunrivermusic.org
Web Site: www.sunrivermusic.org
Officers:
 President: Jim Putney
Management:
 Executive Director: Pamela Beezley
 Office Manager: Vicki Udlock
 Ticket Office Manager: Robin Burford
Mission: To present quality performaces of classical music and support music education programs for the youth of Central Oregon.
Utilizes: Fine Artists; Guest Lecturers; Multimedia; Original Music Scores
Founded: 1971
Specialized Field: Series and Festivals: Classical Music
Status: Non-Profit, Professional
Paid Staff: 3
Volunteer Staff: 4
Budget: $250,000
Income Sources: Private; Business; Grants
Performs At: Great Hall
Annual Attendance: 3,500

5425
YACHATS MUSIC FESTIVAL
2930 Domingo Avenue
Suite 190
Yachats, OR 94705
Phone: 510-845-4444
Fax: 510-549-3504
e-mail: fsa@fsarts.org
Web Site: fsarts.org
Officers:
 President: Kay Adams
 Secretary: Sylvester Brooks
 Treasurer: Anthony Taplin
Management:
 Director: Jesse W Anthony
 Technical Assisstant: William S Kruse
 Assisstant: Barbara A Bauer
Founded: 1981

Pennsylvania

5426
ALLENTOWN COMMUNITY CONCERTS
905 S Cedar Crest Boulevard
Allentown, PA 18103
Phone: 610-432-9143
Officers:
 President: William Lazenberg
Mission: To present four annual concerts with varied programs; membership is open to the public during the annual campaign.
Founded: 1927
Specialized Field: Dance; Vocal Music; Instrumental Music
Status: Nonprofit

Budget: $20,000-35,000
Income Sources: Community Concerts
Organization Type: Educational; Sponsoring

5427
MUHLENBERG COLLEGE CONCERT SERIES
2400 Chew Street
Allentown
Allentown, PA 18104-5586
Phone: 484-664-3100
Fax: 484-664-3633
Web Site: www.muhlenberg.edu
Management:
 President: Randall Helms
 Executive Director: Douglas Ovens
 Theatre Director: Charles Richter
Founded: 1847
Specialized Field: Series & Festivals; Instrumental Music; Vocal Music
Status: Non-Profit, Professional
Paid Staff: 20
Paid Artists: 20

5428
BEAVER VALLEY COMMUNITY CONCERT ASSOCIATION
153 Oak Drive
Beaver Falls, PA 15010
Phone: 724-846-6814
Officers:
 President: EE Bass
Budget: $20,000-35,000

5429
ARTSQUEST
25 W 3rd Street
Bethlehem, PA 18015
Phone: 610-332-1300
Fax: 610-861-2644
e-mail: info@fest.org
Web Site: www.musikfest.org
Officers:
 President: Jeffrey Parks
Management:
 Director of Performing Arts: Patrick Brogan

5430
BETHLEHEM BACH FESTIVAL
440 Heckewelder Place
Bethlehem
Bethlehem, PA 18018
Phone: 610-866-4382
Fax: 610-866-6232
Toll-free: 888-743-3100
e-mail: office@bach.org
Web Site: www.bach.org
Officers:
 President: David G Beckwith
 Vice President: Harold G Black
 Vice President: Paul A Florenz
Management:
 Artistic Director and Conductor: Greg Funfgeld
 Executive Director: Bridget George
 Deputy Executive Director: Karen Glose
 Development Officer: Cheryl Dungan
 Accounting Manager: Bonnie Lindsey
Founded: 1898

5432
BLOOMSBURG UNIVERSITY ARTIST-CELEBRITY SERIES
400 E 2nd Street
Bloomsburg, PA 17815-1301
Phone: 570-389-4000
Fax: 570-389-4201
e-mail: rpress@bloomu.edu
Web Site: www.bloomu.edu
Management:
 President: Jessica Kozloff
 VP Administration/Finance: Richard Rugen
Specialized Field: Higher Education
Status: Non-Profit, Professional
Budget: $60,000-150,000
Performs At: Mitrani Hall; Haas Center for the Arts; Gross Auditorium

5433
MONTGOMERY COUNTY COMMUNITY COLLEGE LIVELY ARTS SERIES
340 Dekalb Pike
Blue Bell
Blue Bell, PA 19422-0796
Phone: 215-641-6300
Fax: 215-641-6645
e-mail: livarts@mc3.edu
Web Site: www.mc3.edu
Officers:
 Chair: Michael J D'Aniello
 President: Dr Karen A Stout
Management:
 Vice Chair: Anthony Disandro
 Executive Director: Peggy Lee Clark
 Executive Assisstant to president: Joshua Schwartz
 Executive Assisstant to Board: Deborah Rogers
Founded: 1972
Paid Staff: 2
Budget: $35,000-60,000
Performs At: Science Center Theater

5434
BRADFORD CREATIVE & PERFORMING ARTS CENTER
10 Marilyn Horne Way
PO Box 153
Bradford, PA 16701
Phone: 814-362-2522
Fax: 814-362-2556
e-mail: arts@bcpac.com
Web Site: www.bcpac.com
Officers:
 President: James D Guelfi
 Treasurer: Marcia Morrison
 Secretary: Pat Ryan
Management:
 Executive Director: James D Guelfi
 VP: Karen Niemic Bucheit
 Marketing Consultant: Tim Zlaukas
 Office Manager: Kathy Peace
 Program Selection Chair: Dean Harten
Founded: 1984
Paid Staff: 1
Volunteer Staff: 15
Paid Artists: 5
Budget: $60,000-150,000
Income Sources: Sales; Grants; Patrons
Annual Attendance: 5,000
Seating Capacity: 1410

SERIES & FESTIVALS / Pennsylvania

5435
CRS NATIONAL FESTIVAL FOR THE PERFORMING ARTS
724 Winchester Road
Broomall, PA 19008
Phone: 215-544-5920
Fax: 215-544-5921
e-mail: crsnews@erols.com
Web Site: www.erols.com/crsnews
Management:
  Artistic Advisor: Milton Babbitt
Mission: To offer performers, composers, teachers, libraries, educational institutions, amateurs, devotees of music and prosepective sponsors cultural enrichment through vast musical sources.
Utilizes: Community Members; Guest Artists; Guest Companies; Scenic Designers; Singers
Founded: 1981
Specialized Field: Dance; Vocal Music; Instrumental Music; Festivals
Status: Professional; Semi-Professional; Nonprofit
Income Sources: Contemporary Record Society
Organization Type: Performing; Touring; Resident; Educational

5436
BRYN MAWR COLLEGE PERFORMING ARTS SERIES
101 N Merion Avenue
Bryn Mawr, PA 19010-2899
Phone: 610-526-5000
Fax: 610-526-7451
e-mail: dalder@brynmawr.edu
Web Site: www.brynmawr.edu
Officers:
  President: Kim Cassidy
Management:
  Executive Director: Linda Caruso Haviland
  Performing Arts Coordinator: Lisa Kraus
Founded: 1985
Specialized Field: Series and Festivals; Dance; Theatre; Chamber Music
Status: Non-Profit, Professional
Paid Staff: 2
Volunteer Staff: 2
Budget: $43,350
Seating Capacity: 800

5437
PENNSYLVANIA SHAKESPEARE FESTIVAL
2755 Station Avenue
Center Valley, PA 18034
Phone: 610-282-9455
Fax: 610-282-2084
e-mail: psf@pashakespeare.org
Web Site: www.pashakespeare.org
Officers:
  President: John Russo
  Vice President: Jo-Ann S Kelly
  Secretary: Kathleen Kund Nolan
Management:
  Producing Artistic Director: Patrick Mulcahy
  General Manager: Casey William Gallagher
  Endowment Director: Gerard J Schubert, OSFS
  Managing Director: Casey William Gallagher
  Production Manager: Matthew Given
  Business Manager: Janice Hein
Founded: 1992
Status: Professional
Paid Staff: 6
Volunteer Staff: 200
Paid Artists: 100
Season: May - August
Type of Stage: Thrust
Stage Dimensions: 38' x 40'
Seating Capacity: 473

5438
WILSON COLLEGE PERFORMING ARTS SERIES
1015 Philadelphia Avenue
Chamebrsburg, PA 17201
Phone: 717-264-4141
Fax: 717-262-2038
e-mail: admissions@wilson.edu
Web Site: www.wilson.edu
Officers:
  President: Dr Barbara K Mistick
Management:
  Cultural Events Director: Kathy Lehman
Mission: Provide series of artistic performances that enrich lives of students, faculty and staff, and to serve as a cultural resource to the Cumberland Valley area.
Utilizes: Artists-in-Residence; Dance Companies; Multimedia; Special Technical Talent
Founded: 1869
Specialized Field: Laird Hall
Status: Non-Profit, Professional
Paid Staff: 3
Volunteer Staff: 4
Paid Artists: 4
Budget: $12,000
Income Sources: Grants; Endowment Funds
Facility Category: Auditorium
Type of Stage: Proscenium
Stage Dimensions: 30'x30'
Seating Capacity: 300

5439
CLARION UNIVERSITY ACTIVITIES BOARD ARTS
840 Wood Street
Clarion
Clarion, PA 16214
Phone: 814-393-2000
Toll-free: 800-672-7171
e-mail: info@clarion.edu
Web Site: www.clarion.edu
Officers:
  Chair: Kurt Weres
  UAB Secretary: Paul Sherer
  UAB Advisor: Brian Hoover
  Vice President: Andromeda Earley
Management:
  Advisor: Jamie Bero-Johnson
  Director: Shawn Hoke
  Assisstant Director: Kelly Ryan
  Administrative Assisstant: Greta Lutz
Budget: $10,000-20,000
Performs At: Marwick - Boyd Auditorium

5440
LEHIGH VALLEY BLUES & JAZZ FESTIVAL
PO Box G
Coplay, PA 18037
Web Site: www.lvbluesfest.org

5441
MUSIC FOR MT.LEBANON
1526 Staunton Drive
Corapolis, PA 15108
Phone: 412-264-3354
Officers:
  President: Paula Bongiorno
  1st Vice President: Marlene Wohleber
  2nd Vice President: Rose Liptak
  Recording Secretary: Fran Ritz
  Scholarship Treasurer: Lynn Hagan
  Keynote Treasurer: Jean Petersen
Management:
  President: Elliot Davis
  Artistic Director: Carl Apone
Founded: 1945
Specialized Field: Series and Festivals: Community Musical Programs
Status: Non-Profit, Professional
Paid Staff: 2

5442
PENNSYLVANIA RENAISSANCE FAIRE
PO Box 685
Cornwall, PA 17016
Phone: 717-665-7021
Fax: 717-664-3466
e-mail: royalspk@parenaissancefaire.com
Web Site: www.parenfaire.com
Management:
  Associate Producer: Thomas Roy
Utilizes: Actors; Artists-in-Residence; Choreographers; Dancers; Designers; Fine Artists; Guest Accompanists; Guest Conductors; Guest Directors; Guest Ensembles; Guest Musical Directors; Guest Musicians; High School Drama; Local Artists; Multimedia; Organization Contracts; Original Music Scores; Resident Artists; Resident Professionals; Selected Students; Sign Language Translators; Singers; Soloists; Student Interns
Founded: 1980
Status: Non-Equity; Commercial
Season: August - October
Annual Attendance: 200,000
Facility Category: Outdoor Festival
Type of Stage: Outdoor
Year Built: 1980

5443
MOUNT ALOYSIUS COLLEGE PERFORMING ARTS SERIES
7373 Admiral Peary Highway
Cresson
Cresson, PA 16630-1999
Phone: 814-886-4131
Fax: 814-886-2978
Toll-free: 888-823-2220
e-mail: jniebauer@mtaloy.edu
Web Site: www.mtaloy.edu
Management:
  Director of Student Activities: Joyce Niebauer
Budget: $10,000-20,000

5444
DELAWARE WATER GAP CELEBRATION OF THE ARTS
PO Box 249
Delaware Water Gap, PA 18327
Phone: 717-424-2210
Web Site: www.welcome.to/cotajazz
Management:
  Director: Richard C Chamberlain

5445
LAFAYETTE COLLEGE CONCERT SERIES
730 High Street
Easton
Easton, PA 18042

SERIES & FESTIVALS / Pennsylvania

Phone: 610-330-5000
Fax: 610-250-8728
Web Site: williamscenter.lafayette.edu
Officers:
President: Alison R Byerly
Management:
Executive Director: Dr. Ellis Finger
Budget: $60,000-150,000
Seating Capacity: 400

5446
EDINBORO UNIVERSITY OF PENNSYLVANIA PERFORMING ARTS SERIES
219 Medville Street
Edinboro
Edinboro, PA 16444
Phone: 814-732-2000
Fax: 814-732-2862
e-mail: aortega@edinboro.edu
Web Site: www.edinboro.edu
Officers:
Chairperson: John E Horan
Vice Chairperson: Dennis R Frampton
President: Dr Julie E Wollman
Secretary: John A Pulice
Student Trustee: Shaquan A Walker
Management:
Director Performing Arts: Ann Ortega
Specialized Field: Choral; Dance; Instrumental Music
Status: Non-Profit, Professional
Budget: $35,000-60,000
Performs At: Memorial Auditorium

5447
MUSIC AT GRETNA
1 Alpha Drive
Elizabethtown, PA 17022
Phone: 717-361-1508
Fax: 717-361-1512
e-mail: music@mtgretna.com
Web Site: gretnamusic.org
Officers:
Founder: Carl Ellenberger, Jr
President: Henry Kenderdine
Management:
President: David Wood
Executive Director: Michael Murray
Development Director: Suzanne Kenderdine
Founded: 1975
Specialized Field: Series & Festivals; Instrumental Music; Vocal Music; Youth; Dance; Ethnic Performances
Status: Non-Profit, Professional
Paid Staff: 3
Budget: $60,000-150,000
Income Sources: Mt. Greten Playhouse; Clyde & Perk Center
Performs At: Leffler Chapel Performance Center
Organization Type: Educational; Sponsoring; Producing

5448
ERIE CIVIC CENTER/ WARNER THEATRE
809 French Street
Erie, PA 16501
Phone: 814-453-7117
Fax: 814-455-9931
Web Site: erieevents.com
Officers:
Chairperson: James T Marnen
Vice Chairperson: Thomas Doolin
Treasurer: Bruce Q Whitehair
Secretary: Gwendolyn White
Management:
Managing Director: John A Wells
Director Of Facilities: Ronald J. Desser
Controller: Cheryl Wodecki
Coordinator Special Events, Publici: Dawn M. Betza
General Manager: Jeff Esposito

5449
ERIE CIVIC MUSIC ASSOCIATION
PO Box 143
Erie, PA 16512
Phone: 814-864-5681
Fax: 814-864-1218
e-mail: butchvick@aol.com
Web Site: www.eriecivicmusic.com
Officers:
President: Garlan Newcomb
VP: Harry Osiecki
Treasurer: Chris Mosier
Executive Secretary: Beatrice Hansen
Management:
Director of Advertising: Vickie Newcomb
Mission: We present the greatest international talent available at the most reasonable costs.
Founded: 1928
Specialized Field: Vocal Music; Instrumental Music; International Dancers and Nostalgia Shows
Status: Nonprofit
Volunteer Staff: 35
Budget: $50,000-90,000
Income Sources: Erie Area Fund for the Arts; Season & Single Tickets Sales
Performs At: Warner Theatre
Annual Attendance: 7,500-9,000
Organization Type: Sponsoring

5450
MESSIAH COLLEGE CULTURAL SERIES
One College Avenue
PO Box 3020
Grantham, PA 17055
Phone: 717-766-2511
Fax: 717-796-5371
e-mail: ehager@messiah.edu
Web Site: www.messiah.edu
Management:
President: Kim Pitts
Founded: 1909
Specialized Field: Series & Festivals; Coral; Dance; Ethnic; Opera; Educational; Instrumental Music; Jazz; Theatre; Music
Status: Non-Profit
Paid Staff: 8
Budget: $20,000-35,000
Performs At: Miller Auditorium

5451
27TH ANNUAL CENTRAL PA COMMERCE BANK JAZZ FESTIVAL
5721 Jonestown Road
Harrisburg, PA 17112
Phone: 717-540-1010
Fax: 717-540-7735
e-mail: dave@pajazz.org
Web Site: www.pajazz.org
Officers:
President: Rosemary Barrett
Management:
Executive Director: David Lazorcik
Founded: 1980
Specialized Field: Series and Festivals: Jazz Music
Status: Non-Profit, Professional
Paid Staff: 1
Paid Artists: 200

5452
HARRISBURG AREA COMMUNITY COLLEGE
1 HACC Drive
Harrisburg, PA 17110-2999
Phone: 717-780-2545
Fax: 717-780-3281
Toll-free: 800-ABC-HACC
Web Site: www.hacc.edu
Officers:
President: John J. Sygielski
Management:
Performing Artist Series Director: Teri Guerrisi
Utilizes: Dance Companies; Multimedia; Original Music Scores; Theatre Companies
Founded: 1975
Specialized Field: Series & Festivals; Dances; Music; Theatre; Family
Status: Non-Profit, Professional
Paid Staff: 6
Volunteer Staff: 30
Budget: $35,000-60,000
Performs At: Rose Lehrman Auditorium
Facility Category: Proscenium
Type of Stage: Hardwood, Spring Floor
Stage Dimensions: 36'x40'
Seating Capacity: 374
Year Built: 1975
Year Remodeled: 1993
Rental Contact: Teri Guerrsi

5453
MARKET SQUARE CONCERTS
225 Market Street
2nd Floor
Harrisburg, PA 17101
Mailing Address: PO Box 1292
Phone: 717-221-9599
Fax: 717-221-9588
e-mail: info@marketsquareconcerts.org
Web Site: www.marketsquareconcerts.org
Officers:
President: David Lehman
Management:
Executive Director: Ya-Ting Chang
Artistic Director: Peter Sirotin
Mission: Presenting a wide range of chamber and solo music presentations by distinguished artists.
Founded: 1982
Specialized Field: Chamber Music
Status: Non-Profit, Professional
Paid Staff: 1
Budget: $60,000-150,000
Performs At: Market Square Church; Rose Lehrman Art Center; Whitaker Ctr.
Organization Type: Educational; Presenting

5454
NEXT GENERATION FESTIVAL
WITF-Inc 1982 Locust Lane
PO Box 2954
Harrisburg, PA 17105-2954
Phone: 717-236-6000
Web Site: www.nextgenerationfestival.org

5455
HERSHEYPARK ARENA/STADIUM
100 W Hersheypark Drive
Hershey, PA 17033

SERIES & FESTIVALS / Pennsylvania

Phone: 717-534-8966
Fax: 717-534-3113
Web Site: www.hersheypa.com
Management:
General Manager: Matthew Ford

5456
JUNIATA PRESENTS
Juniata College
1900 Moore Street
Huntingdon, PA 16652
Phone: 814-641-3608
e-mail: herzog@juniata.edu
Web Site: www.juniatapresents.com
Officers:
President: Thomas R Kepple Jr
Executive Assistant to President: JoAnne Isenberg
Management:
Director of the Performing Arts: Chad Herzog
Mission: Providing the highest quality of liberal education and to awaken students to the empowering richness of the mind and to enable them to lead fulfilling and useful lives.
Utilizes: Actors; Artists-in-Residence; Collaborating Artists; Collaborations; Commissioned Composers; Community Members; Community Talent; Contract Actors; Contract Orchestras; Curators; Dance Companies; Dancers; Educators; Filmmakers; Fine Artists; Grant Writers; Guest Accompanists; Guest Artists; Guest Choreographers; Guest Directors; Guest Ensembles; Guest Soloists; High School Drama; Multi Collaborations; Multimedia; Original Music Scores; Paid Performers; Playwrights; Resident Companies; Scenic Designers; Soloists; Students; Student Interns; Theatre Companies; Visual Designers
Founded: 1876
Specialized Field: Educational
Status: Non-Profit, Professional
Paid Staff: 400
Budget: $35,000-60,000

5457
INDIANA UNIVERSITY OF PENNSYLVANIA ONSTAGE: ARTS AND ENTERTAINMENT
410 Sutton Hall
Indiana, PA 15705
Phone: 724-357-2315
Fax: 724-357-2593
e-mail: destefan@iup.edu
Web Site: www.onstageatiup.com
Management:
Arts/Entertainment Director: Frank Destefano
Mission: Presenting organization
Founded: 1963
Specialized Field: Series; music, theater, dance
Status: Non-Profit, Professional
Paid Staff: 3
Volunteer Staff: 60
Budget: $800,000
Income Sources: Corporate; Grants; Tickets; Donors
Performs At: Fisher Auditorium
Type of Stage: Proscenium
Seating Capacity: 1454
Year Built: 1938
Year Remodeled: 2008
Cost: $12,000,000

5458
LAUREL FESTIVAL OF THE ARTS
PO Box 206
Jim Thorpe, PA 18229
Phone: 570-325-4439
Fax: 570-325-4439
Management:
Artistic Director: Marc Mostaroy
Weeknight Concerts: Randall Perry
Publicity: Herbert Thompson
Marketing: Barbara Loeffler
Mission: To unite the finest performers in working together to present events for the public.
Founded: 1990
Specialized Field: Dance; Vocal Music; Instrumental Music; Festivals; Poetry
Status: Professional; Nonprofit
Performs At: Manch Chunk Opera House
Organization Type: Performing; Resident; Educational

5459
LONGWOOD GARDENS PERFORMING ARTS
1001 Longwood road
Kennett Square, PA 19348
Mailing Address: P.O. Box 501, Kennett Square, PA 19348
Phone: 610-388-1000
Fax: 610-388-3833
e-mail: questions@longwoodgardens.org
Web Site: www.longwoodgardens.org
Management:
Director of Horticulture: Sharon Loving
Director of Guest Experience: Connie McCaw
Director: Paul B Redman
irector of Marketing/CMO: Marnie Conley
Director of Administration/CFO: Dennis Fisher
Mission: To enhance the gardens and follow tradition of founder Pierre S duPont.
Utilizes: Actors; Choreographers; Dance Companies; Dancers; Local Artists; Multimedia; Original Music Scores; Sign Language Translators; Singers; Special Technical Talent; Theatre Companies
Founded: 1906
Specialized Field: Series & Festivals; Instrumental Music; Theatre; Dance
Status: Non-Profit, Professional
Paid Staff: 50
Budget: $60,000-150,000
Income Sources: Ticket Sales
Annual Attendance: 1 Million to Gardens
Facility Category: Outdoor Historic Theatre
Stage Dimensions: 73 x 36
Seating Capacity: 2000
Year Built: 1920
Organization Type: Performing; Educational

5460
KUTZTOWN UNIVERSITY PERFORMING ARTISTS SERIES
Office of Cultural Affairs
Kutztown University
Kutztown, PA 19530
Phone: 610-683-4092
Fax: 610-683-4555
e-mail: kupas@kutztown.edu
Web Site: www2.kutztown.edu
Management:
Director: Robin Zaremski
Patron Services: Amy L. Botwright
Education and Outreach Coordinator: Elaine Bonfitto
Production Manager: Greg Kokolus
Box Office Assistant: Jennifer Pisano
Founded: 1986
Specialized Field: Series & Festivals; Instrumental Music; Vocal Music; Theatre; Youth; Dance; Ethnic Performances
Status: Non-Profit, Professional
Paid Staff: 3
Paid Artists: 30
Budget: $60,000-150,000
Performs At: Schaeffer Auditorium

5461
NEW ARTS PROGRAM
173 W Main Street
PO Box 82
Kutztown, PA 19530
Phone: 610-683-6440
Fax: 610-683-6440
e-mail: napconn@aol.com
Web Site: www.napconnection.com
Officers:
President: James FL Carroll
VP: Michael Kessler
Treasurer: James FL Carroll
Secretary: Joanne P. Carroll
Management:
President: James Carroll
Mission: To present artists from the performing, visual and literary arts in one-to-one consultations; to offer a presentation/performance style collective consultation.
Utilizes: Artists-in-Residence; Choreographers; Dancers; Filmmakers; Fine Artists; Multimedia; Performance Artists; Playwrights; Singers
Founded: 1974
Specialized Field: Series & Festivals; Instrumental Music; Vocal Music; Dance; Ethnic Performances
Status: Non-Profit, Professional
Paid Staff: 1
Volunteer Staff: 2
Paid Artists: 8
Budget: $60,000
Income Sources: PCA, Foundations, Corporations, Individuals
Performs At: Saint Johns UCC
Annual Attendance: 3000
Facility Category: Gallery
Seating Capacity: 76 - 350
Organization Type: Performing; Resident

5462
FRANKLIN & MARSHALL COLLEGE SOUND HORIZONS CONCERT SERIES
PO Box 3003
Lancaster, PA 17604-3003
Phone: 717-291-3911
Fax: 717-358-7168
e-mail: mathew.weaver@fandm.edu
Web Site: www.fandm.edu
Officers:
Chairman Concert Committee: Bruce Gustafson
Management:
Concert Coordinator: Mathew Weaver
Performance Manager: Mark Miskinis
Chair of Concert: John Carbon
Utilizes: Artists-in-Residence; Commissioned Composers; Commissioned Music; Composers-in-Residence; Dance Companies; Dancers; Grant Writers; Guest Accompanists; Guest Companies; Guest Composers; Guest Designers; Guest Directors; Guest Ensembles; Guest Musical Directors; Guest Musicians; Guest Soloists; Local Artists; Multimedia; Music; Original Music Scores; Resident Artists; Sign Language Translators; Singers; Soloists
Founded: 1935

SERIES & FESTIVALS / Pennsylvania

Specialized Field: Series & Festivals; Instrumental Music; Vocal Music; Theatre; Youth; Dance; Ethnic Performances
Status: Non-Profit, Professional
Paid Staff: 6
Volunteer Staff: 6
Budget: $35,000-50,000
Performs At: The Ann & Richard Barshinger Center; Miller Recital Hall
Facility Category: Concert Hall
Seating Capacity: 500
Year Built: 1925
Year Remodeled: 2000

5463
CARIN UNIVERSITY
Philadelphia Biblical University
200 Manor Avenue
Langhorne, PA 19047
Phone: 215-702-4329
Fax: 215-702-4342
Toll-free: 800-366-0049
e-mail: admissions@caim.edu
Web Site: cairn.edu
Officers:
  President: Todd Williams
  Dean: Paul Isensee
Specialized Field: Degrees; Music Degrees; Church Music; Music Education
Status: Non-Profit, Professional
Paid Staff: 3
Paid Artists: 25
Budget: $10,000
Affiliations: NASM
Facility Category: Chapel
Seating Capacity: 750

5464
BUCKNELL UNIVERSITY: WEIS CENTER PERFORMANCE SERIES
Weis Center for the Performing Arts
Bucknell University
Lewisburg, PA 17837
Phone: 570-577-3700
Fax: 570-577-3701
e-mail: boswell@bucknell.edu
Web Site: www.bucknell.edu
Management:
  President: Brian Mitchell
  Executive Director: William Boswell
Mission: To provide the campus and region with opportunity for exposure to the essential cultural and educational values inherent in the great historical an radical traditions of the performing arts.
Founded: 1988
Specialized Field: Series & Festivals: Performing Arts
Status: Non-Profit, Professional
Paid Staff: 120
Budget: $150,000-400,000
Affiliations: APAP, CMA, PA Presenters, Others
Annual Attendance: 9000
Facility Category: Concert Hall
Type of Stage: Sprung Wood Floor
Seating Capacity: 1,200+
Year Built: 1988

5465
THE MIFFLIN-JUNIATA CONCERT ASSOCIATION
P.O. Box 208
Lewiston, PA 17044-0870
Phone: 717-248-5732
Fax: 717-248-2672
e-mail: mjconcert@comcast.net
Web Site: mjconcerts.org
Management:
  Director Emeritus: Allen J Levin
Budget: $20,000-35,000

5466
MANSFIELD UNIVERSITY FINE ARTS SERIES
Music Department
Mansfield, PA 16933
Phone: 570-662-4710
Fax: 570-662-4114
Web Site: www.music.mnsfld.edu
Management:
  President: John Halstead
  Department Chairperson: Adam Brennan
  Manager: Kenneth Sarch
Founded: 1857
Specialized Field: Series & Festivals; Instrumental Music; Vocal Music; Theatre
Status: Non-Profit, Non-Professional
Paid Staff: 24
Budget: $10,000-20,000
Performs At: Steadman Theatre

5467
MUSIC AT FISHS EDDY
875 Welsh Road
Maple Glen, PA 19002
Mailing Address: PO Box 191, Fishs Eddy, NY. 13774
Phone: 607-637-3413
Fax: 607-637-3413
e-mail: fishsmusic@aol.com
Management:
  Artistic Director: Joyce Lindorff

5468
ALLEGHENY COLLEGE PUBLIC EVENTS SERIES
Allegheny College
520 N Main Street
Box V
Meadville, PA 16335
Phone: 814-332-3100
Fax: 814-332-4320
e-mail: info@allegheny.edu
Web Site: www.allegheny.edu
Officers:
  President: Richard Cook
Management:
  Events Director: Patricia Henry
Utilizes: Dance Companies; Dancers; Guest Musical Directors; Multimedia; Original Music Scores; Special Technical Talent; Theatre Companies
Founded: 1815
Specialized Field: Series and Festivals; Instrumental Music; Vocal Music; Theatre; Youth; Dance; Ethnic Performances
Status: Non-Profit, Professional
Paid Staff: 3
Budget: $35,000-60,000
Type of Stage: Proscenium
Seating Capacity: 1,700

5469
BRODHEAD CULTURAL CENTER SUMMER SERIES
Penn State Beaver
100 University Drive
Monaca, PA 15061
Phone: 724-773-3800
Fax: 724-773-3578
e-mail: amk6@psu.edu
Web Site: www.br.psu.edu/Information/10938.htm
Management:
  Executive Director: Amy K Kerbs
Mission: The Brodhead Cultural Center is operated through the Penn State Beaver Offices of University Relations to provide free and low-cost programs for the public.
Founded: 1977
Specialized Field: Series & Festivals: Instrumental Music
Status: Non-Profit, Professional
Paid Staff: 1
Budget: $10,000-20,000
Affiliations: Pennsylvania State
Annual Attendance: 10,000
Facility Category: Outdoor Amphitheater
Type of Stage: Concrete
Seating Capacity: 750
Year Built: 1997

5470
ALLEGHENY VALLEY CONCERT ASSOCIATION
67 River Avenue
Natrona, PA 15065
Phone: 724-226-2155
Officers:
  President: Nora Ann Pastrick
Budget: $20,000-35,000

5471
WESTMINSTER COLLEGE CELEBRITY SERIES
Westminster College
319 South Market Street
New Wilmington, PA 16172
Phone: 724-946-7371
Fax: 724-946-6243
Toll-free: 800-942-8033
e-mail: decatre@westminster.org
Web Site: www.westminster.edu
Management:
  President: Thomas Williamson
  Celebrity Series Director: Gene Decaprio
  VP Admissions and Financial Aid: Thomas H. Stein
  VP Academic Affairs: Jane Wood
  Registrar: June G. Pierce
  VP Finance and Management Services: Kenneth Romig
  Director of Financial Aid: Cheryl Gerber
Founded: 1966
Specialized Field: Series & Festivals: Music and Song and Dance Performers
Status: Non-Profit, Non-Professional
Paid Staff: 2
Budget: $150,000-400,000

5472
PCCA FESTIVAL AT LITTLE BUFFALO
PO Box 354
Newport, PA 17074
Phone: 717-567-7023
Fax: 717-567-7429
e-mail: pcca@perrycountyarts.org
Web Site: www.perrycountyarts.org
Management:
  President: Joni Williamson
Founded: 1983

SERIES & FESTIVALS / Pennsylvania

Specialized Field: Members Gallery and Exhibits; Joint Classes; Workshops
Status: Non-Profit
Paid Staff: 5
Volunteer Staff: 500
Paid Artists: 100
Facility Category: Multi-Cultural

5473
BUCKS COUNTY COMMUNITY COLLEGE CULTURAL PROGRAMMING
Bucks County Community College
275 Swamp Road
Newtown, PA 18940
Phone: 215-968-8000
Fax: 215-504-8530
e-mail: mengersk@storm.bucks.edu
Web Site: www.bucks.edu
Officers:
   Chairman: Blake H. Eisenhart
   Vice-Chair: James M. Dancy, Jr.
   Secretary: Thomas Skiffington
   Assistant Secretary: Elizabeth Fineburg
Management:
   President: James Linksz
Founded: 1964
Specialized Field: Series & Festivals; Instrumental Music; Vocal Music; Theatre; Youth; Ethnic Performances
Status: Non-Profit, Professional
Paid Staff: 100
Budget: $10,000-20,000
Seating Capacity: 345

5474
AMERICAN MUSIC THEATER FESTIVAL/PRINCE MUSIC THEATER
1412 Chestnut Street
Philadelphia, PA 19102
Phone: 215-972-1000
Fax: 215-972-1020
e-mail: info@princemusictheater.org
Web Site: www.princemusictheater.org
Officers:
   Chairman: Herbert Lotman
   President: Robert A. Fox
   Vice-President: Howard Morgan
   Secretary-Treasurer: Lee Tolbert
Management:
   Executive Director: James E. Hines
   Controller: Louis J. Coppola
   Director of Development: Heather S. Giampapa
   Artistic Administrator: Nancy Lee Kathan
   Digital Media and Marketing Manager: Angela Madgin
   Director of Production: Gary Miller
   Lead Technician: Kevin E. Wayns
   Stage Manager: Pamela M. Hobson
Founded: 1984
Specialized Field: Song Driven Musical
Status: Non-Profit, Professional
Paid Staff: 37
Performs At: Prince Music Theater
Facility Category: Theater
Type of Stage: Proscenium
Seating Capacity: 450

5475
CHORAL ARTS PHILADELPHIA
P.O. Box 22445
Philadelphia, PA 19110-2445
Phone: 267-240-2586
e-mail: info@choralarts.com
Web Site: choralarts.com
Officers:
   President: Lisa Barton, Esq.
   Vice President: Alexis Barron, Esq.
   Second Vice President: Meredith Quirin
   Secretary: Joseph J. Leube, Jr.
   Treasurer: Stephen Herbert
Management:
   Artistic Director: Matthew C. Glandorf
   Director of Development: Amanda Schkeeper
Mission: The Bach Festival of Philadelphia is dedicated to enriching the community through concerts and educational programs presented by some of the best Baroque interpreters in the world.
Utilizes: Collaborations; Guest Composers; Guest Directors; Guest Musical Directors; Guest Musicians; Guest Soloists; Multimedia; Original Music Scores; Sign Language Translators; Singers
Founded: 1976
Specialized Field: Series & Festivals; Instrumental Music; Vocal Music; Youth
Status: Non-Profit, Professional
Paid Staff: 3
Volunteer Staff: 8
Paid Artists: 20
Income Sources: Government; Corporate and private foundations; Donations; Ticketsales; Advertising books
Performs At: Churches, Performance halls
Annual Attendance: 2,000-3,000
Organization Type: Educational; Presenting

5476
COMMUNITY EDUCATION CENTER
3500 Lancaster Avenue
Philadelphia, PA 19104-2434
Phone: 215-387-1911
Fax: 215-387-3701
e-mail: cec@libertynet.org
Web Site: www.cec.libertynet.org
Management:
   President: Elaine Simone
   Executive Director: Theresa Shockley
   Artistic Director: Edgar Shockley
Founded: 1973
Specialized Field: Series & Festivals; Theatre; Youth; Dance; Ethnic Performances
Status: Non-Profit, Professional
Paid Staff: 6
Paid Artists: 5

5477
COMMUNITY EDUCATION CENTER
3500 Lancaster Avenue
Philadelphia, PA 19104-2434
Phone: 215-387-1911
Fax: 215-387-3701
Budget: $10,000-20,000
Seating Capacity: 100

5478
WELLS FARGO CENTER
3601 S Broad Street
Philadelphia, PA 19148
Phone: 215-336-3600
Fax: 215-389-9403
Toll-free: 800-298-4200
e-mail: customerservice@neweratickets.com
Web Site: www.wellsfargocenterphilly.com
Management:
   President: Peter Luukko
   VP Event Producer: John Page
Specialized Field: Home of the Philadelphia 76ers (NBA); Philadelphia Flyers (NFHL); and the Philadelphia Wings (NLL)
Seating Capacity: 21,000, 19,500
Year Built: 1996

5479
THE GERMAN SOCIETY OF PENNSYLVANIA
611 Spring Garden Street
Philadelphia, PA 19123
Phone: 215-627-2332
Fax: 215-627-5297
e-mail: info@germansociety.org
Web Site: www.germansociety.org
Officers:
   President: Ernest Weiler
   Executive Vice President: Tony Michels
   Vice President of Culture & Heritag: Maria Sturm
   Vice President of Finance: Lew Volgenau
   Treasurer: Lew Volgenau
   Secretary: Christiane Schmidt
Management:
   Office Manager: Beate Brockman
Mission: Devoted to furthering the understanding of German and German-American contributions to the growth of American history and culture from the past to the present, and into the future.
Founded: 1764
Specialized Field: Series & Festivals; Instrumental Music; Dance; Ethnic Performances
Status: Non-Profit, Professional
Paid Staff: 3
Paid Artists: 10

5480
MARLBORO MUSIC
1528 Walnut Street, Suite 301
Philadelphia, PA 19102
Phone: 215-569-4690
Fax: 215-569-9497
e-mail: info@marlboromusic.org
Web Site: www.marlboromusic.org
Officers:
   Administrator: Anthony P Checchia
Management:
   Artistic Administration: Miles Cohen
   Administrator: Anthony Checchia
   Director of Admissions: Jennifer Loux
   Manager: Philip Maneval
   Director of Development: Jacob Smith
   Box Office Manager: Brian Potter
   Business Manager: Marianne Tierney
   Artistic Director: Mitsuko Uchida
Mission: Artistic development of younger musicians with older, more experienced musicians.
Founded: 1951
Specialized Field: Series & Festivals; Instrumental Music; Vocal Music
Status: Non-Profit, Professional
Paid Staff: 15
Volunteer Staff: 10
Paid Artists: 80
Season: August-June
Performs At: Persons Auditorium
Organization Type: Performing; Touring; Resident; Educational; Sponsoring

SERIES & FESTIVALS / Pennsylvania

5481
MIDATLANTIC ARTS FOUNDATION PENNSYLVANIA PERFORMING ARTS ON TOUR
1811 Chestnut Street, 301
Philadelphia, PA 19103
Phone: 215-496-9424
Fax: 215-496-9585
e-mail: pennpat@erols.com
Web Site: www.libertynet.org/pennpat
Management:
   Director: Katie West

5482
NORTHEAST PHILADELPHIA CULTURAL COUNCIL
Jardel Recreation Center
Penny & Cottman Avenue
Philadelphia, PA 19111
Phone: 215-686-0592
Management:
   Coordinator: James Robb
Budget: $35,000-60,000
Performs At: Small Hall

5483
ANNENBERG CENTER FOR THE PERFORMING ARTS
3680 Walnut Street
Philadelphia, PA 19104-6219
Phone: 215-898-3900
Fax: 215-573-9568
Web Site: www.annenbergcenter.org
Officers:
   Chair: David Brashear
   Vice Chair, Development: Andrew R. Brownstein, Esquire
   Vice Chair, Finance: Richard Feintuch
Management:
   Managing Director: Michael J Rose
   Facilities/Events Manager: Marie Gallagher
   Box Office Manager: Alexander Freeman
   Development Assistant: Laura Mraz
   Director of Finance,Administration: Stuart Jasper
   Business Administrator: John Baji
   Director Marketing & Communications: Dawn Frisby Byers
   Technical Staff Manager: James Cackovich
   Production Flyman: Charles Doherty
Utilizes: Dance Companies; Five Seasonal Concerts; Guest Musicians; Multimedia; Original Music Scores; Selected Students; Singers; Student Interns; Special Technical Talent; Theatre Companies
Founded: 1971
Specialized Field: Series and Performances: Dance
Status: Non-Profit, Professional
Paid Staff: 70
Annual Attendance: 100000+
Facility Category: 5 theaters throughout Univ. of Pennsylvania
Type of Stage: Proscenium, Black Box
Seating Capacity: 120-1270
Year Built: 1971
Rental Contact: Marie Gallagher

5484
PRESIDENTIAL JAZZ WEEKEND
African-American History Museum
701 Arch Street
Philadelphia, PA 19106
Phone: 215-574-0380
Fax: 215-574-3110
Management:
   Jazz Live Director: Rhoda Blount
   Museum Director: Dr. Rowena Stewart
Mission: To celebrate the classical music of African-Americans.
Utilizes: Singers
Founded: 1989
Specialized Field: Vocal Music; Instrumental Music; Festivals; Ethnic
Status: Professional; Semi-Professional; Nonprofit
Income Sources: Greater Philadelphia Cultural Alliance; American Association of Museums; Coalition of Afro-American Organizations
Organization Type: Performing; Educational; Sponsoring

5485
SETTLEMENT MUSIC SCHOOL
416 Queen Street
PO Box 63966
Philadelphia, PA 19147
Phone: 215-320-2600
Fax: 215-551-0483
e-mail: info@smsmusic.org
Web Site: www.smsmusic.org
Officers:
   Chair: Barrie Trimingham
   President: Ellen S. Friedell
   Vice President: Libby S. Harwitz
   Treasurer: Philip N. Russo
   Secretary: Steven N. Haas
Management:
   Executive Director: Helen S. Eaton
   Community Engagement Manager: Joseph P. Nebistinsky
   Director of Communications: Christopher Spangler
   Director of Development: Amelia Schmertz
   Program Coordinator: Marka G. Stepper
   Director of Finance,Administration: Richard Smith
Founded: 1908
Specialized Field: Music Education
Status: Non-Profit, Professional
Paid Staff: 250
Paid Artists: 250
Performs At: PNC Bank-Presser Recital Hall

5486
ST. STEPHEN'S
19 S 10 Street
Philadelphia, PA 19107
Phone: 215-922-3807
Fax: 215-829-4561
e-mail: charlesflood@ststephensphl.org
Web Site: www.ststephensphl.org
Management:
   Program Director: Mark Yurkanin
Performs At: St. Stephen's Sanctuary

5487
TONY WILLIAMS SCHOLARSHIP JAZZ FESTIVAL
PO Box 27116
Philadelphia, PA 19118
Phone: 215-848-3677
Fax: 215-842-3760
e-mail: vwedwards@worldnet.att.net
Web Site: www.maccjazz.org
Officers:
   President: Donald Clark Ph.D
   Ambassador At Large: Thelma Anderson
   Secretary: Joseph Stevenson
Management:
   President: Anthony H Williams
   Festival Director: Greg Williams
Mission: To increase community involvement with our youth. A commitment to helping the youth develop the proper attitude necessary in becoming a productive adult through the expressive arts with special emphasis on jazz, our only American art form.
Founded: 1977
Specialized Field: Instrumental Program
Status: Non-Profit, Professional
Paid Staff: 12
Volunteer Staff: 20
Paid Artists: 12
Non-paid Artists: 20

5488
ALLEGHENY COUNTY SUMMER CONCERT SERIES
101 County Courthouse
436 Grant Street
Pittsburgh, PA 15219-2904
Phone: 412-350-6500
Fax: 412-350-4360
e-mail: executive@county.allegheny.pa.us
Web Site: www.county.allegheny.pa.us
Management:
   County Chief Executive: Dan Onorato
Mission: Enhance quality of life for the people.
Paid Staff: 3
Volunteer Staff: 20
Paid Artists: 500

5489
CARNEGIE-MELLON SCHOOL OF MUSIC
5000 Forbes Avenue
Pittsburgh, PA 15213
Phone: 412-268-4118
Fax: 412-268-1431
e-mail: musicschool@andrew.cmu.edu
Web Site: music.cmu.edu
Officers:
   President: Joseph Waz Jr.
Management:
   Head: Denis Colwell
   Assistant Head: Ross Garin
   Coordinator of Special Music Prog.: Daniel Barrett
   Associate Head: Kenneth Keeling
   Director of Operations: Robert Skavronski
Budget: $20,000-35,000
Performs At: Carnegie Music Hall; Lecture Hall; Exhibition Hall
Seating Capacity: 450

5490
FIRST FRIDAY AT THE FRICK CONCERT SERIES
7227 Reynolds Street
Pittsburgh, PA 15208
Phone: 412-371-0600
Fax: 412-371-6030
e-mail: smartin@frickart.org
Web Site: www.frickart.org
Management:
   Director: Bill Bodine
   Media And Marketing: Greg Langel
   Visitor Services: Peg McLean
   Group Sales & Event Rentals Coord.: Sylvia Ehler
Utilizes: Collaborations; Instructors; Local Artists; Lyricists; Multi Collaborations; Multimedia; Original Music Scores; Playwrights; Sign Language Translators; Singers; Soloists; Student Interns
Founded: 1995

SERIES & FESTIVALS / Pennsylvania

Specialized Field: Series & Festivals; Outdoor Summer Concert Series; Instrumental Music; Vocal Music; Ethnic Performance
Status: Non-Profit, Professional
Paid Staff: 50
Paid Artists: 12
Budget: $20,000
Annual Attendance: 10,000
Facility Category: Outdoor Stage
Type of Stage: Platform
Stage Dimensions: 24x40
Seating Capacity: 3,000

5491
MCJAZZ JUGEND BIGBAND
1815 Metropolitan Street
Pittsburgh, PA 15233
Phone: 412-322-1773
Fax: 412-322-1075
e-mail: experiencemcg@mcg-btc.org
Web Site: www.mcjazz.org
Officers:
  President/CEO: William E. Strickland, Jr
Management:
  Executive Producer, MCG Jazz: Marty Ashby
Mission: To present jazz performances as well as community and educational activities.
Utilizes: Artists-in-Residence; Commissioned Composers; Commissioned Music; Educators; Guest Companies; Guest Directors; Guest Instructors; Guest Lecturers; Guest Musical Directors; Guest Soloists; Lyricists; Multimedia
Founded: 1987
Specialized Field: Series & Festivals: Jazz Concerts
Status: Non-Profit, Professional
Paid Staff: 30
Volunteer Staff: 6
Performs At: Manchester Craftmen's Guild Music Hall
Annual Attendance: 15,000
Facility Category: Concert Hall
Type of Stage: Concert stage
Stage Dimensions: 24x26
Seating Capacity: 350
Year Built: 1987
Organization Type: Educational; Presenting

5492
MUSIC FOR MT. LEBANON
2016 Worcester Drive
Pittsburgh, PA 15243-1542
Phone: 412-258-4814
Fax: 412-344-9054
Web Site: www.musicformtlebanon.org
Officers:
  President: Dave Christopher
  VP: Ben Taylor
  Secretary: Stu Fox
  Treasurer: Paul Mooney
Management:
  Artistic Director: Carl Apone
Budget: $60,000-150,000
Seating Capacity: 1,500

5493
PITTSBURGH ARTS COUNCIL
810 Penn Avenue
Suite 600
Pittsburgh, PA 15222-3401
Phone: 412-391-2060
Fax: 412-394-4280
e-mail: info@pittsburghartscouncil.org
Web Site: www.pittsburghartscouncil.org
Officers:
  Chair: Joseph B. Smith
  Executive Vice Chair: John C. Camillus
  Vice Chair: Kathleen Mulcahy
  Secretary: James Wilkinson
  Treasurer: Victor Dozzi, CPA
Management:
  CEO: Mark Swain
  Director of Communications: Jennifer Saffron
  Artist Relations Coordinator: Christiane Leach

5494
PITTSBURGH PLAYHOUSE
222 Craft Avenue
Pittsburgh, PA 15213
Phone: 412-392-8000
Fax: 412-621-4762
Web Site: www.pittsburghplayhouse.com
Management:
  Artistic Producing Director: Ronald Allan-Lindblom
  Producing Director: Earl Hughes
  Managing Director: David Vinski
  House Manager: Alfred Kirschman
  Director Production, Stage Manag: Kim Martin
Specialized Field: Series & Festivals; Theatre; Dance; and Children's Theatre
Status: Non-Profit, Professional
Performs At: John Hopkins Auditorium & Library Center

5495
THREE RIVERS ARTS FESTIVAL
937 Liberty Avenue
Pittsburgh, PA 15222
Phone: 412-281-8723
Fax: 412-281-7822
e-mail: pearlman@sgi.net
Web Site: www.artsfestival.net
Management:
  Executive Director: Elizabeth Reiss
Founded: 1959
Specialized Field: Series & Festivals; Instrumental Music; Vocal Music; Theatre; Youth; Dance; Ethnic Performances
Status: Non-Profit, Professional
Paid Staff: 6

5496
UNIVERSITY OF PITTSBURGH CONCERT SERIES
Music Building
Room 110
Pittsburgh, PA 15260
Phone: 412-624-4125
Fax: 412-624-4186
e-mail: musicdpt+@pitt.edu
Web Site: www.pitt.edu
Management:
  Chancellor: Mark Notingburd
Founded: 1787
Specialized Field: Series & Festivals; Instrumental Music; Vocal Music; Ethnic Performances
Status: Non-Profit, Professional
Paid Staff: 1
Budget: $10,000
Performs At: Frick Fine Arts Auditorium; William Pitt Union Ballroom

5497
Y MUSIC SOCIETY OF THE JEWISH COMMUNITY CENTER
5738 Forbes Avenue
Pittsburgh, PA 15217
Phone: 412-521-8010
Fax: 412-208-9107
e-mail: mroth@jccpgh.org
Web Site: www.jccpgh.org
Officers:
  Chair: Marc L. Brown
  Vice Chair: Richard Guttman
  Treasurer: Kenneth T. Segel
  Secretary: Hilary Tyson
Management:
  Director: Mayda Roth
Budget: $60,000-150,000
Performs At: Carnegie Music Hall

5498
HILL SCHOOL CENTER FOR THE ARTS LIVELY ARTS SERIES
717 E High Street
Pottstown, PA 19464-5791
Phone: 610-326-1000
e-mail: bmerriam@thehill.org
Web Site: www.thehill.org
Officers:
  President: David Dougherty
Management:
  Executive Director: Burton Merriam
Founded: 1854
Specialized Field: Series & Festivals; Instrumental Music; Vocal Music; Theatre; Youth; Dance; Ethnic Performances
Status: Non-Profit, Non-Professional
Budget: $20,000-35,000
Performs At: The Center Theatre

5499
CABRINI COLLEGE
610 King of Prussia Road
Radnor, PA 19087
Phone: 610-902-8380
Fax: 610-902-8285
e-mail: abethany@cabrini.edu
Web Site: www.cabrinicollege.edu
Officers:
  President: Dr. Marle George
Management:
  Music Dir./Coor. Cultural Events: Dr. Adeline Bethany
Founded: 1957
Specialized Field: Vocal Music: Classical Music
Status: Non-Profit, Professional
Paid Staff: 1
Budget: $10,000
Performs At: Lecture Hall; Mansion Grand Foyer

5500
ALBRIGHT COLLEGE CONCERT SERIES
13th & Bern Streets
PO Box 15234
Reading, PA 19612-5234
Phone: 610-921-7871
Fax: 610-921-7768
e-mail: bbutler@alb.edu
Web Site: www.albright.edu/concertseries
Officers:
  Chair: Jeffrey J. Joyce
  Vice Chair: Kathleen C. Hittner
  Secretary: Karen A. Rightmire
Management:
  President: Patricia Hummel
  Executive Director: Rebecca Butler
Founded: 1995
Specialized Field: Series & Festivals; Instrumental Music; Vocal Music; Ethnic Performances
Status: Non-Profit, Professional

Budget: $10,000
Performs At: Memorial Chapel; Roop Hall

5501
BERKS JAZZ FESTIVAL
Berks Arts Council
PO Box 854
Reading, PA 19603-0854
Phone: 610-655-6374
Fax: 610-655-6378
Toll-free: 800-523-3781
e-mail: info@berksjazfest.com
Web Site: www.berksjazzfest.com
Management:
   President: Jim Landrigan
   Executive Director: Karen Haver
   Marketing: John Ernesto
Founded: 1971
Specialized Field: Arts In Berks County
Status: Non-Profit, Professional
Paid Staff: 9
Volunteer Staff: 200
Paid Artists: 100

5502
STAR SERIES ASSOCIATION
147 N 5th Street
Reading, PA 19601
Phone: 610-373-0141
Fax: 610-376-3336
e-mail: cbreaux@redrose.net
Web Site: www.berks.net
Management:
   Manager: Chip Breaux
Performs At: Rajah Theatre; Albright Coll. Theatre; Albright Coll. Chapel

5503
SCRANTON COMMUNITY CONCERTS
404 N Washington Avenue
Scranton, PA 18503
Phone: 570-342-4137
Fax: 570-342-4856
e-mail: commconcerts@aol.com
Web Site: www.scrantonconcerts.org
Management:
   President: Susan Trussler
   Executive Director: Bridget Fitzpatrick
Mission: To present world-class performing arts in classical, jazz, opera and dance.
Utilizes: Collaborations; Dance Companies; Multimedia; Original Music Scores; Theatre Companies
Founded: 1928
Specialized Field: Series & Festivals: Present Concerts
Status: Non-Profit, Professional
Paid Staff: 2
Budget: $170,000
Income Sources: Grants; Donations
Performs At: Scranton Cultural Center; Mellow Theater

5504
SUSQUEHANNA UNIVERSITY ARTIST SERIES
514 University Avenue
Selinsgrove, PA 17870
Phone: 570-372-4260
Fax: 570-372-2722
Toll-free: 800-326-9672
e-mail: artistseries@susqu.edu
Web Site: www.susqu.edu/artists
Management:
   President: Jay Lemons
Founded: 1902
Budget: $35,000-60,000
Performs At: Weber Chapel Auditorium and Dogenstein Center Theatre

5505
CENTRAL COMMUNITY CONCERTS
52 E Independence Street
Shamokin, PA 17872
Phone: 570-648-3931
Officers:
   President: Irvin R Liachowitz
Budget: $20,000-35,000

5506
SLIPPERY ROCK UNIVERSITY - PERFORMING ARTS SERIES
1 Morrow Way
Slippery Rock, PA 16057
Phone: 724-738-2092
Fax: 724-738-2624
Toll-free: 800-778-9111
e-mail: cheryl.knoch@sru.edu
Web Site: www.sru.edu
Officers:
   Chairman: Guido M. Pichini
   Vice Chair: Laura E. Ellsworth
Management:
   President: Cherly Norton
Performs At: Miller Auditorium; Swope Music hall

5507
CENTRAL PENNSYLVANIA FESTIVAL OF THE ARTS
403 S. Allen Street, Suite 205A
P.O. Box 1023
State College, PA 16804
Phone: 814-237-3682
Fax: 814-237-0708
e-mail: office@arts-festival.com
Web Site: www.arts-festival.com
Officers:
   President: Joyce Robinson
   Vice President: Steve Watson
   Treasurer: Charley DeBow
   Secretary: Sue Haug
   Past President: Katherine Allen
Management:
   Executive Director: Rick Bryant
   Director of Operations: Carol Baney
   Director of Development: Diane Bloom
   Festival Intern: Katrina Oselinsky
   Festival Intern: Katrina Shope
Mission: To offer an annual festival which celebrates all the arts.
Utilizes: Fine Artists; Instructors; Local Artists; Multimedia; Selected Students; Touring Companies
Founded: 1967
Specialized Field: Series & Festivals: Arts Festival
Status: Non-Profit, Professional
Paid Staff: 3
Budget: $490,000
Income Sources: Sponsorship; ticket sales; entry fees
Performs At: Indoor; Auditorium; Outdoor stages
Affiliations: PA Presenters
Annual Attendance: 100,000
Facility Category: Festival
Organization Type: Performing

5508
MUSIC AT PENN'S WOODS
Pennsylvania State School Of Music
Music Building 1
University Park, PA 16802-1901
Phone: 814-865-0431
Fax: 814-865-6785
e-mail: pennswoods@psu.edu
Web Site: mpw.psu.edu
Officers:
   Chair: Cathy Herrera
   Vice Chair: Buzz Graham
   Secretary: Ellie Lewis
Management:
   Music Director: Gerardo Edelstein
   Marketing/Operations: Russell Bloom
   Director: Sue Haug
Mission: Orchestra and chamber music festival
Founded: 1985
Specialized Field: Orchestra; chamber music
Paid Staff: 3
Paid Artists: 45
Budget: $100,000
Performs At: Eisenhower Auditorium
Facility Category: Performing Arts Facility
Seating Capacity: 2500
Year Built: 1972

5509
VILLANOVA UNIVERSITY CHAMBER SERIES
800 E. Lancaster Avenue
Villanova University
Villanova, PA 19085
Phone: 610-519-4500
Fax: 610-519-7596
Toll-free: 888-862-5050
e-mail: brian.meneely@villanova.com
Web Site: www1.villanova.edu
Management:
   Executive Director: John Junphi
   Artistic Director: Peter Marino
   Managing Director: Brian Meneeli
Specialized Field: Series & Festivals; Instrumental Music; Vocal Music; Theatre; Dance
Status: Non-Profit, Non-Professional
Paid Staff: 6
Budget: $20,000-35,000
Performs At: St. Mary's Hall

5510
WILDFLOWER MUSIC FESTIVAL
PO Box 356
White Mills, PA 18473
Phone: 570-253-5500
Fax: 570-253-5196
e-mail: music01@ptd.net
Web Site: www.dorflinger.org
Management:
   Executive Director: Joan Gillner
   Artistic Director: Kyler Brown
Founded: 1982
Specialized Field: Series and Festivals; Instrumental Music; Vocal Music; Ethnic Performances
Status: Non-Profit, Professional
Paid Staff: 3
Paid Artists: 8
Performs At: Outdoor Natural Amphitheater
Annual Attendance: 5,000-8,000
Type of Stage: Concrete W/Shell
Seating Capacity: 800

5511
KING'S COLLEGE EXPERIENCING THE ARTS SERIES
133 N River Street
Wilkes-Barre, PA 18711-0801

SERIES & FESTIVALS / Rhode Island

Phone: 570-208-5900
Fax: 570-208-6023
e-mail: rbmcgoni@kings.edu
Web Site: www.kings.edu
Officers:
　Chairman: Thomas R. Smith
　Vice Chairman: Mark DeCesaris
　Secretary: Karen Keefer
Management:
　President: Rev. John Ryan
　Artistic Director: Robert McGonigle
Utilizes: Actors; Artists-in-Residence; Guest Directors; Guest Musical Directors; Multimedia; Original Music Scores; Sign Language Translators
Founded: 1946
Specialized Field: Education
Status: Non-Profit, Professional
Paid Staff: 1
Paid Artists: 1
Budget: $10,000-20,000
Performs At: Campus Ministry Center; Sheeny-Farmer Campus Center

5512
WILLIAMSPORT COMMUNITY CONCERT ASSOCIATION

1401 Washington Boulevard
Williamsport, PA 17701-5424
Phone: 570-326-2424
Fax: 570-327-7663
Toll-free: 800-432-9382
e-mail: boxoffice@pct.edu
Web Site: www.williamsportcommunityconcerts.org
Officers:
　President: Terry L Ziegler
Management:
　President: Cynthia Staiman Vosk
Budget: $35,000-60,000
Performs At: Scottish Rite Auditorium

5513
ARCADIA THEATER

1418 Graham Avenue
Windber, PA 15963
Phone: 814-467-9070
Fax: 814-467-5646
e-mail: arcadiatheater@floodcity.net
Web Site: www.arcadiatheater.net
Officers:
　Chairman of Board: Frank Consolo
　President: Frank Consolo
　Second Chair: Al Christ
Management:
　Executive Director: Gerald Ledney
　Artistic Director: Elsie Mock
　Asst Artistic Director: Robert Seese
　Children's/Community Theater Dir: Aspen Mock
　Public Relations Director: Amy Moore
　Technical Director: Leon O'Connor
　House and Grounds Director: Dan Hiteshew
Founded: 1998
Specialized Field: Series & Festivals; Vocal Music; Youth; Arts
Status: Non-Profit, Professional
Paid Staff: 4
Budget: $60,000-150,000
Seating Capacity: 710
Year Built: 1921
Year Remodeled: 1998

5514
BUCKS COUNTY PERFORMING ARTRS SERIES

1100 Edgewood Road
Yardley, PA 19067
Phone: 267-274-1100
Fax: 215-968-2475
e-mail: admin@lmt.org
Web Site: www.lmt.org
Management:
　Executive Director: Mary Borkovitz
Founded: 1978
Specialized Field: Series & Festivals; Instrumental Music; Vocal Music; Youth; Dance; Ethnic Performances
Status: Non-Profit, Professional
Volunteer Staff: 10
Paid Artists: 25
Budget: $24,000
Performs At: Township Community Room
Annual Attendance: 1050
Seating Capacity: 175
Year Built: 1976

5515
STRAND-CAPITOL PERFORMING ARTS CENTER SERIES

50 N George Street
York, PA 17401
Phone: 717-846-1111
Fax: 717-843-1208
e-mail: boxoffice@strandcapitol.org
Web Site: www.mystrandcapitol.org
Officers:
　Chair: Joel Menchey
　Vice Chairman: Loren H. Kroh
　Treasurer/Secretary: Darren Welker
　President & CEO: Ken Wesler
Management:
　Operations Director: Dale Elkiss
　Program Director: Carol Oppelaar
　Box Office Manager: Sarah Blask
　General Manager: Anne Sturm
　Business Manager: Trisha Melikian
Founded: 1980
Specialized Field: Performing Arts Facility; Instrumental Music; Vocal Music; Theatre; Youth; Dance; Ethnic Performances
Status: Non-Profit
Paid Staff: 17
Budget: $3 million

Rhode Island

5516
CONCERTS BY THE BAY

101 Ferry Road
Route 114
Bristol, RI 02809
Phone: 401-253-2707
Fax: 401-253-0412
e-mail: info@blitheworld.org
Web Site: www.blithewold.org
Management:
　Site Administrator: Constance Coar

5517
CULTURAL ORGANIZATION OF THE ARTS

PO Box 258
111 Pierce Street
East Greenwich, RI 02818
Phone: 401-886-4530
Management:
　COA Director: Kate Leach
Budget: $10,000

5518
KINGSTON CHAMBER MUSIC FESTIVAL AT URI

PO Box 1733
Kingston, RI 02881
Phone: 401-789-0665
Fax: 401-874-2380
e-mail: kcmfboxoffice@etal.uri.edu
Web Site: www.kingstonchambermusic.org
Officers:
　Vice President: Michelle Little
　Treasurer: Harold Bibb
　Secretary: Joanne Hall Coombs
Management:
　President: Martin Sadd
　Artistic Director: Natalie Zhu
　Managing Director: Bryan Mitchell
Mission: To provide outstanding classical music programs in New England. Offers both summer and winter concerts, and also outreach programs at local area schools.
Utilizes: Guest Musical Directors; Multimedia; Original Music Scores
Founded: 1989
Specialized Field: Series & Festivals; Instrumental Music; Youth; Classical Music
Status: Non-Profit, Professional
Paid Staff: 2
Volunteer Staff: 15
Paid Artists: 20
Budget: $60,000
Income Sources: Donations; Ticket sales
Affiliations: University of Rhode Island
Annual Attendance: 2800

5519
NEW ENGLAND PRESENTERS: UNIVERSITY OF RHODE ISLAND GREAT PERFORMANCES

105 Upper College Road
URI
Kingston, RI 02881
Phone: 401-874-1000
Fax: 401-874-2772
e-mail: rto9302u@postoffice.uri.edu
Web Site: ww2.uri.edu
Management:
　Director: Roxana Tourigny
Budget: $35,000-60,000
Performs At: Veterans Memorial Auditorium; Edwards Hall; Will Theatre

5520
NEWPORT MUSIC FESTIVAL

850 Aquidneck Avenue
Newport, RI 02840
Phone: 401-846-1133
Fax: 401-849-1857
e-mail: staff@newportmusic.org
Web Site: www.newportmusic.org
Officers:
　President: Ms Diane S Hurley
　President Emeritus: Mrs. Marion Oates Charles
　First Vice President: Mrs. Ruth Orthwein
　Second Vice President: Dr. Orest V. Zaklynsky
　Secretary: Mrs. Pamela O. Giroux
Management:
　General Manager: Mark P Malkovich IV

Mission: Presenting chamber music of the Romantic era. 65 concerts per year.
Utilizes: Collaborations; Commissioned Composers; Commissioned Music; Guest Accompanists; Guest Companies; Guest Musical Directors; Guest Musicians; Instructors; Multimedia; Original Music Scores; Sign Language Translators; Singers
Founded: 1969
Specialized Field: Series & Festivals; Vocal Music; Chamber Music
Status: Non-Profit, Professional
Paid Staff: 3
Volunteer Staff: 300
Paid Artists: 50
Budget: $1 Million
Income Sources: Box Office; Donations; Corporate & Foundation Support
Season: July
Performs At: Newport Mansions
Affiliations: Yamaha Corporation of America; Roederer Champagne; Time, Inc.; Lufthansa
Annual Attendance: 28,000
Facility Category: Various Mansions; Churches; Tents
Seating Capacity: 250 - 500
Organization Type: Performing; Sponsoring
Comments: The Newport Music Festival is listed by Cadogen Press in their Ultimate List of 1000 Best Things in America.

5521
CAPITOLARTS PROVIDENCE CULTURAL AFFAIRS
65 Weybosset Street, Mailbox 39
Suite 68
Providence, RI 02903
Phone: 401-265-5051
Fax: 401-621-1883
e-mail: info@caparts.org
Web Site: www.caparts.org
Management:
  President: Randy Kass
  Executive Director: Bob Rizzo
  Choreographer: Nancy Compton
Mission: Dedicated to producing arts events that enliven the cityscape of Providence, Rhode Island; working together with the City of Providence, Parks Department, Office of Cultural Affairs, CapitolArts Providence produces events, both large and small, that appeal to the region's diverse community.
Founded: 1992
Specialized Field: Producing arts events
Status: Nonprofit

5522
CONVERGENCE ARTS FESTIVAL
Providence Parks Department
400 Westminister Street 4th Floor
Providence, RI 02903
Phone: 401-621-1992
Fax: 401-621-1883
Web Site: www.vac.igs.net
Specialized Field: Two-day workshop - poetry of Walt Whitman

5523
FIRST NIGHT PROVIDENCE
10 Dorrance Street
Suite 920
Providence, RI 02903
Phone: 401-521-1166
Fax: 401-273-5630
e-mail: firstnight@firstnightprovidence.org
Web Site: www.firstnightprovidence.org
Management:
  Director: Doris Stephens
  Assistant Director: Annette Robinson
  Artistic Director: Kathleen Fletcher
  Business Director: Carolyn Tick
Mission: Nonalcoholic family celebration of the arts on New Year's Eve.
Utilizes: Actors; Artists-in-Residence; Collaborating Artists; Collaborations; Dance Companies; Dancers; Five Seasonal Concerts; Instructors; Local Artists; Lyricists; Multi Collaborations; Multimedia; Original Music Scores; Playwrights; Sign Language Translators; Special Technical Talent; Touring Companies
Founded: 1985
Specialized Field: Dance; Vocal Music; Instrumental Music; Theater
Status: Nonprofit
Paid Staff: 4
Budget: $550,000
Income Sources: Admission Sales; Corporate Sponsors; Individual Contributions
Performs At: Theaters; Performance Halls; Churches
Annual Attendance: 50,000
Facility Category: Arts festival
Type of Stage: Multi-Purpose
Organization Type: Performing; Educational; Sponsoring

5524
NEWGATE THEATER
PO Box 41311
Providence, RI 02940
Phone: 401-454-0454
e-mail: brien@newgatetheatre.org
Management:
  Artistic Director: Brien Lang
  Managing Director: Joseph Mecca
  Webmaster: Peter Gogol
Mission: Committed to producing new and established works which challenge both artists and audiences.
Utilizes: Guest Companies
Founded: 1982
Specialized Field: June Festival of Short Plays
Status: Semi-Professional; Nonprofit
Income Sources: New England Theatre Conference
Organization Type: Performing; Resident; Producing

5525
PROVIDENCE DIVISION OF PUBLIC PROGRAMMING DEPARTMENTS
Providence Parks Department
400 Westminster Street 4th Floor
Providence, RI 02903-3222
Phone: 401-621-1992
Fax: 401-621-1883
e-mail: info@caparts.org
Web Site: www.caparts.org
Management:
  Public Programming Director: Bob Rizzo
Budget: $60,000-150,000

5526
RHODE ISLAND COLLEGE: PERFORMING ARTS SERIES
600 Mount Pleasant Avenue
301 Roberts Hall
Providence, RI 02908-1991
Phone: 401-456-8000
Fax: 401-456-8269
e-mail: theweb@ric.edu
Web Site: www.ric.edu/pfa
Management:
  Director: Michael Ducharme
Utilizes: Actors; Artists-in-Residence; Dance Companies; Dancers; Educators; Fine Artists; Grant Writers; Guest Accompanists; Guest Artists; Guest Choreographers; Guest Companies; Guest Conductors; Guest Directors; Guest Instructors; Guest Musical Directors; Guest Musicians; Guest Soloists; Instructors; Multimedia; Original Music Scores; Playwrights; Selected Students; Sign Language Translators; Singers; Soloists; Special Technical Talent; Theatre Companies
Founded: 1962
Specialized Field: Series & Festivals; Instrumental Music; Vocal Music; Theatre; Youth; Dance; Ethnic Performances
Status: Non-Profit, Professional
Paid Staff: 9
Volunteer Staff: 24
Paid Artists: 80
Budget: $60,000-$150,000
Performs At: Roberts Auditorium; Sapinsley Hall; Forman Theatre

South Carolina

5527
UNIVERSITY OF SOUTH CAROLINA: AIKEN ETHERREDGE CENTER
471 University Parkway
Aiken, SC 29801
Phone: 803-641-3305
Fax: 803-641-3691
e-mail: jackb@usca.edu
Web Site: web.usca.edu/etherredge-center
Management:
  President: Thomas Hallmen
  Executive Director: Prof. Jack Benjamin
  House Manager: Juanita Palmer
  Technical Director: Chet Longley
Utilizes: Dance Companies; Dancers; Fine Artists; Instructors; Local Artists; Multimedia; Sign Language Translators; Singers; Soloists; Special Technical Talent; Theatre Companies
Founded: 1982
Specialized Field: Series & Festivals; Musical; Dance; Ballads
Status: Non-Profit, Non-Professional
Paid Staff: 3
Budget: $60,000-150,000
Affiliations: University of Saint Gerdina
Facility Category: Theater Complex
Type of Stage: Thrust Proscenium
Stage Dimensions: 38 by 24
Seating Capacity: 687
Year Built: 1986
Rental Contact: Jane Schumacher

5528
ANDERSON UNIVERSITY
316 Boulevard
Anderson, SC 29621
Phone: 864-231-2000
Fax: 864-231-2083
Toll-free: 800-542-3594
e-mail: dlarson@andersonuniversity.edu
Web Site: www.andersonuniversity.edu
  Dean/Visual Performance Arts: David Larson
Management:
  President: Dr. Evans P. Whitaker
  Director Marketing,Communication: Barry D. Ray
Founded: 1911
Specialized Field: Series & Festivals; Instrumental Music; Vocal Music; Theatre
Status: Non-Profit, Non-Professional

SERIES & FESTIVALS / South Carolina

Paid Staff: 3
Volunteer Staff: 20
Paid Artists: 13
Budget: $10,000-20,000
Seating Capacity: 1100; 200; 100

5529
CIVIC CENTER OF ANDERSON
3027 MLK Jr. Blvd
Anderson, SC 29625
Phone: 864-260-4800
Fax: 864-260-4847
e-mail: asec@andersoncountysc.org
Web Site: www.andersonevents.com
Management:
    Manager: Charles Wyatt
    Events Coordinator: Terry Gaines
    Athletic Coordinator: Todd McCormick
Specialized Field: Series & Festivals Instrumental Music; Vocal Music; Theatre; Youth; Dance; Ethnic Performances
Status: Non-Professional
Paid Staff: 15

5530
UNIVERSITY OF SOUTH CAROLINA-BEAUFORT
801 Carteret Street
Beaufort, SC 29902
Phone: 843-521-4100
Fax: 843-379-2789
e-mail: ellenz@hargray.com
Web Site: www.uscb.edu
Management:
    President: John Gettys Smith
    Executive Director: Ellen Zisholtz
Founded: 1991
Status: Non-Profit
Budget: $60,000-150,000
Performs At: Beaufort Waterfront Park

5531
CHARLESTON CONCERT ASSOCIATION
131 King Street
Charleston, SC 29401
Phone: 843-722-7667
Fax: 843-577-5173
e-mail: nicholscca@aol.com
Web Site: www.charlestonconcerts.org
Management:
    President: John Davis
    Director: Jason Nichols
Founded: 1934
Specialized Field: Series & Festivals; Instrumental Music; Vocal Music; Theatre; Youth; Dance; Ethnic Performances
Status: Non-Profit, Professional
Paid Staff: 3
Budget: $150,000-400,000
Performs At: Gaillard Municipal Auditorium

5532
CITADEL FINE ARTS SERIES
The Citadel
171 Moultrie Street
Charleston, SC 29409
Phone: 843-953-5065
Fax: 843-953-6797
e-mail: Grant.Staley@citadel.edu
Web Site: www.citadel.edu/finearts
Officers:
    Chairman: Dr. Grant B Staley
Budget: $10,000-20,000
Performs At: Mark Clark Hall Auditorium

5533
PICCOLO SPOLETO FESTIVAL
Office of Cultural Affairs
180 Meeting Street
Charleston, SC 29401
Phone: 843-724-7305
Fax: 843-720-3967
e-mail: cultural_affairs@ci.charleston.us
Web Site: www.piccolospoleto.com
Management:
    Executive Director: Scott Watson
    Finance Coordinator: Rachel Dewyngaert
    Operations Coordinator: Alicia Evans
    Production Manager: Ray Swagerty
    Development Manager: Gordon Rooney
Founded: 1979
Specialized Field: Series & Festivals; Instrumental Music; Vocal Music; Theatre; Youth; Dance; Ethnic Performances
Status: Non-Profit, Professional
Paid Staff: 9

5534
SPOLETO FESTIVAL USA
14 George Street
Charleston, SC 29401-1524
Phone: 843-722-2764
Fax: 843-723-6383
e-mail: info@spoletousa.org
Web Site: www.spoletousa.org
Officers:
    Chairman: Carlos E. Evans
    President: M. Edward Sellers
    Treasurer: Ronald D. Abramson
Management:
    Artistic Director-Choral Activities: Joseph Flummerfelt
    Director, Chamber Music: Geoff Nuttall
    General Director: Nigel Redden
    Producer: Nunally Kersh
    Director Of Development: Julia Forster
    Director Marketing/Public Relations: Jennifer Scott
    Facilities Manager: Chelsea Mylett
    Director of Production: Rhys Williams
Mission: To present opera, dance, theater, symphonic, choral and chamber music, jazz and visual arts exhibits of the highest quality; to serve as an educational environment for young artists and audiences alike.
Utilizes: Singers
Founded: 1977
Specialized Field: Jazz; Theatrical Dance
Status: Professional; Semi-Professional; Non-Profit
Paid Staff: 18
Budget: $7,000,000
Income Sources: Ticket Revenues; Contributions
Performs At: Gaillard Municipal Auditorium; Dock Street Theater
Annual Attendance: 70,000-80,000
Organization Type: Performing; Educational; Sponsoring

5535
PRESBYTERIAN COLLEGE
503 S Broad Street
Clinton, SC 29325
Phone: 864-833-2820
Fax: 864-833-8600
Toll-free: 800-476-7272
e-mail: lwshealy@presby.edu
Web Site: www.presby.edu
Officers:
    President: Dr. Claude C. Lilly

Management:
    Cultural Events Director: Laura Shealy
    Technical Director: Greg Bruce
Utilizes: Artists-in-Residence; Dance Companies; Guest Directors; Guest Instructors; Guest Musical Directors; Guest Soloists; Multimedia; Original Music Scores; Singers; Soloists
Founded: 1880
Specialized Field: Education
Status: Non-Profit, Non-Professional
Paid Staff: 3
Paid Artists: 10
Non-paid Artists: 30
Budget: $35,000-60,000
Annual Attendance: 25,000
Facility Category: Concert Hall/Recital Hall
Type of Stage: Proscenium
Stage Dimensions: 39'x24'/23'x49'
Seating Capacity: 1,100/335
Rental Contact: Not Available for Rental

5536
CAROLINA PRODUCTIONS, PERFORMING ARTS COMMISSION
Russell House University Union
Room 227
Columbia, SC 29208
Phone: 803-777-0169
Fax: 803-777-7132
Toll-free: 800-922-9755
e-mail: visitor@mailbox.sc.edu
Web Site: www.sc.edu
Officers:
    President: Adam Mayer
    VP Internal Affairs: Allie Anderson
    VP Media Relations: Samantha Wheatley
Specialized Field: Series & Festivals; Instrumental Music; Vocal Music; Theatre; Youth; Dance; Ethnic Performances
Status: Non-Profit, Professional
Performs At: Koger Center for the Arts; Carolina Coliseum

5537
COLUMBIA COLLEGE POWER COMPANY SERIES
1301 Columbia College Drive
Columbia College Dance Department
Columbia, SC 29203
Phone: 803-786-3825
Fax: 803-786-3868
e-mail: mbrim@colacoll.edu
Web Site: www.columbiacollegesc.edu
Officers:
    Dance Department Chair: Susan Haigler-Robles
Management:
    President: Caroline Whitson
    Executive Director: Laurie Hopkins
    Artistic Director: Martha Brim
Utilizes: Artists-in-Residence; Choreographers; Collaborating Artists; Collaborations; Dance Companies; Dancers; Educators; Guest Artists; Guest Soloists; High School Drama; Instructors; Local Artists; Resident Artists; Soloists; Theatre Companies
Founded: 1987
Specialized Field: Series & Festivals: Contemporary Dance
Status: Non-Profit, Professional
Paid Staff: 2
Volunteer Staff: 45
Paid Artists: 5
Budget: $10,000
Performs At: Cottingham Theater, Columbia College

SERIES & FESTIVALS / South Carolina

Affiliations: The Power Company; South Carolina Center for Dance Education
Annual Attendance: 12,000
Facility Category: Theater
Type of Stage: Proscenium
Stage Dimensions: 30 X 40
Seating Capacity: 385
Year Built: 1960
Rental Contact: Patrick Faulds

5538
KOGER CENTER FOR THE ARTS
University of South Carolina
1051 Greene Street
Columbia, SC 29201
Phone: 803-777-7500
Fax: 803-777-9774
Web Site: www.koger.sc.edu
Management:
  Director: Ron Pearson
  Assistant Director: Michael Gaylor
Founded: 1989
Specialized Field: Series and Festivals; Instrumental Music; Vocal Music; Theatre; Youth; Dance; Ethnic Performances
Status: For-Profit, Non-Professional
Paid Staff: 7
Budget: $1,000,000+

5539
ERSKINARTS (THE FINE & PERFORMING ARTS AT ERSKINE COLLEGE)
Erskine College
P.O. Box 338
Due West, SC 29639
Phone: 864-379-8831
Fax: 864-379-3164
Toll-free: 888-359-4358
e-mail: mattman@erskine.edu
Web Site: www.erskine.edu
Officers:
  Chairman: W. D. Conner
  Vice Chairman: W.S. Cain
  Secretary: H.M. Bolin
Management:
  Director Of Choral Activities: Johnn Warre
  Chair Of The Department Of Music: Matthew Manwarr
Founded: 1839
Budget: $20,000-35,000
Performs At: Memorial Hall

5540
FRANCIS MARION UNIVERSITY ARTISTS SERIES
PO Box 100547
Florence, SC 29501-0547
Phone: 843-661-1385
Fax: 843-661-1529
Toll-free: 800-368-7551
e-mail: jfallenger@fmarion.edu
Web Site: www.fmarion.edu
Officers:
  Chairman: George C. McIntyre
  Vice Chairman: L. Franklin Elmore
  Secretary: Kenneth W. Jackson
Management:
  President: Luther F Carter
Founded: 1972
Specialized Field: Series & Festivals; Instrumental Music; Vocal Music; Theatre; Dance; Classical Dance
Status: Non-Profit, Professional
Budget: $10,000-20,000

Performs At: McNair Auditorium

5541
METROPOLITAN ARTS COUNCIL
16 Augusta Street
Greenville, SC 29601
Phone: 864-467-3132
Fax: 864-467-3133
e-mail: mac@greenvilleARTS.com
Web Site: www.greenvillearts.com
Officers:
  Chairman: Charles Ratterree
  Secretary: Kenneth Betsch
  Treasurer: Sandy Watkins
Management:
  Executive Director: Alan Ethridge
  Director of Operations: Kim Sholly
  Director of Arts Education: Hearther Marshall
  Assistant Director of Operations: Erin Turner
Mission: To stimulate and support artistic expression and its appreciation and enjoyment in ways that enrich all citizens, artsits, cultural organizations, and communities of the Metropolitan area.
Utilizes: Actors; Artists-in-Residence; Choreographers; Collaborating Artists; Collaborations; Commissioned Composers; Commissioned Music; Curators; Dance Companies; Dancers; Designers; Educators; Equity Actors; Filmmakers; Fine Artists; Five Seasonal Concerts; Guest Accompanists; Guest Choreographers; Guest Composers; Guest Designers; Guest Ensembles; Guest Lecturers; Guest Musical Directors; Guest Musicians; Guest Teachers; Guild Activities; High School Drama; Instructors; Local Artists; Local Unknown Artists; Lyricists; Multi Collaborations; Multimedia; Music; New Productions; Organization Contracts; Original Music Scores; Performance Artists; Playwrights; Poets; Resident Professionals; Sign Language Translators; Singers; Soloists; Special Technical Talent; Touring Companies; Visual Arts
Founded: 1973
Status: Non-Profit, Non-Professional
Paid Staff: 3
Budget: $450,000
Income Sources: City, State and Federal grants, private donations

5542
GREENWOOD-LANDER PERFORMING ARTS
Lander University
CPO Box 6044
Greenwood, SC 29649
Phone: 864-388-8326
Fax: 864-388-8036
e-mail: glpa@lander.edu
Web Site: www.greenwoodlanderperformingarts.com
Management:
  Executive Director: Cecily Ferguson
  Outreach Program Director: Jackie Counts
Founded: 1946
Specialized Field: Series & Festival; Instrumental Music; Dance
Status: Non-Profit, Professional
Paid Staff: 1
Paid Artists: 250
Budget: $70,000-80,000
Annual Attendance: 3,500- 4,000
Facility Category: Concert Hall
Seating Capacity: 700

5543
HARTSVILLE COMMUNITY CONCERT ASSOCIATION
PO Box 2283
Hartsville, SC 29551
Phone: 866-821-4266
e-mail: HCCA@coker.edu
Web Site: www.hartsvillecokerconcerts.org
Officers:
  President: David M Tavernier
  Secretary: Lisa Jones
  Treasurer: Elizabeth Kremer
Founded: 1945
Budget: $20,000-35,000

5544
ARTS CENTER OF COASTAL CAROLINA
14 Shelter Cove Lane
Hilton Head Island, SC 29928
Phone: 843-686-3945
Fax: 843-842-7877
Toll-free: 888-860-2787
e-mail: info@artshhi.com
Web Site: www.artshhi.com
Officers:
  President/CEO: Kathleen P Bateson
Management:
  President: Kathleen Bateson
  General Manager: Richard Feldman
Mission: Theatre and presenting.
Founded: 1996
Specialized Field: Performing; Visual Gallery; Produce and Present Live Theatre
Status: Non-Profit, Professional
Paid Staff: 35
Paid Artists: 15
Budget: $3.2 million
Performs At: Elizabeth Wallace Theatre
Type of Stage: Proscenium
Seating Capacity: 350
Year Built: 1996
Rental Contact: Richard Feldman

5545
COASTAL CONCERT ASSOCIATION
1107 48 Avenue N
Suite 211-E
Myrtle Beach, SC 29577
Phone: 843-449-7546
Fax: 843-449-9391
e-mail: coastcon@infionline.net
Web Site: www.coastalconcert.com
Officers:
  President: John Trugdeau
  Treasurer: Kelli Shana Felt
  President: B Matt Morris
Management:
  President: Brenda Mancill
  Executive Director: Shirley Cope
  Concert Chairperson: Linda Erwin
Utilizes: Dance Companies; Multimedia; Original Music Scores; Special Technical Talent
Founded: 1972
Specialized Field: Music
Status: Non-Profit, Professional
Paid Staff: 1
Volunteer Staff: 20
Paid Artists: 20
Budget: $35,000-60,000
Performs At: Performing Arts Center
Annual Attendance: 6,000
Seating Capacity: 1900

SERIES & FESTIVALS / South Dakota

5546
ARTS ETC
PO Box 2692 CRS
Rock Hill, SC 29732
Phone: 803-324-8803
Fax: 803-324-8200
e-mail: karenb@infoave.net
Web Site: www.artsetc.org
Management:
    Executive Director: Karen Blankenship
Paid Staff: 5
Budget: $35,000-60,000
Performs At: Byrnes Auditorium
Type of Stage: Proscenium
Seating Capacity: 3,540
Year Built: 1938

5547
WINTHROP UNIVERSITY COLLEGE OF VISUAL & PERFORMING ARTS
College of Visual & Performing Arts
701 Oakland Avenue
Rock Hill, SC 29733
Phone: 803-323-2323
Fax: 803-323-2333
e-mail: rogersd@winthrop.edu
Web Site: www.winthrop.edu
Management:
    Dean: David Wahl
    Chair Of Music/Associate Music Prof: Donald M Rogers
Budget: $35,000-60,000

5548
ARTS PARTNERSHIP OF GREATER SPARTANBURG
200 E St. John Street
Spartanburg, SC 29306-3350
Phone: 864-583-2776
Fax: 864-948-5353
e-mail: sWong@SpartanArts.org
Web Site: www.chapmanculturalcenter.org
Management:
    President & COO: H Perry Mixter
    Director of Facilities: Jan Benjamin
    Director of Development: Jennifer Evins
    Marketing: Steve Wong
    Facility Director: Jeff Pickens
    Ticket Office Manager: Melissa Earley
    Financial Director: Angela Geter
    Arts Education Director: Ava J. Hughes
Mission: The Arts Partnership inspires one true expression and educational discovery in Spartanburg County; and provides strategic and financial leadership to cultural organizations, artists and educators
Founded: 1968
Specialized Field: United Arts Council
Paid Staff: 17
Volunteer Staff: 100
Paid Artists: 12
Budget: $2,000,000
Income Sources: Annual fund; rental; grants
Affiliations: Americans for the Arts
Annual Attendance: 132,000
Facility Category: Cultural Center
Type of Stage: Proscenium
Stage Dimensions: 40 x 80
Seating Capacity: 500
Year Built: 2007
Cost: $47,000,000
Rental Contact: Kathy Campbell

5549
MUSIC FOUNDATION OF SPARTANBURG CONCERT SERIES
385 S Spring Street
Spartanburg, SC 29306
Mailing Address: Box 1274, Spartanburg, SC. 29304
Phone: 864-948-9020
Fax: 864-948-5353
e-mail: music@teleplex.net
Web Site: www.sparklenet.com/musicfoundation
Management:
    President: Robert Rainer
    Executive Director: Dana Gencarelli
Specialized Field: Series & Festivals: Instrumental Music
Status: Non-Profit, Professional
Paid Staff: 3
Budget: $60,000-150,000
Performs At: Twichell Auditorium

5550
FINE ARTS COUNCIL OF SUMTER PERFORMING ARTS SERIES
10 Mood Avenue
Sumter, SC 29150
Phone: 803-775-5580
Fax: 803-778-9664
e-mail: finearts@ftc-i.net
Web Site: www.angelfire.com/sc/finearts
Management:
    Director: Zan Fort
Mission: To enrich the cultural atmosphere of our area by presenting a Performing Arts Series; to reward students of the performing arts by sponsoring a school competition.
Utilizes: Actors; Artists-in-Residence; Dance Companies; Dancers; Fine Artists; Guest Lecturers; Guest Musical Directors; Local Artists; Multimedia; Sign Language Translators; Special Technical Talent; Theatre Companies
Founded: 1986
Paid Staff: 1
Volunteer Staff: 25
Budget: $100,000
Income Sources: Grants; ticket sales
Performs At: Patriot Hall
Facility Category: Auditorium
Type of Stage: Proscenium
Stage Dimensions: 47x21
Seating Capacity: 1,017
Year Remodeled: 1988

5551
NORTH GREENVILLE UNIVERSITY: FINE ARTS SERIES
PO Box 1892
Tigerville, SC 29688
Phone: 864-977-7001
Fax: 864-977-7021
Toll-free: 800-468-6642
e-mail: admissions@ngu.edu
Web Site: www.ngu.edu
Management:
    President: James B Epting
    Dean of Fine Arts/Head of Music: Dr. Jackie Griffin
    Head of Theater: Dr. Dale Savidge
    Head of Visual Arts: Zac Buser
Mission: Quality education in a Christian environment
Founded: 1882
Specialized Field: Music; Visual; Theatre
Status: Accredited; University
Budget: $10,000
Performs At: Fine Arts Center
Affiliations: NASM; SACS
Seating Capacity: 260/Recital; 1600/Auditorium

South Dakota

5552
ABERDEEN COMMUNITY CONCERT ASSOCIATION
PO Box 426
Aberdeen, SD 57402
Phone: 605-226-2452
e-mail: info@aberdeencommunityconcerts.org
Web Site: aberdeencommunityconcerts.org
Officers:
    President: Gene Morsching
Budget: $10,000-20,000
Performs At: Johnson Fine Arts Center

5553
SOUTH DAKOTA STATE UNIVERSITY STUDENT ACTIVITIES
PO Box 2815
Brookings, SD 57007-1599
Phone: 605-688-6129
Fax: 605-688-4973
Management:
    Program Advisor: Adam Karnopp
Budget: $20,000-35,000
Performs At: David B. Doner Auditorium

5554
THE LAURA INGALLS WILDER PAGEANT SOCIETY
PO Box 154
De Smet, SD 57231
Phone: 605-692-2108
Toll-free: 800-880-3383
Web Site: www.desmetpageant.org
Management:
    Managing Director: Portia Potvin
Mission: To present an outdoor pageant depicting The Little House on the Prairie books of Laura Ingalls Wilder. The pageant takes place across from the site of the Ingalls homestead.
Founded: 1971
Specialized Field: Theatre
Status: Nonprofit
Organization Type: Performing

5555
HURON ARENA
150 5th Street SW
Huron, SD 57350
Phone: 605-353-6990
Fax: 605-353-6973
Web Site: www.huron.k12.sd.us/education/district/district.php?sectionid=1
Management:
    Manager: Glen Ulvested

5556
MADISON AREA ARTS COUNCIL
PO Box 147
Madison, SD 57042
Phone: 605-256-5051
Management:
    Arts Coordinator: Eve Fisher
Mission: To promote arts appreciation; to sponsor arts activities; to offer opportunities for arts education to community members.

SERIES & FESTIVALS / Tennessee

Utilizes: Guest Companies
Founded: 1968
Specialized Field: Dance; Vocal Music; Instrumental Music; Theater; Festivals
Status: Nonprofit
Income Sources: South Dakota Arts Council; Community Arts Council Network; South Dakota Alliance
Performs At: Dakota Prairie Playhouse
Organization Type: Educational; Sponsoring

5557
PIERRE COMMUNITY CONCERTS ASSOCIATION
PO Box 519
808 W Pleasant
Pierre, SD 57501
Phone: 605-224-5803
Web Site: www.pierreconcertseries.com
Officers:
    President: Joan Likness
    Vice President: Jerry Wagner
    Secretary: Gail Lyngstad
    Treasurer: Nancy Thomsen
Budget: $10,000-20,000

Tennessee

5558
ATHENS AREA COUNCIL FOR THE ARTS
320 N. White St.
Athens, TN 37371-0095
Phone: 423-745-8781
Fax: 423-745-8635
e-mail: office@athensartscouncil.org
Web Site: www.athensartscouncil.org
Officers:
    President: Sandra Boyd
    Vice President: Jerry Hagaman
    Secretary: Joe Littleton
    Treasurer: Shelley Griffith
Management:
    Program Coordinator: Jennifer Nunley
    Executive Director: Lauren Brown Shepherd
Founded: 1979
Specialized Field: Arts Council
Status: Non-Profit, Professional
Paid Staff: 3
Paid Artists: 30
Budget: $10,000-20,000

5559
RIVERBEND FESTIVAL
Friends of the Festival
180 Hamm Road
Chattanooga, TN 37405
Phone: 423-756-2211
Fax: 423-756-2719
e-mail: info@riverbendfestival.com
Web Site: www.riverbendfestival.com
Management:
    Executive Director: Chip Baker
    Artistic Director: Joe Fuller
    Operations Director: Randy Buckles
    Director Of Sales: Karen Shostak
    Finance Director: Donica Branum
    Director of Public Relations: Amy Morrow
Mission: A huge family-oriented music festival which goes on for 9 nights, with six stages of almost every possible genre of music, fantastic fireworks and a children's village.
Founded: 1981
Specialized Field: Series & Festivals; Instrumental Music; Vocal Music; Theatre; Youth; Dance; Ethnic Performances
Status: Non-Profit, Professional
Paid Staff: 8

5560
UNIVERSITY OF TENNESSEE AT CHATTANOOGA
Fine Arts Center, Department 1351
615 Mccallie Avenue
Chattanooga, TN 37403
Phone: 423-425-4371
Fax: 423-425-5249
e-mail: Bob-Boyer@utc.edu
Web Site: www.utc.edu/finearts
Management:
    Fine Arts Center Manager: Bob Boyer
    Box Office Manager: Sue Carroll
Mission: Patten performances provides the Southeast Tennessee area with a professional showcase of national and international artists who perform and conduct residency activities in music, theatre and dance.
Paid Staff: 3
Paid Artists: 12
Budget: $60,000-150,000
Performs At: Roland Hayes Concert Hall
Annual Attendance: 4,000-5,000
Facility Category: Fine Arts Center
Type of Stage: Modified Proscenium
Seating Capacity: 505
Year Built: 1979
Rental Contact: Sue Carroll

5561
AUSTIN PEAY STATE UNIVERSITY
Center of Excellence for the Creative Arts
PO Box 4666
Clarksville, TN 37044
Phone: 931-221-7876
Fax: 931-221-7149
e-mail: johnsonf@apsu.edu
Web Site: www.apsu.edu
Management:
    President: Cherry Hoppe
    Executive Director: Jim Diehr
    Managing Director: Feleesha Johnson
Founded: 1985
Specialized Field: Series & Festivals; Instrumental Music; Vocal Music; Theater; Youth; Ethnic Performances; Arts
Status: Non-Profit, Non-Professional
Paid Staff: 3
Paid Artists: 5
Budget: $700,000
Income Sources: State
Performs At: Mass Communication Building
Type of Stage: Proscenium
Seating Capacity: 600

5562
LEE UNIVERSITY PRESIDENTIAL CONCERT SERIES
Lee University
1120 North Ocoee Street
Cleveland, TN 37311
Phone: 423-614-8240
Fax: 423-614-8242
e-mail: ngoff@leeuniversity.edu
Web Site: www.leeuniversity.edu
Officers:
    Dean, School Of Music: Stephen W Plate
Management:
    President: Paul Conn
    Vocal Chair: Luktann Holden
    Instrumental Chair: Philip Thomas
    Dean, School Of Music: Stephen Plate
Founded: 1991
Specialized Field: Series and Festivals; Instrumental Music; Vocal Music
Status: Non-Profit, Professional
Paid Staff: 21
Budget: $20,000-35,000
Performs At: Dixon Center
Annual Attendance: 3,000+
Facility Category: Music/Drama Performing Hall
Type of Stage: Full

5563
SOUTHERN ADVENTIST UNIVERSITY
PO Box 370
4881 Taylor Circle
Collegedale, TN 37315
Phone: 423-236-2813
Fax: 423-236-1814
Toll-free: 800-768-8437
e-mail: wohlers@southern.edu
Web Site: www1.southern.edu
Officers:
    Student Services VP: William R Wohlers
Management:
    President: Gordon Bietz
    Executive Director: Bill Wolhers
Founded: 1892
Specialized Field: Series & Festivals; Instrumental Music; Vocal Music; Theatre; Youth; Ethnic Performances & Cultural
Status: Non-Profit, Non-Professional
Budget: $20,000-35,000
Performs At: Physical Education Center; Ackerman Auditorium

5564
BRYAN COLLEGE DEPARTMENT OF MUSIC
Bryan College
PO Box 7000
Dayton, TN 37321
Phone: 423-775-2041
Fax: 423-775-7330
Toll-free: 800-277-9522
e-mail: info@bryan.edu
Web Site: www.bryan.edu
Management:
    President: Stephen Livesay
    Vice President of Finance: Vance Berger
    Vice President of Operations: Tim Hostetler
Founded: 1930
Specialized Field: Series and Festivals; Instrumental Music; Vocal Music; Theatre
Status: Non-Profit, Professional
Paid Staff: 80
Budget: $20,000
Performs At: Rudd Auditorium
Facility Category: Auditorium
Type of Stage: Proscenium
Seating Capacity: 750
Year Built: 1976

5565
ETOWAH ARTS COMMISSION
PO Box 193
Etowah, TN 37331

SERIES & FESTIVALS / Tennessee

Phone: 423-263-7608
Fax: 423-263-1670
e-mail: info@etowaharts.org
Web Site: www.etowaharts.org
Management:
    Chairman: Charles Marta
Founded: 1977
Specialized Field: Series & Festivals; Instrumental Music; Vocal Music; Theater; Youth
Status: Non-Profit, Non-Professional
Paid Staff: 1
Paid Artists: 25
Budget: $10,000
Performs At: Gem Theater

5566
GERMANTOWN PERFORMING ARTS CENTRE
1801 Exeter Road
Germantown, TN 38138
Phone: 901-751-7500
e-mail: info@gpacweb.com
Web Site: www.gpacweb.com
Management:
    Executive Director: Paul Chandler
Founded: 1994
Specialized Field: Series & Festivals: Instumental Music
Status: Non-Profit, Professional
Paid Staff: 14
Paid Artists: 40
Budget: $400,000-1,000,000
Income Sources: Box Office; Member Support

5568
CARSON-NEWMAN COLLEGE CONCERT-LECTURE SERIES
Carson-Newman College
Box 71891
Jefferson City, TN 37760
Phone: 865-471-2000
Fax: 865-471-4849
e-mail: rscruggs@cn.edu
Web Site: www.cn.edu
Officers:
    President: Randall O'Brien
Management:
    Director: Richard Scruggs
Founded: 1917
Specialized Field: Series and Festivals; Instrumental Music; Vocal Music; Theatre; Dance
Status: Non-Profit, Professional
Paid Staff: 2
Budget: $20,000-35,000
Performs At: Henderson Humanities Building

5569
EAST TENNESSEE FINE AND PERFORMING ARTS SCHOLARS
Box 70589
Johnson City, TN 37614-0691
Phone: 423-439-7507
Fax: 423-439-6080
e-mail: arts.scholars@etsu.edu
Web Site: www.etsu.edu/HONORS/arts/default.asp
Management:
    Department Chairman: Terry Countermine
    Assistant Department Chair: Martin Barrett
    Executive Aide: Cathy McGinnis
Specialized Field: Series and Festivals: Instrumental Music
Status: Non-Profit, Professional
Paid Staff: 5
Performs At: Brooks Gym

5570
JOHNSON CITY AREA ARTS COUNCIL
214 E Main Street
Johnson City, TN 37604
Mailing Address: Box 1033, Johnson City, TN. 37605
Phone: 423-928-8229
Fax: 423-928-4511
e-mail: jcarts@mounet.com
Web Site: www.arts.org
Management:
    President: Lee Lay
    Executive Director: Sarah K Davis
    Media Director: Christine Murdock
Mission: Dedicated to preserving the cultural communities in our area.
Founded: 1978
Specialized Field: Art Gallery
Status: Non-Profit, Professional
Paid Staff: 2
Volunteer Staff: 1
Budget: $10,000
Performs At: Small gallery space

5571
JUBILEE COMMUNITY ARTS
Laurel Theater
1538 Laurel Avenue
Knoxville, TN 37916-2016
Phone: 865-522-5851
Fax: 865-522-5386
e-mail: info@jubileearts.org
Web Site: www.jubileearts.org
Management:
    Executive Director: Brent Cantrell
    Concert Manager: Tolby Koosman
Founded: 1969
Specialized Field: Series & Festivals; Instrumental Music; Vocal Music; Dance; Ethnic Performances
Status: Non-Profit, Non-Professional
Paid Staff: 4
Budget: $35,000-60,000

5572
UNIVERSITY OF TENNESSEE AT KNOXVILLE: CULTURAL ARTS
305 University Center
Knoxville, TN 37996
Phone: 865-974-1000
Fax: 865-974-9252
e-mail: ronl@utk.edu
Web Site: www.utk.edu
Management:
    President: Jon Peterson
    Assistant Director: Edee Vaughan
    CEO: Jimmy G. Cheek
Specialized Field: Series & Festivals: Cultural Music And Dance
Status: Non-Profit, Professional
Paid Staff: 3
Budget: $150,000-400,000
Performs At: Clarence Brown Theatre

5573
UNIVERSITY OF TENNESSEE AT MARTIN ARTS COUNCIL
19 McCombs Center
Martin, TN 38238
Phone: 731-881-7436
e-mail: lcrews@utm.edu
Web Site: www.utm.edu/departments/honors/events.php
Management:
    Director: Lionel Crews
Budget: $20,000-35,000
Performs At: Harriet Fulton Performing Arts Theater

5574
CONCERTS INTERNATIONAL
PO Box 770522
Memphis, TN 38177-0522
Phone: 901-527-3067
Fax: 901-682-1928
e-mail: barnbeca@mindspring.com
Web Site: www.concertsinternationalmemphis.org
Officers:
    President: Barbara Blumenthal
    Vice President: Charles Caldwell III
    Secretary: David Blaylock
    Treasurer: Andrew Inglis
Management:
    Executive Director: Stephanie Tatum
    Artistic Director: Julie Schap
Utilizes: Guest Musical Directors; Multimedia; Original Music Scores
Specialized Field: Chamber Music
Paid Staff: 1
Budget: $35,000-60,000
Performs At: Harris Concert Hall; University of Memphis
Seating Capacity: 385
Year Remodeled: 1999

5575
MEMPHIS IN MAY INTERNATIONAL FESTIVAL
56 S Front St
Memphis, TN 38103
Phone: 901-525-4611
Fax: 901-525-4686
e-mail: mim@memphisinmay.org
Web Site: www.memphisinmay.org
Officers:
    Chair: Ronald Coleman
    Chair Elect: Wei Chen
    Vice Chair: Doug Browne
    Treasurer: Andre Fowleks
    Secretary: Roquita Coleman
Management:
    President, CEO: James L. Holt
    VP Finance, CFO: Mack Weaver
    VP Programming: Randy Blevins
    VP Sponsorships: Kevin Grothe
    Director Operations: Nick Hughes
Mission: To promote and celebrate Memphis culture, foster economic growth and enhance international awareness.
Founded: 1976
Specialized Field: Series & Festivals; Instrumental Music; Vocal Music; Youth; Ethnic Performances
Status: Non-Profit, Professional
Paid Staff: 14
Volunteer Staff: 999
Performs At: Tom Lee Park in downtown Memphis, Tennessee and various venues throughout town
Annual Attendance: 300,000+
Organization Type: Educational; Sponsoring

5576
RHODES COLLEGE: MCCOY VISITING ARTIST SERIES
2000 N Parkway
Memphis, TN 38112

SERIES & FESTIVALS / Tennessee

Phone: 901-843-3875
Fax: 901-843-3553
e-mail: templeton@rhodes.edu
Web Site: www.rhodes.edu
Management:
  President: William Troutt
Founded: 1848
Specialized Field: Communications
Status: Professional
Paid Staff: 15
Budget: $10,000

5577
MIDDLE TENNESSEE STATE UNIVERSITY

Music Department
1301 East Main Street
Murfreesboro, TN 37132-0001
Phone: 615-898-2300
Fax: 615-898-5037
e-mail: jperkins@frank.mtsu.edu
Web Site: www.mtsu.edu
Management:
  President: Sidney A Necphee
  Executive Director: George T Riorden
Specialized Field: Series and Festivals; Instrumental Music; Vocal Music; Music Performance
Status: Non-Profit, Professional
Paid Staff: 8
Budget: $10,000-20,000

5578
DAVID LIPSCOMB UNIVERSITY: MUSIC DEPARTMENT

David Lipscomb University
One University Park Drive
Nashville, TN 37204-3951
Phone: 615-269-1000
Fax: 615-386-7620
Toll-free: 800-333-4358
e-mail: reedja@dlu.edu
Web Site: www.lipscomb.edu
Officers:
  Chair: David Scobey
Management:
  President: L. Randolph Lowry III
  Senior Vice President: Candice McQueen
  SVP Finance and Administration: Danny H. Taylor
  VP, Chief Information Officer: Mike Green
  Athletic Director: Philip Hutcheson
Founded: 1891
Specialized Field: Series and Festivals; Instrumental Music; Vocal Music; Theatre; Christian Education
Status: For-Profit, Professional
Budget: $10,000-20,000
Performs At: Ward Lecture Auditorium; Alumni Auditorium

5579
FRIENDS OF MUSIC

PO Box 23593
Nashville, TN 37202-3593
Phone: 931-254-0469
Fax: 931-254-0469
Officers:
  President: Joseph S Johnson, Jr
Budget: $20,000-35,000
Performs At: James K. Polk Theater; Tennessee Performing Arts Center

5580
HOWARD C GENTRY COMPLEX

Tennessee State University
3500 John Merrit Boulevard
Nashville, TN 37209
Phone: 615-963-5000
Fax: 615-963-5911
Management:
  Athletic Director: Bill Thomas

5581
THE NASHVILLE SHAKESPEARE FESTIVAL

161 Rains Avenue
Nashville, TN 37203
Phone: 615-255-2273
Fax: 615-248-2273
e-mail: shellie@nashvilleshakes.org
Web Site: www.nashvilleshakes.org
Officers:
  Chairman: Donald Capparella
  Secretary: Ann Marie Deer-Owens
  Treasurer: Chad Milom
Management:
  President: Donald Capparrella
  Artistic Director: Denice Hicks
  Education Director: Nettie Kraft
  Operations Manager: Robert Marigza
  Development Director: Rickey Chick Marquardt
Mission: Dedicated to community enrichment and arts in education through innovative and relevant presentations of the works of William Shakespeare and other curriculum-based programming. We focus our work to stimulate imagination and inspire conversation, which are essential elements to a healthy society.
Founded: 1988
Specialized Field: Series & Festivals: Theatre
Status: Non-Profit, Professional
Paid Staff: 3
Paid Artists: 30
Season: august
Performs At: Centennial Park Bandshell
Affiliations: Shakespeare Theatre Association of America
Annual Attendance: 14,000
Organization Type: Performing; Resident; Touring; Educational
Comments: Productions are free of charge or at a cost that makes them accesible regardless of socio-economic circumstances; Barrier free and multiculturally cast.

5582
VANDERBILT UNIVERSITY: GREAT PERFORMANCES

207 Sarratt Center
Student Center
Nashville, TN 37240
Phone: 615-322-2471
Fax: 615-343-8081
e-mail: bridgette.kohnhorst@vanderbilt.edu
Web Site: www.vanderbilt.edu/greatperformances
Management:
  Executive Director: Bridgette Kohnhorst
  Art&Cultural Programs Director: Bridgette Kohnhorst
Founded: 1974
Specialized Field: Series and Festivals; Instrumental Music; Vocal Music; Dance; Ethnic Performances; Theatre; Performing Art
Status: Non-Profit, Professional
Paid Staff: 8
Paid Artists: 8

Budget: $150,000-400,000

5583
OAK RIDGE CIVIC MUSIC ASSOCIATION

PO Box 4271
Oak Ridge, TN 37831
Phone: 865-483-5569
Fax: 865-483-5569
e-mail: orcma@korrnet.org
Web Site: www.korrnet.org/orcma
Management:
  Managing Director: Earle Lovering
  Music Director: Serge Fournier
Mission: To provide the community with quality music; to encourage community youth to enjoy good music.
Founded: 1944
Specialized Field: Series and Festivals; Symphony; Orchestra; Classical
Status: Non-Profit, Professional
Paid Staff: 2
Paid Artists: 50
Performs At: Oak Ridge High School Auditorium
Organization Type: Performing; Educational; Sponsoring

5584
SEWANEE SUMMER MUSIC FESTIVAL

University of the South
735 University Avenue
Sewanee, TN 37383-1000
Phone: 931-598-1225
Fax: 931-598-1706
e-mail: ssmf@sewanee.edu
Web Site: www.sewaneemusicfestival.org
Management:
  Managing Director: Katherine Lehman, klehman@sewanee.edu
  Operations Manager: Donna Cotter, ssmf@sewanee.edu
  Production Manager: Jack Ray
  Assistant Director for Marketing: Stephanie Kelley
Mission: Internationally acclaimed summer festival, combining a program for advanced music students and a professional concert series.
Founded: 1957
Specialized Field: Orchestra
Paid Staff: 29
Volunteer Staff: 20
Paid Artists: 5
Income Sources: Tuition, Annual Fund, Endowed Funds, Grants
Annual Attendance: 145
Facility Category: Concert Hall
Seating Capacity: 1,999

5585
SEWANEE FESTIVAL ORCHESTRAS / SEWANEE MUSIC FESTIVAL

735 University Avenue
Sewanee, TN 37383
Phone: 931-598-1000
Fax: 615-598-1145
e-mail: sshrader@sewanee.edu
Web Site: www.sewanee.edu
Management:
  Chairman: Steven Shrader

5586
WATERTOWN JAZZ FESTIVAL

Watertown Bed & Breakfast
116 Depot Avenue
Watertown, TN 37184

SERIES & FESTIVALS / Texas

Phone: 615-237-9999
e-mail: mccomb28@charter.net
Web Site: www.watertownjazz.com
Management:
  President: Sharon McComb
  Artistic Director: Glenn Martin
Founded: 1990
Specialized Field: Series & Festivals; Instrumental Music; Vocal Music; Youth; Ethnic Performances
Status: Non-Profit, Professional

Texas

5587
UNIVERSITY OF TEXAS AT ARLINGTON
Excel Campus Activities
701 South Nedderman Drive
Arlington, TX 76019
Phone: 817-272-2011
Fax: 817-272-2962
e-mail: excel@uta.edu
Web Site: www.uta.edu
Management:
  President: Vistasp M. Karbhari
  Director of Student Activities: Mardie Sorensen
  Artistic Director: Megan Ridley Ridley
Founded: 1992
Specialized Field: Programming
Status: Non-Profit, Non-Professional
Paid Staff: 15
Volunteer Staff: 50
Non-paid Artists: 6
Budget: $20,000-35,000
Performs At: Texas Hall; Rosebud Theatre; Blubonnet Ballroom

5588
AUSTIN CHAMBER MUSIC FESTIVAL
3814 Medical Parkway
Suite 203
Austin, TX 78756
Phone: 512-454-0026
Fax: 512-454-0029
e-mail: info@austinchambermusic.org
Web Site: www.austinchambermusic.org
Officers:
  President: Catherine Wildermuth
  VP: Laura Beussman
  Secretary: Tadd Lanham
  Treasurer: Donald McDaniel
Management:
  Executive Director: Peter Helf
  Artistic Director: Michelle Schumann
  Business Manager: Ora Shay
  Director of Operations: Maureen Cross
  Director of Education: Jeni Gossard
Mission: To enhance the quality of community life by nurturing and expanding knowledge, understanding, and appreciation of chamber music through education, community outreach and performance.
Founded: 1981
Specialized Field: Series & Festivals; Instrumental Music; Vocal Music; Youth; Ethnic Performances; Chamber Music
Status: Non-Profit, Professional
Paid Staff: 4
Paid Artists: 60
Budget: 265,000
Income Sources: Grants; Membership; Corporate Support; Government Funds; Individuals
Facility Category: Varies
Type of Stage: Varies

5589
AUSTIN SHAKESPEARE FESTIVAL
P. O. Box 4589
Austin, TX 78765
Phone: 512-470-4505
e-mail: info@austinshakespeare.org
Web Site: www.austinshakespeare.org
Officers:
  Vice President: Mary B. Nichols
  Treasurer: Catherine Wildermuth
  Secretary: Lisa Jones
Management:
  President: Boyce Cabaniss
  Artistic Director: Ann Ciccolella
  Managing Director: Alex Alford
Mission: To produce professional quality productions of Classical theatre with an emphasis on the plays of William Shakespeare and to entertain and enrich the theatre-going public by presenting productions that are accessible, imaginative, and stimulating, while remaining true to the integrity of the plays and the author.
Founded: 1984
Status: Non-Equity; Nonprofit
Season: September - October
Type of Stage: Outdoor
Stage Dimensions: 50' x 40'
Seating Capacity: 3000

5590
FRANK ERWIN CENTER/ UNIVERSITY OF TEXAS-AUSTIN
1701 Red River
PO Box 2929
Austin, TX 78701
Phone: 512-471-7744
Fax: 512-471-9652
Toll-free: 800-982-2386
e-mail: erwin.center@erwin.utexas.edu
Web Site: www.uterwincenter.com
Management:
  Director: John M Graham
  Associate Director: Jimmy Earl
  Administrative Office Manager: Charly Wallace
  Box Office Manager: Thom Ramirez
  Business Manager: Mike Furtado
  Assistant Director for Marketing: Liz Land
Founded: 1977
Specialized Field: Series & Festivals; Vocal; Instrumental Music; Theatre; Youth; Dance; Ethnic Performances
Status: Non-Profit, Non-Professional
Paid Staff: 2000
Seating Capacity: 17,800, 16,500
Year Built: 1977

5591
SALON CONCERTS, INC.
PO Box 163501
Austin, TX 78716
Phone: 512-342-2516
Fax: 512-342-0515
e-mail: salonconcerts@aol.com
Web Site: www.salonconcerts.org
Officers:
  President: Nan Hampton
  Secretary: Cathy Cocco
Management:
  Artistic Director: Kathryn Mishell
  Executive Director: Beth Beauchamp
Founded: 1992
Specialized Field: Series and Festivals: Chamber Music

Status: Non-Profit, Professional
Paid Staff: 2
Budget: $10,000

5592
BAY CITY FESTIVAL ARTS ASSOCIATION
PO Box 111
Bay City, TX 77404-0111
Phone: 409-245-9062
Fax: 409-245-1622
e-mail: melvine@sat.net
Officers:
  Chairman Selection Committee: Melvin Epstein
Budget: $20,000-35,000
Performs At: Keye Ingram Auditorium

5593
FESTIVAL ARTS ASSOCIATION
PO Box 1794
Bay City, TX 77404-1794
Phone: 409-245-2727
Fax: 409-245-6966
e-mail: mseaman@alphainternet.net
Web Site: www.festarts.org
Management:
  Artistic Director: Mark Seaman

5594
BEAUMONT MUSIC COMMISSION
PO Box 7469
Beaumont, TX 77726
Phone: 409-755-3565
Fax: 409-755-3596
e-mail: bmc@exp.net
Web Site: www.beaumontmusic.org
Officers:
  President: Matthew White
  VP/Chairman: Naaman J Woodland, Jr
  Second VP: David Hitt
  Third VP: J. Robert Madden
  Fourth VP: Virginia Christopher
  Recording Secretary: Gwenn Mercer
Management:
  President: Murray Anderson
  Executive Director: Cathy Theall
Mission: To offer instrumental and vocal artists in small ensembles, recitals/concerts, opera, musicals, dance groups and small orchestras.
Utilizes: Actors; Collaborating Artists; Collaborations; Community Members; Dance Companies; Dancers; Educators; Grant Writers; Guest Artists; Guest Companies; Guest Soloists; Guest Writers; Local Artists; Local Unknown Artists; Lyricists; Multimedia; Music; New Productions; Organization Contracts; Original Music Scores; Special Technical Talent; Theatre Companies; Touring Companies
Founded: 1923
Specialized Field: Dance; Vocal Music; Instrumental Music
Status: Nonprofit
Volunteer Staff: 60
Budget: $128,000
Performs At: Julie Rogers Theatre for the Performing Arts
Annual Attendance: 8,000
Organization Type: Educational; Sponsoring

SERIES & FESTIVALS / Texas

5595
YOUNG AUDIENCES OF SOUTHEAST TEXAS, INC.
700 North St.
Suite G
Beaumont, TX 77701
Phone: 409-835-3884
Fax: 409-835-5504
e-mail: yasetx@aol.com
Web Site: yasetx.org
Officers:
 Vice President: Kim Kiker
 Treasurer: Allison Nathan Golias
 Secretary: Linda Ireland
Management:
 President: Becky Henry
 Executive Director: Stacie Jannise
Mission: To provide students with an opportunity to experience live performances featuring professional artists; to further arts education.
Utilizes: Actors; Artists-in-Residence; Collaborations; Curators; Dance Companies; Educators; Fine Artists; High School Drama; Local Artists; Multimedia; Original Music Scores; Playwrights; Poets; Sign Language Translators; Soloists; Special Technical Talent; Theatre Companies; Touring Companies
Founded: 1973
Specialized Field: Fine Arts Education
Status: Non-Profit, Professional
Paid Staff: 2
Paid Artists: 35
Budget: $155,598
Income Sources: Individual, Corporate, Grants/Foundations
Organization Type: Performing; Educational

5596
UNIVERSITY OF MARY HARDIN: BAYLOR
900 College Street
Box 8012, UMHB Station
Belton, TX 76513
Phone: 254-295-8642
Fax: 254-295-4158
Toll-free: 800-727-8642
e-mail: glayne@umhb.edu
Web Site: www.umhb.edu
Officers:
 Interim Chairman, Dept of Music: Ted Barnes
 President: Dr Randy O'Rear
Founded: 1845
Specialized Field: Series & Festivals; Instrumental Music; Vocal Music; Theatre
Status: Non-Profit, Non-Professional
Paid Staff: 200
Budget: $100,000
Performs At: Hughes Recital Hall

5597
BIG SPRING CULTURAL AFFAIRS COUNCIL
Box 1391
Big Spring, TX 79721
Phone: 931-598-1000
Fax: 915-264-9111
Management:
 Director: Marae Brooks
Mission: To offer balanced cultural activities to the community; to enhance natural cultural resources.
Utilizes: Guest Artists; Singers
Specialized Field: Dance; Vocal Music; Instrumental Music; Theater
Status: Nonprofit
Budget: $10,000
Organization Type: Touring

5598
ARTS COUNCIL OF WASHINGTON COUNTY
701 Milroy Drive
Brenham, TX 77833
Phone: 979-836-3120
Fax: 979-830-4030
Mission: To advance local arts in our community; to bring events to our community that are not locally available.
Utilizes: Guest Artists; Guest Companies; Singers
Founded: 1981
Specialized Field: Vocal Music; Instrumental Music; Theatre
Status: Professional; Semi-Professional; Non-Professional; Nonprofit
Income Sources: TCA
Organization Type: Touring; Resident; Educational; Sponsoring

5599
UNIVERSITY OF TEXAS AT BROWNSVILLE
80 Fort Brown
Brownsville, TX 78520
Phone: 956-544-8247
e-mail: sue.z.urbis@utb.edu
Web Site: www.utb.edu/finearts
Officers:
 President: Juliet Garcia
 Department Chairman: Sue Zanne Williamson Urbis
Management:
 Music Professor: Richard Urbis
Founded: 1992
Specialized Field: Series & Festivals; Instrumental Music; Vocal Music; Youth; Ethnic Performances
Status: Non-Profit, Professional
Paid Staff: 2
Paid Artists: 12
Budget: $10,000

5600
CITY OF BRYAN PARKS AND RECREATION
1309 E. Martin Luther King Blvd.
PO Box 1000
Bryan, TX 77803
Phone: 979-209-5520
Fax: 979-209-5524
e-mail: cmessina@ci.bryan.tx.us
Web Site: www.bryantx.gov
Management:
 Speical Events Coordinator: Linda Giffen
 Managing Director: David Schmitz
 Special Events Coordinator: Ashley Bennett
 Maintenance Supervisor: Billy Ebner
Mission: To provide area residents with quality entertainment.
Utilizes: Singers
Founded: 1890
Specialized Field: Recreation and Part Programming for the City
Status: Non-Profit, Non-Professional
Paid Staff: 60
Performs At: Lake Byrant
Type of Stage: Amphitheatre; Outdoors
Organization Type: Performing; Touring; Resident; Educational; Sponsoring

5601
MONTGOMERY COUNTY PERFORMING ARTS SERIES
PO Box 1714
Conroe, TX 77305
Phone: 936-760-2787
Web Site: www.mcpas.org
Officers:
 President: Peggy Miller
Budget: $20,000-35,000

5602
CATHEDRAL CONCERT SERIES
505 N Upper Broadway
Corpus Christi, TX 78401
Phone: 361-888-6520
Fax: 361-883-1918
e-mail: tccs@cccathedral.com
Web Site: www.goccn.org/ccs
Officers:
 Executive Director: Lee Gwozdz
Mission: Preserve, promote and provide high quality live performances to all segments, cultures and divisions of the community's population at no charge.
Utilizes: Five Seasonal Concerts; Guest Accompanists; Guest Artists; Guest Choreographers; Guest Companies; Guest Composers; Guest Musical Directors; Guest Musicians; Guest Writers; Instructors; Multimedia; Original Music Scores; Sign Language Translators; Singers; Soloists; Student Interns; Theatre Companies
Founded: 1985
Specialized Field: Series & Festivals: Vocal music
Status: Non-Profit, Professional
Paid Staff: 2
Paid Artists: 15
Budget: $101,275.00
Income Sources: Corporate Sponsors; Grants; VIP Memberships
Performs At: Church
Annual Attendance: 6,000
Facility Category: Cathedral
Type of Stage: Portable
Seating Capacity: 1,000
Organization Type: Performing; Touring; Resident

5603
CORPUS CHRISTI LIVE
446 Troy
Corpus Christi, TX 78412
Phone: 361-980-1949
e-mail: info@corpuschristilive.com
Web Site: www.corpuschristilive.com
Founded: 1935

5604
DEL MAR COLLEGE STUDENT CULTURAL PROGRAMS
Del Mar College Music
Music & Drama Department, East Campus
Corpus Christi, TX 78404-3897
Phone: 361-886-1200
Toll-free: 800-652-3357
Web Site: delmar.edu
Budget: $10,000-20,000
Performs At: Nell Bartlett Theater

5605
TEXAS JAZZ FESTIVAL SOCIETY
PO Box 424
Corpus Christi, TX 78403

SERIES & FESTIVALS / Texas

Phone: 361-808-9515
Fax: 361-853-4185
e-mail: tjfspres@email.msn.com
Web Site: www.texasjazz-fest.org/
Management:
   President: Rick Sanchez
Mission: Producing the Texas Jazz Festival to the public annually, free of charge; promoting and preserving American jazz.
Utilizes: Singers
Founded: 1969
Specialized Field: Vocal Music; Instrumental Music; Festivals
Status: Professional; Nonprofit
Performs At: Bayfront Plaza Convention Center
Organization Type: Performing

5606
PINEY WOODS FINE ARTS ASSOCIATION
603 E Goliad
Suite 203
Crockett, TX 75835
Mailing Address: PO Box 1213, Crockett, TX 75835
Phone: 936-544-4276
Fax: 936-546-0927
e-mail: pwfaa@consolidated.net
Web Site: www.pwfaa.org
Officers:
   Vice-President: Patty Meyer
   Secretary: Shirley Michka
   Treasurer: Deborah Porth Blackwell
Management:
   President: Dr. J. Patrick Walker
   Executive Director: J Bryan Lake
   Executive Administrative Assistant: Janae L. Whitehead
   Financial Director: Deborah Porth Blackwell
   Associate Producer: Glenn Barnhart
   Receptionist: Fran Harvey
Utilizes: Actors; Collaborations; Dance Companies; Educators; Guest Instructors; Guest Soloists; Guild Activities; Instructors; Local Artists; Multimedia; Original Music Scores; Poets; Resident Professionals; Sign Language Translators; Soloists; Student Interns; Special Technical Talent; Theatre Companies; Touring Companies; Visual Arts
Founded: 1991
Specialized Field: Series & Festivals; Instrumental Music; Vocal Music; Theatre; Youth; Dance; Ethnic Performances; Performing/Visual Arts
Status: Non-Profit, Professional
Paid Staff: 2
Volunteer Staff: 80
Paid Artists: 4
Non-paid Artists: 1
Performs At: General Purpose

5607
THE BLACK ACADEMY OF ARTS AND LETTERS SERIES
650 S Griffin
Dallas, TX 75202
Phone: 214-743-2440
Fax: 214-743-2451
e-mail: info@tbaal.org
Web Site: www.tbaal.org
Management:
   Founder and President: Curtis King
   Facility Operations Manager: Gwen Hargrove
   Developmental Manager: Ken Rowe
   Membership Developer: Gail Johnson
   Publicist: Marilyn Clark
Mission: Promoting, fostering, cultivating, perpetuating and preserving Black Americans' arts and letters.
Utilizes: Guest Artists; Guest Companies; Singers
Founded: 1977
Specialized Field: Series & Festivals; Dance; Music; Theatre
Status: Non-Profit, Professional
Paid Staff: 100
Organization Type: Performing; Educational

5608
DEEP ELLUM ARTS FESTIVAL
Mei Festivals
2630 E. Commerce St.
Dallas, TX 75226
Phone: 214-885-1881
Fax: 805-456-0303
Toll-free: 800-538-1881
e-mail: info@meifestivals.com
Web Site: www.deepellumartsfestival.com
Management:
   President: Stephen Millard
Founded: 1986

5609
DALLAS SUMMER MUSICALS, INC.
Music Hall at Fair Park
909 1st Avenue Parry
Dallas, TX 75210
Phone: 214-421-5678
Fax: 214-428-4526
e-mail: jcagle@dallassummermusicals.org
Web Site: www.dallassummermusicals.org
Officers:
   Chairman: Richard L. Rogers
   Chairman Elect: Dorsey Baskin
   Vice President - Audit: Brian Dill
   Vice President - Development: Ted Munselle
   Treasurer: David Dienes
   Secretary: Steven C. Metzger
Management:
   President: Michael A Jenkins
   Executive Secretary: Jenny Cagle
   Executive Secretary: Wanda Crow
   Executive Secretary: Patsy Brockway
   Human Resources: Mike Graham
   Director of Marketing: Paulette Hopkins
Mission: To promote the performing arts.
Utilizes: Special Technical Talent; Theatre Companies
Founded: 1940
Specialized Field: Musical Theatre
Status: Non-Profit, Professional
Paid Staff: 50
Season: June - August
Annual Attendance: 400,000+
Facility Category: Performance; Concert Hall
Type of Stage: Proscenium
Stage Dimensions: 100'x39'10'
Seating Capacity: 3,420
Year Built: 1925
Rental Contact: Jayne Basse
Organization Type: Performing

5610
DALLAS SYMPHONY ORCHESTRA
2301 Flora Street
Suite 300
Dallas, TX 75201-2497
Phone: 214-692-0203
Fax: 214-953-1218
e-mail: customerservice@dalsym.com
Web Site: s-s.www.mydso.com
Officers:
   President: Dr. Eugene Bonelli
Management:
   President: Fred Bronstein
   Music Director: Jaap van Zweden
Founded: 1900

5611
DALLAS SUMMER MUSICALS, INC.
PO Box 150188
Dallas, TX 75315
Phone: 214-421-5678
Fax: 214-428-4526
e-mail: cls2nd@aol.com
Web Site: www.dallassummermusicals.org
Officers:
   Chairman: Richard L. Rogers
   Chairman Elect: Dorsey Baskin
   Vice President - Audit: Brian Dill
   Vice President - Development: Ted Munselle
   Treasurer: David Dienes
   Secretary: Steven C. Metzger
Management:
   President: Michael Jenkins
   Executive Secretary: Jenny Cagle
   Executive Secretary: Wanda Crow
   Executive Secretary: Patsy Brockway
   Human Resources: Mike Graham
   Director of Marketing: Paulette Hopkins
Mission: Offers a 277 acre cultural and exhibition park including; Cotton Bowl Stadium; eight museums; the Old Mill Inn Restaurant; five indoor performance halls.
Specialized Field: Series and Festivals: Theatre
Status: Non-Profit, Professional
Seating Capacity: 72,500 (Cotton Bowl)
Year Built: 1936

5612
SHAKESPEARE DALLAS
3630 Harry Hine Boulevard
3rd Floor
Dallas, TX 75219
Phone: 214-559-2778
Fax: 214-559-2782
e-mail: sotg@shakespearedallas.org
Web Site: www.shakespearedallas.org
Officers:
   Chairman: Adam Reed
   Vice Chairman: Darren Dittrich
   Treasurer: Jennifer Green-Moneta
Management:
   Artistic Director: Raphael Parry
   Development & Program Director: Jenni Pittman
   Education & Outreach Manager: Julie Osborne
   Development & Marketing Associate: Devin Overman
   Communications Coordinator: Jessica Helton
   Artistic Associate: Rene Moreno
Utilizes: Singers
Founded: 1971
Status: Non-Profit
Paid Staff: 3
Performs At: Fair Park Band Shell
Organization Type: Performing; Educational

5613
FIREHOUSE ARTS CENTER
4444 Railroad Avenue
Del Rio, TX 94566
Phone: 925-931-4848
Fax: 925-931-4850
e-mail: drcarts@delrio.com
Web Site: www.firehousearts.org
Management:
   Executive Director: Ann Stool

SERIES & FESTIVALS / Texas

Utilizes: Actors; Artists-in-Residence; Curators; Dance Companies; Dancers; Educators; Fine Artists; Guest Accompanists; Guest Choreographers; Guest Ensembles; Guest Musical Directors; Guest Musicians; Guest Soloists; High School Drama; Instructors; Local Artists; Multimedia; Original Music Scores; Sign Language Translators; Singers; Soloists; Special Technical Talent; Theatre Companies; Touring Companies
Founded: 1977
Specialized Field: Performing Arts
Status: Non-Profit, Professional
Paid Staff: 2
Volunteer Staff: 21
Paid Artists: 105
Non-paid Artists: 15
Budget: $250,000
Income Sources: Grants; Ticket Sales; Fundraisers; Corporate Sponsors; City; County; State; Foundation;
Performs At: Theatre, Schools, Fairgrounds, Ampitheaters
Affiliations: Southwest Performing Arts Presenters; Mid-America Arts Alliance, Heartland Fund
Annual Attendance: 16,000
Facility Category: Proscenium
Type of Stage: Wooden floor
Stage Dimensions: 25x27
Seating Capacity: 700
Year Built: 1930
Year Remodeled: 1980

5614
GRAYSON COUNTY COLLEGE HUMANITIES
6101 Grayson Drive
Denison, TX 75020
Phone: 903-465-6030
Web Site: www.grayson.edu
Management:
  Dean: John Dartin
  Chairman: Steve Black
  Manager: Joe Hick
  VP Business Services: Giles Brown
  President: Bill McFatridge
  Vice President: Ralph Jones
  Secretary: Ruby Jo Williams
Founded: 1965
Specialized Field: Series & Festivals: Theatre
Status: Non-Profit, Non-Professional
Paid Staff: 6
Paid Artists: 50
Budget: $35,000-60,000

5615
DENTON ARTS & JAZZ FESTIVAL
Denton Festival Foundation, Inc.
PO Box 2104
Denton, TX 76202
Phone: 940-565-0931
Fax: 940-566-7007
e-mail: artspatron@aol.com
Web Site: www.dentonjazzfest.com
Officers:
  Board President: Jean Stanley
Management:
  Executive Director: Carol Short
  Artistic Manager: Ray Hair
Mission: To plan, promote and produce the annual Denton Arts & Jazz Festival that is free to the public.
Founded: 1980
Specialized Field: Music; Fine Arts, Crafts and Diverse Performances
Status: Non-Profit
Paid Staff: 2
Volunteer Staff: 300
Paid Artists: 250
Budget: $400,000
Income Sources: Sponsors; Grants; Memberships; Booth Space Fees; Concessions; Souvenirs
Affiliations: City of Denton/Denton Convention & Visitors Bureau
Annual Attendance: 200,000
Facility Category: Quakertown Park
Type of Stage: 7 Stages

5616
GREATER DENTON ARTS COUNCIL
400 East Hickory St
Denton, TX 76201
Phone: 940-382-2787
Fax: 940-383-1467
Web Site: www.dentonarts.com
Officers:
  VP Finance: Jan Hillman
  VP Membership: Roni Beasley
  VP Education: Don Edwards
  Treasurer: Judy Willis
  Secretary: Cathy Kerley
Management:
  President: Kristin Johnson
  Executive Director: Margaret Chalfant
  Programs Coordinator: John Riegelman
  Director of Development: Michael Schwerin
  Community Arts Coordinator: Caroline Holley
  Financial Assistant: Mika Slough
Founded: 1975
Specialized Field: Visual Arts in Education
Status: Non-Profit, Non-Professional
Paid Staff: 7
Budget: $10,000

5617
EASTLAND FINE ARTS ASSOCIATION
PO Box 705
108 N Lamar
Eastland, TX 76448
Phone: 254-629-2102
Fax: 254-629-2247
e-mail: majestic@txol.net
Management:
  Manager: Ed Allcorn
Budget: $10,000
Performs At: Majestic Theatre

5618
EL PASO ASSOCIATION FOR THE PERFORMING ARTS
3525 Pershing Boulevard
El Paso, TX 79930
Phone: 915-231-1165
Fax: 915-565-6999
e-mail: VivaEP@Yahoo.com
Web Site: www.viva-ep.org
Management:
  Executive Director: Thea Chambers
  Artistic Director: Babil Gandara
Mission: An outdoor drama emphasizing dance, which celebrates the Western American, Native American, Mexican and Spanish cultures that have influenced El Paso's history. Shakespeare-on-the-Rocks presents four plays in repertory each September.
Founded: 1978
Specialized Field: Dance; Vocal Music; Theater; Ballet; Folkdance
Status: Professional; Nonprofit
Paid Staff: 15
Paid Artists: 100
Income Sources: Institute of Outdoor Drama
Season: June - August
Performs At: McKelligon Canyon Amphitheater
Organization Type: Performing; Resident

5619
EL PASO CHAMBER PRO-MUSICA FESTIVAL
6557 North Mesa
El Paso, TX 79912
Mailing Address: PO Box 133328
Phone: 915-833-9400
Fax: 915-833-9425
e-mail: info@elpasopromusica.org
Web Site: www.elpasopromusica.org
Officers:
  President: Charles Dodds III
  Secretary: Wendy Sudimack
  Treasurer: Jeames Beale
Management:
  Artistic Director: Zuill Bailey
  Executive Director: Felipa Solis
  Office Manager: Marivi Isaac
Founded: 1977
Specialized Field: Series and Festivals: Chamber Music
Status: Non-Profit, Professional
Paid Staff: 3
Paid Artists: 25

5620
IMPACT: PROGRAMS OF EXCELLENCE
444 E Robinson
El Paso, TX 79902
Phone: 915-545-5068
Fax: 915-545-5076
e-mail: INFO@IMPACTPROGRAMSOFEXCELLENCE.ORG
Web Site: www.impactprogramsofexcellence.org
Management:
  Executive Director: Sally Gilbert

5621
MUSEUMS & CULTURAL AFFAIRS DEPARTMENT
2 Civic Center Plaza
6th Floor
El Paso, TX 79901
Phone: 915-541-4481
Fax: 915-541-4902
e-mail: quijanoal@elpasotexas.gov
Web Site: www.elpasotexas.gov
Management:
  Director: Yolanda Alameda
  Deputy City Manager: Debbie Hamlyn
  Artistic Director: Betty Jaraba
Founded: 1984
Specialized Field: Series and Festivals; Instrumental Music; Vocal Music; Theatre; Youth; Dance; Ethnic Performances
Status: Non-Profit, Professional
Paid Staff: 6
Paid Artists: 7
Budget: $150,000-400,000
Performs At: Chamizal National Memorial

5622
BROOKHAVEN COLLEGE CENTER FOR THE ARTS
3939 Valley View Lane
Farmers Branch, TX 75244

All listings are in alphabetical order by state, then city, then organization within the city.

SERIES & FESTIVALS / Texas

Phone: 972-860-4700
Fax: 972-860-4385
e-mail: bhcInfo@dcccd.edu
Web Site: www.brookhavencollege.edu
Management:
   President: Alice Villedsen
   Dean Fine Arts: Rodger Bennett
Founded: 1978
Specialized Field: Community College
Status: Non-Profit, Non-Professional
Paid Staff: 3
Budget: $35,000-60,000
Income Sources: City Grants; Tickets
Annual Attendance: 7,000
Facility Category: Performance Center
Type of Stage: Proscenium
Seating Capacity: 680
Year Built: 1978
Rental Contact: Roger Bennett

5623
FORT HOOD COMMUNITY MUSIC AND THEATER
Building 2803
Fort Hood, TX 76544
Phone: 254-287-1110
Management:
   Mucsical Director/Theater: Jean Zavoina
   Music Director: Roland Gagne
   Technical Director: Fred Baker
   Costumer: Tom Ross
Mission: To provide opportunities for military personnel, their families and other area residents to participate in talent competitions, musicals and shows.
Utilizes: Guest Artists; Guest Companies
Founded: 1950
Specialized Field: Dance; Vocal Music; Instrumental Music; Theater; Festivals
Status: Non-Professional
Organization Type: Performing; Touring

5624
TEXAS GIRL'S CHOIR
4449 Camp Bowie Boulevard
Fort Worth, TX 76107-3834
Phone: 817-732-8161
Fax: 817-732-4774
e-mail: tgc@texasgirlschoir.org
Web Site: www.texasgirlschoir.org
Management:
   Executive Director: Debi Weir
Mission: To bring together childrens choirs from all over the world to share their music in performance.
Utilizes: Arrangers; Collaborating Artists; Collaborations; Community Members; Composers; Dancers; Educators; Five Seasonal Concerts; Grant Writers; Guest Artists; Guest Companies; Guest Composers; Guest Directors; Guest Ensembles; Guest Lecturers; Guest Musical Directors; Guest Speakers; High School Drama; Local Artists; Local Artists & Directors; Multimedia; Music; Organization Contracts; Resident Companies; Sign Language Translators; Volunteer Artists
Founded: 1998
Specialized Field: Children's Choral Music
Status: Non-Profit, Non-Professional
Paid Staff: 10
Volunteer Staff: 55

5625
CLIBURN CONCERTS
Van Cliburn Foundation
2525 Ridgmar Boulevard, Suite 307
Fort Worth, TX 76116
Phone: 817-738-6536
Fax: 817-738-6534
e-mail: clistaff@cliburn.org
Web Site: www.cliburn.org
Management:
   President, CEO: Jacques Marquis
   Director Education: Susan Robertson
   CFO: Alissa Ford
   Office Manager: Marie Giasson
Mission: To produce the Cilburn Piano Series.
Founded: 1962
Specialized Field: Series & Festivals; Instrumental Music; Vocal Music
Status: Non-Profit, Professional
Paid Staff: 13
Paid Artists: 15
Budget: $150,000-400,000
Performs At: Nancy Lee & Perry R. Bass Performance Hall

5626
PERFORMING ARTS FORT WORTH, INC
330 E 4th Street
#300
Fort Worth, TX 76102
Phone: 817-212-4300
Fax: 817-810-9294
e-mail: pbeard@basshall.com
Web Site: www.basshall.com
Management:
   Managing Director: Paul S Beard
   Director Operations: Don Fearing
   Director Communications: Carl Davis
   Sales/Sponsorship Director: Julie Curtis
Utilizes: Dance Companies; Dancers; Fine Artists; Grant Writers; Instructors; Local Artists; Original Music Scores; Resident Artists; Sign Language Translators; Special Technical Talent; Theatre Companies
Founded: 1992
Specialized Field: Series & Festivals; Instrumental Music; Vocal Music; Theatre; Youth; Dance; Ethnic Performances
Status: Non-Profit, Professional
Paid Staff: 35
Volunteer Staff: 750
Budget: $1,000,000+
Income Sources: Ticket Sales; Facility Rental; Donations
Performs At: One 2,056 seat multi-purpose theatre; Two 350 Seat Spaces For Small Productions
Annual Attendance: 500,000 - 600,000
Facility Category: Multi-purpose theater
Type of Stage: Proscenium
Stage Dimensions: see www.basshall.com
Seating Capacity: 2,056
Year Built: 1998
Cost: 67 Million
Rental Contact: Managing Director Paul Beard
Resident Groups: Five local resident companies

5627
FREDERICKSBURG MUSIC CLUB, INC.
PO Box 1214
Fredericksburg, TX 78624
Phone: 830-997-5413
Fax: 830-997-2980
Web Site: www.fredericksburgmusicclub.com
Officers:
   President: Mark Eckhardt
   VP: Judy Hickerson
   Secretary: Kay Daigle
   Treasurer: Carlton Ottmers
Management:
   Artistic Director: Frances Gibson
Founded: 1937
Specialized Field: Classical
Budget: $10,000-20,000
Facility Category: Church; High School Auditorium

5628
GRAND 1894 OPERA HOUSE
2020 Post Office Street
Galveston, TX 77550
Phone: 409-763-7173
Fax: 409-763-1068
Toll-free: 800-821-1894
e-mail: mpatton@thegrand.com
Web Site: www.thegrand.com
Management:
   Executive Director: Maureen M Patton
   Development Director: Virginia Weber
Mission: To present professional performing arts in a restored, historic structure and to maintain that structure; to serve the Galveston and the Greater Houston areas.
Utilizes: Actors; Commissioned Music; Dance Companies; Educators; Original Music Scores; Special Technical Talent; Theatre Companies
Founded: 1974
Specialized Field: Live Theatre
Status: Non-Profit, Professional
Paid Staff: 12
Volunteer Staff: 300
Budget: $3.5 million
Income Sources: Earned and Contributed Revenue
Performs At: The Grand 1894 Opera House
Affiliations: Assoc. of Performing Arts Presenters; League Of Historic American Theatres; SW Performing Arts Presenters
Annual Attendance: 100,000+
Facility Category: Historic Theatre
Type of Stage: Proscenium
Stage Dimensions: 38x36
Seating Capacity: 1,040
Year Built: 1894
Year Remodeled: 1985
Rental Contact: Maureen Patton
Organization Type: Performing; Touring; Resident; Educational; Sponsoring; Presenting
Resident Groups: Galveston Symphony Orchestra

5629
GARLAND SUMMER MUSICALS
PO Box 462049
Garland, TX 75046
Phone: 972-205-2780
Fax: 972-205-2775
e-mail: info@garlandsummermusicals.org
Web Site: www.garlandsummermusicals.org
Officers:
   Chairman: Jerry Prater
   Treasurer: Steve Huber
   Secretary: Vickie Brinkley
Management:
   Producer: Patty Granville
   Director: Buff Shurr
Mission: To bring to the community productions of the highest quality; to continue to provide excellent family entertainment.
Utilizes: Singers
Founded: 1983
Specialized Field: Dance; Vocal Music; Instrumental Music
Status: Semi-Professional; Nonprofit
Income Sources: Actors' Equity Association
Performs At: Garland Center for the Performing Arts
Organization Type: Sponsoring

SERIES & FESTIVALS / Texas

5630
SOUTHWESTERN UNIVERSITY ARTIST SERIES
Southwestern University
1001 E. University Avenue
Georgetown, TX 78626
Phone: 512-863-6511
Fax: 512-863-1422
Web Site: www.southwestern.edu
Management:
 President: Jake Schrum
 Dean: Paul Gaffney
Specialized Field: Series & Festivals; Performing Arts; Musical Concerts
Status: Non-Profit, Professional
Paid Staff: 10
Paid Artists: 10
Budget: $10,000-20,000
Performs At: Alma Thomas Theater

5631
HARLINGEN COMMUNITY CONCERT ASSOCIATION
PO Box 707
Harlingen, TX 78551
Phone: 956-748-3020
Officers:
 President: James Hough
Management:
 Publicity: Joyce Davis-Tucker
Mission: To entertain and influence community adults and students in culture and cultural events.
Founded: 1930
Specialized Field: a variety of cultural programs

5632
RIOFEST: A BLENDING OF THE ARTS AND ENTERTAINMENT
305 E Jackson, Suite 214
PO Box 531105
Harlingen, TX 78550
Phone: 956-425-2705
Fax: 956-440-0476
Toll-free: 800-746-3378
e-mail: riofest@aol.com
Web Site: www.riofest.com
Management:
 President: Gregg Henderson
 Festival Director: Kathy Preddy
Mission: To develop new audiences for the arts and provide access to the arts for all citizens.
Founded: 1982
Specialized Field: Series & Festivals; Instrumental Music; Vocal Music; Theatre; Youth; Dance; Ethnic Performances
Status: Non-Profit, Professional
Paid Staff: 1
Paid Artists: 50
Non-paid Artists: 100
Budget: $305,000
Income Sources: Gate; Sale of food & drink; Sponsors
Performs At: 40 Acre Park, One 1800 Seat Theatre & One 300 Seat Theatre
Affiliations: TFEA; TCA; City of Harlingen
Annual Attendance: 30,000
Facility Category: Multi-Venue; Indoor & Outdoor Theaters

5633
HILL COLLEGE
112 Lamar Drive
Hillsboro, TX 76645
Phone: 254-659-7500
Fax: 254-582-7591
e-mail: plowe@hillcollege.edu
Web Site: www.hillcollege.edu
Management:
 President: Sheryl Kappus
 Coordinator Visual/Performing Arts: Phillip Lowe, plowe@hillcollege.edu
Founded: 1963
Specialized Field: Series & Festivals; Instrumental Music; Vocal Music; Theatre; Youth; Ethnic Performances
Status: Non-Profit, Professional
Paid Staff: 2
Budget: $$8,000-$10,000
Income Sources: Donations
Annual Attendance: 1,200
Seating Capacity: 400

5634
CHILDREN'S THEATRE FESTIVAL
School of Theatre
University of Houston
Houston, TX 77204-4016
Phone: 713-743-3003
e-mail: sjudice@uh.edu
Management:
 Production Director: Sidney Berger
Founded: 1978
Specialized Field: Educational Institution Theater Department
Status: Non-Equity; Nonprofit
Season: June - August
Type of Stage: Proscenium
Stage Dimensions: 40' x 33'
Seating Capacity: 566

5635
DA CAMERA OF HOUSTON
1427 Branard
Houston, TX 77006
Phone: 713-524-7601
Fax: 713-524-4148
Toll-free: 800-233-2226
e-mail: mlaleskie@decamara.com
Web Site: www.dacamera.com
Management:
 Executive Director: Sarah Loudermilk
 Artistic Director: Sarah Rothenberg
 Artistic and General Administrator: Becky Brown
 Development Director: P. Carrigan Byrd, Jr.
 Director of Education: Craig Hauschildt
 Assistant Development Director: James Hays
 Chief Operating Officer: Karen Hendricks
Utilizes: Guest Companies; Multimedia; Original Music Scores; Sign Language Translators
Founded: 1987
Specialized Field: Chamber Music/Jazz
Status: Non-Profit, Professional
Paid Staff: 10
Paid Artists: 100
Budget: $1,200,000
Performs At: Cullen Theater; Wortham Center

5636
JAZZ EDUCATION INC.
3303 S Rice
Suite 107
Houston, TX 77056
Mailing Address: PO Box 8031 Houston, TX 77288
Phone: 713-839-7000
Fax: 713-839-8266
e-mail: jazzed@jazzeducation.org
Web Site: www.jazzeducation.org
Officers:
 President/COO: Dr. James Austin
Management:
 Festival Director: Richard Dabon
Mission: To sponsor a 10-day cultural celebration in an urban setting, focusing on a different country every year.
Founded: 1974
Specialized Field: Performing Series
Status: Non-Profit
Paid Staff: 4
Paid Artists: 19
Income Sources: Cultural Arts Council of Houston; Houston Convention & Visitors Center
Organization Type: Educational; Sponsoring

5637
HOUSTON SHAKESPEARE FESTIVAL
School of Theatre
133 CWM Center
Houston, TX 77204-4016
Phone: 713-743-3003
Fax: 713-743-2648
e-mail: sjudice@uh.edu
Web Site: www.uh.edu/class/theatre-and-dance
Management:
 President: Sidney Berger
 Secretary: Sandy Judice
 Office Manager: Jerry Aven
 Academic Advisor: Molly Dean
 Lighting Designer: John Gow
 Scene Shop Forman: Drew Hoovler
 Costume Production Supervisor: Toni Lovaglia
 Technical Director: Mo Tuttle
Mission: To provide classical theater at no cost to citizens of Houston and surrounding areas.
Founded: 1975
Specialized Field: Series & Festivals: Theater
Status: Non-Profit, Professional
Paid Staff: 100
Paid Artists: 12
Income Sources: University of Houston
Performs At: Miller Outdoor Theatre
Organization Type: Performing

5638
HOUSTON'S ANNUAL ASIAN-AMERICAN FESTIVAL
1714 Tannehill Drive
Houston, TX 77008
Phone: 713-861-8273
Fax: 713-861-3450
Management:
 Festival Director: Glenda Joe
Mission: Promote, preserve, present Asian cultural arts.
Founded: 1980
Specialized Field: Music; Dance; Theatre; Puppetry
Paid Staff: 1
Volunteer Staff: 50
Paid Artists: 1600

5639
THE IMMANUEL & HELEN OLSHAN TEXAS MUSIC FESTIVAL
120 School of Music Bldg
Houston, TX 77204-4017
Phone: 713-743-3313
Fax: 713-743-3166
e-mail: tmf@uh.edu
Web Site: www.uh.edu/music/tmf
Management:

SERIES & FESTIVALS / Texas

General and Artistic Director: Alan Austin, tmf@uh.edu
Assistant Director: Melissa Mccrimmon, mfmccrimmon@uh.edu
Mission: The Texas Music Festival is an orchestral training program for talented young musicians ages 18-30. Performs four orchestral programs under internationally recognized conductors.
Utilizes: Artists-in-Residence; Commissioned Composers; Composers; Educators; Grant Writers; Guest Accompanists; Guest Companies; Guest Composers; Guest Ensembles; Guest Musical Directors; Guest Musicians; High School Drama; Multimedia; Organization Contracts; Original Music Scores; Sign Language Translators; Singers; Soloists; Students
Founded: 1990
Specialized Field: Classical
Paid Staff: 2
Paid Artists: 60
Budget: $800,000+
Performs At: Concert Hall
Affiliations: Univ. of Houston, Moores School of Music, Houston Symphony, Houston Grand Opera Orchestra, Houston Ballet Orchestra, Shepherd School of Music
Annual Attendance: 7,000

5640
EVELYN RUBENSTEIN JEWISH COMMUNITY CENTER
5601 S Braeswood
Houston, TX 77096-3907
Phone: 713-729-3200
Fax: 713-551-7223
Web Site: www.erjcchouston.org
Management:
   Executive Director: Jerry Wische
   Executive Vice President: Joel Dinkin
   Senior Associate Executive Director: Gayle Rockoff
   Associate Executive Director: Alan Lipman
   Chief Financial Officer: Alison Sullivan
Mission: To offer education, leisure activities and recreation to Southwest Houston; to promote the appreciation of theatre.
Utilizes: Guest Companies; Singers
Founded: 1935
Specialized Field: Series & Festivals; Dance; Vocal Music; Instrumental Music; Theater
Status: Non-Profit, Professional
Paid Staff: 50
Income Sources: Texas Nonprofit Theatre; National Council of Jewish Theatres
Performs At: Jewish Community Center; Kaplan Theatre; IW Marks Theatre Center; Joe Frank Theatre
Facility Category: Proscenium Theatre; Black Box Theatre
Type of Stage: Proscenium; Thrust
Seating Capacity: 330; 130
Organization Type: Performing; Educational; Sponsoring

5641
JONES HALL FOR THE PERFORMING ARTS
615 Louisiana Avenue
Houston, TX 77002
Phone: 832-487-7050
Fax: 832-487-7051
Web Site: www.houstonfirsttheaters.com
Management:
   Manager: Vivian Montejano
   Director: Gerald J Tollett

Opened: 1966

5642
THE SHEPHERD SCHOOL OF MUSIC
Rice University
6100 Main Street
Houston, TX 77005
Phone: 713-348-4933
Fax: 713-348-5317
e-mail: littman@rice.edu
Web Site: music.rice.edu
Management:
   Associate Dean of Music: Gary Smith
   Concert Manager: Tom Littman
   Department Coordinator: Susie Schoepf
   Director of Development: Diane McOmie
Mission: Pre-professional training for musicians in a conspiratory environment within a private university.
Founded: 1975
Specialized Field: Series & Festivals; Instrumental Music; Vocal Music; Theater; Youth
Status: Non-Profit, Non-Professional
Paid Staff: 100
Paid Artists: 75
Facility Category: Concert Hall
Seating Capacity: 780
Year Built: 1991
Rental Contact: Tom Littman

5643
JESSE H. JONES HALL
615 Louisiana
Suite 100
Houston, TX 77002
Phone: 713-632-8100
Fax: 713-632-8122
e-mail: mattox@spahouston.org
Web Site: www.spahouston.org
Officers:
   Chair: Melanie Gray
   CEO/President: June Christensen
Management:
   Executive Director: Sally Tyler
   Director Development: Priscilla Larson
   Director Marketing: Allison Lott
   Director Operations: Kathryn Lott
   Director Ticketing Services: Greg Brown
   Development Associate: Ashley Coffey
   Director of Finance, Administration: Karen Whitlock
Mission: To present the world's best in performing arts, whether dance, music or theatre.
Utilizes: Commissioned Composers; Commissioned Music; Dancers; Multimedia; Theatre Companies
Opened: 1966
Specialized Field: Modern; Mime; Ballet; Jazz; Ethnic; Folk
Status: Professional; Nonprofit
Budget: $2,500,000 - $4,000,000
Income Sources: Sales; Contributions
Performs At: Jones Hall; Wortham Theatre Center
Affiliations: ISPA; Arts Presenters; Dance USA
Annual Attendance: 50,000-60,0000
Type of Stage: Sprung Wood
Seating Capacity: 2912
Year Built: 1966
Year Remodeled: 1996
Cost: $9,000,000
Organization Type: Sponsoring

5644
UNIVERSITY OF ST. THOMAS
3800 Montrose
Houston, TX 77006-4626

Phone: 713-522-7911
Fax: 713-942-5912
e-mail: yong@stthom.edu
Web Site: www.stthom.edu
Management:
   President: Robert Ivany
   Artistic Director: Tom Crow
   Department Coordinator: Sue Young
Mission: Enrichment for students, faculty and community.
Founded: 1947
Specialized Field: School of Hire Learning
Status: Non-Profit, Non-Professional
Paid Staff: 1
Paid Artists: 2
Budget: $10,000-20,000

5645
HILL COUNTRY ARTS FOUNDATION
Highway 39
PO Box 1169
Ingram, TX 78025
Phone: 830-367-5121
Fax: 830-367-4332
Toll-free: 800-459-4223
Web Site: www.hcaf.com
Officers:
   Vice President - Visual Arts: Julie Sentell
   Vice President - Theatre: Ann Galland
   Secretary: Kari Short
   Treasurer: Barbara von Brandt-Siemers
Management:
   President: David Howard
   Artistic Director: Jennifer Hayne
   Executive Director: Katharine Schaafs
   Development Director: Rosanne Thrall
   Visual Arts Coordinator: Phyllis Garey
   Box Office Manager: Sarah Derousseau
Mission: Promoting the performing and visual arts.
Utilizes: Guest Artists; Guest Companies; Singers
Founded: 1958
Specialized Field: Series & Festivals; Dance; Vocal Music; Instrumental Music; Theater
Status: Non-Profit, Professional
Paid Staff: 75
Income Sources: American Association of Community Theatres; Texas Nonprofit Theatre
Performs At: Outdoor Amphitheatre
Organization Type: Performing; Educational

5646
ENTERTAINMENT SERIES OF IRVING
3333 N MacArthur Boulevard
Suite 300
Irving, TX 75062
Phone: 972-252-7558
Fax: 972-570-4962
Web Site: www.ci.irving.tx.us
Officers:
   Chairman: Kim Dennis
   Vice-Chairman: Vanessa Bell
   Secretary: Laura Sanner
Management:
   President: Dotty Verept
   Technical Theater Coordinator: Ross Moroney
   Box Office Manager: Andy Pate
   Director Marketing/Publications: Jo Trizila
Founded: 1955
Specialized Field: Series and Festivals; Instrumental Music; Vocal Music; Theatre; Dance
Status: Non-Profit, Professional
Income Sources: Community Concerts
Organization Type: Sponsoring

SERIES & FESTIVALS / Texas

5647
KERRVILLE FOLK FESTIVAL
Quiet Valley Ranch
PO Box 291466
Kerrville, TX 78029
Phone: 830-257-3600
Fax: 830-257-8680
e-mail: info@kerrville-music.com
Web Site: www.kerrville-music.com
Management:
   President: Charlie Land
   Producer and Director: Dalis Allen
Mission: To offer recordings, workshops and music festivals, featuring regional national and international artists and emphasizing acoustic musicians and songwriters.
Utilizes: Singers
Founded: 1972
Specialized Field: Singer/Songwriters Music Outdoor Theatre Concerts
Status: For-Profit, Professional
Paid Staff: 4
Volunteer Staff: 600
Paid Artists: 100
Income Sources: Texas Festivals Association; Texas Music Association
Performs At: Festival Outdoor Theater
Organization Type: Performing

5648
KILGORE COMMUNITY CONCERT ASSOCIATION
PO Box 47
Kilgore, TX 75663-0047
Phone: 903-984-7753
Fax: 903-984-1101
e-mail: jclaudwall@aol.com
Web Site: kilgoreconcerts.com
Officers:
   President: Claud Wallace
   First VP: John Bolton
   Secretary: Greg Collins
   Treasurer: Sheila Smithwick
Budget: $20,000-35,000

5649
TEXAS SHAKESPEARE FESTIVAL
1100 Broadway
Kilgore, TX 75662
Mailing Address: PO Box 2788, Kilgore, TX. 75663
Phone: 903-983-8117
Fax: 903-983-8124
e-mail: info@texasshakespeare.com
Web Site: www.texasshakespeare.com
Management:
   Artistic Director: Raymond Caldwell
   Managing Director: John Dodd
Mission: To serve the community by providing cultural enrichment, educational opportunities and economic benefits.
Founded: 1986
Specialized Field: Series & Festivals: Theatre
Status: Non-Profit, Professional
Paid Staff: 2
Paid Artists: 20
Season: June - July
Type of Stage: Flexible
Stage Dimensions: 30' x 30'
Seating Capacity: 240

5650
LUBBOCK ARTS ALLIANCE
1001 Main Street
Suite 606
Lubbock, TX 79401
Phone: 806-744-2787
Fax: 806-744-2790
e-mail: mail@lubbockarts.org
Web Site: www.lubbockarts.org
Officers:
   President: Robby Vestal
   Festival Chairman: Meredith McAlister
Management:
   President: Meredith McAllister
   Executive Director: Elizabeth Regner
Specialized Field: Promotion of the Arts
Status: Non-Profit, Professional
Paid Staff: 2
Volunteer Staff: 250
Non-paid Artists: 300
Budget: $10,000-20,000
Income Sources: Grants; Corporate Sponsors
Performs At: Lubbock Memorial Civic Center

5651
LUBBOCK CHRISTIAN UNIVERSITY
5601 W 19th Street
Lubbock, TX 79407-2099
Phone: 806-720-7151
Fax: 806-720-7255
Web Site: www.lcu.edu
Management:
   President: Ken Jones
   Artistic Director: Michelle Kraft
   Theatre Director: Don Williams
   Assistant Professor Music: Philip Camp
   Professor Music: Dr. Ruth Holmes
Utilizes: Guild Activities
Founded: 1957
Specialized Field: Series & Festivals; Music; Art; Theatre
Status: Non-Profit, Non-Professional
Paid Staff: 6
Paid Artists: 2
Budget: $10,000
Type of Stage: Proscenium
Stage Dimensions: 35x20
Seating Capacity: 1,200
Year Built: 1967

5652
TEXAS TECH UNIVERSITY ARTISTS & SPEAKERS
TTU
PO Box 45014
Lubbock, TX 79409-5014
Phone: 806-742-5433
Fax: 806-742-0138
e-mail: campusactivitiesinvolvement@ttu.edu
Web Site: www.depts.ttu.edu/centerforcampuslife
Management:
   President: James Whitmore
   Executive Director: Gregory Elkins
   Artistic Director: Jennifer Henley
Specialized Field: Series & Festivals: Concerts and Speakers
Status: Non-Profit, Non-Professional
Paid Staff: 20

5653
MARSHALL REGIONAL ARTS COUNCIL
2501 E End Boulevard S
PO Box C
Marshall, TX 75671-3003
Phone: 903-935-4484
Fax: 903-927-2132
e-mail: marshallartscouncil@gmail.com
Web Site: www.marshallartscouncil.org
Officers:
   President: Frank Lower
   Executive Director: Joyce Weekly
   Secretary: Willa Bose
   Treasurer: Jim Kale
Mission: To support, promote, and encourage participation and involvement of all citizens of the region in quality experiences in both the arts and humanities.
Utilizes: Actors; Artists-in-Residence; Dancers; Instructors; Local Artists; Multimedia; Original Music Scores; Resident Artists; Singers; Special Technical Talent; Theatre Companies
Founded: 1979
Specialized Field: Series & Festivals; Dance; Vocal Music; Instrumental Music; Theatre; Festivals; Grand Opera
Status: Non-Profit, Professional
Paid Staff: 2
Budget: $100,000
Income Sources: Association of Performing Arts Presenters; National Association of Local Arts Agencies; Texas Arts Council; Country Music Association
Performs At: Marshall Convention Center
Facility Category: Convention Center
Type of Stage: Proscenium
Stage Dimensions: 78 x 57
Seating Capacity: 1600
Year Built: 1984
Year Remodeled: 2001
Cost: 1.5 Million
Organization Type: Educational; Sponsoring

5654
MCALLEN PERFORMING ARTS
PO Box 790
McAllen, TX 78505
Phone: 956-631-2545
Fax: 956-631-8571
Management:
   Executive Director: Genevia Crow
Mission: To provide the public with professional touring theatre productions and entertainment not available through local agencies.
Specialized Field: Vocal Music; Theatre; Broadway Musicals
Status: Professional; Nonprofit
Performs At: McAllen Civic Center
Organization Type: Performing; Touring

5655
RIO GRANDE VALLEY INTERNATIONAL MUSIC FESTIVAL
PO Box 2315
McAllen, TX 78502
Phone: 956-618-6085
Officers:
   Chairman: Dean R PhD Canty
   Vice Chairman: Joy Judin
   Secretary/Treasurer: Carol Edrington
   Financial Secretary: Mildred Erhart
Mission: To present a major symphony orchestra annually, in varied concerts for students and adults, with emphasis on education of young listeners.

SERIES & FESTIVALS / Texas

Utilizes: Singers
Founded: 1960
Specialized Field: Dance; Vocal Music; Instrumental Music; Festivals; Grand Opera
Status: Nonprofit
Paid Staff: 14
Performs At: McAllen International Civic Center
Organization Type: Performing; Touring; Educational; Presenting

5656
STEPHEN F AUSTIN UNIVERSITY VISUAL & PERFORMING ARTS
Box 13022 SFA
Nacogdoches, TX 75962
Phone: 936-468-2801
Fax: 936-468-1168
e-mail: jgoodall@sfasu.edu
Web Site: www.finearts.sfasu.edu
Management:
   Dean: A.C. Buddy Himes
   Associate Dean: John W. Goodall
   Assistant to Dean: Lisa Rodrigues
Founded: 1923
Specialized Field: Arts; Music; Theatre
Status: Non-Profit, Professional
Budget: $60,000-150,000

5657
ADVENTURES WITH THE ARTS
602 Motley Drive
Overton, TX 75684-1021
Phone: 903-834-6234
Fax: 903-834-3574
e-mail: awamwc@aol.com
Budget: $35,000-60,000

5658
ROUND TOP FESTIVAL INSTITUTE
James Dick Foundation for the Performing Arts
248 Jaster Road
Round Top, TX 78954
Mailing Address: PO Box 89
Phone: 979-249-3129
Fax: 979-249-5078
e-mail: info@festivalhill.org
Web Site: www.festivalhill.org
Officers:
   President: James Dick
Management:
   Managing Director: Richard Royal
   Program Director: Alain G Declert
   Director Library/Museum: Lamar Lentz
   Bookkeeper: Rhonda Hinkley
   Payroll Administrator: Becky Robinson
Mission: Educational project.
Utilizes: Commissioned Composers; Composers-in-Residence; Educators; Fine Artists; Five Seasonal Concerts; Guest Companies; Guest Composers; Guest Ensembles; Guest Instructors; Guest Soloists; Scenic Designers; Students
Founded: 1971
Specialized Field: Classical Music; Poetry; Theatre; Dance
Status: Non-Profit, Professional
Paid Staff: 14
Paid Artists: 44
Budget: $2 Million
Income Sources: Individual Gifts; Foundations; Grants; Box Office; Gift Shop
Performs At: Festival Concert Hall
Affiliations: Chamber Music of America, League of American Orchestra, American String Teachers Association

Type of Stage: Proscenium
Stage Dimensions: 70 x 50
Seating Capacity: 1,100
Rental Contact: Program Director Alain G Declert

5659
ANGELO STATE UNIVERSITY
2601 W Avenue N
San Angelo, TX 76909
Phone: 325-942-2062
Fax: 915-942-2354
Toll-free: 800-946-8627
e-mail: program@angelo.edu
Web Site: www.angelo.edu/org/ucpc/
Officers:
   President: Naiha Campos
   Vice President for Public Relations: Taylor Price
   VP Marketing & Communications: Mik Samaniego-Lira
Management:
   Assistant Director Programming: Rick E Greig
   Assistant Program Director: Rick E Greig
Mission: The Arts Committee of the University Center Program Council presents performing and visual arts to the ASU and San Angelo communities.
Budget: $20,000-35,000

5660
CACTUS JAZZ & BLUES FESTIVAL
Cactus Hotel
PO Box 2477
San Angelo, TX 76902
Phone: 325-653-6793
Fax: 325-658-6036
e-mail: info@sanangeloarts.com
Web Site: www.sanangeloarts.com
Officers:
   President: Carolyn McEnrue
   VP: Dorothy Noriega
   Treasurer: Mark Stevenson
   Secretary: Cindy Gray

5661
ALAMO CITY PERFORMING ARTS ASSOCIATION
12915 Jones Maltsberger
Suite 200
San Antonio, TX 78247
Phone: 210-495-2787
Fax: 210-495-0872
e-mail: saspa@aol.com
Web Site: www.saspa.org
Management:
   President: Sherrie Aoki
   Executive Director: Nancy Grossenbacher
   Artistic Director: Scott Conway
Mission: To offer the best in music, both national and international, as well as theatre, dance and music to San Antonio year-round.
Utilizes: Actors; Choreographers; Dance Companies; Educators; Guest Accompanists; Guest Artists; Guest Designers; Guest Ensembles; Guest Lecturers; Guest Writers; Local Artists; Original Music Scores; Sign Language Translators; Singers; Soloists
Founded: 1991
Specialized Field: Series & Festivals; Dance; Vocal Music; Instrumental Music; Theatre; Festivals
Status: Non-Profit, Professional
Paid Staff: 10
Budget: $50,000
Income Sources: TCA; National Endowment for the Arts; City of San Antonio; Private Donations
Performs At: Theaters
Annual Attendance: 10,000

Organization Type: Sponsoring
Resident Groups: Alamo City Dance Company

5662
ARTS SAN ANTONIO
418 10th Street
San Antonio, TX 78215
Phone: 210-226-2891
Fax: 210-226-1981
e-mail: Info@ArtsSA.org
Web Site: www.artssa.org
Officers:
   Chairman: Wilhelm E. Liebmann
   Treasurer: Alvin A. Loewenberg
   Secretary: Amy Abbey Robinson
Management:
   President, Executive Director: John A. Toohey
   Director Administration, Education: Delia I. Isunza-Rodriguez
   Director of Development: Lee TinkerLee
   Marketing Manager: Melanie Robinson
Mission: To offer theatre, music, ethnic dance, opera, ballet and family performances; to provide outreach programs.
Utilizes: Sign Language Translators; Singers; Theatre Companies; Visual Arts
Founded: 1992
Specialized Field: Series & Festivals; Arts Presenter; Ballet; Opera; Concerts
Status: Non-Profit, Professional
Paid Staff: 4
Paid Artists: 50
Budget: One million
Income Sources: Ticket sales - concession sales - in school workshops and grants
Performs At: Multiple
Affiliations: SWPAP; ISPA; Association of Performing Arts Presenters
Annual Attendance: 40,000
Seating Capacity: 400 - 5,000

5663
THE CARVER COMMUNITY CULTURAL CENTER
226 N Hackberry
San Antonio, TX 78202
Phone: 210-207-7211
Fax: 210-207-4412
e-mail: yonnie.blanchette@sanantonio.gov
Web Site: www.thecarver.org
Officers:
   Chair: Melanie Cowart
   Vice Chair: Mark Wittig
   Secretary: Sarah McLornan
   Treasurer: Seymour Battle III
Management:
   Executive Director: Yonnie Blanchette
   Education Coordinator: Philip Castillo
   House Manager: Jennifer Gonzalez
   Management Analyst: Tracy Alva
   Administrative Assistant II: Gracie Jimenez
Utilizes: Actors; Artists-in-Residence; Collaborating Artists; Collaborations; Commissioned Composers; Commissioned Music; Dance Companies; Dancers; Fine Artists; Five Seasonal Concerts; Guest Accompanists; Guest Choreographers; Guest Ensembles; Guest Musical Directors; High School Drama; Instructors; Local Artists; Lyricists; Multimedia; Original Music Scores; Poets; Resident Artists; Selected Students; Special Technical Talent; Theatre Companies; Touring Companies
Specialized Field: African American Visual and Performing Arts
Paid Staff: 20

SERIES & FESTIVALS / Texas

Volunteer Staff: 50
Paid Artists: 15
Budget: $400,000-1,000,000
Annual Attendance: 50,000
Facility Category: Theatre and Arts School
Type of Stage: Proscenium
Seating Capacity: 640
Year Built: 1929
Year Remodeled: 2000
Rental Contact: 210-207-7215 Leticia Velazquez

5664
SAN ANTONIO PARKS FOUNDATION
600 Hemistair Plaza Way
Building 247
San Antonio, TX 78205
Phone: 210-212-8423
Fax: 210-212-4376
e-mail: info@saparksfoundation.org
Web Site: www.saparksfoundation.org
Officers:
  President and CEO: Noah Almanza,
  Executive Vice President: Judi Deleon
Founded: 1984

5665
TUESDAY MUSICAL CLUB ARTIST SERIES
5410 Pawtucket Drive
San Antonio, TX 78230
Phone: 210-366-2464
Fax: 210-342-7748
Officers:
  Booking Chairman: Mrs. Harold Cockburn
Utilizes: Fine Artists; Guest Directors; Multimedia; Original Music Scores; Sign Language Translators; Singers
Budget: $20,000-35,000
Income Sources: Tickets
Annual Attendance: 1,000
Facility Category: Chruch

5666
SOUTHWEST TEXAS STATE UNIVERSITY ARTS SERIES
Dance Department
601 University Drive
San Marcos, TX 78666
Phone: 512-245-2194
Fax: 512-245-8181
e-mail: jwli@swt.edu
Web Site: www.txstate.edu
Officers:
  Artist Series Committee Chair: LeAnne Smith-Stedman
  Assistan Chair: Cary Michaels
Budget: $60,000-150,000

5667
TEXAS LUTHERAN UNIVERSITY CULTURAL ARTS EVENTS
1000 W Court
Seguin, TX 78155
Phone: 830-372-8000
Fax: 830-372-8096
Toll-free: 800-771-8521
Web Site: www.tlu.edu
Management:
  President: John Moline
  Provost: John Masterson
  Jackson Auditorium Director: Susan Rinn
Specialized Field: Education
Status: Non-Profit, Professional
Budget: $20,000-35,000

5668
AUSTIN COLLEGE COMMUNITY SERIES
900 N Grand
Suite 61602
Sherman, TX 75090-4440
Phone: 903-813-2000
Fax: 903-813-2273
Web Site: www.austincollege.edu
Officers:
  Chair: Todd A. Williams
  Vice Chair: Becky R. Sykes
  President: Mariorie Hass
Management:
  Manager: Joe Hicks
Utilizes: Actors; Fine Artists; Guest Directors; Guest Instructors; Guest Musical Directors; Guest Musicians; Multimedia; Original Music Scores; Singers; Special Technical Talent
Founded: 1966
Paid Staff: 2
Volunteer Staff: 12
Budget: $35,000-60,000
Performs At: Wynne Chapel
Affiliations: AAAP
Annual Attendance: 7,000

5669
CROSS TIMBERS FINE ARTS COUNCIL
204 River North Boulevard
PO Box 1172
Stephenville, TX 76401
Phone: 254-965-6190
Fax: 254-965-6186
e-mail: info@ctfac.com
Web Site: ctfac.com
Officers:
  President: Lisa Pence
  Vice President: Emily Roberson
  Treasurer: Trent Tidwell
  Secretary: Chris Ireland
Management:
  Executive Director: Julie Crouch
Founded: 1980
Specialized Field: Cultural Arts
Status: Non-Profit, Non-Professional
Paid Staff: 2
Budget: $60,000-150,000
Performs At: Clyde H. Wells Fine Arts Center

5670
TARLETON STATE UNIVERSITY STUDENT PROGRAMMING
Tarleton Station
Box T-0670
Stephenville, TX 76402
Phone: 254-968-9000
Fax: 254-968-9492
e-mail: stuact@tarleton.edu
Web Site: www.tarleton.edu
Management:
  President: Merideth Lincoln
  Executive Director: Donna Strohmeyer
Specialized Field: Programming Opportunities
Status: Non-Profit, Non-Professional
Paid Staff: 3

5671
TEXARKANA REGIONAL ARTS & HUMANITIES COUNCIL
221 Main Street
PO Box 1711
Texarkana, TX 75504-1171
Phone: 903-792-4992
Fax: 903-793-8511
e-mail: artsinfo@trahc.org
Web Site: www.trahc.org
Management:
  Executive Director: Brian W Goesel
  Operations Director: Randal Conry
  Administrative Director: Mary Starrett
  Bookkeeper: Paula Watson
  ArtsSmart/Education Director: Charlotte Smelser
Mission: Mission is to grow people and community through the arts.
Founded: 1978
Opened: 1924
Specialized Field: Series & Festivals; Instrumental Music; Vocal Music; Theatre; Youth; Dance; Ethnic Performances
Status: Non-Profit, Professional
Paid Staff: 17
Budget: $1,602,244
Performs At: Perot Theatre
Affiliations: LHAT; APAP; SWPAP
Annual Attendance: 40,000
Type of Stage: Proscenium
Stage Dimensions: 69x35
Seating Capacity: 1,606
Year Built: 1924
Year Remodeled: 1980
Cost: $2.4 Million (1980)
Rental Contact: Randal Conry

5672
TOMBALL REGIONAL ARTS COUNCIL
PO Box 1321
Tomball, TX 77377-1321
Phone: 713-351-2787
Officers:
  President: Kathi Truex
Management:
  Executive Director: Harriet Fether

5673
TYLER COMMUNITY CONCERT ASSOCIATION
1008 W 4th St
Tyler, TX 75701
Mailing Address: PO Box 131673
Phone: 903-592-6266
e-mail: TylerCCA@aol.com
Web Site: www.tcca.biz
Officers:
  President: Gini Rainey
  Secretary: Diane Sorrels
  Treasurer: Lowell Hinsch
Founded: 1933
Specialized Field: Music; Dance; Instrumental Music; Vocal Music; Performing Arts
Budget: $35,000-60,000

5674
UNIVERSITY OF TEXAS AT TYLER
3900 University Boulevard
Department Of Music
Tyler, TX 75799

SERIES & FESTIVALS / Utah

Phone: 903-566-7000
Fax: 903-566-7068
e-mail: info@uttyler.edu
Web Site: www.uttyler.edu/music
Management:
    Senior Lecturer In Music: Vicki J Conway
    Music Program Coordinator: Jeffrey D Emge
Specialized Field: Series and Festivals; Theatre; Dance; Ethnic Performances
Status: For-Profit, Professional
Paid Staff: 7
Budget: $35,000-60,000
Performs At: Fine & Performing Arts Center

5675
UVALDE ARTS COUNCIL
104 W North Street
Uvalde, TX 78801
Phone: 830-278-4184
Fax: 830-278-1658
e-mail: Esther@peppersnet.com
Officers:
    President: Carol Kirlcham
    VP: Michael Box
    Treasurer: Esther Trevino
Management:
    Managing Director: Esther Trevino
Utilizes: Actors; Collaborating Artists; Collaborations; Dance Companies; Dancers; Educators; Guest Accompanists; Guest Designers; Guest Lecturers; Guest Musical Directors; Guest Teachers; Guild Activities; Instructors; Local Artists; Multimedia; Music; Resident Professionals; Sign Language Translators; Soloists; Student Interns; Special Technical Talent; Theatre Companies
Founded: 1981
Paid Staff: 3
Volunteer Staff: 15
Budget: $20,000 - $30,000
Income Sources: memberships, ticket sales
Performs At: Grand Opera House
Annual Attendance: 14,000
Facility Category: Performing Arts & Presenter
Seating Capacity: 370
Year Built: 1891
Year Remodeled: 1981
Cost: 650,000

5676
CULTURAL COUNCIL OF VICTORIA
PO Box 1758
Victoria, TX 77902-1758
Phone: 361-572-2787
Fax: 361-572-6739
e-mail: leee@icsi.net
Web Site: www.ccvtx.org
Management:
    President: Don Truman
    Executive Director: Leolive Rogge
Utilizes: Artists-in-Residence; Collaborations; Educators; Original Music Scores; Soloists; Theatre Companies; Touring Companies
Founded: 1981
Specialized Field: Series & Festivals: Council
Status: Non-Profit, Professional
Paid Staff: 2
Volunteer Staff: 200
Budget: $10,000
Facility Category: Victoria College Auditorium

5677
VICTORIA FINE ARTS ASSOCIATION
700 N. Main St
Victoria, TX 77901
Phone: 361-572-2787
Management:
    Artists Selection Chairman: Joe Hewell
    Artists Selection: Ruth Williams
Founded: 1946
Specialized Field: Series Festival; Youth; Jazz
Status: Non-Profit, Professional
Budget: $35,000-60,000

5678
BAYLOR UNIVERSITY DISTINGUISHED ARTIST SERIES
Baylor University
School of Music
Waco, TX 76798
Phone: 254-710-2112
Fax: 254-710-1191
Toll-free: 800-229-5678
e-mail: john_wilson@baylor.edu
Web Site: www.baylor.edu
Management:
    Distinguished Artist Series Manager: Kathy Johnson
    Interim Provost: David Garland
Budget: $20,000-35,000
Performs At: Jones Concert Hall; Roxy Grove Hall

5679
WHARTON COUNTY JUNIOR COLLEGE THE CENTER FOR THE ARTS SERIES
911 Boling Highway
Wharton, TX 77488
Phone: 979-532-4560
Fax: 979-532-6587
Toll-free: 800-561-9252
e-mail: marjoriek@wcjc.edu
Web Site: www.wcjc.cc.tx.us
Officers:
    President: Betty McCrohan
    Communications Chair: Dr Pam Speights
    Secretary: Jack C. Moses
Management:
    Manager of Student Recruiting: Julie Aaronson
    Director of Continuing Education: Alice Atkins
Founded: 1946
Specialized Field: Series & Festivals; Art; Drama; Music
Status: For-Profit, Non-Professional
Paid Staff: 5
Budget: $10,000
Performs At: Horton Foote Theatre

5680
MIDWESTERN STATE UNIVERSITY: ARTIST LECTURE SERIES
3410 Taft Boulevard
CSC Room 104
Wichita Falls, TX 76308
Phone: 940-397-4000
Fax: 940-397-4938
e-mail: jane.leishner@mwsu.edu
Web Site: www.mwsu.edu
Management:
    President: Jessy Rogers
Founded: 1922
Specialized Field: University; Musical Events
Status: Non-Profit, Professional
Paid Staff: 300
Budget: $10,000-20,000

Utah

5682
UTAH SHAKESPEAREAN FESTIVAL
351 W Center Street
Cedar City, UT 84720
Phone: 435-586-7880
Fax: 435-865-8003
Toll-free: 800-752-9849
e-mail: ussboxoffice@suu.edu
Web Site: www.bard.org
Officers:
    Chair: Mark C. Moench
    Vice Chair and Chair-Elect: Jeffery R. Nelson
Management:
    Founder: Fred Adams
    Artistic Director: David Ivers
    Managing Director: R Scott Phillips
    Associate Artistic Director: Cathleen Conlin
    Marketing Director: Kami Terry Paul
    Production Manager: Ran Inkel
    Director Plays-in-Progress: George Judy
    Education Director: Michael Don Bahr
    Publications Director: Bruce Lee
Mission: To present six classic and Shakespearean works in repertory each summer.
Utilizes: Actors; Guest Conductors; Guest Designers; Guest Writers; Guild Activities; Performance Artists; Resident Professionals; Student Interns
Founded: 1961
Specialized Field: Series and Festivals; Instrumental Music; Vocal Music; Theatre; Dance
Status: Non-Profit, Professional
Paid Staff: 30
Volunteer Staff: 250
Paid Artists: 400
Budget: $5 Million
Income Sources: Box Office Sales; Contributed Income; Endowment Income; Merchandise Sales
Season: June - August
Performs At: Adams Memorial Stage; Randall L. Jones Theatre; University Stage
Affiliations: USA; SSD&C; Actors' Equity Association; LORT; TCG
Annual Attendance: 155,000
Facility Category: Outdoor/Indoor
Type of Stage: Thrust; Proscenium
Stage Dimensions: 50Wx30D; 22Hx42Wx25D; 18Hx44Wx39D
Seating Capacity: 887; 769; 981
Year Remodeled: 1989
Rental Contact: Production Manager Ray Inkel
Organization Type: Performing; Resident; Educational

5683
CACHE VALLEY CENTER FOR THE ARTS
43 S Main Street
Logan, UT 84321-4535
Phone: 435-753-6518
Fax: 435-753-1232
e-mail: wbloss@centerforthearts.us
Web Site: www.cachearts.org
Management:
    Executive Director: Wally Bloss
Utilizes: Actors; Artists-in-Residence; Choreographers; Collaborations; Curators; Dance Companies; Dancers; Designers; Educators; Fine Artists; Five Seasonal Concerts; Grant Writers; Guest Accompanists; Guest Artists; Guest Choreographers; Guest Companies; Guest Composers; Guest Conductors; Guest Designers; Guest Directors; Guest Ensembles; Guest Instructors; Guest Lecturers; Guest Musical Directors; Guest Musicians; Guest Soloists; Guest Teachers; High School Drama; Instructors; Local Artists; Local

SERIES & FESTIVALS / Utah

Unknown Artists; Multimedia; Music; Original Music Scores; Performance Artists; Playwrights; Resident Artists; Resident Professionals; Selected Students; Sign Language Translators; Singers; Soloists; Student Interns; Special Technical Talent; Theatre Companies; Touring Companies; Volunteer Artists
Founded: 1989
Specialized Field: Northern Utah
Paid Staff: 10
Volunteer Staff: 50
Budget: $1,300,000
Income Sources: City and County; Foundations; Corporations and Individuals
Facility Category: Proscenium Theatre
Stage Dimensions: 36'x32'
Seating Capacity: 1,100
Year Built: 1923
Year Remodeled: 1993
Rental Contact: Mary Shope
Resident Groups: Utah Festival Opera, Alliance for the Varied Arts, Paint Utah

5684
UTAH STATE UNIVERSITY PERFORMING ARTS SERIES
Taggart Student Center, UMC-01
Logan, UT 84322-0105
Phone: 435-797-1000
Fax: 435-797-2571
Web Site: www.usu.edu
Management:
  Student Activities Director: Randy Jensen
Budget: $150,000-400,000
Performs At: Chase Fine Arts Center

5685
WASSERMANN PIANO FESTIVAL
Utah State University, Music Department
4015 Old Main Hill
Logan, UT 84322-4015
Phone: 435-797-3000
Fax: 435-797-1862
e-mail: musicdep@cc.usu.edu
Web Site: music.usu.edu
Management:
  President: Bruce Saperston
  Director for Festivals: R Dennis Hirst
Founded: 1965
Specialized Field: Music and Music Therapy
Status: Non-Profit, Professional
Paid Staff: 40
Paid Artists: 15

5686
MORMON MIRACLE PAGEANT
PO Box 155
Manti, UT 84642
Phone: 435-835-3000
Web Site: www.mormonmiracle.org/
Management:
  Pageant Director: Laren Swensen
Mission: Portraying the religious history of the Latter-Day Saints and relating it to national events.
Utilizes: Guest Companies
Founded: 1967
Specialized Field: Theater
Status: Non-Professional; Nonprofit
Performs At: Manti Temple Grounds Amphitheatre
Organization Type: Performing; Resident

5687
CANYONLANDS ARTS COUNCIL
59 S Main Street
#236
Moab, UT 84532
Phone: 435-259-2742
Fax: 435-259-2418
Management:
  Director: Theresa King
Budget: $10,000-20,000

5688
MOAB MUSIC FESTIVAL
58 East 300 South
Moab, UT 84532
Phone: 435-259-7003
Fax: 432-259-7044
e-mail: info@moabmusicfest.org
Web Site: www.moabmusicfest.org
Officers:
  President: Hank Rutter
Management:
  Music Director: Michael Barrett
  Artistic Director: Leslie Tomkins
  Executive Director: Laura E. Brown
  Operations Director: Dave Montgomery
  Box Office Manager: Rhiana Medina
  External Relations Manager: Aubrey Davis
Mission: Produce music festival and provide education outreach program to community schools.
Founded: 1991
Specialized Field: Classical Chamber Music
Status: Non-Profit, Professional
Paid Staff: 8
Volunteer Staff: 1

5689
WEBER STATE UNIVERSITY CULTURAL AFFAIRS
1006 University Circle
Ogden, UT 84408-1006
Phone: 801-626-6003
Fax: 801-626-7922
e-mail: dstern@weber.eduu
Web Site: www.weber.edu
Management:
  Office Cultural Affairs Director: Diane Stern
Budget: $60,000-150,000
Seating Capacity: 1800

5690
AUTUMN CLASSIC MUSIC FESTIVAL
PO Box 354
Park City, UT 84060
Phone: 435-649-5309
e-mail: lharlow@pcmusicfestival.com
Web Site: www.pcmusicfestival.com
Officers:
  President: Russell Harlow
  Director Development: Leslie Blackburn Harlow
Founded: 1984
Specialized Field: Series & Festivals: Chamber Music
Status: Non-Profit, Professional
Paid Staff: 1
Paid Artists: 15

5691
CONTEMPORARY MUSIC CONSORTIUM
PO Box 354
Park City, UT 84060
Phone: 435-649-5309
e-mail: lharlow@pcmusicfestival.com
Web Site: www.cmcconcerts.org

Officers:
  President: Russell Harlow
  Director Development: Leslie Blackburn Harlow
Founded: 1984
Specialized Field: Series & Festivals: Chamber Music
Status: Non-Profit, Professional
Paid Staff: 1
Paid Artists: 15

5692
PARK CITY & SALT LAKE MUSIC FESTIVAL
PO Box 354
Park City, UT 84060
Phone: 435-649-5309
e-mail: lharlow@pcmusicfestival.com
Web Site: www.pcmusicfestival.com
Officers:
  President: Russell Harlow
  Director Development: Leslie Blackburn Harlow
Founded: 1984
Specialized Field: Series & Festivals: Chamber Music
Status: Non-Profit, Professional
Paid Staff: 1
Paid Artists: 15

5693
PARK CITY FILM MUSIC FESTIVAL
PO Box 354
Park City, UT 84060
Phone: 435-649-5309
Web Site: www.pcfmf.com
Officers:
  President: Russell Harlow
  Director Development: Leslie Blackburn Harlow
Founded: 1984
Specialized Field: Series & Festivals: Chamber Music
Status: Non-Profit, Professional
Paid Staff: 1
Paid Artists: 15

5694
PARK CITY JAZZ FESTIVAL
PO Box 680720
Park City, UT 84068-0720
Phone: 435-940-1362
Fax: 435-940-1464
Toll-free: 800-453-1360
e-mail: info@parkcityjazz.com
Web Site: www.parkcityjazz.com
Officers:
  Founder: Lew Fine
  Founder: Arlene Fine
  Interim Chairman: Martin Marmor
Management:
  Chairman: Hans Suegi
  Executive Director: Tom Horrocks
  Assistant To Director: Mike Andrews
Mission: Is committed to promoting jazz music through an annual showcase of national, regional, and local jazz musicians.
Founded: 1998
Specialized Field: Series & Festivals: Jazz Festivals
Status: Non-Profit, Professional
Paid Staff: 2
Volunteer Staff: 186
Paid Artists: 11
Annual Attendance: 15,000
Seating Capacity: 5000

SERIES & FESTIVALS / Utah

5695
BRIGHAM YOUNG UNIVERSITY PERFORMING ARTS SERIES
F-315 Harris Fine Arts Center
Provo, UT 84602
Phone: 801-378-5203
Fax: 801-378-8008
Officers:
   Director: Jon Hollsman
Management:
   Director: Jon Hollsman
Mission: A varied production and concert season in support of academic programs in music, dance and theatre.
Utilizes: Guest Artists; Guest Companies; Singers
Founded: 1875
Specialized Field: Dance; Vocal Music; Instrumental Music; Theatre; Grand Opera
Status: Professional; Semi-Professional; Nonprofit
Paid Staff: 11
Budget: $60,000-150,000
Income Sources: Association of Performing Arts Presenters; Western Alliance of Arts Administrators
Performs At: Harris Fine Arts Center; Brigham Young University
Facility Category: Concert hall
Type of Stage: Proscenium w/hydralic pit
Stage Dimensions: 60 x 45
Seating Capacity: 1960
Year Built: 1963
Organization Type: Performing; Touring; Educational; Sponsoring

5696
CELEBRITY CONCERT SERIES OFFICE
225 S 700 E
Saint George, UT 84770
Phone: 435-652-7994
Fax: 435-656-4080
e-mail: mstephenson@dixie.edu
Web Site: dixie.edu/concerts
Officers:
   President: Bill Ostler
   Chair: Toni Caplin
Management:
   Director: Gail Bunker
Mission: Presents eleven to twelve professional concerts on two consecutive nights each from October through May 2008. Concerts are held in the 1200-seat Cox Performing Arts Center and represent the finest professional artists and companies available representing various genres: opera, symphonic, dance, choral, brass, wind and string ensembles, jazz and string, vocal and piano soloists.
Utilizes: Artists-in-Residence; Collaborations; Dance Companies; Dancers; Fine Artists; New Productions; Original Music Scores; Playwrights; Sign Language Translators; Singers; Special Technical Talent; Theatre Companies
Founded: 1958
Specialized Field: Series & Festivals: Multi-Discipline Performance Arts
Status: Non-Profit, Non-Professional
Paid Staff: 1
Volunteer Staff: 12
Paid Artists: 12
Budget: $150,000-200,000
Income Sources: Season Memberships; Ticket Sales; Grants; Donations; Endowment Income
Performs At: Avenna Center Cox Auditorium
Annual Attendance: 14,200
Facility Category: Theatre
Type of Stage: Proscenium
Seating Capacity: 1,200
Year Built: 1980

5697
THE WISCONSIN CENTER DISTRICT
400 W. Wisconsin Avenue
Salt Lake City, UT 53203
Phone: 414-908-6000
Toll-free: 800-745-3000
e-mail: boxoffice@wcd.org
Web Site: wisconsincenter.org
Management:
   Group Sales Manager: Chris Kroening
   Director of Public Safety: Jeremie Ott
   Director of Sales & Marketing: Trace Goudreau
   Senior Catering Sales Manager: Bridget Gallagher
   Director of Productions: Casey Trotter
Founded: 1991
Specialized Field: Home of the Utah Jazz (NBA) and the Utah Starzz (WNBA).
Seating Capacity: 19,911
Year Built: 1991

5698
EASTERN ARTS INTERNATIONAL DANCE THEATER
PO Box 526362
Salt Lake City, UT 84152
Phone: 801-485-5824
e-mail: kstjohn@burgoyne.com
Web Site: www.easternartists.com
Officers:
   Dance Director: Katherine St John
   Music Director: Lloyd Miller
Management:
   President: Katherine John
Mission: To promote time-honored traditions by offering concerts, lectures, and workshops of cultures from Asia and Eastern Europe.
Founded: 1960
Specialized Field: Series & Festivals: International Music and Dance
Status: Non-Profit, Professional
Paid Staff: 10
Income Sources: Western Alliance of Arts Administrators; Society for Ethno-Musicology; Middle East Studies Association; Society for Dance Ethnology
Organization Type: Performing; Educational; Sponsoring

5699
GINA BACHAUER INTERNATIONAL PIANO COMPETITION & FESTIVAL
138 W Broadway
Suite 220
Salt Lake City, UT 84101
Phone: 801-297-4250
Fax: 801-521-9202
e-mail: gina@bachauer.com
Web Site: www.bachauer.com
Management:
   President of the Board: Brad Beagles
   Artistic Director: Douglas Humpherys
   Manager: Kimi Kawashima
   Director: Paul C Pollei
   Executive Director: Kary Billings
Founded: 1977
Specialized Field: Series and Festivals; Instrumental Music; Youth
Status: Non-Profit, Professional
Paid Staff: 3
Paid Artists: 5

5700
TEMPLE SQUARE CONCERT SERIES
LDS Church Office Building, 20th Floor
50 E North Temple
Salt Lake City, UT 84150
Phone: 801-240-3323
Fax: 801-240-1994
Management:
   Director: Iain B McKay
Performs At: Assembly Hall; Tabernacle at Temple Square
Seating Capacity: 1200; 5500

5701
WESTMINSTER COLLEGE
1840 S 1300 E
Salt Lake City, UT 84105
Phone: 801-484-7651
Fax: 801-484-5579
Toll-free: 800-748-4753
e-mail: wccconcerts@rider.edu
Web Site: www.wcslc.edu
Management:
   President: Michael Bassis
   Artistic Director: Karlyn Bard
Founded: 1874
Specialized Field: Master Programming in Community and Education
Status: Non-Profit, Professional
Paid Staff: 42
Budget: $10,000
Performs At: Jewett Center for the Performing Arts
Seating Capacity: 300

5702
WORLD ARTS/NOON CONCERTS SERIES
PO Box 526362
Salt Lake City, UT 84152
Phone: 801-485-5824
Management:
   Project Coordinator: Lloyd Miller
Founded: 1990
Specialized Field: Series & Festivals; Instrumental Music; Vocal Music; Youth; Dance; Ethnic Performances
Status: Non-Profit, Professional
Paid Staff: 6
Budget: $10,000

5703
AMERICAN WEST HERITAGE FESTIVAL
4025 S Highway 89-91
Wellsville, UT 84339
Phone: 435-245-6050
Fax: 435-245-6052
Toll-free: 800-225-3378
e-mail: info@awhc.org
Web Site: www.awhc.org
Management:
   Executive Director: Matt Dahl
   Artistic Director: Lorraine Bowen
Mission: Educate, entertain, and enlighten guests about life from 1820-1920.
Founded: 1972
Specialized Field: Series & Festivals: Ethnic Performances
Status: Non-Profit, Professional
Paid Staff: 17
Volunteer Staff: 100
Paid Artists: 55
Non-paid Artists: 15

SERIES & FESTIVALS / Vermont

Vermont

5704
BRATTLEBORO MUSIC CENTER
38 Walnut Street
Brattleboro, VT 05301
Phone: 802-257-4523
e-mail: info@bmcvt.org
Web Site: www.bmcvt.org
Officers:
  President: Jean Giddings
  Vice President: William Shakespeare
  Secretary: Alison Schantz
  Treasurer: Patricia Mangan
Management:
  Managing Director: Pam Lierle
  Education Programs Director: Carol Compton
  Administrative Coordinator: Gay Foster
  Bookkeeper: Donna Simpson
  Campaign Director: Eric Russell
Founded: 1952
Specialized Field: Series and Festivals; Instrumental Music; Vocal Music
Status: Non-Profit, Professional
Paid Staff: 5
Paid Artists: 30

5705
BURLINGTON DISCOVER JAZZ FESTIVAL
156 College Street
Suite 202
Burlington, VT 05401
Phone: 802-863-7992
Fax: 802-864-3927
e-mail: info@discoverjazz.com
Web Site: www.discoverjazz.com
Officers:
  Director, Flynn Center: Andrea Rogers
Management:
  Managing Director: Brian Mital
  Chief Programming Officer: Arnie Malina
  Associate Director: Geeda Searfoorce
Mission: Offering the widest possible range of jazz and music educational programs; ticketed and free events.
Utilizes: Community Members; Community Talent; Composers; Educators; Guest Directors; Guest Musical Directors; Instructors; Local Artists & Directors; Lyricists; Multimedia; Music; Scenic Designers; Sign Language Translators
Founded: 1984
Specialized Field: Jazz
Status: Non-Profit, Professional
Paid Staff: 2
Volunteer Staff: 350
Budget: $600,000
Income Sources: Burlington City Arts; Flynn Center
Performs At: Multi-disciplinary
Annual Attendance: 45,000
Facility Category: City-wide (Burlington)
Organization Type: Performing; Educational; Sponsoring

5706
UNIVERSITY OF VERMONT: GEORGE BISHOP LANE SERIES
460 S Prospect Street
Burlington, VT 05401-2501
Phone: 802-656-4455
Fax: 802-656-4010
e-mail: lane.series@uvm.edu
Web Site: www.uvm.edu/laneseries
Officers:
  President: Anne Francis
  Vice President: George Dameron
Management:
  Director: Natalie Neuert
  Manager: Rebecca Stone
  Operations: Freda Farrell
  Customer Service: Carol Sankowski
  Stage Manager: Sarah Sherrill
Utilizes: Artists-in-Residence; Collaborations; Commissioned Music; Composers-in-Residence; Dancers; Educators; Fine Artists; Guest Choreographers; Guest Musical Directors; Guest Musicians; Lyricists; Multimedia; Original Music Scores; Sign Language Translators; Singers; Soloists
Founded: 1954
Specialized Field: Presenter
Status: Non-Profit, Professional
Paid Staff: 3
Volunteer Staff: 20
Budget: $500,000
Income Sources: Endowment; Ticket Sales; Fundraising
Performs At: Flynn Theatre

5707
CASTLETON STATE COLLEGE PERFORMING ARTS SERIES
Castleton State College
Castleton, VT 05735
Phone: 802-468-5611
Fax: 802-468-6470
e-mail: mariko.hancock@castleton.edu
Web Site: www.castleton.edu
Management:
  President: David Walk
  Executive Director: James Fuller
  Fine Arts Center Coordinator: Mariko Hancock
Founded: 1787
Specialized Field: Series & Festivals; Instrumental Music; Vocal Music; Theatre; Youth; Dance; Ethnic Performances
Status: Non-Profit, Professional
Budget: $10,000-20,000

5708
GREEN MOUNTAIN FESTIVAL SERIES
PO Box 561
Chester, VT 05143
Phone: 802-875-4473
Fax: 802-875-3989
e-mail: info@greenmountainfestivalseries.com
Web Site: www.greenmountainfestivalseries.com
Management:
  Manager: Ann C. DiBernardo
Mission: Organized to bring quality arts to local schools and communities.
Budget: $20,000-35,000

5709
ST. MICHAEL'S COLLEGE CONCERTS
St Michael's College
One Winooski Park
Colchester, VT 05439
Phone: 802-654-2000
Fax: 802-654-2906
e-mail: admission@smcvt.edu
Web Site: www.smcvt.edu
Management:
  Music Director: Dr. William Tortolano
Budget: $10,000-20,000

5710
DORSET THEATRE FESTIVAL
PO Box 510 Dorset
Dorset, VT 05251
Phone: 802-867-2223
Fax: 802-867-0144
e-mail: theatre@sover.net
Web Site: www.theatredirectories.com
Management:
  President of the Board: Robert Bushnel
  Executive Director: James Faszholz
  Artistic Director: William John Aupperly
Founded: 1976
Specialized Field: Series & Festivals; Instrumental Music; Vocal Music; Theatre; Youth; Ethnic Performances
Status: Non-Profit, Professional
Paid Staff: 5
Paid Artists: 32
Income Sources: Theatre Communications Group
Season: June-September
Performs At: Dorset Playhouse
Type of Stage: Proscenium
Seating Capacity: 218
Organization Type: Performing

5711
WAREBROOK CONTEMPORARY MUSIC FESTIVAL
276 Hillandale Road
Irasburg, VT 05845
Phone: 802-754-6335
Fax: 802-754-2562
e-mail: saracomposer@hotmail.com
Web Site: www.warebrook.org
Management:
  President: Elizabeth Doncaster
  Executive Director: Sarah Doncaster
Founded: 1991
Specialized Field: Chamber and Vocal Music
Status: Non-Profit, Professional
Paid Staff: 3
Paid Artists: 22

5712
FESTIVAL OF THE ARTS
Southern Vermont Arts Center/West Coast
PO Box 672
Manchester, VT 05254
Phone: 802-362-1405
Fax: 802-362-3274
Management:
  Executive Director: Christopher Madkour
Founded: 1929
Specialized Field: All Medium Arts
Status: Non-Profit, Non-Professional
Paid Staff: 9
Performs At: Southern Vermont Arts Center
Organization Type: Sponsoring

5713
MANCHESTER MUSIC FESTIVAL
42 Dillingham Avenue
PO Box 33
Manchester, VT 05254
Phone: 802-362-1956
Fax: 802-362-0711
Toll-free: 800-639-5868
e-mail: mmfvermont@adelphia.net
Web Site: www.mmfvt.org
Management:
  Artistic Director: Ariel Rudiskov
  Executive Director: Margaret Wood-Holmes

SERIES & FESTIVALS / Vermont

Business Manager: Heidi French
Mission: Educating young artists for a professional career.
Utilizes: Commissioned Composers; Composers; Guest Artists; Guest Musical Directors; Original Music Scores; Sign Language Translators; Students
Founded: 1974
Specialized Field: Series & Festivals: Chamber Music Concert
Status: Non-Profit, Professional
Paid Staff: 2
Paid Artists: 15
Budget: $500,000
Income Sources: Ticket sales; contributions
Performs At: The Louise Arkell Pavilion
Annual Attendance: 4,000
Organization Type: Performing; Touring; Educational

5714
MIDDLEBURY COLLEGE CONCERT SERIES
Middlebury College
Middlebury, VT 05753
Phone: 802-443-5307
Fax: 802-443-2084
Management:
  Director: Paul Nelson
Budget: $60,000-150,000
Performs At: Wright Theatre; Dance Performance Hall

5715
ONION RIVER ARTS COUNCIL: CELEBRATION SERIES
41 Elm Street
Montpelier, VT 05602
Phone: 802-229-9408
Fax: 802-229-9408
e-mail: orac@sover.net
Web Site: www.onionriverarts.org
Management:
  Executive Director: Diane Manion
Status: Non-Profit
Budget: $35,000-60,000

5716
YELLOW BARN MUSIC FESTIVAL
63 Main Street
Putney, VT 05346
Phone: 802-387-6637
Fax: 802-419-4855
Toll-free: 800-639-3819
e-mail: info@yellowbarn.org
Web Site: www.yellowbarn.org
Officers:
  President: Douglas Cox
Management:
  Executive Director: Catherine Stephan
  Artistic Director: Seth Knopp
  Administrator: Maurey McNaughton
  Production Manager: Kelsey Ekker
  Box Office Manager: Jamie Mohr
Mission: To offer professional training and a performance festival to talented young chamber artists.
Utilizes: Guest Artists
Founded: 1969
Specialized Field: Chamber music
Status: Nonprofit
Paid Staff: 50
Volunteer Staff: 50+
Paid Artists: 22
Budget: $350,000
Income Sources: Private donations; Grants
Performs At: Concert Hall and touring events

Organization Type: Performing; Educational

5717
WHITE RIVER VALLEY CHAMBER OF COMMERCE
31 VT Route 66
Suite #1
Randolph, VT 05060
Phone: 802-728-9027
Fax: 802-728-4612
e-mail: chandler@innevi.com
Web Site: www.whitervervalleychamber.com
Officers:
  President: Janet Watton
Management:
  Program Director: Rebecca B McMeekin
Mission: Providing opportunities to the community at large for artistic expression and educational pursuit by sponsoring and producing programs in the creative and performing arts in and for Chandler Music Hall.
Utilizes: Actors; Artists-in-Residence; Collaborations; Dance Companies; Educators; Guest Directors; Guild Activities; High School Drama; Instructors; Local Artists; Multimedia; Original Music Scores; Sign Language Translators; Soloists; Touring Companies
Founded: 1978
Paid Staff: 2
Volunteer Staff: 50
Budget: $200,000
Income Sources: Individual and corporate donations; Grants; and Ticket sales
Annual Attendance: 13,000
Facility Category: Music hall and art gallery
Type of Stage: Proscenium
Stage Dimensions: 31'W x 20'H x 21'D
Seating Capacity: 589
Year Built: 1907
Rental Contact: Becky McMeekin

5718
CHAFFEE ART CENTER
16 South Main Street
Rutland, VT 05701
Phone: 802-775-0356
e-mail: director@crossroadsarts.com
Web Site: www.chaffeeartcenter.org
Officers:
  President: William Tracy Carris
  Vice President: Barbara Giancola
  Treasurer: David Pride
  Secretary: Laura Conti
Management:
  Ex-Director: Margaret Creed Barros
  Program Directory: Whitnaey Lamy
Mission: To bring performing artists to the Rutland Region.
Founded: 1971
Specialized Field: Series & Festivals; Performances; Workshop; Educational Programme
Status: Non-Profit, Professional
Paid Staff: 3
Paid Artists: 30
Budget: $225,000
Annual Attendance: 5,000+

5719
KILLINGTON MUSIC FESTIVAL
56 Howe Street
Rutland, VT 05702
Mailing Address: PO Box 386, Rutland, VT. 05702
Phone: 802-773-4003
Fax: 802-773-1168
e-mail: kmfest@sover.net
Web Site: www.killingtonmusicfestival.org

Management:
  Executive Director: Maria Fish
  Artistic Director: Daniel Andai
Mission: To present a series of summer chamber music concerts; To maintain a summer school to train aspiring musicians.
Utilizes: Guest Companies
Founded: 1982
Specialized Field: Series and Festivals; Classical Chamber Music; Residency Program; Concert Series
Status: Non-Profit, Professional
Paid Staff: 2
Paid Artists: 20
Organization Type: Performing; Educational

5720
STOWE PERFORMING ARTS
1250 Waterbury Road
Stowe, VT 05672
Phone: 802-253-7792
Fax: 802-253-7140
e-mail: spa@stowearts.com
Web Site: www.stoweperformingarts.com
Management:
  Executive Director: Lynn Paparella
Mission: Stowe Performing Arts is a non-profit community organization with a volunteer Board of Directors dedicated to bringing high quality performances and opportunities for cultural enrichment through the Performing Arts to the community and surrounding areas.
Utilizes: Fine Artists; Guest Musicians; Instructors; Multimedia; Original Music Scores; Sign Language Translators; Singers
Founded: 1976
Specialized Field: Series and Festivals; Present Concerts in Classical; Country; Pops; Jazz; Chamber Music
Status: Non-Profit, Professional
Paid Staff: 1
Volunteer Staff: 15
Paid Artists: 10
Budget: $100,000
Income Sources: Donations and Ticket Sales
Performs At: Outdoor venue, Church, Ice Arena
Facility Category: Open Stage
Type of Stage: Wooden Platform
Stage Dimensions: 30'x40'
Seating Capacity: 2,200

5721
PENTANGLE COUNCIL ON THE ARTS AND THE WOODSTOCK TOWN HALL THEATRE
31 The Green
PO Box 172
Woodstock, VT 05091
Phone: 802-457-3981
Fax: 802-457-4972
e-mail: info@pentanglearts.org
Web Site: www.pentanglearts.org
Management:
  Executive Director: Sabrina Brown
Mission: To maintain an arts program of high quality for the enrichment of our community and schools.
Utilizes: Artists-in-Residence; Collaborating Artists; Collaborations; Dance Companies; Dancers; Educators; Filmmakers; Guest Instructors; Guild Activities; Local Artists; Multi Collaborations; Multimedia; New Productions; Original Music Scores; Sign Language Translators; Soloists; Special Technical Talent
Founded: 1974

SERIES & FESTIVALS / Virginia

Specialized Field: Series & Festivals; Instrumental Music; Vocal Music; Theatre; Youth; Dance; Ethnic Performances
Status: Non-Profit, Professional
Paid Staff: 3
Paid Artists: 25
Budget: $275,000
Income Sources: Annual Appeal; Membership; Endowment; Ticket Sales; Grants
Performs At: Town Hall Theatre; Little Theatre
Annual Attendance: 12,000
Facility Category: Theatre
Type of Stage: Proscenium
Seating Capacity: 400
Year Built: 1901
Year Remodeled: 1979
Rental Contact: Sabrina Brown

Virginia

5722
ALEXANDRIA RECITAL SERIES

5917 Berkshire Court
Alexandria, VA 22303-1632
Phone: 703-960-0616
Fax: 703-960-6691
e-mail: RecitalSeries@aol.com
Management:
 Program Director: Willis Bennett
Budget: $10,000
Performs At: The Lyceum

5723
INTERNATIONAL CHILDREN'S FESTIVAL

Arts Council of Fairfax County
10604 Judicial Drive
Annandale, VA 22030
Phone: 703-642-0862
Fax: 703-642-1773
e-mail: info@artsfairfax.org
Web Site: www.artsfairfax.org
Management:
 President, CEO: Linda S. Sullivan
 Performing Arts Director: Scott Fridy
 Business Manager: Janay Turner
Utilizes: Selected Students; Sign Language Translators; Singers; Soloists
Founded: 1964
Specialized Field: Arts and artists
Status: Non-Profit, Professional
Paid Staff: 3
Income Sources: Arts Council of Fairfax County, Inc.
Performs At: Wolf Trap Farm Park for the Performing Arts
Annual Attendance: 30,000
Facility Category: Amphitheatre in a park
Seating Capacity: 4,000
Year Built: 1971
Organization Type: Performing; Resident; Sponsoring

5724
ARLINGTON CULTURAL AFFAIRS DIVISION

1100 North Glebe Road
Suite 1500
Arlington, VA 22201
Phone: 703-228-1850
Fax: 703-228-0805
e-mail: arts@arlingtonza.us
Web Site: www.arlingtonarts.org
Management:
 Performing Arts Director: Jon Palmer Claridge
Specialized Field: Series & Festivals; Instrumental Music; Vocal Music; Theatre; Youth; Dance; Ethnic Performances
Paid Staff: 40
Budget: $60,000-150,000

5725
ARLINGTON'S ARTS AL FRESCO & THE INNOVATORS

1100 North Glebe Road
Suite 1500
Arlington, VA 22201
Phone: 703-228-1850
Fax: 703-228-0805
e-mail: arts@arlingtonva.us
Web Site: www.arlingtonarts.org
Management:
 Department Director: Toni Hubbard
 Artistic Director: Jon Claridge
Founded: 1985
Specialized Field: Series and Festivals; Instrumental Music; Vocal Music; Theatre; Dance; Ethnic Performances
Status: Non-Profit, Professional
Paid Staff: 25
Paid Artists: 150
Budget: $60,000-150,000
Performs At: Thomas Jefferson Theatre; Ellipse Art Center

5726
VIRGINIA TECH UNION LIVELY ARTS SEASON

Virginia Tech
325 Squires Student Center (0138)
Blacksburg, VA 24061
Phone: 540-231-7117
Fax: 540-231-7028
e-mail: vtu@vtu.org
Web Site: www.vtu.org.vt.edu
Officers:
 President: Adam Taber
 Vice President: Anisha Thadani
Management:
 Director of Graphic Design: Dag Yeshiwas
 Director of Public Relations: Rachel Brassfield
 Director of Lively Arts: Michaela McNamara
 Director of House and Hospitality: Mitchell Haugen
 Director of Alternative Sounds: Claire Reynolds
Utilizes: Dance Companies; Special Technical Talent; Theatre Companies
Founded: 1969
Specialized Field: Series & Festivals; Vocal Music; Theatre; Dance; Ethnic Performances
Status: Non-Profit, Professional
Paid Staff: 1
Volunteer Staff: 20
Budget: $150,000-400,000
Income Sources: Ticket Sales; Student Activity Fees
Annual Attendance: 14,000
Facility Category: Auditorium
Type of Stage: Proscenium
Stage Dimensions: 58x34x32
Seating Capacity: 2,950
Year Built: 1935

5727
BRIDGEWATER COLLEGE LYCEUM SERIES

402 East College Street
Bridgewater, VA 22812
Phone: 540-828-8000
Fax: 540-828-5637
e-mail: jhopkins@bridgewater.edu
Web Site: www.bridgewater.edu
Management:
 President: Phillip Stone
 Executive Director: P Hopkins
 Director: Jesse E Hopkins
Specialized Field: Series & Festivals; Instrumental Music; Vocal Music; Ethnic Performances
Status: Non-Profit, Professional
Budget: $20,000-35,000
Performs At: Cole Hall

5728
ASHLAWN-HIGHLAND SUMMER FESTIVAL

1941 James Monroe Parkway
Charlottesville, VA 22902
Phone: 804-293-4500
Fax: 804-293-0736
e-mail: summerfestival@avenue.gen.va.us
Web Site: www.avenue.org/summerfestival
Management:
 General Director: Judith H Walker
Founded: 1978
Status: Non-Equity; Nonprofit
Paid Staff: 4
Volunteer Staff: 100
Paid Artists: 80
Non-paid Artists: 25
Season: June - August
Stage Dimensions: 24' x 16'
Seating Capacity: 450

5729
TUESDAY EVENING CONCERT SERIES

108 5th Street SE
Suite 208
Charlottesville, VA 22902
Phone: 434-244-9505
Fax: 434-244-9510
e-mail: kpellon@tecs.org
Web Site: www.tecs.org
Management:
 Executive Director: Karen Pellon
Mission: Chamber music series with artists from around the world.
Utilizes: Guest Musicians; Multimedia
Founded: 1948
Specialized Field: Music
Status: Professional; Nonprofit
Paid Staff: 2
Paid Artists: 30
Budget: $100000+
Income Sources: Tickets; Advertising; Grants; Donations
Performs At: Concert Hall
Annual Attendance: 5,000
Facility Category: Concert Hall
Seating Capacity: 850
Year Built: 1896
Year Remodeled: 1995
Organization Type: Sponsoring

5730
ALLEGHANY HIGHLANDS ARTS COUNCIL/PERFORMING ARTS

PO Box 261
Covington, VA 24426

SERIES & FESTIVALS / Virginia

Phone: 540-962-6220
Fax: 540-962-4911
e-mail: artsco@aol.com
Web Site: www.alleghanyhighlands.com/arts4all
Management:
  President of the Board: Gary Pillow
  Executive Director: Tammy S Scruggs
Founded: 1952
Specialized Field: Series & Festivals; Instrumental Music; Vocal Music; Theater; Youth; Dance; Ethnic Performances
Status: Non-Profit, Professional
Paid Staff: 2
Budget: $35,000-60,000
Performs At: Curfman Hall

5731
AVERETT UNIVERSITY CONCERT-LECTURE SERIES

420 W Main
Danville, VA 24541
Phone: 804-791-5621
Fax: 804-791-5819
e-mail: paul.bryant@averett.edu
Management:
  Dean of Students: Paul A Bryant
Utilizes: Actors; Dance Companies; Dancers; Educators; Fine Artists; Guest Accompanists; Guest Directors; Guest Instructors; Guest Soloists; Local Artists; Original Music Scores; Playwrights; Sign Language Translators; Singers
Budget: $10,000-20,000

5732
DANVILLE AREA ASSOCIATION FOR THE ARTS & HUMANITIES

435 Main Street
PO Box 3581
Danville, VA 24543
Mailing Address: PO Box 3581, Danville, VA. 24543-3581
Phone: 434-792-6965
Fax: 434-792-1307
e-mail: aandh@gamewood.net
Web Site: www.danriverartalliance.com
Officers:
  President: John W Collins
Management:
  Executive Director: Arlyne McDowell
Utilizes: Actors; Dance Companies; Dancers; Guild Activities; Multimedia; Special Technical Talent; Theatre Companies; Touring Companies
Founded: 1981
Status: Non-Profit
Paid Staff: 1
Budget: $35,000-60,000
Income Sources: Box office; Grants; Private donations
Annual Attendance: 5,500
Type of Stage: Proscenium
Stage Dimensions: 40x27
Seating Capacity: 1,119
Year Built: 1955

5733
EMORY & HENRY COLLEGE CONCERT SERIES

PO Box 947
Emory, VA 24327
Phone: 540-944-6846
Fax: 540-944-6259
e-mail: atcoulth@ehc.edu
Web Site: www.ehc.edu/inweb
Management:
  Arts Coordinator: Anita Coulthard
  President: Jake Schrum
Mission: To provide cultural events that support the curriculum of the college.
Specialized Field: College arts organ
Paid Staff: 1
Paid Artists: 20
Non-paid Artists: 5
Budget: $20,000-35,000
Income Sources: College budget and grants
Performs At: Chapel, auditorium
Annual Attendance: 5,000
Facility Category: College campus, chapel and auditorium
Type of Stage: Proscenium
Seating Capacity: Chapel 500; auditorium - 300

5734
COLLEGE OF VISUAL AND PERFORMING ARTS

George Mason University
4400 University Drive, MSN 4C1
Fairfax, VA 22030-4444
Phone: 703-993-8877
Fax: 703-993-8883
e-mail: skruppin@gmu.edu
Web Site: cfa.gmu.edu
Management:
  President: Allan Mertens
  Artistic Director: Richard Davis
  Dean: William Reeder
  Assistant Dean: William Reeder
Specialized Field: Series & Festivals; Instrumental Music; Vocal Music; Theatre; Youth; Dance; Arts
Status: Non-Profit, Professional
Budget: $400,000-1,000,000
Performs At: Harris Theatre
Facility Category: Performing Arts Hall
Type of Stage: Proscenium
Seating Capacity: 1,935

5735
FREDERICKSBURG MUSIC FESTIVAL

PO Box 7816
Fredericksburg, VA 22404
Phone: 540-374-5040
Fax: 540-479-8358
e-mail: theArts@FredFest.org
Web Site: www.fredfest.org
Officers:
  Vice-President: W. Angus Muir, M.D.
  Treasurer: W. Andrew Withers
  Corresponding Secretary: Rebecca Danello, Ed.D.
Management:
  President: Anne M. R. Adams
  Executive Director: Susan Mullane
  Founder And Artistic Director: Heidi Lehwalder
  Artistic Director: Michael Reynolds
Mission: To foster excellence and diversity in the arts in Virginia and to bring world class arts events to the residents of the greater Fredericksburg area.
Founded: 1988
Specialized Field: Chamber Music; Pops; Big Band; Ethnic; Dance
Status: Nonprofit
Paid Staff: 3
Income Sources: Corporate & Individual Donations; Grants
Annual Attendance: 2,500+

5736
HAMPDEN-SYDNEY MUSIC FESTIVAL

Hampden-Sydney College
1 College Road
Hampden-Sydney, VA 23943
Phone: 434-223-6000
Fax: 804-223-6399
Web Site: www.hsc.edu
Management:
  Executive Director: James Kidd

5737
HAMPTON ARTS COMMISSION

4205 Victoria Boulevard
Hampton, VA 23669
Phone: 757-722-2787
Fax: 757-727-1621
Web Site: www.hamptonarts.net
Management:
  Director: Michael P Curry
Mission: Presenting and promoting the finest visual and performing arts.
Utilizes: Actors; Artists-in-Residence; Dance Companies; Fine Artists; Guest Accompanists; Guest Musical Directors; Guest Musicians; Original Music Scores; Special Technical Talent; Theatre Companies
Founded: 1987
Specialized Field: Series and Festivals; Performing Arts; Visual Arts; Theatre
Status: Non-Profit, Non-Professional
Paid Staff: 9
Income Sources: Association of Performing Arts Presenters
Performs At: American Theatre
Annual Attendance: 30,000
Facility Category: Theatre
Type of Stage: Procenium
Seating Capacity: 400
Year Built: 1908
Year Remodeled: 2000
Cost: $2.8 million
Organization Type: Performing; Educational; Sponsoring

5738
HAMPTON JAZZ FESTIVAL

1000 Coliseum Drive
PO Box 7309
Hampton, VA 23666
Phone: 757-838-4203
Fax: 757-838-2595
e-mail: jtsao@hampton.gov
Web Site: www.hamptonjazzfestival.com
Management:
  Executive Director: Joe Tsao
Founded: 1968
Specialized Field: Series and Festivals; Instrumental Music; Vocal Music; Theatre; Youth; Ethnic Performances; Multipurpose
Status: For-Profit, Professional
Paid Staff: 32

5739
JAMES MADISON UNIVERSITY ENCORE SERIES

College of Visual & Performaning Arts
Forbes Center for the Arts
Harrisonburg, VA 22807
Mailing Address: 147 Warsaw Avenue, MSC 5602
Phone: 540-568-6211
Fax: 540-568-2787

SERIES & FESTIVALS / Virginia

Toll-free: 877-201-7543
e-mail: weaverje@jmu.edu
Web Site: www.jmu.edu/jmuartssterpiece
President: Jonathan R. Alger
Utilizes: Actors; Artists-in-Residence; Dance Companies; Dancers; Fine Artists; Grant Writers; Guest Accompanists; Guest Directors; Guest Musical Directors; Guest Musicians; Instructors; Lyricists; Multimedia; New Productions; Organization Contracts; Original Music Scores; Resident Artists; Sign Language Translators; Soloists; Special Technical Talent; Theatre Companies; Touring Companies; Visual Arts
Specialized Field: Series & Festivals; Instrumental Music; Vocal Music; Theatre; Youth; Dance; Ethnic Performances
Status: Non-Profit, Non-Professional
Paid Staff: 6
Budget: $60,000-150,000
Affiliations: Association of Performing Arts Performers
Facility Category: Auditorium
Type of Stage: Proscenium
Stage Dimensions: 34 x 33
Seating Capacity: 1300, 500, 450

5740
SHENANDOAH VALLEY BACH FESTIVAL
Eastern Mennonite University
1200 Park Road
Harrisonburg, VA 22802
Phone: 540-432-4367
Fax: 540-432-4622
e-mail: bach@emu.edu
Web Site: www.emu.edu/bach
Management:
  President, Eastern Mennonite Univ: Loren Swartzentruber
  Executive Director: Mary Kay Adams, mary.adams@emu.edu
  Artistic Director: Kenneth Nafziger
Mission: One week festival honoring the creative spirit of Johann Sebastian Bach with first rate performances for an ever widening audience.
Utilizes: Actors; Collaborating Artists; Commissioned Composers; Community Members; Community Talent; Composers; Contract Orchestras; Educators; Five Seasonal Concerts; Grant Writers; Guest Accompanists; Guest Directors; Guest Ensembles; Guest Musical Directors; Guest Musicians; Guest Soloists; Guest Speakers; High School Drama; Instructors; Local Artists & Directors; Multimedia; Organization Contracts; Original Music Scores; Paid Performers; Scenic Designers; Sign Language Translators; Singers; Soloists; Students; Visual Designers
Founded: 1993
Specialized Field: Series & Festivals, Instrumental Music, Vocal Music, Youth, Classical Music Festival, Chamber Music, Baroque Performance Workshop
Status: Non-Profit, Professional
Paid Staff: 3
Volunteer Staff: 50
Paid Artists: 50
Non-paid Artists: 60
Budget: $185,000
Income Sources: Grants, Private Donations, Business Advertising, Tickets
Performs At: University Auditorium, Church Sanctuary
Affiliations: ASOL
Annual Attendance: 4,000
Seating Capacity: 600/400

5741
TOWN OF HERNDON
PO Box 427
Herndon, VA 20172
Phone: 703-435-6800
Fax: 703-787-7325
e-mail: holly.popple@herndon-va.gov
Web Site: www.herndon-va.gov
Management:
  Executive Director: Arthur Anselelne
Mission: Functions as a talent buyer and events director.
Founded: 1975
Specialized Field: Series & Festivals; Theatre; Youth; Dance
Status: For-Profit, Professional
Paid Artists: 80
Performs At: Industrial Strength Theatre; Worldgate Theatre

5742
WASHINGTON & LEE UNIVERSITY LENFEST SERIES
Lenfest Center, 100 Glasgow Street
Washington & Lee University
Lexington, VA 24450
Phone: 540-458-8000
Fax: 540-463-8041
e-mail: wlunews@wlu.edu
Web Site: www.wlu.edu/lenfest-center
Management:
  Managing Director: Michael Gorman
  Assistant Director: Susan Wager
Mission: Home of Theatre/Music/Dance Departments. Presenter of a few touring attractions.
Utilizes: Actors; Dance Companies; Dancers; Designers; Guest Artists; Guest Choreographers; Guest Composers; Guest Conductors; Guest Designers; Guest Directors; Guest Musical Directors; Guest Musicians; Instructors; Multimedia; Poets; Resident Professionals; Soloists; Student Interns; Theatre Companies
Founded: 1991
Specialized Field: Theatre/Dance/Music
Budget: $35,000-60,000
Income Sources: Endowment/Ticket Sales
Performs At: Keller Theatre
Facility Category: Performing Arts Center
Type of Stage: Proscenium
Seating Capacity: 415
Year Built: 1991

5743
LYNCHBURG COMMUNITY CONCERT ASSOCIATION
PO Box 1332
Lynchburg, VA 24505
Phone: 804-845-3563
Fax: 804-845-3536
Management:
  Manager: Betty Sue Moehlenkamp
Budget: $35,000-60,000
Performs At: E.C. Glass High School Auditorium

5744
TOURING CONCERT OPERA COMPANY: MARTINSVILLE-HENRY COUNTY FESTIVAL OF OPERA
730 Craig Street
Martinsville, VA 24112
Phone: 540-632-5861
Fax: 518-851-6778
e-mail: tcoc@mhonline.com
Officers:
  President: Alberto Figols
  VP: Glenn Wilder
  Secretary/Treasurer: Anne de Figols
Management:
  Managing Director: Alberto Figols
  Managing Director: Alberto Figols
  Public Relations: Ruth Johnson
  Bookkeeper: Alberto Fijolo
Mission: To bring live opera performances to audiences, internationally making it accessible to all.
Utilizes: Actors; Artists-in-Residence; Choreographers; Collaborating Artists; Collaborations; Commissioned Composers; Commissioned Music; Dance Companies; Dancers; Designers; Fine Artists; Grant Writers; Guest Accompanists; Guest Artists; Guest Companies; Guest Composers; Guest Conductors; Guest Designers; Guest Directors; Guest Ensembles; Guest Lecturers; Guest Musical Directors; Guest Musicians; Guest Soloists; Guild Activities; Instructors; Local Artists; Multimedia; New Productions; Organization Contracts; Original Music Scores; Poets; Resident Professionals; Sign Language Translators; Singers; Soloists
Founded: 1977
Specialized Field: Dance; Vocal Music; Instrumental Music; Theater; Lyric Opera; Grand Opera
Annual Attendance: 5,000 - 10,000

5745
SWIFT CREEK ACADEMY OF THE PERFORMING ARTS
2808 Fox Chase Lane
Midlothian, VA 23112
Phone: 804-744-2801
e-mail: info@swiftcreekacademy.org
Web Site: www.swiftcreekacademy.org
Management:
  Owner/Academy Director: Cassandra Lacey
Mission: Performance school
Specialized Field: Dance, Drama, Instrumental & Music classes for all ages; student performances
Paid Staff: 15
Budget: $10,000

5746
CHRISTOPHER NEWPORT UNIVERSITY
1 University Place
Newport News, VA 23606
Phone: 757-594-7000
Fax: 757-594-7389
Web Site: www.cnu.edu
Mission: The Department of Theatre & Dance offers developing theater artists a comprehensive curriculum of rigorous training with a superb faculty of professional actors, directors, play wrights and designers. Within the dedicated atmosphere of a small liberal arts university, the theater majors enjoy a unique spirit of closeness and collaboration teamed with immediate opportunities to perform and/or to work backstage.
Founded: 1960
Specialized Field: Series & Festivals; Instrumental Music; Vocal Music; Theatre; Dance
Status: Non-Profit, Non-Professional
Paid Staff: 100
Paid Artists: 100
Budget: $20,000-35,000
Performs At: John W. Gaines Theatre

SERIES & FESTIVALS / Virginia

5747
NORFOLK FESTEVENTS
Norfolk Festevents
120 W Main Street
Norfolk, VA 23501
Phone: 757-441-2345
Fax: 757-441-5098
e-mail: festevents@festevents.org
Web Site: www.festevents.org
Founded: 1982

5748
TIDEWATER PERFORMING ARTS SOCIETY
PO Box 1140
Norfolk, VA 23501-1140
Phone: 757-627-2314
Fax: 757-622-2803
e-mail: tpas@tpas.org
Web Site: www.tpas.org
Management:
 Executive Director: Karen E Levy
Budget: $35,000-60,000
Performs At: Pavilion Theatre; Wells Theatre; Harrison Opera House

5749
VIRGINIA ARTS FESTIVAL
220 Boush Street
Norfolk, VA 23510
Mailing Address: PO Box 3595, Norfolk, VA 23514
Phone: 757-282-2800
Fax: 757-282-2787
Toll-free: 877-741-2787
e-mail: lori@virginiaartsfest.com
Web Site: www.virginiaartsfest.com
Management:
 Executive Director: Robert W Cross
 Director Operations: Renae Adrian
 Marketing Manager: Lori Gubala
Mission: Brings an imaginative and eclectic line-up of world-renowned performers, complemented by the region's own cultural stars, to the Virginia waterfront. Stages events in seven cities within a 60 mile radius. More than 80 performances in dance, theatre, classical, chamber, jazz and vocalmusic each season.
Founded: 1997
Specialized Field: Series & Festivals; Instrumental Music; Vocal Music; Theatre; Youth; Dance; Ethnic Performances
Status: Non-Profit, Professional
Paid Staff: 22
Volunteer Staff: 300
Paid Artists: 700

5750
BLUEMONT CONCERT SERIES
PO Box 802
Purcellville, VA 22611
Phone: 540-955-8186
Fax: 540-338-4847
e-mail: info@bluemont.org
Web Site: www.bluemont.org
Management:
 Artistic Director: Peter Dunning
 Executive Director: Lily Rose Dunning
 Deputy Director: Nathan Borger
 Technical and Soud Crew Coordinator: Cory Finch
Mission: To offer a wide range of quality arts programs to the community.
Utilizes: Singers
Founded: 1975
Specialized Field: Concert Presenter
Status: Non-Profit, Professional
Paid Staff: 6
Budget: $60,000-400,000
Performs At: Outdoor venues
Organization Type: Educational; Sponsoring

5751
RADFORD UNIVERSITY PERFORMING ARTS SERIES
Box 6980
Radford University
Radford, VA 24142
Phone: 540-831-5265
Fax: 540-831-6313
e-mail: cvpa411@radford.edu
Web Site: www.radford.edu
Officers:
 Dean College/Visual/Performing: Dr. Joe Scartelli
Management:
 President: Douglas Covington
 Technical Director: Doug Mead
 Dean: Joe Scartelli
Mission: Provide high end cultural artistic experiences for the campus and surrounding communities.
Utilizes: Actors; AEA Actors; Artists-in-Residence; Choreographers; Collaborating Artists; Collaborations; Curators; Dance Companies; Dancers; Designers; Educators; Filmmakers; Fine Artists; Guest Accompanists; Guest Artists; Guest Choreographers; Guest Companies; Guest Composers; Guest Conductors; Guest Designers; Guest Directors; Guest Ensembles; Guest Instructors; Guest Musical Directors; Guest Musicians; Guest Soloists; High School Drama; Instructors; Local Artists; Multi Collaborations; Multimedia; Paid Performers; Playwrights; Poets; Resident Professionals; Sign Language Translators; Soloists; Special Technical Talent; Theatre Companies; Touring Companies; Visual Arts
Founded: 1975
Specialized Field: Series and Festivals; Instrumental Music; Vocal Music; Theatre; Youth; Dance; Ethnic Performances
Status: Non-Profit,Professional
Paid Staff: 2
Volunteer Staff: 8
Non-paid Artists: 20
Budget: $60,000-150,000
Income Sources: Student activities fees; Ticket revenues
Annual Attendance: 10,000
Facility Category: Auditorium
Type of Stage: Proscenium
Stage Dimensions: 40 x 25
Seating Capacity: 1500
Year Built: 1960

5752
RESTON COMMUNITY CENTER HUNTERS WOODS
2310 Colt Neck Road
Reston, VA 20191
Phone: 703-476-4500
Fax: 703-476-8617
e-mail: rcccontact@fairfaxcounty.gov
Web Site: www.restoncommunitycenter.com
Management:
 Executive Director: Leila Gordon
 Public Information Officer: Cristin Bratt
 Facility Supervisor: Patricia Farrell
 Deputy Director: Thomas L. Ward
 Customer Service Manager: Pam Leary
Founded: 1979
Specialized Field: General Recreation and Cultural Agency
Status: Non-Profit, Professional
Paid Staff: 284
Budget: $200,000
Income Sources: Government agency
Affiliations: Assoc. of Performing Arts Presenters
Annual Attendance: 25,000 +
Facility Category: Cultural and recreational
Type of Stage: Proscenium
Stage Dimensions: 32W x 18H x 25D
Seating Capacity: 290
Year Built: 1979
Cost: $2 MM

5753
CITYCELEBRATIONS MUSICFEST
200 S 3rd Street
Richmond, VA 23219
Phone: 804-788-6466
Fax: 804-788-6477
e-mail: info@citycelebrations.org
Web Site: www.citycelebrations.org
Officers:
 Chair: Sarah T. Paxton
 Vice Chair: Robert P. Englander, Jr.
 Treasurer: Elizabeth L. Nelson
 Secretary: Julie Joyce
Management:
 Executive Director: K Alferio
 Managing Director: Pamela Wiseman
Founded: 1988
Specialized Field: Series and Festivals; Instrumental Music; Vocal Music; Youth; Dance; Ethnic Performances; Festivals; Event
Status: Non-Profit, Professional
Paid Staff: 6
Paid Artists: 100

5754
MODLIN CENTER FOR THE ARTS
University Of Richmond
28 Westhampton Way
Richmond, VA 23173
Phone: 804-287-6632
Fax: 804-287-6681
Toll-free: 800-700-1662
e-mail: modlinarts@richmond.edu
Web Site: www.oncampus.richmond.edu
Management:
 Executive Director: Kathleen Panoff
Utilizes: Actors; Artists-in-Residence; Dancers; Guest Accompanists; Guest Artists; Guest Designers; Guest Soloists; High School Drama; Instructors; Local Artists; Multimedia; Original Music Scores; Sign Language Translators; Singers; Special Technical Talent; Theatre Companies; Touring Companies
Founded: 1996
Paid Staff: 7
Paid Artists: 30
Non-paid Artists: 15
Budget: $60,000-150,000

5755
RICHMOND SHAKESPEARE FESTIVAL
28 Westhampton Way
Richmond, VA 23173
Phone: 804-270-3310
Fax: 804-232-4400
Toll-free: 888-373-2628
e-mail: cliffick@richmondshakespeare.com
Web Site: www.richmond.edu
Management:
 President: Stephanie Meharg

SERIES & FESTIVALS / Virginia

Managing Director: Cynde Liffick
Specialized Field: Shakespeare Production
Status: Non-Profit, Professional
Paid Staff: 5
Paid Artists: 20

5756
THEATREVIRGINIA
2800 Groove Avenue
Richmond, VA 23221
Phone: 804-353-6100
Fax: 804-353-8799
Web Site: www.theatreva.com
Management:
    Programming Artistic Director: Benny Ambush
    Assistant Director: Karen Brown
    Managing Director: Barbara Wells
Budget: $150,000-400,000

5757
VIRGINIA COMMONWEALTH UNIVERSITY COMMONS COLLEGE
907 Floyd Avenue
Box 842032
Richmond, VA 23284
Phone: 804-828-6500
Fax: 804-828-6182
e-mail: mhorvath@vcu.edu
Web Site: www.students.vcu.edu/commons
Management:
    Executive Director: Timothy Reed
    Artistic Director: Justin Hirsch
    Managing Director: John Leppo
    Activities Coordinator: Mary Beth Horvath
Specialized Field: Series & Festivals; Instrumental Music; Vocal Music; Theatre; Youth; Dance; Ethnic Performances
Status: For-Profit, Non-Professional
Budget: $10,000-20,000
Performs At: University Student Commons Commonwealth Ballroom

5758
HOLLINS UNIVERSITY PERFORMING ARTS SERIES
Presser Hall, 8226 Tinker Lane NE
PO Box 9707
Roanoke, VA 24020
Phone: 540-362-6511
Fax: 540-362-6648
Toll-free: 800-456-9595
e-mail: huadm@hollins.edu
Web Site: www.hollins.edu
Management:
    President: Nancy Gray
    Provost: Wayne Markert
    Chairman of Music Department: Judith Cline
Founded: 1842
Specialized Field: Women's Art Events and Training
Status: Non-Profit, Professional
Paid Staff: 13
Paid Artists: 8
Budget: $10,000

5759
ROANOKE COLLEGE PERFORMING ARTS SERIES
Roanoke College
221 College Lane
Salem, VA 24153
Phone: 540-375-2500
Fax: 540-375-2559
e-mail: arthur@roanoke.edu
Web Site: www.roanoke.edu
Management:
    Administrator: George N Arthur
    President: Michael Creed Maxey
Utilizes: Actors; Artists-in-Residence; Collaborations; Commissioned Music; Dancers; Fine Artists; Multimedia; Poets; Resident Artists; Special Technical Talent
Specialized Field: Performing Arts Events
Status: Non-Profit, Professional
Paid Staff: 2
Budget: $10,000-20,000
Performs At: Olin Hall
Seating Capacity: 404

5760
CARL BROMAN CONCERTS
Mary Baldwin College
Box 1500
Staunton, VA 24402
Phone: 540-887-7019
Fax: 540-885-7887
Toll-free: 800-468-2262
e-mail: info@mbc.edu
Web Site: www.mbc.edu
Officers:
    President: Pamela Fox
    Vice President for Public Relations: Crista Cabe
    Chief Information Officer: Angus McQueen
Management:
    Manager: Robert T Allen III
Founded: 1980
Specialized Field: Series & Festivals; Chambers; Recitals
Status: Non-Profit, Professional
Paid Artists: 12
Budget: $10,000-20,000
Performs At: Francis Auditorium

5761
MIDDLE PENINSULA COMMUNITY CONCERT ASSOCIATION
PO Box 198
Topping, VA 23169
Phone: 804-758-4819
Officers:
    President: Carolyn Shank
Budget: $20,000-35,000

5762
WOLF TRAP FOUNDATION FOR THE PERFORMING ARTS
1645 Trap Road
Vienna, VA 22182
Phone: 703-255-1900
Fax: 703-255-1918
e-mail: wolftrap@wolftrap.org
Web Site: www.wolftrap.org
Officers:
    Chairman: Daniel A. D'Aniello
    Vice Chairman and Secretary: Gil Guarino
Management:
    President and CEO: Arvind Manocha
    Sr Director Comm and Marketing: Lisa Lacamera
    Director Media Relations: Melissa Chotiner
Mission: To provide enrichment, education and enjoyment to diverse audiences through presentation, production and creation of a broad spectrum of performing arts activities.
Utilizes: Artists-in-Residence; Commissioned Music; Dance Companies; Five Seasonal Concerts; Guest Composers; Instructors; Multimedia; Students
Founded: 1971
Specialized Field: Series & Festivals; Instrumental Music; Vocal Music; Theatre; Youth; Dance; Ethnic Performances; Dance
Status: Non-Profit, Professional
Paid Staff: 80
Budget: $20,000,000
Performs At: Filene Center at America's National Park for the Performing Arts
Facility Category: Indoor/Outdoor Amphitheatre
Type of Stage: Proscenium
Seating Capacity: 7,023 with lawn seats
Year Built: 1971
Year Remodeled: 1984
Organization Type: Educational; Sponsoring

5763
GARTH NEWEL MUSIC CENTER
PO Box 240
Warm Springs, VA 24484
Phone: 540-839-5018
Fax: 540-839-3154
Toll-free: 877-558-1689
e-mail: office@garthnewel.org
Web Site: www.garthnewel.org
Management:
    Artistic Director: Evelyn Grau
    Managing Director: Jacod Yarrow
    Executive Director: Christopher Williams
    Director of Operations: Georgia Tennant
Mission: Promoting and performing chamber music.
Utilizes: Guest Artists
Founded: 1973
Specialized Field: Series & Festivals; Youth; Ethnic Performances; Vocal Music; Festivals; Instrumental music; Concert Series; Performance and study of Classical Music
Status: Non-Profit, Professional
Paid Artists: 4
Performs At: Herter Hall
Organization Type: Performing; Touring; Resident; Educational

5764
SPECIAL MUSIC HOLIDAYS
PO Box 240
Warm Springs, VA 24484
Phone: 540-839-5018
Fax: 540-839-3154
Toll-free: 877-558-1689
e-mail: office@garthnewel.org
Web Site: www.garthnewel.org
Management:
    Managing Director: Jacob Yarrow
    Artistic Director: Evelyn Grau
    Executive Director: Christopher Williams
    Director of Operations: Georgia Tennant
Founded: 1973
Specialized Field: Series and Festivals; Instrumental Music; Vocal Music; Youth; Ethnic Performances; Music Classical
Status: Non-Profit, Professional
Paid Staff: 9
Paid Artists: 4
Season: November; December

5765
SUMMER CHAMBER MUSIC FESTIVAL
Garth Newel Music Center
PO Box 240
Warm Springs, VA 24484

SERIES & FESTIVALS / Washington

Phone: 540-839-5018
Fax: 540-839-3154
Toll-free: 877-558-1689
e-mail: office@garthnewel.org
Web Site: www.garthnewel.org
Management:
   Artistic Director: Evelyn Grau
   Managing Director: Jacob Yarrow
   Executive Director: Christopher Williams
   Director of Operations: Georgia Tennant
Mission: A tradition since 1973, the Summer Chamber Music Festival makes Garth Newel the place to be on weekends afternoons. Each concert consist of a unique program featuring members of the Garth Newel Piano Quartet and guest artists. Performances take place in Herter Hall.
Founded: 1973
Specialized Field: Performance and Study of Chamber Music
Status: Non-Profit, Professional
Paid Staff: 7
Paid Artists: 4

5766
VIRGINIA SHAKESPEARE FESTIVAL
College of William and Mary
PO Box 8795
Williamsburg, VA 23187-8795
Phone: 757-221-2683
Fax: 757-221-2636
e-mail: clowen@wm.edu
Web Site: www.wm.edu/as/vsf
Management:
   Producing Artistic Director: Christopher Owens
   Executive Director: Jerry H Bledsoe
   Lighting Designer: Steve Holliday
   Costume Designer: Patricia Wesp
   Scenic Designer: J. David Blatt
Mission: To offer quality Shakespeare performed in the classical manner.
Utilizes: Singers
Founded: 1978
Specialized Field: Series and Festivals; Theatre; Youth; Dance; Festivals
Status: Non-Profit, Professional
Paid Staff: 20
Paid Artists: 25
Income Sources: The College of William & Mary
Season: July - August
Performs At: Phi Beta Kappa Memorial Hall; The College of Williamsburg
Organization Type: Performing; Educational

5767
WILLIAM & MARY CONCERT SERIES
The Campus Center 203
PO Box 8795
Williamsburg, VA 23187-8795
Phone: 757-221-3300
Fax: 757-221-3451
e-mail: mxcons@wm.edu
Web Site: www.wm.edu
Management:
   President: Tim Sullivan
Founded: 1950
Specialized Field: Series & Festivals; Instrumental Music; Vocal Music; Dance; Ethnic Performances
Status: For-Profit, Non-Professional
Paid Staff: 2
Budget: $60,000-150,000
Performs At: Phi Beta Kappa Memorial Hall
Seating Capacity: 763

5768
WINTERGREEN PERFORMING ARTS
Box 816
Wintergreen, VA 22958
Phone: 434-325-8292
Fax: 888-675-8238
e-mail: info@wintergreenperformingarts.org
Web Site: www.wintergreenperformingarts.org
Officers:
   President: Thomas W. Steele
   Vice President: Edith Wittig van Wageningen
   Secretary: Janet R. Jones
   Treasurer: Lawrence Luessen
Management:
   Artistic and Executive Director: Larry Alan Smith
   Marketing Director: Karen S. Quillen
   Finance Manager: Cyndi Michener
   Office Assistant: Lisa Gillmor

5769
WINTERGREEN SUMMER MUSIC FESTIVAL
Wintergreen Performing Arts
PO Box 816
Wintergreen, VA 22958
Phone: 434-325-8292
Fax: 888-675-8238
e-mail: info@wintergreenperformingarts.org
Web Site: www.wintergreenperformingarts.org
Officers:
   President: Thomas W. Steele
   Vice President: Edith Wittig van Wageningen
   Secretary: Janet R. Jones
   Treasurer: Lawrence Luessen
Management:
   Artistic and Executive Director: Larry Alan Smith
   Marketing Director: Karen S. Quillen
   Finance Manager: Cyndi Michener
   Office Assistant: Lisa Gillmor
Mission: Summer Orchestra Concerts.
Founded: 1996
Paid Staff: 2
Volunteer Staff: 40
Paid Artists: 70
Non-paid Artists: 10

5770
SHENANDOAH VALLEY MUSIC FESTIVAL
PO Box 528
Woodstock, VA 22664
Phone: 540-459-3396
Fax: 540-459-3730
Toll-free: 800-459-3396
e-mail: dennismlynch@yahoo.com
Web Site: www.musicfest.org
Officers:
   Executive Director: Dennis M Lynch
Mission: To foster, promote, and increase the musical knowledge of the public by organizing and presenting programs chosen primarily from the literature of symphonic music, and incidentally from folk, bog band, jazz and family programming.
Utilizes: Guest Musicians; Multimedia; Original Music Scores
Founded: 1963
Specialized Field: Series and Festivals: Symphonic Music
Status: Non-Profit, Professional
Paid Staff: 3
Budget: $7,500
Income Sources: Government & private grants
Performs At: Orkney Springs Pavilion

Annual Attendance: 10,000
Organization Type: Sponsoring

Washington

5771
AUBURN ARTS COMMISSION
Auburn City Hall
25 W Main Street
Auburn, WA 98001
Phone: 253-804-5057
Fax: 253-288-3132
Management:
   Cultural Programs Manager: Susan Sagawa
Budget: $60,000-150,000

5772
BELLINGHAM FESTIVAL OF MUSIC
PO Box 818
Bellingham, WA 98227
Phone: 360-201-6621
Fax: 360-647-3521
Toll-free: 800-335-5550
Web Site: www.bellinghamfestival.org
Officers:
   Chairperson: Robert Lynch
   Vice Chair: Karen Berry
   Treasurer: Mary Pat Thuma
   Secretary: John Moffat
Management:
   Assistant Conductor/Pianist: Whitney Reader
   Orchestra Personnel Manager: Marvin Warshaw
   Artistic Director: Micheal Palmer
   Guest Artist Coordinator: Andrew Moquin
   Production Manager: Audrey Kelley
Mission: To provide the area with educational opportunities to experience live music performances at the highest artistic level by nationally and internationally renowned musicians in a concentrated festival format.
Founded: 1993
Specialized Field: Series & Festivals; Summer Music Festival Featuring Classical; Chamber; Jazz; and Ethnic Music
Status: Non-Profit, Professional
Paid Staff: 3
Volunteer Staff: 6
Paid Artists: 50
Budget: $500,000
Income Sources: Grants from City; County; Private Foundations; Local Fund Drive; Ticket Sales
Performs At: Bellwether on the Bay
Annual Attendance: 9,000
Facility Category: Outdoor

5773
WESTERN WASHINGTON UNIVERSITY PERFORMING ARTS CENTER SERIES
Pac, Pa-361
516 High Street
Bellingham, WA 98225-9109
Phone: 360-650-3000
Fax: 360-650-3028
Web Site: cfpa.wwu.edu
Management:
   Dean: Kit Spicer
   Performing Arts Series Coordinator: Tamara McDonald
   Director of Development: Sonja Sather
   Operations Manager: Patricia Lundquist
   Manager of Marketing: Chris Casquilho
Budget: $40,000-55,000
Performs At: PAC Mainstage Theatre, PAC Concert Hall

SERIES & FESTIVALS / Washington

5774
OLYMPIC COLLEGE
Student Programs
1600 Chester Avenue
Bremerton, WA 98337-1699
Phone: 360-792-6050
Fax: 360-475-7454
e-mail: jgallagher@oc.ctc.edu
Web Site: www.oc.ctc.edu
Management:
  President: David Michell
  Artistic Director: Rick White
  Managing Director: Barry Janucsh
  Associate Director: Jean Gallagher
Specialized Field: Medical Training
Status: Non-Profit, Non-Professional
Paid Staff: 250
Budget: $10,000-20,000

5775
LAKE CHELAN BACH FESTIVAL
PO Box 554
Chelan, WA 98816-9522
Phone: 509-667-0904
Fax: 509-682-0901
e-mail: info@bachfest.org
Web Site: www.bachfest.org
Officers:
  Co-President: Ruth Rogers
  Co-President: Kerry Travers
  Secretary: Karen Rich
  Treasurer: Rosemary Easley
Management:
  Executive Director: Beth Jensen
  Artistic Director: Dan Baldwin
  Grant Writer: Ruth Rogers
Mission: To inspire, enrich and educate through live musical performances.
Founded: 1982
Specialized Field: Vocal Music; Instrumental Music; Lyric Opera
Status: Professional; Non-Professional; Nonprofit
Organization Type: Performing; Educational

5776
ORCAS THEATER & COMMUNITY CENTER
917 Mount Baker Road
PO Box 567
East Sound, WA 98245-0567
Phone: 360-376-2281
Fax: 360-376-6822
e-mail: Info@OrcasCenter.org
Web Site: www.orcascenter.org
Officers:
  President: Theron Soderlund
Management:
  Executive/Artistic Director: Kara O'Toole
  Front of House Manager: Artha Kass
  Facilities Manager: Jeffrey Ludwig
  Business Manager: Annie Moss Moore
  Theatre Productions Director: Deborah Sparks
Budget: $35,000-60,000

5777
EDMONDS ARTS COMMISSION
700 Main Street
Edmonds, WA 98020
Phone: 425-771-0228
Fax: 425-771-0253
e-mail: chapin@ci.edmonds.wa.us
Web Site: www.ci.edmonds.wa.us/artscommission
  Vice President: James Wolf
  Secretary: Eska Wilson
  Treasurer: Loreen Arnold
Management:
  Cultural Services Manager: Frances White Chapin
Founded: 1975
Specialized Field: Municipal Organizations Promotes Arts
Status: For-Profit, Non-Professional
Paid Staff: 2
Budget: $10,000-20,000

5778
JAZZ IN THE VALLEY
PO Box 214
Ellensburg, WA 98926
Phone: 509-899-3639
Fax: 509-962-3957
Toll-free: 888-925-2204
e-mail: jazzinfo@jazzinthevalley.com
Web Site: www.jazzinthevalley.com
Management:
  Director: Larry Sharpe
Status: Non-Profit

5779
ENUMCLAW ARTS COMMISSION
1339 Griffin
Enumclaw, WA 98022
Phone: 360-802-0232
Fax: 360-825-1429
Management:
  Cultural Programs Manager: DeNae McGee
Budget: $35,000-60,000
Performs At: City Hall Park (summer)

5781
KENT ARTS COMMISSION
220 4th Avenue S
Kent, WA 98032
Phone: 253-856-5200
Fax: 253-856-6050
e-mail: rbillerbeck@ci.kent.wa.us
Web Site: kentwa.gov/arts
Management:
  Cultural Programs Manager: Ronda Billerbeck
Utilizes: Collaborating Artists; Dance Companies; Fine Artists; Instructors; Local Artists; Multimedia; Original Music Scores; Special Technical Talent; Theatre Companies; Touring Companies
Founded: 1980
Specialized Field: Cultural Programs
Status: Non-Profit, Professional
Paid Staff: 7
Budget: $35,000-60,000
Annual Attendance: 50,000
Facility Category: Performing Arts Center/Outdoor Festival - various

5782
ABBEY CHURCH EVENTS
Saint Martin's Abbey
5300 Pacific Avenue SE
Lacey, WA 98503-1297
Phone: 360-438-4476
Fax: 360-438-4387
Management:
  Director: Boniface V Lazzari, OSB
Budget: $10,000-20,000

5783
ICICLE CREEK MUSIC CENTER
PO Box 2071
Leavenworth, WA 98826
Phone: 509-548-6347
Fax: 509-548-3128
Toll-free: 877-265-6026
e-mail: icicle@icicle.org
Web Site: www.icicle.org
Officers:
  President: Tom Bassett
  Treasurer: John Peterson
  Secretary: Anita Whitney
Management:
  Executive Director: Sheila Hughes
  Artistic Director: Sally Singer
  Artistic Director: Oksana Ezhokino
  General Director: Lisa Bergman
  General Manager: Rebecca Ryker
  Director Marketing & Communications: Lilia Grundy
  Director of Program Development: Michael Caemmerer
Mission: To advance classical music, performing arts and education in a spectacular retreat setting.
Founded: 1995
Specialized Field: Music/Chamber Music
Paid Staff: 5
Volunteer Staff: 20
Paid Artists: 18
Performs At: Classical Music; Performing Arts & Education

5784
LYNNWOOD JAZZ FESTIVAL AT EDMONDS COMMUNITY COLLEGE
20000 68th Avenue W
Lynnwood, WA 98036
Phone: 425-640-1650
Fax: 425-640-1083
e-mail: kmarcy@edcc.edu
Web Site: www.edcc.edu
Management:
  Festival Director: Randi Irby
Founded: 1975
Specialized Field: Series & Festivals; Instrumental Music; Vocal Music; Theatre; Youth; Dance; Ethnic Performances
Status: For-Profit, Non-Professional
Paid Artists: 3

5785
MERCER ISLAND ARTS COUNCIL
2040 84th Avenue SE
Mercer Island, WA 98040
Phone: 206-236-3545
Fax: 206-236-3631
e-mail: miparks@ci.mercer-island.wa.us
Web Site: www.mercergov.org
Management:
  Chairman: Barry Massoudi
  Recreation Supervisor: Jennifer Berner
Mission: To present cultural arts programs to the citizens of Mercer Island and to advocate for the arts and Mercer Island artists.
Founded: 1985
Specialized Field: Arts Council
Status: For-Profit, Non-Professional
Paid Staff: 2
Volunteer Staff: 12
Budget: $20,000-35,000

All listings are in alphabetical order by state, then city, then organization within the city.

SERIES & FESTIVALS / Washington

5786
EVERGREEN STATE COLLEGE
EVERGREEN EXPRESSIONS
Communications Building
2700 Evergreen Parkway NW
Olympia, WA 98505
Phone: 360-867-6000
Fax: 360-866-6794
Toll-free: 877-787-9721
Web Site: www.evergreen.edu
Management:
    Performing/Media Arts Manager: John Robbins
    Technical Director: Jeremy Reynolds
Founded: 1967
Specialized Field: Series & Festivals; Instrumental Music; Vocal Music; Theater; Ethnic Performances
Status: For-Profit, Non-Professional
Paid Staff: 50
Paid Artists: 10
Budget: $20,000-35,000

5787
JUAN DE FUCA FESTIVAL OF THE ARTS
101 W. Front St., Suite 101
PO Box 796
Port Angeles, WA 98362
Phone: 360-457-5411
Fax: 360-457-5411
e-mail: danmaguire@jffa.org
Web Site: jffa.org
Officers:
    President: Nancy Vivolo
    Vice President: Clark Driese
    Treasurer: Melody Charno
Management:
    Executive Director: Dan Maguire
    Office Manager, Ad sales: Carol Pope
    Volunteer Coordinator: Sam Calhoun

5788
DANCE FESTIVAL: CENTRUM FESTIVAL
PO Box 1158
Port Townsend, WA 98368
Phone: 360-385-3102
Fax: 360-385-2470
Toll-free: 800-733-3608
e-mail: info@centrum.org
Web Site: www.centrum.org
Management:
    President: Cindy McBride
    Executive Director: Robert Birman
    Marketing & Communications Manager: Megan Claflin
    Director of Development: Karen Gose Clemens
    Finance Manager: Lisa Johnson
    Director of Operations: Lisa Waipio Werner
Mission: To assist those who seek creative and intellectual growth and to present visual, literary and performing arts to the public.
Founded: 1973
Specialized Field: Arts Workshop
Status: Non-Profit, Professional
Paid Staff: 18
Volunteer Staff: 60
Paid Artists: 200

5789
JAZZ PORT TOWNSEND: CENTRUM FESTIVAL
PO Box 1158
Port Townsend, WA 98368
Phone: 360-385-3102
Fax: 360-385-2470
Toll-free: 800-733-3608
e-mail: info@centrum.org
Web Site: www.centrum.org
Management:
    President: Cindy McBride
    Executive Director: Robert Birman
    Marketing & Communications Manager: Megan Claflin
    Director of Development: Karen Gose Clemens
    Finance Manager: Lisa Johnson
    Director of Operations: Lisa Waipio Werner
Mission: To assist those who seek creative and intellectual growth and to present visual, literary and performing arts to the public.
Founded: 1973
Specialized Field: Arts and Education
Status: Non-Profit, Professional
Paid Staff: 18
Volunteer Staff: 60
Paid Artists: 200

5790
PORT TOWNSEND BLUES HERITAGE FESTIVAL: CENTRUM FESTIVAL
PO Box 1158
Port Townsend, WA 98368
Phone: 360-385-3102
Fax: 360-385-2470
Toll-free: 800-733-3608
e-mail: info@centrum.org
Web Site: www.centrum.org
Officers:
    Vice President: Steve Fetter
Management:
    President: Cindy McBride
    Executive Director: Robert Birman
    Marketing & Communications Manager: Megan Claflin
    Director of Development: Karen Gose Clemens
    Finance Manager: Lisa Johnson
    Director of Operations: Lisa Waipio Werner
Mission: To assist those who seek creative and intellectual growth and to present visual, literary and performing arts to the public.
Founded: 1973
Specialized Field: Arts and Education
Status: Non-Profit, Professional
Paid Staff: 18
Volunteer Staff: 60
Paid Artists: 200

5791
WASHINGTON STATE UNIVERSITY
Washington State University
Pullman, WA 99164-1710
Phone: 509-335-2241
Fax: 509-335-3853
Web Site: www.wsu.edu
Management:
    Executive Director: Leo Udy
    President: Elson S. Floyd
Founded: 1974
Specialized Field: Series & Festivals: Performing Arts
Status: Non-Profit, Professional
Paid Staff: 200
Budget: $10,000
Performs At: Performing Arts Coliseum Theatre

5792
CORNISH COLLEGE: CORNISH SERIES
1000 Lenora Street
Seattle, WA 98121
Phone: 206-726-5030
Fax: 206-720-5183
Toll-free: 800-726-2787
Web Site: www.cornish.edu
Officers:
    Music Department Chairperson: Laura Kaminsky
Management:
    President: Sergei Tschernisch
    Department Chairman: Carol Shiffman
Founded: 1914
Specialized Field: Series and Festivals: Performing in Visual Arts
Status: Non-Profit, Non-Professional
Budget: $20,000-35,000
Performs At: Poncho Concert Hall
Seating Capacity: 200
Year Remodeled: 2000

5793
EARLY MUSIC GUILD INTERNATIONAL SERIES/RECITALS
2366 Eastlake Avenue E
Suite #335
Seattle, WA 98102
Phone: 206-325-7066
Fax: 206-860-9151
e-mail: emg@earlymusicguild.org
Web Site: www.earlymusicguild.org
Officers:
    President: JoLynn Edwards
    Vice President: Peter Seibert
    Secretary: Jamia Hansen-Murray
    Treasurer: Richard Ginnis
Management:
    Executive Director: August Denhard
    Office Manager/Education: Ben Albritton
    Operations Manager: Ann Stickney
    Marketing Director: Hayley Woldseth
Founded: 1977
Paid Staff: 2
Volunteer Staff: 11
Paid Artists: 30
Budget: $35,000-60,000

5794
EARSHOT JAZZ FESTIVAL
3429 Fremont Place
#309
Seattle, WA 98103
Phone: 206-547-6763
Fax: 206-547-6286
e-mail: jazz@earshot.org
Web Site: www.earshot.org
Management:
    Executive Director: John Gilbreath
    Managing Director: Karen Caropepe
    Programs Assistant: Caitlin Peterkin
Founded: 1984
Status: Non-Profit

5795
GOVERNORS CHAMBER MUSIC SERIES
205 Mcgraw Street
Seattle, WA 98109
Phone: 206-281-8292
Fax: 206-285-7610
Management:
    Artistic Director: Judith Cohen
Specialized Field: Only Use Pacific Northwest Artists
Budget: $10,000-20,000
Performs At: State Theatre, Olympia, Washington and the Governor's

SERIES & FESTIVALS / Washington

5796
LADIES MUSICAL CLUB
P.O. Box 94337
Seattle, WA 98124-6637
Phone: 206-622-6882
Fax: 206-622-0791
Web Site: www.lmcseattle.org
Officers:
   VP Development: Regina Thomas
   VP Communications: Emily J. Black
   Recording Secretary: Betsy Chamberlin
   Corresponding Secretary: Lynn Muehleisen
   Treasurer: Candice Chin
Management:
   President: Rena Ilumin
Mission: To grant scholarships to deserving music students; to sponsor a yearly International Artists Series; to foster music among its members and the community.
Utilizes: Singers
Founded: 1891
Specialized Field: Classical
Status: Non-Profit, Professional
Paid Staff: 1
Performs At: Meany Hall; University of Washington
Organization Type: Performing; Resident; Educational; Sponsoring

5797
NORTHWEST FOLKLIFE FESTIVAL
158 Thomas St #32
Seattle, WA 98109
Phone: 206-684-7300
Fax: 206-684-7190
e-mail: folklife@nwfolklife.org
Web Site: www.nwfolklife.org
Officers:
   Vice President: Harvey Niebulski, M.D.
   Vice President: Karen White
   Secretary: Michael Richardson
   Treasurer: Ann Suter
Management:
   President: Luther F. Black
   Executive Director: Michael Herschensohn
   Artistic Director: Deborah Fant
   Managing Director: Mea Fischelis
   Arts and Education Project Manager: Lara D. Clark
Mission: Preserving and presenting traditional and ethnic arts; fostering cultural understanding.
Founded: 1971
Specialized Field: Series & Festivals; Instrumental Music; Vocal Music; Theatre; Youth; Dance; Ethnic Performances; Classical
Status: Non-Profit, Professional
Paid Staff: 14
Budget: $2,200,000
Income Sources: Fees; Commissions; Donations; Grants
Performs At: Seattle Center
Annual Attendance: 200,000
Organization Type: Performing; Touring; Educational; Sponsoring

5798
OLYMPIC MUSIC FESTIVAL
PO Box 45776
Seattle, WA 98145-0776
Phone: 206-527-8839
Fax: 206-526-8621
Web Site: www.olympicmusicfest.org
Management:
   Executive Director: Alan Iglitzin
Founded: 1982
Specialized Field: Series & Festivals; Instrumental Music; Vocal Music
Status: Non-Profit, Professional
Paid Staff: 2
Paid Artists: 30

5799
ON THE BOARDS
100 W Roy Street
Seattle, WA 98119
Mailing Address: PO Box 19515 Seattle, WA 98109
Phone: 206-217-9886
Fax: 206-217-9887
e-mail: info@ontheboards.org
Web Site: www.ontheboards.org
Officers:
   Board President: Tyler Engle
   Vice President: John Behnke
   Vice President: Ruth Lockwood
   Treasurer: John Robinson
   Secretary: Tom Israel
Management:
   Artistic Director: Lane Czaplinski
   Managing Director: Sarah Wilke
   Technical Director: Rich Bresnahan
   Communications/Design Director: Erin Jorgensen
   Operations Manager: Shasti Walsh
Mission: Presentation oragnization featuring contemporary performance artists in dance, theater, music, multimedia and visual arts from around the globe.
Utilizes: Actors; Artists-in-Residence; Choreographers; Collaborating Artists; Composers-in-Residence; Dance Companies; Dancers; Instructors; Local Artists; Multimedia; Performance Artists; Poets; Special Technical Talent; Theatre Companies
Founded: 1978
Specialized Field: Series & Festivals: Contemporary Avanta Grade Performance
Status: Non-Profit, Professional
Paid Staff: 12
Budget: $1,200,000
Type of Stage: Black Box; Proscenium
Rental Contact: Operations Manager Brett McDowell

5800
SEATTLE CHAMBER MUSIC FESTIVAL
10 Harrison Street
Suite 306
Seattle, WA 98109-4509
Phone: 206-283-8710
Fax: 206-283-8826
e-mail: info@seattlechambermusic.org
Web Site: www.seattlechambermusic.org
Officers:
   President: Diana K. Carey
   1st Vice President: Laurence Herron
   2nd Vice President: Erica Hamlin
   Secretary/Treasurer: Bob Mangino
   Immediate Past President: John F. Cramer
Management:
   Executive Director: Connie Cooper
   Artistic Director: James Ethens
   Director of Operations: Jeremy Jolley
   Director of Marketing: Seneca Garber
Mission: To present a four-week summer series of twelve outstanding chamber-music concerts annually.
Founded: 1982
Specialized Field: Series & Festivals; Chamber Music; String Music
Status: Non-Profit, Professional
Paid Staff: 5
Budget: $500,000
Performs At: Lakeside School; Saint Nicholas Hall; Benareya Recital Hall
Organization Type: Performing

5801
SEATTLE INTERNATIONAL CHILDREN'S FESTIVAL
305 Harrison Street
Seattle, WA 98109
Phone: 206-684-7338
Fax: 206-233-3944
e-mail: info@seattleinternational.org
Web Site: www.seattleinternational.org
Management:
   Executive Director: Andrea Wagner
   Artistic Director: Brian Faker
   Director Education: Chris Jeffries
Mission: To offer an international festival of performing arts for children.
Founded: 1987
Specialized Field: Series & Festivals: International Performing Arts Festival
Status: Non-Profit, Professional
Paid Staff: 6
Paid Artists: 100
Income Sources: Western Alliance of Arts Administrators; International Association of Theatre for Children and Youth
Performs At: Seattle Center
Organization Type: Performing; Educational

5802
SEATTLE SHAKESPEARE FESTIVAL
1219 Westlake Avenue North
Suite 109
Seattle, WA
Phone: 206-286-0736
Fax: 206-286-0843
Web Site: www.seanet.com/~ssf/
Management:
   Producing Artistic Director: Stephanie Shine
Mission: To serve the community by presenting plays essential to our common culture in stagings that are vital and accesible to all.

5803
SEATTLE YOUTH SYMPHONY ORCHESTRA'S MARROWSTONE MUSIC FESTIVAL
11065 5th NE
Seattle, WA 98125
Phone: 206-362-2300
Fax: 206-361-9254
e-mail: info@syso.org
Web Site: www.syso.org
Officers:
   President: Dean Willard
   Vice President: John Neeleman
   Secretary: Charles E. Johnson
   Treasurer: Satoru Tashiro
Management:
   Executive Director: Dan Pettersen
   Music Director: Stephen Rogers Radcliffe
   Finance Director: Aimee Tan
   Orchestra Coordinator: Janice Gatti
   Director of Education: Kathleen Allen
Founded: 1942
Specialized Field: Series & Festivals: Instrumental Music
Status: Non-Profit, Non-Professional
Paid Staff: 8

All listings are in alphabetical order by state, then city, then organization within the city.

SERIES & FESTIVALS / West Virginia

5804
TEATRO ZINZANNI
PO Box 9750
Seattle, WA 98109-0750
Phone: 206-281-7788
Fax: 206-281-7799
e-mail: rduff@onereel.org
Web Site: www.zinzannil.org
Management:
    President/CEO/Artistic Director: Norman Langill
    Associate Artistic Director: Reenie Duff
Budget: $400,000-1,000,000

5805
WATER MUSIC FESTIVAL
PO Box 524
Seaview, WA 98644-0524
Phone: 360-261-1598
Fax: 360-642-5812
Toll-free: 800-451-2542
Web Site: watermusicfestival.com
Management:
    President: Susan Spence
    Board VP: Diane Marshall
    Board Secretary: Diana Thompson
    Board Treasurer: Rita Nicely
    Grants, Advertising: Una Boyle
Founded: 1984
Specialized Field: Chamber Music
Volunteer Staff: 50

5806
CONNOISSEUR CONCERTS ASSOCIATION
315 W Mission Avenue
#21
Spokane, WA 99201-2325
Phone: 509-326-4942
e-mail: g.m.harvey@comcast.net
Web Site: www.nwbachfest.com
Officers:
    President: Mart K. Craft
    Vice President: Verne Windham
Management:
    Executive Director: Gertrude Harvey
    Artistic Director: Gunther Schuller
Specialized Field: Instrumental Music; Festivals
Budget: $35,000-60,000
Income Sources: Washington State Arts Commission; donations
Performs At: Metropolitan Performing Arts Center

5808
BROADWAY CENTER FOR THE PERFORMING ARTS
901 Broadway
7th Floor
Tacoma, WA 98402
Phone: 253-591-5890
Fax: 253-591-2013
e-mail: administration@broadwaycenter.org
Web Site: www.broadwaycenter.org
Officers:
    President: Sara Kendall
    Vice President: Warren Willoughby
    Secretary: Tiffany Harmon
    Treasurer: Meng Li Che
Management:
    Executive Director: David Fischer, dfischer@broadwaycenter.org
    Operations Director: Scott Painter, spainter@broadwaycenter.org
    Box Office Manager: Sean Nash
    Director of Development: Becky Johnson
    Director of Marketing: Lacey Leffler
Utilizes: Actors; Collaborating Artists; Collaborations; Dance Companies; Dancers; Educators; Fine Artists; Grant Writers; High School Drama; Instructors; Local Artists; Lyricists; Multimedia; Original Music Scores; Resident Artists; Selected Students; Sign Language Translators; Singers; Theatre Companies
Founded: 1983
Specialized Field: Series & Festivals; Instrumental Music; Vocal Music; Theatre; Youth; Dance; Ethnic Performances
Status: Non-Profit, Professional
Paid Staff: 25
Volunteer Staff: 100
Budget: $5 Million
Performs At: Pantages Theater; Rialto Theater; Theatre on the Square
Seating Capacity: 1169; 735; 302
Year Built: 1918
Year Remodeled: 1979
Cost: $25 Million
Rental Contact: Brenda Ramsey
Resident Groups: Tacoma Actors Guild

5809
EVERGREEN MUSIC FESTIVAL: TACOMA YOUTH SYMPHONY ASSOCIATION
901 Broadway Plaza
Suite 500
Tacoma, WA 98402-4415
Phone: 253-627-2792
Fax: 253-627-1682
e-mail: info@tysamusic.org
Web Site: www.tysamusic.org
Management:
    Festival Music Director: Dr. Paul-Elliot Cobbs
    Executive Director: Dr. Loma Mosley
    Marketing Manager: Kristina Thomas
Mission: To provide an intense musical experience for younger students at the first session, and pre-professionals at the second session.
Founded: 1984
Specialized Field: Music

5810
PACIFIC LUTHERAN UNIVERSITY PROGRAM BOARD
Pacific Lutheran University
12180 Park Avenue S.
Tacoma, WA 98447-0003
Phone: 253-535-7602
Fax: 253-535-8669
Toll-free: 877-254-7001
e-mail: music@plu.edu
Web Site: www.plu.edu
Management:
    President: Lorin Anderson
Founded: 1890
Specialized Field: Series and Festivals; Instrumental Music; Vocal Music; Theatre; Youth; Ethnic Performances
Status: Non-Profit, Non-Professional
Budget: $10,000
Performs At: Lutheran Concert Hall

5811
UNIVERSITY OF PUGET SOUND CULTURAL EVENTS
1500 N Warner
Tacoma, WA 98416
Phone: 253-879-3366
Fax: 253-879-2671
e-mail: ssolidarios@ups.edu
Web Site: www.pugetsound.edu
Management:
    Public Events Director: Margaret Throndill
    Director of Student Programs: Serni Solidarios
Founded: 1888
Specialized Field: Education
Status: Non-Profit, Non-Professional
Budget: $20,000-35,000

West Virginia

5812
BETHANY COLLEGE
Renner Union
PO Box 37
Bethany, WV 26032
Phone: 304-829-7000
Fax: 304-829-7434
Web Site: www.bethanywv.edu
Officers:
    Chair: Gregory B. Jordan
    Vice Chair: Robert J. McCann
    Treasurer: John W. Mullen
    Secretary: Janet A. Long
Management:
    President: Scott D. Miller
Utilizes: Commissioned Music; Dance Companies; Educators; Fine Artists; Grant Writers; Guest Directors; Guest Instructors; Guest Musical Directors; Guest Musicians; Guest Soloists; Instructors; Multimedia; Organization Contracts; Original Music Scores; Performance Artists; Playwrights; Sign Language Translators; Singers; Soloists; Touring Companies
Founded: 1860
Specialized Field: Students Activities
Status: Non-Profit, Non-Professional
Budget: $10,000-20,000
Income Sources: Private
Performs At: Sstage; Steinman Hall of Fine Arts; Hummel Field House
Annual Attendance: 750
Facility Category: College

5813
BLUEFIELD STATE COLLEGE
219 Rock Street
Bluefield, WV 24701-2198
Phone: 304-327-4000
Fax: 304-325-7747
Toll-free: 800-344-8892
Web Site: bluefieldstate.edu
Management:
    Campus Life Director: JD Carpenter
    President: Marsha V. Krotseng
Budget: $10,000

5814
JEWISH CULTURAL SERIES
3828 Virginia Avenue SE
Charleston, WV 25304
Phone: 304-925-5112
Officers:
    Chairman: Dr. Steve Jubelirer
Budget: $10,000-20,000
Performs At: Temple Israel; B'nai Jacob Synagogue

SERIES & FESTIVALS / West Virginia

5815
GLENVILLE STATE COLLEGE CULTURAL AFFAIRS COMMISSION
Glenville State College
Glenville, WV 26351-1292
Phone: 304-462-7361
Fax: 304-462-4407
Toll-free: 800-924-2010
Web Site: www.glenville.edu
Officers:
 Chairman Fine Arts: John S McKinney
Management:
 President: Robert Freeman
 Executive Director: Robert Hardman
 Artistic Director: Duane Chapman
Founded: 1872
Specialized Field: Education
Status: Non-Profit, Non-Professional
Paid Staff: 200
Budget: $10,000-20,000

5816
MARSHALL ARTISTS SERIES
Jomie Jazz Center
One John Marshall Drive
Huntington, WV 25755-2210
Phone: 304-696-6656
Fax: 304-696-6658
e-mail: artistsseries@marshall.edu
Web Site: www.marshall.edu
Officers:
 President: J Wade Gilley
Management:
 Executive Director: Penny Watkins
Mission: To aid, promote and contribute to the educational and cultural life of Marshall University and the surrounding area.
Founded: 1936
Specialized Field: Performing Arts
Status: Non-Profit, Professional
Paid Staff: 3
Paid Artists: 50
Budget: $150,000-400,000
Income Sources: Marshall University
Performs At: Keith-Albee Theatre
Organization Type: Educational; Sponsoring

5817
WEST VIRGINIA STATE UNIVERTISY MUSIC SERIES
Campus Box 4
PO Box 1000
Institute, WV 25112-1000
Phone: 304-766-3194
Fax: 304-766-5100
Toll-free: 800-987-2112
e-mail: cgiles@wvstateu.edu
Web Site: www.wvstateu.edu
Officers:
 Music Department Chairperson: Charlotte Giles
 Chair: Thomas Susman
 Vice Chair: Ann Brothers Smith
 Secretary: L. Vincent Williams
Management:
 President: Hazo Carter Jr
Founded: 1891
Specialized Field: Liberal Arts
Status: Non-Profit, Professional
Paid Staff: 4
Budget: $35,000-60,000

5818
CARNEGIE HALL
881 Seventh Avenue
Lewisburg, WV 10019
Phone: 212-247-7800
Web Site: www.carnegie-hall.com
Officers:
 Chairman: Sanford I. Weill
 Vice Chairman: Mercedes T. Bass
 Secretary: Kenneth J. Bialkin
 Treasurer: Edward C. Forst
Management:
 Executive and Artistic Director: Clive Gillinson
 Community Relations Director: Susan Bell
 Director: Richard Malenka
 Director: Susan J. Brady
Founded: 1983
Paid Staff: 12
Volunteer Staff: 150
Budget: $35,000-60,000

5819
FAIRMONT CHAMBER MUSIC SOCIETY
407 Jackson Street
Morgantown, WV 26554-2941
Phone: 304-291-8277
Fax: 304-367-4248
e-mail: ashtonjohn@comcast.net
Web Site: www.thomassmith.us/charity/fcms/
Officers:
 President: John Ashton
 Vice President: Brenda Giannis
 Treasurer: Ruth Brooks
 Secretary: Marcella Yarenhuk
Mission: To present the finest of classical chamber music in the North Central West Virginia area.
Founded: 1982
Specialized Field: Chamber Music; Classical
Volunteer Staff: 8
Budget: $11,000
Performs At: St. Peter's Church
Seating Capacity: 700

5820
WVU ARTS SERIES
PO Box 6017
Morgantown, WV 26506-6017
Phone: 304-293-4406
Fax: 304-293-7574
Web Site: www.events.wvu.edu
Budget: $150,000-400,000

5821
WEST VIRGINIA UNIVERSITY AT PARKERSBURG
W Virginia University at Parkersburg
300 Campus Drive
Parkersburg, WV 26104-8647
Phone: 304-424-8000
Fax: 304-424-8315
e-mail: hg.young@mail.wvu.edu
Web Site: www.wvup.edu
Management:
 President: Marie Gnage
 Executive Director: Tom Yencha
 Artistic Director: H G Young III
Founded: 1961
Specialized Field: Series & Festivals; Vocal Music; Theatre
Status: Non-Profit, Non-Professional
Paid Staff: 1
Budget: $35,000-60,000

5822
CONTEMPORARY AMERICAN THEATER FESTIVAL
PO Box 429
Shepherdstown, WV 25443
Phone: 304-876-3473
Fax: 304-876-5443
Toll-free: 800-999-2283
e-mail: info@catf.org
Web Site: www.catf.org
Officers:
 Vice President: Ann Harkins
 Secretary: Michael Proffitt
 Treasurer: Karen Rice
Management:
 President: Jenny Ewing Allen
 Managing Director: James Mcneel
 Producing Director: Ed Herendeen
 Director of Production: Patrick H. Wallace
 Production Supervisor: Trent Kugler
Founded: 1990
Specialized Field: Theater Festival
Status: Non-Profit
Performs At: Main Stage, Studio Theater
Type of Stage: Proscenium, Black Box
Seating Capacity: 350, 99

5823
PERFORMING ARTS SERIES AT SHEPHERD
Shepherd College
101 College Center
Shepherdstown, WV 25443
Phone: 304-876-5113
Fax: 304-876-5137
e-mail: rmeads@shepherd.edu
Web Site: www.shepherd.edu/passweb
Officers:
 Chairperson: Rachael Meads
Management:
 President: Rachael Meads
 Production Director: Patrick Wallac
Founded: 1982
Specialized Field: Series & Festivals; Instrumental Music; Vocal Music; Theatre; Dance; Ethnic Performances; Folk Art
Status: Non-Profit, Professional
Paid Staff: 2
Paid Artists: 35
Budget: $35,000-60,000

5824
CHARLESTON COMMUNITY MUSIC ASSOCIATION
PO Box 8008
South Charleston, WV 25303
Phone: 304-744-1400
Fax: 304-343-7058
Officers:
 President: JB Wollenberger
Mission: Presenter.
Founded: 1933
Specialized Field: Music; Dance
Volunteer Staff: 100
Budget: $150,000
Income Sources: Ticket Sales; Contributions
Performs At: Concert Hall
Annual Attendance: 2,800-3,100
Type of Stage: Procenium
Seating Capacity: 3,450
Year Built: 1939

SERIES & FESTIVALS / Wisconsin

5825
WEST LIBERTY COLLEGE CONCERT SERIES
W Liberty College
Hall of Fine Arts
West Liberty, WV 26074-0335
Phone: 304-336-8006
Fax: 304-336-8056
Web Site: www.wlsc.edu
Officers:
   Concert Committee Chairman: James C Guerriero
Management:
   President: Richard Owens
   VP of Academics: John McCullough
   Chairman of Concert Series: James Gueraiero
Founded: 1964
Specialized Field: Series & Festivals; Instrumental Music; Vocal Music
Status: Non-Profit, Professional
Paid Staff: 1
Paid Artists: 15
Budget: $20,000-35,000

5826
OGLEBAY INSTITUTE
Oglebay Park
1330 National Road
Wheeling, WV 26003
Phone: 304-242-7700
Fax: 304-242-4203
Toll-free: 888-696-4283
e-mail: inspire@oionline.com
Web Site: www.oionline.com
Officers:
   Treasurer: Seth McIntyre
Management:
   President: Valerie Golik
   Director of Performing Arts: Kate Crosbie
   Artistic Director: Harold O'Leary
   Technical Director: P.D. Gregg
   Director of Marketing: Misty Klug
Founded: 1930
Specialized Field: Series & Festivals; Vocal Music; Theatre; Youth; Dance; Ethnic Performances Theatre; Lyric Opera; History
Status: Non-Profit, Professional
Paid Staff: 100
Organization Type: Performing; Touring; Educational

Wisconsin

5827
PERFORMING ARTS AT LAWRENCE
711 E. Boldt Way
Appleton, WI 54911
Phone: 920-832-7000
Fax: 920-832-6783
Web Site: www.lawrence.edu
Management:
   President: Jill Beck
   Executive Director: Gregory Volk
   Managing Director: Shana Shallue
   Associate Director, Development: Rudi Pakendorf
   Associate Director of Admissions: Russell Bold
Founded: 1847
Specialized Field: Series & Festivals; Jazz And Classical Concerts
Status: Non-Profit, Professional
Paid Staff: 2
Paid Artists: 8
Budget: $60,000-150,000

Income Sources: Ticket Revenue; Sponsorship
Annual Attendance: 10,000

5828
AL RINGLING THEATRE: LIVELY ARTS SERIES
PO Box 381
136 Fourth Avenue
Baraboo, WI 53913
Phone: 608-356-8864
Fax: 608-356-0976
e-mail: info@alringling.com
Web Site: www.alringling.com
Officers:
   President: Charlene Flygt
   Vice President: Carol Kratochwill
   Treasurer: Stephanie Potter
   Secretary: Rebecca Oettinger
Management:
   Executive Director: Brian Heller
   Assistant Director: Beth Rozman
Founded: 1915
Status: For-Profit

5829
BELOIT COLLEGE PERFORMING ARTS SERIES
Int'l Performing Arts & Lecture Series
700 College Street
Beloit, WI 53511
Phone: 608-363-2000
Fax: 608-363-2870
Web Site: www.beloit.edu
Officers:
   President: John Burris
   Chair: James R. Sanger
Management:
   Director Special Events: Mary Frey
Founded: 1846
Specialized Field: Liberal Arts Education
Status: Non-Profit, Professional
Paid Staff: 1
Paid Artists: 40
Budget: $20,000-35,000
Income Sources: Beloit College
Performs At: Eaton Chapel

5830
ST. NORBERT COLLEGE PERFORMING ARTS
St. Norbert College
100 Grant Street
De Pere, WI 54115
Phone: 920-403-3950
Fax: 920-403-4081
e-mail: performingarts@snc.edu
Web Site: www.snc.edu/performingarts/
Management:
   Advisor: Garrett Grenz
Utilizes: Dance Companies; Fine Artists; Guest Instructors; Original Music Scores; Soloists
Founded: 1898
Budget: $10,000-20,000
Performs At: Abbot Pennings Hall of Fine Arts
Annual Attendance: 7,000
Facility Category: vantons

5831
HEADWATERS COUNCIL FOR THE PERFORMING ARTS
Box 1481
Eagle River, WI 54521

Phone: 715-477-6206
Fax: 715-477-1736
e-mail: info@hcpapresents.com
Web Site: www.hcpapresents.com
Officers:
   President: Bernie Hupperts
   VP: Linnea Ebann
   Secretary: Susan Fosdick
   Treasurer: Marty Ketterer
Management:
   Community Contact: Nancy Berg
Mission: To bring quality entertainment to our remote community.
Utilizes: Sign Language Translators; Singers; Soloists; Special Technical Talent; Theatre Companies
Founded: 1982
Specialized Field: Dance; Vocal Music; Instrumental Music; Theater
Status: Nonprofit
Volunteer Staff: 15
Budget: $24,000
Income Sources: Ticket Sales; Donations; Grants
Performs At: Northland Pines High School
Facility Category: High School Auditorium
Seating Capacity: 450
Year Built: 1980
Organization Type: Performing

5832
EAU CLAIRE REGIONAL ARTS CENTER
316 Eau Claire Street
Eau Claire, WI 54701
Phone: 715-832-2787
Fax: 715-832-0828
e-mail: info@eauclairearts.com
Web Site: www.eauclairearts.com
Management:
   Executive Director: Ben Richgruber
   Office Coordinator: Meredith Pirazzini
   Production and Facilities Director: Brianna Hotchkiss
   Visual Arts Director: Rose Dolan-Neill
Utilizes: Choreographers; Dance Companies; Dancers; Fine Artists; Five Seasonal Concerts; Grant Writers; Guest Accompanists; Guest Choreographers; Guest Designers; Guest Directors; Guest Musicians; Guest Soloists; High School Drama; Instructors; Local Artists; Lyricists; Original Music Scores; Resident Artists; Student Interns; Special Technical Talent; Theatre Companies; Touring Companies
Founded: 1984
Opened: 1926
Status: Nonprofit
Paid Staff: 7
Budget: $300,000-400,000
Income Sources: Grants; Membership; Ticket Sales; Rentals
Annual Attendance: 80,000+
Facility Category: State Theatre
Type of Stage: Prosenium Theatre
Stage Dimensions: 50x29
Seating Capacity: 1,117
Year Built: 1926
Year Remodeled: 1986
Resident Groups: Chippewa Valley Symphony, Chippewa Valley Theatre Guild, Eau Claire Childrens Theatre

SERIES & FESTIVALS / Wisconsin

5833
UNIVERSITY OF WISCONSIN AT EAU CLAIRE ARTISTS SERIES
University of Wisconsin-Claire
Activities & Programs
P.O. Box 4004
Eau Claire, WI 54702-4004
Phone: 715-836-2787
Fax: 715-836-2521
Toll-free: 800-949-8932
e-mail: brockpjl@uwec.edu
Web Site: www.uwec.edu
Management:
  Arts/Events Coordinator: Jennifer Brockpahler
  Arts/Events Coordinator: Beverly Soll
Utilizes: Dancers; Guest Choreographers; Guest Directors; Guest Instructors; Guest Musicians; Guest Soloists; Multimedia; Original Music Scores; Sign Language Translators; Special Technical Talent; Theatre Companies
Founded: 1967
Specialized Field: Series & Festivals; Instrumental Music; Vocal Music; Theatre; Dance; Ethnic Performances
Status: Non-Profit, Professional
Paid Staff: 5
Budget: $60,000-150,000
Performs At: Zorn Arena; Gantner Concert Hall
Annual Attendance: varies
Facility Category: varies

5834
THE PENINSULA MUSIC FESTIVAL
3045 Cedar Street
PO Box 340
Ephraim, WI 54211
Phone: 920-854-4060
Fax: 920-854-1950
e-mail: musicfestival@musicfestival.com
Web Site: www.musicfestival.com
Officers:
  President: Jack Zilavy
  1st Vice President: Karen Smuda
  2nd Vice President: Orren Bradley
  Treasurer: William Miller
  Secretary: Sue Stone
Management:
  Music Director/Conductor: Victor Yampolsky
  Associate Conductor: Stephen Alltop
Mission: To perform quality music in a casual atmosphere and promote young, new artists.
Utilizes: Singers
Founded: 1953
Specialized Field: Series & Festivals; Instrumental Music; Festivals
Status: Non-Profit, Professional
Paid Staff: 3
Volunteer Staff: 115
Paid Artists: 75
Budget: $650,000
Income Sources: Ticket Sales; Contributions; Endowments
Season: August 6 - August 26, 2000
Performs At: Door Community Auditorium
Annual Attendance: 7,000
Facility Category: Concert Hall
Organization Type: Performing; Educational

5835
DOOR COMMUNITY AUDITORIUM SERIES
3926 Highway 42
PO Box 397
Fish Creek, WI 54212
Phone: 920-868-2728
Fax: 920-868-2590
e-mail: boxoffice@dcauditorium.org
Web Site: www.dcauditorium.org
Officers:
  President: Richard Burress
  Vice President: Larry Thoreson
  Secretary: Linda Laarman
  Treasurer: Michael Serpe
Management:
  Executive Director: Cari Lewis
  Technical Director: Kurt Thomas
  Production and Marketing Manager: Jennifer DuPont
  Office Manager: Amanda Berby
  Box Office Assistant: Dee Hopper
Mission: Door Community Auditorium serves as a center to enrich, entertain and challenge through a balanced combination of performing, visual and literary arts and to provide opportunities for social educational and cultural growth.
Utilizes: Actors; Artists-in-Residence; Choreographers; Collaborating Artists; Collaborations; Dance Companies; Dancers; Educators; Filmmakers; Fine Artists; Five Seasonal Concerts; Grant Writers; Guest Accompanists; Guest Artists; Guest Choreographers; Guest Composers; Guest Designers; Guest Directors; Guest Instructors; Guest Lecturers; Guest Musical Directors; Guest Musicians; Guest Soloists; Guest Teachers; Guest Writers; Guild Activities; Instructors; Local Artists; Local Unknown Artists; Lyricists; Multi Collaborations; Multimedia; Music; New Productions; Organization Contracts; Original Music Scores; Playwrights; Resident Professionals; Sign Language Translators; Singers; Soloists; Theatre Companies; Touring Companies
Founded: 1991
Status: Non-Profit
Paid Staff: 8
Volunteer Staff: 100
Budget: $600,000
Year Built: 1991
Rental Contact: Pete Evans

5836
BROWN COUNTY CIVIC MUSIC ASSOCIATION
PO Box 5243
Green Bay, WI 54115-5243
Phone: 920-338-1801
Fax: 920-338-9702
e-mail: bccivicmusic@gmail.org
Web Site: www.bccivicmusic.org
Officers:
  President: Helen Bintz
  Executive Secretary: R Kilmer
  Vice-president: Brooks Dodson
  Treasurer: Neal Van Ess
  Secretary: Darlene Andre
Management:
  Artistic Director: Roger Bintz
Utilizes: Dance Companies; Dancers; Fine Artists; Guest Musical Directors; Multimedia; Original Music Scores; Sign Language Translators; Singers; Theatre Companies
Founded: 1926
Opened: 1927
Specialized Field: Classical Music Series; Instrumental Music; Vocal Music; Dance; Ethnic Performances
Status: Non-Profit, Professional
Paid Staff: 1
Volunteer Staff: 150
Budget: $50,000
Annual Attendance: 3,000
Facility Category: Auditorium
Seating Capacity: 1,522

5837
GREEN LAKE FESTIVAL OF MUSIC
PO Box 569
Green Lake, WI 54941
Phone: 920-748-9398
Fax: 920-748-6918
Toll-free: 800-662-7097
Web Site: www.greenlakefestival.org
Officers:
  President: David Woods
  Vice-President: Jerry Seaman
  Secretary: Gladys Veidemanis
  Treasurer: Steven Sorenson
Management:
  Executive Director: Jeffrey Harkins
Mission: The Green Lake Festival of Music is a non-profit corporation founded for cultural enrichment through the creation, promotion and public performance of the musical arts.
Founded: 1979
Specialized Field: Series & Festivals: Concert Series And Music Workshop
Status: Non-Profit, Professional
Paid Staff: 3
Paid Artists: 20
Organization Type: Performing; Touring; Resident; Educational; Sponsoring

5838
JANESVILLE PERFORMING ARTS CENTER
408 South Main Street
Janesville, WI 53545
Phone: 608-758-0297
Fax: 608-758-2549
e-mail: boxoffice@janesvillepac.org
Web Site: www.janesvillepac.org
Officers:
  President: Tobin Ryan
  Vice President: Mark Gregory
  Treasurer: Lynn Gardinier
  Secretary: Lisa Stevens
Management:
  Executive Director: Laurel Canan
  Technical Director: Michael Stalsberg
Founded: 1932
Specialized Field: Events for Family Audiences
Status: Non-Profit, Professional
Paid Staff: 1
Budget: $20,000-35,000

5839
COUNCIL FOR THE PERFORMING ARTS
700 W. Milwaukee St.
Jefferson, WI 53549-1717
Phone: 920-674-2179
Fax: 920-674-5140
e-mail: jeffersoncpastaff@gmail.com
Web Site: www.councilfortheperformingarts.org
Officers:
  President: Susie Polk
  Vice President: Denise Tubman-Reichhoff
  Treasurer: Brian Monfre
  Secretary: C.J. O'Neil

All listings are in alphabetical order by state, then city, then organization within the city.

SERIES & FESTIVALS / Wisconsin

Management:
   Executive Director: Nicole Pupanek
   Office Manager: Jamie Magner
Mission: To provide culturally and socially valuable entertainment and educational opportunities for this area.
Utilizes: Actors; Artists-in-Residence; Choreographers; Dance Companies; Guild Activities; Instructors; Multimedia; Music; Poets; Selected Students; Sign Language Translators; Singers; Soloists; Special Technical Talent; Theatre Companies
Founded: 1977
Specialized Field: Series & Festivals; Instrumental Music; Vocal Music; Theatre; Youth; Dance; Ethnic Performances
Status: Non-Profit, Professional
Paid Staff: 3
Volunteer Staff: 100
Paid Artists: 100
Non-paid Artists: 175
Budget: $250,000
Income Sources: Ticket Sales; Grants; Donations
Affiliations: Arts Midwest
Annual Attendance: 15,000
Facility Category: Auditorium
Type of Stage: Proscenium
Stage Dimensions: 66'x44'
Seating Capacity: 996
Year Built: 1977
Organization Type: Performing; Educational

5840
CARTHAGE COLLEGE CHAMBER MUSIC & LECTURE SERIES
2001 Alford Park Drive
Kenosha, WI 53140
Phone: 262-551-8500
Web Site: www.carthage.edu
Management:
   Chair, Music Department: Corinne Ness
Specialized Field: Chamber music, various lectures

5841
KOHLER FOUNDATION
725X Woodlake Road
Kohler, WI 53044
Phone: 920-458-1972
Fax: 920-458-4280
e-mail: terri.yoho@kohler.com
Web Site: www.kohlerfoundation.org
Management:
   President: Ruth Kohler
   Executive Director: Terri Yoho
   Accountant: Wanda Bintzler
   Admin Coordinator: Larry Thomas
Mission: To provide cultural opportunities for the benefit of the community.
Founded: 1940
Specialized Field: Series & Festivals; Art Conservation; Dance; Vocal Music; Instrumental Music; Theatre
Status: Non-Profit, Professional
Paid Staff: 6
Income Sources: Ticket Sales
Performs At: Kohler Memorial Theater
Annual Attendance: 4,000
Type of Stage: Wood Sprung Floor
Year Built: 1968
Organization Type: Performing

5842
GREAT RIVER FESTIVAL OF ARTS
PO Box 1434
La Crosse, WI 54602-1434
Phone: 608-784-3033
e-mail: grff@greatriverfolkfest.org
Web Site: www.greatriverfolkfest.org
Management:
   Administrator: Kathy Fitchuk
Founded: 1959
Specialized Field: Education and Cultural Events
Status: Non-Profit, Professional
Paid Staff: 1
Paid Artists: 20

5843
GREAT RIVER JAZZ FEST
1311 Badger Street #609
La Crosse, WI 54601
Phone: 608-784-7575
e-mail: jazznowt@gmail.com
Web Site: www.lacrossejazz.com
Management:
   Director: Terry Rochester, jazznowt@gmail.com
Status: Non-Profit

5844
PUMP HOUSE REGIONAL ARTS
119 King Street
La Crosse, WI 54601
Phone: 608-785-1434
Fax: 608-785-1432
Web Site: www.thepumphouse.org
Officers:
   President: Timothy Riley
   Vice President: Ryan Soberg
   Treasurer: Julie Deets
   Secretary: Franci Stavropoulos
Management:
   Executive Director: Toni Asher
   Artistic Director: Marti Schwem
Utilizes: Educators; Fine Artists; Five Seasonal Concerts; Guest Accompanists; Guest Musical Directors; Guest Musicians; High School Drama; Instructors; Local Artists; Multimedia; New Productions; Special Technical Talent; Touring Companies
Founded: 1977
Specialized Field: Series & Festivals; Instrumental Music; Vocal Music; Theatre; Youth; Dance; Ethnic Performances
Status: Non-Profit, Professional
Paid Staff: 4
Volunteer Staff: 3
Non-paid Artists: 350
Budget: $98,000
Performs At: Dayton Gallery
Annual Attendance: 12,000
Facility Category: Arts Center
Seating Capacity: 130
Year Built: 1880
Rental Contact: Jodi Bente

5845
UNIVERSITY OF WISCONSIN AT LA CROSSE LECTURES
1725 State Street, La Crosse
La Crosse, WI 54601
Phone: 608-785-8000
Fax: 608-785-6575
e-mail: richter.jara@uwlax.edu
Web Site: www2.uwlax.edu
Management:
   Program Adviser: Jaralee Richter
Budget: $20,000-35,000

5846
VITERBO UNIVERSITY BRIGHT STAR SEASON
900 Viterbo Drive
La Crosse, WI 54601
Phone: 608-796-3000
Fax: 608-796-3736
e-mail: communication@viterbo.edu
Web Site: www.viterbo.edu/fac
Officers:
   President: Richard B. Artman
Management:
   Artistic Director: Michael Ranscht
Utilizes: Artists-in-Residence; Dance Companies; Dancers; Designers; Five Seasonal Concerts; Guest Artists; Guest Conductors; Guest Instructors; Guest Soloists; Local Artists; Multimedia; Music; Resident Professionals; Singers; Soloists; Special Technical Talent; Theatre Companies
Founded: 1890
Specialized Field: Series & Festivals; Instrumental Music; Vocal Music; Theatre; Youth; Dance; Ethnic Performances; General Education
Status: Non-Profit, Professional
Paid Staff: 250
Budget: $200,000 - 250,000
Performs At: Fine Arts Center
Annual Attendance: 65,000
Facility Category: Multi-Disciplinary Arts Center
Type of Stage: Proscenium
Stage Dimensions: 40x30
Seating Capacity: 1,090
Year Built: 1971
Rental Contact: Michael Ranscht

5847
FLAMBEAU VALLEY ARTS ASSOCIATION
PO Box 343
Ladysmith, WI 54848
Phone: 715-532-5594
Web Site: www.flambeauvalley.com
Officers:
   President: Charmaine Johnson
Management:
   President: Karen Ek
   Vice President: Margaret Foss
   Treasurer: Kevin Smith
Mission: To present a season of 6-7 performing arts events to public audiences in their rural county.
Utilizes: Dance Companies; Multimedia; Original Music Scores; Sign Language Translators; Special Technical Talent; Theatre Companies
Founded: 1971
Specialized Field: Performing Arts; Dance; Instrumental Music; Vocal Music
Status: Nonprofit
Volunteer Staff: 3
Budget: $10,000-20,000
Income Sources: Admissions; Wisconsin Arts Board, Performing Arts Fund of Arts Midwest, General Mills Foundation, Land O'Lakes Foundation
Performs At: High School Auditorium
Annual Attendance: 1600-2800
Type of Stage: Multipurpose auditorium w/fly space
Stage Dimensions: 60'x40'
Seating Capacity: 450
Year Built: 1968

5848
MADISON JAZZ SOCIETY
PO Box 8866
Madison, WI 53708-8866

SERIES & FESTIVALS / Wisconsin

Phone: 608-850-5400
Fax: 608-850-5401
e-mail: marsch@chorus.net
Web Site: www.madisonjazz.com
Management:
   President: Linda Marty Schmitz
Founded: 1984
Specialized Field: Series and Festivals: Jazz Music
Status: Non-Profit, Non-Professional

5849
MADISON BLUES FESTIVAL
PO Box 5363
Madison, WI 53705
Phone: 608-836-0020
Fax: 608-836-8555
Web Site: www.madisonblues.com

5850
SILVER LAKE COLLEGE GUEST ARTIST SERIES
2406 S Alverno Road
Manitowoc, WI 54220-9319
Phone: 920-686-6175
Fax: 920-684-7082
Toll-free: 800-236-4752
e-mail: admslc@sl.edu
Web Site: www.sl.edu
Officers:
   Music Department Chairperson: Sr. Marella Wagner
   President: Chris E. Domes
Management:
   Marketing, Graphic Design: Susan Bins
   Controller: Melissa Diener
   Accountant: Shanna Fitzgerald
   Director of Admissions: Jamie Grant
   Office Manager: Lori Salm
Mission: Outreach program bringing quality music performance to the community
Founded: 1935
Specialized Field: Instrumental music; Vocal Music; Piano; Mixed Ensemble
Paid Artists: 5
Budget: $6,000
Income Sources: College Sponsorship & Ticket Sales
Performs At: Silver Lake College Chapel
Annual Attendance: 100-125
Seating Capacity: 250

5851
UNIVERSITY OF WISCONSIN LECTURES AND FINE ARTS
2000 W 5th Street
PO Box 150
Marshfield, WI 54449
Phone: 715-389-6500
Fax: 715-389-6517
e-mail: msfadmit@uwc.edu
Web Site: www.marshfield.uwc.edu
Management:
   Dean: Andy Keogh
   Music Professor: Robert I Biederwolf
   Drama Director: Greg Rindfleisch
   Associate Dean, Associate Professor: Adam Iddi
Mission: Provide performances and lectures for the University and the community.
Founded: 1962
Specialized Field: Series and Festivals; Vocal Music; Theatre; Youth; Dance; Ethnic Performances
Status: Non-Profit, Professional
Paid Staff: 50
Paid Artists: 10
Performs At: University of Wisconsin Marshfield/Wodd County Theater
Type of Stage: Black Box
Organization Type: Educational; Sponsoring

5852
UNIVERSITY OF WISCONSIN CENTER - FOX VALLEY
1478 Midway Road
Menasha, WI 54952-1297
Phone: 920-832-2600
Fax: 920-832-2674
e-mail: jkuepper@uwc.edu
Web Site: www.uwfox.uwc.edu
Management:
   Student Activities Director: Jeff Kuepper
Founded: 1972
Specialized Field: Series & Festivals; Instrumental Music; Vocal Music; Theatre; Dance; Ethnic Performances
Status: Non-Profit, Non-Professional
Budget: $10,000-20,000
Performs At: Fine Arts Theatre
Organization Type: Performing; Educational

5853
CONCORDIA UNIVERSITY WISCONSIN
12800 N Lake Shore Drive
Mequon, WI 53097
Phone: 262-243-5700
Fax: 262-243-4351
Toll-free: 888-628-9472
e-mail: admissions@cuw.edu
Web Site: www.cuw.edu
Officers:
   Music Department Chairperson: Louis A Menchaca
   President: Patrick Ferry
Utilizes: Fine Artists
Specialized Field: Series & Festivals; Instrumental Music; Vocal Music; Theatre; Youth; Dance; Ethnic Performances
Status: Non-Profit, Non-Professional
Budget: $10,000
Performs At: Chapel of Christ Triumphant

5854
MERRILL AREA CONCERT ASSOCIATION
1201 N. Sales St
Merrill, WI 54452
Phone: 715-536-3740
Management:
   Manager: Chad P Premeau
   Contact: Meagan Cihlar
Specialized Field: Instrumental Music; Performing Arts, Vocal Music
Budget: $20,000-35,000

5855
ALVERNO COLLEGE
3400 South 43rd Street
PO Box 343922
Milwaukee, WI 53234-3922
Phone: 414-382-6000
Fax: 414-382-6354
Toll-free: 800-933-3401
e-mail: webinfo@alverno.edu
Web Site: www.alverno.edu
Officers:
   Chair: Mary Beth Berkes
   Vice Chair: Howard J. Jacob
   Secretary: Sister Pacis Meservey
   Treasurer: Ronald L. Blake
Management:
   President: Mary Meehan Ph D
Mission: Alverno Presents, the performing arts series of Alverno College has presented the finest artists of all disciplines since 1960. Emphasis is on contemporary dance and world music. Artists perform in one of three theatre spaces or various locations throughout Milwaukee. Mission is to engage our community in stimulating arts experiences with both established and emerging artists from a variety of perspectives and cultural backgrounds.
Utilizes: Actors; Artists-in-Residence; Collaborating Artists; Collaborations; Dance Companies; Dancers; Educators; Fine Artists; Local Artists; Lyricists; Multimedia; Original Music Scores; Playwrights; Special Technical Talent; Theatre Companies
Founded: 1887
Specialized Field: Presenter
Paid Staff: 3
Annual Attendance: 5000
Facility Category: Performing Arts Venue
Type of Stage: Proscenium
Stage Dimensions: 40'x30'
Seating Capacity: 930
Year Built: 1951
Rental Contact: Jan Kellogg

5857
CARDINAL STRITCH UNIVERSITY SCHOOL OF VISUAL AND PERFORMING ARTS
6801 N Yates Road
Milwaukee, WI 53217-3965
Phone: 414-410-4000
Fax: 414-410-4111
Toll-free: 800-347-8822
e-mail: admissions@stritch.edu
Web Site: www.stritch.edu
Officers:
   Chairman: Thomas A. Myers
   Vice President, Secretary: Anthea L. Bojar,
   Treasurer: Tammy M. Howard
Management:
   President: James P. Loftus
Utilizes: Actors; Educators; Fine Artists; Guest Composers; Guest Musical Directors; Guest Soloists; Instructors; Local Artists; Multimedia; New Productions; Organization Contracts; Playwrights; Sign Language Translators; Singers; Soloists; Special Technical Talent; Touring Companies
Specialized Field: Art; Music; Theatre; Dance; Film; Photography
Facility Category: Art Gallery
Type of Stage: Proscenium Arch
Seating Capacity: 400
Year Built: 1997
Comments: Theatre is air conditioned, handicapped accessible, infra-red hearing enhanced.

5858
EARLY MUSIC NOW
759 N Milwaukee Street
Suite 420
Milwaukee, WI 53202-1810
Phone: 414-225-3113
Fax: 414-225-3787
e-mail: info@earlymusicnow.org
Web Site: www.earlymusicnow.org
Officers:
   President: Donald Stacy
   Vice President: Donald Cress
   Secretary: David Houser

SERIES & FESTIVALS / Wisconsin

Treasurer: Ian Lambert
Management:
　Executive & Artistic Director: Charles Q Sullivan
Utilizes: Guest Directors; Guest Instructors; Guest Soloists; Multimedia; Original Music Scores
Founded: 1986
Specialized Field: Series & Festivals: Vocal And Instrumental-Renaissance
Status: Non-Profit, Professional
Paid Staff: 3
Budget: $225,000
Income Sources: Ticket sales; donations; grants
Annual Attendance: 2,000-3,000
Facility Category: Various halls and churches
Seating Capacity: 300-1,000

5859
WISCONSIN CONSERVATORY OF MUSIC

1584 N Prospect Avenue
Milwaukee, WI 53202
Phone: 414-276-5760
Fax: 414-276-6076
e-mail: info@wcmusic.org
Web Site: www.wcmusic.org
Officers:
　President: Karen Deschere
Management:
　President: Karen Deschere
Mission: Music education and performance opportunities.
Founded: 1899
Specialized Field: Music Education
Status: Non-Profit, Professional
Paid Staff: 16
Volunteer Staff: 50
Paid Artists: 100
Budget: $2,400,000
Performs At: Recital Hall
Affiliations: NASM; NGCSA
Annual Attendance: 5,000
Seating Capacity: 115
Year Built: 1903

5860
LAKELAND PERFORMING ARTS ASSOCIATION

PO Box 1279
Minocqua, WI 54548
Phone: 715-356-5645
e-mail: Info@lakelandperformingarts.org
Web Site: www.lakelandperformingarts.org
Management:
　President: Deane Galloway
Specialized Field: Vocal Music; Instrumental Music; Festivals; Lyric Opera
Budget: $10,000

5861
UNIVERSITY OF WISCONSIN AT OSHKOSH CHAMBER ARTS SERIES

Department of Music
800 Algoma Blvd.
Oshkosh, WI 54901
Phone: 920-424-4224
Fax: 920-424-1266
e-mail: music@uwosh.edu
Web Site: www.uwosh.edu/music
Management:
　President: Beverly Hassel
Mission: To offer the highest quality series of four professional classical music performances each season.
Founded: 1967
Specialized Field: Series & Festivals; Instrumental Music; Vocal Music; Music Education
Status: Non-Profit, Professional
Volunteer Staff: 10
Budget: $20,000-35,000
Income Sources: Student Allocations and Box Office
Affiliations: University of Wisconsin-Oshkosh
Annual Attendance: 2,000
Facility Category: University Recital Hall
Type of Stage: Open
Stage Dimensions: 43'x 23'
Seating Capacity: 500
Year Built: 1970

5862
UNIVERSITY OF WISCONSIN-PLATTEVILLE

Center for the Arts
1 University Plaza, Platteville
Platteville, WI 53818
Phone: 608-342-1491
Fax: 608-342-1478
Web Site: www.uwplatt.edu
Management:
　Director: Michael J. Breitner
Specialized Field: Series & Festival; Instrumental Music
Status: Non-Profit; Professional
Budget: $35,000-60,000
Performs At: Center for the Arts-Concert Hall

5863
PRAIRIE PERFORMING ARTS CENTER

4050 Lighthouse Drive
Racine, WI 53402
Phone: 262-752-2500
Fax: 262-260-3790
Web Site: www.prairieschool.com
Management:
　President: Mark Murphy
Founded: 1965
Budget: $10,000

5864
NORTHWOODS CONCERT ASSOCIATION

1960 Larsen Director
Rhinelander, WI 54501
Phone: 715-362-4912
Officers:
　President: Meredith Pirazzini
Budget: $20,000-35,000

5865
RIPON COLLEGE: CAESTECKER FINE ARTS SERIES

300 Seward Street
PO Box 248
Ripon, WI 54971
Phone: 920-748-8164
Fax: 920-748-7243
Toll-free: 800-947-4766
e-mail: adminfo@ripon.edu
Web Site: www.ripon.edu
Officers:
　President: Zach Messitte
　Vice Chair: Ronald R. Peterson
　Secretary: Doreen C. Chemerow
　Treasurer: Mark J. Wright
　Special Assistant: Margaret Carne
　Vice President for Finance: Thomas Ponto
　Vice President for Advancement: Wayne Webster
Mission: To present four to five performing and visual artists, representing diverse backgrounds and arts areas each season for the college and surrounding Ripon community.
Founded: 1800
Specialized Field: Series & Festivals; Dance; Vocal Music; Instrumental Music; Theatre
Status: Non-Profit, Non-Professional
Performs At: Benstead Theater; Demmer Recital Hall
Organization Type: Sponsoring

5866
UNIVERSITY OF WISCONSIN RIVER FALLS: WYMAN CONCERTS & LECTURES SERIES

River Falls 410 S 3rd Street
River Falls, WI 54022
Phone: 715-425-4911
Fax: 715-425-3296
e-mail: dots@uwrf.edu
Web Site: www.uwrf.edu
Management:
　Assistant Director Of Leadership: Kaye Schendel
　Assistant Director of Leadership: Vicky Hajewski
Specialized Field: Series & Festivals: Variety
Status: Non-Profit
Paid Staff: 1

5867
JOHN MICHAEL KOHLER ARTS CENTER: FOOTLIGHTS

608 New York Avenue
Sheboygan, WI 53081
Phone: 920-458-6144
Fax: 920-458-4473
e-mail: jzufeltbarnes@jmkac.org
Web Site: www.jmkac.org
Management:
　Executive Director: Ruth DeYoung Kohler
　Deputy Director Operations: Patti Sherman-Cisler
　Marketing Manager: Julie Frinzi
Specialized Field: Visual and Performing Arts
Status: Non-Profit, Professional
Paid Staff: 30
Budget: $35,000-60,000

5868
LAKELAND COLLEGE KRUEGER FINE ARTS SERIES

Lakeland College
PO Box 359
Sheboygan, WI 53082-0359
Phone: 920-565-1000
Fax: 920-565-1206
Toll-free: 800-569-2166
Web Site: www.lakeland.edu
Officers:
　Chair: Robert T. Melzer
　Sr. Vice Chair, Treasurer: Peter N. Reddin
　Recording Secretary: William C. Sheldon
Management:
　President: Daniel Eck
　Artistic Director: Bill Weidner
　Kraeger Fine Arts Coordinator: Debra Fale
　Assistant to the President: Ann Flad-Jesion
　Vice President for Finance: Carole Robertson
Founded: 1846
Specialized Field: Liberal Arts College.
Status: For-Profit, Non-Professional
Paid Staff: 100
Volunteer Staff: 4
Paid Artists: 5
Budget: $20,000-35,000

Performs At: Bradley Building
Seating Capacity: 495

5869
SHELL LAKE ARTS CENTER
802 1st Street
PO Box 315
Shell Lake, WI 54871-9700
Phone: 715-468-2414
Fax: 715-468-4570
e-mail: info@shelllakeartscenter.org
Web Site: www.shelllakeartscenter.org
Officers:
   President of Board: William Taubman
   VP: Jeanne Chamberlain
Management:
   Director: Jill Johnson
   Assistant Director: Tara Heckel
Mission: To provide creative arts education and enrichment experiences for diverse populations of youth and adult learners.
Founded: 1968
Specialized Field: Instrumental & Chorus Music; Visual Arts; Arts Education
Paid Staff: 4
Volunteer Staff: 104
Paid Artists: 60

5870
LUCIUS WOODS PERFORMING ARTS CENTER: MUSIC IN THE PARK
PO Box 295
Solon Springs, WI 54873
Phone: 715-378-4272
e-mail: luciuswoods@lwmusic.org
Web Site: www.lwmusic.org
Management:
   Executive Director: Pat Pluntz
Founded: 1994
Specialized Field: Musical Arts Presenter
Status: Non-Profit, Professional
Paid Staff: 1
Paid Artists: 300

5871
UNIVERSITY OF WISCONSIN AT STEVENS POINT PERFORMING ARTS
1108 Fremont Street Room 102
Stevens Point, WI 54481-3897
Phone: 715-346-3265
Fax: 715-346-4655
e-mail: cseefeld@uwsp.edu
Web Site: www.uwsp.edu
Management:
   Manager: Chris Seefeldt
Founded: 1934
Specialized Field: Series & Festivals; Instrumental Music; Vocal Music; Theater; Youth; Dance; Ethnic Performances
Status: Non-Profit, Professional
Paid Staff: 2
Budget: $35,000-60,000
Performs At: Michelsen Concert Hall; Sentry Theatre

5872
UNIVERSITY OF WISCONSIN: SUPERIOR UNIVERSITY
P.O. Box 2000
Superior, WI 54880-2898
Phone: 715-394-8115
Fax: 715-394-8454
Web Site: www.uwsuper.edu
Management:
   Chairman: D Greg Kehl Morre
Founded: 1893
Specialized Field: Series and Festivals; Instrumental Music; Vocal Music; Theatre; Youth; Dance; Ethnic Performances
Status: Non-Profit, Non-Professional
Paid Staff: 1
Paid Artists: 26
Budget: $10,000

5873
WAUPACA FINE ARTS FESTIVAL
Box 55
Waupacu, WI 54981
Phone: 715-842-1676
Fax: 715-848-4314
Officers:
   Chairman: Gerald Knoepfel
   Co-Chairman: Charles Spanhauer
   Treasurer: Blanche Fanik
Mission: Encouragement of active participation of musicians, artists and listeners/viewers of all the fine arts.
Founded: 1962
Specialized Field: Dance; Vocal Music; Instrumental Music; Theater
Status: Nonprofit
Paid Staff: 300
Income Sources: Wisconsin Art Council
Performs At: High School Auditorium
Organization Type: Performing

5874
PERFORMING ARTS FOUNDATION
401 4th Street
Wausau, WI 54403
Phone: 715-842-0988
Fax: 715-842-8715
Toll-free: 888-239-0421
e-mail: joconnell@grandtheater.org
Web Site: www.grandtheater.org
Management:
   Executive Director: Jim O'Connell
   General Manager/Associate Director: Merry Little
   Development Director: Megan Krueger
   Development Assistant: Susan Rupnow
   Marketing Director: Martha Kudick
   Technical Director: Mark Weiss
Utilizes: Artists-in-Residence; Dance Companies; Educators; Guest Soloists; Instructors; Multimedia; Special Technical Talent; Theatre Companies
Founded: 1972
Specialized Field: Series & Festivals; Instrumental Music; Vocal Music; Theatre; Youth; Dance; Ethnic Performances; Multi-Disciplinary
Status: Non-Profit, Professional
Paid Staff: 15
Volunteer Staff: 200
Paid Artists: 30
Budget: $2,000,000
Income Sources: Ticket Sales; Theater Rental; Annual United Arts Fund Drive
Performs At: Proscenium Theater; Multi-purpose Room
Affiliations: Arts Presenters; Wisconsin Presenter's Network; Art's Wisconsin
Annual Attendance: 100,000+
Facility Category: Performing Arts Center
Type of Stage: Proscenium
Stage Dimensions: 42 x 42
Seating Capacity: 1214
Year Built: 1927
Year Remodeled: 2002
Cost: $13.1 Million
Rental Contact: Merry Little

5875
UNIVERSITY OF WISCONSIN MARATHON COUNTY
518 S 7th Avenue
Wausau, WI 54401
Phone: 715-261-6234
Fax: 715-261-6333
Web Site: uwmc.uwc.edu
Management:
   Program Coordinator: Jean Greenwood
Utilizes: Artists-in-Residence; Guest Accompanists; Guest Instructors; Guest Soloists; Instructors; Local Artists; Multimedia; Original Music Scores; Playwrights; Sign Language Translators; Singers; Soloists; Special Technical Talent; Theatre Companies; Touring Companies
Paid Staff: 1
Budget: $15,000-25,000
Income Sources: Grants, student fees
Annual Attendance: 2500
Facility Category: Proscenium Stage
Stage Dimensions: 26 x 36
Seating Capacity: 240

5876
UNIVERSITY OF WISCONSIN AT WHITEWATER
Irvin L Young Auditorium
University of Wiscocsin at Whitewater
Whitewater, WI 53190-1790
Phone: 262-472-1234
Fax: 262-472-4400
e-mail: youngaud@mail.uww.edu
Web Site: www.uww.edu
Management:
   Program Director: Ken Kohberger
   Technical Director: David Nees
   Audience Services Manager: Michael Morrissey
   Marketing Director: Leslie LaMuro
Mission: Performing arts series for community, on-school-time presentations for school children and academic facility for the university arts students.
Utilizes: Actors; AEA Actors; Artists-in-Residence; Dance Companies; Multimedia; Original Music Scores; Selected Students; Theatre Companies
Founded: 1896
Specialized Field: Series & Festivals; Instrumental Music; Vocal Music; Theatre; Youth; Dance; Ethnic Performances
Status: Non-Profit, Professional
Paid Staff: 6
Volunteer Staff: 200
Paid Artists: 50
Budget: $150,000-400,000
Facility Category: Multi-Purpose Auditorium
Type of Stage: Proscenium
Stage Dimensions: 48'x30'
Seating Capacity: 1,335
Year Built: 1993
Rental Contact: Malinda Hunter

5877
ARTS COUNCIL OF SOUTH WOOD COUNTY
240 Johnson Street
PO Box 818
Wisconsin Rapids, WI 54495-0818
Phone: 715-421-4552
Fax: 715-421-4245
e-mail: swcarts.wctc.net
Management:

SERIES & FESTIVALS / Wyoming

Administrator: Mary Beth Rokus
Utilizes: Artists-in-Residence; Dance Companies; Fine Artists; Multimedia; Original Music Scores; Theatre Companies
Founded: 1976
Budget: $10,000-20,000
Performs At: Library Fine Arts Center; Performing Arts Center
Annual Attendance: 10,000
Seating Capacity: 800

Wyoming

5878
ARTCORE
PO Box 874
Casper, WY 82602
Phone: 307-265-1564
e-mail: ARTCOREWY@aol.com
Web Site: www.artcorewy.com
Management:
  Executive Director: Carolyn Deuel
  President: Richard Turner
  Vice President: Chuck Wilson
  Secretary-Treasurer: Jim Brown
Specialized Field: Instrumental Music; Vocal Music; Dance; Children's Performances
Volunteer Staff: 1
Budget: $20,000-35,000

5879
WYOMING ARTS COUNCIL
2320 Capitol Avenue
Cheyenne, WY 82002
Phone: 307-777-7742
Fax: 307-777-5499
Web Site: www.wyoarts.com
Officers:
  Chairman: Jim Willms
Management:
  Director: John G Coe
  Literature Manager: Mike Shay
  Visual Arts Manager: Liliane Francuz
  Visual Arts Manager: Liliane Francuz
  Grants Data Manager: Donna French
  Fiscal Officer: Justine Morris
  Office Manager: Evangeline Bratton
Mission: Promoting performing and literary and visual arts in Wyoming.
Utilizes: Artists-in-Residence; Community Talent; Curators; Guest Accompanists; Guest Musical Directors; Guest Soloists; Guest Teachers; Instructors; Original Music Scores; Playwrights; Selected Students; Students
Founded: 1967
Specialized Field: Dance; Vocal Music; Instrumental Music; Theater; Festivals; Lyric Opera; Grand Opera
Status: Nonprofit
Paid Staff: 10
Income Sources: National Endowment for the Arts; National Association of State Arts Agencies; WESTAF; Americans for the Arts
Organization Type: Educational; Sponsoring

5880
UNIVERSITY OF WYOMING CULTURAL PROGRAMS
Box 3951 University Station
Fine Arts Buiding, Room 113
Laramie, WY 82071
Phone: 307-766-5139
Fax: 307-766-2560
Web Site: www.uwadmnweb.uwyo.edu/culturalprograms
Management:
  President: Cedric Reverand
  Managing Director: Wendy Fanning
Utilizes: Actors; Artists-in-Residence; Dance Companies; Dancers; Fine Artists; Guest Accompanists; Guest Choreographers; Guest Composers; Guest Designers; Guest Musical Directors; Guest Musicians; Multimedia; Original Music Scores; Special Technical Talent; Theatre Companies
Founded: 1979
Specialized Field: Series & Festivals; Instrumental Music; Vocal Music; Theatre; Dance
Status: Non-Profit, Professional
Paid Staff: 3
Volunteer Staff: 6
Paid Artists: 25
Budget: $60,000-$150,000
Annual Attendance: 5,000 - 6,000
Facility Category: Concert Hall
Type of Stage: Concert Stage
Seating Capacity: 699
Year Built: 1974
Year Remodeled: 2001

5881
WESTERN ARTS MUSIC FESTIVAL
University of Wyoming Department of Music
PO Box 3037
Laramie, WY 82071
Phone: 307-766-5242
Management:
  Chairman Music Department: Fredrick Gersten
Mission: To offer quality music to audiences during the summer.
Founded: 1972
Specialized Field: Vocal Music; Instrumental Music; Festivals; Lyric Opera
Status: Professional; Nonprofit
Income Sources: Wyoming Council of the Arts
Performs At: The Fine Arts Council Hall; University of Wyoming
Organization Type: Performing; Touring; Resident; Educational

5882
NORTHWEST COLLEGE
Northwest College
231 W 6th Street
Powell, WY 82435
Phone: 307-754-6307
Fax: 307-754-6245
Toll-free: 800-560-4692
e-mail: neil.hansen@northwestcollege.edu
Web Site: area10.northwestcollege.edu
Management:
  Music Coordinator: Neil Hansen
Budget: $10,000-$20,000

5883
WESTERN WYOMING COLLEGE
2500 College Drive
Rock Springs, WY 82901
Phone: 307-382-1729
Fax: 307-382-7665
e-mail: jyoung@wwcc.wy.edu
Web Site: www.wwcc.wy.edu
Officers:
  Chairman Cultural Affairs: Billy Smith
Management:
  President: Tex Boggs
  Executive Director: Jamie Young
Founded: 1989
Specialized Field: Theatre: Musical
Status: Non-Profit, Non-Professional
Paid Staff: 34
Paid Artists: 4
Budget: $20,000-$35,000

5884
GRAND TETON MUSIC FESTIVAL
4015 W Lake Creek Drive #100
Wilson, WY 83014
Phone: 307-733-3050
Fax: 307-739-9043
e-mail: gtmf@gtmf.org
Web Site: www.gtmf.org
Officers:
  President: Margaretha Walk
Management:
  Music Director: Donald Runnicles
  Executive Director: Andrew Palmer Todd
  Dir of Artistic Planning/Ops: Liz Kintz
  Director Marketing: Susan Scarlata
  Managing Dir Artistic Operations: Steve Friedlander
  Finance Associate: Steffan Larson
  Facilities Manager: Doug Henderson
  Artistic Associate: Marty Camino
  Development Associate: Andy Mahoney
Mission: To establish a resident ensemble of like-minded artists to perform in small ensembles in a superb symphony orchestra; to bring the musical resources of a great metropolis to the Northern Rocky Mountain region for the summer season.
Utilizes: Guest Accompanists; Guest Composers; Guest Directors; Guest Musical Directors; Guest Musicians; Original Music Scores; Singers; Theatre Companies
Founded: 1962
Specialized Field: Music: Classical
Status: Non-Profit, Professional
Paid Staff: 9
Volunteer Staff: 100
Paid Artists: 200
Budget: 1,900,00
Income Sources: Donations; Sales
Performs At: Walk Festival Hall
Affiliations: ASOL; Jackson Hole Chamber of Commerce
Annual Attendance: 50,000
Facility Category: Concert Hall
Stage Dimensions: 60'wx 40'd
Year Built: 1974
Organization Type: Performing; Sponsoring

FACILITIES / Alabama

Alabama

5885
ANNISTON MUSEUM OF NATURAL HISTORY
PO Box 1587
Anniston, AL 36202-1587
Mailing Address: P.O. Box 1587, Anniston, AL 36202-1587
Phone: 256-237-6766
Fax: 256-237-6776
e-mail: info@annistonmuseum.org
Web Site: www.annistonmuseum.org
Management:
  Executive Director: Cheryl H Bragg
  Marketing Manager: Margie Conner
  Development Director: Lindie K Brown
Founded: 1929
Status: Non-Profit, Professional
Paid Staff: 30
Budget: $10,000
Annual Attendance: 85,000
Seating Capacity: 175-200

5886
ALABAMA THEATRE
1817 Third Avenue N
Birmingham, AL 35203
Mailing Address: 1817 Third Avenue North, Birmingham, AL 35203
Phone: 205-252-2262
Fax: 205-776-1623
e-mail: jhanks6349@aol.com
Web Site: www.alabamatheatre.com
Management:
  Executive Director: Brant Beene
  House Manager/Event Coordinator: Kathi Glasscox
  Hill Event Center Director: Cindy Mullins
  Technical Director: Bert Trotman
  Business Manager: Susan Darby
Founded: 1927
Seating Capacity: 2,174
Year Built: 1927

5887
ALYS ROBINSON STEPHENS PERFORMING ARTS CENTER
1200 10th Ave S
Birmingham, AL 35205
Mailing Address: ASC, 1720 2nd Avenue South, Birmingham, AL 35294-1261
Phone: 205-975-9540
Fax: 205-975-2341
Toll-free: 877-278-8457
Web Site: www.alysstephens.org
Officers:
  President: Russell M. Cunningham IV
  Chairman: Theresa H. Bruno
  Treasurer: Lilian Glass
  Secretary: Rahul Thadani
Management:
  Executive Assistant to the Director: Chuck Evans
  Development Director: Lili Anderson
  Stage Manager: Kenny Crayton
  Senior Director: Laura Kelly
  Director of Operations: Bryan Jones
Utilizes: Artists-in-Residence; Dance Companies; Dancers; Guest Accompanists; Guest Choreographers; Multimedia; Original Music Scores; Resident Artists; Sign Language Translators; Singers; Special Technical Talent; Theatre Companies
Founded: 1996

Status: Non-Profit, Professional
Paid Staff: 23
Seating Capacity: 1,330

5888
B & A WAREHOUSE
1531 First Avenue South
Birmingham, AL 35233
Mailing Address: 1531 First Avenue South, Birmingham, AL 35233
Phone: 205-326-4220
Fax: 205-326-0233
e-mail: info@bawarehouse.com
Web Site: www.bawarehouse.com
Management:
  Associate Director: Kristen Farmer Hall
  Executive Director: Anne G. Miller
Seating Capacity: 2,235

5889
BIRMINGHAM-JEFFERSON CONVENTION COMPLEX ARENA
2100 Richard Arrington Jr Boulevard N
Birmingham, AL 35203
Phone: 205-458-8400
Fax: 205-458-8438
Toll-free: 877-843-2522
e-mail: info@bjcc.org
Web Site: www.bjcc.org
Officers:
  CEO: Jack Fields
Management:
  Sales/Marketing Director: Susette Hunter, susette.hunter@bjcc.org
Founded: 1970
Paid Staff: 150
Performs At: Concerts; Meetings; Conventions; Exhibits
Affiliations: ArenaNetwork; IAAM; IEBA; ACAE; Pollstar; RCMA
Annual Attendance: 413,044
Facility Category: Arena
Type of Stage: Varies
Seating Capacity: 18,000
Year Built: 1973
Year Remodeled: 2009
Rental Contact: Contract Specialist/Administrator Tara Roseberry

5890
BIRMINGHAM-JEFFERSON CONVENTION COMPLEX CONCERT HALL
2100 Richard Arrington Jr Boulevard N
Birmingham, AL 35203
Mailing Address: 2100 Richard Arrington Jr. Blvd. North, Birmingham, AL 35203
Phone: 205-458-8400
e-mail: info@bjcc.org
Web Site: www.bjcc.org
Officers:
  CEO: Jack Fields
Management:
  Executive Director: Jack Fields, susette.hunter@bjcc.org
  IT Director: Tad Snider
Founded: 1973
Facility Category: Concert Hall
Seating Capacity: 3,000
Rental Contact: Sales/Marketing Director Susette Hunter

5891
BIRMINGHAM-SOUTHERN COLLEGE THEATRE
Birmingham Southern College
900 Arkadelphia Road
PO Box 549026
Birmingham, AL 35254
Mailing Address: 900 Arkadelphia Road, Birmingham, AL 35254
Phone: 205-226-4600
Fax: 205-226-3044
Toll-free: 800-523-5793
e-mail: admission@bsc.edu
Web Site: www.bsc.edu
Officers:
  Chair: Michael Flowers
Management:
  Director: Ruth S Henry
  Artistic Director: Mira Popovich
  Director of Sports Information: Sarah Erreca
  Visual Identity and Publications Di: Tracy Thoma
  Communications Director: Hannah Wolfson

5892
BIRMINGHAM-SOUTHERN COLLEGE THEATRE
Birmingham Southern College
900 Arkadelphia Road
PO Box 549026
Birmingham, AL 35254
Mailing Address: 900 Arkadelphia Road, Birmingham, AL 35254
Phone: 205-226-4600
Fax: 205-226-3044
Toll-free: 800-523-5793
e-mail: admission@bsc.edu
Web Site: www.bsc.edu
Officers:
  Chair: Michael Flowers
Management:
  Director: Ruth S Henry
  Artistic Director: Mira Popovich
  Director of Sports Information: Sarah Erreca
  Visual Identity and Publications Di: Tracy Thoma
  Communications Director: Hannah Wolfson
Type of Stage: Split-Revolve-Lift Stage

5893
HARRISON THEATRE
Samford University
800 Lakeshore Drive
Birmingham, AL 35229
Mailing Address: 800 Lakeshore Drive, Birmingham, Alabama 35229
Phone: 205-726-2011
e-mail: wanunnel@samford.edu
Web Site: www.samford.edu
Officers:
  Chair: Dr Don Sandley
Management:
  Theatre Director: Dr Don Sandley
  Director of media and public relati: William Nunnelley
  President: Andrew Westmoreland
  Executive Assistant to President: Darlene Kuhn
  Assistant to President: Michael Morgan
Opened: 1976
Specialized Field: Dance; Theatre
Type of Stage: Proscenium Thrust
Seating Capacity: 288

FACILITIES / Alabama

5894
LEGION FIELD STADIUM
400 Graymont Avenue W
Birmingham, AL 35204
Mailing Address: 400 Graymont Avenue West, Birmingham, Alabama 35204
Phone: 205-254-2391
Web Site: www.informationbirmingham.com
Management:
  Director: Melvin Miller
  Stadium Manager: Walter Garrett
Founded: 1926
Status: Non-Profit, Professional
Paid Staff: 12
Seating Capacity: 80,673
Year Built: 1927
Year Remodeled: 1991

5895
SLOSS FURNACES NATIONAL HISTORIC THEATER
McMillan Associates
1923 3rd Avenue N
Suite 900
Birmingham, AL 35203
Mailing Address: 1923 3rd Avenue N. Birmingham, AL 35203
Phone: 205-324-6881
Fax: 205-323-7074
Web Site: www.mcmillan-associates.com
Officers:
  President: George DH McMillan
Management:
  Executive Director: Denise Lovoy Koch
Seating Capacity: 2,600

5896
THE LESLIE WRIGHT CENTER
Samford University
800 Lakeshore Drive
Birmingham, AL 35229
Mailing Address: 800 Lakeshore Drive, Birmingham, Alabama 35229
Phone: 205-726-2011
Fax: 205-726-2243
e-mail: dvhartle@samford.edu
Web Site: www.samford.edu
Management:
  Managing Director: David Hartley
  President: Andrew Westmoreland
  Executive Assistant to President: Darlene Kuhn
  Assistant to President: Michael Morgan
Seating Capacity: 2,640

5897
UAB ARENA
University of Alabama
1701 11th Ave. S.
Birmingham, AL 35294-4412
Mailing Address: 1701 11th Ave. S., Birmingham, AL 35294-4412
Phone: 205-934-8221
Fax: 205-975-7114
Toll-free: 800-421-8743
e-mail: chooseuab@uab.edu
Web Site: www.uab.edu
Officers:
  President: Carol Garrison
Management:
  Director: Steve Mitchell
Founded: 1987
Status: Non-Profit, Non-Professional
Paid Staff: 5
Paid Artists: 5
Type of Stage: Concert Stage
Seating Capacity: 9,000

5898
PRINCESS THEATRE CENTER FOR THE PERFORMING ARTS
112 2nd Avenue NE
Decatur, AL 35601
Mailing Address: 112 Second Avenue NE, Decatur, Alabama 35601
Phone: 256-350-1745
Fax: 256-350-1712
e-mail: debbie@princesstheatre.org
Web Site: www.princesstheatre.org
Management:
  Executive Director: Lindy Ashwander
  Office Manager: Debbie Nieberlein
  Technical Director: Penny Linville
  Box Office Manager: Gail Williams
Founded: 1983
Paid Staff: 5
Volunteer Staff: 250
Budget: $500,000
Affiliations: SAF
Annual Attendance: 60,000
Facility Category: Proscenium
Seating Capacity: 677
Year Built: 1919

5899
DOTHAN CIVIC CENTER
126 N Saint Andrews Street
Room 214, PO Box 2128
Dothan, AL 36303
Mailing Address: 126 N. Saint Andrews Street, P.O. Box 2128, Dothan, AL 36302
Phone: 334-615-3000
Fax: 334-615-3179
e-mail: civiccenter@dothan.org
Web Site: www.dothan.org
Management:
  Director: Chris Fredeman
Utilizes: Actors; AEA Actors; Dance Companies; Dancers; Educators; Grant Writers; Guest Artists; Guest Composers; Guest Designers; Guest Directors; Guest Musical Directors; Guest Soloists; Guild Activities; Instructors; Multi Collaborations; Multimedia; Original Music Scores; Sign Language Translators; Singers; Soloists; Special Technical Talent; Theatre Companies; Touring Companies
Founded: 1975
Status: For-Profit, Professional
Paid Staff: 12
Budget: $1,600,000
Income Sources: Municipal
Performs At: Proscenium Stages
Annual Attendance: 296,000
Facility Category: Arena and Opera House
Type of Stage: Proscenium
Seating Capacity: 3,100

5900
WALLACE HALL FINE ARTS CENTER
Gadsden State Community College
1001 George Wallace Drive
Gadsden, AL 35903
Mailing Address: PO BOX 227, Gadsden, AL 35902
Phone: 256-549-8475
Fax: 256-549-9637
e-mail: wallacehall@gadsdenstate.edu
Web Site: www.gadsdenstate.edu
Officers:
  President: Raymond W. Staats
Management:
  House Manager & Box Office Coordi: Hannah Lloyd
  Lighting Specialist: Tanner Ford
  Audio Engineer: Dalton Gargus
  Event Specialist: James Watkins
  Theatre Specialist: John Longshore
Mission: The mission of Wallace Hall Fine Arts Center is to serve as a meeting place for the community to engage in educational opportunities and enhance understanding and enjoyment of life through the creation and presentation of performing and visual arts.
Founded: 1968
Opened: 1968
Stage Dimensions: 40'W, 20'H, 30'D
Seating Capacity: 1,213
Year Built: 1966
Year Head Theatre Renovated: 2000
Cost: $450,000

5901
VON BRAUN CIVIC CENTER PLAYHOUSE
700 Monroe Street
Huntsville, AL 35801
Mailing Address: 700 Monroe Street Huntsville, Alabama 35801
Phone: 256-533-1953
Fax: 256-551-2203
e-mail: vbcinfo@vonbrauncenter.com
Web Site: www.vonbrauncenter.com
Officers:
  Chairman: Gordon Dykes
  President & Ceo: Steven J. Greil
Management:
  Executive Director: Steve Maples
  Operations Director: Ron Grimes
  Director of Sales and Marketing: Marie Arighi
  Director of Special Projects: Johnny Hunkapiller
  Director of Facilities: Byron Clanton
  Event Coordination: Brian Boggs
  Novelties and Concessions: Kevin Glouner
  Production: Lynn Broad
  Box Office Services: Jessica Owen
Founded: 1965
Income Sources: Private and Corporate Donations, Endowment Fund
Seating Capacity: 8,748

5902
VON BRAUN CIVIC CENTER ARENA
700 Monroe Street
Huntsville, AL 35801
Mailing Address: 700 Monroe Street Huntsville, Alabama 35801
Phone: 256-533-1953
Fax: 256-551-2203
e-mail: vbcinfo@vonbrauncenter.com
Web Site: www.vonbrauncenter.com
Officers:
  Chairman: Gordon Dykes
  President & Ceo: Steven J. Greil
Management:
  Executive Director: Steve Maples
  Operations Director: Ron Grimes
  Director of Sales and Marketing: Marie Arighi
  Director of Special Projects: Johnny Hunkapiller
  Director of Facilities: Byron Clanton
  Event Coordination: Brian Boggs
  Novelties and Concessions: Kevin Glouner
  Production: Lynn Broad
  Box Office Services: Jessica Owen
Founded: 1965
Seating Capacity: 10,000

FACILITIES / Alabama

5903
VON BRAUN CIVIC CENTER CONCERT HALL
700 Monroe Street
Huntsville, AL 35801
Mailing Address: 700 Monroe Street Huntsville, Alabama 35801
Phone: 256-533-1953
Fax: 256-551-2203
e-mail: vbcinfo@vonbrauncenter.com
Web Site: www.vonbrauncenter.com
Officers:
   Chairman: Gordon Dykes
   President & Ceo: Steven J. Greil
Management:
   Executive Director: Steve Maples
   Operations Director: Ron Grimes
   Director of Sales and Marketing: Marie Arighi
   Director of Special Projects: Johnny Hunkapiller
   Director of Facilities: Byron Clanton
   Event Coordination: Brian Boggs
   Novelties and Concessions: Kevin Glouner
   Production: Lynn Broad
   Box Office Services: Jessica Owen
Founded: 1965
Seating Capacity: 2,153

5904
VON BRAUN CIVIC CENTER EXHIBIT HALL
700 Monroe Street
Huntsville, AL 35801
Mailing Address: 700 Monroe Street Huntsville, Alabama 35801
Phone: 256-533-1953
Fax: 256-551-2203
e-mail: vbcinfo@vonbrauncenter.com
Web Site: www.vonbrauncenter.com
Officers:
   Chairman: Gordon Dykes
   President & Ceo: Steven J. Greil
Management:
   Executive Director: Steve Maples
   Operations Director: Ron Grimes
   Director of Sales and Marketing: Marie Arighi
   Director of Special Projects: Johnny Hunkapiller
   Director of Facilities: Byron Clanton
   Event Coordination: Brian Boggs
   Novelties and Concessions: Kevin Glouner
   Production: Lynn Broad
   Box Office Services: Jessica Owen
Founded: 1965

5905
PAUL SNOW MEMORIAL STADIUM
Jacksonville State University
700 Pelham Road N
Jacksonville, AL 36265-1602
Mailing Address: 700 Pelham Road North, Jacksonville, AL 36265-1602
Phone: 256-782-5781
Fax: 256-782-5953
Toll-free: 800-231-5291
e-mail: info@jsu.edu
Web Site: www.jsu.edu
Officers:
   President: Bill Meeham
   VP, Academic and Student Affairs: Rebecca Turner
   VP, Administrative and Business Aff: Clint Carlson
   VP, Institutional Advancement: Charles Lewis
   VP, Information Technology: Vinson Houston
Management:
   Athletic Director: Jim Fuller
   Public Relations Director: Patty Hobbs
   Public Relations Specialist: Angie Finley
Founded: 1883
Status: Non-Profit, Professional
Paid Staff: 50
Seating Capacity: 14,000

5906
PETE MATHEWS COLISEUM
Jacksonville State University
JSU Athletic Dept
700 Pelham Road N
Jacksonville, AL 36265-1602
Mailing Address: 700 Pelham Road North, Jacksonville, AL 36265-1602
Phone: 256-782-5781
Fax: 256-782-5953
Toll-free: 800-231-5291
e-mail: info@jsu.edu
Web Site: www.jsu.edu
Officers:
   President: Bill Meeham
   VP, Academic and Student Affairs: Rebecca Turner
   VP, Administrative and Business Aff: Clint Carlson
   VP, Institutional Advancement: Charles Lewis
   VP, Information Technology: Vinson Houston
Management:
   Athletic Director: Jim Fuller
   Public Relations Director: Patty Hobbs
   Public Relations Specialist: Angie Finley
Seating Capacity: 6,000

5907
ARTHUR R OUTLAW MOBILE CONVENTION CENTER
1 S Water Street
Mobile, AL 36602
Mailing Address: 1 S Water Street, Mobile, AL 36602
Phone: 251-208-2100
Fax: 251-208-2150
e-mail: bbrazier@mobileconventions.com
Web Site: www.mobileconventions.com
Management:
   General Manager: Bob Brazier
   Event Coordinator: Cristin Bolt
   Director of Sales: Cheryl Gee
   Sales Manager: Melanie Pierce
   Senior Director of Finance: Sharee Self
Facility Category: Convention Center
Seating Capacity: 6,000

5908
MITCHELL CENTER
University of South Alabama
5950 Old Shell Road
Mobile, AL 36688
Mailing Address: 5950 Old Shell Road, Mobile, AL 36688
Phone: 251-461-1632
Fax: 251-461-1634
e-mail: vcohen@southalabama.edu
Web Site: www.mitchellcenter.com
Management:
   Arena Manager: Victor Cohen
Specialized Field: Sports, Career fairs, youth concerts, adult lectures
Facility Category: Sport Arena
Seating Capacity: 10,000

5909
MOBILE CIVIC CENTER
401 Civic Center Drive
Mobile, AL 36602-0204
Mailing Address: 401 Civic Center Drive, Mobile, AL 36602-0204
Phone: 251-208-7261
Fax: 334-208-7551
e-mail: mlmccrory@mobilecivicctr.com
Web Site: www.mobilecivicctr.com
Management:
   General Manager: Bob Brazier
   Operations Director: Joe Delaronde
   Director of Sales: Cheryl Gee
   Senior Director of Finance: Sharee Self
   Marketing Manager: Cheryl Gee
   Stage Manager: Paul Buchanan
Mission: Conceived from the ground up as a venue for major events
Specialized Field: professional hockey and Division I basketball tournaments to rock concerts and monster truck rallies

5910
MOBILE THEATRE GUILD
14 N Lafayette Street
Mobile, AL 36606-2206
Mailing Address: P.O. Box 1265, Mobile, AL 36633
Phone: 251-433-7513
e-mail: mtg.boxoffice@gmail.com
Web Site: www.mobiletheatreguild.org
Officers:
   President: Barney March
   VP: Buffi Peter
   Secretary: Sherrick Sandy
   Treasurer: Bob Peter

5911
USA SAENGER THEATRE
401 Civic Center Drive
Mobile, AL 36602-0204
Phone: 251-208-7261
Fax: 251-208-5607
e-mail: cla.williams@cityofmobile.org
Web Site: www.mobilesaenger.com
Officers:
   Chairman: Mike Rogers
   Treasurer: Meg McGovern
Management:
   General Manager: Bob Brazier
   Operations Director: Joe Delaronde
   Director of Sales: Cheryl Gee
   Senior Director of Finance: Sharee Self
   Production/Facilities Manager: Mitch Teeple
Founded: 1927

5912
CHICHESTER BLACK BOX THEATRE
University of Montevallo
College Of Fine Arts
Station 6663
Montevallo, AL 35115
Mailing Address: University of Montevallo, Station 6663 Montevallo, AL 35115
Phone: 205-665-6000
Fax: 205-665-6058
e-mail: shackelc@montevallo.edu
Web Site: www.montevallo.edu
Officers:
   President: Philip C Williams
   VP, Academic Affairs: Mary B Horton
   Vice President Student Affairs: Karen Lynn Willingham

FACILITIES / Alabama

Management:
- **Director of Public Relations:** Cynthia K Shackelford
- **Public Relations Asst:** Diane Kennedy
- **Payroll Manager:** Mitzi C Bentley
- **Staff Accountant:** Melissa L Higgins
- **Payroll Technician:** Tammy Lynn Plier

Specialized Field: plays and musicals
Type of Stage: Black Box
Seating Capacity: 50

5913
PALMER THEATRE
University of Montevallo
College of Fine Arts
Station 6663
Montevallo, AL 35115
Mailing Address: University of Montevallo, Station 6663 Montevallo, AL 35115
Phone: 205-665-6000
Fax: 205-665-6058
e-mail: shackelc@montevallo.edu
Web Site: www.montevallo.edu
Officers:
- **President:** Philip C Williams
- **VP, Academic Affairs:** Mary B Horton
- **Vice President Student Affairs:** Karen Lynn Willingham

Management:
- **Director of Public Relations:** Cynthia K Shackelford
- **Public Relations Asst:** Diane Kennedy
- **Payroll Manager:** Mitzi C Bentley
- **Staff Accountant:** Melissa L Higgins
- **Payroll Technician:** Tammy Lynn Plier

Specialized Field: musicals and an occasional play
Type of Stage: Balcony Proscenium Auditorium
Orchestra Pit: Y
Seating Capacity: 1200

5914
REYNOLDS STUDIO THEATRE
University of Montevallo
College Of Fine Arts
Station 6663
Montevallo, AL 35115
Mailing Address: University of Montevallo, Station 6663 Montevallo, AL 35115
Phone: 205-665-6000
Fax: 205-665-6058
e-mail: shackelc@montevallo.edu
Web Site: www.montevallo.edu
Officers:
- **President:** Philip C Williams
- **VP, Academic Affairs:** Mary B Horton
- **Vice President Student Affairs:** Karen Lynn Willingham

Management:
- **Director of Public Relations:** Cynthia K Shackelford
- **Public Relations Asst:** Diane Kennedy
- **Payroll Manager:** Mitzi C Bentley
- **Staff Accountant:** Melissa L Higgins
- **Payroll Technician:** Tammy Lynn Plier

Specialized Field: main stage shows
Orchestra Pit: Y
Seating Capacity: 160
Year Stage Renovated: 2004

5915
ALABAMA SHAKESPEARE FESTIVAL - FESTIVAL STAGE
1 Festival Drive
Montgomery, AL 36117
Mailing Address: 1 Festival Drive Montgomery, AL 36117
Phone: 334-271-5353
Fax: 334-271-5348
Toll-free: 800-841-4273
e-mail: mlewis@asf.net
Web Site: www.asf.net
Officers:
- **COO:** Michael Vigilant
- **Chairman:** Dr. Laurie Jean Wei
- **Vice Chairman:** Gordon G. Martin
- **Secretary:** Gene C. Crane
- **Treasurer:** Eugene Stanaland

Management:
- **Producing Artistic Director:** Geoffrey Sherman
- **Production Manager:** Ahkim Church
- **Associate Director:** Nancy Rominger
- **Marketing Manager:** David Roberson
- **Development Director:** Eve Loeb

Mission: principal performance space within the Carolyn Blount Theatre, designed to be used in either proscenium or thrust-staging mode.
Founded: 1985
Specialized Field: 14 world-class productions annually
Status: Non-Profit, Professional
Annual Attendance: 300,000
Seating Capacity: 750

5916
ALABAMA SHAKESPEARE FESTIVAL - OCTAGON
1 Festival Drive
Montgomery, AL 36117
Mailing Address: 1 Festival Drive Montgomery, AL 36117
Phone: 334-271-5353
Fax: 334-271-5348
Toll-free: 800-841-4273
e-mail: mlewis@asf.net
Web Site: www.asf.net
Officers:
- **COO:** Michael Vigilant
- **Chairman:** Dr. Laurie Jean Wei
- **Vice Chairman:** Gordon G. Martin
- **Secretary:** Gene C. Crane
- **Treasurer:** Eugene Stanaland

Management:
- **Producing Artistic Director:** Geoffrey Sherman
- **Production Manager:** Ahkim Church
- **Associate Director:** Nancy Rominger
- **Marketing Manager:** David Roberson
- **Development Director:** Eve Loeb

Founded: 1985
Specialized Field: 14 world-class productions annually
Status: Non-Profit, Professional
Annual Attendance: 300,000
Seating Capacity: 225

5917
GARRET COLISEUM
1555 Federal Drive
PO Box 70026
Montgomery, AL 36107
Mailing Address: Agricultural Center Board, Garrett Coliseum, P.O. Box 70026
Phone: 334-356-6866
Fax: 334-272-6835
e-mail: GCRC@TheGarrettColiseum.com
Web Site: www.thegarrettcoliseum.com
Officers:
- **Executive Secretary:** Dianne Hall

Management:
- **Executive Director:** William H Johnson III
- **Assistant Director:** Ed Wesson

Mission: family entertainment that includes Rodeos, Concerts, Social Events, Expositions, Trade Shows, Sports Events, Horse and Cattle Shows and Sales, Circuses and Conventions.
Founded: 1951
Status: For-Profit, Professional
Paid Staff: 10

5918
JOE L REED ACADOME
Alabama State University
Carter Hill Road
915 S. Jackson Street
Montgomery, AL 36104
Mailing Address: Carter Hill Road, PO Box 271, Montgomery, AL 36101-0271
Phone: 334-229-4100
Fax: 334-229-4988
e-mail: admissions@alasu.edu
Web Site: www.alasu.edu
Officers:
- **President:** Joseph H. Silver
- **Executive Vice President/COO:** John F. Knight
- **Associate Executive Vice President:** Bernadette Chapple
- **Interim Vice President:** Eric Thornton
- **VP, Business and Finance:** Freddie Gallot

Management:
- **Director:** Gina Jobe-Ishman
- **Associate Executive Director:** Lavonette Bartley

Mission: physical education instruction, entertainment activities, conventions, cultural events and commencement exercises
Seating Capacity: 7,400

5919
TULANE UNIVERSITY NEWCOMB DEPARTMENT OF MUSIC
102 Dixon Hall
New Orleans, AL 70118-5683
Mailing Address: 102 Dixon Hall, New Orleans, LA 70118-5683
Phone: 504-865-5267
Fax: 504-865-5270
e-mail: music@tulane.edu
Web Site: www.tulane.edu/~music
Officers:
- **Chair:** B Michael Howard

Management:
- **Artisitic Director:** B Michael Howard
- **Office Manager:** Charlie Farve Hayes
- **Project Assistant:** Diane C. Banfell
- **Production Manager:** Michael Batt
- **Production Assistant/ Box Office Ma:** James Velasquez

Status: Non-Profit, Non-Professional

5920
OZARK CIVIC CENTER
320 E College Street
PO Box 789
Ozark, AL 36361
Mailing Address: 320 East College Street, PO Box 789, Ozark, AL 36361
Phone: 334-774-2618
Toll-free: 877-622-2322
Web Site: www.ozarkalabama.us
Officers:
- **Chairman:** E M Collier
- **Vice Chairman:** Herman F. Jackson
- **Secretary/Treasurer:** Donald K. Hallford

Management:
- **General Manager:** Donald K Hallford
- **Director:** Stanley Enfinger

FACILITIES / Alabama

Divisions Manager/Programs: Denise Ellis
Mission: concerts, circuses, wrestling and boxing events. We are also available for conventions, expos, pageants, trade shows, etc.
Founded: 1975
Status: Non-Profit, Non-Professional
Paid Staff: 2
Type of Stage: Concert Stage
Seating Capacity: 4,000

5921
CLAUDIA CROSBY THEATRE
Troy University
University Avenue
Troy, AL 36082
Mailing Address: 132 Malone Hall, Troy University
Phone: 334-808-6142
Fax: 334-670-3395
Web Site: www.troytheatre.org
Officers:
  Department Secretary: Jane Barwood
Management:
  Department Director: Adeena Moree
  Repertory Ensemble Coorinator: Deborah Chappell Hicks
  Instructor, Technical Direction: Mike Schafer
  Associate Professor: John Patton
  Departmental Secretary: Jane Barwood
Mission: plays, pageants, ceremonies, and commencement exercises
Type of Stage: Proscenium
Stage Dimensions: 22'H x 43'6W
Seating Capacity: 939

5922
TROJAN/ADAMS CENTER PERFORMING ARTS THEATRE
Troy University
University Avenue
Troy, AL 36082
Mailing Address: 132 Malone Hall, Troy University
Phone: 334-808-6142
Fax: 334-670-3395
Toll-free: 800-551-9716
Web Site: www.troytheatre.org
Officers:
  Department Secretary: Jane Barwood
Management:
  Department Director: Adeena Moree
  Repertory Ensemble Coorinator: Deborah Chappell Hicks
  Instructor, Technical Direction: Mike Schafer
  Associate Professor: John Patton
  Departmental Secretary: Jane Barwood
Specialized Field: classical, contemporary, drama, comedy, children's theatre, and musical theatre
Type of Stage: Proscenium
Stage Dimensions: 19'H x 30'W
Seating Capacity: 296

5923
BAMA THEATRE PERFORMING ARTS CENTER
Bama Theatre
600 Greensboro Avenue
PO Box 1117
Tuscaloosa, AL 35401
Mailing Address: PO Box 1117, Tuscaloosa, AL 35403
Phone: 205-758-5195
Fax: 205-345-2787
e-mail: director@tuscarts.org
Web Site: www.tuscarts.org
Officers:
  President: Ann Bourne
  Vice President: Brenda Randall
  Secretary: Amy Ahmed
  Treasurer: Debbie Watson
Management:
  Executive Director: Sandra Wolfe
  Theatre Manager: David Allgood
  Education Director: Sharron Rudowski
  Marketing Coordinator: Meghan Hawkes
  Publicity: Kevin Ledgewood
Founded: 1976
Status: Non-Profit, Non-Professional
Paid Staff: 4
Seating Capacity: 1,094

5924
BRYANT DENNY STADIUM
University of Alabama
Box 870323
Tuscaloosa, AL 35487
Mailing Address: Box 870323, Tuscaloosa, AL 35487
Phone: 205-348-3600
Fax: 205-348-2196
Web Site: www.rolltide.com
Officers:
  CFO: Finus Gaston
  Deputy Director/Chief Operating Off: Shane Lyons
Management:
  Athletic Director: Mal Moore
  Associate Athletics Director/Busine: Carol Park
  Support Services: Kevin Almond
  Administrative Specialist: Judy Tanner
  Academic Program Advisor: Evan Cardwell
Founded: 1929
Seating Capacity: 92,138

5925
COLEMAN COLISEUM
University of Alabama
Box 870323
Tuscaloosa, AL 35487
Mailing Address: Box 870323, Tuscaloosa, AL 35487
Phone: 205-348-3600
Fax: 205-348-2196
Web Site: www.rolltide.com
Officers:
  CFO: Finus Gaston
  Deputy Director/Chief Operating Off: Shane Lyons
Management:
  Athletic Director: Mal Moore
  Associate Athletics Director/Busine: Carol Park
  Support Services: Kevin Almond
  Administrative Specialist: Judy Tanner
  Academic Program Advisor: Evan Cardwell
Founded: 1968
Seating Capacity: 15,043

5926
FRANK MOODY MUSIC BUILDING
University of Alabama
810 Second Avenue
Tuscaloosa, AL 35487-0366
Mailing Address: 810 Second Avenue, Tuscaloosa, AL 35487
Phone: 205-348-7110
Fax: 205-348-1473
e-mail: ssnead@music.ua.edu
Web Site: www.music.ua.edu
Management:
  Music Director: Charles Snead
  Associate Director of Bands: Randall Coleman
  Coordinator of Music Administration: Pam Penick
  Administrative Specialist: Pam Woodard
  Office Associate Senior: Cathie Daniels
Founded: 1987
Seating Capacity: 1,000

5927
GALLAWAY THEATRE
University of Alabama
Department of Theatre & Dance
PO Box 870239
Tuscaloosa, AL 35487-0239
Phone: 205-348-7007
Fax: 205-348-0272
e-mail: olin@ua.edu
Web Site: www.as.ua.edu
Officers:
  Department Chair: William Teague
  Administrative Secretary: Sharron Skipper
  Dean: Dr. Robert F. Olin
Management:
  Dance Director: Cornelius Carter
  Director of Financial Affairs: Jimmy Vail
  Accounting Specialist: Gayle Lind
  Senior Accountant: Christina L. Crawford
  Development Director: Kathy Yarbrough

5928
HUEY RECITAL HALL
University of Alabama
Frank Moody Music Building
PO Box 870366
Tuscaloosa, AL 35487-0366
Mailing Address: 810 Second Avenue, Tuscaloosa, AL 35487
Phone: 205-348-7110
Fax: 205-348-1473
e-mail: ssnead@music.ua.edu
Web Site: www.music.ua.edu
Management:
  Music Director: Charles Snead
  Associate Director of Bands: Randall Coleman
  Coordinator of Music Administration: Pam Penick
  Administrative Specialist: Pam Woodard
  Office Associate Senior: Cathie Daniels
Seating Capacity: 140

5929
MARIAN GALLAWAY THEATRE
The University of Alabama
Department of Theatre & Dance
Box 870239
Tuscaloosa, AL 35487-0239
Phone: 205-348-5283
Fax: 205-348-9048
e-mail: theatre.dance@ua.edu
Web Site: www.theatre.ua.edu
Officers:
  Department Chair: William Teague
  Administrative Secretary: Sharon Skipper
Management:
  Theatre Management Director: Christopher Montpetit
  Assistant Professor, Music: Stacy Alley
  Associate Professor of Dance: Sarah M. Barry
  Assistant Professor of Dance: Qianping Guo
  Technical Supervisor: Lyndell McDonald
Mission: The mission of the Department of Theatre and Dance is to offer excellent teaching and resultant dynamic learning on the graduate (theatre only) and undergraduate levels of education.

FACILITIES / Alaska

Utilizes: Choreographers; Dancers; Designers; Educators; Guest Instructors; Guest Soloists; High School Drama; Resident Professionals; Soloists
Paid Staff: 25
Facility Category: University Theatre & Dance Space
Type of Stage: Proscenium
Seating Capacity: 305
Year Built: 1954

5930
MORGAN AUDITORIUM
University of Alabama
Department of Theatre & Dance
Box 870239
Tuscaloosa, AL 35487-0239
Phone: 205-348-7007
Fax: 205-348-0272
e-mail: olin@ua.edu
Web Site: www.as.ua.edu/theatre
Officers:
    Department Chair: William Teague
    Dean: Dr. Robert F. Olin
Management:
    Dance Director: Cornelius Carter
    Director of Financial Affairs: Jimmy Vail
    Accounting Specialist: Gayle Lind
    Senior Accountant: Christina L. Crawford
    Development Director: Kathy Yarbrough
Type of Stage: Proscenium
Seating Capacity: 600

5931
THE ALLEN BALES THEATRE
University of Alabama
Department of Theatre & Dance
Box 870239
Tuscaloosa, AL 35487-0239
Phone: 205-348-5283
Fax: 205-348-9048
e-mail: theatre.dance@us.edu
Web Site: www.theatre.us.edu
Officers:
    Department Chair: William Teague
    Administrative Secretary: Sharon Skipper
Management:
    Theatre Management Director: Christopher Montpetit
    Assistant Professor, Music: Stacy Alley
    Associate Professor of Dance: Sarah M. Barry
    Assistant Professor of Dance: Qianping Guo
    Technical Supervisor: Lyndell McDonald
Utilizes: Actors; Choreographers; Dancers; Designers; Guest Artists; Guest Soloists; High School Drama; Resident Professionals
Paid Staff: 25
Type of Stage: Black Box
Seating Capacity: 170

5932
CLEVE L ABBOTT MEMORIAL ALUMNI STADIUM
Tuskegee University
1200 W. Montgomery Rd.
Tuskegee, AL 36088
Mailing Address: Tuskegee University, Tuskegee, AL 36088
Phone: 334-727-8503
Fax: 334-727-8202
e-mail: media@tuskegee.edu
Web Site: www.tuskegee.edu/Global/story.asp?S=1323231
Officers:
    President: Gilbert L. Rochon, Ph.D., MPH
    VP for Academic Affairs: Luther S. Williams, Ph.D.
    VP for Finance and CFO: Cecil Lucy
    VP for Development: Cheryl M. Thomas
    VP for Capital Projects and Facilit: Harold Tate
    Chair: Charles E. Williams
    First Vice Chair: Bernard E. Anderson
Management:
    Chief of Staff: Shamima Amin
    Sports Information Director: Arnold Houston
    Faculty Athletic Representative: Luther Williams
    Compliance Officer: George Johnson
Founded: 1924
Specialized Field: Sports Facility
Seating Capacity: 10,000

Alaska

5933
ALMA PERFORMING ARTS CENTER
103 E Main St
Po Box 2359
Alma, AK 72921
Phone: 479-632-2129
Fax: 479-632-4793
e-mail: tschlabach@almasd.net
Web Site: www.almapac.org
Officers:
    Executive Director: Teresa Schlabach
Facility Category: Theatre
Type of Stage: Proscenium
Stage Dimensions: 1500

5934
ALASKA CENTER FOR THE PERFORMING ARTS
621 W 6th Avenue
Anchorage, AK 99501
Phone: 907-263-2900
Fax: 907-263-2927
e-mail: fdesk@alaskapac.org
Web Site: www.myalaskacenter.com
Officers:
    President/COO: Nancy Harbour
    VP: Julie Millington
    Treasurer: Bob Klein
    Chair: Micky Becker
    Vice Chair/Secretary: Henry Penney
Management:
    Development Director: Jayna Combs
    Accounting: Adele Hamey
    Director of Ticketing: John Fraser
    Box Office Manager: Richard Tillman
Founded: 1988
Status: Non-Profit, Non-Professional
Paid Staff: 30
Annual Attendance: 250,000
Type of Stage: Proscenium

5935
GEORGE M SULLIVAN SPORTS ARENA
1600 Gambell Street
Anchorage, AK 99501
Mailing Address: 1600 Gambell Street, Anchorage, AK 99501
Phone: 907-279-0618
Fax: 907-274-0676
Toll-free: 800-745-3000
Web Site: www.sullivanarena.com
Management:
    Region General Manager: Joe Wooden
    Operations Director: Ernest Jackson
    Marketing Director: Tanya Pont
    Director of Finance: Penny McKibbon
    Box Office Manager: Beth Rosenbaum
    Accounting Manager: Jason Sarate
Mission: designed to be a multi-use facility
Founded: 1983
Opened: 1983
Specialized Field: Olympic-size ice rink for hockey, with an insulated floor covering for basketball, concerts, and trade shows.
Facility Category: Arena
Seating Capacity: 9,000

5936
UAA RECITAL HALL
University of Alaska Anchorage
University of Alaska Anchorage
3211 Providence Drive
Anchorage, AK 99508
Mailing Address: University of Alaska Anchorage, 3211 Providence Drive, Ancho
Phone: 907-786-1800
Fax: 907-786-1799
e-mail: theatre@uaa.alaska.edu
Web Site: www.uaa.alaska.edu
Officers:
    Department Chair: Tom T Skore
Management:
    Director: David Edgecomb
    Director: Tom T Skore
    Building Manager: Cedar Cussins
Specialized Field: Music concerts
Type of Stage: Convertible Thrust

5937
WELLS FARGO SPORTS COMPLEX
University of Alaska Anchorage Athletics
3211 Providence Drive
Anchorage, AK 99508
Mailing Address: 3211 Providence Drive, Anchorage, Alaska 99508
Phone: 907-786-1800
e-mail: athletics@uaa.alaska.edu
Web Site: www.uaa.alaska.edu
Management:
    Athletic Director: Steve Cobb
    General Manager: Kevin Silver
Mission: exists primarily to enhance the educational athletic experience available on the Anchorage campus
Founded: 1978
Specialized Field: Gym, Swimming Pool, Ice Rink, Fitness Center, Jogging Track and Dance Studio
Status: Non-Profit, Non-Professional
Paid Staff: 40
Seating Capacity: 1,250

5938
ALASKALAND CIVIC CENTER & THEATRE
Parks & Recreation FNSB
PO Box 71267
Fairbanks, AK 99707-1267
Mailing Address: PO Box 71267, Fairbanks, AL 99707
Phone: 907-459-1087
Web Site: fairbanks-alaska.com
Mission: theater, art gallery and exhibition room.
Seating Capacity: 384

5939
CHARLES W DAVIS CONCERT HALL
Fairbanks Symphony Association
312 Tanana Dr
Room 234
Fairbanks, AK 99775

FACILITIES / Arizona

Mailing Address: PO Box 82104, Fairbanks, AK 99708
Phone: 907-474-5733
e-mail: symphony@fairbankssymphony.org
Web Site: www.fairbankssymphony.org
Officers:
  President: Chuck Lemke
  VP: Paul Schneider
  Treasurer: David McDowell
  Secretary: Martha Springer
Management:
  Executive Director: Laura Berghn
  Marketing Director: George Rydlinski
  Operations Director: Jenni Warren
Utilizes: Educators; Multimedia
Founded: 1984
Status: Nonprofit, Professional
Paid Staff: 2
Paid Artists: 23
Stage Dimensions: 30x60
Seating Capacity: 950
Year Built: 1968

5940
CHILKAT CENTER FOR THE ARTS
PO Box 1128
Haines, AK 99827
Mailing Address: Box 1128, Haines, AK 99827
Phone: 907-766-3573
Fax: 907-766-3574
e-mail: chamber@haineschamber.org
Web Site: www.chilkatcenter.org
Officers:
  Chairman: Tara Bicknell
  Sec/Treas: Annette Smith
  Vice-Chairman: Lorraine Dudzik
Management:
  Business Manager: Georgia Giacobbe
  General Manager: Judy Ereckson
  Director: Lorraine Dudzik
  Director: Janet Kurz
  Director: Joe Parnell
Status: Non-Profit, Professional
Paid Staff: 2
Paid Artists: 20
Type of Stage: Flexible

5941
PIER ONE THEATRE
PO Box 894
Homer, AK 99603
Mailing Address: PO BOX 894, Homer, AK 99603-0894
Phone: 907-235-7333
e-mail: info@pieronetheatre.net
Web Site: www.pieronetheatre.org
Officers:
  President: Nancy Lander
  Vice President: Phil Morin
  Treasurer: Julia Clymer
  Secretary: Mellisa Nill
Management:
  Artistic Director: Lance Petersen

5942
CENTENNIAL HALL CONVENTION CENTER
101 Egan Drive
Juneau, AK 99801
Mailing Address: 101 Egan Drive, Juneau, Alaska 99801
Phone: 907-586-5283
Fax: 907-586-1135
Toll-free: 800-587-2201
e-mail: centennial_hall@ci.juneau.ak.us
Web Site: www.juneau.org/centennial
Management:
  Manager: Wendi Marriott
Founded: 1985
Status: For-Profit, Professional
Seating Capacity: 3,106

5943
KODIAK ARTS COUNCIL
PO Box 1792
Kodiak, AK 99615-1792
Mailing Address: P.O. Box 1792, Kodiak, AK 99615-1792
Phone: 907-486-4782
Fax: 907-486-5591
Toll-free: 800-789-4782
e-mail: kodiak-arts-council@gci.net
Web Site: www.kodiak.org
Officers:
  President: Mike Wall
  VP: Mike Pfeffer
  Secretary: Ginny Shank
  Treasurer: Andrew Ott
Management:
  Executive Director: Nancy Kemp
Utilizes: Artists-in-Residence; Collaborating Artists; Dance Companies; Dancers; Educators; Fine Artists; Guest Accompanists; Guest Directors; Guest Instructors; Guest Lecturers; Guest Musical Directors; Guest Musicians; Guest Soloists; High School Drama; Instructors; Local Artists; Lyricists; Multi Collaborations; Multimedia; Music; New Productions; Original Music Scores; Resident Professionals; Selected Students; Sign Language Translators; Singers; Soloists; Theatre Companies; Touring Companies
Founded: 1963
Status: Non-Profit, Professional
Paid Staff: 3
Paid Artists: 100
Budget: $190,000
Income Sources: Grants; membership; ticket sales
Facility Category: Auditorium
Type of Stage: Proscenium
Stage Dimensions: 40'x35'
Seating Capacity: 750
Year Built: 1986
Cost: 10,000,000

5944
HARRIGAN CANTENNO HALL
330 Harbor Drive
Sitka, AK 99835
Phone: 907-747-3225
Fax: 907-747-8495
e-mail: donk@cityofsitka.com
Web Site: www.cityofsitka.com/government/departments/centennial/index.html
Management:
  Building Manager: Don Kouting
  Building Supervisor: Dave Patt
Founded: 1967
Status: Non-Profit, Non-Professional
Paid Staff: 5
Seating Capacity: 500

5945
VALDEZ CONVENTION AND CIVIC CENTER
212 Chenega Ave.
Valdez, AK 99686
Phone: 907-835-4313
Fax: 907-835-2992
e-mail: plunt@ci.valdez.ak.us
Web Site: www.ci.valdez.ak.us
Management:
  Facility Manager: Pamela Lunt

Arizona

5946
CHANDLER CENTER FOR THE ARTS
250 N Arizona Avenue
Chandler, AZ 85225
Mailing Address: 250 N. Arizona Avenue, Chandler, Arizona 85225
Phone: 480-782-2683
Fax: 480-782-2684
e-mail: info@chandlercenter.org
Web Site: www.chandlercenter.org
Management:
  General Manager: Katrina Pappas
  Development Director: Bill Harrison
  Marketing Coordinator: Judi Johnson
  Development Coordinator: Joe Pastori
  Financial Specialist: Debbie Lawless
  Box Office Supervisor: Patricia Carroll
Status: Non-Profit, Professional
Paid Staff: 15
Seating Capacity: 1,550

5947
PAC AUDITORIUM
Chandler-Gilbert Community College
2626 E Pecos Road
Chandler, AZ 85225-2499
Mailing Address: 2626 East Pecos Road, Chandler, Arizona 85225-2499
Phone: 480-732-7000
Fax: 480-732-7090
e-mail: mary.day@cgcmail.maricopa.edu
Web Site: www.cgc.maricopa.edu
Officers:
  Administrative Secretary: Iris Ishikawa
  President: Linda Lujan
  Vice President, Academic Affairs: William Guerriero
  Vice President, Administrative Serv: Jacalyn Askin
  Vice President, Student Affairs: William Crawford III
Management:
  Director of Research Planning & Dev: Mary Day
Mission: faculty and staff offices, and performance support facilities including costuming and make-up areas, dressing rooms, a full-scale set building shop, storage and classroom space
Founded: 2000
Specialized Field: Vocal and Instrumental Music, Dance, Theater and Musical Theater.
Seating Capacity: 299

5948
RAWHIDE PAVILION & RODEO ARENA
5700 W N Loop Road
Chandler, AZ 85226
Mailing Address: 5700 West North Loop Rd, Chandler, AZ 85226
Phone: 480-502-5600
Fax: 480-502-1301
Toll-free: 800-527-1880
e-mail: info@rawhide.com
Web Site: www.rawhide.com
Management:

FACILITIES / Arizona

President: Jerry Hirche
General Manager: Steve Feld
Entertainment Director: Rob Jensen
Director Sales & Marketing: Floy Kennedy
Operations Manager: Patty Kearney
Founded: 1971
Status: For-Profit, Professional
Paid Staff: 200
Annual Attendance: 960,000
Seating Capacity: 4,500

5949
ARDREY AUDITORIUM
Northern Arizona University
Building 37A
PO Box 6040
Flagstaff, AZ 86011-6040
Mailing Address: NAU Ardrey Auditorium, P. O. Box 6040, Flagstaff, AZ 86011-6
Phone: 928-523-4120
Fax: 928-523-2056
e-mail: Kathleen.Battali@nau.edu
Web Site: www.nau.edu
Management:
    Facility Manager: Kathy Battali
    Technical Director: Janice Gary
    Director-Community Relations: Molly Munger
    Administrative Director: David Isbell
    Fiscal Operations Manager: Kathy McConnell
Mission: performing arts auditorium
Seating Capacity: 1400

5950
ASHURST AUDITORIUM
Northern Arizona University
Building 37A
PO Box 6040
Flagstaff, AZ 86011-6040
Mailing Address: NAU Ardrey Auditorium, P. O. Box 6040, Flagstaff, AZ 86011-6
Phone: 928-523-4120
Fax: 928-523-2056
e-mail: Kathleen.Battali@nau.edu
Web Site: www.nau.edu
Management:
    Facility Manager: Kathy Battali
    Technical Director: Janice Gary
    Administrative Director: David Isbell
    Fiscal Operations Manager: Kathy McConnell
    Director-Community Relations: Molly Munger
Mission: recital stage/banquet hall
Founded: 1918
Specialized Field: Musical perfomances
Seating Capacity: 300

5951
CLIFFORD E WHITE THEATRE
Northern Arizona University
1115 S Knoles Dr
PO Box 6040
Flagstaff, AZ 86011
Mailing Address: Department of Theatre, PO Box 6040, Building 37/Room 120, Fl
Phone: 928-523-3781
Fax: 928-523-5111
e-mail: Theatre@nau.edu
Web Site: www.nau.edu
Officers:
    Department Chair: Kathleen M McGeever
Management:
    Technical Director/Facility Manager: Ben Grohs
    Technical Director: Ben Alexander
    Costume Shop Manager: Nancy Parr
    Professor of Theatre: Robert Yowell
    Assistant Professor: Kate Ellis
Mission: Main Stage shows are held
Founded: 1998
Seating Capacity: 600
Year Remodeled: 1998

5952
COCONINO CENTER FOR THE ARTS
Po Box 296
2300 North Fort Valley Road
Flagstaff, AZ 86002
Mailing Address: PO Box 296, Flagstaff, AZ 86002
Phone: 928-779-2300
Fax: 928-779-7197
e-mail: info@culturalpartners.Org
Web Site: flagartscouncil.org
Officers:
    President: Jean Hockman
    VP: Holly Taylor
    Treasurer: Maxie Inigo
    Secretary: Erin Evans
Management:
    Executive Director: John Tannous
    Office Manager: Jillian Asplund
    Program Coordinator: Damon Taylor
    Marketing Coordinator: Sarah Smallwood
    Box Office Manager: Whitney Packer
    Marketing Assistant: Robyn Shipton
Seating Capacity: 200

5953
J LAWRENCE WALK-UP SKYDOME
Northern Arizona University
PO Box 15096
Flagstaff, AZ 86011
Mailing Address: PO Box 15096, Flagstaff, AZ 86011
Phone: 928-523-3449
Fax: 928-523-7588
e-mail: dave.brown@nau.edu
Web Site: www.nau.edu
Management:
    Skydome Director: Dave Brown
    Athletic Director: Jim Fallis
    Marketing: Ashley Hammerstrom
Founded: 1977

5954
PROCHNOW AUDITORIUM
Northern Arizona University
PO Box 15096
Suite 152
Flagstaff, AZ 86011
Mailing Address: PO Box 15096, Flagstaff, AZ 86011
Phone: 928-523-5638
Fax: 928-523-9219
Web Site: www.nau.edu
Management:
    Operations: Rachel Cole
Mission: University movie theater
Specialized Field: comedians, concerts and weekend movies.
Facility Category: Theatre Hall
Seating Capacity: 900

5955
STUDIO THEATRE
Northern Arizona University
1115 S Knoles Dr
PO Box 6064
Flagstaff, AZ 86011
Mailing Address: Department of Theatre, PO Box 6040, Building 37/Room 120, Fl
Phone: 928-523-3781
Fax: 928-523-5111
e-mail: Theatre@nau.edu
Web Site: www.nau.edu
Officers:
    Department Chair: Kathleen M McGeever
Management:
    Technical Director/Facility Manager: Ben Grohs
    Technical Director: Ben Alexander
    Costume Shop Manager: Nancy Parr
    Professor of Theatre: Robert Yowell
    Assistant Professor: Kate Ellis
Mission: Second Stage shows are held
Founded: 1998
Seating Capacity: 150
Year Built: 1998

5956
GCC PERFORMING ARTS CENTER
Glendale Community College
6000 W Olive Avenue
Glendale, AZ 85302
Mailing Address: 6000 W. Olive Ave., Glendale AZ 85302
Phone: 623-845-3000
e-mail: info@gccaz.edu
Web Site: www2.gccaz.edu
Officers:
    Department Chair: Donald Smith
    Department Secretary: Alyssa Beach
    President: Irene Kovala
Mission: dedicated to producing students capable of succeeding in today's highly competitive professional world

5957
MCC PERFORMING ARTS CENTER
Mohave Community College
1971 Jagerson Avenue
Kingman, AZ 86409
Mailing Address: 1971 Jagerson Ave., Kingman, AZ 86409
Phone: 928-757-4331
Fax: 928-757-0837
Toll-free: 866-664-2832
e-mail: de@mohave.edu
Web Site: www.mohave.edu
Officers:
    President: Julie Bare
    Secretary: Vance Miller
Management:
    Data Analyst: Shelly Castaneda
    Admissions and Recruitment Coordina: Brandi Colbert
    Systems Analyst: Clint Colbert
    Representative: Keisha Cordice
    Operations Specialist: Gloria Cordier
Founded: 1971

5958
MESA CONVENTION CENTER
263 N Center Street
Mesa, AZ 85201
Mailing Address: 263 N Center Street, Mesa, AZ 85201
Phone: 480-644-2178
Fax: 480-644-2617
e-mail: rhett.evans@cityofmesa.org
Web Site: mesaconventioncenter.com
Management:
    Director: J.D. Dockstader
    Sales/Marketing Manager: Dyan Dwyer Seaburg
    Events & Operations Supervisor: Felix Imadiyi
    Sales Manager: Karen Davis
    Events Coordinator: Jose Ramirez

FACILITIES / Arizona

Utilizes: Multimedia
Paid Staff: 23
Facility Category: Amphitheatre
Seating Capacity: 4,200
Year Built: 1978

5959
MESA CONVENTION CENTER-MESA AMPHITHEATRE
263 N Center Street
Mesa, AZ 85201
Mailing Address: 263 N Center Street, Mesa, AZ 85201
Phone: 480-644-2178
Fax: 480-644-2617
e-mail: rhett.evans@cityofmesa.org
Web Site: mesaconventioncenter.com
Management:
  Director: J.D. Dockstader
  Sales/Marketing Manager: Dyan Dwyer Seaburg
  Events & Operations Supervisor: Felix Imadiyi
  Sales Manager: Karen Davis
  Events Coordinator: Jose Ramirez
Founded: 1978
Paid Staff: 80
Type of Stage: Outside Stages
Seating Capacity: 4,200
Rental Contact: Sales Specialist (480) 644-4906 Heather Murray

5960
THEATRE OUTBACK
Mesa Community College
1833 W Southern Avenue
Mesa, AZ 85202
Mailing Address: 1833 West Southern Ave, Mesa, AZ 85202
Phone: 480-461-7000
e-mail: dutson@mc.maricopa.edu
Web Site: www.mesacc.edu
Management:
  Theatre Director: Lyn Dutson
  Director: Gary Stephens
Seating Capacity: 250

5961
PEORIA SPORTS COMPLEX
16101 N 83rd Avenue
Peoria, AZ 85382
Mailing Address: 16101 N. 83rd Avenue, Peoria, AZ 85382
Phone: 623-773-8700
Fax: 623-412-4255
Toll-free: 800-409-1511
e-mail: sportscomplex@peoriaaz.com
Web Site: www.peoriasportscomplex.com
Management:
  Operations Manager: Chris Easom
  Marketing Supervisor: Melissa Melton
Founded: 1994
Status: Non-Profit, Professional
Paid Staff: 30
Volunteer Staff: 486
Annual Attendance: 450,000
Seating Capacity: 18,000
Year Built: 1994

5962
ARIZONA VETERANS MEMORIAL COLISEUM
1826 W McDowell Street
Phoenix, AZ 85007
Mailing Address: 1826 W. McDowell Rd, Phoenix, AZ 85007
Phone: 602-252-6771
Fax: 602-495-1302
e-mail: info@azstatefair.com
Web Site: www.azstatefair.com
Management:
  Executive Director: Don West
  Deputy Director: Wanell Costello
  Marketing Director: Kristi Walsh
  Purchasing Director / Operations Ma: Jack Bell
  Sales Manager: Mary Evanson
  Accountant: Lacy Mason
Facility Category: Arena
Seating Capacity: 14,500

5963
CELEBRITY THEATRE
440 N 32nd Street
Phoenix, AZ 85008
Mailing Address: 440 N 32nd Street, Phoenix AZ 85008
Phone: 602-267-1600
Fax: 602-267-4882
e-mail: gsmanager@celebritytheatre.com
Web Site: www.celebritytheatre.com
Management:
  General Manager: Alycia Klein
  Administration: Steve Gorewitz
  Box Office Manager: Kit Pope
  Production Manager: Kelli Kereny
Founded: 1963
Type of Stage: Proscenium
Seating Capacity: 2,651
Year Built: 1963
Year Remodeled: 1997
Rental Contact: Reed Glick

5964
CHASE FIELD
401 E Jefferson Street
PO Box 2095
Phoenix, AZ 85001
Mailing Address: 401 E. Jefferson St., Phoenix, AZ 85004
Phone: 602-462-6500
Fax: 602-514-8699
Toll-free: 888-777-4664
e-mail: tomt@chasefieldevents.com
Web Site: www.azchasefield.com
Officers:
  President: Derrick Hall
  CFO: Tom Harris
Management:
  Business Operations: Tom Grlfinkel
  Senior Marketing Director: Karina Bohn
  Vice President of Stadium Operation: Tom Tygett
Mission: Baseball
Founded: 1998
Specialized Field: Sports Facility
Status: For-Profit, Professional
Paid Staff: 450
Seating Capacity: 49,500
Year Built: 1998

5965
CRICKET PAVILION
400 West Washington Street
Phoenix, AZ 85003
Mailing Address: 400 West Washington Street, Phoenix, AZ 85003
Phone: 602-379-2800
Fax: 602-379-2801
Web Site: www.livenation.com
Officers:
  Executive Director: Brandon Sirochman
  Director of Sponsor Sales: Sterling Dortch
  Box Office Manager: Deidra Warstler
  Controller: Tonya Riley
Management:
  Premium Seats Director: Shelby Burdick
  Sponsorship Coordinator: Hollie Robbins
  Asst to the Executive Director: Tiffany Green
  Operations Manager: Billy Royal
  Director of Ticket Sales & Service: Linzy Jones
Mission: Concert venue
Performs At: Amphitheater
Affiliations: Live Nation
Annual Attendance: 300,000
Facility Category: Amphitheater
Seating Capacity: 20,000
Rental Contact: Brandon Sirochman

5966
DODGE THEATRE
400 West Washington
Phoenix, AZ 85003
Mailing Address: 400 West Washington Street, Phoenix, AZ 85003
Phone: 602-379-2800
Fax: 602-379-2801
Web Site: www.livenation.com
Officers:
  General Manager: Paige Peterson
  VP Entertainment Services: Ralph Marchetta
  VP Marketing/Advertising: Cathey Moses
  Box Office Manager: Maria Kimaszewski
  Director of Theatre Operations: Maggie Harvey
Management:
  Theatre Events Manager: Bryan White
  Production Manager: Shaun Schultz
Facility Category: Theatre
Type of Stage: Wood
Stage Dimensions: 100x50
Seating Capacity: 5,000
Year Built: 2002
Rental Contact: Ralph Marchetta

5967
ETHINGTON AUDITORIUM
Grand Canyon University
3300 W Camelback Road
Phoenix, AZ 85017-1097
Phone: 602-589-2482
Fax: 602-589-2492
Toll-free: 800-800-9776
Management:
  Chairperson Music Department: Dr. Sheila Corley
  Piano Area Coordinator: Dr. Judy Lively
  Instrumental Area Coordinator: Joe Lloyd
  Choral Activities: Dr. Keith Whitlock
  Director Vocal Activities: Nathan Wight
Budget: $10,000
Seating Capacity: 300
Rental Contact: Nathan Wight

5968
JOBING.COM ARENA
9400 W Maryland
Phoenix, AZ 85303
Phone: 623-772-3200
Fax: 623-772-3201
e-mail: guest.services@jobingarena.com
Web Site: www.jobingarena.com.com
Facility Category: Arena
Seating Capacity: 20,000

FACILITIES / Arizona

5969
LEWIS AUDITORIUM
203 West Adams Street
Phoenix, AZ 85003
Phone: 602-252-9678
Fax: 602-252-1223
e-mail: phoenix.convention.center@phoenix.gov
Web Site: www.phoenixconventioncenter.com
Management:
  Executive Director: Joan Weil
  Director: Robert Allen
  Facilities Department Director: Jay Green
Mission: The 1,364-seat Orpheum audience chamber—now known as the Lewis Auditorium, dedicated to Jewell and Delbert Lewis and family—has 1,062 seats on orchestra level, 302 in the balcony.
Founded: 1929
Paid Staff: 3

5970
PHOENIX CONVENTION CENTER - BALLROOMS
100 N 3rd Street
Phoenix, AZ 85004
Mailing Address: 100 N. 3rd Street, Phoenix, Arizona 85004
Phone: 602-262-6225
Fax: 602-495-3642
Toll-free: 800-282-4842
e-mail: phoenix.convention.center@phoenix.gov
Web Site: www.phoenixconvention
Management:
  Director: Jay Green
  Marketing Director: Kevin Hill
  Event Manager: Caron Bernard
  Assistant Sales Director: Diana McCullough
Status: Non-Profit, Non-Professional
Volunteer Staff: 120
Seating Capacity: 8,210

5971
PHOENIX STAGES
203 West Adams Street
Phoenix, AZ 85003
Phone: 602-534-4874
Fax: 602-534-5622
e-mail: phoenix.convention.center@phoenix.gov
Web Site: www.phoenixconventioncenter.com
Management:
  Director: Jay Green
  Assistant Director: Tracey Short
  Marketing Director: Kevin Hill
  Sales Director: Diane McCullough
  Music Director: Hermann Michael
Mission: Division of the city of Phoenix which manages the Lewis Auditorium and Symphony Hall.
Founded: 1996
Status: Non-Profit, Professional
Paid Staff: 50
Volunteer Staff: 500

5972
PVCC CENTER FOR THE PERFORMING ARTS
Paradise Valley Community College
Division Of Fine & Performing Arts
18401 North 32nd Street
Phoenix, AZ 85032
Mailing Address: Center for the Performing Arts, Paradise Valley Community Co
Phone: 602-787-6500
e-mail: Julia.devous@pvmail.maricopa.edu
Web Site: www.pvc.maricopa.edu
Officers:
  Division Chair: Christopher Scinto
  President: Mary Kay Kickles PhD
  Division Secretary: Daral Alonzo
Management:
  Director Theatre: Alan Tonget
  Director of Development and Communi: Julia Devous
Mission: PAC will now provide a showplace for theater, music, dance, literature, and the visual arts.
Founded: 2005
Specialized Field: music, theater, dance productions and film presentations. In addition, the lobby space serves as an art gallery
Seating Capacity: 300
Architect: Westlake Reed Leskosky
Cost: $7.8 million

5973
SMCC PERFORMING ARTS CENTER
South Mountain Community College
7050 S. 24th Street
South Mountain Community College
Phoenix, AZ 85042
Mailing Address: 7050 South 24th Street, Phoenix, Arizona 85042
Phone: 602-243-8000
Fax: 602-243-8329
e-mail: students@southmountaincc.edu
Web Site: www.southmountaincc.edu
Officers:
  President: Shari L. Olson
Management:
  Theatre Faculty: Julie Holston
Mission: SMCC offers a full range of theatre classes to meet your needs, whether you plan to major in theatre at the university level or simply take theatre classes on the side while pursuing another major. Our program offers a wide variety of courses to give you both the broad background you need in theatre, as well as the focused study of your artistic and/or technical skills.
Type of Stage: Auditorium
Seating Capacity: 350

5974
SMCC STUDIO THEATRE
South Mountain Community College
7050 S. 24th Street
South Mountain Community College
Phoenix, AZ 85042
Mailing Address: 7050 South 24th Street, Phoenix, Arizona 85042
Phone: 602-243-8000
Fax: 602-243-8329
e-mail: students@southmountaincc.edu
Web Site: www.southmountaincc.edu
Officers:
  President: Shari L. Olson
Management:
  Theatre Faculty: Julie Holston
Mission: SMCC offers a full range of theatre classes to meet your needs, whether you plan to major in theatre at the university level or simply take theatre classes on the side while pursuing another major. Our program offers a wide variety of courses to give you both the broad background you need in theatre, as well as the focused study of your artistic and/or technical skills.
Type of Stage: Black Box
Seating Capacity: 100

5975
PHOENIX CONVENTION CENTER - SYMPHONY HALL
203 West Adams Street
Phoenix, AZ 85003
Phone: 602-534-4874
Fax: 602-534-5622
e-mail: phoenix.convention.center@phoenix.gov
Web Site: www.phoenixconventioncenter.com
Management:
  Director: Jay Green
  Assistant Director: Tracey Scott
  Marketing Director: Kevin Hill
  Information Officer/Symphony Hall: Sina Matthes
  Sales Director: Diane McCullough
Founded: 1972
Seating Capacity: 2,387

5976
U S AIRWAYS CENTER
201 East Jefferson Street
PO Box 433
Phoenix, AZ 85004
Mailing Address: PO Box 433, Phoenix, AZ 85001
Phone: 602-379-2000
Fax: 602-379-2002
e-mail: webmaster@phxses.com
Web Site: www.usairwayscenter.com
Officers:
  President: Jerry Cooangelo
Management:
  Executive Director: Paige Peterson
  Director Ticket Operations: John Walker
  Sales Manager: Chris Montgomery
Founded: 1992
Status: For-Profit, Professional

5977
JOHN PAUL THEATRE
Phoenix College
1202 W. Thomas Road
Phoenix,, AZ 85013
Mailing Address: 1202 W. Thomas Road, Phoenix, AZ 85013
Phone: 602-285-7500
Fax: 602-285-7309
e-mail: geoffrey.eroe@pcmail.maricopa.edu
Web Site: www.phoenixcollege.edu
Officers:
  Department Chair: Liz O'Brien
  President: Anna Solley EdD
Management:
  Coordinator Performing Arts Center: Gary Imel
  club advisor: Geof Eroe
Mission: campus club for students interested in theatre. The Phoenix College Theatre & Film Department, one of the oldest and most respected theatre programs in Arizona, offers students the opportunity to earn an undergraduate AA transferable degree with an emphasis in acting, directing, technical work and design.
Type of Stage: Modified Thrust
Seating Capacity: 300

5978
YAVAPAI COLLEGE PERFORMANCE HALL
Yavapai College
1100 East Sheldon
Prescott, AZ 86301
Mailing Address: 1100 E Sheldon Avenue, Prescott AZ, 86301
Phone: 928-776-2000

FACILITIES / Arizona

Fax: 520-776-2032
Toll-free: 877-928-4253
Web Site: www.ycpac.com
Management:
   Community Events Mamager: Debbie McCasland
Mission: To present a broad variety of music, dance and theatre.
Founded: 1976
Paid Staff: 4
Paid Artists: 300
Income Sources: Ticket Sales; Grants
Annual Attendance: 30,000
Facility Category: Theater
Type of Stage: Proscenium; Thurst
Stage Dimensions: 40'x50'
Seating Capacity: 1100
Year Built: 1992
Cost: $6.5 Million
Rental Contact: Garry Charter

5979
SCOTTSDALE CENTER FOR THE PERFORMING ARTS
7380 E 2nd Street
Scottsdale, AZ 85251
Mailing Address: 7380 E. 2nd Street, Scottsdale, AZ 85251
Phone: 480-994-2787
Fax: 480-874-4699
e-mail: info@sccarts.org
Web Site: www.scottsdaleperformingarts.org
Officers:
   Chair: Laura R. Grafman
   Accounting Coordinator: Chris Keal
   Human Resource Manager: Valerie James
   Director of Retail Operations: Janice Bartczak
   Facility Rentals Manager: Andrea Anderson
   Director of Marketing: Ted Ciccone
   Public Relations Manager: William Thompson
Utilizes: Artists-in-Residence; Dance Companies; Dancers; Educators; Guest Soloists; Multimedia; Student Interns; Theatre Companies
Founded: 1975
Specialized Field: Performing Arts
Status: Non-Profit, Professional
Paid Staff: 60
Annual Attendance: 300,000
Facility Category: Multi-Disciplinary
Type of Stage: Proscenium/Thrust
Seating Capacity: 853
Year Built: 1975
Year Remodeled: 2009
Rental Contact: Kasey Croxton

5980
SCOTTSDALE COMMUNITY COLLEGE PERFORMING ARTS CENTER
9000 East Chaparral
Scottsdale, AZ 85256-2626
Mailing Address: 9000 E. Chaparral Road Scottsdale, AZ 85256
Phone: 480-423-6000
Fax: 480-423-6365
Web Site: www.scottsdalecc.edu
Management:
   Theatre Arts Director: Kimb Williamson
   Associate Theatre Arts Director: Elaine Moe
   President: Jan L. Gehler. Ed.D
Founded: 1970

5981
SEDONA CULTURAL PARK
250 Cultural Park Place
Sedona, AZ 86336
Phone: 928-282-0747
Fax: 928-220-1633
Web Site: www.sedonaculturalpark.org
Officers:
   Production Director: Dallas Taylor
   Operations Director: Lisa Rhodes
Seating Capacity: 5,000

5982
BUENA PERFORMING ARTS CENTER
5225 Buena School Blvd.
Sierra Vista, AZ 85635
Mailing Address: 5225 Buena School Blvd., Sierra Vista, AZ 85635
Phone: 520-515-2820
Fax: 520-515-2874
e-mail: msneary@ci.sierra-vista.az.us
Web Site: www.buenapac.org
Management:
   Community Managers: Rick Klein
   Community Managers: Margaret Klein
   Assistant Manager: Duane Chun
   Production Supervisor: Carrie Duerk
Status: Professional
Budget: $35,000-$60,000
Type of Stage: Flexible
Seating Capacity: 1,366

5983
SIERRA VISTA THEATRE HALL
Cochise College
Cochise College
901 North Colombo Avenue
Sierra Vista, AZ 85635-2315
Mailing Address: 901 North Colombo Avenue, Sierra Vista, AZ 85635-2317
Phone: 520-515-0500
Toll-free: 800-966-7943
e-mail: contact@cochise.edu
Web Site: www.cochise.edu
Management:
   Manager: M David Meeker
   Cultural/Music Events Coordinator: Carol Rivera
   Director Cultural Events: Marc C Bellassai
   Creative Services Dir, Marketing/Cr: Colin Boyd
Mission: as a source of personal growth and selfexpression, to fulfill general education requirements for associate's or baccalaureate degrees, to successfully transfer credit to four-year institutions.
Founded: 1961
Specialized Field: music, theater, and visual arts

5984
SUNDOME CENTER
19403 RH Johnson Blvd, Sun City West, AZ, USA
19403 RH Johnson Boulevard
Sun City West, AZ 85375
Phone: 623-584-3118
Fax: 623-584-7947
e-mail: SMOKEY.RENEHAN@asu.edu
Web Site: www.asusundome.com
Management:
   Director: M Smokey Renehan
   Technical Director: Rob Neyman
   Event / Rental Coordinator: Melissa Schwartz
Paid Staff: 35
Volunteer Staff: 250
Paid Artists: 35
Non-paid Artists: 60
Affiliations: Arizona State University; APAP; WAA
Annual Attendance: 300,000
Facility Category: Performing Arts
Type of Stage: Proscenium
Seating Capacity: 7036
Year Built: 1978
Rental Contact: Melissa Schwartz

5985
GALVIN PLAYHOUSE
Arizona State University
Herberger College of Fine Arts
PO Box 872002
Tempe, AZ 85287-2002
Mailing Address: Herberger College of Fine Arts, PO Box 872002, Tempe, AZ 852
Phone: 480-965-5337
Fax: 480-965-5351
e-mail: theatre@asu.edu
Web Site: theatrefilm.asu.edu
Management:
   Technical Director: Stephanie Armenta
   Business Manager: Cynthia Noldy
   Student Affairs Coordinator: Joya Scott
   Program Coordinator: John Tang
Mission: To educate imaginative, knowledgeable, skilled, and responsible artists, teachers, scholars, audience members, and advocates for the future of theatre and film arts.
Type of Stage: Proscenium
Stage Dimensions: 101' x 52'10
Orchestra Pit: Y
Seating Capacity: 500

5986
GAMMAGE AUDITORIUM
Arizona State University
Corner of Mill Avenue & Apache Boulevard
Tempe, AZ 85287
Mailing Address: PO Box 870105, Tempe, AZ 85287-0105
Phone: 480-965-5062
Fax: 480-965-3583
e-mail: boxoffice@asugammage.com
Web Site: www.asugammage.com
Management:
   Executive Director Public Events: Colleen Jennings-Roggensack
   Senior Director Operations: Terri Cranmer
   Senior Director of Operations: Terri Cranmer
   Events Coordinator: Larry Kovac
   Director of Audience Services: Karie Lurie
Founded: 1962
Type of Stage: Concert Stage; Flexible
Seating Capacity: 3,000

5987
LYCEUM THEATRE
Arizona State University
Herberger College of Fine Arts
PO Box 872002
Tempe, AZ 85287-2002
Mailing Address: Herberger College of Fine Arts, PO Box 872002, Tempe, AZ 852
Phone: 480-965-5337
Fax: 480-965-5351
e-mail: theatre@asu.edu
Web Site: theatrefilm.asu.edu
Management:
   Technical Director: Stephanie Armenta
   Business Manager: Cynthia Noldy
   Student Affairs Coordinator: Joya Scott
   Program Coordinator: John Tang

FACILITIES / Arizona

Mission: To educate imaginative, knowledgeable, skilled, and responsible artists, teachers, scholars, audience members, and advocates for the future of theatre and film arts.
Type of Stage: Proscenium
Seating Capacity: 164
Year Built: 1917

5988
MARQUEE THEATRE
730 North Mill Avenue
Tempe, AZ 85281
Phone: 480-829-1300
Fax: 480-829-1552
e-mail: orion@luckymanonline.com
Web Site: www.luckymanonline.com
Officers:
  Owner: Tom LaPenna
  GM: Mike Lee
  Talent Buyer: Will Anderson
  Owner/ Event Booking: Tom LaPenna
Specialized Field: Music concerts
Facility Category: Concert Hall
Seating Capacity: 1,001

5989
PRISM THEATRE
Arizona State University
Herberger College of Fine Arts
PO Box 872002
Tempe, AZ 85287-2002
Mailing Address: Herberger College of Fine Arts, PO Box 872002, Tempe, AZ 852
Phone: 480-965-5337
Fax: 480-965-5351
e-mail: theatre@asu.edu
Web Site: theatrefilm.asu.edu
Management:
  Technical Director: Stephanie Armenta
  Business Manager: Cynthia Noldy
  Student Affairs Coordinator: Joya Scott
  Program Coordinator: John Tang
Mission: To educate imaginative, knowledgeable, skilled, and responsible artists, teachers, scholars, audience members, and advocates for the future of theatre and film arts.
Type of Stage: Flexible Black Box
Seating Capacity: 74

5990
SUN DEVIL STADIUM
500 East Stadium Drive
PO Box 872405
Tempe, AZ 85287-2505
Mailing Address: 500 E. Veterans Way, Tempe, AZ 85287-2505
Phone: 480-965-3482
Fax: 480-965-8154
Toll-free: 888-786-3857
e-mail: athletics.director@asu.edu
Web Site: www.thesundevils.com
Management:
  Vice President University Athletics: Lisa Love
  Asst Athletic Director/Operations: Bill Givens
  Marketing Manager: Mike Bosewell
  Athletics Business Manager: Brian Milhorn
  Events Coordintor: Tyrone Figaro
Founded: 1968
Specialized Field: Facility
Seating Capacity: 74,000

5991
FINE ARTS CENTER AUDITORIUM
Eastern Arizona College
615 N. Stadium Avenue
Thatcher, AZ 85552
Mailing Address: 615 N Stadium Ave, Thatcher, AZ 85552
Phone: 928-428-8472
Toll-free: 800-678-3808
e-mail: webmaster@eac.edu
Web Site: www.eac.edu
Officers:
  President: Mark Bryce
  Chairman: Richard W. Mattice
  Secretary: Lois Ann Moody
Management:
  Director, Marketing and PR: Todd Haynie
  Theatre Arts Faculty: Rice John
Mission: Eastern Arizona College boasts one of the most active and distinguished Fine Arts programs in Arizona. Opportunities to showcase your talents abound here, and class credits are fully transferable to universities.
Founded: 1972
Specialized Field: Music and in Theatre and Cinematic Arts
Seating Capacity: 960

5992
LEE LITTLE THEATRE
Eastern Arizona College
615 N. Stadium Avenue
Thatcher, AZ 85552
Mailing Address: 615 N Stadium Ave, Thatcher, AZ 85552
Phone: 928-428-8472
Toll-free: 800-678-3808
e-mail: webmaster@eac.edu
Web Site: www.eac.edu
Officers:
  President: Mark Bryce
  Chairman: Richard W. Mattice
  Secretary: Lois Ann Moody
Management:
  Director, Marketing and PR: Todd Haynie
  Theatre Arts Faculty: Rice John
Mission: Eastern Arizona College boasts one of the most active and distinguished Fine Arts programs in Arizona. Opportunities to showcase your talents abound here, and class credits are fully transferable to universities.
Seating Capacity: 305

5993
DINE COLLEGE
One Circle Drive
Route 12
Tsaile, AZ 86556
Phone: 928-724-6609
Fax: 928-724-6613
e-mail: info@dinecollege.edu
Web Site: www.dinecollege.edu
Officers:
  Vice President: Laurence Gishey
  Treasurer: Loretta Draper
  Secretary: Theresa Hatathlie
Management:
  President: Maggie George
Founded: 1968
Status: Non-Profit, Professional

5994
TUBAC CENTER OF THE ARTS
9 Plaza Road
PO Box 1911
Tubac, AZ 85646
Mailing Address: PO Box 1911, Tubac, AZ 85646
Phone: 520-398-2371
Fax: 520-398-9511
Web Site: www.tubacarts.org
Officers:
  President: Mike Jacoby
  Vice President: Kim Roseman
  Treasurer: Tom Potter
  Secretary: Dennis Eshleman
Management:
  Marketing & Exhibitions Manager: Karon Leigh
  Education Coordinator: Paula Kim
  Weekend Supervisor: Linda Patmore
  Executive Director: Karin Topping
  Gallery Shop Manager: Bonnie Jaus
Utilizes: Actors; Collaborations; Commissioned Music; Dance Companies; Educators; Fine Artists; Five Seasonal Concerts; Guest Accompanists; Guest Ensembles; Guest Soloists; Guild Activities; High School Drama; Instructors; Local Artists; Multimedia; Original Music Scores; Playwrights; Sign Language Translators; Soloists; Special Technical Talent
Founded: 1972
Status: Non-Profit, Professional
Paid Staff: 4
Volunteer Staff: 200
Budget: $10,000
Performs At: Auditorium
Annual Attendance: 36,000
Facility Category: Regional Art Center
Type of Stage: Flexible
Seating Capacity: 175
Year Built: 1972
Year Remodeled: 1999

5995
ARIZONA STADIUM
University of Arizona
Tucson, AZ 85721
Mailing Address: The University of Arizona Athletics, McKale Center, 1 Nation
Phone: 520-621-2287
Fax: 520-621-2419
Toll-free: 800-452-2287
e-mail: schev@arizona.edu
Web Site: www.arizcats.com
Management:
  President: Peter Likens
  Artistic Director: Jim Livengood
  Director of Marketing and Licensing: Shawn Chevreux
  Assistant Dirctor of Marketing/Lice: Alixe Holcomb
Mission: Football
Founded: 1928
Specialized Field: Sports Facility
Status: For-Profit, Professional
Affiliations: NCAA, Home to University of Arizona athletics, football season games
Seating Capacity: 56,136
Year Built: 1979

5996
CENTENNIAL HALL
University of Arizona
1020 East University Boulevard
Tucson, AZ 85721-0029

FACILITIES / Arizona

Mailing Address: 1020 E. University Blvd., P.O. Box 210029, Tucson, AZ 85721-
Phone: 520-621-3341
Fax: 520-621-8991
e-mail: uapresents@arizona.edu
Web Site: www.uapresents.org
Management:
  Executive Director: Charles Tennes
  Development/Managing Director: Itzik Becher
  Marketing Director: Jo Alenson
  Programming Development Coordinator: Staci Santa
  Information Technology Manager: Phil McElfresh
  Production Manager: Gary Lotze
  Artist Relations Coordinator: Aspen Green
Seating Capacity: 2,456

5997
CROWDER HALL
University of Arizona
1017 N Olive Rd.
Tucson, AZ 85721-0004
Mailing Address: College of Fine Arts, PO Box 210004
Phone: 520-621-1302
Fax: 520-621-1307
e-mail: sevigny@u.arizona.edu
Web Site: cfa.arizona.edu
Officers:
  Dean: Jory Hancock
Management:
  Senior Director of Development: Ellen E. Bussing
  Accountant: Steven Froehlich
  Program Coordinator: Brittany K Churchill
Mission: Faculty and student music and dance recitals
Utilizes: Collaborations; Guest Accompanists; Guest Companies; Guest Composers; Guest Directors; Guest Ensembles; Guest Instructors; Guest Musical Directors; Guest Musicians; Guest Soloists; High School Drama; Instructors; Multimedia; Sign Language Translators; Singers; Soloists
Founded: 1934
Paid Staff: 2
Performs At: Recital Hall
Seating Capacity: 544

5998
FOX TUCSON THEATRE
17 W. Congress St.
Tucson, AZ 85701
Mailing Address: Po Box 1008
Phone: 520-624-1515
Fax: 520-624-5855
e-mail: foxinfo@foxtucsontheatre.org
Web Site: www.foxtucsontheatre.org
Officers:
  Board Chairman: Bill Holmes
  Vice President: Renee Morton
  Treasurer: Kevin Yeanoplos
  Secretary: Dan Cavanagh
Management:
  Executive Director: Craig Sumberg
  Accounting & Finance Manager: Cathie Bacia
  Box Office Manager: Rachel Miranda Wedig
  House Manager: Tamara Mack
  Development Assistant: Kim McDowell
Facility Category: Theatre
Seating Capacity: 1164

5999
HI CORBETT FIELD
3400 East Camino Campestre
Tucson, AZ 85716
Mailing Address: Colorado Rockies, Coors Field, 2001 Blake Street, Denver, CO
Phone: 520-327-2621
Toll-free: 520-327-2371
Web Site: http://mlb.mlb.com/NASApp/mlb/col/news/spring_training_ballpark.jsp
Officers:
  Chairman & Chief Executive Officer: Charles K Monfort
  Vice Chairman: Richard L Monfort
  Executive Vice Presidnet/Gen. Mgr.: Daniel J O'Dowd
  SVP/CFO and General Counsel: Harold R Roth
Management:
  Director Baseball Operations: Jeff Bridich
  Business Operations: Donna Reed
  Director Medical Operations: Tom Probst
  Engineering/Facility Asst Director: James Wiener
  AVP Commmunications/PR: Irma Thumin
Mission: Baseball
Specialized Field: Sports Facility
Seating Capacity: 8,665

6000
HOLSCLAW RECITAL HALL
University of Arizona
Theatre Arts, Drama Bldg, Room 239
1017 N Olive Rd.
Tucson, AZ 85721-0004
Mailing Address: P.O. Box 210004, 1017 N Olive Rd, Music Bldg, Rm 111, Tucson
Phone: 520-621-1302
Fax: 520-621-1307
e-mail: finearts@email.arizona.edu
Web Site: cfa.arizona.edu
Officers:
  Dean: Jory Hancock
Management:
  Senior Director of Development: Ellen E. Bussing
  Accountant: Steven Froehlich
  Program Coordinator: Brittany K Churchill
Mission: The mission of the School of Theatre Arts at the University of Arizona is to provide professional training and education leading to careers in acting, musical theatre, theatre design and technology, theatre education and outreach, and theatre history and dramaturgy. The School is dedicated to educating students through a highly visible production program enriching the university and Tucson communities.
Specialized Field: Organ chamber music hall
Seating Capacity: 204

6001
MCKALE MEMORIAL CENTER
University of Arizona Athletics
1721 E Enke Dr
Tucson, AZ 85721
Mailing Address: 1721 E Enke Dr, Tucson, AZ 85721
Phone: 520-621-2200
Fax: 520-621-9690
e-mail: schev@arizona.edu
Web Site: www.arizona.edu
Management:
  Athletics Director: Jim Livengood
  Community Relations: Phoebe Chalk
  Operations: Suzy Mason
  Sales Director: Galen Hungate
  Information Technology: Greg Shaffer
Specialized Field: Sports Facility
Seating Capacity: 20,000

6002
MUSIC RECITAL HALL
Pima Community College
4905 E. Broadway Blvd.
Tucson, AZ 85709-1010
Mailing Address: 4905 E. Broadway Blvd., Tucson, AZ 85709-1010
Phone: 520-206-4500
Fax: 520-206-6719
e-mail: infocenter@pima.edu
Web Site: www.pima.edu
Officers:
  Chancellor: Roy Flores PhD
Mission: The Theatre Arts program is house in the Center for the Arts at the West Campus. The program provides extensive experience and training in performance and all aspects of theatre production.
Specialized Field: Small-Group or Solo Performances, Readings and Lectures.
Type of Stage: Curved Amphitheater-Style
Seating Capacity: 75-120

6003
OLD TUCSON STUDIOS
201 South Kinney Road
Tucson, AZ 85735
Mailing Address: 201 S. Kinney Road, Tucson, AZ, 85735
Phone: 520-883-0100
Fax: 520-578-1269
e-mail: GuestRelations@OldTucson.com
Web Site: www.oldtucson.com
Officers:
  Marketing Manager: Jeff Anderson
Facility Category: Film Studio Set
Seating Capacity: 4,000

6004
TEMPLE OF MUSIC & ART
343 S. Scott Avenue
Tucson, AZ 85701
Mailing Address: 343 S. Scott Avenue, PO Box 1631, Tucson AZ, 8570
Phone: 520-884-8210
Fax: 520-628-9129
e-mail: info@arizonatheatre.org
Web Site: www.arizonatheatre.org
Officers:
  Facilities Manager: Eileen Bagnall
  President: Robert Glaser
  Chairman: Michael Seiden
  Vice President: Beth A. Bank
  Treasurer: Eileen W. Lamse
Management:
  Artistic Director: David Ira Goldstein
  Associate Artistic Director: Stephen Wrentmore
  Artistic Associate: Tim Toothman
  Company Manager: Robyn Lambert
  Managing Director: Jessica Andrews
Founded: 1927
Opened: 1990
Facility Category: Theatre
Seating Capacity: 623

6005
TUCSON CONVENTION CENTER - ARENA
260 South Church Avenue
Tucson, AZ 85701
Mailing Address: 260 S. Church Ave., Tucson, AZ 85701
Phone: 520-791-4101

All listings are in alphabetical order by state, then city, then organization within the city.

FACILITIES / Arizona

Fax: 520-791-5572
e-mail: richard.singer@tucsonaz.gov
Web Site: www.tucsonaz.gov
Management:
   Director: Richard Singer
   General Manager: Rich Henkel
   Administration: Elizabeth O'Hara Walker
   Marketing/Sales Director: Kate Breck Calhoun
   Event Manager: Andrew Brown
Mission: The Tucson Arena floor can also be utilized as 33,750 square feet of exhibit or banquet space.
Founded: 1981
Paid Staff: 100
Facility Category: Arena
Type of Stage: Flexible
Seating Capacity: 9,505
Year Built: 1971
Rental Contact: Marketing/Sales Director Kate Breck Calhoun

6006
TUCSON CONVENTION CENTER - EXHIBITION HALL
260 South Church Avenue
Tucson, AZ 85701
Mailing Address: 260 S. Church Ave., Tucson, AZ 85701
Phone: 520-791-4101
Fax: 520-791-5572
e-mail: richard.singer@tucsonaz.gov
Web Site: www.tucsonaz.gov
Management:
   Director: Richard Singer
   General Manager: Rich Henkel
   Event Manager: Andrew Brown
   Marketing/Sales Director: Kate Breck Calhoun
   Administration: Elizabeth O'Hara Walker
Mission: The Tucson Convention Center has a total of five (5) Exhibit Hall spaces that will provide 147,690 square feet of contiguous floor space. Each space is equipped with wireless Internet, electrical outlets, concession stands and load-in doors.
Founded: 1981
Paid Staff: 100
Facility Category: Exhibition Hall
Year Built: 1981
Rental Contact: Marketing/Sales Director Kate Breck Calhoun

6007
TUCSON CONVENTION CENTER - LEO RICH THEATRE
260 South Church Avenue
Tucson, AZ 85701
Mailing Address: 260 S. Church Ave., Tucson, AZ 85701
Phone: 520-791-4101
Fax: 520-791-5572
e-mail: richard.singer@tucsonaz.gov
Web Site: www.tucsonaz.gov
Management:
   Director: Richard Singer
   General Manager: Rich Henkel
   Event Manager: Andrew Brown
   Markting/Sales Director: Kate Breck Calhoun
   Administration: Elizabeth O'Hara Walker
Founded: 1981
Paid Staff: 100
Type of Stage: Proscenium
Seating Capacity: 501
Rental Contact: Marketing/Sales Director Kate Breck Calhoun

6008
TUCSON CONVENTION CENTER - MUSIC HALL
260 South Church Avenue
Tucson, AZ 85701
Mailing Address: 260 S. Church Ave., Tucson, AZ 85701
Phone: 520-791-4101
Fax: 520-791-5572
e-mail: richard.singer@tucsonaz.gov
Web Site: www.tucsonaz.gov
Management:
   Director: Richard Singer
   General Manager: Rich Henkel
   Events Manager: Andrew Brown
   Marketing/Sales Director: Kate Breck Calhoun
   Administration: Elizabeth O'Hara Walker
Mission: The auditorium has a permanent seating capacity of 2277 (1489 - orchestra level, 386 - lower balcony, 402 - upper balcony). An additional 77 seats may be added in the orchestra pit when lowered to house level bringing the total seating capacity to 2,354.
Founded: 1981
Paid Staff: 100
Facility Category: Music Hall
Type of Stage: Concert Stage
Seating Capacity: 2,354
Rental Contact: Marketing/Sales Director Kate Breck Calhoun

6009
TUCSON ELECTRIC PARK
2500 East Ajo Way
Tucson, AZ 85713
Mailing Address: 2500 East Ajo Way, Tucson, AZ 85713
Phone: 520-434-1000
Fax: 520-434-1159
e-mail: info@kinosportscomplex.com
Web Site: www.kinosportscomplex.com
Officers:
   Director: Kate O'Rielly
   Stadium Business Manager: Tom Taylor
   President: Mike Feder
Management:
   Genral Manager: Mike Feder
Facility Category: Sports Arena
Seating Capacity: 17,500

6010
UAPRESENTS CENTENNIAL HALL
1020 E University Boulevard
PO Box 210029
Tucson, AZ 85721-0029
Mailing Address: 1020 E. University Blvd., P.O. Box 210029, Tucson, AZ 85721-
Phone: 520-621-3341
Fax: 520-621-8991
e-mail: uapresents@arizona.edu
Web Site: www.uapresents.org
Management:
   Executive Director: Charles Tennes
   Development/Managing Director: Itzik Becher
   Marketing Director: Jo Alenson
   Programming Development Coordinator: Staci Santa
   Information Technology Manager: Phil McElfresh
   Production Manager: Gary Lotze
   Artist Relations Coordinator: Aspen Green
Specialized Field: Theater

6011
ARIZONA WESTERN COLLEGE AMPHITHEATRE
2020 S Avenue 8 E
PO Box 929
Yuma, AZ 85366
Mailing Address: 2020 S. Avenue 8E, PO Box 929, Yuma, AZ 85365
Phone: 928-317-6000
Fax: 928-344-7730
Toll-free: 888-293-0392
e-mail: deborah.leal@azwestern.edu
Web Site: www.azwestern.edu
Management:
   President: Donald Schoening
   Theatre Department: Forrest A Straley
   Senior Secretary: Lupe Fuentes
   Field Coordinator: Paige C Anderson
   Financial Aid Technician: Angelica M. Audelo
Founded: 1963
Status: For-Profit, Professional
Budget: $60,000-$150,000
Seating Capacity: 600

6012
DESERT SUN STADIUM
1440 Desert Hills Drive
Yuma, AZ 85365
Phone: 928-373-5040
Fax: 928-344-9121
e-mail: ycc@ci.yuma.az.us
Web Site: www.yumaaz.gov
Officers:
   Events/Booking Supervisor: Kathy Anderson
   Box Office Manager: Stephanie McMillin
   Operations Supervisor: Joe Baro
Founded: 1970
Paid Staff: 12
Volunteer Staff: 25
Income Sources: 2% Hospitality Tax; City Of Yuma
Affiliations: Owned And Operated By The City Of Yuma
Facility Category: Outdoor Stadium
Type of Stage: Portable
Stage Dimensions: varies depending on event needs
Seating Capacity: 6,000
Year Built: 1970
Rental Contact: Kathy Anderson

6013
RAY KROC BASEBALL COMPLEX
Yuma Civic Center
1440 Desert Hills Drive
Yuma, AZ 85365
Phone: 928-344-3800
Fax: 928-344-9121
e-mail: ycc@ci.yuma.az.us
Web Site: www.yumaconventioncenter.com/complex_facilities.htm
Management:
   Director: Anthony Guerrera
   Complex Supervisor: Joel Hubbard
   Marketing Rep: Mary Jane Chambers
   Booking Manager: Becky Franks
Seating Capacity: 6,590

6014
YUMA CIVIC CENTER
1440 W Desert Hills Drive
Yuma, AZ 85365
Mailing Address: 1440 W Desert Hills Drive, Yuma, AZ 85365
Phone: 928-373-5040

FACILITIES / Arkansas

Fax: 928-344-9121
e-mail: ycc@ci.yuma.az.us
Web Site: www.yumaconventioncenter.com
Management:
  Park and Recreation Director: Becky Chavez
  Assistant Director: Roberta Ukura
  Events/Booking Supervisor: Kathy Anderson
Utilizes: Instructors; Multimedia; Sign Language Translators; Theatre Companies
Founded: 1973
Status: For-Profit, Non-Professional
Paid Staff: 20
Budget: $1.2 million
Income Sources: Earned Revenue, Hospitality Tax
Affiliations: IAAM, MPI, SGMP
Type of Stage: Portable
Stage Dimensions: 30x40
Seating Capacity: 2,000
Year Built: 1973
Cost: 900

Arkansas

6015
JONES PERFORMING ARTS CENTER
Ouachita Baptist University
410 Ouachita Street
Arkadelphia, AR 71998
Mailing Address: 410 Ouachita St., Arkadelphia, AR 71998
Phone: 870-245-5000
Fax: 870-245-5500
Toll-free: 800-DIA- OBU
e-mail: hosclaws@.obu.edu
Web Site: www.obu.edu/thearts
Officers:
  President: Rex M. Horne
Management:
  Department Chair: Scott Holsclaw
  Production Manager Technical Direct: Joey Licklider
Mission: Ouachita's theatre arts department provides the students with practical experience which is enhanced by classroom instruction. Though rehearsals and performance, students engage in the collaborative process and continue to develop their skills under faculty direction.
Specialized Field: chapel, music events, campus social club shows, and touring productions/concerts
Type of Stage: Proscenium
Stage Dimensions: 54' X 28'
Seating Capacity: 1500

6016
OUACHITA BAPTIST UNIVERSITY HARVEY & BERNICE JONES PERFORMING ARTS CENTER
410 Ouachita Street
Arkadelphia, AR 71998
Mailing Address: 410 Ouachita St., Arkadelphia, AR 71998
Phone: 870-245-5000
Fax: 870-245-5500
Toll-free: 800-DIA- OBU
Web Site: www.obu.edu/music/facilities.asp
Officers:
  President: Rex M. Horne
Management:
  President: Andy Westmoreland
  Executive Director: Charles Fuller
  Department Chair: Scott Holsclaw
  Technical Director: Joey Licklider
Founded: 1886
Status: Non-Profit, Professional
Paid Staff: 41
Paid Artists: 41
Seating Capacity: 1,500

6017
VERSER THEATER
Ouachita Baptist University
410 Ouachita Street
Arkadelphia, AR 71998
Mailing Address: 410 Ouachita St., Arkadelphia, AR 71998
Phone: 870-245-5000
Fax: (87-0) -245-
Toll-free: 800-DIA- OBU
e-mail: hosclaws@.obu.edu
Web Site: www.obu.edu/thearts
Officers:
  President: Rex M. Horne
Management:
  Department Chair: Scott Holsclaw
  Production Manager: Joey Licklider
Mission: Ouachita's theatre arts department provides the students with practical experience which is enhanced by classroom instruction. Though rehearsals and performance, students engage in the collaborative process and continue to develop their skills under faculty direction.
Specialized Field: Dramatic productions
Type of Stage: Proscenium Modified Thrust Stage
Stage Dimensions: 36' X 18'
Seating Capacity: 200

6018
CENTRE STAGE
University of Central Arkansas
Silas D. Snow Fine Arts Building
201 Donaghey Ave, Harrin Hall 222
Conway, AR 72035
Mailing Address: 201 Donaghey Ave., Harrin Hall 222, Conway, AR 72035
Phone: 501-450-5000
Fax: 501-450-3296
e-mail: jdmiller@uca.edu
Web Site: www.uca.edu/cfac/mct/theatre
Officers:
  Dean: Rollin R. Potter
  Interim Associate Dean: Gayle Seymour
  Co-Chairman: Joseph Anderson
Management:
  President: Tom Courtway
  Admissions and Advising Director: Dianna Flippo
  Administrative Specialist III: Eddie Fugatt
  Administrative Specialist II: Joshua Miller
Mission: The Department of Mass Communication and Theatre offers programs that combine art and technology in four areas of emphasis: digital filmmaking, journalism, television, and theatre.
Type of Stage: Proscenium
Seating Capacity: 307

6019
DONALD W. REYNOLDS AUDITORIUM
University of Central Arkansas
Silas D. Snow Fine Arts Building
201 Donaghey Ave, Harrin Hall 222
Conway, AR 72035
Mailing Address: 201 Donaghey Ave., Harrin Hall 222, Conway, AR 72035
Phone: 501-450-5000
Fax: 501-450-3296
e-mail: jdmiller@uca.edu
Web Site: www.uca.edu/cfac/mct/theatre
Officers:
  Dean: Rollin R. Potter
  Interim Associate Dean: Gayle Seymour
  Co-Chairman: Joseph Anderson
Management:
  President: Tom Courtway
  Admissions and Advising Director: Dianna Flippo
  Administrative Specialist III: Eddie Fugatt
  Administrative Specialist II: Joshua Miller
Mission: The Department of Mass Communication and Theatre offers programs that combine art and technology in four areas of emphasis: digital filmmaking, journalism, television, and theatre.
Opened: 2000
Type of Stage: Performance Hall
Orchestra Pit: Y
Seating Capacity: 1200
Cost: $22 million

6020
STUDIO THEATRE
University of Central Arkansas
Silas D. Snow Fine Arts Building
201 Donaghey Ave, Harrin Hall 222
Conway, AR 72035
Mailing Address: 201 Donaghey Ave., Harrin Hall 222, Conway, AR 72035
Phone: 501-450-5000
Fax: 501-450-3296
e-mail: jdmiller@uca.edu
Web Site: www.uca.edu/cfac/mct/theatre
Officers:
  Dean: Rollin R. Potter
  Interim Associate Dean: Gayle Seymour
  Co-Chairman: Joseph Anderson
Management:
  President: Tom Courtway
  Admissions and Advising Director: Dianna Flippo
  Administrative Specialist III: Eddie Fugatt
  Administrative Specialist II: Joshua Miller
Mission: The Department of Mass Communication and Theatre offers programs that combine art and technology in four areas of emphasis: digital filmmaking, journalism, television, and theatre.
Type of Stage: Black Box
Seating Capacity: 150

6021
EL DORADO MUNICIPAL AUDITORIUM
City of El Dorado
P.O. Box 2170
El Dorado, AR 71730
Phone: 870-862-7911
Fax: 870-881-4164
e-mail: mayor@eldoradoar.org
Web Site: www.eldoradoar.org/auditorium.html
Management:
  Mayor: Bobby Beard
  Judge Union County Courthouse: Bobby Edmonds
Specialized Field: Concerts, theater, weddings

6022
SOUTH ARKANSAS ARTS CENTER
110 East 5th Street
Suite 206
El Dorado, AR 71730
Phone: 870-862-5474
Fax: 870-862-4921
e-mail: info@saac-arts.org
Web Site: www.saac-arts.org
Officers:
  President Board of Directors: Tela Webb
  Vice President: Mark Southall

FACILITIES / Arkansas

Secretary: Sam Allen
Treasurer: Scott Enzor
Management:
 Executive Director: Jack Wilson
 Marketing: Colleen Means
 Media Relations: Darrin Riley

6023
CARLSON CENTER
Ogden Entertainment
2010 2nd Avenue
Fairbanks, AR 99701
Mailing Address: 2010 2nd Avenue Fairbanks, AL 99701
Phone: 907-451-7800
Fax: 907-451-1195
e-mail: info@carlson-center.com
Web Site: www.carlson-center.com
Management:
 General Manager: David Welborn
 Production Supervisor: Brian Palmer
 Marketing/Box Office Manager: Kristin Bayer
 Operations Manager: Phil Wheeler
Mission: Event Facility
Utilizes: Actors; Artists-in-Residence; Collaborating Artists; Commissioned Music; Dance Companies; Dancers; Designers; Educators; Filmmakers; Guest Companies; Guest Conductors; Guest Directors; Guest Ensembles; Guest Instructors; Guest Lecturers; Guest Musical Directors; Guest Musicians; Guest Soloists; Guest Writers; Guild Activities; Instructors; Local Artists; Multi Collaborations; Multimedia; Music; New Productions; Original Music Scores; Poets; Resident Artists; Resident Professionals; Selected Students; Sign Language Translators; Singers; Soloists; Student Interns; Special Technical Talent; Theatre Companies; Touring Companies; Visual Arts
Founded: 1990
Paid Staff: 100
Type of Stage: Concert Stage; Portable; Sico
Seating Capacity: 3,470; 6,539

6024
BUD WALTON ARENA
University of Arkansas
Fayetteville, AR 72701
Mailing Address: PO Box 7777
Phone: 479-575-2000
Fax: 501-575-3716
Web Site: www.uark.edu
Officers:
 President Razorbacks Foundation: Chuck Dicus
 Vice Presidient Razorbacks Foundtn: Norm DeBriyn
 Chief Financial Officer: Jackie Rollins
Management:
 Arena Manager: Fred Vorsanger
 Concession Manager: Mike Holbrook
 Donor Relations: Charlotte Faucette
Specialized Field: Sports Arena
Seating Capacity: 19,500

6025
STELLA BOYLE SMITH CONCERT HALL
UALR Music Department
University of Arkansas at Fayetteville
525 Old Main
Fayetteville, AR 72701
Mailing Address: MB 201, University of Arkansas, Fayettville AR 72701
Phone: 479-575-4801
Fax: 479-575-5409
e-mail: Fulbright@uark.edu
Web Site: www.music.uark.edu

Officers:
 Department Chairman: Dr. Ronda Mains
 Dean: Todd Shields
Management:
 Chancellor of University: Dave Gearhart
 Administrative Support Supervisor: Jennifer Atchley White
 Administrative Specialist III: Rachel Collins
 Administrative Specialist II: Debbie Power
 Administrative Support Supervisor: Connie Vick
Status: Non-Profit, Professional
Paid Staff: 30
Paid Artists: 30
Facility Category: Concert Hall

6026
WALTON ARTS CENTER
229 N School Street
PO Box 3547
Fayetteville, AR 72702
Mailing Address: Walton Arts Center, P.O. Box 3547. Fayetteville, AR 72702
Phone: 479-443-5600
Fax: 479-443-9024
e-mail: info@waltonartscenter.org
Web Site: www.waltonartscenter.org
Officers:
 Chair: Greg W. Lee
 Vice Chair: David Banks
 Secretary/Treasurer: Jerry Walton
Management:
 Director of Production: Pete Croken
 Production Administrator: Sundi Tyler
 Booking & Events Coordinator: Meisha Stewart
 Volunteer Coordinator: Mel Philips
 Finance Manager: Sandy Dilbeck
 President/CEO: Peter B. Lane
Mission: Visual and performing arts center.
Utilizes: Artists-in-Residence; Collaborations; Curators; Dance Companies; Educators; Fine Artists; High School Drama; Instructors; Multimedia; Original Music Scores; Theatre Companies; Touring Companies
Founded: 1992
Status: Non-Profit, Professional
Paid Staff: 47
Volunteer Staff: 300
Non-paid Artists: 50
Budget: $4 million
Income Sources: Ticket Sales, Corporate Sponsors, Members, Grants
Performs At: 1200 Seat Hall; 200 Seat Black Box
Affiliations: APAP, Midwest Arts Alliance
Annual Attendance: 150,000+
Type of Stage: Proscenium
Stage Dimensions: 58 x 40
Seating Capacity: 1,200
Year Built: 1992
Cost: $9 Million

6027
BREEDLOVE AUDITORIUM WESTARK COMMUNITY COLLEGE
5210 Grand Avenue
PO Box 3649
Fort Smith, AR 72913-3649
Mailing Address: 5210 Grand Avenue, P.O. Box 3649, Fort Smith, AR 72913-3649
Phone: 479-788-7000
e-mail: information@uafortsmith.edu
Web Site: www.uafortsmith.edu
Officers:
 Vice Chancellor for University Rela: Mark Horn
 Chancellor: Paul B. Beran
 Provost and Senior Vice Chancellor: Ray Wallace

 Vice Chancellor for Finance: Darrell Morrison
 Vice Chancellor for Student Affairs: Lee Krehbiel
Management:
 Director/EEO Officer: Beverly L. McClendon
 HR Manager: Jeanne Stevens
 HR Specialist: Melissa Brown
 Administrative Analyst: Tammy Spencer
 Benefits Coordinator: Tracy Hester
Founded: 1928
Status: Non-Profit, Non-Professional

6028
FORT SMITH CONVENTION CENTER
55 S 7th Street
Fort Smith, AR 72901
Mailing Address: 55 South 7th Street, Fort Smith, AR 72901
Phone: 479-788-8932
Fax: 479-788-8930
e-mail: jrichey@fortsmithar.gov
Web Site: www.fortsmithconventioncenter.org
Management:
 Director of Convention Center: Frankie Hamilton
 Sales Director: Karen Hobbs
 Sales Director: Jeremy Richey
 General Manger: Tim Seeberg
 Event Coordinator: Bob Reykers
Mission: Multipurpose facility for conventions, tradeshows, banquets, meetings, PAC performances and 40,000 square feet Exhibit Hall with riser seating.
Founded: 2001
Status: Operational
Paid Staff: 12
Income Sources: Concerts; Tradeshows; Conventions; Banquets; Rental Facilities
Annual Attendance: 500,000
Facility Category: Convention Center
Type of Stage: Hardwood on plywood substrate
Stage Dimensions: 58 x 42
Seating Capacity: 1330; 4700
Year Built: 1966
Year Remodeled: 2000
Cost: $27 Million
Rental Contact: Melanie Jordin

6029
FORT SMITH LITTLE THEATRE
401 North 6th Street
Fort Smith, AR 72913
Mailing Address: PO Box 3752, Fort Smith, AR 72913
Phone: 479-783-2966
Fax: 479-783-1295
Web Site: fslt.org
Officers:
 President Board of Directors: Cecelia Woods-McDonald
 Vice President Board of Directors: Rham Cunningham
 Secretary Board of Directors: Lora Rice
 Treasurer Board of Directors: Paula Sharum
Founded: 1948

6030
KAY ROGERS PARK
4400 Midland Boulevard
Fort Smith, AR 72904
Mailing Address: P.O. Box 4145, Fort Smith, AR 72914
Phone: 479-783-2393
Fax: 501-782-9944
Toll-free: 800-364-1080
e-mail: rebecca@kayrogerspark.com
Web Site: www.kayrogerspark.org
Management:

FACILITIES / Arkansas

Director: Denny Flynn
Accounting: Beverly Sharp
Administration: Cindy
Seating Capacity: 13,000

6031
HOT SPRINGS CONVENTION SUMMIT CENTER
134 Convention Boulevard
Hot Springs, AR 71901
Mailing Address: P.O. Box 6000, Hot Springs National Park, AR 71902
Phone: 501-321-2277
Fax: 501-321-2136
Toll-free: 800-543-2284
e-mail: hscvbsales@hotsprings.org
Web Site: www.hotsprings.org
Management:
  Executive Director: Steve Arrison
  Deputy Director: Gordon Manoney
  Box Office Manager: Brian Leonard
  Catering Sales Manager: Kim Hamilton
Status: Nonprofit, Professional
Paid Staff: 75
Seating Capacity: 6,500

6032
FORUM
115 East Monroe
Jonesboro, AR 72401
Mailing Address: 115 East Monroe Ave, Jonesboro, AR 72401
Phone: 870-935-2726
Fax: 870-277-9505
e-mail: info@foajonesboro.org
Web Site: www.foajonesboro.org
Officers:
  Chair: Dr. Rebecca Evans
  Vice Chair: Dana Kelley
  Treasurer: Robin Martin
  Secretary: Debra Sharp
Management:
  Executive Director: Sherri Beatty
  Customer Service Associate: LeeAnn Knierim
  Director of Education: Rob Spencer
  Customer Service Associate: Ceola Dockery
  Development Coordinator: Vicki Pillow
  Associate Executive Director: Amanda Drennon
Founded: 1926
Seating Capacity: 658

6033
FOUNDATION OF ARTS
115 East Monroe
PO Box 310
Jonesboro, AR 72403
Mailing Address: 115 East Monroe Ave, Jonesboro, AR 72401
Phone: 870-935-2726
Fax: 870-277-9505
e-mail: info@foajonesboro.org
Web Site: www.foajonesboro.org
Officers:
  Chair: Dr. Rebecca Evans
  Vice Chair: Dana Kelley
  Treasurer: Robin Martin
  Secretary: Debra Sharp
Management:
  Executive Director: Sherri Beatty
  Associate Executive Director: Amanda Drennon
  Technical Director: Gaylon Tyner
  Director of Education: Heather Intres
  House Manager: Kent O'Daniel
  Development Coordinator: Vicki Pillow

Status: Non-Profit, Non-Professional
Paid Staff: 5
Paid Artists: 5
Performs At: Auditorium
Seating Capacity: 658

6034
FOWLER CENTER AT ARKANSAS UNIVERSITY
201 Olympic Drive
PO Box 2339
Jonesboro, AR 72467
Phone: 870-972-3471
Fax: 870-972-3748
e-mail: fowlercenter@astate.edu
Web Site: www.yourfowlercenter.com
Management:
  Director: Jeff Brown
  Bradbury Gallery Director: Les Christensen
  Technical Director: Jeff McLaughlin
  Assitant Technical Director: Jason Henson
  Adminstratve Assistan 2: Barbara Pearson
  Assistant Technical Director: Evan Palumbo
Founded: 2001
Specialized Field: Music; Theatre; Visual Art
Status: Nonprofit
Paid Staff: 5
Budget: $100,000
Income Sources: Arkansas State University; Endowments; Ticket Sales
Facility Category: Concert Hall/Drama Theatre
Type of Stage: Proscenium
Seating Capacity: 975; 342
Year Built: 2000
Rental Contact: Director Jeff Brown

6035
HAISLIP ARENA THEATRE
University of Arkansas Little Rock
2801 South University Avenue
Little Rock, AR 72204
Mailing Address: University of Arkansas Little Rock, 2801 S. University Avenu
Phone: 870-972-2037
Fax: 870-972-2830
e-mail: asutheatre@astate.edu
Web Site: www.ualr.edu
Officers:
  Department Chair: Jay Raphael Ph.D
Management:
  Chancellor: Joe Anderson
  Executive Director: Robert Hupp
  Technical Director: Carl Wick
Status: Non-Profit, Non-Professional
Paid Staff: 10

6036
RAY WINDER FIELD
400 W. Broadway
Little Rock, AR 72114
Mailing Address: 400 W. Broadway, North Little Rock, AR 72114
Phone: 501-664-1555
Fax: 501-664-1834
e-mail: travs@travs.com
Web Site: www.travs.com
Officers:
  President: Bert Parke
Management:
  Executive Director: Bill Valentine
  Assistant General Manager: Pete Laven
  Superintendant: Greg Johnson
  Director Stadium Operations: Mike Green
  Assistant Park Supervisor: Reggi Temple

Director Media Relations: Phil Elson
Director of Tickets: David Kay
Director of Group Sales: Paul Allen
Founded: 1932
Status: Non-Profit, Professional
Paid Staff: 8
Seating Capacity: 6,083

6037
RITZ CIVIC CENTER
1 Capitol Mall
Little Rock, AR 72201
Mailing Address: 1 Capitol Mall, Little Rock, Arkansas 72201
Phone: 501-762-1744
Fax: 501-763-1950
Web Site: www.arkansas.com
Management:
  Director: Rae Glidewell

6038
ROBINSON CENTER MUSIC HALL
Markham and Broadway
PO Box 3232
Little Rock, AR 72203
Mailing Address: P.O. Box 3232, Little Rock, AR 72203
Phone: 501-376-4781
Fax: 501-374-2255
Toll-free: 800-844-4781
e-mail: lrcvb@littlerock.com
Web Site: www.littlerock.com
Officers:
  President / CEO: Gretchen Hall
  Senior Vice President / CFO: Leisa Pulliam
  Vice President of Sales and Service: Alan Sims
  VP of Marketing and Communications: John Mayner
Management:
  Chief Operating Officer: Jim Rice
  Chief Executive Officer: Barry Travis
Affiliations: Arkansas Symphony Orchestra Celebrity Attractions
Year Built: 1939
Year Remodeled: 1989
Rental Contact: Lisa Simmons

6039
WAR MEMORIAL STADIUM
Markham and Van Buren Street
1 Stadium Drive
Little Rock, AR 72225
Mailing Address: 1 Stadium Drive, PO Box 250222, Little Rock, AR 72225
Phone: 501-663-0775
Fax: 501-663-6387
e-mail: jerry.cohen@arkansas.goc
Web Site: www.wmstadium.com
Management:
  Stadium Manager: Charlie Staggs
  Assistant Stadium Manager: Jerry Cohen
  Office Manager: Nancy Toland
  Marketing Manager: Danny-Joe Crofford
  Concession Supervisor: Greg Segalla
  Stadium Fiscal Manager: Dinah Soderling
Mission: Football
Founded: 1948
Specialized Field: Sports facility, concerts
Status: Non-Profit, Non-Professional
Paid Staff: 5
Seating Capacity: 53,727

FACILITIES / Arkansas

6040
WILDWOOD PARK FOR THE PERFORMING ARTS
20919 Denny Road
Little Rock, AR 72223-9279
Mailing Address: 20919 Denny Road, Little Rock, Arkansas 72223-9279
Phone: 501-821-7275
Fax: 501-821-7280
Toll-free: 888-821-7225
e-mail: info@wildwoodpark.org
Web Site: www.wildwoodpark.org
Officers:
   Secretary: Margaret A. Johnston
   Vice Chairman: Ray Dillon
   Treasurer: Tom Galek
   Chairman: Melissa Thoma
Management:
   Director: Cliff Fannin Baker
   Founder/Artistic Director: Ann Chotard
   Director of Finance: Benny Cagle
   Public Relations Coordinator: Kristen Vandaveer
   Managing Director: Leslie Golden
Utilizes: AEA Actors; Artists-in-Residence; Collaborations; Commissioned Composers; Commissioned Music; Dancers; Designers; Educators; Fine Artists; Five Seasonal Concerts; Grant Writers; Guest Accompanists; Guest Artists; Guest Choreographers; Guest Composers; Guest Conductors; Guest Designers; Guest Instructors; Guest Lecturers; Guest Musical Directors; Guest Musicians; Guest Soloists; Guest Writers; Guild Activities; Instructors; Local Artists; Lyricists; Multimedia; Music; New Productions; Organization Contracts; Original Music Scores; Poets; Resident Artists; Resident Professionals; Sign Language Translators; Singers; Soloists; Student Interns; Special Technical Talent; Touring Companies; Visual Arts
Founded: 1991
Status: Non-Profit, Professional
Paid Staff: 6
Paid Artists: 10
Budget: $1.2 million
Income Sources: Friends of Wildwood, Grants, City and State Fundings
Affiliations: Opera America
Annual Attendance: 3,750
Facility Category: Opera House
Type of Stage: Thrust
Seating Capacity: 625
Year Built: 1996
Cost: $6 Million

6041
WILKINS STADIUM
Southern Arkansas University
100 East University
Magnolia, AR 71753-5000
Mailing Address: 100 E. University, Magnolia, AR 71753-5000
Phone: 870-235-4000
Fax: 870-235-5005
e-mail: muleriders@saumag.edu
Web Site: web.saumag.edu
Management:
   Executive Assistant to President: Ronnie Birdsong
   Director Development: Sharon Eichenberger
   University Editor: Mark Trout
   Athletic Director: Jay Adcox
   Assistant Athletic Director: Houston Taylor
   Sports Information Director: Houston Taylor
   Director Wellness Center: Leonard Biddle
Seating Capacity: 6,000

6042
ARTS AND SCIENCE CENTER FOR SOUTHEAST ARKANSAS
701 S Main Street
Pine Bluff, AR 71601
Mailing Address: 701 South Main Street, Pine Bluff, AR 71601
Phone: 870-536-3375
Fax: 870-536-3380
e-mail: info@asc701.org
Web Site: www.asc701.org
Management:
   Executive Director: Lenore Shoults
   Director of Operations: Raven Harris
   Education Coordinator: Alexandra Pearson
   Director of Member Services: Laurie Pascale
   Receptionist: Cassundra Haynes
   Administrative Support: Ashley Smith
Utilizes: Actors; Choreographers; Curators; Dance Companies; Dancers; Designers; Educators; Grant Writers; Guest Artists; Guest Conductors; Guest Designers; Guest Ensembles; Guest Musical Directors; Guest Musicians; Guild Activities; High School Drama; Instructors; Local Artists; Multimedia; Music; Resident Professionals; Sign Language Translators; Soloists; Student Interns; Theatre Companies; Touring Companies
Founded: 1966
Status: Non-Profit, Non-Professional
Paid Staff: 10
Volunteer Staff: 300
Paid Artists: 3
Non-paid Artists: 80
Budget: $110,000
Income Sources: Ticket Sales; Sponsorship; Grants
Annual Attendance: 5,500
Facility Category: Multi-use
Seating Capacity: 232
Year Built: 1994

6043
GOLDEN LION STADIUM
University of Arkansas Pine Bluff
1200 North University Drive
Pine Bluff, AR 71601
Phone: 870-575-8000
Fax: 870-575-4607
Web Site: www.uapb.edu
Management:
   President: Lawrence Davis Jr/Ph.D
   Athletic Director: Craig Cury
   Sports Information Director: Carl Whimper
   Faculty Athletic Representative: George Herts
   Senior Women's Administrator: Betty Hayes
Founded: 2000
Status: Non-Profit, Non-Professional

6044
HESTAND STADIUM
One Convention Center Plaza
Pine Bluff, AR 71601
Mailing Address: One Convention Center Plaza, Pine Bluff, AR 71601
Phone: 870-536-7600
Fax: 870-850-2105
Toll-free: 800-536-7660
e-mail: pbinfo@pinebluff.com
Web Site: www.pineblufcvb.org
Officers:
   President: Dale Dixon
Management:
   Director: Greg Gustek
   Executive Director: Pier Ponder
   Managing Director: Brent Lacy
   Convention Center Event Booking Mgr: Marian Anderson
   Convention Meeting Information Mgr: Sheri Storie
   City/Tourist/Information: Susie Madsen
Status: Non-Profit, Professional
Paid Staff: 6
Paid Artists: 6
Seating Capacity: 7,000

6045
PINE BLUFF CONVENTION CENTER AUDITORIUM
One Convention Center Plaza
Pine Bluff, AR 71601
Mailing Address: One Convention Center Plaza, Pine Bluff, AR 71601
Phone: 870-536-7600
Fax: 870-850-2105
Toll-free: 800-536-7660
e-mail: pbinfo@pinebluff.com
Web Site: www.pineblufcvb.org
Management:
   President: Bob Purvis
   Festival/Special Events Information: Greg Gustek
   Tourist Information: Susie Madsen
   Event Booking Information: Sheri Storie
   Convention Meeting Information: Sheri Storie
Founded: 1976
Status: Non-Profit, Non-Professional
Paid Staff: 28

6046
PINE BLUFF CONVENTION CENTER ARENA
1 Convention Center Plaza
Pine Bluff, AR 71601
Mailing Address: One Convention Center Plaza, Pine Bluff, AR 71601
Phone: 870-536-7600
Fax: 870-850-2105
Toll-free: 800-536-7660
e-mail: pbinfo@pinebluff.com
Web Site: www.pineblufcvb.org
Officers:
   President: Dale Dixon
Management:
   Tourist/Travel Information: Susie Madsen
   Festival/Special Events Manager: Greg Gustek
   Convention/Meeting Manager: Sheri Storie
   Events Manager: Marion Anderson
   Convention Meeting Information Mgr: Sheri Storie
Paid Staff: 26
Seating Capacity: 9,000

6047
ARKANSAS RIVER VALLEY ARTS CENTER
340 N. Escondido Blvd.
Russellville, AR 92025
Phone: 760-839-4138
Toll-free: 800-988-4253
e-mail: artscenter@centurytel.net
Web Site: www.artcenter.org
Officers:
   President: John Gale
Management:
   Executive Director: Betty Lagrone
   Artistic Director: Winston Taylor
Founded: 1981

FACILITIES / California

Opened: 1981
Status: Non-Profit, Professional
Paid Staff: 4
Paid Artists: 2
Annual Attendance: 5,000
Seating Capacity: 400

6048
JOHN E TUCKER COLISEUM
Arkansas Tech Athletic Department
Tucker Coliseum, 1604 Coliseum Drive
Russellville, AR 72801
Phone: 479-968-0389
Fax: 479-964-0829
Web Site: athletics.atu.edu
Management:
- President: Robert Brown
- Athletic Director: Steve Mullins
- Faculty Athletic Representative: Thomas DeBlack Ph.D
- Director Corporate Relations: Kelly Davis

Founded: 1976
Seating Capacity: 3,500

6049
WITHERSPOON ARTS ARENA
Arkansas Tech University
1505 North Boulder Avenue
Russellville, AR 72801
Phone: 479-968-0368
Fax: 501-964-0812
Web Site: htp://lfa.atu.edu/music.htm
Management:
- Music Department Head: Andy Anders
- Director of Bands: Hal Cooper
- Director of Choirs: Gary Morris

6050
ARTS CENTER OF THE OZARKS
214 South Main Street
PO Box 725
Springdale, AR 72765-0725
Mailing Address: PO Box 725, Springdale AR 72765
Phone: 479-751-5441
Fax: 479-927-0308
e-mail: info@artscenteroftheozarks.org
Web Site: www.acozarks.org
Management:
- President: James Blount
- Executive Director: Cathy Blundell
- Theatre Director: Harry Blundell
- Music Director: Bill Burrows
- Administrative Director: Kathi Blundell
- Director of Operations: Erin West
- Visual Arts Director: Eve Smith
- Technical Director: Stephen Pigman

Mission: To provide opportunities to be or see the arts in Northwest Arkansas, Southwest Missouri, Northeast Oklahoma and Southeast Kansas.
Founded: 1967
Specialized Field: Multi Disciplinary; Performing; Visual Arts
Status: Non-Profit, Non-Professional
Paid Staff: 9
Paid Artists: 3
Budget: $500,000

6051
THE CONVOCATION CENTER
Arkansas State University
217 Olympic Drive
State University, AR 72467
Mailing Address: P.O. Box 880, State University, AR 72467
Phone: 870-972-3870
Fax: 870-972-3825
e-mail: timd@astate.edu
Web Site: www.astateconvo.com
Management:
- Associate Director: Kenny Brewer
- Booking Coordinator: Lesa Carmack
- Marketing Director: Brad Pietz
- Director: Tim L Dean
- Director of Concessions: Debbie Honeycutt

Founded: 1987
Budget: $1 million
Annual Attendance: 350,000
Facility Category: Arena
Type of Stage: Sico
Stage Dimensions: 60'x40'
Seating Capacity: 10,500
Year Built: 1987
Year Remodeled: 2001
Cost: $18.6 million
Rental Contact: Tim Dean

6052
THE RIALTO THEATRE
318 E. Congress St
Tucson, AR 85702
Mailing Address: Po Box 1728
Phone: 520-740-1000
Fax: 520-740-0071
e-mail: cmccrary@rialtotheatre.com
Web Site: www.rialtotheatre.com
Officers:
- Exective Director: Curtis McCrary

Management:
- General Manager: Curtis McCrary
- Booking: Kris Kerry
- Production Manager: Bruce Momich
- Operations Manager: Mark Martinez
- Graphic Design: Ryan Trayte
- Marketing: Kristin Evans
- Accounting: Mohamed Omar-Makram

Facility Category: Theatre
Seating Capacity: 900/1444 standing

California

6053
SOKA PERFORMING ART CENTER
Soka University Of America
1 University Drive
Aliso Viejo, CA 92656
Phone: 949-480-4000
Fax: 949-480-4278
e-mail: dpalmer@soka.edu
Web Site: www.performingarts.soka.edu
Management:
- General Manager: David Palmer

Mission: Multiple performance venues, theatre and dance studios, class rooma and academic office housed in the Soka Performing Arts Center
Founded: 2009
Opened: 2011
Year Built: 2009
Architect: ZGF Architects LLP

6054
ANAHEIM CONVENTION CENTER - ARENA
800 West Katella Avenue
Anaheim, CA 92802
Mailing Address: 800 West Katella Avenue, Anaheim CA 92802
Phone: 714-765-8950
Fax: 714-765-8965
e-mail: slowry@anaheim.net
Web Site: www.anaheimconventioncenter.com/
Management:
- City Manager: David M Morgan
- Assistant City Manager: Thomas J Wood
- Deputy City Manager: Joel Fick

Mission: The Anaheim Convention Center houses 815,000 square feet of exhibit space; Meeting and Ballroom space totals 130,000, Arena Capacities are 28,140 total square feet and the seating capacity is 9,100.
Opened: 1967

6055
EDISON INTERNATIONAL FIELD OF ANAHEIM
2000 Gene Autry Way
Anaheim, CA 92806
Mailing Address: 2000 Gene Autry Way, Anaheim, CA 92806
Phone: 714-634-2000
Fax: 714-940-2001
Toll-free: 888-796-4256
Web Site: losangeles.angels.mlb.com/mlb/official_info/index.jsp
Officers:
- Executive Vice President, Business: Tim Brosnan
- Executive VP, Economics: Rob Manfred
- Chief Financial Officer: Jonathan Mariner
- Chief Information Officer: John McHale Jr.
- VP/General Manager: Bill Stoneman
- VP/Communications: Tim Mead
- VP/Finance: Molly Taylor

Management:
- Manager Baseball Operation: Abe Flores
- Director Player Development: Tony Reagins
- Assistant General Manager: Ken Forsch
- Communications Director: Nancy Mazmanian
- Marketing Director: Robert Alvarado

Founded: 1966
Specialized Field: Home to the Anaheim Angels (MLB) and many other events and consumer shows.
Seating Capacity: 45,050
Year Built: 1966
Year Remodeled: 1998

6056
CABRILLO CROCKER THEATER
Cabrillo College
6500 Soquel Drive
Aptos, CA 95003
Mailing Address: 6500 Soquel Drive, Aptos, CA 95003
Phone: 831-479-6100
Fax: 831-464-8382
e-mail: mahopkins@cabrillo.edu
Web Site: www.cabrillo.edu
Management:
- Theatre Manager: Mark Hopkins
- Marketing & Communications: Jana Marcus
- President: Laurel Jones
- Assistant Theatre Manager: Anya Finke
- Theatre Manager: Sean C McCullough

Founded: 1959
Opened: 2009
Specialized Field: Music/Theater/Dance
Seating Capacity: 527
Year Built: 2009

FACILITIES / California

6057
CENTERARTS
Humboldt State University
1 Harpst Street
Arcata, CA 95521-8299
Mailing Address: 1 Harpst Street, Arcata, CA 95521
Phone: 707-826-4411
Fax: 707-826-5980
e-mail: rmf7001@humboldt.edu
Web Site: www.humboldt.edu
Management:
  President: Rollin Richmond
  Director: Roy Furshpan
  Event Coordinator: Michael Moore Jr
  Technical Director: Dan Stockwell
  Administrative Coordinator: Tiffany O'Connell
  Ticket Officer Manager: Jason Henry
  Technical Director: Greta Welsh
Mission: Facilities include the Van Duzer Theatre with a seating capacity of 862; Fulkerson Recital Hall With a seating capacity of 201; and the Kate Buchanan Room with a seating capacity of 600.

6058
EAST GYMNASIUM
Humboldt State University
1 Harpst Street
Arcata, CA 95521
Mailing Address: Humboldt State University, 1 Harpst Street, Arcata, CA 95521
Phone: 707-826-4411
Fax: 707-826-5980
e-mail: rmf7001@humboldt.edu
Web Site: www.humboldt.edu
Officers:
  Provost and VP, Academic Affairs: Robert A Snyder
  VP, Administrative Affairs: Burt Nordstrom
  President: Rollin C. Richmond
Management:
  Director: Roy Furshpan
  Event Coordinator: Michael Moore Jr
  Director, Academic Resources: Volga Koval
  Administrative Support Assistant: Taylor Baker
  Ticket Office Manager: Jason Henry
  Technical Director: Greta Welsh
Seating Capacity: 1,400

6059
FULKERSON RECITAL HALL
Humboldt State University
1 Harpst Street
Arcata, CA 95521
Mailing Address: Humboldt State University, 1 Harpst Street, Arcata, CA 95521
Phone: 707-826-4411
Fax: 707-826-5980
e-mail: rmf7001@humboldt.edu
Web Site: www.humboldt.edu
Officers:
  Provost and VP, Academic Affairs: Robert A Snyder
  VP, Administrative Affairs: Burt Nordstrom
  President: Rollin C. Richmond
Management:
  Director: Roy Furshpan
  Event Coordinator: Michael Moore Jr
  Director, Academic Resources: Volga Koval
  Administrative Support Assistant: Taylor Baker
  Technical Director: Greta Welsh
Seating Capacity: 201

6060
JOHN VAN DUZER THEATRE
Humboldt State University
1 Harpst Street
Arcata, CA 95521
Mailing Address: Humboldt State University, 1 Harpst Street, Arcata, CA 95521
Phone: 707-826-4411
Fax: 707-826-5980
e-mail: rmf7001@humboldt.edu
Web Site: www.humboldt.edu
Officers:
  Provost and VP, Academic Affairs: Robert A Snyder
  VP, Administrative Affairs: Burt Nordstrom
  President: Rollin C. Richmond
Management:
  Director: Roy Furshpan
  Event Coordinator: Michael Moore Jr
  Director, Academic Resources: Volga Koval
  Administrative Support Assistant: Taylor Baker
  Ticket Office Manager: Jason Henry
  Technical Director: Greta Welsh
Seating Capacity: 862

6061
KATE BUCHANAN ROOM
Humboldt State University
1 Harpst Street
Arcata, CA 95521
Mailing Address: Humboldt State University, 1 Harpst Street, Arcata, CA 95521
Phone: 707-826-4411
Fax: 707-826-5980
e-mail: rmf7001@humboldt.edu
Web Site: www.humboldt.edu
Officers:
  Provost and VP, Academic Affairs: Robert A Snyder
  VP, Administrative Affairs: Burt Nordstrom
  President: Rollin C. Richmond
Management:
  Director: Roy Furshpan
  Event Coordinator: Michael Moore Jr
  Director, Academic Resources: Volga Koval
  Administrative Support Assistant: Taylor Baker
  Ticket Office Manager: Jason Henry
  Technical Director: Greta Welsh
Seating Capacity: 600

6062
CLARK CENTER FOR THE PERORMING ARTS
487 Fair Oaks Ave
Arroyo Grande, CA 93420
Phone: 805-489-9444
Fax: 805-489-4287
e-mail: info@clarkcenter.org
Web Site: www.clarkcenter.org
Officers:
  President: Stephen Hughes
  Vice-President: Iris Swisher
  Treasurer: Jack Smith
  Secretary: Randy Voss
Management:
  Business Manager: Wendy Marie Foerster
  Executive Director: Connie O'Henley
  Marketing and Operations Director: Jamie Maraviglia-Manalo
  Box Office Manager: Ryan C. Loyd
  Technical Director: Rick Pierce
Mission: Two theatres used by professional and community productions. The hall and lobby are used as a venue for local artists.

6063
APU THEATER
Azusa Pacific University
901 E. Alosta Ave
PO Box 7000
Azusa, CA 91702-7000
Mailing Address: PO Box 7000, Azusa, CA 91702-7000
Phone: 626-815-6000
e-mail: tft@apu.edu
Web Site: www.apu.edu/theater
Management:
  Director Theater Arts: Bart McHenry
  General Manager Theater Arts: Brian Mercer
Mission: APU Theater offers, on average, six quality productions a semesters, featuring a combination of family-friendly comedy, drama, and musical performances.
Seating Capacity: 450

6064
RABOBANK ARENA, THEATER AND CONVENTION CENTER
1001 Truxton Avenue
Bakersfield, CA 93301
Phone: 661-852-7300
Fax: 661-861-9904
Toll-free: 888-255-2200
Web Site: www.rabobankarena.com
Management:
  Executive Director: Jim Foss
  Event Manager: Adam Miller
  Marketing Director: Scott Norton
  Operations Director: Claudia Goodsell
  Director of Security: Sam Cornejo
  Finance Director: Steve Womack
Mission: Convention Hall has a seating capacity of 3,000, Convention Arena has a seating capacity of 2,200.
Seating Capacity: 3,000

6065
DORE THEATRE/MADIGAN GALLERY
California State University
Theatre Department, Music Bldg 102
9001 Stockdale Hwy
Bakersfield, CA 93311-1022
Mailing Address: 9001 Stockdale Hwy., Bakersfield, CA. 93311-1022
Phone: 661-654-3093
Fax: 661-665-6901
e-mail: excellence@csub.edu
Web Site: www.csub.edu
Management:
  President: Ray Finnell
  Stage Technician: Frank Robinson
  Adminstrative Coordinator: Kathryn Plunkett
  Custodial Supervisor: Wilfredo Hernandez
  Facilities Manager: Tom Velasquez
Founded: 1977
Specialized Field: Theatre
Seating Capacity: 500

6066
BENJIMAN IDE WHEELER AUDITORIUM
University of California, Berkeley
101 Zellerbach Hall
Suite 4800
Berkeley, CA 94720-4800

FACILITIES / California

Mailing Address: 101 Zellerbach Hall # 4800,
Berkeley, CA, 94720-4800
Phone: 510-642-0212
Fax: 510-643-6707
e-mail: tickets@calperformances.org
Web Site: calperformances.org
Officers:
  Chair: Gail Rubinfeld
  Chief Financial Officer: Calvin D. Eng
  Vice Chair: Tim Gallagher
  Vice Chair & Treasurer: Susan Graham Harrison
  Secretary: Deborah Van Nest
Management:
  Executive and Artistic Director: Matjas Tarnopolsky
  Event Operations Manager: Rob Bean
  Production Manager: Alan Herro
  Development Director: Sarah Sobey
  Information Systems Manager: Andrew Kraus
Mission: The mission of Cal Performances is to inspire, nurture and sustain a lifelong appreciation for the performing arts.
Specialized Field: Concerts, Dance, Music, Theatre, and other performing arts disciplines
Status: Nonprofit, Professional
Paid Staff: 50
Type of Stage: Proscenium
Stage Dimensions: 15' X 30'
Seating Capacity: 760

6067
BERKELEY COMMUNITY THEATRE
Berkley High School
1930 Allston Way
Berkeley, CA 94710
Phone: 415-346-7222
Fax: 415-771-9719
e-mail: rcagan@berkeley.k12.ca.us
Web Site: www.premiertickets.com/berkeley
Management:
  President: Bryan Rotton
  Lead Teacher: Ray Cagan
Founded: 2003
Specialized Field: Concerts, theater
Status: Non-Profit, Professional
Paid Staff: 87

6068
JULIA MORGAN CENTER FOR THE ARTS
2640 College Avenue
Berkeley, CA 94704
Mailing Address: 2640 College Avenue, Berkeley, CA 94704
Phone: 510-845-8542
Fax: 510-845-3133
Web Site: berkeleyplayhouse.org
Management:
  President: Timothy Choate
  Founding Artistic Director: Elizabeth McKoy
  Production Manager: Leighland Hooks
  Managing Director: Lauren Hewitt
  Operations Manager: Linell Ragsdale
  Producing Director: Daren A.C. Carollo
  Communications Director: Ken Levin
Mission: The Julia Morgan Center for the Arts is a home for artists, educators, learners and the community.
Founded: 1980
Status: Non-Profit, Professional
Paid Staff: 8
Budget: $700,000
Type of Stage: Proscenrum
Stage Dimensions: 39'4 x 31'6"
Seating Capacity: 400

Year Built: 1908
Year Remodeled: 1990
Cost: $650-$1250
Rental Contact: Bridget Frederick

6069
LA PENA CULTURAL CENTER
3105 Shattuck Avenue
Berkeley, CA 94705
Mailing Address: 3105 Shattuck Avenue, Berkeley, CA 94705 USA
Phone: 510-849-2568
Fax: 510-849-9397
e-mail: info@lapena.org
Web Site: lapena.org
Officers:
  President: Paul Chin
  Secretary: Amelia Gonzalez
Management:
  Executive Director: Kristen Sbrogna
  Technical Director: Oscar Autie
  Development Director: Manuel Alonso
  Development Associate: Nico Cabrera
  Programmer: Cece Carpio
  Communications Manager: Anna Leal
  Programs Manager: Nico Cabrera
Mission: To present cultural educational programs that increase understanding of different cultures and support efforts to build a more just society based on respect for human, social and economic rights for all people; to operate a multi-use cultural center/community gathering place where people of all races and cultures can share the rich and diverse heritages of the Americas and learn about conditions in the US, Latin American and the world.
Utilizes: Artists-in-Residence; Dancers; Filmmakers; Guest Directors; Guest Musical Directors; Instructors; Lyricists; Original Music Scores; Playwrights
Founded: 1973
Specialized Field: Latin American Music
Status: Non-Profit, Professional
Paid Staff: 7
Volunteer Staff: 20
Paid Artists: 4
Annual Attendance: 25,000
Facility Category: Black Box
Type of Stage: Raised Platform
Stage Dimensions: 24'x14'
Seating Capacity: 170
Year Built: 1932
Year Remodeled: 1990
Cost: $100,000
Rental Contact: Paul Chin

6070
WILLIAM RANDOLPH HEARST GREEK THEATRE
University of California, Berkeley
101 Zellerbach Hall
Suite 4800
Berkeley, CA 94720-4800
Mailing Address: 101 Zellerbach Hall, Berkeley, CA, 94720-4800
Phone: 510-642-0212
Fax: 510-643-6707
e-mail: tickets@calperformances.org
Web Site: calperformances.org
Officers:
  Chair: Gail Rubinfeld
  Chief Financial Officer: Calvin D. Eng
  Vice Chair: Tim Gallagher
  Vice Chair & Treasurer: Susan Graham Harrison
  Secretary: Deborah Van Nest
Management:
  Executive and Artistic Director: Matjas Tarnopolsky
  Event Operations Manager: Rob Bean
  Production Manager: Alan Herro
  Development Director: Sarah Sobey
  Information Systems Manager: Andrew Kraus
Mission: The mission of Cal Performances is to inspire, nurture and sustain a lifelong appreciation for the performing arts.
Specialized Field: Concerts, Dance, Music, Theatre, and other performing arts disciplines
Status: Nonprofit, Professional
Paid Staff: 50
Type of Stage: Amphitheater
Stage Dimensions: 127' X 28'
Seating Capacity: 8500

6071
ZELLERBACH AUDITORIUM
University of California, Berkeley
101 Zellerbach Hall
Suite 4800
Berkeley, CA 94720-4800
Mailing Address: 101 Zellerbach Hall, Berkeley, CA, 94720-4800
Phone: 510-642-0212
Fax: 510-643-6707
e-mail: tickets@calperformances.org
Web Site: calperformances.org
Officers:
  Chair: Gail Rubinfeld
  Chief Financial Officer: Calvin D. Eng
  Vice Chair: Tim Gallagher
  Vice Chair & Treasurer: Susan Graham Harrison
  Secretary: Deborah Van Nest
Management:
  Executive and Artistic Director: Matjas Tarnopolsky
  Event Operations Manager: Rob Bean
  Production Manager: Alan Herro
  Development Director: Sarah Sobey
  Information Systems Manager: Andrew Kraus
Mission: The mission of Cal Performances is to inspire, nurture and sustain a lifelong appreciation for the performing arts.
Specialized Field: Concerts, Dance, Music, Theatre, and other performing arts disciplines
Status: Nonprofit, Professional
Paid Staff: 50
Type of Stage: Proscenium
Stage Dimensions: 63'x30'
Orchestra Pit: y
Seating Capacity: 2,089

6072
ZELLERBACH PLAYHOUSE
University of California, Berkeley
101 Zellerbach Hall
Suite 4800
Berkeley, CA 94720-4800
Mailing Address: 101 Zellerbach Hall, Berkeley, CA, 94720-4800
Phone: 510-642-0212
Fax: 510-643-6707
e-mail: tickets@calperformances.org
Web Site: calperformances.org
Officers:
  Chair: Gail Rubinfeld
  Chief Financial Officer: Calvin D. Eng
  Vice Chair: Tim Gallagher
  Vice Chair & Treasurer: Susan Graham Harrison
  Secretary: Deborah Van Nest
Management:

FACILITIES / California

Executive and Artistic Director: Matjas Tarnopolsky
Event Operations Manager: Rob Bean
Production Manager: Alan Herro
Development Director: Sarah Sobey
Information Systems Manager: Andrew Kraus
Mission: The mission of Cal Performances is to inspire, nurture and sustain a lifelong appreciation for the performing arts.
Specialized Field: Concerts, Dance, Music, Theatre, and other performing arts disciplines
Status: Nonprofit, Professional
Paid Staff: 50
Type of Stage: Proscenium or Thrust
Seating Capacity: 547

6073
BEVERLY HILLS PLAYHOUSE
254 South Robertson Boulevard
Beverly Hills, CA 90211
Mailing Address: 254 South Robertson Boulevard, Beverly Hills, CA 90211
Phone: 310-855-1556
Fax: 310-652-4889
e-mail: interviewer@bhplayhouse.com
Web Site: www.bhplayhouse.com
Officers:
  Founder/President: Milton Katselas
Management:
  Executive Director: Allen Barton
  Producing Director: Gary Grossman
  Director of Student Affairs: Art Cohan
Paid Staff: 10
Paid Artists: 10
Season: Year Round
Type of Stage: Proscenium

6074
WALLIS ANNENBERG CENTER FOR THE PERFORMING ARTS
470 N. Canon Drive
Beverly Hills, CA 90210
Mailing Address: 9911 West Pico Blvd Suite 680 Los Angeles CA 90035
Phone: 310-246-3800
Fax: 310-557-9827
Web Site: www.bhculturalcenter.com
Officers:
  Executive Director: Lou Moore
Mission: Goldsmith Theatre: theatre classes, studio theater and 500 seat performance theatre. Opens 2013
Seating Capacity: 500

6075
BIG BEAR LAKE PERFORMING ARTS CENTER
39707 Big Bear Boulevard
PO Box 10000
Big Bear Lake, CA 92315
Mailing Address: 39707 Big Bear Blvd. P.O. Box 10000. Big Bear Lake, CA 92315
Phone: 909-866-5381
Fax: 909-878-6766
Web Site: www.citybigbearlake.com/bblpac/index.htm
Management:
  Theatre Director: Don Gavitte
  City Manager: Jeff Mathieu
  Assistant City Manager: Kathy Jefferies
Utilizes: Dance Companies; Guild Activities; Local Artists; Original Music Scores; Playwrights; Resident Artists; Special Technical Talent; Theatre Companies
Founded: 1987
Status: Non-Profit, Professional

Paid Staff: 3
Volunteer Staff: 10
Annual Attendance: 18,000
Facility Category: Performing Arts Center
Type of Stage: Wood
Stage Dimensions: 40'x55'
Seating Capacity: 398
Year Built: 1988
Cost: $3 million
Rental Contact: Manager Don Gavitte

6076
CURTIS THEATRE
1 Civic Center Circle
Brea, CA 92821
Mailing Address: 1 Civic Center Circle, Brea, CA 92821
Phone: 714-990-7600
Fax: 714-990-7635
e-mail: curtistheatre@ci.brea.ca.us
Web Site: www.ci.brea.ca.us
Officers:
  Chairman: Roy Moore
Management:
  HR Manager: Emily Keller
  Technical Director: Kevin Clowes
  Box Office Manager: Vertira Johns
Utilizes: Actors; AEA Actors; Dance Companies; Dancers; Guest Accompanists; Guest Artists; Guest Choreographers; Guest Designers; Guild Activities; Original Music Scores; Selected Students; Soloists; Theatre Companies
Founded: 1980
Status: Non-Profit, Professional
Paid Staff: 10
Paid Artists: 10
Affiliations: Western Arts Alliance; California Presenters; Association of Performing Arts
Facility Category: Theatre
Type of Stage: Procenium
Stage Dimensions: 42W X 36D
Seating Capacity: 199
Year Built: 1981
Rental Contact: Manager Christian Wolf

6077
AIA ACTOR'S STUDIO
2210 W. Olive Ave.
Suite #320
Burbank, CA 91505
Mailing Address: 2210 W. Olive Ave. Suite #320, Burbank, CA 91505
Phone: 818-563-4142
Fax: 818-563-4318
e-mail: info@aiastudios.com
Web Site: www.aiastudios.com
Officers:
  VP/Director: Emily Yost
Management:
  President: Katy Wallin
  Executive Director: Anita Jhonson
  Managing Director: Autrey Legassik
Mission: Mission is help actors achieve professional excellence. Has sucessfully integrated the business of acting with formal training. Instructors from the worlds of casting, producing, directing, writing and acting teach a diverse array of classes.
Utilizes: Actors; Educators; Filmmakers; Guest Instructors; Guest Soloists; Guest Teachers; Guild Activities; High School Drama
Founded: 1990
Status: For-Profit, Professional
Paid Staff: 10
Facility Category: Actor's Studio

Rental Contact: VP/Director Emily Yost

6078
SUNSET CULTURAL CENTER
PO Box 1950
San Carlos Street at Ninth Avenue
Carmel, CA 93921
Mailing Address: San Carlos Street at Ninth Avenue, PO Box 1950, Carmel, CA 9
Phone: 831-620-2048
Fax: 831-624-0147
e-mail: info@sunsetcenter.org
Web Site: www.sunsetcenter.org
Officers:
  President: Dave Parker
  Chairman: Elece Otten Leverone
  Vice Chairman: Kathleen Bang
  Treasurer: Lisa Boardman
  Secretary: Stan Meresman
Management:
  Executive Director: Christine Sandin
  Finance Director: Agha Bilal
  Event Manager: Mary Carrieri
  Operations Manager: Rollie Weaver
  Facilities: Mauricio Castro
  Development Manager: Barbara Davison
  Marketing and Event Coordinator: Sasha Swift
Mission: To provide performing arts experiences to the greater Monteray County area.
Founded: 2004
Specialized Field: Concerts; Recitals; Dance; Theater; Lectures
Paid Staff: 12
Paid Artists: 50
Budget: $1,850,000
Income Sources: Ticket Sales; Rent; Office Leases; Sponsorships; Governmental Supports

6079
CERRITOS CENTER FOR THE PERFORMING ARTS
12700 Center Court Drive
Cerritos, CA 90703
Mailing Address: 12700 Center Court Drive, Cerritos, CA 90703
Phone: 562-916-8510
Fax: 562-916-8514
Toll-free: 800-300-4345
e-mail: TicketOffice@CerritosCenter.com
Web Site: www.cerritoscenter.com
Management:
  Executive Director: Dianne Cheney
  Marketing Manager: Lauriey Kajiwana
  Operations: Tom Hamilton
  Performance Manager: Michael Wolfe
  Event Sales Manager: Cynthia Doss
Utilizes: Special Technical Talent; Theatre Companies
Founded: 1993
Specialized Field: Present Pop; Jazz; Classical; Opera; Dance; Broadway; Holiday; Special Attractions
Status: For-Profit, Professional
Paid Staff: 100
Volunteer Staff: 500
Paid Artists: 100
Budget: $11,000,000
Income Sources: Ticket Sales; Rental Revenue
Affiliations: California Presenters; Western Arts Alliance; APAP; ISPA; IAAM; IATT
Annual Attendance: 200,000
Facility Category: Multi-configuration auditorium
Seating Capacity: 950-1800
Year Built: 1992
Cost: $105,000,000
Rental Contact: Cynthia Doss

FACILITIES / California

6080
HARLEN ADAMS THEATRE
California State University, Chico
400 West First Street
Chico, CA 95929
Mailing Address: California State University, 400 West First Street, Chico, C
Phone: 530-898-4636
Fax: 530-898-6824
e-mail: darangoodsell@csuchico.edu
Web Site: www.csuchico.edu
Officers:
  President: Paul Zingg
Management:
  Production Manager: Michael Johnson
  Performing Arts Technician: Sandra L. Barton
  Scenic Artist: David Neal Beasley
  Costume Shop Supervisor: Sandra L. Barton
  Production Manager: Michael L. Johnson
Mission: Harlen Adams Theatre is used for cultural offerings in drama, opera, recitals, and choral programs.
Specialized Field: Dance, Music, Theatre
Type of Stage: Traditional Proscenium
Stage Dimensions: 40 foot
Orchestra Pit: y
Seating Capacity: 507

6081
LARRY WISMER THEATRE
California State University, Chico
400 West First Street
Chico, CA 95929
Mailing Address: California State University, 400 West First Street, Chico, C
Phone: 530-898-4636
Fax: 530-898-6824
e-mail: darangoodsell@csuchico.edu
Web Site: www.csuchico.edu
Officers:
  President: Paul Zingg
Management:
  Production Manager: Michael Johnson
  Performing Arts Technician: Sandra L. Barton
  Scenic Artist: David Neal Beasley
  Costume Shop Supervisor: Sandra L. Barton
  Production Manager: Michael L. Johnson
Mission: Harlen Adams Theatre is used for cultural offerings in drama, opera, recitals, and choral programs.
Specialized Field: Dance, Music, Theatre
Type of Stage: Black Box
Seating Capacity: 200

6082
LAXSON AUDITORIUM
California State University, Chico
400 West First Street
Chico, CA 95929
Mailing Address: California State University, 400 West First Street, Chico, C
Phone: 530-898-4636
Fax: 530-898-6824
e-mail: darangoodsell@csuchico.edu
Web Site: www.csuchico.edu
Officers:
  President: Paul Zingg
Management:
  Production Manager: Michael Johnson
  Performing Arts Technician: Sandra L. Barton
  Scenic Artist: David Neal Beasley
  Costume Shop Supervisor: Sandra L. Barton
  Production Manager: Michael L. Johnson
Mission: The Theatre Arts Department produces its spring musical in Laxson Auditorium. Many theatre students gain valuable experience as stage hands for the many events which are produced in Laxson.
Founded: 1931
Specialized Field: Dance, Music, Theatre
Type of Stage: Proscenium
Orchestra Pit: y
Seating Capacity: 1200

6083
ROLAND TAYLOR THEATRE
California State University-Chico
400 West 1st Street
Chico, CA 95929
Mailing Address: 400 West First St., Chico, CA 95929-805
Phone: 530-898-5152
Fax: 530-898-4797
e-mail: mus@csuchico.edu
Web Site: www.csuchico.edu
Officers:
  President: Paul Zingg
  Chairman: David J Colson
Management:
  Director: Dan De Wayne
  Managing Director Music: James Bankhead
  Administrative Support Assistant II: Adrienne Glatz
  Student Assistant: Kadie Wallace
Utilizes: Actors; Artists-in-Residence; Choreographers; Collaborating Artists; Collaborations; Commissioned Composers; Commissioned Music; Dance Companies; Dancers; Guest Accompanists; Guest Artists; Guest Instructors; Guild Activities; Instructors; Lyricists; Multi Collaborations; Multimedia; Original Music Scores; Sign Language Translators; Singers; Soloists; Special Technical Talent
Founded: 1887
Status: Nonprofit, Non-Professional
Budget: $400,000-$1,000,000
Performs At: Laxson Auditorium; Adams Theatre
Facility Category: Pit Stage; Proscenium
Seating Capacity: 1300; 500

6084
ROWLAND-TAYLOR RECITAL HALL
California State University, Chico
400 West First Street
Chico, CA 95929
Mailing Address: California State University, 400 West First Street, Chico, C
Phone: 530-898-4636
Fax: 530-898-6824
e-mail: darangoodsell@csuchico.edu
Web Site: www.csuchico.edu
Officers:
  President: Paul Zingg
Management:
  Production Manager: Michael Johnson
  Performing Arts Technician: Sandra L. Barton
  Scenic Artist: David Neal Beasley
  Costume Shop Supervisor: Sandra L. Barton
  Production Manager: Michael L. Johnson
Mission: Ruth Rowland-Taylor Recital Hall is presently used for operas, recitals, concerts, choral workshops, performance art shows, and other university gatherings.
Specialized Field: Dance, Music, Theatre
Seating Capacity: 218

6085
GARRISON THEATRE
Scripps College
1030 Columbia Avenue
Claremont, CA 91711-3948
Mailing Address: 1030 Columbia Avenue, Claremont California, 91711
Phone: 909-621-8000
Fax: 909-621-8890
e-mail: James_Taylor@pomona.edu
Web Site: www.scrippscol.edu
Officers:
  President: Lori Bettison-Varga
  VP for Enrollment: Victoria Romero
  Planning & Research Director: Janel Hastings
  Vice President Business Affairs: James Manifold
  Chair Theatre/Dance Department: James P Taylor
  Chair: Linda Davis Taylor
  Co Chair: Mark R. Herron
Management:
  Chair Theatre/Dance Department: James P Taylor
  Operations Assistant: Yvette Fahim
  Transfer Coordinator: Tina Brooks
  Director of Admission: Laura Stratton
  Executive Assistant to President: Christine Costanza
Comments: Scripps College purchased Garrison Theater in 1999.

6086
MABEL SHAW BRIDGES AUDITORIUM
Claremont College
450 North College Way
Claremont, CA 91711
Mailing Address: 333 North College Way, Claremont, CA 91711-6312
Phone: 909-621-8031
Fax: 909-621-8398
Web Site: www.cuc.claremont.edu/bridges/contact/index.html
Officers:
  President: David W. Oxtoby
  VP for Academic Affairs: Cecilia Conrad
  VP and Dean of Students: Miriam Feldblum
  VP and Treasurer: Karen Sisson
  VP of Planning: Richard Fass
Management:
  Director: Tim Morrison
  Events Manager: Sharon Kuhn
  Production Manager: Kurt Beardsley
Mission: 60,000 square feet of inside floor space; 14,000 square feet of porches and walks; seating of 2,494.

6087
THATCHER MUSIC BUILDING
450 N. College Way
Polona College
Claremont, CA 91711
Phone: 909-621-8031
Fax: 909-607-7774
e-mail: music@pomona.edu
Web Site: www.pomona.edu
Officers:
  President: David Oxtoby
  Secretary: Teresa Shaw
  Vice President and Treasurer: Karen Sisson
Management:
  Chair Music Department: Genevieve Lee
  Music Facilities Director: Graydon Beeks
  Rentals: Jan O'Neill, 9096218373
  Director: Christopher Waugh
  Production Manager: Kurt Beardsley

FACILITIES / California

Technical Director: Matt Pavey
Events Manager: Sharon Kuhn
Mission: Houses 3 venues, music library, practice rooms, office and studios for the music department

6088
SLEEP TRAIN PAVILLION AT CONCORD
2000 Kirker Pass Road
Concord, CA 94521
Mailing Address: 2000 Kirker Pass Road, Concord, CA 94521
Phone: 925-676-8742
Fax: 925-676-8742
Web Site: www.livenation.com/venues/14806/concord-pavilion-formerly-sleep-train-pavil
Management:
  General Manager: Trevor Ralph
  Director Premium Seat Sales: Javier Olazaba
  Director Promotions: Aaron Siuda
  Director of Sponsorship Sales: Molly Manin
  Box Office Manager: Jozee Perrelli
  Office Manager: Loretta Hill
Opened: 1975

6089
WILLOWS THEATRE
1425 Gasoline Alley
Concord, CA 94520
Phone: 925-798-1300
Fax: 925-676-5726
e-mail: info@willowstheatre.org
Web Site: www.willowstheatre.org
Management:
  Artistic Director: Richard Elliot
  Managing Director: Andrew Holtz
  Development Director: Barbara Grant
  Production Manager: Chris Butler
  Education/Casting Director: Cassidy Brown
  Patron Services Director: Dan Uroff
  Associate Director Education: Becky Potter
  Box Office Manager: Jonathan Spencer
  Technical Director: Adam Puglieli
Founded: 1975
Status: Non-Profit, Professional
Paid Staff: 9
Paid Artists: 50
Season: January - December
Annual Attendance: 48,000
Type of Stage: Proscenium; Amphitheater
Stage Dimensions: 40' x 26'
Seating Capacity: 210; 1200

6090
SEGERSTROM CENTER FOR THE ARTS
600 Town Center Drive
Costa Mesa, CA 92626
Mailing Address: 600 Town Center Drive, Costa Mesa, CA 92626
Phone: 714-556-2121
Fax: 714-556-8984
Web Site: www.scfta.org
Officers:
  Chairman: Lawrence M. Higby
  President: Terrence W. Dwyer
  Treasurer/ Vice Chairman: Roger T. Kirwan
  Secretary: Marta S. Bhathal
Management:
  Artistic Director: Paul Solino
  VP Programming: Judy Morr
Founded: 1986
Status: Non-Profit, Professional
Paid Staff: 75

6091
SOUTH COAST REPERTORY SEGERSTROM AUDITORIUM
655 Town Center Drive
Costa Mesa, CA 92628-2197
Mailing Address: PO Box 2197
Phone: 714-708-5500
Fax: 714-545-0391
e-mail: theatre@scr.org
Web Site: www.scr.org
Officers:
  Chairman: Michael S Gordon
  President: Damien M. Jordan
  Treasurer: John R Evans
Management:
  Artistic Director: Marc Masterson
  Managing Director: Paula Tomei
  Founding Artistic Director: David Emmes
  Development Director: Susan C. Reeder
  Marketing/Communications Director: Bill Schroeder
  Production Manager: Joshua Marchesi
  Operations Manager: Luis De La Cruz
  Casting Director: Joanne DeNaut
  Literary Director: Kelly L. Miller
Founded: 1954
Status: Non-Profit, Professional
Paid Staff: 75
Seating Capacity: 507

6092
VETERAN'S MEMORIAL COMPLEX
4117 Overland Avenue
Culver City, CA 90230
Mailing Address: 4117 Overland Ave., Culver City, CA, 90232
Phone: 310-670-4471
Fax: 310-253-6629
Web Site: www.culvercity.org/citygov/humanservices/fac_reserv.html
Management:
  City Parks & Recreation Director: Don Rogers
  Veteran's Memorial Complex Manager: Pam Robinson
  City Recreation Manager: Marty Nicholson
  City Parks Supervisor: Taks Matsurra
  City Senior Management Analyst: Patti Mooney
Mission: The Veterans' Memorial Complex is a Community and Recreation facility that includes a 1500 seat auditorium, 13 meeting and banquet rooms, a basketball court, a Teen Center and a Senior Citizens Center.
Founded: 1917
Status: For-Profit, Non-Professional

6093
FLINT CENTER FOR THE PERFORMING ARTS
De Anza College
21250 Stevens Creek Boulevard, 4th Floor
Cupertino, CA 95015
Mailing Address: PO Box 1897, Cupertino, CA 95015
Phone: 408-864-8820
Fax: 408-864-8918
Web Site: www.flintcenter.com
Officers:
  Dean Creative Arts Department: Nancy J Canter, Ph.D
Management:
  General Manager: Paula J Davis
Founded: 1971
Annual Attendance: 265,000
Type of Stage: Proscenium
Seating Capacity: 2,300

6094
BARBARA K & W TURRENTINE JACKSON HALL
Mondavi Center
One Shields Avenue
Davis, CA 95616-8543
Mailing Address: One Shields Avenue, Davis, CA, 95616-8543
Phone: 530-752-9041
Fax: 530-752-3055
e-mail: dkholoman@ucdavis.edu
Web Site: hector.ucdavis.edu/ucdso/04Always/AboutJacksonMondavi.htm
Management:
  Executive Director: Don Roth Ph.D
  Programming Director: Jeremy Genter
  Campus Engagement Director: David Webbs
  Marketing Manager: Rebecca Summers
  Arts Education Community Director: Joyce Donaldson
  Director of Development: Silvia M H Lester
  Director of Technology Services: Shaun Owens
  Director Audience Services: Kelly Denny
  Facility Director: John Dorsey
Founded: 1977
Status: Non-Profit, Non-Professional
Paid Staff: 240
Seating Capacity: 1,801

6095
ROBERT & MARGRIT MONDAVI CENTER FOR THE PERFORMING ARTS
Mondavi Center Admin Bldg
One Shields Avenue
Davis, CA 95616-8543
Mailing Address: One Shields Avenue, Davis, CA, 95616-8543
Phone: 530-754-2787
Fax: 530-754-5519
e-mail: droth@ucdavis.edu
Web Site: www.mondaviarts.org
Management:
  Executive Director: Don Roth
  Programming Director: Jeremy Ganter
  Director Campus Engagement: David Webb
  Marketing Manager: Rebecca Summers
  Director of Development: Silvia M H Lester
  Ticketing Manager: Rickey Booker
  Facility Director: John Dorsey
  Director Business Services: Debbie Armstrong
  Director Technology Services: Shaun Owens
Founded: 1961
Status: Non-Profit, Professional
Paid Staff: 5
Annual Attendance: 50,000
Seating Capacity: 200

6096
STUDIO THEATRE
University of California, Davis
Administration Building
One Shields Avenue
Davis, CA 95616-8543
Mailing Address: One Shields Avenue, Davis, CA, 95616-8543
Phone: 530-754-2787
Fax: 530-754-5519
e-mail: mcrentals@ucdavis.edu
Web Site: www.mondaviarts.org

FACILITIES / California

Officers:
President: Garry P. Maisel
Executive Director: Don Roth, PhD
Director Programming: Jeremy Ganter
Director of Facilities: John Dorsey
Management:
Production Stage Manager: Steve Lorick
Assistant Production Manager: Rick Berger
Mission: Presents a full range of campus-based and international musical, theatrical and dance performances and is a learning laboratory for students of the performing arts.
Utilizes: Resident Artists
Specialized Field: Dance, Music, Theatre
Type of Stage: Adaptable Stage
Seating Capacity: 250
Year Built: 2002

6097
VETERANS' MEMORIAL THEATRE
203 East 14th Street
Davis, CA 95616
Mailing Address: 203 E. 14th St., Davis, CA 95616
Phone: 530-757-5626
Fax: 530-758-9218
Web Site: www.davisvisitor.com/brochures/Facility%20Guide%20and%20Map
Management:
Executive Director: Robert Stephenson
Seating Capacity: 325

6098
W. TURRENTINE AND BARBARA K. JACKSON HALL
University of California, Davis
Administration Building
One Shields Avenue
Davis, CA 95616-8543
Mailing Address: One Shields Avenue, Davis, CA, 95616-8543
Phone: 530-754-2787
Fax: 530-754-5519
e-mail: mcrentals@ucdavis.edu
Web Site: www.mondaviarts.org
Officers:
President: Garry P. Maisel
Executive Director: Don Roth, PhD
Director Programming: Jeremy Ganter
Director of Facilities: John Dorsey
Management:
Production Stage Manager: Steve Lorick
Assistant Production Manager: Rick Berger
Mission: Presents a full range of campus-based and international musical, theatrical and dance performances and is a learning laboratory for students of the performing arts.
Utilizes: Resident Artists
Specialized Field: Classical
Type of Stage: Adaptable Stage
Seating Capacity: 1800
Year Built: 2002

6099
EAST COUNTY PERFORMING ARTS CENTER - THEATRE
210 E Main Street
El Cajon, CA 92020
Phone: 619-440-2277
Fax: 619-440-6429
Web Site: www.ecpac.com
Officers:
President/CEO: Dick Zellner
Management:
Executive Director: Paul Russell
Managing Director: Cathie Stanner
Operations Director: Melissa Hill
Technical Director: Kristina Claar
Marketing Director: Roxanne Fulkerson
Mission: Performing arts presenter and rental house. We book nationally and internationally recognized performers, from the Dixie Chicks to Bob Newhart, from Alvin Ailey to Dave Kue.
Utilizes: Artists-in-Residence; Dance Companies; Fine Artists; Instructors; Local Artists; Multimedia; Original Music Scores; Special Technical Talent; Theatre Companies
Founded: 1977
Specialized Field: Concert Presenter; Arts Education; Visual Arts; Touring Theatres
Status: Non-Profit, Professional
Paid Staff: 8
Budget: $1,900,000
Income Sources: Ticket revenues; Corporate sponsors; Individual donors; Foundations
Performs At: East County Performing Arts Center
Affiliations: Western Alliance of Arts Admistrators, International Association ofAuditorium Managers
Annual Attendance: 100,000
Facility Category: Concert Hall
Type of Stage: Proscenium
Stage Dimensions: 40 x 70
Seating Capacity: 1,142
Year Built: 1977
Year Remodeled: 1998
Rental Contact: Director of Operations Melissa Hill

6100
SOUTHWEST PERFORMING ARTS THEATRE
2001 Ocotillo Drive
El Centro, CA 92243
Mailing Address: 2001 Ocotillo Drive, El Centro, CA 92243
Phone: 760-336-4228
Fax: 760-336-4244
e-mail: theatres@cuhsd.net
Web Site: www.southwesttheatre.com
Management:
President: Orland Foote
Theatre Manager: Ron Newhouse
Founded: 1996
Status: Non-Profit, Non-Professional
Paid Staff: 2
Seating Capacity: 1,150

6101
CALIFORNIA CENTER FOR THE ARTS-ESCONDIDO
340 N Escondido Boulevard
Escondido, CA 92025
Mailing Address: 340 North Escondido Boulevard, Escondido, CA 92025
Phone: 760-839-4138
Fax: 760-739-0205
Toll-free: 800-988-4253
e-mail: info@artcenter.org
Web Site: www.artcenter.org
Officers:
VP/General Manager: Vicky Basehore
Performing Arts Director: Joanne Ewan-Kroeger
Utilizes: Actors; Dance Companies; Multimedia; Singers; Student Interns; Special Technical Talent; Theatre Companies; Touring Companies
Founded: 1994
Status: Non-Profit, Professional
Paid Staff: 100

6102
FONTANA PERFORMING ARTS CENTER
8353 Sierra Ave.
Fontana, CA 92335
Mailing Address: 8353 Sierra Ave., Fontana, CA 92335
Phone: 909-350-7600
Fax: 909-428-2546
e-mail: kherron @ fontana.org
Web Site: www.fontana.org/main/parks_rec/rec_home.htm
Management:
Director: Ken Herron
Manager: Ray Gonzales
Management Services: Lisa Strong
Community Services Supervisors: Michael Wright
Community Services Supervisors: Mariana Mitchell
Status: Non-Profit, Professional
Paid Staff: 15

6103
GARY SOREN SMITH CENTER FOR THE FINE AND PERFORMING ARTS
43600 Mission Boulevard
Fremont, CA 94539
Mailing Address: 43600 Mission Boulevard, Fremont, CA 94539-5847
Phone: 510-659-6031
Fax: 510-659-6188
e-mail: boxoffice@ohlone.edu
Web Site: www.ohlone.edu
Management:
Dean Fine Arts: Walter B. Birkedahl
Director Theatre Operations: Christopher Booras
Technical Coordinator: Jasper Gong
Technical Assistant: Adam Fresquez
Box Office Manager: Maria Gonzalez
Mission: The Gary Soren Smith Center for the Fine and Performing Arts houses the G. Craig Jackson main stage theater with a seating capacity of 405, the NUMMI studio theater, the Louie Art Gallery, an outdoor amphitheater, a dance studio, television studios, and a radio station.
Founded: 1995
Opened: 1995
Specialized Field: Performing Arts

6104
BULLDOGS STADIUM
5305 North Campus Drive NG27
Fresno, CA 93740
Phone: 559-278-2643
Fax: 559-278-6611
Web Site: www.gobulldogs.com
Management:
Director Athletics Department: Thomas Boeh
Facilities Operations Director: John Kriebs
Athletic Development Director: Gregory Walaitis
Operations Manager: Richard Enns
Athletic Compliance Director: John Lucier
Marketing Director: Sarah Teachey
Director Media Relations: Steve Weakland
Director External Affairs: Paul Ladwig
Founded: 1980
Seating Capacity: 41,031

FACILITIES / California

6105
FRESNO CONVENTION & ENTERTAINMENT CENTER
848 M Street
2nd Floor
Fresno, CA 93721
Mailing Address: 848 M Street, 2nd Floor, Fresno, CA 93721
Phone: 559-445-8100
Fax: 559-445-8110
e-mail: bill.overfelt@fresno.gov
Web Site: www.fresnoconventioncenter.com
Management:
  Director Finance: Lyn Higginson
  General Manager: William Overfelt
  Director Sales Marketing: Claudia Arguelles Miller
  Director Events Services: Wilhelmina Santana
  Director Operations: Theresa Kraus
  Box Office Manager: Matt Heinks
  Sales Manager: Shannon Stewart
Mission: Robert A. Schoettler Conference Center, with a 13,129 square foot ballroom which can accommodate 1,200 theatre style seats or 900 for a banquet; William Saroyan Theatre With 2,353 luxuriously upholstered seats; Convention Center features 67,000 square feet of uninterrupted exhibit space with an additional 16,000 square feet of available exhibit space in the first and second floor lobbies; and the Selland Arena with a seating capacity of 11,300.
Founded: 1966
Paid Staff: 60
Volunteer Staff: 150
Budget: $2 million
Income Sources: Rentals
Performs At: Performing Arts Theater
Year Built: 1966
Year Remodeled: 1992
Cost: $ 3 Million
Rental Contact: Mercy Tritian

6106
RATCLIFFE STADIUM
1101 East University Avenue
Fresno, CA 93741
Mailing Address: 1101 East University Ave, Fresno, CA 93741
Phone: 559-442-4600
Fax: 559-489-2281
Toll-free: 866-245-3276
e-mail: susan.yates@fresnocitycollege.edu
Web Site: www.fresnocitycollege.edu
Officers:
  President: Tony Cantu
Management:
  Athletic Director: Susan Yates
  Sports Publicist: Woody Wilk
  Communications/Marketing Director: Cris Monahan Bremer
  Public Information Officer: Kathleen Bonilla
  Business Manager: Michael Guerra
Founded: 1926
Seating Capacity: 13,500

6107
TOWER THEATER FOR THE PEFORMING ARTS
815 E Olive Ave
Fresno, CA 93728
Phone: 559-485-9050
Fax: 559-485-3941
e-mail: snev@sbcglobal.net
Web Site: www.towertheatrefresno.org
Management:
  Theatre Director: Lawrence Abbate
  Rental Facility Agent: Susan Neville
Facility Category: Theatre
Seating Capacity: 761

6108
WARNOR'S THEATER
1400 Fulton Street
Fresno, CA 93721
Mailing Address: 1400 Fulton Street, Fresno CA 93721
Phone: 559-264-2848
Fax: 559-264-5643
e-mail: paul@warnors.com
Web Site: www.warnors.com
Management:
  General Manager: Paul Fountaine
Mission: Warnors Theatre, located in downtown Fresno, has a rich heritage reaching back to its inaugural year of 1928, having a seating capacity of 2,100.
Founded: 1928

6109
WHALBERG RECITAL HALL
5201 N. Maple Ave. M/S SA46
2380 East Keats
Fresno, CA 93740-8027
Mailing Address: 5201 N. Maple Ave. M/S SA46, Fresno, CA 93740-8027
Phone: 559-278-3987
Fax: 559-278-7215
Web Site: www.fresnostate.edu
Management:
  Costume Shop Supervisor: Stephanie Bradshaw
  Business & Promotions Manager: Pamela Dyer
  Scene Shop Supervisor: Michael Hansen
  Costume Shop Technician: Kelly Pantzlaff Curry
  Administrative Support Coordinato: Cathie r Salanitro
  Director Publications/New Media: Bruce Whitworth
  Director Campaign Communications: Shannon Puphal
Mission: Theatre Arts students work side-by-side with faculty to create exciting productions
Founded: 1911
Specialized Field: Dance, Music, Theatre
Status: For-Profit, Professional
Seating Capacity: 100

6110
HALLBERG THEATRE
California State University, Fullerton
800 N. State College Blvd
Fullerton, CA 92831-3599
Mailing Address: P.O. Box 6850, Fullerton, CA 92834-6850
Phone: 657-278-3628
Fax: 657-278-7041
e-mail: gaildawson@fullerton.edu
Web Site: www.fullerton.edu/arts
Officers:
  President: Milton A. Gordon
  Dean, College of the Arts: Dr. Joseph Arnold
Management:
  Chair: Marc R. Dickey
  Department Administrative Coordinat: Gail Dawson
  Department Chair: Larry Johnson
  Director: Julie Bussell
  Box Office Manager & Systems Admini: Sandra Clark
Mission: The new performing arts center will expand the theatre, dance and music programs' physical capabilities, but allow imaginations to soar and explore new artistic possibilities.
Specialized Field: Experimental Productions and will showcase new plays, ballet
Type of Stage: Black Box
Seating Capacity: 150
Architect: Pfeiffer Partners

6111
MENG CONCERT HALL
California State University, Fullerton
800 N. State College Blvd
Fullerton, CA 92831-3599
Mailing Address: P.O. Box 6850. Fullerton, CA 92834-6850
Phone: 657-278-3628
Fax: 657-278-7041
e-mail: gaildawson@fullerton.edu
Web Site: www.fullerton.edu/arts
Officers:
  President: Milton A. Gordon
  Dean, College of the Arts: Dr. Joseph Arnold
Management:
  Chair: Marc R. Dickey
  Department Administrative Coordinat: Gail Dawson
  Department Chair: Larry Johnson
  Director: Julie Bussell
  Box Office Manager & Systems Admini: Sandra Clark
Mission: The new performing arts center will expand the theatre, dance and music programs' physical capabilities, but allow imaginations to soar and explore new artistic possibilities.
Specialized Field: Choral and Instrumental Ensembles
Seating Capacity: 800
Architect: Pfeiffer Partners

6112
THE MUCKENTHALER CULTURAL CENTER
1201 W Malvern Avenue
Fullerton, CA 92833
Mailing Address: 1201 West Malvern Avenue, Fullerton, California 92833
Phone: 714-738-6595
Fax: 714-738-6366
Toll-free: 866-411-1212
e-mail: info@themuck.org
Web Site: www.themuck.org
Officers:
  President: Fred Ouweleen
  Vice President: Marianne Dolan
  Vice President: Craig Walker
  Treasurer: Marcia Ryan
  Treasurer: Andy Ersek
Management:
  Executive Director: Zoot Velasco
  Director Of Exhibitions: Matthew Leslie
  Marketing Director: Allison Town
  Lead Artist: Willie Tabath
  Events Manager: Stefan Tatarowski
Mission: To provide our community experiences that stimulate creativity and imagination, and to conserve the heritage and architecture of the Muckenthaler estate.
Founded: 1965
Specialized Field: Multi-Cultural/Multi Discipline
Status: For-Profit, Professional
Paid Staff: 11
Volunteer Staff: 600
Paid Artists: 9

Budget: $724,968
Income Sources: City, Corporation and Foundation Grants; Generated Revenue
Performs At: Outdoor Amphitheatre
Annual Attendance: 25,000
Facility Category: Historic Mansion

6113
FCLO MUSIC THEATRE
218 W, Commonwealth Avenue
Fullerton, CA 92832
Phone: 714-870-2813
Fax: 714-992-1193
e-mail: marilyn@fclo.com
Web Site: www.fclo.com
Officers:
   President: John Bedell
   Vice President: Norma Jones
   Secretary: Doris Winters
   Treasurer: Gordon Haag, MD
Management:
   General Manager: Griff Duncan
   Artistic Director: Jan Duncan
   Resident Stage Manager: Donna Parsons
   Costume Rental Manager: Faye Robinson
   Scenic Operations Manager: Larry Knigge
   Public Relations/Marketing/Sales: Marilyn Gianetti
Mission: Plummer Auditorium is home to the Fullerton Civic Light Opera, the mission of which is to present live stage musicals for the enjoyment and cultural enrichment of the general public at affordable prices. A key focus of their mission is to educate youth in this distinctly American art form, and create a lasting interest and appreciation for it in addition to providing access for under priviledged youth and adults.
Founded: 1930
Specialized Field: Theater, Musicals
Status: non- profit
Annual Attendance: r
Seating Capacity: 1,300

6114
YOUNG THEATRE
California State University, Fullerton
800 N. State College Blvd
Fullerton, CA 92831-3599
Mailing Address: P.O. Box 6850. Fullerton, CA 92834-6850
Phone: 657-278-3628
Fax: 657-278-7041
e-mail: ddombrow@fullerton.edu
Web Site: www.fullerton.edu/arts
Officers:
   President: Milton A. Gordon
   Dean, College of the Arts: Dr. Joseph Arnold
Management:
   Chair: Marc R. Dickey
   Department Administrative Coordinat: Debbie Dombrow
   Department Chair: Bruce Goodrich
   Director: Julie Bussell
   Box Office Manager & Systems Admini: Sandra Clark
Mission: The new performing arts center will expand the theatre, dance and music programs' physical capabilities, but allow imaginations to soar and explore new artistic possibilities.
Specialized Field: Dramatic Productions from the Classics to Contemporary
Type of Stage: Thrust Stage Theatre
Seating Capacity: 250
Architect: Pfeiffer Partners

6115
ALEX THEATRE
216 North Brand Boulevard
Glendale, CA 91203
Mailing Address: 216 North Brand Boulevard, Glendale, California 91203
Phone: 818-243-2539
Fax: 818-243-3622
e-mail: info@alextheatre.org
Web Site: www.alextheatre.org
Officers:
   Chairman: Harry Hull
   Vice Chairman: Peter Ciulla
   Treasurer: Patrick Karapetian
   Secretary: Joylene Wagner
   VP Membership: Marcia Hanford
Management:
   Executive Director: Barry McComb
   General Manager: Jack Allaway
   CEO: Elissa Glickman
   Director of Marketing & Events: Maria Sahakian
   Box Office Manager: Judith Baker
   Controller: Sandy Leitao
   Maintenance Supervisor: Hector Martinez
   Master Electrician: David Robkin
   Event Services Manager: Betty Jean Morris
Founded: 1925
Seating Capacity: 1,460

6116
HAUGH PERFORMING ARTS CENTER
Citrus College
1000 West Foothill Boulevard
Glendora, CA 91741
Mailing Address: 1000 West Foothill Boulevard, Glendora, CA 91741-1899
Phone: 626-963-9411
Fax: 626-335-4715
e-mail: hpac@citruscollege.edu
Web Site: www.haughpac.com
Officers:
   President: Dr Geraldine Perri
Management:
   Interim Performing Arts Director: John Vaughan
   Marketing & Operations: Linda Graves
   Technical Director: Dan Vilter
   Graphic Designer: Diane Berendes
   Scene Shop Supervisor: John Patrick
   Administrative Secretary: Sharol Carter
Founded: 1971
Status: Nonprofit, Non-Professional
Paid Staff: 6
Paid Artists: 10
Annual Attendance: 100,000
Type of Stage: Flexible; Proscenium
Seating Capacity: 1,400

6117
THE CENTER FOR THE ARTS
314 W Main St
Grass Valley, CA 95945
Phone: 530-274-8384
Fax: 530-272-7084
e-mail: info@thecenterforthearts.org
Web Site: www.thecenterforthearts.org
Officers:
   Executive Director: Julie Baker
Management:
   Booking And Production Manager: Nancy Solyan
   Director of Facilities, Operations: David Spellman
   Executive Director: Julie Baker
   Marketing Manager: Pamela Roberts
   Technical Director: John Taber
Mission: Cutural and educational facility promoting literary, visual and performing arts.

6118
CALIFORNIA STATE UNIVERSITY-HAYWARD - MAIN THEATRE
Theatre & Dance Department
25800 Carlos Bee Boulevard
Hayward, CA 94542
Mailing Address: 25800 Carlos Bee Boulevard, Hayward, CA 94542
Phone: 510-885-3000
Fax: 510-885-4748
e-mail: applycsh@csuhayward.edu
Web Site: www20.csueastbay.edu
Officers:
   President: Norma Reese
   Department Chairman: Thomas Hird
   College/Department Dean: Alden Reimonenq, Ph.D
Management:
   Director New Music Theatre: Darryl V Jones
   Artistic Director: Timothy Smith
Mission: Built in 1971, the theatre building houses two theatres - the 480-seat main University Theatre and the flexible Studio Theatre, which can seat between 150 to 250.
Status: Non-Profit, Non-Professional
Paid Staff: 35
Paid Artists: 18

6119
CHABOT COLLEGE PERFORMING ARTS CENTER
Chabot College
25555 Hesperian Boulevard
Hayward, CA 94545
Mailing Address: 25555 Hesperian Blvd., Hayward CA 94545
Phone: 510-723-6976
Fax: 510-723-7157
e-mail: kmcallister@chabotcollege.edu
Web Site: www.chabotcollege.edu/PAC/
Officers:
   Dean: Gary Carter
Management:
   Theatre Manager: Kari McAllister
   Stage Technician: Gene Hale
   Community Education Specialist: Judy Vetters
   Director Community Education/Mrktng: Susan May
Mission: First opened in 1967, the Performing Arts Center is a 1,432-seat auditorium, which functions as a full featured theater. The Little Theater, located in Building 1200, is a 200 seat capacity intimate viewing space that is ideal for meetings, movies and other smaller scaled productions.
Founded: 1967
Status: Non-Profit, Professional
Paid Staff: 15
Income Sources: Rentals
Annual Attendance: 100,000
Type of Stage: Proscenium
Stage Dimensions: 36'x45'
Seating Capacity: 1,432
Year Built: 1967
Cost: $1.8 million

FACILITIES / California

6120
STUDIO THEATRE
California State University, East Bay
Theatre And Dance Department
25800 Carlos Bee Boulevard
Hayward, CA 94542
Mailing Address: 25800 Carlos Bee Boulevard,
Hayward, CA 94542
Phone: 510-885-3000
e-mail: thomas.hird@csueastbay.edu
Web Site: www20.csueastbay.edu
Officers:
   President: Mo Qayoumi
Management:
   Department Chair: Tom Hird
Mission: Performance at Cal State is an important aspect of the department's undergraduate curriculum. The program leading to the Bachelor or Arts in Theatre degree provides comprehensive instruction in the theatre arts.
Specialized Field: Dance, Music, Theatre
Type of Stage: Flexible
Seating Capacity: 250

6121
UNIVERSITY THEATRE
California State University, East Bay
Theatre And Dance Department
25800 Carlos Bee Boulevard
Hayward, CA 94542
Mailing Address: 25800 Carlos Bee Boulevard,
Hayward, CA 94542
Phone: 510-885-3000
e-mail: thomas.hird@csueastbay.edu
Web Site: www20.csueastbay.edu
Officers:
   President: Mo Qayoumi
Management:
   Department Chair: Tom Hird
Mission: Performance at Cal State is an important aspect of the department's undergraduate curriculum. The program leading to the Bachelor or Arts in Theatre degree provides comprehensive instruction in the theatre arts.
Specialized Field: Dance, Music, Theatre
Seating Capacity: 480

6122
RAMONA BOWL AMPHITHEATRE
27400 Ramona Bowl Road
Hemet, CA 92544
Mailing Address: 27400 Ramona Bowl Road, Hemet California 92544
Phone: 951-658-3111
Fax: 909-658-2695
Toll-free: 800-645-4465
e-mail: ramona@ramonabowl.com
Web Site: www.ramonabowl.com
Officers:
   President: Myrna Rohr
   Vice President: Al Cordova
   Secretary: Amelia Hippert
   Treasurer: Mary Wright
Management:
   General Manager: Linda Hoogestraat
   Artistic Director: Dennis Anderson
   Business Manager: Kathy Long
   Ticket Office Manager: Julie Weidemann
   Maintenance Manager: Jose Torres
   Ticket Office Assistant: Stephanie Parssinen
Mission: To promote and produce The Ramona Pageant, America's longest running outdoor drama; to promote the Ramona Bowl Amphitheatre for events.
Founded: 1927
Status: Non-Profit, Non-Professional
Seating Capacity: 6,500

6123
COORS AMPHITHEATRE
7060 Hollywood Blvd.
11th Floor
Hollywood, CA 90028
Mailing Address: 7060 Hollywood Blvd., 11th Floor, Hollywood, CA 90028
Phone: 323-769-4600
Fax: 303-220-7407
Web Site: www.hob.com
Management:
   General Manager: Kyle Svanda
   Operations Manager: Jack Ahrens
   Assistant Operations Manager: Trevor Herasingh
   Administration: Christian Lewis
Founded: 1988
Specialized Field: Concerts
Seating Capacity: 16,283

6124
HOLLYWOOD BOWL
2301 N Highland Avenue
Hollywood, CA 90078
Mailing Address: 2301 North Highland Avenue, Hollywood, CA 90068
Phone: 323-850-2000
Fax: 323-850-2155
e-mail: dborda@laphil.org
Web Site: www.hollywoodbowl.com
Officers:
   Chairman: David C. Bohnett
   Secretary: Alan Wayte
Management:
   President, CEO: Debra Borda
   Director Development: Evie DiCiaccio
   Chief Operating Officer: Gail Samuel
   Controller/Treasurer: Ida Chan
   Marketing Coordinator: Katie Airey
   Assistant Manager: Nick Gianopoulos
   Stage Manager: Drew Flaherty
   Senior Publicist: Lisa Bellamore
Founded: 1922
Status: For-Profit, Professional
Seating Capacity: 18,000

6125
HOLLYWOOD COMPLEX THEATRE
6476 Santa Monica Boulevard
Hollywood, CA 90038
Mailing Address: 6476 Santa Monica Blvd., Hollywood, CA 90038
Phone: 323-465-0383
Fax: 323-469-5408
e-mail: complexhollywood@hotmail.com
Web Site: www.complexhollywood.com
Management:
   President/Director: Matt Chait
Mission: The Hollywood Complex Theatres consists of: the Ruby Theatre with a seating capacity of 55; Dorie Theatre - seating capacity of 55; Flight Theatre - seating capacity of 49; Theatre 6470 - seating capacity of 42; and the East Theatre with a seating capacity of 49.
Founded: 1989
Status: For-Profit, Non-Professional
Paid Staff: 1
Paid Artists: 1

6126
HOLLYWOOD PALLADIUM
6215 W Sunset Boulevard
Hollywood, CA 90028
Phone: 323-962-7600
Fax: 323-962-7502
Web Site: www.livenation.com/venues/14586/hollywood-palladium
Management:
   President: Allan Shuman
Mission: We are an all purpose revue that has music acts as well as conventions and dinner events.
Founded: 1940
Status: For-Profit, Non-Professional

6127
JOHN ANSON FORD THEATRES
2580 Cahauga Boulevard E
Hollywood, CA 90068
Mailing Address: 2580 Cahuenga Blvd. East, Hollywood, CA 90068
Phone: 323-461-3673
Fax: 323-871-5904
e-mail: boxoffice@arts.lacounty.gov
Web Site: www.fordamphitheatre.org
Management:
   Managing Director: Adam Davis
   Director Development: Louanne Brazil
   Event Services Manager: William Berry
   Director of Communications: Leticia Rhi Buckley
   Box Office Manager: Eve Cakar
   Operations Manager: Marah Morris
Founded: 1920
Status: Volunteer
Facility Category: Amphitheatre/ Black Box
Seating Capacity: 1245/87
Rental Contact: David Pier

6128
KODAK THEATRE
6801 North Hollywood Boulevard
Suite 180
Hollywood, CA 90028
Mailing Address: 6801 Hollywood Boulevard, Hollywood, CA 90028
Phone: 323-308-6300
Fax: 323-308-6381
e-mail: info@kodaktheatre.com
Web Site: www.kodaktheatre.com
Management:
   VP and General Manager: Jay Thomas
   Marketing/Event Services Manager: Natalie Vo
   Box Office Manager: Ly Pham
   Technical Director: Alys Holden
Mission: Kodak Theatre is the crown jewel of the Hollywood & Highland Center retail, dining and entertainment complex located in the heart of historic Hollywood.
Founded: 2001
Specialized Field: Concerts, Comedians, American Ballet Theatre and various touring Broadway productions, award events
Seating Capacity: 3.4

6129
RICARDO MONTALBAN THEATER
Will and Company
1615 North Vine Street
Hollywood, CA 90028

Mailing Address: 1615 North Vine Street, Hollywood, CA 90028
Phone: 323-871-2420
e-mail: gilbertsmith@themontalban.com
Web Site: www.themontalban.com
Officers:
   President: Jerry G Velasco
   1st Vice President: Felipe Alejandro
   2nd Vice President: Jesse Arranda
   Chair, Secretary: Gilbert Smith
   VP, Treasurer: Margarita Martinez
Management:
   Artistic Director: Margarita Cannon
   Managing Producer: Gilbert A. Smith
   American Latino Film Festival Mgr: Felipe Alejandro
   Showcase/E-Group Manager: Jesse Aranda
   Artistic Director: Margarita Cannan
   House Manager: Ricardo Ortiz-Barreto
   Producer: Tom Quinn
Mission: The program, designed to inspire children's imaginations through reading and live performance
Founded: 1926
Specialized Field: Movies, theater, concerts, sports, award ceremonies.
Seating Capacity: 1,200

6130
THEATRE EAST
6760 Lexington Avenue
Hollywood, CA 90038
Phone: 323-957-5720
Web Site: www.theatreeast.com/interface/index.php?action=home
Officers:
   President: Chris White
   Director: Leif Gantvoort
   Director: Peter Haskell
   Director: Alan Naggar
   Director: Walter Novak
   Director: Tabatha Sheltra
   Director: Pag Shirley
Mission: Theatre East was founded in 1960 to provide a forum and workshop for professional artists in the theatrical and allied arts to develop their talents and skills through live performance and evaluation. The Lex, where Theate East is housed, is a versatile, 49-seat black-box theatre space that can be variously configured to suit your staging requirements.
Founded: 1960

6131
GOLDEN WEST COLLEGE MAINSTAGE THEATRE
15744 Golden West Street
Huntington Beach, CA 92647-2748
Mailing Address: 15744 Golden West Street, Huntington Beach, CA 92647-2748
Phone: 714-895-8150
Fax: 714-895-8784
e-mail: tamen@gwc.cccd.edu
Web Site: www.gwctheater.com/
Management:
   Director: Tom Amen
   Director: Martie Ramm
   Stage Crew/Set Construction: Sigrid Wolf
   Costuming/Makeup: Susan Babb
   Division Administrative Coordinator: Lynn Schramm
   Usher: Ann Yarchin
Status: Non-Profit, Professional
Paid Staff: 800
Seating Capacity: 367

6132
BREN EVENTS CENTER
University of California, Irvine
100 Bren Events Center
Irvine, CA 92697
Mailing Address: 100 Bren Events Center, Irvine, CA 92697-1500
Phone: 949-824-5000
Fax: 949-824-5097
e-mail: dspitzer@uci.edu
Web Site: www.bren.uci.edu
Management:
   Director: Bernadette Strobel-Lopez
   Business Manager: Kristina Engel
   Office Manager: Sheryl Suarez
   Technical Manager: David Da Costa
   Maintenance Supervisor: Jack Brooks
   Production/Events Manager: Carla Gonzalez
   Booking Manager: Jeff Grady
   Events/Operations Manager: Daniel Spitzer
   Manager: Marko Popovich
Mission: The Bren Center has a maximum capacity of 5,700 for concert and entertainment events with 4,984 for court sports such as basketball and volleyball. There are 2,610 fixed seats, 2,374 in retracting or telescopic bleachers.
Founded: 1987
Status: For-Profit, Non-Professional
Paid Staff: 80
Annual Attendance: 175,000
Type of Stage: Portable
Rental Contact: Danny Spitzer

6133
CLAIRE TREVOR SCHOOL OF THE ARTS
University of California, Irvine
4000 Mesa Road
Irvine, CA 92697-2775
Mailing Address: 4000 Mesa Rd., Irvine, CA 92697-2775
Phone: 949-824-4339
e-mail: artsinfo@uci.edu
Web Site: www.arts.uci.edu
Management:
   Artistic Director: David Familian
   Program Manager: Samantha Younghans-Haug
   Box Office Manager: David Walker
   Director of Financial Operations: Alan Doig
   Sr. Financial Analyst: Leo Ixcamey
Mission: Dedicated to the study of the visual and performing arts.
Specialized Field: Arts; Live Music; Performance; Stage; Theater
Type of Stage: Proscenium
Seating Capacity: 285

6134
IRVINE BARCLAY THEATRE
4242 Campus Drive
Suite 680
Irvine, CA 92612
Mailing Address: PO Box 5646, Irvine, CA 92616-5646
Phone: 949-854-4646
e-mail: info@thebarclay.org
Web Site: www.thebarclay.org
Officers:
   President: Douglas C. Rankin
   Vice President: Domenick Ietto
   General Manager: Chris Burrill
   Dir Communications/Program Dvlpment: Karen Drews Hanlon
   Production Manager: Jim Laird
Management:
   General Manager: Christopher Burrill
   Marketing Assistant: Helena Danovich
   Director of Communications: Karen Drews Hanlon
   Chief Development Officer: Julia Baumgarten Foster
   Director of Finance: Gary Payne
Mission: The mission of the Irvine Barclay Theatre is to be a presenter featuring the work of diverse and exceptional artists and providing a state-of-the-art venue for community cultural organizations and University programs, thus broadening the scope, availability and appreciation of the performing arts in Orange County.
Specialized Field: Dance; Music; Theatre
Status: Private, Not-for-Profit
Type of Stage: Proscenium
Stage Dimensions: 87'3W x 40'6D
Orchestra Pit: Y
Seating Capacity: 756
Year Built: 1990

6135
CLAIRE TREVOR SCHOOL OF THE ARTS
University of California
4000 Mesa Road
Irvine, CA 92697-2775
Mailing Address: 4000 Mesa Rd., Irvine, CA 92697-2775
Phone: 949-824-4339
e-mail: elmartin@uci.edu
Web Site: www.arts.uci.edu
Officers:
   Director Marketing: Wendy Day-Brown
   Director Development: Ryan Marsh
   Production Manager: Toby F. Weiner
   Facilities Manager: Anthony E. Marquez
Management:
   Artistic Director: David Familian
   Program Manager: Samantha Younghans-Haug
   Box Office Manager: David Walker
   Director of Financial Operations: Alan Doig
   Sr. Financial Analyst: Leo Ixcamey
Mission: Dedicated to the study of the visual and performing arts.
Specialized Field: Arts; Live Music; Performance; Stage; Theater
Type of Stage: Modified Thrust Platform Stage
Seating Capacity: 230

6136
ATHENAEUM MUSIC & ARTS LIBRARY
1008 Wall Street
La Jolla, CA 92037
Mailing Address: 1008 Wall St., La Jolla, CA 92037
Phone: 858-454-5872
Fax: 858-454-5835
e-mail: athlib@pacbell.net
Web Site: ljathenaeum.org
Management:
   Managing Director: Erika Torri
   Program Director: Geoffrey Brooks
Utilizes: Artists-in-Residence; Commissioned Composers; Commissioned Music; Curators; Fine Artists; Grant Writers; Guest Companies; Guest Directors; Guest Ensembles; Guest Instructors; Guest Musical Directors; Guest Musicians; Guest Soloists; High School Drama; Instructors; Local Artists; Multi Collaborations; Multimedia; Organization Contracts; Original Music Scores; Playwrights; Sign Language Translators; Singers; Touring Companies
Founded: 1898
Status: Non-Profit, Professional
Paid Staff: 20

FACILITIES / California

Volunteer Staff: 150
Paid Artists: 80
Non-paid Artists: 20
Budget: $1.2 million
Income Sources: Memberships; Donations
Performs At: Athenaem; Neurosciences Institute
Facility Category: Library
Seating Capacity: 140; 350
Rental Contact: Susan Dilts

6137
DANCE STUDIO 3
University of California, San Diego
9500 Gilman Drive MC0344
La Jolla, CA 92093
Mailing Address: 9500 Gilman Drive MC0344, La Jolla, CA 92093
Phone: 858-534-3791
Fax: 858-534-1080
e-mail: promotions@ucsd.edu
Web Site: www-theatre.ucsd.edu/facilities
Officers:
  Chancellor: Marye Anne Fox
Management:
  Production Manager: Michael D. Francis
  Financial Manager: Hedi Jafari
  Undergraduate Coordinator: Laura Jimenez
  Graduate Student Coordinator: Marybeth Ward
  Promotions Director: Aimee Zygmonski
Mission: UCSD's theatre and dance facilities are among the best. We share our home, The Mandell Weiss Center for the Performing Arts, with the La Jolla Playhouse.
Specialized Field: Dance, Theatre
Type of Stage: Black Box
Seating Capacity: 120

6138
GALBRAITH HALL STUDIO THEATRE 157
University of California, San Diego
9500 Gilman Drive MC0344
La Jolla, CA 92093
Mailing Address: 9500 Gilman Drive MC0344, La Jolla, CA 92093
Phone: 858-534-3791
Fax: 858-534-1080
e-mail: promotions@ucsd.edu
Web Site: www-theatre.ucsd.edu/facilities
Officers:
  Chancellor: Marye Anne Fox
Management:
  Production Manager: Michael D. Francis
  Financial Manager: Hedi Jafari
  Undergraduate Coordinator: Laura Jimenez
  Graduate Student Coordinator: Marybeth Ward
  Promotions Director: Aimee Zygmonski
Mission: UCSD's theatre and dance facilities are among the best. We share our home, The Mandell Weiss Center for the Performing Arts, with the La Jolla Playhouse.
Specialized Field: Dance, Theatre
Type of Stage: Thrust
Seating Capacity: 99

6139
MANDELL WEISS FORUM STUDIO
University of California, San Diego
9500 Gilman Drive MC0344
La Jolla, CA 92093
Mailing Address: 9500 Gilman Drive MC0344, La Jolla, CA 92093
Phone: 858-534-3791
Fax: 858-534-1080
e-mail: promotions@ucsd.edu
Web Site: www-theatre.ucsd.edu/facilities
Officers:
  Chancellor: Marye Anne Fox
Management:
  Production Manager: Michael D. Francis
  Financial Manager: Hedi Jafari
  Undergraduate Coordinator: Laura Jimenez
  Graduate Student Coordinator: Marybeth Ward
  Promotions Director: Aimee Zygmonski
Mission: UCSD's theatre and dance facilities are among the best. We share our home, The Mandell Weiss Center for the Performing Arts, with the La Jolla Playhouse.
Specialized Field: Dance, Theatre
Type of Stage: Black Box
Seating Capacity: 100

6140
MANDELL WEISS FORUM
University of California, San Diego
9500 Gilman Drive MC0344
La Jolla, CA 92093
Mailing Address: 9500 Gilman Drive MC0344, La Jolla, CA 92093
Phone: 858-534-3791
Fax: 858-534-1080
e-mail: promotions@ucsd.edu
Web Site: www-theatre.ucsd.edu/facilities
Officers:
  Chancellor: Marye Anne Fox
Management:
  Production Manager: Michael D. Francis
  Financial Manager: Hedi Jafari
  Undergraduate Coordinator: Laura Jimenez
  Graduate Student Coordinator: Marybeth Ward
  Promotions Director: Aimee Zygmonski
Mission: UCSD's theatre and dance facilities are among the best. We share our home, The Mandell Weiss Center for the Performing Arts, with the La Jolla Playhouse.
Specialized Field: Dance, Theatre
Type of Stage: Thrust
Seating Capacity: 400
Architect: Antoine Predock

6141
MANDELL WEISS THEATRE
University of California, San Diego
9500 Gilman Drive MC0344
La Jolla, CA 92093
Mailing Address: 9500 Gilman Drive MC0344, La Jolla, CA 92093
Phone: 858-534-3791
Fax: 858-534-1080
e-mail: promotions@ucsd.edu
Web Site: www-theatre.ucsd.edu/facilities
Officers:
  Chancellor: Marye Anne Fox
Management:
  Production Manager: Michael D. Francis
  Financial Manager: Hedi Jafari
  Undergraduate Coordinator: Laura Jimenez
  Graduate Student Coordinator: Marybeth Ward
  Promotions Director: Aimee Zygmonski
Mission: UCSD's theatre and dance facilities are among the best. We share our home, The Mandell Weiss Center for the Performing Arts, with the La Jolla Playhouse.
Specialized Field: Dance, Theatre
Type of Stage: Proscenium
Stage Dimensions: 40'x 23'
Orchestra Pit: y
Seating Capacity: 500

6142
MANDEVILLE THEATRE
University of California San Diego
Department of Theatre and Dance
La Jolla, CA 92093
Phone: 858-534-3791
Fax: 858-534-1080
e-mail: promotions@ucsd.edu
Web Site: www-theatre.ucsd.edu/facilities
Management:
  Production Manager: Michael D. Francis, j3flores@ucsd.edu
  Financial Manager: Hedi Jafari, mfahey@ucsd.edu
  Production Manager: Tom Aberger
  Graduate Student Coordinator: Marybeth Ward
Mission: The Mandeville Center has two theatres; the Auditorium, which seats 785 and the Recital Hall, which seats 150.
Founded: 1963
Status: Non-Profit, Non-Professional
Paid Staff: 35
Paid Artists: 50

6143
SHEILA & HUGHES POTIKER THEATRE
University of California, San Diego
Department of Theatre and Dance
9500 Gilman Drive MC0344
La Jolla, CA 92093
Mailing Address: 9500 Gilman Drive MC0344, La Jolla, CA 92093
Phone: 858-534-3791
Fax: 858-534-1080
e-mail: promotions@ucsd.edu
Web Site: www-theatre.ucsd.edu/facilities
Officers:
  Chancellor: Marye Anne Fox
Management:
  Production Manager: Michael D. Francis
  Financial Manager: Hedi Jafari
  Undergraduate Coordinator: Laura Jimenez
  Graduate Student Coordinator: Marybeth Ward
  Promotions Director: Aimee Zygmonski
Mission: UCSD's theatre and dance facilities are among the best. We share our home, The Mandell Weiss Center for the Performing Arts, with the La Jolla Playhouse.
Specialized Field: Dance, Theatre
Type of Stage: Thrust, Round, Proscenium, Traverse
Stage Dimensions: 70' x 80'
Seating Capacity: 417

6144
SHERWOOD AUDITORIUM
700 Prospect Street
La Jolla, CA 92037
Phone: 858-454-3541
Fax: 858-729-0912
e-mail: events@mcasd.org
Web Site: www.mcasd.org
Management:
  Events Assistant: Starr Lopez
  Manager: Eric Reichman
Founded: 1940
Status: Non-Profit, Professional
Paid Staff: 50
Performs At: Auditorium
Type of Stage: Proscenium
Stage Dimensions: 45' X 25'
Seating Capacity: 492

FACILITIES / California

6145
BIOLA UNIVERSITY
13800 Biola Avenue
La Mirada, CA 90639
Mailing Address: 13800 Biola Ave. La Mirada, CA 90639-0001
Phone: 562-903-6000
Fax: 562-903-4746
e-mail: georgeboesflug@truth.biola.edu
Web Site: www.biola.edu
Officers:
   President: Clide Cook
Management:
   Music Department Chairman: George Boespflug
Founded: 1908
Income Sources: Ticket sales
Performs At: Lansing Auditorium
Seating Capacity: 450

6146
LA MIRADA THEATRE FOR THE PERFORMING ARTS
14900 La Mirada Boulevard
La Mirada, CA 90638
Mailing Address: 14900 La Mirada Boulevard, La Mirada, CA 90638
Phone: 714-994-6310
Fax: 714-994-5796
e-mail: jbrown@lamiradatheatre.com
Web Site: www.lamiradatheatre.com
Management:
   Executive Director: Jeff Brown
   Ticketing Services Manager: Debbie J Walker
   Technical Director: David Cruise
   Theatre Operations: Jane Lynch
   House Manager: Devis Andrade
Founded: 1947
Status: City Owned Professional Theatre
Paid Staff: 50
Volunteer Staff: 100
Annual Attendance: 200,000
Facility Category: Performing Arts
Type of Stage: Proscenium
Stage Dimensions: 46'x26'x40'
Seating Capacity: 1,251
Year Built: 1977
Year Remodeled: 1999
Rental Contact: Laura Moore

6147
LAGUNA PLAYHOUSE
606 Laguna Canyon Road
Laguna Beach, CA 92651
Mailing Address: P.O. Box 1747, Laguna Beach, CA 92652
Phone: 949-497-2787
Fax: 949-376-8185
Toll-free: 800-946-5556
Web Site: www.lagunaplayhouse.com
Management:
   Executive Director: Karen Wood
   General Manager: Michael Barker
   Artistic Director: Ann E. Wareham
   Operations Director: Jim Prodger
   Director Development/Marketing: Greg Patterson
   Director Youth Theatre: Donna Inglima
   Production Manager: Jim Ryan
Founded: 1920
Annual Attendance: 100,000
Type of Stage: Open Proscenium
Seating Capacity: 420

6148
LANDCASTER PERFORMING ARTS CENTER
750 West Lancaster Boulevard
Lancaster, CA 93534
Fax: 661-723-5945
Web Site: www.ipac.org
Management:
   Manager: Mary Tanner
   Marketing Manager: Danise Baker
   Technical Director: Rodney Stickrod
   Business Operation Manager: Judy Kepa
   Education/Rental Coordinator: Tanya Stows
Seating Capacity: 792

6149
LONG BEACH CONVENTION AND ENTERTAINMENT CENTER
300 East Ocean Boulevard
Long Beach, CA 90802
Phone: 562-436-3636
Fax: 562-436-9491
e-mail: dspellens@longbeachcc.com
Web Site: www.longbeachcc.com/mainmenu.asp
Management:
   Director of Facilities: Ray Blanton, rblanton@longbeachcc.com
   General Manager: Charles Beirne, cbeirne@longbeachcc.com
   Box Office Manager: Kenda Neumann, kneumann@longbeachcc.com
   Director Of Event Services: Marcellus Taylor
   Sales Manager: Pamela Still
   Convention Sales Director: Ellen Scwartz
   Director-Theatres & Entertainment: Dan Spellins
   Assistant General Manager: Dan Lee
Mission: The Convention & Entertainment Center's Arena has seating capacity of 13,500, and 46,000 square feet of exhibit space and the Arena Concourse has 29,000 square feet of exhibit space. There are also 3 exhibit halls providing 224,0000 square feet of space for all types of conventions, tradeshows, consumer shows and special events; the Terrace Theatre, a full production proscenium theatre that seats 3,051 and a thrust stage seating 825.
Utilizes: Actors; Choreographers; Dance Companies; Dancers; Grant Writers; Guest Composers; Guest Designers; Guest Instructors; Guest Lecturers; Guest Musical Directors; Guest Musicians; Multimedia; Music; Original Music Scores; Resident Artists; Selected Students; Sign Language Translators; Singers; Special Technical Talent; Theatre Companies
Facility Category: Performing Arts Center
Type of Stage: Permanent; Proscenium
Stage Dimensions: 66 x 35
Year Built: 1928
Year Remodeled: 1999
Rental Contact: Director-Theatres & Entertainment Dan Spellens

6150
LONG BEACH PLAYHOUSE
5021 East Anaheim Street
Long Beach, CA 90804
Mailing Address: 5021 E Anaheim St, Long Beach, CA 90804
Phone: 562-494-1014
Fax: 562-961-8616
e-mail: boxoffice@lbplayhouse.org
Web Site: www.lbplayhouse.org
Officers:
   Co President: Bart DeLio
   Co President: Roxanne Patmor
   Vice President: Tony Diaz
   Treasurer: Shirley Guy
   Secretary: Cheryl Avirom
Management:
   Managing Director: Lauren Morris
   Artistic Director: Andrew Vonderschmitt
   Business & Operations Manager: Madison Mooney
   Designer/Costume Shop Manager: Donna Fritsche
   Head Ticket Services: Christa Svorinich
   Public Relations Manager: Cort Huckabone
   Community Outreach: Michael Ross
Mission: To nuture and cultivate new and traditional audiences, as well as emerging and established artists; encourage the participation of all interested individuals; maintain a strong theater which includes traditional plays and classics, new works and thought-provoking, socially significant productions, and is accessible to our socially and economically diverse community.
Founded: 1929
Status: Non-Profit, Professional
Paid Staff: 12
Volunteer Staff: 200
Budget: $700,000
Income Sources: Ticket Sales; Grants; Individual Contributions
Performs At: Main Stage
Annual Attendance: 34,000
Type of Stage: Proscenium
Seating Capacity: 200

6151
RICHARD & KAREN CARPENTER PERFORMING ARTS CENTER
6200 Atherton Street
Long Beach, CA 90815-4500
Mailing Address: 6200 Atherton St., Long Beach, CA 90815
Phone: 562-985-7000
Fax: 562-985-7023
e-mail: cpac@carpenterarts.org
Web Site: www.carpenterarts.org
Management:
   Stage Supervisor: Ken Beaupre
   Executive Director: Michele Roberge
   Production Manager: Kathryn Havey
   Graphic Designer: Patti Laurrell
   Ticket Office Manager: Jill Mather
Mission: Presenting organization. Also, home to four resident companies.
Utilizes: Actors; AEA Actors; Artists-in-Residence; Choreographers; Collaborating Artists; Collaborations; Commissioned Composers; Commissioned Music; Dance Companies; Dancers; Designers; Educators; Filmmakers; Five Seasonal Concerts; Guest Accompanists; Guest Artists; Guest Choreographers; Guest Conductors; Guest Designers; Guest Musical Directors; Guest Soloists; Instructors; Local Artists; Lyricists; Multi Collaborations; Multimedia; Music; Original Music Scores; Poets; Resident Artists; Selected Students; Sign Language Translators; Soloists; Special Technical Talent; Theatre Companies; Visual Arts
Founded: 1994
Status: Non-Profit, Professional
Paid Staff: 15
Paid Artists: 40
Budget: $1,800,000
Income Sources: Individual Donor; Corporations; Rental Clients; Ticket Buyers
Performs At: Performing Arts Center with continental seating.
Affiliations: CSALB

FACILITIES / California

Annual Attendance: 150,000
Type of Stage: Proscenium
Stage Dimensions: 70'x70'
Seating Capacity: 1,065
Year Built: 1994
Rental Contact: 562-985-7047 Glennis Watceman

6152
RICHARD AND KAREN CARPENTER PERFORMING ARTS CENTER

California State University, Long Beach
1250 Bellflower Boulevard
Long Beach, CA 90840
Phone: 562-985-4274
Fax: 562-985-7203
e-mail: cpac@carpenterarts.org
Web Site: www.csulb.edu/depts/theatre/
Officers:
   Executive Director: Peter Lesnick
   Events Manager: Aimee Bramble
   Director Development: Michelle Sprokkereef
Management:
   Chair: Joanne Garden
   Production Manager: Kathryn Harvey
Mission: The mission of the Richard and Karen Carpenter Performing Arts Center is to quarantee the citizens of Long Beach, CSULB students, faculty, and staff, and surrounding communities access to the entire spectrum of performing arts experiences through resident companies, arts outreach, and unique programming.
Specialized Field: Cabaret, Comedy, Dance, Music
Seating Capacity: 1074

6153
ROBERT C SMITHWICK THEATRE

12345 El Monte Road
Los Altos Hills, CA 94022-4599
Phone: 650-949-7252
Toll-free: 888-892-4599
e-mail: thomaslori@foothill.edu
Web Site: www.foothill.edu/fa/theater/smithwick.html
Officers:
   Fine Arts Facilities Coordinator: Kay Thornton
   Fines Arts Communications Division: Mark Anderson
Management:
   Publications/Publicity Coordinator: Lori Thomas
   Assoc VP of External Relations: Kurt Hueg
Utilizes: Actors; Collaborations; Community Members; Dancers; Designers; Educators; Guest Composers; Guest Designers; Guest Soloists; Multi Collaborations; Performance Artists; Playwrights; Resident Artists
Seating Capacity: 950

6154
BING THEATRE

University of Southern California
School of Theatre
1029 Childs Way
Los Angeles, CA 90089-0791
Mailing Address: School of Theatre, 1029 Childs Way, Los Angeles, CA 90089-07
Phone: 213-821-2744
Fax: 213-740-8888
e-mail: thtrinfo@usc.edu
Web Site: www.usc.edu
Officers:
   Dean: Madeline Puzo
   President: C. L. Max Nikias
   CFO: Robert Abeles
   Senior VP: Dennis F. Dougherty
   VP, Finance: Margo Steurbaut
Management:
   Dean School of Theater: Robert Scales
   Chief of Staff: Dennis Cornell
   Managing Director: Jeffery A. Fischer
   Business Manager: Elizabeth G. Divine
   Special Project Manager: M. Jeffrey Sawada
Mission: The School of Theatre offers professional and scholarly training in the theatre, stressing the interdependence of production experience with academic knowledge .
Founded: 1945
Specialized Field: Concerts, Theatre
Type of Stage: Proscenium
Stage Dimensions: 20' x 47'6
Orchestra Pit: y
Seating Capacity: 551

6155
CELEBRATION THEATRE

7985 Santa Monica Boulevard
#109-1
Los Angeles, CA 90046
Mailing Address: 7985 Santa Monica Boulevard, Los Angeles, CA 90046
Phone: 323-957-1884
Fax: 323-957-1826
e-mail: info@celebrationtheatre.com
Web Site: www.celebrationtheatre.com/
Officers:
   President: Cameron Faber
   Vice President: Bill Stoddard
   Treasurer: Nicholas Caprio
   Secretary: Jen McGlone
Management:
   Artistic Director: Michael Matthews
   Managing Director: David Tarlow
   Technical Director: Matthew Denman
   Associate Managing Director: Michael O'Hara
   Literary Director: Charls Hall
   Facilities Manager: Timothy Swiss
   Grants Coordinator: Luke Sandler
Founded: 1982

6156
DODGER STADIUM

1000 Elysian Park Avenue
Los Angeles, CA 90012
Phone: 323-224-1500
Fax: 323-224-1833
Web Site: losangeles.dodgers.mlb.com
Officers:
   Chairman: Frank McCourt
   Vice Chairman/President: Jamie McCourt
   Special Advisor to the Chairman: Tommy Lasorda
   Chief Operating Officer: Martin Greenspun
   General Manager: Ned Colletti
   SVP/Chief Financial Officer: Cristine Hurley
   SVP/Public Affairs: Howard Sunkin
   SVP/Communications: Camille Johnston
   Vice President/Sales & Marketing: Serfio Del Prado
Management:
   Director Public Relations: Josh Rawitch
   Director Community Relations: Don Newcombe
   Vice President/Stadium Operations: Lon Rosenberg
   Director Ticket Operations: Bill Hunter
   Director Sponsorship Sales: Karen Marumoto
   Director Premium Sales: David Siegel
   Publications Director: Jorge Martin
   Publications Editor/Team Historian: Mark Langill
   Director Accounting: Mike Litvack
Mission: Baseball and concerts
Founded: 1962
Specialized Field: Home of the Los Angeles Dodgers (MLB). Available For Rental And Concerts.
Seating Capacity: 56,000
Year Built: 1962

6157
FORD AMPHITHEATRE

2580 Cahuenga Boulevard East
Los Angeles, CA 90068
Mailing Address: 2580 Cahuenga Blvd. East, Hollywood, CA 90068
Phone: 323-461-3673
Fax: 323-871-5904
e-mail: boxoffice@arts.lacounty.gov
Web Site: www.fordamphitheatre.com
Officers:
   Chairman: David C. Bohnett
   Secretary: Alan Wayte
Management:
   Managing Director: Adam Davis
   Director Development: Louanne Champag Brazil
   Event Services Manager: William Berry
   Director of Communications: Leticia Rhi Buckley
   Box Office Manager: Eve Cakar
   Interim Productions Marketing Manag: Kim Glann
Mission: Its programs nurture artists, arts organizations and community, and provide a gateway for the people of greater Los Angeles to discover and appreciate cultures of their region and the world.
Founded: 1964
Specialized Field: music, dance and film events
Seating Capacity: 1,241

6158
GETTY CENTER

1200 Getty Center Drive
Los Angeles, CA 90049-1679
Mailing Address: 1200 Getty Center Drive, Los Angeles, CA 90049-1679
Phone: 310-440-7300
Fax: 310-440-7751
e-mail: communications@getty.edu
Web Site: www.getty.edu
Officers:
   Chairman: Mark S Siegel
   Vice Chairman: Neil L Rudenstine
   Interim President/CEO: James Cuno
   VP/Chief Investment Offcr/Treasurer: James M Williams
   Secretary/VP/General Counsel: Stephen Clark
Management:
   Managing Director: Benjamin Liou
   Asst Director Museum Advancement: Mikka Gee Conway
   Asst Director Educational Programs: Peggy Fogelman
   Asst Director Public Programs: Quincy Houghton
   Associate Director Administration: Thomas Rhoads
Founded: 1953

6159
GREEK THEATRE

2700 North Vermont Avenue
Los Angeles, CA 90027
Mailing Address: 2700 North Vermont Ave., Los Angeles, CA 90027
Phone: 323-665-5857
Fax: 323-666-8202
e-mail: yourcontact@greektheatrela.com
Web Site: www.greektheatrela.com/
Management:
   Owner/President/Chairman: James M Nederland

FACILITIES / California

Marketing/Sales/Public Relations: James L Nederland
General Manager: Mike Garcia
Director of Corporate Partnerships: Kim Hawkins
Founded: 1929
Seating Capacity: 6,162

6160
HARRIET & CHARLES LUCKMAN FINE ARTS COMPLEX
California State University, Los Angeles
5151 State Unviersity Drive
Los Angeles, CA 90032
Mailing Address: 5151 State University Drive, Los Angeles, CA, 90032
Phone: 323-343-6600
Fax: 323-343-6423
e-mail: info@luckmanarts.org
Web Site: www.luckmanarts.org
Management:
  Executive Director: Wendy A Baker
  Marketing Director: Nicholas A Viski Mestas
  Business Manager: Hennry Harris
  Technical Director: Andy Barth
  Box Office Manager: Rogelio Ramirez
Mission: The Luckman Theatre, home of the Luckman Jazz Orchestra, seats up to 1,152, and, the Intimate Theatre has a seating capacity of 250.
Utilizes: Choreographers; Community Talent; Contract Orchestras; Curators; Dance Companies; Designers; Fine Artists; Five Seasonal Concerts; Grant Writers; Guest Artists; Guest Choreographers; Guest Composers; Guest Directors; Guest Lecturers; Guest Musical Directors; Guest Soloists; Guest Speakers; Guest Writers; Instructors; Multi Collaborations; Multimedia; Paid Performers; Sign Language Translators; Special Technical Talent; Theatre Companies; Touring Companies
Founded: 1994
Seating Capacity: 1,152 in Theatre/250 in Luckman Intimate

6161
HARRIET AND CHARLES LUCKMAN FINE ARTS COMPLEX
California State University, Los Angeles
5151 State University Drive
Los Angeles, CA 90032
Mailing Address: 5151 State University Drive, Los Angeles, CA, 90032
Phone: 323-343-6600
Fax: 323-343-6423
e-mail: info@luckmanarts.org
Web Site: www.luckmanarts.org
Officers:
  Executive Director: Wendy A. Baker
Management:
  Executive Director: Wendy A Baker
  Marketing Director: Nicholas A Viski Mestas
  Business Manager: Hennry Harris
  Technical Director: Andy Barth
  Box Office Manager: Rogelio Ramirez
Mission: Cal State L.A. is more than academics it offers students music, dance and theatre performances.
Specialized Field: Dance, Film, Music, Theatre, Video, Visual Arts
Type of Stage: Proscenium
Stage Dimensions: 60 foot wide
Orchestra Pit: y
Seating Capacity: 1,152
Year Built: 1994
Architect: Luckman Partnership

6162
INTIMATE THEATRE
California State University, Los Angeles
5151 State University Drive
Los Angeles, CA 90032
Mailing Address: 5151 State University Drive, Los Angeles, CA, 90032
Phone: 323-343-6600
Fax: 323-343-6423
e-mail: info@luckmanarts.org
Web Site: www.luckmanarts.org
Officers:
  Executive Director: Wendy A. Baker
Management:
  Executive Director: Wendy A Baker
  Marketing Director: Nicholas A Viski Mestas
  Business Manager: Hennry Harris
  Technical Director: Andy Barth
  Box Office Manager: Rogelio Ramirez
Mission: Cal State L.A. is more than academics it offers students music, dance and theatre performances.
Specialized Field: Dance, Jazz
Type of Stage: Flexible Stage
Seating Capacity: 250
Year Built: 1994
Architect: Luckman Partnership

6163
JAPANESE AMERICAN CULTURAL & COMMUNITY CENTER
244 South San Pedro Street
Los Angeles, CA 90012
Mailing Address: 244 S. San Pedro Street, Los Angeles, CA 90012
Phone: 213-628-2725
Fax: 213-617-8576
e-mail: info@jaccc.org
Web Site: www.jaccc.org
Officers:
  Chairman: Henry Y Ota
  Vice Chairman: Nancy Matsui
  Chair Elect: George Tanaka
  Secretary: Helen Hashimoto
  Treasurer: Gary Kawaguchi
Management:
  Artistic Director: Hirokagu Kosaka
  Chief Engineer: Arthur Granados
  Office Manager: Marlene Lee
  Director of Development: Liliane Ribeiro
  Media Art Director: Wakana Kimura
  Chief Engineer: Arthur Granados
  Board/Donor Relations: Robert Hori
Founded: 1971
Status: Non-Profit, Professional
Paid Staff: 30
Performs At: Japan America Theatre; Plaza
Seating Capacity: 878; 2000

6164
KECK THEATRE
Occidental College
1600 Campus Road
Los Angeles, CA 90041
Mailing Address: 1600 Campus Road, Los Angeles, CA 90041
Phone: 323-259-2500
Fax: 323-341-2958
e-mail: beatrice@oxy.edu
Web Site: www.oxy.edu/
Officers:
  Dean: Kenyon S. Chan
  President: Jonathan Veitch
  Chair: Chris Calkins
Chief Investment Officer: Peter Adamson
Senior VP: Carl A Ballton
Management:
  Production Manager: Brian Fitzmorris
  Human Resources Assistant/Reception: Gisselle Cornejo
  Associate Director of Human Resourc: Jacalyn Feigelman
  Human Resources Coordinator: Marivel Santos
  Employment Manager: Karen Salce
Mission: Students explore the art of theater through theory, performance, and production. Our students develop a rich understanding of the enactment of the written word and of various forms of theatrical expression, with each student combining theoretical studies with intensive performance and production experiences.
Specialized Field: Theatre
Type of Stage: Adjustable Lambda Platforms
Seating Capacity: 412
Year Built: 1987

6165
L'ERMITAGE FOUNDATION STAGE
11724 Gwynne Lane
Los Angeles, CA 90077
Phone: 310-472-3330
Fax: 310-476-8003
e-mail: reneelcherniak@aol.com
Web Site: lermitagefoundation.org
Management:
  Executive Director: Renee Cherniak
Utilizes: Dancers; Guest Accompanists; Guest Companies; Guest Instructors; Guest Lecturers; Guest Musical Directors; Guest Musicians; Guest Soloists; Instructors; Multimedia; Sign Language Translators; Singers
Income Sources: Member Donations
Performs At: Salon Setting
Annual Attendance: 100
Facility Category: Hotel Salon
Seating Capacity: 200-250

6166
LOS ANGELES COUNTY MUSEUM OF ART
5905 Wilshire Boulevard
Los Angeles, CA 90036
Phone: 323-857-6000
Fax: 323-932-5874
e-mail: publicinfo@lacma.org
Web Site: www.lacma.org
Officers:
  President: Michael Govan
  Co-Chairman: Andrew Brandon Gordon
  Co-Chairman: Terry Semel
  Vice Chairman: William H Ahmanson
  Vice Chairman: Willow Bay
Management:
  Director Music Programs: Mitch Glickman
  Sundays Live Programs: Bill Vestal
  Music Programs Coordinator: Ryan Zwahlen
  Music Programs Coordinator: Gregory Milliren
  CFO: Ann Rowland
Mission: To produce concerts of chamber music and jazz.
Utilizes: Guest Artists; Singers
Founded: 1939
Specialized Field: Arts Museum
Status: Non-Profit, Non-Professional
Income Sources: Los Angeles County Museum of Art
Performs At: Leo S. Bing Theatre
Seating Capacity: 600
Organization Type: Performing

FACILITIES / California

6167
LOS ANGELES MEMORIAL COLISEUM & SPORTS ARENA
3939 South Figueroa Street
Los Angeles, CA 90037
Mailing Address: 3939 South Figueroa Street, Los Angeles, CA 90037
Phone: 213-747-7111
Fax: 213-746-9346
e-mail: lacsainfo@usc.edu
Web Site: www.lacoliseum.com
Management:
  General Manager: Patrick J Lynch
  Assistant General Manager: Ron Lederkramer
  Marketing/Sales Director: Jonathan Lee
  Event Coordinator: 7rene Asalde
  Event Director: Todd Destefano
Mission: Sports/Entertainment
Founded: 1959
Status: Non-Profit, Non-Professional
Paid Staff: 32
Type of Stage: Proscenium
Seating Capacity: 16,500
Year Built: 1923
Year Remodeled: 1994
Comments: Main office is located at 3911 South Figueroa Street.

6168
LOS ANGELES PERFORMING ARTS THEATRES
201 North Figueroa Street
Suite 1400
Los Angeles, CA 90012
Mailing Address: 201 North Figueroa Street, Suite 1400, Los Angeles, CA 9001
Phone: 213-202-5500
Fax: 213-202-5517
Web Site: www.culturela.org
Management:
  Assisstant General Manager: Matthew Rudnick
  Director of Marketing: Wiil Caperton Y Montoya
  Public Art Division Director: Felicia Filer
  Grants Administration Director: Joe Smoke
  Community Arts Director: Leslie Thomas
Founded: 1925
Specialized Field: Theatre; Dance; Music; Variety
Volunteer Staff: 12
Budget: $13.2 million
Income Sources: Rentals, Ticket Sales, Municipal Fund
Performs At: Theatre, 1; 2; 3; 4; Madrid Theatre; Warner Grand Theatre
Affiliations: Theatre LA; CALAA
Annual Attendance: 80,000
Facility Category: Theatre Complex
Type of Stage: Trust; Proscenium
Seating Capacity: 500; 296; 323; 90; 471; 1500

6169
LOS ANGELES TENNIS CENTER
555 Westwood Plaza Los Angeles
Los Angeles, CA 90095
Mailing Address: 555 Westwood Plaza Los Angeles, CA 90095
Phone: 310-825-8699
Fax: 310-825-5775
e-mail: jhenson@ucla.edu
Web Site: uclabruins.cstv.com/genrel
Officers:
  Chancellor: Gene Block
Management:
  Executive Director: David Sefton
  Director Rental Events: John Henson
  Director of Athletics: Daniel G. Guerrero
  Director of Executive Relations: Marc Dellins
  Senior Learning Specialist: Sabrina Youmans
  Patron Services Manager: David McGrath
  Box Office Manager: Matthew Poe
  Technical Director: David Muller
  House Audio Engineer: Keith Endo
Seating Capacity: 6,800

6170
MARK TAPER FORUM
Center Theatre Group
601 W Temple Street
Los Angeles, CA 90012
Mailing Address: 601 W. Temple St., Los Angeles, CA 90012
Phone: 213-628-2772
Fax: 213-628-2796
e-mail: tickets@ctgla.com
Web Site: www.taperahmanson.com
Officers:
  Chairman: Martin Massmann
  President Board of Directors: William H Ahmanson
  VP: Ava Fries
  Secretary: Amy R. Forbes
  Treasurer: Dr Steven Nagelberg
Management:
  Artistic Director: Michael Ritchie
  Managing Director: Charles Dillingham
Mission: To serve the diverse audiences of Los Angeles by producing and presenting theatre of the highest caliber, by nurturing new artists, by attracting new audiences, and by developing youth outreach and arts education programs. This mission is based on a belief that the art of theatre is a cultural force with the capacity to transform the lives of individuals and society at large.
Utilizes: Actors; AEA Actors; Arrangers; Artists-in-Residence; Choreographers; Collaborating Artists; Collaborations; Community Members; Contract Actors; Dancers; Designers; Educators; Equity Actors; Five Seasonal Concerts; Guest Accompanists; Guest Artists; Guest Companies; Guest Composers; Guest Conductors; Guest Designers; Guest Lecturers; Guest Musical Directors; Guest Teachers; Instructors; Local Artists; Local Artists & Directors; Local Unknown Artists; Lyricists; Multi Collaborations; Multimedia; Music; Organization Contracts; Original Music Scores; Paid Performers; Performance Artists; Poets; Resident Artists; Resident Companies; Resident Professionals; Scenic Designers; Selected Students; Sign Language Translators; Singers; Soloists; Students; Student Interns; Special Technical Talent; Theatre Companies; Touring Companies; Visual Arts; Visual Designers; Volunteer Directors & Actors; Writers
Founded: 1967
Opened: 1967
Specialized Field: Musical; Comedy; Drama
Status: Non-Profit, Professional
Paid Artists: 100
Affiliations: Ahmanson Theatre, Kirk Douglas Theatre
Annual Attendance: 750,000
Facility Category: Music Center of Los Angeles
Type of Stage: Thrust
Stage Dimensions: 190Wx47Dx67H; 40Wx28H
Seating Capacity: 739
Year Built: 1967
Year Remodeled: 2008

6171
MARTIN MASSMAN THEATRE
University of Southern California
1029 Childs Way
Los Angeles, CA 90089-0791
Mailing Address: School of Theatre, 1029 Childs Way, Los Angeles, CA 90089-07
Phone: 213-821-2744
Fax: 213-740-8888
e-mail: thtrinfo@usc.edu
Web Site: www.usc.edu
Officers:
  Dean: Madeline Puzo
  President: C. L. Max Nikias
  CFO: Robert Abeles
  Senior VP: Dennis F. Dougherty
  VP, Finance: Margo Steurbaut
Management:
  Dean School of Theater: Robert Scales
  Chief of Staff: Dennis Cornell
  Managing Director: Jeffery A. Fischer
  Business Manager: Elizabeth G. Divine
  Special Project Manager: M. Jeffrey Sawada
Mission: The School of Theatre offers professional and scholarly training in the theatre, stressing the interdependence of production experience with academic knowledge.
Founded: 1945
Specialized Field: Theatre
Type of Stage: Black Box
Seating Capacity: 65

6172
MUNICIPAL ART GALLERY THEATER
201 North Figueroa Street
Suite 1400
Los Angeles, CA 90012
Mailing Address: 201 North Figueroa Street, Suite 1400, Los Angeles, CA 9001
Phone: 213-202-5500
Fax: 213-202-5517
Web Site: www.culturela.org
Management:
  Assisstant General Manager: Matthew Rudnick
  Director of Marketing: Wiil Caperton Y Montoya
  Public Art Division Director: Felicia Filer
  Grants Administration Director: Joe Smoke
  Community Arts Director: Leslie Thomas

6173
MUSIC CENTER/ PERFORMING ARTS CENTER OF LOS ANGELES COUNTY
135 North Grand Avenue
Los Angeles, CA 90012
Phone: 213-972-7406
Fax: 213-481-1176
e-mail: general@musiccenter.org
Web Site: www.musiccenter.org
Officers:
  Chairman: Lisa Specht
  President & CEO: Stephen D Rountree
  Vice Chair: Michael J Pagano
  Secretary: Karen Kay Platt
  Treasurer: Thomas R Weinberger
Management:
  Artistic Director: Barbara Leonard
  Managing Director of Education: Michael Solomon
  Director of Programming: Ming Ng
  Director of Production: Chris Christel
  Director of Engineering: Keith McTague
  Press Director Center Theatre Group: Nancy Hereford

FACILITIES / California

Sr Press Associate Mark Taper Forum: Phyllis Moberly
Publicist L A Chorale: Libby Huebner
Mission: The Music Center of Los Angeles, which encompasses the Dorothy Chandler Pavilion (capacity of 3,189), the Ahmanson Theatre (capacity of 2,115) and the Mark Taper Forum (capacity of 747), and the Walt Disney Concert Hall (capacity 2,265), lies at the heart of downtown Los Angeles.
Founded: 1964
Specialized Field: Los Angeles Philharmonic; Los Angeles Opera; Los Angeles Master Chorale; Center Theatre Group (Mark Taper & Ahmanson Theatre)

6174
PAULEY PAVILION
University California - Los Angeles/UCLA
555 Westwood Plaza Los Angeles
Los Angeles, CA 90095
Mailing Address: 555 Westwood Plaza Los Angeles, CA 90095
Phone: 310-825-4546
Fax: 310-825-5775
Web Site: uclabruins.cstv.com
Management:
  Executive Director: David Sefton
  Athletics Director: Daniel G Guerrero
  Facilities Director: Kevin Borg
  Management Information Systems: Bob Park
  Asst. Director Events Operations: Paul Brown
  Sports Information Director: Marc Dellins
  Marketing/New Revenues: Scott Mitchell
  External Relations: Ross Bjork
  Compliance Director: Rich Herczog
Mission: Pauley Pavilion contains 10,337 permanent upholstered seats and retractable bleachers for 2,482 spectators.
Founded: 1965
Specialized Field: Recreation, concerts, basketball, volleyball, award shows

6175
PLAZA GRAND PERFORMANCES
350 South Grand Avenue
Suite A-4
Los Angeles, CA 90071
Mailing Address: 350 S. Grand Ave., Suite A-4, Los Angeles, CA 90071
Phone: 213-687-2159
Fax: 213-687-2191
e-mail: comments@grandperformances.org
Web Site: www.grandperformances.org
Officers:
  Chairman: Karen Molleson
  Vice Chair: Janice Geringer
  Secretary: Anahita Ferasat
  Treasurer: Karim Teymourtache
Management:
  Executive Director: Michael Alexander
  Technical Manager: Mark Baker
  Programming Director: Leigh Ann Hahn
  Development Associate: Kate Harmatz
  General Manager: Lee Lawlor
  Marketing Director: Dean Porter
  Production Manager: Fred Stites
Founded: 1986
Specialized Field: Southern California
Paid Staff: 10
Volunteer Staff: 3
Paid Artists: 40
Annual Attendance: 70,000
Type of Stage: Amphitheater; Thrust-Style
Seating Capacity: 6,500

6176
SCENE DOCK THEATRE
University of Southern California
1030 West 37th Street
Los Angeles, CA 90089
Mailing Address: 1030 West 37th Street, Los Angeles, CA 90089
Phone: 213-821-2744
Fax: 213-740-8888
e-mail: thtrinfo@usc.edu
Web Site: www.usc.edu
Officers:
  Dean: Madeline Puzo
  President: C. L. Max Nikias
  CFO: Robert Abeles
  Senior VP: Dennis F. Dougherty
  VP, Finance: Margo Steurbaut
Management:
  Dean School of Theater: Robert Scales
  Chief of Staff: Dennis Cornell
  Managing Director: Jeffery A. Fischer
  Business Manager: Elizabeth G. Divine
  Special Project Manager: M. Jeffrey Sawada
Mission: The School of Theatre offers professional and scholarly training in the theatre, stressing the interdependence of production experience with academic knowledge .
Founded: 1945
Specialized Field: Theatre
Type of Stage: Proscenium, Round, Thrust
Seating Capacity: 100

6177
SHRINE AUDITORIUM AND EXPOSITION CENTER
665 West Jefferson Boulevard
Los Angeles, CA 90007
Phone: 213-748-5116
Fax: 213-742-9922
Web Site: www.shrineauditorium.com/expo.html
Management:
  Operations Manager: Andy Stamatin
  Administration: Kimberly Walker
  Ticket Coordinator: Andrew Johnston
Mission: The Shrine Auditorium seats atotal of 6,300 with 3,044 on the main floor and 3,256 in the balcony. The Expo Center features over 54,000 square feet, with 34,000 square feet on the main floor and another 20,000 on the mezzanine. The center will accommodate up to 4,000 people, approximately 250 booths; has a 21,160 square foot dance floor; accommodates banquet dining for 1,800 and has a ceiling height of 49 feet.
Utilizes: Actors; AEA Actors; Choreographers; Collaborations; Dance Companies; Dancers; Designers; Educators; Filmmakers; Fine Artists; Guest Accompanists; Guest Artists; Guest Companies; Guest Composers; Guest Conductors; Guest Designers; Guest Directors; Guest Instructors; Guest Lecturers; Guest Musical Directors; Guest Musicians; Guest Soloists; Guest Writers; Guild Activities; High School Drama; Instructors; Local Artists; Lyricists; Multi Collaborations; Multimedia; Music; New Productions; Organization Contracts; Original Music Scores; Performance Artists; Playwrights; Resident Professionals; Selected Students; Sign Language Translators; Singers; Soloists; Student Interns; Special Technical Talent; Theatre Companies; Touring Companies; Visual Arts
Founded: 1920
Specialized Field: Los Angeles
Facility Category: Auditorium with adjoining Expo Center
Type of Stage: Concerts; Masonite; Wood
Stage Dimensions: 193'x73'
Year Built: 1926
Cost: $2,500,000
Rental Contact: Douglas Worthington

6178
STAPLES CENTER
1111 South Figueroa Street
Los Angeles, CA 90015
Mailing Address: 1111 S. Figueroa Street, Los Angeles, CA 90015
Phone: 213-742-7100
Fax: 213-624-3054
e-mail: media@staplescenter.com
Web Site: www.staplescenter.com
Management:
  President: Tim Leiweke
  SVP/General Manager: Bobby Goldwater
  Community Development: Jackie Baca Geary
Seating Capacity: 16,096

6179
THORNE HALL
1600 Campus Road
Los Angeles, CA 90041
Mailing Address: 1600 Campus Road, Los Angeles, CA 90041
Phone: 323-259-2700
Fax: 323-259-2958
e-mail: abart@oxy.edu
Web Site: www.oxy.edu
Officers:
  President: Jonathan Veitch
  Chair: Christopher C Calkins
  Vice Chair: David W Berkus
  Treasurer: Amos Himmelstein
  Secretary: Rozita Afar
Management:
  President: Ted Mitchell
  Artistic Director: Allen Freeman
  Human Resources Assistant/Reception: Gisselle Cornejo
  Associate Director of Human Resourc: Jacalyn Feigelman
  Human Resources Coordinator: Marivel Santos
Founded: 1938
Status: Non-Profit, Non-Professional
Seating Capacity: 835

6180
TOM BRADLEY INTERNATIONAL HALL
330 De Neve Drive
Suite L-16
Los Angeles, CA 90095-1492
Mailing Address: 330 De Neve Drive Los Angeles, CA 90095-1372
Phone: 213-627-6500
Fax: 213-847-3169
e-mail: aisportalteam@it.ucla.edu
Web Site: map.ais.ucla.edu/portal/site/UCLA/menuitem
Officers:
  Acting Chancellor: Norman Abrams
  Executive Vice Chancellor/Provost: Daniel Neuman
  Administrative Vice Chancellor: Jack Powazek
  Vice Chancellor, External Affairs: Rhea Turteltaub
  Vice Chancellor, Legal Affairs: Kevin Reed
Management:
  Business/Administrative Services: Sam Morabito
  Capital Programs: Peter Blackman
  External Affairs: Rhea Turteltaub
  Academic Personnel: Thomas H Rice

FACILITIES / California

Mission: The 5,270 square foot International Room is divisible into six smaller salons. The East and West Galleries are excellent locations for meeting registration, poster sessions, or refreshment breaks. Several multi-purpose rooms are versatile spaces for smaller events.
Type of Stage: Black Box; Flexible
Seating Capacity: 1836
Rental Contact: John Henson

6181
UCLA PERFORMING ARTS
Royce Hall, B100
PO Box 951529
Los Angeles, CA 90095-1529
Mailing Address: B100 Royce Hall, Box 951529, Los Angeles, CA 90095-1529
Phone: 310-825-4401
Fax: 310-206-3843
e-mail: info@cap.ucla.edu
Web Site: www.uclalive.org
Management:
   Executive and Artistic Director: Kristy Edmunds
   Production Manager: Owen Lewis
   Director of Operations: Steve Keeley
   Event Coordinator: Matthew Poe
   Venue Manager: Lorrie P. Snyder
Founded: 1929
Status: Non-Profit, Professional
Paid Staff: 60
Annual Attendance: 200,000
Seating Capacity: 1,818

6182
UNIVERSITY OF SOUTHERN CALIFORNIA
School of Theatre
1029 Childs Way
Los Angeles, CA 90089-0791
Mailing Address: 1029 Childs Way Los Angeles, CA 90089-0791
Phone: 213-821-1286
Fax: 213-740-8888
e-mail: thtrinfo@theatre.usc.edu
Web Site: www.usc.edu
Officers:
   President: Jonathan Veitch
   Chair: Christopher C Calkins
   Vice Chair: David W Berkus
   Treasurer: Amos Himmelstein
   Secretary: Rozita Afar
Management:
   Technical Theatre Manager: Sue Brandt
   Theatre Reservations: Alexandra Bristrow
Mission: The School's active production program utilizes the Bing Theatre, a traditional proscenium 575-seat house; the Massman Theatre, a flexible space that seats 50-75; and the Scene Dock Theatre, which is also a flexible space, with seating for 99 people.
Founded: 1880
Specialized Field: Dance; Theatre; Drama
Status: For-Profit, Non-Professional

6183
VETERANS WADSWORTH THEATRE
11611 San Vincente Boulevard, Suite 204
Suite 204
Los Angeles, CA 90049
Mailing Address: 11661 San Vicente Blvd., Suite 204, Los Angeles, CA 90049
Phone: 310-820-5366
Fax: 310-820-1486
e-mail: info@veteransparkconservancy.org
Web Site: www.veteransparkconservancy.org/wadsworth.h
Officers:
   Chairperson: Sandra Krause
   CFO: Lester Stein
Management:
   Executive Director: Sue Young
Mission: The Wadsworth Theatre is owned by the West Los Angeles Department of Veteran's Affairs and is located on the Veteran's Administration campus. Built in 1939, in Spanish Colonial/Mission Revival architectural style, with its stucco finish and red clay tile roofing, makes the Wadsworth not only aesthetically pleasing, but also a historic landmark.
Founded: 1919
Seating Capacity: 1,356

6184
WILSHIRE EBELL THEATRE
4401 W Eighth St
Los Angeles, CA 90005-3856
Phone: 323-939-1128
Fax: 323-939-0132
e-mail: wilshireebelltheatre@ebellla.com
Web Site: www.ebellla.com
Officers:
   President: Patty Hill
Management:
   Theatre General Manager: Michael O'Connor
Seating Capacity: 1270

6185
PEPPERDINE UNIVERSITY SMOTHERS THEATRE
24255 Pacific Coast Highway
Malibu, CA 90263
Mailing Address: 24255 Pacific Coast Highway, Malibu, CA 90263
Phone: 310-506-4000
Fax: 310-506-4998
e-mail: pr@pepperdine.edu
Web Site: www.pepperdine.edu
Officers:
   President: Andrew K. Benton
Management:
   Director: Jerry Derloshon
   Assistant Director: Wileen Wong
   Public Relations Specialist: Jaclyn Tully
   University Photographer: Ron Hall
Utilizes: Actors; Dance Companies; Dancers; Fine Artists; Guest Accompanists; Guest Choreographers; Guest Designers; Guest Directors; Guest Musical Directors; Guest Musicians; Guest Writers; Instructors; Multimedia; Original Music Scores; Sign Language Translators; Singers; Soloists; Special Technical Talent; Theatre Companies; Touring Companies
Founded: 1937
Seating Capacity: 450
Year Built: 1980
Rental Contact: Managing Director Marnie Mitze

6186
HELEN SCHOENI THEATER
45200 Little Lake Street
Mendocino, CA 95460
Mailing Address: P.O. Box 765, Mendocino, CA 95460
Phone: 707-937-5818
Fax: 707-937-4625
Toll-free: 800-653-3328
e-mail: register@mendocinoartcenter.org
Web Site: www.mendocinoartcenter.org
Officers:
   Acting President: John Cornacchia
   Vice President: Patrick Keller
   Treasurer: Mark Adler
   Secretary: Dale Moyer
Management:
   Executive Director: Lindsay Shields
   Communications Director: Michael McDonald
   Music Events Coordinator: Gayle Caldwell
   Gallery Exhibitions: Megan Smithyman
   Education Director: Karen Bowers
Founded: 1959
Status: Non-Profit, Professional
Paid Staff: 15

6187
GALLO CENTER FOR THE ARTS
1000 I St
Modesto, CA 95354
Mailing Address: 1000 I Street Modesto CA 95354
Phone: 209-338-2100
Fax: 209-338-5006
e-mail: info@galloarts.org
Web Site: www.galloarts.org
Officers:
   Chairman: Britta Foster
   President: Marie D Gallo
   Vice President: June A Rogers
   Treasurer: Doug Vilas
   CEO: Lynn Dickerson
Management:
   Director Of Production/Tech. Ops: Erik Vose
   Director Of Tecnology/Theatre Ops: Al Poulus
Mission: Performing arts center with two venues
Type of Stage: Proscenium

6188
MODESTO JUNIOR COLLEGE PERFORMING ARTS CENTER
435 College Avenue
Modesto, CA 95350
Mailing Address: 435 College Avenue, Modesto, CA 95350
Phone: 209-575-6550
Fax: 209-575-6630
e-mail: hoilel@mjc.edu
Web Site: mjc.yosemite.cc.ca.us
Officers:
   President: Jill Stearns
Management:
   Interim Dean: Michael Sundquist
Mission: Recital Hall 300 seats.
Founded: 1967
Status: For-Profit, Non-Professional
Paid Staff: 80

6189
STARLITE PATIO THEATRE
5111 Benito Street
Montclair, CA 91763
Mailing Address: 5111 Benito Street. Montclair, CA 91763
Phone: 909-626-8571
Fax: 909-399-9751
e-mail: webmaster@cityofmontclair.org
Web Site: www.cityofmontclair.org
Management:
   Community Development Director: Robert W Clark
   Administrative Services Director: Edward C Starr
   Redevelopment Director: Marilyn J Staats
   Facility Supervisor: Shirley Wofford
   Manager: Harve Edwards
   Benefits Coordinator: Leslie Phillips
Specialized Field: Concerts

FACILITIES / California

6190
MOUNTAIN VIEW CENTER FOR THE PERFORMING ARTS
500 Castro Street
Post Office Box 7540
Mountain View, CA 94039-7540
Mailing Address: Post Office Box 7540, Mountain View, CA 94039-7540
Phone: 650-903-6000
Fax: 650-962-9900
e-mail: performingarts@mvcpa.com
Web Site: www.mvcpa.com
Management:
   Marketing/Public Relations Manager: Michele Roberts
   Business Manager: Cindy Miksa
   Technical Services Manager: Bernadette Fife
   Executive Director: W. Scott Whisler
   Operations Manager: Patrick Skelton
   Community Services Director: David Muela
Mission: Seeks to enrich Silicon Valley audiences through enjoyment, celebration and interaction with the arts.
Founded: 1991
Paid Staff: 50
Volunteer Staff: 300
Budget: $1.3 million
Performs At: Theaters
Affiliations: United States Institute for Theater Technolgies Inc., International Assocation of Auditorium Managers
Annual Attendance: 170,000
Type of Stage: Black Box; Mainstage-proscenium
Seating Capacity: Mainstage 600, Black Box 200, Park 300
Year Built: 1991
Rental Contact: Booking Coordinator Jenn Poret
Resident Groups: Theatre Works, Peninsula Youth Theatre

6191
NAPA VALLEY OPERA HOUSE
1030 Main Street,
Napa, CA 94559
Mailing Address: 1030 Main Street, Napa, CA 94559
Phone: 707-226-7372
Fax: 707-226-5392
e-mail: info@nvoh.org
Web Site: www.nvoh.org
Officers:
   Chairman: Bob Almeida
Management:
   Executive/Artistic Director: Peter Williams, evy@nvoh.org
   Executive Director: Jessica Thomason, gg@zbbs.com
   Office Manager: Lisa Thompsom
   House Manager/Artist Services: Lisa Thompson
   Maintenance Manager: Ed Rapp
Mission: The Napa Valley Opera House enriches the cultural experience of a diverse community - offering distinctive performing arts and preserving a unique historic theater.
Utilizes: Collaborating Artists; Collaborations; Community Members; Community Talent; Dance Companies; Guest Accompanists; Guest Designers; Guest Instructors; Guest Musicians; Guest Soloists; Guild Activities; Instructors; Local Artists & Directors; Lyricists; Multi Collaborations; Scenic Designers; Soloists; Students; Student Interns; Special Technical Talent
Founded: 1879
Opened: 2003
Specialized Field: Multi-Disciplinary
Budget: $2.1 million
Income Sources: Revenue; Donations; Grants
Annual Attendance: 65,000
Type of Stage: Proscenium, Thrust
Stage Dimensions: 80' x 12'
Seating Capacity: 467; 150
Year Built: 1879
Year Remodeled: 2003
Cost: $16+ Million
Rental Contact: Artistic Director Evy Warshawski

6192
GREAT WESTERN FORUM
3900 W/ Manchester Blvd Inglewood
New York, CA 90305
Phone: 310-330-7300
Fax: 310-679-2375
e-mail: info@thelaforum.com
Web Site: www.fabulousforum.com
Officers:
   Executive Chairman: James L. Dolan
   President and Chief Executive Offic: Hank Ratner
   Executive Vice President: Lawrence Burian
   Chief Technology Officer: Sean O'Donoghue
   Chief Financial Officer: Robert Pollichino
Management:
   General Manager: Gene Felling
   Director Event Services: Denise Williams
   Director Finance: Richard Nissenbaum
   Director Operations: Bill Rydum
   Human Resources: Molly Pascucci
Mission: The venue now serves as the home of Faithful Central Bible Church's congregation as well as a gathering place for concerts and community events
Founded: 1968
Opened: 1968
Specialized Field: Home of the Los Angeles Sparks (WNBA)
Seating Capacity: 18,000

6193
BALBOA PERFORMING ARTS THEATER
PO Box 752
707 E. Balboa Blvd
Newport Beach, CA 92661
Mailing Address: PO Box 752, Newport Beach, CA 92661
Phone: 949-673-0895
Fax: 949-673-0838
e-mail: info@thebalboatheater.org
Web Site: www.balboavillagetheatre.org
Officers:
   Chairman: Dr. Donald Hecht
   President: Dr. Steven Beazley
   Vice Chairman: Judy Posnikoff
   Treasurer & Secretary: Craig Smith
   Treasurer: Bill Wren
Management:
   Executive Director: Mary Lynch
   Marketing/Development Director: Christopher Trela
   Operations Director: Shana Bannert
Seating Capacity: 350

6194
EL PORTAL THEATRE
5269 Lankershim Boulevard
North Hollywood, CA 91601
Mailing Address: 11206 Weddington St., North Hollywood, CA 91601
Phone: 818-508-4200
Fax: 818-508-5113
e-mail: THE ELPORTAL@AOL.COM
Web Site: www.elportaltheatre.com
Officers:
   President: Thomas H Cole
   Vice President: Carol Rowen
   Secretary: Sunny Caine
Management:
   Artistic Director: Jeremiah Morris
   Managing Director: Robert Caine
Utilizes: Guest Companies; Singers
Founded: 1971
Specialized Field: Theater
Status: Professional; Nonprofit
Paid Staff: 65
Income Sources: Los Angeles Theatre Alliance; California Theater Council
Performs At: Alley Theater (Pavilion, Circle Forum)
Type of Stage: Proscenium, Thrust, Flexible
Seating Capacity: 350, 99, 42
Organization Type: Performing; Resident

6195
PLAZA DEL SOL PERFORMANCE HALL
California State University, Northridge
18111 Nordhoff Street
Northridge, CA 91330
Mailing Address: 18111 Nordhoff Street, Northridge, CA 91330
Phone: 818-677-1200
e-mail: theatre@csun.edu
Web Site: www.csun.edu/theatre
Officers:
   President: Jolene Koester
Management:
   Theatre Manager: William Taylor
   Administrative Support Assistant II: Sterling Davis
   Scene Shop Supervisor: Efren Delgadillo
   Department Technical Director: Scott McKim
   Financial Manager: Rachel Valiensi
Mission: Bachelor of Arts in theatre at California State University, Northridge offers an integrative, balanced program of studies that prepares students to enter the field of theatre, to undertake specialized graduate study, or to draw upon their theatre education in other fields and pursuits.
Specialized Field: Theatre
Seating Capacity: 500

6196
HENRY J KAISER CONVENTION CENTER
10 10th Street
Oakland, CA 94607
Phone: 510-238-7765
Fax: 510-238-7767
Web Site: www.hjkevents.com
Management:
   Facility Manager: Michael Lange
   Booking Manager: Gwendolyn Singleton
   Finance Director: Neil Mitchell
   Operations Manager: Albert M Plaza
   Event Manager: Rose Goodrich
   House Technician: Elijah Morgan
   Security Chief: Michael A Campbell
Mission: The Henery J Kaiser Convention Center is a sophisticated, diverse avenue which can accomodate all types of events from pefformimg arts, to entertainment, sports and private receptions. Arena: 25,000 square feet floor space; Ballroom seating capacity: reception/350, banquet/150, dance/200, theatre/325, classroom/120.
Founded: 1984

FACILITIES / California

Specialized Field: multi - use facility with theatre and arena space

6197
MCAFEE COLISEUM
7000 Coliseum Way
Oakland, CA 94621
Mailing Address: McAfee Coliseum, 7000 Coliseum Way, Oakland, CA 94621
Phone: 510-638-4900
Fax: 510-569-4246
Web Site: oakland.athletics.mlb.com/NASApp/mlb/oak/ballpark/index.jsp
Officers:
   President: Michael Crowley
Management:
   Stadium Operations Director: David Avila
   Stadium Operations Events Manager: Kristy Ledbetter
   Public Relations Director: Jim Young
   Finance Director: Kasey Miraglia
   Information Systems Manager: Debbie Dean
   Vice President Marketing/Sales: Jim Leahy
   Vice President/General Manager: Billy Beane
   General Counsel: Steve Johnston
Founded: 1966
Specialized Field: Sports Events Stadium (Oakland Athletics/Oakland Raiders)
Status: For-Profit, Professional
Seating Capacity: 63,146

6198
MILLS COLLEGE CONCERT HALL
5000 Macarthur Boulevard
Oakland, CA 94613
Phone: 510-430-2255
Fax: 510-430-3314
e-mail: music@mills.edu
Web Site: www.mills.edu/academics/undergraduate/mus/center_contemporary_music.php
Management:
   Department Head: Maggi Payne
   Technical Director: Les Stuck
   Faculty Administrator: Kathleen Baumgardner
   Concert Coordinator: Steed Cowart
Founded: 1852
Status: Non-Profit

6199
PARAMOUNT THEATRE
2025 Broadway
Oakland, CA 94612
Mailing Address: 2025 Broadway, Oakland, CA, 94612
Phone: 510-465-6400
Fax: 510-893-2300
e-mail: lstewart@paramounttheatre.com
Web Site: www.paramounttheatre.com
Officers:
   President: Michael Panico
   Vice President: Ed Thomas
   Treasurer: Tom Hart
   Secretary: Ronald R. McClain
Management:
   General Manager: Leslee Stewart
   Operations Manager: Jeffrey Ewald
   Box Office Manager: Gina Bishop
   Stage Manager: Larry Hunter
   House Organist: Jerry Nagano
Founded: 1931
Status: Non-Profit, Professional
Paid Staff: 7

6200
OROVILLE STATE THEATER
1489 Myers Street
Oroville, CA 95965
Mailing Address: 1489 Myers Street, Oroville, CA 95965
Phone: 530-538-2470
Fax: 530-534-1609
e-mail: orovillestatetheatre@ncen.org
Web Site: www.orovillestatetheatre.org
Management:
   Manager: Jim Christensen, jschristensen@ncen.org
Founded: 1928
Seating Capacity: 608

6201
OXNARD CIVIC AUDITORIUM
800 Hobson Way
Oxnard, CA 93030
Mailing Address: 800 Hobson Way Oxnard, CA 93030
Phone: 805-486-2424
Fax: 805-483-7303
Web Site: www.oxnardpacc.com
Officers:
   Vice President: Dale Belcher
   Treasurer: Gary Blum
Management:
   Executive Director: Bob Holden
   Box Office Manager: Dan Crouse
   Chief Engineer: Victor Rasmussen
   Business Services Manager: Cindy Crowell
   Box Office Manager: Dan Crouse
   Event Coordinator: Bevera Skelton
   House Senior Manager: Jessie Lucio
Founded: 1968
Specialized Field: Concert-Plays-Meetings
Status: Non-Profit, Professional
Paid Staff: 55
Seating Capacity: 1,604

6202
MCCALLUM THEATRE FOR THE PERFORMING ARTS
73000 Fred Waring Drive
Palm Desert, CA 92260
Mailing Address: 73000 Fred Waring Drive, Palm Desert, CA 92260
Phone: 760-346-6505
Fax: 760-341-9508
Toll-free: 866-889-2787
e-mail: information@mccallum-theatre.org
Web Site: www.mccallumtheatre.co
Officers:
   President/CEO: Mitch Gershenfeld
Management:
   Assistant Development Director: Liz Chambers
   Manager of Marketing & Sales: Rick Darius
   Box Office Manager: Sophia Perrone
   Marketing/Sales Manager: Rick Darius
   Director of Operations: Kalsa Thuresson Frary
   Assistant Development Director: Marcia Stone
   Education Director: Kajsa Thuresson Frary
   Manager of Special Events: Judi Pofsky
   Box Office Manager: Barbara Dawson
Utilizes: Actors; Collaborating Artists; Collaborations; Dance Companies; Educators; Local Artists; Original Music Scores; Soloists; Student Interns; Special Technical Talent; Theatre Companies
Founded: 1988
Paid Staff: 64
Volunteer Staff: 425
Income Sources: Earned; Contributed revenues
Performs At: Presenting Theatre
Annual Attendance: 250,000
Type of Stage: Proscenium
Stage Dimensions: 41'D x 84'W
Seating Capacity: 1,127

6203
ANNENBERG THEATER
Palm Springs Art Museum
101 Museum Drive
Palm Springs, CA 92262
Mailing Address: 101 Museum Drive, Palm Springs, CA 92262-5659
Phone: 760-322-4800
Fax: 760-327-5069
Web Site: www.psmuseum.org/performances_venue.shtml
Management:
   Executive Director: Janice Lyle
   Chief Curator/Liaison: Katherine Hough
   Development Director: Scott Schroeder
   Communications Director: Kimberly Nichols
   Education Director: Robert Brasier
   Director Theater Operations: John Finkler
   Business Services Director: Fred Clewell
   Publications Manager: Roy Komassa
Founded: 1976
Status: Non-Profit, Professional
Affiliations: APAP
Stage Dimensions: 50x30
Seating Capacity: 433
Year Built: 1976
Year Remodeled: 1999
Rental Contact: Bill Witte

6204
PALM SPRINGS CONVENTION CENTER
277 North Avenida Caballeros
Palm Springs, CA 92262
Mailing Address: 277 N Avenida Caballeros, Palm Springs CA 92262
Phone: 760-325-6611
Fax: 760-778-4102
Toll-free: 800-333-7535
Web Site: www.palmspringscc.com
Management:
   Executive Director: James Canfield
   Director of Sales: Rick Leson
   Marketing Director: Mary Perry
   Director of Catering: Lynne Toles
   Director of Operations: Mike Cross
Seating Capacity: 6.5

6205
SPANGENBURG THEATRE
Gunn High School
780 Arastradero Road @ Foothill Expressway
Palo Alto, CA 94306
Phone: 650-354-8263
Fax: 650-354-8277
Web Site: www.spangenbergtheatre.com
Management:
   Theatre Manager: Jorgen Wedseltoft
Founded: 1965
Specialized Field: Movie House
Status: Non-Profit, Non-Professional
Paid Staff: 1
Facility Category: Performance Center; Art House; Cinema
Type of Stage: Proscenium
Seating Capacity: 953
Year Remodeled: 2002

FACILITIES / California

6206
PARADISE PERFORMING ARTS CENTER
777 Nunneley Rd
P O Box 1124
Paradise, CA 95967
Mailing Address: Po Box 1124
Phone: 530-872-8454
Fax: 530-872-0809
e-mail: parartscen@sbcglobal.net
Web Site: www.paradiseperformingarts.com
Officers:
  President: Harvey Parrott
  Vice President: Bert Chumbler
  Secretary: Margo Yerman
  Tresurer: Becky Decottignes
Seating Capacity: 762

6207
CALIFORNIA INSTITUTE OF TECHNOLOGY PERFORMING ARTS CENTER
332 S. Michigan Ave.
Pasadena, CA 91106
Mailing Address: 332 S. Michigan Ave., Pasadena, CA 91106
Phone: 626-395-6811
Fax: 626-577-0130
Toll-free: 888-222-5832
e-mail: yokon@caltech.edu
Web Site: events.caltech.edu/preview/venues/adp
Officers:
  Chairman & CEO: Andrew N Liverls
  Chairman: Robert B Chess
  President: Thomas F Rosenbaum
  CEO: Alexander Lldow
  Director & Secretary-Treasurer: Camllla C Frost
Management:
  President: David Baltimore
  Grant Manager: Alexander Abramyan
  Operations Coordinator: Deborah White
  Senior Research Scientist: Benjamin Deverman
  Network Administrator: Dwayne Miles
  Senior House Manager: Chuck Barnes
  Marketing/Outreach Manager: Cara Stemen
  Associate Director: Chris Harcourt
Mission: Provides a broad spectrum of high quality multi-disciplinary cultural, educational and information programs. These programs are designed to compliment the Caltech experience of Institutes, students, faculty and staff, as well as serving as cultural enhancement to the greater Pasadena community.
Founded: 1891
Status: Non-Profit, Professional
Paid Staff: 60
Paid Artists: 100

6208
PASADENA CIVIC AUDITORIUM
300 East Green Street
Pasadena, CA 91101
Mailing Address: 300 E Green Street, Pasadena, CA 91101
Phone: 626-449-7360
Fax: 626-395-7132
e-mail: boxoffice@thepasadenacivic.com
Web Site: www.thepasadenacivic.com
Management:
  CEO Pasadena Center Operations: Michael Ross
Founded: 1931
Opened: 1932
Seating Capacity: 3,029
Year Built: 1931

6209
PASADENA PLAYHOUSE - MAINSTAGE THEATRE
39 S El Molino Avenue
Pasadena, CA 91101
Mailing Address: 39 S. El Molino Avenue, Pasadena, CA 91101
Phone: 626-356-7529
Fax: 626-204-7399
e-mail: boxoffice@pasadenaplayhouse.org
Web Site: www.pasadenaplayhouse.org
Officers:
  Chairman: Sheila Grether Marion
  Vice Chairman: David DiCristofaro
  Treasurer: Tony Phillips
  Secretary: Linda Boyd Griffey
  President: Valerie Amidon
Management:
  Artistic Director: Sheldon Epps
  Executive Director: Elizabeth Doran
  Director of Finance: Meredith Min
  Director of Management: Jan Saiget
  Associate Artistic Director: Seema Sueko
Founded: 1917
Seating Capacity: 682
Year Built: 1925
Rental Contact: Thomas Ware

6210
ROSE BOWL STADIUM
1001 Rose Bowl Drive
Pasadena, CA 91103
Mailing Address: 1001 Rose Bowl Drive, Pasadena, CA 91103
Phone: 626-577-3100
Fax: 626-405-0992
Web Site: www.rosebowlstadium.com
Officers:
  President: William E Thomson Jr
  Vice President: Fred Claire
  Treasurer: Robert Monk
  Secretary: Ann Marie Hickambottom
  CEO: Andy Meyers
  Chief Operations Officer: Jess Waiters
Management:
  General Manager: Darryl Dunn
  Asst General Manager/Operations: Jess Waiters
  Corporate Communications: Charles Thompson Jr
  Event Manager: Julie Benavidez
  Maintenance Superintendent: Will Schnell
Founded: 1921
Status: Non-Profit, Professional
Seating Capacity: 92,542

6211
CALIFORNIA POLYTECHNIC UNIVERSITY THEATRE
3801 West Temple Avenue
Building 5, Room 158
Pomona, CA 91768
Mailing Address: 3801 West Temple Ave., Pomona, California 91768
Phone: 909-869-3500
Fax: 909-869-3184
e-mail: dlogan@csupomona.edu
Web Site: www.class.csupomona.edu/th/cpframes.htm
Officers:
  Department Chairman: Bill Morse
Management:
  Director Technical Facilities: Dennis Logan
  Director Scenic Operations: Joyce Ehrenberg
  Publicity: Kellee Flanders
Mission: University theatre with continental seating - university theatre arts education, concerts, dance, on-campus activities and outside lease.
Founded: 1972
Seating Capacity: 516

6212
POWAY CENTER FOR THE PERFORMING ARTS
15498 Espola Road
Poway, CA 92064
Mailing Address: 15498 Espola Road. Poway, CA 92064
Phone: 858-668-4693
Fax: 858-748-0826
e-mail: foundation@powayarts.org
Web Site: www.powayarts.org
Officers:
  Chairperson: Jay Riordan
  Treasurer: Robert Lakosil
  Secretary: Jim Roth
  Incoming Chairman: Dennis Naas
Management:
  Marketing Manager: Yvonne Dows
  Executive Director: Michael Rennie
  Controller: Arlene Lund
  Administration: Lynn Wolsey
  Sales: Tom Johnson
Founded: 1990
Status: For-Profit, Non-Professional
Performs At: Poway Center for the Performing Arts
Seating Capacity: 815

6213
REDDING CIVIC AUDITORIUM
777 Cypress Avenue
Redding, CA 96001
Mailing Address: PO Box 496071, Redding, CA 96001
Phone: 530-225-4060
Fax: 530-225-4354
Toll-free: 800-874-7562
e-mail: kstarman@ci.redding.ca.us
Web Site: www.ci.redding.ca.us/cm/major_pr/civic_cent
Management:
  Executive Director/City Manager: Kurt Starman
  Senior Redevelopment Project Drctor: Larry Morgon
  Services Supervisor: Teresa Rudolph
  Assistant City Manager: Randy Bachman

6214
SHASTA COLLEGE FINE ARTS THEATRE
11555 Old Oregon Trail
P.O. Box 496006
Redding, CA 96049-6006
Mailing Address: P.O. Box 496006, Redding, CA 96049-6006
Phone: 530-242-7500
Fax: 530-225-4763
e-mail: info@shastacollege.edu
Web Site: www.shastacollege.edu
Officers:
  VP Administration Services: Morris Rodrigue
  VP Human Resource: Laura Cyphers Benson
  Board President: Duane K Miller
  Board Vice President: Robert M Steinacher
Management:
  Dean: Ronald G Johnson
  Human Resources Technician: Pearl Alworth
  Managing Director: Robert Soffian
  Personnel Recruitment Assistant: Courtney Vigna
  Research and Planning Director: Marc Beam
Founded: 1948

FACILITIES / California

Status: Non-Profit, Non-Professional
Paid Staff: 230

6215
GLENN WALLICHS THEATRE
University of Redlands
1200 East Colton Avenue
P.O. Box 3080
Redlands, CA 92373-0999
Mailing Address: 1200 E. Colton Ave. P.O. Box 3080, Redlands, CA 92373-0999
Phone: 909-793-2121
Fax: 909-793-2029
Web Site: www.redlands.edu
Officers:
  President: Dr. Ralph W Kuncl
  Chair: Carole Beswick
  Senior VP: Fran Inman
  CEO Fdelity: Leland C Launer
Management:
  Professor Theatre: Nephelie Andonyadis
  Professor Theatre: Chris Beach
  Director of Public Safety: Jeff Talbott
Mission: Seeks to provide opportunities for all students who enjoy the theater to be more involved on campus.
Founded: 1907
Specialized Field: Departmental and Guest Artist Productions
Status: Private
Seating Capacity: 326

6216
REDLANDS BOWL AMPHITHEATRE
168 South Eureka Street
Redlands, CA 92373-4620
Mailing Address: 168 South Eureka Street Redlands 92373-4620
Phone: 909-793-7316
Fax: 909-793-5086
e-mail: info@redlandsbowl.org
Web Site: www.redlandsbowl.org
Officers:
  Chairman: Jeffrey L Waldron
  President: Robert Dawes
  Vice President: Jan Hudson
  Treasurer: Joan Benson
  Secretary: Susan Sequeria
Management:
  Executive Director: Beverly Noerr
  Program Director: Marsha Gebara
Mission: Providing a range of performing arts to residents of Redlands at no admission charge.
Utilizes: Dance Companies; Dancers; Grant Writers; Guest Accompanists; Guest Musical Directors; Guest Musicians; Multimedia; Music; Original Music Scores; Singers; Special Technical Talent
Founded: 1923
Specialized Field: Series & Festivals; Instrumental; Opera; Choral; Traditional Jazz; Dance; Childrens'
Status: Non-Profit, Non-Professional
Paid Staff: 2
Volunteer Staff: 100
Budget: $150,000-$400,000
Income Sources: Freewill Donations; Underwriting; Grants
Season: Late June - Late August
Performs At: Redlands Open-air Amphitheatre (Festival Site)
Affiliations: Redlands Bowl
Annual Attendance: 80,000 to 100,000
Seating Capacity: 3,750
Organization Type: Performing; Sponsoring

6217
REDLANDS COMMUNITY MUSIC ASSOCIATION
168 South Eureka Street
Redlands, CA 92373-4620
Mailing Address: 168 South Eureka Street Redlands 92373-4620
Phone: 909-793-7316
Fax: 909-793-5086
e-mail: info@redlandsbowl.org
Web Site: www.redlandsbowl.org
Officers:
  President: Eric Gruenler
  Vice President: Paul W. Brubacher
  Secretary: Joan Benson
  Secretary: Robert Dawes
Management:
  Executive Director: Beverly Noerr
  Office Manager: Kristi Marnell
  Communications Coordinator: Jerri Graham
  Technical Director: Tim Mahoney
  Stage Manager: Nathan Prince
Founded: 1923
Status: Non-Profit, Professional
Paid Staff: 2
Seating Capacity: 6,000

6218
REDONDO BEACH PERFORMING ARTS CENTER
415 Diamond Street
Redondo Beach, CA 90278
Mailing Address: 415 Diamond Street, Redondo Beach, CA 90277
Phone: 310-372-1171
Fax: 310-643-0096
e-mail: john.larockr@redondo.org
Web Site: www.rbpac.com
Management:
  Theatre Manager: John La Rock
  Technical Director: Jack Meyer
Utilizes: Actors; AEA Actors; Choreographers; Collaborating Artists; Commissioned Composers; Commissioned Music; Dance Companies; Dancers; Designers; Educators; Filmmakers; Fine Artists; Grant Writers; Guest Accompanists; Guest Artists; Guest Choreographers; Guest Companies; Guest Composers; Guest Conductors; Guest Designers; Guest Directors; Guest Lecturers; Guest Musical Directors; Guest Musicians; Guest Soloists; High School Drama; Instructors; Local Artists; Local Unknown Artists; Multimedia; Music; Original Music Scores; Playwrights; Poets; Resident Professionals; Sign Language Translators; Singers; Soloists; Student Interns; Theatre Companies
Founded: 2003
Specialized Field: Performing Arts Center
Status: For-Profit, Professional
Paid Staff: 10
Type of Stage: Proscenium
Seating Capacity: 1,457

6219
MATEEL COMMUNITY CENTER
59 Rusk Ln.
P.O. Box 1910
Redway, CA 95560
Mailing Address: PO Box 1910, Redway, CA 95560
Phone: 707-923-3368
Fax: 707-923-3370
e-mail: office@mateel.org
Web Site: www.mateel.org
Officers:
  President: Bruce Champie
  Vice President: Garth Epling
  Treasurer: Bob Stern
  Secretary: Elena Worley
Management:
  Executive Director: Taunya Stapp
  Hall Manager: John Jennings
  Marketing: Justin Crellin
  Administrative Manager: Katz Boose
  General Manager: Justin Crellin
Founded: 1978
Status: Non-Profit
Annual Attendance: 45,000
Seating Capacity: 300

6220
RICHMOND MEMORIAL CONVENTION CENTER
403 Civic Center Plaza
Side Rooms, 2533 Nevin Avenue
Richmond, CA 94804
Mailing Address: 450 Civic Center Plaza, Richmond, CA 94804
Phone: 510-620-6509
Fax: 510-620-6583
Web Site: www.ci.richmond.ca.us/index.asp?NID=425
Management:
  Reservations/Rental Coordinator: Jerry Anderson
  Economic Development: Janet Johnson
Mission: to be a focal point for the Community of Richmond. This magnificent facility has played host to a number of different activities including concerts, car shows, boxing exhibitions, basketball games, mixed martial arts events, and a host of others.
Founded: 1949
Specialized Field: dance, reunion, reception, concert, pageant, party, sporting event, or banquet

6221
ARTS PERFORMANCE LAB
University Of California, Riverside
900 University Avenue
Arts 121
Riverside, CA 92521-0324
Mailing Address: 900 University Avenue, ARTS 121, Riverside, CA 92521-0324
Phone: 951-827-7193
Fax: 951-827-1255
e-mail: kathleen.deatley@ucr.edu
Web Site: www.theatre.ucr.edu
Officers:
  Chair: Stuart Krieger
  Facilities Manager: Paul Richardson
  Financial & Administrative Officer: Reasey Heang
Management:
  Production Manager: Marc Longlois
  Program Promotions Manager: Kathleen DeAtley
  Financial & Administrative Officer: Reasey Heang
  Production Manager: Carmen Gomez
  Program Promotions Manager: Kathy DeAtley
Mission: Theatre students have the opportunity and are encouraged to perform, direct, and design for departmental productions and student playwrights have their work staged in the annual Playworks Festival.
Specialized Field: Dance, Theatre
Type of Stage: Adaptable
Seating Capacity: 140

FACILITIES / California

6222
BARN THEATRE
University Of California, Riverside
900 University Avenue
Arts 121
Riverside, CA 92521-0324
Mailing Address: 900 University Avenue, ARTS 121,
Riverside , CA 92521-0324
Phone: 951-827-7193
Fax: 951-827-1255
e-mail: kathleen.deatley@ucr.edu
Web Site: www.theatre.ucr.edu
Officers:
   Chair: Stuart Krieger
   Facilities Manager: Paul Richardson
   Financial & Administrative Officer: Reasey Heang
Management:
   Production Manager: Marc Longlois
   Program Promotions Manager: Kathleen DeAtley
   Financial & Administrative Officer: Reasey Heang
   Production Manager: Carmen Gomez
   Program Promotions Manager: Kathy DeAtley
Mission: Theatre students have the opportunity and are encouraged to perform, direct, and design for departmental productions and student playwrights have their work staged in the annual Playworks Festival.
Specialized Field: Movement Classes in Tap and Dances of Mexico
Seating Capacity: 50

6223
DANCE STUDIO THEATRE
University Of California, Riverside
900 University Avenue
Arts 121
Riverside, CA 92521-0324
Mailing Address: 900 University Avenue, ARTS 121,
Riverside , CA 92521-0324
Phone: 951-827-7193
Fax: 951-827-1255
e-mail: kathleen.deatley@ucr.edu
Web Site: www.theatre.ucr.edu
Officers:
   Chair: Stuart Krieger
   Facilities Manager: Paul Richardson
   Financial & Administrative Officer: Reasey Heang
Management:
   Production Manager: Marc Longlois
   Program Promotions Manager: Kathleen DeAtley
   Financial & Administrative Officer: Reasey Heang
   Production Manager: Carmen Gomez
   Program Promotions Manager: Kathy DeAtley
Mission: Theatre students have the opportunity and are encouraged to perform, direct, and design for departmental productions and student playwrights have their work staged in the annual Playworks Festival.
Specialized Field: Movement Classes
Type of Stage: Adaptable
Seating Capacity: 130

6224
RIVERSIDE CONVENTION CENTER
3750 University Avenue
Suite 175
Riverside, CA 92501
Mailing Address: 3750 University Avenue, Suite 175,
Riverside, CA 92501
Phone: 951-222-4700
Fax: 909-222-4706
e-mail: info@RiversideCVB.com
Web Site: www.riversidecb.com
Officers:
   Senior VP: Debbi Guthrie
Management:
   President: Scott Megna
   Executive Director: Debbie Megna, dmegna@riversidecvb.com
   Sales Manager: Anne Seymour
   Visitor Center Manager: Pam Seinturier
   Sales Manager: Anne Seymour
Status: For-Profit, Non-Professional
Paid Staff: 200
Facility Category: Convention Center
Seating Capacity: 2,000
Rental Contact: Pamela Sturrock

6225
RIVERSIDE MUNICIPAL AUDITORIUM
3485 Mission Inn Avenue
Riverside, CA 92501
Phone: 909-787-7678
Fax: 909-682-8464
Web Site: www.riversidemunicipalauditorium.com
Officers:
   President: Robert Stein
   Executive Director: Carlos Vonfrankemberg
Founded: 1987
Status: For-Profit, Professional
Paid Staff: 8
Annual Attendance: 50,000
Type of Stage: Proscenium
Seating Capacity: 1,776

6226
UNIVERSITY THEATRE
University Of California, Riverside
900 University Avenue
Arts 121
Riverside, CA 92521-0324
Mailing Address: 900 University Avenue, ARTS 121,
Riverside , CA 92521-0324
Phone: 951-827-7193
Fax: 951-827-1255
e-mail: kathleen.deatley@ucr.edu
Web Site: www.theatre.ucr.edu
Officers:
   Chair: Stuart Krieger
   Facilities Manager: Paul Richardson
   Financial & Administrative Officer: Reasey Heang
Management:
   Production Manager: Marc Longlois
   Program Promotions Manager: Kathleen DeAtley
   Financial & Administrative Officer: Reasey Heang
   Production Manager: Carmen Gomez
   Program Promotions Manager: Kathy DeAtley
Mission: Theatre students have the opportunity and are encouraged to perform, direct, and design for departmental productions and student playwrights have their work staged in the annual Playworks Festival.
Specialized Field: Art History, Dance, Music, Studio Art, and Theatre
Type of Stage: Proscenim
Seating Capacity: 484
Year Built: 2001
Architect: Israel, Callas, Shortridge Design Associates of Los Angeles
Cost: $35 Million

6227
NORRIS CENTER FOR THE PERFORMING ARTS
27570 Norris Centre Drive
Rolling Hills Estates, CA 90274
Phone: 310-544-0403
Fax: 310-377-2997
e-mail: emarketing@norristheatre.org
Web Site: www.norriscenter.com
Officers:
   President: Julie Moe Reynolds
   Vice President: Greg Zikos
   Treasurer: Denise Van Deuren
   Secretary: Jana Kelly
Management:
   Executive Director: James W Gruessing
   Sales Director: Nancy Nassimbene
   Finance and HR Director: Susan Henry
   Public Relations Director: Kelly Schmocker
   Technical Director: Greg Forbess
Mission: The Norris Theatre is a 450-seat, state of the art facility that has become the cornerstone of the performing arts on the Palos Verdes Peninsula, bringing leading entertainers and performing artists to the region and reinforcing these efforts with high-quality educational outreach programs for children and adults.
Utilizes: Actors; Dance Companies; Educators; Fine Artists; Guest Choreographers; Guest Composers; Guest Designers; Guest Ensembles; Guest Instructors; Guest Lecturers; Guest Soloists; High School Drama; Instructors; Multimedia; Music; Original Music Scores; Soloists; Student Interns; Special Technical Talent; Theatre Companies; Touring Companies
Founded: 1978
Specialized Field: All Performing Arts - Presenting House
Status: Non-Profit, Professional
Paid Staff: 7
Volunteer Staff: 80
Income Sources: Private donations and ticket sales
Annual Attendance: 14,000
Facility Category: Presenting; Producing; Rental
Type of Stage: Proscenium
Year Built: 1983
Rental Contact: Box Office Manager David Barr

6228
ARCO ARENA
One Sports Parkway
Sacramento, CA 95834
Phone: 916-928-3650
Fax: 916-928-6936
e-mail: tickets@arcoarena.com
Web Site: www.arco.com
Officers:
   President: John Thomas
Management:
   SVP/Business Operations: John Rinehart
   SVP Arena Services: Mark Stone
   SVP Sales/Service: Jeff Morander
   VP Marketing/Business Operations: Public Relation Leighton
   VP Service Development: Tom Peterson
   VP Strategic Alliances: Tom Hunt
   VP Human Resources: Donna Ruiz
Founded: 1988
Specialized Field: Sports Facility Also hosts Numerous Concerts; Ice Shows; Festivals; and Other Family Events.
Affiliations: Home of the Sacramento Kings, Sacramento Monarchs and Sacramento Knights.
Seating Capacity: 17,317
Year Built: 1985

FACILITIES / California

6229
ARDEN PLAYHOUSE
5640 Roseville Road
Suite D
Sacramento, CA 95842
Mailing Address: 5640 Roseville Road Suite D,
Sacramento, CA 95842
Phone: 916-332-2582
Fax: 916-782-1072
e-mail: admin@ardenplayhouse.com or
arden@ardenplayhouse.com
Web Site: www.ardenplayhouse.com
Management:
  Owner/Producer: Michael Messmer
  Marketing Director: Barbara Messmer
Mission: We will continue our tradition of presenting the best in comedy, including some original plays, for your entertainment.
Founded: 1998
Specialized Field: comedies and farces

6230
CROCKER ART MUSEUM BALLROOM
216 O Street
Sacramento, CA 95814
Mailing Address: 216 O Street, Sacramento, CA 95814
Phone: 916-264-5423
Fax: 916-264-7372
Toll-free: 800-735-2929
e-mail: cam@cityofsacramento.org
Web Site: www.crockerartmuseum.org
Officers:
  President: Steve Mills
  Vice President: David Townsend
  Treasurer: Rhea Brunner
  Secretary: Garry Maisel
Management:
  Executive Director: Lial Jones
  Director of Administration: Cheri Johnson
  Finance Director: David Separovich
  Development Director: Lynn Upchurch
  Marketing/Communications Director: LeAnne Ruzzamenti
  Human Resoureces Manager: Laurie Rodriguez
Mission: Providing performances in an intimate museum setting.
Founded: 1885
Specialized Field: Dance; Vocal Music; Instrumental Music; Theater
Status: Non-Profit, Non-Professional
Performs At: Crocker Museum Ballroom
Annual Attendance: 140,000
Organization Type: Sponsoring

6231
SACRAMENTO COMMUNITY CENTER THEATRE
City Of Sacramento
1301 L Street
Sacramento, CA 95814
Mailing Address: 1030 15th Street, Sacramento CA 95814
Phone: 916-808-5481
Fax: 916-808-7687
e-mail: conventioncenter@cityofsacramento.org
Web Site: www.sacramentoconventioncenter.com
Management:
  Theater Manager: Bryan Chatterton
  Director Convention/Culture/Leisure: Barbara E Bonebrake
  General Manager: Judy Goldbar
  Deputy General Manager: Matthew Voreyer
  Facility & Operations Manager: Dan Goodwater
Founded: 1974
Opened: 1974
Performs At: Variety
Annual Attendance: 350,000
Type of Stage: Proscenium Arch
Seating Capacity: 2,350
Year Built: 1974
Rental Contact: Theater Manager Bryan Chatterton

6232
SACRAMENTO CONVENTION CENTER
1030 15th Street
Suite 100
Sacramento, CA 95814
Mailing Address: 1030 15th Street, Sacramento, CA 95814
Phone: 916-449-5291
Fax: 916-264-7687
e-mail: conventioncenter@cityofsacramento.org
Web Site: www.sacramentoconventioncenter.com
Management:
  Deputy General Manager: Matthew W. Voreyer
  General Manager: Judy Goldbar
  Administrative Officer: Tina McCarty
  Box Office Manager: Jeanne Sapunor
  Facility & Operations Manager: Dan Goodwater
Mission: The Sacramento Convention Center includes 134,000 square feet of contiguous exhibit space, 31 meeting rooms, an outdoor garden terrace adjacent to an elegant 24,000 square-foot ballroom, and two separate 10,000 square-foot regisration/prefunction areas. The complex also includes the 4,000 seat Memorial Auditorium and the 2,452 seat Community Center Theatre. All venues are located conveniently near City parking facilities.
Founded: 1926
Type of Stage: Proscenium Arch

6233
COUSSOULIS ARENA
Californaia State University, San Bernardino
5500 University Pkwy
San Bernadino, CA 92407
Phone: 909-537-7390
Fax: 909-880-7162
e-mail: arena@csusb.edu
Web Site: www.arena.csusb.edu

6234
CALIFORNIA THEATRE OF PERFORMING ARTS
562 West 4th Street
San Bernardino, CA 92402-0270
Mailing Address: P.O. Box 270, San Bernardino, CA 92402-0270
Phone: 909-885-5152
Fax: 909-885-8672
Toll-free: 800-511-6449
e-mail: jbond007@gmail.com
Web Site: www.theatricalarts.com
Management:
  President: Joseph Hansen
  Executive Director: Alan Edenson
Founded: 1998
Status: Non-Profit, Professional

6235
STURGES CENTER FOR FINE ARTS
780 N. E St
San Bernardino, CA 92410
Mailing Address: Po Box 1303 San Bernardino 92402
Phone: 909-384-5415
Fax: 909-384-5449
e-mail: sturgescenter@gmail.com
Web Site: www.sturgescenter.org

6236
BALBOA PARK RECITAL HALL
202 C Street
San Diego, CA 92101
Mailing Address: 202 C Street, San Diego, CA 92101
Phone: 619-544-7827
Fax: 619-544-7832
e-mail: boxoffice@starlighttheatre.org
Web Site: www.sandiego.gov/park-and-recreation/parks/balboa/recitalhall.shtml
Management:
  Executive Director: Cecilia Soriano
  Box Office Manager: Stephan Lewicki
  Finance Manager: Karen Dalton
  Artistic/Production Director: Brian Wells
  Marketing/Community Relations: Annette Grieshaber
Mission: The Recital Hall is located in the Palisades Building, a historic building which was built for the second exposition. There is one large, open hall with a stage and high truss beamed ceiling. It is approximately 5,400 sq ft. Maximum Capacity: 200 banquet-style, 300 meeting.

6237
BALBOA PARK STARLIGHT THEATER
PO Box 3519
San Diego, CA 92163
Phone: 619-544-7800
e-mail: info@starlighttheatre.org
Web Site: www.starlighttheatre.org
Management:
  Executive Director: Cecilia Soriano
  Producing Artistic Director: Brian Wells
  Finance Manager: Karen Dalton
  Marketing/Community Relations: Annette Grieshaber
Founded: 1945

6238
CAFE DEL REY MORO
1649 El Prado
Suite 3
San Diego, CA 92101
Mailing Address: 1649 El Prado, Suite 3. San Diego, CA 92101-1611
Phone: 619-232-6203
e-mail: ngeorge@sandiegohistory.org
Web Site: www.sandiegohistory.org/bpbuildings/hospitality.htm
Officers:
  President: Thompson Fetter
  Vice President: Robert F. Adelizzi
  Secretary: Helen Kinnaird
  Treasurer: Woody Ledford
  Past President: Hal Sadler
Management:
  Executive Director: Charlotte Cagan
  Business Manager: Maria Howard
  Facilities Manager: Oscar Urrutia
  Education Director: Naomi Ostwald Kawamura
  Development Director: Lori Gremel

6239
COX ARENA AT AZTEC BOWL
5500 Canyon Crest Drive
San Diego, CA 92182

FACILITIES / California

Phone: 619-594-0234
Fax: 619-594-6423
Web Site: www.cox-arena.com/welcome.html
Management:
  Director: John Kolek
  Assistant Director: Tim Ripke
  Operations Manager: Tom Granucci
  Event Services Manager: Aaron Woods
  Facility Operations: Adrian Munoz
  Facility Services: Julio Pina
  Financial Administrator: Stacy Desmond
  Ticket Office Manager: June Barreras
Mission: Facility - 12,000 seat multi-purpose area.
Founded: 1997
Status: Professional
Seating Capacity: 12,000

6240
DON POWELL THEATRE
San Diego State University
5500 Campanile Drive
San Diego, CA 92182-7601
Mailing Address: 5500 Campanile Drive, San Diego, CA 92182-7601
Phone: 619-594-5091
Fax: 619-594-7431
e-mail: aparkhur@mail.sdsu.edu
Web Site: http://ttf.sdsu.edu/
Officers:
  Director: Nick Reid
  Facilities Manager: Peter Nordyke
Management:
  TTF Coordinator: Angie Parkhurst
  Business Manager: Mark Anderson
  Interim School Director: D.J. Hopkins
  Scene Designer: Ralph Funicello
  Costume Shop Manager: Teri Tavares
Mission: The Theatre Program provides its students with an understanding of the great legacy of dramatic literature, technical skills as they relate to public performance, training in critical thinking and the means to express themselves with clarity and grace.
Specialized Field: Theatre
Type of Stage: Proscenium
Seating Capacity: 500

6241
EXPERIMENTAL THEATRE
San Diego State University
5500 Campanile Drive
San Diego, CA 92182-7601
Mailing Address: 5500 Campanile Drive, San Diego, CA 92182-7601
Phone: 619-594-5091
Fax: 619-594-7431
e-mail: aparkhur@mail.sdsu.edu
Web Site: http://ttf.sdsu.edu/
Officers:
  Director: Nick Reid
  Facilities Manager: Peter Nordyke
Management:
  TTF Coordinator: Angie Parkhurst
  Business Manager: Mark Anderson
  Interim School Director: D.J. Hopkins
  Scene Designer: Ralph Funicello
  Costume Shop Manager: Teri Tavares
Mission: The Theatre Program provides its students with an understanding of the great legacy of dramatic literature, technical skills as they relate to public performance, training in critical thinking and the means to express themselves with clarity and grace.
Specialized Field: Theatre
Type of Stage: Flexible
Seating Capacity: 175

6242
LYCEUM THEATRES COMPLEX
San Diego Repertory Theatre
79 Horton Plaza
San Diego, CA 92101-6144
Phone: 619-231-3586
Fax: 619-235-0939
e-mail: artistic@sandiegorep.com
Web Site: www.sandiegorep.com
Management:
  Artistic Director: Sam Woodhouse
  Managing Director: Karen Wood
  Associate Artistic Director: Todd Salovey
Founded: 1976
Annual Attendance: 50,000
Seating Capacity: 545

6243
PRADO AT BALBOA PARK
1649 El Prado
Suite 3
San Diego, CA 92101
Mailing Address: 1649 El Prado, Suite 3. San Diego, CA 92101-1611
Phone: 619-557-9441
Web Site: www.sandiegohistory.org/bpbuildings/hospitality.htm
Officers:
  President: Thompson Fetter
  Vice President: Robert F. Adelizzi
  Secretary: Helen Kinnaird
  Treasurer: Woody Ledford
  Past President: Hal Sadler
Management:
  Executive Director: Charlotte Cagan
  Business Manager: Maria Howard
  Facilities Manager: Oscar Urrutia
  Education Director: Naomi Kawamura
  Development Director: Lori Gremel
Mission: The Prado, an award-winning, full-service restaurant located in the House of Hospitality, offers charming indoor and outdoor dining
Specialized Field: Theater, Ballet, Symphonies, Weddings, Dance,
Status: Non profit

6244
QUALCOMM STADIUM
202 C Street
San Diego, CA 92101
Mailing Address: 202 C Street, San Diego, CA 92101
Phone: 619-236-5555
Fax: 619-283-0460
e-mail: stadium@sandiego.gov
Web Site: www.sandiego.gov/qualcomm/index.shtml
Management:
  General Manager: Mike McSweeney
  Centerplate: Scott Marshall
  Director Sales: Lynn Abramson
Founded: 1967
Specialized Field: Stadium; Performances
Status: Non-Profit, Professional
Paid Staff: 38
Performs At: Football Stadium
Facility Category: Stadium
Seating Capacity: 70,500
Year Remodeled: 1997
Rental Contact: General Manager Michael McSweeney

6245
SAN DIEGO CIVIC THEATRE
1100 Third Avenue
San Diego, CA 92101
Mailing Address: 1100 Third Avenue, San Diego, CA 92101
Phone: 619-570-1100
Fax: 619-615-4001
e-mail: info@sandiegotheatres.org
Web Site: www.sandiegotheatres.org
Officers:
  Chair: M Faye Wilson
  Vice Chair: Cheryl Kendrick
  President & CEO: Donald M. Telford
  Director: Bob Nelson
  Director: Matthew Strauss
Management:
  Event Manager: Cindy Bowers
  Ticket Sales Manager: Debbie McDonald
  Production Services Manager: Carolyn Satter
  Director: Chris Cramer
Founded: 1965
Annual Attendance: 282800
Seating Capacity: 2,976

6246
SAN DIEGO MUSEUM OF ART AUDITORIUM
1450 El Prado
Balboa Park
San Diego, CA 92101
Mailing Address: PO Box 122107, San Diego, CA. 92112-2107
Phone: 619-232-7931
Fax: 619-232-9367
e-mail: information@sdmart.org
Web Site: www.sdmart.org
Officers:
  President: Frank Rogozienski
  Vice-President: Gordon Brodfuehrer
  Vice-President: Rob Hayes
  Treasurer: Doug Carlson
  Secretary: Chuck Hellerich
Management:
  Executive Director: Derrick Curtwright
  Interim Director Communications: Chris Zook
Utilizes: Dance Companies; Dancers; Filmmakers; Guest Choreographers; Guest Instructors; Guest Soloists; Multi Collaborations; Multimedia; Original Music Scores; Playwrights; Special Technical Talent; Touring Companies
Founded: 1925
Specialized Field: Visual
Status: Non-Profit, Professional
Paid Staff: 85
Budget: $9 million
Performs At: James Copley Auditorium
Annual Attendance: 400,000
Facility Category: Auditorium
Type of Stage: Proscenium
Seating Capacity: 425
Year Remodeled: 1999

6247
SAN DIEGO SPORTS ARENA
3500 Sports Arena Boulevard
San Diego, CA 92110-4919
Mailing Address: 3500 Sports Arena Blvd, San Diego, CA 92110-4919
Phone: 619-224-4171
Fax: 619-224-3010
e-mail: info@valleyviewcasinocenter.com
Web Site: www.sandiegoarena.com

FACILITIES / California

Management:
   President: Ron Hahn
   General Manager: Ernie Hahn
   VP: Bob Brown
   Director Public Relations: Stephanie Coolich
   VP/Operations: John Sanders
   Event Manager: Jason Lebdetter
   Marketing & Sponsorship Director: Kathy Padilla
   Marketing Coordinator: Dana Cappello
Founded: 1967
Status: Non-Profit, Professional
Paid Staff: 60
Affiliations: Clear Channel Entertainment
Facility Category: Arena
Stage Dimensions: 60' x 40'
Seating Capacity: 14,000
Year Built: 1966
Cost: 6.4 million
Rental Contact: Sean Saadeh

6248
SAN DIEGO THEATRES/BALBOA & CIVIC THEATRES
1100 Third Avenue
San Diego, CA 92101
Mailing Address: 1100 Third Avenue, San Diego, CA 92101
Phone: 619-615-4000
Fax: 619-615-4001
e-mail: info@sandiegotheatres.org
Web Site: www.sandiegotheatres.org
Officers:
   Chair: M Faye Wilson
   Vice Chair: Cheryl Kendrick
   President & CEO: Donald M. Telford
Management:
   Event Manager: Cindy Bowers
   Production Services Manager: Carolyn Satter
   Director: Chris Cramer
Paid Staff: 43
Annual Attendance: 282800

6249
AFRICAN AMERICAN ART AND CULTURE COMPLEX
762 Fulton Street
Suite 300
San Francisco, CA 94102
Mailing Address: 762 Fulton Street, San Francisco, CA 94102
Phone: 415-922-2049
Fax: 415-922-5130
e-mail: info@aaacc.org
Web Site: www.aaacc.org
Officers:
   President: Nichole Jordan
   Vice-President: Annemarie Conroy
   Treasurer: Patty-Jo Rutland
   Secretary: Arnold Townsend
Management:
   Executive Director: Kimberly Hayes
   Program Manager: Tamika Chenier
   Office Manager: Melorra Green
   Case Manager: Brandon Banks
   Youth Coordinator: Nicola Figgins
   Office Manager: Tamiko Johnson
Mission: Mission is to empower our community through Afro-centric artistic and cultural expression, mediums, education and programming. Dedicated to inspiring children and youth to serve as agents of change, cultivating their leadership skills and fostering a commitment to community service and activism.
Founded: 1989

Status: Non-Profit, Professional
Paid Staff: 10

6250
ALCAZAR THEATRE
650 Geary Street
San Francisco, CA 94102
Phone: 415-441-6655
Fax: 415-441-9567
e-mail: AlcazarTheatre@aol.com
Web Site: www.southcamdentheatre.org
Management:
   Artistic Director: Steve Dobbins
   Administrative Director: Alan Ramos
   Casting Director: Kim Parolari
   House Manager: Bernadette Lopes
Utilizes: Actors; AEA Actors; Choreographers; Designers; Grant Writers; Guest Accompanists; Guest Artists; Guest Companies; Guest Designers; Guest Teachers; Instructors; Local Artists; Lyricists; Multimedia; Organization Contracts; Original Music Scores; Resident Professionals; Sign Language Translators; Soloists; Special Technical Talent
Founded: 1978
Status: Commercial
Volunteer Staff: 3
Budget: $10,000-$50,000
Season: Year Round
Performs At: Commercial, For-Profit Theatre
Annual Attendance: 200,000
Type of Stage: Proscenium
Stage Dimensions: 45'x31'
Seating Capacity: 520
Year Built: 1917
Year Remodeled: 1991
Cost: $2.5 million
Rental Contact: Artistic Director Steve Dobbins

6251
AT&T PARK
24 Willie Mays Plaza
San Francisco, CA 94107
Mailing Address: 24 Willie Mays Plaza, San Francisco, CA 94107
Phone: 415-972-2000
Toll-free: 866-800-1275
Web Site: sanfrancisco.giants.mlb.com/NASApp/mlb/sf/ballpark/index.jsp
Officers:
   President: Peter A Magowan
   EVP/Chief Operating Officer: Laurence M Baer
   VP/Chief Information Officer: Bill Schlough
   SVP/Chief Financial Officer: John F Yee
   SVP/General Counsel: Jack F Bair
Management:
   SVP/General Manager: Brian R Sabean
   SVP/Ballpark Operations: Jorge Costa
   VP Communications: Staci A Slaughter
   Public Affairs/Community Relations: Shana Daum
   SVP Consumer Marketing: Tom McDonald
   Vice President Finance: Lisa Pantages
Mission: Open aired baseball park
Founded: 2000
Specialized Field: Concerts
Status: For-Profit, Professional
Paid Artists: 25
Seating Capacity: 41,503

6252
BAYVIEW OPERA HOUSE
4705 3rd Street
San Francisco, CA 94124

Mailing Address: 4705 Third Street, San Francisco, CA 94124
Phone: 415-824-0386
Fax: 415-824-7124
Toll-free: 877-227-5544
e-mail: info.bvoh@bvoh.org
Web Site: www.bvoh.org
Officers:
   President: Jerald Joseph
   Secretary: Theo Ellington
   Treasurer: Willie B. Kennedy
Management:
   Executive Director: Shelley Bradford-Bell
   Program Director: Eugene Steptoe
Utilizes: Actors; Artists-in-Residence; Collaborating Artists; Collaborations; Dance Companies; Dancers; Designers; Educators; Filmmakers; Fine Artists; Five Seasonal Concerts; Guest Directors; Guest Lecturers; High School Drama; Local Artists; Lyricists; Multi Collaborations; Multimedia; Music; Original Music Scores; Performance Artists; Playwrights; Sign Language Translators; Soloists; Student Interns; Special Technical Talent; Touring Companies; Visual Arts
Founded: 1968
Specialized Field: Series & Festivals; Dance; Instrumental Music; Musical Theatre; Theatrical Group; Vocal Music
Status: Non-Profit, Non-Professional
Seating Capacity: 300

6253
BILL GRAHAM CIVIC AUDITORIUM
99 Grove Street
San Francisco, CA 94102
Mailing Address: 99 Grove Street, San Francisco, CA 94102
Phone: 415-974-4000
Fax: 415-974-4073
e-mail: miendaro@moscone.com
Web Site: www.billgrahamcivic.com
Management:
   General Manager: Richard Shaff
   Sales Director: Melody Lendaro
   Communications Manager: Naina Ayya
Seating Capacity: 7,000

6254
COMMUNITY MUSIC CENTER
544 Capp Street
San Francisco, CA 94110
Mailing Address: 544 Capp Street, San Francisco, CA 94110
Phone: 415-647-6015
Fax: 415-647-3890
e-mail: info@sfcmc.org
Web Site: www.sfcmc.org
Officers:
   Chairperson: Kay Kleinerman
   President: Patricia Taylo Lee
   Vice President: Catharine L. Kalin
   Treasurer: Paul Sussman
   Secretary: David J. Neuman
Management:
   Executive Director: Christopher Borg
   Program Director: Sylvia Sherman
   Development Director: John Robinson
   Marketing Director: Sonia Caltvedt
   Development Associate: Ashley Coyle
   Registrar: Kathy Cole
Founded: 1921
Status: Non-Profit, Professional
Paid Staff: 137
Paid Artists: 125

FACILITIES / California

Type of Stage: Proscenium
Seating Capacity: 90

6255
COW PALACE
2600 Geneva Street
PO Box 34206
San Francisco, CA 94134-0206
Mailing Address: 2600 Geneva Avenue, PO Box 34206, Daly City, CA 94014
Phone: 415-404-4111
Fax: 415-469-6111
e-mail: info@cowpalace.com
Web Site: www.cowpalace.com
Officers:
  President: Henry Kuechler
  1st Vice President: Mara Kopp
  2nd Vice President: Barbara Wanvig
  Chief Executive Officer: Walter Haub
Management:
  Director: Mike Treacy
  Managing Director: William Mendes
Founded: 1941
Specialized Field: Home of the Grand National Rodeo; Horse and Stock Show. Hosts ice events; basketball; motorcycle races
Status: Non-Profit, Non-Professional
Paid Staff: 25
Type of Stage: Proscenium
Seating Capacity: 8,849
Year Built: 1941

6256
COWELL THEATER
2 Marina Blvd at Buchanan St.
Building A
San Francisco, CA 94123
Mailing Address: Marina Blvd and Buchanan St., San Francisco, CA 94123
Phone: 415-345-7500
Fax: 415-441-3405
e-mail: contact@fortmason.org
Web Site: www.fortmason.org
Officers:
  Corporate communications consultant: Sally P McNulty
  President: David Becker
  Vice Chair: Courtney Damkroger
Management:
  Executive Director: Rich Hillis
  Sales Manager: William Enright
  Marketing Director: Pat Schultz Kilduff
  Marketing Associate: Claudia Willen
  Director of Events: Patrick Hajduk
Mission: Support-reflect the evolving cultural fabric of the San Francisco Bay Area.
Founded: 1976
Specialized Field: Dance; Theater; Music; Film
Status: Non-Profit, Professional
Paid Staff: 30
Annual Attendance: 1.7 Million
Facility Category: Cultural Center
Stage Dimensions: 40' x 30' 20'
Seating Capacity: 437
Year Built: 1989
Rental Contact: Amanda Matthews

6257
CURRAN THEATRE
445 Geary Street
San Francisco, CA 94102
Mailing Address: 445 Geary Street, San Francisco, CA 94102
Phone: 415-512-7770
Fax: 415-431-5052
Toll-free: 888-746-1799
e-mail: feedback@shnsf.com
Web Site: www.shnsf.com
Officers:
  CEO: Greg Holland
  President: Carole Shorenstein Hays
  VP, Ticketing: David Cushing
  VP, Production and Theatre Operatio: Regina Guggenheim
  Chief Marketing Officer: Scott Kane
Management:
  Public Relations/Communications: Anne Abrams
  Ticket Manager: David Cushing
  Operations: Regina Guggenheim
  Marketing/Sales: Scott Kane
Mission: The officail site of broadway in San Francisco
Founded: 1922
Specialized Field: Theater
Seating Capacity: 1,667

6258
FLORENCE GOULD THEATRE
100 34th Avenue
San Francisco, CA 94121
Mailing Address: 50 Hagiwara Tea Garden Drive San Francisco, CA 94118
Phone: 415-750-3600
e-mail: contact@famsf.org
Web Site: legionofhonor.famsf.org
Officers:
  President: Diane B. Wilsey
  Vice President: Belva Davis
Management:
  Facility Rental Manager: Shannon Murphy
  Director: Colin B. Bailey
Mission: Originally called the Little Theater, the Florence Gould Theater opened at the California Palace of the Legion of Honor in 1924. The Gould Theater hosts numerous concerts, plays, operas, lectures, and symposiums, and has seen performances by such diverse artists as Andrés Segovia, Marcel Marceau, Joan Baez, the Philharmonia Baroque Orchestra, and Duke Ellington.
Opened: 1924
Seating Capacity: 316

6259
GOLDEN GATE THEATRE
1 Taylor Street
San Francisco, CA 94102
Mailing Address: 1 Taylor St., San Francisco, CA 94102
Phone: 415-512-7770
Fax: 415-431-5052
Toll-free: 888-746-1799
e-mail: feedback@shnsf.com
Web Site: www.shnsf.com
Officers:
  President: Carole Shorenstein Hays
  VP, Ticketing: David Cushing
  VP, Production and Theatre Operatio: Regina Guggenheim
  Chief Marketing Officer: Scott Kane
Management:
  CEO: Greg Holland
Founded: 1922
Specialized Field: Theater
Seating Capacity: 2,297

6260
HERBEST THEATRE
401 Van Ness Avenue
Room 110
San Francisco, CA 94102
Mailing Address: 401 Van Ness Avenue, Room 110, San Francisco, CA 94102
Phone: 415-621-6600
Fax: 415-621-5091
e-mail: info@sfwmpac.org
Web Site: www.sfwmpac.org
Officers:
  President: MajGen J. Michael Myatt
  Vice President: Wilkes Bashford
Management:
  Assistant Managing Director: Jennifer E. Norris
  Managing Director: Elizabeth Murray
  Assistant Director: Greg Ridenour
  Catering Sales Manager: Susan Serpanchy
Founded: 1932
Status: For-Profit, Professional
Paid Staff: 100
Affiliations: Owned and operated by the War Memorial, a department of the city of San Francisco
Annual Attendance: 127,000
Facility Category: theatre
Type of Stage: proscenium
Stage Dimensions: 33 x 40
Seating Capacity: 916
Year Built: 1937
Year Remodeled: 1979
Rental Contact: Jennifer Norris

6261
NOB HILL MASONIC CENTER
1111 California Street
San Francisco, CA 94108
Mailing Address: 1111 California Street, San Francisco, CA 94108
Phone: 415-776-7457
Fax: 415-776-3945
Toll-free: 877-598-8497
Web Site: www.sfmasoniccenter.com
Management:
  Executive Director: Michael Grive
  Director of Sales: Tara Porter
  General Manager: Matt Prieshoff
  Operations Manager: Megan Pyron
Founded: 1958
Status: Non-Profit, Professional
Paid Staff: 10
Facility Category: Event Center

6262
ODC THEATRE
351 Shotwell Street
San Francisco, CA 94110
Mailing Address: 3153 17th Street San Francisco CA 94110
Phone: 415-863-6606
Fax: 415-863-9833
e-mail: info@odctheater.org
Web Site: www.odctheater.org
Officers:
  President: Tim Schroeder
  Vice President: Becky Saeger
  Vice President: Mary Margaret Jones
  Treasurer: Paul Webb
  Secretary: Samantha Test Cauthen
Management:
  Executive Director: Victor Gotesman
  Artistic Director: Brenda Way
  Marketing Director: Francis Aviani

FACILITIES / California

Production Manager: David Coffman
Managing Director: Lori Laqua
Theater Manager: Brittany Brown Ceres
Theater Publicist: Lori Perkovich
Seating Capacity: 187

6263
ORPHEUM THEATRE
1192 Market Street
San Francisco, CA 94102
Mailing Address: 1192 Market Street., San Francisco, CA 94102
Phone: 415-512-7770
Fax: 415-431-5052
Toll-free: 888-746-1799
e-mail: feedback@shnsf.com
Web Site: www.shnsf.com
Officers:
  CEO: Greg Holland
Management:
  President: Carole Shorenstein Hays
  Chief Executive Officer: Greg Holland
  VP Public Relations/Communications: Anne Abrams
  VP Ticketing: David Cushing
  VP Production/Theatre Operations: Regina Guggenheim
  VP Marketing & Sales: Scott Kane
Founded: 1926
Specialized Field: Theater
Seating Capacity: 2,203

6264
PALACE OF FINE ARTS THEATRE
3301 Lyon Street
San Francisco, CA 94123
Mailing Address: 3301 Lyon Street, San Francisco, CA 94123
Phone: 415-563-6504
Fax: 415-567-4062
e-mail: info@palaceoffinearts.org
Web Site: www.palaceoffinearts.org
Officers:
  President: Jerry Firedman
Management:
  Executive Director: Kevin J O'Brien
  Technical Director: Kevin Taylor
  House Manager: David Young
Founded: 1970
Specialized Field: Multidiscipliary; Multi-Use
Paid Staff: 15
Income Sources: Rental and concession fees
Performs At: Rental Theatre
Annual Attendance: 120,000
Facility Category: Theatre
Type of Stage: Proscenium
Stage Dimensions: 73'x54'
Seating Capacity: 1,000
Year Built: 1970
Rental Contact: Kevin O'Brien

6265
SAN FRANCISCO COUNTY FAIR ARENA
Lincoln Way & 9th Avenue
Golden Gate Park
San Francisco, CA 94122
Mailing Address: San Francisco Recreation and Park Commission, 501 Stanyan St
Phone: 415-666-7079
Fax: 415—22-1-80
e-mail: recpark.commission@sfgov.org
Web Site: www.sfgov.org
Officers:
  Director Sales: Melody Lendaro

General Manager: Richard Shaff
Building Manager: Thaddeus Watkins
Mission: Special events.
Utilizes: Student Interns; Theatre Companies
Founded: 1961
Affiliations: City of San Francisco
Annual Attendance: 300,000
Facility Category: Multi-Use Arena
Type of Stage: Flexible
Seating Capacity: 7,000
Year Built: 1918
Year Remodeled: 1986
Rental Contact: Melody Lendaro

6266
SAN FRANCISCO WAR MEMORIAL AND PERFORMING ARTS CENTER
401 Van Ness Ave
Room 110
San Francisco, CA 94102
Mailing Address: 401 Van Ness Avenue, Room 110, San Francisco, CA 94102
Phone: 415-621-6600
Fax: 415-621-5091
e-mail: info@sfwmpac.org
Web Site: www.sfwmpac.org
Officers:
  President: MajGen J. Michael Myatt
  Vice President: Wilkes Bashford
Management:
  Managing director: Elizabeth Murray, elizabeth.murray@sfgov.org
  Booking Director: Stephanie Smith, stephanie.smith@sfgov.org
  Assistant Managing Director: Jennifer E. Norris
Mission: Houses multiple venues including an opera house, symphony hall and performing arts locations

6267
YERBA BUENA CENTER FOR THE ARTS
701 Mission Street at 3rd Street
San Francisco, CA 94103-3138
Mailing Address: 701 Mission Street 3rd st., San Francisco, CA 94103-3138
Phone: 415-978-2700
Fax: 415-978-9635
e-mail: press@ybca.org
Web Site: www.ybca.org
Officers:
  President: Diana Cohn
  VP, Finance Chairperson: Erik Mayo
  VP, Governance Chairperson: Berit Ashla
  VP and Audit Chairperson: Johann Zimmern
  Development Chairperson: Vicki Shipkowitz
Management:
  Executive Director: Deborah M. Cullinan
  Managing Director: Scott Rowitz
  Finance Director: Claire SunSpiral
  Community Engagement Director: Joel Tan
  Development Director: Charles Ward
  Events Manager: Lisa Elliot
  Assistant Facility Manager: Adil Fartas
  Production Manager: Jose Maria Francos
  Visual Arts Director: Rene De Guzman
Mission: Theater has a seating capacity of 757 and The Forum and East Garden have 6,700 square feet of space.
Utilizes: Artists-in-Residence; Collaborating Artists; Collaborations; Commissioned Music; Curators; Dance Companies; Fine Artists; Instructors; Local Artists; Multi Collaborations; Selected Students; Student Interns; Special Technical Talent; Theatre Companies; Touring Companies
Founded: 1993

Status: Non-Profit, Non-Professional
Paid Staff: 55
Volunteer Staff: 100
Budget: $7,300,000
Income Sources: Contributions; Rental Revenue; Ticket Revenue
Affiliations: LATSE
Annual Attendance: 205,000
Facility Category: Theater ; Multi-Use Forum
Type of Stage: Proscenium and Flexible
Stage Dimensions: 43'x93'
Year Built: 1993

6268
HP PAVILION AT SAN JOSE
525 W Santa Clara Street
San Jose, CA 95113
Mailing Address: 525 W. Santa Clara Street, San Jose, CA 95113
Phone: 408-287-7070
Fax: 408-999-5797
Toll-free: 800-755-5050
Web Site: www.sapcenteratsanjose.com
Officers:
  Vice President of Building Operatio: Rich Sotelo
Management:
  President: Greg Jamison
  General Manager: Jim Goddard
  Director Booking/Events: Steve Kirsner
  Facility Technical Director: Greg Carrolan
  Event Conversion Manager: Bruce Tharaldson
Founded: 1993
Specialized Field: concerts and sporting events
Status: For-Profit, Professional
Paid Staff: 35
Performs At: Sports/Entertainment Arena
Affiliations: IAAM; Arena Network; MPI
Facility Category: Arena
Type of Stage: Portable
Seating Capacity: 4,500-18,000
Year Built: 1995
Rental Contact: Steve Kirsner

6269
MONTGOMERY THEATRE
271 South Market Street
San Jose, CA 95113
Mailing Address: 271 S. Market St., San Jose, CA 95113
Phone: 408-792-4540
Fax: 408-277-3535
Toll-free: 888-726-5673
e-mail: tickets@sanjose.org
Web Site: http://sanjosetheaters.org/theaters/montgome
Management:
  General Manager: John Ciulla
  Theater Event Services Manager: Leticia Pena
  Theater Operations Manager: Jesse Hernandez
  Theater Sales Coordinator: Jennifer Anson
  Production Coordinator: Elaine Lee
Mission: home of the San Jose Children's Musical Theater, the Montgomery Theater hosts a variety of cultural and performing arts events
Founded: 1936
Specialized Field: cultural and performing arts events
Seating Capacity: 475
Year Built: 1936

6270
SAN JOSE CENTER FOR THE PERFORMING ARTS
255 Almaden Boulevard
San Jose, CA 95113

FACILITIES / California

Mailing Address: 255 Almaden Blvd., San Jose, CA, 95113
Phone: 408-792-4540
Fax: 408-277-3535
Toll-free: 800-533-2345
e-mail: tickets@sanjose.org
Web Site: http://sanjosetheaters.org/theaters/montgom
Officers:
  Chairman: Patrick J D'Angelo
  President: Stewart Slater
  Immediate Past-Chairman: Frank S Greene, Jr
Management:
  General Manager: John Ciulla
  Theater Event Services Manager: Leticia Pena
  Theater Operations Manager: Jesse Hernandez
  Theater Sales Coordinator: Jennifer Anson
  Production Coordinator: Elaine Lee
  Director: Dan Fenton
Status: Nonprofit, Non-Professional
Paid Staff: 150
Seating Capacity: 2,677

6271
SAN JOSE MUNICIPAL STADIUM
588 East Alma Avenue
San Jose, CA 95112
Mailing Address: P.O. Box 21727, San Jose, CA 95151
Phone: 408-297-1435
Fax: 408-297-1453
e-mail: info@sjgiants.com
Web Site: sanjose.giants.milb.com
Officers:
  President/CEO: Daniel Orum
  Chairman: Bill Schlough
  Chief Operating Office: Mark Wilson
  Chief Marketing Officer: Juliana Paoli
  Vice President of Stadium: Zach Walter
Management:
  General Manager/COO: Mark Wilson
  Director of Player Personnel: Linda Pereira
  Marketing Coordinator: Sarah Carpenter
  Director of Ticketing: Kellen Minteer
  Director of Broadcasting: Joe Ritzo
Founded: 1988
Status: For-Profit, Professional
Annual Attendance: 154,324
Type of Stage: Baseball Stadium
Seating Capacity: 4,500

6272
SAN JOSE STATE UNIVERSITY THEATRE
One Washington Square
San Jose, CA 95192-0098
Phone: 408-924-4530
Fax: 408-924-4574
e-mail: info@tvradiofilmtheatre.com
Web Site: www.tvradiofilmtheatre.com
Officers:
  President/Chairman: Mike Adams
Management:
  Executive Director: Barnaby Dallas
  Artistic Director: Laura Long
  Technology Director: Jim Lefever
Founded: 1904
Status: Non-Profit, Non-Professional
Paid Staff: 30

6273
CAL POLY STATE UNIVERSITY PERFORMING ARTS CENTER
1 Grand Avenue,
San Luis Obispo, CA 93407

Mailing Address: 1 Grand Avenue, San Luis Obispo, CA 93407-0441
Phone: 805-756-7222
Fax: 805-756-6088
Toll-free: 800-289-8425
e-mail: mrklemin@calpoly.edu
Web Site: www.pacslo.org
Management:
  Managing Director: Ron Regler
  Ticketing Services Manager: Terri Hopson
  Technical Services Manager: Stephanie Roberson
  Theatre Operations Manager: Nancy Cochran
  Technical Coordinator: Eli Zabala
Mission: The Artistic Mission of the Performing Arts Center is to:,To actively encourage full, broad-based facility use, featuring a schedule of varied, high quality arts events designed to serve diverse audience interests. ,To actively support local arts groups, providing a range of quality services, which encourage and enable them to reach their maximum potential. ,To promote use of the Center and its services to potential clients from outside the commu
Founded: 1996
Seating Capacity: 1277

6274
SAN MATEO PERFORMING ARTS CENTER
600 North Delaware Avenue
San Mateo, CA 94401
Mailing Address: 600 North Delaware Avenue, San Mateo, CA 94401
Phone: 650-762-0258
Fax: 650-762-0218
e-mail: info@peninsulasymphony.org
Web Site: www.peninsulasym.org/locations.html
Management:
  Executive Director: Margrit Rinderknecht
  Marketing Associate: Trudy Taliaferro
  Development Associate: Emily Carr
Founded: 1968
Status: Non-Profit, Professional
Paid Staff: 12
Paid Artists: 2
Seating Capacity: 1,600

6275
ANGELS GATE CULTURAL CENTER
3601 South Gaffey Street
San Pedro, CA 90731
Mailing Address: 3601 South Gaffey Street, San Pedro, California 90731
Phone: 310-519-0936
Fax: 310-519-8698
e-mail: info@angelsgateart.org
Web Site: www.angelsgateart.org
Management:
  President of the Board: Rae Wyman
  Executive Director: Deborah Lewis
  Director of Development: Oscar Garcia
  Volunteer Coordinator: Delora Bertsch
  Director of Education: Amy Eriksen
Mission: Angels Gate Cultural Center, a nonprofit corporation, serves to develop an active environment mutually nourishing to the growth of artists, cultural arts and the community.
Founded: 1982
Status: Non-Profit, Non-Professional
Paid Staff: 4
Volunteer Staff: 6
Paid Artists: 15

6276
WARNER GRAND THEATRE
478 West 6th Street
San Pedro, CA 90731
Mailing Address: 478 West 6th Street, San Pedro, CA 90731
Phone: 310-548-7672
Fax: 310-548-2498
Web Site: www.warnergrand.org
Mission: Built in 1931, the Warner Grand is the only one of the three Warner Brothers art deco theaters in Los Angeles that is still intact and fully functioning with a calendar of events appealing to a wide range of interests, including classic and foreign films, youth programs, and contemporary and classical music.
Status: Non-Profit, Non-Professional
Seating Capacity: 1,500
Year Built: 1931
Rental Contact: Theatre Manager Lee Sweet

6277
DOMINICAN COLLEGE AUDITORIUM
50 Acacia Avenue
San Rafael, CA 94901
Mailing Address: 50 Acacia Avenue, San Rafael, CA 94901
Phone: 415-457-4440
Fax: 415-485-3205
Toll-free: 888-323-6763
e-mail: chilly@dominican.edu
Web Site: www.dominican.edu
Officers:
  Chair: Andrew P. Barowsky
  Vice Chair: Timothy Blackburn
  Vice Chair: John Boneparth
  VP of Finance and Administration: Michele Hinken
  President: Mary B Marcy
Management:
  Operations Manager: Crystal Anderson
  Administrative Asst., Academic Affa: Marcia Tilford
  Administrative Coordinator: June Caminiti
  Procurement Manager: Arian Ahmadi
Founded: 1890

6278
MARIN CENTER SHOWCASE THEATRE
10 Avenue of the Flags
San Rafael, CA 94903
Phone: 415-499-6400
Fax: 415-499-3700
e-mail: webmaster@co.marin.ca.us
Web Site: www.marincenter.org
Management:
  Director: Jim Farley
  Deputy Director: Marion Boyd
  Senior Events Coordinator: Christian Gutt
  Technical Coordinator: Tony Taubert
Founded: 1971
Status: For-Profit, Professional
Paid Staff: 214
Performs At: Theatre
Seating Capacity: 348

6279
ARLINGTON CENTER FOR THE PERFORMING ARTS
1317 State Street
Santa Barbara, CA 93101

All listings are in alphabetical order by state, then city, then organization within the city.

813

FACILITIES / California

Mailing Address: 1317 State St., Santa Barbara, CA 93101
Phone: 805-963-4408
Fax: 805-966-4688
Web Site: thearlingtontheatre.com
Management:
   Manager: Karen Killingsworth
   Webmaster, House Photographer: A Arthur Fisher
Founded: 1931
Facility Category: Theatre
Seating Capacity: 2,018
Year Built: 1931
Year Remodeled: 1977
Rental Contact: Karen Killingsworth

6280
ELLEN PORTER HALL
Westmont College
955 La Paz Road
Santa Barbara, CA 93108
Mailing Address: 955 La Paz Road, Santa Barbara, CA 93108
Phone: 805-565-6040
e-mail: theater@westmont.edu
Web Site: www.westmont.edu
Officers:
   President: Gayle D. Beebe
   VP For Administration & Planning: Chris Call
   Dean Of Admissions: Silvio Vazquez
Management:
   Professor of Theatre Arts: John Blondell
   Associate Professor Theatre Arts: Erlyne Whiteman
   Adjunct Instructor Theatre Arts: Victoria Finlayson
   Administrative Asst: Mariah Velasquez
   Admissions Counselor: Jessica Bennett
Mission: The program is distinct for many reasons. We couple traditional theatrical methods with innovative practices, engaging in a dynamic and lively approach to the study and practice of the art of the theatre.
Specialized Field: Theatre
Type of Stage: Auditorium
Seating Capacity: 180

6281
HARDER STADIUM
University of California,
Santa Barbara, CA 93106-1030
Mailing Address: UC Santa Barbara, Santa Barbara CA 93106
Phone: 805-893-4156
Fax: 805-893-8640
e-mail: customer.service@pf.ucsb.edu
Web Site: www.facilities.ucsb.edu
Officers:
   Senior Associate Vice Chancellor: Marc Fisher
Management:
   Acting Director: Jon Cook
   Associate Director/Operations: Jim Dewey
   Athletics Director: Gary Cunningham
   Associate Athletic Director: Bobby Castagna
   Development Director: Gil Picciotto
   Assistant Athletic Director & Media: Bill Mahoney
   Assist. Athletic Director & Finance: Sally Orsua
   Facilities/Operations Manager: Joe Ballesteros
   Assistant Director & Marketing: Jeff Kim
Opened: 1966
Seating Capacity: 17,000

6282
HATLEN THEATRE
University of California, Santa Barbara
UC Santa Barbara
Santa Barbara, CA 93106-7060
Mailing Address: Department of Theater & Dance, University of California, San
Phone: 805-893-3241
Fax: 803-893-7029
e-mail: smcmillan@theaterdance.ucsb.edu
Web Site: www.theaterdance.ucsb.edu
Officers:
   Chair: Debra Vance
   Chief Administrative Officer: Eric Mills
Management:
   Senior Scene Technician: Paul . Barnes
   Technical Director: Neil Reda
   Graduate Program Assistant: Mary Tench
   Undergraduate Advisor: Lauren C. Ward
   Asst. Public Events Manager: Ellen Anderson
Mission: Dedicated to the study and practice of theatre in all its phases, the Department of Dramatic Art offers a wide range of classes appropriate for non-majors pursuing a liberal arts education and for majors preparing for a professional or educational career.
Specialized Field: Dance, Theatre
Type of Stage: Proscenium
Orchestra Pit: y
Seating Capacity: 340

6283
LOBERO THEATRE FOUNDATION
33 East Canon Perdido Street
Santa Barbara, CA 93101
Mailing Address: 33 East Canon Perdido Street, Santa Barbara, CA 93101
Phone: 805-966-4946
Fax: 805-963-8752
Toll-free: 888-456-2376
Web Site: www.lobero.com
Officers:
   President: Jeff DeVine
   Vice President: Amy MacLeod
   Secretary: Melissa Fassett
   Treasurer: William J. Nasif
Management:
   Executive Director: David Asbell
   Marketing & Communications: Angie Bertucci
   Box Office Manager: Genevieve Rhiger
   Sound Engineer: J.O. Davis
   Director of Development: Jim Dougherty
Utilizes: Collaborating Artists; Collaborations; Commissioned Music; Dance Companies; Educators; Lyricists; Multimedia; Original Music Scores; Resident Artists; Theatre Companies
Founded: 1873
Specialized Field: California Central Coast
Status: Non-Profit, Professional
Paid Staff: 15
Volunteer Staff: 100
Paid Artists: 2
Affiliations: APAP WAA Ca. Presenters
Annual Attendance: 100,000
Seating Capacity: 680
Year Built: 1924
Year Remodeled: 1996
Cost: 3 Million

6284
MUSIC THEATER OF SANTA BARBARA
1216 State Street
Suite 200
Santa Barbara, CA 93101
Mailing Address: P.O. Box 1028, Santa Barbara CA
Phone: 805-962-1922
Fax: 805-963-3510
Web Site: www.santabarbara.com/community/art/sb_theater/
Management:
   Executive Producer: Anthony Rhine
Mission: To enrich the community through musical theater.
Founded: 1989
Paid Staff: 15
Volunteer Staff: 20
Paid Artists: 100
Budget: $5 million
Income Sources: Tickets and Donations
Performs At: Granada Theater
Affiliations: National Association of Musical Theatre
Annual Attendance: 120,000
Facility Category: Theater
Type of Stage: Proscenium
Stage Dimensions: 60x40
Seating Capacity: 953
Year Built: 1908
Resident Groups: Santa Barbara Civic Light Opera

6285
PERFORMING ARTS THEATRE
University of California, Santa Barbara
Department of Theater & Dance, University of Santa Barbara, CA 93106-7060
Mailing Address: Department of Theater & Dance, University of California, San
Phone: 805-893-5515
Fax: 803-893-7029
e-mail: mrklemin@calpoly.edu
Web Site: www.theaterdance.ucsb.edu
Officers:
   Chair: Debra Vance
   Chief Administrative Officer: Eric Mills
Management:
   Senior Scene Technician: Paul . Barnes
   Technical Director: Neil Reda
   Graduate Program Assistant: Mary Tench
   Undergraduate Advisor: Lauren C. Ward
   Asst. Public Events Manager: Ellen Anderson
Mission: Dedicated to the study and practice of theatre in all its phases, the Department of Dramatic Art offers a wide range of classes appropriate for non-majors pursuing a liberal arts education and for majors preparing for a professional or educational career.
Opened: 1996
Specialized Field: Acting and Directing Classes
Type of Stage: Black Box
Seating Capacity: 150

6286
SANTA BARBARA CONTEMPORARY ARTS FORUM
653 Paseo Nuevo
Santa Barbara, CA 93101
Mailing Address: 653 Paseo Nuevo, Santa Barbara, CA 93101
Phone: 805-966-5373
Fax: 805-962-1421
e-mail: sbcaf@sbcaf.org
Web Site: www.mcasantabarbara.org
Officers:
   President: Jacquelyn Klein-Brown
   1st Vice President: Josh Blumer
   Secretary: Carolyn Glasoe
   Treasurer: Mary Lynn Harms
   Trustee: Lesley Cunningham
Management:
   Executive Director: Miki Garcia

FACILITIES / California

Gallery Manager: Dena Beard
Director of Development: Frederick Janka
Assistant Curator: Elizabeth Lovero
Head Preparator: Saul Gray Hildenbrand
Mission: To provide an arena for the presentation, documentation and support of a broad variety of visual, media and performing arts representing a wide range of attitudes.
Founded: 1976
Specialized Field: Visual and Performing Arts Organization
Status: Non-Profit, Professional
Paid Staff: 6
Volunteer Staff: 30
Budget: $300,000
Income Sources: Membership; Business Sponsorship
Performs At: Center Stage Theater
Facility Category: Black Box
Year Built: 1990

6287
STUDIO THEATRE
University of California, Santa Barbara
Department of Theater & Dance, University of Santa Barbara, CA 93106-7060
Mailing Address: Department of Theater & Dance, University of California, San
Phone: 805-893-5515
Fax: 803-893-7029
e-mail: mrklemin@calpoly.edu
Web Site: www.theaterdance.ucsb.edu
Officers:
 Chair: Debra Vance
 Chief Administrative Officer: Eric Mills
Management:
 Senior Scene Technician: Paul . Barnes
 Technical Director: Neil Reda
 Graduate Program Assistant: Mary Tench
 Undergraduate Advisor: Lauren C. Ward
 Asst. Public Events Manager: Ellen Anderson
Mission: Dedicated to the study and practice of theatre in all its phases, the Department of Dramatic Art offers a wide range of classes appropriate for non-majors pursuing a liberal arts education and for majors preparing for a professional or educational career.
Specialized Field: Acting and Directing Classes

6288
THE GRANADA
1214 State Street
Sanata Bar
Santa Barbara, CA 93101
Phone: 805-899-3000
Fax: 805-899-3081
e-mail: unfo@granada.org
Web Site: www.granadasb.org
Officers:
 Executive Director: Craig Springer
Management:
 Marketing Director: Vince Coranado, vcoranado@granadasb.org

6289
FESS PARKER STUDIO THEATRE
Santa Clara University
500 El Camino Real
Santa Clara, CA 95053-0341
Mailing Address: 500 El Camino Real, Santa Clara, CA 95053
Phone: 408-554-4565
Fax: 408-554-2171
e-mail: RJigour@scu.edu
Web Site: www.scu.edu/cpa
Officers:
 Asst VP for Operations and Campaign: Caroline Chang
 Assistant VP for Development: Mike Wallace
 Class Giving Officer: Natasha Pedroza
 Class Giving Officer: Jimmy Shoven
Management:
 Chair Dept of Theatre: Aldo Billingslea
 Director: Butch Coyne
 Managing Director: Lisa Rademacher
 Director, Reunion Giving: Trevor Hansen
 Director of Foundation Relations: Matt Hendricks
Mission: Santa Clara University's Center of Performing Arts presents a diverse season of dance, music, and theatre events featuring the talent and artistry of our students and faculty.
Specialized Field: Theatre
Type of Stage: Black Box
Seating Capacity: 130

6290
LOUIS B. MAYER THEATRE
Santa Clara University
500 El Camino Real
Santa Clara, CA 95053-0341
Mailing Address: 500 El Camino Real, Santa Clara, CA 95053
Phone: 408-554-4565
Fax: 408-554-2171
e-mail: RJigour@scu.edu
Web Site: www.scu.edu/cpa
Officers:
 Asst VP for Operations and Campaign: Caroline Chang
 Assistant VP for Development: Mike Wallace
 Class Giving Officer: Natasha Pedroza
 Class Giving Officer: Jimmy Shoven
Management:
 Chair Dept of Theatre: Aldo Billingslea
 Director: Butch Coyne
 Managing Director: Lisa Rademacher
 Director, Reunion Giving: Trevor Hansen
 Director of Foundation Relations: Matt Hendricks
Mission: Santa Clara University's Center of Performing Arts presents a diverse season of dance, music, and theatre events featuring the talent and artistry of our students and faculty.
Specialized Field: Theatre
Type of Stage: Proscenium
Orchestra Pit: y
Seating Capacity: 500

6291
EXPERIMENTAL THEATER
University of California, Santa Cruz
J-106 Theater Arts Center
Santa Cruz, CA 95064
Mailing Address: J-106 Theater Arts Center, Santa Cruz, CA 95064
Phone: 831-459-2974
Fax: 831-459-5359
e-mail: theater@ucsc.edu
Web Site: theater.ucsc.edu/contact/
Management:
 Production Manager: Scott Anderson
 Costume Shop Assistant: Giusi Capella
 Equipment Coordinator: Eric Mack
 Technical Operations Director: Joe Weiss
 Event Manager: Jenaro Ordo¤ez
Mission: The Theater Arts Department combines drama, dance, critical studies, and theater design, technology offering students an intensive, unified undergraduate program.
Specialized Field: Theatre
Type of Stage: Black Box
Seating Capacity: 200

6292
KUUMBWA JAZZ CENTER
320-2 Cedar Street
Santa Cruz, CA 95060
Mailing Address: 320-2 Cedar Street, Santa Cruz, CA 95060
Phone: 831-427-2227
Fax: 831-427-3342
e-mail: kuumbwa@kuumbwajazz.org
Web Site: kuumbwajazz.org
Officers:
 President: Drew Miller
 Vice-President: John Livingston
 Secretary: Tim Jackson
 Treasurer: Mary Jo Walker
Management:
 Artistic Director: Tim Jackson
 Managing Director: Bobbi Todaro
 Marketing Director: Sandy Sloan
 Production Coordinator: Jeff Sloan
 Education Coordinator: Melody Korkos
Mission: To present jazz and educational opportunities to Santa Cruz County and surrounding areas.
Utilizes: Commissioned Music; Educators; Grant Writers; Guest Ensembles; Guest Musical Directors; Guest Musicians; Instructors; Local Artists; Multimedia; Music; Sign Language Translators; Singers; Soloists; Touring Companies
Founded: 1975
Specialized Field: Jazz Music
Status: Non-Profit
Paid Staff: 7
Volunteer Staff: 50
Budget: $950,000
Income Sources: Membership; Grants
Performs At: Music
Stage Dimensions: 20'x14'6"", "",200""
Cost: Sandy
Year Stage Renovated: Sloa

6293
MAINSTAGE THEATER
University of California, Santa Cruz
J-106 Theater Arts Center
Santa Cruz, CA 95064
Mailing Address: J-106 Theater Arts Center, Santa Cruz, CA 95064
Phone: 831-459-2974
Fax: 831-459-5359
e-mail: theater@ucsc.edu
Web Site: theater.ucsc.edu/contact
Officers:
 Event Manager: Trink Praxell
Management:
 Production Manager: Scott Anderson
 Costume Shop Assistant: Giusi Capella
 Equipment Coordinator: Eric Mack
 Technical Operations Director: Joe Weiss
 Event Manager: Tracye Lawson
Mission: The Theater Arts Department combines drama, dance, critical studies, and theater design, technology offering students an intensive, unified undergraduate program.
Specialized Field: Theatre
Type of Stage: Proscenium, Thrust
Seating Capacity: 528

6294
MUSIC CENTER RECITAL HALL
University of California, Santa Cruz
J-106 Theater Arts Center
Santa Cruz, CA 95064

FACILITIES / California

Mailing Address: J-106 Theater Arts Center, Santa Cruz, CA 95064
Phone: 831-459-2974
Fax: 831-459-5359
e-mail: theater@ucsc.edu
Web Site: theater.ucsc.edu/contact
Officers:
  Event Manager: Trink Praxell
Management:
  Production Manager: Scott Anderson
  Costume Shop Assistant: Giusi Capella
  Equipment Coordinator: Eric Mack
  Technical Operations Director: Joe Weiss
  Event Manager: Tracye Lawson
Mission: The Theater Arts Department combines drama, dance, critical studies, and theater design, technology offering students an intensive, unified undergraduate program.
Opened: 1997
Specialized Field: Dance
Type of Stage: Variable
Seating Capacity: 396

6295
SANTA CRUZ CIVIC AUDITORIUM
307 Church Street
Santa Cruz, CA 95060
Phone: 831-420-5240
Fax: 831-420-5261
e-mail: civic@cityofsantacruz.com
Web Site: www.cityofsantacruz.com
Management:
  Auditorium Supervisor: Andrea Botsford
Founded: 1940
Affiliations: Owned and operated by the City of Santa Cruz
Annual Attendance: 87,000
Type of Stage: Proscenium
Seating Capacity: 1,957

6296
SECOND STAGE
University of California, Santa Cruz
J-106 Theater Arts Center
Santa Cruz, CA 95064
Mailing Address: J-106 Theater Arts Center, Santa Cruz, CA 95064
Phone: 831-459-2974
Fax: 831-459-5359
e-mail: theater@ucsc.edu
Web Site: theater.ucsc.edu/contact
Officers:
  Event Manager: Trink Praxell
Management:
  Production Manager: Scott Anderson
  Costume Shop Assistant: Giusi Capella
  Equipment Coordinator: Eric Mack
  Technical Operations Director: Joe Weiss
  Event Manager: Tracye Lawson
Mission: The Theater Arts Department combines drama, dance, critical studies, and theater design, technology offering students an intensive, unified undergraduate program.
Specialized Field: Student Dance and Theater Productions
Seating Capacity: 231

6297
STANLEY-SINSHEIMER FESTIVAL GLEN
University of California, Santa Cruz
Shakespeare Santa Cruz
Theater Arts/UCSC, 1156 High Street
Santa Cruz, CA 95064
Mailing Address: 1156 High Street, Santa Cruz, CA 95064
Phone: 831-459-5810
e-mail: theater@ucsc.edu
Web Site: shakespearesantacruz.org
Officers:
  Director Development: Matt Henry
  President: Nancy K. Austin
Management:
  Artistic Director: Marco Barricelli
  Managing Director: Kyle Clausen
  Company Manager: Maria Frangos
  Production Administrator: Jessica Bond
  Operations Director: Geoff Girard
Mission: The Theater Arts Department combines drama, dance, critical studies, and theater design, technology offering students an intensive, unified undergraduate program.
Specialized Field: Theatre
Type of Stage: Amphitheater
Seating Capacity: 625

6298
UNIVERSITY OF CALIFORNIA SANTA CRUZ PERFORMING ARTS CENTER
1156 High Street
Santa Cruz, CA 95064
Mailing Address: 1156 High Street, Santa Cruz, CA 95064
Phone: 831-459-0111
Fax: 831-459-3502
e-mail: staffadv@ucsc.edu
Web Site: www.ucsc.edu
Management:
  Director of Media Services: Henry J Burnett Ed.D
  Business Administration Services: Don Calerdine
  Business & Administrative Services: Valerie Chase
  Internal Audit & Advisory Services: Deb Collins
  Information Technology Services: Shawn Duncan
Founded: 1965
Seating Capacity: 527

6299
PACIFIC CONSERVATORY OF THE PERFORMING ARTS
800 S College Drive
PO Box 1700
Santa Maria, CA 93454
Phone: 805-928-7731
Fax: 805-928-7506
Toll-free: 800-727-2123
e-mail: pcpa@pcpa.org
Web Site: www.pcpa.org
Management:
  Artistic Director: Mark Booher
  Managing Director: Mike Black
  Marketing Director: Maria Centrella
Founded: 1964
Specialized Field: Professional Live Theatre; Conservatory Training Program

6300
MORGAN-WIXSON THEATRE
2627 Pico Boulevard
Santa Monica, CA 90405
Mailing Address: 2627 Pico Boulevard, Santa Monica, CA 90405
Phone: 310-828-7519
Fax: 310-828-6209
e-mail: info@morgan-wixson.org
Web Site: www.morgan-wixson.org
Officers:
  Chairman: Thomas Brown
  President: Joe Anderson
  Executive Vice President: Saul Saladow
  First VP Marketing: Marc Ostroff
  Second VP Production: Larry Gesling
  Treasurer: Anne Gesling
  Secretary: Al Barlaan
Management:
  Marketing/Development Director: Joshua Schulz
  Volunteer/Membership Coordinator: Thomas A Brown
  Volunteer Coordinator: Tom Laskey
  Volunteer Coordinator: Mary Beth Sciarabba
  Box Office: Taylor Pyles

6301
SANTA MONICA CIVIC AUDITORIUM
1855 Main Street
Santa Monica, CA 90401-3209
Mailing Address: 1685 Main Street, Santa Monica, CA 90401
Phone: 310-458-8411
Fax: 310-394-3411
e-mail: carole.curtin@smgov.net
Web Site: www.smgov.net
Management:
  Manager: Carole Curtin
  Business Administrator: Glennis Waterman

6302
WELLS FARGO CENTER FOR THE ARTS
50 Mark West Springs Road
Santa Rosa, CA 95403
Phone: 707-527-7006
Fax: 707-545-0518
e-mail: rentals@wellsfargocenterarts.org
Web Site: www.wellsfargocenterarts.org
Officers:
  Chairman: Sherry Swayne
  First Vice Chairman: Paul Wilcock
  Secretary: Kevin McCullough
  Treasurer: Bruce DeCrona
Management:
  Executive Director: Richard Nowlin
  Director of Programming: Anita Wiglesworth
  Human Resources Manager: Patricia Rinere
  Rentals Manager: Shekeyna Black
  Executive Assisstant: Candice Day
Mission: Enrich, Educate, Entertain
Utilizes: Actors; Community Members; Dancers; Five Seasonal Concerts; Guest Accompanists; Guest Artists; Guest Companies; Guest Composers; Guest Designers; Guest Directors; Guest Instructors; Guest Musical Directors; Guest Musicians; Guest Teachers; Guest Writers; Guild Activities; Local Talent; Music; New Productions
Founded: 1981
Performs At: Performing Arts, Small Concert Venue
Facility Category: Performing Arts Center
Seating Capacity: R.F. Finley-1600; Metro-399; Cabaret-220

6303
FALLON HOUSE THEATRE
Sierra Repetory Theatre
PO Box 3030
Sonora, CA 95370
Mailing Address: P.O. Box 3030, Sonora, California 95370
Phone: 209-532-3120

FACILITIES / California

Fax: 209-532-7270
e-mail: admin@sierrarep.org
Web Site: www.sierrarep.org
Officers:
  President: Bill Green
  Vice President: Mike Jones
  Treasurer: Eric Carlson
Management:
  Producing Director: Dennis Jones
  Artistic Director: Scott Viets
  Managing Director: Sara Jones
  Development Director: Amy Nilson
  Marketing Director: Harmony Wheeler
  Resident Stage Manager: Doug Brennan
  Production Manager: Benjamin Loverin
  Technical Director: Patrick Conley
  Box Office Manager: Bert Simonis
Mission: To produce a year-round season of professional theatre including musicals, drama and comedy.
Founded: 1980
Specialized Field: Theatre
Status: Non-Profit, Professional
Paid Staff: 25
Paid Artists: 200
Annual Attendance: 50,000
Type of Stage: Proscenium
Seating Capacity: 270

6304
ANNENBERG AUDITORIUM
Stanford University
Stanford, CA 94305-2018
Mailing Address: 435 Lasuen Mall, Stanford, CA 94305
Phone: 650-723-3404
Fax: 650-725-0140
e-mail: eimboden@stanford.edu
Web Site: www.stanford.edu
Officers:
  Chairman: Joel Leivick
  President: John Hennessy
Management:
  Department Administrator: Elis Imboden
  Facilities Administrator: Rory Brown
  Studio Manager: Moira Murdock
  Academic Technology Specialist: Michael Gonzalez
  Publicist: Lisa Vestal
Seating Capacity: 351

6305
BING CONCERT HALL
Stanford University
356 Lasuen St, 2nd Floor
Littlefield Center, MC2250
Stanford, CA 94305
Phone: 650-723-2551
Fax: 650-723-8231
e-mail: binghall@stanford.edu
Web Site: www.binghall.stanford.edu
Mission: Opens January 2013

6306
CAMPBELL RECITAL HALL
Stanford University
Braun Music Center
Stanford, CA 94305-3076
Mailing Address: 541 Lasuen Mall, Stanford, CA 94305-3076
Phone: 650-723-3811
Fax: 650-725-2686
e-mail: marioch@stanford.edu
Web Site: music.stanford.edu/DeptInfo/index.html
Officers:
  Chairman: Stephen M Sano
  Financial Officer: Velda Williams
  Chairman Secretary: Debbie Barney
Management:
  Administrative Director: Mario Champagne
  Facilities/Production Manager: Mark Dalrymple
  Publicist: Beth Youngdoff
  Academic Administrator: Debbie Barney
  Financial Officer: Velda Williams
Seating Capacity: 221

6307
DINKELSPIEL AUDITORIUM
Stanford University
Braun Music Center
Stanford, CA 94305-3076
Mailing Address: 541 Lasuen Mall, Stanford, CA 94305-3076
Phone: 650-723-3811
Fax: 650-725-2686
e-mail: sano@stanford.edu
Web Site: music.stanford.edu/DeptInfo/index.html
Officers:
  Chairman: Stephen M Sano
  Financial Officer: Velda Williams
  Chairman Secretary: Debbie Barney
Management:
  Administrative Director: Mario Champagne
  Technical Services Director: Scott Kepley
  Academic Administration: Debbie Barney
  Financial Officer: Velda Williams
  Publicist: Beth Youngdoff
Performs At: Multi-Use Auditorium
Seating Capacity: 716
Year Built: 1957

6308
MEMORIAL AUDITORIUM
Stanford University
Memorial Hall
Stanford, CA 94305-5010
Mailing Address: 551 Serra Mall Stanford, CA 94305
Phone: 650-725-2576
Fax: 650-723-0843
Web Site: www.stanford.edu/dept/drama/spaces.html
Management:
  Department Administrator: Ron Davies
  Technical Director/Operations: Ross Williams
  Financial Administrator: Mitzi Woods
  Academic Technology Specialist: Michael Gonzalez
Seating Capacity: 2000

6309
STANFORD UNIVERSITY DEPARTMENT OF MUSIC
Stanford University Braun Music Center
541 Lasuen Mall
Stanford, CA 94305-3076
Mailing Address: 541 Lasuen Mall, Stanford, CA 94305-3076
Phone: 650-723-3811
Fax: 650-725-2686
e-mail: sano@stanford.edu
Web Site: www.music.stanford.edu
Officers:
  Professor & Chair, Dept Of Music: Stephen M Sano
  Financial Officer: Velda Williams
  Chairman Secretary: Debbie Barney
Management:
  Administrative Director: Mario Champagne
  Technical Services Director: Scott Kepley
  Academic Administration: Debbie Barney
  Financial Officer: Velda Williams
  Publicist: Beth Youngdoff
Utilizes: Arrangers; Artists-in-Residence; Collaborating Artists; Collaborations; Commissioned Composers; Community Members; Community Talent; Composers; Contract Orchestras; Educators; Fellows of Institute; Guest Accompanists; Guest Companies; Guest Composers; Guest Directors; Guest Ensembles; Guest Instructors; Guest Musical Directors; Guest Musicians; Guest Soloists; Guest Speakers; Guest Writers; Instructors; Local Artists & Directors; Multi Collaborations; Multimedia; Music; Organization Contracts; Original Music Scores; Resident Companies; Scenic Designers; Sign Language Translators; Singers; Students; Student Interns
Founded: 1947
Specialized Field: Music
Performs At: Auditorium; Recital Halls; Church; Concert Hall

6310
FAYE SPANOS CONCERT AND RECITAL HALLS
3601 Pacific Avenue
Stockton, CA 95211
Mailing Address: 3601 Pacific Avenue, Stockton, California 95211
Phone: 209-946-2285
e-mail: sperdicaris@pacific.edu
Web Site: www.pacific.edu/conservatory/facilities.asp
Officers:
  Dean: Giulio M. Ongaro
  Assistant Dean: David Chase
Management:
  Operations Manager: Stephens Perdicaris
  Technical Director: James Gonzales
  Director of Development: Holly Stanco
  Administration: Patricia Eckert
  Budget Manager: Jose Quijano
Mission: Located within the Conservatory of Music, the Faye Spanos Concert Hall has a seating capacity of 950 and the Recital Hall seats 120.
Utilizes: Actors; Artists-in-Residence; Collaborating Artists; Commissioned Music; Educators; Grant Writers; Guest Accompanists; Guest Artists; Guest Designers; Guest Lecturers; Guild Activities; High School Drama; Music; Organization Contracts; Resident Professionals; Sign Language Translators; Soloists
Founded: 1927
Non-paid Artists: 19
Income Sources: Tickets, University
Annual Attendance: 1,800
Facility Category: Black Box
Type of Stage: Flexible

6311
LONG THEATRE
3601 Pacific Avenue
Stockton, CA 95211
Mailing Address: University of the Pacific, 3601 Pacific Avenue, Stockton, CA
Phone: 209-946-2285
Fax: 209-946-2118
Web Site: www.pacific.edu
Management:
  Theatre Manager: Jack Platt
  Dean: Giulio M. Ongaro
Utilizes: Actors; Choreographers; Dance Companies; Dancers; Designers; Educators; Grant Writers; Guest Accompanists; Guest Artists; Guest Designers; Guild Activities; High School Drama; Instructors; Multimedia;

FACILITIES / California

Performance Artists; Resident Professionals; Sign Language Translators; Singers; Soloists; Student Interns
Founded: 1976
Paid Staff: 1
Non-paid Artists: 19
Performs At: Proscenium
Annual Attendance: 8-10,000
Facility Category: Proscenium
Type of Stage: Proscenium
Stage Dimensions: 40 x 80
Seating Capacity: 400
Year Built: 1950
Year Remodeled: 1998

6312
WARREN ATHERTON AUDITORIUM
5151 Pacific Avenue
Stockton, CA 95207
Mailing Address: 5151 Pacific Ave, Stockton, CA 95207
Phone: 209-954-5151
Fax: 209-954-5600
Web Site: www.deltacollege.edu
Management:
  Managing Director: Don Bennett
Mission: Atherton Auditorium is one of the finest theater facilities in California. It maintains an independent staff of technical personnel who coordinate the productions presented on stage.
Specialized Field: Performing arts facility
Status: Non-Profit, Non-Professional
Type of Stage: Proscenium
Stage Dimensions: 60 W x 26 L x 40 D
Seating Capacity: 1,456
Year Built: 1977
Rental Contact: Philenia Francis

6313
PREUS-BRANDT FORUM
60 West Olsen Road
Thousand Oaks, CA 91360-2700
Mailing Address: 60 West Olsen Road, Thousand Oaks, CA 91360-2787
Phone: 805-493-3051
Fax: 805-493-3645
e-mail: www@clunet.edu
Web Site: www.callutheran.edu/event_services/venues/
Officers:
  President: Chris Kimball
  Vice President for Academic Affairs: Leanne Neilson
  Vice President for Administration: Karen Davis
  Vice President for Student Affairs: William Rosser
  Vice President for Enrollment: Matthew Ward
Management:
  Facility Operations/Planning: Ryan Van Ommeren
  Facility Operations Assistant: Diane Noble
  General Manager: Mary Olson
  Special Assistant to the President: James McHugh
  Director of Church Relations: Arne Bergland
Seating Capacity: 200

6314
THOUSAND OAKS CIVIC ARTS PLAZA
2100 Thousand Oaks Boulevard
Thousand Oaks, CA 91362
Mailing Address: 2100 Thousand Oaks Boulevard, Thousand Oaks, CA 91362
Phone: 805-449-2100
Fax: 805-449-2750
e-mail: tmitze@toaks.org
Web Site: www.civicartsplaza.com
Management:
  Technical Director: Gary Mintz
  Box Office Supervisor: Sharon Lauritzen
  Theatre House Supervisor: Nancy Loncto
  Marketing Manager: Vanessa Pellegrino
  Library Services Director: Stephen R. Brogden
Utilizes: Community Talent; Dance Companies; Dancers; Equity Actors; Fine Artists; Grant Writers; Guest Accompanists; Guest Choreographers; Guest Instructors; Guest Musical Directors; Instructors; Local Artists & Directors; Multi Collaborations; Multimedia; Original Music Scores; Resident Artists; Selected Students; Sign Language Translators; Student Interns; Special Technical Talent; Theatre Companies; Touring Companies
Founded: 1994
Performs At: Performing Arts Center
Affiliations: City of Thosand Oaks
Annual Attendance: 300,000+
Facility Category: Performing Arts Center
Type of Stage: Proscenium
Seating Capacity: 1800; 400
Year Built: 1994
Rental Contact: Tom Mitze
Resident Groups: Cabrillo Music Theatre and New West Symphony

6315
EL CAMINO COLLEGE CENTER FOR THE ARTS
16007 Crenshaw Boulevard
Torrance, CA 90506
Phone: 310-329-5345
Fax: 310-660-3734
Toll-free: 800-832-2787
e-mail: artstickets@elcamino.edu
Web Site: www.elcamino.edu
Officers:
  President: Tom Fallow
  Dean of Fine Arts: Connie Fitzsimons
Management:
  Executive Director: Bruce Spain
  Production Manager: Nancy Adler
  Stage Manager: Jerry Root
  Theatre Manager: Barbara Riser
  Event Specialist: Georgi Levine
  Promotions Specialist: Hector Salazar
  Ticket Office Manager: Terri Dixon
Mission: The El Camino College Center for the Arts consists of Marsee Auditorium, a 2,000 seat, multi-purpose performance facility, the 350 seat Campus Theatre and the 180 seat Robert Haag Recital Hall.
Founded: 1967
Organization Type: Performing; Educational

6316
JAMES R ARMSTRONG THEATRE
Torrance Cultural Arts Center
3330 Civic Center Drive
Torrance, CA 90503-9998
Mailing Address: 3330 Civic Center Drive, Torrance, CA 90503
Phone: 310-781-7150
Fax: 310-618-2399
e-mail: Info@TorranceArts.com
Web Site: www.ci.torrance.ca.us/9028.htm
Officers:
  President: Jean Adelsman
Management:
  Executive Director: Ray Solley
  Facility Booking Manager: Lisa Morales
  Cultural Services Manager: Robert Myers
Utilizes: Collaborations; Curators; Educators; Guest Writers; High School Drama; Local Artists; Organization Contracts; Soloists; Touring Companies
Founded: 1991
Status: Non-Profit, Professional
Paid Staff: 50
Volunteer Staff: 200
Income Sources: Facility rentals
Performs At: Theatre, Visual & Performing Arts Studios(dance,crafts,etc)
Affiliations: City of Torrance, Torrance Cultural Arts Center Foundation
Facility Category: Multi-purpose complex (theater, art studios, rental)
Type of Stage: Proscenium
Stage Dimensions: 47 Feet Wide
Seating Capacity: 502
Year Built: 1991
Cost: $12 Million

6317
CALIFORNIA STATE UNIVERSITY STANISLAUS PERFORMING ARTS CENTER
801 W Monte Vista Avenue
Turlock, CA 95382
Mailing Address: 801 W. Monte Vista Avenue Turlock, CA 95382
Phone: 562-951-4060
Fax: 209-667-3782
e-mail: summerarts@calstate.edu
Web Site: blogs.calstate.edu/summerarts/
Officers:
  Chancellor: Charles B. Reed
  Vice Chancellor/CFO: Benjamin F. Quillian
  Vice Chancellor, Human Resource: Gail E. Brooks
  Chief Academic Officer: Ephraim P. Smith
  General Counsel: Christine Helwick
Management:
  Chancellor: Charles B Reed
  Director: Rachel Lee Nardo
  Business Manager: Laura Schultz
  Production Manager: Shannon Pringle
  Community Relations Specialist: Rob Klevan
Founded: 1986
Seating Capacity: 50-800

6318
VISALIA CONVENTION CENTER ROTARY THEATRE
303 East Acequia Avenue
Visalia, CA 93291
Mailing Address: 303 E. Acequia, Visalia, CA 93291
Phone: 559-713-4000
Fax: 559-713-4804
Toll-free: 800-225-2277
e-mail: vcc@ci.visalia.ca.us
Web Site: www.visalia.org
Management:
  Convention Center Manager: Wally Roeben
  Sales Manager: Leticia Garcia
  Convention Center Bureau Sales Rep: Danika Heatherly
  Sr. Convention Center Technician: Anthony Morfin
  Box Office Manager: Teresa Villarreal
Mission: The Visalia Convention Center offes over 114,000 square feet of flexible meeting and convention space and is adjacent to The marriott Hotel.
Seating Capacity: 2,000 to 4,000 telescopic seating

FACILITIES / Colorado

6319
MOONLIGHT AMPHITHEATRE
1200 Vale Terrace Drive
Vista, CA 92084
Mailing Address: 200 Civic Center Drive, Vista CA 92084
Phone: 760-639-6199
Fax: 760-643-2897
e-mail: moonlight@ci.vista.ca.us
Web Site: www.moonlightstage.com
Management:
   Artistic Director: Kathy Brombacher
   Managing Director: Daniel Kays
   Technical Director: Justin Hall
   Marketing Specialist: Fred Tracey
   Office Manager: Maureen Stroud
   Rental Coordinator: Alex Scollon
Founded: 1976
Paid Staff: 4
Paid Artists: 20
Seating Capacity: 899

6320
COLLEGE OF THE SISKIYOUS THEATRE
800 College Avenue
Weed, CA 96094
Mailing Address: 800 College Avenue Weed CA 96094
Phone: 530-938-5366
Fax: 530-938-5227
Toll-free: 888-397-4339
Web Site: www.siskiyous.edu/theatre/
Management:
   Theatre Manager: Eric Siems
   Head of Department: Anna Budd
   Technical Director/Theater Manager: Neil Carpentier-Alting
   Costume Designer: Sharon Swingle
Mission: Facilities include the Kenneth W. Ford Theater with 584 permanent seats and the Studio Theater, a small black box studio theater that can accomodate up to 100 people.
Founded: 1969
Status: Non-Profit, Non-Professional
Paid Staff: 4

6321
MERTON WRAY THEATRE
3600 Workman Mill Road
Whittier, CA 90601
Mailing Address: 3600 Workman Mill Road Whittier CA 90601
Phone: 562-692-0921
Fax: 562-908-3446
e-mail: slohr@riohondo.edu
Web Site: www.riohondo.edu/facilities/rentals.htm
Management:
   Facilities Services Director: Steven Lohr Ph.D
   Facilities Services Asst. Director: Gus Gonzalez
   Facilities Rentals/Scheduler: Eva Cabral
   Transportation Coordinator: Liz Haney
   Manager Mechanical Services: Stephen J Gabriel
   Manager Grounds/Parking/Security: George Lopez
Status: Non-Profit, Non-Professional

6322
PICO RIVERA SPORTS ARENA
11003 Rooks Road
Whittier, CA 90605
Mailing Address: 11003 Rooks Road, Whittier, CA 90605
Phone: 562-695-0509
Fax: 562-699-0005
Web Site: www.lasports.org/lafacilities/list.php?s=Arena
Management:
   President/Manager: Ralph Hauser Jr
   Assistant Manager/Director: Elaine Hauser
   Marketing Director: Malu Elizondo
   Concessions Manager: Anothony Hauser
   Sound Engineer: Daniel Esparza
Opened: 1979
Status: For-Profit, Professional
Paid Staff: 4
Paid Artists: 1
Seating Capacity: 5,000

6323
ROBINSON THEATRE
Whittier College
Ruth B. Shannon Center
13406 Philadelphia
Whittier, CA 90608-0634
Mailing Address: 13406 Philadelphia St. Whittier, CA 90608
Phone: 562-907-4202
Fax: 562-698-4067
e-mail: lwagner@whittier.edu
Web Site: http://web.whittier.edu/academic/Theatre
Officers:
   Dean: Susan D. Gotsch
Management:
   Assistant Professor Theatre Arts: Jennifer Holmes
   Associate Professor Theatre Arts: Brian Allan Reed
   Media Services: Rich Cheatham
   Assistant Professor: Gil Gonzalez
   Costume Designer & Instructor: Carin Jacobs
Mission: The Department of Theatre and Communication Arts offers a wide array of courses in the areas of performance, directing, theatre history and dramatic literature, and stage design and technology.
Specialized Field: Theatre
Type of Stage: Proscenium
Seating Capacity: 400

6324
STUDIO THEATRE
Whittier College
Ruth B. Shannon Center
13406 Philadelphia
Whittier, CA 90608-0634
Mailing Address: 13406 Philadelphia St. Whittier, CA 90608
Phone: 562-907-4202
Fax: 562-698-4067
e-mail: lwagner@whittier.edu
Web Site: http://web.whittier.edu/academic/Theatre
Officers:
   Dean: Susan D. Gotsch
Management:
   Assistant Professor Theatre Arts: Jennifer Holmes
   Associate Professor Theatre Arts: Brian Allan Reed
   Media Services: Rich Cheatham
   Assistant Professor: Gil Gonzalez
   Costume Designer & Instructor: Carin Jacobs
Mission: The Department of Theatre and Communication Arts offers a wide array of courses in the areas of performance, directing, theatre history and dramatic literature, and stage design and technology.
Specialized Field: Theatre
Type of Stage: Black Box
Seating Capacity: 100

6325
WOODLAND OPERA HOUSE
340 2nd Street
PO Box 1425
Woodland, CA 95776
Phone: 530-666-9617
Fax: 530-666-4783
e-mail: operahouse@afes.com
Web Site: www.wohtheatre.org/
Officers:
   President: Chris Taloff
   Vice President: Nancy Lohse
   Secretary: Gus Bush
   Treasurer: Becky Kleinhans
Management:
   Executive Director: Jeff Kean
   Education Director: Angela Shellhammer
   Manager: Cathy Oliver
   Costume Manager: Laurie Everly Klassen
   Box Office Coordinator: Rosemary O'Brien
   House Manager: Pam McCullaugh
Founded: 1885

6326
YREKA COMMUNITY THEATRE CENTER
1000 South Main
Yreka, CA 96097
Phone: 530-842-1649
e-mail: info@yrekachamber.com
Web Site: yrekachamber.com
Management:
   Community Theatre Center Manager: Jeff Shinn
   Director City of Yreka: David Phillipe
Seating Capacity: 300

Colorado

6327
ARVADA CENTER FOR THE ARTS AND HUMANITIES
6901 Wadsworth Boulevard
Arvada, CO 80003-9985
Mailing Address: 6901 Wadsworth Blvd., Arvada, Colorado 80003-9985
Phone: 720-898-7200
Fax: 720-898-7204
e-mail: info@arvadacenter.org
Web Site: www.arvadacenter.org
Management:
   Executive Director: Philip Sneed
   Artistic Producer: Rod A. Lansberry
   Production Manager: Adam Stolte
   Technical Director: Nick Cimyotte
   Sound Technician: Grant Evenson
Founded: 1976
Status: Non-Profit, Professional
Paid Staff: 30
Paid Artists: 50
Seating Capacity: 500

6328
ASPEN MUSIC FESTIVAL AND SCHOOL
225 Music School Road
Aspen, CO 81611
Phone: 970-925-3254
Fax: 970-925-3802
Web Site: www.aspenmusicfestival.com
Officers:
   Vice President of Development: Alexander Brose
   Development Officer: Jenny Lyons

FACILITIES / Colorado

VP for Finance and Administration: Mike Stoll
VP and Dean of Students: Jennifer Johnston
VP for Artistic Administration: Asadour Santourian
Management:
President/CEO: Alan Fletcher
Artistic Director: David Zinman
General Director: Daniel Song
Office Manager: Erich Grueter
Director of Housing: Ingrid Grueter
Director of Finance/Administration: Jennifer Brown Elliot
Manager of Information Services: Fritz Grueter
Director of Development: Mimi Teschner
Communications/Corporate Support: Laura Smith
Founded: 1949
Status: Non-Profit, Professional
Paid Staff: 30
Seating Capacity: 2,050

6329
WHEELER OPERA HOUSE
320 E Hyman Avenue
Aspen, CO 81611
Mailing Address: 320 East Hyman Avenue, Aspen, Colorado 81611
Phone: 970-920-5770
Fax: 970-920-5780
Toll-free: 866-449-0464
e-mail: grams@ci.aspen.co.us
Web Site: www.wheeleroperahouse.com
Officers:
Chairperson: Brian O'Neil
Vice-Chairperson: Richard Cohen
Secretary: Christine Benedetti
Management:
Executive Director: Gram Slaton
Senior Manager For Operations: Amy Kaiser
Senior Manager for Finance: Rose Bennett
Marketing Coordinator: Lauren Pierce
Production Manager: Brad Spooner
Founded: 1889
Specialized Field: Raoring Folk Valley
Status: Non-Profit, Professional
Paid Staff: 12
Performs At: Proc Theatre
Facility Category: Theatre
Type of Stage: Proscenium
Stage Dimensions: 28'x28'
Seating Capacity: 503
Year Built: 1889
Year Remodeled: 2006
Rental Contact: Operations Manager Gail Mason

6330
AURORA FOX ARTS CENTER
15151 E. Alameda Pkwy
PO Box 9
Aurora, CO 80010
Mailing Address: 15151 E. Alameda Pkwy, Aurora, CO 80012
Phone: 303-739-7000
Fax: 303-361-2909
e-mail: foxbox@auroragov.org
Web Site: www.auroragov.org/AuroraGov/Departments/index.htm
Management:
Executive Director: Robert Salisbury
President: Charles Packard
Box Office/House Manager: Bobbie Rubin
Vice President: Lisa Mumpton
Technical Director: Mike Haas

Mission: The Aurora Fox Arts Center, a historic landmark, is a 245-seat performing arts facility, with attached rehearsal and scenery shop facilities. A former movie theatre that was built in 1946, the Aurora Fox was completely renovated and reopened in March of 1985 and currently serves as the home for the Aurora Fox Theatre Company, and the Aurora Fox Children's Theatre Company.

6331
BICENTENNIAL ART CENTER
15151 E. Alameda Pkwy
Aurora, CO 80012
Mailing Address: 15151 E. Alameda Pkwy, Aurora, CO 80012
Phone: 303-739-7000
Fax: 303-341-7985
e-mail: culturalservices@auroragov.org
Web Site: www.auroragov.org/AuroraGov/Departments/index.htm
Officers:
President: Charles Packard
Vice President: Lisa Mumpton
Mission: The Bicentennial Art Center was originally a satellite building operated as part of the Lowery Air Force Base. Now this facility is a fully functioning pottery studio. The staff at Bicentennial not only coordinates pottery programs but also coordinate music and fine arts programs, held at City of Aurora libraries and recreation centers.

6332
BOULDER MUSEUM OF CONTEMPORARY ART GALLERIES AND THEATER
1750 13th Street
Boulder, CO 80302
Mailing Address: 1750 13th Street, Boulder, CO 80302
Phone: 303-443-2122
Fax: 303-447-1633
e-mail: info@bmoca.org
Web Site: www.bmoca.org
Officers:
President: Tracey Bradshaw
Vice President: Jeff Gaillard
Treasurer: Josh White
Secretary: Beth Isacke
Management:
Executive Director: David Dadone
Director of Education: Shannon M. Crothers
Operations Manager: Laura Post
Events & Membership Coordinator: Rendl Clark
Marketing Assistant: Valerie Amend
Associate Curator: Kirsten Gerdes
Finance/Membership Coordinator: Kent Nowlin
Director of the Collection: Keleigh Asbury
Performance Coordinator: Judson Webb
Mission: The Boulder Museum of Contemporary Art was originally called the Boulder Arts Center. It was founded in 1972 by a group of local artists as a venue to showcase and promote the visual arts in Boulder. The West Gallery has a capacity of 125; East Gallery capacity of 75; Union Works Gallery capacity of 50, and Theatre 13 has a seating capacity of 100.
Founded: 1972
Status: Non-Profit, Professional

6333
FOLSOM FIELD/COORS EVENTS CONFERENCE CENTER/STADIUM CLUB
University of Colorado, Boulder
Colorado & Folsom
Boulder, CO 80309

Mailing Address: University of Colorado, UCB Boulder, CO 80309
Phone: 303-492-5318
e-mail: Gail.Pederson@Colorado.edu
Web Site: www.CUBuffs.com
Officers:
Director of Marketing: Prema Khanna
Management:
Scheduling: Karl Eggert
Office of Athletic Director: Gail Pederson
Office Manager: Rosi Hauber
Internet Marketing Manager: Sam Neumann
Chief of Staff: Gail Pederson

6334
MACKY AUDITORIUM CONCERT HALL
University of Colorado
UCB 285
Boulder, CO 80309
Mailing Address: 17th Street & University Avenue, 285 UCB, Boulder, CO 80309
Phone: 303-492-8423
Fax: 303-492-1651
e-mail: macky@colorado.edu
Web Site: macky.colorado.edu
Management:
Director: Rudy Betancourt
Assistant Director: Sara Krumwiede
Technical Director: JP Osnes
Assistant Technical Director: Rhett Snyder
House Manager: Rojana Savoye
Mission: Offers a broad range of performances including University ensembles of band, choir, and orchestra, the Artist Series, the Boulder Philharmonic, internationally known jazz, dance, classical, pop artists, and lectures.
Facility Category: Concert Hall
Type of Stage: Proscenium
Stage Dimensions: 37x28
Seating Capacity: 2,047
Year Built: 1914
Year Remodeled: 1986

6335
NAROPA UNIVERSITY PERFORMING ARTS CENTER
2130 Araphoe Avenue
Boulder, CO 80302
Mailing Address: 2130 Arapahoe Avenue, Boulder, CO 80302
Phone: 303-444-0202
Fax: 303-444-0410
Toll-free: 800-772-6951
e-mail: infodesk@naropa.edu
Web Site: www.naropa.edu
Officers:
President: Charles G. Lief
Management:
Technical Director: David Ortolano
PAC Production Manager: Donald Stikeleather
Founded: 1974
Status: Nonprofit, Professional
Performs At: Performing Arts Center

6336
BRECKENRIDGE BACKSTAGE THEATRE
The Breckenridge Theatre
121 South Ridge Street
Breckenridge, CO 80424
Mailing Address: PO Box 297, Breckenridge, CO 80424
Phone: 970-453-0199

FACILITIES / Colorado

Fax: 970-453-4382
e-mail: info@backstagetheatre.org
Web Site: www.backstagetheatre.org
Officers:
- **President:** Frankie Hood
- **Vice President:** Phil Kopp
- **Treasurer:** Laurie Rambaud
- **Secretary:** Pam O'Neil

Management:
- **Artistic Director:** Christopher Willard
- **Business Manager:** Jean Krak
- **Reservation Manager:** Sandra Willis
- **Business Manager:** Alicia Dineen
- **Ticketing and Special Events Manage:** Kim Lineaweaver

Founded: 1974

6337
COORS EVENTS CONFERENCE CENTER
Regent Drive & 28th Street
Colorado, CO 80309
Mailing Address: Regent Drive & 28th Street, Boulder, CO 80309
Phone: 303-492-5316
Fax: 303-492-4801
e-mail: info@totalsite.com
Web Site: www.totalboulder.com/resources/8.html
Management:
- **Director:** Steve Wells
- **Asst Director Facilities Scheduling:** Karl Eggert
- **Technical Coordinator:** Brett McQueen

Mission: The facility features 37,000 square feet of meeting space.

6338
ARNOLD HALL THEATER UNITED STATES AIR FORCE
2302 Cadet Drive
Suite 12
Colorado Springs, CO 80840
Mailing Address: 2302 Cadet Drive Suite 12, U.S. Air Force Academy, CO 80840
Phone: 719-472-4497
Fax: 719-333-6771
Web Site: www.usafa.af.mil/10abw/10msg/svk/cadets/concerts.cfm?catname=10abw
Management:
- **Director of Staff:** Colonel Douglas Kreulen
- **Director of Communications:** Johnny Whitaker
- **Director of Public Affairs:** John Bryan

Specialized Field: Theater, concerts
Seating Capacity: 3,000

6339
COLORADO SPRINGS CITY AUDITORIUM
221 East Kiowa Street
Colorado Springs, CO 80903
Mailing Address: 221 E. Kiowa Street Colorado Springs, CO 80903
Phone: 719-385-5969
Fax: 719-385-6584
e-mail: jcarricato@springsgov.com
Web Site: www.springsgov.com/page.aspx?NavID=3616
Officers:
- **Chief of Staff/Chief Administrative:** Laura Neumann

Management:
- **Manager:** Bob Lillie

Founded: 1923
Paid Staff: 4
Volunteer Staff: 6
Annual Attendance: 125,000
Type of Stage: Raised Stage
Seating Capacity: 2,500

6340
FINE ARTS CENTER COLORADO SPRINGS
30 West Dale Street
Colorado Springs, CO 80903
Phone: 719-634-5583
Fax: 719-634-0570
e-mail: info@csfineartscenter.org
Web Site: www.csfineartscenter.org
Officers:
- **Chair:** Jim Raughton
- **Vice Chair:** Ann Winslow
- **Treasurer:** Kimberley Sherwood
- **Secretary:** Kate Faricy
- **CFO:** Debbie Linster

Management:
- **Director of Operations:** Mathew Holdt
- **Executive Director of Advancement a:** Erin Hannan
- **Creative Director:** Serena Wolford
- **Production Manager/Technical Direct:** Christopher Sheley
- **Executive Director of Education:** Tara Thomas
- **Director of Facilities:** Chuck Broughton
- **Grant Manager:** Laura Hines
- **Director of Patron Services:** Winter Davis

Founded: 1936
Status: Non-Profit, Professional
Paid Staff: 65
Seating Capacity: 400

6341
PIKES PEAK CENTER
190 S. Cascade Ave.
Colorado Springs, CO 80903
Phone: 719-477-2121
Fax: 719-477-2199
e-mail: anyquist@worldarena.com
Web Site: www.pikespeakcenter.org
Management:
- **Director of Event Services:** Dennis Lucero
- **Director Sales/Marketing/Promotions:** Andrea Nyquist
- **Group Sales Manager:** Kimberly Barberi
- **General Manager:** Dorothea Lischick
- **Assistant General Manager:** Tuesday Heslop

Mission: The El Pomar Great Hall is the main auditorium of the Pikes Peak Center. Continental seating on all three levels will accommodate 2,000 patrons for performances. Annual performances at the Center cover the entire entertainment spectrum: symphony, opera, musical theatre, drama, rock, country, variety, and ballet.

Utilizes: Theatre Companies
Founded: 1982
Status: Non-Profit, Non-Professional
Paid Staff: 10
Annual Attendance: 200,000
Facility Category: Theat7e
Type of Stage: Proscenium
Seating Capacity: 2,000
Year Built: 1982
Cost: 13.2 Million
Rental Contact: Booking Manager Cindy Ballard

6342
SKY SOX STADIUM
4385 Tutt Boulevard
Security Service Field
Colorado Springs, CO 80922
Mailing Address: 4385 Tutt Blvd, Security Service Field, Colorado Springs, CO
Phone: 719-597-1449
Fax: 719-597-2491
e-mail: info@skysox.com
Web Site: www.skysox.com
Officers:
- **EVP:** Rai Henniger

Management:
- **Stadium Operations Director:** Kevin Bannan

Founded: 1988
Status: For-Profit, Professional
Paid Staff: 14
Annual Attendance: 265,000
Facility Category: Baseball Stadium
Seating Capacity: 8,500
Year Remodeled: 2005
Cost: $7 million

6343
CREEDE REPERTORY THEATRE
124 North Main Street
PO Box 269
Creede, CO 81130
Mailing Address: P.O. Box 269, Second Floor, Creede, Colorado 81130
Phone: 719-658-2540
Fax: 719-658-2343
Toll-free: 866-658-2540
e-mail: info@creederep.com
Web Site: www.creederep.com
Officers:
- **President:** Robert W Slater
- **Vice President:** Arvin VanRy
- **VP/Secretary:** Charlene Ameel
- **VP/Treasurer:** Tom Brummett
- **VP/Community Relations:** Stan Letz
- **VP/Development:** Phil Lack

Management:
- **Artistic Director:** Jessica Jackson
- **MD & Production Stage Manager:** Jonathan D. Allsup
- **Production Manager:** Ryan Prince
- **Education Director:** Renee Stynchula
- **Executive Director:** Catherine Augur

Founded: 1966
Type of Stage: Black Box; Proscenium
Seating Capacity: 313

6344
CRESTED BUTTE MOUNTAIN THEATRE
403 Second Street
PO Box 611
Crested Butte, CO 81224
Mailing Address: P. O. Box 611, Crested Butte, CO 81224
Phone: 970-349-0366
e-mail: office_mttheatre@crestedbutte.net
Web Site: www.cbmountaintheatre.org
Officers:
- **President:** Laura Martineau
- **Vice President:** Suzanne Hadley

Management:
- **Managing/Artistic Director:** Harry Woods
- **Technical/Administrative Assistant:** September Sack
- **Director:** Sam Porter
- **Director:** Sandy Dorf
- **Advisory Council:** Jo Ann Macy
- **Treasurer:** Kristi Hargrove

Mission: To entertain, educate and enrich the Crested Butte community and greater Gunnison Valley providing a well-balanced theatrical season of high quality every year.

FACILITIES / Colorado

Utilizes: Choreographers; Collaborating Artists; Collaborations; Community Members; Community Talent; Dancers; Designers; Five Seasonal Concerts; Grant Writers; Guest Designers; Guest Musical Directors; Guest Speakers; Guest Teachers; Guild Activities; Instructors; Local Artists; Local Artists & Directors; Local Talent; Lyricists; Multimedia; Music; Performance Artists; Playwrights; Resident Professionals; Scenic Designers; Sign Language Translators; Singers; Students; Student Interns; Visual Designers; Volunteer Artists
Founded: 1972
Specialized Field: Community Theatre
Status: Non-Profit
Paid Staff: 1
Budget: $100,000
Income Sources: Ticket Sales; Grants; Donations; Member/Friends
Affiliations: AACT; SWCCT; RMTA
Annual Attendance: 4,000
Facility Category: Modified Black Box
Stage Dimensions: 22' x 12'
Seating Capacity: 100
Year Built: 1883
Year Remodeled: 2008

6345
THE BUTTER THEATER
139 East Bennett Avenue
Cripple Creek, CO 80813
Mailing Address: POB 430, Cripple Creek, CO 80813
Phone: 719-689-6402
Fax: 719-689-1008
e-mail: bjmac@peakinet.net
Web Site: www.buttetheater.com
Management:
  Theater Manager: Mel Moser
  Marketing Director: Ruth Zalewski
  Art Director: Mickey Burdick
  Board Member: Rick Wood
  Board Member: Bob Jeffries
  Board Member: Butch Ward
Seating Capacity: 174

6346
AUGUSTANA ARTS
5000 E. Alameda Avenue
Denver, CO 80246
Mailing Address: 5000 E. Alameda Avenue, Denver, CO 80246
Phone: 303-388-4962
Fax: 303-388-1338
Web Site: www.augustanaarts.org
Officers:
  President: John Richardson
  VP: Jerry Sanders
  Secretary: Joel Haas
Management:
  City Strings Director: Robyn Sosa
  Executive Director: Donna E. Smith
  Principal Conductor: Jennifer Ferguson
  Music Director: David Rutherford
  Principal Conductor: Jennifer Ferguson
  Secretary: Tom Virtue
Mission: To enhance the cultural life of the Denver Community: by supporting the efforts of local performing artists; by presenting performers of international renown; and performing arts outreach and educational programming.
Utilizes: Actors; Collaborating Artists; Collaborations; Fine Artists; Grant Writers; Guest Accompanists; Guest Composers; Guest Designers; Guest Lecturers; Guest Musical Directors; Guest Musicians; High School Drama; Local Artists; Multimedia; Music; Organization Contracts; Poets; Sign Language Translators; Singers; Soloists
Founded: 1997
Specialized Field: Series & Festivals; Music Instrumental; Vocal; Opera
Status: Non-Profit, Professional
Paid Staff: 6
Paid Artists: 6
Budget: $250,000
Income Sources: Ticket Sales; Grants; Donations
Performs At: Primary - Church
Annual Attendance: 8,000
Seating Capacity: 700

6347
DENVER PERFORMING ARTS COMPLEX
1345 Champa St.
First Floor
Denver, CO 80204
Mailing Address: 1245 Champa Street, Denver, CO 80204
Phone: 720-865-4220
Fax: 303-640-2397
Toll-free: 800-641-1222
e-mail: dwitherspoon@dcpa.org
Web Site: www.artscomplex.com
Management:
  Venue Director: Mark Najarian
  Security Operations Coordinator: Eugene Wade
  Superintendent: Jon Graham
  Manager of Booking & Events: Elizabeth Miller
  Patron Services Manager: Nancy May
Mission: Dedicated to excellence in the arts, The Denver Center for the Performing Arts (DCPA) is a showcase for live theatre, a nurturing ground for new plays, a preferred stop on the Broadway touring circuit, an award-winning multi-media production facility, a national training school for actors, and the site of a voice clinic and research facility.
Founded: 1972
Specialized Field: Theatre
Status: Not-For-Profit
Facility Category: Concert Hall
Type of Stage: 360-Degree-Surround
Orchestra Pit: y
Seating Capacity: 2,700
Year Built: 1978
Rental Contact: Susan Hennessy

6348
COORS FIELD
2001 Blake Street
Denver, CO 80205
Phone: 303-292-0200
Fax: 303-312-2116
e-mail: tickets@rockies.mlb.com
Web Site: colorado.rockies.mlb.com/col/ballpark/
Officers:
  Chairman & Chief Executive Officer: Charles K Monfort
  Vice Chairman: Richard L Monfort
  President: Keli S McGregor
  EVP/General Manager: Daniel J O'Dowd
  SVP/Business Operations: Gregory D Feasel
  SVP/Chief Financial Officer: Harold R Roth
  VP/Communications/Public Relations: Jay Alves
Management:
  Director Stadium Operations: Paul Egins
  Director Administration/Development: Dave Moore
  Director Senior Scouting: Bill Schmidt
  Information Systems Director: Bill Stephani
  Promotions/Broadcasting Sr Director: Alan Bossart
  Operations/Service Senior Director: Kevin G Fenton
  Facilities Director: Scott Amerman
Founded: 1960
Annual Attendance: 7,701,861
Seating Capacity: 50,445
Year Built: 1995

6349
DENVER BOTANIC GARDENS
1007 York Street
Denver, CO 80206
Mailing Address: 909 York Street, Denver, Colorado 80206
Phone: 720-865-3500
Fax: 720-865-3713
e-mail: pr@botanicgardens.org
Web Site: www.botanicgardens.org
Management:
  Interim CEO: Linda Greene
  Facility Rentals: Daphne Webb
  Marketing/Public Relatons: Rhetta Shead
  Board Chair: Jandel Allen-Davis
  Vice-Chair: Richard Clark
  Treasurer: Shawn A. Simmons
  Secretary: Christine Grawemeyer
Mission: Denver Botanic Gardens offers a broad range of programs for all ages. Choose from hands-on workshops, certificate courses, public lectures, professional development seminars or learning for personal enrichment
Founded: 1951
Seating Capacity: 2,200

6350
THE DENVER BRASS
2253 Downing St.
Denver, CO 80205
Mailing Address: 2253 Downing St. Denver, CO 80205
Phone: 303-832-4676
Fax: 303-829-4676
e-mail: info@denverbrass.org
Web Site: www.denverbrass.org
Management:
  Executive Directory: Kathleen Aylsworth Brantigan
Founded: 1908
Affiliations: Colorado Ballet, Colorado Symphony, Center Attractions
Annual Attendance: 1,500,000
Seating Capacity: 2,100
Year Built: 1908
Rental Contact: Bobbi McFarland

6351
DENVER BRONCOS FOOTBALL CLUB
1701 Bryant St.
Suite 100
Denver, CO 80204
Mailing Address: 1701 Bryant St. Suite 100. Denver, CO 80204
Phone: 720-258-3333
Fax: 720-258-3335
Web Site: www.denverbroncos.com/
Officers:
  Chairman: Pat Bowlen
Management:
  EVP/Business Operations: Joe Ellis
  General Manager: Ted Sundquist
  VP Stadium Operations: Mac Freeman
  VP Public Relations: Jim Saccomano
  VP Marketing: Greg Carney
  VP Finance: Jim Barlow

FACILITIES / Colorado

VP Community Development: Cindy Galloway Kellogg
VP Operations: Chip Conway
VP Information Technology: Rick Schoenhals
Founded: 1999
Status: Non-Profit, Non-Professional
Paid Staff: 1
Seating Capacity: 76,125

6352
DENVER CENTER FOR THE PERFORMING ARTS
1101 13th St.
Denver, CO 80204
Phone: 303-893-4000
e-mail: denvercenter@dcpa.org
Web Site: www.denvercenter.org
Officers:
  Chairman/CEO: Daniel L. Ritchie
  President/COO: Randy Weeks
  First Vice Chair: W. Leo Kiely III
  Chief Financial Officer: Vicky Miles
  Secretary/Treasurer: William Dean Singleton
Management:
  Artistic Director: Kent Thompson
  Director, Information Services: Bruce Montgomery
  Director, Accounting: Jennifer Siemers
  Director, Education: Tam Dalrymple Frye
  Director, Publications: Sylvie Drake
Founded: 1972
Status: Nonprofit; Professional
Seating Capacity: 1,577

6353
DENVER PERFORMING ARTS COMPLEX
1345 Champa St
Denver, CO 80204
Phone: 720-865-4220
Web Site: www.artscomplex.com
Officers:
  Executive Director: Kent Rice
  Deputy Director: Ginger White-Brunetti
  Director of M&C: Brian Kitts
  Asst. Director, M&C: Dan Rowland
  M&C Coordinator: Amber Fochi
Management:
  Venue Director: Mark Najarian, kent.rice@denvergov.org
  Security Operations Coordinator: Eugene Wade, mark.najarian@denvergov.org
  Superintendant: Jon Graham, elisabeth.miller@denvergov.org
  Manager of Booking & Events: Elizabeth Miller
  Patron Services Manager: Nancy May
Mission: The complex showcases theatre, modern dance, ballet, broadway shows, opera, the symphony and much more in its 9 venues

6354
DENVER VICTORIAN PLAYHOUSE
4201 Hooker Street
Denver, CO 80211
Phone: 303-433-4343
e-mail: tawx@msn.com
Web Site: www.denvervic.com/about.htm
Management:
  Owner/Producer: Wade P Wood
  Office Manager: Terry Ann Watts
Mission: Presenting a season of plays with five productions, including a variety of comedy and drama.
Utilizes: Guest Companies
Founded: 1911
Specialized Field: Community; Theatrical Group
Status: Semi-Professional; Nonprofit; Commercial
Paid Staff: 30
Season: Year Round
Seating Capacity: 73
Organization Type: Performing; Sponsoring

6355
EL CENTRO SU TEATRO
721 Santa Fe Dr.
Denver, CO 80204
Mailing Address: 721 Santa Fe Dr. Denver, CO 80204
Phone: 303-296-0219
Fax: 303-296-4614
e-mail: elcentro@suteatro.org
Web Site: www.suteatro.org
Management:
  Executive Artistic Director: Tony Garcia
  Development Director: Tanya Marina Mote
  Organizational Manager: Mica Garcia de Benavidez
  Office Manager: Valarie Castillo
  Graphic Designer: Archie Villeda
Founded: 1971

6356
ELIZABETH ERIKSEN BYRON THEATRE
University of Denver
The Robert And Judi Newman Center for Perform
2344 East Iliff Avenue
Denver, CO 80208
Mailing Address: 2344 E. Iliff Ave. Denver, CO 80208
Phone: 303-871-7720
Fax: 303-871-6507
e-mail: newman_center@du.edu
Web Site: www.newmancenterrental.com
Officers:
  Associate Professor/Chair: William Temple Davis
Management:
  Event Coordinator: Andrea Copland
  Assistant Director,Patron Services: Dee Getchel
  Assistant Director, Production Serv: Garret Glass
  Event & Community Outreach Manager: Sarah Johnson
Mission: At the University of Denver, you will explore a broad spectrum of theatre crafts and theories within the context of a liberal arts education.
Specialized Field: Theatre
Type of Stage: Alley. Thrust
Seating Capacity: Bench/modular seating
Architect: Mark Rodgers

6357
ELLIE CAULKINS OPERA HOUSE
Denver Performing Arts Complex
1345 Champa Street
First Floor
Denver, CO 80204
Mailing Address: 1345 Champa Street, Denver, CO 80204
Phone: 720-865-4220
Fax: 720-865-4246
Toll-free: 800-641-1222
e-mail: jeannette.murrietta@ci.denver.co.us
Web Site: www.artscomplex.com
Management:
  Venue Director: Mark Najarian
  Security Operations Coordinator: Eugene Wade
  Superintendent: Jon Graham
  Manager of Booking & Events: Elizabeth Miller
  Patron Services Manager: Nancy May
Mission: Dedicated to excellence in the arts, The Denver Center for the Performing Arts (DCPA) is a showcase for live theatre, a nurturing ground for new plays, a preferred stop on the Broadway touring circuit, an award-winning multi-media production facility, a national training school for actors, and the site of a voice clinic and research facility.
Founded: 1972
Specialized Field: Opera
Status: Not-For-Profit
Facility Category: Opera House
Type of Stage: Proscenium
Stage Dimensions: 20' x 40'
Orchestra Pit: y
Seating Capacity: 2,245
Year Restored: 1979
Rental Contact: Susan Hennessy

6358
THE HISTORIC PARAMOUNT THEATRE
352 Cypress St.
Denver, CO 79601
Phone: 325-676-9620
Fax: 325-676-0642
e-mail: theatre@paramount-abilene.org
Web Site: www.paramount-abilene.org
Management:
  Executive Director: Jim Sprinkle
  Executive Director: Betty Hukill
  Theatre Artistic Director: Barry Smoot
  Business Manager: Sara McKnight
  Technical Director: Taylor Compton
Founded: 1930
Seating Capacity: 2,000

6359
HOUSTON FINE ARTS CENTER
Lamont School of Music
7111 Montview Boulevard
Denver, CO 80220
Mailing Address: 7111 Montview Blvd., Denver, CO 80220
Phone: 303-871-6404
Fax: 303-871-3118
e-mail: nryan@du.edu
Web Site: www.du.edu/maps/houston.html
Management:
  Marketing director: Natalie Kate Ryan
  Event & Community Outreach Mgr: Deirdre A. Lopez
  Executive Director: Stephen Seifert
Specialized Field: play, an opera or a musical
Rental Contact: Jennifer L. Olcott
Resident Groups: The Climb ((jazz), Davinici Quartet string ensemble)

6360
JONES THEATRE
Denver Center for the Performing Arts
Helen Bonfils Theatre Complex
1101 13th St
Denver, CO 80204
Mailing Address: 1101 13th St, Denver, CO 80204
Phone: 303-893-4000
Fax: 303-640-2397
Toll-free: 800-641-1222
e-mail: info@dcpa.org
Web Site: www.artscomplex.com
Officers:
  Chairman Emeritus: Donald R. Seawell
  President/COO: Randy Weeks
  Director Events/Facilities: Susan Hennessy
  Secretary/Treasurer: William Dean Singleton
  First Vice Chair: W. Leo Kiely III
  Second Vice Chair: Robert S. Slosky
Management:
  Executive Director: Kent Rice
  Deputy Director: Ginger White

FACILITIES / Colorado

Director of Facilities: Mark Najarian
Director of Marketing & Communicati: Brian Kitts
Production Manager: Nancy May
Director, Information Services: Bruce Montgomery
Director, Accounting: Jennifer Siemers
Director, Education: Tam Dalrymple Frye
Associate Director, Corporate Spons: Jeremy Anderson

Mission: Dedicated to excellence in the arts, The Denver Center for the Performing Arts (DCPA) is a showcase for live theatre, a nurturing ground for new plays, a preferred stop on the Broadway touring circuit, an award-winning multi-media production facility, a national training school for actors, and the site of a voice clinic and research facility.
Founded: 1972
Opened: 1979
Specialized Field: Theatre
Status: Not-For-Profit
Facility Category: Concert Hall
Type of Stage: Thrust
Seating Capacity: 200
Year Built: 1978
Rental Contact: Susan Hennessy

6361
MAY BONFILS STANTON CENTER FOR THE PERFORMING ARTS

3001 S Federal Boulevard
Denver, CO 80110
Phone: 303-935-9110

6362
DENVER BRONCOS

1701 Bryant Street
Suite 100
Denver, CO 80204
Mailing Address: 1701 Bryant St. Suite 100. Denver, CO 80204
Phone: 720-258-3333
Fax: 720-258-3335
e-mail: tickets@broncos.nfl.com
Web Site: www.denverbroncos.com
Management:
  President: Pat Bowlen
  Director Operations: Gary Jones
Founded: 1970
Seating Capacity: 76,098

6363
MIZEL ARTS & CULTURE CENTER

350 S Dahlia Street
Denver, CO 80246
Phone: 303-316-6323
Fax: 303-320-0042
e-mail: info@jccdenver.org
Web Site: www.maccjcc.org
Management:
  Executive Director: Steve Wilson
  Technical Director: C J Hosier
  Education Director: Roberta Bloom
  Arts Center Director: Joanne Kauvar
Utilizes: Actors; Choreographers; Commissioned Composers; Curators; Designers; Educators; Fine Artists; Grant Writers; Guest Artists; Guest Companies; Guest Composers; Guest Conductors; Guest Designers; Guest Directors; Guest Ensembles; Guest Instructors; Guest Lecturers; Guest Soloists; Guild Activities; High School Drama; Instructors; Local Artists; Multimedia; Original Music Scores; Resident Professionals; Selected Students; Sign Language Translators; Soloists; Student Interns; Touring Companies
Status: Non-Profit
Paid Staff: 6
Budget: $300,000
Income Sources: Ticket Sales; Grants; City; State
Annual Attendance: 20,000
Type of Stage: Proscenium; Thrust
Seating Capacity: 300; 95
Year Built: 1970
Year Remodeled: 1995

6364
THE ROBERT AND JUDI NEWMAN CENTER FOR THE PERFORMING ARTS

University Of Denver
2344 East Iliff Avenue
Denver, CO 80208
Mailing Address: 2344 East Iliff Avenue, Denver, Co 80208
Phone: 303-871-6200
Fax: 303-871-6507
e-mail: newman_center@du.edu
Web Site: www.du.edu/newmancenter
Management:
  Executive Director: Stephen W Seifert
  Operations Director: Tracy Wagner
  Event Coordinator: Andrea Copland
  Assistant Director, Patron Services: Dee Getchel
  Assistant Director, Production Servi: Garret Glass
  Event & Community Outreach Manager: Sarah Johnson
Mission: To assist music and theater schools in performances; to rent theaters to community organizations; to select and present performing artists from around the world.
Founded: 2002
Specialized Field: Multi-Disciplinary
Paid Staff: 12
Volunteer Staff: 160
Budget: $1.4 million
Performs At: Multi-Purpise; Multi-Venue Performing Arts Center
Facility Category: Theatre
Type of Stage: Proscenium
Stage Dimensions: 49'widex50'd; 90' to the grid
Seating Capacity: 977
Year Built: 2002
Cost: $65 Million
Rental Contact: Tracy Wagner

6365
PEPSI CENTER

1000 Chopper Place
Denver, CO 80204
Mailing Address: 1000 Chopper Circle, Denver, CO 80204
Phone: 303-405-1100
Fax: 303-893-6685
e-mail: webmaster@pepsicenter.com
Web Site: www.pepsicenter.com
Officers:
  President and CEO: Jim Martin
  Executive VP and CFO: Bruce Glazer
  Senior VP, Venues: Doug Ackerman
  President & Governor: Josh Kroenke
  EVP and Chief Operating Officer: Matt Hutchings
  EVP and Chief Marketing Officer: Tom Philand
  EVP and General Counsel: Stephen Stieneker
  Senior Vice President, Finance: Mark Waggoner
Management:
  Owner and Governor: E Stanley Kroenke
  Executive VP: David Ehrlich
  Senior VP: Doug Ackerman
  VP Business Affairs: Mike Benson
Founded: 1999
Type of Stage: Concert Stage
Seating Capacity: 20,000

6366
RED ROCKS AMPHITHEATRE & VISITOR CENTER

18300 West Alameda Parkway
Denver, CO 80465
Mailing Address: 18300 West Alameda Parkway, Morrison, CO 80465
Phone: 720-865-2494
Fax: 720-865-2467
e-mail: jeannette.murrietta@ci.denver.co.us
Web Site: www.redrocksonline.com
Management:
  Director Theatres/Arenas: Jack Finlaw
  Marketing Director: Erik Dyce
  Director Event Services: Tad Bowman
  Booking Manager: Jeannette Murrietta
Founded: 1941
Status: Non-Profit, Professional
Paid Staff: 26

6367
RICKETSON THEATRE

Denver Center for the Performing Arts
Helen Bonfils Theatre Complex
1101 13th St
Denver, CO 80204
Mailing Address: 1101 13th Street, Denver, CO 80204
Phone: 303-893-4000
Fax: 303-640-2397
Toll-free: 800-641-1222
e-mail: info@dcpa.org
Web Site: www.artscomplex.com
Officers:
  Chairman Emeritus: Donald R. Seawell
  President/COO: Randy Weeks
  Director Events/Facilities: Susan Hennessy
  Secretary/Treasurer: William Dean Singleton
  First Vice Chair: W. Leo Kiely III
  Second Vice Chair: Robert S. Slosky
Management:
  Executive Director: Kent Rice
  Deputy Director: Ginger White
  Director of Facilities: Mark Najarian
  Director of Marketing & Communicati: Brian Kitts
  Production Manager: Nancy May
  Director, Information Services: Bruce Montgomery
  Director, Accounting: Jennifer Siemers
  Director, Education: Tam Dalrymple Frye
  Associate Director, Corporate Spons: Jeremy Anderson
Mission: Dedicated to excellence in the arts, The Denver Center for the Performing Arts (DCPA) is a showcase for live theatre, a nurturing ground for new plays, a preferred stop on the Broadway touring circuit, an award-winning multi-media production facility, a national training school for actors, and the site of a voice clinic and research facility.
Founded: 1972
Opened: 1979
Specialized Field: Theatre
Status: Not-For-Profit
Facility Category: Concert Hall
Type of Stage: Proscenium
Seating Capacity: 250
Year Built: 1978
Rental Contact: Susan Hennessy

FACILITIES / Colorado

6368
SPACE THEATRE
Denver Center for the Performing Arts
Helen Bonfils Theatre Complex
1101 13th St
Denver, CO 80204
Mailing Address: 1101 13th Street, Denver, CO 80204
Phone: 303-893-4000
Fax: 303-640-2397
Toll-free: 800-641-1222
e-mail: info@dcpa.org
Web Site: www.artscomplex.com
Officers:
- **Chairman Emeritus:** Donald R. Seawell
- **President/COO:** Randy Weeks
- **Director Events/Facilities:** Susan Hennessy
- **Secretary/Treasurer:** William Dean Singleton
- **First Vice Chair:** W. Leo Kiely III
- **Second Vice Chair:** Robert S. Slosky

Management:
- **Executive Director:** Kent Rice
- **Deputy Director:** Ginger White
- **Director of Facilities:** Mark Najarian
- **Director of Marketing & Communicati:** Brian Kitts
- **Production Manager:** Nancy May
- **Director, Information Services:** Bruce Montgomery
- **Director, Accounting:** Jennifer Siemers
- **Director, Education:** Tam Dalrymple Frye
- **Associate Director, Corporate Spons:** Jeremy Anderson

Mission: Dedicated to excellence in the arts, The Denver Center for the Performing Arts (DCPA) is a showcase for live theatre, a nurturing ground for new plays, a preferred stop on the Broadway touring circuit, an award-winning multi-media production facility, a national training school for actors, and the site of a voice clinic and research facility.
Founded: 1972
Opened: 1979
Specialized Field: Theatre
Status: Not-For-Profit
Facility Category: Concert Hall
Seating Capacity: 450
Year Built: 1978
Rental Contact: Susan Hennessy

6369
STAGE THEATRE
Denver Center for the Performing Arts
Helen Bonfils Theatre Complex
1101 13th St
Denver, CO 80204
Mailing Address: 1101 13th Street, Denver, CO 80204
Phone: 303-893-4000
Fax: 303-640-2397
Toll-free: 800-641-1222
e-mail: info@dcpa.org
Web Site: www.artscomplex.com
Officers:
- **Chairman Emeritus:** Donald R. Seawell
- **President/COO:** Randy Weeks
- **Director Events/Facilities:** Susan Hennessy
- **Secretary/Treasurer:** William Dean Singleton
- **First Vice Chair:** W. Leo Kiely III
- **Second Vice Chair:** Robert S. Slosky

Management:
- **Executive Director:** Kent Rice
- **Deputy Director:** Ginger White
- **Director of Facilities:** Mark Najarian
- **Director of Marketing & Communicati:** Brian Kitts
- **Production Manager:** Nancy May
- **Director, Information Services:** Bruce Montgomery
- **Director, Accounting:** Jennifer Siemers
- **Director, Education:** Tam Dalrymple Frye
- **Associate Director, Corporate Spons:** Jeremy Anderson

Mission: Dedicated to excellence in the arts, The Denver Center for the Performing Arts (DCPA) is a showcase for live theatre, a nurturing ground for new plays, a preferred stop on the Broadway touring circuit, an award-winning multi-media production facility, a national training school for actors, and the site of a voice clinic and research facility.
Founded: 1972
Opened: 1979
Specialized Field: Theatre
Status: Not-For-Profit
Facility Category: Concert Hall
Type of Stage: Thrust
Seating Capacity: 778
Year Built: 1978
Rental Contact: Susan Hennessy

6370
TEMPLE HOYNE BUELL THEATRE
Denver Center for the Performing Arts
Quigg Newton Denver Municipal Auditorium
1101 13th St
Denver, CO 80204
Mailing Address: 1101 13th Street, Denver, CO 80204
Phone: 303-893-4000
Fax: 303-640-2397
Toll-free: 800-641-1222
e-mail: info@dcpa.org
Web Site: www.artscomplex.com
Officers:
- **Chairman Emeritus:** Donald R. Seawell
- **President/COO:** Randy Weeks
- **Director Events/Facilities:** Susan Hennessy
- **Secretary/Treasurer:** William Dean Singleton
- **First Vice Chair:** W. Leo Kiely III
- **Second Vice Chair:** Robert S. Slosky

Management:
- **Executive Director:** Kent Rice
- **Deputy Director:** Ginger White
- **Director of Facilities:** Mark Najarian
- **Director of Marketing & Communicati:** Brian Kitts
- **Production Manager:** Nancy May
- **Director, Information Services:** Bruce Montgomery
- **Director, Accounting:** Jennifer Siemers
- **Director, Education:** Tam Dalrymple Frye
- **Associate Director, Corporate Spons:** Jeremy Anderson

Mission: Dedicated to excellence in the arts, The Denver Center for the Performing Arts (DCPA) is a showcase for live theatre, a nurturing ground for new plays, a preferred stop on the Broadway touring circuit, an award-winning multi-media production facility, a national training school for actors, and the site of a voice clinic and research facility.
Founded: 1972
Specialized Field: Theatre
Status: Not-For-Profit
Facility Category: Theatre
Type of Stage: Proscenium
Stage Dimensions: 20' x 67'
Orchestra Pit: y
Seating Capacity: 2,884
Year Built: 1978
Rental Contact: Susan Hennessy

6371
FORT LEWIS COLLEGE COMMUNITY CONCERT HALL
1000 Rim Drive
College Heights
Durango, CO 81301
Mailing Address: 1000 Rim Drive Durango, CO 81301
Phone: 970-247-7657
Fax: 970-247-7058
e-mail: concerthall@fortlewis.edu
Web Site: www.durangoconcerts.com
Management:
- **Director:** Charles Leslie
- **Production Manager/Technical Direct:** LeAnn Brubaker
- **Downtown Ticket Office Manager:** Deahna Geehan
- **Downtown Ticket Office Agent:** Dixie Reed

Mission: To provide Durango, CO and the Four Corners with an eclectic presenting program and to provide a high-quality, low-cost production venue for our community
Founded: 1997
Specialized Field: Southwest Colorado; Four Corners
Status: Non-Profit, Professional
Paid Staff: 3
Volunteer Staff: 200
Annual Attendance: 35,000-40,000
Facility Category: Presenting & Rental
Type of Stage: Proscenium
Stage Dimensions: 46W x 28D
Seating Capacity: 1200
Year Built: 1997
Rental Contact: Technical Director LeAnn Brubaker

6372
COLORADO STATE UNIVERSITY THEATRE
1778 Campus Delivery
Fort Collins, CO 80523
Mailing Address: 1778 Campus Delivery, Fort Collins, CO 80523
Phone: 970-491-5529
Fax: 970-493-4363
e-mail: mtdinfo@colostate.edu
Web Site: www.theatre.colostate.edu
Management:
- **President:** Larry Penley
- **Director of marketing:** Jennifer Clary
- **Production manager:** Jimmie Robinson
- **Scene Shop Technician:** Hannah Baldus
- **Office Manager, Music, Theatre and:** Heather Bellotti
- **Publicity, Alumni & Donor Relations:** Carrie Care
- **Marketing Director:** Jennifer Clary
- **University Center for the Arts:** Heather James

Mission: The Theatre Program at Colorado State University offers a curriculum that allows students numerous opportunities to study, train, and explore theatre in all performance and design/technical fields
Specialized Field: Theater
Status: Non-Profit, Non-Professional
Paid Staff: 8
Type of Stage: Black Box

6373
HUGHES STADIUM
Colorado State University
McGraw Athetic Building
Fort Collins, CO 80523
Mailing Address: 1800 South Overland Trail, Fort Collins, CO 80526
Phone: 970-491-6211

FACILITIES / Colorado

Fax: 970-491-1348
e-mail: ben.chulick@colostate.edu
Web Site: www.csurams.com
Management:
  Assistant Athletic: Doug Max
  Director of marketing and sales: Ben Chulick
  Assistant director of marketing and: Michelle Farger Clark
Founded: 1968
Specialized Field: Concerts

6374
LINCOLN CENTER
417 W Magnolia
Fort Collins, CO 80521
Mailing Address: Lincoln Center, 417 W. Magnolia, Fort Collins, CO 80521
Phone: 970-221-6735
Fax: 970-221-6373
e-mail: lcinfo@fcgov.com
Web Site: www.lctix.com
Management:
  Director: Gill Stilwell
Mission: The mission of the Lincoln Center is to be a leader in cultural experience and make it an essential value to the community
Founded: 1979
Specialized Field: professional theatre, dance, music, visual arts and children's programs
Status: Non-Profit, Professional
Year Remodeled: 2011

6375
UNIVERSITY CENTER FOR THE ARTS
Colorado State University
1400 Remington Street
Fort Collins, CO 80524
Mailing Address: 1778 Campus Delivery, Fort Collins, CO 80523-1778
Phone: 970-491-5529
Fax: 970-491-7541
e-mail: mtdinfo@colostate.edu
Web Site: www.sota.colostate.edu
Officers:
  Chair, Department of Music, Theatre: Todd Queen
  Chair, Department of Art: Gary Voss
  Assistant Chair of the Department o: Walt Jones
Management:
  Chair, Department of Music, Theatre: Todd Queen
  Director of Marketing, University C: Jennifer Clary
  Event Director: Eileen Kirby
  Office Manager, Music, Theatre and: Heather Bellotti
  Director of Event Operations, Unive: Eileen May Krebs
  Audio Engineer: Dan Butcher
  Publicity and Development Coordinat: Carrie Care
  Director of Recruiting: Tom Krebs
  Budget Director: Sheryl Highsmith
Utilizes: Actors; Artists-in-Residence; Choreographers; Collaborating Artists; Commissioned Composers; Commissioned Music; Composers; Composers-in-Residence; Curators; Dance Companies; Dancers; Designers; Educators; Fine Artists; Grant Writers; Guest Accompanists; Guest Artists; Guest Companies; Guest Composers; Guest Designers; Guest Directors; Guest Ensembles; Guest Instructors; Guest Lecturers; Guest Musical Directors; Guest Musicians; Guest Soloists; High School Drama; Local Unknown Artists; Lyricists; Multimedia; Original Music Scores; Performance Artists; Poets; Resident Professionals; Scenic Designers; Sign Language Translators; Singers; Soloists; Students; Student Interns; Theatre Companies; Touring Companies; Visual Arts; Volunteer Directors & Actors; Writers
Founded: 1870
Opened: 2008
Specialized Field: University Center for the Arts
Performs At: Concert Hall, Theatre, Dance Theatre, Museums
Annual Attendance: 35,000
Type of Stage: 5 Performance Spaces
Year Remodeled: 2008
Cost: $45,000,000

6376
LINCOLN PARK STOCKER STADIUM
250 N 5th Street
Grand Junction, CO 81501
Phone: 970-244-1542
Fax: 970-242-1637
e-mail: cross@mesastate.edu
Web Site: www.mesastate.edu
Management:
  Director: Erik Joe Stevens
Seating Capacity: 6,600

6377
MESA EXPERIMENTAL THEATRE
Mesa State College
Moss Performing Arts Center
1100 North Avenue
Grand Junction, CO 81501
Mailing Address: 1100 North Avenue, Grand Junction, CO 81501-3122
Phone: 970-248-1020
Toll-free: 800-982-6372
Web Site: www.coloradomesa.edu/theatre/met_perform.html
Officers:
  President: Tim Foster
Management:
  Associate Professor Theatre Arts: Richard R. Cowden
  Professor Theatre Arts: David M. Cox
  Director of Human Resources: Barbara Case King
  Benefits and Compensation Manager: Jill Knuckles
  Technician III: Shannon Mims
Mission: Our mission is to prepare students for careers in theatre and from your first day on campus there are abundant opportunities for you to gain the experience you need to take your place in the American Theatre scene.
Specialized Field: Drama
Type of Stage: Black Box

6378
MESA RECITAL HALL
Mesa State College
Moss Performing Arts Center
1100 North Avenue
Grand Junction, CO 81501
Mailing Address: 1100 North Avenue, Grand Junction, CO 81501-3122
Phone: 970-248-1604
Toll-free: 800-982-6372
Web Site: http://www.mesastate.edu/index.htm
Officers:
  President: Tim Foster
Management:
  Associate Professor Theatre Arts: Richard R. Cowden
  Professor Theatre Arts: David M. Cox
  Director of Human Resources: Barbara Case King
  Benefits and Compensation Manager: Jill Knuckles
  Technician III: Shannon Mims
Mission: Our mission is to prepare students for careers in theatre and from your first day on campus there are abundant opportunities for you to gain the experience you need to take your place in the American Theatre scene.
Specialized Field: Chamber Music, Piano, Vocalists
Seating Capacity: 300

6379
WALTER WALKER AUDITORIUM
Mesa College
1100 N Avenue
Grand Junction, CO 81501
Phone: 970-248-1233
Fax: 970-248-1159
e-mail: chofer@mesastate.edu
Web Site: www.mesastate.edu
Management:
  Head of Department: Calvin Hofer
Founded: 1974
Status: For-Profit, Professional
Paid Staff: 36
Paid Artists: 36

6380
WILLIAM S. ROBINSON THEATRE
Mesa State College
Moss Performing Arts Center
1100 North Avenue
Grand Junction, CO 81501
Mailing Address: 1100 North Avenue, Grand Junction, CO 81501-3122
Phone: 970-248-1604
Toll-free: 800-982-6372
Web Site: http://www.mesastate.edu/index.htm
Officers:
  President: Tim Foster
Management:
  Associate Professor Theatre Arts: Richard R. Cowden
  Professor Theatre Arts: David M. Cox
  Director of Human Resources: Barbara Case King
  Benefits and Compensation Manager: Jill Knuckles
  Technician III: Shannon Mims
Mission: Our mission is to prepare students for careers in theatre and from your first day on campus there are abundant opportunities for you to gain the experience you need to take your place in the American Theatre scene.
Specialized Field: Dance, Music, Theatre
Seating Capacity: 600
Cost: $5.1 Million

6381
FRAZIER HALL
University of Northern Colorado
501 20th Street
Greeley, CO 80639
Mailing Address: 501 20 St., Greeley, CO 80639
Phone: 970-351-1890
Fax: 303-351-1923
Web Site: www.unco.edu
Management:
  Director of Faculty Development: Deborah Romero
Founded: 1954

FACILITIES / Colorado

6382
UNION COLONY CIVIC CENTER
701 10th Avenue
Greeley, CO 80631
Mailing Address: 701 10th Avenue, Greeley, CO 80631
Phone: 970-356-5000
Fax: 970-336-4001
Toll-free: 800-315-2787
Web Site: www.ucstars.com
Management:
   Cultural Affairs Director: Jill Rosentrater
   Programming Coordinator: Mari Beegle
   Financial Services Coordinator: Jill Droetemueller
   Asst. Ticket Office Coordinator: Nico Ruscitti
   Asst. Ticket Office Coordinator: Kandice Peterson
   Lead House Manager: Jessica Rivera
   Technical Director: Neal Johnson
Utilizes: Actors; Artists-in-Residence; Collaborations; Fine Artists; Grant Writers; Guest Soloists; Guest Writers; Guild Activities; Local Artists; Lyricists; Multimedia; Organization Contracts; Original Music Scores; Sign Language Translators; Soloists; Student Interns; Special Technical Talent; Theatre Companies; Touring Companies
Founded: 1988
Status: Non-Profit, Non-Professional
Paid Staff: 14
Volunteer Staff: 250
Budget: $1.5 million
Income Sources: Ticket Sales; Rentals; Sponsorships; City Subsidy
Annual Attendance: 110,000
Facility Category: Concert Hall; Auditorium; Performance
Stage Dimensions: 50 x 60
Seating Capacity: 1660
Year Built: 1988
Cost: $9.2 Million
Rental Contact: Julie Givan

6383
UNIVERSITY OF NORTHERN COLORADO
College of Performing and Visual ARTS
501 20th Street, Campus Box 30
Greeley, CO 80639
Mailing Address: Campus Box 30, University of Northern Colorado, Greeley, CO
Phone: 970-351-2515
Fax: 970-351-1923
e-mail: susan.nelson@unco.edu
Web Site: www.arts.unco.edu
Management:
   Community Arts Director: Susan Nelson
   Director, School Art & Design: Dennis Morimoto
   Box Office Manager: Diane Cays
   Student Services Specialist: Di Smice
   Director, Marketing and Community R: Susan Nelson
Founded: 1954

6384
THE OTERO PLAYERS
1802 Colorado
La Junta, CO 81050
Mailing Address: 1802 Colorado Ave., La Junta, CO 81050
Phone: 719-384-6831
Fax: 719-384-6933
e-mail: information@ojc.edu
Web Site: www.ojc.edu
Management:
   President: Jim Rizzugo
   VP: Brad Franz
   Theatre Arts Director: Ben Sisler
   Managing Director: Tom Armstrong
   Athletic Director: Gary Addington
   Arts Department Chair: RuAnn Keith
   Director of Theatre: Stephen Simpson
Founded: 1941
Status: Non-Profit, Professional
Paid Staff: 100
Paid Artists: 5

6385
PICKETWIRE PLAYERS
802 San Juan Avenue
La Junta, CO 81050
Mailing Address: Picketwire Players, 802 San Juan/ P.O. Box 912, La Junta, CO
Phone: 719-384-8320
e-mail: info@picketwireplayers.org
Web Site: www.picketwireplayers.org
Mission: WHEREAS, there being a group of individuals desiring to produce, direct, act and otherwise participate in a theater group, we do hereby organize and establish ourselves as the Picketwire Players.
Founded: 1968
Status: Non- profit
Seating Capacity: 350-394
Year Built: 1968

6386
TOWN HALL ARTS CENTER
2450 West Main Street
Littleton, CO 80120
Mailing Address: 2450 West Main Street, Littleton, CO 80120
Phone: 303-794-2787
Fax: 303-794-6580
e-mail: thac@townhallartscenter.org
Web Site: www.townhallartscenter.org
Officers:
   President: Jeff Kirkendall
   Vice President: Linda Scott
   Secretary/Treasurer: David Taylor
Management:
   Executive Director: Cheryl McNab
   Education Director: Seth Maisel
   Development Coordinator: Carol Petitmaire
   Theatre Technician: Greg Kendall
   House Manager: Patty Haas
   Box Office Manager: Kim Drennan
   Sales & Volunteer Manager: Corey Brown
   Marketing and PR Director: Leslie Rutherford
Mission: Offering live broadway musicals in an intimate setting for families.
Specialized Field: Live Theater; Art Gallery

6387
DICKENS OPERA HOUSE
302 Main Street
Longmont, CO 80501
Mailing Address: 300 Main St. Longmont, CO 80501
Phone: 303-834-9384
Fax: 303-651-7774
e-mail: info@dickensoperahouse.com
Web Site: www.dickensoperahouse.com
Founded: 1879
Specialized Field: live music
Year Built: 1881

6388
BUDWEISER EVENTS CENTER
5290 Arena Circle
Loveland, CO 80538
Mailing Address: 5290 Arena Circle, Loveland, CO 80538
Phone: 970-619-4100
Fax: 970-619-4123
Toll-free: 877-544-8499
e-mail: malloka@budweisereventscenter.com
Web Site: www.budweisereventscenter.com
Management:
   General Manager: Rick Hontz
   Assistant General Manager/ Director: Tim Savona
   Director of Marketing: Alissa Cunningham
   Director of Operations: Mark Tinklenberg
   Director of Corporate Sales: Dave Namesnik
   Director of Finance: Mary Lou Henson
Founded: 2003
Paid Staff: 20
Facility Category: Multi-Purpose
Type of Stage: Stage Right Rolling Stage
Seating Capacity: 6,500
Year Built: 2003
Rental Contact: Shane Cadwell

6389
SANGRE DE CRISTO ARTS AND CONFERENCE CENTER
210 N Santa Fe Avenue
Pueblo, CO 81003
Mailing Address: 210 N Santa Fe Avenue, Pueblo, CO 81003
Phone: 719-295-7200
Fax: 719-543-0134
e-mail: mail@sdc-arts.org
Web Site: www.sdc-arts.org
Management:
   Executive Director: JIM RICHERSON
   Fund Development Manager/Marketing: Jenny Kemp
   Controller: DONA SKAGGS
   Artistic Director of Dance: Stephen Wynne
   Marketing Manager: Nicky Hart
   Marketing Coordinator: Alyssa Parga
   Curator of Buell Children's Museum: Donna StinchComb
   Curator of Visual Arts: Elizabeth Szabo
   Interim Visual Arts Coordinator: Meghan Bocsh
Founded: 1972

6390
NORTHEASTERN JUNIOR COLLEGE THEATRE
Northeastern Junior College
100 College Avenue
Sterling, CO 80751
Mailing Address: 100 College Ave., Sterling CO, 80751
Phone: 970-521-6600
Fax: 970-521-6703
Toll-free: 800-626-4637
e-mail: melissa.bornhoft@njc.edu
Web Site: www.njc.edu
Officers:
   President: Jay Lee
   Vice President of Academic Services: Stanton Gartin
   Vice President of Finance: Tyler Kelsch
   Executive Assistant to the Presiden: Shawn Rose
   Vice President of Student Services: Steven Smith
Management:
   Sales Manager: Randy Pauletto
   Director of Marketing: Barbara Baker
   Athletic Director: Marci Henry

FACILITIES / Connecticut

Executive Director of NJC Foundatio: Gail Laforce
Director of Human Resources: Anglea Anderson
Type of Stage: Proscenium
Seating Capacity: 566

6391
MICHAEL D. PALM THEATRE
721 W. Colorado Ave.
Telluride, CO 81435
Mailing Address: 721 W. Colorado Ave., Telluride, CO 81435
Phone: 970-369-5669
Fax: 970-369-5670
e-mail: info@telluridepalm.com
Web Site: www.telluridepalm.com
Management:
   Director: Heather Know Rommel
   Artistic Director: Scott Doser
   Facility Manager: Kathy Jepson
   Technical Director: Tree Priest
Seating Capacity: 650

Connecticut

6392
ARENA AT HARBOR YARD
600 Main Street
2nd Floor
Bridgeport, CT 06604
Mailing Address: 600 Main Street - 2nd Floor, Bridgeport, CT 06604
Phone: 203-345-2300
Fax: 203-335-1719
e-mail: booking@arenaatharboryard.com
Web Site: www.arenaatharboryard.com
Management:
   General Manager: Lynn Carlotto
   Booking Manager: Stephanie Panico
   Director Of Operations: Tom Saunders
Founded: 2001
Facility Category: Arena
Seating Capacity: 10,000
Rental Contact: Booking Manager Stephanie Panico

6393
BERNHARD CENTER
University of Bridgeport
84 Iranistan Avenue
Bridgeport, CT 06604
Mailing Address: 84 Iranistan Avenue, Bridgeport, CT 06604
Phone: 203-576-4000
Fax: 203-576-4051
e-mail: nas@bridgeport.edu
Web Site: www.bridgeport.edu
Founded: 1971

6394
DOWNTOWN CABARET THEATRE
263 Golden Hill Street
Bridgeport, CT 06604
Mailing Address: 263 Golden Hill Street, Bridgeport, CT 06604
Phone: 203-576-1636
Fax: 203-576-1444
e-mail: tickets@mycabaret.org
Web Site: www.DowntownCabaret.org
Management:
   Executive Producer: Hugh Hallinan
   Production Manager: Phill Hill
   Group Sales Coordinator: Rosemary Martin Hayduk
   House Manager: Vicki Keiffer-Rinkerman
   Technical Director/Front Of House M: Steve Swatt
   Press Representative: Richard P. Pheneger
   Bookkeeper: Karen Rizzo
   Box Office Manager: Tondrea Mabins
Utilizes: Actors; AEA Actors; Choreographers; Dancers; Designers; Guest Artists; Guest Lecturers; Guild Activities; Local Artists; Music; Original Music Scores; Resident Professionals; Student Interns
Founded: 1975
Status: Non-Profit, Professional
Paid Staff: 12
Season: Year Round
Annual Attendance: 80,000
Type of Stage: Proscenium
Seating Capacity: 276
Year Remodeled: 1995

6395
KLEIN MEMORIAL AUDITORIUM
910 Fairfield Avenue
Bridgeport, CT 06605
Mailing Address: 910 Fairfield Avenue, Bridgeport, CT 06605
Phone: 203-576-8115
Fax: (20-3) -259-
Toll-free: 800-424-0160
e-mail: kleinmemorial@fairfieldtheatre.org
Web Site: www.theklein.org
Officers:
   President: James O'Donnell
   Treasurer: Thomas Errichetti
Management:
   Executive Director: Karl Gasteyer
   Director of Development: Cara Bertini
   Bookkeeper/Accountant: George Comer
Founded: 1940
Specialized Field: symphonies, operas, and theatre, to local dance recitals, graduations, and union meetings

6396
CHARLES IVES CENTER PAVILION
PO Box 2957
Danbury, CT 06813
Mailing Address: P.O. Box 2957 Danbury, CT 06813
Phone: 203-837-9227
Fax: 203-837-9230
e-mail: ivescenter@aol.com
Web Site: www.ivesconcertpark.com
Officers:
   Chairman: Steve Greenberg
Management:
   Board of Director: Robert Parker
   Executive Director: Phyllis Cortese
Founded: 1974
Status: Non-Profit, Professional
Paid Staff: 2
Type of Stage: Concert Stage
Seating Capacity: 5,500

6397
O'NEILL CENTER
Western Connecticut State University
Lake Avenue & University Boulevard
Danbury, CT 06810
Mailing Address: 181 White Street, Danbury, CT 06810
Phone: 203-837-8343
Fax: 203-837-8345
Toll-free: 877-837-9278
e-mail: murphyj@wcsu.edu
Web Site: www.wcsu.edu
Management:
   President: James Schmotter
   Managing Director: Jan Murphy
Founded: 1995
Status: Non-Profit, Professional
Paid Staff: 5
Seating Capacity: 3,500

6398
GOODSPEED OPERA HOUSE
Route 82
PO Box A
East Haddam, CT 06423
Mailing Address: PO Box A, East Haddam, CT 06423-0281
Phone: 860-873-8664
Fax: 860-873-2329
e-mail: info@goodspeed.org
Web Site: www.goodspeed.org
Officers:
   President: Francis G. Adam
   Vice President: Robert Landino
   Vice President: Jeffrey S. Hoffman
   Secretary: Eric D. Ort
   Treasurer: Mark Masselli
Management:
   Executive Director: Michael P Price
   General Manager: Harriett Kittner
   Associate Producer: Robert Alwine
   Theatre Manager: Edward C. Blaschik
   Systems Administrator: Jeffrey Mays
   Line Producer: Donna Lynn Cooper Hilton
   Assistant to Mr. Price: Donna Tafel
   Director of Finance: William F. Nivison
   Payroll Manager: Joanne D'Amato
Founded: 1963
Specialized Field: Opera House
Status: Non-Profit, Professional
Performs At: Goodspeed Opera House, Goodspeed-at-Chester
Type of Stage: Proscenium, Adaptable Proscenium
Seating Capacity: 400, 200

6399
EDGERTON CENTER FOR THE PERFORMING ARTS
Sacred Heart University
5151 Park Avenue
Fairfield, CT 06825-1000
Mailing Address: 5151 Park Avenue, Fairfield, Connecticut 06825-1000
Phone: 203-371-7908
Fax: 203-365-4858
e-mail: edgertoncenter@sacredheart.edu
Web Site: www.edgertoncenter.org
Officers:
   Chairman: James T. Morley
   Vice Chairman: Frank R. Martire
   Secretary: Christopher K. McLeod
   Treasurer: Teresa Ressel
Mission: Dedicated to creating and presenting high quality programming for families, students and the community that will entertain, educate and challenge.
Opened: 1986
Specialized Field: Jazz, Musical, Theatre
Status: professional
Type of Stage: Proscenium
Seating Capacity: 776

FACILITIES / Connecticut

6400
REGINA A. QUICK CENTER FOR THE ARTS
Fairfield University
Regina A Quick Center for the Arts
1073 N Benson Road
Fairfield, CT 06824
Mailing Address: 1073 North Benson Road, Fairfield, CT 06824
Phone: 203-254-4000
Fax: 203-254-4113
Toll-free: 877-278-7396
e-mail: info@quickcenter.com
Web Site: www.quickcenter.com
Officers:
  President: Rev Jeffrey P von Arx SJ
Management:
  Events Coordinator: Christian Kaplan, rentals@quickcenter.com
  VP Marketing/Communications: Rama Sudhakar
  Media Relations Director: Mark Gregorio
  Program Director: Meredith Kazer
  Track Coordinator: Sheila Grossman
Mission: Department of Visual and Performing Arts, theatre program classes examine the history, theory, and literature of theatre while considering artistic methods and techniques. We put that knowledge to work in our theatre laboratory, Theatre Fairfield.
Specialized Field: Dance; Music; Theatre
Seating Capacity: 860
Year Built: 1990
Rental Contact: Events Manager Christian Kaplan

6401
PEPSICO THEATRE
Fairfield University
1073 N Benson Road
Fairfield, CT 06824
Mailing Address: 1073 North Benson Road, Fairfield, CT 06824
Phone: 203-254-4000
Fax: 205-254-4167
e-mail: webmaster@fairfield.edu
Web Site: www.fairfield.edu
Officers:
  President: Rev Jeffrey P von Arx SJ
Management:
  Professor Theatre: Lynne Porter
  Department Coordinator: Caitlin Doyle
  Media Relations Director: Mark Gregorio
  Chief of Staff: Mark C. Reed
Mission: Department of Visual and Performing Arts, theatre program classes examine the history, theory, and literature of theatre while considering artistic methods and techniques. We put that knowledge to work in our theatre laboratory, Theatre Fairfield.
Specialized Field: Theatre
Seating Capacity: 70
Year Built: 1922

6402
QUICK CENTER FOR THE ARTS
Fairfield University
1073 N Benson Road
Fairfield, CT 06824
Mailing Address: 1073 North Benson Road, Fairfield, CT 06824
Phone: 203-254-4000
Fax: 203-254-4113
Toll-free: 877-278-7396
e-mail: info@quickcenter.com
Web Site: www.quickcenter.com
Officers:
  President: Rev Jeffrey P von Arx SJ
Management:
  Events Manager: Christian Kaplan
  VP Marketing/Communications: Rama Sudhakar
  Media Relations Director: Mark Gregorio
  Program Director: Meredith Kazer
  Track Coordinator: Sheila Grossman
Mission: A year round Regional Arts Center that provides professional performances in all disciplines, outreach and educational programs and a 6'exhibit visual arts gallery.
Utilizes: AEA Actors; Artists-in-Residence; Choreographers; Collaborating Artists; Collaborations; Commissioned Composers; Commissioned Music; Dance Companies; Dancers; Designers; Educators; Fine Artists; Grant Writers; Guest Accompanists; Guest Artists; Guest Companies; Guest Composers; Guest Conductors; Guest Designers; Guest Directors; Guest Ensembles; Guest Instructors; Guest Musical Directors; Guest Musicians; Guest Soloists; Guest Teachers; High School Drama; Instructors; Local Artists; Lyricists; Multi Collaborations; Multimedia; New Productions; Original Music Scores; Performance Artists; Playwrights; Poets; Resident Professionals; Selected Students; Sign Language Translators; Singers; Soloists; Student Interns; Special Technical Talent; Theatre Companies; Visual Arts
Founded: 1990
Specialized Field: University Owned; Performing; and Visual Educational
Status: Non-Profit, Professional
Paid Staff: 10
Volunteer Staff: 100
Budget: $2 million
Income Sources: Ticket Revenue; Rentals; Sponsorships; Donations; Grants
Performs At: Kelley Theatre, Wien Experimental Theatre, Walsh Art Gallery
Affiliations: New England Presenters, National Association of Gallerys, Museums, Connecticut Dance Alliance, Association of Preforming Arts Presenters
Annual Attendance: 90,000
Facility Category: Two theatres
Type of Stage: Proscenium & Black Box
Seating Capacity: 741
Year Built: 1990
Rental Contact: Events Manager Christian Kaplan

6403
WIEN EXPERIMENTAL THEATRE
Fairfield University
Regina A Quick Center for the Arts
1073 N Benson Road
Fairfield, CT 06824
Mailing Address: 1073 North Benson Road, Fairfield, CT 06824
Phone: 203-254-4000
Fax: 203-254-4113
Toll-free: 877-278-7396
e-mail: info@quickcenter.com
Web Site: www.quickcenter.com
Officers:
  Chair: Jesus Escobar
  President: Rev. Jeffrey P Von Arx, S.J.
  Director Media Relations: Nancy Habetz
Management:
  Events Manager: Christian Kaplan, rentals@quickcenter.com
  VP Marketing/Communications: Rama Sudhakar
  Media Relations Director: Mark Gregorio
  Program Director: Meredith Kazer
  Track Coordinator: Sheila Grossman
Mission: Department of Visual and Performing Arts, theatre program classes examine the history, theory, and literature of theatre while considering artistic methods and techniques. We put that knowledge to work in our theatre laboratory, Theatre Fairfield.
Founded: 1990
Specialized Field: Dance; Music; Theatre
Type of Stage: Black Box
Seating Capacity: 150
Year Built: 1990
Rental Contact: Events Manager Christian Kaplan

6404
ALBANO BALLET AND PERFORMING ARTS CENTER
15 Girard Avenue
Hartford, CT 06105
Mailing Address: Albano Ballet, 15 Girard Avenue, Hartford, Connecticut 06105
Phone: 860-232-8898
e-mail: albanoballet@netzero.net
Web Site: www.albanoballet.org
Management:
  Artistic Director: Joseph Albano
Founded: 1971
Specialized Field: ballet

6405
AUSTIN ARTS CENTER
Trinity College
300 Summit Street
Hartford, CT 06106
Mailing Address: 300 Summit Street, Hartford, CT 06106
Phone: 860-297-2000
Fax: 860-297-5380
Web Site: www.trincoll.edu/Arts/Pages/AustinArtsCenter.aspx
Management:
  Austin Arts Center Director: Jeffrey Walker
Mission: The Austin Arts Center (AAC) is Trinity College's premier venue for the performing and visual arts. Centrally-located on campus, it houses two performance spaces (Goodwin Theater and Garmany Hall) and the Widener Gallery. Annually presenting over 40 public events featuring guest artists, facility and students, programming can range from the creation of Tibetan mandalas to modern opera to political theater.
Paid Staff: 4
Facility Category: Performing; Visual Arts
Type of Stage: Proscenium; Black Box

6406
BUSHNELL CENTER FOR THE PERFORMING ARTS
166 Capitol Avenue
Hartford, CT 06106-1621
Mailing Address: 166 Capitol Avenue, Hartford CT 06106-1621
Phone: 860-987-6000
Fax: 860-987-6070
Toll-free: 888-824-2874
e-mail: info@bushnell.org
Web Site: www.bushnell.org
Management:
  Executive Director: David Fay
  Associate Executive Director: Donna Reynolds
  Programs Director: Dorothy Bertoni
  Programs Coordinator: Megan Fitzgerald
  Service Director/Facility Sales: Paige Rubino
  Marketing Director: Carolynn Hebert
  Box Office Manager: Margaret Rush
Founded: 1930

FACILITIES / Connecticut

Status: Non-Profit, Professional
Paid Staff: 100
Volunteer Staff: 700
Annual Attendance: 350,000
Facility Category: Performing Arts Center
Type of Stage: Proscenium
Seating Capacity: 2,800
Year Built: 1929
Year Remodeled: 2001
Rental Contact: Jodi Arnmark

6407
CHARTER OAK CULTURAL CENTER
21 Charter Oak Avenue
Hartford, CT 06106
Mailing Address: 21 Charter Oak Avenue Hartford, CT 06106
Phone: 860-310-2580
Fax: 860-524-8014
e-mail: info@charteroakcenter.org
Web Site: www.charteroakcentre.org
Officers:
   Board President: Molly O'Neill Louden
   Vice President: J. Michael Wells
   Treasurer: Jeffrey Digel
   Secretary: Karen Gantt
Management:
   Executive Director: Rabbi Donna Berman PhD
Utilizes: Artists-in-Residence; Collaborations; Dance Companies; Five Seasonal Concerts; Playwrights; Touring Companies
Specialized Field: Dance; Visual Arts; Music; Theatre; Exhibits; Film
Status: Non-Profit, Non-Professional
Paid Staff: 2
Volunteer Staff: 1
Budget: $200,000
Income Sources: Private Foundations; Grants; Business and Individual Donations; Box Office; Government; Endowments
Affiliations: Greater Hartford Arts Council; Dance Connecticut
Annual Attendance: 2,500
Facility Category: Former Synagogue
Type of Stage: Stage and Dance Floor
Stage Dimensions: 40'x60'
Seating Capacity: 200
Year Built: 1876

6408
HARTFORD CIVIC CENTER
One Civic Center Plaza
Hartford, CT 06103
Mailing Address: One Civic Center Plaza, Hartford, CT 06103
Phone: 860-249-6333
Fax: 860-241-4210
e-mail: xlcenterinfo@xlcenter.com
Web Site: www.xlcenter.com
Officers:
   Senior Vice President & General Man: Chuck Steedman
   Vice President, Finance & Administr: Lisa Bagley
   Vice President, Operations: Tony Vail
   Vice President, Sales & Marketing: Michael Kassa
Management:
   Director Faciluty Booking: Corey Humpage
   Manager, Event Service: Anthony Rosati
   Assistant Manager, Event Services: Mike Kravec
   Assistant Manager, Guest Services &: Mike Sobieraj
   Assistant Manager, Operations: Carl Zaparanick
Founded: 1977

Status: For-Profit, Professional
Paid Staff: 400
Seating Capacity: 16,500
Year Built: 1978
Year Remodeled: 1998

6409
HORACE BUSHNELL MEMORIAL HALL
166 Capitol Avenue
Hartford, CT 06106-1621
Mailing Address: 166 Capitol Avenue, Hartford CT 06106-1621
Phone: 860-987-6000
Fax: 860-987-6070
Toll-free: 888-824-2874
e-mail: info@bushnell.org
Web Site: www.bushnell.org
Management:
   CEO: David Fay
Founded: 1929
Status: For-Profit, Non-Professional
Annual Attendance: 350,000
Type of Stage: Flexible; Proscenium

6410
MASHANTUCKET PEQUOT MUSEUM & RESEARCH CENTER
110 Pequot Trail
PO Box 3180
Mashantucket, CT 06338-3180
Mailing Address: P.O. Box 3180, Mashantucket, CT 06338-3180
Phone: 860-396-6835
Fax: 860-396-6570
Toll-free: 800-411-9671
e-mail: museumwebmaster@pequotmuseum.org
Web Site: www.pequotmuseum.org
Management:
   Executive Director: Kimberly Hatcher-White
   Head Curator: Steven Cook
   Marketing/Development Director: Steve Dennin
   Director of Research: Kevin A. McBride
   Head of Conservation: Doug Currie
Founded: 1998
Status: Non-Profit, Professional
Paid Staff: 80
Paid Artists: 75
Annual Attendance: 300,000
Seating Capacity: 320

6411
CENTER FOR THE ARTS
Wesleyan University
283 Washington Terrace
Middletown, CT 06459
Mailing Address: 283 Washington Terrace, Middletown, CT, 06459
Phone: 860-685-3355
Fax: 860-685-2061
e-mail: cfa@wesleyan.edu
Web Site: www.wesleyan.edu/cfa
Management:
   President: Douglas Bennet
   Events Manager: Barbara Ally
   Director: Pamela Tatge
   Art Director: John Elmore
   Program Manager: Erinn Roos-Brown
Utilizes: Artists-in-Residence; Collaborating Artists; Collaborations; Dance Companies; Dancers; Guest Companies; Lyricists; Multi Collaborations; Multimedia; Singers; Special Technical Talent; Theatre Companies; Touring Companies
Founded: 1973
Specialized Field: Music; dance; theatre; visual arts

Status: Non-Profit, Professional
Paid Staff: 20
Performs At: Crowell Concert Hall/Theater
Annual Attendance: 41,000
Facility Category: Concert Hall, Theatre
Type of Stage: Flexible
Seating Capacity: 1,799
Year Built: 1973

6412
CFA THEATER
Wesleyan University
Center for the Arts
Wesleyan Station
Middletown, CT 06459-0442
Mailing Address: 45 Wyllys Avenue, Middletown, CT 06459-0442
Phone: 860-685-2695
Fax: 860-685-2061
e-mail: boxoffice@wesleyan.edu
Web Site: www.wesleyan.edu/cfa/about/index.html
Officers:
   President: Douglas J. Bennett
   Director Facilities: Mark Gawlak
Management:
   Professor of Theater: John F. Carr
   Director: Pamela Tatge
   Assistant Technical Director: Suzanne Sadler
   Costume Shop Manager: Christian Milik
   Associate Director for Programming: Barbara Ally
   Associate Director for Facilities a: Mark Gawlak
   Art Director: John Elmore
   Press and Marketing Director: Andrew R. Chatfield
Mission: Wesleyan sponsors an active program in the dramatic arts within the Theater Department, which produces theater in a liberal arts setting.
Specialized Field: Art, Dance, Music, Theater
Type of Stage: Proscenium, Thrust
Seating Capacity: 400-550
Year Built: 1973
Architect: John Dinkeloo Architects

6413
CROWELL CONCERT
Wesleyan University
Center for the Arts
Wesleyan Station
Middletown, CT 06459-0442
Mailing Address: 45 Wyllys Avenue, Middletown, CT 06459-0442
Phone: 860-685-2695
Fax: 860-685-2061
e-mail: boxoffice@wesleyan.edu
Web Site: http://www.wesleyan.edu/theater
Officers:
   President: Douglas J. Bennett
   Director Facilities: Mark Gawlak
Management:
   Professor of Theater: John F. Carr
   Director: Pamela Tatge
   Assistant Technical Director: Suzanne Sadler
   Costume Shop Manager: Christian Milik
   Associate Director for Programming: Barbara Ally
   Associate Director for Facilities a: Mark Gawlak
   Art Director: John Elmore
   Press and Marketing Director: Andrew R. Chatfield
Mission: Wesleyan sponsors an active program in the dramatic arts within the Theater Department, which produces theater in a liberal arts setting.
Specialized Field: Lectures and Music Performances

FACILITIES / Connecticut

Seating Capacity: 414

6414
WORLD MUSIC HALL
Wesleyan University
Center for the Arts
Wesleyan Station
Middletown, CT 06459-0442
Mailing Address: 45 Wyllys Avenue, Middletown, CT 06459-0442
Phone: 860-685-2695
Fax: 860-685-2061
e-mail: boxoffice@wesleyan.edu
Web Site: http://www.wesleyan.edu/theater
Officers:
  President: Douglas J. Bennett
  Director Facilities: Mark Gawlak
Management:
  Professor of Theater: John F. Carr
  Director: Pamela Tatge
  Assistant Technical Director: Suzanne Sadler
  Costume Shop Manager: Christian Milik
  Associate Director for Programming: Barbara Ally
  Associate Director for Facilities a: Mark Gawlak
  Art Director: John Elmore
  Press and Marketing Director: Andrew R. Chatfield
Mission: Wesleyan sponsors an active program in the dramatic arts within the Theater Department, which produces theater in a liberal arts setting.
Specialized Field: Music Performances
Seating Capacity: 175-250

6415
BLACK BOX THEATRE
Central Connecticut State University
Department of Theatre
1615 Stanley Street
New Britain, CT 06050
Mailing Address: 1615 Stanley Street, New Britain CT, 06050
Phone: 860-832-3150
e-mail: v.clarkebligh@ccsu.edu
Web Site: http://www.theatre.ccsu.edu
Officers:
  Department Chair: Thomas J. Callery Jr.
  Secretary: Jackie Colon
Management:
  Director of the Dance: Catherine J. Fellows
  Interim Executive Director: Jackie Coleman
  Technical Director: Scott Bartley
  University Assistant: Bryan Kopp
  Scene Shop Manager: Peggy Messerschmidt
Mission: Dedicated to forging the highest quality graduates in all aspects of theatre.
Specialized Field: Classical Works, Dance/Musicals, Modern, Realism, and Originals
Type of Stage: Thrust
Seating Capacity: 100

6416
THADDEUS TORP THEATRE
Central Connecticut State University
Department of Theatre
1615 Stanley Street
New Britain, CT 06050
Mailing Address: 1615 Stanley Street, New Britain CT, 06050
Phone: 860-832-3150
e-mail: v.clarkebligh@ccsu.edu
Web Site: http://www.theatre.ccsu.edu
Officers:
  Chair: Lani Johnson
Management:
  Director of the Dance: Catherine J. Fellows
  Interim Executive Director: Jackie Coleman
  Technical Director: Scott Bartley
  University Assistant: Bryan Kopp
  Scene Shop Manager: Peggy Messerschmidt
Mission: Dedicated to forging the highest quality graduates in all aspects of theatre.
Specialized Field: Classical Works, Dance/Musicals, Modern, Realism, and Originals
Type of Stage: Proscenium

6417
INGALLS RINK
Yale University
20 Tower Parkway
New Haven, CT 06511
Mailing Address: P.O. Box 208216, New Haven, CT 06520-8216
Phone: 203-432-4747
Fax: 203-432-7772
e-mail: thomas.beckett@yale.edu
Web Site: www.yale.edu/athletic
Management:
  Director of Athletics: Thomas Beckett
  Assistant to the Director: Jennifer O'Neil
  Senior Associate Athletics Director: Amy Backus
  Sr. Administrative Assistant: Sheila DeChello
  Ingalls Rink Operations Lead Assist: George Arnoutis
Founded: 1958
Status: Non-Profit, Non-Professional
Seating Capacity: 3,486

6418
KENDALL DRAMA LAB
Southern Connecticut State University
John Lyman Center for the Performing Arts
501 Crescent Street
New Haven, CT 06515
Mailing Address: 501 Crescent Street, New Haven, CT 06515
Phone: 203-392-6100
Fax: 203-392-6158
e-mail: fordr2@southernct.edu
Web Site: www.southernct.edu
Officers:
  President: Cheryl J. Norton
Management:
  Administrative Support: Rebecca Ford
  Director of Public Affairs: Patrick Dilger
Mission: The John Lyman Center for the Performing Arts is a multi-use performing arts facility. It consists of two performing spaces and a lobby art gallery. It is also home to the Department of Theatre with its costume and scenery shops.
Specialized Field: Drama
Type of Stage: Black Box
Seating Capacity: 125

6419
LONG WHARF THEATRE STAGE II
222 Sargent Drive
New Haven, CT 06511
Mailing Address: 222 Sargent Drive New Haven, CT 06511
Phone: 203-787-4282
Fax: 203-776-2287
Toll-free: 800-782-8497
e-mail: info@longwharf.org
Web Site: www.longwharf.org
Officers:
  Chair: R. Sanford Stoddard
  Vice-Chair: David I. Scheer
  Secretary: Gail Brekke
  Treasurer: Elwood B. Davis
  Founder Trustee: Ruth Lord
Management:
  Artistic Director: Gordon Edelstein
  Managing Director: Joshua Borenstein
  Associate Artistic Director: Eric Ting
  Literary Manager: Elizabeth Nearing
Founded: 1960
Annual Attendance: 100,000
Type of Stage: Thrust; Proscenium
Seating Capacity: 487; 201

6420
JOHN LYMAN CENTER FOR THE PERFORMING ARTS
Southern Connecticut State University
501 Crescent Street
New Haven, CT 06515
Mailing Address: 501 Crescent Street, New Haven, CT 06515
Phone: 203-392-6161
Fax: 203-392-6158
e-mail: tomascak@southernct.edu
Web Site: www.southernct.edu
Management:
  Director: Cynthia Disano
Status: Non-Profit, Professional
Paid Staff: 4
Type of Stage: Thrust
Seating Capacity: 1,568

6421
MAIN STAGE
Southern Connecticut State University
John Lyman Center for the Performing Arts
501 Crescent Street
New Haven, CT 06515
Mailing Address: 501 Crescent Street, New Haven, CT 06515
Phone: 203-392-6100
Fax: 203-392-6158
e-mail: fordr2@southernct.edu
Web Site: www.southernct.edu
Officers:
  President: Cheryl J. Norton
Management:
  Box Office and Business Services: Vincent Ferrie
  Event Technical Direction and Produ: A.J. Bilotta
  Associate Director: David Starkey
  Programming, Marketing, Event Manag: Larry Tomascak
  Department Secretary, John Lyman Ce: Arlene Lucibello
Mission: The John Lyman Center for the Performing Arts is a multi-use performing arts facility. It consists of two performing spaces and a lobby art gallery. It is also home to the Department of Theatre with its costume and scenery shops.
Specialized Field: Broadway, Dance, Drama, Music
Type of Stage: Thrust
Seating Capacity: 1,568

6422
NEW HAVEN VETERANS MEMORIAL COLISEUM
275 South Orange Street
New Haven, CT 06510

FACILITIES / Connecticut

Mailing Address: 275 S Orange Street, New Haven, CT, 06510
Phone: 203-772-4200
Fax: 203-495-7745
Web Site: www.nhcoliseum.com
Management:
  Executive Director: James E Perillo
  Marketing: Jan Barese
  Assistant Director: Stephanie Panico
  Facility Coordinator: Jason Smith
Founded: 1972
Seating Capacity: 11,000

6423
PALACE THEATRE
100 East Main Street
New Haven, CT 06702
Mailing Address: Palace Theater, 100 East Main Street, Waterbury, CT 06702
Phone: 203-789-2120
Fax: 203-773-0478
Web Site: http://www.palacetheaterct.org/
Officers:
  Chairman: Ronald Pugliese
  Vice Chairman: Dr. Peter Jacoby
  Vice Chairman II: Nancy Becker
  Secretary: Paul Pernerewski
  Treasurer: Peter Ferraro
Management:
  Marketing & Public Relations Office: Sheree Marcucci
  Finance Associate: Jennifer Mellitt
  Communications Manager: Audra Bouffard
  Technical Director: Dave Flowers
  Development Officer: Natalie Lawlor
Mission: The Palace Theater's vision is to stimulate a cultural and economic renaissance in the region through the celebration of arts, education and community. Our mission is to build a strong sense of community and an appreciation for the arts by operating, maintaining and sustaining the Palace Theater as a financially viable not-for-profit performing arts center that provides positive artistic, cultural, educational, social and financial impact to the
Founded: 1922
Specialized Field: Broadway, comedy, lecture, celebrity, education and family programming
Status: Non-Profit

6424
SHUBERT THEATER
247 College Street
New Haven, CT 06510
Mailing Address: 247 College St, New Haven, CT 06510
Phone: 203-562-5666
Fax: 203-789-2286
Toll-free: 800-228-6622
Web Site: www.shubert.com
Officers:
  Chair: Kevin Burke
  Vice Chair: Karen L. Chute
  Treasurer: Anthony Scilla
  Secretary: Matthew Susman
  Chairman Emeritus: Don Chaffee
Management:
  Executive Director: John F. Fisher
  General Manager: Sheri Kaplan
  Director of Development & Comm: Elisabeth Verrastro
  Volunteer Coordinator: Kathy Apuzzo
  Director of Ticketing: Susan Jacobson
Status: Non-Profit, Professional
Facility Category: Theater
Type of Stage: Proscenium
Seating Capacity: 1,655
Year Built: 1914
Year Remodeled: 1997
Rental Contact: Debbi Rosenthal

6425
YALE BASEBALL STADIUM
Yale University
20 Tower Parkway
New Haven, CT 06511
Mailing Address: P.O. Box 208216, New Haven, CT 06520-8216
Phone: 203-432-4747
Fax: 203-432-7772
e-mail: thomas.beckett@yale.edu
Web Site: www.yale.edu/athletic
Management:
  Director of Athletics: Thomas Beckett
  Assistant to the Director: Jennifer O'Neil
  Senior Associate Athletics Director: Amy Backus
  Sr. Administrative Assistant: Sheila DeChello
  Ingalls Rink Operations Lead Assist: George Arnoutis
Founded: 1928
Status: Non-Profit, Professional
Seating Capacity: 6,200

6426
YALE BOWL
Yale University
20 Tower Parkway
PO Box 208216
New Haven, CT 06511
Mailing Address: P.O. Box 208216, New Haven, CT 06520-8216
Phone: 203-432-4747
Fax: 203-432-7772
e-mail: thomas.beckett@yale.edu
Web Site: www.yale.edu/athletic/
Management:
  Director of Athletics: Thomas Beckett
  Assistant to the Director: Jennifer O'Neil
  Senior Associate Athletics Director: Amy Backus
  Sr. Administrative Assistant: Sheila DeChello
  Ingalls Rink Operations Lead Assist: George Arnoutis
Founded: 1914
Seating Capacity: 64,269

6427
YALE REPERTORY THEATRE
1120 Chapel Street
New Haven, CT 06520-8244
Mailing Address: P.O. Box 208244, New Haven, CT 06520-8244
Phone: 203-432-1234
Fax: 203-432-6423
Toll-free: 800-824-9710
e-mail: yalerep@yale.edu
Web Site: www.yalerep.org
Management:
  Artistic Director: James Bundy
  Managing Director: Victoria Nolan
  Associate Artistic Director: Jennifer Kiger
  Literary Manager: Amy Boratko
  Director of Education and Accessibi: Ruth M. Feldman
Founded: 1966
Seating Capacity: 487

6428
GARDE ARTS CENTER
325 State Street
New London, CT 06320
Mailing Address: 325 State StreetNew London, CT 06320
Phone: 860-444-6766
Fax: 860-447-0503
Toll-free: 888-061-2033
e-mail: info@gardearts.org
Web Site: www.gardearts.org
Officers:
  President: Phil Michalowski
  Vice-President: John Devine
  Treasurer: Louis B. Shoor
  Secretary: Karen J. Ricciardi
Management:
  Executive Director: Steve Sigel
  Marketing & Development Director: Jeanne Sigel
  Accounting Manager: Linda Kaminski
  Communications & Social Media: Rita Rivera
Founded: 1976
Status: Non-Profit, Non-Professional
Paid Staff: 15
Volunteer Staff: 200
Budget: $2,200,000
Income Sources: Ticket Sales; Sponsorships
Affiliations: Easter Connecticut Symphony Orchestra; Summer Music
Annual Attendance: 72,000
Type of Stage: Proscenium
Stage Dimensions: 41'x 36'
Seating Capacity: 1,471
Year Built: 1926
Year Remodeled: 1999
Cost: $13,000,000
Organization Type: Proscenium Theatre

6429
PALMER AUDITORIUM
Connecticut College
270 Mohegan Avenue
New London, CT 06320
Mailing Address: 270 Mohegan Ave., New London, CT, 06320
Phone: 860-447-1911
Fax: 860-439-2595
Toll-free: 888-553-8760
e-mail: dthol@conncoll.edu
Web Site: www.conncoll.edu
Officers:
  President: Katherine Bergeron
Management:
  President: Norman Sainscein
  Executive Director: Linda Herr
  Associate Director: Tom Hobaica
  Manager: Steve George
Founded: 1911
Specialized Field: Theatre
Status: Non-Profit, Non-Professional
Paid Staff: 4

6430
THE RIDGEFIELD PLAYHOUSE
80 East Ridge Avenue
Ridgefield, CT 06877
Mailing Address: 80 East Ridge, Ridgefield, CT 06877
Phone: 203-438-5795
Fax: 203-438-4543
e-mail: info@ridgefieldplayhouse.org
Web Site: www.ridgefieldplayhouse.org
Officers:
  President: Scott Schneider

Vice-President: Patricia Minskoff Breede
Secretary: Steve Carlson
Treasurer: David Lyons
Management:
 Chief Development Officer: Suzanne Brennan
 Executive Director: Allison Stockel
 Finance Director: Julie Paltauf
 Marketing Manager: Lisa Barrett
 Events Coordinator: Nicki Crai
Founded: 1938
Seating Capacity: 509

6431
THE SHERMAN PLAYHOUSE
5 Route 39 North
PO Box 471
Sherman, CT 06784
Mailing Address: PO Box 471. Sherman, CT 06784
Phone: 860-354-3622
e-mail: information@theshermanplayhouse.org
Web Site: www.shermanplayers.org
Officers:
 President: Robin Frome
 Vice President: Al Chiappetta
 Vice President: Valerie Lorimer
 Secretary: Ann Brennan
 Treasurer: Betsy Sholze
Founded: 1926
Annual Attendance: 3,200
Type of Stage: Proscenium
Seating Capacity: 120

6432
THEATRE PROJECT CONSULTANTS
47 Water Street
South Norwalk, CT 06854
Mailing Address: 25 Elizabeth Street South Norwalk, CT 06854
Phone: 203-299-0830
Fax: 203-299-0835
Web Site: www.theatreprojects.com
Officers:
 President: Victor Gotesman
Management:
 President: Richard Pilbrow
 Senior Consultant: Carol Allen
 Finance Director: Marion Daehms
 Director: Tom Davis
 Director: Michael Ferguson
Mission: We are stage managers, theatre technicians, designers, producers, arts administrators and architects.
Founded: 1947
Specialized Field: Theater
Status: For-Profit, Non-Professional
Paid Staff: 20

6433
SOUTHINGTON COMMUNITY THEATRE INC.
1237 Marion Ave.
Southington, CT 06444
Mailing Address: P.O. Box 411, Southington, CT 06849
Phone: 860-276-1961
Web Site: www.southingtoncommunitytheatre.org
Officers:
 President: Heidi Bass-Lamberto
 Vice President: Tony Lamberto
 Treasurer: Christopher Palmieri
 Recording Secretary: Patricia Hackett
Management:
 President: Chad E Valk
 VP: Adrianne Giammatteo

Technical Director: Tom Harwood
Founded: 1957

6434
THE PALACE
Stamford Center for the Arts
61 Atlantic Street
Stamford, CT 06901
Mailing Address: 61 Atlantic Street, Stamford, CT 06901
Phone: 203-358-2305
Fax: 203-358-2313
e-mail: jpowers@scalive.org
Web Site: http://www.stamfordcenterforthearts.org/home.cfm
Officers:
 Chairman: Michael L. Widland
 Vice President: James K. Goodwin
 Secretary: Ernest A. DiMattia
 Treasurer: Lori T. Charlton
 Vice Chairman: Sandra Goldstein
Management:
 Producing Artistic Director: B.T. McNicholl
 Director of Education: Carol Bryan
 Executive Director: Michael E. Moran, Jr.
 Associate Artistic Director: Nick Stimler
 Audience Services Manager: Elisabeth Sinniger
Founded: 1992
Specialized Field: Broadway, comedy, lecture, celebrity, education and family programming
Status: Non-Profit
Type of Stage: Proscenium
Seating Capacity: 757

6435
STAMFORD CENTER FOR THE ARTS
61 Atlantic Street
Stamford, CT 06901
Mailing Address: 61 Atlantic Street, Stamford, CT 06901
Phone: 203-358-2305
Fax: 203-358-2313
e-mail: jpowers@scalive.org
Web Site: http://www.stamfordcenterforthearts.org/home.cfm
Officers:
 Chairman: Michael L. Widland
 Vice President: James K. Goodwin
 Secretary: Ernest A. DiMattia
 Treasurer: Lori T. Charlton
 Vice Chairman: Sandra Goldstein
Management:
 Producing Artistic Director: B.T. McNicholl
 Director of Education: Carol Bryan
 Executive Director: Michael E. Moran, Jr.
 Associate Artistic Director: Nick Stimler
 Audience Services Manager: Elisabeth Sinniger
 Production Manager: Gene Ricciardi
Mission: Dedicated to serving as the region's center for performing arts. Operates two facilities, the Palace Theatre and the Rich Forum.
Founded: 1927
Specialized Field: Broadway, comedy, lecture, celebrity, education and family programming
Status: Non-Profit
Seating Capacity: 1,580

6436
HARRIET S. JORGENSEN THEATRE
University of Connecticut
Jorgensen Center For The Performing Arts
2132 Hillside Road, Unit 3014
Storrs, CT 06269-310

Mailing Address: University of Connecticut, Storrs, CT 06269
Phone: 860-486-4226
Fax: 860-486-3110
Web Site: www.uconn.edu
Officers:
 President: Susan Herbst
 Facilities Manager: Gary Yakstis
Management:
 Dean: Brid Grant
 Director: Rodney Rock
 Ticket Manager: Jennifer Darius
 Box Office Assistant: Amanda Salas
Mission: Jorgensen Center for the Performing Arts has presented the communities of eastern New England with the best the world of the performing arts has to offer, from world-renowned masters to rising stars.
Specialized Field: Ballet, Comedy, Dance, Music, Symphony, Theatre
Status: Nonprofit, Professional
Paid Staff: 10
Type of Stage: Proscenium
Seating Capacity: 500

6437
JORGENSEN CENTER FOR THE PERFORMING ARTS
University of Connecticut
2132 Hillside Road Unit 3104
Storrs, CT 06269-3104
Mailing Address: 2132 Hillside Road, Unit 3104 , Storrs, CT 06269-3104
Phone: 860-486-4226
Fax: 860-486-6781
e-mail: rodney.rock@uconn.edu
Web Site: www.jorgensen.uconn.edu
Management:
 Dean: Brid Grant
 Director: Rodney Rock
 Ticket Manager: Jennifer Darius
 Box Office Assistant: Amanda Salas
Mission: Through the presentation fo the performing arts, enlightens, entertains and inspires the intellectual curiosity in the university's students, faculty and staff, as well as the community at large.
Founded: 1955
Specialized Field: Multi-Disciplinary
Status: Non-Profit, Professional
Paid Staff: 13
Volunteer Staff: 8
Paid Artists: 50
Budget: $2 million
Income Sources: Sales; University Fees; Grants
Performs At: Jorgensen Center For The Performing Arts; Von Der Mehden Recital Hall
Affiliations: NEP, APAP
Annual Attendance: 70,000
Facility Category: Auditorium
Type of Stage: Proscenium
Seating Capacity: 2,630/500

6438
UNIVERSITY OF CONNECTICUT SPORTS COMPLEX - HARRY A GAMPEL PAVILION
The UConn Club Office
2111 Hillside Road, Unit 1078
Storrs, CT 6269-1078
Mailing Address: 2095 Hillside Road Unit 1173, Storrs, CT 06269
Phone: 860-486-3530

FACILITIES / Connecticut

Fax: 860-486-1204
e-mail: mike.enright@uconn.edu
Web Site: www.uconnhuskies.com
Officers:
 President: Paul Young
 Vice President: Kim Demsey
 Treasurer: Steve Germaine
 Assistant Treasurer: Barry Botticello
 Secretary: Michael Cartona
Management:
 Assistant Athletics Director: Jim Donohue
 Assistant Athletics Director: Mike Morrison
 Director of Major Giving: Meg Culmo
 Development Coordinator: Nicole Barkley
 Director of Annual Giving: Ashley Bruton
Mission: The Harry A. Gampel Pavilion, opened in January of 1990, totals more than 171,000 square feet in the domed area of the entire UConn Sports Center Complex with a seating capacity of 10,127. The entire UConn Sports Center Complex measures 320 feet in diameter in the circular domed arena area. The brilliant aluminum dome of the Gampel Pavilion towers more than 130 feet in the air from ground level.
Founded: 1881
Status: Non-Profit

6439
VON DER MEHDEN RECITAL HALL
University of Connecticut
875 Coventry Road
Storrs, CT 06269-1128
Mailing Address: 830 Bolton Road, U-1128, Storrs, CT 06269-1128
Phone: 860-486-4228
Fax: 860-486-1979
Web Site: http://www.sfa.uconn.edu/vdm
Officers:
 President: Philip E. Austin
 Facilities Manager: Gary Yakstis
Management:
 Director: Rod Rock
 Artistic Director: Gary English
 Contact: Patricia Thurber
Mission: Jorgensen Center for the Performing Arts has presented the communities of eastern New England with the best the world of the performing arts has to offer, from world-renowned masters to rising stars.
Specialized Field: Concerts
Status: Nonprofit, Professional
Paid Staff: 10
Type of Stage: Proscenium
Seating Capacity: 488

6440
COE PARK CIVIC CENTER
101 Litchfield Street
Torrington, CT 06790
Mailing Address: Torrington Armory, 153 South Main Street, Torrington, CT 067
Phone: 860-489-2274
Fax: 489—25-88
e-mail: BRETT_SIMMONS@Torringtonct.org
Web Site: http://www.coeparkgardens.com/ and http://ww
Management:
 Superintendent of Parks & Recreatio: J. Brett Simmons
 Recreation director: Donna Winn
Founded: 1973
Specialized Field: Summer Concerts-on-the-Green

6441
WARNER THEATRE
68 Main Street
PO Box 1012
Torrington, CT 06790
Mailing Address: 68 Main Street, Torrington, CT 06790
Phone: 860-489-7180
Fax: 860-482-4076
e-mail: info@warnertheatre.org
Web Site: www.warnertheatre.org
Officers:
 Chairman: Brian Mattiello
 Vice Chairman: Andrew Smith
 Treasurer: Patricia Shishkov
Management:
 Executive Director: Lynn Gelormino
 Business Manager: Al September
 Business Associate: Sandra Gagnon
 Development Manager: Donna Marconi
 Development Coordinator: Kayle Crowley
Founded: 1931
Status: Non-Profit, Professional
Paid Staff: 16
Annual Attendance: 10,000
Seating Capacity: 80

6442
OAKDALE THEATRE
95 South Turnpike Road
Wallingford, CT 06492
Mailing Address: 95 South Turnpike Road, Wallingford, CT 06492
Phone: 203-265-1501
Fax: 203-284-1816
Web Site: www.oakdale.com
Management:
 Booking: Anna Cappala
 Marketing: Jim Bozzi
Seating Capacity: 4,800

6443
PAUL MELLON ARTS CENTER
Choate Rosemary Hall
333 Christian Street
Wallingford, CT 06492
Mailing Address: 333 Christian Street, Wallingford, CT 06492
Phone: 203-697-2000
Fax: 203-697-2396
e-mail: rbrandt@choate.edu
Web Site: www.choate.edu
Management:
 Director: Ray Diffley
 Associate Director: Joanne Bailey
 Admission Campus Visit Coordinator: Meredith Berman
 Admission Office Manager: Anne W. Nations
 Admission Officer: Carolyn M. Traester
Founded: 1890
Annual Attendance: 45,000
Type of Stage: Proscenium
Seating Capacity: 750

6444
HOFFMAN AUDITORIUM
University of Saint Joseph
1678 Asylum Avenue
West Hartford, CT 06117
Phone: 860-232-4571
Fax: 860-231-8396
e-mail: rsmith@sjc.edu
Web Site: www.usj.edu/arts/carol-autorino-center-arts-humanities/
Officers:
 Director: Dr. Robert Smith
 Events Assistant: Andrea Hotes
Mission: The Center serves both the academic needs of the College and the cultural needs of the greater community. In keeping with the College's rich tradition in the liberal arts, students attend and participate in a wide variety of artistic and cultural events.
Opened: 2001
Specialized Field: Ballet, Classical Guitar, Concert Opera, Dance, Gospel, Theatre
Season: Year Round
Seating Capacity: 365

6445
LINCOLN THEATRE
The Hartt School
University of Hartford
200 Bloomfield Avenue
West Hartford, CT 6117-1599
Mailing Address: 200 Bloomfield Avenue, West Hartford, CT 06117
Phone: 860-768-4454
Fax: 860-768-4229
e-mail: dbell@mail.hartford.edu
Web Site: www.hartford.edu
Officers:
 Managing Director: David Bell
 Director Audience Services: Robert Thompson
Management:
 Dean: Aaron A. Flagg
 Executive Assistant to the Dean: Philip Grover
 Academic Advisor and Evaluator: Lynn Wronker
 Academic Advisor and Evaluator: Patrick Veronneau
 Director of Admissions: Megan Abernathy
Facility Category: Concert Hall
Seating Capacity: 1,100

6446
UNIVERSITY OF HARTFORD SPORTS CENTER
200 Bloomfield Avenue
West Hartford, CT 06117
Mailing Address: University of Hartford Sports Center, 200 Bloomfield Ave., W
Phone: 860-768-4536
Fax: 860-768-4229
e-mail: tstavropo@hartford.edu
Web Site: uhaweb.hartford.edu/sportsctr/home%20page.html
Management:
 Director: Daivd Bell
 Sports Center Director: Ted Stavropoulos
 Assistant Facility Director: Kelli Cullen
 Assistant Facility Director/Events: Chris Wilk
 Assistant Facility Director/Evening: Shaun Krafthofer
Seating Capacity: 3,545

6447
LEVITT PAVILION FOR THE PERFORMING ARTS
260 South Compo Road
Westport, CT 06880
Mailing Address: 260 South Compo Road Westport, CT 06880
Phone: 203-226-7600
Fax: 203-226-2330
e-mail: levitt@westportct.gov
Web Site: www.levittpavilion.com
Management:
 Executive Director: Freda Walsh

FACILITIES / Delaware

Mission: The Pavilion provides over 50 nights of diverse, top-quality entertainment every summer, at no charge, plus 1-5 special ticketed events, to the residents of Connecticut and beyond.
Utilizes: Actors; Dance Companies; Dancers; Grant Writers; Guest Accompanists; Guest Choreographers; Guest Composers; Guest Lecturers; Guest Musical Directors; Guest Musicians; Multimedia; Original Music Scores; Playwrights; Sign Language Translators; Singers; Special Technical Talent
Founded: 1973
Specialized Field: Performing Arts
Status: Nonprofit
Paid Staff: 6
Volunteer Staff: 20
Budget: $490,000
Income Sources: Fundraising Events; Foundation Grants; Corporate Donations; Individual Donations
Affiliations: Friends of the Levitt Pavilion and the Town of Westport
Annual Attendance: 50,000
Facility Category: Outdoor
Type of Stage: Proscenium
Stage Dimensions: 26'x45'
Seating Capacity: 2,500
Year Built: 1973
Year Remodeled: 1990

6448
WESTPORT COMMUNITY THEATRE
110 Myrtle Avenue
Westport, CT 06880
Mailing Address: 110 Myrtle Avenue, Westport, CT 06880
Phone: 203-226-1983
Web Site: http://www.westportcommunitytheatre.com/
Management:
    President: Rob Watts
Founded: 1978
Specialized Field: theater

6449
WESTPORT COUNTRY PLAYHOUSE
25 Powers Court
Westport, CT 06880
Mailing Address: 25 Powers Court, Westport, CT 06880
Phone: 203-227-4177
Fax: 203-454-3238
Toll-free: 888-927-7529
e-mail: info@westportplayhouse.org
Web Site: www.westportplayhouse.org
Management:
    Artistic Director: Mark Lamos
    Managing Director: Michael Ross
    Associate Artistic Director: David Kennedy
    Company Manager: Bruce Miller
    Artistic & Management Coordinator: Chad Kinsman
Founded: 1931
Seating Capacity: 707

Delaware

6450
SCHWARTZ CENTER FOR THE ARTS
226 S. State Street
Dover, DE 19901
Mailing Address: PO Box 1449, Dover, DE 19901
Phone: 302-678-3583
Fax: 302-678-1267
Toll-free: 800-778-5078
e-mail: thearts@schwartzcenter.com
Web Site: www.schwartzcenter.com
Officers:
    Chairman: Sylvia Cowell
    Vice Chair: Honorable Robert Young
    Treasurer: Constance Welde
Management:
    Executive Director: Sylvia Cowell
    Accountant: Kim Ritter
    Marketing Coordinator: Heather Moore
    Technical Coordinator: John Moller
Mission: In 2004, a strategic alliance was formed to partner the resources of Wesley College, Delaware State University, The Grand Opera House and The Friends of the Capital Theater, to maximize usage and position the historic treasure as the premiere performing arts center south of Wilmington.
Founded: 2001
Specialized Field: Comedy, Dance, Music, Theater
Status: Non-Profit, Professional
Paid Staff: 2
Volunteer Staff: 50
Seating Capacity: 600
Year Built: 1904
Year Restored: 2001
Cost: $8.3 Million

6451
BOB CARPENTER CENTER
University of Delaware
631 S. College Avenue
Newark, DE 19716
Mailing Address: University of Delaware, 631 S. College Avenue. Newark, DE 1
Phone: 302-831-4016
Fax: 302-831-4019
e-mail: bcc-admin@udel.edu
Web Site: www.udel.edu/bcc
Officers:
    President: Patrick Harker
Management:
    Managing Director: Domenick Sicilia
    Box Office Manager: Denita Patrick
Mission: To provide a venue for University of Deleware home basketball games, convocations, entertainment and special events.
Founded: 1992
Specialized Field: Rock; Pop; Country; Contemprary and Christian Concerts; Rock
Status: Non-Profit, Professional
Paid Staff: 25
Volunteer Staff: 5
Paid Artists: 3
Facility Category: Arena
Rental Contact: Domenick B Sicilia

6452
CFA STUDIO
University of Delaware
413 Academy Street
Second Floor
Newark, DE 19716
Mailing Address: REP/UD Dept. of Theatre, Newark, DE 19716
Phone: 302-831-2201
Fax: 302-831-3673
e-mail: dpugh@udel.edu
Web Site: http://www.udel.edu/theatre
Officers:
    President: Patrick Harker
Management:
    Media contact: Nadine Howett
Mission: The University of Delaware Professional Training Program/Resident Ensemble Players is a powerful and unique marriage of a resident professional acting company and a conservatory training program.
Specialized Field: Theatre
Type of Stage: Black Box

6453
CFA THOMPSON THEATRE
University of Delaware
413 Academy Street
Second Floor
Newark, DE 19716
Mailing Address: REP/UD Dept. of Theatre, Newark, DE 19716
Phone: 302-831-2201
Fax: 302-831-3673
e-mail: dpugh@udel.edu
Web Site: http://www.udel.edu/theatre
Officers:
    President: Patrick Harker
Mission: The University of Delaware Professional Training Program/Resident Ensemble Players is a powerful and unique marriage of a resident professional acting company and a conservatory training program.
Specialized Field: Theatre
Type of Stage: Proscenium
Seating Capacity: 450

6454
HARTSHORN THEATER
University of Delaware
413 Academy Street
Second Floor
Newark, DE 19716
Mailing Address: REP/UD Dept. of Theatre, Newark, DE 19716
Phone: 302-831-2201
Fax: 302-831-3673
e-mail: dpugh@udel.edu
Web Site: http://www.udel.edu/theatre
Officers:
    President: Patrick Harker
Mission: The University of Delaware Professional Training Program/Resident Ensemble Players is a powerful and unique marriage of a resident professional acting company and a conservatory training program.
Specialized Field: Theatre
Type of Stage: Black Box

6455
DUPONT THEATRE
DuPont Building
1007 North Market Street
Wilmington, DE 19801
Mailing Address: 1007 North Market Street, Wilmington, DE 19801
Phone: 302-656-4401
Fax: 302-594-1437
Toll-free: 800-338-0881
e-mail: Carolyn.F.Grubb@usa.dupont.com
Web Site: www.duponttheatre.com
Management:
    General Manager: John Gardner
    Marketing Manager: Carolyn Grubb
    Box Office Manager: Barbara Slavin
    Technical Director: Terry Gray
Founded: 1913
Status: For-Profit, Professional
Paid Staff: 17
Seating Capacity: 1,251

FACILITIES / District of Columbia

6456
GRAND OPERA HOUSE
818 North Market Street
Wilmington, DE 19801
Mailing Address: 818 North Market Street, Wilmington, DE 19801
Phone: 302-658-7897
Fax: 302-652-5346
e-mail: grandopera@grandopera.org
Web Site: www.grandopera.org
Management:
   Executive Director: Stephen M Bailey
   Associatge Director/Booking: Stephen Baile
   Marketing Director: Mary K Davis
   Box Office Manager: Terru Cruz
   Managing Director: Mark Fields
   Director of Administration: Christine Molino
   Director of Finance: Paula DiGuglielmo
   Payroll and Benefits Manager: Teresa Crawford
   Bookkeeper: Maryetta Binder
Seating Capacity: 7,000

6457
GRAND OPERA HOUSE
818 N Market Street
Wilmington, DE 19801
Mailing Address: 818 North Market Street, Wilmington, DE 19805
Phone: 302-658-7897
Fax: 302-652-5346
e-mail: grandopera@grandopera.org
Web Site: www.grandopera.org
Management:
   Executive Director: Stephen M Bailey
   Associate Director: Stephen Bailey
   Controller: Barbara Kell
   Assistant Controller: Ismay Dacosta
   Managing Director: Mark Fields
   Director of Administration: Christine Molino
   Director of Finance: Paula DiGuglielmo
   Payroll and Benefits Manager: Teresa Crawford
   Bookkeeper: Maryetta Binder
Founded: 1871
Type of Stage: Proscenium
Seating Capacity: 1,190

District of Columbia

6458
AMERICAN UNIVERSITY - MCDONALD RECITAL HALL
4400 Massachusetts Avenue NW
Washington, DC 20016
Mailing Address: 4400 Massachusetts Avenue, NW, Washington, DC 20016
Phone: 202-885-3075
Fax: 202-885-1092
Web Site: www.american.edu
Management:
   Athletic Director: Benjamin Ladner
   Assistant Athletic Director: Ed McLaughlin

6459
BAIRD AUDITORIUM
Smithsonian National Museum of Natural History
Constitution Avenue
10th Street, NW
Washington, DC 20560-0139
Mailing Address: Office of Special Events,P.O. Box 37012,NMNH 2209, MRC 139,W
Phone: 202-633-1650
Fax: 202—35-7-16
e-mail: nhevents@si.edu
Web Site: www.mnh.si.edu
Officers:
   Chair of the Board: Kathryn S. Fuller
   Vice-Chair of the Board: Roger W. Sant
   Board Member: Bruce Babbitt
   Board Members: Dr. Jane Buikstra
   Board Members: Dr. Scott Edwards
Management:
   Sant Director: Kirk Johnson
   Associate Director for Science: Dr.Jonathan A. Coddington
   Associate Director for Public Engag: Elizabeth Duggal
   Associate Director for Operations: Mike McCarthy
   Campaign Director: Tracy LaMondue

6460
BENDER ARENA
American University
4400 Massachusetts Avenue NW
Washington, DC 20016
Mailing Address: 4400 Massachusetts Avenue, NW, Washington, DC 20016
Phone: 202-885-3075
Fax: 202-885-3033
Web Site: www.aueagles.com
Management:
   Athletic Director: Benjamin Ladner
   Assistant Athletic Director: Ed McLaughlin
   Director of Athletics & Recreation: Dr. Billy Walker
   Senior Associate AD / Business Oper: Josephine Harrington
   Associate AD / SWA: Athena Argyropoulos
   Associate AD / External Relations: David Bierwirth
   Associate AD / Compliance & Interna: Jessica Hegmann
Founded: 1988
Seating Capacity: 5,000 to 6,000

6461
CARMICHAEL AUDITORIUM
Smithsonian Institution
10th and Constitution Avenue NW
Washington, DC 20560
Mailing Address: P.O. Box 37012 Smithsonian Inst., Washington D.C., 20013-701
Phone: 202-357-1300
e-mail: info@si.edu
Web Site: www.mnh.si.edu
Officers:
   Chief of Collections: Carol Butler
   Chairman: Kathryn S. Fuller
Management:
   Director: Kirk Johnson
   Associate Director for Science: Jonathan A. Coddington
   Associate Director for Operations: Greg Bettwy
   Associate Director for Public Engag: Elizabeth Duggal
   Campaign Director: Tracy LaMondue

6462
CHARLES E SMITH CENTER
The George Washington University
2121 Eye Street, NW
Washington, DC 20052
Mailing Address: 600 22nd Street NW Washington, D.C. 20052
Phone: 202-994-1000
Fax: 202-994-6818
e-mail: gwsports@gwu.edu
Web Site: www.gwu.edu
Officers:
   VP for Academic Affairs: Steven Lerman
   Executive VP and Treasurer: Louis H. Katz
   Senior VP and General Counsel: Beth Nolan
   VP for Development and Alumni Relat: Michael J. Morsberger
   VP for Research: Leo M. Chalupa
Management:
   Athletic Director: Jack Kvancz
Status: Non-Profit, Professional
Paid Staff: 100

6463
CONSTITUTION HALL
National Society Daughters of the American Revolution
1776 D Street NW
Washington, DC 20006
Mailing Address: 1776 D Street, NW, Washington, DC 20006-5303
Phone: 202-628-1776
Fax: 202-628-2570
Web Site: www.dar.org/conthall
Management:
   President: Merry Ann T. Wright
Founded: 1929
Specialized Field: theater, concerts
Status: Non-Profit, Professional

6464
CRAMTON AUDITORIUM
Howard University
2455 Sixth NW
Washington, DC 20059
Mailing Address: 2455 Sixth Street, NW Washington, DC 20059
Phone: 202-806-7194
Fax: 202-806-9183
e-mail: ddsaunders@howard.edu
Web Site: www.howard.edu
Officers:
   Interim Executive Director: Steven G. Johnson
   Technical Director: Michael C. Stepowany
   Production Manager: Charles Coward
   House Operations Coordinator: Kim E. Banks
   Chief Academic Officer: Wayne Frederick
Management:
   Manager: Denise Saunders Thompson
Mission: Cramton Auditorium has provided the Institution and the community with the means to enrich the lives of both students and visitors academically, culturally, and socially.
Opened: 1961
Specialized Field: Theatre
Performs At: Performing Arts; Educational Event; Keynote Speakers
Affiliations: Association of Performing Arts Presenters
Type of Stage: Proscenium
Seating Capacity: 1,508

6465
DC ARMORY
2400 E Capitol Street, SE
Washington, DC 20003
Mailing Address: 2400 East Capitol Street, SE, Washington, D.C. 20003
Phone: 202-547-9077
Fax: 202-547-7460
e-mail: RFKoutreach@eventsdc.com
Web Site: www.dcsportsent.com
Officers:
   Senior VP and Managing Director: Erik A. Moses

FACILITIES / District of Columbia

Vice President, Event Operations: Troy Scott
Management:
- Deputy General Counsel: Nicole Jackson
- Staff Attorney: Ryan Malet
- Event Manager: Rebecca Stirrett
- Director, Event Operations: Candace Johnson
- Director, Communications: Teri Washington

Seating Capacity: 10,000

6466
DEPARTMENT OF THEATRE ARTS
Howard University
2455 Sixth Street NW
Washington, DC 20059
Mailing Address: 2455 Sixth Street, NW Washington, DC 20059
Phone: 202-806-7050
Fax: 202-806-9193
e-mail: ddsaunders@howard.edu
Web Site: www.howard.edu
Officers:
- Chair: Kim James Bey
- Technical Director: Michael C. Stepowany
- Production Manager: Charles Coward
- House Operations Coordinator: Kim E. Banks
- Chief Academic Officer: Wayne Frederick

Management:
- Administrative Aide: Janet Johnson
- Costume Assistant: Luqman Salim
- Theatre Manager: Denise Saunders Thompson
- Master Electrician: T.W. Starnes
- Technical Director: Michael Stepowany

Mission: The Department continues to present a rich mix of high quality theatre productions to the greater Washington community.
Opened: 1961
Specialized Field: Theatre
Performs At: Performing Arts; Educational Event; Keynote Speakers
Affiliations: Association of Performing Arts Presenters
Type of Stage: Proscenium

6467
FOLGER CONSORT
Folger SHAKESPEARE LIBRARY
201 East Capitol Street, SE
Washington, DC 20003
Mailing Address: 201 East Capitol Street, SE, Washington, DC 20003
Phone: 202-544-4600
Fax: 202-544-4623
e-mail: webmaster@folger.edu
Web Site: www.folger.edu
Officers:
- Chair: Louis R. Cohen
- Vice-Chair: Philip J. Deutch

Management:
- Director: Michael Witmore
- Director: Michael Witmore

Founded: 1970

6468
GASTON HALL
Georgetown University
37th and O Streets NW
Washington, DC 20003
Mailing Address: 37th and O Streets NW, Washington, DC 20003
Phone: 202-687-4081
Fax: 202-687-2191
e-mail: lignellr@georgetown.edu
Web Site: www.folger.edu
Management:
- Manager: Susanne Oldham

Director: Michael Witmore
Founded: 1789
Annual Attendance: 15,000
Type of Stage: Black Box
Seating Capacity: 728

6469
GEORGETOWN UNIVERSITY PERFORMING ARTS CENTER
Davis Arts Center
108 Davis Performing Arts Center
Washington, DC 20005-1063
Mailing Address: Box 571063,Box 571063,Washington D.C. 20057-1063
Phone: 202-687-3838
Fax: 202-687-5757
e-mail: lignellr@georgetown.edu
Web Site: www.college.georgetown.edu
Officers:
- Dean: Chester Gillis
- Sr Assoc Dean: Jeffery Connor-Linton
- Assistant Dean: Marlene Canlas
- Senior Associate Dean: Thomas Chiarolanzio
- Assistant Dean: Jessica Ciani-Dausch

Management:
- President: Jack Degioia
- Executive Director: Maya Rag
- Administrative Director: Ron Lignelli

Utilizes: Artists-in-Residence; Choreographers; Collaborating Artists; Collaborations; Dance Companies; Dancers; Guest Artists; Guest Directors; Guest Musical Directors; Guest Musicians; High School Drama; Instructors; Multimedia; Music; Original Music Scores; Performance Artists; Sign Language Translators; Soloists; Student Interns
Founded: 1989
Specialized Field: All
Status: Non-Profit, Professional
Paid Staff: 40
Performs At: 2 Music Halls, 4 Theatres, 1 Multipurpose
Annual Attendance: 20,000
Facility Category: Black Box, Recital, Concert Hall, Multipurpose

6470
IRA ALDRIDGE THEATER
Howard University
2455 6th Street NW
Washington, DC 20059
Mailing Address: 2455 Sixth Street, NW Washington, DC 20059
Phone: 202-806-7050
Fax: 202-806-9183
e-mail: ddsaunders@howard.edu
Web Site: www.howard.edu
Officers:
- Chair: Kim James Bey
- Technical Director: Michael C. Stepowany
- Production Manager: Charles Coward
- House Operations Coordinator: Kim E. Banks
- Chief Academic Officer: Wayne Frederick

Management:
- Administrative Aide: Janet Johnson
- Costume Assistant: Luqman Salim
- Theatre Manager: Denise Saunders Thompson
- Master Electrician: T.W. Starnes
- Technical Director: Michael Stepowany

Mission: The Department continues to present a rich mix of high quality theatre productions to the greater Washington community.
Opened: 1961
Specialized Field: Theatre
Performs At: Performing Arts; Educational Event; Keynote Speakers
Affiliations: Association of Performing Arts Presenters
Type of Stage: Proscenium
Seating Capacity: 300

6471
THE JOHN F KENNEDY CENTER FOR THE PERFORMING ARTS
2700 F Street, NW
Washington, DC 20566
Mailing Address: 2700 F Street, NW Washington, DC 20566
Phone: 202-467-4600
Fax: 202-416-8018
Toll-free: 800-444-1324
Web Site: www.kennedy-center.org
Officers:
- Chairman: David M. Rubenstein
- President: Michael M. Kaiser
- Founding Chairman: Roger L. Stevens
- Secretary: Helen Lee Henderson
- Treasurer: Michael F. Neidorff

Management:
- Music Director, NSO & Kennedy Cente: Christoph Eschenbach
- Senior Counsel: Robert Barnett
- Program Director/ SR/Youth/Family: Kim Peter Kovac
- Program Manager/Performance Plus: Marlene Cooper

Mission: The Kennedy Center is America's living memorial to President Kennedy-presenting the greatest performers and performances from across America and around the world, nurturing new works and young artists, and serving as a leader in arts education.
Founded: 1971
Specialized Field: Theatre Dance Musics; Commercial Arts
Status: Non-Profit, Professional

6472
LINCOLN THEATRE
1215 U Street NW
Washington, DC 20009
Mailing Address: 1215 U Street, NW, Washington, DC 20009
Phone: 202-888-0050
Fax: 202-328-9245
e-mail: info@thelincolndc.com
Web Site: www.thelincolntheatre.org
Management:
- General Manager: Darlene Brown
- Facility Booking: Darlene Brown

Founded: 1922
Seating Capacity: 1,250

6473
LISNER AUDITORIUM
Lisner Auditorium
730 21st Street NW
Washington, DC 20052
Mailing Address: 730 21st Street, NW , Washington, DC 20052
Phone: 202-994-6800
Fax: 202-994-6906
e-mail: lisner@gwu.edu
Web Site: lisner.gwu.edu
Management:
- Theatre Manager: Cassandra Lammers
- Programming Manager: Anne Kogan
- Marketing Manager: Adah Pittman-DeLancey
- Artist Marketing Liaison: Katherine Jones
- Assistant Manager, Ticket and Box O: Nicole Langway

Status: Non-Profit, Professional

FACILITIES / District of Columbia

Paid Staff: 10
Paid Artists: 75
Affiliations: George Washington University
Annual Attendance: 200,000
Facility Category: Auditorium
Seating Capacity: 1490
Year Built: 1942
Year Remodeled: 1990
Rental Contact: Rosanna Ruscetti

6474
MCDONALD RECITAL HALL
American University
4400 Massachusetts Avenue NW
Washington, DC 20016
Mailing Address: 4400 Massachusetts Avenue, NW,
Washington, DC 20016
Phone: 202-885-3420
Fax: 202-885-1092
Web Site: www.american.edu
Management:
  Athletic Director: Benjamin Ladner
  Assistant Athletic Director: Ed McLaughlin

6475
VERIZON CENTER
601 F Street NW
Washington, DC 20004
Mailing Address: Verizon Center, 601 F Street, NW,
Washington, DC 20004
Phone: 202-628-3200
Fax: 301-808-3002
Web Site: http://www.verizoncenter.com/
Officers:
  President: John Stranix
  Chairman, CEO: Ted Leonsis
  Vice Chairman, COO: Dick Patrick
  Vice Chairman: Raul Fernandez
Management:
  VP/Executive Director: Nancy Lacy
  Booking Director: Patt Darr
  Assistant General Manager: Fritz Smith
  Director Executive Seating: Bernie Deluca
Mission: sports and entertainment arena
Founded: 1997
Specialized Field: Sports and concerts
Seating Capacity: 19,000

6476
NEW LECTURE HALL
American University
4400 Massachusetts Avenue NW
Washington, DC 20016
Mailing Address: 4400 Massachusetts Avenue, NW,
Washington, DC 20016
Phone: 202-885-3420
Fax: 202-885-1092
Web Site: www.american.edu
Officers:
  President: Cornelius M. Kerwin
  Provost: Scott A. Bass
  Vice President, Communication: Teresa Flannery
  Interim Chief Financial Officer: Doug Kudravetz
  Chief of Staf: David E. Taylor
Management:
  Athletic Director: Benjamin Ladner
  Assistant Athletic Director: Ed McLaughlin
Founded: 1968

6477
SHAKESPEARE THEATRE COMPANY
516 8th Street SE
Washington, DC 20003-2834
Phone: 202-547-1122
Fax: 202-638-3869
Toll-free: 877-487-8849
e-mail: web_admin@shakespearetheatre.org
Web Site: www.shakespearetheatre.org
Officers:
  Chief Development Officer: Ed Zakreski
  Chief Marketing Officer: Michael Porto
  Chief Production Officer: Deborah Vandergrift
Management:
  Artistic Director: Michael Kahn
  Managing Director: Chris Jennings
  Associate Artistic Director: Alan Paul
  Head of Voice and Text: Ellen O'Brien
  Literary Associate: Drew Lichtenberg
Mission: The Theatre's core mission is to present classic theatre in an accessible, skillful, imaginative, American style that honors playwrights' language and intentions while viewing their plays through a 21st-century lens.
Founded: 1986
Status: Non-Profit, Professional
Paid Staff: 90
Paid Artists: 75
Seating Capacity: 451

6478
THEATER J
Jewish Community Center
1529 16th Street NW
Washington, DC 20036
Mailing Address: 1529 16th Street NW, Washington DC 20036
Phone: 202-518-9400
Fax: 202-518-9420
Toll-free: 800-494-8497
e-mail: theaterj@dtheaterj.org
Web Site: www.theaterj.org
Officers:
  Co-Chair: Carolyn Kaplan
  Co-Chair: Mita M. Schaffer
  Vice Co-Chair: Al Munzer
  Vice Co-Chair, Co-Treasurer: Stephen Stern
  Co-Treasurer: Lois Fingerhut
Management:
  Associate Producer: Delia Taylor
  Artistic Director: Ari Roth
  Managing Director: Rebecca Ende
  Associate Producer: Delia Taylor
  Associate Artistic Director: Shirley Serotsky
Mission: Theater J produces thought-provoking, publicly engaged, personal, passionate and entertaining plays and musicals that celebrate the distinctive urban voice and social vision that are part of the Jewish cultural leagacy. Acclaimed as one of the nation's premiere playwrights' theaters, Theater J presents cutting edge contemporary work alongside spirited revivals and is a nurturing home for the development and production of new work.
Utilizes: Actors; AEA Actors; Collaborating Artists; Filmmakers; Guest Conductors; Local Artists; Original Music Scores; Performance Artists
Founded: 1990
Specialized Field: Theater
Status: 501c3
Season: October - May
Annual Attendance: 25,000
Facility Category: Theatre
Type of Stage: Thrust/Proscenium
Stage Dimensions: 20' x 20'
Seating Capacity: 258
Year Built: 1925
Year Remodeled: 1996
Rental Contact: Wanda ChiChester

6479
GEORGETOWN UNIVERSITY DEPARTMENT OF PERFORMING ARTS
Davis Arts Center
108 Davis Performing Arts Center
Washington, DC 20057-1063
Mailing Address: Box 571063, Washington, DC 20057-1063
Phone: 202-687-3838
Fax: 202-687-5757
e-mail: lignellr@georgetown.edu
Web Site: www.performingarts.georgetown.edu
Officers:
  Chairman: Maya E. Roth
Management:
  Artistic Director: Derek Goldman
  Core Faculty, Associate Professor: Soyica Colbert
  Assistant Professor: Christine Evans
  Artistic Adviser to Co-curricular T: Susan Lynskey
  Lecturer: Nadia Mahdi
Type of Stage: Black Box; Masonite
Seating Capacity: 200

6480
WARNER THEATRE
513 13th Street NW
NW Suite 111
Washington, DC 20004
Mailing Address: 513 13th Street NW, Washington, DC 20004
Phone: 202-783-4000
Fax: 202-783-0204
Toll-free: 202-783-4000
Web Site: www.warnertheatredc.com
Mission: Rental facility for local and touring presenters.
Utilizes: Theatre Companies
Founded: 1924
Performs At: Rental
Facility Category: Theater
Type of Stage: Proscenium
Seating Capacity: 1,847
Year Built: 1924
Year Remodeled: 1992
Rental Contact: 202-626-8250 B Newman

6481
WALTER E. WASHINGTON CONVENTION CENTER
801 Mount Vernon Place NW
Washington, DC 20001
Mailing Address: 801 Mount Vernon Place NW, Washington, DC 20001
Phone: 202-249-3000
Fax: 202-249-3133
e-mail: sthomas@eventsdc.com
Web Site: www.dcconvention.com
Officers:
  Vice President, Facility Operations: John Collins
  VP, Communications and Marketing: Chinyere Hubbard
  President and CEO: Gregory A. O'Dell
  Senior Vice President and General M: Samuel R. Thomas, Jr.
  Chief of Staff: Sean Sands
  Senior Vice President and Managing: Erik A. Moses
  Chief Financial Officer: Henry W. Mosley, CPA
Management:
  General Manager: Maceo Jones
  Deputy General Manager: Claud Bailey
  Sales Director: Linda G. Erickson

FACILITIES / Florida

Florida

6482
THE ISLAND PLAYERS THEATRE
10009 Gulf Drive (Corner of Pine Avenue)
Anna Maria, FL 34216
Mailing Address: P.O. Box 2059, Anna Maria, FL 34216
Phone: 941-778-5755
e-mail: hjscan@aol.com
Web Site: www.theislandplayers.org
Officers:
    President: Herb Stump
Management:
    Chairman for Publicity: Hugn Scanlon
Specialized Field: plays and musicals
Status: Non profit

6483
DOLLY HANDS CULTURAL ARTS CENTER
M091920010ge Drive
Belle Glade, FL 33430
Phone: 561-992-6160
Fax: 407-992-6179
Web Site: www.pbcc.cc.fl.us
Management:
    Manager: Leigh Woodham

6484
PALM BEACH COMMUNITY COLLEGE PERFORMING ARTS CENTER
1977 College Drive
Belle Glade, FL 33430
Phone: 561-993-1160
Fax: 561-993-1162
Web Site: www.pbcc.edu
Management:
    President: Dennis P Gallon
    Executive Director: Leigh Woodham
Founded: 1982
Specialized Field: Performing
Status: Non-Profit, Professional
Paid Staff: 2

6485
WT NEAL CIVIC CENTER
1773 NE Pear Street
Blountstown, FL 32424
Phone: 850-674-4500
Fax: 850-674-1714
Management:
    President: Howell Montgomery
Founded: 1983
Status: Non-Profit, Professional
Paid Staff: 4

6486
CENTURY VILLAGE THEATERS
19296 Lyons Road
Boca Raton, FL 33434
Mailing Address: 19296 Lyons Road, Boca Raton, FL 33434
Phone: 561-451-1227
Fax: 561-883-2624
e-mail: scohen@cenrec.com
Web Site: www.centuryvillagetheater.com
Officers:
    VP: Abby Koffler
Management:
    Assistant Entertainment Director: Kittie Midkiff
    Entertainment Secretary: Michele Schultz
    Media Director: Jan Ramsey Brick
Status: For-Profit, Professional

6487
UNIVERSITY CENTER AUDITORIUM
Florida Atlantic University
777 Glades Road
Boca Raton, FL 33431
Mailing Address: 777 Glades Road, Boca Raton, FL 33431
Phone: 561-297-3057
Fax: 561-297-3951
Web Site: www.fau.edu
Officers:
    President & Corporate Secretary: Mary Jane Saunders
Management:
    Director of Housing: Jill Eckardt
Founded: 1987

6488
RUTH ECKERD HALL
1111 McMullen Booth Road
Clearwater, FL 33759
Mailing Address: 1111 McMullen Booth Road, Clearwater, Florida 33759
Phone: 727-791-7400
Fax: 727-724-5976
Web Site: www.rutheckerdhall.com
Officers:
    Chairman: Joshua Magidson
    Sr., Vice Chair: Marcus Greene,
    Treasurer: Michael Bollenback
    Secretary, CFO: Jana L. Jones
    Chief Marketing Officer: Eric Blankenship
Management:
    Director of Special Events: Nancy Dietrich
    Corporate Relations Manager: Katie Abbitt-Hartnett
    Director of Marketing: Megan Brennan
    Tech Director: Tyson Smith
    Sr. Director of Education: Sharon Reid-Kane
Mission: To present major national and international artists and attractions year-round in a fine acoustic hall; to present educational programming, visual arts exhibits and senior citizen programs.
Utilizes: Actors; Artists-in-Residence; Choreographers; Collaborating Artists; Collaborations; Commissioned Music; Dance Companies; Dancers; Fine Artists; Guild Activities; High School Drama; Local Artists; Multi Collaborations; Multimedia; New Productions; Organization Contracts; Original Music Scores; Resident Artists; Selected Students
Founded: 1978
Specialized Field: Series & Festivals; Dance; Vocal Music; Instrumental Music; Theatre
Status: Non-Profit, Professional
Paid Staff: 50
Paid Artists: 120
Budget: $9 million
Income Sources: Association of Performing Arts Presenters; International Society of Performing Arts Administrators; Florida Professional Presenters Association
Annual Attendance: 200,000
Facility Category: Performing Arts Center
Seating Capacity: 2,173
Year Built: 1982
Year Remodeled: 2002
Rental Contact: Gregory Wright

Organization Type: Performing; Educational; Sponsoring

6489
COCOA EXPO SPORTS CENTER
500 Friday Road
Cocoa, FL 32926
Mailing Address: 500 Friday Road, Cocoa, FL 32926
Phone: 321-639-3976
Fax: 407-390-9435
e-mail: gilesmalone@cocoaexpo.com
Web Site: www.cocoaexpo.com
Management:
    President/General Manager: Giles Malone
Utilizes: Local Artists; Multimedia; Original Music Scores
Founded: 1985
Specialized Field: Brevard County/Space Coast
Performs At: 25,000 Square Foot Arena
Annual Attendance: 225,000
Facility Category: Multi-Purpose
Type of Stage: Concert Stage
Seating Capacity: 5000; 1500

6490
THE HISTORIC COCOA VILLAGE PLAYHOUSE
300 Brevard Avenue
Cocoa, FL 32922
Mailing Address: 300 Brevard Avenue, Cocoa, FL 32922
Phone: 321-636-5050
Fax: 321-636-5050
Web Site: www.cocoavillageplayhouse.com
Officers:
    Chairperson: Dewey Harris
    Vice Chairperson: Scott Baughan
    Treasurer: John W. McAnany Jr.
    Secretary: Delores Spearman
Management:
    Executive Director: Dr. Anastacia Hawkins-Smith
    Ticket Office Manager: Judy Lacy
    Associate Artistic Directors: J.Thomas Black
    Administrative Assistants: Jonathon Adler
    Marketing Artist: Benjamin Cox
Founded: 1924
Status: Non-Profit, Non-Professional
Paid Staff: 20
Volunteer Staff: 250
Paid Artists: 35

6491
OMNI AUDITORIUM
Broward College
1000 E Coconut Creek Parkway
Coconut Creek, FL 33066
Mailing Address: 1000 Coconut Creek Boulevard, Coconut Creek, FL 33066
Phone: 954-201-2240
Fax: 954-201-2242
Web Site: www.broward.edu
Mission: true multi-purpose facility, capable of hosting events ranging from opera to basketball tournaments.
Specialized Field: theater, opera
Type of Stage: Flexible
Seating Capacity: 1900+

6492
WYNMOOR RECITAL HALL
1300 Avenue of the Stars
Coconut Creek, FL 33066
Phone: 954-978-2632
Fax: 954-978-2626
Officers:

FACILITIES / Florida

Chairman Fine Arts Committee: Murray Ross
Management:
Chairman: Murray Ross
Utilizes: Dance Companies; Fine Artists; Guest Accompanists; Guest Musical Directors; Guest Musicians; Multimedia; Sign Language Translators; Singers; Theatre Companies
Founded: 1974
Budget: $100,000
Income Sources: Ticket sales
Performs At: Recital Hall
Annual Attendance: 12,000
Facility Category: Concert Hall
Type of Stage: Double thrust
Stage Dimensions: 38' 10' x 21' 9'
Seating Capacity: 950
Year Built: 1979

6493
GUSMAN CONCERT HALL
Universiy Of Miami
P.O. Box 248165
Coral Gables, FL 33124-7610
Phone: 305-284-2438
Fax: 305-284-4237
e-mail: foliveira@miami.edu
Web Site: www.music.miami.edu
Officers:
President: Donna E. Shalala
Management:
Director Of Operations: Felipe Oliveira
Mission: Used for large performances and smaller ensembles, mainly open to the public. Also holds academic offices and a recording studio

6494
BLACK BOX THEATRE
University of Miami
Department Of Theatre Arts
P.O. Box 248273
Coral Gables, FL 33124-4820
Mailing Address: P.O. Box 248273, Coral Gables, FL 33124-4820
Phone: 305-284-4474
Fax: 305-284-5702
e-mail: theatredepartment@miami.edu
Web Site: http://www.as.miami.edu/theatrearts/ring
Officers:
President: Donna E. Shalala
Management:
Provost, Vice Provosts: Thomas J. LeBlanc
General Manager: Kent Lantaff
Stage Management: James P. Birder
Musical Theatre: Gregory M. Brown
Costume Design: Michiko Kitayama
Mission: University of Miami Theatre is strictly an undergraduate training program. Our students study directly with Professors, not graduate assistants. Our Professors remain active in the profession working in the country's leading regional theaters, in New York, and in film and television. Our students do not take a back seat to graduate students in casting, design assignments, directing opportunities, or in research opportunities.
Specialized Field: Musicals, Plays
Type of Stage: Black Box
Seating Capacity: 60

6495
JERRY HERMAN RING THEATRE
University of Miami
1312 Miller Drive
Coral Gables, FL 33146
Mailing Address: P.O. Box 248273, Coral Gables, FL 33124-4820
Phone: 305-284-3355
Fax: 305-284-5702
e-mail: theatredepartment@miami.edu
Web Site: www.as.miami.edu/ringtheatre
Officers:
Chairman: Henry Fonte
Management:
Chair/Artistic Director: Vincent J. Cardinal
General Manager: Kent Lantaff
Stage Management: James P. Birder
Musical Theatre: Gregory M. Brown
Costume Design: Michiko Kitayama
Mission: University of Miami Theatre is strictly an undergraduate training program. Our students study directly with Professors, not graduate assistants. Our Professors remain active in the profession working in the country's leading regional theaters, in New York, and in film and television. Our students do not take a back seat to graduate students in casting, design assignments, directing opportunities, or in research opportunities.
Specialized Field: Musicals, Plays
Type of Stage: Proscenium/Thrust/Arena
Seating Capacity: 311

6496
BANK UNITED CENTER
University of Miami
1245 Dauer Drive
Coral Gables, FL 33146
Phone: 305-284-8686
Fax: 305-284-6547
e-mail: convocationcenter@miami.edu
Web Site: www.bankunitedcenter.com
Officers:
General Manager: Lorenzo Muniz
Marketing Director: Christi Soltz
Management:
Director of Operations: Kevin Retchless
Operations Manage: Jermaine Banks
Event Manager: Andrew Flores
Event Coordinator: Blake Malcom
Operations Supervisor: John Dolphin
Opened: 2003
Seating Capacity: 7,900

6497
CORAL SPRINGS CENTER FOR THE ARTS
2855 Coral Springs Drive
Coral Springs, FL 33065
Mailing Address: 2855 Coral Springs Drive, Coral Springs, FL 33065
Phone: 954-344-5990
Fax: 954-344-5980
e-mail: info@coralspringscenterforthearts.com
Web Site: www.coralspringscenterforthearts.com
Management:
General Manager: Kevin Barrett
Education Director: Linda Hanson
Artistic Director: Cynthia O'Brien
Technical Director: Gerry Regan
Founded: 1989
Specialized Field: Theatre Venue; Museum
Status: For-Profit, Professional
Paid Artists: 1
Annual Attendance: 200,000
Type of Stage: Proscenium
Seating Capacity: 1,456

6498
DAYTONA BEACH COMMUNITY COLLEGE THEATRE CENTER
1200 Volusia Avenue
Daytona Beach, FL 32115
Mailing Address: 1200 W. International Speedway Blvd., Daytona Beach, FL 3211
Phone: 904-254-3000
Fax: 904-254-3044

6499
DAYTONA PLAYHOUSE
100 Jessamine Blvd.
Daytona Beach, FL 32118
Mailing Address: 100 Jessamine Boulevard Daytona Beach, FL 32118
Phone: 386-255-2431
Fax: 386-255-2432
e-mail: webmaster@daytonaplayhouse.org
Web Site: www.daytonaplayhouse.org
Management:
Director: Kathy Thompson
Founded: 1946
Status: Non-Profit, Non-Professional

6500
JACKIE ROBINSON BALL PARK
Minor League Baseball
105 E. Orange Ave.
Daytona Beach, FL 32114
Mailing Address: 105 E. Orange Ave., Daytona Beach, FL 32114
Phone: 386-257-3172
Fax: 386-523-9490
e-mail: info@daytonacubs.com
Web Site: www.milb.com
Officers:
General Manager: Josh Lawther
Assistant General Manager: Clint Cure
Assistant General Manager: Jim Jaworski
Director of Business Operations: Tammy Devine
Management:
Assistant General Manager of Stadiu: JR Laub
Director of Ticket Operations: Erin Killian
Director of Broad & Media Relations: Robbie Aaron
Director of Community Relations & S: Kasey Blair
Founded: 1914

6501
OCEAN CENTER
101 N Atlantic Ave.
Daytona Beach, FL 32118
Mailing Address: 101 N. Atlantic Ave., Daytona Beach, FL 32118
Phone: 386-254-4500
Fax: 386-254-4512
Toll-free: 800-858-6444
e-mail: FrontDesk@OceanCenter.com
Web Site: www.oceancenter.com
Management:
Director: Don Poor
Assistant Director of Operations: Kristofer Beatty
Daniels : Angela Daniels
Finance Director: Teresa Mitchell
Parking Garage Manager: Jamie Fish
Founded: 1985
Annual Attendance: 525,000
Facility Category: Multi-Purpose
Type of Stage: Sico
Seating Capacity: 9,500

FACILITIES / Florida

Year Built: 1985
Rental Contact: Sales Manager Tim Buckley

6502
PEABODY AUDITORIUM
600 Auditorium Boulevard
Daytona Beach, FL 32118
Mailing Address: P.O. Box 2451, Daytona Beach, FL 32115
Phone: 386-671-3462
Fax: 904-258-3169
e-mail: scottb@CODB.US
Web Site: http://www.peabodyauditorium.org
Management:
  Director: Helen Riger
  Assistant Director: Jill Jaquet
  Box Office Manager: Ben Scott
  Group Services: Christy Forrester
  Marketing & Public Relations: Helen Riger
Founded: 1919
Specialized Field: Broadway, concerts, opera, drama, and comedy shows
Seating Capacity: 2,560

6503
DELRAY BEACH PLAYHOUSE
950 NW 9th Street
Delray Beach, FL 33444
Mailing Address: 950 NW 9th Street, Delray Beach, Florida 33444
Phone: 561-272-1281
Fax: 561-272-5884
e-mail: delraybeachplayhouse@gmail.com
Web Site: www.delraybeachplayhouse.com
Founded: 1948
Status: Non-Profit
Seating Capacity: 238

6504
MESA PARK ARENA
100 Mesa Park Boulevard
Fellsmere, FL 32948
Phone: 954-777-4091
Fax: 954-777-4197
e-mail: barbara.kelleher@dot.state.fl.us
Web Site: www.dot.state.fl.us/emo/scenichwy/designated/indianriver/activities.htm
Management:
  Public Information Officer FDOT: Barbara Kelleher
  Director Transportation Operations: Hesham Ali
  Director Transportation Development: Gery O'Reilly
Mission: This 50-acre park features an amphitheater, festival area, Mesa Village and the motorsport arena. Mesa Park also provides a venue of events such as a Bluegrass/Fiddler's convention, a Valentine's Day Tea Dance, Cinco de Mayo Festival, Fourth of July Extravaganza, a Blues Festival and a Special Christmas Showcase.

6505
BAILEY CONCERT HALL
Broward College
3501 SW Davie Road
Fort Lauderdale, FL 33314
Phone: 95-420-1680
Fax: 954-424-3154
Toll-free: 888-475-6884
e-mail: tjones@broward.edu
Web Site: www.broward.cc.fl.us

6506
BROWARD CENTER FOR THE PERFORMING ARTS
201 SW Fifth Avenue
Fort Lauderdale, FL 33312
Mailing Address: 201 SW Fifth Avenue, Fort Lauderdale, Florida 33312
Phone: 954-522-5334
Fax: 954-468-3282
Toll-free: 800-564-9539
e-mail: BoxOffice@browardcenter.org
Web Site: www.browardcenter.org
Officers:
  Chair: George I. Platt
  Vice Chair: Anne Scherer
  Secretary: Barbara H. Jones
  Treasurer: Charles L. Palmer
Management:
  President: Mark Nerenhausen
  General Manager: Kelley Shanley
  Director of Production: Tim Lessig
Founded: 1991
Specialized Field: Series & Festivals; Dance; Instrumental Music; Musical Theater; Theatrical Group; Vocal Music
Status: Non-Profit, Professional
Type of Stage: Concert Stage
Seating Capacity: 2,700

6507
FORT LAUDERDALE STADIUM
Lockhart Stadium
1401 NW 55th Street
Fort Lauderdale, FL 33309
Phone: 954-828-4980
Fax: 305-938-4979
Web Site: www.ci.ftlaud.fl.us
Management:
  Stadium Manager: Vincent Gizzi
Founded: 1962

6508
PARKER PLAYHOUSE
707 NE 8th Street
PO Box 4603
Fort Lauderdale, FL 33304
Mailing Address: 707 NE 8th Street, Fort Lauderdale, FL 33304
Phone: 954-764-1441
Fax: 954-524-9952
e-mail: info@parkerplayhouse.com
Web Site: http://www.parkerplayhouse.com/
Founded: 1967
Status: Non-Profit, Professional
Paid Staff: 2
Seating Capacity: 1,200

6509
WAR MEMORIAL AUDITORIUM
800 NE 8th Street
Fort Lauderdale, FL 33301
Mailing Address: 800 NE 8th Street, Fort Lauderdale, FL 33304
Phone: 954-761-5380
Fax: 954-763-1769
Web Site: www.ci.ftlaud.fl.us/warmemorial.com
Management:
  Manager: Robert Stried
Founded: 1949
Seating Capacity: 2,110

6510
SQUITIERI STUDIO THEATRE
Florida Gulf Coast University
FGCU Arts Complex South
10501 FGCU Blvd
Fort Meyers, FL 33965-6565
Mailing Address: Phillips Center, 315 Hull Road, PO Box 112750, Gainesville,
Phone: 239-590-7268
e-mail: adouglas@performingarts.ufl.edu
Web Site: http://www.fgcu.edu/CAS/blackbox/
Officers:
  President: Bill Merwin
Management:
  Marketing Director: Amy Douglas
Mission: Theatre at Florida Gulf Coast University provides students with opportunities to experience performance and production as artists completing a major in theatre to prepare themselves for graduate study or professional work.
Founded: 1992
Specialized Field: Theater and dance
Type of Stage: Black Box
Seating Capacity: 120

6511
BARBARA B MANN PERFORMING ARTS HALL
13350 Edison Parkway
Fort Myers, FL 33919
Mailing Address: 13350 Edison Parkway, Fort Myers, FL 33919
Phone: 239-481-4849
Fax: 239-489-0326
Toll-free: 800-440-7469
Web Site: www.bbmannpah.com
Management:
  General Manager: Mary Bensel
  Director Marketing: Peg Welty
  Operations Manager: Eva Calhoun
  Technical Director: Robb McCoy
  Group Sales Manager: Lois Soscia
Mission: The Barbara B. Mann Performing Arts Hall countinues to improve the quality and accessiblity of touring broadway and star performing artists to the communities of Southwest Florida.
Founded: 1985
Specialized Field: Broadway; variety theatre
Paid Staff: 9
Volunteer Staff: 150
Paid Artists: 500
Affiliations: League of American Theatres & Producers; Florida Facility Managers; Southern Arts, APAP
Facility Category: Performing Arts Hall
Type of Stage: Non-Sprung
Stage Dimensions: 160'x47'
Seating Capacity: 1,753
Year Built: 1985
Year Remodeled: 1998

6512
FORT MYERS HARBORSIDE
1375 Monroe Street
Fort Myers, FL 33901
Mailing Address: P.O. Box 9204, Fort Myers, FL 33902
Phone: 239-321-8110
Fax: 239-344-5926
Web Site: www.fmharborside.com
Management:
  General Manager: Rose Bernal-Rundle
  Operations Manager: Lincoln Roberts
  Senior Staff Assistant: Jane Brant

FACILITIES / Florida

Technical Services Coordinator: Tim Scobee
Event Coordinator: Sue Robbins

6513
HARBORSIDE EVENT CENTER
Po Box 9204
Fort Myers, FL 33902
Mailing Address: 1375 Monroe Street, Fort Myers, FL 33901
Phone: 239-321-8110
Fax: 239-344-5926
Toll-free: 800-294-9516
e-mail: HarborsideSales@cityftmyers.com
Web Site: www.harborsideevents.com
Officers:
   Owner: Jim Harmon
Management:
   General Manager: Peter Koralewicz, rrundle@cityftmyers.com
   Assitant General Manager: Andrew Thompson, athompson@cityftmysers.com
   Operations Manager: Lincoln Roberts, lroberts@cityftmyers.com
Seating Capacity: 3200

6514
WILLIAM H HAMMOND STADIUM
Lee County Government Southwest Florida
2115 Second St.
Fort Myers, FL 33901
Mailing Address: 3410 Palm Beach Bl., Fort Myers, FL. 33916
Phone: 239-533-2111
Fax: 941-339-3333
Web Site: www.lee-county.com
Management:
   Director: John Yardbrough
   Manager: Ed McLntyre
Seating Capacity: 7,600

6515
WILLIAM R FRIZZELL CULTURAL CENTRE CLAIBORNE & NED FOULDS THEATRE
Lee County Alliance for the Arts
10091 McGregor Boulevard
Fort Myers, FL 33919
Phone: 239-939-2787
Fax: 239-939-0794
e-mail: administration@artinlee.org
Web Site: www.artinlee.org/visit/about-us/history-and-organization
Management:
   Executive Director: Lydia Black
Founded: 1975
Opened: 1985
Status: Non-Profit
Paid Staff: 5
Volunteer Staff: 2
Budget: $700,000
Performs At: Amphitheatre; Indoor theater; Studio space
Rental Contact: Jamie Golob

6516
SAINT LUCIE COUNTY
2300 Virginia Avenue
Fort Pierce, FL 34982
Mailing Address: 2300 Virginia Avenue, Fort Pierce, FL 34982
Phone: 772-462-1538
Fax: 772-462-1526
Web Site: www.stlucieco.gov
Management:
   Clerk of the Circuit Court: Joseph E. Smith
   Property Appraisal: Ken Pruitt
   Supervisor of Elections: Gertrude Walker
   Sheriff: Ken J. Mascara
   Tax Collector: Chris Craft
Seating Capacity: 4,000

6517
SUNRISE THEATRE
117 South Second Street
Fort Pierce, FL 34950
Phone: 772-461-4884
Fax: 772-461-8373
e-mail: exec@sunrisetheatre.com
Web Site: www.sunrisetheatre.com
Management:
   Executive Director: John Wilkes
   Techinical Director: Marty Petlock
   Public Relations & Dev Director: Anne W. Satterlee
   Marketing Director: Susan Hunt
   Marketing Assistant: Stephanie LaBella
Mission: Historic fully retsored theatre that presents touring broadway shows, full orchestras, comedy acts, ballet and symphony. Thetheatre is the main venue but there are more located with in it.
Seating Capacity: 1200

6518
ROSE AND ALFRED MINIACI PERFORMING ARTS CENTER ON THE NOVA SOUTHEASTERN UNIVERSITY
3100 Ray Ferrero Jr Blvd
Ft. Lauderdale, FL 33314
Mailing Address: 3100 Ray Ferrero Jr. Blvd., Ft. Lauderdale, Fl. 33314
Phone: 954-262-5480
Fax: 954-262-3809
e-mail: boxoffice@ticketflorida.com
Web Site: www.miniacipac.com
Management:
   Theatre Manager: Chris Henry
   Technical Director: Roger Predmore
   Event Manager: Ben Loeb
Mission: Our mission is to provide more cultural programming opportunities for Broward County residents and university students and faculty members.
Seating Capacity: 500

6519
HIPPODROME STATE THEATRE, INC.
25 SE 2nd Place
Gainesville, FL 32601
Mailing Address: 25 SE 2nd Place, Gainesville, FL 32601
Phone: 352-373-5968
Fax: 352-371-9130
e-mail: groupsales@thehipp.org
Web Site: www.thehipp.org
Management:
   Managing Director: Jessica Hurov
   Artistic Director: Lauren Caldwell
   Director of Operations: Nicole Nicole
   Artistic Associate Costume Designer: Marilyn A. Wall
   Information Systems Director: Rusty Salling
Mission: To explore the truth of human experience and the human spirit through the examination and presentation of dramatic work. Our purpose is to accomplish this through our commitment to create an artistic home.
Utilizes: Actors; AEA Actors; Artists-in-Residence; Choreographers; Collaborating Artists; Commissioned Composers; Commissioned Music; Dancers; Designers; Educators; Five Seasonal Concerts; Grant Writers; Guest Accompanists; Guest Artists; Guest Companies; Guest Conductors; Guest Designers; Guest Ensembles; Guest Lecturers; Guest Musical Directors; High School Drama; Instructors; Local Artists; Multi Collaborations; Music; Original Music Scores; Poets; Resident Professionals; Selected Students; Sign Language Translators; Soloists; Touring Companies; Visual Arts
Founded: 1973
Specialized Field: Theatre
Status: Professional; Nonprofit
Paid Staff: 38
Volunteer Staff: 63
Budget: $243 million
Income Sources: Ticket sales; Concession sales; Corporate support, Federal, State and local grants
Season: Year round
Performs At: Hippodrome
Annual Attendance: 167,000
Facility Category: Live stage and movie theatre
Type of Stage: Thrust
Seating Capacity: 266
Year Built: 1911
Year Remodeled: 1980
Architect: $1.5 Million
Rental Contact: General Manager Mark Sexton
Organization Type: Performing; Touring; Resident; Educational; Sponsoring

6520
PHILLIPS CENTER
University of Florida
Performing Arts
3201 Hull Road, PO Box 112750
Gainesville, FL 32611-2750
Mailing Address: Curtis M. Phillips Center, 315 Hull Road, PO Box 112750, Gai
Phone: 352-392-1900
Fax: 352-392-3775
Toll-free: 800-905-2787
e-mail: adouglas@performingarts.ufl.edu
Web Site: http://ww
Officers:
   Director: Michael Blachly
   Assistant Director: Elizabeth Auer
   Accounting Coordinator: J.A. Lopez
   Human Resources/Accounting: Vivian Royer
   Financial Assistant: Derek Wohlust
Management:
   Development Associate: Katherine Davies
   Development Assistant: Ashley Clarke
   Box Office Manager: Robbie Stevens
   Assistant Box Office Manager: James Kersey
   Operations Director: Matt Cox
Mission: To provide an unparalleled experience where the very best performing artists create and share knowledge to serve the students, residents and visitors to North Central Florida.
Founded: 1992
Opened: 1992
Specialized Field: Theatre
Type of Stage: Proscenium
Seating Capacity: 1,754
Architect: Flad & Associates

6521
SAMUEL P HARN MUSEUM OF ART
University of Florida
3259 Hull Road
Gainesville, FL 32611-2700

FACILITIES / Florida

Mailing Address: PO Box 112700, Gainesville, Florida 32611-2700
Phone: 352-392-9826
Fax: 352-392-3892
e-mail: chale@harn.ufl.edu
Web Site: www.harn.ufl.edu
Management:
- Director: Rebecca M Nagy Ph.D
- Marketing/Public Relations Director: Tami Wroath
- Assistant to the Director: Coral Stimac
- Marketing and Public Relations Coor: Megan Pugh
- Director of Finance and Operations: Mary Yawn

Mission: The Samuel P. Harn Museum of Art promotes the power of the arts to inspire and educate people and enrich their lives. To this purpose the museum builds and maintains exemplary art collections and produces a wide variety of challenging, innovative exhibitions and stimulating educational programs. In addition, the Mary Ann Harn Cofrin Pavilion has 11,620 square feet of exhibition gallery and 7,800 square feet of cafe and curatorial spaces.
Founded: 1987
Specialized Field: Art Museum
Status: Non-Profit, Non-Professional
Paid Staff: 45

6522
STEPHEN C O'CONNELL CENTER
University of Florida
250 Gale Lemerand Dr.
Gainesville, FL 32611
Mailing Address: PO Box 115850 Gainesville, FL 32611-5850
Phone: 352-392-5500
Fax: 352-392-7106
e-mail: scoc-marketing@ufl.edu
Web Site: www.oconnellcenter.ufl.edu
Management:
- Director: Lynda Reinhart
- Associate Director: Renee Musson
- Director of Operations: Jeremy Cynkar
- Assitant Director of Production: Kevin Burgess
- Assistant Director: David Lucier

Founded: 1980
Specialized Field: Entertainment - Concets-Indoor Sports-Shows
Status: Non-Profit, Non-Professional
Paid Staff: 12
Budget: $2.3 million
Performs At: Multi-Purpose Arena
Facility Category: Multi-Purpose/Arena
Type of Stage: Portable
Seating Capacity: 12,000
Year Built: 1980
Year Remodeled: 1998
Cost: $16.5 million
Rental Contact: Associate Director Darius Dunn

6523
YOUNG CIRCLE PARK AND BANDSHELL
Art and Cultural center of hollywood
City of Hollywood
P.O. Box 229045
Hollywood, FL 33022-9045
Mailing Address: P. O. Box 229045, Hollywood, FL 33022-9045
Phone: 954-921-3500
Fax: 305-921-3233
e-mail: alesh@artandculturecenter.org
Web Site: http://www.hollywoodfl.org/parks_rec/Cultloc.htm
Management:
- Director: Steeve Joseph

Deputy Director, Operations: Francois Domond
Deputy Director, Finance: Mark Moore
Assistant Director for Engineering: Jitendra Patel
Assistant Director for Engineering: Raelin Storey
Specialized Field: Theater and musicals

6524
HOMESTEAD SPORTS COMPLEX
1601 SE 28th Avenue
Homestead, FL 33030
Mailing Address: CURRENTLY VACANT
Phone: 305-247-1801
Fax: 305-246-3200
Management:
- Director Parks/Recreation: Alan Ricke

Founded: 1991

6525
EVERBANK FIELD
One Alltel Stadium Place
Jacksonville, FL 32202
Mailing Address: One EverBank Field Drive, Jacksonville, FL 32202
Phone: 904-633-6100
Fax: 904-633-6113
Web Site: www.jaguars.com/alltelstadium
Management:
- President: Bob Downey
- Managing Director: Tracy Evans
- General Manager: Robert Downing

Founded: 1995
Status: Non-Profit, Professional
Seating Capacity: 80,000
Year Built: 1995
Resident Groups: Home to the Jacksonville Jaguars

6526
FLORIDA NATIONAL PAVILION
Metropolitan Park
1410 E Adams Street
Jacksonville, FL 32202
Mailing Address: Metropolitan Park, 1410 Gator Bowl Blvd., Jacksonville, Flor
Phone: 904-630-0837
Fax: 904-630-0538
e-mail: cgoodell@coj.net
Web Site: http://www.coj.net/Departments/Recreation+and+Community+

6527
FLORIDA THEATRE
128 East Forsyth Street
Suite 300
Jacksonville, FL 32202
Mailing Address: 128 East Forsyth Street, Suite 300, Jacksonville FL 32202
Phone: 904-355-2787
Fax: 904-358-1874
e-mail: info@floridatheatre.com
Web Site: www.floridatheatre.com
Officers:
- President: Numa C. Saisselin
- Chairman: Dave Henry
- Vice Chair: Kelly Diaz
- Treasurer: Kellie Hardee
- Secretary: Vince McCormack

Management:
- House Manager: Jennifer Dobrowoiski
- Finance Director: Tracy Duffy
- Director of Development: Holly Hammond
- Interim Director of Marketing: Cheryl Hays

Founded: 1927
Status: Non-Profit, Professional

Paid Staff: 13
Annual Attendance: 250,000
Type of Stage: Flexible

6528
GATOR BOWL
1 Alltel Stadium Place
Jacksonville, FL 32202
Mailing Address: One Gator Bowl Blvd., Jacksonville, FL 32202
Phone: 904-690-0335
Fax: 904-633-6113
e-mail: erik@gatorbowl.com
Web Site: www.gatorbowl.com
Officers:
- President/CEO: Richard M. Catlett
- Executive Vice-President/CAO: Cheri O'Neill
- Vice President/CFO: Robert Leverock

Management:
- Director of Marketing: Katie Cox
- Vice President of Marketing: Erik Dellenback
- Committee Relations Manager: LeAnne Crabtree
- Ticket Manager: Bret Guice
- Events Manager: Tom Norton

Mission: The Gator Bowl Association's mission is to provide Northeast Florida with the very best in college athletics and related activities in order to maximize positive impact on the area's economy, national image and community pride.
Founded: 1945

6529
TIMES-UNION CENTER FOR THE PERFORMING ARTS
JaxEvents.com
300 West Water Street
Jacksonville, FL 32202
Phone: 904-630-3900
Fax: 904-633-6190
e-mail: sbartlo@smgjax.com
Web Site: www.jaxevents.com
Management:
- General Manager: Bill McConnell
- Arena Director & AGM: W. Zane Collings
- Event Manager: Jamie Nice
- Operations/Production Manager: Lyle Klemmt
- Box Office Manager: Sandy Avery

Mission: 3 venue building supporting both visual and performing arts

6530
UNF ARENA
University of North Florida
1 UNF Drive
Jacksonville, FL 32224
Mailing Address: 4567 St. Johns Bluff Road, South Jacksonville, FL 32224-2675
Phone: 904-620-1000
Fax: 904-620-1705
Web Site: www.unf.edu/groups/osprod/
Officers:
- Arena Manager: Becky Purser
- Programming Coordinator: Lindsay Bryant

Management:
- Director: John Chwalisz
- Assistant Director: Zahni Thuzar
- Graphics Program Assistant: Stormy Goodman
- Office Program Assistant: Katie Jackson
- Event Coordinator: Vivian Taylor

Facility Category: Sports Arena
Seating Capacity: 6,000

FACILITIES / Florida

6531
UNIVERSITY OF NORTH FLORIDA FINE ARTS CENTER
The Lazzara Performance Hall
1 UNF Drive
Jacksonville, FL 32224
Phone: 904-620-1000
Fax: 904-620-1897
e-mail: unfce@unf.edu
Web Site: www.unf.edu
Management:
  Director: George Androuin, gandroui@unf.edu
Mission: The center combines world class performing arts with space for up and coming artists and students
Seating Capacity: 1300

6532
VETERANS MEMORIAL ARENA
JaxEvents.com
300 A. Philip Randolph Boulevard
Jacksonville, FL 32202
Mailing Address: 300 A. Philip Randolph Boulevard, Jacksonville, FL 32202
Phone: 904-630-3900
Fax: 904-630-3913
e-mail: rtimothy@coj.net
Web Site: www.jaxevents.com
Management:
  General Manager: Bill McConnell
  Event Manager: Jamie Nice
  Operations/Production Manager: Lyle Klemmt
  Box Office Manager: Sandy Avery
  Director of Sales & Marketing: Alex Alston
Status: For-Profit, Professional
Seating Capacity: 10,276

6533
TENNIS CENTER AT CRANDON PARK
Miami-Dade County
6747 Crandon Boulevard
Key Biscayne, FL 33149
Mailing Address: 7300 Crandon Blvd, Key Biscayne, FL 33149
Phone: 305-361-5421
Fax: 305-365-2327
e-mail: parks@miamidade.gov
Web Site: www.miamidade.gov/parks/crandon.asp
Management:
  Financial/Grant Manager: Jesus Guerra
Seating Capacity: 14,000

6534
SOUTH FLORIDA CENTER FOR THE ARTS
P.O. Box 2540
Key Largo, FL 33037
Mailing Address: P.O. Box 2540, Key Largo, Florida 33037
Phone: 350-304-9059
Fax: 305-664-2090
e-mail: info@sfca-arts.org
Web Site: www.sfca-arts.tix.com

6535
RED BARN THEATRE
319 Duval Street (rear)
Rear Key West
Key West, FL 33040
Mailing Address: Box 707 Key West, Fl. 33041
Phone: 305-296-9911
Fax: 305-293-3035
Toll-free: 866-870-9911
Web Site: www.redbarntheatre.com
Officers:
  President: Kim Works
  Vice President: Michele Grahl
  Secretary: Mimi McDonald
  Treasurer: Lisa Van Gilder
Status: Non-Profit
Seating Capacity: 88

6536
TENNESSEE WILLIAMS THEATRE
5901 College Road
Key West, FL 33040
Mailing Address: 5901 College Road, Key West, FL 33040
Phone: 305-296-1520
Fax: 305-292-3725
e-mail: info@twstages.com
Web Site: www.tennesseewilliamstheatre.com
Officers:
  Chair: Ann Reynolds
  Treasurer: Bryan Green
Management:
  Executive Director: Frank Wood
  Technical Director: Matthew Rawls
  Resident Lighting Designer: Matthew Rawls
  Accounting Manager: Mary Hunter
  House Management: Jim Cameron
Founded: 1977
Specialized Field: Performing Arts
Status: Non-Profit, Professional
Paid Staff: 6
Affiliations: Performing Arts Centers for Key West
Rental Contact: Rebecca Tomlinson

6537
OSCEOLA CENTER FOR THE ARTS
2411 East Irlo Bronson Highway
Kissimmee, FL 34744
Mailing Address: 2411 E. Irlo Bronson Hwy., Kissimmee, FL 34744
Phone: 407-846-6257
Fax: 407-846-7902
Web Site: www.ocfta.com
Officers:
  Chief Executive Officer: Brandon Arrington
  Chief Operating Officer: Jeremiah Krivinchuk
  Front Office Manager: Jennifer Panzella
Management:
  Youth Theater Manager: Stephanie Day
  Accounting: Norma Shelton
  Technical Department: Erin Mohr
  Technical Department: Matt Mundell
  Technical Department: Derek Parkins
Mission: To promote, cultivate and foster interest and participation in the arts by providing affordable and accessible programs and facilities that encourage artistc expression in the diverse community we serve.
Founded: 1963
Specialized Field: Visual Arts; Music; Craft; Local Art Council
Status: Non-Profit, Non-Professional
Paid Staff: 6
Volunteer Staff: 150
Paid Artists: 240
Non-paid Artists: 125
Budget: $580,000
Performs At: Theatre; Tours
Affiliations: Artexhibits
Facility Category: Art Center
Seating Capacity: 250
Year Built: 1913
Year Remodeled: 2002

6538
OSCELOA COUNTY STADIUM & SPORTS COMPLEX
631 Heritage Park Way
Kissimmee, FL 34744
Phone: 321-697-3201
Fax: 407-847-6237
Web Site: www.osceolastadium.com/#sthash.TTXMrOsS.dpbs
Management:
  Facility Superintendent: Erik Anderson
Mission: Florida home of the Houston Astros.
Seating Capacity: 5,200

6539
WALT DISNEY WIDE WORLD OF SPORTS STADIUM
700 Victory Way
Lake Buena Vista, FL 34747-1000
Phone: 407-939-7810
Fax: 407-363-7000
e-mail: wdw.disney.sports.travel@disney.com
Web Site: www.disneyworldsports.com
Management:
  President: Al Weiss
  Vice President Walt Disney Sports: Reggie Williams
  Director/Event Programming: Mike Millay
  Manager Sports Programming: John Bisignano
  CEO: Michael Eisner
Founded: 1998
Status: For-Profit, Professional

6540
DUNCAN THEATRE
Palm Beach Community College
4200 Congress Avenue
Lake Worth, FL 33461
Mailing Address: 4200 Congress Avenue, Lake Worth, FL 33461
Phone: 561-868-3350
Fax: 561-868-3317
Toll-free: 866-576-7222
e-mail: echeverh@palmbeachstate.edu
Web Site: www.palmbeachstate.edu
Management:
  Theatre Manager: Mark Alexander
Founded: 1986
Status: Non-Profit/Professional/Collegiate
Paid Staff: 6
Type of Stage: Proscenium
Seating Capacity: 720

6541
BRANSCOMB MEMORIAL AUDITORIUM
Florida Southern College
111 Lake Hollingsworth Drive
Lakeland, FL 33801
Mailing Address: 111 Lake Hollingsworth Drive, Lakeland, FL 33801-5698
Phone: 863-680-4111
Fax: 813-680-3758
Toll-free: 800-274-4131
e-mail: campusweb@flsouthern.edu
Web Site: www.flsouthern.edu
Officers:
  President: Anne B. Kerr
  Chief Executive Officer: Ed Goodemotte
Management:
  President: Anne Kerr
  Executive Director: Anthony Harris
  Artistic Director: Robert MacDonald
  Office Manager: Cathy Criswell

Founded: 1959
Status: Non-Profit
Paid Staff: 4
Annual Attendance: 2,000
Type of Stage: Proscenium
Seating Capacity: 1,700

6542
BUCKNER THEATRE
Florida Southern College
111 Lake Hollings Worth Drive
Lakeland, FL 33801
Mailing Address: 111 Lake Hollingsworth Drive, Lakeland, FL 33801-5698
Phone: 863-680-4111
Fax: 863-680-4120
Web Site: www.flsouthern.edu
Officers:
    President: Anne B. Kerr
    Chief Executive Officer: Ed Goodemotte
Management:
    Office Manager: Kity Oelker
    Department Chair: James Beck
    Costumer/Faculty: Mary Albright
    Office Manager: Cathy Criswell
Status: Student Theater
Paid Staff: 3
Budget: $30,000
Income Sources: College/Academic Budget
Affiliations: Florida Southern College
Facility Category: Line Theatre Production
Year Built: 1971
Year Remodeled: 2000

6543
LAKELAND CENTER
Lakeland Center
701 West Lime Street
Lakeland, FL 33815
Mailing Address: 701 West Lime Street, Lakeland, FL 33815
Phone: 863-834-8100
Fax: 863-834-8101
e-mail: allen.johnson@lakelandgov.net
Web Site: www.thelakelandcenter.com
Management:
    Executive Director: Mike LaPan
    Assistant Director/Booking Director: Scott Sloman
    Executive Administrative Assistant: Lindsay Hansen
    Receptionist: Peggy LaChance
    Director of Sales: Lori Powell
Founded: 1880
Seating Capacity: 10,000

6544
KING CENTER FOR THE PERFORMING ARTS
Eatern Florida State College
3865 N. Wickham Road
Melbourne, FL 32935
Phone: 321-242-2219
Fax: 321-433-5817
e-mail: sjanicki@kingcenter.com
Web Site: www.kingcenter.com
Officers:
    Chairperson: Alan H Landman
    Vice Chairperson: Dewey L Harris
    EFSC President: James H Richey
    BCC President:
Founded: 1988
Paid Staff: 10
Volunteer Staff: 400
Type of Stage: Proscenium
Seating Capacity: 2,001

6545
MELBOURNE AUDITORIUM
625 East Hibiscus Blvd.
Melbourne, FL 32901
Phone: 321-674-5700
Fax: 321-953-6287
e-mail: auditorium@melbourneflorida.org
Web Site: www.melbourneflorida.org
Management:
    chairman: Al Beyer
    City Engineer: Jenni Lamb
    Planning and EconomicDevelopment Di: Cindy Dittmer
    Recording Secretary: Angela Howard
Founded: 1964
Specialized Field: Civic Events; Dance; Instrumental Music; Musical Theatre; Theatrical Group; Vocal Music
Status: Non-Profit
Paid Staff: 12

6546
AMERICAN AIRLINES ARENA
601 Biscayne Boulevard
Miami, FL 33132
Phone: 786-777-1000
Fax: 786-777-4080
e-mail: guestservices@heat.com
Web Site: www.aaarena.com
Management:
    Director of Human Resources: Sarah Moran
    Staffing Coordinator: Octavia Lake
    General Manager: Alex M Diaz
Founded: 1999
Status: For-Profit, Professional
Paid Staff: 250
Paid Artists: 20
Seating Capacity: 20,000

6547
DADE COUNTY AUDITORIUM
2901 W Flagler St
Miami, FL 33131
Phone: 305-547-5414
Fax: 305-541-7782
Web Site: www.orlando@miamidade.gov
Management:
    General Manager: Orlando Castellano
    Asst. General Manager: Patricia Arbeluez
Founded: 1951
Paid Staff: 11
Budget: $1,000,000
Performs At: Performing Arts Theatre
Affiliations: IAAM; FPPC
Annual Attendance: 125,000
Facility Category: Fixed Seat Theatre
Type of Stage: Proscenium
Stage Dimensions: 60'X40'
Seating Capacity: 2,372
Year Built: 1951
Year Remodeled: 2009

6548
GOLDEN PANTHER SPORTSPLEX
Florida International University
Room 255 University Park
Miami, FL 33199
Mailing Address: Florida International University, Golden Panther SportsPlex
Phone: 305-348-2756
Fax: 305-348-2963
Web Site: www.fiu.edu/
Management:
    Athletic Director: Jose Sotolongo
    Chairman: Albert Maury
    Vice Chairman: Michael M Adler

6549
GUSMAN CENTER FOR THE PERFORMING ARTS
174 E Flagler Street
Miami, FL 33131
Phone: 305-374-2444
Fax: 305-374-0303
e-mail: mwharton@gusmancenter.org
Web Site: www.gusmancenter.org
Management:
    Executive Director: Robert Geitner
    Technical Manager: Issac Taylor
    House Manager: Lucia Cosenza
    Box Office Manager: Angela McCall
Founded: 1970
Specialized Field: Series and Festivals; Dance; Instrumental Music; Musical Theatre; Theatrical Group; Vocal Music
Status: For-Profit, Professional
Paid Staff: 5
Seating Capacity: 1,700

6550
JAMES L KNIGHT CENTER
400 2nd Avenue
Miami, FL 33131
Phone: 305-372-4633
Fax: 305-350-7910
e-mail: info@jlkc.com
Web Site: www.jlkc.com
Management:
    General Manager: Bob Murray
    Box Office Manager: Carlos M. Djaz
    Senior Sales Manager: Kate James
    Director of Finance/HR Manager: Jackie Rowley
    Senior Convention Sales Manager: Amy Issersohn
Founded: 1982
Specialized Field: Music; Theatre; Dance

6551
MIAMI ARENA
701 Arena Boulevard
Suite 415
Miami, FL 33136
Mailing Address: DEMOLISHED IN 2008
Phone: 305-530-4400
Fax: 305-530-4429
Web Site: www.miamiarena.com
Management:
    President: Jim Jenkins
    Assistant Director Entertainment: Brenda Carter
Founded: 1989
Specialized Field: Concerts; Family Shows; Exhibitions
Status: Non-Profit, Professional
Paid Staff: 30
Facility Category: Arena
Seating Capacity: 15,500
Year Built: 1986
Rental Contact: Mike Carr

6552
ORANGE BOWL STADIUM
1501 NW 3rd Street
Suite 415
Miami, FL 33125

FACILITIES / Florida

Phone: 305-643-7100
Fax: 305-643-7115
Web Site: www.orangebowlstadium.com
Management:
   President: Ileana Gomez
Founded: 1937
Specialized Field: Bowling; Sports
Status: Professional
Seating Capacity: 82,000

6553
PERFORMING ARTS CENTER OF GREATER MIAMI FOUNDATION
1300 Biscayne Boulevard
Miami, FL 33132
Phone: 786-468-2000
Fax: 786-468-2001
e-mail: info@carnivalcenter.org
Web Site: www.pacfmiami.org
Officers:
   Executive Director/CEO: Tom Tomlinson
Management:
   President/CEO: Michael C Hardy
   Chief Of Staff: Valerie Riles-Robinson
Status: Non-Profit, Non-Professional
Paid Staff: 8

6554
JACKIE GLEASON THEATER
1700 Washington Avenue
Miami Beach, FL 33139
Phone: 305-673-7300
Fax: 305-938-2560
Web Site: www.gleasontheater.com
Management:
   Managing Director: Mitchell Morales
Founded: 1950
Status: For-Profit, Professional
Paid Staff: 20
Annual Attendance: 185,000
Type of Stage: Proscenium
Seating Capacity: 2,705

6555
MOBILE CIVIC CENTER - EXPOSITION HALL
401 Civic Center Drive
Mobile, FL 33602
Mailing Address: 401 Civic Center Drive, Mobile, AL 36602-0204
Phone: 251-208-7261
Fax: 334-208-7551
e-mail: mlmccrory@mobilecivicctr.com
Web Site: www.mobilecivicctr.com
Management:
   Director of Operations: Joe Delaronde
   Stage Manager: Paul Buchanan
   Event Coordinator: Cristin Bolt
   Director Of Sales: Cheryl Gee
   Parking Manager: Mike Smitherman
Mission: Expo Hall is the Mobile Civic Center's multi-use facility. The portable stage and public address system, along with retractable seating, allow for maximum flexibility in event planning. Expo Hall is the perfect venue for exhibits, conventions, dances and sporting events.
Specialized Field: exhibits, conventions, dances and sporting events
Type of Stage: Concert Stage; Portable
Seating Capacity: 3,000

6556
MOBILE CIVIC CENTER - THEATRE
401 Civic Center Drive
Mobile, FL 33602
Mailing Address: 401 Civic Center Drive, Mobile, AL 36602-0204
Phone: 251-208-7261
Fax: 334-208-7551
e-mail: mlmccrory@mobilecivicctr.com
Web Site: www.mobilecivicctr.com
Management:
   Director of Operations: Joe Delaronde
   Stage Manager: Paul Buchanan
   Event Coordinator: Cristin Bolt
   Director Of Sales: Cheryl Gee
   Parking Manager: Mike Smitherman
Mission: Mobile Civic Center Theater is a comfortably elegant location for performances ranging from solo artists to symphony orchestras.
Specialized Field: Concerts
Seating Capacity: 1,940

6557
MONTICELLO OPERA HOUSE, INC.
185 West Washington Street
PO Box 518
Monticello, FL 32345
Mailing Address: PO Box 518 Monticello, FL 32345
Phone: 904-997-4242
Fax: 904-997-7142
e-mail: office@monticellooperahouse.org
Web Site: www.monticellofloridaoperahouse.com
Officers:
   Chair: Denise Vogelgesang
   Vice Chair: Ron Cichon
   Secretary: Bill Hatcher
   Treasurer: Linda Schrader
   Treasurer: Kevin Carr

6558
NAPLES PHILHARMONIC
5833 Pelican Bay Boulevard
Naples, FL 34108-2740
Phone: 239-597-1900
Fax: 239-597-7856
Toll-free: 800-597-1900
e-mail: info@thephil.org
Web Site: www.thephil.org
Officers:
   Chairman of the Board: Ned C. Lautenbach
   CEO and President: Kathleen Van Bergen
   Senior Executive Assistant to CEO a: Dianne Sponseller
   Chief Advancement Officer: Mary Deissler
   Assistant to CAO: Crystal Diggs
Management:
   Event Services Manager: Kristen Carlson
   Assistant Cafe Supervisor: Karen Gelinas
   Event Services Supervisor: Erin Perez
   Senior Major Gifts Officer: Mary Frank Madera
   Assistant Annual Fund Manager: Kelly Colligan
Mission: To enlighten, educate and entertain people of alla ges and backgrounds in Southwest Florida by presenting the very best of the visual and performing arts.
Founded: 1989
Opened: 1989
Seating Capacity: 1,421

6559
PASCO SCHOOLS CENTER FOR THE ARTS AT RIVER RIDGE
11646 Town Center Road
New Port Richey, FL 34654
Phone: 727-774-7386
Fax: 727-774-7389
Web Site: rrhs.pasco.k12.fl.us/theater/cfa_welcome.html
Management:
   Theater Director: Thomas J. Gale
   Office and Ticketing Manager: Faith Brooks
   House Technician: William Richardson
Performs At: Auditorium

6560
ATLANTIC CENTER FOR THE ARTS
1414 Art Center Avenue
New Smyrna Beach, FL 32168
Phone: 386-427-6975
Fax: 386-427-5669
Toll-free: 800-393-6975
e-mail: program@atlanticcenterforthearts.org
Web Site: www.atlanticcenterforthearts.org
Management:
   Residency Director: Nick Conroy
   Marketing and Membership Director: Kathryn Peterson
   Co-Executive Director: Nancy Lowden Norman
   Co-Executive Director: Jim Frost
   Gallery Director: Meghan Martin
Utilizes: Artists-in-Residence; Choreographers; Collaborations; Filmmakers; Fine Artists; Guest Artists; Guest Companies; Multi Collaborations; Playwrights; Touring Companies
Founded: 1977
Specialized Field: Florida; National; All disciplines
Status: Non-Profit, Professional
Paid Staff: 14
Volunteer Staff: 15
Budget: $1 million
Income Sources: Grants; Donations; Fundraisers
Annual Attendance: 250
Facility Category: 5 studios
Type of Stage: Black Box
Year Built: 1996
Rental Contact: Frankie Robert

6561
ARTS CENTER
Okaloosa Walton College
100 College Boulevard
Niceville, FL 32578
Phone: 850-678-5111
Fax: 850-729-5286
Toll-free: 888-838-2787
Web Site: www.owc.edu/arts
Management:
   Executive Director: Clifford Herron

6562
LEE CIVIC CENTER
11831 Bayshore Road
North Fort Myers, FL 33917
Phone: 239-543-8368
Fax: 239-543-4110
Web Site: www.leeciviccenter.com
Management:
   General Manager: Alta Mosley
   Operations Manager: Simon Train
Seating Capacity: 7,800

FACILITIES / Florida

6563
LEE CIVIC CENTER - SMALL THEATER
11831 Bayshore Road
North Fort Myers, FL 33917
Phone: 239-543-8368
Fax: 239-543-4110
Web Site: www.leeciviccenter.com
Seating Capacity: 7,800

6564
LITTMAN THEATER & CONFERENCE CENTER
17011 NE 19th Avenue
North Miami Beach, FL 33162
Phone: 305-787-6005
Fax: 305-787-6037
e-mail: info@littmantheater.com
Web Site: www.littmantheater.com

6565
BLACK BOX
University of Central Florida
UCF Conservatory Theatre, UCF Campus
4000 Central Florida Blvd.
Orlando, FL 32826
Phone: 407-823-2862
Web Site: www.cas.ucf.edu/theatre
Officers:
  Interim Chair: Diane Chase
  Interim Associate Chair: Joseph Rosnock
Management:
  Interim Artistic Director: Kate Ingram
Mission: The UCF Conservatory Theatre seeks to develop theatre artists of the highest quality. We provide our students with the training, education, and experiences necessary for the successful pursuit of professional theatre careers
Specialized Field: Theatre
Type of Stage: Black Box
Seating Capacity: 200

6566
BLACK BOX THEATER
Valencia Community College
East Campus, 701 North Econlockhatchee Trail
Orlando, FL 32825
Mailing Address: P.O. BOX 3028, Orlando, Florida 32802-3028
Phone: 407-299-5000
Fax: 407-277-0621
Web Site: www.valenciacc.edu

6567
BOB CARR PERFORMING ARTS CENTER
401 W Livingston St,
Orlando, FL 03280
Phone: 407-246-4262
Fax: 407-849-2329
e-mail: sharon.clayton@cityoforlando.net
Web Site: www.orlandocentroplex.com
Management:
  Director: Allan Johnson
  Deputy Director: Jon Dorman
  Box Office Manager: Sharon Clayton
  Advertising/Promotions Manager: Tanya Bowley
Mission: This fully functional theatre/concert hall features continental style seating for 2518. It's acoustics and sound capabilities make it ideal for concerts, Broadway presentations, the Symphony, Ballet and Opera as well as a business conference or general session.
Founded: 1926
Status: For-Profit, Non-Professional
Paid Staff: 6
Type of Stage: Proscenium

6568
MAIN STAGE
University of Central Florida
UCF Conservatory Theatre, UCF Campus
4000 Central Florida Blvd.
Orlando, FL 32826
Phone: 407-823-2862
Web Site: www.cas.ucf.edu/theatre
Officers:
  Interim Chair: Diane Chase
  Interim Associate Chair: Joseph Rosnock
Management:
  Interim Artistic Director: Kate Ingram
Mission: The UCF Conservatory Theatre seeks to develop theatre artists of the highest quality. We provide our students with the training, education, and experiences necessary for the successful pursuit of professional theatre careers
Specialized Field: Theatre
Type of Stage: Proscenium
Orchestra Pit: y

6569
ORANGE COUNTY CONVENTION CENTER
9400 Universal Boulevard
Orlando, FL 32819
Mailing Address: P.O. Box 691509, Orlando, FL 32869-1509
Phone: 407-685-9800
Toll-free: 800-345-9845
e-mail: Info@occc.net
Web Site: www.occc.net
Officers:
  Chief Financial Officer: Kris Shoemaker
Management:
  Executive Director: Kathie Canning
  Deputy General Manager: Yulita Osuba
  Deputy General Manager: Jan Addison
  Guest & Community Relations Manager: Lex Veech
  Security Manager: Greg Forehead
Utilizes: New Productions
Founded: 1996
Status: For-Profit, Professional
Income Sources: Conventions, Tradeshows, Seminars/Workshops, Tourist Development Tax
Affiliations: Orange County Government
Facility Category: Performance Auditorium
Type of Stage: Performance Stage with Dock Access
Stage Dimensions: 26'x145'5x49'6"""'
Seating Capacity: 2,643
Year Built: 1983
Year Remodeled: 1996
Rental Contact: Sales Assistant Willie Nelson

6570
ORLANDO CENTROPLEX
600 W Amelia Street
Orlando, FL 32801
Phone: 407-849-2000
Fax: 407-849-2329
Web Site: www.orlandocentroplex.com
Management:
  Director: Allan Johnson
  Deputy Director: Bill Becker
  Events Manager: Michael Thompson
  Convention Sales/Booking: Robin R Handlan
Status: For-Profit, Non-Professional
Seating Capacity: 17,500
Year Built: 1989

6571
AMWAY ARENA
Orlando Centroplex
600 W Amelia Street
Orlando, FL 32801
Mailing Address: CLOSED SEPTEMBER 30, 2010
Phone: 407-849-2000
Fax: 407-849-2329
Web Site: www.orlandocentroplex.com
Management:
  Director: Allen Johnson
  Concessions Manager: Jim Breig
  Deputy Director: Jon Dorman
  Business Manager: Cindy Mitchum
Founded: 1989
Status: For-Profit, Professional
Paid Staff: 60
Seating Capacity: 17,320

6572
UCF ARENA
12777 Gemini Blvd N
PO Box 161500
Orlando, FL 32816
Mailing Address: PO Box 161500
Phone: 407-823-3070
Fax: 407-823-0248
Web Site: www.ucfarena.com
Management:
  General Manager: Brian Hixenbaugh
  Director Of Marketing: Julian Bowman
  Chief Engineer: Robbie Balenger
  Event Manager: Ryan Fitzgerald
Founded: 1991
Status: For-Profit, Non-Professional
Seating Capacity: 10,000
Year Built: 2007

6573
UNIVERSITY THEATRE
University of Central Florida
UCF Conservatory Theatre, UCF Campus
Orlando, FL 32816-1500
Phone: 407-823-2862
Web Site: www.cas.ucf.edu/theatre
Officers:
  Interim Chair: Diane Chase
  Interim Associate Chair: Joseph Rosnock
Management:
  General Manager: Brian Hixenbaugh
  Assistant General Manager: Lavar Smith
  Operations Manager: Mike Terrell
  McDade: Eric McDade
  Event Manager: Ryan Fitzgerald
Mission: The UCF Conservatory Theatre seeks to develop theatre artists of the highest quality. We provide our students with the training, education, and experiences necessary for the successful pursuit of professional theatre careers
Specialized Field: Musical Concerts
Type of Stage: Concert
Seating Capacity: 867
Year Built: 1920

6574
VALENCIA COLLEGE PERFORMING ARTS CENTER
PO Box 3028
Orlando, FL 32802-302
Mailing Address: P.O. BOX 3028, Orlando, Florida 32802-3028
Phone: 407-299-5000

FACILITIES / Florida

Fax: 407-277-0621
e-mail: alapietra@valenciacc.edu
Web Site: www.valenciacc.edu
Management:
  Chair of Performing Arts: Ann Stichler
Founded: 1967

6575
FLAGLER AUDITORIUM
5500 East Hwy 100
Palm Coast, FL 32164
Phone: 386-437-7547
Fax: 386-437-7551
Toll-free: 866-352-4537
e-mail: flaglerpromotion@aol.com
Web Site: www.flaglerauditorium.org
Officers:
  President: Jack Marcussen
  President Elect: Charles Ebel
  Vice President: Joel Schwalb
  Secretary: Sandra Madden
  Treasurer: Beverly Alleman
Management:
  Executive Director: Lisa McDevitt
Mission: Provide a favorable, healthy climate for the simulation, promotion and growth of culture and the arts.
Founded: 1989
Status: Non-Profit, Professional
Paid Staff: 6
Type of Stage: Concert Stage
Seating Capacity: 1,000

6576
MARINA CIVIC CENTER
8 Harrison Ave.
Panama City, FL 32401
Phone: 850-763-4696
Fax: 850-785-5165
Web Site: www.marinaciviccenter.com
Management:
  General Manager/Booking: Chris Cockrill
  Executive Director: Jennifer Jones
  House Manager: Carol Cheshire
  Technical Director: Shawn Perry
Seating Capacity: 2,500

6577
PENSACOLA BAY CENTER
201 E. Gregory St.
Pensacola, FL 32502
Phone: 850-432-0800
Fax: 850-432-1707
e-mail: webmaster@pensacolaciviccenter.com
Web Site: www.pensacolaciviccenter.com
Management:
  General Manager: Cyndee Pennington
  Assistant General Manager: Casey Sparks
  Box Office Manager: Steven Jette
  Box Office Assistant Manager: Tina Burnham
Founded: 1985
Paid Staff: 219
Facility Category: Arena
Seating Capacity: 10,000

6578
PENSACOLA JUNIOR COLLEGE PERFORMING ARTS CENTER
Music and Drama Department
1000 College Boulevard
Pensacola, FL 32504
Phone: 850-484-1000
Fax: 850-484-1835
Toll-free: 888-897-3605
e-mail: dsnowden@pjc.edu
Web Site: www.pensacolastate.edu/department_page.asp?DeptID=6703
Officers:
  President: Edward Meadows
Management:
  President: Tom Delaino
  Executive Director: Stan Dean
Founded: 1958
Status: Non-Profit, Non-Professional
Paid Staff: 35
Performs At: Ashmore Fine Arts Auditorium
Annual Attendance: 7,000
Type of Stage: Proscenium
Seating Capacity: 314
Year Built: 1990

6579
SAENGER THEATRE
118 South Palafox Place
Pensacola, FL 32502
Phone: 850-595-3880
Fax: 850-444-7684
e-mail: info@pensacolasaenger.com
Web Site: www.pensacolasaenger.com
Management:
  Executive Director: Doug Lee
Utilizes: Dance Companies; Multimedia; Original Music Scores; Theatre Companies
Founded: 1925
Annual Attendance: 150,000
Facility Category: performing arts theatre
Type of Stage: Proscenium
Seating Capacity: 1,802
Year Built: 1925
Year Remodeled: 1981
Rental Contact: Douglas Lee

6580
UNIVERSITY OF WEST FLORIDA CENTER FOR FINE & PERFORMING ARTS
Art, Music, and Theatre Departments
Building 82, 11000 University Pkwy
Pensacola, FL 32514
Phone: 850-857-6057
Fax: 850-474-3247
e-mail: cfpa@uwf.edu
Web Site: www.uwf.edu/cfpa
Officers:
  President: Judith A. Bense
  Vice President: Kimberly Brown
  Chair: Lewis Bear
  Vice Chair: Mort O'Sullivan
Management:
  Asst. Dir for Fine/Performing Arts: Jerre Brisky
  Program Director: John Markowitz
  Chair of Music: Joseph Spaniola
  Chair of Theatre: Charles Houghton
  Art Gallery Director: Amy Bowman
Mission: To support and educate the students and the community.
Utilizes: Actors; Designers; Educators; Fine Artists; Guest Conductors; Guest Ensembles; Guest Soloists; High School Drama; Multi Collaborations; Multimedia; Music; Resident Professionals; Sign Language Translators; Singers; Soloists; Student Interns; Special Technical Talent; Touring Companies
Founded: 1970
Status: Non-Profit, Professional
Paid Staff: 3
Volunteer Staff: 10
Paid Artists: 5
Budget: $40,000
Income Sources: SGA Funds; State and Private Donations; Black Box Theatre
Performs At: Music Hall; Concert Hall
Annual Attendance: 33,000
Facility Category: Performance
Type of Stage: Proscenium; Black Box
Seating Capacity: 309
Year Built: 1992
Rental Contact: Asst. Director Fine/Performing Arts Jerre Brisky
Organization Type: Education

6581
CHARLOTTE HARBOR EVENT AND CONFERENCE CENTER
75 Taylor Street
Punta Gorda, FL 33950
Phone: 941-833-5444
Fax: 941-833-5451
Toll-free: 800-329-9988
e-mail: amy.issersohn@charlottefl.com
Web Site: www.charlotteharborecc.com
Management:
  General Manager: Jim Finch
  Event Manager: Clare Riggs
  Director of Finance: Sharon Markham
  Event Manager: Natalie Clark
  Director of Sales and Event Service: Sandy Darna
Seating Capacity: 2,000
Year Built: 2009
Rental Contact: Sales Manager Amy Issersohn
Organization Type: a Multipurpose 19,000 Sq Ft Ballroom with full rigging, lighting and multiple staging configurations. 18,000 Sq Ft Great Lawn with full performance capabilities along the waters edge.

6582
SEMINOLE COUNTY GOVERNMENT
1101 East First Street
Sanford, FL 32771
Phone: 407-665-0000
Fax: 407-665-7958
Web Site: www.co.seminole.fl.us
Management:
  Sports/Events Manager: John Giantonio

6583
ED SMITH STADIUM SPORTS COMPLEX
The City of Sarasota
City Hall 1565
1St Street
Sarasota, FL 34236
Phone: 941-365-2200
Fax: 941-365-1587
Web Site: www.sarasotagov.com
Management:
  Sports Facility Manager: Patrick M Calhoon
Founded: 1839

6584
FLORIDA STUDIO THEATRE
1241 North Palm Avenue
Sarasota, FL 34236
Phone: 941-366-9017
Fax: 941-955-4137
e-mail: info@floridastudiotheatre.org
Web Site: www.floridastudiotheatre.org
Officers:
  President: Dennis McGillicuddy
  Vice President: Richard Hopkins
  Secretary/Treasurer: Tom Hayes

FACILITIES / Florida

Trustee: Kate Alexander
Trustee: Carol Buchanan
Management:
   Casting/Hiring Coordinator: James Ashford
   Artistic Director: Richard Hopkins
   Associate Director: Kate Alexander
   Managing Director: Rebecca Hopkins
   Production Manager: Bruce Price
Founded: 1973
Paid Staff: 40
Volunteer Staff: 100
Paid Artists: 70

6585
THE PLAYERS THEATRE
838 N. Tamiami Trail
Sarasota, FL 34236
Phone: 941-365-2494
Fax: 941-954-0282
e-mail: info@theplayers.org
Web Site: www.theplayers.org
Officers:
   Chair: Leona Collesano
   Vice Chair: Lyn Wiley
   Treasurer: Michael G Brown
   Secretary: Barbara Johnson
   Financial Advisor: Shelley I. Cairo
Management:
   Managing Director: Michelle Bianchi Pingel
   Director of Operations: Jolie Schroeder
   Artistic Director: Jeffery Kin
   Production Manager/Director of Musi: Berry Ayers
   Evening Box Office Manager: Patty Campbell
Founded: 1930
Status: Non-Profit, Non-Professional
Paid Staff: 7
Volunteer Staff: 700
Budget: $1.2 million
Income Sources: Earned Income; Donations
Performs At: Community Theatre
Annual Attendance: 65,000
Type of Stage: Proscenium
Seating Capacity: 497
Year Built: 1970

6586
VAN WEZEL PERFORMING ARTS HALL
777 N. Tamiami Trail
Sarasota, FL 34236
Phone: 941-955-7676
Fax: 941-951-1449
Toll-free: 800-826-9303
Web Site: www.vanwezel.org
Management:
   Executive Director: Mary Bensel
   Marketing Director: Julia Mays
   Events Coordinator: Charmaine McVicker
   Technical Director: Stephen Brown
   Education Director: Robert Warren
   General Manager/Box Office Manager: Loreda Williams
   Business Manager: Anthony Becich
Mission: Present a broad spectrum of the world's finest artists, educational outreach programs for the community and provide a quality home for the other local groups.
Utilizes: AEA Actors; Dance Companies; Dancers; Guest Accompanists; Guest Choreographers; Guest Ensembles; Guest Musicians; Multimedia; Original Music Scores; Singers; Special Technical Talent; Theatre Companies
Founded: 1970
Specialized Field: Theatre; Dance; Music; Education; Comedy
Status: Non-Profit, Professional
Paid Staff: 100
Volunteer Staff: 300
Paid Artists: 500
Budget: $9,000,000
Income Sources: Ticket Sales; Grants; Donations; Sponsorships; Food & Beverage rentals
Performs At: Performing Arts Hall
Affiliations: Broadway League, Florida Facilities Managers, City of Sarasota, Fla Presents
Annual Attendance: 200,000
Facility Category: Performing Arts Hall
Type of Stage: Proscenium
Stage Dimensions: 60' wide x 30' high x 49' deep
Seating Capacity: 1709
Year Built: 1969
Year Remodeled: 2000
Rental Contact: Charmaine McVicker

6587
SPRINGSTEAD THEATRE
3300 Mariner Boulevard
Spring Hill, FL 34609
Phone: 352-797-7010
Fax: 352-797-7110
Web Site: www.springsteadtheatre.com
Management:
   President: Mark Pennington
Founded: 1976
Status: Non-Profit, Non-Professional
Paid Staff: 2

6588
MAHAFFEY THEATRE/DUKE ENERGY CENTER FOR THE ARTS
400 First Street South
St Petersburg, FL 33701
Phone: 727-893-7111
Fax: 727-892-5102
e-mail: lauren.kleinfeld@stpete.org
Web Site: www.themahaffey.com
Management:
   Director Facilities: Michael R Barber
   Booking/Marketing Manager: Lauren Kleinfeld
   Mayor: Bill Foster
   Fire Chief: Jim Large
   City Administrator: Tish Elston
Facility Category: Theatre/Arena

6589
TROPICANA FIELD
One Tropicana Drive
St Petersburg, FL 33705
Phone: 888-326-7297
Fax: 727-825-3167
e-mail: dugout1@verizon.net
Web Site: www.devilrays.com
Management:
   VP Operations/Facilities: Rick Nafe
   Event Manager: Rick Nafe
   VP Sales/Marketing: John Brown
   President: Matthew Silverman
   Principal Owner: Stuart Sternberg
Seating Capacity: 45,200

6590
MAINSTAGE THEATRE
Flagler College
Theatre Arts Department
74 King Street
St. Augustine, FL 32084
Phone: 904-829-6481
Fax: 904-826-0094
Toll-free: 800-304-4208
e-mail: theatredept@flagler.edu
Web Site: www.flagler.edu
Officers:
   President: William Abare
Management:
   Adjunct Theatre: Christine Fogarty
   Assistant Professor: Andrea McCook
   Technical Director: Britton Corry
   Advertising/Promotions Manager: Phyllis M. Gibbs
   Advertising/Promotions Manager: Kerry Fradler
Mission: Flagler College's Theatre Arts Department educates students as theatre generalists in the areas of performance, technology, design, literature, history, management and directing.
Specialized Field: Theatre

6591
RAHNER-GIBBS SECOND STAGE THEATRE
Flagler College
Theatre Arts Major or Minor
74 King Street
St. Augustine, FL 32084
Phone: 904-819-6217
Fax: 904-826-0094
e-mail: theatredept@flagler.edu
Web Site: www.flagler.edu
Officers:
   President: William Abare
Management:
   Adjunct Theatre: Christine Fogarty
   Assistant Professor: Andrea McCook
   Technical Director: Britton Corry
   Advertising/Promotions Manager: Phyllis M. Gibbs
   Advertising/Promotions Manager: Kerry Fradler
Mission: Flagler College's Theatre Arts Department educates students as theatre generalists in the areas of performance, technology, design, literature, history, management and directing.
Specialized Field: Theatre

6592
STUDIO THEATRE
Eckerd College
4200 54th Avenue South
St. Petersburg, FL 33711
Mailing Address: Eckerd College, 4200 54th Avenue South, St. Petersburg, Flor
Phone: 727-867-1166
Fax: 727-864-1877
Toll-free: 800-456-9009
Web Site: www.eckerd.edu/academics/theatre/
Officers:
   President: Donald R. Eastman, III
   Chairman: Miles C. Collier
   Vice Chairman: John G. Finneran
   Secretary: Dr. Lisa A. Mets
   Treasurer: Christopher P. Brennan
Management:
   Professor Theater: Cynthia Totten
   Theater Coordinator: Eric Haak
Mission: Theatre at Eckerd is designed to prepare students for the 'real world' of professional theatre, and the varied demands of the global workplace.
Specialized Field: Theatre
Type of Stage: Flexible Black Box
Seating Capacity: 50-80

FACILITIES / Florida

6593
BININGER THEATRE
Eckerd College
4200 54th Avenue South
St. Petersburg, FL 33711
Mailing Address: Eckerd College, 4200 54th Avenue South, St. Petersburg, Flor
Phone: 727-867-1166
Toll-free: 800-456-9009
Web Site: www.eckerd.edu/academics/theatre/
Officers:
    President: Donald R. Eastman, III
    Chairman: Miles C. Collier
    Vice Chairman: John G. Finneran
    Secretary: Dr. Lisa A. Mets
    Treasurer: Christopher P. Brennan
Management:
    Professor Theater: Cynthia Totten
    Theater Coordinator: Eric Haak
Mission: Theatre at Eckerd is designed to prepare students for the 'real world' of professional theatre, and the varied demands of the global workplace.
Specialized Field: Theatre
Type of Stage: Proscenium/Thrust
Seating Capacity: 350

6594
KINGS POINT THEATRE AT THE CLUBHOUSE
1900 Clubhouse Drive
Sun City Center, FL 33573
Phone: 813-634-9229
Fax: 813-633-3759
Management:
    Entertainment Director: Marvin Donner
Specialized Field: Theater

6595
CENTER THEATER COMPANY OF TAMPA BAY
1010 N W.C. MacInnes Place
Tampa, FL 33602
Phone: 813-222-1000
Fax: 813-222-1057
e-mail: rick.criswell@tbpac.org
Management:
    Production Stage Manager: Rick Criswell
Utilizes: Actors; AEA Actors; Artists-in-Residence; Choreographers; Collaborations; Commissioned Composers; Dancers; Designers; Educators; Five Seasonal Concerts; Guest Accompanists; Guest Artists; Guest Companies; Guest Composers; Guest Conductors; Guest Designers; Guest Ensembles; Guest Lecturers; Guest Musical Directors; Guest Musicians; Guest Soloists; Guest Teachers; Instructors; Local Artists; Multi Collaborations; Multimedia; New Productions; Organization Contracts; Original Music Scores; Poets; Resident Companies; Selected Students; Sign Language Translators; Soloists; Student Interns; Special Technical Talent; Touring Companies; Visual Arts
Founded: 1995
Specialized Field: Performing Arts Complex
Status: Nonprofit
Type of Stage: Thrust
Stage Dimensions: 40' x 24'
Seating Capacity: 300
Rental Contact: Bobbi Warnick

6596
TAMPA BAY PERFORMING ARTS CENTER
Straz Center for the Performing Arts
1010 N. W.C. MacInnes Place
PO Box 518
Tampa, FL 33602
Phone: 813-222-1000
Fax: 813-222-1057
Toll-free: 800-955-1045
Web Site: www.tbpac.org
Officers:
    President: Judith Lisi
    Chief Programming and Marketing Off: Georgiana Young
    Chief Operating Officer: Lorrin Shepard
    Chief Financial Officer: Mary Beth Rossi
Management:
    Vice President of Development: Julie Britton
    Director of Corporate Giving and Sp: Marc Brechwald
    Director of Foundations: Donna McBride
    Director of Special Events: Sharon McDonald
    Manager of Individual Giving: Kimberly Bateman
Seating Capacity: 2,550

6597
TAMPA THEATRE
711 N Franklin Street
Tampa, FL 33602
Mailing Address: P.O. Box 172188, Tampa, FL 33672-0188
Phone: 813-274-8286
Fax: 813-274-8978
e-mail: john@tampatheatre.org
Web Site: www.tampatheatre.org
Officers:
    President & CEO: John Bell
Management:
    Director of Development: JL Wagner
    Director of Marketing & Community R: Jill Witecki
    Business Manager / Director of Oper: Cathy Prance
    Projectionist: Gary Dowling
Founded: 1976
Seating Capacity: 1,446

6598
USF SPECIAL EVENTS CENTER
University of South Florida
4202 East Fowler Avenue
Tampa, FL 33620
Phone: 813-574-5538
Fax: 813-574-5466
e-mail: kriegler@admin.usf.edu
Web Site: www.ctr.usf.edu/cab
Officers:
    Program Coordinator: Keri Kriegler
    Reservations: Greg Jackson
Seating Capacity: 1,950

6599
USF SUN DOME
University Of South Florida
4202 E. Fowler Avenue
Sun 130
Tampa, FL 33620
Phone: 813-974-3111
Fax: 813-974-3813
e-mail: receptionist@sundome.org
Web Site: www.sundome.org
Officers:
    Director: Scott Glaser
Management:
    Director, Event Services: Seth Benalt
    Facilities Director: Chris Paras
Founded: 1980
Opened: 1981
Paid Staff: 30
Facility Category: Arena
Seating Capacity: 11,324
Year Built: 1980
Rental Contact: Director Event Services Seth Benalt

6600
RIVERSIDE THEATRE
3250 Riverside Park Drive
Vero Beach, FL 32963
Phone: 772-231-5860
Fax: 772-234-5298
Toll-free: 800-445-6745
e-mail: info@riversidetheatre.com
Web Site: www.riversidetheatre.com
Officers:
    President: Thomas Slaughter
    Vice President: Gay Bain
    Vice President: David Baldwin
    Secretary: Richard Stark
    Treasurer: Fred Wonham
Management:
    Producing Artistic Director: Allen D Cornell
    Managing Director: Jon Moses
    Education Director: Linda Downey
    Production Manager: Kyle Atkins
    I.T. Manager: Rob Botto
Mission: Riverside Theatre is committed to providing a total theatre arts experience that entertains, challenges, and educates both adults and children.
Utilizes: AEA Actors; Arrangers; Choreographers; Collaborating Artists; Composers; Contract Actors; Designers; Equity Actors; Guest Accompanists; Guest Artists; Guest Companies; Guest Conductors; Guest Designers; Guest Instructors; Guest Lecturers; Guest Musical Directors; Guest Musicians; Guest Soloists; Guest Speakers; High School Drama; Local Artists; Local Artists & Directors; Multi Collaborations; Multimedia; Music; New Productions; Original Music Scores; Resident Professionals; Sign Language Translators; Soloists; Students; Student Interns; Visual Arts
Founded: 1973
Status: Non-Profit, Professional
Paid Staff: 75
Volunteer Staff: 600
Paid Artists: 135
Budget: $6,000,000
Income Sources: Corproate and Private Donations; Rentals; Grants; Fund-Raising Events; Ticket Sales
Season: October - May
Affiliations: Florida Professional Theatres Association; Florida Division of Cultural Affairs
Annual Attendance: 100,000
Type of Stage: Proscenium
Seating Capacity: 672 & 250 (2 stages)
Year Built: 1973
Year Remodeled: 2007
Cost: $20 Million
Rental Contact: Jon R Moses
Organization Type: Professional; Regional producing Theatre that occasionally serving as a presenter
Resident Groups: The Acting Company

6601
VERO BEACH CONCERT ASSOCIATION
PO Box 4024
Vero Beach, FL 32967

Phone: 772-231-8441
Fax: 772-388-0455
e-mail: info@VeroBeach.com
Web Site: www.verobeach.com
Officers:
President: Cora Witten

6602
KRAVIS CENTER FOR THE PERFORMING ARTS
The Raymond F. Kravis Center for the Performi
701 Okeechobee Boulevard
West Palm Beach, FL 33401
Phone: 561-833-8300
Fax: 561-833-3901
Toll-free: 800-572-8471
e-mail: kravis@kravis.org
Web Site: www.kravis.org
Officers:
Chair: Jane M. Mitchell
Vice-Chair: Michael J. Bracci
Vice-Chair: Laurie S. Silvers
Treasurer: William A. Meyer
Secretary: Stephen L. Brown
Management:
CEO: Judith A. Mitchell
Development Officer: Thalia E. White
Development Officer: Julie Hetherington
Planned Giving & Endowment Officer: Margaret May Damen
Founded: 1994
Paid Staff: 75
Volunteer Staff: 800
Annual Attendance: 500,000
Facility Category: Performing Arts Center
Type of Stage: Proscenium
Seating Capacity: 2,200
Year Built: 1992
Cost: $68 million
Rental Contact: Shirnette Ball

6603
POMPANO BEACH AMPHITHEATRE
1801 North East 6th Street
West Palm Beach, FL 33060
Phone: 561-832-6397
Fax: 561-832-2043
e-mail: fantasma@fantasma.com
Web Site: www.fantasma.com
Management:
Sponsorship: Randy Lvenla
Marketing/Advisor: Rachel Schrift
Box Office/Operations: Jason Morey
Production: Brian Cutler
Seating Capacity: 3,000

6604
STEPHEN FOSTER STATE FOLK CULTURE CENTER
Post Office Drawer G
White Springs, FL 32096
Mailing Address: Stephen Foster State Folk Culture Center, Post Office Drawer
Phone: 386-397-2733
Fax: 904-397-4262
Toll-free: 800-326-3521
Web Site: www.abfla.com/parks/StephenFoster/stephenfoster.html

6605
ANNIE RUSSELL THEATRE
Rollins College
Department Theatre and Dance
1000 Holt Ave.
Winter Park, FL 32789
Phone: 407-646-2000
Fax: 407-646-2257
e-mail: jnassif@rollins.edu
Web Site: www.rollins.edu/theatre/
Officers:
President: Lewis.M Duncan
VP: Carol.M Bresnahan
Treasurer: Jeffrey.G Eisenbarth
Chair: David Charles
Management:
Administrative Assistant / House Ma: Blair Johnson
Assistant Technical Director/ Resid: Lauren Cushman
Production Manager: Kevin Griffin
Costume Studio Manager: Seth Schrager
Marketing Communications Coordinato: Olivia Horn
Mission: The Rollins College Department of Theatre and Dance provides for the development of imaginative, purposeful, and skilled expression in the theatre, and for students' artistic, intellectual, and personal growth.
Utilizes: Actors; AEA Actors; Artists-in-Residence; Choreographers; Collaborating Artists; Commissioned Music; Dance Companies; Dancers; Designers; Educators; Guest Accompanists; Guest Artists; Guest Lecturers; Guest Soloists; High School Drama; Multimedia; Performance Artists; Poets; Resident Professionals; Sign Language Translators; Singers; Soloists; Visual Arts
Founded: 1932
Opened: 1932
Specialized Field: Comedy, Drama, Musicals
Income Sources: Ticket Sales; Donations
Season: August-April
Performs At: Theatre Stages/Dance Studios
Annual Attendance: 15,000
Type of Stage: Proscenium/Thrust
Seating Capacity: 377
Year Built: 1932
Year Remodeled: 1978
Cost: $1,000,000

6606
FRED STONE THEATRE
Rollins College
Department Theatre and Dance
1000 Holt Ave.
Winter Park, FL 32789
Phone: 407-646-2000
Fax: 407-646-2257
e-mail: jnassif@rollins.edu
Web Site: www.rollins.edu/theatre/
Officers:
President: Lewis.M Duncan
VP: Carol.M Bresnahan
Treasurer: Jeffrey.G Eisenbarth
Chair: David Charles
Management:
Administrative Assistant / House Ma: Blair Johnson
Assistant Technical Director/ Resid: Lauren Cushman
Production Manager: Kevin Griffin
Costume Studio Manager: Seth Schrager
Marketing Communications Coordinato: Olivia Horn
Mission: The Rollins College Department of Theatre and Dance provides for the development of imaginative, purposeful, and skilled expression in the theatre, and for students' artistic, intellectual, and personal growth.
Utilizes: Actors; AEA Actors; Artists-in-Residence; Choreographers; Collaborating Artists; Commissioned Music; Dance Companies; Dancers; Designers; Educators; Guest Accompanists; Guest Artists; Guest Lecturers; Guest Soloists; High School Drama; Multimedia; Performance Artists; Poets; Resident Professionals; Sign Language Translators; Singers; Soloists; Visual Arts
Founded: 1932
Opened: 1932
Specialized Field: Comedy, Drama, Musicals
Income Sources: Ticket Sales; Donations
Season: August-April
Performs At: Theatre Stages/Dance Studios
Annual Attendance: 15,000
Type of Stage: Proscenium/Thrust
Seating Capacity: 377
Year Built: 1932
Year Remodeled: 1978
Cost: $1,000,000

Georgia

6607
COBB ENERGY PERFORMING ARTS CENTRE
2800 Cobb Galleria Parkway
GA 30339
Phone: 770-916-2800
Fax: 770-916-2820
e-mail: info@cobbenergycentre.com
Web Site: www.cobbenergycentre.com
Management:
Managing Director: Michael Taormina
Technical Director: Johannes Pikel
Director of Facility Operations: Jenny Pollock
Director of Marketing & Sponsorship: Tom Rowland
House Manager: Richard Stevens
Mission: Venue for all performing art- opera, broadway, ballet, concerts and more It also houses space for corporate meetings and events

6608
ALBANY JAMES H GRAY SR CIVIC CENTER
100 W Oglethorpe Boulevard
Albany, GA 31706-3189
Mailing Address: P. O. Box 3189, Albany, GA 31706-3189
Phone: 229-430-5200
Fax: 229-430-5163
e-mail: desmith@albany.ga.us
Web Site: www.albanymunicipalauditorium.org
Management:
Deputy Director: Derrell Smith
Event Manager: Roger Burnett
Booking & Sales: Jacque Yeoman
Seating Capacity: 10,240

6609
DEPARTMENT OF FINE ARTS
University at Albany
State University of New York
1400 Washington Avenue
Albany, GA 12222

FACILITIES / Georgia

Mailing Address: University at Albany, State University of New York, 1400 Was
Phone: 518-442-5435
Fax: 518-442-5383
e-mail: ugadmissions@albany.edu
Web Site: www.albany.edu/pac/
Officers:
   Chairman: Dr. Marcia Mitchell Hood
Management:
   Director: Patrick Ferlo
   Assistant Director: Kim Engel
Mission: To provide high quality academic and artistic education for the members of the ASU community. The department's mission is central to the University, because the arts are at the heart of intellectual, social and personal development and human interaction.
Founded: 1903
Specialized Field: theater, concerts
Status: Non-Profit, Professional
Paid Staff: 21
Paid Artists: 32
Performs At: Albany Municipal Auditorium

6610
HUGH MILLS MEMORIAL STADIUM
601 North Van Buren Street
Albany, GA 31701
Phone: 912-431-3308
Fax: 912-431-3309
Management:
   Athletic Director: Frank Orgel
Founded: 1936

6611
THEATRE ALBANY
514 Pine Avenue
Albany, GA 31701
Mailing Address: PO Box 552 Albany, GA 31702
Phone: 229-439-7193
e-mail: mcostello@theatrealbany.com
Web Site: www.theatrealbany.com
Management:
   Artistic Director: Mark Costello
   Technical Director: Steve Felmet
Mission: To expose young people to the art of live performance.
Founded: 1932
Seating Capacity: 314

6612
HUGH HODGSON CONCERT HALL
The University of Georgia
230 River Road
Athens, GA 30605
Mailing Address: 212 Performing Arts Center, UGA, Athens GA 30605
Phone: 706-542-1668
Toll-free: 888-289-8497
e-mail: ugaarts@uga.edu
Web Site: www.uga.edu/pac
Management:
   Director: George C. Foreman
   General Manager: Erin E. Tatum
   Business Manager: Kellie Pless
   Director of Development: Caitlin M. Hubbard
   House Manager: Katherine Garcia
Mission: The Performing Arts Center serves as a showcase for world-class performers and ensembles. It also provides a home for UGA's faculty and student performers.
Type of Stage: Concert Hall
Seating Capacity: 1,100

6613
RAMSEY CONCERT HALL
The University of Georgia
230 River Road
Athens, GA 30605
Mailing Address: 212 Performing Arts Center, UGA, Athens GA 30605
Phone: 706-542-1668
Toll-free: 888-289-8497
e-mail: ugaarts@uga.edu
Web Site: www.uga.edu/pac
Management:
   Director: George C. Foreman
   General Manager: Erin E. Tatum
   Business Manager: Kellie Pless
   Director of Development: Caitlin M. Hubbard
   House Manager: Katherine Garcia
Mission: The Performing Arts Center serves as a showcase for world-class performers and ensembles. It also provides a home for UGA's faculty and student performers.
Specialized Field: Solo Recitals, Chamber Music
Type of Stage: Concert Hall
Seating Capacity: 360

6614
SANFORD STADIUM
University of Georgia
110 Field Street
Athens, GA 30602
Mailing Address: 110 Field Street, Athens, GA 30602
Phone: 706-542-1231
Fax: 706-542-9388
Toll-free: 877-542-1231
Web Site: www.georgiadogs.com/facilities/sanford-stadium
Mission: To continue to be the world-famous home of the University of Georgia Bulldogs football team and to continue to rank in the top five in the country among on-campus stadium venues.
Founded: 1929
Seating Capacity: 86,117

6615
THE CLASSIC CENTER
300 N. Thomas Street
Athens, GA 30601
Phone: 706-208-0900
Fax: 706-548-0870
e-mail: maureen@classiccenter.com
Web Site: www.classiccenter.com
Management:
   Convention Sales Manager: Alicia Brasher
   Theatre Director/Booking: Philip Verrastro, philipclassiccenter.com
   Director Of Sales: Maureen Baker, maureen@classiccenter.com
   Outside Sales Manager: Marvin Nunnally
   Director of Operations: Shannon McCullough
Mission: convention and arts center

6616
UNIVERSITY OF GEORGIA PERFORMING ARTS CENTER
The University of Georgia
230 River Road
Athens, GA 30605
Phone: 706-542-1668
Fax: 706-542-8497
e-mail: ugadmissions@albany.edu
Web Site: www.uga.edu/pac
Management:
   Director: George C. Foreman
   General Manager: Erin E. Tatum
   Business Manager: Kellie Pless
   Director of Development: Caitlin M. Hubbard
   House Manager: Katherine Garcia
Mission: The UGA Performing Arts Center serves as a showcase for world class performers and ensembles. It also provides a home for UGA's faculty and student performers.
Status: Non-Profit, Professional
Paid Staff: 10
Paid Artists: 30
Performs At: Hugh Hodgson Concert Hall; Ramsey Concert Hall; Fine Arts Theatre; UGA Chapel; Franklin College Chamber Music Series
Seating Capacity: 1100

6617
14TH STREET PLAYHOUSE
173 14th Street
Atlanta, GA 30309
Phone: 404-733-4754
e-mail: 14thplay@woodruffcenter.org
Web Site: www.14thstplayhouse.org
Mission: A thriving three-theatre complex is open to performing artists work and corporate events alike.
Specialized Field: Performing Arts; Corporate Venues

6618
ATLANTA CIVIC CENTER
395 Piedmont Ave., NE
Atlanta, GA 30309
Phone: 404-523-6275
Fax: 404-525-4634
e-mail: information@atlantaciviccenter.com
Web Site: www.atlantaciviccenter.com
Management:
   Director: Ann Marie Moraitakis
   Special Events Coordinator: Joyce Whisenant, jessica.coale@gmail.com
   Accounting Specialist: Constance Glover
   Auditorium Supervisor: Clifford Bacon
Mission: The civic center holds a 4600 seat performing arts center and 5800 more square feet for private receptions and corporate meetings

6619
BOBBY DODD STADIUM AT GRANT FIELD
Georgia Institute Of Technology
North Avenue
Atlanta, GA 30332
Phone: 404-894-2000
Fax: 40-489-4951
e-mail: admission@gatech.edu
Web Site: www.gatech.edu
Officers:
   President: G. P. Bud Peterson
   Assistant Vice President: Lynn Durham
   Executive Assistant to the Presiden: Stephanie Johnston
Management:
   Faculty Athletics Representative: Dr. Sue Ann Allen
   Administrative Professional Senior: Valarie Thomas
   Administrative Professional II: Ashley Riggs
   Event & Admin Coordinator: Stephanie Sigler
   President's Speechwriter: Patti Futrell
Mission: Georgia Tech's storied football facility has been a cornerstone of college football for nearly a century. Cozily nestled among Atlanta's skyscrapers, Bobby Dodd Stadium at Historic Grant Field is easily one of the nation's most unique settings for college football.

FACILITIES / Georgia

Founded: 1913
Specialized Field: Concerts

6620
DELTA CLASSIC CHASTAIN PARK AMPHITHEATRE
4469 Stella Dr North West
Atlanta, GA 30342
Phone: 404-733-4900
Fax: 404-733-4999
e-mail: asogroups@woodruffcenter.org
Web Site: www.classicchastain.com
Officers:
   President: James W. Wagner
   Assoc VP Arts/Sciences Development: John Ingersoll
   Media Relations/PR/Marketing: Sally Corbett
Management:
   Director: Janice Akers
   Associate Professor: John Ammerman
   Managing Director: Rosalind Staib
Mission: The venue's cozy confines create the perfect rendezvous for spreading out with friends and family, hanging out with a group of co-workers or members of a special group; entertaining clients; or getting away for a romantic idyll amid music and moonlight.
Founded: 1973
Seating Capacity: 6,900

6621
FERST CENTER FOR THE ARTS
Georgia Tech
349 Ferst Drive
Atlanta, GA 30332-0468
Phone: 404-894-2787
Fax: 404-864-9864
e-mail: info@ferstcenter.org
Web Site: www.ferstcenter.gatech.edu
Management:
   Interim Director/Business Manager: Dedra Gillett
   Operations Manager/Technical Direct: Paul Cottongim
   Client and Patron Services Manager: Chris Dreger
   Mark And PR Director: Stephanie Lee
Mission: As a presenter, the Ferst Center for the Arts is dedicated to bringing to the Georgia Tech Campus world class performances and artist residency programs that will enhance the total learning experience of the Georgia Tech student body, serve as a bridge to the surrounding Atlanta community and engage artists in a way that is uniquely Georgia Tech.
Utilizes: Actors; Artists-in-Residence; Choreographers; Collaborating Artists; Dance Companies; Dancers; Designers; Educators; Guest Directors; Guest Instructors; Guest Soloists; Instructors; Multimedia; Original Music Scores; Resident Professionals; Soloists; Special Technical Talent
Founded: 1992
Performs At: 1,155 seat theatre
Annual Attendance: 60,000
Facility Category: Theatre & 2 galleries
Type of Stage: Proscenium
Stage Dimensions: 37x52
Seating Capacity: 1,155
Rental Contact: Tori Wallingford

6622
FOX THEATRE
660 Peachtree Street NE
Atlanta, GA 30308
Phone: 404-881-2100
Fax: 404-872-2972
Toll-free: 855-285-8499
e-mail: information@foxtheatre.org
Web Site: www.foxtheatre.org
Officers:
   President and Chief Executive Offic: Allan C. Vella
Management:
   Publicity Manager: Deborah Garner
Mission: Known throughout the Southeast as the premier venue for musicals, plays, concerts and ballets.
Founded: 1928
Status: Non-Profit, Professional
Paid Staff: 100
Seating Capacity: 4,000

6623
GEORGIA DOME
One Georgia Dome Drive
Atlanta, GA 30313-1591
Phone: 404-223-9200
Fax: 404-223-4011
e-mail: info@gadome.com
Web Site: www.gadome.com
Management:
   Director of Business Development: Julia Karrenbauer
   Director of Facility Operations: Adam Straight
   Director of Event Operations: Erik Waldman
   Administration Manager: Harriet Thomas
   Assistant to the Director of Event: Anna Shoemake
Mission: To constantly earn our reputation as one of the worlds finest convention, sports and entertainment venues.
Founded: 1992
Status: For-Profit, Professional
Paid Staff: 120
Seating Capacity: 71,500
Year Built: 1992

6624
OGLETHORPE UNIVERSITY THEATRE
Oglethorpe University
4484 Peachtree Road NE
Atlanta, GA 30319
Mailing Address: 4484 Peachtree Road NE, Atlanta, GA 30319
Phone: 404-261-1441
Toll-free: 800-428-4484
e-mail: vweiss@oglethorpe.edu
Web Site: www.oglethorpe.edu/arts/theatre
Officers:
   President: Lawrence Schall
Management:
   Theatre Department Director: Deborah Merola
   Director of Musical Activities: Dr W Irwin Ray Jr
Mission: Oglethorpe is committed to supporting the success of all students in a diverse community characterized by civility, caring, inquiry and tolerance.
Utilizes: Resident Artists
Opened: 1997
Specialized Field: Theatre
Type of Stage: Modified-Thrust
Seating Capacity: 511

6625
PHILIPS ARENA
1 Philips Drive
Atlanta, GA 30303
Phone: 404-878-3000
Toll-free: 800-326-4000
e-mail: philipsarena-questions@atlantaspirit.com
Web Site: www.philipsarena.com
Officers:
   President: Bob Williams
   Senior VP: Trey Feazell
   Chief Executive Officer: Steeve Koonin
   Executive Vice President and CFO: Phil Ebinger
   Sr. VP and Chief Revenue Officer: Andrews Steinberg
Management:
   VP Operations: Barry Henson
   VP Guest Services: Jason Parker
   VP Marketing & Business Dev: Kevin Preast
   Executive Assistant to President &: Janice Koon
   Executive Assistant & Booking Manag: Rita Cobb
Mission: To leave a lasting impression upon the public before, during and after the events hosted at the Arena.
Founded: 1999
Specialized Field: Arena
Seating Capacity: 20,000

6626
RIALTO CENTER FOR THE ARTS
Georgia State University
80 Forsyth Street NW
Atlanta, GA 30303
Mailing Address: P.O. Box 3965 Atlanta, GA 30302-3965
Phone: 404-413-2000
Fax: 404-651-1332
e-mail: info@rialtocenter.org
Web Site: www.rialtocenter.org
Officers:
   President: Mark P. Becker
Management:
   Marketing Manager: Kara Keene Cooper
   Assistant Director: Jennifer Moore
   Director: Leslie Gordon
Mission: To inspire, educate and entertain diverse audiences by presenting innovative and exceptional arts programming and cultivating community partnerships.
Founded: 1916
Status: Non-Profit, Professional

6627
7 STAGES THEATRE
1105 Euclid Avenue N.E.
Atlanta, GA 30307
Mailing Address: 7 Stages Theatre, 1105 Euclid Avenue, Atlanta, GA, 30307
Phone: 404-522-0911
Fax: 404-522-0913
Web Site: www.7stages.org
Officers:
   Board Chair: Gregory N. Pierce
   Secretary: Sarah Muldin
   Treasurer: Susan Roe
   Co-Vice Chair: Pamela Benson
   President & CEO: Andjela Kessler
Management:
   Artistic Director: Heidi S. Howard
   Co-Founder: Faye Allen
   Managing Direct: Mack Headrick
   Director Of Marketing: Charles Swint
   Co-Founder: Del Hamilton
Mission: devoted to engaging artists and audiences by focusing on the social, political, and spiritual values of contemporary culture. 7 Stages gives primary emphasis

FACILITIES / Georgia

to international work and the support and development of new plays, new playwrights, and new methods of collaboration.
Specialized Field: Theater
Status: Non profit
Volunteer Staff: 2
Paid Artists: 65
Budget: $850,000
Income Sources: Theatre Communications Group; National Endowment for the Arts; Georgia Council of the Arts; City of Atlanta Bureau of Cultural Affairs; Trust for Mutual Understanding; AT&T
Affiliations: Theatre Communications Group; Atlanta Coalition for the Performing Arts
Annual Attendance: 15,000
Facility Category: 2 Performing Arts Theatres
Type of Stage: Black Boxes
Seating Capacity: 99; 202
Year Built: 1928
Year Remodeled: 1994
Architect: $1.6 million
Rental Contact: Del Hamilton

6628
THE BOISEFEUILLET JONES ATLANTA CIVIC CENTER
395 Piedmont Ave., NE
Atlanta, GA 30309
Phone: 404-523-6275
Fax: 404-525-4634
e-mail: information@atlantaciviccenter.com
Web Site: www.atlantaciviccenter.com
Management:
  Director: Ann Marie Moraitakis
  Special Events Coordinator: Joyce Whisenant
  Accounting Specialist: Constance Glover
  Auditorium Supervisor: Clifford Bacon
Mission: The Atlanta Civic Center has played host to some of the worlds most highly anticipated productions. In 2001, the Atlanta Civic Center was renamed as a lasting tribute to on of Atlanta's most beloved philanthropists, Boisfeuillet Jones.
Facility Category: procenium theatre
Type of Stage: Proscenium
Seating Capacity: 86,520
Year Built: 1968
Year Remodeled: 2001
Cost: 2 million
Rental Contact: Joyce Whisenant

6629
THEATER AT EMORY
Emory University
Donna and Marvin Schwartz Center
1602 Fishburne Drive
Atlanta, GA 30322
Mailing Address: Theater Studies, Theater at Emory, or Theater Emory, Rich Me
Phone: 404-727-6123
e-mail: hhanger@emory.edu
Web Site: www.theater.emory.edu
Management:
  Artistic Director: Janice Akers
  Associate Professor: John Ammerman
  Managing Director: Rosalind Staib
  Company Manager, Theater Emory: Emma Yarbrough
  Professor, Resident Dramaturg: Michael Evenden
Mission: a professional theater company in residence at the University, undergraduates collaborate on significant and challenging artistic projects and plays with professional artists: directors, actors, designers, playwrights, dramaturgs, technicians, and stage managers, including the Departmentjs core faculty

Founded: 1982
Specialized Field: theater
Status: Professional
Seating Capacity: 135
Architect: Michael Dennis and Associates
Cost: $35 Million
Acoustical Consultant: Kirkegaard and Associates

6630
TURNER FIELD
755 Hank Aaron Drive
Atlanta, GA 30315
Phone: 404-522-7630
Web Site: www.mlb.mlb.com/atl/ballpark
Officers:
  President: John Schuerholz
Founded: 1997
Specialized Field: Baseball Stadium
Seating Capacity: 52,007

6631
WOODRUFF ARTS CENTER
1280 Peachtree St. NE
Atlanta, GA 30309
Mailing Address: Woodruff Arts Center, 1280 Peachtree St. NE, Atlanta, GA 303
Phone: 404-733-4200
Web Site: www.woodruffcenter.org
Officers:
  President & CEO: Virginia Hepner
  VP, Strategy & Operations: Tara Perry
  Executive VP/CFO: Stephen P. Merz
Management:
  Artistic Director: Susan Booth
Specialized Field: Theater, symphony, art
Status: Non-Profit, Professional
Paid Staff: 200
Paid Artists: 125

6632
AUGUSTA ENTERTAINMENT COMPLEX
James Brown Arena
601 Seventh Street
Augusta, GA 30901
Mailing Address: James Brown Arena, 601 Seventh Street, Augusta GA 30901
Phone: 706-722-3521
Fax: 706-724-7545
e-mail: kwells@arccc.com
Web Site: www.augustaentertainmentcomplex.com
Management:
  Director of Marketing: Katie Cason
  General Manager: Chris Bird
  Assistant General Manager: Linda Roberts
  Box Office Manager: Jessica Henley
  Group Sales Manager: Vicki Johnson
Specialized Field: Concerts
Type of Stage: Proscenium
Seating Capacity: 8500 Arena, 2690 Auditorium
Year Built: 1979
Rental Contact: Mike McGhee (713)623-4583

6633
GROVER C. MAXWELL PERFORMING ARTS THEATRE
Augusta State University
2500 Walton Way
Augusta, GA 30904
Mailing Address: Augusta State University, 1120 15th Street, Augusta, GA 309
Phone: 706-667-4100
Fax: 706-667-4916
e-mail: kthoma12@aug.edu
Web Site: www.gru.edu/maxwelltheatre

Management:
  Director of Marketing: Katie Wells
  General Manager: Monty Jones
  Assistant General Manager: Linda Roberts
  Box Office Manager: Scott Montgomery
Mission: The Grover C. Maxwell Performing Arts Theatre is the cultural heart of the ASU campus, and students take center stage
Specialized Field: Theater
Type of Stage: Proscenium/Thrust
Orchestra Pit: y
Seating Capacity: 750

6634
IMPERIAL THEATRE
749 Broad Street
Augusta, GA 30901
Mailing Address: The Imperial Theatre, 749 Broad St, Augusta GA
Phone: 706-722-8341
Web Site: www.imperialtheatre.com
Management:
  Executive Director: Charles Scavullo
  Box Office Manager: Daniella Maynard
  Technical Director: Tim Campbell
Founded: 1918

6635
ACADEMY THEATRE
119 Center Street
Avondale Estates, GA 30002
Phone: 404-525-4111
Fax: 404-296-9511
e-mail: academytheatre@mindspring.com
Web Site: www.academytheatre.org
Officers:
  Board Chair: Jimmy Gough
  Vice President and Chief Operating: Jeffrey A. Cooper
Management:
  Managing Director: Lorenne Fey
  Artistic Director: Robert Drake
  Director of the Human Service Prog: Brenda Porter
  Director of the Thoroughly Modern S: Mira Hirsch
  Director of Development: David Burt
Mission: To enrich the metropolitan community by providing a space for the exploration of the arts, producing educational youth focused outreach and nurturing appreciation for the performing and visual arts through presentation of quality professional artistic work.
Founded: 1956
Status: Non-Profit, Professional
Paid Staff: 6
Paid Artists: 4

6636
TOWNSEND CENTER FOR THE PERFORMING ARTS
University of West Georgia
1601 Maple Street
Carrollton, GA 30118-1400
Phone: 678-839-4722
Fax: 678-839-4805
e-mail: tcpa@westga.edu
Web Site: www.townsendcenter.org
Management:
  Artistic Director: Robert Jennings
  Technical Director and Safety Offic: David E. Manuel
  Business Services Manager: Renet Jones
  Patron Services Manager: Misty Parham
Founded: 1989

FACILITIES / Georgia

Specialized Field: Performing Arts
Facility Category: Performing Arts Center
Type of Stage: Procenium & Black Box
Seating Capacity: 250
Year Built: 1989
Rental Contact: Business Manager Renet Jones

6637
CEDARTOWN CIVIC AUDITORIUM
205 East Avenue
Cedartown, GA 30125
Phone: 770-748-4168
e-mail: gm@ccauditorium.com
Web Site: www.cedartownshows.com
Management:
  Director: Patrick Moore
Utilizes: Actors; AEA Actors; Collaborating Artists; Collaborations; Community Members; Community Talent; Contract Actors; Contract Orchestras; Dance Companies; Designers; Educators; Equity Actors; Fine Artists; Grant Writers; Guest Accompanists; Guest Choreographers; Guest Directors; Guest Ensembles; Guest Musical Directors; Guest Soloists; Guild Activities; High School Drama; Instructors; Local Artists & Directors; Local Talent; Multi Collaborations; Multimedia; New Productions; Original Music Scores; Paid Performers; Resident Professionals; Selected Students; Soloists; Students; Student Interns; Special Technical Talent; Theatre Companies; Touring Companies; Visual Arts; Visual Designers; Volunteer Artists
Paid Staff: 3
Volunteer Staff: 30
Income Sources: City of Cedartown; Ticket Sales; Donations; Grants
Performs At: Auditorium; Performing Arts Theatre; Professional Touring Shows
Affiliations: City of Cedartown; Georgia Council for the Arts; Southeast Arts Federation
Type of Stage: Proscenium
Seating Capacity: 940
Year Built: 1976
Year Remodeled: 1992
Rental Contact: Director Patrick Moore

6638
MARVIN COLE AUDITORIUM
Georgia Perimeter College
555 North Indian Creek Drive
Clarkston, GA 30021-2361
Mailing Address: 555 N. Indian Creek Dr., Bldg. CF-2230, Clarkston, GA 30021
Phone: 678-891-3200
e-mail: jjenkins@gpc.edu
Web Site: www.gpc.edu/~clafa/
Management:
  Chair Of Fine Arts: David Koffman
  Facilities Manager: Jennifer Jenkins
Mission: transform the lives of students to thrive in a global society by providing them with outstanding instruction, excellent facilities and technology, and opportunities within a diverse liberal arts environment
Utilizes: Resident Artists
Type of Stage: Proscenium
Orchestra Pit: y
Seating Capacity: 500

6639
COLUMBUS CIVIC CENTER
400 4th Street
Columbus, GA 31901
Mailing Address: Columbus Civic Center, 400 4th Street, (also known as Victor
Phone: 706-653-4482
Fax: 706-653-4841
e-mail: ross@columbusga.org
Web Site: www.columbusciviccenter.org
Management:
  Director: Ross D. Horner
  Operations Manager: Brian Giffin
  Marketing Manager: Robin Wallace
  Director's Assistant: Sammy Eugenio
  Box Office Manager: Lisa Thomas-Cutts
  Assistant Box Office Manager: Al Moore
Founded: 1996
Seating Capacity: 10,000

6640
RIVERCENTER FOR THE PERFORMING ARTS
900 Broadway
Columbus, GA 31901
Mailing Address: PO Box 2425 Columbus GA 31902-2425
Phone: 706-256-3620
Fax: 706-653-8664
e-mail: information@rivercenter.org
Web Site: www.rivercenter.org
Management:
  Executive Director: William Bullock
  Director of Business Affairs & CFO: Jannina Mcpherson
  Technical Director: John Camp
  Development Director: Lauren Pastwik Minter
  Program & Education Director: Jim Rutland
Founded: 2002
Specialized Field: Multi-Disciplinary
Seating Capacity: 1,988

6641
THREE ARTS THEATRE
1020 Talbotton Road
Columbus, GA 31901
Phone: 706-653-4183

6642
AGNES SCOTT COLLEGE
141 E. College Ave.
Decatur, GA 30030
Phone: 404-471-6000
Fax: 404-868-8602
Toll-free: 800-868-8602
e-mail: info@agnesscott.edu
Web Site: www.agnesscott.edu
Officers:
  President: Elizabeth Kiss
  Chairperson: Clyde C. Tuggle
  Vice Chairperson: Portia O. Morrison '66
  Secretary: Lea Ann Grimes Hudson '76
Management:
  Chairperson: Harriet King
  Special Events/Conferences Director: Demetrice Parks
Founded: 1889

6643
DANA FINE ARTS BUILDING
Agnes Scott College
141 E. College Ave.
Decatur, GA 30030
Phone: 404-471-6285
Fax: 404-471-6298
Toll-free: 800-868-8602
e-mail: info@agnesscott.edu
Web Site: www.agnesscott.edu
Officers:
  President: Elizabeth Kiss
  Chairperson: Clyde C. Tuggle
  Vice Chairperson: Portia O. Morrison '66
  Secretary: Lea Ann Grimes Hudson '76
Management:
  Cultural Programs Coordinator: James Boynton
  Special Events/Conferences Director: Demetrice Parks
Founded: 1889
Performs At: Gaines Chapel

6644
GWINNETT CENTER
6400 Sugarloaf Parkway
Duluth, GA 30097
Phone: 770-813-7500
Fax: 770-813-7501
Toll-free: 800-224-6422
e-mail: info@gwinnettcenter.com
Web Site: www.gwinnettcenter.com
Officers:
  Executive Director: Joseph Dennis, Jr.
Management:
  General Manager: Joseph L. Dennis
  Assistant General Manager: Ron Jackson
  Assistant General Manager: JoAnne Craig
  Human Resources Manager/Executive A: Cheryl Alicea
  Box Office Manager: Kim Kettler
Founded: 1992
Status: For-Profit, Professional
Income Sources: Ticket Sales
Annual Attendance: 75,000
Type of Stage: Proscenium
Seating Capacity: 702
Rental Contact: Sales Manager Chris Muller

6645
WILD BILL'S ATLANTA
2075 Market St.
Duluth, GA 30096
Phone: 678-473-1000
Fax: 678-417-0477
e-mail: info@wildbillsatlanta.com
Web Site: www.wildbillsatlanta.com
Management:
  Marketing Manager: Tom Siliven
  Event Planner: Amanda Edwards
  Event Planner: Tammie Nielson
Seating Capacity: 5,127

6646
ED CABELL THEATRE
Gainesville Theatre Alliance
3820 Mundy Mill Road
Gainesville, GA 30566
Mailing Address: PO Box 1358 Gainesville GA 30503
Phone: 678-717-3624
Fax: 678-717-3675
Web Site: www.gainesvilletheatrealliance.org
Management:
  Artistic Director: Jim Hammond
  Director of Theatre: Dr. Ann Demling
  Resident Designer: Stuart Beaman
  Resident Director: Elisa Carlson
  Design & Technical Theatre Coordina: Larry E. Cook
Mission: Gainesville Theatre Alliance will provide its artists and audiences quality theatrical experiences that educate, inspire, enrich and unite
Specialized Field: Theater
Budget: $400,000
Annual Attendance: 20,000
Type of Stage: Thrust
Seating Capacity: 225

FACILITIES / Georgia

6647
GEORGIA MOUNTAINS CENTER
301 Main Street SW
PO Box 2496
Gainesville, GA 30501
Phone: 770-534-8420
Fax: 770-534-8425
e-mail: tlee@brenau.edu
Web Site: www.georgiamountainscenter.com
Management:
  Director of Special Events: Tamara Lee
  Assistant Director of Special Event: Vicki Wineland
Seating Capacity: 300

6648
HOSCH THEATRE
Brenau University\ Gainesville State College
John S. Burd Center for the Performing Arts
500 Washington St. SE
Gainesville, GA 30501
Mailing Address: PO Box 1358 Gainesville GA 30503
Phone: 770-718-5337
Fax: 770-718-5338
Toll-free: 800-252-5119
e-mail: admissions@brenau.edu
Web Site: www.gainesvilletheatrealliance.org
Officers:
  President: Ed Schrader
  Senior Vice President & CFO: David L. Barnett
Management:
  Senior Vice President, Enrollment M: Scott Briell
  Provost and Vice President, Academi: Nancy Krippel
  Vice President, Com & Publications: David Morrison
  Vice President, External Relations: Matt Thomas
  Vice President, Financial Services: Toby Hinton
Mission: Gainesville Theatre Alliance will provide its artists and audiences quality theatrical experiences that educate, inspire, enrich and unite
Specialized Field: Theater
Type of Stage: Proscenium
Seating Capacity: 350

6649
PEARCE AUDITORIUM
Brenau University\ Gainesville State College
500 Washington Street SE
Gainesville, GA 30501
Mailing Address: PO Box 1358 Gainesville GA 30503
Phone: 770-718-5337
Fax: 770-718-5338
Toll-free: 800-252-5119
e-mail: admissions@brenau.edu
Web Site: www.gainesvilletheatrealliance.org
Officers:
  President: Ed Schrader
  Senior Vice President & CFO: David L. Barnett
Management:
  Senior Vice President, Enrollment M: Scott Briell
  Provost and Vice President, Academi: Nancy Krippel
  Vice President, Com & Publications: David Morrison
  Vice President, External Relations: Matt Thomas
  Vice President, Financial Services: Toby Hinton
Mission: Gainesville Theatre Alliance will provide its artists and audiences quality theatrical experiences that educate, inspire, enrich and unite
Specialized Field: theater
Seating Capacity: 750
Year Head Theatre Renovated: 1981

Year Restored: 1984

6650
CENTER FOR THE CREATIVE & PERFORMING ARTS
Wesleyan College
4760 Forsyth Road
Macon, GA 31210
Phone: 478-757-5259
Toll-free: 800-447-6610
e-mail: communications@wesleyancollege.edu
Web Site: www.wesleyancollege.edu
Officers:
  President: Ruth A Knox
  Vice President: Vivia Fowler
  Vice President: Deborah Smith
Management:
  Director of Communications: Susan Welsh
Utilizes: Actors; Artists-in-Residence; Collaborating Artists; Curators; Designers; Educators; Fine Artists; Five Seasonal Concerts; Grant Writers; Guest Composers; Guest Directors; Guest Ensembles; Guest Lecturers; Guest Musical Directors; Guest Musicians; Guest Soloists; Guest Speakers; Guest Teachers; High School Drama; Instructors; Local Artists; Local Artists & Directors; Multimedia; Music; Playwrights; Poets; Sign Language Translators; Soloists; Students; Student Interns; Touring Companies; Volunteer Directors & Actors; Writers
Founded: 1836
Opened: 2008
Specialized Field: Music; Theatre; Studio Arts
Paid Staff: 12
Paid Artists: 10
Income Sources: Tuitions; Grants; Donations
Performs At: Multi-use Fine Arts Center
Type of Stage: Auditorium; Black Box
Seating Capacity: 1,200

6651
THE GRAND OPERA HOUSE
A Performing Arts Center of Mercer University
651 Mulberry Street
Macon, GA 31201
Mailing Address: The Grand Opera House, 651 Mulberry Street, Macon, GA U.S.A.
Phone: 478-301-5470
Web Site: www.thegrandmacon.com
Management:
  Executive Director: Roseann Swiergosz
  Director of Operations: Phil Banze
  Vice President, Com & Publications: Robert Mavity
  Marketing Coordinator: J. Cindy Hill
  Asst. Box Office Coordinator: Nikki Vincent
Mission: The Grand has hosted vaudeville performances, Broadway touring companies, community theatre, concerts, movies, and numerous other events
Founded: 1884
Specialized Field: Theater

6652
MADISON MORGAN CULTURAL CENTER
434 S. Main St.
Madison, GA 30650
Phone: 706-342-4743
Fax: 706-342-1154
Toll-free: 877-233-0598
Web Site: www.mmcc-arts.org
Officers:
  Chairman: Steve Schaefer
  Vice-Chairman: Bob Hughes
  Treasurer: Sarah Burbach
  Secretary: Mary Jones
Management:
  Managing Director: Ruth Bracewell
  Grant Writer: Sue Chappell

6653
THEATRE IN THE SQUARE
11 Whitlock Avenue
Marietta, GA 30064
Mailing Address: Theatre in the Square- 11 Whitlock Ave. - Marietta, GA 30064
Phone: 770-422-8369
Fax: 770-424-2637
Web Site: www.theatreinthesquare.com
Management:
  Producing Director: Palmer Wells
  Managing Director: Raye Varney
  Assistant Artistic Director: Jessica Phelps West
  Marketing: Andrea Gardenhire
Utilizes: Actors; AEA Actors; Artists-in-Residence; Choreographers; Collaborating Artists; Collaborations; Dancers; Designers; Educators; Grant Writers; Guest Artists; Guest Companies; Guest Conductors; Guest Designers; Guest Lecturers; Guest Musical Directors; Guest Writers; Guild Activities; High School Drama; Instructors; Lyricists; Multimedia; Music; Original Music Scores; Performance Artists; Resident Professionals; Sign Language Translators; Soloists; Student Interns
Founded: 1982
Specialized Field: Theater

6654
SPIVEY HALL
Clayton State University
2000 Clayton State Blvd
Morrow, GA 30260
Phone: 678-466-4200
Fax: 628-466-4494
e-mail: JohnShiffert@clayton.edu
Web Site: www.spiveyhall.org
Management:
  Executive/Artistic Director: Sam Dixon
  Education Manager: Melanie E. Darby
  Marketing Director: Susan Volkert
  Patron Services Manager: Tammy Moore
  Business Manager: Sherry Echols
Mission: Spivey Hall is home to the award-winning Spivey Hall Children's Choir and Spivey Hall Young Artists
Founded: 1991
Specialized Field: Concerts
Performs At: Music Only, No Theatre, Dance Or Attractions
Seating Capacity: 392

6655
COLQUITT COUNTY ARTS CENTER
401 7th Ave Southwest
Moultrie, GA 31768
Phone: 229-985-1922
Fax: 229-890-6746
e-mail: info@colquittcountyarts.com
Web Site: www.colquittcountyarts.com
Management:
  Executive Director: Jeffery Ophime
  Assistant Director: Lin Sheffield
  Artistic Director: Jane Simpson
  Book-Keeping: Maryann Robinson
  Curator: Lydia Tyler
Mission: A creative and cultural resource that makes quality visual and performing art available to a diverse population. Provides engaging arts education for

children and adults, acts as a steward of permanent collections, and maintains a landmark facility that enriches the whole community.
Paid Staff: 3

6656
FREDERICK BROWN JR AMPHITHEATER
201 McIntosh Trail
Peachtree City, GA 30269
Mailing Address: Frederick Brown Jr. Amphitheater, 201 McIntosh Trail, Peac
Phone: 770-631-0630
Fax: 770-631-0430
e-mail: info@amphitheater.org
Web Site: www.amphitheater.org
Management:
  Manager: Nancy Price
  Facilities Manager: Billy Burke
  Box Office Manager: Sarah Davenport
Mission: The Fred has established itself as one of the leading outdoor entertainment venues in the metro Atlanta area and has hosted hometown favorites, national and touring acts for more than thirty years
Seating Capacity: 2,213

6657
ROME CITY AUDITORIUM
601 Broad Street
Rome, GA 30162-1433
Mailing Address: PO Box 1433 Rome, GA 30162-1433
Phone: 706-236-4416
Web Site: www.romega.us
Management:
  City Manager: John Bennett
  Assistant City Manager: Sammy Rich
Facility Category: Auditorium
Type of Stage: Wood
Seating Capacity: 1,112

6658
ARMSTRONG STATE COLLEGE FINE ARTS AUDITORIUM
Armstrong Atlantic State University
Fine Arts Hall, Room 125
11935 Abercorn Street
Savannah, GA 31419-1997
Phone: 912-344-2556
Fax: 912-344-3419
Toll-free: 800-633-2349
e-mail: finearts@armstrong.edu
Web Site: www.finearts.armstrong.edu
Management:
  Department Head: Dr. Tom L. Cato
  Senior Secretary: Sherrye Beckett
  Instructor of Art - Art : Cynthia Costa
  Associate Professor of Art - Graphi: Angela Horne
  Associate Professor of Art - Painti: Pang Chieh Hsu
Status: Non-Profit, Non-Professional
Paid Staff: 40
Paid Artists: 40
Seating Capacity: 1,000

6659
JENKINS THEATRE
Armstrong Atlantic State University
11935 Abercorn Street
Savannah, GA 31419-1997
Phone: 912-344-2556
Fax: 912-344-3419
Toll-free: 800-633-2349
e-mail: finearts@mail.armstrong.edu
Web Site: www.finearts.armstrong.edu
Management:
  Department Head: Dr. Tom L. Cato
  Senior Secretary: Sherrye Beckett
  Instructor of Art - Art : Cynthia Costa
  Associate Professor of Art - Graphi: Angela Horne
  Associate Professor of Art - Painti: Pang Chieh Hsu
Type of Stage: Black Box
Seating Capacity: 200

6660
LUCAS THEATRE FOR THE ARTS
Savannah College of Art and Design
32 Abercorn St.
Savannah, GA 31401
Mailing Address: 32 Abercorn St., Savannah, GA 31401 USA
Phone: 912-525-5040
Fax: 915-525-5030
e-mail: carter@lucastheatre.com
Web Site: www.lucastheatre.com
Officers:
  Production Manager: David Harris
  Executive Director: Kenneth F. Carter, Jr.
Management:
  Director: David Harris
  Production Coordinator Community Re: Erin L. Muller
  Technical Director: Bryan Bailey
  House Manager: Shea Caruso
Founded: 1921
Season: Year Round
Annual Attendance: 12,000
Type of Stage: Proscenium
Stage Dimensions: 48.3 x 26.11
Orchestra Pit: y
Seating Capacity: 1,237
Year Built: 1921
Architect: C.K. Howell
Cost: $14 Million

6661
SAVANNAH CIVIC CENTER
301 W Ogelthorpe Ave.
Savannah, GA 31401
Mailing Address: 301 West Oglethorpe Avenue, Savannah, Georgia 31401
Phone: 912-651-6550
Fax: 912-651-6552
Web Site: www.savannahcivic.com
Management:
  Director: Lamont Yogi Holman
  Assistant Director: Kelli Johnson
  Event Planner: Mary Bickerton
  Event Planner: Deborah Kicklighter
  Production Manager: Marc Williams
Mission: The facility has two venues: The Martin Luther King Arena and the Johnny Mercer Theater
Founded: 1974
Seating Capacity: 3,500-9,600

6662
TRUSTEES THEATER
Savannah College of Art and Design
216 E. Broughton St.
Savannah, GA 31401
Phone: 912-525-5051
Fax: 912-525-5052
e-mail: trusteestheater@scad.edu
Web Site: www.trusteestheater.com
Management:
  Executive Director: Christina Routhier
  Director of Operations: Joshua Lotz
  Programming Director: Sheila Lynne Bolda
  Programming Coordinator: Amanda Fretz
  Box Office Manager : Matthew Terry
Season: Year Round
Type of Stage: Proscenium
Stage Dimensions: 26' H x 35' W
Seating Capacity: 1,105

6663
GEORGIA SOUTHERN UNIVERSITY PERFORMING ARTS CENTER
847 Plant Drive
Statesboro, GA 30458
Mailing Address: Performing Arts Center, Georgia Southern University, PO Box
Phone: 912-478-7999
Fax: 912-478-1480
e-mail: pac@georgiasouthern.edu
Web Site: www.academics.georgiasouthern.edu/pac/
Management:
  Director: Carol Thompson
  Technical Director: Pete Davis
  House Manager: Stacie McDaniel
  Box Office Manager: Juanita Smith
  Box Office Assistant: Jennifer Zellner
Specialized Field: Dance, Music, Theater
Paid Staff: 8

6664
THOMASVILLE CENTER FOR THE ARTS
600 E. Washington St.
Thomasville, GA 31799
Mailing Address: Thomasville Cultural Center, 600 East Washington Street, P.O
Phone: 229-226-0588
Fax: 229-226-0599
Web Site: www.thomasvilleculturalcenter.com
Officers:
  President: Bruce Grube
Management:
  Executive Director: Charles Glassick
  Director of Development: Susan O'Neal
Mission: The Thomasville Cultural Center is dedicated to enriching creative life through the visual, performing, literary, and applied arts
Paid Staff: 12
Performs At: Thomasville Cultural Center
Seating Capacity: 500

6665
SAWYER THEATRE
Valdosta State University
1500 N. Patterson St.
Valdosta, GA 31698
Mailing Address: 1500 N. Patterson St. Valdosta, GA 31698
Phone: 229-333-5800
Fax: 229-249-2602
e-mail: dguthrie@valdosta.edu
Web Site: www.valdosta.edu
Management:
  Managing Director: H Duke Guthrie
  Artistic Director: Jacque Wheeler
Seating Capacity: 225

6666
WHITEHEAD AUDITORIUM
Valdosta State University
1500 N. Patterson St.
Valdosta, GA 31698

FACILITIES / Hawaii

Mailing Address: 1500 N. Patterson St. Valdosta, GA 31698
Phone: 229-333-5800
Toll-free: 800-618-1878
Web Site: www.valdosta.edu
Management:
    Managing Director: H Duke Guthrie
    Artistic Director: Jacque Wheeler
Founded: 1970
Specialized Field: Theater, Symphony
Type of Stage: Proscenium
Seating Capacity: 773

6667
DOBBS THEATRE
Young Harris College
1 College Street
Young Harris, GA 30582
Mailing Address: 1 College Street, Po Box 68, Young Harris, GA 30582
Phone: 706-379-5176
Toll-free: 800-241-3754
Web Site: www.yhc.edu
Officers:
    President: Cathy Cox
Management:
    Director of Athletics: Randy Dunn
    Vice President for Campus Technolog: Ken Faneuff
    VP for Student Development: Angi Smith, J.D.
    Vice President for Enrollment Manag: Clinton G. Hobbs
    Vice President for Advancement: Jay T. Stroman
Mission: Utilized by Theatre Young Harris, the 175-seat Dobbs Theatre is a state-of-the-art flexible space that can be easily adjusted for arena or thrust staging
Specialized Field: Theater
Type of Stage: Thrust
Seating Capacity: 175

6668
HILDA D GLENN AUDITORIUM
Young Harris College
1 College Street
Young Harris, GA 30582
Mailing Address: 1 College Street, Po Box 68, Young Harris, GA 30582
Phone: 706-379-5176
Toll-free: 800-241-3754
Web Site: www.yhc.edu
Officers:
    President: Cathy Cox
Management:
    Director of Athletics: Randy Dunn
    Vice President for Campus Technolog: Ken Faneuff
    VP for Student Development: Angi Smith, J.D.
    Vice President for Enrollment Manag: Clinton G. Hobbs
    Vice President for Advancement: Jay T. Stroman
Mission: The Clegg Building contains the Hilda D. Glenn Auditorium with a seating capacity of 1,060 and a large stage and orchestra pit for theatre and music presentations. In addition, the Clegg Fine Arts Building houses fully-equipped scenery and costume shops.
Specialized Field: Theater
Type of Stage: Proscenium
Seating Capacity: 1,200

Hawaii

6669
UHH THEATRE
University of Hawaii at Hilo
UH Hilo Performing Arts Center
200 W Kawili Street
Hilo, HI 96720-4091
Mailing Address: University of Hawaii at Hilo, 200 W. Kawili St., Hilo, HI 96
Phone: 808-932-7490
Fax: 808-932-7494
Toll-free: 800-897-4456
e-mail: artsctr@hawaii.edu
Web Site: www.artscenter.uhh.haw
Management:
    Technical Director: Robert H Abe
    General Manager: Lee Dombroski
    Performing Arts Department Chair: Jaquelyn Johnson
Season: Year Round
Type of Stage: Proscenium
Stage Dimensions: 40 ft x 20 ft
Orchestra Pit: y
Seating Capacity: 600

6670
ALOHA STADIUM
99-500 Salt Lake Boulevard
Honolulu, HI 96818
Mailing Address: PO Box 30666 Honolulu HI 96820-0666
Phone: 808-483-2500
Fax: 808-483-2823
e-mail: alohastadium@hawaii.gov
Web Site: www.alohastadium.hawaii.gov
Management:
    Stadium Manager: Scott Chan
    Deputy Manager: Lois Manin
    Chairperson: Kevin Chong Kee
Mission: Honolulu's largest outdoor arena in the State of Hawaii
Founded: 1975
Specialized Field: large concerts and events
Affiliations: NCAA; NFL Pro Bowl; Hawaii Bowl Concerts
Seating Capacity: 50,419
Year Built: 1975
Rental Contact: Edwin K. Hayashi

6671
ANDREWS OUTDOOR THEATRE
University of Hawaii at Manoa
2600 Campus Road
Honolulu, HI 96822
Phone: 808-956-8111
Toll-free: 800-823-9771
e-mail: uhmanoa.admissions@hawaii.edu
Web Site: www.manoa.hawaii.edu
Officers:
    President: David McClain
Management:
    Director of Education: Richard Hogeboom
    Marketing/Communications Director: Xina Ma
Seating Capacity: 3,800

6672
HAWAII THEATRE CENTRE
1130 Bethel Street
Honolulu, HI 96813
Phone: 808-528-5535
e-mail: burtonwhite@hawaiitheatre.com
Web Site: www.hawaiitheatre.com

Officers:
    President: Sarah M Richards
Management:
    Artistic Director/General Manager: Burton White
    Executive Assistant to the General: Elizabeth O'Brian
    VP for Student Development: Janet Sablan
    Box Office Senior Clerk: Lisa Lee
    House Manager: Matt James
Seating Capacity: 1,400

6673
HONOLULU ACADEMY OF ARTS
900 S Beretania Street
Honolulu, HI 96814-1495
Mailing Address: 900 South Beretania St., Honolulu, HI 96814
Phone: 808-532-8700
Fax: 808-532-8787
e-mail: ksumner@honoluluacademy.org
Web Site: www.honoluluacademy.org
Officers:
    Chairman: Violet S.W. Loo
    Vice Chairman: Josh Feldman
    Chairman Emeritus: Samuel A. Cooke
Management:
    Executive Director: Stephen Little
    Managing Director: Robert White
Mission: The Academy is accredited by the American Association of Museums and registered as a National and State Historical site. In 1990, the Academy Art Center was opened to provide a program of studio art classes and workshops. In 2001, the Henry R. Luce Pavilion Complex opened with the Pavilion Caf,, Academy Shop, and Henry R. Luce Wing with 8,000 square feet (740 m2) of gallery space. In 2005, the Asian Painting Conservation Center was opened to prov
Founded: 1922
Paid Staff: 80
Annual Attendance: 250,000

6674
KENNEDY THEATRE
University of Hawaii at Manoa
Department of Theatre and Dance
1770 East-West Road
Honolulu, HI 96822
Phone: 808-956-7677
Fax: 808-956-4234
e-mail: theatre@hawaii.edu
Web Site: www.hawaii.edu/theatre
Officers:
    Chairman: Gregg Lizenbery
Management:
    Director: Dennis Carroll
    Technical Director: Gerald R. Kawaoka
    General Manager: Marty Myers
Mission: Provide performance component for theatre and dance students
Specialized Field: Theatre; Dance
Annual Attendance: 15,000
Facility Category: Educational/College
Type of Stage: Proscenium
Seating Capacity: 600
Year Built: 1963
Architect: I.M. Pei

6675
NEAL S BLAISDELL CENTER
777 Ward Avenue
Honolulu, HI 96814

FACILITIES / Idaho

Mailing Address: Department of Enterprise Services, City & County of Honolulu
Phone: 808-527-5400
Fax: 808-527-5433
e-mail: blaisdellinfo@honolulu.gov
Web Site: www.blaisdellcenter.com
Management:
  Director Enterprise Services: George Miyamoto
  Deputy Director: Randy Leong
  Director of Production: Mary E Lewis
Mission: The multi-purpose complex is composed of an internationally renowned arena, concert hall, conference rooms, galleria and exhibition hall. It was remodeled and expanded in 1994. It is also the home of the Hawaii Basketball League Honolulu Bandits.
Founded: 1964
Specialized Field: multi functional space
Paid Staff: 150

6676
SAINT LOUIS CENTER FOR THE PERFORMING ARTS
3142 Waialae Avenue
Honolulu, HI 96816-1579
Phone: 808-739-4886
Fax: 808-739-4821
e-mail: mamiya@saintlouishawaii.org
Web Site: www.saintlouishawaii.org
Officers:
  Chairman: T. Michael Hogan, Jr.
  Vice Chairman: P. Gregory Frey '79
  Treasurer/Secretary: Darrel R. Hoke '83
Management:
  Provincial Superior: Rev. Martin Solma
  Assistant Provincial: Bro. Joseph Kamis
  Assistant for Religious Life: Rev. William Meyer
  Assistant for Education: Bro. Edward Brink
  Assistant for Temporalities: Rev. Paul Marshall

6677
MAUI ARTS & CULTURAL CENTER
One Cameron Way
Kahului, HI 96732
Phone: 808-242-2787
Fax: 808-242-4665
Web Site: www.mauiarts.org
Officers:
  President: Karen A Fischer
  Executive VP: Art Vento
Management:
  Marketing Director: Barbara Trecker
  Development Director: Lisa Varde
Utilizes: Actors; Collaborations; Curators; Dance Companies; Dancers; Educators; Fine Artists; Five Seasonal Concerts; Guest Choreographers; Guest Directors; Guest Musical Directors; Guild Activities; Instructors; Local Artists; Multimedia; Original Music Scores; Sign Language Translators; Student Interns; Special Technical Talent; Theatre Companies; Touring Companies
Annual Attendance: 250,000
Facility Category: Visual and performing arts
Type of Stage: Proscenium and open air
Seating Capacity: 5,000 + 1,200 + 300
Year Built: 1994
Cost: $32 million
Rental Contact: Candace Croteau

6678
KAHILU THEATRE FOUNDATION
67 1186 Lindsey Road
Kamuela, HI 96743
Mailing Address: PO Box 549 Kamuela HI 96743
Phone: 808-885-6017
Fax: 808-885-0546
e-mail: janet@kahilutheatre.org
Web Site: www.kahilutheatre.org
Officers:
  President: Mimi Kerley
  VP Internal Affairs: Monique Allison
  Secretary: Vicki McManus
  VP Development: Carolyn Stewart
Management:
  Managing and Artistic Director: Tim Bostock
  Operations Director: Alva Kamalani
  Marketing/Development Director: Dayva Keolanui
  Box Office Manager: Molly Hui
  Director: Jennifer Buddenhagen
Mission: the theatre serves as a center for residents and visitors alike to come to experience other cultures and explore the incredibly rich, diverse, imaginative and exciting realm of artistic expression.
Utilizes: Actors; Artists-in-Residence; Dance Companies; Dancers; Educators; Fine Artists; Guest Accompanists; Instructors; Lyricists; Multimedia; Organization Contracts; Original Music Scores; Poets; Resident Artists; Resident Professionals; Selected Students; Sign Language Translators; Singers; Soloists; Special Technical Talent; Theatre Companies; Visual Arts
Founded: 1981
Specialized Field: Theater
Paid Staff: 15
Volunteer Staff: 10
Budget: $1.2 million
Performs At: Proscenium Theatre
Affiliations: WA; APAP
Annual Attendance: 12,000
Facility Category: Theater
Type of Stage: Proscenium
Stage Dimensions: 35 x 65
Seating Capacity: 490
Year Built: 1981
Rental Contact: Operations Director Alva Kamalani
Organization Type: Performing; Sponsoring

6679
PAUL AND VI LOO THEATRE
Hawaii Pacific University
45-045 Kamehameha Highway
Kaneohe, HI 96744-5297
Mailing Address: Hawai'i Pacific University, 1164 Bishop Street, Suite #200,
Phone: 808-544-0200
Toll-free: 866-225-5478
e-mail: KArchibald@hpu.edu
Web Site: www.hpu.edu
Officers:
  President: Chatt G Wright
Management:
  Theater Manager: Karen Archabald
  Theater Director: Joyce Maltby
Specialized Field: Theater

6680
LAHAINA CIVIC CENTER
County of Maui Hawai'i
1840 Hanopilani Hwy
Lahaina, HI 96761
Mailing Address: 1840 Honoapiilani Hwy, Lahaina, HI 96761
Fax: 808-661-9316
Web Site: www.co.maui.hi.us
Officers:
  Chair: Gladys Coelho Baisa
  Vice Chair: Robert Carroll
Management:
  Council Member: Elle Cochran
  Booking: Robbie Wares
Mission: The Lahaina Civic Center is a sports, convention and entertainment complex
Seating Capacity: 2,500

6681
DAVID O MCKAY AUDITORIUM
Brigham Young University Hawaii
55-220 Kulanui Street
Laie, HI 96762-1294
Mailing Address: Brigham Young University-Hawaii, 55-220 Kulanui Street, Laie
Phone: 808-675-3211
Web Site: www.byuh.edu
Officers:
  President: Steven C. Wheelwright
  VP of Academics: Max L Checketts
  VP of Administrative Services: Michael B Bliss
  VP of Student Development & Affairs: Debbie Hippolite Wright
  Vice President, Construction, Facil: David A. Lewis
Management:
  President: Steven C. Wheelwright
Specialized Field: Concerts
Type of Stage: Auditorium
Orchestra Pit: y
Seating Capacity: 800
Architect: Paul Louie & Associates
Cost: $6 Million

6682
THE LEEWARD THEATRE
Leewood Community College
96-045 Ala Ike
Pearl City, HI 96782
Phone: 808-455-0380
Fax: 808-455-0384
e-mail: lcctheatre@lcc.hawaii.edu
Web Site: www.lcctheatre.hawaii.edu
Officers:
  Chancellor: Manuel Cabral
  VC: Michael Pecsok
Management:
  Theatre Manager: Joe Patti
  Technical Director: Don Ranney
Paid Staff: 5
Seating Capacity: 50-65
Year Built: 1974

Idaho

6683
DANNY PETERSON THEATRE
Boise State University
Morrison Center for the Performing Arts
1910 University Drive
Boise, ID 83725
Mailing Address: 1910 University Drive, Boise ID 83725-1050
Phone: 208-426-3957
Fax: 208-426-3021
e-mail: scottbodmer@boisestate.edu
Web Site: www.theatrearts.boisestate.edu/performance-facilities/danny-pete
Officers:
  Department Chair/Director: Richard Klautsch
Management:
  Dramatic Writing: Phill Atlakson

All listings are in alphabetical order by state, then city, then organization within the city.

FACILITIES / Idaho

Design/Technical Theatre: Michael Baltzell
Lighting Design, Scenic Design: Raquel Davis
Theatre History, Dramaturgy: Leslie Durham
Department Chair, Acting, Directing: Richard Klautsch
Mission: the Morrison Center for the Performing Arts is to encourage cultural and intellectual activities for the benefit and enjoyment of all Idaho citizens
Utilizes: Resident Artists
Founded: 1984
Type of Stage: Flexible Black Box
Seating Capacity: 200

6684
MORRISON CENTER FOR THE PERFORMING ARTS
Boise State University
1910 University Drive
Boise, ID 83725
Mailing Address: 1910 University Drive, Boise ID 83725-1050
Phone: 208-426-3957
Fax: 208-426-3021
Web Site: www.mc.boisestate.edu
Officers:
   Department Chair/Director: Richard Klautsch
Management:
   Dramatic Writing: Phill Atlakson
   Design/Technical Theatre: Michael Baltzell
   Lighting Design, Scenic Design: Raquel Davis
   Theatre History, Dramaturgy: Leslie Durham
   Department Chair, Acting, Directing: Richard Klautsch
Mission: the Morrison Center for the Performing Arts is to encourage cultural and intellectual activities for the benefit and enjoyment of all Idaho citizens
Founded: 1984
Specialized Field: Concerts, ballet, theater
Paid Staff: 50
Type of Stage: Proscenium
Seating Capacity: 2,000

6685
CENTURY LINK ARENA BOISE
233 S Capitol Boulevard
Boise, ID 83702
Mailing Address: 455 N. 10th Street, Omaha, NE 68102
Phone: 208-424-2200
Fax: 208-424-2222
e-mail: etrapp@idahosteelheads.com
Web Site: www.centurylinkarenaboise.com
Officers:
   President of Idaho Steelheads at Ce: Eric Trapp
   VP Idaho Sports Properties: Michael DiPalma
Management:
   Assistant GM - Operations and Produ: Mark Zaborski
   Assistant GM - Booking and Event Se: Sean Rhodes
   Guest Services Manager: Jennifer Westerdoll
   Box Office Manager: Andrew Hoffman
   Creative Services & Game Day Operat: Matthew Johnson
Mission: Qwest Arena (formerly Bank of America Centre) is multi-purpose arena in Boise, Idaho. It holds 5,300 fans for ice hockey and basketball, 5,732 for end-stage concerts, 6,400 for boxing and up to 6,800 for center-stage concerts
Founded: 1997
Specialized Field: Concerts
Seating Capacity: 5,000
Year Built: 1997

6686
STUDENT UNION SPECIAL EVENTS CENTER
Boise State University
1910 University Drive
Boise, ID 83725
Mailing Address: 1910 University Drive, Boise ID 83725-1050
Phone: 208-426-3957
Fax: 208-426-3021
e-mail: scottbodmer@boisestate.edu
Web Site: www.sub.boisestate.edu/special-events-center
Officers:
   Department Chair/Director: Richard Klautsch
Management:
   Dramatic Writing: Phill Atlakson
   Design/Technical Theatre: Michael Baltzell
   Lighting Design, Scenic Design: Raquel Davis
   Theatre History, Dramaturgy: Leslie Durham
   Department Chair, Acting, Directing: Richard Klautsch
Mission: the Morrison Center for the Performing Arts is to encourage cultural and intellectual activities for the benefit and enjoyment of all Idaho citizens
Utilizes: Resident Artists
Type of Stage: Proscenium
Seating Capacity: 400

6687
TACO BELL ARENA
Boise State University
1910 University Drive
Boise, ID 83725
Mailing Address: Taco Bell Arena at Boise State University, 1910 University D
Phone: 208-426-1900
Fax: 208-426-1998
e-mail: mcolsen@boisestate.edu
Web Site: www.tacobellarena.com
Management:
   Executive Director: Lisa Cochran
   Director, Booking and Scheduling: John Roberts
   General Manager: Ron Janeczko
   Director of Safety and Security: Tim Deck
   Senior Accountant: Shannon Reed
Founded: 1980
Seating Capacity: 13,000

6688
VELMA V. MORRISON CENTER FOR THE PERFORMING ARTS
Boise State University
1910 University Drive
Boise, ID 83725
Mailing Address: 1910 University Drive, Boise ID 83725-1050
Phone: 208-426-1609
Fax: 208-426-3021
e-mail: morrisoncenter@boisestate.edu
Web Site: www.mc.boisestate.edu
Management:
   Dramatic Writing: Phill Atlakson, rosemaryreinhardt@boisestate.e
   Design/Technical Theatre: Michael Baltzell
   Lighting Design, Scenic Design: Raquel Davis
   Theatre History, Dramaturgy: Leslie Durham
   Department Chair, Acting, Directing: Richard Klautsch
Utilizes: Resident Artists
Founded: 1984
Type of Stage: Proscenium
Orchestra Pit: y
Seating Capacity: 2000
Rental Contact: Virginia Treat

6689
VELMA V. MORRISON CENTER FOR THE PERFORMING ARTS
Boise State University
Morrison Center for the Performing Arts
2201 Cesar Chavez Lane
Boise, ID 83725
Mailing Address: 1910 University Drive, Boise ID 83725-1050
Phone: 208-426-1609
Fax: 208-426-3021
e-mail: jamespatrick@boisestate.edu
Web Site: www.mc.boisestate.edu
Officers:
   Department Chair/Director: Richard Klautsch
Management:
   Executive Director: James Patrick
   Business Director: Scott Bodmer
   Director of Ticketing Relations: Deborah Eidson
   Education Director: Carole Whiteleather
   Event Operations Manager: Ron Ujiiye
Utilizes: Resident Artists

6690
AMPHITHEATRE
The College of Idaho
2112 Cleveland Blvd
Caldwell, ID 83605
Mailing Address: Theatre, Box #111, 2112 Cleveland Blvd., Caldwell, ID 83
Phone: 208-459-5011
Fax: 208-459-5175
Toll-free: 800-244-3246
e-mail: mhartwell@collegeofidaho.edu
Web Site: www.collegeo
Officers:
   President: Marvin Henberg
   Chair: Joe Golden
Management:
   Student Account Representative: Gricelda Blanco
   VP for Finance & Administration: Petra Carver
   Business Office Assistant: Kean-San Choo
   Financial Analyst: Brandi Clark
   Staff Accountant: Gena McLamore
Mission: This beautiful space is used by students for quiet study and is utilized by the Program Council for staging outdoor band concerts. While the theatre department has yet to produce a play here, the opportunity exists for staging classical Greek works in this setting! Wait and see!

6691
EROS THEATRE
The College of Idaho
2112 Cleveland Blvd
Caldwell, ID 83605
Mailing Address: Theatre, Box #111, 2112 Cleveland Blvd., Caldwell, ID 83
Phone: 208-459-5011
Fax: 208-459-5175
Toll-free: 800-244-3246
e-mail: mhartwell@collegeofidaho.edu
Web Site: www.collegeo
Officers:
   President: Robert Hoover
   Chair: Joe Golden
Management:
   Student Account Representative: Gricelda Blanco
   VP for Finance & Administration: Petra Carver
   Business Office Assistant: Kean-San Choo
   Financial Analyst: Brandi Clark

FACILITIES / Idaho

Staff Accountant: Gena McLamore
Mission: The Eros is a versatile space where seats can be arranged or removed depending upon the director's and designer's vision
Founded: 1998

6692
JEWETT AUDITORIUM
The College of Idaho
2112 Cleveland Blvd
Caldwell, ID 83605
Mailing Address: Theatre, Box #111, 2112 Cleveland Blvd., Caldwell, ID 83
Phone: 208-459-5011
Fax: 208-459-5175
e-mail: mhartwell@collegeofidaho.edu
Web Site: www.collegeofidaho.edu
Officers:
    President: Robert Hoover
    Chair: Joe Golden
Management:
    Student Account Representative: Gricelda Blanco
    VP for Finance & Administration: Petra Carver
    Business Office Assistant: Kean-San Choo
    Financial Analyst: Brandi Clark
    Staff Accountant: Gena McLamore
Mission: The college hold various ceremonies in the hall as well as music concerts, guest speakers and other functions. The Caldwell Fine Arts organization frequently brings in touring companies who perform on stage.
Type of Stage: Proscenium
Seating Capacity: 850

6693
RECITAL HALL
The College of Idaho
2112 Cleveland Blvd
Caldwell, ID 83605
Mailing Address: Theatre, Box #111, 2112 Cleveland Blvd., Caldwell, ID 83
Phone: 208-459-5011
Fax: 208-459-5175
e-mail: mhartwell@collegeofidaho.edu
Web Site: www.collegeofidaho.edu
Officers:
    President: Robert Hoover
    Chair: Joe Golden
Management:
    Student Account Representative: Gricelda Blanco
    VP for Finance & Administration: Petra Carver
    Business Office Assistant: Kean-San Choo
    Financial Analyst: Brandi Clark
    Staff Accountant: Gena McLamore
Mission: The Recital Hall is a 200-seat, proscenium performance space designed for optimum sound quality. The CofI Theatre and Music departments have joined forces to stage musicals and operas in this lovely theatre
Type of Stage: Proscenium
Seating Capacity: 200

6694
STUDIO THEATRE
The College of Idaho
2112 Cleveland Blvd
Caldwell, ID 83605
Mailing Address: Theatre, Box #111, 2112 Cleveland Blvd., Caldwell, ID 83
Phone: 208-459-5011
Fax: 208-459-5175
e-mail: mhartwell@collegeofidaho.edu
Web Site: www.collegeofidaho.edu
Officers:
    President: Robert Hoover
    Chair: Joe Golden
Management:
    Student Account Representative: Gricelda Blanco
    VP for Finance & Administration: Petra Carver
    Business Office Assistant: Kean-San Choo
    Financial Analyst: Brandi Clark
    Staff Accountant: Gena McLamore
Mission: This Black Box Theatre located in the Langroise Center for the Performing and Fine Arts converts to thrust, stadium and arena configurations with movable seating sections. The Studio Theatre serves as the primary playing space for Mainstage Theatre productions and classroom work for acting and directing classes at CofI
Type of Stage: Thrust, Stadium, Arena
Stage Dimensions: 50' X 52'
Seating Capacity: 90 - 145

6695
BARRUS AUDITORIUM- CONCERT HALL
Brigum Young University-Idaho
BYU-I Music Department
525 South Center St.
Idaho, ID 83460
Phone: 208-496-1152
Fax: 208-496-4953
e-mail: music@byui.edu
Web Site: www.byui.edu
    Booking Director: Don Spearhawk

6696
CIVIC AUDITORIUM
308 Constitution Way
Idaho Falls, ID 83402
Mailing Address: 501 S. Holmes, P.O. Box 50220, Idaho Falls, Idaho 83405
Phone: 208-612-8396
Web Site: www.idahofallsidaho.gov/city/the-civic-auditorium.html
Officers:
    Mayor: Rebecca Casper
    Council President: Michael Lehto
Management:
    Manager: Ed Morgan
Paid Staff: 2
Seating Capacity: 1,892

6697
COLONIAL THEATRE
498 A Street
Idaho Falls, ID 83402
Phone: 208-522-0471
Web Site: www.idahofallsarts.org
Officers:
    Chair: Steve Carr
    Vice Chair: Laurel Sayer
    Secretary: Kerry Martin
    Treasurer: Tracy Hoart
Management:
    Executive Director: Jill Barnes
    Development Director: Gina Stevenson
    Technical Director: Brad Higbee
Seating Capacity: 970

6698
SUN VALLEY CENTER FOR THE ARTS
191 Fifth Street E
Ketcham, ID 83340
Mailing Address: PO Box 656, Sun Valley ID 83353
Phone: 208-726-9491
Fax: 208-726-2344
e-mail: information@sunvalleycenter.org
Web Site: www.sunvalleycenter.org
Officers:
    President: John Gaeddert
    VP: Katherine Rixon
    Treasurer: Kirk Riedinger
    Secretary: Kathleen M. Jones
Management:
    Artistic Director: Kristin Poole
    Marketing Manager: Holly Bornemeier
    Marketing Director: Kristine Bretall
    Development Associate: Jackie Costello
    Special Events Fundraising Manager: Christine Davis-Jeffers
Mission: Our mission is to provoke and stimulate the imagination while opening hearts and minds through excellence in diverse arts programming. We do this by offering exhibitions, lectures, classes and performing arts events that touch on issues relevant to our times and by bringing some of the world's most interesting artists, writers and thinkers to our small community in central Idaho.
Founded: 1971
Paid Staff: 12
Budget: $60,000-$150,000
Performs At: Sun Valley Center for the Arts and Humanities
Organization Type: Presenting

6699
HARTUNG THEATRE
University of Idaho
Department of Theatre & Film
875 Perimeter Drive
Moscow, ID 83844
Mailing Address: PO Box 443074, Moscow ID 83844-2008
Phone: 208-885-6465
Fax: 208-885-2558
e-mail: theatre@uidaho.edu
Web Site: www.uidaho.edu
Officers:
    Chair: Dean Panttaja
Management:
    Professor of Theatre: Robert C. Caisley
    Professor of Costume Design, Head o: Ann Hoste
    Professor of Performance: David Lee-Painter
    Professor and Department Chair: Dean Panttaja
    Professor of Performance; Head of A: Kelly Quinnett
Utilizes: Resident Artists
Type of Stage: Semi-Thrust Proscenium
Seating Capacity: 417
Year Built: 1973

6700
KIBBIE-ASUI ACTIVITY CENTER
University of Idaho
PO Box 442302
Moscow, ID 83844-2302
Mailing Address: Christopher Cooney, P.O. Box 443221, Moscow, ID 83844-3221
Phone: 208-885-6466
e-mail: drew@uidaho.edu, ccooney@uidaho.edu
Web Site: www.govandals.com
Management:
    Athletic Director: Rob Spear
    General Manager: Tom Morris
    Senior Director of Marketing: Christopher Coonet
Mission: multi-purpose indoor athletic stadium in Moscow, Idaho, on the campus of the University of Idaho
Founded: 1975
Paid Staff: 75
Seating Capacity: 8,500

FACILITIES / Idaho

6701
KIVA THEATRE
University of Idaho
Department of Theatre & Film
875 Perimeter Drive
Moscow, ID 83844
Mailing Address: PO Box 443074, Moscow ID 83844-3074
Phone: 208-885-6465
Fax: 208-885-2558
e-mail: theatre@uidaho.edu
Web Site: www.uidaho.edu
Officers:
   Chair: Dean Panttaja
Management:
   Professor of Theatre: Robert C. Caisley
   Professor of Costume Design, Head o: Ann Hoste
   Professor of Performance: David Lee-Painter
   Professor and Department Chair: Dean Panttaja
   Professor of Performance; Head of A: Kelly Quinnett
Utilizes: Resident Artists
Type of Stage: Theatre-In-The-Round
Seating Capacity: 125
Year Built: 1973

6702
UNIVERSITY OF IDAHO THEATRE ARTS
University of Idaho
875 Perimeter Drive
Moscow, ID 83844
Mailing Address: PO Box 443074 Moscow ID 83844-2008
Phone: 208-885-6465
Fax: 208-885-2558
e-mail: theatre@uidaho.edu
Web Site: www.uitheatre.com
Officers:
   Chair: Dean Panttaja
Management:
   Professor of Theatre: Robert C. Caisley
   Professor of Costume Design, Head o: Ann Hoste
   Professor of Performance: David Lee-Painter
   Professor and Department Chair: Dean Panttaja
   Professor of Performance; Head of A: Kelly Quinnett
Utilizes: Actors; Artists-in-Residence; Choreographers; Collaborations; Community Members; Contract Actors; Dancers; Designers; Educators; Fine Artists; Guest Artists; Guest Choreographers; Guest Lecturers; Guest Soloists; Guest Teachers; Guest Writers; High School Drama; Instructors; Local Artists; Local Unknown Artists; Multimedia; Paid Performers; Performance Artists; Resident Artists; Resident Professionals; Sign Language Translators; Soloists; Students; Student Interns; Special Technical Talent; Visual Arts; Volunteer Directors & Actors; Writers
Specialized Field: Theatre
Type of Stage: Black Box
Seating Capacity: 50
Year Built: 1973

6703
MOUNTAIN HOME ARTS COUNCIL
PO Box 974
Mountain Home, ID 83647
Phone: 208-587-3706
e-mail: mh-arts@qwestoffice.net
Web Site: www.mharts.org
Officers:
   President: Denise Barresi
   Vice President: Linda Kirkendall
   Treasurer: Chris DeVore
   Secretary: Frank Monasterio
   Performing Arts Chair: Betty Ashcraft
Management:
   Executive Director: Sally Cruser
   Marketing Committee: Scotta Groggett
   Marketing Committee: Christy Groggett
Paid Staff: 1

6704
GRAND LOBBY
Northwest Nazarene University
623 S University Boulevard Nampa
Nampa, ID 83686
Mailing Address: Northwest Nazarene University, 623 S University Boulevard, N
Phone: 208-467-8011
e-mail: hmlindner@nnu.edu
Web Site: www.nnu.edu
Officers:
   President: Dr David Alexander
   VP for Enrollment and Marketing: Stacey Berggren
   Director of Leadership Development: Dr. Carey Cook
   VP for Spiritual and Leadership Dev: Dr. Fred Fullerton
   VP for Financial Affairs: David Tarrant
Management:
   Marketing Director: Hollie Lindner
Mission: The 9,000 square-foot Grand Lobby is a beautiful setting for your banquet or annual meeting. With seating for up to 250, fresh and unique menues from Sodexho, and our signature customer service, your banquet will be an event to remember
Type of Stage: Auditorium
Seating Capacity: 1,500

6705
IDAHO CENTER
16200 Idaho Center Blvd.
Nampa, ID 83687
Mailing Address: 16114 Idaho Center Boulevard Suite 2, Nampa ID 83687
Phone: 208-468-1000
Fax: 208-442-3312
Web Site: www.idahocenter.com
Management:
   Executive Director: Ron Oroson
Mission: The Idaho Center, at the Crossroads of the Northwest, is one of the most versatile and accessible facilities of its kind in the West. Whether you're attending a Convention, a Sporting Event, a Concert, a Trade Show, a Conference, an Equestrian Event, or a Theatrical Production
Seating Capacity: 13,500

6706
NAMPA CIVIC CENTER
311 3rd Street S
Nampa, ID 83651
Phone: 208-468-5500
Fax: 208-465-2255
e-mail: info@nampaciviccenter.com
Web Site: www.nampaciviccenter.com
Management:
   Director: Stacey Mooney
   Event Coordinator: James Brown
   Project & Marketing Coordinator: Deidre Friedli
   Tech Staff: Bob Law
   Tech Staff: Bob Crisman
Paid Staff: 23
Seating Capacity: 640

6707
SWAYNE AUDITORIUM
Northwest Nazarene University
623 S University Boulevard Nampa
Nampa, ID 83686
Mailing Address: Northwest Nazarene University, 623 S University Boulevard, N
Phone: 208-467-8011
e-mail: hmlindner@nnu.edu
Web Site: www.nnu.edu
Officers:
   President: Dr David Alexander
   VP for Enrollment and Marketing: Stacey Berggren
   Director of Leadership Development: Dr. Carey Cook
   VP for Spiritual and Leadership Dev: Dr. Fred Fullerton
   VP for Financial Affairs: David Tarrant
Management:
   Marketing Director: Hollie Lindner
Mission: With over 1,500 plush theatre seats, complete backstage support spaces, state of the art technology, and a production staff dedicated to providing our clients with a quality experience, Swayne Auditorium is the ideal venue for your concert, graduation ceremony, organization-wide training session, or theatrical performance.
Type of Stage: Auditorium
Seating Capacity: 1,500

6708
BILYEU THEATRE
Idaho State University
921 South 8th Avenue
Pocatello, ID 83209
Mailing Address: Theatre/Dance ISU, 921 S 8th Ave, Stop 8006 | Pocatello, ID
Phone: 208-282-3173
Fax: 208-282-6281
Web Site: www.isu.edu/theatreisu/index.shtml
Officers:
   President: Arthur C. Vailas
   Coordinator: Allyson Johnson
Mission: The Bilyeu Theatre, previously called Frazier Auditorium, is a 790-seat proscenium theatre housed in Frazier Hall. Since its completion in 1924, Frazier has been the site for numerous theatre productions.
Utilizes: Poets
Founded: 1924
Specialized Field: Theater
Type of Stage: Proscenium
Seating Capacity: 790
Cost: $34 Million

6709
BISTLINE FAMILY THEATRE
Idaho State University
921 S. 8th Avenue
Pocatello, ID 83209
Mailing Address: Theatre/Dance ISU, 921 S 8th Ave, Stop 8006 | Pocatello, ID
Phone: 208-282-0211
Web Site: www.isu.edu
Officers:
   President: Arthur C. Vailas
   Coordinator: Allyson Johnson
Utilizes: Poets
Type of Stage: Thrust
Seating Capacity: 450
Cost: $34 Million

6710
BEVERLY B. BISTLINE THRUST THEATRE
Idaho State University
921 South 8th Avenue
Pocatello, ID 83209
Mailing Address: Theatre/Dance ISU, 921 S 8th Ave, Stop 8006 | Pocatello, ID
Phone: 208-282-0211
e-mail: caspgeor@isu.edu
Web Site: www.isu.edu/stephens/bistline.shtml
Officers:
    President: Arthur C. Vailas
Management:
    Director of Events: George Casper
    Building Facility Foreman: William Bill' Stanton
    Senior Accountant: Kristy Carpenter
    Event Technical Coordinator: Kai Manzo
    Box Office Manger: Paula Corbin
Paid Staff: 8
Performs At: Student Union Ballroom
Affiliations: Alpha Psa Omega
Type of Stage: Proscenium Thurst

6711
GORANSON HALL
Idaho State University
Fine Art Building
921 S 8th Avenue
Pocatello, ID 83209
Phone: 208-282-0211
Fax: 208-282-4884
e-mail: caspgeor@isu.edu
Web Site: www.isu.edu/events/goranson.shtml
Officers:
    President: Arthur C Vailas
Management:
    Director of Events: George Casper
    Director of Ticketing: Erin Joy-Fisk
    Box Office Manager: Paula Corbin
    Senior Accountant: Kristy Carpenter
Type of Stage: Proscenium
Seating Capacity: 446

6712
HOLT ARENA
Idaho State University
921 S 8th Avenue
Pocatello, ID 83209
Mailing Address: Theatre/Dance ISU, 921 S 8th Ave, Stop 8006 | Pocatello, ID
Phone: 208-236-2831
Web Site: www.isu.edu/events/holtarena.shtml
Management:
    Director of Events: George Casper
    Director of Ticketing: Erin Joy-Fisk
    Box Office Manager: Paula Corbin
    Senior Accountant: Kristy Carpenter

6713
IDAHO STATE UNIVERSITY
921 S 8th Avenue
PO Box 8281
Pocatello, ID 83209
Phone: 208-282-0211
Fax: 208-282-4741
e-mail: kovarudo@isu.edu
Web Site: www.isu.edu
Officers:
    President: Arthur C. Vailas
Founded: 1900
Status: Non-Profit, Professional
Paid Staff: 650

6714
POWELL LITTLE THEATRE
Idaho State University
921 S 8th Avenue
Pocatello, ID 83209-8026
Mailing Address: Theatre/Dance ISU, 921 S 8th Ave, Stop 8006 | Pocatello, ID
Phone: 208-282-3595
Web Site: www.isu.edu
Officers:
    Chair: Sherri R Dienstfrey
Management:
    Technical Director: Chad Gross
    Dance Director: Lauralee Zimmerly

6715
JAMES E. AND ROGERS BLACK BOX THEATRE
Idaho State University
1002 Sam Nixon Ave.
Building 88
Pocatello, ID 83209
Mailing Address: 1002 Sam Nixon Ave., Building 88 Pocatello, ID 83209
Phone: 208-282-3595
e-mail: caspgeor@isu.edu
Web Site: www.isu.edu/stephens/rogers.shtml
Officers:
    Chair: Sherri R Dienstfrey
Management:
    Director of Events: George Casper
    Director of Ticketing: Erin Joy-Fisk
    Box Office Manager: Paula Corbin
    Senior Accountant: Kristy Carpenter
Paid Staff: 8
Performs At: Student Union Ballroom
Affiliations: Alpha Psa Omega
Type of Stage: Proscenium Thurst

6716
L. E. AND THELMA E. STEPHENS PERFORMING ARTS CENTER
Idaho State University
1002 Sam Nixon Ave.
Building 88
Pocatello, ID 83209
Mailing Address: 1002 Sam Nixon Ave., Building 88 Pocatello, ID 83209
Phone: 208-282-3595
e-mail: caspgeor@isu.edu
Web Site: www.isu.edu/stephens
Officers:
    Chair: Sherri R Dienstfrey
Management:
    Director of Events: George Casper
    Director of Ticketing: Erin Joy-Fisk
    Box Office Manager: Paula Corbin
    Senior Accountant: Kristy Carpenter

6717
ELIZA R SNOW PERFORMING ARTS CENTER
Bringham Young University-Idaho
525 South Center St.
Rexburg, ID 83466
Mailing Address: Snow Building 126, Rexburg, ID 83460-1215
Phone: 208-496-1411
Fax: 208-496-1249
e-mail: ask@byui.edu
Web Site: www.byui.edu
Officers:
    President: Kim B
Management:
    Managing Director: Wayne Clark
    Facilities Director: Eric Conrad
    Grounds Supervisor: Jeff Wynn
Mission: The building is home to the Music and Performing Arts departments of BYU-Idaho, as well as the famed Barrus Concert Hall.
Utilizes: Dancers; Guest Lecturers; Guest Musical Directors; Multimedia; Sign Language Translators; Theatre Companies
Specialized Field: Theater, Music, dance
Paid Staff: 21
Income Sources: Church Of Jesus Christ Of Latter-Day Saints; Donations
Facility Category: Concert Hall
Type of Stage: Raised
Stage Dimensions: 53'x 48'
Seating Capacity: 700
Year Built: 1981
Rental Contact: Denise Green

Illinois

6718
METROPOLIS PERFORMING ARTS CENTRE
111 W Campbell St.
Arlington Heights, IL 60005
Mailing Address: 111 W. Campbell St., Second Floor, Arlington Heights, IL 600
Phone: 847-818-6393
Web Site: www.metropolisarts.com
Officers:
    President: Joseph Lynn
    VP: Thomas O'Rourke
    Treasurer: Carl R. Anfenson
    Secretary: Kathy Grossman
    First VP - Legal, Equity Residentia: Denise Boklach Beihoffer
Management:
    Executive Director: Charlie Beck
    Director of Production: Joe Mohamed
    Producer: Robin Hughes
Mission: Each year, Metropolis produces 4 shows for our Subscription Series. We also present a wide variety of shows including music performances (such as cabaret nights), comedy shows (including shows from The Second City), and family and holiday programming.
Founded: 2000
Specialized Field: Theater
Paid Staff: 25

6719
PARAMOUNT THEATRE
23 East Galena Boulevard
Aurora, IL 60506
Mailing Address: Paramount Theatre, 23 East Galena Boulevard, Aurora, IL 6050
Phone: 630-896-6666
Fax: 630-892-1084
e-mail: melissam@paramountarts.com
Web Site: www.paramountaurora.com
Officers:
    President: Tim Rater
    VP Development/Sponsorship: Katie Arko
    VP Marketing/Sales: Jim Jarvis
    VP Production: Val Devine
    VP Audience Services and Front of H: Amie Granger
Management:
    Artistic Director: Jim Corti
    Office Manager: Margie Isaacson
    Technical Director: Lou Ann Cates

FACILITIES / Illinois

Events Site Manager: Jennifer Hahn
Mission: The theatre continues to be an anchor in the city bringing in approximately $3.3 million in ancillary revenue as well as hosting many free community events including the Midwest Literary Festival, the Air Force Band Concert, the Aurora Idol Competition and staging the annual Fox Valley Park District children's production.
Founded: 1931
Specialized Field: Theater, General Entertainment.
Seating Capacity: 1,794

6720
MCPHERSON THEATRE
Illinois Wesleyan University
1312 Park Street
Bloomington, IL 61701
Phone: 309-556-1000
e-mail: webmaster@iwu.edu
Web Site: www.iwu.edu
Officers:
  President: Richard F Wilson
  Chair: George A. Vinyard
  Vice Chair: Thomas L. Brown
  Secretary: Jean M. Baird
  Treasurer: Robert E. Field
Management:
  Director of Volunteer Services: Phyllis Barker
  Executive Committee: Cathy T. Carswell
  Managing Director: Sundeep V. Mullangi
  Managing Partner: J. William Roberts
Paid Staff: 38
Seating Capacity: 300
Year Built: 1963

6721
WESTBROOK AUDITORIUM
Illinois Wesleyan University
Presser Hall
1312 Park Street
Bloomington, IL 61701
Phone: 309-556-1000
e-mail: webmaster@iwu.edu
Web Site: www.iwu.edu
Officers:
  President: Richard F Wilson
  Chair: George A. Vinyard
  Vice Chair: Thomas L. Brown
  Secretary: Jean M. Baird
  Treasurer: Robert E. Field
Management:
  Director of Volunteer Services: Phyllis Barker
  Executive Committee: Cathy T. Carswell
  Managing Director: Sundeep V. Mullangi
  Managing Partner: J. William Roberts
Paid Staff: 38
Seating Capacity: 600

6722
SHRYOCK AUDITORIUM AND ARENA PROMOTIONS
Southern Illinois University Carbondale
1263 Lincoln Drive
Carbondale, IL 62901-6899
Phone: 618-453-2121
Fax: 618-453-8164
e-mail: shryock@siu.edu
Web Site: www.siuc.edu
Officers:
  President: Glenn Poshard
Management:
  Director: Bryan L Rives
  Production Manager: Seth Kohlhaas
Founded: 1917
Status: Non-Profit, Non-Professional
Seating Capacity: 1,249

6723
SIU ARENA
Southern Illinois University Carbondale
1263 Lincoln Drive
Carbondale, IL 62901-6899
Phone: 618-453-3379
Fax: 618-453-8164
e-mail: shryock@siu.edu
Web Site: www.siuc.edu
Officers:
  President: Glenn Poshard
Management:
  Director: Bryan L Rives
  Production Manager: Seth Kohlhaas
Status: Non-Profit, Professional
Seating Capacity: 10,014

6724
ASSEMBLY HALL
University of Illinois
1800 S First Street
Champaign, IL 61820
Mailing Address: University of Illinois Assembly Hall, 1800 South First Stree
Phone: 217-333-5000
Fax: 217-244-8003
e-mail: slyman@illinois.edu
Web Site: www.uofiassemblyhall.com
Officers:
  President: B Joseph White
Management:
  Director: Kevin Ullestad
  Marketing Director: Jennifer Larson
  Marketing Director: Sue Lyman
  Marketing: Jennifer Larson
Founded: 1963
Specialized Field: General Entertainmnet
Paid Staff: 42
Seating Capacity: 16,000 to 17,200

6725
LANTZ ARENA
Eastern Illinois University
600 Lincoln Avenue
Charleston, IL 61920
Mailing Address: Eastern Illinois Athletic Department, 600 Lincoln Avenue, Ch
Phone: 217-581-6014
e-mail: rlmoser@eiu.edu
Web Site: www.eiupanthers.com/sports/2007/6/25/Lantz%20Arena%20Complex.aspx?id=23
Officers:
  President: William L Perry
Management:
  Interim Athletic Director: Dr. Dan Nadler
  Senior Associate Athletic Director: Mark Bonnstetter
  Assistant Athletic Director: Ryan Hastings
  Assistant Athletic Director/Special: Dave Kidwell
  Associate Athletic Director/Media &: Rich Moser
Founded: 1967
Seating Capacity: 5,200

6726
O'BRIEN FIELD
Eastern Illinois University
600 Lincoln Avenue
Charleston, IL 61920
Mailing Address: Eastern Illinois Athletic Department, 600 Lincoln Avenue, Ch
Phone: 217-581-6014
e-mail: rlmoser@eiu.edu
Web Site: www.eiupanthers.com/sports/2007/7/6/obrien%20stadium.aspx
Officers:
  President: William L Perry
Management:
  Interim Athletic Director: Dr. Dan Nadler
  Senior Associate Athletic Director: Mark Bonnstetter
  Assistant Athletic Director: Ryan Hastings
  Assistant Athletic Director/Special: Dave Kidwell
  Associate Athletic Director/Media &: Rich Moser
Founded: 1970
Seating Capacity: 10,000

6727
APOLLO THEATER
2540 N Lincoln Avenue
Chicago, IL 60614
Phone: 773-935-6100
Fax: 773-935-6214
e-mail: info@apollochicago.com
Web Site: www.apollochicago.com
Officers:
  President: Rob Kolson
Utilizes: Actors; Collaborations; Designers; Instructors; Local Artists; Multimedia; Music; New Productions; Original Music Scores; Resident Professionals; Selected Students; Sign Language Translators; Student Interns; Special Technical Talent; Theatre Companies
Income Sources: League of Chicago Theatres
Facility Category: Theater
Type of Stage: thrust
Seating Capacity: 450
Rental Contact: Rob Kolson
Organization Type: Sponsoring; Presenting

6728
ARIE CROWN THEATRE
Lakeside Center/McCormick Place
2301 South Lake Shore Drive
Chicago, IL 60616
Phone: 312-791-6516
Toll-free: 800-745-3000
e-mail: dgilmore@mpea.com
Web Site: www.ariecrown.com
Management:
  Booking and Calendar: Dulcie Gilmore
  Business Office/Operations Manager: Rory Rice
  Production Manager: Shelly Krevitt
  Technical Director: John Baker
Founded: 1967
Status: Non-Profit, Non-Professional
Paid Staff: 3
Type of Stage: Proscenium

6729
ATHENAEUM THEATRE
2936 N Southport Avenue
Chicago, IL 60657
Phone: 773-935-6860
Fax: 773-935-6878
Toll-free: 800-433-7285
Web Site: www.athenaeumtheatre.com
Management:
  Business Manager: Jerry Kennedy
  General Manager: Allan Chambers
  Webmaster: Scott Kauffman
  Marketing & Development Director: Jeff Delong
  Box Office Manger: Beth Bullock

FACILITIES / Illinois

Founded: 1972
Status: Non-Profit, Professional
Paid Staff: 21
Paid Artists: 100
Annual Attendance: 20,000+
Type of Stage: Proscenium
Seating Capacity: 1,325

6730
AUDITORIUM THEATRE
Roosevelt University
50 E Congress Parkway
Chicago, IL 60605
Phone: 312-341-2310
Fax: 312-431-2360
e-mail: info@auditoriumtheatre.org
Web Site: www.auditoriumtheatre.org
Officers:
   Chief Development Officer : Judie Moore Green
   Chief Marketing Officer: Colleen Flanigan
   Chief Operating Officer: C.J. Dillon
Management:
   Director of Finance: Kim Backe
   Controller: Denise Cosman
   Accountant: Vanessa Moreno
   Asst. to the Executive Director/Boa: Kathy Bliss
Utilizes: Resident Artists
Founded: 1945
Type of Stage: Flexible Configuration
Seating Capacity: 1,400
Year Built: 1889
Architect: Louis Sullivan and Dankmar Adler

6731
BANK OF AMERICA THEATRE
Broadway In Chicago
17 North State Street
Suite 810
Chicago, IL 60602
Phone: 312-977-1720
Fax: 312-977-0519
e-mail: customerservice@broadwayinchicago.com
Web Site: www.broadwayinchicago.com
Officers:
   President: Lou Raizin
   Vice President: Suzanne Bizer
   Vice President: Eileen LaCario
Founded: 1906

6732
BEVERLY ARTS CENTER
2407 W 111th Street
Chicago, IL 60655
Phone: 773-445-3838
Fax: 773-445-0386
e-mail: bac@beverlyartcenter.org
Web Site: www.beverlyartscenter.org
Officers:
   President: Barbara O'Malley
   VP: Judee Olechno
   Secretary: Steven Golden
   Treasurer: Tim Enright
Management:
   Executive Director: Heather Ireland Robinson
   Artistic Director: Shellee Frazee
   Finance Director: Mary Callaghan
   Director of Operations: Nora Ferstead
   Director of Outreach : Emily Dugan
Founded: 1968
Seating Capacity: 422

6733
CHICAGO SYMPHONY ORCHESTRA ASSOCIATION
220 S Michigan Ave.
Chicago, IL 60604
Mailing Address: 220 S. Michigan Avenue, Chicago, IL, 60604
Phone: 312-294-3000
Fax: 312-294-3329
Toll-free: 800-223-7114
e-mail: patronservices@cso.org
Web Site: www.cso.org
Officers:
   President: Deborah F Rutter
   Chairman: William A Osborn
Management:
   Music Director: Riccardo Muti
   Choral Director: Duain Wolfe
Founded: 1891
Specialized Field: Orchestra

6734
COURT THEATRE
University of Chicago
5535 S Ellis Ave.
Chicago, IL 60637
Phone: 773-702-7005
Fax: 773-834-1897
e-mail: info@courttheatre.org
Web Site: www.courttheater.org
Officers:
   Chair: Marilyn Fatt Vitale
   Vice Chairs: Linda Patton
   Vice Chairs: Margaret Maxwell Zagel
   Secretary: Joan Coppleson
   Treasurer: Michael McGarry
Management:
   Artistic Director: Charles Newell
   Executive Director: Stephen J. Albert
   Resident Artist: Ron OJ Parson
   Casting Director/Artists-in-the-Sch: Cree Rankin
   Director of Production: Jennifer Gadda
Utilizes: Guest Companies; Singers
Paid Staff: 18
Budget: $2.7 million
Income Sources: Actors' Equity Association; League of Chicago Theatres; Theatre Communications Group; Producers Association of Chicago Area Theatres
Performs At: Court Theatre
Annual Attendance: 35,000
Seating Capacity: 250
Organization Type: Performing; Educational

6735
CURTISS HALL
410 S Michigan Avenue
Suite 904
Chicago, IL 60605
Phone: 312-939-3380
e-mail: wwinters@iastate.edu
Web Site: www.fpm.iastate.edu
Management:
   General Manager: Kyle Walsh
   Director: Blake Biggerstaff
   Building Supervisor: Wendy Wintersteen
Founded: 1912
Specialized Field: Music
Paid Staff: 1

6736
DANCE CENTER
Columbia College Chicago
600 S.Michigan Avenue
Chicago, IL 60605
Mailing Address: Columbia College Chicago, 600 S. Michigan Avenue, Chicago, I
Phone: 312-639-8350
e-mail: skauffman@colum.edu
Web Site: www.colum.edu
Officers:
   Chair: Bonnie Brooks
Management:
   Executive Director: Phil Reynolds
   Marketing Director: Liqia Himebaugh
Mission: The mission of The Dance Center of Columbia College Chicago is to provide our students with a superior contemporary dance education in the context of higher learning. We fulfill this mission through the work of a qualified, professional faculty, a comprehensive curriculum that offers both Bachelor of Arts and Bachelor of Fine Arts tracks, world-class guest artists, and a nationally recognized dance performance season
Seating Capacity: 275
Year Built: 1930

6737
ENSEMBLE ESPANOL
Northeastern Illinois University
5500 N St Louis Avenue
Chicago, IL 60625
Phone: 773-442-5930
Fax: 773-442-5908
e-mail: ensemble-espanol@neiu.edu
Web Site: www.ensembleespanol.org
Management:
   Executive Director: Jorge Perez
   Founder & Artistic Director: Dame Libby Komaiko
   Associate Artistic Director: Irma Suarez Ruiz
   Manager of Operations: Giuseppa DiCesare
   Associate Artistic Director: Sara Samuels
Mission: The preservation, presentation and promotion of the classical, folkloric, Flamenco and contemporary traditions of Spain which includes the exploration of the countty's hisotry and identifies its influence on Latin American arts heritage as living sources of cultural pride and education.
Founded: 1976
Specialized Field: Dance
Status: Non-Profit
Paid Staff: 7
Volunteer Staff: 25
Paid Artists: 40

6738
HARRIS THEATER FOR MUSIC AND DANCE
205 E. Randolph Drive
Chicago, IL 60601
Phone: 312-334-7777
e-mail: info@harristheaterchicago.org
Web Site: www.harristheaterchicago.org
Officers:
   Chairman: James L. Alexander
   Executive Vice Chair: Alexandra C. Nichols
   Vice Chair: Caryn Harris
   Vice Chair: Elizabeth Haritgan Connelly
   Secretary: David Snyder
Management:
   Director of Operations and Producti: Lori Dimun
   Operations Coordinator: Emily Macaluso
   Technical Coordinator: Dawn Wilson

FACILITIES / Illinois

Manager of Community Engagement & P: Meghan McNamara
Assistant to the President & Managi: Jake Anderson
Mission: Can be used for music or dance performances as well as specials events, lectures, corporate meetings. Tailor it to fit your needs
Facility Category: Theater For Music And Dance
Seating Capacity: 1525

6739
KATHLEEN MULLADY MEMORIAL THEATRE
Loyola University
Lake Shore Campus Department of Theatre
1032 W,Sheridan Road
Chicago, IL 60660
Phone: 773-274-3000
e-mail: webmaster@luc.edu
Web Site: www.luc.edu
Officers:
President: Michael J Garanzini SJ
Management:
Director: Mark Lococo
Type of Stage: Proscenium
Seating Capacity: 297

6740
LYRIC OPERA OF CHICAGO
The Civic Opera House
20 N Wacker Drive
Chicago, IL 60606
Mailing Address: 20 N. Wacker Drive,Chicago, IL 60606
Phone: 312-332-2244
Fax: 312-419-8345
e-mail: jzimmerman@lyricopera.org
Web Site: www.lyricopera.org
Management:
General Director: Anthony Freud
Development Director: Mary Ladish Selander
Creative Consultant: Ren,e Fleming
Deputy General Director: Drew Landmesser
Director of Finance: Brent Fisher
Founded: 1952
Specialized Field: Opera

6741
THE MERLE RESKIN THEATRE
DePaul University
The Theatre School
60 E Balbo Drive
Chicago, IL 60605
Mailing Address: Anna Ables, Director of Marketing/Public Relations
Phone: 773-325-7917
Fax: 773-325-7920
e-mail: jculbert@depaul.edu
Web Site: theatre.depaul.edu
Officers:
President: Rev Dennis H Holtschneider CM
Management:
Theatre Manager: Leslie Shook
Marketing Director: Anna Ables
Development Director: Vacant
Founded: 1925
Specialized Field: Theater

6742
MILLENIUM PARK
Jay Pritzker Pavilion
201 E. Randolph St
Chicago, IL 60602
Phone: 312-744-6050
e-mail: millenium-park@cityofchicago.org
Web Site: www.milleniumpark.org

6743
NEW STUDIO THEATRE
Columbia College Chicago
600 S Michigan Avenue
Chicago, IL 60605
Mailing Address: Theater Office:, 3rd Floor Room 300, 72 East 11th Street, Ch
Phone: 312-369-6240
Fax: 312-369-8078
Web Site: www.colum.edu
Officers:
President: Warrick L Carter
Chairman: Richard Dunscomb
Management:
Executive Director: HE Baccus
Opened: 2000
Specialized Field: Instrumentals, Recitals
Seating Capacity: 40-70

6744
O'ROURKE CENTER FOR THE PERFORMING ARTS
Truman College
1145 West Wilson Ave
Chicago, IL 60640
Mailing Address: O'Rourke Center, Truman College, 1145 West Wilson Avenue, Ch
Phone: 773-907-4000
Web Site: www.trumancollege.edu
Officers:
Chief Advisor to the Board: Leah Heinecke Krumhus
Founded: 1984

6745
ORCHESTRA HALL
Chicago Symphony Orchestra Association
220 S. Michigan Ave.
Chicago, IL 60604
Phone: 312-294-3333
Fax: 312-294-3329
e-mail: email through website
Web Site: www.cso.org
Management:
president: Deborah Rutter
Vice President & Building Operation: Vanessa Moss

6746
PATRICK L O'MALLEY THEATRE
Roosevelt University
430 S. Michigan Ave
Chicago, IL 60605
Phone: 312-341-3500
e-mail: theatre@roosevelt.edu
Web Site: www.roosevelt.edu
Officers:
President: Chuck Middleton
Dean: Rudy Marcozzi
Management:
General Manager: Kelley Kendall
Production Manager: Emily Humphreys
Founded: 1945
Status: Non-Profit, Non-Professional
Paid Artists: 50

6747
PETRILLO MUSIC SHELL
City of Chicago
235 S Columbus Drive
Chicago, IL 60604
Mailing Address: 235 S. Columbus Dr., Chicago
Phone: 312-742-4763
Web Site: www.centerstagechicago.com/music/clubs/petrillo-music-shell.html
Officers:
Mayor: Richard M Daley
Management:
General Manager: Tracy Jones
Director: Miguel Del Valle
Mission: It serves as host to many large annual music festivals in the city such as Chicago Blues Festival, Chicago Jazz Festival, Taste of Chicago and Lollapalooza
Founded: 1933
Specialized Field: Music Festivals

6748
RECITAL HALL
Northeastern Illinois University
Fine Arts Department
5500 North St. Louis Avenue
Chicago, IL 60625-4699
Mailing Address: Northeastern Illinois University, 5500 N. St. Louis, Chicago
Phone: 773-583-4050
Fax: 773-442-4900
e-mail: B-Harms1@neiu.edu
Web Site: www.neiu.edu
Officers:
President: Sharon K Hahs
Secretary: Gladys Yvette Lopez
Dean: Michael T Kelly
Chair: Dr R Shayne Cofer
Management:
Director: Jorge Perez
Specialized Field: Theater

6749
SOLDIER FIELD
1410 S.
Museum Campus Drive
Chicago, IL 60605
Phone: 312-235-7000
Fax: 312-235-7030
e-mail: kmcgregor@soldierfield.net
Web Site: www.soldierfield.net
Officers:
Mayor, City of Chicago: Richard M Daley
Management:
General Manager: Tim LeFevour
Director of Operations: Michael Ortman
Director of Event Services: Kate McGregor
Assistant General Manager, Finance: Marty McAndrew
Director of Sponsorship & Media: Luca Serra
Founded: 2003
Seating Capacity: 66,950

6750
STAGE CENTER THEATRE
Northeastern Illinois University
5500 N Street Louis Avenue
Chicago, IL 60625-4699
Phone: 773-583-4050
Fax: 773-442-4900
e-mail: a-antaramian@neiu.edu
Web Site: www.neiu.edu

FACILITIES / Illinois

Officers:
President: Sharon K Hahs
Secretary: Gladys Yvette Lopez
Dean: Michael T Kelly
Chair: Dr R Shayne Cofer
Management:
Artistic/Managing Director: Anna Antaramian
Type of Stage: Thrust
Orchestra Pit: y
Seating Capacity: 100

6751
STUDIO THEATRE
Loyola University
1032 W. Sheridan Rd
Chicago, IL 60660
Mailing Address: 1032 W. Sheridan Road, Chicago, IL 60660
Phone: 773-508-3000
e-mail: webmaster@luc.edu
Web Site: www.luc.edu
Officers:
President: Michael J Garanzini SJ
Board President/General Manager: Joseph J Ahern
Chair: Sarah Gabel PhD
Management:
Director: Mark Lococo
Utilizes: Resident Artists
Type of Stage: Black Box
Seating Capacity: 50

6752
SYMPHONY CENTER
Chicago Symphony Orchestra Association
220 S Michigan Avenue
Chicago, IL 60604
Phone: 312-294-3333
Fax: 312-294-3329
e-mail: patronservices@cso.org
Web Site: www.cso.org
Officers:
President: Deborah Rutter
Management:
Director of Programming: James M Fahey
Rental Events Manager: Michael Lavin
VP Marketing: Kevin Giglinto
Box Office Manager: Joe Garnett
Seating Capacity: 2,521

6753
THE CHICAGO THEATRE
175 N State Street
Chicago, IL 60601
Mailing Address: 175 N. State Street, Chicago, IL 60601
Phone: 312-462-6300
Fax: 312-462-6364
Toll-free: 888-235-2990
Web Site: www.thechicagotheatre.com
Officers:
Chairman: James L. Dolan
Vice Chairman: Hank Ratner
President and Chief Executive Offic: Tad Smith
Executive Vice President, General C: Lawrence Burian
Executive Vice President, Facilitie: Steve Collins
Management:
Chief Technology Officer: Sean O'Donoghue
Founded: 1921
Specialized Field: General Entertainmnet
Seating Capacity: 3,604

6754
THE MUSIC CENTER
Columbia College Chicago
600 S Michigan Avenue
Chicago, IL 60605
Phone: 312-369-6240
Fax: 312-369-8078
e-mail: music@colum.edu
Web Site: www.colum.edu
Officers:
President: Warrick L. Carter
Chairman: Allen M Turner
Treasurer: Tom Kallen
Secretary: Averill Leviton
Type of Stage: Concert Hall
Seating Capacity: 125
Year Built: 1912

6755
STAGE 773
1225 W. Belmont Ave.
Chicago, IL 60657
Phone: 773-929-5252
e-mail: info@stage773.com
Web Site: www.stage773.com
Officers:
Chair: Laura Michaud
Treasurer: Alex Meyer
Secretary: Brian Posen
Management:
Artistic Director: Brian Posen
Director Of Operations: Jill Valentine
Director Of Facilities: Brian Peterlin
Executive Director: Kristin Larsen
Director of Grant and Tenant Servic: Jack Short
Utilizes: Actors; AEA Actors; Choreographers; Collaborations; Commissioned Composers; Five Seasonal Concerts; Guest Soloists; High School Drama; Instructors; Local Artists; Local Unknown Artists; Lyricists; Multimedia; Music; Organization Contracts; Original Music Scores; Performance Artists; Resident Artists; Resident Professionals; Sign Language Translators; Soloists; Student Interns; Special Technical Talent; Theatre Companies
Founded: 1969
Specialized Field: Theater
Paid Staff: 10
Volunteer Staff: 800
Paid Artists: 200
Non-paid Artists: 107
Budget: $1,000,000
Annual Attendance: 35,000
Facility Category: multiplex
Type of Stage: 3 black box
Seating Capacity: 444
Year Built: 1962
Year Remodeled: 2002
Cost: 100,000
Rental Contact: Lorraine Townsend

6756
UIC PAVILION
University of Illinois at Chicago
525 S Racine Avenue
Chicago, IL 60607
Phone: 312-413-5700
Web Site: www.uicpavilion.com
Officers:
President: B Joseph White
Management:
Director: Kevin O'Finn
Manager: Matt Liskh
Box Office Manager: Tammy Bender
Mission: The Pavilion provides an adaptable setting for a variety of educational, recreational, cultural, entertainment and civic events. These may include university events, e.g., commencements and athletic events, or non-university events
Seating Capacity: 10,000

6757
UIC THEATRE
University of Illinois at Chicago
Department of Performing Arts EPASW Building
1040 West Harrison Street MC-255
Chicago, IL 60607
Mailing Address: UIC Department of Performing Arts, College of Architecture
Phone: 312-996-2977
Fax: 312-996-0954
e-mail: dpa@uic.edu
Web Site: www.uic.edu
Officers:
President: B Joseph White
Secretary: Michele M Thompson
Chair: Michael J Anderson
Management:
Events Director: Neal McCollam
Chancellor: Paula Allen
Vice Chancellor: Lon S. Kaufman
Mission: The Theatre curriculum emphasizes a balance between practice and theory from originating impulse or idea to realization in performance. The areas of Acting, Voice, Movement, Physical Theatre Techniques, Directing, Playwriting, and Design within the context of their artistic, social, political, and historical environments form the nucleus of the curriculum.
Specialized Field: Theater
Type of Stage: Black Box
Seating Capacity: 250

6758
UNITED CENTER
1901 W Madison Street
Chicago, IL 60612
Phone: 312-455-4500
e-mail: sschanwald@bulls.com
Web Site: www.unitedcenter.com
Management:
General Manager: Jim Koehler
Marketing Director: Steve Schanwald
Operations Director: Terry Savarise
Operations Manager: Erica Schisler
Seating Capacity: 20,500

6759
US CELLULAR FIELD
Chicago White Sox
333 W 35th Street
Chicago, IL 60616
Phone: 312-674-1000
Web Site: www.whitesox.com
Officers:
Chairman: Jerry Reinsdorf
Secretary: Gerald Penner
Management:
Chief Marketing Officer: Brooks Boyer
Seating Capacity: 44,321
Year Built: 1991

6760
VICTORY GARDENS THEATER
2433 North Lincoln Avenue
Chicago, IL 60614

867

FACILITIES / Illinois

Phone: 773-549-5788
e-mail: information@victorygardens.org
Web Site: www.victorygardens.org
Officers:
    President: Steven N. Miller
    Vice President: Gabrielle Griffin
    Secretary: Pamella Capitanini
    Treasurer: David Glasner
Management:
    Artistic Director: Chay Yew
    Managing Director: Chris Mannelli
    Literary Manager: Isaac Gomez
    Artistic Programs Manager: Monty Cole
    Access Project Coordinator: Mike Ervin
Founded: 1974
Paid Staff: 24
Annual Attendance: 60,000
Type of Stage: Black Box; Thrust
Seating Capacity: 195

6761
WRIGLEY FIELD
1060 W Addison Street
Chicago, IL 60613
Phone: 773-404-2827
Web Site: www.chicago.cubs.mlb.com
Officers:
    Chairman: Crane Kenney
Management:
    Director: Scott Nelson
    Marketing Director: Matthew Wszolek
    Manager: Chuck Wasserstrom
    Facility Director: Carl Rice
Founded: 1914
Seating Capacity: 38,710

6762
CONVOCATION CENTER
North Illinois University
1525 Lincold Highway
DeKalb, IL 60115
Phone: 815-752-6800
Fax: 815-752-6830
e-mail: convocenter@niu.edu
Web Site: www.niuconvo.com
Officers:
    President: John G Peters
    Chair: Robert T Boey
Management:
    Director: John A Gordon
    Marketing Director: Heather Priest
Mission: As the center for social, academic, and athletic events on campus, the Convocation Center is the single venue that can bring the university community together at one place and one time to share an experience: the very definition of community.
Seating Capacity: 10,000

6763
EGYPTIAN THEATRE
135 N Second Street
DeKalb, IL 60115
Mailing Address: PO Box 385, DeKalb IL 60115
Phone: 815-758-1215
Fax: 815-748-3292
e-mail: info@egyptiantheatre.org
Web Site: www.egyptiantheatre.org
Officers:
    President: Kathy Love
    VP: Travis Shaffer
    Treasurer: Kay Riley
    Secretary: Kay Shelton
Management:
    Executive Director: Alex Nerad

Marketing Director: Derek Gibbs
Box Office Manager: Nora Reeves
Custodian/Maintenance: Patrick Mlady
Seating Capacity: 1,475

6764
O'CONNELL THEATRE
Northern Illinois University
1425 W Lincoln Hwy
DeKalb, IL 60115-2828
Phone: 815-753-1334
Fax: 815-753-8415
e-mail: UnivInfo@niu.edu
Web Site: www.niu.edu
Officers:
    President: Doug Baker
Management:
    Director: Alexander Gelman
    Marketing Director: David W Booth
Specialized Field: Theatre
Seating Capacity: 450

6765
PLAYERS THEATRE
Northern Illinois University
1425 W Lincoln Hwy
DeKalb, IL 60115-2828
Phone: 815-753-1334
Fax: 815-753-8415
e-mail: UnivInfo@niu.edu
Web Site: www.niu.edu
Officers:
    President: Doug Baker
Management:
    Director: Alexander Gelman
    Marketing Director: David W Booth
Type of Stage: Black Box
Seating Capacity: 180

6766
SCHOOL OF THEATRE AND DANCE
Northern Illinois University
Stevens Building, Gable Hall
DeKalb, IL 60115
Phone: 815-753-1334
Fax: 815-753-8415
e-mail: theatreinfo@niu.edu
Web Site: www.niu.edu/theatre/
Officers:
    President: Dr. John G. Peters
    Director: Alexander Gelman
    Assistant Director: Terrence McClellan
Management:
    Technical Director: Tracy Nunnally
    Director Of Marketing: David W. Booth
Mission: Provides intensive artistic & academic training for students preparing for careers in theatre & theatre-related areas. The course of study is rigorous and realistic, designed to develop, challenge & broaden the skills and attitudes off all theatre students, but especially the highly motivated student who takes responsibility for his/her own growth. Each year we present a full season of stage productions on three stages.
Specialized Field: Performance Theatre; Classical; Modern Dance
Status: Educational; Performance
Performs At: Education; Performing
Affiliations: University/Resident Theatre Assoc.; National Assoc. of Schools of Theatre; Illinois Arts Council; American Assoc. of Community Theatre
Type of Stage: Proscenium, Black Box, 1/4 Round
Seating Capacity: Theatre - 443; Corner Theatre - 145
Rental Contact: Technical Director Tracy Nunnally

6767
ALBERT TAYLOR THEATRE
Millikin University
Kirkland Fine Arts Center
1184 West Main Street
Decatur, IL 62522-2084
Mailing Address: Kirkland Fine Arts Center, 1184 West Main St, Decatur, IL 62
Toll-free: 800-373-7733
Web Site: www.millikin.edu
Officers:
    President: Dr. Patrick White
    Chief of Staff and Board Secretary: Marilyn Davis
    Provost: Dr. Jeffery Aper
    VP, Finance & Business Affairs: Ruby Brase
    VP, University Development: Dave Brandon
Management:
    Dean, College of Arts & Sciences: Dr. Randy Brooks
    Dean, College of Fine Arts: Laura Ledford
    Dean, College: Dr. Deborah Slayton
    Dean, Tabor School of Business: Dr. Susan Kruml
    University Registrar: Jason Wickline
Mission: The Albert Taylor Theatre has served as the main stage for many Millikin University activities from the opening of the University in 1903 on through to today.
Utilizes: Artists-in-Residence; Dance Companies; Fine Artists; Local Artists; Lyricists; Multimedia; Music; Original Music Scores; Resident Artists; Selected Students; Soloists; Special Technical Talent; Theatre Companies; Touring Companies
Founded: 1903
Specialized Field: Theater
Paid Staff: 6
Volunteer Staff: 12
Paid Artists: 20
Annual Attendance: 60,000
Facility Category: Fine Arts Center
Seating Capacity: 750
Architect: Patton and Miller
Year Restored: 2006

6768
KIRKLAND FINE ARTS CENTER
Millikin University
1184 W Main Street
Decatur, IL 62522
Mailing Address: Kirkland Fine Arts Center, 1184 West Main St, Decatur, IL 62
Toll-free: 800-373-7733
Web Site: www.millikin.edu
Officers:
    President: Harold Jeffcoat
    Chief of Staff and Board Secretary: Marilyn Davis
    Provost: Dr. Jeffery Aper
    VP, Finance & Business Affairs: Ruby Brase
    VP, University Development: Dave Brandon
Management:
    Dean, College of Arts & Sciences: Dr. Randy Brooks
    Dean, College of Fine Arts: Laura Ledford
    Dean, College: Dr. Deborah Slayton
    Dean, Tabor School of Business: Dr. Susan Kruml
    University Registrar: Jason Wickline
Mission: houses several music and choral facilities, lecture halls, art galleries, and other multipurpose rooms.
Utilizes: Actors; Artists-in-Residence; Dance Companies; Dancers; Fine Artists; Guest Writers; Instructors; Local Artists; Lyricists; Multimedia; Music;

Original Music Scores; Resident Artists; Selected Students; Soloists; Special Technical Talent; Theatre Companies; Touring Companies
Founded: 1969
Specialized Field: Theater, Dance, Musical
Paid Staff: 6
Volunteer Staff: 12
Paid Artists: 20
Annual Attendance: 60,000
Facility Category: Fine Arts Center
Type of Stage: Proscenium
Stage Dimensions: 53' x 23'
Orchestra Pit: y
Seating Capacity: 1,902
Rental Contact: Scheduling & Events Coordinator Lynne Kickle

6769
PIPE DREAMS STUDIO THEATRE
West Towne Square Plaza
1099 W Wood Street
Decatur, IL 62522
Mailing Address: Pipe Dreams Studio Theatre 1099 West Wood Street
Toll-free: 800-373-7733
Web Site: www.pdtheatre.com
Officers:
  President: Douglas E Zemke
  Chair: Laura Ledford
Management:
  Artistic Director: Grace Barnett
  Managing Director: Blanca Hernandez
  Production Manager: Tyler Hixson
  Marketing Director: Ashlee Estabrook
  Development Director: Hannah Krull
Mission: student operated business with help and guidance by Department of Theatre & Dance faculty
Utilizes: Artists-in-Residence; Dance Companies; Fine Artists; Local Artists; Lyricists; Multimedia; Music; Original Music Scores; Resident Artists; Selected Students; Soloists; Special Technical Talent; Theatre Companies; Touring Companies
Specialized Field: Theater, Dance
Paid Staff: 6
Volunteer Staff: 12
Paid Artists: 20
Annual Attendance: 60,000
Facility Category: Fine Arts Center

6770
ROSEMONT THEATRE
5400 N River Road
Des Plaines, IL 60018
Phone: 847-671-5100
Fax: 847-671-6405
Toll-free: 800-852-7771
e-mail: info@akootheatre.com
Web Site: www.rosemonttheatre.com
Management:
  Event Operations Director: George Theo
  Finance Manager: Keith Krumwiede
  Operations Director: Ed Balogh
Seating Capacity: 4,300

6771
DUNHAM HALL THEATER
Southern Illinois University at Edwardsville
6 S State Route 157
Edwardsville, IL 62026
Mailing Address: College of Arts and Sciences, Campus Box 1608, Southern Illi
Phone: 618-650-2000
Toll-free: 888-328-5168
e-mail: Kbozark@siue.edu
Web Site: www.siue.edu
Officers:
  Chair: Peter Cocuzza
  Secretary: Debbie Brown-Thompson
Management:
  Director: Kathryn Bentley
  Marketing Director: Mr. Kim Bozark
  General Manager: Valerie Goldston
Mission: Katherine Dunham Hall houses the departments of Theater and Dance, Music, and Mass Communications. Plays, musicals, recitals, band concerts and choral clinics are held here. Students make make use of the building's TV studio, multimedia computer lab, video editing lab and photojournalism dark room.
Specialized Field: Dance
Type of Stage: Proscenium
Orchestra Pit: y
Seating Capacity: 400

6772
JAMES F METCALF STUDENT EXPERIMENTAL THEATER
Southern Illinois University at Edwardsville
6 S State Route 157
Edwardsville, IL 62026
Mailing Address: College of Arts and Sciences, Campus Box 1608, Southern Illi
Phone: 618-650-2000
Toll-free: 888-328-5168
e-mail: Kbozark@siue.edu
Web Site: www.siue.edu
Officers:
  Chair: Peter Cocuzza
  Secretary: Debbie Brown-Thompson
Management:
  Director: Kathryn Bentley
  Marketing Director: Mr. Kim Bozark
  General Manager: Valerie Goldston
Founded: 1984
Seating Capacity: 200

6773
ELGIN COMMUNITY COLLEGE VISUAL & PERFORMING ARTS CENTER
Elgin Community College
1700 Spartan Drive
Elgin, IL 60123-7193
Mailing Address: 1700 Spartan Drive, Elgin, IL 60123-7193
Phone: 847-622-0300
e-mail: marketing@elgin.edu
Web Site: www.elgin.edu
Officers:
  President: David Sam PhD JD
Management:
  Director: Steven A Duchrow
  Marketing Director: Paula Amenta MS
  Operations/Theater Director: Cynthia Gaspardo
Mission: The Visual and Performing Arts Center provides residents of Chicago's Fox Valley with a refreshingly different arts experience than can be found in the city or other regional arts center. Our CenterStage lineup avoids tired reruns in favor of fresh, artistically relevant acts. Only the ECC Arts Center pairs club amenities-including gourmet dinners and a wine bar-with performances of the highest caliber. We aim to inspire, engage and spark your cr
Paid Staff: 20
Volunteer Staff: 80
Paid Artists: 15
Annual Attendance: 40,000
Type of Stage: Proscenium
Seating Capacity: 662

6774
THE HEMMENS CULTURAL CENTER
45 Symphony Way
Elgin, IL 60120
Phone: 847-931-5900
e-mail: hemmens@cityofelgin.org
Web Site: www.hemmens.org
Officers:
  Chair: Kathleen A Weber
  Secretary: Cathy Malm
  Treasurer: Jeff Grosser
Founded: 1969
Paid Staff: 33
Volunteer Staff: 35
Type of Stage: Proscenium Arch
Seating Capacity: 1,200

6775
BECKER AUDITORIUM
Eureka College
Donald B Cerf Center
300 E College Ave.
Eureka, IL 61530
Mailing Address: Eureka College, 300 East College Avenue, Eureka, Illinois 61
Phone: 309-467-6350
Toll-free: 888-438-7352
Web Site: www.eureka.edu
Officers:
  Chairman: David Adams
  Vice Chairman: Jim Hengst
  Secretary:: Ed Holderle
Management:
  Senior Manager, Facilities Services: Harry A. Williams
  Attorney: Rodney Gould
  General Manager: Robert Heitzman
  Civic Leader: Florence Banwart
  Retirement Services Manager: Mickeisha Armstrong
Mission: nested at the heart of the Cerf Center, this largest of Eureka's performance spaces seats over 400.
Seating Capacity: 400

6776
PRITCHARD THEATER
Eureka College
Pritchard Hall
300 E College Avenue
Eureka, IL 61530
Mailing Address: Eureka College, 300 East College Avenue, Eureka, Illinois 61
Phone: 309-467-6350
Toll-free: 888-438-7352
Web Site: www.eureka.edu
Officers:
  Chairman: David Adams
  Vice Chairman: Jim Hengst
  Secretary:: Ed Holderle
Management:
  Senior Manager, Facilities Services: Harry A. Williams
  Attorney: Rodney Gould
  General Manager: Robert Heitzman
  Civic Leader: Florence Banwart
  Retirement Services Manager: Mickeisha Armstrong

FACILITIES / Illinois

Mission: is a flexible, 300 seat, black box theater. This is the space used for most productions and is located within Pritchard Hall, near the center of Eureka's academic halls
Type of Stage: Black Box
Seating Capacity: 300
Year Restored: 1995

6777
RAYMOND F MCCALLISTER HALL
Eureka College
300 E College Avenue
Eureka, IL 61530
Mailing Address: Eureka College, 300 East College Avenue, Eureka, Illinois 61
Phone: 309-467-6350
Toll-free: 888-438-7352
Web Site: www.eureka.edu
Officers:
  Chairman: David Adams
  Vice Chairman: Jim Hengst
  Secretary:: Ed Holderle
Management:
  Senior Manager, Facilities Services: Harry A. Williams
  Attorney: Rodney Gould
  General Manager: Robert Heitzman
  Civic Leader: Florence Banwart
  Retirement Services Manager: Mickeisha Armstrong
Mission: is a 300 seat performance space that has been used for such productions as The Little Red Devils improv troupe. It is ideal for cabaret settings and one person shows.
Seating Capacity: 300

6778
RINKER OUTDOOR AMPHITHEATRE
Eureka College
300 E College Avenue
Eureka, IL 61530
Mailing Address: Eureka College, 300 East College Avenue, Eureka, Illinois 61
Phone: 309-467-6350
Toll-free: 888-438-7352
Web Site: www.eureka.edu
Officers:
  Chairman: David Adams
  Vice Chairman: Jim Hengst
  Secretary:: Ed Holderle
Management:
  Senior Manager, Facilities Services: Harry A. Williams
  Attorney: Rodney Gould
  General Manager: Robert Heitzman
  Civic Leader: Florence Banwart
  Retirement Services Manager: Mickeisha Armstrong
Mission: seats well-over 900, features ideal natural acoustics and a topiary, backdrop, and wings.Used most commonly now for convocations and graduation ceremonies, Rinker was an interegral part of Woodford County's traditional pageantry.
Type of Stage: Amphitheatre
Seating Capacity: 900

6779
CAHN AUDITORIUM
Northwestern University
633 Clark Street
Evanston, IL 60208
Phone: 847-491-3741
Web Site: www.northwestern.edu
Officers:
  President: Henry S Bienen
Management:
  Director: Joseph Appelt
  Managing Director: Barbara Butts
Mission: The largest performance space on campus, the Cahn Auditorium seats more than a thousand people and contains an orchestra pit and a balcony. The annual Waa-Mu Show, Northwestern's large-scale student musical revue that has spawned international talent throughout the years, is staged here, as are many other productions each year
Opened: 1980
Orchestra Pit: y
Seating Capacity: 1,000

6780
ETHEL M BARBER THEATRE
Northwestern University
633 Clark Street
Evanston, IL 60208
Phone: 847-491-3741
Fax: 847-467-2019
Web Site: www.northwestern.edu
Officers:
  President: Henry S Bienen
Management:
  Director: Joseph Appelt
  Managing Director: Barbara Butts
Type of Stage: Thrust
Seating Capacity: 439

6781
JOSEPHINE LOUIS THEATER
Northwestern University
633 Clark Street
Evanston, IL 60208
Mailing Address: 20 Arts Circle Drive Evanston 60208
Phone: 847-491-3741
Fax: 847-467-2019
Web Site: www.northwestern.edu
Officers:
  President: Henry S Bienen
Management:
  Director: Joseph Appelt
  Managing Director: Barbara Butts
Type of Stage: Proscenium
Seating Capacity: 369

6782
MARJORIE WARD MARSHALL DANCE CENTER
Northwestern University
633 Clark Street
Evanston, IL 60208
Phone: 847-491-3741
Fax: 847-467-2019
Web Site: www.northwestern.edu
Officers:
  President: Henry S Bienen
Management:
  Director: Joseph Appelt
  Managing Director: Barbara Butts
Mission: The Marjorie Ward Marshall Dance Center is a state-of-the-art teaching and performance facility that contains two dance studios used for productions and classes. It forms part of the Theatre and Interpretation Center. In addition to presenting regular student concerts, the Marjorie Ward Marshall Dance Center hosts exciting master classes and performance residencies by alumni and visiting international artists.
Opened: 1980

6783
PICK-STAIGER CONCERT HALL
Northwestern University
50 Arts Circle Drive
Evanston, IL 60208
Mailing Address: Pick-Staiger Concert Office, 50 Arts Circle Drive, Evanston,
Phone: 847-491-5441
Fax: 847-491-1831
e-mail: pick-staiger@northwestern.edu
Web Site: www.pickstaiger.com
Officers:
  President: Henry S Bienen
Management:
  Director: Joseph Appelt
  Managing Director: Barbara Butts
Mission: Since its inception the hall has functioned as both a classroom and performance facility for Bienen School of Music performing ensembles, Music/Theater productions, faculty recitals, festivals and professional guest artists. A typical season of programming includes Orchestral, Choral, Opera, Chamber, Jazz, Contemporary, Brass, and Percussion concerts as well as solo recitals, lectures, master classes, and other related events.
Founded: 1975
Paid Staff: 50

6784
RYAN FIELD
Northwestern University
1501 Central Street
Evanston, IL 60201
Phone: 847-491-7887
Web Site: www.nusports.com
Officers:
  President: Henry S Bienen
  Secretary: Debbie Robert
Management:
  Athletic Director: Jim Phillips
  Administrative Assistant to the VP: Anne Marie Adams
  Department Assistant: Rachel Gunn
  Deputy Director of Athletics (Exter: Mike Polisky
Founded: 1942

6785
HARBACH THEATER
Knox College
Ford Center for the Fine Arts
2 East South Street
Galesburg, IL 61401-4999
Mailing Address: Knox College, 2 East South Street, Galesburg, IL 61401-4999
Phone: 309-341-7000
e-mail: kheartle@knox.edu
Web Site: www.knox.edu
Officers:
  President: Roger Taylor
  Executive Secretary: Denise Bailey
  Chair: Janet M Koran
  Secretary: Deborah S DeGraff
Management:
  Marketing Director: Kathleen Heartlein
Mission: Knox's main stage theatre. It is a dual-configuration space: the stage and a section of the audience are situated on a 72 ft diameter turntable, capable of rotating 180 degrees to provide a proscenium configuration that seats 600 and a thrust configuration that seats 450. Designers over the years have developed many unique and non-traditional ways of working with the space.
Specialized Field: Theater

FACILITIES / Illinois

Type of Stage: Revolving Proscenium and Thrust
Seating Capacity: 400-600

6786
KNOX COLLEGE
Knox College
2 E South Street
2 East South Street
Galesburg, IL 61401-4999
Mailing Address: Knox College, 2 East South Street, Galesburg, IL 61401-4999
Phone: 309-341-7000
e-mail: kheartle@knox.edu
Web Site: www.knox.edu
Officers:
  President: Teresa Arnott
  Executive Secretary: Denise Bailey
  Chair: Dushan Petrovich
  Secretary: Laurel L Andrew
Management:
  Chief Communications Officer: Megan Scott
Mission: Knox College's Ford Center for the Fine Arts is a superbly endowed facility for art, theatre, dance, and music
Utilizes: Artists-in-Residence; Commissioned Composers; Community Talent; Composers; Composers-in-Residence; Dancers; Equity Actors; Filmmakers; Fine Artists; Guest Composers; Guest Directors; Guest Ensembles; Guest Instructors; Guest Lecturers; Guest Musical Directors; Guest Musicians; Local Unknown Artists; Multimedia; Music; Paid Performers; Singers

6787
KRESGE RECITAL HALL
Knox College
Ford Center for the Fine Arts
2 East South Street
Galesburg, IL 61401-4999
Mailing Address: Knox College, 2 East South Street, Galesburg, IL 61401-4999
Phone: 309-341-7000
e-mail: kheartle@knox.edu
Web Site: www.knox.edu
Officers:
  President: Roger Taylor
  Executive Secretary: Denise Bailey
  Chair: Janet M Koran
  Secretary: Deborah S DeGraff
Management:
  Marketing Director: Kathleen Heartlein
Mission: Kresge is home to music ensemble concerts including the Knox College Choir, Jazz Band, Concert Band, and Jazz Ensemble and to student recitals as well as numerous visiting performance groups and events
Specialized Field: Music
Seating Capacity: 325

6788
STUDIO THEATRE
Knox College
Ford Center for the Fine Arts
2 East South Street
Galesburg, IL 61401-4999
Mailing Address: Knox College, 2 East South Street, Galesburg, IL 61401-4999
Phone: 309-341-7000
e-mail: kheartle@knox.edu
Web Site: www.knox.edu
Officers:
  President: Roger Taylor
  Executive Secretary: Denise Bailey
  Chair: Janet M Koran
  Secretary: Deborah S DeGraff
Management:
  Marketing Director: Kathleen Heartlein
Mission: black box theatre-a room within which the arrangement possibilities are nearly endless, seating about 100 people on average. Studio Theatre is student run, directed, and designed. This space also occasionally plays home to visiting companies and productions for the edification and enjoyment of the campus at large. Studio productions range from simple bare-stage shows to full-length productions complete with specific scenery and lighting.
Specialized Field: Theater
Type of Stage: Flexible Black Box
Stage Dimensions: 40ft x 60ft
Seating Capacity: 100

6789
MCANINCH ARTS CENTER THEATER 2
College of DuPage
425 Fawell Blvd
Glen Ellyn, IL 60137
Mailing Address: McAninch Arts Center at College of DuPage, Fawell and Park B
Phone: 630-942-4000
Fax: 630-790-9806
e-mail: raffel@cod.edu
Web Site: www.cod.edu
Officers:
  President: Robert L Breuder
Management:
  Director: Stephen Cummins
  Marketing Director: Roland Raffel
  Artistic Director: Kirk Muspratt
Mission: This unique facility has presented theater, music, dance and visual arts to more than 1.5 million people
Founded: 1986
Specialized Field: Theater

6790
MCANINCH ARTS CENTER MAINSTAGE
College of DuPage
425 Fawell Blvd
Glen Ellyn, IL 60137
Mailing Address: McAninch Arts Center at College of DuPage, Fawell and Park B
Phone: 630-942-4000
Fax: 630-790-9806
e-mail: raffel@cod.edu
Web Site: www.cod.edu
Officers:
  President: Robert L Breuder
  Board Chairman Wheaton: Erin Birt
  Vice Chairman Hinsdale: Kathy Hamilton
  Board Secretary Winfield: Allison O'Donnell
  Co-Vice Chairman Naperville: Joseph C. Wozniak
Management:
  Director: Stephen Cummins
  Marketing Director: Roland Raffel
  Artistic Director: Kirk Muspratt
Utilizes: Actors; AEA Actors; Dance Companies; Educators; Multimedia; Sign Language Translators; Soloists; Special Technical Talent; Theatre Companies
Founded: 1986
Specialized Field: Theater
Seating Capacity: 793

6791
MCANINCH ARTS CENTER STUDIO THEATRE
College of DuPage
425 Fawell Blvd
Glen Ellyn, IL 60137
Mailing Address: McAninch Arts Center at College of DuPage, Fawell and Park B
Phone: 630-942-4000
Fax: 630-790-9806
e-mail: raffel@cod.edu
Web Site: www.cod.edu
Officers:
  President: Robert L Breuder
  Board Chairman Wheaton: Erin Birt
  Vice Chairman Hinsdale: Kathy Hamilton
  Board Secretary Winfield: Allison O'Donnell
  Co-Vice Chairman Naperville: Joseph C. Wozniak
Management:
  Director: Stephen Cummins
  Marketing Director: Roland Raffel
  Artistic Director: Kirk Muspratt
Utilizes: Actors; Educators; Soloists
Founded: 1986
Specialized Field: Theater
Type of Stage: Black Box
Seating Capacity: 75
Resident Groups: Buffalo Theatre Ensemble

6792
SOUTHEASTERN ILLINOIS COLLEGE VISUAL & PERFORMING ARTS CENTER
3575 College Road
Harrisburg, IL 62946
Mailing Address: Southeastern Illinois College, 3575 College Rd, Harrisburg,
Phone: 618-252-5400
Toll-free: 866-338-2742
e-mail: info@sic.edu
Web Site: www.sic.cc.il.us
Officers:
  President: Raymond V Cummiskey PhD
  Board Chairman Wheaton: Erin Birt
  Vice Chairman Hinsdale: Kathy Hamilton
  Board Secretary Winfield: Allison O'Donnell
  Co-Vice Chairman Naperville: Joseph C. Wozniak
Management:
  Director: Allan Kimball
  Marketing Director: Donna Patton
Mission: The George T. Dennis Visual and Performing Arts Center serves as the artistic home of the Department of Theatre at SIC featuring a wide variety of productions ranging from traditional drama, to children's theatre, to Broadway musicals

6793
SIBERT THEATRE
Illinois College
1101 West College Avenue
Jacksonville, IL 62650
Phone: 214-245-3000
Fax: 217-245-3034
e-mail: info@mail.ic.edu
Web Site: www.ic.edu
Officers:
  President: Barbara A. Farley
  Chair: Joy French Becker
  Vice Chair: Robert E. Chipman
  Secretary: Susan L. Pratt
  Treasurer: Robert B. Thomson
Management:
  Security Officer: Douglas Allgaier
  Professor Of Music: Garrett Allman
  Professor Of Mathematics: Jeremy Alm
Type of Stage: Modified Thrust
Seating Capacity: 250

FACILITIES / Illinois

6794
RIALTO SQUARE THEATRE
15 E. Van Buren St.
Joliet, IL 60432
Phone: 815-726-7171
e-mail: information@rialtosquare.com
Web Site: www.rialtosquare.com
Management:
  General Manager: Randall Green
  Marketing Director: Annette Parker
  Administrative Secretary: Jan Gilligan
  Building Operations Manager: Michael Biedron
  Marketing Assistant/Receptionist: Patti Fitzpatrick
Utilizes: Actors; AEA Actors; Collaborations; Dancers; Educators; Five Seasonal Concerts; Guest Musical Directors; Guild Activities; Lyricists; Multi Collaborations; Original Music Scores; Selected Students; Special Technical Talent; Theatre Companies
Paid Staff: 11
Volunteer Staff: 300
Paid Artists: 40
Budget: $2,000,000
Income Sources: Corporate; Individual; Foundations
Facility Category: Performing Arts
Type of Stage: Proscenium
Stage Dimensions: 52' 0 wide x 23' 6"" high""
Seating Capacity: 1,000
Year Built: 1926
Year Remodeled: 1981
Cost: $7,000,000
Rental Contact: Mary Beth DeGrush

6795
ALLAN CARR THEATRE
Lake Forest College
Hixon Hall
555 North Sheridan Rd
Lake Forest, IL 60045
Phone: 847-234-3100
Web Site: www.lakeforest.edu
Officers:
  President: Stephen D Schutt
  Chairman: William U. Parfet
  Vice-Chairman: Daniel D. Dolan Jr.
  Vice-Chairwoman: Lorna S. Pfaelzer
  Secretary: William A. Lowry
Management:
  Marketing Director: Elizabeth Libby
  Director: D Ohlandt
Year Built: 1912

6796
DAVID ADLER MUSIC AND ARTS CENTER
1700 North Milwaukee Avenue
Libertyville, IL 60048
Mailing Address: The David Adler Music and Arts Center, 1700 North Milwaukee
Phone: 847-367-0707
Fax: 847-367-0804
e-mail: amy@adlercenter.org;
Web Site: www.adlercenter.org
Officers:
  Chairman: Dr. Guy Schumacher
  Vice- Chairman: Ben Johnson
  Treasurer: F. Brian Smith
Management:
  Executive Director: Amy Williams
  Operations Manager: Michelle Adams
Mission: dedicated to promoting music and the arts as an integral part of everyday life. Its year-round activities are designed to foster critical thinking and interpretation, participation, entertainment, and achievement in music and the arts for the people
Organization Type: Performing; Edcuational

6797
HORRABIN HALL THEATRE
Western Illinois University
Horrabin Hall
1 University Circle
Macomb, IL 61455
Phone: 309-298-1543
Fax: 309-298-2695
e-mail: info@wiu.edu
Web Site: www.wiu.edu
Officers:
  President: Alvin Goldfarb
  Chairman: David E Patrick
  Secretary: Wendi Mattson
Management:
  President: Alvin Goldfarb
  Executive Director: Eugene Kozlowski
  Artistic Director: David Patrick
Type of Stage: Thrust
Seating Capacity: 161
Year Restored: 1995

6798
SIMPKINS THEATRE
Western Illinois University
Simpkins Hall
1 University Circle
Macomb, IL 61455
Phone: 309-298-1543
Fax: 309-298-2695
e-mail: info@wiu.edu
Web Site: www.wiu.edu
Officers:
  President: Alvin Goldfarb
  Chairman: David E Patrick
  Secretary: Wendi Mattson
Management:
  President: Alvin Goldfarb
  Executive Director: Eugene Kozlowski
  Artistic Director: David Patrick
Type of Stage: Proscenium/Thrust

6799
WESTERN ILLINOIS UNIVERSITY THEATRE AND DANCE DEPARTMENT
Western Illinois University
Browne Hall
1 University Circle
Macomb, IL 61455
Phone: 309-298-1543
Fax: 309-298-2695
e-mail: info@wiu.edu
Web Site: www.wiu.edu
Officers:
  President: Alvin Goldfarb
  Chairman: David E Patrick
  Secretary: Wendi Mattson
Management:
  President: Alvin Goldfarb
  Executive Director: Eugene Kozlowski
  Artistic Director: David Patrick
Type of Stage: Proscenium
Seating Capacity: 387

6800
MARION CULTURAL AND CIVIC CENTER
800 Tower Square Plaza
Marion, IL 62959
Mailing Address: P O Box 51, Marion, IL 62959
Phone: 618-997-4030
Fax: 618-993-5614
Web Site: www.marionccc.org
Officers:
  Chairman: Yolonde Peterson
  Vice-Chairman: Art Pratt
  Secretary: Martha Stinson
  Treasurer: Louetta Butler
Management:
  Executive Director: Joshua S Benson
  Technical Coordinator: Vincent G. Elliott
  Maintenance Manager: JW Eibeck
  Custodian: Mike Wade
Utilizes: Dance Companies; Guild Activities; New Productions; Special Technical Talent
Founded: 2004
Paid Staff: 4
Budget: $200,000
Income Sources: Donations
Annual Attendance: 52,000
Type of Stage: Proscenium
Stage Dimensions: 45'x36'
Seating Capacity: 1,100
Year Built: 2004
Cost: $8 Million

6801
I WIRELESS CENTER
1201 River Drive
Moline, IL 61265
Mailing Address: i wireless Center, 1201 River Drive, Moline, IL. 61265
Phone: 309-764-2001
Fax: 309-764-2192
Web Site: www.iwirelesscenter.com
Management:
  Executive Director: Scott Mullen
  Marketing Director: Gary Baron
Specialized Field: General Entertainment
Paid Staff: 450
Annual Attendance: 700,000
Seating Capacity: 12,000

6802
WELLS THEATER
Monmouth College
700 E Broadway
Monmouth, IL 61462
Phone: 309-457-2340
Fax: 309-457-2310
e-mail: info@monm.edu
Web Site: www.monm.edu
Officers:
  President: Dr Mauri Ditzler
Management:
  Director: Douglas B Rankin
  Lecturer: Erin Alderson
  Director: Philip Betz
Founded: 1790
Paid Staff: 2
Budget: $15,000
Income Sources: Budget Allocation From Institution
Type of Stage: Proscenium
Stage Dimensions: 32' X 25'
Seating Capacity: 175
Year Built: 1990
Year Remodeled: 2010
Cost: 1.6 Million

FACILITIES / Illinois

Rental Contact: Douglas Raneiu

6803
BARBARA PFEIFFER MEMORIAL HALL
North Central College
310 E Benton Avenue
Naperville, IL 60540
Mailing Address: North Central College, 30 N. Brainard Street, Naperville, IL
Phone: 630-637-5100
Toll-free: 800-411-1861
e-mail: omc@noctrl.edu
Web Site: www.northcentralcollege.edu
Officers:
  President: Troy D. Hammond
  Chair: Steven H. Hoeft
  Vice President: Paul Loscheider
  Vice President: R. Devadoss Pandian
Management:
  Director: Brian T Lynch
  Assistant Director: Elizabeth Appleyard
  Admission Counselor: Jessica s Avila-Cueva
  Associate Director: Heather Breed
Mission: The DuPage Symphony Orchestra and Naperville-North Central College Performing Arts Association have called it home for decades, as have numerous community arts groups, schools, churches, organizations and the College's musical and theatrical programs. Recitals, choral and instrumental performances, and theatrical productions are hosted throughout the year
Founded: 1926
Type of Stage: Proscenium
Seating Capacity: 1,055
Year Built: 1926

6804
HEININGER AUDITORIUM
North Central College
Larrance Academic Center
309 E School Street
Naperville, IL 60540
Mailing Address: North Central College, 30 N. Brainard Street, Naperville, IL
Phone: 630-637-5100
Toll-free: 800-411-1861
e-mail: omc@noctrl.edu
Web Site: www.northcentralcollege.edu
Officers:
  President: Troy D. Hammond
  Chair: Steven H. Hoeft
  Vice President: Paul Loscheider
  Vice President: R. Devadoss Pandian
Management:
  Director: Brian T Lynch
  Assistant Director: Elizabeth Appleyard
  Admission Counselor: Jessica s Avila-Cueva
  Associate Director: Heather Breed
Mission: Great for small group presentations, dance instruction and performance rehearsals
Specialized Field: Dance
Seating Capacity: 100

6805
BRADEN AUDITORIUM
Illinois State University
100 N University Street
Normal, IL 61761-4441
Mailing Address: Bone Student Center, Campus Box 2640, 100 N University St, N
Phone: 309-438-4636
Fax: 309-438-3147
e-mail: Infocentre@illinoisState.edu
Web Site: www.bsc.ilstu.edu
Officers:
  President: Larry Dietz
Management:
  Director: Michelle S. Paul
  Assistant Director: Barb Dallinger
  Office Manager: Shirley McCauley
  Manager: Rick Holmes
  Technical Director: Chuck Fudge
Mission: Braden hosts Broadway shows, touring companies, concerts, ballets, conferences and much more
Performs At: Auditorium
Affiliations: Illinois State University
Seating Capacity: 3,457
Rental Contact: Coordinator Jennifer Booher

6806
HANCOCK STADIUM
Illinois State University
College Avenue and Main Street
Normal, IL 61761
Phone: 309-438-8000
Fax: 309-438-3513
Web Site: www.goredbirds.cstv.com
Officers:
  President: Dr Al Bowman
Management:
  Athletic Director: Dr Sheahon Zenger
  Marketing Director: Brad Ledford
  Operations Director: Peyton Deterding
  Development Director: Doug Banks
Founded: 1963
Seating Capacity: 15,000

6807
MABEL CLAIRE ALLEN THEATRE
Illinois State University College of Fine Arts
School of Theatre
100 N University Street
Normal, IL 61790-5700
Mailing Address: Campus Box 5700 Normal Il 61790-5700, Office of the Dean, C
Phone: 309-438-8783
Fax: 309-438-5806
Web Site: www.ilstu.edu
Officers:
  President: Larry Dietz
Management:
  Director: John Poole
  Marketing Director: Christopher Peak
Mission: The Allen Theatre offers black box opportunities for performance. The space serves as a rehearsal hall and classroom building for dance classes
Type of Stage: Black Box

6808
MFA DIRECTING STUDIO
Illinois State University College of Fine Arts
School of Theatre
100 N University Street
Normal, IL 61790-5700
Mailing Address: Campus Box 5700 Normal Il 61790-5700, Office of the Dean, C
Phone: 309-438-8783
Fax: 309-438-5806
Web Site: www.ilstu.edu
Officers:
  President: Larry Dietz
Management:
  Director: John Poole
  Marketing Director: Christopher Peak
Type of Stage: Proscenium
Seating Capacity: 50

6809
REDBIRD ARENA
Illinois State University
College Avenue and Main Street
Normal, IL 61790-2660
Mailing Address: Campus Box 2660 Normal IL 61790-2660
Phone: 309-438-8000
Web Site: www.goredbirds.cstv.com
Officers:
  President: Larry Dietz
Management:
  Athletic Director: Dr Sheahon Zenger
  Marketing Director: Brad Ledford
  Operations Director: Peyton Deterding
  Development Director: Doug Banks
Seating Capacity: 10,500

6810
THEATRE AT EWING
Illinois State University College of Fine Arts
School of Theatre
100 N University Street
Normal, IL 61790-5700
Mailing Address: Campus Box 5700 Normal Il 61790-5700, Office of the Dean, C
Phone: 309-438-8783
Fax: 309-438-5806
Web Site: www.ilstu.edu
Officers:
  President: Larry Dietz
Management:
  Director: John Poole
  Marketing Director: Christopher Peak
Type of Stage: Proscenium
Seating Capacity: 450

6811
WESTHOFF EXPERIMENTAL THEATRE
Illinois State University College of Fine Arts
School of Theatre
100 N University Street
Normal, IL 61790-5700
Mailing Address: Campus Box 5700 Normal Il 61790-5700, Office of the Dean, C
Phone: 309-438-8783
Fax: 309-438-5806
Web Site: www.ilstu.edu
Officers:
  President: Larry Dietz
Management:
  Director: John Poole
  Marketing Director: Christopher Peak
Type of Stage: Proscenium
Orchestra Pit: y
Seating Capacity: 525

6812
SHEELY CENTER FOR THE PERFORMING ARTS
Glenbrook North High School
2300 Shermer Road
Northbrook, IL 60062
Phone: 847-272-6400
e-mail: info@glenbrook225.org
Web Site: www.glenbrook225.org/gbn/Home
Officers:
  President: Paul Pryma

FACILITIES / Illinois

6813
MORAINE VALLEY COMMUNITY COLLEGE FINE & PERFORMING ARTS CENTER
9000 W College Parkway
Palos Hills, IL 60465-0937
Mailing Address: 9000 W. College Pkwy., Palos Hills, IL 60465-2478
Phone: 708-974-4300
Fax: 708-974-9556
Web Site: www.morainevalley.edu
Officers:
  President: Dr Vernon O Crawley
  Chairman: Nicholas Thomas
Management:
  Managing Director: Tommy Hensel
Mission: The mission of the Fine and Performing Arts center, through its public presentations of dance, music, theater and the visual arts, is to enrich the members of the college community by providing opportunities for people of all ages to experience and grow through the arts.
Founded: 1994
Specialized Field: Theater, Dance, Music
Seating Capacity: 780

6814
FREEDOM HALL: NATHAN MANILOW THEATRE
410 Lakewood Boulevard
Park Forest, IL 60466
Phone: 708-747-0580
e-mail: tickets@freedomhall.org
Web Site: www.freedomhall.org
Management:
  General Manager: Naomi Ferr
Mission: Freedom Hall is proud to bring you childrens theatre, musical theatre, senior theatre and performances for all ages
Founded: 1976
Specialized Field: Theater
Paid Staff: 4
Paid Artists: 50

6815
LAB THEATRE
Bradley University
Hartmann Center for the Performing Arts
1501 W Bradley Avenue
Peoria, IL 61625
Phone: 309-676-7611
Fax: 309-677-3505
Toll-free: 800-447-6460
e-mail: theatre@bradley.edu
Web Site: www.theatre.bradley.edu
Officers:
  President: Joanne K Glasser
  Chairman: Gerald L Shaheen
  Secretary: Debbie Perry
Management:
  Director: George H Brown
  Manager: Marty Burgeson
Type of Stage: Black Box
Seating Capacity: 70

6816
MEYER JACOBS THEATRE
Bradley University
Hartmann Center for the Performing Arts
1502 W Bradley Avenue
Peoria, IL 61625
Phone: 309-676-7611
Fax: 309-677-3505
Toll-free: 800-447-6460
e-mail: theatre@bradley.edu
Web Site: www.theatre.bradley.edu
Officers:
  President: Joanne K Glasser
  Chairman: Gerald L Shaheen
  Secretary: Debbie Perry
Management:
  Director: George H Brown
  Manager: Marty Burgeson
Seating Capacity: 250-275

6817
PEORIA CIVIC CENTER
201 SW Jefferson Street
Peoria, IL 61602-1448
Mailing Address: Peoria Civic Center, 201 SW Jefferson Ave. Peoria, IL 61602
Phone: 309-673-8900
Fax: 309-673-9223
e-mail: info@peoriaciviccenter.com
Web Site: www.peoriaciviccenter.com
Management:
  Director Marketing: Marc Burnett
  General Manager: Debbie Ritschel
  Director Operations: Will Kenney
  Director Event Services: Jim Weatherington
  Asst. General Manager: Shaun Schoonover
Founded: 1982
Specialized Field: Musical; Comedy; Youth Theater; Dinner Theater; Ethnic Theater; Community Theater; Classic; Contemporary
Paid Staff: 450

6818
PEORIA CIVIC CENTER
201 SW Jefferson Street
Peoria, IL 61602-1448
Mailing Address: Peoria Civic Center, 201 SW Jefferson Ave., Peoria, IL 61602
Phone: 309-673-8900
e-mail: mburnett@peoriaciviccenter.com
Web Site: www.peoriaciviccenter.com
Management:
  General Manager: Debbie Ritschel
  Marketing Director: Mark Burnettl
  Operations Director: Will Kenney
Founded: 1982
Specialized Field: General Entertainment
Paid Staff: 450
Annual Attendance: 20,000
Facility Category: Theater
Seating Capacity: 2127

6819
BERGMAN THEATRE
Concordia University Chicago
7400 Augusta Street
River Forest, IL 60305-1499
Mailing Address: 7400 Augusta St, River Forest, IL 60305-1402
Phone: 708-771-8300
e-mail: pr@CUChicago.edu
Web Site: www.cuchicago.edu
Officers:
  President: Rev. Daniel Lee
  Chair: Eunice R Eifert
Management:
  General Manager: Julie E Hinz
  Marketing Director: Krisse L Paulson
Mission: Provides a more intimate setting for smaller scale productions, student one-acts, as well as space for classroom lab opportunities. As a truly flexible performance space, past productions have enjoyed arena, alley and proscenium stagings
Type of Stage: Alley, Arena, Proscenium

6820
ELOISE MARTIN RECITAL HALL
Dominican University
Fine and Performing Arts
7900 Division Street
River Forest, IL 60305
Mailing Address: Performing Arts Center, 7900 West Division St., River Forest,
Phone: 708-366-2490
Fax: 708-524-5990
Web Site: www.dom.edu
Officers:
  President: Donna M Carroll
  Secretary: Alexandra Garcia
  SVP, Finance: Amy McCormack
  VP, Mission and Ministry: Claire Noonan
  VP, University Advancement: Grace Cichomska
  VP, CIO: Jill Albin-Hill
Management:
  Artistic Director: Krista Hansen
  Managing Director: Leslie Rodriguez
Seating Capacity: 200

6821
LUND AUDITORIUM
Dominican University
Fine and Performing Arts
7900 Division Street
River Forest, IL 60305
Mailing Address: Performing Arts Center, 7900 West Division St., River Forest,
Phone: 708-366-2490
Fax: 708-524-5990
Web Site: www.dom.edu
Officers:
  President: Donna M Carroll
  Secretary: Alexandra Garcia
  SVP, Finance: Amy McCormack
  VP, Mission and Ministry: Claire Noonan
  VP, University Advancement: Grace Cichomska
  VP, CIO: Jill Albin-Hill
Management:
  Artistic Director: Krista Hansen
  Managing Director: Leslie Rodriguez
Seating Capacity: 1,200

6822
WERNER AUDITORIUM
Concordia University Chicago
7400 Augusta Street
River Forest, IL 60305-1499
Mailing Address: 7400 Augusta St, River Forest, IL 60305-1402
Phone: 708-771-8300
e-mail: pr@CUChicago.edu
Web Site: www.cuchicago.edu
Officers:
  President: Rev. Daniel Lee
  Chair: Eunice R Eifert
Management:
  General Manager: Julie E Hinz
  Marketing Director: Krisse L Paulson
Mission: is a proscenium space dedicated to bringing large scale productions to life. Many off campus groups utilize this space in conjunction with our campus chapel
Type of Stage: Proscenium

6823
ROBERT M COLLINS CENTER
Triton College
2000 Fifth Avenue
River Grove, IL 60171
Phone: 708-456-0300
e-mail: triton@triton.edu
Web Site: www.triton.edu
Officers:
   President: Dr Patricia Granados
   Chairman: Mark R Stephens
   Secretary: Diane Viverito
   VP, Academic and Student Affairs: Douglas Olson
Management:
   Director, Marketing services: Sam Tolia

6824
TRITON COLLEGE PERFORMING ARTS CENTER
Triton College
2001 Fifth Avenue
River Grove, IL 60171
Phone: 708-456-0300
e-mail: triton@triton.edu
Web Site: www.triton.edu
Officers:
   President: Dr Patricia Granados
   Chairman: Mark R Stephens
   Secretary: Diane Viverito
   VP, Academic and Student Affairs: Douglas Olson
Management:
   Department Chair: Angelee Johns, ajohns39@triton.edu
   Director, Marketing services: Sam Tolia
Mission: Education and entertainment of students and public
Utilizes: Actors; Dance Companies; Dancers; Guest Choreographers; Guest Musical Directors; High School Drama; Instructors; Local Artists; Multimedia; Original Music Scores; Sign Language Translators; Singers; Soloists; Special Technical Talent; Theatre Companies
Specialized Field: Music; Theatre
Paid Staff: 10
Volunteer Staff: 10
Paid Artists: 25
Non-paid Artists: 20
Income Sources: College Budget; Ticket Sales
Performs At: Mid-Size Auditorium; Black Box Theatre
Facility Category: Performing Arts Center
Type of Stage: Proscenium; Thrust
Seating Capacity: 412; 75
Rental Contact: Manager Maria Correa

6825
AUGUSTANA THEATRE
Augustana College
Department of Theatre Arts
639 38th Street
Rock Island, IL 61201
Mailing Address: 639 38th Street, Rock Island, IL 61201
Phone: 309-794-7307
Toll-free: 800-988-00
Web Site: www.augustana.edu
Officers:
   President: Steven C Bahls
   Chair: Jeffrey L Coussens
   Secretary: Anna Hurty
   VP, Advancement: Julie Crockett
Management:
   Director, Annual Giving: Susan Horan
   Secretary, Annual Giving: Chris Loula
   Director, Development Research: Chris Myers
   Director, Alumni & Parent Relations: Kelly Noack
Specialized Field: Theatre
Type of Stage: Modified Thrust
Seating Capacity: 150
Year Restored: 1998

6826
CENTENNIAL HALL
Augustana College
639 38th Street
Rock Island, IL 61201
Mailing Address: 639 38th Street, Rock Island, IL 61201
Phone: 309-794-7000
Toll-free: 800-988-00
Web Site: www.augustana.edu
Officers:
   President: Steven C Bahls
   VP, Advancement: Julie Crockett
Management:
   Director, Annual Giving: Susan Horan
   Secretary, Annual Giving: Chris Loula
   Director, Development Research: Chris Myers
   Director, Alumni & Parent Relations: Kelly Noack

Founded: 1860

6827
STUDIO THEATRE
Augustana College
Department of Theatre Arts
639 38th Street
Rock Island, IL 61201
Mailing Address: 639 38th Street, Rock Island, IL 61201
Phone: 309-794-7000
Toll-free: 800-988-00
Web Site: www.augustana.edu
Officers:
   President: Steven C Bahls
   Chair: Jeffrey L Coussens
   Secretary: Anna Hurty
   VP, Advancement: Julie Crockett
Management:
   Director, Annual Giving: Susan Horan
   Secretary, Annual Giving: Chris Loula
   Director, Development Research: Chris Myers
   Director, Alumni & Parent Relations: Kelly Noack
Specialized Field: Theatre
Year Restored: 1998

6828
CHEEK THEATRE
Rockford College
Clark Arts Center
5050 E State Street
Rockford, IL 61108
Mailing Address: Rockford College, Performing Arts, J263Clark Arts Center, 50
Phone: 815-226-4000
Web Site: www.rockford.edu
Officers:
   President: Dr Robert Head
   Chair: Noel Rennerfeldt
Management:
   Commissioner: Charles Box
   Attorney: Dawn R. Hallsten
Mission: Cheek Theatre is a 40' by 50' flexible seating black box theater. The department produces faculty directed and student directed shows, our Three-Penny Theatre, in Cheek Theatre annually.
Specialized Field: Theater
Type of Stage: Flexible Black Box
Stage Dimensions: 40' by 50'

6829
CORONADO PERFORMING ARTS CENTER
314 N Main Street
Rockford IL
Rockford, IL 61101-0476
Mailing Address: PO Box 1976 Rockford IL 61110-0476
Phone: 815-968-2722
Fax: 815-968-1318
e-mail: hstorm@smgrockford.com
Web Site: www.coronadopac.org
Management:
   Director, Facilities: Mike Walsh
   Technical Director: Luis Lara
   Box Office Manager: Chrissy Bartik
Founded: 2006
Paid Staff: 5314
Volunteer Staff: 100
Budget: $1.1 million
Type of Stage: Proscenium
Stage Dimensions: 53' x 45'
Seating Capacity: 2,309
Year Built: 1927
Year Remodeled: 2001
Rental Contact: Janice Bartik

6830
MADDOX THEATRE
Rockford College
Clark Arts Center
5050 E State Street
Rockford, IL 61108
Mailing Address: Rockford College, Performing Arts, J263Clark Arts Center, 50
Phone: 815-226-4000
Web Site: www.rockford.edu
Officers:
   President: Dr Robert Head
   Chair: Noel Rennerfeldt
Management:
   Manager: Elizabeth Drog
Mission: Maddox Theatre is a fully equipped 572 seat proscenium theater which is home to a variety of performing arts events. Each year the department produces faculty directed shows, choral concerts and recitals in Maddox Theatre. It also hosts the College forum series and many community cultural events
Specialized Field: Theater
Type of Stage: Proscenium
Seating Capacity: 572

6831
ROCKFORD METROCENTRE
300 Elm Street
Rockford, IL 61101
Phone: 815-968-5600
Fax: 815-968-5451
e-mail: info@thebmoharrisbankcenter.com
Web Site: www.metrocentre.com
Officers:
   Chairman: Mike Dunn
   Treasurer: John Phelps
   Secretary: Lori Burke
   VP, Head of Media operation: Jim Kappel
Management:

FACILITIES / Illinois

General Manager: Gordon Kaye
Marketing Director: Matt Mohr
Operations Director: Susan Campbell
Seating Capacity: 9,952

6832
PHILIP LYNCH THEATRE
Lewis University
1 University Parkway
Romeoville, IL 60446-2200
Mailing Address: One University Parkway, Romeoville, IL 60446
Phone: 815-838-0500
Toll-free: 800-979-00
Web Site: www.lewisu.edu
Officers:
President: Br James Gaffney FSC
EVP: Wayne Draudt
VP, Student Services: Joseph T. Falese
SVP,CFO: Robert C. DeRose
Management:
Dean: Bonnie Bondavalli
Dean: Rami Khasawneh
Paid Staff: 1
Budget: $6,000
Performs At: Philip Lynch Theatre
Facility Category: Educational Theatre
Type of Stage: 3/4 Thrust
Seating Capacity: 240
Year Built: 1976

6833
ALLSTATE ARENA
6920 N Mannheim Road
Rosemont, IL 60018
Mailing Address: 6920 N. Mannheim Road, Rosemont, IL 60018
Phone: 847-635-6601
Web Site: www.allstatearena.com
Officers:
President: Edward M Liddy
Management:
Marketing Director: Phil Chihoski
Founded: 1980
Paid Staff: 400
Annual Attendance: 1,500,000
Seating Capacity: 18,500

6834
PRAIRIE CENTER FOR THE ARTS
201 Schaumburg Court
Schaumburg, IL 60193
Mailing Address: 201 Schaumburg Court, Schaumburg, IL 60193-1899
Phone: 847-895-3600
Fax: 847-895-1837
e-mail: rpileckis@ci.schaumburg.il.us
Web Site: www.prairiecenter.org
Management:
Director: Betsy Armstead
Development Director: Lucinda Floodin
PR: Rob Pileckis
Mission: The Prairie Center for the Arts is an ideal venue to see a concert, play or musical. A full season of entertainment including music, dance and theatre and a free, outdoor summer concert series.
Founded: 1986
Specialized Field: Concert, play, musicals
Paid Staff: 20
Volunteer Staff: 50
Paid Artists: 100
Budget: $1 million
Income Sources: Tickets; Rentals; Foundation Support
Annual Attendance: 75,000

Type of Stage: Proscenium
Year Built: 1986
Rental Contact: Pat DeBartolo

6835
NORTHSHORE CENTER FOR THE PERFORMING ARTS
9501 Skokie Boulevard
Skokie, IL 60077
Phone: 847-679-9501
e-mail: customerservice@northshorecenter.org
Web Site: www.northshorecenter.org
Management:
General Manager: Michael Pauken
Operations Manager: Adrelle K. Winston
Marketing & Communications Manager: Joseph Alaimo
Office Manager: Carolyn Adams
Event Manager: Betty Boduch
Technical Director: Frank Rose
Utilizes: Dancers; Educators; Original Music Scores; Special Technical Talent; Theatre Companies
Paid Staff: 4
Volunteer Staff: 8
Seating Capacity: 848
Year Built: 1996

6836
MUSIC HALL
Springfield College
1500 N Fifth Street
Springfield, IL 62702
Phone: 217-525-1420
Toll-free: 800-635-7289
e-mail: springweb@ben.edu
Web Site: www.sci.edu
Officers:
President: William J Carroll
Paid Staff: 70

6837
SANGAMON AUDITORIUM
University Of Illinois At Springfield
MSPAC 397
Springfield, IL 62703-5407
Mailing Address: One University Plaza, MS PAC 397
Springfield, IL 62703-5407
Phone: 217-206-6160
Fax: 217-206-6391
Toll-free: 800-207-6960
e-mail: info@sangamonauditorium.org
Web Site: www.uis.edu/s
Management:
Director: Bob Vaughn

6838
STUDIO THEATRE
University of Illinois at Springfield
Sangamon Auditorium
One University Plaza Springfield, Illinois
Springfield, IL 62703-5407
Phone: 217-206-6160
Fax: 217-206-6391
Toll-free: 800-207-6961
Web Site: www.uis.edu
Officers:
President: B Joseph White
Management:
Director: Robert Vaughn
Type of Stage: Flexible
Seating Capacity: 100-318

6839
NORRIS CULTURAL ARTS CENTER
1040 Dunham Road
St Charles, IL 60174
Mailing Address: PO Box 3340 St Charles IL 60174
Phone: 630-584-7200
Fax: 630-584-7262
e-mail: businessoffice@norrisculturalarts.com
Web Site: www.norrisculturalarts.com
Officers:
President: James L Collins
Secretary: Joanne deSimone
Treasurer: Mark D Smith
Management:
Operations Director: JoAnne Granquist
Technical Director: John Mizanin
Founded: 1978
Paid Staff: 4
Volunteer Staff: 10
Budget: $300,000
Income Sources: Tickets Sales; Rentals; Donors; Grants
Performs At: Live Theatre
Annual Attendance: 20,000
Facility Category: Performing Arts & Gallery
Type of Stage: Persimon
Stage Dimensions: 40x50
Seating Capacity: 1,052
Year Built: 1978
Year Remodeled: 2001
Rental Contact: JoAnne Granquist

6840
STERLING CENTENNIAL AUDITORIUM
Sterling High School
1608 4th Avenue
Sterling, IL 61081
Phone: 815-625-6800
Web Site: www.centennialauditorium.org
Management:
Director: Chuck Price
Development Director: Tim Schlegel

6841
MAINSTAGE
Governors State University
The Center for Performing Arts
1 University Parkway
University Park, IL 60466-0975
Mailing Address: 1 University Parkway, University Park, IL 60484-0975
Phone: 708-235-2222
Fax: 708-235-2121
e-mail: tickets@govst.edu
Web Site: www.centertickets.net
Officers:
President: Elaine P Maimon PhD
Management:
Executive Director: Lana Rogachevskaya
Theatre Manager: Jon Cobb
Technical Director: Michael Krull
Box Office Manager: Patricia Guy
Marketing Director: Sharon Banaszak
Founded: 1994
Specialized Field: Dance; Music; Drama; Broadway
Annual Attendance: $45,000
Facility Category: Professional Venue
Type of Stage: Proscenium
Seating Capacity: 1,176
Year Built: 1994
Cost: $8.5 Million
Rental Contact: Theatre Manager Jon Cobb

6842
THE CENTER FOR THE PERFORMING ARTS
Governors State University
1 University Parkway
University Park, IL 60466-0975
Phone: 708-235-2222
Fax: 708-235-2121
e-mail: tickets@govst.edu
Web Site: www.centertickets.net
Officers:
    President: Elaine P Maimon PhD
Management:
    Director: Lana Rogachevskaya
    Theatre Manager: Jon Cobb
    Technical Director: Michael Krull
    Box Office Manager: Patricia Guy
    Marketing Director: Sharon Banaszak
Utilizes: Actors; Dance Companies; Five Seasonal Concerts; Guest Accompanists; Guest Choreographers; Guest Directors; Guest Musical Directors; Guest Musicians; Guild Activities; Instructors; Local Artists; Multimedia; New Productions; Original Music Scores; Student Interns; Special Technical Talent; Theatre Companies
Founded: 1995
Paid Staff: 7
Volunteer Staff: 50
Paid Artists: 40
Budget: $975,000
Income Sources: Tickets; Rentals; Donations; Sales
Annual Attendance: 60,000
Facility Category: Theater
Type of Stage: Proscenium
Stage Dimensions: 45'x35'
Seating Capacity: 1,171
Year Built: 1995
Cost: $8,000,000
Rental Contact: Les Alberts
Organization Type: Performing

6843
KRANNERT CENTER FOR THE PERFORMING ARTS - THEATRE 3
500 S Goodwin Avenue
Urbana, IL 61801-3788
Phone: 217-333-6280
Fax: 217-244-7469
e-mail: kran-tix@illinois.edu
Web Site: www.krannertcenter.com
Officers:
    President: B Joseph White
Management:
    Attendant: Robin Baker
    Performance Supervisor: Bunny Berg
    Accounting Staff: Lynn Bierman
    Assistant Director, FAA IT: Gary Bernstein
    Art Director: Vanessa Burgett
Founded: 1969
Type of Stage: Proscenium
Seating Capacity: 4,000

6844
KRANNERT CENTER FOR THE PERFORMING ARTS - STUDIO
500 S Goodwin Avenue
Urbana, IL 61801-3789
Phone: 217-333-6280
Fax: 217-244-7469
e-mail: kran-tix@illinois.edu
Web Site: www.krannertcenter.com
Officers:
    President: B Joseph White
Management:
    Attendant: Robin Baker
    Performance Supervisor: Bunny Berg
    Accounting Staff: Lynn Bierman
    Assistant Director, FAA IT: Gary Bernstein
    Art Director: Vanessa Burgett

6845
KRANNERT CENTER FOR THE PERFORMING ARTS - THEATRE 2
500 S Goodwin Avenue
Urbana, IL 61801-3790
Phone: 217-333-6280
Fax: 217-244-7469
e-mail: kran-tix@illinois.edu
Web Site: www.krannertcenter.com
Officers:
    President: B Joseph White
Management:
    Attendant: Robin Baker
    Performance Supervisor: Bunny Berg
    Accounting Staff: Lynn Bierman
    Assistant Director, FAA IT: Gary Bernstein
    Art Director: Vanessa Burgett
Type of Stage: Proscenium
Seating Capacity: 4,000; (200 to 2,094)

6846
ODEUM SPORTS & EXPO CENTER
1033 N Villa Avenue
Villa Park, Illinois
Villa Park, IL 60181
Phone: 630-941-9292
Fax: 630-831-9183
e-mail: phil@odeumexpo.com
Web Site: www.odeumexpo.com
Officers:
    President: Phil Greco
Management:
    Facility Manager: Brad Walsh
    Director of soccer: Tony Dallas
Seating Capacity: 5,500

6847
JACK BENNY CENTER FOR THE ARTS
39 Jack Benny Drive
Waukegan, IL 60087
Phone: 847-360-4740
Fax: 847-662-0592
Web Site: www.waukeganparks.org
Officers:
    President: Terry Duffy
    VP: Patricia Pat Foley
    Treasurer: Janet E. Kilkelly
    Commissioner: William Bill Sarocka
    Commissioner: George Bridges
Management:
    Executive Director: Greg Petry, CPRE
    Superintendent of Finance: Jim Glogovsky, CPRP
    Superintendent of Parks: Mike Trigg, CPRP
    Superintendent of Recreation: Jay Lerner, CPRP, CPP
    Superintendent of Cultural Arts: Claudia Freeman, CPRP
Mission: provides fine arts instruction for music, dance, theatre, art, and traditional craft and lecture programming through the Bowen Heritage Circle.
Founded: 1986
Seating Capacity: 100

6848
ARENA THEATER
Wheaton College
501 College Avenue
Wheaton, IL 60187-5593
Phone: 630-752-5000
Web Site: www.wheaton.edu
Officers:
    President: Dr Philip Graham Ryken
    Chairman: David Geiser
    Secretary: Jeffrey Meyer
    VP, Student Development: Paul Chelsen
    Interim VP: Cindra Taetzsch
Management:
    Executive Director: Ken Chase PhD
Founded: 1973

6849
EDMAN CHAPEL
Wheaton College
501 College Avenue
Wheaton, IL 60187-5593
Phone: 630-752-5000
Web Site: www.wheaton.edu
Officers:
    President: Dr Philip Graham Ryken
    Chairman: David Geiser
    Secretary: Jeffrey Meyer
    VP, Student Development: Paul Chelsen
    Interim VP: Cindra Taetzsch
Founded: 1860

6850
DILLER STREET THEATER
North Shore Country Day School
310 Green Bay Road
Winnetka, IL 60093
Phone: 847-446-0674
Fax: 847-446-0675
Web Site: www.nscds.org
Officers:
    President: Tom Doar III
Management:
    Development Director: Molly Ingram McDowell
    Marketing Director: Tura Cottingham
    Operations Director: Cindy Hooper
Founded: 1919
Seating Capacity: 480

6851
WOODSTOCK OPERA HOUSE
121 Van Buren Street
Woodstock, IL 60098
Phone: 815-338-4212
Fax: 815-334-2287
e-mail: jscharres@woodstockil.gov
Web Site: www.woodstockoperahouse.com
Management:
    MD: John Scharres
    Building Manager: Mark Greenleaf
    Box Office Manager: Daniel Campbell
Mission: Providing McHenry County, Illinois with a cultural center; showcasing Illinois artists as well as American and international performers; working closely with the local Woodstock community.
Utilizes: Dance Companies; Dancers; Fine Artists; Guild Activities; Local Artists; Multi Collaborations; Multimedia; Original Music Scores; Resident Professionals; Sign Language Translators; Student Interns; Special Technical Talent; Theatre Companies
Founded: 1890
Specialized Field: Opera; Musical Theatre
Status: Non-Profit, Professional

FACILITIES / Indiana

Paid Staff: 15
Volunteer Staff: 20
Income Sources: International Society of Performing Arts Administrators; Association of Performing Arts Presenters
Performs At: Woodstock Opera House
Annual Attendance: 55,000
Facility Category: Theatre
Type of Stage: Proscenium
Stage Dimensions: 24'x26'
Seating Capacity: 420
Year Built: 1890
Year Remodeled: 1974
Organization Type: Performing; Resident; Educational; Sponsoring

6852
CHRISTIAN ARTS AUDITORIUM
2500 Dowie Memorial Drive
Zion, IL 60099
Phone: 847-746-1411
Fax: 847-746-1452
e-mail: frontoffice@ccczion.org
Web Site: www.ccczion.org
Officers:
  Chairman: Ken Langley
  Secretary: Katy Lee
Management:
  Music Director: Dean LaBelle
  Senior Pastor: Ken Langley
Seating Capacity: 522

Indiana

6853
REARDON AUDITORIUM
1100 E Fifth Street
Anderson, IN 46012
Phone: 765-641-4080
Fax: 765-641-4091
Toll-free: 800-286-14
e-mail: Info@anderson.edu
Web Site: www.anderson.edu
Officers:
  President: Dr James L Edwards
  Treasurer: Sena Landey
Management:
  Director Of Admissions: Joe Davis
  Associate Director: Jill Cooper
  Operations Manager: Ruth Oliver
Founded: 1983
Paid Staff: 4
Paid Artists: 4
Income Sources: University Administration; Facility Rental
Facility Category: Auditorium
Stage Dimensions: 52' x 75'
Seating Capacity: 23,000
Year Built: 1983
Cost: $5.1 million

6854
ASSEMBLY HALL
1001 E 17th Street
Bloomington, IN 47405-7000
Phone: 812-855-4848
Web Site: www.iuhoosiers.edu
Officers:
  President: Michael A McRobbie
Management:
  Director: Kevin Ullested
  Box Office: Cam McKinley
  Group Sales: Rose Munds

Performs At: Athletics Arena
Facility Category: Intercollegiate Athletics
Type of Stage: Basketball Court
Seating Capacity: 17,466
Year Built: 1971
Cost: $14.6 Million
Rental Contact: Assistant Director Facilities Chuck Crabb

6855
B C PLAYHOUSE
Indiana University
Department of Theatre & Drama
275 North Jordan
Bloomington, IN 47405-1101
Phone: 812-855-4535
Web Site: www.theatre.indiana.edu
Officers:
  Chair: Jonathan Michaelsen
  Associate Chair: Dale McFadden
  Secretary: Catherine Richards
  MD: Drew Bratton
Management:
  Assistant Professor: Paul Brunner
  Associate Professor: Fred M. Duer
  Fiscal Officer: James Barrow
  Director, Marketing: Amy Osajima
Paid Staff: 20
Paid Artists: 30
Type of Stage: Black Box
Orchestra Pit: y

6856
MUSICAL ARTS CENTER
Indiana University
Jacobs School of Music
1201 E Thrid Street
Bloomington, IN 47405
Phone: 812-855-1583
e-mail: musicpub@indiana.edu
Web Site: www.music.indiana.edu
Officers:
  Dean: Gwyn Richards
Management:
  Marketing Director: Alain Barker
  Development Director: Melissa Korzec
  General Manager: Tridib Pal
Founded: 1972
Paid Staff: 60
Annual Attendance: 88,390
Type of Stage: Proscenium Arch
Seating Capacity: 3,200

6857
RUTH N HALLS THEATRE
Indiana University
Department of Theatre & Drama
275 North Jordan
Bloomington, IN 47405-1101
Phone: 812-855-4535
Web Site: www.theatre.indiana.edu
Officers:
  Chair: Jonathan Michaelsen
  Associate Chair: Dale McFadden
  Secretary: Catherine Richards
  MD: Drew Bratton
Management:
  Assistant Professor: Paul Brunner
  Associate Professor: Fred M. Duer
  Fiscal Officer: James Barrow
  Director, Marketing: Amy Osajima
Paid Staff: 20
Paid Artists: 30
Type of Stage: Proscenium

Orchestra Pit: y
Seating Capacity: 443

6858
WELLS-METZ THEATRE
Indiana University
Department of Theatre & Drama
275 North Jordan
Bloomington, IN 47405-1101
Phone: 812-855-4535
Web Site: www.theatre.indiana.edu
Officers:
  Chair: Jonathan Michaelsen
  Associate Chair: Dale McFadden
  Secretary: Catherine Richards
  MD: Drew Bratton
Management:
  Assistant Professor: Paul Brunner
  Associate Professor: Fred M. Duer
  Fiscal Officer: James Barrow
  Director, Marketing: Amy Osajima
Paid Staff: 20
Paid Artists: 30
Type of Stage: Flexible
Orchestra Pit: y
Seating Capacity: 236

6859
WORKSHOP THEATRE
Indiana University
Department of Theatre & Drama
275 N Jordan
Bloomington, IN 47405-1101
Phone: 812-855-4535
e-mail: theatre@indiana.edu
Web Site: www.theatre.indiana.edu
Officers:
  Chair: Jonathan Michaelsen
  Associate Chair: Dale McFadden
  Secretary: Catherine Richards
  MD: Drew Bratton
Management:
  Assistant Professor: Paul Brunner
  Associate Professor: Fred M. Duer
  Fiscal Officer: James Barrow
  Director, Marketing: Amy Osajima
Utilizes: Actors; AEA Actors; Designers; Educators; Fine Artists; Guest Accompanists; Guest Ensembles; Guest Instructors; Guest Soloists; Guild Activities; High School Drama; Original Music Scores; Performance Artists; Resident Professionals; Soloists
Specialized Field: Theatre and drama

6860
THE CENTER FOR THE PERORMING ARTS
355 City Center Dr
Carmel, IN 46032
Phone: 317-660-3373
Fax: 317-660-3374
e-mail: info@thecenterfortheperformingarts.org
Web Site: www.thecenterfortheperformingarts.org
Officers:
  President/CEO: Tania C Moskalenko
  Chairman: Frank M. Basile
  Vice Chairman: Donald Gottwald
  Treasurer: Traci L. Dossett
  Secretary: Randi Bellner
Management:
  Director Of Production: Kyle Lemoi
  General Manager: Douglas Tatum
  Artistic Director: Michael Feinstein

FACILITIES / Indiana

Mission: The center houses three venues of various sizes that are perfect for special events ranging from cocktail parties and weddings to speakers or concerts

6861
BALL THEATER
Wabash College
PO Box 352
Crawfordsville, IN 47933
Phone: 765-361-6100
e-mail: webmaster@wabash.edu
Web Site: www.wabash.edu
Officers:
   President: Patrick White
   Treasurer: Larry Griffith
Management:
   Artistic Director: Michael S Abbott
Type of Stage: Proscenium
Seating Capacity: 370

6862
EXPERIEMNTAL THEATER
Wabash College
PO Box 352
Crawfordsville, IN 47933
Phone: 765-361-6100
e-mail: webmaster@wabash.edu
Web Site: www.wabash.edu
Officers:
   President: Patrick White
   Treasurer: Larry Griffith
Management:
   Artistic Director: Michael S Abbott
Type of Stage: Black Box
Seating Capacity: 125

6863
SALTER CONCERT HALL
Wabash College
PO Box 352
Crawfordsville, IN 47933
Phone: 765-361-6100
e-mail: webmaster@wabash.edu
Web Site: www.wabash.edu
Officers:
   President: Patrick White
   Treasurer: Larry Griffith
Management:
   Artistic Director: Michael S Abbott
Seating Capacity: 275

6864
EVANSVILLE AUDITORIUM AND CONVENTION CENTRE
715 Locust Street
Evansville, IN 47708
Phone: 812-435-5770
Web Site: www.smgevansville.com
Management:
   General Manager: Todd Denk
   Operations Director: Harry Cochran
   Marketing Director: Kathy Embry
Paid Staff: 40

6865
HELEN MALLETTE STUDIO THEATRE
University of Southern Indiana
Liberal Arts Center
8600 University Boulevard
Evansville, IN 47712-3596
Phone: 812-464-8600
Web Site: www.usi.edu
Officers:
   President: H Ray Hoops
   Chair: Elliot H Wasserman
Type of Stage: Black Box
Seating Capacity: 100

6866
LINCOLN AMPHITHEATRE: MUSICAL OUTDOOR DRAMA
University of Southern Indiana
8600 University Boulevard
Evansville, IN 47712-3596
Mailing Address: P.O. Box 7-21, Lincoln City, Indiana 47552
Phone: 812-465-1668
Fax: 812-464-0029
Toll-free: 800-264-4223
Web Site: www.lincolnamphitheatre.org
Officers:
   Marketing Coordinator: Stacy A Brown
   LBDA President: Fr. Jeremy King, OSB
   LBDA Vice-President and Treasurer: Bud Schaaf
Management:
   Artistic Director: Elliot H Wasserman
   Managing Director: M Christopher Boyer
   Executive Director: Dan Wilkinson
   Producer: Tom Wilhelmus
   Communications Director: Brandi Weyer
Founded: 1987
Specialized Field: Musical; Youth Theater; Community Theater; Classic; Contemporary; Outdoor Theater
Status: Non-Profit, Non-Professional
Paid Staff: 20
Volunteer Staff: 20
Paid Artists: 40
Non-paid Artists: 10
Season: June - August
Stage Dimensions: 150' x 80'
Seating Capacity: 150

6867
ROBERTS MUNICIPAL STADIUM
2600 Division Street
Evansville, IN 47714
Phone: 812-476-1383
Web Site: www.smgevansville.com
Management:
   General Manager: Todd Denk
   Operations Director: Kevin McAlister
   Marketing Director: Kathy Embry
Seating Capacity: 12,500

6868
SOLDIERS & SAILORS MEMORIAL COLISEUM
300 Court Street
Evansville, IN 47708
Phone: 812-424-5879
Fax: 812-424-2798
Web Site: www.ssmcoliseum.org
Management:
   Director: Mark Acker
   General Manager: Jay Ball
Seating Capacity: 4,055

6869
VICTORY THEATRE
600 Main Street
Evansville, IN 47708
Mailing Address: 1 S.E. Martin Luther King, Jr. Blvd.
Evansville, IN 47708
Phone: 812-422-1515
e-mail: Information@thefordcenter.com
Web Site: www.victorytheatre.com
Management:
   General Manager: Ben Bolander
   Operations Director: Ed Mason
   Marketing Director: Kathy Embry
   Executive Director: Scott Schoenike
Seating Capacity: 1,950

6870
EMBASSY CENTRE
125 West Jefferson Boulevard
Fort Wayne, IN 46802
Phone: 260-424-6287
Fax: 260-424-4806
e-mail: etflori@embassycentre.org
Web Site: www.embassycentre.org
Management:
   Executive Director: Lori Lobsinger
   Business Manager/Booking: Mahlon Houihan
   Marketing/Advisor: Eileen Ahlersmeyer
   Box Office Manager: Colette Conrad
Founded: 1928
Seating Capacity: 2,477

6871
FOELLINGER THEATER IN FRANKE PARK
705 E. State Blvd
Fort Wayne, IN 46805
Phone: 260-427-6000
Fax: 260-427-6020
Web Site: www.fortwayneparks.org
Management:
   Director: AL Moll
Founded: 1949
Annual Attendance: 52,000

6872
PERFORMING ARTS CENTER
303 E Main Street
Fort Wayne, IN 46802
Phone: 219-422-8641
Fax: 219-422-6699
Web Site: www.fwcvb.org
Seating Capacity: 150

6873
SCOTTISH RITE CENTER
431 W Berry Street
Fort Wayne, IN 46802
Phone: 260-423-2593
Fax: 260-426-4126
Toll-free: 877-480-8020
Web Site: www.srcenter.org
Management:
   President: Hans Sheridan
   Artistic Director: Samantha Teter
   Managing Director: Colleen O'Linger
Utilizes: Dance Companies; Multimedia; Original Music Scores; Special Technical Talent; Theatre Companies
Founded: 1925
Status: Non-Profit, Professional
Paid Staff: 8
Volunteer Staff: 20
Facility Category: Theater, Ballroom, Banquet Rooms
Type of Stage: Proscenium
Stage Dimensions: 90 w x 30 d
Seating Capacity: 50 to 2,086
Year Built: 1928
Year Remodeled: 2001
Rental Contact: Director of Marketing & Events Samantha Teter

FACILITIES / Indiana

6874
WILLIAMS THEATRE
Indiana University-Purdue
Department of Theatre
2101 E. Coliseum Blvd
Fort Wayne, IN 46805-1499
Phone: 260-481-6551
Fax: 260-481-6707
Toll-free: 800-324-4739
e-mail: schultzj@ipfw.edu
Web Site: www.ipfw.edu/vpa/theatre/
Officers:
   Chair: John O'Connell
   Secretary: Joanne Schultz-Ithier
   Box office Supervisor: Reuben Albaugh
Management:
   Box Office Supervisor: Reuben Albaugh
   Maintenance Mechanic: Lee Hoggard
Mission: Degree programs offered by the Department of Theatre provide comprehensive training for the theatre profession and explore theatre's 2,000-year history and literature.
Specialized Field: Broadway, Shakespeare Musicals
Type of Stage: Thrust
Seating Capacity: 299

6875
THEATRE MARGOT
Franklin College
Johnson Center for Fine Arts
101 Branigin Boulevard
Franklin, IN 46131
Phone: 317-738-8000
Toll-free: 800-852-0232
Web Site: www.franklincollege.edu
Officers:
   President: James Moseley
Management:
   Director: Robin Roberts
Mission: Students not only play most of the roles in campus production, but they also get a taste of set and prop construction, lighting and sound design, costume management, state management, front-of-house management and publicity.
Founded: 1834
Specialized Field: Comedies, Drama, Historic Classics, Modern Plays, Musicals
Paid Staff: 65
Type of Stage: Black Box
Seating Capacity: 200
Year Built: 2001

6876
ALLEN COUNTY WAR MEMORIAL COLISEUM
4000 Parnell Avenue
Ft. Wayne, IN 46805
Phone: 260-482-9502
Fax: 260-484-1637
e-mail: rbrown@memorialcoliseum.com
Web Site: www.memorialcoliseum.com
Officers:
   EVP & General Manager: Randy Brown
   VP, Finance & COO: C.J. Steigmeyer
   VP, operation: Bryan Christie
   VP, Sales: Nathan Dennison
   Vice President of Event Services: Michele Remenschneider
Management:
   Assistant Operations: Eric Lonsbury
   Plant Facilities Manager: Rich Thoma
   Systems & Technology Manager: Brad Riehle
   Contract Administrator: Deborah Dambra
   Event Coordinator: Amanda Gehl
Founded: 1952
Specialized Field: Concerts; Family Shows; Trade/Consumer Shows; Private Meetings and Banquets
Status: Professional
Paid Staff: 300
Annual Attendance: 1.1 Million
Facility Category: Complex
Type of Stage: Stageright
Stage Dimensions: variable
Seating Capacity: 13,000
Year Built: 1952
Year Remodeled: 202
Cost: $34.5 Million
Rental Contact: Garnett Miller

6877
IUDONS
3400 Broadway
PO Box 64622
Gary, IN 46408
Phone: 219-980-7120
Fax: 219-981-4208
Toll-free: 888-968-7486
e-mail: vesmith@iun.edu
Web Site: www.iun.edu
Officers:
   President: Michael A. McRobbie
   EVP: Charles R. Bantz
   VP: CRAIG BRATER
Founded: 1963
Budget: $5,000-$10,000
Annual Attendance: 2,000
Facility Category: University Auditorium
Type of Stage: Professional
Seating Capacity: 2,000; 300
Year Built: 1980

6878
JOHN S. UMBLE CENTER
Goshen College
1700 South Main Street
Goshen, IN 46526
Phone: 574-535-7000
Fax: 574-535-7609
Toll-free: 800-348-7422
e-mail: info@goshen.edu
Web Site: www.goshen.edu/theater
Officers:
   President: James E. Brenneman
Management:
   Department Chair: Doug Caskey
   Production Manager: Brian Mast
Mission: The theater program at Goshen College has a strong liberal arts emphasis grounded in communication and performance theory.
Founded: 1894
Specialized Field: Operas, Plays, Theatre
Status: Private, Co-Educational
Facility Category: Theatre
Type of Stage: Proscenium/Thrust
Stage Dimensions: 70'x40'
Orchestra Pit: y
Seating Capacity: 419
Year Built: 1978

6879
KRESGE AUDITORIUM
DePauw University
Performing Arts Center
701 S. College Ave.
Greencastle, IN 46135-0037
Mailing Address: P.O. Box 37, Greencastle IN 46135-0037
Phone: 765-658-4800
e-mail: pacboxoffice@depauw.edu
Web Site: www.depauw.edu/pac/generalinfo
Officers:
   President: Brain W. Casey
   Coordinator Publicity/Marketing: Gigi Fenlon
Management:
   Managing Director: Kenneth Coquilette
   Director, Women Studies: Haris Anne
   Consultant: Janet Johns
   Event Coordinator: Janice Bagwell
Mission: The DePauw University Performing Arts Center strives to create a place of learning, appreciation and love for the arts by providing artistically diverse, stimulating and accessible programs to the university, local and regional communities.
Specialized Field: Concerts, Theatre
Seating Capacity: 1,500

6880
MOORE THEATER
DePauw University
Performing Arts Center
701 S. College Ave.
Greencastle, IN 46135-0037
Phone: 765-658-4800
e-mail: pacboxoffice@depauw.edu
Web Site: www.depauw.edu/pac/generalinfo
Officers:
   President: Brain W. Casey
   Coordinator Publicity/Marketing: Gigi Fenlon
Management:
   Managing Director: Kenneth Coquilette
   Director, Women Studies: Haris Anne
   Consultant: Janet Johns
   Event Coordinator: Janice Bagwell
Mission: The DePauw University Performing Arts Center strives to create a place of learning, appreciation and love for the arts by providing artistically diverse, stimulating and accessible programs to the university, local and regional communities.
Utilizes: Resident Artists
Specialized Field: Theatre
Type of Stage: Wrap-Around Stage
Seating Capacity: 400

6881
THOMPSON RECITAL HALL
DePauw University
Performing Arts Center
701 S. College Ave.
Greencastle, IN 46135-0037
Phone: 765-658-4800
e-mail: pacboxoffice@depauw.edu
Web Site: www.depauw.edu/pac/generalinfo
Officers:
   President: Brain W. Casey
   Coordinator Publicity/Marketing: Gigi Fenlon
Management:
   Managing Director: Kenneth Coquilette
   Director, Women Studies: Haris Anne
   Consultant: Janet Johns
   Event Coordinator: Janice Bagwell
Mission: The DePauw University Performing Arts Center strives to create a place of learning, appreciation and love for the arts by providing artistically diverse, stimulating and accessible programs to the university, local and regional communities.
Specialized Field: Recitals
Type of Stage: 40 Foot Semi-Circular
Seating Capacity: 220

FACILITIES / Indiana

6882
EASTERN HOWARD PERFORMING ARTS SOCIETY
421 South Harrison Street
Greentown, IN 46936
Mailing Address: P.O Box 351, Greentown, IN 46936
Phone: 765-628-4025
Fax: 765-628-5017
Toll-free: 888-649-2787
Web Site: ehpas.tripod.com
Management:
    Executive Director: Kelli Austin
Mission: Be catalysts for the cultural enrichment of the community by presenting performing arts programs to entertain and enrich all audiences: futhermore, the society hopes to foster intrest and development of the arts in the schools.
Founded: 1999
Status: Non-Profit
Paid Staff: 2
Volunteer Staff: 27
Type of Stage: Proscenium
Year Built: 1999

6883
FITZGIBBON RECITAL HALL
Hanover College
Lynn Center For Fine Arts
484 Ball Drive
Hanover, IN 47243
Mailing Address: PO Box 108, Hanover IN 47243
Phone: 812-866-7110
Web Site: www.hanover.edu/theatre/facilities
Officers:
    President: Sue DeWine
Management:
    Department Chair: Jim Stark
    Director: Paul Hildebrand
    Production Supervisor: Rob Doenges
Mission: The Hanover College Theatre approach to theatre training is production-intensive. Our curriculum includes courses in acting, directing, playwriting, design, technical theatre, history, and literature.
Specialized Field: Concerts, Recitals, Soloists
Seating Capacity: 300

6884
PARKER AUDITORIUM
Hanover College
484 Ball Drive
Hanover, IN 47243
Mailing Address: PO Box 108, Hanover IN 47243
Phone: 812-866-7110
Web Site: www.hanover.edu/theatre/facilities
Officers:
    President: Sue DeWine
Management:
    Department Chair: Jim Stark
    Director: Paul Hildebrand
    Production Supervisor: Rob Doenges
Mission: The Hanover College Theatre approach to theatre training is production-intensive. Our curriculum includes courses in acting, directing, playwriting, design, technical theatre, history, and literature.
Specialized Field: Theatre
Type of Stage: Arena, Thrust, Stadium Stages
Seating Capacity: 750

6885
UNIVERSITY THEATRE
Valparaiso University
Center for the Arts
1709 Chapel Dr
Hayward, IN
Phone: 219-464-5213
Fax: 219-464-5244
Web Site: www.valpo.edu/theatre
Officers:
    Chair: Lee F. Orchard
    President: Mark A. Heckler
Management:
    Associate Professor: Ann Kessler
Founded: 1859
Specialized Field: Musicals, Operas, Plays
Status: Private
Orchestra Pit: y
Seating Capacity: 280

6886
ZURCHER AUDITORIUM
Huntington College
Merillat Centre for the Arts
2303 College Avenue
Huntington, IN 46750
Phone: 260-356-6000
Web Site: www.huntington.edu/mca/theatre
Management:
    Athletics Director: Lori Culler
    Athletics Secretary: Cynthia Clore
Mission: Our Department of Theatre Arts offers degree programs in general Theatre, Performance, Design/Technology and Theatre Education. As a theatre student at Huntington University, you will combine classroom study, studio work and production experience to gain a balanced education.
Specialized Field: Theatre
Type of Stage: Proscenium
Seating Capacity: 697

6887
PEPSI COLISEUM
Indiana State Fairgrounds
1202 East 38th Street
Indianapolis, IN 46205
Phone: 317-927-7536
Fax: 317-927-7695
e-mail: dhummel@indianastatefair.com
Web Site: www.indianastatefair.com
Officers:
    VP, COO: Samantha Cross
    VP: Justin Armstrong
    CFO: Dave Ellis
Management:
    Executive Director: William Stinson
    Operations Director: Dave Hummel
    Executive Director: Cindy Hoye
    Director, Strategy: Kristen Gaddis
    Marketing Manager: Anna Whelchel
    Brand manager: Kelly Kough
Seating Capacity: 7,000

6888
BUTLER UNIVERSITY
Jordan College of Fine Arts
4600 Sunset Avenue
Indianapolis, IN 46208
Phone: 317-940-9231
Fax: 317-940-9658
Toll-free: 800-368-6852
e-mail: info@butler.edu
Web Site: www.butler.edu
Officers:
    Chair: Craig E. Fenneman
    Vice Chair: Keith W. Burks
    President: James Danko
Management:
    Dean, Jordan College of Fine Arts: Peter Alexander
Founded: 1928
Status: Non-Profit, Non-Professional
Paid Staff: 50

6889
CLOWES MEMORIAL HALL
Butler University
4602 Sunset Avenue
Indianapolis, IN 46208-3485
Phone: 317-940-6444
Fax: 317-940-9820
e-mail: info@cloweshall.org
Web Site: www.cloweshall.org
Officers:
    President: Dr Bobby Fong
Management:
    Executive Director: Elise J Kushigian
    Operations Director: Karen Steele
    Business Manager: Lisa Whitaker
    Director of Marketing: Joshua Lingenfelter
Mission: Clowes Memorial Hall of Butler University, a professional performing arts facility, is dedicated to lifelong learning in and through the arts. Our mission is to educate, enrich and entertain the citizens of Indiana and the Butler University community by presenting, promoting and hosting culturally, artistically and internationally diverse programs, events and collaborations.
Utilizes: Resident Artists
Founded: 1963
Specialized Field: Ballet, Concerts, Musical, Theatre
Paid Staff: 22
Volunteer Staff: 165
Budget: $3,417,714
Income Sources: Admissions plus Developed Income
Performs At: Auditorium
Annual Attendance: 162,431
Facility Category: Auditorium
Type of Stage: Proscenium
Orchestra Pit: y
Seating Capacity: 2,172
Year Built: 1963
Cost: $3 Million
Rental Contact: Karen Steele

6890
EIDSON-DUCKWALL RECITAL HALL
Butler University
Lilly Hall, Room 152
4600 Sunset Avenue
Indianapolis, IN 46208-3485
Phone: 317-940-9659
Fax: 317-940-9930
e-mail: info@butler.edu
Web Site: www.butler.edu/theatre/
Officers:
    President: Dr. Bobby Fong
    Chairman: Diane Timmerman
Management:
    Department Chair: John C. Green, PhD
    Technical Director: Glen Thoreson
Mission: The program of study in theatre combines stage experience with core studies in: acting, directing, voice, movement, playwriting; scenic, lighting and costume design; stagecraft and make-up; theatre history, play analysis and critical theory.
Founded: 1885

FACILITIES / Indiana

Specialized Field: Recitals
Seating Capacity: 140
Year Built: 2004
Architect: Browning Day Mullins Dierdorf
Cost: #3 Million

6891
EITELJORG MUSEUM
500 W Washington Street
Indianapolis, IN 46204
Phone: 317-636-9378
Fax: 317-264-1724
Web Site: www.eiteljorg.org
Officers:
  President: John Vanausdall
  VP, Developemnt: Susie Maxwell
Management:
  Development Manager: Sally Dickson
  VP/Chief Curator: James Nottage
  Director Education: Cathy Burton
  Assistant President: Molly Sass
Mission: To inspire an appreciation and understanding of the arts, history and cultures of the American West and the indigenous people of North America. The Eiteljorg Museum collects and preserves Western art and Native American art cultural objects of the highest quality, and serves the public through ongoing exhibitions, educational programs, cultural exchanges, and entertaining special events.
Founded: 1989
Specialized Field: American Indian and Western Art
Status: Non-Profit, Professional

6892
HILBERT CENTER THEATRE
45 Monument Circle
Indianapolis, IN 46204-2919
Phone: 317-231-6498
Fax: 317-262-1157
e-mail: fheavrin@indianapolissymphony.org
Web Site: www.hilbertcircletheatreindy.org
Management:
  Rental Coordinator: Frances Heavrin
Mission: 5 venues to be used for private parties, speakers, events

6893
HINKLE FIELDHOUSE
Butler University
4602 Sunset Avenue
Indianapolis, IN 46208
Phone: 317-940-6444
Fax: 317-940-9734
Web Site: www.butler.edu/
Management:
  Executive Director: Elise J Kushigian
  Operations Director: Karen Steele
  Business Manager: Lisa Whitaker
  Director of Marketing: Joshua Lingenfelter
Founded: 1928

6894
INDIANAPOLIS ARTS GARDEN
Arts Council of Indianapolis
924 N Pennsylvania Street
Indianapolis, IN 46204
Phone: 317-631-3301
Fax: 317-624-2559
e-mail: indyarts@indyarts.org
Web Site: www.indyarts.org
Management:
  Public Art Coordinator: Lindsey Lord
  Artsgarden Director: Mike Prusa
  Marketing Coordinator: Maureen Saul
  Director, Grant Services: Ernest Britton
Mission: To enable a large and diverse audience to see, understand and enjoy the best of the worlds visual arts; to this end, the Museum collects, preserves, exhibits and interprets original works of art.
Founded: 1995

6895
LILLY HALL STUDIO THEATRE
Butler University
Performing Arts Complex
4603 Clarendon Rd.
Indianapolis, IN 46208-3485
Phone: 317-940-9659
Fax: 317-940-9930
e-mail: info@butler.edu
Web Site: www.butler.edu/theatre/
Officers:
  Chair: William Fisher
Management:
  Department Chair: William Fisher
  Professor: Owen Schaub
Mission: The program of study in theatre combines stage experience with core studies in: acting, directing, voice, movement, playwriting; scenic, lighting and costume design; stagecraft and make-up; theatre history, play analysis and critical theory.
Founded: 1885
Specialized Field: Student Directed Productions
Type of Stage: Black Box
Seating Capacity: 350
Year Built: 2003
Architect: Browning Day Mullins Dierdorf

6896
MARKEY SQUARE ARENA
Pacers Basketball Corporation
300 E Market Street
Indianapolis, IN 46204
Phone: 317-639-6411
Fax: 317-261-6299
Web Site: www.marketsquaresarena.com
Management:
  VP/General Manager: Rick Fuson
  Communications Manager: Jeff Johnson
  VP/Scheduling/Production Manager: Jeff Bowen
  Concessions Manager: Rich Kapp
Seating Capacity: 16,900

6897
OLD NATIONAL CENTRE
502 North New Jersey Street
Indianapolis, IN 46204
Phone: 317-231-0000
Fax: 317-231-9410
Web Site: www.livenation.com/oldnationalcentre
Management:
  Executive Director/Booking: Terry Hennessey
  Events Director: Debbie Hennessey
  Box Office Manager: Chris O'Connor
  Production Manager: Chris Dicke
Mission: The Old National Centre, formerly the Murat Centre, is a multi-purpose facility offering great versatility for events of all sizes.
Seating Capacity: 2,600

6898
PIKE PERFORMING ARTS CENTER
6701 Zionsville Road
Indianapolis, IN 46268
Phone: 317-216-5450
Fax: 317-216-5460
e-mail: ppac@pike.k12.in.us
Web Site: www.pikePAC.org
Management:
  Executive Director: Don Steffy
  Technical Director: Kyle Bredehoeft
  Box Office Manager: Lorna Startzman
  Bookkeeper: Sue Thatcher
Mission: To offer quality performances and educational activities for the enjoyment and enlightenment of its public.
Utilizes: Actors; Collaborations; Dance Companies; Guest Musical Directors; Guild Activities; Local Artists; Multimedia; Special Technical Talent; Theatre Companies
Founded: 1996
Paid Staff: 5
Budget: $200,000
Income Sources: Box Office, Grants, Sponsors
Affiliations: Association of Performing Arts Presenters; Indiana Presenters Network; League of Indianapolis Theatres
Annual Attendance: 7,800
Facility Category: Performance Center
Type of Stage: Proscenium
Stage Dimensions: 52'w x 24'h x 36'8"d
Seating Capacity: 1,449
Year Built: 1997

6899
RANSBURG AUDITORIUM
University of Indianapolis
Esch Hall Theatre
1400 East Hanna Avenue
Indianapolis, IN 46227
Phone: 317-788-3368
Toll-free: 800-232-8634
e-mail: arts@uindy.edu
Web Site: www.arts.uindy.edu
Officers:
  Chair: Thomas C. Martin
  Vice Chair: Yvonne H. Shaheen
  President: Robert Manuel
  VP, CFO: Michael P. Holstein
  Secretary: Stephen F. Fry
Management:
  Dir Christel DeHann Fine Arts Ctr: Christie Beckmann
  Department Chair: Jim Ream
  Director Theatre: Brad Bright
  Technical Director: Jeffrey Barnes
  Administrative Asst Theatre Dept: Deb Denning
  Faculty Box Office Manager: Jennifer Alexander
Mission: The goal of the Department of Theatre at the University of Indianapolis is to develop the skills, crafts, and imaginations of our students within the liberal arts context.
Founded: 1902
Specialized Field: Bands, Choir Concerts, Conferences, Dance Productions, Lectures, Theatrical
Type of Stage: Traditional Proscenium
Seating Capacity: 780
Year Restored: 1997

6900
RCA DOME
100 S Capitol Avenue
Indianapolis, IN 46225
Phone: 317-262-3403
Fax: 317-262-3455
Web Site: www.iccrd.com
Management:
  Executive Director: Barney Levengood
  Marketing Director: Linda Addaman
  Stadium Director: Micheal A Fox
  Suites/Special Services Manager: Heidi Mallin

FACILITIES / Indiana

General Manager/Volume Service: Dennis Cullinane
Ticket Manager: Mary Dyer
Founded: 1972
Status: Non-Profit, Non-Professional
Paid Staff: 140
Seating Capacity: 60,500

6901
RUTH LILLY PERFORMANCE HALL
University of Indianapolis
Christel DeHaan Fine Arts Center
1400 East Hanna Avenue
Indianapolis, IN 46227
Phone: 317-788-3368
Toll-free: 800-232-8634
e-mail: arts@uindy.edu
Web Site: www.arts.uindy.edu
Officers:
  Chair: Thomas C. Martin
  Vice Chair: Yvonne H. Shaheen
  President: Robert Manuel
  VP, CFO: Michael P. Holstein
  Secretary: Stephen F. Fry
Management:
  Civic Volunteer: Murvin Enders
  Director: Holbrook Hankinson
  Consultant: Charles Johnson
Mission: The goal of the Department of Theatre at the University of Indianapolis is to develop the skills, crafts, and imaginations of our students within the liberal arts context.
Founded: 1902
Opened: 1994
Specialized Field: Chamber, Classical, Jazz Music
Type of Stage: Proscenium
Seating Capacity: 600

6902
STUDIO THEATRE
University of Indianapolis
Esch Hall Theatre
1400 East Hanna Avenue
Indianapolis, IN 46227
Phone: 317-788-3368
Toll-free: 800-232-8634
e-mail: arts@uindy.edu
Web Site: www.arts.uindy.edu
Officers:
  Chair: Thomas C. Martin
  Vice Chair: Yvonne H. Shaheen
  President: Robert Manuel
  VP, CFO: Michael P. Holstein
  Secretary: Stephen F. F. Fry
Management:
  Civic Volunteer: Murvin Enders
  Director: Holbrook Hankinson
  Consultant: Charles Johnson
Mission: The goal of the Department of Theatre at the University of Indianapolis is to develop the skills, crafts, and imaginations of our students within the liberal arts context.
Founded: 1902
Specialized Field: Faculty, Student Productions
Type of Stage: 3/4 Thrust Black Box
Seating Capacity: 80

6903
VICTORY FIELD: INDIANAPOLIS BASEBALL CLUB
501 W Maryland Street
Indianapolis, IN 46225
Mailing Address: Victory Field, 501 West Maryland Street Indianapolis, IN 46
Phone: 317-269-3542
Fax: 317-269-3541
Web Site: www.indyindians.com
Officers:
  Chairman: Max B. Schumacher
  Vice Chair: Alan R. Kimbell
  Secretary: Max W. Hittle, Jr.
Management:
  Chairman/President: Max B Schumacher
  General Manager: D Cal Burleson
  Business Manager: Brad Morris
  Assistant General Manager: Randy Lewandowski
  Office Manager: Scott Rubin
  Media Relations Director: Tim Harms
  Director Advertising: Daryle Keith
  Director Special Projects: Bruce Schumacher
  Director Ticket Operations: Mike Schneider
Founded: 1887
Status: For-Profit, Professional
Paid Staff: 15
Seating Capacity: 15,500

6904
WARREN PERFORMING ARTS CENTER
9500 East 16th Street
Indianapolis, IN 46229
Phone: 317-532-6280
Fax: 317-532-6440
e-mail: pmitchel@warren.k12.in.us
Web Site: www.warrenpac.org
Management:
  Manager: Penny Miritell
Mission: Providing education and cultural programs for the students and community of Warren Township and Greater Indianapolis.
Performs At: Grand Stage Auditorium, Studio Theatre
Type of Stage: Flexible
Seating Capacity: 1000; 150

6905
JASPER ARTS CENTER
951 College Avenue
Jasper, IN 47546
Phone: 812-482-3070
Fax: 812-634-6997
e-mail: jasperarts@psci.net
Web Site: www.jasperarts.org
Officers:
  President: Michael Jones
  VP: Gary Moeller
  Secretary: Linda Khele
Founded: 1975
Type of Stage: Proscenium

6906
HAVENS AUDITORIUM
Indiana University Kokomo
Main Building
2300 S. Washington Street
Kokomo, IN 46904-9003
Phone: 765-453-2000
Web Site: www.iuk.edu/~koautrm/
Officers:
  Chancellor: Susan Sciame-Giesecke
  CIO: Elizabeth Van Gordon
  Vice chancellor: Jan Halperin
Management:
  Technical Director: Jeffrey Gegner
  Executive Director: Gerry G. Stroman
  Director, Physical activity: John Sarber
  Director, HR: Cathy Valcke
Mission: Havens Auditorium is a community cultural center, used for dramatic presentations, concerts, lectures.
Founded: 1945
Opened: 1965
Specialized Field: Concerts, Lectures, Theatre
Type of Stage: Proscenium
Stage Dimensions: 50' x 24'
Orchestra Pit: y
Seating Capacity: 868

6907
LA PORTE CIVIC AUDITORIUM
1001 Ridge St
La Porte, IN 46350
Phone: 219-362-2325
e-mail: info@laportcivicauditorium.com
Web Site: www.laportcivicauditorium.com
Mission: 9 venues for use in the civic center

6908
LONG CENTER FOR THE PERFORMING ARTS
111 N 6th Street
Lafayette, IN 47902
Phone: 765-742-5664
Fax: 765-742-1724
Toll-free: 877-490-7761
e-mail: info@longcentertheater.com
Web Site: www.longcentertheater.com
Officers:
  President: Steve Stucky
  VP: Dave Vorbeck
  Treasurer: Michael Strauch
  Secretary: Mark Hermodson
Management:
  Executive Director: Doug Kern
  Secretary/Ticket Sales: Brenda Shultz
  Accountant: Shelly McConnaughey
  Operations: Shannon Sabel
Mission: Performing Arts Center that enhances the community's cultural life.
Founded: 1921
Specialized Field: Series & Festivals; Dance; Instrumental Music; Musical Theatre; Theatrical Group; Vocal Music
Status: Non-Profit, Professional
Paid Staff: 15
Volunteer Staff: 40
Budget: $250,000
Income Sources: Rentals; Donations
Performs At: Theater, Performing Arts
Annual Attendance: 40,000
Facility Category: Theater, Performing Arts
Type of Stage: Wood
Stage Dimensions: 35' x 30'
Seating Capacity: 1190
Year Built: 1921
Year Remodeled: 2000
Rental Contact: Doug Kern

6909
HERMAN BAKER RECITAL HALL
Indiana Wesleyan University
Phillippe Performing Arts Center
4201 S. Washington St.
Marion, IN 46953
Phone: 765-674-6901
Toll-free: 866-468-6498
Web Site: www.indwes.edu
Officers:
  President: David Wright
  EVP: Audrey Hahn
  VP: Diane McDaniel

FACILITIES / Indiana

VP, CFO: Nancy Schoonmaker
Management:
  Pastor: John A. Bray
  Senior Pastor: Steve DeNeff
  Co Founder: Barbara Green
Mission: Our goal continues to be to provide a diversity of music and theater programming for the enjoyment of students, friends and neighbors of all ages.
Opened: 1996
Specialized Field: Chamber Music, Senior Recitals, Student Performances
Orchestra Pit: y
Seating Capacity: 176

6910
PHILLIPPE AUDITORIUM
Indiana Wesleyan University
Phillippe Performing Arts Center
4201 S. Washington St.
Marion, IN 46953
Phone: 765-674-6901
Toll-free: 866-468-6498
Web Site: www.indwes.edu
Officers:
  President: David Wright
  EVP: Audrey Hahn
  VP: Diane McDaniel
  VP, CFO: Nancy Schoonmaker
Management:
  Pastor: John A. Bray
  Senior Pastor: Steve DeNeff
  Co Founder: Barbara Green
Mission: Our goal continues to be to provide a diversity of music and theater programming for the enjoyment of students, friends and neighbors of all ages.
Opened: 1996
Specialized Field: Recitals, Theatre
Type of Stage: Versatile
Orchestra Pit: y
Seating Capacity: 1,155

6911
RCA BLACK BOX THEATRE
Indiana Wesleyan University
Phillippe Performing Arts Center
4201 S. Washington St.
Marion, IN 46953
Phone: 765-674-6901
Toll-free: 866-468-6498
Web Site: www.indwes.edu
Officers:
  President: David Wright
  EVP: Audrey Hahn
  VP: Diane McDaniel
  VP, CFO: Nancy Schoonmaker
Management:
  Pastor: John A. Bray
  Senior Pastor: Steve DeNeff
  Co Founder: Barbara Green
Mission: Our goal continues to be to provide a diversity of music and theater programming for the enjoyment of students, friends and neighbors of all ages.
Opened: 1996
Specialized Field: Theatre
Type of Stage: Black Box
Orchestra Pit: y
Seating Capacity: 125

6912
STAR PLAZA THEATRE
I-65 & US 30
8001 Deleware Place
Merrillville, IN 46410
Phone: 219-769-6311
Fax: 219-756-0604
Web Site: www.starplazatheatre.com
Officers:
  President: Charles Blum
Management:
  President: Charles Blum
  General Manager: Mark Bishop
Founded: 1979
Specialized Field: Musical
Status: For-Profit, Professional
Facility Category: Theatre
Seating Capacity: 3400
Year Built: 1979

6913
EVEREST-ROHRER AUDITORIUM
Bethel College
Fine Arts Center
1001 Bethel Circle
Mishawaka, IN 46545
Phone: 574-807-7000
Toll-free: 800-422-4101
Web Site: www.bethelcollege.edu/academics/undergrad/theatr
Officers:
  President: Gregg A. Chenoweth
Management:
  Director: Barbara Stith
  Technical Director: Derek Null
  Production Manager: Lisa Staples
Mission: An evangelical Christian college affiliated with the Missionary Church, Bethel is uniquely qualified to provide educational opportunities for all students, traditional and adult, who are interested in a liberal arts program of studies with career and personal growth orientations.
Specialized Field: Comedy, Drama, Musical, Theatre
Type of Stage: Proscenium
Stage Dimensions: 48' x 32'
Orchestra Pit: y
Seating Capacity: 860
Year Built: 1996
Cost: $5 Million

6914
OCTORIUM
Bethel College
Fine Arts Center
1001 Bethel Circle
Mishawaka, IN 46545
Phone: 574-807-7000
Toll-free: 800-422-4101
Web Site: www.bethelcollege.edu/academics/undergrad/theatr
Officers:
  President: Gregg A. Chenoweth
Management:
  Director: Barbara Stith
  Technical Director: Derek Null
  Production Manager: Lisa Staples
Mission: An evangelical Christian college affiliated with the Missionary Church, Bethel is uniquely qualified to provide educational opportunities for all students, traditional and adult, who are interested in a liberal arts program of studies with career and personal growth orientations.
Specialized Field: Plays
Type of Stage: Black Box
Seating Capacity: 160

6915
CAVE THEATRE
Ball State University
Department of Theatre and Dance, AC 306
2000 West University Avenue
Muncie, IN 47306
Phone: 765-285-8740
Fax: 765-285-4030
Toll-free: 800-828-40
e-mail: theatrestu@bsu.edu
Web Site: www.bsu.edu/theatre
Officers:
  President: Jo Ann M. Gora
  Chair: Bill Jenkins
Management:
  Instructor of Theatre: Joe Court
  Technical Director: Curtis Mortimore
  Administrative Coordinator: Melissa Tinsley
Mission: Ball State University's Department of Theatre and Dance is a program of choice for the serious undergraduate theatre and dance student. Our theatre major features options in acting, musical theatre, design and technology, production (directing and stage management), theatrical studies, and theatre education.
Specialized Field: Classes, Student Productions
Paid Staff: 15

6916
EDWARD S. STROTHER THEATRE
Ball State University
Department of Theatre and Dance, AC 306
2000 West University Avenue
Muncie, IN 47306
Phone: 765-285-8740
Fax: 765-285-4030
Toll-free: 800-828-40
e-mail: theatrestu@bsu.edu
Web Site: www.bsu.edu/theatre
Officers:
  President: Jo Ann M. Gora
  Chair: Bill Jenkins
Management:
  Instructor of Theatre: Joe Court
  Technical Director: Curtis Mortimore
  Administrative Coordinator: Melissa Tinsley
Mission: Ball State University's Department of Theatre and Dance is a program of choice for the serious undergraduate theatre and dance student. Our theatre major features options in acting, musical theatre, design and technology, production (directing and stage management), theatrical studies, and theatre education.
Specialized Field: Theatre
Paid Staff: 15
Type of Stage: Black Box
Seating Capacity: 100

6917
EMENS AUDITORIUM
Ball State University
2000 West University Avenue
Muncie, IN 47306
Phone: 765-289-1241
Fax: 765-285-3719
Toll-free: 800-828-40
Web Site: www.bsu.edu
Officers:
  President: Jo Ann M. Gora
  Chair: Bill Jenkins
Management:
  Instructor of Theatre: Joe Court
  Technical Director: Curtis Mortimore
  Administrative Coordinator: Melissa Tinsley

FACILITIES / Indiana

Mission: To provide cultural, fine arts and enterainment opportunities for East Central Indiana.
Founded: 1964
Status: Nonprofit, Professional
Paid Staff: 10
Performs At: Emens Auditorium
Type of Stage: Black Box
Seating Capacity: 3,581

6918
UNIVERSITY THEATRE
Ball State University
Department of Theatre and Dance, AC 306
2000 West University Avenue
Muncie, IN 47306
Phone: 765-285-8740
Fax: 765-285-4030
Toll-free: 800-828-40
e-mail: theatrestu@bsu.edu
Web Site: www.bsu.edu/theatre
Officers:
 President: Jo Ann M. Gora
 Chair: Bill Jenkins
Management:
 Instructor of Theatre: Joe Court
 Technical Director: Curtis Mortimore
 Administrative Coordinator: Melissa Tinsley
Mission: Ball State University's Department of Theatre and Dance is a program of choice for the serious undergraduate theatre and dance student. Our theatre major features options in acting, musical theatre, design and technology, production (directing and stage management), theatrical studies, and theatre education.
Specialized Field: Dance, Theatre
Paid Staff: 15
Seating Capacity: 410

6919
CENTER FOR VISUAL AND PERFORMING ARTS
1040 Ridge Road
Theatre At The Center
Munster, IN 46321
Phone: 219-836-1930
Fax: 219-836-3269
e-mail: cgessert@comhs.org
Web Site: www.cvpa.org
Management:
 Production Manager: Chuck Gessert
 Artistic Director: William Pullinsi
Mission: To touch, enrich and entertain human beings with live professional theatre.
Founded: 1989
Type of Stage: Thrust
Seating Capacity: 450

6920
BROWN COUNTY PLAYHOUSE
Indiana University at Bloomington
Theatre & Drama
70 Van Buren St South
Nashville, IN 47448
Phone: 812-988-2123
Fax: 812-856-0698
Web Site: www.indiana.edu/~thtr
Officers:
 Department Chair: Jonathan R. Michaelson
 Associate Chair: Dale McFadden
Management:
 Technical Director: Paul Brunner
 Assistant Technical Director: I. Christopher Berg
 Production Manager: Thomas Quintas
 Director of Marketing: Amy Osajima
Mission: The Brown County Playhouse, a professional theatre operated in conjunction with the Indiana University Department of Theatre and Drama, is located in the center of scenic Nashville.
Founded: 1949
Specialized Field: Comedy, Contemporary, Theatre
Status: Non-Profit, Professional
Paid Staff: 20
Paid Artists: 30
Seating Capacity: 400

6921
AMPHITHEATRE
Indiana University Southeast
Knobview Hall
4201 Grant Line Road
New Albany, IN 47150
Phone: 812-941-2333
Fax: 812-941-2660
e-mail: setheatr@ius.edu
Web Site: www.ius.edu/Theater/
Officers:
 Chair: Patrick J. O'Connor
 Quinn: Thao Brieanna
 Mahuron: Secretary Jack
Management:
 Assistant Professor: Rebekkah Meixner
 Adjunct Lecturer Theatre: Natalie Bowman
 Adjunct Lecturer Theatre: Daniel Hill
 Manager: Sandra Herron
Mission: The Theatre program at Indiana University Southeast is committed to providing a wide variety of opportunities for students to explore and develop expertise in performance and design.
Specialized Field: Graduation
Seating Capacity: 6,000
Cost: $12 Million

6922
PAUL G. ROBINSON THEATER
Indiana University Southeast
Paul W. Ogle Cultural and Community Center
4201 Grant Line Road
New Albany, IN 47150
Phone: 812-941-2333
Fax: 812-941-2660
e-mail: setheatr@ius.edu
Web Site: www.ius.edu/Theater/
Officers:
 Chair: Patrick J. O'Connor
 Quinn: Thao Brieanna
 Mahuron: Secretary Jack
Management:
 Assistant Professor: Rebekkah Meixner
 Adjunct Lecturer Theatre: Natalie Bowman
 Adjunct Lecturer Theatre: Daniel Hill
 Manager: Sandra Herron
Mission: The Theatre program at Indiana University Southeast is committed to providing a wide variety of opportunities for students to explore and develop expertise in performance and design.
Specialized Field: Dance, Theatre
Type of Stage: Thrust
Seating Capacity: 340
Cost: $12 Million

6923
PAUL W OGLE CULTURAL & COMMUNITY CENTER
Indiana University Southeast
4201 Grant Line Road
New Albany, IN 47150-6405
Phone: 812-941-2333
e-mail: oglemail@ius.edu
Web Site: www.ius.indiana.edu
Officers:
 Chair: Patrick J. O'Connor
 Quinn: Thao Brieanna
 Mahuron: Secretary Jack
Management:
 Assistant Professor: Rebekkah Meixner
 Adjunct Lecturer Theatre: Natalie Bowman
 Adjunct Lecturer Theatre: Daniel Hill
 Manager: Sandra Herron
Founded: 1996
Status: Non-Profit, Non-Professional
Paid Staff: 11
Volunteer Staff: 15
Performs At: Concert Hall

6924
RECITAL HALL
Indiana University Southeast
Paul W. Ogle Cultural and Community Center
4201 Grant Line Road
New Albany, IN 47150
Phone: 812-941-2333
Fax: 812-941-2660
e-mail: setheatr@ius.edu
Web Site: www.ius.edu/Theater/
Officers:
 Chair: Patrick J. O'Connor
 Quinn: Thao Brieanna
 Mahuron: Secretary Jack
Management:
 Assistant Professor: Rebekkah Meixner
 Adjunct Lecturer Theatre: Natalie Bowman
 Adjunct Lecturer Theatre: Daniel Hill
 Manager: Sandra Herron
Mission: The Theatre program at Indiana University Southeast is committed to providing a wide variety of opportunities for students to explore and develop expertise in performance and design.
Specialized Field: Community Meetings, Conferences, Faculty and Student Recitals
Seating Capacity: 96
Cost: $12 Million

6925
RICHARD K. STEM CONCERT HALL
Indiana University Southeast
Paul W. Ogle Cultural and Community Center
4201 Grant Line Road
New Albany, IN 47150
Phone: 812-941-2333
Fax: 812-941-2660
e-mail: setheatr@ius.edu
Web Site: www.ius.edu/Theater/
Officers:
 Chair: Patrick J. O'Connor
 Quinn: Thao Brieanna
 Mahuron: Secretary Jack
Management:
 Assistant Professor: Rebekkah Meixner
 Adjunct Lecturer Theatre: Natalie Bowman
 Adjunct Lecturer Theatre: Daniel Hill
 Manager: Sandra Herron
Mission: The Theatre program at Indiana University Southeast is committed to providing a wide variety of opportunities for students to explore and develop expertise in performance and design.
Specialized Field: Concerts, Drummer Series, Music Department
Type of Stage: Proscenium
Orchestra Pit: y
Seating Capacity: 500

FACILITIES / Indiana

Cost: $12 Million

6926
CORDIER AUDITORIUM
Manchester College
604 East College Avenue
North Manchester, IN 46962
Phone: 260-982-5000
Fax: 219-982-6868
Web Site: www.manchester.edu
Officers:
   President: Jo Young Switzer
   Chair: Scott K. Strode
Management:
   Dir Performing Art Technologies: Matt Unger
   Event Specialist: Alexis Leininger
   Facilities Coordinator: Paula Finton
Mission: As a primarily undergraduate, residential, liberal arts community rooted in the tradition of the Church of the Brethren, Manchester College values: Learning, Faith, Service, Integrity, Diversity, Community.
Founded: 1889
Specialized Field: Presentations, Theatre Productions
Seating Capacity: 1,300
Year Built: 1978

6927
CHRIS AND ANNE REYES ORGAN AND CHORAL HALL
University of Notre Dame
Marie P. Debartolo Performing Arts Center
100 Performing Arts Center
Notre Dame, IN 46556
Phone: 574-631-2800
Web Site: www.performingarts.nd.edu
Officers:
   President: Rev. John I. Jenkins, CSC
   EVP: John F. Affleck-Graves
   Provost: Thomas G. Burish
Management:
   Executive Director: Anna M. Thompson
   Senior Associate Director: Ted Barron
   Program Manager: Tom Barkes
   Events Program Manager: Denise Sullivan
Mission: The DeBartolo Center for the Peforming Arts was carefully designed for both public performance and for teaching and learning. Our mission is rooted in the conviction that the arts are an indispensable element of a liberal education and an enlightened society.
Opened: 2004
Specialized Field: Sacred Music
Seating Capacity: 80

6928
EDMUND P. JOYCE ATHLETIC & CONVOCATION CENTER
University of Notre Dame
Marie P. Debartolo Performing Arts Center
101 Performing Arts Center
Notre Dame, IN 46556
Phone: 574-631-6107
Fax: 574-631-8596
e-mail: develop@nd.edu
Web Site: www.nd.edu
Management:
   Assistant Business Manager: Heidi Uebelhor
Founded: 1842
Status: Non-Profit, Professional
Paid Staff: 13
Seating Capacity: 9,800

6929
JUDD AND MARY LOU LEIGHTON CONCERT HALL
University of Notre Dame
Marie P. Debartolo Performing Arts Center
100 Performing Arts Center
Notre Dame, IN 46556
Phone: 574-631-2800
Web Site: www.performingarts.nd.edu
Officers:
   President: Rev. John I. Jenkins, CSC
Management:
   Executive Director: Anna M. Thompson
   Senior Associate Director: Ted Barron
   Program Manager: Tom Barkes
Mission: The DeBartolo Center for the Peforming Arts was carefully designed for both public performance and for teaching and learning. Our mission is rooted in the conviction that the arts are an indispensable element of a liberal education and an enlightened society.
Opened: 2004
Specialized Field: Choir, Jazz Band, Shakespeare, Symphony Orchestra
Type of Stage: Concert Hall Stage
Stage Dimensions: 58' x 40'
Orchestra Pit: y
Seating Capacity: 952

6930
MARIE P. DEBARTOLO CENTER FOR THE PERFORMING ARTS
University of Notre Dame
100 Performing Arts Center
Notre Dame, IN 46556
Phone: 574-631-2800
Fax: 574-631-9411
e-mail: performingarts.nd.edu
Web Site: www.performingarts.nd.edu
Officers:
   Executive Director: Anna M. Thompson
   Business Program Manager: Tom Barkes
   Senior Associate Director: Ted Barron
Management:
   Executive Director: Anna M. Thompson
   Senior Associate Director: Ted Barron
   Program Manager: Tom Barkes
Mission: The Marie P. DeBartolo center for the Performing Arts facilitates learning reflective of the University of Notre Dame's distinctive liberal arts tradition through the informed exploration of universal truth and beauty. We serve to encourage and celebrate the human spirit through the performing and cinematic arts, which connect, stimulate and enrich our communities.
Utilizes: Dance Companies; Touring Companies
Founded: 2004
Specialized Field: Professional Music/Dance Theatre; Academic Music Dance Theatre; Art House Cinema
Paid Staff: 24
Volunteer Staff: 55
Paid Artists: 25
Budget: $2-3 million
Income Sources: Ticket Sales; Endowment; Grants; Donations; University Support
Performs At: Regis Philbin Studio Theatre, Judd and Mary Lou Leighton Concert Hall, Patricia George Decio Mainstage Theatre
Affiliations: ISPA; APAP; CMA; Dance USA; INMX; Cavco; Cavort
Annual Attendance: 50,000
Facility Category: Concert Hall; Proscenium; Black Box; Cinema; Organ Hall
Type of Stage: Proscenium; Black Box

Seating Capacity: 100, 900, 350
Year Built: 2004
Cost: $64 Million

6931
MICHAEL BROWNING FAMILY CINEMA
University of Notre Dame
Marie P. Debartolo Performing Arts Center
104 Performing Arts Center
Notre Dame, IN 46556
Phone: 574-631-2800
Web Site: www.performingarts.nd.edu
Officers:
   President: Rev. John I. Jenkins, CSC
   EVP: John F. Affleck-Graves
   Provost: Thomas G. Burish
Management:
   Executive Director: Anna M. Thompson
   Senior Associate Director: Ted Barron
   Program Manager: Tom Barkes
   Production Manager: Jenny Goetz
Mission: The DeBartolo Center for the Peforming Arts was carefully designed for both public performance and for teaching and learning. Our mission is rooted in the conviction that the arts are an indispensable element of a liberal education and an enlightened society.
Opened: 2004
Specialized Field: Art House Theatre, Current and Historic Films
Type of Stage: Cinema
Seating Capacity: 202

6932
NOTRE DAME STADIUM
University of Notre Dame
Marie P. Debartolo Performing Arts Center
105 Performing Arts Center
Notre Dame, IN 46556
Phone: 574-631-2800
Fax: 574-631-6772
e-mail: develop.1@nd.edu
Web Site: www.und.com
Officers:
   President: Rev. John I. Jenkins, CSC
   EVP: John F. Affleck-Graves
   Provost: Thomas G. Burish
Management:
   Executive Director: Anna M. Thompson
   Senior Associate Director: Ted Barron
   Program Manager: Tom Barkes
   Events Program Manager: Denise Sullivan
Seating Capacity: 80,530

6933
PATRICIA GEORGE DECIO THEATRE
University of Notre Dame
Marie P. Debartolo Performing Arts Center
106 Performing Arts Center
Notre Dame, IN
Phone: 574-631-2800
Web Site: www.performingarts.nd.edu
Officers:
   President: Rev. John I. Jenkins, CSC
   EVP: John F. Affleck-Graves
   Provost: Thomas G. Burish
Management:
   Executive Director: Anna M. Thompson
   Senior Associate Director: Ted Barron
   Program Manager: Tom Barkes
   Events Program Manager: Denise Sullivan

FACILITIES / Indiana

Mission: The DeBartolo Center for the Peforming Arts was carefully designed for both public performance and for teaching and learning. Our mission is rooted in the conviction that the arts are an indispensable element of a liberal education and an enlightened society.
Opened: 2004
Specialized Field: Professional and Amateur Productions
Type of Stage: Proscenium
Stage Dimensions: 32' and 42' x 24'
Orchestra Pit: y
Seating Capacity: 360

6934
REGIS PHILBIN STUDIO THEATRE
University of Notre Dame
Marie P. Debartolo Performing Arts Center
107 Performing Arts Center
Notre Dame, IN
Phone: 574-631-2800
Web Site: www.performingarts.nd.edu
Officers:
  President: Rev. John I. Jenkins, CSC
  EVP: John F. Affleck-Graves
  Provost: Thomas G. Burish
Management:
  Executive Director: Anna M. Thompson
  Senior Associate Director: Ted Barron
  Program Manager: Tom Barkes
  Events Program Manager: Denise Sullivan
Mission: The DeBartolo Center for the Peforming Arts was carefully designed for both public performance and for teaching and learning. Our mission is rooted in the conviction that the arts are an indispensable element of a liberal education and an enlightened society.
Opened: 2004
Specialized Field: Classes, Workshops, Rehearsals, and Impromptu Performances
Type of Stage: Black Box
Stage Dimensions: 53'3 x 43'8
Seating Capacity: 100

6935
WASHINGTON HALL AUDITORIUM
University of Notre Dame
Marie P. Debartolo Performing Arts Center
108 Performing Arts Center
Notre Dame, IN
Phone: 574-631-2800
Web Site: www.performingarts.nd.edu
Officers:
  President: Rev. John I. Jenkins, CSC
  EVP: John F. Affleck-Graves
  Provost: Thomas G. Burish
Management:
  Executive Director: Anna M. Thompson
  Senior Associate Director: Ted Barron
  Program Manager: Tom Barkes
  Events Program Manager: Denise Sullivan
Mission: The DeBartolo Center for the Peforming Arts was carefully designed for both public performance and for teaching and learning. Our mission is rooted in the conviction that the arts are an indispensable element of a liberal education and an enlightened society.
Opened: 2004
Specialized Field: Musicals, Theatre
Type of Stage: Semi Thrust Stage
Stage Dimensions: 26'8 x 25'
Seating Capacity: 571

6936
OLE OLSEN MEMORIAL THEATRE
154 South Broadway
Peru, Indiana
Peru, IN 46970
Phone: 765-472-3680
e-mail: postmaster@oleolsen.org
Web Site: www.oleolsen.org
Officers:
  President: Dick Schaffhausen
  Executive VP: Cheryl Jaquay
  Secretary: Michelle Boswell
  Treasurer: Sue Malloy
Management:
  Publicity: Kelly Voss
Mission: Purpose of this organization shall be to promote and encourage interest in the theatrical arts on a non-profit basis.
Founded: 1964
Specialized Field: Community Theater
Status: Non-Professional; Nonprofit
Income Sources: Indiana Community Theatre League; Division of Indiana Theaters
Performs At: High School Auditorium
Organization Type: Performing

6937
CIVIC HALL PERFORMING ARTS CENTER
380 Hub Etchison Parkway
Richmond, IN 47374
Phone: 765-973-3350
Fax: 765-973-3346
Toll-free: 888-484-42
e-mail: boxoffice@civichall.com
Web Site: www.civichall.com
Officers:
  Box Office Secretary: Cindy Cate
Management:
  Facilities Director: Jeffrey Thorne
  Technical Director: Mike Rogan
Founded: 1993
Specialized Field: Multi-discipline; School System; Entertainment
Status: Non-Profit, Professional
Paid Staff: 5
Volunteer Staff: 150
Seating Capacity: 924

6938
RICHMOND CIVIC THEATRE
1003 E Main Street
Richmond, IN 47374
Phone: 765-962-1816
Fax: 765-939-2572
e-mail: office@richmondcivictheatre.org
Web Site: www.richmondcivictheatre.org
Officers:
  President: Ghlee Jewison
  VP: Jaclyn Bartlemay
  Secretary: Kari Kinsey
Mission: To produce high quality theatrical productions that will engage, entertain, educate, and inspire the people of Richmond and the surrounding community, participants and audience alike.
Founded: 1941
Specialized Field: A Community Theatre
Status: Non-Profit, Non-Professional
Paid Staff: 3
Type of Stage: Concert Stage

6939
CENTURY CENTER RECITAL HALL
120 S St. Joseph Street
South Bend, IN 46601
Phone: 574-235-9711
Fax: 574-235-9185
Web Site: www.centurycenter.com
Management:
  Executive Director: Andrew Delgado
  Program Director: Noe Zuniga
  Project Coordinator: Xandie Groves

6940
CENTURY CENTER CONVENTION HALL
120 S St. Joseph Street
South Bend, IN 46601
Phone: 574-235-9711
Fax: 574-235-9185
Web Site: www.centurycenter.com
Management:
  Executive Director: Andrew Delgado
  Program Director: Noe Zuniga
  Project Coordinator: Xandie Groves
Founded: 1977
Type of Stage: Thrust
Seating Capacity: 694

6941
MORRIS PERFORMING ARTS CENTER
211 N Michigan Street
South Bend, IN 46601
Mailing Address: Morris Performing Arts Center, 211 North Michigan Street, So
Phone: 574-235-9190
Fax: 574-235-5604
Toll-free: 800-376-15
e-mail: info@morriscenter.org
Web Site: www.morriscenter.org
Officers:
  Executive Director: Dennis J. Audres
  Asst. Director/Admin & Marketing: Mary Ellen Smith
Management:
  Operation Superior: Denise Zigler
  Executive Director: Dennis J. Andres
  Marketing Manager: Anita Beachy
  Facility Maintenance Manager: Jim Monroe
  Director Marketing: Mary Ellen Smith
Mission: It is the mission of the Morris Performing Arts Center to be the premier performing arts center in the region; to provide a cornucopia of diverse events throughout the year fulfilling the needs and wishes of all who might use the facilities; and to be recognized as one of the best theatre rental venues in the nation.
Founded: 1921
Specialized Field: Live Entertainment; National Broadway Touring Shows; Concerts; Symphony; Comedians; Family Shows
Status: Professional
Paid Staff: 11
Volunteer Staff: 150
Performs At: Theater
Affiliations: Register Of Historic Places; Ranked By Pollstar Magazine Top 100; Facilities Magazine; IAAM; League Of American Historic Theatres
Facility Category: Restored 1921 Vaudeville Theatre With Ballroom
Type of Stage: Proscenium, Orchestra
Stage Dimensions: 54'X25"",''',2
Seating Capacity: 1921
Year Built: 2000
Year Stage Renovated: Deni

FACILITIES / Indiana

6942
COMMUNITY THEATRE OF TERRE HAUTE
1431 S 25th Street
Terre Haute, IN 47803
Phone: 360-373-5152
Fax: 360-373-6754
Web Site: www.mama.indstate.edy
Officers:
   President: Sonni Crawford
   VP: Tim Porter
   Secretary: Marti Cornelius
   Treasurer: Wayne Huston

6943
DREISER THEATRE
Indiana State University
Department of Theatre
540 North 7th Street
Terre Haute, IN 47809
Phone: 812-237-3337
Fax: 812-237-3342
Web Site: www.web.indstate.edu/theatre/
Officers:
   President: Daniel Bradley
   Treasurer: Dainn E. McKee
   VP: Biff Williams
Management:
   Department Chairperson: Sherry McFadeen
   Dramaturgy Concentration Head: Christopher Berchild
   Technical Director: David G. Del Colletti
   Acting Concentration Head: Julie Dixon
Mission: At ISU Theater, our goal is to offer our students a challenging artistic and academic environment which allows them to grow as both theater artists and people. Our course offerings are diverse, exposing our students to a number of exciting concentrations and fields of study.
Specialized Field: Theatre
Type of Stage: Thrust/Arena
Seating Capacity: 200

6944
HULMAN CENTER
Indiana State University
200 N 8th Street
Terre Haute, IN 47809
Phone: 812-237-3737
Fax: 812-237-3741
Toll-free: 800-745-3000
Web Site: www.indstate.edu/hctaf
Management:
   Director: Cliff Lambert
   Facility Marketing/Ticket Sales: Jennifer Cook
   Operations/Event Services Manager: Judy Price
   Technical Services Supervisor: Don Knott
Founded: 1973
Specialized Field: Multi Purpose Venue
Seating Capacity: 11,000
Year Built: 1973

6945
NEW THEATER
Indiana State University
Department of Theatre
540 North 7th Street
Terre Haute, IN 47809
Phone: 812-237-3337
Fax: 812-237-3342
Web Site: www.web.indstate.edu/theatre/
Officers:
   President: Daniel Bradley
   Treasurer: Dainn E. McKee
   VP: Biff Williams
Management:
   Department Chairperson: Sherry McFadeen
   Dramaturgy Concentration Head: Christopher Berchild
   Technical Director: David G. Del Colletti
   Acting Concentration Head: Julie Dixon
Mission: At ISU Theater, our goal is to offer our students a challenging artistic and academic environment which allows them to grow as both theater artists and people. Our course offerings are diverse, exposing our students to a number of exciting concentrations and fields of study.
Specialized Field: Theatre
Type of Stage: Proscenium
Seating Capacity: 240

6946
STUDIO THEATRE
Valparaiso University
1700 Chapel Drive
Valparaiso, IN 46383-5244
Phone: 219-464-5213
Fax: 219-464-5244
Web Site: www.valpo.edu
Officers:
   President: Mark A Heckler
   Chair: Lee F Orchard
Management:
   Development Director: Markus Jennings
Type of Stage: Black Box
Stage Dimensions: 40' x 40'
Seating Capacity: 65

6947
HONEYWELL CENTER
275 W Market Streeet
Wabash, IN 46992
Phone: 260-563-1102
Fax: 260-563-0873
Toll-free: 800-266-45
Web Site: www.honeywellcenter.org
Officers:
   President: Bruce Ingraham
   VP: Steve Downs
   Treasurer: Tom Hodson
Mission: Serve the local and surrounding communities through cultural and educational programs.
Utilizes: Actors; Choreographers; Dance Companies; Dancers; Fine Artists; Grant Writers; Guest Accompanists; Guest Artists; Guest Choreographers; Guest Companies; Guest Composers; Guest Directors; Guest Instructors; Guest Lecturers; Guest Musical Directors; Guest Musicians; Guest Soloists; Instructors; Local Artists; Multimedia; Original Music Scores; Playwrights; Sign Language Translators; Singers; Soloists; Special Technical Talent; Theatre Companies
Founded: 1940
Status: Nonprofit
Paid Staff: 24
Volunteer Staff: 150
Budget: $3,100,000
Income Sources: Earned
Annual Attendance: 30,000
Facility Category: cultural arts/ conference
Type of Stage: Proscenium
Stage Dimensions: 50' x 30' x45'
Seating Capacity: 1500
Year Built: 1994
Year Remodeled: 1994
Cost: $17,000,000
Rental Contact: Shannon Shrider

6948
CAROLE AND GORDON MALLETT THEATRE
Purdue University Main Campus
Yue-Kong Pao Hall of Visual & Performing Arts
552 W. Wood Street
West Lafayette, IN 47907-2002
Phone: 765-494-3074
Fax: 765-494-1766
e-mail: theatre@purdue.edu
Web Site: www.cla.purdue.edu/theatre
Officers:
   President: Martin C. Jischke
   Secretary: Stephanie Brackett
Management:
   Dean Liberal Arts: John J. Contreni
   Theatre Division Mktging Relations: Peggy Felix
   Director, Marketing: David Lageveen
   Operation Manager: Rosie Starks
Mission: There are three readily identifiable components of the Theatre Division: the undergraduate program, the graduate program and the production program. The latter also serves as a laboratory for the whole division. Each program has distinct goals, although the objectives of all the programs are inter-related.
Opened: 2006
Specialized Field: Theatre
Type of Stage: Arena, Thrust, End Stage
Seating Capacity: 100-150

6949
ELLIOTT HALL OF MUSIC
Purdue University
Hovde Hall, 601 Purde Mall
West Lafayette, IN 47907
Phone: 765-494-4600
Fax: 317-494-6621
e-mail: sdhall@purdue.edu
Web Site: www.purdue.edu
Officers:
   President: Mitchell E. Daniels Jr
   Chair: Thomas Spurgeon
   Vice Chairman: Michael Berghoff
   Secretary: Janice Indrutz
   Treasurer: Al Diaz
Management:
   Assistant Director, Administrative: Jennifer Molden
   Director: Steve Hall
   Assistant Director: Jim Chapman
   Box Office Manager: Carolanne Robinson
   Fiscal Administrator: Michael Smolen
   Account Clerk: Kay Gohn
   House Manager: Joyce Banta
Mission: To serve our customers in West Lafayette, IN by providing an environment which enhances their Purdue university experience while supporting the University's overall objectives of Education, Research, and Service.
Founded: 1940
Type of Stage: Proscenium
Seating Capacity: 6,025

6950
MACKEY ARENA
Purdue University
1790 Mackey Arena
West Lafayette, IN 47907
Phone: 765-494-4600
Fax: 765-784-4497
Web Site: www.purdue.edu
Officers:

FACILITIES / Iowa

President: Mitchell E. Daniels Jr
Chair: Thomas Spurgeon
Vice Chairman: Michael Berghoff
Secretary: Janice Indrutz
Treasurer: Al Diaz
Management:
   Athletic Director: Morgan Burke
Seating Capacity: 14,121

6951
NANCY T. HANSEN THEATRE
Purdue University Main Campus
Yue-Kong Pao Hall of Visual & Performing Arts
552 W. Wood Street
West Lafayette, IN 47907-2002
Phone: 765-494-3074
Fax: 765-494-1766
Web Site: www.cla.purdue.edu/theatre
Officers:
   President: Martin C. Jischke
   Secretary: Stephanie Brackett
Management:
   Dean Liberal Arts: John J. Contreni
   Theatre Division Mktging Relations: Peggy Felix
   Director, Marketing: David Lageveen
   Operation Manager: Rosie Starks
Mission: There are three readily identifiable components of the Theatre Division: the undergraduate program, the graduate program and the production program. The latter also serves as a laboratory for the whole division. Each program has distinct goals, although the objectives of all the programs are inter-related.
Opened: 2006
Specialized Field: Theatre
Type of Stage: Proscenium
Stage Dimensions: 36' x 28'
Orchestra Pit: y
Seating Capacity: 300

6952
ROSS-ADE STADIUM
Purdue University
West Lafayette, IN 47907
Mailing Address: Mackey Arena, Room 2200,900 John R. Wooden Drive, West Lafay
Phone: 765-494-3248
Fax: 765-496-1280
Toll-free: 800-213-2239
e-mail: jpc@purdue.edu
Web Site: www.purduesports.com
Management:
   Athletic Director: Morgan Burke
   Senior Associate Athletic Director: Glenn Tompkins
   Senior Associate Athletic Director: Nancy Cross
   Associate Athletic Director: Roger Blalock
Founded: 1869
Seating Capacity: 67,332

Iowa

6953
AMES CITY AUDITORIUM
Ames Parks & Recreation
515 Clark Avenue
Ames, IA 50010
Mailing Address: 515 Clark Avenue
Phone: 515-239-5265
Fax: 515-239-5325
e-mail: MKing@city.ames.ia.us
Web Site: www.amesparkrec.org/Auditorium.htm
Management:
   Director: Jane Cox
   Technical Director: Derek Hisek
   Costume Designer: Kelly Schaefer
Mission: To enrich lives by providing exceptional parks, facilities and programs for current and future generations.
Utilizes: Instructors; Local Talent; Resident Professionals; Student Interns; Special Technical Talent
Founded: 1990
Opened: 1992
Specialized Field: Theater Music
Status: Non-Profit, Non-Professional
Paid Staff: 17
Budget: $85,000
Income Sources: Rental; City Subsidy; Ticket Sales
Affiliations: IAAM
Facility Category: Proscenium Theater
Type of Stage: Concert Stage
Stage Dimensions: 37' x 24'
Seating Capacity: 881
Year Built: 1938
Year Remodeled: 1992
Rental Contact: Mike King

6954
BENTON AUDITORIUM
Iowa State University
Iowa State Center
Scheman Building, Suite 4, 2130 Pearson Hall
Ames, IA 50011-1113
Mailing Address: 100 Enrollment Services Center, Ames, IA 50011-2011
Phone: 515-294-2624
Fax: 515-294-2624
Toll-free: 877-432-68
e-mail: isutheatre@iastate.edu
Web Site: www.theatre.iastate.edu
Officers:
   Secretary: Liese VanderBroek
   president: steven Leath
Management:
   Director: Jane Cox
   Technical Director: Derek Hisek
   Costume Designer: Kelly Schaefer
Mission: To provide a comprehensive undergraduate education in Theatre and the Performing Arts. This program prepares the student for graduate school, professional theatre training programs, and the teaching of Theatre at the secondary education level.
Specialized Field: Social Events
Seating Capacity: 450
Year Built: 1969

6955
FISHER THEATRE
Iowa State University
Iowa State Center
Scheman Building, Suite 4, 2130 Pearson Hall
Ames, IA 50011-1113
Mailing Address: 101 Enrollment Services Center, Ames, IA 50011-2011
Phone: 515-294-2624
Fax: 515-294-2624
Toll-free: 877-432-68
e-mail: isutheatre@iastate.edu
Web Site: www.theatre.iastate.edu
Officers:
   Secretary: Liese VanderBroek
   president: steven Leath
Management:
   Director: Jane Cox
   Technical Director: Derek Hisek
   Costume Designer: Kelly Schaefer
Mission: To provide a comprehensive undergraduate education in Theatre and the Performing Arts. This program prepares the student for graduate school, professional theatre training programs, and the teaching of Theatre at the secondary education level.
Specialized Field: Dance, Drama, ISU Theatre Productions
Type of Stage: Proscenium
Orchestra Pit: y
Seating Capacity: 451

6956
HILTON COLISEUM
Iowa State University
Iowa State Center
Scheman Building, Suite 4, 2130 Pearson Hall
Ames, IA 50011-1113
Mailing Address: 102 Enrollment Services Center, Ames, IA 50011-2011
Phone: 515-294-2624
Fax: 515-294-2624
Toll-free: 877-432-68
e-mail: isutheatre@iastate.edu
Web Site: www.theatre.iastate.edu
Officers:
   Secretary: Liese VanderBroek
   president: steven Leath
Management:
   Director: Jane Cox
   Technical Director: Derek Hisek
   Costume Designer: Kelly Schaefer
Mission: To provide a comprehensive undergraduate education in Theatre and the Performing Arts. This program prepares the student for graduate school, professional theatre training programs, and the teaching of Theatre at the secondary education level.
Specialized Field: Concerts
Type of Stage: Arena Circle, Portable
Seating Capacity: 14,500

6957
IOWA STATE CENTER
Iowa State University
Scheman Building, Suite 102
Ames, IA 50011-1113
Phone: 515-294-3347
Fax: 515-294-3349
Toll-free: 877-432-68
e-mail: isutheatre@iastate.edu
Web Site: www.center.iastate.edu
Officers:
   Secretary: Liese VanderBroek
   president: steven Leath
Management:
   Director: Jane Cox
   Technical Director: Derek Hisek
   Costume Designer: Kelly Schaefer
   Director Operations: Randy Baumeister
   Director Programing: Mark E Ewalt
   Technical Director: James B Ewalt Ewalt
Mission: To develop and support the programming facilities and services necessary to establish the Iowa State Center as the premier university public assembly complex in the United States.
Type of Stage: Concert Stage; Flexible
Seating Capacity: 3,650
Year Built: 1971

6958
STEPHENS AUDITORIUM
Iowa State University
Iowa State Center
Scheman Building, Suite 103
Ames, IA 50011-1113

FACILITIES / Iowa

Phone: 515-294-3347
Fax: 515-294-3349
Toll-free: 877-432-68
e-mail: isutheatre@iastate.edu
Web Site: www.center.iastate.edu
Officers:
  Secretary: Liese VanderBroek
  president: steven Leath
Management:
  Director: Jane Cox
  Technical Director: Derek Hisek
  Costume Designer: Kelly Schaefer
Mission: To provide a comprehensive undergraduate education in Theatre and the Performing Arts. This program prepares the student for graduate school, professional theatre training programs, and the teaching of Theatre at the secondary education level.
Specialized Field: Broadway Musicals, Concerts, Dance, Music, Orchestras, Theatre
Type of Stage: Proscenium
Stage Dimensions: 70' x 30'
Orchestra Pit: y
Seating Capacity: 2,747
Year Built: 1969

6959
STEPHENS AUDITORIUM
Iowa State University
Scheman Building, Suite 104
Ames, IA 50011-1113
Phone: 515-294-3347
Fax: 515-294-3349
Toll-free: 877-432-68
e-mail: isutheatre@iastate.edu
Web Site: www.center.iastate.edu
Officers:
  Secretary: Liese VanderBroek
  president: steven Leath
Management:
  Director: Jane Cox
  Technical Director: Derek Hisek
  Costume Designer: Kelly Schaefer
Seating Capacity: 2,750

6960
BURLINGTON MEMORIAL AUDITORIUM
200 Front Street
Burlington, IA 52601
Phone: 319-753-8128
Fax: 319-753-8166
e-mail: morlanb@burlingtonauditorium.com
Web Site: www.burlingtonauditorium.com
Management:
  Stage Manager/Marketing Director: Michael Courtney
  Building Manager: Bredyn Hill
Seating Capacity: 2,311

6961
BERTHA MARTIN THEATRE
University of Northern Iowa
Department of Theatre
1227 West 27th Street
Cedar Falls, IA 50614
Phone: 319-273-2311
e-mail: strayer-wood@uni.edu
Web Site: www.uni.edu/theatre/
Officers:
  President: Benjamin J. Allen
  Department secretary: Tange Kole
  Secretary, Financial Services: Lisa Althof
  VP, Development: Frank Esser
Management:
  Director. Development: Nate Clapham
  Technical Director: Ron Koinzan
  Director Mktg/Production Manager: Jascenna Haislet
  Assiatant, President: Brenda Buzynski
Mission: The mission of the Department of Theatre is to provide university students with an experiential, liberal arts education in theatre through coursework and productions which are diverse, creative and participatory.
Founded: 1876
Specialized Field: Theatre
Type of Stage: Modular Black Box
Seating Capacity: 126

6962
GALLAGHER BLUEDORN PERFORMING ARTS CENTER
University of Northern Iowa
8201 Dakota Street
Cedar Falls, IA 50613
Phone: 319-273-3660
Fax: 319-273-7470
Toll-free: 877-497-69
e-mail: gbpac@uni.edu
Web Site: www.uni.edu/gbpac
Officers:
  Finance Director: Jocelyn Moeller
  Department secretary: Tange Kole
  Secretary, Financial Services: Lisa Althof
  VP, Development: Frank Esser
Management:
  Director, Finance: Jocelyn Moeller
  Development Director: Dianne Campbell
  Technical Services Director: Sandy Nordahl
  Assistant Technical Director: Tuzicka
  Education Director: Amy Hunzelman
  Assistant House Manager: Vee Shaffer
  Audio Engineer: Travis Duncan
  Programming Assistant: Molly Hackenmiller
  Marketing Director: Janelle Darst
Founded: 2000
Specialized Field: Present Arts
Paid Staff: 10
Volunteer Staff: 350
Type of Stage: Tongue-in-groove oak
Stage Dimensions: 55'W X 40'H
Seating Capacity: 1,680
Year Built: 2000
Rental Contact: Chris Kremer

6963
STRAYER-WOOD THEATRE
University of Northern Iowa
Department of Theatre
1227 West 27th Street
Cedar Falls, IA 50614
Phone: 319-273-6381
Web Site: www.uni.edu/theatre/
Officers:
  President: Benjamin J. Allen
  Department secretary: Tange Kole
  Secretary, Financial Services: Lisa Althof
  VP, Development: Frank Esser
Management:
  Director. Development: Nate Clapham
  Technical Director: Ron Koinzan
  Director Mktg/Production Manager: Jascenna Haislet
  Assiatant, President: Brenda Buzynski
Mission: The mission of the Department of Theatre is to provide university students with an experiential, liberal arts education in theatre through coursework and productions which are diverse, creative and participatory.
Founded: 1876
Specialized Field: Theatre
Type of Stage: Proscenium, Thrust
Seating Capacity: 525

6964
STRAYER-WOOD THEATRE
University of Northern Iowa
1227 West 27th Street
Cedar Falls, IA 50614-0371
Phone: 319-273-6386
Fax: 319-273-6390
e-mail: eric.lange@uni.edu
Web Site: www.uni.edu
Officers:
  President: Benjamin J. Allen
  Department secretary: Tange Kole
  Secretary, Financial Services: Lisa Althof
  VP, Development: Frank Esser
Management:
  Director. Development: Nate Clapham
  Technical Director: Ron Koinzan
  Director Mktg/Production Manager: Jascenna Haislet
  Assiatant, President: Brenda Buzynski
Mission: To create theatre which excites, and which illuminates the human condition in ways that are relevant to students, audiences, community members, teachers and guest artists. Offers coursework and productions that are diverse, creative and particpatory, serving students who want to prepare for a life in the theatre and also students who want to prepare a place for theatre in their lives. We create theatre and, in this process, educate.
Utilizes: Actors; Collaborations; Designers; Educators; Five Seasonal Concerts; Guest Accompanists; Guest Artists; Guest Conductors; Guest Ensembles; Guest Lecturers; Performance Artists; Resident Companies; Resident Professionals
Founded: 1976
Specialized Field: Theatre
Paid Staff: 3
Paid Artists: 11
Facility Category: Theater house
Type of Stage: Proscenium
Stage Dimensions: 22 x 84 x 39
Seating Capacity: 500
Year Built: 1978
Rental Contact: Eric Lange

6965
UNI-DOME
University of Northern Iowa
2501 Hudson Road
Cedar Falls, IA 50613
Phone: 319-273-6334
Fax: 319-273-2913
e-mail: gerald.peterson@uni.edu
Web Site: www.uni.edu
Officers:
  President: Benjamin J. Allen
  Department secretary: Tange Kole
  Secretary, Financial Services: Lisa Althof
  VP, Development: Frank Esser
Management:
  Director. Development: Nate Clapham
  Technical Director: Ron Koinzan
  Director Mktg/Production Manager: Jascenna Haislet
  Assiatant, President: Brenda Buzynski
  Assistant Operations Coordinator: Ryan McKernan
Founded: 1976
Seating Capacity: 25,000

FACILITIES / Iowa

Rental Contact: Ryan McKernan

6966
DOW THEATRE
Coe College
Dows Fine Arts Center
1220 1st Avenue NE
Cedar Rapids, IA 52402
Phone: 319-399-8500
e-mail: coeboxoffice@coe.edu
Web Site: www.coe.edu/academics/TheatreArts
Officers:
   Chair: Gene Henderson
   Vice Chair: John R. Girotto
   Secretary: David Gehring
   President: David McInally
Management:
   Professor of Theatre: Susan Wolverton
   Associate Professor of Theatre: Steven Marc Weiss
   Assistant Professor of Theatre: Dennis Barnett
Mission: Coe offers a Theatre Arts degree with emphasis in Acting, Directing or with Technical & Design Production emphasis. Additionally, students may opt to focus on the Playwriting or Dramaturgy areas of study.
Founded: 1851
Opened: 1974
Specialized Field: Plays, Musicals
Status: Private
Paid Staff: 80
Seating Capacity: 300
Year Built: 1974
Year Remodeled: 1994

6967
US SAILORS CENTER
370 1st Avenue NE
Cedar Rapids, IA 52401
Phone: 319-398-5211
Fax: 319-362-2102
e-mail: s.cummins@ussailorscenter.com
Web Site: www.ussailorscenter.com
Management:
   President: Steve Peters
   Executive Director: Sharon Cummins
   Director Marketing: Sarah Madalinski
   Director, finance: Nicole Wright
Founded: 1979
Status: For-Profit, Professional
Paid Staff: 200
Paid Artists: 150
Type of Stage: Wood
Seating Capacity: 1,901
Year Built: 1979

6968
MILLS EXPERIMENTAL THEATRE
Coe College
Dows Fine Arts Center
1220 1st Avenue NE
Cedar Rapids, IA 52402
Phone: 319-399-8500
e-mail: coeboxoffice@coe.edu
Web Site: www.coe.edu/academics/TheatreArts
Officers:
   Chair: Gene Henderson
   Vice Chair: John R. Girotto
   Secretary: David Gehring
Management:
   Professor of Theatre: Susan Wolverton
   Associate Professor of Theatre: Steven Marc Weiss
   Assistant Professor of Theatre: Dennis Barnett
Mission: Coe offers a Theatre Arts degree with emphasis in Acting, Directing or with Technical & Design Production emphasis. Additionally, students may opt to focus on the Playwriting or Dramaturgy areas of study.
Founded: 1851
Opened: 1974
Specialized Field: Dance
Status: Private
Paid Staff: 80
Seating Capacity: 50

6969
PARAMOUNT THEATRE
123 3rd Avenue SE
Cedar Rapids, IA 52401
Mailing Address: 370 1st Avenue NE Cedar Rapids IA, 52401
Phone: 319-398-5226
Fax: 319-362-2102
Web Site: www.uscellularcenter.com
Management:
   Executive Director: Sharon Cummins
   Assistant Executive Director: Thomas Fesenmey
   General Manager: Tim Westemeier
Affiliations: Home of Cedar Rapids Symphony Orchestra, Cedar Rapids Area Theatre Organ Society, Community Concerts, Broadway Series, School Programming Series

6970
SINCLAIR AUDITORIUM
Coe College
1220 1st Avenue NE
Cedar Rapids, IA 52402
Phone: 319-399-8500
e-mail: coeboxoffice@coe.edu
Web Site: www.coe.edu/academics/TheatreArts
Officers:
   Chair: Gene Henderson
   Vice Chair: John R. Girotto
   Secretary: David Gehring
Management:
   Professor of Theatre: Susan Wolverton
   Associate Professor of Theatre: Steven Marc Weiss
   Assistant Professor of Theatre: Dennis Barnett
Mission: Coe offers a Theatre Arts degree with emphasis in Acting, Directing or with Technical & Design Production emphasis. Additionally, students may opt to focus on the Playwriting or Dramaturgy areas of study.
Founded: 1851
Status: Private
Paid Staff: 80
Seating Capacity: 1,100

6971
US CELLULAR CENTER
370 1st Avenue NE
Cedar Rapids, IA 52401
Phone: 319-398-5211
Fax: 319-362-2102
Web Site: www.uscellularcenter.com
Management:
   President: Steve Peter
   Executive Director: Sharon Cummins
   Director Marketing: Sarah Madalinski
   Director, finance: Nicole Wright
Founded: 1979
Status: Non-Profit
Paid Staff: 100
Facility Category: Arena
Type of Stage: Stageright
Seating Capacity: 914
Year Built: 1978
Rental Contact: R Nowers

6972
RIVERVIEW STADIUM
PO Box 1295
Clinton, IA 52733
Phone: 563-242-0727
Fax: 563-242-1433
e-mail: lumberkings@lumberkings.com
Web Site: www.lumberkings.com
Officers:
   President: Paul Davis
   Treasurer: George Chaney
   Treasurer: Paul Schnack
   VP: Dale Dalton
Management:
   General Manager: Ted Tornow
   Director Of Broadcasting: Chad Seely
   Office Manager: Ryan Marcum
Founded: 1937
Status: For-Profit, Professional
Paid Staff: 50
Seating Capacity: 3,600

6973
THE ARTS CENTER
Iowa Western Community College
2700 College Rd
Council Bluffs, IA 51503
Phone: 712-388-7140
Fax: 712-388-7144
e-mail: mnoon@iwcc.edu
Web Site: www.artscenter.iwcc.edu
Management:
   Director: Molly Noon
   Box Office Coordinator: Dc Etta Robison, drobison@iwcc.edu
   Technical Director: Keith Christie, kchristie@iwcc.edu

6974
ALLAERT AUDITORIUM
St. Ambrose University
518 West Locust Street
Davenport, IA 52803
Phone: 563-333-6000
Fax: 563-333-6243
Toll-free: 800-383-2627
e-mail: webmaster@sau.edu
Web Site: www.sau.edu
Officers:
   President: Joan Lescinski
   Executive Administrative Assistant: Jan Stafford
   Executive Administrative Assistant: Jan Stafford
Mission: We are committed to the richness of the liberal arts tradition through quality instruction that fosters development of a broad awareness of humanity in all its dimensions. Ambrosians use their knowledge, talents, and career skills in service to others.
Founded: 1882
Specialized Field: Musicals, Performing Arts Series, Theatre
Status: Private
Paid Staff: 292
Budget: $70,000,000
Seating Capacity: 1,200
Year Remodeled: 1971

FACILITIES / Iowa

6975
GALVIN FINE ARTS CENTER
Saint Ambrose College
518 West Locust Street
Davenport, IA 52803
Phone: 563-333-6427
Web Site: www.web.sau.edu/theatre
Officers:
  President: Joan Lescinski
  Executive Administrative Assistant: Feb Stafford
  Executive Administrative Assistant: Jan Stafford
Founded: 1971

6976
LYCEUM HALL
Palmer College of Chiropractic
1000 Brady Street
Davenport, IA 52803
Phone: 563-884-5000
Fax: 563-884-5414
Toll-free: 800-223-48
e-mail: pcadmit@palmer.edu
Web Site: www.palmer.edu
Officers:
  President: Donald Kern DC PhC
  Dean: Daniel Weinert MS DC
Seating Capacity: 4,000

6977
QUAD CITY RIVER BANDITS BASEBALL STADIUM
PO Box 3496
209 S Gaines Street
Davenport, IA 52808
Phone: 563-324-3000
Fax: 319-324-3109
e-mail: bandit@riverbandits.com
Web Site: www.riverbandits.com
Officers:
  General Manager: Andrew Chesser
  VP, Sales: Shawn Brown
Management:
  Finance Manager: Dustin Miller
  Director, Group Sales: Joe Kubly
  Marketing Director: Matt Beatty
  Production Manager: Stacy Issen
Seating Capacity: 6,200

6978
RIVER CENTER/ADLER THEATRE
136 E 3rd Street
Davenport, IA 52801
Phone: 319-326-8500
Fax: 319-326-8505
Web Site: www.adlertheatre.com/
Management:
  Executive Director: Mike Hartman
Specialized Field: Theater

6979
STUDIO THEATRE
St. Ambrose University
Galvin Fine Arts Center
518 West Locust Street
Davenport, IA 52803
Phone: 563-333-6255
Web Site: www.web.sau.edu/theatre/
Officers:
  President: Joan Lescinski
  Executive Administrative Assistant: Jan Stafford

Mission: We are committed to the richness of the liberal arts tradition through quality instruction that fosters development of a broad awareness of humanity in all its dimensions. Ambrosians use their knowledge, talents, and career skills in service to others.
Founded: 1882
Specialized Field: Theatre
Status: Private
Paid Staff: 292
Budget: $70,000,000
Type of Stage: Black Box
Seating Capacity: 50

6980
JEWEL THEATRE
Luther College
Center for the Arts
700 College Drive
Decorah, IA 52101
Phone: 563-387-2000
Fax: 563-387-2158
Toll-free: 800-588-37
e-mail: infodesk@luther.edu
Web Site: www.theatre.luther.edu/contactus
Officers:
  Vice President: Scot Schaeffer
  President: David Tiede
  VP, Marketing & communication: Rob Larson
Management:
  Executive Director: Sherry Alcock
  Director: Jon Christy
  Athletic Director: Joe Thompson
  Manager: Brad Phillips
Mission: Drawing from the two distinctive art forms of theatre and dance, the Luther College Theatre/Dance Department focuses on empowering and enlivening the creative imagination in self and community. In so doing, the department is a partner within a liberal arts environment that seeks to develop whole persons who emerge as informed artists and capable, passionate, accountable citizens.
Founded: 1861
Specialized Field: Theatre
Paid Staff: 191
Type of Stage: Flexible
Seating Capacity: 225

6981
LUTHER COLLEGE
Luther College Center For The Arts
700 College Drive
Decorah, IA 52101
Phone: 563-387-2000
Fax: 563-387-2158
Toll-free: 800-588-37
e-mail: infodesk@luther.edu
Web Site: www.theatre.luther.edu/contactus
Officers:
  Vice President: Scot Schaeffer
  President: David Tiede
  VP, Marketing & communication: Rob Larson
Management:
  Executive Director: Sherry Alcock
  Director: Jon Christy
  Athletic Director: Joe Thompson
  Manager: Brad Phillips
Mission: Drawing from the two distinctive art forms of theatre and dance, the Luther College Theatre/Dance Department focuses on empowering and enlivening the creative imagination in self and community. In so doing, the department is a partner within a liberal arts environment that seeks to develop whole persons who emerge as informed artists and capable, passionate, accountable citizens.
Founded: 1861
Specialized Field: Theatre
Paid Staff: 191
Performs At: Flexible Theatre
Seating Capacity: 1,600
Year Built: 1978

6982
RECITAL HALL
Luther College
Center for Faith and Life
700 College Drive
Decorah, IA 52101
Phone: 563-387-2000
Fax: 563-387-2158
Toll-free: 800-588-37
e-mail: infodesk@luther.edu
Web Site: www.theatre.luther.edu/contactus
Officers:
  Vice President: Scot Schaeffer
  President: David Tiede
  VP, Marketing & communication: Rob Larson
Management:
  Executive Director: Sherry Alcock
  Director: Jon Christy
  Athletic Director: Joe Thompson
  Manager: Brad Phillips
Mission: Drawing from the two distinctive art forms of theatre and dance, the Luther College Theatre/Dance Department focuses on empowering and enlivening the creative imagination in self and community. In so doing, the department is a partner within a liberal arts environment that seeks to develop whole persons who emerge as informed artists and capable, passionate, accountable citizens.
Founded: 1861
Specialized Field: Theatre
Paid Staff: 191
Seating Capacity: 200
Year Built: 1978

6983
WESTON H. NOBLE RECITAL HALL
Luther College
Jenson-Noble Hall of Music
700 College Drive
Decorah, IA 52101
Phone: 563-387-2000
Fax: 563-387-2158
Toll-free: 800-588-37
e-mail: infodesk@luther.edu
Web Site: www.theatre.luther.edu/contactus
Officers:
  Vice President: Scot Schaeffer
  President: David Tiede
  VP, Marketing & communication: Rob Larson
Management:
  Executive Director: Sherry Alcock
  Director: Jon Christy
  Athletic Director: Joe Thompson
  Manager: Brad Phillips
Mission: Drawing from the two distinctive art forms of theatre and dance, the Luther College Theatre/Dance Department focuses on empowering and enlivening the creative imagination in self and community. In so doing, the department is a partner within a liberal arts environment that seeks to develop whole persons who emerge as informed artists and capable, passionate, accountable citizens.
Founded: 1861
Specialized Field: Music
Paid Staff: 191
Type of Stage: Black Box
Seating Capacity: 300

FACILITIES / Iowa

6984
CIVIC CENTER OF GREATER DES MOINES
Des Moines Performing Arts
221 Walnut Street
Des Moines, IA 50309
Phone: 515-246-2300
Fax: 515-246-2305
e-mail: info@desmoinesperformingarts.org
Web Site: www.civiccenter.org
Officers:
   President: Jeff Chelesvig
   VP & COO: Laura Sweet
Management:
   General Manager: Bill McElrath
   Director, Finance: Heidi Watkins
   Business Director: Bill McElrath
   Accountant: Barbara Hanson
Mission: Engage the Midwest in world-class entertainment, education and cultural activities.
Founded: 1979
Opened: 1979
Status: Non-Profit, Professional
Paid Staff: 30
Volunteer Staff: 40
Budget: $14 million
Income Sources: Ticket Sales; Rentals; Concessions; Sponsorship; Public & Private Support
Performs At: Theater
Annual Attendance: 300,000
Facility Category: Theater
Type of Stage: Proscenium
Seating Capacity: 2,744
Year Built: 1979
Year Remodeled: 2007
Cost: $12.5 Million
Rental Contact: General Manager Bill McElrath

6985
DES MOINES WOMEN'S CLUB
Hoyt Sherman Place
1501 Woodland Avenue
Des Moines, IA 50309
Phone: 515-244-0507
Fax: 515-237-3582
Web Site: www.hoytsherman.org
Officers:
   President: Rusty Goode
   VP: Marilyn Kramme
   Treasurer: Tom Slaughter
   Secretary: Chris Conyers
Management:
   Executive Director: Leisha Barcus
Founded: 1875
Specialized Field: Theatre
Status: Non-Profit, Professional
Paid Staff: 10
Annual Attendance: 200,000
Type of Stage: Proscenium
Seating Capacity: 1,400

6986
DRAKE STADIUM
Drake University
2507 University Avenue
Des Moines, IA 50311
Phone: 515-271-2889
Fax: 515-271-3015
Toll-free: 800-443-7253
Web Site: www.drakebulldogs.org
Officers:
   President: Dr. David Maxwell
   VP, Finance: Deborah Newsom
   Provost: Deneese Jones
Management:
   Athletic Director: Sandy Clubb
   Business Manager: Sue Tygeson
Founded: 1925
Seating Capacity: 18,000

6987
HARMON FINE ARTS CENTER
Drake University
2507 University Avenue
Des Moines, IA 50311-4505
Phone: 515-271-2018
Fax: 515-271-3977
Toll-free: 800-443-7253
e-mail: Marilyn.dean@drake.edu
Web Site: www.drake.edu
Officers:
   President: Dr. David Maxwell
   VP, Finance: Deborah Newsom
   Provost: Deneese Jones
Management:
   Athletic Director: Sandy Clubb
   Business Manager: Sue Tygeson
   Facilities Manager: Marilyn Dean
   Director Marketing/Communications: Brooke Benschoter
   Director Public Relations: Lisa Lacher
Mission: The mission of the College of Arts & Sciences is to provide an exceptional learning environment for students to develop the talents and skills necessary for personal and professional success.
Founded: 1881
Specialized Field: Musicals, Theatre
Paid Staff: 246
Seating Capacity: 460

6988
JORDAN STAGE
Drake University
Sheslow Auditorium
2507 University Avenue
Des Moines, IA 50311-4505
Phone: 515-271-2018
Fax: 515-271-3977
Toll-free: 800-443-7253
e-mail: Marilyn.dean@drake.edu
Web Site: www.drake.edu
Officers:
   President: Dr. David Maxwell
   VP, Finance: Deborah Newsom
   Provost: Deneese Jones
Management:
   Athletic Director: Sandy Clubb
   Business Manager: Sue Tygeson
   Facilities Manager: Marilyn Dean
   Director Marketing/Communications: Brooke Benschoter
   Director Public Relations: Lisa Lacher
Mission: The mission of the College of Arts & Sciences is to provide an exceptional learning environment for students to develop the talents and skills necessary for personal and professional success.
Founded: 1881
Specialized Field: Concerts, Recitals
Paid Staff: 246
Seating Capacity: 773

6989
SHESLOW AUDITORIUM IN OLD MAIN
Drake University
2507 University Avenue
Des Moines, IA 50311
Phone: 515-271-3939
Fax: 515-271-3977
Toll-free: 800-443-7253
e-mail: lisa.lacher@drake.edu
Web Site: www.drake.edu
Officers:
   President: Dr. David Maxwell
   VP, Finance: Deborah Newsom
   Provost: Deneese Jones
Management:
   Athletic Director: Sandy Clubb
   Business Manager: Sue Tygeson
Mission: Drake's mission is to provide an exceptional learning environment that prepares students for meaningful personal lives, professional accomplishments, and responsible global citizenship. The Drake experience is distinguished by collaborative learning among students, faculty, and staff and by the integration of the liberal arts and sciences with professional preparation.
Founded: 1881
Status: Non-Profit, Professional
Paid Staff: 25
Seating Capacity: 100-200

6990
VETERANS MEMORIAL AUDITORIUM
Regional Facilities, Polk County
111 Court Avenue
Des Moines, IA 50309
Phone: 515-286-3000
Fax: 515-323-5225
e-mail: info@polkcountyiowa.gov
Web Site: www.co.polk.ia.us
Management:
   General Manager: Andy Long
   Director: F Michael Grimaldi
   Managing Director: Joy Giudicossi
Founded: 1954
Status: Non-Profit, Professional
Paid Staff: 40
Facility Category: Arena
Type of Stage: Concert
Seating Capacity: 7,200
Year Built: 1954
Year Remodeled: 1997

6991
FIVE FLAGS CENTER ARENA
405 Main Street
Dubuque, IA 52001
Phone: 563-589-4254
Fax: 563-589-4351
Toll-free: 888-129-58
e-mail: info@fiveflagscenter.com
Web Site: www.fiveflagscenter.com
Officers:
   General Manager: Joyce White
Management:
   Marketing Coord/Admin Support: Ali Levasseur
   Concessions Man: Angie Cross
   Supervisor: Ron Swift
   Technical Director: Dan Haltkamp
Mission: To provide the best entertainment to Dubuque Area; including all national touring, regional and local talent
Founded: 1971
Status: Non-Profit, Professional
Paid Staff: 80
Affiliations: A SMG Managed Facility
Facility Category: Historical Theater & Sporting Arena
Seating Capacity: 5,200

All listings are in alphabetical order by state, then city, then organization within the city.

FACILITIES / Iowa

6992
FIVE FLAGS CENTER - THEATRE
50 West 13th Street
Dubuque, IA 52001
Phone: 563-589-4100
Fax: 563-589-0890
Web Site: www.cityofdubuque.org

6993
MAHARISHI UNIVERSITY PERFORMING ARTS CENTER
1000 North Fourth Street
Maharishi University of Management, SU 361
Fairfield, IA 52557
Phone: 641-472-1104
Fax: 641-472-7000
e-mail: student_activities@mum.edu
Web Site: www.mum.edu
Management:
    Administrator: David Stried
Founded: 1971
Status: Non-Profit, Non-Professional

6994
HAROLD AND CHARLOTTE SMTIH THEATRE
Waldorf College
Thorson Hall
106 South 6th Street
Forest City, IA 50436
Phone: 641-585-2450
Toll-free: 800-921-03
Web Site: www.waldorf.edu/finearts/theatre
Officers:
    President: Bob Alsop
Management:
    Director: Jim Amelsberg
    Library Assistant: Cindy Fitzgerald
    Director, Marketing: Barrows Barbara
Mission: As a liberal arts college Waldorf offers a core curriculum to help students develop a broad base of knowledge in a variety of disciplines, an interest in intellectual pursuits, the ability to reason and communicate, and a growing awareness of the global community.
Founded: 1903
Opened: U
Specialized Field: Fheatre
Status: KF
Paid Staff: 925
Seating Capacity: 180

6995
RECITAL HALL
Waldorf College
Odvin Hagen Music Center
106 South 6th Street
Forest City, IA 50436
Phone: 641-585-2450
Toll-free: 800-921-03
Web Site: www.waldorf.edu/finearts/theatre
Officers:
    President: Bob Alsop
Management:
    Director: Jim Amelsberg
    Library Assistant: Cindy Fitzgerald
    Director, Marketing: Barrows Barbara
Mission: As a liberal arts college Waldorf offers a core curriculum to help students develop a broad base of knowledge in a variety of disciplines, an interest in intellectual pursuits, the ability to reason and communicate, and a growing awareness of the global community.
Founded: 1903
Specialized Field: Music
Seating Capacity: 129

6996
OLD CREAMERY THEATRE
39 38th Avenue
Suite 200
Garrison, IA 52203
Phone: 319-622-6194
Toll-free: 800-352-6262
Web Site: www.oldcreamery.com
Officers:
    President-Amana: Bruce Eickhacker
    VP-Cedar Rapids: Richard Welch
    Secretary - Vinton: Ron Baldwin
    Treasurer-Amana: Vic Rathje
    General Manager: Pat Wagner
Management:
    Producing and Artistic Director: Thomas P Johnson
    Associate Artistic Director: Meg Merckens
    Associate Artistic Director: Sean McCall
    Marketing Manager: Lily Allen
    Director, Finance: Darby Geiger
Founded: 1971
Status: Non-Profit
Seating Capacity: 275

6997
HALLIE B. FLANAGAN STUDIO THEATRE
Grinnell College
Bucksbaum Center for the Arts
1115 8TH AVE
Grinnell, IA 50112-1690
Phone: 641-269-4000
Fax: 641-269-4420
Web Site: www.web.grinnell.edu/theatre/facilities
Officers:
    President: Raynard Kington
    Secretary : Susan Schoen
    VP: Angela Voos
Management:
    Department Chair: Lesley Delmenico
    Technical Director: Erik Sanning
    President Assistant: Tammy D. Prusha
Mission: The study of theatre and movement at Grinnell embraces all aspects of the dramatic art as part of a liberal arts education.
Founded: 1846
Specialized Field: Theatre
Status: Private
Seating Capacity: 126

6998
ROBERTS THEATRE
Grinnell College
Bucksbaum Center for the Arts
1116 8TH AVE
Grinnell, IA 50112-1690
Phone: 641-269-4000
Fax: 641-269-4420
Web Site: www.web.grinnell.edu/theatre/facilities
Officers:
    President: Raynard Kington
    Secretary : Susan Schoen
    VP: Angela Voos
Management:
    Department Chair: Lesley Delmenico
    Technical Director: Erik Sanning
    President Assistant: Tammy D. Prusha
Mission: The study of theatre and movement at Grinnell embraces all aspects of the dramatic art as part of a liberal arts education.
Founded: 1846
Specialized Field: Theatre
Status: Private
Type of Stage: Semi-Thrust
Seating Capacity: 450
Year Remodeled: 2000
Architect: Cesar Pelli and Associates

6999
WALL PERFORMANCE LAB
Grinnell College
Bucksbaum Center for the Arts
1117 8TH AVE
Grinnell, IA 50112-1690
Phone: 641-269-4000
Fax: 641-269-4420
Web Site: www.web.grinnell.edu/theatre/facilities
Officers:
    President: Raynard Kington
    Secretary : Susan Schoen
    VP: Angela Voos
Management:
    Department Chair: Lesley Delmenico
    Technical Director: Erik Sanning
    President Assistant: Tammy D. Prusha
Mission: The study of theatre and movement at Grinnell embraces all aspects of the dramatic art as part of a liberal arts education.
Founded: 1846
Specialized Field: Student Productions
Status: Private
Type of Stage: Black Box
Seating Capacity: 72

7000
BARNUM STUDIO THEATRE
Simpson College
Blank Performing Arts Center
701 North C Street
Indianola, IA 50125
Phone: 515-961-6251
Fax: 515-961-1758
Toll-free: 800-622-54
e-mail: admiss@simpson.edu
Web Site: www.simpson.edu/theatre
Officers:
    President: Jay Simmons
    CEO: Jay Byers
Management:
    Technical Assistant: Rick Goetz
    Adjunct Faculty: Jed Alexander
    Media Manager: Sheila Allbee
Mission: Theatre Simpson is a dynamic community that views theatre as an avenue for personal discovery, self-discipline, creative expression and artistic excellence. Departmental courses and projects provide students with dynamic cultural and artistic experiences and help develop their abilities to observe, reflect, think critically and express themselves.
Founded: 1860
Specialized Field: Theatre
Type of Stage: Flexible Black Box
Seating Capacity: 125

7001
POTE THEATRE
Simpson College
Blank Performing Arts Center
701 North C Street
Indianola, IA 50125

FACILITIES / Iowa

Phone: 515-961-6251
Fax: 515-961-1758
Toll-free: 800-622-54
e-mail: admiss@simpson.edu
Web Site: www.simpson.edu/theatre
Officers:
   President: Jay Simmons
   CEO: Jay Byers
Management:
   Technical Assistant: Rick Goetz
   Adjunct Faculty: Jed Alexander
   Media Manager: Sheila Allbee
Mission: Theatre Simpson is a dynamic community that views theatre as an avenue for personal discovery, self-discipline, creative expression and artistic excellence. Departmental courses and projects provide students with dynamic cultural and artistic experiences and help develop their abilities to observe, reflect, think critically and express themselves.
Founded: 1860
Specialized Field: Opera, Theatre Arts
Type of Stage: Proscenium/Thrust
Seating Capacity: 500

7002
SVEN AND MILDRED LEKBERG RECITAL HALL

Simpson College
Amy Robertson Music Center
701 North C Street
Indianola, IA 50125
Phone: 515-961-6251
Fax: 515-961-1758
Toll-free: 800-622-54
e-mail: admiss@simpson.edu
Web Site: www.simpson.edu/theatre
Officers:
   President: Jay Simmons
   CEO: Jay Byers
Management:
   Technical Assistant: Rick Goetz
   Adjunct Faculty: Jed Alexander
   Media Manager: Sheila Allbee
Mission: Theatre Simpson is a dynamic community that views theatre as an avenue for personal discovery, self-discipline, creative expression and artistic excellence. Departmental courses and projects provide students with dynamic cultural and artistic experiences and help develop their abilities to observe, reflect, think critically and express themselves.
Founded: 1860
Opened: 1983
Specialized Field: Jazz Ensembles, Music Convocations, Student Recitals
Seating Capacity: 200

7003
DAVID THAYER THEATRE

University of Iowa
Department of Theatre Arts
107 Theatre Building
Iowa City, IA 52242-1705
Phone: 319-335-2700
Fax: 319-335-3568
Toll-free: 800-534-92
e-mail: theatre@uiowa.edu
Web Site: www.theatre.uiowa.edu/people/david-l-thayer
Officers:
   Interim President: Gary C. Fethke
   Chair: David L. Thayer
Management:
   Acting: John Cameron
   Design: Eric Stone
   Directing: Eric Forsythe
   Stage Manager: David McGraw
   Marketing coordinator: Kristan Hellige
Mission: The purpose of the Division of Performing Arts is to support the mission, objective, and visibility of the Department of Dance, the School of Music, and the Department of Theatre Arts through coordinated artistic activities, academic activities, public communications and outreach, student recruitment, and fundraising.
Opened: 1985
Specialized Field: Artistry, Dance, Drama, Music
Type of Stage: Semiflexible
Seating Capacity: 150-225
Year Built: 1935
Year Remodeled: 1985
Cost: $6.7 Million
Rental Contact: Stage Manager Daivd McGraw

7004
HANCHER AUDITORIUM

University of Iowa
PO Box 4550
Iowa City, IA 52244
Phone: 319-335-3305
Toll-free: 806-869-3
Web Site: www.uifoundation.org/hancher
Officers:
   Secretary : Tim Meier
Management:
   Executive Director: Charles Swanson
   Programming Director: Jacob Yarrow
   Director, Marketing: Rob Cline
   Director, Graphic Design: Zo‰ Woodworth
Founded: 1972
Status: Nonprofit, Professional
Annual Attendance: 20,000+

7005
KINNICK STADIUM

University of Iowa
157 Carver-Hawkeye Arena
Iowa City, IA 52242
Phone: 319-335-9411
Fax: 319-335-9333
e-mail: gohawks@hawkeyesports.com
Web Site: www.hawkeyesports.com
Management:
   President: David Skorton
   Facility Manager: Damian Simcox
Founded: 1847
Specialized Field: Home of University of Iowa Athletics
Status: Non-Profit, Non-Professional
Seating Capacity: 70,111

7006
MABIE THEATRE

University of Iowa
Department of Theatre Arts
107 Theatre Building
Iowa City, IA 52242-1705
Phone: 319-335-2700
Fax: 319-335-3568
Toll-free: 800-536-2
e-mail: theatre@uiowa.edu
Web Site: www.theatre.uiowa.edu
Officers:
   Interim President: Gary C. Fethke
   Chair: David L. Thayer
Management:
   Acting: John Cameron
   Design: Eric Stone
   Directing: Eric Forsythe
   Stage Manager: David McGraw
   Marketing coordinator: Kristan Hellige
Mission: The purpose of the Division of Performing Arts is to support the mission, objective, and visibility of the Department of Dance, the School of Music, and the Department of Theatre Arts through coordinated artistic activities, academic activities, public communications and outreach, student recruitment, and fundraising.
Opened: 1936
Specialized Field: Artistry, Dance, Drama, Music
Type of Stage: Proscenium
Seating Capacity: 477
Year Built: 1935
Year Remodeled: 1985
Cost: $6.7 Million
Rental Contact: Stage Manager Daivd McGraw

7007
STUDIO THEATRE

University of Iowa
Department of Theatre Arts
107 Theatre Building
Iowa City, IA 52242-1705
Phone: 319-335-2700
Fax: 319-335-3568
Toll-free: 800-536-2
e-mail: theatre@uiowa.edu
Web Site: www.theatre.uiowa.edu
Officers:
   Interim President: Gary C. Fethke
   Chair: David L. Thayer
Management:
   Acting: John Cameron
   Design: Eric Stone
   Directing: Eric Forsythe
   Stage Manager: David McGraw
   Marketing coordinator: Kristan Hellige
Mission: The purpose of the Division of Performing Arts is to support the mission, objective, and visibility of the Department of Dance, the School of Music, and the Department of Theatre Arts through coordinated artistic activities, academic activities, public communications and outreach, student recruitment, and fundraising.
Specialized Field: Theatre
Type of Stage: Flexible
Seating Capacity: 50
Year Built: 1935
Year Remodeled: 1985
Cost: $6.7 Million
Rental Contact: Stage Manager Daivd McGraw

7008
THEATRE B

University of Iowa
Department of Theatre Arts
107 Theatre Building
Iowa City, IA 52242-1705
Phone: 319-335-2700
Fax: 319-335-3568
Toll-free: 800-536-2
e-mail: theatre@uiowa.edu
Web Site: www.theatre.uiowa.edu
Officers:
   Interim President: Gary C. Fethke
   Chair: David L. Thayer
Management:
   Acting: John Cameron
   Design: Eric Stone
   Directing: Eric Forsythe
   Stage Manager: David McGraw
   Marketing coordinator: Kristan Hellige
Mission: The purpose of the Division of Performing Arts is to support the mission, objective, and visibility of the Department of Dance, the School of Music, and the

FACILITIES / Iowa

Department of Theatre Arts through coordinated artistic activities, academic activities, public communications and outreach, student recruitment, and fundraising.
Opened: 1985
Specialized Field: Workshop Productions
Type of Stage: Black Box
Seating Capacity: 144
Year Built: 1935
Year Remodeled: 1985
Cost: $6.7 Million
Rental Contact: Stage Manager Daivd McGraw

7009
SHAW CENTER AUDITORIUM
Graceland University
Shaw Center for the Performing Arts
1 University Place
Lamoni, IA 50140
Phone: 641-784-5000
Fax: 641-784-5487
Toll-free: 816-833-0524
e-mail: finearts@graceland.edu
Web Site: www.graceland.edu/finearts/theatre
Officers:
  President: John Seller
  Secretary: Michael Morain
Management:
  Coordinator: Rebecca M. Foster
  Director: Robert A. Hamel
Mission: The Department of Theatre in the Division of Fine Arts at Graceland University offers a Bachelor of Arts in Theatre as well as a Theatre minor. Theatre students develop creative skills, practice critical thinking and problem solving, and develop personal discipline through coursework and production.
Founded: 1895
Specialized Field: Theatre
Seating Capacity: 800

7010
STUDIO THEATRE
Graceland University
Shaw Center for the Performing Arts
1 University Place
Lamoni, IA 50140
Phone: 641-784-5000
Fax: 641-784-5487
Toll-free: 816-833-0524
e-mail: finearts@graceland.edu
Web Site: www.graceland.edu/finearts/theatre
Officers:
  President: John Seller
  Secretary: Michael Morain
Management:
  Coordinator: Rebecca M. Foster
  Director: Robert A. Hamel
Mission: The Department of Theatre in the Division of Fine Arts at Graceland University offers a Bachelor of Arts in Theatre as well as a Theatre minor. Theatre students develop creative skills, practice critical thinking and problem solving, and develop personal discipline through coursework and production.
Founded: 1895
Specialized Field: Theatre
Seating Capacity: 150

7011
CHARLES H MACNIDER ART MUSEUM
303 2nd Street SE
Mason City, IA 50401
Phone: 641-421-3666
Fax: 641-422-9612
Web Site: www.macniderart.org
Management:
  Director: Sheila Perry
  Education Coordinator: Linda Willeke
  Financial Secretary: Audrey Gabel
Founded: 1966
Status: Non-Profit, Non-Professional
Paid Staff: 9

7012
NORTH IOWA COMMUNITY AUDITORIUM
500 College Drive
Mason City, IA 50401-7299
Phone: 641-423-1264
Fax: 641-423-1711
Toll-free: 888-466-4222
e-mail: request@niacc.edu
Web Site: www.niacc.edu
Officers:
  President: Steven Schulz
Management:
  Artistic Director: Elizabeth Gales
Founded: 1918
Status: Non-Profit, Professional

7013
KIMMEL THEATRE
Cornell College
Armstrong Hall of Fine Arts
600 First Street West
Mount Vernon, IA 52314
Phone: 319-895-4000
e-mail: theatre@cornellcollege.edu
Web Site: www.cornellcollege.edu/theatre/
Officers:
  President: Jonathan Brand
  VP, Academic Affairs: Joe Dieker
Management:
  Department Chair: Mark Hunter
  Technical Director: Ben Alexander
  Production Manager: Scott Olinger
Mission: Cornell College endorses liberal education as an end in itself and as a means of empowering students for leadership through productive careers and humane service in the global community.
Founded: 1853
Specialized Field: Jazz, Theatre
Paid Staff: 76
Seating Capacity: 266
Cost: $8.9 Million
Year Restored: 2003

7014
PLUM FLEMING STUDIO THEATRE
Cornell College
Armstrong Hall of Fine Arts
600 First Street West
Mount Vernon, IA 52314
Phone: 319-895-4000
e-mail: theatre@cornellcollege.edu
Web Site: www.cornellcollege.edu/theatre/
Officers:
  President: Jonathan Brand
  VP, Acadamic Affairs: Joe Dieker
Management:
  Department Chair: Mark Hunter
  Technical Director: Ben Alexander
  Production Manager: Scott Olinger
Mission: Cornell College endorses liberal education as an end in itself and as a means of empowering students for leadership through productive careers and humane service in the global community.
Founded: 1853
Specialized Field: Theatre
Paid Staff: 76
Type of Stage: Black Box
Cost: $8.9 Million
Year Restored: 2003

7015
DEWITT THEATRE ARTS CENTER
Northwestern College
101 7th Street Southwest
Orange City, IA 51041
Phone: 712-707-7000
Web Site: www.nwciowa.edu
Officers:
  President: Gregory Christy
  Vice President: Doug Beukelman
  Provost: Jasper Lesage
Management:
  Artistic Director: Tim McGarvey
Mission: To provide a distinctively Christian liberal arts education of recognized quality in a primarily undergraduate, co-educational, multicultural, residential environment.
Founded: 1882
Status: Nonprofit, Professional
Paid Staff: 250
Paid Artists: 24

7016
MAIN STAGE THEATRE
Central College
Kruidenier Center for Theatre
812 University
Pella, IA 50219
Phone: 641-628-9000
Toll-free: 877-623-87
Web Site: www.departments.central.edu/theatre/
Management:
  Department Chair: Mary Jo Sodd
  Professor of Theatre/Production Mgr: Treva Reimer
  Technical Director: Tom E. Thatcher
  Theatre Arts Associate: Ann Wilkinson
Mission: Theatre Central offers a broad range of course work across the theatre discipline. We believe that the undergraduate student should learn the whole of theatre within the larger context of the world. That is why we are very proud of the liberal arts emphasis which encourages broader thinking and creativity for the theatre artist.
Founded: 1853
Specialized Field: Theatre
Type of Stage: Black Box
Seating Capacity: 200

7017
STUDIO THEATRE
Central College
Kruidenier Center for Theatre
812 University
Pella, IA 50219
Phone: 641-628-9000
Toll-free: 877-623-87
Web Site: www.departments.central.edu/theatre/
Management:
  Department Chair: Mary Jo Sodd
  Professor of Theatre/Production Mgr: Treva Reimer
  Technical Director: Tom E. Thatcher
  Theatre Arts Associate: Ann Wilkinson
Mission: Theatre Central offers a broad range of course work across the theatre discipline. We believe that the undergraduate student should learn the whole of theatre within the larger context of the world. That is why we are very proud of the liberal arts emphasis which encourages broader thinking and creativity for the theatre artist.

FACILITIES / Iowa

Founded: 1853
Specialized Field: Theatre
Type of Stage: Black Box
Seating Capacity: 75

7018
B.J. HAAN AUDITORIUM
Dordt College
498 4th Avenue NE
Sioux Center, IA 51250-1606
Phone: 712-722-6002
Fax: 712-722-1198
Toll-free: 800-436-38
e-mail: lmoerman@dordt.edu
Web Site: www.dordt.edu/arts/theatre
Officers:
  President: Erik Hoekstra
  President, Executive Secretary: LeeAnn Moerman
Management:
  Department Chair: Teresa Ter Haar
  Assistant Professor of Theatre: Josiah Wallace
  Technical Director: Laura Berkompas
  Theatre Arts Secretary: Karen Vreugdenhil
Mission: Dordt's Theatre Arts Department is small but very active theatre program serves our community with two fully mounted mainstage shows each year, as well as numerous smaller student-directed or classroom-based projects.
Founded: 1937
Specialized Field: Concerts, Organ Recitals
Seating Capacity: 1,500
Year Built: 1979

7019
KLINGER-NEAL THEATRE
Morningside College
1501 Morningside Avenue
Sioux Center, IA 51106
Phone: 712-274-5000
Fax: 712-274-5101
Toll-free: 800-831-0806
e-mail: skewis@morningside.edu
Web Site: www.morningside.edu
Officers:
  President: John C. Reynders
Management:
  Department Chair: Bette Skewis-Arnett
  Assistant Professor of Theatre: Arthur H. Moss
Mission: The theatre curriculum includes courses emphasizing the inter-dependence of all aspects of production: acting, directing, and technical theatre.
Specialized Field: Ballets, Musicals, Plays, Recitals
Type of Stage: Proscenium, Thrust, Arena
Seating Capacity: 360
Year Built: 1964

7020
NEW WORLD THEATRE
Dordt College
498 4th Avenue NE
Sioux Center, IA 51250-1606
Phone: 712-722-6002
Fax: 712-722-1198
Toll-free: 800-436-38
e-mail: lmoerman@dordt.edu
Web Site: www.dordt.edu/arts/theatre
Officers:
  President: Erik Hoekstra
  President, Executive Secretary: LeeAnn Moerman
Management:
  Department Chair: Teresa Ter Haar
  Assistant Professor of Theatre: Josiah Wallace
  Technical Director: Laura Berkompas
  Theatre Arts Secretary: Karen Vreugdenhil
Mission: Dordt's Theatre Arts Department is small but very active theatre program serves our community with two fully mounted mainstage shows each year, as well as numerous smaller student-directed or classroom-based projects.
Founded: 1937
Specialized Field: Theatre
Type of Stage: Black Box

7021
TE PASKE THEATRE
Dordt College
498 4th Avenue NE
Sioux Center, IA 51250-1606
Phone: 712-722-6002
Fax: 712-722-1198
Toll-free: 800-436-38
e-mail: lmoerman@dordt.edu
Web Site: www.dordt.edu/arts/theatre
Officers:
  President: Erik Hoekstra
  President, Executive Secretary: LeeAnn Moerman
Management:
  Department Chair: Teresa Ter Haar
  Assistant Professor of Theatre: Josiah Wallace
  Technical Director: Laura Berkompas
  Theatre Arts Secretary: Karen Vreugdenhil
Mission: Dordt's Theatre Arts Department is small but very active theatre program serves our community with two fully mounted mainstage shows each year, as well as numerous smaller student-directed or classroom-based projects.
Founded: 1937
Specialized Field: Theatre
Type of Stage: Modified Thrust
Seating Capacity: 414

7022
BRIAR CLIFF THEATRE
Briar Cliff University
Department of Theatre
3303 Rebecca Street
Sioux City, IA 51104
Phone: 712-279-5542
Toll-free: 800-622-3303
Web Site: www.briarcliff.edu/departments/theatre
Officers:
  President: Beverly A. Wharton
Management:
  Director, Theater: Richard L. Poole
Mission: The goal of the Theatre Department is to provide students with theatre training to prepare them for a life in professional, community or educational theatre.
Founded: 1930
Specialized Field: Theatre

7023
ROBERTS STADIUM
2600 Division Street
PO Box 3183
Sioux City, IA 47711
Phone: 712-279-6651
Fax: 712-279-6651
Web Site: www.robertstadium.com
Management:
  Manager Public Schools: Ray Rowe
Seating Capacity: 7,000

7024
BLACK HAWK CHILDREN'S THEATRE
PO Box 433
Waterloo, IA 50704
Phone: 319-235-0367
Fax: 319-235-7489
Web Site: www.cedarnet.org/wcpbhct
Officers:
  President: Bryan Molinaro-Blonigan
  VP Fund Developement: Stephen Saladrigas
  VP Marketing: Beverly McCusker
  Secretary: Linda Neese
  Treasurer: Chad Abbas
Management:
  Artistic/Managing Director: Charles Stilwill
  Production Manager: Katrina Sanddik
  Marketing/Development Director: Kristin Teig-Torres
Founded: 1916
Status: Non-Profit, Non-Professional
Paid Staff: 15

7025
WATERLOO RIVERFRONT STADIUM
850 Park Road
Waterloo, IA 50704
Phone: 319-232-5633
Fax: 319-232-6140
Management:
  Manager: Eric Snider
Seating Capacity: 4,000

7026
MCCASKEY LYCEUM
Wartburg College
100 Wartburg Boulevard
Waverly, IA 50677
Phone: 319-352-8691
Toll-free: 800-722-85
e-mail: webmaster@wartburg.edu
Web Site: www.wartburg.edu/vtour/vr/neumann.html
Officers:
  Art Department Chairman: Thomas Payne
  President: Darrel Colson
Management:
  Music Department Chair: Karen Black, PhD
  Art Department Chair: Thomas Payne
Seating Capacity: 1,400

7027
NEUMANN AUDITORIUM
Wartburg College
100 Wartburg Boulevard
Waverly, IA 50677
Phone: 319-352-8691
Toll-free: 800-722-85
e-mail: webmaster@wartburg.edu
Web Site: www.wartburg.edu/vtour/vr/neumann.html
Officers:
  Art Department Chairman: Thomas Payne
  President: Darrel Colson
Management:
  Music Department Chair: Karen Black, PhD
  Art Department Chair: Thomas Payne
Seating Capacity: 1,400

7028
CHARLES KOCH ARENA
1845 Fairmount
Wichita, IA 67260
Fax: 316-978-3443
Web Site: www.goshockers.com
Management:

FACILITIES / Kansas

Facilities Manager: Jesse Torres
Assistant Facilities Director: Roland Banks
Media Relations Director: Larry Rankin
Athletics Director: Rege Klitze
Seating Capacity: 10,400

Kansas

7029
MEMORIAL AUDITORIUM
101 S Lincoln
PO Box 907
Chanute, KS 66720
Phone: 620-431-5200
Fax: 620-431-5209
Toll-free: 800-355-29
e-mail: city@chanute.org
Web Site: www.chanute.org
Management:
  Auditorium Manager: Ruth Ports
Founded: 1925
Paid Staff: 2
Seating Capacity: 1,243

7030
FLORAL HALL
PO Box 1629
Coffeyville, KS 67337
Phone: 316-251-9794
Stage Dimensions: 8x15 (meters)

7031
DODGE CITY FESTIVALS
PO Box 818
311 W Spruce
Dodge City, KS 67801
Phone: 620-227-9501
Fax: 620-338-8734
Toll-free: 800-813-90
e-mail: jknight@dodgedev.org
Web Site: www.dodgedev.org
Management:
  Executive Director: Joann Knight
  Development Corporation: Chelsey Dawson
Founded: 1999

7032
ALBERT TAYLOR HALL
Emporia State University
Plumb Hall
1 Kellogg Circle Emporia
Emporia, KS 66801
Phone: 620-341-5256
e-mail: idambro@emporia.edu
Web Site: www.emporia.edu/theatre
Officers:
  President: Dr Michael R Lane
Management:
  Director Theatre: Jim Bartruff
  Administrative Specialist : Barbara Ternes
Mission: Campus venue for convocations, theatre performances and road shows.
Founded: 1863
Opened: 1916
Specialized Field: Concerts, Dance, Productions
Type of Stage: Proscenium
Stage Dimensions: 40' x 18'
Orchestra Pit: y
Seating Capacity: 1,281

7033
KARL C. BRUDER THEATRE
Emporia State University
King Hall
3 Kellogg Circle Emporia
Emporia, KS 66801
Phone: 620-341-5256
e-mail: esutheatre@emporia.edu
Web Site: www.emporia.edu/theatre
Officers:
  President: Micheal Shonrock
Management:
  Director Theatre: Jim Bartruff
  Technical Director: Doug Dion
  Administrative Specialist : Barbara Ternes
Mission: At ESU, students can earn a BFA or BA in theatre, or gain certification to become a secondary teacher in our BSE program in speech and theatre. We are proud to be a part of an outstanding department, Communication and Theatre.
Specialized Field: Theatre
Type of Stage: Proscenium
Stage Dimensions: 39'6 x 18'
Orchestra Pit: y
Seating Capacity: 402
Year Built: 1967

7034
RONALD Q. FREDERICKSON THEATRE
Emporia State University
Roosevelt Hall
4 Kellogg Circle Emporia
Emporia, KS 66801
Phone: 620-341-5256
e-mail: esutheatre@emporia.edu
Web Site: www.emporia.edu/theatre
Officers:
  President: Michael Shonrock
Management:
  Director Theatre: Jim Bartruff, jbartruf@emporia.edu
  Technical Director: Doug Dion
  Administrative Specialist : Barbara Ternes
Mission: At ESU, students can earn a BFA or BA in theatre, or gain certification to become a secondary teacher in our BSE program in speech and theatre. We are proud to be a part of an outstanding department, Communication and Theatre.
Utilizes: Choreographers; Designers; Educators; Guest Accompanists; Guest Conductors; Music; Soloists; Students
Founded: 2001
Opened: 2001
Specialized Field: Theatre
Type of Stage: Black Box
Seating Capacity: 100-125

7035
BEACH-SCHMIDT PERFORMING ARTS CENTER
Fort Hays State University
Sheridan Hall
600 Park Street
Hays, KS 67601-4099
Phone: 785-628-3478
Fax: 785-628-4227
Web Site: www.fhsu.edu/communication/theatreinfo
Officers:
  President: Edward H. Hammond
Management:
  Chair Communications Studies: Carrol Haggard, PhD
  Assistant Professor: Bruce Bardwell
  Executive Assistant, President: Todd Powell
Mission: Theatre provides you with an opportunity to excel on stage. You can develop your talents in acting, directing, costuming, stage design and theatre management. You may take part in up to five major productions each year and a variety of one-act plays. In addition to performance, a broad range of courses are offered in acting, directing, stagecraft, and dramatic literature.
Specialized Field: Concerts, Recitals
Seating Capacity: 1,100
Year Remodeled: 1998

7036
FELTEN-START THEATRE
Fort Hays State University
Malloy Hall
600 Park Street
Hays, KS 67601-4100
Phone: 785-628-3478
Fax: 785-628-4227
Web Site: www.fhsu.edu/communication/theatreinfo
Officers:
  President: Edward H. Hammond
Management:
  Chair Communications Studies: Carrol Haggard, PhD
  Assistant Professor: Bruce Bardwell
  Executive Assistant, President: Todd Powell
Mission: Theatre provides you with an opportunity to excel on stage. You can develop your talents in acting, directing, costuming, stage design and theatre management. You may take part in up to five major productions each year and a variety of one-act plays. In addition to performance, a broad range of courses are offered in acting, directing, stagecraft, and dramatic literature.
Specialized Field: Music, Theatre
Seating Capacity: 350

7037
FELTON CENTER
Fort Hays State University
600 Park Street
Hays, KS 67601
Phone: 785-628-5801
Fax: 785-628-4007
Web Site: www.fhsu.edu
Management:
  Chair Communications Studies: Carrol Haggard, PhD
  Assistant Professor: Bruce Bardwell
  Executive Assistant, President: Todd Powell

7038
HAL PALMER RECITAL HALL
Fort Hays State University
Malloy Hall
600 Park Street
Hays, KS 67601-4102
Phone: 785-628-3478
Fax: 785-628-4227
Web Site: www.fhsu.edu/communication/theatreinfo
Officers:
  President: Edward H. Hammond
Management:
  Chair Communications Studies: Carrol Haggard, PhD
  Assistant Professor: Bruce Bardwell
  Executive Assistant, President: Todd Powell
Mission: Theatre provides you with an opportunity to excel on stage. You can develop your talents in acting, directing, costuming, stage design and theatre management. You may take part in up to five major

FACILITIES / Kansas

productions each year and a variety of one-act plays. In addition to performance, a broad range of courses are offered in acting, directing, stagecraft, and dramatic literature.
Specialized Field: Student Recitals
Seating Capacity: 115

7039
FOX THEATRE
18 East First Avenue
Hutchinson, KS 67501
Phone: 620-663-5861
Fax: 620-663-5371
Toll-free: 877-697-69
e-mail: thefox@hutchinsonfox.com
Web Site: www.hutchinsonsonfox.com
Management:
  Executive Director: Mary Hemmings
  Technical Director: John Davies
  Box Office Manager: Shelby Haug
  Technical Assistant: John Depew
Seating Capacity: 1,221

7040
KANSAS STATE FAIR - GRANDSTAND
2000 N Poplar Street
Hutchinson, KS 67502-5562
Phone: 620-669-3600
Fax: 620-669-3640
Toll-free: 800-623-47
Web Site: www.kansasstatefair.com
Officers:
  General Manager: Denny Stoecklein
Management:
  Finance Director: Anita Walkar
  Plant Supervisor: Keith Schroeder
  Assistant Manager: Lori Hart
  Events and Sponsorship Director: Connie Schmitt
Mission: The annual Kansas State Fair is held annually beginning the Friday following Labor Day and lasts for 10 days at the Kansas State Fairgrounds in Hutchinson, Kansas. The largest single event in the State, the Fair annually attracts approximately 350,000 people from all 105 Kansas counties and several other states.
Founded: 1913
Status: Non-Profit, Professional
Paid Staff: 25
Paid Artists: 20

7041
BOWLUS FINE ARTS CENTER
205 E Madison
Iola, KS 66749
Phone: 620-365-4765
Web Site: www.bowluscenter.org/index/home&
Officers:
  President: Tony Leavitt
  VP: Don Snavely
Management:
  Executive Director: Susan Rains
  Facility Manager: Jeff Jordon
  Assistant Technical Director: John Higginbotham
  Marketing and Volunteer Coordinator: Judy Cochran
Mission: Attracts nationally-acclaimed performers to the area. Also houses a fine arts education center. The Bowlus provides display areas for local and visiting artists, while maintaining a permanent collection of distinctive paintings.

7042
ALLEN FIELDHOUSE
University of Kansas
1651 Naismith Drive, Lawrence
Lawrence, KS 66045
Phone: 785-864-3143
Fax: 785-864-5517
e-mail: KUAthletics@KU.edu
Web Site: www.kuathletics.cstv.com/facilities/kan-allen-fieldhouse.html
Management:
  Chancellor: Robert Hemenway
  Athletics Director: Lew Perkins
Founded: 1955
Seating Capacity: 16,300

7043
CRAFTON-PREYER THEATRE
University of Kansas
317 Murphy Hall, 1530 Naismith Drive, Murphy
Lawrence, KS 66045
Phone: 785-864-3381
Fax: 785-864-6007
e-mail: cjenkins@ku.edu
Web Site: www.kutheatre.com
Officers:
  Chair: Mechele Leon
  Chancellor: Bernadette Gray-Little
Management:
  Executive Vice Chancellor: Jeffrey S. Vitter
  Executive Vice Chancellor: Doug Girod
  Vice Chancellor: Dave Cook
Utilizes: Collaborations; Guest Accompanists; Guest Conductors; Guest Designers; Guest Writers; Multi Collaborations; Soloists
Founded: 1923
Specialized Field: Theatre
Paid Staff: 13
Income Sources: State of Kansas and Box Office
Annual Attendance: 65,000
Facility Category: University Theatre
Type of Stage: Proscenium
Seating Capacity: 1,188
Year Built: 1957
Rental Contact: Tech Director Jim Peterson

7044
LIED CENTER OF KANSAS
University of Kansas
1600 Stewart Drive, Lawrence
Lawrence, KS 66045
Phone: 785-864-2787
Fax: 785-864-5450
e-mail: lied@ku.edu
Web Site: www.lied.ku.edu
Officers:
  Honorary President: Christina Hixson
  President: Marilyn McCleary
  Treasurer: Kara Bhala
Management:
  Art Director: Meghan Bahn
  Associate Director: Karen Lane Christilles
  Assistant Technical Director: Erika Eden
  Executive Director: Derek S. Kwan
Founded: 1993
Specialized Field: Presenting
Status: Non-Profit, Professional
Paid Staff: 100
Type of Stage: Proscenium
Seating Capacity: 2,018

7045
XAVIER HALL THEATRE
University of Saint Mary
4100 S 4th Street
Leavenworth, KS 66048
Phone: 913-682-5151
Fax: 913-758-6140
Toll-free: 913-527-43
e-mail: enroll@stmary.edu
Web Site: www.stmary.edu
Officers:
  President: Diane Steel
  Executive Administrative Assistant: Katherine Tatom
  VP, Acadamic affairs: Bryan Le Beau
Management:
  Community Director: Maureen Hall
  Instructor/Fine Arts-Theatre: Danielle Trebus
Mission: Seeks to prepare students for value-centered lives and careers that contribute to the well being of the global society.
Founded: 1859
Specialized Field: Greater Kansas City Metropolitan Area
Status: Non-Profit, Non-Professional
Paid Staff: 2
Paid Artists: 6
Budget: $10,000
Income Sources: Annual budget provided by the University plus Gifts; Donations; Season Tickets and Single Ticket Revenue
Performs At: Theatre
Annual Attendance: 4,000
Facility Category: Theatre
Type of Stage: Proscenium/Thrust
Stage Dimensions: 40' x 20'
Seating Capacity: 349
Year Built: 1918
Year Remodeled: 2007

7046
BURNETT THEATRE
Bethany College
Burnett Center for Religion & Performing Arts
335 E.Swensson Street
Lindsborg, KS 67456
Phone: 785-227-3380
Fax: 785-227-2004
Toll-free: 800-262-81
e-mail: legaultg@bethanylb.edu
Web Site: www.bethanylb.edu
Officers:
  President: Edward Leonard III
  Custodian: Korena Anderson
  Controller: John Coykendall
  Director Operations: Jeff Barkman
Mission: Bethany College offers a small but highly flexible hands-on Theater Program.
Founded: 1881
Specialized Field: Theatrical
Status: Non-Profit, Professional
Seating Capacity: 250
Year Built: 1974

7047
FRED BRAMLAGE COLISEUM
Kansas State University
1800 College Avenue Suite 137
Manhattan, KS 66502
Phone: 785-532-7600
Fax: 785-532-7655
e-mail: bramlage@ksu.edu
Web Site: www.k-state.edu/bramlage

FACILITIES / Kansas

Management:
  Executive Director: Charles E Thomas
  Artistic Director: James Muller
Founded: 1988
Status: Non-Profit, Professional
Paid Staff: 200
Type of Stage: Concert Stage
Seating Capacity: 14,000

7048
MANHATTAN ARTS CENTER
1520 Poyntz Avenue
Manhattan, KS 66502
Phone: 785-537-4420
Fax: 785-539-3356
e-mail: office@manhattanarts.org
Web Site: www.manhattanarts.org
Officers:
  President: Steve Galitzer
  VP: Rebecca Gould
  Secretary: Dennis Hemmendinger
  Treasurer: Sheldon Edelman
Management:
  Executive Director: Penny Senften
  Office Manager: Sandy Mead
  Development Director: Amy Gross
  Marketing Director: Kim Belanger
Mission: To make arts activities available to all.
Utilizes: Actors; Collaborations; Community Members; Community Talent; Designers; Educators; Fine Artists; Five Seasonal Concerts; Grant Writers; Guest Accompanists; Guest Musical Directors; Guild Activities; High School Drama; Local Artists; Local Artists & Directors; Local Talent; Multimedia; Music; Original Music Scores; Paid Performers; Resident Professionals; Sign Language Translators; Soloists; Special Technical Talent; Theatre Companies; Touring Companies; Visual Designers; Volunteer Directors & Actors; Writers
Founded: 1996
Specialized Field: Galleries; Live Theatre; Concerts; Classes
Status: Non-Profit, Non-Professional
Paid Staff: 3
Volunteer Staff: 75
Budget: $290,000
Income Sources: Kansas Arts Commission; City of Manhattan; Foundations; Private Donations; Admissions; Tuition
Performs At: Multi-use Arts Center
Annual Attendance: 11,000
Type of Stage: Black Box
Seating Capacity: 145-160
Year Remodeled: 1996
Organization Type: Educational; Sponsoring

7049
MCCAIN AUDITORIUM
Kansas State University
207 McCain Auditorium
Manhattan, KS 66506
Phone: 785-532-6428
Fax: 785-532-5870
e-mail: mccain@k-state.edu
Web Site: www.ksu.edu
Officers:
  President: Barbara Gatewood
  President-Elect: Peggy Anderson
Management:
  Executive Director: Todd Holmberg
  Associate Director: Terri Lee
  Technical Director: Kyle McGuffin
  Ticket Services Manager: Stefani Schrader
Mission: The mission of the theatre program is to develop human potential, expand knowledge, and enrich cultural understanding and expression through high quality undergraduate and graduate education.
Founded: 1858
Specialized Field: Dance, Theatre
Orchestra Pit: y
Seating Capacity: 900-1,800
Year Built: 1970

7050
NICHOLS THEATRE
Kansas State University
109 McCain Auditorium
Manhattan, KS 66506
Phone: 785-532-7540
Web Site: www.k-state.edu/sctd/theatre/
Officers:
  President: Jon Wefald
Management:
  Executive Director: Todd Holmberg
  Associate Director: Terri Lee
  Technical Director: Kyle McGuffin
  Ticket Services Manager: Stefani Schrader
Mission: The mission of the theatre program is to develop human potential, expand knowledge, and enrich cultural understanding and expression through high quality undergraduate and graduate education.
Founded: 1858
Specialized Field: Theatre
Type of Stage: Arena-Thrust
Seating Capacity: 240-280
Year Built: 1985

7051
PURPLE MASQUE
Kansas State University
110 McCain Auditorium
Manhattan, KS 66506
Phone: 785-532-7540
Web Site: www.k-state.edu/sctd/theatre/
Officers:
  President: Jon Wefald
Management:
  Executive Director: Todd Holmberg
  Associate Director: Terri Lee
  Technical Director: Kyle McGuffin
  Ticket Services Manager: Stefani Schrader
Mission: The mission of the theatre program is to develop human potential, expand knowledge, and enrich cultural understanding and expression through high quality undergraduate and graduate education.
Founded: 1858
Specialized Field: Student Productions
Type of Stage: Thrust
Orchestra Pit: y
Seating Capacity: 100

7052
BROWN AUDITORIUM
McPherson College
1600 East Euclid
McPherson, KS 67460
Mailing Address: PO Box 1402
Phone: 316-241-0731
Fax: 316-241-8443
Toll-free: 800-657-02
e-mail: admiss@mcpherson.edu
Web Site: www.mcpherson.edu
Officers:
  President: Michael P. Schneider
  VP: Barrett David
Management:
  Computer Services Director: David D Gitchell
  Business Manager: Shirley Reissig
  Library/Media Services Director: Rowena Olsen
  Director of Student Success: Barr Carole
Founded: 1887

7053
NEODESHA ARTS ASSOCIATION
PO Box 65
5th Street & Indiana
Neodesha, KS 66757
Phone: 316-325-3422
Fax: 316-325-3122
e-mail: neodeshaart@yahoo.com
Management:
  Executive: Teresa Railsback
Mission: The mission is to improve the quality of life in Neodesha and surrounding area through presentation of culutral activities in which the arts flourish.
Founded: 1973
Paid Staff: 1
Volunteer Staff: 13
Paid Artists: 1
Non-paid Artists: 3

7054
OTTAWA MUNICIPAL AUDITORIUM
301 S Hickory Street
PO Box 462
Ottawa, KS 66067 - 04
Phone: 785-242-8810
Fax: 785-229-3760
e-mail: sstitt@ottawaks.gov
Web Site: www.ottawamunicipalauditorium.com
Management:
  Administration Manager: Shonda Stitt
Founded: 1890
Status: Non-Profit, Professional
Paid Staff: 9
Paid Artists: 100
Seating Capacity: 840

7055
PERFORMING ARTS SERIES
Johnson County Community College
12345 College Boulevard
OVERLAND PARK
Overland Park, KS 66210
Phone: 913-469-8500
Fax: 913-469-2252
e-mail: tickets@jccc.edu
Web Site: www.jccc.edu/TheSeries
Officers:
  Chairperson: Melody Royt
  Vice Chair: Jon Stewart
  President: Terry A. Calaway
Management:
  General Manager: Emily Behrmann, ebehrman@jccc.edu
  Director of Operations: Anthony Perry, aperry@jccc.edu
  Event Manager: Christina Wright, cwright@jccc.edu
Founded: 1990
Opened: 1990
Specialized Field: Multi-discipline, performing arts presenter
Paid Staff: 15
Volunteer Staff: 150
Budget: $22,000,000
Income Sources: Ticket revenue, private donations, institutional support
Performs At: Yardley Hall, Polsky Theatre
Affiliations: APAP, INTIX, KS Arts Alliance/Kennedy Center

FACILITIES / Kansas

Annual Attendance: 100,000
Type of Stage: Proscenium & Thrust
Orchestra Pit: y
Seating Capacity: Polsky-400; Yardley-1300
Year Built: 1990
Cost: $22,000,000
Rental Contact: Anthony Perry

7056
CARNIE SMITH STADIUM
Pittsburg State University
1701 S Broadway street
Pittsburg, KS 66762
Phone: 620-231-7000
Fax: 316-235-4661
e-mail: acad@pittstate.edu
Web Site: www.pittstate.edu
Officers:
    President: Steve Scott
    Provost: Lynette J. Olson
    Assistant, President: Jaime Dalton
Management:
    Athletic Director: Chuck Broyles
Annual Attendance: 238,911
Seating Capacity: 8,343

7057
MEMORIAL AUDITORIUM AND CONVENTION CENTER
City Hall, 201 W. 4th St
Pittsburg, KS 66762
Phone: 620-231-4100
Fax: 316-231-5967
Web Site: www.pittks.org
Management:
    Manager: Judy Collins
    Office Manager: Janice Arthur
    Technical Director: David Stubbs
Founded: 1925
Paid Staff: 5
Annual Attendance: 10,000
Facility Category: Concert Hall, Children's theater
Type of Stage: Proscenium
Stage Dimensions: 90 x 37
Seating Capacity: 1588
Year Built: 1923
Year Remodeled: 1984
Architect: Seidler, Owsley and Associates
Cost: $3.4 million
Rental Contact: Manager Judy Collins

7058
WEEDE ARENA
Pittsburgh State University
1701 South Broadway
Pittsburg, KS 66762
Phone: 316-235-4646
Fax: 316-235-4661
Web Site: www.oitstate.edu
Management:
    Athletic Director: Chuck Broyles
    Sports Information Director: Dan Wilkes
Seating Capacity: 6,000

7059
SALINA BICENTENNIAL CENTER
800 The Midway
PO Box 1727
Salina, KS 67402
Phone: 785-826-7200
Fax: 785-826-7207
Toll-free: 888-826-7469
Web Site: www.bicentennial.org
Officers:
    President: Steve Scott
    Provost: Lynette J. Olson
    Assistant, President: Jaime Dalton
Management:
    President: Keith Rawlings
Founded: 1979
Status: For-Profit, Non-Professional
Paid Staff: 20
Seating Capacity: 2,000

7060
STIEFEL THEATRE FOR THE PERFORMING ARTS
151 South Santa Fe
Po Box 1871
Salina, KS 67401
Phone: 785-827-1998
Fax: 785-827-3478
Web Site: www.stiefeltheatre.com
Management:
    Executive Director: Michele Douglas
Seating Capacity: 1,286

7061
KANSAS EXPOCENTRE
One Expocentre Drive
Topeka, KS 66612
Phone: 785-235-1986
Fax: 785-235-2967
e-mail: roym@ksexpo.com
Web Site: www.ksexpo.com
Officers:
    Managing Manager: HR Cook
Management:
    Director of Finance: Donna Starin
    Director Operations: Roy Mitchell
    Director Marketing: Shannon Reilly
    Marketing Manager: Phil Thompson
Founded: 1986
Specialized Field: Multi-Purpose Facility
Status: For-Profit, Professional
Paid Staff: 200
Seating Capacity: 10,000
Year Built: 1987

7062
LEE ARENA
Washburn University
1700 College Avenue
Topeka, KS 66621
Phone: 785-670-1010
Fax: 785-670-1091
Web Site: www.washburn.edu
Officers:
    President: Jery Farley
Management:
    Athletic Director: Loren Ferre
    Facilities Manager: Gilbert Herrera
Seating Capacity: 3,804

7063
TOPEKA PERFORMING ARTS CENTER
214 Se 8th Avenue
Topeka, KS 66603
Phone: 785-234-2787
Fax: 785-234-2307
Web Site: www.tpactix.org
Management:
    Executive Director: Robert Seitz
    Development Director: John Esau
    Marketing Manager: Abby Howard
    Business Manager: Linda Nedved
Founded: 1990
Seating Capacity: 4,200

7064
KANSAS COLISEUM
1229 E 85th Street N
Park City
Valley Center, KS 67147
Phone: 316-440-0888
Fax: 316-440-0928
e-mail: info@kansascoliseum.com
Web Site: www.kansascoliseum.com
Management:
    Managing Director: John W Nath
    Assistant Director: David Rush
Founded: 1975
Specialized Field: Multi-Purpose Arena; Home of the Wichita Thunder (CHL); and Wichita Stealth
Status: For-Profit, Professional
Paid Staff: 50
Annual Attendance: 700,000
Seating Capacity: 9,600; 12,400
Year Built: 1978

7065
COLUMBIAN THEATRE: MUSEUM & ART CENTER
521 Lincoln Avenue
PO Box 72
Wamego, KS 66547
Phone: 785-456-2029
Fax: 785-456-9498
Toll-free: 800-991-93
e-mail: boxoffice@columbiantheatre.com
Web Site: www.columbiantheatre.com
Officers:
    President: Lance White
Management:
    Executive Director: Client Stueve
    Artistic Director: Ariane Chapman
    Marketing/Events Director: Kayla Oney
    Administrative Coordinator: Brooke Rindt
Founded: 1989
Status: Non-Profit, Non-Professional
Paid Staff: 4
Annual Attendance: 12,000
Rental Contact: Marketing/Events Director Kayla Oney

7066
WELLINGTON MEMORIAL AUDITORIUM
317 S. Washington
Wellington, KS 67152
Phone: 620-326-3631
Fax: 620-326-8506
Web Site: cityofwellington.net/memorialauditorium.html
Management:
    Manager: Ellen McCue

7067
CENTURY II CIVIC CENTER EXHIBITION HALL
225 W Douglas Avenue
Wichita, KS 67202
Phone: 316-264-9121
Fax: 316-268-9268
Web Site: www.century2.org
Management:
    Manager: John D'Angelo
    Event Manager: Barney Byard
    Technical Director: John Hale
Type of Stage: 62,500 Sq Ft
Seating Capacity: 2,000

FACILITIES / Kentucky

7068
CENTURY II CIVIC CENTER MARY JANE TEALL THEATRE
225 W Douglas Avenue
Wichita, KS 67202
Phone: 316-264-9121
Fax: 316-268-9268
Web Site: www.century2.org
Management:
  Manager: John D'Angelo
  Event Manager: Barney Byard
  Technical Director: John Hale
Type of Stage: Proscenium
Seating Capacity: 646

7069
CENTURY II PERFORMING ARTS & CONVENTION CENTER
225 W Douglas Avenue
Wichita, KS 67202-3100
Phone: 316-264-9121
Fax: 316-268-9268
e-mail: DLWILLIAMS@wichita.gov
Web Site: www.century2.org
Management:
  Manager: John D'Angelo
  Event Manager: Barney Byard
  Technical Director: John Hale
Founded: 1960
Status: Non-Profit, Non-Professional
Paid Staff: 35
Seating Capacity: 5,244; 2,178
Rental Contact: Kathy Pearson

7070
HENRY LEVITT ARENA
Wichita State University
1845 Fairmount Street
Wichita, KS 67260
Mailing Address: Campus Box 12
Phone: 316-978-3456
Fax: 316-978-3336
Web Site: www.twsu.edu
Management:
  Director: Eric L. Sexton

7071
MILLER CONCERT HALL
Wichita State University
Duerksen Fine Arts Center
1845 Fairmount Street
Wichita, KS 67260
Phone: 316-978-3456
e-mail: webmaster@wichita.edu
Web Site: www.wichita.edu
Officers:
  President: John W. Bardo
  VP: Marry Herrin
  Provost: Tony Vizzini
  VP: Wade Robbinson
Management:
  Director: Eric L. Sexton
Founded: 1895
Seating Capacity: 10,432

7072
WIEDEMANN RECITAL HALL
Wichita State University
1845 Fairmount Street
Wichita, KS 67260
Phone: 316-978-3456
e-mail: webmaster@wichita.edu
Web Site: www.wichita.edu

Officers:
  President: John W. Bardo
  VP: Marry Herrin
  Provost: Tony Vizzini
  VP: Wade Robbinson
Management:
  Director: Eric L. Sexton
Founded: 1895
Seating Capacity: 10,432

7073
WILNER AUDITORIUM
Wichita State University
1845 Fairmount Street
Wichita, KS 67260
Phone: 316-978-3456
e-mail: webmaster@wichita.edu
Web Site: www.wichita.edu
Officers:
  President: John W. Bardo
  VP: Marry Herrin
  Provost: Tony Vizzini
  VP: Wade Robbinson
Management:
  Director: Eric L. Sexton
Founded: 1895
Seating Capacity: 10,432

Kentucky

7074
PARAMOUNT ARTS CENTER
1300 Winchester Avenue
PO Box 1546
Ashland, KY 41105
Phone: 606-324-3175
Fax: 606-324-1233
e-mail: jenny@paramountartscenter.com
Web Site: www.paramountartscenter.com
Management:
  Executive Director: Bruce Marquis
  Marketing Director: Jenny Holmes,
  Jenny@paramountartscenter.com
  Development Director: Jody Collins
Mission: Originally designed and built to show talking pictures, has provided an intimate venue for a variety of performaning arts since it re-opened in 1972.
Utilizes: Collaborations; Dance Companies; Dancers; Guest Accompanists; Guest Musical Directors; Guest Soloists; Guest Writers; Guild Activities; Instructors; Local Artists; Lyricists; Multimedia; New Productions; Original Music Scores; Playwrights; Sign Language Translators; Soloists; Special Technical Talent; Theatre Companies; Touring Companies
Founded: 1931
Specialized Field: Multi Disciplinary Presenter
Status: Nonprofit, Professional
Paid Staff: 10
Volunteer Staff: 100
Annual Attendance: 115,000
Facility Category: Performing Arts
Type of Stage: Proscenium
Stage Dimensions: 46x52
Seating Capacity: 1400
Year Built: 1931
Year Remodeled: 2001
Cost: $ 9 Million
Rental Contact: Cindy Collins

7075
STEPHEN FOSTER PRODUCTIONS
PO Box 546, Bardstown
Bardstown, KY 40004

Phone: 502-348-5971
Fax: 502-349-0574
Toll-free: 800-626-1563
e-mail: info@stephenfoster.com
Web Site: www.stephenfoster.com
Management:
  General Manager: Betty Kelley
Founded: 1959
Status: Non-Profit, Professional
Paid Staff: 100
Paid Artists: 60
Season: June - August
Seating Capacity: 1450
Year Built: 1959
Year Remodeled: 1997
Cost: $1.6 million

7076
PHELPS-STOKES AUDITORIUM AT BEREA COLLEGE
Berea College Campus
CPO 2220
Berea, KY 40404
Phone: 895-985-3000
Fax: 606-985-3512
Toll-free: 800-265-48
e-mail: linda_avery@berea.edu
Web Site: www.berea.edu

7077
CAPITOL ARTS CENTER
416 E Main Street
Bowling Green, KY 42101
Mailing Address: P.O. Box 748, Bowling Green
Phone: 270-904-5000
Fax: 270-782-2804
Toll-free: 877-942-87
e-mail: info@theskypac.com
Web Site: www.capitolarts.com
Management:
  Executive Director: Karen Hume
  Technical Director: Rob Hatcher
  Accounting: Patti Reagle
Founded: 1981
Status: Non-Profit, Professional
Paid Staff: 9

7078
DIDDLE ARENA
Western Kentucky University
1906 College Heights Blvd. Bowling Green
Bowling Green, KY 42101
Phone: 270-745-0111
Fax: 502-745-6187
Web Site: www.wku.edu/athletics
Officers:
  President: Gary A. Ransdell
Management:
  Executive Director: Karen Hume
  Technical Director: Rob Hatcher
  Accounting: Patti Reagle
  Executive Administrative Assistant: Torie Cockriel
  Executive Legal Assistant: Lauren Ossello
Founded: 1963

7079
LT SMITH STADIUM
Western Kentucky University
1906 College Heights Blvd. Bowling Green
Bowling Green, KY 42101
Phone: 270-745-0111
Fax: 502-745-6187
Web Site: www.wku.edu/athletics.html

Officers:
   President: Gary A. Ransdell
Management:
   Executive Director: Karen Hume
   Technical Director: Rob Hatcher
   Accounting: Patti Reagle
   Executive Administrative Assistant: Torie Cockriel
   Executive Legal Assistant: Lauren Ossello
Founded: 1968
Seating Capacity: 17,000

7080
MADISON THEATER
730 Madison Avenue
Covington, KY 41011
Phone: 859-491-2444
Fax: 859-655-4808
e-mail: info@madisontheateronline.com
Web Site: www.madisontheateronline.com
Management:
   Owner: Ester Johnson
   Operations: Howard Hodge
Founded: 1912
Seating Capacity: 1,200
Year Remodeled: 2001

7081
NORTON CENTER FOR THE ARTS
Centre College
600 W Walnut Street, Danville
Danville, KY 40422
Phone: 859-238-5200
Fax: 859-238-5448
Toll-free: 877-487-69
e-mail: chafin@centre.edu
Web Site: www.centre.edu/nc
Officers:
   President: John Rosh
   Managing Director: George Foreman
   Associate VP: Jamey Leahey
Management:
   President, Secretary: Cindy Arnold
Founded: 1973
Status: Non-Profit, Professional
Seating Capacity: Newlin Hall-1500; Weisiger Theatre-360
Year Built: 1973
Year Remodeled: 1994

7082
HENDERSON FINE ARTS CENTER
2660 S Green Street Center
Henderson, KY 42420
Phone: 270-827-1867
Fax: 270-831-9802
Toll-free: 800-969-58
Web Site: www.hencc.kctcs.edu
Officers:
   President: Kris Williams
   Chair: Cassidy Wilson, III
   Vice Chair: Rose Marie Shouse
   Provot: David Brauer
   CIO: Kim Conley
Management:
   Director: Rachael Baar
Founded: 1993
Status: Non-Profit, Professional
Paid Staff: 3

7083
COMMONWEALTH STADIUM
University of Kentucky
University Drive, Room 23
Lexington, KY 40506
Phone: 859-257-3838
Fax: 859-323-4310
Web Site: www.ukathletics.com
Management:
   President: Lee Todd
   Executive Director: Mitch Barnhart
   Managing Director: Rodney Stiles
Mission: Home of Kentucky Wildcats
Founded: 1973
Status: For-Profit, Non-Professional
Paid Staff: 250
Seating Capacity: 67,530
Year Built: 1973

7084
LEXINGTON CENTER
430 W Vine Street
Lexington
Lexington, KY 40507
Phone: 859-233-4567
Fax: 859-253-2718
e-mail: webmaster@rupparena.com
Web Site: www.lexingtoncenter.com
Officers:
   President/CEO: William B Owen
Management:
   Director Arena Management: Carl Hall
   Marketing Director: Sheila Kenny
   HR, Director: Chester maull
   Technical Service Manager: Bob Stoops
   Group Sales: Jana Hatton
Seating Capacity: 23,500

7085
LEXINGTON OPERA HOUSE
430 W Vine Street
Lexington
Lexington, KY 40507
Phone: 859-233-4567
Fax: 859-253-2718
Web Site: www.lexingtonoperahouse.com
Officers:
   President/CEO: Bill Owen
Management:
   Marketing Director: Sheila Kenny
   Technical Service Manager: Bob Stoops
   Group Sales: Jana Hatton
Founded: 1886
Status: For-Profit, Professional
Paid Staff: 3
Seating Capacity: 1,000
Year Built: 1886
Year Remodeled: 1972

7086
LUCILLE C LITTLE THEATER
Transylvania University
300 North Broadway
Lexington, KY 40508
Phone: 859-233-8300
Fax: 859-233-8797
Toll-free: 800-726-98
e-mail: admissions@transy.edu
Web Site: www.transy.edu
Officers:
   President: R. Owen Williams
Management:
   President: Charles Shearer
   Artistic Director: Tim Soulis
   Managing Director: Devin Query
Founded: 1780

7087
MITCHELL FINE ARTS CENTER
Transylvania University
300 N Braodway
Lexington, KY 40508
Phone: 859-233-8300
Fax: 859-233-8797
Toll-free: 800-726-98
e-mail: admissions@transy.edu
Web Site: www.transy.edu
Officers:
   President: R. Owen Williams
Management:
   President: Charles Shearer
   Artistic Director: Tim Soulis
   Managing Director: Devin Query
Founded: 1780
Status: Non-Profit, Non-Professional
Paid Staff: 250

7088
SINGLETARY CENTER FOR THE ARTS
University of Kentucky
405 Rose Street, Lexington
Lexington, KY 40503-0241
Phone: 859-257-1706
Fax: 859-323-9991
Web Site: www.uky.edu/SCFA/
Management:
   Director: Michael Grice
   Office Manager: Elizabeth Navarra
   Production Director: Tanya Harper
   Fiscal Affairs Officer: Sam Woolery
Mission: Host over 350 programs a year.
Founded: 1979
Paid Staff: 71
Volunteer Staff: 70
Annual Attendance: 112,000
Seating Capacity: Concert Hall-1500; Recital Hall-400

7089
UNIVERSITY OF KENTUCKY MEMORIAL COLISEUM
Lexington Avenue
Room 111
Lexington, KY 40506
Phone: 859-257-8000
Fax: 859-257-6303
Toll-free: 800-282-87
e-mail: mbarn@uky.edu
Web Site: www.ukathletics.com
Management:
   President: Lee T Todd Jr
   Athletic Director: Mitch Barnhart
   Associate Director Athletics: Kathleen DeBoer
   Associate Director: Bob Bradley
Founded: 1950
Seating Capacity: 8,500

7090
CARDINAL STADIUM
Kentucky Fair & Exposition Center
937 Phillips Lane
Louisville, KY 40209-1398
Mailing Address: PO Box 37130
Phone: 502-367-5000
Fax: 502-367-5139
Web Site: www.kyfairexpo.org
Management:
   President/CEO: Harold Workman

FACILITIES / Kentucky

Operations Director: Larry Faue
VP Sales/Marketing: Linda Edwards
Founded: 1900
Specialized Field: Sports Stadium for baseball and NCAA
Status: For-Profit, Non-Professional
Seating Capacity: 47,925
Year Built: 1956
Year Remodeled: 1981

7091
FREEDOM HALL ARENA
Kentucky Fair & Exposition Center
937 Phillips Lane
Louisville, KY 40209-1398
Mailing Address: PO Box 37130 Louisville, KY 40233
Phone: 502-367-5000
Fax: 502-367-5139
Web Site: www.kyfairexpo.org
Management:
  President/CEO: Harold Workman
  Operations Director: Larry Faue
  VP Sales/Marketing: Linda Edwards
Founded: 1956
Specialized Field: Home of University of Louisville Athletics (NCAA)
Status: For-Profit, Professional
Paid Staff: 300
Seating Capacity: 19,169
Year Built: 1956
Year Remodeled: 1984

7092
KENTUCKY CENTER FOR THE ARTS ROBERT S WHITNEY HALL
501 West Main Street
Louisville, KY 40202
Phone: 502-562-0100
Fax: 502-562-0150
Toll-free: 800-757-77
e-mail: info@kentuckycenter.org
Web Site: www.kentuckycenter.org
Officers:
  President: Kim Baker
  SVP: Heather Weston Bell
  SVP, Business Affairs: Christopher Roberts
Management:
  Director: Harry Hinkel
  Associate Director: Abby Shue
Mission: A 2,406-seat, multipurpose concert facility, Whitney Hall can accommodate everything from the most elaborate touring Broadway extravaganzas to the more modest requirements of a chamber music ensemble. Named for the eminent former conductor of the Louisville Orchestra, this theater has exemplary acoustics, comfortable seats and uninterrupted sight lines to ensure that every patron enjoys their theatrical experience to the fullest.
Founded: 1984
Status: Non-Profit, Professional
Rental Contact: Vickie Dorsey

7093
KENTUCKY CENTER FOR THE ARTS BOMHARD THEATRE
502 West Main Street
Louisville, KY 40202
Phone: 502-562-0100
Fax: 502-562-0150
Toll-free: 800-757-77
e-mail: info@kentuckycenter.org
Web Site: www.kentuckycenter.org
Officers:
  President: Kim Baker
  SVP: Heather Weston Bell
  SVP, Business Affairs: Christopher Roberts
Management:
  Director: Harry Hinkel
  Associate Director: Abby Shue
Seating Capacity: 619

7094
LOUISVILLE MEMORIAL AUDITORIUM
970 SOUTH FOURTH STREET
Louisville, KY 40203
Phone: 502-584-4911
Fax: 502-574-1487
Web Site: www.louisvillememorialauditorium.com/index.aspx
Management:
  Executive, Director: Dale Royer
Founded: 1929
Specialized Field: Gospel Shows; Stage Plays; Small Concerts; Children's Shows; Dance and Talent Competitions
Status: Non-Profit, Professional
Paid Staff: 3
Annual Attendance: 100,000
Facility Category: Auditorium
Stage Dimensions: 50' x 85'
Year Built: 1929
Rental Contact: Dale Royer

7095
LOUISVILLE PALACE THEATRE
625 Fourth Avenue
Louisville, KY 40202
Phone: 502-583-4555
Fax: 502-583-9955
Web Site: www.louisvillepalace.com
Management:
  General Manager/Booking: David Bartlett
  Sales/Marketing Director: Jennifer Crutcher
  Box Office Manager: Cindy Brown
  Production Manager: Casey Clark
  Operations Manager: Christie Lunsford
  Accounting: Jennifer Hunt
Seating Capacity: 2,715

7096
W L LYONS BROWN THEATRE
315 West Broadway
Louisville, KY 40202
Phone: 502-562-0100
Fax: 502-581-9213
e-mail: wrichards@kentuckycenter.org
Web Site: www.kentuckycenter.org
Officers:
  President: Kim Baker
  SVP: Heather Weston Bell
  SVP, Business Affairs: Christopher Roberts
Management:
  Director: Harry Hinkel
  Associate Director: Abby Shue
Seating Capacity: 1381

7097
GLEMA MAHR CENTER FOR THE ARTS
Madisonville Community College
2000 College Drive
Madisonville, KY 42431
Phone: 270-824-8651
Fax: 270-824-1868
e-mail: bradley.downall@kctcs.edu
Web Site: www.glemacenter.org
Management:
  Director: Bradley Downall
  Technical Director: Rob Blumrick
Mission: To enhance the quality of life in Madisonville and surrounding communities by developing and presenting a wide range of arts programming and arts education opportunities for all ages and interests.
Founded: 1990
Status: Non-Profit, Professional
Paid Staff: 7
Facility Category: Performing & Visual Arts Center
Type of Stage: Proscenium
Seating Capacity: 1017

7098
JAYNE STADIUM
100 Admission Center
Morehead, KY 40351
Phone: 606-783-5038
Fax: 606-783-5035
Toll-free: 800-585-6781
e-mail: t.stevens@moreheadstate.edu
Web Site: www.morehead-st.edu
Officers:
  President: Dr Wayne Andrews

7099
MURRAY STATE UNIVERSITY LOVETT AUDITORIUM
102 Curris Center
PO Box 9
Murray, KY 42071
Phone: 270-762-5577
Fax: 270-762-5511
Toll-free: 800-724-78
e-mail: rsec@murraystate.edu
Web Site: www.murraystate.edu
Officers:
  Chair: Constantine W. Curris
  President: John P. Young
  VP: Laura Lohr
  Treasurer: Sheri Riddle
Management:
  Facility Manager: Jason Pittman
Founded: 1926
Facility Category: Auditorium

7100
RACER ARENA
Murray State University
Athletic Department
Murray, KY 42071
Phone: 502-762-6800
Fax: 270-762-5498
Toll-free: 800-724-78
e-mail: webmaster@murraystate.edu
Web Site: www.murraystate.edu
Officers:
  Chair: Constantine W. Curris
  President: John P. Young
  VP: Laura Lohr
  Treasurer: Sheri Riddle
Management:
  Facility Manager: Jason Pittman
Founded: 1997
Seating Capacity: 5,500

7101
REGIONAL SPECIAL EVENTS CENTER
Murray State University
1401 State Route 121 North
Murray, KY 42071

FACILITIES / Louisiana

Phone: 270-762-5577
Fax: 270-762-5511
Toll-free: 800-724-78
e-mail: rsec@murraystate.edu
Web Site: www.murraystate.edu
Officers:
  Chair: Constantine W. Curris
  President: John P. Young
  VP: Laura Lohr
  Treasurer: Sheri Riddle
Management:
  Facility Manager: Jason Pittman
Founded: 1998
Status: Non-Profit, Professional
Paid Staff: 30
Seating Capacity: 8,600

7102
ROY STEWART STADIUM
Murray State University
Murray, KY 42071
Mailing Address: Box 2002 University Station
Phone: 270-762-6951
Fax: 270-762-6952
Toll-free: 800-724-78
e-mail: jeanie.morgan@murraystate.edu
Web Site: www.murraystate.edu
Officers:
  Chair: Constantine W. Curris
  President: John P. Young
  VP: Laura Lohr
  Treasurer: Sheri Riddle
Management:
  Facility Manager: Jason Pittman
Opened: 1973
Facility Category: Sports Arena
Seating Capacity: 16,800

7103
OWENSBORO SPORTS
200 East 3rd Street
PO Box 825
Owensboro, KY 42302
Phone: 270-926-1860
Fax: 270-687-8787
Web Site: www.owensboro.com
Management:
  Facility Manager: Hal L Mischel
Seating Capacity: 5,000

7104
RIVERPARK CENTER
101 Daviess Street
Owensboro
Owensboro, KY 42303
Phone: 270-687-2770
Fax: 270-687-2775
e-mail: info@riverparkcenter.org
Web Site: www.riverparkcenter.org
Officers:
  President: Zev Buffman
  Chairman: Jeff Danhauer
  Treasurer: Jeff Ebelhar
  Secretary: Doug Field
Management:
  Executive Director: Roxi Witt, rwitt@riverparkcenter.org
  Technical Director: Phillip Poe, pope@riverparkcenter.org
  Box Office Manager: Dana Wheeler, dwheeler@riverparkcenter.org

Mission: Riverpark Center is a non-profit organization seeking to improve the quality of life by hosting and presenting diverse arts and civic events, focusing on arts and education.
Founded: 1992
Status: Non-Profit
Paid Staff: 16
Volunteer Staff: 200
Performs At: State-Of-The-Art Broadway Style Theater In Addition To A Cabaret Theater And Reception Areas.
Facility Category: Performing Arts
Seating Capacity: 1,497/300 in cabaret theater
Year Built: 1992

7105
CARSON CENTER
100 Kentucky Ave
Paducah, KY 42003
Phone: 270-443-9932
Fax: 270-443-9947
e-mail: boxoffice@thecarsoncenter.org
Web Site: www.thecarsoncenter.org
Management:
  Production Manager: Joe Searcy
  Director, Opeation: Jeff Foreman
  Building Services Manager: Bill Fox
  Box Office Manager: Andrea James
Status: 501c-3 Non-Profit

7106
FOUR RIVERS CENTER FOR THE PERFORMING ARTS
101 Kentucky Ave
Paducah, KY 42003
Phone: 270-443-9932
Fax: 270-443-9947
Web Site: www.fourriverscenter.org
Officers:
  Chairman: Ted Borodofsky
  Vice Chairman: Mike Livingston
  Treasurer: Linda Miller
  Secertary: Anne Gwinn
Management:
  Production Manager: Joe Searcy
  Director, Opeation: Jeff Foreman
  Building Services Manager: Bill Fox
  Box Office Manager: Andrea James
Founded: 1996
Specialized Field: Performing Arts
Status: Non-Profit, Non-Professional
Paid Staff: 19
Seating Capacity: 1,800

7107
PADUCAH COMMUNITY COLLEGE FINE ARTS CENTER
4810 Alben Barkley Drive
PO Box 7380
Paducah, KY 42002-7380
Phone: 270-554-9290
Fax: 270-552-6310
e-mail: PCC.PR@kctcs.edu
Web Site: www.pccky.com
Management:
  Chairman/Director: Gail Robinson
Founded: 1983
Performs At: Auditorium
Type of Stage: Proscenium
Seating Capacity: 500

7108
EATSERN KENTUCKY UNIVERSITY ALUMNI COLISEUM
521 Lancaster Avenue
Richmond, KY 40475
Phone: 859-622-2122
Fax: 859-622-5108
Web Site: www.ekusports.com
Management:
  Athletic Director: John J Shafer
  Busines Manager: David Parke
Founded: 1963
Paid Staff: 2
Volunteer Staff: 4

Louisiana

7109
RAPIDES COLISEUM
5600 Coliseum Boulevard
Alexandria, LA 71303
Phone: 318-442-9581
Fax: 318-442-9582
Web Site: www.louisianarangers.com
Management:
  Executive Director: Don Guillory
Seating Capacity: 6,000

7110
ALEX BOX STADIUM
Louisiana State University
S Stadium Drive
Baton Rouge, LA 70803
Phone: 225-578-8226
Fax: 225-578-2430
e-mail: jkersh2@lsu.edu
Web Site: www.lsu.sports.net
Officers:
  President: F. King Alexander
Management:
  General Manager: Michael Derr
Founded: 1938
Status: Non-Profit, Professional
Seating Capacity: 7,760

7111
LSU UNION THEATER
Louisiana State University
Raphael Semmes Road
Baton Rouge, LA 70803-2504
Phone: 225-578-5128
Fax: 225-578-0612
e-mail: mderr@lsu.edu
Web Site: www.lsu.edu
Officers:
  President: F. King Alexander
Management:
  General Manager: Michael Derr
Mission: The generation, preservation, dissemination, and application of knowledge and cultivation of the arts for the benefit of the people of the state, the nation, and the global community.
Founded: 1861
Seating Capacity: 1,250

7112
PETE MARAVICH ASSEMBLY CENTER
Louisiana State University
N Stadium Drive
Baton Rouge, LA 70803

FACILITIES / Louisiana

Phone: 225-578-8205
Fax: 225-578-8437
e-mail: jkersh2@lsu.edu
Web Site: www.lsu.sports.net
Officers:
    President: F. King Alexander
Management:
    General Manager: Michael Derr
Founded: 1972
Status: For-Profit, Non-Professional
Paid Staff: 15
Seating Capacity: 4,500 - 14,164

7113
RIVER CENTER ARENA
275 S River Road
Baton Rouge, LA 70802
Phone: 225-389-3030
Fax: 225-389-4954
Web Site: www.brcentroplex.com
Seating Capacity: 8,500 - 12,000

7114
RIVER CENTER EXHIBITION HALL
275 S River Road
Baton Rouge, LA 70810
Phone: 225-389-3030
Fax: 225-389-4954
Web Site: www.brcentroplex.com
Type of Stage: 70,000 Sq Ft

7115
RIVER CENTER GRAND BALLROOM
275 S River Road
Baton Rouge, LA 70810
Phone: 225-389-3030
Fax: 225-389-4954
Web Site: www.brcentroplex.com
Seating Capacity: 2,100

7116
RIVER CENTER THEATRE FOR PERFORMING ARTS
275 S River Road
Baton Rouge, LA 70802
Phone: 225-389-3030
Fax: 225-389-4954
Web Site: www.brcentroplex.com
Founded: 1977
Seating Capacity: 1,900

7117
TIGER STADIUM
Louisiana State University
Athletic Department
Baton Rouge, LA 70894-5095
Mailing Address: LSU Athletics Administration Building, Baton Rouge, LA 70803
Phone: 225-578-8001
Fax: 225-388-2430
e-mail: jkersh2@lsu.edu
Web Site: www.lsu.sports.net
Officers:
    President: F. King Alexander
Management:
    General Manager: Michael Derr
Founded: 1924
Seating Capacity: 91,600

7118
EUNICE PLAYERS THEATRE
PO Box 306
Eunice, LA 70535
Phone: 337-546-0163
Fax: 337-457-3081
Management:
    President: David Manuel
Founded: 1970
Status: Non-Profit, Non-Professional

7119
GRAMBLING UNIVERSITY MEMORIAL GYMNASIUM
403 Main Street
PO Box 1193
Grambling, LA 71245
Phone: 318-247-3811
Fax: 318-274-6053
Toll-free: 800-694-14
e-mail: admission@gram.edu
Web Site: www.gram.edu
Officers:
    President: Frank G. Pogue
Management:
    University President: Horece Judson
    Human Resources Director: Karen Emmanuel
    Facility Director: Mark Blake
    Associate Director: Betty Jones
Founded: 1901
Status: Non-Profit, Professional
Paid Staff: 15
Seating Capacity: 2,200

7120
SOUTHEASTERN LOUISIANA UNIVERSITY STRAWBERRY STADIUM
910 Galloway Drive
Hammond, LA 70402
Mailing Address: PO Box 309
Phone: 504-549-2253
Fax: 504-549-2253
Management:
    Director: Tom Douple
Founded: 1936
Seating Capacity: 7,400

7121
SOUTHEASTERN LOUISIANA UNIVERSITY CENTER
800 W University Avenue
SLU 10309
Hammond, LA 70402
Phone: 985-549-3819
Fax: 985-549-5383
Web Site: www.southeastern.edu/admin/uc/
Officers:
    President: Micheeal R. Moffett
Management:
    Head Basketball Coach (M): Bill Kennedy
    Director: Larry M Hymel
    Athletic Director: Frank Pergolizzi
    Head Basketball Coach (W): Lori Davis Jones
    Event Operations Coordinator: Tiffany Rauschkolb
Founded: 1982
Status: Nonprofit, Non-Professional
Paid Staff: 60
Seating Capacity: 7,500

7122
HOUMA TERREBONNE CIVIC CENTER
346 Civic Center Boulevard
Houma, LA 70360
Phone: 985-850-4657
Fax: 985-850-4663
Toll-free: 888-714-22
e-mail: info@houmaciviccenter.com
Web Site: www.houmaciviccenter.com
Management:
    Director: Janel Ricca
    Buisness Manager: Christopher Moore
    Event Coordinator: Stacey Martin
    Marketing Manager: Celeste Breaux
Utilizes: Original Music Scores; Theatre Companies
Paid Staff: 15
Annual Attendance: 200,000+
Facility Category: Civic Center
Type of Stage: Portable
Stage Dimensions: 40x80x150
Seating Capacity: 5,000
Year Built: 1999
Cost: $20 million
Rental Contact: Linda McCarthy

7123
BLACKHAM COLISEUM
University of Louisiana
2330 Johnston Street
Lafayette, LA 70506
Phone: 337-482-2001
Fax: 337-482-5830
Web Site: facilities.louisiana.edu/resource-center/building-physical-addresses
Management:
    General Manager: Joseph Evans
Founded: 1894
Status: Non-Profit, Non-Professional
Seating Capacity: 9,800

7124
CAJUN STADIUM
University of Southwestern Louisiana
Lafayette, LA 70506

Management:
    General Manager: Mike Broussard
Mission: UL football
Founded: 1971
Seating Capacity: 31,000

7125
CAJUNDOME AND CONVENTION CENTER
444 Cajundome Boulevard
Lafayette, LA 70506
Phone: 337-265-2100
Fax: 337-265-2311
e-mail: pdeville@cajundome.com
Web Site: www.cajundome.com
Management:
    Business Director: Giselle Cormier
    Assistant Director: Pam DeVille
    Marketing Manager: Heidi Champagne
Founded: 1984
Seating Capacity: 13,232

7126
HEYMANN PERFORMING ARTS CONVENTION CENTER
1373 South College Road
Lafayette, LA 70503
Phone: 337-291-5540
Fax: 337-291-5580
e-mail: eplumbar@lafayettegov.net
Web Site: www.heymann-center.com/

FACILITIES / Louisiana

Management:
  Manager: Frank Bradshaw
  Box Office Manager: Elnora Plumbar
  Event Coordinator: Phillip Lukinovich
  Stage Manager: Dennis Skerrett
Mission: Located within the center of Lafayette, the Heymann Performing Arts Center is a theatre with a seating capacity of 2,230. Located adjacent to Lafayette's Oil Center, the auditorium provides bi-monthly performances by the Acadiana Symphony, a Broadway series and dozens of other community functions throughout the year.
Status: Non-Profit, Non-Professional
Paid Staff: 10

7127
LAFAYETTE COMMUNITY THEATRE
529 Jefferson Street
Lafayette, LA 70501
Phone: 318-235-1532

7128
ARTISTS CIVIC THEATRE AND STUDIO
One Reid Street
PO Box 278, Lake Charles
Lake Charles, LA 70601
Phone: 337-433-2287
e-mail: mail@actstheatre.com
Web Site: www.actstheatre.com
Officers:
  President: Mark Bowling
  VP: David Hamilton
  Treasurer: Anita Fields-Gold
  Secretary: Anjo Elsbury
Management:
  Director: Kris Perez Webster
  Guest Director: Walt Kiser
Specialized Field: Community Theatre
Organization Type: Performing; Educational

7129
BURTON COLISEUM
McNeese State University
7001 Gulf Highway
Lake Charles, LA 70607
Phone: 337-562-4040
Fax: 337-562-4070
Toll-free: 800-223-52
e-mail: webmaster@mcneese.edu
Web Site: www.mcneesesports.cstv.com/facilities/mcne-mbb.html
Officers:
  President: Philip Williams
  VP & Provost: Jeanne Daboval
Management:
  Executive Director: Mark Ethridge
  CHIEF DIVERSITY OFFICER: Michael Snowden
  Internal Auditor: Victoria Roach
Founded: 1976
Status: Non-Profit, Non-Professional
Paid Staff: 10
Seating Capacity: 8,000

7130
COWBOY STADIUM
McNeese State University
4205 Ryan Street, Lake Charles
Lake Charles, LA 70609
Phone: 337-475-5000
Fax: 337-475-5202
Toll-free: 800-622-3352
Web Site: www.mcneese.edu
Officers:
  President: Philip Williams
  VP & Provost: Jeanne Daboval
Management:
  Director: John Suydam
  CHIEF DIVERSITY OFFICER: Michael Snowden
  Internal Auditor: Victoria Roach

7131
LAKE CHARLES CIVIC CENTER - JAMES E SUDDUTH COLISEUM
900 Lakeshore Drive
PO Box 900, Lake Charles
Lake Charles, LA 70602
Phone: 337-491-1256
Fax: 337-491-1534
e-mail: mayorsactionline@cityoflc.us
Web Site: www.cityoflakecharles.com
Management:
  Director: Joe Toups
  Operations: Don Zimmerman
  Building Supervisor: Roger Sensat
  Marketing Manager: James Mayo
Seating Capacity: 7,450

7132
LAKE CHARLES CIVIC CENTER - EXHIBITION HALL
900 Lakeshore Drive
PO Box 900, Lake Charles
Lake Charles, LA 70602
Phone: 337-491-1256
Fax: 337-491-1534
e-mail: mayorsactionline@cityoflc.us
Web Site: www.cityoflakecharles.com
Management:
  Director: Joe Toups
  Operations: Don Zimmerman
  Building Supervisor: Roger Sensat
  Marketing Manager: James Mayo
Mission: The Civic Center structure is a 3-level, 3-part complex housing the Rosa Hart Theatre, which has a fixed seating capacity of 2000, the Contraband and Jean Lafitte Rooms have a capacity of up to 500 each, the Buccaneer has a capacity of up to 1000, the Exhibition Hall has a capacity of up to 1400, and the James E. Sudduth Coliseum has a capacity of 8000.

7133
LAKE CHARLES CIVIC CENTER - ROSA HART THEATRE
900 Lakeshore Drive
PO Box 900, Lake Charles
Lake Charles, LA 70602
Phone: 337-491-1256
Fax: 337-491-1534
e-mail: mayorsactionline@cityoflc.us
Web Site: www.cityoflakecharles.com
Management:
  Director: Joe Toups
  Operations: Don Zimmerman
  Building Supervisor: Roger Sensat
  Marketing Manager: James Mayo
Seating Capacity: 2,050

7134
FANT-EWING COLISEUM
University of Louisiana at Monroe
700 University Avenue
Monroe, LA 71209
Phone: 318-342-1000
Web Site: www.ulmathletics.com
Officers:
  President: James E Cofer Sr
Management:
  Athletic Director: Bobby Staub
  Marketing Director: Patti Thrumon
  Executive Director: Toni Bacon
Paid Staff: 50
Type of Stage: Wood
Seating Capacity: 8,000

7135
MALONE STADIUM
University of Louisiana at Monroe
700 University Ave
Monroe, LA 71209
Phone: 318-342-1000
Fax: 318-342-5367
Web Site: www.nlu.edu
Officers:
  President: Nick J. Bruno
  VP: Eric Pani
Management:
  Chief Business Officer: William T. Graves
  Director Of Athletics: Bobby Staub
Mission: Named in memory of James L Malone, the University of Louisiana/Monroe's winningest football coach, the first game was played on September 16, 1978. The seating capacity of the stadium is 30,427.
Founded: 1978
Status: Non-Profit, Professional
Paid Staff: 50
Paid Artists: 10

7136
MONROE CIVIC CENTER
401 Lea Joyner Memorial Expressway
Monroe, LA 71201
Phone: 318-329-2225
Fax: 318-329-2548
Web Site: www.ci.monroe.la.us/civiccenter.php
Management:
  Director: Charles Tomas
  Marketing Manager: Melissa Thaxton
  Event Coordinator: Sharon Traxler
  Office Administrator: Katrina Chilton
  Technical Director: Chris Kidd
Mission: The Arena provides 44,000 square feet of exhibit space and seats 5,600 (Standard Concert Configuration). Larger Capacities available for events in the round. The Arena may be used for a multitude of events including Concerts, Large Banquets, Basketball, Circuses, Ice Events, Trade Shows, and Rodeos.

7137
PRATHER COLISEUM
NSU Athletic Department
Natchitoches, LA 71497
Phone: 318-357-5251
Fax: 318-357-4221
Web Site: www.nsudemons.com
Management:
  Director of Athletic Facilities: Charles Bourg
  Director of Sports Information: Doug Ireland
  Vice President External Affairs: Jerry Pierce
Mission: Prather Coliseum, an athletic facility for sporting events in basketball, volleyball and soccer, is the home of the Louisiana Sports Hall of Fame and the Graduate N Club Hall of Fame.
Founded: 1894
Status: For-Profit, Professional
Paid Staff: 80
Seating Capacity: 3,500

FACILITIES / Louisiana

7138
TURPIN STADIUM
Northweatern Stare University
Nsu Athletic Field House
Natchitoches, LA 71497
Phone: 318-357-5251
Fax: 318-357-4221
Web Site: www.nsudemons.com
Management:
   VP: Jerry Pierce
   Director Athletics: Greg Burke
   Associate Director: Donnie Cox
   Business Manager: Roxanne Freeman
Seating Capacity: 16,000

7139
CONTEMPORARY ARTS CENTER
900 Camp Street
New Orleans, LA 70130
Phone: 504-528-3805
Fax: 504-528-3828
e-mail: info@cacno.org
Web Site: www.cacno.org
Officers:
   CEO: Neil Barclay
   VP: Stephanie Huger
   Chair: Steve Dumez
   Vice Chair: Gregg Porter
   Treasurer: Debbie Brockley
   Secretary: Stephanie Huger
Management:
   Executive Director: Jay Weigel
   CFO: Glenn W. Gruber
   Associate Director: Merit Shalett
   External Affairs Coordinator: Allison Abney
Founded: 1976
Status: Non-Profit, Professional
Paid Staff: 30
Type of Stage: Concert Stage; Flexible
Seating Capacity: 200-3,500

7140
KIEFER UNO LAKEFRONT ARENA
University of New Orleans
6801 Franklin Avenue
New Orleans, LA 70122
Phone: 504-280-7171
Fax: 540-280-7178
e-mail: arena@uno.edu
Web Site: www.arena.uno.edu
Officers:
   General Manager: Marco A. Perez
Management:
   Assistant General Manager: David P. Armond
   Facilities Manager: David L. Lendermon
   Business Manager: Stephanie Parrino
   Concessions Manager: Lucas Funderburk
Seating Capacity: 10,000

7141
LE PETIT THEATRE DU VIEUX CARRE
616 St Peter
New Orleans, LA 70116
Phone: 504-522-2081
Fax: 504-524-9027
e-mail: info@lepetittheatre.com
Web Site: www.lepetittheatre.com
Officers:
   Chair: Bruce R. Hoefer
   Vice - Chair: Jackie Clarkson
   Secretary: Kathleen Van Horn
   Treasurer: Leon Contavesprie
Management:
   Executive Director: Cassie Steck Worley
   Managing Director: Jim Word
   Executive Artistic Director: Sonny Borey
   Technical Director: Bill Walker
   Box Office Manager: Jenny Richardson
   House Manager: Linda Wegmann
Founded: 1917
Specialized Field: Community/Regional Theatre
Status: Non-Profit, Non-Professional
Paid Staff: 11
Seating Capacity: 325

7142
LOUIS J. ROUSSEL PERFORMANCE CENTER
Loyola University
6363 Saint Charles Avenue
New Orleans, LA 70118
Phone: 504-865-3240
Toll-free: 800-569-52
e-mail: music@loyno.edu
Web Site: www.loyno.edu
Officers:
   President: Kevin Wildes
Management:
   Finance And Administration: Jay Calamia
   Financial Affairs: Leon Mathes
   Director: Ric Bell
   Bursar: Shannon Duplantis
Seating Capacity: 600

7143
LOUISIANA SUPERDOME
Sugar Bowl Drive
New Orleans
New Orleans, LA 70112
Phone: 504-587-3663
Fax: 504-587-3848
Toll-free: 800-567-74
Web Site: www.superdome.com
Management:
   General Manager: Glenn Menard
   Assistant General Manager: Danny Vincens
   Media Relations Coordinator: Bill Curl
Founded: 1975
Type of Stage: Concert Stage
Seating Capacity: 87,500
Year Built: 1975
Year Remodeled: 1997

7144
LOYOLA UNIVERSITY THEATRE
Loyola University
Loyola University
6363 Saint Charles Avenue
New Orleans, LA 70118
Phone: 504-865-3240
Fax: 504-865-2284
Toll-free: 800-569-52
e-mail: drama@loyno.edu
Web Site: www.loyno.edu
Officers:
   President: Kevin Wildes
Management:
   Finance And Administration: Jay Calamia
   Financial Affairs: Leon Mathes
   Director: Ric Bell
   Bursar: Shannon Duplantis
Mission: The mission of the Department of Theatre Arts and Dance at Loyola University New Orleans is to educate and develop the whole person, focusing on undergraduate education that prepares students for meaningful lives, professional accomplishments, and responsible world citizenship. The Department distinguishes itself as a noteworthy center of learning by creating and structuring a collaborative learning environment.
Specialized Field: Theatre Arts; Dance
Status: Non-Profit, Non-Professional
Paid Staff: 14
Affiliations: ATHE; USITT
Type of Stage: Proscenium; Flexible Theatre
Seating Capacity: 150

7145
MAHALIA JACKSON THEATRE OF PERFORMING ARTS
New Orleans Cultural Center
1419 Basin Street
New Orleans, LA 70116
Phone: 504-287-0351
Fax: 504-565-7477
e-mail: kturner@neworleansculturalcenter.com
Web Site: www.mahaliajacksontheater.com/
Management:
   General Manager: David Skinner
   Director Operations: E.P. Miller
   Office Manager: Margo Baum
Seating Capacity: 2,300

7146
MORRIS FX JEFF SR MUNICIPAL AUDITORIUM
New Orleans Cultural Center
1201 Saint Peter Street
New Orleans, LA 70116
Phone: 504-218-0150
Fax: 504-218-0160
Management:
   Executive Director: Gene Blaun
Founded: 1930
Status: Non-profit, Professional
Paid Staff: 20
Seating Capacity: 6,500

7147
SMOOTHIE KING CENTER
1501 Dave Dixon Drive
New Orleans, LA 70113
Mailing Address: PO Box 52439 New Orleans, LA 70152
Phone: 504-587-3663
Fax: 504-587-3848
Toll-free: 800-756-7074
e-mail: comments@smgneworleans.com
Web Site: www.neworleansarena.com
Management:
   Assistant General Manager: Mike Schilling
   General Manager: Glenn Menard
Founded: 1999
Seating Capacity: 17,232

7148
SAENGER THEATRE
1111 Canal St.
New Orleans, LA 70112
Phone: 504-525-1052
Fax: 504-569-1533
e-mail: dskinner@acetheatregroup.com
Web Site: www.saengernola.com
Management:
   Booking Manager: Patricia Baham
   General Manager: David Skinner
   Associate General Manager: Debra Gonzales
   Office Manager: Kimmie Tubre
   Director of Marketing - Concerts &: Kym Atkins
   Director of Marketing - Broadway: Jean McIver

FACILITIES / Louisiana

Founded: 1927
Status: For-Profit, Professional
Paid Staff: 14
Seating Capacity: 2,794
Year Built: 1927
Year Remodeled: 2013

7149
STATE PALACE THEATRE
1108 Canal Street
PO Box 55278
New Orleans, LA 70112
Fax: 504-522-5880
e-mail: brunet-co@att.net
Web Site: www.statepalace.com
Management:
  Director/Booking: Robert Brunet
  Theatre Manager: Douglas Castro
Seating Capacity: 3,000

7150
TULANE UNIVERSITY ALBERT LUPIN EXPERIMENTAL THEATRE
Department of Theatre and Dance
215 McWilliams Hall
New Orleans, LA 70118
Phone: 504-314-7760
Fax: 504-865-6737
Toll-free: 800-873-9283
e-mail: tutd@tulane.edu
Web Site: www.tulane.edu
Officers:
  Managing Director, Shakespeare Fest: Clare Moncrief
  Executive Secretary for Theatre Pro: Gaynell Robinson-Watkins
  Executive Secretary for Dance Progr: Elizabeth Stewart-Ackers
Management:
  CFO: Anthony Lorino
  Executive Assistnat: Frances Vickers
  Costume Shop Supervisor: Cassandra Paine
  Production and Operations Manager: Ardice Cotter
  Assistant Technical Director/Scene: David Raphel
Founded: 1937
Performs At: Albert Lupin Experimental Theatre, Dixon Hall
Type of Stage: Proscenium; Black Box
Seating Capacity: 1,000

7151
TULANE UNIVERSITY DEPARTMENT OF THEATRE AND DANCE
Tulane University
6823 St. Charles Avenue
215 McWilliams Hall
New Orleans, LA 70118
Phone: 504-314-7760
Fax: 504-865-6737
Toll-free: 800-873-9283
e-mail: tutd@tulane.edu
Web Site: www.tulane.edu/liberal-arts/theatre-dance/
Officers:
  Managing Director, Shakespeare Fest: Clare Moncrief
  Executive Secretary for Theatre Pro: Gaynell Robinson-Watkins
  Executive Secretary for Dance Progr: Elizabeth Stewart-Ackers
Management:
  CFO: Anthony Lorino
  Executive Assistnat: Frances Vickers
  Costume Shop Supervisor: Cassandra Paine
  Production and Operations Manager: Ardice Cotter
  Assistant Technical Director/Scene: David Raphel
Founded: 1834
Seating Capacity: 3,600

7152
UNIVERSITY OF NEW ORLEANS PERFORMING ARTS CENTER
Lakefront
2000 Lakeshore Drive
New Orleans, LA 70148
Phone: 504-280-6317
Fax: 504-280-6318
Toll-free: 888-514-4275
e-mail: cola@uno.edu
Web Site: www.uno.edu
Officers:
  President: Peter J. Fos
Management:
  Business Manager: Donna Burroughs
  Director: Lindsey Hamlin
Founded: 1956

7153
AILLET STADIUM
1450 W Alabama
Ruston, LA 71272
Phone: 318-257-3144
Fax: 318-257-3456
Management:
  Director Athletic Facilities: Tommy Sisemore
Founded: 1968
Seating Capacity: 30,200

7154
HOWARD CENTER FOR PERFORMING ARTS
Louisiana Tech University
Corner of Arizona & Adams
Ruston, LA 71272
Mailing Address: PO Box 8608
Phone: 318-257-3036
Fax: 318-257-4571
e-mail: krobbins@latech.edu
Web Site: www.performingarts.latech.edu
Management:
  Executive Director: Erica Griessel
  Associate Director: Eileen McMillen
  Director: Mark Guinn
  Coordinator of Music: Randall Sorensen
  SPA Administrative Assistant: Mary Roberts
  Band Administrative Assistant: Toni Troiano
  Associate Director of Bands: Lawrence Gibbs
Founded: 1898
Paid Staff: 6
Annual Attendance: 2,000
Type of Stage: Proscenium
Seating Capacity: 150
Year Built: 1938
Year Remodeled: 2001

7155
THOMAS ASSEMBLY CENTER
Louisiana Tech University
PO Box 3042
Ruston, LA 71272
Phone: 318-257-4111
Fax: 318-257-4437
Management:
  Manager: Tommy Sisemore
Seating Capacity: 8,698

7156
CENTENARY COLLEGE RECITAL HALL
Hurley School of Music
2911 Centenary Blvd
Shreveport, LA 71104
Phone: 318-869-5235
Fax: 318-869-5248
Toll-free: 800-234-4448
e-mail: music@centenary.edu
Web Site: www.centenary.edu
Officers:
  President: David Rowe
Management:
  Provost: Michael Hemphill
  Dean: Melva Williams
  Director: Edward Ragan
Founded: 1852
Status: Non-Profit, Professional
Paid Staff: 35
Paid Artists: 12

7157
HIRSCH MEMORIAL COLISEUM
State Fair of Louisiana
3701 Hudson Avenue
Shreveport, LA 71109
Phone: 318-635-1361
Fax: 318-631-4909
e-mail: info@statefairoflouisiana.com
Web Site: www.statefairoflouisiana.com
Officers:
  President: Chris Giordano
  Chairman: Bill Montgomery
  Secretary/Treasurer: James Elrod
Management:
  General Manager: Chris Giordano
  Livestock Manager: Mohamed Shamsie
Mission: To serve as the State Fair of Louisiana's prime facility; to host-year round events such as major concerts, circuses, rodeos, ice shows, sporting events and motor thrill shows.
Founded: 1954
Status: Non-Profit
Paid Staff: 10
Budget: $80,000
Income Sources: Concerts; Rodeos; Circuses
Annual Attendance: 300,000
Facility Category: Multi-Purpose
Type of Stage: Portable
Seating Capacity: 10,300
Year Built: 1954
Year Remodeled: 1994
Cost: $300,000
Rental Contact: Mary M Gasper

7158
RIVERVIEW HALL & THEATER
600 Clyde Fant Parkway
Shreveport, LA 71101
Phone: 318-673-5100
Fax: 318-673-5105
e-mail: spar@ci.shreveport.la.us
Web Site: www.ci.shreveport.la.us
Management:
  Airport Authority: William Cooksey
  Finance: Charles Madden
Specialized Field: Municipal Performance Theater
Status: Non-Profit, Professional
Paid Staff: 50
Type of Stage: Proscenium
Stage Dimensions: 49 x 41

FACILITIES / Maine

Seating Capacity: 1,725
Year Built: 1965
Year Remodeled: 1997

7159
SHREVEPORT MUNICIPAL AUDITORIUM
705 Elvis Presley Avenue
Shreveport, LA 71101
Phone: 318-841-4000
Fax: 318-841-4040
e-mail: eroberts@shreveportcenter.com
Web Site: www.shreveportmunicipalauditorium.com
Officers:
   President: Louise Burton
   VP: Janie Landry
   Secretary: Becky Johnson
Founded: 1900
Status: Non-Profit, Professional
Type of Stage: Proscenium
Stage Dimensions: 58'x 29'x 37'
Seating Capacity: 3,007
Year Built: 1929

7160
STRAND THEATRE
619 Louisiana Avenue
PO Box 1547
Shreveport, LA 71165
Phone: 318-226-1481
Fax: 318-424-5434
Toll-free: 800-313-6373
e-mail: strand@thestrandtheatre.com
Web Site: www.thestrandtheatre.com
Officers:
   President: Ron Weems
   Executive Director: Danny Fogger
Management:
   Technical Director: Bill Gaston
   Assistant Director: Lily Herd
   Executive Director: Danny Fogger
   General Manager: Jenifer Hill
   Administration: Teresa Carmack
   Director of Finance: Cheri Holley
   BOX OFFICE MANAGER: Stacy Dickerson
Founded: 1925

7161
NICHOLLS STATE UNIVERSITY GYM
906 East 1st St
Thibodaux, LA 70310
Mailing Address: P. O. Box 2701, Thibodaux, LA 70310
Phone: 985-493-2746
Fax: 985-493-2740
Toll-free: 877-642-6557
e-mail: rachel.dufrene@nicholls.edu
Web Site: www.nicholls.edu
Officers:
   President: Dr. Bruce T. Murphy
Management:
   Director: Michael Matherne
   Assistant Director: Sabrina Laurent
   Fitness and Wellness Coordinator: Kat Harrell Slosarek
   Intramural Coordinator: Kristen Fillmore
   Administrative Coordinator: Rachel Dufrene
Founded: 1948
Seating Capacity: 15,500

Maine

7162
AUGUSTA CIVIC CENTER NORTH STAGE
16 Cony Street
Augusta, ME 04330
Mailing Address: City of Augusta,City Center Plaza, 16 Cony Street, Augusta,
Phone: 207-626-2405
Fax: 207-626-5968
e-mail: info@augustaciviccenter.org
Web Site: www.augustaciviccenter.org
Management:
   Director: Dana Colwill
   Office Manager: Betty L Brann
   Reservation Coordinator: Nancy M Dumont
Mission: To promote and facilitate various events and group functions in order to enhance area trade and commerce.
Seating Capacity: 6,433

7163
AUGUSTA CIVIC CENTER ARENA CENTER STAGE
16 Cony Street
Augusta, ME 04330
Mailing Address: City of Augusta,City Center Plaza, 16 Cony Street, Augusta,
Phone: 207-626-2405
Fax: 207-626-5968
e-mail: info@augustaciviccenter.org
Web Site: www.augustaciviccenter.org
Management:
   Director: Dana Colwill
Seating Capacity: 7,264

7164
AUGUSTA CIVIC CENTER HALF HOUSE CONCERT STAGE
16 Cony Street
Augusta, ME 04330
Mailing Address: City of Augusta,City Center Plaza, 16 Cony Street, Augusta,
Phone: 207-626-2405
Fax: 207-626-5968
e-mail: info@augustaciviccenter.org
Web Site: www.augustaciviccenter.org
Management:
   Director: Dana Colwill
Seating Capacity: 3,653

7165
BANGOR CIVIC CENTER & AUDITORIUM
515 Main Street
Bangor, ME 04401
Phone: 207-947-5555
Fax: 207-947-5105
Toll-free: 800-745-300
Web Site: www.bangorciviccenter.com
Management:
   General Manager: Joe Imbriaco
   Box Office Manager: Chris Sun
   Event Manager: Jake Crumb
   Event Manager: Dan Gearin
Mission: To serve as Maine's premier multi-purpose convention, tradeshow, meeting and entertainment show place.
Founded: 1954
Type of Stage: Portable
Seating Capacity: 6,000

7166
MORRELL GYM
Bowdoin College Department of Athletics
9000 College Station
Brunswick, ME 04011
Phone: 207-725-3326
Fax: 207-725-3019
e-mail: jcaton@bowdoin.edu
Web Site: www.bowdoin.edu
Officers:
   President: Barry Mills
Management:
   Director of Athletic Training: Dan Davies
   Head Coach: Mike Connnolly
   Assistant Coach: KJ Krasco
Seating Capacity: 2,000

7167
PICKARD THEATRE
Bowdoin College
9000 College Station
Brunswick, ME 04011
Phone: 207-725-3326
Fax: 207-725-3019
e-mail: jcaton@bowdoin.edu
Web Site: www.bowdoin.edu/theater-dance/facilities/pickard-theater.shtml
Officers:
   President: Don Gerrish
   VP: Robert Magnus
Management:
   Assistant Professor of Dance: Charlotte Griffin
   Senior Lecturer in Dance Performanc: Gwyneth Jones
   Visiting Assistant Professor of Dan: Nyama McCarthy-Brown
   Senior Lecturer in Dance Performanc: Paul Sarvis
   Visiting Assis Professor: Kathryn Syssoyeva
Mission: Historic Pickard Theater, located on the beautiful Bowdoin College campus within walking distance of downtown Brunswick, was originally constructed to honor the memory of the Bowdoin students who served on both sides during the Civil War. Maine State Music Theatre had its genesis at The Pickard in 1959. The theatre is air-conditioned and offers comfortable seating with an excellent view of the stage.
Founded: 1794
Status: Non-Profit, Non-Professional
Paid Staff: 10
Type of Stage: Proscenium
Seating Capacity: 600

7168
CAMDEN OPERA HOUSE
29 Elm St.
Camden, ME 04843
Mailing Address: PO Box 1207, Camden, ME. 04843
Phone: 207-236-7963
Fax: 207-236-7956
e-mail: dmorrison@camdenmaine.gov
Web Site: www.camdenoperahouse.com
Officers:
   President: Jean Friedman White
Management:
   Manager: Kerry Hadley
Mission: Elegant, historic yet practical facility for rental; providing affordable space for local nonprofit groups to perform and meet; conference and meeting facility, wedding parties.
Founded: 1894

FACILITIES / Maine

Specialized Field: Theatre; Concerts; and Conference Rentals
Status: Non-Profit, Professional
Paid Staff: 2
Volunteer Staff: 12
Budget: $100,000
Income Sources: Rentals; Show Production
Performs At: Proscenium Stage w/Thrust
Annual Attendance: 12,000
Facility Category: Performing Arts
Type of Stage: Thrust
Stage Dimensions: 37'x34'
Seating Capacity: 500
Year Built: 1894
Year Remodeled: 1994
Cost: $250-$800+
Rental Contact: Kenny Hedley
Resident Groups: Maine Grand Opera

7169
OLIN ARTS CENTER
Bates College
2 Andrews Road
Lewiston, ME 04240
Phone: 207-786-6255
Fax: 207-786-8335
Web Site: www.bates.edu/music/about/olin-arts-center
Officers:
   President: A. Clayton Spencer
   VP for Academic Affairs: Matthew Auer
   Vice President for College Advancem: Sarah R. Pearson
   Chief of Staff to the President and: Michael S. Hussey
   Vice President for Finance & Admini: Terry J. Beckmann
Management:
   Dean of Students: Tedd R. Goundle
   Associate Vice President for Commun: Margaret B. Kimmel
   Dean of Admission and Financial Aid: Leigh A. Weisenburger
Mission: addition to the Bates College Museum of Art and a 300-seat concert hall, Olin houses a slide library, classrooms, faculty offices, individual and group practice rooms for musicians, art studios (including a drawing studio with a panoramic view of Lake Andrews), and two photographic darkrooms.
Year Built: 1986

7170
UNIVERSITY OF MAINE PERFORMING ARTS CENTER
University of Maine at Machias
116 O'Brien Avenue
Machias, ME 04654
Phone: 207-255-1200
Fax: 207-255-4864
e-mail: stewartb@maine.edu
Web Site: www.umm.maine.edu
Officers:
   President: Cynthia E. Huggins
Mission: Host to many campus and community meetings, seminars, festivals and performing arts. Also the home of the UMM Theater and Music Programs, as well as the Down River Theater production company and the Maine Youth Summer Theater Institute. Presents a variety of dramas, comedies and musicals.
Founded: 1909
Facility Category: Amphitheater
Seating Capacity: 358
Organization Type: Amphitheater Auditorium

7171
JOHN LANE'S OGUNQUIT PLAYHOUSE
10 Main Street - Rt 1
Ogunquit, ME 03907
Mailing Address: PO Box 1510, Ogunquit, ME 03907
Phone: 207-646-2402
Fax: 207-646-4732
e-mail: boxoffice@ogunquitplayhouse.org
Web Site: www.ogunquitplayhouse.org
Officers:
   President: Fran Spechts
   President: Eileen Eberhart
   Treasurer: Mark K. Forsyth
   Clerk/Secretary: Michael O. Severance
Management:
   Executive Artistic Director: Bradford T Kenney
   Director of Finance and Administrat: Leslie Randazzo M.S.
   Director of Facilities and Real Est: Peter Lewis
   Asstnt Executive Artistic Director: Jean Benda
   Front of House Coordinator: Sandi Clark
Founded: 1933
Year Built: 1933

7172
COLLINS CENTER FOR THE ARTS
Universty Of Maine
5746 Collins Center For The Arts
Orono, ME 04469
Phone: 207-581-1805
Fax: 207-581-1837
Toll-free: 877-486-2364
e-mail: john.patches@umit.maine.edu
Web Site: www.collinscenterforthearts.com/index.php
Management:
   Executive Director: Daniel Williams
   Associate Director, CCA: Adele Adkins
   Managre Of Theater Operations: Joe Cota
   Ticket Services Director: Mary Addison
   Box Office Assistant: Susan Melvin
Mission: Venue located in the center thatis available is the itchins Concert Hall

7173
MAINE CENTER FOR THE ARTS AT THE UNIVERSITY OF MAINE
5746 Maine Center for the Arts
Orono, ME 04469
Phone: 207-581-1755
Fax: 207-581-1837
Toll-free: 877-486-2364
e-mail: CCATIX@umit.maine.edu
Web Site: www.ume.maine.edu/mca
Officers:
   President: Paul W. Ferguson
Management:
   Executive Director: Daniel Williams
   Associate Director, CCA: Adele Adkins
   Managre Of Theater Operations: Joe Cota
   Ticket Services Director: Mary Addison
   Box Office Assistant: Susan Melvin
Mission: Hosts a wide variety of events, presenting classical and contemporary music, dance, theatre, comedy and lectures.
Founded: 1986
Specialized Field: Performing Arts
Paid Staff: 10
Volunteer Staff: 60
Seating Capacity: 1,629

7174
UNIVERSITY OF MAINE ALUMNI STADIUM
Memorial Gymnasium
Orono, ME 04469
Phone: 207-581-1110
Fax: 207-581-3070
e-mail: CCATIX@umit.maine.edu
Web Site: www.umaine.edu
Officers:
   President: Paul W. Ferguson
Management:
   Administrative and Fiscal Coordinat: Heidi Carlow
   Special Assistant to the President: Suzi Miller
   Administrative Specialist: Alisha Lukas

7175
CUMBERLAND COUNTY CIVIC CENTER
1 Civic Center Square
Portland, ME 04101
Phone: 207-775-3481
Fax: 207-828-8344
Web Site: www.theciviccenter.com
Officers:
   Chair: Dale Olmstead, Jr
   Vice Chair: Neal Pratt
   Treasurer: Richard Ranaghan, Jr
Management:
   General Manager: Steve Crane
   Controller: Mark Eddy
   Box Office Manager: Mark Warner
   Operations Manager: James Leo
   Event Services Director: Roberta Wright
Mission: A multi-purpose entertainment and sports facility that hosts a wide variety of family shows, concerts, sporting events, and trade shows.
Founded: 1977
Paid Staff: 212

7176
HADLOCK FIELD
389 Congress St.
Portland, ME 04101
Phone: 207-874-8200
Fax: 207-874-8130
e-mail: arl@portlandmaine.gov
Web Site: www.portlandevents.com
Management:
   City Manager: Mark Rees
   City Mayor: Michael F. Brennan
   Finance Director: Ellen Sanborn
Founded: 1994
Facility Category: Arena
Type of Stage: Sports Arena
Stage Dimensions: 60x40
Seating Capacity: 7,000
Year Built: 1915
Year Remodeled: 1990

7177
MERRILL AUDITORIUM
389 Congress St.
Portland, ME 04101
Phone: 207-874-8200
Fax: 207-874-8130
Web Site: www.portlandevents.com
Management:
   City Manager: Mark Rees
   City Mayor: Michael F. Brennan
   Finance Director: Ellen Sanborn
Founded: 1997
Status: Non-Profit, Professional

FACILITIES / Maryland

Facility Category: Upscale Arts Facility
Type of Stage: Proscenium
Seating Capacity: 1900
Year Built: 1912
Year Remodeled: 1996

7178
PORTLAND EXPOSITION BUILDING
389 Congress St.
Portland, ME 04101
Phone: 207-874-8200
Fax: 207-874-8130
Web Site: www.portlandevents.com
Officers:
   Division Director: Arthur Stephenson
Management:
   City Manager: Mark Rees
   City Mayor: Michael F. Brennan
   Finance Director: Ellen Sanborn
Founded: 1915
Specialized Field: Series & Festivals; Dance; Instrumental Music; Musical Theatre; Theatrical Group; Vocal Music
Status: Non-Profit, Professional
Facility Category: Arena
Type of Stage: Portable
Stage Dimensions: 60' wide x 40' deep
Seating Capacity: 3,000
Year Built: 1914

7179
STATE THEATRE
609 Congress Street
PO Box 4152
Portland, ME 04101
Phone: 207-780-8265
Web Site: www.liveatthestate.com
Management:
   Owner: Grant Wilson
   House Manager: John Octera
Seating Capacity: 1,750

7180
ROCKPORT OPERA HOUSE
Central St
Rockport, ME 04856
Phone: 207-236-2514
Web Site: www.town.rockport.me.us/operahouse
Management:
   Executive Director: Thomas Wolf
   Administrative Director: Ann Tani
   Director Marketing: Kathy Maloney
Mission: Music, dance, poetry and plays are performed in the air-conditioned auditorium.
Founded: 1961
Type of Stage: Flexible
Seating Capacity: Auditorium 400; Meeting Room 100
Year Built: 1891
Year Remodeled: 1993
Cost: $1 million

7181
CELEBRATION BARN THEATER
190 Stock Farm Road
South Paris, ME 04281
Phone: 207-743-8452
e-mail: info@celebrationbarn.com
Web Site: www.celebrationbarn.com
Officers:
   President: Davis Robinson
   VP: Fritz Grobe
   Secretary: Kavi Montanaro
   Treasurer: Kelsey Goldsmith
   Executive Director: Amanda Huotari
Management:
   Executive Director: Amanda Huotari
Mission: Celebration Barn is a center for creating or performing original theatre. Performances, workshops and residencies are offered May-October.
Utilizes: Actors; Artists-in-Residence; Collaborating Artists; Collaborations; Community Members; Contract Actors; Dance Companies; Dancers; Five Seasonal Concerts; Guest Choreographers; Guest Designers; Guest Directors; Guest Ensembles; Guest Speakers; High School Drama; Instructors; Local Artists; Local Artists & Directors; Local Talent; Lyricists; Multi Collaborations; Original Music Scores; Paid Performers; Poets; Resident Artists; Resident Companies
Founded: 1972
Seating Capacity: 125
Year Built: 1902

7182
STRIDER THEATER
Colby College
4520 Mayflower Hill
Waterville, ME 04901-8845
Phone: 207-859-4520
Fax: 207-859-4533
Web Site: www.colby.edu/theater
Officers:
   Chair: Lynne Conner
Management:
   Chair: Lynne Conner
   Professor: Todd Coulter
   Technical Director: John D. Ervin
Mission: To promote the historical, theoretical, and experiential study of these performing arts as vital and important areas of inquiry for liberal arts students.
Founded: 1817
Status: Non-Profit, Non-Professional
Paid Staff: 9
Facility Category: Proscenium
Type of Stage: Proscenium
Seating Capacity: 262
Year Built: 1976

7183
WATERVILLE OPERA HOUSE
93 Main St.
Waterville, ME 04901
Phone: 207-873-7000
Fax: 207-861-7096
e-mail: operainfo@operahouse.org
Web Site: www.operahouse.com
Officers:
   Chairman: Earle Bessey III
   President: Tom Misner
   Treasurer: Kathleen Livollen
Management:
   Executive Director: Diane Bryan
   Office Manager: Bridgett Campbell
   Development Director: Barbara Allen
   Production Coordinator: Joan Phillips-Sandy
Mission: The purpose of which is to maintain, restore and enhance the Opera House as a public facility for the Arts and cultural enrichment of the community.
Founded: 1902
Status: Nonprofit, Professional
Annual Attendance: 80,000
Type of Stage: Proscenium
Seating Capacity: 924

Maryland

7184
FRANCIS SCOTT KEY AUDITORIUM
60 College Avenue
St. John's College
Annapolis, MD 21401
Phone: 410-626-2547
Fax: 410-626-2885
Web Site: www.sjca.edu/college
Management:
   Facilities Director: Diane Ensor
Founded: 1657
Status: Non-Profit, Non-Professional
Paid Staff: 200
Seating Capacity: 600
Year Built: 1958

7185
MARYLAND HALL FOR THE CREATIVE ARTS
801 Chase Street
Annapolis, MD 21401
Phone: 410-263-5544
Fax: 410-263-5114
Toll-free: 866-438-3808
e-mail: info@mdhallarts.org
Web Site: www.marylandhall.org
Officers:
   President and CEO: Linnell Bowen
   Chairman: Sean M. Looney
   Secretary: Emily (Penny) Evans
   Treasurer: Brian E. Lees
Management:
   Marketing Coordinator: Carling Belden
   Facilities Manager: Dennis Coughlin
   Performing Arts Coordinator: Rebecca Daubney
   Technical Coordinator: Jeanie McAlpine
   Education Coordinator: Leslie Mills
Mission: Provides a broad range of arts-related programming for people of all ages, backgrounds and socio-economic levels.
Founded: 1972
Specialized Field: Theatre; School
Status: Non-Profit, Professional
Paid Staff: 20
Year Built: 1979

7186
US NAVAL ACADEMY ALUMNI HALL
US Naval Academy
121 Blake Road
Annapolis, MD 21402
Phone: 410-293-2234
Fax: 410-293-3218
Web Site: www.usna.edu
Management:
   Manager: Gregory B Zingler
Founded: 1845
Status: Non-Profit, Non-Professional

7187
ARENA PLAYERS PLAYHOUSE
801 McCulloh Street
Baltimore, MD 21201
Phone: 410-728-6500
Fax: 410-383-2692
Web Site: arenaplayersinc.com
Officers:
   Chairman: Edward Smith
Management:
   Managing Director: Rodney Orange
   Artistic Director: Donald Owens

FACILITIES / Maryland

Associate Artistic Director: David D. Mitchell
Youtheater Director: Catherine Orange
Assistant. Youtheater Director: Charlene Williamson

7188
CENTER STAGE
700 North Calvert Street
Baltimore, MD 21202
Phone: 410-986-4000
Fax: 410-539-3912
e-mail: info@centerstage.org
Web Site: www.centerstage.org
Management:
  Associate Managing Director: Del W. Risberg
  Special Assistant to the Managing D: Kevin Maroney
  Artistic Director: Hana Sharif
  Box Office Manager: Mandy Benedix
Mission: An artistically driven institution, producing and developing an eclectic repertory in collaboration with leading theater artists for a diverse audience, interested in challenging, bold, thought-provoking work.
Utilizes: Actors; AEA Actors; Artists-in-Residence; Guest Accompanists; Guest Companies; Guest Conductors; Guest Designers; Guest Instructors; Guest Lecturers; Guest Musical Directors; Guest Soloists; Instructors; Original Music Scores; Performance Artists; Selected Students; Student Interns
Founded: 1963
Budget: $6.2 million
Affiliations: BACVA, Baltimore Tourism Association, Baltimore Theatre Alliance, TCG, AEA
Type of Stage: Semi-Thrust and Flexible
Stage Dimensions: 40'x36' and 67'x118'
Seating Capacity: 541 and 850
Year Remodeled: 2000
Rental Contact: Harry Delair

7189
DUNBAR PERFORMING ARTS CENTER
1400 Orleans Street
Baltimore, MD 21231
Phone: 410-534-6614

7190
FIRST MARINER ARENA
201 W. Baltimore Street
Baltimore, MD 21201
Phone: 410-347-2020
Fax: 410-347-2042
Web Site: www.firstmarinerarena.com
Management:
  General Manager: Donna P Julian
  Contracts Coordinator: Trish Howerton
Founded: 1999
Status: For-Profit, Professional
Performs At: Entertainment; Sports
Seating Capacity: 14,000
Year Built: 1962
Year Remodeled: 1984

7191
JOHNS HOPKINS
Johns Hopkins University
Wolman House
3213 N Charles Street
Baltimore, MD 21218
Phone: 410-516-7159
e-mail: thehop@jhu.edu
Web Site: www.jhu.edu/
Officers:
  President: Ronald J. Daniels
  Vice President and Chief of Staff: Kerry A. Ates
  VP for Communications: Glenn M. Bieler
  VP Investments: Kathryn J. Crecelius
  VP for Facilities and Real Estate: Alan Fish
Management:
  Director: Suzanne Pratt

7192
JOHNS HOPKINS UNIVERSITY HOMEWOOD FIELD
3400 N Charles Street
Baltimore, MD 21218
Phone: 410-516-7490
Fax: 410-516-7482
e-mail: andrew.harrington@jhu.edu
Web Site: www.hopkinssports.com
Officers:
  President: Ronald J. Daniels
  Vice President and Chief of Staff: Kerry A. Ates
  VP for Communications: Glenn M. Bieler
  VP Investments: Kathryn J. Crecelius
  VP for Facilities and Real Estate: Alan Fish
Management:
  Managing Director: Andrew Harrington
  Athletic Director: Tom Calder
Founded: 1876
Specialized Field: Education
Status: Non-Profit, Non-Professional

7193
JOSEPH MEYERHOFF SYMPHONY HALL
1212 Cathedral Street
Baltimore, MD 21201
Phone: 410-783-8100
e-mail: tblumenthal@bsomusic.org
Web Site: www.bsomusic.org
Officers:
  President: Marge Penhallegon
  Secretary: Florence McLean
  Treasurer: Barbara Kelly
  Vice President of Communications an: Kitty Allen
  Vice President of Education: Regina Hartlove
Management:
  Director of Orchestra Personnel: Nishi Badhwar
  Artistic Coordinator : Patrick Chamberlain
  Operations Manager: Anna Harris
  Director of Operations and Faciliti: Tabitha Pfleger
  Assistant Personnel Manager : David George

7194
KRAUSHAAR AUDITORIUM
Goucher College
1021 Delaney Valley Road
Baltimore, MD 21204
Phone: 410-769-5054
Fax: 410-337-6123
Web Site: www.goucher.edu/conferenceservices
Officers:
  Director: Margaret Ermer
  Assistant Director: Ann Grabenstein
Management:
  Director: Margaret Ermer
  Assistant Director: Ann Grabenstein
Seating Capacity: 980

7195
LECLERC AUDITORIUM
College Of Notre Dame Of Maryland
4701 North Charles Street
Baltimore, MD 21210
Phone: 410-532-5732
Fax: 410-532-5790
e-mail: kyendell@ndm.edu
Web Site: www.ndm.edu
Officers:
  President: Joan Develin Coley
  Chair: Patricia J. Mitchell
  Vice Chair: Brenda Jews
  Administrative Coordinator: Laura Beattie-Hoang
  Special Assistant to the President: Candace Caraco
  VP Enrollment Management: Heidi Fletcher
  VP Mission: Eileen O'Dea

7196
LYRIC OPERA HOUSE
140 W Mount Royal Avenue
Baltimore, MD 21201
Phone: 410-685-5086
Fax: 410-332-8234
Web Site: www.lyricoperahouse.com
Management:
  President: Sandy Ichmond
  Executive Director: Tim Kormberger
Founded: 1896
Status: Non-Profit, Professional

7197
MCMANUS THEATER
Loyola College
4501 N Charles Street
Baltimore, MD 21210
Phone: 410-617-2031
Fax: 410-617-5216
Toll-free: 800-221-9107
Web Site: www.loyola.edu
Officers:
  President: Fr Brian Linnane, SJ
Management:
  Event Services Director: Jospeh Bradley
Founded: 1852
Specialized Field: Series & Festivals
Status: Non-Profit, Non-Professional

7198
MEYERHOFF SYMPHONY HALL
1212 Cathedral Street
Baltimore, MD 21201
Phone: 410-783-8000
Fax: 410-783-8004
e-mail: darmor@baltimoresymphony.org
Web Site: www.baltimoresymphony.org
Officers:
  Chair: Barbara Bozzuto
  Secretary: Kathleen A. Chagnon
  Vice Chair: Lainy eBow-Sachs
  President & CEO: Paul Meecham
  Treasurer: Steven R. Schuh
Management:
  House Manager: Allen McCallum
  Facility Booking: Dori Armor
  Box Office Manager: Kathy Marciano
Seating Capacity: 2,443

7199
MODELL PERFORMING CENTER AT THE LYRIC
140 W. Mount Royal Ave.
Baltimore, MD 21201
Phone: 41-090-0115
e-mail: rentals@lyricoperahouse.com
Web Site: www.lyricoperahouse.com
Management:
  President & Director: Sandy Richmond

All listings are in alphabetical order by state, then city, then organization within the city.

FACILITIES / Maryland

Finance Director: Laura Wiesle
Marketing Director: Nicoletta Macris
Operations Manager: Rick Gerhardt
Mission: The facility can be used for receptions, rehearsals and private events. The theater/auditorium can be used for performances, concerts, recitals, civic gatherings, corporate meetings and community programs
Seating Capacity: theater:2564; facility:1000

7200
REITZ ARENA
Loyola College Maryland
4501 North Charles Street
Baltimore, MD 21210
Phone: 410-617-2031
Fax: 410-617-5216
Toll-free: 800-221-9107
e-mail: jfillynn@loyola.com
Web Site: www.loyola.edu
Management:
  Director Event Services: Joan Flynn
Specialized Field: Series & Festivals
Seating Capacity: 3,500

7201
BOWIE STATE UNIVERSITY MARTIN LUTHER KING JR. CENTER
14000 Jericho Park Road
Bowie, MD 20715-9465
Phone: 301-464-3441
Toll-free: 877-772-6943

7202
PRINCE GEORGE'S STADIUM
Bowie Baysox
4101 Crain Highway
Bowie, MD 20716
Phone: 301-805-6000
Fax: 301-464-4911
e-mail: info@baysox.com
Web Site: www.baysox.com
Management:
  General Manager: Brian Shallcross
  Assistant General Manager: Phil Wrye
  Book Keeper: Carol Terwilliger
  Director Of Marketing: Brandan Kaizer
Founded: 1993
Opened: 1993
Facility Category: Minor League Baseball Facility
Seating Capacity: 10,000
Rental Contact: Brian Shallcross

7203
CLARICE SMITH PERFORMING ARTS CENTER
University of Maryland
Clarice Smtih Performing Arts Center
Suite 3800
College Park, MD 20742-1625
Phone: 301-405-7794
Fax: 301-405-5977
e-mail: contact.claricesmith@umd.edu
Web Site: www.claricesmithcenter.umd.edu
Management:
  Creative Strategy Senior Manager: Kelly Andrews
  Director of Development: Edward J. Lewis
  Director, Artistic Initiatives: Paul Brohan
  Stage Operations Manager: Bill Brandwein
Mission: The Clarice Smith Performing Arts Center transforms lives through sustained engagement with the arts.
Utilizes: Artists-in-Residence; Choreographers; Collaborations; Commissioned Composers; Educators; Five Seasonal Concerts; Instructors; Paid Performers; Soloists; Students; Student Interns
Founded: 2001
Paid Staff: 50
Budget: $6.1 million
Performs At: 6 Venues
Year Built: 2001
Rental Contact: Nicholas Roberts
Organization Type: The Clarice Smith Performing Arts Center has six performance venues. In addition to offering a presenting series, the Center serves as home to the UM School of Music, Departments of Dance and Theatre, and the Michelle Smith Perf

7204
TOBY'S DINNER THEATRE
5900 Symphony Woods Road
PO Box 1003
Columbia, MD 21044
Phone: 410-730-8311
Fax: 410-730-8311
Toll-free: 800-888-6297
e-mail: info@tobysdinnertheatre.com
Web Site: www.tobysdinnertheatre.com
Founded: 1980

7205
JOHN ADDISON CONCERT HALL
10701 Livingston Road
Fort Washington, MD 20744
Phone: 301-203-6070
Fax: 301-203-6071
Web Site: www.pgparks.com
Management:
  Managing Director: Lawrence J Knowles
Founded: 1989
Status: Non-Profit, Non-Professional

7206
MARYLAND THEATRE
21 South Potomac Street
Hagerstown, MD 21740
Phone: 301-790-3500
Fax: 301-791-6114
e-mail: tix@mdtheatre.org
Web Site: www.mdtheatre.org
Management:
  Executive Director: Brian Sullivan
  Operations Manager: Jessica Green
Mission: Performances include country artists, comedians, orchestra concerts, children's shows, musicians, recitals, stage shows, and others.
Founded: 1915
Seating Capacity: 1,300

7207
COLLEGE OF SOUTHERN MARYLAND FINE ARTS CENTER
8730 Mitchell Road
La Plata, MD 20646
Phone: 301-934-2251
Fax: 301-934-7682
Toll-free: 800-933-9177
e-mail: askme@csmd.edu
Web Site: www.csmd.edu
Officers:
  Chair Communication Arts/Humanities: Ronald Brown
Management:
  Vice Chair: Mike Middleton
  President: Bradley Gottfried
Founded: 1959
Status: Non-Profit, Professional
Paid Staff: 100
Paid Artists: 100
Type of Stage: Proscenium
Seating Capacity: 404
Year Built: 1983

7208
STRATHMORE
5301 Tuckerman Lane
North Bethesda, MD 20852
Phone: 301-581-5200
Fax: 301-581-5201
e-mail: csr@strathmore.org
Web Site: www.strathmore.org
Officers:
  Chief Executive Officer: Eliot Pfanstiehl
  President: Monica Jeffries Hazangeles
  Executive Assistant to the Presiden: Carol Maryman
Management:
  Chief Executive Officer: Eliot Pfanstiehl
  President: Monica Jeffries Hazangeles
  Director Of Finance: Jasper Cox
Mission: Presents a lively and diverse program of art exhibitions, concerts and performing arts programs, and literary lectures and events.
Founded: 1983
Status: Non-Profit, Professional
Paid Staff: 30

7209
ROLAND E POWELL CONVENTION CENTER
4001 Coastal Highway
40th Street
Ocean City, MD 21842
Phone: 410-289-8311
Fax: 410-289-0058
Toll-free: 800-626-2326
Web Site: www.ococean.com
Management:
  Director: Mike Noah
Status: For-Profit, Professional
Paid Staff: 75

7210
GORDON CENTER FOR PERFORMING ARTS
3506 Gwynbrook Avenue
Owings Mills, MD 21117
Phone: 410-356-7469
Fax: 410-356-7605
e-mail: info@gordoncenter.com
Web Site: www.gordoncenter.com
Management:
  Managing Director Arts & Culture: Randi Benesch
  Theater Manager: Dave Eske
Mission: To offer professional, high-quality performances in all genres to all ages.
Utilizes: Dance Companies; Dancers; Filmmakers; Guest Accompanists; Guest Companies; Guest Soloists; Multi Collaborations; Multimedia; Original Music Scores; Singers; Special Technical Talent; Theatre Companies; Touring Companies
Founded: 1995
Specialized Field: Varied
Status: Nonprofit
Income Sources: Grants; Endowments
Annual Attendance: 35,000
Facility Category: Performing Arts Center
Type of Stage: Proscenium

FACILITIES / Massachusetts

Stage Dimensions: 70'x 40'
Seating Capacity: 550
Year Built: 1995
Rental Contact: Nancy Goldberg

7211
GILDENHORN/SPEISMAN CENTER FOR THE ARTS
Jewish Community Center of Greater Washington
6125 Montrose Road
Rockville, MD 20852
Phone: 301-881-0100
Fax: 301-881-5512
Web Site: www.jccgw.org
Officers:
  Chief Executive Officer: Michael Feinstein
  Chief Financial Officer: Ruth Carski
  Chief Program Officer: Tracey E. Dorfmann
  Chief Marketing Officer: Treva Bustow
  Chief Operating Officer: Amy I. Gantz
  President: Bradley C. Stillman
Management:
  President: Marcy Cohen
  CEO: Arnie Sohniki
  Director Adult Services: Selma Sweetbaum
  Chief Executive Officer: Michael Feinstein
Founded: 1923
Status: Non-Profit, Professional
Paid Staff: 60
Performs At: Gliddenhorn/Speisman Center for the Arts

7212
MONTGOMERY COLLEGE ROBERT E PARILLA PERFORMING ARTS CENTER
51 Mannakee Street
Rockville, MD 20850-1195
Phone: 301-251-5301
Fax: 301-251-7542
e-mail: boffice@montgomerycollege.edu
Web Site: www.montgomerycollege.edu/PAC/
Management:
  President: Charlene Munley
  Executive Director: William Campbell
  Artistic Director: Deborah Fyodorov
Mission: The theater facility of Montgomery College hosts visiting artists as well as collegiate productions. Fully handicapped accessible.
Founded: 1984
Status: Non-Profit, Non-Professional
Paid Staff: 7
Paid Artists: 10

7213
WICOMICO CIVIC CENTER
500 Glen Avenue
Salisbury, MD 21804
Phone: 410-548-4900
Fax: 410-546-0490
Web Site: www.wicomicociviccenter.org
Management:
  Director: Gary Mackes
  Deputy Director: Andy Wisk
  Manager: Charles R Rousseau
  Assistant Building Manager: Joe Harbinson
  Box Office Manager: Alan Gravenor
Founded: 1950
Status: Non-Profit, Professional
Paid Staff: 25

7214
STEPHENS AUDITORIUM
Towson State University
8000 York Road
Towson, MD 21252
Phone: 410-704-2792
Fax: 410-830-3914
e-mail: theatre@towson.edu
Web Site: www.towson.edu/theatre
Management:
  Assistant Manager Of Costume Shop: Julie Gerhardt
  Administrative Assistant I: Catie Mickletz
  Assistant Technical Director/Master: Brandon Ingle
Founded: 1915
Year Remodeled: 1991

7215
TOWSON CENTER ARENA
Towson University
8000 York Road
Towson, MD 21252
Phone: 410-704-2000
Fax: 410-704-5069
Web Site: www.towson.edu
Officers:
  Director: Bill Murphy
  Ticket Office Manager: Joanne Repasi
Management:
  Assistant Manager Of Costume Shop: Julie Gerhardt
  Administrative Assistant I: Catie Mickletz
  Assistant Technical Director/Master: Brandon Ingle
Opened: 1976
Seating Capacity: 5,000

Massachusetts

7216
AMHERST COLLEGE LEFRAK GYM
Amherst College
220 S Pleasant Street
PO Box 5000
Amherst, MA 01002-5000
Mailing Address: P.O. Box 5000, Amherst, MA 01002-5000
Phone: 413-542-2000
Fax: 413-542-5845
e-mail: info@amherst.edu
Web Site: www.amherst.edu
Officers:
  President: Biddy Martin
  Chairman: Jide J Zeitlin
Management:
  Director: Suzanne Coffey
  President: Biddy Martin
  Chairman: Culley Murphy
Seating Capacity: 2,400

7217
UNIVERSITY OF MASSACHUSETTS FINE ARTS CENTER
35 Fine Arts Center
Amherst, MA 01003-9336
Phone: 413-545-3670
Fax: 413-545-2018
Web Site: www.fineartscenter.com
Management:
  Director: Dr Willie L Hill Jr
  Associate Director: Dennis Conway
  Technology Manager: Christine Texiera
  Manager: Steven Coombs
Utilizes: Artists-in-Residence; Collaborations; Dance Companies; Lyricists; Multi Collaborations; Multimedia; Theatre Companies; Touring Companies
Founded: 1975
Status: Non-Profit
Paid Staff: 50
Facility Category: Concert Hall; Bowker Auditorium
Type of Stage: Proscenium
Seating Capacity: 1980; 700

7218
WILLIAM D MULLINS MEMORIAL CENTER
University of Massachusetts
200 Commonwealth Avenue
2nd Floor
Amherst, MA 01003
Phone: 413-545-3001
Fax: 413-545-3005
Web Site: www.mullinscenter.com
Management:
  General Manager: Bob Weiss
  Operations: J R Westveer
  Marketing: Scott Sasenbury
Founded: 1994
Status: For-Profit, Professional
Seating Capacity: 10,500

7219
BERKLEE PERFORMANCE CENTER
Berklee College of Music
136 Massachusetts Avenue
Boston, MA 02115
Phone: 617-747-2261
Fax: 617-375-9228
e-mail: bpc@berklee.edu
Web Site: www.berkleebpc.com
Officers:
  President: Roger H Brown
  Chair: Jeff Shames
Management:
  Manager: Ed Liberatore
Seating Capacity: 1,220

7220
BOSTON CENTER FOR THE ARTS PLAZA THEATRE
539 Tremont Street
Boston, MA 02116
Phone: 617-426-5000
Fax: 617-426-5336
e-mail: info@bcaonline.org
Web Site: www.bcaonline.org
Officers:
  Chair: Philip Lovejoy
  President/CEO: Veronique Le Melle
Management:
  Director Development/Marketing: Anne Norton
  Individual Giving Manager: Kelly Teer
  Director of Events & Community Rel: Kristi keefe
  Associate Director of Education & P: Cynthia Woo
Mission: A nonprofit performing and visual arts complex that supports working artists to create, perform and exhibit new work; builds new audiences; and connects arts to community
Founded: 1968
Status: Non-Profit, Professional

FACILITIES / Massachusetts

7221
BOSTON OPERA HOUSE
539 Washington St
Boston, MA 02111-1718
Phone: 617-259-3400
e-mail: dkirk@bohvllc.com
Web Site: www.bostonoperahouse.com
Mission: 7 venues in the opera house can be used privately or the entire opera house can be rented for a private function

7222
CITI PERFORMING ART CENTER WANG THEATRE
270 Tremont Street
Boston, MA 02116
Phone: 866-348-9738
Fax: 617-451-1436
Toll-free: 800-982-2787
e-mail: info@citicenter.org
Web Site: www.citicenter.org
Officers:
   Chair: Lorraine C. Wang
   Vice Chair: David E. Goel
   Treasurer: Michael Bell
   President & CEO: Josiah A. Spaulding, Jr.
Management:
   Vice President & General Manager: Michael Szczepkowski
   Director of Theatre Operations: Eric Neill
   Chief Financial Officer: John Perkins
   Director Of Education: Corey Evans
Utilizes: Community Members; Community Talent; Educators; High School Drama; Scenic Designers; Theatre Companies
Founded: 1988
Status: Non-Profit, Professional
Paid Staff: 50
Facility Category: Theatre
Type of Stage: Proscenium
Stage Dimensions: 80 x 60
Seating Capacity: 3561
Year Built: 1910
Year Remodeled: 1996

7223
CUTLER MAJESTIC THEATRE AT EMERSON COLLEGE
219 Tremont Street
Boston, MA 02116-4117
Phone: 617-824-8000
Fax: 617-824-3209
Toll-free: 800-233-3123
e-mail: majestic@emerson.edu
Web Site: www.maj.org
Management:
   Administration/Production Director: Jonathan S. Miller
   Director of Artistic Programs: David Dower
   Director of External Affairs: Rita McAteer
   Administration/Production Director: Jonathan S. Miller
Founded: 1984
Status: Non-Profit, Non-Professional
Paid Staff: 40
Volunteer Staff: 40
Annual Attendance: 150,000
Facility Category: Opera/Dance Theatre
Type of Stage: Proscenium
Stage Dimensions: 40'x 40'
Seating Capacity: 1,000
Year Built: 1903
Year Remodeled: 2003

Rental Contact: Manager Lance Olson
Resident Groups: Dance Umbrella, World Music, BAM Opera, Celebrity Series, Jose Mateo's Ballet Theatre, The Revels...

7224
HUNTINGTON THEATRE COMPANY
Boston University
264 Huntington Avenue
Boston, MA 02115
Phone: 617-266-0800
Fax: 617-421-9674
e-mail: thehuntington@huntingtontheatre.org
Web Site: www.huntingtontheatre.org
Management:
   General Manager: Sondra R. Katz
   Associate General Manager: Justin Haslett
   Associate Company Manager: Ali Leskowitz
   Assistant to the Managing Director: Allison McDonough
Utilizes: Guest Accompanists; Guest Companies; Guest Composers; Guest Musical Directors; Guest Soloists; Instructors; Sign Language Translators; Soloists
Founded: 1982
Status: Non-Profit; Professional

7225
ISABELLA STEWART GARDNER MUSEUM
280 The Fenway
Boston, MA 02115
Phone: 617-566-1401
Fax: 617-566-7653
e-mail: information@isgm.org
Web Site: www.gardnermuseum.org
Officers:
   Chef/Owner: Peter Crowley
Management:
   Director of Marketing and Communica: David Franke
   Director of Development: Lisa Bevilaqua
   Development Assistant: Alejandra Bennett
   Store Manager and Buyer: M.K. Wong
Utilizes: Artists-in-Residence; Composers-in-Residence; Fine Artists; Grant Writers; Guest Directors; Guest Instructors; Guest Soloists; Multimedia; Original Music Scores; Sign Language Translators; Touring Companies
Founded: 1903
Status: Nonprofit
Budget: $130,000
Performs At: Museum Gallery
Annual Attendance: 200,000
Facility Category: Museum
Seating Capacity: 250
Organization Type: Sponsoring

7226
JORDAN HALL AT NEW ENGLAND CONSERVATORY
290 Huntington Avenue
Boston, MA 02115
Phone: 617-585-1260
Fax: 617-585-1270
Web Site: www.newenglandconservatory.edu
Management:
   Director: Brian Yankee
Founded: 1903
Annual Attendance: 125,000
Facility Category: Performance Hall
Seating Capacity: 1,013
Year Remodeled: 1995

Architect: Ann Beha Associates
Cost: $8.2 million

7227
SYMPHONY HALL
301 Massachusetts Avenue
Boston, MA 02115
Phone: 617-266-1492
Fax: 617-637-9367
Toll-free: 800-266-1492
e-mail: customerservice@bso.org
Web Site: www.bso.org
Officers:
   Chairman: Ed Linde
   CFO: Thomas May
Management:
   Managing Director: Mark Volpe
   Artistic Director: Anthony Fogg
   Director of Development: Bart Reidy
Founded: 1881
Status: Non-Profit, Professional

7228
TD BANKNORTH GARDEN
100 Legends Way
Boston, MA 02114
Phone: 617-624-1050
Fax: 617-624-1818
e-mail: customerservice@tdgarden.com
Web Site: www.tdbanknorthgarden.com
Officers:
   Chairman/CEO: Jeremy Jacobs
   President: Charles Moran Jr
Management:
   Principal: Jerry Jacob
   Principal: Lou Jacob
   Principal: Charlie Jacob
Founded: 1995
Status: For-Profit, Professional
Paid Staff: 1000
Seating Capacity: 18,600
Year Built: 1995
Year Restored: 2006

7229
AGASSIZ THEATRE
10-12 Holyoke Street
Cambridge, MA 02138
Phone: 617-495-1000
Fax: 617-495-8728
e-mail: theatre@fas.harvard.edu
Web Site: www.fas.harvard.edu
Management:
   Director: Thomas Morgan
   Dean: Nina Gasper
Founded: 1904

7230
CONSTELLATIONCENTER
43 Thorndike Street
Suite 301
Cambridge, MA 02142
Phone: 617-939-1900
Fax: 617-939-0190
e-mail: development@constellationcenter.org
Web Site: www.constellationcenter.org
Officers:
   President: Glenn Knickrehm
Mission: Four main halls for private use

7231
LOEB DRAMA CENTER
64 Brattle Street
Cambridge, MA 02138

FACILITIES / Massachusetts

Phone: 617-495-2668
Fax: 617-495-1705
e-mail: information@amrep.org
Web Site: www.amrep.org
Officers:
 Chairman: Steven Johnson
 Co-Chair: Ann Gund
Management:
 Artistic Director: Dianne Paulus
 Producer: Diane Borger
 Director: Scott Zigler
Founded: 1960
Status: Non-Profit, Professional
Paid Staff: 60
Paid Artists: 30
Type of Stage: Proscenium
Stage Dimensions: 26 x 60
Seating Capacity: 556
Year Built: 1960

7232
BOSTON COLLEGE ALUMNI FIELD STADIUM
140 Commonwealth Avenue
Chestnut Hill, MA 02467
Phone: 617-552-3004
Fax: 617-552-4903
e-mail: mahonebe@bc.edu
Web Site: www.bceagles.com
Management:
 General Manager: Barry McNulty
 Athletic Director: Gene Defillippo
Founded: 1957
Seating Capacity: 8,606

7233
MARGARET L JACKSON ARTS CENTER
Bristol Community College
777 Elsbree Street
Fall River, MA 02720
Phone: 508-678-2811
Fax: 508-730-3284
e-mail: president@bristol.mass.edu
Web Site: www.bristolcc.edu
Officers:
 President: John J Sbrega
Status: Non-Profit, Professional

7234
HIGHFIELD THEATRE
Cape Cod Conservatory of Music
60 Highfield Drive
PO Box 233
Falmouth, MA 02540
Phone: 508-540-0611
Fax: 508-495-0025
Web Site: www.capecodconservatory.org
Officers:
 Chairman: John A. Ketchum
 Treasurer: William Thomas
 Secretary: Douglas MacDonald
Management:
 Managing Director: Stephanie Weaver
 Director: George Scharr
 Artistic Director: Jung-Ho Park

7235
ORPHEUM THEATRE
Bay Colony Productions
1 School Street
PO Box 266
Foxboro, MA 02035

Mailing Address: P.O. Box 266, Foxboro, MA 02035
Phone: 508-543-4434
e-mail: info@orpheum.org
Web Site: www.orpheum.org
Officers:
 President: Gail Gilman
Management:
 Executive Director: Bill Cunningham
 Education Directo: Michael Hammond
Founded: 1993
Status: Nonprofit

7236
THE MAHAIWE PERFORMING ARTS CENTER THEATRE
14 Castle Street
Great Barrington, MA 01230
Phone: 413-644-9040
Fax: 413-528-8352
Web Site: www.mahaiwe.org
Management:
 Executive Director: Beryl Jolly
 General Manager: Karin Watkins
Founded: 1904
Opened: 1905
Status: Non-Profit; Professional

7237
HINGHAM HIGH SCHOOL AUDITORIUM
17 Union Street
Hingham, MA 02043
Phone: 781-741-1500
Fax: 781-741-1515
Web Site: www.hinghamschools.com
Officers:
 Chair: Christine Smith
Status: Non-Profit, Non-Professional

7238
TANGLEWOOD MUSIC CENTER
297 West Street
Lenox, MA 01240
Phone: 413-637-1600
Fax: 413-637-5100
e-mail: customerservice@bso.org
Web Site: www.bso.org
Officers:
 Chairman: James Levine
Management:
 Managing Director: Mark Volpe
Founded: 1940
Seating Capacity: 18,000

7239
LOWELL MEMORIAL AUDITORIUM
50 East Merrimack Street
Lowell, MA 01852
Phone: 978-937-8688
Fax: 978-452-7342
e-mail: boxoffice@lowellauditorium.com
Web Site: www.lowellauditorium.com
Management:
 Director: Peter Lally
 Manager: Thomas McKay
Status: For-Profit, Professional
Paid Staff: 20
Seating Capacity: 3,000

7240
UNIVERSITY OF MASSACHUSETTS CENTER FOR THE ARTS
35 Wilder Street
Suite 1
Lowell, MA 01854-3081
Phone: 978-934-4444
Fax: 978-934-2017
Web Site: www.uml.edu
Management:
 Director: Christine Heaton Brown
 Marketing: Joan Sherman

7241
THE LYNN AUDITORIUM.
Lynn City Hall
Room 311
Lynn, MA 01901
Phone: 781-599-7469
Fax: 781-477-7026
e-mail: jmarsh@ci.lynn.ma.us
Web Site: www.lynnauditorium.com
Management:
 General Manager & Booking Agent: James Marsh
 Production Manager: Henry Ryan
 Box Office Manager: Joanna Mills
 House Manager: Anne Marie Leonard
Opened: 1948

7242
TWEETER CENTER FOR THE PERFORMING ARTS
885 S Main Street
Mansfield, MA 02048
Phone: 508-339-2331
Fax: 508-339-0550
Web Site: www.livenation.com
Facility Category: Open Air Amphitheater
Seating Capacity: 19,900

7243
ZEITERION THEATRE
684 Purchase Street
New Bedford, MA 02740
Phone: 508-997-5664
Fax: 508-999-5956
e-mail: info@zeiterion.org
Web Site: www.zeiterion.org
Officers:
 CEO: Katherine Knowles
Management:
 Co-Director: Rosemary Gill
 Patron and Business Partnerships Ma: Dori Legge
 Marketing Manager: Penny Pimental
 Office Manager: Matt Gomes
Founded: 1923
Status: Non-Profit, Professional

7244
FIREHOUSE CENTER FOR THE ARTS
Market Square
Newburyport, MA 01950
Phone: 978-462-7336
Fax: 978-462-9911
e-mail: info@firehouse.org
Web Site: www.firehouse.org
Officers:
 President: Louis Rubenfeld
 Vice President: Lois Honegger
 Treasurer: Peter Kelly
 Secretary: Victor Atkins
Management:

FACILITIES / Massachusetts

Director of Productions: Kimm Wilkinson
Director of Development: Beth Falconer
Production Assistant: Caron Nardi
Box Office Manager: Nancy Oagasapian
Founded: 1991
Seating Capacity: 195
Year Remodeled: 1991

7245
MASSACHUSETTS MUSEUM OF CONTEMPORARY ART
MASS MoCA
87 Marshall Street
North Adams, MA 01247
Mailing Address: 1040 MASS MoCA Way, North Adams, MA 01247
Phone: 413-662-2111
Fax: 413-663-8548
e-mail: info@massmoca.org
Web Site: www.massmoca.org
Officers:
    Chairman: Duncan Brown
Management:
    Director: Joseph C Thompson
Founded: 1999
Status: Non-Profit, Professional

7246
CALVIN THEATRE AND PERFORMANCE ARTS CENTER
19 King Street
Northampton, MA 01060
Phone: 413-584-1444
Fax: 413-586-1162
Web Site: www.iheg.com
Management:
    Creative Director: Jordi Herold

7247
JOHN M GREENE HALL
Smith College
30 Balmont Avenue
Northampton, MA 01063
Phone: 413-584-2700
Fax: 413-585-6990
e-mail: events@email.smith.edu
Web Site: www.smith.edu
Officers:
    President: Carol T Christ
    Chair: Elizabeth Mugar Eveillard
Management:
    Director: Gail Norskey
    Dean: Deb Shaver
    Athletic Director: Lynn Oberbling
Seating Capacity: 2,046

7248
ACADEMY PLAYHOUSE
120 Main Street
Orleans, MA 02653
Phone: 508-255-3075
Fax: 508-255-8704
e-mail: academyplayhouse@apacape.org
Web Site: www.apacape.org
Management:
    Artistic Director: Peter Earle
    Marketing: Gayle Kenerson
Founded: 1975
Status: Non-Profit, Non-Professional
Paid Staff: 10
Volunteer Staff: 150
Facility Category: Arena Theatre
Type of Stage: Arena

Seating Capacity: 164

7249
KOUSSEVITZKY PERFORMING ARTS CENTER
Berkshire Community College
1350 West Street
Pittsfield, MA 01201
Phone: 413-236-1000
Fax: 413-496-9511
Toll-free: 800-816-1233
Web Site: www.berkshirecc.edu
Officers:
    President: Ellen Kennedy
    VP: Frances Feinerman
Management:
    Staff Assistant: Alyson Weathwax
    Director: Denise Johns
Founded: 1960
Status: Non-Profit, Professional
Type of Stage: Proscenium
Stage Dimensions: 56'x46'x66'
Comments: Best contact method for info on Theatre is by telephone.

7250
GRISWOLD THEATRE
American International College
1000 State Street
Springfield, MA 01109
Phone: 413-747-6393
Fax: 413-737-2803
Toll-free: 800-242-3142
Web Site: www.aic.edu
Officers:
    President: Dr. Vincent Maniaci
    Chairman: Peter J. Bittel
    Vice Chairman: Frank Colaccino
    Treasurer: Craig Brown
    President, Abdow Corporation: Ronald J. Abdow
Management:
    Director: Ronald J. Abdow
    Director: David Adams

7251
MASSMUTUAL CENTER
1277 Main Street
Springfield, MA 01103
Phone: 413-787-6610
Fax: 413-787-6645
e-mail: mmeinfo@massconvention.com
Web Site: www.massmutualcenter.com
Management:
    General Manager: Matt Hollander
    Assistant General Manager: Joe Flanagan
    Sales Manager: Ami Vieceli
Founded: 1972
Status: For-Profit, Professional
Affiliations: Global Spectrum
Facility Category: Arena & Convention Center
Type of Stage: Various
Seating Capacity: 8,000
Year Remodeled: 2005

7252
SPRINGFIELD SYMPHONY HALL
One Columbus Center
Springfield, MA 01103
Phone: 413-788-7646
Fax: 413-737-9991
e-mail: tickets@citystage.symphonyhall.com
Web Site: www.symphonyhall.com
Officers:
    President: Tina D'Agostino

Management:
    Box Office Manager: Brian Askin
    Technical Director: Chad LaBumbard
    Group Sales: Sue Prairie
    House Manager: Amanda Spear
Founded: 1912
Type of Stage: Proscenium
Orchestra Pit: Y
Seating Capacity: 2,611
Year Built: 1912
Year Remodeled: 2004

7253
GOSMAN SPORTS & CONVOCATION CENTER
Brandeis University
415 South St.
Waltham, MA 02453
Phone: 781-736-2000
Fax: 781-736-4305
e-mail: vnlevin@brandeis.edu
Web Site: www.brandeis.edu
Officers:
    President: Fredrick M. Lawrence
Management:
    Executive Assistant to the Presiden: Celia D. Harris
    Special Assistant to the President: Vicky N. Levin
    Department Administrator: Lindsay Hage
    Director, Office of Special Events: Meredith Walsh

7254
SPINGOLD THEATER CENTER
Brandeis University
415 South St.
Waltham, MA 02453
Phone: 781-736-2000
Fax: 781-736-3408
e-mail: vnlevin@brandeis.edu
Web Site: www.brandeis.edu
Officers:
    President: Fredrick M. Lawrence
    Chair: Susan Dibble
Management:
    Executive Assistant to the Presiden: Celia D. Harris
    Special Assistant to the President: Vicky N. Levin
    Department Administrator: Lindsay Hage
    Director, Office of Special Events: Meredith Walsh

7255
CAPE COD CONSERVATORY OF MUSIC & ARTS
Barnstable Campus
2235 Iyannough Road
Route 132
West Barnstable, MA 02668
Phone: 508-362-2772
Fax: 508-362-4071
e-mail: info@capecodconservatory.org
Web Site: www.capecodconservatory.org
Officers:
    Chairman: John A. Ketchum
    Treasurer: William Thomas
    Secretary: Douglas MacDonald
Management:
    Managing Director: Stephanie Weaver
    Director: George Scharr
    Artistic Director: Jung-Ho Park

FACILITIES / Michigan

Founded: 1956
Status: Non-Profit, Professional

7256
REGIS COLLEGE FINE ARTS CENTER
235 Wellesley Street
Weston, MA 02493
Phone: 781-768-7000
Fax: 781-768-7030
e-mail: admission@regiscollege.edu
Web Site: www.regiscollege.edu
Officers:
- President: Antoinette Haya
- Chair: Joan Shea
- Vice Chair: Lee Hogan
- Secretary: Maureen Doherty
- Treasurer: Christina McCann

Management:
- Special Assistant to the President: Mary Jane Doherty
- Dean, School of Nursing, Science, a: Penelope Glynn
- Trustee Emeritus: Richard W. Young

Opened: 1993
Status: Non-Profit, Professional

7257
PRISCILLA BEACH THEATRE
800 Rocky Hill Road
White Horse Beach, MA 02360
Mailing Address: Priscilla Beach Theatre, PO Box 424, White Horse Beach, MA 0
Phone: 508-224-4888
e-mail: info@pbtheatre.org
Web Site: www.thinktheatre.org
Officers:
- Founder: Franklin Trask PhD

Founded: 1937

7258
CHAPIN HALL
University of Chicago
1313 East 60th Street
Williamstown, MA 60637
Phone: 773-256-5100
Fax: 413-597-3100
Web Site: www.chapinhall.org
Officers:
- Chair: John (Mark) Hansen
- Executive VP The Field Museum: Jim Croft
- VP & Secretary of the University: David B. Fithian
- Senior Vice President: Sunil (Sonny) Garg

Management:
- Educational Consultant: Adrienne Y. Bailey
- Dean: Neil B. Guterman
- Dean and Professor: Colm A. O'Muircheartaigh

Founded: 1910
Status: Non-Profit, Professional

7259
STERLING & FRANCINE CLARK ART INSTITUTE
225 South Street
Williamstown, MA 01267
Mailing Address: 225 South Street, Williamstown, Massachusetts 01267
Phone: 413-458-2303
Fax: 413-458-2318
e-mail: info@clarkart.edu
Web Site: www.clarkart.edu
Officers:
- President: Morton Owen Schapiro PhD

Management:
- Executive Director: Michael Conforti

Founded: 1955
Status: Non-Profit, Professional
Performs At: Auditorium
Annual Attendance: 200,000
Seating Capacity: 320
Year Built: 1973

7260
MECHANICS HALL
321 Main Street
Worcester, MA 01608
Phone: 508-752-5608
Fax: 508-754-8442
e-mail: info@mechanicshall.org
Web Site: www.mechanicshall.org
Management:
- Executive Director: Robert M Kennedy

Mission: To preserve Mechanics Hall as a world-class performance center and community meeting space.
Founded: 1857
Status: Non-Profit, Non-Professional
Paid Staff: 8
Volunteer Staff: 20
Budget: $1 million
Income Sources: Rental Income; Membership; Foundations; Businesses
Annual Attendance: 200,000
Type of Stage: Thrust
Seating Capacity: 16,484
Year Built: 1857
Year Remodeled: 2000
Cost: $8 Million

7261
PERFORMING ARTS SCHOOL OF WORCESTER
29 High Street
Worcester, MA 01608
Phone: 508-755-8246
Fax: 508-795-0640
e-mail: info@pasow.org
Web Site: www.pasow.org
Officers:
- Chair: Christine Cuccaro
- Treasurer: Nigel Belgrave
- Secretary: Todd Gleason

Management:
- Acting Executive Director/CEO: Fred Dowling
- Production Manager: Pieter Struyk
- Registrar: Sheryl Gordon
- Artistic Director of Dance: Jennifer Agbay
- Artistic Director of Music: Greg Shannon

Utilizes: Actors; Choreographers; Collaborations; Commissioned Composers; Commissioned Music; Dancers; Educators; Five Seasonal Concerts; Grant Writers; Guest Companies; Guest Composers; Guest Ensembles; Guest Instructors; Guest Soloists; Guest Writers; High School Drama; Instructors; Lyricists; Music; New Productions; Organization Contracts; Sign Language Translators; Student Interns
Status: Non-Profit, Non-Professional

Michigan

7262
THE CROSWELL OPERA HOUSE & FINE ARTS ASSOCIATION
129 East Maumee St.
Adrian, MI 49221
Phone: 517-263-6868
Fax: 517-263-5130
e-mail: jrighter@croswell.org
Web Site: www.croswell.org
Management:
- Artistic Director: Jere Righter
- Box Office Manager: Ashley Brainered
- Graphic Design & Marketing: Nate Clark
- Costume Designer: Emily Gifford
- Technical Assistant: Terry Hissong

Facility Category: Theatre
Seating Capacity: 659

7263
DAWSON AUDITORIUM
Adrian College
110 S Madison St.
Adrian, MI 49221
Phone: 517-265-5161
Fax: 517-264-3331
Toll-free: 800-877-2246
e-mail: jdocking@adrian.edu
Web Site: www.adrian.edu
Officers:
- President: Jeffrey R Docking PhD
- VP Enrollment & Student Affairs: Dr.Frank J. Hribar
- VP & Dean, Academic Affairs: Dr. Agnes Caldwell
- VP Business Affairs: Jerry Wright
- VP Development: Jim Mahony

Founded: 1962
Seating Capacity: 1,000
Year Built: 1962
Year Remodeled: 2004

7264
COMMUNITY THEATRE ASSOCIATION OF MICHIGAN
4619 W Van Buren Road
Alma, MI 48801-9556
Phone: 989-463-1252
e-mail: w.heine@mediamajik.net
Web Site: www.communitytheatre.org
Officers:
- President: Mary Lou Britton
- Vice President: Larry Nielsen
- Treasurer: Christy Frick
- Secretary: David Wahr

Management:
- Director: Jill Patchin
- Director: Bill Anderson
- Director: Jonanne Berry
- Director: Kristen Chesak
- Director: Tracy Tiffany
- Executive Secretary: Nancy Peska

Founded: 1951
Status: Non-Profit, Non-Professional
Affiliations: Arts Council For Chautauqa County
Annual Attendance: 5000
Organization Type: Service Organization

7265
ARTHUR MILLER THEATRE
Univeristy of Michigan
School of Music, Theatre & Dance
E.V. Moore Building,1100 Baits Dr.
Ann Arbor, MI 48109-1265
Phone: 734-764-0583
Fax: 734-763-5097
e-mail: sberritt@umich.edu
Web Site: www.music.umich.edu
Officers:
- President: Mary Sue Coleman

Management:

FACILITIES / Michigan

Manager: Shannon Rice
Manager: Barry LaRue
Founded: 1997
Affiliations: UM School of music
Type of Stage: Black Box

7266
CRISLER ARENA
University of Michigan
G002 Michigan Union
530 South State st.
Ann Arbor, MI 48109
Phone: 734-764-0247
Fax: 734-936-8942
e-mail: mtickets@umich.edu
Web Site: www.mgoblue.com
Officers:
    President: Mary Sue Coleman
Management:
    Director: William C Martin
Founded: 1967
Seating Capacity: 13,750

7267
HILL AUDITORIUM
University of Michigan
G002 Michigan Union
530 South State st.
Ann Arbor, MI 48109
Phone: 734-763-3333
Fax: 734-763-5097
Web Site: www.muto.umich.edu
Officers:
    President: Mary Sue Coleman
Management:
    Manager: Shannon Rice
Opened: 1913
Seating Capacity: 4,163

7268
KERRYTOWN CONCERT HOUSE
415 North Fourth Avenue
Ann Arbor, MI 48104
Phone: 734-769-2999
Fax: 734-769-7791
e-mail: kch@kerrytown.com
Web Site: www.kerrytownconcerthouse.com
Management:
    Director of Operations: Allison Halerz
    Asstnt Director of Operations: Priscilla Johnson
    House Manager & Marketing Asstnt: Abby Dotz
    Director: Jennifer Goltz
Founded: 1984
Status: Non-Profit, Professional

7269
LYDIA MENDELSSOHN THEATRE
University of Michigan
School of Music, Theatre & Dance
E.V. Moore Building, 1100 Baits Dr.
Ann Arbor, MI 48109-2085
Phone: 734-764-0583
Fax: 734-763-5097
Web Site: www.music.umich.edu
Officers:
    President: Mary Sue Coleman
Management:
    Manager: Shannon Rice
Founded: 1929
Performs At: Intimate, shoe-box theatre with a cyclorama.
Type of Stage: Proscenium
Stage Dimensions: 29'11 x 16'10"""
Seating Capacity: 640

Year Built: 1929
Year Remodeled: 1995

7270
MICHIGAN THEATER
603 E Liberty Street
Ann Arbor, MI 48104
Phone: 734-668-8397
Fax: 734-668-7136
e-mail: info@michtheater.org
Web Site: www.michtheater.com
Officers:
    Executive Director & CEO: Russ Collins
    Chief Development Officer: Lee Berry
Management:
    Executive Director & CEO: Russell Collins
    Marketing Director: Emily Mathews
    Development: Laura Barnes-Gabriel
    Director, Finance & Administration: Chris Tabaczka
    Director, Programming & Education: Amanda Bynum
    Facility & Programming Manager: Brian Hunter
Founded: 1928
Status: Non-Profit
Paid Staff: 12
Volunteer Staff: 300
Paid Artists: 3
Non-paid Artists: 4
Budget: $2 million
Income Sources: 20% Membership; Contributions; Grants
Affiliations: National Association of Theater Owners
Annual Attendance: 2,100,000
Facility Category: Historic Movie Palace
Type of Stage: Proscenium
Stage Dimensions: 55x30
Seating Capacity: 1710
Year Built: 1928
Year Remodeled: 2000
Cost: $ 8.4 Million

7271
POWER CENTER FOR THE PERFORMING ARTS
University of Michigan
1100 Baits Drive
Ann Arbor, MI 48109-2085
Phone: 734-764-0583
Fax: 734-763-5097
e-mail: ckndll@umich.edu
Web Site: www.music.umich.edu
Management:
    Facilities Coordinator/Manager: Perry Titus
    Facilities/Booking Manager: Shannon Rice
    Business Administrator: Scott Ward
    Coordinator Financial Services: Jeanette Bierkamp
    Coordinator HR Services: Amy Truckey
    Manager: Greg Laman
    Performing Arts Sound and Recording: Roger Arnett
Mission: Most technically sophisticated performance space. It is a fully functioning theatre able to handle the most complex sales meetings, product roll-outs, and corporate presentations.
Founded: 1971
Status: For-Profit, Non-Professional

7272
YOST ICE ARENA
University of Michigan
1000 S State Street
Ann Arbor, MI 48109

Phone: 734-764-4600
Fax: 734-764-4597
e-mail: yostice@umich.edu
Web Site: www.umich.edu
Management:
    Manager: Craig Wotta
Founded: 1923
Status: For-Profit, Professional
Seating Capacity: 6,637

7273
PALACE AT AUBURN HILLS
Palace Sports & Entertainment
5 Championship Drive
Auburn Hills, MI 48326
Phone: 248-377-0100
e-mail: feedback@palacenet.com
Web Site: www.palacenet.com
Officers:
    President/CEO: Dennis Mannion
    EVP, OPERATIONS: Mario Etemad
    EVP, CHIEF MARKETING AND COMMUNICAT: Charlie Metzger
    EVP, CHIEF FINANCIAL OFFICER: Bob Feller
    EVP, BUSINESS OPERATIONS & STRATEGY: Jim Ross
Management:
    Director: Laura Passariello
    Marketing: Dave Neitzer
Status: For-Profit, Professional
Seating Capacity: 21,454

7274
BATTLE CREEK CIVIC THEATRE
PO Box 519
Battle Creek, MI 49106
Phone: 269-660-9659
e-mail: info@bccivic.org
Web Site: www.bccivic.org
Officers:
    President: Andy Helmboldt
    Treasurer: Steve Parks

7275
CO BROWN STADIUM
189 Bridge Street
Battle Creek, MI 49017
Phone: 269-962-0735
Fax: 269-962-0741
e-mail: info@battlecreekbombers.com
Web Site: www.battlecreekbombers.com
Management:
    General Manager: Brian Colopy
Founded: 1990
Status: For-Profit, Professional

7276
KELLOGG ARENA
One McCamly Square
Battle Creek, MI 49017
Phone: 269-963-4800
Fax: 269-968-8840
e-mail: tdearing@kelloggarena.com
Web Site: www.kelloggarena.com
Management:
    Interim General Manager: Ted Dearing
    Operations Manager: Ben Randels
    Sales and Marketing Manager: Lindsay Lerette
    Director of Finance: Bob Bengtsson
Status: Non-Profit, Professional
Paid Staff: 50
Seating Capacity: 6,000

FACILITIES / Michigan

7277
MENDEL CENTER
Lake Michigan College
2755 East Napier Avenue
Benton Harbor, MI 49022
Phone: 269-927-1000
Fax: 269-927-6710
e-mail: martinda@lakemichigancollege.edu
Web Site: www.themendelcenter.com
Management:
 Manager: Deedy Fowler
 Director, Conference & Event Servic: Tonya Martindale
 Manager: Amanda Rodriguez
 Event Manager: Christine Coble
 Conference Coordinator: Christine Anderson
Seating Capacity: 1,505

7278
WINK ARENA
Ferris State University
210 Sports Drive
Big Rapids, MI 49307
Phone: 231-591-2860
Fax: 231-591-2869
Web Site: www.ferris.edu
Officers:
 President: David L Eisler
 Chair: James K Haverman Jr
Management:
 Director: Tom Kirinovic
 Development: Tarrance Price
Facility Category: Sports Arena
Seating Capacity: 2,434

7279
CALUMET THEATRE COMPANY
340 Sixth Street
PO Box 167
Calumet, MI 49913
Phone: 906-337-2166
Fax: 906-337-3763
e-mail: BoxOffice@calumetTheatre.com
Web Site: www.calumettheatre.com
Management:
 Executive Director: Laura Miller
 Artistic/Technical Director: Davey Holmbo, techdirector@calumettheatre.co
Mission: Hosting and sponsoring performing events.
Founded: 1900
Specialized Field: Musical; Comedy; Community Theater; Classic; Contemporary; Musical; Ethnic Theater
Status: Non-Profit, Non-Professional
Paid Staff: 5
Income Sources: Michigan Association of Community Arts Agencies
Organization Type: Educational; Sponsoring

7280
CHEBOYGAN OPERA HOUSE
403 N Huron Street
Cheboygan, MI 49721
Phone: 231-627-5432
Fax: 231-627-2643
e-mail: pam@theoperahouse.org
Web Site: www.theoperahouse.org
Officers:
 President: Jane Roe
 Treasurer: Alice Barron
Management:
 Executive Director: Pam Westover
 Box Office: Dolores Kozlowski
 Box Office Manager: Patty Corkwell
 Technicians/Custodians: Leo Cocciarelli
 Technicians/Custodians: Matt Block
Founded: 1877
Status: Non-Profit, Professional
Paid Staff: 6
Budget: $250,000
Income Sources: Ticket Sales; Contributions; Annual Campaigns; Grants
Affiliations: Association of Performing Arts Presenters
Type of Stage: Proscenium
Stage Dimensions: 34 x 23
Seating Capacity: 582
Year Built: 1877
Year Remodeled: 1984
Rental Contact: Executive Director Pamela Westover

7281
MACOMB CENTER FOR THE PERFORMING ARTS
44575 Garfield Road
Clinton Township, MI 48038-1139
Phone: 586-286-2141
Fax: 586-286-3130
e-mail: macombarts@macomb.edu
Web Site: www.macombcenter.com
Management:
 Director: Christine Guarino
 Operations: Elaine Adams
 Marketing: Sandy Hazelton
 Operations Coordinator: Lori Wingert
 Manager: Lois Jackman
 Education & Enrichment Assistant: Maria Hunciag
 Education & Enrichment Assistant: Jessica Trepton
Opened: 1982
Status: Professional
Type of Stage: Proscenium
Stage Dimensions: 48'-6 X 29""
Orchestra Pit: Y
Seating Capacity: 1,273

7282
COBO ARENA
301 Civic Center Drive
Detroit, MI 48226
Phone: 313-471-6606
Fax: 313-396-7998
Web Site: www.olympiaentertainment.com
Officers:
 President: Dana Warg
Seating Capacity: 12,200
Year Built: 1959

7283
DETROIT SYMPHONY ORCHESTRA HALL
3711 Woodward Avenue
Detroit, MI 48201
Phone: 313-576-5111
Fax: 313-576-5101
Web Site: www.detroitsymphony.com
Officers:
 Chairman: James B Nicholson
 President and CEO: Anne Parsons
 Executive Vice President: Paul W Hogle
 Chief Financial Officer: Linda Lutz
 Managing Director of Special Events: Anne Wilczak
Management:
 Executive Director: Anne Parsons
 Artistic Director: Charles Burke
 Marketing: Ross Binnie
 General Manager and Artistic Admini: Erik R"nmark
 Artistic Manager: Kathryn Ginsburg
 Assistant Artistic Administrator: Jessica Ruiz
 Artistic & Community Engagement Coo: Katherine Curatolo
 Orchestra Manager: Alice Sauro
Founded: 1914
Status: Non-Profit, Professional
Paid Staff: 60
Paid Artists: 100

7284
FISHER THEATRE
3011 W Grand Boulevard
Detroit, MI 48202
Phone: 313-872-1000
Fax: 313-872-0632
e-mail: contact@broadwayindetroit.com
Web Site: www.nederlanderdetroit.com
Management:
 Operations: Ray Harris
Utilizes: Theatre Companies
Status: For-Profit, Professional
Paid Staff: 12
Income Sources: Box Office
Facility Category: Live Stage Theater
Type of Stage: Proscenium House
Stage Dimensions: 50' 0 x 32' 6"""
Seating Capacity: 2,089
Year Remodeled: 2001
Architect: Rapp & Rapp of Chicago

7285
FORD FIELD
2000 Brush Street
Suite 200
Detroit, MI 48226
Phone: 313-262-2000
Fax: 313-262-2239
e-mail: guestservices@detroitlions.com
Web Site: www.detroitlions.com/ford-field/index
Management:
 Manager: Connie Kladja
Seating Capacity: 65,000

7286
FOX THEATRE
2211 Woodward Avenue
Detroit, MI 48201
Phone: 313-471-6611
Fax: 313-471-3220
Toll-free: 800-745-3000
Web Site: www.olympiaentertainment.com
Officers:
 President: Dana Warg
Status: For-Profit, Professional

7287
JOE LOUIS ARENA
600 Civic Center Drive
Detroit, MI 48226
Phone: 313-471-7000
Fax: 313-396-7998
Web Site: www.olympiaentertainment.com
Officers:
 President: Dana Warg
Status: For-Profit, Professional
Seating Capacity: 19,965
Year Built: 1979

FACILITIES / Michigan

7288
MASONIC TEMPLE THEATRE
500 Temple Avenue
Detroit, MI 48201
Phone: 313-832-7100
Fax: 313-832-2292
Web Site: www.olympiaentertainment.com
Management:
　President: Dana Wang
Status: Professional

7289
MUSIC HALL CENTER FOR THE PERFORMING ARTS
350 Madison
Detroit, MI 48226
Phone: 313-887-8500
Fax: 313-887-8502
e-mail: KarenM@MusicHall.org
Web Site: www.musichall.org
Officers:
　President: Vincent Paul
Management:
　Director of Events: Karen McBride
Founded: 1928
Seating Capacity: 1701
Year Built: 1928
Year Remodeled: 1995
Rental Contact: Director of Events Karen McBride
Organization Type: Performing

7290
UNIVERSITY OF DETROIT MERCY CALIHAN HALL
4001 W McNichols
Detroit, MI 48221-3038
Phone: 313-993-1700
Fax: 313-993-2449
Web Site: www.udmercy.edu
Officers:
　University President: Antoine M. Garibaldi, Ph.D.
　Provost and VP for Academic Affairs: Pamela Zarkowski, J.D., M.P
　VP for Business and Finance: Vincent Abatemarco, C.P.A.,
　VP for University Advancement: Barbara S. Milbauer, M.B.A
　Assistant to the President for Miss: John Staudenmaier, S.J.,
　Executive Assistant to the President: Joy Crawford
Management:
　Operations: Tamara Batcheller
　Marketing: Elizabeth Patterson
　Development: Gregory Cascione
Founded: 1877
Status: Non-Profit, Professional

7291
MAGGIE ALLESEE DEPARTMENT OF THEATRE AND DANCE
4841 Cass Avenue
Suite 3226
Detroit, MI 48202
Phone: 313-577-3508
Fax: 313-577-0935
e-mail: theatre_dance@wayne.edu
Web Site: theatre.wayne.edu
Officers:
　President: Jay Noren
Management:
　Director: Blair Anderson
　Professor and Dean: Matthew W. Seeger
　Interim Senior Associate Dean: Dennis J. Tini
　Interim Associate Dean: Judith A. Moldenhauer
　Assistant Dean: Joan Ferguson
　Information Management Specialist: Karin Abel
Utilizes: Actors; AEA Actors; Artists-in-Residence; Choreographers; Collaborating Artists; Collaborations; Commissioned Composers; Commissioned Music; Composers-in-Residence; Curators; Dance Companies; Dancers; Designers; Educators; Filmmakers; Fine Artists; Five Seasonal Concerts; Grant Writers; Guest Accompanists; Guest Artists; Guest Choreographers; Guest Companies; Guest Composers; Guest Conductors; Guest Designers; Guest Directors; Guest Ensembles; Guest Instructors; Guest Lecturers; Guest Musical Directors; Guest Musicians; Guest Soloists; Guest Teachers; High School Drama; Instructors; Local Artists; Local Unknown Artists; Lyricists; Multi Collaborations; Multimedia; Music; Organization Contracts; Original Music Scores; Performance Artists; Playwrights; Poets; Resident Artists; Resident Professionals; Selected Students; Sign Language Translators; Singers; Soloists; Student Interns; Special Technical Talent; Theatre Companies; Touring Companies; Visual Arts

7292
JACK BRESLIN STUDENT EVENTS CENTER
534 Birch Road
East Lansing, MI 48824
Phone: 517-432-1989
Fax: 517-432-1510
e-mail: bement@msu.edu
Web Site: www.breslincenter.com
Management:
　Sales Manager: Nanci Yeadon
　Stage Manager: Joel Wilkiins
　Acting Breslin Center Manager: Ken Horvath
Founded: 1989
Status: Non-Profit
Performs At: Sports & Entertainment
Seating Capacity: 15,085

7293
SPARTAN STADIUM
Michigan State University
200 Spartan Way
East Lansing, MI 48824
Phone: 517-355-1610
Fax: 800-464-7336
Toll-free: 800-467-8273
Web Site: www.msuspartans.com
Management:
　Director: Mark Hollis
　Operations: Peggy Brown
　Development: Chuck Sleeper
Seating Capacity: 72,027

7294
WHARTON CENTER FOR PERFORMING ARTS
Michigan State University
750 E Shaw LN
East Lansing, MI 48824
Mailing Address: 750 E Shaw LN, East Lansing 48824
Phone: 517-432-2000
Fax: 517-353-5329
Toll-free: 800-942-7866
e-mail: wharton@msu.edu
Web Site: www.whartoncenter.com
Management:
　Executive Director: Mike Brand, brandmi@msu.edu
　Programming Manager: D Bryan Jao, jao@msu.edu
　Director of Development: Doug Miller, mille756@msu.edu
　Dir. of Marketing & Communications: Diane E. Willcox
　Director of Institute for Arts & Cr: Bert Goldstein
　Senior Production Manager: Sandy Thomley
　Director of Patron Services: Nina Silbergleit
　General Manager: Diana Baribeau
Utilizes: Artists-in-Residence; Choreographers; Collaborating Artists; Collaborations; Commissioned Composers; Composers; Contract Actors; Contract Orchestras; Dance Companies; Educators; Equity Actors; Five Seasonal Concerts; Guest Accompanists; Guest Artists; Guest Choreographers; Guest Conductors; Guest Designers; Guest Directors; Guest Instructors; Guest Musical Directors; Guest Musicians; Guest Soloists; Guest Speakers; Lyricists; Multimedia; Original Music Scores; Paid Performers; Performance Artists; Resident Artists; Selected Students; Singers; Soloists; Students; Special Technical Talent; Theatre Companies
Founded: 1982
Opened: 1982
Status: Non-Profit
Paid Staff: 30
Volunteer Staff: 300
Budget: $12,000,000-$17,000,000
Income Sources: Ticket Sales, Funding, Rentals
Performs At: Great Hall
Affiliations: Michigan State University; APAP; ISPA; IAAM
Annual Attendance: 250,000
Facility Category: Performing Arts Center
Type of Stage: Proscenium; Thrust; Auditorium
Seating Capacity: 2,420, 600, 3739
Year Built: 1982
Year Remodeled: 2009
Rental Contact: Baribeau@msu.edu Diana S Baribeau

7295
1515 BROADWAY PERFORMANCE VENUE
29205 Greening Boulevard
Farmington Hills, MI 48334
Phone: 248-932-0090
Fax: 248-932-8763
Toll-free: 877-683-4452
Web Site: www.the-feds.com
Management:
　President: Chris Jazczak
　Managing Director: Joseph S Ajlouny Jr
　Marketing Director: Angela Booterbaugh
Mission: Urban performance venue.
Founded: 1990
Specialized Field: Music; Theatre
Status: Non-Profit, Non-Professional
Paid Staff: 3
Volunteer Staff: 10
Budget: $160,000
Income Sources: Tickets; Sponsorship
Annual Attendance: 4,000
Facility Category: Independent Theater
Type of Stage: Proscenium; In-the-Round; Black Box
Stage Dimensions: 18' x 16' with Thrust
Seating Capacity: 120
Year Built: 1979
Year Remodeled: 1989

7296
FLINT INSTITUTE OF MUSIC
1025 E Kearsley Street
Flint, MI 48503

FACILITIES / Michigan

Phone: 810-238-1350
Fax: 810-238-6385
Toll-free: 800-395-4849
e-mail: fim@fim.com
Web Site: www.flintinstituteofmusic.com
Officers:
  FIM President and CEO: Paul Torre
  Director of Donor Relations: Sheila Zorn
  Director of Donor Administration an: Tinna Immink
Management:
  Marketing Director: Andrew Ward
  Senior Graphic Designer: Janeane Bady
  Mark Coordinator & Project Manager: Pam Howe Bailey
  Graphic Designer: Michelle Delecki
Founded: 1917
Status: Non-Profit, Non-Professional
Performs At: Whiting Auditorium
Annual Attendance: 3,500

7297
PERANI ARENA AND EVENT CENTER
3501 Lapeer Road
Flint, MI 48503
Phone: 810-744-0580
Fax: 810-744-2906
e-mail: info@peraniarea.com
Web Site: www.peraniarena.com
Officers:
  President: Khaled Shukairy
Management:
  General Manager: Jaremy Torrey
  Business & Box Office Manager: Mary Nagy
  Concession Manager: Shamika Roots
  Operations Supervisor: Bob Salazar
Founded: 1969

7298
CITY OF GRAND HAVEN COMMUNITY CENTER
519 Washington Ave
Grand Haven, MI 49417
Phone: 616-842-3210
Fax: 616-844-5287
Web Site: www.grandhaven.org
Officers:
  Mayor: Geri McCaleb
  Council Member: Michael D. Fritz
  Council Member: John Hierholzer
  Council Member: Robert Monetza
  Council Member: Dennis Scott
Management:
  Manager: Sandy Katt
Status: Non-Profit, Non-Professional
Paid Staff: 8
Seating Capacity: 450
Year Remodeled: 2006

7299
CALVIN COLLEGE FINE ARTS CENTER
3201 Burton SE
Grand Rapids, MI 49546-4404
Phone: 616-526-6000
Fax: 616-526-6266
Toll-free: 800-688-0122
e-mail: info@calvin.edu
Web Site: www.calvin.edu
Management:
  Marketing: Melissa Reiffer
Founded: 1966
Status: Non-Profit, Professional
Paid Staff: 45
Seating Capacity: 1,065

7300
DELTAPLEX ARENA & CONFERENCE CENTER
2500 Turner Ave
Grand Rapids, MI 49544
Phone: 616-364-9000
Fax: 616-559-8001
e-mail: plexdesk@deltaplex.com
Web Site: www.deltaplex.com
Officers:
  President: Joel Langlois
Management:
  Event Director: Erin Bowen
  Event Codinatior: Christine Welsh
  Director: Chirs Hudson
  Marketing Manager: Carlie Zervan
Status: For-Profit, Professional
Stage Dimensions: 60'x56'
Seating Capacity: 6,500

7301
DEVOS PERFORMANCE HALL
303 Monroe Avenue NW
Grand Rapids, MI 49503
Phone: 616-742-6500
Fax: 616-742-6590
e-mail: webmaster@smggr.com
Web Site: www.devosperformancehall.com
Management:
  General Manager: Richard MacKeigan
  Marketing Director: Lynne Ike, like@smggr.com
  Operations Manager: Ryan Schultz
  Facilities Director: Rod Weeber
  Director of Finance: Chris Machuta
Founded: 1980
Opened: 1980
Paid Staff: 34
Income Sources: Performing Arts Groups; Touring Productions
Affiliations: Grand Rapids Symphony, Opera Grand Rapids, Broadway Grand Rapids & Grand Rapids Ballet
Facility Category: Performing Arts Theater
Type of Stage: Proscenium
Stage Dimensions: 58'9 x 33' x 42'5"""
Seating Capacity: 2,404
Year Built: 1980
Year Remodeled: 2002
Cost: $5 Million
Rental Contact: Director of Finance Chris Machuta

7302
FOUNTAIN STREET CHURCH
24 Fountain Street NE
Grand Rapids, MI 49503
Phone: 616-459-8386
Fax: 616-459-4809
e-mail: office@fountainstreet.org
Web Site: www.fountainstreet.org
Management:
  Adult Choir Director: Stephen Barton
  Account/HR Manager: Melissa Hoezee
Founded: 1879
Status: Non-Profit, Non-Professional

7303
URBAN INSTITUTE FOR CONTEMPORARY ARTS
2 Fulton West
Grand Rapids, MI 49503
Phone: 616-454-7000
Fax: 616-459-9395
e-mail: info@uica.org
Web Site: www.uica.org
Officers:
  President: Scott Vander Leek
  Secretary: Luanne Datema
Management:
  Executive Director: Miranda Krajniak
  Associate Director: Megan Bylsma
  Volunteer and Event Coordinator: Taylor Greenfield
  Exhibitions Curator: Alexander Paschka
  Exhibitions Preparator: Brandon Alman
Founded: 1977
Status: Non-Profit, Professional
Paid Staff: 6

7304
VAN ANDEL ARENA
130 West Fulton
Grand Rapids, MI 49503
Phone: 616-742-6600
Fax: 616-742-6197
e-mail: webmaster@smggr.com
Web Site: www.vanandelarena.com
Management:
  Regional General Manager: Richard MacKeigan
  General Manager: Jim Watt
  Facilities Director: Rod Weeber
Founded: 1996
Status: For-Profit, Professional
Paid Staff: 29
Performs At: Sports & Entertainment Arena
Affiliations: AHL & AFL
Annual Attendance: 1 million
Facility Category: Arena
Type of Stage: Varies
Stage Dimensions: varies
Seating Capacity: 12,048
Year Built: 1996
Rental Contact: Rich MacKeigan

7305
HOPE COLLEGE THEATRE
141 E 12 Street
Holland, MI 49423
Phone: 616-395-7600
Fax: 616-395-7180
e-mail: chesnut@hope.edu
Web Site: www.hope.edu
Officers:
  Chairperson of Theatre Department/P: Daina Robins
Management:
  Director of Theatre: Michelle Bombe
  Costume Shop Manager: Darlene Veenstra
  Visiting Assistant Professor: Jean Bahle
  Professor of Theatre: John Tammi
  Office Manager: Reagan Chesnut
Founded: 1866
Status: Non-Profit, Professional
Type of Stage: Proscenium; Thrust

7306
INTERLOCHEN CENTER FOR THE ARTS KRESGE AUDITORIUM
4000 Highway M-137
PO Box 199
Interlochen, MI 49643-0199
Phone: 231-276-7200
Fax: 231-276-6321
e-mail: admission@interlochen.org
Web Site: www.interlochen.org
Officers:
  Chair: Steve Hayden
Facility Category: Open Sided Ampitheatre
Type of Stage: Proscenium

FACILITIES / Michigan

Stage Dimensions: 64'x 20'
Seating Capacity: 3,943
Year Built: 1940

7307
INTERLOCHEN CENTER FOR THE ARTS DENDRINOS CENTER
4000 Highway M-137
PO Box 199
Interlochen, MI 49643-0199
Phone: 231-276-7200
Fax: 231-276-6321
e-mail: admission@interlochen.org
Web Site: www.interlochen.org
Officers:
    Chair: Steve Hayden
Founded: 1981
Seating Capacity: 200
Year Built: 1981

7308
IRONWOOD THEATRE
109 E Aurora Street
Ironwood, MI 49938
Phone: 906-932-0618
Fax: 906-932-0457
Web Site: www.ironwoodtheatre.net
Officers:
    President: Tom Williams
    Vice President: Betsy Wesselhoft
    Secretary: Sam Filippo
Management:
    Managing Director: Deb Kallunki Gotham
Founded: 1928
Status: Non-Profit, Non-Professional
Paid Staff: 2
Budget: $125,000
Income Sources: Grants; State of Michigan; Fund Raisers
Performs At: Auditorium
Affiliations: Michigan Council for Arts-Cultural Affairs
Annual Attendance: 20,000
Facility Category: Performing Arts Center
Type of Stage: Proscenium
Stage Dimensions: 28'6wx23'l
Seating Capacity: 732
Year Built: 1928
Year Remodeled: 1983
Cost: $160,000

7309
JACKSON ACADEMY PERFORMING ARTS CENTER
4908 RidgewoodRoad
Jackson, MI 39211
Phone: 601-362-9676
e-mail: INFO@JACKSONACADEMY.ORG
Web Site: www.japac.net
Management:
    Rental Contact: Stacy Hontzas

7310
POTTER CENTER
Jackson Community College
2111 Emmons Road
Jackson, MI 49201-8399
Phone: 517-787-0800
Web Site: www.jccmi.edu
Management:
    Director: Cindy Allen
Seating Capacity: 1,543

7311
JAMES W MILLER AUDITORIUM
1903 West Michigan Avenue
Kalamazoo, MI 49008-5344
Phone: 269-387-2311
Fax: 269-387-2317
Toll-free: 800-228-9858
e-mail: miller-comments@wmich.edu
Web Site: www.millerauditorium.com
Management:
    Director of Business Operations AE: Rob Pennock
    Office Coordinator/Marketing Assist: Thomasina Emory
    Business Manager: Faith Wicklund
    Director of Marketing & Development: Tracey Lawie
    Assistant Director of Marketing: Bethany Gauthier
Mission: To enlighten, entertain and educate
Founded: 1968
Specialized Field: Southwest Michigan
Status: Non-Profit, Non-Professional
Paid Staff: 20
Facility Category: Auditorium
Seating Capacity: 3423

7312
KALAMAZOO CIVIC AUDITORIUM
329 S Park Street
Kalamazoo, MI 49007
Phone: 616-343-1313
Fax: 616-343-0532
Web Site: www.kazoocivic.com
Management:
    Box Office Manager: LYN Albert
    Production Stage Manager: Mike Artis
    Resident Properties Manager: Stacy Bartell
    Box Office Associate: Kim Chandler
    Managing Director: Kristen Chesak

7313
NELDA K BALCH PLAYHOUSE
Kalamazoo College Theatre Department
1200 Academy Street
Kalamazoo, MI 49006
Phone: 269-337-7000
Fax: 269-337-7305
Toll-free: 800-253-3602
Web Site: www.kzoo.edu
Management:
    Director: Ed Menta
Founded: 1833
Status: Non-Profit, Non-Professional
Paid Staff: 400

7314
WINGS STADIUM
3600 Vanrick Drive
Kalamazoo, MI 49001
Phone: 269-345-1125
Fax: 269-383-8029
e-mail: ppickard@wingsstadium.com
Web Site: www.wingsstadium.com
Officers:
    President: Paul Pickard
Management:
    Facility Manager: Kathy Rosner
    Public Relations Director: Mike Modugno
Founded: 1974
Seating Capacity: 5,113
Year Built: 1974

7315
BERRY EVENTS CENTER
Northern Michigan University
1401 Presque Isle Avenue
Marquette, MI 49855
Phone: 906-227-2850
e-mail: webhelp@nmu.edu
Web Site: www.nmu.edu
Officers:
    University President: Les Wong
Management:
    Athletic Director: Ken Godfrey
    Facilities Director: Carl Bammert
    Operations Director: Steve Reed
Founded: 1999
Seating Capacity: 3,800
Year Built: 1999

7316
LAKEVIEW ARENA
Marquette Parks and Recreation
401 E Fair Avenue
Marquette, MI 49855
Phone: 906-228-0460
Fax: 906-228-0493
e-mail: parks@mqtcty.org
Web Site: www.mqtcty.org
Management:
    Director: Karl Zueger
    Manager: Doug Smith
Paid Staff: 5
Seating Capacity: 600

7317
MIDLAND CENTER FOR THE ARTS
1801 W St Andrews Road
Midland, MI 48640-2695
Phone: 989-631-5930
Toll-free: 800-523-7649
e-mail: info@mcfta.org
Web Site: www.mcfta.org
Officers:
    President/CEO: Michael Hayes
    Chair: Lee Rouse
    Immediate Past Chair: David Ramaker
    Vice-Chair: Bill Collins
    Treasurer: Brain Rodgers
    Secretary: Melissa Barnard
Management:
    Marketing Director: Linda Basque
    Facilities Mangager: Larry Salva
Founded: 1966
Status: Non-Profit
Paid Staff: 100

7318
RIVER RAISIN CENTRE FOR THE ARTS
114 S Monroe Street
Monroe, MI 48161
Phone: 734-242-7722
Fax: 734-242-9238
e-mail: rrca@riverraisincentre.org
Web Site: www.riverraisincentre.org
Officers:
    President: Denny Miller
    Immediate Past President: Chris Durocher
    Board: Kris Zuckerman
    Board: Joe Bellino
Management:
    Treasurer: Joe Bellion
Founded: 1988
Status: Non-Profit

FACILITIES / Michigan

7319
KELLY SHORTS STADIUM
Central Michigan University Athletics
100 Rose Center
Mount Pleasant, MI 48859
Phone: 989-774-3041
e-mail: heeke1dw@cmich.edu
Web Site: www.cmuchippewas.com
Officers:
   President: Michael Rao
Management:
   Athletics Director: Dave Heeke
   Marketing Director: Mike Dabbs
Founded: 1892
Status: Non-Profit, Professional
Paid Staff: 10
Paid Artists: 100
Seating Capacity: 30,000

7320
PLACHTA AUDITORIUM
Central Michigan University
1200 S. Franklin St
Mount Pleasant, MI 48859
Phone: 989-774-4000
Fax: 517-774-7957
e-mail: Robert.J.Ebner@cmich.edu
Web Site: www.cmich.edu
Officers:
   President: Michael Rao
Management:
   University Events Director: Robert Ebner

7321
ROSE ARENA
Central Michigan University
100 Rose Center
Mount Pleasant, MI 48859
Phone: 989-774-3041
e-mail: heeke1dw@cmich.edu
Web Site: www.cmuchippewas.com
Officers:
   University President: Michael Rao
Management:
   Athletics Director: Dave Heeke
   Marketing Director: Mike Dabbs
Status: Non-Profit, Non-Professional
Paid Staff: 6
Seating Capacity: 5,200

7322
FRAUENTHAL CENTER FOR THE PERFORMING ARTS
425 W Western Avenue
Muskegon, MI 49440
Phone: 231-722-2890
e-mail: info@frauenthal.org
Web Site: www.frauenthal.org
Management:
   Building Manager: Scott Bartoszek
   Special Projects: Polly Doctor
   Event Coordinator: Heather Hansen
Utilizes: Lyricists; Special Technical Talent; Theatre Companies
Founded: 1974
Status: Non-Profit, Professional
Paid Staff: 7
Volunteer Staff: 385
Budget: $890,000
Income Sources: Ticket Sales; Endowments
Affiliations: League of Historic American Theatres; American Association of Arts Presenters
Annual Attendance: 185,000
Facility Category: Historic Theater
Type of Stage: Proscenium
Stage Dimensions: 41'6'x30H
Seating Capacity: 1,748
Year Built: 1930
Year Remodeled: 1998
Cost: $8,500,000
Rental Contact: Linda Medema
Organization Type: Performing; Resident; Educational; Sponsoring; Presenter
Resident Groups: Muskegon Community Concert Association, Muskegon Civic Theatre, Cherry County Playhouse, West Shore

7323
OVERBROOK THEATER
Muskegon Community College
221 S Quarterline Road
Muskegon, MI 49442
Phone: 231-773-9131
Fax: 231-777-0324
Toll-free: 866-711-4622
e-mail: webmaster@muskegoncc.edu
Web Site: www.muskegoncc.edu
Officers:
   President: David Rule
Management:
   Artistic Director: Sheila Kulp Wahamaki
Founded: 1926
Specialized Field: Fine Arts
Status: Non-Profit, Professional
Paid Staff: 12
Paid Artists: 5
Seating Capacity: 344

7324
L.C WALKER ARENA
955 Fourth Street
Muskegon, MI 49440
Phone: 231-726-2939
Fax: 231-726-4620
Web Site: www.lcwalkerarena.com
Management:
   Director: Neil Hawryliw
Seating Capacity: 6,400

7325
MCMORRAN PLACE THEATRE
701 McMorran Boulevard
Port Huron, MI 48060
Phone: 810-985-6166
Fax: 810-985-3358
Toll-free: 800-858-6166
Web Site: www.mcmorran.com
Management:
   General Manager: Larry Krabach
   Operations Director: Jerry Hamilton
Founded: 1957
Specialized Field: Theatre; Community; Theatrical Group
Status: Non-Profit, Professional
Paid Staff: 10
Income Sources: College
Facility Category: Performing Arts
Type of Stage: Procenium
Stage Dimensions: 50x30
Seating Capacity: 1159
Year Built: 1959

7326
KIRTLAND CENTER FOR THE PERFORMING ARTS
Kirtland Community College
10775 N Saint Helen Road
Roscommon, MI 48653
Phone: 989-275-6777
e-mail: kcpa@kirtland.edu
Web Site: www.kirtlandcenter.com
Officers:
   President: Thomas Quinn
Management:
   Director: Jomarie Gurnow
   Event Coordinator: Beth Petrik
   Technical Director: Tony Fantozzi
Utilizes: Actors; Artists-in-Residence; Collaborations; Dance Companies; Educators; Grant Writers; Guest Accompanists; Guest Artists; Guest Companies; Guest Conductors; Guest Ensembles; Guild Activities; Instructors; Original Music Scores; Selected Students; Sign Language Translators; Soloists; Student Interns; Special Technical Talent; Theatre Companies
Founded: 1966
Status: Non-Profit
Paid Staff: 4
Volunteer Staff: 30
Budget: $300,000
Income Sources: Ticket Sales; Donations; College Funding
Affiliations: Arts Midwest; APAP; USITT; MACAA
Annual Attendance: 30,000
Facility Category: Theatre
Type of Stage: Modified Thrust
Seating Capacity: 846
Year Built: 1966
Rental Contact: Director Gary Carlton

7327
HERITAGE THEATER
Dow Event Center
303 Johnson Street
Saginaw, MI 48607
Phone: 989-759-1320
Fax: 989-759-1322
e-mail: info@DowEventCenter.com
Web Site: www.doweventcenter.com
Officers:
   Director of Finance: Matthew Rick
Management:
   General Manager: Matt Blasy
   General Manager Sales and Marketing: Regina Demski
   Director of Finance: Matthew Rick
Utilizes: Dancers; Local Artists; Multimedia; Original Music Scores; Theatre Companies
Founded: 1970
Status: Non-Profit, Professional
Paid Staff: 200
Facility Category: Theater, Arena
Seating Capacity: 2,276
Year Built: 1970
Year Remodeled: 2002
Rental Contact: Matt Blasy

7328
FREEDOM HILL AMPHITHEATRE
14900 Metropolitan Parkway
Sterling Heights, MI 48312
Phone: 586-268-9700
Fax: 586-268-9753
e-mail: info@freedomhill.net
Web Site: www.freedomhill.net
Officers:

FACILITIES / Minnesota

President: Joe Bolanca
Management:
   Box Office Manager: Christa Bolleber
   Product Manager: Jeff Davey
   Administration: Kristine Kamlay
Status: Professional
Seating Capacity: 7,000

7329
TECUMSEH CENTER FOR THE ARTS
400 N Maumee Street
Tecumseh, MI 49286
Phone: 517-423-6617
Fax: 517-423-3610
e-mail: boxoffice@theTCA.org
Web Site: www.thetca.org
Management:
   Cultural & Leisure Director: Shelley Lim
   Marketing Director: Rebecca Peach
   Sales & Marketing Assistant: Joanna Gall
Status: Profit
Seating Capacity: 572

7330
DENNOS MUSEUM CENTER MILLIKEN AUDITORIUM
Northwest Michigan College
1701 E Front Street
Traverse City, MI 49686
Phone: 231-995-1595
Fax: 231-995-1597
e-mail: boxoffice@nmc.edu
Web Site: www.dennosmuseum.org
Officers:
   President: Timothy Nelson
Management:
   Museum Director: Eugene Jenneman
   Operations Manager: Gale Cook
Utilizes: Actors; Collaborations; Curators; Dance Companies; Dancers; Educators; Fine Artists; Grant Writers; Guest Accompanists; Guest Artists; Guest Choreographers; Guest Directors; Guest Ensembles; Guest Instructors; Guest Musical Directors; Guest Musicians; Guest Soloists; High School Drama; Instructors; Local Artists; Lyricists; Multimedia; Sign Language Translators; Singers; Soloists; Special Technical Talent; Theatre Companies; Touring Companies; Visual Arts
Founded: 1991
Specialized Field: Visual & Performing Arts
Status: Non-Profit
Paid Staff: 9
Volunteer Staff: 160
Paid Artists: 12
Budget: $900,000
Affiliations: Northwestern Michigan College
Annual Attendance: 600,000
Facility Category: Museum & Concert Hall
Stage Dimensions: 30' X 50'
Seating Capacity: 367
Year Built: 1991
Rental Contact: Assistant to the Director Judith Albers

7331
PARK PLACE HOTEL
300 E State Street
Traverse City, MI 49684
Phone: 231-946-5000
Fax: 231-946-2772
e-mail: hotel@park-place-hotel.com
Web Site: www.park-place-hotel.com
Management:
   General Manager: Amy Parker
   Marketing Director: Margaret Morse

Founded: 1930
Status: For-Profit, Professional

7332
JAMES E O'NEIL JR ARENA
Saginaw Valley State University
7400 Bay Road
University Center, MI 48710
Phone: 989-964-4000
e-mail: sid@svsu.edu
Web Site: www.svsu.edu
Officers:
   President: Eric Gilbertson
Management:
   Athletic Director: Mike Watson
   Operations: Matt Oberlin
Status: Non-Professional

7333
JEWISH COMMUNITY CENTER OF METROPOLITAN DETROIT
D Dan & Betty Kahn Building
6600 W Maple Road
West Bloomfield, MI 48322-3002
Phone: 248-661-1000
e-mail: mlit@jccdet.org
Web Site: www.jccdet.org
Officers:
   President: Todd Sachse
Management:
   Executive Director: Mark A Lit
   Development: Wendy Strip
   Marketing Director: Suzanne Lichtman
Founded: 1926
Status: Non-Profit
Paid Staff: 491
Volunteer Staff: 999

7334
YACK ARENA
3131 Third Street
Wyandotte, MI 48192
Phone: 734-324-7290
e-mail: recreation@wyan.org
Web Site: www.wyandotte.net
Officers:
   Chairman: Molly Exner
Management:
   Operations: Fred Pischke
Founded: 1800
Status: Non-Profit, Non-Professional
Paid Staff: 150
Seating Capacity: 3,800

7335
EASTERN MICHIGAN UNIVERSITY CONVOCATION CENTER
799 N Hewitt Road
Ypsilanti, MI 48197
Phone: 734-487-5386
Fax: 734-487-6898
e-mail: mmonahan@emich.edu
Web Site: www.emich.edu
Officers:
   President: Susan Martin
Management:
   Director: Mark Monahan
   Marketing Director: Marcy Szabo
   Sr. Account: Jeanne Torok
   Operations Supervisor: Dave Keller
   Coordinator Indoor: Kara Corwin
Founded: 1998
Seating Capacity: 9,500

Minnesota

7336
ALBERT LEA CITY ARENA
701 Lake Chapeau Drive
Albert, MN 56007
Phone: 507-377-4370
e-mail: jhutchison@city.albertlea.org
Web Site: www.city.albertlea.org
Management:
   Facility Manager: Robert Furland
   Director: Jay Hutchison
Founded: 1976
Specialized Field: 377-4370 work
Status: Non-Profit, Non-Professional
Paid Staff: 12
Paid Artists: 6

7337
ALBERT LEA COMMUNITY THEATRE
Marion Ross Performing Arts Center
147 N Broadway
Albert Lea, MN 56007
Phone: 507-377-4372
e-mail: mrpac@charterinternet.com
Web Site: www.city.albertlea.org
Management:
   Theatre Manager: Patrick Rasmussen
   Director: Jay Hutchison
Utilizes: Actors; Guest Artists; Guest Designers; Guest Instructors; Guest Soloists; Guild Activities; Instructors; Local Artists; Playwrights; Resident Artists; Special Technical Talent; Theatre Companies
Status: Profit
Paid Staff: 1
Facility Category: Theatre
Type of Stage: Proscenium
Stage Dimensions: 29' 6 x 23' x 28''''
Seating Capacity: 255
Year Remodeled: 1989

7338
RIVERSIDE ARENA
501 2nd Avenue NE
Austin, MN 55912
Phone: 507-433-1881
Fax: 507-433-9078
Management:
   Director: Kim A Underwood
Status: Non-Professional
Facility Category: Arena
Type of Stage: Portable
Seating Capacity: 4,200

7339
BEMIDJI STATE UNIVERSITY THOMPSON RECITAL HALL
Bangsberg Fine Arts Complex
1500 Birchmont Drive NE
Bemidji, MN 56601-2699
Phone: 218-755-2001
Fax: 218-755-4048
Toll-free: 800-475-2001
e-mail: plogan@bemidjistate.edu
Web Site: www.bemidjistate.edu
Officers:
   Chair: P Bradley Logan
   President: Jon Quistgaard
Specialized Field: Fine Arts
Status: Non-Professional
Type of Stage: Main Stage; Black Box

FACILITIES / Minnesota

7340
NATIONAL SPORTS CENTER
1700 105th Avenue NE
Blaine, MN 55449
Phone: 763-785-5600
Fax: 763-785-5699
e-mail: webmaster@nscsports.org
Web Site: www.nscsports.com
Management:
  Executive Director: Paul Erickson
  Chief Administrative Officer: Kris Bjerkness
  Senior Director: Neil Ladd
  Director of Finance: Darin Thompson
  Accounting: Patti Pellow
Founded: 1990
Status: Non-Profit, Non-Professional
Paid Staff: 150
Seating Capacity: 12,000

7341
ARTS IN THE PARKS PORTABLE STAGE
2215 W Old Shakopee Road
Bloomington, MN 55431
Phone: 952-948-3925
Fax: 612-887-9695

7342
BROOKLYN CENTER COMMUNITY CENTER
6301 Shingle Creek Parkway
Brooklyn Center, MN 55430
Phone: 763-569-3300
Fax: 763-569-3494
e-mail: info@ci.brooklyn-center.mn.us
Web Site: www.cityofbrooklyncenter.org
Management:
  Director: Jim Glasoe
Status: Non-Profit

7343
NORTH HENNEPIN COMMUNITY COLLEGE THEATER
7411 85th Avenue North
Brooklyn Park, MN 55445
Phone: 763-488-0391
Fax: 763-424-0929
Toll-free: 800-818-0395
e-mail: info@nhcc.edu
Web Site: www.nhcc.edu
Officers:
  Dean: Jane Wilson
Status: Non-Professional

7344
DULUTH ENTERTAINMENT CONVENTION CENTER
350 Harbor Drive
Duluth, MN 55802
Phone: 218-722-5573
Fax: 218-722-4247
Toll-free: 800-628-8385
Web Site: www.decc.org
Management:
  Executive Director: Dan Russel
  Assistant Executive Director: Chelly Townsend
  Financial Director: Caty kaups
Founded: 1990
Status: For-Profit, Professional

7345
ST LOUIS COUNTY HERITAGE AND ARTS CENTER
Duluth Depot
506 W Michigan Street
Duluth, MN 55802
Phone: 218-727-8025
Web Site: www.duluthdepot.org
Management:
  Executive Director: Ken Buehler
Founded: 1892

7346
FAIRMONT OPERA HOUSE
45 Downtown Plaza
PO Box 226
Fairmont, MN 56031
Phone: 507-238-4900
e-mail: director@fairmontoperahouse.com
Web Site: www.fairmontoperahouse.com
Officers:
  President: Bonnie Taplin
  VP: Erica Volikir
Management:
  Managing Director: Tom Dodge
Founded: 1901
Status: Non-Profit, Professional
Paid Staff: 2
Paid Artists: 10

7347
GRAND CASINO HINCKLEY AMPHITHEATER
777 Lady Luck Drive
P.O. Box 343
Hinckley, MN 55037
Toll-free: 800-472-6321
Web Site: www.grandcasinomn.com
Seating Capacity: 5,644

7348
PRAIRIE ARTS CENTER
PO Box 94
310 1st Avenue North
Long Prairie, MN 56347
Phone: 320-732-6080
Officers:
  President: Linda Kielty

7349
ELIAS J HALLING RECITAL HALL
Minnesota State University
202 Performing Arts Center
Mankato, MN 56001
Phone: 507-389-2118
Fax: 507-389-2922
e-mail: music@mnsu.edu
Web Site: www.intech.mnsu.edu
Management:
  Events Coordinator/Music: Dale Haefner
Utilizes: Artists-in-Residence; Educators; Fine Artists; Guest Musical Directors; Guest Musicians; Instructors; Multimedia; Original Music Scores
Founded: 1867
Paid Staff: 13
Paid Artists: 11
Budget: $55,000
Income Sources: Gate Receipts; Grants; Advertising; Corporate Contributions
Annual Attendance: 14,000
Facility Category: Performing Arts Center
Type of Stage: Proscenium
Stage Dimensions: 80'x40'
Seating Capacity: 350
Year Built: 1968
Rental Contact: 507-398-5549 Dale Haefner

7350
MIDWEST WIRELESS CIVIC CENTER
One Civic Center Plaza
Mankato, MN 56001
Phone: 507-389-3000
Fax: 507-345-1627
Web Site: www.midwestwirelesscivicenter.com
Management:
  Executive Director: Burt Lyman
  Marketing Manager: Mona Will
  Operations Manager: Dave Randalls
Seating Capacity: 7,310

7351
GUTHRIE THEATER
818 South 2nd Street
Minneapolis, MN 55415
Phone: 612-225-6000
Fax: 612-225-6004
Toll-free: 877-447-8243
e-mail: boxoffice@guthrietheater.org
Web Site: www.guthrietheater.org
Officers:
  President: Douglas M Steenland
  VP: Randall Hogan
  Treasurer: Jay Kiedrowski
  Secretary: Robert A Rosenbaum
Management:
  Director: Joe Dowling
  Associate Artistic Director: John Miller-Stephany
  Production Director: Frank Butler
Mission: An American center for theater performance, production, education and professional training. By presenting both classical literature and new work from diverse cultures, the Guthrie illuminates the common humanity connecting Minnesota to the peoples of the world.
Founded: 1963
Status: Non-Profit, Professional
Paid Staff: 326
Seating Capacity: 1,293
Year Built: 1963

7352
HENNEPIN CENTER FOR THE ARTS
528 Hennepin Avenue
Minneapolis, MN 55403
Phone: 612-206-3600
Fax: 612-332-8131
Web Site: www.thecowlescenter.org
Management:
  Executive Director: Lynn A. Von Eschen
  General Manager: Randy Ingram
  Marketing Director: Dana Munson
  Director of Education: Jessi Fett
  Senior Staff Accountant: Kim Upsher
Founded: 1979
Status: Non-Profit, Professional
Paid Staff: 6

7353
HISTORIC ORPHEUM THEATRE
910 Hennepin Avenue
Minneapolis, MN 55403
Phone: 612-455-9500
Fax: 612-455-9502
e-mail: Info@HennepinTheatreTrust.org
Web Site: www.hennepintheatretrust.org
Officers:
  Chairperson: Dan Cramer

FACILITIES / Minnesota

   Vice Chairperson: Scott Benson
   President/CEO: Tom Hoch
   Business Partnerships Manager: Julie Gotlieb
   Accounting Associate: Deborah Hunt
   Sponsorship Manager: Scott Mayer
   Artist Relationship Manager: Kari Schloner
Founded: 1921
Seating Capacity: 2,579

7354
HISTORIC STATE THEATRE
805 Hennepin Avenue
Minneapolis, MN 55402
Phone: 612-373-5600
Fax: 612-252-0601
e-mail: Info@HennepinTheatreTrust.org
Web Site: www.hennepintheatretrust.org
Officers:
   Chairperson: Dan Cramer
   Vice Chairperson: Scott Benson
   President/CEO: Tom Hoch
   Business Partnerships Manager: Julie Gotlieb
   Accounting Associate: Deborah Hunt
   Sponsorship Manager: Scott Mayer
   Artist Relationship Manager: Kari Schloner
Status: For-Profit, Non-Professional
Paid Staff: 100

7355
HORTON GRAND THEATRE
1407 Nicollet Ave
Minneapolis, MN 55403
Mailing Address: 1407 Nicollet Ave , Minneapolis, MN 55403
Phone: 612-874-1100
Fax: 612-767-4947
e-mail: BoxOffice@MusicBoxMpls.com
Web Site: www.tripleespresso.com
Management:
   President/Executive Producer: Dennis Babcock
   Associate Producer: Rosalie Miller
   Operations Manager: Hector Roberts
   Group Sales Manager: Emilia Zellmer
   Marketing Manager: Megan Paulek
   Controller: Greg Triplett
   Audience Services Manager: Ben Netzley
   Artistic Director: William Partlan
Utilizes: Actors; Designers; Educators; Fine Artists; Guest Accompanists; Guest Musical Directors; Guest Soloists; High School Drama; Instructors; Local Unknown Artists; Multimedia; Original Music Scores; Performance Artists; Resident Artists; Resident Professionals; Sign Language Translators; Special Technical Talent; Theatre Companies; Visual Arts
Founded: 1985
Paid Staff: 20
Paid Artists: 20
Income Sources: Ticket Sales
Affiliations: San Diego Performing Arts League; San Diego Chamber of Commerce; San Diego Convention & Visitors Bureau
Annual Attendance: 50,000
Facility Category: Rental house
Type of Stage: Proscenium
Stage Dimensions: 29'9 x 18'x22'6"""
Seating Capacity: 250
Year Built: 1983
Rental Contact: General Manager Matt Boden

7356
HUBERT H HUMPHREY METRODOME
900 South Fifth Street
Minneapolis, MN 55415
Phone: 612-332-0386
Fax: 612-332-8334
e-mail: lesterb@msfc.com
Web Site: www.msfc.com
Management:
   Executive Director: William J Lester
   Director Operations: Dennis Alfton
Founded: 1982
Status: For-Profit, Non-Professional
Seating Capacity: 65,000 (football), 55,500 (basketball)
Year Built: 1982

7357
MACPHAIL CENTER FOR THE ARTS
1128 LaSalle Avenue
Minneapolis, MN 55403
Phone: 612-321-0100
Management:
   Assistant Director: Joanna Cortright
Mission: Lessons and classes in music to both adults and children.
Founded: 1907
Specialized Field: Vocal Music; Instrumental Music
Status: Semi-Professional; Nonprofit
Income Sources: University of Minnesota; National Guild of Community Schools of Music
Organization Type: Educational

7358
NORTHROP AUDITORIUM
University of Minnesota
84 Church Street Southeast
Minneapolis, MN 55455
Phone: 612-625-6600
Fax: 612-626-1750
e-mail: northrop@umn.edu
Web Site: www.northrop.umn.edu
Officers:
   GM: Dale Schatzlein
   Publicity Office: Linda Brandt
Management:
   Director: Christine Tschida
   Operating Director: Sally Dischinger
   Business Manager: Robin Sauerwein
Founded: 1928
Seating Capacity: 4,767

7359
ORCHESTRA HALL
1111 Nicollet Mall
Minneapolis, MN 55403
Phone: 612-371-5600
Toll-free: 800-292-4141
e-mail: info@mnorch.com
Web Site: www.minnesotaorchestra.org
Officers:
   CEO: Gordon M. Sprenger
   Vise Chaiperson: Karen Himle
   President and CEO: Michael Hudson
Management:
   Executive Assistant to the Presiden: Julie Stemmler
   General Manager: Robert Meu
Mission: To enrich lives with great music.
Founded: 1903
Status: Non-Profit, Professional
Paid Staff: 150
Paid Artists: 100
Budget: $28,000,000
Annual Attendance: 400,000
Facility Category: Concert Hall
Type of Stage: Proscenium
Seating Capacity: 2,450
Year Built: 1974

7360
TARGET CENTER
600 First Avenue North
Minneapolis, MN 55403-1416
Phone: 612-673-1600
Fax: 612-673-1370
e-mail: info@targetcenter.com
Web Site: www.targetcenter.com
Management:
   Executive Director: Steve Mattson
   VP: Kevin McHale
   Marketing Director: Sandy Sweetser
   Concessions Manager: Ajay Sekhran
Mission: There are 18,467 theatre-style permanent seats in Target Center and in addition there are over 114 wheelchair and accessible seating located on all concourse levels of Target Center. The Minnesota Timberwolves played their first game in their new home, Target Center, on October 16, 1990 vs. the Philadelphia 76ers.
Founded: 1990
Status: For-Profit, Non-Professional
Paid Staff: 500

7361
TED MANN CONCERT HALL
University of Minnesota
2106 Fourth Street South
Minneapolis, MN 55455
Phone: 612-624-5740
Fax: 612-624-8001
e-mail: mnmusic@umn.edu
Web Site: www.tedmann.umn.edu
Officers:
   Facilities Manager: Craig Carnahan
Seating Capacity: 1,100

7362
THEATRE IN THE ROUND PLAYERS
245 Cedar Avenue
Minneapolis, MN 55454-1054
Phone: 612-333-3010
e-mail: Admin@TheatreintheRound.org
Web Site: www.theatreintheround.org
Management:
   Assistant Administrator: Greg Johnson
   Executive Director: Steven Antenucci
Mission: To produce excellent theatre in, with, and for the community.
Founded: 1952
Status: Non-Profit, Non-Professional
Paid Staff: 3
Paid Artists: 9
Seating Capacity: 249

7363
UNIVERSITY OF MINNESOTA SPORTS PAVILLION
1923 University Avenue SE
Minneapolis, MN 55455
Phone: 612-625-5804
Fax: 612-624-5887
Management:
   Director/Athletic Facilities: Scott P Ellison
   Assistant Program Director: Leon Freese
Seating Capacity: 5,700

7364
WALKER ART CENTER
1750 Hennepin Avenue
Minneapolis, MN 55403

Phone: 612-375-7600
Fax: 612-375-7618
e-mail: info@walkerart.org
Web Site: www.walkerart.org
Mission: A catalyst for the creative expression of artists and the active engagement of audiences, examines the questions that shape and inspire us as individuals, cultures, and communities.
Founded: 1927

7365
NEW HOPE OUTDOOR THEATRE
4401 Xylon Avenue N
New Hope, MN 55428
Phone: 763-531-5100
Fax: 763-531-5136
Web Site: www.ci.new-hope.mn.us
Management:
 Director Arts Creation: Shery French
Founded: 1970
Status: Non-Profit

7366
MARTIN LUTHER COLLEGE LYCEUM
1995 Luther Court
New Ulm, MN 56073
Fax: 507-354-8225

7367
MAYO CIVIC CENTER ARENA
30 Civic Center Drive SE
Rochester, MN 55904
Phone: 507-328-2220
Fax: 507-328-2221
Toll-free: 800-422-2199
e-mail: info@mayociviccenter.com
Web Site: www.mayociviccenter.com
Management:
 Executive Director: Donna Drews
 Operations Manager: David Silker
 Managing Director: Andy Krogstad
 Operations Supervisor: Randy Blake
 Director of Sales: Matt Esau

7368
MAYO CIVIC CENTER AUDITORIUM THEATRE
30 Civic Center Drive SE
Rochester, MN 55904
Phone: 507-328-2220
Fax: 507-328-2221
Toll-free: 800-422-2199
e-mail: info@mayociviccenter.com
Web Site: www.mayociviccenter.com
Management:
 Executive Director: Donna Drews
 Managing Director: Andy Krogstad
 Operations Manager: David Silker

7369
PARAMOUNT THEATER VISUALS & ARTS CENTER
913 West Saint Germain Street
Saint Cloud, MN 56301
Phone: 320-259-5463
e-mail: boxoffice@paramountarts.org
Web Site: www.paramountarts.org
Officers:
 Vice President: Helga Bauerly
 Secretary: Rebecca Billig
 Counsel: Robert Kalenda
 President: Greg Murray
 Treasurer: Paul Thompson
Management:
 Executive Director: Tony Goddard
 Performing Arts Director: Laurie Johnson
 Sound Engineer/Maintenance Manager: Paul Deutsch
 Visual Arts Director: Melissa Gohman
 Finance Director: Cindy O'Konek
Founded: 1998
Performs At: Historic Theatre
Seating Capacity: 700

7370
BENEDICTA ARTS CENTER
College of Saint Benedict
37 South College Avenue
Saint Joseph, MN 56374
Phone: 320-363-5777
Fax: 320-363-6097
Web Site: www.csbsju.edu/finearts
Management:
 Executive Director: Brian Jose
 Technical Director: Adam Dahl
 Facility Operations Manager: Eric Geier
 Production Manager: Kevin Knodi
 Gallery Manager: Jill Dubbeldee Kuhn
 Box Office Systems Manager: Deb Wolford
Utilizes: Actors; Artists-in-Residence; Choreographers; Collaborating Artists; Collaborations; Commissioned Music; Dance Companies; Dancers; Designers; Educators; Filmmakers; Fine Artists; Five Seasonal Concerts; Grant Writers; Guest Accompanists; Guest Artists; Guest Choreographers; Guest Companies; Guest Composers; Guest Conductors; Guest Designers; Guest Directors; Guest Ensembles; Guest Instructors; Guest Lecturers; Guest Musical Directors; Guest Musicians; Guest Soloists; Guest Teachers; High School Drama; Instructors; Local Artists; Lyricists; Multimedia; Music; Organization Contracts; Original Music Scores; Performance Artists; Playwrights; Resident Artists; Selected Students; Sign Language Translators; Singers; Soloists; Student Interns; Special Technical Talent; Theatre Companies; Touring Companies; Visual Arts
Paid Staff: 13
Volunteer Staff: 20
Paid Artists: 9
Non-paid Artists: 400
Income Sources: NEA, MSAB, Heartland Arts Fund, Target Stores, local corporations, fees and tickets
Annual Attendance: 15,000
Facility Category: Performing Arts Center
Type of Stage: Proscenium
Stage Dimensions: 59' X 38
Seating Capacity: 1,084
Year Built: 1963
Cost: 2.5 million
Rental Contact: Mary Darnall

7371
FITZGERALD THEATER
10 E Exchange Street
Saint Paul, MN 55101
Phone: 651-290-1200
Fax: 651-290-1195
e-mail: fitzgerald@mpr.org
Web Site: www.fitzgeraldtheater.org
Management:
 President: Brian Sanderson
 Production Manager: Thomas Campbell
 Box Office Manager: Shane Wethers
Mission: The theater has, over the years, played host to Broadway musicals, vaudeville shows, film festivals, and concerts of all sorts.
Utilizes: AEA Actors; Choreographers; Collaborations; Dance Companies; Dancers; Designers; Guest Choreographers; Multimedia; Music; Resident Professionals; Sign Language Translators; Special Technical Talent; Theatre Companies
Founded: 1980
Specialized Field: Concerts; Theater; Broadcasting; Dance
Status: Non-Profit, Professional
Paid Staff: 15
Volunteer Staff: 15
Budget: $350,000
Income Sources: Box Office; Rent; Concession; Grant from Parent Company
Facility Category: Rental-Performing Arts
Type of Stage: Sprung Floor
Stage Dimensions: 36'x30'
Year Built: 1910
Year Remodeled: 1986
Rental Contact: Manager, General Services Shane Wethers

7372
LEGENDARY ROY WILKINS AUDITORIUM AT SAINT PAUL RIVERCENTRE
175 W Kellogg Boulevard
Suite 501
Saint Paul, MN 55102
Phone: 651-265-4800
Fax: 651-265-4899
e-mail: info@rivercentre.org
Web Site: www.theroy.org
Management:
 Vice President/General Manager: Jim Ibister
 Director Booking: Susan Hubbard
Founded: 1930
Facility Category: Auditorium with flat floor and balcony seating
Type of Stage: portable
Stage Dimensions: 6' x 8'x 8' sections
Seating Capacity: 5,500
Year Built: 1931
Year Remodeled: 1984

7373
MIDWAY STADIUM
1771 Energy Park Drive
Saint Paul, MN 55108
Phone: 651-644-3517
Fax: 651-644-1627
e-mail: funsgood@saintsbaseball.com
Web Site: www.saintsbaseball.com
Officers:
 VP/Owner: Jeff Goldklang
 VP: Tom Whaley
Management:
 Assistant General Manager: Chris Schwab
 Assistant General Manager: Scott Bush
 Box Office Manager: Alex Harkaway
Seating Capacity: 14,000

7374
O'SHAUGHNESSY THEATRE
St. Catherine University
2004 Randolph Avenue F-24
Saint Paul, MN 55105
Phone: 651-690-6700
Fax: 651-690-6769
e-mail: oshuaghnessy@stkate.edu
Web Site: www.stkate.edu/oshaughnessy
Officers:
 Managing Director: Brandie Greig

FACILITIES / Mississippi

Production Manager: Greg Morrissey
Founded: 1970
Status: Nonprofit. Professional
Paid Staff: 11
Paid Artists: 20
Seating Capacity: 1,817

7375
ORDWAY CENTER FOR THE PERFORMING ARTS
345 Washington Street
Saint Paul, MN 55102
Phone: 651-282-3000
Fax: 651-224-5319
e-mail: jpetrie@ordway.org
Web Site: www.ordway.org
Officers:
 President and CEO: Patricia Mitchell
 Chair: Thomas Handley
 Vice Chair: Robert Cattanach
Management:
 Director of Production and Construc: Andy Luft
 Assistant Production Manager: Julia Erickson
 Production Stage Manager: Janet Huyck
Founded: 1985
Paid Staff: 80
Volunteer Staff: 100
Performs At: Ordway Music McKnight Theatre

7376
RIVERCENTER
175 West Kellogg Boulevard
Saint Paul, MN 55102
Phone: 651-265-4800
Fax: 651-265-4899
e-mail: info@rivercentre.org
Web Site: www.rivercentre.org
Management:
 Managing Director: Jim Ivester
 Interim Director: Erich Mische
Founded: 1996
Status: For-Profit, Professional
Paid Staff: 200
Seating Capacity: 16,000

7377
XCEL ENERGY CENTER
175 West Kellogg Blvd
Suite 501
Saint Paul, MN 55102
Phone: 651-265-4800
Fax: 652-654-899
e-mail: info@rivercentre.org
Web Site: www.wild.com
Management:
 President: Doug Raisebrough
 Executive Director: Jack Larson
 Director Marketing: Peter Johns
 Arena Project Director: Ray Chandler
Founded: 1997
Status: Professional
Seating Capacity: 18,600

7378
SCHAEFFER FINE ARTS CENTER
Gustavus Adolphus College
800 W College Avenue
Saint Peter, MN 56082
Phone: 507-933-7363
Fax: 507-933-6253
e-mail: al@gac.edu
Web Site: www.gustavus.edu
Management:
 President: James Peterson

Fine Arts Director: Alan Behrends
Founded: 1862
Status: Non-Profit, Professional
Paid Staff: 700
Paid Artists: 32

7379
I-90 EXPO CENTER
1010 70th Avenue
Sherburn, MN 56171
Phone: 507-764-4025
Fax: 507-764-4990
e-mail: codi@i90expocenter.com
Web Site: www.i90expocenter.com
Officers:
 Co-Owner: Mike Johnson
 Co-Owner: Greg Johnson
Seating Capacity: 7,000

7380
LAKESHORE PLAYHOUSE
4820 Stewart Avenue
White Bear Lake, MN 55110
Phone: 651-426-3275
Fax: 651-429-5674
e-mail: office@lakeshoreplayers.com
Web Site: www.lakeshoreplayers.com
Officers:
 President: Frank Mabley
Founded: 1952
Status: Non-Profit, Non-Professional
Paid Staff: 4

Mississippi

7381
DEPOT THEATRE
110 Magnolia Street
Belzoni, MS 39038
Phone: 662-247-1976
Season: June - September

7382
BEAU RIVAGE THEATRE
875 Beach Boulevard
Biloxi, MS 39530
Mailing Address: PO Box 7777
Phone: 228-386-7111
Fax: 228-386-7619
Toll-free: 888-750-7111
Web Site: www.beaurivage.com
Officers:
 Executive Director Of Entertainment: Anthony Gibson
Founded: 1999
Seating Capacity: 1,500
Year Built: 2006

7383
HARLEY OUTDOOR AMPHITHEATRE
942 Cedar Lake Road
Biloxi, MS 39532
Phone: 228-547-4239
Fax: 985-646-1662
Management:
 GM: Shannon Elias
Seating Capacity: 20,000

7384
SAENGER THEATRE OF THE PERFORMING ARTS
170 Reynoir Street
PO Box 775
Biloxi, MS 39530
Phone: 228-432-1601
e-mail: rchester@biloxi.ms.us
Web Site: www.biloxi.ms.us/saenger/
Management:
 Manager: Ron Chester
 Technical Director: Bob Montgomery
Founded: 1929

7385
BOLOGNA PERFORMING ARTS CENTER
Delta State University
PO Box 3213
Cleveland, MS 38733
Phone: 662-846-4625
Fax: 662-846-4627
e-mail: ddallas@deltastate.edu
Web Site: www.bolognapac.com
Management:
 Executive Director: David Dallas
 Production Coordinator: Paula H Lindsey
 Arts Education Coordinator: Tennie Lester
 Asst Dir/Audience Dev Coordinator: Jolana R Gibbs
 Senior Secretary: Kimberly Potts
Mission: The center attracts quality programming, superb artists and powerful performances to enrich, entertain and strengthen our Delta community. In addition, the Bologna Center has demonstrated its commitment to arts education and developed the Janice Wyatt Mississippi Summer Arts Institute, which provides a comprehensive training program in all arts disciplines.
Founded: 1994
Specialized Field: Education; Dance; Speakers; Musical Shows; Broadway Shows; Performances
Status: Non-Profit, Professional
Paid Staff: 10
Paid Artists: 12

7386
WHISTLE STOP PLAYHOUSE
Cleveland Community Theatre
PO Box 44
Cleveland, MS 38732
Phone: 601-843-3096

7387
COLUMBIA EXPOSITION CENTER
150 Industrial Park Drive
Columbia, MS 39429
Phone: 601-736-6204
Fax: 601-736-6259
e-mail: expocenter@cblink.com
Management:
 Manager: Linda Martin
 Manager: Paul Pounds
Seating Capacity: 3,200

7388
PRINCESS THEATRE
5th Street S
Columbus, MS 39701
Phone: 662-328-7860

FACILITIES / Mississippi

7389
COLISEUM CIVIC CENTER
404 Taylor Street
PO Box 723
Corinth, MS 38834
Phone: 662-287-6079
Fax: 662-286-0903

7390
LEFLORE COUNTY CIVIC CENTER
Highway 7 N
PO Box 1659
Greenwood, MS 38930
Phone: 662-453-4065
Fax: 662-453-4067
Management:
    Executive Director: Andrew McQueen
    Booking: Flo Long
Founded: 1979
Status: Non-Profit, Professional
Paid Staff: 5
Budget: $350,000
Income Sources: Leflore County
Facility Category: Arena/Meeting Rooms
Type of Stage: Proscenium
Seating Capacity: 3000
Year Built: 1980

7391
SAENGER THEATRE
201 Forrest Street
Hattiesburg, MS 39401
Phone: 601-584-4888
Fax: 601-296-7740
e-mail: saenger@hattiesburg.org
Web Site: www.hattiesburgmsaenger.com
Mission: To accommodate both live performancesamd film and to evoke images of romantic for away places
Utilizes: Actors; Collaborating Artists; Collaborations; Dance Companies; Dancers; Grant Writers; Guest Accompanists; Guest Artists; Guest Composers; Guest Designers; Guest Instructors; Guest Lecturers; Guest Musical Directors; Guest Musicians; Guest Soloists; Guild Activities; Instructors; Local Artists; Multimedia; Music; New Productions; Original Music Scores; Sign Language Translators; Singers; Soloists; Special Technical Talent; Theatre Companies
Paid Staff: 13
Volunteer Staff: 10
Paid Artists: 10
Budget: $100,000
Income Sources: Revenue Taxes
Annual Attendance: 100,000+
Facility Category: Theatre
Seating Capacity: 1000
Year Built: 1929
Year Remodeled: 2000
Cost: $3.75 Million
Rental Contact: H. Allen Sanders

7392
UNIVERSITY OF SOUTHERN MISSISSIPPI SCHOOL OF MUSIC
118 College Drive
#5081
Hattiesburg, MS 39406-0001
Phone: 601-266-1000
Fax: 601-266-6427
e-mail: music@usm.edu
Web Site: www.usm.edu\music
Officers:
    President: Rodney D. Bennett
    Vice President-Advancement: Bob Pierce
    Vice President-Finance & Administra: Douglas Vinzant
Management:
    Director: Dr Michael Miles, michael.a.miles@usm.edu
    Associate Director: Dr Jennifer Shank, jennifer.shank@usm.edu
Mission: Recognized for its eminence in musical artistry, education and community service. Provides a wealth of valuable opportunities for the professional and artistic growth of the students.
Founded: 1920
Specialized Field: Orchestra; Chamber; Ensemble; Choral; Band
Status: Non-Profit, Non-Professional
Paid Staff: 150
Seating Capacity: 1,000

7393
INDIANOLA LITTLE THEATRE
Main and Sunflower Avenue
Indianola, MS 38751
Phone: 662-887-9920
Management:
    President: Andy Dineals
    Executive Director: Wildon Aultman
    Managing Director: Kathreen Parcel
Founded: 1978
Status: Non-Profit, Non-Professional
Paid Staff: 30

7394

Jackson, MS

7395
BELHAVEN COLLEGE CENTER FOR THE ARTS
Belhaven College
1500 Peachtree Street
Jackson, MS 39202-1789
Phone: 601-968-5940
Fax: 601-968-9998
Toll-free: 800-960-5940
e-mail: cfta@belhaven.edu
Web Site: www.belhaven.edu
Officers:
    Music Department Chairman: Christopher Shelt
Management:
    Coach/Athletics Administration: John Aiken, fdolansky@belhaven.edu
    Asst. Coordinator, Men's Basketball: Alex Ainsworth
    Housekeeper: Chandra Alexander
    Security Officer: Jerome Anderson
    Executive Assistant to the Associat: Sheri Anderson

7396
JACKSON MUNICIPAL AUDITORIUM THALIA MARA HALL
225 E. Pascagoula St.
Jackson, MS 39201
Mailing Address: PO Box 288
Phone: 601-960-1537
Fax: 601-960-1583
Web Site: www.jacksonms.gov
Management:
    Director: Michael Raff
    Deputy Director: Louis Armstrong
    Secretary: Andrew Burns
Mission: Theatre style venue for operas, ballets, symphony, plays, small seminars, concerts and broadway musicals.
Founded: 1968
Status: For-Profit, Non-Professional
Paid Staff: 4
Affiliations: City of Jackson
Annual Attendance: 160,000
Facility Category: Theatre
Seating Capacity: 2,350
Year Built: 1968
Rental Contact: Vicki Carter

7397
MISSISSIPPI VETERANS MEMORIAL STADIUM
2531 N State Street
Jackson, MS 39296
Phone: 601-354-6021
Fax: 601-354-6019
Web Site: www.ms-veteransstadium.com
Management:
    Director: Matt Watley
Seating Capacity: 60,492

7398
THALIA MARA HALL
255 E Pascagoula St
Jackson, MS 39201
Phone: 601-960-1537
e-mail: email through website
Web Site: www.jacksonms.gov
Mission: Venue for nationally and internationally known performers including ballet, opera and symphony performances; plays, concerts and presentations by localperforming ats organizations. Available for non-profit and for-profit organizations for theater-style priductions and suitable special events.
Founded: 1968
Facility Category: Theater
Type of Stage: Proscenium
Seating Capacity: 2362

7399
WOOD COLLEGE THEATRE
Wood College Road
PO Box 289
Mathiston, MS 39752
Phone: 662-263-5352
Fax: 662-263-4964

7400

Meridian, MS

7401

Meridian, MS

7402
MERIDIAN COMMUNITY COLLEGE THEATRE
910 Highway 19 N
Meridian, MS 39307
Phone: 601-483-8241
Fax: 601-482-3936
Web Site: www.mcc.cc.ms.us
Management:
    Chair/Fine Arts: Ronnie Miller
Founded: 1937
Specialized Field: Visual Arts; Music; Theatre

FACILITIES / Missouri

Paid Staff: 5

7403
MSU RILEY CENTER
2200 Fifth St
Meridian, MS 39301
Phone: 601-696-2200
Fax: 601-696-2300
e-mail: dsankovich@riley.msstate.edu
Web Site: www.msrileycener.com
Officers:
 Executive Director: Dennis Sankovich
Management:
 Conference Sales: Suzanne Helveston, shelveston@riley.msstate.edu
 Education Director: Charlotte Tabereaux Ph.D, ctabereaux@riley.msstate.edu
 Technical Director: William Nix, wnix@riley.msstate.edu
Opened: 2006
Specialized Field: Performing Arts, Conference Center And Education
Facility Category: Conference Center/Performing Arts Center
Seating Capacity: opera house:950; theater:200

7404
HUMPHREY COLISEUM
Mississippi State University
College View Street
Mississippi State, MS 39762
Mailing Address: PO Box HY
Phone: 662-325-4201
Fax: 662-325-7456
Web Site: www.humphreycoliseum.msstate.edu
Officers:
 Director: Todd Hunt
 Assistant Director: Raymond Brooks
Opened: 1974
Seating Capacity: 11,000

7405
FULTON CHAPEL
University of Mississippi
Oxford, MS 38677
Phone: 662-232-7411
Fax: 662-232-5082
Web Site: www.olemiss.edu
Founded: 1927
Seating Capacity: 915
Year Built: 1927

7406
MEEK AUDITORIUM
University of Mississippi
Oxford, MS 38677
Phone: 662-232-7268
Fax: 662-915-7443
e-mail: music@olemiss.edu

7407
UNIVERSITY OF MISSISSIPPI STUDIO THEATRE
PO Box 1848
Oxford, MS 38677
Phone: 662-232-7411
Fax: 662-232-5082
Web Site: www.olemiss.edu

7408
PANOLA PLAYHOUSE
212 S Main Street
PO Box 43
Sardis, MS 38666
Phone: 662-487-3975
Fax: 662-487-1421
e-mail: lee@panola.com
Web Site: www.panolaplayhouse.com
Mission: To provide an outlet for entertainment and performance for the mostly rural area of Panola County and the surrounding area of North Mississippi.
Founded: 1963
Specialized Field: Community Theatre
Status: Active
Paid Staff: 2
Volunteer Staff: 3
Budget: $20,000
Income Sources: Membership; Donations; Box Office; Fundraising
Affiliations: Mississippi Arts Commission
Annual Attendance: 1,200
Seating Capacity: 163
Year Built: 1946
Year Remodeled: 1970
Rental Contact: Lee Dixon

7409
BANCORPSOUTH ARENA AND CONFERENCE CENTER
375 East Main Street
Tupelo, MS 38804
Mailing Address: PO Box 7288
Phone: 601-841-6573
Fax: 601-841-6413
e-mail: dskinner@bcsarena.com
Web Site: www.bcsarena.com/
Management:
 Executive Director: Todd Hunt
 Director of Operations: Craig Russell
 Director of Marketing: Kevan Kirkpatrick
 Director of Ticketing: Jeanie Friday
 Assistant Director of Operations: Stennis Harrison
Mission: The spacious 32,000 square foot arena seats nearly 10,000 for concerts and 8,000 for sporting events. The arena floor can accommodate wood, ice or dirt for events ranging from basketball to skating to rodeos.

7410
GERTRUDE C. FORD CENTER FOR THE PERFORMING ARTS
University Of Mississippi
100 University Hall
Po Box 1848
University, MS 38677-1848
Phone: 662-915-2787
Fax: 662-915-1217
e-mail: fordcenter@olemiss.edu
Web Site: www.fordcenter.org
Management:
 Director: Norman S. Eastbrook, ebrook@olemiss.edu
 Marketing: Kate Meacham, kmeacham@olemiss.edu
 Technical: Matt Zerangue, mattzolemiss.edu
Opened: 2003
Seating Capacity: 1250

7411
TRIANGLE CULTURAL CENTER
322 North Main Street
Yazoo City, MS 39194
Phone: 662-746-2273
Fax: 662-746-2838
Toll-free: 800-381-0662
e-mail: kkyazoo@gmail.com
Web Site: www.triangleculturalcenter.com
Management:
 Director: K K Hill
Mission: To provide the community with a venue for performing arts.
Founded: 1978
Paid Staff: 3
Paid Artists: 1
Non-paid Artists: 3
Seating Capacity: 200

Missouri

7412
LYCEUM THEATRE
114 High Street
PO Box 14
Arrow Rock, MO 65320
Phone: 660-837-3311
Fax: 660-837-3112
e-mail: lyceumtheatre@lyceumtheatre.org
Web Site: www.lyceumtheatre.org
Officers:
 President: Dick Malon
 VP: Robert Lamn
 Treasurer: John Fletcher
 Secretary: Bea Smith
Management:
 Artistic Director: Quin Gresham
 Managing Director: Steve Bertani
 Marketing Director: Erin Willis
 Box Office Manager: Alice Roselius
Mission: To provide the loyal audience with the best theatrical experience possible.
Status: Professional
Seating Capacity: 408

7413
CULVER-STOCKTON COLLEGE PERFORMING ARTS HALL
One College Hill
Canton, MO 63435
Phone: 573-288-6352
Fax: 573-288-6614
Toll-free: 800-537-1883
e-mail: admission@culver.edu
Web Site: www.culver.edu
Officers:
 Chairman: Ronald W Leftwich
 President: Richard D Valentine
 Assistant to the President: Doris Briscoe
Management:
 President: William Fox
Mission: Private liberal Arts college with a strong progam in Art, Theatre and Music.
Utilizes: Actors; AEA Actors; Dancers; Designers; Educators; Fine Artists; Five Seasonal Concerts; Grant Writers; Guest Accompanists; Guest Artists; Guest Choreographers; Guest Companies; Guest Composers; Guest Conductors; Guest Directors; Guest Ensembles; Guest Instructors; Guest Lecturers; Guest Musicians; Guest Soloists; Guild Activities; High School Drama; Instructors; Local Artists; Local Unknown Artists; Multi Collaborations; Multimedia; Music; New Productions; Playwrights; Resident Professionals; Sign Language Translators; Singers; Soloists; Student Interns; Special Technical Talent; Theatre Companies; Touring Companies; Visual Arts
Founded: 1853

Specialized Field: Art; Music; Theatre
Status: Non-Profit, Non-Professional
Paid Staff: 12
Paid Artists: 8
Budget: $10,000-$20,000
Performs At: Alexander Campbell Auditorium; Meriallat Recital Hall
Annual Attendance: 5,000
Facility Category: College Campus
Type of Stage: Recital Hall; Proscenium; Black Box
Stage Dimensions: 60'x40'
Seating Capacity: 200; 969; 150
Year Built: 1966
Year Remodeled: 1990
Rental Contact: 217-231-6346 Judy Garkie

7414
SHOW ME CENTER
1333 N Sprigg Street
Cape Girardeau, MO 63701
Phone: 573-651-2297
Fax: 573-651-5054
e-mail: dross@semo.edu
Web Site: www.showmecenter.biz
Officers:
  Business Manager/Executive Director: Greg Talbut
Management:
  Director: David Ross, dross@semo.edu
  Operations Supervisor: Jim Barbatti, jbarbatti@semo.edu
  Marketing Director: Shannon Buford, sbuford@semo.edu
Founded: 1987
Opened: 1987
Paid Staff: 13
Facility Category: Multi-Purpose Arena
Type of Stage: Portable SICO Stage
Stage Dimensions: 60'x40'
Seating Capacity: 7,000
Year Built: 1987
Cost: $16.5 Million
Rental Contact: David Ross

7415
FAUROT FIELDHOUSE
University of Missouri
600 Stadium Boulevard, Room 260
Columbia, MO 65211
Phone: 573-882-2056
Fax: 573-882-4298
e-mail: hickmantl@missouri.edu
Web Site: www.mutigers.com
Management:
  Director: Timothy L Hickman
Facility Category: Stadium
Stage Dimensions: 67,000 sq ft

7416
HEARNES CENTER
University of Missouri
600 Stadium Boulevard
Columbia, MO 65203
Phone: 573-882-2056
Fax: 573-882-4298
Web Site: www.missouri.edu
Management:
  Director: Timothy L Hickman
  Operations Manager: Jeff Roberts
Seating Capacity: 13,500
Year Built: 1972

7417
JESSE AUDITORIUM
University of Missouri
311 Jesse Hall
Columbia, MO 65211
Phone: 573-884-9044
Fax: 573-884-5446
e-mail: murrayjs@missouri.edu
Web Site: www.missouri.edu/~jesseaud
Management:
  Booking Contact: John Murray
  Events Assistant: Marlys Johnson
Seating Capacity: 1,798

7418
MISSOURI THEATRE
203 S Ninth St
Columbia, MO 65201
Phone: 573-875-0600
Fax: 573-449-4214
e-mail: info@motheatre.org
Web Site: www.motheatre.org
Officers:
  President: Doug Moore
  President-Elect: Cortney Wright
  Secretary: Jeff Keevil
  Treasurer: Jim Weaver
  Past President: Nancy Bedan
Management:
  Executive Director: David A White, III
Mission: Providing an artistic home for the visual and performing arts - produced by local, regional and nationally-recognized arts organizations; Providing arts education for the community's youth and adults; Preserving the community's cultural heritage within the timeless structure of the historic Missouri Theatre; Enhancing downtown Columbia's economic base.

7419
OKOBOJI SUMMER THEATRE
Stephens College
1200 E Broadway
Columbia, MO 65215
Mailing Address: Box 341, Spirit Lake, IA. 51360
Phone: 573-442-2211
Toll-free: 800-876-7207
e-mail: bleonard@stephens.edu
Web Site: www.stephens.edu/news/stephensevents/okoboji.php
Management:
  Box Office/Tickes Manager: Beth Leonard
Mission: Stephens College began operating the Okoboji Summer Theatre in 1958 for the purpose of providing commercial summer stock experience for advanced theatre students.
Founded: 1833

7420
ELIZABETH T CHAMP AUDITORIUM
Westminster College
501 Westminster Avenue
Fulton, MO 65251
Phone: 573-592-5319
Fax: 573-592-5138
e-mail: webmaster@westminster-mo.edu
Web Site: www.westminster-mo.edu/explore/about/buildings.html
Management:
  President: Dr. Fletcher M Lamkin
Mission: The Elizabeth T. Champ Auditorium, built in 1966, seats 1,400 persons for concerts, lectures, dramatic productions, movies and other college events such as Commencement. The lower level houses the bookstore, an audio-visual classroom and the Office of Enrollment Services.
Founded: 1851

7421
WILLIAM WOODS COLLEGE CAMPUS CENTER DULANY AUDITORIUM
200 W 12th Street
Fulton, MO 65251
Phone: 573-642-2251
Fax: 612-690-3279
Toll-free: 800-995-3159
Web Site: www.williamwoods.edu
Officers:
  President: Jahnae H Barnett
  Vice-President University Advanceme: Diedriech Dan
Management:
  President: Jahnae Barnett
  VP: Robert Fredler
  Artistic Director: Joe Potter
Founded: 1825
Status: Non-Profit, Professional
Paid Staff: 200
Paid Artists: 10

7422
WINSTON CHURCHILL MEMORIAL HALL
Westminster College
7th and Westminster
Fulton, MO 65251
Phone: 314-642-3361

7423
AMERICAN ROYAL CENTER KEMPER ARENA
Global Spectrum
1800 Genessee
Kansas City, MO 64102
Phone: 816-513-4000
Fax: 816-513-4001
e-mail: jlewis@kemperarenakc.com
Web Site: www.kemperarenakc.com
Officers:
  Media/Public Relations Manager: Ken Gies
  Executive Director: William Lamette
Management:
  General Manager: Larry Hovick
  Assistant General Manager: Todd Mitchell
  Director of Operations: Thom Jones
  Box Office Manager: Brian Wholf
  Event Manager: Danny Burns
  Marketing Manager: Ryan McCarthy
Founded: 1973
Specialized Field: Sports and Entertainment Arena. Home of the Kansas City Comets (Misl)
Status: For-Profit, Professional
Paid Staff: 60
Seating Capacity: 19,500
Year Built: 1974
Year Remodeled: 1997

7424
FOLLY THEATER
300 West 12th Street
Kansas City, MO 64105
Mailing Address: PO Box 26505 Kansas City, MO 64196
Phone: 816-474-4444
Fax: 816-842-8709
Web Site: www.follytheater.com
Management:

FACILITIES / Missouri

Executive Director: Gale Tallis
Director of Development: Martha Atlas
Events Manager: Stephanie Spatz-Ornburn
Manager of Ticketing & Administrati: Linda Bowlen
Mission: The Folly is the premier Kansas City showplace for business meetings, events, and performances.
Founded: 1981
Status: Non-Profit, Professional
Paid Staff: 5
Seating Capacity: 1,078

7425
GOPPERT THEATRE
Avila College
11901 Wornall Road
Kansas City, MO 64145
Phone: 816-501-2411
Fax: 816-501-2442
Toll-free: 800-462-8452
e-mail: Robert.Foulk@Avila.edu
Web Site: www.avila.edu/theatre/goppert.htm
Officers:
  Dean of the College Performing Arts: Dr. Charlene Gould
Management:
  Theatre Director: Robert Foulk
  Director Design & Technical Theatre: Jason Harris
Mission: Avila University offers state of the art performance facilities including the newly remodeled Goppert Theatre providing an exceptional performance venue.
Founded: 1973
Specialized Field: Goppert Theatre
Budget: $10,000
Performs At: Goppert Theater

7426
KANSAS CITY MUNICIPAL AUDITORIUM MUSIC HALL
301 W 13th Street
Suite 100
Kansas City, MO 64105
Mailing Address: 301 West 13th Street, Suite 100, Kansas City, MO 64105
Phone: 816-513-5000
Fax: 816-513-5001
Toll-free: 800-821-7060
Web Site: www.kcconvention.com
Management:
  Executive Director: Oscar McGaskey Jr
  Executive Assistant to the Director: Kathleen Keens
  Deputy Director: Dean Barrett
  Director of Sponsorship Sales: Audrey DeGrandpre
  Director of Sales: Gemma Zook
  Senior Sales Manager: Jacque Stock
  Senior Sales Manager: Janet O'Hagan
Utilizes: Dance Companies; Dancers; Fine Artists; Grant Writers; Guest Accompanists; Guest Composers; Guest Instructors; Guest Soloists; Instructors; Local Artists; Multimedia; Original Music Scores; Singers; Special Technical Talent; Theatre Companies
Founded: 1936
Paid Staff: 120
Income Sources: Rental and User Fees
Performs At: Performance Hall
Facility Category: Fine Arts Performing Arts
Type of Stage: Proscenium
Stage Dimensions: 85'6wx35'lx46'h"'
Seating Capacity: 2,400

Year Built: 1936
Year Remodeled: 1981
Architect: $1,200,000
Rental Contact: Sales Associate Sue Hodes

7427
KANSAS CITY MUNICIPAL AUDITORIUM
Convention Center
301 W 13th Street Suite 100
Kansas City, MO 64105
Mailing Address: 301 West 13th Street, Suite 100, Kansas City, MO 64105
Phone: 816-513-5000
Fax: 816-513-5001
Toll-free: 800-821-7060
Web Site: www.kcconvention.com
Management:
  Executive Director: Oscar McGaskey Jr
  Executive Assistant to the Director: Kathleen Keens
  Deputy Director: Dean Barrett
  Marketing Manager: Liz Bowman
Seating Capacity: 10,700

7428
KAUFFMAN STADIUM
One Royal Way
Kansas City, MO 64129
Mailing Address: PO Box 419969 Kansas City, MO 64141-6969
Phone: 816-921-8000
Fax: 816-921-1366
Toll-free: 800-676-9257
Web Site: www.kcroyals.com
Founded: 1969
Specialized Field: Home of the Kansas City Royals (MLB)
Status: For-Profit, Professional
Paid Staff: 88
Seating Capacity: 40,625
Year Built: 1973

7429
STARLIGHT THEATRE
4600 Starlight Road
Kansas City, MO 64132
Phone: 816-363-7827
Fax: 816-361-6398
Toll-free: 800-776-1730
Web Site: www.kcstarlight.com
Officers:
  President and CEO: Richard Baker
  Concerts Director: Bill Waugh
  Concert Sponsorship: Jeff Miller
Seating Capacity: 8,108

7430
UNICORN THEATRE
3828 Main Street
Kansas City, MO 64111
Phone: 816-531-7529
Fax: 816-531-0421
e-mail: unicornnews@unicorntheatre.org
Web Site: www.unicorntheatre.org
Management:
  Producing Artistic Director: Cynthia Levin
  Managing Director: Jason Kralicek
  Production Director: Johnny Wolfe
  Development Director: Julie E Milner
  Technical Supervisor: Jeffrey Cady
  Box Office Manager: Paula Simkins

Mission: Exists to enhance the cultural life of Kansas City by producing professional contemporary, thought-provoking theater, which inspires emotional response and stimulates discussion.

7431
LIBERTY PERFORMING ARTS THEATRE
1600 S Withers Road
Liberty, MO 64068-4604
Phone: 816-439-4373
Fax: 816-439-4377
e-mail: info@lpat.org
Web Site: www.lpat.org
Management:
  Mayor: Steven Hawkins
  Recreation Director: Chris Deal
  Managing Director: Paul Miler
  Technical Director: Hunter Burgess
Mission: A rental venue hosting a wide range of dance, music, drama, ceremonial, and other special events; striving to provide the best in personnel, services, and equipment. The theatre also serves as a co-presenter of high quality, family-oriented art events.
Utilizes: Collaborations; Guest Directors; Guild Activities; Instructors; Local Artists; Multimedia; Original Music Scores; Soloists; Student Interns; Theatre Companies
Founded: 1992
Specialized Field: All performing Arts Disciplines
Status: Non-Profit, Professional
Paid Staff: 10
Budget: $110,000
Income Sources: Rental Sales; Ticket Revenue; Private Donations
Performs At: Liberty Performing Arts Theatre
Affiliations: Kansas City Jazz Ambassadors, Plain Presenters Consortium, local Chamber of Commerce
Annual Attendance: 80,000
Facility Category: Multi-discipline Theatrical Space
Type of Stage: Proscenium
Stage Dimensions: 85x41
Seating Capacity: 725 (700 permanent)
Year Built: 1992
Cost: $1.5 milion
Rental Contact: Theatre Coordinator Paul Miller

7432
UMB BANK PAVILION
14141 Riverport Drive
Maryland Heights, MO 63043
Phone: 314-962-4000
Fax: 314-291-4719
Web Site: www.umbbankpavilion.com
Management:
  Executive Director: Eric Blockie
  Box Office Manager: Larry Pearson
Seating Capacity: 21,202

7433
MARY LINN PERFORMING ARTS CENTER
Northwest Missouri State University
800 University Drive
Maryville, MO 64468
Phone: 660-562-1212
Fax: 660-562-1346
Toll-free: 800-633-1175
e-mail: music@mail.nwmissouri.edu
Web Site: www.nwmissouri.edu
Officers:
  President: Dean Hubbart
Management:
  Department Chair/Music: Dr. Ernest Woodruff
Mission: Educational

FACILITIES / Missouri

Founded: 1905
Specialized Field: Instrumental Music; Vocal Music
Affiliations: National Association of Schools of Music

7434
PRICE CUTTER PARK
4400 North 19th Street
Ozark, MO 65721
Mailing Address: PO Box 1472
Phone: 417-581-2868
Fax: 417-581-8342
e-mail: tclegg@centurytel.net
Web Site: www.ducksprobaseball.com
Management:
  GM: Tim Clegg
Seating Capacity: 6,000

7435
GRAHAM TYLER MEMORIAL CHAPEL
Park College
8700 N.W. River Park Dr.
Parkville, MO 64152
Phone: 816-741-2000
Web Site: www.park.edu
Management:
  President: Beverly Byer Pevitts
Founded: 1875
Status: Non-Profit, Non-Professional

7436
PARK COLLEGE ALUMNI HALL THEATRE
8700 River Park Drive
Parkville, MO 64152
Phone: 816-741-2000
Fax: 816-587-5585
Web Site: www.park.edu
Management:
  President: Beverley Byers-Pevitts
  Executive Director: Michael Droge
  Artistic Director: Marsha Morgan
Founded: 1875
Specialized Field: Series & Festivals; Intrumental Music; Vocal Music; Theaterical Group
Status: Non-Profit, Non-Professional
Paid Staff: 10

7437
JONES AUDITORIUM
College of the Ozarks
PO Box 17
Point Lookout, MO 65726
Phone: 417-334-6411
Fax: 417-335-2618
Web Site: www.coso.edu
Management:
  President: Jerry Davis
Founded: 1906
Status: For-Profit, Non-Professional

7438
LEACH THEATRE
103 Castleman Hall
400 W. 10th St.
Rolla, MO 65409-1550
Phone: 573-341-6964
Fax: 573-341-6983
e-mail: leach@mst.edu
Web Site: www.leachtheatre.mst.edu
Officers:
  Chair Campus Performing Arts: Paula M Lutz
Management:
  Managing Director: Emily Brickler
  Marketing Representative: Roy Jacobs
  Technical Director: Kevin Shaw
  Box Office Supervisor: Sliri Ginless
Utilizes: Dance Companies; Multimedia; Special Technical Talent; Theatre Companies
Budget: $60,000-$150,000
Income Sources: Box Office; Subscriptions; Grants
Affiliations: Plains Presenters
Annual Attendance: 3,900
Facility Category: Theater/Concert Hall
Type of Stage: Proscenium
Stage Dimensions: 45'x21'
Seating Capacity: 656
Year Built: 1991
Rental Contact: House Manager Barbara Griffen

7439
UNIVERSITY OF MISSOURI PERFORMING ARTS SERIES
University of Missouri
College of Arts & Sciences
121 Fulton
Rolla, MO 65409-1130
Phone: 573-341-4141
Fax: 573-341-6127
Web Site: www.campus.umr.edu/cpas
Management:
  Dean: Paula Lutz
  Production Manager: Shelley Dotson
Founded: 1873
Status: Non-Profit, Non-Professional

7440
MISSOURI THEATER
715 Edmond Street
Saint Joseph, MO 64501
Phone: 816-271-4628
Fax: 816-232-9213
Toll-free: 800-821-5052
e-mail: info@missouritheater.org
Web Site: www.stjoearts.org/missouri_theater
Management:
  Manager: Kathy Brock
  Maintenance/Operations: Steve O'Neal
  Assistant: Carolyn Hitchings
Founded: 1980
Specialized Field: Performing Art Association
Paid Staff: 5
Income Sources: City Owned Facility
Facility Category: Performing Arts Facility
Type of Stage: Permanent
Seating Capacity: 1,200
Year Built: 1927
Year Remodeled: 1995
Resident Groups: Robidouk Resident Theatre

7441
MISSOURI WESTERN STATE COLLEGE FINE ARTS THEATRE
Music Department
4525 Downs Drive
Saint Joseph, MO 64507
Phone: 816-271-4200
Fax: 816-271-5974
e-mail: music@missouriwestern.edu
Web Site: www.missouriwestern.edu/Music/
Management:
  President: James Scaoom
  Music Department Chair: Matt Gilmour
Mission: The Thompson E. Potter Fine Arts Building houses the Departments of Art, Music, and Theatre. The music wing, recently receiving an acoustic renovation, houses the Fine Arts Theatre and the Kemper Recital Hall.
Founded: 1969
Status: Non-Profit, Professional
Paid Staff: 30
Paid Artists: 5
Budget: $10,000

7442
SAINT JOSEPH CIVIC ARENA
1100 Frederick Ave.
Saint Joseph, MO 64501
Phone: 81-627-1473
Fax: 816-232-9213
Toll-free: 800-821-5052
Web Site: www.ci.st-joseph.mo.us
Management:
  Manager: Kathy Brock
  Assistant: Carolyn Hitchings
  Operations Supervisor: Chad Dumphrey
Founded: 1980
Specialized Field: Music; Trade Shows
Status: For-Profit, Non-Professional
Paid Staff: 4
Income Sources: City Owned Facility/Arena
Facility Category: multi-use facility/arena
Type of Stage: Portable
Stage Dimensions: 36'x48'
Seating Capacity: 5000
Year Built: 1980
Year Remodeled: 1997

7443
AMERICAN THEATRE
1401 S Brentwood Boulevard
Suite 700
Saint Louis, MO 63144
Phone: 314-962-4000
Fax: 314-436-0483

7444
BUSCH STADIUM
Saint Louis Cardinals
700 Clark Street
Saint Louis, MO 63102
Phone: 314-421-3060
Fax: 314-425-0640
Web Site: www.stlcardinals.com
Management:
  President: Mark Lamping
  General Manager: Walt Jocketty
  Director: Marian Rhodes
  VP Stadium Operations: Joe Abernathky
Specialized Field: Operated by St. Louis Cardinals
Status: Non-Profit, Professional
Paid Staff: 500
Paid Artists: 100
Seating Capacity: 49,625
Year Built: 1966
Year Remodeled: 1997

7445
BUSCH STUDENT CENTER
Saint Louis University
20 North Grand Suite 335
Saint Louis, MO 63103
Phone: 314-977-2820
Fax: 314-977-7177
e-mail: BSC@SLU.EDU
Web Site: www.slu.edu
Officers:
  Activities Coordinator: Chris Grabau
Opened: 2003
Seating Capacity: 2,900

FACILITIES / Missouri

7446
CATHEDRAL OF SAINT LOUIS
4431 Lindell Boulevard
Saint Louis, MO 63108-2496
Phone: 314-373-8200
Fax: 314-533-2844
e-mail: concerts@cathedralstl.org
Web Site: www.cathedralstl.org
Management:
    Business Manager: Tom Fasl
    Operations and Events Manager: Laura Voegelie

7447
CENTER OF CREATIVE ARTS
524 Trinity Avenue
Saint Louis, MO 63130
Phone: 314-725-6555
Fax: 314-725-6222
e-mail: info@cocastl.org
Web Site: www.cocastl.org
Management:
    Executive Director: Erin Smith
    Executive Director: Kelly Pollock
Mission: Provides meaningful arts experiences to St. Louisans and their family for nearly two decades. COCA has become the largest multidisciplinary arts institution and one of the most valuable community assets in the St. Louis metropolitan area
Founded: 1986
Status: Non-Profit, Professional
Paid Staff: 20
Paid Artists: 5

7448
EDISON THEATRE
Washington University
One Brookings Dr
Saint Louis, MO 63130-4899
Mailing Address: Campus Box 1119
Phone: 314-935-6543
Fax: 314-935-7362
e-mail: edison@artsci.wustl.edu
Web Site: http://edisontheatre.wustl.edu
Management:
    Executive Director: Charlie Robin
    Operations Manager: Bill Larson
    Marketing Manager: Jennifer Killion
    Technical Director/Facility Manager: Michael Hensley
Mission: To provide the highest caliber national and international artists in music, dance and theater, performing new works as well as innovative interpretations of classical material not otherwise seen in St. Louis. Focusing on presentations that are interdisciplinary, multicultural and/or experimental, Edison Theatre presents work intended to challenge, educate and inspire.
Founded: 1971
Status: Non-Profit, Professional
Paid Staff: 30
Seating Capacity: 656

7449
FABULOUS FOX THEATRE
Grand Center
527 N Grand Boulevard
Saint Louis, MO 63103
Phone: 314-534-1111
Fax: 314-534-8702

7450
GRAND CENTER GRANDEL THEATRE
3526 Washington Ave.
2nd Floor
Saint Louis, MO 63103
Phone: 314-289-1500
Fax: 314-533-3345
e-mail: info@grandcenter.org
Web Site: www.grandcenter.org
Officers:
    President/CEO: Vincent Schoemehl, Jr
Management:
    Manager: Merrell Wiegraffe
Budget: $60,000-$150,000
Seating Capacity: 450

7451
HILTON CENTER FOR THE ARTS
Webster University
130 Edgar Road
Saint Louis, MO 63119
Phone: 314-968-6933
Fax: 314-963-6102
e-mail: luekinar@webster.edu
Management:
    Director: Arthur L. Lueking
Founded: 1963
Specialized Field: Theater and Opera
Status: Non-Profit, Professional
Paid Staff: 110
Paid Artists: 300

7452
JEWISH COMMUNITY CENTER OF SAINT LOUIS
Cultural Arts Department
2 Millstone Campus Drive
Saint Louis, MO 63146
Phone: 314-432-5700
Fax: 314-432-5825
Management:
    Theatre Coordinator: Kathleen Sitzer

7453
MISSOURI BOTANICAL GARDEN AMPHITHEATRE
4344 Shaw Boulevard
Saint Louis, MO 63110
Phone: 314-577-5100
Toll-free: 800-642-8842
e-mail: firstname.lastname@mobot.org
Web Site: www.mobot.org
Management:
    Director: Peter H Raven
    Senior Development Manager: Sharon Cognac Mertzlufft
    Develpoments Event Manager: Brenda Zonola
Mission: To discover and share knowledge about plants and their environment, in order to preserve and enrich life.
Founded: 1859
Paid Staff: 385
Volunteer Staff: 99+
Income Sources: Admission Charges; Membership Fees; Grants; Private Donations
Annual Attendance: 750,000
Facility Category: Auditorium; Outdoor Amphitheatre
Type of Stage: Proscenium
Seating Capacity: 300

7454
MUNY AMPHITHEATRE
#1 Theatre Drive
Saint Louis, MO 63112
Phone: 314-361-1900
Fax: 314-361-0009
e-mail: munyinfo@muny.org
Web Site: www.muny.com
Officers:
    President and CEO: Dennis Reagan
    Vice President: Raymond R. Fournie
    Treasurer: Douglas H. Yaeger
    Assistant Treasurer: Louis A. Cella
    Secretary: Stephen C. Jones
Management:
    Company Manager: Sue Greenberg
    Artistic Director & Executive Produ: Mike Isaacson
    Director of Corporate Partnerships: Bill Borger
    Director of Group Sales: Diane Church
Mission: Broadway-style musical theatre productions
Founded: 1919
Specialized Field: Theatre
Status: Non-Profit, Professional
Paid Staff: 550
Paid Artists: 200
Non-paid Artists: 200
Season: June - August
Annual Attendance: 400,000
Facility Category: Outdoor Amphitheatre
Type of Stage: Traditional
Seating Capacity: 11,000
Year Built: 1919
Year Remodeled: 2000

7455
POWELL SYMPHONY HALL
Grand Center
718 N Grand Boulevard
Saint Louis, MO 63103
Phone: 314-533-2500
Fax: 314-286-4142
Toll-free: 800-232-1880
Web Site: www.slso.org
Officers:
    Executive Assistant to the Presiden: Darwin Dianne
    CFO: Garrone JM
    VP Maketing: Robertson Jonna
    VP Development: Easley John
    VP/Orchestra Manager: Robert McGrath
    Director of Communications: Jeff Trammel
    VP Education/Community Partnerships: Marc C Thayer
Management:
    Executive Director: Randy Adams
Founded: 1880
Specialized Field: Symphony Music; Classical Music
Status: Non-Profit, Professional
Paid Staff: 150
Paid Artists: 92
Seating Capacity: 2,689

7456
SCOTTRADE CENTER
1401 Clarke Avenue
Saint Louis, MO 63103
Phone: 314-622-5400
Fax: 314-589-5981
e-mail: webmaster@gw.kiel.com
Web Site: www.scottradecenter.com
Management:

FACILITIES / Missouri

Sr VP/General Manager Savis Center: Dennis Petrullo
Sr VP Marketing: Jim Woodcockne
VP/Operations: Fred Corsi
Box Office Director: Carol Chilton
Boc Offive Manager: Debra Freking
Publicity/Special Events Manager: Cindy Underwood
Director Manager: Gayle Leonard
Marketing Manager: Michele Peck
Seating Capacity: 20,000
Year Built: 1994

7457
SHELDON CONCERT HALL AND BALLROOM
3648 Washington Boulevard
Saint Louis, MO 63108
Phone: 314-533-9900
Fax: 314-533-2958
Web Site: www.sheldonconcerthall.org
Management:
  Executive Director: Paul Reuter
  Assistant Director: Julie A. Plowman
  Director of Development: Lauren Wihite
  Development Assistant: Meghan Horvath
Mission: To present concerts of jazz, folk and classical music, art exhibits in the Sheldon Galleries and community events in 500 and 250 seat rental spaces.
Founded: 1912
Specialized Field: Series & Festivals: Instrumental and Vocal Concerts
Status: Non-Profit
Paid Staff: 14
Budget: $2.4 million
Income Sources: Subscriptions; Rentals; Contributions
Annual Attendance: 100,000
Facility Category: Concert Hall
Type of Stage: Flexible; Platform
Stage Dimensions: 17 x 24
Seating Capacity: 702
Year Built: 1912
Year Remodeled: 1998
Rental Contact: Director Events Laurie Hasty

7458
TRANSWORLD DOME AT AMERICAS' CENTER
701 Convention Plaza
Saint Louis, MO 63101
Phone: 314-342-5036
Fax: 314-342-5040
Management:
  Director: Bruce Sommer
  Director Sports Entertainment: Jack Croghan
  General Manager/Sports Service: Tom Schlaker
  Executive Suites Director/Catering: Gregory Lee
Seating Capacity: 65,600

7459
UNION AVENUE OPERA THEATRE
733 North Union Boulevard
Saint Louis, MO 63108
Phone: 314-361-8844
Fax: 314-361-3036
Web Site: www.union-avenue.org/uaot.
Officers:
  President: Clela Anderson
  First Vice President: Catherine Davis
  Second Vice President: Roger Duncan
  Secretary: George Sublette
  Finance: Eric Koch
Management:
  Senior Minister: Suzannne Webb
  Associate Minister: Meredith Jackson
Mission: The mission of the Union Avenue Opera Theatre is to provide a professional level opera experience for talented singers, directors, orchestra musicians, and technicians pursuing careers in the theater, and to provide quality, affordable opera for the metropolitan St. Louis community. The company operated under the auspices of the Arts Group of Union Avenue Christian Church until gaining not-for-profit status in 2003.

7460
HAMMONS STUDENT CENTER
661 S John Q Hammons Parkway
Springfield, MO 65807
Phone: 417-836-5240
Fax: 417-836-6344
Web Site: www.missouristate.edu/hsc
Management:
  Executive Director: Randy Blackwood
  Director: Keith Boaz
  Assistant Director: Laree Moore
  Administrative Secretary: Brenda O'Connell
Mission: The mission of HSC is continually supporting the recreational needs of enrolled Missouri State University students, faculty and staff members, and supporting the intramural and intercollegiate athletic programs.
Founded: 1976
Status: Non-Profit, Professional
Paid Staff: 10
Seating Capacity: 8,846

7461
JUANITA K HAMMONS HALL
Missouri State University
901 South National
Springfield, MO 65897
Phone: 417-836-6776
Fax: 417-836-6891
Toll-free: 888-476-7849
e-mail: jackwheeler@missouristate.edu
Web Site: www.hammonshall.com
Management:
  Events Coordinator: Jack Wheeler
Founded: 1992
Paid Staff: 15
Volunteer Staff: 250
Budget: $400,000-$1,000,000
Annual Attendance: 125,000
Type of Stage: Proscenium
Seating Capacity: 2,215
Year Built: 1992
Cost: $17.3 million
Rental Contact: Jack Wheeler

7462
SPRINGFIELD LITTLE THEATRE AT THE LANDERS
311 E Walnut Avenue
Springfield, MO 65806
Phone: 417-869-3869
Fax: 417-869-4047
Web Site: www.landerstheatre.org
Officers:
  President: Robert Grosser
  First VP: Mike Bridges
  Second VP: Dawn Cosby
  Third VP: Cary Cummings
  Secretary: Cindy Lear
  Treasurer: Steve Bullard
  Immediate Past President: Jason Brown
Management:
  Artistic Director: Beth Domann
  Education Director: Lorianne Dunn
  Designer/Technical Director: John R Rogers
  Technical Director: Jamie Bower
  Community Relations Director: Annie Carlyn
  Marketing Director: Rachel Peacock-Young
  Box Office Manager: Leah Macioce
  Admin Asst/Volunteer Coordinator: Heather Shannon
Mission: A volunteer driven organization, energized by the highest artistic ideals, that strives to entertain, educate and involve the community in live productions and in the preservation of the historic Landers Theatre.
Utilizes: Actors; AEA Actors; Choreographers; Commissioned Composers; Dance Companies; Dancers; Designers; Grant Writers; Guest Artists; Guest Companies; Guest Conductors; Guest Designers; Guest Lecturers; Local Artists; Music; Original Music Scores; Resident Professionals
Founded: 1934
Specialized Field: Southwest Missouri
Status: Non-Profit, Non-Professional
Paid Staff: 9
Budget: $750,000
Income Sources: Tickets; Underwriting; Grants
Annual Attendance: 35,000
Facility Category: Theatre
Type of Stage: Proscenium

7463
FAMILY ARENA
2002 Arena Parkway
St. Charles, MO 63303
Phone: 636-896-4200
Fax: 636-896-4205
Web Site: www.familyarena.com
Management:
  Director: Steven R. Rosenblatt
Founded: 1999
Specialized Field: Arena/Facility
Status: Non-Profit, Professional
Paid Staff: 100
Income Sources: Tickets; Concessions; Suites; Advertising
Affiliations: St. Charles County Government
Annual Attendance: 750,000
Facility Category: Arena
Type of Stage: Stageright
Seating Capacity: 11,000
Year Built: 1999
Cost: $32 million

7464
BLANCHE M. TOUHILL PERFORMING ARTS CENTER
University of Missouri-St.Louis
8001 Natural Bridge Road
St. Louis, MO 63121-4400
Phone: 314-516-4949
Fax: 314-516-4110
Toll-free: 866-516-4949
e-mail: ticket@umsl.edu
Web Site: www.touhill.org
Officers:
  Vice Chancellor Univer. Relations: Dixie Kohn
  Director Operations: John Cattanach
  Director Development: Bill George
  Director Stage Services: Jason Stahr
  Assistant Director Marketing: Rachel Queen
  Events Services Manager: Patrick McKeon
Management:
  Managing Director: John Cattanach
  Business Manager: Alberta Breckinridge
  Executive Associate: Sara Ross

FACILITIES / Montana

Engagement Manager: Michael Sieveking
Administrative Associate: Julia Gleason
Mission: The Touhill Performing Arts Center at the University of Missouri-St. Louis creates opportunities for the people of our region to experience, appreciate and embrace the transformational power of the performing arts. It is a welcoming place, a leading cultural partner in our community and a symbol of this University's commitment to integrate education, innovation and excellence.
Specialized Field: Classical; Soloists; Ensemble
Status: Non Profit
Performs At: Anheuser-Busch Performance Hall, E. Desmond and Mary Ann Lee Theater
Type of Stage: Proscenium
Seating Capacity: 1625, 360
Architect: Wischmeyer Architects/Pei Cobb Freed & Partners
Acoustical Consultant: Kirkegaard & Associates

7465
MULE BARN THEATRE
224 Main
Tarkio, MO 64491
Phone: 660-736-4430

7466
COGER THEATRE
Southwest Missouri State University
128 Garfield
West Plains, MO 65775
Phone: 417-836-5000
Fax: 417-257-7682
e-mail: marktempleton@missouristate.edu OR jimgrider@missouristate.edu
Web Site: www.theatreanddance.missouristate.edu
Management:
  Associate Professor: Ruth Barnes
  Per Course Faculty: Susan Bennett
  Associate Professor: Sara Brummel
  Per Course Faculty: Julie M Bubalo
  Assistant Professor: Darryl K. Clark
Mission: A performing arts center theatre located within Craig Hall on the campus of Southwest Missouri State University.
Budget: $20,000-$35,000

Montana

7467
BIGFORK CENTER FOR THE PERFORMING ARTS
526 Electric Avenue
Bigfork, MT 59911
Mailing Address: PO Box 1230, Bigfork, Montana 59911
Phone: 406-837-4885
e-mail: info@bigforkcenter.org
Web Site: www.bigforktheater.org

7468
ALBERTA BAIR THEATRE FOR THE PERFORMING ARTS
PO Box 1556
Billings, MT 59103
Phone: 406-256-8915
Fax: 406-256-5060
Toll-free: 877-321-2074
e-mail: hbergeson@albertabairtheater.org
Web Site: www.albertabairtheatre.org
Management:
  Executive Director: Bill Fisher
  Artistic Director: Corby Skinner
  Technical Director: Tom Lund
Mission: In its brief history, the Alberta Bair Theater has brought to audiences the finest performers in every discipline of the performing arts, including classical and popular music, country music and jazz, opera, ballet, modern and ethnic dance, comedy, drama and musical theater.
Utilizes: Actors; Collaborations; Dance Companies; Dancers; Educators; Guest Accompanists; Guest Artists; Guest Choreographers; Guest Composers; Guest Directors; Guest Ensembles; Guest Instructors; Guest Musical Directors; Guest Soloists; Guest Teachers; High School Drama; Instructors; Local Artists; Lyricists; Multimedia; Original Music Scores; Playwrights; Resident Artists; Selected Students; Sign Language Translators; Singers; Special Technical Talent; Theatre Companies
Founded: 1983
Status: Non-Profit, Professional
Paid Staff: 15
Volunteer Staff: 200
Budget: $1.2 million
Income Sources: Ticket Sales
Annual Attendance: 123,000
Facility Category: Performing Arts
Type of Stage: Proscenium
Stage Dimensions: 54 x 30
Seating Capacity: 1416
Year Remodeled: 1987
Cost: $ 5-6 million
Rental Contact: Bill Fisher

7469
METRAPARK
308 6th Avenue N
PO Box 2514
Billings, MT 59103
Phone: 406-256-2400
Fax: 406-254-2479
Toll-free: 800-366-8538
e-mail: shawke@metrapark.com
Web Site: www.metrapark.com
Officers:
  President: Brian Cebull
  Vice President: Lisa Harmon
  Chairman: Jim Reno
Management:
  General Manager: Bill Dutcher
  Senior Secretary: Sue Watts
  Marketing Director: Ray Massie
  Operations Director: Jeff Seward
Seating Capacity: 12,000

7470
BREENDEN FIELD HOUSE/WORTHINGTON ARENA
Montna State University, Sports Facilities
PO Box 3380
Bozeman, MT 59717-3380
Phone: 406-994-7117
Fax: 406-994-4400
Web Site: www.montana.edu/wwwsfac
Management:
  Sports Facilities Director: Melanie Stocks
  Events/Operations Manager: Brad Murphy
  Event Coordinator: Brooks Phillips
Founded: 1956
Status: Professional

7471
RENO H SALES STADIUM
Montana State University Sports Facilities
1 Bobcat Circle
Bozeman, MT 59717
Phone: 406-994-4221
Fax: 406-994-2278
Web Site: www.montana.edu
Management:
  President: Jeffery Gamble
  Director Sports Facilities: Melanie Stocks
  Operations Manager: Brad Murphy
  Sports Information Director: Tom Schulz
Status: Non-Profit, Non-Professional
Paid Staff: 60
Seating Capacity: 12,500

7472
BUTTE CENTER FOR THE PERFORMING ARTS
General Business Office
316 West Park Street
Butte, MT 59701
Mailing Address: Po Box 552 Butte MT 59703
Phone: 406-723-3602
Fax: 406-782-2362
e-mail: inco@buttearts.org
Web Site: www.buttearts.org
Management:
  Managing Director: Robin Busch, markarmstrong@buttearts.org
  Business Manager: Robin Busch, robin@buttearts.org
  Facilities Director: Mike Shelton, mike.nance@buttearts.org
Mission: Built to restore the Mother Lode theatre and the Orphan Girl theatre. The Mother Lode theatre is used for local, regional and national touring productions and community events. The Orphan Girl theatre is a childrens theatre.
Seating Capacity: Mother Lode theatre:1202; Orpahan Girl: 106

7473
BUTTE CIVIC CENTER
1340 Harrison Avenue
Butte, MT 59701
Phone: 406-497-6400
Fax: 406-497-6404
Toll-free: 800-555-8989
e-mail: bmelvin@bsb.mt.gov
Web Site: www.buttciviccenter.com
Management:
  Manager: Bill Melvin
Performs At: Multi-Purpose
Seating Capacity: 7,200

7474
FOUR SEASONS ARENA
400 3rd St NW
Great Falls, MT 59404
Mailing Address: PO Box 1888 Great Fall, MT 59403
Phone: 406-727-8900
Fax: 406-452-8955
Web Site: www.goexpopark.com
Management:
  Director of Events: Susan Shannon
  Marketing and Sales Director: Kim Lander
  Box Office Manager: Janet Connolly
  Box Office Manager: Debby Wigger
  Marketing/Development: Lori Cox
  Event Coordinator: Amy Robbins

FACILITIES / Nebraska

Mission: Events include concerts, trade shows, rodeos, circuses, wrestling and boxing, basketball tournaments and ice shows.
Status: For-Profit, Non-Professional
Paid Staff: 18
Seating Capacity: 6,134

7475
GREAT FALLS CIVIC CENTER THEATER
PO Box 5021
Great Falls, MT 59403
Phone: 406-454-3915
Fax: 406-454-3468

7476
CARROLL COLLEGE THEATRE
1601 N Benton Ave
Helena, MT 59625
Phone: 406-442-3450
Fax: 406-447-4533
Toll-free: 800-942-3648
Web Site: www.carroll.edu

7477
HELENA CIVIC CENTER
340 Neill Avenue
Helena, MT 59601
Phone: 406-447-8481
Fax: 406-447-8480
Web Site: www.ci.helena.mt.us
Management:
  Manager: Diane Stavnes
  Director Communications/Technical: Gery Carpenter
Founded: 1936
Status: Non-Profit, Non-Professional
Paid Staff: 7
Income Sources: City of Helena; Ticket Sales; Rental Income.
Performs At: Auditorium
Facility Category: Rental
Stage Dimensions: 45'x38'x17'6"",'"',2
Seating Capacity: 1921
Year Built: 1995
Year Stage Renovated: Dian
Rental Contact: Stavnes Manager

7478
HELENA CIVIC CENTER AUDITORIUM
340 Neill Avenue
Helena, MT 59601
Phone: 406-447-8481
Fax: 406-447-8480
Web Site: www.ci.helena.mt.us
Management:
  Manager: Diane Stavnes
  Director Comm Facility/Tech Direct: Gery Carpenter
Founded: 1936
Paid Staff: 7
Performs At: Auditorium
Facility Category: Rental
Stage Dimensions: 25'x15'x12'
Seating Capacity: 2,000
Year Built: 1920
Year Remodeled: 1995
Rental Contact: Manager Diane Stavnes

7479
MYRNA LOY CENTER
15 North Ewing
Helena, MT 59601
Phone: 406-443-0287
Fax: 406-443-6620
e-mail: myrnaloy@mt.net
Web Site: www.myrnaloycenter.com
Officers:
  President: Brett Jakovac
  Immediate Past President: Ali Bovingdon
  VP Business: Shalon Hastings
  VP Program: Robin Shropshire
  Secretary: Annie Hull
  Treasurer: Bob Shepard
Management:
  Executive Director: Ed Noonan
  Film Programmer, Box Office Manager: Peter Ruzevich
  Program Associate: Zac Lachenbruch
  Marketing and Graphics: Ali Zackheim
Mission: To present the arts, including media, performing, literary and visual, in an educational context, challenging and culturally enriching programs that would not otherwise appear in the Helena area or in Montana.
Utilizes: Actors; Artists-in-Residence; Collaborating Artists; Commissioned Music; Dance Companies; Dancers; Educators; Filmmakers; Fine Artists; Guest Teachers; Instructors; Local Artists; Lyricists; Multi Collaborations; Multimedia; Original Music Scores; Performance Artists; Playwrights; Poets; Sign Language Translators; Soloists; Student Interns; Special Technical Talent; Theatre Companies
Founded: 1976
Specialized Field: Series & Festivals; Dance; Vocal Music; Instrumental Music; Theater; Festivals; Lyric Opera; Film House
Status: Non-Profit, Professional
Paid Staff: 12
Budget: $400,000
Income Sources: Ticket Sales; Grants; Fundraising
Affiliations: NPN
Annual Attendance: 8000
Facility Category: Media and Performance Center
Type of Stage: Proscenium
Seating Capacity: 250
Year Built: 1875
Year Remodeled: 1990
Cost: $ 1.6 Million
Rental Contact: Rental Coordinator Christy Stile
Organization Type: Performing; Touring; Resident; Educational; Sponsoring

7480
MAJESTIC VALLEY ARENA
3630 Highway 93 North
Kalispell, MT 59901
Phone: 406-755-5366
Fax: 406-755-5399
e-mail: bparker@majesticvalleyarena.com
Web Site: www.majesticvalleyarena.com
Management:
  GM: Bob Parker
  Booking: Jim Volke
Opened: 2002
Seating Capacity: 4,000

7481
ADAMS EVENT CENTER
University of Montana-Missoula
Adams Center 103
Missoula, MT 59812
Phone: 406-243-5355
Fax: 406-243-4265
Toll-free: 888-666-8262
e-mail: bettyjo.miller@mso.umt.edu
Web Site: www.adamseventcenter.com
Management:
  Executive Director: Mary Muse
  Asst Director Operations: Jackie Hedtke
Mission: The premier multi-use facility in Western Montana, providing first-class customer service in support of a broad range of quality events for the public, the University of Montana and the public.
Founded: 1955
Specialized Field: Sports; Concerts; Flatshows; Special Events
Status: Non-Profit, Professional
Paid Staff: 12
Budget: $1.5 million
Income Sources: Rent; Services
Facility Category: Arena
Seating Capacity: 7,500
Year Built: 1955
Year Remodeled: 1999
Cost: $15,000,000
Rental Contact: Director Mary Muse

7482
UNIVERSITY OF MONTANA THEATRE
School of Theatre & Dance
The University of Montana
Missoula, MT 59812-8136
Phone: 406-243-4581
Fax: 406-243-5726
Web Site: www.umtheatredance.org
Utilizes: Actors; AEA Actors; Dance Companies; Designers; Educators; Guest Conductors; Guest Designers; Guest Ensembles; High School Drama; Instructors; Local Artists; Original Music Scores; Resident Artists; Resident Professionals; Soloists; Student Interns

7483
WILMA THEATRE
131 South Higgins Avenue
Room 200
Missoula, MT 59802
Phone: 406-728-2521
Fax: 406-728-7903
Web Site: www.thewilma.com
Management:
  General Manager: Bill Emerson
Seating Capacity: 1,100

Nebraska

7484
COMMUNITY PLAYERS THEATER
412 Ella Street
Beatrice, NE 68310
Phone: 402-228-1801
Fax: 402-228-9121
Web Site: www.beatricene.com/communityplayers/
Management:
  Artistic Director: Jamie Ulmer
Founded: 1975
Status: Non-Profit, Non-Professional
Paid Staff: 2
Paid Artists: 1

7485
BELLEVUE LITTLE THEATRE
203 Mission Avenue
Bellevue, NE 68005
Phone: 402-291-1554
Fax: 402-291-3809
e-mail: cyberma609@aol.com
Web Site: www.bellevuelittletheatre.com
Officers:

FACILITIES / Nebraska

President: Curtis Leach
Vice President: Robin Klushmire
Recording secretary: Joey Lorincz
Management:
President: Edward Roche, ebroche@cox.net
Mission: To create a superior environment for the promotion of the performing arts through the presentation of comedy, drama and musical theatre productions; and to stimulate educational and recreational programs in the technical and artistic venues of the performing arts for the citizens of the city of Bellevue, Sarpy County, and the Greater Omaha Metropolitan Area.
Founded: 1968
Specialized Field: Musical; Comedy; Ethnic Theatre; Community Theatre; Contemporary
Status: Non-Profit, Non-Professional
Seating Capacity: 244
Year Built: 1942

7486
BLADEN OPERA HOUSE
Main Street
Bladen, NE 68928

7487
CHADRON STATE COLLEGE MEMORIAL HALL
1000 Main Street
Chadron, NE 69337
Toll-free: 800-242-3766
Web Site: www.csc.edu

7488
UNIVERSITY OF NEBRASKA THEATRE
2506 12th Avenue
Kearney, NE 68849
Phone: 308-865-8618
Fax: 308-865-8806
Web Site: www.unk.edu
Management:
President: Doug Kristensen
Founded: 1905
Status: Non-Profit, Professional
Paid Staff: 800

7489
UNK SPORTS CENTER
University of Nebraska
2506 12th Avenue
Kearney, NE 68849
Phone: 308-865-8514
Fax: 308-865-8806
e-mail: jamesonj@unk.edu
Web Site: www.unk.edu
Management:
Chancellor: Doug Kristensen
Vice Chancellor: Finnie Murray
Vice Chancellor Finances: Randy Haack
Music Professor: Nathan Buckner
Founded: 1905
Status: Non-Profit, Professional
Paid Staff: 24
Seating Capacity: 5,842

7490
BOB DEVANEY SPORTS CENTER
University of Nebraska-Lincoln
103 South Stadium
Lincoln, NE 68588-0119
Phone: 402-472-4224
Fax: 402-472-9675
Web Site: www.huskerwebcast.com

Management:
Director Athletic Facilities: John M Ingram

7491
LIED CENTER FOR PERFORMING ARTS
12th and R Streets
PO Box 880151
Lincoln, NE 68588-0151
Phone: 402-472-4700
Fax: 402-472-4730
Toll-free: 800-432-3231
Web Site: www.liedcenter.org
Management:
Executive Director: Bill Stephan
Artistic Director: Anna Chang
Marketing and Sales Manager: Matthew Borlng
Communications Coordinator: Carrle Christensen
Director of Business Services: Natalle Stroud
Founded: 1988
Status: Non-Profit, Non-Professional
Paid Staff: 80

7492
LINCOLN MEMORIAL STADIUM
University of Nebraska-Lincoln
118 South Stadium
Lincoln, NE 68588-0119
Phone: 402-472-1960
Fax: 402-472-4662
Web Site: www.huskerwebcast.com
Management:
Director Athletic Facilities: John M Ingram
Director Athletics Events: Butch Hug
Seating Capacity: 73,650

7493
PERSHING CENTER
226 Centennial Mall South
Lincoln, NE 68508
Phone: 402-904-4444
Fax: 402-441-7913
e-mail: info@pershingauditorium.com
Web Site: www.pershingcenter.com
Officers:
Vice Chairman: Daivd McBride
Management:
General Manager: Thomas Lorenz
Marketing Director: Derek Andersen
Event Director: Sharon Mandery
Operations Director: Fred McCoy
Assistant General Manager: Terre Stickey
Founded: 1956
Paid Staff: 12
Performs At: Multi-purpose arena and exhibit hall
Stage Dimensions: 42'x105'
Seating Capacity: 6,818
Year Built: 1956
Rental Contact: Manager Tom Lorenz

7494
UNIVERSITY OF NEBRASKA-LINCOLN: KIMBALL RECITAL HALL
University of Nebraska-Lincoln
108 Westbrook
PO Box No 880100
Lincoln, NE 68588-0100
Phone: 402-475-5775
Fax: 402-472-2997
e-mail: rbowlin1@unl.edu
Web Site: www.unl.edu/music
Management:
Professor/Director School of Music: John W. Richmond, PhD
Events Coordinator, School of Music: Ron Bowlin

Founded: 1894
Status: Non-Profit, Non-Professional
Paid Staff: 50
Paid Artists: 50

7495
AL CANIGLIA STADIUM
University of Nebraska-Omaha
6001 Dodge
Omaha, NE 68182
Phone: 402-554-2305
Fax: 402-554-3694
Web Site: www.cidunomaha.edu/cyberman/
Management:
Sports Information Director: Gary Anderson
Athletic Director: Bob Danenhauer
Head Football Coach: Pat Behrns
Head Basketball Coach (M): Kevin McKenna
Seating Capacity: 3,800

7496
HOLLAND PERFORMING CENTER-ORPHEUM THEATER
Omaha Performing Arts
13th And Douglas St
Omaha, NE 68102
Phone: 402-345-0202
Fax: 402-345-0222
e-mail: info@omahaperformingarts.org
Web Site: www.omahaperformingarts.org
Officers:
Chairman: John Gottschalk
Vice Chairman: Richard D Holland
Management:
President: Joan Squires, jsquires@omahaperformingartsce
Event Coordinator: Tim Dickmeyer, tdickmeyer@omahaperformingartc
Direcetor Of Perfprmance Rentals: Ed Hurd, ehurd@omahaperformingartcenter
Production Manager: Kate Williams
Mission: 2 venues used for a variety of performing arts events. Also available for outside use by the community: The Peter Kiewit Concert hall and the Suzanne Walter Scott Recital hall. There is also an outside area the is used for a music/movies series during the summer.
Seating Capacity: concert hall:2000; recital hall: 400

7497
JEWISH COMMUNITY CENTER OF OMAHA
333 South 132nd Street
Omaha, NE 68154
Phone: 402-334-8200
Fax: 402-334-6466
e-mail: info@jewishomaha.org
Web Site: www.jewishomaha.org
Officers:
President: Michael W Miller
Chief Executive Officer: Mike Silverman
Chief Financial Officer: Jordana Glazer
Management:
Associate Director: Julee Katzman
Associate Executive Director: Lisa Shkolnick
Mission: To create a positive Jewish environment in which to build, strengthen and preserve Jewish identity and traditions. The Center reaches out to the Jewish community and provides its members with the unique opportunity to associate through a variety of social, cultural, recreational, educational and physical fitness programs, activities and services.
Budget: $10,000

FACILITIES / Nevada

7498
OMAHA CIVIC AUDITORIUM
1804 Capitol Avenue
Omaha, NE 68102
Phone: 402-444-3353
Fax: 402-444-4739
e-mail: info@omahacivic.com
Web Site: www.omahacivic.com
Management:
- Manager: Lawrence Lahaie
- Manager: Jeff Treney

Seating Capacity: 10,950

7499
ORPHEUM THEATER
Omaha Performing Arts
409 South 16th St
Omaha, NE 68102
Phone: 40-234-5060
Fax: 402-345-6224
Toll-free: 866-434-8587
e-mail: info@omahaperformingarts.org
Web Site: www.omahaperformingarts.org
Management:
- President: Joan Squires, jsquires@omahaperformingartsce
- Event Coordinator: Tim Dickmeyer, tdickmeyer@omahaperformingartc
- Direcetor Of Perfprmance Rentals: Ed Hurd, ehurd@omahaperformingartcenter
- Production Manager: Kate Williams

Mission: 2 venues used for a variety of performing arts events. Also available for outside use by the community: The Peter Kiewit Concert hall and the Suzanne Walter Scott Recital hall. There is also an outside area the is used for a music/movies series during the summer.
Seating Capacity: 2600

7500
ORPHEUM THEATRE
409 South 16th Street
Omaha, NE 68102
Phone: 402-661-8501
Fax: 402-884-6224
Web Site: www.omahaperformingarts.org
Officers:
- Chairman: John Gottschalk
- Vice Chairman: Richard D. Holland
- Secretary: John K. Boyer

Management:
- Accountant: Rita Conver
- Retail and Event Manager: Georgia Gruenler
- Facilities Manager: Randall Ward
- Event Coordinator: Cailin Fuller
- Development Coordinator: Nicole Tromler

7501
CENTURYLINK CENTER OMAHA
455 North 10th Street
Omaha, NE 68102
Phone: 402-341-1500
Fax: 402-991-1501
e-mail: info@omahameca.com
Web Site: www.centurylinkcenteromaha.com
Officers:
- President/CEO: Roger Dixon

Management:
- VP Corporate Sales: Tom O'Gorman

Seating Capacity: 17,000

7502
WEST NEBRASKA ARTS CENTER
106 East 18th Street
Scottsbluff, NE 69363-0062
Mailing Address: PO Box 62
Phone: 308-632-2226
Fax: 308-632-2226
e-mail: wneartsed@earthlink.net OR wneartsmb@earthlink.net
Web Site: www.nebraskarts.com
Officers:
- President: Pamela Kabalin
- Vice President: Steve Frederick
- Secretary: Christie Shaver
- Treasurer: Clark Wisniewski

Management:
- Executive Director: Peggy Millay
- Assistant Director: Mason Burbach
- Office Manager: Jo Haslow

Mission: The West Nebraska Arts Center (WNAC) is a regional cultural center, committed to the awareness and the fostering of excellence in the arts.
Budget: $10,000-$20,000

7503
PAVILION & EVENTS CENTER INC.
1580 County Road K
Wahoo, NE 68502
Phone: 402-560-9230
Fax: 402-474-5055
Web Site: www.thepavilioninc.com
Officers:
- President/CEO: Paul Ramirez

Management:
- Events Director: Bob Glantz

Seating Capacity: 35,000

7504
WAYNE STATE COLLEGE ARENA
1111 Main Street
Wayne, NE 68787
Phone: 402-375-7517
Fax: 402-375-7120
Toll-free: 800-228-9972
e-mail: studentfinance1@wsc.edu
Web Site: www.wsc.edu
Management:
- President: Richard Collings
- Athletic Director: Eric Schoh
- Assistant Athletic Director: Mike Barry
- Head Football Coach: Scott Hoffman
- Head Basketball Coach (M): Greg McDermott

Founded: 1910
Status: Non-Profit, Non-Professional
Paid Staff: 30
Seating Capacity: 6,000

Nevada

7505
BREWERY ARTS CENTER
449 West King Street
Carson City, NV 89703
Phone: 775-883-1976
Fax: 775-883-1922
Web Site: www.breweryarts.org
Officers:
- President: Chirs Bayer

Management:
- Executive Director: John Procaccini
- Senior Administrator: Laura Guberman
- Program Manager/Rentals: Christopher Wilson
- Technical Services: Eric Klug

Mission: Facilities include the 1864 Grand Ballroom that accomdates meetings, receptions, intimate performances up to 100 people; and the Performance Hall that accomodates 300 people.
Founded: 1976
Budget: $10,000
Performs At: Carson City Community Center

7506
CAESARS PALACE
3570 Las Vegas Boulevard South
Las Vegas, NV 89109
Phone: 866-227-5938
Fax: 702-731-7328
Toll-free: 800-342-7724
Web Site: www.caesarspalace.com
Management:
- Director: Charry Kennedy

7507
CHARLESTON HEIGHTS ARTS CENTER
800 S Brush
Las Vegas, NV 89107
Phone: 702-229-6383
Fax: 702-258-8286
Web Site: www.artslasvegas.org
Management:
- Cultural Supervisor: Linda Leos

Budget: $35,000-$60,000
Facility Category: Ballroom; Theater
Seating Capacity: 365
Year Built: 1979
Year Remodeled: 1989
Rental Contact: 702-229-5256 Roy Ramirez

7508
HUNTRIDGE THEATRE
1208 East Charleston Boulevard
Las Vegas, NV 89104
Phone: 702-678-6800
Fax: 702-678-6808
Web Site: www.thehuntridge.com
Management:
- Talent Buyer: Eli Mizrachi
- Marketing Manager: Kim Garcia

Seating Capacity: 1,090

7509
LAS VEGAS CONVENTION AND VISITORS AUTHORITY
3150 Paradise Road
Las Vegas, NV 89109
Phone: 702-892-0711
Fax: 702-386-7126
Toll-free: 877-847-4858
Web Site: www.lvcva.com
Management:
- President: Rossi Ralenkotter
- Managing Director: Phil Simmons

Founded: 1959
Status: Non-Profit, Non-Professional
Paid Staff: 112

7510
MANDALAY BAY EVENTS CENTER
Mandalay Bay Resort & Casino
3950 Las Vegas Boulevard South
Las Vegas, NV 89119
Phone: 702-632-7551
Fax: 702-632-7508
Web Site: www.mandalaybay.com
Management:
- Executive Director: H. C. Rowe

FACILITIES / Nevada

VP Entertainment: Glenn Medas
Seating Capacity: 12,000

7511
MGM GRAND GARDEN ARENA
3799 Las Vegas Boulevard South
Las Vegas, NV 89109
Phone: 877-880-0880
Fax: 702-891-7831
Toll-free: 800-299-10
e-mail: guestservices@lv.mgmgrand.com
Web Site: www.mgmgrand.com
Officers:
  President: Terry Lanni
  Vice President: Mark W. Prows
  Executive Director: Karen Prescia
  Assistant Vice President: Rich Baccellieri
  Senior Event Manager: Dick Hill
Founded: 1993
Status: For-Profit, Professional
Seating Capacity: 15,200

7512
REED WHIPPLE CULTURAL ARTS CENTER
821 Las Vegas Boulevard N
Las Vegas, NV 89101
Phone: 702-229-6211
Fax: 702-382-5199
Web Site: www.lasvegasnevada.gov
Management:
  Director of Dept: Barbara Jackson
  Supervisor: Dale Barbeau
  Manager Cultural Division: Nancy Deaner
Founded: 1975
Status: Non-Profit, Professional
Paid Staff: 30
Paid Artists: 100

7513
SAM BOYD STADIUM
4505 Maryland Parkway
Las Vegas, NV 89145-0003
Phone: 702-895-3716
Fax: 702-895-1099
e-mail: customer.service@unlvtickets.com
Web Site: www.samboydstadium.com
Management:
  Director: Patrick J Christenson
  Assistant Director: Robert P Anderson
  Assistant Director/Booking: Daren Libonati
  Assistant Director/Sports Marketing: Steve Stallworth
  Assistant Director Operations: Rick Picone
  Promotions/Public Relations Manager: Cliff Clinger
Seating Capacity: 42,500

7514
THE SMITH CENTER FOR THE PERFORMING ARTS
361 Symphony Park Avenue
Las Vegas, NV 89106
Phone: 702-749-2012
Toll-free: 800-326-6868
e-mail: patronservices@thesmithcenter.com
Web Site: www.thesmithcenter.com
Officers:
  President/CEO: Myron G. Martin
  Chairman: Donald D Snyder
  Vice Chairman: Keith Boman
  Secretary: Kim Sinatra
Mission: 3 venues: cabaret jazz, large concert hall, smaller venues perfect for gatherings, rehearsals

7515
THOMAS & MACK CENTER
4505 Maryland Parkway
Box 450003
Las Vegas, NV 89154-0003
Mailing Address: 4505 S Maryland Parkway, Box 450003, Las Vegas, NV 89154-000
Phone: 702-895-3761
Fax: 702-895-1099
e-mail: customer.service@unlvtickets.com
Web Site: www.thomasandmack.com
Management:
  Executive Director: Mike Newcomb
  Artistic Director: Nevada Colwell
  Associate Director Operations: Rick Picone
  Public Relations: Angela Gomes
  Event Services Director: Todd Clawson
  Event Services Manager: Mike Newcomb
  Event Coordinator: Jim Sanders
  External Coordinator: Kenny Sasaki
Founded: 1983
Status: For-Profit, Professional
Paid Staff: 100
Seating Capacity: 18,500

7516
UNIVERSITY OF NEVADA-LAS VEGAS PERFORMING ARTS CENTER ARTEMUS HAM CONCERT HALL
4505 Maryland Parkway
Box 455005
Las Vegas, NV 89154-5005
Phone: 702-895-3011
Fax: 702-895-4714
e-mail: henley@ccmail.nevada.edu
Web Site: www.unlv.edu/maps/hch
Management:
  Director Artistic Programming: Larry Henley
  Technical Director: Trent Downing
Founded: 1976
Specialized Field: Present World's Greatest Talent
Status: Non-Profit, Professional

7517
CHURCH OF FINE ARTS
University of Nevada-Reno
1664 N. Virginia Street
Reno, NV 89557
Phone: 775-784-1110
Web Site: www.unr.edu

7518
LAWLOR EVENTS CENTER
University of Nevada Athletic Department
1500 N Virginia St
Reno, NV 89557
Phone: 775-784-4659
Fax: 775-784-4428
e-mail: lawlor@unr.edu
Web Site: www.unr.edu
Management:
  Director: Ann Larson
  Programming Manager: John Tipton
  Operations Manager: Kevin Fields
  Events Technician/Operations Superv: Parker Shonnard
Seating Capacity: 12,400

7519
MACKEY STADIUM
University of Nevada
Legacy Hall 232
Reno, NV 98557
Phone: 775-784-6900
Fax: 775-784-4497
Web Site: www.nevadawolfpack.com
Management:
  Athletic Director: Chris Ault
Seating Capacity: 30,000

7520
PIONEER CENTER FOR THE PERFORMING ARTS
100 S Virginia Street
Reno, NV 89501
Phone: 702-686-6010
Fax: 702-686-6630
e-mail: admin@pioneercenter.com
Web Site: www.pioneercenter.com
Management:
  Executive Director: Willis Allen
  Technical Director: Italo Crocco

7521
RENO LITTLE THEATER
147 East Pueblo Street
Reno, NV 89502
Mailing Address: P.O. Box 7071, Reno, NV 89510
Phone: 775-329-0661
e-mail: info@renolittletheater.org
Web Site: www.renolittletheater.org
Officers:
  Chairman: Moria Bengochea
  Vice-Chairman: Paul Malikowski
  Chair Elect: Nettie Oliverio
  Secretary: Margaret Jacques

7522
RENO SPARKS CONVENTION CENTENNIAL COLISEUM
4590 South Virginia Street
Reno, NV 89502
Phone: 775-827-7620
Fax: 775-825-3726
Toll-free: 800-367-7366
Web Site: www.visitrenotahoe.com/facilities/reno_sparks_cc/tours/
Officers:
  President/CEO: Ellen Oppenheim
Management:
  Director of Operations, Levy Restau: Dave Marguth
  Event Services Manager: Tracy Legarza
  Audio Visual Manager: Dan Hogan
  Senior Sales Manager: Tracy Sousa
  Assistant General Manager: Joe Walther
Mission: Facility overview of the Reno Convention Center includes 500,000 square feet of fully adaptable exhibition and meeting space; 53 meeting rooms with 110,000 square feet of space; and 381,000 square feet of contiguous exhibit space.
Status: For-Profit, Professional
Paid Staff: 400

7523
PIPER'S OPERA HOUSE
12 N B Street
PO Box J
Virginia City, NV 89440

FACILITIES / New Hampshire

Phone: 775-847-0433
Fax: 775-847-9668
e-mail: info@piperslivevc.com
Web Site: www.piperslivevc.com
Management:
    President: Ron Waicul
    Executive Director: Sam Folio
    Artistic Director: William Beeson
Founded: 1878
Status: Non-Profit, Non-Professional
Paid Staff: 2
Paid Artists: 2

New Hampshire

7524
CLAREMONT OPERA HOUSE
City Hall on Tremont Square
PO Box 664
Claremont, NH 03743
Phone: 603-542-4433
Fax: 603-542-7014
e-mail: office@claremontoperahouse.org
Web Site: www.claremontoperahouse.com
Management:
    Executive Director: Louanne Lewit
Mission: Multi-use performing arts center.
Utilizes: Guest Accompanists; Guest Musical Directors; Local Artists; Multimedia; Original Music Scores; Soloists; Special Technical Talent; Theatre Companies
Opened: 1977
Status: Non-Profit, Professional
Paid Staff: 1
Budget: $150,000
Income Sources: Tickets; Membership; Sponsors
Affiliations: APAP; APNNE
Annual Attendance: 15,000
Facility Category: Theatre
Type of Stage: Proscenium
Seating Capacity: 780
Year Built: 1897
Year Remodeled: 1975

7525
CAPITOL CENTER FOR THE ARTS
44 South Main Street
Concord, NH 03301
Phone: 603-225-1111
Fax: 603-224-3408
e-mail: mtmennino@ccanh.com
Web Site: www.ccanh.com
Management:
    Executive Director: Mary-Therese Mennino
Mission: To inspire, educate and entertain audiences by providing both the finest venue for the performing arts and a wide range of professioanlly excellent and artistically significant presentations.
Founded: 1995
Status: Non-Profit, Professional
Paid Staff: 15
Budget: $1.8 million
Annual Attendance: 100,000
Seating Capacity: 1300
Year Built: 1927
Year Remodeled: 1995

7526
CONCORD CITY AUDITORIUM
The Friends of the Concord City Auditorium
2 Prince Street
Concord, NH 03301
Mailing Address: PO Box 652 Concord, NH 03302-0652
Phone: 603-228-2793
e-mail: inf0@concordcityauditorium.org
Web Site: www.theaudi.org
Officers:
    Treasurer: Merwyn Bagan
Management:
    Friends Information Chair: David Murdo, nhdm40@comcast.net
    Friends Marketing Chair: Carol Bagan, carolbagam@comcast.net
Mission: To restore and renovate our historic theatre and to foster its use for the benefit of all the people in our community. The Friends of the Audi will assist all presenters who wish to book the City Auditorium.
Utilizes: Actors; Arrangers; Choreographers; Collaborating Artists; Collaborations; Community Members; Community Talent; Composers; Contract Actors; Contract Orchestras; Dance Companies; Dancers; Designers; Educators; Filmmakers; Five Seasonal Concerts; Grant Writers; Guest Accompanists; Guest Choreographers; Guest Companies; Guest Conductors; Guest Designers; Guest Directors; Guest Ensembles; Guest Instructors; Guest Lecturers; Guest Musical Directors; Guest Musicians; Guest Soloists; Guest Speakers; Guild Activities; Instructors; Local Artists; Local Artists & Directors; Local Talent; Local Unknown Artists; Multi Collaborations; Multimedia; Music; New Productions; Organization Contracts; Original Music Scores; Paid Performers; Performance Artists; Playwrights; Poets; Resident Artists; Resident Professionals; Scenic Designers; Selected Students; Sign Language Translators; Singers; Soloists; Students; Student Interns; Special Technical Talent; Theatre Companies; Touring Companies; Visual Arts; Visual Designers; Volunteer Artists; Volunteer Directors & Actors;
Founded: 1904
Specialized Field: Theatre; Music; Dance; Series; Community Based A and E
Status: Non-Profit, Professional
Performs At: Auditorium; Adjoining Reception Lobby
Annual Attendance: 75,000
Facility Category: Municipal Theatre
Type of Stage: Proscenium
Stage Dimensions: 25'x 25'
Seating Capacity: 850
Year Built: 1904
Year Remodeled: 1991
Rental Contact: 230-3851 Nina Piroso

7527
BRATTON RECITAL HALL
University of New Hampshire-Durham
4 Ballard Street
Durham, NH 03824
Phone: 603-862-3038
Fax: 603-862-3038

7528
HENNESSY CENTER
University of New Hampshire-Durham
4 Ballard Street
Durham, NH 03824
Phone: 603-862-3038
Fax: 603-862-3038
Web Site: www.unh.edu/theatre-dance
Seating Capacity: 150

7529
PAUL CREATIVE ARTS CENTER
University of New Hampshire-Durham
30 College Road
Durham, NH 03824-2617
Phone: 603-862-7222
Fax: 603-862-2191
Toll-free: 800-735-2964
e-mail: museum.of.art@unh.edu
Web Site: www.unh.edu/moa
Management:
    Interim Director: Weston LaFountain
    Assistant Director: Astrida Schaeffer
    Education & Publicity Coordinator: Catherine A Mazur
    Administrative Assistant III: Cindy Farrell
Mission: A professional managed museum providing exhibitions and programs in the visual arts, the Museum of Art is a vitally important component of the University of New Hampshire. Role encompasses two major areas: academic and community outreach. As a teaching unit, the Museum provides the opportunity for universitystudents to gain knowledge and experience in dealing with works of art on a first hand basis.
Founded: 1960
Paid Staff: 4
Volunteer Staff: 6
Affiliations: AAM; AAMG
Annual Attendance: 6,846
Year Built: 1960
Year Remodeled: 1973
Cost: $2.5 Million

7530
WHITTEMORE CENTER
University of New Hampshire
128 Main St
Durham, NH 03824
Phone: 603-862-4057
Fax: 603-862-4069
Web Site: www.unh.edu/athletics
Management:
    Athletic Director: Judith Ray
    Marketing Director: Dan Raposa
    Media Relations Director: Scott Stapin
Seating Capacity: 6,000

7531
HAMPTON PLAYHOUSE THEATRE ARTS WORKSHOP
357 Winnacunnet Road
Hampton, NH 03842
Phone: 603-926-3073

7532
HAMPTON BEACH CASINO BALLROOM
169 Ocean Boulevard
Hampton Beach, NH 03842
Phone: 603-929-4100
Fax: 603-926-9505
e-mail: info@Casinoballroom.com
Web Site: www.casinoballroom.com
Management:
    General Manager: Fred Schaake Jr
    Marketing Director: Andrew Herrick
    Operations Manager: Adam Lacasse
Seating Capacity: 2,200

7533
MEMORIAL STADIUM
Dartmouth College
7 Lebanon Street, Suite 201
Hanover, NH 03755

FACILITIES / New Hampshire

Phone: 603-646-3661
Fax: 603-646-2850
e-mail: office.of.public.affairs@dartmouth.edu
Web Site: www.dartmouth.edu
Management:
  President: James Wright
  Director Athletics: Joann Harper
  Director Sports Information: Kathy Slattery
  Dean: James Larimore
Founded: 1969
Seating Capacity: 20,416

7534
COLONIAL THEATRE
95 Main Street
Keene, NH 03431
Mailing Address: P.O. Box 77 Keene
Phone: 603-357-1233
Fax: 603-357-7817
e-mail: email@thecolonial.org
Web Site: www.thecolonial.org
Officers:
  Executive Director: Alec Doyle
  Director Of Marketing: Jessica Reeves
Management:
  Executive Director: Alec Doyle
  House Manager: Georgia Fletcher
  Director of Marketing: Jessica Reeves
  Director of Finance & Administratio: Gale Saleski
Founded: 1924
Status: Non-Profit
Paid Staff: 12
Volunteer Staff: 150
Season: year round
Annual Attendance: 60,000
Type of Stage: Proscenium
Stage Dimensions: 24X60
Seating Capacity: 900
Year Built: 1924
Year Remodeled: 1998
Rental Contact: Executive Director Alec Doyle

7535
REDFERN ARTS CENTER ON BRICKYARD POND
Keene State College
229 Main Street
Keene, NH 03435-2401
Phone: 603-358-2167
Fax: 603-358-2145
e-mail: bmenezes@keene.edu
Web Site: www.keene.edu/racbp
Management:
  Director: Shannon Mayers
  Production Manager: Cheryl A Perry
  Assistant Director: Sharon Fantl
Mission: Educational
Founded: 1979
Specialized Field: Theatre; Dance; Music
Status: Non-Profit, Non-Professional
Paid Staff: 4
Budget: $250,000
Income Sources: Tickets Sales, College Subscriptions, Corparate Sponsors, Private Donations
Affiliations: Green Mountain Consortium; New England Presenters; Associated Performing Arts Presenters
Annual Attendance: 15,000
Facility Category: Multipurpose
Type of Stage: Proscenium
Stage Dimensions: 36'x 30'x 56'
Seating Capacity: 572
Year Built: 1979
Rental Contact: B Denehy

7536
LEBANON OPERA HOUSE
51 North Park Street
PO Box 384
Lebanon, NH 03766
Phone: 603-448-0400
Fax: 603-448-0444
e-mail: info@lebanonoperahouse.org
Web Site: www.lebanonoperahouse.org
Officers:
  President: Eric Janson
  Vice President: Paul Olsen
  Secretary: Steven Therriault
Management:
  Executive Director: Heather J. Clow
  Facilities Manager: Dan Merlo
  Assistant Director: Joe Gleason
Founded: 1991
Specialized Field: Series and Festivals; Music; Theatre; Dance
Status: Non-Profit, Professional
Paid Staff: 5

7537
LOON MOUNTAIN
60 Loon Mountain Rd
Lincoln, NH 03251
Phone: 603-745-8111
Fax: 603-745-8214
Toll-free: 800-229-5666
e-mail: info@loonmtn.com
Web Site: www.loonmtn.com
Management:
  Events Coordinator: Stacey Lopes
Seating Capacity: 6,000

7538
NCCA PAPERMILL THEATRE
34 Papermill Drive
Lincoln, NH 03251
Mailing Address: PO Box 1060
Phone: 603-745-6032
Fax: 603-745-2564
e-mail: info@jeans-playhouse.com
Web Site: jeans-playhouse.com
Officers:
  President: David Yager
  Vice Presidemt: Andrew Noyes
  Treasurer: Warren Bahr
  Secretary: Maureen Polimeno
Management:
  Producing Director: Scott H. Severance
  Business Manager: Christa Hollingsworth
  Technical Director: Kyle Trumble
  Director of Community Relations and: Vicki Etchings
Mission: To provide theatre, cultural programming and theatre education for children and adults.
Utilizes: Guest Companies
Founded: 1986
Specialized Field: Theater; Festivals; Touring Children's Theatre; Art Gallery
Status: Non-Profit, Professional
Paid Staff: 3
Volunteer Staff: 50
Paid Artists: 50
Non-paid Artists: 20
Organization Type: Performing; Touring; Educational

7539
PALACE THEATRE
80 Hanover Street
Manchester, NH 01301
Phone: 603-668-5588
Fax: 603-668-5804
e-mail: info@palacetheatre.org
Web Site: www.palacetheatre.org
Officers:
  President: Quentin W Keefe
  Vice Chair: Alexander J Walker Jr.
  Secretary: J. Michael Perrella
Management:
  Office Manager/Theatre Renta Contac: Beth Mortensen
  Production Manager: Whit Privette, whitprivettepalacetheatre.org
Mission: Offers performances produced by the theatre, presnted by the theatre or events performed at the theatre by outside groups renting the space.
Seating Capacity: 840

7540
VERIZON WIRELESS ARENA
555 Elm Street
Manchester, NH 03101
Phone: 603-644-5000
Fax: 603-644-1575
Web Site: www.verizonwirelessarena.com
Management:
  General Manager: Timothy Bechert
  Director Sales/Marketing: Jason Perry
Founded: 2001
Paid Staff: 300
Performs At: Sports & Entertainment
Affiliations: Manchester Monarch; Manchester Wolves
Annual Attendance: 550,000
Facility Category: Arena
Type of Stage: Standard
Stage Dimensions: various
Seating Capacity: 11,000
Year Built: 2001
Cost: $70 million

7541
NEW LONDON BARN PLAYHOUSE
84 Main Street
New London, NH 03257
Mailing Address: PO Box 9, New London, NH 03257
Phone: 603-526-6570
Fax: 603-526-2849
e-mail: info@nlbarn.org
Web Site: www.nlbarn.com
Management:
  Producing Artistic Director: carol Dunne
  Managing Director: Milena Zuccotti
  Business Manager: Beth Perregaux
  Education Director: Joshua Feder
Mission: The New London Barn Playhouse in New London, New Hampshire has operated continuously since 1933 and functions as a true summer stock theatre.
Season: June - August

7542
EASTERN SLOPE INN PLAYHOUSE
Main Street
PO Box 265
North Conway, NH 03860
Phone: 603-356-5776
Fax: 603-356-8357
e-mail: SuzieLaskin@gmail.com
Web Site: www.mwvtheatre.org
Mission: To keep the tradition of line performance, especially musical.

7543
MUSIC HALL
28 Chestnut Street
Portsmouth, NH 03801-4078
Phone: 603-433-3100
Fax: 603-431-4103
Web Site: www.themusichall.org
Management:
  Executive Director: Patricia Lynch
  Executive Administrative Assistant: Todd Hunter
  Senior Accountant: Suzanne Patrakis
  Director of Marketing: Monte Bohanan
Founded: 1876
Specialized Field: Seacoast, NH
Status: Non-Profit, Professional
Paid Staff: 12
Volunteer Staff: 274

New Jersey

7544
BAYONNE VETERANS MEMORIAL STADIUM
W 26th Street
Bayonne, NJ 07002
Phone: 201-858-6164
Fax: 201-858-6092
Management:
  Director: Steve Gallo

7545
ARMSTRONG HIPKINS CENTER FOR THE ARTS
Blair Academy
2 Park Street
Blairstown, NJ 07825
Mailing Address: PO Box 600
Phone: 908-362-6121
Fax: 908-362-2029
e-mail: habers@blair.edu
Web Site: www.blair.edu/performing_arts
Officers:
  Chairman: Douglas W. Kimmelman
  Vice Chair: Dominick J. Romano
  Secretary: Anne E. Cramer
Management:
  President: Chandler Chardwick
  Executive Director: Sam Backon
  Artistic Director: Craige Evens
  Managing Director: Jim Frick
Mission: Educational insititution.
Founded: 1997
Status: Non-Profit, Professional
Paid Staff: 150
Type of Stage: Black Box
Seating Capacity: 500

7546
CALDWELL COLLEGE STUDENT UNION BUILDING
120 Bloomfield Avenue
Caldwell, NJ 07006
Phone: 973-618-3000
Fax: 201-228-3851
Web Site: www.caldwell.edu

7547
RUTGERS-CAMDEN CENTER FOR THE ARTS GORDON THEATER
Rutgers University Fine Arts Building
314 Linden Street
Camden, NJ 08102-1403
Phone: 856-225-6676
Fax: 856-225-6597
e-mail: arts@camden.rutgers.edu
Web Site: www.rcca.camden.rutgers.edu
Management:
  Director: Cyril Reade
  Associate Director of Exhibitions: Nancy Maguire
Founded: 1996
Status: Non-Profit, Professional
Paid Staff: 8
Paid Artists: 50

7548
WALT WHITMAN CULTURAL ARTS CENTER
2nd and Cooper Streets
Camden, NJ 08102
Phone: 856-964-8300
Fax: 856-964-2953
Web Site: www.waltwhitmancenter.org/
Management:
  Executive Director: Pamela Bridgeforth
  Artistic Director: Ozzie Jones
  Finance & Administration Director: Tony Lewis
  Public Relations/External Affairs: Maureen L Mullin
Mission: The Walt Whitman Arts Center, a non-profit, multi-cultural literary, performing and visual arts center in Camden, New Jersey, is dedicated to continuing its namesake's legacy of artistic excellence. The organization also is committed to ensuring that its programming is accessible to Camden and its surrounding communities.
Founded: 1975
Status: Non-Profit, Professional
Paid Staff: 7
Budget: $60,000-$150,000

7549
MID-ATLANTIC CENTER FOR THE ARTS & HUMANITIES
1048 Washington Street
PO Box 340
Cape May, NJ 08204
Mailing Address: PO Box 340, Cape May NJ 08204
Phone: 609-884-5404
Fax: 609-884-0574
Toll-free: 800-275-4278
e-mail: mstewart@capemaymac.org
Web Site: www.capemaymac.org
Officers:
  CFO: Melissa Zeides
Management:
  Director: Michael Zuckerman, mstewart@capemaymac.org
  Assistant to the Director: Anna Ieeper
Mission: Dedicated to promoting preservation, awareness and interpretation of the Victorian era and its customs, heritage and architecture, as well as striving to promote the performing arts.
Utilizes: Community Members; Curators; Educators; Five Seasonal Concerts; Guest Directors; Original Music Scores
Founded: 1970
Opened: 1990
Specialized Field: Series & Festivals; Instrumental Music; Special Events
Status: Non-Profit, Professional
Paid Staff: 25
Volunteer Staff: 50
Paid Artists: 100
Performs At: Cape May Convention Hall
Organization Type: Sponsoring

7550
MIDDLE TOWNSHIP PERFORMING ARTS CENTER
1 Penkethman Way
Cape May, NJ 08210
Phone: 609-463-1924
Fax: 609-463-1928
Management:
  Executive Director: Richard Ludwig
Founded: 1992
Status: Non-Profit, Professional
Paid Staff: 4
Budget: $60,000-$150,000

7551
CRANFORD DRAMATIC CLUB THEATRE
78 Winans Avenue
PO Box 511
Cranford, NJ 07016
Mailing Address: PO Box 511,Cranford, N.J. 07016
Phone: 908-276-7611
e-mail: info@cdctheatre.org
Web Site: www.cdctheatre.org

7552
DOVER LITTLE THEATRE
Elliott Street
PO Box 82
Dover, NJ 07801
Phone: 973-328-9202
Web Site: www.doverlittletheater.org

7553
CONTINENTAL AIRLINES ARENA
Meadowlands
50 Route 120
East Rutherford, NJ 07073
Phone: 201-460-4374
Fax: 201-507-8122
e-mail: mbell@njsea.com
Web Site: www.meadowlands.com
Management:
  President/CEO: George Zoffinger
  Senior VP/General Manager: Timothy D Hassett
  VP Event Booking: Ron Vandeveen
Founded: 1976
Status: For-Profit, Non-Professional
Paid Staff: 300
Budget: $3 million
Facility Category: Arena
Seating Capacity: 20,029
Year Built: 1981
Rental Contact: Ron VanDeVeen

7554
GIANTS STADIUM
Meadowlands
50 Route 120
East Rutherford, NJ 07073
Phone: 201-460-4355
Fax: 201-460-4294
e-mail: webmaster@meadowlands.com
Web Site: www.meadowlands.com
Management:
  President/CEO: George Zoffinger

FACILITIES / New Jersey

Senior VP/CFO: Joseph Consolazio
Senior VP Sales/Marketing: Kathleen Francis
Senior VP/Stadium Arena GM: Timothy D Hassett
Mission: Home of the New York Giants and the New York Jets, The Metro Stars, college football and concerts.
Founded: 1971
Status: For-Profit, Professional
Paid Staff: 100
Seating Capacity: 80,242
Year Built: 1976

7555
MEADOWLANDS THEATER
Meadowlands
50 Route 120
East Rutherford, NJ 07073-0700
Phone: 201-240-4038
Fax: 201-507-8130
Web Site: www.meadowlands.com
Management:
  President/CEO: George Zoffinger
  General Manager: Timothy D Hassett
Mission: For smaller, more intimate venues.
Founded: 2004

7556
APPEL FARM ARTS AND MUSIC CENTER
457 Shirley Road
P.O. Box 888
Elmer, NJ 08318
Phone: 609-358-2472
Fax: 609-358-6513
Web Site: www.appelfarm.org
Officers:
  President: Denise Hayman-Loa
  Vice President: Ronnie Cimprich
  Secretary: Franklin Moore, Esq
  Treasurer: Anita Zippert
Management:
  Executive Director: Cori Solomon
  Summer Arts Camp Director: Jennie Quinn
  Summer Arts Camp Assistant Director: Rachel Chadwin
  Director of Arts Education and Outr: Kerri Sullivan
  Arts Education Assistant: Millie Struve

7557
JOHN HARMS CENTER FOR THE ARTS
30 N Van Brunt Street
Englewood, NJ 07631
Phone: 201-567-5797
Fax: 201-567-7357
Web Site: www.johnharms.org
Management:
  Executive Director: Jessica Finkelberg
  Business Manager: Steve Nemiroff
  Director Education: Cathy Roy
  Communications/Marketing: Ed Kirchdoerffer
Founded: 1976
Status: Nonprofit
Paid Staff: 14
Volunteer Staff: 150
Paid Artists: 250
Budget: $3,000,000
Income Sources: Foundations, Grants, Corporate Support, Individuals, Earned
Annual Attendance: 300,000
Facility Category: Theater
Type of Stage: Proscenium
Stage Dimensions: 33 x 30
Seating Capacity: 1322
Year Built: 1926

7558
GLASSBORO CENTER FOR THE ARTS
Rowan University
Wilson Hall, Room 211
Glassboro, NJ 08028
Phone: 856-256-4548
Fax: 856-256-4919
e-mail: fields@rowan.edu
Web Site: www.users.rowan.edu/~benson/centerart/
Management:
  Office Manager: Ginny Allen
  Director: Mark Fields
Mission: To provide several different professional cultural events for the Southern New Jersey area.
Utilizes: Collaborations; Dance Companies; Guest Choreographers; Guest Directors; Guest Musical Directors; Guest Musicians; Multimedia; Original Music Scores; Singers; Special Technical Talent; Theatre Companies
Founded: 1989
Specialized Field: Dance; Vocal Music; Instrumental Music; Theater; Lyric Opera; Grand Opera; Jazz
Status: Professional
Budget: $950,000
Income Sources: New Jersey State Council on the Arts; Bergen Foundation; PSEG;
Performs At: Wilson Concert Hall
Annual Attendance: 35,000
Facility Category: Auditorium
Type of Stage: Proscenium
Stage Dimensions: 50' X 35'
Seating Capacity: 895
Year Built: 1971
Rental Contact: Stu McKee
Organization Type: Performing; Touring; Resident; Educational; Sponsoring

7559
ORRIE DE NOOYER AUDITORIUM
Bergen County Academic
200 Hackensack Avenue
Hackensack, NJ 07601
Phone: 201-343-6000
Fax: 201-343-8884
Web Site: www.bergen.org
Management:
  Principal: Patricia Cosgroze
Founded: 1990
Status: For-Profit, Non-Professional

7560
RICHARD L SWIG ARTS CENTER
Peddie School
201 South Main Street
Highstown, NJ 08520
Phone: 609-944-7500
Fax: 609-944-7901
Web Site: www.peddie.org
Officers:
  CEO: Christopher J. Acito
  President: John J. Burke
  Chairman: Robert Kaye
Management:
  Director: Karen Buroojy
  Bond Manager: Jon N. Eckert
Founded: 2000
Status: Non-Profit, Professional
Paid Staff: 3

7561
NORTHERN STAR ARENA
Six Flags Great Adventure
Route 537
Jackson, NJ 08527
Mailing Address: P.O. Box 120
Phone: 732-928-2000
Fax: 732-928-0937
Web Site: www.sixflags.com
Management:
  Entertainment Director: Bob O'Neill
Seating Capacity: 10,000

7562
LIBERTY SCIENCE CENTER
222 Jersey City Boulevard
Liberty State Park
Jersey City, NJ 07305-4699
Phone: 201-200-1000
Fax: 201-451-6383
e-mail: events@lsc.org OR guestcomments@lsc.org
Web Site: www.lsc.org
Management:
  President: Emlyn Koster
  Events/Rentals Director: Alison Marcon
Mission: The Central Railroad of New Jersey (CRRNJ) Concourse Hall is suitable for a wide variety events, from dinners and festivals to trade shows and fund-raisers and more and can hold up to 1,000 people.
Founded: 1993
Status: Non-Profit, Non-Professional
Paid Staff: 200

7563
STRAND THEATRE
400 Clifton Avenue
Lakewood, NJ 08701
Phone: 732-367-7789
Fax: 732-367-7819
Web Site: www.strand.org
Management:
  Executive Director: Theresa Beaugard
  Event Manager: Patti Curtis
  Technical Director: Chris Staton
  Office Manager: Judy Jensen
  House Manager: Jose Pastrana
Utilizes: Collaborations; Five Seasonal Concerts; Guest Writers; Guild Activities; Instructors; Local Artists; Multi Collaborations; Multimedia; Special Technical Talent; Theatre Companies
Founded: 1922
Status: Non-Profit, Professional
Paid Staff: 25
Volunteer Staff: 30
Non-paid Artists: 80
Income Sources: Rentals; Grants; Ticket Sales
Facility Category: Theatre
Seating Capacity: 1,042
Year Built: 1922
Year Remodeled: 2001
Cost: $5,000,000
Rental Contact: Linda Hassa

7564
YVONNE THEATER
Rider University
2083 Lawrenceville Road
Lawrenceville, NJ 08648
Phone: 609-896-500
Fax: 609-896-5232
e-mail: millsm@rider.edu
Web Site: www.rider.edu
Management:

FACILITIES / New Jersey

Theater Director: Tharyle Prather
Professor: Miriam Mills
Mission: To produce outstanding Theater, Dance and Music events for the university and the surrounding communities. This venue provides the university with the opportunity to learn the theater process from concept to performance. In addition, the theater also offers outside cultural and intellectual events, as time permits.
Specialized Field: Theater; Dance; Music
Type of Stage: Proscenium
Seating Capacity: 440
Rental Contact: Tharyle Prather

7565
BOWNE THEATRE
Drew University
36 Madison Avenue
Madison, NJ 07940
Phone: 908-272-0100
Fax: 908-272-3949
e-mail: info@dgdco.com

7566
BERRIE CENTER FOR PERFORMING AND VISUAL ARTS
Ramapo College of New Jersey
505 Ramapo Valley Road
Mahwah, NJ 07430
Phone: 201-684-7500
Fax: 201-684-7979
e-mail: eeloi@ramapo.edu
Web Site: www.ramapo.edu/berriecenter/index.html
Management:
  Manager of Berrie Center Operations: Edonard A Eloiffer
  Theater Technical Director: Jason Hughes
  Assistant Technical Director: Jonathan Ginnow
  Gallery Director: Sidney O Jenkins
Mission: Constructed in 1999, the Performing Arts Center houses the Sharp Theater, a 350-seat proscenium theater engineered without obstructions to visibility or sound; the Myron and Elaine Adler Theater, a blackbox theater which can seat up to 100; The Kresge and Pascal Art Galleries, mounting exhibitions of museum, international, student, faculty, and community artwork; and The Curtain Call Cafe serving beverages and light fare.
Status: For-Profit, Professional
Paid Staff: 30
Paid Artists: 50

7567
PAPER MILL PLAYHOUSE
Brookside Drive
Millburn, NJ 07041
Phone: 973-379-3636
Fax: 973-376-2359
e-mail: info@papermill.org
Web Site: www.papermill.org
Management:
  President: Michael Gennaro
  Casting Director: Alison Franck
  Associate Artistic Director: Mark S Hoebee
  Director Development: Nina S Jacobs

7568
BICKFORD THEATRE AT THE MORRIS MUSEUM
6 Normandy Heights Road
Morristown, NJ 07960
Phone: 978-921-5706
Fax: 973-538-0154
e-mail: info@morrismuseum.org
Web Site: www.bickfordtheatre.org
Management:
  Artistic Director: Eric Hafen
  Public Relations Manager: Stephen Kantrowitz
Mission: A 312-seat professional theatre located within the Morris Museum. The theatre produces 4 main stage productions each year that include classic and contemporary comedies, mysteries and musicals. The company is affiliated with the Actors Equity Association and the Society of Stage Directors and Choreographers. In addition, Bickford Theatre presents year-round Children's theatre, music concerts and the acclaimed Wyeth Jazz Concert Series.
Utilizes: Actors; AEA Actors; Choreographers; Curators; Dance Companies; Dancers; Educators; Guest Conductors; Guest Designers; Guest Instructors; Guest Lecturers; Guest Soloists; Instructors; Original Music Scores; Touring Companies
Founded: 1983
Specialized Field: Theatre; Performing Arts
Status: For-Profit, Professional
Paid Staff: 20
Type of Stage: Proscenium
Stage Dimensions: 40x80
Seating Capacity: 300
Year Built: 1975
Year Remodeled: 1987
Rental Contact: Rental Coordinator Kristin Granade
Resident Groups: The Bickford Theatre

7569
COMMUNITY THEATRE
100 South Street
Morristown, NJ 07960
Phone: 973-539-0345
Fax: 973-455-1607
Web Site: www.communitytheatrenj.org
Officers:
  President: Mary Lou Britton
  Vice President: Larry Nielsen
  Treasurer: Christy Frick
  Secretary: David Wahr
Management:
  Director: Bill Anderson
  Director: Joanne Berry
  Director: Kristen Chesak
  Director: Jill Patchin
  Executive Secretary: Nancy Peska
Founded: 1994
Status: Non-Profit, Professional
Paid Staff: 12

7570
WILLIAM G MENNEN SPORTS ARENA
161 E Hanover Avenue
Morristown, NJ 07962
Phone: 973-326-7651
Fax: 973-829-8698
Web Site: www.morrisparks.net
Management:
  Executive Director: Dave Helmer
  Skating School Director: Jackie Kulik
Founded: 1975
Status: For-Profit, Professional
Paid Staff: 70
Seating Capacity: 3,500

7571
HISTORIC PALACE THEATRE
Route 183
7 Ledgewood Avenue
Netcong, NJ 07857
Mailing Address: PO Box 36, Netcong, NJ 07857
Phone: 973-347-4946
Fax: 973-691-7069
e-mail: exdir@growingstage.com
Web Site: www.growingstage.com
Officers:
  President: William H. Byrnes Jr
  Vice President: Theresa Scarpone
  Secretary: Manny Fernandes
  Treasurer: Michael Kochan
Management:
  Executive Director: Stephen L Fredericks
  Managing Director: Thomas J. Romano
  Education Director: Lori B. Lawrence
  Development Director: Joanne Miceli
  Production Manager: Steve Graham
Utilizes: Special Technical Talent; Theatre Companies
Founded: 1995

7572
RUTGERS ARTS CENTER
George Street and Route 18
New Brunswick, NJ 08903
Phone: 732-932-4636

7573
STATE THEATRE
15 Livingston Avenue
New Brunswick, NJ 08901-1903
Mailing Address: 11 Livingston Avenue
Phone: 732-246-7469
Fax: 732-745-5653
e-mail: info@statetheatrenj.org
Web Site: www.statetheatrenj.org
Officers:
  Chairman, Board of Trustees: Warren Zimmerman
  President & CEO: John S. Fitzgerald
  Senior Vice President National Acco: Ann H. Asbaty
Management:
  Director of Operations: Dave Hartken
  COO: Marlon Combs
  VP of Marketing: Daniel Grossman
  VP of Education: Lian Farrer
  Director of Production: Larry Dember
  Ticket Office Manager: Don McKim
Mission: Exists to enrich the lives of people from diverse backgrounds in New Jersey and to contribute to a vital urban environment by: presenting the finest national and international performing artists; providing arts education programs to inform and build future audiences; and to providing a major performing arts venue in central New Jersey that encourages and enables members of the community to have a life-long association with the performing arts.
Utilizes: Artists-in-Residence; Guest Musicians; Guest Soloists; Multimedia; Original Music Scores; Special Technical Talent; Theatre Companies
Founded: 1921
Specialized Field: Music; Dance; Live Performing Arts
Status: Non-Profit, Professional
Paid Staff: 45
Volunteer Staff: 20
Paid Artists: 100
Budget: $5 million
Income Sources: Individuals, Government, Corporations

FACILITIES / New Jersey

Affiliations: League of Historic Theatres New Brunswick Cultural Center, others
Annual Attendance: 275,000
Facility Category: Performing Arts Center
Type of Stage: Procenium
Stage Dimensions: 45'x28'
Seating Capacity: 1,800
Year Built: 1921
Year Remodeled: 1988
Rental Contact: David Hartkern

7574
NEW JERSEY PERFORMING ARTS CENTER
1 Center Street
Newark, NJ 07102
Phone: 973-642-8989
Fax: 973-648-6724
Toll-free: 888-466-5722
e-mail: ldenmark@njpac.org
Web Site: www.njpac.org
Officers:
   President/CEO: John Schreiber
   Vice President, Development: Peter H. Hansen
   VP/CFO: Warren Tranquada
   Treasurer: Marc E. Berson
   Secretary: Michael R. Griffinger, Esq.
   Founding Chair: Raymond G. Chambers
   Chair Emeritus: Arthur E. Ryan
Mission: To be a world class cultural complex and center stage for New Jersey's best performing artists; to aid in providing economic revitalization in Newark.
Utilizes: Actors; AEA Actors; Artists-in-Residence; Collaborating Artists; Collaborations; Commissioned Composers; Commissioned Music; Community Talent; Composers; Contract Actors; Contract Orchestras; Curators; Dance Companies; Dancers; Designers; Educators; Guest Accompanists; Guest Choreographers; Guest Composers; Guest Designers; Guest Instructors; Guest Musical Directors; Guest Musicians; Guest Soloists; Guest Teachers; High School Drama; Instructors; Local Artists; Lyricists; Multimedia; Music; Original Music Scores; Performance Artists; Scenic Designers; Sign Language Translators; Singers; Students; Special Technical Talent; Theatre Companies
Founded: 1988
Specialized Field: Series & Festivals; Classical; Jazz; Pop; Broadway Dramatic Theatre; Modern and Classical Dance
Status: Non-Profit, Professional
Paid Staff: 130
Budget: $22 million
Income Sources: Earned Revenue: Ticket Sales, Fees, Parking, Restaurant Commission and Philanthropy
Performs At: New Jersey Performing Arts Center
Annual Attendance: 550,000
Type of Stage: Proscenium
Stage Dimensions: 37'x 39'4'x 3'2'/116' x 49'x 3'6'
Seating Capacity: 514/2,750
Year Built: 1997
Year Remodeled: N/A
Cost: $187 million
Organization Type: Performing, Resident, Educational, Sponsoring, Touring

7575
NEWARK SYMPHONY HALL
1030 Broad Street
Newark, NJ 07102
Phone: 973-643-8009

7576
THEATRE AT RARITAN VALLEY COMMUNITY COLLEGE
Raritan Valley Community College
Route 28 and Lamington Road
North Branch, NJ 08876-1265
Mailing Address: The Theatre at RVCC, PO Box 3300, Somerville, NJ 08876-1265
Phone: 908-725-3420
e-mail: theatre@rvccarts.org
Web Site: www.rvccArts.org
Management:
   Director Theatre: Alan Liddell
Founded: 1985
Status: Non-Profit, Professional
Paid Staff: 4
Seating Capacity: 1,000

7577
GREAT AUDITORIUM
Pilgrim Pathway
54 Pitman Avenue
Ocean Grove, NJ 07756
Mailing Address: PO Box 248
Phone: 732-775-0035
Fax: 732-775-5689
e-mail: information@oceangrove.org
Web Site: www.oceangrove.org
Management:
   GM: David Shotwell
   Entertainment Director: Shelley Bellusar
Seating Capacity: 5,500

7578
LOUIS BROWN ATHLETIC CENTER
Rutgers University
83 Rockafeller Road
Piscataway, NJ 08854
Phone: 732-445-4220
Fax: 732-445-4623
Web Site: www.scarletknights.com
Management:
   President: Richard McCormick
   Athletic Director: Bob Mulcahy
Founded: 1776
Status: Non-Profit, Professional
Seating Capacity: 8,400

7579
RUTGERS ATHLETIC CENTER
Rutgers University
83 Rockefeller Road
Piscataway, NJ 08854
Phone: 732-932-9360
Fax: 732-445-2990
Web Site: www.recreation.rutgers.edu
Management:
   Dean: Diane Bunano
Founded: 1766
Status: Non-Profit, Professional
Paid Staff: 75
Seating Capacity: 9,000

7580
RUTGERS STADIUM
Rutgers University
PO Box 1149
Piscataway, NJ 08855-1149
Phone: 732-445-4223
Fax: 732-445-2990
Management:
   Assistant Athletic Director: Douglas S Kokoskie
Seating Capacity: 42,000

7581
SILVER CENTER FOR THE ARTS
Plymouth State University
114 Main Street
Plymouth, NJ 3264-1595
Phone: 603-535-2787
Fax: 603-535-2917
e-mail: silver-center@plymouth.edu
Web Site: www.plymouth.edu
Management:
   Director of the Silver Center: Diane Jeffrey
   House Manager: Ginny Fisher
   Technical Operations Manager: Stuart Crowell
   Box Office Manager: Trudy Pelletier
   Events Coordinator: Melissa Furbish
Founded: 1992
Status: Non-Profit, Non-Professional
Paid Staff: 7

7582
STOCKTON PERFORMING ARTS CENTER
Jim Leeds Road
PO Box 195
Pomona, NJ 08240-0195
Phone: 609-652-4607
Fax: 609-626-5523
Web Site: www.stocktonpac.org
Officers:
   President: Herman Saatkamp
Management:
   Executive Director: Michael Cool
   Artistic Director: Harley Halpern
   Director Ticketing Services: David T. Buzza
Founded: 1963
Status: Non-Profit, Professional
Paid Staff: 8
Budget: $150,000-$400,000

7583
JADWIN GYMNASIUM
Princeton University
Princeton, NJ 08544
Phone: 609-258-3000
Fax: 609-258-4477
Web Site: www.nj.com/princeton/basketball/stadium
Management:
   President: Shirley Tilghman
   Athletic Director: Gary D Walters
Founded: 1969
Status: Non-Profit, Non-Professional
Paid Staff: 80

7584
MCCARTER THEATRE
91 University Place
Princeton, NJ 08540
Phone: 609-258-6500
Fax: 609-497-0369
Toll-free: 888-ART-SWEB
e-mail: sales@mccarter.org
Web Site: www.mccarter.org
Management:
   Assistant General Manager: Tim Walling
   Director of Finance: Judy Leventhal
   Finance Assistant: Alex Kornberg
   Payroll Assistant: Karen Fink
Founded: 1929
Status: For-Profit, Professional
Paid Staff: 80
Paid Artists: 10

FACILITIES / New Jersey

7585
RICHARDSON AUDITORIUM
Princeton University
Alexander Hall
Princeton, NJ 08544
Phone: 609-258-4239
Fax: 609-258-6793

7586
UNION COUNTY ARTS CENTER
1601 Irving Street
Rahway, NJ 07065
Phone: 732-499-0441
Fax: 732-499-8227
Web Site: ucpac.org
Management:
  Executive Director: Sandy Erwin
Mission: Dedicated to providing world class entertainment that is exciting, educational, affordable and responsive to the diverse interests of the communities we serve.
Specialized Field: Performing Arts Presenter
Status: Non-Profit, Professional
Paid Staff: 8
Volunteer Staff: 50
Budget: $1.5 million
Performs At: 1,350 Seat Historic Theatre
Seating Capacity: 1,350
Year Built: 1928
Year Remodeled: 1996

7587
COUNT BASIE THEATRE
99 Monmouth Street
Red Bank, NJ 07701
Phone: 732-842-9000
Fax: 732-842-9323
e-mail: info@countbasietheatre.org
Web Site: www.countbasietheatre.org
Officers:
  Chief Executive Officer: Adam Philipson
  Vice President of Operations: Izzy Sackowitz
  Chair: Tom Widener
Management:
  Executive Assistant/Project : Ann Marie Keenan
  Event Manager: Joe Pulito
  Technical Director: MIke Jacoby
  General Manager: Vantony Jenkins
Utilizes: Collaborations; Dance Companies; Fine Artists; Soloists; Special Technical Talent
Founded: 1991
Specialized Field: Dance; Theatre; Vocal Music; Instrumental Music
Status: Non-Profit, Non-Professional
Paid Staff: 109
Seating Capacity: 1,400
Year Built: 1926
Rental Contact: Annette Bartolomeo

7588
WILLIAMS CENTER FOR THE ARTS NEWMAN THEATRE
One Williams Plaza
Rutherford, NJ 07070
Phone: 201-939-6969
Fax: 201-939-0843
Web Site: www.williamscenter.org
Officers:
  President: Joseph Desazio
  Treasurer: Evelyn Spath-Mercado
Management:
  Executive Director: G W McLuckey

Mission: To provide programs of artistic excellence at affordable prices.
Utilizes: Actors; AEA Actors; Dance Companies; Local Artists; Multimedia; Original Music Scores; Student Interns; Theatre Companies
Founded: 1978
Paid Staff: 22
Budget: $650,000
Income Sources: Ticket Sales; Grants; Sponsorships; Rentals
Annual Attendance: 50,000
Facility Category: Performing Arts Center
Type of Stage: Black Box; Proscenium Arch
Seating Capacity: 200; 642
Year Built: 1922
Year Remodeled: 1992

7589
TD BANK ARTS CENTRE
519 Hurffville-Crosskeys Road
Sewell, NJ 08080
Phone: 856-256-8660
Fax: 856-256-8659
e-mail: jweiner@wtps.org
Web Site: www.tdbankarts.com
Management:
  Theatre Manager: James Weiner
  Technical Direector: Mike Simpson, mike@simpsonsound.net
Founded: 1998
Specialized Field: Philadelphia; Southern New Jersey
Paid Staff: 5
Volunteer Staff: 40
Facility Category: Indoor Performing Arts Center
Seating Capacity: 2,450

7590
KAPLAN JCC ON THE PALISADES
JCC School of Performing Arts
411 E Clinton Avenue
Tenafly, NJ 07670
Phone: 201-569-7900
Fax: 201-569-7448
e-mail: droberts@jccotp.org
Web Site: www.jcconthepalisades.org
Management:
  Artistic Director: Deborah Roberts, droberts@jccotp.org
  Program Director: Carol Leslie, cleslie@jccotp.org
Mission: The JCC School of Performing Arts offers classes, workshops and performance opportunities for the pre-professional as well as the recreational student from early childhood to adult. The School is ethnically diverse and welcomes serious students of all backgrounds and walks of life. Instructors are at the top of their profession, in collaboration with Strasberg and New York City's working professionals.Agents & Managers attend programs each year
Founded: 1981
Opened: 1982
Specialized Field: Theatre; Musical Theatre; Private Singing; Dance
Status: Non-Profit, Professional
Paid Staff: 3
Volunteer Staff: 3
Paid Artists: 20
Non-paid Artists: 4
Performs At: Fixed-seat 188 Seat Theatre; Auditorium That Seats 700
Affiliations: Kaplan JCC on the Palisades
Type of Stage: Proscenium
Stage Dimensions: 23'x18'; 28'x40'
Seating Capacity: 700; 188
Year Built: 1994

Year Remodeled: 2003
Rental Contact: Artistic Director Deb Roberts

7591
NEW JERSEY STATE MUSEUM AUDITORIUM
205 W State Street
PO Box 530
Trenton, NJ 08625-0530
Phone: 609-292-6464
Fax: 609-599-4098
e-mail: feedback@sos.state.nj.us
Web Site: www.state.nj.us/state/museum/
Officers:
  President: Kenneth Newcomb
  Vice President: Doug Setzer
  Treasurer: Charles Moseley
  Secretary: Louise Barrett
Management:
  Acting Director: Lorraine E Williams
Mission: To produce the historical outdoor drama From This Day Forward annually; to produce Dickens' A Christmas Carol annually; to produce other dramas, engage in outreach activities, and sponsor workshops and cultural events.
Founded: 1895

7592
PATRIOTS THEATER AT THE WAR MEMORIAL
PO Box 232
Trenton, NJ 08625
Phone: 609-984-8484
Fax: 609-777-0581
Toll-free: 800-955-5566
e-mail: thewarmemorial@sos.state.nj.us
Web Site: www.thewarmemorial.com
Management:
  Executive Director: Molly S McDonough
  Production Coordinator: Bill Nutter
  Ticketing/Sales Director: Andrew Burkett
  Ticketing/Sales Director: Rebecca Jensen
Mission: Proudly hosts a diverse and exciting array of theatrical and concert events — from comedy to ballet, from opera to gospel, from international to jazz, from classical to country to rock, pop, and folk.
Founded: 1932
Status: Non-Profit, Professional
Paid Staff: 20
Volunteer Staff: 100
Income Sources: State of New Jersey
Affiliations: State of New Jersey, Department of State Division of War Memorial
Facility Category: Theater
Type of Stage: Proscenium
Stage Dimensions: 50 x 30
Seating Capacity: 1800; 12,000 sq ft
Year Built: 1932
Year Remodeled: 1998
Cost: $ 34.5 Million
Rental Contact: Executive Director Molly S. McDonough
Resident Groups: New Jersey Symphony, Greater Trenton Sympony, Boheme Opera, American Repertory Ball

7593
SUN NATIONAL BANK CENTER
81 Hamilton Ave. at Rt. 12
Trenton, NJ 08611
Phone: 609-656-3200
Fax: 609-656-3201
Web Site: www.sunnationalbankcenter.com

FACILITIES / New Mexico

Management:
   Director of Marketing: Jen Grinspan
   Director of Corporate Partnerships: Andrew Sklarz
   Director of Finance: Christine Fritz
   Director of Marketing: Jen Grinspan
   Assistant Director of Finance: Colleen Banfe
Mission: Theatre events, concerts, sports, family shows and community events.
Founded: 1999
Seating Capacity: 8,600
Year Built: 1999

7594
WILKENS THEATRE
Kean College of New Jersey
1000 Morris Avenue
Union, NJ 07083
Phone: 908-737-7469
Fax: 908-527-8345
Web Site: www.kean.edu
Mission: To offer theatre to all citizens in our county, primarily through the schools, providing one selected offering annually.

7595
PARK THEATRE PERFORMING ARTS CENTRE
560 32nd Street
Union City, NJ 07087
Phone: 201-865-6980
Fax: 201-865-5339
Web Site: www.passionplayusa.org
Management:
   Artistic Director: Meriam Lobel
   Theatre Director: Sixto Perez
   Executive Director: Kevin Ashe
Founded: 1983
Status: Non-Profit, Professional
Paid Staff: 3
Budget: $400,000
Income Sources: Earned Income; State Grants; Private Funds
Stage Dimensions: 70x40
Seating Capacity: 1400
Year Built: 1933

7596
MONTCLAIR STATE COLLEGE MEMORIAL AUDITORIUM
1 Normal Avenue
Upper Montclair, NJ 07043
Phone: 973-655-4000
Fax: 973-655-7371
Toll-free: 800-624-7780
e-mail: webmaster@montclair.edu
Web Site: www.montclair.edu
Officers:
   President: Susan Cole
Mission: Producing and promoting high quality, accessible, professional theater; training and developing the talents of musicians, actors and technicians.
Status: For-Profit, Professional

7597
HUNZIKER BLACK BOX THEATER
William Patterson University
300 Pompton Road
Wayne, NJ 07470
Phone: 973-720-2000
Web Site: ww2.wpunj.edu
Officers:
   President: Mary Harper
   Treasurer: Leslie Madigan
   Immediate Past President: Janet Bondurant
Mission: Children's Theatre Board provides opportunities for students, educators and families to experience and participate in the performing arts. CTB offers multidisciplinary, culturally diverse programs to foster sensitivity and acceptance.

7598
POLLAK THEATRE
Monmouth University
400 Cedar Avenue
West Long Branch, NJ 07764
Phone: 732-571-3400
Fax: 732-263-5262
e-mail: vpeck@monmouth.edu
Web Site: www.monmouth.edu/performingarts
Management:
   Director: Vaune Peck
   Assistant Director: Alice Arnts
Seating Capacity: 700

7599
MAURICE LEVIN THEATER
Jewish Community Center Metrowest
760 Northfield Avenue
West Orange, NJ 07052
Phone: 973-736-3200
Fax: 973-736-6871
Web Site: www.jccmetrowest.org
Officers:
   Chief Executive Officer: Alan Feldman
   VP of Finance: Jennifer Helprin
   Marketing & Membership Director: Marcy Burach
Management:
   Program Supervisor: Jo Golstein
   Program Assistant: Marsha Fleisch
Mission: To provide for all within the community an avenue for education and development in all aspects of theatrical arts and to provide entertainment for the community by offering a series of well-staged performances of live theatre.
Founded: 1877
Specialized Field: Vocal Music; Instrumental Music; Theater; Festivals; Film Series
Status: Non-Profit, Non-Professional
Paid Staff: 6
Paid Artists: 8

7600
BARRON ARTS CENTER
582 Rahway Avenue
Woodbridge, NJ 07095
Phone: 732-634-0413
Fax: 732-634-8633
e-mail: barronarts@twp.woodbridge.nj.us
Officers:
   President: Sigmund Molis
Management:
   Executive Director: Cynthia Knight
Mission: To offer professional music and spoken word performances free of charge to the central New Jersey community.
Founded: 1976
Status: Non-Profit, Professional
Paid Staff: 3
Volunteer Staff: 30
Income Sources: Municipal & Not-For-Profit Organization
Performs At: Small Multipurpose Building Used As An Center For The Arts Featuring Concerts, Poetry Readinga & Art Exhibits.
Annual Attendance: 10,000
Facility Category: Small Victorian Building
Type of Stage: Temporary 6 Riser Stage""
Seating Capacity: 95
Year Built: 1877

New Mexico

7601
FLICKINGER CENTER FOR PERFORMING ARTS
1110 New York Avenue
Alamogordo, NM 88310
Phone: 505-437-2202
Fax: 505-434-0067
e-mail: flickinger@zianet.com
Web Site: www.flickingercenter.com
Officers:
   President, Board of Directors: Lonnie Jarrett
Management:
   Executive Director: Doug Gibson
   Marketing: Karla Davis
   Technical Director: Kelly Lynch
Utilizes: Dance Companies; Guest Writers; Guild Activities; Lyricists; New Productions; Original Music Scores; Special Technical Talent; Theatre Companies; Touring Companies
Founded: 1988
Status: Non-Profit, Professional
Paid Staff: 5
Volunteer Staff: 60
Non-paid Artists: 200
Facility Category: Performing Arts Center
Type of Stage: Proscenium
Stage Dimensions: 30 x 40
Seating Capacity: 675
Year Built: 1954
Year Remodeled: 1991
Rental Contact: Vicki Rogers

7602
ALBUQUERQUE CONVENTION CENTER
401 Second Street NW
Albuquerque, NM 87102
Phone: 505-768-4575
Fax: 505-768-3239
e-mail: info@albuquercc.com
Web Site: www.albuquercc.com
Paid Staff: 56
Facility Category: Convention Center; Ballroom; Auditorium
Type of Stage: Flexible, Platform/Proscenium
Seating Capacity: 3000
Year Built: 1972
Year Remodeled: 1990
Rental Contact: Scheduling Manager Carol Chavez

7603
JOURNAL PAVILION
5601 University Boulevard Southeast
Albuquerque, NM 87105
Phone: 505-452-5100
Fax: 505-452-0900
Web Site: www.journalpavilion.com
Management:
   Executive Director: Laura Loghry
   Marketing Director: Christine Lorello
Seating Capacity: 12,000

7604
KIMO THEATRE
423 Central Ave NW
Albuquerque, NM 87102

FACILITIES / New Mexico

Phone: 505-768-3522
Fax: 505-768-3542
e-mail: kwright@cabq.gov
Web Site: www.kimotickets.com
Management:
    Operations Manager: Craig Rivera
Seating Capacity: 650

7605
NATIONAL HISPANIC CULTURAL CENTER OF NEW MEXICO
Quickel Building
600 Central SW, Suite 201
Albuquerque, NM 87102-3194
Phone: 505-246-2261
Fax: 505-246-2613
e-mail: rlove@state.nm.us
Web Site: www.nmhcc.org
Management:
    President: Tom Kevis
    Artistic Director: Reve Love
    Managing Director: Gene Hemley
Founded: 1987
Status: Non-Profit, Professional
Paid Staff: 52
Paid Artists: 12

7606
POPEJOY HALL
University of New Mexico
Center for the Arts
Albuquerque, NM 87131-3176
Phone: 505-277-3824
Fax: 505-277-7353
e-mail: customerservice@popejoypresents.com
Web Site: www.popejoypresents.com
Officers:
    President: Carol Leevers
    VP: Jane Traynor
    Treasurer/Secretary: Dean Petska
Management:
    Director: Tom Tkach
    Public Relations Manager: Terry Davis
    Technical Director: Billy Tubb
    Artistic Director: Judy Ryan
Mission: To present Touring Broadway, plus national as well as international music and dance.
Paid Staff: 12
Volunteer Staff: 200
Budget: $2,000,000
Income Sources: State Legislature; Event Revenue
Affiliations: University of New Mexico-Center for the Arts
Annual Attendance: 100,000
Seating Capacity: 2044
Year Built: 1966
Year Remodeled: 1996
Rental Contact: Thomas Tkach
Resident Groups: Musical Theatre Southwest & New Mexico Symphony Orchestra

7607
SANTA FE OPERA HOUSE
301 Opera Drive
Albuquerque, NM 87506
Mailing Address: PO Box 2408, Santa Fe, NM 87504-2408
Phone: 505-986-5955
Fax: 505-986-5999
Toll-free: 800-280-4654
e-mail: boxoffice@santafeopera.org
Web Site: www.santafeopera.org
Management:
    Administrative Director: Tom Morris

Founded: 1957
Seating Capacity: 2,234

7608
SOUTH BROADWAY CULTURAL CENTER
1025 Broadway SE
Albuquerque, NM 87102
Phone: 505-848-1320
Fax: 505-848-1329
e-mail: lulibarri@cabq.gov
Web Site: www.cabq.gov/sbec
Management:
    Director: Linda Ulibarri
    Technical Director: Antonio Aragon
    Gallery Curator: John Peterson
Mission: To produce theatrical productions reflecting a high degree of professionalism; to develop artists in the theatre as well as responsive audiences.
Founded: 1970
Status: Non-Profit, Non-Professional
Paid Staff: 8

7609
TINGLEY COLISEUM
300 San Pedro NE
Albuquerque, NM 87108
Mailing Address: PO Box 8546, Albuquerque, NM 87198
Phone: 505-222-9700
Fax: 505-266-7784
Web Site: exponm.com
Officers:
    Chief Financial Officer: Bill Nordin
Management:
    General Manager: Dan Mourning
    Deputy Manager: John C. Jaramillo
    Operations Manager: Ken Salazar
    Senior Manager: Sally Mayer
    Parking Director: Susan Rebman
Founded: 1942
Status: For-Profit, Professional

7610
UNIVERSITY OF NEW MEXICO STADIUM
1414 University Boulevard SE
Albuquerque, NM 87131
Phone: 505-925-5500
Fax: 505-925-5559
Web Site: www.enm.edu/lobo
Management:
    Sports Information: Greg Remington
    Head Football Coach: Rocky Long
    Head Basketball Coach: Fran Fraschilla
    Head Basketball Coach (M): Don Flanahan
Seating Capacity: 18,018

7611
SPENCER THEATER FOR THE PERFORMING ARTS
108 Spencer Road
Alto, NM 88312
Phone: 505-336-4800
Fax: 575-336-0055
Toll-free: 888-818-7872
e-mail: ccentilli@spencertheater.com
Web Site: www.spencertheater.com
Management:
    Executive Director: Charles Centilli
    Box Office Manager: Donna Clarke
    House Manager: Sharon Davis

Utilizes: Actors; Artists-in-Residence; Dance Companies; Dancers; Educators; Five Seasonal Concerts; Guest Soloists; Guest Writers; Guild Activities; Original Music Scores; Resident Professionals; Sign Language Translators; Singers; Soloists; Student Interns; Special Technical Talent; Theatre Companies; Visual Arts
Founded: 1997
Status: Non-Profit, Professional
Paid Staff: 13
Volunteer Staff: 30
Income Sources: Private Contributions
Annual Attendance: 5,000
Facility Category: Theater
Stage Dimensions: 50 x 80
Seating Capacity: 514
Year Built: 1979
Cost: $22 Million
Rental Contact: Charles Centilli

7612
FARMINGTON CIVIC CENTER
Two Black Knight Drive
Farmington, NM 63640
Phone: 573-756-0900
Fax: 505-599-1146
Toll-free: 877-599-3331
e-mail: lparks@fmtn.org
Web Site: www.farmington-mo.gov
Officers:
    Foundation President: Melissa Sharpe
Management:
    Supervisor: Loretta J Parks
Mission: To further promote the cultural enrichment of the citizens of the City of Farmington and surrounding area.
Utilizes: Actors; Dance Companies; Dancers; Educators; Fine Artists; Guest Instructors; Guest Soloists; Guild Activities; High School Drama; Local Artists; Multimedia; Original Music Scores; Playwrights; Sign Language Translators; Singers; Soloists; Theatre Companies; Touring Companies
Founded: 1976
Specialized Field: Performing and Visual
Status: Non-Profit, Professional
Paid Staff: 16
Budget: $571,000
Income Sources: Division of City of Farmington Tax Revenue
Performs At: Broadway Musicals, SJ Community Concert & Symphony League
Affiliations: WAA and IAAM
Annual Attendance: 150,000
Facility Category: Performing Arts Theatre & Convention Center
Type of Stage: Proscenium
Stage Dimensions: 52 w x 72 deep
Seating Capacity: 1200
Year Built: 1976

7613
AMERICAN SOUTHWEST CENTER
New Mexico State University
PO Box 3072
Las Cruces, NM 88003
Phone: 505-646-4517
Fax: 505-646-5767
Toll-free: 800-525-2782
Web Site: www.nmsutheatre.com
Management:
    President: Michael Martin
    Artistic Director: Michael Wise
    Managing Director: Ruth Cantrell
Status: Non-Profit, Professional

All listings are in alphabetical order by state, then city, then organization within the city.

FACILITIES / New York

Paid Staff: 10
Paid Artists: 10

7614
PAN AMERICAN CENTER
New Mexico State University
PO Box 30001
Las Cruces, NM 88003
Phone: 505-646-4413
Fax: 505-646-3605
Web Site: www.panam.nmsu.edu
Management:
    President: Will Lofdahl
    Artistic Director: Gary Rachele
    Box Office Manager: Patrick Kennedy
Founded: 1968
Status: For-Profit, Professional
Paid Staff: 600
Seating Capacity: 13,007

7615
DUANE SMITH AUDITORIUM
1300 Diamond Drive
Los Alamos, NM 87544
Mailing Address: Los Alamos Concert Association
Phone: 505-662-9000
Web Site: www.losalamosconcert.org
Management:
    Artistic Director: Rosalie Heller
Utilizes: Dance Companies; Fine Artists; Multimedia; Sign Language Translators
Founded: 1946
Volunteer Staff: 30
Paid Artists: 5

7616
PEARSON AUDITORIUM
New Mexico Military Institute
101 W College Boulevard
Roswell, NM 88201
Phone: 505-622-6250
Fax: 505-624-8459
Web Site: www.nmmi.cc.nm.us
Officers:
    President: Ken Haarstad
    VP: Shirley Olson
    Secretary: Lori Garnes
    Treasurer: Jerry Jorgenson
Mission: Community theatre to promote adult education and provide theatre arts to surroundings communities children's educational performing arts.
Income Sources: State Education Funds
Annual Attendance: 20,000
Facility Category: Auditorium
Seating Capacity: 1,100

7617
GREER GARSON THEATRE CENTER
College of Santa Fe
1600 Saint Michael's Drive
Santa Fe, NM 87505
Phone: 505-473-6439
Fax: 505-473-6016
Toll-free: 800-456-2673
Web Site: www.ccsf.edu
Officers:
    President: John Rizzo
    VP: Anita Grier
Management:
    Assistant Director: Jennifer Kilbourn
    Chair: John Weckesser
Mission: Provide undergraduate degrees, BA and BFA in Theatre, Acting, Music Theatre, Design Tech and Theatre Management.

Founded: 1936
Specialized Field: Acting; Musical Theatre; Technical Theatre; Theatre Management; Stage Management
Paid Staff: 25

7618
GUADALUPE HISTORIC FOUNDATION (SANTUARIO DE GUADALUPE) DINNER THEATER
100 S Guadalupe Street
Santa Fe, NM 87501
Phone: 505-988-2027
Management:
    Owner/President: Prescott F Griffith
Mission: Elegant dinner theatre featuring live Broadway musical productions.

7619
LENSIC PERFORMING ARTS CENTER
211 W. San Francisco St
Santa Fe, NM 87501
Phone: 505-988-7050
Fax: 505-988-4370
e-mail: email through website
Web Site: www.lensic.org
Management:
    Executive Director: Robert Martin, rmartin@lensic.org
    Production Manager: Sarah Leblanc, slebanc@lensic.org
    Operations Director: Steph Smith, ssmith@lensic.org
Mission: Home to tickets Santa Fe—community box office serving over 35 organizations and venues; provide technical education to high school student; provide a venue for non-profit performace art organizations

7620
SANTA FE CONVENTION AND VISITORS BUREAU SWEENEY CENTER
201 W Marcy
PO Box 909
Santa Fe, NM 87501
Phone: 505-955-6200
Fax: 505-955-6222
Toll-free: 800-777-2489
e-mail: santafe@santafenm.gov
Web Site: www.santafe.org
Management:
    Executive Director: Darlene Greigo
Status: Non-Profit, Non-Professional
Paid Staff: 12

7621
SANTA FE STAGES
422 W San Francisco Street
Santa Fe, NM 87501
Phone: 505-982-6680
Fax: 505-982-6682
e-mail: info@santastages.org
Web Site: www.santafestages.org
Management:
    Technical Director: Mike Curtis
    Development Manager: Susan Apker
    Marketing Director: Aimee Gwynne Franklyn
    Producing Director: Craig Strong
Founded: 1994

New York

7622
ALBANY PERFORMING ARTS CENTER
SUNY
1400 Washington Avenue
Albany, NY 12222
Phone: 518-442-3995
Fax: 518-442-4206
Facility Category: Recital Hall; Theater

7623
CAPITAL REPERTORY THEATRE
111 N Pearl Street
Albany, NY 12207
Phone: 518-462-4531
Fax: 518-881-1823
e-mail: info@capitalrep.org
Web Site: www.capitalrep.org
Management:
    Production Manager: Brandon Curry
    Artistic Director: Margaret Mancinelli-Cahill
    Managing Director: Elizabeth Doran
Utilizes: Actors; Choreographers; Designers; Guest Accompanists; Guest Lecturers; Music; Original Music Scores; Resident Professionals; Theatre Companies
Founded: 1981
Status: Non-Profit, Professional
Paid Staff: 25
Budget: $2.1 million
Income Sources: Corporate Sponsors; Individual Donors; Subscriptions; Ticket Sales
Season: July - May
Affiliations: LORT
Annual Attendance: 63,000+
Facility Category: Theatre
Type of Stage: Thrust
Seating Capacity: 285

7624
EGG-EMPIRE STATE PERFORMING ARTS CENTER
Empire State Plaza
PO Box 2065
Albany, NY 12220
Phone: 518-473-1061
Fax: 518-473-1848
e-mail: info@theegg.org
Web Site: www.theegg.org
Management:
    Executive Director: Peter Lesser
    Operation Assistant: Jeff Becker
    Operations & Production Manager: Bill Darcy
    Business Manager: Matthew Moross
Founded: 1978
Status: Professional
Paid Staff: 20

7625
PALACE PERFORMING ARTS CENTER
19 Clinton Avenue
Albany, NY 12207
Phone: 518-465-3334
Fax: 518-427-0151
Web Site: www.palacealbany.com
Officers:
    Vice Chair: Jeffrey Sperber
    Treasurer: Steve Fischer
Management:
    House Manager: Bill O'Donnell
    Director Of Development: George P Kansas
Founded: 1931

FACILITIES / New York

7626
PEPSI ARENA
51 S Pearl Street
Albany, NY 12207
Phone: 518-487-2000
Fax: 518-487-2020
e-mail: info@pepsiarena.com
Web Site: www.timesunioncenter-albany.com
Management:
   General Manager: Robert Belber
Seating Capacity: 17,000

7627
UNIVERSITY AT ALBANY PERFORMING ARTS CENTER (PAC)
SUNY
1400 Washington Avenue
Albany, NY 12222
Phone: 518-442-5435
Fax: 518-442-5383
e-mail: ugadmissions@albany.edu
Web Site: www.albany.edu/pac/
Management:
   Executive Director: Patrick Ferlo
   Assistant Director: Kim Engel
   Technical Operations Director: Bryan Robinson
   Event Supervisor: Frank Barone
Mission: The mission at the University at Albany Performing Arts Center is to maintain a state-of-the-art facility that enhances the quality of learning for University of Albany students as well as one that offers cultural opportunities to all in the Capital Region. The Main Theatre auditorium seats 500 people; the Recital Hall seats 242 people; the Arena Theatre auditorium seats 196; the Studio Theatre seats 153 people; and the Lab Theatre seats 200.
Founded: 1983
Status: Non-Profit, Professional
Paid Staff: 4
Budget: $10,000

7628
MERRILL FIELD
Alfred University, Saxon Drive
1 Saxon Drive
Alfred, NY 14802-1205
Phone: 607-871-2115
Fax: 607-871-2293
Web Site: www.alfred.edu
Officers:
   President: Charles Edmondson
Management:
   Director: William T Emrick
Founded: 1836
Seating Capacity: 3,000

7629
MUSICAL FARE THEATRE
Daemen College
4380 Main Street, Suite 810
Amherst, NY 14226
Phone: 716-839-8540
Fax: 716-839-8539
e-mail: musicalfare@daemen.edu
Web Site: www.musicalfare.com
Officers:
   President: Cheryl A Wasson
   Vice President: Francis A. Balcerzak
   Treasurer: Paul B. Kieffer
Management:
   Executive Director: Randall Kramer
   Marketing Coordinator: Doug Weyand
   Administrative Director: Debbie Pappas
Mission: To bringing quality musical theatre to Western NY, and to becoming a significant regional theatre with national prominence by developing and presenting new musicals, new versions of traditional musicals and area premieres.
Founded: 1990
Specialized Field: Musical Theatre
Status: Non-Profit, Professional
Paid Staff: 5
Paid Artists: 50
Affiliations: AEA; SSDC; Buffalo Theatre Alliance
Annual Attendance: 20,000
Facility Category: Theatre
Type of Stage: Proscenium
Seating Capacity: 13
Year Built: 2000

7630
RICHARD B FISHER CENTER FOR THE PERFORMING ARTS AT BARD COLLEGE
60 Manor Avenue
Annadale-on-Hudson, NY 12504
Phone: 845-758-7914
Fax: 845-758-7920
e-mail: fishercenter@bard.edu
Web Site: www.fishercenter.bard.edu
Officers:
   Chair: Jeanne Donovan Fisher
   Managing Director: Nancy Cook
   Director Communications: Mark Primoff
   Production Manager: Robert Airhart
Mission: This facility will be devoted primarily to teaching and college events during the academic year and used as a public performing arts facility and venue for the college's graduate programs in the arts during the summer months.
Opened: 2003
Specialized Field: Dance; Music; Theater
Status: Non-Profit
Season: Summer
Performs At: Sosnoff Theater, Theater Two
Facility Category: Academics Facilities
Type of Stage: Proscenium
Orchestra Pit: Y
Seating Capacity: 900, 200
Year Built: 2003
Architect: Frank O Gehry & Associates
Cost: $62 Million

7631
US MILITARY ACADEMY
Wells College
Student Activities
Aurora, NY 13026
Phone: 315-364-3330
Fax: 315-364-3325

7632
JUNE COMPANY
28 Coolidge Way
Averil Park, NY 12018
Phone: 518-447-5414
Fax: 518-447-5446

7633
QUEENSBOROUGH COMMUNITY COLLEGE THEATER
222-05 56th Avenue Bayside
Bayside, NY 11364-1497
Phone: 718-631-6311
Fax: 718-631-6033
e-mail: agin@qcc.cuny.edu
Web Site: www.qcc.cuny.edu
Management:
   Executive Director: Sophie Foglia
Founded: 1965
Status: For-Profit, Professional
Paid Staff: 5
Annual Attendance: 15,000+
Facility Category: Conventional Theatre
Type of Stage: Proscenium
Stage Dimensions: 40x40
Seating Capacity: 875
Year Built: 1970

7634
BROOME COUNTY VETERANS MEMORIAL ARENA
1 Stuart Street
Binghamton, NY 13901
Phone: 607-778-1528
Fax: 607-778-6041
e-mail: bhoffman@co.broome.ny.us
Web Site: www.gobroomecounty.com
Management:
   Arena Manager: Brian Hoffman
Founded: 1972
Status: Non-Profit, Professional
Paid Staff: 55
Budget: $800,000
Income Sources: Sports; Concerts, Government; State; County; Concessions; Trade Shows
Performs At: Multipurpose
Affiliations: AHL Binghamton Senators
Facility Category: Arena

7635
STATE UNIVERSITY OF NEW YORK-BINGHAMPTON: ANDERSON CENTER FOR THE ARTS
Binghamton University
4400 Vestal Parkway East
Binghamton, NY 13902-6000
Phone: 607-777-2000
Fax: 607-777-6771
e-mail: mmack@binghamton.edu
Web Site: www.binghamton.edu
Management:
   Director: Floyd Herzog
   Assistant Director: Mary Mack
   Adiministrative Assistant: Patricia J Benjamin
   Development Director: Marcia Steinbrecher
Mission: Designed to meet the needs of every performing group such as soloists, chamber ensembles, symphonies, dance or large theatrical productions complemented by a full scale orchestra.
Founded: 1986
Status: Non-Profit, Non-Professional
Paid Staff: 10

7636
ADIRONDACK LAKES CENTER FOR THE ARTS
Route 28
PO Box 205
Blue Mountain Lake, NY 12812
Phone: 518-352-7715
Fax: 518-352-7333
e-mail: stephen@adirondackarts.org
Web Site: www.adirondackarts.org
Officers:
   President: Jamie Strader
   Vice President: Donna Pohl
   Trustee: Pat Benton
   Secretary: Joanna Pine
Management:

FACILITIES / New York

Artistic Director: Stephen Svoboda
Executive Director: Alex Harris
Artistic Associate: Danielle Melendez
Production Manager: Joe Perreault
Graphic Designer: Jessie Dobrzynski
Mission: To promote visual and performing arts through programs and services in our region, to serve established professional and aspiring artists.
Utilizes: Dancers; Educators; Fine Artists; High School Drama; Local Artists; Multimedia; Original Music Scores; Selected Students; Sign Language Translators; Soloists; Student Interns; Special Technical Talent; Theatre Companies; Touring Companies
Founded: 1967
Status: Non-Profit, Professional
Paid Staff: 5
Income Sources: Membership; grants; admission fees
Annual Attendance: 3,500
Facility Category: Concert Hall; Performance Center; Theatre
Type of Stage: Platform
Stage Dimensions: varible
Seating Capacity: 170
Year Remodeled: 1991

7637
SPECIAL OLYMPICS STADIUM
SUNY
350 New Campus Drive
Brockport, NY 14420-2989
Phone: 716-395-2218
Fax: 716-395-2160
e-mail: mandriat@brockport.edu
Web Site: www.brockport.edu
Management:
  Sports Information Director: Kelly Vergin
Seating Capacity: 10,000

7638
TOWER FINE ARTS CENTER AND HARTWELL HALL
Suny Brockport
350 New Campus Drive
Brockport, NY 14420-2983
Phone: 716-395-2797
Fax: 716-395-5872
e-mail: ssoloway@brockport.edu
Web Site: www.brockport.edu/finearts
Type of Stage: procenium/dance stage/black box
Stage Dimensions: 45'x30'
Seating Capacity: 400; 270; 100
Year Built: 1968
Year Remodeled: 1999

7639
LEHMAN CENTER FOR THE PERFORMING ARTS
250 Bedford Park Boulevard West
Bronx, NY 10468
Phone: 718-960-8833
Fax: 718-960-8233
e-mail: eva.bornstein@lehman.cuny.edu
Web Site: www.lehmancenter.org
Officers:
  Chair: Father Richard Gorman
  Vice Chair: Valerie Washington
  Treasurer: Janice Page
  Secretary: Gary Weinberg
Management:
  Executive Director: Eva Bornstein
Utilizes: Actors; Dance Companies; Dancers; Educators; Grant Writers; Guest Accompanists; Guest Artists; Guest Choreographers; Guest Companies; Guest Directors; Guest Instructors; Guest Musical Directors; Guest Musicians; Guest Soloists; Instructors; Local Artists; Multimedia; Original Music Scores; Singers; Special Technical Talent; Theatre Companies
Founded: 1980
Status: Non-Profit, Professional
Paid Staff: 10
Budget: $400,000-$1 million
Facility Category: Concert Hall
Type of Stage: Proscenium
Seating Capacity: 2,310
Year Built: 1979
Rental Contact: Operations Manager Janet Sanchez

7640
YANKEE STADIUM
One East 161st Street
Bronx, NY 10451
Phone: 718-293-4300
Fax: 718-293-7431
Web Site: www.yankees.com
Management:
  SVP/General Manager: Brian Cashman
  SVP Marketing: Deborah Tymon
  SVP Community Relations: Brian Smith
  SVP Marketing: Deborah Tymon
  Senior Director Stadium Operations: Michael Bonner
  Senior Director Ticket Operations: Irfan Kirimica
  Director, Non-Baseball Events: Emily Hamel
Mission: Home stadium of the New York Yankees major league baseball team.
Facility Category: Baseball Stadium
Seating Capacity: 50,086
Year Built: 2009
Architect: Populous
Cost: $1.5 billion

7641
BROOKLYN ACADEMY OF MUSIC: CAREY PLAYHOUSE
30 Lafayette Avenue
Brooklyn, NY 11217
Phone: 718-636-4100
Fax: 718-857-2021
e-mail: info@bam.org
Web Site: www.bam.org
Officers:
  President: Karen Books
Management:
  President: Carron Hopkins
Founded: 1851
Status: Non-Profit, Professional
Paid Staff: 150

7642
BROOKLYN ACADEMY OF MUSIC: CAREY PLAYHOUSE
30 Lafayette Avenue
Brooklyn, NY 11217
Phone: 718-636-4100
Fax: 718-857-2021

7643
BROOKLYN ACADEMY OF MUSIC: OPERA HOUSE
30 Lafayette Avenue
Brooklyn, NY 11217
Phone: 718-636-4100
Fax: 718-857-2021

7644
BROOKLYN CENTER FOR THE PERFORMING ARTS
Broolyn College
Campus Road & Hillel Place
Brooklyn, NY 11210
Mailing Address: PO Box 100163
Phone: 718-951-4600
Fax: 718-951-4343
e-mail: info@brooklyncenter.org
Web Site: www.brooklyncenter.com
Officers:
  Chair: Karen L. Gould
  President: Yvonne Riley-Tepie
  VP: Renee McClure
  Treasurer: Cliff Luster
  Secretary: Joshua Schneps
Management:
  Director: Jon Yanofsky
  Marketing & Communications Director: Rick Berube
  Education Manager / Patron Services: Joyce Disner
  Institutional Giving Manager: Noreen Collins
Budget: $400,000-$1 million
Performs At: Walt Whitman Hall
Seating Capacity: 2,400
Rental Contact: Director/General Manager Richard Grossberg

7645
BROOKLYN CONSERVATORY OF MUSIC
58 7th Avenue
Brooklyn, NY 11217
Phone: 718-622-3300
Fax: 718-622-3957
e-mail: info@bqcm.org
Web Site: www.bqcm.org
Officers:
  Chair: Joel Kress
  Vice Chair: Jerri Sines Mayer
  Secretary: Brian Cogan
  Treasurer: Janson Tepper
Management:
  Executive Director: Karan Geer
  Managing Director: Pete Robbins
  Director of Marketing and Communica: Arlene Kriv
  Director of Suzuki Division: Julianne Carney
Founded: 1897

7646
PRATT INSTITUTE: AUDITORIUM
200 Willoughby Avenue
Brooklyn, NY 11205
Phone: 718-636-3600
Fax: 718-399-4578
e-mail: info@pratt.edu
Web Site: www.pratt.edu
Management:
  President: Thomas Shutte
Founded: 1887
Status: Non-Profit, Professional

7647
SAINT JOSEPH'S COLLEGE CENTER FOR ARTS
Brooklyn Campus
245 Clinton Avenue
Brooklyn, NY 11205
Phone: 718-940-5300
e-mail: suffolkas@sjcny.edu
Web Site: www.sjcny.edu

FACILITIES / New York

Officers:
President: Elizabeth A Hill
Vice President of Academic Affairs: Loretta McGrann
Chair: Sheila Baird
Vice Chairman: Frank Lourenso
Secretary: Stephan Hochberg
Mission: Providing a strong academic and value-oriented education at the undergraduate and graduate levels, a liberal arts tradition that supports provision for career preparation and enhancement.
Founded: 1916

7648
HICKOX FIELD
CW Post Campus
Brookville, NY 11548
Phone: 516-299-2289
Fax: 516-299-3155
Management:
Athletic Director: Vincent Salamone

7649
AFRICAN-AMERICAN CULTURAL CENTER: PAUL ROBESON HALL
350 Masten Avenue
Buffalo, NY 14209
Phone: 716-884-2013
Fax: 716-885-2590
Web Site: www.aaccbuffalo.org
Management:
Executive Director: Agnes M. Bain

7650
BUFFALO STATE COLLEGE PERFORMING ARTS CENTER
1300 Elmwood Avenue
Rockwell Hall 210
Buffalo, NY 14222
Phone: 716-878-3005
Fax: 716-878-4234
e-mail: rhpac@buffalostate.edu
Web Site: www.buffalostate.edu
Management:
Director Operations: Jeff Marsha
Technical Director: Thomas Kostusiak
Mission: To provide a first class professional performing arts facility that enhances the quality of life for the campus and the citizens of Western New York.
Founded: 1987
Specialized Field: Series & Festivals; Music; Dance; Theatre
Status: Non-Profit, Non-Professional
Paid Staff: 5

7651
GREATER BUFFALO YOUTH BALLET THEATER
328 Kenmore Avenue
Buffalo, NY 14223
Phone: 716-835-3585
e-mail: GBYBallet@hotmail.com
Web Site: www.gbyballet.org
Management:
Artistic Director: Elizabeth DiStasio-Waddell
Mission: A pre-professional ballet company which provides western New York dancers with a quality education in the performing art of dance. Offering children of diverse ethnic and socioeconomic backgrounds the opportunity to achieve artistic excellence through dance.
Founded: 1997

7652
FIRST NIAGARA CENTER
One Seymour H. Knox III Plaza
Buffalo, NY 14203-3096
Phone: 716-855-4100
Fax: 716-855-4122
Toll-free: 888-467-2273
e-mail: info@firstniagaracenter.com
Web Site: www.firstniagaracenter.com
Management:
Director Building Operations: Stan Makowski
Director Arena Booking: Jennifer Van Rysdam
Status: For-Profit, Professional

7653
KLEINHANS MUSIC HALL
3 Symphony Circle
Buffalo, NY 14201
Phone: 716-885-5000
Fax: 716-883-7430
e-mail: boxoffice@bpo.org
Web Site: www.kleinhansbuffalo.org
Officers:
Vice Chair: Chris Brown
Mayor of the City of Buffalo: Byron Brown
Chair: Catherine Schweitzer
Management:
Event Manager: Brian Seibel
Building Services Manager: Maggie Shea
Director of Marketing and Comm: Susan Schwartz
Communications Coordinator: Kate Jenkins
Chief Engineer: Charlie McDonald
Founded: 1941
Status: Non-Profit, Professional
Paid Staff: 40
Paid Artists: 3
Facility Category: Music Hall/Theater
Seating Capacity: 2,839
Rental Contact: Kristen R Carlsen

7654
LIPPES CONCERT HALL IN SLEE HALL
University at Buffalo
105 Slee Hall Music Department
Buffalo, NY 14260-4800
Phone: 716-645-2921
Fax: 716-645-3175
e-mail: rehard@buffalo.edu
Web Site: www.slee.buffalo.edu
Management:
Assistant Concert Manager: Alana Janus
Concert Manager: Phil Rehard
Mission: Dedicated to performing both new and traditional chamber music in an intimate setting.
Founded: 1955
Specialized Field: Classical
Status: Non-Profit, Professional
Paid Staff: 11
Volunteer Staff: 15
Paid Artists: 13
Income Sources: Endowment; State
Affiliations: Chamber Music America; ECMEA
Annual Attendance: 10,000
Facility Category: 670 Seat Concert Hall; 215 Seat Recital Hall
Rental Contact: Concert Manager Phil Rehard

7655
MARINE MIDLAND ARENA
1 Seymour H Knox III Plaza
Buffalo, NY 14203-3007

Phone: 716-855-4100
Fax: 716-855-4120
e-mail: info@hsbcarena.com
Web Site: www.firstniagaracenter.com
Management:
Director Building Operations: Stan Makowski
Director Arena Booking: Jennifer Stich
Founded: 1969
Status: For-Profit, Professional
Paid Staff: 100

7656
SHEA'S PERFORMING ARTS CENTER
646 Main Street
Buffalo, NY 14202
Mailing Address: Shea's Performing Arts Center, PO Box 1130, Buffalo, New York
Phone: 716-847-1410
Fax: 716-847-1644
Web Site: www.sheas.org
Officers:
President: Anthony Conte
Management:
Development Manager: Linda Sroka
Production Manager: Bill Hendrick
Marketing Manager: Lisa Grisanti
Founded: 1926
Status: Non-Profit

7657
SUNY CENTER FOR THE ARTS
Department of Theatre and Dance
285 Alumni Arena
Buffalo, NY 14260
Phone: 716-645-6898
Fax: 716-645-6992
e-mail: clwhelan@buffalo.edu
Web Site: www.cas.buffalo.edu/depts/theatredance
Management:
Department Chairman: Robert Knopf
Director Music Theater: Lynne Kurdziel-Formato
Utilizes: Dance Companies; Dancers; Designers; Educators; Guest Artists; Guest Designers; Guest Directors; Guest Ensembles; Guest Instructors; Guest Musical Directors; Guest Soloists; High School Drama; Local Artists; Multimedia; Resident Artists; Soloists
Status: Non-Profit, Non-Professional
Paid Staff: 5
Paid Artists: 28
Affiliations: Irish Classical Theatre Company; Shakespeare in Delaware Park; Kavinoky; Musical Fare; Art Park
Type of Stage: Proscenium; Black Box
Seating Capacity: 120; 388
Year Built: 1995
Cost: $500,000,000
Rental Contact: S. Fazekas

7658
UNIVERSITY AT BUFFALO CENTER FOR THE ARTS
103 Center for the Arts
Buffalo, NY 14260-6000
Phone: 716-645-6259
Fax: 716-645-6973
e-mail: kmangel@buffalo.edu
Web Site: www.ubcfa.org
Management:
Executive Director: Thomas B. Burrows
Assistant Director: Rob Falgiano
Director of Finance: Pamela Garvey
Director of Events & Outreach: Katherine Trapanovski
Director of Marketing: David Wedekindt

FACILITIES / New York

Mission: Mission is to create an environment for the visual and performing arts to flourish through education, exploration, collaboration, and presentation, while enriching cultural opportunities for the surrounding community.
Utilizes: Actors; Artists-in-Residence; Dance Companies; Original Music Scores; Singers; Special Technical Talent; Theatre Companies
Founded: 1994
Status: Non-Profit, Professional
Paid Staff: 30
Volunteer Staff: 300
Budget: $2 million
Income Sources: Rental, ticket sales, 60% salaries.
Affiliations: State University of New York at Buffalo
Annual Attendance: 130,000
Facility Category: Performing and Visual Arts
Type of Stage: Proscenium
Stage Dimensions: 42' X 102'
Seating Capacity: 1,748
Year Built: 1994
Cost: $2,500 commercial & labor
Rental Contact: Katherine Trapanovski
Organization Type: Mainstage 1748; Drama Theatre 388; Screening Room 210; Black Box 185.

7659
AUGSBURY CENTER
Saint Lawrence University
23 Romoda Drive
Canton, NY 13617
Phone: 315-229-5423
Fax: 315-229-5589
Toll-free: 800-285-1856
Web Site: www.stlawu.edu
Management:
  Associate Director Athletics: Randolph W LaBrake
  Athletic Director: Margie Strait
  Sports Information Director: Walter Johnson
  Head Football Coach: Chris Phelps
  Head Basketball Coach (M): Chris Downs
  Head Basketball Coach (W): GP Bromacki
Seating Capacity: 3,500

7660
NORTON HALL
Chautauqua Institution
Chautauqua, NY 14722
Phone: 716-357-6000
Fax: 716-357-4175

7661
HAMILTON COLLEGE: MINOR THEATRE
198 College Hill Road
Clinton, NY 13323
Phone: 31-585-9401
Fax: 315-859-4457
Toll-free: 800-843-2655
e-mail: admission@hamilton.edu
Web Site: www.hamilton.edu
Officers:
  President: Joan Hinde Stewart
  Chairman: Stuart Scott
  Vice Chairman: Chester Siuda
  Executive Assistant to the Presiden: Meredith Harper Bonham
Management:
  Events Coordinator: Sue Campanie
Mission: A liberal arts college with an emphasis on individualized instruction and independent research and a national leader in teaching effective writing and persuasive speaking.
Status: Non-Profit, Non-Professional

7662
KIRKLAND ART CENTER
9 1/2 East Park Row
PO Box 213
Clinton, NY 13323-0213
Phone: 315-853-8871
Fax: 315-853-2076
e-mail: info@kacny.org
Web Site: www.kacny.org
Officers:
  Co-President: Carol Drogus
  VP: Chris Willemsen
  Secretary: Damhnait McHugh
  Treasurer: Bill Eichinger
Management:
  Executive Director: Gina Murtaugh
  Operation Manager: Jennifer Walker
Founded: 1961
Specialized Field: Series & Festivals; Dance; Instrumental Music; Musical Theatre; Theatrical Group; Vocal Music
Status: Non-Profit, Professional
Paid Staff: 5

7663
171 CEDAR ARTS CENTER
171 Cedar Street
Corning, NY 14830
Phone: 607-936-4647
Fax: 607-936-2081
Web Site: www.171cedararts.org
Management:
  Executive Director: Susan O'Leary
Founded: 1968
Status: Non-Profit, Professional
Paid Staff: 10
Paid Artists: 50
Budget: $60,000-$150,000

7664
DARIEN LAKE PERFORMING ARTS CENTER
9993 Allegheny Road
Darien Center, NY 14040
Phone: 585-599-4641
Fax: 585-599-3444
Web Site: www.darienlakeconcerts.com
Management:
  GM: Peter O'Donnell
  Operations: Joan Passarro
Seating Capacity: 21,000

7665
MERCY COLLEGE: LECTURE HALL
555 Broadway
Dobbs Ferry, NY 10566
Phone: 914-693-9455

7666
EARLVILLE OPERA HOUSE
6-22 East Main Street
Earlville, NY 13332
Phone: 315-691-3550
Fax: 315-691-4111
e-mail: info@earlvilleoperahouse.com
Web Site: www.earlvilleoperahouse.com
Officers:
  President: Putter Cox
Management:
  Executive Director: Patti Lockwood Blais
Mission: To promote the arts in a rural region of Central New York State by offering programs of cultural, educational and historical significance.
Founded: 1970
Status: Non-Profit, Professional
Paid Staff: 1
Volunteer Staff: 2
Paid Artists: 79
Non-paid Artists: 600
Performs At: Multi-Arts Center w/Galleries, Workshops, Arts Cafe, Gift Shop
Affiliations: NYMACC, NYS Arts, NYSCa
Facility Category: Multi Arts Center
Type of Stage: Proscenium
Stage Dimensions: 20' x 20'
Seating Capacity: 300
Year Built: 1892

7667
CLEMENS CENTER
207 Clemens Center Parkway And Gray Street
PO Box 1046
Elmira, NY 14901
Mailing Address: Clemens Center, P.O. Box 1046, Elmira, NY 14902-1046
Phone: 607-733-5639
Fax: 607-737-1162
Toll-free: 800-724-0159
e-mail: info@clemenscenter.com
Web Site: www.clemenscenter.com
Management:
  President: Jerald M Stemerman
  Executive Director: Thomas Weidemann
  Associate Executive Director: Julie Kriston
  Director Facility: Julie Kriston
  Marketing Director: Jensen Monroe
Mission: To enhance the performing arts and the entertainment experiences for the people of our region by providing superior facilities and programs.
Founded: 1977
Specialized Field: Year-Round Presenter 10; 5 Canty Region; Resident Companies And Rentals
Paid Staff: 17
Volunteer Staff: 200

7668
GIBSON THEATRE
Elmira College
1 Park Place
Elmira, NY 14901
Phone: 607-735-1814
Fax: 607-735-1757
Toll-free: 800-935-6472
e-mail: jseeley@elmira.edu
Web Site: www.elmira.edu
Officers:
  Vice President: Deborah McKinzie
Management:
  Director of Alumni Relations: Lindsay Petrillose
  Coordinator of Alumni Programs: Ellen Himmelreich
Mission: Performing Arts program established as a graduation requirement for freshmen and sohomores. We want to keep the arts alive through making them a necessary part of their college education. Community patrons may purchase tickets also.
Founded: 1855
Status: Educational Institution
Paid Staff: 4
Volunteer Staff: 25
Income Sources: Course Fees; Ticket Sales
Type of Stage: Proscenium
Stage Dimensions: 28'x30'x15'
Seating Capacity: 448
Year Remodeled: 1995

FACILITIES / New York

7669
WESTCHESTER BROADWAY THEATRE
One Broadway Plaza
Elmsford, NY 10523
Phone: 91-459-2222
Fax: 914-592-6917
Toll-free: 800-729-7469
e-mail: hgiarlo@cloud9.net
Web Site: www.broadwaytheatre.com
Management:
 Owner/Executive Producer: Bob Funking
 Owner/Executive Producer: Bill Stutler
 Director: Carol Waaser
Founded: 1974
Status: For-Profit, Professional

7670
ARTHUR ASHE STADIUM
USTA National Tennis Center
Flushing Meadows, Corona Park
Flushing, NY 11368
Phone: 718-760-6200
Fax: 718-592-9488
Web Site: www.usta.com
Management:
 Executive Director: Lee Hamilton
 Facility Managing Director: Dan Zausner Dan Zausner

7671
BROOKLYN CONSERVATORY OF MUSIC
58 Seventh Avenue
Flushing, NY 11217
Phone: 718-622-3300
Fax: 71-862-2395
e-mail: info@bqcm.org
Web Site: www.bqcm.org
Officers:
 Chair: Joel Kress
 Vice Chair: Jerri Sines Mayer
 Janson: Cogan Secretary
Management:
 Executive Director: Karan Geer
 Managing Director: Pete Robbins
 Executive Assistant and HR Manager: Madeleine Davidson
Founded: 1955
Specialized Field: Music
Status: Non-Profit, Professional

7672
CITI FIELD
12301 Roosevelt Ave
Flushing, NY 11368
Phone: 718-507-6387
Fax: 718-507-6395
Toll-free: 800-221-1155
Web Site: www.mets.com
Management:
 President: Saul Katz
 Chairman: Fred Wilpon
 EVP: Dave Howard
 SVP/Treasurer: Harry O'Shaughnessy
 VP/Ticket Sales/Service: Bill Ianniciello
 Director Media Relations: Jay Horowitz
 VP Venue Services: Mike Landeen
 VP Facilities: Karl Smolarz
 VP Guest Services: Pat McGovern
Mission: Home stadium for New York Mets major league baseball team.
Opened: 2009
Status: For-Profit, Professional
Seating Capacity: 41,800
Year Built: 2009
Architect: Populous
Cost: $900 million

7673
COLDEN CENTER FOR THE PERFORMING ARTS
65-30 Kissena Boulevard
Kissena Boulevard
Flushing, NY 11367-1597
Phone: 718-544-2996
Fax: 718-261-7063
Web Site: www.kupferbergcenter.org
Management:
 Director: Vivian Charlop
 Operations Manager: Michael Kelleher
 Technical Director: Craig Platt
 Box Office Manager: Stephanie McWoods
Utilizes: Collaborations; Dance Companies; Dancers; Fine Artists; Multimedia; Original Music Scores; Sign Language Translators; Singers; Special Technical Talent; Theatre Companies
Founded: 1961
Status: Non-Profit
Paid Staff: 9
Performs At: Auditorium w/permanent acoustical shell
Facility Category: Performing Arts
Seating Capacity: 2143
Year Built: 1961
Rental Contact: Stephen Mallalieu

7674
MICHAEL C ROCKEFELLER ARTS CENTER
SUNY Fredonia
280 Central Ave.
Fredonia, NY 14063
Phone: 716-673-3217
Fax: 716-673-3617
e-mail: arts.center@fredonia.edu
Web Site: www.fredonia.edu/rac
Officers:
 President: Ginny Horvath
Management:
 Artistic Director: Jefferson Westwood
Founded: 1969
Specialized Field: Pop Series; Family Caladoscope Series; Travelog Series Dance; Theatrical Group; Vocal Music; Musial Theatre
Status: Non-Profit, Professional
Paid Staff: 6
Volunteer Staff: 100
Budget: $400,000
Income Sources: State Of New York; Ticket Sales; Gifts
Performs At: Multi Arts Venue
Annual Attendance: 58,000
Seating Capacity: 1,145; 400; 200

7675
WADSWORTH AUDITORIUM
SUNY-Geneseo
1 College Circle
Geneseo, NY 14454
Phone: 716-245-5855
Fax: 716-245-4500
Web Site: www.geneseo.edu

7676
SMITH OPERA HOUSE
82 Seneca Street
Geneva, NY 14456
Phone: 315-789-5483
Fax: 315-789-6360
Toll-free: 866-355-LIVE
e-mail: boxoffice@thesmith.org
Web Site: www.thesmith.org
Officers:
 Chair: Murray P. Heaton
 Vice Chair: Michael E. Rusinko
 Treasurer: Mitchell Wilber
 Secretary: Sandy Bissell
Management:
 Executive Director: Kelly A. Bradley
 Office Manager: Jessica Allen
Mission: A 107-year-old, fully restored, acoustically perfect performing arts venue and movie theatre catering to college students, senior citizens, families, and children.
Founded: 1894
Specialized Field: Series & Festivals; Music; Theatre; Dance; Film; Childrens Programing
Status: Non-Profit, Non-Professional
Paid Staff: 4
Paid Artists: 80

7677
GLENS FALLS CIVIC CENTER
1 Civic Center Plaza
Glens Falls, NY 12801
Phone: 518-798-0366
Fax: 518-793-7750
Toll-free: 855-432-2849
Web Site: www.glensfallscc.com
Management:
 General Manager: Jeremy Huelsing
 Finance Manager: Justin Reed
 Event Manager: Chris Johnson
 Event Manager: Nic Broussard
 Box Office Manager: Avery Giroux
Founded: 1979
Status: Non-Profit, Non-Professional
Paid Staff: 30

7678
TILLES CENTER FOR THE PERFORMING ARTS
Long Island University
720 Northern Boulevard
Greenvale, NY 11548-1300
Phone: 516-299-2752
Fax: 516-299-2520
e-mail: george.lindsay@liu.edu
Web Site: www.tillescenter.org
Management:
 Executive Director: Elliott Sroka
 General Manager: George N. Lindsay, Jr.
 Business Manager: Marc Courtade
 Director of Marketing and Communica: Susanna Stickley
 Production Manager: Robert Goida
Seating Capacity: 2,200

7679
ANDY KERR STADIUM
Colgate University
Hamilton, NY 13346
Phone: 315-228-7611
Fax: 315-228-7008
Web Site: www.athletics.colgate.edu
Management:
 Athletic Director: Mark Murphy

FACILITIES / New York

7680
DANA ARTS CENTER UNIVERSITY THEATRE
Colgate University
13 Oak Drive
Hamilton, NY 13346
Phone: 315-228-1000
Fax: 315-228-7932
e-mail: admission@mail.colgate.edu
Web Site: www.colgate.edu
Management:
  President: Rebecca Chopp
Founded: 1819
Status: Non-Profit, Professional
Paid Staff: 267

7681
HOFSTRA UNIVERSITY STADIUM & ARENA
200 Hofstra University
Room 112
Hempstead, NY 11549
Phone: 516-463-6625
Fax: 516-463-6520
Web Site: www.hofstra.edu
Management:
  Associated Director: Ann Baller

7682
FAIR & EXPO CENTER
2695 E Henrietta Road
Henrietta, NY 14467
Phone: 585-334-4000
Fax: 585-334-3005
e-mail: mcfair@rochester.rr.com
Web Site: www.fairandexpocenter.org
Officers:
  President: Bruce Radley
  VP: Sharlene Reeves
  Secretary: Carolyn Gauvin
  Treasurer: Christine Miller
Management:
  Executive Director: Frances Tepper
  Events Director: Michael Wettach
  Marketing/Development Director: Tom Gamble
Mission: To build community through the affirmation, advancement and support of youth, agriculture and technology culminating in the annual celebration of the Monroe County Fair
Utilizes: Dancers; Guest Directors; Guest Musical Directors; Guest Musicians; Guest Soloists; Local Artists; Multimedia; Original Music Scores; Sign Language Translators; Singers; Soloists; Theatre Companies
Founded: 1823
Status: Non-Profit, Professional
Paid Staff: 11
Volunteer Staff: 256
Budget: $1,172,000
Income Sources: Trade Shows
Performs At: Arena
Affiliations: IAFE; OABA
Annual Attendance: 300,000
Facility Category: Arena
Type of Stage: Portable
Stage Dimensions: varied
Seating Capacity: 3200
Year Built: 1973
Year Remodeled: 2006
Rental Contact: Executive Director Fran Tepper

7683
WESLEY CHAPEL
Houghton College
One Willard Avenue
Houghton, NY 14744
Phone: 585-567-9400
Fax: 716-567-9517
Toll-free: 800-777-2556
e-mail: music@houghton.edu
Web Site: www.houghton.edu
Officers:
  President: Shirley A. Mullen
Management:
  Executive Director: Ben King
Founded: 1960
Status: Non-Profit, Professional
Paid Staff: 300

7684
INTER-MEDIA ART CENTER
370 New York Avenue
Huntington, NY 11743
Phone: 631-549-9666
Fax: 631-549-9423
Web Site: www.imactheater.org
Management:
  President: Michael Rothbard
Founded: 1973
Status: Non-Profit, Professional
Paid Staff: 25

7685
ALICE STATLER HALL
Statler School of Hotel Administration
189 Statler Hall
Ithaca, NY 14853-6902
Phone: 607-255-8702
Fax: 607-255-9243
e-mail: communications@sha.cornell.edu
Web Site: www.hotelschool.cornell.edu

7686
BEN LIGHT GYM
Ithaca College
319 Egbert Hall
Ithaca, NY 14850
Phone: 607-274-3222
Fax: 607-274-1725
e-mail: boc@ithaca.edu
Web Site: www.ithaca.edu/boc
Management:
  Advisor: Karen Coleman
Seating Capacity: 3,000

7687
HANGAR THEATRE
Cass Park
PO Box 205
Ithaca, NY 14851
Phone: 607-273-8588
Fax: 607-273-4516
e-mail: info@hangartheatre.org
Web Site: www.hangartheatre.org
Officers:
  President: Shelley S. Semmler
  VP: Margaret Shackell
  Treasurer: Paul Kirk
  Secretary: Judith Pastel
Management:
  Managing Director: Josh Friedman
  Artistic Director: Jen Waldman
  Business Director: Jennifer D. Anderson
  Production Manager: Adam Zonder
Founded: 1975

7688
DILLINGHAM CENTER FOR THE PERFORMING ARTS
Ithaca College
226 Dillingham Center
Ithaca, NY 14850
Phone: 607-274-3345
Fax: 607-274-3672
e-mail: theatrearts@ithaca.edu
Web Site: www.ithaca.edu/theatre
Officers:
  Chair: Catherine Weidner
  Associate Chair: Steve TenErck
Management:
  Coordinator of Theatre Operations: Mary Scheidegger
Founded: 1962
Specialized Field: Theatre Education
Status: Non-Profit, Professional
Paid Staff: 25
Paid Artists: 3

7689
JIM BUTTERFIELD STADIUM
201 Ceracchie Athletic Center
Ithaca College
Ithaca, NY 14850-7198
Phone: 607-274-3209
Fax: 607-274-1667
Web Site: www.ithaca.edu
Management:
  President: Peggy Williams
  Director of Athletics: Ken Kutler
Founded: 1892
Specialized Field: Education for College
Status: Non-Profit, Non-Professional

7690
ALUMNI HALL GYMNASIUM
Saint John's University
8000 Utopia Parkway
Jamaica, NY 11439
Phone: 718-990-6217
Management:
  Director: Edward J Manetta
  Sr Associate Director: Kathleen Meehan
  Associate Director: Charlie Elwood
  Sports Information Director: Dominic Scianna
Seating Capacity: 6,008

7691
JAMAICA CENTER FOR THE PERFORMING & VISUAL ARTS
161-04 Jamaica Avenue
Jamaica, NY 11432
Phone: 718-658-7400
Fax: 718-658-7922
Web Site: www.jcal.org
Officers:
  President: Tonya L. Cantlo-Cockfield
  1st Vice President: Michael James
  2nd Vice President: Peter Magnani
  Treasurer: Shanqua Harrison
  Secretary: Philippa L. Karteron
Management:
  Executive Director: Cathy Hung
  Senior Program & Development Direct: Akua-Akilah Anokye
  Facility Support Staff: Aaron Boone
  Director of Finance & Administratio: Jennifer Chiang

FACILITIES / New York

Founded: 1972
Status: Non-Profit, Professional
Paid Staff: 24

7692
ST. JOHN'S UNIVERSITY
8000 Utopia Parkway
Jamaica, NY 11439
Phone: 718-990-2000
Fax: 718-990-2075
e-mail: sjcug@stjohns.edu
Web Site: www.stjohns.edu
Officers:
   President: Conrado Gempesaw, Ph.D.
   EVP, COO & Treasurer: Martha K. Hirst, M.U.P.
   EVP for Mission: Rev. Gerard Luttenberger, C.M.
   VP for Enrollment Management: Beth M. Evans, M.P.A.
   VP & and University Secretary: Dorothy E. Habben, Ph.D.
Status: Non-Profit, Non-Professional
Paid Staff: 30
Paid Artists: 25

7693
LUCILLE BALL LITTLE THEATRE OF JAMESTOWN
18 East Second Street
Jamestown, NY 14701
Phone: 716-483-1095
Fax: 716-483-1099
e-mail: lblittletheatre@juno.com
Web Site: www.lucilleballlittletheatre.org
Officers:
   President: Carla Kayes
Management:
   Office Manager: Autumn Eccles
   Director: Helen Merrill
Mission: Produce five plays and musicals from September through May.
Utilizes: Actors
Founded: 1936
Status: Non-Profit, Non-Professional
Paid Staff: 4
Budget: $150,000
Income Sources: Ticket sales, grants
Annual Attendance: 12,000
Facility Category: Auditorium theatre house
Type of Stage: Proscenium
Stage Dimensions: 80 x 40 x 24
Seating Capacity: 400
Year Built: 1925
Year Remodeled: 1968
Cost: $230,000

7694
CARAMOOR CENTER FOR MUSIC AND THE ARTS VENETIAN THEATRE
149 Girdle Ridge Road
Katonah, NY 10536
Phone: 914-232-5035
Fax: 914-232-5521
e-mail: admin@caramoor.org
Web Site: www.caramoor.org
Officers:
   President/CEO: Erich Vollmer
Management:
   Executive Director: Howard Herring
   Managing Director: Paul Rosenblum
   Director Development: Susan Shine
   Director Operations: Melissa Montera
   Box Office Manager: Sal Vaccaro
Mission: To offer a performing arts venue in Bedford and New York State.
Founded: 1945
Specialized Field: Vocal Music; Instrumental Music; Festivals
Status: Professional; Nonprofit
Performs At: Museum Music Room Venetian Theatre
Organization Type: Performing; Educational; Sponsoring

7695
ULSTER PERFORMING ARTS CENTER
601 Broadway
Kingston, NY 12401
Phone: 845-339-6088
Fax: 845-339-3814
Web Site: www.upac.org
Officers:
   President: Karen Strain Smythe
   VP: Steven Chickery
   Treasurer: Nan Greenwood
   Secretary: Robert A. Kallman
Management:
   Facilities Director: Will Pittmant
   Technical Director: Todd Renedette
   Assistant to the Executive Director: Jodi Longto
   Executive Artisitic Director: Ron Marquette
Year Remodeled: 2001
Rental Contact: Jodi Longto

7696
LAKE GEORGE DINNER THEATRE
2223 Route 9
PO Box 266
Lake George, NY 12845
Phone: 518-668-5781
Fax: 518-668-9213
Web Site: www.lakegeorgedinnertheatre.com
Management:
   Producer: Victoria Eastwood
Founded: 1968

7697
LAKE PLACID CENTER FOR THE ARTS THEATER
17 Algonquin Drive
Lake Placid, NY 12946
Phone: 518-523-2512
Fax: 518-523-2521
e-mail: info@lakeplacidarts.org
Web Site: www.lakeplacidarts.org
Officers:
   President: Cathy Johnston
   VP: Diane Fish
   Treasurer: James Maswick
   Secretary: Caroline welsh
Management:
   Executive Director: James Lemons
   Development Director: Macie Huwiler
   Office Manager: Anya Villeneuve
   Maintenance Manager: Cade Grady
Mission: Dedicated to presenting and fostering quality arts which inspire, enrich, educate and entertain people of all ages.
Founded: 1972
Specialized Field: Multi-Purpose Arts Center
Status: Non-Profit, Professional
Paid Staff: 8
Volunteer Staff: 50
Budget: $750,000
Income Sources: Grants; Rentals
Annual Attendance: 35,000
Facility Category: Theatre/Gallery/Studio
Type of Stage: Proscenium
Seating Capacity: 355
Year Built: 1971
Rental Contact: Nadine Danaime

7698
OLYMPIC CENTER
Olympic Regional Development Authority
2634 Main Street
Lake Placid, NY 12946
Phone: 518-523-1655
Fax: 518-523-9275
Toll-free: 800-462-6236
Web Site: www.orda.org
Management:
   President: Ted Blazer
   General Manager: Dennis R Allen
Status: Non-Profit, Professional
Paid Staff: 150
Paid Artists: 150
Seating Capacity: 11,100

7699
LANCASTER NEW YORK OPERA HOUSE
21 Central Avenue
Lancaster, NY 14086
Phone: 716-683-1776
Fax: 716-683-8220
e-mail: dbondrow@lancopera.org
Web Site: www.lancopera.org
Officers:
   President: John Trojanowsky
   Vice President: Linda Koziol
   Treasurer: Aurelius Marc Chaves, Jr
   Secretary: David Bondrow
Management:
   Technical Director: Kirkland Gilmer
   Artistic Director: David Bondrow
   House Manager: Kristy Paradowski
Founded: 1981
Status: Non-Profit, Non-Professional
Paid Staff: 10

7700
ARTPARK
450 Soth 4th Street
Lewiston, NY 14092
Phone: 716-754-9000
Fax: 716-754-2741
e-mail: email through website
Web Site: www.artpark.net
Officers:
   President: George D Osborne
   Director Finance: Jean Stopa
   Productions Manager: Susan Stimson
Management:
   President: George Osborne, gosborne@artpark.net
   Operations Manager: Steve Bewlay, sbewlay@artpark.net
   Production Manager: Susan Stimson
   Director OF Development: Carrie Veltri
Mission: To provide arts education and programming to nuture and develop the talents of visual and performing artists; to provide quality volunteer experiences in the arts; to produce and present a series of theatre productions and concert events that will entertain and enrich the residents of Western New York, southeastern Canada, and area tourists.
Utilizes: Actors; AEA Actors; Artists-in-Residence; Choreographers; Dance Companies; Dancers; Designers; Fine Artists; Local Artists; Multimedia; Music; Original Music Scores; Resident Professionals; Sign Language Translators; Soloists; Touring Companies; Visual Arts
Founded: 1974

FACILITIES / New York

Specialized Field: Series & Festivals; Dance; Vocal Music; Instrumental Music; Festivals
Status: Non-Profit, Professional
Paid Staff: 100
Volunteer Staff: 300
Paid Artists: 200
Budget: $4 Million
Income Sources: Tickets; Grants; Sponsors
Season: June - September
Affiliations: Actors' Equity Association; International Association of Theatrical Stage Employees; American Guild of Musical Artists
Annual Attendance: 300,000
Facility Category: Theater & Ampi-Theater
Type of Stage: Sprung
Seating Capacity: 2,324
Year Built: 1974
Cost: $7,200,000
Rental Contact: Productions Manager Susan Stimson
Organization Type: Performing; Resident; Sponsoring

7701
BETHEL WOODS CENTER FOR THE ARTS
Po Box 222
Liberty, NY 12754
Fax: 845-295-2444
Toll-free: 866-781-2922
e-mail: info@bethelwoodscenter.org
Web Site: www.bethelwoodscenter.org
Management:
  Education And Community Outreach: Jodi Kane, jkane@bethelwoodscenter.org
Mission: Located at the site of the original 1969 woodstock festival, Bethel Woods combines a museum, farmers market and the Pavilion stage for a unique cultural experience

7702
STUDIO THEATRE
141 S Wellwood Avenue
Lindenhurst, NY 11757
Phone: 631-226-1833

7703
MOHAWK VALLEY CENTER FOR THE ARTS
401 S Ann Street
Little Falls, NY 13365
Phone: 315-823-0808
e-mail: director@mohawkvalleyarts.org
Web Site: www.mohawkvalleyarts.org
Officers:
  President: Michael Guidice
  VP: Jo Gloo
  Secretary: Daivd Van Meter
  Treasurer: Margaret Goldman
  Executive Director: Marjorie Balder
Founded: 1983
Status: Non-Profit, Non-Professional
Paid Staff: 1
Paid Artists: 220

7704
KENAN CENTER
433 Locust Street
Lockport, NY 14094
Phone: 716-433-2617
Fax: 716-433-6645
e-mail: info@kenancenter.org
Web Site: www.kenancenter.org
Officers:
  President: Selena Truax
Management:
  Executive Director: Susan Przybyl
Founded: 1969
Status: Non-Profit, Professional
Paid Staff: 20

7705
LAGUARDIA PERFORMING ARTS CENTER
31-10 Thomson Avenue
Room E-241
Long Island City, NY 11101
Phone: 718-482-5151
Fax: 718-482-5155
e-mail: lpac@lagcc.cuny.edu
Web Site: www.lagcc.cuny.edu/lpac
Officers:
  President: Gale Mellow
Management:
  Managing Director: Steven Hitt
  General Director: Barbara Carson
  Assistant Artistic Director: Handan Ozbilgin
  Finance Officer: Crayn Campo
Status: Non-Profit, Professional
Paid Staff: 15
Paid Artists: 75
Budget: $60,000-$150,000
Performs At: Little Theatre

7706
EMELIN THEATRE FOR THE PERFORMING ARTS
Library Lane
Mamaroneck, NY 10543
Mailing Address: P.O. Box 736, Mamaroneck, NY 10543-0736
Phone: 914-698-3045
Fax: 914-698-1404
e-mail: info@emelin.org
Web Site: www.emelin.org
Management:
  Production Manager: Bryan McPartlan
  Development Director: Soledad Fernadez
  Marketing Director: Michelle Zern

7707
HARLEM STAGE
Harlem Stage Gatehouse
150 Convent Avenue
New York, NY 10031
Phone: 212-281-9240
Fax: 212-281-9318
e-mail: boxoffice@harlemstage.org
Web Site: www.harlemstage.org
Officers:
  President: Tamara Tunie
  Vice President: Jenette Kahn
  Secretary: Michael Young
  Treasurer: Leon Henderson Jr.
Management:
  Executive Director: Patricia Cruz
  Managing Director: James King
  Director of Programming: Brad Learmonth
  Production Manager: Amanda Ringger
  Operations Manager: Rodney Bissessar
Specialized Field: Series & Festivals; Dance; Instrumental Music; Musical Theatre; Theatrical Group; Vocal Music
Status: Non-Profit, Professional
Performs At: Marian Anderson Theater

7708
AMBASSADOR THEATRE
215 W 49th Street
New York, NY 10019
Phone: 212-944-3700

7709
AMERICAN PLACE THEATRE
One East 53rd Street
8th Floor
New York, NY 10022
Phone: 212-594-4482
Fax: 212-594-4208
e-mail: edu@americanplacetheatre.org
Web Site: www.americanplacetheatre.org
Management:
  Executive Director: David Kener
  Artistic Director: Wynn Handman
  Managing Director: Jennifer Barnette
Status: Non-Profit, Professional
Paid Staff: 3
Annual Attendance: 90,000
Facility Category: Three Theatres; Cabaret; Black Box
Seating Capacity: 74/74/350
Year Built: 1971

7710
ANPSACHER STAGE
Public Theater
425 Lafayette Street
New York, NY 10003
Phone: 212-539-8500
Fax: 212-539-8705
e-mail: press@publictheater.org
Web Site: www.publictheater.org
Management:
  Artistic Director: Oskar Eustis
  Executive Director: Andrew D Hamingson
  General Manager: Andrea Nellis
Mission: The Public Theater is dedicated to achieving artistic excellence while developing an American thester that is accessible and relevant to all people through productions of challenging new plays, musicals and innovative stagings of the classics.
Founded: 1967
Specialized Field: Plays, Musicals, Shakespeare
Performs At: LuEsther Hall, Martinson Hall, Shiva Theater, Newman Theater
Type of Stage: Thrust
Stage Dimensions: 23' X 32'
Seating Capacity: 275

7711
APOLLO THEATRE
253 W 125th Street
New York, NY 10027
Phone: 212-531-5300
Fax: 212-749-2743

7712
ASCAP
One Lincoln Plaza
New York, NY 10023
Phone: 212-621-6000
Fax: 212-724-9064
Toll-free: 800-652-7227
e-mail: ascapfoundation@ascap.com
Web Site: www.ascap.com
Officers:
  President and Chairman: Paul Williams
  Vice Chairman: Jimmy Webb
  Treasurer: James M. Kendrick
Management:

FACILITIES / New York

President: Marilyn Bergman
Chairman and CEO: Irwin Robins

7713
BAKER FIELD
Columbia University
533 W 218th Street
New York, NY 10027
Phone: 212-942-0431
Fax: 212-854-2988
Web Site: www.columbia.edu

7714
BERNARD B JACOBS THEATRE
242 W 45th Street
New York, NY 10036
Phone: 212-239-6200
Seating Capacity: 1,068
Year Built: 1927

7715
BOOTH THEATRE
222 W 45th Street
New York, NY 10036
Phone: 212-239-6200

7716
BROADHURST THEATRE
235 W 44th Street
New York, NY 10035
Phone: 212-239-6200
Web Site:
www.shubertorganization.com/theatres/broadhurst.asp

7717
BROADWAY THEATRE
1681 Broadway
New York, NY 10019
Phone: 212-239-6200

7718
BROOKS ATKINSON THEATRE
256 W 47th Street
New York, NY 10036
Phone: 212-719-4099
Web Site: brooksatkinsontheater.com

7719
CARNEGIE HALL CORPORATION
881 Seventh Avenue
New York, NY 10019
Phone: 212-903-9600
Fax: 212-581-6539
Web Site: www.carnegiehall.org
Officers:
  Chairman: Sanford I. Weill
  Vice Chair: Mercedes T. Bass
  Secretary: Kenneth J. Bialkin
  Treasurer: Edward C. Forst
Management:
  Artistic Director: Clive Gillinson
  Director: Richard Malenka
Mission: To continue to be one of the world's leading institutions in presenting great music and in promoting music education, music creation and music enjoyment in landmark concert hall.
Founded: 1891
Specialized Field: Arts
Status: Non-Profit, Professional
Paid Staff: 250
Volunteer Staff: 150

7720
CENTER FOR TRADITIONAL MUSIC & DANCE
32 Broadway
Suite 1314
New York, NY 10004
Phone: 212-571-1555
Fax: 212-571-9052
e-mail: traditions@ctmd.org
Web Site: www.ctmd.org
Management:
  Executive Director: Peter Rushefsky
  Artistic Director: Ehtel Raim
Mission: Works to preserve and present the performing arts traditions of New Yor's immigrant communities through research-based educational programming, public performance and community partnerships.
Founded: 1976
Specialized Field: World Music; Dance
Status: Non-Profit, Professional
Paid Staff: 8
Volunteer Staff: 2

7721
CIRCLE IN THE SQUARE THEATER SCHOOL
1633 Broadway
New York, NY 10019
Phone: 212-307-0388
Fax: 212-307-0257
e-mail: admissions@circleinthesquare.org
Web Site: www.circlesquare.org
Officers:
  President: Paul Libin
Management:
  Executive Director: E Colin O'Leary
  Artistic Director: Theodore Mann
Mission: School of training.
Founded: 1961
Status: Non-Profit, Non-Professional
Paid Staff: 25
Facility Category: Broadway Theatre

7722
CITY CENTER OF MUSIC AND DRAMA
70 Lincoln Central Plaza
4Th Floor
New York, NY 10023
Phone: 212-870-4266
Fax: 212-870-4286
Management:
  Director Finance: Michael Edwards
Mission: To provide ballet, theatre and opera for the community at low cost or no charge.
Founded: 1943
Specialized Field: Dance; Vocal Music; Instrumental Music; Theatre
Status: Professional; Nonprofit
Performs At: New York State Theater
Organization Type: Performing; Touring; Educational

7723
CORT THEATRE
138 West 48th Street
New York, NY 10036
Phone: 212-239-6200
Fax: 212-239-5134
Web Site:
www.shubertorganization.com/theatres/cort.asp

7724
DANCE THEATER WORKSHOP
219 W 19th Street
New York, NY 10011
Phone: 212-691-6500
Fax: 212-633-1974
Web Site: www.dtw.org
Management:
  Executive Director: Marion Dienstag
  Artistic Director: Cathy Edwards
  Senior Associate Producer: David Sheingild
Founded: 1965
Specialized Field: Dance; Theater
Status: Non-Profit, Professional
Paid Staff: 30

7725
DELACORTE THEATER IN CENTRAL PARK
81st Street at Central Park W
New York, NY 10003
Phone: 212-539-8750
Fax: 212-839-8505
Web Site: www.publictheater.org
Officers:
  Producer: George C Wolfe
  Managing Director: Mark Litvin
Management:
  Executive Director: Mara Manus
  General Manager: Michael Hurst
Founded: 1954
Season: June - September
Facility Category: Amphitheatre (open air)
Type of Stage: Thrust
Seating Capacity: 1900
Year Built: 1962
Year Remodeled: 1999
Rental Contact: General Manager Michael Hurst
Comments: The Delacorte Theater is operated by the Joseph Papp Public Theater/New York Shakespeare Festival Shakespeare productions. Free tickets are distributed starting at 1 PM on days of performances.

7726
EDEN'S EXPRESSWAY
537 Broadway
New York, NY 10012
Phone: 212-226-8988

7727
ENSEMBLE STUDIO THEATRE
549 West 52nd Street
2nd Floor
New York, NY 10019
Phone: 212-247-4982
Fax: 212-664-0041
Toll-free: 866-811-4111
e-mail: est@ensemblestudiotheatre.org
Web Site: www.ensemblestudiotheatre.org
Officers:
  Treasurer, Chairman Emeritus: G. H. Denniston
  Chai: Bob Jaffe
  Vice Chair: Ann Sachs
  Secretary: Susan Vitucci
Management:
  Artistic Director: William Carden
  Executive Director: Paul A. Slee
  Finance Director: Randee Smith
  Associate Artistic Director: Graeme Gillis
  Co-Artistic Director: Rj Tolan
Founded: 1972

FACILITIES / New York

Specialized Field: Theatre; Marathon; one act plays; Open Theatre; focousing on developing news plays; Festivals
Status: Non-Profit, Professional

7728
ETHEL BARRYMORE THEATRE
243 West 47th Street
New York, NY 10036
Phone: 212-239-6200
Web Site: www.shubertorganization.com/theatres/barrymore.asp

7729
FREDERICK P ROSE HALL
3 Columbus Circle
12th Floor
New York, NY 10019
Phone: 212-258-9800
Fax: 212-258-9900
e-mail: customerservice@jalc.org
Web Site: www.jalc.org
Officers:
 Chairman: Lisa Schiff
 Vice Chair: Diane M Coffey
 Vice-Chair: Shahara Ahmad-Llewellyn
 Treasurer: Alan D Cohn
 Secretary: Michael D Fricklas
Management:
 Artistic Director: Wynton Marsalis
 Executive Director: Adrian Ellis
Mission: Features three distinct concert or performance venues: Rose Theater, Allen Room seats 300-600 and Dizzy's Club Coca Cola seats 140.
Utilizes: Artists-in-Residence; Poets; Resident Artists
Founded: 2004
Status: Professional
Income Sources: Private and Corporate Donations, Endowment Fund
Type of Stage: Proscenium
Stage Dimensions: 100x43
Seating Capacity: 1,100-1,231
Organization Type: Resident, Performing

7730
GERALD SCHOENFELD THEATRE
236 W 45th Street
New York, NY 10036
Phone: 212-239-6200
Web Site: www.shubertorganization.com/theatres/schoenfeld.asp
Seating Capacity: 1080
Year Built: 1917
Comments: Formerly Plymouth Theater

7731
GERSHWIN THEATRE
222 West 51st Street
New York, NY 10019
Phone: 212-586-6510
e-mail: customerservice@nederlander.com
Web Site: www.gershwintheatre.com

7732
GOETHE-INSTITUT NEW YORK/GERMAN CULTURAL CENTER
72 Spring Street
11th Floor
New York, NY 10012
Phone: 212-439-8700
Fax: 212-439-8705
Toll-free: 877-463-8431
e-mail: info@newyork.goethe.org
Web Site: www.goethe.de/newyork
Officers:
 President: Klaus-Dieter Lehmann
Management:
 Director: Christoph Bartmann
 Deputy Executive Director: Ulrich Linder
 Assistant to the Director: Meret Hofer
Founded: 1951
Status: Non-Profit, Professional
Paid Staff: 25
Budget: $10,000

7733
HAMMERSTEIN BALLROOM
Manhattan Center Studios
311 West 34th Street
New York, NY 10001
Phone: 212-279-7740
Fax: 212-564-1072
e-mail: info@mcstudios.com
Web Site: www.mcstudios.com
Management:
 Director of Sales & Marketing: Jessica Rothste Berman
 Sales & Marketing Executive: Tara Cohn
Founded: 1906
Stage Dimensions: 54' x 24'
Seating Capacity: 2,200

7734
HB PLAYWRIGHTS FOUNDATION THEATRE HOUSE
124 S Bank Street
New York, NY 10014
Phone: 212-989-6540
Fax: 212-627-4288

7735
IMPERIAL THEATRE
249 W 45th Street
New York, NY 10036
Phone: 212-944-3700

7736
JEWISH MUSEUM
1109 5th Avenue at 92nd street
New York, NY 10128
Phone: 212-423-3200
Fax: 212-423-3232
e-mail: info@thejm.org
Web Site: www.thejewishmuseum.org
Management:
 Media and Public Programs Director: Aviva Weintraub

7737
JOE'S PUB AT THE PUBLIC THEATER
425 Lafayette Street
New York, NY 10003
Phone: 212-539-8500
Fax: 212-539-8507
e-mail: info@joespub.com
Web Site: www.joespub.com
Management:
 Director: Shanta Thake
 Managing Director: Kevin Abbott
 Associate Director: Alex knowlton
Mission: One of New York City's most celebrated and in-demand showcase venues for live music and performance. With its genre-blind booking and vast diversity of interests, the stage at Joe's Pub gives voice to a world of varied and stellar artists.
Founded: 1998
Performs At: Newman Theater, Anspacher Theater, Martinson Hall, LuEsther Hall, Shiva Theater
Type of Stage: Thrust
Stage Dimensions: 23' X 32'
Seating Capacity: 275

7738
JOHN GOLDEN THEATRE
252 W 45th Street
New York, NY 10036
Phone: 212-944-4136
Officers:
 Chair: J. Kerry Clayton
 Vice chair: Steven M. Pesner
 Secretary: Anh-Tuyet Nguyen
 Treasurer: Stephine R. Breslow

7739
JOYCE THEATER
175 Eighth Avenue
New York, NY 10011
Phone: 212-691-9740
e-mail: staff@joyce.org
Web Site: www.joyce.org
Officers:
 Chair: J. Kerry Clayton
 Vice Chair: Steven M. Pesner
 Secretary: Anh-Tuyet Nguyen
 Treasurer: Stephanie R. Breslow
 Chair Emeritus: David D. Holbrook
Management:
 Executive Director: Linda Shelton
 Director of Marketing: Martha Cooper
 Director of Development: Anni Luneau
 Director of Finance: Margeret Hollenbeck
 Director of Education: Joanne Robinson Hill
Mission: To serve and support the art of dance and choreography, promote the richness and variety of the art form in its fullest expression, and enhance the public interest in, and appreciation of, dance and the allied arts of music, design, and theater
Founded: 1982
Specialized Field: Dance
Annual Attendance: 136,000
Facility Category: Theater
Type of Stage: Proscenium
Stage Dimensions: 64x35
Seating Capacity: 472
Year Built: 1930
Year Remodeled: 1982

7740
KATHRYN BACHE MILLER THEATRE
Columbia University, 2960 Broadway
Mail Code 1801
New York, NY 10027
Phone: 212-854-1633
Fax: 212-854-7740
e-mail: miller-arts@columbia.edu
Web Site: www.millertheatre.com
Management:
 Executive Director: Melissa Smey
 Director Of Marketing: Charlotte Levitt
 Director of Production: Barbara J George Jones
Mission: To provide high quality presentations of contemporary, classical and early music to the greater New York City audience.
Founded: 1998
Specialized Field: Theater
Facility Category: Concert Hall
Seating Capacity: 688
Rental Contact: Gary Caruana

FACILITIES / New York

7741
KAYE PLAYHOUSE AT HUNTER COLLEGE
695 Park Avenue
New York, NY 10021
Phone: 212-772-4471
Fax: 212-650-3919
e-mail: kayeinfo@hunter.cuny.edu
Web Site: www.kayplayhouse.hunter.cuny.edu
Management:
  General Manager: Nancy B Dodds
Status: Non-Profit, Non-Professional

7742
KAZUKO HIRABAYASHI DANCE THEATRE
330 Broome Street
New York, NY 10002
Phone: 212-966-6414

7743
THE KITCHEN
512 West 19th Street
New York, NY 10011
Phone: 212-255-5793
Fax: 212-645-4258
e-mail: info@thekitchen.org
Web Site: www.thekitchen.org
Officers:
  Chairman: Philip Glass
  President: Chris Ahearn
  VP: Melissa Schiff Soros
  Vice-Chairman: Molly Davis
  Treasurer: Greg S Feldman
  Secretary: Douglas A Hand
Management:
  Executive Director/Chief Curator: Debra Singer
  Associate Director: Kerry Scheidt
  Marketing Director: Justin Neal
Mission: A non-profit, interdisciplinary organization that provides innovative artists working in the media, literary, and performing arts with exhibition and performance opportunities to creat and present new work. Identifies, supports, and presents emerging and under-recognized artists who are making significant contributions to their perspectives fields as well as serves as a safe space for mre established artists to take unusual creative risks.
Founded: 1971
Specialized Field: Dance; Music; Performance; Literature; Film and Video; New Media Arts
Status: Non-Profit, Professional
Paid Staff: 20
Volunteer Staff: 10
Paid Artists: 40

7744
LAMB'S THEATRE
130 W 44th Street
New York, NY 10036
Phone: 212-997-1780
Fax: 212-997-1082

7745
LEHMAN CENTER FOR THE PERFORMING ARTS
250 Bedford Park Boulevard West
New York, NY 10468
Phone: 718-960-8833
Fax: 718-960-8233
e-mail: eva.bornstein@lehman.cuny.edu
Web Site: www.lehmancenter.org
Management:
  Executive Director: Eva Bornstein
  Associate Director: Carter Van Pelt
  Operations Manager & House Manager: Janet SanChez
Founded: 1980
Status: Non-Profit; Professional
Paid Staff: 10
Type of Stage: Proscenium
Seating Capacity: 2,310
Year Built: 1979
Rental Contact: Operations Manager Janet Sanchez

7746
LINCOLN CENTER THEATER
150 West 65th Street
New York, NY 10023
Phone: 212-362-7600
Fax: 212-873-0761
Toll-free: 800-331-0472
e-mail: customerservice@lct.org
Web Site: www.lct.org
Officers:
  Chairman: J Tomlinson Hill
  President: Eric M Mindich
  Vice Chairman: Daryl Roth
  Treasurer: John W Rowe
  Secretary: Brooke Garber Neidich
Management:
  Artistic Director: Andre Bishop
  Executive Producer: Bernard Gersten
  General Manager: Adam Siegel
  Production Manager: Jeff Hamlin
  Marketing Director: Linda Mason Ross
Founded: 1985
Specialized Field: Theater
Performs At: Vivian Beaumont, Mitzi E. Newhouse
Type of Stage: Thrust
Seating Capacity: 1000, 300

7747
LONGACRE THEATRE
220 West 48th Street
New York, NY 10036
Phone: 212-239-6200
Web Site: www.shubertorganization.com/theatres/longacre.asp

7748
LUCILLE LORTEL THEATRE
121 Christopher Street
New York, NY 10014
Phone: 212-924-2817
Fax: 212-939-0036
Web Site: www.lortel.org
Management:
  General Manager: Beer Nancy
  House Manager: Crigler Rebecca
  Executive Director: Frobes Georger

7749
LUESTHER HALL
Public Theater
425 Lafayette Street
New York, NY 10003
Phone: 212-539-8500
Fax: 212-539-8705
e-mail: marketing@publictheater.org
Web Site: www.publictheater.org
Management:
  Artistic Director: Oskar Eustis
  Executive Director: Andrew D Hamington
  General Manager: Andrea Nellis
Mission: The Public Theater is dedicated to achieving artistic excellence while developing an American theater that is accessible and relevant to all people through productions of challenging new plays, musicals and innovative stagings of the classics.
Founded: 1967
Specialized Field: Plays, Musicals, Shakespeare
Performs At: Newman Theater, Anspacher Theater, Martinson Hall, LuEsther Hall, Shiva Theater
Type of Stage: Loft Space
Stage Dimensions: 67' X 27'
Seating Capacity: 160

7750
LUNT-FONTANNE THEATRE
205 W 46th Street
New York, NY 10036
Phone: 212-575-9200
Mission: To promote and increase awareness and interest in the theatre and performing arts locally, nationally and globally.
Founded: 1955
Status: For-Profit, Professional

7751
LYCEUM THEATRE
149 W 45th Street
New York, NY 10036
Phone: 212-239-6200

7752
MADISON SQUARE GARDEN
4 Pennsylvania Plaza
New York, NY 10001
Phone: 212-465-6741
Fax: 212-465-6029
e-mail: feedback.msg@thegarden.com
Web Site: www.thegarden.com
Officers:
  Executive Chairman: James L Dolan
  President/CEO: Hank J Ratner
  Executive VP/CFO: Robert M Pollichino
Mission: Madison Square Garden is part of Madison Square Garden, L.P. Cablevision Systems Corporation owns a majority interest in MSG.

7753
MAJESTIC THEATRE
245 W 44th Street
New York, NY 10036
Phone: 212-239-6200

7754
MANHATTAN THEATRE CLUB
261 W 47th Street
8th Floor
New York, NY 10036
Phone: 212-239-6200
Fax: 212-399-4329
e-mail: questions@mtc-nyc.org
Web Site: www.mtc-nyc.org
Management:
  General Manager: Florie Seery
  Artistic Director: Lynne Meadow
  Executive Producer: Barry Grove
  Production Manager: Kurt Gardner
  Theatre Manager: Jim Joseph
Mission: To produce a season of innovative work with a series of productions as broad and diverse as New York itself; to encourage significant new work by creating an environment in which writers and theatre artists are supported by the finest professionals producing theatre today; to nurture new talent in playwriting, musical

All listings are in alphabetical order by state, then city, then organization within the city.

FACILITIES / New York

composition, directing, acting and design; and to reach out to young audiences with innovative programs in education
Founded: 1970

7755
MARQUIS
211 W 45th Street
New York, NY 10036
Phone: 212-382-0100

7756
MARTIN BECK THEATER
302 W 45th Street
New York, NY 10036
Phone: 212-239-6200

7757
MARTINSON THEATRE
Public Theater
425 Lafayette Street
New York, NY 10003
Phone: 212-539-8500
Fax: 212-539-8705
e-mail: press@publictheater.org
Web Site: www.publictheater.org
Management:
  Artistic Director: Oskar Eustis
  Executive Director: Andrew D Hamingson
  General Manager: Andrew Nellis
Mission: The Public Theater is dedicated to achieving artistic excellence while developing an American theater that is accessible and relevant to all people through productions of challenging new plays, musicals and innovative stagings of the classics.
Founded: 1967
Specialized Field: Plays, Musicals, Shakespeare
Performs At: Newman Theater, Anspacher Theater, Martinson Hall, LuEsther Hall, Shiva Theater
Type of Stage: Set Black Box
Stage Dimensions: 68' X 28'
Seating Capacity: 199

7758
MARYMOUNT MANHATTAN COLLEGE
221 E 71st Street
New York, NY 10021
Phone: 212-517-0400
Fax: 212-517-0541
Toll-free: 800-627-9686
Web Site: www.mmm.edu
Management:
  President: Judson Shaver PhD
Founded: 1961
Status: Non-Profit, Non-Professional

7759
MERKIN CONCERT HALL AT KAUFMAN CENTER
Goodman House
129 West 67Th Street
New York, NY 10023
Phone: 212-501-3330
Fax: 212-501-3317
e-mail: boxoffice@kaufmanmusiccenter.org
Web Site: www.kaufmanmusiccenter.org
Officers:
  Honorary Chair: Leonard Goodman
  Honorary Chair: Elaine Kaufman
  Chairman: Bethany Millard
Management:
  Executive Director: Lydia Kontos
  Booking Manager: Andrea Murray
Mission: To awaken and enhance appreciation of and participation in music and other arts; seeks to further this mission as an independent concert hall. Merkin Hall's programming reflects a diverse society and encompasses a breath of musical styles, periods, and traditions, with emphasis on new work, new artists, events and programs which draw on our rich Jewish cultural heritage.
Utilizes: Actors; AEA Actors; Artists-in-Residence; Collaborating Artists; Collaborations; Commissioned Composers; Commissioned Music; Composers; Dance Companies; Educators; Fine Artists; Five Seasonal Concerts; Grant Writers; Guest Accompanists; Guest Choreographers; Guest Companies; Guest Composers; Guest Designers; Guest Directors; Guest Ensembles; Guest Instructors; Guest Lecturers; Guest Musical Directors; Guest Musicians; Guest Soloists; Guild Activities; High School Drama; Instructors; Local Unknown Artists; Multimedia; Music; Organization Contracts; Original Music Scores; Resident Artists; Resident Professionals; Singers; Soloists
Founded: 1952
Specialized Field: Concert Hall
Status: Professional; Nonprofit
Paid Staff: 19
Paid Artists: 500
Budget: $720,000
Income Sources: Earned and Contributed; Foundation; Individual; Government Support
Performs At: Merkin Concert Hall
Affiliations: Chamber Music America
Annual Attendance: 60,000
Facility Category: Professional Concert Hall
Type of Stage: Fixed Proscenium
Stage Dimensions: 35'x57'x20'
Seating Capacity: 443
Year Built: 1978
Rental Contact: Booking Manager Andrea Murray
Resident Groups: Poppyseed Players

7760
MICHAEL SCHIMMEL CENTER FOR THE ARTS
3 Spruce Street, Pace University
1 Pace Plaza
New York, NY 10038
Phone: 212-346-1715
Fax: 212-346-1645
e-mail: galleries@pace.edu
Web Site: www.pace.edu/culture
Management:
  Director for Cultural Affairs: Martin I. Kagan
  Theater Manager: Joy Besozzi
  Box Office Manager: Nora Mae Lyng
  Technical Director: John Fistos
Mission: Presents a wide range of cultural progrtams and public events for the campus and surrounding community. In addition to student productions and special events, the Center also hosts professional theatre, music and dance, as well as international companies such as the Beijing People's Art Theatre.
Founded: 1969
Specialized Field: Series & Festivals; Dance; Jazz; Theatrical Student Productions; Location for Film and TV
Status: Non-Profit, Professional
Paid Staff: 5
Seating Capacity: 743

7761
MINETTA LANE THEATRE
18 Minetta Lane
New York, NY 10012
Phone: 212-420-8000
Fax: 212-254-4963
Management:
  President: Margaret Carter
Status: For-Profit, Professional
Paid Staff: 10

7762
MINSKOFF THEATRE
200 W 45th Street
New York, NY 10036
Phone: 212-869-0550
Fax: 212-944-8644
Status: Professional
Seating Capacity: 1685

7763
MUSIC BOX
239 W 45th Street
New York, NY 10036
Phone: 212-239-6200

7764
NEDERLANDER THEATRE
208 W 41st Street
New York, NY 10036
Phone: 212-921-8000
Web Site: www.siteforrent.com

7765
NEIL SIMON THEATRE
250 W 52nd Street
New York, NY 10019
Phone: 212-757-8646
Fax: 212-262-2400
Seating Capacity: 1334

7766
NEW DRAMATISTS
424 West 44th Street
New York, NY 10036
Phone: 212-757-7960
Fax: 646-390-8705
Web Site: www.newdramatists.org
Officers:
  Chairman: Seth Gelblum
  President: Isobel Robins Konecky
  VP/Secretary: Robet Kuchner
  VP: Robin lynn
  Treasurer: David C. Rosenzweig
Management:
  Executive Director: Joel Ruark
  Artistic Director: Todd London
Founded: 1949
Status: Non-Profit, Professional
Paid Staff: 8

7767
NEW VICTORY THEATER
209 W 42nd Street
New York, NY 10036
Phone: 646-223-3010
Fax: 646-562-0175
e-mail: info@new42.org
Web Site: www.newvictory.org
Officers:
  President: Cora Cahan
Founded: 1995
Specialized Field: Musical; Comedy; Ethnic Theater; Classic; Contemporary; Children's Theater
Status: Non-Profit, Professional
Paid Staff: 150

7768
NEW YORK CITY CENTER
130 W 56th Street
New York, NY 10019
Phone: 212-581-1212
Fax: 212-541-7979
e-mail: elowery@nycitycenter.org
Web Site: www.nycitycenter.org
Officers:
  Co-Chairman: Stacey Mindich
  President/CEO: Arlene Shuler
  Chairman Emeritus: Raymond A. Lamontagne
Management:
  Managing Director: Stacy Bash-Polley
  Founder andArtistic Director: Rose Caiola
  President & Executive Director: Theodore S. Chapin
  Director of Production: Mark Mongold
Mission: To make the finest in the performing arts accessible to the broadest possible audience, while insuring that its landmark facility remains an active and welcoming venue to both audiences and artists throughout the year.
Founded: 1943
Status: Non-Profit, Professional
Paid Staff: 32
Budget: $1,000,000
Income Sources: Ticket Sales; Donations
Annual Attendance: 200,000
Facility Category: Theater
Type of Stage: Proscenium
Stage Dimensions: 43'x45'
Seating Capacity: 2,684
Year Built: 1923
Rental Contact: Eugene Lowery

7769
NEWMAN STAGE
Public Theater
425 Lafayette Street
New York, NY 10003
Phone: 212-539-8500
Fax: 212-539-8705
e-mail: marketing@publictheater.org
Web Site: www.publictheater.org
Management:
  Artistic Director: Oskar Eustis
  Executive Director: Andrew D Hamingson
  General Manager: Andrea Nellis
Mission: The Public Theater is dedicated to achieving artistic excellence while developing an American theater that is accessible and relevant to all people through productions of challenging new plays, musicals and innovative stagings of the classics.
Founded: 1967
Specialized Field: Plays, Musicals, Shakespeare
Performs At: Newman Theater, Anspacher Theater, Martinson Hall, LuEsther Hall, Shiva Theater
Type of Stage: Proscenium
Stage Dimensions: 40' X 36'
Seating Capacity: 299

7770
OPEN EYE: NEW STAGINGS
270 W 89th Street
New York, NY 10024
Phone: 212-226-8435
Fax: 212-343-1065

7771
ORPHEUM THEATRE
126 2nd Avenue
New York, NY 10003
Phone: 212-477-2477
Fax: 212-871-9094
Management:
  President: Margaret Carter
Founded: 1980
Status: For-Profit, Professional

7772
PALACE THEATRE
1564 Broadway
New York, NY 10036
Phone: 212-730-8200
Fax: 212-730-7932
Web Site: palacetheatreonbroadway.com

7773
PAN AMERICAN MUSICAL ART RESEARCH
644 West 185th St.
Suite 6B
New York, NY 10033
Phone: 646-701-0010
Fax: 212-688-6862
e-mail: info@pamar.org
Web Site: www.pamar.org
Officers:
  Honorary President: Placido Domingo
  Chairman: Diego Recalde
  Vice Chairman: Daniel Doura
  Secretary: Aurora Belliard
  Treasurer: Roberto Krell
Management:
  Founder/Artistic Director: Polly Ferman
Mission: A non-profit organization seeking to promote a better knowledge, understanding and coexistence, between the various cultures and countries of the americas, primarily through an ongoing and vital exchange of their artistic fields including music, dance, theater, film, visual arts and literature, and through educational programs.
Founded: 1984
Status: Non-Profit

7774
PERFORMANCE SPACE 122
67 West Street #315
New York, NY 11222
Phone: 212-477-5829
Fax: 212-353-1315
e-mail: ps122@ps122.org
Web Site: www.ps122.org
Officers:
  President: Ivan Martinez
  Treasurer: Jason C Tsou
Management:
  Artistic Director: Vallejo Ganter
  Director of Production: Derek Lloyd
  Marketing/Communications Director: Carliegh Welsh
Mission: Dedicated to supporting and presenting artists whose work challenges the traditional boundaries of dance, theatre, music and performance. Committed to exploring innovative form as well as material, PS 122 is steadfast in its search for pioneering artists from a diversity of cultures and points of view.
Founded: 1979
Status: Non-Profit, Professional
Paid Staff: 16

7775
PROMENADE THEATRE
2162 Broadway
New York, NY 10023
Phone: 212-707-8270
Fax: 212-707-8775

7776
QUEBEC GOVERNMENT HOUSE
1 Rockefeller Plaza
26th Floor
New York, NY 10020
Phone: 212-843-0950
Fax: 212-376-8984
Web Site: www.quebecusa.org
Management:
  General Delegate: Michel Robicaille
Founded: 1940
Status: Non-Profit, Non-Professional
Paid Staff: 35

7777
RADIO CITY MUSIC HALL
1260 Avenue of the Americas
New York, NY 10020
Phone: 212-247-4777
e-mail: group.sales@msg.com
Web Site: www.radiocity.com
Mission: Since 1932, Radio City Hall has been synonymous with the very in entertainment.
Founded: 1933
Resident Groups: Radio City Rockettes

7778
RICHARD ROGERS THEATRE
226 W 46th Street
New York, NY 10036
Phone: 212-221-1211
Web Site: www.richardrodgerstheatre.com
Management:
  President: James Nederlander
Founded: 1965
Status: For-Profit, Professional

7779
SAINT CLEMENT'S CHURCH
423 W 46th Street
New York, NY 10036
Phone: 212-246-7277
Fax: 212-307-1442
Web Site: www.saintclement'snyc.org
Management:
  Incharge of Theater Operations: Rob Alberson
  President: Pamela J Nelson
Founded: 1860
Status: Non-Profit, Professional
Paid Staff: 10
Paid Artists: 200

7780
SAINT JAMES THEATER
246 W 44th Street
New York, NY 10036
Phone: 212-239-6200

7781
SHIVA THEATRE
Public Theater
425 Lafayette Street
New York, NY 10003
Phone: 212-539-8500
Fax: 212-539-8705
e-mail: marketing@publictheater.org
Web Site: www.publictheater.org
Officers:
  Chair: Arielle Tepper Madover
  Vice Chair: Pat Fili-Krushel
  Treasurer: Jim Steinberg

FACILITIES / New York

Secretary: Gail Merrifield Papp
Management:
  Artistic Director: Oskar Eustis
  Executive Director: Patrick Willingham
  General Manager: Andrea Nellis
Mission: The Public Theater is dedicated to achieving artistic excellence while developing an American theater that is accessible and relevant to all people through productions of challenging new plays, musicals and innovative stagings of the classics.
Founded: 1967
Specialized Field: Plays, Musicals, Shakespeare
Performs At: Newman Theater, Anspacher Theater, Martinson Hall, LuEsther Hall, Shiva Theater
Type of Stage: Black Box
Stage Dimensions: 58' X 40'
Seating Capacity: 99

7782
SHUBERT THEATRE
225 W 45th Street
New York, NY 10036
Phone: 212-239-6200
Seating Capacity: 1,513

7783
SOHO REP
401 Broadway
Suite 300
New York, NY 10013
Phone: 212-941-8632
Fax: 212-941-7148
e-mail: sohorep@sohorep.org
Web Site: www.sohorep.org
Officers:
  Chair: Jon Dembrow
Management:
  Artistic Director: Sarah Benson
  Executive Director: Cynthia Flowers
  Company Manager: Nathan Shreeve
  Production/Facilities Manager: Robbie Saenz de Viteri
Mission: Committed to nuturing innovative and umcompromising new york from first impulse through fully mounted production.
Founded: 1975
Status: Non-Profit, Professional
Season: March - August
Stage Dimensions: 25' x 35'
Seating Capacity: 99

7784
SULLIVAN STREET PLAYHOUSE
181 Sullivan Street
New York, NY 10012
Phone: 212-674-3838
Fax: 212-674-4706
Seating Capacity: 153

7785
SUPPER CLUB THEATER
240 W 47th Street
New York, NY 10036
Phone: 212-921-1940
Web Site: www.thesupperclub.com
Management:
  Operations Manager: Kevin Sharpe
  Executive Chef: Peter Garst
  Technical Director: Jeremy Schaffer
Status: For-Profit, Professional

7786
SURDNA FOUNDATION
330 Madison Avenue
30Th Floor
New York, NY 10017
Phone: 212-557-0010

7787
SYMPHONY SPACE
2537 Broadway
New York, NY 10025-6947
Phone: 212-864-5400
Fax: 212-864-4551
e-mail: boxoffice@symphonyspace.org
Web Site: www.symphonyspace.org
Officers:
  President and CEO: Cynthia Elliott
  Senior VP: Peg Wreen
Management:
  Director of Marketing: Johanna H. Thomsen
  Assistant Director of Marketing: Mary Shimkin
  SM of Interactive Mark & Media: Loelia Santos
Mission: 2 theatres, a recording studio, a studio room and a bar all available for use at Symphony Space
Founded: 1978
Specialized Field: Series and Festivals; Instrumental Music; Vocal Music; Theatre; Youth; Dance
Status: Non-Profit, Professional
Facility Category: Theater
Rental Contact: Jeff Goad

7788
TISCH CENTER FOR THE ARTS
92nd Street Y
1395 Lexington Avenue
New York, NY 10128
Phone: 212-415-5500
Fax: 212-415-5738
Web Site: www.92ndsty.org
Officers:
  President: Stuart J. Ellman
  Chairman of Boards: Thomas S. Kaplan
  VP: Laurence D. Belfer
  Treasurer/Chairman of the Finance C: Paul Levy
  Secretary: Marcia Eppler Colvin
Management:
  Director: Hanna Arie-Gaifman
Budget: $400,000-$1,000,000
Performs At: Theresa L. Kaufmann Concert Hall

7789
TOWN HALL CONCERT HALL
123 W 43rd Street
New York, NY 10036
Phone: 212-997-1003
Fax: 212-997-1929
e-mail: info@the-townhall-nyc.org
Web Site: www.the-townhall-nyc.org
Officers:
  President of the Board: Tom M. Wirtshafter
  VP of the Board: Alfred H. Horowitz
  Treasurer: Andrew T. Miltenberg
  President Emeritus: Marvin Leffler
Management:
  Executive Director: Lawrence C Zucker
  Marketing Director: E A Kafkalas
Mission: To offer affordable entertainment to all ages.
Utilizes: Dance Companies; Dancers; Educators; Filmmakers; Guest Instructors; Guest Musical Directors; Guest Soloists; Guild Activities; Multimedia; Playwrights; Soloists; Theatre Companies
Founded: 1921
Status: Non-Profit, Non-Professional
Paid Staff: 20
Annual Attendance: 500,000
Facility Category: Concert Hall
Type of Stage: Proscenium
Seating Capacity: 1,500
Year Built: 1921

7790
TRIBECA PERFORMING ARTS CENTER
199 Chambers Street
Suite S110c
New York, NY 10007
Phone: 212-220-1459
e-mail: info@tribecapac.org
Web Site: www.tribecapac.org
Officers:
  President of the Board: Richard Kennedy
  VP of the Board: Grace L Anderson-Spivey
  Secretary: Dr Sadie Bragg
  Treasurer: G Scott Anderson
Management:
  Executive Director: Linda Herring
  Operations Director: Carol Cleveland
  Marketing Director: Eli Abdallah
Mission: Strives to present a broad global perspective through the presentation of high quality artistic work in music, theatre, dance, film and visual arts. Supports emerging and established artists who create works that inspire creativity and imagination, celebrate diversity and change as well as instill emotional, social and political awareness.
Utilizes: Artists-in-Residence; Dance Companies; Soloists; Special Technical Talent; Theatre Companies
Founded: 1983
Specialized Field: Performing Arts
Paid Staff: 14
Paid Artists: 5
Budget: $600,000
Income Sources: Earned Income; Rental Income; Charitable Contributions
Affiliations: TCG; ART New York
Annual Attendance: 40,000
Facility Category: Multi-theatre Performing Arts
Type of Stage: Proscenium; Thrust
Seating Capacity: 913/262
Year Built: 1983
Rental Contact: Carol Cleveland

7791
UNION SQUARE THEATRE
126 2nd Avenue
New York, NY 10003
Phone: 212-505-0700
Fax: 212-477-7732

7792
UNIVERSITY SETTLEMENT
184 Eldridge Street
New York, NY 10002
Phone: 212-674-9120
Fax: 212-475-3278
e-mail: info@universitysettlement.org
Web Site: www.universitysettlement.org
Officers:
  Chairman: Alan P Winters
  Treasurer: Paul W Brandow
  Secretary: Nancy Drosd
Management:
  Executive Director: Michael H Zisser PhD
  Director of Development: Nicole P Sharpe
Mission: Serves people of all ages, from infants to senior citizens throughout the multi-racial and multi-ethnic community.
Founded: 1886

FACILITIES / New York

Status: Non-Profit, Professional

7793
VIRGINIA THEATER
245 W 52nd Street
New York, NY 10019
Phone: 212-840-8181

7794
WALTER KERR THEATRE
219 W 48th Street
New York, NY 10036

7795
WEB CONCERT HALL
2565 Broadway
Suite 316
New York, NY 10025
Phone: 212-280-8187
Fax: 212-280-8187
e-mail: webconcerthall@usa.com
Web Site: www.webconcerthall.com
Management:
    Producer/Director: Dr Yoon-Il Auh
    Music Director: Dr Mi-Jung Im
Budget: $10,000

7796
WESTBETH STUDIO THEATRE
111 W 17th Street
3rd Floor
New York, NY 10011
Phone: 212-691-2272
Fax: 212-924-7185
Web Site: www.westbeththeatre.com
Officers:
    President: Arnold Engelman
    Marketing Director: Neil Turton
    Social Media Director: Laura Vogel
Season: Year-Round
Type of Stage: Thrust and Arena
Seating Capacity: 60-300

7797
WESTBETH THEATRE CENTER
151 Bank Street
New York, NY 10014
Phone: 212-691-2272
Fax: 212-924-7185
Web Site: www.westbeththeatre.com

7798
WESTSIDE THEATRE
407 W 43rd Street
New York, NY 10036
Phone: 212-315-2302
Fax: 212-315-2307
Type of Stage: proscenium/ thrust
Stage Dimensions: 40'x 26' 6"/ 40'x 18'3"
Seating Capacity: 299/ 250
Organization Type: Theatre Complex; Performance Center; Commercial Rental Theatre

7799
WHITNEY MUSEUM OF ART THEATER
120 Park Avenue at 42 Street
New York, NY 10017
Phone: 212-878-2475
Fax: 212-907-5770

7800
WIEN STADIUM
Columbia University, Dodge Fitness Center
3030 Broadway, Mail Code 1902
New York, NY 10027
Phone: 212-854-2538
Fax: 212-854-2988
Management:
    Athletic Director: John Reeves
Seating Capacity: 3,405

7801
WINTER GARDEN THEATRE
1634 Broadway
New York, NY 10019
Phone: 212-944-3700

7802
HERSHELL CARROUSEL FACTORY MUSEUM
180 Thompson Street
PO Box 672
North Tonawanda, NY 14120
Phone: 716-693-1885
Fax: 716-743-9018
e-mail: info@carrouselmuseum.org
Web Site: www.carrouselmuseum.org
Founded: 1915
Status: For-Profit

7803
HELEN HAYES PERFORMING ARTS CENTER
PO Box 229
Nyack, NY 10960
Phone: 914-358-2847
Management:
    Artistic Director: Rod Kaats
    Managing Director: Joel Warren
Founded: 1996
Status: Nonprofit
Season: October - July
Type of Stage: Proscenium
Stage Dimensions: 60' x 28'
Seating Capacity: 600

7804
RALPH WILSON STADIUM
One Bills Drive
Orchard Park, NY 14127
Phone: 716-648-1800
Fax: 716-649-6446
Web Site: www.buffalobills.com
Management:
    President: Tom Donahoe
    VP Operations: William G Munson
    VP Marketing: Russ Brandon
    Director Stadium Operations: Joe Frandina
Founded: 1960
Status: For-Profit, Professional
Seating Capacity: 79,902

7805
PARAMOUNT CENTER FOR THE ARTS
1008 Brown Street
Peekskill, NY 10566
Phone: 914-739-2333
Fax: 914-736-9674
e-mail: info@paramountcenter.org
Web Site: www.paramountcenter.org
Management:
    President: Paul Rubin
    Executive Director: Jon Yanofsky
Mission: To provide quality programming in live perfromance and the visual arts. Serving the interest of the Hudson Valley and raising the level of cultural enrichment of all who enter this unique theater.
Founded: 1930
Status: Non-Profit
Seating Capacity: 1024
Year Built: 1930

7806
THEATRE THREE PRODUCTIONS SECOND STAGE
412 Main Street
PO Box 512
Port Jefferson, NY 11777
Phone: 631-928-9202
Fax: 631-928-9120
Facility Category: Theatre House
Rental Contact: Vivian Koutrakas

7807
HELEN M. HOSMER CONCERT HALL
SUNY Potsdam
Snell Music Theater
Potsdam, NY 13676
Phone: 315-267-2775
Fax: 315-267-2413
e-mail: crane@potsdam.edu
Web Site: www.potsdam.edu
Management:
    Dean: Michael Sitton, sittonmr@potsdam.edu

7808
BARDAVON 1869 OPERA HOUSE
35 Market Street
Poughkeepsie, NY 12601-9990
Phone: 845-473-5288
Fax: 845-473-4259
e-mail: slamarca@bardavon.org
Web Site: www.bardavon.org
Management:
    President: Patrick Moore
    Executive Director: Chris Silva
    Managing Director: Ameri Foust
    Managing Director Production: Stephen Lamarca
Utilizes: Actors; AEA Actors; Artists-in-Residence; Choreographers; Dance Companies; Dancers; Designers; Educators; Filmmakers; Five Seasonal Concerts; Grant Writers; Guest Accompanists; Guest Artists; Guest Choreographers; Guest Companies; Guest Composers; Guest Conductors; Guest Designers; Guest Directors; Guest Ensembles; Guest Instructors; Guest Lecturers; Guest Musical Directors; Guest Musicians; Guest Soloists; Guest Teachers; Guild Activities; Instructors; Local Artists; Lyricists; Multi Collaborations; Multimedia; New Productions; Organization Contracts; Original Music Scores; Performance Artists; Playwrights; Resident Professionals; Sign Language Translators; Singers; Soloists; Student Interns; Special Technical Talent; Theatre Companies
Founded: 1979
Status: Non-Profit, Professional
Paid Staff: 17
Volunteer Staff: 80
Paid Artists: 270
Seating Capacity: 944
Year Built: 1869

7809
MID-HUDSON CIVIC CENTER
14 Civic Center Plaza
Poughkeepsie, NY 12601

FACILITIES / New York

Phone: 845-454-9800
Fax: 845-454-5877
Web Site: www.midhudsonciviccenter.com
Management:
   President: John S Morgan
   Executive Director: Amy Sloan
   Controller: Chris Sasser
Status: Non-Profit, Professional
Paid Staff: 100

7810
PURCHASE COLLEGE PERFORMING ARTS CENTER
735 Anderson Hill Road
Purchase, NY 10577-0140
Mailing Address: MPO Box 140
Phone: 914-251-6222
Fax: 914-251-6171
e-mail: brian.mccurdy@purchase.edu
Web Site: www.artscenter.org
Officers:
   Executive Director: Wiley Hausam
Management:
   General Manager: Harry McFadden
   Director Of Operations: Dan Sedgwick

7811
BLUE CROSS ARENA
1 War Memorial Square
Rochester, NY 14614
Phone: 585-758-5330
Fax: 716-758-5327
Web Site: www.bluecrossarena.com
Management:
   General Manager: Jeffrey E Calkins

7812
EASTMAN THEATRE
University of Rochester
26 Gibbs Street
Rochester, NY 14604
Phone: 585-274-1110
Fax: 585-274-1073
e-mail: concerts@esm.rochester.edu
Web Site: www.rochester.edu/eastman
Management:
   Director Concert Operations: Andrew Green
   Assistant Director: Julia Ng
   Professor of Violin: Agostini Federico
   Associate Professor Musicology: Michael Alan
   English Professor: Baldo Johnathan
Founded: 1921
Seating Capacity: 3,094

7813
FRONTIER FIELD
333 N Plymounth Avenue
Rochester, NY 14608
Phone: 716-262-2009
Fax: 716-232-3453
Management:
   Director: Jim Lebeau
Seating Capacity: 10,500

7814
NAZARETH ARTS CENTER
Nazareth College
4245 East Avenue
Rochester, NY 14618
Phone: 716-586-2483

7815
PYRAMID ARTS CENTER
Cultural Quarter
Palmyra Square South
Rochester, NY 14603
Phone: 192-544-2345
Fax: 912-544-2888
e-mail: pyramid@warrington.gov.uk
Web Site: www.pyramidparrhall.com
Management:
   Administration Manager: Richard Fleming
   Event Coordinator: Vicky Turner
   Drama Development Officer: Owen Hutchings
   Music Development Officer: Stuart Smith

7816
STRONG THEATRE
University of Rochester-River Campus
Rochester, NY 14627
Phone: 716-275-2330
Fax: 716-273-5306

7817
CAPITOL THEATRE
220 W Dominick Street
Rome, NY 13440
Phone: 315-337-6277
Fax: 315-337-6277
Management:
   President: Eileen Prnoeis
   Executive Director: Art Pierce
Founded: 1928
Status: Non-Profit, Professional
Paid Staff: 4
Paid Artists: 150

7818
RYE ARTS CENTER
51 Milton Road
Rye, NY 10580
Phone: 914-967-0700
Fax: 914-967-4495
e-mail: ryearts@bestweb.net
Web Site: www.ryeartscenter.org
Management:
   President: Marilyn Gasparini
   Executive Director: Peggy Hill
Founded: 1960
Status: Non-Profit, Non-Professional
Paid Staff: 6

7819
SARATOGA PERFORMING ARTS CENTER
Saratoga Spa State Park
Hall of Springs
Saratoga Springs, NY 12866
Phone: 518-584-9330
Fax: 518-584-0809
Web Site: www.spac.org
Officers:
   Vice Chairman: Wallace A Graham
   Chairman: Charles E Matter
   President: Herbert A Chesbrough
   Secretary/Treasurer: Edward P. Swyer
Mission: To host performing arts events.
Utilizes: Singers
Founded: 1966
Specialized Field: Series & Festivals; Dance; Vocal Music; Instrumental Music; Theatre; Opera
Status: Non-Profit, Professional
Paid Staff: 13
Budget: $11 million
Income Sources: International Association of Auditorium Managers; New York Performing Arts Association; Membership ticket sales
Affiliations: Summer home of New York City Ballet, Philadelphia Orchestra and Saratoga Chamber Music Festival
Annual Attendance: 350,000
Facility Category: Ampitheatre
Type of Stage: Proscenium
Stage Dimensions: 80 W x 60 D
Seating Capacity: 5100
Year Built: 1966
Organization Type: Performing; Educational; Sponsoring

7820
PROCTOR'S THEATRE
432 State Street
Schenectady, NY 12305
Phone: 518-382-3884
Fax: 518-346-2468
Web Site: www.proctors.org
Officers:
   President: Ronald Backer
   Guild President: Patricia Barney
   Chairman of Power Technology: Lionel Barthold
   Executive VP: Jeffery Lawrence
   President: Morris Massry
Management:
   CEO: Philip Morris
   Director Annual Programs: Dan Hanifin
   Finance Director: Kathleen Cetnar
   Production Manager: Dan Sheehan
Founded: 1926

7821
SCHENECTADY CIVIC PLAYERS THEATER
12 S Church Street
Schenectady, NY 12305
Phone: 518-382-2081

7822
SHEA THEATRE
Suffolk County Community College
533 College Road
Selden, NY 11784
Phone: 631-451-4163
Fax: 631-451-4601
Web Site: www.sunysuffolk.edu
Management:
   Theatre Director: Charles Wittreich
Status: Non-Profit, Non-Professional

7823
LONG ISLAND UNIVERSITY: FINE ARTS THEATRE
Southampton Campus
Montauk Highway
Southampton, NY 11968
Phone: 516-283-4000

7824
REILLY CENTER ARENA
St Bonaventure University
PO Box BZ
St. Bonaventure, NY 14778
Phone: 716-375-2514
Fax: 716-375-3583
Web Site: www.fbu.edu
Management:
   President: Margaret Carney
   Director: Steve Pleasec

FACILITIES / New York

Founded: 1960
Status: Non-Profit, Professional
Seating Capacity: 6,500

7825
CENTER FOR THE ARTS RECITAL HALL
College of Staten Island
2800 Victory Boulevard
Staten Island, NY 10314
Mailing Address: Building 1P-116
Phone: 718-982-2787
Fax: 718-982-2251
e-mail: Michele.Walsh@csi.cuny.edu
Web Site: www.csi.cuny.edu/arts
Officers:
   President: Marlene Springer
   Director: John Jankowaski
Management:
   Managing/Artistic Director: Lisa Reilly
   Technician: David Loncle
   Marketing Manager: Michele Walsh
   Box Office Manager: Annie Varghese
   Production Manager: Christina Werkmeister
Mission: An intimate room seating 150, The Recital Hall is the Center's space for chamber music, solo recitals, and lectures.
Founded: 1996
Paid Staff: 10
Budget: $850,000
Income Sources: Ticket sales; other earned revenue; grants and contributions
Affiliations: Association of Performing Arts Presenters, onsortium of Eastern Regional Theatres
Annual Attendance: 100,000
Facility Category: Performing Arts Center
Type of Stage: Theatre
Seating Capacity: 150
Year Built: 1996
Cost: $35 million
Resident Groups: Staten Island Symphony; Staten Island Ballet, NeverLand Theatre Company; Enrichment Through the Arts

7826
CENTER FOR THE ARTS LECTURE HALL
College of Staten Island
2800 Victory Boulevard
Staten Island, NY 10314
Mailing Address: Building 1P-116
Phone: 718-982-2787
Fax: 718-982-2251
e-mail: Michele.Walsh@csi.cuny.edu
Web Site: www.csi.cuny.edu/arts
Officers:
   President: Marlene Springer
   Director: John Jankowaski
Management:
   Managing/Artistic Director: Lisa Reilly
   Technician: David Loncle
   Marketing Manager: Michele Walsh
   Box Office Manager: Annie Varghese
   Production Manager: Christina Werkmeister
Mission: An intimate room seating 150 and equipped with the latest audio- visual equipment, The Lecture Hall is the Center's venue for academic programs, and is also a frequent site of public hearings.
Founded: 1996
Paid Staff: 10
Budget: $850,000
Income Sources: Ticket sales; other earned revenue; grants and contributions
Affiliations: Association of Performing Arts Presenters, onsortium of Eastern Regional Theatres
Annual Attendance: 100,000
Facility Category: Performing Arts Center
Type of Stage: Lecture Hall
Seating Capacity: 150
Year Built: 1996
Cost: $35 million
Resident Groups: Staten Island Symphony; Staten Island Ballet, NeverLand Theatre Company; Enrichment Through the Arts

7827
SNUG HARBOR CULTURAL CENTER
1000 Richmond Terrace
Staten Island, NY 10301-1116
Phone: 718-448-2500
Fax: 718-442-8534
Management:
   Presentations Director: Ellen Kodadek
   Presentations Associate: Elizabeth LaCause
Budget: $60,000-$150,000
Performs At: Veterans Memorial Hall; Performance Meadow; Cabaret

7828
VETERANS MEMORIAL HALL
1000 Richmond Terrace
Staten Island, NY 10301
Phone: 718-448-2500
Fax: 718-442-8534

7829
SPORTS COMPLEX
Stony Brook University
Stony Brook, NY 11794-3500
Phone: 516-632-7174
Fax: 516-632-7122
Management:
   Managing Director: Kay Don
Seating Capacity: 5,000

7830
STALLER CENTER FOR THE ARTS
SUNY Stony Brook
Staller Center For The Arts
Room 2030A
Stony Brook, NY 11794
Phone: 631-632-7235
Fax: 631-632-7354
e-mail: webmaster@stallercenter.com
Web Site: www.staller.sunysb.edu
Mission: venue for theatre, music, dance, jazz, comedy, family and MET live. Pleases contact the webmaster for questions or to contact staff: webmaster@stallercenter.com

7831
ALLIANCE BANK STADIUM
One Tex Simone Drive
Syracuse, NY 13208
Phone: 315-474-7833
Fax: 315-474-2658
e-mail: baseball@syracusechiefs.com
Web Site: www.syracusechiefs.com
Officers:
   President: Tex Simone
Management:
   Director Group Sales: Victor Gallucci
   General Manager: John Simone
Founded: 1961
Specialized Field: Professional Baseball Club
Status: For-Profit, Professional
Paid Staff: 12
Seating Capacity: 11,071

7832
CARRIER DOME
Syracuse University
900 Irving Avenue
Syracuse, NY 13244
Phone: 315-443-4634
Fax: 315-443-5203
Web Site: www.carrierdome.syr.edu
Officers:
   General Manager: Jason Smorol
   Assistant GM: Jason Horbal
   Corporate Sales Manager: Julie Cardibali
   Group Sales Director: Brandon Massey
   Multimedia Production Director: Anthony Cianchetta
Management:
   Managing Director: Patrick M Campbell
Seating Capacity: 50,000 Football, 32,000 Basketball
Year Built: 1980

7833
CIVIC CENTER OF ONONDAGA COUNTY CROUSE-HIND HALL
411 Montgomery Street
Syracuse, NY 13202
Phone: 315-435-2121
Fax: 315-435-8099

7834
CIVIC CENTER OF ONONDAGA COUNTY CARRIER THEATRE
411 Montgomery Street
Syracuse, NY 13202
Phone: 315-435-2121
Fax: 315-435-8099

7835
GOLDSTEIN AUDITORIUM
Syracuse University
303 University Place
Syracuse, NY 13244
Phone: 315-443-2044
Fax: 315-443-5458
Web Site: www.syracuse.edu/ets/goldstein/html
Management:
   Talent Buyer: Alison Weinflash
Seating Capacity: 1,500

7836
MULROY CIVIC CENTER
800 S State Street
Syracuse, NY 13202
Phone: 315-435-8000
Fax: 315-435-8099
e-mail: C_Tucciarone@oncenter.org
Web Site: www.oncentercomplex.com
Officers:
   President/CEO: Jerry Gallagher
Management:
   Director Of Sales/Marketing: Christine Tucciarone
   Account Executive: Mike Spaulding
Founded: 1976
Specialized Field: Onondage County / Central New York
Status: Non-Profit, Professional
Paid Staff: 100
Volunteer Staff: 300
Paid Artists: 200
Non-paid Artists: 250

FACILITIES / New York

7837
SYRACUSE AREA LANDMARK THEATRE
362 S Salina Street
Syracuse, NY 13202
Phone: 315-475-7979
Fax: 315-473-7993
e-mail: denise@landmarktheatre.org
Web Site: www.landmarktheatre.org
Officers:
   President: James Albanese
   VP: Paula Deckman
   VP: Jamie Williams
   VP & Foundation: David Muolo
Management:
   Patron Service Assistant: Marguerite Beebe
   Executive Director: Thomas T. Kazmierczak III
   Facility Manager: Gregg Discenza
   Patron Service Manager: Nick Pallotta
Status: Non-Profit, Professional
Paid Staff: 12

7838
KNICKERBACKER RECREATIONAL FACILITY AND ICE ARENA
191 103rd Street
Troy, NY 12180
Phone: 518-235-7761
Fax: 518-235-0219
Web Site: www.troynet.net
Officers:
   President: Bruce Arnold
   VP: Steven Angle
Management:
   Facility Manager: Irma A Magee
Mission: To provide the public with recreation and special events in a healthy atmosphere.
Founded: 1990
Specialized Field: Figure Skating; Speed Skaters; Hockey
Status: Non-Profit, Professional
Paid Staff: 10
Income Sources: City of Troy
Season: Year Round
Affiliations: City of Troy
Facility Category: Ice arena, baseball field, softball fields
Rental Contact: Facility Manager Irma Magee
Organization Type: Ice arena, baseball and softball fields, tennis courts, pool, basketball courts, 400 meter oval, out-door rink, street hockey suface, sand volleyball courts, children's playground
Resident Groups: Predominantly Figure Skaters

7839
RENSSELAER POLYTECHNIC INSTITUTE: HOUSTON FIELD HOUSE
1900 Peoples Avenue
Troy, NY 12180
Phone: 518-276-6262
Fax: 518-276-2833
Management:
   President: Sherly Jackson
   Manager: Norris A Pearson
   Box Office Manager: Dorothy Conroy
   Department Specialist: Kim M Forette
Status: Non-Profit, Professional
Seating Capacity: 6,900

7840
RENSSELAER NEWMAN FOUNDATION CHAPEL AND CULTURAL CENTER
2125 Burden Avenue
Troy, NY 12180
Phone: 518-274-7793
Fax: 518-274-5945
Management:
   President: Eric Smith
Founded: 1968
Status: Non-Profit, Professional
Paid Staff: 5

7841
TROY SAVINGS BANK MUSIC HALL
7 State Street
Troy, NY 12180-3920
Phone: 518-273-0038
Fax: 518-273-1564
e-mail: info@troymusichall.org
Web Site: www.troymusichall.org
Management:
   Executive Director: Laura Kratt
Founded: 1875
Status: Non-Profit, Professional
Paid Staff: 6

7842
NASSAU VETERANS MEMORIAL COLISEUM
1255 Hempstead Turnpike
Uniondale, NY 11553
Phone: 516-794-9303
Fax: 516-794-9389
Web Site: www.nassaucoliseum.com
Management:
   General Manager: Scott Mullen
Founded: 1972
Seating Capacity: 16,285

7843
STANLEY PERFORMING ARTS CENTER
259 Genesee Street
Utica, NY 13501
Phone: 315-724-5919
Fax: 315-724-3854
Web Site: www.cnyarts.com
Management:
   Owner: Ronald Puerte
   Manager: John Fausaut
Founded: 1928
Status: Non-Profit, Non-Professional

7844
UTICA MEMORIAL AUDITORIUM
400 Oriskany Street W
Utica, NY 13502
Phone: 315-738-0164
Fax: 315-738-9597
e-mail: uticaaud@aol.com
Management:
   Executive Director: Will Berkeiser
   Director Operations: Frank Labella
   Arena Administrator: Betsy Woish
Utilizes: Dance Companies; Multimedia; Original Music Scores; Sign Language Translators; Soloists
Founded: 1996
Status: Non-Profit,Non-Professional
Paid Staff: 90
Facility Category: Arena
Type of Stage: Wenger
Stage Dimensions: 56x44
Year Built: 1959
Rental Contact: Will Berkheiser/Gen.Mgr.

7845
EUGENE O'NEILL THEATER CENTER
305 Great Neck Road
Waterford, NY 06385
Phone: 860-443-5378
Fax: 860-443-9653
e-mail: info@theoneill.org
Web Site: www.theoneill.org
Management:
   Executive Director: Amy Sullivan
   Artistic Director: Richard Kuranda
Founded: 1964
Status: Non-Profit,Professional

7846
JEFFERSON COMMUNITY COLLEGE MCVEAN STUDENT CENTER
Jefferson Community College
Watertown, NY 13601
Phone: 315-786-2289
Fax: 315-788-0716
Web Site: www.sunyjefferson.edu
Management:
   President: Joseph Olson
   Asst Director Student Development: Mary Kinne
Status: Non-Profit, Non-Professional
Paid Staff: 1

7847
LUMIERE BALLET
64 East Nancy Street
West Babylon, NY 11704
Phone: 631-643-6549
Web Site: www.lumiereballet.net
Management:
   Founder/Artistic Director: Svetlana Caton-Noble
   Co-Founder/Artistic Director: Ventzislav Petrov
Mission: To foster excellence in present and future generations of talented young people and promote the appreciation for classical music and dance. The organization has initiated a fully graded training program and a performing youth ballet company which has become important and respected in the dance community.

7848
US MILITARY ACADEMY MICHIE STADIUM
Odia Building 639
West Point, NY 10996
Phone: 914-938-3002
Fax: 914-938-2210
Web Site: www.usma.com
Officers:
   President: Don Heitmeier
Management:
   Director: Ben Russell
Seating Capacity: 41,000

7849
KLEINERT/JAMES ARTS CENTER
34 Tinker Street
Woodstock, NY 12498
Phone: 845-679-2079
Fax: 845-679-4529
e-mail: info@woodstockguild.org
Web Site: www.woodstockguild.org
Officers:
   Secretary: Susan Auchincloss
   VP: Nancy Azara
   President: Byron Bell
   Chairman: Henry T. Ford
   Executive VP: Kerrie Buitrago
Management:
   Counsel: Joseph W. Belluck
   Executive Director: Matthew Leaycraft
   Artist Educator: Mark Kanter

Mission: The Woodstock Byrdcliffe Guild (WBG) provides the opportunity for people to discover and develop their creative and artistic spirit. We are dedicated to the preservation of the Byrdcliffe Arts Colony as an arts haven, natural enviornment, and historic site. Our goal is to present and foster the creative arts for the enjoyment and education of the people of Woodstock, the region, and beyond.
Founded: 1939
Status: Non-Profit, Professional
Paid Staff: 4
Budget: $25,000
Income Sources: Concerts; Rentals
Annual Attendance: 1,500
Facility Category: Indoor
Seating Capacity: 135
Year Built: 1957
Year Remodeled: 1994
Rental Contact: Carla Smith

7850
MAVERICK CONCERT HALL
PO Box 102
Woodstock, NY 12498
Phone: 845-679-8217

7851
HUDSON RIVER MUSEUM
511 Warburton Avenue
Yonkers, NY 10701-1899
Phone: 914-963-4550
Fax: 914-963-8558
Web Site: www.hrm.org
Management:
  Managing Director: Dan Gillespe
  President: Michael Botwinick
Founded: 1919
Status: Non-Profit, Professional
Paid Staff: 40
Volunteer Staff: 100
Paid Artists: 200
Season: Seasonal

North Carolina

7852
STANLY COUNTY AGRI-CIVIC CENTER
26032-B Newt Road
Albemarle, NC 28001
Phone: 704-986-3666
Fax: 704-986-3817
Web Site: www.stanlyciviccenter.com
Management:
  Director: Edmund Roush
  Secretary: Lee Thompson
Utilizes: Actors; Dance Companies; Dancers; Educators; Grant Writers; Guest Soloists; Guest Writers; Guild Activities; Instructors; Local Artists; Multimedia; Sign Language Translators; Soloists; Special Technical Talent; Theatre Companies
Founded: 1988
Specialized Field: Music; Theater; Dance; Meetings
Status: Non-Profit, Non-Professional
Paid Staff: 3
Performs At: Performing Arts Theatre
Facility Category: Performing Arts Theatre
Type of Stage: Pine
Stage Dimensions: 53 x 38
Seating Capacity: 1200
Year Built: 1988
Rental Contact: Tim Harris

7853
ASHEVILLE CIVIC CENTER
87 Haywood Street
Asheville, NC 28801
Phone: 828-259-5544
Fax: 828-259-5777
Web Site: www.ashvilleciviccenter.com
Officers:
  GM: Chris Corl
  Operation Manager: Dan Dover
  Box Office Manager: Nobert Irvine
  Marketing Coordinator: Jared Bullock
Management:
  Director: David Pisha
Status: For-Profit, Professional

7854
DIANA WORTHAM THEATRE AT PACK PLACE
2 S. Pack Place
Asheville, NC 28801
Phone: 828-257-4530
Fax: 828-251-5652
e-mail: jellis@dwtheatre.com
Web Site: www.dwtheatre.com
Management:
  Managing Director: John Ellis, jellis@dwtheatre.com
  Operations Manager: Tiffany Santiago, tiffany@dwtheatre.com
Mission: Individuals and groups can rent this venue for performances, meetings, rehearsals, workshops and presentations. riority is given to local groups, main stage users and first time, casual users
Seating Capacity: 500

7855
HAYES AUDITORIUM
Lees McRae College
Main Street
Banner Elk, NC 28604
Phone: 828-898-5241
Fax: 704-898-8814
e-mail: joslinp@lmc.edu
Web Site: www.lmc.edu
Officers:
  President: Dr Barry M Buxton
  VP Advancement: Caroline Hart
Management:
  Artistic Director: Dr Janet Barton Speer
  Assistant to Summer Theatre: Pam Wilder Joslin
  Executive Director, Summer Theatre: Dr Kacy Crabtree
Founded: 1884
Status: Non-Profit, Non-Professional
Paid Staff: 13
Paid Artists: 15
Seating Capacity: 700

7856
FARTHING AUDITORIUM
Appalachian State University
Rivers Street
Boone, NC 28608
Phone: 704-262-6372
Fax: 704-262-2848

7857
KIDD BREWER STADIUM
Appalachian State University
Department of Athletics
Boone, NC 28608
Phone: 828-262-4010
Fax: 828-651-2556
Management:
  Director: Rachel Laney
Seating Capacity: 18,000

7858
THE HOLMES CENTER
Appalachian State University
111 Rivers Street
Boone, NC 28608
Mailing Address: ASU Box 32141
Phone: 828-262-7890
Fax: 828-262-7894
e-mail: parkerjc@appstate.edu
Web Site: www.theholmescenter.com
Management:
  Director: Eddie Crawford
  Assistant Director: Jason Parker
Founded: 1968
Seating Capacity: 8,325

7859
PORTER CENTER FOR PERFORMING ARTS
Brevard College
1 Brevard College Drive
Brevard, NC 28712
Phone: 828-884-8330
Fax: 828-883-4185
Web Site: www.brevard.edu/portercenter
Management:
  Managing Director: Steve MacQueen
Budget: $20,000-$35,000
Performs At: The Concert Hall; Porter Center for Performing Arts

7860
STRAUS AUDITORIUM
Brevard Music Center
Probart Street
Brevard, NC 28712
Mailing Address: PO Box 592
Phone: 704-884-2011
Fax: 704-884-2036

7861
WHITTINGTON-PFOHL AUDITORIUM
Brevard Music Center
1000 Probart Street
Brevard, NC 28712
Mailing Address: PO Box 312
Phone: 828-862-2100
Fax: 828-884-2036
Toll-free: 888-848-82
e-mail: bmc@brevardmusic.org
Web Site: www.brevardmusic.org
Management:
  President: John Candler
  Artistic Director: David Effron
Founded: 1936
Status: Non-Profit
Paid Staff: 100

7862
J. CLYDE TURNER AUDITORIUM
PO Box 567
414 Judge Taylor Road
Buies Creek, NC 27506
Mailing Address: PO Box 95
Phone: 910-893-1554
Fax: 910-893-1534
Toll-free: 800-344-11
Web Site: www.campbell.edu

FACILITIES / North Carolina

Management:
   Director Student Activities: Tracie Renfrow
Seating Capacity: 1,066

7863
CAMP THEATER
Building 19
Camp Lejeune, NC 28542
Phone: 919-451-1759
Fax: 919-451-1879

7864
TOWN OF CARY CULTURAL ARTS DIVISION
PO Box 8005
Cary, NC 27512-8005
Phone: 919-469-4061
Fax: 919-469-4344
Web Site: www.townofcary.org
Management:
   Artistic Director: Deb Royals
   Cultural Arts Supervisor: Lyman Collins
Mission: Present high quality cultural arts events musical and theatrical in the Town of Cary.
Founded: 1994
Specialized Field: Music; Classical; Jazz; Pop
Status: For-Profit, Non-Professional
Paid Staff: 6

7865
DEANE E SMITH CENTER
University of North Carolina-Chapel Hill
Chapel Hill, NC 27515
Phone: 919-962-7777
Fax: 919-966-3173
Web Site: www.smithcenter.unc.edu
Management:
   Managing Director: Angelyn S Bitting

7866
KENAN STADIUM
University of North Carolina-Chapel Hill
Chapel Hill, NC 27515-2126
Mailing Address: PO Box 2126
Phone: 919-966-2575
Fax: 919-962-0393
Web Site: www.tarheelblue.com
Officers:
   Chairperson: W.Lowry Caudill
   Vice Chair: Alston Gardner
   Secretary: Sallie Shupping
Management:
   Athletic Director Game Operations: William Scroggs
   Associate Athletic Director: Bob Savod
   Ticket Manager: Darren Lucas
Specialized Field: Home of University of North Carolina football (NCAA)
Seating Capacity: 60,000
Year Built: 1927
Year Remodeled: 1997

7867
AFRO-AMERICAN CULTURAL CENTER
401 N Myers Street
Charlotte, NC 28202-2910
Phone: 704-374-1565
Fax: 704-374-9273
Web Site: www.aacc-charlotte.org
Officers:
   President: Michael Vaughn
   VP: Angeline Clinton
   Second VP: Dee Merrill
   Treasurer: Chris Carter
Management:
   Executive Director: Beverley Cureton
   Director Operations: Lisa Rowland
   Direct External Affairs: Sherry Walter
   Director Development: Alecia Bracy
Mission: To preserve, promote and present African-American art, history and culture.
Founded: 1976
Specialized Field: Multi-disciplinary
Status: Non-Profit, Professional
Paid Staff: 7
Paid Artists: 200
Budget: $35,000-$60,000

7868
BANK OF AMERICA STADIUM
800 S Mint Street
Charlotte, NC 28202
Phone: 704-358-7407
Fax: 704-358-7619
e-mail: pauls@panthers.nfl.com
Web Site: www.panthers.com
Management:
   President: Mark Richardson
   Executive Director: Jackie Jeffries
   Director Tickets: Phil Youtsey
Founded: 1995
Specialized Field: Home of the Carolina Panthers (NFL)
Status: For-Profit, Professional
Paid Staff: 200
Seating Capacity: 73,250
Year Built: 1996

7869
BELK THEATER
PO Box 37322
Charlotte, NC 28237
Phone: 704-333-4686
Fax: 704-376-2289
Web Site: www.blumenthalcenter.org
Officers:
   President: Tom Gabbart
   Marketing: Wendy Oglesby
   Education: Ralph Beck
   Communication: Elise Esasky
   Promotion: Lauren Platts
Status: Non-Profit, Professional

7870
CHARLOTTE COLISEUM
100 Paul Buck Boulevard
Charlotte, NC 28217
Phone: 704-357-4701
Fax: 704-357-4757
Web Site: www.charlottecoliseum.com
Management:
   Managing Director: Michael E Crum
   Director Marketing: Ereka Crawford
Mission: Home of the Charlotte Hornets and the Charlotte Sting. Also hosts family shows, motorsports and concert events.
Founded: 1959
Status: Professional
Seating Capacity: 23,698

7871
CRICKET ARENA
2700 E Independent Boulevard
Charlotte, NC 28205
Phone: 704-372-3600
Fax: 704-335-3118
Web Site: www.cricketarenacharlotte.com
Management:
   Managing Director: Michael E Crum
   Director Marketing: Eric Scott
   Director Marketing: Ereka Cranford
Founded: 1955
Status: For-Profit, Non-Professional
Paid Staff: 25

7872
GRADY COLE CENTER
310 North Kings Drive
Charlotte, NC 28204
Phone: 704-336-8979
Fax: 704-336-3876
Web Site: www.parkandrec.com
Management:
   Facility Manager: Greg Clemmer
   Customer Service: Shirley Floyd
Seating Capacity: 3,000

7873
HALTON ARENA
UNC Charlotte
9201 University City Boulevard
Charlotte, NC 28223
Phone: 704-687-4805
Fax: 704-687-4803
e-mail: ndsimmon@uncc.edu
Web Site: www.haltonarena.com
Management:
   Event Director: Nina Simmons
   Associate Director: Forrest Shook
   Associate Director: Trend Barnes
   Building Manager: Melissa Barnett
Seating Capacity: 10,000

7874
NORTH CAROLINA BLUMENTHAL PERFORMING ARTS CENTER
PO Box 37322
Charlotte, NC 28237
Phone: 704-379-1279
Fax: 704-444-2111
Web Site: www.performingartsctr.org
Officers:
   President: Judith Allen
Management:
   President: Tom Gabbard

7875
OVENS AUDITORIUM
2700 E Independence Boulevard
Charlotte, NC 28205
Phone: 704-372-3600
Fax: 704-372-3620

7876
SPIRIT SQUARE CENTER FOR THE ARTS
345 N College Street
Charlotte, NC 28202
Phone: 704-333-4686
Fax: 704-377-9808

7877
SUMMER THEATRE
Central Piedmont Community College
Box 55009
Charlotte, NC 28235-5009
Phone: 704-330-2722
Web Site: www.cpcc.edu
Management:
   President: Tony Ziess
Status: For-Profit, Professional

FACILITIES / North Carolina

7878
VERIZON WIRELESS AMPHITHEATRE
707 Pavilion Boulevard
Charlotte, NC 28262
Phone: 704-549-1292
Fax: 704-549-1043
Web Site: www.blockconcerts.com
Management:
    Executive Director: Della Rowser
    Director Sponsorships: Shiela Fletcher
Seating Capacity: 18,500

7879
RAMSEY REGIONAL ACTIVITY CENTER
Western Carolina University
Cullowhee, NC 28723
Phone: 828-227-7677
Fax: 828-227-7680
Toll-free: 866-928-3378
Web Site: www.ramsey.wcu.edu
Management:
    Director: Bill Clarke
    Operations Manager: Jim Irvin
    Ticket Office Manager: Laura Sellers
Founded: 1986
Status: Non-Profit, Professional
Paid Staff: 10
Budget: $35,000-$60,000
Annual Attendance: 100,000
Facility Category: Multipurpose
Seating Capacity: 8000
Year Built: 1986

7880
DURHAM PERFORMING ARTS CENTER
123 Vivian St
Durham, NC 27701
Phone: 919-688-3722
e-mail: email through website
Web Site: www.dpacnc.com
Management:
    General Manager: Bob Klaus
    Technical Director: Josh Anderson
    Director Of Operations: Adrienne Quick-Wright
Mission: Broadway, concerts, family, comedy— has everything for everyone
Seating Capacity: 2700

7881
ST. JOSEPH'S HISTORIC FOUNDATION/HAYTI HERITAGE CENTER
804 Old Fayetteville Street
Durham, NC 27701
Mailing Address: PO Box 543, Durham, NC. 27702
Phone: 919-683-1709
Fax: 919-682-5869
e-mail: hayti@hayti.org
Web Site: www.hayti.org
Officers:
    President/CEO: Dianne Pledger
    Programs Director: Darrell Stover
Utilizes: Actors; Artists-in-Residence; Choreographers; Collaborating Artists; Collaborations; Dance Companies; Dancers; Educators; Filmmakers; Fine Artists; Guest Instructors; Guest Musical Directors; Guest Musicians; Guest Teachers; Instructors; Local Artists; Lyricists; Multi Collaborations; Multimedia; Original Music Scores; Performance Artists; Playwrights; Sign Language Translators; Soloists; Special Technical Talent; Theatre Companies; Touring Companies
Founded: 1975
Status: Non-Profit, Professional
Paid Staff: 10
Budget: $1.2 million
Seating Capacity: 450

7882
COA COMMUNITY AUDITORIUM
College of the Albemarle
1208 North Road Street
Elizabeth City, NC 27909
Phone: 252-335-9050
Fax: 252-337-6622
Web Site: www.albemarle.edu
Officers:
    Chair: J.Fletcher Willey
    Vice Chair: Marion Haris Jr.
    President: Dr. Kandi W. Deitemeyer
    COO: Joseph Turner
    CFO: Susan Gentry
Management:
    GM: Sam Johnson
    Superintendent: Sandra Boyce
Seating Capacity: 1,000

7883
CUMBERLAND COUNTY COLISEUM COMPLEX
1960 Coliseum Drive
PO Drawer 64549
Fayetteville, NC 28306
Phone: 910-323-5088
Fax: 919-323-0489
Web Site: www.crowncoliseum.com
Management:
    President: Rick Reno
    Executive Director: Max Peers
Founded: 1997
Status: For-Profit, Non-Professional
Paid Staff: 20
Seating Capacity: 13,500
Year Built: 1997

7884
AYCOCK AUDITORIUM
University of North Carolina at Greensboro
Greensboro, NC 27412
Phone: 919-334-5800
Fax: 919-334-3008

7885
CAROLINA THEATRE
310 S Greene Street
Greensboro, NC 27401
Phone: 336-333-2600
Fax: 336-333-2604
e-mail: comments@carolinatheatre.com
Web Site: www.carolinatheatre.com
Officers:
    Chairperson: Eleanor Schaffner
    Vice Chair: David Ball
    Treasurer: Sandy Shelton
    Secretary: Jim Roskelly
    Honorary Chair: Elizabeth W. Cone
Management:
    Executive Director: Brian Gray
    Marketing Director: Meagan Kopp
Founded: 1927
Annual Attendance: 83,000+
Seating Capacity: 1075
Year Built: 1927

7886
GREENSBORO COLISEUM: WAR MEMORIAL AUDITORIUM
1921 W Lee Street
PO Box 5447
Greensboro, NC 27403
Phone: 336-373-7400
Fax: 336-373-2170
Web Site: www.greensborocoliseum.com
Management:
    Deputy Director: Scott Johnson
    Booking Assistant: Robin Crews
    Production Manager: Scott Polkinhorn
Founded: 1959
Income Sources: City
Performs At: Multi-Purpose
Seating Capacity: 23,500
Year Built: 1959
Year Remodeled: 1994

7887
HENDRIX THEATRE
Mendenhall Student Center
Greenville, NC 27858
Phone: 919-757-4702
Fax: 919-757-4778

7888
WRIGHT AUDITORIUM
E Carolina University
Campus Circle
Greenville, NC 27858
Phone: 919-757-6269
Fax: 919-757-4778

7889
LENOIR - RHYNE COLLEGE FACILITIES
7th Avenue and 8th NE
Hickory, NC 28601
Phone: 828-328-7254
Fax: 828-328-7329
Web Site: www.irc.edu
Management:
    Director: Caroline Cauthen
    Athletic Facilities Coordinator: Joe Fisher
Seating Capacity: 3,000

7890
HIGH POINT THEATRE AND EXHIBITION CENTER
220 E Commerce Street
High Point, NC 27260
Phone: 336-883-3401
Fax: 336-883-3533
Web Site: www.ci.high-point.nc.us
Management:
    Executive Director: Louisa Hart
Utilizes: Actors; Collaborations; Dance Companies; Guest Instructors; Instructors; Local Artists; Original Music Scores; Special Technical Talent; Theatre Companies
Annual Attendance: 60,000+
Facility Category: Theatre and Exhibition Center
Seating Capacity: 967
Year Built: 1975
Rental Contact: Louisa Hart

7891
HIGHLANDS PLAYHOUSE
PO Box 896
Highlands, NC 28741
Phone: 828-526-9443
Web Site: www.highlandsplayhouse.org

FACILITIES / North Carolina

Management:
  President: Dwight E Bryant
Founded: 1939
Status: Non-Profit, Professional
Paid Staff: 10
Paid Artists: 30
Season: June - August

7892
GRAINER STADIUM
400 E Grainer Avenue
Kinston, NC 28501
Phone: 252-527-9111
Fax: 919-527-2328
Web Site: www.kinstinindians.com
Management:
  Director/Manager: North Johnson

7893
JE BROYHILL CIVIC CENTER
Caldwell Community College
1913 Hickory Boulevard Southeast
Lenoir, NC 28645
Mailing Address: PO Box 600
Phone: 828-726-2401
Fax: 828-726-2405
e-mail: dbriggs@caldwell.cc.nc.us
Web Site: www.broyhillcenter.com
Management:
  Director: David Briggs
  Program Assistant: Cheryl Bolt
  Director: Jeff Bentley
  Scheduling & Billing: Cheryl Bolt
  Box Office: Martha Schauman
Utilizes: Collaborations; Dance Companies; Dancers; Educators; Guild Activities; Instructors; Lyricists; Multimedia; New Productions; Original Music Scores; Selected Students; Singers; Theatre Companies
Founded: 1993
Paid Staff: 7
Budget: $350,000
Income Sources: Tickets, local and state support, sponsors and advertising.
Annual Attendance: 80,000
Facility Category: Performing Arts/ Meeting Center
Type of Stage: Procenium
Stage Dimensions: 42W X 45D X 22H
Seating Capacity: 999
Year Built: 1993
Cost: 6.1 million
Rental Contact: Jean Rondeau

7894
LINCOLN CULTURAL CENTER
403 E Main Street
Lincolnton, NC 28092
Phone: 704-732-9055
Fax: 704-732-9057
Management:
  Executive Director: Valarie King
  Artistic Director: Andrea Tripvoi
Status: Non-Profit, Non-Professional
Paid Staff: 4

7895
MOORE AUDITORIUM
Mars Hill College
Marshall Highway
Mars Hill, NC 28754
Phone: 704-689-1260
Fax: 704-689-1474

7896
CITY OF MORGANTON MUNICIPAL AUDITORIUM
401 S College Street
PO Box 3448
Morganton, NC 28680
Phone: 828-438-5294
Fax: 828-438-5246
Toll-free: 800-939-7469
Web Site: www.ci.morganton.nc.us
Management:
  Director: John W Wilson III
Founded: 1986
Status: For-Profit, Professional
Paid Staff: 5

7897
MOUNT AIRY FINE ARTS CENTER
ANDY GRIFFITH PLAYHOUSE
218 Rockford Street
Mount Airy, NC 27030
Phone: 336-786-7998
Fax: 919-986-9822

7898
MCDOWELL COLUMNS AUDITORIUM
Chowan College
Jones Drive
Murfreesboro, NC 27855
Phone: 919-398-4101
Fax: 919-398-1190

7899
GIVENS PERFORMING ARTS CENTER
University of North Carolina-Pembroke
PO Box 1510
Pembroke, NC 28372-1510
Mailing Address: PO Box 1510
Phone: 910-521-6287
Fax: 910-521-6552
e-mail: gpac@uncp.edu
Web Site: www.uncp.edu/gpac
Officers:
  Technical Operations Manager: Lenea Barela
Management:
  Executive Director: Patricia S.Fields
  Assistant Director: David Thaggard
  Marketing Director: Chad Locklear
  Box Office Manager: Dedra Sanderson
  Technical Director: Gary Trembley
Seating Capacity: 1,636

7900
A.J. FLETCHER OPERA THEATER
Progress Energy Ctr for the Performing Arts
2 East South Street
Raleigh, NC 27601
Phone: 919-831-6011
Fax: 919-831-6661
e-mail: holly.jacques@raleighconvention.com
Web Site: www.progressenergycenter.com
Management:
  Booking Coordinator: Holly Jacques

7901
CARTER FINLEY STADIUM
2500 Warren Carroll Drive
Campus Box 8502
Raleigh, NC 27695
Phone: 919-515-3050
Fax: 919-515-1161
Web Site: www.athletics.ncsu.edu

7902
JS DORTIN ARENA
1025 Blue Ridge Boulevard
Raleigh, NC 27607
Phone: 919-733-2626
Fax: 919-733-5079
Web Site: www.arg.state.nc.us/fair
Management:
  Manager: Wesley Rowley

7903
KENNEDY THEATRE
Progress Energy Ctr for the Performing Arts
2 East South Street
Raleigh, NC 27601
Phone: 919-996-8700
Fax: 919-831-6661
e-mail: holly.jacques@raleighconvention.com
Web Site: www.progressenergycenter.com
Management:
  Booking Coordinator: Holly Jacques

7904
MEMORIAL AUDITORIUM
Progress Energy Ctr for the Performing Arts
2 East South Street
Raleigh, NC 27601
Phone: 919-996-8700
Fax: 919-831-6661
e-mail: holly.jacques@raleighconvention.com
Web Site: www.progressenergycenter.com
Management:
  Booking Coordinator: Holly Jacques

7905
MEYMANDI CONCERT HALL
Progress Energy Ctr for the Performing Arts
2 East South Street
Raleigh, NC 27601
Phone: 919-996-8700
Fax: 919-831-6661
e-mail: holly.jacques@raleighconvention.com
Web Site: www.progressenergycenter.com
Management:
  Booking Coordinator: Holly Jacques

7906
NORTH CAROLINA STATE UNIVERSITY CENTER STAGE
Campus Box 7306
Raleigh, NC 27695-7306
Mailing Address: 4630 Mail Service Center, Raleigh, NC. 27699-4630
Phone: 919-513-3030
Fax: 919-515-1390
e-mail: centerstage@ncsu.edu
Web Site: www.ncsu.edu/arts
Management:
  Interim Director: Dennis Kekas
Utilizes: Actors; Artists-in-Residence; Choreographers; Collaborations; Commissioned Composers; Composers-in-Residence; Curators; Dance Companies; Dancers; Designers; Educators; Filmmakers; Fine Artists; Five Seasonal Concerts; Grant Writers; Guest Accompanists; Guest Artists; Guest Choreographers; Guest Companies; Guest Composers; Guest Conductors; Guest Designers; Guest Directors; Guest Ensembles; Guest Instructors; Guest Musical Directors; Guest Musicians; Guest Soloists; High School Drama; Instructors; Local Artists; Lyricists; Multi Collaborations; Multimedia; Original Music Scores; Playwrights; Poets;

FACILITIES / North Carolina

Selected Students; Sign Language Translators; Singers; Soloists; Student Interns; Theatre Companies; Touring Companies
Specialized Field: Multi-Disciplinary
Volunteer Staff: 50
Budget: $275,000
Income Sources: Ticket; Sponsorships
Performs At: Outdoor Theatre
Affiliations: NC Museum of Art
Annual Attendance: 40,000+
Facility Category: Outdoor Theatre/cinema
Type of Stage: Open Air/Concert
Seating Capacity: 3,000
Year Built: 1997
Cost: 3,000,000

7907
RALEIGH CIVIC CENTER COMPLEX
500 Fayetteville Street Mall
Raleigh, NC 27601
Phone: 919-831-6011
Fax: 919-831-6013
Web Site: www.raleighconvention.com
Management:
   Executive Director: Roger Krupa
   Marketing/Promotions Director: James G Lavery
Founded: 1977
Status: Non-Profit, Non-Professional
Paid Staff: 35
Seating Capacity: 3,800

7908
RALEIGH LITTLE THEATRE
301 Pogue Street
PO Box 5637
Raleigh, NC 27607
Phone: 919-821-4579
Fax: 919-821-7961
e-mail: info@raleighlittletheatre.org
Web Site: www.raleighlittletheatre.com
Officers:
   President, Board Of Directors: Scott Sutton
Management:
   Managing Director: Ellen Landau
   Artistic Director: Haskell Fitz-Simons
Mission: The purpose is to enrich, educate and entertain our community by providing a superior theatrical experience. The professionally directed, non-profit community theatre produces a variety of productions each season with 11 fully-staged shows, ranging from Broadway and Off-Broadway style musicals and non-musicals to family programs.
Founded: 1936
Specialized Field: Performing Arts - Theatre
Paid Staff: 15
Volunteer Staff: 600
Paid Artists: 40
Non-paid Artists: 160
Budget: $850,000
Income Sources: Ticket Sales; Corporate & Individual Contributions
Performs At: Two Indoor Theatres; Outdoor Amphitheatre
Annual Attendance: 36,000
Facility Category: Live Theatre
Type of Stage: Proscenium; Blackbox; Amphitheatre
Year Built: 1940
Year Remodeled: 1989
Rental Contact: Office Manager Wayne Olsen

7909
RBC CENTER
1400 Edwards Mill Road
Raleigh, NC 27607
Phone: 919-467-7825
Fax: 919-462-7030
Toll-free: 888-645-8494
Web Site: www.caneshockey.com
Management:
   President: Peter Karmanos
   General Manager: Jim Rutherford
Founded: 1999
Status: For-Profit, Professional
Paid Staff: 100
Seating Capacity: 19,000

7910
REYNOLDS COLISEUM
North Carolina State University-Raleigh
103 Dunn Avenue
Raleigh, NC 27695
Phone: 919-515-3050
Fax: 919-515-1161
Web Site: www.ecsu.edu
Officers:
   Staff Senate Chairperson: Parnell D.Bartlet
Management:
   Athletic Director: Les Robinson
Seating Capacity: 11,400

7911
THEATRE IN THE PARK
107 Pullen Road
Raleigh, NC 27607
Phone: 919-831-6936
Fax: 919-831-9475
Web Site: www.theatreinthepark.com
Founded: 1947
Status: Non-Profit, Professional
Paid Staff: 4

7912
DUNN CENTER FOR THE PERFORMING ARTS
Wesleyan College
3400 North Wesleyan Boulevard
Rocky Mount, NC 27804
Phone: 252-985-5248
Fax: 252-985-5249
e-mail: dunnevents@ncwc.edu
Web Site: www.dunncenter.com
Management:
   Executive Director: Don Briscar
Seating Capacity: 1,180

7913
CATAWBA COLLEGE COMMUNITY CENTER THEATRE
2300 W Inves Street
Salisbury, NC 28144
Phone: 704-637-4200
Fax: 704-637-4211
Toll-free: 800-228-2922
Web Site: www.catawba.edu
Officers:
   President: Brian Lewis
Management:
   Artistic Director: Woody Hood
   Managing Director: Christopher Zinc
   Professor of Religion: Barry Sang
   Professor of History: Gary Freeze
   Professor of Biology: Steve Coggin
Utilizes: Actors; Dance Companies; Educators; Fine Artists; Grant Writers; Guest Instructors; Guest Soloists; Guild Activities; High School Drama; Multimedia; New Productions; Original Music Scores; Resident Professionals; Selected Students; Soloists; Special Technical Talent
Founded: 1851
Status: Non-Profit, Non-Professional
Paid Staff: 5
Annual Attendance: 20,000+
Facility Category: Theatre
Type of Stage: Proscenium
Stage Dimensions: 48'x35'
Seating Capacity: 1,451
Year Built: 1963
Year Remodeled: 1998
Rental Contact: Clark Current

7914
TEMPLE THEATRE COMPANY
120 Carthage Street
PO Box 1391
Sanford, NC 27331-1391
Phone: 919-774-4512
Fax: 919-774-7531
Toll-free: 800-752-2765
Web Site: www.transoftinc.com/temple
Management:
   President: Jerry Sitt
   Managing Director: Sheila Bruer
Founded: 1982
Status: Non-Profit, Professional
Paid Staff: 6
Paid Artists: 50

7915
ISOTHERMAL COMMUNITY COLLEGE PERFORMING ARTS CENTER
286 ICC Loop Road
PO Box 804
Spindale, NC 28160
Phone: 828-286-3636
Fax: 828-287-8090
e-mail: pacc@isothermal.edu
Web Site: www.isothermal.edu
Officers:
   Chair: Grady Franklin
   Vice Chair: John Condrey
   Secretary: Jacqueline Godlock
Management:
   President: Willard Lewis
   Director: Russell J Wicker
Founded: 1999
Status: Non-Profit, Non-Professional
Paid Staff: 5

7916
TRYON FINE ARTS CENTER
208 Melrose Avenue
Tryon, NC 28782
Phone: 828-859-8322

7917
JOHN A WALKER COMMUNITY CENTER
PO Box 120
Wilkesboro, NC 28697-0120
Phone: 336-838-6133
Fax: 336-838-6277
Web Site: www.walkercenteronline.org
Officers:
   President: Arnold Lakey
Mission: To provide an entertainment facility, and banquet & meeting facility.
Founded: 1985
Specialized Field: Dance; Vocal Music; Instrumental Music; Theater; Festivals
Status: Non-Profit, Non-Professional

All listings are in alphabetical order by state, then city, then organization within the city.

FACILITIES / North Dakota

Budget: $150,000-$400,000
Income Sources: Association of Performing Arts Presenters; North Carolina Arts Council
Organization Type: Performing; Touring; Resident; Educational; Sponsoring

7918
KENAN MEMORIAL AUDITORIUM
University Of North Carolina- Wilmington
601 S. College Rd
Wilmington, NC 28403
Phone: 910-962-7527
Fax: 910-962-7008
e-mail: summersj@uncw.edu
Web Site: www.uncw.edu/kenan
Management:
- Operations Manager: Jeremy Summers, summersj@uncw.edu

Mission: 1000 seat venue used by civic groups, churches, arts organizations, corporations in hosting concerts, large sacle meetings, lectures and performances.
Seating Capacity: 1000

7919
LEGION STADIUM
PO Box 1810
Wilmington, NC 28402
Phone: 910-341-7855
Fax: 910-341-7854
Web Site: www.ci.wilmington.nc.us
Management:
- Manager Director: Gary Shell

Status: Non-Profit, Professional
Seating Capacity: 6,500

7920
THALIAN HALL CENTER FOR THE PERFORMING ARTS
310 Chestnut Street
Wilmington, NC 28401
Phone: 910-632-2241
Fax: 910-343-3662
Toll-free: 800-523-2820
e-mail: trivenbark@thalianhall.org
Web Site: www.thalianhall.org
Officers:
- President: Ronna Zimmer

Management:
- Executive Director: Tony Rivenbark
- Finance Director: Sarah N Daniel
- Development Director: Lauren Daley
- Marketing Director: Gary Tucker
- Technology Director: Mike Jones

Founded: 1858
Status: Non-Profit, Non-Professional
Paid Staff: 17
Annual Attendance: 75,000
Facility Category: Historic Theatre
Type of Stage: Proscenium
Stage Dimensions: 32' x 32'
Seating Capacity: 546
Year Built: 1858
Year Remodeled: 2010

7921
BOWMAN GRAY STADIUM
Winston-Salem Entertainment-Sports Complex
2825 University Parkway
Winston-Salem, NC 27105
Phone: 336-725-5635
Fax: 336-727-2922
e-mail: info@wscvb.com
Web Site: www.ljvm.com
Management:
- Coliseum Director: Benjamin Dame
- Assistant Dir Booking/Marketing: Gerry Duncan

Seating Capacity: 15,290

7922
CE GAINES COMPLEX
Winston Salem State University
601 Martin Luther King Drive
Winston-Salem, NC 27110
Mailing Address: Campus Box 19529
Phone: 336-750-2000
Fax: 336-750-2144
Web Site: www.wssu.edu
Management:
- Chancellor: Harolt Martin

Status: Non-Profit, Non-Professional

7923
DIXIE CLASSIC FAIRGROUNDS
Winston-Salem Entertainment-Sports Complex
2825 University Parkway
Winston-Salem, NC 27105
Phone: 336-725-5635
Fax: 336-727-2922
e-mail: jeffsalisbury@img.com
Web Site: www.ljvm.com
Management:
- Coliseum Director: Benjamin Dame
- Assistant Dir Booking/Marketing: Gerry Duncan

Seating Capacity: 15,290

7924
ERNIE SHORE FIELD
Winston-Salem Entertainment-Sports Complex
2825 University Parkway
Winston-Salem, NC 27105
Phone: 336-725-5635
Fax: 336-727-2922
e-mail: jeffsalisbury@img.com
Web Site: www.ljvm.com
Management:
- Coliseum Director: Benjamin Dame
- Assistant Dir Booking/Marketing: Gerry Duncan

Seating Capacity: 15,290

7925
GROVES STADIUM
Wake Forest University
499 Deacon Boulevard
Winston-Salem, NC 27105
Phone: 336-759-5000
Fax: 336-759-6090
Management:
- Athletic Director: Ron Wellman

7926
K.R. WILLIAMS AUDITORIUM
Winston-Salem State University
601 Martin Luther King Jr Drive
Winston-Salem, NC 27110
Mailing Address: PO Box 19402
Phone: 336-750-3350
Fax: 336-750-3355
Management:
- Thompson Center Director: Willie A Cumbo

Budget: $20,000-$35,000

7927
LAWRENCE JOEL VETERANS MEMORIAL COLISEUM
Winston-Salem Entertainment-Sports Complex
2825 University Parkway
Winston-Salem, NC 27105
Phone: 336-725-5635
Fax: 336-727-2922
e-mail: jeffsalisbury@img.com
Web Site: www.ljvm.com
Management:
- Coliseum Director: Benjamin Dame
- Assistant Dir Booking/Marketing: Gerry Duncan

Seating Capacity: 15,290

7928
NORTH CAROLINA SCHOOL OF THE ARTS - ROGER
1533 South Main Street
Winston-Salem, NC 27127-2188
Phone: 336-770-3399
Fax: 336-722-7240
Web Site: www.ncarts.edu/stevens_center
Annual Attendance: 175,000
Facility Category: Theatre
Seating Capacity: 1,380
Year Built: 1979
Year Remodeled: 1983
Rental Contact: Scott Spencer

7929
REYNOLDS MEMORIAL AUDITORIUM
301 N Hawthorne Road
Winston-Salem, NC 27104
Phone: 336-727-2061
Fax: 336-727-2053

7930
STEVENS CENTER
University Of North Carolina School Of The Arts
405 W. Forth St.
Winston-Salem, NC 27101
Phone: 336-723-6320
Fax: 336-722-7240
Web Site: www.uncsa.edu/stevenscenter

7931
CASWELL COUNTY CIVIC CENTER
Intersection of Highway 158 & Highway 62
PO Box 609
Yanceyville, NC 27379
Phone: 910-694-4591
Fax: 910-694-5675

North Dakota

7932
BISMARK CIVIC CENTER
601 E Sweet Avenue
PO Box 1075
Bismarck, ND 58504-5660
Phone: 701-222-6487
Fax: 701-222-6599
e-mail: bccdp@btinet.net
Web Site: www.bismarckciviccenter.com
Management:
- President: Richard L Petersen
- Sales/Marketing Director: Ross Horner
- General Manager: Dick Petersen
- Events Coordinator: Darla Pelton
- Operations Manager: Ron Staiger

Founded: 1969
Status: Non-Profit, Professional
Paid Staff: 20

FACILITIES / Ohio

7933
FARGODOME
1800 N University Drive
Fargo, ND 58102
Phone: 701-241-9100
Fax: 701-237-0987
Web Site: www.fargodome.com
Management:
 President: Keith Bjerke
 VP: Marilyn Guy
Founded: 1992
Status: Non-Profit

7934
FESTIVAL CONCERT HALL
University of North Dakota
1241 North University Drive
Fargo, ND 58105
Phone: 701-231-8011
Fax: 701-237-8043

7935
ALERUS CENTER
1200 42nd Street South
Grand Forks, ND 58201
Phone: 701-792-1200
Fax: 701-746-6511
Web Site: www.aleruscenter.com
Management:
 Executive Director: Charles Jeske
 Marketing Director: Kellie Snaith
Seating Capacity: 22,000

7936
CHESTER FRITZ AUDITORIUM
University of North Dakota
Grand Forks, ND 58202-9028
Mailing Address: 3475 University Avenue Stop 9028
Phone: 701-777-3076
Fax: 701-777-4710
Web Site: www.cfa.und.edu
Management:
 Director: Betty Allan
 Box Office Manager/Asst Director: Tom Swanglier
Founded: 1972
Status: Non-Profit, Professional
Paid Staff: 6

7937
HYSLOP SPORTS CENTER
University Sports Center
Grand Forks, ND 58202
Mailing Address: PO Box 9013
Phone: 701-777-2234
Fax: 701-777-4352
Web Site: www.fightingsioux.com
Management:
 Director: Roger Thomas

7938
CITY OF JAMESTOWN NORTH DAKOTA
102 Third Avenue Southeast
PO Box 389
Jamestown, ND 58401
Phone: 701-252-5900
Fax: 701-252-5903
e-mail: jmstnd@jamestownnd.com
Web Site: www.jamestownnd.com
Officers:
 President: Lori Anderson
Management:
 City Administrator: Jeff Fuchs
 Deputy Auditor: Jay Sveum
 Licensing: Lynette Stoddart
 Marketing/Sales Manager: Fred Walker
Founded: 1973
Status: Non-Profit, Professional
Paid Staff: 5
Seating Capacity: 5,500
Year Built: 1973

7939
BURNING HILLS AMPHITHEATRE
3422 Chateau Road
Medora, ND 58645
Mailing Address: P.O. Box 198, Medora, ND 58645
Phone: 701-623-4444
Fax: 701-623-4494
e-mail: medora@medora.com
Web Site: www.medora.com
Management:
 PR/Marketing Director: Wade Weston
 Marketing Assistant: Daniel Gannarelli
Seating Capacity: 2,854

7940
ALL SEASONS ARENA
2005 Burdick Expressway East
Minot, ND 58701
Mailing Address: PO Box 1796, Minot, ND
Phone: 701-857-7620
Fax: 701-857-7622
e-mail: ndsf@minot.com
Web Site: www.ndstatefair.com
Management:
 Manager: Renae Korslien
 Marketing Director: Shannon Pearson
Seating Capacity: 6,200

Ohio

7941
AKRON CIVIC THEATRE
182 S Main Street
Akron, OH 44308
Phone: 330-535-3179
Fax: 234-525-6467
Toll-free: 800-745-3000
e-mail: hparr@akroncivic.com
Web Site: www.akroncivic.com
Officers:
 President: Ralph Palmisano
 VP: Mark Watkins
Management:
 Executive Director: Howard Parr
 Assistant Director/Finance Admin: Brian Cummings
Status: Non-Profit

7942
EJ THOMAS PERFORMING ARTS HALL
University of Akron
198 Hill Street
Akron, OH 44325-0501
Phone: 330-972-7570
Fax: 330-972-2700
Web Site: www.ejthomashall.com
Management:
 Executive Director: Dan Dahl
 Managing Director: Cynthia Hollis
 Marketing Manager: Nancy Logan Barton
Founded: 1973
Opened: 1973
Status: Non-Profit, Non-Professional
Paid Staff: 15

7943
DAIRY BARN CULTURAL ARTS CENTER
8000 Dairy Lane
Athens, OH 45701
Mailing Address: P.O. Box 747, Athens, Ohio 45701
Phone: 740-592-4981
Fax: 740-592-5090
e-mail: artsinfo@dairybarn.org
Web Site: www.dairybarn.org
Officers:
 President: David Reiser
Management:
 Executive Director: Jane Forrest Redfern
 Education Director: Lyn Smith
 Exhibitions & Rental Coordinator: Courtney Kessel
 Facility Manager: Reid Secoy
 Facility & Gallery Shop Assistant: April Boggs
Utilizes: Artists-in-Residence; Curators; Educators; Fine Artists; Guest Accompanists; Guest Conductors; Guest Soloists; Instructors; Local Artists; Multimedia; Original Music Scores; Playwrights; Soloists; Touring Companies
Founded: 1977
Specialized Field: Arts; Crafts; Cultural
Status: Non-Profit
Paid Staff: 6
Paid Artists: 24
Budget: $320,000
Income Sources: Grants, membership, private donations
Annual Attendance: 15,000
Facility Category: Cultural Arts Center
Type of Stage: wood/rented
Seating Capacity: 200
Year Built: 1914
Year Remodeled: 2000
Rental Contact: Mark Rice

7944
OHIO UNIVERSITY: SCHOOL OF MUSIC CENTER
1 Ohio University
Athens, OH 45701-2979
Phone: 740-593-1000
Fax: 740-593-0560
e-mail: webteam@ohio.edu
Web Site: www.ohiou.edu
Officers:
 Graduate Chair: Richard Wetzel
 President: Roderick J. McDavis
 EVP and Provost: Pam Benoit
 Vice President: J. Bryan Benchoff
 Executive Director: Jennifer Bowie
Management:
 Director: W Michael Parkinson
Founded: 1917
Status: Non-Profit, Non-Professional
Paid Staff: 42

7945
CALICO THEATRE
UC Clermont College
4200 Clermont College Drive
Batavia, OH 45103
Phone: 513-732-5200
Web Site: www.ucclermont.com
Officers:
 President: Michael Carroll
 VP: William Mulvill
 Secretary/Treasurer: William Henrich

FACILITIES / Ohio

Utilizes: Collaborations; Dance Companies; Educators; Fine Artists; Guest Writers; Guild Activities; Instructors; Lyricists; Soloists; Special Technical Talent; Touring Companies
Opened: 1972
Specialized Field: Musical; Theatre; Dance
Status: Non-Profit
Paid Staff: 1
Income Sources: Grants; Ticket Sales
Facility Category: Auditorium
Type of Stage: procenium
Stage Dimensions: 20x30
Seating Capacity: 400
Rental Contact: Katie Turning

7946
HUNTINGTON PLAYHOUSE
28601 Lake Road, Bay Village
Bay Village, OH 44140
Phone: 440-871-8333
Fax: 216-221-9495
e-mail: huntingtonplayhouse@huntingtonplayhouse.com
Web Site: www.huntingtonplayhouse.com
Management:
  Managing Director: Tom Meyrose
Founded: 1971
Status: Non-Profit

7947
MANDEL JEWISH COMMUNITY CENTER OF CLEVELAND
Mandel JCC
26001 S Woodland Road
Beachwood, OH 44122
Phone: 216-831-0700
Fax: 216-831-7796
e-mail: info@mandeljcc.org
Web Site: www.mandeljcc.org
Officers:
  President: Arthur A. Weisman
  Vice President: Greg Marcus
  Vice President: Keith Polster
  Vice President: William Schonberg
  Vice President: Alan Semel
Management:
  Executive Director: Michael Hyman
  Chief Operating Officer: Gil Rubanenko
  Chief Financial Officer: Deborah Ackerman
  Chief Mark & Membership Officer: Debra Posner
Mission: To provide opportunities through the arts for persons of all ages to explore and strengthen Jewish identity, arts expertise, and human-relation skills.
Utilizes: Actors; AEA Actors; Choreographers; Collaborations; Dancers; Designers; Educators; Fine Artists; Grant Writers; Guest Artists; Guest Companies; Guest Conductors; Guest Designers; Guest Directors; Guest Instructors; Guest Lecturers; Guest Musical Directors; Guest Soloists; Instructors; Local Artists; Lyricists; Music; Original Music Scores; Performance Artists; Playwrights; Resident Professionals; Selected Students; Sign Language Translators; Soloists; Student Interns; Touring Companies; Visual Arts
Founded: 1889
Status: Professional, Non Professional, Nonprofit
Income Sources: Jewish Community Center; Ohio Arts Council
Annual Attendance: 10,000
Facility Category: Theatre; Community Theatre
Type of Stage: Proscenium
Stage Dimensions: 29x35
Seating Capacity: 270
Year Built: 1960
Organization Type: Performing; Resident; Educational

7948
KULAS MUSICAL ARTS
Baldwin Wallace College
275 Eastland Road
Berea, OH 44017
Phone: 440-826-2900
e-mail: info@bw.edu
Web Site: www.bw.edu/con
Management:
  Director: Peter Landgren
  Intern: Steven Brown
  Dir of ACES: Jay Hairston
  Graduate Intern: Christopher Malkowski
Mission: To educate and train undergraduate musicians.
Utilizes: Commissioned Composers; Commissioned Music; Composers-in-Residence; Educators; Grant Writers; Guest Accompanists; Guest Companies; Guest Composers; Guest Designers; Guest Directors; Guest Ensembles; Guest Instructors; Guest Musicians; High School Drama; Instructors; Local Artists; Multimedia; Original Music Scores; Sign Language Translators; Singers
Founded: 1845
Specialized Field: Music
Paid Staff: 4
Performs At: Recital Hall
Affiliations: United Methodist Church
Facility Category: Conservatory of Music
Type of Stage: Concert
Stage Dimensions: 35x41
Seating Capacity: 650
Year Built: 1913
Year Remodeled: 1988
Rental Contact: Ellen Hansen-Ellis

7949
ANDERSON ARENA
Bowling Green State University
14 College Park
Bowling Green, OH 43403-0001
Phone: 419-372-2531
e-mail: online@bgsu.edu
Web Site: www.bgsu.edu
Officers:
  VP/CFO: Sherideen S Stoll
Management:
  Athletic Director: Gregory Christopher
  Chief Human Resources Officer: Rebecca C. Ferguson
  Associate Director: Viva Mccarver
  Benefits Manager: Sandra Heck
Opened: 1910

7950
DOYT L PERRY FIELD
Sebo Atheletic Center
1610 Stadium Drive
Bowling Green, OH 43403
Phone: 419-372-2401
Fax: 419-372-6015
Web Site: www.bgsufalcons.com
Officers:
  Interim Unviersity President: Carol Cartwright
Management:
  Student Affairs/Asst Vice President: Gregory Christopher

7951
CANTON MEMORIAL CIVIC CENTER
1101 Market Avenue N
Canton, OH 44702
Phone: 330-489-3090
Fax: 330-471-8840
Web Site: www.cantonciviccenter.com
Management:
  General Manager: Blake Schilling
  Assistant General Manager: Geoff M Thompkins
  Operation Manager: Steve Meadows
  Box Office Manager: Monica Johnson
  Finance Manager: Wilbur Allen
Status: For-Profit, Professional
Seating Capacity: 4500

7952
THE CARTON PALACE THEATRE ASSOCIATION
605 Market Avenue North
Canton, OH 44702
Phone: 330-454-8172
Fax: 330-994-0530
e-mail: info@cantonpalacetheatre.org
Web Site: www.cantonpalacetheatre.org
Officers:
  Chairperson: Laura A. Baloun
  President: Cathy Wyatt
  Executive Vice President: Mary Beth Medford
  Vice President: Carla Derr
  Vice President: Rodney Conrad
Management:
  Executive Director: Georgia Paxos, georgia@cantonpalacetheatre.or
  Marketing and Membership Coord: Laura Strader
  Technical Director: Christopher Lesho
Mission: Hosts lives events, personal life events, corporate events and private screenings

7953
CINCINNATI MUSIC HALL
1241 Elm Street
Cincinnati, OH 45202
Phone: 513-744-3344
Fax: 513-744-3345
e-mail: info@cincinnatiarts.org
Web Site: www.cincinnatiarts.org
Officers:
  President & Executive Director: Stephen A. Loftin
  Vice President, Finance: Tina Loeb Carroll
Management:
  Development Director: Deborah A. Morgan
  Director of Education: Stephen D. Finn
  Director of Human Resources: Brenda A. Carter
  Director of Marketing & Public Rel: Van Ackerman
  Marketing Manager: Curtis L. Trefz
Founded: 1992
Status: Non-Profit, Professional
Performs At: Concert Hall
Annual Attendance: 270,000
Stage Dimensions: 48x112
Seating Capacity: 3,500
Year Built: 1875
Rental Contact: 513-744-3242 Terri Kidney
Organization Type: Performing; Touring; Resident; Educational

7954
CINTAS CENTER
Xavier University
1624 Herald Avenue
Cincinnati, OH 45207
Phone: 513-745-3900
e-mail: jonesp@xu.edu
Web Site: cintascenter.com
Management:

FACILITIES / Ohio

Director: Mr. Michael Dunn
Director for Business Operations: Mr. Andy Barry
Conference Coordinator: Ms. Megan Tracey
Director of the Schiff Conference: Mrs. Marsha Burton
Assistant Technical Director: Mr. David Overbeck
Facility Category: Arena
Seating Capacity: 10,250
Year Built: 2000
Cost: $50 MM
Rental Contact: Phillip Jones

7955
CORBETT AUDITORIUM
University of Cincinnati
Corbett Center for the Performing Arts
Cincinnati, OH 45221-0003
Mailing Address: PO Box 210003,Cincinnati OH 45221-0003
Phone: 513-556-6638
Web Site: www.ccm.uc.edu
Officers:
  Dean: Peter Landgren
  Assistant: Jane Whipple
  Dean: Terrell Finney
  Assistant: Tondra Holt
  Assistant Dean: Paul Hillner
Management:
  Box Office Manager: Jeanne Rose
  Admissions Officer: Kathryn Zajac
  Director of Business Affairs: Diane White
  Financial Administrator: Cassandra Wittwer
  Director: Kristin Suess
Founded: 1867
Seating Capacity: 380

7956
PAUL BROWN STADIUM
Two Paul Brown Way
Cincinnati, OH 45202
Phone: 513-455-4800
Fax: 513-455-4801
Toll-free: 866-621-8383
Web Site: www.paulbrownstadium.com
Officers:
  President: Mike Brown
  SVP - Player Personnel: Pete Brown
  Executive Vice President: Katie Blackburn
  Vice President - Player Personnel: Paul Brown
  Vice President: John Sawyer
Management:
  Managing Director: Eric J Brown
  Business Manager: Bill Connelly
  Director of Business Development: Bob Bedinghaus
  Director of Security: Rusty Guy
  Director: Brian Sells
Founded: 2000
Status: For-Profit, Professional
Seating Capacity: 65,600

7957
RIVERBEND MUSIC CENTER
6295 Kellogg Avenue
Cincinnati, OH 45230
Phone: 513-232-6220
Fax: 513-232-7577
Toll-free: 800-745-3000
Web Site: www.riverbend.org

7958
MARY EMERY HALL
University of Cincinnati
PO Box 210003
Cincinnati, OH 45221-0003
Mailing Address: PO Box 210003,Cincinnati OH 45221-0003
Phone: 513-556-6638
Web Site: www.ccm.uc.edu
Officers:
  Dean: Peter Landgren
  Assistant: Jane Whipple
  Dean: Terrell Finney
  Assistant: Tondra Holt
  Assistant Dean: Paul Hillner
Management:
  Box Office Manager: Jeanne Rose
  Admissions Officer: Kathryn Zajac
  Director of Business Affairs: Diane White
  Financial Administrator: Cassandra Wittwer
  Director: Kristin Suess

7959
US BANK ARENA
100 Broadway
Cincinnati, OH 45202
Phone: 513-421-4111
Fax: 513-333-3040
e-mail: info@usbankarena.com
Web Site: www.usbankarena.com
Officers:
  President: Kristen Ropp
Management:
  General Manager: Kristen Ropp
  Corporate Sales: Chris Parsons
  Corporate Sales: Kevin Olthaus
Founded: 1975
Status: Non-Profit, Professional
Performs At: Arena
Seating Capacity: 17,566
Year Built: 1975
Year Remodeled: 1997

7960
CLEVELAND BROWNS STADIUM
76 Lou Groza Boulevard
Cleveland, OH 44114
Phone: 440-891-5000
Fax: 440-891-5009
Web Site: www.clevelandbrowns.com
Officers:
  Owner: Jimmy Haslam
  President: Alec Scheiner
  Executive Vice President, General C: Sashi Brown
  Chief Financial Officer: David A. Jenkins
  Executive Vice President, Chief Rev: Brent Stehlik
Management:
  Staff Writer: Zac Jackson
  Assistant Athletic Trainer: Andre Tucker
  Head Equipment Manager: Brad Melland
  Director, Player Engagement: Dr. Jamil Northcutt
Founded: 1999
Specialized Field: Home of the Cleveland Browns
Status: For-Profit, Professional
Paid Staff: 135
Seating Capacity: 62m799
Year Built: 1999

7961
CLEVELAND INSTITUTE OF MUSIC
11021 East Blvd Cleveland
Cleveland, OH 44106
Phone: 216-791-5000
Fax: 216-791-3063
e-mail: lxw21@cim.edu
Web Site: www.cim.edu
Officers:
  Chairman: A. Malachi Mixon
  Vice Chairman: Brent M. Buckley
  President and Chief Executive Offic: Joel Smirnoff
  Vice President, Chief Operating Off: Eric W. Bower
  Vice President for Institutional Ad: Karin Stone
Management:
  Director Concerts And Events: Lori Wright, lxw21@cim.edu
  Events Manager: Ashley Davonport, add36@cim.edu
  Concert Facilities Coordinator: Whitney Clair, wxc189@cim.edu
  Director of Marketing and Communica: Susan Iler
  Communications Manager: Margaret Hagan
Mission: To provide talented students with a professional, world-class education in the art of music.
Utilizes: Artists-in-Residence; Collaborations; Guest Accompanists; Guest Composers
Founded: 1920
Specialized Field: Educational; Classical Music; World Music
Budget: $13,175,000
Affiliations: Cleveland International Piano Competition; Art Song Festival; Western Reserve University
Annual Attendance: 47,000
Facility Category: Music
Seating Capacity: 550
Year Built: 1961
Rental Contact: Lori Wright
Resident Groups: Faculty and Student Performers

7962
CLEVELAND MUSEUM OF ART: GARTNER AUDITORIUM
11150 E Boulevard
Cleveland, OH 44106
Phone: 216-421-7350
Fax: 216-707-6867
Toll-free: 877-262-4748
e-mail: info@clevelandart.org
Web Site: www.clevelandart.org
Officers:
  Chairman: R. Steven Kestner
  Vice Chair and Secretary: Sarah S. Cutler
  President: Alfred M Rankin
  VP: Sarah S Cutler
  Secretery: Stephen J Knerly Jr
  Treasurer: Janet Ashe
Management:
  Director: Timothy Rub
  Interim Director: Fred Bidwell
  Incoming Director: William M. Griswold
Founded: 1916
Status: Non-Profit, Professional
Paid Staff: 500

7963
CLEVELAND PLAY HOUSE
Allen Theater Complex
1407 Euclid Avenue
Cleveland, OH 44115

FACILITIES / Ohio

Mailing Address: 1901 E. 13th Street, Suite 200,
Cleveland, OH 44114
Phone: 216-400-7000
Fax: 216-795-7005
e-mail: mbloom@clevelandplayhouse.com
Web Site: www.clevelandplayhouse.com
Officers:
   Chair: H. Alexander Pendleton
   Vice-Chair: Nancy Hancock Griffith
   Vice President: Marilyn K. Brown
   Treasurer/Finance Chair: Kenneth M. Haffey
   Secretery: Raymond M. Malone
Management:
   Director: Jsssie O'Neill Arose
   Artistic Director: Laura Kepley
   National Director: Alan Alda
   Managing Director: Kevin Moore
   Associate Producer: Corey Atkins
Founded: 1915
Specialized Field: theatrical
Status: Non-Profit,Professional
Paid Staff: 175

7964
CLEVELAND PLAY HOUSE BOLTON THEATRE

Allen Theater Complex
1407 Euclid Avenue
Cleveland, OH 44115
Mailing Address: 1901 E. 13th Street, Suite 200,
Cleveland, OH 44114
Phone: 216-400-7000
Fax: 216-795-7005
e-mail: mbloom@clevelandplayhouse.com
Web Site: www.clevelandplayhouse.com
Officers:
   Chair: H. Alexander Pendleton
   Vice-Chair: Nancy Hancock Griffith
   Vice President: Marilyn K. Brown
   Treasurer/Finance Chair: Kenneth M. Haffey
   Secretery: Raymond M. Malone
Management:
   Artistic Director: Laura Kepley
   Managing Director: Kevin Moore
   Associate Producer: Corey Atkins
   Director: Jsssie O'Neill Arose
   National Director: Alan Alda
Founded: 1915

7965
CLEVELAND PLAY HOUSE BROOKS THEATRE

Allen Theater Complex
1407 Euclid Avenue
Cleveland, OH 44115
Mailing Address: 1901 E. 13th Street, Suite 200,
Cleveland, OH 44114
Phone: 216-400-7000
Fax: 216-795-7005
e-mail: mbloom@clevelandplayhouse.com
Web Site: www.clevelandplayhouse.com
Officers:
   Chair: H. Alexander Pendleton
   Vice-Chair: Nancy Hancock Griffith
   Vice President: Marilyn K. Brown
   Treasurer/Finance Chair: Kenneth M. Haffey
   Secretery: Raymond M. Malone
Management:
   Artistic Director: Laura Kepley
   Managing Director: Kevin Moore
   Associate Producer: Corey Atkins
   Director: Jsssie O'Neill Arose
   National Director: Alan Alda
Founded: 1915

7966
CLEVELAND PLAY HOUSE DRURY THEATRE

Allen Theater Complex
1407 Euclid Avenue
Cleveland, OH 44115
Mailing Address: 1901 E. 13th Street, Suite 200,
Cleveland, OH 44114
Phone: 216-400-7000
Fax: 216-795-7005
e-mail: MBLOOM@CLEVELANDPLAYHOUSE.COM
Web Site: www.cleavelandplayhouse.com
Officers:
   Chair: H. Alexander Pendleton
   Vice-Chair: Nancy Hancock Griffith
   Vice President: Marilyn K. Brown
   Treasurer/Finance Chair: Kenneth M. Haffey
   Secretery: Raymond M. Malone
Management:
   Artistic Director: Laura Kepley
   Managing Director: Kevin Moore
   Associate Producer: Corey Atkins
   Director: Jsssie O'Neill Arose
   National Director: Alan Alda
Founded: 1915

7967
CLEVELAND PUBLIC THEATRE

6415 Detroit Avenue
Cleveland, OH 44102
Phone: 216-631-2727
Fax: 216-631-2575
e-mail: info@cptonline.org
Web Site: www.cptonline.org
Officers:
   President: Marcia Levine
   Vice President: Philip Oliss
   Treasure: Ann Rowlett
   Secretary: Kristofer Spreen
Management:
   Executive Artistic Director: Raymond Bobgan
   Associate Artistic Director: Beth Wood
   New Play Associate: Caitlin Lewins
   General Manager: Denis M. Griesmer
   Assistant General Manager: James Kosmatka
Founded: 1981
Status: Non-Profit, Professional

7968
CLEVELAND STATE UNIVERSITY: CONVOCATION CENTER

2121 Euclid Avenue
Cleveland, OH 44115-2214
Phone: 216-687-2000
Web Site: www.csuohio.edu
Officers:
   President: Ronald M. Berkman
Management:
   Chief of Staff: Michael Artbauer
   Executive Assistant to the Presiden: Shane Connor
   Director Special Events: Barbara E. Smith
   Administrative Coordinator: Brenda Darkovich
Founded: 1991
Status: Non-Profit, Non-Professional

7969
ELDRED HALL

Case Western Reserve University
Department of Theater
10900 Euclid Avenue
Cleveland, OH 44106-7077
Phone: 216-368-4868
Fax: 216-368-5184
Toll-free: 800-421-3681
e-mail: ksg@po.cwru.edu
Web Site: www.case.edu/artsci/thtr
Officers:
   Chair, Dept of Theater/Dance: Ron Wilson
Utilizes: Choreographers; Dancers; Designers; Educators; Grant Writers; Guest Accompanists; Guest Artists; Guest Conductors; Guest Designers; Guest Ensembles; Guest Musical Directors; Guest Soloists; Guest Speakers; High School Drama; Instructors; Resident Professionals; Soloists; Student Interns; Visual Arts
Opened: 1826
Status: Nonprofit
Performs At: College Theater
Type of Stage: Proscenium
Seating Capacity: 152
Year Built: 1898
Year Remodeled: 1997

7970
GUND ARENA

Cavaliers Operating Company, LLC
1 Center Court
Cleveland, OH 44115-4001
Phone: 216-420-2000
Fax: 216-420-2260
Toll-free: 888-894-9424
e-mail: Contactus@Cvs.com
Web Site: www.theqarena.com
Management:
   Executive VP/General Manager: Roy Jones
   Senior VP Sales/Marketing: Jim Kahler
Mission: Home of the Cleveland Cavaliers and the Cleveland Lumberjacks.
Seating Capacity: 20,600
Year Built: 1994

7971
JACOBS FIELD

Cleveland Indians
2401 Ontario Street
Cleveland, OH 44115-4003
Phone: 216-420-4200
Fax: 216-420-4430
Web Site: www.indian.com
Management:
   President: Larry Dolan
   Director Ballpark Operations: Jim Folk
   Senior Director Corporate Marketing: Jon Starrett
   Concession General Manager: Charlie Henningsen
Mission: Home of the Cleveland Indians. Offers ballpark signage and branded products opportunities.
Founded: 1901
Seating Capacity: 43,368
Year Built: 1994

7972
KARAMU HOUSE PERFORMING ARTS THEATRE: PROSCE HALL

2355 E 89th Street
Cleveland, OH 44106

FACILITIES / Ohio

Phone: 216-795-7070
Fax: 216-795-7073
Web Site: www.karamu.com
Officers:
  Chair: Vickie Eaton Johnson
  Treasurer: Michael Beedless
  Secretary: Anelia Smith
Founded: 1915

7973
KARAMU HOUSE PERFORMING ARTS THEATRE: AMPHITHEATRE
2355 E 89th Street
Cleveland, OH 44106
Phone: 216-795-7070
Fax: 216-795-7073
Web Site: www.karamu.com
Officers:
  Chair: Vickie Eaton-Johnson
  Treasurer: Michael Beedles
  Secretary: Anelia Smith
Founded: 1915

7974
KARAMU HOUSE PERFORMING ARTS THEATRE: ARENA
2355 E 89th Street
Cleveland, OH 44106
Phone: 216-795-7070
Fax: 216-795-7073
Web Site: www.karamu.com
Officers:
  Chair: Vickie Eaton-Johnson
  Treasurer: Michael Beedles
  Secretary: Anelia Smith
Founded: 1915

7975
PLAYHOUSE SQUARE CENTER: OHIO THEATRE
1501 Euclid Avenue
Suite 200
Cleveland, OH 44115
Phone: 216-771-4444
Fax: 216-771-0217
Web Site: www.playhousesquare.com
Officers:
  Chairman: David S. Goodman
  President and CEO: Art J. Falco
  Vice Chairs, Community Engagement a: James R. Pender
  Vice Chairs, Development: Paul Carleton
  Vice Chair, Finance: Richard H. Fearon
Management:
  Director: Terry Adelman
  Director: Thomas W. Adler
  Director: Warren E. Anderson
  Director: John D. Andrica
  Director: Brent D. Ballard
Founded: 1921
Status: Non-Profit, Non-Professional

7976
PLAYHOUSE SQUARE CENTER: PALACE THEATRE
1501 Euclid Avenue
Suite 200
Cleveland, OH 44115
Phone: 216-771-4444
Fax: 216-771-0217
e-mail: reeds@playhousesquare.com
Web Site: www.playhousesquare.com
Officers:
  Chairman: David S. Goodman
  President and CEO: Art J. Falco
  Vice Chairs, Community Engagement a: James R. Pender
  Vice Chairs, Development: Paul Carleton
  Vice Chair, Finance: Richard H. Fearon
Management:
  Director: Terry Adelman
  Director: Thomas W. Adler
  Director: Warren E. Anderson
  Director: John D. Andrica
  Director: Brent D. Ballard
Founded: 1921

7977
PLAYHOUSE SQUARE CENTER: STATE THEATRE
1501 Euclid Avenue
Suite 200
Cleveland, OH 44115
Phone: 216-771-4444
Fax: 216-771-0217
e-mail: reeds@playhousesquare.com
Web Site: www.playhousesquare.com
Officers:
  Chairman: David S. Goodman
  President and CEO: Art J. Falco
  Vice Chairs, Community Engagement a: James R. Pender
  Vice Chairs, Development: Paul Carleton
  Vice Chair, Finance: Richard H. Fearon
Management:
  Director: Terry Adelman
  Director: Thomas W. Adler
  Director: Warren E. Anderson
  Director: John D. Andrica
  Director: Brent D. Ballard
Founded: 1921

7978
SEVERANCE HALL
Cleveland Orchestra
11001 Euclid Avenue
Cleveland, OH 44106-1796
Phone: 216-231-1111
Fax: 216-231-4038
Toll-free: 800-686-1141
e-mail: info@clevelandorchestra.com
Web Site: www.clevelandorchestra.com
Management:
  Executive Director: Gary Hanson
  Operations: Charles Laszlo
  Development: Christina Walker
  Director of Individual Support and: Grace Sipusic
  Director of Institutional Giving: Erin Gay

7979
CAIN PARK THEATRE
Cleveland Heights City Hall
40 Severance Circle
Cleveland Heights, OH 44118
Phone: 216-291-5796
Fax: 216-291-3705
e-mail: cainpark@clvhts.com
Web Site: www.cainpark.com
Utilizes: Actors; AEA Actors; Choreographers; Curators; Dance Companies; Dancers; Designers; Educators; Fine Artists; Grant Writers; Guest Artists; Guest Companies; Guest Lecturers; Local Artists; Multimedia; Music; Original Music Scores; Resident Professionals; Selected Students; Sign Language Translators; Touring Companies
Founded: 1938
Status: For-Profit, Professional
Budget: $630,000
Income Sources: Ticket sales; Grants; City of Cleveland Heights
Performs At: Evans Amphitheater; Alma Theater
Affiliations: Ohio Arts Council; Arts Midwest; Association of Performing Arts Presenters; Ohio Arts Presenters Network
Annual Attendance: 125,000+
Facility Category: Summer outdoor, covered open-air theatres
Type of Stage: Proscenium, Thrust
Seating Capacity: 1,222 + lawn; 262
Year Built: 1938
Year Remodeled: 1989
Organization Type: Sponsoring

7980
DOBAMA THEATRE
2340 Lee Road
Suite 325
Cleveland Heights, OH 44118
Phone: 216-932-6838
Fax: 216-932-3259
e-mail: dobama@dobama.org
Web Site: www.dobama.org
Officers:
  President: Jennifer Stapleton
  Vice President: Donna Korn
  Treasurer: Jimmy Forbes
  Secretary: Margi Herwald Zitelli
Management:
  Artistic Director: Nathan Motta
  Managing Director: Julie Friedman
  Artistic Associate - Production: Dianne Boduszek
  Administrative Assistant and co-Hou: Mindi Bonde
  Associate Managing Director: Jonathan Wilhelm
Founded: 1959
Status: Non-Profit, Professional
Paid Staff: 1

7981
CREW STADIUM
One Black & Gold Boulevard
Columbus, OH 43211
Phone: 614-447-2739
Fax: 614-447-4109
Web Site: www.thecrew.com
Officers:
  Chairman: Anthony Precourt
  President: John Wagner
  VP: Tom Patton
Management:
  General Manager: Mark McCullers
  Sporting Director & Head Coach: Gregg Brehalter
  Director of Soccer Operations: Asher Mendelsohn
  Assistant Coach: Robert Maaskant
  Assistant Coach: Pat Onstad
Founded: 1999
Status: For-Profit, Professional

7982
FRANKLIN COUNTY VETERANS MEMORIAL
300 W Broad Street
Columbus, OH 43215
Phone: 614-221-4341
Fax: 614-221-8422
e-mail: info@fcvm.com
Web Site: www.fcvm.com
Officers:
  President: John P. Raphael

FACILITIES / Ohio

Vice President: William A. Goldman
Management:
   Board Member: Ronald J. Koltak
   Board Member: Shay Anthony
   Board Member: Russell C. Goodwin, Jr.
   Board Member: Warren E. Motts
   Board Member: Robert Thurman
Budget: $1.6 million
Income Sources: Self Generator Revenue
Facility Category: Auditorium and Exhibition Facility
Type of Stage: Proscenium
Stage Dimensions: 32'x26'
Seating Capacity: 3916
Year Built: 1955
Year Remodeled: 2000
Cost: $11.5 million
Rental Contact: Richard Nolan

7983
JEROME SCHOTTENSTEIN CENTER
Ohio State University
555 Borror Drive
Columbus, OH 43210
Phone: 614-292-3231
Fax: 614-292-5067
Toll-free: 800-ARE-A 01
e-mail: osuarena@osu.edu
Web Site: www.schottensteincenter.com
Management:
   Director: Michael Gatto
Founded: 1996
Annual Attendance: 1,000,000
Facility Category: Arena
Type of Stage: Portable
Stage Dimensions: 60x80
Seating Capacity: 20,000
Year Built: 1998
Rental Contact: Sharon Rone

7984
NATIONWIDE ARENA
200 W Nationwide Boulevard
Columbus, OH 43215
Phone: 614-246-2000
Fax: 614-246-1800
Web Site: www.nationwidearena.com
Management:
   General Manager: Eric Granger
   Marketing Manager: Jim Riley
Mission: Multi-purpose sports and entertainment venue.
Founded: 2000
Performs At: Arena
Annual Attendance: 1+ Million
Facility Category: Arena
Seating Capacity: 18,500
Year Built: 2000
Cost: $150 Million

7985
OHIO STADIUM
Ohio State University
411 Woody Hayes Drive
Columbus, OH 43210
Phone: 614-292-7572
Fax: 614-292-0506
e-mail: penner.2@osu.edu
Web Site: www.ohiostatebuckeyes.com
Management:
   Sr Assoc Athletic Director: Ben Jay, jay.21@osu.edu
   Associate Athletics Director: Mike Penner, penner.2@osu.edu
   Asst Direcetor Event Management: Brittan Roth, roth.199@osu.edu
Seating Capacity: 98,000

7986
OHIO THEATRE
55 E State Street
Columbus, OH 43215-4264
Phone: 614-469-1045
Fax: 614-461-0429
Web Site: www.capa.com
Officers:
   Chairman: Michael Petrecca
   Vice Chairman: Lawrence L. Fisher
   Secretary: Barbara B. Lach
   Treasurer: Stephanie E. Green
Management:
   General Manager: Sheri Kaplan
   Marketing Director: Elisabeth Rivers
   Group and Organization Ticketing: JoLane Campbell
   Director of Ticketing: John Sherwood
   Facility Rental: Elena Perantoni
Opened: 1928
Seating Capacity: 2,779

7987
WEXNER CENTER FOR THE ARTS
Ohio State University
1871 N High Street
Columbus, OH 43210-1393
Phone: 614-292-0330
Fax: 614-292-3369
Web Site: www.wexarts.org
Officers:
   Chairman: Leslie H Wexner
Management:
   Director: Sherri Geldin
   Deputy Director: Jack Jackson
   Director of Education: Shelly Casto
   Director of Patron Services: Megan Cavanaugh
   Director of Marketing and Communica: Jerry Dannemiller
Opened: 1989
Budget: $150,000-$400,000
Performs At: Mershon Auditorium; Weigel Hall Auditorium
Type of Stage: Black Box
Rental Contact: Claudia Bonham

7988
POMERENE CENTER FOR THE ARTS
317 Mulberry St. Coshocton
Coshocton, OH 43812
Phone: 740-622-0326
Fax: 740-622-0326
e-mail: acornell@pomereneartsorg
Web Site: www.pomerenearts.org
Officers:
   President: Mike Mc Cullough
   VP: Ed Keifer
   Treasurer: Roger Eastman
Management:
   Director: Anne Cornell
   Office Manager: Katheleen Goode
Founded: 1984
Status: Non-Profit, Professional
Paid Staff: 3
Paid Artists: 2
Budget: $10,000
Seating Capacity: 75-900

7989
BLOSSOM MUSIC CENTER
1145 W. Steels Corners Rd
Cuyahoga Falls, OH 44223
Phone: 330-920-8040
Toll-free: 800-745-3000
Web Site: www.theblossommusiccenter.com
Facility Category: Outdoor Amphitheatre
Seating Capacity: 5763; 13500 on lawn

7990
DAYTON HARA ARENA
1001 Shiloh Springs Road
Dayton, OH 45414
Phone: 937-278-4776
Fax: 937-278-4633
e-mail: harapr@haracomplex.com
Web Site: www.haracomplex.com
Management:
   Marketing Director: Karen Wampler
   Assistant Director of Marketing: Brooke Folkerth-Jett
   Event Coordinator: Kimberly Wampler
   Home Show Manager: Jim Kelly
Founded: 1964
Facility Category: Arena; Exhibtion Centers
Seating Capacity: 7,000
Year Built: 1964
Year Remodeled: 1997
Rental Contact: Corey Rose

7991
DAYTON PLAYHOUSE
1301 E Siebenthaler Avenue
Dayton, OH 45414
Phone: 937-424-8477
Fax: 937-424-0062
e-mail: box.office.dayton.playhouse@gmail.com
Web Site: wordpress.thedaytonplayhouse.com
Officers:
   Chair: Brain P. Sharp
   Vice Chairman: Daniel Hall
   President: Becky Lamb
   Treasurer: Kelli Locker
   Secretary: Stephanie Lindsley
Management:
   Executive Director: Amy Brown
   Board Member: Jim Garvey
   Board Member: Ron Kindell
   Board Member: Bob Kovach
   Board Member: Fran Pesch
Founded: 1959

7992
WRIGHT STATE UNIVERSITY'S NUTTER CENTER
3640 Colonel Glenn Highway
Suite 430
Dayton, OH 45435-0001
Phone: 937-775-3498
Fax: 937-775-2060
e-mail: nutterguest@wright.edu
Web Site: www.nuttercenter.com
Management:
   Executive Director: Jim Brown
   Assistant Director - Operations: John Cox
   Marketing Manager: Misty Cox
   Patron Services Manager: Chris Bethel
   Business Manager: Becky Sparks
Seating Capacity: 12,000
Year Built: 1990

FACILITIES / Ohio

7993
VICTORIA THEATRE ASSOCIATION
138 N Main Street
Dayton, OH 45402
Phone: 937-228-7591
Fax: 937-449-5068
e-mail: info@victoriatheatre.com
Web Site: www.victoriatheatre.com
Officers:
  President/CEO: Ken Neufeld
  VP - Ticketing & Hospitality: Lisa Wagner
  VP - Development: Ricia Ballas
  VP- Facilities: Jo Ann Brown
  CFO: David Schrodi
Management:
  Human Resource Director: Rhonda Hess
  Director- Advancement: Karen Meade
  Director-Education: Gary Minyard
  Controller: David Becker
  Manager: Robert Suchland
Status: Non-Profit
Budget: $1,000,000
Performs At: Victoria Theatre; Schuster Performing Arts Center
Annual Attendance: 375,000
Facility Category: Theatre
Type of Stage: Proscenium
Seating Capacity: 1,154/2,319
Year Built: 1868
Year Remodeled: 1990
Rental Contact: Mechele Pritchard

7994
DELAWARE COUNTY CULTURAL ARTS CENTER
190 W Winter Street
Delaware, OH 43015
Phone: 740-369-2787
Fax: 740-363-2733
e-mail: INFO@ARTSCASTLE.ORG
Web Site: www.artscastle.org
Officers:
  President: Ralph Hodges
  Vice President: Brandon Feller
  Treasurer: Tiffany Rankin
  Secretary: Walt Abood
Management:
  Executive Director: Daine Hodges
  Director Finance & Administration: Kathy A. Cope
  Manager of Admin and Reg: Lora Kruse
  Program Coordinator : Karen McCulloch
  Graphics Coordinator : Cindy Smith
Founded: 1989
Status: Non-Profit, Non-Professional
Budget: $10,000
Seating Capacity: 2,000

7995
MEMORIAL ATHLETIC & CONVOCATION CENTER
Kent State University
800 E. Summit St.
Kent, OH 44240
Phone: 330-672-3000
e-mail: info@kent.edu
Web Site: www.kent.edu
Officers:
  President: Beverly Warren
  VP: Gregg S. Floyd
  Provost & Senior Vice President: Todd A. Diacon
  Vice President: Alfreda Brown
  Vice President: Greg Jarvie
Management:
  Athletic Director: Joel Nielsen
Founded: 1910
Seating Capacity: 6,327

7996
FRAZE PAVILION FOR THE PERFORMING ARTS
Lincoln Park Center
695 Lincoln Park Boulevard
Kettering, OH 45429
Phone: 937-296-3300
Fax: 937-296-3302
e-mail: fraze@ketteringoh.org
Web Site: www.fraze.com
Management:
  General Manager: Karen Durham
Utilizes: Guest Accompanists; Guest Lecturers; Instructors; Local Artists; Multimedia; Original Music Scores
Founded: 1991
Status: For-Profit, Professional
Paid Staff: 300
Budget: $400,000-$1,000,000
Income Sources: Ticket sales
Annual Attendance: 200,000
Facility Category: Amphitheatre
Seating Capacity: 4,300
Year Built: 1991

7997
KENNETH C BECK CENTER FOR THE PERFORMING ARTS
17801 Detroit Avenue
Lakewood, OH 44107
Phone: 216-521-2540
e-mail: grumio85@aol.com
Web Site: www.beckcenter.org
Officers:
  President/CEO: Lucinda B Einhouse
  Vice Chair: Mary Anne Crampton
  Vice Chair & Treasurer: Richard Fox
  Vice Chair: Douglas Hoffman
  Secretary: Thomas C. Wagner
Management:
  Artistic Director: Scott Spence
  Director of Finance & Business Admi: Larry Goodpaster
  Controller: Hope McGuan
  Accountant: Judi Votypka
  Associate Director, Dance: Melanie Szucs
Founded: 1930
Status: Non-Profit, Non-Professional

7998
VETERANS MEMORIAL CIVIC AND CONVENTION CENTER
7 Town Square
Lima, OH 45801
Phone: 419-224-5222
Fax: 419-224-6964
e-mail: jrohr@limaciviccenter.com
Web Site: www.limaciviccenter.com
Officers:
  President: Greg Wannemacher
  First Vice President: Jeff Tracy
  Second Vice President: Cheryl Morgan
  CEO: Cindy Wood
  Treasurer: Steve Bryan
Management:
  Marketing Services Manager: Jenni Rohr
  Office Coordinator: Christy Van Buskirk
  Director of Event Services: Tina Moenter
  Technical Services Manager: Paul Ring
  Customer Service Specialist: Jennifer Demellweek
Specialized Field: Performing Arts
Status: Non-Profit, Professional
Income Sources: 50% earned; 50% subsidy
Affiliations: I.A.A.M.
Annual Attendance: 250,000
Facility Category: Multi-Purpose
Type of Stage: Proscenium
Stage Dimensions: 60'x40'
Seating Capacity: 1700
Year Built: 1984
Cost: $9 Million
Rental Contact: Joe Shaffnerr
Resident Groups: Lima Symphony Orchestra

7999
PALACE CIVIC CENTER
617 Broadway Ave
Lorain, OH 44052
Phone: 440-245-2323
Fax: 440-246-6076
e-mail: suzanne@lorainpalace.com
Web Site: www.lorainpalace.org
Officers:
  President: Gary Fisher
  Vice President: Ben Zientarski
  Treasurer: Scott Muska
Founded: 1928

8000
MARION PALACE THEATRE
276 W Center Street
Marion, OH 43302
Phone: 740-383-2101
Fax: 740-387-3425
e-mail: info@marionpalace.org
Web Site: www.marionpalace.org
Officers:
  President: Brenda Johnston
  VP: Don Smith
  Secretary: Jill Frey
Management:
  Executive Director: Ben Ford
  Director of Finance: Veronica Bodine
  Technical Director: Steve Beltz
  Marketing Manager: Lisa Brammer
  Facility use Coordinator: Jill Rinker
Founded: 1928
Status: Non-Profit, Professional

8001
JEANNE B. MCCOY COMMUNITY CENTER FOR THE ARTS
100 West Dublin Granville Road
New Albany, OH 43054
Mailing Address: PO Box 508, New Albany, OH 43054
Phone: 614-245-4701
Fax: 614-245-4705
e-mail: contact through website
Web Site: www.mccoycenter.org
Officers:
  Chair: David Martin
  Vice Chair: Jill Beckett-Hill
  Treasurer: Chad Palmer
  Secretary: Eloise DiPietra
Management:
  Director Of Marketing: Mindy Hayward
Mission: Multiple venues available for any occasion

FACILITIES / Ohio

8002
TRUMBULL NEW THEATRE
5883 Youngstown-Warren Road
Niles, OH 44446
Phone: 330-652-1103
e-mail: webmaster@trumbullnewtheatre.com
Web Site: www.trumbullnewtheatre.com
Officers:
   President: John Timmins
   1st Vice President: B Bunker
   2nd Vice President: D. Nuhfer
   Treasurer: Susan Gillespie
   Secretary: Lisa Bennett
Founded: 1948
Status: Non Profit

8003
FAIRMOUNT CENTER FOR THE CREATIVE AND PERFORMING ARTS
8400 Fairmount Road
Novelty, OH 44072
Phone: 440-338-3171
Fax: 440-338-4218
e-mail: info@fairmountcenter.org
Web Site: www.fairmountcenter.org
Officers:
   Founder: Ron Kumin
   Founder: Jan Kumin
Management:
   Artistic Director: Tom Fulton
   Director: Fred Sternfeld
   Office Manager: Sarah Lenk
Founded: 1970
Status: Non-Profit, Professional

8004
MILLETT HALL
501 E High Street
Oxford, OH 45056
Phone: 513-529-1809
Officers:
   President: David Hodge
   Secretary: S Kay Geiger
   Treasurer: David Herche
Founded: 1809
Status: Non-Profit, Non-Professional
Seating Capacity: 10,000

8005
CUYAHOGA COMMUNITY COLLEGE: WESTERN CAMPUS THEATRE
700 Carnegie Avenue
Western Campus
Parma, OH 44115
Phone: 866-933-5175
Toll-free: 800-954-8742
Web Site: www.tri-c.edu
Officers:
   Chairman: Jerry L. Kelsheimer
   Vice Chairman: Nadine H. Feighan
   President: Alex Johnson
   Vice President: Peter Mac Ewan
   Board of Trustees: Nadine H Feighan
Management:
   Artistic Director: Robert Ellis
Founded: 1966
Status: Non-Profit, Professional

8006
SOUTHERN OHIO MUSEUM & CULTURAL CENTER
825 Gallia Street
PO Box 990
Portsmouth, OH 45662
Phone: 740-354-5629
Fax: 740-354-4090
e-mail: info@somacc.com
Web Site: www.somacc.com
Officers:
   Assosiate Director: Darren Baker
Management:
   Executive Director: Mark Chepp
   Artistic Director: Charlotte Gordon
   Senior Curator: Sarah Johnson
   Assistant to Director: Pegi Wilkes
   Visitor Services: Beverly Reeder
Founded: 1979
Status: Non-Profit, Professional

8007
VERN RIFFE CENTER FOR THE ARTS
940 2nd Street
Portsmouth, OH 45662
Phone: 740-351-3600
Fax: 740-351-3414
e-mail: info@vrcfa.org
Web Site: www.vrcfa.org
Officers:
   President: Stephen Rodeheffer
   Vice President: Barbara Pratt
   Treasurer: Lee Kasper
   Secretary: Rhoni Maxwell
Management:
   Executive Director: Carl Daehler
   Box Office Manager: Casey Glenn
   Technical Director: Leo Schlosser
   Box Office Manager: Casey Glenn
Founded: 1995
Paid Staff: 4
Volunteer Staff: 110
Paid Artists: 50
Budget: $720,000
Performs At: Proscenium Theater Concert Hall
Affiliations: AAPA, OAPN
Annual Attendance: 75,000
Type of Stage: Proscenium and Concert Hall
Stage Dimensions: 58'x 30'
Seating Capacity: 1,139
Year Built: 1995
Cost: $16,000,000
Rental Contact: Regina Bradley

8008
CLARK STATE PERFORMING ARTS CENTER
PO Box 570
Springfield, OH 45501-0570
Phone: 937-325-0691
Fax: 937-328-3879
Web Site: www.clarkstate.edu
Officers:
   Chairman: James N. Doyle
   Vice Chairman: Peggy Noonan
   President: Andy Bell
   Vice President: Heather A. Corbin
   President and CEO: Mike McDorman
Management:
   Director: Corey Holliday
   Trustee: Elise Spriggs
   Executive Director: Pam Strickler
Founded: 1962
Status: Non-Profit, Professional
Budget: $660,000
Income Sources: Box Office, Rentals, Grants, Sponsorships, Donations
Performs At: Kuss Auditorium; Turner Studio Theatre
Affiliations: Association of Performing Arts Presenters; Ohio Arts Performers Network
Annual Attendance: 90,000
Facility Category: Auditorium Studio Theatre
Type of Stage: Proscenium/ Studio Theatre
Stage Dimensions: 55'x 40'
Seating Capacity: 1,500/200
Year Built: 1993
Cost: $15.1 million
Rental Contact: Operations Manager Karen Clark
Organization Type: Arts Center

8009
FRANCISCAN CENTER OF LOURDES UNIVERSITY
6832 Convent Boulevard
Sylvania, OH 43560
Phone: 419-824-3975
Fax: 419-882-2981
Web Site: www.franciscancenter.org
Officers:
   President: Robert Helmer
   Chairman: Larry Ulrich
   Secretary: Ann Anderson Stranahan
   Treasurer: William Carroll
Management:
   Advising Director: Mary Douglas
Founded: 1958
Status: Non-Profit, Professional

8010
THE RITZ THEATRE
30 S Washington St
Tiffin, OH 44883
Phone: 419-448-8544
Fax: 419-448-7410
e-mail: michael@ritztheatre.org
Web Site: www.ritztheatre.org
Management:
   Executive Director: Michael Strong
   Marketing Director: Bruce Hannom, bruce@ritztheatre.org
   Finance Director: Nancy Betz
   Development Director: Jessica Dickey
   Production Manager: Lukas Frey
Mission: 2 venues: the Ritz and the National theatres. The Ritz is ideal for large events while the National is perfect for small such as a graduation party.

8011
COLLINGWOOD ARTS CENTER
2413 Collingwood Boulevard
Toledo, OH 43620
Phone: 419-244-2787
Fax: 419-244-2820
e-mail: info@collingwoodartscenter.org
Web Site: www.collingwoodartscenter.org
Officers:
   President: Micahael Szuberla
   Treasurer: Dr Robert Brundage
   Secretary: Laura Gerdenich
Management:
   Programming Director: John Dorsey
   Manager: Marlon Harris
Status: Non-Profit

FACILITIES / Ohio

8012
GLASS BOWL STADIUM
The University of Toledo
2801 W Bancroft
Toledo, OH 43606-3390
Phone: 419-530-4226
Fax: 419-530-4428
Toll-free: 800-586-5336
e-mail: charles.lehnert@utoledo.edu
Web Site: www.utoledo.edu
Officers:
- Chairman: Joseph H. Zerbey
- Vice Chair: Sharon Speyer
- President: Nagi Naganathan
- Executive Vice President of Finance: David R. Morlock
- Vice President of Corporate Relatio: Charles Lehnert

Founded: 1872

8013
JOHN F SAVAGE HALL
The University of Toledo
2801 W Bancroft
Toledo, OH 43606-3390
Phone: 419-530-4226
Fax: 419-530-4428
Toll-free: 800-586-5336
e-mail: charles.lehnert@utoledo.edu
Web Site: www.utoledo.edu
Officers:
- Chairman: Joseph H. Zerbey
- Vice Chair: Sharon Speyer
- President: Nagi Naganathan
- Executive Vice President of Finance: David R. Morlock
- Vice President of Corporate Relatio: Charles Lehnert

Founded: 1872
Seating Capacity: 9,600

8014
SEAGATE CONVENTION CENTRE
401 Jefferson Avenue
Toledo, OH 43604
Phone: 419-255-3300
Fax: 419-255-7731
Web Site: www.toledo~seagate.com
Officers:
- Chairman: Scott Shook
- CFO: Terry Dachenhaus

Management:
- General Manager: Steve Miller
- Director of Sales: Carol Dupuis
- Event Co ordinator: Brany Cramer
- Director of Operations: James Thielman
- Director of Event Services: Kelly O'Boyle

Founded: 1987
Status: Non-Profit, Professional
Seating Capacity: 7,500

8015
STRANAHAN THEATER GREAT HALL
4645 Heather Downs Boulevard
Toledo, OH 43614
Phone: 419-381-8851
Fax: 419-381-9525
Toll-free: 866-381-7469
Web Site: stranahantheater.org
Management:
- Executive Director: Steve Hyman
- Marketing Director: Elizabeth Gladieux
- Box Office Manager: Cherie Byrne
- Business Agent: Pat Thayer
- Controller: Laura Contos

Founded: 1965
Specialized Field: Music; Dance; Theatre
Facility Category: Performing Arts
Type of Stage: Proscenium
Stage Dimensions: 60 x 46
Seating Capacity: 2424
Year Built: 1969
Year Remodeled: 2000
Cost: $1,900
Rental Contact: General Manager Ward Whiting

8016
TOLEDO CULTURAL ARTS CENTER VALENTINE THEATRE
410 Adams Street
Toledo, OH 43604-1402
Phone: 419-242-3490
Fax: 419-242-2791
Web Site: www.valentinetheatre.com
Officers:
- Finance Manager: Rutte Kille

Management:
- Executive Director: Jori Jex
- Technical Director: Tim Durham
- Finance Manager: Ruth Kille
- Events and Catering Manager: Dan Heberling
- Marketing Director: Matt Lentz

Specialized Field: Theater
Paid Staff: 20
Volunteer Staff: 185
Paid Artists: 20

8017
TOLEDO MUSEUM OF ART
PO Box 1013
Toledo, OH 43697
Phone: 419-255-8000
Fax: 419-254-5089
Toll-free: 800-644-6862
e-mail: information@toledomuseum.org
Web Site: www.toledomuseum.org
Officers:
- Chair of the Board: David K. Welles, Jr.
- Vice Chair of the Board: George L. Chapman
- Vice Chair of the Board: Sara Jane DeHoff
- President, Director and CEO: Brian P. Kennedy
- Chief Operating Officer: Carol Bintz

Management:
- President/Director/CEO: Brian P Kennedy
- COO: Carol Bintz
- Collections Director: Carolyn Putney
- Development Director: Susan Palmer
- Communications Director: Kelly Garrow

Mission: Through our collection and programs, we strive to integrate art into the lives of people.
Founded: 1901
Specialized Field: Painting; Sculpture; Glass; Works on Paper; Decorative Arts
Status: Nonprofit
Paid Staff: 232
Volunteer Staff: 531

8018
HOBART ARENA
255 Adams Street
Troy, OH 45373
Phone: 937-339-2911
Fax: 937-335-0046
Web Site: www.hobartarena.com
Management:
- Director: Charles R Sharrett
- Arena Manager: Ken Siler
- Arena Office Manager: Cheryl Terry
- Operations Manager: Phill Noll

Status: For-Profit, Non-Professional

8019
TROY HAYNER CULTURAL CENTER
301 W Main Street
Troy, OH 45373
Phone: 937-339-0457
Fax: 937-335-6373
e-mail: troyhaynercenter@troyhayner.org
Web Site: www.troyhayner.org
Management:
- Executive Director: Linda Lee Jolly
- Artistic Director: Theresa Boehringer
- Assistant Director: Terri Boehringer
- Exhibit Coordinator: Leona Sargent
- Facilities Coordinator: Susan Kremer

Founded: 1976
Status: Non-Profit, Professional
Paid Staff: 8
Paid Artists: 25

8020
W.D. PACKARD MUSIC HALL
1703 Mahoning Ave NW
Warren, OH 44483-2066
Phone: 330-841-2936
Fax: 330-393-5348
e-mail: cstephenson@warren.org
Web Site: www.packardmusichall.com
Management:
- Manager: Christopher Stephenson, cstephenson@warren.org
- Assistant Auditorium Manager: Cherie Celedonia

8021
BEEGHLY GYM
1 University Plaza
Youngstown, OH 44555
Phone: 330-941-3000
Toll-free: 877-468-6978
Web Site: www.ysu.edu
Officers:
- President: Cynthia E. Anderson
- Vice Presidnt: Delores Crawford

Management:
- Executive Director: Ron Strollo

8022
DEYOR PERFORMING ARTS CENTER
Youngstown Symphony Society
260 W Federal Street
Youngstown, OH 44503-1256
Phone: 330-744-4269
Fax: 330-744-1441
e-mail: symphony@youngstownsymphony.com
Web Site: www.youngstownsymphony.com
Officers:
- Executive Secretary: Mari Ann Cann

Management:
- Director: Randall Craig Fleischer
- Academic Advisor: Justin Edward
- Academic Advisor: Mrs. Mary Lou Weingart

Status: Non-Profit, Professional

8023
FORD THEATRE
Youngstown State University
One University Plaza
Youngstown, OH 44555
Phone: 330-941-3625
e-mail: theatre@cc.ysu.edu
Web Site: web.ysu.edu

FACILITIES / Oklahoma

Officers:
  Department Chair: Frank Castronovo
  Dean : Dr. Bryan DePoy, D.M.
  Associate Dean : Dr. Cary Wecht
Management:
  Director: Leslie Brothers
  Senior Academic Advisor : Mary Lou Weingart
  Academic Advisor : Justin Edwards
  Coordinator: Lori Factor
  Director: Michele Lepore-Hagan

8024
SPOTLIGHT ARENA
Youngstown State University
One University Plaza
Youngstown, OH 44555
Phone: 330-941-3625
e-mail: theatre@cc.ysu.edu
Web Site: web.ysu.edu
Officers:
  Department Chair: Frank Castronovo
  Dean : Dr. Bryan DePoy, D.M.
  Associate Dean : Dr. Cary Wecht
Management:
  Director: Leslie Brothers
  Senior Academic Advisor : Mary Lou Weingart
  Academic Advisor : Justin Edwards
  Coordinator: Lori Factor
  Director: Michele Lepore-Hagan

8025
STAMBAUGH AUDITORIUM
1000 5th Avenue
Youngstown, OH 44504-1603
Phone: 330-747-5175
Fax: 330-747-1981
e-mail: info@stambaughauditorium.com
Web Site: www.stambaughonline.com
Officers:
  President: Douglas Wittenauer
  VP: William Conti
  Secretary: Jeanne Simeone
  Treasurer: David Konik
Management:
  Executive Director: Phil Cannaits
  Box Office: Bernadette Lim
Mission: To present events for the enjoyment, entertainment and education of the people of Youngstown and the surrounding communities.
Founded: 1926
Paid Staff: 6
Volunteer Staff: 30

8026
SECREST AUDITORIUM
334 Shinnick Street
Zanesville, OH 43701
Phone: 740-454-6851
Fax: 740-454-6852
e-mail: auditorium@coz.org
Web Site: www.secrestonline.com
Management:
  Manager: Ann Combs
  Marketing Director: Ann Combs
Status: Non-Profit, Non-Professional
Paid Staff: 2

8027
ZANESVILLE ART CENTER
620 Military Road
Zanesville, OH 43701
Phone: 740-452-0741
Web Site: www.zanesvilleartcenter.org
Officers:
  Secretary: Vanessa Brosie
Management:
  Director: Susan Talbot-Stanaway
Utilizes: Collaborations; Commissioned Composers; Curators; Dancers; Educators; Filmmakers; Fine Artists; Guest Accompanists; Guest Composers; Guest Designers; Guest Ensembles; Guest Instructors; Guest Musical Directors; Guest Musicians; Guest Writers; High School Drama; Instructors; Lyricists; Multi Collaborations; Multimedia; New Productions; Organization Contracts; Poets; Sign Language Translators; Singers; Soloists; Special Technical Talent; Touring Companies
Paid Staff: 7
Volunteer Staff: 50
Paid Artists: 5
Budget: $300,000
Income Sources: Multiple Sources
Annual Attendance: 15,000
Facility Category: Auditorium
Stage Dimensions: 30'x
Seating Capacity: 80
Year Built: 1984
Rental Contact: Debbie Lowe

Oklahoma

8028
DOROTHY I SUMMERS AUDITORIUM
East Central University
1100 E 14th Street
Ada, OK 74820
Phone: 580-332-8000
Fax: 580-436-3329
Web Site: www.ecok.edu
Officers:
  President: John R. Hargrave
  Provost and Vice President: Duane C. Anderson
  Vice President: Jessica A. Boles
  Vice President: Jerry Forbes
  Executive Secretary: Ms. Meredith L. Jones
Management:
  Police Officer: Larame Adams
  LPN/Clinician: Lisa Albert
  Dean's Secretary: Janet Alexander
  Professor and Chair: Richard Alfrod
  Adjunct: Jody Alfrod
Utilizes: Educators; Soloists
Founded: 1911
Status: Non-Profit, Non-Professional
Paid Staff: 3
Annual Attendance: 1200 - 1500
Seating Capacity: 430

8029
ALVA PUBLIC LIBRARY AUDITORIUM
415 4th Street
Alva, OK 73717
Phone: 580-327-1340
Fax: 580-327-5329
e-mail: lthorne@alva.lib.ok.us
Web Site: www.alvaok.org
Officers:
  Office Manager: Joyce Hibbs
Management:
  Director: Larry Thorne
  Police Chief: Gary Sanderson
  Fire Chief: Kirk Trekell
  Supervisor: Chad Campbell
  Mayor: Arden Chaffee

8030
BARTLESVILLE COMMUNITY CENTER
300 SE Adams Boulevard
Bartlesville, OK 74003
Toll-free: 800-618-2787
Web Site: www.bartlesvilleok.com
Officers:
  Chairman: Bob Fraser
  Vice Chairman: Dan Stope
  Secretary: Bud Sexson
  Treasurer: Sherry Musselman-Cox
Management:
  Managing Director: Bud Sexson
  Facility Manager: Pat Patterson
  Marketing Director: Jo Yates Baughman
Utilizes: Actors; Artists-in-Residence; Choreographers; Collaborations; Dance Companies; Dancers; Educators; Fine Artists; Five Seasonal Concerts; Grant Writers; Guest Accompanists; Guest Artists; Guest Choreographers; Guest Companies; Guest Composers; Guest Designers; Guest Ensembles; Guest Instructors; Guest Lecturers; Guest Musical Directors; Guest Musicians; Guest Soloists; Guest Teachers; Guest Writers; Guild Activities; Instructors; Local Artists; Lyricists; Multi Collaborations; Multimedia; Music; New Productions; Organization Contracts; Original Music Scores; Performance Artists; Playwrights; Poets; Resident Professionals; Selected Students; Sign Language Translators; Singers; Soloists; Student Interns; Special Technical Talent; Theatre Companies; Touring Companies; Visual Arts
Founded: 1982
Specialized Field: Performing Arts Hall and Rental Facility
Status: Non-Profit, Non-Professional
Paid Staff: 15
Volunteer Staff: 400
Budget: $860,000
Income Sources: Interest Income; Endowment; Rental Income; Hotel/Motel Tax Revenue; Donations; Admissions; Rentals
Affiliations: City of Bartlesville
Annual Attendance: 130,000
Facility Category: Performing Arts Hall; Rental Facility
Type of Stage: Proscenium
Stage Dimensions: 40-60wx30d
Seating Capacity: 1,702
Year Built: 1982
Cost: $13,000,000
Rental Contact: Events Coordinator Shallan John

8031
BROKEN ARROW PERFORMING ARTS CENTER
701 S. Main St
Broken Arrow
Broken Arrow, OK 74012
Phone: 918-259-5778
e-mail: mark@brokenarrowpac.com
Web Site: www.thepacba.com
Management:
  Technical Director: Scott Heberling
  Event Manager: Whitney Rose
  Box Office Manager: Kate Pike
  Marketing Manager: Adam J. Foreman
  Public Relation Manager: Christina Dixon
Seating Capacity: 1500

8032
CARL WOOTEN STADIUM
Oklahoma Panhandle State University
PO Box 430
Goodwell, OK 73939

FACILITIES / Oklahoma

Phone: 580-349-2611
Fax: 580-349-2302
Toll-free: 800-664-6778
e-mail: webmaster@opsu.edu
Web Site: www.opsu.edu
Officers:
  President: David Bryant
  VP: Kim Peterson
  Secretary: Dr. Doris Looper
Management:
  Director: David Steele
  Head Basketball Coach: Steve Appel
  Interim Visiting Instructor: Michael Ask
  Program Facilitator: Reyna Baez
  English Instructor: Margie Bailey
Founded: 1909
Status: Non-Profit, Non-Professional

8033
GREAT PLAINS COLISEUM
Comanche County Fairgrounds
920 Sheridan Road
Lawton, OK 73505
Phone: 580-357-1483
Fax: 580-357-1192
e-mail: gpc64@swbell.net
Web Site: www.gpcoliseum.com
Officers:
  Chairman: David Dorrell
  Treasurer: Jerry Krasser
Management:
  Executive Director: Phillip Humble
  Office Manager: Joe Kirk
  Catering Staff: Ellen Fisher
  Catering Staff: Sarah Stonerock
Status: For-Profit, Professional
Paid Staff: 10

8034
MCCAHON MEMORIAL AUDITORIUM
801 NW Ferris
Lawton, OK 73507
Phone: 580-581-3472
e-mail: amorman@city.lawton.ok.us
Web Site: www.cityf.lawton.ok.us/mma
Management:
  Arts & Humanities Administrator: Billie A. Whipp
  Auditorium Coordinator: Andrea Morman
  Maintainence: Robert Torres
  House Manager: Stavis Morman
  Part Time Maintainence: Manuel Smith

8035
MCMAHON MEMORIAL AUDITORIUM
801 NW Ferris
Lawton, OK 73507
Phone: 580-917-0707
Web Site: www.lawtonok.com
Officers:
  Co-Founder: Louise McMahon
Founded: 1954
Affiliations: Lawton Philharmonic Society
Type of Stage: Proscenium
Stage Dimensions: 92'Wx40'D
Orchestra Pit: 1
Architect: Paul Harris
Rental Contact: Jim McCarthy

8036
ROSE STATE COLLEGE PERFORMING ARTS THEATRE
6420 SE 15th Street
Midwest City
Midwest City, OK 73110-2704
Phone: 405-733-7673
Toll-free: 866-621-0987
Web Site: www.rose.edu
Officers:
  President: Terry Britton
  Chair: James Howell
  Secretary: Aarone Corwin
  Treasurer: Robert Croak
Management:
  Director: John Cain
  Marketing: Donna Syth
Seating Capacity: 1,400

8037
MUSKOGEE CIVIC CENTER
229 W Okmulgee Ave
PO Box 2361
Muskogee, OK 74401
Phone: 918-684-6300
Fax: 918-684-6299
Toll-free: 888-687-6137
e-mail: cassandra.gaines@muskogeeciviccenter.com
Web Site: www.cityofmuskogee.com
Officers:
  Mayor: Bob Coburn
Management:
  Manager: Cassandra Gaines
Seating Capacity: 3,710

8038
MUSKOGEE LITTLE THEATRE
325 Cincinnati
PO Box 964
Muskogee
Muskogee, OK 74403
Mailing Address: PO Box 964, Muskogee, OK 74402
Phone: 918-683-5332
Web Site: www.muskogeelittletheatre.com
Management:
  Executive Director: Coni Wetz

8039
LLYOD NOBLE CENTER
University of Okhlahoma
660 Parrington Oval
Norman, OK 73019-0390
Phone: 405-325-0311
Fax: 405-325-7605
Web Site: www.ou.edu
Officers:
  Chairman: Tom Clark
  Vice Chairman: Jon R. Stuart
  President: David L Boren
  VP: Kyle Harper
  CFO: Chris Kwitsky
Founded: 1975
Seating Capacity: 12,000

8040
UNIVERSITY THEATRE
University of Oklahoma
660 Parrington Oval
Norman, OK 73019-0310
Phone: 405-325-0311
Fax: 405-325-7605
Web Site: www.ou.edu
Officers:
  Chairman: Tom Clark
  Vice Chairman: Jon R. Stuart
  President: David L Boren
  VP: Kyle Harper
  CFO: Chris Kwitsky
Management:
  Director: James Garner
Marketing: Sandra Bent
Budget: $8,000
Seating Capacity: 600; 144

8041
BLACK LIBERATED ARTS CENTER
PO Box 11014
Oklahoma City, OK 73136
Phone: 405-524-3800
Web Site: www.blacinc.org
Officers:
  Founder: Dr. John Smith
  President: F E Berroughs
Management:
  Executive Director: Anita G Arnold
Founded: 1970
Status: Non-Profit, Professional
Paid Staff: 1
Budget: $35,000-$60,000
Performs At: Civic Center Music Hall

8042
BURG THEATRE
Oklahoma City University
2501 N Blackwelder
Oklahoma City, OK 73106-1493
Phone: 405-208-5000
e-mail: visitocu@okcu.edu
Web Site: www.okcu.edu
Officers:
  President: Dr Tom J McDaniel
  Chair: William F Shdeed
  Secretary: Josephine Freede
  Treasurer: Roy W Chandler
Management:
  Theatre Department Director: Donald Childs

8043
CIVIC CENTER MUSIC HALL
201 N Walker Avenue
Oklahoma City, OK 73102
Phone: 405-297-2584
Fax: 405-297-3890
Web Site: www.okcciviccenter.com
Officers:
  President: Lee Symcox
  VP: Joe Hodges
  Tressurer: Jim Shaw
  Secretary: Jane Thompson
  Ex-Offio: Carol Troy
Management:
  General Manager: Jim Brown
  Operations: John Siska
  Marketing: Jennifer Lindsey-McCintock
  Technical Director: Brent Winters
  Technical Director: Donna Monarch

8044
COX CONVENTION CENTER
One Myriad Gardens
Oklahoma City
Oklahoma City, OK 73102-9219
Phone: 405-602-8500
Fax: 405-602-8505
e-mail: info@coxconventioncenter.com
Web Site: www.coxconventioncenter.com
Officers:
  Executive Director: Kim Wimmer
Management:
  General Manager: Gary Desjardins
  Operations Director: David Ellsworth
  Marketing Director: Tim Linville
  Box Office Manager: Valory Dalton
  Event Manager: Steve Bray

FACILITIES / Oklahoma

Founded: 1972
Seating Capacity: 14,380

8045
KIRKPATRICK AUDITORIUM
Oklahoma City University
2501 N Blackwelder
Oklahoma City, OK 73106-1493
Phone: 405-208-5000
e-mail: visitocu@okcu.edu
Web Site: www.okcu.edu
Officers:
  President: Dr Tom J McDaniel
  Chair: William F Shdeed
  Secretary: Josephine Freede
  Treasurer: Roy W Chandler
Management:
  Theatre Department Director: Donald Childs

8046
OKLAHOMA CITY ZOO AMPHITHEATRE
2000 Remington Place
Oklahoma City, OK 73111
Mailing Address: 2101 NE 50th Street
Phone: 405-424-3344
Web Site: www.okczoo.com
Officers:
  President: Howard Pollack
  VP: Cesar Morales
  CFO: Tom Schadegg
Management:
  Promotions Director: David Beerley

8047
PONCA PLAYHOUSE
301 S First Street
PO Box 1414
Ponca City, OK 74601
Phone: 580-765-5360
e-mail: PoncaPlayhouse@gmail.com
Web Site: www.poncaplayhouse.com
Officers:
  President: Dave Gunin
  VP: Stephen Long
  Treasurer: Ardeth Mason
  Secretary: Paula Coppock
Management:
  Board Member: Ruslyn Hermanson
  Board Member: Meghann Borum
  Board Member: Karen Brown
  Board Member: Ginger Duval
  Board Member: Kelli Graves
Opened: 1959

8048
STILLWATER COMMUNITY CENTER
City of Stillwater
315 W 8th Street
Stillwater, OK 74076-1449
Mailing Address: P.O. Box 1449
Phone: 405-372-0025
Fax: 405-533-8022
e-mail: CityHall@stillwater.org
Web Site: www.stillwater.org
Officers:
  Executive Director: Patti Osmus
Management:
  Manager: Stephanie Walker
  Internal Service Manager: Rob Baker
Status: Non-Profit, Professional
Budget: $10,000
Performs At: Continental Auditorium

8049
MABEE CENTER ARENA
Oral Roberts University
7777 S Lewis Avenue
Tulsa, OK 74171
Phone: 918-495-6400
Fax: 918-495-6478
e-mail: twinters@oru.edu
Web Site: www.mabeecenter.com
Management:
  Operations Director: Crispin Ngenda
  Managing Director: Tony Winters
  Marketing Manager: James D Smith
  Events Coordinator: Olivia Whaley
  Events Coordinator: Jonnah Ogle
Founded: 1972
Status: Non-Profit, Professional
Seating Capacity: 11,763

8050
MOHAWK PARK
175 E 2nd Street
Suite 690
Tulsa, OK 74103
Phone: 918-596-2100
Web Site: www.tulsaparks.org
Officers:
  Secretary: R. Louis Reynold
Management:
  Director: Monica Hamilton
  Manager: Kim MacLeod
Seating Capacity: 30,000

8051
RIVER PARKS AMPHITHEATRE
2424 E. 21st St.
Suite 300
Tulsa, OK 74114
Phone: 918-596-2001
Fax: 918-596-2004
e-mail: staff@riverparks.org
Web Site: www.riverparks.org
Officers:
  Chairman: Robin Flint Ballenger
  Vice Chairman: Phil Frohlich
  Treasurer: Jamie Marchsano
Management:
  Executive Director: Matt Meyer, staff@riverparks.org
  Administrative Manager: Janet Kendall
  Park Superintendent: Michael Crumb
  Community Relations Director: Tonja Carrigg
  Public Events Coordinator: John Graham
Founded: 1974
Seating Capacity: 3,000

8052
GOLDEN HURRICANE CLUB
The University of Tulsa
800 South Tucker Drive
Westby Hall
Tulsa, OK 74104-3189
Phone: 918-631-2342
Fax: 918-631-2049
e-mail: ghc@utulsa.edu
Web Site: www.tulsahurriccane.com
Officers:
  President: Jennifer Salcher
  VP: Kent Mayberry
  Treasurer: Chris Kaiser
  Secretary: Karen Ham
Management:
  Athletic Director: Brain Scisio
  Director: Connor Meier
  Assistant Director: Ashley Davidson
  Department Assistant: Marni Stilson
  Development Assistant: Matt Wittiq
Seating Capacity: 40,235

8053
TULSA PERFORMING ARTS CENTER
110 E 2nd Street
Tulsa, OK 74103
Phone: 918-596-7122
Fax: 918-596-7144
Toll-free: 800-364-7122
e-mail: NHERMANN@cityoftulsa.org
Web Site: www.tulsapac.com
Management:
  Director: John E Scott
  Assistant Director: Janet Rockefeller
Opened: 1977

8054
TULSA PERFORMING ARTS CENTER: JOHN H WILLIAM HALL
110 E 2nd Street
Tulsa, OK 74103
Phone: 918-596-7122
Fax: 918-596-7144
e-mail: NHERMANN@cityoftulsa.org
Web Site: www.tulsapac.com
Management:
  Director: John E Scott
  Assistant Director: Janet Rockefeller
Opened: 1977

8055
TULSA PERFORMING ARTS CENTER: DOENGES THEATER
110 E 2nd Street
Tulsa, OK 74103
Phone: 918-596-7122
Fax: 918-596-7144
e-mail: NHERMANN@cityoftulsa.org
Web Site: www.tulsapac.com
Management:
  Director: John E Scott
  Assistant Director: Janet Rockefeller
Opened: 1977

8056
TULSA PERFORMING ARTS CENTER: STUDIO II
110 E 2nd Street
Tulsa, OK 74103
Phone: 918-596-7122
Fax: 918-596-7144
e-mail: NHERMANN@cityoftulsa.org
Web Site: www.tulsapac.com
Management:
  Director: John E Scott
  Assistant Director: Janet Rockefeller
Opened: 1977

8057
TYRRELL HALL
University of Tulsa
800 South Tuker Drive
Tulsa, OK 74104-9700
Phone: 918-631-2000
Fax: 918-631-5003
Toll-free: 800-331-3050
e-mail: schoolofmusic@utulsa
Web Site: www.utulsa.edu
Officers:

President: Dr Steadman Upham
Dean: Henry Kendall

8058
WALTER ARTS CENTER
Holland Hall
5666 E 81 Street
Tulsa, OK 74137-2099
Phone: 918-481-1111
Fax: 918-481-1193
Web Site: hollandhall.org
Officers:
   Chairman: Roger B. Collins
   Vice Chairman: Robert L. Hughes
   President: James F. Adelson
   Secretary: David Keglovits
   Treasurer: Charles K. Lamson
Management:
   Director: Olivia Martin
   Coordinator: Pam Lieber
Utilizes: Artists-in-Residence; Guild Activities; High School Drama; Instructors; Soloists; Touring Companies
Founded: 1922
Budget: $10,000
Performs At: Branch Theatre
Facility Category: Arts Education
Type of Stage: Proscenium
Seating Capacity: 1,119
Year Built: 1992
Rental Contact: Jackie Hewitt

8059
TULSA COMMUNITY COLLEGE PERFORMING ARTS CENTER FOR EDUCATION
10300 E 81st Street
Tusla, OK 74133
Phone: 918-595-7000
e-mail: webteam@tcc
Web Site: www.tulsacc.edu
Officers:
   President and CEO: Dr. Leigh Goodson
   VP: Ric Baser
   VP for External Affairs: Lauren Brookey
   VP for Student Affairs: Dr. Jan Clayton
   Comptroller and CEO: Shane Netherton
Management:
   Associate Vice President for Academ: Dr. Donna Wood

8060
MILAN STADIUM
Southwestern Oklahoma State University
100 Campus Drive
Weatherford, OK 73096
Phone: 580-774-3063
Fax: 580-774-7101
Web Site: www.swosu.edu
Officers:
   President: John M Hayes
Management:
   Executive Director for Institutiona: Lynne Thurman
Founded: 1903
Seating Capacity: 9,000

Oregon

8061
ONE WORLD PERFORMING ARTS
Southern Oregon University
1250 Siskiyou Boulevardity
Ashland, OR 97520
Phone: 541-552-7672
Fax: 541-552-6440
Web Site: www.sou.edu
Officers:
   President: Mary Cullinan
   VP: James M. Klein
Management:
   Associate Provost: Susan Walsh

8062
OREGON SHAKESPEARE FESTIVAL
15 S Pioneer
PO Box 158
Ashland, OR 97520
Phone: 541-482-2111
Fax: 541-482-0446
Toll-free: 800-219-8161
e-mail: administration@osfashland.org
Web Site: www.osfashland.org
Officers:
   President: Sid DeBoer
   VP: Kathryn Ma
   Secretary: Gail Lopes
   Tressurer: Susan Cain
Management:
   Artistic Director: Bill Rauch
   Executive Director: Cynthia Rider
   General Manager: Ted DeLong, media@osfashland.org
   Director Marketing/Communications: Mallory Pierce
   Director Administration/Finance: Jerry Roos
Founded: 1935
Specialized Field: Shakespeare; Classic; Contemporary
Status: Non-Profit; Professional
Paid Staff: 550
Volunteer Staff: 600
Budget: $23,000,000
Income Sources: Earned; Contributions
Performs At: Angus Bowmer Theatre; New Theatre; Elizabethan Theatre
Affiliations: Actors' Equity Association; ATA; University/Resic Theatre Association; Theatre Communications Group
Annual Attendance: 400,000
Type of Stage: Thrust Stage; Black Box; Outdoors
Seating Capacity: 601; 275; 1188

8063
OREGON SHAKESPEARE FESTIVAL: BLACK SWAN THEATER
15 S Pioneer
Ashland, OR 97520
Phone: 541-482-2111
Fax: 541-482-0446
e-mail: administration@osfashland.org
Web Site: www.osfashland.org
Officers:
   President: Sid DeBoer
   VP: Kathryn Ma
   Secretary: Gail Lopes
   Tressurer: Susan Cain
Management:
   Artistic Director: Bill Rauch
   Executive Director: Cynthia Rider
   General Manager: Ted DeLong
   Director Marketing/Communications: Mallory Pierce
   Director Administration/Finance: Jerry Roos
Founded: 1935

8064
SOUTHERN OREGON UNIVERSITY
1250 Siskiyou Boulevard
Ashland, OR 97520
Phone: 541-552-7672
Fax: 541-552-6440
Toll-free: 800-482-7672
Web Site: www.sou.edu
Officers:
   President: Mary Cullinan
   VP: James M. Klein
Management:
   Associate Provost: Susan Walsh

8065
CLATSOP COMMUNITY COLLEGE PERFORMING ARTS CENTER
1651 Lexington Avenue
Astoria, OR 97103
Phone: 503-325-0910
Toll-free: 866-252-8767
e-mail: admissions@clatsopcc.edu
Web Site: www.clatsopcc.edu
Officers:
   Chairman: Rosemary Baker
   Vice Chairman: Patrick Wingard
   President: Dr. Lawrence Galizio
Management:
   Direcor: Dirk Rohne
Facility Category: Theatre
Type of Stage: Plywood
Seating Capacity: 255
Year Built: 1920

8066
COASTER THEATRE
108 N Hemlock
PO Box 643
Cannon Beach, OR 97110
Phone: 503-436-1242
Fax: 503-436-9653
e-mail: boxoffice@coastertheatre.com
Web Site: www.coastertheatre.com
Management:
   Artistic Director: Craig Shepherd
Founded: 1972
Status: Non-Profit; Professional

8067
GILL COLISEUM
Oregon State University
123 Gill Coliseumersity
Corvallis, OR 97331
Phone: 541-737-2370
Fax: 541-737-2929
e-mail: rfrank@oregonstate.edu
Web Site: www.osubeavers.com
Officers:
   President: Anjeanette Brown
   VP: Ray Brooks
   Treasurer: Jim Renton

8068
LASELLS STEWART CENTER
Oregon State University
600 Kerr Administration Building
Corvallis, OR 97331-2128

FACILITIES / Oregon

Phone: 541-737-1000
Fax: 541-737-3033
e-mail: life@osu
Web Site: www.oregonstate.edu
Officers:
   President: Dr Edward Ray
Management:
   Executive Director: Elizabeth Grubb
Income Sources: Rental And Fees
Performs At: Concert Hall
Facility Category: Auditorium
Type of Stage: Hardwood Concert
Stage Dimensions: 53x42
Seating Capacity: 1200
Year Built: 1981
Rental Contact: Vi Anderson

8069
RESER STADIUM
Oregon State University
123 Gill Coliseum
Corvallis, OR 97331
Phone: 541-737-2370
Fax: 541-737-2929
e-mail: rfrank@oregonstate.edu
Web Site: www.osubeavers.com
Officers:
   President: Anjeanette Brown
   VP: Ray Brooks
   Treasurer: Jim Renton
Seating Capacity: 35,000

8070
AUTZEN STADIUM
University of Oregon
2727 Leo Harris Parkway
Eugene, OR 97401
Phone: 541-346-4481
Fax: 541-346-5051
Web Site: www.goducks.com
Officers:
   President: Dave Frohamayer
Management:
   Atheletics Director: Rob Mullens
   Assistant Director: Mark Ruckwardt
   Business Office: Sharon Bonin
   Development Director: Franklin Algeria
   Event Manager: Ashley McCrea

8071
BEALL CONCERT HALL
UO School of Music and Dance
961 E. 18th Ave
Eugene, OR 97403-1225
Mailing Address: 1225 University of Oregon
Phone: 541-346-3761
Fax: 541-346-0723
e-mail: mushelp@uoregon.edu
Web Site: www.music.uoregon.edu
Officers:
   Director: Brad Foley
   Manager: Laura Littlejohn
Management:
   Technology Consultant: Marc Levy
   Receptionist: Woddy Karen
   Admission Assistant: Spicer Sara
   Recrding Tecnician: Miller Lance
Mission: Educational/professional
Founded: 1921
Opened: 1921
Specialized Field: Miscellaneous
Paid Staff: 4
Volunteer Staff: 1
Paid Artists: 200
Non-paid Artists: 200
Income Sources: Ticket Revenues; Grants; Donors
Performs At: Concert Hall
Affiliations: University Of Oregon
Type of Stage: Proscenium
Stage Dimensions: 38 X 42
Seating Capacity: 520
Year Built: 1921
Year Remodeled: 1978

8072
COMMUNITY CENTER FOR THE PERFORMING ARTS
WOW Hall
291 W 8th Avenue
Eugene, OR 97401
Phone: 541-687-2746
Fax: 541-687-1664
e-mail: info@wowhall.org
Web Site: www.wowhall.org
Officers:
   Chair: Aaron Dietrich
   Secretary: Sara Shmigelsky
   Treasurer: Craig Lawrence
Management:
   Manager: Lily Lamadore
   Coordinator: Bob F.
   Program Coordinator: Calyn K.
   Office Manager: Donna C.
   Concessions Manager: Angela L.
Founded: 1975
Status: Non-Profit, Professional

8073
HULT CENTER FOR THE PERFORMING ARTS
One Eugene Center
Eugene, OR 97401
Phone: 541-682-5087
Fax: 541-682-5426
Toll-free: 1 8-0 7-5 29
e-mail: hultcenter@ci.eugene.or.us
Web Site: www.hultcenter.org
Management:
   Manager: Karm Hagedorn
   Facilities Services Manager: Mark D Loigman
   Marketing & PR Manager: Libby Tower
Founded: 1982
Status: City Owned Venue
Income Sources: City of Eugene; Lodging Tax
Seating Capacity: 2,500; 500

8074
JAQUA CONCERT HALL
John C Shedd Institute for the Arts
868 High Street
PO Box 1497
Eugene, OR 97401-1497
Phone: 541-687-6526
Fax: 541-687-1589
e-mail: info@ofam.net
Web Site: www.ofam.org
Management:
   Executive Director: Ken Peplowski
   Faculty: Lou Crist
Status: Non-Profit, Professional
Facility Category: Concert Hall; Recital Hall; Gymnasium
Seating Capacity: 750; 175; 300
Year Built: 1926
Year Remodeled: 3-Fe
Rental Contact: Erik Martin

8075
FLORENCE EVENTS CENTER
Florence Events Center
715 Quince Street
Florence, OR 97439
Phone: 541-997-1994
Fax: 541-902-0991
Toll-free: 888-968-4086
e-mail: kevin@eventcenter.org
Web Site: www.eventcenter.org
Officers:
   Administrative: Angela Palmer
Management:
   Director: Kevin Rhodes, kevin@eventcenter.org
   Marketing: Paula Becker, paula@eventcenter.org
   Maintenance Technician: Dino Raviolo
   Office Coordinator: Jennifer Anderson
Founded: 1996
Status: Non-Profit, Non-Professional
Paid Staff: 4
Volunteer Staff: 50
Stage Dimensions: 33' x 44', 20' x 40' proscenium
Seating Capacity: 457
Year Built: 1996
Rental Contact: Kevin Rhodes

8076
TAYLOR-MEADE PERFORMING ARTS CENTER
Pacific University
2034 College Way
Forest Grove, OR 97116
Phone: 503-352-6151
Fax: 503-352-2056
Toll-free: 877-722-8648
e-mail: tuomis1@pacificu.edu
Web Site: www.pacificu.edu
Officers:
   Chair: Scott Tuomi PhD
   President: Lesley M. Hallick
   VP: John Miller
   VP: Mike Mallery
   VP: Mark E Ankeny
Management:
   Director: Bryce Seliger PhD
   Program Director: Linda Hunt, Ph.D
   Business Manager: Julie B. Baker

8077
THEATRE IN THE GROVE
2028 Pacific Avenue
Forest Grove, OR 97116
Mailing Address: PO Box 263
Phone: 503-359-5349
e-mail: info@theatreinthegrove.org
Web Site: www.theatreinthegrove.org
Officers:
   Chairman: Jeff Zimmerman
   Treasurer: Dana Lommen
   Secretary: Jessica Stephens
Management:
   Manager: Jeanna Van Dyke
   Volunteer Coordinator : Susan Dieter-Robinson
   Building Manager: Ken Centers
   Technical Manager: Zachary Centers
   Publicity Manager: McKenzie Brock

8078
TOM MILES THEATRE
Pacific University
2043 College Way
Forest Grove, OR 97116

FACILITIES / Oregon

Phone: 503-352-6151
Fax: 503-352-2056
Toll-free: 877-722-8648
e-mail: theatredance@pacificu.edu
Web Site: www.pacificu.edu
Officers:
  Chair: Scott Tuomi PhD
  President: Lesley M. Hallick
  VP: John Miller
  VP: Mike Mallery
  VP: Mark E Ankeny
Management:
  Director: Bryce Seliger PhD
  Program Director: Linda Hunt, Ph.D

8079
ROSS RAGLAND THEATER & CULTURAL CENTER
218 N 7th Street
Klamath Falls, OR 97601
Phone: 541-884-0651
Fax: 541-884-8574
Toll-free: 888-627-5484
e-mail: media@rrtheater.org
Web Site: www.rrtheater.org
Officers:
  Board Chair: Lynne Butterworth
  Vice Chair: John Novak
  Treasurer: Brian Menefee
  Secretary: Nancy Pratt
Management:
  Executive Director: Mark R. McCrary, MBA, CAE
  Marketing Coordinator: Crystal Muno
  Technical Director: Steve Ayola
  Office Manager: Deborah Jones
  Facility Manager: Christy Ruegger
Founded: 1989
Status: Non-Profit, Professional
Budget: $600,000
Facility Category: Performing Arts Center
Type of Stage: Proscenium
Stage Dimensions: 51x45
Seating Capacity: 700
Year Remodeled: 1989
Rental Contact: Kelly Buckles

8080
LAKE OSWEGO PARKS & REC
380 A Avenue
Lake Oswego, OR 97304
Mailing Address: PO Box 369
Phone: 503-636-9673
Fax: 503-697-6579
e-mail: cic@ci.oswego.or.us
Web Site: www.ci.oswego.or.us
Officers:
  Manager: David Donalson
  President: Tom Bland
Management:
  Attorney: David D. Powell
  Managing Director: Kim Gilmer
  Assistant Manager: Brant Williams
Status: For-Profit, Professional
Paid Staff: 75
Paid Artists: 1

8081
LAKEWOOD CENTER FOR THE ARTS
368 S State Street
Lake Oswego, OR 97034
Phone: 503-635-3901
Fax: 503-635-2002
e-mail: center.info@lakewood-center.org
Web Site: www.lakewood-center.org
Officers:
  President: Michelle Dorman
  Treasurer: Don Irving
Management:
  Executive Director: Andrew Edwards
  Executive Producer: Kay Vega
  Education Coordinator: Steve Knox
  Development Director: Peter Jurney
Founded: 1952

8082
YAMHILL COUNTY FAIRGROUNDS
2070 Lafayette Avenue
McMinnville, OR 97128
Phone: 503-434-7524
Fax: 503-435-1860
e-mail: ycec@onlinemac.com
Web Site: www.co.yamhill.or.us.com
Officers:
  Board Member: Bruce Distler
  Fair Board Chairman: Larry Collver
  Secretary: Gary Wetz
  Fair Board Vice Chairman: Russ Christensen
Management:
  Fairgrounds Manager: Darcie Vanderyacht
  Maintenance Foreman: Kevin Rose
Mission: Yamhill County Fair and rodeo, horse shows, weddings, wedding receptions, horse boarding, concerts, canine training, master gardeners test garden, saturday market, talent contests during Yamhill County Fair, flea maret and rodeo.
Founded: 1854
Paid Staff: 2
Volunteer Staff: 6
Income Sources: Horseshows; Horseboarding; Fairs & Rodeos; USDA or Lottery; Receptions; Weddings; Banquets
Performs At: Fairgrounds
Seating Capacity: 4,000
Rental Contact: Darcie Vanderyacht

8083
BRITT PAVILION
Britt Festivals
216 W Main Street
Medford, OR 97501
Mailing Address: PO Box 1124
Phone: 541-773-6077
Fax: 541-776-3712
Toll-free: 800-882-7488
Web Site: www.brittfest.org
Officers:
  Chairman: Matt Pattern
  Vice Chairman: Mike Burrill
  President and CEO: Donna Briggs
  Vice-President: Matt Patten
  Secretary: Kelsey Ausland
  Treasure: Dave Bernard
Management:
  Executive Director: Jim Fredericks
  Development Director: Mark Knippel
  Box Office Manager: Marie Carbone
  Marketing Director: Sara K. Cole
  Sales Associate: Bobby Abernathy
Seating Capacity: 2,200

8084
CRATERIAN GINGER ROGERS THEATER
23 S. Central Ave
Medford, OR 97501
Phone: 541-779-3000
Fax: 541-779-8175
e-mail: stephen@craterian.org
Web Site: www.craterian.org

Officers:
  President: Steve Erb
  Vice President: Judy Gambee
  Secretary: Judy Chiosso-Glass
  Treasurer: Ron Silverman
Management:
  Executive Director: Stephen McCandless
  Development & Communications Manage:
  Maureen Esser
  Office Manager: Darla DenHerder
  Box Office Manager: Colette Tidball
  Event Manager: Eric Strahl
Status: Non-Profit, Non-Professional

8085
MCARTHUR SPORTS FIELD
Western Oregon University
345 N Monmouth Avenue
Monmouth, OR 97361
Phone: 503-838-8000
Fax: 503-838-8370
Toll-free: 877-877-1593
e-mail: webmaster@wou.edu
Web Site: www.wou.edu
Officers:
  Chair: Diane Baxter PhD
  President: Mark D. Weiss
Management:
  Director: Jon Carey
  Marketing: Denise Visuano
  Atletics: Linsay Bouman
  Director: Judy Vanderburg
  Office Coordinato: Kayla Fordham
Seating Capacity: 2,500

8086
RICE AUDITORIUM
Western Oregon University
345 N Monmouth Avenue
Monmouth, OR 97361
Phone: 503-838-8000
Fax: 503-838-8370
Toll-free: 877-877-1594
e-mail: webmaster@wou.edu
Web Site: www.wou.edu
Officers:
  President: Mark D. Weiss
  Chair: Diane Baxter PhD
Management:
  Marketing: Denise Visuano
  Marketing: Denise Visuano
  Atletics: Linsay Bouman
  Director: Judy Vanderburg
  Office Coordinato: Kayla Fordham

8087
NEWPORT PERFORMING ARTS CENTER
777 W Olive Street
PO Box 1315
Newport, OR 97365
Phone: 541-265-9231
Fax: 541-265-9464
Toll-free: 888-701-7123
e-mail: occa@coastarts.org
Web Site: coastarts.org
Officers:
  President: Kay Moxness
  Secretary: Wayne Belmont
  VP: Sandi Williams
Management:
  Executive Director: Catherine Rickbone
  Manager: Polly Ivers
  Operations: Ron Miller

FACILITIES / Oregon

Utilizes: Actors; Artists-in-Residence; Choreographers; Collaborating Artists; Collaborations; Commissioned Composers; Commissioned Music; Curators; Dance Companies; Dancers; Designers; Educators; Filmmakers; Fine Artists; Five Seasonal Concerts; Grant Writers; Guest Accompanists; Guest Artists; Guest Choreographers; Guest Companies; Guest Composers; Guest Conductors; Guest Designers; Guest Directors; Guest Ensembles; Guest Instructors; Guest Lecturers; Guest Musical Directors; Guest Musicians; Guest Soloists; Guest Teachers; Guest Writers; Guild Activities; High School Drama; Instructors; Local Artists; Local Unknown Artists; Lyricists; Multi Collaborations; Multimedia; Music; New Productions; Organization Contracts; Original Music Scores; Performance Artists; Playwrights; Resident Artists; Resident Professionals; Sign Language Translators; Singers; Soloists; Student Interns; Special Technical Talent; Theatre Companies; Touring Companies; Visual Arts
Facility Category: Live performance venue
Type of Stage: Proscenium
Stage Dimensions: 23 x 42
Seating Capacity: 393
Year Built: 1988
Year Remodeled: 2000
Rental Contact: Jan Eastman
Resident Groups: 8 major resident presenting organizations

8088
PENDLETON CONVENTION CENTER
500 SW Dorion Ave
Pendleton, OR 97801
Phone: 541-966-0201
Fax: 541-278-1317
Toll-free: 800-863-9358
e-mail: tracy.bosen@ci.pendleton.or.us
Web Site: www.pendleton.or.us
Officers:
   Human Resources Manager: Andrea Denton
   Mayor: Phillip Houk
Management:
   Development Director: Tracy Bosen
   Manager: Robb Corbett
   Administrative Services Officer: Andrea Denton
   Police Assistant: Dianna Assistant
Status: Non-Profit, Professional
Paid Artists: 3
Seating Capacity: 128,193

8089
ARLENE SCHNITZER CONCERT HALL
Portland Center for the Performing Arts
1111 SW Broadway
Portland, OR 97205
Phone: 503-248-4335
Fax: 503-274-7490
e-mail: info@pcpa.com
Web Site: www.pcpa.com
Officers:
   Chairman: Ronald K. Ragan
Management:
   Executive Director: Robyn Williams
   Public Relations Coordinator: Alicia Loos
   Assistant Executive Director: Lori Leyba Kramer
   Box Office Manager: Stephanie Viegas
Opened: 1984
Budget: $8 million
Income Sources: Hotel/Motel Tax; City; County & Regional Government
Affiliations: Oregon Symphony
Annual Attendance: 300,000
Facility Category: Concert Hall
Type of Stage: Proscenium
Stage Dimensions: 54'x40'
Seating Capacity: 2,992
Year Built: 1928
Year Remodeled: 1984
Cost: $10,000,000
Rental Contact: Lori Kramer
Resident Groups: Oregon Symphony Orchestra

8090
COLUMBIA MEADOWS
63701 Southwest Columbia River Highway
Portland, OR 97054
Phone: 503-221-0288
Fax: 503-227-4418
e-mail: lowell@doubletree.com
Web Site: www.doubletree.com
Officers:
   President: David Leiken
Management:
   GM: Lowell MacGregor
Seating Capacity: 25,000

8091
COMMUNITY MUSIC CENTER
923 SW Washington Portland
Portland, OR 97202
Mailing Address: 503
Phone: 530-823-3177
Fax: 503-228-7034
e-mail: symphony@orsymphony.org
Web Site: www.orsymphony.org
Officers:
   Chairman: Karl Smith
   Vice Chairman: J. Clayton Hering
   Vice Chairman: Walter E. Weyler
   Treasurer: Ted Austin
Management:
   General Manager: Mary Crist
   Operations: Susan Nielsen
   Marketing: Michael Granados
   Operations Manager: Jacob Wade
   Director: Laura Fay

8092
DOLORES WINNINGSTAD THEATRE
Portland Center for the Performing Arts
1111 SW Broadway
Portland, OR 97205
Phone: 503-248-4335
Fax: 503-274-7490
e-mail: info@pcpa.com
Web Site: www.pcpa.com
Officers:
   Chairman: Ronald K Ragen
Management:
   Executive Director: Robyn Williams
   Public Relations Coordinator: Alicia Loos
   Assistant Executive Director: Lori Leyba Kramer
   Box Office Manager: Stephanie Viegas
Budget: $8 million
Income Sources: City; County; Regional Government; Hotel-Motel Tax
Annual Attendance: 200,000
Facility Category: Black box
Type of Stage: Black Box
Seating Capacity: 292
Year Built: 1987

8093
EARLE A CHILES CENTER
University of Portland
5000 N Willamette Boulevard
Portland, OR 97203-5798
Phone: 503-943-7525
Fax: 503-943-7451
Toll-free: 800-227-4568
e-mail: williams@up.edu
Web Site: www.portlandpilots.com
Officers:
   President: E William Beauchamp
Management:
   Director: Larry Williams
   Marketing: Tricia Miller
   Athletic Director: Scott Leykam
   Associate Athletic Director: Buzz Stroud
   Operations Manager: Tony Ortiz
Status: Non-Profit, Non-Professional

8094
EVANS AUDITORIUM
Lewis and Clark College
0615 Palatine Hill Road
Portland, OR 97219
Phone: 503-768-7000
Fax: 503-768-7475
e-mail: music@lclark.edu
Web Site: www.lclark.edu
Officers:
   Chair: David Becker
   President: Barry Glassner
Management:
   Artistic Director: Amy Drill
   Marketing: Joe Becker

8095
MEMORIAL COLISEUM
1 Center Court
Suite 150
Portland, OR 97227
Phone: 503-797-9619
Fax: 507-736-2182
e-mail: rq.boxoffice@rosequarter.com
Web Site: www.rosequarter.com
Officers:
   President: Paul G Allen
   CEO: Tod Leiweke
Management:
   General Manager: Mike Scanlon
Seating Capacity: 12,500

8096
NEWMARK THEATRE
Portland Center for the Performing Arts
1111 SW Broadway
Portland, OR 97205
Phone: 503-248-4335
Fax: 503-274-7490
e-mail: info@pcpa.com
Web Site: www.pcpa.com
Officers:
   Chairman: Ronald K Ragen
Management:
   Executive Director: Robyn Williams
   Public Relations Coordinator: Alicia Loos
   Assistant Executive Director: Lori Leyba Kramer
   Box Office Manager: Stephanie Viegas
Budget: $8 million
Income Sources: City; County; Regional Government; Hotel-Motel Tax
Performs At: Theatre, dance, choral, chamber music
Affiliations: Oregon Symphony Orchestra
Annual Attendance: 200,000
Facility Category: Concert Hall
Type of Stage: Proscenium
Stage Dimensions: 48'6 x 56'""
Orchestra Pit: 1
Seating Capacity: 880

FACILITIES / Pennsylvania

Year Built: 1987
Architect: Rapp & Rapp
Cost: $18,000,000

8097
PGE PARK
1844 SW Morrison Street
Portland, OR 97205
Phone: 503-553-5400
Fax: 503-553-5405
e-mail: info@pgepark.com
Web Site: www.pgepark.com
Officers:
   President: Merritt Paulson
Management:
   Operations: Ken Puckett
   Development: Ryan Brach
   Marketing: Cory Dolich
Seating Capacity: 30,500

8098
PIONEER COURTHOUSE SQUARE
715 SW Morrison Street
Suite 702
Portland, OR 97205
Phone: 503-223-1613
Fax: 503-222-7425
e-mail: webmaster@pioneercourthousesquare.org
Web Site: www.thesquarepdx.org
Management:
   Executive Director: Jennifer Polver
   Production Director: Shannon Weisinger
   Marketing Director: Theresa Vetsch-Sandoval
   Development Manager: Maren Jones
   Administrative Coordinator: Travis Brumet
Budget: $400,000-$1,000,000
Annual Attendance: 7.6 million
Facility Category: Outdoor
Seating Capacity: 3,000

8099
PORTLAND CENTER FOR THE PERFORMING ARTS
Portland Center for the Performing Arts
1111 SW Broadway
Portland, OR 97205
Phone: 503-248-4335
Fax: 503-274-7490
e-mail: info@pcpa.com
Web Site: www.pcpa.com
Officers:
   Chairman: Ronald K Ragen
Management:
   Executive Director: Robyn Williams
   Public Relations Coordinator: Alicia Loos
   Assistant Executive Director: Lori Leyba Kramer
   Box Office Manager: Stephanie Viegas
Annual Attendance: 400,000
Facility Category: Theatre
Type of Stage: Proscenium
Seating Capacity: 2,992
Year Built: 1952
Year Remodeled: 1968
Rental Contact: Booking Manager Lori Kramer

8100
PORTLAND INSTITUTE FOR CONTEMPORARY ART
224 NW 13th Avenue
Suite 305
Portland, OR 97209
Phone: 503-242-1419
Fax: 503-243-1167
e-mail: pica@pica.org
Web Site: www.pica.org
Officers:
   Chair: Michael Tingley
   Treasurer: Nancy Barrows
   Secretary: Sally Lawrence
   Vice Chair: Eric Philps
Management:
   Executive Director: Victoria Frey
   Glass: Philip
Founded: 1995
Status: Non-Profit, Professional

8101
REED THEATRE
Reed College
3203 SE Woodstock Boulevard
Portland, OR 97202
Phone: 503-777-7356
Fax: 503-777-7769
e-mail: worleyk@reed.edu
Web Site: www.reed.edu
Officers:
   Chairman: Daniel B Greenberg
   President: Colin Diver
   Treasurer: Edwin McFarlane
   Secretary: E Randolph Labbe
Management:
   General Manager: Kathleen Worley
   Director: Jan Kurtz

8102
ROSE QUARTER
1 Center Court
Suite 150
Portland, OR 97227
Phone: 503-797-9619
Fax: 503-736-2182
e-mail: rq.boxoffice@rosequarter.com
Web Site: www.rosequarter.com
Officers:
   President: Paul G Allen
   CEO: Tod Leiweke
Management:
   General Manager: Mike Scanlon
Status: For-Profit, Professional
Seating Capacity: 12,000

8103
WILSON CENTER FOR THE PERFORMING ARTS
1111 SW 10th
Portland, OR 97205
Phone: 503-746-9293

8104
HISTORIC ELSINORE THEATRE
170 High St
Salem, OR 97301
Phone: 503-375-3574
Fax: 503-375-0284
e-mail: steve@elsinoretheatre.com
Web Site: www.elsinoretheatre.com
Management:
   Executive Director: Stephen Martin
   Events Director: Sharon McCurry
   Technical Director: Greg Rieder
   Facilities Manager: John Riches
   Managment Assistant: TJ Lowdon
   Volunter Coordinator/Events Ass't: Amber Limb
Mission: Promote, protect and enhance the Historic Elsinore Theatre asa historic national landmark and performing arts center
Seating Capacity: 1200

8105
SEASIDE CIVIC AND CONVENTION CENTER
415 1st Avenue
Seaside, OR 97138
Phone: 503-738-8585
Fax: 503-738-0198
Toll-free: 800-394-3303
e-mail: sales@seasideconvention.com
Web Site: www.seasideconvention.com
Management:
   Manager: Karen Murray
Status: Non-Profit, Non-Professional

8106
BROADWAY ROSE THEATRE
12850 SW Grant Avenue
Tigard, OR 97281
Phone: 503-620-5262
Fax: 503-670-8512
e-mail: brisa@broadwayrose.com
Web Site: www.broadwayrose.com
Officers:
   President: Lisa Francolini
   VP: Scott Schiefelbein
   Treasurer: Jennifer Dale
   Secretary: Dave Cutz
Management:
   Executive Director: Brisa Trinchero
   Artistic Director: Sharon Maroney
   Marketing: Alan Anderson
Founded: 1992

Pennsylvania

8107
ALLENTOWN SYMPHONY HALL
23 N 6th Street
Allentown, PA 18101
Phone: 610-432-6715
Fax: 610-432-6735
Web Site: www.allentownsymphony.org
Officers:
   President: Kristine Burfeind
   Secretary: Frank Heston
   Treasurer: Joan B Cole
Management:
   Development Director: Maureen S Joly
   Marketing: Lucy Bloise
   Manager: Tracy Damiani
   Executive Director: Sheila Evans
   Development Director: Robin Flores
Opened: 1953
Status: Non-Profit, Professional

8108
J BIRNEY CRUM STADIUM
31 S Penn Street
Allentown, PA 18105
Phone: 484-765-4000
Fax: 610-871-6052
e-mail: webmaster@allentownsd.org
Web Site: www.allentownsd.org
Officers:
   President: Robert E. Smith
   Vice President: Julie Ambrose
   Chief Academic Officer: Tina M. Belardi, Ph.D.
   Chief Financial Officer: John R Clark

FACILITIES / Pennsylvania

Chief Operations Officer: David M. Wildonger
Management:
  Executive Director: Kristin Kruger
  Executive Director: Christina Mazzella
  Director: Jos, Rosado
  Director of Assessment: Karen Baurkot
  Director of Child Nutrition: Ellen O'Brien

8109
MISHLER THEATRE
1212 12th Avenue
Altoona, PA 16601
Phone: 814-949-2787
Fax: 814-949-3909
e-mail: blrartsorg@aol.com
Web Site: www.mishlertheatre.org
Officers:
  President: Diane Osgood
  Treasurer: Gerald Hymes
  Secretary: Jane Hite
  Vice President: Jane Hite
Management:
  Executive Director: Katherine Shaffer
  Development Director: Karen Volpe
  Executive Director: Kate Shaffer
Founded: 1906
Status: Non-Profit; Professional

8110
ARTS GUILD AT NEUMANN COLLEGE
Neumann College
1 Neumann Drive
Aston, PA 19014-1298
Phone: 610-459-0905
Fax: 610-459-1370
e-mail: dimarinn@neumann.edu
Web Site: www.neumann.edu
Officers:
  President: Rosalie Mirenda
Management:
  Marketing: Stephen T Bell
  Director: Sara Melisi
  Health Services: Kim Agozzino
  Education: Jenelle Abnett
  Arts and Science Faculty: Kristen Acosta

8111
FRED P MEAGHER THEATRE
Neumann College
One Neumann Drive
Aston, PA 19014-1298
Phone: 610-459-0905
Fax: 610-459-1370
Web Site: www.neumann.edu
Officers:
  President: Rosalie Mirenda PhD
Management:
  Director: Sara Melisi
  Marketing: Stephen T Bell
  Health Services: Kim Agozzino
  Education: Jenelle Abnett
  Arts and Science Faculty: Kristen Acosta

8112
TD BANK AMPHITHEATER
2400 Bayberry Rd
Bensalem, PA 19020
Phone: 215-633-3604
Fax: 215-633-3629
e-mail: tdbaevents@bensalem-township.org
Web Site: www.tdbankamphitheater.com
Management:
  Manager: Dawn Davis
Facility Category: Outdoor Amphitheater

Seating Capacity: 2500

8113
MORAVIAN COLLEGE: MUSIC INSTITUTE
1200 Main Street
Bethlehem, PA 18018
Phone: 610-861-1320
Fax: 610-861-1657
Toll-free: 800-441-3191
e-mail: music@moravian.edu
Web Site: www.moravian.edu
Officers:
  Chair: Larry Lipkis
  President: Bryon L. Grigsby
  Secretary: Debbie Hinkel
  Chief Human Resource Officer: Jon Conard
  Chief Research Officer: Carole Reese
Management:
  Operations: Blair Flintom
  Assoiate Professor: Daniel Jasper
  Assistant: Deborah L. Evans
Founded: 1742

8114
STABLER ARENA
Leghigh University
124 Goodman Drive
Bethlehem, PA 18015
Phone: 610-758-3770
Fax: 610-866-8070
e-mail: info@stablerarena.com
Web Site: www.lehighsports.com
Officers:
  President: Alice P Gast
Management:
  Director: Karen Adams
  Dean of Athletics: Joe Sterrett
  Associate Director: Bill Griffin
  Associate Director: Jack Foley
  Assistant Athletic Dorector: Greg Strobel
Founded: 1979
Seating Capacity: 6,700

8115
TOUCHSTONE THEATRE
321 E 4th Street
Bethlehem, PA 18015
Phone: 610-867-1689
e-mail: touchstone@touchstone.org
Web Site: www.touchstone.org
Officers:
  President: Alex Shade
  Vice President: Jeanne B. Shook
  Treasurer: John Fallock
  Secretary: Alexis Leon
Management:
  Managing Director/Ensemble Member: Lisa Jordan
  Artistic Manager/Ensemble Member: James P Jordan
  Touring Manager/Ensemble Member: Bill George
  General Manager: Emma Chong
  Coodinator: Mary Wright
Founded: 1981
Opened: 1981
Status: Non-Profit, Professional

8116
ZOELLNER ARTS CENTER
Lehigh University
420 E Packer Avenue
Bethlehem, PA 18015

Phone: 610-758-2787
Fax: 610-758-6537
e-mail: els7@lehigh.edu
Web Site: www.zoellnerartscenter.org
Officers:
  Executive Director: Elizabeth Scofield
Management:
  Development Director: Maureen Connelley
  Program Director: Deborah Sacaratis
Utilizes: Artists-in-Residence; Collaborations; Composers-in-Residence; Dance Companies; Dancers; Fine Artists; Five Seasonal Concerts; Guest Choreographers; Guest Musical Directors; Guest Musicians; Instructors; Local Artists; Multi Collaborations; Original Music Scores; Sign Language Translators; Singers; Soloists; Special Technical Talent; Theatre Companies
Founded: 1997
Status: Non-Profit, Professional
Paid Staff: 20
Volunteer Staff: 180
Paid Artists: 20
Budget: $2.2 million
Income Sources: Ticket Sales; Rentals; Development; Playbill
Performs At: Baker Hall; Diamond Theater; Black Box Theatre; Presenting Series
Affiliations: Lehigh University
Annual Attendance: 30,000
Type of Stage: Proscenium & Thrust
Stage Dimensions: 37x25
Seating Capacity: 1,000
Year Built: 1997
Architect: 33,000,000
Rental Contact: Annette Stolte

8117
BRADFORD CREATIVE & PERFORMING ARTS CENTER
10 Marilyn Home Way
PO Box 153
Bradford, PA 16701
Phone: 814-362-2522
Fax: 814-362-2556
e-mail: arts@bcpac.com
Web Site: www.bcpac.com
Officers:
  President: Shane Oschman
  Vice President: Jeannine Schoenecker
  Treasurer: Marcia Morrison
  Secretary: Pat Ryan
  Co Chair: Terri Leven
Management:
  Executive Director: James D Guelfi
  Marketing: Tim Ziaukas
  Assistant Manager: Christin Davis
  Program Selection Chair: Dean Harten
  Office Manager: Kathy Peace
Founded: 1984
Status: Non-Profit
Paid Staff: 17
Budget: $275,000
Income Sources: Grants; Corporate & Individual Donations Ticket Sales
Annual Attendance: 6,000

8118
ALUMNI AUDITORIUM
Widener University
14th and Chestnut Street
One University Place
Chester, PA 19013

FACILITIES / Pennsylvania

Phone: 610-499-4000
Fax: 610-499-4196
e-mail: cmmccormick@widener.edu
Web Site: www.widener.edu
Officers:
   President: James T Harris III
   Provost of Academic Affairs: Stephen C. Wilhite
   Senior Vice President: Joseph J. Baker
   Senior Vice President: Linda S. Durant
   Chief Community Engagement and Dive: Marcine Pickron-Davis
Management:
   Executive Director: Cecilia M McCormick
   Operations: Carl G Pierce
Founded: 1961

8119
MARWICK BOYD AUDITORIUM
Clarion University
840 Wood Street
Clarion, PA 16214-1232
Phone: 814-393-2000
Fax: 814-393-2039
Toll-free: 800-672-7171
e-mail: info@clarion.edu
Web Site: www.clarion.edu
Officers:
   President: Joe Grunenwald
   Chair: R Lee James
   Secretary: Richard Hilinski
Management:
   Director: James Stockman
   Marketing: David Love

8120
UPPER DARBY PERFORMING ARTS CENTER
601 N Lansdowne Avenue
Drexel Hill, PA 19026
Phone: 610-622-1189
Fax: 610-622-6960
e-mail: udpac@mac.com
Web Site: www.udpac.org
Management:
   Executive Director: Harry Dietzler

8121
STATE THEATRE CENTER FOR THE ARTS
453 Northampton Street
Easton, PA 18042-3562
Phone: 610-252-3132
Fax: 610-258-2570
Toll-free: 800-999-7828
e-mail: info@statetheatre.org
Web Site: www.statetheatre.org
Officers:
   President/CEO: Shelley Brown
   Vice President: Jamie Balliet
   VP, Production and Operation: Mark Rafinski
   Vice President of Development: Denise Smith
Management:
   Operations: Mark Rafinski
   Marketing: Jamie Balliet
   Box Office Manager: Karey Roberts
   Sound Engineer: Mike Healy
   Accountant: Cindy Kemmerer
Annual Attendance: 10,000
Facility Category: Performing Arts Theatre
Seating Capacity: 1,400
Year Built: 1922
Year Remodeled: 2000

8122
ERIE CIVIC CENTER: LJ TULLIO ARENA
809 French Street
Erie, PA 16501
Phone: 814-453-7117
Fax: 814-455-9931
e-mail: casey@erieevents.com
Web Site: www.erieevents.com
Officers:
   Chair: James T. Maren
   Vice Chair: Thomas Doolin
   Treasurer: Bruce Q Whitehair
   Secretary: Gwendolyn White
Management:
   Executive Director: John A Casey Wells
   Operations: Barry Copple
   General Manager: Jeff Esposito
   Director of Finance and Administrat: Charles Iverson
Founded: 1983
Status: Professional
Budget: $600,000
Annual Attendance: 140,000
Facility Category: Historic Performing Arts Center
Type of Stage: Proscenium
Stage Dimensions: 60x32
Seating Capacity: 2506
Year Built: 1931
Cost: $ 1.5 Milion

8123
MARY D'ANGELO PERFORMING ARTS CENTER
Mercyhurst College
501 E 38th Street
Erie, PA 16546
Phone: 814-824-2000
Fax: 814-824-3098
Toll-free: 800-825-1926
e-mail: mfuhrman@mercyhurst.edu
Web Site: www.mercyhurst.edu
Officers:
   Chairman: Marlene D. Mosco
   Vice Chair: Richard A. Lanzillo
   Vice Chair: Sister JoAnne K Courneen
   President: Thomas J. Gamble, Ph.D.
   CEO: Terrence Cavanaugh
Management:
   Director: Michael Fuhrman
   Marketing: Michelle Ellia
   Manager: Annette Gardner
Status: Non-Profit, Professional

8124
TOTEM POLE PLAYHOUSE
9555 Golf Course Road
PO Box 603
Fayetteville, PA 17222-0603
Phone: 717-352-2164
Fax: 717-352-8870
Toll-free: 888-805-7056
e-mail: boxoffice@totempoleplayhouse.org
Web Site: www.totempoleplayhouse.org
Officers:
   President: Dana Witt
   Treasurer: Judy Kaufman
Management:
   Managing Director: Sue McMurtray
   Artistic Director: Rowan Joseph
   General Manager: Daphne Blair
   Associate Producer: Chris Russo
   Box Office Manager: Renee Rankin
Founded: 1950
Specialized Field: Professional Theatre
Status: Non-Profit, Professional
Paid Staff: 4
Volunteer Staff: 30
Paid Artists: 50
Budget: $1,100,000
Income Sources: Ticket Sales; Tax Deductible Gifts; Corporate Sponsors
Affiliations: Actors Equity Association
Annual Attendance: 29,000
Facility Category: Air-Conditioned Enclosure
Type of Stage: Proscenium
Year Built: 1969

8125
MUSSELMAN STADIUM
Gettysburg College
300 N Washington Street
Gettysburg, PA 17325
Phone: 717-337-6300
Fax: 717-337-6528
e-mail: dwright@gettysburg.edu
Web Site: www.gettysburg.edu
Officers:
   President: Janet Morgan Riggs
Management:
   Director: David Wright
   Associate Provost for Faculty Devel: Robert E. Bohrer
   Administrative Services Assistant: Kara Flythe
   Assistant Provost for Scholarship: Maureen E. Forrestal
   Administrative Services Assistant: Suzanne Gockowski
Founded: 1965
Status: Non-Profit
Seating Capacity: 6,000

8126
PALACE THEATRE
21 W Otterman Street
Greensburg, PA 15601
Phone: 724-836-8000
Fax: 724-836-5833
e-mail: palace@earthlink.net
Web Site: www.thepalacetheatre.org
Officers:
   President: Michael J Langer
   Chairman: T Terrance Reese
   Treasurer: Sean Cassidy
   Secretary: Jamie McHugh
Management:
   Manager: Linda Kubas
   Marketing/Programming Director: Teresa Baughman
Founded: 1926
Specialized Field: Pittsburgh Metro
Status: Non-Profit, Non-Professional
Paid Staff: 10
Volunteer Staff: 80
Performs At: Multi-disciplinary; In-House & Rentals
Annual Attendance: 60,000
Facility Category: Performing Arts Center
Type of Stage: Proscenuim
Stage Dimensions: 40' x 37'
Seating Capacity: 1369
Year Built: 1926
Year Remodeled: 2010
Rental Contact: Teresa Baughman

FACILITIES / Pennsylvania

8127
FARM SHOW COMPLEX AND EXPO CENTER
2300 N Cameron Street
Harrisburg, PA 17110-9443
Phone: 717-787-5373
Fax: 717-783-8710
e-mail: farmshow@state.pa.us
Web Site: www.pafarmshowcomplex.com
Management:
  Executive Director: Michael Waugh
  Assistant Director: Heidi Crager
  Senior Advisor: Patrick Kerwin
  Director of Sales: Sharon S. Altland
  Show Manager: Morgan Firestine
Mission: To host a full lineup of exciting events including arena events, business meetings, conferences and expositions.
Status: For-Profit, Professional
Facility Category: Expo and Conference Center
Seating Capacity: 7,400
Year Built: 1938
Rental Contact: Heidi Cragera

8128
STATE MUSEUM OF PENNSYLVANIA
300 N Street
Harrisburg, PA 17120-0024
Phone: 717-787-4980
Fax: 717-783-4558
e-mail: ra-statemuseum@pa.gov
Web Site: www.statemuseumpa.org
Officers:
  President: Franklin D. Roosevelt
Management:
  Marketing: Howard Pollman
Facility Category: Auditorium

8129
WHITAKER CENTER FOR SCIENCE AND THE ARTS
222 Market Street
Harrisburg, PA 17101
Phone: 717-214-2787
Fax: 717-214-2791
e-mail: info@whitakercenter.org
Web Site: www.whitakercenter.org
Officers:
  Chairman: Gary D. St. Hilaire
  Vice Chairman: Terry Lehman
  President/CEO: Michael L Hanes PhD
  Vice President: Steve Bishop
  Chief Financial Officer: Jacqueline Wolpert
Management:
  Operations: Lisa Kreider
  Development: Michele Holloway
  Marketing: Kathleen Keller
  Director of Marketing & Sales: Michael Chapaloney
Utilizes: Original Music Scores; Resident Artists; Theatre Companies; Touring Companies
Opened: 1999
Status: Non-Profit, Non-Professional
Facility Category: Theater
Type of Stage: Proscenium
Stage Dimensions: 45 x 80
Seating Capacity: 636
Year Built: 1997

8130
HERSHEY THEATRE
15 E Caracas Avenue
PO Box 395
Hershey, PA 17033
Phone: 717-534-3405
Fax: 717-533-2882
e-mail: pseeley@hersheypa.com
Web Site: www.hersheytheatre.com
Management:
  Operations: Rod Underkoffler
  Marketing: Andy Longenberger
  Events & Programming: Amanda Haffly
  Educational Outreach: Mariella Trosko
  Event Services: Sarah Measley
Founded: 1933
Status: Non-Profit, Professional

8131
FISHER AUDTORIUM
Indiana University Of Pennsylvania
403 South 11th St
Indiana, PA 15705
Phone: 724-357-2548
Fax: 724-357-7899
Web Site: www.iup.edu/fisher
Management:
  Technical Dir. College Of Fine Arts: David Surtasky
  Assoc. Technical Director: Andrew Niedziela
Seating Capacity: 1460

8132
MOUNTAIN PLAYHOUSE
7690 Somerset Pike
PO Box 205
Jennerstown, PA 15547
Phone: 814-629-9201
Fax: 814-629-9201
e-mail: info@mountainplayhouse.com
Web Site: www.mountainplayhouse.org
Officers:
  Chair: Dr.Joseph Beer
  Vice Chair: Jason E. Miller
  Treasurer: Kevin McQuillan
  Secretary: Marcene Glover
Management:
  Development: Erica Roslonski
  Manager: Lori Kishlock
  Marketing: Mary Louise Stoughton
Status: Non-Profit, Professional

8133
CAMBRIA COUNTY WAR MEMORIAL ARENA
326 Napoleon
Johnstown, PA 15901
Phone: 814-536-5156
Fax: 814-536-3670
Toll-free: 800-243-8499
e-mail: gm@warmemorialarena.com
Web Site: www.warmemorialarena.com
Management:
  President: Larry Giannone
  Executive Director: James Vautar
  Managing Director: Tom Grenell
Mission: Sports and entertainment
Founded: 1950
Specialized Field: Hockey
Status: Non-Profit, Professional
Paid Staff: 9
Paid Artists: 12
Budget: 1.5 million
Income Sources: Rental Events
Annual Attendance: 275,000
Facility Category: Arena
Type of Stage: Portable
Seating Capacity: 5,000
Year Built: 1950
Year Remodeled: 2003
Cost: $85 million
Rental Contact: Jim Vautar

8134
PASQUERILLA PERFORMING ARTS CENTER
University of Pittsburgh at Johnsontown
450 Schoolhouse Road
Johnstown, PA 15904-2990
Phone: 814-269-7200
Fax: 814-269-7240
Toll-free: 800-846-2787
e-mail: upjarts@pitt.edu
Web Site: www.upj.pitt.edu/artscenter
Officers:
  Chair: Barbara Parkins
  Scott: Jodie S Novak
  Richard: Becker CEO
Management:
  Executive Director: Michael Bodolosky
  Office Manager: Beverly Walerysiak
  Technical Director: Thomas Brubaker
Founded: 1991
Status: Non-Profit, Professional
Paid Staff: 3
Volunteer Staff: 39
Seating Capacity: 1001

8135
PASQUERILLA PERFORMING ARTS CENTER
University of Pittsburgh at Johnstown
450 Schoolhouse Road
Johnstown, PA 15904-2990
Phone: 814-269-7200
Fax: 814-269-7240
Toll-free: 800-846-2787
e-mail: upjarts@pitt.edu
Web Site: www.upj.pitt.edu/artscenter
Officers:
  Chair: Barbara Parkins
  Scott: Jodie S Novak
  Richard: Becker CEO
Management:
  Executive Director: Michael Bodolosky
  Office Manager: Beverlyh Walerysiak
  Technical Director: Thomas Brubaker
Founded: 1991
Status: Non-Profit, Professional
Paid Staff: 3
Volunteer Staff: 39
Seating Capacity: 1001

8136
POINT STADIUM
City Hall Recreation Department
401 Main Street
Johnstown, PA 15901
Phone: 814-533-2104
Fax: 814-533-2111
Management:
  Director: Clifford Kitner
Founded: 1926
Status: Non-Profit, Non-Professional
Paid Staff: 151
Seating Capacity: 10,500

FACILITIES / Pennsylvania

8137
LONGWOOD GARDENS
PO Box 501
Kennett Square, PA 19348
Phone: 610-388-1000
Fax: 610-388-3833
e-mail: emoody@longwoodgardens.org
Web Site: www.longwoodgardens.org
Officers:
  President: Marie Viallet
Management:
  Director: Paul B. Redman
  Chief Financial Officer: Dennis Fisher
Status: Non-Profit, Professional
Paid Staff: 200

8138
LONG'S PARK AMPHITHEATRE
630 Janet Avenue
Lancaster, PA 17602
Mailing Address: PO Box 1553
Phone: 717-295-7054
Fax: 717-290-7123
e-mail: info@longspark.org
Web Site: www.longspark.org
Officers:
  President: Richard Kurtz
  VP: David L. Wauls
  Treasurer: Kimberly Wefelmeyer
  Secretary: William (Bill) Wright
  Immediate Past President: Timothy Ardinger
Management:
  Music Director: Stella Reno
  Operations Manager: Carol Barton
Income Sources: Donations; Sponsorships
Seating Capacity: 30,000

8139
WEIS CENTER FOR THE PERFORMING ARTS
Lewisburg, PA
Lewisburg, PA 17837-2005
Mailing Address: 1 Dent Drive Lewisburg, 18737
Phone: 570-572-000
Fax: 570-577-3701
e-mail: boswell@bucknell.edu
Web Site: http://www.departments.bucknell.edu
Officers:
  President: John C. Bravman
Management:
  Director Cultural Events: William Boswell
Mission: To provide the campus and region with opportunity for exposure to the essential cultural and educational values inherent in the great historical and radical traditions of the performing arts.
Founded: 1846
Budget: $150,000-$400,000
Affiliations: APAP, CMA, PA Presenters, Others
Annual Attendance: 9000
Facility Category: Concert Hall
Type of Stage: Sprung Wood Floor
Seating Capacity: 1,200+
Year Built: 1988

8140
SHAFER AUDITORIUM
Allegheny College
Box H
Meadville, PA 16335
Phone: 814-332-2754
Web Site: www.allegheny.edu
Officers:
  VP: Brain F. Dalton
  Sr. Associate Director: Bob Baldwin
  Admission Counselor: Anne Leonard
  Admission Counselor: Loni Benzvi
  Assistant Director: Richel Dingman
Management:
  Director Student Activities: Ellen Kauffman
Seating Capacity: 1,750

8141
MILLBROOK PLAYHOUSE
Country Club Lane
PO Box 161
Mill Hall, PA 17751
Phone: 570-748-8083
Fax: 570-748-0925
e-mail: info@millbrookplayhouse.org
Web Site: www.millbrookplayhouse.org
Officers:
  President: Erla Mae Frederick
  VP: Jason Brown
  Treasurer: Jacqui Conklin
  Secretary: Joanne Hoberman
Management:
  Member: Mary Lins
Founded: 1952
Status: Non-Profit
Season: May - August

8142
LACKAWANNA COUNTY STADIUM
235 Montage Mountain Road
Moosic, PA 18507
Phone: 570-969-2255
Fax: 570-963-6564
Web Site: www.redbarons.com
Officers:
  President: Rob Crain
Management:
  General Manager: Tom Vanschaak
  Staff Accountant: William Steiner
  Corporate Services Manager: Karen Luciano
  Ticket Operations Manager: Seth Atkinson
  Vice President of Ticket Sales: Doug Augis
Founded: 1989
Status: Non-Profit, Professional
Paid Staff: 200
Seating Capacity: 10,800

8143
POCONO PLAYHOUSE
Playhouse Lane
Mountainhome, PA 18342
Phone: 570-595-7456
Fax: 570-595-7465

8144
BUCKS COUNTY PLAYHOUSE
70 S Main
PO Box 313
New Hope, PA 18938
Phone: 215-862-2041
Fax: 215-862-0220
e-mail: mail@buckscountyplayhouse.com
Web Site: www.buckscountyplayhouse.com
Management:
  President: Ralph Miller
Founded: 1938
Status: Professional

8145
BEEGHLY THEATER
Westminster College
New Wilmington, PA 16172
Phone: 724-946-8761

8146
WILL W ORR AUDITORIUM
Westminster College
Market Street
New Wilmington, PA 16172
Phone: 724-946-7270
Fax: 724-946-6270
Toll-free: 800-942-8033
Web Site: www.westminster.edu/music
Officers:
  President: Dr. Richard H. Dorman
  Associate Professor Music: Dr. Anne Bentz
  Associate Professor Music: Dr. Nancy DeSalvo
  Associate Professor Music: Dr. Daniel Perttu
  Associate Professor Music: Dr. Robin Lind
Management:
  Artistic Director: Nancy Desalvo
Status: Non-Profit, Professional
Paid Staff: 200
Paid Artists: 50

8147
ACADEMY OF MUSIC: MAIN AUDITORIUM
Broad and Locust Streets
Philadelphia, PA 19102
Phone: 215-893-1935
Fax: 215-545-4588

8148
ANNENBERG CENTER
University of Pennsylvania
3680 Walnut Street
Philadelphia, PA 19104
Phone: 212-898-6702
Fax: 215-573-9568
e-mail: mjrose@pobox.upenn.edu
Web Site: www.annenbergcenter.org
Officers:
  Vice President: Kira Strong
Management:
  Managing Director: Dr. Michael J Rose
  Facilities/Events Manager: Marie Gallagher
  Kamp: Jane
Founded: 1971
Seating Capacity: 2,500

8149
CURTIS INSTITUTE OF MUSIC
1726 Locust Street
Philadelphia, PA 19103
Phone: 215-893-5252
Fax: 215-893-9065
Web Site: www.curtis.edu
Officers:
  President: Roberto Diaz
Management:
  Department of Performance Studies: David Ludwig
Founded: 1924
Specialized Field: classical music conservatory
Status: Non-Profit, Professional

8150
ESTHER BOYER PERFORMING ARTS CENTER
Temple University
Philadelphia, PA 19122
Phone: 215-204-8301
Fax: 215-204-4957
Officers:
  Associate Dean: Steven Kreinberg

All listings are in alphabetical order by state, then city, then organization within the city.

FACILITIES / Pennsylvania

8151
FOLKLIFE CENTER OF INTERNATIONAL HOUSE
3701 Chestnut Street
Philadelphia, PA 19104
Phone: 215-387-5125
Fax: 215-895-6550
e-mail: helen@ihphilly.org
Web Site: www.ihousephilly.org
Officers:
  Chairperson: James M. Papada
  Vice Chair: David C.Prichard
  Vice Chair: Zoltan Kerekes
  Treasurer: Yelena Barychev
  Secretary: Janet Wishchnia
Management:
  President: Osagie Imasogie
Founded: 1977
Specialized Field: Traditional Arts (ethnic)
Paid Artists: 50

8152
FORREST THEATRE
1114 Walnut Street
Philadelphia, PA 19107
Phone: 215-923-1515
Web Site: www.forrest-theatre.com
Management:
  President: Philip Smith
  Managing Director: Mark Schweppe
Founded: 1928
Specialized Field: Broadways Production
Status: For-Profit, Professional

8153
FRANKLIN FIELD
University of Pennsylvania
235 South 33rd Street
Philadelphia, PA 19104
Phone: 215-898-9231
Fax: 215-573-2161
e-mail: kowalski@pobox.upenn.edu
Web Site: www.pennathletics.com
Management:
  Director: Dave Bryan
  Associate Director: Peggy Kowalski
Specialized Field: Home of University of Pennsylvania athletics (NCAA); Site of the Penn Relays; one of the largest track and field events in the country.
Seating Capacity: 52,593
Year Built: 1996

8154
IRVINE AUDITORIUM
University of Pennsylvania
3451 Walnut Street
Philadelphia, PA 19104
Phone: 215-573-5000
Fax: 215-898-2143
Web Site: www.upenn.edu
Officers:
  President: Dr. Amy Gutmann
  Provost: Vincent Price
Management:
  Event Coordinator: Laura Carney
Seating Capacity: 1,246

8155
KIMMEL CENTER FOR THE PERFORMING ARTS
1500 Walnut Street
Suite 901
Philadelphia, PA 19102
Phone: 215-790-5800
Fax: 215-790-5801
e-mail: patronservices@ticketphiladelphia.org
Web Site: www.kimmelcenter.org
Officers:
  President: Anne C. Ewers
  Sr. VP: J. Edward Cambron
  VP Operations: David Theile
  VP Sales & Marketing: Crystal Brewe
  CFO: Stan Applegate
Management:
  VP Programming/Education: Mervon Mehta
  VP Theatrical Presentations: Jordan Fiksenbaum
  Production Director: Joseph Dillon
  Facility Manager: Matt Suydam
  Production Manager: Nicole Thornton
Mission: The Regional Performing Arts Center manages The Kimmel Center for the Performing Arts Academy of Music in Philadelphia, and presents a wide variety of programming including jazz, dance, theatre, classical and world music.
Founded: 2001
Specialized Field: Facility/Presenter
Status: Non-Profit, Professional
Paid Staff: 350

8156
MANN CENTER FOR THE PERFORMING ARTS
5201 Parkside Avenue
Suite 1930
Philadelphia, PA 19131
Phone: 215-546-7900
Fax: 215-546-9524
e-mail: info@manncenter.org
Web Site: www.manncenter.org
Officers:
  President: Catherine M. Cahill
  Vice President: Thomas J. Metz
  Executive Assistant to the CEO and: Alayna Sands
Management:
  President: Peter B Lane
  General Manager: Jerry W Gralbey
  Director Marketing: Rosie Vergilio
  Director Development: Nancy Newman
Founded: 1925
Specialized Field: Presenter; venue address; 52nd and Parkside
Status: Nonprofit
Paid Staff: 7
Budget: $4.2 million
Income Sources: Ticket sales, grants, sponsorships
Annual Attendance: 275,000
Facility Category: Amphitheatre
Type of Stage: Proscenium
Stage Dimensions: 263 x 200 x 107
Year Remodeled: 1975
Rental Contact: Director Marketing & Dprogramming Rosie Vergilio

8157
MCCARTHY STADIUM
Lasalle University
1900 W Oleny Avenue
Philadelphia, PA 19141-1199
Phone: 215-951-1694
Fax: 215-951-1694
e-mail: athletics@lasalle.edu
Web Site: www.lasalle.edu
Officers:
  President: Michael J. McGinniss
  Chair: William R. Sautter
Management:
  Director Athletics: Tom Brennan
  Advisor: Louis A. Petroni
Seating Capacity: 7,500

8158
MERRIAM THEATER
250 S Broad Street
Philadelphia, PA 19102
Phone: 215-732-5446
Fax: 215-732-1396
Toll-free: 888-451-5761
Web Site: www.broadwayseries.com
Management:
  General Manager: DeVida Jenkins
  Marketing Director: Collie Andrew
Utilizes: Dance Companies; Multimedia; Special Technical Talent; Theatre Companies
Founded: 1987
Paid Staff: 35
Income Sources: Ticket Sales
Performs At: Procenium Theater
Annual Attendance: 301,847
Facility Category: Road House
Type of Stage: Proscenium
Stage Dimensions: 45'x25',44'x85'
Seating Capacity: 1870
Year Built: 1910
Year Remodeled: 1986
Rental Contact: General Manager DeVida Jenkins

8159
PAINTED BRIDE ART CENTER
230 Vine Street
Philadelphia, PA 19106
Phone: 215-925-9914
Fax: 215-925-7402
e-mail: info@paintedbride.org
Web Site: www.paintedbride.org
Officers:
  Chair: Harriet Rubenstein
  Vice Chair: Jennifer E. Jordan
  Treasurer: Gene Muller
  Secretary: Joan K. Sloan
  Controller: Lisa Solis
Management:
  Executive Director: Laurel Raczka
  Associate Director: Lisa Nelson
  Director Programs: Ellen Rosenholtz
  Marketing: LaNeshe Miller White
  Rental Manager: Siobhan Groves
Mission: The Painted Bride Art Center works with artists to create and present programs that affirm the intrinsic values of all cultures, the inspirational and healing powers of the arts, and their ability to effect social change.
Founded: 1969
Specialized Field: Multi-Disciplinary
Status: Non-Profit, Professional
Paid Staff: 15
Paid Artists: 20

8160
SOCIETY HILL PLAYHOUSE
507 S 8th Street
Philadelphia, PA 19147
Phone: 215-923-0210
Fax: 215-923-1789
e-mail: shp@erols.com
Web Site: www.societyhillplayhouse.com
Management:
  Director: Deen Kogan
Mission: To present works of the finest contemporary American and European writers.
Founded: 1959

FACILITIES / Pennsylvania

Opened: 1959
Specialized Field: New American Works; Classic; International
Status: Professional; Non-Profit
Performs At: Society Hill Playhouse
Affiliations: Theatre Communications Group; American Arts Alliance; Theatre Alliance
Annual Attendance: 100,000
Type of Stage: Proscenium; Black Box
Seating Capacity: 250; 99
Year Built: 1900
Year Remodeled: 1979
Rental Contact: Lee Vaughn

8161
THE PALESTRA
University of Pennsylvania
235 South 33rd Street
Philadelphia, PA 19104
Phone: 215-898-6121
Fax: 215-898-6117
Web Site: www.upenn.edu/athletics
Officers:
  Athletics Director: M Grace Calhoun
  Deputy Director of Athletics: Alanna Shanahan
  Sr. Associate Director: Tony Vecchione
  Sr. Advisor to Athletics Director: Decker Uhlhorn
Management:
  Athletic Director: Steve Bilsky
Seating Capacity: 8,700

8162
WACHOVIA SPECTRUM
3601 S Broad Street
Philadelphia, PA 19148
Phone: 215-336-3600
Fax: 215-389-9506
Web Site: www.wellsfargocenterphilly.com
Management:
  President: Peter Luukko
  VP Marketingducer: Bob Schwartz
Founded: 1967
Status: For-Profit, Professional
Paid Staff: 750
Paid Artists: 65
Seating Capacity: 18,000
Year Built: 1965

8163
WALNUT STREET THEATRE
825 Walnut
Philadelphia, PA 19107
Phone: 215-574-3550
Fax: 215-574-3598
Web Site: www.walnutstreettheatre.org
Officers:
  President and Producing Artistic Di: Bernerd Hardward
  Managing Director: Mark D. Sylvester
Management:
  Production Manager: Joel Markus
  Director of Marketing and Public Re: Ralph Weeks
  Director of Institutional Advanceme: Rebekah Sassi
  Director of Education: Thomas P. Quinn
  Box Office Treasurer: Rick Dougherty

8164
WALNUT STREET THEATRE: MAINSTAGE
825 Walnut
Philadelphia, PA 19107
Phone: 215-574-3550
Fax: 215-574-3598
Web Site: www.walnutstreettheatre.org
Officers:
  President and Producing Artistic Di: Bernerd Hardward
  Managing Director: Mark D. Sylvester
Management:
  Production Manager: Markus
  Director of Marketing and Public Re: Ralph Weeks
  Director of Institutional Advanceme: Rebekah Sassi
  Director of Education: Thomas P. Quinn
  Box Office Treasurer: Rick Dougherty

8165
WALNUT STREET THEATRE: STUDIO 3
825 Walnut
Philadelphia, PA 19107
Phone: 215-574-3550
Fax: 215-574-3598
Web Site: www.walnutstreettheatre.org
Officers:
  President and Producing Artistic Di: Bernerd Hardward
  Managing Director: Mark D. Sylvester
Management:
  Production Manager: Markus
  Director of Marketing and Public Re: Ralph Weeks
  Director of Institutional Advanceme: Rebekah Sassi
  Director of Education: Thomas P. Quinn
  Box Office Treasurer: Rick Dougherty

8166
WALNUT STREET THEATRE: STUDIO 5
825 Walnut
Philadelphia, PA 19107
Phone: 215-574-3550
Fax: 215-574-3598
Web Site: www.walnutstreettheatre.org
Officers:
  President and Producing Artistic Di: Bernerd Hardward
  Managing Director: Mark D. Sylvester
Management:
  Production Manager: Markus
  Director of Marketing and Public Re: Ralph Weeks
  Director of Institutional Advanceme: Rebekah Sassi
  Director of Education: Thomas P. Quinn
  Box Office Treasurer: Rick Dougherty

8167
A.J. PALUMBO CENTER
Duquesne University
1304 Forbes Avenue
Pittsburgh, PA 15282
Phone: 412-396-0000
Fax: 412-396-5855
Web Site: www.duq.edu
Officers:
  President: Charles J. Dougherty, Ph.D.
  Provost and Vice President of Acade: Ralph Pearson
Management:
  Executive Director: David DiPetro
  Associate Director: Scott Richards
  Event Coordinator: Tamia Pringle
Seating Capacity: 6,200

8168
BENEDUM CENTER
803 Liberty Avenue
Pittsburgh, PA 15222
Phone: 412-471-6070
Fax: 412-456-6666
e-mail: ciavarra@pgharts.org
Web Site: www.pgharts.org
Officers:
  President: Kevin McMahon
  Assistant President: Cheryl Schnippert
  Operations Manager: Jacob Bacharach
Management:
  Director of Board Relations and C: Lorene Vinsk
  Executive Director: Jude Rau
  Programming Director: Fran Egler
Utilizes: Guild Activities; Selected Students; Touring Companies
Founded: 1981
Specialized Field: Performing Arts
Status: Non-Profit, Professional
Paid Staff: 18
Volunteer Staff: 550
Facility Category: Proscenium theater
Type of Stage: FIR
Stage Dimensions: 75x142
Seating Capacity: 2,889
Year Built: 1927
Year Remodeled: 1987
Cost: $42 million
Rental Contact: Gene Ciavarra

8169
CARNEGIE: LECTURE HALL
4400 Forbes Avenue
Pittsburgh, PA 15213
Phone: 412-622-3114
Fax: 412-622-1923
Web Site: http://calliopehouse.org/
Officers:
  President and Director: Mary Frances Cooper
  Deputy Director: Susan Banks
Management:
  President: Susan Brladhust
  Executive Director: Herd Lish
  Director: Linda Barsevich
Founded: 1895
Status: Non-Profit, Non-Professional

8170
CARNEGIE: MUSEUM OF ART THEATRE
4400 Forbes Avenue
Pittsburgh, PA 15213
Phone: 412-622-3131
Fax: 412-688-8664
Web Site: www.carnegiemuseum.org
Officers:
  Vice President for Development: Dolly Ellenberg
Management:
  Director of Development: Ronald Gruca
  Director of Development: Alyssa Deluca
  Senior Director of Development: Sally Davoren
Founded: 1895
Status: Non-Profit, Non-Professional

8171
CARNEGIE: MUSIC HALL
4400 Forbes Avenue
Pittsburgh, PA 15213
Phone: 412-622-3131
Fax: 412-688-8664
Web Site: www.carnegiemuseum.org
Officers:

FACILITIES / Pennsylvania

Vice President for Development: Dolly Ellenberg
Management:
 Director of Development: Ronald Gruca
 Director of Development: Alyssa Deluca
 Senior Director of Development: Sally Davoren

8172
FITZGERALD FIELDHOUSE
University of Pittsburgh
Pittsburgh, PA 15213
Phone: 412-648-8200
Fax: 412-648-8306
Management:
 Athletic Director: Steve Pederson

8173
HEINZ HALL FOR THE PERFORMING ARTS
600 Penn Avenue
Pittsburgh, PA 15222
Phone: 412-392-4839
Fax: 412-392-4909
Web Site: www.pittsburghsymphony.org
Officers:
 President: Lawrence Tamburri
Management:
 Music Director: Manfred Honeck
Founded: 1927
Status: Non-Profit, Professional

8174
MANCHESTER CRAFTSMEN'S GUILD
1815 Metropolitan Street
Pittsburgh, PA 15233
Phone: 412-323-4000
Fax: 412-322-1075
e-mail: experiencemcg@mcg-btc.org
Web Site: www.mcgjazz.org
Officers:
 President: William E Strickland Jr
 Marketing Manager: Amy Kline
 Associate Producer: Renee Govanucci
 EVP: Jesse Fefe
 Artistic Director: Marty Ashby
 Production Manager: Eric Granata
Founded: 1986
Status: Non-Profit, Professional
Paid Staff: 100

8175
MELLON ARENA
23679 Calabasas Road
Pittsburgh, PA 91302
Phone: 412-642-2062
Fax: 412-562-9913
Toll-free: 818-712-8500
Web Site: www.civiccenter.com
Officers:
 President: Monica Garcja
Management:
 Director: Rich Engler
Seating Capacity: 18,000

8176
PITT STADIUM
University of Pittsburgh
PO Box 7436
Pittsburgh, PA 15213-0436
Phone: 412-648-8200
Fax: 412-648-8306
Management:
 Athletic Director: Steve Pederson
 Excutive Athletic Director: Marc Boehm

Senior Associate Athletic Director: Carol Sprague
Associate Athletics for Business: Jim Earle
Seating Capacity: 56,500

8177
PITTSBURGH CIVIC ARENA
Gate Number 9
66 Mario Lemieux Place
Pittsburgh, PA 15219
Phone: 412-642-1800
Fax: 412-642-1925
Web Site: www.civicarena.com
Management:
 General Manager: Hank Abate
 Director Operations: Jay Roberts
 Comcessions Manager: Rob Sunday
Seating Capacity: 17,500

8178
PNC PARK
115 Federal Street
PO Box 7000
Pittsburgh, PA 15212
Phone: 412-323-5000
Fax: 412-323-5009
Toll-free: 800-289-2827
Web Site: www.pirateball.com
Management:
 President: Kevin McClatchy
 Executive Vice President: Tim Brosnan
 Executive Vice President: Rob Manfred
Founded: 1887
Paid Staff: 75
Seating Capacity: 38,127

8179
RAJAH THEATRE
136 North Sixth Street
Reading, PA 19601
Phone: 610-371-8820
Fax: 610-371-8691

8180
SOVEREIGN CENTER
700 Penn Street
Reading, PA 19602
Phone: 610-898-7469
Fax: 610-898-1141
e-mail: jberney@sovereigncenter.com
Web Site: www.sovereigncenter.com
Management:
 GM: Robert Cavalieri
 Marketing Director: Dolly Vogt
 Senior Sales and Marketing Manager: Heather Adams
 Director of Finance: Hope J. Parkin, CPA
 Event Manager: Steve Quinn
Seating Capacity: 9,146

8181
SCRANTON CULTURAL CENTER AT THE MASONIC TEMPLE
420 North Washington Avenue
Scranton, PA 18503
Phone: 570-346-7369
Fax: 570-346-7365
e-mail: info@scrantonculturalcenter.org
Web Site: www.scrantonculturalcenter.org
Officers:
 Technical Director: John Cardoni
 Operation Assistant: Larry Hickernell
 Facility Manager: Fran McMullen
Management:

Executive Director: Jo Ann Fremiotti
Facilities/Technical Director: John Cardoni
Box Office Manager: Jason Helman
Business Manager: Donna Kunda
Utilizes: AEA Actors; Artists-in-Residence; Collaborating Artists; Dancers; Designers; Filmmakers; Five Seasonal Concerts; Guest Accompanists; Guest Choreographers; Guest Directors; Guest Ensembles; Guest Musical Directors; Guest Soloists; High School Drama; Instructors; Local Artists; Multimedia; New Productions; Original Music Scores; Performance Artists; Resident Professionals; Selected Students; Sign Language Translators; Soloists; Student Interns; Special Technical Talent; Theatre Companies
Founded: 1996
Specialized Field: Mid Atlantic
Status: Non-Profit, Professional
Paid Staff: 12
Volunteer Staff: 100
Paid Artists: 50
Annual Attendance: 140,000+
Facility Category: Theatre
Type of Stage: Proscenium
Stage Dimensions: 48x32x64
Seating Capacity: 1,866
Year Built: 1927

8182
LAUREL ARTS/THE PHILIP DRESSLER CENTER
214 S Harrison Avenue
PO Box 414
Somerset, PA 15501-0414
Phone: 814-443-2433
Fax: 814-443-3870
e-mail: arts@laurelarts.org
Web Site: www.laurelarts.org
Officers:
 Board of Directors: Hank Parke
Management:
 President: Hank Parke
 Executive Director: Mike Oliver
 Support Staff : Tracey Dunmyer
Founded: 1976
Status: Non-Profit, Non-Professional
Paid Staff: 14

8183
MOUNTAIN LAUREL CENTER FOR PERFORMING ARTS
1 Tamiment Rd
Tamiment, PA 18371
Phone: 570-588-2522
Toll-free: 866-448-7849
e-mail: email through website
Web Site: www.mountlaurelpac.com
Facility Category: Amphitheatre
Seating Capacity: 2500 under cover; 7500 on lawn

8184
BEAVER STADIUM
Penn State University
201 Old Main
University Park, PA 16802
Phone: 814-865-4700
Fax: 814-863-8569
Toll-free: 877-564-6778
Web Site: www.psu.edu
Management:
 President: Michelle Kramer-Fitzgerald
 Assistant: Anne Zirkare
 Director: Paula R Ammerman

FACILITIES / Rhode Island

Specialized Field: Home Of Penn State University Athletics.

8185
BRYCE JORDAN CENTER
127 Bryce Jordan Center
University Park, PA 16802
Phone: 814-863-5500
Fax: 814-863-1820
Toll-free: 800-863-3336
e-mail: jordancenter@psu.edu
Web Site: www.bjc.psu.edu
Management:
   President: Graham Stanier
   Executive Director: Bob Howard
Founded: 1996
Specialized Field: Music

8186
EISENHOWER AUDITORIUM
Pennsylvania State University
University Park, PA 16802
Phone: 814-863-0255
Fax: 814-865-5340
e-mail: cfpa@psu.edu
Web Site: www.cpa.psu.edu
Officers:
   Director: George Trudeau
Management:
   Calendar Coordinator: Lisa Faust
   Marketing Director: Laura Sullivan
   Assistant Director: Lea Asbell-Swanger
   Advisor: Deb Latta
Founded: 1974
Status: Non-Profit, Professional
Paid Staff: 135
Volunteer Staff: 150
Facility Category: Auditorium (Continental Seating)
Seating Capacity: 2,500
Year Built: 1974

8187
PENNSYLVANIA CENTRE STAGE
106 Arts Building
University Park, PA 16802
Phone: 814-865-7588
Fax: 814-863-7327
Web Site: www.theatre.psu.edu
Officers:
   Chair: Nancy VanLandingham
   Vice Chair: Lam Hood
Management:
   Manager: Janet Bergamaschi
   Production Manager: Ronda Craig
Season: June - August

8188
FARREL STADIUM
West Chester University
West Chester, PA 19383
Phone: 610-436-1000
Fax: 610-436-2171
e-mail: jberkowitz@wcupa.edu
Web Site: www.wcupa.edu
Management:
   President: Madeleine Edler
   Associate Provost and Graduate Dean: Dr. Darla Spence Coffey
Status: Non-Profit, Professional
Paid Staff: 1

8189
DOROTHY DICKSON DARTE CENTER
84 West South Street
Wilkes-Barre, PA 18766
Phone: 717-824-4651
Fax: 717-408-7842
Web Site: www.wilkes.edu
Officers:
   President: Dr. Patrick F. Leahy

8190
FM KIRBY CENTER FOR THE PERFORMING ARTS
71 Public Square
Wilkes-Barre, PA 18701
Mailing Address: PO Box 486, Wilkes-Barre, PA. 18703
Phone: 570-823-4599
Fax: 570-823-4890
Web Site: www.kirbycenter.org
Officers:
   Board Chairman: Robert Cioruttoli
   Vice Chairman: Denise Ceasare
   Treasurer: Dr. Wallace Steitler
Management:
   Executive Director: Marilyn Santarelli
   Program Manager: Mark Thomas
   Technical Director: Fran McMullen
   Director Operations: Brew Taylor
Mission: To promote and present the performing arts in our region.
Founded: 1986
Status: Non-Profit, Professional
Paid Staff: 15
Budget: $400,000-$1,000,000
Performs At: Film, concerts, broadway
Type of Stage: Proscenium
Stage Dimensions: 47'3 x 30' x 30' deep30'"''
Seating Capacity: 1800
Year Built: 1936
Year Remodeled: 1986
Rental Contact: Director of Operations John Domzalski

8191
STRAND-CAPITOL PERFORMING ARTS CENTER
50 N George Street
York, PA 17401
Phone: 717-846-1111
Fax: 717-843-1208
e-mail: boxoffice@strandcapitol.org
Web Site: www.strandcapitol.org
Officers:
   Chair: Joel Menchey
   Vice Chairman: Loren H. Kroh
   Treasurer/Secretary: Darren Welker
   President: Ken Wesler
Management:
   General Manager: Carol Oppelaar
   Customer Service Agent: Wyatt Oerman
Status: Non-Profit, Professional
Paid Staff: 20

Rhode Island

8192
RYAN CENTER
1 Lincoln Almond Plaza
Kingston, RI 02881
Phone: 401-788-3220
Fax: 401-788-3210
e-mail: tickets@theryancenter.com
Web Site: www.theryancenter.com
Management:
   GM: Terry Butler
   Facilities Director: James Hathaway
   General Manager: Leah Becki
   Assistant: Jeff Kuhn
Seating Capacity: 7,700

8193
UNIVERSITY OF RHODE ISLAND FINE ARTS CENTER
105 Upper College Road
Fine Arts Center
Kingston, RI 02881
Phone: 401-874-1000
Fax: 401-874-5618
Web Site: www.uri.edu
Officers:
   President: David M. Dooley
   Vice President: Donald H. DeHayes
Management:
   Chairman: Paula McGlasson
Founded: 1950
Paid Staff: 4
Volunteer Staff: 20
Paid Artists: 10
Non-paid Artists: 10
Type of Stage: Proscenium; Black Box
Rental Contact: Bonnie Besworth

8194
NEWPORT YACHTING CENTER
4 Commercial Wharf
Newport, RI 02840
Mailing Address: PO Box 550
Phone: 401-846-1600
Fax: 401-847-7754
e-mail: gm@newportyachtingcenter.com
Web Site: www.newportfestivals.com
Management:
   GM: Michele Maker Palmieri
   Director Sales/Marketing: Gail Alofsin
Seating Capacity: 2,000

8195
AS220
115 Empire Street
Providence, RI 02903
Phone: 401-831-9327
Fax: 401-454-7445
e-mail: info@as220.org
Web Site: www.as220.org
Officers:
   President and Ceo: Sean Ally
Management:
   Artistic Director: Umberto Crenca
   Managing Director: Shawn Wallace
Founded: 1984
Status: Non-Profit
Paid Staff: 25

8196
BROWN STADIUM
235 Hope Street
Providence, RI 02912
Phone: 401-863-2295
Fax: 401-863-1436
Web Site: www.as220.org
Management:
   Athletic Director: David Roach

FACILITIES / South Carolina

8197
PERISHABLE THEATRE
95 Empire Street
PO Box 23132
Providence, RI 02903
Phone: 401-331-2695
Fax: 401-331-7811
e-mail: info@perishable.org
Management:
 Artistic Director: Mark Lerman
 Managing Director: Carol Drowne
 PR Director: Marya Jones
 PR Director: Marilyn Dubois
Mission: Perishable Theatre brings together artists from all media and provides them with the opportunity to perform and develop their craft. The theatre offers a mainstage season of new plays, a theatre arts school, and touring children's theatre.
Utilizes: Actors; AEA Actors; Artists-in-Residence; Choreographers; Collaborating Artists; Collaborations; Commissioned Composers; Dancers; Designers; Educators; Five Seasonal Concerts; Guest Artists; Guest Choreographers; Guest Companies; Guest Conductors; Guest Designers; Guest Directors; Guest Ensembles; High School Drama; Instructors; Local Artists; Lyricists; Multi Collaborations; Music; Original Music Scores; Performance Artists; Poets; Resident Professionals; Selected Students; Sign Language Translators; Soloists; Student Interns; Special Technical Talent; Theatre Companies; Visual Arts
Founded: 1982
Status: Non-Profit, Professional
Paid Staff: 5
Volunteer Staff: 4
Paid Artists: 20
Budget: $500,000
Performs At: Theatre Arts Center
Affiliations: TCG
Annual Attendance: 3,000
Facility Category: Performing Arts Center
Type of Stage: Black Box
Seating Capacity: 75

8198
PROVIDENCE DUNKIN DONUTS CENTER
1 Lasalle Square
Providence, RI 02903
Phone: 401-331-0700
Fax: 401-751-6792
e-mail: dtolselli@dunkindonutscenter.com
Web Site: www.dunkindonutscenter.org
Management:
 Executive Director: Larry Lapore
 Ceo: Ed Anderson
Status: Non-profit, Professional
Seating Capacity: 14,500

8199
PROVIDENCE PERFORMING ARTS CENTER
220 Weybosset Street
Providence, RI 02903
Phone: 401-421-2997
Fax: 401-421-5767
e-mail: info@ppacri.org
Web Site: www.ppacri.org
Officers:
 Chair: Joseph W. Walsh
 First Chairman: Mark T. Ryan
 Second Chairman: Thomas A. Tanury
 Secretary: Ellen Barnes
 Treasurer: J. Joseph Kruse
 Technical Director: William Darckett
 General Manager: Alan Chille
Specialized Field: Touring Broadway; Concerts; Film
Status: Non-Profit, Professional
Paid Staff: 50

8200
TRINITY ARTS CENTER
55 Locust Street
Providence, RI 02906
Phone: 423-926-6048
Web Site: www.trinityartscenter.com
Management:
 Executive Director: Jamin Rathbun
 Artistic Director: Tanya Rathbun

8201
VETERANS MEMORIAL AUDITORIUM
1 Avenue of the Arts Providence
Providence, RI 02903
Phone: 401-222-1467
Fax: 401-277-1466
Web Site: www.vmari.com
Officers:
 Security Director: David Luongo
 House Manager: Patricia Lynch
 Concession Manager: Matthew Pawlik
 Technical Director: Todd Snow
Management:
 President: Terriann Greenwood
 General Manager: Daniel Schwartz
 Box Office Manager: Tara Edwards
 Promotion Manager: Michael Gravison
Founded: 1950
Status: Non-Profit, Non-Professional
Paid Staff: 6

8202
STADIUM THEATRE PERFORMING ARTS CENTER
28 Monument Square
PO Box 665
Woonsocket, RI 02895
Phone: 401-762-4545
Fax: 401-765-4949
e-mail: info@stadiumtheatre.com
Web Site: www.stadiumtheatre.com
Officers:
 Marketing Director: Jeffrey Polucha
 President: Robert P Picards
 Events Chairman/First VP: Jean Rondeau
 Second VP: Joan Gahan
 Secretary: Donna Palreiro
Management:
 Ceo: John Walker
 Executive Director: Adell Marchbank
 Managing Director: Anne Choquette
Utilizes: Actors; Community Talent; Contract Orchestras; Educators; Filmmakers; Guest Accompanists; Guest Companies; Guest Musical Directors; Guest Musicians; Guest Soloists; Instructors; Multimedia; Original Music Scores; Performance Artists; Resident Artists; Sign Language Translators; Singers; Special Technical Talent; Theatre Companies
Founded: 1996
Specialized Field: Perfoming Arts
Status: Non-Profit, Professional
Paid Staff: 2
Volunteer Staff: 200
Income Sources: Rentals; Donations; Grants; Box Office
Performs At: Live theatre, classic films, local & national entertainment
Affiliations: Encore Repertory Company
Annual Attendance: 60,000-100,000
Facility Category: Performing arts center
Seating Capacity: 1100
Year Built: 1926
Year Remodeled: 2000
Cost: $2.5 Million
Rental Contact: Jean Rondeau
Resident Groups: Encore Reportory Company

South Carolina

8203
ABBEVILLE OPERA HOUSE
Court Square
PO Box 247
Abbeville, SC 29620
Phone: 864-366-2157
Fax: 803-459-9266
e-mail: operahouse@wctel.net
Web Site: www..theabbevilleoperahouse.com
Officers:
 President: Ruth Freeman
 VP: Evelyn Horton
 Secretary: Mark Meyers
 Treasurer: David Eller
Management:
 Executive Director: Micheal Genevie
 Managing Director: Kathy Genevie
Founded: 1908
Status: Non-Profit, Non-Professional
Paid Staff: 3

8204
ANDERSON SPORTS CENTER
3027 Mall Road
Anderson, SC 29625
Phone: 864-260-4800
Fax: 864-260-4847
e-mail: asec@andersoncountysc.org
Web Site: www..andersonevents.com
Management:
 Director: Charles Wyatt
 Assistant Manager: Dan Brawley
Seating Capacity: 15,000

8205
FINE ARTS CENTER OF KERSHAW COUNTY
810 Lyttleton Street Camden
Camden, SC 29020
Phone: 803-425-7676
Fax: 803-425-7679
Web Site: www.fineartscentre.com
Officers:
 President: Karen Eckford
 VP: Sheila McKinney
 Secretary: Linda Shaylor
 Treasurer: Jim Watt
Management:
 Executive Director: Kristin Cobb
 Executive Director: Susan Duplessis
 Artistic Director: Steve Levan
 Managing Director: Diane Edward
Founded: 1974
Status: Non-Profit, Non-Professional
Paid Staff: 5
Paid Artists: 40

8206
DOCK STREET THEATRE
135 Church Street
Charleston, SC 29401

Phone: 843-720-3968
Fax: 843-720-3967
Web Site: www.charlestonstage.org
Officers:
  Founder: Julian Wiles
Management:
  Associate Artistic Director: Marybeth Clark
  Director of Sales: Allison Schnake

8207
DRAYTON HALL
University of South Carolina
3380 Ashley River Road
Charleston, SC 29414
Phone: 843-769-2600
Fax: 843-766-0878
e-mail: info@draytonhall.org
Web Site: www.draytonhall.org
Officers:
  Finance Director: Paula Marian
  Financial Assistant: Michael Johanek
Management:
  President: Andrew Sorensen
  Chairman: Jim Hunter
  Executive Director: George W McDaniel
  Deputy Director: Carter C. Hudgins
Status: Non-Profit, Non-Professional

8208
FOOTLIGHT PLAYERS THEATRE
20 Queen Street
PO Box 62
Charleston, SC 29401
Phone: 843-722-7521
Fax: 843-722-3777
e-mail: info@footlightplayers.net
Web Site: www.footlightplayers.net
Officers:
  President: Christy Loftin
  Vice President: Tracey Todd
  Business Manager: Gail Pike
Founded: 1931
Specialized Field: Theatre
Status: Non-Profit, Non-Professional
Paid Staff: 2

8209
GAILLARD MUNICIPAL AUDITORIUM
77 Calhoun Street
Charleston, SC 29401
Phone: 843-577-7400
Fax: 843-724-7389
Web Site: www.charlestoncity.info
Management:
  Executive Director: Cam Patterson
Founded: 1969
Status: For-Profit, Non-Professional
Paid Staff: 17

8210
JOHNSON HAGOOD STADIUM
The Citadel Athletic Department
P. O. Box 652
Charleston, SC 29402
Phone: 843-957-7697
Fax: 843-953-6727
e-mail: rileyj@charleston-sc.gov
Web Site: www.ci.charleston.sc.us
Officers:
  Mayor: Joseph P. Riley, Jr
Management:
  President: John Granold
  Executive Director: Ray Whiteman
  Artistic Director: Robbie Bennet

Athletic Director: Les Robinson
Founded: 1842
Status: Non-Profit, Non-Professional
Seating Capacity: 22,500

8211
MCALISTER FIELDHOUSE
The Citadel Athletic Department
171 Moultrie Street
Charleston, SC 29409
Phone: 843-225-3294
Fax: 843-953-6727
Web Site: www.citadel.edu
Officers:
  President: John W. Rosa
  Vice President: Thomas J. Elzey
  Provost and Dean of the College: Samuel M. Hines, Jr., Ph.D
Management:
  Assocaite Athletic Director: Robert Bennett
Seating Capacity: 6,000

8212
BROOKS CENTER FOR THE PERFORMING ARTS
Clemson University
Box 340526
Clemson, SC 29634-0526
Phone: 864-656-3043
Fax: 864-656-1013
e-mail: harderl@clemson.edu
Web Site: www.clemson.edu
Officers:
  Chair: David Hartmann
Management:
  Director: Lillian U Harder

8213
CLEMSON MEMORIAL STADIUM
Clemson University
602 University Union
Clemson, SC 29634
Mailing Address: PO Box 344056
Phone: 864-656-5827
Fax: 864-656-1858
e-mail: mkern@clemson.edu
Web Site: www.clemson.edu/Brooks
Officers:
  Chair: David Hartmann
Management:
  Director: Lillian U Harder
Mission: Successfully produce area shows with capacity of 20,000-70,000

8214
LITTLEJOHN COLISEUM
Clemson University
1 Avenue of Champions Clemson
Clemson, SC 29632
Mailing Address: PO Box 31
Phone: 864-646-1935
Fax: 864-646-0299
Web Site: www.majorevents.clemson.edu
Management:
  Director Programs/Services: Michael Arnold
  Business Manager: Cecilia Vazquez
  Associate Director Event Planning &: Dixie Wilson
Seating Capacity: 10,820

8215
TILLMAN AUDITORIUM
Clemson University
210 Hendrix Student Center
Clemson, SC 29364-4056
Phone: 864-656-6676
Fax: 864-656-1414
e-mail: mkern@clemson.edu
Web Site: www.clemsonmajorevents.com
Management:
  Director Major Events: Marty S Kern
  Marketing Director: Tina LeMay
  Associate Director of Operations: Kevin Burgess
Seating Capacity: 800

8216
CAPITOL CITY STADIUM
301 South Assemble Street
Columbia, SC 29201
Mailing Address: PO Box 1328
Phone: 803-254-3474
Fax: 803-254-4482
e-mail: info@blowfishbaseball.com
Web Site: www.blowfishbaseball.com
Officers:
  CEO: Michael Savit
  President: Bill Shanahan
Management:
  GM: Tim Swain
  Ticketing Director: Luis Gonzalez
  Assistant Director: Skip Anderson
Seating Capacity: 10,000

8217
CAROLINA COLISEUM
University of South Carolina
701 Assembly Street
Columbia, SC 29201
Phone: 803-777-5113
Fax: 803-777-5114
Web Site: www.coliseum.sc.edu
Management:
  Director: John Bolin
  Business Manager: Dick Marks
Specialized Field: Home to USC basketball.
Seating Capacity: 12,500
Year Built: 1969

8218
KOGER CENTER FOR THE ARTS
University of South Carolina
1051 Greene Street
Columbia, SC 29208
Phone: 803-777-7500
Fax: 803-777-5774
Web Site: www.koger.su.edu

8219
LONGSTREET THEATRE
University of South Carolina
Green and Sumter Streets
Columbia, SC 29208
Phone: 803-777-4288

8220
WILLIAMS-BRICE STADIUM
University of South Carolina
701 Assembly Street
Columbia, SC 29201
Phone: 704-223-8193
Fax: 704-233-8170
Management:
  Head Basketball Coach (W): Johnny Jacumin

FACILITIES / South Carolina

Managing Director/CEO: John C Bondi
Director Marketing: Connie O Scrivens
Athletic Director: Beth Lawrence
Sports Information Director: David Sherwood
Head Football Coach: Doug Malone
Head Basketball Coach (M): Jeff Reynolds
Seating Capacity: 72,000

8221
FLORENCE CIVIC CENTER
North Carolina
Florence, SC 28174
Phone: 704—23-3-80
Fax: 843-679-9429
e-mail: info@florenceciviccenter.com
Web Site: www.wingate.edu
Officers:
  President: Dr. Jerry E. McGee
  Executive Assistant to the Preside: Dr. Heather Campbell
  Executive Secretary: Ms. Betty Manus
Management:
  General Manager: Kendell Wall, kwall@florenceciviccenter.com
  Director Of Operations: Russell Infinger
  Director Sales/Marketing: Tina Dean, tdean@florenceciviccenter.com
  Director Sales/Marketing: Karen Johnson
Mission: The Florence Civic Center is the hub for entertainment, exhibitions & civic events for the Florence area. With over 50,000 square feet of multi-purpose space, the center can accomodate events of all shapes, types and sizes. The facility is also close to dozens of national chain hotels, and is located across the street from Florence's premier shopping plaza.
Opened: 1993
Specialized Field: Theatre Ballroom
Affiliations: Ticketmaster
Annual Attendance: 245,000
Facility Category: Adaptable to nearly any events needs
Seating Capacity: 1,400 - 10,000
Year Built: 1993
Year Remodeled: 2008
Rental Contact: Director Of Sales & Marketing Tina Dean

8222
CHARLOTTE KNIGHTS BASEBALL STADIUM
2280 Deerfield Drive
Ft. Hill, SC 29715
Phone: 803-548-8050
Fax: 803-548-8055
Web Site: www.florenceciviccenter.com
Officers:
  Ovations Office Manager: Jessi Brienzi
Management:
  President: Don Beaver
  Assistant General Manager/Facility: Jon Percival
  BoxOff Manager: Brian Davison
  Event Coordinator: Mark Wade
  Event Service Manager: Rod Saavendra
Status: For-Profit, Professional
Paid Staff: 20
Seating Capacity: 10,000
Year Built: 1990

8223
BI-LO CENTER
650 N Academy Street
Greenville, SC 29601
Phone: 864-241-3800
Fax: 864-250-4939
Web Site: www.bi-locentre.com
Officers:
  President: Roger Newton
Management:
  Executive Director: Ed Rubenstein
  Director Operations: Steve Chastain
  Marketing Director: Jill Weninger
Founded: 1998
Specialized Field: Sports and entertainment arena in upstate South Carolina.
Status: For-Profit, Professional
Paid Staff: 100
Seating Capacity: 16,000
Year Built: 1998

8224
BOB JONES UNIVERSITY
1700 Wade Hampton Boulevard
Greenville, SC 29614
Phone: 864-242-5100
Fax: 864-770-1375
e-mail: finearts@bju.edu
Web Site: www.bju.edu
Officers:
  President: Dr Stephen Jones
Management:
  Dean Fine Arts/Communication: Dr Darren Lawson
Mission: dual venues: perfomance hall- used for student productions; Rodeheaver Hall-used for classic players performances,annual opera; Founders Memorail Auditorium
Founded: 1927
Status: For-Profit, Professional
Budget: $35,000-60,000
Performs At: Founder's Memorial Auditorium
Seating Capacity: 7,000

8225
GREENVILLE MUNICIPAL STADIUM
One Braves Avenue
Greenville, SC 29607
Phone: 864-241-3800
Fax: 864-250-4939
Web Site: www.bilocenter.com
Officers:
  President: Roger Newton
Management:
  General Manager: Steve Desalvo

8226
MCALISTER AUDITORIUM
Furman University
3300 Poinsett Highway
Greenville, SC 29613
Phone: 864-294-2000
Fax: 864-294-3035
Web Site: www2.furman.edu
Officers:
  Board Member: Ann Brayon
  Board Member: Robert H. Buckman
  Board Member: C Jordan Clark
  Board Member: Richard Cullin
  Board Member: Francie Heller
Management:
  President: David E Shi
  VP: Tom Kazee
  Artistic Director: Bill Thomas
Founded: 1826
Specialized Field: vocal music
Status: Non-Profit, Professional
Paid Staff: 700
Paid Artists: 50

8227
PEACE CENTER FOR THE PERFORMING ARTS
300 South Main Street Greenville
Greenville, SC 29601
Phone: 864-467-3000
Fax: 864-467-3040
Toll-free: 800-888-7768
e-mail: administration@peacecenter.org
Web Site: www.furman.edu
Officers:
  President: Megan Riegel
  Chairman: Rick Timmons
Mission: Providing a world-class home for Resident Companies
Founded: 1985
Specialized Field: Performing
Paid Staff: 130
Volunteer Staff: 57
Budget: $400,000
Income Sources: Board, Edowment, Patrons
Annual Attendance: 97,000
Facility Category: Performing Arts7
Type of Stage: Proscenium
Stage Dimensions: 34' x 58'
Seating Capacity: 2089
Year Built: 1985
Year Remodeled: 2002
Cost: 4 million
Rental Contact: Tom Bugg

8228
TIMMONS ARENA
Furman University
3300 Poinsett Highway
Greenville, SC 29613
Phone: 864-294-3267
Fax: 864-294-3269
e-mail: timmonsarena@furman.edu
Web Site: www.timmonsarena.org
Management:
  GM: Mike Arnold
  Booking/Business Manager: Todd Duke
Seating Capacity: 5,000

8229
GREENWOOD CIVIC CENTER
PO Box 740
Greenwood, SC 29648
Phone: 864-942-8606
Fax: 864-942-8595
e-mail: timmonsarena@furman.edu
Web Site: www.timmonsarena.com
Management:
  Executive Director: Ron Plemmons
  Managing Director: Tracy Upton
Founded: 1978
Status: For-Profit, Non-Professional
Paid Staff: 7

8230
CENTER THEATER
212 N 5th Street
Hartsville, SC 29550
Phone: 843-332-5721
Web Site: www.centertheater.org
Management:
  Executive Director: Den Latham
Founded: 1936
Status: Non-Profit, Non-Professional
Paid Staff: 1

FACILITIES / South Dakota

8231
THE PALACE THEATRE
21 West Otterman Street
Myrtle Beach, SC 15601
Phone: 724-836-8000
Fax: 843-626-9659
e-mail: admin@palacetheatremyrtlebeach.com
Web Site: www.thepalacetheatre.org
Management:
 GM: Cynthia Sweeney
Founded: 1995
Seating Capacity: 2,638
Rental Contact: Cheryl Holowacz

8232
NEWBERRY OPERA HOUSE
1201 McKibben Street
Newberry, SC 29108
Phone: 803-276-5179
Fax: 803-276-9993
e-mail: debra@newberryoperahouse.com
Web Site: www.newberryoperahouse.com
Management:
 Executive Director: Debra Smith
 Technical Director: Jason Osborne
 Lighting Director: Denise Simpson-Osborne
Utilizes: Artists-in-Residence; Commissioned Composers; Dance Companies; Dancers; Five Seasonal Concerts; Grant Writers; Guest Accompanists; Guest Choreographers; Guest Composers; Guest Designers; Guest Musical Directors; Guest Musicians; Guest Writers; Instructors; Local Artists; Multimedia; Original Music Scores; Resident Professionals; Sign Language Translators; Singers; Soloists; Student Interns; Special Technical Talent; Theatre Companies
Founded: 1881
Status: Non-Profit
Budget: $400,000-$1,000,000
Stage Dimensions: 29'x25'
Seating Capacity: 426
Year Built: 1881
Year Remodeled: 1996

8233
NORTH CHARLESTON PERFORMING ARTS CENTER
5001 Coliseum Drive
North Charleston, SC 29418
Phone: 843-529-5000
Fax: 843-529-5010
e-mail: IHaveaQuestion@northcharlestoncoliseumpac.com
Web Site: www.northcharlestoncoliseumpac.com
Management:
 General Manager: Dave Holscher, dholscher@northcharlestoncolis
 Assistant General Manager: John Trinki
 Director of Operation: Wes Dickerson
 Marketing Manager: Alan Coker
 Facility Parking: Mark Cruse
Founded: 1993
Status: For-Profit, Non-Professional
Type of Stage: Proscenium
Seating Capacity: 2254
Year Built: 1999
Rental Contact: Dave Holscher

8234
OLIVER C DAWSON STADIUM
South Carolina State University
300 College Avenue
Orangeburg, SC 29115
Phone: 803-536-8998
Fax: 803-533-3661
Web Site: www.coliseumpac.com
Management:
 Athletics Director: Timothy Autry
Seating Capacity: 2,500

8235
JAMES F BYRNES AUDITORIUM
South Carolina State University
129 Conservatory
Rock Hill, SC 29117
Mailing Address: 300 College Street NE
Phone: 803-536-7000
Fax: 803-323-2343
Toll-free: 800-260-5956
e-mail: rogersd@winthrop.edu
Web Site: www.scsu.edu
Officers:
 President: Cynthia Warrick
Management:
 Chairman of the Department: Donald Rogers
Status: Non-Profit, Non-Professional
Paid Staff: 30
Paid Artists: 2

8236
SPARTANBURG MEMORIAL AUDITORIUM: THEATRE
385 North Church Street
Po Box 1410
Spartanburg, SC 29303
Phone: 864-582-8107
Fax: 803-583-9850
Toll-free: 800-745-3000
Web Site: www.crowdpleaser.com
Management:
 General Manager: Steve Jones
 Assistant General Manager: Jonathan Pitts
 Operations Manager: Atlee Pettit
 Office Manager: Sandy Henson

8237
SPARTANBURG MEMORIAL AUDITORIUM: ARENA
385 North Church Street
PO Box 1410
Spartanburg, SC 29303
Phone: 864-582-8107
Fax: 803-583-9850
Toll-free: 800-745-3000
Web Site: www.crowdpleaser.com
Management:
 General Manager: Steve Jones
 Assistant General Manager: Jonathan Pitts
 Operations Manager: Atlee Pettit
 Office Manager: Sandy Henson

8238
SUMTER COUNTRY GALLERY OF ART
200 Hasel Street
Sumter, SC 29150
Mailing Address: PO Box 1316, Sumter, SC 29151
Phone: 803-775-0543
Fax: 803-436-2258
e-mail: patriot_hall@sumtercountysc.org
Web Site: www.sumtergallery.org
Management:
 Executive Director: Karen Watson
 Assistant Director: Frank McCauley
 Art Education Director: Trevor Bauknight
Founded: 1974
Status: For-Profit, Non-Professional
Paid Staff: 3
Paid Artists: 3
Income Sources: Sumter County Government
Facility Category: Auditorium
Type of Stage: Proscenium
Stage Dimensions: 47wx21hx26-38l
Seating Capacity: 1,013
Year Built: 1935
Year Remodeled: 1986
Cost: $4 million
Rental Contact: Martha Greenway

8239
MCCELVEY CENTER OF YORK
212 East Jefferson Street
York, SC 29745
Phone: 803-684-3948
Fax: 803-684-0230
e-mail: lifundbrburk@chmuseums.org
Web Site: www.chmuseums.org/mccelvey/
Management:
 Executive Director: Mary Norton
 Managing Director: Liz Funderburk
Founded: 1988
Status: Non-Profit, Professional
Paid Staff: 2
Paid Artists: 12

South Dakota

8240
COUGHLIN ALUMNI STADIUM
16th Avenue and 11th Street
Brookings, SD 57007
Phone: 605-688-5625
Fax: 605-688-5999
Web Site: www.chmuseums.org
Officers:
 Assitent Director: Carree Tilley
Management:
 President: Peggy Miller
 Athletic Director: Fred Oien
 Chambell: Richard
Founded: 1881
Specialized Field: Engineering
Status: Non-Profit, Non-Professional

8241
SOUTH DAKOTA ART MUSEUM
936 Medary Ave.
Box 2250
Brookings, SD 57007
Phone: 605-688-5423
Fax: 605-688-4445
Web Site: www.sdstate.edu/southdakotaartmuseum/
Officers:
 President: Marilyn DeLong
 Vice President: Tim Dougherty
 Treasurer: Jack Stengel
 Secretary: Maree Larson
Management:
 Director: Lynn Verschoor
 Coordinator/Curator of Exhibitions: Jodi Undgren
 Coordinator/Curator of Collections: Lisa Scholten
 Museum Store Manager/Program Assist: Pam Adler
 Marketing and Development Coordinat: Stacy Buehner

8242
SWIFTEL CENTER
824 32nd Avenue
Brookings, SD 57006

FACILITIES / Tennessee

Phone: 605-692-7539
Fax: 605-697-6393
e-mail: swiftelcenter@swiftelcenter.com
Web Site: www.swiftelcenter.com
Management:
　Executive Director: Tom Richter
　Operations Manager: Dave Biteler
　Director of Operations: Scott Smith
　Box Office Manager: Molly Nagelhout
　Director of Sales/Marketing: Jenny Hammrich
Seating Capacity: 7,000

8243
CORN PALACE
601 N. Main
PO Box 1026
Mitchell, SD 57301
Phone: 605-996-6223
Fax: 605-996-8273
e-mail: mschilling@cornpalace.com
Web Site: www.visitmitchell.com
Management:
　Director: Jacki Miskimins
　Marketing Coordinator: Katie Knutson
Founded: 1892
Opened: 1892
Status: Non-Profit, Professional
Paid Staff: 25
Volunteer Staff: 75
Paid Artists: 4
Budget: $1,809,000
Income Sources: Rentals; Commissions; Donations
Annual Attendance: 500,000
Stage Dimensions: 32x70
Seating Capacity: 3,148
Year Built: 1921
Year Remodeled: 1965
Rental Contact: Mark Schilling

8244
RUSHMORE PLAZA CIVIC CENTER
444 Mount Rushmore Road N
Rapid City, SD 57701
Phone: 605-394-4115
Fax: 605-394-4119
Toll-free: 800-468-6463
Web Site: www.gotmine.com
Management:
　Asst General Manager / Finance: Tracy Heitsch
　Accounting & Administration Manager: Jarrett Breuninger
　Asst General Manager / Events: Jayne Kraemer
　Events Services Manager: Tanya Tanya
　Life Safety & Events Coordinator: Larry Dale
Founded: 1977
Status: For-Profit, Professional
Paid Staff: 300
Seating Capacity: 11,000

8245
SIOUX FALLS ARENA
Odgen Entertainment
1201 N. West Avenue Sioux Falls
Sioux Falls, SD 57104
Phone: 605-367-7288
Fax: 605-338-1463
Toll-free: 800-338-3177
e-mail: info@sfarena.com
Web Site: www.sfarena.com
Officers:
　General Manager: Brian Maliske
Management:
　General Manager: Terry Torkildson
　Director of Operations: Jeff Gortmaker
　Box Office Superviso: Lucy Albers
　Event Manager: Holly Anderson
　Box Office Manager: Nicole Fred
Specialized Field: Concerts; sporting events; trade shows
Status: For-Profit, Professional
Paid Staff: 300
Seating Capacity: 8,000

8246
SIOUX FALLS COMMUNITY PLAYHOUSE
315 N. Phillips Ave
PO Box 767
Sioux Falls, SD 57104
Phone: 605-360-4800
Fax: 605-336-2243
Web Site: www.siouxfallstheatre.com
Management:
　General Manager: Terry Torkildson
　Director of Operations: Jeff Gortmaker
　Box Office Superviso: Lucy Albers

8247
WASHINGTON PAVILION OF ARTS & SCIENCE
301 South Main Avenue
Sioux Falls, SD 57104
Mailing Address: PO Box 984, Sioux Falls, SD. 57101-0984
Phone: 605-367-6000
Fax: 605-367-7399
Toll-free: 877-927-4728
e-mail: info@washingtonpavilion.org
Web Site: www..washingtonpavilion.org
Officers:
　Co-President: Larry Toll
　Co-President: Scott Petersen
　Vice President: Ben Arndt
　CEO/President: William L. Baker
Management:
　Director, Community Learning Center: Rose Ann Hofland
　Director, Kirby Science Discovery C: Erica Lacey
　Vice President of Operations: Jon Loos
　Director, Visual Arts Center: Sheila Agee
　Manager Husby Performing Arts Cente: Regina Ruhberg
Mission: To educate, entertain and inspire community by making arts and science part of our lives.
Founded: 1999
Specialized Field: South Dakota; Northwest Iowa; Southwest Minnesota; Northeast Nebraska
Paid Staff: 85
Volunteer Staff: 200
Budget: $5 million
Income Sources: Donors; Grants; Ticket Sales
Affiliations: APAP; AAM; ASTC; IAAM
Annual Attendance: 100,000
Facility Category: Theater, Science Center, Visual Arts Center
Type of Stage: Proscenium
Seating Capacity: 1,904
Year Built: 1999
Year Remodeled: 1999
Cost: $32 Million
Rental Contact: Regina Ruhberg

8248
DAKOTA DOME
University of South Dakota
414 E. Clark St.
Vermillion, SD 57069
Phone: 877-269-6837
Fax: 605-677-5618
e-mail: urelate@usd.edu
Web Site: www.usd.edu
Officers:
　VP: Royce Engstrom
　President: James W. Abbott
Management:
　Athletic Director: Kelly Higgins
Founded: 1862

8249
NATIONAL MUSIC MUSEUM
414 E Clark Street
Vermillion, SD 57069
Phone: 877-269-6837
Fax: 605-677-6995
e-mail: nmm@usd.edu
Web Site: www.usd.edu
Officers:
　Chairman: Tom Lillibridge
　Vice Chairman: Kevin V. Schieffer
　Secretary: Marilyn Nyberg
　Treasurer: Jack Powell
Management:
　Assistant to the Director: Barbara Stark
　Director: Andre Larson
Mission: The NMM serves the people of South Dakota and the world as an international center for collecting and conserving musical instruments of all cultures and bringing people together to study, enjoy, and understand our diverse musical heritage.
Founded: 1973
Specialized Field: Musical instruments
Status: Non-Profit, Professional
Paid Staff: 12
Performs At: Concert Hall
Seating Capacity: 125

8250
SLAGLE AUDITORIUM
University of South Dakota
414 E. Clark St.
Vermillion, SD 57069
Phone: 877-269-6837
Fax: 605-677-5988
Web Site: www.usd.edu
Officers:
　President: James W. Abbott

8251
WARREN M LEE CENTER
University of South Dakota
414 E. Clark St.
Vermillion, SD 57069
Phone: 877-269-6837
Fax: 605-677-5988
Web Site: www.usd.edu
Officers:
　President: James W. Abbott

Tennessee

8252
THE PARAMOUNT CENTER FOR THE ARTS
518 State Street
Bristol, TN 37620
Phone: 423-274-8920
Fax: 423-274-8937
e-mail: info@theparamountcenter.com
Web Site: www.theparamountcenter.com
Seating Capacity: 750

FACILITIES / Tennessee

8253
VIKING HALL CIVIC CENTER
1100 Edgemont Avenue
Bristol, TN 37620
Mailing Address: P.O. Box 3563,Bristol, TN 37625
Phone: 423-764-0188
Fax: 423-765-3299
Web Site: www.vikinghall.com
Management:
 Department Manager: Terrie Talbert
 Box Office Manager: Angie Rutherford
 Office Manager: Lisa Beckner
 Box Office Manager: Angie Rutherford
 Venue Manager: Darlene Cole
Founded: 1981
Status: Non-Profit, Professional
Paid Staff: 100
Seating Capacity: 6,200

8254
ROLAND HAYES CONCERT HALL
University of Tennessee
615 McCallie Ave
Chattanooga, TN 37403
Phone: 423-425-4111
Fax: 615-755-5249
Web Site: www.utc.edu/utcarena
Officers:
 Interim Chancellor: E. Grady Bogue

8255
TIVOLI THEATRE
399 McCallie Avenue
Chattanooga, TN 37402
Phone: 423-757-5050
Fax: 615-757-5326
e-mail: onstage@chattanooga.gov??
Web Site: www.chattanoogaonstage.com
Management:
 Manager: Wolly Robinson
Founded: 1921
Status: For-Profit, Non-Professional
Paid Staff: 15

8256
UTC MCKENZIE ARENA
University of Tennessee-Chattanooga
615 McCallie Avenue, Department 3403
Chattanooga, TN 37403
Phone: 423-425-4706
Fax: 423-425-4783
e-mail: ken-kapelinski@utc.edu
Web Site: www.chattanooga/showplaces.gov
Officers:
 Interim Chancellor: E. Grady Bogue
Management:
 Executive Director of Entertainment: Obie Webster
 Technical Director: Kyle Askew
 Operations Coordinator: Arland Jenkins
 Event Coordinator/Accounting: Sandra Farris
 Box Office Supervisor: Brent McMillan
Founded: 1982
Paid Staff: 11
Volunteer Staff: 30
Budget: $.8 million
Income Sources: Rental, Concessions, Services
Affiliations: University of Tennessee, Chatanooga
Annual Attendance: 240,000
Facility Category: Arena
Type of Stage: Flexible
Stage Dimensions: 64 x 48
Seating Capacity: 12,000
Year Built: 1982
Rental Contact: Ken Kapelinski

8257
APSU CONCERT HALL
Austin Peay State University
Center of Excellence for the Creative Arts
615 McCallie Avenue
Clarksville, TN 37403
Phone: 423-755-4269
Fax: 931-221-7149
e-mail: burawac@apsu.edu
Web Site: www.utc.edu/utcarena
Officers:
 Interim Chancellor: E. Grady Bogue
Management:
 Director: Christopher Burawa, burawac@apsu.edu
Mission: To inspire an appreciation of the creative arts with APSu students and the Clarksville community.
Utilizes: Artists-in-Residence; Choreographers; Collaborations; Commissioned Composers; Community Members; Composers; Curators; Dancers; Educators; Five Seasonal Concerts; Guest Accompanists; Guest Companies; Guest Directors; Guest Musicians; Guest Soloists; Guest Teachers; Instructors; Multimedia; Music; Organization Contracts; Paid Performers; Playwrights; Poets; Resident Companies; Sign Language Translators; Singers; Soloists; Students; Volunteer Directors & Actors; Writers
Founded: 1985
Facility Category: Concert Hall; Dance and Theatre Venue

8258
HOOPER EBLEN CENTER
601 College Street
Cookeville, TN 37044
Mailing Address: PO Box 5057
Phone: 931-221-7011
Fax: 931-372-3114
Toll-free: 187-861-PSU
e-mail: gov@apsu.edu
Web Site: www.apsu.edu/creativearts
Officers:
 President: Timothy L. Hall
Management:
 Athletic Director: David Larimore
 Administrative Assistant : Christina Harvey
 Department Of Music: Gregory Wolynec

8259
TULANE UNIVERSITY
Tennessee Tech University
6823 St. Charles Avenue
Cookeville, TN 70118
Phone: 504-865-5000
Fax: 931-372-3114
e-mail: website@tulane.edu
Web Site: www.tulane.edu
Management:
 Director: David Lorimore

8260
GATLINBURG CONVENTION CENTER
234 Historic Nature Trail Gatlinburg
Gatlinburg, TN 37738
Phone: 865-436-2392
Fax: 865-436-3704
e-mail: debbieo@ci.gatlinburg.tn.us
Web Site: www.gatlinburgconferencecenter.com
Management:
 Director: Vickie Blake
 Event Manager: Pattie Baker
Seating Capacity: 28,767

8261
TEX TURNER ARENA
Lincoln Memorial University
Highway 25 East
Harrogate, TN 37752
Phone: 423-869-6311
Fax: 423-869-6356
Toll-free: 800-250-00
e-mail: lcarter@lmunet.edu
Web Site: www.lmurailsplitters.com
Management:
 Director Special Events: Larry Carter
 Operations Director: Travis Moody
 Head Coach: Josh Schertz
Seating Capacity: 5,500

8262
JACKSON CIVIC CENTER
400 South Highland Avenue
Jackson, TN 38301
Phone: 901-425-8580
Fax: 901-425-8385
e-mail: info@cityofjackson.net
Web Site: www.cityofjackson.net/venues/CivicCenterMain.htm

8263
LAMBUTH THEATRE
Lambuth College
705 Lamburth Boulevard
Jackson, TN 38301
Phone: 731-425-7982
Fax: 901-423-3493
e-mail: lambuth@memphis.edu.
Web Site: www.memphis.edu/lambuth

8264
AMAN ARENA
City of Jackson
179 Lane Avenue
Jackson, TN 38301
Phone: 901-425-8390
Fax: 701-425-8390
Management:
 Manager: Martha A Pope
Seating Capacity: 5,612

8265
DERTHICK THEATRE
Milligan College
Johnson City, TN 38301
Mailing Address: PO Box 210
Phone: 731-423-6020
Fax: 423-461-8755
Web Site: www.cj.jacksoin.tn.us

8266
FREEDOM HALL CIVIC CENTER
601 E. Main Street
Johnson City, TN 37601
Phone: 423-434-6000
Fax: 423-461-4867
e-mail: director@freedomhall-tn.com
Web Site: www.johnsoncitytn.com/freedomhall/
Officers:
 City Manager: M. Denis Peterson
 Assistant City Manager: Charles Stahl
Management:
 Administration/City Manager : Pete Peterson
 Administration/Assistant City Manag: Charlie Stahl
 Administration/Assistant City Manag: Bob Wilson

FACILITIES / Tennessee

Finance: Janet Jennings
Human Resources: Kevin Bratton
Mission: To provide venue space for public assembly, cultural arts, sports and entertainment opportunities.
Founded: 1974
Status: For-Profit, Professional
Paid Staff: 6
Performs At: Arena
Affiliations: City Of Johnson City, TN
Annual Attendance: 150,000
Facility Category: Arena
Type of Stage: Wenger Portable
Seating Capacity: 7,500

8267
MINI DOME
E Tennessee State University
Johnson City, TN 37614
Phone: 423-439-4343
Fax: 423-439-5294
Web Site: www.freedomhall-tn.com
Management:
  Director: Bill Toohey
Seating Capacity: 16,000

8268
SEEGER CHAPEL CONCERT HALL
Milligan College
Johnson City, TN 37682
Mailing Address: PO Box 500
Phone: 423-461-8700
Fax: 423-461-8755
Web Site: www.milligan.edu/community/spiritual/Seeger.html
Officers:
  President: Dr.Bill Gear
  VP: Mark Fox
  Director of Campus Activities: Kristal Dove
  Campus Minister: Brad Wallace
  Director of Residence Life & Housin: Kate Anderson
  Director of Calling and Career Expl: Beth Anderson

8269
BIJOU THEATRE
PO Box 1746
803 South Gay Street
Knoxville, TN 37901-1746
Mailing Address: P.O. Box 1746
Phone: 865-522-0832
Fax: 865-522-0238
Toll-free: 800-738-0832
e-mail: info@knoxbijou.com
Web Site: www.knoxbijou.com
Management:
  General Manager: Tom Bugg
  Assistant Manager: Jeanine Fowler
  Technical Director: Lee Vanham
  Development Manager: Amanda Womac
Utilizes: Theatre Companies
Founded: 1984
Specialized Field: Theater
Paid Staff: 7
Volunteer Staff: 60
Paid Artists: 40
Budget: $35,000-$60,000
Facility Category: Performing Arts
Type of Stage: Proscenium
Stage Dimensions: 35'x 51'
Seating Capacity: 750
Year Built: 1909
Year Remodeled: 1998

8270
BIJOU THEATRE CENTER
PO Box 1747
Knoxville, TN 37901-1747
Phone: 865-522-0832
Fax: 865-522-0238
Web Site: www.knoxbijou.com
Management:
  Producer: Laura Williams
  Director: Beverly Snukals

8271
KNOXVILLE CIVIC AUDITORIUM AND COLISEUM-AUDITORIUM
500 Howard Baker Jr. Ave
PO Box 37901
Knoxville, TN 37915
Mailing Address: P.O. Box 2603, Knoxville, TN 37901
Phone: 865-215-8900
Fax: 865-215-8989
e-mail: coliseumboxoffice@cityofknoxville.org
Web Site: www.knoxvillecoliseum.com
Officers:
  Executive Secretary: Jamie Cunningham
Management:
  Director of Public Facilities: Greg Mackay
  General Manager: Dale Dunn
  Assistant General Manager / Booking: Robbie Sandoval
  Operations Manager: Doug Simmons
  Box Office Manager: Robby Scheuermann
Utilizes: Actors; AEA Actors; Artists-in-Residence; Choreographers; Collaborating Artists; Commissioned Composers; Commissioned Music; Composers-in-Residence; Curators; Dance Companies; Dancers; Designers; Educators; Filmmakers; Fine Artists; Five Seasonal Concerts; Grant Writers; Guest Accompanists; Guest Artists; Guest Choreographers; Guest Companies; Guest Composers; Guest Conductors; Guest Designers; Guest Directors; Guest Ensembles; Guest Instructors; Guest Lecturers; Guest Musical Directors; Guest Musicians; Guest Soloists; Guest Teachers; Guest Writers; Guild Activities; High School Drama; Instructors; Local Artists; Local Unknown Artists; Lyricists; Multi Collaborations; Multimedia; Music; New Productions; Organization Contracts; Original Music Scores; Performance Artists; Playwrights; Resident Artists; Resident Professionals; Selected Students; Sign Language Translators; Singers; Soloists; Student Interns; Special Technical Talent; Theatre Companies; Touring Companies; Visual Arts
Founded: 1962
Status: Non-Profit, Professional
Paid Staff: 20
Facility Category: Auditorium and Arena
Stage Dimensions: Auditorium 57x57x27, Arena 60x40
Seating Capacity: Auditorium- 2,500 Arena- 6,000
Year Built: 1961
Year Remodeled: 1987
Rental Contact: Robbie Sandoval

8272
NEYLAND STADIUM
1235 Phillip Fulmer Way
Knoxville, TN 37996
Phone: 723-974-9053
Fax: 423-974-2800
Web Site: www.utsports.com/facilities/neyland_stadium.html
Management:
  Manager: Tim Reese
  Associtae Director Athletics: Robert J Dobell
Seating Capacity: 102,455

8273
TENNESSEE THEATER
604 South Gay Street
Knoxville, TN 37902
Mailing Address: P.O. Box 272, Knoxville, TN 37901-0272
Phone: 865-684-1200
Fax: 865-684-1201
e-mail: info@tennesseetheatre.com
Web Site: www.tennesseetheatre.com
Management:
  Executive Director: Becky Hancock
  General Manager: Tom Bugg
  Assistant General Manager: Heather Seiber
  Assistant Manager: Travis Monday

8274
THOMPSON-BOLING ARENA
1600 Phillip Fulmer Way
Suite 202
Knoxville, TN 37996
Phone: 423-974-0953
Fax: 423-974-2800
Web Site: www.tbarena.com
Management:
  Manager: Timothy L Reese
Seating Capacity: 24,451

8275
UNIVERSITY OF TENNESSEE MUSIC HALL
1600 Phillip Fulmer Way
Suite 202
Knoxville, TN 37996
Phone: 865-656-4444
Toll-free: 977-959-61
Web Site: www.knoxvilletickets.com

8276
CUMBERLAND UNIVERSITY AUDITORIUM
1 Cumberland Square
Lebanon, TN 37087
Phone: 615-444-2562
Fax: 615-444-2569
Toll-free: 800-467-0562
Web Site: www.cumberland.edu
Management:
  President: Harvill Eaton
  Artistic Director: Steve Farnsley
Founded: 1842
Status: Non-Profit, Professional
Paid Staff: 30
Paid Artists: 10

8277
SKYHAWK ARENA
University of Tennessee-Martin
1 Cumberland Square
Martin, TN 37807
Phone: 800-467-0562
Fax: 901-587-7725
Web Site: www.cumberland.edu
Management:
  Interim Director Campus Recreation: Gina Warren
Seating Capacity: 6,600

FACILITIES / Tennessee

8278
MARYVILLE COLLEGE
502 E Lamar
Alexander Parkway
Maryville, TN 37804
Phone: 731-881-7000
Fax: 865-981-8010
Toll-free: 800-597-2687
Web Site: www.maryvillecollege.edu
Management:
    President: Gerald Gibson
Founded: 1819
Status: Non-Profit, Professional

8279
WILSON CHAPEL COMPLEX
502 E. Lamar Alexander Pkwy
Maryville, TN 37804
Phone: 865-597-2687
Fax: 865-981-8001
Toll-free: 800-597-2687
Web Site: www.maryvillecollege.edu
Officers:
    President: Dr. William T. Tom Bogart
    Chair: Mr. James N. Proffitt
Management:
    Senior Consultant: Ms. Elizabeth A. Bulette
    Managing Editor & Exec.: Nancy B. Cain

8280
EWING CHILDREN'S THEATRE
2599 Avery Avenue
Memphis, TN 38112
Phone: 901-452-3968
Fax: 901-452-3805
Utilizes: Actors; Choreographers; Collaborations; Dancers; Guest Accompanists; Guest Choreographers; Guest Conductors; Guest Designers; Guest Ensembles; Guild Activities; Local Artists; Multimedia; Music; Organization Contracts; Performance Artists; Resident Professionals; Sign Language Translators; Soloists; Student Interns; Theatre Companies
Founded: 1949
Income Sources: Memphis Park Services
Annual Attendance: 10,000
Facility Category: Theatre
Type of Stage: Proscenium
Seating Capacity: 193
Year Built: 1982
Rental Contact: Kay Lightfoot

8281
LIBERTY BOWL MEMORIAL STADIUM
335 South Hollywood Street
Memphis, TN 38104
Phone: 901-729-4344
Fax: 901-276-2756
Web Site: www.libertybowlstadium.com
Management:
    General Manager: Art Davis
    Event Manager: Alex Hall
Founded: 1965
Paid Staff: 5
Seating Capacity: 64,000
Year Built: 1963
Year Remodeled: 1965

8282
MEMPHIS COOK CONVENTION CENTER COMPLEX
Cannon Center for the Performing Arts
255 North Main Street
Memphis, TN 38103
Phone: 901-576-1200
Fax: 901-576-1212
Toll-free: 800-726-0915
e-mail: tknight@memphisconvention.com
Web Site: www.memphistravel.com/conventions/memphis-cook-center/contact-us
Officers:
    Chairman: Harold Graeter
Management:
    Vice President/General Manager: Pierre Landaich
    Director, Convention Center Sales: Nicole Seltzer
    Director, Event Services: Yvonne Joiner
    Director, Finance: Chuck Jabbour
    Technical Director: Cory Hoffman
Mission: They are a full service convention center with a performing arts center.
Founded: 1974
Status: For-Profit, Non-Professional
Paid Staff: 40
Seating Capacity: 2,100
Year Built: 2002

8283
MID-SOUTH COLISEUM
996 Early Maxwell Boulevard
Memphis, TN 38104
Phone: 901-274-3982
Fax: 901-276-8653
Web Site: www.memphisconvention.com
Management:
    Managing Director: Steve Fox
Founded: 1964
Status: For-Profit, Professional
Seating Capacity: 12,000

8284
MUD ISLAND RIVER AMPHITHEATRE
125 North Front Street
Memphis, TN 38103
Phone: 901-576-7241
Fax: 901-576-6666
Toll-free: 800-076-07
e-mail: trey@mudisland.com
Web Site: www.mudisland.com
Management:
    GM: Trey Giuntini
    Operations Manager: Alisa Bradley
Seating Capacity: 5,061

8285
ORPHEUM THEATRE
842s Broadway
PO Box 3370
Memphis, TN 90014
Phone: 877-677-4386
Fax: 213-622-1939
e-mail: info@laorpheum.com
Web Site: www.laorpheum.com
Officers:
    Chief Administrative Officer: Donna Darwin
Management:
    President: Pat Halloran
    Director Education/Programs: Alica Donohoe
    Technical Director: Richard Reinach
Founded: 1978
Status: Non-Profit, Non-Professional
Paid Staff: 25

8286
THEATRE MEMPHIS
630 Perkin Extended
Memphis, TN 38117
Phone: 901-682-8323
Fax: 901-763-4096
Web Site: www.theatrememphis.org
Officers:
    President: Sarah Norton
    VP: Dabney Coors
    Treasurer: Brayn W. Ford
    Vice President: Joe Lackie
    Vice President: Barclay Roberts
Management:
    Executive Producer: Debbie Litch
    Artistic Director: Kell Christie
    Operations Manager: Lisa Hayes
    Executive Direc: Debbi Litch
Utilizes: Actors; Artists-in-Residence; Choreographers; Dancers; Designers; Grant Writers; Guest Accompanists; Guest Artists; Guest Conductors; Guest Designers; Guest Ensembles; Guest Lecturers; Guest Musical Directors; Guest Writers; Guild Activities; High School Drama; Local Artists; Music; Organization Contracts; Original Music Scores; Performance Artists; Resident Artists; Resident Professionals; Student Interns
Founded: 1920
Specialized Field: Theatre
Status: Non-Profit, Non-Professional
Paid Staff: 13
Paid Artists: 4
Budget: $1,100,000
Income Sources: Ticket sales, Contributions, Foundation
Season: Year-Round
Performs At: Live Theatre
Annual Attendance: 40,000
Type of Stage: Proscenium; Flexible
Seating Capacity: 400
Year Built: 1975
Year Remodeled: 2004
Rental Contact: Mimi Morgrey

8287
THEATRE GUILD
314 S Hill Street
Morristown, TN 37814
Phone: 423-586-9260
Web Site: theatreguildinc.org
Officers:
    Chairman: Bill Crawford
    Vice Chairman: Key Flockhart
    Treasurer: Larry McGowan

8288
CHARLES M MURPHY ATHLETIC CENTER
Murphy Center Room G100
Middle Tennessee State University
Murfreesboro, TN 37132
Mailing Address: PO Box 203
Phone: 615-904-8258
Fax: 615-904-8101
e-mail: rita.whitaker@mtsu.edu
Web Site: www.mtsu.edu
Officers:
    Secretary: Kim Scutero
Management:
    Director: Darrell Towe
    Manager: Rita Whitaker
    Manager: Boniface Amuzu
    Admin Assistant & Office Manager: Sherrie Murray
    Event Coordinator: Chris Gannar

FACILITIES / Tennessee

8289
JOHNNY 'RED' FLOYD STADIUM
MTSU Box 20
Murfreesboro, TN 37132
Phone: 615-898-2450
Fax: 615-898-2873
e-mail: cdoman@mtsu.edu
Web Site: www.goblueraiders.com
Officers:
  Secretary: Cindy Kloss
Management:
  Asso Dir/Coordinator of Life Skills: Wynnifred Counts
  Director: Todd Wyant
  Assistant Director: Angel Nathan
  Director of Athletics: Chris Massaro
  Associate Athletic Director/SWA: Diane Turnham
Seating Capacity: 31,000

8290
ADELPHIA STADIUM
1 Titans Way
Nashville, TN 37213
Phone: 615-565-4000
Fax: 615-565-4444
Web Site: www.titansonline.com
Officers:
  CEO: K.S. Adams
  VP: Mike Reinfeldt
Management:
  Managing Director: Dempsey Henderson
  Head Coach: Mike Munchak
Founded: 1999
Status: For-Profit, Professional
Paid Staff: 300

8291
ALLEN ARENA
Lipscomb University
One University Park Drive
Nashville, TN 37204
Phone: 615-279-1000
Fax: 615-279-7071
Toll-free: 800-334-4358
Web Site: www.lipscomb.edu
Officers:
  President: L. Randolph Lowry III
Management:
  GM: Trish Stapp
  Box Office Manager: Janet Grimes
Seating Capacity: 5,534

8292
CHAFFIN'S BARN DINNER THEATRE
8204 Highway 100
Nashville, TN 37221
Phone: 615-646-9977
Fax: 615-662-5439
Toll-free: 800-282-2276
e-mail: chaffinsboxoffice@yahoo.com
Web Site: www.dinnertheatre.com
Officers:
  Owners/ Producers: John Chaffin
  Owners/ Producers: Janie Chaffin
Management:
  Artistic Director: Martha Wilkinson
  Group Sales: Vanessa Wynn
  Stage Manager: Liz Fletcher
  Box Office: Kim Nygren
  Box Office: Annie Cavender
Mission: Offers a package price for professional non-equity theatre and buffet dining. The dinner theatre was Nashville's first professional theatre and continues to produce high quality productions.
Utilizes: Guest Companies
Founded: 1967
Specialized Field: Musical; Dinner Theatre
Status: Non-Profit, Professional
Performs At: Chaffin's Barn
Organization Type: Performing

8293
CURB EVENT CENTER
Belmont University
2002 Belmont Boulevard
Nashville, TN 37212
Phone: 615-460-8500
Fax: 615-460-8010
e-mail: eventservices@belmont.edu
Web Site: www.belmont.edu/curbeventcenter/
Management:
  Director: Jeff Hunter
  Booking Coordinator: Liz Parris
Seating Capacity: 5,900

8294
BRIDGESTONE ARENA
501 Broadway
Nashville, TN 37203
Phone: 615-770-2000
Fax: 615-770-2010
Web Site: www.bridgestonearena.com
Management:
  General Manager/COO: Hugh Lombardi
  Senior Director Booking: Brock James
Specialized Field: Home of the Nashville Predators (NHL) and the Nashville Kats (AFL)
Seating Capacity: 17,298, 20,000
Year Built: 1996

8295
GORDON JEWISH COMMUNITY CENTER
801 Percy Warner Boulevard
Nashville, TN 37205
Phone: 615-356-7170
Fax: 615-353-2659
e-mail: info@nashvillejcc.org
Web Site: www.nashvillejcc.org
Officers:
  President: Didi Biesman
  President-Elect: Howard Kirshner
  Executive Director: Eric Goldstein
  Treasurer: Frank Gordon
  Secretary: Raymond Jacobs
Management:
  Executive Director: Leslie M. Sax
  Director of Finance: Jaclyn Walters
  Athletics Director: Blayne Lipman
  Health & Wellness Director: Harriet Shirley
  Adult Director: Meryl Kraft
Founded: 1902
Status: Non-Profit, Non-Professional

8296
GRAND OLE OPRY HOUSE
2804 Opryland Drive
Nashville, TN 37214
Phone: 615-871-6612
Fax: 615-871-5719
Toll-free: 800-SEE-OPRY
Web Site: www.opry.com
Management:
  General Manager: Pete Fisher
  Event Manager: Sally Williams
Founded: 1974
Status: For-Profit, Professional
Facility Category: Theatre
Type of Stage: Procenium
Stage Dimensions: 80w x 60d
Seating Capacity: 4400
Year Built: 1974
Cost: 4,500 vs 12% gbr

8297
GREER STADIUM
534 Chestnut Street
Nashville, TN 37203
Phone: 615-690-HITS
Fax: 615-256-5684
e-mail: admin@minorleaguebaseball.com
Web Site: www.milb.com
Officers:
  President & CEO: Pat O'Conner
  Vice President: Stan Brand
  SVP, Legal Affairs: Scott Poley
  Special Counsel: George Yund
  VP, Baseball & Business Operations: Tim Brunswick
Management:
  Executive Director, Communications: Steve Densa
  Director, Finance and Accounting: Sean Brown
  Director, Information Technology: Rob Colamarino
  Director, Licensing: Sandie Hebert
  Director, Business Development: Scott Kravchuk
Founded: 1978
Paid Staff: 20

8298
HERSCHEL GREER STADIUM
534 Chestnut Street
Nashville, TN 37203
Phone: 615-690-4487
Fax: 615-256-5684
e-mail: info@nashvillesounds.com
Web Site: www.milb.com
Officers:
  Executive Director: Frank Ward
  President: Masahiro Honzawa
  Vice President / General Manager: Brad Tammen
  VP - Ticket Sales & Service: Eric Rowley
  VP Corp Partnerships & Marketing: Jason Franke
Management:
  Director of Accounting: Barb Walker
  Head Groundskeeper: Thomas Trotter
  Director of Community Relations: Shannon Lapsley
  Stadium Operations Manager: Chad Green
  Stadium Operations Assistant: Jeremy Wells
Founded: 1978
Status: Non-Profit, Non-Professional

8299
NASHVILLE CONVENTION CENTER
601 Commerce Street
Nashville, TN 37203
Phone: 615-742-2000
Fax: 615-742-2014
e-mail: conventioncenter@nashville.gov
Web Site: www.nashvilleconventionctr.com
Management:
  Executive Director: Theresa Horgon
Founded: 1987
Status: For-Profit, Non-Professional
Paid Staff: 45

FACILITIES / Tennessee

8300
NASHVILLE MUNICIPAL AUDITORIUM
417 4th Avenue N
Nashville, TN 37201
Phone: 615-862-6390
Fax: 615-862-6394
Toll-free: 800-745-3000
e-mail: sharon.hill@nashville.gov
Web Site: www.nashvilleauditorium.com
Officers:
  Chairman: John Lander
  Vice Chair: Adrrenne Newman
Management:
  Director of Operations: Jim Raver
  Director of Sales & Marketing: Sharon Hill
  General Manager: Bob Skoney
  Box Office Manager: Taneisha Alexander
Mission: To provide the highest degree of patron services in a cost effective manner in order to promote the macimum use of the venue.
Founded: 1962
Specialized Field: Concerts
Status: For-Profit, Non-Professional
Paid Staff: 8
Volunteer Staff: 1
Budget: $1.5 million
Income Sources: Ticket Sales
Affiliations: Nashville Convention & Visitors Bureau
Annual Attendance: 232,000
Facility Category: Arena
Type of Stage: Portable
Stage Dimensions: 60' x 40'
Seating Capacity: 9,600
Year Built: 1962
Year Remodeled: 2005
Cost: $5 million
Rental Contact: Sharon Hill

8301
RYMAN AUDITORIUM
116 Fifth Avenue North
Nashville, TN 37219
Phone: 615-458-8700
Fax: 615-458-8701
e-mail: jyost@ryman.com
Web Site: www.ryman.com
Management:
  Marketing & Advertising: Jamie Yost
  Public Relations & Filming Requests: Lisaann Dupont
  Daytime Tours & Ryman History: Joshua Bronnenberg
  Rentals & Special Events: David Collier
  Group Sales: Wayne Chandler
Utilizes: Actors; Artists-in-Residence; Choreographers; Collaborating Artists; Commissioned Music; Dance Companies; Educators; Fine Artists; Grant Writers; Guest Accompanists; Guest Artists; Guest Choreographers; Guest Companies; Guest Composers; Guest Conductors; Guest Designers; Guest Directors; Guest Instructors; Guest Lecturers; Guest Musical Directors; Guest Musicians; Guest Soloists; Local Artists; Lyricists; Multi Collaborations; Multimedia; Music; New Productions; Organization Contracts; Original Music Scores; Performance Artists; Sign Language Translators; Singers; Soloists; Special Technical Talent; Theatre Companies
Founded: 1892
Specialized Field: Museum; Concert Hall
Status: For-Profit, Professional
Paid Staff: 100
Year Built: 1892
Year Remodeled: 1994
Rental Contact: Brian Gavron

8302
SCHERMERHORN SYMPHONY CENTER
1 Symphony Place
Nashville, TN 37201-2031
Phone: 615-687-6500
Fax: 615-687-6530
e-mail: events@nashvillesymphony.com
Web Site: www.schermerhorncenter.com
Officers:
  President and CEO: Alan D. Valentine
  COO: Mark A. Blakeman
  CFO: Chad Boyd
  V.P. of Development: Jonathan Norris
  V.P. of Marketing: Daniel B. Grossman
Management:
  Director of Events: Hays McWhirter
  Director of Artistic Administration: Laurence Tucker
  Director of Data Standards: Tony Exler
  Director of Human Resources: Ashley Skinner SPHR
  Dir of Advertising and Promotions: Misty Cochran
Seating Capacity: 1862

8303
TENNESSEE PERFORMING ARTS CENTER
505 Deaderick Street
PO Box 190660
Nashville, TN 37343
Phone: 615-782-4000
Fax: 615-782-4001
e-mail: sgreil@tpac.org
Web Site: www.tpac.org
Officers:
  Chairman: Claire Tucker
  Vice Chairman: Dale Allen
  Treasurer: Ron Corbin
  Secretary: Larry Stessel
  Director: Brent Hing

8304
TENNESSEE PERFORMING ARTS CENTER: ANDREW JACKSON HALL
505 Deaderick Street
Nashville, TN 37343
Phone: 615-782-4000
Fax: 615-782-4001
Web Site: www.tpac.org
Officers:
  Chairman: Claire Tucker
  Vice Chairman: Dale Allen
  Treasurer: Ron Corbin
  Secretary: Larry Stessel
Management:
  Director: Brent Hing

8305
VANDERBILT STADIUM
25th & Kensington Place
Nashville, TN 37212
Phone: 615-322-4727
Fax: 615-343-1805
Management:
  Chancellor: Gordon Gee
  Vice Chancellor: David Williams
Status: Non-Profit, Non-Professional
Seating Capacity: 41,203

8306
VANDERBILT UNIVERSITY: MEMORIAL GYM
2601 Jess Neely Drive
Nashville, TN 37212
Phone: 615-322-4653
Fax: 615-343-8738
e-mail: elizabeth.wright@vanderbilt.edu
Web Site: www.zucomodores.com
Management:
  Director of Baseball Operations: Drew Fann
  Director of Operations: Dan Cage
  Director of Video Operations: Julian Terrell
  Director of Academic Support: Elizabeth Wright
  Senior Academic Counselor: Nate Bell
Founded: 1873
Status: Non-Profit, Non-Professional
Paid Staff: 200
Paid Artists: 300
Seating Capacity: 15,626

8307
W.J. HALE STADIUM
Tennessee State University
3500 John Merrit Boulevard
Nashville, TN 37240
Phone: 615-322-7311
Web Site: www.vanderbilt.edu
Management:
  Athletic Director: Bill Thomas
Seating Capacity: 16,500

8308
LOUISE MANDRELL THEATER
2046 Parkway
Pigeon Forge, TN 37203
Phone: 615-327-3400
Fax: 865-453-9641
e-mail: web@louisemandrell.com
Web Site: www.louisemandrell.com
Management:
  GM: Sande Weiss
  Facility Contact: Debbie Glandon
Seating Capacity: 1,400

8309
SIOUX FALLS STADIUM
1001 North West Avenue
Sioux Falls, TN 57104
Phone: 605-336-6060
e-mail: info@sfcanaries.com
Web Site: sfcanaries.com
Management:
  President: Jeff Loeble
  GM: John Hindle
Seating Capacity: 20,000

8310
SOUTH JACKSON CIVIC CENTER
404 South Jackson Street
Tullahoma, TN 37388
Phone: 931-455-5321
Fax: 931-455-9340
e-mail: sojack@lighttube.net
Web Site: www.southjackson.org
Management:
  President: Shirley Moore
  Managing Director: Patty Wimsatt
Founded: 1977
Status: Non-Profit, Professional
Paid Staff: 1

FACILITIES / Texas

Texas

8311
ABILENE CIVIC CENTER: THEATER
555 Walnut St
PO Box 60
Abilene, TX 79604
Phone: 325-676-6200
Fax: 915-676-6343
e-mail: abilene@abilenetx.com
Web Site: www.abilenetx.com

8312
ABILENE CIVIC CENTER: EXHIBIT HALL
555 Walnut St
PO Box 60
Abilene, TX 79604
Phone: 325-676-6200
Fax: 915-676-6343
e-mail: abilene@abilenetx.com
Web Site: www.abilenetx.com

8313
AZTEC
2 Railroad Street
PO Box 2017
Albany, TX 76430
Phone: 915-762-3838
Fax: 915-762-3125
e-mail: fandangle@bitstreet.com
Web Site: www.fortgriffinfandangle.org

8314
FORT GRIFFIN FANDANGLE OUTDOOR THEATRE
2 Railroad Street
PO Box 2017
Albany, TX 76430
Phone: 915-762-3838
Fax: 915-762-3125
e-mail: fandangle@bitstreet.com
Web Site: www.fortgriffinfandangle.org

8315
OLD JAIL ART CENTER
201 S 2nd Street
Albany, TX 76430
Phone: 915-762-2269
Fax: 915-762-2260
e-mail: director@theoldjailartcenter.org
Web Site: www.theoldjailartcenter.org
Management:
 Executive Director: James Peck
 Education Director: Erin Whitmore
 Business Manager: Dorothy Walker
 Curator of Exhibitions: Patrick Kelly
 Education Outreach: Mary Schrader
Mission: To serve as an educational and cultural center focused on the visual arts through collections, interpretation, programs and regional history resources to enhance the education of the audience.
Founded: 1980
Specialized Field: Art Meseum
Paid Staff: 8
Volunteer Staff: 89
Paid Artists: 28
Non-paid Artists: 20

8316
AMARILLO CIVIC CENTER: MUSIC HALL
PO Box 2047
Amarillo, TX 76430
Phone: 325-762-2525
Fax: 325-762-3125
Web Site: www.albanytexas.com
Management:
 Managing Director: Chris Miller
Paid Staff: 25
Affiliations: Western Professional Hockey League
Seating Capacity: 4900 Sporting Events, 7000 Concerts
Year Built: 1968

8317
AMARILLO CIVIC CENTER: ARENA
PO Box 2047
Amarillo, TX 76430
Phone: 325-762-2525
Fax: 325-762-3125
Web Site: www.albanytexas.com

8318
BALLPARK IN ARLINGTON
1000 Ballpark Way
Suite 400
Arlington, TX 76011
Phone: 817-273-5222
Fax: 817-273-5174
Management:
 VP Event Services: Tim Murphy
 Director Facility Event Operations: Kevin Jimison
Specialized Field: Sports Facility; home of the Texas Rangers; Also includes a baseball museum; youth baseball park; amphitheatre; and an office building.
Seating Capacity: 49,166
Year Built: 1994

8319
MAVERICK STADIUM
University of Texas at Arlington
1409 W Mitchell Street
Arlington, TX 76013
Phone: 817-272-2261
Fax: 817-272-5037
Web Site: texas.rangers.mlb.com/help/index.jsp?c_id=tex
Management:
 Athletic Director: Pete Carlon
 Director: Kathryn Beeler
Mission: Pre-professional training program for theatre.
Utilizes: Actors; Artists-in-Residence; Choreographers; Collaborating Artists; Designers; Educators; Grant Writers; Guest Accompanists; Guest Artists; Guest Companies; Guest Designers; Guest Instructors; Guest Lecturers; Guest Soloists; Performance Artists; Resident Professionals; Soloists; Student Interns
Affiliations: University of Texas system
Facility Category: Mainstage Theater; Black Box Theater
Type of Stage: Proscenium; Black Box
Seating Capacity: 12,800

8320
MUSIC MILL AMPHITHEATRE
2201 Road To Six Flags
Arlington, TX 76011
Mailing Address: PO Box 191
Phone: 817-640-8900
Fax: 817-607-6144
Web Site: www.sixflags.com
Seating Capacity: 10,200

8321
THEATRE ARLINGTON
305 W Main Street
Arlington, TX 76010
Phone: 817-275-7661
Fax: 817-275-3370
e-mail: info@theatrearlington.org
Web Site: www.theatrearlington.org
Management:
 Executive Director: Norman Ussery
 Education Director: Cindy Honeycutt
 Outreach Manager: Jacque Campbell Disher
 Box Office/Office Manager: Troy Stidham
 Marketing Manager/Volunteer Coor: Gary Payne
Mission: Dedicated to the cultural enrichment, education and entertainment of the citizenry of Arlington and the North Texas community.
Founded: 1973
Status: Non-Profit, Professional
Paid Staff: 6
Volunteer Staff: 100
Paid Artists: 3

8322
DARRELL K ROYAL-TEXAS MEMORIAL STADIUM
University of Texas Athletics
405 E. 23rd St.
Austin, TX 78712
Mailing Address: The University of Texas at Austin, P.O. Box 7399, Austin TX
Phone: 512-471-9405
Fax: 512-471-+130
e-mail: streaming@sidearmsports.com
Web Site: www.texassports.com
Officers:
 Chief Revenue Officer: Steve Hank
Management:
 Athletics Director: Steve Patterson
 Assistant Athletics Director: Larry Falk
 Assistant Director of Annual Fund: Kevin Collins
 Special Assistant to the President: DeLoss Dodds
 Deputy Director: Butch Worley
Specialized Field: Home of University of Texas athletics (NCAA).
Seating Capacity: 79,450
Year Built: 1924
Year Remodeled: 1998

8323
FRANK ERWIN CENTER
1701 Red River
PO Box 2929
Austin, TX 78701
Phone: 512-471-7744
Fax: 512-471-9652
e-mail: comments@erwin.utexas.edu
Web Site: www.uterwincentre.com
Management:
 Assistant Director for Marketing: Liz Land
 Athletics Director: John M. Graham
 Associate Director: Jimmy Earl, CFE
 Administrative Office Manager: Charly Wallace
 Box Office Manager: Thom Ramirez
Founded: 1977
Status: Non-Profit, Professional
Paid Artists: 2

8324
ONE WORLD THEATRE
7701 Bee Caves Road
Austin, TX 78746
Phone: 888-616-0522
Fax: 512-330-9600
e-mail: BoxOffice@OneWorldTheatre.org
Web Site: www.oneworldtheatre.org
Officers:

FACILITIES / Texas

Chief Operating Officer: Albert Magara
Management:
  Executive Director & Co Founder: Hartt Stearns
  Co Founder: Nada Stearns
  Director of Production: Marcus Hutsell
  Lighting Designer: Andrew Van Osselaer
Founded: 1999
Status: Non-Profit, Non-Professional
Paid Staff: 6

8325
PARAMOUNT THEATER FOR THE PERFORMING ARTS
713 Congress Avenue
Austin, TX 78701
Phone: 512-472-5470
Fax: 512-472-5824
Web Site: www.austintheatrealliance.org
Officers:
  President: Duff M. Stewart
  Secretary: Grace F. Renbarger
  Treasurer: Sharon Francia
Management:
  Artistic Director: Ken Tein
  Director Programming: Paul Bewtel
Mission: Presenting performing arts and film.
Founded: 1975
Status: Non-Profit, Professional
Paid Staff: 25
Volunteer Staff: 200
Paid Artists: 40
Performs At: Proscenium Theatre
Affiliations: APAP; LHAT
Type of Stage: Proscenium
Seating Capacity: 1,300
Year Built: 1915
Year Remodeled: 1980
Rental Contact: Paul Bentel

8326
UNIVERSITY OF TEXAS AT AUSTIN PERFORMING ARTS CENTER
PO Box 7818
Austin, TX 78713-7818
Phone: 512-477-6060
Fax: 512-471-3636
e-mail: info@texasperformingarts.org
Web Site: www.texasperformingarts.org
Officers:
  President: Larry Faulkner
  Executive Director: Pebbles Wadsworth
  Assistant /Associate Director: JB Tuttle
  Assistant Director: Suzanne Cooper
  Production Manager: Charles Leslie
  Associate Director: Neil Barclay
  Events Manager: Peter Melnick
Management:
  Director and Associate Dean: Kathy Panoff
  Associate Director, Administration: April Holmes
  Judith: Rachel Durkin-Drga
Mission: The University of Texas at Austin Performing Arts Center is a fully professional presenter of the performing arts. The PAC also seeks to educate, enlighten and entertain residents of the state with diverse and innovative programs that reflect the traditional and evolving culture of the United States and of the world.
Founded: 1981
Status: Non-Profit, Professional
Paid Staff: 70
Budget: $1,000,000
Performs At: Bass Concert Hall; Bates Recital Hall; McCullough Theatre
Facility Category: Performance Center; Opera House
Type of Stage: Proscenium
Stage Dimensions: 30'Wx36'D; 30'Wx18'H
Rental Contact: Pebbles Wadsworth

8327
UNIVERSITY OF TEXAS AT AUSTIN: THEATRE ROOM
2247 Guadalupe Street Austin
Austin, TX 78713
Phone: 512-471-6636
Fax: 512-471-0824
Web Site: www.utexas.edu

8328
OLD BASTROP OPERA HOUSE
711 Spring Street
PO Box 691
Bastrop, TX 78602
Phone: 512-321-6283
e-mail: Chester@BastropOperaHouse.com
Web Site: www.bastropoperahouse.com
Management:
  Executive Director: Chester Eitze

8329
BEAUMONT CIVIC CENTER COMPLEX: JULIE ROGERS THEATRE
765 Pearl Street
Beaumont, TX 77701
Phone: 409-838-3435
Fax: 409-838-3715
Toll-free: 800-782-3081
e-mail: lcaballero@ci.beaumont.tx.us
Web Site: www.beaumont-tx-complex.com
Officers:
  Secretary: Amy Franklin
Management:
  Event Facilities Director: Lenny Caballero
  Operations Manager: Tommie Minkins
  Sales and Marketing Coordinator: Emily Wheeler
  Production Coordinator: Shon Hodgkinson

8330
CARDINAL STADIUM
1 Cardinals Drive
4400 MLK Parkway
Beaumont, TX 85305
Phone: 623-433-7101
Fax: 623-433-7199
Toll-free: 800-745-3000
Web Site: www.universityofphoenixstadium.com
Management:
  Athletic Director: Dean Billick
  Event Manager: David Widoff

8331
CIVIC CENTER COMPLEX
765 Pearl Street
Beaumont, TX 77701
Mailing Address: PO Box 3827, Beaumont TX 77704
Phone: 409-838-3435
Fax: 409-838-3715
Toll-free: 800-782-3081
e-mail: lcaballero@ci.beaumont.tx.us
Web Site: www.beaumont-tx-complex.com
Officers:
  Secretary: Amy Franklin
Management:
  Event Facilities Director: Lenny Caballero, marrington@ci.beaumont.tx.us
  Operations Manager: Tommie Minkins, tminkins@ci.beaumont.tx.us
  Sales and Marketing Coordinator: Emily Wheeler, chawking@ci.beaumont.tx.us
  Production Coordinator: Shon Hodgkinson

8332
LAMAR UNIVERSITY STUDIO THEATRE
765 Pearl Street
Beaumont, TX 77701
Phone: 409-838-3435
Fax: 409-838-3715
Toll-free: 800-782-3081
e-mail: lcaballero@ci.beaumont.tx.us
Web Site: www.beaumont-tx-complex.com
Officers:
  Secretary: Amy Franklin
Management:
  Event Facilities Director: Lenny Caballero
  Operations Manager: Tommie Minkins
  Sales and Marketing Coordinator: Emily Wheeler
  Production Coordinator: Shon Hodgkinson
Mission: Educational
Specialized Field: Theatre
Paid Staff: 5

8333
MONTAGNE CENTER
4400 MLK Blvd
PO Box 10009
Beaumont, TX 77710
Phone: 409-880-7011
Fax: 409-880-8990
e-mail: admissions@lamar.edu
Web Site: www.lamar.edu
Officers:
  President: Dr. Kenneth Evans
  Provost and Vice President: Dr. Stephen Doblin
  VP for Finance and Operations: Dr. Cruse Melvin
  VP for University Advancement: Camille Mouton
  VP for Information Technology: Priscilla Parsons
Management:
  Athletic Director: Jason Henderson
  Executive Assistant to President: Dr. Jack Hopper
Seating Capacity: 10,080

8334
GERTRUDE RUSSELL JONES AUDITORIUM
440 Wilchester Blvd
3800 Charco Road
Beeville, TX 77079
Phone: 713-932-1639
Fax: 361-358-3971
e-mail: info@houstonaudubon.org
Web Site: www.cbc.cc.tx.us
Officers:
  Performing Arts Division Chair: James L Lee
  President: Mary Carte
  Treasurer: Kay Medford
  Secretary: Bernice Hotman
Management:
  Education Director: Mary Anne Weber
  Interim Executive Director: Jim Winn
  Development Director: Jessica Jubin
  Coordinator: Bethany Foshee

8335
BELL COUNTY EXPO CENTER
301 West Loop 121
PO Box 206
Belton, TX 76512

FACILITIES / Texas

Phone: 254-933-5353
Fax: 254-933-5354
e-mail: info@bellcountyexpo.com
Web Site: www.bellcountyexpo.com
Management:
   General Manager: Tim Stephens
   Assistant Director: John Dungan
Founded: 1987
Specialized Field: Concerts
Paid Staff: 16
Budget: $1.4 million
Income Sources: County
Performs At: Arena
Affiliations: IAVM; IEBA; IAFE
Annual Attendance: 400,000+
Facility Category: Arena
Stage Dimensions: 60' x 40'
Seating Capacity: 8,000
Year Built: 1987
Cost: $12 million
Rental Contact: Tim Stephens

8336
CAMILLE PLAYHOUSE
1 Dean Porter Park
Brownsville, TX 78520
Phone: 956-542-8900
Fax: 956-542-0567
e-mail: camilleplayhouse@aol.com
Web Site: www.camilleplayhouse.org
Officers:
   President: Stephen Shull
   Vice President: Lecia Chaney
   Secretary: Ana Rodriguez
   Treasurer: Jaime Lucio
Management:
   Executive Artistic Director: Eric A. Vera
   Business Manager: Penny Bridger
Mission: To stimulate an interest in the performing arts through the presentation of live theatre, utilizing the talents of the entire Valley community.
Founded: 1963
Specialized Field: Live theatre
Status: Non-Profit, Non-Professional
Paid Staff: 2
Volunteer Staff: 3
Facility Category: Theatre house
Type of Stage: Thrust, proscenium
Stage Dimensions: 20 x 48 x 28
Seating Capacity: 301
Year Built: 1964
Rental Contact: Executive Director Joel Humphries

8337
BROWNWOOD AREA CHAMBER OF COMMERCE
600 E. Depot St.
Brownwood, TX 76801
Phone: 325-646-9535
Fax: 915-646-0938
Web Site: www.brownwoodchamber.org
Officers:
   CEO: Laura Terhune
Management:
   General Manager: David Withers
   Facility Manager: Kevin Dearling
   Marketing: Ray Tipton
   Office Manager: Dawn Norway
Facility Category: Arena; Multy- Purpose
Type of Stage: flexible
Stage Dimensions: 60 4'x 8' stage segments
Seating Capacity: 3,000
Year Built: 1963
Rental Contact: David Withers

8338
KIMBROUGH MEMORIAL STADIUM
West Texas A&M University
PO Box 60049
Canyon, TX 79016
Phone: 806-651-2069
Fax: 806-651-2688
Management:
   Athletic Director: Ed Harris
Seating Capacity: 20,000

8339
PIONEER AMPHITHEATRE
Palo Duro Canyon State Park
PO Box 268
Canyon, TX 79015
Phone: 806-488-2421
Fax: 806-655-7425

8340
WTAMU THEATRE
West Texas A&M University
2403 Russell Long Blvd
Canyon, TX 79015
Phone: 806-651-2799
Fax: 806-651-2818
e-mail: rbrantley@wtamu.edu
Web Site: www.wtamu.edu/bit
Officers:
   President: J. Patrick O'Brien, Ph.D.
Management:
   Theatre Director: Royal Brantley
   Technical Director: John Landon
Mission: Education of theatre educators and professionals of the Texas Panhandle
Founded: 1910
Specialized Field: Theatre; Performace; Technical Theatre; Music Theatre; Theatre Education
Status: Non-Profit, Non-Professional
Paid Staff: 6
Budget: $70,000
Income Sources: Student Fees; Box Office
Performs At: University Theatre
Affiliations: TETA; USITT; APO
Annual Attendance: 6,000
Facility Category: Performing Arts
Type of Stage: Pro Arch & Black Box
Stage Dimensions: 38x70; 51x51
Seating Capacity: 304/100
Year Built: 2006
Cost: $33 Million
Rental Contact: Perry Crafton

8341
G ROLLIE WHITE COLISEUM
Texas A&M University
Athletic Department
College Station, TX 77843-1128
Phone: 409-845-2313
Fax: 409-845-6825
Web Site: sports.tamu.edu
Management:
   Athletic Director: Wally Groff

8342
KYLE FIELD
12th Man Foundation
P.O. Box 2800
College Station, TX 77841-2800
Phone: 979-845-5725
Fax: 979-845-0564
Toll-free: 855-687-5953
e-mail: dsouth@athletics.tamu.edu
Web Site: kylefield.com/?DB_OEM_ID=27300
Management:
   Associate Athletic Director: Dave South
   Sr Associate Athletic Director: Billy Pickard
Specialized Field: Home of Texas A&M University athletics NCAA
Seating Capacity: 58,000
Year Built: 1927
Year Remodeled: 1998

8343
UNIVERSITY CENTER THEATRE COMPLEX AND CONFERENCE CENTER
Texas A&M University
College Station, TX 77843
Phone: 979-845-8903
Fax: 979-845-7312
Web Site: www.tamus.edu
Officers:
   President: Robert Gates
   President: Robert Gates
   Managing Director: Bill Bielamowicz
Founded: 1975
Status: Non-Profit, Non-Professional
Paid Staff: 30

8344
BAYFRONT PLAZA CONVENTION CENTER: AUDITORIUM
Texas A&M University
Corpus Christi, TX 77843
Phone: 979-845-8903
Fax: 979-845-7312
Web Site: www.tamus.edu
Management:
   General Manager: Mark Solis
Status: For-Profit, Professional
Paid Staff: 30

8345
PEFORMING ARTS CENTER
Texas A&M University- Corpus Christi
6300 Ocean Drive
Unit #5722
Corpus Christi, TX 7842-5722
Phone: 361-825-2316
Fax: 361-825-2250
e-mail: university.theatre@tamucc.edu
Web Site: cla.tamucc.edu
Officers:
   Visual/Performing Arts Dept. Chair: Carey Rote
Management:
   Events Coordinator: Olivia Ross
   Professor of Theatre: Dr. Terry Lewis
   Assis Professor of Costume Design: Rosa Lazaro
   Asstant Professor of Dance: Jilissa Cotton
Founded: 1947
Status: Non-Profit, Professional
Paid Staff: 6
Paid Artists: 30
Budget: $10,000-20,000
Performs At: Warren Theatre

8346
AMERICAN BANK CENTER
1901 N. Shoreline Blvd
Corpus Christi, TX 78401

FACILITIES / Texas

Phone: 361-826-4700
Fax: 361-826-4905
e-mail: americanbankcenter@cctexas.com
Web Site: www.americanbankcenter.com
Management:
  Director of Marketing & Sales: Eric Jaramillo
  Director of Convention Center Sales: Donna Canatella
  Sales Account Executive: April Smith
  General Manger: Karen Graham

8347
WAREHOUSE LIVING ARTS CENTER
119 West 6th Avenue
Corsicana, TX 75110
Phone: 903-872-5421
Fax: 903-875-1068
e-mail: info@warehouselivingartscenter.com
Web Site: www.warehouselivingartscenter.com
Management:
  Executive Director: Sandra McClure Mahood
  Box Office: Betty Bowden
Founded: 1971
Status: Non-Profit, Non-Professional
Paid Staff: 3

8348
DISCOVER HOUSTON COUNTY VISITORS CENTER: MUSEUM
303 S 5st
Crockett, TX 75835
Phone: 936-544-9520
Web Site: www.corsicanaarts.com

8349
AT&T PERORMING ARTS CENTER
2100 Ross Ave
Suite 650
Dallas, TX 75201
Phone: 214-954-9925
Fax: 214-954-9936
e-mail: info@attpac.org
Web Site: www.attpac.org
Officers:
  President and CEO: Doug Curtis
  Chief Financial Officer: Amber Kinney
  Executive Vice President: Albert Milano
  Vice President of External Affairs: Chris Heinbaugh
  Vice President of Operations: Russell Read

8350
BATH HOUSE CULTURAL CENTER
521 E Lawther Drive
Dallas, TX 75218
Phone: 214-670-8749
Fax: 214-670-8751
Web Site: www.bathhousecultural.com
Management:
  Visual Arts Coordinator/Curator: Enrique Fernand
  Manager: David Fisher
  Coordinator: Theresa Furphy
Utilizes: Actors; Artists-in-Residence; Collaborating Artists; Collaborations; Curators; Dance Companies; Fine Artists; Guest Conductors; Local Artists; Performance Artists; Playwrights; Student Interns; Special Technical Talent; Touring Companies; Visual Arts
Founded: 1930
Paid Staff: 3
Facility Category: Art/Cultural Center
Type of Stage: Thrust
Stage Dimensions: 13' x 20'
Seating Capacity: 120

Year Built: 1930
Year Remodeled: 1997
Rental Contact: Manager David Fisher

8351
BIBLICAL ARTS CENTER
7500 Park Lane
Dallas, TX 75225
Phone: 214-691-4622
Fax: 214-361-1365
e-mail: info@biblicalarts.org
Web Site: www.biblicalarts.org
Management:
  Executive Director: Scott Peck
  Director: R J Machacek
Status: Non-Profit, Professional

8352
BOB HOPE THEATRE
Southern Methodist University
Owen Fine Arts Center, 6101 Bishop
Dallas, TX 75205
Phone: 214-768-2000
Fax: 214-692-4138
Web Site: www.smu.edu/Meadows/About/Facilities/OwenArtsCenter/BobHopeTheatre

8353
BRONCO ARENA
2600 Fort Worth Avenue
Dallas, TX 75211
Phone: 214-943-1777
Fax: 214-943-2014
Management:
  Director: Susan Palmer

8354
CARUTH AUDITORIUM
Southern Methodist University
Owen Fine Arts Center, 6101 Bishop
Dallas, TX 75205
Phone: 214-768-2000
Fax: 214-692-4138
Web Site: www.smu.edu/Meadows/About/Facilities/OwenArtsCenter/CaruthAuditorium

8355
COTTON BOWL/FAIR PARK
1121 First Avenue
PO Box 159090
Dallas, TX 75210
Phone: 214-670-3400
Fax: 214-426-0737
e-mail: jason@fairpark.org
Web Site: www.fairpark.org
Management:
  General Manager: Eddie Hueston
  Sales/Event Manager: Leslie Studard
Seating Capacity: 22,528 Soccer, 67,000 Football
Year Built: 1935

8356
KAY BAILEY HUTCHISON CONVENTION CENTER
650 S. Griffin St.
Dallas, TX 75202
Phone: 214-939-2750
Fax: 214-939-2795
Toll-free: 877-850-2100
e-mail: info@dallasconventioncenter.com
Web Site: www.dallasconventioncenter.com
Founded: 1970

8357
KAY BAILEY HUTCHISON CONVENTION CENTER
650 S. Griffin St.
Dallas, TX 75202
Phone: 214-939-2750
Fax: 214-939-2795
Toll-free: 877-850-2100
e-mail: info@dallasconventioncenter.com
Web Site: www.dallasconventioncenter.com

8358
DALLAS THEATER CENTER: KALITA HUMPHREYS THEATRE
651 South Griffin
Dallas, TX 75202
Phone: 214-939-2700
Fax: 214-939-2795
Toll-free: 877-502-00
Web Site: www.dallasconventioncenter.com

8359
MAJESTIC THEATRE
1925 Elm Street
Dallas, TX 75201
Phone: 214-880-0137
Fax: 214-880-0097
e-mail: jwilborn@dallassummermusicals.org

8360
MCFARLIN MEMORIAL
6405 Boaz Lane
Suite 101
Dallas, TX 75275
Mailing Address: PO Box 750152 , Dallas, TX 75275-0152
Phone: 214-768-3139
Fax: 214-768-4763
e-mail: jdbricker@smu.edu
Web Site: www.smu.edu/BusinessFinance/CampusServices/McFarlin/About%20McFarlin/Contac
Officers:
  Chairman: Darrell Jordan
  Vice President: Dorsey Baskin
  President & Managing Directo: Michael A. Jenkins
Management:
  Director of Operations: J. Denton Bricker
  Production Manager: Rhonda Miller

8361
MOODY COLISEUM
Southern Methodist University
6405 Boaz Lane, Suite 101
Dallas, TX 75275
Phone: 214-768-2864
Fax: 214-768-2044
Web Site: www.smumustangs.com/facilities/moody-coliseum.html
Management:
  Assistant Manager: Kevin Diggs
Status: Non-Profit,Non-Professional
Seating Capacity: 9,500

8362
MORTON H MEYERSON SYMPHONY CENTER
2301 Flora Street
PO Box 26207
Dallas, TX 75100

All listings are in alphabetical order by state, then city, then organization within the city.

FACILITIES / Texas

Phone: 214-871-4000
Fax: 214-670-4334
e-mail: customerservice@dalsym.com
Web Site: www.casamanana.org
Officers:
    Concertmaster/Chair: Alexander Kerr
    President & CEO: Jonathan Martin
    Vice President of Finance: Randy Leiser
    VP of People and Facilities: Debi Pena
    Vice President of Marketing: Sean Kelly
Management:
    Music Director: Jaap van Zweden
    Principal Pops Conductor: Jeff Tyzik
    Pops Conductor Laureate: Richard Kaufman
    Director, Dallas Symphony Chorus: Joshua Habermann
    Senior Principal Asso Concertmaster: Gary Levinson
Founded: 1900
Status: Non-Profit, Professional
Paid Staff: 100

8363
MUSIC HALL AT FAIR PARK
909 1st Avenue
Dallas, TX 75210
Phone: 214-565-1116
Fax: 214-565-0071
Web Site: www.liveatthemusichall.com
Paid Staff: 10

8364
SOUTH DALLAS CULTURAL CENTER
3400 South Fitzhugh
Dallas, TX 75210
Phone: 214-939-2787
Fax: 214-670-8118
Web Site: www.dallasculture.org/sdculturalcenter/
Management:
    Manager: Vicki Meek
    Performing Arts Coordinator: Harold Steward
    Marketing/PR Coordinator: Sondra Roney
    Coordinator II/Events: Marilyn Clark
Founded: 1986
Status: Non-Profit, Non-Professional
Paid Staff: 4

8365
THANKSGIVING SQUARE: COURTYARD AT THANKSGIVING
PO Box 131770
Dallas, TX 75313-1770
Phone: 214-969-1977
Fax: 214-754-0152
Web Site: www.dallasblack.com
Management:
    President/CEO: Tatiana Anderson
Founded: 1977
Status: Non-Profit, Non-Professional
Paid Staff: 7

8366
DECATUR CIVIC CENTER THEATRE
2010 W US 380
PO Box 894
Decatur, TX 76234
Phone: 940-393-0280
Fax: 940-267-6400
e-mail: info@decaturciviccenter.com
Web Site: www.decaturciviccenter.com
Management:
    Director: Duffy Terry
    Sales Director: Krista Lewis
    Receptionist: Araceli Perez

Founded: 1854

8367
DECATUR CIVIC CENTER - VENUE
2010 W US 380
PO Box 894
Decatur, TX 76234
Phone: 940-393-0280
Fax: 940-267-6400
e-mail: info@decaturciviccenter.com
Web Site: www.decaturciviccenter.com
    Director: Duffy Terry
    Receptionist: Araceli Perez

8368
REDBUD THEATRE
Redbud Theatre P.O. Box 1311
TWU Station
Denton, TX 95573
Mailing Address: PO Box 23865
Phone: 817-898-2500
Fax: 817-898-3198
e-mail: info@redbudtheatre.com
Web Site: www.redbudtheatre.com

8369
UNIVERSITY OF NORTH TEXAS PERFORMING ARTS CENTER
PO Box 310710
Denton, TX 76203-0710
Phone: 940-565-3815
Fax: 940-565-3773
e-mail: Keffer@unt.edu
Web Site: www.unt.edu
Officers:
    Chairman: Lindsay Keffer
    President: Dr. V. Lane Rawlins
    VP: Dr. Warren Burggren
Management:
    Director: Rick Villarreal
Founded: 1924
Specialized Field: Performing; Visual; Literary
Paid Staff: 1
Volunteer Staff: 9
Budget: $60,000-$150,000
Income Sources: Grants; Ticket Sales; Underwriting; Student Service Fees
Affiliations: A.A; APA
Type of Stage: Thrust; Proscenium
Seating Capacity: 200/8,000

8370
UNIVERSITY OF TEXAS-PAN AMERICAN: THEATER
1201 West University Drive
Edinburg, TX 78539
Phone: 512-381-3581
Fax: 956-381-3472
Web Site: www.portal.utpa.edu

8371
CHAMIZAL NATIONAL MEMORIAL: THEATER
800 South San Marcial Street
PO Box 722
El Paso, TX 79905-4123
Phone: 915-532-7273
Fax: 915-532-7240
Web Site: www.nps.gov
Management:
    Artistic Director: Virginia Nef
Founded: 1967
Status: Non-Profit, Non-Professional

Paid Staff: 26

8372
COHEN STADIUM
9700 Gateway North Boulevard
El Paso, TX 79924
Phone: 915-755-2000
Fax: 915-757-0671
Web Site: www.nps.gov/cham
Management:
    General Manager: Jimmy Hicks
Founded: 1989
Status: For-Profit, Non-Professional
Paid Staff: 32

8373
DON HASKINS CENTER
9700 Gateway North Blvd
500 W University Avenue
El Paso, TX 79924
Phone: 915-755-2000
Fax: 915-757-0671
e-mail: dhc@utep.edu
Web Site: www.diablos.com
Management:
    President: Diana Natalicio
    Executive Director: Mike Spence
Utilizes: Dance Companies; Designers; Educators; Guest Accompanists; Soloists; Student Interns; Theatre Companies
Status: Non-Profit, Professional
Paid Staff: 9
Affiliations: University of Texas at El Paso
Facility Category: SICO
Seating Capacity: 12,000
Year Remodeled: 2001
Rental Contact: (915)747-5481 Carol Roberts-Spence

8374
EL PASO CIVIC CENTER: EXHIBITION HALL
1 Civic Center Plaza
El Paso, TX 79901
Phone: 915-534-0600
Fax: 915-534-0687
Toll-free: 800-351-6024
e-mail: info@destinationelpaso.com
Web Site: www.elpaso.com

8375
EL PASO CIVIC CENTER: THEATRE
1 Civic Center Plaza
El Paso, TX 79901
Phone: 915-541-4920
Fax: 915-534-0686
Web Site: www.elpaso.com

8376
EL PASO CONVENTION & PERFORMING ARTS CENTER
1 Civic Center Plaza
El Paso, TX 79901
Phone: 915-534-0600
Fax: 915-534-0687
Toll-free: 800-351-6024
e-mail: info@destinationelpaso.com
Web Site: www.elpaso.com
Management:
    General Manager: William Blaziek
    Facility Sales Manager: Esther Portillo
Founded: 1972
Status: Non-Profit, Professional

FACILITIES / Texas

8377
EL PASO COUNTY COLISEUM
4100 East Paisano Drive
El Paso, TX 79905
Phone: 915-534-4229
Fax: 915-532-4048
e-mail: Contact@countycoliseum.com
Web Site: www.countycoliseum.com
Officers:
   Vice President of Operations: James Smith
Management:
   Ticketing Director: Isela Inungaray
   Administrator: Lacey Hernandez
   Event Staffing Supervisor: Veronica Enriquez
   National Concessions: Maria Elena Megret
Founded: 2003
Status: Non-Profit, Professional
Paid Staff: 15

8378
MAGOFFIN AUDITORIUM
151 Glory Road
302 Union East
El Paso, TX 79908
Phone: 915-747-5481
Fax: 915-532-4048
Web Site: www.utepspecialevents.com
Officers:
   President: Bryan Kennedy
Management:
   Exe Director of Special Events: Jorge Vazquez
   Director: Mike Spence
   Assistant Director: Ricky Nichols
   Business Manager: Eileen Laidler
   Marketing Coordinator: Julian E. Valdes
Seating Capacity: 1,200

8379
SUN BOWL
151 Glory Road
El Paso, TX 79908
Phone: 915-747-5481
Fax: 915-747-5228
e-mail: events@utep.edu
Web Site: www.utepspecialevents.com
Management:
   Exe Director of Special Events: Jorge Vazquez
   Director: Mike Spence
   Assistant Director: Ricky Nichols
   Business Manager: Eileen Laidler
   Marketing Coordinator: Julian E. Valdes
Founded: 1913
Status: Non-Profit, Professional
Paid Staff: 3000
Seating Capacity: 52,000

8380
UNIVERSITY OF TEXAS AT EL PASO: MAIN PLAYHOUSE
2501 Montana
El Paso, TX 79903
Phone: 915-532-1317
Fax: 915-747-5228
e-mail: elpasoplayhouse@sbcglobal.net
Web Site: www.elpasoplayhouse.com
Officers:
   President: Dr. Diana Natalicio
Management:
   Department Chairman: Mimi Gladstein
   Department Chairman: Mimi Gladstein
Status: Non-Profit, Non-Professional

8381
AMOIN G CARTER STADIUM
2850 Stadium Drive
Fort Worth, TX 76129
Phone: 915-747-5481
Fax: 915-747-5228
Toll-free: 817-257-7000
e-mail: stadium@tcu.edu
Web Site: www.stadium.tcu.edu
Management:
   Athletic Director: Eric Hyman
   Department Chairman: Mimi Gladstein
   Athletic Director: Eric Hyman

8382
BASS PERFORMANCE HALL
4th and Calhoun Streets
Fort Worth, TX 76102
Phone: 817-212-4325
Toll-free: 877-212-4280
e-mail: info@basshall.com
Web Site: www.basshall.com
Management:
   Director of Education: Sue Buratto
   Director of Information Technology: Chris De Leon
   Director of Front of House: Chris Sanders
   Director of Development: Patricia H. Schutts
   Director of Mark & Sponsorships: Jason Wise
Mission: Houses three performance venues

8383
CARAVAN OF DREAMS
312 Houston Street
Fort Worth, TX 76102
Phone: 817-877-3000
Fax: 817-877-3752
Web Site: www.gofrogs.com

8384
CASA MANANA THEATRE
3101 West Lancaster Avenue
Fort Worth, TX 76107
Phone: 817-332-2272
Fax: 817-332-5711
Web Site: vwww.casamanana.org
Officers:
   Chairman: Rob Hood
   Immediate Past Chairman: Taylor Gandy
   Secretary: Daniel Washburn
   Treasurer: Connie Fagg
   Vice Chair, Development Committee: Karen Denney
Season: june - august

8385
DANIEL-MEYER COLISEUM
Texas Christian University
2800 S University Drive
Fort Worth, TX 76129
Phone: 817-257-7000
Fax: 817-257-7656
Management:
   Chancellor: Victor Boschini

8386
ED LANDRETH AUDITORIUM
Texas Christian University
TCU Box 297510
Fort Worth, TX 76129
Phone: 817-921-7625
Fax: 817-921-7333
Web Site: www.tcu.edu
Officers:
   Chair: Mr. Clarence Scharbauer III
   Vice Chair: Mr. Mark L Johnson
   Secretary: Ms. Karen M. Baker
Management:
   Costume Studio Supervisor: Michele Alford
   Scenic Studio Supervisor: Philip Zielke

8387
FORT WORTH COMMUNITY ARTS CENTER
WE Scott Theater
1300 Gendy Drive
Fort Worth, TX 76107
Phone: 817-738-1938
Fax: 817-738-3766
e-mail: marla@fwcac.org
Web Site: www.fwcac.com
Management:
   Special Events and Theatre Rentals: Marla Fleischmann Owen
   Director of Operations: Mary Montalvo
   Gallery Manager: Elaine Taylor
Mission: To provide accessible and affordable exhibition, performance, workshop, classroom space to artists and arts organizations in the region and to serve the community in a user friendly environment.
Founded: 1964
Specialized Field: Theater
Status: Non-Profit, Professional
Paid Staff: 8
Paid Artists: 50
Facility Category: Rental Facility

8388
HIP POCKET THEATRE
1950 Silver Creek Road
Fort Worth, TX 76108
Mailing Address: P.O. Box 136758, Fort Worth, TX 76136
Phone: 817-246-9775
Fax: 817-246-5651
e-mail: hippockettheatre@aol.com
Web Site: www.hippocket.org
Management:
   Executive Director: Diane Simons, mdmolemo@aol.com
   Artistic Director: Johnny Simons, hippockettheatre@aol.com
Mission: Produce live theatre events
Utilizes: Actors; AEA Actors; Artists-in-Residence; Choreographers; Collaborating Artists; Collaborations; Commissioned Composers; Community Members; Community Talent; Composers; Dancers; Designers; Educators; Equity Actors; Filmmakers; Five Seasonal Concerts; Guest Accompanists; Guest Conductors; Guest Designers; Guest Musical Directors; Local Artists; Local Artists & Directors; Lyricists; Multi Collaborations; Music; Organization Contracts; Original Music Scores; Paid Performers; Performance Artists; Poets; Resident Artists; Sign Language Translators; Soloists; Visual Designers
Founded: 1977
Status: Non-Profit, Professional
Paid Staff: 10
Income Sources: Grants, Box Office

8389
SOUTHWESTERN BAPTIST THEOLOGICAL SEMINARY
2001 W. Seminary Drive
Fort Worth, TX 76115

FACILITIES / Texas

Phone: 817-923-1921
Fax: 817-921-8762
Toll-free: 800-792-8701
e-mail: scmusic@swbts.edu
Web Site: www.swbts.edu
Officers:
   Dean, School of Church Music: Stephen P Johnson
   Assoc Dean, Academic Division: William Colson
   Assoc Dean, Performance Division: William MacDavis
   President: Paige Patterson
   Exec VP/Provost: Craig Blaising
   Assoc Dean, Undergraduate Music: Tom Song
Founded: 1908
Specialized Field: Sacred Music
Status: Non-Profit, Professional
Paid Staff: 60
Paid Artists: 20
Performs At: Graduate School Recital Hall
Facility Category: Concert Halls, Auditorium, Studio
Seating Capacity: 500
Year Built: 1933
Year Remodeled: 1960
Rental Contact: Ext 3130 William MacDavis

8390
TEXAS WESLEYAN COLLEGE: FINE ARTS

Rosedale and Wesleyan
PO Box 50010
Fort Worth, TX 76105
Phone: 817-531-4443
Fax: 817-531-6583
Web Site: www.swbts.edu
Officers:
   President: Dr. Paige Patterson

8391
GRAND 1894 OPERA HOUSE

2020 Postoffice Street
Galveston, TX 77550
Phone: 409-765-1894
Fax: 409-763-1068
Toll-free: 800-821-1894
e-mail: tickets@thegrand.com
Web Site: www.thegrand.com
Management:
   Director of Ticketing Services: Judy Webb
   Assistant Director: Kimberly Mayee
   Executive Director: Maureen M. Patton
   Development Director: Virginia Weber
   Marketing Director: Kathy Van Dewalli

8392
MOODY CIVIC CENTER: EXHIBITION HALL

2100 Seawall Boulevard
Galveston, TX 77550
Phone: 409-762-8626
Fax: 406-762-8911

8393
GARLAND GRANVILLE ARTS CENTER

300 N. Fifth Street
Garland, TX 75040
Phone: 972-205-2780
Fax: 972-205-2775
e-mail: arts@garlandtx.gov
Web Site: www.garlandtx.gov

8394
GRANBURY OPERA HOUSE

116, South Houston Street Granbury
PO Box 297
Granbury, TX 76048
Phone: 817-573-9191
Fax: 817-573-9717
Toll-free: 866-572-0881
Web Site: www.texasfamilymusicals.com
Management:
   President: Max Jones
   Executive Producer: Marty Van Kleeck
Founded: 1975
Status: Non-Profit, Professional
Paid Staff: 8

8395
CAPITAL BASEBALL STADIUM

116, South Houston Street Granbury
1204 Fair Park Boulevard
Harlingen, TX 76048
Phone: 817-573-9191
Fax: 817-573-9717
Toll-free: 866-572-0882
e-mail: harlingenarts@xanadu2.net
Web Site: www.texasfamilymusicals.com
Officers:
   President: Max Jones
Management:
   Director: Susan Thomae-Morphew
   Executive Director: Joel Humphries
Founded: 1992
Status: Non-Profit, Professional
Paid Staff: 3

8396
HARLINGEN CULTURAL ARTS CENTER: AUDITORIUM

576'76 Drive
PO Box 609
Harlingen, TX 78551
Phone: 210-423-9736
Web Site: www.harlingenarts.org

8397
ALLEY THEATRE: HUGO V NEUHAUS ARENA STAGE

615 Texas Avenue
Houston, TX 77002
Phone: 713-200-5700
Fax: 713-222-6542
e-mail: webmaster@alleytheatre.org
Web Site: www.alleytheatre.org
Officers:
   President/CEO: Mike Puryear
Management:
   Artistic Director: Gregory Boyd
   Managing Director: Paul Tetreault
   Direction Production: Sean Skeeman
   Managing Director: Dean Gladden
   Stage Superior: Becca Duhaime
Year Remodeled: 2001

8398
ALLEY THEATRE

615 Texas Avenue
Houston, TX 77002
Phone: 713-200-5700
Fax: 713-222-6542
e-mail: webmaster@alleytheatre.org
Web Site: www.alleytheatre.org
Officers:
   President/CEO: Mike Puryear
Management:
   Artistic Director: Gregory Boyd
   Managing Director: Dean R. Gladden
   Associate Director: James Black
   Managing Director: Dean R. Gladden
   Stage Supervisor: Eric Breikjern

8399
ALLEY THEATRE: LARGE STAGE

615 Texas Avenue
Houston, TX 77002
Phone: 713-200-5700
Fax: 713-222-6542
e-mail: webmaster@alleytheatre.org
Web Site: www.alleytheatre.org
Officers:
   President/CEO: Mike Puryear
Management:
   Artistic Director: Gregory Boyd
   Managing Director: Dean R. Gladden
   Associate Director: James Black
   Managing Director: Dean R. Gladden
   Stage Supervisor: Eric Breikjern

8400
ASTRODOME

615 Texas Avenue
Houston, TX 77002
Phone: 713-200-5700
Fax: 713-222-6542
e-mail: webmaster@alleytheatre.org
Web Site: www.alleytheatre.org
Management:
   Managing Director: Dean R. Gladden
   Associate Director: James Black
   Artistic Director: Gregory Boyd
   Managing Director: Dean R. Gladden
   Stage Supervisor: Eric Breikjern
Seating Capacity: 53,000 (Stadium, 6,000 [Arena])
Year Built: 1963
Year Remodeled: 1988

8401
COMMUNITY MUSIC CENTER

3100 Cleburne
Houston, TX 77004
Phone: 713-523-9710
Fax: 713-523-0507
Web Site: www.astros.com
Management:
   President of the Board: Kathy Wilson
   Executive Director: Gary Wilkins
   Music Director: Anne Lundy
Founded: 1979
Status: Non-Profit, Professional
Paid Staff: 2
Paid Artists: 100

8402
CULLEN PERFORMANCE HALL

University Of Houston
4800 Calhoon Road
Houston, TX 77204-2003
Phone: 713-743-2255
Fax: 713-743-5194
Toll-free: 832-842-3100
e-mail: cphinfo@uh.edu
Web Site: www.uh.edu/cph
Officers:
   President: Renu Khattar
   VP: John J. Antel
   Executive Vice Chancellor for Admin: Carl Carlucci
Management:

FACILITIES / Texas

Acting Manager/Technical Director: Charlie Matthew
Founded: 1949
Paid Staff: 10
Budget: $400,000
Income Sources: Facility Rental
Performs At: Rental Facility
Affiliations: University Of Houston
Annual Attendance: 125,000
Facility Category: Rental
Type of Stage: Proscenium Theatre
Seating Capacity: 1,536
Year Built: 1949
Year Remodeled: 1987
Rental Contact: Acting Manager Charlie Matthew

8403
DELMAR STADIUM COMPLEX
2020 Magnum
Houston, TX 77092
Phone: 713-957-7700
Fax: 713-957-7704
Web Site: www.houstonisd.org
Management:
  Director: Mike Truelove

8404
DIVERSEWORKS
4102 Fannin Street
Suite 200
Houston, TX 77004
Phone: 713-223-8346
Fax: 713-223-4608
e-mail: info@diverseworks.org
Web Site: www.diverseworks.org
Management:
  Director of Development: Jordan Dupuis
  Director of External Affairs: Jennifer Gardner
  Executive Director: Elizabeth Dunbar
  Finance Manager: Stephanie Atwood
  Associate Curator: Rachel Cook
Mission: Dedicated to presenting new visual, performing, and literary art. A place where the process of creating art is valued and where artists can test new ideas in the public arena. By encouraging the investigation of current artistic, cultural and social issues, they build, educate, and sustain audiences for contemporary art.
Founded: 1982
Specialized Field: Multidisciplinary Performance and Visual
Status: Non-Profit, Professional
Paid Staff: 7
Paid Artists: 2

8405
ENRON FIELD
PO Box 288
Houston, TX 77001-0288
Phone: 713-799-9500
Fax: 713-799-9881
Web Site: www.astros.com
Management:
  Facility Manager: Don Collins
  Senior VP Marketing Advertising: Pam Gardner
Founded: 1962
Specialized Field: Home of the Houston Astros (MLB).
Seating Capacity: 42,000
Year Built: 2000

8406
HAMMAN HALL
Rice University
PO Box 1892
Houston, TX 77251-1892
Phone: 713-348-7529
Fax: 713-348-4609
e-mail: hamman@rice.edu
Web Site: www.rice.edu/players
Management:
  Theatre Director: Trish Rigdon
  Baradino: Mike
Founded: 1914
Status: Non-Profit, Non-Professional
Paid Staff: 3

8407
HOBBY CENTER FOR THE PERFORMING ARTS
800 Bagby Street
Suite 300
Houston, TX 77002
Phone: 713-305-2400
Fax: 713-315-2402
e-mail: email specific staff members through website
Web Site: www.thehobbycenter.org
Officers:
  President: Fran Macferran
Management:
  Director of Donor Programs: Julie Anderson-Smith
  Director of Marketing: Sheri Johnson
  Director of Operations: Denise Wright
  Sarofim Hall Technical Director: Michael Metzdorf
  Zilkha Hall Technical Director: Russell Buonasera
Mission: provides 2 venues the work for meetings, perming arts, television shoots and much more

8408
HOFHEINZ PAVILION
4800 Calhoun Rd. Houston
Houston, TX 77004
Phone: 713-743-2255
Fax: 713-743-9375
Web Site: www.uh.edu
Officers:
  President: Renu Khattar
  VP: John J. Antel
  Executive Vice Chancellor for Admin: Carl Carlucci
Management:
  President: Jay Gague
  Athletic Director: Dave Maggard
Status: Non-Profit, Non-Professional
Paid Staff: 100

8409
HOUSTON CIVIC CENTER: GUS WORTHAM THEATER
510 Preston 4th Floor
Houston, TX 77002
Phone: 713-237-1439
Fax: 713-237-9313
Management:
  Building Director: Down Ullrich
Founded: 1987
Status: Non-Profit, Professional
Paid Staff: 13

8410
HOUSTON CIVIC CENTER: JESSE H JONES HALL FOR THE PERFORMING ARTS
615 Louisiana
Houston, TX 772002
Phone: 832-487-7000
Fax: 83-248-7700
Web Site: www.worthamcenter.org

8411
HOUSTON CIVIC CENTER: GEORGE R BROWN CONVENTION CENTER
1001 Avenida De Las Americas
Houston, TX 77010
Phone: 713-853-8000
Fax: 713-583-8090
Toll-free: 800-427-4697
e-mail: ccinfo@houstonfirst.com
Web Site: www.houstonconventionctr.com
Officers:
  President and CEO: Dawn Ullrich
  Chief Operating Officer: Luther Villagomez
Management:
  Director of Sales: Kenny King

8412
JESSE H. JONES HALL FOR THE PERFORMING ARTS
615 Louisiana
Houston, TX 77002
Phone: 832-487-7050
Fax: 832-487-7051
Web Site: www.houstonfirsttheaters.com
Mission: Houston 1st Corporation owns Jones Hall, the Wortham Center, Houston 1st Outdoors and the Miller outdoor theatre in downtown houston.ÆEach can be rented for personal use.

8413
MILLER OUTDOOR THEATRE
6000 Hermann Park Drive
Houston, TX 77030
Mailing Address: P.O. Box 66267, Houston, TX 77266-6267
Phone: 832-487-7102
Fax: 713-942-0863
Web Site: www.milleroutdoortheatre.com
Management:
  Managing Director: Cissy Segall Davis
  Director of Finance & Operations: Reg Burns
  Director of Advancement: Colin Brokaw
  Facility Manager: Shawn Hauptmann
  Public Relations: Lydia Baehr

8414
RICE STADIUM
Rice University
6100 S Main Street
Houston, TX 77005
Phone: 713-527-4077
Fax: 713-527-6019
Web Site: www.riceowls.com
Management:
  Athletic Director: Bobby May
Seating Capacity: 70,000

8415
ROBERTSON STADIUM
University of Huston
3100 Cullen Boulevard
Houston, TX 7137439444

FACILITIES / Texas

Phone: 713-743-9370
Fax: 713-743-9375
Web Site: www.uh.edu
Officers:
   Chair: Rodney Nathan
   Secretary: Miriam Meyers
   Treasurer: Allen Ueckert
Seating Capacity: 22,000

8416
STAGES REPERTORY THEATRE
3201 Allen Parkway
Suite 101
Houston, TX 77019
Phone: 713-527-0123
Fax: 713-527-8669
e-mail: kmclaughlin@stagestheatre.com
Web Site: www.stagestheatre.com
Management:
   Producing Artistic Director: Kenn McLaughlin
   Associate Artistic Director: Josh Morrison
   Artistic Associate: Mitchell Greco
   Marketing Director: Lise Bohn
   Development Manager: Dwight Clark
Mission: To present new works, interpret established works in new ways, and encourage and cultivate culture for the community.

8417
THEATRE SUBURBIA
4106 Way Out West Dr
Suite N
Houston, TX 77092
Mailing Address: PO Box 920518, Houston, TX 77292-0518
Phone: 713-682-3525
e-mail: info@theatresuburbia.org
Web Site: www.theatresuburbia.org

8418
BERNARD G JOHNSON COLISEUM
800 Bowers Blvd.
Huntsville, TX 77340
Mailing Address: PO Box 2387, Huntsville, TX 77341
Phone: 936-294-1740
Fax: 936-294-4833
e-mail: rca_elc@shsu.edu
Web Site: www.shsu.edu
Management:
   Associate Director Facilities: Ed Chatal
   Associate Director: Jaron Rider
   Associate Director: Melissa Fadler
   Special Programs: David Yebra
   Office Supervisor: Cindy Allbright
Founded: 1976
Status: For-Profit, Professional
Paid Staff: 18

8419
SAM HOUSTON STATE UNIVERSITY THEATRE
Theatre & Dance Department
Box 2297
Huntsville, TX 77341-2297
Phone: 936-294-1329
Fax: 936-294-4833
e-mail: theatre@shsu.edu
Web Site: www.shsu.edu
Officers:
   President: James Gartner
   Chair, Theatre and Musical Theatre: Penelope A. Hasekoester
Utilizes: Grant Writers; Guest Artists; Guest Conductors; Guest Designers; Guest Instructors; Guest Lecturers; Guest Soloists
Founded: 1871
Status: Non-Profit, Non-Professional
Paid Staff: 20
Type of Stage: Proscenium and Thrust
Seating Capacity: 396, 96
Year Built: 1976
Year Remodeled: 2001

8420
IRVING ARTS CENTER
3333 North MacArthur Blvd.
Irving, TX 75062
Phone: 972-252-ARTS
Fax: 936-294-4833
Web Site: www.irvingartscenter.com
Officers:
   President: James Gartner
Management:
   Executive Director: Richard E Huff
   Director of Exhibitions: Marcie Inman
   Assistant Executive Director: Kass Price
   Assistant Executive Director: Rosie Meng
   Sr. Security Officer: Chris Bailey
Mission: To serve the citizens of Irving through the support and development of artistic opportunities.
Founded: 1986
Status: Non-Profit, Professional
Paid Staff: 25
Volunteer Staff: 800
Affiliations: City of Irving
Annual Attendance: 100,000
Type of Stage: Proscenium; Black Box
Seating Capacity: 700; 450; 500
Year Built: 1990

8421
KERRVILLE OUTDOOR THEATRE
Quiet Valley Ranch
120 Point Theatre Road S
Kerrville, TX 78025
Phone: 830-367-5121
Fax: 830-257-8680
Toll-free: 800-435-8429
Web Site: www.hcaf.com/
Management:
   President: Charlie Land
   Managing Director: Dalis Allen
Founded: 1970
Status: For-Profit, Professional
Paid Staff: 5

8422
ALLEN THEATRE
Texas Tech University
15th Street & Akron Avenue
Lubbock, TX 79409
Mailing Address: PO Box 42031
Phone: 806-742-3636
Fax: 806-742-0655
e-mail: james.drake@ttu.edu
Web Site: www.depts.ttu.edu/sub/allentheatre/
Management:
   Manager, Theatre Operations: James Drake
   Coordinator, Theatre Operations: Mark Nazworth
Utilizes: Actors; AEA Actors; Choreographers; Collaborating Artists; Dance Companies; Dancers; Designers; Educators; Filmmakers; Grant Writers; Guest Accompanists; Guest Artists; Guest Choreographers; Guest Companies; Guest Composers; Guest Conductors; Guest Designers; Guest Directors; Guest Ensembles; Guest Instructors; Guest Lecturers; Guest Musical Directors; Guest Musicians; Guest Soloists; Guest Teachers; High School Drama; Instructors; Local Artists; Local Talent; Local Unknown Artists; Multimedia; Music; Original Music Scores; Performance Artists; Playwrights; Resident Professionals; Sign Language Translators; Singers; Soloists; Student Interns; Special Technical Talent; Theatre Companies; Visual Arts
Paid Staff: 10
Facility Category: rental
Type of Stage: proeswien
Stage Dimensions: 60 x 20
Seating Capacity: 928
Year Built: 1976

8423
JONES AT&T STADIUM
6th & Boston
Lubbock, TX 79409
Phone: 806-742-3355
Fax: 806-742-1970
e-mail: chris.cook@ttu.edu
Web Site: www.texastech.com/facilities/fac-jones-stadium.html
Seating Capacity: 52,882
Year Built: 1947
Year Remodeled: 2003

8424
LUBBOCK MEMORIAL CIVIC CENTER THEATER
1501 MacDavis Lane
Lubbock, TX 79401
Phone: 806-775-2242
Fax: 806-775-3240
e-mail: DebraJustice@mylubbock.us
Web Site: www.mylubbock.us
Officers:
   Chancellor: Kent Hance
   President: Brian May
Management:
   Director: Freddy Chavez
   Assistant Director: Debra Justice
   Senior Events Coordinator: Julia Gonzalez
   Stage/Tech Coordinator: John James
   Event Coordinator: Justine Fulton
Founded: 1976
Specialized Field: Performance
Status: Non-Profit, Professional
Paid Staff: 31
Performs At: Theatre; Auditorium
Affiliations: IAAM
Annual Attendance: 500,000+
Facility Category: Convention Center
Type of Stage: Proscenium
Stage Dimensions: 40x80; 96x45
Seating Capacity: 1397; 2803
Rental Contact: Leslie Timmons

8425
LUBBOCK MEMORIAL CIVIC CENTER BANQUET HALL
1501 MacDavis Lane
Lubbock, TX 79401
Phone: 806-775-2242
Fax: 806-775-3240
Web Site: www.mylubbock.us
Management:
   Director: Freddy Chavez
   Assistant Director: Debra Justice
   Senior Events Coordinator: Julia Gonzalez
   Technical Coordinator: John James
   Event Coordinator: Justine Fulton

FACILITIES / Texas

8426
LUBBOCK MEMORIAL CIVIC CENTER COLISEUM
1501 MacDavis Lane
Lubbock, TX 79401
Phone: 806-775-2242
Fax: 806-775-3240
Web Site: www.mylubbock.us
Management:
 Director: Freddy Chavez
 Assistant Director: Debra Justice
 Senior Events Coordinator: Julia Gonzalez
 Technical Coordinator: John James
 Event Coordinator: Justine Fulton

8427
LUBBOCK MEMORIAL CIVIC CENTER EXHIBIT HALL
1501 MacDavis Lane
Lubbock, TX 79401
Phone: 806-775-2242
Fax: 806-775-3240
Web Site: www.mylubbock.us
Management:
 Director: Freddy Chavez
 Assistant Director: Debra Justice
 Senior Events Coordinator: Julia Gonzalez
 Technical Coordinator: John James
 Event Coordinator: Justine Fulton

8428
LUBBOCK MEMORIAL CIVIC CENTER MUNICIPAL AUDITORIUM
1501 MacDavis Lane
Lubbock, TX 79401
Phone: 806-775-2242
Fax: 806-775-3240
Web Site: www.mylubbock.us
Management:
 Director: Freddy Chavez
 Assistant Director: Debra Justice
 Senior Events Coordinator: Julia Gonzalez
 Technical Coordinator: John James
 Event Coordinator: Justine Fulton

8429
TEXAS TECH UNIVERSITY PERFORMING ARTS CENTER
18th and Boston
Box 42033
Lubbock, TX 79409-2033
Phone: 806-742-2270
Fax: 806-742-2294
e-mail: cvpa@ttu.edu
Web Site: www.ttu.edu/~music
Officers:
 President: Jo Moore

8430
UNITED SUPERMARKETS ARENA
Texas Tech University
1701 Indiana Avenue
Lubbock, TX 42200
Phone: 806-742-7362
Fax: 806-742-7557
e-mail: unitedspiritarena@ttu.edu
Web Site: www.unitedspiritarena.com
Management:
 Director: Kent Meredith
 Assistant Director: Cindy Harper
Seating Capacity: 15,000

8431
MARSHALL CIVIC CENTER
One John Marshall Drive
Marshall, TX 25755
Phone: 304-696-2372
Fax: 903-935-0538
e-mail: jcarpenter@marshalltexas.net
Web Site: www.marshallphysics.com
Management:
 Managing Director: Jennifer Carpenter
 Event Facilites Director: Ardis Wright
Founded: 1976
Status: Non-Profit, Non-Professional
Paid Staff: 5
Paid Artists: 5

8432
RESISTOL ARENA/RODEO CENTER EXHIBIT HALL
SW Sports Group
1818 Rodeo Drive
Mesquite, TX 75149
Phone: 972-285-8777
Fax: 972-289-2999
Web Site: www.mesquiterodeo.com
Officers:
 President: Jack B Beckman
Management:
 President: Mark Miller
Status: For-Profit, Professional
Paid Staff: 20
Seating Capacity: 5,300

8433
CHAPARRAL CENTER
Midland College
3600 North Garfield
Midland, TX 79705
Phone: 915-685-4584
Fax: 915-685-4740
e-mail: mstevens@midland.edu
Web Site: www.midland.edu/about_mc/facilities_chapcenter.php
Management:
 Director: Michael J Stevens
Founded: 1978
Affiliations: Midland College
Facility Category: Small arena with curtain system
Type of Stage: Stageright Portable
Stage Dimensions: 60' x 40'
Seating Capacity: 1800; 2400; 5000
Year Built: 1978

8434
MIDLAND CENTER
105 N. Main Street
Midland, TX 79701
Phone: 432-682-6234
Fax: 915-686-9830
e-mail: irece@visitmidlandtx.com
Web Site: www.themidlandcenter.com
Management:
 Manager: Irece Jordan
Seating Capacity: 1,400

8435
HOMER BRYCE STADIUM
Stephen F. Austin State University
PO Box 13010, SFA Station
Nacogdoches, TX 75962
Phone: 409-468-3501
Fax: 936-468-4070
Web Site: www.visitmidlandtx.com
Management:
 Athletic Director: Steve McCarty
 Athletic Operations Director: Jeremy Stolfa

8436
WILLIAM R JOHNSON COLISEUM
Stephen F Austin State University
PO Box 13010-SFA Station
Nacogdoches, TX 75962
Phone: 936-468-3501
Fax: 936-468-4070
Web Site: www.visitmidlandtx.com
Management:
 Athletic Operations Director: Jeremy Stolfa
 Athletic Director: Steve McCarty
Founded: 1973
Type of Stage: Portable
Seating Capacity: 7,200

8437
LUTCHER THEATER
707 W Main Street
Orange, TX 77630
Phone: 409-886-5535
Fax: 409-886-5537
Toll-free: 800-828-5535
e-mail: lutcher@exp.net
Web Site: www.lutcher.org

8438
PALESTINE CIVIC CENTER COMPLEX
825 W Spring St
Palestine, TX 75801
Phone: 903-723-3014
Fax: 903-729-6067
Toll-free: 800-659-3484
e-mail: VisitorCenter@palestine-tx.org
Web Site: www.visitpalestine.com
Management:
 Events Coordinator: Heather Hrebec
Founded: 1986
Status: For-Profit, Non-Professional
Paid Staff: 3

8439
MK BROWN MEMORIAL AUDITORIUM & CIVIC CENTER
1100 W Coronado Drive
Pampa, TX 79066-2499
Mailing Address: PO Box 2499
Phone: 806-669-5750
Fax: 806-669-5787
e-mail: ecabrales@cityofpampa.org
Web Site: www.cityofpampa.org
Management:
 Auditorium Manager: Enrique Cabrales
Founded: 1972
Status: Non-Profit, Non-Professional
Paid Staff: 10
Stage Dimensions: 3,150 square feet
Seating Capacity: 1,500

8440
PARIS JUNIOR COLLEGE
2400 Clarksville St.
Paris, TX 75460
Phone: 903-785-7661
Fax: 903-784-9370
Toll-free: 800-232-5804
Web Site: www.parisjc.edu
Officers:
 President: Curtis Fendley
 VP: Louise Taylor
 Secretary: Berdie Gibson

All listings are in alphabetical order by state, then city, then organization within the city.

FACILITIES / Texas

8441
SLOCOMB AUDITORIUM
San Jacinto College Central
8060 Spencer Highway
Pasadena, TX 77501-2007
Mailing Address: PO Box 2007
Phone: 281-998-6150
Fax: 281-476-1892
Web Site: www.sjtd.edu
Management:
    President: Jerry Ivin
    Executive Director: Jerry Dyess
    Artistic Director: Bob Robert
    Managing Director: Louie Sal
Founded: 1969
Status: For-Profit, Professional
Paid Staff: 236
Paid Artists: 240

8442
CHARLES W. EISEMANN CENTER FOR PERFORMING ARTS & CORPORATE PRESENTATIONS
2351 Performance Drive
Richardson, TX 75082
Phone: 972-744-4650
Fax: 972-744-5823
e-mail: bruce.macpherson@cor.gov
Web Site: www.eisemanncenter.com
Management:
    Managing Director: Bruce MacPherson
    Marketing & Development Manager: Sarah R. Nesbit
    Administrative & Events Manager: Philip Nelson
    Event Services Manager: Hillary W. Adams
    Event Services Manager: Abram Rankin

8443
ROUND TOP FESTIVAL INSTITUTE
James Dick Foundation for the Performing Arts
248 Jaster Road
Round Top, TX 78954
Mailing Address: PO Box 89
Phone: 979-249-3129
Fax: 979-249-5078
e-mail: info@festivalhill.org
Web Site: www.festivalhill.org
Management:
    Managing Director: Richard R. Royal
    Program Director: Alain G Declert
    Associate Managing Director: Lamar Lentz
    Founder and Artistic Director: James C. Dick
    Director of Gardens: Henry Flowers
Mission: Educational project.
Utilizes: Commissioned Composers; Composers-in-Residence; Educators; Fine Artists; Five Seasonal Concerts; Guest Companies; Guest Composers; Guest Ensembles; Guest Instructors; Guest Soloists; Scenic Designers; Students
Founded: 1971
Specialized Field: Classical Music; Poetry; Theatre; Dance
Status: Non-Profit, Professional
Paid Staff: 14
Paid Artists: 44
Budget: $2 million
Income Sources: Individual Gifts; Foundations; Grants; Box Office; Gift Shop
Performs At: Orchestral and Chamber Music Concerts, Theatre, Dance
Affiliations: Chamber Music of America, League of American Orchestra, American String Teachers Association
Annual Attendance: 20,000
Type of Stage: Proscenium
Stage Dimensions: 70 x 50
Seating Capacity: 1100
Rental Contact: Program Director Alain G. Declert

8444
ANGELO STATE UNIVERSITY AUDITORIUM
2601 W Avenue N
San Angelo, TX 76909
Phone: 915-942-2021
Fax: 915-942-2229
Toll-free: 800-946-8627
e-mail: web.oversight@angelo.edu
Web Site: www.angelo.edu
Officers:
    President: Dr. Brian J. May
Management:
    Library Director: Maurice Fortin
    Assistant Director, Special Events: Jessica Manning
    Events Manager: Ashley Wallace

8445
HOUSTON HARTE UNIVERSITY CENTER
Angelo State University
2601 W Avenue N
San Angelo, TX 76909
Phone: 325-942-2021
Fax: 325-942-2229
e-mail: david.rosipal@angelo.edu
Web Site: www.angelo.edu/services/specialevents/hhuc.php
Officers:
    Executive Director, Business Svcs.: Greg Pecina
    Associate Director, Special Events: David Rosipal
Management:
    Assistant Director, Special Events: Jessica A. Manning
    Events Manager: Justin Segura
    Events Manager: Don Cheek
    Events Manager: Gary Jarrod Stackhouse
    Senior Scheduling Coordinator: Kailee Sunshine Malleck
Mission: To support the mission of Angelo State University
Status: Student Union
Paid Staff: 9
Income Sources: Student Fees; Rentals
Performs At: Conference Center
Type of Stage: Portable
Stage Dimensions: 20'x8' sections
Seating Capacity: 900
Year Remodeled: 2000
Year Restored: 2000
Rental Contact: Shayna Lopez

8446
SAN ANGELO CITY AUDITORIUM
72 W. College Avenue
72 West College
San Angelo, TX 76903
Phone: 915-653-9577
Fax: 915-659-0900
Web Site: www.sanangelotexas.org

8447
ALAMODOME
100 Montana
San Antonio, TX 78203
Phone: 210-207-3663
Fax: 210-207-3646
Toll-free: 800-884-3663
e-mail: dmarketing@alamodome.com
Web Site: www.alamodome.com
Management:
    Director: Goerge Abington
    Operations Manager: Jim Mery
    Booking Manager: Carol Pollock
Founded: 1993
Status: For-Profit, Professional
Paid Staff: 50
Type of Stage: Stadium
Seating Capacity: 65,000

8448
ARNESON RIVER THEATRE
418 Villita Street
San Antonio, TX 78205
Phone: 210-207-8614
Fax: 210-299-8444
e-mail: lavillita@sanantonio.gov
Web Site: www.lavillita.com

8449
BEETHOVEN HALL: SAN JOSE CONVENTION CENTER
200 E Market
San Antonio, TX 78205
Phone: 210-299-8500
Fax: 210-223-1495

8450
CARVER COMMUNITY CULTURAL CENTER
226 N Hackberry
San Antonio, TX 78202
Phone: 210-207-7211
Fax: 210-207-4412
e-mail: yonnie.blanchette@sanantonio.gov
Web Site: www.thecarver.org
Officers:
    Chair: Melanie Cowart
    Vice Chair: Mark Wittig
    Secretary: Sarah McLornan
    Treasurer: Seymour Battle III
    Immediate Past Chair: Jelynne LeBlance Burley
Management:
    Executive Director: Yonnie Blanchette
    Education Coordinator: Philip Castillo
    Administrative Assistant II: Gracie Jimenez
    House Manager: Jennifer Gonzalez
    Management Analyst: Tracy Alva
Mission: To celebrate the diverse cultures of our world, nation and community, with emphasis on its African American heritage by providing challenging artistic presentations, community outreach activities and educational programs.
Founded: 1976
Specialized Field: Multi-ethnic and multi-cultural performing and visual arts center
Status: Non-Profit, Professional
Paid Staff: 18
Paid Artists: 10

8451
CARVER COMPLEX
226 N Hackberry
San Antonio, TX 78202
Phone: 210-207-7211
Fax: 210-207-4412
e-mail: yonnie.blanchette@sanantonio.gov
Web Site: www.thecarver.org

FACILITIES / Texas

Officers:
- **Chair:** Melanie Cowart
- **Vice Chair:** Mark Wittig
- **Secretary:** Sarah McLornan
- **Treasurer:** Seymour Battle III
- **Immediate Past Chair:** Jelynne LeBlance Burley

Management:
- **Executive Director:** Yonnie Blanchette
- **Education Coordinator:** Philip Castillo
- **Administrative Assistant II:** Gracie Jimenez
- **House Manager:** Jennifer Gonzalez
- **Management Analyst:** Tracy Alva

8452
FREEMAN COLISEUM
3201 E Houston
PO Box 200283
San Antonio, TX 78219
Phone: 210-226-1177
Fax: 210-226-5081
e-mail: news@freemancoliseum.com
Web Site: www.freemancoliseum.com

Management:
- **Executive Director:** Derrick Howard
- **General Manager:** JC Hrubetz
- **Marketing Director:** Jeanne Janes
- **Events Director:** Anna Harrier
- **Executive Assistant/Booking:** Cindy Alvarado

Mission: Multi-purpose concert and performance facility
Founded: 1949
Specialized Field: Dance; Music; Facility

8453
HENRY B. GONZALEZ CONVENTION CENTER & LILA COCKRELL THEATRE
200 E. Market Street
San Antonio, TX 78205
Mailing Address: P.O. Box 1809, San Antonio, Texas 78296
Phone: 210-207-8500
Fax: 210-223-1495
Toll-free: 877-504-8895
e-mail: cseinfo@sanantonio.gov
Web Site: www.sahbgcc.com

8454
LAURIE AUDITORIUM
Trinity University
One Stadium Drive
San Antonio, TX 78212
Phone: 210-736-8117
Fax: 210-736-8100
e-mail: khawkins@trinity.edu
Web Site: web.trinity.edu/about-us/our-facilities/laurie-auditorium

Officers:
- **Chairman:** Mr. John C. Korbell
- **Vice Chair:** Mr. Douglas D. Hawthorne
- **Treasurer:** Mr. Thomas R. Semmes
- **Secretary:** Mr. E. Carey Joullian IV

Management:
- **Director:** Kevin Hawkins
- **Technical Coordinator:** Travis Stampley
- **Box Office Manager:** Sandra Hernandez

8455
MUNICIPAL AUDITORIUM
417 4th Ave. N, Nashville
San Antonio, TX 37201
Phone: 615-862-6390
Fax: 210-223-1495
Toll-free: 877-504-8895
e-mail: municipal.auditorium@nashville.gov
Web Site: www.nashvilleauditorium.com

Management:
- **Director of Operations:** Jim Raver
- **Box Office Manager:** Taneisha Alexander
- **General Manager:** Bob Skoney
- **Director of Sales & Marketing:** Sharaon Hill

Founded: 1926
Status: Non-Profit

8456
NELSON W WOLFF MUNICIPAL STADIUM
5757 New Highway 90 W
San Antonio, TX 78227
Phone: 210-675-7275
Fax: 210-670-8251
e-mail: tmcafee@alamodome.com
Web Site: www.sanantonio.missions.milb.com

Management:
- **Director:** Mike Abingeon
- **Stadium Manager:** James G Mery

Founded: 1994
Status: Non-Profit, Professional
Paid Staff: 5
Seating Capacity: 6,100

8457
SAN ANTONIO CONVENTION CENTER LILA COCKRELL HALL
200 E Market Street
San Antonio, TX 78205
Mailing Address: P.O. Box 1809, San Antonio, Texas 78296
Phone: 210-207-8500
Fax: 210-223-1495
e-mail: CSEFinfo@sanantonio.gov
Web Site: www.sahbgcc.com

8458
SUNKEN GARDEN AMPHITHEATRE
3875 North Saint Mary's
San Antonio, TX 78212
Phone: 210-735-4824
Fax: 210-735-4850
Web Site: www.sanantonio.gov

Management:
- **Supervisor:** Peter Georgiev
- **Vincent:** Kathy Director

Seating Capacity: 4,800

8459
THE MAJESTIC AND CHARLINE MCCOMBS EMPIRE THEATRES
208 East Houston St
San Antonio, TX 78205
Phone: 210-226-5700
Fax: 210-226-3377
e-mail: info@majesticempire.com
Web Site: www.majesticempire.com

Management:
- **General Manager:** Michael Rilley
- **Associate General Manager:** Isabel A. Rodriguez
- **Director of Marketing - Broadway:** Jean McIver
- **Director of Marketing - Concerts:** Emily Smith
- **Marketing Coordinator:** Brittney Garcia

8460
STRAHAN COLISEUM
700 Aquarena Springs Drive
San Marcos, TX 78666
Phone: 512-245-2023
Fax: 512-245-8387
e-mail: athletics@txstate.edu
Web Site: www.txstatebobcats.com/sports/2010/7/29/MBB_0729100618.aspx?tab=strahancoli

Management:
- **Director Facility/Game Operations:** Chris Hannah
- **Assis Director Facility/Game Oper:** Adam Alonzo
- **Assistant Athletic Director:** Jeremy Stolfa
- **Facilities and Game Operations Coor:** Kyle Katcher
- **Director of Athletics:** Dr. Larry Teis

Seating Capacity: 7,739

8461
JACKSON AUDITORIUM
1000 W. Court St.
Seguin, TX 78155
Phone: 210-372-8180
Fax: 210-372-8096
Toll-free: 830-372-8000
e-mail: admissions@tlu.edu
Web Site: www.tlu.edu

Officers:
- **President:** Stuart Dorsey

8462
CULTURAL ACTIVITIES CENTER
3011 North Third Street
Temple, TX 76501
Phone: 254-773-9926
Fax: 254-773-9929
e-mail: director@cacarts.org
Web Site: www.cacarts.org

Officers:
- **President:** Jean Thorp

Management:
- **Visual Arts Director / Curator:** Marilyn Ritchie
- **Marketing Director:** Jane Boone
- **Technical Director:** Byron Lovelace
- **Facilities Supervisor:** James Stewart
- **Business Manager:** Brock Boone

Mission: Provide area residents, especially children, with opportunities to expirence visual and performing arts.
Utilizes: Actors; Artists-in-Residence; Collaborations; Dance Companies; Dancers; Educators; Fine Artists; Guest Accompanists; Guest Directors; Guest Instructors; Instructors; Local Artists; Multi Collaborations; Multimedia; Original Music Scores; Resident Artists; Sign Language Translators; Soloists; Special Technical Talent; Touring Companies; Visual Arts
Founded: 1958
Specialized Field: Visual Arts; Performing Arts
Status: Non-Profit, Professional
Paid Staff: 10
Budget: $500,000
Income Sources: Heartland Fund; Texas Commission on the Arts; Foundations; Grants; Memberships
Affiliations: Southwest Performing Arts Presenters; Texas Association of Museums; Texas Alliance for Education & The Arts
Annual Attendance: 80,000
Facility Category: Auditorium
Type of Stage: Proscenium
Stage Dimensions: 38Wx30D
Seating Capacity: 487

FACILITIES / Utah

Year Built: 1978
Rental Contact: Aileen Snyder
Organization Type: Performing; Touring; Resident; Educational; Sponsoring

8463
TEMPLE CIVIC THEATRE
2413 South 13th St.
Temple, TX 76504
Phone: 254-778-4751
Fax: 254-778-4980
e-mail: tct@ArtsTemple.com
Web Site: www.artstemple.com
Officers:
  President: Jody Donaldson
  Vice-President, Production: Jacob Duncan
  Vice-President, Front of House: Chris Ling
  Treasurer: Al Dobos
  Secretary: Natasha Tolleson
Management:
  Technical Director: Dustin Ozment
  Office Manager: Hope Brown
Founded: 1977
Status: Non-Profit, Non-Professional
Paid Staff: 4

8464
PEROT THEATRE
221 Main Street
PO Box 1171
Texarkana, TX 75501
Phone: 903-792-4992
Fax: 903-793-8510
e-mail: mstarrett@trahc.org
Web Site: www.artstemple.com
Management:
  Operations Director: Randal Conry
  Executive Director: Brian Goesl, artsinfo@trahc.org
  Administrative Director: Mary Starrett, mstarrett@trahc.org
Mission: To enrich the human experience in the region by increasing public awareness of, exposure to and participation in the arts and humanities in their many diverse forms.
Utilizes: Artists-in-Residence; Community Talent; Five Seasonal Concerts; Guest Writers; Guild Activities; Local Artists; Original Music Scores; Student Interns; Touring Companies
Founded: 1981
Status: Non-Profit, Professional
Paid Staff: 14
Volunteer Staff: 114
Paid Artists: 3
Year Built: 1924
Year Remodeled: 1980
Cost: $2.4 Million
Rental Contact: Operations Director Randall Conroy

8465
CYNTHIA WOODS MITCHELL PAVILION
2005 Lake Robbins Drive
The Woodlands, TX 77380
Phone: 281-363-3300
Fax: 281-364-3011
e-mail: info@woodlandscenter.org
Web Site: www.woodlandscenter.org
Officers:
  President/CEO: Jerry MacDonald
  VP: Jeff Young
  Treasurer: Lori Figaro
  Chairman of the Board: Joseph P. Ash
  Vice Chairman: Carol P. Garner
Founded: 1990
Status: Non-Profit, Professional
Paid Staff: 19
Paid Artists: 70
Performs At: Amphitheatre
Annual Attendance: 500,000
Facility Category: Amphitheatre/Fine Arts Theatre
Type of Stage: Proscenium
Stage Dimensions: 60x40
Seating Capacity: 16,500
Year Built: 1990
Year Remodeled: 2008

8466
REGIONAL ARTS CENTER
333 South Cherry Street
500 Malone, Suite B
Tomball, TX 77375
Phone: 281-351-2787
Fax: 281-351-2702
Web Site: www.regional-arts.org
Management:
  President: Elaine Chrisnan
Founded: 1987
Specialized Field: Theatre: Community Performances
Status: Non-Profit, Professional
Paid Staff: 1

8467
COWAN FINE & PERFORMING ARTS CENTER
University of Texas at Tyler
3900 University Boulevard
Tyler, TX 75701
Phone: 903-566-7424
Fax: 903-566-7264
e-mail: smorphew@uttyler.edu
Web Site: www.cowancenter.org
Management:
  Executive Director: Susan Thomas-Morphew
  Assistant Director: Terri Holland
  Administrative Associate: Melanie Mogle
  Technical Director: Bob Patterson
  Business Manager: Mark Wilson
Founded: 1997
Paid Staff: 6
Performs At: Theatre
Seating Capacity: 2,036
Year Built: 1997

8468
TRINITY MOTHER FRANCES ROSE STADIUM
700 Fair Park Dr.
Tyler, TX 75701
Phone: 903-531-3602
Fax: 765-496-1280
Web Site: www.kylgrafx.com/raiders/rose.htm
Management:
  Athletic Director: Billy Hall
Seating Capacity: 14,000

8469
FERREL CENTER
Baylor University
150 Bear Run
Waco, TX 76711
Phone: 254-710-1011
Fax: 254-710-1968
Toll-free: 800-BAY-LORU
Web Site: www.baylor.edu
Officers:
  President: Kenn Starr
  VP: Elizabeth Davis
Management:
  President: Robert B Sloan Jr
  Associate Athletic Director: Jim Trego
Founded: 1845
Status: For-Profit, Non-Professional

8470
WACO CONVENTION CENTER CHISHOLM HALL
100 Washington Avenue
PO Box 2570
Waco, TX 76701
Mailing Address: PO Box 2570, Waco, Texas 76712-2570
Phone: 245-750-5810
Fax: 817-750-5801
Toll-free: 800-321-9226
e-mail: lizt@ci.waco.tx.us
Web Site: www.wacoheartoftexas.com
Officers:
  Chair: Elaine Seeber
  Vice Chair: Patrick Nowotny
Management:
  Director: Elizabeth A. Taylor
  Director of Sales & Internet Devel: Carla Pendergraft, CMP
  Convention Services Manager: Rhonda Bailey, CMP
  Convention Center Sales: Sandi Lane, CMP

8471
WACO HIPPODROME
724 Austin Avenue
Waco, TX 76701
Phone: 254-752-7745
Fax: 254-752-9806
Toll-free: 800-701-2787
Web Site: wacohippodrometheatre.com
Management:
  Executive Director: Teresa Ford
  Artistic Director: Richard Aslanian
  Technical Director: Len Howard
Mission: To preserve the historic Waco Hippodrome, originally a vaudeville show house; to provide quality Broadway entertainment and nationally known children's shows based on children's literature at an affordable price.
Founded: 1913
Status: Non-Profit, Professional
Paid Staff: 5
Volunteer Staff: 60
Budget: $150,000-$400,000
Annual Attendance: 21,000-35,000
Facility Category: Performing Arts Center
Seating Capacity: 943
Rental Contact: Facilities Manager Len Howard

8472
MEMORIAL AUDITORIUM
1300 7th Street
Wichita Falls, TX 76307
Phone: 940-716-5500
Fax: 940-716-5509
Management:
  Manager: George Casper

Utah

8473
CENTRUM ARENA
Southern Utah University
351 West University Boulevard
Cedar City, UT 84720

All listings are in alphabetical order by state, then city, then organization within the city.

FACILITIES / Utah

Phone: 435-586-7700
Fax: 435-865-8542
e-mail: benson_m@suu.edu
Web Site: www.suu.edu
Management:
   Director Student Activities: Mindy Benson
   Box Office: Shron Spevak
Seating Capacity: 5,022

8474
ECCLES COLISEUM
Southern Utah University
351 West University Boulevard
Cedar City, UT 84720
Phone: 435-586-7700
Fax: 435-586-5444
Web Site: www.suu.edu
Management:
   Athletic Director: Tom Douple
   Benson: Mindy
   Spevak: Director Studen Shron

8475
HERITAGE CENTER
105 North 100 East
Cedar City, UT 84720
Phone: 435-865-2896
Fax: 435-865-2898
e-mail: NOSPAMtechdirector@heritagectr.org
Web Site: www.heritagectr.org
Management:
   Managing Director: Jason Clark
   Front Of House Manager: Dallen Olcott
Type of Stage: Proscenium With Fly
Seating Capacity: 1000

8476
LAGOON ENTERTAINMENT DIVISION
375 N Lagoon Drive
Farmington, UT 84025
Mailing Address: P.O. Box 696, Farmington, Utah 84025
Phone: 801-451-8000
Fax: 801-451-8015
Toll-free: 800-748-5246
e-mail: info@lagoonpark.com
Web Site: www.lagoonpark.com
Status: For-Profit, Professional
Paid Staff: 15
Paid Artists: 30

8477
CAINE LYRIC THEATRE
Utah State University Caine College of the Arts
28 West Center
Logan, UT 84322-4030
Phone: 435-797-3040
Fax: 435-797-0107
e-mail: jarrod.larsen@usu.edu
Web Site: cca.usu.edu/venues/venue.cfm?vid=3
Management:
   Director: Jarrod Larsen, jarrod.larsen@usu.edu
   Technical Director: Timothy North, timothy.north@usu.edu
   Scheduling Director: Kris Bushman, kris.bushman@usu.edu
   Scheduling Coordinator: Gwen Scott
   Marketing Director/Box Office Mgr: Denise Albiston
Mission: Connect the artist work of students with audiences
Utilizes: Actors; Artists-in-Residence; Collaborations; Community Members; Composers; Contract Orchestras; Dancers; Educators; Five Seasonal Concerts; Guest Artists; Guest Composers; Guest Directors; Guest Lecturers; Guest Soloists; Guest Teachers; Guest Writers; Instructors; Local Talent; Lyricists; Multi Collaborations; Paid Performers; Scenic Designers; Soloists; Theatre Companies; Touring Companies; Volunteer Directors & Actors; Writers
Founded: 1913
Opened: 1913
Specialized Field: Theatre; Music; Lectures; Dance
Status: Non-Profit; Non-Professional
Paid Staff: 5
Volunteer Staff: 100
Paid Artists: 40
Budget: $600,000
Income Sources: Ticket Sales; Rental Revenue; Grants; Donations; State-Appropriated Funds
Annual Attendance: 10,000
Type of Stage: Proscenium
Stage Dimensions: 21'x21'x14'
Seating Capacity: 378
Year Built: 1913
Year Remodeled: 1996
Cost: $5 million
Rental Contact: Gwen Scott

8478
CHASE FINE ARTS CENTER
Utah State University
4030 Old Main Hill
Logan, UT 84322
Phone: 435-797-8022
Fax: 435-797-0107
Web Site: arts.usu.edu
Management:
   Director: Jarrod Larsen
   Technical Director: Timothy North
   Scheduling Director: Kris Bushman
   Scheduling Coordinator: Gwen Scott
   Marketing Director/Box Office Mgr: Denise Albiston

8479
D GLEN SMITH SPECTRUM
Utah State University
7400 Old Main Hill
Logan, UT 84322-7400
Phone: 435-797-1850
Fax: 435-797-2615
Management:
   Director: Rance Pugmire
   Marketing Director: Michelle Wilson
Seating Capacity: 10,270

8480
KENT CONCERT HALL
Utah State University Caine College of the Arts
CCA Production Services
4030 Old Main Hill
Logan, UT 84322-4030
Phone: 435-797-3040
Fax: 435-797-0107
e-mail: jarrod.larsen@usu.edu
Web Site: cca.usu.edu/venues/venue.cfm?vid=1
Management:
   Director: Jarrod Larsen, jarrod.larsen@usu.edu
   Technical Director: Timothy North, timothy.north@usu.edu
   Scheduling Director: Kris Bushman, kris.bushman@usu.edu
   Scheduling Coordinator: Gwen Scott
   Marketing Director/Box Office Mgr: Denise Albiston
Utilizes: Actors; Artists-in-Residence; Collaborations; Community Members; Composers; Contract Orchestras; Dancers; Educators; Five Seasonal Concerts; Guest Artists; Guest Composers; Guest Directors; Guest Lecturers; Guest Soloists; Guest Teachers; Guest Writers; Instructors; Local Talent; Lyricists; Multi Collaborations; Paid Performers; Scenic Designers; Soloists; Theatre Companies; Touring Companies; Volunteer Directors & Actors; Writers
Founded: 1967
Opened: 1967
Specialized Field: Theatre; Music; Lectures; Dance
Status: Non-Profit; Professional
Paid Staff: 5
Volunteer Staff: 100
Paid Artists: 40
Income Sources: Ticket Sales; Rental Revenue; Grants; Donations; State-Appropriated Funds
Type of Stage: Proscenium
Stage Dimensions: 72'x46'x21'
Seating Capacity: 2168
Cost: $4 million
Rental Contact: Gwen Scott

8481
MANON CAINE RUSSELL KATHRYN CAINE WANLASS PERFORMANCE HALL
Utah State University Caine College of the Arts
CCA Production Services
4030 Old Main Hill
Logan, UT 84322-4030
Phone: 435-797-3040
Fax: 435-797-0107
e-mail: jarrod.larsen@usu.edu
Web Site: cca.usu.edu/venues/venue.cfm?vid=4
Management:
   Director: Jarrod Larsen, jarrod.larsen@usu.edu
   Technical Director: Timothy North, timothy.north@usu.edu
   Scheduling Director: Kris Bushman, kris.bushman@usu.edu
   Scheduling Coordinator: Gwen Scott
   Marketing Director/Box Office Mgr: Denise Albiston
Mission: Connect the artist work of students with audiences
Utilizes: Actors; Artists-in-Residence; Collaborations; Community Members; Composers; Contract Orchestras; Dancers; Educators; Five Seasonal Concerts; Guest Artists; Guest Composers; Guest Directors; Guest Lecturers; Guest Soloists; Guest Teachers; Guest Writers; Instructors; Local Talent; Lyricists; Multi Collaborations; Paid Performers; Scenic Designers; Soloists; Theatre Companies; Touring Companies; Volunteer Directors & Actors; Writers
Founded: 2006
Opened: 2006
Specialized Field: Theatre; Music; Lectures; Dance
Status: Non-Profit; Non-Professional
Paid Staff: 5
Volunteer Staff: 100
Paid Artists: 40
Budget: $600,000
Income Sources: Ticket Sales; Rental Revenue; Grants; Donations; State-Appropriated Funds
Annual Attendance: 45,000
Type of Stage: Proscenium
Stage Dimensions: 30'x30'
Seating Capacity: 421
Year Built: 2006
Cost: $13 million
Rental Contact: Gwen Scott

FACILITIES / Utah

8482
MORGAN THEATRE
Utah State University Caine College of the Arts
CCA Production Series
4030 Old Main Hill
Logan, UT 84322-4030
Phone: 435-797-3040
Fax: 435-797-0107
e-mail: jarrod.larsen@usu.edu
Web Site: cca.usu.edu/venues/venue.cfm?vid=2
Officers:
  Department Chair: William Teague
Management:
  Dance Director: Cornelius Carter
Utilizes: Actors; Artists-in-Residence; Collaborations; Community Members; Composers; Contract Orchestras; Dancers; Educators; Five Seasonal Concerts; Guest Artists; Guest Composers; Guest Directors; Guest Lecturers; Guest Soloists; Guest Teachers; Guest Writers; Instructors; Local Talent; Lyricists; Multi Collaborations; Paid Performers; Scenic Designers; Soloists; Theatre Companies; Touring Companies; Volunteer Directors & Actors; Writers
Founded: 1967
Opened: 1967
Specialized Field: Theatre; Music; Lectures; Dance
Status: Non-Profit, Non-Professional
Paid Staff: 5
Volunteer Staff: 100
Paid Artists: 40
Budget: $600,000
Income Sources: Ticket Sales; Rental Revenue; Grants; Donations; State-Appropriated Funds
Annual Attendance: 30,000
Type of Stage: 3/4 Round Modified Thrust
Stage Dimensions: Full 72'x72'; Thrust 42'x50'
Seating Capacity: 669
Year Built: 1967
Year Remodeled: 2001
Cost: $4.5 Million
Rental Contact: Gwen Scott

8483
MANTI TEMPLE GROUNDS AMPHITHEATRE
Manti, UT 84642
Phone: 435-835-3000
Web Site: arts.usu.edu

8484
DEE EVENTS CENTER
4400 Harrison Boulevard Ogden
Ogden, UT 84403
Phone: 801-626-8500
Fax: 801-626-7190
e-mail: jlake@weber.edu
Web Site: community.weber.edu/deeeventscenter/default.asp
Management:
  Manager: Jody G Lake
  Director: Jody Lake
  Ticket Office Manager: Terry Shaw
Founded: 1977
Status: Non-Profit, Non-Professional
Paid Staff: 30

8485
ECCLES COMMUNITY ART CENTER
2580 Jefferson Avenue
Ogden, UT 84401
Phone: 801-392-6935
e-mail: patpoce@ogden4arts.org
Web Site: www.ogden4arts.org
Management:
  Executive Director: Pat Poce
  Assistant Director: Debra Muller
  Saturday Rental Coordinator: Travis Pate
Founded: 1959
Specialized Field: Visual Arts
Status: Non-Profit, Non-Professional
Paid Staff: 3

8486
PEERY'S EGYPTIAN THEATRE
2415 Washington Boulevard
Ogden, UT 84401-2315
Phone: 801-689-8700
Fax: 801-698-8651
Toll-free: 866-472-4627
e-mail: boxoffice@peerysegyptiantheater.com
Web Site: egyptiantheaterogden.com
Management:
  Technical Director: H C Sorensen
  Smith: Marty
  Griffeth: Executive Direc Gary
Mission: Performing arts and movie theater.
Utilizes: AEA Actors
Founded: 1920
Paid Staff: 8
Budget: $60,000-$150,000
Season: June - August
Facility Category: Historic Theater
Type of Stage: Proscenium
Stage Dimensions: 36' x 40'
Seating Capacity: 850
Year Built: 1924
Year Remodeled: 1997
Rental Contact: Director Kathryn Maguet

8487
VAL A BROWNING CENTER FOR THE PERFORMING ARTS
Weber State University
1901 University Circle
Ogden, UT 84408-1901
Phone: 801-626-7000
Fax: 801-626-8901
e-mail: browningcenter@weber.edu
Web Site: www.browningcenter.org
Officers:
  President: Chales A. Wight
Management:
  Executive Director: Scott Jemson
Status: Non-Profit

8488
DEER VALLEY RESORT AMPHITHEATRE
2250 Deer Valley Drive South
Park City, UT 84060
Mailing Address: PO Box 1525
Phone: 435-649-1000
Fax: 435-645-6939
Toll-free: 800-424-3337
e-mail: emarketing@deervalley.com
Web Site: www.deervalley.com
Management:
  Events Manager: Carrie Budding
Seating Capacity: 5,000

8489
MARRIOTT CENTER/COUGAR STADIUM
Brigham Young University
PO Box 20530
Provo, UT 84602-0530
Phone: 801-422-1211
Fax: 801-378-2042
Toll-free: 800-322-2981
Web Site: www.byu.edu
Officers:
  President: Cecil O. Samuelson
Management:
  Executive Director: Larry R Duffin
  Assistant Manager: Mary Jean Draper
Founded: 1964
Status: Non-Profit, Non-Professional
Paid Staff: 13
Seating Capacity: 65,524

8490
DIXIE COLLEGE FINE ARTS CENTER
225 S 700th E
Saint George, UT 84770
Phone: 435-652-7790
Fax: 435-656-4021
Web Site: www.dixie.edu
Officers:
  VP: Stan Plewe
Management:
  President: Robert Huddleston
  Artistic Director: Eric Young
  Lamoreaux: Marilyn
Status: Non-Profit, Non-Professional

8491
DIXIE COLLEGE ARENA THEATRE
225 S 700th E
Saint George, UT 84770
Phone: 435-652-7790
Fax: 435-656-4021
Web Site: www.dixie.edu
Officers:
  VP: Stan Plewe
Management:
  President: Robert Huddleston
  Artistic Director: Eric Young
  Lamoreaux: Marilyn

8492
DIXIE COLLEGE PROSCENIUM THEATRE
225 S 700th E
Saint George, UT 84770
Phone: 435-652-7790
Fax: 435-656-4021
Web Site: www.dixie.edu
Officers:
  VP: Stan Plewe
Management:
  President: Robert Huddleston
  Artistic Director: Eric Young
  Lamoreaux: Marilyn

8493
TUACAHN AMPHITHEATRE
1100 Tuacahn Drive
Saint George, UT 84738
Phone: 435-652-3200
Fax: 435-652-3227
Toll-free: 800-746-9882
e-mail: give@tuacahn.org
Web Site: www.tuacahn.org
Officers:
  Chief Executive Officer: Kevin Smith
  Chairman of the Board: Jonathan O. Hafen
  Foundation Chair: Carol Hansen
  Vice Chairman: Hyrum W. Smith
Management:
  Managing Director: Kevin Warnick
  Artistic Director: Scott Anderson

FACILITIES / Vermont

Exec. Dir. Marketing and PR: Scott Raine
I.T. Director: Shane Hale
Technical Director: Wes Hamblin
Mission: Was established to awaken the mobility of the hman soul and transmit light and hope to people everywhere through the arts and education. The theatre wishes to preserve and project the legacy of the American Musical into the 21st century.
Founded: 1992
Specialized Field: Theater
Status: Nonprofit
Season: June - September
Facility Category: Ampitheatre; Highschool
Type of Stage: Proscenium
Stage Dimensions: 75' x 60'
Seating Capacity: 1920

8494
ABRAVANEL HALL
123 West South Temple
Salt Lake City, UT 84101
Phone: 801-323-6871
Fax: 801-538-2272
Toll-free: 888-451-2787
Web Site: www.arttix.org
Management:
  Event Coordinator: Terri McGhee
  Event Coordinator: Mindy Nielson
  Executive Director: Chris Crowley
Seating Capacity: 2,800

8495
ABRAVANEL SYMPHONY HALL
123 W South Temple
Salt Lake City, UT 84101
Phone: 801-323-6871
Fax: 801-538-2272
Toll-free: 888-451-2787
Web Site: www.arttix.org
Management:
  Executive Director: Chris Crowley
  McGhee: Terri
  Nielson: Event Coordinat Mindy
Status: Non-Profit, Professional
Paid Staff: 200

8496
CAPITOL THEATRE
48 W Second S
Salt Lake City, UT 84101
Phone: 888-451-2787
Fax: 801-538-2272
Web Site: www.arttix.org

8497
ENERGY SOLUTIONS ARENA
301 W South Temple
Salt Lake City, UT 84101
Phone: 801-325-2000
Fax: 801-325-2516
Web Site: www.energysolutionsarena.com
Officers:
  President: Randy Rigby
  CFO/Facilities Executive VP: Bob Hyde
Management:
  Senior VP Marketing: Jim Olson
  VP Event Services: Mark Powell
Founded: 1990
Facility Category: Sports & Entertainment
Seating Capacity: 20,400

8498
JON M HUNTSMAN CENTER
451 South 1400 East
Suite 600
Salt Lake City, UT 84112
Phone: 801-581-5445
Fax: 801-585-1417
e-mail: info@stadium.utah.edu
Web Site: www.stadium.utah.edu
Management:
  Director: Richard L James
  Box Office Supervisor: Jon Jabobsen
Founded: 1969
Specialized Field: Athletics and Concerts
Status: For-Profit, Non-Professional
Seating Capacity: 15,000

8499
KINGSBURY HALL
University of Utah
1395 East Presidents Circle, Room 190
Salt Lake City, UT 84112-0040
Phone: 801-581-7100
Fax: 801-585-5464
e-mail: sheri.jardine@kingsbury.utah.edu
Web Site: www.kingsburyhall.org
Management:
  Director: Greg Gailmann
  Manager Events/Operations: Lynda Christensen
  Development Director: Kathleen Harmon Gardner
  Technical Director: Randy Rasmussen
Utilizes: Dance Companies; Guest Instructors; Guest Soloists; Special Technical Talent; Theatre Companies
Founded: 1930
Specialized Field: Performing Arts Center
Paid Staff: 20
Income Sources: Rentals
Affiliations: University of Utah Music Department
Annual Attendance: 200,000
Facility Category: Auditorium
Type of Stage: Proscenium
Stage Dimensions: 120 x 48 x 72
Seating Capacity: 1,913
Year Built: 1930
Year Remodeled: 1996
Rental Contact: Manager of Events & Operations Lynda Christensen
Resident Groups: University of Utah Associated Students (Ballet, Organization theaters, operat, etc.)

8500
RICE-ECCLES STADIUM
University of Utah
451 South 1400 East, Suite 600
Salt Lake City, UT 84112
Phone: 801-581-5445
Fax: 801-585-1417
e-mail: mburk@stadium.utah.edu
Web Site: www.rice-ecclesstadium.com
Management:
  Director: Mark Burk
  Event Services: Kristy Holt
Seating Capacity: 45,734

8501
SALT LAKE COUNTY CENTER FOR THE ARTS
50 West 200 South
Salt Lake City, UT 84101
Phone: 385-468-1010
e-mail: email through website
Web Site: www.slccfa.org
Mission: comprised of 3 separate venues

Vermont

8502
BARRE OPERA HOUSE
6 N Main Street
PO Box 583
Barre, VT 05641
Phone: 802-476-8188
Fax: 802-476-5648
e-mail: staff@barreoperahouse.org
Web Site: www.barreoperahouse.org
Management:
  Executive Director: Carol Dawes
Utilizes: Dance Companies; Instructors; Local Artists; Poets; Student Interns; Special Technical Talent; Theatre Companies
Paid Staff: 2
Annual Attendance: 22,000
Facility Category: Performance Hall
Type of Stage: Proscenium
Stage Dimensions: 32x30
Seating Capacity: 645
Year Built: 1899
Year Remodeled: 1993
Rental Contact: Carol Dawes

8503
BURLINGTON MEMORIAL AUDITORIUM
250 Main Street
Burlington, VT 05401
Phone: 802-864-6044
Fax: 802-863-4322
e-mail: memorial@ci.burlington.vt.us
Web Site: www.bma-live.com
Management:
  President: Peter Clazelle
  Executive Director: Alan Campbell
Founded: 1928
Status: Non-Profit, Professional
Paid Staff: 3

8504
FLYNN CENTER FOR THE PERFORMING ARTS
153 Main Street
Burlington, VT 05401
Phone: 802-652-4500
Fax: 802-863-8788
e-mail: box@flynncenter.org
Web Site: www.flynncenter.org
Officers:
  Chair: Peter M. Bernhardt
  Vice Chair: Sara Byers
  Secretary: Leigh Keyser Phillips
  Treasurer: Michael R. Tuttle
Management:
  Executive Director & CEO: John R. Killacky
  Director of Information Services: Gloria Ormsby
  Development Director: Regina Haddock
  Director of Education: Christina Weakland
  Facilities Director: Jack Galt
Utilizes: Actors; Artists-in-Residence; Choreographers; Collaborating Artists; Collaborations; Commissioned Composers; Commissioned Music; Dance Companies; Dancers; Educators; Guest Writers; Guild Activities; High School Drama; Instructors; Local Artists; Multimedia; Original Music Scores; Resident Artists; Sign Language Translators; Soloists; Special Technical Talent; Theatre Companies
Founded: 1981
Status: Non-Profit, Non-Professional
Paid Staff: 35
Volunteer Staff: 300

FACILITIES / Virginia

Annual Attendance: 100,000+
Facility Category: 150 Seat Modular Black Box
Type of Stage: Proscenium
Seating Capacity: 1,450; 150
Year Built: 1930
Year Remodeled: 2000
Rental Contact: Aimee Petrin

8505
UNIVERSITY OF VERMONT: RECITAL HALL
460 South Prospect Street
Redstone Campus - S Prospect Street
Burlington, VT 05401
Phone: 802-656-4455
Web Site: www.uvm.edu
Officers:
   President: Anne Francis
   VP: George Dameron
Management:
   Manager: Rebecca J. Stone
   Executive Director: Andrea Rogers
   Artistic Director: Arnie Malina

8506
DEPARTMENT OF THEATRE AND DANCE
Middlebury College
Middlebury, VT 05753
Phone: 802-443-5000
Fax: 802-443-2137
Web Site: www.middlebury.edu
Officers:
   President: Ken Pierce
   VP: Ashley Calkins
   Secretary: Cathy Tester
Management:
   Chair: Mark Evancho
Status: For-Profit, Non-Professional
Performs At: Seeler Studio Theatre, Wright Memorial Theatre

8507
YELLOW BARN
63 Main Street
Putney, VT 05346
Phone: 802-387-6637
Fax: 802-419-4855
e-mail: info@yellowbarn.org
Web Site: www.yellowbarn.org
Officers:
   Acting President: Mary Louise Montgomery
   Treasurer: Robert Dionne
   Secretary: John Leppman
Management:
   Artistic Director: Seth Knopp
   Executive Director: Catherine Stephan
   Production Manager: Kelsey Ekker
   Special Projects: Carole Gaddis
   Box Office Manager: Jamie Mohr
Founded: 1969
Status: Non-Profit, Professional

8508
CHANDLER MUSIC HALL AND CULTURAL CENTER
71-73 Main Street
Randolph, VT 05060
Phone: 802-728-9878
e-mail: director@chandler-arts.org
Web Site: www.chandler-arts.org
Officers:
   President: Janet Watton
Management:
   Executive Director: Becky McMeekin
   Rentals: Kathy Corrao
   Technical Director: Emily Crosby
   Volunteer Coordinator: Marda Donner
   Box Office: Kathy Corrao

8509
THE GREEN AT SHELBURNE MUSEUM
Shelburn Museum
6000 Shelburne Road
Shelburne, VT 05482
Mailing Address: P.O. Box 10, Shelburne, VT 05482
Phone: 802-985-3346
Fax: 802-985-2331
e-mail: info@shelburnemuseum.org
Web Site: www.shelburnemuseum.org
Officers:
   Chairman: Peter Martin
   Vice Chair: Frances von Stade Downing
   Vice Chair: Charles Granquist
   Vice Chair: Michael Polemis
   Secretary: Alice Cooney Frelinghuysen
Seating Capacity: 3,000

Virginia

8510
BARTER PLAYHOUSE/THEATRE HOUSE
1214 Williston Road
PO Box 867
Abingdon, VA 05403
Phone: 802-652-0777
Fax: 540-676-6064
e-mail: info@highergroundmusic.com
Web Site: www.highergroundmusic.com/shelburne

8511
RACHEL M. SCHLESINGER CONCERT HALL AND ARTS CENTER
Northern Virginia Community College, Alexandr
3001 North Beauregard Street
Alexandria, VA 22311-5097
Phone: 703-845-6156
Fax: 703-845-6154
e-mail: lvitello@nvcc.edu
Web Site: www.schlesingercenter.com
Management:
   Marketing/PR Manager: Linda M Vitello
   Production Manager: Stephen Shetler
   Managing Director: Dr Leslie White
Founded: 2001
Opened: 2001
Specialized Field: Washington, DC Metropolitan Area; Northern Virginia
Performs At: Rental Venue Providing Concert Hall Space For Vocal, Instrumental, Dance And Drama Performances.
Facility Category: Concert Hall And Arts Center
Type of Stage: Proscenium
Seating Capacity: 1,000 concert hall/80 reception areas

8512
BURRUSS AUDITORIUM
Virginia Tech University
225 Squires Center
Blacksburg, VA 24061
Phone: 703-231-5431
Fax: 703-231-5430

8513
CASELL COLISEUM
Virginia Tech University
Washington Street
Blacksburg, VA 24061
Phone: 540-231-6796
Fax: 540-231-3060
e-mail: caraw@vt.edu
Web Site: www.hokiesports.com
Management:
   President: Charles Steger
   Director Athletics: Jim Weaver
   Senior Associate Director Athletics: Sharon McCloskey
   Associate Director Athletics: Tom Gabhard
   Associate Director Athletics: Jon Jaudon
   Director Fiance Affairs: Randy Butt
Founded: 1872
Status: For-Profit, Non-Professional

8514
LANE STADIUM
285 Spring Road
Blacksburg, VA 24061
Phone: 540-231-6796
Fax: 540-231-3060
Web Site: www.hokiesports.com
Officers:
   President: Charles Steger
Management:
   Director Athletics: Jim Weaver
   Senior Associate Director Athletics: Sharon McCloskey
   Associate Director Athletics: Tom Gabhard
   Associate Director Athletics: Jon Jaudon
   Director Fiance Affairs: Randy Butt
   Assistant Director Athletics: Tim East
Specialized Field: Athletics
Status: Non-Profit, Professional
Paid Staff: 500
Volunteer Staff: 250
Seating Capacity: 50,000

8515
JIFFY LUBE LIVE
7800 Cellar Door Drive
Bristow, VA 20136
Phone: 703-754-6400
Fax: 703-754-6429
e-mail: boxoffice@nissanpavilion.com
Web Site: www.thejiffylubelive.com
Management:
   GM: Bruce Edwards
Seating Capacity: 25,000

8516
SAINT ANNE'S-BELFIELD SCHOOL SUMMER MUSIC ACADEMY
2132 Ivy Road Charlottesville
Charlottesville, VA 22903
Phone: 804-295-160
Fax: 804-963-9964
Web Site: www.stab.org
Management:
   Executive Director: Susan Black
   Assistant Director: Kai'li Millner

8517
SCOTT STADIUM
University of Virginia
PO Box 3785
Charlottesville, VA 22903

FACILITIES / Virginia

Phone: 804-982-5100
Fax: 804-982-5213
Web Site: www.virginiasports.com
Management:
  Athletic Director: M Terry Holland
Seating Capacity: 61,500

8518
UNIVERSITY OF VIRGINIA HALL
University of Virginia
PO Box 400000
Charlottesville, VA 22904-4846
Phone: 434-924-7231
Fax: 804-982-5212
Web Site: www.virginia.edu
Management:
  Associate Athletic Director: Mark Fletcher
  Athletic Director: Craig Littlepage
  Sports Information Director: Rich Murray
  Head Football Coach: George Welsh
  Head Men's Basketball Coach: Pete Gillen
  Head Women's Basketball Coach: Debbie Ryan
  Associate Athletic Director: Mike Thomas
  Ticket Manager: Dick Mathias
Seating Capacity: 8,450

8519
GEORGE MASON UNIVERSITY DEPARTMENT OF THEATER
Mason School of Theater
4400 University Drive
Fairfax, VA 22030
Phone: 703-993-1120
Toll-free: 888-945-2468
e-mail: theater@gmu.edu
Web Site: www.theater.gmu.edu
Officers:
  Department Chair: Ken Elston
  Associate Dean, AASA: Ken Elston Miller
  Chair: Ken Elston
Management:
  Director, School of Theater: Ken Elston
  Costume Shop Manager: Laurel Dunayer
  Scene Shop Manager: Ethan Osborne
  Office Manager: Libby Stevens
Mission: Provides a rigorous, creative and nuturing environment where we encourage conceptual and cultural diversity. Students establish a professional work ethic, collaborate with others, and take responsibility for individuals as well as group efforts as they prepare for a life and career beyond graduation.
Founded: 1990
Opened: 1990
Status: Non-Profit, Professional
Performs At: TheaterSpace, Black Box Theater, Harris Theater
Seating Capacity: 150, 460

8520
PATRIOT CENTER
4500 Patriot Circle
Fairfax, VA 22030
Phone: 703-993-3000
Fax: 703-993-3079
e-mail: bgeisler@gmu.edu
Web Site: patriotcenter.monumentalnetwork.com/about-patriot-center
Management:
  President: Paolin Abe
  General Manager: Barry H Geisler
  Director Operations: John Gabbert
Founded: 1985
Seating Capacity: 10,000

8521
FORT EUSTIS MUSIC AND VIDEO CENTER - JACOBS THEATRE
ATZF-PRC-MT BUILDING 224
Fort Eustis, VA 23604
Phone: 757-878-3436

8522
RIVERSIDE CENTER DINNER THEATER AND CONFERENCE FACILITY
95 Riverside Parkway
Fredericksburg, VA 22406
Phone: 540-370-4300
Fax: 540-370-4304
Toll-free: 888-999-8527
e-mail: riverside@aol.com
Web Site: www.riversidedt.com
Founded: 1998
Specialized Field: Musical Theatre
Status: For-Profit, Professional

8523
INNSBROOK PAVILION
4901 Lake Brook Dr
Glen Allen, VA 23060
Phone: 804-423-1775
Fax: 804-217-8802
e-mail: events@innsbrook.com
Web Site: www.innsbrook.com
Officers:
  President: Bruce Kay
  Treasurer: Toby Leslie
Management:
  Executive Director: Denise Kranich
Seating Capacity: 6,000

8524
HAMPTON COLISEUM
1000 Coliseum Drive
PO Box 7309
Hampton, VA 23666-0309
Phone: 757-838-5650
Fax: 757-838-2595
e-mail: jtsao@hampton.gov
Web Site: www.hamptoncoliseum.org
Management:
  Director: Joe Tsao
Founded: 1969
Status: Non-Profit, Professional
Paid Staff: 200

8525
HAMPTON UNIVERSITY
121 Holland Hall
Hampton, VA 23668
Mailing Address: 100 E. Queen St., Hampton, VA 23668
Phone: 757-727-5000
Fax: 757-728-6995
Web Site: www.hamptonu.edu
Officers:
  Executive Vice President: Dr. JoAnn W. Haysbert
  VP for Administrative Services: Dr. Rodney D. Smith
  Vice President for Development: Mr. Laron Clark
  Vice President & General Counsel: Atty. Faye Hardy-Lucas
  VP of Business Affairs & Treasurer: Doretha J. Spells
Management:
  Director of Athletics: Lonza Hardy Jr
  Business Manager: Petra Klimplova
  Asst AD/SWA: Tianna Scott

Founded: 1868
Status: For-Profit, Non-Professional
Paid Staff: 200
Paid Artists: 50

8526
BRIDGEFORTH STADIUM
251 Bluestone Dr
Harrisonburg, VA 22801
Phone: 540-568-6164
Fax: 540-568-6598
Web Site: www.jmusports.com
Officers:
  President: Linwood Rose
Management:
  Athletic Director: Jeffrey Boume
  Athletic Facilities Director: Ty Phillips
Founded: 1908
Status: Non-Profit, Professional

8527
EXPERIMENTAL THEATRE
James Madison University
Theatre II Building
Theatre II, MSC 5601
Harrisonburg, VA 22807
Phone: 540-568-6342
Fax: 540-568-6598
e-mail: buckwj@jmu.edu
Web Site: www.jmu.edu/theatre
Management:
  Director: William Buck
  Technical Director: Charlie Lawlor
Mission: The James Madison University Theatre program has a liberal arts orientation directed specifically toward undergraduate students. We have three basic emphases: instruction in the theory and history of drama; instruction in the practice of theatre arts; and a full production program.
Status: Professional
Type of Stage: Black Box
Seating Capacity: 150

8528
LATIMER-SHAEFFER THEATRE
James Madison University
Duke Hall
Theatre II, MSC 5601
Harrisonburg, VA 22807
Phone: 540-568-6342
Fax: 540-568-6598
e-mail: buckwj@jmu.edu
Web Site: www.jmu.edu/theatre
Management:
  Director: William Buck
  Technical Director: Charlie Lawlor
Mission: The James Madison University Theatre program has a liberal arts orientation directed specifically toward undergraduate students. We have three basic emphases: instruction in the theory and history of drama; instruction in the practice of theatre arts; and a full production program.
Status: Professional
Type of Stage: Proscenium
Seating Capacity: 324
Year Built: 1967
Year Restored: 1988

8529
ALUMNI MEMORIAL FIELD
Virginia Military Institute
North Main Street
Lexington, VA 24450

FACILITIES / Virginia

Phone: 540-464-7529
Fax: 540-464-7622
Toll-free: 866-539-3387
e-mail: brannerwh@vmi.edu
Web Site: www.vmi.edu
Officers:
   President: J H Binford Peay, III
Management:
   Director Communications/Marketing: COL Grover O Craven, Jr
   Sports Information Director: Wade Branner
Founded: 1839
Opened: 1962
Status: Non-Profit, Non-Professional
Paid Staff: 103
Seating Capacity: 10,000
Cost: $250,000
Year Restored: 1985

8530
CAMERON HALL
North Main Street
North Main Street
Lexington, VA 24450
Phone: 540-464-7529
Fax: 540-646-7622
Toll-free: 866-539-3387
Web Site: www.vmi.edu
Management:
   President: J Binford Peay
   Executive Director: Dennis Toney
   Director: Donny White
Founded: 1839
Status: Non-Profit, Professional
Paid Staff: 50
Seating Capacity: 5800

8531
VINES CENTER
Liberty University
1971 University Boulevard
Lynchburg, VA 24502
Phone: 434-582-2064
Fax: 434-582-2076
Toll-free: 800-543-5317
Web Site: www.liberty.edu
Officers:
   VP: Dr. Todd Campo
Management:
   EVP: Dave Young
   Director: Woody Galbreath
Founded: 1971
Status: Non-Profit, Non-Professional
Seating Capacity: 8,085

8532
WILLIAM STADIUM
Liberty University
1971 University Boulevard
Lynchburg, VA 24502
Phone: 434-582-2000
Fax: 804-582-2076
Web Site: www.liberty.edu
Officers:
   VP: Dr. Todd Campo
Management:
   Director: Woody Galbreath
Seating Capacity: 12,000

8533
PRINCE WILLIAM COUNTY STADIUM
14420 Bristow Road
Manassas, VA 22191
Phone: 703-792-7060
Fax: 703-792-4219
Management:
   Director: Rich Artenian
   Sports Marketing Coordinator: Marvin Vann
Seating Capacity: 6,000

8534
TULTEX CORPORATION
101 Commonwealth Boulevard
Martinsville, VA 24112
Phone: 540-632-2961
Fax: 510-632-9123

8535
ALDEN THEATRE AT MCLEAN COMMUNITY CENTER
1234 Ingleside Avenue
McLean, VA 22101
Phone: 703-790-0123
Fax: 703-556-0547
e-mail: clare.kiley@fairfaxcounty.gov
Web Site: www.mcleancenter.org
Management:
   Executive Director: Bill Bersie
   Artistic Director: Clare Kiley
Founded: 1975
Status: Non-Profit, Non-Professional
Paid Staff: 30

8536
ATTUCKS THEATRE
City of Norfolk
1010 Church Street
Norfolk, VA 23510
Phone: 757-664-6464
Fax: 757-664-6990
e-mail: info@sevenvenues.com
Web Site: www.sevenvenues.com
Management:
   Director: John Rhamstine
   Events Manager: Scott Warren
   Marketing Manager: Melissa Skinner
Mission: To present the best in sports, family and cultural entertainment.
Founded: 2004
Opened: 2004
Status: Non-Profit, Professional
Paid Staff: 56
Budget: $400,000
Income Sources: City Budget
Facility Category: Theater
Type of Stage: Proscenium
Seating Capacity: 624
Year Built: 1919
Year Remodeled: 2002
Cost: $8 Million
Rental Contact: John Rhamstine

8537
CHRYSLER HALL
City of Norfolk
215 St Pauls Boulevard
Norfolk, VA 23510
Phone: 757-664-6464
Fax: 757-664-6990
e-mail: info@sevenvenues.com
Web Site: www.sevenvenues.com
Management:
   Director: John Rhamstine
   Events Manager: Scott Warren
   Marketing Manager: Melissa Skinner
Mission: To present the best in sports, family and cultural entertainment.
Founded: 1971
Specialized Field: Concerts, Theatre
Status: Non-Profit, Professional
Paid Staff: 56
Budget: $6 million
Income Sources: City Budget
Annual Attendance: 200,000
Facility Category: Performing Arts Theater
Type of Stage: Proscenium
Orchestra Pit: y
Seating Capacity: 2,500
Year Built: 1969
Cost: $33 Million
Rental Contact: John Rhamstine

8538
CONSTANT CONVOCATION CENTER
Old Dominion College
4320 Hampton Boulevard
Norfolk, VA 23529
Phone: 757-683-4444
Fax: 757-683-6544
e-mail: tedconstantcenter@gmail.com
Web Site: www.constantcenter.com
Management:
   General Manager: Doug Higgons
   Assistant General Manager: Mike Fryling
   Director of Events and Operations: Jack Ligon
   Director of Marketing: Amy Stephen
   Operations Manager: Adam Fisher
Seating Capacity: 8,500
Year Built: 2002

8539
GENERIC THEATER
215 St. Paul's Blvd.
Norfolk, VA 23510
Mailing Address: PO BOX 566, Norfolk, VA 23501
Phone: 757-441-2160
Fax: 757-441-2729
e-mail: contact@generictheater.org
Web Site: www.generictheater.org
Management:
   President: Jeff Russell
   Artistic Director: Staci Robbins
   Technical Director: Patricia S Ellison
Founded: 1981
Status: Non-Profit, Professional
Paid Staff: 5

8540
HARBOR PARK STADIUM
City Of Norfolk
150 Park Avenue
Norfolk, VA 23504
Phone: 757-664-6464
Fax: 757-664-6990
e-mail: info@sevenvenues.com
Web Site: www.sevenvenues.com
Management:
   Director: John Rhamstine
   Events Manager: Scott Warren
   Marketing Manager: Melissa Skinner
   Marketing Manager: Melissa Skinner
Mission: To present the best in sports, family and cultural entertainment.
Founded: 1993
Opened: 1993
Specialized Field: Professional AAA Baseball Facility
Status: Non-Profit, Professional
Paid Staff: 56
Budget: $6 million
Performs At: Stadium
Annual Attendance: 400,000

FACILITIES / Virginia

Seating Capacity: 12,067
Year Built: 1993
Cost: $16 Million
Rental Contact: Director John Rhamstine

8541
HARRISON OPERA HOUSE
City of Norfolk
160 Virginia Beach Blvd.
Norfolk, VA 23510
Phone: 757-664-6464
Fax: 757-664-6990
e-mail: info@sevenvenues.com
Web Site: www.sevenvenues.com
Management:
   Director: John Rhamstine
   Events Manager: Scott Warren
   Marketing Manager: Melissa Skinner
Mission: To present the best in sports, family and cultural entertainment.
Founded: 1994
Opened: 1994
Specialized Field: Opera
Status: Non-Profit, Professional
Paid Staff: 56
Budget: $6 million
Income Sources: City Budget
Annual Attendance: 100,000
Facility Category: Opera House
Type of Stage: Proscenium
Seating Capacity: 1,632
Year Built: 1945
Year Remodeled: 1994
Cost: $10 Million
Rental Contact: John Rhamstine

8542
LITTLE THEATRE OF NORFOLK
801 Claremont Avenue
Norfolk, VA 23507
Phone: 757-627-8551
e-mail: info@ltnonline.org
Web Site: www.ltnonline.org

8543
NORFOLK SCOPE ARENA
City of Norfolk
201 E Brambleton Avenue
Norfolk, VA 23510
Phone: 757-664-6464
Fax: 757-664-6990
e-mail: info@sevenvenues.com
Web Site: www.sevenvenues.com
Management:
   Director: John Rhamstine
   Events Manager: Scott Warren
   Marketing Manager: Melissa Skinner
Mission: To present the best in sports, family and cultural entertainment.
Founded: 1971
Opened: 1971
Specialized Field: Series & Festivals; Instrumental Music; Vocal Music; Theatre; Performing Series; Sports; Concerts
Status: Non-Profit, Professional
Paid Staff: 56
Budget: $6 million
Income Sources: City Budget
Annual Attendance: 500,000
Facility Category: Arena
Type of Stage: Wegner
Stage Dimensions: adjustable
Seating Capacity: 12600
Year Built: 1969

Cost: $33 Million
Rental Contact: John Rhamstine

8544
WELLS THEATRE
110 E. Tazwell Street
Norfolk, VA 23510
Phone: 757-664-6464
Fax: 757-664-6990
e-mail: info@sevenvenues.com
Web Site: www.sevenvenues.com
Management:
   Director: John Rhamstine
   Events Manager: Scott Warren
   Marketing Manager: Melissa Skinner
Mission: To present the best in sports, family and cultural entertainment.
Founded: 1971
Status: Non-Profit, Professional
Paid Staff: 56
Seating Capacity: 600

8545
ROGERS STADIUM
108 E. Tazewell St.
PO Box 9058
Petersburg, VA 23510
Phone: 804-524-5030
Fax: 804-524-5763
Web Site: www.vastage.com
Officers:
   President: Tyler Leinbach
   VP: Dwight Handforth
Management:
   President: Eddie N Moore Jr
   Interim Athletic Director: Peggy Davis
Founded: 1882
Status: Non-Profit, Non-Professional
Seating Capacity: 13,500

8546
RADFORD UNIVERSITY THEATRE
1 Hayden Dr., Petersburg
PO Box 6969
Radford, VA 23806
Phone: 804-524-5000
Fax: 540-831-6313
Web Site: www.vsu.edu
Management:
   President: Douglas Covington
   Training: Riss Mason
Status: Non-Profit, Non-Professional
Paid Staff: 7

8547
CENTER STAGE
East Main St.
Reston, VA 24142
Phone: 540-831-5000
Fax: 540-831-5128
e-mail: admissions@radford.edu
Web Site: www.radford.edu
Officers:
   President: Penelope W. Kyle, J.D
   Provost and Vice President for Acad: Dr. Sam Minner
   Chief Financial Officer and Vice Pr: Mr. Richard Alvarez
   Special Assistant to the President: Ms. Jo Ann Kiernan
Management:
   Executive Director: Dennis Kern
   Artistic Director: Leila Gordon
Founded: 1979

Status: For-Profit, Professional

8548
CARPENTER CENTER FOR THE PERFORMING ARTS
600 E Grace Street
Richmond, VA 23219
Phone: 804-225-9000
Fax: 804-649-7402
Web Site: www.carpentercenter.com
Management:
   President: Martin Rust
   Executive Director: Joel Katz
   Business Manager: Maria Donaldson
   Director Marketing: Torra Holnan
   Facility Manager: Joe Yarborough
Founded: 1983
Status: Non-Profit, Non-Professional
Paid Staff: 10
Annual Attendance: 180,000
Type of Stage: proscenium
Stage Dimensions: width 76'6 inch, depth 26'6 inch
Seating Capacity: 2,041
Year Built: 1928
Year Remodeled: 1983
Rental Contact: Joel Katz

8549
EMPIRE THEATRE COMPLEX
Theatre IV
114 W Broad Street
Richmond, VA 23220
Phone: 804-344-8040
Fax: 804-643-2671
e-mail: j.daugherty@theatreivrichmond.org
Web Site: www.theatreivrichmond.org
Officers:
   President: Anne Murphy Douglas
Management:
   Artistic Director: Bruce Miller
   Managing Director: Thomas H. Tullidge, Jr
   Business Development Manager: Thomas Hogg
Mission: We provide outstanding educational entertainment designed to tour and innovative instructional programs that enrich our nation's schools.
Founded: 1975
Opened: 1911
Specialized Field: Broadway
Status: Non-Profit, Professional
Paid Staff: 50
Paid Artists: 30
Annual Attendance: 80,000

8550
EMPIRE THEATRE COMPLEX: EMPIRE STAGE
118 W Broad Street
Richmond, VA 23220
Phone: 804-344-8040
Fax: 804-643-2671
Web Site: www.theatreivrichmond.org

8551
EMPIRE THEATRE COMPLEX: LITTLE THEATRE
114 W Broad Street
Richmond, VA 23220
Phone: 804-783-1688
Fax: 804-775-2325

FACILITIES / Virginia

8552
GREATER RICHMOND CONVOCATION CENTER
403 North 3rd Street
Richmond, VA 23219
Phone: 804-783-7300
Fax: 804-225-0508
e-mail: info@greaterrichmondcc.com
Web Site: www.richmondcenter.com
Management:
   GM: Michael A Meyers
   Assistant GM: Carmen Barefoot
   Executive Asst.: Kathy Johnson
   Director of Finance & Administratio: Donna Reid
   Staff Accountant: Kelly Ralston
Seating Capacity: 10,000

8553
JAMES L CAMP MEMORIAL
University of Richmond
28 Westhampton Way
Richmond, VA 23173
Phone: 804-289-8592
Fax: 804-287-1841
e-mail: dmullin@richmond.edu
Web Site: theatre.richmond.edu
Officers:
   Chair: Dorothy J. Holland
Management:
   Assistant Director of Costume: Heather Hogg
   Associate Professor of Theatre: Chuck Mike
   Administrative Coordinator: Debbie Mullin
   Associate Professor of Theatre: Johann Stegmeir
   Assistant Professor of Dance: Matthew thornton
Status: Non-Profit, Non-Professional
Paid Staff: 10
Paid Artists: 2

8554
RICHMOND COLISEUM
City of Richmond
601 East Leigh Street
Richmond, VA 23219
Phone: 804-780-4970
Fax: 804-780-4606
e-mail: info@richmondcoliseum.net
Web Site: www.richmondcoliseum.net
Management:
   Regional General Manager: Dolly Vogt
   General Manager: Dwight Johnson
   Director of Operations: Glenn Major
   Director of Finance: Jeff LaSante
Founded: 1979
Status: For-Profit, Professional
Paid Staff: 25
Seating Capacity: 15,523

8555
RICHMOND STADIUM
University of Richmond
28 Westhampton Way
Richmond, VA 23173
Phone: 804-289-8000
Fax: 804-289-8820
Toll-free: 800-700-1662
e-mail: athletic@richmond.edu
Web Site: www.richmond.edu/athletics/
Management:
   President: William Cooper
   Athletic Director: Jim Miller
Founded: 1830
Status: Non-Profit, Non-Professional
Seating Capacity: 22,319

8556
ROBINS CENTER
University of Richmond
28 Westhampton Way
Richmond, VA 23173
Phone: 804-289-8000
Fax: 804-289-8820
Toll-free: 800-700-1662
Web Site: www.richmond.edu/athletics/
Management:
   Athletic Director: Charles S Boone
   Head Basketball Coach (M): John Beilein
   Head Football Coach: Jim Reid
   Head Basketball Coach (W): Bob Foley
Seating Capacity: 9,171

8557
STUART C. SIEGEL CENTER
Virginia Commonwealth University
1200 West Broad Street
Richmond, VA 23284
Mailing Address: PO Box 843013
Phone: 804-827-1000
Fax: 804-827-1001
e-mail: events@vcu.edu
Web Site: www.siegelcenter.com
Management:
   GM: Tim Lampe
   Assistant GM: Nate Doughty
Seating Capacity: 8,000

8558
THEATREVIRGINIA
Virginia Museum of Fine Arts
2800 Grove Avenue
Richmond, VA 23221-2466
Phone: 804-354-7074
Fax: 804-353-8799
Toll-free: 877-353-6161
Web Site: www.ramortheatre.com
Management:
   Administrator: Nuala McCabe
   Manager: Mary Hanley
   Technical Manager: Paddy Farrelly
   Front of House Manager: Pat Sharkey
Utilizes: Guest Companies; Singers
Founded: 1955
Specialized Field: Ballet
Status: Professional; Nonprofit
Income Sources: League of Resident Theatres; Actors' Equity Association; Society for Stage Directors and Choreographers
Organization Type: Performing; Resident

8559
JEFFERSON THEATRE CENTER
541 Luck Avenue
Suite 221
Roanoke, VA 24016
Phone: 540-343-2624
Fax: 540-343-3744
Toll-free: 866-345-2550
e-mail: info@jeffcenter.org
Web Site: www.jeffcenter.org
Officers:
   President: Bruce Houghton
   Treasurer: Philip B. Nelson
   Vice Chair: Susan P Frantz
   Chairman: David Tenzer
Management:
   Production Manager & Technical Dire: Rob Bessolo
   Director of Finance: John Bingham
   Development Assistant: Kaitlyn Chase
   Volunteer Coordinator: Sandra Coan
   Music Lab Studio Engineer: Nick Corrigan
Mission: Strives to be the destination of choice in the Blue Ridge for cultural and artistic opportunities within a dynamic environment that nurtures creativity, facilitates community events and presents diverse programming.
Founded: 1924
Specialized Field: Theater
Status: Non-Profit

8560
ROANOKE CIVIC CENTER
710 Williamson Road Northeast
PO Box 13005
Roanoke, VA 24016
Mailing Address: PO Box 13005, Roanoke, VA 24030-3005
Phone: 540-853-5483
Fax: 540-853-6583
e-mail: tickets@roanokeciviccenter.com
Web Site: www.roanokeciviccenter.com
Management:
   Executive Director: Willhomina Boyd
   Head of Department: Menna Boyd
   Booking Manager: Susan Owens
   Business Manager: Mae Huff
   Event Services Manager: Lisa Moorman
   Catering Manager: Jed McCracken
   Box Office Manager: Judy Jennings
   Operations Superintendent: Gary Hannabass
Utilizes: Dancers; Soloists; Special Technical Talent; Theatre Companies
Founded: 1971
Status: Non-Profit, Non-Professional
Paid Staff: 35
Annual Attendance: 500,000
Facility Category: Public Assembly - Coliseum, Auditorium, Ex. Hall
Seating Capacity: 11,000
Year Built: 1971
Cost: $14 million
Rental Contact: Booking Manager Tricia Downie

8561
SALEM CIVIC CENTER
James E. Taliaferro Sports/Entertainment Complex
1001 Roanoke Boulevard
PO Box 886
Salem, VA 24153
Phone: 540-375-3004
Fax: 540-375-4011
e-mail: sales@salemciviccenter.com
Web Site: www.salemciviccenter.com
Management:
   Director of Tourism: Carey Harveycutter
   Director: John Saunders
   Events Manager: Brian Horsely
   Events Manager: Paul Bowles
   Sales Manager: Wendy Delano
   Box Office Manager: Hank Luton
Mission: Multi-purpose entertainment facility with arena, ballroom and parlors.
Founded: 1967
Status: Non-Profit, Non-Professional
Paid Staff: 25

8562
BABCOCK AUDITORIUM
Sweet Briar College
134 CHAPEL ROAD
Sweet Briar, VA 24595

FACILITIES / Washington

Phone: 434-381-6100
Fax: 804-381-6173
e-mail: INFO@SBC.EDU
Web Site: www.sbc.edu
Officers:
　Chair : Paul G Rice
　Vice-Chair: Elizabeth H.S Wyatt
　Secretary : Elvira McMillan Mannelly
　President : Jo Ellen Parker
Management:
　Manager: Loretta Whittman
　Chair of the Board: Paul G. Rice
　Vice Chair: Elizabeth H.S. Wyatt '69, M.B.A.

8563
WOLF TRAP FARM PARK FOR THE PERFORMING ARTS
1645 Trap Road
Vienna, VA 22182
Phone: 703-255-1900
Fax: 703-255-1918
Web Site: www.wolftrap.org
Management:
　President: Terrence Jones
　CEO: Charles Walters
　Service President Performing Arts: Ann McKee
Status: Non-Profit, Professional
Paid Staff: 480

8564
VIRGINIA BEACH PAVILION CONVENTION CENTER
2101 Parks Avenue Virginia Beach
Virginia Beach, VA 23451
Phone: 757-385-2000
Fax: 804-422-8860
Web Site: www.visitvirginiabeach.com
Management:
　Manager: Courtney Dyer, CFE
　Assistant Manager: Bryan Miller, MBA, CMP

8565
CARY FIELD
College of William & Mary
Williamsburg, VA 23187
Mailing Address: P.O. Box 8795, Williamsburg, VA 23187-8795
Phone: 757-221-4000
Fax: 413-545-3412
Web Site: www.wm.edu
Management:
　President: Timothy J Sullivan
　Director: Bettie S Adams

8566
WILLIAM & MARY HALL
College of Williams & Mary
PO Box HC
Williamsburg, VA 23187
Mailing Address: P.O. Box 8795, Williamsburg, VA 23187-8795
Phone: 757-221-4000
Fax: 413-545-3412
Web Site: www.wm.edu
Officers:
　President: Timothy J Sullivan
Management:
　Director: Bettie S Adams
Seating Capacity: 11,300

Washington

8567
BISHOP CENTER FOR PERFORMING ARTS
Grays Harbor College
1620 Edward P Smith Drive
Aberdeen, WA 98520
Phone: 360-538-4026
Fax: 360-538-4299
Toll-free: 800-562-4830
e-mail: mhood@ghc.edu
Web Site: www.ghc.ctc.edu/bishop
Officers:
　President: Edward Brewster
Management:
　Director Public Relations: Jane Goldberg
Founded: 1974
Specialized Field: Grays Harbor Symphony Orchestra, Ballet, Opera, Jazz, Theater, Classical and Popular Music
Status: Non-Profit, Non-Professional
Paid Staff: 5
Seating Capacity: 440

8568
INTERURBAN CENTER FOR THE ARTS
12401 SE 320th Street
Auburn, WA 98092-3699
Phone: 253-833-9111
Fax: 253-288-3359
e-mail: pthomas@greenriver.edu
Web Site: www.interurbancenterforthearts.org
Officers:
　President: Dr. Eileen Ely
　Chair: Tom Campbell
　Vice Chair: Linda Cowan
Management:
　President: Rich Rukowski
　Executive Director: Patricia Thomas
Founded: 1978
Status: Non-Profit, Professional
Paid Staff: 1
Budget: $10,000

8569
WHITE RIVER AMPHITHEATRE
40601 Auburn Enumclaw Road
Auburn, WA 98092
Phone: 360-825-6200
Fax: 360-825-6203
Web Site: www.whiteriverconcerts.com
Management:
　Executive Director: Lance Miller
　VP Booking: Alex Kochan
Seating Capacity: 20,000

8570
THEATRE AT MEYDENBAUER
11100 NE 6th Street
Bellevue, WA 98004
Phone: 425-450-3810
Fax: 425-637-0166
e-mail: theatre@meydenbauer.com
Web Site: www.meydenbauer.com/theatre
Officers:
　Chair: Rick Carlson
　Vice Chair: Dan Watson
　Treasurer: Laurie Tish
Management:
　Director: Roger Anderson
　Director: John Christison
　Director: Ron Hofilena
Executive Director: Stacy Graven
Deputy Director of Operations: Tim Carr
Founded: 1989
Specialized Field: Theater

8571
CITY OF BELLINGHAM FACILITIES
210 Lottie Street
Bellingham, WA 98225
Phone: 360-677-8800
Fax: 360-778-8001
e-mail: info@cob.org
Web Site: www.cob.org
Management:
　Director: Jack Gamer

8572
MOUNT BAKER THEATRE
104 Norht Commercial
Bellingham, WA 98225
Phone: 360-733-5793
Fax: 360-671-0114
e-mail: tickets@mountbakertheatre.com
Web Site: www.mountbakertheatre.com
Officers:
　President: John Pedlow
　Secretary: Jane Carten
　VP: Edwin H. Williams
　Treasurer: Mark Thoma
Management:
　Executive Director: Brad Burdick
　Deputy Director: Kim Laskey
　Deputy Director: Kim Laskey
　Finance Director: Sharon Cassidy
　Technical Director: Jim Zoehrer
　Associate Director of Development: Kristin Costanza
Mission: To provide arts, entertainment and social interaction through a wide variety of programs, results in personal enrichment, enjoyment and a sense of community, for diverse audiences in the region, and to preserve the restored historic Mount Baker Theatre as a home for local performing arts organizations, film, a venue for touring performers, and community events.
Founded: 1927
Status: Non-Profit, Professional
Paid Staff: 20
Volunteer Staff: 175

8573
OLD MAIN THEATER
Western Washington University
CFPA Performing Arts Center
516 High Street
Bellingham, WA 98225
Phone: 360-650-3000
Fax: 360-650-3028
Toll-free: 800-998-2372
e-mail: courtney.hiatt@wwu.edu
Web Site: www.wwu.edu/cfpa
Officers:
　Dean: Carol D. Edwards, PhD
　Assistant to Dean: Jane M. Friesen
Management:
　CFPA Media/PAC Series Manager: Courtney M. Hiatt
　Facilities Operations Manager: Fred Ramage
Mission: Our College is committed to a central mission of quality arts education for Western students through the mentoring and creative talents of our dedicated faculty.
Founded: 1975
Opened: 1950
Type of Stage: Proscenium

FACILITIES / Washington

Stage Dimensions: 30'x11'
Seating Capacity: 200

8574
PAC CONCERT HALL
Western Washington University
CFPA Performing Arts Center
516 High Street
Bellingham, WA 98225
Phone: 360-650-3000
Fax: 360-650-3028
Toll-free: 800-998-2372
e-mail: courtney.hiatt@wwu.edu
Web Site: www.wwu.edu/cfpa
Officers:
   Dean: Carol D. Edwards, PhD
   Assistant to Dean: Jane M. Friesen
Management:
   CFPA Media/PAC Series Manager: Courtney M. Hiatt
   Facilities Operations Manager: Fred Ramage
Mission: Our College is committed to a central mission of quality arts education for Western students through the mentoring and creative talents of our dedicated faculty.
Founded: 1975
Opened: 1950
Type of Stage: Amphitheater Style
Seating Capacity: 700

8575
PAC MAINSTAGE THEATER
Western Washington University
CFPA Performing Arts Center
516 High Street
Bellingham, WA 98225
Phone: 360-650-3000
Fax: 360-650-3028
Toll-free: 800-998-2372
e-mail: courtney.hiatt@wwu.edu
Web Site: www.wwu.edu/cfpa
Officers:
   Dean: Carol D. Edwards, PhD
   Assistant to Dean: Jane M. Friesen
Management:
   CFPA Media/PAC Series Manager: Courtney M. Hiatt
   Facilities Operations Manager: Fred Ramage
Mission: Our College is committed to a central mission of quality arts education for Western students through the mentoring and creative talents of our dedicated faculty.
Founded: 1975
Opened: 1950
Type of Stage: Proscenium
Stage Dimensions: 40' x 21'
Seating Capacity: 1,100

8576
UNDERGROUND THEATRE
Western Washington University
CFPA Performing Arts Center
516 High Street
Bellingham, WA 98225
Phone: 360-650-3000
Fax: 360-650-3028
Toll-free: 800-998-2372
e-mail: courtney.hiatt@wwu.edu
Web Site: www.wwu.edu/cfpa
Officers:
   Dean: Carol D. Edwards, PhD
   Assistant to Dean: Jane M. Friesen
Management:
   CFPA Media/PAC Series Manager: Courtney M. Hiatt
   Facilities Operations Manager: Fred Ramage
Mission: Our College is committed to a central mission of quality arts education for Western students through the mentoring and creative talents of our dedicated faculty.
Founded: 1975
Opened: 1950
Type of Stage: Thrust
Seating Capacity: 104

8577
WESTERN WASHINGTON UNIVERSITY MAIN STAGE
Performing Arts Center
516 High Street
Bellingham, WA 98225
Phone: 360-650-6146
Fax: 206-676-3028
e-mail: boxoffice@wwu.edu
Web Site: www.wwu.edu

8578
WESTERN WASHINGTON UNIVERSITY OLD MAIN THEATRE
High Street
517 High Street
Bellingham, WA 98225
Phone: 360-650-6146
e-mail: boxoffice@wwu.edu
Web Site: www.wwu.edu

8579
CORBET THEATRE
Centralia College
600 Centralia College Boulevard
Centralia, WA 98531
Phone: 360-736-9391
Fax: 360-330-7501
e-mail: webmaster@centralia.edu
Web Site: www.centralia.edu
Officers:
   Chair: Stuart Halsan
   Vice Chair: Joe Dolezal
Management:
   Artistic Director: Tony Petzold
   Events Coordinator: Candy Lunke
Founded: 1925
Status: Non-Profit, Non-Professional
Paid Staff: 225

8580
EWU PAVILION
Eastern Washington University
526 5th St
Cheney, WA 99004
Phone: 509-359-6200
Fax: 509-359-4673
e-mail: sennis@mail.ewu.edu
Web Site: www.ewu.edu
Officers:
   President: Dr. Rodolfo Arevalo
Management:
   Director Facilities: Karry Pease
   Booking Contact: Stephanie Ennis
Mission: Dr. Rodolfo
Seating Capacity: 5,000

8581
EDMONDS CENTER FOR THE ARTS
410 Fourth Avenue North
Edmonds, WA 98020
Phone: 425-275-9595
Fax: 425-771-0252
e-mail: boxoffice@ec4arts.org
Web Site: www.edmondscenterforthearts.org
Officers:
   President: David Brewster
   Treasurer: Mike Meeks
   VP: Susan Dunn
   Secretary: Susan Hoppe
Management:
   Executive Director: Joseph McIalwain
   Development Manager: Amy Stone
   Production Manager: TJ Loehman
   Box Office Lead: Cara Roper
   Marketing & Communications Manage: Tina Stryker
Mission: A cultural resource for the entire region, Edmonds Center for the Arts inspires creativity, learning and growth through performing arts presentations, community partnerships and education outreach programs.
Opened: 2006
Status: Non-Profit
Annual Attendance: 80,000
Seating Capacity: 700

8582
EVERETT CIVIC AUDITORIUM
2710 Wetmore Avenue Everett, W
Everett, WA 98201
Phone: 425-257-8600
Fax: 425-339-4675
Web Site: www.villagetheatre.org

8583
EVERETT PARKS AND RECREATION DEPARTMENT
802 E. Mukilteo Blvd.
Everett, WA 98203
Phone: 425-257-8399
Fax: 425-257-8325
e-mail: recreation@everettwa.gov
Web Site: www.everettwa.org/parks
Officers:
   President: Paul Robert
   VP: Jeff Moore
Management:
   Director: Susan Francisco
Mission: The Everett Cultural Commission was established by city ordinance in 1974 to provide focus, visibility and direction for arts and cultural related activities of the City of Everett.

8584
7TH STREET THEATRE
313 7th Street
Hoquiam, WA 98550
Phone: 360-537-4000
e-mail: info@7thstreettheatre.com
Web Site: www.7thstreettheatre.com
Officers:
   President: Ray Kahler
   Vice President: Mickey Thurman
   Secretary: Ginger Akers
   Treasurer: Sandie Pennant
Management:
   Manager: Jamie Brand

8585
TRI-CITIES COLISEUM
7000 West Grandridge Boulevard
Kennewick, WA 99336

FACILITIES / Washington

Phone: 509-737-3700
Fax: 509-735-4699
Web Site: www.yourtoyotacenter.com
Management:
  Executive Director: Corey Pearson
  Director of Finance: Joe Potts
  Director of Operations: Rob Gierke
  Event Manager: Roni Gierke
Seating Capacity: 7,587

8586
KIRKLAND PERFORMANCE CENTER
350 Kirkland Avenue
Kirkland, WA 98033-6504
Mailing Address: 350 Kirkland Avenue, Kirkland, WA 98033
Phone: 425-828-0422
Fax: 425-889-9827
e-mail: info@kpcenter.org
Web Site: www.kpcenter.org
Officers:
  Executive Director: Daniel Mayer
Mission: KPC provides cultural enrichment by offering a home for the presentation, support and promotion of the performing arts.
Founded: 1998
Specialized Field: Series & Festivals; Theatre; Dance; Music
Status: Non-Profit, Professional
Paid Staff: 12
Paid Artists: 120
Seating Capacity: 402

8587
MCCLELLAND ARTS CENTER
390 McClelland Drive
Longview, WA 3910
Phone: 397-891-671
Fax: 613-978-9161
e-mail: info@mcclellandgallery.com
Web Site: www.mcclellandgallery.com
Officers:
  Chairman: Lyn Williams
  Deputy Chair: Mary Delahunty
  Deputy Chair: Susie Hamson
  Treasurer: David Pitt
Management:
  Director: Robert Lindsay
  Deputy Director: Lyn Johnson
  Development Manager: Phillip A Jones
  Business Manager: Robyn Feher

8588
LINCOLN THEATRE CENTER
712 S 1st Street
PO Box 2312
Mt. Vernon, WA 98273
Phone: 360-333-6895
Fax: 360-336-2408
e-mail: info@lincolntheatre.org
Web Site: www.lincolntheatre.org
Officers:
  Ray: Hunt President
  Ragina: Horak VP
  Penny: Gray Secretary
Management:
  Executive Director: Carol Hays
  Artistic Director: Vicky Young
Mission: Jan
Founded: 1987
Status: Non-Profit, Professional
Paid Staff: 5

8589
WHIDBEY PLAYHOUSE
730 Southeast Midway Boulevard Oak Harbor,
Oak Harbor, WA 98277
Mailing Address: PO Box 571, Oak Harbor, WA 98277
Phone: 360-679-2237
e-mail: playhouse@whidbey.net
Web Site: www.whidbeyplayhouse.com

8590
BLACK BOX
South Puget Sound Community College
Kenneth J. Minnaert Center for the Arts
2011 Mottman Rd. SW
Olympia, WA 98512
Phone: 360-754-7711
Fax: 360-664-0780
Web Site: www.spscc.ctc.edu
Management:
  Director: Cassie Welliver
  Program Coordinator: Davis Mary
  Chief Human Resource: Emery Sheila
Mission: The Minnaert Center provides an important point of contact for the college and the community. It serves as a community resource and asset, and offers an additional choice for spectators and patrons of the arts.
Founded: 1962
Type of Stage: Flexible
Stage Dimensions: 38'x38'
Seating Capacity: 100

8591
MAIN STAGE
South Puget Sound Community College
Kenneth J. Minnaert Center for the Arts
2011 Mottman Rd. SW
Olympia, WA 98512
Phone: 360-754-7711
Fax: 360-664-0780
Web Site: www.spscc..ctc.edu
Management:
  Director: Cassie Welliver
  Program Coordinator: Davis Mary
  Chief Human Resource: Emery Sheila
Mission: The Minnaert Center provides an important point of contact for the college and the community. It serves as a community resource and asset, and offers an additional choice for spectators and patrons of the arts.
Founded: 1962
Type of Stage: Proscenium
Orchestra Pit: y
Seating Capacity: 500

8592
WASHINGTON CENTER FOR THE PERFORMING ARTS
512 Washington Street SE
Olympia, WA 98501
Phone: 360-753-8585
Fax: 360-754-1177
e-mail: info@washingtoncenter.org
Web Site: www.washingtoncenter.org
Officers:
  Executive Director: Thomas Iovanne
Founded: 1985
Status: Non-Profit, Professional
Paid Staff: 25
Type of Stage: Proscenium
Seating Capacity: 1,000
Year Remodeled: 1985
Rental Contact: Janet Freeman

8593
BEASLEY PERFORMING ARTS COLISEUM
Washington State University
1 North Fairway Road
Pullman, WA 99164
Mailing Address: PO Box 641710
Phone: 509-335-3525
Fax: 509-335-3853
e-mail: udy@mail.wsu.edu
Web Site: www.beasley.wsu.edu
Officers:
  Secretary: Joni Parkard
Management:
  Director: Leo A. Udy
  Assistant Director: Russ Drive
  Staff Technician I: Chris VanHarn
  Tech Service Manager: Patrick Starr
  Stage Technician III: Shawn S. Paulson
Seating Capacity: 12,000

8594
GORGE AMPHITHEATRE
754 Silica Road Northwest
Quincy, WA 98848
Phone: 425-990-0222
Fax: 425-990-0221
Web Site: www.gorgeamphitheatre.net
Management:
  GM: Bill Parsons
  Marketing Director: Russ McGrath
Seating Capacity: 20,000

8595
RAYMOND THEATER
323 Third Street
Raymond, WA 98577
Phone: 360-942-4127
Fax: 360-942-5616
e-mail: raymondtheatre@willapabay.org
Web Site: www.raymondtheater.com
  Manager: Rebecca Watson
Specialized Field: Theater; Community Center

8596
MARYMOOR AMPHITHEATRE
6046 West Lake Sammamish Parkway
Redmond, WA 98073
Phone: 425-990-0222
Fax: 425-990-0221
e-mail: jeff.trisler@hobconcerts.com
Web Site: www.concertsatmarymoor.com
Management:
  House of Blues Concerts: Dave Litrell
  House of Blues Concerts: Jeff Trisler
Seating Capacity: 5,000

8597
A CONTEMPORARY THEATRE
P.O. Box 5256
Seattle, WA 75505
Phone: 206-292-7660
Fax: 206-292-7676
Web Site: www.tickets.com/venue_info
Officers:
  President: Mt. Rushmore

8598
BATHHOUSE THEATRE
7312 W Greenlake Drive N
Seattle, WA 98103

FACILITIES / Washington

Phone: 206-524-1300
Fax: 206-527-1942
e-mail: boxoffice@seattlepublictheater.org
Web Site: www.seattlepublictheater.org
Officers:
　President: Neill Warfield
　VP: Wendy Woolery
　Treasurer: Greg Piantanida
　Secretary: Rebekah Hewitt
　Attorney: Aaron Keyt
Management:
　Assistant Director: Shana Bestok
　Managing Director: Zo‰ Alexis Scott
　Artistic & Education Director: Shana Bestock
　Development Manager: Heather Beasley
　Communications & PR Manager: Cole Hornaday

8599
HEC EDMUNDSON PAVILION
University of Washington
2035 Corte del Nogal
Seattle, WA 92009
Mailing Address: Box 354070
Phone: 206-543-7373
Fax: 206-616-1523
Web Site: www.gohuskies.com
Management:
　Assistant Athletic Director: Chip Lydum
　Event Manager: Steve Harper
　Chief Financial Officer: Robert Sasaki
　Faculty Athletic Representative: Pete Dukes
　Receptionist and Marketing Assistan: Janet Sukraw
Year Built: 1927
Year Remodeled: 1999

8600
HUSKY STADIUM
University of Washington
2035 Corte del Nogal
Seattle, WA 92009
Mailing Address: Box 35407
Phone: 206-543-7373
Fax: 206-616-1523
Web Site: www.gohuskies.com
Management:
　Assistant Athletics: Chip Lydum
　Event Manager: Steve Harper
　Chief Financial Officer: Robert Sasaki
　Faculty Athletic Representative: Pete Dukes
　Receptionist and Marketing Assistan: Janet Sukraw
Mission: Home of the University of Washington athletics (NCAA).
Seating Capacity: 72,484
Year Built: 1920

8601
KEYARENA AT SEATTLE CENTER
305 Harrison Street
Seattle, WA 98109
Phone: 206-684-7200
Fax: 206-684-7366
Toll-free: 206-847-00
e-mail: sccomm@seattle.gov
Web Site: www.seattlecenter.com
Management:
　Director: Virginia Anderson
　Director Event Producer: John Rhamstine
　Associate Director: Margaret Wetter
Mission: Home to Seattle Supersonics (NBA) and Seattle Thunderbirds (WHL).
Seating Capacity: 15,000, 6000
Year Built: 1995

8602
MERCER ARENA AT SEATTLE CENTER
305 Harrison Street
Seattle, WA 98109
Phone: 206-684-7200
Fax: 206-684-7366
Toll-free: 206-847-00
e-mail: eventsales.seattlecenter@ci.seattle.wa.us
Web Site: www.seattlecenter.com
Management:
　Director: Virginia Anderson
　Associate Director: Margaret Wetter
　Chief Financial Officer: Robert Sasaki
　Faculty Athletic Representative: Pete Dukes
　Receptionist and Marketing Assistan: Janet Sukraw

8603
NESHOLM FAMILY LEATURE HALL
Marion Oliver McCaw Hall at Seattle Center
305 Harrison Street
Seattle, WA 98109
Phone: 206-684-7200
Fax: 206-684-7366
Toll-free: 206-847-00
e-mail: eventsales.seattlecenter@ci.seattle.wa.us
Web Site: www.seattlecenter.com
Management:
　Sr Event Sales Representative: Alison McGuire
　Director Event Producer: John Rhamstine
　Chief Financial Officer: Robert Sasaki
　Faculty Athletic Representative: Pete Dukes
　Receptionist and Marketing Assistan: Janet Sukraw
Utilizes: Actors; Choreographers; Commissioned Composers; Contract Orchestras; Curators; Dance Companies; Dancers; Designers; Educators; High School Drama; Multi Collaborations; Multimedia; Original Music Scores; Performance Artists; Resident Artists; Sign Language Translators; Singers; Soloists; Special Technical Talent; Theatre Companies
Founded: 1962
Opened: 2003
Specialized Field: Multi-Media
Status: For-Profit, Professional
Seating Capacity: 400

8604
SAFECO FIELD
1250 1st Avenue South Seattle
Seattle, WA 98134
Phone: 206-346-4001
Fax: 206-346-4400
Web Site: www.seattle.mariners.mlb.com
Management:
　President: Chuck Armstrong
　Chairman: Howard Lincoln
　General Manager: Bill Batasi
　Manager Events Services: Toni Pereira
　VP/Ballpark Planning: John Palmer
　VP/Ballpark Operations: Neil Campbell
Founded: 1977
Status: For-Profit, Professional
Paid Staff: 170
Seating Capacity: 47,000

8605
SEATTLE CENTER OPERA HOUSE
1020 John Street Seattl
Seattle, WA 98109
Phone: 206-684-7600
Fax: 206-615-7651
Web Site: www.seattleopera.org
Officers:
　Chair: John F. Nesholm
　President: William T. Weyerhaeuser
　Treasurer: Gary Houlahan
　Secretary: Jonathan Caves
Management:
　General Director: Speight Jenkins
　Executive Director: Kelly Tweeddale
　Production Administrator: Andrea Reay
　Assistant Master Stage Carpenter: Jack F. Harrison
　Head Flyman: Justin Lloyd
Seating Capacity: 17,000

8606
SEATTLE REPERTORY THEATRE
155 Mercer Street
PO Box 900923
Seattle, WA 98109-9982
Phone: 206-443-2222
Fax: 206-443-2379
Toll-free: 877-900-9285
e-mail: info@seattlerep.org
Web Site: www.seattlerep.org
Officers:
　President: Mary Robinson
　VP: Jean Pierre Green
Management:
　Artistic Director: Sharon Ott
　Managing Director: Ben Moore
Founded: 1963

8607
SUSAN BROTMAN AUDITORIUM
Marion Oliver McCaw Hall at Seattle Center
305 Harrison Street
Seattle, WA 98109
Phone: 206-684-7202
Fax: 206-684-7366
e-mail: alison.mcguire@seattle.gov
Web Site: www.seattlecenter.com
Management:
　Sr Event Sales Representative: Alison McGuire
　MD: Bruce Allardice
Mission: Marion Oliver McCaw Hall is a renovation of the Opera House at Seattle Center.
Utilizes: Actors; Choreographers; Commissioned Composers; Contract Orchestras; Curators; Dance Companies; Dancers; Designers; Educators; High School Drama; Multi Collaborations; Multimedia; Original Music Scores; Performance Artists; Resident Artists; Sign Language Translators; Singers; Soloists; Special Technical Talent; Theatre Companies
Founded: 1962
Opened: 2003
Specialized Field: Concerts
Status: For-Profit, Professional
Paid Staff: 200
Type of Stage: Proscenium
Stage Dimensions: 60'x35'
Orchestra Pit: y
Seating Capacity: 2,900
Organization Type: Grand Lobby available for special events

8608
UW WORLD SERIES
University of Washington
305 Harrison Street
Seattle, WA 98109
Phone: 206-543-7340
Fax: 206-685-2759
e-mail: krashan@u.washington.edu
Web Site: www.uwworldseries.org

FACILITIES / Washington

Officers:
 Executive Director: Michelle Witt
Management:
 Director: Matthew Krashan
 MD: Rita Calabro
 Education Assistant: Robert Babs
Founded: 1974
Paid Staff: 26

8609
AVISTA STADIUM
602 N Havana
Spokane, WA 99202
Phone: 509-535-2922
Fax: 509-534-5368
e-mail: mail@spokaneindiansbaseball.com
Web Site: www.spokaneindiansbaseball.com
Officers:
 General Manager & Vice President: Chris Duff
Management:
 President: Andy Billig
 Managing Director: Paul Barbeau
 MD: Bobby Brett
Founded: 1985
Status: For-Profit, Professional
Paid Staff: 10

8610
INB PERFORMING ARTS CENTER
Spokane Public Facilities District
334 W Spokane Falls Boulevard
Spokane, WA 99201
Phone: 509-324-7000
Fax: 509-324-7050
e-mail: kbooth@spokanepfd.org
Web Site: www.spokanecenter.com
Management:
 General Manager: Johnna Boxley
 Marketing Manager: Kelsey Booth
 Tech Specialist: Mike Tucker
Mission: To operate as a community facility - providing first class performing and meeting surroundings with excellent service at affordable use rates to local performing arts groups, event presenters, meeting planners and school districts, thereby enhancing the quality of life for all citizens and serving the economic well-being of the community and enhancing the quality of life.
Opened: 1995
Specialized Field: Symphony Concerts, Ballet, Grand Opera, Country and Rock Music, Musical Stage Productions
Status: For-Profit, Professional
Paid Staff: 30
Seating Capacity: 2,700

8611
METROPOLITAN PERFORMING ARTS CENTER
111 West Campbell Street Arlington Heights
Spokane, WA 60005
Phone: 847-577-5982
Web Site: www.metropolisarts.com
Officers:
 President: Joseph Lynn
 VP: Kathy Grossman
 Treasurer: Carl R. Anfenson
 Secretary: Dennis Collins

8612
RUSSELL THEATRE
Gonzaga University
Jundt Art Center and Museum
502 East Boone Avenue
Spokane, WA 99258
Phone: 800-986-9585
Fax: 509-323-5718
Web Site: www.gonzaga.edu
Officers:
 President: Fr. Robert J. Spritzer, S.J.
Management:
 Professor Theatre Arts: Dr. Kevin Bradshaw
 Associate Professor Theatre Arts: John Hofland
Founded: 1887
Specialized Field: Theatre
Status: Non-Profit, Non-Professional
Paid Staff: 6
Paid Artists: 6
Type of Stage: Black Box
Seating Capacity: 200

8613
SPOKANE CONVENTION CENTER
334 W Spokane Falls Boulevard
Spokane, WA 99201
Phone: 509-324-7000
Fax: 509-324-7050
Web Site: www.spokanecenter.com
Management:
 Executive Director: Kevin Twohig
 General Manager: Johnna Boxley
 Marketing Manager: Kelsey Booth
 Tech Specialist: Mike Tucker
Founded: 1974
Status: Non-Profit, Professional

8614
SPOKANE OPERA HOUSE
334 W Spokane Falls Boulevard
Spokane, WA 99201
Phone: 509-324-7000
Fax: 509-324-7050
Web Site: spokanecenter.com
Management:
 Director: Johnna Boxley
 Events Manager: Maxey Adams
 General Manager: Johnna Boxley
 Marketing Manager: Kelsey Booth
 Tech Specialist: Mike Tucker
Performs At: Performing Arts
Annual Attendance: 315,000
Facility Category: Performing Arts
Type of Stage: Wood
Stage Dimensions: 149.5'x59'
Seating Capacity: 2,700
Year Built: 1974
Rental Contact: Events Manager Maxey Adams

8615
SPOKANE VETERANS MEMORIAL ARENA
West 720 Mallon Avenue
Spokane, WA 99201
Phone: 509-324-7000
Fax: 509-324-7050
e-mail: kbooth@spokanepfd.org
Web Site: www.spokanearena.com
Management:
 Executive Director: Kevin J Twohig
 Manager Events/Booking: Matt Gibson
 Marketing Manager: Kelsey Booth
 Operations Director: Dave Gebhardt
Opened: 1995
Specialized Field: Multi-Purpose Arena
Status: For-Profit, Professional
Paid Staff: 30
Seating Capacity: 12,500

8616
STAR THEATRE
Spokane Veterans Memorial Arena
West 720 Mallon Avenue
Spokane, WA 99201
Phone: 509-324-7000
Fax: 509-324-7050
e-mail: kbooth@spokanepfd.org
Web Site: www.spokanearena.com
Management:
 Executive Director: Kevin J Twohig
 Manager Events/Booking: Matt Gibson
 Marketing Manager: Kelsey Booth
 Operations Director: Dave Gebhardt
Opened: 1995
Specialized Field: Theatre, Concerts, Broadway, Family Shows
Status: For-Profit, Professional
Paid Staff: 30
Seating Capacity: 5,900

8617
CHENEY STADIUM
Tacoma Rainiers Baseball Club
2502 South Tyler Street
Tacoma, WA 98405
Phone: 253-752-7707
Fax: 253-752-7135
Toll-free: 800-281-3834
Web Site: www.tacomarainiers.com
Officers:
 President: Aaron Artman
 Vice President of Business Develop: Jim Flavin
 Director of Administration, Assist: Patti Stacy
Management:
 General Manager: Dave Lewis
 Chief Financial Officer: Laurie Yarbroug
 Director Marketing: Rachel Marecle
Mission: The rental of the stadium, parking area and/or meeting rooms for as many outside events as possible. Includes concerts, car shows, travelling performers, etc.
Founded: 1960
Facility Category: Baseball Stadium
Rental Contact: Philip Cowan

8618
TACOMA DOME
2727 East D Street
Tacoma, WA 98421
Phone: 253-272-3663
Fax: 253-593-7620
Web Site: www.tacomadome.org
Management:
 Executive Director: Mike Combs
 Assistant Director: Jody Hodgson
 Marketing Manager: Beth Sylves
 Director: Rob Henson
Founded: 1983
Status: Non-Profit, Professional
Paid Staff: 45
Seating Capacity: 20,200

8619
UPS FIELDHOUSE
University of Puget Sound
1500 North Warner
Tacoma, WA 98416

FACILITIES / West Virginia

Phone: 253-879-3366
Fax: 253-879-2671
e-mail: ssolidarios@ups.edu
Web Site: www.ups.edu
Management:
　Director Student Programs: Serni Solidarios
　Box Office Manager: Kristi Maplethorpe
Seating Capacity: 3,400

8620
CORDINER HALL
Whitman College
345 Boyer
Walla Walla, WA 99362
Phone: 509-527-5279
Fax: 509-522-4406
e-mail: help@whitman-college.org
Web Site: www.whitmancollege.org
Management:
　President: Timothy Cromin
　Artistic Director: Nancy Simon
　Managing Director: Tom Hines
Founded: 1823
Status: Non-Profit, Non-Professional
Paid Staff: 8

8621
CAPITOL THEATRE
13 Campbell Street
PO Box 102
Yakima, WA 2000
Phone: 293-205-000
Fax: 292-126-014
e-mail: arts@capitoltheatre.org
Web Site: www.capitoltheatre.org
Management:
　CEO: Steven J Caffery
　President: Keith Riffe
　VP: Darell Blue
　VP: Brian Roberts
　Manager: Tatjana Vaupel
Specialized Field: Theater
Budget: $400,000-$1,000,000

8622
YAKIMA VALLEY SUNDOME
1301 S Fair Avenue
Yakima, WA 98901
Phone: 509-248-7160
Fax: 509-248-8093
Web Site: www.fairfund.com
Officers:
　President: Greg Stewart
　Chairman: Jake Jundt
　Vice Chairman: Trent Marquis
Management:
　General Manager: Greg Stewart
　Assistant General Manager: Greg Lybeck
　Events Manager: Ray Mata
Seating Capacity: 8,000

West Virginia

8623
ATKINSON AUDITORIUM
West Virginia Wesleyan College
9500 Gilman Drive
Buckhannon, WV 92093
Phone: 858-822-4998
Fax: 858-534-2129
e-mail: info@calit2.net
Web Site: www.atkinsonhall.calit2.net

8624
OLD OPERA HOUSE THEATRE COMPANY
204 N George Street
Charles Town, WV 25414
Phone: 304-725-4420
Fax: 304-725-4420
Toll-free: 888-900-7469
e-mail: ooh@oldoperahouse.org
Web Site: www.oldoperahouse.org
Management:
　Manager/Artistic Director: Steven Brewer
　Box Office Manager: Christina Smith
Founded: 1973
Status: Non-Profit, Non-Professional
Paid Staff: 1

8625
CAPITOL CENTER
West Virginia State College
P.O. Box 1000
Charleston, WV 25112
Phone: 304-342-6522
Fax: 304-766-5718
Toll-free: 800-987-2112
Web Site: www.wvstateu.edu
Management:
　President: Hazo Carter
　Program Coordinator: Laura McCullough
Founded: 1840
Status: Non-Profit, Non-Professional
Paid Staff: 2

8626
CHARLESTON CIVIC CENTER
200 Civic Center Drive
Charleston, WV 25301
Phone: 304-345-1500
Fax: 304-345-3492
Web Site: www.charlestonwvciviccenter.com
Management:
　Executive Director: John D Robertson
　Business Manager: Bitty Tinny
　Box Office: Regima Bare
　Event Coordinator: Laura Buckalew
Founded: 1959
Status: Non-Profit, Professional
Paid Staff: 25

8627
CLAY CENTER FOR THE ARTS & SCIENCES
1 Clay Square
Charleston, WV 25301
Phone: 304-561-3570
Fax: 304-561-3599
e-mail: lcook@theclaycenter.org
Web Site: www.theclaycenter.org
Officers:
　President: Judith L. Wellington, Ph.D.
　Programming Director: Lakin Cook
Management:
　Manager/Artistic Director: Traci West-McCombs
　Chief Development Officer: Kathy Bush-Morris
Opened: 2003
Seating Capacity: 1,883

8628
GEARY AUDITORIUM
2300 MacCorkle Avenue SE
Charleston, WV 25304
Phone: 304-357-4807
Fax: 304-357-4915

8629
LAIDLEY FIELD ATHLETIC RECREATIONAL CENTER
200 Elizabeth Street
Charleston, WV 25311
Phone: 304-348-1134
Fax: 304-348-6559
Toll-free: 877-446-10
Web Site: www.uniquevenues.com
Officers:
　President: Chuck Salem
Management:
　Facility Director: Lou Ann Lanham
Seating Capacity: 22,000

8630
WATT POWELL STADIUM
35th Street & Mac Corkle Avenue
Charleston, WV 25304
Phone: 304-925-8222
Fax: 304-344-0083
Web Site: www.charlestonallycats.com
Management:
　General Manager: Tim Bordein
Seating Capacity: 7,500

8631
BIG SANDY SUPER STORE ARENA
1 Civic Center Plaza
Huntington, WV 25701
Phone: 304-696-5990
Fax: 304-696-4463
Web Site: www.bigsandyarena.com
Management:
　President: Elliot Murnick
　Director Marketing: Pete Wenzel
　Director of Operations: Steve Kessick
　Ticket Director: Martha Lunsford
　General Manager: Brian R. Sipe
Utilizes: Dance Companies; Guest Soloists; Instructors; Multimedia; Original Music Scores; Sign Language Translators; Singers; Special Technical Talent; Theatre Companies
Founded: 1976
Status: Non-Profit, Professional
Paid Staff: 120
Facility Category: civic arena\ conference center
Year Built: 1977
Year Remodeled: 1999
Rental Contact: Pete Wenzel

8632
CAM HENDERSON CENTER
Marshall University
400 Hal Greer Boulevard
Huntington, WV 25755
Phone: 304-696-3170
Fax: 304-696-6448
Web Site: www.marshall.edu
Management:
　Athletic Director: Lance West

8633
HUNTINGTON CIVIC ARENA
Ogeden Entertainment
One Civic Center Plaza
Huntington, WV 25701
Phone: 304-696-5990
Fax: 305-696-4463
Web Site: www.hcarena.com
Management:
　Executive Director: Steven J Haver

FACILITIES / West Virginia

8634
HUNTINGTON MUSEUM OF ART AUDITORIUM
2033 McCoy Road
Huntington, WV 25701
Phone: 304-529-2701
Fax: 304-529-7447
e-mail: jgillisp@hmoa.org
Web Site: www.hmoa.org
Management:
  Executive Director: Margaret Mary Layne
  Director of Development: Carol Bailey
  Conservatory Director: Mike Beck
  Education Director: Katherine Cox
Mission: To provide services and education in the fine and performing arts.
Founded: 1952
Status: Non-Profit, Professional
Paid Staff: 27
Volunteer Staff: 400
Budget: $1.9 million
Income Sources: Endowment; Gifts; Grants
Affiliations: AAM Accredited
Annual Attendance: 60,000
Facility Category: Museum with 300-seat auditorium
Type of Stage: Proscenium
Seating Capacity: 300
Year Built: 1970
Cost: $1 million
Rental Contact: Jennifer Wheeler

8635
JOAN C EDWARDS PLAYHOUSE
Marshall University
One John Marshall Drive
Huntington, WV 25755
Phone: 304-696-3170
Fax: 304-696-6582
Toll-free: 800-642-3463
e-mail: admissions@marshall.edu
Web Site: www.marshall.edu
Management:
  Chair: Howard Lang Reynolds
  Director Theatre Facilities: James Morris-Smith
  Technical Director: Edward Leo Murphy

8636
JOAN C. EDWARDS PERFORMING ARTS CENTER
Marshall University
Department of Theatre
One John Marshall Drive
Huntington, WV 25755
Phone: 304-696-3170
Fax: 304-696-6582
Toll-free: 800-642-3463
e-mail: reynoldsh@marshall.edu
Web Site: www.marshall.edu
Management:
  Chair: Howard Lang Reynolds
  Director Theatre Facilities: James Morris-Smith
  Technical Director: Edward Leo Murphy
Mission: The Marshall University Theatre Department offers students opportunities to earn a Bachelor of Fine Arts Degree in Fine Arts with a major in Theatre in two areas of emphasis: Performance and Production.
Opened: 1992
Status: Non-Profit, Professional
Paid Staff: 30
Type of Stage: Auditorium
Seating Capacity: 530

8637
KEITH-ALBEE THEATRE
925 4th Avenue
Huntington, WV 25720
Phone: 304-525-4440
Fax: 304-558-1189
Web Site: www.keithalbeearts.org

8638
JOAN C EDWARDS STADIUM
Marshall Athletics
2001 3rd Avenue
Huntington, WV 25703
Phone: 304-696-6448
Fax: 304-676-6448
Web Site: www.herdzone.com
Management:
  Athletic Director: Lance A West
Seating Capacity: 30,000

8639
SMITH RECITAL HALL
Marshall University
Department of Theatre
One John Marshall Drive
Huntington, WV 25755
Phone: 304-696-3170
Fax: 304-696-6582
e-mail: reynoldsh@marshall.edu
Web Site: www.marshall.edu
Management:
  Chair: Howard Lang Reynolds
  Director Theatre Facilities: James Morris-Smith
  Technical Director: Edward Leo Murphy
Mission: The Marshall University Theatre Department offers students opportunities to earn a Bachelor of Fine Arts Degree in Fine Arts with a major in Theatre in two areas of emphasis: Performance and Production.
Opened: 1967
Status: Non-Profit, Professional
Paid Staff: 30
Seating Capacity: 490

8640
VETERANS MEMORIAL FIELD HOUSE
PO Box 5455
Huntington, WV 25703
Phone: 304-528-5173
Fax: 304-528-5185
Management:
  Manager: Donald S Ewanus
Seating Capacity: 6,800

8641
WEST VIRGINIA STATE COLLEGE THEATRE
Fine Arts Building
P.O. Box 1000
Institute, WV 25112
Phone: 304-766-3186
Fax: 304-768-9842
Toll-free: 800-987-2112
e-mail: walkercr@wvstateu.edu
Web Site: www.wvstateu.edu
Management:
  President: Hazo W Carter Jr
Founded: 1890
Status: Non-Profit, Non-Professional

8642
CARNEGIE HALL
881 7th Avenue New York
Lewisburg, WV 10019
Phone: 212-247-7800
Fax: 304-645-5228
Web Site: www.carnegiehall.org
Management:
  Executive and Artistic Director: Clive Gillinson
  Executive Assistant : Catherine Schaefer
  Director: Richard Malenka
  Coordinator: Melissa Monterosso
  Chief Engineer : Hugh McCloy

8643
ANTOINETTE E. FALBO THEATRE
West Virigina University
College of Creative Arts
PO Box 6111, One Evansdale Drive
Morgantown, WV 26506-6111
Phone: 304-293-4841
Fax: 304-293-6896
e-mail: mark.oreskovich@mail.wvu.edu
Web Site: www.ccarts.wvu.edu
Management:
  Dean/Director: J Bernard Schultz
  Associate Dean: William Winsor
  Assistant Director: Mark S. Oreskovich
Mission: Educational facility.
Utilizes: Actors; AEA Actors; Artists-in-Residence; Choreographers; Commissioned Composers; Community Members; Composers; Composers-in-Residence; Contract Actors; Curators; Dance Companies; Dancers; Designers; Educators; Equity Actors; Fine Artists; Grant Writers; Guest Accompanists; Guest Artists; Guest Companies; Guest Composers; Guest Conductors; Guest Designers; Guest Directors; Guest Ensembles; Guest Instructors; Guest Lecturers; Guest Musical Directors; Guest Musicians; Guest Soloists; Guest Speakers; High School Drama; Instructors; Multi Collaborations; Multimedia; Music; Organization Contracts; Paid Performers; Performance Artists; Poets; Resident Professionals; Selected Students; Sign Language Translators; Singers; Soloists; Students; Student Interns; Theatre Companies; Touring Companies; Visual Arts
Founded: 1969
Opened: 1969
Specialized Field: Visual Art & Design; Music; Theatre & Dance
Performs At: Black Box
Affiliations: NASAD, NAST, NASM
Annual Attendance: 3,000
Facility Category: Educational
Type of Stage: Black Box
Stage Dimensions: 5000 sq. ft.
Seating Capacity: 104
Year Built: 1972

8644
BLOCH LEARNING AND PERFORMANCE HALL
College of Creative Arts
PO Box 6111
Morgantown, WV 26506-6111
Phone: 304-293-4841
Fax: 304-293-6896
e-mail: mark.oreskovich@mail.wvu.edu
Web Site: www.ccarts.wvu.edu
Management:
  Assistant Director: Mark Oreskovich, mark.oreskovich@mail.wvu.edu
  Chairman, Division of Music: Keith Jackson
  Associate Director, Finance: Vicki Grim
  Interim Chairman Division Music: David Bess
  Associate Director/Finance: Linda Queen
Mission: Educational facility.

FACILITIES / West Virginia

Utilizes: Actors; AEA Actors; Artists-in-Residence; Choreographers; Commissioned Composers; Community Members; Composers; Composers-in-Residence; Contract Actors; Curators; Dance Companies; Dancers; Designers; Educators; Equity Actors; Fine Artists; Grant Writers; Guest Accompanists; Guest Artists; Guest Companies; Guest Composers; Guest Conductors; Guest Designers; Guest Directors; Guest Ensembles; Guest Instructors; Guest Lecturers; Guest Musical Directors; Guest Musicians; Guest Soloists; Guest Speakers; High School Drama; Instructors; Multi Collaborations; Multimedia; Music; Organization Contracts; Paid Performers; Performance Artists; Poets; Resident Professionals; Selected Students; Sign Language Translators; Singers; Soloists; Students; Student Interns; Theatre Companies; Touring Companies; Visual Arts
Founded: 1969
Opened: 1969
Specialized Field: Visual Art; Design; Music; Theatre; Dance
Income Sources: Stage and private
Performs At: Concert Theatre
Affiliations: National Association of Schools of Theatre; National Association of Schools of Art and Design, NASM
Annual Attendance: 200,000
Facility Category: Educational
Type of Stage: Proscenium
Stage Dimensions: 58 x 42
Seating Capacity: 1441
Year Built: 1968

8645
CHORAL RECITAL HALL
College of Creative Arts
1 Evandale Drive
Morgantown, WV 26506-6111
Mailing Address: PO Box 6111
Phone: 304-296-0111
Fax: 304-293-6896
e-mail: mark.oreskovich@mail.wvu.edu
Web Site: www.ccarts.wvu.edu
Management:
    Assistant Director: Mark Oreskovich
    Chairman, Division of Music: Keith Jackson
    Associate Director, Finance: Vicki Grim
    Interim Chairman Division Music: David Bess
    Associate Director/Finance: Linda Queen
Mission: Educational facility
Utilizes: Actors; AEA Actors; Artists-in-Residence; Choreographers; Collaborating Artists; Commissioned Music; Community Talent; Composers; Curators; Dance Companies; Dancers; Designers; Educators; Guest Accompanists; Guest Artists; Guest Companies; Guest Composers; Guest Designers; Guest Directors; Guest Instructors; Guest Lecturers; Guest Speakers; High School Drama; Instructors; Multimedia; Music; Original Music Scores; Paid Performers; Performance Artists; Sign Language Translators; Singers; Students; Special Technical Talent; Theatre Companies; Visual Arts
Specialized Field: Visual art; music theatre; dance
Income Sources: Stage and private
Performs At: Choral Recital Hall
Affiliations: NASM - National Association of Schools of Theatre - NASAD
Annual Attendance: 22,500
Facility Category: Educational
Type of Stage: Indoor amphitheatre
Stage Dimensions: 18 x 56
Seating Capacity: 180
Year Built: 1968
Year Remodeled: 2000
Cost: $500,000

8646
GLADYS G. DAVIS THEATRE
West Virigina University
College of Creative Arts
PO Box 6111, One Evansdale Drive
Morgantown, WV 26506-6111
Phone: 304-293-4841
Fax: 304-293-6896
e-mail: mark.oreskovich@mail.wvu.edu
Web Site: www.ccarts.wvu.edu
Management:
    Dean/Director: J Bernard Schultz
    Associate Dean: William Winsor
    Assistant Director: Mark S. Oreskovich
    Interim Chairman Division Music: David Bess
    Associate Director/Finance: Linda Queen
Mission: Educational facility.
Utilizes: Actors; AEA Actors; Artists-in-Residence; Choreographers; Commissioned Composers; Community Members; Composers; Composers-in-Residence; Contract Actors; Curators; Dance Companies; Dancers; Designers; Educators; Equity Actors; Fine Artists; Grant Writers; Guest Accompanists; Guest Artists; Guest Companies; Guest Composers; Guest Conductors; Guest Designers; Guest Directors; Guest Ensembles; Guest Instructors; Guest Lecturers; Guest Musical Directors; Guest Musicians; Guest Soloists; Guest Speakers; High School Drama; Instructors; Multi Collaborations; Multimedia; Music; Organization Contracts; Paid Performers; Performance Artists; Poets; Resident Professionals; Selected Students; Sign Language Translators; Singers; Soloists; Students; Student Interns; Special Technical Talent; Theatre Companies; Touring Companies; Visual Arts
Founded: 1969
Opened: 1969
Specialized Field: Visual Art & Design; Music; Theatre & Dance
Income Sources: Stage and private
Performs At: Concert Theatre
Affiliations: National Association of Schools of Theatre; National Association of Schools of Art and Design, NASM
Annual Attendance: 200,000
Facility Category: Educational
Type of Stage: Proscenium
Stage Dimensions: 58 x 42
Seating Capacity: 1441
Year Built: 1968

8647
LYELL B CLAY CONCERT THEATRE
West Virigina University
College of Creative Arts
PO Box 6111, One Evansdale Drive
Morgantown, WV 26506-6111
Phone: 304-293-4841
Fax: 304-293-6896
e-mail: mark.oreskovich@mail.wvu.edu
Web Site: www.ccarts.wvu.edu
Management:
    Dean/Director: J Bernard Schultz
    Associate Dean: William Winsor
    Assistant Director: Mark S. Oreskovich
    Interim Chairman Division Music: David Bess
    Associate Director/Finance: Linda Queen
Mission: Educational facility.
Utilizes: Actors; AEA Actors; Artists-in-Residence; Choreographers; Commissioned Composers; Community Members; Composers; Composers-in-Residence; Contract Actors; Curators; Dance Companies; Dancers; Designers; Educators; Equity Actors; Fine Artists; Grant Writers; Guest Accompanists; Guest Artists; Guest Choreographers; Guest Companies; Guest Composers; Guest Conductors; Guest Designers; Guest Directors; Guest Ensembles; Guest Instructors; Guest Lecturers; Guest Musical Directors; Guest Musicians; Guest Soloists; Guest Speakers; High School Drama; Instructors; Multi Collaborations; Multimedia; Music; Organization Contracts; Paid Performers; Performance Artists; Resident Professionals; Selected Students; Sign Language Translators; Singers; Soloists; Students; Student Interns; Special Technical Talent; Theatre Companies; Touring Companies; Visual Arts
Founded: 1969
Opened: 1969
Specialized Field: Visual Art& Design; Music; Theatre & Dance
Performs At: Concert Theatre
Affiliations: NASAD, NAST, NASM
Annual Attendance: 200,000
Facility Category: Educational
Type of Stage: Proscenium
Stage Dimensions: 58 x 42
Seating Capacity: 1441
Year Built: 1968
Year Remodeled: 2003
Cost: $1.4M

8648
MONTAINEER FIELD
West Virginia University
Room 107
Morgantown, WV 26507-0877
Phone: 307-293-5621
Fax: 717-337-6528
Web Site: www.msnsportsnet.com
Management:
    Athletic Director: Oliver Luck
Seating Capacity: 63,500

8649
VIVIAN DAVIS MICHAEL LABORATORY THEATRE
West Virigina University
College of Creative Arts
PO Box 6111, One Evansdale Drive
Morgantown, WV 26506-6111
Phone: 304-293-4841
Fax: 304-293-6896
e-mail: mark.oreskovich@mail.wvu.edu
Web Site: www.ccarts.wvu.edu
Management:
    Dean/Director: J Bernard Schultz
    Associate Dean: William Winsor
    Assistant Director: Mark S. Oreskovich
    Interim Chairman Division Music: David Bess
    Associate Director/Finance: Linda Queen
Mission: Educational facility.
Utilizes: Actors; AEA Actors; Artists-in-Residence; Choreographers; Community Members; Community Talent; Composers; Composers-in-Residence; Contract Actors; Curators; Dance Companies; Dancers; Designers; Educators; Equity Actors; Fine Artists; Grant Writers; Guest Accompanists; Guest Artists; Guest Companies; Guest Composers; Guest Conductors; Guest Designers; Guest Directors; Guest Ensembles; Guest Instructors; Guest Lecturers; Guest Musical Directors; Guest Musicians; Guest Soloists; Guest Speakers; Guild Activities; High School Drama; Instructors; Local Unknown Artists; Multi Collaborations; Multimedia; Music; Organization Contracts; Original Music Scores; Paid Performers; Performance Artists; Poets; Resident Professionals; Selected Students; Sign

FACILITIES / Wisconsin

Language Translators; Singers; Soloists; Students; Student Interns; Special Technical Talent; Theatre Companies; Touring Companies; Visual Arts
Founded: 1969
Opened: 1969
Specialized Field: Visual Art & Design; Music; Theatre & Dance
Performs At: Classroom Lab
Affiliations: NASAD, NAST, NASM
Annual Attendance: 500
Facility Category: Educational
Type of Stage: Proscenium
Stage Dimensions: 24 x 18
Seating Capacity: 50
Year Built: 1968

8650
WEST VIRGINIA UNIVERSITY COLISEUM
West Virginia University
PO Box 6017
Morgantown, WV 26506-6017
Phone: 304-293-4406
Fax: 304-293-6896
Web Site: www.events.wvu.edu
Management:
  Program Manager: Eric Andrews
  Schultz: Bernard
  Oreskovich: Dean Mark
Seating Capacity: 15,000

8651
WEST VIRGINIA UNIVERSITY CREATIVE ARTS CENTER
One Evansdale Drive
PO Box 6111
Morgantown, WV 26506-6111
Phone: 304-296-0111
Fax: 304-293-6896
e-mail: mark.oreskovich@mail.wvu.edu
Web Site: www.wvu.edu
Management:
  Dean: Bernard Schultz
  Assistant Director: Mark Oreskovich
Mission: Educational facility
Utilizes: Actors; AEA Actors; Artists-in-Residence; Choreographers; Collaborating Artists; Commissioned Composers; Community Members; Community Talent; Composers; Composers-in-Residence; Contract Actors; Contract Orchestras; Curators; Dance Companies; Dancers; Designers; Educators; Equity Actors; Fine Artists; Five Seasonal Concerts; Grant Writers; Guest Accompanists; Guest Artists; Guest Choreographers; Guest Companies; Guest Composers; Guest Conductors; Guest Designers; Guest Directors; Guest Ensembles; Guest Instructors; Guest Lecturers; Guest Musical Directors; Guest Musicians; Guest Soloists; Guest Speakers; High School Drama; Instructors; Local Artists & Directors; Lyricists; Multi Collaborations; Multimedia; Music; New Productions; Organization Contracts; Paid Performers; Performance Artists; Poets; Resident Professionals; Selected Students; Sign Language Translators; Singers; Soloists; Students; Student Interns; Theatre Companies; Touring Companies; Visual Arts; Volunteer Directors & Actors; Writers
Founded: 1969
Opened: 1969
Specialized Field: Visual Art & Design; Music; Theatre & Dance
Status: Professional
Annual Attendance: 300,000
Facility Category: Performing and Educational Arts Center
Year Built: 1968

Year Remodeled: 2003
Cost: $9,000,000

8652
SUNSHINE DAYDREAMS CAMPGROUND
Terra Alta, WV 26764
Mailing Address: Route 2 Box 6E
Phone: 304-789-2292
Web Site: www.sunshinedreams.com
Management:
  Owner: Kevin Trip McClenny
Seating Capacity: 7,000

8653
CAPITOL MUSIC HALL & JAMBOREE USA
13 Campbell Street
PO Box 102
Wheeling, WV 2000
Phone: 293-205-000
Fax: 292-126-014
e-mail: arts@capitoltheatre.org
Web Site: www.capitoltheatre.org
Officers:
  VP/General Manager: Larry Anderson
Management:
  CEO: Steven J Caffery
  President: Keith Riffe
  VP: Darell Blue
  VP: Brian Roberts
  Manager: Tatjana Vaupel
Mission: Entertainment from country music artists, Broadway productions, comedy acts, Las Vegas-style acts and pop groups.
Utilizes: Dancers; Multimedia; Theatre Companies
Specialized Field: Theater
Budget: $400,000-$1,000,000
Seating Capacity: 2,500
Year Built: 1928

8654
WHEELING CIVIC CENTER
Two 14th Street
Wheeling, WV 26003
Phone: 304-223-7000
Fax: 304-233-7001
Web Site: www.wesbancoarena.com
Management:
  Executive Director: Dennis R Magruder
  Assistant Director: Philip D Campbell
  Operations Director: Mark A George
Seating Capacity: 8,000

8655
WHEELING ISLAND STADIUM
S Front Street
Wheeling, WV 26003
Phone: 304-243-0431
Fax: 304-243-0328
e-mail: rconaway@access.k12.wv.us
Web Site: www.wphs.ohio.k12.wv.us
Management:
  Executive Director: George Krelis
  Manager: Robert Conaway
Founded: 1987
Status: Non-Profit, Non-Professional
Seating Capacity: 10,000

Wisconsin

8656
FOX CITIES PERFORMING ARTS CENTER
400 W. College Ave
Appleton, WI 54911
Phone: 920-730-3782
Fax: 920-130-3794
e-mail: info@foxcitiespac.com
Web Site: www.foxcitiespac.xom

8657
LAWRENCE UNIVERSITY MUSIC-DRAMA CENTER
711 E. Boldt Way
PO Box 599
Appleton, WI 54911
Phone: 920-832-7000
Fax: 920-832-6633
Web Site: www.lawrence.edu
Officers:
  President: Jill Beck
Status: Non-Profit, Professional

8658
AL RINGLING THEATRE
136 4th St
Po Box 381
Baraboo, WI 53913
Phone: 608-356-8864
Fax: 608-356-0976
e-mail: info@alringling.com
Web Site: www.alringling.com
Management:
  Executive Director: Brian Heller
Seating Capacity: 750

8659
CEDARBURG PERFORMING ARTS CENTER
W 68 N 611 Evergreen Boulevard
Cedarburg, WI 53012
Phone: 262-376-6162
Fax: 262-376-6163
e-mail: kkoster@cedarburg.k12.wi.us
Web Site: www.cedarburgpac.com
Management:
  Technical Director: Paul Thur
Founded: 1999
Status: Non-Profit, Professional
Paid Staff: 2
Volunteer Staff: 40
Paid Artists: 8
Income Sources: Ticket Revenue; District Funding
Performs At: School District Functions; Tear 1 &2 Arts; Local Talent
Annual Attendance: 50,000
Facility Category: Performing Arts Center
Stage Dimensions: 50x22x34
Seating Capacity: 580
Year Built: 1998
Cost: 1.5 million
Rental Contact: Kathleen Pier

8660
NORTHLAND PINES HIGH SCHOOL
1800 Pleasure Island Road
PO Box 1269
Eagle River, WI 54521
Phone: 715-479-4473
Fax: 715-479-7633
Web Site: www.npsd.k12,wi.us

FACILITIES / Wisconsin

Management:
   Advisor for Drama Club: David Strong
Status: Non-Profit, Non-Professional
Paid Staff: 1

8661
ALPINE VALLEY MUSIC THEATRE
2699 Highway D
East Troy, WI 53120
Mailing Address: PO Box 921
Phone: 262-642-4400
Fax: 414-223-4531
Web Site: www.alpinevalleymusic.com
Management:
   VP: Karl Adams
   Executive Director: David Shaw
Seating Capacity: 35,144

8662
WL ZORN ARENA
University of Wisconsin: Eau Claire
105 Garfield Avenue
Eau Claire, WI 54702
Phone: 715-836-4636
Fax: 715-836-4268
e-mail: admissions@uwec.edu
Web Site: www.uwec.edu
Management:
   Conference Manager: Karen Stuber
Seating Capacity: 3,200

8663
BIRCH CREEK MUSIC PERFORMANCE CENTER
PO Box 230
Egg Harbor, WI 54209
Phone: 920-868-3763
Fax: 920-868-1643
e-mail: mainoffice@birchcreek.org
Web Site: www.birchcreek.org
Officers:
   President: Gregory Mox
Management:
   Executive Director: Kaye Wagner
Mission: To provide intensive, performance-based instruction to promising young musicians by immersing them in a professional, mentoring environment.
Utilizes: Artists-in-Residence; Collaborating Artists; Community Members; Composers; Educators; Five Seasonal Concerts; Guest Musical Directors; High School Drama; Instructors; Local Talent; Multimedia; Music; Paid Performers; Poets; Resident Companies; Scenic Designers; Singers; Soloists; Students; Student Interns
Founded: 1976
Opened: 1976
Specialized Field: Music Education & Performance
Status: Non-Profit, Professional
Paid Staff: 6
Volunteer Staff: 150
Paid Artists: 95
Budget: $808,565
Income Sources: Ticket Sales; Student Tuition
Affiliations: League of American Orchestras
Annual Attendance: 6,000
Facility Category: Live Music: Symphony, Percussion/Steel Band, Jazz
Type of Stage: Thrust
Seating Capacity: 300; 500
Year Built: 1897
Year Remodeled: 1976
Rental Contact: Executive Director Kaye Wagner

8664
BROWN COUNTY ARENA
University of Wisconsin
2420 Nicolet Drive
Green Bay, WI 54311-7001
Phone: 920-494-6868
Fax: 920-465-2178
Management:
   Director: Les Raduenz

8665
COFRIN FAMILY HALL
Weidner Center for the Performing Arts
2420 Nicolet Drive
Green Bay, WI 54311-7001
Phone: 920-465-2726
Fax: 920-465-2619
Toll-free: 800-922-9272
e-mail: nevermab@uwgb.edu
Web Site: www.weidnercenter.com
Management:
   General Manager: Brock Neverman
   Event Manager: Kasha Huntowski
   Technical Director: Josh Koleske
Mission: To present cultural entertaining and educational programs to Northeast Wisconsin and serve as home for university and local performing arts organizations.
Opened: 1993
Facility Category: Road House
Type of Stage: Proscenium
Stage Dimensions: 54'4 x 48'""
Seating Capacity: 2,021
Year Built: 1993
Rental Contact: Kasha Huntowski
Organization Type: Performing

8666
FORT HOWARD HALL
University of Wisconsin-Green Bay
Weidner Center for the Performing Arts
2420 Nicolet Drive
Green Bay, WI 54311-7001
Phone: 920-465-2726
Fax: 920-465-2619
Toll-free: 800-922-9272
e-mail: nevermab@uwgb.edu
Web Site: www.uwgb.edu/weidner/
Management:
   General Manager: Brock Neverman
   Director Of Events: Kasha Huntowski
   Technical Director: Josh Koleski
Mission: To present cultural entertaining and educational programs to Northeast Wisconsin and serve as home for university and local performing arts organizations.
Opened: 1993
Specialized Field: Recitals; Lectures
Stage Dimensions: 45 x 54
Seating Capacity: 200
Organization Type: Performing

8667
LAMBEAU FIELD
Green Bay Packers
1265 Lombardi Avenue
Green Bay, WI 54304
Phone: 920-496-5700
Fax: 920-496-5712
Web Site: www.packers.com
Management:
   President: Robert Harland
   Public Relations Executive Director: Lee Remmel
   Stadium Manager: Ted Eisenreich
   Marketing Director: Jeff Cieply
Specialized Field: Home of the Green Bay Packers
Seating Capacity: 60,790
Year Built: 1957
Year Remodeled: 1990

8668
P BROWN COUNTY ARENA
University of Wisconsin
2420 Nicolet Drive
Green Bay, WI 54311-7001
Phone: 920-494-6868
Fax: 920-465-2178
Management:
   Director: Les Raduenz

8669
STUDIO ONE
University of Wisconsin-Green Bay
Weidner Center for the Performing Arts
105 Garfield Avenue
Green Bay, WI 54311
Phone: 715-836-4636
Fax: 920-465-2619
Toll-free: 800-922-9272
e-mail: admissions@uwec.edu
Web Site: www.uwgb.edu/weidner
Management:
   General Manager: Brock Neverman
   Event Manager: Kasha Huntowski
   Stage Manager: Josh Koleske
Mission: To present cultural entertaining and educational programs to Northeast Wisconsin and serve as home for university and local performing arts organizations.
Founded: 1993
Opened: 1993
Stage Dimensions: 34 x 34
Seating Capacity: 100
Organization Type: Performing

8670
PHIPPS CENTER FOR THE ARTS
109 Locust Street
Hudson, WI 54016
Phone: 715-386-8409
Fax: 715-381-2177
e-mail: info@thephipps.org
Web Site: www.thephipps.org
Officers:
   President: Sarah J Andersen
   VP: Mark J Gherty
   Secretary: Roberta Pominville
   Treasurer: James Steel
Management:
   Executive Director: John H Potter
   Artistic Director: Anastasia Shartin
Mission: To celebrate the creative spirit.
Founded: 1981
Specialized Field: Multi-Disciplinary
Status: Non-Profit, Non-Professional
Paid Staff: 7
Volunteer Staff: 500
Paid Artists: 100
Non-paid Artists: 200
Budget: $900,000
Income Sources: Earned and Contributed
Affiliations: Wisconsin Presenters Network
Annual Attendance: 22,500
Facility Category: Arts Center
Type of Stage: Proscenium
Stage Dimensions: 36' x 34'/247
Year Built: 1983

FACILITIES / Wisconsin

Year Remodeled: 1992
Cost: $7 million
Rental Contact: Executive Director John H Potter

8671
COMMUNICATION ARTS THEATRE
University of Wisconsin at Parkside
900 Wood Road
Kenosha, WI 53141-2000
Mailing Address: Box 2000
Phone: 262-595-2345
Fax: 262-595-2202
Web Site: www.uwp.edu
Officers:
    President: Nikki Kulas
Management:
    Activities Assistant Director: Stephanie Sirovatka
Founded: 1968
Status: Non-Profit, Professional
Paid Staff: 2
Budget: $35,000-$60,000
Performs At: Communication Arts Theatre

8672
MITCHELL HALL GYMNASIUM
University of Wisconsin-Lacrosse
1725 State Street
La Crosse, WI 54601
Phone: 608-785-8000
Fax: 608-785-8674
e-mail: webmaster@uwlax.edu
Web Site: www.uwlax.edu
Officers:
    Vice Chancellor for Administration: Bob Hetzel
    Chancellor: Joe Gow
Management:
    President: Katharine C Lyall
Seating Capacity: 3,400

8673
VITERBO UNIVERSITY FINE ARTS CENTER
929 Jackson St
La Crosse, WI 54601
Mailing Address: 900viterbo Drive
Phone: 608-796-3737
Fax: 608-796-3736
e-mail: finearts@viterbo.edu
Web Site: www.viterbo.edi/fac
Management:
    Director Fine Arts Center: Michael Ranscht, mranscht@viterbo.edu
    Production coordinator: Chris Scheuermann, cmscheuermann@viterbo.edu
    Director Of Event Operations: Carter Martin, chmartin@viterbo.edu

8674
CAMP RANDALL STADIUM
1440 Monroe Street
Madison, WI 53711
Phone: 608-262-1866
Fax: 608-265-3036
e-mail: webmaster@uwbadgers.com
Web Site: www.uwbadgers.com
Management:
    Interim Athletic Director: Andrea Nilsen
    Facility Director: Barry Fox
Specialized Field: Home of University of Wisconsin athletics.
Seating Capacity: 77,745
Year Built: 1917
Year Remodeled: 1968

8675
FREDRIC MARCH PLAY CIRCLE
University of Wisconsin-Madison
Memorial Union
800 Langdon St
Madison, WI 53706
Phone: 608-262-2201
Fax: 608-265-5084
e-mail: rfrusso@wisc.edu
Web Site: http://www.uniontheater.wisc.edu/
Management:
    Cultural Arts Directory: Ralph Russo
    Technical Directory: Jeff Macheel
    Operations Manager: Bruce Ehlinger
    Marketing/Communications Manager: Esty Dinur
    Box Office Manager: Ted Harks
Mission: The Department of Theatre and Drama/University Theatre is a collaborative community of artists and scholars — faculty, staff and students — aiming to achieve the highest level of excellence in their teaching and learning, research and creative endeavors, and outreach to the community and the state.
Opened: 1939
Specialized Field: Films, Plays
Seating Capacity: 168

8676
GILBERT V. HEMSLEY THEATRE
University of Wisconsin-Madison
Department of Theatre and Drama
821 University Avenue
Madison, WI 53706-1497
Phone: 608-263-2329
Fax: 608-263-2463
e-mail: gradsec@theatre.wisc.edu
Web Site: www.theatre.wisc.edu
Officers:
    Chair: Ann M. Archbold
Management:
    Director: Tony Simotes
    General Manager: Michele Traband
    Production Manager: David Stewart
    Technical Director: Dan Lisowski
Mission: The Department of Theatre and Drama/University Theatre is a collaborative community of artists and scholars — faculty, staff and students — aiming to achieve the highest level of excellence in their teaching and learning, research and creative endeavors, and outreach to the community and the state.
Specialized Field: Drama, Theatre
Type of Stage: Black Box
Seating Capacity: 125

8677
KOHL CENTER
601 W Dayton Street
Madison, WI 53711
Phone: 608-263-5645
Fax: 608-265-4700
Toll-free: 800-223-4377
Web Site: www.uwbadgers.com
Management:
    Managing Director: Douglas Beard
    Associate Athletic Director: Jamie Pollard
    Facility Director: Barry Fox
Founded: 1848
Status: Non-Profit, Non-Professional
Seating Capacity: 17,142
Year Built: 1998

8678
NORMAN MITBY THEATER
Madison Area Technical College
Truax Campus
1701 Wright Street
Madison, WI 53704-2599
Phone: 608-246-6100
Fax: 608-243-6880
Toll-free: 800-322-6282
e-mail: dhelser@matcmadison.edu
Web Site: www.madisoncollege.edu
Officers:
    President: Bettsey L. Barhorst, PhD
Management:
    Managing Director: D Corey Helser
    Technical Coordinator: Matt Breaux
    Box Office: Dee Traxler
Founded: 1932
Specialized Field: Concerts, Theater
Status: Non-Profit, Professional
Paid Staff: 11
Type of Stage: Contemporary Proscenium
Orchestra Pit: y
Seating Capacity: 976

8679
OVERTURE CENTER FOR THE ARTS
201 State Street
Madison, WI 53703-2214
Phone: 608-258-4177
Fax: 608-258-4971
Web Site: www.overturecenter.com
Officers:
    President/CEO: Ted Deedee
    VP Finance: Reynold Peterson
    Director Marketing/Public Relations: Anna Hahm
    Director Education/Outreach: Susan Crofton
    Director Building Facilities/Ops: Glenn Weihert
    Building Systems Manager: Rick Bidlingmaier
    Director Theatre Ops/Facilities: Rudy Lienau
    Technical Director: Steve Schroeder
    Rental Contact: Brenda Malisch
Management:
    Group Sales Manager: Heather Mern
Mission: Presenting internationally acclaimed jazz, classical, opera, musicals, dance, world music, family entertainment and more. The Overture Center is currently home to seven resident performing arts organizations adn two visual arts organizations. The Playhouse seats 350, Capitol Theater seats 400-600.
Seating Capacity: 2,251
Organization Type: Resident, Presenters

8680
RONALD E. MITCHELL THEATRE
University of Wisconsin-Madison
Department of Theatre and Drama
821 University Avenue
Madison, WI 53706-1497
Phone: 608-263-2329
Fax: 608-263-2463
e-mail: gradsec@theatre.wisc.edu
Web Site: www.theatre.wisc.edu
Officers:
    Chair: Ann M. Archbold
Management:
    Director: David Furumoto
    Technical Director: Dan Lisowski
Mission: The Department of Theatre and Drama/University Theatre is a collaborative community of artists and scholars — faculty, staff and students — aiming to achieve the highest level of excellence in their

FACILITIES / Wisconsin

teaching and learning, research and creative endeavors, and outreach to the community and the state.
Specialized Field: Drama, Theatre
Type of Stage: Thrust
Seating Capacity: 321

8681
UNION THEATER
University of Wisconsin
800 Langdon Street
Madison, WI 53706
Phone: 608-262-2202
Fax: 608-265-5084
e-mail: bruce@wut.org
Web Site: www.union.wisc.edu/theater
Management:
 Director: Ralph Russo
 Facility Booking Contact: Bruce Ehlinger
 Marketing & Communications Director: Esty Dinur
 Operations Manager: Bruce Ehlinger
 Marketing & Communications Directo: Esty Dinur
Seating Capacity: 1,300

8682
UNIVERSITY OF WISCONSIN FIELDHOUSE
University of Wisconsin
1450 Monroe Street
Madison, WI 53711
Phone: 608-262-3354
Fax: 608-265-3036
Web Site: www.uwbadgers.com
Management:
 Facilities Manager: Glenn Betts
Seating Capacity: 11,500

8683
WISCONSIN UNION THEATRE
University of Wisconsin-Madison
Memorial Union
800 Langdon St
Madison, WI 53706
Phone: 608-262-2202
Fax: 608-265-5084
e-mail: edinur@wisc.edu
Web Site: www.union.wisc.edu/theater
Management:
 Cultural Arts Directory: Ralph Russo
 Technical Directory: Jeff Macheel
 Operations Manager: Bruce Ehlinger
 Marketing/Communications Manager: Esty Dinur
 Box Office Manager: Ted Harks
Mission: The Department of Theatre and Drama/University Theatre is a collaborative community of artists and scholars — faculty, staff and students — aiming to achieve the highest level of excellence in their teaching and learning, research and creative endeavors, and outreach to the community and the state.
Founded: 1939
Specialized Field: Classical, World, Jazz and other music, drama, dance
Status: Non-Profit; Professional
Type of Stage: Proscenium
Stage Dimensions: 36'x23'7
Orchestra Pit: y
Seating Capacity: 1,300

8684
CAPITOL CIVIC CENTRE
913 S 8th Street
PO Box 399
Manitowoc, WI 54220
Phone: 920-683-2184
Fax: 920-683-0272
e-mail: ccc@cccshows.org
Web Site: www.cccshows.org
Management:
 Executive Director: Jian Paul Morelli
 Assistant Director: Peggy Krey
 Marketing & Communications Director: Lori Kirby
 Box Office Manager: Doretta Klein
Utilizes: Actors; Artists-in-Residence; Commissioned Composers; Dance Companies; Dancers; Instructors; Local Artists; Multimedia; Original Music Scores; Sign Language Translators; Soloists; Special Technical Talent; Theatre Companies
Founded: 1987
Status: Non-Profit, Professional
Paid Staff: 9
Budget: $60,000-$150,000
Seating Capacity: 1,150
Year Built: 1921
Year Remodeled: 1987

8685
SILVER LAKE COLLEGE
2406 S Alverno Road
Manitowoc, WI 54220
Phone: 920-684-6691
Fax: 920-684-7082
Toll-free: 800-236-4752
Web Site: www.sl.edu
Management:
 President: Sr. Marella Wagner
 VP: Wendy Schuler
Mission: Outreach program bringing quality music performance to the community
Founded: 1935
Specialized Field: Instrumental Music; Vocal Music; Piano; Mixed Ensemble
Status: Non-Profit, Professional
Paid Staff: 5
Paid Artists: 10
Budget: $6,000
Income Sources: College Sponsorship & Ticket Sales
Performs At: Chapel
Annual Attendance: 100-125

8686
MUSIC LIBRARY ASSOCIATION
8551 Research Way
Suite 180
Middletown, WI 53562
Phone: 608-836-5825
Fax: 608-831-8200
e-mail: mla@areditions.com
Web Site: www.musiclibraryassoc.org
Officers:
 President: Jerry L. McBride
 VP: Michael Colby
 Treasurer/Executive Secretary: Laura Gayle Green
 Recording Secretary: Lynn Gullickson
Founded: 1931
Status: Non-Profit, Professional

8687
BRADLEY CENTER
1001 North Fourth Street
Milwaukee, WI 53203
Phone: 414-227-0400
Fax: 414-227-0497
Web Site: www.bradleycenter.com
Management:
 CEO: David Skiles
 GM: Stephen Costello
Founded: 1986
Opened: 1988
Seating Capacity: 20,000

8688
COOLEY AUDITORIUM
Milwaukee Area Technical College
700 West State Street
Milwaukee, WI 53233
Phone: 414-297-6600
Fax: 414-271-2195

8689
MARCUS CENTER FOR THE PERFORMING ARTS
929 N Water Street
Milwaukee, WI 53202-3122
Phone: 414-273-7121
Fax: 414-273-5480
Toll-free: 888-612-3500
e-mail: hlofy@marcuscenter.org
Web Site: www.marcuscenter.org
Officers:
 President: Paul Mathews
 Operations VP: Richard Hecht
 Finance/Human Resource VP: Carol Hayden
 Sales & Marketing VP: Heidi Lofy
Management:
 Director of Programming: John Hassig
 Director of Facility Relations: Jerold Fox
Mission: To serve the community, offer facilities and services of the highest quality, also makes a wide range of performing arts available.
Utilizes: Actors; Artists-in-Residence; Choreographers; Collaborating Artists; Collaborations; Commissioned Composers; Dance Companies; Dancers; Designers; Educators; Fine Artists; Five Seasonal Concerts; Grant Writers; Guest Accompanists; Guest Artists; Guest Choreographers; Guest Companies; Guest Composers; Guest Conductors; Guest Designers; Guest Directors; Guest Ensembles; Guest Instructors; Guest Lecturers; Guest Musical Directors; Guest Musicians; Guest Soloists; Guest Teachers; Guest Writers; High School Drama; Instructors; Local Artists; Lyricists; Multimedia; Music; New Productions; Original Music Scores; Performance Artists; Poets; Resident Artists; Resident Professionals; Selected Students; Sign Language Translators; Singers; Soloists; Special Technical Talent; Theatre Companies; Touring Companies; Visual Arts
Income Sources: Technical income; County grants; Facility Rental
Affiliations: Milwaukee Ballet Company; Florentine Opera Company; First Stage Children's Theatre; Milwaukee Youth Symphony Orchestra
Resident Groups: Milwaukee Ballet Co.; Florentine Opera Co.; Milwaukee Symphony Orch.; First Stage Children's Theater

8690
MILWAUKEE RIVERSIDE THEATER
Milwaukee Center Complex
116 West Wisconsin Avenue
Milwaukee, WI 53202
Phone: 414-286-3663
Fax: 414-286-2154
Toll-free: 800-511-1552
e-mail: gwitt@pabsttheater.org
Web Site: www.pabsttheater.org

FACILITIES / Wisconsin

Officers:
   President: Michael Cudahy
Management:
   Executive Director: Gary Witt
Founded: 1895
Specialized Field: Broadway, Pop, Country Artists
Paid Staff: 12
Orchestra Pit: y
Seating Capacity: 2,460

8691
MILWAUKEE THEATRE
Wisconsin Center District
400 West Wisconsin Avenue
Milwaukee, WI 53203
Phone: 414-908-6000
Fax: 414-908-6010
e-mail: slange@wcd.org
Web Site: www.milwaukeetheatre.com
Officers:
   President: Richard A Geyer
Management:
   Director Marketing/Sales: Sandra A Lange
   Director Event Services: David Anderson
   Box Office Manager: Donna Piotrowski
   Director Business Development: Richard Freiberg
Facility Category: Theatre
Type of Stage: Proscenium
Seating Capacity: 4,200
Year Built: 1905
Year Remodeled: 2002
Cost: $34 million
Rental Contact: Director Marketing/Sales Sandra Lange

8692
PABST THEATRE
Milwaukee Center Complex
144 E Wells Street
Milwaukee, WI 53202
Phone: 414-286-3663
Fax: 414-286-2154
Toll-free: 800-511-1552
e-mail: gwitt@pabsttheater.org
Web Site: www.pabsttheater.org
Officers:
   President: Michael Cudahy
Management:
   Executive Director: Gary Witt
Founded: 1895
Specialized Field: Chamber Music
Status: Non-Profit, Professional
Paid Staff: 12
Type of Stage: Proscenium
Orchestra Pit: y
Seating Capacity: 1,279

8693
PITMAN THEATRE
Pitman Theatre
3400 South 43rd Street
Milwaukee, WI 53234
Mailing Address: PO Box 343922
Phone: 414-382-6000
Fax: 414-382-6354
e-mail: boxoffice@alverno.edu
Web Site: www.alverno.edu
Officers:
   President: Mary J. Meehan, Ph.D
Management:
   Director: Amanda Lang
   Assistant Director: Jan Kellogg

Utilizes: Actors; Artists-in-Residence; Collaborating Artists; Collaborations; Dance Companies; Dancers; Educators; Fine Artists; Local Artists; Lyricists; Multimedia; Original Music Scores; Playwrights; Special Technical Talent; Theatre Companies
Paid Staff: 3
Annual Attendance: 5000
Facility Category: Performing Arts Venue
Type of Stage: Proscenium
Stage Dimensions: 40' x 30'
Seating Capacity: 930
Year Built: 1951
Rental Contact: Jan Kellogg

8694
U.S. CELLULAR ARENA
400 W Kilbourn Avenue
Milwaukee, WI 53203
Phone: 414-908-6000
Fax: 414-908-6010
e-mail: rgeyer@wcd.org
Web Site: www.uscellulararena.com
Officers:
   President: Richard A Geyer
Management:
   Sales Manager: Tony Dynicki
   Production/Operations: Jason Borders
   Box Office Manager: Donna Hrobsky
   Group Sales: Molly Powell
   PR/Promotions: David Snyder
Mission: The US Cellular Arena, home to decades of sports legends and rock and roll history, has undergone over $13 million in technilogical, accessibility and aesthetic improvements since 1998, maintaining its place as a vibrant center for Milwaukee entertainment, sports and culture
Opened: 1998
Seating Capacity: 4,087

8695
US CELLULAR ARENA
Wisconsin Center District
400 W Winconsin Avenue
Milwaukee, WI 53203
Phone: 414-908-6000
Fax: 414-908-6010
Web Site: www.uscellulararena.com
Officers:
   President: Richards A Geyer
Management:
   Box Office Manager: Donna Piotrowski
   Director Marketing/Sales: Sandra A Lange
   Director Event Services: David Anderson
   Director Business Development: Richard Freiberg
   PR/Promotions: David Snyder
Seating Capacity: 12,600

8696
MONROE ARTS CENTER
PO Box 472
Monroe, WI 53566
Phone: 608-325-5700
Fax: 608-325-5701
e-mail: info@monroeartscenter.com
Web Site: www.monroeartscenter.com
Management:
   President: Barbara Woodriff
   Executive Director: Richard Daniels
   Assistant Director: Lori Grinnell
Founded: 1976
Status: Non-Profit, Professional
Paid Staff: 5
Paid Artists: 18

8697
GRAND OPERA HOUSE
100 High Avenue
PO Box 1004
Oshkosh, WI 54901
Phone: 920-424-2350
Fax: 920-424-2357
Toll-free: 866-964-7263
e-mail: grandinfo@grandoperahouse.org
Web Site: www.grandoperahouse.org
Officers:
   President: Kelly Laux
   President-Elect: Ron Johnson
   Secretary: James Macy
   Treasurer: Randy Hedge
Management:
   Executive Director: Joseph A Ferlo
   Development Manager: Jeff Potts
   Event Manager: David Lange
Founded: 1883
Specialized Field: All
Status: Non-Profit, Professional
Paid Staff: 7
Volunteer Staff: 100
Non-paid Artists: 20
Budget: $500,000
Income Sources: Public; Private
Affiliations: City of Oshkosh
Stage Dimensions: 30'x30'
Seating Capacity: 668
Year Built: 1883
Year Remodeled: 1986
Rental Contact: Merry Little

8698
PIONEER FIELD
University of Wisconsin
1 University Plaza
Platteville, WI 53818-3099
Phone: 608-342-1125
Fax: 608-342-1122
Toll-free: 800-362-5515
e-mail: admit@uwplatt.edu
Web Site: www.uwplatt.edu
Officers:
   President: Martin Hubman
   VP: Haley Norpel
   Secretary: Brandom Mackesey
   Treasurrer: Dr. Joanne Wilson
Management:
   Athletic Director: Mark Wolesworth
   Director Performing/Visual Arts: John Hassig
   Public Relations: Krystle Kurdi
   Krystle: Hassig Director Performing/
Seating Capacity: 10,000

8699
RICHARD & HELEN BRODBECK CONCERT HALL
University of Wisconsin-Platteville
Center for the Arts
One University Plaza
Platteville, WI 53818-3099
Phone: 608-342-1125
Fax: 608-342-1122
Toll-free: 800-362-5515
e-mail: admit@uwplatt.edu
Web Site: www.uwplatt.edu
Officers:
   President: Martin Hubman
   VP: Haley Norpel
   Secretary: Brandom Mackesey
   Treasurrer: Dr. Joanne Wilson

All listings are in alphabetical order by state, then city, then organization within the city.

FACILITIES / Wyoming

Management:
   Director Performing/Visual Arts: John Hassig
   Public Relations: Krystle Kurdi
   Athletic Director: Mark Wolesworth
   Athletic Director: Mark Wolesworth
Mission: The Center for the Arts (CFA) provides a professional performing arts environment for the campus and community to experience the arts through classroom learning and quality cultural and performing arts performances.
Founded: 1866
Specialized Field: Dance, Drama, Children's Theater, Orchestra Concerts, Choral, Jazz, Recitals, Performing Arts Series, and the Heartland Festival
Paid Staff: 1
Income Sources: Box office, grants, student support
Facility Category: Concert Hall, Theatre House
Type of Stage: Proscenium
Orchestra Pit: y
Seating Capacity: 565

8700
THEATER
University of Wisconsin-Platteville
Center for the Arts
One University Plaza
Platteville, WI 53818-3099
Phone: 608-342-1125
Fax: 608-342-1122
Toll-free: 800-362-5515
e-mail: admit@uwplatt.edu
Web Site: www.uwplatt.edu
Officers:
   President: Martin Hubman
   VP: Haley Norpel
   Secretary: Brandom Mackesey
   Treasurrer: Dr. Joanne Wilson
Management:
   Director Performing/Visual Arts: John Hassig
   Public Relations: Krystle Kurdi
   Athletic Director: Mark Wolesworth
   Athletic Director: Mark Wolesworth
Mission: The Center for the Arts (CFA) provides a professional performing arts environment for the campus and community to experience the arts through classroom learning and quality cultural and performing arts performances.
Founded: 1866
Specialized Field: Dance, Drama, Children's Theater, Orchestra Concerts, Choral, Jazz, Recitals, Performing Arts Series, and the Heartland Festival
Paid Staff: 1
Income Sources: Box office, grants, student support
Facility Category: Concert Hall, Theatre House
Type of Stage: Flexible
Orchestra Pit: y
Seating Capacity: 200

8701
RACINE CIVIC CENTER- FESTIVAL HALL & PARK &MEMORIAL HALL
5 5th St
Racine, WI 53403
Phone: 262-636-9229
Fax: 262-619-2518
e-mail: info@racinecc.com
Web Site: www.racinecc.com
Mission: multipurpose auditorium space
Seating Capacity: 1530

8702
DEMMER RECITAL HALL
Ripon College
Rodman Arts Center, 300 Seward Street
Ripon, WI 54971
Mailing Address: Box 248
Phone: 414-748-8120
Fax: 414-748-9262

8703
FINE ARTS THEATRE
36 Biltmore Avenue
Sheboygan, WI 28801
Phone: 414-459-6600
Fax: 920-459-6602
Toll-free: 828-232-1568
Web Site: www.fineartheater.com

8704
JOHN MICHAEL KOHLER ARTS CENTER
608 New York Avenue
Sheboygan, WI 53081
Phone: 920-458-6144
Fax: 920-458-4473
e-mail: rkohler@jmkac.org
Web Site: www.jmkac.org
Management:
   President: Marty Crneckiy
   Director: Ruth Deyoung
Founded: 1967
Status: Non-Profit, Professional
Paid Staff: 35

8705
LUCILLE TACK CENTER FOR THE ARTS
300 School Street
PO Box 337
Spencer, WI 54479
Phone: 715-659-5347
Fax: 715-659-5470
Web Site: www.spencer.k12.wi.us/ltca
Management:
   Executive Director: Deborah Janz
Mission: To provide an environment that encourage a variety of opportunities to enlighten, enrich and develop activity growth for community members of all ages.
Founded: 1995
Status: Non-Profit, Professional
Paid Staff: 1
Volunteer Staff: 50
Seating Capacity: 500

8706
ST. CROIX FESTIVAL THEATRE
PO Box 801
St. Croix Falls, WI 54024
Phone: 715-483-3387
Web Site: www.festivaltheatre.org
Founded: 1990
Specialized Field: Theater
Status: Non-Equity; Nonprofit
Season: July - December
Type of Stage: Thrust
Seating Capacity: 260

8707
QUANDT FIELDHOUSE
2100 Main Street Stevens Point
2050 Fourth Avenue
Stevens Point, WI 54481
Phone: 715-346-0123
Fax: 715-346-4365
e-mail: gdiekroe@uwsp.edu
Web Site: www.uwsp.edu
Management:
   Assistant Director: Greg Diekroeger
   Chancellor: Bernie L. Patterson
   Interim Provost: Greg Summers
Seating Capacity: 3,500

8708
MANION THEATRE
University of Wisconsin-Superior
Superior, WI 54880
Mailing Address: PO Box 2000
Phone: 715-394-8369
Fax: 715-394-8065
Web Site: www.uwsuperior.edu
Management:
   Theatre Director: Cathy Fank
Status: Non-Profit, Non-Professional

8709
WAUKESHA CIVIC THEATRE
Margaret Brate Bryant Civic Theatre
264 W Main Street
Waukesha, WI 53186
Phone: 262-547-4911
Fax: 262-547-8454
e-mail: planious@waukeshacivictheatre.com
Web Site: ww.waukeshacivictheatre.com
Founded: 1957

8710
IRVIN L. YOUNG AUDITORIUM
University of Wisconsin-Whitewater
930 West Main Street
Whitewater, WI 53190
Phone: 262-472-2222
Fax: 262-472-4400
e-mail: youngaud@uww.edu
Web Site: www.uww.edu/youngauditorium
Management:
   Director: Ken Kohberger
   Marketing: Leslie LaMuro
   Assistant Manager: Malina Hunter
Opened: 1991
Seating Capacity: 1,289

8711
WARHAWK STADIUM
University of Wisconsin
800 W Main Street
Whitewater, WI 53190
Phone: 414-472-1234
Fax: 414-472-2791
e-mail: myersw.wwwvax.uww.edu
Web Site: www.uww.edu
Officers:
   Provost & Vice Chancellor: Beverly Kopper
Management:
   Athletic Director: Willie Myers
   Athletic Director/Women's: Dianne Jones
Seating Capacity: 11,500

Wyoming

8712
CASPER EVENTS CENTER
1 Events Drive
PO Box 128
Casper, WY 82601

FACILITIES / Wyoming

Phone: 307-235-8400
Fax: 307-235-8445
Toll-free: 800-442-2256
e-mail: tcanepa@cityofcasperwy.com
Web Site: www.caspereventscenter.com
Management:
   Director: Max Torbert
   Marketing Director: Tiffine Canepa
   Box Office Manager: Carmen Mills
   Operations Manager: Bud Dovala
Seating Capacity: 10,452
Year Built: 1982

8713
DURHAM HALL
Casper College
125 College Drive
Casper, WY 82601
Phone: 307-268-2110
Fax: 307-268-3023
Toll-free: 800-442-2963
Web Site: www.caspercollege.edu
Management:
   Executive Director: Eric Unruh
   Director: Kyla Foltz
Founded: 1940
Status: Non-Profit, Professional
Paid Staff: 23

8714
CHEYENNE CIVIC CENTER
2101 O'Neil Avenue
Cheyenne, WY 82001
Phone: 307-637-6363
Fax: 307-637-6365
e-mail: drohla@cheyennecity.org
Web Site: www.cheyenneciviccenter.org
Management:
   Executive Director: Dru A Rohla
Founded: 1981
Status: Non-Profit, Professional
Paid Staff: 105

8715
FRONTIER PARK
4610 Carey Avenue
Cheyenne, WY 82001
Mailing Address: PO Box 2477
Phone: 307-778-7200
Fax: 307-778-7213
e-mail: dave@cfdrodeo.com
Web Site: www.cfdrodeo.com
Management:
   Director: Dave Johansen
   Marketing Manager: Nicole Gamst
Seating Capacity: 24,000

8716
THE IKON CENTER
1530 West Lincolnway
Cheyenne, WY 82001
Phone: 307-433-0024
Fax: 307-433-0027
Web Site: www.ikoncenter.com
Management:
   GM: Ron Byrne
Opened: 2000
Seating Capacity: 2,500

8717
CAM-PLEX HERITAGE CENTER
1635 Reata Drive
Gillette, WY 82718
Phone: 307-682-0552
Fax: 307-682-8418
Toll-free: 800-358-1897
e-mail: camplex@vcn.com
Web Site: www.cam-plex.com
Management:
   Theatre Manager: Phyllis Colpitts
   GM: Dan Barks
   Marketing: Elle Picket
   Operations Manager: Jimmy Williama

8718
UNIVERSITY OF WYOMING: ARTS AND SCIENCES AUDITORIUM
109 Knight Hall
Laramie, WY 82071
Phone: 307-766-3073
Fax: 307-766-4010
e-mail: udss@uwyo.edu
Web Site: www.uwyo.edu
Management:
   Head Football Coach: Vick Koenning
   Head Basketball Coach (M): Steve McClain
   Head Basketball Coach (W): Cindy Fisher
   Athletic Director: Lee Moon
   Associate Athletic Director: Keener Fry

8719
UNIVERSITY OF WYOMING: FINE ARTS CONCERT HALL
110 Knight Hall
Laramie, WY 82071
Phone: 307-766-3073
Fax: 307-766-4010
e-mail: udss@uwyo.edu
Web Site: www.uwyo.edu
Management:
   Head Football Coach: Vick Koenning
   Head Basketball Coach (M): Steve McClain
   Head Basketball Coach (W): Cindy Fisher
   Athletic Director: Lee Moon
   Associate Athletic Director: Keener Fry

8720
WAR MEMORIAL STADIUM (WY)
University of Wyoming
Dept 3414, 1000 E University Avenue
Laramie, WY 82071
Phone: 307-766-2292
Fax: 307-766-5414
e-mail: wyosid@uwyo.edu
Web Site: www.wyomingathletics.com
Officers:
   President: Tom Buchanan
Management:
   President: Philip Dubois
   Athletic Director: Gary A Barta
   Sports Informations Director: Kevin McKinney
Founded: 1869
Status: For-Profit, Non-Professional
Paid Staff: 100
Seating Capacity: 33,500

8721
COMMUNITY FINE ARTS CENTER
400 C Street
Rock Springs, WY 82901
Phone: 307-362-6212
Fax: 307-352-6657
Web Site: www.cfac4art.com
Officers:
   Chairman: Kim Lopiccolo
   Vice Chairman: Kari Martin
   Secretary: Katie Pastor
   Treasurer: David Kathka
Management:
   Executive Director: Debra Soule
   Messer: Jennifer
   Christoffersen: Assistant Doris
Founded: 1970
Specialized Field: American Art Work
Status: Non-Profit, Professional
Paid Staff: 3

8722
WYO THEATER
42 North Main Street
PO Box 528
Sheridan, WY 82801
Phone: 307-672-9083
Fax: 307-672-8074
e-mail: execdir@wyotheater.com
Web Site: www.wyotheater.com
Officers:
   Chairman: Jerry Pilch
   Vicechairman: Liana Huey
   Secretary: Rock Sathre
   Treasurer: Cheri Wilson
Management:
   Executive Director: Nick Johnson
   Technical Director: Pam Thompson
   Box Office Manager: Curt Sare
   Business Office: Carlyn King
Mission: Since reopening in 1989 the WYO has brought countless hours of live entertainment, cultural enrichment, and educational opportunities to the greater Sheridan community.
Founded: 1923
Status: Non-Profit, Professional
Paid Staff: 1

INFORMATION RESOURCES / Associations

Associations

8723
Academy of Country Music
5500 Balboa Blvd
Suite 200
Encino, CA 91316-1505
818-788-8000
FAX 818-788-0999
E-Mail: info@acmcountry.com
Home Page: www.acmcountry.com

Gayle Holcomb, Chairman
David Young, Director Operations
Tiffany Moon, Secretary
Brandi Brammer, Project Manager
Tree Paine, Director Marketing

Involved in numerous events and activities promoting country music. Presents annual awards.
4M Members
Founded in 1964

8724
Academy of Motion Picture Arts and Sciences
8949 Wilshire Blvd
Beverly Hills, CA 90211-1972
310-247-3000
FAX 310-271-3395
Home Page: www.oscars.org
Social Media: *Facebook, Twitter, LinkedIn, Youtube*

The Academy was founded to advance the arts and sciences of motion pictures; foster cooperation among creative leaders for cultural, educational and technological progress; recognize outstanding achievments; cooperate on technical research and improvement of methods and equipment; provide a common forum and meeting ground for various branches and crafts; represent the viewpoint of actual creators of the motion picture. Hosts annual Academy Awards.
6000 Members
Founded in 1927

8725
Academy of Science Fiction Fantasy and Horror Films
334 W 54th St
Los Angeles, CA 90037-3806
323-752-5811
FAX 323-752-5811
E-Mail: scifiacademy@ca.rr.com
Home Page: www.saturnawards.org

Robert Holguin, President
Roger Fenton, VP
Michael Laster, Director

Culminated from the Count Dracula Society, the Academy hosts the annual Science Fiction Film Awards, called the Saturn Awards.
Founded in 1972

8726
Accordian Federation of North America
14126 E Rosencrans Boulevard
Santa Fe Springs, CA 90670
562-921-5058
E-Mail: afna@musician.org
Home Page: www.afnafestival.org
Social Media: *Facebook, Twitter,*

Madeleine D'Ablaing, President
Debbie Gray, VP
Oakley Yale, Secretary
Prisscilla Martinez, Treasurer
Larry Demian, Parliamentarian

Members are primarily teachers and music school owners with the primary purpose to encourage young people to pursue their music study. Holds festivals and competitions
75 Members
Founded in 1972

8727
Accordion Teachers Guild
10349 Century,Lane
Overland Park, KS 66215
913-722-5625
E-Mail: Betty@BettyJoSimon.com
Home Page: www.accordions.com/atg

Betty Jo Simon, President
Liz Finch, First VP
Amy Jo Sawyer, Second VP
Joan C. Sommers, Executive Secretary
John Neu, Treasurer

ATG members are accordion teachers and professionals committed to furthering the progress of the accordion by improving teaching standards, music and all phases of music education.
Founded in 1940

8728
Acoustical Society of America
2 Huntington Quadrangle
Suite 1NO1
Melville, NY 11747-4502
516-576-2360
FAX 516-576-2377
E-Mail: asa@aip.org
Home Page: www.acousticalsociety.org

David Bradley, President
Michael Stinson, Vice President
David Feit, Treasurer
Paul Shomer, Standards Director
Charles Schmid, Executive Director

Premier international scientific society in acoustics, dedicated to increasing and diffusing the knowledge of acoustics and its practical applications.

8729
Actors Equity Association
165 W 46th St
New York, NY 10036-2500
212-869-8530
FAX 212-719-9815
Home Page: www.actorsequity.org

Alan Eisenberg, CEO
Mark Zimmerman, President
David Lotz, National Director of Communications
Mary Lou Westerfield, Natioanl Director Policy
Flora Stamatiades, National Director Organizing

A labor union that represents Actors and Stage Managers in the United States. Seeks to advance, promote and foster the art of live theatre as an essential component of our society. Negotiates wages and working conditions and provides a wide range of benefits, including health and pension plans.
45000 Members
Founded in 1913

8730
American Alliance for Theatre and Education
4908 Auburn Avenue
Bethesda, MD 20814-3474
301-200-1944
FAX 301-280-1682
E-Mail: info@aate.com
Home Page: www.aate.com
Social Media: *Facebook,*

Jo B.Gonzalez, President
Rachel Prouty, Treasurer
Amy P.Jenson, Advocacy Director
Jeremy Kisling, Communications Director
Mitch Mattson, Planning Director

The national voice for theatre and education, representing artists and educators serving young people in theatre and education. Its members play a vital role in advocating for the interests of children who benefit from theatre in their communities and classrooms. AATE embraces diversity and encourages inclusion of all races, social classes, ages, genders, religions, sexual orientations, national organizations and abilities.
700 Members
Founded in 1986

8731
American Association of Community Theatre
1300 Gendy St Forth Worth
Lago Vista, TX 76107
817-732-3177
866-687-2228
FAX 817-732-3178
E-Mail: info@aact.org
Home Page: www.aact.org

Julie Crawford, Executive Director
Linda Lee, President
Gary Walker, Executive VP
Frank Peot, Secretary
Tim Jebsen, Treasurer

The national voice of community theatre, representing the interests of its members and over 7,000 theatres across the US and with the armed services overseas. Its mission is to foster the encouragement and development of, and commitment to, the highest standards by community theatres, including standards of excellence for production, management, governance, community relations and service.
1800 Members
Founded in 1986

8732
American Choral Directors Association
545 Couch Drive
Oklahoma City, OK 73102
405-232-8161
FAX 405-232-8162
Home Page: www.acdaonline.org

Timothy Sharp, Executive Director
Jerry Mccoy, President
Haiary Aphelstadt, VP
Jo-Ann Miller, Treasurer

Nonprofit music-education organization whose central purpose is to promote excellence in choral music through performance, composition, publication, research and teaching. In addition, ACDA strives to elevate choral music's position in American society through arts advocacy. Holds annual convention.
Cost: $90
19500 Members
Founded in 1959

8733
American Cinema Editors
100 Universal City Plaza
Verna Fields Building 2282 Room 190
Universal City, CA 91608
818-777-2900
FAX 818-733-5023
E-Mail: americancinema@earthlink.net

INFORMATION RESOURCES / Associations

Home Page: www.ace-filmeditors.org
Social Media: Facebook, Twitter,

Alan Heim, President
Stephen Rivkin, VP
Lillian Bennson, Secretary
Ed Abroms, Treasurer
Jan Ambler, A.C.E

A non-profit corporation committed to the encouragement of mutually-beneficial dialogue with other members of the motion picture industry and to educating the general public. Holds the annual ACE Eddie Awards honoring the nominees for the Film Editing Award given by the Academy of Motion Pictures Arts and Sciences.
Founded in 1950

8734
American College of Musicians
PO Box 1807
Austin, TX 78767
512-478-5775
FAX 512-478-5843
E-Mail: ngpt@pianoguild.com
Home Page: www.pianoguild.com

Richard Allison, President
Julia Kruger, VP

Provides student awards and teachers benefits.
Founded in 1931

8735
American Dance Therapy Association
10632 Little Patuxent Pkwy
Suite 108
Columbia, MD 21044-3263
410-997-4040
FAX 410-997-4048
E-Mail: info@adta.org
Home Page: www.adta.org

Gloria Farrow, Manager
Jody Wager, VP
Gloria J Farrow, Operations Director
Meghan Dempsey, Treasurer
Ty Tedmon Jones, Secretary

Professional organization of dance movement therapists, with members both nationally and internationally; offers training, research findings, and a newsletter. Holds annual conference.
1.1M Members
Founded in 1966

8736
American Disc Jockey Association
20118 N 67th Avenue
Suite 300-605
Glendale, AZ 85308
888-723-5776
888-723-5776
FAX 866-310-4676
E-Mail: office@adja.org
Home Page: www.adja.org
Social Media: Facebook, Twitter, YouTube

Rob Snyder, Director

An association of professional mobile entertainers. Encourages success for its members through continuous education, camaraderie, and networking. The primary goal is to educate Disc Jockeys so that each member acts ethically and responsibly.

8737
American Federation of Musicians of the United States and Canada
1501 Broadway
Suite 600
New York, NY 10036-5501
212-869-1330
FAX 212-764-6134
E-Mail: info@afm.org
Home Page: www.afm.org

Thomas Lee, President
Linda Patterson, Executive Secreatry to President

AFM is an association of professional musicians united through their locals so that they can live and work in dignity; produce work that will be fulfilling and compensated fairly; have a meaningful voice in decisions that affect them; have the opportunity to develop their talents and skills; whose collective voice and power will be realized in a democratic and progressive union; and who oppose the forces of exploitation through their union solidarity.
10K Members
Founded in 1896

8738
American Federation of Violin and Bow Makers
1121 East Avenue
Red Wing, MN 55066
507-396-3411
E-Mail: info@afvbm.org
Home Page: www.afvbm.com

Peter Seman, President
Yung Chin, Vice President
William Scott, Treasurer
Lisbeth N.Butler, Secretary

Members are those with recognized professional abilities and experience in either making or repairing violins and bows. They are elected to the Federation and are entitled to all privileges and duties of membership. The Federation has designed programs to held develop the technical skills and knowledge of the membership through seminars and regular meeting events. The Federation sponsors exhibitions as a forum for makers, musicians and the general public.
Cost: $300
Founded in 1980

8739
American Guild of Music
PO Box 599
Warren, MI 48090
248-686-1975
E-Mail: agm@americanguild.org
Home Page: www.americanguild.org

Barry Carr, President
Joanne Darby, Treasurer
Lorelei Eccleston Dart, First VP
Steve Petrunak, Second VP

The worls's oldest international music organization. Its membership is oipen to independent music teachers, music store owners and their teaching staffs, music publishers and instrument manufacturers and music students.
6000 Members

8740
American Guild of Musical Artists
1430 Broadway
14th Floor
New York, NY 10018-3308
212-265-3687
FAX 212-262-9088
E-Mail: agma@musicalartists.org
Home Page: www.musicalartists.org
Social Media: Facebook,

Alan S.Gordon, Executive Director
Gerry Angel, Director of Operations
Deborah A.Maher, Associate Executive Director
Gerry Angel, Director of Operations

AGMA is a labor union. It negotiates collective bargaining agreements for its members that provide them with these vital benefits: guaranteed salaries; rehearsal and overtime pay; regulated work hours; vacation and sick pay; access to low-cost health benefits; good-faith resolution of disputes; and protection of their legal and contractual rights.
5700 Members
Founded in 1936

8741
American Guild of Organists
475 Riverside Drive
Suite 1260
New York, NY 10115-0055
212-870-2310
FAX 212-870-2163
E-Mail: info@agohq.org
Home Page: www.agohq.org

James Thomashower, Executive Director
Marcia Van Oyen, Director

Membership in the American Guild of Organists is primarily through local chapters, which hold regular meetings featuring performances, lectures, seminars, and discussions on a wide variety of topics. Many chapters also offer monthly newsletters, scholarship programs, musician placement services, and substitute referrals to employing institutions. Membership can also be without chapter affiliation.
20000 Members
Founded in 1896

8742
American Harp Society
PO Box 278
Greenfield Center, NY 12833
518-893-7495
E-Mail: elizabetharp@juno.com
Home Page: www.harpsociety.org

Delaine Fedson, President
Randall Pratt, 1st VP
Lillian Lau, 2nd VP
Jaymee Haefner, Secretary
Ashanti Pretlow, Executive Secretary

Promotes and fosters the appreciation of the harp as a musical instrument, to encourage the composition of music for the harp and to improve the quality of performance of harpists.
Cost: $50
3000 Members
Founded in 1962

8743
American Indian Registry for the Performing Arts
1717 N Highland
Suite 614
Los Angeles, CA 90028
213-962-6574
Home Page: www.afn.org/~native/orgnztns.htm

Organization of American Indian performers and technical personnel in the entertainment field.

1049

INFORMATION RESOURCES / Associations

8744
American Institute of Organ Builders
PO Box 35306
Canton, OH 44735
330-806-9011
E-Mail: robert_sullivan@pipeorgan.org
Home Page: www.pipeorgan.org
Social Media: *Twitter,*

Matthew M Bellocchio, President
Patrick J. Murphy, Vice President
Louis E Patterson, Secretary
Charles R Eames, Treasurer

Sponsors training seminars, quarterly journal and annual convention for pipe organ builders and service technicians.
385 Members
Founded in 1974
Mailing list available for rent: 350 names at $250 per M

8745
American Music Therapy Association
8455 Colesville Rd
Suite 1000
Silver Spring, MD 20910-3392
301-589-3300
FAX 301-589-5175
E-Mail: info@musictherapy.org
Home Page: www.musictherapy.org

Andrea Farbman, Executive Director
Brian Abrams, Mid Atlantic Region President

The mission of the American Music Therapy Association is to advance public awareness of the benefits of music therapy and increase access to quality music therapy services in a rapidly changing world.
3800 Members
Founded in 1998

8746
American Musical Instrument Society
1106 Garden Street
Hoboken, NJ 07030
201-656-0107
E-Mail: amis@guildassoc.com
Home Page: www.amis.org
Social Media: *Facebook,*

Albert R Rice, President
Carolyn Bryant, Vice-President
Deborah Check Reeves, Secretary
Joanne Kopp, Treasurer

Promotes better understanding of all aspects of history, design, construction, restoration, and usage of musical instruments in all cultures and from all periods. The membership of AMIS includes collectors, historians, curators, performers, instrument makers, restorers, dealers, conservators, teachers, students, and many institutional members.
Founded in 1971

8747
American Musicological Society
6010 College Station
Brunswick, ME 04011-8451
207-798-4243
877-679-7648
FAX 877-679-7648
E-Mail: ams@ams-net.org
Home Page: www.ams-net.org

Robert Judd, Executive Director

Advances research in the various fields of music as a branch of learning and scholarship.
3600 Members
Founded in 1934

8748
American Orff-Schulwerk Association
PO Box 391089
Cleveland, OH 44139-8089
440-543-5366
FAX 440-600-7332
E-Mail: info@aosa.org
Home Page: www.aosa2.org

Katharine P. Johnson, Executive Director
Jo Ella Hug, President
Julie Scott, VP
Jennifer Hartman, Treasurer

Professional organization of music and movement educators dedicated to the creative teaching approach developed by Carl Orff and Gunild Keetman.
Cost: $70

8749
American School Band Directors Association
227 N 1st Street
PO Box 696
Guttenberg, IA 52052-0696
563-252-2500
FAX 563-252-2500
E-Mail: asbda@alpinecom.net
Home Page: www.asbda.com
Social Media: *Facebook,*

Kebin Beaber, President
Valerie Gaffney, Secretary
Blair Callaway, Treasurer
Dennis Hanna, Manager
Russ Hilton, Treasurer

Nationwide organization dedicated to the support of professional and college band conductors. Membership by invitation only.
1200 Members
Founded in 1953

8750
American Society of Cinematographers
1782 N Orange Drive
PO Box 2230
Hollywood, CA 90028
323-969-4333
800-448-0145
FAX 323-882-6391
E-Mail: office@theasc.com
Home Page: www.theasc.com
Social Media: *Facebook,*

Daryn Okadaan, President
Michael Negrin, Secretary
Victor J Kemper, Treasurer

The ASC is not a labor union or guild, but is an educational, cultural and professional organization. Membership is possible by invitation and is extended only to directors of photography with distinguished credits in the industry. Publishes 'American Cinematographer' magazine.
Founded in 1919

8751
American Society of Composers, Authors and Publishers (ASCAP)
1 Lincoln Plaza
New York, NY 10023-7097
212-621-6000
FAX 212-621-8453
E-Mail: info@ascap.com
Home Page: www.ascap.com

Paul Williams, President/Chairman
James M Kendrick, Treasurer
Kathyr Spanberger, Secretary
John Lofrumento, CEO

Performing rights organization created and controlled by composers, songwriters and music publishers. Protects the rights of its members by licensing and distributing royalties for the non-dramatic public performances of their copyrighted works. An online newsletter is also available filled with the most up-to-date information about professional opportunities, legislative issues, member benefits and more.
26000 Members
Founded in 1914

8752
American Society of Music Arrangers and Composers
5903 Noble Ave
Van Nuys, CA 91411-3026
818-994-4661
FAX 818-994-6181
E-Mail: asmac@theproperimageevents.com
Home Page: www.asmac.org
Social Media: *Facebook, Twitter, LinkedIn, Youtube*

Scherr Lillico, Executive Director
Duane L Tatro, Vice President
Ray Charles, Vice President

Professional society for arrangers, composers, orchestrators, and musicians. Monthly meetings with great speakers from the music industry.
500 Members
Founded in 1938

8753
American String Teachers Association
4155 Chain Bridge Rd
Fairfax, VA 22030-4102
703-279-2113
FAX 703-279-2114
E-Mail: asta@astaweb.com
Home Page: www.astaweb.com

Donna Hale, Executive Director
Beth Danner-Knight, Deputy Director
Mary Jane Dye, Deputy Director

A membership organization for string and orchestra teachers and players, helping them to develop and refine their careers. Members range from budding student teachers to artist-status performers, businesses who supply goods and services to the string and orchestra world plus colleges, universities, music programs and conservatories.
11300 Members
Founded in 1946

8754
American Viola Society
14070 Proton Rd
Suite 100
Dallas, TX 75244-3601
972-233-9107
FAX 972-490-4219
E-Mail: info@avsnationaloffice.org
Home Page: www.americanviolasociety.org
Social Media: *Facebook, Twitter,*

Nokunthula Ngwenyama, President
Madeline Crouch, General Manager
Karin Brown, Secretary
Michelle Sayles, Treasurer

An association for the promotion of viola performance and research. AVS membership is accompanied by two print issues of the Journal of the American Viola Society (JAVS) each year.
1000 Members

INFORMATION RESOURCES / Associations

8755
Art Directors Guild
11969 Ventura Blvd
Suite 200
Studio City, CA 91604-2619
818-762-9995
FAX 818-762-9997
E-Mail: lydia@artdirectors.org
Home Page: www.adg.org
Social Media: *Facebook, Twitter,*

Scott Roth, Executive Director
Lisa Frazza, Secretary
Michael Baugh, Treasurer
Alexandra Schaaf, Manager Membership Department

The creative talents that concieve and manage the background and settings for most films and television projects are members of the Art Directors Guild, Local 800. They and most other crafts of the entertainment industry are members of the International Alliance of Theatrical Stage Employees, Moving Picture Technicians, Artists and Allied Crafts of the United States, its Territories and Canada.
935 Members
Founded in 1937

8756
Assistant Directors Training Program
15301 Ventura Blvd.
Bldg E #1075
Sherman Oaks, CA 91403
818-386-2545
FAX 818-386-2876
E-Mail: mail@dgptp.org
Home Page: www.trainingplan.org

Tom Joyner, Chair

Provides motion picture and television industry training as directed by the Alliance of Motion Picture and Television Producers and the Directors Guild of America.
Founded in 1965

8757
Associated Pipe Organ Builders of America
PO Box 155
Chicago Ridge, IL 60415
800-473-5270
800-473-5270
Home Page: www.apoba.com

Bob Rusczyk, Executive Director
Richard Parsons, President
Paul Lytle, Vice President
Randall Dyer, Secretary
Seth Marshall, Treasurer

A professional association of North American firms engaged in building traditional pipe organs. Members are a select group of organbuilders who have passed stringent membership requirements which include commitment to principles regarding the use of electronic technology in organ building.
27 Members

8758
Association for Theatre in Higher Education
PO Box 1290
Boulder, CO 80306-1290
303-530-2167
888-284-3737
FAX 303-530-2168
E-Mail: info@athe.org
Home Page: www.athe.org

Bill Doane, President
Terry Brino Dean, Secretary
Nina Lenoir, Treasurer

ATHE serves the interests of its diverse individual and organization members. Its vision is to advocate for the field of theatre and performance in higher education. It serves as an intellectual and artistic center for producing new knowledge about theatre and performance-related disciplines. cultivating vital alliances with other scholarly and creative disciplines, linking with professional and community-based theatres, and promoting access and equity.
1700 Members
Founded in 1986

8759
Association of Arts Administration Educators
Bolz Center for Arts Administration
N4460 Allan Rd
Portage, WI 53901
608-561-2040
FAX 608-265-2735
E-Mail: info@artsadministration.org
Home Page: www.artsadministration.org

Andrew Taylor, President/Director
John McCann, VP
Phyllis Johnson, Treasurer
Stephen Boyle, Secretary

The Association of Administration Educators (AAAE) is an international organization incorporated as a nonprofit institution within the United States. Its mission is to represent college and university graduate and undergraduate programs in the arts administration, encompassing training in the management of visual, performing, literary, media, cultural and arts service organizations.
Founded in 1975

8760
Association of Cinema and Video Laboratories
Bev Wood C/O Deluxe Laboratories
1377 North Serrano Avenue
Hollywood, CA 90027
323-462-6171
FAX 206-682-6649
E-Mail: beverly.wood@bydeluxe.com
Home Page: www.acvl.org

Bev Wood, President
Chip Wilkenson, First VP
John Carlson, Second VP
Kevin Dillon, Treasurer
Bob Olson, Secretary

Provides opportunities for discussion and exchange of ideas in connection with administrative, technical and managerial problems in the motion picture and video industry. The Association is concerned with improvements in technical practices and procedures, public and industry relations, product specifications to vendors, the impact of current and impending governmental regulations, and any and all other areas of interest to the laboratory industry.
80 Members
Founded in 1953

8761
Association of Concert Bands
6613 Cheryl Ann Drive
Independence, OH 44131-3718
800-726-8720
FAX 216-524-1897
Home Page: www.acbands.org

Allen Beck, President
Nada Vencl, Secretary
Mike Montgomery, CIO
Howard Habenicht, Treasurer

The purpose of ACB is to encourage and foster adult concert community, municipal, and civic bands and to promote the performance of the highest quality traditional and contemporary literature for band.
750 Members
Founded in 1977

8762
Association of Hispanic Arts
P.O.Box 1169
El Barrio, NY 10029
212-876-1242
888-876-1240
FAX 212-876-1285
E-Mail: informacion@latinoarts.org
Home Page: www.latinoarts.org

Nicholas L Arture, Executive Director
Julia L Gutierrez-Rivera, Program Officer/Arts Service Coord.
Crystal Chaparro, Office Assistant
Gregory Castro, Comptroller
Brenda L Jiminez, Board Chair

A nonprofit arts service organization serving the Latino arts and cultural community. AHA was established out of the need to create funding and presenting opportunities for individual Latino artists and cultural organizations whose contributions were unrecognized and whose efforts were underserved by mainstream public and private institutions.
Founded in 1975

8763
Association of Performing Arts Presenters
1211 Connecticut Ave NW
Suite 200
Washington, DC 20036-2716
202-833-2787
888-820-2787
FAX 202-833-1543
E-Mail: info@artspresenters.org
Home Page: www.artspresenters.org
Social Media: *Facebook, Twitter,*

Sandra Gibson, President
Josh Labelle, Chair
Terri Trotter, Vice Chairman
Johann Zietsman, Vice Chair

A national membership and advocacy organization dedicated to bringing performing artists and audiences together.
1900 Members
Founded in 1957

8764
Association of Talent Agents
9255 Sunset Blvd
Suite 930
Los Angeles, CA 90069-3317
310-274-0628
FAX 310-274-5063
E-Mail: shellie@agentassociation.com
Home Page: www.agentassociation.com

Sandy Bresler, President
Sheldon Sroloff, VP
Jim Gosnell, Secretary/Treasurer
Karen Stuart, Executive Director
Shellie Jetton, Administrative Director

A non-profit trade association representing talent agencies in the industry. ATA is the voice of unified talent and

INFORMATION RESOURCES / Associations

literary agencies. ATA agencies represent the vast majority of working artists, including actors, directors, writers, and other artists in film, stage, television, radio, commercial, literary work, and other entertainment enterprises.
Founded in 1937

8765
Blues Foundation
421 S.Main St
Memphis, TN 38103-4464
901-527-2583
FAX 901-529-4030
E-Mail: jay@blues.org
Home Page: www.blues.org
Social Media: *Facebook, Twitter, LinkedIn, YouTube, RSS*

Jay Sieleman, President
Joey Whitmer, DeputuDirector
Cindy James, Membership
Chadd Webb, Treasurer

A nonprofit corporation which serves as the hub for the worldwide passion for Blues Music.
Founded in 1980

8766
Broadcast Music Incorporated BMI
7 World Trade Center
250 Greenwich Street
New York, NY 10007-0030
212-220-3000
FAX 212-246-2163
E-Mail: newyork@bmi.com
Home Page: www.bmi.com
Social Media: *Facebook, Twitter,*

Del Bryant, CEO
John E Cody, COO/Executive VP

American performing rights organization that represents approximately 300,000 songwriters, composers and music publishers in all genres of music. The nonprofit company collects license fees on behalf of those American creators it represents, as well as thousands of creators from around the world who chose BMI for representation in the US. These fees are then distributed as royalties to the writers, composers and copyright holders it represents.
300m Members
Founded in 1939

8767
Casting Society of America
606 N Larchmont Blvd
Los Angeles, CA 90004-1309
323-463-1925
FAX 323-463-4753
E-Mail: info@castingsociety.com
Home Page: www.castingsociety.com

Larry Raab, Manager

CSA is the largest professional association of Casting Directors in the world. They work in all areas of entertainment in film, television and theatre. CSA continually seeks to expand their standing in the industry by providing information and opportunities that support is members.
500+ Members
Founded in 1982

8768
Chamber Music America
99 Madison Avenue
5th Floor
New York, NY 10016
212-242-2022
FAX 646-430-5667
Home Page: www.chamber-music.org

Susan Dadian, Program Director
Margaret M Lioi, CEO
Louise Smith, Chair

Promotes artistic excellence and economic stability within the profession and to ensure that chamber music is a vital part of American life. Their vision is that chamber music serves as a model of cooperation and collaboration, that audiences become more committed to supporting chamber music and the professionals who devote their lives to this art form, and that opportunities for the performance of chamber music increase in traditional concert venues and beyond.
Founded in 1977

8769
Children in Film
11271 Ventura Blvd.
Studio City, CA 91604
818-432-7400
800-902-9001
E-Mail: contact@childreninfilm.com
Home Page: www.childreninfilm.com

Toni Casala, Founder & President
Trisha Noble, Director, Permit Services
Heather Broeker, Director, Marketing

To provide tools and information needed to successfully employ a child in the entertainment industry while also lending a healthy, positive view into the world of child actors.
Founded in 2000

8770
Chinese Music Society of North America
PO Box 5275
Woodridge, IL 60517-0275
630-910-1551
FAX 630-910-1561
Home Page: www.chinesemusic.net

Sin-Yan Shen, President
Kok-Koon Ng, VP
Yuan-Yuan Lee, Executive Director
Billie Jefferson, Artistic Administrator
Der-Tung Yuan, Membership

A national nonprofit organization founded to increase and diffuse the knowledge of Chinese music and performing arts. Today it has grown to become the national association of Chinese musicians and scholars and National and International organization specializing in Research and Educational Material in English concerning Music/Theater/Dance and Musical Instruments from China and Non-Western Cultures.
Founded in 1969

8771
Chorus America
1156 15th St NW
Suite 310
Washington, DC 20005-1747
202-331-7577
FAX 202-331-7599
E-Mail: service@chorusamerica.org
Home Page: www.chorusamerica.org
Social Media: *Facebook, Twitter, Youtube*

Ann Meier Baker, President & Chief Executive Officer
Rollo Dilworth, Chairman
Michael McCarthy, Treasurer

Chorus America's mission is to build a dynamic and inclusive choral community so that more people are enriched by the beauty and power of choral singing.
2100 Members
Founded in 1977

8772
Classical Action
165 W 46th St
Suite 1300
New York, NY 10036-2514
212-997-7717
FAX 212-840-0551
E-Mail: classicalaction@broadwaycares.org
Home Page: www.classicalaction.org
Social Media: *Facebook, Twitter,*

Charles Hamlen, Founding Director
Chris Kenney, Associate Director

Since 1993, Classical Action has provided a unified voice for all those within the performing arts community to help combat HIV/AIDS and the devastating effects of this epidemic.
Founded in 1993

8773
College Music Society
312 E Pine St
Missoula, MT 59802-4624
406-721-9616
FAX 406-721-9419
E-Mail: cms@music.org
Home Page: www.music.org
Social Media: *Facebook, Twitter,*

Robby D Gunstream, Executive Director
David B. Williams, President

A consortium of college, conservatory, university and independent musicians and scholars interested in all disciplines of music. Its mission is to promote music teaching and learning, musical creativity and expression, research and dialogue, and diversity and interdisciplinary interaction.
9500 Attendees
Founded in 1958

8774
Conductors Guild
719 Twinridge Ln
Richmond, VA 23235
804-553-1378
FAX 804-553-1876
E-Mail: guild@conductorsguild.org
Home Page: www.conductorsguild.org

Amanda Burton Winger, Executive Director
Scott Winger, Assistant Director
David Leibowitz, Editor
Rufus Jones Jr, Editor

The Conductors Guild is the only music service organization devoted exclusively to the advancement of the art of conducting and to serving the artistic and professional needs of conductors.
1850+ Members
Founded in 1975

8775
Congress on Research in Dance
SUNY College of Brockport
3416 Primm Lane
Birmingham, AL 35216
205-823-5517
FAX 205-823-2760
E-Mail: ashanti@cordance.org
Home Page: www.cordance.org

Marta Savigliano, President
Helen Thomas, Chair, Editorial Board

INFORMATION RESOURCES / Associations

A not-for-profit, interdisciplinary organization with an open, international membership. Its purposes are: to encourage research in all aspects of dance, including related fields; to foster the exchange of ideas, resources, and methodology, through publication, international and regional conferences and workshops; to promote the accessibility of research materials.
Cost: $35
750 Members
Founded in 1965
Mailing list available for rent

8776
Contemporary Record Society
724 Winchester Road
Broomall, PA 19008
610-544-5920
FAX 610-544-5920
E-Mail: crsnews@verizon.net
Home Page:
www.mysite.verizon.net/vzeeewvp/contemporaryrecordsociety/

Caroline Hunt, Contact

Promotes both a fellowship in the musical arts between artists, composers and presenters and commercial recordingsa of participants in this endeavor. The intent of the Society is to advance the cause of music in the United States and throughout the world, promoting an association among its constituents. The scope of the Society's repertoire includes the musical masterworks of both well-known and relatively unknown composers of all periods.
Cost: $45
Founded in 1981

8777
Country Dance & Song Society
116 Pleasant St
Suite 345
Easthampton, MA 01027-2759
413-203-5467
FAX 413-203-5471
E-Mail: office@cdss.org
Home Page: www.cdss.org

Rima Dael, Executive/Artistic Director
Carol Compton, Financial Manager
Christine Dadmun, Membership Admin
Bob Blondin, Business Manager
Robin Hayden, Development Director

A national organization dedicated to the preservation and promotion of English and Anglo-American traditional and historical folk dance, music and song. Composed of individual members and affiliate groups, it functions both as an international service bureau and as a facilitator in building and maintaining local and regional dance, music and song communities. It exists to meed needs for community-based activity, for active participation, and for sharing and keeping historical and folk
3400 Members
Founded in 1915

8778
Country Music Association
One Music Circle S
Nashville, TN 37203
615-244-2840
FAX 615-242-4783
Home Page: www.cmaworld.com

Gary Overton, Chairman
Troy Tomlison, President
Jessie Schmidt, Secretary/Treasurer
Steve Moore, CEO

CMA is dedicated to bringing the poetry and emotion of Country Music to the World. They will continue a tradition of leadership and professionalism, promotoing the music and recognizing excellence in all its forms. They foster a spirit of community and sharing, and respect and encourage creativity and the unique contributions of everyone. It is a place to have fun and celebrate success.
5000+ Members
Founded in 1958

8779
Country Radio Broadcasters
819 18th Ave S
Nashville, TN 37203-3218
615-327-4487
FAX 615-329-4492
E-Mail: news@crb.org
Home Page: www.crb.org

Ed Salamon, Executive Director
Chasity Crouch, Business Manager
Bill Mayne, VP
Carole Bowen, Secretary
Jeff Walker, Treasurer

A nonprofit eductional organization. It is the principal entity that brings Country radio together with the Country music industry for learning opportunities that promote growth.
Founded in 1969

8780
Creative Musicians Coalition
PO Box 6205
Peoria, IL 61601-6205
309-685-4843
800-882-4262
FAX 309-685-4879
E-Mail: aimcmc@aol.com
Home Page: www.creativemusicianscoalition.com

Ronald Wallace, Founder/President

An international organization dedicated to the advancement of new music and the success of independent musicians.
1000 Members
Founded in 1984

8781
Dance Critics Association
Old Chelsea Station
PO Box 1882
New York, NY 10011
732-643-4008
E-Mail: dancecritics@hotmail.com
Home Page: www.dancecritics.org

Kena Herod, Co-Chair
Linda Traiger, Co-Chair

Encourages excellence in dance criticism through education, research and the exchange of ideas. Produces quarterly newsletter.
Cost: $50
300 Members
Founded in 1974

8782
Dance Educators of America
3340 S.E Federal Highway
Suite262
Stuart, FL 34997
914-636-3200
800-329-3868
FAX 914-636-5895
E-Mail: info@dancedea.com

Home Page: http://usadance.dancedea.com/
Social Media: *Facebook, Twitter, Youtube*

Vickie Sheer, Executive Director
Fran Peters, President
Charles Kelley, Treasurer
Robyn Bourdeau, Chief FinancialOfficer
Stephen Ball, Events and DEA Coordinator

Dedicated to improving the quality and teaching abilities of its member teachers and enhancing their education of students, as well as furthering the professional and ethical standards in the performing arts and of dance in all its form. Membership is limited to qualified teachers.
Cost: $150
1800 Members
Founded in 1932

8783
Dance Films Association
48 W 21st St
Suite 907
New York, NY 10010-6989
212-727-0764
FAX 212-727-0765
E-Mail: info@dancefilms.org
Home Page: www.dancefilms.org

Deidra Towers, Executive Director
Latika Young, Education Director
Anna Brady Nuse, Festival Coordinator
Julian Barnett, Research/Development

Supports all those professionals in both the dance and the film community. Publishes bi-monthly magazine.
Cost: $50
Founded in 1956

8784
Dance Masters of America
PO Box 610533
Bayside, NY 11361
718-255-4013
FAX 718-225-4293
E-Mail: dmamann@aol.com
Home Page: www.dma-national.org

Shely Pack Manning, National President
Robert Mann, National Executive Secretary
Charleen Locascio, National Treasurer

An international organization of dance educators who have been certified by test to teach whose main focus is advancing the art of dance and improving the practice of its teaching.
2.5M Members
Founded in 1884

8785
Dance USA
1111 16th St NW
Suite 300
Washington, DC 20036-4830
202-833-1717
FAX 202-833-2686
E-Mail: danceusa@danceusa.org
Home Page: www.danceusa.org
Social Media: *Facebook, Twitter,*

Amy Fitterer, Executive Director
Tom Thielen, Director Finance/Operations
Katherine Fabian, Membership Manager

Provides a forum for the discussion of issues of concern to members and a support network for exchange of information.
400 Members
Founded in 1982

INFORMATION RESOURCES / Associations

8786
Directors Guild of America
7920 W Sunset Blvd
Los Angeles, CA 90046-3347
310-289-2000
800-421-4173
FAX 310-289-2029
E-Mail: LDavis@dga.org
Home Page: www.dga.org

Jay Roth, President
Steven Soderbergh, National VP
Gilbert Cates, Secretary/Treasurer

The DGA represents Film and Television Directors, Unit Production Managers, First Assistant Directors, Second Assistant Directors, Technical Coordinators and Tape Associate Directors, Stage Managers and Production Assistants.

8787
Dramatists Guild of America
1501 Broadway
Suite 701
New York, NY 10036-5505
212-398-9366
FAX 212-944-0420
E-Mail: igor@dramaguild.com
Home Page: www.dramatistsguild.com

Ralph Sevush, Executive Director Business Affairs
Gary Garrison, Executive Director Creative Affairs
Abby Marcus, Managing Director
Roland Tec, Director of Membership

The Dramatists Guild of America was established over eighty years ago, and is the only professional association that advances the interests of playwrights, composers, lyricists and librettists writing for the living stage.
6000+ Members
Founded in 1964

8788
East-2-West Marketing & Promotion
559 Wanamaker Road
Jenkintown, PA 19046-2219
215-884-3308
FAX 215-884-1083

Jackie Paul, President/CEO

Marketing and promotion.
Mailing list available for rent

8789
Educational Theatre Association
2343 Auburn Ave
Cincinnati, OH 45219-2819
513-421-3900
FAX 513-421-7077
Home Page: www.schooltheatre.org
Social Media: Facebook, Twitter,

Jay Seller, President
Frank Pruet, VP
Julie Woffington, Executive Director
Jim Flanagan, Director of Operations
Ginny Butsch, Community Manager

EdTA is a professional organization for theatre educators. In addition to providing professional development, advocacy, and networking support to its members, Edta oprtates the International Society, an honorary organization for high school and middle school theatre students.
4600+ Members
Founded in 1929

8790
Esperanza Performing Arts Association
Po Box 502591
San Diego, CA 92150
858-391-1311
E-Mail: info@esperanzaarts.org
Home Page: www.esperanzaarts.org

Alan Cox, Executive Director
Adam Stout, Assistant Director

8791
Film Society of Lincoln Center
70 Lincoln Center Plz
New York, NY 10023-6595
212-875-5601
FAX 212-875-5636
E-Mail: webmaster@filmlinc.com
Home Page: www.filmlinc.com
Social Media: Facebook, Twitter,

Serge Joseph, Manager
Daniel H Stern, President
Wendy Keys, Secreaty
James Bouras, Treasurer
Claudia Bonn, Executive Director

Celebrates American and international cinema, recognizes and supports new filmmakers, and enhances awareness, accessibility and understanding of the art among a broad and diverse film going audience. The Film Society is best known for two international festivals - the New York Film Festival and the New Directors/New Films festival.
Founded in 1969

8792
Folk Alliance
510 S Main St
First Floor
Memphis, TN 38103-6417
901-522-1170
FAX 816-221-3658
E-Mail: fa@folk.org
Home Page: www.folkalliance.org

Lewis Meyers, Executive Director
Van Denn, VP
Alan Korolenko, Secretary
Mark Moss, Treasurer

The service association for the field, working on behalf of the folk music and dance industry year round. They offer a business directory of contacts for members, and a non-profit group exemption program for US-based organizations.
Cost: $70
Founded in 1989

8793
Folklife Center Of International House
3701 Chestnut Street
Philadelphia, PA 19104
215-387-5125
FAX 215-895-6550

Osagie Imasogie, President
Tanya Steinberg, Executive Director
William Parker, Director Of Communications Events

To present the highest caliber of traditional arts.

8794
Fritz and Lavinia Jensen Foundation
Foundation for the Carolinas
220 N Tryon Street
Charlotte, NC 28202
704-973-4500
FAX 704-973-4599
E-Mail: info@jensenfoundation.org
Home Page: www.jensenfoundation.org

Ann Todd, Competition Coordinator

Sponsors voice competitions supporting opera and other classical singers.

8795
Gina Bachauer International Piano Foundation
138 W Broadway
Suite 220
Salt Lake City, UT 84101-1913
801-297-4250
FAX 801-521-9202
E-Mail: info@bachauer.com
Home Page: www.bachauer.com
Social Media: Facebook, Twitter, Flickr

Thomas Holst, Manager
Kimi Kawashima, Manager
Arlo McGinn, Secretary
Nathan Morgan, Treasurer

The mission of the Foundation is to further the pianistic art, foster excellence in performance and teaching, develop opportunities for pianists beyond the scope of the organization and offer leadership in developing a musically-educated community.
Founded in 1976

8796
Gospel Music Association
741 cool Springs Blvd.
Franklin, TN 37067
615-242-0303
FAX 615-254-9755
E-Mail: service@gospelmusic.org
Home Page: www.gospelmusic.org
Social Media: Facebook, Twitter, LinkedIn, Youtube

John Styll, President
Scott Brickell, Director
Charles Dorris, Founder/Chairman
Ed Harper, Director
Ed Leonard, Direcotr

Our mission is to expose, promote and celebrate the gospel through music. GMA serves as a voice for the Christian music community. It provides an atmosphere in which artists, industry leaders, retail stores, radio stations, concert promoters and local churches can coordinate their efforts for the purpose of benefitting the industry as a whole, while remaining true to the purpose of communicating the gospel message.
Cost: $85
5000 Members
Founded in 1964

8797
Greek Americans in the Arts and Entertainment
3916 Sepulveda Blvd
Suite 107
Culver City, CA 90230
323-651-3507
FAX 310-933-0250
E-Mail: info@americanhellenic.org
Home Page: www.americanhellenic.org
Social Media: Facebook, Twitter,

Michael Galanakis, President
Alexander Mizan, Executive Director
Michael Sarris, VP, finance

Follows the legacy of Greek-Americans in the arts and entertainment field.

INFORMATION RESOURCES / Associations

8798
Guild of American Luthiers
8222 S Park Ave
Tacoma, WA 98408-5226
253-472-7853
FAX 253-472-7853
E-Mail: orders@luth.org
Home Page: www.luth.org
Social Media: Facebook,

Debra G Olsen, Executive Director
Tim Olsen, Editor
Kurt Kendall, Membership

Manufacturers and repairs stringed instruments; offers quarterly journal and triennial meeting.
Cost: $45
3000 Members
Founded in 1972

8799
Guitar Accessory and Marketing Association (GAMA)
Po Box 757
New York, NY 10033
212-795-3630
FAX 212-795-3630
E-Mail: assnhdqs@earthlink.net
Home Page: www.discoverguitar.com

Membership is comprised of guitar and guitar accessory manufacturers and various consumer magazines.
Founded in 1933

8800
Guitar Foundation of America
P.O.Box 171269
Austin, TX 78717
877-570-1651
FAX 877-570-3409
E-Mail: info@guitarfoundation.org
Home Page: www.guitarfoundation.org
Social Media: Facebook, Twitter,

Brian Head, President
Jill Winchell, Operations Manager
Martha Masters, Executive VP
Jeff Cogan, VP
Robert Lane, Vice President/Secretary

Provides its members the combined advantages of a guitar society, a library, a publisher, a continuing education resource, and an artis council. The GFA is a non-profit educational and literacy organization devoted to furthering the knowledge of and interest in the guitar and its music.
Cost: $40
Founded in 1973

8801
Historians Film Committee
Rural Route 3
Box 80
Cleveland, OK 74020-9515
918-243-7637
FAX 202-544-8307
E-Mail: rollinspc@aol.com
Home Page: www.filmandhistory.org

Peter C Rollins, Editor-in-Chief

The Committee exists to further the use of film sources in teaching and research, to disseminate information about film and film use to historians and other social scientists, to work for an effective system of film preservation so that scholars may have ready access to film archives, and to organize periodic conferences dealing with film.
Founded in 1970

8802
Hollywood Arts Council
PO Box 931056
Hollywood, CA 90093
323-462-2355
FAX 323-465-9240
E-Mail: admin@hollywoodartscouncil.org
Home Page: www.hollywoodartscouncil.org
Social Media: Facebook,

Nyla Arslanian, President
Nancy J Brown, VP
Steve Tronson, Treasurer
Shauna McClure, Executive Director

Promotes, nurtures and supports the arts in Hollywood. Has served the community through advocacy, coalition building, free public arts events and after school programs.
400 Members
Founded in 1978

8803
Independent Film & Television Alliance
10850 Wilshire Blvd
9th Floor
Los Angeles, CA 90024-4628
310-446-1000
FAX 310-446-1600
E-Mail: info@ ifta-online.org
Home Page: www.ifta-online.org

Jean Prewitt, CEO
Jonathan Wolfe, Executive VP/Managing Director
Michael Ryan, Chairman
Lew Horwitz, Vice Chairman Finance

A non-profit association whose mission is to provide the independent film and television industry with high-quality marketplace-oriented services and worldwide representation. The Alliance actively lobbies the United States and Eurpoean governments and the international organizations on measures that impact production and distribution.
Founded in 1980

8804
International Animated Film Society
2114 W Burbank Blvd
Burbank, CA 91506-1232
818-842-8330
FAX 613-232-6315
E-Mail: info@asifa-hollywood.org
Home Page: www.animationarchive.org

Amtran Manoogian, President

A California nonprofit organization established to promote and encourage the art and craft of animation. They support and encourage animation education, supports the preservation and critical evaluation of animation history, recognize achievement of excellence in the art and field of animation, strive to increase the public awareness of animation, act as a liaison to encourage the free exchange of ideas within the animation community, as well as a variety of other goals.
350 Members
Founded in 1974

8805
International Association of Electronic Keyboard Manufacturers
305 Maple Avenue
Wyncote, PA 19095-3228
617-747-2816
Home Page: www.iaekm.org

An association that comprises the global manufacturers of electronic keyboards and affiliated software and publications.

8806
International Association of Jazz Education
PO Box 724
Manhattan, KS 66505
785-776-8744
FAX 785-776-6190
E-Mail: bill@iage.org
Home Page: www.iaje.org

Bill McFarlin, Executive Director
Chuck Owen, President
Ronald Carter, VP
Laura Johnson, Treasurer
Brian Coyle, Secretary

To ensure the continued development and growth of jazz through education and outreach.
Cost: $70
8000 Members
Founded in 1989

8807
International Association of Round Dance Teachers
176 S Cole Road
Boise, ID 83709-0932
208-377-1232
800-346-7522
FAX 208-377-1236
E-Mail: roundalab@roundalab.org
Home Page: www.roundalab.org

Gil & Judy Martin, General Chairman
Jeanne & Warren Shane, Vice Chairman
Chuck & Becky Jaworski, Marketing Membership

Supports all those involved in the field of square dancing. Publishes quarterly magazine.
Founded in 1976
Mailing list available for rent

8808
International Bluegrass Music Association
608 West, Irish Drive
Nashville, TN 37204
615-256-3222
888-438-4262
FAX 615-256-0450
E-Mail: info@ibma.org
Home Page: www.ibma.org
Social Media: Facebook, Twitter, LinkedIn, Youtube

Dan Hayes, Executive Director
Stan Zdonik, Vice Chair/Associations
Peter D'Addario, Treasurer
Lee Michael Demsey, Secretary

IBMA works together for high standards of professionalism, a greater appreciation for our music, and the success of the worldwide bluegrass community.

8809
International Cinematographers Guild
7755 W Sunset Boulevard
Hollywood, CA 90046
323-876-0160
FAX 323-876-6383
E-Mail: admin@camerguild.com
Home Page: www.cameraguild.com

Steven Poster, President
Tom Weston, National VP

1055

INFORMATION RESOURCES / Associations

Paul V Ferrazzi, Secretary/Treasurer
Bruce C Doering, Executive Director

The International Cinematographers Guild welcomes camera professionals from across the United States and around the world.

8810
International Clarinet Association
14070 Proton Rd
Suite 100 LB9
Dallas, TX 75244
972-233-9107
FAX 972-490-4219
E-Mail: membership@clarinet.org
Home Page: www.clarinet.org

John Cipolla, President
Tod Kerstetter, Treasurer
Caroline Hartig, Secretary
So Rhee, Executive Director

A community of clarinetists and clarinet enthusiasts that supports projects that will benefit clarinet performance; provides opportunities for the exchange of ideas, materials and information among its members; fosters the composition, publication, recording, and distribution of music for the clarinet; encourages the research and manufacture of a more definitive clarinet; and encourages and promotes the perfomance and teaching of a wide variety of repertoire for the clarinet.
4000 Members
Founded in 1990

8811
International Computer Music Association
1819 Polk Street
Suite 330
San Francisco, CA 94109
FAX 734-878-3031
E-Mail: icma@umich.edu
Home Page: www.computermusic.org
Social Media: *Facebook,*

Tae Hong Park, President
Margaret Schedel, VP Of Conference

The International Computer Music Association is an international affiliaton of individuals and institutions involved in the technical, creative, and performance aspects of computer music. It serves composers, engineers, researchers and musicians who are interested in the integration of music and technology.
Cost: $63.52
450 Members

8812
International Documentary Association
3470 Wilshire Blvd
Suite 980
Los Angeles, CA 90010
213-232-1660
FAX 213-232-1669
E-Mail: michael@documentary.org
Home Page: www.documentary.org
Social Media: *Facebook, Twitter, LinkedIn, Youtube*

Michael Lumpkin, Executive Director
Cindy Chyr, Development Director
Andrew Kaiser, Development Associate
Jina Chung, Associate
Amy Halpin, Manager

A nonprofit membership organization dedicated to supporting the efforts of nonfiction film and video makers throughout the United States and the world; promoting the documentary form; and expanding opportunities for the production, distribution, and exhibition of documentary.

2800+ Members
Founded in 1982

8813
International Festivals and Events Association
2603 W Eastover Ter
Boise, ID 83706-2800
208-433-0950
FAX 208-433-9812
E-Mail: nia@ifea.com
Home Page: www.ifea.com

Steven Schmader, President
Nia Hovde, VP/Marketing

A voluntary association of events, event producers, event suppliers, and related professionals and organizations whose common purpose is the production and presentation of festivals, events, and civic and private celebrations.
2000 Members
Founded in 1956

8814
International Horn Society
E-Mail: exec-secretary@hornsociety.org
Home Page: www.hornsociety.org

Frank Lloyd, President
Joseph Ognibene, VP
Marian Hesse, Secretary/Treasurer
Heidi Vogal, Executive Secretary
Cost: $35
3500 Members
Founded in 1970

8815
International Music Products Association NAMM
5790 Armada Drive
Carlsbad, CA 92008-4608
760-438-8001
800-767-6266
FAX 760-438-7327
E-Mail: info@namm.org
Home Page: www.namm.org

Larry Morton, President
Mark Goff, President/Owner
Robin Walents, President/CEO
Chris Martin, Chairman/CEO
Joe Lamond, President/CEO

An association whose mission is to unify, lead and strengthen the international music products industry and increase active participation in music making.
9000 Members
Founded in 1901

8816
International Piano Guild
PO Box 1807
Austin, TX 78767
512-478-5775
E-Mail: ngpt@pianoguild.com
Home Page: www.pianoguild.com

Richard Allison, President

A division of the American College of Musicians Professional society of piano teachers and music faculty members. Its primary function is to establish definite goals and awards for students of all levels, from the earliest beginner to the gifted prodigy. Its purpose is to encourage growth and enjoyment through the study of piano.
118m Members
Founded in 1929

8817
International Planned Music Association
5900 S Salina Street
Syracuse, NY 13205
315-469-7711
FAX 315-469-8842
Home Page: www.ipmanet.com

Roy Salgado, President
Steve Seiden, VP
Larry Zaiser, Secretary
Jon Baker, Treasurer

IPMA is a trade organization made up of providers of planned and programmed music services and key vendors. The Associatin exists to provide members with a common ground on which to share informatio about running exciting, profitable franchises and to provide associate members with opportunities to expand their sales in markets all over the world.
200 Members

8818
International Polka Association
4608 S Archer Ave
Chicago, IL 60632-2932
773-254-7771
800-867-6552
E-Mail: ipa@internationalpolka.com
Home Page: www.internationalpolka.com

Dave Ulczycki, President
Rick Rzeszutko, First VP
Fred Kenzierski, Second VP
Marlene Gill, Secretary
Linda Niewierowski, Treasurer

An educational and charitable organization for the preservation, promulgation and advancement of polka music and to promote, maintain and advance public interest in polka entertainment; to advance mutual interests and encourage greater cooperation among its members who are engaged in polka entertainment; and to encourage and pursue the study of polka music, dancing and traditional folklore. Responsible for the continued operation and growth of the Polka Music Hall of Fame and Museum.
Cost: $15
8M Members
Founded in 1968

8819
International Society for the Performing Arts
630 9th Avenue
Suite 213
New York, NY 10036-4752
212-206-8490
FAX 212-206-8603
E-Mail: info@ispa.org
Home Page: www.ispa.org
Social Media: *Facebook,*

Martha H Jones, Chair
Willem Brans, Treasurer
Horacio Lecona, Secretary
Johann Zietsman, CEO
Lynne Caruso, Membership Manager

A nonprofit organization of executives and directors of concert and performance halls, festivals, performing companies, and artists competitions; government cultural officials; artists' managers; and other interested parties with a professional involvement in the performing arts around the world, and in every arts disciplie. The purpose of ISPA is to develop, nurture, energize and educate an international network of arts leaders

INFORMATION RESOURCES / Associations

and professionals who are dedicated to advancing its field.
600 Members
Founded in 1949

8820
International Society of Folk Harpers and Craftsmen
1614 Pittman Drive
Missoula, Mt 59803
406-542-1976
E-Mail: harps@thorharp.com
Home Page: www.folkharpsociety.org

Dave Kolacny, President
Timothy Habinski, First VP
Verlene Schermer, Second VP
Alice Williams, Secretary
Barbra Bailey Bradley, Treasurer

The mission of the ISFHC is: to promote the playing and enjoyment of the folk harp by all; to promote education, creation and development in the building of the folk harp; to increase awareness of professional folk harpers; and to increase public awareness of the music and joys of the folk harp.
Cost: $30
Founded in 1985

8821
International Stunt Association
11331 Ventura Boulevard
Suite 100
Studio City, CA 91604
818-760-2072
FAX 818-501-5656
E-Mail: info@isastunts.com
Home Page: www.isastunts.com
Social Media: *Facebook, Twitter,*

Leading the industry in exciting action while holding safety above all else, ISA is a fraternal organization whose membership is by invitation only. It is comprised of the top stuntment, stunt coordinators and second unit directors that Hollywood has to offer and a safety record that is second to none.
Founded in 1980

8822
International Theatre Equipment Association
770 Broadway
5th Floor
New York, NY 10003-9595
646-654-7680
FAX 212-257-6428
E-Mail: info@itea.com
Home Page: www.itea.com

Robert Sunshine, Executive Director
Barry Ferrell, President
Jack Panzeca, VP
Joe DeMeo, Treasurer
Sarah Fuller, Secretary

Fosters and maintains professional, business and social relationships among its members within all segments of the motion picture industry. Bestows annual Teddy Award to manufacturer of the year and the annual Rodney Award to dealer of the year.
Cost: $375
180 Members
Founded in 1971

8823
International Ticketing Association
One College Park, 8910 Purdue Road
Suite 480
Indianapolis, IN 46268
212-629-4036
FAX 212-628-8532
E-Mail: info@intix.org
Home Page: www.intix.org
Social Media: *Facebook,*

Jena L Hoffman, President
Kathleen O'Donnell, Director

Non-profit association committed to the improvement, progress and advancement of ticket management. Provides educational programs, trade shows, conducts surveys, conference proceedings, and its valuable membership directory.
1200 Members
Founded in 1979

8824
Jazz Education
3303 South Rice, Suite 107
PO Box 8031
Houston, TX 77056
713-839-7000
FAX 715-839-8266
E-Mail: jazzed@jazzedcation.org
Home Page: www.jazzeducation.org
Social Media: *Facebook, LinkedIn,*

Tracy Scott, Executive Director

Nonprofit music organization providing worthwhile educational activities for school-aged youth in the field of music. Includes many subjects not covered by school systems. Promotes appreciation and understanding of Jazz.
Founded in 1970

8825
Keyboard Teachers Association International
361 Pin Oak Lane
Westbury, NY 11590-1941
516-333-3236
FAX 516-997-9531
Home Page: www.musiciansnetwork.com

Dr. Albert DeVito, President

8826
League of American Ochestras
33 W 60th Street
New York, NY 10023-7905
212-262-5161
FAX 212-262-5198
E-Mail: league@symphony.org
Home Page: www.symphony.org

Henry Fogel, CEO
Jesse Rosen, President/CEO
Aja Stephens, Assistant to President
Peter D Cummings, Vice Chair
Heather Noonan, Vice Chair

Provides leadership and service to American orchestras while communicating to the public the value and importance of orchestras and the music they perform. The League links a national network of thousands of musicians, conductors, managers, board members, volunteers, staff members and business partners, providing a wealth of services, information, and educational opportunities to its members.
1200 Members
Founded in 1942
Mailing list available for rent

8827
League of American Theatres and Producers
729 Seventh Avenue
5th Floor
New York, NY 10019
212-764-1122
FAX 212-944-2136
E-Mail: league@broadway.org
Home Page: www.livebroadway.com
Social Media: *Facebook, Twitter, LinkedIn, Pinterest*

Charolette St Martin, Executive Director
Colin Gibson, Director Finance
Jane Svendsen, Director Marketing
Ed Sandler, Director Membership Services

National trade association for the commercial theatre industry whose principal activity is negotiation of labor contracts and government relations.
400 Members
Founded in 1930

8828
League of Historic American Theatres
2105 Laurel Bush Rd
Suite 201
Bel Air, MD 21015
443-640-1058
877-627-0833
FAX 443-640-1031
E-Mail: info@lhat.org
Home Page: www.lhat.org

Frances Holden, Executive Director
Thomas Johnson, VP
Lance Olson, Treasurer

The League of Historic American Theatres, a nonprofit membership association, promotes the rescue, rehabilitation and sustainable operation of historic theatres throughout North America. Founded in 1976, the League serves its members through educational programs, publications, specialized services and an annual conference and theatre tour.
500+ Members
Founded in 1976

8829
Literary Managers and Dramaturgs of the Americas
PO Box 36
New York, NY 10129
212-561-0315
800-680-2148
E-Mail: lmdanyc@hotmail.com
Home Page: www.lmda.org

Cynthia M SoRelle, Chair
Vicki Stroich, President
Danielle Carroll, Administrative Director
Beth Blickers, Treasurer

The mission of the LMDA is to affirm the role of dramaturg, to expand the possibilities of the field to other media and institutions and to cultivate, develop and promote the function of dramaturgy and literary management.
500 Members

8830
Metropolitan Opera Guild
70 Lincoln Center Plz
New York, NY 10023-6593
212-769-7000
FAX 212-769-7007
E-Mail: info@metguild.org
Home Page: www.metoperafamily.org/guild/

INFORMATION RESOURCES / Associations

David Dik, Manager

Seeks to encourage the appreciation of opera and to support the Metropolitan Opera. The guild provides programs and services in many areas designed to further these goals. Publishes monthly magazine and organizes special events throughout the year to raise funds.
100M Members
Founded in 1935

8831
Mid-Atlantic Arts Foundation
201 N Charles Street
Suite 401
Baltimore, MD 21201-4102
410-539-6656
FAX 410-837-5517
E-Mail: info@midatlanticarts.org
Home Page: www.midatlanticarts.org

Alan Cooper, Executive Director
E Scott Johnson, Secretary

MAAF celebrates, promotes and supports the richness and diversity of the region's art resources and works to increase access to the arts and other cultures of the region and the world.
40000 Members
Founded in 1979
Mailing list available for rent: 30,000 names

8832
Midland Center For The Arts Midland Music And Concert Series
1801 W. St Andrews Road
Midland, MI 48640
989-631-8250
FAX 989-631-7890
E-Mail: hohmeyer@mcfta.org
Home Page: www.mcfta.org
Social Media: Facebook, Twitter, LinkedIn, Youtube

Michael Tiknis, President
James Hohmeyer, Artistic Director
Robb Wouose, Managing Director
Mark Bachman, Director
David Blakemore, Director

encourage concert audiences; Providing students with opportunities to experience professional performances.

8833
Motion Picture Association of America
15301 Ventura Boulevard
Building E
Sherman Oaks, CA 91403
818-995-6600
FAX 818-285-4403
Home Page: www.mpaa.org

Christopher J Dodd, President/CEO

Serves as the voice and advocate of the American motion picture, home video and television industries. The association advocates for strong protection of the creative works produced and distributed by the industry, fights copyright theft around the world, and provides leadership in meeting new and emerging industry challenges.
7 Members
Founded in 1922

8834
Motion Picture Editors Guild
7715 Sunset Boulevard
Suite 200
Hollywood, CA 90046
323-876-4770
800-705-8700
FAX 323-876-0861
E-Mail: webmester@editorsguild.com
Home Page: www.editorsguild.com
Social Media: Facebook,

Lisa Zeno Churgin, President
Carol Littleton, VP
Martin Levenstein, Second Vice Presdient
Diane Adler, Secretary
Rachel B Igel, Treasurer

A national labor organization representing freelance and staff post-production professionals. MPED negotiates new collective bargaining agreements and enfoces exisiting agreements with employers involved in post-production. They provide assistance for securing better conditions, including but not limted to financial, medical, safety and artistic concerns.
6000 Members
Founded in 1937

8835
Motion Picture Pilots Association
7435 Valjean Avenue
Van Nuys, CA 91406
818-947-5454
E-Mail: moviepilots@cox.net
Home Page: www.moviepilots.com

Cliff Fleming, Board Director
Dirk Vahle, Board Director
Rick Shuster, Board Director
Neil Looy, Board Director
Kevin LaRosa, Board Director

The MPPA promotes aviation safety and the interest of aviators working in the motion picture, television and entertainment industries; establishes, conducts and maintains such activities which promote higher aviation standards and better business methods as may assist in the advancement of aviation in the Entertainment Aviation Profession; cooperates with those government agencies, industry organizations, entities or association whose objective is the betterment or advancement of the industry.
Founded in 1997

8836
Music Distributors Association
14070 Proton Rd
Suite 100 LB9
Dallas, TX 75244-3601
972-233-9107
FAX 972-490-4219
E-Mail: office@musicdistributors.org
Home Page: www.musicdistributors.org

International, nonprofit trade association representing and serving manufacturers, wholesalers, importers and exporters of musical instruments and accessories, sound reinforcement products and published music.
Cost: $675
Founded in 1939

8837
Music Library Association
8551 Research Way
Suite 180
Middleton, WI 53562
608-836-5825
FAX 608-831-8200
E-Mail: mla@areditions.com
Home Page: www.musiclibraryassoc.org
Social Media: Facebook,

Michael Colby, President
Pamela Bristah, Secretary
Paul Cary, Admin Officer
Linda W.Blair, Admin Officer

Provides a forum for issues surrounding music, music in libraries, and music librarianship.
Cost: $90
Founded in 1931

8838
Music Performance Fund
1501 Broadway
Suite 600
New York, NY 10036
212-391-3950
FAX 212-221-2604
E-Mail: lwilliamson@musicpf.org
Home Page: www.musicpf.org
Social Media: Facebook,

Den Beck, Trustee
Al Elvin, Director of Finance
Linda Williamson, Manager

A nonprofit public service organization headquartered in New York City. MPF is the world's largest sponsor of live, admission-free musical programs.
Founded in 1948

8839
Music Publishers Association
243 5th Ave
Suite 236
New York, NY 10016-8728
212-675-7354
FAX 212-675-7381
E-Mail: mpa-admin@mpa.org
Home Page: www.mpa.org

Kathleen Marsh, President
Bryndon Bay, Treasurer
Todd Vunderink, Secretary
Lauren Keiser, Second VP

The MPA fosters communication among publishers, dealers, music educators, and all ultimate users of music. It is a nonprofit association which addresses Itself to issues pertaining to every area of music publishing with an emphasis on the issues relevant to the publishers of print music for concert and educational purposes.
75 Members
Founded in 1895

8840
Music Teachers National Association
441 Vine St
Suite 3100
Cincinnati, OH 45202-3004
513-421-1420
888-512-5278
FAX 513-421-2503
E-Mail: mtnanet@mtna.org
Home Page: www.mtna.org
Social Media: Facebook, Twitter,

Gary L Ingle, Executive Director
Gail Berenson, President
Janice Wenger, VP

The mission of the MTNA is to advance the value of music study and music making to society and to support the professionalism of music teachers.
24000 Members
Founded in 1876
Mailing list available for rent: 23,000 names at $85 per M

8841
Music for All Foundation
39 W Jackson Place
Suite 150
Indianapolis, IN 46225

INFORMATION RESOURCES / Associations

317-636-2263
FAX 317-524-6200
E-Mail: info@music-for-all.org
Home Page: www.musicforall.org

Eric Martin, President/CEO
Nancy H.Carlson, Executive VP/CFO
Carolyn Ealy, Education and Office Manager
Tonya Bullock, Accounting manager

Committed to expanding the role of music and the arts in education, to heightening the public's appreciation of the value of music and arts education, and to creating a positive environment for the arts through societal changes.
Founded in 1975
Mailing list available for rent

8842
Musical Box Society International
MBSI Member Registration
PO Box 10196
Springfield, MO 65808-0196
FAX 417-886-8839
Home Page: www.mbsi.org
Social Media: *Facebook, Twitter, Digg, Yahoo, Reddit, StumbleUp*

A nonprofit organization dedicated to the enjoyment, sstudy and preservation of all automatic musical instruments. Members receive the bimonthly scholarly journal, Mechanical Music, covering educational articles, relevant events, activities, news, information, and advertisements and the biennial, Directory of Members, Museums and Dealers. Hosts annual convention.
Cost: $55
2.8M Members
Founded in 1949

8843
Musicians Foundation
875 Sixth Avenue
Suite 2303
New York, NY 10001-3507
212-239-9137
FAX 212-239-9138
E-Mail: info@musiciansfoundation.org
Home Page: www.musiciansfoundation.org

BC Vermeersch, Executive Director
Hans E Tausig, President
Joseph Hertzberg, Treasurer

Representing interests on the condition and social welfare of professional musicians and their families. Provides emergency financial assistance to meet current living, medical and allied expenses.
Founded in 1914

8844
National Association for Drama Therapy
44365 Premier Plaza
Suite 220
Ashburn, VA 20147
585-381-5618
FAX 571-223-6440
E-Mail: nadt.office@nadt.org
Home Page: www.nadt.org

Nisha Sajnani, President
Lisa Merrell, VP
Gary Raucher, Secretary
Mary Caligiure, Treasurer
Nancy Sondag, Membership

A nonprofit association which establishes and upholds high standards of professional competence and ethics among drama therapists; to develop criteria for training and registration; to sponsor publications and conferences; and to promote the profession of drama therapy through information and advocacy.
Founded in 1979

8845
National Association for Music Education MENC
1806 Robert Fulton Drive
Reston, VA 20191
703-860-4000
800-336-3768
FAX 703-860-1531
Home Page: www.menc.org

John J Mahlmann, Executive Director
Lynn Brinckmeyer, President

Mission is to advance music education by encouraging the study and making of music by all.
Founded in 1907

8846
National Association of Band Instrument Manufacturers
2026 Eagle Road
PO Box 51
Normal, IL 61761
309-452-4257
FAX 309-452-4825
E-Mail: napbirt@napbirt.org
Home Page: www.napbirt.org
Social Media: *Facebook,*

Jerome Hershman, Contact

A trade association of band instrument manufacturers, importers and distributors including accessories selling to the trade only.
34 Members
Founded in 1976

8847
National Association of College Wind and Percussion Instructor
Division of Fine Arts
Truman State University
Kirksville, MO 63501
660-785-4442
FAX 660-785-7463
E-Mail: cmoore@fsu.edu
Home Page: www.nacwpi.org

Chris Moore, President
Michael Dean, VP
Richard K Weerts, Executive Secretary/Treasurer

A forum for communication within the profession of applied music on the college campus. The Association is composed of university, college, and conservatory teachers.
Cost: $35
600 Members
Founded in 1951

8848
National Association of Negro Musicians Inc
931 Monroe Drive NE
Suite A102-159
Atlanta, GA 30308
404-647-7217
FAX 404-745-0128
E-Mail: info@nanm.org
Home Page: www.nanm.org

David E Morrow, President
Byron J. Smith, First VP
Glenn L Jones, Second VP
Ona B Campbell, Executive Secretary
Daniel.J Long, Treasurer

Dedicated to the preservation, encouragement and advocacy of all genres of the music of African Americans. Holds a national convention in a different city eac year, offering a chance to participate in workshops, seminars, lectures and performances. NANM invites the professional artists, the educator, the student, the amateur, the lover of music to become a part of this organization's 'Pride in a Cultural Heritage.'
2.5M Members
Founded in 1919

8849
National Association of Pastoral Musicians
962 Wayne Ave
Suite 210
Silver Spring, MD 20910-4461
240-247-3000
FAX 240-247-3001
E-Mail: npmsing@npm.org
Home Page: www.npm.org

J Michael Mc Mahon, President
Kathleen Haley, Director Membership Services
Lowell Hickman, Office Manager/Executive Assistant
Joseph Lively, Comptroller

Fosters the art of musical liturgy. The members of NPM serve the Catholic Church in the United States as musicians, clergy, liturgists, and other leaders of prayer.
9000 Members
Founded in 1976

8850
National Association of Professional Band Instrument Repair Technicians
2026 Eagle Road
PO Box 51
Normal, IL 61761
309-452-4257
FAX 309-452-4825
E-Mail: napbirt@napbirt.org
Home Page: www.napbirt.org
Social Media: *Facebook,*

Bill Mathews, President

A nonprofit international educational association dedicated to the advancement of the craft of band instrument repair. Their mission is to promote the highest possible standards of band instrument repair, restoration and maintenance by providing members with multi-level professional development by offering technical training, continuing education and the publication of their bi-monthky trade journal.
Cost: $95
1300 Members
Founded in 1976

8851
National Association of Recording Merchandisers
9 Eves Drive
Suite 120
Marlton, NJ 08053-3130
856-596-2221
FAX 856-596-3268
E-Mail: donio@narm.com
Home Page: www.narm.com

Sue Peterson, Chair
Scott Wilson, Vice Chairman
Bob Schneider, Treasurer
Rachelle Friedman, Secretary
Jim Donio, President

INFORMATION RESOURCES / Associations

A not-for-profit trade association that serves the music retailing community in the areas of networking, advocacy, information, education and promotion. Membership includes music and other entertainment retailers, wholesalers, distributorsm record labels, multimedia suppliers, and suppliers of related products and services, as well as individual professionals and educators in the music business field.
Founded in 1958

8852
National Association of Schools of Music
11250 Roger Bacon Drive
Suite 21
Reston, VA 20190-5248
703-437-0700
FAX 703-437-6312
E-Mail: info@arts-accredit.org
Home Page: www.arts-accredit.org

Don Gibson, President
Mark Wait, VP
Mellasenah Y Morris, Treasurer

An organization of schools, conservatories, colleges and universities. NASM provides information to potential students and parents, consultations, stastistical information, professional development and policy analysis. It is the national accrediting agency for music and music-related disciplines.
635 Members
Founded in 1924

8853
National Association of Teachers of Singing
9957 Moorings Drive
Suite 401
Jacksonville, FL 32257-2416
904-992-9101
FAX 904-262-2587
E-Mail: info@nats.org
Home Page: www.nats.org
Social Media: *Facebook, Twitter, LinkedIn,*

Allen Henderson, Executive Director
Deborah Guess, Director of Operations

To encourage the highest standards of the vocal art and of ethical principles in the teaching of singing; and to promote vocal education and research at all levels, both for the enrichment of the general public and for the professional advancement of the talented.
7000 Members
Founded in 1944

8854
National Ballroom and Entertainment Association
PO Box 274
Decorah, IA 52101-7600
563-382-3871
E-Mail: nbea@q.com
Home Page: www.nbea.com

John Matter, Executive Director

National nonprofit association which advocates that social dancing is a life-long activity that contributes to the physical, mantal, and social well-being of an individual. They believe that social dancing should be preserved for current and future generations and introduced to today's youth as an alternate form of social interaction.
450 Members
Founded in 1947

8855
National Band Association
Membership Office
745 Chastain Road-Ste 1140
PO Box 102
Kennesaw, GA 30144
601-297-8168
FAX 601-266-6185
E-Mail: info@nationalbandassociation.org
Home Page: www.nationalbandassociation.org

Roy Holder, President
Richard Good, First VP
Scott Casagrande, Second VP
Linda Moorehouse, Secretary/Treasurer
David Gregory, Advisor to the President

The purpose of the NBA to promote the musical and educational significance of bands and is dedicated to the attainment of a high level of excellence for bands and band music. It is open to anyone and everyone interested in bands, regardless of the length if his/her experience, type of position held, or the specific area at which he/she works. The membership roster includes men and women from every facet of the band world.
3M Members
Founded in 1960

8856
National Costumers Association
121 N Bosart Avenue
Indianapolis, IN 46201-3729
317-351-1940
800-622-1321
FAX 317-351-1941
E-Mail: office@costumers.org
Home Page: www.costumers.org

Janie Westendorf, President
Deborah Meredith, First Vive President
Linda Adams Foat, Second VP
Jennifer Skarstedt, Secretary/Treasurer

The objectives on the NCA are to establish and maintain professional and ethical standards of business in the costume industry. They encourage and promote a greater and more diversified use of costumes in all fields of human activity. They provide trade information, cooperation and friendship among its members together with a sound public relations policy.
400 Members
Founded in 1923

8857
National Dance Association
1900 Association Dr
Reston, VA 20191-1502
703-476-3400
800-213-7193
FAX 703-476-9527
E-Mail: nda@aahperd.org
Home Page: www.aahperd.org/nda
Social Media: *Facebook, Twitter,*

Colleen Dean, Manager
Marcey E Siegel, VP Dance Education
Mary Ann Laverty, VP Dance Performance

A nonprofit service organization dedicated to increasing knowledge, improving skills and encouraging sound professional practices in dance education while promoting and supporting creative and healthy lifestyles through high quality dance programs.
2000 Members
Founded in 1932

8858
National Dance Education Organization
8609 2nd Avenue
Suite 203 B
Silver Spring, MD 20910
301-585-2880
FAX 301-585-2888
E-Mail: info@ndeo.org
Home Page: www.ndeo.org

Susan McGreevy-Nichols, Executive Director
Patricia Cohen, Treasurer

A nonprofit organization dedicated to promoting standards of excellence in dance education.
2000 Members
Founded in 1998

8859
National Endowment for the Arts
1100 Pennsylvania Ave NW
Washington, DC 20506
202-682-5400
FAX 202-682-5611
E-Mail: webmgr@arts.gov
Home Page: www.arts.endow.gov
Social Media: *Facebook, Twitter,*

Dana Gioia, CEO
Guilomar Barbi, Scheduler
Sarah Cook, Executive Assistant
Jon P Peede, Counselor to the Chairman
Sydney Smith, Administrative Specialist

The National Endowment for the Arts, an investment in America's living heritage, serves the public good by nurturing the expression of human creativity, supporting the cultivation of community spirit, and fostering the recognition and appreciation of the excellence and diversity of our nation's artistic accomplishments.

8860
National Federation of Music Clubs
1646 W Smith Valley Rd
Greenwood, IN 46142-1550
317-882-4003
FAX 317-882-4019
E-Mail: info@nfmc-music.org
Home Page: www.nfmc-music.org
Social Media: *Facebook, Twitter, LinkedIn, Youtube*

Carolyn Nelson, President
Michael Edwards, First VP
Kay Hawthorne, Secretary
Barbara Hildebrand, Treasurer
Jennifer Keller, Administrative Manager

NFMC provides opportunities for musical study, performance and appreciation to more than 200,000 senior, student and junior members in 6,500 music-related clubs and organizations nationwide. Members are professional and amateur musicians, vocalists, composers, dancers, performing artists, arts and music educators, music students, generous music patrons and benefactors, and music lovers of all ages.
170M Members
Founded in 1898

8861
National Music Publishers Association
101 Constitution Avenue NW
Suite 705 East
Washington, DC 20001
202-742-4375
FAX 202-393-6673
E-Mail: pr@nmpa.org
Home Page: www.nmpa.org

Martin Bandier, President/CEO
John Eastman, Director

The NMPA is committed to promoting and advancing the interests of music publishers and their songwriting partners. Their goal is to foster a business climate that allows its members to thrive creatively and financially.

INFORMATION RESOURCES / Associations

800 Members
Founded in 1917

8862
National Opera Association
PO Box 60869
Canyon, TX 79016-0869
806-651-2857
FAX 806-651-2958
Home Page: www.noa.org

Robert Hansen, Executive Director
JoElyn Wakefield-Wright, President
Carole Notestine, Secretary
Robert Thieme, Editor Opera Journal
Philip Hagemann, Treasurer

The NOA seeks to promote a greater appreciation of opera and music theatre, to enhance pedagogy and performing activities, and to increase performance opportunities by supporting projects that improve the scope and quality of opera. Members in the United States, Canada, Europe, Asia and Australia participate in a wide array of activities in support of this mission.
775 Members
Founded in 1955
Mailing list available for rent

8863
National Piano Travelers Association
401 Sawkill Road
PO Box 2264
Kingston, NY 12401-2264
845-338-1464
FAX 845-338-5751
Home Page: www.pianotravelers.com

Roy Chandler, President
Bob dove, VP
Dawn Demars, Secretary/Treasurer

Buys and sells pianos.
110 Members

8864
New England Theatre Conference
215 Knob Hill Drive
Hamden, CT 06518
617-851-8535
FAX 203-288-5938
E-Mail: mail@netconline.org
Home Page: www.netconline.org

Sabine Klein, President
Jeffrey Watts, Executive VP
Charles Emmons, VP Administration/Finance

Non-profit corporation, composed of individuals and organizations in the six-State region of New England, who are active and interested in the performing arts. The NETC promotes excellence in theatre for their region, and supports quality theatre and performance in all of its diversity.
500 Members
Founded in 1952

8865
North American Performing Arts Managers and Agents
459 Columbus Ave
Suite 133
New York, NY 10024-5129
212-362-8304
800-867-3281
E-Mail: info@napama.org
Home Page: www.napama.org

Richard Baird, Owner
David Wannen, VP
Jerry Ross, VP
Susan Endrizzi Moris, Secretary
Robin Pomerance, Treasurer

National nonprofit trade association dedicated to promoting the professionalism of its members and the vitality of the performing arts. NAPAMA promotes the mutual advancement and the best interests of performing arts managers and agents; promotes open discourse among members and within the larger field; gives active consideration and expression of opinion on questions affecting the industry and develops and encourages ethical and sound business practices.
Cost: $150
Founded in 1979

8866
Opera America
330 7th Ave
16th Floor
New York, NY 10001-5248
212-796-8620
FAX 212-796-8631
E-Mail: frontdesk@operaamerica.org
Home Page: www.operaamerica.org

Marc A Scorca, President
Frayda B. Lindemann, Chairman
Timothy O'Leary, Treasurer
James W Wright, Secretary
Rebecca Ackerman, Membership Manager

Opera America serves and strengthens the field of opera by providing a variety of informational, technical, and administrative resources to the greater opera community. Its fundamental mission is to promote opera as exciting and accessible to individuals from all walks of life.

8867
Oratorio Society of New York
1440 Broadway
23rd Floor
New York, NY 10018-9759
212-400-7255
E-Mail: president@oratoriosocietyofny.org
Home Page: www.oratoriosocietyofny.org
Social Media: *Facebook, Twitter, Youtube*

Richard A Pace, President/Chairman
Mary J.Knight, Vice President
Marie Gangemi, Treasurer
Jay Jacobson, Secretary
Kent Tritle, Music Director

New York City's second oldest cultural organization. On December 25, 1874 the society began what has become an unbroken tradition of annual performances of Handel's Messiah (at Carnegie Hall since its opening in 1891).
Founded in 1873

8868
Organization of American Kodaly Educators
10951 Pico Blvd
Suite 405
Los Angeles, CA 90064
310-441-3555
FAX 310-441-3577
E-Mail: info@oake.org
Home Page: www.oake.org

Joan Dahlin, Manager
Penny Whalen, VP
Paul Baumann, Secretary
Greg Williams, Treasurer
Joan Dahlin, Administrative Director

The purpose of this organization is to promote Zoltan Kodaly's concept of Music for Everyone, through the improvment of music education in schools.
Founded in 1973

8869
Pedal Steel Guitar Association
PO Box 20248
Floral Park, NY 11002-0248
516-616-9214
FAX 516-616-9214
E-Mail: bobpsga@optonline.net
Home Page: www.psga.org

Kelly Foster Griffin, President
Jane Smith, VP
Kathy Hickey, Treasurer
David Gadberry, Secretary
Doug Mack, Newsletter Editor

A nonprofit organization whose primary purpose is to share information on playing the steel guitar and in particular the pedal steel guitar. Publishes the Pedal Steel Newsletter ten times per year
1540 Members
Founded in 1973

8870
Percussive Arts Society
110 W Washington Street
Suite A
Indianapolis, IN 46204
317-974-4488
FAX 317-974-4499
E-Mail: percarts@pas.org
Home Page: www.pas.org

Lisa Rogers, President
Steve Houghton, VP
Julie Hill, Secretary
Michael Balter, Treasurer
Larry Jacobson, Executive Director

A music service organization promoting percussion education, research, performance and appreciation throughout the world. Offers two print publications, the Percussive Arts Society International Headquarters/Museum and the annual Percussive Arts Society International Convention.
Cost: $85
7000 Members
Founded in 1961

8871
Performing Arts Association
719 Edmond St
St Joseph, MO 64501-2268
816-279-1225
E-Mail: info@paastjo.org
Home Page: www.paastjo.org

David Cripe, President
Elaine Smith, VP
Debbie Demuth, Secretary
Kim Lueger, Treasurer

Mission is to provide a diverse selection of performing arts in the St. Joseph area by presenting programs that foster, increase and promote public knowledge and appreciation of music, theatre and dance and lectures on subjects of cultural interests.
Founded in 1979

8872
Performing Arts Medicine Association
PO Box 117
Englewood, CO 80151
303-808-5643
FAX 866-408-7069

1061

INFORMATION RESOURCES / Associations

E-Mail: webmaster@artsmed.org
Home Page: www.artsmed.org

Julie Massaro, Executive Director
Mary Fletcher, Consultant
John Chong, President
Dorry Allen, Manager of Member Services

Organization for physicians and other professionsl persons who are involved in treatment and/or research in the field of Performing Arts Medicine.
Founded in 1989

8873
Piano Manufacturers Association
14070 Proton Road
Suite 100
Dallas, TX 75244
972-233-9107
FAX 972-490-4219
Home Page: www.pianonet.com

Donald W Dillon, Executive Director

Piano industry trade association.
Founded in 1991

8874
Piano Technicians Guild
4444 Forest Ave
Kansas City, KS 66106
913-432-9975
FAX 913-432-9986
E-Mail: ptg@ptg.org
Home Page: www.ptg.org

Barbara Cassaday, Executive Director
Allan Gilreath RPT, President
Jim Coleman Jr RPT, VP

A nonprofit organization serving piano tuners, technicians, and craftsmen throughout the world, organized to promote the highest possible service and technical standards among piano tuners and technicians.
4100 Members
Founded in 1957

8875
Producers Guild of America
8530 Wilshire Blvd
Suite 450
Beverly Hills, CA 90211-3115
310-358-9020
FAX 310-358-9520
E-Mail: info@producersguild.org
Home Page: www.producersguild.com

Marshall Herskovitz, President
Vance Van Paten, Executive Director
Grant Stoner, Director Membership
Courtney Cowan, Treasurer
Gale Ann Hurd, Secretary

The PGA represents, protects and promotes the interests of all members of the producing team by providing employment opportunities and health and welfare benefits for all members of the producing team; combating deceptive or uneraned credits within the producing team; and representing the interests of the entire producing team. The producing team consists of all those whose interdependency and support of each other are necessary for the creation of motion pictures and television programs.
500 Members
Founded in 1950

8876
Production Music Library Association
8551 Research Way
Suite 180
Middleton, WI 53562
608-836-5825
FAX 608-831-8200
E-Mail: mla@areditions.com
Home Page: www.musiclibraryassoc.org

Jerry L McBride, President
Michael Colby, VP
Pamela Bristah, Secretary

Provides a forum for issues surrounding music, music in libraries, and music librarianship. Members include music librarians, librarians who work with music as part of their responsibilities, composers and music scholars, and others interested in the program of the association.
20 Members
Founded in 1931

8877
Professional Women Singers Association
PO Box 231162
New York, NY 10023
212-969-0590
FAX 928-395-2560
E-Mail: info@womensingers.org
Home Page: www.womensingers.org
Social Media: *Facebook,*

Elissa Weiss, President
Allison Atteberry, First VP
Sarah Downs, Second VP
Ruth Ann Cunningham, Secretary
Mary Lou Zobel, Treasurer

Non-profit networking organization for professional women singers. The group sponsors concerts, master classes and seminars for both singers and the community at large.
40 Members
Founded in 1982

8878
Retail Print Music Dealers Association
2650 Midway Rd
Suite 230
Carrolton, TX 75006
972-818-1333
FAX 214-483-7004
E-Mail: cwilbur@penders.com
Home Page: www.printmusic.org

Madeleine Crouch, Owner
Myrna Sislen, VP/Secretary
Christie Smith, VP/Treasurer

A professional trade organization founded to address the special needs and interests of the print music industry. RPMDA provides a common meeting ground for the congenial interchange of ideas among print music dealers; promotes ethical standards and policies in dealing with music publishers; promotes better dealer/publisher relations; serves the public and encourages music education; provides association-sponsored activities and publications that help its members prepare for future trends.
275 Members
Founded in 1976

8879
Rhythm and Blues Foundation
P.O.Box 22438
Philadelphia, PA 19101
215-985-4822
FAX 215-985-1195
E-Mail: info@rhythmblues.org
Home Page: www.rhythm-n-blues.org

Patricia Wilson Aden, Executive Director
Jim Fifield, Vice Chairman
Jeff Harleston, Treasurer
Kenneth Gamble, Secretary

Nonprofit service organization dedicated to the historical and cultural preservation of Rhythm and Blues music. The Foundation provides financial support, medical assistance and educational outreach through various grants and programs to support R&B amd Motown artists of the 40s, 50s, 60s and 70s.
Founded in 1988

8880
Screen Actors Guild
5757 Wilshire Blvd
7th Floor
Los Angeles, CA 90036-3600
323-954-1600
855-724-2387
FAX 323-549-6792
Home Page: www.sag.org

Allen Rosenburg, President
Kent McCord, First VP
Paul Christie, Second VP
Steve Fried, Third Vice President
Connie Stevens, Secretary/Treasurer

Labor union affiliated with AFL-CIO which represents actors in film, television and commercials. The Guild exists to enhance actors' working conditions, compensation and benefits and to be a powerful, unifed voice on behalf of artists' rights.
120M Members
Founded in 1933

8881
Society for Cinema & Media Studies
640 Parrington Oval
Wallace Old Science Hall Room 300
Norman, OK 73019
405-325-8075
FAX 405-325-7135
E-Mail: office@cmstudies.org
Home Page: www.cmstudies.org
Social Media: *Facebook, Twitter,*

Stephen Prince, President
Eric Schaefer, Secretary
Amy Villarejo, Treasurer
Jane Dye, Administrative Coordinator

A professional organization of college and university educators, filmmakers, historians, critics, scholars, and others devoted to the study of the moving image. The gaols of SCMS are to promote all areas of media studies within universities and two- and four-year colleges; to encourage and reward excellence in scholarship and writing; to facilitate and improve the teaching of media studies as disciplines and to advance multi-cultural awareness and interaction.
1M Members
Founded in 1959

8882
Society of American Magicians
PO Box 510260
Saint Louis, MO 63151-0260
314-846-5659
FAX 314-846-5659
E-Mail: rmblowers@aol.com
Home Page: www.magicsam.com

J.Christopher Bontjes, President
Bruce Kalver, First VP
Mike Miller, Second VP

INFORMATION RESOURCES / Associations

Chuck Lehr, Secretary
Mary Ann Blowers, Treasurer

Founded to promote and maintain harmonious fellowship among those interested in magic as an art, to improve ethics of the magical profession, and to foster, promote and improve the advancement of magical arts in the field of amusement and entertainment. Membership includes professional and amateur magicians, manufacturers of magical apparatus and collectors.
5.5M Members
Founded in 1902

8883
Society of Camera Operators
PO Box 2006
Toluca Lake, CA 91610
818-382-7070
FAX 323-856-9155
E-Mail: info@soc.org
Home Page: www.soc.org

Dan Dodd, Director

Non-profit organization which advances the art and creative contribution of the operating cameraman in the Motion Picture and Television Industries.
Founded in 1979
Mailing list available for rent

8884
Society of Motion Picture & Television Engineers
3 Barker Ave
5th Floor
White Plains, NY 10601-1509
914-761-1100
FAX 914-761-3115
Home Page: www.smpte.org
Social Media: *Facebook, Twitter, LinkedIn, Youtube*

Barbara Lange, Executive Director
Sally-Ann D'Amato, Director Operations
Roberta Gorman, Manager
Peter Symes, Director Engineering
Amiee Ricca, Marketing and Communications

The SMPTE is the leading technical society for the motion imaging industry. It was founded to advance theory and development in the motion imaging field. Today, it publishes ANSI-approved Standards, Recommended Practices, and Engineering Guidelines. SMPTE holds conferences and local Section meetings to bring people and ides together, allowing for useful interaction and information exchange.
100 Members
Founded in 1916

8885
Society of Professional Audio Recording Services
9 Music Square S
Suite 222
Nashville, TN 37203
800-771-7727
FAX 214-722-1422
E-Mail: spars@spars.com
Home Page: www.spars.com

Karen Brinton, President
Eric W Johnson, Secretary
Andrew Kautz, Treasurer

SPARS is dedicated to excellence through innovation, education and communication.
200 Members
Founded in 1979
Mailing list available for rent

8886
Society of Stage Directors and Choreographers
1501 Broadway
Suite 1701
New York, NY 10036-5653
212-391-1070
800-541-5204
FAX 212-302-6195
E-Mail: info@ssdc.org
Home Page: www.ssdc.org
Social Media: *Facebook,*

Laura Penn, Executive Director
Sue Lawless, Secretary
Doug Hughes, Treasurer
Barbara Hauptman, Executive Director
Gretchen M Michelfeld, Membership Coordinator

An independent labor union representing directors and choreographers in American theatre.
1700 Members
Founded in 1959
Mailing list available for rent

8887
Songwriters Guild of America
5120 Virginia Way
Suite C22
Brentwood, TN 37027
615-742-9945
800-524-6742
FAX 615-630-7501
E-Mail: corporate@songwritersguild.com
Home Page: www.songwritersguild.com

Joe Whitt, Manager

Provides agreements between songwriters, composers and publishers. The SGA will take such lawful actions as will advance, promote and benefit the profession.
4000 Members
Founded in 1931

8888
Southern Arts Federation
1800 Peachtree St NW
Suite 808
Atlanta, GA 30309-2512
404-874-7244
FAX 404-873-2148
Home Page: www.southarts.org

Susie Surkamer, Executive Director
Stephanie Conner, Secretary
Ken May, Treasurer
David Batley, Marketing/Communications Director

In partnership with nine state arts agencies: promotes and supports arts regionally, nationally and internationally; enhances the artistic excellence and professionalism of Southern Arts Organizations and artists; serves the diverse population of the south.
Founded in 1975

8889
Stuntmen's Association of Motion Pictures
5200 Lankershim Blvd.
Suite 190
North Hollywood, CA 91601
818-766-4334
FAX 818-766-5943
E-Mail: hq@stuntmen.com
Home Page: www.stuntmen.com

Chris Doyle, Manager
Jeff Wolfe, First VP
Alex Daniels, Second VP
Toby Holguin, Secretary
Hugh Aodh O'Brien, Treasurer

Seeks to improve working conditions for stuntmen. Encourages members to uphold high professional standards.
135 Members
Founded in 1961

8890
Stuntwomen's Association of Motion Pictures
3760 Cahuenga Blvd
Suite 104
Studio City, CA 91604-2411
818-588-8888
888-817-9267
FAX 818-762-0907
E-Mail: INFO@STUNTWOMEN.COM
Home Page: www.stuntwomen.com
Social Media: *Facebook,*

Jane Austin, President

A professional association for stuntwomen and stunt coordinators which seeks to uphold professional standards and improve working conditions.
Founded in 1967

8891
Sundance Institute
1825 Three Kings Drive
PO Box 684429
Park City, UT 84060
435-658-3456
FAX 435-658-3457
E-Mail: Institute@sundance.org
Home Page: www.sundance.org

Robert Redford, President
Kerl Putnam, Executive Director
Geoffrey Gilmore, Director Sundance Film Festival
Brooke McAffee, Director Finance
Ellen Oh, Associate Director Marketing

Non-profit organization dedicated to the discovery and development of independent artists and audiences. The Institute seeks to discover, support, and inspire independent film and theatre artists from the United States and around the world, and to introduce audiences to their new work. The Institutes programs include the annual Sundance Film Festival, held in Park City, Utah each January.
Founded in 1981

8892
Sweet Adelines International
PO Box 470168
Tulsa, OK 74147-0168
918-622-1444
800-992-7464
FAX 918-665-0894
E-Mail: admin@sweetadelineintl.org
Home Page: www.sweetadelineintl.org

Donna Kerley, Dicector Finance/Administration
Kelly Kirchoff, Director Communications
Jane Hanson, Marketing/Membership Coordinator

A worldwide organization of women singers committed to advancing the musical art form of barbershop harmony through education and performances. Their motto is to 'Harmonize the World.'
27000 Members
Founded in 1945

8893
Theatre Authority
165 West 46th Street
New York, NY 10036

1063

INFORMATION RESOURCES / Newsletters

212-869-8530
FAX 212-719-9815
Home Page:
www.actorsequity.org/benefits/theatreauthority.asp
Presides over theatrical agencies and performing arts organizations.

8894
Theatre Bay Area
1663 Mission Street
Suite 525
San Francisco, CA 94103
415-430-1140
FAX 415-430-1145
E-Mail: tba@theatrebayarea.org
Home Page: www.theatrebayarea.org
Social Media: *Facebook, Twitter, YouTube*

Karen Mc Kevitt, Executive Director
Dale Albright, Director, Member Services
Clayton Lord, Director, Audience Development

Theatre Bay Area's mission is to unite, strengthen and promote the theatre community in the San Francisco Bay Area, working on behalf of their conviction that the performing arts are an essential public good, critical to a healthy and truly democratic society, and invaluable as a source of personal enrichment and growth.
3,000 Members
Founded in 1976

8895
Theatre Communications Group
520 8th Ave
24th Floor
New York, NY 10018-8666
212-609-5900
FAX 212-609-5901
E-Mail: tcg@tcg.org
Home Page: www.tcg.org
Social Media: *Facebook, Twitter,*

Theresa Eyring, Executive Director
Jennifer Cleary, Director of Membership

The mission of the TCG is to strengthen, nurture and promote the professional not-for-profit American theatre. TCG believes that their diversity as a field is their greatest strength. They celebrate differences in aesthetic, culture, organizational structure, and geography. They believe that every theatre makes a contribution to the greater field as a whole, that every performance expands the artistic vocabulary for us all, and that we all benefit from one another's presence.
Cost: $39.95
14000 Members
Frequency: Monthly
Founded in 1961

8896
Theatre Development Fund
520 Eight Avenue
Suite 801
New York, NY 10018-6507
212-912-9770
E-Mail: info@tdf.org
Home Page: www.tdf.org
Social Media: *Facebook, RSS*

Earl D. Weiner, Chairman
Sandra Kresch, Vice Chairman
Robert T. Goldm Treasurer, Deborah
Hartnett Secretary

Not-for-profit service organization for the performing arts. TDF administers a wide range of audience development and financial assistance programs that encourage production of new plays and musicals and enable more New Yorkers and visitors to enjoy the riches and variety of the city's theatre, dance and music.
Cost: $25
Founded in 1968

8897
US Institute for Theatre Technology
315 S Crouse Ave
Suite 200
Syracuse, NY 13210-1835
315-463-6463
800-938-7488
FAX 315-463-6525
E-Mail: info@.usitt.org
Home Page: www.usitt.org
Social Media: *Facebook, LinkedIn,*

Carol Carrigan, Manager
Patricia Dennis, Secretary
Travis DeCastro, Treasurer

Association of design, production and technology professionals in the performing arts and entertainment industry whose mission is to promote the knowledge and skills of its members. International in scope, USITT draws its board of directors from across the US and Canada. Sponsors projects, programs, research, symposia, exhibits and annual conference. Disseminates information on aesthetic and technical developments.
3700 Members
Founded in 1960

8898
USA Dance Inc
PO Box 152988
Cape Coral, FL 33915-2988
800-447-9047
FAX 239-573-0946
E-Mail: central-office@usadance.org
Home Page: usadance.org
Social Media: *Facebook, Twitter, LinkedIn,*

Lydia Scardina, National President
Bill Rose, Sr.Vice President
Greg Warner, National Secretary
Esther Freeman, National Treasurer
Ken Richards, VP, Dance Sports

Nonprofit organization working to promote ballroom dancing, both as a recreational activity and as a competitive sport, and to educate the public about the mental, physical and social benefits of dance.
23000 Members
Founded in 1965

8899
University Film and Video Association
UFVA Membership Office C/O Cheryl Jestis
University of Illinois Press
1325 South Oak Street
Champaign, IL 61820-6903
217-244-0626
866-244-0626
FAX 217-244-9910
E-Mail: ufvahome@gmail.com
Home Page: www.ufva.org
Social Media: *Facebook, Twitter,*

Karla Berry, President
Thomas Tomasulo, Executive VP
Beverly Seckinger, Secretary
Peter Bukalski, Treasurer
Cheryl Jestis, Membership Coordinator

Supports those interested in the fields of film and video production, history, criticism, and aesthetics. Provides training, education, and a quarterly magazine.
Cost: $75
Founded in 1947

8900
Women in Film
6100 Wilshire Blvd
Suite 710
Los Angeles, CA 90048-5107
323-935-2211
FAX 323-935-2212
E-Mail: info@wif.org
Home Page: www.wif.org

Tichi Wilkerson-Kassel, Founder
CiCi Holloway, President
Glen Alpert, VP Membership
Nicole Katz, CFO
Gayle Nachlis, Executive Director

WIFs purpose is to empower, promote, nurture, and mentor women in the industry through a network of valuable contacts, events, and programs.
10000 Members
Founded in 1974

8901
Women in the Arts Foundation
C/O E Butler
PO Box 1258
New York, NY 10276
212-941-0130
E-Mail: reginas@anny.org
Home Page: www.anny.org/2/orgs/womeninarts/

Regina Stewart, Executive Director
Eric Butler, Executive Coordinator
Linda Butti, Executive Coordinator
Sari Menna, Financial Coordinator

WIA works to overcome discrimination against women artists. They provide information to help women function effectively as professional artists. WIA is open to all women interested in the arts.
150 Members
Founded in 1971

8902
World Piano Competition/AMSA
441 Vine St
Suite 1030
Cincinnati, OH 45202-2832
513-421-5342
FAX 513-421-2672
E-Mail: info@amsa-wpc.orgm
Home Page: www.amsa-wpc.org

Gloria Ackerman, Founder, CEO
William Selnick, Treasurer
Stanley Aronoff, Event Chair
Leon Fleisher, President

Provides an continuum of services and role models to assist youth in need. Their task is to provide a venue of excitement and compassion to teach them to do their best to prepare for the enormous challenges they will face as they approach adulthood.
2.5M Members
Founded in 1956
Newsletters

Newsletters

8903
American Academy of Arts & Sciences Bulletin
American Academy of Arts & Sciences
136 Irving Street
Cambridge, MA 02138
617-576-5000
FAX 617-576-5050

INFORMATION RESOURCES / Newsletters

E-Mail: vsp@amacad.org
Home Page: www.amacad.org

Leslie Berkowitz, President
Mark Robinson, Director, Operations
Paul Karoff, Director, Communications

Features the following departments: Academy News; Around the Country; Noteworthy; and Remembrance.
Frequency: 2x/year

8904
American Dance
240 West 14th Street
New York, NY 10011
212-932-2789
E-Mail: info@americandanceguild.org
Home Page: www.americandanceguild.org
Social Media: Facebook,

Gloria McLean, President
Tina Croll, VP

Contains articles on member news, dance, and education.
Frequency: 4 per year
Founded in 1956

8905
American Guild Associate News Newsletter
American Guild of Music
PO Box 599
Warren, MI 48090-4905
248-686-1975
FAX 630-968-0197
E-Mail: agm@americanguild.org
Home Page: www.americanguild.org

Richard Chizmadia, Editor-in-Chief

Offers information and news for professionals in the music profession.
Cost: $25
5000 Members
Frequency: Quarterly
Founded in 1901

8906
American Music Center Opportunity Update
American Music Center
322 8th Ave
Suite 1001
New York, NY 10001-6774
212-366-5263
FAX 212-366-5265
E-Mail: center@amc.net
Home Page: www.amc.net

Joanne Cossa, Executive Director

A listing of composition competitions, calls for scores, workshops, and other opportunities delivered every month via e-mail to members of the American Music Center.
Frequency: Monthly
Founded in 1939

8907
American Musical Instrument Society Newsletter
AMIS
1106 Garden Street
Hoboken, NJ 07030
201-656-0107
E-Mail: amis@guildassoc.com
Home Page: www.amis.org

Albert R Rice, President
Carolyn Bryant, Vice-President

Deborah Check Reeves, Secretary
Joanne Kopp, Treasurer

Official notices and news of the Society's activites; short articles and communications; recent acquisition lists from member institutions; news of members; and classified ads.
Frequency: 2x/Year

8908
American Musicological Society Inc
University of Iowa
6010 College Station
Brunswick, ME 04011-8451
207-798-4243
877-679-7648
FAX 207-798-4254
E-Mail: ams@ams-net.org
Home Page: www.ams-net.org

Peter Alexander, Editor
Robert Judd, Executive Director
Al Hipkins, Office Manager
Melissa Kapocius, Secretary

The AMS Newsletter is published simiannually in February and August. The February Newsletter is mailed with the new Directory and Ballot each year. The August Newsletter is mailed with the Annual Meeting information and registration form each year.
Frequency: Semi-Annually
Founded in 1934

8909
American School Band Directors Association Newsletter
American School Band Directors Association
227 N 1st Street
PO Box 696
Guttenberg, IA 52052-0696
563-252-2500
FAX 563-252-2500
E-Mail: asbda@alpinecom.net
Home Page: www.asbda.com

Monte Dunnum, President
Valerie Gaffney, Secretary
Blair Callaway, Treasurer

Reports and information for members of the ASBDA
Frequency: Quarterly
Founded in 1953
Printed in 2 colors on matte stock

8910
American Viola Society Newsletter
American Viola Society
14070 Proton Rd
Suite 100
Dallas, TX 75244-3601
972-233-9107
FAX 972-490-4219
E-Mail: stemple@comcast.net
Home Page: www.madcrouch.com

Madeleine Crouch, President

A monthly e-newsletter. It contains announcements from the AVS, upcoming local chapter events, and other important items.
Frequency: Monthly

8911
Artsearch
Theatre Communications Group
520 8th Ave
Suite 305
New York, NY 10018-4156
212-609-5900
FAX 212-609-5901

E-Mail: tcg@tcg.org
Home Page: www.tcg.org

Theresa Eyring, Executive Director

Artsearch is divided into five main categories: Administration, Artistic, Production/Design, Career Development, and Education.
Cost: $75
Frequency: Bi-Monthly
ISSN: 0730-9023
Founded in 1961
Printed in on newsprint stock

8912
Banjo Newsletter
PO Box 3418
Annapolis, MD 21403-0418
800-759-7425
FAX 410-263-6503
E-Mail: bnl@infionline.net
Home Page: www.banjonews.com

Newletter focusing on Bluegrass banjo music.
Mailing list available for rent

8913
Bluegrass Music Profiles
Bluegrass Publications
PO Box 850
Nicholasville, KY 40340-0850
859-333-6456
E-Mail: info@bluegrassmusicprofiles.com
Home Page: www.bluegrassmusicprofiles.com
Social Media: Facebook, Twitter,

Information on Bluegrass music.

8914
Bluegrass Now
PO Box 2020
Rolla, MO 65402
573-341-7335
E-Mail: Bgn@fidnet.com
Home Page: www.bluegrassnow.com

Information on Bluegrass music.

8915
Bluegrass Unlimited
PO Box 771
Warrenton, VA 20188-0771
540-349-8181
800-258-4727
E-Mail: info@bluegrassmusic.com
Home Page: www.bluegrassmusic.com

Information on Bluegrass music.
Mailing list available for rent

8916
Broadside
Theatre Library Association
New York Public Library for Performing Arts
40 Lincoln Center Plaza
New York, NY 10023
E-Mail: info@tla-online.org
Home Page: www.tla-online.org/publications/broadside.html

Nancy Friedland, President
Angela Weaver, VP
Rebecca Lord, Executive Secretary
Collen Reilly, Treasurer

Features articles and news items related to exhibitions and collections, information about TLA-sponsored events, book reviews, and other items of interest in the fields of theatre, film, and dance.

INFORMATION RESOURCES / Newsletters

ISSN: 0068-2748
Founded in 1937

8917
Brooklyn Institute for Studies in American Music
Brooklyn College
2900 Bedford Ave
Brooklyn, NY 11210-2889
718-951-5000
Home Page:
www.brooklyn.cuny.edu/bb/fac/american.htm

Karen L Gould, President

Music news and Academy activities.
Frequency: Semi-Annual
Founded in 1861

8918
CMS Newsletter
College Music Society
312 E Pine Street
Missoula, MT 59802
406-721-9616
FAX 406-721-9419
E-Mail: cms@music.org
Home Page: www.music.org

Robby D Gunstream, Executive Director

8919
Country Dance and Song Society News
Country Dance and Song Society
116 Pleasant St
Suite 345
Easthampton, MA 01027-2759
413-203-5467
FAX 413-203-5471
E-Mail: news@cdss.org
Home Page: www.cdss.org

Caroline Batson, Editor
Rima Dael, Executive Director
Bob Blondin, Business Manager

A selection of articles, letters and poems. CDSS News is available as a benefit of membership in the Country Dance and Song Society.
ISSN: 1070-8251
Founded in 1915

8920
DNBulletin
151 W 30th Street
Suite 202
New York, NY 10001
212-564-0985
FAX 212-216-9027
E-Mail: dnbinfo@dancenotation.org
Home Page: www.dancenotation.org

Senta Driver, Editor

Dance news for consumers and professionals.
Founded in 1940
Printed in 2 colors on matte stock

8921
Dancedrill
3101 Poplarwood Court
Suite 310
Raleigh, NC 27604-1010
919-872-7888
FAX 919-872-6888

Susan Wershing, Publisher
Kay Crawford, Editor

Publication informs members of dance drill teams and their directors.

Frequency: 4 per year

8922
Dirty Linen
PO Box 6660
Baltimore, MD 21239-6600
410-583-7973
E-Mail: office@dirtylinen.com
Home Page: www.dirtylinen.com

Information on Bluegrass music.

8923
Dramatists Guild Newsletter
Dramatists Guild of America
1501 Broadway
Suite 701
New York, NY 10036-5505
212-398-9366
FAX 212-944-0420
Home Page: www.dramaguild.com

Ralph Sevush, Executive Director

Supplement to 'The Dramatist,' available only to Guild members, includes bi-monthly reports from New York and Los Angeles, advice from the Business Affairs Department, the latest information on submission and career development opportunities, and reminders of approaching deadlines.

8924
Early Music Newsletter
New York Recorder Guild
145 W 93 Street
New York, NY 10025-7559
212-662-2946
E-Mail: mzumoff@nyc.rr.com
Home Page: www.priceclan.com/nyrecorderguild/

Michael Zumoff, Executive Director

A publication of the New York Recorder Guild
10 Pages
Frequency: Monthly

8925
Festival Rag
541 Main Street
Union, WV 24983
FAX 888-813-5457
E-Mail: markus@kemek.com
Home Page:
www.kemek.com/independent-film/the-festival-rag

Markus Varjo, Publisher
Cil Ripley, Editor-In-Chief
Dave Roberts, Managing Editor
Carl Merrick, Content & Development

Dedicated to true independent filmmaking and filmmakers, and broadcast to thousands of media-industry subscribers. Provides information on film festivals worldwide, including interviews with filmmakers and programmers.

8926
Film Advisory Board Monthly
Film Advisory Board
263 W Olive Avenue
#377
Burbank, CA 91502
323-461-6541
FAX 323-469-8541
Home Page: www.filmadvisoryboard.org
Social Media: Facebook, Twitter, LinkedIn,

Janet Stokes, President

Information and news on the entertainment industry.

Frequency: Monthly
Founded in 1975
Printed in one color on glossy stock

8927
Flatpicking Guitar
High View Publications
PO Box 2160
Pulaski, VA 24301
540-980-0338
800-413-8296
FAX 540-980-0557
E-Mail: info@flatpickingmercantile.com
Home Page: www.flatpick.com

Information on Bluegrass music and the Flatpick guitar.
Mailing list available for rent

8928
GMA Update
Gospel Music Association
PO Box 22697
Nashville, TN 37202
615-242-0303
FAX 615-254-9755
E-Mail: info@gospelmusic.org
Home Page: www.gospelmusic.org

John Styll, President
Jackie Patillo, Executive Director

GMA's industry e-newsletter available to any non-GMA member who wishes to receive it. Sent out once a month, GMA Update contains the latest news about the Christian music industry and valuable information about the GMA.
Frequency: Monthly
Mailing list available for rent

8929
GMAil
Gospel Music Association
PO Box 22697
Nashville, TN 37202
615-242-0303
FAX 615-254-9755
Home Page: www.gospelmusic.org

John Styll, President

E-newsletter sent weekly to GMA members. Includes weekly music sales, charts, news, links to valuable resources, and information about upcoming GMA and industry events.
Frequency: Weekly
Founded in 1964

8930
Girl Groups Gazette
PO Box 69A04
Department HSND
West Hollywood, CA 90069-0066

Louis Wendruck, Editor/Publisher

For fans of girl groups and female singers of the 1960's and 70's including photos, discographies, records, t-shirts, postcards, and videos.
Cost: $20
Frequency: Quarterly
Founded in 1988

8931
Hollywood Arts Council
PO Box 931056
Hollywood, CA 90093
323-462-2355
FAX 323-465-9240
E-Mail: bianca@hollywoodartcouncil.org
Home Page: www.hollywoodartscouncil.org

Promotes, nurtures and supports the arts field in Hollywood. Newsletter is included with membership.
Founded in 1978
Printed in 4 colors on glossy stock

8932
INTIX Bulletin
International Ticketing Association
One College Park, 8910 Purdue Road
Suite 480
Indianapolis, IN 46268
212-629-4036
FAX 212-628-8532
E-Mail: info@intix.org
Home Page: www.intix.org

Jena L Hoffman, President
Kathleen O'Donnell, Director

E-bulletin provides news from the International Ticketing Association including information about upcoming events, conferences and exhibitions, industry news.
1200 Members
Frequency: Monthly
ISSN: 1071-6254
Founded in 1979
Printed in 4 colors on glossy stock

8933
In Focus
National Association of Theatre Owners
13190 SW 68th Parkway
Suite 200
Portland, OR 97223-8368
503-207-4700
877-388-8385
FAX 503-207-1937
Home Page: http://www.infocus.com

8934
In Theater
Parker Publishing & Communications
214 Sullivan St
Suite 2C
New York, NY 10012-1354
212-228-1225
FAX 212-719-4477
E-Mail: intheater@aol.com
Home Page: www.parkerhodges.com

Emily Parker, President

Offers the reader a behind-the-scenes perspective of how a show is technically conceived, rehearsed and staged. Regular departments center on drama and musical reviews, listings of shows in major cities and columnist options.
Cost: $78
Frequency: Weekly
Circulation: 71,068

8935
In the Groove
Michigan Antique Phonograph Society
60 Central St
Battle Creek, MI 49017-3704
269-968-1299
E-Mail: ITG@michiganantiquephonographsociety.org
Home Page:
www.michiganantiquephonographsociety.org

Phil Stewart, Editor
Eileen Stewart, Editor

The Newsletter of the Michigan Antique Phonograph Society. Includes show, sales and auction announcements, MAPS chapter news, President's message, monthly feature articles, letters to the editor, and swap shop.
Cost: $25
24 Pages
Frequency: Monthly
Founded in 1976

8936
InLEAGUE
League of Historic American Theatres
2105 Laurel Bush Rd
Suite 201
Bel Air, MD 21015
443-640-1058
877-627-0833
FAX 443-640-1031
E-Mail: info@lhat.org
Home Page: www.lhat.org

Frances Holden, Executive Director
John Bell, VP
Darlene Smolik, Treasurer
Edward Kelsey, Secretary

Quarterly newsletter which reports news from historic theatre progects around the country and features articles on all facets of historic theatre restoration and operation. The newsletter solicits articles and information from the membership.
Frequency: Quarterly
Founded in 1976

8937
International Bluegrass Music Association
IBMA
2 Music Cir S
Suite 100
Nashville, TN 37203-4381
615-256-3222
888-438-4262
FAX 615-256-0450
E-Mail: info@ibma.org
Home Page: www.ibma.org

Dan Hays, Executive Director

Information on Bluegrass music from the IBMA

8938
Job Contact Bulletin
Southeastern Theatre Conference
1175 Revolution Mill Dr.
Studio 14
Greensboro, NC 27405
336-272-3645
FAX 336-272-8810
E-Mail: arpil@setc.org
Home Page: www.setc.org

April J'C Marshall, Contact
Jack Benjamin, President
H. Duke Guthrie, Treasurer

On-line employment listing of Classified Ads for theatrical positions, auditions, and more.
Founded in 1949

8939
Music for the Love of It
67 Parkside Drive
Berkeley, CA 94705-2409
510-654-9134
FAX 510-654-4656
E-Mail: tedrust@musicfortheloveofit.com
Home Page: www.musicfortheloveofit.com

Edgar Rust, Publisher/Editor
Janet Telford, Co-Editor

A newsletter for people everywhere who love making music. Every issues brings new enthusiasm, new ideas and new opportunities for making music.
Frequency: Bi-Monthly
ISSN: 0898-8757
Founded in 1988
Printed in on matte stock

8940
National Music Museum Newsletter
National Music Museum
414 E Clark St
Vermillion, SD 57069-2307
605-677-5306
FAX 605-677-6995
E-Mail: smm@usd.edu
Home Page: www.usd.edu/smm/

Andre Larson, Director

Quarterly Newletter which includes feature articles written by the curatorial staff and lists recent acquisitions. Published in February, May, August and November. It is available with basic museum membership.
Cost: $35
Printed in 4 colors

8941
No Depression
908 Halcyon Avenue
Nashville, TN 37204
615-292-7084
Home Page: www.nodepression.net

Information on Bluegrass music
Founded in 1995

8942
Notes a Tempo
West Virginia University
Fairmount State University
1201 Locust Avenue
Fairmont, WV 26554
304-293-4841
Home Page:
www.wvmea.tripod.com/Notes_a_Tempo_Winter_10.pdf

David Bess, Co-Editor
Becky Terry, Co-Editor

The official publication of the West Virginia Music Educators. Published Fall, Winter and Spring
20-32 Pages
Frequency: 3 per year
Circulation: 1115

8943
Old Time Herald
P.O.Box 61679
Durham, NC 27715-1679
919-286-2041
E-Mail: info@oldtimeherald.org
Home Page: www.oldtimeherald.org

Sarah Bryan, Editor-in-chief
Peter Honig, Business Director

Information on Bluegrass music
Mailing list available for rent

8944
Pedal Steel Newsletter
Pedal Steel Guitar Association
PO Box 20248
Floral Park, NY 11002-0248
516-616-9214
FAX 516-616-9214
E-Mail: bobpsga@optonline.net
Home Page: www.psga.org

INFORMATION RESOURCES / Newsletters

Doug Mack, Editor
Bob Maickel, President

Dedicated to the art of playing pedal steel guitar. Every issue contains tablature arrangements of songs for the steel guitar as well as coming events, record reviews, product reports and news concerning the instrument.
Frequency: 10 x Per Year
ISSN: 1088-7954
Founded in 1973
Mailing list available for rent

8945
Percussion News
Percussive Arts Society
**110 W Washington Street
Suite A
Indianapolis, IN 46204**
317-974-4488
FAX 317-974-4499
E-Mail: percarts@pas.org
Home Page: www.pas.org

Rick Mattingly, Editor
Hillary Henry, Art Director
Lisa Rogers, President

Newsletter devoted to membership activities. This colorful newsletter also features a Classified Advertising section. Percussion News is published in January, March, May, July, September and November.
Frequency: 6 Editions Per Year
Founded in 1961
Mailing list available for rent

8946
Performing Arts Insider
PAI C/O Total Theater
**PO Box 31
Greeley, CO 80632**
970-405-3077
E-Mail: totalpost@totaltheater.com
Home Page: performingartsinsider.com

A leading source of information about the perfoming arts in New York City and around the country. Each issue includes day-by-day calendar listings of shows on broadway, off and off-off broadway, plus dance, opera, cabaret and special events. Also includes comprehensive theatre guides, listing the author, director, cast, designers, synopsis, theater and box office details, as well as contact information for producers, press agents, general managers and casting directors.
Cost: $275
Frequency: Monthly+9 Mid-Month Updat
Founded in 1944
Printed in on matte stock

8947
Preview Family Movie & TV Review
Movie Morality Ministries
**6302 Riverside Dr
Irving, TX 75039**
972-409-9960
800-807-8071
FAX 785-255-4316
E-Mail: preview@fni.com
Home Page: www.merchantcircle.com

Dave Haverty, President
Greg Shull, Editor
Susan Haverty, Desktop Publisher/Office Manager

Reviews current films and TV series from a Christian and family values perspective.
Cost: $34
Frequency: Monthly
ISSN: 0892-6468
Printed in 2 colors on matte stock

8948
Rolling Stone
Rolling Stone Magazine
**1290 Ave of the Americas
2nd Floor
New York, NY 10104-0298**
212-484-1616
800-283-1549
FAX 212-484-1771
E-Mail: rollingstone@real.com
Home Page: www.rssoundingboard.com
Social Media: *Facebook, Twitter, YouTube, RSS, Foursqare*

Jann Wenner, President

A monthly newsletter geared for marketing, advertising and music exexecutives. It includes information on such matters as rock tours and musician endorsements, ad campaigns and rock contests.
Cost: $50
Frequency: Monthly
Founded in 1967
Mailing list available for rent

8949
Roots and Rhythm Newsletter
Roots and Rhythm
**PO Box 837
El Cerrito, CA 94530**
510-526-8373
888-766-8766
FAX 510-526-9001
E-Mail: roots@toast.net
Home Page: www.rootsandrhythm.com

Frank Scott, Owner
Nancy Scott-Noennig, Co-Owner

Lists, reviews and makes available for sale, recordings of blues, rhythm and blues, rockabilly, country, folk, ethnic, nostalgia and jazz music. Each newsletter reviews about 400 items and lists another 500 without reviews.
Frequency: Bi-Monthly
Circulation: 10000
Founded in 1974
Printed in 2 colors on newsprint stock

8950
SETC News
Southeastern Theatre Conference
**1175 Revolution Mill Dr.
Studio 14
Greensboro, NC 27405**
336-272-3645
FAX 336-272-8810
E-Mail: deanna@setc.org.net
Home Page: www.setc.org

Deanna Thompson, Editor
Jack Benjamin, President
H. Duke Guthrie, Treasurer

Provides news and important information to members of the Southeaster Theatre Conference on upcoming SETC events, advocacy efforts, awards and competitions as well as items of special interest to the various divisions and interest areas. In addition, SETC News publishes news about people and organizations based in the Southeast.
Circulation: 4000
Founded in 1949

8951
Sing Out!
**PO Box 5460
Bethlehem, PA 18015-0460**
610-865-5366
FAX 215-895-3052
E-Mail: info@singout.org
Home Page: www.singout.org

Information on Bluegrass music
Mailing list available for rent

8952
Spotlight
American Association of Community Theatre
**1300 Gendy St Forth Worth
Forth Worth, TX 76107**
817-732-3177
866-687-2228
FAX 817-732-3178
E-Mail: info@aact.org
Home Page: www.aact.org
Social Media: *Facebook, Twitter,*

Julie Angelo, Executive Director
John Sullivan, President

News and updates on issues pertinent to community theatre.
Cost: $2
24 Pages
Circulation: 2000
Founded in 1958
Mailing list available for rent: 9,500 names at $180 per M
Printed in on matte stock

8953
Technical Brief
Yale School of Drama
**222 York Street
PO Box 208244
New Haven, CT 06520**
203-432-8188
FAX 203-432-8129
E-Mail: bronislaw.sammler@yale.edu
Home Page: www.technicalbrief.org

Ben Sammler, Editor
Dan Harvey, Editor

Produced for technical managers in theater. Written by professionals for professionals, its purpose is simple: communication. Technical Brief provides a dailogue between technical practitioners from the several performing arts who all share similar problems.
Cost: $15
Frequency: 3 X Year
Founded in 1924

8954
Tempo
Academy of Country Music
**5500 Balboa Blvd
Suite 200
Encino, CA 91316-1505**
818-788-8000
FAX 818-788-0999
E-Mail: info@acmcountry.com
Home Page: www.acmcountry.com

Butch Waugh, Chairman

Devoted exclusively to the country music industry.
12 Pages
Frequency: Quarterly
Circulation: 4500
Founded in 1964

8955
The Voice
**1156 15th St NW
Suite 310
Washington, DC 20005-1747**
202-331-7577
FAX 202-331-7599

INFORMATION RESOURCES / Magazines & Journals

E-Mail: service@chorusamerica.org
Home Page: www.chorusamerica.org

Ann Meier Baker, President & Chief Executive Officer
1600 Members
Frequency: Quarterly
Circulation: 5000
ISSN: 1074-0805
Founded in 1977

8956
Westfield Center
Westfield Center for Early Keyboard Studies
726 University Ave, Room 102
Cornell University
Ithaca, NY 14850-3914
607-255-3065
E-Mail: info@westfield.org
Home Page: www.westfield.org

Annette Richards, Executive Director
Maja Anderson, Program Coordinator
Evan Cortens, Administrative Assistant

E-newsletter providing information to professional keyboard musicians.
12 Pages
Frequency: Monthly
Founded in 1979

8957
Women in Bluegrass Newsletter
PO Box 2498
Winchester, VA 22604
800-227-2357
E-Mail: Nmhentry@visuallink.com
Home Page:
www.murphymethod/com/womeninbluegrass.cfm

Information on women in bluegass music

8958
Women in the Arts Bulletin
Women in the Arts Foundation
32-35 30th Street
D24
Long Island City, NY 11106
212-941-0130
E-Mail: reginas@anny.org
Home Page: www.womenintheartsfoundation.org

Erin Butler, Editor
Regina Stewart, Executir Director
Sandra Cockerham, President

Gallery information and reviews. Women in the Arts Foundation works to overcome discrimination against women artists.
Frequency: Monthly
Founded in 1971
Magazines & Journals

Magazines & Journals

8959
Advanstar
Advanstar Communications
641 Lexington Ave
Suite 8
New York, NY 10022-4503
212-951-6600
FAX 212-951-6793
E-Mail: info@advanstar.com
Home Page: www.advanstar.com

Joseph Loggia, CEO

News and features emphasize innovation in equipment technology and creative technique for editing, graphics, and special effects. Covers all budget levels from desktop post to feature films.
130 Pages
Frequency: Monthly
Circulation: 31464
Founded in 1986

8960
AfterTouch: New Music Discoveries
Music Discovery Network
PO Box 6205
Peoria, IL 61601-6205
309-685-4843
800-882-4262
FAX 309-685-4878
E-Mail: aimcmc@aol.com
Home Page: www.musicdiscoveries.com

Ronald Wallace, Editor

A magazine for music lovers who would like to experience new sights and sounds and would like to keep their fingers on the pulse of the music industry.
Frequency: Annual
Circulation: 10,000
Founded in 1984
Printed in on glossy stock

8961
American Cinematographer
American Society of Cinematographers
1782 North Orange Drive
PO Box 2230
Hollywood, CA 90078-2230
323-969-4333
800-448-0145
FAX 323-876-4973
E-Mail: office@theasc.com
Home Page: www.theasc.com

Covers feature films, television, commercials, music videos, digital video, new equipment, DVD and book releases and much more. An exploration and a reflection of today's cinematography. A publication of the American Society of Cinematographers.
Cost: $29.95
Frequency: Monthly
Circulation: 42000
Founded in 1919
Mailing list available for rent

8962
American Dancer
USA Dance
PO Box 152988
Cape Coral, FL 33915-2988
800-447-9047
FAX 239-573-0946
Home Page: www.usadance.org

Shawn Fisher, Editor

News of interests to dance enthusiasts.
Cost: $25
Frequency: Bi-Monthly
Circulation: 23000

8963
American Music
University of Illinois Press
1325 South Oak Street
MC-566
Champaign, IL 61820-6903
217-244-0626
866-244-0626
FAX 217-244-8082
E-Mail: journals@uillinois.edu
Home Page: www.press.uillinois.edu

Michael Pisani, Editor
Jeff McArdle, Journals Marketing/Advertising Mgr.

Publishes articles on American composers, performers, publishers, institutions, events, and the music industry as well as book and recording reviews, bibliographies, and discographies.
Cost: $45
Frequency: Quarterly
Circulation: 1650
ISSN: 0734-4392
Founded in 1981
Mailing list available for rent: 1,650 names at $100 per M
Printed in 2 colors on glossy stock

8964
American Music Teacher
Music Teachers National Association
441 Vine St
Suite 505
Cincinnati, OH 45202-2813
513-421-1420
888-512-5278
FAX 513-421-2503
E-Mail: mtnanet@mtna.org
Home Page: www.mtna.org

Gary L Ingle, Executive Director
Gail Berenson, President
Janice Wenger, VP

Provides articles, reviews and regular columns that inform, educate and challenge music teachers and foster excellence in the music teaching profession.
Cost: $30
Circulation: 35000
Founded in 1876
Mailing list available for rent: 24000 names at $85 per M
Printed in 4 colors on glossy stock

8965
American Organist
American Guild of Organists
475 Riverside Dr
Suite 1260
New York, NY 10115-0055
212-870-2310
800-246-5115
FAX 212-870-2163
E-Mail: info@agohq.org
Home Page: www.agohq.org
Social Media: Facebook,

James Thomashower, Executive Director

Most widely read journal devoted to organ and choral music in the world. Officialjournal of the American Guild of Organists, the Royal Canadian College of Organists, and the Associated Pipe Organ Builders of America.
Cost: $ 52
Frequency: Monthly
Circulation: 24000
ISSN: 0164-3150
Founded in 1967

8966
American String Teachers Journal
American String Teachers Association
4155 Chain Bridge Rd
Fairfax, VA 22030-4102
703-279-2113
FAX 703-279-2114
E-Mail: asta@astaweb.com
Home Page: www.astaweb.com

Donna Hale, Executive Director
Beth Danner-Knight, Deputy Director

INFORMATION RESOURCES / Magazines & Journals

Available to members. Provides an overview of current articles featured in the journal. Also answers questions about content, advertising, and contact information.
Cost: $90
Frequency: Quarterly
Circulation: 11,300
Mailing list available for rent: 10M+ names

8967
American Theatre Magazine
Theatre Communications Group
520 8th Ave
Suite 305
New York, NY 10018-8666
212-609-5900
FAX 212-609-5901
E-Mail: custserve@tcg.org
Home Page: www.tcg.org

Jim O'Quinn, Editor in Chief
Nicole Estvanik Taylor, Managing Editor
Cost: $35

8968
American Viola Society Journal
American Viola Society
14070 Proton Rd
Suite 100LB
Dallas, TX 75244-3601
972-233-9107
FAX 972-490-4219
E-Mail: info@avsnationaloffice.org
Home Page: www.americanviolasociety.org

Nokuthula Ngwenyama, President
Karin Brown, Secretary
Michelle Sayles, Treasurer
Kathryn Steely, Webmaster

Peer reviewed journal which promotes interest in the viola.
Cost: $42
Frequency: Annually
Circulation: 1500
Founded in 1984

8969
Animation Magazine
Animation Magazine
26500 W.Agoura Rd
Suite 102
Calabasas, CA 91302
818-883-2884
FAX 818-883-3773
E-Mail: info@animationmagazine.net
Home Page: www.animationmagazine.net

Jean Thoren, President

Promotes the art and business of animation and gives recognition to those animators and technicians who make the world of animation what it is today.
Cost: $50
Frequency: Monthly
Circulation: 30000
ISSN: 1041-617X
Founded in 1986
Printed in 4 colors on glossy stock

8970
Applause Magazine
Denver Center for Performing Arts
1101 13th St
Denver, CO 80204-5319
303-893-3272
800-641-2222
FAX 303-893-3206
Home Page: www.denvercenter.org

Randy Weeks, President
Daniel L. Ritchie, Chairman &CEO

A publication of the Denver Center Theatre Company and Dever Center Attractions
Frequency: 8-10 per year
Founded in 1988
Printed in 4 colors on glossy stock

8971
Asian Pacific American Journal
Asian American Writers Workshop
16 W 32nd St
Suite 10A
New York, NY 10001-1093
212-494-0061
FAX 212-494-0062
E-Mail: desk@aaww.org
Home Page: www.aaww.org

Ken Chen, Executive Director
Jeannie L Wong, Adminstrative Director
Anjali Goyal, Programs Assistant
Jeffrey Lin, Designer
Hanya Yanagihara, Journal Editor

Features include short fiction, poems, essays, stage scripts, translations and artwork.
Frequency: Semi-Annual
ISSN: 1067-778X
Founded in 1992

8972
BMI Musicworld
Broadcast Music
7 World Trade Center
250 Greenwich Street
New York, NY 10007-0030
212-220-3000
FAX 212-246-2163
Home Page: www.bmi.com

Del Bryant, CEO
John E Cody, COO/EVP

Performing rights organization. Articles of interest to the songwriting community.
Founded in 1985

8973
Back Stage
770 Broadway 7th Floor
New York, NY 10003
212-493-4420
800-658-8372
E-Mail: advertising@backstage.com
Home Page: www.backstage.com

Charles Weiss, Manager
Jamie Painter Young, Editor-in-Chief
Jenelle Riley, Film/TV Editor
Leonard Jacobs, Theatre Editor
Sherry Eaker, Editor-at-Large

Four print, four interactive and two face-to-face publications. Provides casting, news, articles and other resources for working actors, cingers, dancers and behind-the-scenes staff and crew.
Cost: $84
Circulation: 30,000
Founded in 1960
Mailing list available for rent

8974
Billboard Magazine
Prometheus Global Media
770 Broadwaye Blvd.
New York, NY 10003-9595
212-493-4100
FAX 646-654-5368

Home Page: www.prometheusgm.com
Social Media: Facebook, Twitter,

Richard D. Beckman, CEO
James A. Finkelstein, Chairman
Madeline Krakowsky, Vice President Circualtion
Tracy Brater, Executive Director Creative Service

Packed with in-depth music and entertainment features including the latest in new media and digital music, global coverage, music and money, touring, new artists, radio news and retail reports.
Cost: $149
Frequency: Weekly
Founded in 1894

8975
Bomb Magazine
New Art Publications
80 Hanson Pl
Suite 703
Brooklyn, NY 11217-1506
718-636-9100
866-354-0334
FAX 718-636-9200
E-Mail: info@bombsite.com
Home Page: www.bombsite.com
Social Media: Facebook, Twitter, YouTube

Betsy Sussler, Publisher/Editor
Mary-Ann Monforton, Associate Publisher
Nell McClister, Senior Editor
Lucy Raven, Managing Editor
Paul W Morris, Director Marketing/Special Projects

Focuses on contemporary art, literature, theater, film, music.
Cost: $495
Frequency: Quarterly
Circulation: 60,000
Founded in 1981
Mailing list available for rent
Printed in 4 colors on matte stock

8976
BoxOffice Magazine
BoxOffice Media
9107 Wilshire Blvd.
Suite 450
Beverly Hills, CA 90210-4241
310-876-9090
Home Page: www.boxoffice.com

Peter Crane, Publisher
Kenneth James Bacon, Creative Director
Phil Contrino, Editor
Amy Nicholson, Editor

The premier trade magazine covering the latest developments in the movie industry, from films in production to digital cinema and everything in between.
Founded in 1948

8977
CCM Magazine
Salem Publishing
402 BNA Drive
Suite 400
Nashville, TN 37217
615-386-3011
FAX 615-386-3380
E-Mail: info@ccmcom.com
Home Page: www.ccmmagazine.com
Social Media: Facebook, Twitter, RSS

Jim Cumbee, President

The voice of Contemporary Christian Music. Each monthly issue features music news, exclusive interviews, and an in-depth look at the spiritual lives of to-

INFORMATION RESOURCES / Magazines & Journals

day's leading Christian music artists.
Cost: $19.95
Frequency: Monthly
Founded in 1978
Printed in 4 colors on glossy stock

8978
Callaloo
Johns Hopkins University Press
2715 N Charles St
Baltimore, MD 21218-4363
410-516-6900
800-537-5487
FAX 410-516-6998
Home Page: www.press.jhu.edu/journals/callaloo

William Brody, President
Kyle G Dargan, Managing Editor

Journal of African and African-American issues. Content includes original works by, and critical studies of, black writers worldwide. Offers a rich mixture of fiction, poetry, plays, critical essays, cultural studies, interviews, and visual art, as well as special thematic issues.
Frequency: Quarterly
Circulation: 2,500
ISSN: 0161-2492
Founded in 1976

8979
Callboard
Theatre Bay Area
1663 Mission St
Suite 525
San Francisco, CA 94103-2487
415-430-1140
FAX 415-430-1145
E-Mail: tba@theatrebayarea.org
Home Page: www.theatrebayarea.org
Social Media: Facebook, Twitter, YouTube

Karen Mc Kevitt, Manager

Provides trade information for professionals in the Bay Area. The magazine contains the following departments: Letterbox, Inside the Industry, Community News, How Did They Do That, Keep An Eye On, Editors' Picks and Encore.
Cost: $65
Frequency: Monthly
ISSN: 1064-0703
Founded in 1976
Printed in 2 colors on matte stock

8980
Canadian Theatre Review
University of Toronto Press
5201 Dufferin Street
Toronto, ON M3H-5T8
416-667-7810
800-221-9985
FAX 416-667-7881
E-Mail: journals@utpress.utoronto.ca
Home Page: www.utpjournals.com
Social Media: Facebook, Twitter, Blog

Anne Marie Corrigan, VP
Audrey Greenwood, Advertising/Marketing Coordinator

Provides critical analysis and innovative coverage of current developments in Canadian theatre. Advocates new issues and artists. Publishes at least one significant new playscript per issue. Each issue includes at least one complete playscript related to the issue theme, insightful articles, and informative reviews.
Cost: $40
Frequency: Quarterly
ISSN: 0315-0836

Founded in 1974
Mailing list available for rental $250 per M

8981
Celebrity Service
8833 W Sunset Boulevard
Suite 401
Los Angeles, CA 90069-2171
213-883-3671
FAX 310-652-9244

Robert Dean, Manager/Director

A listing of celebrities names and addresses. Publisher of the Celebrity Bulletin informing the entertainment and news industry of which celebrities are traveling to Hollywood and New York
Frequency: Bi-Monthly

8982
Chamber Music Magazine
Chamber Music America
UPS Box 458
243 Fifth Avenue
New York, NY 10016
212-242-2022
FAX 212-242-7955
Home Page: www.chamber-music.org

Susan Dadian, Program Director
Margaret M Lioi, CEO
Louise Smith, Chair
Cost: $5.95
Frequency: Bi-Monthly
Circulation: 6000
Founded in 1977

8983
Choral Journal
American Choral Directors Association
545 Couch Drive
Oklahoma City, OK 73102
405-232-8161
FAX 405-232-8162
Home Page: www.acdaonline.org

Carroll Gonzo, Editor
Ron Granger, Managing Editor

Contains articles and columns of a scholarly and practical nature in addition to reviews of newly released CD recordings, books, and printed music.
Frequency: Monthly

8984
Cineaste
Cineaste Magazine
243 5th Ave
Suite 706
New York, NY 10016
212-366-5720
FAX 212-366-5724
E-Mail: cineaste@cineaste.com
Home Page: www.cineaste.com

Gary Crowdus, Editor-in-Chief
Cynthia Lucia, Editor
Richard Porton, Editor
Dan Georgakas, Consulting Editor
Vicki Robinson, Production Assistant

An internationally recognized independent film magazine. Features contributions from many of America's most articulate and outspoken writers, critics and scholars. Focussing on both the art and politics of the cinema.
Cost: $ 20
Frequency: Quarterly
Circulation: 11000
ISSN: 0009-7004

Founded in 1967
Mailing list available for rent

8985
Cinefantastique
CFQ Media
PO Box 34425
Los Angeles, CA 90034-0425
310-204-0825
FAX 310-204-5882
E-Mail: info@cfq.com
Home Page: www.cfq.com

Frederick Clarke, Editor

Provides coverage of genre entertainment. Each issue features in-depth coverage of sci-fi, fantasy and horror films, TV, DVDs, games, toys, books, comics and more.
Cost: $34.95
Frequency: Monthly
Circulation: 40,000

8986
Cinefex
79 Daily Drive
#309
Camarillo, CA 93010
805-383-0800
FAX 805-383-0803
E-Mail: advertising@cinefex.com
Home Page: www.cinefex.com

A quarterly magazine devoted to motion picture special effects.
Cost: $32
180 Pages
Frequency: Quarterly
Circulation: 30000
ISSN: 0198-1056
Founded in 1980
Printed in 4 colors

8987
Cinema Journal
University of Texas Press
2100 Comal
PO Box 7819
Austin, TX 78713-7819
512-471-7233
800-252-3206
FAX 512-232-7178
E-Mail: utpress@uts.cc.utexas.edu
Home Page: www.utexas.edu/utpress

Sponsored by the Society for Cinema and Media Studies. The journal presents recent scholarship by SCMS members. It publishes essays on a wide variety of subjects from diverse methodological perspectives. A 'Professional Notes' section informs Society of Cinema and Media Studies readers about upcoming events, research opportunities, and the latest published research. Cinema Journal is a member of the CELJ, the Conference of Editors of Learned Journals.
Cost: $42
144 Pages
Frequency: Quarterly
Circulation: 2800
ISSN: 0009-7101
Founded in 1950
Printed in on matte stock

8988
Clarinet Journal
International Clarinet Society
PO Box 5039
Wheaton, IL 60189-5039
630-665-3602
FAX 630-665-3848

INFORMATION RESOURCES / Magazines & Journals

E-Mail: info@clarinet.org
Home Page: www.clarinet.org

James Gillespie, Editor
So Rhee, Executive Director
Maxine Ramey, President
Caroline Hartig, Secretary
Tod Kerstetter, Treasurer

Contains articles in wide variety of areas written by performers and scholars.
Cost: $25
Frequency: Quarterly
Circulation: 3000

8989
Clavier
Instrumentalist Publishing Company
200 Northfield Road
Northfield, IL 60093-3390
847-446-5000
888-446-6888
FAX 847-446-6263
E-Mail: editor@theinstrumentalist.com
Home Page: www.instrumentalistmagazine.com
Social Media: Facebook,

James Rohner, Publisher
Judy Nelson, Editor

Provides new ideas and advice for piano teachers from leading educators. The focus of each issue is to offer practical advice for teachers. Articles include interviews with prominent performers, teachers and composers, the latest teaching methods, tributes to great artists of the past, and reviews of newly publshed music, educational software and videos.
Cost: $17
Frequency: 10X Per Year
Circulation: 16000
Founded in 1965
Mailing list available for rent

8990
Close Up Magazine
Country Music Association
One Music Circle S
Nashville, TN 37203
615-244-2840
FAX 615-242-4783
E-Mail: international@cmaworld.com
Home Page: www.cmaworld.com

Profiles of country music artists, various songwriters and industry news. Members of the Association receive the magazine as a benefit of their membership.
Circulation: 8000
Founded in 1958

8991
Confrontation
CW Post Campus English Department
720 Northern Blvd
Greenvale, NY 11548-1300
516-626-0099
FAX 516-299-3566
E-Mail: confrontation@liu.edu
Home Page: www.liunet.bkstore.com

Jayne Mo, Manager

Brings new talent to light in the shadows cast by well-known authors. Each issue contains orignal work by famous and by lesser known writers.
Cost: $10
Frequency: Twice Yearly
Founded in 1968

8992
Contact Quarterly Journal of Dance and Improvisation
Contact Collaborations
PO Box 603
Northampton, MA 01061
413-586-1181
FAX 413-586-9055
E-Mail: info@contactquarterly.com
Home Page: www.contactquarterly.com

Lisa Nelson, Co-Editor
Nancy Stark Smith, Co-Editor
Melinda Buckwalter, Associate Editor
Kristin Horrigan, Operations Manager/Advertising
Bill McCully, Development/Marketing

A journal of dance, improvisation, performance and contemporary movement arts. Presents materials that spring from the experience of doing. Encourages articulation and dialogue and stimulates activity and exploration within the field of movement and its performance.
Cost: $22
Frequency: BiAnnual
Founded in 1978

8993
Country Weekly Magazine
American Media Inc
1000 American Media Way
T-Rex Technology Center
Boca Raton, FL 33464-1000
561-997-7733
FAX 561-989-1298
Home Page: www.nationalenquirer.com

David J Pecker, CEO

Devoted to country music and entertainment. Packed with feature articles and photos of country music personalities, music and video reviews, tour dates and late breaking news from the world of country music.
Cost: $34.95
Frequency: Bi-Weekly

8994
Cue Magazine
PO Box 2027
Burlingame, CA 94011-2027
415-348-8004
FAX 650-348-7781
Home Page: www.cuemagazines.com

Devoted to the Northern California, Seattle and Portland commercial film, video and multimedia industries and locations that support production.
Frequency: Monthly

8995
DJ Times
Testa Communications
25 Willowdale Avenue
Port Washington, NY 11050-3779
516-767-2500
800-937-7678
FAX 516-767-9335
E-Mail: djtimes@testa.com
Home Page: www.djtimes.com

Jim Tremayne, Editor-in-Chief
Steve Thorakos, Production Manager

Colorful tabloid magazine dedicated to professional mobile and club DJs. Specialized music sections, new product departments for sound and lighting, record reviews, business columns, informative entertainer profiles and more.
Cost: $19.40
Frequency: Monthly
Circulation: 30000
Founded in 1988

8996
Daily Variety/Gotham
360 Park Avenue South
New York, NY 10010-3659
646-746-7001
FAX 646-746-6977
E-Mail: vtccustserv@cdsfulfillment.com
Home Page: www.variety.com

Peter Bart, Editor-in-Chief
Timothy M Gray, Editor
Ted Johnson, Managing Editor
Kathy Lyford, Managing Editor
Phil Gallo, Associate Editor

Focus is on Broadway theater, network television headquarters, regional music business, and local film production. Explores the role of New York City in relation to the national and global entertainment industries.
Cost: $259
Frequency: Daily
Founded in 1905

8997
Daily Variety/LA
5900 Wilshire Boulevard
Suite 3100
Los Angeles, CA 90036-3659
323-617-9100
FAX 323-857-0494
E-Mail: vtccustserv@cdsfulfillment.com
Home Page: www.variety.com

Peter Bart, Editor-in-Chief
Timothy M Gray, Editor
Ted Johnson, Managing Editor
Kathy Lyford, Managing Editor
Phil Gallo, Associate Editor

Focus is on Hollywood, network television headquarters, regional music business, and local film production. Explores the role of Hollywood in relation to the national and global entertainment industries.
Cost: $259
Frequency: Daily
Founded in 1905

8998
Dance Chronicle
Taylor & Francis Group
270 Madison Ave
Floor 4
New York, NY 10016-0601
212-679-3853
FAX 212-564-7854
Home Page: www.summitcom.com

George Dorris, Co-Editor
Jack Anderson, Co-Editor
Edwin Bayrn, Associate Editor

Covers a wide variety of topics, including dance and music, theater, film, literature, painting and aesthetics.
Cost: $465
Frequency: TriAnnual
ISSN: 0147-2526

8999
Dance Magazine
Macfadden Performing Arts Media
333 7th Avenue
11th Floor
New York, NY 10001
212-979-4800
Home Page: www.dancemagazine.com

INFORMATION RESOURCES / Magazines & Journals

Amy Cogan, VP/Group Publisher
Karen Hildebrand, VP Editorial
Jessi Petrov, Publishing/Marketing Director
Wendy Perron, Editor-in-Chief

The must read magazine for professional and aspiring dancers. From Broadway to ballet and tap to hip hop, not other magazine keeps you in touch with what is going on in all disciplines of dance.
Cost: $34.95
Frequency: Monthly
Circulation: 300,000
ISSN: 0011-6009
Founded in 1927
Printed in 4 colors on glossy stock

9000
Dance Research Journal
Congress on Research in dance
3416 Primm Lane
Birmingham, AL 24702-6170
205-823-5517
FAX 205-823-2760
E-Mail: ashanti@cordance.org
Home Page: www.cordance.org

Ann Dils, Co-Editor
Jill Green, Co-Editor

Published twice a year by the Congress on Research in Dance, this journal carries scholarly articles, book reviews, lists of books and journals received, and reports of scholarly conferences, archives and other projects of interest to the field.
Cost: $65
Frequency: Bi-annually
ISSN: 0149-7677
Founded in 1965
Mailing list available for rent: 750+ names at $75 per M

9001
Dance Spirit
Macfadden Performing Arts Media, LLC
333 7th Avenue
11th Floor
New York, NY 10001
212-979-4800
Home Page: www.dancespirit.com

Amy Cogan, VP/Group Publisher
Karen Hildebrand, VP Editorial
Jessi Petrov, Publishing/Marekting Director
Kayte Lydon, Editor-in-Chief

Dedicated to inspiring the next generation of dancers. Packed with expert advice on dance techniques and performing, health and nutrition tips and the latest styles to keep you looking your best from studio to stage to school.
Cost: $16.95
Frequency: 10 Per Year
Founded in 1980

9002
Dance Teacher Magazine
Macfadden Performing Arts Media
333 7th Avenue
11th Floor
New York, NY 10001
212-979-4800
FAX 646-459-4900
Home Page: www.dance-teacher.com

Amy Cogan, VP/Group Publisher
Karen Hildebrand, VP Editorial/Editor-in-Chief
Jessie Petrov, Publishing/Marketing Director

The only magazine written just for dance professionals. Packed with useful ideas that will help you and your students become better dancers.
Cost: $24.95
Frequency: Monthly
Circulation: 60000
Founded in 1979
Printed in 4 colors

9003
Dance on Camera Journal
Dance Films Association
48 W 21st St
Suite 907
New York, NY 10010-6989
212-727-0764
FAX 212-727-0764
E-Mail: info@dancefilms.org
Home Page: www.dancefilms.org
Social Media: *Facebook, Twitter,*

Deidra Towers, Executive Director
Marta Renzi, President
Harry Streep, VP
Amy Meharg, Treasurer
Nolini Barretto, Secretary

Subjects range from reviews and essays, news items regarding dance films, festivals, opportunites, and issues facing artists
Frequency: Bi-Monthly
Founded in 1956

9004
Dance/USA Journal
Dance/USA
1111 16th St Nw
Suite 300
Washington, DC 20036-4830
202-833-1717
FAX 202-833-2686
E-Mail: danceusa@danceusa.org
Home Page: www.danceusa.org

Andrea Snyder, Executive Director
Tom Thielen, Director Finance/Operations
Katherine Fabian, Membership Manager

The journal features articles on issues of importance to the dance community; news stories relating to arts and dance; essays from leaders in the dance field; notes on changes, transitions and opportunities in the field; calendar of up coming events; and highlights of Dance/USA sponsored events. Subscription is free to members of Dance/USA.
Cost: $40
28-36 Pages
Frequency: Quarterly
Founded in 1982
Printed in 2 colors on glossy stock

9005
Descant
50 Baldwin Street
PO Box 314 Station P
Toronto, ON M5S-2S8
416-593-2557
FAX 416-593-9362
E-Mail: info@descant.ca
Home Page: www.descant.on.ca
Social Media: *Facebook,*

Karen Mulhallen, Editor-in-Chief
Vera DeWaard, Managing Editor
Mary Newberry, Project Manager
Stacey May Fowles, Circulation Manager
Pasha Malla, Director of Outreach

A quarterly journal publishing new and established contemporary writers and visual artists from Canada and around the world. Devoted to the discovery and development of new writers, and places their work in the company of celebrated writers.
Cost: $28
Frequency: Quarterly
Circulation: 1200
ISSN: 0382-909X
Founded in 1970
Mailing list available for rent

9006
Diapason
Scranton Gillette Communications
3030 W Salt Creek Lane
Suite 201
Arlington Heights, IL 60005-5025
847-391-1000
FAX 847-390-0408
E-Mail: jbutera@sgcmail.com
Home Page: www.thediapason.com

Jerome Butera, Editor/Publisher
Joyce Robinson, Associate Editor

Devoted to the organ, the harpsichord, the carillon, and church music. Includes feature articles, reviews, reports, news, organ specifications, and a calendar, as well as classified advertisements.
Cost: $35
Frequency: Monthly
ISSN: 0012-2378
Founded in 1909

9007
Discoveries
700 East State Street
Ioal, WI 54990-0001
715-445-2214
800-258-0929
FAX 715-445-4087
E-Mail: wayne.youngblood@fwpubs.com
Home Page: www.discoveriesmag.com

Mark Wlilliams, Publisher
Wayne Youngblood, Editorial Director
Cathy Bernardy, Associate Editor
Todd Whitesel, Associate Editor
Trevor Lauber, Advertising Sales Manager

Keeps close watch on market trends for collectible records, CDs and memorabilia. The Market Watch pages serve to interpret the mass of information available online and break it down to the most useful data collectors need. Each monthly issue is full of personality and opinion, with many reviews to help you determine where to spend your money. Coverage includes rock 'n' roll, rhythm &'blues, pop, doo-wop, classic jazz and country western recordings.
Cost: $28
Frequency: Monthly
Circulation: 10,859
Founded in 1988

9008
Downbeat
102 N Haven Road
PO Box 906
Elmhurst, IL 60126
630-941-2030
800-554-7470
FAX 630-941-3210
E-Mail: service@downbeat.com
Home Page: www.downbeat.com

Kevin Maher, CEO

Monthly magazine includes such features as Readers Poll results, festival reviews, CD reviews, feature articles and more.
Cost: $29.95

1073

INFORMATION RESOURCES / Magazines & Journals

Frequency: Monthly
Mailing list available for rent

9009
Drama Review
MIT Press
55 Hayward Street
Cambridge, MA 02142-1493
617-253-5646
800-207-8354
FAX 617-258-6779
E-Mail: journals-info@mit.edu
Home Page: www.mitpress.mit.edu
Social Media: Facebook, Twitter, RSS

Rebbecca Mc Leod, Owner

TDR focuses on performances in their social, economic, and political conctexts. It emphasizes experimental, avant-garde, intercultural and interdisciplinary performance. TDR covers dance, theatre, performance art, visual art, popular entertainment, media, sports, rituals, and performance in politics and everyday life.
Frequency: Quarterly
Founded in 1955

9010
Dramatics Magazine
Educational Theatre Association
2343 Auburn Ave
Cincinnati, OH 45219-2819
513-421-3900
FAX 513-421-7077
E-Mail: jpalmarini@schooltheatre.org
Home Page: schooltheatre.org
Social Media: Facebook, Twitter,

Donald A Corathers, Publications Director
James Palmarini, Editor

Dramatics is the only magazine that is edited exclusively for students and teachers of theatre. Contents include practical articles about acting, directing, playwriting, design, and technical theatre; interviews with working professionals that illuminate the process of becoming a theatre artist; options for higher education and training in theatre; playscripts; reports on new shows and other important events in the theatre world; book, video, and CD-ROM reviews, and more.
Cost: $27
4000 Members
Frequency: 9x/ A Year
Circulation: 34100
ISSN: 0012-5989
Founded in 1929

9011
Electronic Musician
PRIMEDIA
6400 Hollis Street
Suite 12
Emeryville, CA 94608-1086
510-653-3307
E-Mail: emeditorial@prismb2b.com
Home Page: www.emusician.com
Social Media: Facebook, Twitter,

Steve Oppenheimer, Editor-in-Chief
Joe Perry, Associate Publisher
Marie Briganti, List Manager

Magazine for musicians recording and producing music in a home or personal studio environment. They are a source of user-friendly technical information for musicians. Features include: Tech Page, ProFile, Working Musician, Sound Design Workshop, Making Tracks, Square One, Reviews, What's New, Master Class, Final Mix, and Editors Choice Awards.
Cost: $23.97

Frequency: Monthly
Circulation: 61102
Founded in 1986
Mailing list available for rent

9012
Encore Performance Publishing
PO Box 95567
South Jordan, UT 84095-0567
801-282-8159
E-Mail: encoreplay@aol.com
Home Page: www.encoreplay.com

Michael C Perry, President

Publishes a variety of publications for those professionals in the performing arts industry.

9013
Film & History
Historians Film Committee
Lawrence University,Memorial Hall B5
711 E Boldt Way
Appleton, WI 54911
920-832-6649
E-Mail: centre@filmandhistory.org
Home Page: www.h-net.org/~filmhis

Peter C Rollins, Director
Deborah Carmichael, Editor-in-Chief
Cynthia Miller, Associate Editor-in-Chief

An Interdisciplinary Journal of Film and Television Studies concerned with the impact of motion pictures on our society. Film and History focuses on how feature films and documentary films both represent and interpret history. Types of articles include: Analysis of individual films and/or television programs from a historical perspective, survey of documents related to the production of films, or analysis of history as explored through film.
Cost: $50
Frequency: Bi-annually
Circulation: 1000
ISSN: 0360-3695
Founded in 1970

9014
Film & Video Magazine
110 William Street
11th Floor
New York, NY 10038
212-621-4900
FAX 212-621-4635
Home Page: www.studiodaily.com/filmandvideo

Bryant Frazer, Editor-in-Chief
Pete Putman, Senior Editor
Alison Johns, Editor-in-Chief
Scott Gentry, Group Publisher
Jarrett Cory, Classified Sales

Covers new ideas in creating entertainment by focusing on technique in the production and finishing of features, TV programming, music videos and commercials. No longer publishes print copies, magazine is 100% digital
Frequency: Monthly
Founded in 1983
Printed in 4 colors

9015
Film Journal International
VNU Business Media
770 Broadway,7th Floor
New York, NY 10003-9595
212-493-4097
FAX 646-654-7694
E-Mail: subscriptions@filmjournal.com
Home Page: www.filmjournal.com

Penny Vane, President
Sid Holt, Editorial Director
Robert Sunshine, Publisher/Editor
Robin Klamfoth, Advertising Director
Kevin Lally, Executive Editor

A trade publication covering the motion picture industry, including theatrical exhibition, production, distribution, and allied activities. Articles report on US and international news, with features on current production, industry trends, theatre design, equipment, concessions, sound, digital cinema, screen advertising, and other industry-related news. Each issue also includes the Buying and Booking Guide, with comprehensive feature film reviews.
Cost: $65
Frequency: Monthly
Founded in 1934
Mailing list available for rent

9016
Film Threat
Film Threat International Headquarters
5042 Wilshire Boulevard
PMB 1500
Los Angeles, CA 90036
FAX 310-274-7985
E-Mail: advertise@filmthreat.com
Home Page: www.filmthreat.com
Social Media: Facebook, Twitter,

Mark Bell, Editor-in-Chief
Eric Campos, Senior Contributing Editor
Chris Gore, Founder/Publishjer

The print edition of Film Threat retired in 1997, but the legend has lived on as an internet journalism mainstay. FilmThreat.com delivers film reviews, film festival coverage, exclusive filmmaker interviews and original video content.
Cost: $10.50
Frequency: Bi-Monthly
Circulation: 100,000
Founded in 1985

9017
Flute Talk
Instrumentalist Company
200 Northfield Road
Northfield, IL 60093-3390
847-446-5000
888-446-6888
FAX 847-446-6263
E-Mail: fteditor@instrumentalistmagazine.com
Home Page: www.instrumentalistmagazine.com
Social Media: Facebook,

Flute Talk is written for professional flute players, teachers, and advanced students. Frequent topics include performance analyses of flute repertoire, current teaching techniques, piccolo articles, interviews with prominent performers and teachers, and reviews of new music, recordings, and books for flutists.
Cost: $13
Frequency: 10 x Per Year
Circulation: 12000
Founded in 1981

9018
Goldmine
700 E State Street
Iola, WI 54990-0001
715-445-2214
800-258-0929
FAX 715-445-4087
E-Mail: susan.sliwicki@fwmedia.com
Home Page: www.goldminemag.com
Social Media: Facebook, YouTube, RSS, Pinterest

INFORMATION RESOURCES / Magazines & Journals

Jeff Pozorski, Publisher
Brian Earnest, Editorial Director
Peter Lindblad, Associate Editor
Tim Neely, Research Director
Trevor Lauber, Advertising Sales Manager

The world's largest marketplace for collectible records, CDs, and music memorabilia covering Rock N' Roll, Blues, Country, Folk, and Jazz. Large volumes of For Sale and Wanted ads are placed by collectors and dealers. Includes articles on recording stars of the past and present with discographies listing all known releases, a listing of upcoming record-and-CD-collector conventions, album reviews, hobby and music news, a collecting column, a letters section, and Collector Mania (Q&A).
Cost: $39.95
Frequency: Bi-Weekly
Circulation: 17026
Founded in 1974
Mailing list available for rent

9019
Gospel Today
Gospel Today
PO Box 800
Fairburn, GA 30213
770-719-4825
FAX 770-716-2660
E-Mail: admin@gospeltoday.com
Home Page: www.gospeltoday.com

Dr Teresa Hairston, Publisher

To provide a quality publication to inspire, educate, inform, and empower readers towards standards of Godly excellence.
Cost: $17.97
Frequency: 8 Per Year
Circulation: 250000
Founded in 1989
Printed in 4 colors on glossy stock

9020
Guitar One
Cherry Lane Magazines
6 E 32nd St
Suite 11
New York, NY 10016-5422
212-561-3000
800-825-4942
FAX 212-447-6885
E-Mail: guitarshop@worldnet.att.net
Home Page: www.guitarmag.com

Peter W Primont, CEO
Jonathan Simpson-Bint, President
Holly Klingel, VP Circulation
Steve Aaron, Publishing Director
Greg Di Benedetto, Publisher

Information on everything from the guitar equipment evaluations to news on the latest trends and technological developments to special insider pieces covering the sound secrets of today's top players.
Cost: $24.95
Frequency: Monthly
Circulation: 105,000
Founded in 1985

9021
Guitar Review
Albert Augustine Limited
151 W 26th St
Suite 4
New York, NY 10001-6810
917-661-0220
FAX 917-661-0223
E-Mail: mail@guitarreview.com
Home Page: www.albertaugustine.com

Steven Griesgraber, President
Eliot Fisk, Associate Editor
David Starobin, Associate Editor
Ian Gallagher, Music Editor
Matthew Hough, Circulation

Scholarly articles related to the classical guitar.
Cost: $28
48 Pages
Frequency: Quarterly
Circulation: 4000
Founded in 1946

9022
HipHop Weekly
Z & M Media
401 Broadway
New York, NY
212-696-0831
Home Page: www.hiphopweekly.com
Social Media: Facebook, Twitter,

Covers the entire hip hop culture.

9023
Hispanic Arts News
Association of Hispanic Arts
1025 Connecticut Ave
Suite 1000
Washington, DC 20036
202-657-5158
888-876-1240
FAX 202-478-2767
E-Mail: informacion@latinoarts.org
Home Page: www.hispanics.einnews.com
Social Media: Facebook, Twitter,

Features in depth articles on the local and national arts community, including artist profiles and a calendar of events.
Frequency: 9 Per Year
Mailing list available for rent: 5000 names at $80 per M

9024
Hollywood Life
Movieline Magazine
10537 Santa Monica Blvd
Suite 250
Los Angeles, CA 90025-4952
310-234-9501
FAX 310-234-0332
E-Mail: hollywoodlife@pcspublink.com
Home Page: www.hollywoodlive.net

Anne Volokh, President

Formerly called Movieline, an entertainment lifestyle featuring interviews with stars, directors and producers; as well as information on celebrity shopping, up and coming talent, soundtracks, electronics and fashion associated with hollywood style and trends.
Cost: $13.75
Frequency: Monthly
Founded in 1989
Printed in 4 colors on glossy stock

9025
Hollywood Reporter
Prometheus Global Media
770 Broadway
New York, NY 10003-9595
212-493-4100
FAX 646-654-5368
Home Page: www.prometheusgm.com
Social Media: Facebook, Twitter, YouTube

Richard D. Beckman, CEO
James A. Finkelstein, Chairman
Madeline Krakowsky, Vice President Circulation
Tracy Brater, Executive Director Crative Service

Gives fresh ideas for film and TV. Covers the full spectrum of craft and commerce in the entertainment industry.
Cost: $199
Frequency: Weekly
Circulation: 34770

9026
Instrumentalist
Instrumentalist Company
200 Northfield Road
Northfield, IL 60093-3390
847-446-5000
888-446-6888
FAX 847-446-6263
E-Mail: insteditor@instrumentalistmagazine.com
Home Page: www.instrumentalistmagazine.com
Social Media: Facebook,

A magazine school band and orchestra directors can depend on for practical information to use for then ensembles. The articles written by veteran directors and performers cover a wide range of topics, including rehearsal techniques, conducting tips, programming ideas, instrument clinics, repertoire analyses, and much more. Monthly new music reviews guide directors to selecting the best music for their students.
Cost: $21
Frequency: Monthly
Circulation: 16,000
Founded in 1945
Printed in 4 colors

9027
International Cinematographers Guild Magazine
7755 W Sunset Blvd
Suite 300
Los Angeles, CA 90046-3911
323-876-0160
FAX 323-876-6383
E-Mail: info@icgmagazine.com
Home Page: www.cameraguild.com

Steven Poster, President
John McCarthy, Marketing

Serves as the journal of 'how to' for film and digital techniques. It incorporates a wide range of editorial for specific job categories in relation to cinematography for Film/Hi-Def/Digital production and defines the tools and technology necessary for advancement in this field. The magazine is written for members of the International Cinematographers Guild, including cinematographers, camera operators, camera assistants, still photographers, publicists, film loaders, and others in the field.
Cost: $48
Frequency: Monthly
Founded in 1929

9028
International Documentary Magazine
International Documentary Association
Ste M270
1201 W 5th St
Los Angeles, CA 90017-1476
213-534-3600
FAX 213-534-3610
E-Mail: tom@documentary.org
Home Page: www.documentary.org

Thomas White, Editor
Tamara Krinsky, Associate Editor

INFORMATION RESOURCES / Magazines & Journals

Jodi Pais Montgomery, Manager Advertising Sales
Michael Lumpkin, Executive Director

Devoted exclusively to nonfiction media.
Frequency: Monthly
Founded in 1982
Printed in 4 colors on glossy stock

9029
International Musician
American Federation of Musicians
1501 Broadway
Suite 600
New York, NY 10036-5501
212-869-1330
FAX 212-764-6134
E-Mail: info@afm.org
Home Page: www.afm.org

Thomas Lee, President

Delivers the latest happenings in music. Focuses on the overall well-being of all musicians. Provides news pertaining to symphonic, rock, freelance, recording and touring musicians. IM features aricles on pressing issues sich as piracy, legislation, on-the-job struggles, and the effects of technology.
Cost: $25
Frequency: Monthly
Circulation: 110000
Founded in 1896
Printed in on n stock

9030
JAMIA
American Musical Instrument Society
389 Main Street
Suite 202
Malden, MA 02148
781-397-8870
FAX 781-397-8887
E-Mail: amis@guildassoc.com
Home Page: www.amis.org

Stewart Carter, President
Joanne Kopp, Treasurer

Presents peer-reviewed articles that assist in both professionals and students to develop and apply biomedical and health informatics to patient care, teaching, research, and health care administration.
Frequency: Bi-Monthly
Founded in 1971

9031
Jazz Education Journal
JazzTimes Magazine,Madavor Media
85 Quincy Ave
Suite 2
Quincy, MA 02169
617-706-9110
FAX 617-536-0102
E-Mail: karen@iage.org
Home Page: www.jazztimes.com

Leslie M Sabina, Editor
Karen Mayse, Advertising

Provides news and information in the field of jazz education. Contains information of today's top jazz artists, reviews, transcriptions, industry news, and articles on improvisation, teaching techniques, history, performance, composition, arranging and music business.
Cost: $23.95
100 Pages
Circulation: 10,000
Founded in 1968
Mailing list available for rent
Printed in on glossy stock

9032
JazzTimes
JazzTimes Magazine
Madavor Media,85 Quincy Ave
Suite 2
Quincy, MA 02169
617-706-9110
800-437-5828
FAX 617-536-0102
Home Page: www.jazztimes.com

Glen Sabin, CEO
Eric Wynne, Consumer Advertising Director

JazzTimes contains extensive news coverage, award winning jazz journalism, hundreds of CD, Book and Video reviews, World class photography and award winning graphics, informative features and columns, special theme issues, special directories, readers poll and critic pics, and sound$weeps giveaways and prizes.
Cost: $23.95
Frequency: 10 Issues per y
Circulation: 86000
Founded in 1980

9033
Journal of American Organbuilding
American Institute of Organ Builders
PO Box 35306
Canton, OH 44735
330-806-9011
E-Mail: robertsullivan@pipeorgan.org
Home Page: www.pipeorgan.org

Jeffrey L Weiler, Editor

Features technical articles, product and book reviews, and a forum for the exchange of building and service information and techniqes. Subscriptions are provided free to AIO members, and are available to non-members for $24 per year.
Cost: $24
Frequency: Quarterly
Founded in 1974
Mailing list available for rent: 350 names at $250 per M
Printed in on glossy stock

9034
Journal of Arts Management, Law, Society
Heldref Publishers
325 Chestnut Street
Suite 800
Philadelphia, PA 19106
215-625-8900
800-354-1420
FAX 202-296-5149
E-Mail: customer.service@taylorandfrancis.com
Home Page: www.heldref.org

James Denton, Executive Director

A resource for arts policymakers and analysts, sociologists, arts and cultural administrators, educators, trusteed, artists, lawyers, and citizens concerned with the performing, visual, and media arts as well as cultural affairs. Articles, commentaries, and reviews of publications address marketing, intellectual property, arts policy, arts law, governance, and cultural production and dissemination, from a variety of philosophical, disciplinary, and national and international perspectives.
Cost: $79
Frequency: Monthly
ISSN: 1063-2921
Founded in 1956

9035
Journal of Dance Education
National Dance Education Organization
8609 2nd Avenue
Suite 203 B
Silver Spring, MD 20910
301-585-2880
FAX 301-585-2888
E-Mail: info@ndeo.org
Home Page: www.ndeo.org
Social Media: *Facebook, Twitter,*

Susan McGreevy-Nichols, Executive Director
Jane Bonbright EdD, Executive Director
Patricia Cohen, Treasurer
Cost: $90
Frequency: Quarterly
Circulation: 2000
ISSN: 1529-0824

9036
Journal of Film and Video
University Film and Video Association
University of Illinois Press
1325 S Oak Street
Champaign, IL 61820
217-244-0626
866-244-0626
FAX 217-244-9910
E-Mail: journals@uiuc.edu
Home Page: www.ufva.org

Stephen Tropiano, Editor
Cheryl Jestis, Membership

Focuses on scholarship in the fields of film and video production, history, criticism, and aesthetics. Topics include film and related media, education in these fields, and the function of film and video in society.
Cost: $40
Frequency: Quarterly
Circulation: 1200

9037
Journal of Music Theory
Yale University
Department of Music
PO Box 208310
New Haven, CT 06520-8310
203-432-2985
FAX 203-432-2983
E-Mail: jmt.editor@yale.edu
Home Page: www.yale.edu/jmt/

Ian Quinn, Editor
David Clampitt, Associate Editor
Richard Cohn, Associate Editor
Daniel Harrison, Associate Editor
Patrick McCreless, Associate Editor

Publishes peer-reviewed reseach in Music Theory.
Cost: $30
Frequency: Annual
Founded in 1957

9038
Journal of Music Therapy
American Music Therapy Association
8455 Colesville Rd
Suite 1000
Silver Spring, MD 20910-3392
301-589-3300
FAX 301-589-5175
E-Mail: info@musictherapy.org
Home Page: www.musictherapy.org

Andrea Farbman, Executive Director

INFORMATION RESOURCES / Magazines & Journals

Research in the area of music therapy and rehabilitation, a forum for authoratative articles of current music therapy research and theory, use of music in the behavioral sciences, book reviews, and guest editorials.
Cost: $120
Frequency: Quarterly
Circulation: 6000
ISSN: 0022-2917
Founded in 1998

9039
Journal of Popular Film and Television
Heldref Publications
**1319 18th St Nw
Suite 2
Washington, DC 20036-1802**
202-296-6267
800-365-9753
FAX 202-296-5149
E-Mail: subscribe@heldref.org
Home Page: www.heldref.org

James Denton, Executive Director
Gary Edgerton, Co-Executive Director

Articles discuss networks, genres, series and audiences, as well as celebrity stars, directors and studios. Regular features include essays on the social and cultural background of films and television programs, filmographies, bibliographies, and commisioned book and video reviews.
Cost: $51
Frequency: Quarterly
ISSN: 0195-6051
Founded in 1956

9040
Journal of Research in Music Education
MENC Subscription Office
**PO Box 1584
Birmingham, AL 35201**
800-633-4931
E-Mail: menc@ebsco.com
Home Page: www.menc.org
Social Media: *Facebook, Twitter,*

Keeps members informed of the latest music education research. Offers a collection of reports that includes thorough analyses of theories and projects by respected music researchers. Issued four times yearly.
Frequency: Quarterly
Founded in 1907
Printed in on matte stock

9041
Journal of Singing
National Association of Teachers of Singing
**9957 Moorings Dr
Suite 401
Jacksonville, FL 32257-2416**
904-992-9101
FAX 904-262-2587
E-Mail: info@nats.org
Home Page: www.nats.org

Richard Dale Sjoerdsma, Editor-in-Chief

Provides current information regarding the teaching of singing as well as results of recent research in the field. The Journal serves as a historical record and a venue for teachers of singing and other scholars to share the resilts of their work in areas such as history, diction, voice science, medicine, and voice pedagogy.
Frequency: 5x times/year

9042
Journal of the American Musicological Society
University of California Press, Journals Division
**2000 Center Street Way
Suite 203
Berkeley, CA 94704-1223**
510-643-7154
FAX 510-642-9917
E-Mail: journals@ucpress.edu
Home Page: www.ucpressjournals.com

Bruce Alan Brown, Editor
Louise Goldberg, Assistant Editor
Julie Cumming, Book Review Editor

The JAMS publishes scholarship from all fields of musical inquiry: from historical musicology, critical theory, music analysis, iconography and organology, to performance practice, aesthetics and hermeneutics, ethnomusicology, gender and sexuality, popular music and cultural studies. Each issue includes articles, book reviews, and communications.
Cost: $42
Frequency: Tri-Annual
Circulation: 5000
ISSN: 0003-0139
Founded in 1893

9043
Jukebox Collector Magazine
**2545 SE 60th Court
Pleasant Hill, IA 50327-5099**
515-265-8324
FAX 515-265-1980
E-Mail: JukeboxCollector@att.net
Home Page: www.jukeboxmagazine.com

Rick Botts, Editor

Focuses on collectors of jukeboxes from the 40's, 50's, and 60's. There are approximately 150 jukeboxes for sale each month, along with show events information. Accepts advertising.
Cost: $33
36 Pages
Frequency: Monthly
Circulation: 1800
Founded in 1977

9044
Keyframe Magazine
DMG Publishing
**2756 N Green Valley Pkwy
Suite 261
Henderson, NV 89014-2120**
702-990-8656
FAX 702-992-0471
E-Mail: info@dmgpublishing.com
Home Page: www.dmgpublishing.com

Dariush Derakhshani, Editor-in-Chief
Cheri Madison, Managing Editor
Charles Edgin, Editorial Director
Alice Edgin, Executive Editor

In response to reader requests, Keyframe is adding to its LightWave and Photoshop tutorials and content additional bonus pages covering other tools used by digital artists. As Keyframe evolves into this larger, better magazine, its new title with be HDRI 3D.
Cost: $54
Circulation: 9000
Founded in 1997

9045
Lighting Dimensions
Primedia Business

**249 W 17th St
New York, NY 10011-5382**
212-206-1894
800-827-3322
FAX 212-514-3719
Home Page: lightingdimensions.com

Doug MacDonald, Group Publisher
David Johnson, Associate Publisher/Editorial
Marian Sandberg-Dierson, Editor
Mark Newman, Managing Editor
Jennifer Hirst, Director

Trade publication for lighting professionals in film, theatre, television, concerts, clubs, themed environments, architecctural, commercial, and industrial lighting. Sponsors of the LDI Trade Show and the Broadway Lighting Master Classes.
Cost: $34.97
Frequency: 12/year
Circulation: 14,177
Founded in 1989

9046
Live Sound International
**111 Speen Street
Framingham, MA 01701**
415-387-4009
800-375-8015
FAX 866-449-3761
E-Mail: amclean@livesoundint.com
Home Page: www.livesoundint.com

Mark Herman, Publisher
Jeff MacKay, Editor
Mitch Gallagher, Associate Editor
Sara Elliott, Advertising

The editorial focus is performance audio and event sound. Contains audio production techniques, new products, equipment applications and associated commercial concerns.
Cost: $60
Frequency: Monthly
Circulation: 20,000
Mailing list available for rent
Printed in on glossy stock

9047
Mid-Atlantic Events Magazine
**1800 Byberry Road
Suite 901
Huntingdon Valley, PA 19006**
215-947-8600
800-521-8588
FAX 215-947-8650
E-Mail: editor@eventsmagazine.com
Home Page: www.eventsmagazine.com
Social Media: *Facebook, Twitter, YouTube*

Jim Cohn, Publisher
Rich Kupka, Editor
Fred Cohn, VP Sales
Katie O'Connell, Director Sales/Marketing
Dana Kurtbek, Production

Focused on Hospitality in the Mid-Atlantic area. It assists the Associations, Corporations, Government, Group and Independent Meeting, Event and Travel Planners who are responsible for arranging Conventions, Trade Shows, Hotel Accommodations, Corporate/Group Travel, Meetings, Seminars, Conferences, Symposiums, Site Selections, Special Events, Banquets, Entertainment, Corporate Golf Outings and Golf Tournaments, Company Picnics, Team Building, Retreats, Board Meetings, Training & Development.
Circulation: 26000
ISSN: 0896-3967
Founded in 1987

1077

INFORMATION RESOURCES / Magazines & Journals

Mailing list available for rent
Printed in 8 colors on glossy stock

9048
Millimeter Magazine
PO Box 2100
Skokie, IL 60076-7800
847-763-9504
866-505-7173
FAX 847-763-9682
E-Mail: millimeter@pbinews.com
Home Page: www.millimeter.com

Cynthia Wisehart, Editor

In a fast-changing and challenging industry, Millimeter anticipates the future. Its early coverage of important technology-driven trends such as 24p production, desktop post, and digital cinema has helped readers remain competitive and plan their business investments. Millimeter is an authoritative resource for professionals in production, postproduction, animation, streaming, and visual effects for motion pictures, television and commercials.
Cost: $70
Frequency: Monthly

9049
Mix
Prism Business Media
6400 Hollis St
Suite 9
Emeryville, CA 94608-1052
510-658-3793
866-860-7087
FAX 510-653-5142
E-Mail: mixeditorial@prismb2b.com
Home Page: www.mixonline.com

Melinda Paras, Owner
Erika Lopez, Associate Publisher
Tom Kenny, Editor
John Pledger, Publisher
Christen Pocock, Marketing Director

Mix covers a wide range of topics including: recording, live sound and production, broadcast production, audio for film and video, and music technology. In addition, Mix includes coverage of facility design and construction, location recording, tape/disc manufacturing, education, and other topics of importance to audio professionals. Distributed in 94 countries.
Cost: $35.97
Frequency: Monthly
Circulation: 45244
Founded in 1977

9050
Modern Drummer
Modern Drummer Publications
12 Old Bridge Rd
Cedar Grove, NJ 07009-1288
973-239-4140
FAX 973-239-7139
E-Mail: mdinfo@moderndrummer.com
Home Page: www.moderndrummer.com

Isabel Spagnardi, Owner
Tracy A Kearns, Associate Publisher
Bill Miller, Editor-in-Chief
Rick Van Horn, Senior Editor
Adam Budofsky, Managing Editor

Every issue of Modern Drummer includes interviews with the world's leading drummers, a full roster of columns on all facets of drumming, complete drum charts, solos and patterns performed by your favorite players, insightful reviews on the hottest new geat, the best in CDs, books, and DVDs for drummers, and giveaways worth thousands of dollars.
Cost: $29.97
Frequency: Monthly
Circulation: 6000
ISSN: 1078-1757
Founded in 1993
Mailing list available for rent
Printed in 4 colors on glossy stock

9051
Movie Collectors World
Arena Publishing
PO BOX 309
Fraser, MI 48026
586-774-4311
FAX 703-940-4566
E-Mail: mail@mcwonline.com
Home Page: www.mcwonline.com

Brian Bukantis, Editor

Leading collector's publication for collectors of movie memorabilia, with an emphasis on collectible movie posters. Each issue is filled with ads from dealers and collectors all over the world. In any monthly issue, you will find movie posters common and rare - everything from the 'Golden Age' to today's blockbusters.
Cost: $36
36-44 Pages
Frequency: Monthly
Circulation: 6000

9052
MovieMaker
MovieMaker Magazine
8328 De Soto Ave.
Canoga Park, CA 91304
310-742-7214
888-881-5861
FAX 818-349-9922
Home Page: www.moviemaker.com

Timothy Rhys, Publisher/Editor-in-Chief
Jennifer M Wood, Editor
Phillip Williams, Editor at Large
Ian Bage, New Marketing Services
Liza Kelley, Production Manager

MovieMaker is the world's most widely - read independent movie magazine that focuses on the art and business of making movies. Its editorial mix is a progressive mix of in depth interviews and criticism combined by practical techniques and advice on financing, distribution and production strategies.
Cost: $18
Frequency: Quarterly
Circulation: 54000
Founded in 1993
Mailing list available for rentat $175 per M

9053
Music
102 N Haven Road
PO Box 906
Elmhurst, IL 60126-2932
630-941-2030
FAX 630-941-3210
E-Mail: subscriptions@musicncmag.com
Home Page: www.musicincmag.com

Zach Phillip, Editor
Kevin Maher, CEO
John Cahill, Eastern Advertising
Tom Burns, Western Advertising
Chris Maher, Classified Ads

Offered free to those involved in music products retailing. Delivers news you can use for the musical products industry. Geared toward store owners and managers in musical product retail and repair shops in the United States and Canada.
Frequency: 11 Per Year
Circulation: 8,949
Founded in 1934

9054
Music & Sound Retailer
Testa Communications
25 Willowdale Avenue
Port Washington, NY 11050
516-767-2500
800-937-7678
FAX 516-767-9335
E-Mail: testa@testa.com
Home Page: www.testa.com

Brian Berk, Editor

News magazine serving owners, managers and sales personnel in retail musical-instument and sound-product dealerships. The magazine's emphasis is on full-line and combo dealerships offering guitars, drums, electronic keyboards and digital pianos, recording and sound-reinforcement products, lighting, DJ equipment, software, print and accessories. Recurring features include 'MI Spy,' 'Top Ten,' 'Veddatorial,' 'Selling Points,' and editor's letter
Cost: $18
Frequency: Monthly
Circulation: 11000
Founded in 1985

9055
Music Row
1231 17th Avenue S
PO Box 158542
Nashville, TN 37215-8542
615-321-3617
FAX 615-329-0852
E-Mail: sales@musicrow.com
Home Page: www.musicrow.com

David M Ross, CEO/President

Written for people who work in the music business. Contents include record reviews, current news items, timely interviews or discovering hot talent first. Music Row subscriptions include six print issues per year, daily Afternoon News updates via e-mail and @Musicrow reports every Tuesday, Thursday and Friday via e-mail.
Cost: $159
Frequency: Six Per Year
Circulation: 14000
Founded in 1981
Printed in 4 colors on glossy stock

9056
Music Trades Magazine
Music Trades
80 West Street
Englewood, NJ 07631-0432
201-871-1965
800-423-6530
FAX 201-871-0455
E-Mail: music@musictrades.com
Home Page: www.musictrades.com

Brian Majeski, Publisher
Richard T Watson, Managing Editor
Juanita Hampton, Circulation Manager

A blend of industry news, hard sales and marketing data, trend analysis and management tips in every issue. Target audience is retailers, distributors, and manufacturers of musical instruments, professional audio equipment and related products, worldwide.
Cost: $16

INFORMATION RESOURCES / Magazines & Journals

Frequency: Monthly
Circulation: 7500
Founded in 1890
Mailing list available for rent

9057
Music and Sound Journal
912 Carlton Road
Tarpon Spring, FL 34689
727-938-0571
E-Mail: sound@masj.com
Home Page: www.masj.com

Don Kulak, Founder/Owner

Brings readers the future of sound today, with new music, experimental sound, cutting edge audio and acoustics and alternative media. MSJ is written for people who are discriminating about music, audio, and sound - people who want to improve their sonic environments on all levels, without having to study pages of data - people who want to more fully understand the profound impact sound has on every aspect of their daily lives.
ISSN: 1541-8545
Founded in 1988

9058
Musical Merchandise Review
21 Highland Circle
Suite One
Needham, MA 02494
781-453-9310
800-964-5150
FAX 781-453-9389
E-Mail: mprescott@symphonypublishing.com
Home Page: www.mmrmagazine.com

Lee Zapis, President
Sidney L Davis, Group Publisher
Richard E Kessel, Publisher/Advertising Sales
Maureen Johan, Classified Sales

Serves retailers of musical instruments, accessories, and related services as well as wholesalers, importers/exporters and manufacturers of related products. Its purpose is to communicate facts and ideas that will benefit musical merchandisers and their daily business operations as well as help them enhance their growth. Its editorial approach includes features on industry trends and innovations, new product promotion, in-store display techniques, financing, planning and dealer surveys.
Cost: $32
Frequency: Monthly
Founded in 1879
Mailing list available for rentat $100 per M
Printed in 4 colors

9059
National Squares
National Square Dance Convention
C/O Gene and Connie Triplett
2760 Polo Club Boulevard
Matthews, NC 28105
704-847-1265
E-Mail: Richp27890@aol.com
Home Page: www.nationalsquaredanceconvention.com

Dick/Linda Peterson, Editors
Gene/Connie Triplett, Circulation Managers
Dick/Linda Peterson, Public Relations

A national square dance magazine published by the National Executive Committee of the National Square Dance Convention.
Cost: $7
Frequency: Quarterly

9060
New England Theatre Journal
New England Theatre Conference
215 Knob Hill Drive
Hamden, CT 06518
617-851-8535
FAX 203-288-5938
E-Mail: mail@netconline.org
Home Page: www.netconline.org

Sabine Klein, President
Jeffrey Watts, Executive VP
Charles Emmons, VP Administration/Finance

Scholarly publication produced once per year. Includes book and theatre reviews, historical analyses, and other well-written articles by noted authors. Free to NETC members. Specifically designed to provide members, and others interested in live theatre arts, with the information and resources they need to enhance their careers, promote their groups, and sharpen their theatre skills.
Cost: $10
Frequency: Annual
Founded in 1952

9061
New on the Charts
Music Business Reference
70 Laurel Place
New Rochelle, NY 10801-7105
914-632-3349
FAX 914-633-7690
E-Mail: lenny@notc.com
Home Page: www.notc.com

Leonard Kalikow, Publisher/Editor

Circulation limited to professionals only, provides major signings, contracts and directories.
Cost: $365
Frequency: Monthly
Circulation: 5,000
ISSN: 0276-7031
Founded in 1976

9062
Notes
Music Library Association
8551 Research Way
Suite 180
Middleton, WI 53562
608-836-5825
FAX 608-831-8200
E-Mail: mla@areditions.com
Home Page: www.musiclibraryassoc.org

Michael Colby, President
Jane Gottlieb, Editor

9063
Nouveau Magazine
Barbara Tompkins
5933 Stoney Hill Rd
New Hope, PA 18938-9602
215-794-5996
FAX 215-794-8305
E-Mail: info@nouveaumagazine.com
Home Page: www.nouveaumagazine.com

Barbara Tompkins, Publisher

Features theater reviews.
Frequency: Monthly
Founded in 1981
Printed in 4 colors on glossy stock

9064
OffBeat
OffBeat
421 Frenchmen St
Suite 200
New Orleans, LA 70116-2039
504-944-4300
877-944-4300
FAX 504-944-4306
E-Mail: offbeat@offbeat.com
Home Page: www.offbeat.com
Social Media: Facebook, Twitter, Flickr

Jan Ramsy, Publisher
Joseph L Irrera, Managing Editor
Bunny Matthews, Senior Editor
Michael Jastroch, Magazine Design/Production
Doug Jackson, Distribution Manager

Consumer-oriented music magazine focusing on New Orleans and Louisiana music. Regular columns on Cajun music, zydeco, traditional and contemporary jazz, brass band (Mardi Gras second-line music), New Orleans R & B, Louisiana and delta blues, Gospel, modern and roots rock and our internationally-appreciated culture and cusine. Information on music fairs and festivals in the region is given.
Cost: $29
Frequency: Monthly
Circulation: 50000
ISBN: 1-090081-0 -
Founded in 1985
Mailing list available for rent: 15000 names
Printed in 4 colors on newsprint stock

9065
Opera America Newsline
Opera America
330 7th Ave
Suite 1600
New York, NY 10001-5248
212-796-8620
FAX 212-796-8631
E-Mail: info@operaamerica.org
Home Page: www.operaamerica.org

Marc Scorca, President

Provides company news from around the world, articles on issues affecting the field, professional opportunities, and updates on OPERA America programs and activities. Complimentary subscription with all membership levels, excluding stand-alone professional subscriptions.
Frequency: 10X Per Year
Founded in 1970

9066
Opera News
Metropolitan Opera Guild
70 Lincoln Center Plz
New York, NY 10023-6577
212-769-7000
FAX 212-769-7007
E-Mail: info@metguild.org
Home Page: www.metoperafamily.org

David Dik, Manager

Monthly magazine that reports on opera around the world. Issues include reviews of commercial recordings and live performances, profiles of artists and articles by eminent writers on the music scene.
Cost: $29.95
Frequency: Monthly
Circulation: 60000
Founded in 1883

INFORMATION RESOURCES / Magazines & Journals

9067
Percussive Notes
Percussive Arts Society
110 W Washington Street
Suite A
Indianapolis, IN 46204
317-974-4488
FAX 317-974-4499
E-Mail: percarts@pas.org
Home Page: www.pas.org

Rick Mattingly, Editor
Hillary Henry, Managing Editor

The official journal of the Percussive Arts Society. Published in February, April, June, August, October and December, this magazine features a variety of articles and advertising aimed at professional and student percussionists. Regular sections are devoted to drumset, marching percussion, world percussion, symphonic percussion, technology, keyboard, health and wellness, research and reviews.
Cost: $85
Frequency: 6 Times Per Year
Circulation: 8000
Founded in 1961
Mailing list available for rent

9068
Performing Arts Insider Magazine
PAI C/O Total Theater
PO Box 31
Greeley, CO 80632
970-405-3077
E-Mail: paipress@aol.com
Home Page: www.performingartsinsider.com

David Lefkowitz, Publisher/Editor
Richmond Shepard, Publisher
J. Weil, Advertising Sales

Includes day-by-day calendar listings of shows on Broadway, Off and Off-Off Broadway, plus dance, opera, cabaret and special events. Also included are comprehensive theater guides, listing the author, director, cast, designers, synopsis, theater and box office details, as well as contact information for producers, press agents, general managers and casting directors.
Cost: $275
Frequency: Monthly+9 Updates
Circulation: 2000
Founded in 1944

9069
Performing Arts Resources
Theatre Library Association
New York Public Library for Performing Arts
40 Lincoln Center Plaza
New York, NY 10023
E-Mail: info@tla-online.org
Home Page: www.tla-online.org/publications/par.html

Nancy Friedland, President
Angela Weaver, VP
Rebecca Lord, Executive Secretary
Colleen Reilly, Treasurer

Features articles on resource materials in the fields of theatre, popular entertainment, film, television and radio, information on public and private collections, and essays on conservation and collection management of theatre arts materials.
Cost: $30
Frequency: Irregular
Circulation: 500
ISSN: 0360-3814
Founded in 1974

9070
Piano Guild Notes
Piano Guild Publications
PO Box 1807
Austin, TX 78767-1807
512-478-5775
FAX 512-478-5843
E-Mail: ngpt@pianoguild.com
Home Page: www.pianoguild.com

Richard Allison, President

Music industry publication focusing on Piano Guild members and activities.
Cost: $16
Frequency: Quarterly
Circulation: 11000
Founded in 1929
Printed in 2 colors

9071
Piano Technicians Journal
Piano Technicians Guild
4444 Forest Avenue
Kansas City, KS 66106
913-432-9975
FAX 913-432-9986
E-Mail: ptg@ptg.org
Home Page: www.ptg.org

Barbara Cassaday, Executive Director
Jim Coleman Jr RPT, President
Norman R Cantrell RPT, VP

Monthly technical magazine covering all phases of working on pianos. Articles explore new tools, industry news and organizational issues. Feature articles range from setting up a repair shop to rebuilding techniques.
Cost: $ 150
Frequency: Monthly
Circulation: 4300
ISSN: 0031-9562

9072
Pitch Pipe
Sweet Adelines International
9110 S Toledo
PO Box 470168
Tulsa, OK 74137-0168
918-622-1444
800-992-7464
FAX 918-665-0894
E-Mail: Joey@sweetadelineintl.org
Home Page: www.sweetadelineintl.org

Pat LeVezu, President
Joey Mechell Stenner, Editor
Kelly Kirchhoff, Director Communications

Official publication of Sweet Adelines International, the world's largest singing performance and music education organization for women. The Pitch Pipe informs, educates and recognizes the members who have made the organization a success. The subscription price for members is included in the annual per capita fee.
Cost: $12
Frequency: Quarterly
Circulation: 30,000
Founded in 1947
Mailing list available for rent: 30M names
Printed in 4 colors on glossy stock

9073
Playback
American Society of Composers, Authors & Publisher
1 Lincoln Plz
New York, NY 10023-7097
212-621-6027
800-952-7227
FAX 212-362-7328
E-Mail: Playback@ascap.com
Home Page: www.ascap.com

Marilyn Bergman, President
Phil Crossland, Executive Editor
Jin Moon, Deputy Editor
Mike Barsky, Advertising
David Pollard, Design

The Society's magazine is loaded with full-color photos, features the latest news on ASCAP events, new member listings, legislative updates, feature articles on members, distribution info, upcoming workshops and showcases and much more.
Cost: $12
Frequency: Annual
Circulation: 100,000
ISSN: 1080-1391

9074
Playbill
34-15 61st Street
Woodside, NY 11377
212-557-5757
FAX 212-682-2932
E-Mail: agans@playbill.com
Home Page: www.playbill.com

Andrew Gans, Editor

The exclusive magazine for Broadway and Off-Broadway theatregoers, providing the information necessary for the understanding and enjoyment of each show, including features articles and columns by and about theatre personalities, entertainment, travel, fashion, dining and other editorial pieces geared to the lifestyle of the upscale, active theatre attendee. Playbill also serves New York's three most prominent performing arts venues - the Metropolitan Opera House, Lincoln Center and Carnegie Hall
Cost: $24
Frequency: Monthly
Founded in 1884

9075
Plays: Drama Magazine for Young People
Plays Magazine
PO Box 600160
Newton, MA 02460
617-630-9100
800-630-5755
FAX 617-630-9101
E-Mail: lpreston@playsmag.com
Home Page: www.playsmag.com

Elizabeth Preston, Editor

Includes eight to ten royalty-free one-act plays, arranged by age level. Modern and traditional plays for the celebration of all important holidays and occasions. Adaptable to all cast sizes with easy to follow instructions for settings and costumes. A complete source of original plays and programs for school-age actors and audiences.
Cost: $39
Frequency: 7 X Per Year
Circulation: 6000
Founded in 1940
Printed in on matte stock

9076
Pointe Magazine
Macfadden Performing Arts Media LLC
333 7th Avenue
11th Floor
New York, NY 10001
212-979-4800
Home Page: www.pointemagazine.com

INFORMATION RESOURCES / Magazines & Journals

Amy Cogan, VP/Group Publisher
Karen Hildebrand, VP Editorial
Jessie Petrov, Publishing/Marketing Director

Dedicated exclusively to the world of ballet.
Frequency: Bi-Monthly
Circulation: 120000

9077
Pollstar: Concert Hotwire
Pollstar
4697 W Jacquelyn Ave
Fresno, CA 93722-6443
559-271-7900
FAX 559-271-7979
E-Mail: info@pollstar.com
Home Page: www.pollstar.com

Gary Smith, COO
Shari Rice, VP
Gary Bongiovanni, CEO

Trade publication for the concert industry offering global coverage and information including concert tour schedules, ticket sales information and more.
Cost: $449
Frequency: Weekly
Circulation: 20000
Printed in 4 colors

9078
Premiere Magazine
Hachette Filipacchi Media US Inc
1633 Broadway
Suite 41
New York, NY 10019-6708
212-767-6000
FAX 212-481-6428
Home Page: www.premiere.com

Jessica Letkemann, Editor
Jennifer Cooper, Producer

A magazine for young adults, which focuses on the art and commerce of the film industry. Premiere's feature articles, profiles and monthly columns include original photography, interviews with Hollywood's A-list and up-and-coming talent, studio heads and producers.

9079
Pro Audio Review
IMAS Publishing
28 East 28th Street
12th Floor
New York, NY 22041
212-378-0400
FAX 212-378-0470
E-Mail: letters@proaudioreview.com
Home Page: www.proaudioreview.com

John Gatski, Publisher/Executive Editor
Brett Moss, Managing Editor
Claudia Van Veen, Advertising

Reviews of the latest new equipment written by audio professionals in the field, from bench tests checking the specs, to new product announcements.
Cost: $24.95
Frequency: Monthly
Circulation: 26000
ISSN: 1083-6241
Founded in 1995
Mailing list available for rent: 30,000 names at $145 per M
Printed in 4 colors on glossy stock

9080
Pro Sound News
United Business Media
28 East 28th Street
12th Floor
New York, NY 10019
212-378-0400
FAX 212-378-2160
E-Mail: sedorusa@optonline.net
Home Page: www.governmentvideo.com

Gary Rhodes, International Sales Manager

Provides timely and accurate news, industy analysis, features and technology updates to the expanded professional audio community.
Cost: $30
Frequency: Monthly
Circulation: 250003
Printed in 4 colors

9081
Produced By
The Producers Guild of America
8530 Wilshire Blvd
Suite 450
Beverly Hills, CA 90211-3115
310-358-9020
FAX 310-358-9520
E-Mail: info@producersguild.org
Home Page: www.producersguild.com

Vance Van Petter, Executive Director
Audra Whaley, Director Operations
Kyle Katz, Director Member Benefits
Chris Greenr, Director Communications
Dan Dodd, Advertising

Provided as a benefit with membership to the Producers Guild of America.
Frequency: Quarterly
Circulation: 325
Founded in 1962

9082
Producer
Testa Communications
25 Willowdale Avenue
Port Washington, NY 11050-3779
516-767-2500
FAX 516-767-9335
Home Page: avvproducersguide.com

Randi Altman, Editor
Sande Seidman, Advertising Manager

Magazine aimed at producers, directors and creative people in the image and sound realms, with production stories on feature films, television, commercials, documentary, and corporate video projects. Accent is on the creative application of technology, following producers into the field and onto the studio set.
Cost: $15
Frequency: Bi-Monthly
Circulation: 18,300

9083
RePlay Magazine
PO Box 572829
Tarzana, CA 91357-7004
818-776-2880
FAX 818-776-2888
E-Mail: editor@replaymag.com
Home Page: www.replaymag.com

Edward Adlum, President
Barry Zweben, Marketing

A trade publication for those within the coin-operated amusement machine industry, primarily distributors, manufacturers and operators of jukeboxes and games.
Cost: $65
Frequency: Monthly
Circulation: 36000
ISSN: 1534-2328
Founded in 1975
Mailing list available for rent
Printed in 4 colors on glossy stock

9084
Rolling Stone Magazine
1290 Ave of the Americas
Floor 2
New York, NY 10104-0295
212-484-1616
FAX 212-484-1771
Home Page: www.rssoundingboard.com
Social Media: *Facebook, Twitter,*

Jann Wenner, President

Covers pop culture, politics etc in a massive amount of music articles, interviews, news, reviews, photos, and sound clips.

9085
SMPTE Journal
Society of Motion Picture & Television Engineers
3 Barker Ave
Suite 5
White Plains, NY 10601-1509
914-761-1100
FAX 914-761-3115
E-Mail: smpte@smpte.org
Home Page: www.smpte.org
Social Media: *Facebook, Twitter,*

Kimberly Maki, Executive Director
Charlie Barone, Administrative Assistant

Featuring industry-leading papers and standards, each month the Journal keeps its members on the cutting edge of the industry. Each issue provides the latest research and papers, ranging in style from technical, scientific, and tutorial, to applications/practices. Readers are kept up-to-date on events and meetings, the latest publications and brochures, and new products and developments.
Cost: $140
Frequency: Monthly
Circulation: 10000
Founded in 1916
Printed in on glossy stock

9086
San Francisco Cinematheque
San Francisco Cinematheque
145 Ninth Street
Suite 240
San Francisco, CA 94103
415-552-1990
FAX 415-552-2067
E-Mail: sfc@sfcinematheque.org
Home Page: www.sfcinematheque.org

Stephen Anker, Executive Director
Alfonso Alvarez, Board Director
Gina Basso, Board Director
Aimee Friberg, Board Director
Jeff Lambert, Board Director

Supports risk-taking art, cutting edge artists and the boundless potential of creative expression.
Cost: $15
Frequency: Monthly
Founded in 1961

9087
Script
Forum
5638 Sweet Air Road
Baldwin, MD 21013-9009

INFORMATION RESOURCES / Magazines & Journals

410-592-3466
888-245-2228
FAX 410-592-8062
E-Mail: scriptmag@fwmedia.com
Home Page: www.scriptmag.com
Social Media: Facebook, YouTube, RSS

Mark Madnick, Publisher
David Geatty, Founding Publisher
Shelly Mellot, Editor-in-Chief
Andrew Schneider, Managing Editor
Maureen Green, Editor

A leading source of information on the crage and business of writing for film and television. Each issues delivers informative articles on writing, developing and marketing screenplays and television scripts. Most articles are written by working writers. Additionally, development executives, agents, managers and entertainment attorneys contribute regularly.
Cost: $24.95
Frequency: Bi-Monthly
Circulation: 12000

9088
Shakespeare Bulletin
University of North Carolina
Department of English
9201 University City Boulevard
Charlotte, NC 28223
E-Mail: sbeditor@email.uncc.edu
Home Page: www.shakespeare-bulletin.org

Seymour Isenberg, Founding Editor
Andrew James Hartley, Editor
Jeremy Lopez, Theatre Review Editor
Genevieve Love, Book Review Editor
Kirk Melnikoff, Shakespeare on Film Editor

A peer-reviewed journal of performance and criticism and scholarship which provides commentary on Shakespeare and Renaissance drama through feature articles, thatre and film reviews, and book reviews. The journal is a member of the Conference of Editors of Learned Journals.
Cost: $35
Frequency: Quarterly
ISSN: 0748-2558
Founded in 1982
Mailing list available for rent
Printed in on matte stock

9089
Sheet Music Magazine
PO Box 58629
Boulder, CO 80323
914-244-8500
800-759-3036
FAX 914-244-8560
Home Page: www.sheetmusicmagazine.com

Ed Shanaphy, Publisher

Features actual reproduction of popular songs, both words and music, articles on various aspects of musical performance and interest for many types of musicians, and self improvement features for keyboard and fretter instrument players. A single year's subscription brings you at least 66 great songs best-loved standards and today's most lyrical hits.
Cost: $22.97
Frequency: Bi-Monthly
Circulation: 50,000

9090
Show Music
Po Box A
East Haddam, CT 06423-0466
860-873-8664
FAX 860-873-2329
E-Mail: rklink@goodspeed.org
Home Page: www.showmusic.org

Ryan Klink, Managing Editor
Maz O Preeo, Editor-In-Chief

Internationally acclaimed by professionals and fans as the premier magazine covering musical theatre around the world. Show music combines insightful interviews and reviews of productions, recordings, videos and books.

9091
Society News
Contemporary Record Society
724 Winchester Road
Broomall, PA 19008
610-544-5920
FAX 915-808-4232
E-Mail: crsnews@verizon.net
Home Page: www.mysite.verizon.net/vzeeewvp/contemporaryrecordsociety/id3.

Jack M Shusterman, Advertising

Offers opportunities to CRS consitituents, progress notes on its associates, various awards and performance possibilities. The Society News offers feature articles of renowned composers/performers and reviews of music, recordings and music books.
Founded in 1983

9092
Sondheim Review
PO Box 11213
Chicago, IL 60611-0213
773-275-4254
800-584-1020
FAX 773-275-4254
E-Mail: info@sondheimreview.com
Home Page: www.sondheimreview.com

Dedicated to the work of the musical theater and Broadway's foremost composer and lyricist, Stephen Sondheim. Each issue contains news, interviews, upcoming productions in the area, puzzles and more.
Cost: $19.95
Frequency: Quarterly
Circulation: 40000
ISSN: 1076-450X
Founded in 1994
Mailing list available for rent: 6,000 names at $105 per M
Printed in on glossy stock

9093
Southern Theatre
Southeastern Theatre Conference
1175 Revolution Mill Dr.
Studio 14
Greensboro, NC 27405
336-272-3645
FAX 336-272-8810
E-Mail: setc@setc.org
Home Page: www.setc.org

Elizabeth Baun, Executive Director
April J'Callahan Marshall, Professional Theatre Services Mgr
Hardy Koenig, Educational Services Manager

Spotlights people, places and organizations within the region that are paving new paths in theatre. Includes low-cost strategies for design success, tips on hot markets for playwrights, new books of special interest, innovative ideas for marketing theatre, inside track on new trends and some of the region's up-and-coming theatre stars. Subscription is free with SETC membership.
Cost: $18.75
Frequency: Quarterly
Circulation: 4000+
Founded in 1949

9094
Southwestern Musician
Texas Music Educators Association
7900 Centre Park
PO Box 140465
Austin, TX 78714-0465
512-452-0710
888-318-8632
FAX 512-451-9213
E-Mail: rfloyd@tmea.org
Home Page: www.tmea.org

Robert Floyd, Executive Director
Karen Kneten, Communications Manager
Tesa Harding, Advertising/Exhibit Manager
Laura Kocian, Financial Manager
Rita Ellinger, Membership Assistant

The official magazine of the TMEA. Publsihed monthly August through May. Included with membership. A President's newsletter is published each June when necessary to provide an update on TMEA activities. The purposed of this publication is to serve the music educators of Texas as a means of communication or professional philosophy and action and to promote the field of music education within the state.
Circulation: 14000
Founded in 1938
Mailing list available for rent: 10,000 names
Printed in 4 colors on glossy stock

9095
Spectrum
110 S Jefferson Street
Dayton, OH 45402-3412
937-220-1600
800-247-1614
FAX 937-220-1642
E-Mail: comments@thinktv.org
Home Page: www.thinktv.org
Social Media: Facebook, Twitter, YouTube

Jerry Kathman, President&CEO
Brad Mays, Treasurer
Alisa Poe, Secretary

ThinkTV's monthly member magazine. Contains program listings for both ThinkTV 16 and ThinkTV14 as well as interesting feature stories, station news and more.
Frequency: Weekly
Circulation: 18000
Founded in 1959

9096
Stage of the Art
American Alliance for Theatre and Education
4908 Auburn Avenue
Bethesda, MD 20814-3474
301-200-1944
FAX 301-280-1682
E-Mail: info@aate.com.edu
Home Page: www.aate.com
Social Media: Facebook, Twitter, RSS

David Young, Editor
JoBeth Gonzalez, Director Publications/Research

Published by the American Alliance for Theatre and Education.
Mailing list available for rent: 700 names at $150 per M

INFORMATION RESOURCES / Magazines & Journals

9097
Stagebill
Stagebill
144 E 44th Street
New York, NY 10017
212-476-0640
FAX 212-983-5976
E-Mail: bmattison@stagebill.com
Home Page: www.avant-rus.com/stagebill

Fred B Tarter, Chairman/President/CEO
Gerry Byrne, Chairman/President/CEO
Ben Mattison, Editorial Contact

Publisher of the program magazines for the leading, theaters, symphonies, dance companies and performing arts centers in the United States. A national performing arts magazine.
Frequency: Monthly
Founded in 1924

9098
Stages
Curtains
301 W 45th Street
Apartment 5A
New York, NY 10036-3825
FAX 201-836-4107

Frank Scheck, Editor
Cost: $20
Frequency: Monthly
Circulation: 35,000

9099
Starlog
1372 Broadway
2nd Floor
New York, NY 10018
212-689-2830
800-934-6788
E-Mail: rita@starloggroup.com
Home Page: www.starlog.com

David McDonnel, Editor
Norman Jacobs, Founder

Information on science fiction happenings in the movies and television industries.
Cost: $56.97
Frequency: Monthly
Circulation: 350000

9100
Symphony Magazine
American Symphony Orchestra League
33 W 60th St
Suite 5
New York, NY 10023-7905
212-262-0638
FAX 212-262-5198
E-Mail: editor@symphony.org
Home Page: www.symphony.org

Henry Fogel, CEO
Stephen Alter, Advertising Manager
Michael Rush, Production Manager

Bimonthly magazine of the American Symphony Orchestra League. Discusses issues critical to the orchestra community and communicates the value and importance of orchestras and the music they perform. Publishes articles on compelling issues and trends relevant to the entire orchestra field. Its readers include professional staff, musicians, and board members in the orchestra industry and related fields; orchestra patrons and volunteers; and music critics and arts and media professionals.
Cost: $22
Frequency: Bi-Monthly
Circulation: 18000
Founded in 1942
Mailing list available for rent
Printed in 4 colors

9101
Symposium
312 E Pine Street
Missoula, MT 59802
406-721-9616
800-729-0235
FAX 406-721-9419
E-Mail: cms@music.org
Home Page: www.music.org

Robby D Gunstream, Executive Director
Cynthia Taggart, President
Glenn Stanley, Editor

Serves as a vehicle for the dissemination of information and ideas on music in higher education. The content of the publication highlights concerns of general interest and reflects the work of the Society in the areas of music represented on its Board of Directors.
Frequency: One Per Year
Circulation: 8000
Founded in 1968
Printed in one color on matte stock

9102
TD & T: Theatre Design & Technology
US Institute for Theatre Technology
315 South Crouse Avenue
Suite 200
Syracuse, NY 13210
315-463-6525
FAX 315-463-6525
E-Mail: info@.usitt.org
Home Page: www.usitt.org
Social Media: *Facebook, Twitter,*

David Roger, Editor
Arnold Wengrow, Book Review Editor
Michelle Smith, Membership/Advertising Manager
N Deborah Hazlett, Art Director

Published by United States Institute for Theatre Technology. Focuses on USITT's ten interest areas: architecture, costume design and technology, education, engineering, health and safety, lighting, management, scene design, sound design, and technical production.
3700 Members
Frequency: Quarterly

9103
Teaching Theatre Journal
Educational Theatre Association
2343 Auburn Ave
Cincinnati, OH 45219-2819
513-421-3900
FAX 513-421-7077
E-Mail: jpalmarini@schooltheatre.org
Home Page: schooltheatre.org
Social Media: *Facebook, Twitter,*

Donald A Corathers, Publications Director
James Palmarini, Editor

For professional theatre educators. A typical issue includes an article on acting, directing, playwriting, or technical theatre; a profile of an outstanding educationl theatre program; a piece on curriculum design, assessment, or teaching methodology; and reports on current trends or issues in the field, such as funding, standards, or certification.
4000 Members
Frequency: Quarterly
Circulation: 4000
ISSN: 1077-2561
Founded in 1929

9104
Technical Brief
Yale School of Drama
222 York Street
PO Box 208244
New Haven, CT 06520
203-432-8188
FAX 203-432-8129
E-Mail: bronislaw.sammler@yale.edu
Home Page: www.technicalbrief.org

Ben Sammler, Co-Editor
Don Harvey, Co-Editor

Written by professionals for professionals, providing a dialogue between technical practitioners from the several performing arts. The succinct articles, complete with mechanical drawings, represent the best solutions to recurring technical problems. Published October, January and April.
Cost: $15
Frequency: 3X Per Year
Founded in 1924

9105
Theater Magazine
Yale School of Drama
1120 Chapel Street
P.O Box 1257
New Haven, CT 06505
203-432-1234
FAX 203-432-6423
E-Mail: yalerep@yale.edu
Home Page: www.yale.edu/drama

Tom Sellar, Editor
Laraine Sammler, Business Manager
Alex Grennan, Director of Business/Comm

Periodicals, essays and articles of the Yale School of Drama.
Cost: $22
Frequency: Annual+
Circulation: 2500
Founded in 1924
Mailing list available for rent: 1.5M names
Printed in one color on matte stock

9106
Theatre Bay Area Magazine
1663 Mission Street
Suite 525
San Francisco, CA 94103
415-430-1140
FAX 415-430-1145
E-Mail: tba@theatrebayarea.org
Home Page: www.theatrebayarea.org
Social Media: *Facebook, Twitter, YouTube*

Karen Mc Kevitt, Executive Director
Dale Albright, Director, Member Services
Clayton Lord, Director, Audience Development
Cost: $5.95
Frequency: Monthly
Circulation: 4500

9107
Theatre Bill
Jerome Press
332 Congress St
Suite 2
Boston, MA 02210-1217
617-423-3400
FAX 617-423-7108
Home Page: www.showofthemonthtravel.com

INFORMATION RESOURCES / Trade Shows

Jerome Rosenfeld, Owner

9108
Theatre Journal
Johns Hopkins University Press
2715 N Charles St
Baltimore, MD 21218-4363
410-516-6900
800-537-5487
FAX 410-516-6968
E-Mail: webmaster@jhupress.jhu.edu
Home Page: www.press.jhu.edu

William Brody, President
David Z Saltz, Co-Editor
Sonja Arsham Kuftinec, Performance Review Editor
James Peck, Book Review Editor
Bob Kowkabany, Managing Editor

One of the most authoritative and useful publications of theatre studies available today. Theatre Journal features social and historical studies, production reviews, and theoretical inquiries that analize dramatic texts and production. Official journal of the Association for Theatre in Higher Education.
Cost: $40
Frequency: Quarterly
Circulation: 2492
ISSN: 0192-2882
Founded in 1878
Mailing list available for rent

9109
Theatre Symposium
Auburn University
1175 Revolution Mill Dr.
Studio 14
Greensboro, NC 27405
336-272-3645
FAX 336-272-8810
E-Mail: setc@setc.org
Home Page: www.setc.org

M Scott Phillips, Editor

An annual publication of works of scholarship resulting from a single topic meeting held on a southeastern university campus each year. Available to adult members only. A copublication of the Southeaster Theatre Conference and the University of Alabama Press.

9110
Theatre Topics
Johns Hopkins University Press
2715 N Charles St
Baltimore, MD 21218-4363
410-516-6900
800-537-5487
FAX 410-516-6998
E-Mail: webmaster@jhupress.jhu.edu
Home Page: www.press.jhu.edu

William Brody, President
Sandra G Shannon, Co-Editor
DeAnna Toten Beard, Book Review Editor
Elanore Lampners, Managing Editor
Beverley Pevitts, Founding Editor

Focuses on performance studies, dramaturgy, and theatre pedagogy. Concise and timely articles on a broad array of practical, performance-oriented subjects, with special attention to topics of current interest to the profession. Keeps readers informed of the latest developments on the stage and in the classroom. The official journal of the Association for Theatre in Higher Education. Published in March and September.
Cost: $32
Frequency: Semi-Annually
Circulation: 1528
ISSN: 1054-8378
Founded in 1878
Mailing list available for rent

9111
Variety
Reed Business Information
5700 Wilshire Boulevard
Suite 120
Los Angeles, CA 90036-3659
323-857-6600
866-698-2743
FAX 323-857-0494
E-Mail: VTCCustserv@cdsfulfillment.com
Home Page: www.variety.com

Charles C Koones, Publisher
Peter Bart, Editor-in-Chief
Timothy Gray, Editor
Kathy Lyford, Managing Editor
Christopher Wessel, Circulation Director

Variety covers all aspects of film, television and cable, homevideo, music, new media and technolgy, theater and finance. Topics run from people, companies, products and performances, to development, financing, distribution, regulation and marketing.
Cost: $259
Frequency: Weekly
Circulation: 35168
Founded in 1905

9112
Vibe
E-Mail: vbecustserv@cdsfulfillment.com
Home Page: www.vibe.com

Mimi Valdez, Editor-In-Chief

Covers the trends, the events, and culture of the urban scene. Film, fashion and art to politics and music-pop, jazz, R&B, dance, hip hop, rap, house and more.
Cost: $11.95
Frequency: Monthly

9113
Youth Theatre Journal
American Alliance for Theatre and Education
4908 Auburn Ave
Bethesda, MD 20814
301-200-1944
FAX 301-235-7108
E-Mail: info@aate.com
Home Page: www.aate.com

A scholarly journal dedicated to advancing the study and practice of theatre and drama with, for, and by the people of all ages. It is concerned with all forms of scholarship of the highest quality that inform the fields of theatre for young audiences and drama/theatre education.
Cost: $25
Frequency: 2x/Year
Circulation: 1000
ISSN: 0892-9092
Mailing list available for rent: 700 names at $150 per M
Trade Shows

Trade Shows

9114
ASTA National Conference
American String Teachers Association
4155 Chain Bridge Road
Fairfax, VA 22030
703-279-2113
FAX 703-279-2114
E-Mail: asta@astaweb.com
Home Page: www.astaweb.com

Donna Sizemore Hale, Executive Director
Beth Danner-Knight, Deputy Director
Jody McNamara, Deputy Director

Recognizing the wealth of our rich traditions as well as offer members new horizons in teaching and performing strings. Cost of attendance begins at $255. 150 exhibitors.
2000 Attendees
Frequency: Annual/March

9115
American Choral Directors Association National Conference
American Choral Directors Association
545 Couch Drive
Oklahoma City, OK 73102
405-232-8161
FAX 405-232-8162
Home Page: www.acdaonline.org

Dr Tim Sharp, Executive Director

4 full days of concerts, interest sessions, exhibits, and networking.
Frequency: Annual/March

9116
American Film Institute Festival: AFI Fest
American Film Institute
2021 N Western Avenue
Los Angeles, CA 90027-1657
323-856-7896
866-234-3378
FAX 323-856-9118
E-Mail: AFIFEST@AFI.com
Home Page: www.afifest.com

Jennifer Morgerman, Publicity Director
Stacey Leinson, Publicity Manager
Lagan Sebert, Publicity Coordinator
John Wildman, Filmmaker Press Liaison
Alison Deknatel, Director Communications

A 10-day event held each November, the festival features a rich slate of films from emerging filmmakers, nightly red-carpet gala premieres and global showcases of the latest work from the great film masters. AFI runs concurrently with the American Film Market. Together, AFT Fest and AFM provide the film industry with the only concurrent festival/market event in North America.
60000 Attendees
Frequency: November
Founded in 1986

9117
American Guild of Organists, National Conference
475 Riverside Drive
Suite 1260
New York, NY 10115
212-870-2310
FAX 212-870-2163
E-Mail: info@agohq.org
Home Page: www.agohq.org

James Thomashower, Executive Director
Jennifer Madden, Manager Membership
Harold Calhoun, Mgr Competitions

Over 20 exhibits and a workshop for professional, amatuer and student organists.
Frequency: Biennial

INFORMATION RESOURCES / Trade Shows

9118
American Harp Society National Conference
3416 Primm Lane
Birmingham, AL 35216
205-795-7130
FAX 205-823-2760
E-Mail: execsecretary@harpsociety.org
Home Page: www.harpsociety.org

Christa Grix, National Conference Chair
Lynne Aspnes, Conference Program Advisory Chair
Delaine Fedson, President

Conference will explore the mind-body-music connection, the creative process, and the connection between creativity and learning. The conference will include multiple disciplines including educators, composers, performers, therapists and practioners.
300 Attendees
Frequency: Annual
Founded in 1962

9119
American Institute of Organbuilders Annual Convention
American Institute of Organ Builders
PO Box 130982
Houston, TX 77219
713-529-2212
FAX 713-529-2212
E-Mail: pipes@pipeorgan.org
Home Page: www.convention.pipeorgan.org

Rene Marceau, Convention Committee Chairman

Annual convention includes supplier exhibits, technical lectures, sight-seeing tours, professional examinations, lectures and organ demonstrations.
Frequency: October
Founded in 1974
Mailing list available for rent: 350 names at $250 per M

9120
American Music Therapy Conference
National Music Therapy Association
8445 Colesville Road
Suite 1000
Silver Spring, MD 20910
301-589-3300
FAX 301-589-5175
Home Page: www.musictherapy.org

Seminar and exhibits of publications, musical instruments, books, learning aids and recordings.
Frequency: November

9121
American Musical Instrument Society
1106 Garden Street
Hoboken, NJ 07030
202-656-0107
E-Mail: amis@guildassoc.com
Home Page: www.amis.org

Susan Thompson, Program Co-Chair
Kathryn Libin, Program Co-Chair

A broad range of topics include the history, design, use, care and acoustics of musical instruments in all cultures and from all periods.
Frequency: Annual

9122
American Musicological Society Annual Meeting
American Musicological Society
6010 College Station
Brunswick, ME 04011-8451
207-798-4243
877-679-7648
FAX 877-679-7648
E-Mail: ams@ams-net.org
Home Page: www.ams-net.org

Robert Judd, Executive Director

A society of professional musicologists and university educators. The annual meetings are held in the fall each year; 2007- Quebec; 2008- Nashville; 2009- Philadelphia.
2000 Attendees
Frequency: Annual
Founded in 1948
Mailing list available for rent: 3515 names at $100 per M

9123
American Orff-Schulwerk Association National Conference
American Orff-Schulwerk Association
PO Box 391089
Cleveland, OH 44139-8089
440-543-5366
FAX 440-600-7332
E-Mail: info@aosa.org
Home Page: www.aosa2.org

Karen Medley, Conference Chair

One hundred exhibits of music, music books, software, insturments, and gifts in addition to National Conference of 2000+ music educators.
2400 Attendees
Frequency: November
Founded in 1969

9124
American Symphony Orchestra League National Conference
33 W 60th Street
5th Floor
New York, NY 10023
212-262-5161
FAX 212-262-5198
E-Mail: league@symphony.org
Home Page: www.symphony.org

Stephen Alter, Advertising and Meetings Manager
Meghan Whitbeck, Advertising/Meetings Coordinator
Henry Fogel, President/CEO

Ninety booths incorporating all facets of classical music industries including industry suppliers, music publishers and computer technology.
1200 Attendees
Frequency: June

9125
CMS National Conference
College Music Society
312 E Pine Street
Missoula, MT 59802
406-721-9616
FAX 406-721-9419
E-Mail: cms@music.org
Home Page: www.music.org

Robby D Gunstream, Executive Director

Presents higher education's broadest array of topics dealing with music. Attendees are faculty, administrators, graduate students, independent scholars, composers, publishers, and music business personnel who share a common interest and dedication to the improvement of music and its relationship to the other academic disciplines of higher education.
450 Attendees
Frequency: Annual/October

9126
Chamber Music America National Conference
Chamber Music America
305 7th Avenue
5th Floor
New York, NY 10001
212-242-2022
FAX 212-242-7955
Home Page: www.chamber-music.org

Susan Dadian, Program Director
Margaret M Liol, CEO
Louise Smith, Chair
700 Attendees
Frequency: Annual

9127
Chorus America Annual Conference
910 17th Street NW
Washington, DC 20006
202-776-0215
FAX 202-776-0224
E-Mail: service@chorusamerica.org
Home Page: www.chorusamerica.org

Ann Meier Baker, President/CEO
Melanie Garrett, Membership Services Manager

This four day conference offers seminars, workshops, concerts, expert consultations and peer-group meetings in a friendly, dynamic environment.
500 Attendees
Frequency: June
Printed in 2 colors on matte stock

9128
CinemaCon
National Association of Theatre Owners
750 1st St NE
Suite 1130
Washington, DC 20002-4241
202-962-0054
FAX 202-962-0370
E-Mail: nato@natodc.com
Home Page: www.natoonline.org

John Fithian, President
Gary Klein, VP
Kathy Conroy, Executive Director

A gathering of cinema owners and operators.
4000 Members
Frequency: Annual/March

9129
Country Radio Seminar
Country Radio Broadcasters
819 18th Avenue S
Nashville, TN 37203
615-327-4487
FAX 615-329-4492
E-Mail: info@crb.org
Home Page: www.crb.org

Ed Salamon, Executive Director
Chasity Crouch, Business Manager
Carole Bowen, Secretary

Conference attendess include major radio groups and record labels as well as independents, Features include exhibits, seminars and shows.
2300 Attendees
Frequency: Annual
Founded in 1969

9130
EXPO
Theatre Bay Area

1085

INFORMATION RESOURCES / Trade Shows

870 Market Street
Suite 375
San Francisco, CA 94102-3002
415-430-1140
FAX 415-430-1145
E-Mail: dale@theatrebayarea.org
Home Page: www.theatrebayarea.org

Dale Albright, Director of Individual Services

Theatre Bay Area's EXPO is where attendees can meet those kinds of businesses that might offer services to the theatre community: theatre companies, actors, etc. There are also break-out sessions discussing issues of interest to the theatre community.
500+ Attendees
Frequency: May

9131
EdTA Thespian Festival
Educational Theatre Association
2343 Auburn Ave
Cincinnati, OH 45219-2819
513-421-3900
FAX 513-421-7077
Home Page: www.schooltheatre.org
Social Media: Facebook, Twitter,

Michael Peitz, Executive Director
Gloria McIntyre, President
Jay Seller VP

The premiere showcase for high school theatre, drawing students and teachers from throughout the United States and abroad.
3000 Attendees

9132
Educational Theatre Association Conference
Educational Theatre Association
2343 Auburn Ave
Cincinnati, OH 45219-2819
513-421-3900
FAX 513-421-7077
Home Page: www.schooltheatre.org
Social Media: Facebook, Twitter,

Michael Peitz, Executive Director
Gloria McIntyre, President
Jay Seller VP
400 Attendees
Frequency: Annual

9133
Folk Alliance Annual Meeting
Folk Alliance
510 South Main
1st Floor
Memphis, TN 38103
901-522-1170
FAX 816-221-3658
E-Mail: fa@folk.org
Home Page: www.folkalliance.org

200+ artists, 4 nights of show cases, four days of feature concerts, exhibit hall parties, panels, workshops, clinics and much more all under one roof.
3000 Attendees

9134
Gospel Music Week
Gospel Music Association
PO Box 22697
Nashville, TN 37202
615-242-0303
FAX 615-254-9755
E-Mail: info@gospelmusic.org
Home Page: www.gospelmusic.org

Jackie Patillo, Executive Director

Listen to new music as you experience over 100 eclectic performances throughout the week from today's top artists and tomorrow's hit-makers, invent new waysof enhancing your ministry through educational opportunities found in over 100 seminars and panels and through the sharing of your ideas with colleagues. Connect with your industry peers and friends at various networking opportunities including receptions, roundtables and more.
3,000 Attendees
Frequency: April
Founded in 1964

9135
Gospel Music Workshop America
PO Box 34635
Detroit, MI 48208
313-898-6900
FAX 313-898-4520
E-Mail: manager@gmwnational.org
Home Page: www.gmwanational.org

Rev Albert L Jamison, Sr, Chair, Board of Directors
Sheila Smith, Director Operations
Mark Smith, Convention Manager

Conferences open with a highly spirited service including Sacraments, music from choirs within the GMWA, Psalmists and the preached Word. This is followed by lectures, speakers, preachers and over 100 courses offered during the week. Nightly musicals include chapter choirs and national recording artists. Midnight services are held which include music, preaching and various recordings by the Women's Division, Men's Division, Youth/Young Adult division and a service by Bishop Richard White.
16M Attendees
Frequency: August
Founded in 1967

9136
Horns Over the Sea
Central Washington University Music Department
400 E University Way
Ellensburg, WA 98926-7458
509-963-1226
FAX 509-963-1239
E-Mail: gross@music.ucsb.edu
Home Page: www.hornsociety.org

Jeffrey Snedeker, President
Steven Gross, Conference Coordinator
Heidi Vogel, Membership Coordinator

Features renowned hornists, guest ensembles, recitals and master classes
450 Attendees
Frequency: August

9137
International Association of Jazz Educators Conference
International Association of Jazz Education
PO Box 724
Manhattan, KS 66505
785-776-8744
FAX 785-776-6190
E-Mail: info@iage.org
Home Page: www.iaje.org

Bill McFarlin, Executive Director

This four-day conference fatures a 75,000 square-food music industry exposition, commission premieres, technology presentations, research papers, award ceremonies, and performances by over 500 of the world's most respected professional jazz groups and musicians.
8000 Attendees
Frequency: Annual

9138
International Association of Venue Managers
International Association of Assembly Managers
635 Fritz Drive
Suite 100
Coppell, TX 75019-4442
972-906-7441
800-935-4226
FAX 972-906-7418
E-Mail: mike.meyers@iaam.org
Home Page: www.iaam.org

Steven Peters, President
Robyn Williams, First Vice President
Frequency: Annual

9139
International Cinema Equipment (ICECO) Showest
Magna-Tech Electronic Company
5600 NW 32nd Avenue
Miami, FL 33142
305-573-7339
FAX 305-573-8101
E-Mail: iceco@iceco.com
Home Page: www.showest.com

Steven H Krams, President
Dara Reusch, VP
Julio Urbay, VP International Sales/Marketing
Fancisco Blanco, VP Technical Services
Arturo Quintero, Architectural Design/Development

Annual convention for the Motion Picture industry. It is an international gathering devoted exclusively to the movie business. It is also the single largest international gathering of motion picture professionals and theatre owners in the world, with delegates from more than 50 countries in attendance each year.
Frequency: March
Founded in 1975

9140
International Cinema Equipment Company ICECO Show East
Magna-Tech Electronic Company,Inc.
1998 NE 150th Street
North Miami, FL 33181
305-573-7339
FAX 305-573-8101
E-Mail: iceco@aol.com
Home Page: www.iceco.com

Steven H Krams, President
Dara Reusch, VP
Julio Urbay, VP International Sales/Marketing
Francisco Blanco, VP/Technical Services
Arturo Quintero, Architectural Design & Development

This annual convention brings together over 1300 colleagues from the motion picture industry in the United States, Latin America and the Caribbean. The convention provides information on industry trends, screen films and product reels, state-of-the-art theatre equipment along with services and technologies vital to the industry.
1300 Attendees
Founded in 1975

9141
International Computer Music Conference
International Computer Music Association

INFORMATION RESOURCES / Trade Shows

1819 Polk Street
Suite 330
San Francisco, CA 94109
FAX 734-878-3031
E-Mail: icma@umich.edu
Home Page: www.computermusic.org
Social Media: Facebook,

Tae Hong Park, President
Margaret Schedel, VP of Conference
Chryssie Nanou, Treasurer/Secretary
Tom Erbe, VP, Membership
Sandra Neal, Administrative Assistant

The International Computer Music Association is an international affiliation of individuals and institutions involved in the technical, creative, and performance aspects of computer music. It serves composers, engineers, researchers and musicians who are interested in the integration of music and technology.
Founded in 1974

9142
International Horn Competition of America
BGSU Continuing and Extended Education
14 College Park
Bowling Green, OH 43403-0200
509-963-1226
FAX 509-963-1239
Home Page: www.ihcamerica.org

Jeffrey Snedeker, President
Andrew Pelletier, Host

International competition specifically for the horn as a solo instrument.
450 Attendees
Frequency: July

9143
International Steel Guitar Convention
College Music Society
312 East Pine Street
Missoula, MT 59802
406-721-9616
FAX 406-721-9419
E-Mail: cms@music.org
Home Page: www.music.org
Social Media: Facebook, Twitter, YouTube, RSS

Dewitt Scott Sr, President
Mary Scott, Secretary

Sixty-five booths that provide entertainment from steel guitarists and various instruments including the bass guitar.
3M Attendees
Frequency: August

9144
Mid-South Horn Conference
Central Washington University Music Department
400 E University Way
Ellensburg, WA 98926-7458
509-963-1226
FAX 509-963-1239
E-Mail: campbellel@umkc.edu
Home Page: www.hornsociety.org

Jeffrey Snedeker, President
Ellen Campbell, Event Host
Heidi Vogel, Membership Coordinator

Features renowned hornists, guest ensembles, recitals and master classes
450 Attendees
Frequency: March

9145
Midwest International Band & Orchestra Clinic
Midwest International Band & Orchestra Clinic
111 E Touhy Ave
Suite 250
Des Plaines, IL 60018
847-424-4163
FAX 773-321-1509
E-Mail: info@midwestclinic.org
Home Page: www.midwestclinic.org

The purpose to the clinic is to raise the standards of music education, to develop new teaching techniqes, to examine, analyze, analyze and appraise literature dealing with music, demonstrations for the betterment of music education. 350 exhibitors, 565 booths, 30 concerts, and 50 instructional clinics.
12000 Attendees
Frequency: December

9146
Moondance Film Festival
970 9th Street
Boulder, CO 80302
303-545-0202
E-Mail: director@moondancefilmfestival.com
Home Page: www.moondancefilmfestival.com

Elizabeth English, Festival Founder/Executive Director
Kyle/Erica Saylors, Festival Director/Event Coordinator
Karina Pyudik, Registration Coordinator
Douglis C Garvin, Special Events Coordinator
Roy Bodner, Publicist/Media Relations

The Festival's primary goal is to present films and scripts which have the power to raise awareness about vital social issues, educating writers and filmmakers, as well as festival audiences, and inspiring them to take positive action. The Festival's objective is to promote and encourage independent filmmakers, screenwriters and playwrights, and the best works in films, screenplays, stageplays, TV scripts, radioplays, film scores, lyrics, librettos, music videos, and short stories.
Frequency: Annual

9147
Music Teachers National Association Convention
441 Vine Street
Suite 3100
Cincinnati, OH 45202
513-421-1420
888-512-5278
FAX 513-421-2503
E-Mail: mtnanet@mtna.org
Home Page: www.mtna.org

Gary L Ingle, Executive Director
Gail Berenson, President
Janice Wenger, VP

Atendees include independent music teachers, college faculty, students and parents from all over North America.
2500 Attendees
Frequency: Annual
Founded in 1876
Mailing list available for rent: 23000 names at $85 per M

9148
NAMM: International Music Products Association
5790 Armada Drive
Carlsbad, CA 92008-4608
760-438-8001
800-767-6266
FAX 760-438-7327
E-Mail: tradeshow@namm.com
Home Page: www.thenammshow.com

Joe Lamond, President

NAMM's trade shows are all about the experience. The experience of checking out the latest gear, of networking with other music product professionals, of attending free business-boosting classes. From the cook exhibits to the sizzling hot nightlife, music and music making always take center stage.
80000 Attendees
Frequency: January

9149
NATS National Conference
National Association of Teachers of Singing
9957 Moorings Dr
Suite 401
Jacksonville, FL 32257-2416
904-992-9101
FAX 904-262-2587
E-Mail: info@nats.org
Home Page: www.nats.org

Allen Henderson, Executive Director
Deborah L Guess, Director of Operations
Frequency: June/July

9150
NDEO National Conference
National Dance Education Organization
8609 2nd Avenue
Suite 203 B
Silver Spring, MD 20910
301-585-2880
FAX 301-585-2888
E-Mail: info@ndeo.org
Home Page: www.ndeo.org

Susan McGreevy-Nichols, Executive Director
Jane Bonbright EdD, Executive Director
Patricia Cohen, Treasurer

Provides 200+ professional development sessions for artists, educators and administrators teaching or supporting dance education programs in PreK-12, colleges/universities, private studio/schools of dance, community centers and performing arts organizations.
800 Attendees
Frequency: Annual

9151
National Association for Music Education Conference
1806 Robert Fulton Drive
Reston, VA 20191-4348
703-860-4000
800-336-3768
FAX 703-860-1531
Home Page: www.menc.org
Social Media: Facebook, Twitter, LinkedIn,

John J Mahlmann, Executive Director
Margaret Jamborsky, Director Meetings/Conventions
Elizabeth Lasko, Director Public Relations/Marketing
Amanda Kidwell, Membership Director

To advance music education by encouraging the study and making of music by all.
5M Attendees
Frequency: April

INFORMATION RESOURCES / Trade Shows

9152
National Association of Pastoral Musicians Convention
National Association of Pastoral Musicians
962 Wayne Avenue
Suite 210
Silver Spring, MD 20910-4461
240-247-3000
FAX 240-247-3001
E-Mail: npmsing@npm.org
Home Page: www.npm.org

J Michael McMahon, President
Kathleen Haley, Membership Services Director
Paul H Colloton, Continuing Education Director
Lowell Hickman, Executive Assistant/Office Manager

200 workshop sessions, 5 major addresses, music education classes, clinics, new music showcases and exhibits, musical performances, prayer and songs, adult and children's choirs, handbells, youth gatherings, Liturgical Space Tour.
4000 Attendees
Frequency: July

9153
National Association of Recording Merchandising Trade Show
9 Eves Drive
Suite 120
Marlton, NJ 08053-3130
856-596-2221
FAX 859-596-3268
E-Mail: still@narm.com
Home Page: www.narm.com
Social Media: *Facebook, Twitter, RSS*

Jim Donio, President
Pat Daly, Meeting Planner
Evelyn Dichter, Membership Coordinatorsusan, VP Communications/Marketing

One-on-One meeting opportunities, welcome reception, keynote speakers, marketplace exhibits, live performances, forums, receptions and awards dinner
3M Attendees
Frequency: April/May

9154
National Association of Schools of Music Annual Meeting
National Association of Schools of Music
11250 Roger Bacon Drive
Suite 21
Reston, VA 20190-5248
703-437-0700
FAX 703-437-6312
E-Mail: info@arts-accredit.org
Home Page: www.arts-accredit.org

Don Gibson, President
Mark Wait, VP
Mellasenah Y Morris, Treasurer
Frequency: November

9155
National Black Theatre Festival
610 Coliseum Drive
Suite 1
Winston-Salem, NC 27106
336-723-2266
E-Mail: nbtf@bellsouth.net
Home Page: www.nbtf.org

Patrice Toney, President
Frequency: Annual, Winston-Salem

9156
National Opera Association Conference
National Opera Association
PO Box 60869
Canyon, TX 79016
806-651-2857
FAX 806-651-2958
E-Mail: rhansen@mail.wtamu.edu
Home Page: www.noa.org
Social Media: *Facebook, RSS*

Robert Hansen, Executive Director
Robert Thieme, Editor

Annual conference and exhibits of opera related equipment, supplies and services.
775 Attendees
Frequency: Annual
Founded in 1954

9157
National Square Dance Convention
PO Box 5790
Topeka, KS 66605-5790
317-635-4455
Home Page: www.57nsdc.com

Ernie Stone, Executive Committee
Barbara Stone, Executive Committee

250 booths and 250 exhibitors.
20M+ Attendees
Frequency: June

9158
New England Theatre Conference
215 Knob Hill Drive
Hamden, CT 06518
617-851-8535
FAX 203-288-5938
E-Mail: mail@netconline.org
Home Page: www.netconline.org

Sabine Klein, President
Jeffrey Watts, Executive VP
Charles Emmons, VP Administration/Finance

Promoting excellence in theatre, a conference of New England's oldest, largest regional theatre association.
800+ Attendees
Frequency: November
Founded in 1952

9159
New York Film Festival
Film Society of Lincoln Center
70 Lincoln Center Plaza
New York, NY 10023
212-875-5610
888-313-6085
E-Mail: filminfo@filmlinc.com
Home Page: www.filmlinc.com
Social Media: *Facebook, Twitter,*

Rose Kuo, Executive Director
Richard Pena, Program Director
Lesli Klainberg, Managing Director

Celebrates American and international cinema and recognizes and supports new filmmakers.
Frequency: Annual

9160
North Carolina Southeastern Theatre Conference
1175 Revolution Mill Drive
Suite 14
Greensboro, NC 27405-0868
336-272-3645
FAX 336-272-8810
E-Mail: info@setc.org
Home Page: www.setc.org

Betsey Baun, Executive Director
April Marshall, Contact/Pro. Theatre Services

Join over 4,000 Theatre Artists for education, exchanges, ideas, products, networking and great theatre. Convention activities include keynote speakers, auditions, guest speakers, festivals, design competition, commercial and educational expo exhibits, scholarship awards, social events and workshops.
4000+ Attendees

9161
Northeast Horn Workshop
Central Washington University Music Department
400 E University Way
Ellensburg, WA 98926-7458
509-963-1226
FAX 509-963-1239
E-Mail: rdodsonw@mansfield.edu
Home Page: www.hornsociety.org

Jeffrey Snedeker, President
Rebecca Dodson, Workshop Host
Heidi Vogel, Membership Coordinator

Features renowned hornists, guest ensembles, recitals and master classes
450 Attendees
Frequency: February

9162
Opera America Conference
Opera America
330 7th Avenue
16th Floor
New York, NY 10001-5248
212-796-8620
FAX 212-796-8631
Home Page: www.operaamerica.org
Social Media: *RSS*

Session topics include identifying ways to harness the power of the best new technologies, how to reach current and prospective audiences, how to gain support from donors, and how to enrich the lives of children and adults who are now downloading podcasts, reading blogs, and designing their own multimedia communications.
275 Attendees
Frequency: April

9163
Piano Technicians Guild Annual Convention
Piano Technicians Guild
4444 Forest Avenue
Kansas City, KS 66106
913-432-9975
FAX 913-432-9986
E-Mail: ptg@ptg.org
Home Page: www.ptg.org

Barbara J Cassaday, Executive Director
Jim Coleman Jr RPT, President
Norman R Cantrell RPT, VP

Come for the learning: find a hands-on class for your skill level; pick from sessions covering every type of piano service; squeeze in a mini-tech; prepare for the RPT exams; see the latest and greatest piano products.
650 Attendees
Frequency: June

INFORMATION RESOURCES / Directories & Databases

9164
Prescott Park Arts Festival
105 Marcy Street
PO Box 4370
Portsmouth, NH 03802-4370
603-436-2848
FAX 603-436-1034
E-Mail: info@prescottpark.org
Home Page: www.prescottpark.org
Social Media: *Facebook,*

Ben Anderson, Executive Director
John Moynihan, General Manager
Catherine Wejchert, Development Coordinator

Provide a financially accessible, quality multi-arts festival to a diverse audience.

9165
Sundance Film Festival
Sundance Institute
1825 Three Kings Drive
PO Box 684426
Park City, UT 84060
435-658-3456
FAX 435-658-3457
E-Mail: Institute@sundance.org
Home Page: www.sundance.org

Robert Redford, Founder
Keri Putnam, Executive Director
Jill Miller, Managing Director

Annual festival held in Park City, Utah as a US showcase for American and International independent film. The Institute is dedicated to the development of artists of independent vision and the exhibition of their new work. Since its inception, the Institute has grown into an internationally recognized resource for thousands of independent artists.
Frequency: January
Founded in 1981

9166
Sweet Adelines International Convention
Sweet Adelines International
PO Box 470168
Tulsa, OK 74147-0168
918-622-1444
800-992-7464
FAX 918-665-0894
Home Page: www.sweetadelineintl.org

Kathy Hayes, Director Meetings/Corporate Service
Ruth Cameron, Meetings/Exhibits Coordinator
Jane Hanson, Marketing Coordinator
Connie Heyer, Membership Registrar
Kellye Kirchhoff, Director Communications

Heart-pounding chorus competitions, the rush and excitement of the quartet competition, education classes, shopping in the Harmony Bazaars and good times with old friends and new are all included in the International Convention.
8M Attendees
Frequency: October

9167
TCG National Conference
Theatre Communications Group
520 8th Ave
24th Floor
New York, NY 10018-4156
212-609-5900
FAX 212-609-5901
E-Mail: tcg@tcg.org
Home Page: www.tcg.org

Theresa Eyring, Executive Director
Jennifer Cleary, Membership Director

9168
Telluride Film Festival
National Film Preserve
800 Jones Street
Berkeley, CA 94710
510-665-9494
FAX 510-665-9589
E-Mail: mail@telluridefilmfestival.org
Home Page: www.telluridefilmfestival.org

Bill Pence, Founder
Stella Pence, Founder

Well situated on the international film festival calendar, Terruride takes place in Telluride, Colorado, and is defined by sense of purity and commitment.
Founded in 1974

9169
Toronto International Film Festival
TIFF Bell Lightbox
350 King Street West
Toronto
888-599-8433
Home Page: www.tiff.net

William Marshall, Founder
Piers Handling, Director & CEO
Noah Cowan, Artistic Director, Bell Lightbox
Cameron Bailey, Co-Director

Publicly attended film festival that takes place each September in Toronto, Ontario, Canada, showing upwards of 400 films from more than 60 countries. The festival is currently headquartered at TIFF Bell Lightbox, which opened in 2010.
Founded in 1976
Mailing list available for rent

9170
US Institute for Theatre Technology Annual Conference & Stage Expo
USITT
315 S Crouse Avenue
Suite 200
Syracuse, NY 13210
315-463-6463
800-938-7488
FAX 315-463-6525
E-Mail: info@usitt.org
Home Page: www.usitt.org
Social Media: *Facebook, Twitter, LinkedIn,*

Carl Lefko, President
Patricia Dennis, Secretary
Travis DeCastro, Treasurer

The Conference offers over 175 sessions featuring design, technology, costume, sound, architecture, management, engineering, and production. The Stage Expo showcases businesses, products, services, and eductional opportunities in the performing arts and entertainment industry. With over 150 exhibitors, Stage Expo provides conference attendees with the opportunity to see the newest and best products and services on the market today.
3700 Members
3800 Attendees
Frequency: March
Founded in 1960

9171
Winter Music Conference
3450 NE
12th Terrace
Fort Lauderdale, FL 33334

954-563-4444
FAX 954-563-1599
E-Mail: info@wintermusicconference.com
Home Page: www.wintermusicconference.com

Regarded as the singular networking event in the dance music industry, attracting professionals from over 60 different countries.

9172
World of Bluegrass
International Bluegrass Music Association
2 Music Circle South
Suite 100
Nashville, TN 37203
615-256-3222
888-438-4262
FAX 615-256-0450
E-Mail: info@ibma.org
Home Page: www.ibma.org

Dan Hays, Executive Director
Nancy Cardwell, Special Projects Coordinator
Jill Snider, Member/Convention Services

Build relationships with event producers, record label reps, agents and managers, broadcasters, association leaders, educators, the media, instrument builders, artists and composers. Educational and networking events like seminars, facilitated discussions and workshops are the primary focus of the conference. Browse through 100+ booths in the Exhibit Hall. You will hear bluegrass music around the clock for seven days. The Highpoint of the Conference is the International Bluegrass Music Awards.
1,800 Attendees
Frequency: October
Directories & Databases

Directories & Databases

9173
Academy Players Directory
2210 W Olive Avenue
Suite 320
Burbank, CA 91506
310-247-3058
FAX 310-550-5034
E-Mail: info@playersdirectory.com
Home Page: www.playersdirectory.com

The Players Directory appeared in 1937 as the first reliable casting directory that listed both featured stars and extras. Today, more than 16,000 actors are included.
Cost: $75
Founded in 1937

9174
American Association of Community Theatre Membership Directory
1300 Gendy St Forth Worth
St Forth Worth, TX 76107
817-732-3177
866-687-2228
FAX 817-732-3178
E-Mail: info@aact.org
Home Page: www.aact.org

Julie Angelo, Executive Director
Linda Lee, President
Carole Ries, VP Public Relations
Frank Peot, Secretary
Tim Jebsen, Treasurer

The database includes addresses for over 7,000 community theatre organizations in the USA. Only available to members.

INFORMATION RESOURCES / Directories & Databases

Mailing list available for rent: 10000 names at $180 per M

9175
American Music Center Directory
American Music Center
90 John Street
Suite 312
New York, NY 10038
212-645-6949
FAX 212-366-5265
E-Mail: library@newmusicusa.org
Home Page: www.amc.net

Joanne Cossa, Executive Director
Lyn Liston, Director New Music Information Svce
Peter Shavitz, Director Development
Lisa Taliano, Director Information Technology
Carlos Camposeco, Director Finance and Administration

Mailing lists include all United States members; all International and United States members; Composer Members in the United States; Members in the New York City Metropolitan area; and Members in the United States and Canada.

9176
American Society of Composers, Authors and Publishers
American Soc. of Composers, Authors & Publishers
1 Lincoln Plz
New York, NY 10023-7097
212-621-6027
FAX 212-621-8453
E-Mail: ACE@ascap.com
Home Page: www.ascap.com

Marilyn Bergman, President
Johnny Mandel, Writer Vice Chairman
Jay Morgenstern, Publisher Vice Chairman
Arnold Broido, Treasurer
Kathy Spanberger, Secretary

ASCAP created the dial-up ACE system as a useful tool for music professionals. An enhanced World Wide Web version of this database is now available. The database contains information on all compositions in the ASCAP repertory which have appeared in any of ASCAP's domestic surveys, including foreign compositions licensed by the ASCAP in the United States.
Frequency: Annual
Founded in 1993

9177
Americans for the Arts Field Directory
Americans for the Arts
1 E 53rd St
2nd Floor
New York, NY 10022-4242
212-223-2787
FAX 212-980-4857
Home Page: www.artsactionfund.org
Social Media: *Facebook, Twitter, RSS, You Tube*

Suzanne Niemeyer, Editor
Robert L Lynch, President/CEO
Liz Bartolomeo, Public Relations/Marketing Coord
Chad Bauman, Director Print/Multimedia Commun
Graham Dunstan, Assoc Director Publication Sales

A must-have resource for anyone working in the arts and community development. The directory provides contact information for local, state, regional, and national arts service organizations-more than 4,000 entries broken down by state and region. Also includes contact information for professional consultants working in the nonprofit arts field. A great networking tool.
Cost: $35

262 Pages

9178
Annual Index to Motion Picture Credits
Academy of Motion Picture Arts and Sciences
8949 Wilshire Blvd
Beverly Hills, CA 90211-1972
310-247-3000
FAX 310-271-3395
Home Page: www.oscars.org

The Index is closely tied to the annual Academy Awards presentation. As part of the Academy Awards process, the Academy of Motion Picture Arts and Sciences gathers credits for each film hoping to qualify for awards. These credits, compiled and verified by the film's producer or distributor, are the core of the Annual Index and IMPC database. In addition to personal credits, IMPC also records index production and releasing dates, MPAA ratings, running times, color, language, and more.
Frequency: Annual
ISBN: 0-942102-37-1
ISSN: 0163-5123
Founded in 1934

9179
Association of Performing Arts Presenters Membership Directory
APAP
1211 Connecticut Ave NW
Suite 200
Washington, DC 20036-2716
202-833-2787
888-820-2787
FAX 202-833-1543
E-Mail: info@artspresenters.org
Home Page: www.artspresenters.org

Sandra Gibson, President
Sean Handerhan, Marketing

An invaluable resource for keeping in touch with colleagues. Puts more than 1,450 presenters, service organizations, artists, management companies, consultants, and vendors at your fingertips. An excellent networking tool for everyone on your staff.
1900 Members
Frequency: Annual
Founded in 1957

9180
AudArena International Guide
Billboard Directories
PO Box 15158
North Hollywood, CA 91615
818-487-4582
800-562-2706
E-Mail: info@billboard.com
Home Page: www.orderbillboard.com

Arkady Fridman, Inside Sales Manager

Complete data on over 4,400 venues worldwide, including Amphitheaters, Arenas, Stadiums, Sports Facilities, Concert Halls and New Constructions. Also includes complete listings of companies offering services to the touring industry in the Facilty Buyer's Guide. The guide features contact names, phone and fax numbers, e-mail and web site addresses, market population, facility capacities and staging configurations, and rental fees and ticketing rights.
Cost: $99
325 Pages
Frequency: Annual

9181
Billboard Subscriber File
Edith Roman Associates
PO Box 1556
Pearl River, NY 10965
845-620-9000
800-223-2194
FAX 845-620-9035
E-Mail: john.logiudice@edithroman.com
Home Page: www.edithroman.com

Steve Roberts, President
Wayne Nagrowski, E-Mail List Info Contact

Directory listees include booking agencies and agents, clubs, music publishers, promoters, radio stations, record labels, sound and lighting services, retailers, video, venues, wholesalers, equipment and manufacturing and general services.
Frequency: Annual

9182
Blu-Book Production Directory
Hollywood Creative Directory
5055 Wilshire Blvd
Los Angeles, CA 90036-6103
323-525-2369
800-815-0503
FAX 323-525-2398
E-Mail: hcdcustomerservice@hcdonline.com
Home Page: www.hcdonline.com

Valencia McKinley, Manager

A comprehensive directory for professionals in the production and post-production industries. Provides current contact information needed to produce a film, TV program, commercial, or music video. The directory contains a special tabbed section on premier below-the-line craft professionals, along with selective credits, and has been expanded to include New York production facilities and services, making it one of the only bi-coastal resources of its kind.
Cost: $39.95
450 Pages
Frequency: Annual
ISBN: 1-928936-44-X

9183
Bluegrass Resource Directory
International Bluegrass Music Association
2 Music Cir S
Suite 100
Nashville, TN 37203-4381
615-256-3222
888-438-4262
FAX 615-256-0450
E-Mail: info@ibma.org
Home Page: www.ibma.org

Member Directory can only be accessed by IBMA members.
Cost: $25
88 Pages
Frequency: Annual

9184
Boxoffice: Circuit Giants
Boxoffice
PO Box 1634
Des Plains, IL 60019
212-627-7000
Home Page: www.boxoffice.com

Peter Cane, Publisher
Joe Policy, CEO
Annlee Ellingson, Editor
Francesca Dinglasan, Senior Editor
Bob Vale, VP Advertising and Sales

INFORMATION RESOURCES / Directories & Databases

Directory of the largest exhibition chains. Available to subscribers of Boxoffice magazine
Cost: $59.95
Frequency: Annual
Founded in 1990

9185
Boxoffice: Distributor Directory
Boxoffice
PO Box 1634
Des Plains, IL 60019
212-627-7000
Home Page: www.boxoffice.com

Peter Cane, Publisher
Joe Policy, CEO
Annlee Ellingson, Editor
Francesca Dinglasan, Senior Editor
Bob Vale, VP Advertising and Sales

Listings of studio and independent film suppliers. Available to subscribers of Boxoffice magazine
Cost: $59.95
Frequency: Annual
Founded in 1990

9186
Complete Catalogue of Plays
Dramatists Play Service
440 Park Ave S
New York, NY 10016-8012
212-683-8960
FAX 212-213-1539
E-Mail: webmasters@dramatists.com
Home Page: www.dramatists.com
Social Media: *Facebook,*

Stephen Fultan, President
Rafael J Rivera, VP Finance/Administration
Michael Q Fellmeth, VP Publications/IT
Tamra Feifer, Director Operations

The Complete Catalogue is published in odd years and the Supplement of New Plays in even years. Both books are distributed, without charge, to current customers in the Fall of each year.
412 Pages
Founded in 1936

9187
Costume Designers Guild Directory
Costumer Designers Guild
4730 Woodman Avenue
Suite 430
Sherman Oaks, CA 91423-2400
818-905-1557
FAX 818-905-1560
E-Mail: cdgia@earthlink.net
Home Page: www.costumedesignersguild.com

Cheryl Downey, Executive Director
Deborah N Landis, President

Directory includes members' names, classification, and other statistical information.
Frequency: Annual

9188
Dance Annual Directory
Dance Magazine
333 7th Ave
11th Floor
New York, NY 10001-5109
212-979-4800
FAX 212-979-4817
E-Mail: emacel@dancemagazine.com
Home Page: www.dancemagazine.com

Karla Johnson, Publisher
Emily Macel, Editor

Karen Hildebrand, Editorial Director
Wendy Perron, Editor-in-Chief
Hanna Rubin, Managing Editor

Reach 300,000+ dancers, dance teachers, and dance professionals in the dance world.
Cost: $100
Frequency: Annual

9189
Dance Magazine College Guide
Dance Magazine
333 7th Ave
11th Floor
New York, NY 10038-3900
212-979-4800
FAX 212-979-4817
E-Mail: subscriptions@dancemagazine.com
Home Page: www.dancemagazine.com

Karla Johnson, President
Karen Hildebrand, Editorial Director
Wendy Perron, Editor-in-Chief
Hanna Rubin, Managing Editor
Kate Lydon, Education Editor

With over 500+ listings, Dance Magazine College Guide is a comprehensive source for dance degree programs in higher education. Find application deadlines and audition dates. Get student perspectives and career advice. Online database offers the ability to identify programs that match an individual's personal criteria for degree, type of dance, location, department size, tuition and more.
Cost: $29.95
Frequency: Annual

9190
Dance Magazine: Summer Dance Calendar Issue
Dance Magazine
33 W 60th Street
Floor 10
New York, NY 10023-7905
212-245-9050
800-331-1750
Home Page: www.dancemagazine.com

A list of dance workshops and special programs for students are listed.
Cost: $3.95
Frequency: Annual
Circulation: 100,000

9191
Dance/USA Annual Directory and List-Serv
Dance/USA
1111 16th St NW
Suite 300
Washington, DC 20036-4830
202-833-1717
FAX 202-833-2686
E-Mail: danceusa@danceusa.org
Home Page: www.danceusa.org

Andrea Snyder, Executive Director
Tom Thielen, Director Finance/Operations
Katherine Fabian, Membership Manager

On-going list-servs keep many peer councils in touch throughout the year, by providing a quick and easy connection to peer counseling when members have an immediate question or problem. Information about dance companies, schools, presenters, service organizations and commercial suppliers is included in the annual copy of Dance Annual Directory.
Frequency: Annual
Circulation: 400+

9192
Directors Guild of America Directory of Members
Directors Guild of America
7920 W Sunset Blvd
Los Angeles, CA 90046-3347
310-289-2000
800-421-4173
FAX 310-289-2029
Home Page: www.dga.org

Jay Roth, President
Morgan Rumpf, Director Communications/Media Relat
Paul Zepp, Membership Administrator
Darrell L Hop, Editor DGA Monthly/Website
Michael Apted, Secretary

The DGA represents Film and Television Directors, Unit Production Managers, First Assistant Directors, Second Assistant Directors, Technical Coordinators and Tape Associate Directors, Stage Managers and Production Associates. The Directory is available in print and on-line
Cost: $25
Frequency: Annual

9193
Directory of Theatre Training Programs
Theatre Directories
P.O.Box 2409
Manchester Center, VT 05255-2409
802-867-9333
FAX 802-867-2297
E-Mail: info@theatredirectories.com
Home Page: www.theatredirectories.com

Peg Lyons, Editor
PJ Tumielewicz, Editor

Profiles admissions, tuition, faculty, curriculum, facilities, productions and philosophy of training at 475 programs in the US, Canada and abroad: Colleges, Universities, Conservatories, Undergraduate and Graduate degrees. Includes Combined Auditions information. Indexed by degrees offered in each program.
Cost: $39.50
ISBN: 0-933919-61-1

9194
Dramatics College Theatre Directory
Educational Theatre Association
2343 Auburn Ave
Cincinnati, OH 45219-2815
513-421-3900
FAX 513-421-7077
Home Page: www.edta.org
Social Media: *Facebook, Twitter,*

Michael Peitz, Executive Director
Gloria McIntyre, President
Jay Seller, VP

Lists more than 250 college, university, and conservatory theatre programs, offering a sketch of each based on information provided by the schools. The listings can be used to measure each school against one's own criteria for location, setting, courses of study, admission requirements, and cost. Find out which programs offer merit scholarships and grants and how those funds are awarded. Use the contact information to get in touch with the programs that seem to offer the best fit for your needs
Cost: $9
Frequency: Annual

INFORMATION RESOURCES / Directories & Databases

9195
Dramatics Magazine: Summer Theatre Directory
Educational Theatre Association
2343 Auburn Ave
Cincinnati, OH 45219-2815
513-421-3900
FAX 513-421-7077
Home Page: www.edta.org
Social Media: *Facebook, Twitter,*

Michael Peitz, Executive Director
Gloria McIntyre, President
Jay Seller, VP

Lists nearly 200 summer theatre programs and stock companies, offering a sketch of each based on factual information provided by the schools, camps, and theatre companies. The listings can be used to measure each program against one's own criteria for location, setting, housing, courses of study, admission requirements and fees.
Cost: $9
Frequency: Annual

9196
Dramatist's Sourcebook
Theatre Communications Group
520 8th Ave
24th Floor
New York, NY 10018-4156
212-609-5900
FAX 212-609-5901
E-Mail: tcg@tcg.org
Home Page: www.tcg.org

Theresa Eyring, Executive Director
Kelly Haydon, Database Manager
Jennifer Cleary, Director Membership
Terence Nemeth, Publisher
Kathy Sova, Editorial Director

Completely revised, with more than 900 opportunities for playwrights, translators, composers, lyricists, and librettists, as well as opportunities for screen, radio, and television writers. Thoroughly indexed, with a calendar of deadlines. The Sourcebook contains scrip-submission procedures for more than 350 theatres seeking new plays; guidelines for more than 150 prizes; and sections on agents, fellowships and residencies.
Cost: $22.95
Frequency: Annual
ISBN: 1-559362-94-4
Founded in 1980

9197
Dramatists Guild Annual Resource Directory
Dramatists Guild of America
1501 Broadway
Suite 701
New York, NY 10036-5505
212-398-9366
FAX 212-944-0420
Home Page: www.dramaguild.com

Ralph Sevush, Executive Director

The Resource Directory is an annual sourcebook available only to Guild members, sent automatically as one of the privileges of Guild members. It includes lists of conferences and festivals, contests, producers, publishers, agents and attorneys, fellowships and grants, and workshops throughout the US and the world.
Frequency: Annual

9198
Editors Guild Directory
Motion Picture Editors Guild
7715 Sunset Boulevard
Suite 200
Hollywood, CA 90046
323-876-4770
800-705-8700
FAX 323-876-0861
E-Mail: info@editorsguild.com
Home Page: www.editorsguild.com

Ron Kutak, Executive Director
Tomm Carroll, Publications Director
Serena Kungr, Director Membership Services
Adriana Iglesias-Dietl, Membership Administrator
Tris Carpenter, Manager

An invaluable resource for producers, directors and post production professionals alike. It lists contact, credit, award and classification information for all of the Guild's active members at the time of publication, as well as a list of Oscar and Emmy winners for every year since the awards began. It also includes a retirees section.
Cost: $25
Frequency: Bi-Annual
Founded in 1994

9199
Encyclopedia of Exhibition
National Association of Theatre Owners
750 1st St Ne
Suite 1130
Washington, DC 20002-4241
202-962-0054
FAX 202-962-0370
E-Mail: nato@natodc.com
Home Page: www.natoonline.org

John Fithian, President
Gary Klein, VP
Kathy Conroy, Executive Director

Packed with information on film grosses, upcoming releases, and filmgoer demographics. Also features a directory of international and domestic exhibitors and distributors, cinema companies ranked by screen count, trade publications and more
Cost: $500
Frequency: Annual

9200
Fame Index
Hollywood Madison Group
11684 Ventura Boulevard
#258
Studio City, CA 91604-2499
818-762-8008
FAX 818-762-8089
Home Page: holllywood-madison.com

Jonathan Holiff, Founder/President/CEO

Search over 10,000 celebrities from actors to athletes to find every performer who meets your needs. The Index has more than 250 searchable criteria including: age, sex, children, birthplace, genre, fees, ethnicity/heritage, biography, statistics, interests, hobbies, sports, personality attributes, charity affiliations, medical conditions, and endorsement histories. Contact information includes: agent, manager, publicist, business manager, attorney, and personal assistant.
Founded in 1996

9201
Feedback Theatrebooks and Prospero Press
Feedback Theatrebooks & Prospero Press
PO Box 174
Brooklin, ME 04616
207-359-2781
FAX 207-359-5532

Publishes theatre histories, cookbooks, directories, anthologies of plays, plays published before WWII, and format guidelines for playwrights.

9202
Film Journal: Distribution Guide Issue
Film Journal International
770 Broadway
5th Floor
New York, NY 10003-9595
646-654-7680
FAX 646-654-7694
Home Page: www.filmjournal.com

Robert Sunshine, Publisher/Editor
Kevin Lally, Executive Editor
Rex Roberts, Associate Editor
Andrew Sunshine, Advertising Director
Katey Rich, Editorial Assistant

The International Distribution and subdistribition Guide supplements the regular monthly Buying and Booking Guide. It is designed to furnish ready reference information on the who, what, where and how of theatrical sales. It lists the names, addresses, personnel, telephone numbers and product of domestic and international distributors, both major and independent, along with similar information on regional exchanges together with national companies they handle.
Frequency: Annual

9203
Film Journal: Equipment Guide
Film Journal International
770 Broadway
5th Floor
New York, NY 10003-9595
646-654-7680
FAX 646-654-7694
Home Page: www.filmjournal.com

Robert Sunshine, Publisher/Editor
Kevin Lally, Executive Editor
Robin Klamfoth, Advertising Director
Rex Roberts, Associate Editor
Katey Rich, Editorial Assistant

The Equipment, Concessions and Services Guide is designed to provide ready reference information on the theatrical equipment and concessions industry. It lists in detail the company names, addresses, telephone numbers, personnel, affiliations and products of equipment and concession manufacturers and service companies, along with similar information on US and foreign service dealers and suppliers, arranged in alphabetical order according to state or country.
Frequency: Annual

9204
Film Journal: Exhibition Guide
Film Journal International
770 Broadway
5th Floor
New York, NY 10003-9595
212-493-4097
FAX 646-654-7694
E-Mail: subscriptions@filmjournal.com
Home Page: www.filmjournal.com

INFORMATION RESOURCES / Directories & Databases

Robert Sunshine, Publisher/Editor
Kevin Lally, Executive Editor
Robin Klamfoth, Advertising Director
Rex Roberts, Associate Editor
Sarah Sluis, Editorial Assistant

The exhibition Guide is an alphabetical listing designed to provide ready reference information on the leading theatrical motion picture circuits. It lists in comprehensive detail such data as company names, addresses and phone numbers, total screens and new screens projected, division office locations, top personnel, recent circuit acquisitions, and a state-by-state breakdown of screens.
Frequency: Annual
Founded in 1934
Mailing list available for rent

9205
Film Superlist: Motion Pictures in the Public Domain
Hollywood Film Archive
8391 Beverly Blvd
Ste. 321
Los Angeles, CA 90048-2633
323-655-4968

Richard Baer, Executive Director

Created by Walter E. Hurst and updated by Richard Baer. 1992-1994. Three volumes to date, covering 50,000 films from the years 1894-1939, 1940-1949 and 1950-1959.

9206
Gospel Music Industry Directory
Gospel Music Association
P.O Box 22697
Nashville, TN 37202
615-242-0303
FAX 615-254-9755
E-Mail: info@gospelmusic.org
Home Page: www.gospelmusic.org
Social Media: *Facebook, YouTube*

John Styll, President
Scott Brickell, Director
Ed Harper, Director

Formerly called the Networking Guide, the GMA Music Industry Directory is a comprehensive listing of Christian and Gospel music artists, managers, booking agents, record companies, publishing companies and more. Active GMA Professional members get a copy of the directory free. Associate and Student GMA members can purchase one for a discounted rate.

9207
Grey House Performing Arts Directory
Grey House Publishing
4919 Route 22
PO Box 56
Amenia, NY 12501
518-789-8700
800-562-2139
FAX 845-373-6390
E-Mail: books@greyhouse.com
Home Page: www.greyhouse.com
Social Media: *Facebook, Twitter,*

Leslie Mackenzie, Publisher
Richard Gottlieb, Editor

The most comprehensive resource covering the Performing Arts. This directory provides current information on over 8,500 Dance Companies, Instrumental Music Programs, Opera Companies, Choral Groups, Theater Companies, Performing Arts Series, Performing Arts Facilities and Artist Management Groups.
Cost: $185
1200 Pages
Frequency: Annual
ISBN: 1-592373-76-3
Founded in 1981

9208
Grey House Performing Arts Directory - Online Database
Grey House Publishing
4919 Route 22
PO Box 56
Amenia, NY 12501
518-789-8700
800-562-2139
FAX 518-789-0556
E-Mail: gold@greyhouse.com
Home Page: www.gold.greyhouse.com
Social Media: *Facebook, Twitter,*

Leslie Mackenzie, Publisher
Richard Gottlieb, Editor

The Grey House Performing Arts Directory - Online Database provides immediate access to dance companies, orchestras, opera companies, choral groups, theater companies, series, festivals and perfoming arts facilities across the country, or in their region, state, or in your own backyard. It offers unequaled coverage of the Performing Arts - over 8,500 listings - of the major performance organization, facilities, and information resources.
Frequency: Annual
Founded in 1981

9209
International Buyers Guide
Billboard Directories
PO Box 15158
North Hollywood, CA 91615
818-487-4582
800-562-2706
E-Mail: info@billboard.com
Home Page: www.billboard.com/directories

Arkady Fridman, Inside Sales Manager

A must-have resource for doing business in the music industry, covers every aspect of the recording business worldwide. The latest edition includes contact information on: record labels, video and digital music companies, distributors and importers/exporters; music publishers and rights organizations - blank media manufacturers, pressing plants and services; manufacturers of jewel boxes and other packaging and equipment services; and suppliers of store fixtures, security and accessories.
Cost: $179
340 Pages
Frequency: Annual

9210
International Motion Picture Alamanc
Quigley Publishing Company
64 Wintergreen Lane
Groton, MA 01450
860-228-0247
800-231-8239
FAX 860-228-0157
E-Mail: quigleypub@aol.com
Home Page: www.quigleypublishing.com

William J Quigley, President/Publisher
Eileen Quigley, Editor

Contains over 400 pages of biographies and 500 pages of reference material. From 1928 to the present day, the complete set contains the biography of everyone who has ever been of importance to the Industry. Each edition includes thousands of company listings, credits for current films and films released in the prior ten years, statistics and awards and complete coverage of all aspects of the industry, including production, distribution and exhibition.
Cost: $175
Frequency: Annual

9211
International Talent and Touring Guide
Billboard Directories
PO Box 15158
North Hollywood, CA 91615
818-487-4582
800-562-2706
E-Mail: info@billboard.com
Home Page: www.billboard.com/directories

Arkady Fridman, Inside Sales Manager

A reference guide for anyone who books, promotes or manages talent. Features over 30,000 listings, including 12,900 artists, managers and agents worldwide, including the USA and Canada. The guide includes contact names, phone and fax numbers, e-mail and website addresses, artists and their record labels, managers and agents, tour services and merchandise, sound and lighting vendors, equipment and instrument rentals, limo rentals, security services, plus national promoters and their key personnel
Cost: $139
242 Pages
Frequency: Annual

9212
International Television and Video Almanac
Quigley Publishing Company
64 Wintergreen Lane
Groton, MA 01450
860-228-0247
800-231-8239
FAX 860-228-0157
E-Mail: quigleypub@aol.com
Home Page: www.quigleypublishing.com

William J Quigley, President/Publisher
Eileen Quigley, Editor

Each edition contains over 400 pages of biographies and an additional 500 pages of reference material on television programs, broadcast, cable and satellie, production services, the video industry, statistics and awards. Included are detailed listings for thousands of companies, as well as coverage outside the United States.
Cost: $175
Frequency: Annual
Founded in 1955

9213
Keyboard Teachers Association International
Dr. Albert DeVito
361 Pin Oak Lane
Westbury, NY 11590-1941
516-333-3236
FAX 516-997-9531

Albert DeVito, President

Music teachers and those related to keeping members updated as to activity going on in music world.
Frequency: Quarterly
Founded in 1963

9214
MLA Membership Handbook
Music Library Association

1093

INFORMATION RESOURCES / Directories & Databases

8551 Research Way
Suite 180
Middleton, WI 53562
608-836-5825
FAX 608-831-8200
E-Mail: mla.areditions.com
Home Page: www.musiclibraryassoc.org

Philip Vandermeer, President

A mailing list that is available for rental in a variety of formats.
Cost: $25
Founded in 1931

9215
Mini Reviews
Cineman Syndicate
31 Purchase St
Suite 203
Rye, NY 10580-3013
914-967-5353
Home Page: www.minireviews.com

John P McCarthy, Editor

An easy to read, easy to use guide for movie watchers updated weekly.
Frequency: Weekly
Founded in 2000

9216
Money for Film and Video Artists
Americans for the Arts
1 E 53rd St
2nd Floor
New York, NY 10022-4242
212-223-2787
FAX 212-980-4857
Home Page: www.artsactionfund.org
Social Media: *Facebook, Twitter, RSS, You Tube*

Suzanne Niemeyer, Editor
Robert L Lynch, President/CEO
Liz Bartolomeo, Public Relations/Marketing Coord
Chad Bauman, Director Print/Multimedia Commun
Graham Dunstan, Assoc Director Publication Sales

A comprehensive resource guide to fellowships, grants, awards, low-cost facilities, emergency assistance programs, technical assistance, and support services. Entries include contact information; type of award and/or scope of service; eligibilty requirements; application procedures; deadlines and more.
Cost: $14.95
317 Pages
ISBN: 1-879903-09-1

9217
Money for International Exchange in the Arts
Americans for the Arts
1 E 53rd St
2nd Floor
New York, NY 10022-4242
212-223-2787
FAX 212-980-4857
Home Page: www.artsactionfund.org
Social Media: *Facebook, Twitter, RSS, You Tube*

Suzanne Niemeyer, Editor
Robert L Lynch, President/CEO
Liz Bartolomeo, Public Relations/Marketing Coord
Chad Bauman, Director Print/Multimedia Commun
Graham Dunstan, Assoc Director Publication Sales

This resource includes grants, fellowships and awards for travel and work abroad; support and technical assistance for international touring and exchange; international artists' residencies; programs that support artists' professional development, and more. Indexed by region, discipline and type of support.
Cost: $14.95
122 Pages
ISBN: 1-879903-01-6

9218
Money for Performing Artists
Americans for the Arts
1 E 53rd St
2nd Floor
New York, NY 10022-4242
212-223-2787
FAX 212-980-4857
Home Page: www.artsactionfund.org
Social Media: *Facebook, Twitter, RSS, You Tube*

Suzanne Niemeyer, Editor
Robert L Lynch, President/CEO
Liz Bartolomeo, Public Relations/Marketing Coord
Chad Bauman, Director Print/Multimedia Commun
Graham Dunstan, Assoc Director Publication Sales

Lists awards, grants, fellowships, competitions, auditions, workshops, and artists' colonies, as well as emergency and technical assistance programs.
Cost: $12
240 Pages
ISBN: 0-915400-96-0
Founded in 1991

9219
Money for Visual Arts
Americans for the Arts
1 E 53rd St
2nd Floor
New York, NY 10022-4242
212-223-2787
FAX 212-980-4857
Home Page: www.artsactionfund.org
Social Media: *Facebook, Twitter, RSS, You Tube*

Suzanne Niemeyer, Editor
Robert L Lynch, President/CEO
Liz Bartolomeo, Public Relations/Marketing Coord
Chad Bauman, Director Print/Multimedia Commun
Graham Dunstan, Assoc Director Publication Sales

A guide to grants, fellowships, awards, artist colonies, emergency and technical assistance, and support services. Entries include contact information; type of award and/or scope of service; eligibility requirements; application procedures; deadlines, and more.
Cost: $14.95
340 Pages

9220
Motion Picture TV and Theatre Directory
Motion Picture Enterprises
PO Box 276
Tarrytown, NY 10591-0276
212-245-0969
FAX 212-245-0974
Home Page: www.mpe.net

Neal R Pilzer, Publisher

The Guide is mailed to members of 59 trade associations, unions and professional societies; decision-makers at advertising agencies, production companies, TV stations, and government agencies; faculty and students of nearly 200 film schools; and other prime purchasers of film and TV equipment and services nationwide. Companies are listed both by category and company name. Listings include company name, address and telephone number as well as fax numbers, e-mail addresses, and web site URLs.
Cost: $18.80

335 Pages
Frequency: Annual
Circulation: 82500
Founded in 1963

9221
Movie World Almanac
Hollywood Film Archive
8391 Beverly Blvd
PMB 321
Los Angeles, CA 90048-2633
323-655-4968

Richard Baer, Executive Director

Lists over 200 major American and foreign film distributors who handle old and contemporary films.

9222
Music Library Association Membership Directory
Music Library Association
8551 Research Way
Suite 180
Middleton, WI 53562
608-836-5825
FAX 608-831-8200
E-Mail: mla@areditions.com
Home Page: www.musiclibraryassoc.org

Jerry L. McBride, President

The MLA mailing list is available for rental in a variety of formats. Members include music librarians, librarians who work with music as part of their responsibilities, composers and music scholars, and others interested in the program of the association.

9223
Musical America Directory
Musical America
PO Box 1330
Highstown, NJ 08520
609-448- 334
800-221-5488
FAX 609-371-7879
E-Mail: info@musicamerica.com
Home Page: www.musicamerica.com
Social Media: *Facebook, Twitter, YouTube*

Joyce Wasserman, Subscription Information
Bob Hudoba, Contact

Provides thousands of names, phone numbers, addresses, and Email and Web site addresses for manangers, orchestras, opera companies, festivals, presenters, venues and more around the world.
Cost: $125
Mailing list available for rent

9224
Musical America International Directory of the Performing Arts
Commonwealth Business Media
50 Millstone Rd
Suite 200
East Windsor, NJ 08520-1418
609-371-7700
800-221-5488
FAX 609-371-7879
E-Mail: info@musicamerica.com
Home Page: www.cbizmedia.com

Stephanie Challener, Publisher
Sedgwick Clark, Editor
Susan Elliot, News Editor
Bob Hudoba, Data Editor

Features over 14,000 detailed listings of worldwide arts organizations, including key contact information such as

name, address, phone, fax, Web site and E-mail addresses, budget category, type of event and seating capacity. In addition, through advertising, over 10,000 artists are indexed in the alphabetical and categorical indexes. Categories include artist managers, orchestras, opera companies, concert series, festivals, competitions, music schools and departments, record companies, and more.
Founded in 1898

9225
Musician's Guide
Billboard Directories
PO Box 15158
North Hollywood, CA 91615
818-487-4582
800-562-2706
E-Mail: info@billboard.com
Home Page: www.billboard.com/directories

Arkady Fridman, Inside Sales Manager

Everything the working musician needs to book gigs, contact record labels, find a manager, and locate tour services. The latest edition includes A & R Directory, Music Business Services, and City by City listings.
Cost: $15.95
170 Pages
Frequency: Annual

9226
NYC/On Stage
Theatre Development Fund
520 Eight Avenue
Suite 801
New York, NY 10018-6507
212-912-9770
E-Mail: info@tdf.org
Home Page: www.tdf.org
Social Media: *Facebook,*

Earl D. Weiner, Chair
Sandra Kresch, Vice Chairman
Robert T. Goldman, Treasurer
Deborah Hartnett, Secretary

Theater, dance, and music companies and performing arts centers in New York City.
Founded in 1995

9227
National Network For Artist Placement
National Network for Artist Placement
935 W Avenue 37
Los Angeles, CA 90065
323-222-4035
800-354-5348
E-Mail: NNAPnow@aol.com
Home Page: www.artistplacement.com

Warren Christensen, Consultant

Internship opportunities in dance, music, theatre, art and film.
Cost: $85
375 Pages
Frequency: Bi-Annual
ISBN: 0-945941-13-7

9228
National Opera Association Membership Directory
PO Box 60869
Canyon, TX 79016-0869
806-651-2857
FAX 806-651-2958
E-Mail: rhansen@mail.wtamu.edu
Home Page: www.noa.org
Social Media: *Facebook, RSS*

Robert Hansen, Executive Director
JoElyn Wakefield Wright, President
Edith Kirkpatrick Vrenios, VP Resources
Philip Hageman, Treasurer
Carol Notestine, Recording Secretary

Members of the National Opera Association are entitled to receive the NOA Freelance Artists and Production Resources databases, the NOA membership directory, and access to the NOA e-mail listserve.
Frequency: Annual
Mailing list available for rent

9229
Opera America Membership Directory
Opera America
330 7th Ave
16th Floor
New York, NY 10001-5248
212-796-8620
FAX 212-796-8631
E-Mail: info@operaamerica.org
Home Page: www.operaamerica.org
Social Media: *YouTube*

Marc Scorca, President

Directory of Opera America's Company, Business, Library, and Affilliate Members, indexed alphabetically and geographically. Includes the Annual Report to Members, a description of Opera America's programs and services, and a list of individual members.
Cost: $25
Frequency: Annual

9230
Orion Blue Book: Guitars and Musical Instruments
Orion Research Corporation
14555 N Scottsdale Rd
Suite 330
Scottsdale, AZ 85254-3487
480-951-1114
FAX 480-951-1117
E-Mail: sales@UsedPrice.com
Home Page: www.orionbluebook.com

Roger Rohrs, Owner

77,834 products listed; products listed from 1970s to present; over 450 manufacturers listed; 2 volumes - hardbound or on CD-ROM. Lists musical instruments from Accordians to Xylophones
Cost: $195
Frequency: Annual
Founded in 1981

9231
Orion Blue Book: Professional Sound
Orion Research Corporation
14555 N Scottsdale Rd
Suite 330
Scottsdale, AZ 85254-3487
480-951-1114
800-844-0759
FAX 480-951-1117
E-Mail: sales@UsedPrice.com
Home Page: www.orionbluebook.com

Roger Rohrs, Owner

Features over 48,964 products from the 1950's to present. Over 350 manufacturers listed. Comes in hardbound or on CD-ROM. Lists products from Cartridge Players to Wireless Microphone Systems.
Cost: $150
970 Pages
Frequency: Annual
Founded in 1973

9232
Orion Blue Book: Vintage Guitar
Orion Research Corporation
14555 N Scottsdale Rd
Suite 330
Scottsdale, AZ 85254-3487
480-951-1114
800-844-0759
FAX 480-951-1117
E-Mail: sales@UsedPrice.com
Home Page: www.orionbluebook.com

Roger Rohrs, Owner

Features more than 11,413 products from the 1800's to present. Over 30 manufacturers listed. Comes in hardbound or CD-ROM, Lists products from Banjos to Ukuleles.
Cost: $50
Frequency: Quarterly
Founded in 1990

9233
Plays and Playwrights
International Society of Dramatists
1638 Euclid Avenue
Miami Beach, FL 33139-7744
305-882-1864
Home Page: http://blog.nytesmallpress.com/

Offers valuable information on over 1,000 dramatists producing works in English.
Cost: $29.95
200 Pages
Frequency: Annual
Circulation: 10,000

9234
Record Retailing Directory
Billboard Directories
PO Box 15158
North Hollywood, CA 91615
818-487-4582
800-562-2706
E-Mail: info@billboard.com
Home Page: www.billboard.com/directories

Arkady Fridman, Inside Sales Manager

Over 5,500 listings covering the entire retailing community. Provides access to major chain headquarters and local outlets; complete coverage of independent retailers; hard-to-find audiobook retailers; and the booming world of online record retailing, plus store genre or specialization; executives, owners, buyers and planners; address, phone, fax, email and web.
Cost: $215
Frequency: Annual

9235
Reel Directory
Lynetta Freeman
PO Box 1910
Boyes Hot Springs, CA 95416
415-531-9760
FAX 707-581-1725
E-Mail: info@reeldirectory.com
Home Page: www.reeldirectory.com

Lynetta Freeman, Manager
Keith Marsalis, Director
Katie Carney, Director of Marketing

Source for Film, Video and Multimedia in Northern California.
Cost: $25
700 Pages
Frequency: Annual

INFORMATION RESOURCES / Industry Web Sites

Circulation: 5,000
Founded in 1979

9236
Regional Theatre Directory
Theatre Directories
P.O.Box 2409
Manchester Center, VT 05255-2409
802-867-9333
FAX 802-867-2297
Home Page: www.theatredirectories.com

Peg Lyons, Editor
PJ Tumielewicz, Editor

Profiles over 400 theatres including dinner theatres, equity and non-equity. Find out when/where auditions are held, when resumes shoul be sent, housing and transportation policy, and general description of company. If you want to find a job or an internship as an actor, designer, technician or staff in a professional regional or dinner theatre anywhere in the country, this directory can help you.
Cost: $29.50
Frequency: Annual
ISBN: 0-933919-63-8
Founded in 1984

9237
ShowBiz Bookkeeper
Theatre Directories
P.O.Box 2409
Manchester Center, VT 05255-2409
802-867-9333
FAX 802-867-2297
E-Mail: info@theatredirectories.com
Home Page: www.theatredirectories.com

The tax record-keeping system for professionals working in the arts.
Cost: $22.95

9238
Source Directory of Books, Records and Tapes
Sutton's Super Marketplace
153 Sutton Lane
Fordsville, KY 42343
270-276-9880
E-Mail: mtsutton32@earthlink.net
Home Page: www.pubdisco.com

Jerry Sutton, Owner/Founder

Publishers, recording studios, wholesalers, distributors, manifacturers and importers. Approximatley 450 records. Changes daily as updated.
Cost: $55.20

9239
Source Directory of Musical Instruments
Sutton's Super Marketplace
153 Sutton Lane
Fordsville, KY 42343
270-276-9880
E-Mail: mtsutton32@earthlink.net
Home Page: www.pubdisco.com

Jerry Sutton, Owner/Founder

Listings in directory include names, addresses, phone and fax numbers, and product descriptions from wholesale distributors, Importers, Manufacturers, Close-out houses and Liquidators. Updated daily.
Cost: $55.20

9240
Stars in Your Eyes...Feet on the Ground
Theatre Directories
P.O.Box 2409
Manchester Center, VT 05255-2409
802-867-9333
FAX 802-867-2297
E-Mail: info@theatredirectories.com
Home Page: www.theatredirectories.com

PJ Tumielewicz, Editor
Peg Lyons, Editor

For teens who want to act...Practical advice for young actors: learning how show business works; agents and managers; local cable shows and television commercials; auditioning for stage, student films and TV; choosing a school; dealing with rejection; parental support and more. Written by a 19-year old professional actress.
Cost: $16.95
ISBN: 0-933919-42-5

9241
Student's Guide to Playwriting Opportunities
Theatre Directories
P.O.Box 2409
Manchester Center, VT 05255-2409
802-867-9333
FAX 802-867-2297
E-Mail: info@theatredirectories.com
Home Page: www.theatredirectories.com

Michael Write, Directory Editor
Christi Pyland, Directory Editor
PJ Tumielewicz, Theatre Directories, Inc Editor
Peg Lyons, Theatre Directories, Inc Editor

An essential tool for every high shool or college student with an interest in playwriting. Comprehensive listings of 79 academic programs and another 80 professional development programs geared for the young writer. New essays on the art, process and business of playwriting.
Cost: $23.95
128 Pages
ISBN: 0-933919-53-0

9242
Studio Report: Film Development
Hollywood Creative Directory
5055 Wilshire Blvd
Los Angeles, CA 90036-6103
323-525-2369
800-815-0503
FAX 323-525-2398
E-Mail: hcdcustomerservice@hcdonline.com
Home Page: www.hcdonline.com

Valencia McKinley, Manager

The only directory of its kind, in print for the first time. A complete breakdown of film development project tracking. A-Z listings by title, spec screenplays sold, hot studio projects, cross-referenced by studio, production company and genre. The directory's main body consists of an alphabetical listing of all in-development projects that have achieved a forward-moving milestone some time in the last five months. Subsequent sections sort and cross-reference the information to highlight aspects
Cost: $19.95
190 Pages
ISBN: 1-928936-49-0

9243
Summer Theatre Directory
Theatre Directories
P.O.Box 2409
Manchester Center, VT 05255-2409
802-867-9333
FAX 802-867-2297
E-Mail: info@theatredirectories.com
Home Page: www.theatredirectories.com

Opportunities at over 350 summer theatres, theme parks, and summer training programs.
Cost: $29.50

9244
Theatre Profiles Database
Theatre Communications Group
520 8th Ave
24th Floor
New York, NY 10018-4156
212-609-5900
FAX 212-609-5901
E-Mail: tcg@tcg.org
Home Page: www.tcg.org

Theresa Eyring, Executive Director
Kelly Haydon, Database Manager
Jennifer Cleary, Director Membership
Terence Nemeth, Publisher
Kathy Sova, Editorial Director

Online database of more than 400 theatre members in 47 states, 17,000 individual members, 100 Trustee Leadership Network members and a growing number of University, Funder and Business Affiliates.
Frequency: Annual

9245
Whole Arts Directory
Midmarch Arts Press
300 Riverside Dr
Apartment 8A
New York, NY 10025-5279
212-666-6990
FAX 212-865-5510
E-Mail: info@midmarchpress.org
Home Page: www.midmarchartspress.org

Cynthia Navaregga, Manager

Directory to arts resources, organiztions, museums, galleries, colonies, retreats, art therapy, information services, and much more. Highly useful material for all artists, students, organizations and institutions.
Cost: $12.95
175 Pages
ISBN: 0-960247-67-x
Founded in 1987
Printed in on matte stock
Industry Web Sites

Industry Web Sites

9246
http://gold.greyhouse.com
G.O.L.D Grey House OnLine Databases

Grey House Publishing's online database platform, GOLD, offers Quick Search, Keyword Search and Expert Search for most business sectors including motion picture and entertainment markets. The GOLD platform makes finding the information you need quick and easy - whether you're a novice searcher or an experienced database user. All of Grey House's directory products are available for subscription on the GOLD platform.

9247
www.aact.org
American Association of Community Theatre

Non-profit corporation fostering excellence in community theatre productions and governance through community theatre festivals, educational opportunity publications, network, resources, and website.

INFORMATION RESOURCES / Industry Web Sites

9248
www.aahperd.org/nda
National Dance Association

A nonprofit service organization dedicated to increasing knowledge, improving skills and encouraging sound professional practices in dance education while promoting and supporting creative and healthy lifestyles through high quality dance programs.

9249
www.aate.com
American Alliance for Theatre and Education

Members are artists, teachers and professionals who serve youth theatres and theatre educational programs.

9250
www.absolutewrite.com
Absolute Write

Advice for writers, including playwrights.

9251
www.acdaonline.org
American Choral Directors Association

Nonprofit music-education organization whose central purpose is to promote excellence in choral music through performance, composition, publication, research and teaching.

9252
www.acmcountry.com
Academy of Country Music

Involved in numerous events and activities promoting country music. Presents annual awards.

9253
www.actioncutprint.com
Action-Cut-Print

Website for filmmakers. filmmaking resources, free ezine for directors, film and TV bookstore. The Director's Chair magazine by director Peter D. Marshall.

9254
www.actorsequity.org
Actors Equity Association

Labor union affiliated with AFL-CIO which represents actors in film, television and commercials.

9255
www.actorsite.com
Actor Site

Audition and other information.

9256
www.actorsource.com
Actorsource

Extensive information and resources for actors.

9257
www.actorstheatre.org
Actors Theatre of Louisville

Supports new playwrights. For information on entering a play, click Humana Festival.

9258
www.adta.org
American Dance Therapy Association

Founded in 1966; professional organization of dance movement therapists, with members both nationally and internationally; offers training, research findings, and a newsletter.

9259
www.afm.org
American Federation of Musicians of the United States and Canada

Union representing over 100,000 professional musicians, performing in all genres of music.

9260
www.afvbm.com
American Federation of Violin and Bow Makers

Strives to elevate professional standards of craftsmanship and ethical conduct among members. Helps members develop technical skills and knowledge.Research and study organization.

9261
www.agohq.org
American Guild of Organists

Promotes the organ in its historic and evolving roles and provides a forum for mutual support, inspiration, education and certification.

9262
www.aislesay.com
Aislesay

Internet magazine of stage reviews and opinions.

9263
www.americandanceguild.org
American Dance Guild

Non-profit membership organization; sponsors professional seminars, workshops, a student scholarship and other projects and institutes programs of national significance in the field of dance.

9264
www.americantheaterweb.com
American Theater Web

Find theaters, Broadway shows and musicals.

9265
www.answers4dancers.com
Answers for Dancers

Dance Magazine sponsors this site.

9266
www.artdirectors.org
Art Directors Guild

Conceive and manage the background and settings for most films and television projects.

9267
www.artsmed.org
Performing Arts Medicine Association

Organization for physicians and professionals interested in the research of Performing Arts Medicine.

9268
www.artspresenters.org
Association of Performing Arts Presenters

Celebrates rich and diverse performing arts to the public.

9269
www.artstabilization.org
National Arts Strategies

Offers training and technical assistance to arts organizations.

9270
www.asatalent.com
ASA/Affordable Services

Entertainment services are brought to you as you need them and when you need them at the best price available. Security services, studio teachers, and medical services.

9271
www.ascap.com
American Society of Composers Authors & Publishers

Membership association of more than 260,000 US composers, song writers, lyricists and music publishers.

9272
www.asmac.org
American Society of Music Arrangers and Composers

Professional society for arrangers, composers, orchestrators, and musicians. Monthly meetings with great speakers from the music industry.

9273
www.bachauer.com
Gina Bachauer International Piano Foundation

Produce a yearly piano international competition

9274
www.backstage.com
Backstage.com

Information for actors, casting calls, film reviews, auditions and acting jobs.

9275
www.backstagejobs.com
Theatre Design and Technical Jobs Page

Employment opportunities.

9276
www.backstageworld.com
Backstage World

Post your resume and search for design and technical job opportunities worldwide.

9277
www.billboard.com

The ultimate music industry research tool and information source. The Member Service database is state-of-the-art electronic information service, enabling users to efficiently access information from a variety of music industry databases via the World Wide Web.

9278
www.bmi.com
BMI

Secures the rights of songwriters/composers. Collects license fees for the public performance of music and pays royalties to its copyright owners.

9279
www.castingsociety.com
Casting Society of America

An organization representing casting directors.

9280
www.catf.org
Contemporary American Theater Festival

Dedicated to providing and developing new American Theater.

1097

INFORMATION RESOURCES / Industry Web Sites

9281
www.chorusamerica.org
Chorus America
National service for orchestral choruses, independent choruses and professional choruses.

9282
www.cincinnatiarts.org
Cincinnati Arts Association
Dedicated to supporting performing and visual arts.

9283
www.clarinet.org
International Clarinet Association
Seeks to focus attention on the importance of the clarinet and to foster communication of the fellowship between clarinetists.

9284
www.classicalaction.org
Classical Action
Provides a unified voice for all those within the performing arts community to help combat HIV/AIDS.

9285
www.cmaworld.com
Country Music Association
Promotes and publicizes country music.

9286
www.computermusic.org
International Computer Music Association
Supports the performance aspects of computer music; publishes newsletter and holds annual conferance.

9287
www.conductorsguild.org
Conductors Guild
Dedicated to encouraging the highest standards in the art and profession of conducting. Founded in 1975.

9288
www.contactimprov.net
Contact Improv
Improvisation for dancers.

9289
www.costume-con.org
Costume Connections
Costume conferences.

9290
www.costume.org
International Costumers' Guild
An affiliation of amateur hobbyist and professional costumers.

9291
www.costumegallery.com
Costume Gallery
A central location on the web for fashion and costume since 1996.

9292
www.costumers.org
National Costumers Association
Seeks to establish and maintain professional and ethical standards of business in the costume industry.

9293
www.costumes.org
Costumer's Manifesto
Online book, information and links.

9294
www.costumesocietyamerica.com
Costume Society of America
Education, research, presentation and design.

9295
www.creativedir.com
Creative Directory Services
Directory of suppliers for costumes, sets, special effects and stunts.

9296
www.creativemusicalcoalition.com
Creative Musician Coalition
A national organization that brings the world of new music to its readers. Includes in depth music reviews, informative artist interviews, interesting articles and feature columns, and valuable resource material.

9297
www.criticaldance.com
Dance Critics Association
Critical dance forum and ballet dance magazine

9298
www.csulb.edu/~jvancamp/copyrigh.html
Csulb.edu
Copyrighting choreographic works.

9299
www.csusa.org/face/index.htm
Friends of Active Copyright Education
Playwrights should click on Words, then Copyright Basics.

9300
www.cyberdance.org
Cyber Dance
Collection of links to modern dance and classical ballet resources.

9301
www.danceart.com/edancing
Danceart.com
Ballet and dance art, features, chat and more.

9302
www.dancenotation.org
Dance Notation Bureau
Notation basics, Notated Theatrical Dances Catalogue and links.

9303
www.dancepages.com
Dance Pages.com
Offers resources to dance teachers.

9304
www.dancer.com/dance-links
Dance Links
Links to many dance sites.

9305
www.danceusa.org
Dance/USA
Provides a forum for the discussion of issues of concern to membersand a support network for exchange of information; also bestows awards.

9306
www.deadance.com
Dance Educators of America
Promotes the education of teachers in the performing arts.

9307
www.discoverhollywood.com
Hollywood Arts Council
Promotes, nurtures and supports the arts field in Hollywood. Discover Hollywood on line.

9308
www.dma-national.org
Dance Masters of America
An organization of dance teachers.

9309
www.documentary.org
International Documentary Association
A nonprofit association founded to promote non-fiction film and video, to support the efforts of documentary film and video makers around the world, and to increase public appreciation and demand for the documentary.

9310
www.dramaguild.com
Dramatists Guild
Comprehensive organization that deals solely with Broadway and off-Broadway producers, off-off-Broadway groups, agents, theatres and sources of grants.

9311
www.dramaleague.org
Drama League
Seeks to strengthen American theatre through the nurturing of stage directors.

9312
www.dtw.org
Dance Theater Workshop
Identifies, presents and supports independent contemporary artists and dance companies to advance dance and live performances in New York and worldwide.

9313
www.edta.org
Educational Theater Association
Theater educators working to increase support for theater programs in the educational system.

9314
www.esperanzaarts.org
Esperanza Performing Arts Association

9315
www.etecnyc.net
Entertainment Technology Online
For employment in design and technical theatre, click on Classifieds. Also offers resources and buyers guides for theatrical lighting.

9316
www.flmusiced.org
Florida Music Educators Association
Florida Music Educators Association and Florida School Music Association.

1098

INFORMATION RESOURCES / Industry Web Sites

9317
www.folkharpsociety.org
International Society of Folk Harpers and Craftsmen

Conducts technical and artistic programs and promotes craft exchange.

9318
www.gmn.com
Global Music Network

Go backstage, watch rehearsals, listen to performances of classical and jazz artists.

9319
www.goldmime.com
Goldston Mime Foundation: School for Mime

Holds summer seminars and workshops.

9320
www.gospelmusic.org
Gospel Music Association

Dedicated to providing leadership, direction and unity for all facets of the gospel music industry. Through education, communication, information, promotion and recognition, the GMA is striving to help those involved in gospel music.

9321
www.greyhouse.com
Grey House Publishing

Authoritative reference directories for most business sectors including motion picture and entertainment markets. Users can search the online databases with varied search criteria allowing for custom searches by product category, geographic area, sales volume, keyword, subject and more. Full Grey House catalog and online ordering also available.

9322
www.guitarfoundation.org
Guitar Foundation of America

Supports the serious studies of the guitar.

9323
www.harada-sound.com/sound/handbook
Kai's Sound Handbook

Information for sound designers.

9324
www.harpsociety.org
American Harp Society

Improves the quality of the instrument and performance.

9325
www.hawaii.edu
Association for Theatre in Higher Education

Promotes quality in theatre education.

9326
www.heniford.net/1234
Small Cast One-Act Guide Online

List of short plays.

9327
www.horndoggie.com/horn
International Horn Society

A national organization that focuses on music industry news and information.

9328
www.iaekm.org
International Association of Electronic Keyboard Manufacturers

Global manufacturers of electronic keyboards and affiliated software and publications.

9329
www.ibma.org
World of Bluegrass

IBMA: working together for high standards of professionalism, a greater appreciation for our music, and the success of the world-wide bluegrass community.

9330
www.ifea.com
International Festivals and Events Association

Network for planning events and exchange programs; publishes quarterly magazine.

9331
www.imeamusic.org
Indiana Music Educators Association

Supports and advances music education in Indiana.

9332
www.internationalpolka.com
International Polka Association

Educational organization concerned with the preservation and advancement of polka music. Operates the Polka Music Hall of Fame and Museum, and presents the International Polka Fesitval every year during the complete first weekend of August.

9333
www.intix.org
International Ticketing Association

Not-for-profit association representing 22 countries worldwide and more than 1,200 members. Committed to the improvement, progress and advancement of ticket management, and to reach this goal provides educational programs, trade shows, conducts surveys and conference proceedings and produces a membership directory.

9334
www.iqfilm.org
International Quorum of Film and Video Producers

Fosters the exchange of information and ideas. Seeks to raise professional standards. Disseminates information on new concepts and technology.

9335
www.ispa.org
International Society for the Performing Arts Foundation

Supports international cooperation, facilitates networking and enhances professional dialogue.

9336
www.jensenfoundation.org
Fritz and Lavinia Jensen Foundation

Sponsors competitions.

9337
www.latinoarts.org
Association of Hispanic Arts

A multidisciplary organization which supports Hispanic arts organizations and individual artists with technical assistance. The organization facilitates projects and programs designed to foster the appreciation, growth, and well being of the Latino cultural community. It's quarter publication, AHA; Hispanic Arts News, features in depth articles on the local and national arts community, including artist profiles and a calendar of events.

9338
www.lib.colum.edu/costwais.html
Costume Image Database

Access costume images.

9339
www.light-link.com
Lightsearch.com

Lists of lighting equipment suppliers.

9340
www.livebroadway.com
League of American Theatres and Producers

National trade association for the commercial theatre industry whose principal activity is negotiation of labor contracts and government relations.

9341
www.lmda.org
Literary Managers and Dramaturgs of the Americas

Voluntary membership organization.

9342
www.luth.org
Guild of American Luthiers

Manufacturers and repairs stringed instruments; offers quarterly journal and triennial meeting.

9343
www.lycos.com
Lycos

Click Arts and Entertainment, then Dance, Theatre or Performing Arts.

9344
www.magicsam.com
Society of American Magicians

Founded to promote and maintain harmonious fellowship among those interested in magic as an art, to improve ethics of the magical profession, and to foster, promote and improve the advancement of magical arts in the field of amusement and entertainment. Membership includes professional and amateur magicians, manufacturers of magical apparatus and collectors.

9345
www.makeupmag.com
Make-Up Artist Magazine

Make-up artist magazine online.

9346
www.members.aol.com/thegoop/gaff.html
Gaff Tape Webring

Tech theatre.

9347
www.metguild.org
Metropolitan Opera Guild

Seeks to promote greater understanding and interest in opera.

9348
www.midatlanticarts.org
Mid Atlantic Arts Foundation

Provides leadership and support for artists and arts organizations in the Mid-Atlantic region and beyond.

INFORMATION RESOURCES / Industry Web Sites

9349
www.milieux.com/costume
Costume Source

Provides online sources for materials, costumes, accessories and books.

9350
www.millimeter.com
Millimeter Magazine

Authoritative resource for more than 33,000 qualified professionals in production, postproduction, animation, streaming and visual effects for motion pictures, television and commercials.

9351
www.mpa.org
Music Publishers Association of the United States

Encourages understanding of the copyright laws and works to protect musical works against infringements and piracy.

9352
www.mpaa.org
Motion Picture Association of America

Promotes high moral and artistic standards in motion picture production. Maintains Motion Picture Association Political Action Committee.

9353
www.mtishows.com
Music Theatre International

Scripts, cast recordings, study guides, production slides and other resources.

9354
www.mtna.org
Music Teachers National Association

This is a nonprofit organization of independent and collegiate music teachers committed to furthering the art of music through teaching, performance, composition and scholarly research.

9355
www.music.org
College Music Society

The Society is a national service organization for college conservatory and university music teachers.

9356
www.musicalamerica.com
Musicalamerica.com

Late-breaking industry news, full search capabilities, immediate interaction between Presenter and Artist Manager/Artist.

9357
www.musicalartists.org
American Guild of Musical Artists

Exclusive bargaining agent for all concert musical artists.

9358
www.musicdistributors.org
Music Distributor Association

A trade association of 160 manufactures, importers, wholesalers of musical instruments and accessories, domestic and international selling to the trade only

9359
www.musicianshealth.com
Chiropractic Performing Arts Association

To educate amateur and professional entertainers, musicians and dancers about reaching optimum health potential through natural, drug-free, conservative chiropractic care.

9360
www.musiclibraryassoc.org
Music Library Association

Promotes growth and establishment in the use of music libraries, musical instruments and musical literature.

9361
www.nacwpi.org
National Association of College Wind and Percussion Instructors

Teachers of wind and percussion instruments in American colleges and universities.

9362
www.nadt.org
National Association for Drama Therapy

Promotes the profession of Drama Therapy.

9363
www.namm.org
NAMM-International Music Products Association

Offers professional development seminars; sells musical instruments and allied products.

9364
www.napama.org
North American Performing Arts Managers and Agents

A cooperative voice in a competitive business.

9365
www.napbirt.org
National Association of Professional Band Instrument Repair Technicians

Promotes technical integrity in the craft. Surveys tools and procedures to improve work quality. Makes available emergency repair of band instruments. Provides placement services.

9366
www.narm.com
National Association of Recording Merchandisers

Not-for-profit trade association that represents the retailers, wholesalers, and distributors of prerecorded music in the United States.

9367
www.natoonline.org
National Association of Theatre Owners

Exhibition trade organization, representing more than 30,000 movie screens in all 50 states, and additional cinemas in 50 countries worldwide.

9368
www.nats.org
National Association of Teachers of Singing

To encourage the highest standards of the vocal art and of ethical principals in the teaching of singing; and to promote vocal education and research at all levels, both for the enrichment of the general public and for the professional advancement of the talented.

9369
www.nbea.com
National Ballroom and Entertainment Association

Provides exchange for owners and operators of ballrooms.

9370
www.nbtf.org
National Black Theatre Festival

9371
www.netconline.org
New England Theatre Conference

Non-profit educational corporation founded to develop, expand and assist theatre activity in community, educational and professional levels in New England. Holds annual auditions.

9372
www.netsword.com/stagecombat.html
Netsword

Lessons on stage combat.

9373
www.newplaysforchildren.com
New Plays Online

Plays for children and young adults.

9374
www.nmpa.org
National Music Publishers' Association

Publishes a quarterly newsletter and holds an annual meeting.

9375
www.noa.org
National Opera Association

To advance the appreciation, composition and production of opera.

9376
www.npm.org
National Association of Pastoral Musicians

Membership organization primarily composed of musicians, musician-liturgist, clergy, and other leaders of prayer devoted to serving the life and mission of the Church through fostering the art of musical liturgy in Roman Catholic worshiping communities in the United States.

9377
www.ntcp.org
Non-Traditional Casting Project

Promotes inclusive practices in television, theatre and film.

9378
www.nyfa.com
New York Film Academy

Educational institution devoted to providing focused filmmaking and acting instructions. Geared to offer an intensive, hands-on experience which gives students the opportunity to develop their creative skills to the fullest extent possible.

9379
www.nyfa.org
New York Foundation for the Arts

Employment openings in the arts.

9380
www.nypl.org/reseach/lpa/lpa.html
New York Public Library for the Performing Arts

Primary research collection.

9381
www.nyssma.org
New York State School Music Association

INFORMATION RESOURCES / Industry Web Sites

Advocates and improves the education in music of all people in New York State.

9382
www.nytimes.com
New York Times on the Web

Arts and Theatre contains play reviews.

9383
www.oobr.com
Off-Off-Broadway Review

Lists information on off-off broadway shows such as: title of show, author, director, producing company, theatre, address, box-office phone number, dates and times, admission price and contact info.

9384
www.opencasting.com
Open Casting

Bulletin board containing auditions, crew calls, casting notices and links.

9385
www.oscars.org
Academy of Motion Picture Arts and Sciences

Current information on motion pictures, the arts and sciences, events and screenings.

9386
www.paastjo.org
Performing Arts Association

Provides a diverse selection of performing arts.

9387
www.pas.org
Percussive Arts Society

Promotes drums and percussion through a viable network of performers, teachers, students, enthusiasts and sustaining members. Offers publications, a worldwide network of the World Percussion Network, the Percussive Arts Society International Headquarters/Museum and the annual Percussive Arts Society International Convention.

9388
www.pen.org
PEN: American Center

Site of the international literary community organization.

9389
www.performingarts.net
Performing Arts Online

Dedicated to the perpetuation of quality performing arts.

9390
www.pianoguild.com
International Piano Guild

A division of the American College of Musicians Professional society of piano teachers and music faculty members. Sponsers national examinations.

9391
www.pianonet.com
Piano Manufacturers Association International

Manufacturers and suppliers of pianos and parts; holds annual trade show.

9392
www.pipeorgan.org
American Institute of Organ Builders

Sponsers training seminars, quarterly journal and annual convention for pipe organ builders and service technicians.

9393
www.plasa.org
Professional Lighting and Sound Association

Web site for PLASA, a leading trade body for Lighting and Sound Professionals.

9394
www.playbill.com
Playbill Online

Listings for Broadway and off Broadway theatre productions. Also guides for sites, including summer stock, national touring shows and regional theatres worldwide.

9395
www.playwrights.org
Playwrights Center of San Francisco

Playwrites directory.

9396
www.playwrightshorizons.org
Playwrights Horizon

At home page click arrow. On next page click working with PH. You will see Writing Submissions.

9397
www.playwrightsproject.com
Playwrights Project

Promotes literacy, creativity and communication skills in young people through drama-based activities.

9398
www.press.jhu.edu/press/journals/paj
Johns Hopkins University Press

A journal of performance and art.

9399
www.press.jhu.edu/press/journals/tj
Johns Hopkins University Press

Theatre Journal

9400
www.press.jhu.edu/press/journals/tt
Johns Hopkins University Press

Theatre Topics

9401
www.printmusic.org
Retail Print Music Dealers Association

The voice of the print music industry.

9402
www.producersguild.com
Producers Guild of America

Members are producers of motion pictures and television shows mainly in the Los Angeles area.

9403
www.proppeople.com
Proppeople.com

Online home for props professionals.

9404
www.ptg.org
Piano Technicians Guild

Conducts technical institutes at conventions and seminars. Promotes public education in piano care. Bestows awards. Publishes monthly technical journal by subscriptions.

9405
www.renfaire.com/Language/index.html
Renfaire.com

Lessons on proper Elizabethan accents.

9406
www.resumegenie.com

Motion Pictures job listings, salary information and job search tips.

9407
www.rigging.net
Rigger's Page

Technical information on stage rigging equipment.

9408
www.roundalab.org
Roundalab

A professional international society of individuals who teach round dancing at any phase.

9409
www.safd.org
Society of American Fight Directors

Promotes safety in directing staged combat and theatrical violence.

9410
www.sag.org
Screen Actors Guild

Labor union affiliated with AFL-CIO which represents actors in film, television and commercials.

9411
www.sapphireswan.com/dance
Dance Directory

Dance resources.

9412
www.setc.org
Southeastern Theatre Conference

Annual conventions include auditions.

9413
www.sfballet.org
San Francisco Ballet Association

Provides a repertoire of classical and contemporary ballet; to provide educational opportunities for professional dancers and choreographers; to excel in ballet, artistic direction and administration.

9414
www.smpte.org
Society of Motion Picture & Television Engineers

Advances the practice and theory of engineering in television and film industry.

9415
www.southarts.org
Southern Arts Federation

Serves as the leadership voice to increase the regional, national and international awareness and prominence of Southern arts. Creates mechanisms and partnerships to expand local, regional, national and international markets for Southern arts.

9416
www.spars.com
Society of Professional Audio Recording Services

Members are individuals, companies and studios connected with the professional recording industry.

1101

INFORMATION RESOURCES / Industry Web Sites

9417
www.spolin.com
Spolin Center
Information on improvisational theatre.

9418
www.ssdc.org
Society of Stage Directors and Choreographers
An independent labor union representing directors and choreographers in American theatre.

9419
www.stage-directions.com
Stage Directions Magazine
The practical and technical side of theatrical operations.

9420
www.stageplays.com/markets.htm
Playwrights Noticeboard
Information on contests, publishing and production opportunities.

9421
www.stetson.edu/csata/thr_guid.html
McCoy's Guide to Theatre and Performance Studies
A brief guide to internet resources in theatre and performance studies put out by Stetson University.

9422
www.stuntnet.com
International Stunt Association
Represents those involved in stunt work for the entertainment industry.

9423
www.stuntwomen.com
Stuntwomen's Association of Motion Pictures
A professional association for stuntwomen and stunt coordinators which seeks to uphold professional standards and improve working conditions.

9424
www.summertheater.com
Directory of Summer Theater in the United States
Search for summer theater opportunities by alphabetized listings or geographic region.

9425
www.sundance.org
Sundance Institute
Nonprofit corporation dedicated to the support and development of emerging screenwriters and directors of vision. Hosts the Sundance Film Festival.

9426
www.symphony.org
American Symphony Orchestra League
The national nonprofit service and educational organization dedicated to strengthening symphony and chamber orchestras. It provides artistic, organizational and financial leadership and service to orchestral conductors, managers, volunteers and staff.

9427
www.talkinbroadway.com
Talkin' Broadway
Theatrical events and information on and off Broadway and other selected geographical locations.

9428
www.tcg.org
Theatre Communications Group
Supports alliances among playwrights, theatres and communities. Promotes not-for-profit theatre and offers resources to jobseekers. Offers financial support to designers and directors through its Career Development Program.

9429
www.tdf.org
Theatre Development Fund
Not-for-profit service organization. Provides support for every area of the dance, music and professional theatre field. Founded 1968.

9430
www.teleport.com/~bjscript/index.htm
Essays on the Craft of Dramatic Writing
Essays on writing a screenplay, play or novel.

9431
www.theatre-resource.com
Theatre Resource
Career and employment information.

9432
www.theatrebayarea.org
Theatre Bay Area
Serving more than 400 member theatre companies and 3,000 individual members in the San Francisco Bay Area and Northern California, Theatre Bay Area provides monthly classes, workshops, events, information and publications.

9433
www.theatrecrafts.com
Theatrecrafts.com
Practical information about technical theatre techniques for theatre folk at any level.

9434
www.theatrejobs.com
Theatrejobs.com
Online job placement. Festival listings, summer stock, assistantships, apprenticeships, fellowships and internships.

9435
www.theatrelibrary.org/links
Performing Arts Links
General resources including applied and interactive theatre, performing arts data service and art sites. Digital librarian includes glossary of technical theatre terms.

9436
www.theatrelibrary.org/links/index.html
Theatrelibrary.org
Master categories are Theatre, Dance, Cinema and Reviews.

9437
www.thecastingnetwork.com/webring.html
Casting Network.com
By and for actors.

9438
www.theplays.org
Electronic Literature Foundation
William Shakespeare's plays online.

9439
www.tmea.org
Texas Music Educators Association
Promoting excellence in music education.

9440
www.top20performingarts.com
Top 20 Performing Arts
Online directory for Perfoming Arts education.

9441
www.towson.edu/worldmusiccongresses
World Music Congresses
1997-2010 World Cello Congress' II-V, 2004 The First World Guitar Congress and 2008 World Guitar Congress II. Celebrations of music with international gatherings of the world's greatest musicians, composers, conductors, instrument manufacturers students, and music lovers from around the globe.

9442
www.unc.edu/depts/outdoor
Institute of Outdoor Drama
Summer jobs for all theatrical personnel.

9443
www.ups.edu/professionalorgs/dramaturgy
Dramaturgy Northwest
Relevant information for all dramaturgs.

9444
www.urta.com
University/Resident Theatre Association
Coalition of theatre training programs. Sponsors unified auditions.

9445
www.usabda.org
USA Dance
Non-profit organization working to promote ballroom dancing, both as a recreational activity and as a competetive sport.

9446
www.usitt.org
United States Institute for Theatre Technology
The association of design, production and technology professionals in the performing arts and entertainment industry whose mission is to promote the knowledge and skills of its members. International in scope, USITT draws its board of directors from across the US and Canada. Sponsors projects, programs, research, symposia, exhibits, and annual conference. Disseminates information on aesthetic and technical developments.

9447
www.variety.org
Variety
e-version of the show business newspaper.

9448
www.vcu.edu/artweb/playwriting
Playwriting Seminars
An opinionated web companion on the art and craft of playwriting for theatre and dance.

9449
www.vl-theatre.com
WWW Virtual Library
Links to theatre and drama resources. Updated daily.

INFORMATION RESOURCES / Industry Web Sites

9450
www.wif.org
Women in Film

For global entertainment, communication and media industries. Focuses on contemporary issues facing women and provides an extensive network of valuable contacts, educational programs, scholars, film finishing funds, grants, community outreach, advocacy and practical services that promote, nurture and mentor women to achieve their highest potential.

9451
www.writersguild.com
Writers Guild of America

List of Agents and information on Mentor program.

9452
www.wwar.com
World Wide Arts Resources

Links to Theatre and Dance.

9453
www2.sundance.org
Sundance Institute

Information on the Sundance Theatre Laboratory summer workshop for directors, playwrights, choreographers, solo performers and composers. For information on submitting a play, click Theatre Program on home page.

Entry Index

A

A Contemporary Theatre, 8597
A Festival of Art, 5065
A Good Old Summer Time's Genesee Street Festival, 5212
A Noise Within, 2490
A.D. Players, 3980
A.J. Fletcher Opera Theater, 7900
A.J. Palumbo Center, 8167
Aai Productions, 3416
Abbeville Opera House, 8203
Abbey Bach Festival, 5423
Abbey Church Events, 5782
Abendmusik Series, 4944
Aberdeen Community Concert Association, 5552
Aberdeen Community Theatre, 3883
Abhinaya Dance Company, 98
Abilene Civic Center: Exhibit Hall, 8312
Abilene Civic Center: Theater, 8311
Abilene Philharmonic Association, 1698
Abingdon Theatre Company, 3460
About Face Theatre, 2903
Abravanel Hall, 8494
Abravanel Symphony Hall, 8495
Acacia Theatre, 4119
Academy Concerts, 4377
Academy of Music: Main Auditorium, 8147
Academy of Performing Arts, 3168
Academy of Saint Elizabeth Performing Arts Series, 5000
Academy of Vocal Arts Opera Theatre, 2305
Academy Playhouse, 7248
Academy Theatre, 2847, 6635
Acadia Repertory Theatre, 3100, 3101
Acadiana Symphony Orchestra, 1138
Act II Playhouse, 3793
Act Theatre, 4078
Acting Company, 3461
Acting Company of Riverside Theatre, 2836
Acting Studio, 3462
Acting Up Theatre Company, 3205
Actor's Express Theatre, 2848
Actor's Theatre of Charlotte, 3646
Actors & Playwrights' Initiative, 3208
Actors Art Theatre, 2491
Actors Cabaret/Mainstage Theatre Company, 3774
Actors Co-Op, 3901
Actors Comedy Lab, 3673
Actors for Themselves, 2492
Actors Forum Theatre, 2530
Actors Repertory Theatre, 3338
Actors Repertory Theatre at Santa Monica Playhouse, 2618
Actors Studio, 3285
Actors Theatre of Houston, 3981
Actors Theatre of Louisville, 3068
Actors Theatre of Nantucket, 3162
Actors Theatre of Phoenix, 2426
Actors' Guild of Lexington, 3064
Actors' Playhouse at the Miracle Theatre, 2764
Actors' Theatre Company, 3719
Adam Miller Dance Project, 129
Adams Event Center, 7481
Adams Mystery Playhouse, 2652
Adelphia Stadium, 8290
Adelphian Players, 3417
Adirondack Festival of American Music, 5199
Adirondack Lakes Center for the Arts, 7636
Adirondack Theatre Festival, 3442, 5080
Admiral Theatre Foundation, 4065
Adobe Theater, 3397
Adobe Theatre Company, 3398
Adrian College Events Series, 4816
Adrian Symphony Orchestra, 1220, 2018
Adventure Theatre: Glen Echo Park, 3124
Adventures With the Arts, 5657
Aeolian Ballet Theatre, 36
Aeolian Chamber Players, 1405
African American Art and Culture Complex, 6249
African American Cultural Centre, 3423
African American Dance Ensemble, Inc., 508
African American Drama Company, 2572
African Continuum Theatre Company (Actco), 2730
African-American Cultural Center, 374, 5056

African-American Cultural Center: Paul Robeson Hall, 7649
Afrikan Poetry Theatre, 3449
Afro-American Cultural Center, 7867
Agassiz Theatre, 7229
Agnes Scott College, 6642
Agnes Scott College: Department of Theatre and Dance, 2871
Ahmanson Theatre, 2493
Aia Actor's Studio, 6077
Aiken Community Playhouse, 3867
Ailey II, 381
Aillet Stadium, 7153
Aisha Ali Dance Company, 37
Ajkun Ballet Theatre, 382
Akron Civic Theatre, 7941
Akron Symphony Orchestra, 1513
Akron Youth Symphony Orchestra, 1514
Al Caniglia Stadium, 7495
Al Ringling Theatre, 8658
Al Ringling Theatre Lively Arts Series, 4106
Al Ringling Theatre: Lively Arts Series, 5828
Alabama Ballet, 1
Alabama Dance Theatre, 5
Alabama Shakespeare Festival, 4148
Alabama Shakespeare Festival - Festival Stage, 5915
Alabama Shakespeare Festival - Octagon, 5916
Alabama Symphony Orchestra, 707
Alabama Theatre, 5886
Alameda Civic Ballet, 16
Alamo City Performing Arts Association, 5661
Alamodome, 8447
Alaska Center for the Performing Arts, 5934
Alaska Chamber Singers, 1843
Alaska Dance Theatre, 8
Alaskaland Civic Center & Theatre, 5938
Albano Ballet and Performing Arts Center, 6404
Albany Berkshire Ballet, 280
Albany James H Gray Sr Civic Center, 6608
Albany Performing Arts Center, 7622
Albany Pro Musica, 2201
Albany Symphony Orchestra, 1002, 1361
Albany Symphony Orchestra American Fesitval, 5039
Albert Lea City Arena, 7336
Albert Lea Community Theatre, 7337
Albert Mcneil Jubilee Singers of Los Angeles, 1881
Albert Taylor Hall, 7032
Albert Taylor Theatre, 6767
Alberta Bair Theater, 3313
Alberta Bair Theatre for the Performing Arts, 7468
Albion Performing Artist & Lecture Series, 4817
Albright College Concert Series, 5500
Albuquerque Convention Center, 7602
Albuquerque Little Theatre, 3399
Alcazar Theatre, 6250
Alden Theatre at Mclean Community Center, 8535
Alden Theatre Series, 4041
Alea III, 1175
Aleph Movement Theatre, 3317
Alerus Center, 7935
Alex Box Stadium, 7110
Alex Theatre, 6115
Alexandra Ballet, 304
Alexandria Festival of the Lakes, 4865
Alexandria Recital Series, 5722
Alexandria Symphony Orchestra, 1773
Alfred University Performing Arts, 5041
Algonquin Arts, 4999
Alhambra Dinner Theatre, 2784
Alhambra Performing Arts, 4196
Alice Lloyd College Caney Convocation Series, 4700
Alice Statler Hall, 7685
All American Boys Youth Chorus, 1875
All Newton Music School, the Andrew Wolf Concert Series, 4810
All Seasons Arena, 7940
All Seasons Chamber Players, 1328
Allaert Auditorium, 6974
Allan Carr Theatre, 6795
Allan Hancock College Dance Program, 108
Alleghany Highlands Arts Council/Performing Arts, 5730

Allegheny Ballet Company, 567
Allegheny Civic Symphony, 1638
Allegheny College Public Events Series, 5468
Allegheny County Summer Concert Series, 5488
Allegheny Valley Concert Association, 5470
Allegro Ballet of Houston, 633
Allen Arena, 8291
Allen County War Memorial Coliseum, 6876
Allen Fieldhouse, 7042
Allen Philharmonic, 1699
Allen Theatre, 8422
Allenberry Resort Inn and Playhouse, 3797
Allentown Community Concerts, 5426
Allentown Symphony Association, 1616
Allentown Symphony Hall, 8107
Alley Theatre, 3982, 8398
Alley Theatre: Hugo V Neuhaus Arena Stage, 8397
Alley Theatre: Large Stage, 8399
Alleyway Theatre, 3424
Alliance Bank Stadium, 7831
Alliance Repertory Theatre Company, 3386
Alliance Theatre Company, 2849
Alliance World Festival of Women Singing, 4666
Allied Concert Services, 4874
Allied Theatre Group/Stage West, 3967, 3968
Allnations Dance Company, 383
Allstate Arena, 6833
Alma College Performing Arts Series, 4819
Alma Dance Experience, 544
Alma Performing Arts Center, 5933
Alma Symphony Orchestra, 1221
Aloha Performing Arts Company, 2891
Aloha Stadium, 6670
Alonzo King Lines Ballet, 71
Alpha Omega Theatrical Dance Company, 384
Alpine Valley Music Theatre, 8661
Alton Symphony Orchestra, 1053
Altoona Symphony Orchestra, 1617
Alumni Auditorium, 8118
Alumni Hall Gymnasium, 7690
Alumni Memorial Field, 8529
Alva Public Library Auditorium, 8029
Alverno College, 5855
Alvin Ailey American Dance Theater, 385
Alys Robinson Stephens Performing Arts Center, 5887
Am Productions Series, 4996
Aman Arena, 8264
Amarillo Civic Center: Arena, 8317
Amarillo Civic Center: Music Hall, 8316
Amarillo Little Theatre, 3925
Amarillo Opera, 2335
Amarillo Symphony, 1700
Amas Musical Theatre, 3464
Ambassador Theatre, 7708
Ambler Symphony, 1618
American Academy of Dramatic Arts/Hollywood, 2472
American Airlines Arena, 6546
American Artists Series, 4829
American Atlantic Chorale, 2179
American Bach Soloist, 1911
American Balalaika Symphony, 1775
American Ballet Theatre, 386
American Bank Center, 8346
American Bolero Dance Company, 378
American Boychoir, 2186
American Center for Stanislavski Theatre Art, 3465
American Classical Orchestra, 924
American College Theater Festival, 4415
American Composers Orchestra, 1406
American Conservatory Theatre, 2573
American Dance Festival, 5233
American Ensemble Company, 3119
American Family Theater, 3824
American Festival of Microtonal Music, 5110
American Folklore Theatre, 4110
American Indian Community House Series, 5111
American Indian Dance Theatre, 2574
American International College Series, 4804
American International Lyric Theatre, 2214
American Landmark Festivals, 5112
American Magic-Lantern Theater, 2682
American Music Festival, 4416
American Music Theater Festival/Prince Music Theater, 3825, 5474

American Opera Music Theater, 2215
American Opera Projects Inc, 2205
American Philharmonic - Sonoma County, 1877
American Place Theatre, 3466, 7709
American Players Theatre, 4135
American Repertory Ballet, 339
American Repertory Theatre, 2494
American Royal Center Kemper Arena, 7423
American Southwest Center, 7613
American Spiritual Ensemble, 2078
American Stage Festival Peacock Players, 4970
American Symphony Orchestra, 1407
American Tap Dance Foundation, 387
American Theater Arts for Youth, 3826
American Theater Company, 2905
American Theatre, 2906, 7443
American Theatre of Actors, 3467
American Theatre Works, 4020
American University - Mcdonald Recital Hall, 6458
American University Theatre Program, 2731
American West Heritage Festival, 5703
American Youth Symphony, 801
American-International Lyric Theatre, 2216
Ames City Auditorium, 6953
Ames Town and Gown Chamber Music Association, 1099
Amherst Ballet Theatre Company Inc, 269
Amherst College Lefrak Gym, 7216
Amherst Symphony Orchestra, 1474
Amoin G Carter Stadium, 8381
Amphitheatre, 6690, 6921
Amsterdam Area Community Concert Association, 5043
Amway Arena, 6571
Amy Marshall Dance Company, 351
An Appalachian Summer Festival, 5223
Anaheim Ballet, 20
Anaheim Convention Center - Arena, 6054
Anam Cara Theatre Company, 3654
Anchorage Community Theatre, 2415
Anchorage Concert Association, 4156
Anchorage Concert Chorus, 1844
Anchorage Festival of Music, 4157
Anchorage Opera Company, 1845
Anchorage Symphony Orchestra, 717
Anchorage Youth Symphony, 718
And Toto Too Theatre Company, 2653
Anderson Arena, 7949
Anderson Sports Center, 8204
Anderson Symphony Orchestra, 1677
Anderson Symphony Orchestra Association, 1075
Anderson University, 5528
Anderson Young Ballet Theatre, 225
Andrews Outdoor Theatre, 6671
Andy Kerr Stadium, 7679
Andy's Summer Playhouse, 3356
Angeles Chorale, 1943
Angelo State University, 5659
Angelo State University Auditorium, 8444
Angels Gate Cultural Center, 6275
Anima Singers, 2054
Ann Arbor Blues & Jazz Festival, 4821
Ann Arbor Dance Works, 282
Ann Arbor Summer Festival, 4770, 4822
Ann Arbor Symphony Orchestra, 1222
Ann Lacey School of American Dance and Arts Management, 551
Anna Myer and Dancers, 275
Annabella Gonzalez Dance Theater, 388
Annapolis Chamber Orchestra, 1152
Annapolis Opera, 2091
Annapolis Summer Garden Theatre, 3110
Annenberg Auditorium, 6304
Annenberg Center, 8148
Annenberg Center for the Performing Arts, 5483
Annenberg Theatre, 6203
Annie Russell Theatre, 6605
Anniston Museum of Natural History, 5885
Annual Chicago Jazz Festival, 4548
Annual Ocean Grove Choir Festival, 5007
Anpsacher Stage, 7710
Antenna Theater, 2622
Antoinette E. Falbo Theatre, 8643
Apollinaire Theatre Company, 3148
Apollo Chorus of Chicago, 2036
Apollo Theater, 6727

1105

Entry Index

Apollo Theatre, 7711
Apollo's Banquet, 389
Apollo's Fire: the Cleveland Baroque Orchestra, 1541
Appalachian Ballet Company, 617
Appalachian State University Performing Arts & Forum Series, 5224
Appalachian Youth Jazz-Ballet Company, 695
Appel Farm Arts and Music Center, 4989, 7556
Apple Alley Players, 4099
Apple Hill Center for Chamber Music, 1318
Apsu Concert Hall, 8257
Apu Theater, 6063
Aracoma Story, 4101
Arapahoe Philharmonic, 915
Arbor Chamber Music Society, 1350
Arcadia Theater, 5513
Arcady Music Society, 1146
Arch-Opera House of Sandwich, 2060
Arco Arena, 6228
Arden Playhouse, 6229
Arden Theatre Company, 3827
Ardrey Auditorium, 5949
Area Stage Company, 2765
Arena at Harbor Yard, 6392
Arena Civic Theatre, 3154
Arena Dinner Theatre, 3007
Arena Players, 3111
Arena Players Playhouse, 7187
Arena Players Repertory Theatre Company of Long Island, 3431
Arena Stage, 2732
Arena Theater, 6848
Argen Tango Dancers, 336
Aria Dance Company, 677
Arie Crown Theatre, 6728
Arizona Broadway Theatre, 2424
Arizona Early Music Society, 739
Arizona Exposition & State Fair, 4171
Arizona Friends of Chamber Music, 740
Arizona Jazz Festival, 734
Arizona Opera, 1852, 1857
Arizona Stadium, 5995
Arizona State University Public Events, 4177
Arizona State University Theatre, 2428
Arizona Theatre Company, 2430
Arizona Veterans Memorial Coliseum, 5962
Arizona Western College Amphitheatre, 6011
Ark Theatre Company, 2631
Arka Ballet, 265
Arkansas Arts Center Children's Theater, 2438
Arkansas Chamber Singers, 1863
Arkansas Repertory Theatre, 2439
Arkansas River Valley Arts Center, 6047
Arkansas Shakespeare Theatre, 2433
Arkansas State Music Programs, 749
Arkansas Symphony Orchestra, 755
Arlene Schnitzer Concert Hall, 8089
Arlington Center for the Performing Arts, 6279
Arlington Cultural Affairs Division, 5724
Arlington Dance Theatre, 658
Arlington's Arts Al Fresco & the Innovators, 5725
Armstrong Atlantic State University, 4519
Armstrong Chamber Concerts, 4409
Armstrong Hipkins Center for the Arts, 7545
Armstrong State College Fine Arts Auditorium, 6658
Army Entertainment Program, 2882
Arneson River Theatre, 8448
Arnold Hall Theater United States Air Force, 6338
Arrow Rock Lyceum Theatre, 3278
Ars Musical Chorale & Orchestra, 2185
Ars Nova Musicians Chamber Orchestra, 1374
Art Association of East Alabama, 4149
Art of Motion Inc., 342
Art Song Festival, 5314
Art Station Theatre, 2879
Artcore, 5878
Arthur Ashe Stadium, 7670
Arthur Miller Theatre, 7265
Arthur R Outlaw Mobile Convention Center, 5907
Artist Series at Wheaton College, 4603
Artists Civic Theatre and Studio, 7128
Artists Collective, 2685
Artists in Concert Series, 4685
Artists Repertory Theatre, 3783
Artists Showcase West, 4570

Artists Theatre Association, 2725
Artists' Civic Theatre and Studio, 3080
Artpark, 5100, 7700
Artreach: a Division of the Children's Theatre of Cincinnati, 3703
Arts & Culture Alliance of Greater Knoxville, 3902
Arts and Science Center for Southeast Arkansas, 6042
Arts Association in Newton County, 4512
Arts at Argonne Music Series, 4544
Arts at St. Ann's, 5052
Arts Center, 6561
Arts Center of Coastal Carolina, 5544
Arts Center of the Ozarks, 6050
Arts Center/Old Forge, 5177
Arts Council, 4515
Arts Council for Chautauqua County, 5094
Arts Council for the Northern Adirondacks, 5216
Arts Council Lake Erie West, 5368
Arts Council of Fayetteville/Cumberland County, 5242
Arts Council of Macon County, 5243
Arts Council of Moore County, 5267
Arts Council of Oklahoma City, 5386
Arts Council of South Wood County, 5877
Arts Council of the Morris Area, 5001
Arts Council of Tuscaloosa Fanfare, 4152
Arts Council of Washington County, 5598
Arts Etc, 5546
Arts for the Schools, 4339
Arts Guild at Neumann College, 8110
Arts in The Academy, National Academy of Sciences, 4417
Arts in The Parks Portable Stage, 7341
Arts International, 5113
Arts Midwest, 3235
Arts Ncstate, 5259
Arts on Tour Series, 4543
Arts Partnership of Greater Hancock County, 5343
Arts Partnership of Greater Spartanburg, 5548
Arts Performance Lab, 6221
Arts Place, Inc., 4629
Arts San Antonio, 5662
Artscape-Baltimore's Festival of the Arts, 4749
Artscenter, 3642
Artsplosure: 2003 Spring Jazz & Art Festival, 5260
Artspower National Touring Theatre, 3374
Artspree, 4191
Artsquest, 5429
Arundel Barn Playhouse, 3091
Arvada Center for the Arts and Humanities, 6327
As220, 8195
Asbury College Artist Series, 4701
Asbury Park Jazz Festival, 4983
Ascap, 7712
Asheville Chamber Music Series, 1477, 5218
Asheville Civic Center, 7853
Asheville Community Theatre, 3636
Asheville Lyric Opera, 2260
Asheville Symphony Orchestra, 1478
Ashland Folk Music Club, 5399
Ashland Symphony Orchestra, 1515
Ashlawn-Highland Summer Festival, 5728
Ashtabula Chamber Orchestra, 1516
Ashurst Auditorium, 5950
Asia America Symphony Orchestra, 833
Asia Society, 5114
Asian American Arts Centre, 390
Asian American Theater Company, 2575
Asolo Repertory Theatre, 2821
Asolo Theatre Festival, 4480
Aspen Music Festival and School, 4351, 6328
Aspen Opera Theater Center, 1944
Aspen Santa Fe Ballet, 347
Assembly Hall, 6724, 6854
Associated Students of Montana State University, 4930
Aston Magna Festival, 4791
Aston Magna Foundation, 922, 4383
Astors Beechwood Mansion, 3858
Astrodome, 8400
At&T Park, 6251
At&T Perorming Arts Center, 8349
Athenaeum Music & Arts Library, 6136
Athenaeum Theatre, 6729
Athens Area Council for the Arts, 5558

Athens Theatre, 2772
Atkinson Auditorium, 8623
Atlanta Ballet, 179
Atlanta Boy Choir, 2019
Atlanta Chamber Players, 1004
Atlanta Civic Center, 6618
Atlanta Downtown Festival and Tour, 4501
Atlanta Festival Ballet Company and School, 190
Atlanta Jazz Festival, 4502
Atlanta Opera, 2020
Atlanta Symphony Orchestra, 1005
Atlanta Symphony Orchestra Chorus, 2021
Atlanta Symphony Youth Orchestra, 1006
Atlanta Young Singers of Callanwolde, 2022
Atlantic Center for the Arts, 6560
Atlantic City Ballet, 326
Atlantic Coast Theatre, 2760
Atlantic Contemporary Ballet, 327
Atlantic Shakespeare Festival, 4492
Atlantic Stage, 3880
Atlantic Theater Company, 3468
Attic / New Center Theatre, 3196
Attic Ensemble, 3368
Attic Theatre Centre, 2494
Attucks Theatre, 8536
Auburn Arts Commission, 5771
Auburn Chamber Orchestra, 1364
Auburn Players Community Theatre, 3409
Auburn Symphony, 1866
Auburn University Montgomery Theatre, 2412
Auburn University Theatre, 2400
Auditorium Chamber Music Series, 4535
Auditorium Theatre, 6730
Auditorium Theatre of Roosevelt University, 2907
Augsburg Choir, 2142
Augsbury Center, 7659
Augusta Arts Council/Augusta Historic Theatre, 3041
Augusta Civic Center Arena Center Stage, 7163
Augusta Civic Center Half House Concert Stage, 7164
Augusta Civic Center North Stage, 7162
Augusta Entertainment Complex, 6632
Augusta Opera Association, 2026
Augusta Players, 2868
Augustana Arts, 6346
Augustana Choir, 2059
Augustana Symphony Orchestra, 1063
Augustana Theatre, 6825
Aurora Fox Arts Center, 6330
Aurora Fox Children's Theatre Company, 2644
Aurora Players, 3436
Aurora Singers, 1960
Aurora Symphony Orchestra, 896
Aurora Theatre, 2874
Aurora Theatre Company, 2447
Austin Arts Center, 6405
Austin Chamber Music Center, 1701
Austin Chamber Music Festival, 5588
Austin Classical Guitar Society, 1702
Austin College Community Series, 5668
Austin Lyric Opera, 2336
Austin Musical Theatre, 3928
Austin Peay State University, 5561
Austin Shakespeare Festival, 5589
Austin Symphony Orchestra Society, 1703
Austin Theatre for Youth, 3929
Autumn Classic Music Festival, 5690
Autzen Stadium, 8070
Avenue Theater, 2654
Averett University Concert-Lecture Series, 5731
Avista Stadium, 8609
Avodah Dance Ensemble, 391
Axis Company, 3469
Axis Dance Company, 51
Aycock Auditorium, 7884
Aztec, 8313

B

B & a Warehouse, 5888
B C Playhouse, 6855
B Street Theater, 2552
B.J. Haan Auditorium, 7018
Babcock Auditorium, 8562
Babcock Season, 4057
Bach Choir of Pittsburgh, 2316
Bach Festival of Central Florida, 4458

Bach Festival of Philadelphia, 1639
Bach Festival Society of Kalamazoo, 4852
Bach Society Houston, 2351
Bach Society of Saint Louis, 2162
Bach Vespers at Holy Trinity, 2217
Bach Week Festival in Evanston, 4576
Bachanalia Chamber Orchestra, 1408
Bachs Festival Society of Winter Park, 4496
Back Bay Chorale, 2103
Backhausdance, 55
Bailey Concert Hall, 6505
Bailiwick Repertory, 2908
Bainbridge Performing Arts, 4060
Baird Auditorium, 6459
Baker Field, 7713
Bakersfield Symphony Orchestra, 757
Balboa Park Recital Hall, 6236
Balboa Park Starlight Theater, 6237
Balboa Performing Arts Theater, 6193
Baldwin-Wallace College Academic & Cultural Events Series, 5293
Baldwin-Wallace College Symphony Orchestra, 1521
Baldwin-Wallace University, 5292
Ball Theater, 6861
Ballet Academy East, 392
Ballet Arizona, 11
Ballet Arkansas, Inc., 15
Ballet Austin, 621
Ballet Chicago, 198
Ballet Concerto, 630
Ballet Excel Ohio, 529
Ballet Florida, 174
Ballet Folclorico Do Brasil, 72
Ballet Hispanico of New York, 393
Ballet Idaho, 194
Ballet in Cleveland, 518
Ballet Internationale, 230
Ballet Long Island, 500
Ballet Memphis, 618
Ballet Mississippi, 302
Ballet Montana, 313
Ballet Nebraska, 316
Ballet North, 307
Ballet Ny, 497
Ballet Palm Beach, 165
Ballet Pensacola, 166
Ballet Quad Cities, 221
Ballet San Jose, 99
Ballet Tech, 394
Ballet Tennessee, 611
Ballet Theatre of Maryland, 253
Ballet Theatre of Ohio, 537
Ballet West, 651
Ballet Western Reserve, 546
Ballethnic Dance Company, 180
Balletmet Dance Centre, 525
Ballpark in Arlington, 8318
Baltimore Actors' Theatre, 3112
Baltimore Chamber Orchestra, 1153
Baltimore Choral Arts Society, 2092
Baltimore Classical Guitar Society, 1154
Baltimore Consort, 1631
Baltimore Opera Company, 2093
Baltimore Symphony Chorus, 2094
Baltimore Symphony Orchestra, 1155
Baltimore Symphony Orchestra Summer Music Fest: Oregon Ridge Concert Series, 4750
Baltimore-Washington Jazzfest, 4760
Bama Theatre Performing Arts Center, 5923
Banafsheh Sayyad and Namah, 110
Bancorpsouth Arena and Conference Center, 7409
Bang on A Can, 5115
Bangor Ballet, 248
Bangor Civic Center & Auditorium, 7165
Bangor Symphony Orchestra, 1145
Banjo Dan and The Mid-Nite Plowboys, 1771
Bank of America Stadium, 7868
Bank of America Theatre, 6731
Bank United Center, 6496
Banyan Theater Company, 2822
Bar Harbor Music Festival, 4727
Barat College Performing Arts Center Season, 4584
Barbara B Mann Performing Arts Hall, 6511
Barbara K & W Turrentine Jackson Hall, 6094
Barbara Pfeiffer Memorial Hall, 6803

Entry Index

Bard Music Festival, 5044
Bardavon 1869 Opera House, 7808
Bargemusic, 1369
Barksdale Theatre, 4049
Barn Players Theatre, 3048
Barn Theatre, 3192, 6222
Barnstormers, 3354
Barnum Studio Theatre, 7000
Barre Opera House, 8502
Barrington Stage Company, 3169
Barron Arts Center, 7600
Barrow Group, 3470
Barrow-Civic Theatre, 3804
Barrus Auditorium- Concert Hall, 6695
Barter Playhouse/Theatre House, 8510
Barter Theatre - State Theatre of Virginia, 4028
Bartlesville Community Center, 8030
Bartlesville Symphony Orchestra, 1576
Barton International, 5275
Bas Bleu Theatre Company, 2669
Basketball City, 5102
Bass Performance Hall, 8382
Bassett Arts Council, 4941
Bastrop Opera House, 3936
Bat Theatre Company, 3471
Bates Dance Festival, 250, 4735
Bath House Cultural Center, 8350
Bathhouse Theatre, 4079, 8598
Baton Rouge Ballet Theater, 244
Baton Rouge Little Theater, 3077
Baton Rouge Symphony Orchestra, 1137
Battery Dance Company, 395
Battle Creek Civic Theatre, 7274
Battle Creek Symphony Orchestra, 1224
Bay Area Harbour Playhouse, 3964
Bay Area Houston Ballet & Theatre, 634
Bay Arts Alliance, 4472
Bay Arts Council, 4826
Bay Chamber Concerts, 252, 1151, 2090, 4746
Bay City Festival Arts Association, 5592
Bay City Players, 3193
Bay Colony Productions, 3152
Bay Shore-Brightwaters Library Performing Arts Series, 5050
Bay Street Players, 2775
Bay Street Theatre, 3615
Bay View Music Festival, 4827
Bay-Atlantic Symphony, 1325
Bayfront Plaza Convention Center: Auditorium, 8344
Baylor University Distinguished Artist Series, 5678
Bayonne Veterans Memorial Stadium, 7544
Baytown Little Theater, 3937
Bayview Opera House, 6252
Beach Cities Symphony Association, 830
Beach-Schmidt Performing Arts Center, 7035
Beaches Fine Arts Series, 4456
Beacon Dance Company, 184
Beall Concert Hall, 8071
Bear Valley Music Festival, 4201
Beasley Performing Arts Coliseum, 4076, 8593
Beau Rivage Theatre, 7382
Beaufort County Community Concerts Association, 5220
Beaumont Civic Center Complex: Julie Rogers Theatre, 8329
Beaumont Civic Opera, 2340
Beaumont Music Commission, 5594
Beaver Stadium, 8184
Beaver Valley Community Concert Association, 5428
Bebe Miller Company, 396
Beck Center for the Cultural Arts, 3739
Becker Auditorium, 6775
Beef and Boards Dinner Theatre, 3010
Beeghly Gym, 8021
Beeghly Theater, 8145
Beethoven by The Beach, 4444
Beethoven Festival, 1398, 5101
Beethoven Hall: San Jose Convention Center, 8449
Bel Canto Chorus, 2397
Bel Canto Company, 2264
Belhaven College Center for the Arts, 7395
Belhaven College Preston Memorial Series, 4888
Belk Theater, 7869
Belknap Mill Society, 4967

Bell Atlantic Jazz Festival, 5116
Bell County Expo Center, 8335
Bella Voce, 2037
Belle Voix, 1978
Belleayre Music Festival, 5086
Belleville Philharmonic Orchestra, 1029
Bellevue Little Theatre, 3321, 7485
Bellingham Festival of Music, 5772
Belmont Dramatic Club, 3133
Belmont Playhouse, 3414
Beloit College Performing Arts Series, 5829
Beloit Janesville Symphony Orchestra, 1821
Bemidji State University Thompson Recital Hall, 7339
Bemidji Symphony Orchestra, 1257
Ben Light Gym, 7686
Bender Arena, 6460
Benedicta Arts Center, 7370
Benedum Center, 8168
Benjiman Ide Wheeler Auditorium, 6066
Bentley College Bowles Performance Series, 4807
Benton Auditorium, 6954
Berea College Convocation Series, 4686
Bergen Philharmonic Orchestra, 1344
Bergman Theatre, 6819
Berkeley Ballet Theater, 24
Berkeley Community Chorus and Orchestra, 1867
Berkeley Community Theatre, 2448, 6067
Berkeley Festival & Exhibition, 4203
Berkeley Opera, 1868
Berkeley Repertory Theatre, 2449
Berkeley Symphony Orchestra, 758
Berkeley Youth Orchestra, 814
Berklee Performance Center, 7219
Berks Jazz Festival, 5501
Berkshire Choral Festival, 4801
Berkshire Lyric Theatre, 2123
Berkshire Opera Company, 2116
Berkshire Theatre Festival, 3176, 4806
Berkshire-Hudson Valley Festival of Opera, 2203
Bermerton Community Theatre, 4066
Bernard B Jacobs Theatre, 7714
Bernard G Johnson Coliseum, 8418
Bernard Schmidt Productions, Inc, 407
Bernhard Center, 6393
Berrie Center for Performing and Visual Arts, 7566
Berry College Theatre Company, 2802
Berry Events Center, 7315
Bertha Martin Theatre, 6961
Best of Broadway, 3472
Bethany College, 5812
Bethany Lutheran College Concerts & Lectures, 4869
Bethel College Fine Arts Series, 4626
Bethel Woods Center for the Arts, 7701
Bethlehem Bach Festival, 5430
Beverly Arts Center, 6732
Beverly B. Bistline Thrust Theatre, 6710
Beverly Hills Playhouse, 6073
Bi-Lo Center, 8223
Bi-Okoto Cultural Institute, 514
Biblical Arts Center, 8351
Bicentennial Art Center, 6331
Bickford Theatre at the Morris Museum, 7568
Big Arts: Great Performers Series, 4478
Big Bear Lake Performing Arts Center, 6075
Big Bend Community Chorus, 998
Big Dance Theater Inc, 357
Big League Theatricals, Inc., 3473
Big Mess Theatre, 3828
Big Noise Theatre Company, 2961
Big Sandy Super Store Arena, 8631
Big Spring Cultural Affairs Council, 5597
Big Spring Symphony Orchestra, 1640
Bigfork Center for the Performing Arts, 7467
Bigfork Summer Playhouse, 3312
Bijou Theatre, 8269
Bijou Theatre Center, 8270
Bilingual Foundation of the Arts, 2495
Bill Evans Dance Company, 353
Bill Graham Civic Auditorium, 6253
Bill T Jones/Arnie Zane Dance Company, 397
Bill Young/Colleen Thomas and Dancers, 398
Billie Holiday Theatre, 3418
Billings Symphony Orchestra & Chorale, 2166

Billings Symphony Society, 1296
Bilyeu Theatre, 6708
Bing Concert Hall, 6305
Bing Theatre, 6154
Binghamton Philharmonic Orchestra, 1367
Binghamton Summer Music Festival, 5048
Bininger Theatre, 6593
Biola University, 6145
Biotzetik Basque Choir, 2032
Birch Creek Music Performance Center, 8663
Birmingham Children's Theatre, 2401
Birmingham International Center, 4140
Birmingham Music Club, 1839
Birmingham-Bloomfield Symphony, 1226
Birmingham-Jefferson Convention Complex Arena, 5889
Birmingham-Jefferson Convention Complex Concert Hall, 5890
Birmingham-Southern College Theatre, 5891, 5892
Bishop Center for Performing Arts, 8567
Bismarck-Mandan Symphony Orchestra, 1510
Bismark Civic Center, 7932
Bistline Family Theatre, 6709
Bits 'n Pieces Giant Puppet Theatre, 2830
Bix Biederbecke Memorial Jazz Festival, 4646
Black Box, 6565, 8590
Black Box Theater, 6566
Black Box Theatre, 6415, 6494
Black Ensemble Theater, 2909
Black Experience Ensemble, 3407
Black Hawk Children's Theatre, 7024
Black Hills Community Theatre, 3885
Black Hills Passion Play, 3888
Black Hills Playhouse, 3886
Black Hills Symphony Orchestra, 1687
Black Liberated Arts Center, 8041
Black Repertory Group, 2450
Black Spectrum, 3474
Black Swan Theater, 3637
Blackfriars Theatre, 3608
Blackham Coliseum, 7123
Bladen Opera House, 7486
Blair Thomas & Co., 2910
Blanche M. Touhill Performing Arts Center, 7464
Blanco Performing Arts Foundation, 399
Blank Theatre Company, 2473
Bleecker Street Opera, 2218
Blind Parrot Productions, 2911
Bloch Learning and Performance Hall, 8644
Bloomfield Mandolin Orchestra, 1323
Bloomingdale School of Music, 1409
Bloomingdale School of Music Concert Series, 5117
Bloomington County Playhouse, 2999
Bloomington Early Music Festival, 4609
Bloomington Symphony Orchestra, 1076
Bloomsburg Theatre Ensemble, 3796
Bloomsburg University Artist-Celebrity Series, 5432
Blossom Music Center, 7989
Blowing Rock Stage Company, 3641
Blue Cross Arena, 7811
Blue Jacket, First Frontier, 3754
Blue Lake Repertory Theatre, 3217
Blue Spruce Theatre, 3179
Bluefield State College, 5813
Bluemont Concert Series, 5750
Bluffton University Artist Series, 5294
Bob Baker Marionette Theatre, 2496
Bob Carpenter Center, 6451
Bob Carr Performing Arts Center, 6567
Bob Devaney Sports Center, 7490
Bob Hope Theatre, 8352
Bob Jones University, 8224
Bob Jones University Concert, Opera & Drama Series, 3876
Bobby Dodd Stadium at Grant Field, 6619
Boca Ballet Theatre, 150
Body Politic Theatre, 2912
Bodyvox, 560
Boheme Opera, 2180
Boise Chamber Music Series, 1023, 4532
Boise Contemporary Theater, 2894
Boise Master Chorale, 2033
Boise Philharmonic Association, 1024
Boise State University Classical Guitar Society, 1025

Bologna Performing Arts Center, 7385
Bond Street Theatre Coalition, 3475
Bonk Festival of New Music, 4481
Book-It Repertory Theatre, 4080
Booth Productions, 3186
Booth Theatre, 7715
Bopi's Black Sheep/Dance by Kraig Patterson, 5118
Boston Ballet, 271
Boston Baroque, 1173
Boston Camerata, 2104
Boston Center for the Arts Plaza Theatre, 7220
Boston Chamber Music Society, 1185
Boston Children's Theatre, 3135
Boston Civic Symphony Orchestra of Boston, 1216
Boston Classical Orchestra, 1202
Boston College Alumni Field Stadium, 7232
Boston Conservatory, 4773
Boston Dance Company, 276
Boston Early Music Festival, 4783
Boston Globe Jazz & Blues Festival, 4784
Boston Modern Orchestra Project, 1200
Boston Musica Viva, 1186
Boston Opera House, 7221
Boston Philharmonic Orchestra, 1187
Boston Pops Orchestra, 1176
Boston Symphony Chamber Players, 1177
Boston Symphony Orchestra, 1178
Boulder Bach Festival, 897, 4353
Boulder City Arts Council, 4954
Boulder International Music Festival for Young Performers, 4354
Boulder Museum of Contemporary Art Galleries and Theater, 6332
Boulder Philharmonic Orchestra, 898, 899
Bowdoin College Concert Series, 4730
Bowdoin International Music Festival, 4731
Bowdoin Summer Music Festival, 4732
Bowen Park Theatre & Opera, 2990
Bowie State University Martin Luther King Jr. Center, 7201
Bowling Green State University Festival Series, 5296
Bowling Green State University: New Music & Art Festival, 5295
Bowling Green-Western Symphony Orchestra, 1125
Bowlus Cultural Attractions Series, 4675
Bowlus Fine Arts Center, 7041
Bowman Gray Stadium, 7921
Bowne Theatre, 7565
Boychoir of Ann Arbor, 2128
Braden Auditorium, 4590, 6805
Bradford Creative & Performing Arts Center, 5434, 8117
Bradley Center, 8687
Braintree Choral Society, 2109
Brandeis Symphony Orchestra, 1214
Brandeis University Department of Music, 1215
Brandeis University Spingold Theater Center Series, 4808
Brandywine Ballet, 586
Brandywine Baroque, 948
Branscomb Memorial Auditorium, 6541
Brattleboro Music Center, 2369, 5704
Bratton Recital Hall, 7527
Brava! for Women in The Arts, 2576
Brave New Workshop, 3236
Bravo! Vail Valley Music Festival, 4378
Brazos Valley Symphony Orchestra, 1705
Brazosport Symphony Orchestra, 1706
Bread and Circus Theatre, 3962
Breakthrough Theatre, 2841
Breatriz Rodriguez, 199
Breckenridge Backstage Theatre, 2649, 6336
Breckenridge Music Festival Orchestra, 901, 4361
Breckenridge Music Institute Orchestra, 900
Brecksville Little Theatre, 3698
Breedlove Auditorium Westark Community College, 6027
Breenden Field House/Worthington Arena, 7470
Bremerton Symphony Orchestra, 1789
Bren Events Center, 6132
Brenda Angel Aerial Dance Company, 73
Brentwood-Westwood Symphony Orchestra, 875
Brevard Music Festival, 5226

1107

Entry Index

Brevard Symphony Orchestra, 975
Brewery Arts Center, 3336, 7505
Brewton-Parker College Fine Arts Council, 4518
Briar Cliff Theatre, 7022
Bridgeforth Stadium, 8526
Bridgehampton Chamber Music Festival, 5119
Bridgeport Theatre Company, 2678
Bridgestone Arena, 8294
Bridgewater College Lyceum Series, 5727
Bridgewater State College Program Committee, 4781
Brigham Young University, 4538
Brigham Young University Performing Arts Series, 5695
Brigham Young University: Hawaii Performance Series, 4531
Brighton Ballet Theatre Company, Inc., 358
Brigit Saint Brigit Theatre Company, 3329
Bristol Riverside Theatre, 3798
Bristol Valley Theater, 3455
Britt Festivals, 1598, 3780, 5414
Britt Pavilion, 8083
Broad Stage, 2619
Broadhollow Players Limited, 3614
Broadhurst Theatre, 7716
Broadway Center for the Performing Arts, 5808
Broadway Center Stage, 2183
Broadway in Chicago, 2913
Broadway in Fort Lauderdale, 4445
Broadway Live at the Opera House, 3065
Broadway Palm Dinner Theatre, 2778
Broadway Rose Theatre, 8106
Broadway Rose Theatre Company, 3791
Broadway San Diego, 2559
Broadway Series: Indianapolis, 4612
Broadway Theatre, 2408, 7717
Broadway Theatre League of Pueblo, 2676
Broadway Theatre League of South Bend, 3022
Broadway Theatre League of the Quad-Cities, 3031
Broadway Theatre League of Utica, 3630
Broadway Tomorrow, 3476
Brockton Symphony Orchestra, 1184
Brodhead Cultural Center Summer Series, 5469
Brody Theater, 3784
Broken Arrown Performing Arts Center, 8031
Bronco Arena, 8353
Bronx Arts Ensemble, 1368
Brooke Hills Playhouse, 4105
Brookhaven College Center for the Arts, 5622
Brookings Chamber Music Society, 1685
Brooklyn Academy of Music, 5053
Brooklyn Academy of Music: Carey Playhouse, 7641, 7642
Brooklyn Academy of Music: Opera House, 7643
Brooklyn Arts Exchange, 359
Brooklyn Ballet, 360
Brooklyn Center Community Center, 7342
Brooklyn Center for the Performing Arts, 7644
Brooklyn Conservatory of Music, 7645, 7671
Brooklyn Friends of Chamber Music, 1370
Brooklyn Philharmonic Orchestra, 1371
Brooklyn Symphony Orchestra, 1372
Brooks Atkinson Theatre, 7718
Brooks Center for the Performing Arts, 8212
Broom Street Theater, 4113
Broome County Veterans Memorial Arena, 7634
Broward Center for the Performing Arts, 6506
Brown Auditorium, 7052
Brown County Arena, 8664
Brown County Civic Music Association, 5836
Brown County Playhouse, 3020, 6920
Brown Grand Theatre, 3044
Brown Stadium, 8196
Brown Summer Theatre, 3860
Brown University Orchestra, 1674
Brown University Theatre, 3861
Brownville Concert Series, 4947
Brownwood Area Chamber of Commerce, 8337
Bryan College Department of Music, 5564
Bryan Symphony Orchestra, 1690
Bryant Denny Stadium, 5924
Bryce Jordan Center, 8185
Bryn Mawr College Performing Arts Series, 5436
Bucknell University: Weis Center Performance Series, 5464
Buckner Theatre, 6542

Bucks County Community College Cultural Programming, 5473
Bucks County Performing Artrs Series, 5514
Bucks County Playhouse, 3822, 8144
Bud Walton Arena, 6024
Budweiser Events Center, 6388
Buena Performing Arts Center, 5982
Buena Vista University Academic & Cultural Events Series, 4664
Buffalo Chamber Music Society, 1375
Buffalo Philharmonic Chorus & Chamber Singers, 2207
Buffalo Philharmonic Orchestra, 1376
Buffalo State College Performing Arts Center, 7650
Buglisi Dance Theatre, 400
Bull Durham Blues Festival, 5234
Bullard School of Dance, 287
Bulldogs Arena, 6104
Bullshed Theatre Project, 3755
Burg Theatre, 8042
Burklyn Ballet Theatre, 656
Burlington Civic Music Association, 4639
Burlington Discover Jazz Festival, 1768, 5705
Burlington Memorial Auditorium, 6960, 8503
Burnett Theatre, 7046
Burning Coal Theatre Company, 3674
Burning Hills Amphitheatre, 7939
Burruss Auditorium, 8512
Burton Coliseum, 7129
Bus Barn Stage Company, 2489
Busch Stadium, 7444
Busch Student Center, 7445
Bushfire Theatre of Performing Arts, 3829
Bushnell Center for the Performing Arts, 6406
Butler County Symphony, 1620
Butler University, 6888
Butler University Symphony Orchestra, 1082
Butte Center for the Performing Arts, 7472
Butte Civic Center, 7473

C

Cabaret at the Columbia Club, 3011
Cabbages and Kings, 3944
Cabrillo Crocker Theater, 6056
Cabrillo Festival of Contemporary Music, 4327
Cabrini College, 5499
Cache Valley Center for the Arts, 5683
Cactus Jazz & Blues Festival, 5660
Cadence Theatre Company, 4050
Caesars Palace, 7506
Cafe Del Rey Moro, 6238
Cahn Auditorium, 6779
Cain Park Theatre, 3717, 7979
Caine Lyric Theatre, 8477
Cajun Stadium, 7124
Cajundome and Convention Center, 7125
Cal Poly Arts Presents & Great Performances, 4317
Cal Poly State University Performing Arts Center, 6273
Caldwell College Student Union Building, 7546
Caldwell Fine Arts Series, 4534
Caldwell Theatre Company, 2756
Calico Theatre, 7945
California Ballet Company, 65
California Center for the Arts-Escondido, 6101
California Chamber Orchestra & Chamber Opera, 1869
California E.A.R. Unit, 772
California Institute of Music, 4272
California Institute of Technology Performing Arts Center, 6207
California Institute of the Arts: School of Theater, 2637
California Lutheran University Music Series, 4340, 4341
California Musical Theatre, 2553
California Philharmonic Orchestra, 865
California Polytechnic University Theatre, 6211
California Repertory Company, 2485
California Riverside Ballet, 61
California Shakespeare Theater, 2538, 4204
California State Polytechnic University: Department of Theatre and Dance, 2545
California State Summer School for the Arts, 4282

California State University East Bay, 4223
California State University Stanislaus Performing Arts Center, 6317
California State University, Bakersfield: Theatre Program, 2446
California State University, Dominguez Hills: Department of Theatre, 2456
California State University, Fresno: Theatre Arts Department, 2468
California State University, Fullerton: Department of Theatre and Dance, 2469
California State University, Long Beach: Department of Theatre, 2486
California State University, Northridge: Department of Theatre, 2534
California State University, Sacramento: Department of Theatre and Dance, 2554
California State University, Stanislaus, 2635
California State University-Hayward - Main Theatre, 6118
California State University-Los Angeles - Players, 2497
California Symphony, 889
California Theatre Center, 2633
California Theatre of Performing Arts, 6234
California Youth Symphony, 820
Caltech Public Events Series, 4267
Calumet Theatre Company, 3194, 7279
Calvin College Fine Arts Center, 7299
Calvin Theatre and Performance Arts Center, 7246
Cam Henderson Center, 8632
Cam-Plex Heritage Center, 8717
Cambria County War Memorial Arena, 8133
Cambridge Society for Early Music: Chamber Music Series, 1188, 4785
Camden Opera House, 7168
Camellia Symphony Orchestra, 835
Camelot Theatre Company, 3790
Camerata Musica, 1613
Camerata Philadelphia Inc, 1665
Cameratas Singers of Monterey County, 1904
Cameron Hall, 8530
Cameron University: Lecture & Concert Series, 5384
Cameron University: Theatre Arts Department, 3758
Camille Players, 3939
Camille Playhouse, 8336
Camp Randall Stadium, 8674
Camp Theater, 7863
Campbell Recital Hall, 6306
Campbell University Community Concert Series, 5227
Candlelight Concert Society, 1162
Cantabile Youth Singers, 1891
Cantata Singers, 2105
Canterbury Choral Society, 2219, 2294
Canterbury Summer Theatre/The Festival Players Guild, 4625
Canticum Novum Singers, 2220
Canton Ballet, 513
Canton Memorial Civic Center, 7951
Canton Symphony Orchestra, 1523
Canton Youth Symphony, 1524
Cantori Domino, 1938
Canyon Concert Ballet, 127
Canyon Industries, 4265
Canyonlands Arts Council, 5687
Cape & Islands Chamber Music Festival, 4796
Cape Ann Symphony Orchestra, 1195
Cape Cod Chamber Music Festival, 1204, 4797
Cape Cod Conservatory of Music & Arts, 7255
Cape Cod Melody Tent, 3156
Cape Cod Symphony Orchestra, 1219
Cape Fear Regional Theatre, 3655
Cape May Jazz Festival, 4986
Cape May Music Festival, 4987
Cape May Stage, 3361
Capistrano Valley Symphony, 779
Capital Baseball Stadium, 8395
Capital City Council on The Arts, 4901
Capital City Symphony, 952
Capital Jazz Festival, 4767
Capital Repertory Theatre, 7623
Capital Stage Company, 2555
Capitol Arts Alliance, 4687
Capitol Arts Center, 7077

Capitol Center, 8625
Capitol Center for the Arts, 7525
Capitol Chamber Artists, 1362
Capitol City Opera, 2023
Capitol City Stadium, 8216
Capitol Civic Centre, 8684
Capitol Music Hall & Jamboree Usa, 8653
Capitol Opera Sacramento, 1878
Capitol Theatre, 7817, 8496, 8621
Capitol Theatre Summerstage, 3613
Capitolarts Providence Cultural Affairs, 5521
Cappella Romana, 2299
Caramoor Center for Music and The Arts, 5096
Caramoor Center for Music and The Arts Venetian Theatre, 7694
Caramoor International Music Festival, 5097
Caravan of Dreams, 8383
Cardinal Stadium, 7090, 8330
Cardinal Stritch University School of Visual and Performing Arts, 5857
Carin University, 5463
Carl Broman Concerts, 5760
Carl Wooten Stadium, 8032
Carleton College Concert Series, 4878
Carlsbad Community Concert Association, 5028
Carlson Center, 6023
Carmel Bach Festival, 766, 4211
Carmel Dance Arts-Indy Latin Dance, 226
Carmel Music Society, 4212
Carmel Symphony Orchestra, 1077
Carmel Valley Library Concert Series, 4273
Carmichael Auditorium, 6461
Carnegie Chamber Players, 1410
Carnegie Hall, 5818, 8642
Carnegie Hall Corporation, 7719
Carnegie-Mellon School of Music, 5489
Carnegie: Lecture Hall, 8169
Carnegie: Museum of Art Theatre, 8170
Carnegie: Music Hall, 8171
Carnie Smith Stadium, 7056
Carole and Gordon Mallett Theatre, 6948
Carolina Ballet, 511
Carolina Ballet Theatre, 606, 610
Carolina Coliseum, 8217
Carolina Lugo's & Carole Acuna's Ballet Flamenco & Dance Center, 27
Carolina Pro Musica, 1482
Carolina Productions, Performing Arts Commission, 5536
Carolina Theatre, 7885
Carolina Theatre of Durham, 3650
Carolina Union Performing Arts Series, 5228
Carolina Voices, 2261
Carolina Youth Symphony, 1680
Carolinas Concert Association, 5229
Carolyn Dorfman Dance Company, 343
Carolyn Lord and Company, 401
Carousel Dinner Theatre, 3695
Carousel Music Theatre, 3094
Carpenter Center for the Performing Arts, 8548
Carpetbag Theatre, 3903
Carrier Dome, 7832
Carroll College Theatre, 7476
Carrollwood Players Community Theater, 2831
Carson Center, 7105
Carson City Symphony Association, 1311
Carson-Dominguez Hills Symphony, 771
Carson-Newman College Concert-Lecture Series, 5568
Carter Finley Stadium, 7901
Carthage Chamber Music Series, 1824
Carthage College Chamber Music & Lecture Series, 5840
Caruth Auditorium, 8354
Carver Community Cultural Center, 8450
Carver Complex, 8451
Cary Field, 8565
Casa De Unidas Series, 4834
Casa Italiana Opera Company, 1872
Casa Manana Musicals, 3969
Casa Manana Playhouse, 3970
Casa Manana Theatre, 8384
Cascade Festival of Music, 5401
Cascade Head Music Festival, 5412
Cascade Symphony Orchestra, 1790
Cascades Theatrical Company, 3773
Casell Coliseum, 8513
Casper Events Center, 8712

Entry Index

Cass County Arts Council, 4638
Castillo Theatre, 3477
Castle Rock Players, 2650
Castleman Quartet Programs, 1461
Castleton State College Performing Arts Series, 5707
Caswell Council for the Arts, 5280
Caswell County Civic Center, 7931
Catalina Island Jazztrax Festival, 4266
Catamount Film and Arts Company, 4025
Catawba College Community Center Theatre, 7913
Catco (Contemporary American Theatre Company), 3720
Cathedral Arts, 5120
Cathedral Arts Project Series, 4948
Cathedral Basilica of the Sacred Heart Concert Series, 1335, 5004
Cathedral Choral Society, 1982
Cathedral Concert Series, 5602
Cathedral of Saint Louis, 7446
Catholic University of America: Drama Department, 2733
Catskill Symphony Orchestra, 1449
Cave Theatre, 6915
Cayuga Chamber Orchestra, 1394
Ccm Philharmonia & Concert Orchestra, 1526
Ce Gaines Complex, 7922
Cecilia Chorus of New York, 2221
Cedar Lake Dance, 402
Cedar Point Live Entertainment, 3749
Cedar Rapids Community Concerts Association, 4641
Cedar Rapids Opera Theatre, 2069
Cedar Rapids Symphony Orchestra, 1102
Cedarburg Performing Arts Center, 8659
Cedarhurst Chamber Music, 1057
Cedarville University Artist Series, 5299
Celebrate Brooklyn Festival, 5054
Celebration Barn Theater, 7181
Celebration Team, 403
Celebration Theatre, 2640, 6155
Celebrity Concert Series Office, 5696
Celebrity Presentations, 4232
Celebrity Theatre, 5963
Centenary College Recital Hall, 7156
Centenary Stage Company, 3365
Centenary Stage Company and Performing Arts Guild, 4994
Centennial Hall, 5996, 6826
Centennial Hall Convention Center, 5942
Centennial Theater Festival, 4406
Center City Opera Theater, 2306
Center for Contemporary Opera, 2222
Center for Puppetry Arts, 2850
Center for the Arts, 6411
Center for the Arts Lecture Hall, 7826
Center for the Arts Recital Hall, 7825
Center for the Creative & Performing Arts, 6650
Center for the Visual and Performing Arts, 4258
Center for Traditional Music & Dance, 7720
Center for Visual and Performing Arts, 6919
Center of Creative Arts, 7447
Center Stage, 3113, 3330, 7188, 8547
Center Theater, 8230
Center Theater and The Training Center, 2914
Center Theater Company of Tampa Bay, 6595
Centerarts, 6057
Centerstage, Osher Marin Jewish Community Center, 4321
Central California Ballet, 17
Central City Opera, 1950, 1953
Central College Community Orchestra, 1113
Central Community Concerts, 5505
Central Connecticut State University: Department of Theatre, 2693
Central Florida Ballet, 162
Central Florida Cultural Endeavors, 4441
Central Iowa Symphony, 1100
Central Kentucky Arts Series, 4688
Central Kentucky Youth Orchestras, 1126
Central Methodist College Convocations, 4898
Central Missouri State University Symphony Orchestra, 1295
Central Ohio Symphony Orchestra, 1552
Central Ohio Technical College, 5359
Central Oklahoma Concert Series, 5381

Central Park Summerstage, 5121
Central Pennsylvania Festival of the Arts, 5507
Central Pennsylvania Friends of Jazz, 1626
Central Pennsylvania Youth Ballet, 569
Central Piedmont Community Theatre, 3647
Central Presbyterian Church, 5019
Central Standard, 2075
Central West Ballet, 47
Central Wisconsin Symphony Orchestra, 1835
Centralia Philharmonic Orchestra, 1030
Centre Stage, 6018
Centre Stage-South Carolina, 3877
Centrum Arena, 8473
Century Center Convention Hall, 6940
Century Center Recital Hall, 6939
Century II Civic Center Exhibition Hall, 7067
Century II Civic Center Mary Jane Teall Theatre, 7068
Century II Performing Arts & Convention Center, 7069
Century Link Arena Boise, 6685
Century Village Theaters, 6486
Centurylink Center Omaha, 7501
Cerritos Center for the Performing Arts, 6079
Cfa Studio, 6452
Cfa Theater, 6412
Cfa Thompson Theatre, 6453
Chabot College Performing Arts Center, 6119
Chaddick Dance Theater, 622
Chadron State College Memorial Hall, 7487
Chaffee Art Center, 5718
Chaffin's Barn Dinner Theatre, 3912, 8292
Chagrin Valley Little Theatre, 3701
Chamber Arts Society, 1487
Chamber Dance Company, 679
Chamber Music Albuquerque Presents the June Music Festival, 5026
Chamber Music America, 1411
Chamber Music at Rodef Shalom With Stephen Starkman & Friends, 1457
Chamber Music Columbus, 1544
Chamber Music Concerts, 1587
Chamber Music Connection, 5373
Chamber Music Corvallis, 1589
Chamber Music Festival of the East, 5106
Chamber Music Hawaii, 1017
Chamber Music Houston, 1730
Chamber Music in Napa Valley, 838, 4286
Chamber Music in Oklahoma, 1582
Chamber Music International, 1711
Chamber Music Masters, 4293
Chamber Music Monterey Bay, 767
Chamber Music Northwest, 1600, 5417
Chamber Music of Charlotte, 1483
Chamber Music Plus Southwest, 741
Chamber Music Sedona, 733, 4174
Chamber Music Society of Bethlehem, 1619
Chamber Music Society of Central Kentucky, 1127
Chamber Music Society of Detroit, 1231
Chamber Music Society of Lincoln Center, 1412
Chamber Music Society of Oregon, 1601
Chamber Music Society of Salt Lake City, 1758
Chamber Music Society of the North Shore, 1052
Chamber Music Society of Utica, 1473
Chamber Music Tulsa, 1585
Chamber Music Yellow Springs, 1574
Chamber Orchestra of Albuquerque, 1353
Chamber Orchestra of the South Bay, 834
Chamber Orchestra of the Triangle, 1481
Chamber Players International, 1475
Chamber Singers of the Colorado Springs Chorale, 1948
Chamizal National Memorial: Theater, 8371
Champaign Urbana Theatre Company, 2989
Champaign-Urbana Symphony Orchestra, 1031
Chandler Center for the Arts, 5946
Chandler Music Hall and Cultural Center, 8508
Chandler Symphony Orchestra, 725
Changing Scene Theater, 2655
Chanhassen Dinner Theatre, 3223
Channing Players, 3983
Chanticleer, 1912
Chanticleer String Quartet, 1094
Chanute Community Theatre, 3042
Chaparral Center, 8433
Chapin Hall, 7258

Chapman University Symphony Orchestra & Chamber Orchestra, 817
Charles E Smith Center, 6462
Charles H Macnider Art Museum, 7011
Charles Ives Center Pavilion, 6396
Charles Koch Arena, 7028
Charles M Murphy Athletic Center, 8288
Charles River Concert Series, 4774
Charles W Davis Concert Hall, 5939
Charles W. Eisemann Center for Performing Arts & Corporate Presentations, 8442
Charleston Chamber Music Society, 1816
Charleston Civic Center, 8626
Charleston Civic Chorus, 2391
Charleston Community Music Association, 5824
Charleston Concert Association, 5531
Charleston Heights Arts Center, 7507
Charleston Symphony Orchestra, 1678
Charlestown Working Theater, 3147
Charlie Christian International Jazz Festival, 5387
Charlotte Ballet, 507
Charlotte Center City Partners, 5230
Charlotte Coliseum, 7870
Charlotte Harbor Event and Conference Center, 6581
Charlotte Knights Baseball Stadium, 8222
Charlotte Philharmonic Orchestra and Chorus, 1484
Charlotte Players, 2817
Charlotte Symphony, 1485
Charlottesville Classical Guitar Society, 1777
Charter Oak Cultural Center, 6407
Chase Field, 5964
Chase Fine Arts Center, 8478
Chastian Park Amphitheatre Atlanta Symphony Orchestra Festival Pops, 1007, 4503
Chattanooga Ballet, 612
Chattanooga Boys Choir, 2328
Chattanooga Symphony and Opera, 1689
Chattanooga Symphony and Opera Association, 2329
Chautauqua Institution, 5059
Chautauqua Opera, 2252
Chautauqua Summer Schools of Fine and Performing Arts, 2208
Chautauqua Symphony Orchestra, 1378
Cheboygan Area Arts Council/Opera House, 2132, 4833
Cheboygan Opera House, 7280
Cheek Theatre, 6828
Chelsea Opera, 2223
Chen Dance Center, 404
Chenango County Council for the Arts, 5174
Cheney Stadium, 8617
Cherokee National Historical Society, 3767
Cherry Creek Arts Festival, 4366
Cheshire Community Theatre, 2679
Chester Fritz Auditorium, 7936
Chester Theatre Company, 3149
Chestnut Brass Company, 1641
Chestnut Hill Concerts, 4387
Cheyenne Civic Center, 8714
Cheyenne Little Theatre Players, 4137
Cheyenne Symphony Orchestra, 1837
Chicago a Cappella, 2038
Chicago Actors Ensemble, 2915
Chicago Chamber Orchestra, 1033
Chicago Children's Choir, 2039
Chicago Chorale, 2040
Chicago City Limits, 3478
Chicago College of Performing Arts Music Conservatory Series, 4549
Chicago Dramatists, 2916
Chicago Festival Ballet, 218
Chicago Opera Theater, 2041
Chicago Philharmonic, 1048
Chicago Shakespeare Theater on Navy Pier, 2917
Chicago Sinfonietta, 1034
Chicago Studio of Professional Singing Performance Series, 4550
Chicago Symphony Chorus, 2042
Chicago Symphony Orchestra, 1035
Chicago Symphony Orchestra Association, 6733
Chicago Tap Theatre, 201
Chicago Youth Symphony Orchestra, 1036
Chichester Black Box Theatre, 5912

Chico Performances, 2458
Child's Play Touring Theatre, 2918
Children's Aid Society Chorus, 2224
Children's Chorus of Maryland & School of Music, 2101
Children's Concert Society of Akron, 5285
Children's Musical Theater-San Jose, 2598
Children's National Medical Center, New Horizons Program, 4418
Children's Opera Theater, 2346
Children's Performing Arts Series, 5396
Children's Theater Company, 3237
Children's Theatre Board, 3685
Children's Theatre Festival, 5634
Children's Theatre of Charlotte, 3648
Children's Theatre of Eden, 3653
Childsplay, 2429
Chilkat Center for the Arts, 5940
China Dance School & Theatre, 74
China Music Project, 5315
Chinese Classical Orchestra and Educational Program, 1072
Chinese Folk Dance Company, 405
Chinese Music Ensemble of New York, 1413
Chinese Theatre Works, 3453
Chipola College Artist Series, 4463
Chippewa Valley Theatre Guild, 4107
Chisholm Trail Arts Council, 5380
Chitresh Das Dance Company, 75
Chocolate Church Arts Center Festival, 4728
Chookasian Armenian Concert Ensemble, 31, 784
Choral Arts Philadelphia, 5475
Choral Arts Society of New Jersey, 2195
Choral Arts Society of Philadelphia, 2307
Choral Arts Society of Washington, 1984
Choral Guild of Atlanta, 2024
Choral Recital Hall, 8645
Choral Society of Greensboro, 2265
Choral Society of Pensacola, 2008
Chorus America, 1985
Chorus Austin, 2337
Chorus of Westerly, 2326
Chris and Anne Reyes Organ and Choral Hall, 6927
Christian Arts Auditorium, 6852
Christian Community Theater, 2465
Christopher Caines Dance Company, 406
Christopher Newport University, 5746
Chronos Theatre Group, 2560
Chrysalis Repertory Dance Company, 635
Chrysler Hall, 8537
Church of Fine Arts, 7517
Churchill Arts Council, 4956
Cimarron Circuit Opera Company, 2292
Cimarron Opera, 2293
Cincinnati Arts Association: Aronoff Center for the Arts, 5301
Cincinnati Ballet, 515
Cincinnati Boychoir, 2277
Cincinnati Chamber Orchestra, 1527
Cincinnati Folk Life Series, 5302
Cincinnati Gardens, 5303
Cincinnati May Festival, 5304
Cincinnati Music Hall, 7953
Cincinnati Opera, 2278
Cincinnati Opera Association Summer Festival, 5305
Cincinnati Orchestra, 1528
Cincinnati Playhouse in The Park, 3704
Cincinnati Shakespeare Festival, 5306
Cincinnati Symphony Youth Orchestra, 1529
Cinnabar Theater, 2543
Cintas Center, 7954
Circa '21 Dinner Playhouse, 2984
Circle in The Square Theater School, 7721
Circle Theatre, 3202, 3331, 3971
Circuit Playhouse, 3908
Citadel Fine Arts Series, 5532
Citadel Theatre Company, 2972
Citi Field, 7672
Citi Performing Art Center Wang Theatre, 7222
Citicorp Summerfest, 4916
Citrus College Haugh Performing Arts Center, 4221
City Arts Drama Center, 3659
City Ballet, 615
City Ballet of Houston, 636

1109

Entry Index

City Ballet San Diego, 66
City Center of Music and Drama, 7722
City Lights Theatre Company, 2599
City Lit Theater Company, 2919
City of Albany Parks and Recreation Department, 5397
City of Albuquerque Kimo Theatre, 3400
City of Bellingham Facilities, 8571
City of Bryan Parks and Recreation, 5600
City of Gaithersburg Cultural Arts Division, 4765
City of Grand Haven Community Center, 7298
City of Gulf Shores Entertainment Series, 4145
City of Jamestown North Dakota, 7938
City of Los Angeles Cultural Affairs Department, 4236
City of Morganton Municipal Auditorium, 7896
City Players, 2761
City Theater Company, 2726
City Theatre Company, 3841
City Theatre of Independence, 3284
Citycelebrations Musicfest, 5753
Citydance Ensemble, 141
Civic Auditorium, 6696
Civic Center Complex, 8331
Civic Center Music Hall, 8043
Civic Center of Anderson, 5529
Civic Center of Greater Des Moines, 6984
Civic Center of Onondaga County Carrier Theatre, 7834
Civic Center of Onondaga County Crouse-Hind Hall, 7833
Civic Dance Company, 67
Civic Hall Performing Arts Center, 6937
Civic Morning Musicals, 5207
Civic Music Association of Des Moines, 4649
Civic Orchestra of Minneapolis, 1262
Civic Orchestra of Tucson, 742
Civic Theatre & School of Theatre, 3203
Claire Trevor School of the Arts, 6133, 6135
Clancyworks Dance Company, 264
Claremont Opera House, 2172, 7524
Claremont Symphony Orchestra, 773
Clarence Brown Theatre Company, 3904
Clarice Smith Performing Arts Center, 7203
Clarion Concerts in Columbia County, 5064
Clarion Music Society, 5122
Clarion University Activities Board Arts, 5439
Clarita & the Arte Flamenco Dance Theatre, 19
Clark Center for the Perorming Arts, 6062
Clark State Performing Arts Center, 8008
Clarke College Cultural Events Series, 4652
Classic Stage Company, 3479
Classical Frontiers, 5184
Classical Guitar Series, 5307
Classical Piano Series, 5308
Classical Quartet, 1414
Classical Symphony Orchestra & the Protege Philharmonic, 1037
Classicfest: Pensacola Summer Music Festival, 4474
Classics on Stage!, 2920
Clatsop Community College Performing Arts Center, 8065
Claudia Crosby Theatre, 5921
Clay Center for the Arts & Sciences, 8627
Clear Lake Symphony, 1727
Clearwater Jazz Holiday, 4438
Clearwater's Great Hudson River Revival, 5191
Clemens Center, 7667
Clemson Memorial Stadium, 8213
Cleo Parker Robinson Dance, 121
Clermont Philharmonic Orchestra, 1517
Cleve L Abbott Memorial Alumni Stadium, 5932
Cleveland Browns Stadium, 7960
Cleveland Chamber Music Society, 1542
Cleveland Chamber Symphony, 1531
Cleveland Institute of Music, 1532, 7961
Cleveland Jazz Orchestra, 1533
Cleveland Museum of Art Performing Arts Series, 5316
Cleveland Museum of Art: Gartner Auditorium, 7962
Cleveland Music School Settlement Artists Concert Series, 5317
Cleveland Octet, 1534
Cleveland Orchestra, 1535
Cleveland Orchestra Chorus, 2279
Cleveland Orchestra Youth Orchestra, 1536

Cleveland Philharmonic Orchestra, 1537
Cleveland Play House, 3711, 7963
Cleveland Play House Bolton Theatre, 7964
Cleveland Play House Brooks Theatre, 7965
Cleveland Play House Drury Theatre, 7966
Cleveland Pops Orchestra, 1518
Cleveland Public Theatre, 3712, 7967
Cleveland Shakespeare Festival, 5318, 5351
Cleveland Signstage Theatre, 3713
Cleveland State University Dance Company, 519
Cleveland State University: Convocation Center, 7968
Cleveland Women's Orchestra, 1567
Cliburn Concerts, 1722, 5625
Clifford E White Theatre, 5951
Climb Theatre, 3231
Climb Theatre - Creative Learning Ideas, 3265
Clinton Area Showboat Theatre, 3030
Clinton Symphony Orchestra, 1103
Clockwise Theatre, 2991
Clockwork Repertory Theatre, 2703
Clog America, 655
Close Encounters With Music Series, 4792
Clowes Memorial Hall, 6889
Co Brown Stadium, 7275
Co' Motion Dance Theater, 235
Coa Community Auditorium, 7882
Coa Community Center Auditorium, 5238
Coach House Players, 3451
Coastal Carolina Community College, 5253
Coastal Concert Association, 5545
Coaster Theatre, 8066
Cobb Energy Performing Arts Centre, 6607
Cobb Symphony Orchestra, 1013
Cobo Arena, 7282
Cockpit in Court Summer Theatre, 3114
Cocoa Expo Sports Center, 6489
Coconino Center for the Arts, 5952
Coe College Jazz Summit, 4642
Coe College Marquis Series, 4643
Coe Park Civic Center, 6440
Coeur D'alene Summer Theatre/Carousel Players, 2897
Coffee County Arts Alliance, 4143
Coffeyville Community Theatre, 3043
Coffeyville Cultural Arts Council Inc, 4669
Cofrin Family Hall, 8665
Coger Theatre, 7466
Cohan/Suzeau Dance Company, 237
Cohen Stadium, 8372
Colby Music Series, 4747
Colby-Sawyer College, 4972
Colden Center for the Performing Arts, 7673
Colden Center Performances, 5072
Colder by The Lake Comedy Theatre, 3224
Coleman Chamber Concerts, 4268
Coleman Chamber Music Association, 822
Coleman Coliseum, 5925
Coleman Puppet Theatre, 2976
Colgate University Concert Series, 5085
Coliseum Civic Center, 7389
College Light Opera Company, 2114, 2288
College of Creative Arts, 4102
College of Lake County - Performing Arts Building, 4579
College of Marin, 795
College of New Jersey Center for the Arts, 4991
College of Southern Maryland Fine Arts Center, 7207
College of St. Scholastica Mitchell Auditorium, 4867
College of the Siskiyous Performing Arts Series, 4347
College of the Siskiyous Theatre, 6320
College of Visual and Performing Arts, 5734
College-Community Arts Council, 5300
Collegiate Chorale, 2225
Collegium Westchester, 1451
Collingwood Arts Center, 8011
Collins Center for the Arts, 7172
Colonial Symphony, 1321
Colonial Theatre, 6697, 7534
Colony Theatre Company, 2453
Colorado Ballet, 122
Colorado Children's Chorale, 1951
Colorado College Dance Festival, 4363
Colorado Council on The Arts, 4367
Colorado Mahlerfest, 4355

Colorado Music Festival & Rocky Mountain Center for Musical Arts, 4356
Colorado Shakespeare Festival, 4357
Colorado Springs Chorale, 1949
Colorado Springs City Auditorium, 6339
Colorado Springs Fine Arts Center Performing Arts Series, 4364
Colorado Springs Philharmonic, 903
Colorado State University Orchestra, 909
Colorado State University Theatre, 6372
Colorado Symphony Orchestra, 905
Colquitt County Arts Center, 6655
Columbia City Ballet, 597
Columbia College Power Company Series, 5537
Columbia Community Arts Centre, 599
Columbia Exposition Center, 7387
Columbia Festival of the Arts, 4761
Columbia Gorge Repertory Theatre, 4095
Columbia Meadows, 8090
Columbia Orchestra, 1163
Columbia Pro Cantare, 2098
Columbia Stage Society at Town Theatre, 3873
Columbia Theatre for the Performing Arts, 4073
Columbia Theatre/Fanfare, 3079
Columbia University Orchestra, 1415
Columbia's Ballroom Company, 600
Columbian Theatre: Museum & Art Center, 3050, 7065
Columbiana Summer Concert Association, 5323
Columbine Chorale, 1952
Columbus Area Arts Council, 4613
Columbus Arts Festival, 5324
Columbus Association for the Performing Arts: Signature Series, 5325
Columbus Children's Theatre, 3721
Columbus Civic Center, 6639
Columbus Friends of Music Association, 4942
Columbus Indiana Philharmonic, 1078
Columbus Symphony Chorus, 2282
Columbus Symphony Orchestra, 1010, 1545
Columbus Symphony Orchestra: Picnic With the Pops, 5326
Columbus Symphony Youth Orchestras, 1546
Comic Opera Guild, 2129
Commedia Theater Company, 3238
Commodores, 960
Common Stage Theatre Company, 3635
Commonweal Theatre Company, 3232
Commonwealth Ballet Company, 268
Commonwealth Opera, 2115
Commonwealth Stadium, 7083
Communication Arts Theatre, 8671
Community Actors' Studio Theatre Inc., 2399
Community Arts and Music Association of Santa Barbara-Cama, 4322
Community Arts Partnership Series With Peddie School, 4995
Community Center for the Performing Arts, 8072
Community Children's Theatre of Peoria Park District, 4592
Community Concerts of Bartlesville, 5378
Community Education Center, 5476, 5477
Community Fine Arts Center, 8721
Community Music Center, 6254, 8091, 8401
Community Opera, 2193
Community Performance Series, 5189
Community Players of Concord, 3343
Community Players Theater, 7484
Community Theatre, 7569
Community Theatre Association of Michigan, 7264
Community Theatre of Clay County, 3000
Community Theatre of Greensboro, 3660
Community Theatre of Terre Haute, 6942
Company of Fools, 2898
Company One, 3136
Concert Artists Guild New York Recital Series, 5123
Concert Artists of Baltimore, 1156, 4751
Concert Association of Florida, 4468
Concert Socials, 5124
Concertime, 5392
Concerto Soloists, 1642
Concerts at the Cloisters, 5125
Concerts by The Bay, 5516
Concerts International, 5574
Concerts West, 4330
Concerts-At-The-Common, 4812

Concesco Fieldhouse, 4619
Concord Band, 1192
Concord City Auditorium, 7526
Concord Orchestra, 1193
Concord Singers of New Ulm, 2150
Concordia College Cultural Events Series, 4875
Concordia University Concert Series, 4952
Concordia University Wisconsin, 5853
Conejo Pops Orchestra, 884
Conejo Recreation & Park District Summer Concert Series, 4342
Coney Island Usa, 3419
Congo Square Theatre Company, 2921
Conklin's Barn 2 Dinner Theatre, 2971
Connecticut Ballet, 131
Connecticut Choral Artists, 1966
Connecticut Choral Society, 1971
Connecticut Classical Guitar Society, 927
Connecticut College Department of Theatre, 2701
Connecticut College: on Stage, 4398
Connecticut Concert Opera, 1976
Connecticut Conservatory of the Performing Arts, 2702
Connecticut Early Music Festival, 4399
Connecticut Grand Opera and Orchestra, 1972
Connecticut Opera, 1964
Connecticut Repertory Theatre, 2709
Connecticut Theater Festival, 4407
Connecticut Theatre Company, 2694
Connecticut Youth Symphony, 945
Connersville Area Artists Series, 4614
Connoisseur Concerts Association, 5806
Conroe Symphony Orchestra, 1707
Conservatory of Music, 880
Conspirare, Craig Hella Johnson & Company of Voices, 2338
Constant Convocation Center, 8538
Constellationcenter, 7230
Constitution Hall, 6463
Contemporary American Theater Festival, 4104, 5822
Contemporary Arts Center, 7139
Contemporary Ballet Dallas, 627
Contemporary Dance of Sinclair, 530
Contemporary Dance Oklahoma, 549
Contemporary Dance Theater, 516
Contemporary Dance/Fort Worth, 631
Contemporary Music Consortium, 5691
Contemporary Music Forum, 953
Continental Airlines Arena, 7553
Continental Ballet Company, 292
Convergence Arts Festival, 5522
Convergence Dance Theatre, 191
Converse Symphony Orchestra, 1684
Convocation Center, 6762
Conway Symphony Orchestra, 750
Cooley Auditorium, 8688
Cooper Stadium, 5327
Cooperstown Concert Series, 5062
Cooperstown Theatre & Music Festival, 5063
Coors Amphitheatre, 6123
Coors Events Conference Center, 6337
Coors Field, 6348
Coquille Performing Arts, 5403
Coral Ridge Presbyterian Church Concert Series, 4446
Coral Springs Center for the Arts, 6497
Corbet Theatre, 8579
Corbett Auditorium, 7955
Cordier Auditorium, 6926
Cordiner Hall, 8620
Core Performance Company, 185
Corinth Theatre-Arts, 3274
Corn Palace, 8243
Corn Productions at Conservatory, 2922
Cornell Concert Series, 5091
Cornell University Theatre, Film & Dance Department, 3445
Cornerstone Theater Company, 2498
Cornerstone Theatre Company, 2818
Corning-Painted Post Civic Music Association, 5066
Cornish College: Cornish Series, 5792
Corona Symphoney Orchestra, 1874
Coronado Performing Arts Center, 6829
Corpus Acrobatic Theatre, 4294
Corpus Christi Ballet, 626

Entry Index

Corpus Christi Chamber Music Society, 1709
Corpus Christi Live, 5603
Corpus Christi Symphony Orchestra, 1708
Corsicana Community Playhouse, 3943
Cort Theatre, 7723
Cortland Repertory Theatre, 3435
Corvallis-Oregon State University Music Association, 5404
Coterie Theatre, 3286
Cottey Lecturers & Artists Super Series, 4913
Cotton Bowl/Fair Park, 8355
Coughlin Alumni Stadium, 8240
Council for the Arts of Greater Lima, 5353
Council for the Performing Arts, 5839
Count Basie Theatre, 7587
Country Current/Us Navy Band, 961
Country Dinner Playhouse, 2673
Court Theatre, 2923, 6734
Coussoulis Arena, 6233
Covenant Ballet Theatre of Brooklyn, 362
Cow Palace, 6255
Cowan Fine & Performing Arts Center, 8467
Cowboy Stadium, 7130
Cowell Theater, 6256
Cox Arena at Aztec Bowl, 6239
Cox Convention Center, 8044
Crabpot Players, 3879
Crafton-Preyer Theatre, 7043
Cramton Auditorium, 6464
Cranbrook Music Guild Concert Series, 4830
Crane River Theater Company, 3324
Crane School of Music Annual Spring Festival of the Arts, 5190
Cranford Dramatic Club, 3362
Cranford Dramatic Club Theatre, 7551
Crash, Burn and Die Dance Company, 21
Craterian Ginger Rogers Theater, 8084
Crawford County Community Concert Association, 5297
Creach/Company, 408
Creation Production Company, 3480
Creative Arts Team, 3481
Creative Arts Theatre and School, 3926
Creative Theatre, 3381
Creative Time Series, 5126
Creede Repertory Theatre, 2651, 6343
Crescent Concerts, 5012
Cresson Lake Playhouse, 3802
Crested Butte Chamber Music Festival, 4365
Crested Butte Mountain Theatre, 6344
Crested Butte Music Festival, 904
Crew Stadium, 7981
Cricket Arena, 7871
Cricket Pavilion, 5965
Crisler Arena, 7266
Crocker Art Museum Ballroom, 6230
Crooked Tree Arts Council, 4857
Cross Timbers Fine Arts Council, 5669
Crossroads Performance Group, 10
Crossroads Repertory Theatre, 3023
Crossroads Theatre Company, 3377
Crosssound, 4160
Crowder Hall, 5997
Crowell Concert, 6413
Crown Point Community Theatre, 3005
Crs National Festival for the Performing Arts, 5435
Cruisers, 962, 1999
Crystal Ballroom Concert Association Series, 4551
Cso Presents, 1038
Csun Youth Orchestras, 813
Cu Coors Events, 4358
Cuesta College Performing Arts, 4318
Cullen Performance Hall, 8402
Cultural Activities Center, 8462
Cultural Council of Victoria, 5676
Cultural Organization of the Arts, 5517
Cultural Resources Council of Syracuse, 5208
Culver City Symphony Orchestra, 777
Culver Military Academy Concert Series, 4615
Culver-Stockton College Performing Arts Hall, 7413
Cumberland County Civic Center, 7175
Cumberland County Coliseum Complex, 7883
Cumberland County Friends of the Orchestra, 1491
Cumberland County Playhouse, 3895

Cumberland Players, 3393
Cumberland Theatre, 3123
Cumberland University Auditorium, 8276
Curb Event Center, 8293
Curious Theatre Company, 2656
Curran Theatre, 6257
Curtain Players, 3737
Curtis Institute of Music, 8149
Curtis Theatre, 6076
Curtiss Hall, 6735
Cutler Majestic Theatre at Emerson College, 7223
Cutter Theatre, 4074
Cuyahoga Community College: Western Campus Theatre, 8005
Cw Post Chamber Music Festival, 5055
Cygnet Theatre, 2561
Cynthia Woods Mitchell Pavilion, 8465
Cypress Pops Orchestra, 778
Cyrano's Theatre Company, 2416

D

D Glen Smith Spectrum, 8479
Da Camera of Houston, 5635
Dad's Garage Theatre Company, 2851
Dade County Auditorium, 6547
Dairy Barn Cultural Arts Center, 7943
Dakota Dome, 8248
Dallas Bach Society, 1712
Dallas Black Dance Theatre, 628
Dallas Brass, 1725
Dallas Chamber Music Society, 1713
Dallas Children's Theater, 3945
Dallas Metropolitan Ballet, 629
Dallas Opera, 2342
Dallas Puppet Theater, 3946
Dallas Summer Musicals, Inc., 5609, 5611
Dallas Symphony Chorus, 2343
Dallas Symphony Orchestra, 5610
Dallas Theater Center, 3947
Dallas Theater Center: Kalita Humphreys Theatre, 8358
Dallas Wind Symphony, 1714
Dame Myra Hess Memorial Concert Series, 4552
Dana Arts Center University Theatre, 7680
Dana Fine Arts Building, 6643
Dana Tai Soon Burgess & Company, 142
Dance 1 Studio, 609
Dance Affiliates, 575
Dance Alive National Ballet, 153
Dance Alloy Theater, 579, 3842
Dance Baltimore, 255
Dance Brigade, 76
Dance Center, 6736
Dance Center of Columbia College, 202
Dance Collective New York, 409
Dance Delbello, 570
Dance Exchange, 266
Dance Festival: Centrum Festival, 5788
Dance June Lewis and Company, 410
Dance Kaleidoscope, 231
Dance Now! Miami, 157
Dance Place, 143
Dance Prism, 272
Dance Program, 680, 696
Dance Saint Louis, 310
Dance Station, 594
Dance Studio 3, 6137
Dance Studio Theatre, 6223
Dance Theater Workshop, 7724
Dance Theatre Etcetera, 369
Dance Theatre of Harlem, 411, 430
Dance Theatre of Lynchburg, 663
Dance Theatre of Oregon, 556
Dance Theatre of Tennessee, 619
Dance Through Time, 77
Dance Wisconsin, 705
Dancecircus, 701
Dancecleveland, 520
Dancers' Group, 78
Dances Patrelle, 412
Dancevert, 521
Dancevision Inc., 341
Dancewave, 363
Dancing Cat Productions, Inc, 106
Dancing in The Streets, 413
Dancing on Common Ground, 181

Dancing People Company, 555
Daniel-Meyer Coliseum, 8385
Danny Peterson Theatre, 6683
Danspace Project, 414
Danville Area Association for the Arts & Humanities, 5732
Danville Symphony Orchestra, 1044
Danza Floricanto/Usa, 56
Darien Lake Performing Arts Center, 7664
Darius Milhaud Society, 5319
Darkhorse Theater, 3913
Darrell K Royal-Texas Memorial Stadium, 8322
Dartmouth College Hopkins Center Performing Series, 4965
Das Puppenspiel Puppet Theater, 3633
David Adler Music and Arts Center, 6796
David Lipscomb University Theater, 3914
David Lipscomb University: Music Department, 5578
David O Mckay Auditorium, 6681
David Thayer Theatre, 7003
Dawson Auditorium, 7263
Dawson Wallace Dance Project, 126
Dayton Ballet, 531
Dayton Classical Guitar Society, 1525
Dayton Contemporary Dance Company, 532
Dayton Hara Arena, 7990
Dayton Opera Association, 2284
Dayton Philharmonic Orchestra Association, 1549
Dayton Philharmonic Youth Orchestra, 1550
Dayton Playhouse, 3732, 7991
Dayton's Jazz at the Bend Festival, 5334
Daytona Beach Community College Theatre Center, 6498
Daytona Beach International Festival, 4442
Daytona Beach Symphony Society, 967
Daytona Playhouse, 2770, 6499
Dc Armory, 6465
Dc Sports & Entertainment Commission, 4419
Dc Youth Orchestra Program, 954
De La Dance Company, 517
Deane E Smith Center, 7865
Dearborn Highlands Arts Council Series, 4608
Dearborn Orchestral Society / Dearborn Symphony, 1228
Deborah Riley Dance Projects, 144
Debra Weiss Dance Company, 495
Decatur Civic Center - Venue, 8367
Decatur Civic Center Theatre, 8366
Dee Events Center, 8484
Deep Dish Theater Company, 3643
Deep Ellum Arts Festival, 5608
Deep Vision Dance Company, 267
Deer Valley Resort Amphitheatre, 8488
Dekalb Symphony Orchestra, 1015
Del Mar College Student Cultural Programs, 5604
Del Norte Association for Cultural Awareness, 4215
Del Valle Fine Arts Concert Series, 4235
Del-Se-Nango Olde Tyme Fiddlers Association, 1403
Delacorte Theater in Central Park, 7725
Delaware Chamber Music Festival, 4414
Delaware County Cultural Arts Center, 7994
Delaware Dance Company, 138
Delaware Symphony Orchestra, 949
Delaware Theatre Company, 2727
Delaware Valley Opera Company, 2308
Delaware Water Gap Celebration of the Arts, 5444
Deleware Dance Alliance, Llc, 137
Delius Festival, 4451
Dell'arte International School of Physical Theatre, 2452
Delmar Stadium Complex, 8403
Delray Beach Playhouse, 2773, 6503
Delta Center Stage, 3275
Delta Classic Chastain Park Amphitheatre, 6620
Delta Festival Ballet, 245
Delta Symphony Orchestra, 1862
Deltaplex Arena & Conference Center, 7300
Demetrius Klein Dance Company, 536
Demmer Recital Hall, 8702
Denison University Vail Series, 5344
Dennos Museum Center Milliken Auditorium, 7330

Denton Arts & Jazz Festival, 5615
Denton Community Campus Theatre, 3963
Denver Botanic Gardens, 6349
Denver Broncos, 6362
Denver Broncos Football Club, 6351
Denver Center for the Performing Arts, 6352
Denver Center Theater Company, 2657
Denver Civic Theatre, 2658
Denver Municipal Band, 906
Denver Performing Arts Complex, 6347, 6353
Denver Puppet Theater, 2659
Denver Victorian Playhouse, 6354
Denver Young Artists Orchestra, 907
Department of Fine Arts, 6609
Department of Theatre and Dance, 8506
Department of Theatre Arts, 6466
Depaul University Merle Reskin Theatre, 2924
Depauw University Chamber Symphony, 1081
Depauw University Performing Arts Series, 4617
Depot Theatre, 7381
Derby Dinner Playhouse, 3004
Derthick Theatre, 8265
Des Moines Choral Society, 2071
Des Moines Community Orchestra, 1110
Des Moines Metro Opera, 2072
Des Moines Symphony, 1107
Des Moines Women's Club, 6985
Des Plaines Theatre Guild, 2962
Desert Dance Theatre, 12
Desert Foothills Musicfest, 4164
Desert Sun Stadium, 6012
Desert Symphony, 819
Desert Voices, 1858
Detroit Chamber Winds & Strings, 1253
Detroit Festival of the Arts, 4835
Detroit Repertory Theatre, 3197
Detroit Symphony Orchestra, 1229
Detroit Symphony Orchestra Hall, 7283
Devos Performance Hall, 7301
Dewitt Theatre Arts Center, 7015
Deyor Performing Arts Center, 8022
Diablo Ballet, 117
Diablo Light Opera Company, 1939
Diablo Symphony Association, 775
Diamond Circle Melodrama, 2668
Diamond Head Theatre, 2884
Diamond State Chorus of Sweet Adelines, 1977
Diana Wortham Theatre at Pack Place, 3638, 7854
Diavolo, 39
Dickens Opera House, 6387
Dickinson Theatre Organ Society, 950
Diddle Arena, 7078
Dietsch Artists International, 2191
Diller Street Theater, 6850
Dillingham Center for the Performing Arts, 7688
Dillon Community Concert Association, 4931
Dimensions Dance Theater, 52
Dine College, 5993
Dinizulu African Dancers, Drummers and Singers, 377
Dinkelspiel Auditorium, 6307
Dinosaur Annex Music Ensemble, 1179
Discover Houston County Visitors Center: Museum, 8348
Discovery Orchestra, 1348
Discovery Theater, 2734
Disney Theatrical Productions, 3482
District Curators, 4420
Diverseworks, 8404
Dixie Classic Fairgrounds, 7923
Dixie College Arena Theatre, 8491
Dixie College Fine Arts Center, 8490
Dixie College Proscenium Theatre, 8492
Dixie Stampede, 3922
Dixieland Monterey, 4254
Dixon Place, 3483
Do Gooder Productions, 3484
Dobama Theatre, 3718, 7980
Dobbs Theatre, 6667
Dock Street Theatre, 8206
Dodge City Festivals, 7031
Dodge Theatre, 5966
Dodger Stadium, 6156
Dolly Hands Cultural Arts Center, 6483
Dolores Winningstad Theatre, 8092
Dolphin Players, 3782
Dominic Walsh Dance Theater, 637

1111

Entry Index

Dominican College Auditorium, 6277
Dominican University Performing Arts Center, 4596
Don Haskins Center, 8373
Don Powell Theatre, 6240
Don Quixote Children's Theatre, 3485
Dona Ana Arts Council, 5029
Donald W. Reynolds Auditorium, 6019
Donald Williams, 415
Donna Sternberg & Dancers, 109
Donna Uchizono Company, 416
Door Community Auditorium Series, 5835
Dore Theatre/Madigan Gallery, 6065
Dorian Music Festivals, 2070
Dorothy Dickson Darte Center, 8189
Dorothy I Summers Auditorium, 8028
Dorothy Taubman Seminar at Lincoln Center, 5105
Dorset Theatre Festival, 5710
Dothan Civic Center, 5899
Doug Elkins Dance Company, 417
Doug Hamby Dance, 256
Doug Varone and Dancers, 418
Douglas Dunn and Dancers, 419
Dover Little Theatre, 7552
Dow Theatre, 6966
Down in Front Theater, 2814
Downers Grove Choral Society, 2053
Downers Grove Concert Association Series, 4571
Downey Symphony Orchestra, 781
Downriver Council for the Arts, 4862
Downriver Theatre Company, 3098
Downtown Art Company, 3486
Downtown Cabaret Theatre, 6394
Doyt L Perry Field, 7950
Dr. Schaffer and Mr. Stern Dance Ensemble, 107
Dragon Productions, 2546
Drake County Center for the Arts, 5355
Drake Stadium, 6986
Drake Symphony Orchestra, 1108
Drama Circle Theatre, 3948
Drama Department, 3487
Drayton Hall, 8207
Dream Theatre Company, 2925
Dreamcatcher Repertory Theatre, 3387
Dreiser Theatre, 6943
Dreiske Performance Company, 2926
Drury Lane Oakbrook Terrace, 2982
Duane Smith Auditorium, 7615
Dubuque Symphony Orchestra, 1109
Duke University Union Broadway Committee / on Stage Committee, 5235
Duluth Entertainment Convention Center, 7344
Duluth-Superior Symphony Orchestra, 1258
Duluth-Superior Youth Orchestras & Sinfonia, 1259
Dumbarton Concert, 4421
Dunbar Performing Arts Center, 7189
Duncan Lawton City Ballet, 548
Duncan Theatre, 6540
Dundalk Community Theatre, 3115
Dunham Hall Theater, 6771
Dunn Center for the Performing Arts, 7912
Dupage Opera Theater, 2055
Dupage Symphony, 1049
Dupont Theatre, 6455
Durango Choral Society, 1956
Durham Civic Choral Society, 2263
Durham Hall, 8713
Durham Performing Arts Center, 7880
Durham Symphony Orchestra, 1488
Dusk Till Dawn Blues Festival, 5388
Duson Tynek Dance Theatre, 364

E

Earle a Chiles Center, 8093
Earlham College Guest Artist Series, 4630
Earlville Opera House, 7666
Early Music Colorado Fall Festival of Early Music, 4359
Early Music Guild International Series/Recitals, 5793
Early Music Guild of Seattle, 1798
Early Music in Columbus, 5328
Early Music in Marin, 4205

Early Music New York (Em/Ny), 1416, 2226, 5128
Early Music Now, 5858
Earshot Jazz Festival, 5794
Earthen Vessels, 640
East Carolina University Rudolph Alexander Performing Art Series, 5249
East County Performing Arts Center - Theatre, 6099
East Gymnasium, 6058
East Tennessee Fine and Performing Arts Scholars, 5569
East Texas Symphony Orchestra, 1755
East West Music and Dance, 858
East West Players, 2499
East-West Fusion Theatre, 2680
Eastern Arizona College- Community Orchestra, 738
Eastern Arts International Dance Theater, 1759, 5698
Eastern Connecticut Symphony, 935
Eastern Howard Performing Arts Society, 6882
Eastern Michigan University Convocation Center, 7335
Eastern Music Festival & School, 5244
Eastern New Mexico University, 5033
Eastern Oregon State College Performing Arts Program, 5410
Eastern Shore Chamber Music Festival, 4762
Eastern Slope Inn Playhouse, 7542
Eastern Symphony Orchestra, 1032
Eastland Fine Arts Association, 5617
Eastman Philharmonia, 1459
Eastman School of Music, 5193
Eastman Theatre, 7812
Eatsern Kentucky University Alumni Coliseum, 7108
Eau Claire Children's Theatre, 4108
Eau Claire Regional Arts Center, 5832
Eccles Coliseum, 8474
Eccles Community Art Center, 8485
Echo Theater Company, 2500
Echo Theatre, 3949
Eckerd College Theatre Department, 2825
Eclectic Orange Festival, 4229
Eclipse Chamber Orchestra, 1774
Eclipse Theatre Company, 2927
Ed Cabell Theatre, 6646
Ed Landreth Auditorium, 8386
Ed Smith Stadium Sports Complex, 6583
Eden's Expressway, 7726
Edgecombe County Arts Council, 5269
Edgerton Center for the Performing Arts, 6399
Edinboro University of Pennsylvania Performing Arts Series, 5446
Edison Arts Society, 4988
Edison International Field of Anaheim, 6055
Edison Theatre, 3297, 7448
Edman Chapel, 6849
Edmonds Arts Commission, 5777
Edmonds Center for the Arts, 8581
Edmund P. Joyce Athletic & Convocation Center, 6928
Edward S. Strother Theatre, 6916
Edyvean Repertory Theatre, 3012
Egg-Empire State Performing Arts Center, 7624
Eglevsky Ballet, 352
Egyptian Theatre, 6763
Eidson-Duckwall Recital Hall, 6890
1812 Productions, 3823
1891 Fredonia Opera House, 2210
Eiko and Koma, 420
Eisenhower Auditorium, 8186
Eisenhower Dance Ensemble, 291
Eiteljorg Museum, 6891
Ej Thomas Performing Arts Hall, 7942
El Camino College Center for the Arts, 6315
El Camino Youth Symphony, 821
El Centro Su Teatro, 6355
El Dorado Municipal Auditorium, 6021
El Paso Association for the Performing Arts, 5618
El Paso Association for the Performing Arts/Viva El Paso!, 3965
El Paso Chamber Pro-Musica Festival, 5619
El Paso Civic Center: Exhibition Hall, 8374
El Paso Civic Center: Theatre, 8375

El Paso Convention & Performing Arts Center, 8376
El Paso County Coliseum, 8377
El Paso Opera, 2345
El Paso Pro-Musica, 1720
El Paso Symphony Orchestra, 1721
El Portal Theatre, 6194
El Teatro Campesino, 2606
El Teatro De La Esperanza, 2577
Elaine Kaufman Cultural Center Presentations, 5129
Eldred Hall, 7969
Electric Symphony Festival, 4771
Elgin Community College Visual & Performing Arts Center, 6773
Elgin Symphony Orchestra, 1046
Elias J Halling Recital Hall, 7349
Elisa Monte Dance, 421
Eliza R Snow Performing Arts Center, 6717
Elizabeth City State University Lyceum Series, 5239
Elizabeth Eriksen Byron Theatre, 6356
Elizabeth T Champ Auditorium, 7420
Elkhart Civic Theatre, 3001
Ellen Porter Hall, 6280
Ellie Caulkins Opera House, 6357
Elliott Hall of Music, 6949
Elm Shakespeare Company, 2696
Elmhurst College Jazz Festival, 4574
Elmhurst Symphony Orchestra, 1047
Elmwood Playhouse, 3601
Eloise Martin Recital Hall, 6820
Elon University Lyceum Committee, 5240
Embassy Centre, 6870
Embassy Series, 4422
Emelin Theatre for the Performing Arts, 5103, 7706
Emens Auditorium, 4627, 6917
Emerald Chamber Players, 1591
Emerging Artists Theatre Company, 3488
Emmanuel Music Bach Cantata Series, 4775
Emory & Henry College Concert Series, 5733
Emory Symphony Orchestra, 1008
Empire Opera Inc, 2227
Empire Theatre Company, 3694
Empire Theatre Complex, 8549
Empire Theatre Complex: Empire Stage, 8550
Empire Theatre Complex: Little Theatre, 8551
Emporia Arts Council Performing Arts/Concert/Children's Series, 4670
Emporia Symphony Orchestra, 1118
Empty Space Theatre, 4081
En Garde Arts, 3489
Enchanted Forest Summer Theatre, 3792
Encore Players, 2974
Energy Solutions Arena, 8497
Enfield Cultural Arts Commission, 4385
Enid-Phillips Symphony Orchestra, 1578
Enron Field, 8405
Ensemble 21 Artists, 1417
Ensemble Espanol, 6737
Ensemble Espanol Spanish Dance Theater, 2928
Ensemble Music Society of Indianapolis Series, 4620, 4794
Ensemble Studio Theatre, 3490, 7727
Ensemble Theatre, 3984
Ensemble Theatre Company of Santa Barbara, 2610
Ensemble Theatre of Cincinnati, 3705
Entertainment Series of Irving, 5646
Enumclaw Arts Commission, 5779
Ergo Theatre Company, 3491
Erica Essner Performance Co-Op, 365
Erie Civic Center/ Warner Theatre, 5448
Erie Civic Center: Lj Tullio Arena, 8122
Erie Civic Music Association, 5449
Erie Philharmonic, 1621
Ernest Bloch Music Festival at Newport, 5416
Ernesta Corvino's Dance Circle Company, 422
Ernie Shore Field, 7924
Eros Theatre, 6691
Erskinarts (The Fine & Performing Arts at Erskine College), 5539
Esoterics, 2383
Essential Theatre, 2852
Esther Boyer Performing Arts Center, 8150
Eta Creative Arts Foundation, 2929
Ethan Brown, 423

Ethel Barrymore Theatre, 7728
Ethel M Barber Theatre, 6780
Ethington Auditorium, 5967
Ethnic Dance Theatre, 301
Etowah Arts Commission, 5565
Eugene Ballet Company, 557
Eugene James Dance Company, 424
Eugene O'neill Theater Center, 7845
Eugene Opera, 2298
Eugene Symphony Association, 1592
Eunice Players Theatre, 7118
Eureka Theatre Company, 2578
Eva Dean Dance Company, 366
Evangel University Artists & Lectureship Series, 4925
Evans Auditorium, 8094
Evansville Auditorium and Convention Centre, 6864
Evansville Dance Theatre, 227
Evansville Philharmonic Orchestra, 1079
Evelyn Rubenstein Jewish Community Center, 5640
Everbank Field, 6525
Everest-Rohrer Auditorium, 6913
Everett Civic Auditorium, 8582
Everett Dance Theatre, 592
Everett Parks and Recreation Department, 8583
Everett Theatre, 4067
Evergreen City Ballet, 678
Evergreen Music Festival: Tacoma Youth Symphony Association, 5809
Evergreen State College Evergreen Expressions, 5786
Everyman Theatre, 3116
Ewing Children's Theatre, 3909, 8280
Ewu Pavilion, 8580
Experiemntal Theater, 6862
Experimental Theater, 6291
Experimental Theatre, 6241, 8527

F

Fabrefaction Theatre Conservatory, 2853
Fabulous Fox Theatre, 7449
Fair & Expo Center, 7682
Fair Lawn Summer Festival, 4992
Fairbanks Choral Society, 1846
Fairbanks Concert Association Master Series, 4158
Fairbanks Light Opera Theatre, 1847
Fairbanks Red Hackle Pipe Band, 719
Fairbanks Summer Arts Festival, 4159
Fairbanks Symphony Association, 720
Fairfax Symphony Orchestra, 1778
Fairfield City Arts, 4218
Fairfield County Chorale, 1962
Fairfield County Stage Company, 2717
Fairfield University: Department of Visual & Performing Arts, 2684
Fairmont Chamber Music Society, 5819
Fairmont Opera House, 7346
Fairmount Center for the Creative and Performing Arts, 8003
Falcon Ridge Folk Festival, 4404
Fall Arts Festival/Jewish Folk Festival, 5309
Fallon House Theatre, 6303
Family Arena, 7463
Family Caregiver Alliance, 4246
Famous Door Theatre, 2930
Fanfare Festival, 4704
Fant-Ewing Coliseum, 7134
Far-Off Broadway Players, 3060
Fargo-Moorhead Community Theatre, 3689
Fargo-Moorhead Opera Company, 2275
Fargo-Moorhead Symphony Orchestra, 1267
Fargodome, 7933
Farm Show Complex and Expo Center, 8127
Farmington Civic Center, 7612
Farmville Community Arts Council, 5241
Farrel Stadium, 8188
Farthing Auditorium, 7856
Faurot Fieldhouse, 7415
Faye Spanos Concert and Recital Halls, 6310
Fclo Music Theatre, 6113
Federal Way Symphony, 1791
Felice Lesser Dance Theater, 425
Felten-Start Theatre, 7036
Felton Center, 7037

Entry Index

Fermilab Arts Series, 4546
Ferndale Repertory Theatre, 2467
Ferrel Center, 8469
Ferris State University-Arts & Lectures Series, 4828
Ferst Center for the Arts, 6621
Fess Parker Studio Theatre, 6289
Festival Arts Association, 5593
Festival at Sandpoint, 4540
Festival Ballet Providence and School, 593
Festival Concert Hall, 7934
Festival International De Louisiane, 4707
Festival Miami, 4439
Festival Mozaic, 4319
Festival Music Society of Indiana, 4621
Festival of Baroque Music, 5083
Festival of New American Music, 4283
Festival of New Music, 5130
Festival of Orchestras, 4497
Festival of the Arts, 4842, 5179, 5712
Festival Opera, 1940
Fiddlehead Theatre Company, 3167
Fiesta Colorado Dance Company, 128
1515 Broadway Performance Venue, 7295
52nd Street Project, 3459
Figures of Speech Theatre, 3096
Fiji Company, 3492
Filament Theatre, 2931
Filipiniana Dance Company, 688
Fine Arts Center Auditorium, 5991
Fine Arts Center Colorado Springs, 6340
Fine Arts Center of Kershaw County, 8205
Fine Arts Chorale, 2125
Fine Arts Council of Sumter Performing Arts Series, 5550
Fine Arts Council of Trumbull County, 5370
Fine Arts Theatre, 8703
Finest Asian Performing Arts, 4284
Firefly Festival for the Performing Arts, 4631
Firehouse Arts Center, 5613
Firehouse Center for the Arts, 7244
Firethorn Dance Academy, 173, 175
First Arts Series, 4449
First Folio Shakespeare Festival, 4591
First Friday at the Frick Concert Series, 5490
First Mariner Arena, 7190
First Niagara Center, 7652
First Night Boston, 4776
First Night Hartford, 4389
First Night Providence, 5523
First Night Raleigh, 5261
First Presbyterian Theater, 3008
First Stage Children's Theater, 4120
First State Ballet Theatre, 140
Fisher Audtorium, 8131
Fisher Theatre, 6955, 7284
Fitzgerald Fieldhouse, 8172
Fitzgerald Theater, 7371
Fitzgibbon Recital Hall, 6883
Five Flags Center - Theatre, 6992
Five Flags Center Arena, 6991
Flagler Auditorium, 6575
Flagstaff Festival of the Arts, 4167
Flagstaff Symphony Orchestra, 726
Flambeau Valley Arts Association, 5847
Flashpoint Studios, 2735
Flat Rock Playhouse, 3657
Flathead Festival of the Arts, 4939
Flathead Valley Festival, 4935
Fleetboston Celebrity Series, 4777
Fleetwood Stage, 3458
Flickinger Center for Performing Arts, 7601
Flint Center for the Performing Arts, 6093
Flint Institute of Music, 4839, 7296
Flint School of Performing Arts: Youth Ensembles, 1232
Flint Symphony Orchestra, 1233
Floral Hall, 7030
Florence Civic Center, 8221
Florence Events Center, 8075
Florence Gould Theatre, 6258
Florentine Opera Company, 2398
Florida Arts Concert Series, 4447
Florida Atlantic University: Department of Theatre, 2757
Florida Ballet at Jacksonville, 154
Florida Dance Association, 158
Florida Grand Opera, 2005

Florida International Festival Featuring the London Symphony Orchestra, 4443
Florida International University: Department of Theatre and Dance, 2797
Florida National Pavilion, 6526
Florida Orchestra, 997
Florida Repertory Theatre, 2779
Florida Southern College, 4459
Florida Southern College: Department of Theatre Arts, 2790
Florida Stage, 2792
Florida State Opera at Florida State University, 2013
Florida State University: School of Theatre, 2828
Florida Studio Theatre, 2823, 6584
Florida Suncoast Puppet Guild, 2832
Florida Symphony Youth Orchestra, 983
Florida Theatre, 6527
Florida Theatre Performing Arts Series, 4452
Florida West Coast Symphony Series, 4482
Florissant Civic Center Theater, 3283
Flushing Council on Culture & the Arts, 5073
Fly-By-Night Dance Theater, 426
Flynn Center for the Performing Arts, 8504
Fm Kirby Center for the Performing Arts, 8190
Foellinger Theater in Franke Park, 6871
Folger Consort, 6467
Folger Shakespeare Library, 2736
Folger Theatre, 2737
Folklife Center of International House, 8151
Folksbiene Yiddish Theatre, 3493
Folly Theater, 3287, 7424
Folsom Field/Coors Events Conference Center/Stadium Club, 6333
Fond Du Lac Symphonic Band, 1822
Fontana Chamber Arts, 1243
Fontana Festival of Music & Art, 4853
Fontana Performing Arts Center, 6102
Fools Company, 5131
Foothill Theatre Company, 2529
Foothills Art Festival, Southern Hills Arts Council, 5347
Foothills Community Theatre, 3667
Foothills Theatre Company, 3187
Footlight Club, 3158
Footlight Players Theatre, 8208
Footlight Players, Inc., 3017
Ford Amphitheatre, 6157
Ford Detroit International Jazz Festival, 4836
Ford Field, 7285
Ford Theatre, 8023
Ford's Theatre Society, 2738
Forest Hills Symphony Orchestra, 1384
Forestburgh Playhouse, 3441
Forrest Theatre, 8152
Fort Bend Symphony Orchestra, 1753
Fort Collins Symphony Orchestra, 910
Fort Eustis Music and Video Center - Jacobs Theatre, 8521
Fort Griffin Fandangle Association, 3924
Fort Griffin Fandangle Outdoor Theatre, 8314
Fort Hays State University Encore Series, 4672
Fort Hood Community Music and Theater, 5623
Fort Howard Hall, 8666
Fort Lauderdale Children's Theatre, 2776
Fort Lauderdale Stadium, 6507
Fort Lewis College Community Concert Hall, 6371
Fort Myers Community Concert Association Series, 4448
Fort Myers Harborside, 6512
Fort Salem Theatre, 3616
Fort Smith Convention Center, 6028
Fort Smith Little Theatre, 2436, 6029
Fort Smith Symphony, 754
Fort Totten Little Theatre, 3693
Fort Wayne Ballet, 228
Fort Wayne Civic Theatre, 3009
Fort Wayne Dance Collective, 229
Fort Wayne Parks & Recreation Festival, 4616
Fort Wayne Philharmonic Orchestra, 1080
Fort Worth Community Arts Center, 8387
Fort Worth Opera Association, 2347
Fort Worth Symphony Orchestra, 1723
Fort Worth Theatre, 3972
Forte: the University Union Performing Arts Series, 4500
Forum, 6032

Forum Series, 4745
Forum Theatre, 3372
Fostoria Footlighters, 3736
Found Theatre, 2487
Foundation for Baroque Music, 1392
Foundation of Arts, 2437, 6033
Fountain Square Players, 3055
Fountain Street Church, 7302
Fountain Theatre, 2501
Fountain/Warren Musical Arts Series, 4607
451st Army Band, 1270
Four Rivers Center for the Performing Arts, 7106
Four Seasons Arena, 7474
Four Seasons Concerts, 4206
Four Seasons Orchestra, 1865
Four Seasons Theatre, 4114
4th Street Theater, 3003
14th Street Playhouse, 6617
Foust Artist Series, 4690
Fowler Center at Arkansas State University, 4190
Fowler Center at Arkansas University, 6034
Fox Associates, 4917
Fox Cities Performing Arts Center, 8656
Fox Theatre, 6622, 7039, 7286
Fox Tucson Theatre, 5998
Fox Valley Repertory, 2985
Fox Valley Symphony, 1820
Francis Marion University Artists Series, 5540
Francis Scott Key Auditorium, 7184
Franciscan Center of Lourdes University, 8009
Francisco Martinez Dance Theatre, 115
Frank Erwin Center, 8323
Frank Erwin Center/ University of Texas-Austin, 5590
Frank Moody Music Building, 5926
Franklin & Marshall College Sound Horizons Concert Series, 5462
Franklin County Veterans Memorial, 7982
Franklin Field, 8153
Franklin Pierce College Crimson-Grey Cultural Series, 4980
Frauenthal Center for the Performing Arts, 7322
Fraze Pavilion for the Performing Arts, 7996
Frazier Hall, 6381
Fred Bramlage Coliseum, 7047
Fred P Meagher Theatre, 8111
Fred Stone Theatre, 6606
Freddick Bratcher & Company, 167
Frederick Brown Jr Amphitheater, 6656
Frederick Chorale, 2099
Frederick Community College Arts Series, 4763
Frederick P Rose Hall, 7729
Fredericksburg Music Club, Inc., 5627
Fredericksburg Music Festival, 5735
Fredric March Play Circle, 8675
Free Street Programs, 2932
Freedom Hall Arena, 7091
Freedom Hall Civic Center, 8266
Freedom Hall: Nathan Manilow Theatre, 6814
Freedom Hill Amphitheatre, 7328
Freedom Repertory Theatre, 3830
Freeman Coliseum, 8452
Fremont Symphony Orchestra, 783
French Institute Alliance Francaise, 5132
Fresno Convention & Entertainment Center, 6105
Fresno Philharmonic, 785
Frick Collection Concert Series, 5133
Friday Night Concert Series, 4657
Friday Noon Concert Series, 4553
Friends of Chamber Music, 881, 1281, 1602, 1603
Friends of Chamber Music of Miami, 976
Friends of Chamber Music of Troy, 1470
Friends of Good Music, 5178
Friends of Historic Boonville Performing Arts, 4894
Friends of Music, 5579
Friends of Music of Charlotte County Concert Series, 4477
Friends of Music Orchestra, 1386
Friends of Music Series, 4721
Friends of the Arts Regional Art Council, 4975
Friends of the Music Hall Concert Series, 4977
Friends of the Performing Arts, 4790
Friends University Miller Fine Arts Series, 4683
Frontera, 3930
Frontier Field, 7813

Frontier Park, 8715
Frostburg State University Cultural Events Series, 4764
Frostburg State University Dance Company, 259
Fujitsu-Concord Jazz Festival, 4213
Fulkerson Recital Hall, 6059
Full Radius Dance, 182
Fullerton Civic Light Opera, 1880
Fullerton Friends of Music, 4220
Fulton Chapel, 7405
Fulton Opera House, 2303
Fulton Opera House/Actor's Company of Pennsylvania, 3811
Fusionworks Dance Company, 588
Fuzion Dance Artists Inc., 168

G

G Rollie White Coliseum, 8341
Gabbies Puppets, 2844
Gablestage, 2766
Gadsden Symphony Orchestra, 709
Gaillard Municipal Auditorium, 8209
Gainesville Chamber Orchestra, 970
Gainesville Symphony Orchestra, 1011
Gala Hispanic Theatre, 2739
Galbraith Hall Studio Theatre 157, 6138
Gallagher Bluedorn Performing Arts Center, 6962
Gallaudet Dance Company, 145
Gallaway Theatre, 5927
Gallery of Art & Design, 5262
Gallery Theatre of Oregon, 3779
Gallim Dance, 367
Gallo Center for the Arts, 6187
Galveston Outdoor Musicals, 3976
Galvin Fine Arts Center, 6975
Galvin Playhouse, 5985
Gammage Auditorium, 5986
Gamper Festival of Contemporary Music, 4733
Garde Arts Center, 6428
Garden State Philharmonic Symphony Orchestra, 1345
Garden State Philharmonic Symphony Youth Orchestra, 1324
Garden Variety Shakespeare, 2402
Gardner-Webb University Distinguished Artist Series, 5222
Garland Civic Theatre, 3977
Garland Granville Arts Center, 8393
Garland Summer Musicals, 5629
Garland Symphony Orchestra, 1726
Garret Coliseum, 5917
Garrison Theatre, 6085
Garth Fagan Dance, 498
Garth Newel Music Center, 5763
Gary Soren Smith Center for the Fine and Performing Arts, 6103
Gaslight Baker Theatre, 3995
Gaston Hall, 6468
Gateway Performance Productions, 2854
Gateway Playhouse, 3413
Gatlinburg Convention Center, 8260
Gator Bowl, 6528
Gay Men's Chorus of Los Angeles, 1942
Gay Men's Chorus of Washington, 1986
Gaylord Area Council for the Arts, 4841
Gcc Performing Arts Center, 5956
Geary Auditorium, 8628
Geffen Playhouse, 2502
Generic Theater, 4044, 8539
Genesee Community College, 5046
Genesee Symphony Orchestra, 1366
Geneseo Symphony Orchestra, 1387
Geneva Concerts, 5079
George Coates Performance Works, 2579
George M Sullivan Sports Arena, 5935
George Mason University Department of Theater, 8519
George Street Playhouse, 3378
George Washington University Symphony Orchestra, 955
George Washington University: Department of Theatre and Dance, 2740
George Washington's Series at Mount Vernon College, 4423
Georgetown University Department of Performing Arts, 6479

1113

Entry Index

Georgetown University Performing Arts Center, 6469
Georgia Ballet, 187
Georgia Dance Conservatory, 188
Georgia Dome, 6623
Georgia Ensemble Theatre, 2878
Georgia Mountains Center, 6647
Georgia Perimeter College Guest Artist Series, 4511
Georgia Repertory Theatre, 2845
Georgia Shakespeare, 2855
Georgia Shakespeare Festival, 4504
Georgia Southern University Performing Arts Center, 6663
Georgia Southwestern State University Chamber Concert Series, 1003, 4499
Gerald Schoenfeld Theatre, 7730
Germantown Community Theatre, 3898
Germantown Performing Arts Centre, 5566
Germantown Theatre Guild, 3831
Germinal Stage Inc, 2660
Gershwin Theatre, 7731
Gertrude C. Ford Center for the Performing Arts, 7410
Gertrude Russell Jones Auditorium, 8334
Getty Center, 6158
Geva Theatre, 3609
Giants Stadium, 7554
Gibson Theatre, 7668
Gila Valley Arts Council, 4172
Gilbert Studio of Dance Arts, 605
Gilbert Theater, 3656
Gilbert V. Hemsley Theatre, 8676
Gildenhorn/Speisman Center for the Arts, 7211
Gill Coliseum, 8067
Gilma Bustillo, 427
Gilmer Arts & Heritage Association Series, 4514
Gina Bachauer International Piano Competition & Festival, 5699
Gina Bachauer International Piano Foundation, 1760
Gina Gibney Dance, 428
Ginsberg Productions, 2787
Giordano Dance Chicago, 217
Givens Performing Arts Center, 7899
Gladys G. Davis Theatre, 8646
Glass Bowl Stadium, 8012
Glassboro Center for the Arts, 7558
Glema Mahr Center for the Arts, 7097
Glendale Centre Theatre, 2471
Glendale Symphony Orchestra Association, 789
Glendale Youth Orchestra, 790
Glenn Miller Festival, 4645
Glenn Wallichs Theatre, 6215
Glens Falls Civic Center, 7677
Glens Falls Symphony Orchestra, 1390
Glenville State College Cultural Affairs Commission, 5815
Glimmerglass Opera, 2209
Glines, 3494
Globe of the Great Southwest Theatre, 3998
Gloriae Dei Artes Foundation, 2122
Gloucester Stage Company, 3153
Glyde Recitals: New York Viola Society, 5082
Go for Baroque, 1583
Goethe-Institut New York/German Cultural Center, 7732
Gold Coast Opera, 2003
Gold Coast Theatre, 2800
Golden Gate International Children's Choral Festival, 4270
Golden Gate Men's Chorus, 1913
Golden Gate Opera, 1934
Golden Gate Theatre, 6259
Golden Hurricane Club, 8052
Golden Lion Stadium, 6043
Golden Panther Sportsplex, 6548
Golden Thespians, 2782
Golden West College Mainstage Theatre, 6131
Goldenrod Showboat Dinner Theatre, 3308
Goldstein Auditorium, 7835
Goliard Chamber Soloists, 1363
Good Theater, 3104
Goodland Arts Council, 4671
Goodman Theatre, 2933
Goodspeed Musicals, 2683
Goodspeed Opera House, 4384, 6398
Gooseberry Park Players, 3260

Gopherwood Concert Series, 4831
Goppert Theatre, 7425
Goranson Hall, 6711
Gordon Center for Performing Arts, 7210
Gordon Jewish Community Center, 8295
Gorge Amphitheatre, 8594
Gosman Sports & Convocation Center, 7253
Gotham Chamber Opera, 2228
Gotham Early Music Scene, 5134
Gothenburg Community Playhouse, 3323
Governors Chamber Music Series, 5795
Grace Cathedral Concerts, 4295
Grace Church Choral Society, 2229
Grady Cole Center, 7872
Graham Tyler Memorial Chapel, 7435
Grainer Stadium, 7892
Grambling University Memorial Gymnasium, 7119
Gramercy Brass Orchestra of New York, 1418
Granbury Opera House, 8394
Granbury Opera House Theatre, 3979
Grand 1894 Opera House, 5628, 8391
Grand Canyon Music Festival, 4169
Grand Casino Hinckley Amphitheater, 7347
Grand Center Grandel Theatre, 7450
Grand Junction Musical Arts Association, 912
Grand Lobby, 6704
Grand Ole Opry House, 8296
Grand Opera House, 3035, 6456, 6457, 8697
Grand Opera House Season at the Grand, 2027
Grand Performances, 4237
Grand Prairie Festival of the Arts, 4194
Grand Rapids Ballet Company, 285
Grand Rapids Symphony, 1234
Grand Rapids Youth Symphony, 1235
Grand Teton Music Festival, 5884
Grand Valley State University Arts at Noon Series, 4818
Grand View College-Nielsen Concert Series, 4650, 4651
Grand Youth Chorus, 1979
Grande Olde Players Theatre Company, 3332
Grande Ronde Symphony Orchestra, 1597
Granite Youth Symphony, 1761
Grant Park Music Festival, 4554
Grayson County College Humanities, 5614
Great American Brass Band Festival, 4689
Great American Children's Theatre Company, 4121
Great American History Theatre, 3266
Great American Melodrama and Vaudeville, 2536
Great Auditorium, 7577
Great Bay Academy of Dance, 324
Great Connecticut Jazz Fest, 4382
Great Falls Civic Center Theater, 7475
Great Falls Symphony Association, 1298
Great Gorge Festival, 4984
Great Lakes Chamber Music Festival, 4861
Great Lakes Theater, 5320
Great Neck Philharmonic, 1391
Great Performers in Westchester Series, 5068
Great Plains Coliseum, 8033
Great Plains Theatre Festival, 4668
Great River Festival of Arts, 5842
Great River Jazz Fest, 5843
Great Waters Music Festival, 4982
Great Western Forum, 6192
Greater Akron Musical Association, 5286
Greater Augusta Arts Council, 4510
Greater Boston Youth Symphony Orchestras, 1180
Greater Bridgeport Symphony Orchestra, 921
Greater Bridgeport Symphony Youth Orchestra, 923
Greater Buffalo Youth Ballet Theater, 7651
Greater Dallas Youth Orchestra Association, 1715
Greater Denton Arts Council, 5616
Greater Grand Forks Symphony Orchestra, 1511
Greater Hazard Area Performing Arts Series, 4691
Greater Miami Youth Symphony, 977
Greater New Britain Opera Association, 1967
Greater Princeton Youth Orchestra, 1340
Greater Richmond Convocation Center, 8552
Greater Trenton Symphony Orchestra, 1346
Greater Twin Cities Youth Symphonies, 1263
Greater York Youth Ballet, 587

Greece Performing Arts Society Series, 5173
Greece Symphony Orchestra, 1460
Greek Theatre, 2503, 6159
Greeley Philharmonic Orchestra, 913
Green Bay Symphony Orchestra, 1823
Green Earth Players, 3233
Green Lake Festival of Music, 5837
Green Mountain Festival Series, 5708
Green Mountain Guild, 4024
Greenbrier Valley Theatre, 4100
Greensboro Ballet, 509
Greensboro Children's Theatre, 3661
Greensboro Coliseum: War Memorial Auditorium, 7886
Greensboro Opera Company, 2266
Greensboro Symphony Orchestra/Carolina Pops, 1493
Greenville Ballet School and Company, 607
Greenville College Guest Artist Series, 4580
Greenville Municipal Stadium, 8225
Greenville Symphony Orchestra, 1681
Greenville Symphony Society, 1624
Greenwich Choral Society, 1963
Greenwich House Arts: North River Music, 5135
Greenwich Symphony Orchestra, 925
Greenwood Civic Center, 8229
Greenwood-Lander Performing Arts, 5542
Greer Garson Theatre Center, 7617
Greer Stadium, 8297
Gretna Productions, 3819
Griffin Theatre Company, 2934
Grinnell College Music Department Concert Series, 4656
Griswold Theatre, 7250
Grosse Pointe War Memorial, 4844
Grounding Point Dance Company, 46
Groundling Theatre, 2504
Groundworks Dance Theater, 522
Group at the Strasberg Acting Studio, 2641
Group Repertory Theatre, 2531
Grove Theatre Center, 2454
Grover C. Maxwell Performing Arts Theatre, 6633
Groves Stadium, 7925
Growing Stage Theatre Company, 3376
Guadalupe Cultural Arts Center, 4000
Guadalupe Dance Academy, 646
Guadalupe Historic Foundation (Santuario De Guadalupe) Dinner Theater, 7618
Guilford College Arts, 5245
Gulf Coast Opera Theatre, 2155
Gulf Coast Symphony, 1273
Gund Arena, 7970
Gusman Center for the Performing Arts, 6549
Gusman Concert Hall, 6493
Gustavus Adolphus College Artist Series, 4885
Guthrie Theater, 3239, 7351
Gwinnett Center, 6644

H

H.T. Chen Dance Company, Inc., 429
Hackmatack Playhouse, 3093
Haddonfield Symphony, 1329
Hadlock Field, 7176
Haislip Arena Theatre, 6035
Hal Palmer Recital Hall, 7038
Halau Hula Ka No'eau, 4530
Hale Centre Theatre, 2423
Hale Centre Theatre at Harman Hall, 4016
Hallberg Theatre, 6110
Hallie B. Flanagan Studio Theatre, 6997
Halton Arena, 7873
Hamilton College: Minor Theatre, 7661
Hamilton-Fairfield Symphony & Chorale, 2285
Hamilton-Fairfield Symphony Orchestra, 1553
Hamman Hall, 8406
Hammerstein Ballroom, 7733
Hammons Student Center, 7460
Hampden-Sydney Music Festival, 5736
Hampton Arts Commission, 5737
Hampton Beach Casino Ballroom, 7532
Hampton Coliseum, 8524
Hampton Jazz Festival, 5738
Hampton Playhouse, 3345
Hampton Playhouse Theatre Arts Workshop, 7531
Hampton Roads Civic Ballet, 661

Hampton University, 8525
Hancher Auditorium, 7004
Hancock Stadium, 6806
Handel and Haydn Society, 1181, 2106
Handel Choir of Baltimore, 2095
Hangar Theatre, 3446, 7687
Hannah Kahn Dance Company, 123
Hannibal Concert Association, 4900
Hanover College Community Artist Series, 4618
Hanover Symphony Orchestra, 1625
Harbach Theater, 6785
Harbor Arts Jazz Night: Portsmouth Jazz Festival, 4978
Harbor Park Stadium, 8540
Harbor Theatre, 3495
Harborside Event Center, 6513
Harder Stadium, 6281
Hardin County Playhouse, 3058
Harding University Concert & Lyceum Series, 4192
Harford Ballet Company, 261
Harlan County Arts Council, 4940
Harlem Artists Development League, 3496
Harlem Stage, 7707
Harlen Adams Theatre, 6080
Harlequin Productions, 4075
Harley Outdoor Amphitheatre, 7383
Harlingen Community Concert Association, 5631
Harlingen Cultural Arts Center: Auditorium, 8396
Harmon Fine Arts Center, 6987
Harmonia Baroque Players, 894
Harold and Charlotte Smtih Theatre, 6994
Harriet & Charles Luckman Fine Arts Complex, 6160
Harriet and Charles Luckman Fine Arts Complex, 6161
Harriet S. Jorgensen Theatre, 6436
Harrigan Cantenno Hall, 5944
Harriman-Jewell College, 4910
Harris Theater for Music and Dance, 6738
Harrisburg Area Community College, 5452
Harrisburg Symphony Association, 1627
Harrisburg Symphony Orchestra, 1628
Harrison Opera House, 8541
Harrison Theatre, 5893
Hartford Civic Center, 6408
Hartford Jazz Society, 920
Hartford Stage Company, 2686
Hartford Symphony Orchestra, 928
Hartshorn Theater, 6454
Hartsville Community Concert Association, 5543
Hartt School Concert Series, 4410
Hartung Theatre, 6699
Hartwick College Foreman Creative & Performing Arts Series, 5180
Harvard Musical Association in Boston, 4778
Harvard-Radcliffe Orchestra, 1189
Harwich Junior Theatre, 3182
Hastings Symphony Orchestra, 1301
Hatlen Theatre, 6282
Haugh Performing Arts Center, 6116
Hauser Dance Company, 294
Havens Auditorium, 6906
Havre Community Concert Association, 4933
Hawaii Chamber Orchestra Society, 1018
Hawaii Concert Society, 4526
Hawaii Ecumenical Chorale, 2028
Hawaii Opera Theatre, 2029
Hawaii Theatre, 2885
Hawaii Theatre Centre, 6672
Hawaii Youth Symphony Association, 1019
Hayes Auditorium, 7855
Hays Symphony Orchestra, 1119
Haywood Arts Regional Theatre, 3682
Hb Playwrights Foundation Theatre House, 7734
Headwaters Council for the Performing Arts, 5831
Headwaters Dance Company, 314
Healdsburg Jazz Festival, 4224
Hearnes Center, 7416
Heart of America Shakespeare Festival, 4903
Heartland Men's Chorus, 2159
Heartland Symphony Orchestra, 1260
Heartland Theatre Company, 2978
Hec Edmundson Pavilion, 8599
Hedgerow Theatre, 3815
Heidi Duckler Dance Theatre, 38
Heights Chamber Orchestra, 1543

Entry Index

Heininger Auditorium, 6804
Heinz Hall for the Performing Arts, 8173
Helander Dance Theater, 118
Helen Hayes Performing Arts Center, 7803
Helen M. Hosmer Concert Hall, 7807
Helen Mallette Studio Theatre, 6865
Helen Schoeni Theater, 6186
Helena Civic Center, 7477
Helena Civic Center Auditorium, 7478
Helena Symphony Society, 1299
Helicon Foundation, 5136
Henderson Fine Arts Center, 7082
Hendersonville Symphony Orchestra, 1496
Hendrix Theatre, 7887
Henley Street Theatre, 4051
Hennepin Center for the Arts, 7352
Hennessy Center, 7528
Henry B. Gonzalez Convention Center & Lila Cockrell Theatre, 8453
Henry J Kaiser Convention Center, 6196
Henry Levitt Arena, 7070
Henson International Festival of Puppet Theatre, 5137
Herbest Theatre, 6260
Here Arts Center, 3498
Heritage Center, 8475
Heritage Days Festival, 4946
Heritage Theater, 7327
Herman Baker Recital Hall, 6909
Herschel Greer Stadium, 8298
Hershell Carrousel Factory Museum, 7802
Hershey Symphony Orchestra, 1629
Hershey Theatre, 3807, 8130
Hersheypark Arena/Stadium, 5455
Hersheypark Entertainment, 3808
Hesperus, 1776
Hesston/Bethel Performing Arts Series, 4673
Hestand Stadium, 6044
Heymann Performing Arts Convention Center, 7126
Hi Corbett Field, 5999
Hickory Community Theatre, 3662
Hickox Field, 7648
Hidden Theatre, 3240
Hidden Valley Music Seminar, 1873
High Point Community Theatre, 3664
High Point Theatre and Exhibition Center, 7890
Highfield Theatre, 7234
Highland British Brass Band Association, 1492
Highland Summer Theatre, 3234
Highlands Cashiers Chamber Music Festival, 5252
Highlands Playhouse, 7891
Hilberry Theatre, Wayne State University, 3198
Hilbert Center Theatre, 6892
Hilda D Glenn Auditorium, 6668
Hill & Hollow Music, 5198
Hill Auditorium, 7267
Hill College, 5633
Hill Country Arts Foundation, 5645
Hill Country Arts Foundation/Point Theatre, 3991
Hill School Center for the Arts Lively Arts Series, 5498
Hillsdale College Community Orchestra, 1238
Hilo Community Players, 2883
Hilton Center for the Arts, 7451
Hilton Coliseum, 6956
Hilton Head Symphony Orchestra, 1682
Hinge Dance Company, 303
Hingham High School Auditorium, 3155, 7237
Hinkle Fieldhouse, 6893
Hip Pocket Theatre, 3973, 8388
Hippodrome State Theatre, Inc, 6519
Hiram College Concert & Artist Series, 5346
Hirsch Memorial Coliseum, 7157
Hispanic Organization of Latin Actors, 3499
Hispanic-American Lyrical Theatre, inc, 2006
Historic Brass Society - Early Brass Festival, 5138
Historic Elsinore Theatre, 8104
Historic Orpheum Theatre, 7353
Historic Palace Theatre, 7571
Historic State Theatre, 7354
History Making Productions, 3180
Hixon Dance, 526
Hobart Arena, 8018
Hobby Center for the Performing Arts, 8407

Hobson Union Programing Board Performing Artists Series, 4866
Hoffman Auditorium, 6444
Hofheinz Pavilion, 8408
Hofstra University Stadium & Arena, 7681
Hole in The Wall Theatre, 2695
Holland Area Arts Council, 4846
Holland Chamber Orchestra, 1239
Holland Chorale, 2138
Holland Performing Center-Orpheum Theater, 7496
Holland Symphony Orchestra, 1240
Hollins University Performing Arts Series, 5758
Hollywood Bowl, 6124
Hollywood Bowl Orchestra, 792
Hollywood Bowl Summer Festival, 4227
Hollywood Complex Theatre, 2505, 6125
Hollywood Palladium, 6126
Hollywood Playhouse, 2783
Holmdel Theatre Company, 3367
Holsclaw Recital Hall, 6000
Holt Arena, 6712
Homer Bryce Stadium, 8435
Homestead Sports Complex, 6524
Honeywell Center, 6947
Honolulu Academy of Arts, 6673
Honolulu Chamber Music Series, 1020, 4527
Honolulu Children's Opera Chorus, 2030
Honolulu Dance Studio, 192
Honolulu Symphony Orchestra, 1021
Honolulu Theatre for Youth, 2886
Hooper Eblen Center, 8258
Hope College Great Performance Series, 4847
Hope College Orchestra, 1241
Hope College Theatre, 7305
Hope Summer Repertory Theatre, 3206
Horace Bushnell Memorial Hall, 6409
Horizon Theatre Company, 2856
Horizons Theatre, 4032
Horn in The West, 5225
Hornell Area Arts Council, 5087
Horrabin Hall Theatre, 6797
Horse Cave Theatre, 3063
Horsefeathers & Applesauce Summer Dinner Theatre, 3053
Horton Grand Theatre, 2562, 7355
Hosch Theatre, 6648
Hot City Theatre, 3298
Hot Springs Convention Summit Center, 6031
Hot Springs Music Festival Chamber Orchestra, 4189
Hot Steamed Jazz Festival, 4386
Houghton College Artist Series, 5088
Houma Terrebonne Civic Center, 7122
Houston Ballet, 638
Houston Chamber Choir, 2352
Houston Civic Center: George R Brown Convention Center, 8411
Houston Civic Center: Gus Wortham Theater, 8409
Houston Civic Center: Jesse H Jones Hall for the Performing Arts, 8410
Houston Civic Symphony Orchestra, 1728
Houston Early Music, 1729
Houston Fine Arts Center, 6359
Houston Grand Opera, 2353
Houston Harte University Center, 8445
Houston Masterworks Chorus, 2354
Houston Shakespeare Festival, 3985, 5637
Houston Symphony, 1731
Houston Symphony Chorus, 2355
Houston's Annual Asian-American Festival, 5638
Howard C Gentry Complex, 5580
Howard Center for Performing Arts, 7154
Howard Hanger Jazz Fantasy, 1479
Howard University Department of Theatre Arts, 2741
Hp Pavilion at San Jose, 6268
Hubbard Street Dance Chicago, 203
Hubert H Humphrey Metrodome, 7356
Hudson Community Arts Series, 4793
Hudson Guild Theatre, 3500
Hudson Highlands Music Festival, 5077
Hudson River Festival, 5139
Hudson River Museum, 7851
Hudson Theatre, 2474
Hudson Valley Community College Cultural Affairs Program, 5211

Hudson Valley Philharmonic, 1455
Hudson Valley Shakespeare Festival, 3433, 5061
Huey Recital Hall, 5928
Hugh Hodgson Concert Hall, 6612
Hugh Mills Memorial Stadium, 6610
Hughes Stadium, 4285, 6373
Hulman Center, 6944
Hult Center for the Performing Arts, 8073
Humbolt State University: Department of Theatre, Film and Dance, 2445
Humphrey Coliseum, 7404
Huntington Arts Council, 5089
Huntington Beach Playhouse, 2477
Huntington Civic Arena, 8633
Huntington Museum of Art Auditorium, 8634
Huntington Playhouse, 7946
Huntington Summer Arts Festival, 5090
Huntington Symphony Orchestra, 1818
Huntington Theatre, 3697
Huntington Theatre Company, 3137, 7224
Huntridge Theatre, 7508
Huntsville Ballet Company, 3
Huntsville Chamber Music Guild, 710
Huntsville Opera Theater, 1841
Huntsville Symphony Orchestra, 711
Huntsville Youth Orchestra, 712
Hunziker Black Box Theater, 7597
Huron Arena, 5555
Husky Stadium, 8600
Hutchinson Symphony Association, 1120
Hyslop Sports Center, 7937

I

I Cantori Di New York, 2230
I Wireless Center, 6801
I-90 Expo Center, 7379
Iai Presentations, 4271
Ice Theatre of New York, 431
Icehouse Theatre, 2803
Icicle Creek Music Center, 5783
Idaho Center, 6705
Idaho Dance Theatre, 195
Idaho Falls Arts Council Colonial Theater, 2899
Idaho Falls Symphony, 1026
Idaho Repertory Theatre Company, 2900
Idaho Shakespeare Festival, 2895
Idaho State Civic Symphony, 1027
Idaho State University, 6713
Idiom Theater, 4061
Idyllwild Arts-Academy & Summer Program, 4228
Igloo, the Theatrical Group, 3501
Illinois Central College Subscription Series, 4572
Illinois Chamber Symphony, 1069
Illinois Institute of Technology, Union Board Concerts, 4555
Illinois Philharmonic Orchestra, 1060
Illinois Shakespeare Festival, 2979, 4589
Illinois Symphony Orchestra, 1068
Illusion Theater, 3241
Illustrated Stage Company, 2580
Imagination Celebration - Kennedy Center Performances for Young People, 4424
Imagination Stage, 3120
Imagination Theater, 2935
Imago, the Theatre Mask Ensemble, 3604
Immaculata Symphony, 1630
Impact: Programs of Excellence, 5620
Imperial Symphony Orchestra, 974
Imperial Theatre, 6634, 7735
Imperial Valley Symphony, 782
Impossible Players, 2677
Impresario's Choice-The Broadway Series at the Monroe Civic Theatre, 4724
Impulse Theater, 2661
In the Heart of the Beast Puppet and Mask Theatre, 3242
Inb Performing Arts Center, 8610
Inca Son: Music and Dance of the Andes, 277
Independence Symphony Orchestra, 1280
Independent Eye, 2623
Independent Presbyterian Church-November Organ Recital Series, 4141
Indian Hill Symphony, 1199
Indian River Theatre of the Performing Arts, 3832
Indian Wells Valley Concert Association, 4280

Indiana Ballet Theatre, 233
Indiana Repertory Theatre, 3013
Indiana State University Summer Stage, 3024
Indiana University of Pennsylvania Onstage: Arts and Entertainment, 5457
Indiana University Summer Music Festival, 4610
Indianapolis Arts Garden, 6894
Indianapolis Chamber Orchestra, 1083
Indianapolis Opera, 2065
Indianapolis Symphonic Choir, 2066
Indianapolis Symphony Orchestra, 1084
Indianola Little Theatre, 7393
Indy Jazz Festival, 4622
Ingalls Rink, 6417
Inland Pacific Ballet, 48, 49
Inlet Dance Theatre, 523
Innsbrook Pavilion, 8523
Insight Theatre Company, 3311
Inspiration Point Fine Arts Colony, 4186
Institute of Musical Traditions, 2100
Institute of Outdoor Drama, 3644
Intar Theatre, 3502
Inter-Media Art Center, 7684
Interact Story Theatre, 3130
Interact Theatre Company, 3833
Interborough Repertory Theater, 3503
Interlochen Center for Arts, 4850
Interlochen Center for the Arts, 286
Interlochen Center for the Arts Dendrinos Center, 7307
Interlochen Center for the Arts Kresge Auditorium, 7306
Intermedia Arts, 4870
Intermountain Opera Bozeman, 2167
International Children's Festival, 5723
International Concerts Exchange, 4208
International Dance Theater, 652
International Festival of Arts & Ideas, 4396
International Institute of Music Festival, 4274
International Music Network, 1194
International Offestival, 5140
International Seejong Soloists, 1419
International Violin Competition of Indianapolis, 1085
Interplayce, 54
Interplayers Ensemble Theatre, 4090
Interschool Orchestras of New York, 1420
Interurban Center for the Arts, 8568
Intiman Theatre Company, 4082
Intimate Theatre, 6162
Into Salsa Dance Studio, 232
Inventions, 2993
Iowa Arts Festival, 4658
Iowa City Jazz Festival, 4659
Iowa Dance Theatre, 236
Iowa Picture Show, 4660
Iowa State Center, 6957
Iowa State University Performing Arts Council Series, 4637
Iowa Summer Repertory, 3036
Ira Aldridge Theater, 6470
Irina Dvorovenko, 4296
Irish Arts Centre Theatre, 3504
Irish Classical Theatre Company, 3425
Irish Theatre of Florida, 2774
Irondale Ensemble Project, 3420, 3505
Ironwood Theatre, 3207, 7308
Irvin L. Young Auditorium, 8710
Irvine Auditorium, 8154
Irvine Barclay Theatre, 6134
Irving Arts Center, 8420
Irving Ballet Company, 641
Irving Chorale, 2357
Irving Community Theater, 3992
Irving S Gilmore International Keyboard Festival, 4854
Irving Symphony Orchestra Association, 1734
Isabella Stewart Gardner Museum, 7225
Isadora Duncan Dance Foundation, 432
Island Moving Company, 591
Island Players, 2755
Islip Arts Council Chamber Music Series, 1382, 5071
Isothermal Community College Performing Arts Center, 7915
Ithaca Ballet, 376
Ithaca College Concerts, 5092
Iudons, 6877

1115

Entry Index

J

J Birney Crum Stadium, 8108
J Howard Wood Theatre, 2820
J Lawrence Walk-Up Skydome, 5953
J. Clyde Turner Auditorium, 7862
Jack Benny Center for the Arts, 6847
Jack Breslin Student Events Center, 7292
Jackalope Theatre Company, 2936
Jackie Gleason Theater, 6554
Jackie Robinson Ball Park, 6500
Jackson Academy Performing Arts Center, 7309
Jackson Auditorium, 8461
Jackson Civic Center, 8262
Jackson Concert Series, 4662
Jackson County Community Theatre, 3002
Jackson Marionette Productions, 3243
Jackson Municipal Auditorium Thalia Mara Hall, 7396
Jackson Symphony Association, 1691
Jackson Theatre Guild, 3900
Jacksonville Ballet Theatre, 155
Jacksonville Symphony Orchestra, 972
Jacksonville University Master-Class & Artists Series, 4453
Jacob's Pillow Dance, 270
Jacob's Pillow Dance Festival, 4772
Jacobs Field, 7971
Jadwin Gymnasium, 7583
Jafrika, 2662
Jam and Company, 3506
Jamaica Center for the Performing & Visual Arts, 7691
James E O'neil Jr Arena, 7332
James E. and Rogers Black Box Theatre, 6715
James F Byrnes Auditorium, 8235
James F Metcalf Student Experimental Theater, 6772
James L Camp Memorial, 8553
James L Knight Center, 6550
James Madison University Encore Series, 5739
James R Armstrong Theatre, 6316
James Sewell Ballet, 295
James W Miller Auditorium, 7311
Jamestown Concert Association, 1396, 5095
Jan Van Dyke Dance Group, 510
Jane Franklin Dance, 659
Janesville Performing Arts Center, 5838
Janis Brenner and Dancers, 433
Janlyn Dance Company, 28
Japan Society Performing Arts Series, 5141
Japanese American Cultural & Community Center, 6163
Japanese American Cultural and Community Center, 40
Jaqua Concert Hall, 8074
Jasper Arts Center, 6905
Jasper Community Arts, 4624
Jayne Stadium, 7098
Jazz Arts Group of Columbus, 1547
Jazz Aspen Snowmass, 4352
Jazz at Drew Legacy Music & Cultural Marketplace, 4238
Jazz at Lincoln Center's Essentially Ellington Jazz Festival, 1421
Jazz at Lincoln Center: Essentially Ellington Jazz Festival, 5142
Jazz Club of Sarasota, 990
Jazz Education Inc., 5636
Jazz Guitar Series, 5310
Jazz in July, 5143
Jazz in June, 1580, 5385
Jazz in The Grove, 4886
Jazz in The Sangres, 4380
Jazz in The Valley, 5778
Jazz Institute of Chicago, 4556
Jazz It Up Festival, 5022
Jazz on The Lake: People Productions, 4277
Jazz Piano Series, 5311
Jazz Port Townsend: Centrum Festival, 5789
Jazz Society of Pensacola, 987
Jazz Tap Ensemble, 41
Je Broyhill Civic Center, 7893
Jean Cocteau Repertory, 3507
Jeanne B. Mccoy Community Center for the Arts, 8001
Jeannette Neill Dance Studio, 273
Jeff Davis Arts Council, 4706
Jefferson Academy of Music, 5329
Jefferson Community College Mcvean Student Center, 7846
Jefferson Performing Arts Society, 4713
Jefferson Symphony Orchestra, 911
Jefferson Theatre Center, 8559
Jekyll Island Musical Theatre Festival, 4524
Jenkins Theatre, 6659
Jennifer Muller: the Works, 434
Jenny Wiley Theatre, 3075
Jerome Schottenstein Center, 7983
Jerry Herman Ring Theatre, 6495
Jesse Auditorium, 7417
Jesse H. Jones Hall, 5643
Jesse H. Jones Hall for the Performing Arts, 8412
Jet Theatre, 3218
Jette Performance Company, 5021
Jewel Theatre, 6980
Jewett Auditorium, 6692
Jewish Community Center of Metropolitan Detroit, 7333
Jewish Community Center of Omaha, 7497
Jewish Community Center of Saint Louis, 7452
Jewish Community Center Symphony, 1171
Jewish Cultural Series, 5814
Jewish Ensemble Theatre, 3219
Jewish Museum, 7736
Jewish Theatre of New England, 3165
Jiffy Lube Live, 8515
Jim Butterfield Stadium, 7689
Joan C Edwards Playhouse, 8635
Joan C Edwards Stadium, 8638
Joan C. Edwards Performing Arts Center, 8636
Joan Miller Dance Players, 435
Jobing.Com Arena, 5968
Jocelyn Clark, 722
Jody Oberfelder Dance Projects, 436
Joe Goode Performance Group, 79
Joe L Reed Acadome, 5918
Joe Louis Arena, 7287
Joe's Pub at the Public Theater, 7737
Joel Hall Dancer Center, 204
Joffrey Ballet, 205
John a Walker Community Center, 7917
John Addison Concert Hall, 7205
John Anson Ford Theatres, 6127
John Brown University Lyceum Concert Series, 4193
John Chookasian International Folk Ensemble, 786
John Drew Theater at Guild Hall, 3437
John E Tucker Coliseum, 6048
John F Savage Hall, 8013
John Gardner, 437
John Golden Theatre, 7738
John Harms Center for the Arts, 4990, 7557
John Lane's Ogunquit Playhouse, 7171
John Lyman Center for the Performing Arts, 6420
John M Greene Hall, 7247
John Michael Kohler Arts Center, 8704
John Michael Kohler Arts Center: Footlights, 5867
John Paul Theatre, 5977
John S. Little Center, 6878
John Van Duzer Theatre, 6060
Johnny 'red' Floyd Stadium, 8289
Johns Hopkins, 7191
Johns Hopkins University Homewood Field, 7192
Johnson City Area Arts Council, 5570
Johnson City Symphony Orchestra, 1692
Johnson Hagood Stadium, 8210
Johnson/Long Dance Company, 623
Johnston Community College on Stage Concert Series, 5266
Johnstown Symphony Orchestra, 1632
Jolinda Menendez, 438
Jon M Huntsman Center, 8498
Jones At&T Stadium, 8423
Jones Auditorium, 7437
Jones Hall for the Performing Arts, 5641
Jones Performing Arts Center, 6015
Jones Theatre, 6360
Jordan Hall at New England Conservatory, 7226
Jordan Stage, 6988
Jorgensen Center for the Performing Arts, 6437
Jose Greco II Flamenco Dance Company, 80
Jose Mateo Ballet Theatre, 278
Joseph Meyerhoff Symphony Hall, 7193
Josephine Louis Theater, 6781
Journal Pavilion, 7603
Joyce Theater, 7739
Joyful Noise, 1975
Jpas Children's Chorus/Youth Chorale, 2083
Js Dortin Arena, 7902
Juan De Fuca Festival of the Arts, 5787
Juanita K Hammons Hall, 7461
Jubilee Community Arts, 5571
Jubilee Theatre, 3974
Judd and Mary Lou Leighton Concert Hall, 6929
Judith Svalander School Ballet, 215
Judson Theatre, 3671
Juilliard School, 440
Julia Morgan Center for the Arts, 6068
Julian Theatre, 2581
Julius Forstmann Library Second Sunday Series, 5010
Jump-Start Performance Company, 4001
June Company, 7632
June in Buffalo, 5057
Juneau Arts & Humanities Council, 4161
Juneau Jazz and Classics, 723
Juneau Lyric Opera, 1849
Juneau Oratorio Choir, 1850
Juneau Symphony, 724
Junebug Productions, 3082
Juneteenth Heritage & Jazz Festival, 4918
Jungle Theater, 3244
Junior Players, 3950
Junior Theatre, 3032
Just Us Theater Company, 2857
Jvc Jazz Festival New York, 5144

K

K Dance, 669
K.R. Williams Auditorium, 7926
Kahilu Theatre Foundation, 6678
Kalamazoo Civic Auditorium, 7312
Kalamazoo Civic Players, 3209
Kalamazoo Singers, 2139
Kalamazoo Symphony Orchestra, 1244
Kaleidoscope Theatre, 2791
Kanawha Players, 4097
Kanopy Dance Company, 697
Kansas City Ballet, 308
Kansas City Blues & Jazz Festival, 4904
Kansas City Chamber Orchestra, 1282
Kansas City Municipal Auditorium, 7427
Kansas City Municipal Auditorium Music Hall, 7426
Kansas City Renaissance Festival, 4905
Kansas City Symphony, 1283
Kansas City Symphony Chorus, 2161
Kansas City Young Audiences Series, 4906
Kansas City Youth Symphony Association of Kansas, 1293
Kansas Coliseum, 7064
Kansas Expocentre, 7061
Kansas Regional Ballet, 239
Kansas State Fair - Grandstand, 7040
Kansas State University Mccain Performance Series, 4676
Kansas University Theatre, 3045
Kaplan Jcc on The Palisades, 7590
Karamu House, 3714
Karamu House Performing Arts Theatre: Amphitheatre, 7973
Karamu House Performing Arts Theatre: Arena, 7974
Karamu House Performing Arts Theatre: Prosce Hall, 7972
Karl C. Bruder Theatre, 7033
Kate Buchanan Room, 6061
Kathak Ensemble & Friends/Caravan, 441
Kathleen Mullady Memorial Theatre, 6739
Kathryn Bache Miller Theatre, 7740
Kathy Burks Theatre of Puppetry Arts, 3951
Kathy Dunn Hamrick Dance Company, 624
Kathy Harty Gray Dance Theatre, 4029
Kathy Rose, 442
Kauai International Theatre, 2890
Kauffman Stadium, 7428
Kavinoky Theatre, 3426
Kay Bailey Hutchison Convention Center, 8356, 8357
Kay Rogers Park, 6030
Kaye Playhouse at Hunter College, 7741
Kazuko Hirabayashi Dance Theatre, 7742
Kearney Area Symphony Orchestra, 1302
Kearney Community Theatre, 3325
Keck Theatre, 6164
Kei Takei's Moving Earth, 443
Keigwin + Company, 444
Keiser Concert Series, 4961
Keith-Albee Theatre, 8637
Kellogg Arena, 7276
Kelly Shorts Stadium, 7319
Kelsonarts Performances, 4195
Kenai Peninsula Orchestra, 721
Kenan Center, 7704
Kenan Memorial Auditorium, 7918
Kenan Stadium, 7866
Kendall Drama Lab, 6418
Kennedy Center American College Theatre, 2742
Kennedy Center Annual Open House Arts Festival, 4425
Kennedy Center Opera House Orchestra, 956
Kennedy Center/Mary Lou Williams Women in Jazz Festival, 4426
Kennedy Theatre, 6674, 7903
Kenneth C Beck Center for the Performing Arts, 7997
Kennett Symphony, 1634
Kenosha Symphony Association, 1825
Kent Arts Commission, 5781
Kent Concert Hall, 8480
Kent County Theatre Guild, 2722
Kent/Blossom Music, Kent State University, 5348
Kentfest, 5349
Kentucky Ballet Theatre, 241
Kentucky Center for the Arts Bomhard Theatre, 7093
Kentucky Center for the Arts Robert S Whitney Hall, 7092
Kentucky Opera, 2079
Kentucky Shakespeare Festival, 3069, 4696
Kentucky Symphony Orchestra, 1133
Kerrville Folk Festival, 5647
Kerrville Outdoor Theatre, 8421
Kerrville Performing Arts Society, 643
Kerrytown Concert House, 7268
Keshet Chaim Dance Ensemble, 111
Keshet Dance Company, 345
Keweenaw Symphony Orchestra of Michigan Technological University, 1242
Key Chorale, 2010
Key West Contemporary Dance Company, 156
Key West Council on The Arts Series, 4457
Key West Music Festival, 4464
Key West Players, 2788
Key West Symphony, 973
Keyarena at Seattle Center, 8601
Keystone Repertory Theater, 3809
Kibbie-Asui Activity Center, 6700
Kidd Brewer Stadium, 7857
Kids 4 Broadway, 2480
Kids on Broadway, 2615
Kidstock Creative Theater Education Center, 3185
Kiefer Uno Lakefront Arena, 7140
Kilgore Community Concert Association, 5648
Killington Music Festival, 5719
Kim Robards Dance, 124
Kimbrough Memorial Stadium, 8338
Kimmel Center for the Performing Arts, 8155
Kimmel Theatre, 7013
Kimo Theatre, 7604
Kincaid Regional Theatre, 3059
King Center for the Performing Arts, 6544
King Richard's Faire, 4789
King's Chapel Concert Series, 4779
King's College Experiencing the Arts Series, 5511
Kings Point Theatre at the Clubhouse, 6594
Kingsbury Hall, 8499
Kingston Chamber Music Festival at the University of Rhode Island, 1672
Kingston Chamber Music Festival at Uri, 5518
Kingsville Symphony Orchestra, 1737
Kinnick Stadium, 7005

Entry Index

Kirk Douglas Theatre, 2463
Kirkland Art Center, 7662
Kirkland Fine Arts Center, 6768
Kirkland Performance Center, 8586
Kirkpatrick Auditorium, 8045
Kirkwood Symphony Orchestra, 1287
Kirtland Center for the Performing Arts, 7326
Kitchen Dog Theater, 3952
Kitchen Theatre Company, 3447
Kitka Women's Vocal Ensemble, 1894
Kitsap Opera, 2381
Kiva Theatre, 6701
Klamath Community Concerts, 5409
Klein Memorial Auditorium, 6395
Kleinert/James Arts Center, 7849
Kleinhans Music Hall, 7653
Klezmer Conservatory Band, 1190, 2110
Klinger-Neal Theatre, 7019
Kneisel Hall Chamber Music Festival, 4729
Knickerbacker Recreational Facility and Ice Arena, 7838
Knox College, 6786
Knox-Rootabaga Jamm Jazz Festival, 4578
Knoxville Civic Auditorium and Coliseum-Auditorium, 8271
Knoxville Opera Company, 2330
Knoxville Symphony Orchestra, 1694
Knutzen Family Theatre - City of Federal Way, 4069
Ko-Thi Dance Company, 702
Kodak Theatre, 6128
Kodiak Arts Council, 4162, 5943
Koger Center for the Arts, 5538, 8218
Kohav Theatre Foundation, 3509
Kohl Center, 8677
Kohler Foundation, 5841
Kokomo Symphony, 1088
Koresh Dance Company, 576
Koussevitzky Performing Arts Center, 7249
Krannert Center for the Performing Arts - Studio, 6844
Krannert Center for the Performing Arts - Theatre 2, 6845
Krannert Center for the Performing Arts - Theatre 3, 6843
Krannert Center Marquee Series, University of Illinois, 4601
Kraushaar Auditorium, 7194
Kravis Center for the Performing Arts, 6602
Kresge Auditorium, 6879
Kresge Recital Hall, 6787
Kronos Quartet, 846
Kularts, 81
Kulas Musical Arts, 7948
Kumu Kahua Theatre, 2887
Kutztown University Performing Artists Series, 5460
Kuumba Fest, 4454
Kuumbwa Jazz Center, 6292
Kyle Field, 8342

L

L'ensemble Chamber Music, 5040
L'ermitage Foundation Stage, 6165
L'opera Francais De New York, 2231
L'opera Piccola, 2043
L. E. and Thelma E. Stephens Performing Arts Center, 6716
L.C Walker Arena, 7324
L/A Arts, 4736
La Compania De Teatro De Albuquerque, 3401
La Connection Comedy Theatre, 2624
La Danserie, 26
La Gran Scena Opera Company, 2232
La Jolla Music Society, 796
La Jolla Music Society Summerfest, 4233
La Jolla Playhouse, 2481
La Jolla Symphony & Chorus, 797
La Mama Experimental Theatre, 3510
La Marca American Variety Chorus Singers, 1937
La Mirada Theatre for the Performing Arts, 6146
La Musica Festival, 4483
La Pena Cultural Center, 6069
La Porte Civic Auditorium, 6907
Lab Theatre, 6815

Laban/Bartenieff Institute of Movement Studies, 445
Labco Dance, 580
Labyrinth Theater Company, 3511
Lackawanna County Stadium, 8142
Lacma Monday Evening Concerts, 4241
Ladies Musical Club, 5796
Lafayette College Concert Series, 5445
Lafayette Community Concerts Series, 4708
Lafayette Community Theatre, 7127
Lafayette Symphony, 1089
Lagoon Entertainment Division, 8476
Laguardia Performing Arts Center, 7705
Laguna Playhouse, 2484, 6147
Lahaina Civic Center, 6680
Laidley Field Athletic Recreational Center, 8629
Lake Charles Civic Center - Exhibition Hall, 7132
Lake Charles Civic Center - James E Sudduth Coliseum, 7131
Lake Charles Civic Center - Rosa Hart Theatre, 7133
Lake Charles Symphony, 1139
Lake Chelan Bach Festival, 5775
Lake Forest Symphony, 1056
Lake George Chamber Orchestra, 1456
Lake George Dinner Theatre, 3452, 7696
Lake George Jazz Weekend, 1397, 5098
Lake George Opera at Saratoga, 2254
Lake Oswego Festival of the Arts, 5411
Lake Oswego Parks & Rec, 8080
Lake Placid Center for the Arts Theater, 7697
Lake St. Clair Symphony Orchestra, 1255
Lake Superior State University Cultural Events Series, 4859
Lake Union Civic Orchestra, 1799
Lakeland Center, 4460, 6543
Lakeland Civic Orchestra, 1555
Lakeland College Krueger Fine Arts Series, 5868
Lakeland Performing Arts Association, 5860
Lakes Region Summer Theatre, 3348
Lakeshore Players, 3272
Lakeshore Playhouse, 7380
Lakeside Chatauqua, 5350
Lakeside Symphony, 1556
Lakeview Arena, 7316
Lakewood Center for the Arts, 3778, 8081
Lakewood Theater, 3107
Lamar University Studio Theatre, 8332
Lamb's Players Theatre, 2460
Lamb's Theatre, 7744
Lamb's Theatre Company, 3512
Lambda Players, 2556
Lambeau Field, 8667
Lambuth Theatre, 8263
Lamp-Lite Theater, 3997
Lancaster Chorale, 2286
Lancaster Festival, 5352
Lancaster New York Opera House, 7699
Lancaster Opera Company, 2304
Landcaster Performing Arts Center, 6148
Lane Stadium, 8514
Lange Trust, 5364
Lansing Symphony Orchestra, 1245
Lantern Theater Company, 3834
Lantz Arena, 6725
Lar Lubovitch Dance Company, 446
Laredo Philharmonic Orchestra, 1738
Larimer Chorale, 1957
Lark Society for Chamber Music, 1148, 4739
Larry Wismer Theatre, 6081
Las Colinas Symphony Orchestra, 1735
Las Cruces Community Theatre, 3404
Las Cruces Symphony Orchestra, 1356
Las Mascaras Theatre, 2798
Las Vegas Ballet Company, 318
Las Vegas Civic Symphony, 1312
Las Vegas Convention and Visitors Authority, 7509
Las Vegas Little Theatre, 3339
Las Vegas Philharmonic, 1313
Lasells Stewart Center, 8068
Latimer-Shaeffer Theatre, 8528
Latin American Theatre Experiment & Associates, 3513
Laurel Arts/The Philip Dressler Center, 8182
Laurel Festival of the Arts, 5458
Laurie Auditorium, 8454
Lawlor Events Center, 7518

Lawrence Ballet Theatre, 238
Lawrence Joel Veterans Memorial Coliseum, 7927
Lawrence University Music-Drama Center, 8657
Lawton Arts & Humanities Theater, 3759
Lawton Philharmonic Orchestra, 1579
Laxson Auditorium, 6082
Le Centre Du Silence Mime School, 119, 2646
Le Petit Theatre Du Vieux Carre, 3083, 7141
Leach Theatre, 7438
League of Composers-Iscm New York Season, 5145
Leahy Good, 533
Leatherstocking Theatre Company, 3434
Leaven Dance Company, 543
Lebanon Opera House, 7536
Leclerc Auditorium, 7195
Lee Arena, 7062
Lee Civic Center, 6562
Lee Civic Center - Small Theater, 6563
Lee Little Theatre, 5992
Lee University Presidential Concert Series, 5562
Lees-Mcrae College, 3640
Lees-Mcrae College Forum, 5221
Leeward Community College Theatre, 2892
Leflore County Civic Center, 7390
Legend of Daniel Boone/James Harrod Amphitheatre, 3062
Legendary Roy Wilkins Auditorium at Saint Paul Rivercentre, 7372
Legion Arts, 4644
Legion Field Stadium, 5894
Legion Stadium, 7919
Lehigh Valley Blues & Jazz Festival, 5440
Lehigh Valley Chamber Orchestra, 1636
Lehman Center for the Performing Arts, 7639, 7745
Lenoir - Rhyne College Facilities, 7889
Lensic Performing Arts Center, 7619
Les Ballets Grandiva, 447
Les Ballets Trockadero De Monte Carlo, 448
Les Grands Ballets De Loony, 449
Les Guirivoires Dance Company, 354
Levitt Pavilion for the Performing Arts, 6447
Lewis & Clark Theatre Company, 3892
Lewis Auditorium, 5969
Lewisville Lake Symphony Orchestra, 1739
Lexington Center, 7084
Lexington Children's Theatre, 3066
Lexington Opera House, 7085
Lexington Philharmonic Society, 1128
Li Chiao-Ping Dance, 706
Liberty Bowl Memorial Stadium, 8281
Liberty Center, 3306
Liberty Performing Arts Theatre, 7431
Liberty Science Center, 7562
Liberty Symphony Orchestra, 1285
Library of Congress Chamber Music Concert Series, 4427
Licking County Players, 3746
Lied Center for Performing Arts, 4945, 7491
Lied Center of Kansas, 7044
Lifeline Theatre, 2937
Light Opera Oklahoma - Look, 2296, 5393
Light Opera Theatre of Sacramento, 1900
Light Opera Works, 2064
Lightning Strikes Theatre Company, 3514
Lilly Hall Studio Theatre, 6895
Lily Cai Chinese Dance Company, 82, 97
Lima Symphony Orchestra, 1557
Lime Kiln Theater, 4038, 4039
Limelight Theatre, 2827
Lincoln Amphitheatre: Musical Outdoor Drama, 6866
Lincoln Art Council, 5254
Lincoln Center, 6374
Lincoln Center Theater, 7746
Lincoln Civic Orchestra, 1303
Lincoln Community Playhouse, 3326
Lincoln Cultural Center, 7894
Lincoln Friends of Chamber Music, 1304
Lincoln Memorial Stadium, 7492
Lincoln Park Stocker Stadium, 6376
Lincoln Symphony Orchestra, 1305
Lincoln Theatre, 6445, 6472
Lincoln Theatre Center, 8588
Lincoln Youth Symphony, 1306
Lindenwood College Mainstage Season, 4926

Lindenwood Concerts, 2331
Linton Chamber Music Series/Encore, 5312
Linton Chamber Music Series/Encore! Linton, 1530
Linton's Peanut Butter & Jam Sessions, 5313
Lionel Hampton Jazz Festival, 4536
Lipinsky Family San Diego Jewish Arts Festival, 4287
Lippes Concert Hall in Slee Hall, 7654
Lira Chamber Chorus, 2044
Lira Dancers of the Lira Ensemble, 1039
Lira Singers, 2045
Lisner Auditorium, 6473
Litchfield Jazz Festival, 4393
Litchfield Performing Arts Series, 4394
Lithopolis Performing Artists Series, 5298
Little Ballet Theatre, 566
Little Country Theatre, 3690
Little Orchestra Society of New York, 1422
Little Theater of Gastonia, 3658
Little Theatre of Bedford, 2997
Little Theatre of Norfolk, 4045, 8542
Little Theatre of Owatonna, 3263
Little Theatre of the Rockies, 2672
Little Theatre of Winston-Salem, 3686
Little Theatre on The Square, 2988
Littlejohn Coliseum, 8214
Littman Theater & Conference Center, 6564
Live Bait Theatrical Company, 2938
Lively Arts Foundation, 4219
Lively Arts Series: Palace Cultural Arts Association, 5354
Livermore Amador Symphony, 798
Living Stage, 2743
Living Theatre, 3515
Livonia Symphony Orchestra, 1246
Lkb Dance, 340
Lyod Noble Center, 8039
Lmu Guitar Concert & Masterclass Series, 4239
Lobero Theatre Foundation, 6283
Loeb Drama Center, 7231
Logan County Community Concerts, 5291
Long Bay Symphony Orchestra, 1683
Long Beach Convention and Entertainment Center, 6149
Long Beach Opera, 1882
Long Beach Playhouse, 6150
Long Beach Symphony Orchestra, 799
Long Center for the Performing Arts, 6908
Long Island Baroque Ensemble, 1399
Long Island Opera, 2233
Long Island Philharmonic, 1401
Long Island University/Tilles Center, 5084
Long Island University: Fine Arts Theatre, 7823
Long Lake Theater, 3230
Long Theatre, 6311
Long Way Home, 4048
Long Wharf Theatre, 2697
Long Wharf Theatre Stage II, 6419
Long's Park Amphitheatre, 8138
Longacre Theatre, 7747
Longisland Mandolin & Guitar Orchestra, 1400
Longmont Symphony Orchestra, 916
Longmont Theatre Company, 2675
Longstreet Theatre, 8219
Longview Symphony Orchestra, 1740
Longwood Gardens, 8137
Longwood Gardens Performing Arts, 5459
Longwood Opera, 2119
Looking Glass Theatre, 3862
Lookingglass Theatre Company, 2939
Loon Mountain, 7537
Looney's Tavern Productions, 2406
Lorain County Community College: Stocker Arts Center Programming, 5342
Loras College Arts & Lecture Series, 4654
Loren L Zachary Society for the Performing Arts, 763
Lorraine Hansberry Theatre, 2582
Lorraine Productions: East/West, 5045
Los Alamos Concert Association, 5031
Los Angeles Bach Festival, 802, 4240
Los Angeles Ballet, 42
Los Angeles Chamber Orchestra, 803
Los Angeles Chamber Singers & Cappella, 1884
Los Angeles Children's Chorus, 1885
Los Angeles Choreographers and Dancers - Zapped Taps, 45

1117

Entry Index

Los Angeles Concert Opera Association, 1871
Los Angeles County Museum of Art, 6166
Los Angeles Designers' Theatre, 2632
Los Angeles Doctors Symphony Orchestra, 804
Los Angeles Master Chorale, 1886
Los Angeles Memorial Coliseum & Sports Arena, 6167
Los Angeles Opera, 1887
Los Angeles Performing Arts Theatres, 6168
Los Angeles Philharmonic Association, 805
Los Angeles Tennis Center, 6169
Los Angeles Theatre Center: Moving Arts, 2507
Los Angeles Theatre Works, 2639
Los Robles Master Chorale, 1935
Lost Colony, 3666
Lost Nation Theater, 4022
Lotus Fine Arts Productions, 5146
Lotus Music & Dance, 450
Loudoun Ballet Company, 662
Loudoun Symphony, 1779
Louis B. Mayer Theatre, 6290
Louis Brown Athletic Center, 7578
Louis J. Roussel Performance Center, 7142
Louisburg College Concert Series, 5255
Louise Mandrell Theater, 8308
Louisiana Philharmonic Orchestra, 1141
Louisiana Superdome, 7143
Louisiana Tech Concert Association Series, 4720
Louisville Bach, 1129
Louisville Bach Society, 2080
Louisville Ballet, 243
Louisville Chamber Music Society, 1130
Louisville Chorus, 2081
Louisville Memorial Auditorium, 7094
Louisville Orchestra, 1131
Louisville Palace Theatre, 7095
Louisville Youth Orchestra, 1132
Loveland Friends of Chamber Music, 4372
Loveland Stage Company, 3740
Lovland Opera Theatre, 1959
Lowell Memorial Auditorium, 7239
Lower Adirondack Regional Arts Council, 5081
Lowndes/Valdosta Arts Commission, 4525
Loyola Marymount University Theatre Arts Department, 2508
Loyola University Department of Theatre, 2940
Loyola University of Chicago Season Subscription Series, 4557
Loyola University Theatre, 7144
Lsu Union Great Performances Theater Series, 4703
Lsu Union Theater, 7111
Lt Smith Stadium, 7079
Lubbock Arts Alliance, 5650
Lubbock Christian University, 5651
Lubbock Memorial Civic Center Banquet Hall, 8425
Lubbock Memorial Civic Center Coliseum, 8426
Lubbock Memorial Civic Center Exhibit Hall, 8427
Lubbock Memorial Civic Center Municipal Auditorium, 8428
Lubbock Memorial Civic Center Theater, 8424
Lubbock Symphony Orchestra, 1741
Lucas Theatre for the Arts, 6660
Lucille Ball Little Theatre of Jamestown, 7693
Lucille C Little Theater, 7086
Lucille Lortel Theatre, 7748
Lucille Tack Center for the Arts, 8705
Lucius Woods Performing Arts Center: Music in The Park, 5870
Luesther Hall, 7749
Lula Washington Dance Theatre, 43
Lumiere Ballet, 7847
Luna Stage, 3395
Lund Auditorium, 6821
Lunt-Fontanne Theatre, 7750
Lutcher Theater, 8437
Luther College, 6981
Luther College Center Stage Series, 4648
Luther College Symphony Orchestra, 1106
Luzerne Chamber Music Festival, 5099
Lyceum Hall, 6976
Lyceum Theatre, 5987, 7412, 7751
Lyceum Theatres Complex, 6242
Lydia Mendelssohn Theatre, 7269
Lyell B Clay Concert Theatre, 8647

Lynchburg Community Concert Association, 5743
Lynchburg Symphony Orchestra, 1781
Lynn Canal Community Players, 2421
Lynnwood Jazz Festival at Edmonds Community College, 5784
Lyon College Theatre Department, 2432
Lyric Chamber Music Society of New York, 1423
Lyric Opera House, 7196
Lyric Opera of Chicago, 2046, 6740
Lyric Opera of Cleveland, 2280
Lyric Opera of Kansas City, 2160
Lyric Opera Theatre Street, 2309
Lyric Opera Virginia, 2379
Lyric Stage Company of Boston, 3138
Lyric Theatre of Oklahoma, 3761
Lyric Theatre Warehouse, 2613

M

Mabee Center Arena, 8049
Mabel Claire Allen Theatre, 6807
Mabel Shaw Bridges Auditorium, 6086
Mabel Tainter Memorial Theater, 4118
Mabie Theatre, 7006
Mabou Mines, 3516
Mac-Haydn Theatre, 3432
Mackey Arena, 6950
Mackey Stadium, 7519
Macky Auditorium Concert Hall, 6334
Macomb Center for the Performing Arts, 7281
Macomb Symphony Orchestra, 1227
Macon Concert Association, 4516
Macon Symphony Orchestra, 1012
Macphail Center for the Arts, 7357
Mad Cat Theatre Company, 2801
Mad Cow Theatre, 2805
Mad Horse Theatre Company, 3108
Mad River Theater Works, 3753
Madcap Productions Puppet Theatre, 3706
Maddox Theatre, 6830
Madison Area Arts Council, 5556
Madison Blues Festival, 5849
Madison Jazz Society, 5848
Madison Morgan Cultural Center, 6652
Madison Opera, 2395
Madison Repertory Theatre, 4115
Madison Scottish Country Dancers, 698
Madison Square Garden, 7752
Madison Symphony Orchestra, 1826
Madison Theater, 7080
Madison Theatre Guild, 4116
Madlab, 3722
Maggie Allesee Department of Theatre and Dance, 7291
Magic Circle Theater, 62, 2550, 2551
Magic Theatre, 2583
Magic Valley Symphony, 1028
Magical Theatre Company, 3696
Magik Theatre, 4002
Magoffin Auditorium, 8378
Mahaffey Theater, 4488
Mahaffey Theatre/Duke Energy Center for the Arts, 6588
Mahalia Jackson Theatre of Performing Arts, 7145
Maharishi University Performing Arts Center, 6993
Maida Withers Dance Construction Company, 146
Main Stage, 6421, 6568, 8591
Main Stage Theatre, 7016
Main Street Theater, 3986
Maine Arts Series, 4740
Maine Center for the Arts at the University of Maine, 7173
Maine Festival, 4741
Maine Music Society, 1147, 2087
Maine State Ballet, 249
Maine State Music Theatre, 3095
Maine Township Community Concert Association, 4569
Mainly Mozart, 840
Mainly Mozart Festival, 4288
Mainstage, 6841
Mainstage Center for the Arts, 3341
Mainstage Theater, 6293
Mainstage Theatre, 6590

Majestic Theatre, 7753, 8359
Majestic Valley Arena, 7480
Make a Circus: Arco Sports, 2584
Malashock Dance, 68
Malini's Dances of India, 665
Malini's Dances of India Troupe, 664
Mallarme Chamber Players, 1489
Malone Stadium, 7135
Mamadou Diabate, 1379
Mammoth Lakes Jazz Jubilee, 4249
Mamou Cajun Music Festival, 4712
Manatee Players/Riverfront Theatre, 2759
Manbites Dog Theater, 3651
Manchester Choral Society, 2174
Manchester Craftsmen's Guild, 8174
Manchester Music Festival, 5713
Manchester Musical Players, 2690
Manchester Symphony Orchestra/Chorale, 929
Mandalay Bay Events Center, 7510
Mandel Jewish Community Center of Cleveland, 7947
Mandell Weiss Forum, 6140
Mandell Weiss Forum Studio, 6139
Mandell Weiss Theatre, 6141
Mandeville Theatre, 6142
Manhattan Arts Center, 7048
Manhattan Lyric Opera, 2212
Manhattan Tap, 505
Manhattan Theatre Club, 3517, 7754
Manion Theatre, 8708
Mankato Symphony Orchestra, 1261
Mann Center for the Performing Arts, 8156
Mannes College of Music International Keyboard Institute and Festival, 5147
Manon Caine Russell Kathryn Caine Wanlass Performance Hall, 8481
Mansfield Playhouse, 3741
Mansfield Symphony Orchestra, 1558
Mansfield University Fine Arts Series, 5466
Manti Temple Grounds Amphitheatre, 8483
Marathon Community Theatre, 2795
Marcel Marceau Mime Theater, 3518
Marcus Center for the Performing Arts, 8689
Margaret Jenkins Dance Company, 83
Margaret L Jackson Arts Center, 7233
Margolis Brown Theatre Company, 3245
Margot Astrachan Music, 1424
Maria Benitez Teatro Flamenco, 348
Marian Gallaway Theatre, 5929
Marie Hitchcock Puppet Theatre in Balboa, 2563
Marie P. Debartolo Center for the Performing Arts, 6930
Mariemont Players, 3707
Marin Ballet/Center for Dance, 103
Marin Center Showcase Theatre, 6278
Marin Shakespeare Company, 2608
Marin Symphony Orchestra, 866
Marin Symphony Youth Orchestra, 867
Marin Theatre Company, 2526
Marina Civic Center, 6576
Marine Midland Arena, 7655
Marion Cultural and Civic Center, 6800
Marion Palace Theatre, 8000
Marion Philharmonic Orchestra, 1091
Maritime Productions, 3102
Marjorie Liebert, 451
Marjorie Ward Marshall Dance Center, 6782
Mark Degarmo and Dancers, 452
Mark Foehringer Dance Project, 84
Mark Kappel, 453
Mark Morris Dance Group, 368
Mark Taper Forum, 2509, 6170
Mark Twain Outdoor Theatre, 3295
Market House Theatre, 3074
Market Square Concerts, 5453
Markey Square Arena, 6896
Marlboro Music, 5480
Marlboro School of Music, 1643
Marquee Theatre, 5988
Marquis, 7755
Marriott Center/Cougar Stadium, 8489
Marriott's Theatre in Lincolnshire, 2973
Marshall Artists Series, 5816
Marshall Civic Center, 8431
Marshall Regional Arts Council, 5653
Marshall Symphony Orchestra, 1742
Marshfield-Wood Community Symphony, 1829
Martha Graham Dance Company, 454

Martha's Vineyard Chamber Music Society, 1212
Martin Beck Theater, 7756
Martin Community Players, 3683
Martin Luther College Lyceum, 7366
Martin Massman Theatre, 6171
Martinson Theatre, 7757
Marvin Cole Auditorium, 6638
Marwick Boyd Auditorium, 8119
Mary Anthony Dance Theatre, 455
Mary D'angelo Performing Arts Center, 8123
Mary Emery Hall, 7958
Mary Green Singers, 2302
Mary L Welch Theatre, 3856
Mary Linn Performing Arts Center, 7433
Mary Miller Dance Company, 581
Maryland Ballet Theatre, 258
Maryland Hall for the Creative Arts, 7185
Maryland International Chamber Music Festival, 4752
Maryland Symphony Orchestra, 1167
Maryland Theatre, 7206
Maryland Youth Symphony Orchestra, 1165
Marylhurst University Music Department, 5413
Marymoor Amphitheatre, 8596
Marymount Manhattan College, 7758
Maryville College, 8278
Mashantucket Pequot Museum & Research Center, 6410
Masonic Temple Theatre, 7288
Mass Ensemble, 4248
Massachusetts International Festival of the Arts, 4798
Massachusetts Museum of Contemporary Art, 7245
Massachusetts Youth Wind Ensemble, 1182
Massasoit Community College Buckley Arts Center Performance Series, 4782
Massenkoff Russian Folk Festival, 4297
Massmutual Center, 7251
Master Chorale of Orange County, 1876
Master Chorale of Tampa Bay, 2014
Master Singers, 2118
Masters of Harmony, 1932
Masterworks Chorale, 2111
Masterworks Festival, 4636
Matapat, 1380, 2253
Matchbox Children's Theatre, 3221
Mateel Community Center, 6219
Matrix Theatre Company, 3200
Matrix: Midland Festival-Celebration of the Arts, Sciences & Humanities, 4856
Matthews Opera House Society, 3889
Matthews Playhouse, 3669
Maui Academy of Performing Arts, 2893
Maui Arts & Cultural Center, 6677
Maui Community College Series, 4529
Maurice Levin Theater, 7599
Maurice Levin Theater Season, 3396
Maverick Concert Hall, 7850
Maverick Concerts, 1476, 5217
Maverick Stadium, 8319
Maxim Belotserkovsky, 4298
May Bonfils Stanton Center for the Performing Arts, 6361
Mayfair Theatre/Shear Madness, 2941
Mayo Civic Center Arena, 7367
Mayo Civic Center Auditorium Theatre, 7368
Mayville State University (Nd) Fine Arts Series, 5283
Mbt Studio Theatre, 4062
Mcafee Coliseum, 6197
Mcalister Auditorium, 8226
Mcalister Fieldhouse, 8211
Mcallen Performing Arts, 5654
Mcaninch Arts Center Mainstage, 6790
Mcaninch Arts Center Studio Theatre, 6791
Mcaninch Arts Center Theater 2, 6789
Mcarthur Sports Field, 8085
Mcc Performing Arts Center, 5957
Mcc Theater, 3519
Mccahon Memorial Auditorium, 8034
Mccain Auditorium, 7049
Mccallum Theatre for the Performing Arts, 6202
Mccarter Theatre, 3382, 7584
Mccarthy Stadium, 8157
Mccaskey Lyceum, 7026
Mcelvey Center of York, 8239
Mcclelland Arts Center, 8587

Entry Index

Mcdonald Recital Hall, 6474
Mcdowell Columns Auditorium, 7898
Mcfarlin Memorial, 8360
Mcjazz Jugend Bigband, 5491
Mckale Memorial Center, 6001
Mckeesport Symphony Orchestra, 1637
Mckendree College Fine Arts Series, 4585
Mclean Orchestra, 1782
Mcmahon Memorial Auditorium, 8035
Mcmanus Theater, 7197
Mcmorran Place Theatre, 7325
Mcpherson Theatre, 6720
Meadow Brook Theatre, 3213
Meadowlands Theater, 7555
Mechanics Hall, 7260
Media Theatre for the Performing Arts, 3816
Medora Musical, 3246
Meek Auditorium, 7406
Melbourne Auditorium, 6545
Melbourne Chamber Music Society, 971
Melbourne Civic Theatre, 2796
Mellon Arena, 8175
Mellon Jazz in Philadelphia, 5148
Melrose Symphony Orchestra, 1201
Memorial Athletic & Convocation Center, 7995
Memorial Auditorium, 6308, 7029, 7904, 8472
Memorial Auditorium and Convention Center, 7057
Memorial Coliseum, 8095
Memorial Stadium, 7533
Memphis Community Players, 3293
Memphis Cook Convention Center Complex, 8282
Memphis in May International Festival, 5575
Memphis Symphony Orchestra and Youth Symphony Orchestra, 1695
Mendel Center, 7277
Mendelssohn Choir of Pittsburgh, 2317
Mendelssohn Club, 1064
Mendelssohn Club of Philadelphia, 2310
Mendocino Ballet, 114
Mendocino Music Festival, 4251
Mendocino Theatre Company, 2523
Meng Concert Hall, 6111
Menlo Players Guild, 2524
Mentor Performing Artists Concert Series, 5356
Merce Cunningham Dance Company, 456
Mercer Arena at Seattle Center, 8602
Mercer Island Arts Council, 5785
Mercy College: Lecture Hall, 7665
Merian Soto Dance & Performance, 355
Meridian Community College Theatre, 7402
Meridian Symphony Orchestra, 1277
Merkin Concert Hall at Kaufman Center, 7759
Merola Opera Program, 1914
Merriam Theater, 8158
Merrill Area Concert Association, 5854
Merrill Auditorium, 7177
Merrill Field, 7628
Merrimack Repertory Theatre, 3160
Merry-Go-Round Playhouse, 3410
Merton Wray Theatre, 6321
Mesa Convention Center, 5958
Mesa Convention Center-Mesa Amphitheatre, 5959
Mesa County Community Concert Association, 4371
Mesa Experimental Theatre, 6377
Mesa Park Arena, 6504
Mesa Recital Hall, 6378
Mesa State College Theatre Department, 2671
Mesquite Community Theatre, 3996
Messiah 2000, 5270
Messiah College Cultural Series, 5450
Messiah Festival of Music, 4674
Metdance, 639
Metrapark, 7469
Metro Dancers, 561
Metro Lyric Opera, 2175
Metro Theater Company, 3299
Metropolis Performing Arts Centre, 6718
Metropolitan Arts Council, 5541
Metropolitan Ballet Theatre Inc., 262
Metropolitan Museum Concerts and Lectures, 5149
Metropolitan Opera, 2234
Metropolitan Performing Arts Center, 8611
Metropolitan Playhouse, 3520

Metropolitan State College of Denver: Department of Theatre, 2663
Metropolitan Symphony Orchestra, 1264
Metropolitan Youth Symphony, 1254, 1604
Metrostage, 4030
Mettawee Theatre Company, 3617
Meyer Jacobs Theatre, 6816
Meyerhoff Symphony Hall, 7198
Meymandi Concert Hall, 7905
Mfa Directing Studio, 6808
Mgm Grand Garden Arena, 7511
Miami Arena, 6551
Miami Bach Society/Tropical Baroque Music Festival, 966, 4440
Miami City Ballet, 160
Miami Civic Music Association Series, 4465
Miami Classical Guitar Society, 978
Miami Dade Community College, 4466
Miami International Piano Festival, 964, 4435
Miami University Dance Theatre, 540
Miami University Performing Arts Series, 5362
Miami University Symphony Orchestra, 1565
Miami University: Hamilton Artist Series, 5345
Miami Wind Quintet, 1566
Michael Browning Family Cinema, 6931
Michael C Rockefeller Arts Center, 7674
Michael D. Palm Theatre, 6391
Michael Mao Dance, 457
Michael Schimmel Center for the Arts, 7760
Michigan Association of Community Arts Agencies, 4823
Michigan Ballet Theatre, 290
Michigan Classic Ballet Company, 283
Michigan Opera Theatre, 2134
Michigan Renaissance Festival, 4848
Michigan Shakespeare Festival, 4851
Michigan Theater, 7270
Mid Ohio Valley Ballet Company, 694
Mid-America Arts Alliance, 3288
Mid-Atlantic Ballet, 139
Mid-Atlantic Center for the Arts & Humanities, 7549
Mid-Columbia Symphony, 1797
Mid-Hudson Ballet Company, 375
Mid-Hudson Civic Center, 7809
Mid-South Coliseum, 8283
Mid-Texas Symphony Orchestra, 1751
Midamerica Chamber Music Festival, 5340
Midamerica Productions, 5150
Midatlantic Arts Foundation Pennsylvania Performing Arts on Tour, 5481
Middle Peninsula Community Concert Association, 5761
Middle Tennessee State University, 5577
Middle Township Performing Arts Center, 7550
Middlebury College Concert Series, 5714
Middletown Symphony Orchestra, 1559
Midland Center, 8434
Midland Center for the Arts, 7317
Midland Lutheran College Concert: Lecture Series, 4943
Midland Symphony Orchestra, 1247
Midland-Odessa Symphony and Chorale, 1743, 2358
Midsummer Mozart Festival, 847, 4299
Midway Stadium, 7373
Midwest Jazz Heritage Festival, 4593
Midwest Wireless Civic Center, 7350
Midwest Young Artists, 1054
Midwestern State University: Artist Lecture Series, 5680
Milan Stadium, 8060
Mile Square Theatre, 3366
Mill Mountain Theatre, 4055
Mill Valley Chamber Music Society, 809
Millbrook Playhouse, 8141
Millenium Park, 6742
Miller Concert Hall, 7071
Miller Outdoor Theatre, 8413
Millett Hall, 8004
Millikin University Opera Theatre, 2052
Millikin-Decatur Symphony Orchestra, 1045
Mills College Concert Hall, 6198
Mills College Department of Dramatic Arts & Communications, 2535
Mills College Music Department, 4260
Mills Experimental Theatre, 6968
Milwaukee Ballet Company, 703

Milwaukee Chamber Theatre, 4122
Milwaukee Opera Theatre, 2394
Milwaukee Public Theatre, 4123
Milwaukee Repertory Theater, 4124
Milwaukee Riverside Theater, 8690
Milwaukee Symphony Orchestra, 1830
Milwaukee Theatre, 4125, 8691
Milwaukee Youth Symphony Orchestra, 1831
Mimi Garrard Dance Company, 458
Minetta Lane Theatre, 7761
Mini Dome, 8267
Minneapolis Park & Recreation Board-Summer Music in The Parks, 4871
Minnesota Ballet, 293
Minnesota Center Chorale, 2154
Minnesota Chorale, 2143
Minnesota Dance Theatre & Dance Institute, 296
Minnesota Opera, 2144
Minnesota Orchestra, 1265
Minnesota Sinfonia, 1266
Minnesota State Band, 1271
Minnesota State University Moorehead Series, 4876
Minnetonka Chamber Choir, 2148
Minnetonka Symphony Chorus, 2149
Minot Symphony Association, 1512
Minskoff Theatre, 7762
Mint Theater Company, 3521
Miracle Theatre Group, 3785
Mirror Repertory Company, 3522
Mishler Theatre, 8109
Mississippi Arts Commission, 4889
Mississippi Opera, 2156
Mississippi State University Lyceum Series, 4891
Mississippi Symphony Orchestra, 1275
Mississippi Valley Blues Festival, 4647
Mississippi Veterans Memorial Stadium, 7397
Mississippi Youth Symphony Orchestra, 1276
Missoula Children's Theatre, 3318
Missoula Symphony Association, 1300
Missouri Botanical Garden Amphitheatre, 7453
Missouri Contemporary Ballet, 306
Missouri Repertory Theatre, 3289
Missouri River Festival of the Arts, 4895
Missouri Symphony Society, 1279
Missouri Theater, 7440
Missouri Theatre, 7418
Missouri Western State College Fine Arts Theatre, 7441
Mit Guest Artists Series, 4786
Mitchell Center, 5908
Mitchell Fine Arts Center, 7087
Mitchell Hall Gymnasium, 8672
Mixed Blood Theatre Company, 3247
Mizel Arts & Culture Center, 6363
Mk Brown Memorial Auditorium & Civic Center, 8439
Mm Colbert, 699
Moab Music Festival, 5688
Moberly Area Council on The Arts, 4912
Moberly Community Theatre, 3294
Mobile Ballet Inc, 4
Mobile Chamber Music Society, 713
Mobile Civic Center, 5909
Mobile Civic Center - Exposition Hall, 6555
Mobile Civic Center - Theatre, 6556
Mobile Opera, 1842
Mobile Symphony, 714
Mobile Theatre Guild, 5910
Mockingbird Public Theatre, 3915
Modell Performing Center at the Lyric, 7199
Modern-Day Griot Theatre Company, 3421
Modesto Junior College Performing Arts Center, 6188
Modesto Symphony Orchestra, 810
Modlin Center for the Arts, 5754
Moe-Tion Dance Theatre, 344
Mohawk Park, 8050
Mohawk Players, 3411
Mohawk Trail Concerts/Music in Deerfield, 4802
Mohawk Valley Center for the Arts, 7703
Mohawk Valley Community College Cultural Series, 5213
Moline Boys Choir, 2056
Molissa Fenley and Dancers, 459
Momenta, 219
Momentum Dance Company, 151, 642
Momentum Dance Theatre, 147

Momix, 7, 134, 460
Monadnock Music, 4974
Monday Musical Club of Youngstown, Ohio, 5375
Monmouth Symphony Orchestra, 1347
Monroe Arts Center, 8696
Monroe Civic Center, 7136
Monroe Symphony Orchestra, 1140
Montagne Center, 8333
Montaineer Field, 8648
Montana Chorale, 2168
Montana Repertory Theatre, 3319
Montana Shakespeare in The Parks, 3314
Montana Traditional Jazz Festival, 4932
Montclair State College Memorial Auditorium, 7596
Montclair State University, 3391
Montclaire String Quartet, 1817
Monterey Bay Symphony, 768
Monterey Jazz Festival, 4255
Monterey Symphony, 769
Montgomery Ballet, 6
Montgomery College Robert E Parilla Performing Arts Center, 7212
Montgomery County Community College Lively Arts Series, 5433
Montgomery County Performing Arts Series, 5601
Montgomery County Youth Orchestra, 1159
Montgomery Symphony Orchestra, 715
Montgomery Theater, 3854
Montgomery Theatre, 6269
Monticello Opera House, Inc., 6557
Moody Civic Center: Exhibition Hall, 8392
Moody Coliseum, 8361
Moonlight Amphitheatre, 6319
Moore Auditorium, 7895
Moore Community Band, 1480
Moore Theater, 6880
Mooresville Community Theatre, 3670
Moraine Valley Community College Fine & Performing Arts Center, 6813
Moravian College: Music Institute, 8113
Mordine and Company Dance Theatre, 207
Morgan Auditorium, 5930
Morgan Theatre, 8482
Morgan-Wixson Theatre, 6300
Mormon Miracle Pageant, 5686
Mormon Tabernacle Choir, 2363
Morphoses Ltd, 461
Morrell Gym, 7166
Morris Fx Jeff Sr Municipal Auditorium, 7146
Morris Performing Arts Center, 6941
Morrison Artist Series, 4300
Morrison Center for the Performing Arts, 6684
Morrisondance, 524
Morristown Theatre Guild, 3911
Morton H Meyerson Symphony Center, 8362
Mosaic Dance Theater Company, 329
Mostly Mozart Festival, 5151
Mount Airy Fine Arts Center, 7897
Mount Aloysius College Performing Arts Series, 5443
Mount Baker Theatre, 4063, 8572
Mount Hood Festival of Jazz: the Governor Building, 5418
Mount Kisco Concert Association, 5107
Mount Saint Mary's College - the Da Camera Society, 4242
Mount San Antonio College Performing Arts Center, 4346
Mount Vernon Community Children's Theatre, 4031
Mount Vernon Nazarene College: Lecture Artist Series, 5357
Mount Washington Valley Theatre Company, 3350
Mountain Home Arts Council, 4537, 6703
Mountain Laurel Center for Performing Arts, 8183
Mountain Playhouse, 3810, 8132
Mountain View Center for the Performing Arts, 6190
Mountain Winery, 4334
Movement Theatre International, 3857
Mowhawk Valley Ballet, 504
Mozart Classical Orchestra, 776, 793
Mpulse Ann Arbor, 4824
Msu Riley Center, 7403

1119

Entry Index

Mt Desert Festival of Chamber Music, 4737
Mt Hood Jazz Festival, 1596
Mt. Hood Community College, 5408
Mtu/Great Events Series, 4849
Mu Performing Arts, 3248
Mud Island River Amphitheatre, 8284
Muddy River Opera Company, 2058
Muhlenberg College Concert Series, 5427
Muhlenberg Community Theatre, 3061
Mule Barn Theatre, 7465
Mule Barn Theatre of Tarkio College, 3309
Mulroy Civic Center, 7836
Multi-Cultural Music and Art Foundation of Northridge (Mcmafn), 4259
Muna Tseng Dance Projects, 462
Muncie Ballet Studio, 234
Muncie Symphony Orchestra, 1092
Municipal Art Gallery Theater, 6172
Municipal Auditorium, 8455
Municipal Theater Association of Saint Louis, 3300
Munson-Williams-Proctor Arts Institute, 5214
Muntu Dance Theatre of Chicago, 208
Muny Amphitheatre, 7454
Murray Civic Music Association Series, 4698
Murray State University Lovett Auditorium, 7099
Museum of Fine Arts Concerts & Performances, 4780
Museum of Fine Arts Series, 4489
Museums & Cultural Affairs Department, 5621
Music Academy of the West, 869
Music Academy of the West Festival, 4323
Music at Amherst Series, 4769
Music at Fishs Eddy, 5467
Music at Gretna, 5447
Music at Kohl Mansion, 4210
Music at Manoa/University of Hawaii at Manoa Outreach College, 1022
Music at Penn Alps, 1166
Music at Penn's Woods, 5508
Music at Port Milford, 5187
Music Before 1800, 1425, 5152
Music Box, 7763
Music Center of Los Angeles County, 4243
Music Center of South Central Michigan, 1225
Music Center of the Northwest, 1801
Music Center Recital Hall, 6294
Music Center/ Performing Arts Center of Los Angeles County, 6173
Music Festival of the Hamptons, 5042
Music for Mt. Lebanon, 5492
Music for Mt.Lebanon, 5441
Music Foundation of Spartanburg Concert Series, 5549
Music From Angel Fire, 1358
Music From Japan, 5153
Music From Salem, 5197
Music From Stan Hywet, 5287
Music From the Western Reserve, 1554
Music Guild, 4244
Music Hall, 6836, 7543
Music Hall Artist Series, 4475
Music Hall at Fair Park, 8363
Music Hall Center for the Performing Arts, 7289
Music in Motion, 672
Music in Ouray, 4373
Music in The Air, 5330
Music in The Great Hall Series, 4757
Music in The Mountains, 4257
Music in The Mountains Classical Music Festival, 4368
Music in The Park: Third Street Music School Settlement, 5154
Music in The Parks, 4840
Music in The Somerset Hills, 2176
Music in The Vineyards, 811, 4256
Music Institute of Chicago Series, 4604
Music Library Association, 8686
Music Mercer Series, 4517
Music Mill Amphitheatre, 8320
Music Mountain, 4392
Music of the Baroque Chorus & Orchestra, 2047
Music Recital Hall, 6002
Music Society: Midland Center for the Arts, 1248
Music Theater of Santa Barbara, 6284
Music Theatre Associates, 3523
Music Theatre Group at Lenox Arts Center, 3524
Music Theatre Louisville, 3070

Music Theatre of Connecticut, 2718
Music Theatre of Wichita, 3051
Music-Theatre Group, 2235
Musica Angelica, 1933
Musical America, 1893
Musical Arts Center, 6856
Musical Concerts at the Burlingham Inn, 5186
Musical Fare Theatre, 7629
Musical Society of the University Series, 4825
Musical Theatre Southwest, 3402
Musical Theatre Works, 2585
Musicanova, 1856
Musicorda Festival & Summer String Program, 1209
Musicorda Summer Festival, 4803
Muskogee Civic Center, 8037
Muskogee Little Theatre, 8038
Musselman Stadium, 8125
Myart, 2488
Myrna Loy Center, 7479
Mystery Cafe, 2564
Mystery Cafe Series, 4583
Mystery Dinner Playhouse, 4052
Mystic Ballet, 130

N

Nai-Ni Chen Dance Company, 328
Najwa Dance Corps, 209
Nampa Civic Center, 6706
Nancy Karp & Dancers, 85
Nancy T. Hansen Theatre, 6951
Napa Valley Opera House, 6191
Napa Valley Symphony, 895
Naperville-North Central College Performing Arts Series, 4588
Naples Philharmonic, 6558
Naropa University Performing Arts Center, 6335
Nashua Community Concert Association, 4971
Nashville Ballet, 620
Nashville Children's Theatre, 3916
Nashville Convention Center, 8299
Nashville Municipal Auditorium, 8300
Nashville Opera Association, 2333
Nashville Shakespeare Festival, 3917
Nashville Symphony, 1696
Nashville Symphony Chorus, 2334
Nassau Community College Cultural Program, 5076
Nassau Symphony Society, 1472
Nassau Veterans Memorial Coliseum, 7842
Natchez Festival of Music, 4892
National Academy of Sciences Concerts, 4428
National Ballet Company, 254
National Ballet of New Jersey, 338
National Black Arts Festival, 4505
National Black Theatre, 3525
National Black Touring Circuit, 3526
National Conservatory of Dramatic Arts, 2744
National Dance Institute, 463
National Gallery of Art/Concert Series, 4429
National Gallery Orchestra, 957
National Hispanic Cultural Center of New Mexico, 7605
National Improvisational Theatre, 3527
National Lutheran Choir, 2145
National Marionette Theatre, 4018
National Music Museum, 8249
National Musical Arts, 1168
National Orchestral Association, 1426
National Orchestral Institute, 1160
National Repertory Orchestra, 4362
National Shakespeare Company, 3528
National Song and Dance Company of Mozambique, 4301
National Sports Center, 7340
National Symphony Orchestra Association, 958
National Tap Ensemble, 260
National Theater Institute, 2715
National Theatre, 2745
National Theatre Conservatory, 2664
National Theatre of the Deaf, 2687
National Women's Music Festival, 4623
Nationwide Arena, 7984
Natya Dance Theater, 210
Nautilus Music-Theater, 3268
Nazareth Arts Center, 7814
Nazareth College Arts Center Series, 5194

Ncca Papermill Theatre, 7538
Neal S Blaisdell Center, 6675
Near West Theatre, 3715
Nebraska Jazz Orchestra, 1307
Nebraska Repertory Theatre, 3327
Nebraska Shakespeare Festival, 4949
Nebraska Theatre Caravan, 317
Nederlander Theatre, 7764
Negro Ensemble Company, 3529
Neil Simon Theatre, 7765
Nelda K Balch Playhouse, 7313
Nelson W Wolff Municipal Stadium, 8456
Neodesha Arts Association, 7053
Nesholm Family Leature Hall, 8603
Neta Dance Company, 464
Neuer Tanz, 465
Neumann Auditorium, 7027
Nevada Arts Council, 4955
Nevada Ballet Theatre, 319
Nevada Festival Ballet, 321
Nevada Opera, 2171
Nevada Shakespeare Festival, 4959
Nevada Symphony Orchestra, 1314
Nevers' 2nd Regiment Band, 1317
New Albany Symphony, 1560
New American Shakespeare Tavern, 2858
New Amsterdam Singers, 2236
New Arts Program, 5461
New Black Music Repertory Ensemble, 1040
New Britain Symphony Orchestra, 930
New Castle Regional Ballet, 574
New Century Chamber Orchestra, 848
New Century Theatre, 3166
New City Stage Company, 3835
New City Theater, 4083
New Conservatory Center Theatre, 2586
New Day Repertory Company, 3606
New Directions Cello Festival, 1395, 5093
New Dramatists, 3530, 7766
New England College Cultural Events Series, 4966
New England Lyric Operetta, 1961
New England Philharmonic, 1183
New England Presenters: University of Rhode Island Great Performances, 5519
New England String Ensemble, 1213
New Federal Theatre, 3531
New Georges, 3532
New Hampshire Philharmonic Orchestra, 1319
New Hampshire Shakespeare Festival, 4963
New Hampshire Symphony Orchestra, 1320
New Haven Jazz Festival, 4397
New Haven Symphony Orchestra, 932
New Haven Veterans Memorial Coliseum, 6422
New Hope Outdoor Theatre, 7365
New Jersey Association of Verismo Opera, 2181
New Jersey Ballet Company, 334
New Jersey City University Orchestra, 1330
New Jersey Dance Center, 335
New Jersey Festival Orchestra, 1352
New Jersey Intergenerational Orchestra, 1327
New Jersey Music Society, 1331
New Jersey Performing Arts Center, 7574
New Jersey Repertory Company, 3369, 4997
New Jersey State Museum Auditorium, 7591
New Jersey State Opera, 2184
New Jersey State Repertory Opera, 2192
New Jersey Symphony Orchestra, 1336, 1337
New Jersey Symphony Orchestra Amadeus Festival, 5005
New Jersey Tap Ensemble, 325
New Jersey Workshop for the Arts, 1351
New Jersey Youth Symphony, 1334
New Jewish Theatre, 3282
New Jomandi Productions, 2859
New Lecture Hall, 6476
New Life Symphony Orchestra, 1716
New London Barn Playhouse, 7541
New Mexico Ballet Company, 346
New Mexico Jazz Workshop, 5027
New Mexico Symphony Orchestra, 1354
New Music Circle, 1288
New Music Circle Series, 4919
New Music Directions Series, 4726
New Orleans Ballet Association, 246
New Orleans Concert Band, 1142
New Orleans Friends of Music Series, 4716

New Orleans International Piano Competition & Keyboard Festival, 4717
New Orleans Jazz and Heritage Foundation, 1143
New Orleans Opera Association, 2084
New Orleans Recreation Department Theatre, 3084
New Paltz Summer Repertory Theatre, 3457
New Perspectives Theatre Company, 3533
New Philharmonic, 1050
New Phoenix, 3183
New Raft Theater Company, 3534
New Repertory Theatre, 3164
New Rochelle Opera, 2213
New Stage Theatre, 3276
New Studio Theatre, 6743
New Theater, 6945
New Theatre, 3301
New Victory Theater, 7767
New West Symphony Association, 885
New World Symphony, 980
New World Theatre, 7020
New World Youth Symphony Orchestra, 1086
New Year's Fest, 4855
New York Choral Society, 2237
New York City Ballet, 466
New York City Center, 7768
New York City Opera, 2238
New York City Symphony Orchestra, 1427
New York Consort of Viols, 1428
New York Gilbert and Sullivan Players, 2239
New York Grand Opera Company, 2240
New York Harp Ensemble, 1429
New York Opera Project, 2241
New York Philharmonic, 1430
New York Philomusica Chamber Ensemble, 1431
New York Pops, 1432
New York Renaissance Faire, 3629
New York Stage & Film, 3535
New York State Theatre Institute, 3628
New York Street Theatre Caravan, 3450
New York Theatre Ballet/Ballet School of Ny, 467
New York Theatre Workshop, 3536
New York Treble Singers, 2242
New York Youth Symphony, 1433
Newark Museum Association, 5006
Newark Performing Arts Corporation/Newark Symphony Hall, 3379
Newark Symphony Hall, 7575
Newark Symphony Orchestra, 947
Newberry College Theatre, 3881
Newberry Consort, 4558
Newberry Opera House, 8232
Newgate Theater, 5524
Newman Stage, 7769
Newmark Theatre, 8096
Newport Music Festival, 5520
Newport Performing Arts Center, 8087
Newport Yachting Center, 8194
Newton Mid-Kansas Symphony Orchestra, 1121
Newton Symphony Orchestra, 1203
Newtown Friends of Music, 4401
Newvoices, 2393
Next Act Theatre, 4126
Next Generation Festival, 5454
Next Stage Dance Theatre, 691
Next Theatre Company, 2964
Nextstop Theatre Company, 4037
Neyland Stadium, 8272
Nicholls State University Artists & Lecture Series, 4725
Nicholls State University Gym, 7161
Nichols Theatre, 7050
Nina Winthrop and Dancers, 468
Nine O'clock Players, 2511
92nd Street Y, 5198
Nittany Valley Symphony, 1662
Nob Hill Masonic Center, 6261
Nomadics, 1402
Noonday Concerts, 1434
Noonday Concerts at One, 5155
Noontime Concerts-San Francisco's Musical Lunch Break, 4302
Norfolk Chamber Music Festival, 936
Norfolk Chamber Music Festival/Yale Summer School of Music, 4402
Norfolk Festevents, 5747
Norfolk Scope Arena, 8543

Entry Index

Norman Mitby Theater, 8678
Norris Center for the Performing Arts, 6227
Norris Cultural Arts Center, 6839
North Arkansas Symphony Society, 752
North Carolina A&T State University Lyceum Series, 5246
North Carolina Arts Council, 5263
North Carolina Black Repertory Company, 3687
North Carolina Blumenthal Performing Arts Center, 7874
North Carolina Opera Company, 2268
North Carolina School of the Arts - Roger, 7928
North Carolina School of the Arts Symphony Orchestra, 1507
North Carolina School of the Arts: School of Music Performance Series, 5277
North Carolina Shakespeare Festival, 3665, 5251
North Carolina State University Center Stage, 7906
North Carolina Symphony, 1500
North Carolina Theatre, 3675
North Charleston Performing Arts Center, 8233
North Coast Repertory Theatre, 2625
North Country Chamber Players Summer Festival: Music in The White Mountains, 4968
North Country Chorus, 2371
North Dakota Museum of Art, 5282
North Dakota State University Lively Arts Series, 5281
North Florida Community College, 4462
North Georgia College & State University Music Series, 4513
North Greenville University: Fine Arts Series, 5551
North Hennepin Community College Theater, 7343
North Iowa Community Auditorium, 7012
North Orange County Community Concerts Association, 4198
North Shore Music Theatre, 3134
North Shore Philharmonic Orchestra, 1174
North Star Opera, 2153
North/South Consonance, 1435
Northbrook Symphony Orchestra, 1058
Northeast Atlantic Ballet, 186
Northeast Ohio Jazz Society, 1538
Northeast Philadelphia Cultural Council, 5482
Northeastern Junior College Theatre, 6390
Northeastern Oklahoma State University Allied Arts Series, 5391
Northeastern Pennsylvania Philharmonic, 1667
Northeastern State University Sizzlin' Summer Showcase, 3768
Northeastern Theatre, 3139
Northern Arizona University Jazz Madrigal Festival, 4168
Northern Arizona University: Theatre Division, School of Performing Arts, 2422
Northern Ballet Theatre Dance Center, 323
Northern Illinois University Fine Arts Series, 4565
Northern Lights Playhouse, 4112
Northern Ohio Youth Orchestras, 1563
Northern Showcase Concert Association, 4934
Northern Star Arena, 7561
Northland Pines High School, 8660
Northland Symphony Orchestra, 1284
Northlight Theatre, 2986
Northrop Auditorium, 7358
Northrop Dance Season, 297
Northshore Center for the Performing Arts, 6835
Northside Theatre Company, 2600
Northwest Choirs, 2384
Northwest College, 5882
Northwest Corner Young Artists Series, 4405
Northwest Dance Project, 562
Northwest Florida Ballet, 152
Northwest Folklife Festival, 5797
Northwest Indiana Symphony Orchestra and Society, 1093
Northwest Iowa Symphony Orchestra, 1114
Northwest Missouri State University Performing Arts Series, 4911
Northwest Puppet, 4084
Northwest Symphony Orchestra, 1800
Northwestern State University Concert Series, 4715

Northwestern University Summer Drama Festival, 4577
Northwestern University Theatre and Interpretation Center, 2965
Northwoods Concert Association, 5864
Norton Center for the Arts, 7081
Norton Hall, 7660
Norwalk Symphony Orchestra, 937
Norwalk Youth Symphony, 938
Notara Dance Theatre, 585
Notre Dame De Namur Ralston Concert Series, 4202
Notre Dame of Maryland University, 4753
Notre Dame Stadium, 6932
Nova Vista Symphony, 883
Nutmeg Ballet, 133
Nyack College Program of Cultural Events, 5175
Nyc Bhangra Dance Company, 469
Nyk Productions, 4450

O

O'brien Field, 6726
O'connell Theatre, 6764
O'neill Center, 6397
O'rourke Center for the Performing Arts, 6744
O'shaughnessy Theatre, 7374
Oahu Choral Society, 2031
Oak Park Festival Theatre, 2980
Oak Ridge Civic Music Association, 1697, 5583
Oak Ridge Playhouse, 3921
Oakdale Theatre, 6442
Oakland Ballet, 53
Oakland East Bay Symphony, 815
Oakland Opera Theater, 1895
Oakland Youth Chorus, 1896
Oakland Youth Orchestra, 816
Oakmont Concert Series, 4331
Oakwood College Arts & Lectures, 4146
Oberlin Baroque Ensemble, 1564
Oberlin Baroque Performance Institute & Festival, 5360
Oberlin College Conservatory of Music Artist: Recital Series, 5361
Oberlin Theater and Dance Program, 539
Obo Addy Master Drummer, 563
Ocala Symphony Orchestra, 982
Occidental College Artist Series, 4245
Occidental College Department of Theatre, 2512
Ocean Center, 6501
Ocean City Pops, 1338
Ocean County College Fine & Performing Arts Select-A-Series, 5020
Ocean Professional Theatre Company, 3358
Ocean State Theatre, 3866
Ocheami African Dance Company, 681
Octorium, 6914
Odc Theater, 86
Odc Theatre, 6262
Oddfellows Playhouse, 2691
Odeum Sports & Expo Center, 6846
Odyssey Dance Theatre, 649
Odyssey Theatre Ensemble, 2513
Off Broadway Theatre, 4008
Off Square Theatre Company, 4138
Off-Broadway Musical Theatre, 3262
Offstage Theatre, 4034
Ogdensburg Command Performances, 3602, 5176
Oglebay Institute, 5826
Oglethorpe University Theatre, 6624
Oglethorpe University-Arts and Ideas at Oglethorpe, 4506
Ogunquit Playhouse, 3103
Ohio Ballet, 512
Ohio Chamber Orchestra, 1519
Ohio Dance Theatre, 538
Ohio Light Opera, 2290
Ohio Northern University Artist Series, 5284
Ohio Outdoor Historical Drama Association, 5358
Ohio Stadium, 7985
Ohio State University of Dance, 527
Ohio State University-Department of Theatre, 3723
Ohio Theatre, 3537, 7986
Ohio University Performing Arts Series, 5290
Ohio University: School of Music Center, 7944

Ohio Wesleyan University Performing Arts Series, 5341
Oinkari Basque Dancers, 196
Ojai Music Festival, 4262
Ojai Shakespeare Festival, 4263
Oklahoma Baptist University Artist Series, 5389
Oklahoma Children's Theatre, 3762
Oklahoma City Ballet, 552
Oklahoma City Philharmonic Orchestra, 1584
Oklahoma City Zoo Amphitheatre, 8046
Oklahoma Festival Ballet, 550
Oklahoma Mozart International Festival, 1577, 5379
Oklahoma Opera & Musical Theater Company, 3763
Oklahoma Opera and Music Theater Company, 2295
Oklahoma Shakespeare in The Park, 3764
Oklahoma State University Allied Arts, 5390
Okoboji Summer Theatre, 7419
Old Bastrop Opera House, 8328
Old Colony Players, 3681
Old Creamery Theatre, 6996
Old Creamery Theatre Company, 3029
Old First Concerts, 4303
Old Globe, 2565
Old Jail Art Center, 8315
Old Log Theater, 3228
Old Lyric Repertory Company, 4007
Old Main Theater, 8573
Old National Centre, 6897
Old Opera House Theatre Company, 8624
Old Pasadena Jazz Festival - Jazzfest West, 4197
Old Timers Concert Series, 4938
Old Town Playhouse, 3216
Old Tucson Studios, 6003
Oldcastle Theatre Company, 4017
Ole Olsen Memorial Theatre, 6936
Olin Arts Center, 7169
Oliver C Dawson Stadium, 8234
Olney Theatre Center, 3128
Olympia Symphony Orchestra, 1794
Olympic Ballet Theatre, 676
Olympic Center, 7698
Olympic College, 5774
Olympic Music Festival, 5798
Omaha Area Youth Orchestras, 1308
Omaha Civic Auditorium, 7498
Omaha Community Playhouse, 3333
Omaha Symphony, 1309
Omaha Symphony Chamber Orchestra, 1310
Omaha Theatre Company for Young People, 3334
Omilami Productions/People's Survival Theatre, 2860
Omni Auditorium, 6491
Omni Foundation for the Performing Arts, 4304
On the Boards, 5799
171 Cedar Arts Center, 7663
One Way Puppets, 2777
One World Performing Arts, 8061
One World Theatre, 8324
Onion River Arts Council: Celebration Series, 5715
Onondaga Civic Symphony Orchestra, 1365
Onstage in Bedford, 3938
Ontological-Hysteric Theater, 3538
Open Book, 3539
Open Eye Figure Theatre, 3249
Open Eye Theater, 3454
Open Eye: New Stagings, 3540, 7770
Open Fist Theatre Company, 2475
Open Hand Theater, 3625
Open Sky, 4766
Open Stage of Harrisburg, 3805
Openstage Theatre and Company, 2670
Opera a La Carte, 1888
Opera Birmingham, 1840
Opera Boston, 2107
Opera Camerata of Washington, 1989
Opera Carolina, 2262
Opera Circle, 2281
Opera Colorado, 1954
Opera Columbus, 2283
Opera Company of Middlebury, 2370
Opera Company of Philadelphia, 2311
Opera Delaware, 1980

Opera Ebony, 2244
Opera Fairbanks, 1848
Opera for the Young, 2396
Opera Fort Collins, 1958
Opera Grand Rapids, 2136
Opera Guild, 2004
Opera House Theatre Company, 3684
Opera Idaho, 2034
Opera Illinois, 2057
Opera in The Heights, 2356
Opera in The Ozarks at Inspiration Point, 1861
Opera in The Rock, 1864
Opera Lafayette, 4430
Opera Lite, 2135
Opera Louisiane, 2082
Opera Memphis, 2332
Opera Music Theater International, 1990
Opera New England, 2108
Opera North, 2173
Opera Northeast/Children's Opera Theatre, 2245
Opera Omaha, 2169
Opera Omnia, 2211
Opera Orchestra of New York, 2246
Opera Providence, 2325
Opera Roanoke, 2377
Opera San Jose, 1929
Opera Santa Barbara, 1931
Opera Saratoga, 2255
Opera Southwest, 2196
Opera Theatre of No Virginia, 2372
Opera Theatre of Saint Louis, 2163
Opera to Go, 1851
Opera Vivente, 2096
Opera Western Reserve, 2291
Operamission, 2247
Orange Bowl Stadium, 6552
Orange City Arts Council, 4663
Orange Coast College Community Education, 4214
Orange County Convention Center, 6569
Orange County Youth Symphony Orchestra, 818
Orange Park Community Theatre, 2804
Oratorio Society of New York, 2248
Oratorio Society of Utah, 2364
Orcas Theater & Community Center, 5770
Orchard Park Symphony, 1450
Orchestra at Temple Square, 1762
Orchestra Hall, 6745, 7359
Orchestra New England, 933, 946
Orchestra Nova (San Diego), 1905
Orchestra of New Spain, 1717
Orchestra of Northern New York, 1454
Orchestra of St. Luke's, 1436
Orchestra of St. Peter by The Sea, 1322
Orchestra Seattle & Seattle Chamber Singers, 2385
Ordway Center for the Performing Arts, 7375
Oregon Bach Festival, 1593, 5405
Oregon Ballet Theatre, 564
Oregon Children's Theatre, 3786
Oregon Coast Music Festival, 5402
Oregon Contemporary Theatre, 3775
Oregon East Symphony, 1599
Oregon Fantasy Theatre, 3776
Oregon Festival of American Music, 5406
Oregon Mozart Players, 1594
Oregon Shakespeare Festival, 8062
Oregon Shakespeare Festival: Black Swan Theater, 8063
Oregon Shakespearean Festival Association, 3771, 5400
Oregon Symphony, 1605
Organic Theater Company, 2966
Orlando Ballet, 163
Orlando Broadway Dinner Theatre, 2806
Orlando Centroplex, 6570
Orlando Opera, 2007
Orlando Philharmonic Orchestra, 984
Orlando Shakespeare Theater, 2807
Orlando-Ucf Shakespeare Festival, 4469
Ormao Dance Company, 120
Oroville Concert Association, 4264
Oroville State Theater, 6200
Orpheum Theater, 7499
Orpheum Theatre, 2968, 6263, 7235, 7500, 7771, 8285
Orpheus Chamber Orchestra, 1437
Orpheus Male Chorus of Phoenix, 1853

1121

Entry Index

Orpheus Theatre, 3603
Orrie De Nooyer Auditorium, 7559
Osceloa County Stadium & Sports Complex, 6538
Osceola Center for the Arts, 6537
Oshkosh Symphony Orchestra, 1833
Osu-Corvallis Symphony Orchestra, 1590
Oswego Harbor Festivals, 5182
Other Minds Music Festival, 4305
Ottawa Municipal Auditorium, 7054
Ottawa Municipal Auditorium Entertainment Series, 4677
Otterbein University, 5372
Ottumwa Symphony Orchestra, 1112
Ouachita Baptist University Harvey & Bernice Jones Performing Arts Center, 6016
Ouachita Baptist University: Artists Series, 4183
Out North - Vsa Alaska, 2417
Ovens Auditorium, 7875
Overbrook Theater, 7323
Overland Park Arts Commission, 4678
Overture Center for the Arts, 8679
Owensboro Sports, 7103
Owensboro Symphony Orchestra, 1134
Oxnard Civic Auditorium, 6201
Oyster Bay Arts Council, 5104
Ozark Actors Theatre, 3296
Ozark Civic Center, 5920

P

P Brown County Arena, 8668
Pabst Theatre, 8692
Pac Auditorium, 5947
Pac Concert Hall, 8574
Pac Mainstage Theater, 8575
Pacific Boychoir Academy, 1897
Pacific Chamber Symphony, 812
Pacific Chorale, 1930
Pacific Composers Forum, 4882
Pacific Conservatory of the Performing Arts, 6299
Pacific Lutheran University Program Board, 5810
Pacific Northwest Ballet, 682
Pacific Repertory Theatre/Carmel Shakespeare Festival, 2455
Pacific Symphony, 868
Pacific Union College Fine Arts Series, 4200
Pacific University Community Wind Ensemble, 1595
Paddywhack, 1505
Paducah Community College Fine Arts Center, 7107
Paducah Symphony Orchestra, 1135
Painted Bride Art Center, 8159
Pala Opera Association, 2249
Palace at Auburn Hills, 7273
Palace Civic Center, 7999
Palace of Fine Arts Theatre, 6264
Palace Performing Arts Center, 7625
Palace Theatre, 3744, 6423, 7539, 7772, 8126
Palace Theatre of the Arts, 2706
Palestine Civic Center Complex, 8438
Palm Beach Atlantic College: Department of Theatre, 2838
Palm Beach Community College Performing Arts Center, 6484
Palm Beach Opera, 2017
Palm Beach Pops, 1001
Palm Beach Symphony, 986
Palm Springs Convention Center, 6204
Palmer Auditorium, 6429
Palmer Theatre, 5913
Palo Alto Children's Theatre, 2539
Palo Alto Players, 2540
Pampa Civic Ballet, 645
Pan American Center, 5030, 7614
Pan American Musical Art Research, 7773
Pan Asian Repertory Theatre, 3541
Panama City Music Association Series, 4473
Pandora's Box Theatre Company, 3427
Pangea World Theater, 3250
Panida Theatre, 2901
Panola Playhouse, 7408
Panoply Arts Festival, 4147
Paper Bag Players, 3542
Paper Mill Playhouse, 3373, 7567

Papermill Theatre/North County Center for the Arts, 3346
Paradise Performing Arts Center, 6206
Paradise Theatre, 4071
Paradise Valley Jazz Party, 4170
Paramount Arts Center, 7074
Paramount Arts Centre Performing Arts Series, 4545
Paramount Center for the Arts, 7805
Paramount Theater for the Performing Arts, 8325
Paramount Theater Visuals & Arts Center, 7369
Paramount Theatre, 6199, 6719, 6969
Parenthesis Theatre Club, 2875
Paris Junior College, 8440
Park Avenue Theatrical Group, 3543
Park City & Salt Lake Music Festival, 5692
Park City Film Music Festival, 5693
Park City Jazz Festival, 5694
Park College Alumni Hall Theatre, 7436
Park Place Hotel, 7331
Park Playhouse Incorporated, 3408
Park Square Theatre Company, 3269
Park Theatre Performing Arts Centre, 7595
Parker Auditorium, 6884
Parker Playhouse, 6508
Parsons Dance Company, 470
Partial Comfort Productions, 3544
Pasadena Civic Auditorium, 6208
Pasadena Civic Ballet, Inc., 57
Pasadena Conservatory of Music, 823
Pasadena Dance Theatre, 58
Pasadena Playhouse, 2542
Pasadena Playhouse - Mainstage Theatre, 6209
Pasadena Pops Orchestra, 824
Pasadena Symphony, 825
Pasco Schools Center for the Arts at River Ridge, 6559
Pasquerilla Performing Arts Center, 8134, 8135
Passage Theatre Company, 3389
Passaic County Community College Series, 5011
Pat Cannon's Foot & Fiddle Dance Company, 502
Patricia George Decio Theatre, 6933
Patrick G and Shirley W Ryan Opera Center, 2048
Patrick L O'malley Theatre, 6746
Patriot Center, 8520
Patriots Theater at the War Memorial, 3390, 7592
Paul and Vi Loo Theatre, 6679
Paul Brown Stadium, 7956
Paul Bunyan Playhouse, 3222
Paul Creative Arts Center, 7529
Paul Dresher Ensemble, 849
Paul G. Robinson Theater, 6922
Paul Madore Chorale, 2124
Paul Mellon Arts Center, 6443
Paul Snow Memorial Stadium, 5905
Paul Taylor Dance Company, 471
Paul W Ogle Cultural & Community Center, 6923
Pauley Pavilion, 6174
Pavilion & Events Center Inc., 7503
Pawling Concert Series, 5183
Pca Great Performances, 4742
Pcca Festival at Little Buffalo, 5472
Pcpa Theaterfest, 2617
Pdac/Arts for All, 125
Peabody Auditorium, 6502
Peabody Conservatory of Music, 1157
Peace Center for the Performing Arts, 8227
Peach State Summer Theatre, 2880
Pearce Auditorium, 6649
Pearl Theatre Company, 3545
Pearson Auditorium, 7616
Peculiar Works Project, 3546
Peery's Egyptian Theatre, 8486
Peforming Arts Center, 8345
Pegasus Players, 2942
Pegasus Theatre, 3953
Pella Opera House, 2074
Pend Oreille Arts Council, 4541
Pendleton Convention Center, 8088
Pendragon Theatre, 3618
Penfield Smyphony Orchestra, 1453
Penfold Theatre, 3931
Penguin Repertory Company, 3623
Peninsula Ballet Theatre, 100
Peninsula Dance Theatre, 675

Peninsula Players, 2780, 4111
Peninsula Symphony Orchestra, 800
Pennsylvania Academy of Ballet, 573
Pennsylvania Ballet, 577
Pennsylvania Centre Stage, 8187
Pennsylvania Dance Theatre, 584
Pennsylvania Renaissance Faire, 5442
Pennsylvania Shakespeare Festival, 3799, 5437
Pennsylvania Youth Ballet, 568
Pennyroyal Arts Council Series, 4692
Penobscot Theatre Company, 3092
Pensacola Bay Center, 6577
Pensacola Junior College Performing Arts Center, 6578
Pensacola Little Theatre, 2812
Pensacola Opera, 2009
Pensacola Symphony Orchestra, 988
Pentacle Theatre, 3789
Pentangle Council on The Arts and The Woodstock Town Hall Theatre, 5721
Penumbra Theatre Company, 3270
People's Light and Theatre Company, 3814
Peoples' Symphony Concerts, 1438, 5156
Peoria Ballet, 220
Peoria Civic Center, 4594, 6817, 6818
Peoria Players Theatre, 2983
Peoria Sports Complex, 5961
Peoria Symphony Orchestra, 1061
Pepperdine University Orchestra, 808
Pepperdine University Smothers Theatre, 6185
Pepsi Arena, 7626
Pepsi Center, 6365
Pepsi Coliseum, 6887
Pepsico Theatre, 6401
Perani Arena and Event Center, 7297
Performance Network of Ann Arbor, 3190
Performance Riverside, 2547
Performance Space 122, 7774
Performing Arts Association, 4559
Performing Arts Association of Saint Joseph, 4915
Performing Arts at Hamilton, 5060
Performing Arts at Lawrence, 5827
Performing Arts Center, 6872
Performing Arts Center of Greater Miami Foundation, 6553
Performing Arts Chicago, 1041, 2943
Performing Arts Fort Worth, Inc, 5626
Performing Arts Foundation, 5874
Performing Arts Presentations, 4281
Performing Arts School of Worcester, 7261
Performing Arts Series, 7055
Performing Arts Series at Shepherd, 5823
Performing Arts Series for Students, 4566, 4567
Performing Arts Series of Indiana State University, 4632
Performing Arts Society of Acadiana Series, 4709
Performing Arts Society of South Florida, 4436
Performing Arts Theatre, 6285
Peridance Contemporary Dance Company, 472
Perishable Theatre, 8197
Permian Playhouse of Odessa, 3999
Perot Theatre, 8464
Perry Players, 2877
Perseverance Theatre, 2419
Pershing Center, 7493
Persona Grata Productions, 2587
Perspective Dance Theatre/Reno Ballet, 101
Petaluma City Ballet, 59
Pete Maravich Assembly Center, 7112
Pete Mathews Coliseum, 5906
Peter Nero and The Philly Pops, 1644
Peterborough Players, 3351
Petrillo Music Shell, 6747
Petronio, 485
Petrucci's Dinner Theatre, 3125
Pfeiffer University Artist Series, 5257
Pge Park, 8097
Pheasant Run Theatre, 2987
Phelps-Stokes Auditorium at Berea College, 7076
Philadelphia Chamber Music Society, 1645
Philadelphia Classical Guitar Society, 1646
Philadelphia Classical Symphony, 1650
Philadelphia Dance Company, 578
Philadelphia Foundation, 5382
Philadelphia Gay Men's Chorus, 2312

Philadelphia Orchestra, 1647
Philadelphia Singers, 2313
Philadelphia String Quartet, 1648
Philadelphia Theatre Company, 3836
Philadelphia Youth Orchestra, 1649
Philharmonia Baroque Orchestra, 850
Philharmonia of Greensboro, 1494
Philharmonia Virtuosi Corporation, 1448
Philharmonic Center for the Arts, 981
Philharmonic of Southern New Jersey, 1332
Philharmonic Orchestra of Indianapolis, 1087
Philharmonic Society of Orange County, 794
Philip Lorenz Memorial Keyboard Concerts, 787
Philip Lynch Theatre, 6832
Philips Arena, 6625
Phillippe Auditorium, 6910
Phillips Center, 6520
Phillips Collection Sunday Concerts, 4431
Philomusica Choir, 2178
Phipps Center for the Arts, 8670
Phoenix Arts Association Theatre/Westcoast Playwrights Alliance, 2588
Phoenix Bach Choir, 1854
Phoenix Boys Choir, 1855
Phoenix Chamber Music Society, 728
Phoenix Convention Center - Ballrooms, 5970
Phoenix Convention Center - Symphony Hall, 5975
Phoenix Stages, 5971
Phoenix Symphony, 729
Phoenix Theatre, 3014
Phoenix Theatre for Children, 3724
Phyllis Rose Dance Company, 473
Piano Summer at New Paltz, 5108
Pianofest, 5070
Piccadilly Puppets Company, 2872
Piccolo Opera Company, 2002
Piccolo Spoleto Festival, 5533
Pick of the Crop Dance, 501
Pick Up Performance Company, 474
Pick-Staiger Concert Hall, 6783
Pickard Theatre, 7167
Picketwire Players, 2674, 6385
Pickwick Players, 2621
Pico Rivera Sports Arena, 6322
Piedmont Chamber Singers, 2271
Piedmont Opera Theatre, 2272
Piedmont Players Theatre, 3678
Pier One Theatre, 5941
Pierre Community Concerts Association, 5557
Piffaro: the Renaissance Band, 1651
Pike Performing Arts Center, 6898
Pikes Peak Center, 6341
Pikeville Concert Association Series, 4699
Pilgram Theater Research & Performance Collaboration, 3132
Pillsbury House Theatre, 3251
Pilobolus Dance Theatre, 135
Pima Community College for the Arts, 4178
Pinal County Fine Arts Council: Arts in The Desert, 4165
Pinch N' Ouch Theatre, 2861
Pine Bluff Convention Center Arena, 6046
Pine Bluff Convention Center Auditorium, 6045
Pine Bluff Symphony Orchestra, 756
Pine Cone-Piedmont Council of Traditional Music, 5264
Pine Hills Lodge and Dinner Theatre, 2479
Pine Knob Theatre, 3056
Pine Mountain Music Festival, 4845
Pinellas Youth Symphony, 996
Piney Woods Fine Arts Association, 5606
Ping Chong & Company, 3547
Pioneer Amphitheatre, 8339
Pioneer Center for the Performing Arts, 7520
Pioneer Courthouse Square, 8098
Pioneer Dance Arts, 687
Pioneer Field, 8698
Pioneer Playhouse of Kentucky, 3057
Pioneer Theatre Company, 4009
Pioneer Valley Symphony, 1196
Pipe Dreams Studio Theatre, 6769
Piper's Opera House, 7523
Pirate Playhouse, 2819
Pitman Theatre, 8693
Pitt County Arts Council, 5250
Pitt Stadium, 8176

Entry Index

Pittsburg State University Solo & Chamber Music Series, 4679
Pittsburgh Arts Council, 5493
Pittsburgh Ballet Theatre, 582
Pittsburgh Camerata, 2318
Pittsburgh Chamber Music Society, 1654
Pittsburgh Civic Arena, 8177
Pittsburgh Civic Light Opera, 2319
Pittsburgh Concert Chorale, 2320
Pittsburgh Dance Council, 583
Pittsburgh International Children's Theater, 3843
Pittsburgh Irish & Classical Theatre, 3844
Pittsburgh Musical Theater, 3845
Pittsburgh New Music Ensemble, 1655
Pittsburgh Opera, 2321
Pittsburgh Playhouse, 5494
Pittsburgh Public Theater, 3846
Pittsburgh Symphony Orchestra, 1656
Pittsburgh Youth Ballet Company & School, 572
Pittsburgh Youth Symphony Orchestra Association, 1657
Piven Theatre Workshop, 2967
Placer Theatre Ballet, 22
Plachta Auditorium, 7320
Placitas Artists Series, 5032
Plainfield Symphony, 1339
Plan - B Theatre Company, 4010
Plan-B Theatre Company, 4011
Plano Symphony Orchestra, 1744
Plantation Theatre Company, 2815
Playboy Jazz Festival, 4209
Players Guild of Canton, 3700
Players of Utica, 3631
Players Theatre, 2824, 6765
Playhouse on The Square, 3910
Playhouse Square Center: Ohio Theatre, 7975
Playhouse Square Center: Palace Theatre, 7976
Playhouse Square Center: State Theatre, 7977
Playhouse Square Foundation, 3716
Playmakers Repertory Company, 3645
Plays-In-The-Park, 3363
Playtime Productions, 4131
Playwrights Horizons, 3548
Playwrights Project, 2566
Playwrights Theatre of New Jersey, 3370
Playwrights' Arena, 2514
Playwrights' Center, 3252
Plaza Del Sol Performance Hall, 6195
Plaza Grand Performances, 6175
Plaza Theatre Company, 3941
Plum Fleming Studio Theatre, 7014
Plural Arts International, 5157
Plymouth Philharmonic Orchestra, 1207
Plymouth State University, 4976
Plymouth Symphony, 1250
Pnc Park, 8178
Pocket Opera, 1915
Pocket Sandwich Theatre, 3954
Pocono Playhouse, 3821, 8143
Point Loma Nazarene University Cultural Events Series, 4289
Point Park University's Pittsburgh Playhouse, 3847
Point Stadium, 8136
Pointless Theatre, 2746
Polish American Folk Dance Company, 370
Polk Community College Special Performance Series, 4495
Pollak Theatre, 7598
Pollard Theatre, 3756
Pomerene Center for the Arts, 7988
Pomona College Department of Theatre and Dance, 2459
Pomona College Orchestra, 774
Pompano Beach Amphitheatre, 6603
Pompano Players, 2816
Ponca Playhouse, 3766, 8047
Pontine Theatre, 3352
Popejoy Hall, 7606
Poplar Pike Playhouse, 3899
Poppo & the Gogo Boys, 475
Port Angeles Symphony, 1795
Port Huron Civic Theatre, 3211
Port Townsend Blues Heritage Festival: Centrum Festival, 5790
Portage Area Community Theatre, 4132
Porter Center for Performing Arts, 7859

Porterfield Memorial United Methodist Church - Distinguished Artist Series, 4498
Porthouse Theatre Company, 3738
Portland Actors Ensemble, 3787
Portland Ballet Company, 251
Portland Baroque Orchestra, 1606
Portland Center for the Performing Arts, 8099
Portland Center Stage, 3788
Portland Chamber Music Festival, 4743
Portland Chamber Orchestra Association, 1607
Portland Columbia Symphony, 1608
Portland Exposition Building, 7178
Portland Institute for Contemporary Art, 8100
Portland Opera, 2300
Portland Stage Company, 3105
Portland State University Piano Recital Series, 5420
Portland String Quartet Concert Series/Workshop, 1149, 4744
Portland Symphonic Choir, 2088
Portland Symphony Orchestra, 1150
Portland University Portland International: Performance Festival, 5419
Portland Youth Philharmonic Association, 1609
Portopera, 2089
Posey Dance Company, 494
Possum Point Players, 2723
Post Playhouse Incorporated, 3322
Pote Theatre, 7001
Potomac Theatre Project, 4021
Potter Center, 7310
Poway Center for the Performing Arts, 6212
Powder River Symphony Orchestra, 1838
Powell Little Theatre, 6714
Powell Symphony Hall, 7455
Power Center for the Performing Arts, 7271
Powerhouse Theater at Vassar, 3607
Prado at Balboa Park, 6243
Prairie Arts Center, 7348
Prairie Center for the Arts, 6834
Prairie Dance Theatre, 553
Prairie Performing Arts Center, 5863
Prairie Players Civic Theatre, 2969
Prairie Repertory, 3884
Prather Coliseum, 7137
Pratt Institute: Auditorium, 7646
Pregones Theater, 3415
Presbyterian College, 5535
Prescott Fine Arts, 2427
Prescott Park Arts Festival, 4979
Present Music, 1832
Presidential Jazz Weekend, 1652, 5484
Preus-Brandt Forum, 6313
Price Cutter Park, 7434
Primary Stages Company, 3549
Prime Stage, 3848
Prince George's Philharmonic, 1170
Prince George's Stadium, 7202
Prince Music Theater, 3837
Prince William County Stadium, 8533
Princess Theatre, 7388
Princess Theatre Center for the Performing Arts, 2404, 5898
Princess Theatre Professional Series, 4142
Princeton Pro Musica Chorus & Orchestra, 2187
Princeton Rep Company/Princeton Rep Shakespeare Festival, 3383
Princeton Shakespeare Festival, 5013
Princeton Symphony Orchestra, 1341
Princeton University Concerts, 5014
Principia College Concert Series, 4575
Priscilla Beach Theatre, 7257
Prism Opera, 2117
Prism Theatre, 5989
Pritchard Theater, 6776
Pro Arte Chamber Orchestra, 1191
Pro Arte Chamber Singers of Connecticut, 1973
Pro Arte Chorale, 2189
Pro Musica, 4902
Pro Musica Chamber Orchestra of Columbus, 1548
Pro Musica of Detroit, 1230, 1237
Pro Piano New York Recital Series, 5158
Process Studio Theatre, 3550
Prochnow Auditorium, 5954
Proctor's Theatre, 3620, 7820
Professional Ballet School, 23
Professional Performing Arts Series, 5047

Project Artaud, 93
Project Troubador, 4403
Promenade Theatre, 7775
Providence Division of Public Programming Departments, 5525
Providence Dunkin Donuts Center, 8198
Providence Performing Arts Center, 8199
Provincetown Repertory Theatre, 3170
Public Theatre, 3097, 3552
Publick Theatre, 3140
Pueblo Symphony, 917
Puerto Rican Traveling Theatre Company, 3553
Pull-Tight Players, 3896
Pullman Summer Palace, 4077
Pulse Dance Company, 9
Pump House Regional Arts, 5844
Pumpkin Theatre, 3129
Puppet Arts Theatre, 3277
Puppet House Theatre, 2708
Puppet Showplace Theatre, 3144
Puppet Theatre: Dance and Music From Indonesia, 3599
Purchase College Performing Arts Center, 7810
Purdue Professional Summer Theatre, 3028
Purdue University Convocations & Lectures, 4635
Pure Theatre, 3868
Purple Masque, 7051
Purple Rose Theatre Company, 3195
Pushcart Players, 3392
Pushpush Theater, 2873
Putnam Symphony Orchestra, 1377
Pvcc Center for the Performing Arts, 5972
Pyramid Arts Center, 7815

Q

Quad City Arts, 4597
Quad City River Bandits Baseball Stadium, 6977
Quad City Symphony Orchestra Association, 1104
Quad City Youth String Ensemble, 1105
Quad-Cities Jazz Festival, 4587
Qualcomm Stadium, 6244
Quality Hill Playhouse, 3290
Quandt Fieldhouse, 8707
Quantum Theatre, 3849
Quartz Theatre, 3772
Quebec Government House, 7776
Queens College Summer Theatre, 3440
Queens Symphony Orchestra, 1389
Queens University: Queens Friends of Music Chamber Series, 1486, 5231
Queensborough Community College Theater, 7633
Quick Center for the Arts, 6402
Quincy Civic Music Association, 4595
Quincy Symphony Orchestra, 1062, 1218
Quintet of the Americas, 1381

R

Rabobank Arena, Theater and Convention Center, 6064
Racer Arena, 7100
Rachel M. Schlesinger Concert Hall and Arts Center, 8511
Racine Civic Center- Festival Hall & Park &Memorial Hall, 8701
Racine Symphony Orchestra, 1834
Rackham Symphony Choir, 2137
Radcliffe Choral Society, 2112
Radford University Performing Arts Series, 5751
Radford University Theatre, 8546
Radio City Music Hall, 7777
Rahner-Gibbs Second Stage Theatre, 6591
Rainbo Children's Theatre Company, 3271
Rainbow Dance Theatre, 559
Rainier Symphony, 1802
Rajah Theatre, 8179
Rajeckas and Intraub - Movement Theatre, 3581
Rajeckas and Intraub Movement Theatre, 3554
Raleigh Boychoir, 2269
Raleigh Civic Center Complex, 7907
Raleigh Little Theatre, 7908
Raleigh Ringers, 1501
Raleigh Symphony Orchestra, 1502
Ralph Wilson Stadium, 7804

Ramona Bowl Amphitheatre, 4225, 6122
Ramona Hillside Players, 4226
Ramsey Concert Hall, 6613
Ramsey Regional Activity Center, 7879
Randy James Dance Works, 330
Ransburg Auditorium, 6899
Rapides Coliseum, 7109
Rapides Symphony Orchestra, 1136
Raritan River Music, 5008, 5009
Raritan Valley Chorus, 2182
Ratcliffe Stadium, 6106
Rattlestick Theatre, 3555
Raven Theatre Company, 2944
Ravinia Festival, 4581
Rawhide Pavilion & Rodeo Arena, 5948
Ray Kroc Baseball Complex, 6013
Ray Winder Field, 6036
Raymond F Mccallister Hall, 6777
Raymond Theater, 8595
Rb Productions, 3344
Rbc Center, 7909
Rca Black Box Theatre, 6911
Rca Dome, 6900
Reading Community Players, 3852
Reading Symphony Orchestra, 1661
Reality Theatre, 3725
Reardon Auditorium, 6853
Rebecca Kelly Ballet, 476
Rebecca Stenn Company, 477
Recital Hall, 6693, 6748, 6924, 6982, 6995
Red Barn Playhouse, 3214
Red Barn Theatre, 2789, 6535
Red Eye, 3253
Red Herring Theatre Ensemble, 3726
Red Lodge Music Festival, 4929
Red Mountain Chamber Orchestra, 708
Red Octopus Theatre Company, 3781
Red River Revel Arts Festival, 4722
Red Rocks Amphitheatre & Visitor Center, 6366
Redbird Arena, 6809
Redbud Theatre, 8368
Redding Civic Auditorium, 6213
Redfern Arts Center on Brickyard Pond, 7535
Redhouse Arts Center, 3626
Redlands Bowl Amphitheatre, 6216
Redlands Bowl Summer Music Festival, 4276
Redlands Community Music Association, 6217
Redlands Symphony Association, 829
Redondo Beach Performing Arts Center, 6218
Reduxion Theatre Company, 3765
Redwood Art Council, 4261
Redwood Coast Dixieland Jazz Festival, 4217
Redwood Concert Ballet, 30
Redwood Symphony, 831
Reed Marionettes, 4127
Reed Theatre, 8101
Reed Whipple Cultural Arts Center, 4957, 7512
Refuge Dance Company, 176
Regattabar Jazz Festival at the Charles Hotel, 4787
Regina A. Quick Center for the Arts, 6400
Regina Klenjoski Dance Company, 34
Regina Opera Company, 2206
Regional Arts Center, 8466
Regional Arts Music at the Kravis Center for the Performing Arts, 4493
Regional Special Events Center, 7101
Regis College Fine Arts Center, 7256
Regis Philbin Studio Theatre, 6934
Reif Arts Center, 4843
Reif Greenway Series, 4868
Reilly Center Arena, 7824
Reitz Arena, 7200
Relache Ensemble, 1653
Remy Bumppo Theatre Company, 2945
Renaissance and Baroque Society of Pittsburgh, 1658
Renaissance Theaterworks, 4128
Renaissance Theatre, 3742
Reno Chamber Orchestra, 1315
Reno H Sales Stadium, 7471
Reno Little Theater, 7521
Reno Philharmonic, 1316
Reno Sparks Convention Centennial Coliseum, 7522
Rensselaer Newman Foundation Chapel and Cultural Center, 7840

1123

Entry Index

Rensselaer Polytechnic Institute: Houston Field House, 7839
Rep Stage, 3122
Repertorio Espanol, 3556
Repertory Dance Theatre, 653
Repertory People of Evansville, 3006
Repertory Theatre of Saint Louis, 3302
Res Musicamerica Series, 4754
Reser Stadium, 8069
Resident Ensemble Players, 2724
Resistol Arena/Rodeo Center Exhibit Hall, 8432
Reston Community Center Hunters Woods, 5752
Rev. J. Bruce Stewart, 657
Revels, 2126
Revision Theatre, 3357
Reynolds Coliseum, 7910
Reynolds Memorial Auditorium, 7929
Reynolds Studio Theatre, 5914
Rhapsody in Taps, 35
Rhinebeck Chamber Music Society, 1458
Rhode Island Chamber Music Concerts, 1675
Rhode Island Civic Chorale & Orchestra, 1670
Rhode Island Civic Chorale and Orchestra, 2323
Rhode Island College Symphony Orchestra, 1676
Rhode Island College: Performing Arts Series, 5526
Rhode Island Philharmonic Orchestra and Music School, 1671
Rhode Island's Ballet Theatre, 590
Rhodes College: Mccoy Visiting Artist Series, 5576
Rialto Center for the Arts, 6626
Rialto Square Theatre, 6794
Ricardo Montalban Theater, 6129
Rice Auditorium, 8086
Rice Stadium, 8414
Rice-Eccles Stadium, 8500
Richard & Helen Brodbeck Concert Hall, 8699
Richard & Karen Carpenter Performing Arts Center, 6151
Richard and Karen Carpenter Performing Arts Center, 6152
Richard B Fisher Center for the Performing Arts at Bard College, 7630
Richard K. Stem Concert Hall, 6925
Richard L Swig Arts Center, 7560
Richard Rogers Theatre, 7778
Richardson Auditorium, 7585
Richland Performing Arts, 1633
Richmond Ballet, 670
Richmond Children's Theatre, 3076
Richmond Civic Theatre, 6938
Richmond Coliseum, 8554
Richmond Memorial Convention Center, 6220
Richmond Shakespeare Festival, 5755
Richmond Stadium, 8555
Richmond Symphony Orchestra, 1095, 1785
Ricketson Theatre, 6367
Ridge Theater, 3557
Ridgefield Symphony Orchestra, 939
Ridgewood Arts Foundation: Theatre at the Center, 3018
Ridgewood Gilbert and Sullivan Opera Company, 2190
Ridgewood Symphony Orchestra, 1342
Ringwood Friends of Music Series, 5016
Rinker Outdoor Amphitheatre, 6778
Rio Grande Valley Ballet, 644
Rio Grande Valley International Music Festival, 5655
Rio Hondo Symphony Association, 891
Riofest: a Blending of the Arts and Entertainment, 5632
Rioult, 478
Ripon College: Caestecker Fine Arts Series, 5865
Ririe Woodbury Dance Company, 654
Risa Jaroslow and Dancers, 479
Rites and Reason, 3863
Ritz Civic Center, 6037
Ritz Theatre, 3751
Ritz Theatre and La Villa Museum, 2785
River Arts Repertory, 3412
River Center Arena, 7113
River Center Exhibition Hall, 7114
River Center Grand Ballroom, 7115
River Center Theatre for Performing Arts, 7116

River Center/Adler Theatre, 6978
River City Brass Band, 1659
River City Mixed Chorus, 2170
River City Repertory Theatre, 3089
River North Chicago Dance Company, 211
River Oaks Chamber Orchestra (Roco), 1732
River Parks Amphitheatre, 8051
River Raisin Ballet Company, 289
River Raisin Centre for the Arts, 7318
River Rep Theatre Company, 3558
River Rhythms, 5398
Riverbend Festival, 5559
Riverbend Music Center, 7957
Rivercenter, 7376
Rivercenter for the Performing Arts, 6640
Rivercity Jazz Festival, 4275
Riverpark Center, 7104
Riverside Arena, 7338
Riverside Center Dinner Theater, 4036
Riverside Center Dinner Theater and Conference Facility, 8522
Riverside Convention Center, 6224
Riverside County Philharmonic, 832
Riverside Municipal Auditorium, 6225
Riverside Shakespeare Company, 3559
Riverside Symphonia, 1635
Riverside Symphony, 1439
Riverside Theatre, 3038, 6600
Riverview Hall & Theater, 7158
Riverview Stadium, 6972
Roadside Theater, 4047
Roanoke Civic Center, 8560
Roanoke College Performing Arts Series, 5759
Roanoke Island Historical Association, 5256
Roanoke Symphony Orchestra, 1786
Robbins-Zust Family Marionettes, 3171
Robert & Margrit Mondavi Center for the Performing Arts, 6095
Robert C Smithwick Theatre, 6153
Robert Friedman Presents, 88
Robert Ivey Ballet, 595
Robert M Collins Center, 6823
Robert Morris University Colonial Theatre, 3817
Roberts Municipal Stadium, 6867
Roberts Stadium, 7023
Roberts Theatre, 6998
Roberts Wesleyan College, 5195
Robertson Stadium, 8415
Robey Theatre Company, 2515
Robins Center, 8556
Robinson Center Music Hall, 6038
Robinson Theatre, 6323
Rochester Broadway Theatre League, 3610
Rochester Chamber Orchestra, 1462
Rochester City Ballet, 499
Rochester Civic Music, 4880
Rochester Civic Theatre, 3264
Rochester Philharmonic Orchestra, 5196
Rochester Symphony Orchestra & Chorale, 2152
Rock Valley College Lecture/Concert Series, 4598
Rockaway Theatre Company, 3439
Rockford Area Youth Symphony Orchestra, 1065
Rockford Dance Company, 222
Rockford Metrocentre, 6831
Rockford Smyphony Orchestra, 1066
Rockport Chamber Music Festival, 1208, 4800
Rockport Opera House, 7180
Rocky Mountain Ballet Theatre, 315
Rocky Ridge Music Center, 4369
Rod Rodgers Dance Company & Studios, 480
Roger Furman Theatre, 3560
Roger Wagner Chorale, 1936
Rogers Little Theater, 2444
Rogers Stadium, 8545
Rogue Machine Theatre, 2516
Rogue Music Theatre, 3777
Rogue Valley Symphony, 1588
Roland E Powell Convention Center, 7209
Roland Hayes Concert Hall, 8254
Roland Taylor Theatre, 6083
Rollins College: Department of Theatre and Dance, 2842
Rome City Auditorium, 6657
Rome Symphony Orchestra, 1014
Ronald E. Mitchell Theatre, 8680
Ronald Q. Frederickson Theatre, 7034

Roosevelt University Orchestra: Chicago College of Performing Arts, 1042
Rose and Alfred Miniaci Performing Arts Center on The Nova Southeastern University, 6518
Rose Arena, 7321
Rose Bowl Stadium, 6210
Rose City Chamber Orchestra, 1610
Rose Quarter, 8102
Rose State College Performing Arts Theatre, 8036
Rosebriar Shakespeare Company, 3727
Rosemont Theatre, 6770
Rosewood Chamber Ensemble, 1466
Ross Ragland Theater & Cultural Center, 8079
Ross-Ade Stadium, 6952
Roswell Symphony Orchestra, 1357
Roulette Intermedium, 1440
Round House Theatre, 3121
Round Rock Symphony Inc, 1746
Round Top Festival Institute, 5658, 8443
Roundabout Theatre Company, 3561
Rova Saxophone Quartet, 851
Rowland-Taylor Recital Hall, 6084
Roxey Ballet, 333
Roxy Theater, 3894
Roy Stewart Stadium, 7102
Royal Arts Council, 3310, 4927
Roycroft Chamber Music Festival, 5069
Rude Mechanicals, 3932
Rushmore Plaza Civic Center, 8244
Russell Theatre, 8612
Russian Ballet of Orlando, 164
Russian River Blues Festival, 4222
Russian River Chamber Music, 791
Rutgers Arts Center, 7572
Rutgers Athletic Center, 7579
Rutgers Stadium, 7580
Rutgers University Concert Series, 5002
Rutgers-Camden Center for the Arts Gordon Theater, 7547
Ruth Eckerd Hall, 6488
Ruth Lilly Performance Hall, 6901
Ruth N Halls Theatre, 6857
Ryan Center, 8192
Ryan Field, 6784
Ryan Repertory Company at Harry Warren Theatre, 3422
Rye Arts Center, 7818
Ryman Auditorium, 8301

S

Saco River Festival, 4738
Sacramento Ballet, 63
Sacramento Choral Society and Orchestra, 1879
Sacramento Community Center Theatre, 6231
Sacramento Convention Center, 6232
Sacramento Jazz Jubilee, 890, 4348
Sacramento Master Singers, 1901
Sacramento Men's Chorus, 1902
Sacramento Opera Company, 1903
Sacramento Philharmonic Orchestra, 836
Sacramento Symphonic Winds, 770
Sacramento Theatre Company, 2557
Sacramento Youth Symphony & Academy of Music, 837
Sacred Dance Guild, 263
Saddleback College, 2527
Saddleback College Guest Artists Series, 4252
Saeko Ichinohe Dance Company, 481
Saenger Theatre, 2409, 3085, 6579, 7148, 7391
Saenger Theatre of the Performing Arts, 7384
Safeco Field, 8604
Saginaw Bay Symphony Orchestra, 1251
Saginaw Choral Society, 2140
Saginaw Valley State University Concert: Lecture Series, 4863
Saint Anne's-Belfield School Summer Music Academy, 8516
Saint Anselm College Performing Arts Series, 4969
Saint Bart's Players, 3562
Saint Clement's Church, 7779
Saint James Theater, 7780
Saint Joseph Civic Arena, 7442
Saint Joseph Symphony Society, 1286
Saint Joseph's College Center for Arts, 7647
Saint Louis Ballet, 305

Saint Louis Black Repertory Company, 3303
Saint Louis Cathedral Concerts, 4920
Saint Louis Center for the Performing Arts, 6676
Saint Louis Chamber Chorus, 2157
Saint Louis Classical Guitar Society, 1289
Saint Louis Hills Arts Council, 4922
Saint Louis Philharmonic Orchestra, 1290
Saint Louis Symphony Children's Choir, 2164
Saint Louis Symphony Orchestra, 1291
Saint Louis Symphony Youth Orchestra, 1292
Saint Louis Symphony: Classics in The Loop Festival, 4921
Saint Lucie County, 6516
Saint Lukes Chamber Ensemble, 1441
Saint Mary's College Cultural Arts Season, 4628
Saint Olaf College Chorus, 1268
Saint Paul Chamber Orchestra, 1272
Saint Sava Free Serbian Orthodox Church, 2276
Saint Sebastian Players, 2946
Saint Vincent Summer Theatre, 3813
Salem Chamber Orchestra, 1614
Salem Civic Center, 8561
Salem College, 5278
Salem Theatre, 3172
Salia Ni Seydou, 482
Salina Arts & Humanities Commission, 4680
Salina Bicentennial Center, 7059
Salina Community Theatre, 3047
Salisbury Singers, 2127
Salisbury Symphony Orchestra, 1504
Salmon Arts Council, 4539
Salon Concerts, Inc., 5591
Salt and Pepper Mime Company, 3563
Salt Creek Ballet, 224
Salt Lake Acting Company, 4012
Salt Lake County Center for the Arts, 8501
Salt Lake Symphonic Choir, 2365
Salt Lake Symphony, 1763
Salt Marsh Opera, 1974
Salt Marsh Opera Company, 2327
Salter Concert Hall, 6863
Saltworks Theatre Company, 3850
Sam Boyd Stadium, 7513
Sam Houston State University Theatre, 8419
Samahan Filipino American Performing Arts, 29
Sammamish Symphony Orchestra Association, 1792
Samuel P Harn Museum of Art, 6521
San Angelo City Auditorium, 8446
San Angelo Symphony Orchestra and Chorale, 1747, 2359
San Antonio Chamber Music Society, 1748
San Antonio Convention Center Lila Cockrell Hall, 8457
San Antonio Parks Foundation, 5664
San Antonio Symphony, 1749
San Bernardino Symphony Orchestra, 839
San Diego Ballet Company, 64
San Diego Chamber Orchestra, 841
San Diego Children's Choir, 1906
San Diego Civic Theatre, 6245
San Diego Comic Opera/Lyric Opera San Diego, 1907
San Diego Dance Theater, 69
San Diego Early Music Society, 842, 4290
San Diego Junior Theatre, 2567
San Diego Men's Chorus, 1908
San Diego Museum of Art Auditorium, 6246
San Diego Opera, 1909
San Diego Repertory Theatre, 2568
San Diego Sports Arena, 6247
San Diego State University-School of Music and Dance, 4291
San Diego State University: Department of Theatre, 2569
San Diego Symphony Orchestra, 843
San Diego Thanksgiving, Dixieland Jazz Festival, 4292
San Diego Theatres/Balboa & Civic Theatres, 6248
San Diego Youth Symphony, 844
San Fernando Valley Symphony Orchestra, 893
San Francisco Bach Choir, 1917
San Francisco Ballet, 89
San Francisco Blues Festival, 4306
San Francisco Boys Chorus, 1916
San Francisco Chamber Orchestra, 760
San Francisco Choral Artists, 1918, 1919

Entry Index

San Francisco Community Music Center, 852
San Francisco Conservatory of Music, 854
San Francisco Contemporary Music Players, 853
San Francisco County Fair Arena, 6265
San Francisco Early Music Society, 759, 761
San Francisco Ethnic Dance Festival, 90, 4307
San Francisco Fringe Festival, 4308
San Francisco Girls Chorus, 1920
San Francisco Girls Chorus and Association, 1921
San Francisco Jazz Organization, 855
San Francisco Jazz Spring Season, 4309
San Francisco Mime Troupe, 2590
San Francisco Opera, 1926
San Francisco Opera Center, 1922, 1923
San Francisco Performances, 4310
San Francisco Renaissance Voices, 1924
San Francisco Shakespeare Festival, 4311
San Francisco State University: Department of Theatre Arts, 2589
San Francisco Symphony, 856
San Francisco Symphony Chorus, 1925
San Francisco Symphony Youth Orchestra, 857
San Francisco War Memorial and Performing Arts Center, 6266
San Jose Center for the Performing Arts, 6270
San Jose Chamber Music Society, 859
San Jose Children's Musical Theater, 2601
San Jose Jazz Society, 860
San Jose Municipal Stadium, 6271
San Jose Repertory Theatre, 2602
San Jose Stage Company, 2603
San Jose State University Theatre, 6272
San Jose State University: Department of Theatre Arts, 2604
San Jose Taiko Group, 861
San Juan Community Theatre and Arts Center, 4070
San Juan Symphony, 908
San Luis Obispo Mozart Festival, 863, 4320
San Luis Obispo Symphony, 864
San Mateo Performing Arts Center, 6274
San Pedro City Ballet, 102
San Pedro Playhouse, 4003
Sand in The City, 4661
Sandra Feinstein-Gamm Theatre, 3859
Sandstone Productions, 3403
Sandusky Concert Association, 5365
Sandusky State Theatre, 3750
Sanford Maine Stage Company, 3109
Sanford Stadium, 6614
Sangamon Auditorium, 6837
Sangre De Cristo Arts and Conference Center, 4374, 6389
Sangre De Cristo Chorale, 2197
Sanibel Music Festival, 4479
Santa Barbara Chamber Orchestra, 870
Santa Barbara Contemporary Arts Forum, 6286
Santa Barbara Festival Ballet, 4324
Santa Barbara Symphony Association, 871
Santa Cecilia Orchestra, 806
Santa Clara Ballet, 105
Santa Clara University Theatre and Dance Department, 2614
Santa Cruz Ballet Theatre, 112
Santa Cruz Baroque Festival, 873, 4328
Santa Cruz Civic Auditorium, 6295
Santa Cruz County Symphony, 874
Santa Fe Chamber Music Festival, 5034
Santa Fe Concert Association, 5035
Santa Fe Convention and Visitors Bureau Sweeney Center, 7620
Santa Fe Desert Chorale, 2198
Santa Fe Festival Ballet, 349
Santa Fe Opera House, 7607
Santa Fe Pro Musica, 1359
Santa Fe Stages, 7621
Santa Fe Symphony, 1360
Santa Fe Symphony Orchestra and Chorus, 2199
Santa Monica Civic Auditorium, 6301
Santa Monica Symphony Orchestra, 876
Santa Rosa Concert Association, 4332
Santa Rosa Junior College Chamber Concert Series, 877
Santa Rosa Junior College Chamber Music Series, 4333
Santa Rosa Symphony, 878

Sarasota Ballet of Florida, 169
Sarasota Concert, 4484
Sarasota Jazz Festival, 4485
Sarasota Music Festival, 4486
Sarasota Opera Association, 2011
Sarasota Orchestra, 992
Sarasota Orchestra Brass Quintet, 995
Sarasota Orchestra New Artists Piano Quartet, 993
Sarasota Orchestra String Quartet, 991
Sarasota Orchestra Wind Quintet, 994
Sarasota Youth Orchestras, 989
Saratoga International Theater Institute, 3564
Saratoga Performing Arts Center, 1464, 3619, 7819
Saratoga Performing Arts Festival Series, 5200
Saturday Brass Quintet, 1442
Savannah Civic Center, 6661
Savannah Concert Association, 4520
Savannah Music Festival, 4521
Savoyard Light Opera Company, 2113
Sawyer Theatre, 6665
Sc Christian Dance Theater, 601
Scandinavian Fest, 4985
Scarlet Mask Society, 3728
Scene Dock Theatre, 6176
Schaeffer Fine Arts Center, 7378
Schenectady Civic Players, 3621
Schenectady Civic Players Theater, 7821
Schenectady Light Opera Company, 2256
Schenectady Museum: Union College Concert Series, 5202
Schermerhorn Symphony Center, 8302
Schneider Concerts at the New School, 5159
Schola Cantorum, 1892
Schola Cantorum of Texas, 2348
School of Theatre and Dance, 6766
School of Theatre Arts, 2431
Schubert Club International Artist Series, 4883, 4884
Schwartz Center for Performing Arts at Emory, 4507
Schwartz Center for the Arts, 6450
Science Fiction Theatre Company, 3141
Scott Joplin Ragtime Festival, 4924
Scott Stadium, 8517
Scottish Rite Center, 6873
Scottrade Center, 7456
Scottsdale Arts Festival, 4173
Scottsdale Center for the Performing Arts, 5979
Scottsdale Community College Performing Arts Center, 5980
Scottsdale Symphony Orchestra, 732
Scranton Community Concerts, 5503
Scranton Cultural Center at the Masonic Temple, 8181
Sea Chanters, 2000
Seacoast Repertory Theatre, 3353
Seagate Convention Centre, 8014
Seanachai Theatre Company, 2947
Seaside Civic and Convention Center, 8105
Seaside Institute Series, 4487
Seaside Music Theater, 2771
Season of Entertainment, 4187
Seattle Baroque, 1803
Seattle Center Opera House, 8605
Seattle Chamber Music Festival, 5800
Seattle Children's Theatre, 4085
Seattle Choral Company, 2386
Seattle Early Dance, 685
Seattle International Children's Festival, 5801
Seattle Mime Theatre, 4086
Seattle Opera, 2387
Seattle Philharmonic Orchestra, 1804
Seattle Pro Musica, 2388
Seattle Repertory Theatre, 4087, 8606
Seattle Shakespeare Festival, 5802
Seattle Symphony Orchestra, 1805
Seattle Youth Symphony Orchestra, 1806
Seattle Youth Symphony Orchestra's Marrowstone Music Festival, 5803
Second City, 2948
Second Stage, 6296
Second Stage Theatre, 3565
2nd Story Theatre, 3865
2nd Story Theatre Company, 4043
Secrest Auditorium, 8026
Sedona Cultural Park, 5981

Sedona Jazz on The Rocks, 4175
Seeger Chapel Concert Hall, 8268
Segerstrom Center for the Arts, 6090
Selma Community Concert Association, 4150
Sem Ensemble, 1373
Seminole County Government, 6582
Sensedance, 483
Sesame Place, 3812
Settlement Music School, 5485
Seven Angels Theatre, 2713
Seven Dance Company, 528
7 Stages, 2846, 6627
Seven Stages Theatre, 2862
Seven Stories Theatre Company, 4098
Sevenars Concerts Music Festival, 5160
7th Street Theatre, 8584
Severance Hall, 7978
Sewanee Festival Orchestras / Sewanee Music Festival, 5585
Sewanee Summer Music Festival, 5584
Sfjazz, 4312
Sha Sha Higby, 25
Shadow Box Theatre, 3566
Shadow Lawn Summer Stage, 3394
Shadowbox Cabaret, 3729
Shadowland Artists, 3438
Shadowlight Productions, 2591
Shafer Auditorium, 8140
Shaker Symphony Orchestra, 1539
Shakespeare & Company, 3159, 3273
Shakespeare Dallas, 3955, 5612
Shakespeare Festival, 4533
Shakespeare Festival at Tulane, 3086, 4719
Shakespeare in Delaware Park, 3428
Shakespeare on The Green, 3335
Shakespeare Orange County, 2537
Shakespeare Santa Cruz, 2616
Shakespeare Theater of New Jersey, 4998
Shakespeare Theatre Company, 2747, 6477
Shalhavet Festival, 5322
Shandelee Music Festival, 5161
Shark Eat Muffin Theatre Company, 3708
Sharon Community Theatre, 3173
Shasta College Fine Arts Theatre, 6214
Shasta Community Concert Association, 4199
Shasta Symphony Orchestra, 828
Shattered Globe Theater, 2949
Shaw Center Auditorium, 7009
Shawano County Arts Council, 4133
Shawnee Playhouse, 3853
Shawnee Theatre of Greene County, 2998
Shea Theatre, 7822
Shea's Performing Arts Center, 7656
Sheboygan Theatre Company, 4134
Sheely Center for the Performing Arts, 6812
Sheila & Hughes Potiker Theatre, 6143
Sheila-Na-Gig Music, 1443
Sheldon Concert Hall and Ballroom, 7457
Sheldon Theatre, 3212
Shell Lake Arts Center, 5869
Shenandoah Shakespeare, 4056
Shenandoah Valley Bach Festival, 5740
Shenandoah Valley Music Festival, 5770
Shepherd of the Hills, 3279
Sheridan Civic Theatre Guild, 4139
Sherman Players, 2705
Sherman Symphony Orchestra, 1752
Sherwood Auditorium, 6144
Sheslow Auditorium in Old Main, 6989
Shiva Theatre, 7781
Shoestring Productions Limited, 2728
Shoreline Arts Alliance, 4388
Short North Performing Arts Association, 5331
Shotgun Players, 2451
Show Me Center, 7414
Showboat Becky Thatcher, 3743
Showboat Dinner Theatre, 2762
Showboat Majestic, 3709
Shreveport Little Theatre, 3090
Shreveport Metropolitan Ballet, 247
Shreveport Municipal Auditorium, 7159
Shreveport Opera, 2086
Shreveport Symphony Orchestra, 1144
Shrine Auditorium and Exposition Center, 6177
Shriver Hall Concert Series, 4755
Shryock Auditorium and Arena Promotions, 6722
Shua Group, 332
Shubert Theater, 6424

Shubert Theatre, 7782
Sibert Theatre, 6793
Side by Side, 3676
Sideways Contemporary Dance Company, 189
Sierra Repertory Theatre at East Sonora, 2626
Sierra Vista Theatre Hall, 5983
Signature Theatre, 4033
Signature Theatre Company, 3567
Sikeston Little Theatre, 3307
Silk and Bamboo Ensemble, 1073
Silver Center for the Arts, 7581
Silver Lake College, 8685
Silver Lake College Guest Artist Series, 5850
Silver Spring Stage, 3131
Silvermine Guild Art Center Series, 4395
Silvermine Guild Summer Music Series, 931
Simpkins Theatre, 6798
Simulations, 3371
Sinclair Auditorium, 6970
Sinclair Dance, 534
Sinfonia Concertante Orchestra, 1611
Sinfonia Da Camera, 1070
Singing City, 2314
Singletary Center for the Arts, 7088
Sioux City Community Theatre, 3037
Sioux City Symphony Orchestra, 1115
Sioux Falls Arena, 8245
Sioux Falls Community Playhouse, 3887, 8246
Sioux Falls Stadium, 8309
Siouxland Youth Symphony Orchestra, 1116
Sitka Summer Music Festival, 4163
Siu Arena, 6723
651 Arts, 5051
Six Flags Magic Mountain, 2638
Six Flags Over Georgia, 4508
Skagit Opera, 2382
Skagit Symphony, 1793
Skaneateles Festival, 5203
Skidmore Music Department, 5201
Skokie Valley Symphony Orchestra, 1067
Sky Blue Boys, 1772
Sky Sox Stadium, 6342
Skyhawk Arena, 8277
Skylight Opera Theatre, 4129
Skyline Theatre Company, 3364
Slagle Auditorium, 8250
Sleep Train Pavillion at Concord, 6088
Sleuths Mystery Dinner Shows, 2808
Slidell Department of Cultural Affairs, 4723
Slippery Rock University - Performing Arts Series, 5506
Slocomb Auditorium, 8441
Slocum House Theatre Company, 4094
Sloss Furnaces National Historic Theater, 5895
Slow Burn Theatre Co., 2758
Smallbeer Theatre Company, 3127
Smcc Performing Arts Center, 5973
Smcc Studio Theatre, 5974
Smith College Glee Club & Choirs, 2121
Smith College Orchestra, 1205
Smith Opera House, 7676
Smith Recital Hall, 8639
Smithsonian Institution: the Smithsonian Associates, 4432
Smoky Mountain British Brass, 1498
Smoky Mountain Repertory Theatre, 3639
Smoothie King Center, 7147
Smuin Ballet, 91
Snappy Dance Theater, 279
Snow Camp Historical Drama Society, 3680
Snug Harbor Cultural Center, 7827
Society for Chamber Music in Rochester, 1463
Society Hill Playhouse, 3838, 8160
Society of the Cincinnati Concerts at Anderson House, 4433
Society of the Four Arts, 4470
Soho Rep, 7783
Soho Repertory Theatre, 3568
Soirees Musicales Piano Series, 1551, 5336
Soka Performing Art Center, 6053
Solaris Dance Theatre & Video, 484
Soldier Field, 6749
Soldiers & Sailors Memorial Coliseum, 6868
Solid Brass, 1326
Somervell County Expo Center, 3978
Songfest, 4269
Sonoma State University Theater Department, 2549

1125

Entry Index

Sooner Theatre of Norman, 3760
Sorg Opera Company, 2287
Sound of the Rockies, 1946
Sound Symphony Orchestra, 1383
Soundfest Chamber Music Festival, Colorado Quartet, 4993
Soupstone Project, 3569
Source Theatre Company, 2748
South Arkansas Arts Center, 6022
South Arkansas Symphony, 751
South Bay Ballet, 113
South Bay Guitar Society, 862
South Bend Symphony Orchestra, 1096
South Broadway Cultural Center, 7608
South Camden Theatre Company, 3360
South Coast Repertory, 2461
South Coast Repertory Segerstrom Auditorium, 6091
South Dakota Art Museum, 8241
South Dakota State University Civic Symphony, 1686
South Dakota State University Student Activities, 5553
South Dakota Symphony, 1688
South Dallas Cultural Center, 8364
South Florida Center for the Arts, 6534
South Florida Community College Cultural Series, 4437
South Florida Jazz, 4476
South Florida Youth Symphony, 979
South Jackson Civic Center, 8310
South Mountain Concerts, 4799
South of Broadway Theatre Company, 3882
South Orange County Community Theatre, 2607
South Park Theatre, 3794
South Shore Music, 4411
South Texas Symphony Association, 1719
South Valley Symphony, 788
Southeast Alabama Community Theatre, 2405
Southeast Alabama Dance Company, 2
Southeast Community Theatre, 2570
Southeast Iowa Symphony Orchestra, 1111
Southeast Missouri State University: Cultural Series, 4896
Southeast Symphony, 765
Southeastern Community College Performing Arts Series, 5272
Southeastern Illinois College Visual & Performing Arts Center, 6792
Southeastern Louisiana University Arts & Lectures Series, 4705
Southeastern Louisiana University Center, 7121
Southeastern Louisiana University Strawberry Stadium, 7120
Southeastern Ohio Symphony Orchestra, 1561
Southeastern Pennsylvania Symphony Orchestra, 1622
Southeastern Savoyards, 2863
Southeastern School of Ballet, 602
Southern Adventist University, 5563
Southern Appalachian Repertory Theatre, 3668
Southern Appalachian Stages, 2881
Southern Arizona Arts and Cultural Alliance, 4179
Southern Arizona Symphony Orchestra, 743
Southern Arkansas University Theatre & Mass Communications Department, 2442
Southern Connecticut State University: Department of Theatre, 2698
Southern Illinois University Edwardsville Series, 4573
Southern Ohio Museum & Cultural Center, 8006
Southern Oregon University, 8064
Southern Rep, 3087
Southern Rep Theatre, 3081
Southington Community Theatre Inc., 6433
Southwest Chamber Music, 826
Southwest Florida Symphony Orchestra & Chorus Association, 969
Southwest Michigan Symphony Orchestra, 1252
Southwest Performing Arts Theatre, 6100
Southwest Repertory Organization, 3966
Southwest Symphony, 1355
Southwest Symphony Orchestra, 1767
Southwest Texas State University Arts Series, 5666
Southwestern Baptist Theological Seminary, 8389

Southwestern University Artist Series, 5630
Sovereign Center, 8180
Space Theatre, 6368
Spangenburg Theatre, 6205
Spanish Lyric Theater, 2015
Spanish Lyric Theatre, 2833
Spanish Theatre Repertory Company, 3570
Spartan Stadium, 7293
Spartanburg Memorial Auditorium: Arena, 8237
Spartanburg Memorial Auditorium: Theatre, 8236
Speakeasy Stage Company, 3142
Speaking of Stories, 2611
Spearfish Center for the Arts, 3890
Special Music Holidays, 5764
Special Olympics Stadium, 7637
Spectrum Dance Theater, 686
Spelman College Fresh Images Chamber Music Series, 4509
Spencer Theater for the Performing Arts, 7611
Spencers: Theater of Illusion, 4040
Spencertown Academy Performing Series, 5204
Spingold Theater Center, 3178, 7254
Spirit Square Center for the Arts, 7876
Spivey Hall, 6654
Spokane Civic Theatre, 4091
Spokane Convention Center, 8613
Spokane Interplayers Ensemble, 4092
Spokane Opera House, 8614
Spokane Symphony Orchestra, 1807
Spokane Veterans Memorial Arena, 8615
Spoleto Festival Usa, 596, 1679, 3869, 5534
Spooky Action Theatre, 2749
Sports Complex, 7829
Spotlight Arena, 8024
Spring Music Festival: California University of Arts, 4343
Springer Opera House, 2870
Springfield Arts Council, 5366, 5367
Springfield Little Theatre at the Landers, 7462
Springfield Orchestra Association, 1210
Springfield Performing Arts Development Corporation, 4805
Springfield Symphony Hall, 7252
Springfield Symphony Orchestra, 1211, 1294, 1568
Springstead Theatre, 6587
Square One Theatre Company, 2712
Squitieri Studio Theatre, 6510
Sro - a Lyric Theatre Company, 2165
Sro Theatre Company, 3730
St Charles Art & Music Festival, 4600
St Charles Singers, 2061
St Cloud State University Program Board Performing Arts Series, 4881
St Louis County Heritage and Arts Center, 7345
St Martin's Chamber Choir, 1955
St Olaf Choir, 2151
St Petersburg College, 4490
St. Cecilia Music Society, 1236
St. Cloud Symphony Orchestra, 1269
St. Croix Festival Theatre, 8706
St. John Theatre, 3088
St. John's College Concert Series, 4748
St. John's Renaissance Dancers, 337
St. John's University, 7821
St. Joseph's Historic Foundation/Hayti Heritage Center, 7881
St. Mark's Dance Studio, 148
St. Michael's College Concerts, 5709
St. Norbert College Performing Arts, 5830
St. Olaf College Artist Series, 4879
St. Patrick's Cathedral Chamber Music Series, 1444, 5162
St. Philip's in The Hills Friends of Music, 4180
St. Stephen's, 5486
St.Petersburg Opera Company, 2012
Stabler Arena, 8114
Stadium Theatre Performing Arts Center, 8202
Stage 3 Theatre Company, 2627
Stage 773, 6755
Stage Center Theatre, 6750
Stage Coach Theatre, 2896
Stage Left Theatre, 2950
Stage One: the Louisville Children's Theatre, 3071
Stage Theatre, 6369
Stage West, 3975
Stagecenter, 3942

Stagecrafters, 3710
Stageone Productions, 3347
Stages Repertory Theatre, 3987, 8416
Stages St. Louis, 3281
Stages Theatre Center, 2476
Stages Theatre Company, 3229
Stagewest Theater Company, 3034
Stageworks, 3444
Stagewrights, 3571
Staller Center for the Arts, 7830
Stambaugh Auditorium, 8025
Stamford Center for the Arts, 6435
Stamford Symphony Orchestra, 940
Stamford Theatre Works, 2707
Stamford Young Artists Philharmonic, 941
Stanford Jazz Festival & Workshop, 4336
Stanford Lively Arts, 4337
Stanford Symphony Orchestra, 879
Stanford University Department of Music, 6309
Stanley Performing Arts Center, 7843
Stanley-Sinsheimer Festival Glen, 6297
Stanly County Agri-Civic Center, 7852
Stanly County Chorale, 2267
Staples Center, 6178
Star Players Theatre, 3731
Star Plaza Theatre, 3016, 6912
Star Series Association, 5502
Star Theatre, 8616
Starlight Musical Theatre, 1910, 2571
Starlight Theatre, 3291, 7429
Starlite Patio Theater Summer Series, 4253
Starlite Patio Theatre, 6189
Starry Nights Summer Concert Series, 4582
State Ballet of Rhode Island, 589
State Museum of Pennsylvania, 8128
State Palace Theatre, 7149
State Street Ballet, 104
State Theater Company, 3933
State Theatre, 7179, 7573
State Theatre Center for the Arts, 3801, 8121
State Theatre Regional Arts Center at New Brunswick, 5003
State University of New York at Binghamton Performing Arts Series, 5049
State University of New York at Cortland: Campus Artist & Lecture Series, 5067
State University of New York at Stony Brook Concert Series, 5206
State University of New York-Binghampton: Anderson Center for the Arts, 7635
Staten Island Ballet, 503
Staten Island Symphony, 1465
Steep Theatre Company, 2951
Stella Boyle Smith Concert Hall, 6025
Stephen C O'connell Center, 6522
Stephen F Austin University Visual & Performing Arts, 5656
Stephen Foster Productions, 7075
Stephen Foster State Folk Culture Center, 6604
Stephen Foster-Musical, 3054
Stephens Auditorium, 6958, 6959, 7214
Steppenwolf Theatre Company, 2952
Steps Beyond, 486
Sterling & Francine Clark Art Institute, 7259
Sterling Centennial Auditorium, 6840
Sterling College Artist Series, 4681
Sterling Renaissance Festival, 3622, 5205
Stern Grove Festival Association, 4313
Steve Silver Productions, 2592
Stevens Center, 7930
Stiefel Theatre for the Performing Arts, 7060
Stillwater Community Center, 8048
Stockbridge Chamber Concerts at Searles Castle, 1206
Stockton Civic Theatre, 2628
Stockton Performing Arts Center, 7582
Stockton Symphony Association, 882
Stop-Gap, 2609
Stowe Performing Arts, 5720
Strahan Coliseum, 8460
Stranahan Theater Great Hall, 8015
Strand Theatre, 7160, 7563
Strand-Capitol Performing Arts Center, 8191
Strand-Capitol Performing Arts Center Series, 5515
Stratford Festival Theater, 4408
Strathmore, 7208
Straus Auditorium, 7860

Straw Hat Players, 3261
Strawberry Productions, 3150
Strawdog Theatre Company, 2953
Strayer-Wood Theatre, 6963, 6964
Streb Laboratory for Action Mechanics (Slam), 356
Street Theater, 3634
Street Theatre Company, 3918
Strider Theater, 7182
String Orchestra of New York City, 1445
Strings in The Mountains, 918
Strong Theatre, 7816
Struthers Library Theatre, 3855
Stuart C. Siegel Center, 8557
Stuart Pimsler Dance & Theater, 298
Student Union Special Events Center, 6686
Studio Arena Theatre, 3429
Studio One, 8669
Studio Players, 3067
Studio Theatre, 2750, 5955, 6020, 6096, 6120, 6287, 6324, 6592, 6694, 6751, 6788, 6827, 6838, 6902, 6946, 6979, 7007, 7010, 7017, 7702
Sturges Center for Fine Arts, 6235
Su Teatro, 2665
Suburban Symphony Orchestra, 1520
Sue Bennett College, Appalachian Folk Festival, 4695
Suffolk Theater, 5192
Suffolk Y Jcc International Jewish Arts Festival & the Celebration Series, 5075
Suhaila Dance Company & Suhaila Salimpour School of Dance, 18
Sullivan Street Playhouse, 7784
Summer Arts & Music Festival, 4278
Summer Chamber Music Festival, 5765
Summer Fest, 2322
Summer Festival of Chamber Music at Duke University, 5236
Summer Music, 4400
Summer Music Associates Series, 4973
Summer Music Theatre, 2975
Summer Opera Theatre Company, 1991
Summer Repertory Theatre, 2620
Summer Stock at the University of Findlay, 3735
Summer Strings on The Meherrin, 1495
Summer Theatre, 7877
Summer Theatre at Mt. Holyoke College, 3175
Summerdance Santa Barbara, 4325
Summerfest Concerts, 4907
Summergarden, 5163
Summit Chorale, 2194
Summit Jazz Swinging Jazz Concerts, 4370
Summit Music Festival, 5188
Summit Symphony, 1343
Sumter Country Gallery of Art, 8238
Sun Bowl, 8379
Sun Devil Stadium, 5990
Sun National Bank Center, 7593
Sun Valley Center for the Arts, 6698
Sun Valley Opera, 2035
Sun Valley Summer Symphony, 4542
Suncoast Dixieland Jazz Classic, 4461
Sundance Children's Theatre, 4015
Sundance Institute, 4013
Sundome Center, 5984
Sunfest of Palm Beach County, 4494
Sunken Garden Amphitheatre, 8458
Sunrise Theatre, 6517
Sunriver Music Festival, 1615, 5424
Sunset Cultural Center, 6078
Sunset Playhouse, 4109
Sunshine Daydreams Campground, 8652
Suny Center for the Arts, 7657
Suny College at Geneseo Limelight Artist Series, 5078
Supper Club Theater, 7785
Surdna Foundation, 7786
Surflight Theatre, 3359
Surfscape Contemporary Dance Theatre, 161
Surfside Players, 2763
Surry Arts Council, 5258
Susan Brotman Auditorium, 8607
Susan Marshall and Company, 487
Sushi Performance & Visual Art, 70
Susquehanna Symphony Orchestra, 1164
Susquehanna University Artist Series, 5504
Sven and Mildred Lekberg Recital Hall, 7002

Entry Index

Swamp Fox Players, 3875
Swannanoa Chamber Music Festival, 5268
Swayne Auditorium, 6707
Sweet & Hot Summer Music Festival, 4247
Sweet Fanny Adams Theatre & Music Hall, 3897
Swift Creek Academy of the Performing Arts, 5745
Swift Creek Mill Playhouse, 4035
Swiftel Center, 8242
Swine Palace Productions, 3078
Swingdance America, 4314
Symphonicity, 1787
Symphony Center, 6752
Symphony Chorus of New Orleans, 2085
Symphony for United Nations, 1490
Symphony Hall, 7227
Symphony North of Houston, 1733
Symphony of Northwest Arkansas, 753
Symphony of Oak Park & River Forest, 1059
Symphony of Southeast Texas, 1704
Symphony of the Americas, 968
Symphony of the Hills, 1736
Symphony of the Mountains, 1693
Symphony of the Southwest, 727
Symphony on The Sound, 926
Symphony Orchestra, 886, 914
Symphony Orchestra of Augusta, 1009
Symphony Pro Musica, 1197
Symphony Space, 5164, 7787
Synthaxis Theatre Company, 2532
Syracuse Area Landmark Theatre, 7837
Syracuse Friends of Chamber Music, 1467
Syracuse Jazz Festival, 4837
Syracuse Opera, 2258
Syracuse Society for New Music, 5209
Syracuse Stage, 3627
Syracuse Symphony Orchestra, 1468
Syracuse Symphony Youth Orchestra, 1469

T

T Daniel & Laurie Willets, 212
T Daniel Productions, 2994
Taco Bell Arena, 6687
Tacoma Actors Guild, 4093
Tacoma City Ballet, 689
Tacoma Dome, 8618
Tacoma Opera Association, 2389
Tacoma Performing Dance Company, 690
Tacoma Philharmonic, 1808
Tacoma Symphony Orchestra, 1809
Tacoma Youth Symphony, 1810
Tada!, 3572
Taffety Punk Theatre Company, 2751
Taghkanic Chorale, 2259
Tahoe Arts Project, 4335
Tahoe Jazz Festival, 4231
Taipei Theater of Chinese Information & Culture, 1446
Talcott Mountain Music Festival, Summer Series, 4390
Talento Bilingue De Houston, 3988
Talking Band, 3573
Tallahassee Museum, 4491
Tallahassee Symphony Orchestra, 999
Tallgrass Theatre Company, 3040
Tamara and The Shadow Theatre of Java, 3600
Tamburitzans Folk Ensemble, 1660
Tampa Bay Performing Arts Center, 6596
Tampa Bay Symphony, 965
Tampa Theatre, 6597
Tanglewood Festival, 4795
Tanglewood Music Center, 7238
Tannery Pond Concerts, 1404
Taos Art Association, 5037
Taos School of Music, 5038
Tapestry Dance Company, 625
Tapit/New Works Ensemble Theater, 700
Taproot Theatre Company, 4088
Tar River Choral & Orchestral Society, 1503, 2270
Target Center, 7360
Target Margin Theater, 3574
Tarleton State University Student Programming, 5670
Tassajara Symphony Orchestra, 780
Taylor-Meade Performing Arts Center, 8076
Td Bank Amphitheater, 8112

Td Bank Arts Centre, 7589
Td Banknorth Garden, 7228
Te Paske Theatre, 7021
Teaneck New Theatre, 3388
Teatro Avante, 2767
Teatro Hispano De Dallas, 3956
Teatro Shalom, 2528
Teatro Vision, 2605
Teatro Zinzanni, 5804
Tecumseh Center for the Arts, 7329
Tecumseh!, 3702
Ted Mann Concert Hall, 7361
Telluride Chamber Music Festival, 919, 4375
Telluride Jazz Celebration, 4376
Temple Beth Am Series, 4467
Temple Civic Theatre, 4004, 8463
Temple Hoyne Buell Theatre, 6370
Temple Israel, 4412
Temple of Music & Art, 6004
Temple Square Concert Series, 5700
Temple Symphony Orchestra, 1754
Temple Theatre Company, 3679, 7914
Temple Theatre Organ Club, 4858
Tennessee Association of Dance, 613
Tennessee Children's Dance Ensemble, 616
Tennessee Performing Arts Center, 8303
Tennessee Performing Arts Center: Andrew Jackson Hall, 8304
Tennessee Players, 3907
Tennessee Repertory Theatre, 3919
Tennessee Stage Company, 3905
Tennessee Theater, 8273
Tennessee Theatre Company, 3920
Tennessee Williams Theatre, 6536
Tennis Center at Crandon Park, 6533
Terpsicorps Theatre of Dance, 506
Terre Haute Symphony Orchestra, 1097
Tex Turner Arena, 8261
Texarkana Regional Arts & Humanities Council, 5671
Texas A&M University Opera & Performing Arts, 2341
Texas Bach Choir, 2361
Texas Ballet Theater, 632
Texas Boys Choir, 2349
Texas Girl's Choir, 5624
Texas Girls' Choir, 2350
Texas International Theatrical Arts Society, 3957
Texas Jazz Festival Society, 1710, 5605
Texas Lutheran University Cultural Arts Events, 5667
Texas Panhandle Heritage Foundation, 3940
Texas Shakespeare Festival, 3993, 5649
Texas Tech University Artists & Speakers, 5652
Texas Tech University Performing Arts Center, 8429
Texas Wesleyan College: Fine Arts, 8390
Thaddeus Torp Theatre, 6416
Thalia Mara Hall, 7398
Thalia Spanish Theatre, 3624
Thalian Hall Center for the Performing Arts, 7920
Thanksgiving Square: Courtyard at Thanksgiving, 8365
Thatcher Music Building, 6087
Thayer Symphony Orchestra, 1198
The Academy of Ballet Arts, 171
The Actors' Gang Theater, 2462
The Albright Theatre Company, 2902
The Allen Bales Theatre, 5931
The American Mime Theatre, 488
The Antelope Valley Ballet, 33
The Apollo Club, 2141
The Arcadia Chorale, 2301
The Arizona Repertory Singers, 1859
The Art of Black Dance and Music, 281
The Arts Center, 6973
The Atlantic Coast Opera Festival, 2315
The Austin Lyric Opera, 2339
The Black Academy of Arts and Letters Series, 5607
The Boisefeuillet Jones Atlanta Civic Center, 6628
The Bronx Opera Company, 2204
The Butter Theater, 6345
The Carton Palace Theatre Association, 7952
The Carver Community Cultural Center, 5663
The Center for the Arts, 6117
The Center for the Performing Arts, 6842

The Center for the Perorming Arts, 6860
The Charles Moore Dance Theatre, 361
The Charleston Ballet, 693
The Cherry Creek Chorale, 1947
The Chicago Moving Company, 200
The Chicago Theatre, 6753
The Choral Arts Society of Washington, 1983
The City Choir of Washington, 1992
The Classic Center, 6615
The Classical Theatre of Harlem, 3575
The Columbia City Jazz Dance Company & School, 598
The Concert Ballet of Virginia, 668
The Construction Company, 379
The Convocation Center, 6051
The Croswell Opera House & Fine Arts Association, 7262
The Curtainbox Theatre Company, 3033
The Denver Brass, 6350
The Dicapo Opera Theatre, 2250
The Dinner Detective, 3174
The Duluth Playhouse, 3225
The Eba Theatre, 350
The Everyman Repertory Theatre, 3106
The Festival Opera Association Inc, 1941
The Footlight Players, 3870
The Foundation of Arts, 14
The Garden State Opera, 2177
The German Society of Pennsylvania, 5479
The Granada, 6288
The Grand Opera House, 6651
The Greater Middletown Chorale, 1965
The Green at Shelburne Museum, 8509
The Hampstead Stage Company, 3342
The Hartt School, 136
The Haymarket Opera Company, 2049
The Haymarket Theatre, 3328
The Hemmens Cultural Center, 6774
The Historic Cocoa Village Playhouse, 6490
The Historic Paramount Theatre, 6358
The Holmes Center, 7858
The Human Race Theatre Company, 3733
The Ikon Center, 8716
The Immanuel & Helen Olshan Texas Music Festival, 5639
The Island Players Theatre, 6482
The John F Kennedy Center for the Performing Arts, 6471
The Jose Limon Dance Foundation, 439
The Kansas City Chorale, 2158
The Kennedy Dancers, 331
The Kitchen, 7743
The Las Vegas Contemporary Dance Theater, 320
The Laura Ingalls Wilder Pageant Society, 5554
The Leeward Theatre, 6682
The Leslie Wright Center, 5896
The Lexington Ballet, 242
The Lira Ensemble, 206
The Lively Foundation, 92
The Long Beach Chorale and Chamber Orchestra, 1883
The Lynn Auditorium., 7241
The M Ensemble Inc., 2799
The Mahaiwe Performing Arts Center Theatre, 7236
The Majestic and Charline Mcombs Empire Theatres, 8459
The Maple Conservatory of Dance, 32
The Martin City Melodrama & Vaudeville Company Ltd., 3046
The Merle Reskin Theatre, 6741
The Michigan Dance Project, 284
The Mifflin-Juniata Concert Association, 5465
The Montana Ballet Company, 312
The Muckenthaler Cultural Center, 6112
The Music Center, 6754
The Mystical Arts of Tibet, 183
The Nashville Shakespeare Festival, 5581
The National Philharmonic, 1169
The New Group, 3576
The New Orleans Jazz & Heritage Festival and Foundation, Inc., 4718
The New York Virtuoso Singers, 2243
The Opera Orchestra of New York, 2251
The Otero Players, 6384
The Pacific Mozart Ensemble, 1870
The Palace, 6434

The Palace Theatre, 8231
The Palestra, 8161
The Paramount Center for the Arts, 8252
The Pat Graney Company, 683
The Peninsula Music Festival, 5834
The Players Theatre, 6585
The Plaza Theatre, 2793
The Pollard Theatre, 3757
The Providence Singers Inc., 2324
The Purple Moon Dance Project, 87
The Radost Folk Ensemble, 684
The Reno Irish Dance Company, 322
The Rialto Theatre, 6052
The Richard Symphony, 1745
The Ridgefield Playhouse, 6430
The Rising Stars Theatre Company, 2954
The Ritz Theatre, 8010
The Road Theatre Company, 2533
The Robert and Judi Newman Center for the Performing Arts, 6364
The Round Barn Theatre at Amish Acres, 3019
The San Francisco Choral Society, 1927
The Santa Fe Opera, 2200
The Shepherd School of Music, 5642
The Sherman Playhouse, 6431
The Smith Center for the Performing Arts, 7514
The Southern Strutt Studio, 608
The Springfield Ballet Company, 223, 311
The Stage Door Theatre, 2769
The Tallahassee Ballet, 172
The Tin Roof Theatre Company, 3691
The Traveling Bohemians, 60
The Tucson Jazz Soceity, 745
The Ventura County Ballet Company, 116
The Weekend Theater, 2440
The Westchester Ballet Company, 496
The Winnipesaukee Playhouse, 3349
The Wisconsin Center District, 5697
The Wright State University Nutter Center, 5335
The Zoot Theatre Company Inc., 3734
Theater, 8700
Theater at Emory, 6629
Theater Barn, 3456
Theater by The Blind, 3577
Theater Coalition/The Lear Theater, 3340
Theater Emory, 2864
Theater Factory Saint Louis, 3304
Theater for the New City, 3578
Theater Grottesco, 3201
Theater J, 6478
Theater Knoxville, 3906
Theater Latte Da, 3254
Theater of the Stars, 2865
Theater Rhinoceros, 2593
Theater Schmeater, 4089
Theater Works, 2425
Theaterwork, 3405
Theaterworks, 2688
Theatre Albany, 2843, 6611
Theatre Arlington, 3927, 8321
Theatre Artaud, 2594
Theatre Arts Dance Program, 666
Theatre at Ewing, 6810
Theatre at Meydenbauer, 8570
Theatre at Monmouth, 3099
Theatre at Raritan Valley Community College, 3380, 3385, 7576
Theatre B, 3692, 7008
Theatre Bristol, 3893
Theatre Building Chicago, 2955
Theatre Charlotte, 3649
Theatre Club of the Palm Beaches, 2794
Theatre De La Jeune Lune, 3255
Theatre Du Grand-Guignol De Paris, 3579
Theatre East, 6130
Theatre El Dorado, 2544
Theatre First, 2956
Theatre for A New Audience, 3580
Theatre Gael, 2866
Theatre Gemini, 3958
Theatre Guild, 8287
Theatre Harrisburg, 3806
Theatre Hopkins, 3117
Theatre II Company, 2957
Theatre in The Grove, 8077
Theatre in The Park, 3677, 7911
Theatre in The Round, 3256
Theatre in The Round Players, 7362

1127

Entry Index

Theatre in The Square, 2876, 6653
Theatre IV, 4053
Theatre Jacksonville, 2786
Theatre L'homme Dieu, 3220
Theatre Margot, 6875
Theatre Memphis, 8286
Theatre of Western Springs, 2992
Theatre of Youth Company, 3430
Theatre on The Ridge, 3611
Theatre on The Square, 3015, 3699
Theatre Outback, 5960
Theatre Previews at Duke, 3652
Theatre Project, 3118
Theatre Project Consultants, 6432
Theatre Suburbia, 3989, 8417
Theatre Three, 3959
Theatre Three Productions, 3605
Theatre Three Productions Second Stage, 7806
Theatre Tulsa, 3769
Theatre Tuscaloosa, 2414
Theatre Under the Stars, 3990
Theatre West, 2517
Theatre West Virginia, 4096
Theatre Winter Haven, 2839
Theatre Workshop of Nantucket, 3163
Theatre Workshop of Owensboro, 3073
Theatre X, 4130
Theatre-In-The-Works, 2809
Theatrevirginia, 5756, 8558
Theatreworks, 2525, 2541
Theatreworks Usa, 3582
Theatrical Outfit, 2867
Theresa Lang Theatre, 3583
Theron C Bennet Ragtime & Early Jazz Festival, 4914
Thick Description, 2595
Third Street Music School Settlement Faculty Artists Series, 5165
Thodos Dance Chicago, 213
Thomas & Mack Center, 7515
Thomas Armour Youth Ballet, 170
Thomas Assembly Center, 7155
Thomaston-Upson Arts Council Performing Series, 4522
Thomasville Center for the Arts, 6664
Thomasville Entertainment Foundation, 4523
Thompson Recital Hall, 6881
Thompson-Boling Arena, 8274
Thorne Hall, 6179
Thornton Symphony, 807
Thousand Oaks Civic Arts Plaza, 6314
Three Arts Theatre, 6641
Three Rivers Arts Festival, 5495
Threshold Repertory Theatre, 3871
Thunder Bay Arts Council, 4820
Thunder Bay Ensemble, 3584
Thunder Bay Theatre, 3189
Tibbits Opera Foundation and Arts Council, 2133
Ticonderoga Festival Guild, 5210
Tidewater Classical Guitar Society, 1783
Tidewater Performing Arts Society, 5748
Tifereth Israel Community Orchestra, 845
Tiffany Mills Company, 371
Tiger Stadium, 7117
Tilles Center for the Performing Arts, 7678
Tillie Lewis Theater, 2629
Tillman Auditorium, 8215
Timber Lake Playhouse, 2977
Timbers Dinner Theatre, 3820
Timeline Theatre Company, 2958
Times-Union Center for the Performing Arts, 6529
Timmons Arena, 8228
Tingley Coliseum, 7609
Tippecanoe Chamber Music Society, 1090
Tisch Center for the Arts, 1447, 7788
Tivoli Theatre, 8255
Toby's Dinner Theatre, 7204
Toledo Ballet Association, 545
Toledo Cultural Arts Center Valentine Theatre, 8016
Toledo Jazz Society, 1570
Toledo Museum of Art, 8017
Toledo Opera, 2289
Toledo Repertoire Theatre, 3752
Toledo Symphony, 1571
Tom Bradley International Hall, 6180
Tom Miles Theatre, 8078

Tomball Regional Arts Council, 5672
Tony Williams Scholarship Jazz Festival, 5487
Topeka Civic Theatre & Academy, 3049
Topeka Performing Arts Center, 4682, 7063
Topeka Symphony, 1123
Topeka Symphony Chorus, 2076
Totem Pole Playhouse, 3803, 8124
Touchstone Theatre, 3795, 8115
Touring Concert Opera Company: Martinsville-Henry County Festival of Opera, 5744
Tower Fine Arts Center and Hartwell Hall, 7638
Tower Theater for the Peforming Arts, 6107
Town Hall Arts Center, 6386
Town Hall Concert Hall, 7789
Town of Cary Cultural Arts Division, 7864
Town of Herndon, 5741
Town Players, 3891
Towne and Country Players, 3748
Townsend Center for the Performing Arts, 6636
Townsend Opera Players, 1890
Towson Center Arena, 7215
Transworld Dome at Americas' Center, 7458
Traveling Jewish Theatre, 2596
Traverse Symphony Orchestra, 1256
Travesty Dance Group Cleveland, 542
Treasure Coast Concert Association, 4471
Tremont String Quartet, 1388
Trey Mcintyre Project, 197
Tri-C Jazzfest, 5321
Tri-Cities Coliseum, 8585
Tri-Cities Opera Company, 2202
Tri-State Music Festival, 5383
Triangle Cultural Center, 7411
Triangle Productions, 5421
Triangle Theatre Festival, 5237
Triarts Sharon Playhouse, 2704
Tribeca Performing Arts Center, 5166, 7790
Trilakes Community Theatre, 3280
Trinity Arts Center, 8200
Trinity College School of Music, 4568
Trinity College Theatre and Dance Department, 2689
Trinity Irish Dance Company, 216
Trinity Mother Frances Rose Stadium, 8468
Trinity Repertory Company, 3864
Trinkle Brass Works, 1499
Trisha Brown Dance Company, 489
Triton College Performing Arts Center, 6824
Triune Concert Series, 5332
Troika Balalaikes World Artists, 2025
Trojan/Adams Center Performing Arts Theatre, 5922
Tropicana Field, 6589
Troupe America, 3257
Troy Chromatics Concerts, 1471
Troy Hayner Cultural Center, 8019
Troy Savings Bank Music Hall, 7841
Truman State University Lyceum Series, 4909
Trumbull New Theatre, 8002
Trumpet in The Land, 3745
Trustees Theater, 6662
Trustus, 3874
Tryon Concert Association Subscription Series, 5271
Tryon Fine Arts Center, 7916
Tuacahn Amphitheatre, 8493
Tubac Center of the Arts, 5994
Tucson Arizona Boys Chorus, 1860
Tucson Chamber Orchestra, 744
Tucson Convention Center - Arena, 6005
Tucson Convention Center - Exhibition Hall, 6006
Tucson Convention Center - Leo Rich Theatre, 6007
Tucson Convention Center - Music Hall, 6008
Tucson Electric Park, 6009
Tucson Philharmonia Youth Orchestra, 746
Tucson Symphony Orchestra, 747
Tucson Winter Chamber Music Festival, 748, 4181
Tuesday Evening Concert Series, 5729
Tuesday Musical Association, 5288
Tuesday Musical Club Artist Series, 5665
Tuesday Musical Concert Series, 4950
Tulane University, 8259
Tulane University Albert Lupin Experimental Theatre, 7150

Tulane University Department of Theatre and Dance, 7151
Tulane University Newcomb Department of Music, 5919
Tulare County Symphony, 888
Tulsa Ballet, 554
Tulsa Community College Performing Arts Center for Education, 8059
Tulsa Opera, 2297
Tulsa Performing Arts Center, 8053
Tulsa Performing Arts Center Trust, 5394, 5395
Tulsa Performing Arts Center: Doenges Theater, 8055
Tulsa Performing Arts Center: John H William Hall, 8054
Tulsa Performing Arts Center: Studio II, 8056
Tulsa Youth Symphony, 1586
Tultex Corporation, 8534
Tupelo Symphony Orchestra Association, 1278
Turner Field, 6630
Turpin Stadium, 7138
Turtle Creek Chorale, 2344
Tuscaloosa Symphony Orchestra, 716
Tuscarawas Philharmonic, 1562
Tvi Actors Studio, 3585
Tweeter Center for the Performing Arts, 7242
Twentieth Century Unlimited Series, 5036
27th Annual Central Pa Commerce Bank Jazz Festival, 5451
Twilight Cabaret Productions, 3072
Twin Cities Gay Men's Chorus, 2146
Twin Lakes Playhouse, 2443
Twin Mountain Tonesmen, 2360
Two River Theater Company, 3384
Tyler Civic Ballet, 647
Tyler Community Concert Association, 5673
Tyrrell Hall, 8057

U

U S Airways Center, 5976
U.S. Cellular Arena, 8694
Ua Presents, 4182
Uaa Recital Hall, 5936
Uab Arena, 5897
Uapresents Centennial Hall, 6010
Uc Davis Presents, 4216
Uc Santa Cruz Arts & Lectures, 4329
Ucf Arena, 6572
Ucf Civic Theatre, 2810
Ucla Performing Arts, 6181
Ucsb Arts & Lectures, 4326
Uga Ballet Ensemble, 177
Uga Core Concert Dance Company, 178
Uhh Theatre, 6669
Uic Pavilion, 6756
Uic Theatre, 6757
Ukiah Players Theatre, 2636
Ulster Performing Arts Center, 7695
Umb Bank Pavilion, 7432
Umpqua Symphony Association, 1612
Un-Scripted Theater Company, 2597
Una Vocis Choral Ensemble, 2073
Unbound Dance Company, 603
Underground Theatre, 8576
Undermain Theatre, 3960
Unf Arena, 6530
Uni-Dome, 6965
Unicorn Theatre, 3292, 7430
Union Avenue Opera Theatre, 7459
Union Colony Civic Center, 6382
Union County Arts Center, 7586
Union Square Theatre, 7791
Union Theater, 8681
United Arts Council of Greensboro, 5247
United Arts Council of Raleigh and Wake County, 5265
United Black Artists: Usa Series, 4838
United Center, 6758
United States Air Force Band, 951
United States Air Force Singing Sergeants, 1981
United States Navy Band, 963
United Supermarkets Arena, 8430
University at Albany Performing Arts Center (Pac), 7627
University at Buffalo Center for the Arts, 7658
University Center Auditorium, 6487
University Center for the Arts, 6375

University Center Theatre Complex and Conference Center, 8343
University Chamber Orchestra, 736
University Circle Chamber Orchestra, 1540
University Events Office, 4234
University Musical Society Choral Union, 2130
University of Akron: Ej Thomas Hall Series, 5289
University of Alabama School of Music Celebrity Series, 4155
University of Alabama, Birmingham: Department of Theatre, 2403
University of Alaska, Anchorage: Department of Theatre and Dance, 2418
University of Alaska, Fairbanks: Theatre Department, 2420
University of Arkansas at Fayetteville: Department of Drama, 2435
University of Arkansas at Little Rock: Department of Theatre and Dance, 2441
University of California Irvine Cultural Events, 4230
University of California Santa Cruz Performing Arts Center, 6298
University of California, Davis: Department of Dramatic Art, 2464
University of California-Berkeley California, 4207
University of California-Irvine: Department of Drama, 2478
University of California-Los Angeles: Department of Theater, 2518
University of California-Riverside: Department of Theatre, 2548
University of California-San Diego: Department of Theatre and Dance, 2482
University of California-Santa Barbara: Department of Dramatic Art, 2612
University of Central Arkansas Public Appearances, 4185
University of Central Arkansas Theatre Program, 2434
University of Central Florida Orchestra, 985
University of Central Florida: Department of Theatre, 2811
University of Central Missouri, 4928
University of Chicago Professional Instrumental Music Series, 4560, 4561
University of Chicago Symphony Orchestra, 1043
University of Colorado at Boulder: Department of Theatre and Dance, 2647
University of Colorado at Denver: Department of Performing Arts, 2666
University of Colorado Concerts, 4360
University of Connecticut Sports Complex - Harry a Gampel Pavilion, 6438
University of Connecticut: Department of Dramatic Arts, 2711
University of Dayton Arts Series, 5337
University of Delaware Performing Arts Series, 4413
University of Denver Department of Theatre, 2667
University of Detroit Mercy Calihan Hall, 7290
University of Florida: School, Theater and Dance, 2781
University of Georgia Performing Arts Center, 6616
University of Hartford Sports Center, 6446
University of Hartford: Department of Art History, Cinema, Drama, 2716
University of Hawaii Series, 4528
University of Idaho Theatre Arts, 6702
University of Illinois at Chicago Fine Arts Series, 4562
University of Illinois at Springfield Sangamon Performing Arts Series, 4599
University of Illinois: Assembly Hall, 4547
University of Illinois: Summerfest, 4602
University of Kentucky Artists Series, 4694
University of Kentucky Memorial Coliseum, 7089
University of Kentucky Singletary Center for the Arts, 4693
University of Laverne, 2483
University of Louisiana at Lafayette Concert Series, 4710
University of Louisiana at Monroe Performing Arts Series, 4714
University of Maine Alumni Stadium, 7174

Entry Index

University of Maine at Fort Kent, International Performers Series, 4734
University of Maine Performing Arts Center, 7170
University of Mary Hardin: Baylor, 5596
University of Maryland Baltimore County Symphony, 1158
University of Maryland International William Kapell Piano Competition & Festival, 4759
University of Maryland: International William Kapell Piano Competition & Festival, 1161
University of Massachusetts Center for the Arts, 7240
University of Massachusetts Fine Arts Center, 7217
University of Miami: Department of Theatre Arts, 2768
University of Michigan Gilbert and Sullivan, 2131
University of Michigan Symphony Orchestras, 1223
University of Minnesota at Minneapolis Series, 4872
University of Minnesota Duluth: Department of Theatre, 3226, 3227
University of Minnesota Morris Cac Performing Arts Series, 4877
University of Minnesota Sports Pavillion, 7363
University of Mississippi Artist Series, 4893
University of Mississippi Studio Theatre, 7407
University of Missouri Performing Arts Series, 7439
University of Missouri-Kansas City Conservatory Series, 4908
University of Missouri: Columbia Concert Series, 4897
University of Missouri: Saint Louis Premier Performances, 4923
University of Montana Performing Arts Series, 4936
University of Montana Theatre, 7482
University of Montevallo: Division of Theatre, 2411
University of Nebraska at Omaha Music Series, 4951
University of Nebraska Theatre, 7488
University of Nebraska-Lincoln: Kimball Recital Hall, 7494
University of Nevada Performing Arts Center, 4958
University of Nevada-Las Vegas Performing Arts Center Artemus Ham Concert Hall, 7516
University of Nevada: Reno Performing Arts Series, 4960
University of New Hampshire Celebrity Series, 4964
University of New Mexico Stadium, 7610
University of New Orleans Performing Arts Center, 7152
University of North Alabama: Department of Music & Theatre, 2407
University of North Carolina at Asheville Cultural & Special Events, 5219
University of North Carolina at Greensboro Concert/Lecture Series, 5248
University of North Carolina at Wilmington, 5274
University of North Florida Fine Arts Center, 6531
University of North Texas Performing Arts Center, 8369
University of Northern Colorado, 6383
University of Northern Iowa Artists Series, 4640
University of Notre Dame Department of Film, Television & Theatre, 3021
University of Oklahoma Symphony Orchestras, 1581
University of Oregon Chamber Music Series, 5407
University of Oregon Department of Dance, 558
University of Pittsburgh Concert Series, 5496
University of Portland Music at Midweek, 5422
University of Puget Sound Cultural Events, 5811
University of Rhode Island Fine Arts Center, 8193
University of Rhode Island Symphony Orchestra, 1673
University of Rochester Theatre Program, 3612
University of South Alabama, 2410
University of South Carolina-Beaufort, 5530

University of South Carolina: Aiken Etherredge Center, 5527
University of South Florida: School of Theatre, 2834
University of Southern California, 6182
University of Southern California Thornton Opera, 1889
University of Southern California: School of Theatre, 2519
University of Southern Mississippi School of Music, 4887, 7392
University of Southern Mississippi Symphony, 1274
University of Southwestern Louisiana Concert Series, 4711
University of St. Thomas, 5644
University of Tennessee at Chattanooga, 5560
University of Tennessee at Knoxville: Cultural Arts, 5572
University of Tennessee at Martin Arts Council, 5573
University of Tennessee Music Hall, 8275
University of Texas at Arlington, 5587
University of Texas at Austin Performing Arts Center, 8326
University of Texas at Austin: Theatre Room, 8327
University of Texas at Brownsville, 5599
University of Texas at El Paso: Main Playhouse, 8380
University of Texas at Tyler, 5674
University of Texas-Pan American: Theater, 8370
University of the Pacific Conservatory of Music - Resident Artist Series, 4338
University of the Pacific: Department of Theatre Arts, 2630
University of Utah: School of Music, 1764
University of Vermont: George Bishop Lane Series, 5706
University of Vermont: Recital Hall, 8505
University of Virginia Hall, 8518
University of West Florida, 2813
University of West Florida Center for Fine & Performing Arts, 6580
University of Wisconsin at Eau Claire Artists Series, 5833
University of Wisconsin at La Crosse Lectures, 5845
University of Wisconsin at Oshkosh Chamber Arts Series, 5861
University of Wisconsin at Stevens Point Performing Arts, 5871
University of Wisconsin at Whitewater, 5876
University of Wisconsin Center - Fox Valley, 5852
University of Wisconsin Fieldhouse, 8682
University of Wisconsin Lectures and Fine Arts, 5851
University of Wisconsin Marathon County, 5875
University of Wisconsin River Falls: Wyman Concerts & Lectures Series, 5866
University of Wisconsin-Platteville, 5862
University of Wisconsin: Superior University, 5872
University of Wyoming Cultural Programs, 5880
University of Wyoming: Arts and Sciences Auditorium, 8718
University of Wyoming: Fine Arts Concert Hall, 8719
University Productions: University of Michigan, 3191
University Settlement, 7792
University Symphony Orchestra, 737
University Theatre, 6121, 6226, 6573, 6885, 6918, 8040
University Theatre: Summer Show Biz, 2963
Unk Sports Center, 7489
Unto These Hills, 3672
Upper Arlington Cultural Arts Commission, 5369
Upper Catskill Community Council of the Arts, 5181
Upper Darby Performing Arts Center, 8120
Upper Darby Summer Stage, 3800
Ups Fieldhouse, 8619
Upstart Crow Theatre Company, 2648
Uptown Players, 3961
Urban Bush Women, 372
Urban Gateways Series: Center for Arts Education, 4563

Urban Institute for Contemporary Arts, 3204, 7303
Urbanity Dance, 274
Us Bank Arena, 7959
Us Cellular Arena, 8695
Us Cellular Center, 6971
Us Cellular Field, 6759
Us Military Academy, 7631
Us Military Academy Michie Stadium, 7848
Us Naval Academy Alumni Hall, 7186
Us Navy Band, 2001
Us Sailors Center, 6967
Usa Saenger Theatre, 5911
Usdan Center for the Creative & Performing Arts: Festival Concerts, 5167
Usf Special Events Center, 6598
Usf Sun Dome, 6599
Utah Chamber Artists, 2368
Utah Classical Guitar Society, 1765
Utah Festival Opera Company, 2362
Utah Opera Company, 2366
Utah Regional Ballet, 650
Utah Repertory Theater Company, 4014
Utah Shakespearean Festival, 4006, 5682
Utah State University Performing Arts Series, 5684
Utah Symphony, 1766, 2367
Utc Mckenzie Arena, 8256
Utica Memorial Auditorium, 7844
Uvalde Arts Council, 5675
Uw World Series, 8608

V

Vagabond Acting Troupe, 3818
Vail Jazz Festival, 4379
Val a Browning Center for the Performing Arts, 8487
Valdez Convention and Civic Center, 5945
Valdosta Symphony Orchestra, 1016
Valencia College Performing Arts Center, 6574
Vallejo Symphony Association, 887
Valley Artists Series, 5363
Valley Cultural Center Concerts in The Park, 4350
Valley Light Opera, 2102
Valparaiso Theatrical Company, 3025
Valparaiso University Chorale, 2068
Valparaiso University Guest Artists Series, 4633
Valparaiso University Symphony Orchestra, 1098
Van Andel Arena, 7304
Van Wezel Performing Arts Hall, 6586
Vanaver Caravan, 380
Vancouver Symphony Orchestra, 1811
Vanderbilt Stadium, 8305
Vanderbilt University: Great Performances, 5582
Vanderbilt University: Memorial Gym, 8306
Vanguard Concerts, 5338
Vanguard Theatre Ensemble, 2470
Vashon Opera, 2390
Vaudeville Palace, 2826
Vela Luka Croatian Dance Ensemble, 674
Velma V. Morrison Center for the Performing Arts, 6688, 6689
Venice Symphony, 1000
Venice Theatre, 2835
Venti Da Camera, 1522
Ventura Music Festival, 4344
Verb Ballets, 541
Verde Valley Concert Association, 4166
Verge Theater, 3315
Verizon Center, 6475
Verizon Wireless Amphitheatre, 7878
Verizon Wireless Arena, 7540
Vermont Shakespeare Company, 4023
Vermont Stage Company, 4019
Vermont Symphony Orchestra, 1769
Vermont Youth Orchestra Association, 1770
Vern Riffe Center for the Arts, 8007
Vero Beach Concert Association, 6601
Vero Beach Opera Inc, 2016
Vero Beach Theatre Guild, 2837
Veronica's Veil Players, 3851
Verser Theater, 6017
Vesper Chorale, 2067
Veteran's Memorial Complex, 6092
Veterans Memorial Arena, 6532
Veterans Memorial Auditorium, 6990, 8201

Veterans Memorial Civic and Convention Center, 7998
Veterans Memorial Field House, 8640
Veterans Memorial Hall, 7828
Veterans Wadsworth Theatre, 6183
Veterans' Memorial Theatre, 6097
Victoria Fine Arts Association, 5677
Victoria Theatre Association, 7993
Victory Field: Indianapolis Baseball Club, 6903
Victory Gardens Theater, 6760
Victory Gardens Theater at the Biograph, 2959
Victory Theatre, 6869
Vigilante Theatre Company, 3316
Viking Hall Civic Center, 8253
Village Bach Festival, 4832
Village Center for the Arts, 827
Village Players, 3157
Village Players Theater, 2981
Village Repertory Company, 3872
Village Theatre, 4068, 4072
Villanova University Chamber Series, 1663, 5509
Vincennes University Community Series, 4634
Vincennes University Summer Theatre, 3026
Vines Center, 8531
Vineyard Playhouse, 3177
Vineyard Theatre, 3587
Vintage Theatre Productions, 2645
Virginia Arts Festival, 5749
Virginia Ballet Company, 660
Virginia Ballet Theatre, 667
Virginia Beach Pavilion Convention Center, 8564
Virginia Choral Society, 2373
Virginia Commonwealth University Commons College, 5757
Virginia Musical Theatre, 4058
Virginia Opera, 2374
Virginia Repertory Theatre, 4054
Virginia Samford Theatre, 2413
Virginia School of the Arts, 671
Virginia Shakespeare Festival, 4059, 5766
Virginia Stage Company, 4046
Virginia Symphony, 1784
Virginia Symphony Chorus, 2375
Virginia Tech Union Lively Arts Season, 5726
Virginia Theater, 7793
Visalia Convention Center Rotary Theatre, 6318
Visalia Cultural Programs-On Stage Visalia, 4345
Vista Ballroom, 604
Viterbo University Bright Star Season, 5846
Viterbo University Fine Arts Center, 8673
Viva Vivaldi Festival Xxiii, 5058
Vive Les Arts Theatre, 3994
Vivian Beaumont Theater, 3588
Vivian Davis Michael Laboratory Theatre, 8649
Vladimir Issaev's School of Classical Ballet, 159
Vocal Arts Society, 1993
Vocalessence, 2147, 4873
Voce Chamber Singers, 2376
Voices of Change, 1718
Voloshky Ukrainian Dance Ensembles, 571
Von Braun Civic Center Arena, 5902
Von Braun Civic Center Concert Hall, 5903
Von Braun Civic Center Exhibit Hall, 5904
Von Braun Civic Center Playhouse, 5901
Von Der Mehden Recital Hall, 6439
Vortex Repertory Company, 3934
Vox Dance Theater Inc, 44
Vsa Arts, 2752

W

W L Lyons Brown Theatre, 7096
W. Turrentine and Barbara K. Jackson Hall, 6098
W.D. Packard Music Hall, 8020
W.J. Hale Stadium, 8307
Wachovia Spectrum, 8162
Waco Convention Center Chisholm Hall, 8470
Waco Hippodrome, 8471
Waco Symphony Orchestra, 1756
Wadsworth Auditorium, 7675
Wagon Wheel Theatre, 3027
Waimea Community Theatre, 2889
Wake Forest University, 5279
Wake Forest University Symphony Orchestra, 1508
Walden Piano Quartet/Walden Chamber Music Society, 902
Waldorf Community Artists Series, 4655

1129

Entry Index

Walker Art Center, 3258, 7364
Wall Performance Lab, 6999
Walla Walla Symphony, 1812
Wallace Hall Fine Arts Center, 5900
Wallingford Symphony Orchestra, 943
Wallis Annenberg Center for the Performing Arts, 6074
Walnut Street Theatre, 3839, 8163
Walnut Street Theatre: Mainstage, 8164
Walnut Street Theatre: Studio 3, 8165
Walnut Street Theatre: Studio 5, 8166
Walt Disney Wide World of Sports Stadium, 6539
Walt Whitman Cultural Arts Center, 7548
Walter Arts Center, 8058
Walter E. Washington Convention Center, 6481
Walter Kerr Theatre, 7794
Walter Walker Auditorium, 6379
Waltham Community Concert Series, 4809
Walton Arts and Ideas, 4184
Walton Arts Center, 6026
War Memorial Auditorium, 6509
War Memorial Stadium, 6039
War Memorial Stadium (Wy), 8720
Warebrook Contemporary Music Festival, 5711
Warehouse Living Arts Center, 8347
Warehouse Theatre, 3878
Warfield Concerts, 4188
Warhawk Stadium, 8711
Warner Grand Theatre, 6276
Warner Theatre, 6441, 6480
Warnor's Theater, 6108
Warren Atherton Auditorium, 6312
Warren Civic Music Association, 5371
Warren Civic Orchestra, 1664
Warren M Lee Center, 8251
Warren Performing Arts Center, 6904
Wartburg College Artists Series, 4667
Wartburg Community Symphony Orchestra, 1117
Washington & Lee University Lenfest Series, 5742
Washington and Lee University Concert Guild, 1780
Washington Bach Consort, 959, 1994
Washington Ballet, 149
Washington Center for the Performing Arts, 8592
Washington Chorus, 1995
Washington College Concert Series, 4758
Washington Concert Opera, 1996
Washington Hall Auditorium, 6935
Washington Idaho Symphony, 1796
Washington Jewish Theatre, 1172
Washington National Opera, 1997
Washington Pavilion of Arts & Science, 8247
Washington Performing Arts Society, 4434
Washington Savoyards, 1998, 2097
Washington Square Contemporary Music Society, 5169
Washington Square Music Festival, 5168
Washington Stage Guild, 2753
Washington State University, 5791
Wassermann Piano Festival, 5685
Water Music Festival, 5805
Waterbury Symphony Orchestra, 944
Waterford Cultural Council, 4864
Waterloo Community Playhouse & Black Hawk Childrens Theatre, 3039
Waterloo Foundation for the Arts Series, 5018
Waterloo Riverfront Stadium, 7025
Waterloo-Cedar Falls Symphony Orchestra, 1101
Watertower Theatre, 3923
Watertown Jazz Festival, 5586
Watertown Lyric Theater Productions, 3632
Waterville Opera House, 7183
Waterville Valley Foundation Summer Festival, 4981
Watt Powell Stadium, 8630
Waukegan Concert Chorus, 2062
Waukegan Symphony Orchestra & Concert Chorus, 1071, 2063
Waukesha Civic Theatre, 4136, 8709
Waupaca Fine Arts Festival, 5873
Waverly Consort, 1452
Wayne State College Arena, 7504
Wayne State College Special Programs Black & Gold Series, 4953
Wayside Theatre, 4042
Wc Handy Music Festival, 4144
Weatchee Valley Symphony Orchestra, 1813

Weathervane Playhouse, 3747
Weathervane Theatre, 3355
Web Concert Hall, 7795
Weber State University Cultural Affairs, 5689
Weede Arena, 7058
Weis Center for the Performing Arts, 8139
Weissberger Theater Group, 3589
Welk Resort San Diego Theatre, 2466
Wellfleet Harbor Actors Theater, 3181
Wellington Memorial Auditorium, 7066
Wells Fargo Center, 5478
Wells Fargo Center for the Arts, 6302
Wells Fargo Sports Complex, 5937
Wells Theater, 6802
Wells Theatre, 8544
Wells-Metz Theatre, 6858
Wellspring/Cori Terry & Dancers, 288
Werner Auditorium, 6822
Wesley Chapel, 7683
Wesleyan University Theater Department, 2692
West Bay Opera, 1899
West Chester University of Pennsylvania School of Music, 1666
West Coast Chamber Orchestra, 872
West Coast Ensemble, 2520
West End Players Guild, 3305
West Georgia Theatre Company Summer Classic, 2869
West Hawaii Dance Theatre, 193
West Jersey Chamber Music Symphony & Society, 1333
West Liberty College Concert Series, 5825
West Michigan Symphony, 1249
West Nebraska Arts Center, 7502
West Shore Community College Cultural Series, 4860
West Suburban Symphony, 1055
West Valley Arts Council, 4176
West Valley Symphony, 735
West Virginia Dance Company, 692
West Virginia Public Theatre, 4103
West Virginia State College Theatre, 8641
West Virginia State Univertisy Music Series, 5817
West Virginia Symphony Chorus, 2392
West Virginia University at Parkersburg, 5821
West Virginia University Coliseum, 8650
West Virginia University Creative Arts Center, 8651
Westbeth Studio Theatre, 7796
Westbeth Theatre Center, 7797
Westbrook Auditorium, 6721
Westbury Music Fair, 5215
Westchester Broadway Theatre, 7669
Westchester Oratorio Society, 2257
Westchester Philharmonic, 1393
Western Arts Music Festival, 5881
Western Ballet, 50
Western Carolina University Lectures, Concerts & Exhibitions, 5232
Western Connecticut State University: Theatre Arts Department, 2681
Western Illinois University Bca Performing Artist Series, 4586
Western Illinois University Theatre and Dance Department, 6799
Western Nevada Musical Theatre Company, 3337
Western New York Chamber Orchestra, 1385
Western Oklahoma Ballet Theatre, 547
Western Opera Theater, 1928
Western Oregon University Edgar H Smith Fine Arts Series, 5415
Western Piedmont Symphony, 1497
Western Stage, 2558
Western Washington University Main Stage, 8577
Western Washington University Old Main Theatre, 8578
Western Washington University Performing Arts Center Series, 5773
Western Wyoming College, 5883
Westerville Symphony, 1572
Westfield State College Music & More Performing Arts Series, 4811
Westhoff Experimental Theatre, 6811
Westminster Choir College, 2188
Westminster College, 5701

Westminster College Celebrity Series, 5471
Westminster Community Artist Series, 4381
Westmoreland Symphony Orchestra, 1623
Weston H. Noble Recital Hall, 6983
Weston Playhouse, 4026
Westport Community Theatre, 2719, 6448
Westport Country Playhouse, 2720, 6449
Westside Theatre, 7798
Wexner Center for the Arts, 7987
Whalberg Recital Hall, 6109
Wharton Center for Performing Arts, 7294
Wharton County Junior College the Center for the Arts Series, 5679
Whatcom Symphony Orchestra, 1788
Wheaton Symphony Orchestra, 1051
Wheeler Opera House, 1945, 6329
Wheeling Civic Center, 8654
Wheeling Island Stadium, 8655
Wheeling Symphony, 1819
Wheelock Family Theatre, 3143
Whidbey Playhouse, 8589
Whistle Stop Playhouse, 7386
Whitaker Center for Science and The Arts, 8129
White Bird, 565
White Horse Theatre Company, 3590
White River Amphitheatre, 8569
White River Valley Chamber of Commerce, 5717
Whitefish Theatre Company, 3320
Whitehead Auditorium, 6666
Whitney Museum of Art Theater, 7799
Whittemore Center, 7530
Whittier College Bach Festival, 892, 4349
Whittier Junior Theatre, 2642
Whittington-Pfohl Auditorium, 7861
Wichita Community Theatre, 3052
Wichita Contemporary Dance Theatre, 240
Wichita Falls Backdoor Players, 4005, 4027
Wichita Falls Ballet Theatre, 648
Wichita Falls Symphony Orchestra, 1757
Wichita Grand Opera, 2077
Wichita State University Connoisseur Series, 4684
Wichita Symphony, 1124
Wicomico Civic Center, 7213
Wiedemann Recital Hall, 7072
Wien Experimental Theatre, 6403
Wien Stadium, 7800
Wilbur College Cultural Events Series, 4564
Wild Bill's Atlanta, 6645
Wild Space Dance Company, 704
Wildflower Music Festival, 5510
Wildwood Park for the Performing Arts, 6040
Wilkens Theatre, 7594
Wilkins Stadium, 6041
Will Geer Theatricum Botanicum, 2634
Will W Orr Auditorium, 8146
William & Mary Concert Series, 5767
William & Mary Hall, 8566
William D Mullins Memorial Center, 7218
William Ferris Chorale, 2050
William G Mennen Sports Arena, 7570
William H Gile Trust Fund Concert Series, 4962
William H Hammond Stadium, 6514
William Hall Chorale, 1898
William Paterson College: the Jazz Room Series, 5023
William Paterson University Performing & Visual Arts, 1349
William R Frizzell Cultural Centre Claiborne & Ned Foulds Theatre, 6515
William R Johnson Coliseum, 8436
William Randolph Hearst Greek Theatre, 6070
William S. Robinson Theatre, 6380
William Stadium, 8532
William Woods College Campus Center Dulany Auditorium, 7421
William Woods University Concert & Lecture Series, 4899
Williams Center for the Arts, 5017
Williams Center for the Arts Newman Theatre, 7588
Williams Chamber Players, 1217
Williams College Series, 4813
Williams Theatre, 6874
Williams-Brice Stadium, 8220
Williamsburg Ballet Theatre, 673
Williamsport Community Concert Association, 5512

Williamsport Symphony Orchestra, 1668
Williamstown Theatre Festival, 3184, 4814
Willimantic Orchestra, 942
Willowbrook Jazz Festival, 5024
Willows Theatre, 6089
Wilma Theater, 3840
Wilma Theatre, 7483
Wilmington Drama League, 2729
Wilmington Symphony Orchestra, 1506
Wilner Auditorium, 7073
Wilshire Ebell Theatre, 6184
Wilson Center for the Performing Arts, 8103
Wilson Chapel Complex, 8279
Wilson College Performing Arts Series, 5438
Wiltern Theatre, 2521
Wilton Playshop, 2721
Winchester Council for the Arts Series, 4702
Windward Theatre Guild, 2888
Windy City Performing Arts, 2051
Wingate University, 5276
Wings Stadium, 7314
Wings Theatre Company, 3591
Wink Arena, 7278
Winston Churchill Memorial Hall, 7422
Winston-Salem Piedmont Triad Symphony Association, 2273
Winston-Salem Symphony, 1509, 2274
Winter Arts Faire, 4279
Winter Garden Theatre, 7801
Wintergreen Performing Arts, 2380, 5768
Wintergreen Summer Music Festival, 5769
Winthrop University College of Visual & Performing Arts, 5547
Wisconsin Chamber Orchestra, 1827
Wisconsin Conservatory of Music, 5859
Wisconsin Union Theater, 4117
Wisconsin Union Theatre, 8683
Wisconsin Youth Symphony Orchestras, 1828
Witherspoon Arts Arena, 6049
Wittenberg University Department of Music, 1569
Wjct Jacksonville Jazz Festival, 4455
WI Zorn Arena, 8662
Wofa! Percussion and Dance From Guinea, West Africa, 490
Wolf Trap Farm Park for the Performing Arts, 8563
Wolf Trap Foundation for the Performing Arts, 5762
Wolf Trap Opera Company, 2378
Women in Music: Columbus, 5333
Women's Interart Center, 3592
Women's Project & Productions, 3593
Women's Theatre Alliance, 2960
Wood College Theatre, 7399
Woodland Concert Series, 4391
Woodland Opera House, 6325
Woodland Theatre Company, 3161
Woodruff Arts Center, 6631
Woodstock Fine Arts Association - Music for A Sunday Afternoon Series, 4605
Woodstock Mozart Festival, 1074, 4206
Woodstock Opera House, 2995, 6851
Woodward Arts and Theatre Council, 3770
Woolly Mammoth Theatre Company, 2754
Wooster Group, 3594
Wooster Symphony Orchestra, 1573
Worcester Children's Theatre, 3188
Worcester Music Festival, 4815
Word Dance Theater, 257
Working Class Theatre, 3406
Working Theatre Company, 3595
Workshop Theatre, 6859
World Arts Ethnic Festival: West, 4315
World Arts West, 94, 4316
World Arts/Noon Concerts Series, 5702
World Financial Center Arts & Events Program, 5170
World Music Festival, 4788
World Music Hall, 6414
World Music Institute, 491, 5171
World Performance Series: Thalia Mara Foundation, 4890
World Tree Puppet Theater, 3259
Worthington Arts Council, 5374
Wpa Theatre, 3596
Wright Auditorium, 7888
Wright State University Artist Series, 5339
Wright State University's Nutter Center, 7992

Entry Index

Wrigley Field, 6761
Writers' Theatre Chicago, 2970
Wt Neal Civic Center, 6485
Wtamu Theatre, 8340
Wvu Arts Series, 5820
Wwu Summer Stock, 4064
Wylliams/Henry Contemporary Dance Company (Whcdc), 309
Wynmoor Recital Hall, 6492
Wyo Theater, 8722
Wyoming Arts Council, 5879
Wyoming Symphony Orchestra, 1836

Xavier Hall Theatre, 7045
Xcel Energy Center, 7377

Y Music Society of the Jewish Community Center, 5497
Yachats Music Festival, 5425
Yack Arena, 7334
Yadkin Players, 3688
Yaelisa and Caminos Flamencos, 95
Yakima Symphony Orchestra, 1814
Yakima Valley Sundome, 8622
Yakima Youth Orchestra, 1815
Yale Baseball Stadium, 6425
Yale Bowl, 6426
Yale Opera, 1968
Yale Repertory Theatre, 2699, 6427
Yale Russian Chorus, 1969
Yale Schola Cantorum, 1970
Yale School of Drama, 2700
Yale Symphony Orchestra, 934
Yamhill County Fairgrounds, 8082
Yankee Stadium, 7640
Yard, 3151
Yass Hakoshima Mime Theatre, 3375
Yates Performing Arts Series, 5185
Yavapai College Performance Hall, 5978
Yavapai Symphony Association, 730
Yellow Barn, 8507
Yellow Barn Music Festival, 5716
Yellowstone Chamber Players, 1297
Yerba Buena Center for the Arts, 6267
Ym-Ywha of North Jersey Cultural Arts Series, 5025
York Symphony Orchestra, 1669
York Theatre Company, 3597
Yoshiko Chuma and The School of Hard Knocks, 492
Yost Ice Arena, 7272
Young Actors Theatre, 2829
Young Artists Theatre, 3126
Young Audiences of Maryland, 4756
Young Audiences of New Jersey, 5015
Young Audiences of Southeast Texas, Inc., 5595
Young Circle Park and Bandshell, 6523
Young Concert Artists Series, 5172
Young Dancers in Repertory, 373
Young Musicians Foundation Debut Orchestra, 764
Young People's Symphony Orchestra, 762
Young Playwrights, 3598
Young Theatre, 6114
Youngstown State University: Dana Concert Series, 5376
Youngstown Symphony Orchestra, 1575
Youth Orchestra of Greater Fort Worth, 1724
Youth Orchestras of San Antonio, 1750
Youth Symphony Association of Kansas, 1122
Youtheatre, 3215, 3443, 3663
Yreka Community Theatre, 2643
Yreka Community Theatre Center, 6326
Yuba County-Sutter County Regional Arts Council Touring/Presenting Program, 4250
Yueh Lung Shadow Theatre, 3448
Yuma Ballet Theatre & Performing Arts Company, 13
Yuma Civic Center, 6014
Yvonne Theater, 7564

Z

Zaccho Dance Theatre, 96
Zachary Scott Theatre Center, 3935
Zamir Chorale of Boston, 2120
Zanesville Art Center, 8027
Zanesville Concert Association, 5377
Zeiterion Theatre, 7243
Zellerbach Auditorium, 6071
Zellerbach Playhouse, 6072
Zendora Dance Company, 493
Zenon Dance Company and School, 299
Zephyr Dance, 214
Zephyr Theatre, 2522
Zig Zag Ballet, 132
Zion Dance Company, 614
Zion Passion Play, 2996
Zivili Dance Company, 535
Zoellner Arts Center, 8116
Zoronco Famenco Dance Theater and School, 300
Zurcher Auditorium, 6886

Executive Name Index

A

A. Bond, Craig, 2645
A. Bulette, Ms. Elizabeth, 8279
A. Chagnon, Kathleen, 1155
A. Chenoweth, Gregg, 6913, 6914
A. Flagg, Aaron, 6445
A. Kazi, Nadim, 2958
A. Nofsinger, David, 2900
A. Wall, Marilyn, 6519
A.Bradley, Kelly, 7676
Aaoki, Miho, 2420
Aaron, Bert, 2375
Aaron, Gregory, 190
Aarons, Devra, 2596
Aarons, Philip, 5126
Aaronson, Deborah, 3507
Aaronson, Julie, 5679
Aarons, Philip E., 394
Abadiano, Helen, 2693
Abare, William, 6590, 6591
Abate, Hank, 8177
Abate, Stephen, 2556
Abatemarco, C.P.A.,, Vincent, 7290
Abbas, Chad, 7024
Abbate, Lawrence, 6107
Abbe, Dennis, 4224
Abbett, Cybele, 1588
Abbey Robinson, Amy, 5662
Abbitt, Bat, 339
Abbitt, Diana, 1942
Abbitt-Hartnett, Katie, 6488
Abbleggan, Jamie, 50
Abbot, Eric, 3758
Abbott, Caroline, 5393
Abbott, Frank, 3978
Abbott, James W., 8248, 8250, 8251
Abbott, Kevin, 7737
Abbott, Michael S, 6861, 6862, 6863
Abbott, Ramona, 1788
Abbott, Thomas, 966, 4440
Abdallah, Eli, 7790
Abdella, Carolyn, 1277
Abdollahzadeh, Fatemeh, 2693
Abdow, Ronald J., 7250
Abdul-Hanson, Toni, 4238
Abe, Paolin, 8520
Abe, Rob, 4526
Abe, Robert H, 6669
Abel, James K., 2313
Abel, Karin, 7291
Abel, Yves, 2231
Abeles, Robert, 6154, 6171, 6176
Abelin, Jeff, 2167
Abell, Jeff, 200
Abels, Mark, 3305
Aberger, Tom, 6142
Aberlin, Robert E, 471
Aberman, Hugh, 569
Abernathie, Julie, 305
Abernathky, Joe, 7444
Abernathy, Bobby, 3780, 5414, 8083
Abernathy, Brian, 3827
Abernathy, J. J., 1767
Abernathy, Megan, 4410, 6445
Abernathy, Rob, 2903
Abernethy, Robert J., 4243
Abers, David, 3798
Abildsoe, Deborah, 4388
Abillio, David, 4301
Abingeon, Mike, 8456
Abington, Goerge, 8447
Ables, Anna, 6741
Abnett, Jenelle, 8110, 8111
Abney, Allison, 7139
Abney, Laurne, 612
Abo Rabia, Hazza, 2693
Abood, Michael, 5377
Abood, Walt, 7994
Abraham, Braden, 4087
Abraham, Daniel, 2731
Abraham, Dr. Edward, 1508
Abrahamian, Lee, 2234
Abrahams, Michael, 4302
Abrahamsen, Daniel C., 8826
Abrahamsen, Gerri, 8826, 8827
Abrahamson, Jim, 1005, 1006
Abrahamson, Thomas D., 4563

Abramowitz, Arthur, 3359
Abrams, Anne, 6257, 6263
Abrams, Eric, 741
Abrams, Jacqueline, 2291
Abrams, Jim, 1548
Abrams, Linda, 1334
Abrams, Marilyn, 2941
Abrams, Norman, 6180
Abrams, Stephanie, 2584
Abrams, Vicki, 4542
Abramson, Lynn, 6244
Abramson, Ronald D., 1679, 3869, 5534
Abramyan, Alexander, 6207
Abt, Helmut, 740, 4181
Abt, Peggy, 169
Abu Shumays, Sami, 5073
Abuba, Ernest, 429
Abuso, Joe, 1732
Accardi, Sara, 3798
Acebo, Christopher, 3771
Aceti, Diana, 3615
Aceto, Thomas, 4181
Acevedo, David, 2528
Acevedo, Gene, 882
Achorn, Tracy, 1897
Acito, Christopher J., 4995, 7560
Acker, Eunice, 1115, 1116
Acker, Mark, 6868
Ackerley, Dr Julian, 1860
Ackerley, Jennifer, 1860
Ackerman, David, 911
Ackerman, Deborah, 7947
Ackerman, Doug, 6365
Ackerman, Mark, 2918
Ackerman, Melissa, 341
Ackerman, Steve, 3242
Ackerman, Tim, 4910
Ackerman, Van, 7953
Ackert, Stephen, 4416, 4429
Acklin, Liz, 3960
Ackroyd, David, 5196
Acomb, Joanne, 1821
Acord Blackman, Paula, 2354
Acosta, John, 818
Acosta, Kristen, 8110, 8111
Acosta, Rebecca, 244
Acosta, Rick, 2656
Acosta, Viviana, 1163
Acuna, Carole, 27
Acuria, Ana Maria, 4182
Acutanza, Jeanne, 2384
Adair, Nancy, 2186
Adam, Francis G., 6398
Adam, Julia, 618
Adam, Liz, 1339
Adamiak, Diedra, 3806
Adams, Abigail, 2693, 3433, 3814, 5061
Adams, Amy, 1592
Adams, Angie, 620
Adams, Bettie S, 8565, 8566
Adams, Bill, 4292
Adams, Bob, 4191
Adams, Brandon, 3760
Adams, Carolyn, 1067, 6835
Adams, Chelsea, 3382
Adams, Daniel, 5386
Adams, Daria, 4256
Adams, David, 6775, 6776, 6777, 6778, 7250
Adams, Dean, 4406, 4407
Adams, Doug, 903
Adams, Elaine, 7281
Adams, Fred, 5682
Adams, Fred C., 4006
Adams, George, 1027
Adams, Gillian, 1726, 1735
Adams, Hal, 3189
Adams, Heather, 8180
Adams, Hillary W., 8442
Adams, Jason, 1455
Adams, Jean, 705
Adams, Jimi, 2731
Adams, John W, 2970
Adams, John W., 4563
Adams, Jolene, 2491
Adams, Judith, 4742
Adams, Julia, 4739, 4744
Adams, K.S., 8290
Adams, Karen, 8114

Adams, Kari, 4877
Adams, Karl, 8661
Adams, Katie, 2832
Adams, Kay, 3919, 4206, 5425
Adams, Kirk, 4843, 4868
Adams, Larame, 8028
Adams, Lucas, 3070, 3071
Adams, Mark, 621, 749, 4719
Adams, Mary A., 5076
Adams, Mary Kay, 5740
Adams, Maxey, 8614
Adams, Meagan, 755
Adams, Michael, 4256
Adams, Michael & Daria, 811
Adams, Michelle, 6796
Adams, Mike, 6272
Adams, Paul, 3488
Adams, Randy, 1291, 2525, 4916, 4921, 7455
Adams, Rayna, 3798
Adams, Sam, 715, 1833
Adams, Sandra, 1844
Adams, Steve, 1010
Adams, Susan, 1954
Adams, Terry, 4366
Adams, William, 4747
Adams, Yvonne, 2448
Adams III, Thaddeus A, 1495
Adams Jr., Francis G., 4384
Adams Riley, Rev D Wallace, 4474
Adamson, Judy, 3645
Adamson, Kenneth, 2693
Adamson, Peter, 6164
Adaszko, Eva, 2721
Adato, Vanessa, 359
Adcock, Elizabeth, 1297
Adcock, Gregory S., 1755
Adcock, Zilphia, 5266
Adcox, Jay, 6041
Addaman, Linda, 6900
Adderley, Cedric, 5328
Addington, Gary, 6384
Addio, Tanya, 2679
Addison, Anthony, 1542, 1543
Addison, Debbie, 4028
Addison, Jan, 6569
Addison, Jo, 4081
Addison, Wes, 740, 4181
Addison, Mary, 7172, 7173
Adducci, Denise M, 4546
Addy, Obo, 563
Addy, Susan, 563
Ade Brand, Linda, 1861, 4186
Adee, Andrea, 1792
Adekoya, Kevin, 4756
Adelizzi, Robert F., 6238, 6243
Adelle, Chenier, 4419
Adelman, Charles, 461
Adelman, David, 1422
Adelman, Sara, 2498
Adelman, Terry, 7975, 7976, 7977
Adelsman, Jean, 6316
Adelson, James F., 8058
Aderente, David R, 1223
Ades, Thomas, 4795
Adhar, Shruti, 1437
Adhikari, Ani, 1897
Adjmi, David, 3568
Adkins, Amy, 1723
Adkins, Charlotte, 2329
Adkins, Elisabeth, 1774
Adkins, Rob, 261
Adkins, Skip, 4104
Adkins, Adele, 7172, 7173
Adler, Barbara, 5117
Adler, Edward A.K., 5135
Adler, Jeff, 2856, 4032
Adler, Jonathon, 6490
Adler, Joseph, 2766
Adler, Lisa, 2856, 4032
Adler, Mark, 6186
Adler, Michael M, 6548
Adler, Nancy, 886, 6315
Adler, Pam, 8241
Adler, Shane, 461
Adler, Stephen, 621
Adler, Tally, 1026
Adler, Thomas W., 7975, 7976, 7977
Adler, Tiffany, 1142

Administrative Assis, Olonia, 5038
Adrian, Renae, 5749
Adriance, Sarah, 440
Aduddell, Monique, 4598
Afar, Rozita, 6179, 6182
Affentranger, Katie, 3339
Affleck-Graves, John F., 6927, 6931, 6932, 6933, 6934, 6935
Afghani, Sameed S, 982
Aflague, Frank, 4308
Afolayan, LaTanya, 5223
Africa, Jay, 2499
Aftonomos MD, Lefkos, 1916
Agaisse, Lucile, 1730
Agan, Chris, 1998, 2097
Agar, Eunice, 1206
Agarwal, Bij, 4156
Agbay, Jennifer, 7261
Agee, Sheila, 8247
Ager, Christina, 1801
Agin, Marti, 5047
Agin, Susan, 5047
Agins, Bobbi, 2182
Agler, Tim, 55
Agnew, Sue, 4180
Agolini, Susan, 2731
Agozzino, Kim, 8110, 8111
Agresti, Ben, 3939
Agrons, Josh, 2356
Aguiar, Maryann, 1647
Aguilera, Rebecca, 2335
Agustin, Sandy, 4870
Ahamparam, Soori, 1351
Ahearn, Chris, 7743
Ahearn, Matthew, 163
Ahern, Joseph J, 6751
Ahern, Sheryl, 1787
Ahillen, Jerry, 2812
Ahlersmeyer, Eileen, 6870
Ahlin, Marjorie, 3098
Ahlman, Larry, 5220
Ahlquist, Karen, 955
Ahmad-Llewellyn, Shahara, 1421, 5142, 7729
Ahmadi, Arian, 6277
Ahmanson, William A, 2493
Ahmanson, William H, 2463, 2509, 6166, 6170
Ahmed, Amy, 4152, 5923
Ahmed, Kaiser, 2936
Ahmed, Ruth, 1779
Ahn, Hosang, 4559
Ahn, Jooyong, 1125
Aho, Neil, 1897
Ahrens, Anthony, 2731
Ahrens, Elizabeth, 4857
Ahrens, Jack, 6123
Ahrens, Liz, 4857
Ahuja, Tania, 5188
Aibel, Douglas, 3587
Aichele, Rick, 5377
Aidem, Claire, 5164
Aiello, Tony, 1393
Aiges, Scott, 1143, 4718
Aigner, Eva, 1845
Aiken, John, 7395
Aiken, Mary, 2998
Aiken, Steve, 2086
Ailster, Harry, 1339
Ainsworth, Alex, 7395
Ainsworth, Louis R., 1715
Airey, Katie, 6124
Airhart, Robert, 7630
Aito, Suguru, 447
Aja, Ron, 3489
Ajanku, Kibibi, 4749
Ajkun, Chiara, 382
Ajkun, Leonard, 382
Ajlouny Jr, Joseph S, 7295
Akenson, Linda, 3220
Akers, Ginger, 8584
Akers, Janice, 6620, 6629
Akers, Nicole, 715
Akers-Toler, Toneta, 692
Akin, R. Marie, 709
Akina, Henry G, 2029
Akins, Thomas N, 1084
Akiyama, Kazuyoshi, 1468
Akred, Kerry, 1236
Alabastro, Tasi, 2602

1133

Executive Name Index

Alaimo, Joseph, 6835
Alameda, Yolanda, 5621
Alameida, Joseph, 4282
Alan, Michael, 7812
Alan Cohen, Ralph, 4056
Alan Fischer, John, 4447, 4685
Alan Smith, Larry, 5768, 5769
Alancraig, Susan, 5197
Alarcon, Joel, 1511
Albanaese, Emil, 937
Albanese, Alex, 969
Albanese, James, 7837
Albanese, John, 3571
Albanesius, Patrick, 3378
Albano, Joseph, 6404
Albaugh, Reuben, 6874
Albers, Kathleen, 5029
Albers, Lucy, 8245, 8246
Alberson, Rob, 7779
Albert, Crystal Joy, 987
Albert, Heidi, 1531
Albert, Jay, 5321
Albert, Lisa, 8028
ALBERT, LYN, 3209
Albert, LYN, 7312
Albert, Philip, 2881
Albert, PJ, 2807, 4469
Albert, Sharon, 2881
Albert, Stephen, 2923
Albert, Stephen J., 6734
Albert-Loewenberg, Susan, 2639
Alberti, Patricia, 8723
Albertia, Robert, 4035
Albertie, Dante, 3414
Albin, Dr Matha, 5391
Albin, Dr. Martha, 3768
Albin-Hill, Jill, 4596, 6820, 6821
Albiston, Denise, 4007, 8477, 8478, 8480, 8481
Albrecht, Alison, 2153
Albright, Jeff, 923
Albright, Jody, 4749
Albright, John, 4689
Albright, Mary, 6542
Albright, Phil, 3793
Albright, Raymond, 8751
Albritton, Ben, 5793
Albritton, Susan, 3952
Alcaraz, Lonnie, 2478
Alcock, Sherry, 6980, 6981, 6982, 6983
Alcorace, Diana, 58
Alcorn, Janet, 1099
Alcott, Chris, 4880
Alda, Alan, 7963, 7964, 7965, 7966
Aldag, Richard, 895
Alden, Steven M., 5164
Alder, Jac, 3959
Alder, Jack, 3959
Alderete, Fernando, 1738
Alderman, Betty, 1260
Alderman, Lisa, 4028
Alderson, Erin, 6802
Aldinger, Loviah, 2289
Aldredge, Jerry, 4025, 4968
Aldrich, Jonathon, 3105
Aldrich, Kristen, 3654
Aldrich, Nelson, 2327
Aldrich, Richard, 4801
Aldrich, Thomas P., 2089
Aldridge, Alexandra Q., 1653
Aldridge, Ed, 3797
Aldridge, Erin, 1258, 1259
Alegant, Marci, 5361
Alejandro, Felipe, 6129
Alejandro, Jose, 1465
Alemany, Dorothy, 489
Alenson, Jo, 4182, 5996, 6010
Alesandro, Nicholas, 3408
Alexander, Andrew, 2948
Alexander, Ben, 2422, 5951, 5955, 7013, 7014
Alexander, Benjamin, 2310
Alexander, Carol, 2785
Alexander, Chandra, 7395
Alexander, Cindy, 3385
Alexander, Dr David, 6704, 6707
Alexander, F. King, 7110, 7111, 7112, 7117
Alexander, Greg, 3566
Alexander, James L., 6738
Alexander, Jane, 2721
Alexander, Janet, 8028
Alexander, Jed, 7000, 7001, 7002
Alexander, Jennifer, 6899
Alexander, Jim, 3097
Alexander, John, 1930
Alexander, Kate, 2823, 6584
Alexander, Ken, 804
Alexander, Kim, 1683
Alexander, Len, 798
Alexander, Mark, 6540
Alexander, Michael, 1013, 4237, 6175
Alexander, Peter, 6888
Alexander, Sudie, 595
Alexander, Taneisha, 8300, 8455
Alexander, Timothy, 1183, 1185
Alexander Griffin, Janet, 2736
Alexander Robbins, David, 60
Alexandra Johnston, Jennifer, 1507
Alexis,, 1526
Alexis Calzada, Dawn, 139
Alexis Scott, Zo‰, 4079, 8598
Alfandre, Dominique, 591
Alfaro, Alexis, 844
Alfaro, Manny, 3499
Alferio, K, 5753
Alfonso, Sebrina, 973
Alford, Alex, 5589
Alford, David, 3915, 3919
Alford, Mark, 4075
Alford, Michele, 8386
Alfred Wachs, Daniel, 817, 818
Alfree, Charles, 2726
Alfrod, Jody, 8028
Alfrod, Richard, 8028
Alfson, Zac, 4496
Alfton, Dennis, 7356
Alger, Hilary, 577
Alger, Jonathan R., 5739
Alger, Molly, 1418
Algeria, Franklin, 8070
Ali, Aisha, 37
Ali, Hesham, 6504
Aliaga, Nicolas, 1915
Alice Squires, Mary, 2265
Alicea, Cheryl, 6644
Alicea, Cristina, 4019
Aliev, Eldar, 230
Alison Chadwell, Toni, 4452
Alister, Mehdi, 1058
Allan, Betty, 7936
Allan, David, 61
Allan, Doug, 5053
Allan, Mowbray, 4595
Allan, Paul, 3413
Allan-Lindblom, Ronald, 3847, 5494
Allard, Roger, 3175
Allardice, Bruce, 3547, 8607
Allardyce, Frederick, 2578
Allaway, Jack, 6115
Allbee, Sheila, 7000, 7001, 7002
Allbright, Cindy, 8418
Allbritten, James, 2272
Allcorn, Ed, 5617
Allcott, Dan, 1690, 1697
Alle, Martha, 227
Allee, Marty, 3446
Allee, Rockie, 1089
Alleman, Beverly, 6575
Allen, Alice, 1726
Allen, Amy, 3301
Allen, Ann, 1352
Allen, Barbara, 3455, 7183
Allen, Benjamin, 4640
Allen, Benjamin J., 6961, 6963, 6964, 6965
Allen, Brant, 1799
Allen, Brian P., 3104
Allen, Bruce, 3286
Allen, Carmen, 498
Allen, Carol, 6432
Allen, Carolyn, 4173
Allen, Chris, 703, 4085
Allen, Chuck, 4147
Allen, Cindy, 7310
Allen, Claire, 3058
Allen, Dale, 8303, 8304
Allen, Dalis, 5647, 8421
Allen, Daniel, 2210
Allen, Dennis R, 7698
Allen, Eric, 4309
Allen, Faye, 2846, 2862, 6627
Allen, Ginny, 7558
Allen, Hogan, 2156
Allen, Ina, 4757
Allen, James, 2131
Allen, Janet, 3013
Allen, Jerry, 5383
Allen, Jessica, 7676
Allen, Joan, 1354, 1578
Allen, Judith, 7874
Allen, Katherine, 5507
Allen, Kathleen, 1806, 5803
Allen, Kitty, 7193
Allen, Larry, 1933
Allen, LaRue, 454
Allen, Lily, 3029, 6996
Allen, Michael, 3391
Allen, Mike, 308
Allen, Nigel, 2009
Allen, Oliver, 1425
Allen, Paul, 6036
Allen, Paul G, 8095, 8102
Allen, Paula, 6757
Allen, Peter, 2606
Allen, Rebecca, 2836
Allen, Robert, 5969
Allen, Robyn, 2425
Allen, Ronald G, 1909
Allen, Ronald.J, 199, 205
Allen, Rosemary A., 4690
Allen, Russell P., 2374
Allen, Sam, 6022
Allen, Sanford, 5064
Allen, Scott, 5039
Allen, Sharon, 152
Allen, Thomas H., 2387
Allen, Todd, 152
Allen, Todd Eric, 152
Allen, Torrie, 1845
Allen, Wilbur, 7951
Allen, Willis, 7520
Allen Atford, Janie, 5
Allen Baxter, Karen, 3863
Allen Fiske, Dr. Richard, 828
Allen III, Robert T, 5760
Allen III CFE, Mount V., 855
Allen Jarrett, Scott, 2103
Allen Jones, David, 115
Allen Kluge, Kim, 1773
Allen-Davis, Jandel, 6349
Allen-Farley, Anita, 2878
Allenby-Weidner, Jean, 169
Allenton, George, 2773
Alley, David, 4110
Alley, Stacy, 5929, 5931
Allgaier, Douglas, 6793
Allgood, David, 4152, 5923
Allison, Bette, 1747, 2359
Allison, Don, 2360
Allison, Joan, 1709
Allison, Kathleen S, 5382
Allison, Kathy, 1689
Allison, Monique, 6678
Allison, Robert, 4999
Allison, Simin.N, 381, 385
Allman, Eric, 4207
Allman, Garrett, 6793
Allnatt, Steven B, 1426
Allston, Sheelagh M., 4756
Allsup, Jonathan D., 6343
Alltop, Stephen, 1047, 2036, 5834
Allums, Elaine, 1704
Ally, Barbara, 6411, 6412, 6413, 6414
Ally, Sean, 8195
Alm, Jeremy, 6793
Alman, Brandon, 7303
Almanza,, Noah, 5664
Almeida, Bob, 6191
Almeida, Richard J., 3869
Almond, Kevin, 5924, 5925
Almonte, Amanda, 4307, 4315, 4316
Aloe, Verna, 1090
Aloff, Mindy, 406
Alofsin, Gail, 8194
Alonso, Chus, 852
Alonso, Jose, 1911
Alonso, Manuel, 6069
Alonzo, Adam, 8460
Alonzo, Daral, 5972
Alonzo Snyder, Marie, 341
Alpert, Sharon, 150
Alphin, Jack, 5265
Alred Follett, Mary Ruth, 4042
Alrey, a C, 1538
Alrutz, Norma, 3850
Alsedek, Anne L, 3805
Alsedek, Donald, 3805
Alsedek, Donald L, 3805
Alsedek, Gwen, 3805
Alsop, Bob, 6994, 6995
Alsop, Marin, 905, 1155, 4327
Alstad, Michael, 1801
Alston, Alex, 6532
Altemose, Esq., Jennifer L., 568
Altenbernd, Nicholas, 1186
Alter, Burton, 932
Althof, Lisa, 6961, 6962, 6963, 6964, 6965
Atland, Sharon S., 8127
Altman, Gregory, 2953
Altman, Kate, 937
Altman, Kerry, 593
Altman, Lou, 2928
Altman, Peter, 3289
Altman, Scott, 651, 1852
Altman, SueAnn, 648
Altman, Thom, 2839
Altomari, Christine, 2186
Altree Piemme, Karen, 2602
Altshu, Ms Dara, 2930
Altstaff, Judi, 1699
Altus-Buller, Martha, 842, 4290
Alva, Tracy, 5663, 8450, 8451
Alvarado, Cindy, 8452
Alvarado, Elisa Marina, 2605
Alvarado, Robert, 6055
Alvarez, Franklin, 738
Alvarez, John, 3361
Alvarez, Mr. Richard, 8547
Alvarez, Rosa, 679
Alvarez, Steven, 717, 4157
Alves, Dennis, 1176
Alves, Jay, 6348
Alvey, Tracey, 1
Alwar, Tim, 3650
Alwine, Robert, 6398
Alworth, Pearl, 6214
Amadio, Paul, 4263
Amador, Francisca, 1821
Amador, Michelle, 368
Amador, Rosita, 820
Amando, David, 949
Amano, Karen, 2595
Amara, Lucine, 2181
Amaral, Joesph, 3134
Amaral, Joseph, 3134
Amato, John, 3115
Ambramowitz, Jason, 201
Ambrose, Allison, 4967
Ambrose, Jonathan, 4705
Ambrose, Julie, 8108
Ambush, Benny, 5756
Amdall, Sharon, 1061
Amdur, Nurit, 270
Ameel, Charlene, 2651, 6343
Amelan, Bjorn G, 397
Amelsberg, Jim, 6994, 6995
Amen, Tom, 6131
Amend, Valerie, 6332
Amenta MS, Paula, 6773
Amerind, Greg, 1855
Amerman, Scott, 6348
Amerons, Charles, 5257
Ames, Jody, 759, 4205
Ames, Justin, 3878
Amey, Kevin, 308
Amidon, Kevin, 1099
Amidon, Valerie, 2542, 6209
Amin, Shamima, 5932
Amirkhanian, Charles, 4305
Amling, Barbara, 3791
Ammar, Salim, 1748
Ammerman, Alan, 1998, 2097
Ammerman, Angela, 1998, 2097
Ammerman, John, 6620, 6629
Ammerman, Paula R, 8184

Executive Name Index

Amodio, Pamela, 4389
Amodio, Rosio, 359
Amory, Daniel, 3105
Amos, Bob, 4025, 4968
Amos, David, 845
Amos Jr., James H., 1909
Amrhein, Elizabeth, 4755
Amrhein, Jim, 3945
Amster, Clara, 5322
Amsterdam, Mark Russell, 1391
Amsterdam, Susan, 1391
Amstutz, Jennifer, 2201
Amudd, John, 3506
Amundent, Jeffery, 2152
Amundson, Steven, 1268
Amuzu, Boniface, 8288
Amy-Cordero, Jennifer, 557
Amyot, Maribeth, 5307, 5308, 5310, 5311
Amyx, Ira, 2947
An, Elizabeth, 794
Anadu, Margaret, 5051
Anang, Amma, 681
Anang, Kofi, 681
Anastasi, Audrey, 369
Anastasi, Robert, 4432
Anastasio, Robert, 4432
Anastos, Peter, 194, 2033
Anaya, Duce, 155
Ancell, Mary, 4337
Ancona, Teresa, 1309, 1310
and Chief Financial,, 6633
Andai, Daniel, 5719
Anderegg, Dr. David, 1206
Anderer, Joseph, 1436, 1441
Anderle, Jeff, 2930
Anderman, Dr. Mark, 4333
Andersson, Susan, 868
Anders, Andy, 6049
Andersen, Chris, 4303
Andersen, Derek, 7493
Andersen, Gary, 1398
Andersen, Harold W., 4949
Andersen, Ib, 11
Andersen, Lene, 919
Andersen, Sarah J, 8670
Andersen, Robb, 576
Anderson, Alan, 3791, 8106
Anderson, Allie, 5536
Anderson, Amy, 767
Anderson, Andrea, 5979
Anderson, Andy, 1842
Anderson, Anglea, 6390
Anderson, Banks, 1481
Anderson, Barry, 1762
Anderson, Ben, 4979, 4982
Anderson, Bernard E., 5932
Anderson, Beth, 4594, 8268
Anderson, Bill, 564, 7264
Anderson, Blair, 7291
Anderson, Brad, 4680
Anderson, Bradley D, 2438
Anderson, Calvin, 5269
Anderson, Carl, 4985
Anderson, Carol Ann, 1737
Anderson, Cathy, 740, 4181
Anderson, Cheryl, 928
Anderson, Christine, 7277
Anderson, Clela, 7459
Anderson, Crystal, 6277
Anderson, Cynthia E., 8021
Anderson, D'Shaynna, 719
Anderson, David, 8691, 8695
Anderson, Deb, 1838
Anderson, Dennis, 4225, 6122
Anderson, Dewey, 4443
Anderson, Dianne, 1208, 4800
Anderson, Douglas, 2370
Anderson, Duane C., 8028
Anderson, Ed, 8198
Anderson, Edgar A, 3163
Anderson, Ellen, 3814, 6282, 6285, 6287
Anderson, Emily, 4159
Anderson, Eric, 1877
Anderson, Erik, 6538
Anderson, G Scott, 7790
Anderson, Gail, 3358
Anderson, Gary, 7495
Anderson, Gayle, 3768, 5391

Anderson, Glenn, 2705
Anderson, Gloria, 3773
Anderson, Grant, 1186
Anderson, Gretchen, 5242
Anderson, Holly, 8245
Anderson, Jake, 6738
Anderson, James, 3429
Anderson, Jane, 1767
Anderson, Jason, 1598, 4641
Anderson, Jeanette, 4699
Anderson, Jeff, 1838, 6003
Anderson, Jeffrey, 1978
Anderson, Jennifer, 4173, 8075
Anderson, Jennifer D., 3446, 7687
Anderson, Jeremy, 6360, 6367, 6368, 6369, 6370
Anderson, Jerome, 7395
Anderson, Jerry, 6220
Anderson, Jim, 3896
Anderson, Joanne C, 2033
Anderson, Joe, 6035, 6300
Anderson, Joel, 4191
Anderson, John, 4146, 4368
Anderson, John L., 4581
Anderson, Joseph, 6018, 6019, 6020
Anderson, Josh, 7880
Anderson, Joy Rayman, 1111
Anderson, Judith, 5038
Anderson, Justin, 2874
Anderson, Karen, 4904
Anderson, Kate, 8268
Anderson, Kathryn, 268
Anderson, Kathy, 6012, 6014
Anderson, Keith, 4122
Anderson, Kelly, 912
Anderson, Korena, 7046
Anderson, Larry, 8653
Anderson, Laura, 3718
Anderson, Lauren, 2314
Anderson, Laurie, 93, 2594
Anderson, Leighton, 891
Anderson, Leonard A, 2988
Anderson, Lili, 5887
Anderson, Lisa, 2343
Anderson, Lori, 7938
Anderson, Lorin, 5810
Anderson, Marian, 6044
Anderson, Marilyn, 1587
Anderson, Marion, 6046
Anderson, Mark, 6153, 6240, 6241
Anderson, Martin, 1376
Anderson, Mary, 3224
Anderson, Mary Jo, 949
Anderson, Matt, 523
Anderson, Melissa, 2036
Anderson, Michael, 1593
Anderson, Michael J, 6757
Anderson, Michele, 269, 2939, 4324
Anderson, Mike, 4648
Anderson, Murray, 5594
Anderson, Nancy, 1481
Anderson, Paige C, 6011
Anderson, Paul, 1740
Anderson, Peggy, 7049
Anderson, Richard, 1318
Anderson, Richard P., 1571
Anderson, Robert, 50
Anderson, Robert P, 7513
Anderson, Roger, 8570
Anderson, Ron, 2870
Anderson, Sally, 868
Anderson, Sandra, 2894
Anderson, Scott, 6291, 6293, 6294, 6296, 8493
Anderson, Sheri, 7395
Anderson, Skip, 8216
Anderson, Spencer, 478
Anderson, Steven C, 3724
Anderson, Susan, 61, 2094
Anderson, Tatiana, 8365
Anderson, Thelma, 5487
Anderson, Tim, 4938
Anderson, Virginia, 8601, 8602
Anderson, Waldie, 998
Anderson, Walter, 3112
Anderson, Warren E., 7975, 7976, 7977
Anderson, Will, 5988
Anderson Knox, Kahleen, 5038
Anderson McLean, Carol, 967

Anderson Stranahan, Ann, 8009
Anderson-Smith, Julie, 8407
Anderson-Spivey, Grace L, 7790
Anding, Volker, 966, 4440
Andiorio, Jennifer, 4756
Andonyadis, Nephelie, 6215
Andrade, Bob, 3859
Andrade, Devis, 6146
Andrade, Jose, 1438
Andre, Darlene, 5836
Andreas, Michael, 42
Andreass, James, 2696
Andree, Grant, 4573
Andres, Dennis J., 6941
Andres-Schneider, Ellen, 4173
Andress, Madeleine, 319
Andrew, Bill, 2877
Andrew, Collie, 8158
Andrew, Laurel L, 6786
Andrews, Brian, 2460
Andrews, Doug, 4437
Andrews, Douglas, 4437
Andrews, Dr Wayne, 7098
Andrews, Eileen, 2094
Andrews, Elizabeth, 2317
Andrews, Eric, 5820, 8650
Andrews, Jessica, 2430, 6004
Andrews, Julie, 805, 2319
Andrews, Kelly, 1162, 7203
Andrews, Kenneth, 1454, 1468, 1469
Andrews, Larry, 3830
Andrews, Linda, 299
Andrews, Lois, 935
Andrews, Mary, 1518
Andrews, Mike, 5694
Andrews, Opal, 3298
Andrews, Rosa, 5266
Andrica, John D., 7975, 7976, 7977
Andringa, Mel, 4644
Andringa, Steve, 1815
Andriolo, Regina, 328
Andronczyk, Renee, 1834
Androuin, George, 6531
Andrucki, Martin, 3097
Andrucyk, Stanley, 4996
Andrus, Reverend Marc, 1911
Andr,s Montenegro, Paulo, 2739
Andzulis, John, 2835
Aneff, Benjamin, 1622
Anema, Mark, 4883, 4884
Anfenson, Carl R., 8611
Anfin, Larry, 3967
Angel, Albert D., 5005
Angelini, Allegra, 527
Angelini, Marcello, 554
Angelo, Susan, 2634
Angelson, Lynn, 3479
Angermeier, Tom, 3006
Angiel, Brenda, 73
Angle, Eric, 3153
Angle, Jared, 412
Angle, Steven, 7838
Anglin, Daniel, 2332
Anguelov, Ivan, 2191
Angus, David, 2108, 2209
Anich, Debra, 378
Anico, Sabrina, 980
Aniole, Patty, 4453
Ankele, Jason, 3952
Ankele, Jayson, 3952
Ankeny, Mark E, 8076, 8078
Anker, Daniel, 1451
Anker, Peter, 940
Anklan, LeAnne, 1527
Ankrom, David, 4002
Ankrom, Robert, 3660
Anlin, Li, 632
Ann, Mary, 4469
Ann Allen, Dr. Sue, 6619
Ann Aufderheido, Mary, 4873
Ann Bamber, Mary, 4949
Ann Brown, Jo, 7993
Ann Cann, Mari, 8022
Ann Cluff, Cheryl, 4010
Ann Eberlein, Kimberley, 1291, 1292, 4921
Ann Ehishlager, Mary, 4085
Ann Elze-Sussdorff, Carol, 1390
Ann Gambardella, Beth, 2540

Ann Garske, Lee, 3207
Ann Gibson, Lou, 2297
Ann Grose, Lou, 4096
Ann Hahn, Leigh, 4237
Ann Hanson, Mary, 1592
Ann Hirsch, Mary, 1556, 5350
Ann Hofland, Rose, 8247
Ann Howell, Bobbie, 4959
Ann Kearney, Betty, 1671
Ann Kiernan, Ms. Jo, 8547
Ann Lombard, RN, Dee, 253
Ann Molitor, Mary, 4157
Ann Moody, Lois, 738, 5991, 5992
Ann Neely, Patrica, 4399
Ann O'Keefe, Kelsey, 345
Ann Quinson, Mary, 3169
Ann Richardson, Mary, 3804
Ann Russell, Doris, 4692
Ann S. Jones, De, 3675
Ann Shaw, Kathy, 4740, 4741
Ann Stephenson-Love, Sue, 1298
Ann Taylor Kindle, Jo, 1291, 1292
Ann Wiliford, Melanie, 3877
Ann Willetts, Mary, 1471
Anna, Brenda, 1163
Annas, Alicia, 2569
Anne, Haris, 6879, 6880, 6881
Anne, Revanth, 5129
Anne Crampton, Mary, 7997
Anne de Simone, Jo, 4600
Anne Grenfell, Mary, 140
Anne Kenney, Theresa, 4123
Anne Phillips, Ed.D, Mari, 4913
Anne Sadler, Doris, 3011
Anne Servian, Mary, 169
Anne Weber, Mary, 8334
Annegarn, Steven, 572, 582
Annenberg, Wallis, 792, 807, 4243
Annis, Robert, 2188
Annis, Robert L., 1341
Ann Wohlmut, Carol, 3783
Anokye, Akua-Akilah, 7691
Ansah Brew, Kwame, 3130
Ansbacher, Charles A, 4776
Anselelne, Arthur, 5741
Anselmi, Filippo, 8864
Anselmo, Gina, 2932
Ansheles, Beth, 1150
Anslover, Desirae, 346
Anson, Erin, 15
Anson, Jennifer, 6269, 6270
Ansotegui, Dan, 196
Ansotegui, Toni, 196
Antaramian, Anna, 6750
Antel, John J., 8402, 8408
Antelmann, Maria, 468
Antenucci, Steve, 3256
Antenucci, Steven, 3256, 7362
Anthony, Ann Kelly, 2801
Anthony, Ariane, 379, 401
Anthony, Carmen, 3507
Anthony, Cori, 4158
Anthony, Dr. Sofia, 1212
Anthony, Jesse W, 4206, 5425
Anthony, John P., 4399
Anthony, Joseph H., 1245
Anthony, Mary, 455
Anthony, Pam, 4841
Anthony, Scott, 3816
Anthony, Shay, 7982
Anthony, Vincent, 2850
Anthony Jones, Steven, 2582
Antin, Sarah, 2069
Antis, Kristine, 673
Antoline, Marina, 1031
Antolini, Lea, 4994
Anton, Mary, 2923
Antonelli, Cynthia, 3001
Antonian, Nicholas, 2504
Antoniou, Theodore, 1175
Antonlini, Lea, 4994
Antonov, Igor, 670
Antonov, Ivan, 5154
Antosca, Steve, 953
Anwah, Sabrina, 4041
Aoki, Sherrie, 5661
Aotoveoli, Jenna, 2948
Apelgren, Scott, 971

1135

Executive Name Index

Aper, Dr. Jeffery, 6767, 6768
Apker, Susan, 7621
Apland, Erik, 1152
Apone, Carl, 5441, 5492
Appel, Andrew, 1411
Appel, Libby, 3771, 5400
Appel, Robert, 1436, 1441
Appel, Robert J., 1421, 5142
Appel, Steve, 8032
Appelhanz, Julie, 908
Appelhof, Ruth, 3437
Appelt, Joseph, 4577, 6779, 6780, 6781, 6782, 6783
Appenteng, Kofi, 2692
Appenzeller, Rebecca, 531, 1549, 1550
Appiagyei, Kwabena Osei, 508
Apple, Irwin, 2612
Applegate, Stan, 8155
Appler, Kevin, 5200
Applewhite, Andis, 640
Appleyard, Elizabeth, 6803, 6804
Apuzzo, Kathy, 6424
Aragon, Antonio, 7608
Aranda, Jesse, 6129
Aravich, Jr., Robert P., 4533
Arbeluez, Patricia, 6547
Arbogast, Maggie, 3840
Arceneaux, George E, 4708
Arceneaux, Jennifer, 4013, 4015
Arceneaux, John, 3994
Archabal, Nina, 4883, 4884
Archabald, Karen, 6679
Archambealt, Kevin, 3928
Archbold, Ann M., 8676, 8680
Archer, Julie, 3516
Archer, Leslie, 3625
Archer, Linda, 3878
Archer, Neal, 48, 49
Archer, Rickard, 4003
Archer, Sean, 4549
Archuletta, Dave, 79
Archuletta, David, 397
Arciniegas, Diego, 3140
Arden, Lisa, 5089, 5090
Arden, Ron, 2996
Ardinger, Timothy, 8138
Ardito-Martelli, Nick, 4994
Ardolino, Tammy, 1657
Ardueser, Kim, 1112
Aren, Shirley W, 3408
Arena, Maryanne, 5046
Arends, Mildred, 2057
Arensberg, Shirley, 3408
Aresty, Steven, 5164
Arevalo, Dr. Rodolfo, 8580
Arey, Dana, 572
Argo, Cynthia, 3085
Arguelles Miller, Claudia, 6105
Arguijo, Dan, 3988
Argyropoulos, Athena, 6460
Arias, Caitlin, 1441
Arias, Luis, 3553
Arie-Gaifman, Hanna, 1447, 7788
Arighi, Marie, 5901, 5902, 5903, 5904
Arington, Jill, 3799
Arisco, David, 2764
Arko, Katie, 6719
Arlt, Lewis, 3458
Armagnac, Gary, 2630
Armendariz, Gonzalo, 3499
Armenta, Stephanie, 5985, 5987, 5989
Armentrout, Jennifer, 5276
Armentrout, Mary, 78
Armer, Linda, 1359
Arminana, Ruben, 2549
Armitage, Vicki I, 2365
Armond, David P., 7140
Armor, Dori, 7198
Armor, Mary, 102
Armore, Registered Asso, 1607
Armour, LaNell E., 1713
Armstead, Betsy, 6834
Armstrong, Anton, 2151
Armstrong, Chuck, 8604
Armstrong, Debbie, 6095
Armstrong, E Jason, 1942
Armstrong, Helen, 4409
Armstrong, Jean, 122

Armstrong, Justin, 6887
Armstrong, Kara, 4906
Armstrong, Louis, 7396
Armstrong, Michael, 411
Armstrong, Nicholas, 1372
Armstrong, Paul, 4109
Armstrong, Ross, 850
Armstrong, Suzanne, 2054
Armstrong, Tom, 6384
Armstrong, Mickeisha, 6775, 6776, 6777, 6778
Armusik, Emily, 4455
Arn, Dwight, 1281
Arndt, Ben, 8247
Arner, Lucy, 2191
Arnett, David, 2405
Arnett, Roger, 7271
Arney, Randall, 2502
Arnheim, Walter R., 4430
Arnhold, John, 1421, 5142
Arning, David, 3906
Arnn, Larry P, 1238
Arnold, Alexis, 1741
Arnold, Anita G, 5387, 8041
Arnold, Arthur, 1074
Arnold, Bill, 2695
Arnold, Bruce, 7838
Arnold, Cindy, 7081
Arnold, Dr Arline, 1707
Arnold, Dr. Joseph, 6110, 6111, 6114
Arnold, G Brooks, 1938
Arnold, Loreen, 5777
Arnold, Michael, 8214
Arnold, Mike, 8228
Arnold, Sara, 2296, 5393
Arnold, Slee, 5265
Arnold, Soozie, 4373
Arnold, Steve, 3029
Arnold, Tristan, 1877
Arnos, Reed, 1701
Arnott, Teresa, 6786
Arnoutis, George, 6417, 6425, 6426
Arnow, Laura, 4128
Arnts, Alice, 7598
Arntson, Kregg, 3786
Arntz, JoEllen, 91
Aro, Brneda, 2803
Aronchick, Mark, 197
Aronov, Owen, 4148
Aronson, Maure, 4788
Aronstein, Patsy, 1470
Arranda, Jesse, 6129
Arrigotti, Stephanie, 3337
Arrington, Brandon, 6537
Arrington, Darlene, 4035
Arrington, Gigi, 654
Arrington, Mary Elizabeth, 636
Arrison, Steve, 6031
Arroyave, Marcela, 639
Arrufat, Greg, 4329
Arsht, Adrienne, 5151
Artbauer, Michael, 519
Artbauer, Michael, 7968
Artenian, Rich, 8533
Arthur, George N, 5759
Arthur, Janice, 7057
Arthur, Ken, 3582
Arthur, Mary A., 1822
Artiach, Miren, 2032
Artis, Mike, 7312
Artistic Assistant, Botek, 3627
Artistic Director, McDonald, 5038
Artman, Aaron, 8617
Artman, Richard B., 5846
Artz,III, F Allen, 5012
Arunasalam, Chitra, 1894
Aruny, Donita, 4388
Arvidson, Ann, 4623
Arvonio, Pat, 1667
Arzbaecher, Bob, 4120
Asalde, 7rene, 6167
Asbaty, Ann H., 7573
Asbell, David, 4325, 6283
Asbell-Swanger, Lea, 8186
Asbury, Keleigh, 6332
Asch, Leslee, 931, 4395
Asch, Sunny Charla, 4232
Asch, Wilma, 2327
Asebrook, Jen, 3320

Ash, Joseph P., 8465
Ash, Nicholas, 1938
Ash, William, 1289
Ashbahian, Daniella, 2185
Ashbaker, Susan, 2310
Ashby, Claire, 5259, 5262
Ashby, Marty, 5491, 8174
Ashcraft, Betty, 6703
Ashcraft, M.D., Scott, 4903
Ashe, Gregory J, 3714
Ashe, Janet, 7962
Ashe, Kevin, 7595
Ashe, Madeleine, 2543
Asheim, Steve, 915
Asher, Bobby, 1162
Asher, Toni, 5844
Ashford, James, 6584
Ashla, Berit, 6267
Ashley, Douglas, 5013
Ashley, Freddie, 2848
Ashley, Lisa, 1263
Ashly,, 1139
Ashman, Ann, 3688
Ashton, Jack, 3877
Ashton, John, 5819
Ashton, Robert, 3305
Ashton Jr., Kendrick F., 411
Ashwander, Lindy, 4142, 5898
Ashworth, Hal, 1682
Asin, Leslie, 194
Ask, Michael, 8032
Askew, Kyle, 8256
Askew, Mike, 4046
Askew, Penny, 547
Askin, Brian, 4805, 7252
Askin, Glen, 924
Askin, Jacalyn, 5947
Askin, Peter, 3466
Aslanian, Richard, 8471
Asmussen, Jeff, 4900
Aspenlieder, Elizabeth, 3159
Asplund, Jillian, 5952
Assaf, Dennis, 2083
Assaf, Dennis G, 4713
Assante, Claudio, 410
Assink, Brent, 856, 857, 1925
Assistant, Dianna, 8088
Assistant Director, Medley, 8458
Assistant Director,, Rhedin, 8326
Assistant Secretary, Suzanne, 5211
Associate Athletic D, Fry, 8718
Assouliak, Lev, 140
Astin, John, 3117
Astolfi, Cher, 4414
Astrachan, Margot, 1424
Astre, Kerline, 51
Ataee, Behnaz, 2502
Atchley White, Jennifer, 6025
Ates, Kerry A., 7191, 7192
Athaide, Lucas, 6
Athayde, Juliana, 1463
Atherton, David, 840, 4288
Atherton, Nancy, 4180
Athleen, Jane, 1661
Athmann, Sue, 1793
Atiba, Babu, 208
Atkerson, Bill, 1706
Atkerson, Rick, 707
Atkin, Mary, 3302
Atkin, Steven P, 2108
Atkins, Alice, 5679
Atkins, Christopher, 3184, 4814
Atkins, Corey, 7963, 7964, 7965, 7966
Atkins, Kyle, 6600
Atkins, Kym, 7148
Atkins, Nicolette, 803
Atkins, Paul, 4648
Atkins, Steven T., 1404
Atkins, Victor, 7244
Atkinson, Bill, 629
Atkinson, Megan, 2829
Atkinson, Rollie, 4224
Atkinson, Seth, 8142
Atkinson, Susan, 3798
Atkinson Notzold, Tracy, 1897
Atlakson, Phill, 6683, 6684, 6686, 6688
Atland, Hank, 1463

Atlas, Martha, 7424
Atlas, Shannon, 84
Atremova-Schauwecker, Julie, 306
Atria aupt, Karen, 1547
Attar, Yaniv, 1788
Atteberry, Gina, 4902
Attwood, Jr., James A., 5096, 5097
Atwood, James R., 2199
Atwood, Melissa, 2891
Atwood, Stephanie, 8404
Atz, Karen, 1828
Aubel, Leo, 2930
Aubin, Terry, 1136
Aubrey, Robin, 343
AuBuchon, Kathleen J, 1029
Auburn, Mark, 5286
Auburn, Ph.D., Mark, 1513, 1514
Auchincloss, Susan, 7849
Auchincloss Lilley, Eve, 149
Audelo, Angelica M., 6011
Audley, Judith, 1614
Audray, Anne-Julia, 2233
Audres, Dennis J., 6941
Audunson, Janet, 3627
Auer, Elizabeth, 6520
Auer, Matthew, 7169
Auer, Susan, 1849
Auerbach, Carol B., 3468
Auerbach, Ernest, 2336, 2339
Auerbach, Marvin, 330
Aufses, Arthur, 3500
Augello, Christina, 4308
Auger, Giselle A, 1149
Auger, Giselle A/, 1148
Auger, Mary, 1257
Augguire, Javier, 2605
Augis, Doug, 8142
Augur, Catherine, 6343
Augustine, Tracy, 4942
Augustyniak, Shelby, 172
Auh, Dr Yoon-Il, 7795
Auletta, Ken, 856, 857
Ault, Chris, 7519
Aultman, Wildon, 7393
Auman, Elizabeth K., 2958
Aune, Brian, 797
Aune, Gregory, 4674
Aune, Kristine, 197
Aupperly, William John, 5710
Aurisch, Helga, 1729
Aus, Martha, 620
Ausland, Kelsey, 8083
Ausland, Kelsey, 1598
Austen Behan, Jane, 5250
Austensen, Roy A, 4633
Austin, Alan, 5639
Austin, Anjali, 158
Austin, Bob, 1506
Austin, Cindy, 3688
Austin, Debra, 511
Austin, Dr. James, 5636
Austin, Ellen, 1640
Austin, Greg, 1820
Austin, Holly O, 4215
Austin, Jean, 3829
Austin, Kelli, 6882
Austin, Larry, 1401
Austin, Laura, 3626
Austin, Lyn, 3524
Austin, Lyn T., 5266
Austin, Marilyn, 3971
Austin, Nancy, 2616
Austin, Nancy K., 6297
Austin, Philip E., 6439
Austin, Ted, 1605, 8091
Austin, Wanda M., 807
Austin, M.D., John, 5134
Austin, MD, MBA, Rebecca, 1896
Autie, Oscar, 6069
Autry, Timothy, 8234
Auville, Stewart, 4444
AuWerter, Sue, 1609
Avdey, Len, 1327
Avelae II, David, 4704
Aven, Jerry, 3985, 5637
Avent, a William, 2731
Averbach, Ricardo, 1565
Averill, Janet, 577

Executive Name Index

Avery, Alan, 1109
Avery, Gradin, 5067
Avery, Henry, 3399
Avery, Jennifer, 2964
Avery, Kenneth P, 2449
Avery, Larry, 3216
Avery, Sandy, 6529, 6532
Avery, Tricia, 3944
Avganim, Dorit, 3503
Aviani, Francis, 6262
Avila, David, 6197
Avila-Cueva, Jessica s, 6803, 6804
Avirom, Cheryl, 6150
Avis, Alyssa, 4808
Avis, Jack, 4055
Avisar, Eytan, 111
Avital, Samuel, 119, 2646
Avizonis, Dr. Vilija, 651
Awsumb, George, 1014
Axelrod, Joel, 3771
Axelrod, Nancy, 4207
Axford, Theresa, 4457
Axness, Robin, 931
Axt, Tyler, 3919
Axtell, Jamie, 2908
Ayad, Adly, 1934
Ayala, Maria, 4001
Ayala, Shondell, 1979
Ayers, Berry, 6585
Ayers, Debra, 904
Ayers, Evie, 811, 4256
Ayers, Janet, 1696
Ayers, Jim, 4055
Ayers, Lee, 1835
Ayers, Pam, 1557
Ayers, Sue, 4982
Ayling, Ginny, 1585
Aylsworth Brantigan, Kathleen, 6350
Ayola, Steve, 8079
Ayotte, Lisa, 3187
Ayoub, Nancy, 1308
Ayres-Frederick, Linda B, 2588
Ayya, Naina, 6253
Azara, Nancy, 7849
Azaro, Kathy, 341
Azema, Anne, 2104
Azenberg, Karen, 4009
Azer, Karen, 1632
Azevedo, Ann, 2690

B

B, Kim, 6717
B. Kimmel, Margaret, 7169
B. Perkins, Michael B., 3298
B. Schumacher, Max, 6903
B. Skold, Lee, 3239
B. Temper, Lynn, 3202
B. Whiddon, Jerry, 3121
Baad, Debbie, 1900
Baad, Mike, 1900
Baar, Rachael, 7082
Babad, Barbara, 1448
Babb, Kathy M., 754
Babb, Patricia, 1112
Babb, Patty, 1112
Babb, Roger, 3175
Babb, Susan, 6131
Babbitt, Bruce, 6459
Babbitt, Joey, 4313
Babbitt, Milton, 5435
Babbs, Lesli, 213
Babcock, Barbara, 767
Babcock, Bert, 768
Babcock, Dennis, 7355
Babcock, Jeffrey, 4336
Babcock, Jennifer, 790
Babcock, Lawrence, 1279
Babcock, Stover, 947
Babin, L Randolph, 2340
Babler, Stacy J, 2431
Babs, Robert, 8608
Baca, M. Carlota, 1359
Baca Geary, Jackie, 6178
Baccellieri, Rich, 7511
Baccus, HE, 6743
Bachant, Nancy, 2390
Bacharach, Jacob, 583, 8168

Bacheldor, Danny, 347
Bacher, Steve, 3934
Bachman, Randy, 6213
Bachmeier, Mel, 1915
Bachmeier, Yen, 1915
Bachorski, Mary G., 2317
Bachrach, Ben, 1228
Bacia, Cathie, 5998
Backe, Kelsey, 1784
Backe, Kim, 6730
Backer, Ronald, 3620, 7820
Backes, Roy W., 3836
Backhaus, Jennifer, 55
Backon, Sam, 7545
Backus, Amy, 6417, 6425, 6426
Bacolo, Vicki, 5007
Bacon, Brandon, 3202
Bacon, Clifford, 6618, 6628
Bacon, Terry, 4368
Bacon, Toni, 7134
Baczynska, Dorota, 1262
Badalamenti, Barbara, 520
Badami, John, 5254
Badger, J Jeff, 1924
Badger, Jeff J, 1924
Badgett, Darlene, 5056
Badhwar, Nishi, 7193
Bady, Janeane, 7296
Baechle, Simone, 207
Baehr, Lydia, 8413
Baer, Laurence M, 6251
Baer, Maryjane, 3562
Baer, Miriam Reitz, 4369
Baer, Sandra, 1994
Baer Collins, Susan, 3333
Baerenklau, Viviane, 4281
Baeslack III, W. A. Bud, 1540
Baez, Reyna, 8032
Baff, Ella, 270
Bagan, Carol, 7526
Bagan, Merwyn, 7526
Bagasao, Anne, 40
Baggett, Green, 1796
Baggiano, Sebastian, 2208
Bagley, Kathleen, 3381
Bagley, Lisa, 6408
Bagnall, Eileen, 6004
Bagorro, Manuel, 252, 1151, 2090, 4746
Baguyos, Jeremy, 1308
Bagwell, James, 2225, 5304
Bagwell, Janice, 6879, 6880, 6881
Baham, Patricia, 3085, 7148
Bahin, Lila, 1300
Bahiri, Medhi, 497
Bahl, Reggie, 1423
Bahl, Vikrant, 1439
Bahle, Jean, 7305
Bahls, Steven, 2059
Bahls, Steven C, 6825, 6826, 6827
Bahn, Lina, 953
Bahn, Meghan, 7044
Bahnson, Matthew, 2051
Bahr, Sam, 703
Bahr, Warren, 7538
Bahri, Meriem, 2049
Bahto, Rick, 4303
Baier, Kristina, 3445
Baier, Mitchell, 2383
Baier, Stephen, 4097
Baierlein, Ed, 2660
Baierlein, Tad, 2660
Baig, Maryam, 3960
Baile, David, 4559
Baile, Mary Kay, 2877
Baile, Stephen, 6456
Bailey, Ann, 3900
Bailey, Becky, 5176
Bailey, Bill, 5007
Bailey, Bryan, 6660
Bailey, Caleb, 1305
Bailey, Carol, 8634
Bailey, Chase, 3353
Bailey, Chris, 8420
Bailey, Claud, 6481
Bailey, Colin B., 6258
Bailey, Darice, 4240
Bailey, Denise, 6785, 6786, 6787, 6788
Bailey, Erin, 4441

Bailey, Jane, 1193
Bailey, Jennifer, 647
Bailey, Joanne, 6443
Bailey, John Kendall, 816
Bailey, John L., 4585
Bailey, Kacey, 1277
Bailey, Larry, 1716
Bailey, Lauren, 1412, 2278
Bailey, Margie, 8032
Bailey, Margo, 4737
Bailey, Mark, 1969
Bailey, Pam Howe, 7296
Bailey, Rachel, 1836
Bailey, Sarah, 2076, 3747
Bailey, Stephen, 6457
Bailey, Stephen M, 6456, 6457
Bailey, Stephen M., 1979
Bailey, Thomas C., 1243, 4853
Bailey, Tori, 4144
Bailey, William C, 2366
Bailey, Zuill, 1720, 4163, 5619
Bailey, CMP, Rhonda, 8470
Bailey, Jr., Esq,, Lawrence R., 1422
Bailey, Adrienne Y., 7258
Bailis, Rob, 86, 4207
Baillie, Rebecca, 2490
Bain, Agnes M, 5056
Bain, Agnes M., 7649
Bain, Agnes.M, 374
Bain, Donald K, 4367
Bain, Gay, 6600
Bain, George, 5203
Bain, Kris, 680
Bain, Lisa, 1470
Bain, Reginald, 3021
Baine, Thayer, 1995
Baines, Jenine, 1933
Baines, Shaun, 1844
Bair, Irby, 3980
Bair, Jack F, 6251
Bair, Sheldon, 1164
Baird, Connie, 3641
Baird, Heather, 3468
Baird, Jean M., 6720, 6721
Baird, Kenton, 3770
Baird, M Rex, 1314
Baird, Sheila, 7647
Baird, Stacie, 668
Baird, Thomas, 389
Baisden, Charles, 2812
Baisinger, Christy, 1815
Baisley, Elizabeth, 1654
Baji, John, 5483
Bak, Anne, 2137
Bak, Eugene, 2281
Bakardiev, Parvan, 2077
Baker, Adele, 1319
Baker, Angie, 2883
Baker, Ann Meier, 1985
Baker, Antonia, 5355
Baker, Barbara, 6390
Baker, Bryan, 1927
Baker, Carrie, 2420
Baker, Charles, 1123, 2076
Baker, Chip, 5559
Baker, Christopher, 4135
Baker, Cory, 4173
Baker, Daniel, 3013
Baker, Danise, 6148
Baker, Darren, 8006
Baker, David, 4091
Baker, David N., 5093
Baker, Daymara, 753
Baker, Dr Robert Hart, 2260
Baker, Emily, 1743, 2358
Baker, Eric, 1828
Baker, Frank, 411
Baker, Fred, 5623
Baker, Gene, 4843, 4868
Baker, Howard, 5075
Baker, James, 1575
Baker, John, 3544, 6728
Baker, Joseph J., 8118
Baker, Judith, 6115
Baker, Julie, 6117
Baker, Julie B., 8076
Baker, Keith, 3798
Baker, Keith Alan, 2750

Baker, Kendall, 5284
Baker, Kevin, 818
Baker, Kim, 700, 1583, 7092, 7093, 7096
Baker, Laura, 1078
Baker, Lauren, 3437
Baker, Linda S., 1713
Baker, LuAnn, 4007
Baker, Mark, 4237, 6175
Baker, Maureen, 6615
Baker, Mike, 2443
Baker, Ms. Karen M., 8386
Baker, Pamela, 2047
Baker, Pattie, 8260
Baker, Richard, 4917, 7429
Baker, Rob, 8048
Baker, Robin, 6843, 6844, 6845
Baker, Rosemary, 8065
Baker, Samuel, 896
Baker, Scott, 2603
Baker, Stacy, 3353
Baker, Steve, 69
Baker, Susan L, 2225
Baker, Suzanne, 5061
Baker, Suzanne B., 3433
Baker, Taylor, 6058, 6059, 6060, 6061
Baker, Veronica, 2625, 4288
Baker, Wendy A, 6160, 6161, 6162
Baker, Wendy A., 6161, 6162
Baker, Winifred A., 1682
Baker Boris, Leslie, 576
Baker,, John, 3184
Baker-Haines, Janice, 236
Baker-VanCura, Anna, 611
Baker, Doug, 6764, 6765
Baker, William L., 8247
Bakhle, Janaki, 4207
Bakkan, Amy, 1835
Bakken, David, 1835
Bakkila, Brian, 3202
Balance, PhD, Christine, 81
Balanchine, George, 466
Balas, Christina, 325
Balash, Ted, 4956
Balasubramanian, Vishoka, 5065
Balay, Elizabeth, 2143
Balcerzak, Francis A., 7629
Balcom, Derek, 1412
Balcom, Meghan, 3479
Balda, Megan, 1263
Baldassarre, Dr Joseph, 1025
Balder, Marjorie, 7703
Balderston, Megan, 2040
Baldinger, Darlinda, 918
Baldini, Christian, 835
Baldus, Hannah, 6372
Baldwan, Debra, 2441
Baldwin, Aaron, 2897
Baldwin, Adam, 1864
Baldwin, Alison, 211
Baldwin, Bob, 8140
Baldwin, Charles, 3143
Baldwin, Dan, 5775
Baldwin, Daniel, 1106
Baldwin, David, 1243, 4853, 6600
Baldwin, David J, 4755
Baldwin, Elaine, 693
Baldwin, Grace, 839
Baldwin, Lois, 1144
Baldwin, Robert, 1763, 1764
Baldwin, Ron, 6996
Baldwin, Ronald, 1299
Baldwin, Roshada, 43
Baldwin, Susan, 1368
Baldwin, Tery, 1879
Balenger, Robbie, 6572
Baley, Jane, 1243
Baley, Virko, 1314
Balgeman, Thomas, 4121
Balicky, Tommy, 4881
Balkin, Richard, 1388
Ball, Amy, 3994
Ball, Bob, 2033
Ball, David, 7885
Ball, Jancy, 4440
Ball, Jay, 6868
Ball, Maegan, 899
Ball, Michele, 244

1137

Executive Name Index

Ball, Nicole S., 3098
Ball, Steve, 3159
Ball, Teri, 2611
Ball, Thelma, 1745
Ballam, Michael, 2362
Ballard, Brent D., 7975, 7976, 7977
Ballard, Brownie, 6534
Ballard, Carol, 4148
Ballard, H Byron, 3639
Ballard, Jessica, 654
Ballard, Louis, 3054
Ballas, Debi, 2868
Ballas, Ricia, 7993
Ballentine, Emily, 8824
Ballentine, Helen, 5265
Baller, Ann, 7681
Ballesteros, Joe, 6281
Ballew, Tammy, 632
Balliet, Franklin, 5426
Balliet, Jamie, 3801, 8121
Ballinger, June, 3389
Ballou, Joan, 4028
Ballton, Carl A, 6164
Ballver, Bill, 2867
Balm, Michele, 1430
Balog, Amy, 4105
Balog, Gary, 1575
Balogh, Ed, 6770
Balogh, Lajos, 1604
Baloun, Laura A., 7952
Balph, Judy, 2836
Balser, Paul, 3500
Balster, Keith, 1261
Baltar, Joseph, 4726
Balter, Lee, 1431
Baltimore, David, 6207
Baltzell, Michael, 6683, 6684, 6686, 6688
Baltz, Laura, 3015
Balzano, Richard, 5053
Bamberger, Linda, 5177
Bamburg, Marvin, 2599
Bame, Leia, 3737
Bammert, Carl, 7315
Bamrick, Tierney, 2332
Banaszak, Sharon, 6841, 6842
Banchs, William H, 4173
Banda-Rodaz, Maria, 2765
Bandy, Christopher, 506
Bandy, Jeanne, 1956
Baney, Carol, 5507
Banfe, Colleen, 7593
Banfell, Diane C., 5919
Bang, Kathleen, 6078
Bangoura, Kerfala, 1462
Banister, Jan, 4613
Bank, Barbara, 1367
Bank, Beth A., 6004
Bank, Jonathan, 3521
Bankhead, James, 6083
Bankhead, Nancy, 798
Banks, Brandon, 6249
Banks, Carol, 5269
Banks, David, 6026
Banks, Deborah, 2447
Banks, Doug, 6806, 6809
Banks, Eboni, 1368
Banks, Eric, 2383
Banks, Jessica, 394
Banks, Jim, 3316
Banks, Kim E., 6464, 6466, 6470
Banks, Richard, 2610
Banks, Roland, 7028
Banks, Susan, 8169
Bankson, Jeremy, 4944
Bankston, Thomas, 2284
Bankstone, Charley, 2341
Bannan, Kevin, 6342
Banner, Alicia, 374
Banner, Alicia M., 3423
Banner, Alicia., 374
Bannert, Shana, 6193
Banno, Joe, 2748
Bannon, Steve, 3310
Banta, Jody, 3077
Banta, Joyce, 6949
Bantz, Charles R., 6877
Banwart, Florence, 6775, 6776, 6777, 6778
Banze, Phil, 6651

Banzhaf, Lori, 4182
Barabas, Gabor, 3369, 4997
Barabas, Suzanne, 3369, 4997
Baraff, David, 4270
Baragary, Austin, 4910
Barany, Joe, 3890
Barath, Deby, 513
Barathan, Vipin, 1399
Baratta, Leticia D, 446
Barauskas, Madeline, 2782
Barbanell, Ariane, 3145, 3146
Barbara, Barrows, 6994, 6995
Barbaras, Geraldine, 4414
Barbas, Steven, 1192
Barbatti, Jim, 7414
Barbaur, Fredrick, 2667
Barbe, Andre, 2191
Barbeau, Dale, 7512
Barbeau, Paul, 8609
Barbee, Jennifer, 1376
Barbee, Shawna, 2989
Barbee, Victor, 386
Barber, Dave, 4173
Barber, Donna, 4713
Barber, Kim, 3346
Barber, Michael R, 6588
Barber, Nathan, 1621
Barberi, Kimberly, 6341
Barberio, Steve, 3229
Barbieri, Margaret, 169
Barbour, Elizabeth, 2123
Barbre, Beth, 319
Barbu, Simona, 1511
Barclay, Jud, 4674
Barclay, Neil, 7139, 8326
Barclay, Neil A., 4505
Barclay, Steven, 8739
Barcus, Leisha, 6985
Bard, Karlyn, 5701
Bard, Steve, 5071
Bardeen, Tom, 2390
Bardellini, Keith, 2453
Barden, Louise, 1695
Barden, Roland, 4876
Bardo, John W., 7071, 7072, 7073
Bardsley, John, 4682
Bardwell, Bruce, 7035, 7036, 7037, 7038
Bare, Julie, 5957
Bare, Regima, 8626
Barefoot, Carmen, 8552
Bareford, Melissa, 2937
Barela, Lenea, 7899
Barenboim, Thomas S, 3134
Barese, Jan, 6422
Bareuther, Robert, 2228
Barger, Burch, 4141
Barger, Kyle, 1630
Barhorst, PhD, Bettsey L., 8678
Baribeau, Diana, 7294
Barich, Paul T., 4276
Baril, John, 1950, 1953
Barish, Seth, 3470
Barkdoll, Holly, 3696
Barke, Justine, 3066
Barker, Alain, 4610, 6856
Barker, Charles, 582
Barker, Claudette, 4979
Barker, J.C., 714
Barker, John, 4685
Barker, Maureen K., 1953
Barker, Michael, 6147
Barker, Patricia, 285
Barker, Richard, 89
Barker, Rochelle, 2867
Barker, Sherman, 1682
Barker, Stephen, 2478
Barker, Victoria, 2219
Barker, Phyllis, 6720, 6721
Barkes, Tom, 3021, 6927, 6929, 6930, 6931, 6932, 6933, 6934, 6935
Barkley, Byron, 4012
Barkley, Judy, 897
Barkley, Nicole, 6438
Barkley, Sandra, 1258, 1259
Barkman, Jeff, 7046
Barkon, Aaron, 923
Barks, Dan, 8717
Barlaan, Al, 6300

Barlage, Joshua, 1107
Barlament, Jennifer, 1535
Barletta, Richard, 2934
Barlow, Eleanor, 252, 4746
Barlow, Janet H, 5342
Barlow, Jim, 6351
Barlow, Julia, 3235
Barmore, Aleta, 4135
Barnard, Jeff, 1877
Barnard, Melissa, 1247, 1248, 4856, 7317
Barnea, Uri, 2166
Barnell, Robert J, 5291
Barner, Marilyn, 4029
Barnes, Cheri, 2997
Barnes, Chuck, 6207
Barnes, Claire N, 856, 857
Barnes, Ellen, 591, 8199
Barnes, James L., 1547
Barnes, Jeffrey, 6899
Barnes, Jesika, 310
Barnes, Jill, 2502, 6697
Barnes, Joyce, 2148, 2149
Barnes, Kellie M., 4713
Barnes, Lisa, 4657, 4658, 4659, 4660, 4661
Barnes, Lois, 1507
Barnes, Melanie, 1838
Barnes, Pat, 3909
Barnes, Paul, 2612
Barnes, Paul ., 6282, 6285, 6287
Barnes, Philip, 2157
Barnes, Ruth, 7466
Barnes, Sue, 3900
Barnes, Ted, 5596
Barnes, Trend, 7873
Barnes, Warren, 1592
Barnes-Gabriel, Laura, 7270
Barnett, Billie, 554
Barnett, Chris, 4308
Barnett, David L., 6648, 6649
Barnett, Dennis, 6966, 6968, 6970
Barnett, Grace, 6769
Barnett, Jahnae, 4899, 7421
Barnett, Jahnae H, 7421
Barnett, Jennifer, 1694
Barnett, John, 1426
Barnett, Melissa, 7873
Barnett, Nancy, 2792
Barnett, Robby, 135
Barnett, Robert, 6471
Barnette, Jennifer, 3466, 7709
Barney, Dean, 4085
Barney, Debbie, 879, 6306, 6307, 6309
Barney, Patricia, 7820
Barnhart, Frank, 3719
Barnhart, Glenn, 5606
Barnhart, J Kent, 3290
Barnhart, Julia, 4105
Barnhart, Mitch, 7083, 7089
Barnin, Bill, 3393
Barnum, Annette, 1028
Barnwell, David, 2266
Baro, Joe, 6012
Baron, Cristal, 372
Baron, Gary, 6801
Baron, Michael, 3761
Barone, Frank, 7627
Barone, Magaly, 8856
Baroway, Holly, 122
Barowsky, Andrew P., 6277
Barr, Christina, 4959
Barr, Daniel, 4508
Barr, Eric, 2548
Barr, Kathy, 4303
Barr, Linda, 374, 3423
Barr, Lindsey, 1162
Barr, Palmela, 520
Barr, Teresa, 1167
Barrack, Keith D., 3391
Barrack Jr., Thomas J., 807
Barrantes, Camilla, 3105
Barrera, Kerryn, 1730
Barreras, June, 6239
Barreras, Lori, 5324
Barresi, Denise, 4537, 6703
Barresi, Peggy, 3135
Barreto, Julie, 2889
Barrett, Amy, 1956
Barrett, Daniel, 5489

Barrett, Dean, 7426, 7427
Barrett, Jeanne, 4998
Barrett, John, 2552
Barrett, Judy, 1021
Barrett, Kevin, 6497
Barrett, Laura, 2184
Barrett, Leigh, 2950
Barrett, Lisa, 6430
Barrett, Louise, 7591
Barrett, Martin, 5569
Barrett, Melissa, 4582
Barrett, Michael, 5097, 5688
Barrett, Rosemary, 5451
Barricelli, Marco, 2616, 6297
Barrick, Scott, 1762, 2363
Barrios, Bradley, 4539
Barron, Alice, 2132, 4833, 7280
Barron, Eric, 2013
Barron, Michael, 1728
Barron, Ted, 3021, 6927, 6929, 6930, 6931, 6932, 6933, 6934, 6935
Barron, Esq., Alexis, 1639, 2307, 5475
Barrow, Bret, 988
Barrow, James, 6855, 6857, 6858, 6859
Barrow, Kenneth, 1954
Barrows, Nancy, 8100
Barrueto-Cabello, Felipe, 79
Barrus, Andrew, 4016
Barrus, JaceSon, 4016
Barry, Aileen, 403, 463
Barry, Darlin, 2803
Barry, Jane, 2199
Barry, Jerome, 4422
Barry, Joanne, 5067
Barry, Mike, 7504
Barry, Mr. Andy, 7954
Barry, Nancy, 1424
Barry, Sarah M., 5929, 5931
Barry, Tina, 3947
Barry CAE, Douglas, 1320
Barry McCormick, Joan, 339
Barsamian, Sandy, 4107
Barsevich, Linda, 8169
Barstow, Barbara, 1334
Barstow, John, 1191
Barta, Gary A, 8720
Bartczak, Janice, 5979
Bartee, Dr Neale, 1862
Bartee, Dr. Neale King, 2437
Bartee, Neale, 749
Bartel, Carol, 897
Bartel, Matt, 4124
Bartell, Stacy, 7312
Bartels, Brat, 2980
Bartels, Kenneth G., 3479
Barter, Mary, 4368
Barth, Andy, 6160, 6161, 6162
Barth, Charles, 891
Barth, Christina, 3746
Barth, Lue Ann, 891
Barth, Margaret M., 1658
Bartha, Caterina, 396
Barthold, Lionel, 3620, 7820
Bartholomew, Beth, 499
Bartholomew, Cindy, 1608
Bartholomew, David, 2196
Bartholomew, Katie, 800
Bartholomew, Linda, 3883
Bartik, Chrissy, 6829
Bartine, Bill, 4649
Bartkus, Kari, 4356
Bartlemay, Jaclyn, 6938
Bartlett, David, 7095
Bartlett, Lindsay, 1305
Bartley, Lavonette, 5918
Bartley, Scott, 6415, 6416
Bartlo, Sarah K., 2745
Bartmann, Christoph, 7732
Bartner, Bob, 2821, 4480
Bartoldus, Brian, 1992
Bartoletti, Bruno, 2046
Bartolotta, Carl, 3410
Barton, Allen, 6073
Barton, Blythe, 69
Barton, Carol, 8138
Barton, James M., 2209
Barton, Kathy, 1076
Barton, Lisa, 1545, 1546, 5326

Executive Name Index

Barton, Sandra L., 6080, 6081, 6082, 6084
Barton, Stephen, 7302
Barton Speer, Dr Janet, 7855
Barton Speer, Dr. Janet, 3640
Barton, Esq., Lisa, 1639, 2307, 5475
Bartoszek, Scott, 7322
Bartruff, Jim, 7032, 7033, 7034
Bartter, Brit J., 2917
Bartz, Brenda, 2145
Bartz, Paul, 8863, 8911
Barwood, Jane, 5921, 5922
Barychev, Yelena, 8151
Barzilay, Guy, 8834
Basbas, George, 1425
Basbas, Louise, 1425, 1426, 5152
Bascom, Tom, 3356
Basehore, Vicky, 6101
Basel, Kris, 745
Baser, Ric, 8059
Basford, Chris, 1783
Bash-Polley, Stacy, 7768
Basham, Glenn, 977
Bashaw, Mary, 3814
Bashford, Wilkes, 6260, 6266
Bashline, Gary, 3352
Basile, Frank M, 3014
Basile, Frank M., 6860
Baskett, Steve, 3893
Baskin, Dorsey, 5609, 5611, 8360
Basque, Linda, 7317
Bass, Dr. James K., 2014
Bass, Eddie, 2264
Bass, EE, 5428
Bass, Gordon, 4053
Bass, John E D, 39
Bass, Lauren, 2500
Bass, Mercedes T., 1723, 2234, 5818, 7719
Bass, Scott A., 6476
Bass, Thomas, 12
Bass-Lamberto, Heidi, 6433
Bassage Bonfil, Jenn, 55
Bassett, Emma, 374, 3423, 5056
Bassett, Gwendolyn, 374
Bassett, Karen, 15
Bassett, Kay, 1814
Bassett, Ralph, 3168
Bassett, Tom, 5783
Bassila, Andrew, 969
Bassill, Robert, 1054
Bassin, Joel, 3594
Bassion, Mitchell, 4434
Bassis, Michael, 5701
Bassler Sullivan, Alice, 8
Bastid, Pierre.T, 440
Basu, Susan, 5196
Bataller, Linda, 4074
Batasi, Bill, 8604
Batchelder, Anne, 3354
Batcheldor, Toby, 4075
Batcheller, Tamara, 7290
Bate, Anna, 2739
Bate, Judy, 2763
Bateman, Cindy, 2895
Bateman, Danny, 1079
Bateman, Kimberly, 6596
Bateman, Meda, 1044
Bates, Andrea, 1184
Bates, Andy, 5250
Bates, Ann, 312
Bates, Dr. Michael, 756
Bates, Eryn, 4910
Bates, Jamie, 1273
Bates, Julie, 4870
Bates, Linda, 4005, 4027
Bates, Mason, 1035, 1038
Bates, Russel, 1696
Bates, Sheryl, 1842
Batesole, Jeanne, 3220
Bateson, Kathleen, 5544
Bateson, Kathleen P, 5544
Batey, Jessica, 1695
Batezel, Matt, 2488
Batschelet, Bill, 2699
Batson, Justin, 4137
Batt, Michael, 5919
Battali, Kathy, 5949, 5950
Battan, Suzette, 746
Battelani, Laura, 3454

Battenberg, Thomas, 1548
Batterson, Brett, 2907
Batterton, Eric, 1552
Battison, Dr. Sara, 1515
Battle, DeAma, 281
Battle, Drew, 4147
Battle, Erica, 1253
Battle, Robert, 381, 385
Battle III, Seymour, 5663, 8450, 8451
Battles, Patrick, 2422
Baty, Cecelia, 3048
Baty, Janna, 1968
Batzel, Mark, 4058
Bauchens, Robert, 8761
Bauchwitz, Monica, 1445
Bauer, Barbara A, 5425
Bauer, Barbara A., 4206
Bauer, Janice, 323
Bauer, Jeanne, 1730
Bauer, John, 4063
Bauer, Rob, 5197
Bauer-Lyons, Jennifer, 4504
Bauerle, Catherine, 967
Bauerlein, Stacy, 1432
Bauerly, Helga, 7369
Bauers, John, 2661
Baughan, Scott, 6490
Baughman, Jo Yates, 8030
Baughman, Teresa, 8126
Bauknight, Trevor, 8238
Baum, Chris, 4960
Baum, Keith, 4173
Baum, Margo, 7145
Baum, Maude, 350, 373
Bauman, Chad, 4124
Bauman, Maria, 372
Bauman, Phil, 1093
Baumann, Julius, 1753
Baumeister, Randy, 6957
Baumgardner, Kathleen, 6198
Baumgardner, Roger, 4820
Baumgart, Jr, Warren W, 2935
Baumgarten, Hannah, 157
Baumgarten, Michael, 2252, 2262, 4769
Baumgarten Foster, Julia, 6134
Baumgartner, Astrid R., 1406
Baumgartner, Nancy, 1744
Baun, Barbara, 3850
Baunach, Will, 1477
Baur, LauraJane, 4038, 4039
Baurkot, Karen, 8108
Bauwens, Joe, 2035
Bawcombe, Candace, 1713
Baxter, Andy, 1016
Baxter, Jeff, 2021
Baxter, Jessica, 4478
Baxter, Scott W., 1732
Baxter PhD, Diane, 8085, 8086
Bay, John, 3143
Bay, Peter, 1703, 4189
Bay, Willow, 6166
Bayank, Chuck, 3645
Bayer, Chirs, 7505
Bayer, Chris, 3336
Bayer, Kristin, 6023
Bayes, Sammy Dallas, 3603
Bayless, June, 3669
Baylin, Marc, 8883
Baylor, Meghan, 222
Baynard, Nathan, 3607
Bayne, Lorelei, 2554
Bayne Carroll, Valerie, 3130
Bea, Karen, 729
Beach, Alyssa, 5956
Beach, Angela, 4368
Beach, Chris, 6215
Beach, Christopher, 796, 4233
Beach, David, 1834
Beach, Doug, 4574
Beach, Lynn, 1274
Beachnau, Paul, 4841
Beachy, Anita, 6941
Beadell, Lori, 3263
Beadle, Robert, 3088
Beadle, Tony, 1176, 1208
Beagles, Brad, 1760, 5699
Beagley, Craig, 1767
Beal, Suzanne, 3122

Beale, James, 1720
Beale, Jeames, 5619
Beall, Charles, 988
Beam, Marc, 6214
Beaman, Stuart, 6646
Bean, Carole, 1774
Bean, Christa, 3982
Bean, Elizabeth, 3158
Bean, Janet R, 4545
Bean, Rob, 557, 6066, 6070, 6071, 6072
Bean, Virginia, 1704
Beane, Billy, 6197
Bear, Lewis, 6580
Bear, Roger, 2273, 2274
Bear, Stacey, 1669
Bear Jr., Lewis, 2813
Bearce, Amy, 220
Beard, Andrea, 4352
Beard, Beverly, 3088
Beard, Bobby, 6021
Beard, Charles, 1699
Beard, Deb, 387
Beard, Dena, 6286
Beard, Douglas, 8677
Beard, Gary, 2331
Beard, Gayle, 244
Beard, Paul S, 5626
Beard, William, 1860
Bearden, David, 1046
Bearden, Michael, 15
Bearden, Wes, 990
Bearden, Wesley, 4485
Beardsley, Kurt, 6086, 6087
Beardsley-Petit, Karen, 1621
Bears-Bailey, Kim, 578
Beaser, Lawrence J, 5382
Beasley, Ethan, 742
Beasley, Heather, 8598
Beasley, Roni, 5616
Beattie, Ellen, 3372
Beattie, Kurt, 4078
Beattie, Michael, 1275, 1276, 4775
Beattie-Hoang, Laura, 7195
Beatty, Beth, 3702
Beatty, Matt, 6977
Beatty, Max, 3048
Beatty, Sherri, 6032, 6033
Beaubrun, Gerard, 5281
Beauchamp, Beth, 5591
Beauchamp, Bill, 3070
Beauchamp, E William, 8093
Beauchesne, David J., 1671
Beaudry, James, 2977
Beaudry, Suzanne, 708
Beaugard, Theresa, 7563
Beaulieu, John, 179
Beaumant, Maryann, 5101
Beaumont, Andre, 2723
Beaumont, Maryann, 8852
Beaumont, Maryann K, 1398
Beaupre, Ken, 6151
Beaver, Don, 8222
Beaver, John P., 4652
Beaver, Kathy, 3616
Beaver, Robert M., 2940
Beazley, Dr Herschel, 1003
Beazley, Dr. Steven, 6193
Becerra, Tobi, 55
Bechdol, Pat, 507
Becher, Itzik, 5996, 6010, 8788
Bechert, Timothy, 7540
Becich, Anthony, 6586
Beck, Carl, 317, 3333
Beck, Charlie, 6718
Beck, Courtney, 850
Beck, Crafton, 1275, 1276, 1557
Beck, Emily, 4135
Beck, James, 2790, 6542
Beck, James F, 2790
Beck, Jill, 5827, 8657
Beck, Mike, 8634
Beck, Ralph, 7869
Beck Johnson, Lani, 2693
Beckel, Steven L., 4998
Beckenbach, Bill, 3739
Becker, Bill, 6570
Becker, Bryan, 4445
Becker, Carolyn, 1364

Becker, Christine, 3021
Becker, David, 6256, 7993, 8094
Becker, Douglas, 1437
Becker, Jeff, 7624
Becker, Joe, 8094
Becker, Micky, 5934
Becker, Nancy, 6423
Becker, Paula, 8075
Becker, Roberta, 1934
Becker, Rosalind V, 5276
Becker, Stefanie, 1933
Becker, Terri, 2341
Becker, Thomas, 2208
Becker, Thomas M, 5059
Becker, Vanessa, 3724
Becker, Mark P., 6626
Beckerle, Larry, 3601
Beckerman, Shira, 3836
Becker, Joy French, 6793
Beckett, Sherrye, 6658, 6659
Beckett, Thomas, 6417, 6425, 6426
Beckett-Hill, Jill, 8001
Beckham, Hal, 3898
Becki, Leah, 8192
Beckim, Chad, 3544
Beckley, Barbara, 2453
Beckley, Patrick, 1246
Beckman, Jack B, 8432
Beckmann, Christie, 6899
Beckmann, Terry J., 7169
Beckner, Jane, 1575
Beckner, Lisa, 8253
Beckstrand, Sara I., 3269
Beckstrom, Linda, 4123
Beckwith, David G, 5430
Beczala, Piotr, 2281
Bedan, Nancy, 7418
Bedell, John, 6113
Bedford, Dr. Clark, 2320
Bedford, John, 551
Bedford, Mary, 999
Bedinghaus, Bob, 7956
Beebe, Deryl, 5402
Beebe, Gayle D., 6280
Beebe, Marguerite, 7837
Beechly, Linnae, 5402
Beechwood, Jeanne M., 3046
Beeckler, Diane, 3060
Beedles, Michael, 7973, 7974
Beedless, Michael, 7972
Beegle, Mari, 6382
Beekman, Betty, 2687
Beeks, Graydon, 6087
Beeler, Kathryn, 8319
Beeman, Marcus, 2478
Beene, Brant, 5886
Beener, Esq., James F., 1632
Beenhouwer, Maud, 5027
Beeny, Suzanne, 2780
Beer, Beatrice, 2315
Beer, Dr.Joseph, 8132
Beer, Joyce, 2036
Beer, Samantha, 2361
Beerbohm, Darrel, 4713
Beerley, David, 8046
Beerman, Burton, 5295
Beers, John H, 4390
Beers, Larry, 2223, 3595
Beesemyer, Relinda, 790
Beesley, Alison, 146
Beeson, William, 7523
Beezley, Pamela, 1615, 5424
Befleur, Lis B, 5049
Begandy, Cheryl, 3845
Beggs, Cinny, 3679
Beggs, Liz, 827
Beggs, Patricia, 5305
Beggs, Patricia K, 2278
Begley, Greg, 215
Bego, Jim, 4280
Begue, Denise, 651
Behar, Lenore, 1481
Behnke, John, 5799
Behr, Erik, 1463
Behr, Robert, 2980
Behrends, Alan, 4885, 7378
Behrendt, Adrian, 1916
Behrens, Ann, 4108

Executive Name Index

Behrens, Polly, 2092
Behrmann, Emily, 7055
Behrns, Pat, 7495
Beideman, Jeff, 3818
Beierwaltes, Lynda, 1959
Beilein, John, 8556
Beilina, Nina, 1408
Beinlich, Melanie, 2036
Beirne, Charles, 6149
Beischer, Thomas G, 4310
Beisner Warling, Connie, 1313
Bejarno, Judy, 127
Bejjani, Bassem, 1807
Bekeny, Amanda, 1515
Belan, Michelle, 3844
Belanger, A. Douglas, 1807
Belanger, Darlene, 4382
Belanger, Kim, 7048
Belanger, Tammy, 5097
Belanger, Victor, 4786
Belardi, Ph.D., Tina M., 8108
Belasco, Lori, 4999
Belavitch, Kate, 3353
Belber, Robert, 7626
Belbruno, John, 929
Belcher, Dale, 6201
Belcher, Kelly, 1251
Belck, Nancy, 3335
Belden, Carling, 7185
Belding, Steve, 3921
Belfer, Laurence D., 5109, 7788
Belfiglio, Ron, 3149
Belford, Scott, 1485
Belfy, Dr Jeanne, 1023
Belfy, Jeanne, 1023, 4532
Belgrave, Nigel, 7261
Belilove, Jim, 432
Belilove, Lori, 432
Belkin, Robert A, 3588
Belknap, Ian, 3461
Bell, Andy, 8008
Bell, Arzell, 1745
Bell, Beth, 1496
Bell, Bob, 1571
Bell, Byron, 7849
Bell, Camt, 4894
Bell, Chantel, 479
Bell, Charlotte, 1763
Bell, Christine, 2383, 3408
Bell, Colleen, 4243
Bell, Daivd, 6446
Bell, David, 6445
Bell, David H., 2965, 4577
Bell, Debra, 2321
Bell, Deidra S., 1275, 1276
Bell, Elaine, 3978
Bell, Frazier, 593
Bell, Gary, 2197
Bell, Greg, 2650
Bell, Jack, 5962
Bell, Janie, 1708
Bell, Jim, 757
Bell, John, 1708, 6597
Bell, Karen, 5324
Bell, Kristin, 540
Bell, Marilyn, 1741
Bell, Michael, 7222
Bell, Muriel, 2018
Bell, Natalie, 4033
Bell, Nate, 8306
Bell, Nicholas, 2185
Bell, Ric, 7142, 7144
Bell, Richard, 2648
Bell, Robert, 2018
Bell, Stephen T, 8110, 8111
Bell, Stuart, 5256
Bell, Sue, 1943
Bell, Susan, 5818
Bell, Tarvia, 1707
Bell, Vanessa, 5646
Bell, Wishart, 2067
Bellamore, Lisa, 6124
Bellamy, Lou, 3270
Bellamy, Sarah, 3270
Bellante, Jeff, 3413
Bellassai, Marc C, 5983
Beller, Hava, 3509
Bellet, Alain, 1717

Bellevue, Rob, 799
Belliard, Aurora, 7773
Bellinger, Samuel J, 3460
Bellino, Joe, 7318
Bellion, Joe, 7318
Bellner, Randi, 6860
Bello, Tanya, 23
Belloli, Jay, 826
Bellomy, Tony, 2229
Bellotti, Heather, 6372, 6375
Bellows, Brad, 278
Bellrichard, Cindy, 3221
Bellusar, Shelley, 7577
Belmont, Wayne, 8087
Belo, Paul, 4038
Belok, Nancy, 1455
Beloncik Schantz, Anne, 1685, 1686
Belote, Brandon, 4806
Belson, Michele, 2828
Belt, Kathleen, 3302
Belt, Nora Kay, 215
Belth, Samantha, 403
Belton, Erline, 278
Beltran, Victoria, 1833
Beltz, Steve, 3744, 8000
Belusar, Shelley, 5007
Belvel, Kevin, 3343
Bemand, Alice, 2704
Bemelmans, Norman, 5274
Bemis, Rick, 778
Bemis, Stephen, 8779
Ben, Blankley, 3052
Ben Allatt, Hon, 3805
Ben-Dor, Gisele, 871
Benac, Barbara, 1717
Benachowski, Mariyn, 819
Benalt, Seth, 6599
Benaquen, Norma S, 1436
Benavides, Chris, 4233
Benavidez, Julie, 6210
Benavidez, Justin, 1737
Benavidez, Thomas Alex, 4179
Benbow, Anne, 3375
Benchoff, J. Bryan, 7944
Bencini, Barbara, 3244
Benda, Jean, 3103, 3353
Benda, Jean, 7171
Bender, Betsy, 4478
Bender, Elizabeth, 1834
Bender, Jodi, 414
Bender, Stewart, 5325
Bender, Tammy, 6756
Bendeson, Adam, 5075
Bendett, David, 876
Benecke, Jody, 4333
Benedette Snyder, Patricia D, 3628
Benedetti, Christine, 6329
Benedetti, Evangeline, 1409
Benedict, Diane, 2508
Benedict, Michael, 2020
Benedict Brown, Jay, 2669
Benedix, Mandy, 7188
Benefield, Cristi, 679
Benenson, Gladys, 2017
Benerofe, Froma, 470
Benes, Katie, 4843, 4868
Benezra, Steve, 3642
Benfer, David W, 932
Benfield, Brenton, 1170
Benfield, Knolan, 3681
Benford, Alaina R., 3984
Bengtsson, Bob, 7276
Beninato, Barbara L, 1014
Beninoris, Renna, 880
Benish, Neil, 1679
Benitez, Joseph, 5131
Benitez, Maria, 348
Benitz, Cecilio, 348
Benitz, Maria, 348
Benjamin, Adria, 1577
Benjamin, David, 1195
Benjamin, Eric, 1562
Benjamin, Jan, 5548
Benjamin, Lorraine, 445
Benjamin, Mary, 753
Benjamin, Patricia J, 7635
Benjamin, Patricia J., 5049, 5120
Benjamin, Prof. Jack, 5527

Benjamin, Susan M., 4433
Benjamin, Wieke, 1097
Benkovic, Kenneth, 2189
Benn, Connell, 2113
Benn, Douglas J, 2692
Bennahum, Ninotchka, 2612
Benner, Lynnette, 1402
Benner, Paul, 4458
Benner Browne, Marijane, 4790
Bennet, Douglas, 6411
Bennet, Jessica, 1523, 1524
Bennet, Jim, 3163
Bennet, Robbie, 8210
Bennet Herring, Sherrill, 4242
Benneth, Donna, 2938
Bennett, Ashley, 5600
Bennett, Atom, 1
Bennett, Boyce, 5068
Bennett, David, 2228
Bennett, Dick, 800
Bennett, Don, 6312
Bennett, Dorothy, 3903
Bennett, Dottie, 4033
Bennett, Douglas J., 6412, 6413, 6414
Bennett, Ericka, 3029
Bennett, Frances H., 3929, 3933
Bennett, Gail, 578
Bennett, Gerald, 1626
Bennett, Howard, 4713
Bennett, Janice, 1294
Bennett, Jennifer, 524
Bennett, Jessica, 6280
Bennett, Jim, 2455
Bennett, John, 2172, 2263, 6657
Bennett, Josh, 4159
Bennett, Kate, 4758
Bennett, Kevin, 2415
Bennett, Kristy, 4647
Bennett, Lauren, 810
Bennett, Lisa, 8002
Bennett, Mark, 844
Bennett, Phil, 1785
Bennett, Robert, 4510, 8211
Bennett, Robertson H, 1418
Bennett, Rodger, 5622
Bennett, Rodney D., 4887, 7392
Bennett, Rose, 1945, 6329
Bennett, Russell, 3014
Bennett, Samantha, 2475
Bennett, Sara, 3869
Bennett, Sheryl, 2164
Bennett, Susan, 7466
Bennett, Ted, 3377
Bennett, Willis, 5722
Bennett Darwin, Elaine, 796
Bennett-Dellwo, Rena, 3773
Benninga, Carla, 2820
Bennison, Matt, 3932
Benoist, Joan, 2175
Benoit, David, 833
Benoit, Janet, 2047
Benoit, John, 5138
Benoit, Pam, 7944
Benschoter, Brooke, 6987, 6988
Bense, Judith A., 6580
Bensel, Mary, 6511, 6586
Bensignor, Jane, 575
Bensinger, Susan, 246
Benskin, Patty, 1837
Benson, Bix, 228
Benson, Bruce, 2647
Benson, Genie, 111
Benson, Joan, 4276, 6216, 6217
Benson, Joshua S, 6800
Benson, Kevin, 429
Benson, Lois, 2009
Benson, Margaret, 3545
Benson, Martin, 2461
Benson, Meridith, 517
Benson, Mike, 6365
Benson, Mindy, 8473
Benson, Molly, 4082
Benson, Pamela, 2846, 2862
Benson, Pamela, 6627
Benson, Phillip, 4713
Benson, Rosalie, 3603
Benson, Sarah, 3568, 7783
Benson, Scott, 7353, 7354

Benson, Sharon, 4680
Benson, Timothy J., 1830
Benson Schutter, Victoria, 3986
Bent, Kim, 4022
Bent, Sandra, 8040
Bentley, Jeff, 7893
Bentley, Jeffrey J, 308
Bentley, John, 1522
Bentley, Kathryn, 6771, 6772
Bentley, Mitzi C, 5912, 5913, 5914
Bentley, Ron, 2255
Benton, Andrew K., 6185
Benton, Andrew.K, 808
Benton, Pat, 7636
Bentz, Dr.Anne, 8146
Bentz, Kevin, 2367
Benway, Eileen, 775
Benyas, Edward, 1033
Benzaquen, Norman S, 1441
Benzing, Pam, 3074
Benzvi, Loni, 8140
Beracha, Barry H., 1291, 1292, 4921
Beran, Paul B., 4187, 6027
Berberian, George, 4440
Berby, Amanda, 5835
Bercaw, Louise, 1959
Berchild, Chris, 3023
Berchild, Christopher, 6943, 6945
Bercume, Jeff, 2554
Berczik, Daniel, 1655
Berdahl, James, 1944, 4351
Berding, Dennis, 4912
Berdo, Lazlo, 352
Beredesco, Charlie, 1986
Berendes, Diane, 6116
Berg, Al, 1799
Berg, Bunny, 6843, 6844, 6845
Berg, Cassandra, 4135
Berg, Chris, 3694
Berg, Dr. Bradley, 1746
Berg, Gretchen, 4742
Berg, I. Christopher, 6920
Berg, James R., 1749
Berg, Jessica, 4871
Berg, Julia, 4439
Berg, Linda, 2034
Berg, Nancy, 5831
Berg, Paul, 3215
Berg, Rhonda, 4616
Berg, Shelton, 4439
Berg, Tim, 3765
Bergamaschi, Janet, 8187
Bergen, Kathleen Van, 4921
Berger, Barbara, 5280
Berger, Cecilia, 1196
Berger, Ellis, 1418
Berger, Miriam R., 1407
Berger, Rick, 6096, 6098
Berger, Sidney, 5634, 5637
Berger, Sidney L, 3985
Berger, Vance, 5564
Berger, Victoria, 1382, 5071
Bergeret, Albert, 2239
Bergeron, Ann A, 3226, 3227
Bergeron, Katherine, 4440
Berggren, Stacey, 6704, 6707
Bergh, Laura, 720
Berghn, Laura, 5939
Berghoff, Michael, 6949, 6950
Bergin, Sarah, 1682
Bergland, Arne, 6313
Berglund, Jeanine, 4536
Bergman, Cathy, 236
Bergman, Lisa, 5783
Bergman, Marilyn, 7712
Bergman, Terri, 3750
Bergman, Timothy J, 1138
Bergman, Valerie, 559
Bergman, Yaacov, 1607, 1812
Bergner, Bruce, 2647
Bergsma, Paula, 2138
Beriss, Michael, 3121
Berke, Melissa, 4951
Berke, Michael, 4440
Berkeiser, Will, 7844
Berkenblit, Dr. Daniel, 5202
Berkenstein, Catherine, 2926
Berkenstock, Dr. James, 1048

Executive Name Index

Berkman, Ronald M., 7968
Berkompas, Laura, 7018, 7020, 7021
Berkow, Jay, 4024
Berks, Alan, 3251
Berkson, Gary, 819
Berkus, David W, 6179, 6182
Berlew, Timothy, 1825
Berley, Liliane, 467
Berlin, Ernest, 4471
Berlin, Jen, 2680
Berlin, Jr., Russell E., 1343
Berlin, Ricky, 4703
Berlow, Sheldon M., 1373
Berman, Ann, 96
Berman, Carol, 3396
Berman, Jessica Rothste, 7733
Berman, Kathleen, 163
Berman, Meredith, 6443
Berman, Mitchell, 1124
Berman, Nathaniel, 800
Berman, Patricia, 1399
Berman, Richard, 467
Berman PhD, Rabbi Donna, 6407
Bermingham, John, 1833
Bermingham, Ron, 1141
Bermudez, Lisa, 5141
Berna, Linda, 4549
Bernacki, Gary, 2708
Bernal, Janice, 2502
Bernal-Rundle, Rose, 6512
Bernard,, 8650
Bernard, Caron, 5970
Bernard, Dave, 1598, 8083
Bernard, Ellen, 2092
Bernard, Marie-H,IŠne, 1181, 2106, 4354
Bernard Magrinat, Mary, 5244
Bernardo, Don, 5320
Bernardo, Rick, 3242
Bernatchez, Michael, 1198
Bernatowicz, Mariusz, 370
Bernberg, Bruce, 3235
Bernd, Suzanna H., 1390
Bernegger, Sandra, 1379, 1380, 2253
Berner, Barbara, 2164
Berner, Jennifer, 5785
Bernet, Glenn, 4925
Bernet, James, 3467
Bernfeld, Jay, 966, 4440
Bernfield, Susan, 3532
Bernhard, Randy, 4137
Bernhardt, Bonnie, 887
Bernhardt, Elise, 413
Bernhardt, Peter M., 8504
Bernhardt, Robert, 1131, 1689
Bernier, Bill, 717
Bernier, Fred, 249
Bernstein, Adam, 3567, 3576
Bernstein, David C., 3825
Bernstein, Gary, 4601
Bernstein, Jed, 5151
Bernstein, Joanne, 1056
Bernstein, Joe, 1828
Bernstein, Karen, 264
Bernstein, Kenneth, 3960
Bernstein, Louis B., 5164
Bernstein, Mark, 3302
Bernstein, Richard, 2658
Bernstein, Ronald, 922
Bernstein, Sue Renee, 8798
Bernstein, Valerie, 4220
Bernstein Wilt, Johanna, 515
Bernstein-Cohen, Joanne, 1422
Bernstein, Gary, 6843, 6844, 6845
Bernzen, Avril Marie, 2058
Bero-Johnson, Jamie, 5439
Berquist, Guy, 2743
Berrang, Nancy, 3105
Berroughs, F E, 8041
Berry, Andrew, 3124, 3128
Berry, Carl, 2526
Berry, Carolyn A, 1021
Berry, Debra, 4864
Berry, Elizabeth A, 4844
Berry, Gus, 4071
Berry, Joe, 749
Berry, John, 3000
Berry, Jonanne, 7264
Berry, Karen, 5772

Berry, Lee, 7270
Berry, Mike, 3071
Berry, Millicent, 1226
Berry, William, 6127, 6157
Berry II, Thomas W., 4226
Berry Jr, Stafford C, 508
Berryhill, Mark, 4540
Berry, Joanne, 7569
Berseth, John, 1616
Bershad, Jack R, 2310
Bershad, Esq., Jack R., 1645
Bersie, Bill, 8535
Berson, Marc, 3379
Berson, Marc E., 7574
Berssenbrugge, Robert, 1017
Bertani, Niklas, 876
Bertani, Steve, 3278, 7412
Bertaux, Betty, 2101
Bertaux, Dr Betty, 2101
Berthelsdorf, MD, Mildred, 1607
Bertini, Cara, 6395
Bertoia, Pat, 1818
Bertoni, Dorothy, 6406
Bertsch, Delora, 6275
Bertucci, Angie, 6283
Berube, Michael, 100
Berube, Rick, 7644
Berwick, Scott, 5191
Berzansky, Joan M, 1347
Berzok, Robert M., 4806
Besa, Tina, 81
Beshaw, Beth, 1361
Beshore, Rebecca, 4359
Besozzi, Joy, 7760
Bess, David, 8644, 8645, 8646, 8647, 8649
Bess, Robert, 4201
Bessett, Gary, 3150
Bessey, Robb, 4120
Bessey III, Earle, 7183
Bessolo, Rob, 8559
Best, Amy, 1104, 1105
Besl, Charles, 3831, 4441, 4569
Best, Grant, 2202
Best, Reverend David, 3512
Beste, Jeff, 5299
Bestock, Shana, 4079, 8598
Bestok, Shana, 8598
Beston, Dr. Rose Marie, 5194
Bestul, Michelle, 4134
Beswick, Carole, 6215
Beswick, Tim, 878
Beswick, Timothy L, 878
Beswick, Timothy L., 4332
Betancourt, Rudy, 6334
Beth, Liza W., 1985
Beth Berkes, Mary, 5855
Beth Buckley, Karen, 190
Beth Gaffney, Mary, 700
Beth Hughes, Mary, 1819
Beth Johnson, Mary, 1528, 1529
Beth Kuester, Mary, 4133
Beth McFall, Mary, 2195
Beth Rossi, Mary, 6596
Beth Sciarabba, Mary, 6300
Beth Stevens, Mary, 2105
Bethany, Dr. Adeline, 5499
Bethea, Charles Henry, 4945
Bethel, Charles, 3244
Bethel, Chris, 7992
Bethelsen, Maren, 5164
Betof, Nila G., 575
Betsch, Kenneth, 5541
Betsworth, Gary, 1451
Betterton, Ann, 5015
Bettinson, Greg, 2365
Bettis, Alice, 4599
Bettison-Varga, Lori, 6085
Betts, Glenn, 8682
Betts, Kathleen, 4433
Betts, Roland, 956, 958
Betts, Roland H, 4238
Bettwy, Greg, 6461
Betz, Craig M, 3700
Betz, David, 2174
Betz, Nancy, 8010
Betz, Philip, 6802
Betza, Dawn M., 5448
Betzel, Alex, 4556

Betzer, MD, Susan B., 997
Beudert, Mark, 2298
Beukelman, Doug, 7015
Beuning, Sarah L., 223, 311
Beussman, Laura, 1701, 5588
Beussman, Robert, 2150
Beuttler, Jack, 4542
Bevilaqua, Lisa, 7225
Bewlay, Steve, 7700
Bewley, Kingsley, 966, 4440
Bewsher, Erin, 1329
Bewtel, Paul, 8325
Beyer, Al, 6545
Beyer, Peg, 1450
Beyer, Wayne, 1748
Beyrau, Sheri, 4043
Bhala, Kara, 7044
Bhathal, Marta S., 6090
Bhatt, Haren, 1916
Biaggi, Daniel, 2017
Bialkin, Kenneth J., 5818, 7719
Bianchi Pingel, Michelle, 2824, 6585
Bias, Shirley, 4469
Biase, Deanna, 4991
Biasell, Natasha, 4256
Biava, Gayle, 1943
Biava, Luis, 1560
Bibb, Harold, 1672, 5518
Bibelhausen, Keith, 1109
Biberman, Anne, 4158
Bibik, Sara, 211
Bichel, Susan, 3878
Bickel, Jerry, 2830
Bickerton, Mary, 6661
Bicket, Harry, 2200
Bicknell, Marcus, 5131
Bicknell, Tara, 5940
Biddle, Leonard, 6041
Biddle, Ludy, 4026
Biddlecome, James A., 2190
Bidlingmaier, Rick, 8679
Bidwell, Fred, 7962
Bidwoll, Frederick E, 5316
Biebesheimer, Arlene, 1864
Biederman, Ray, 1088
Biederwolf, Robert I, 5851
Biedron, Michael, 6794
Biel, Anne, 1570
Bielamowicz, Bill, 8343
Bielawa, Lisa, 1920, 1921
Bielejeski, Jeanne, 1260
Bieler, Glenn M., 7191, 7192
Bieler, Mel, 2746
Biels, Natasha, 811
Bielski, Michael, 1656
Biemer, Linda, 1367
Bienen, Henry S, 6779, 6780, 6781, 6782, 6783, 6784
Bienkowski, Danek, 4365
Bierhans, Bruce, 3181
Bierkamp, Jeanette, 7271
Bierman, Lynn, 4601, 6843, 6844, 6845
Bierny, Jean-Paul, 4181
Bierwirth, David, 6460
Biesman, Didi B., 8295
Bietz, Gordon, 5563
Bietz, Ted, 797
Bifaro, Anthony J., 3620
Biggers, Joy, 514
Biggerstaff, Blake, 6735
Biggin, Sally, 30
Bigl, Stacie R, 531
Bigos, Elyssa, 324
Bigsbi, Monica, 3678
Bihn, Steve, 5343
Bijelic, Milica, 593
Bikales, Vida, 3048
Bilal, Agha, 6078
Bilfield, Jenny, 4337, 4434
Bilger, Jane R., 4563
Bill, Joseph J., 5150
Bill, Pastor Earl, 2450
Bill Sarocka, William, 6847
Bill' Stanton, William, 6710
Billeci, Celesta, 4326
Billerbeck, Ronda, 5781
Billetter, Leslie, 553
Billick, Dean, 8330

Billig, Andy, 8609
Billig, Rebecca, 7369
Billing, Lisa, 3737
Billings, David, 2320
Billings, Karry, 1760
Billings, Kary, 1760, 5699
Billingslea, Aldo, 6289, 6290
Billmann, Sara, 2130
Billotti, Richard, 2180
Billow, Craig, 326
Bilotta, A.J., 6421
Bilotta, Peter, 5417
Bilotta, CFRE, Peter J., 1600
Bilotti, Richard, 1340
Bilsky, Steve, 8161
Bilyea, Julie K, 4678
Binda, Carrine, 63
Binder, Claude, 199, 205, 4124
Binder, David, 612
Binder, Lara, 68
Binder, Maryetta, 6456, 6457
Binder, Tom, 4179
Bingaman, Robert A., 3360
Bingham, Constance, 2089
Bingham, Joseph, 292
Bingham, Lisa, 4970
Bingham, John, 8559
Binghan, Carolyn, 3133
Binkhuysen, Armand, 1792
Binko, Mike, 750
Binkyuhsen, Armand, 1792
Binnie, Anita, 4881
Binnie, Ross, 1535, 7283
Binns, Lily, 135
Binns, Ralph, 2362
Bins, Susan, 5850
Bintinger, Thomas P., 1321
Bintz, Carol, 8017
Bintz, Helen, 5836
Bintz, Roger, 5836
Bintzler, Wanda, 5841
Birch, Alexandra, 1865
Birchenough, Dave, 5203
Bird, Chris, 6632
Bird, Diane, 1781
Bird, Kathy, 4840
Bird, Kelly, 3367
Bird, Miriam, 473
Bird, Paul S., 5096, 5097
Bird Reynolds, Lindsey, 1837
Birder, James P., 6494, 6495
Birdsong, Ronnie, 6041
Birkedahl, Walter B., 6103
Birkhauser, Robert, 4115
Birkhead, Kathryn, 753
Birman, Robert, 5788, 5789, 5790
Birman, Robert A, 1131
Birmingham, Tom, 2780
Birnbaum, Elaina, 889
Birt, Erin, 6790, 6791, 6792
Bischoff, Chris, 1751
Biscotti, Manrico, 2191
Bishoff, Murray, 4914
Bishop, Andre, 3588, 7746
Bishop, Andrew, 4089
Bishop, Bob, 4025
Bishop, Duane, 655
Bishop, Gina, 6199
Bishop, Mark, 3016, 6912
Bishop, Michelle, 1665
Bishop, Pam, 525
Bishop, Shawnda, 655
Bishop, Steve, 8129
Bishop, Will, 1784
Bishop Hoch, Dr Juliana, 1959
Bisignano, John, 6539
Bisno, Leslie, 870
Bissell, Nancy, 4181
Bissell, Sandy, 7676
Bissell, Stacy, 5081
Bissell, Susan, 1249
Bissessar, Rodney, 7707
Bisset, Joshua, 332
Bisson, Beau, 317
Biswas, Malabika, 450, 5146
Bitetto, Dorothy, 330
Bither, Philip, 3258
Bitner, Shane A, 819

1141

Executive Name Index

Bitonte, Helen, 2291
Bittel, Michael, 4467
Bittel, Peter J., 7250
Bitter, Frances, 1706
Bitting, Angelyn S, 7865
Bittle, Richard, 3279
Bittrick, John, 2345
Bitz, Allison, 5167
Bitz, Kim Patrick, 2912
Bivins, Mrs. John, 2156
Bivins, Wally, 3317
Bixler, Brad, 4068, 4072
Bixler, Harris J., 252, 4746
Bizer, Renee, 43
Bizer, Suzanne, 2913, 6731
Biziewski, Stephanie, 506
Bjaland, Leif, 991, 992, 993, 994, 995
Bjerke, Keith, 7933
Bjerke, Vicki, 2070
Bjerkness, Kris, 7340
Bjork, Larry, 4088
Bjork, Ross, 6174
Blacher, Richard, 1216
Blachere, Brigitte, 2734
Blachford, Erik, 4081
Blachly, Michael, 4451, 6520
Blachowicz, Lee, 1879
Black, Anne T., 2341
Black, Bernard, 1659
Black, Chan. Lendley, 3226, 3227
Black, Charene, 1879
Black, Daniel, 1065, 1066, 1833
Black, Delores, 2340
Black, Dennis, 1376
Black, Emily J., 5796
Black, Harold G, 5430
Black, J.Thomas, 6490
Black, James, 1704, 3982, 8398, 8399, 8400
Black, Jessi, 4597
Black, Jim, 864
Black, Kate, 2950
Black, Luther, 252, 1151, 2090, 4746
Black, Luther F., 5797
Black, Lydia, 6515
Black, Merna, 1899
Black, Michael, 2617
Black, Mike, 6299
Black, Patricia, 5029
Black, Patrick, 4968
Black, Ruth, 4802
Black, Shekeyna, 6302
Black, Steve, 5614
Black, Susan, 4164, 8516
Black, Timuel, 4556
Black, Tony, 3984
Black, PhD, Karen, 7026, 7027
Blackbur, Philip, 4882
Blackburn, Katie, 7956
Blackburn, Timothy, 6277
Blackburn Harlow, Leslie, 5690, 5691, 5692, 5693
Blackledge, Barbara, 3809
Blackman, Gary, 3374
Blackman, Gary W, 8791
Blackman, Mark A, 8791
Blackman, Paul, 1975
Blackman, Peter, 6180
Blackman, Susan, 3848
Blackmon, Pualani, 12
Blacksburg, Nicole, 4321
Blackweldor, Stephen, 1071
Blackwell, Barbara, 799
Blackwell, Caleb, 4042
Blackwell, Courtney, 350, 440
Blackwell, Missy, 3921
Blackwell, Susan, 1543
Blackwood, C. Roy, 4704
Blackwood, Randy, 7460
Blaheta, Don, 2969
Blain, Stuart, 1785
Blain Chaplin, Sarah, 3252
Blaine, Martha, 1582
Blair, Christine, 1231
Blair, Daphne, 3803, 8124
Blair, Ellen L, 2248
Blair, Jena L, 3743
Blair, Kasey, 6500
Blair, Lynne, 79

Blair, Mary, 4058
Blair, Meredith, 8821
Blair, Patricia, 198
Blair, Rebbeca, 2026
Blair Huffman, Ann, 1278
Blair Legow, Christine, 2291
Blais, Donald, 853
Blaising, Craig, 8389
Blaizely, Doris, 2639
Blake, Gregory, 4756
Blake, James N., 1432
Blake, Laurence, 58
Blake, Lynette, 1318
Blake, Mark, 7119
Blake, Nicole, 4999
Blake, Randy, 7367
Blake, Richard, 3926
Blake, Ronald L., 5855
Blake, Rose, 642
Blake, Vickie, 8260
Blakely, Joshua, 2397
Blakeman, Mark A., 8302
Blakemen, Mark A., 2334
Blakemore, Donna, 4309
Blaker, Ken, 4070
Blaker, Sally, 759, 761, 4205
Blakey, Gregory, 2434
Blalock, Roger, 6952
Blanc, George, 4214
Blanc, Nicolas, 199, 205
Blanchard, Charles, 5164
Blanchard, Donna, 2887
Blanchard, Harry, 2887
Blanchard, Joseph, 3987
Blanchard, Judith, 634
Blanchard, Patrick, 2868
Blanchet, Geri, 2859
Blanchette, Aimee, 2326
Blanchette, Terri S., 2317
Blanchette, Yonnie, 5663, 8450, 8451
Blanco, Carol, 399
Blanco, Gricelda, 6690, 6691, 6692, 6693, 6694
Blanco, R Michael, 399
Bland, Steve, 4319, 4320
Bland, Tom, 8080
Blanden, Jeremy, 5117
Blanding, Carrie, 853
Blandino, Michael, 3393
Blandy, Susan, 1470
Blanford, Dave, 4819
Blank, Chef Fritz, 2313
Blank, Martin, 3119
Blank Kelner, Lenore, 3130
Blankemeyer, Ruth, 3358
Blankenship, Eric, 6488
Blankenship, Karen, 5546
Blankenship, Kim, 2069
Blankenstein, Vidal, 4890
Blanks, Jon, 4002
Blanton, Gene, 1716
Blanton, James, 1363
Blanton, Ray, 6149
Blasband, David, 489
Blaschik, Edward C., 6398
Blaschke, Ken, 1150
Blask, Sarah, 5515
Blasy, Matt, 7327
Blatt, J. David, 5766
Blattner, Charles E., 4880
Blau, Nansi, 2362
Blaufuss, Patricia, 2707
Blaun, Gene, 7146
Blavatnik, Len, 1447
Blaylock, David, 5574
Blaylock, Suzy, 3949
Blaylock, William, 2342
Blayney, Kelly, 1779
Blazer, Ted, 7698
Blaziek, William, 8376
Bledsoe, Cindy, 1843
Bledsoe, Jerry H, 5766
Blehm, Julie, 5282
Bleil, Varina, 801
Bleiweis, Leah, 111
Bleiweiss, Rick, 3771
Bleiweiss, Ron, 8811
Blenn, John, 5215
Blessing, Glenna, 264

Blevins, Jennifer, 3664
Blevins, Mary, 4070
Blevins, Michael, 4994
Blevins, Randy, 5575
Bley, Jonathan, 5186
Blezard, Suzanne, 359
Blickenstaff, Rebecca, 3320
Blickers, Beth, 3577
Blight, Andrew, 572
Bline, Amy W., 4962
Blinn, Ken, 3655
Bliss, Kathy, 6730
Bliss, Michael B, 6681
Blitz, Gil, 5015
Blitzer, Judi, 3542
Blixt, Charles A, 5278
Blixt, Janice L, 4851
Blizman, Paul J, 1231
Blobe, Susan, 568
Bloch, Michael, 1453
Bloch, Milton, 5214
Blocher, David M, 1147
Blocher, David M., 2087
Block, Dr. Glenn, 1122
Block, Gene, 6169
Block, Glenn, 1293
Block, Matt, 7280
Block, Mrs James A, 5167
Block, CPA/JD, Paul, 2316
Block, MD, Marian, 2317
Blocker, Jeremy, 3536
Blocker, Robert, 1968
Blocker, Robert L, 934, 936
Blockie, Eric, 7432
Blodgett, Katherine E., 1647
Blodgett, Ruth, 4806
Bloemendaal, Joyce, 4663
Bloise, Lucy, 1616, 8107
Blondell, John, 6280
Blood, Charles, 2174
Blood, Liz, 5386
Bloodgood, Cynthia, 2567
Bloom, Diane, 5507
Bloom, J Lawrie, 4762
Bloom, Jacqueline, 1600, 5417
Bloom, Janice, 1716
Bloom, Katie, 139
Bloom, Kenneth, 1748
Bloom, Lisa, 2067
Bloom, Michael, 3711
Bloom, Naomi, 2779
Bloom, Nicolaus, 4741
Bloom, Olga, 1369
Bloom, Roberta, 6363
Bloom, Russell, 5508
Bloom, Steve, 1021
Bloom, Wendy, 4839
Bloomer, Donna, 907
Bloomfield, Gregg, 3213
Bloomquist, Jean, 1252
Bloss, Wally, 5683
Blount, Derek, 3923
Blount, James, 6050
Blount, Rhoda, 1652, 5484
Blozis, Lisa, 1977
Blue, Darell, 8621, 8653
Blue, Janina, 122
Blue, Sarah, 1541
Blue Hamilton, Margaret, 4815
Bluestein, E. Frank, 3899
Bluett, Valerie, 4317
Blum, Charles, 3016, 6912
Blum, David S., 3839
Blum, Gary, 6201
Blum, Gregory, 2875
Blum, Irene Harriet, 2750
Blum, Linda, 1623
Blum, Marvin E., 1723
Blumberg, Sarah, 1565
Blumenthal, Barbara, 5574
Blumenthal, Liz, 2185
Blumenthal, Saul, 1544
Blumenthal, Toby, 1746, 2094
Blumenthal Phillips, Toby, 1746
Blumer, Josh, 6286
Blumhard, Christopher, 1669
Blumrick, Rob, 7097
Blundell, Cathy, 6050

Blundell, Harry, 6050
Blundell, Kathi, 6050
Blunden-Diggs, Debbie, 532
Blus, Larry, 5404, 5407
Blust, Larry, 200
Bluth, Christina, 649
Blydenburgh, Sal, 3777
Blythe, Amanda, 143, 144
Boal, Peter, 682
Boardman, Donald, 3121
Boardman, Lisa, 6078
Boatman, Linda, 3948
Boatright, Charlie, 4446
Boatright, Joe, 902
Boaz, Keith, 7460
Bob Lamothe, Robert, 3345
Bobbitt, Donald, 4191
Bobbitt, Michael, 3128
Bobbitt, Michael J., 3124
Bobby, Ted, 3846
Bobgan, Raymond, 7967
Bobkowski, Laura, 215
Bobo, Keith, 4355
Bobo, Rowanna, 4355
Bobrick, Elizabeth, 2691
Bobrovsky, Jodi, 3987
Boburka, Robert D, 2920
Bocchicchio, Michael, 798
Bochenek, Neva, 4177
Bock, Barbara, 1912
Bock, Charles, 1661
Bock, Landrie, 3923, 5080
Bocsh, Meghan, 6389
Bodansky, Joel, 4082
Boddie, Lydia, 3610
Boden, Matt, 2562
Bodenstein, Suzanne, 3302
Bodford, Bobby, 3685
Bodig, Joyce, 5133
Bodine, Bill, 5490
Bodine, Blair, 1696
Bodine, Veronica, 3744, 8000
Bodley, Muriel, 1469
Bodley, Sarah, 418
Bodmer, Scott, 6689
Bodnar, Debra, 2713
Bodnar, John, 3370
Bodolosky, Michael, 8134, 8135
Bodony, Adam, 1086
Boduch, Betty, 6835
Boduszek, Dianne, 7980
Boe, Carl, 1918, 1919
Boe, Steven, 1033
Boeh, Thomas, 6104
Boehler, Michelle, 3398
Boehler, Phil, 3397, 3398
Boehlke, Bain, 3244
Boehm, Gari, 648
Boehm, Marc, 8176
Boehmer, Clifford, 4785
Boehne Ehlers, Ashley, 2485
Boehringer, Terri, 8019
Boehringer, Theresa, 8019
Boeren, Lisa L, 3114
Boersma, Susan, 1240
Boespflug, George, 6145
Boettcher, Kayla, 4163
Boey, Robert T, 6762
Bogaev, Bo, 3916
Bogan, Wesley, 4989
Bogard, Norberto, 3556, 3570
Bogart, Anneeen, 3564
Bogart, Richard, 1899
Bogash, Carol, 2094, 4432
Bogats, Catherine, 3846
Bogdanova, Marina, 334
Bogenrief, Abby, 1308
Bogenrief, Richard, 1115, 1116
Boger, Ph.D., Joshua, 4777
Bogert, Margot, 5133
Boggess, Sarah, 5211
Boggioni, Josh, 3529
Boggs, April, 7943
Boggs, Brian, 5901, 5902, 5903, 5904
Boggs, Gary, 711
Boggs, Gil, 122
Boggs, Marcus, 211
Boggs, Tex, 5883

Executive Name Index

Boghossian III, Leon C., 3859
Bognar, Joseph, 1098
Bogner Wong, Betsy, 4853
Bogue, E. Grady, 8254, 8256, 8257
Bogues, Anthony, 3863
Bogusz, Amy, 496
Bogusz, Larry, 1220
Bogza, Sergey, 1260
Bohan, Erin, 4500
Bohan, Scott P., 4961
Bohanan, Monte, 4977, 7543
Boheme, Irene, 5207
Boher, Mark, 2617
Bohling, DeEtta, 4910
Bohmert, Brenda, 1267
Bohn, Karina, 5964
Bohn, Lise, 3987, 8416
Bohnert, Dave, 1166
Bohnett, David C, 805
Bohnett, David C., 6124, 6157
Bohnett, Deborah Borda, 792
Bohnhorst, Brendan, 1240
Bohon, J. Sergio, 832
Bohorquez, Fernando, 439
Bohr, Rob, 4176
Bohrer, Robert E., 8125
Bohrman, Diana, 496
Bohyer, John, 4937
Boico, Daniel, 1430
Boieru, Marin, 511
Boigegrain, Cheryl, 5285
Boin, Jim, 2593
Boiter-Jolley, Bonnie, 598
Boivin, Paul, 590
Bojanic, Nancy Laturno, 4288
Bojar,, Anthea L., 5857
Boklach Beihoffer, Denise, 6718
Bolanca, Joe, 7328
Boland, Hank, 2953
Boland, Maggie, 4033
Boland, Rick, 811, 4256
Bolander, Ben, 6869
Bolar, Gordon, 4852
Bold, Russell, 5827
Bolden Wenger, Kris, 5015
Boles, Jessica A., 8028
Boley, Jon, 5374
Bolin, H.M., 5539
Bolin, John, 8217
Bolingbroke, Christy, 86
Boliard Wilder, Priscilla, 4399
Bolleber, Christa, 7328
Bollenback, Michael, 6488
Bolling, Elana, 5338
Bollinger, Bruce, 5281
Bollinger, Charlotte, 246
Bollinger Vogt, Marie, 545
Bollwinkel-Smith, Jan, 4070
Bolognini, Michael, 1313
Bolshakov, Erin, 604
Bolstad, Iris, 1813
Bolt, Cheryl, 7893
Bolt, Cristin, 5907, 6555, 6556
Bolt, Jennifer, 3905
Bolt, Linda, 4321
Boltman, Jim, 4847
Bolton, Alison, 5039
Bolton, Bruce, 3230
Bolton, Fred C, 1166
Bolton, John, 5648
Bolton, Skip, 4162
Boltz, Lee, 1629
Boltz, Vanessa, 150
Bolz, Terry, 1827
Bolzer, Bill, 2867
Boman, Keith, 7514
Bombaci, Shirley, 4386
Bombardieri, Vanessa R., 3590
Bombe, Michelle, 7305
Bomber, Margaret, 2396
Bonacoroso, Rick, 2600
Bonamico, Joseph, 5358
Bonamico, Margaret M, 5358
Bonamico, Margaret M., 3745
Bonanno, Russell E, 3417
Bonassisa, Requel, 5005
Bond, David, 1896
Bond, Dr. Linwood, 4458

Bond, Emily, 904
Bond, Jessica, 6297
Bond, Laura, 3999
Bond, Robert, 1638
Bond, Timothy, 3627
Bond, Yari, 1410
Bonda, Brett, 670
Bondavalli, Bonnie, 6832
Bonde, Mindi, 7980
Bonder, Amy, 5191
Bondi, John C, 8220
Bondlow, Robert, 198
Bondrow, David, 7699
Bondurant, Janet, 3685, 7597
Bone, Christopher, 4354
Bonebrake, Barbara E, 6231
Bonelli, Dr. Eugene, 5610
Bonenfant, Timothy, 1314
Boneparth, John, 6277
Bonesso, William F., 5089, 5090
Bonfiglio, Robert, 4169
Bonfitto, Elaine, 5460
Bong, Sara, 5150
Bongiorno, Paula, 5441
Bonham, Jr., J. Blaine, 2312
Bonilla, Kathleen, 6106
Bonin, Sharon, 8070
Bonino, Dr. MaryAnn, 4242
Bonis, Fred, 3588
Bonnefoux, Jean-Pierre, 507
Bonnell, Diane, 1353
Bonnelli, Terry, 977
Bonner, Michael, 7640
Bonner, Peter, 1992
Bonnewell, Mia, 1658
Bonnstetter, Mark, 6725, 6726
Boo Johnston, Hattie, 715
Boody, Charles, 1271
Booher, Darle, 1682
Booher, Jennifer, 4590
Booher, Mark, 6299
Booker, Jasmine, 264
Booker, Rickey, 6095
Bookis, John, 268
Books, Karen, 7641
Boolman, Tavia, 4629
Boomer, Judy, 478
Boomgaarden, Jennifer, 1688
Boon, Nigel, 958
Boone, Andrew, 2696
Boone, Brock, 8462
Boone, Charles S, 8556
Boone, Jane, 8462
Boone, Sarah, 2786
Boone, Aaron, 7691
Booras, Christopher, 6103
Boos, Jerry, 279
Boos, Karla, 3849
Boos, Wayne, 785
Boose, Katz, 4278, 4279, 6219
Booterbaugh, Angela, 7295
Booth, Bill, 2759
Booth, David W, 6764, 6765
Booth, David W., 6766
Booth, Faye, 1027
Booth, George, 1278
Booth, Jack, 2784
Booth, Kelsey, 8610, 8613, 8614, 8615, 8616
Booth, Lisa, 8843
Booth, Melanie, 1852
Booth, Richard, 3455
Booth, Susan, 6631
Booth, Susan V, 2849
Booth, Tod, 2784
Booth, Senior, Richard A, 3186
Boothe, Power, 2716
Bootsma, Ken, 1089
Borandi, Leslie, 572
Boratko, Amy, 2699, 6427
Borbolla, III, Henry, 3970
Borchard-Young, Julie, 2234
Borchelt, Mark, 286
Borda, Deborah, 792, 4227
Borda, Debra, 6124
Bordein, Tim, 8630
Bordelon, Lynne L., 2083, 4713
Borden, Betty, 5141
Borden, Debra S., 4763

Borders, Jason, 8694
Bording, Kayla, 747
Bordner, Laura, 1080
Bordner Adams, Laura, 1785
Bordo, Guy Victor, 1095
Boreen, Jean, 2422
Boren, David L, 8039, 8040
Boren, Dr Laura, 5391
Boren, Dr. Laura, 3768
Borenstein, Eric, 1784, 2375
Borenstein, Joshua, 2697, 2700, 6419
Borer, Lennky, 5421
Borey, Sonny, 7141
Borg, Christopher, 852, 6254
Borg, Kevin, 6174
Borgelt, Bruce B, 1314
Borger, Bill, 7454
Borger, CB, 2519
Borger, Diane, 3145, 3146, 7231
Borger, Nathan, 5750
Borges, Wanda, 1962
Borgman, Sequoya, 2397
Borich, Bob, 4473
Boring, Matthew, 4945
Boris, Charry, 2707
Boris, Cherry, 2710, 2711
Boris, Greg, 3318
Borish, Cary, 576
Boriskin, Ronnie, 922
Bork, Paula, 213
Borkovitz, Mary, 5514
Borlng, Matthew, 7491
Bormann, Katherine, 1520
Bormann, Tammy, 372
Bornemann, David, 729
Bornemeier, Holly, 6698
Bornia, Manuel, 4442
Bornick, Lydia, 946
Bornstein, Eva, 7639, 7745
Borodofsky, Ted, 7106
Borowitz, Michael, 2082, 2171, 2290
Borowski, June, 2796
Borreson, Chris, 2482
Borromeo, Venustiano, 3408
Bors, Chris, 811
Bors, Christy, 811, 4256
Borsari, Jim, 3351
Borsnold, David, 1080
Borton, Terry, 2682
Borum, Meghann, 8047
Borut, Donald, 1995
Boryczewski, Julian, 2281
Borysiewicz, Malgorzata, 206, 2044, 2045
Borzoni, Clint, 2247
Bosanquet, N. Thompson, 1207
Boschini, Victor, 8385
Bosco, R. Dean, 4469
Bosco-Lauth, Angela, 1957
Bose, Sharada, 98
Bose, Willa, 5653
Bosen, Tracy, 8088
Bosewell, Mike, 5990
Boskoff, Susan, 4955
Boskovich, Erin, 885
Bossart, Alan, 6348
Bosse, Erik, 4001
Bosse, Joseph B., 4911
Bossy, Michelle, 3549
Bostany, Cecil, 4140
Bostock, Tim, 6678
Boston, Fred, 2360
Boswell, Jody, 4924
Boswell, Michelle, 6936
Boswell, William, 5464, 8139
Bosworth, George, 853
Bosworth, Teal, 127
Botek, Chris, 3627
Botich, Dan, 233
Botkin, John, 2069
Botros, Liz, 3728
Botsford, Andrea, 6295
Botsford, Linda, 4029
Botstein, Leon, 1407, 5044
Bott, Molly, 3247
Bott, Willis, 2185
Botticello, Barry, 6438
Botto, Rob, 6600
Bottomley, Kevin, 3134

Bottoms, Heather, 3896
Botts, Cindy, 5265
Botwinick, Michael, 7851
Botwright, Amy L., 5460
Botyrius, Nijole, 4852
Bouchard, Andre, 347
Bouchard, Joshua, 1601
Bouchard, Lauren, 729
Boucher, Joe, 1150
Bouck, Connie, 3410
Boud, Jan, 1691, 5567
Bouderau, Jim, 3447
Boudreau, Lisa, 3278
Boudreault, Mary, 1497
Boudy, Marsha A., 1143, 4718
Boue, Renate A, 3375
Bouffard, Audra, 6423
Boughton, Audrey, 2226, 5128
Boughton, Leslie, 288
Boughton, William, 932
Boulanger, Paul, 4666
Boulay, Frederic O, 84, 1940, 1941
Boulden, Mazella, 640
Bouldin, Matt, 2266
Boulez, Pierre, 1035, 1038
Bouman, Linsay, 8085, 8086
Bouman, Rhea, 2366
Boume, Jeffrey, 8526
Bounds, Michael, 1724
Bourdeaux, Bob, 3985
Bourdelais, Barb, 3189
Bourdette, Phil, 888
Bourg, Charles, 7137
Bourne, Ann, 4152, 5923
Bourne, Bill, 1900
Bouse, Heidi, 4629
Bousso, Jacob, 1420
Boutiette, Jeff, 3186
Bouwman, Robert, 2922
Bova, Journey, 3990
Bovan-Campbell, Patricia, 1915
Bovingdon, Ali, 7479
Bovington, Betty, 8347
Bowden, Cluadius, 2723
Bowden, David, 1078, 1097
Bowden, Dr. David, 1077
Bowen, Abby, 1956
Bowen, Ann, 1826
Bowen, Elaine, 1028
Bowen, Erin, 7300
Bowen, Gwen, 125
Bowen, Jeff, 6896
Bowen, John, 2096
Bowen, Linnell, 7185
Bowen, Lorraine, 5703
Bowen, Meredith, 2138
Bowen, Polly, 2296, 5393
Bowen, Sylvia, 896
Bower, Betty, 1755
Bower, Cindy, 3660
Bower, Eric, 1532
Bower, Eric W, 5314
Bower, Eric W., 7961
Bower, Jamie, 7462
Bower, Marilyn, 4608
Bowermeister, Kenneth, 1000
Bowers, Cindy, 6245, 6248
Bowers, Karen, 2901, 6186
Bowers, Linda, 221
Bowers, Lucy, 2183
Bowers, Martha, 369
Bowers, Richard, 1855
Bowersock, Karin, 3455
Bowes, Paulette, 4810
Boweyer, Ann Marie, 3812
Bowie, Jennifer, 7944
Bowker, Scott, 2865
Bowlby, Katy, 531
Bowlen, Linda, 7424
Bowlen, Pat, 6351, 6362
Bowler, Gail, 4621
Bowles, Dane, 3060
Bowles, John, 62
Bowles, Paul, 8561
Bowles, William, 1928
Bowley, Tanya, 6567
Bowlin, Ron, 7494
Bowlin, TJ, 5026

1143

Executive Name Index

Bowling, Danny, 4693, 4694
Bowling, Gayle, 4096
Bowling, JC, 2803
Bowling, Mark, 7128
Bowling, Scott, 3048
Bowling, Nick, 2958
Bowman, Amy, 6580
Bowman, Denvy A, 5328
Bowman, Dr Al, 6806
Bowman, Jamie, 1979
Bowman, Joan C, 471
Bowman, Judith, 2515
Bowman, Julian, 6572
Bowman, Liz, 7427
Bowman, Lory, 3302
Bowman, Mark, 4038, 4039
Bowman, Natalie, 6921, 6922, 6923, 6924, 6925
Bowman, Pattie, 2297
Bowman, Tad, 6366
Bowns, Kate, 2419
Bowron, Jr., William A., 707
Bowyer, Crystal, 2039
Box, Charles, 6828
Box, Michael, 5675
Boxhil, Dr. Carlton, 5155
Boxley, Johnna, 8610, 8613, 8614
Boy, Christian, 2802
Boyce, Sandra, 7882
Boyd, Byron, 4520
Boyd, Carol, 1543
Boyd, Chad, 2334, 8302
Boyd, Charles/Chief, 3767
Boyd, Colin, 5983
Boyd, Dorian, 2835
Boyd, Dr. Brad, 33
Boyd, Gregory, 3982, 8397, 8398, 8399, 8400
Boyd, Heidi, 4126
Boyd, James, 1141
Boyd, Julianne, 3169
Boyd, Karen, 1960
Boyd, Linda, 1267
Boyd, Marion, 6278
Boyd, Menna, 8560
Boyd, Randy, 3789
Boyd, Sandra, 5558
Boyd, Sondra, 1518
Boyd, Thomas, 638
Boyd, Willhomina, 8560
Boyer, Bob, 5560
Boyer, Brooks, 6759
Boyer, John K., 7500
Boyer, M Christopher, 6866
Boyer, Maria, 2299
Boyer, Michael, 2788
Boyer, Robert, 2357
Boyer, Scott, 668
Boyer, Yvette, 1548
Boyer Cochran, Nicole, 4078
Boyko, Lisa, 523
Boylan, Llyena, 1636
Boylan, Marie, 30
Boylan, Roberta, 1298
Boyle, Briget, 1894
Boyle, Danny, 1210, 1211
Boyle, David, 1366
Boyle, Dennis, 2178
Boyle, Rick, 2599
Boyle, Una, 5805
Boyler, Mike, 4646
Boynton, James, 6643
Boynton, Katy, 2919
Boyse, Carol, 5377
Boyter, Mary, 1745
Bozark, Mr. Kim, 6771, 6772
Bozarth, Dr. Mimi, 4473
Bozeman, Gene, 3090
Bozic, Joe, 3236
Bozzi, Jim, 6442
Bozzuto, Barbara, 1155
Bracci, Michael J., 4493
Bracci, Michael J., 6602
Brace, Nancy, 4356
Bracero, Walter, 3624
Bracewell, Ruth, 6652
Brach, Ryan, 8097
Bracilano, Peter, 680
Bracken, Michael, 1756
Brackett, Norm, 3105

Brackett, Stephanie, 6948, 6951
Brackett, Ted, 3542
Bracy, Alecia, 7867
Bradac, Thomas F, 2537
Bradburd, Douglas, 3183
Bradburn, Carrie, 4494
BRADBURY, DOUGLAS, 2821
Bradbury, Jeff, 2218
Bradbury, Richard, 3120
Bradbury, Susan M, 3000
Bradbury III, William, 1622
Braddock, Beverly J., 2188
Braddock, Steven, 3188
Braden, Bruce, 91
Braden, Susan, 4055
Bradenburg, Don, 3870
Bradfield MM, David, 771
Bradford, Ann, 2439
Bradford, Barlow, 2368
Bradford, Chris M., 109
Bradford, Leslie, 3970
Bradford Bohl, John, 1995
Bradford-Bell, Shelley, 6252
Bradham, Sharon, 1057
Bradley, Alisa, 8284
Bradley, Bob, 7089
Bradley, Carol, 3770
Bradley, Cynthia, 102
Bradley, Daniel, 6943, 6945
Bradley, David, 716
Bradley, Douglas, 843
Bradley, Gary, 3802
Bradley, Jessica, 3859
Bradley, Joe, 3002
Bradley, Jospeh, 7197
Bradley, Karen, 445
Bradley, Nancy, 3331
Bradley, Orren, 5834
Bradley, Patrick, 102, 339
Bradley, Pete, 929
Bradley, Robert, 3331
Bradley, Sean, 4242
Bradley, Thomas, 2716
Bradshaw, Dr. Kevin, 8612
Bradshaw, Frank, 7126
Bradshaw, Rob, 3466
Bradshaw, Stephanie, 2468, 6109
Bradshaw, Tracey, 6332
Bradwell, Carol, 143, 144
Brady, Dorothy, 2679
Brady, Ed, 1517
Brady, Glenn, 4159
Brady, Joseph, 2939
Brady, Kim, 1136
Brady, Peter, 1393
Brady, Susan J., 5818
Brady Donohue, Therese, 269
Bragg, Cheryl H, 5885
Bragg, Colin, 1008
Bragg, Dr Sadie, 7790
Bragg, Jane, 248
Bragg, Robert, 1562
Brailean, Karen, 4233
Braim, Victoria, 3149
Brainard, Jayne, 3940
Brainered, Ashley, 7262
Brainin, Risa, 2612
Braithwaite, Tony, 3793
Brambila, Noelle, 4071
Bramble, Aimee, 6152
Brammer, Lisa, 8000
Branagan, Alexis, 339
Branam, Travis, 1951
Brancato, Joe, 3623
Branch, Cynthia, 1678
Branch, John Watusi, 3449
Branch, Sekou, 3449
Brand, Carole, 1151, 2090
Brand, Claire, 308
Brand, Jamie, 8584
Brand, Jonathan, 7013, 7014
Brand, Mike, 7294
Brand, Morrie, 1623
Brand, Morris A, 1623
Brand, Stan, 8297
Brandeberry, Donald, 1751
Brandenberg, Kent, 814
Brander, Beau, 2275

Brandesky, Emily, 1749
Brandolino, Dr Tony, 1285
Brandon, Belinda B., 2260
Brandon, Carl, 2173
Brandon, Dave, 6767, 6768
Brandon, Kimmy, 2650
Brandon, Mark, 3688
Brandon, Russ, 7804
Brandow, Paul W, 7792
Brandt, Daniel, 917
Brandt, Joyce, 5019
Brandt, Kate, 3160
Brandt, Kelton, 1787
Brandt, Kirsten, 2602
Brandt, Linda, 7358
Brandt, Loraine, 1763
Brandt, Nicole, 2065
Brandt, Sarah, 3302
Brandt, Sue, 6182
Brandt, William A., 2940
Brandt James, Kirsten, 3950
Brandwein, Bill, 1162, 7203
Brann, Betty L, 7162
Brannen, Carrie, 1243
Branner, Wade, 8529
Brannigan, Catherine, 2593
Brannon, Lance, 166
Branson, Cynthia, 2389
Branstetter, James, 2373
Brant, Bill, 4715
Brant, Jane, 6512
Brantley, Royal, 8340
Branum, Donica, 5559
Brase, Ruby, 6767, 6768
Brashear, Craig, 476
Brashear, Craig D., 476
Brashear, David, 5483
Brashear, William R, 4830
Brasher, Earlene, 2024
Brasher, Jennifer, 2525
Brasier, Robert, 6203
Braso, Ken, 306
Brass, Lietza, 3929
Brassfield, Rachel, 5726
Brastow, Carin, 1980
Braswell, Marcie, 2401
Bratcher, David, 3067
Bratcher, Freddick, 167
BRATER, CRAIG, 6877
Braton, Dave, 1101
Bratt, Cristin, 5752
Brattain Hansen, Marla, 195
Bratton, Drew, 6855, 6857, 6858, 6859
Bratton, Evangeline, 5879
Bratton, Jim, 3988
Bratton, Kevin, 8266
Brauchli, Bernard, 4785
Brauer, David, 7082
Brault, Gregory, 1813
Braum, Jeff D, 900, 901
Braun, Claire, 2725
Braun, David, 2567
Braun, Jerry, 1606
Braun, Luise, 4527
Braun, Mark, 2154
Braun, PhD, Joseph, 805
Braunreuther, James, 1678
Bravman, John C., 8139
Bravo, Leonardo, 4243
Bravo-Gleicher, Luz, 3859
Bravos, Meta, 1848
Brawley, Dan, 8204
Braxton, Gwen, 3829
Braxton, Shirley, 3047
Bray, Honore, 315
Bray, Jim, 1877
Bray, John A., 6909, 6910, 6911
Bray, Laura, 3938
Bray, MaryAnn Kelly, 1014
Bray, Miguel, 2889
Bray, Steve, 8044
Bray Ricks, Christy, 1958
Braymer, John W., 1785
Brayon, Ann, 8226
Braz, Evandro, 4026
Braza, James E., 4124
Brazakis, Debora, 1228
Braziel, Connie, 3266, 3267

Brazier, Bob, 5907, 5909, 5911
Brazil, Louanne, 6127
Brazil, Louanne Champag, 6157
Breaux, Celeste, 7122
Breaux, Chip, 5502
Breaux, Matt, 8678
Brechwald, Marc, 6596
Breck Calhoun, Kate, 6005, 6006, 6007, 6008
Breckenridge, John C., 3990
Breckner, Scott, 5029
Bredehoeft, Kyle, 6898
Breden, Mary, 4239
Breder, Caroline, 2794
Breder-Albright, Stefanie, 1589
Breed, Ellen, 3352
Breed, Heather, 6803, 6804
Breed, John, 695
Breen, Riza, 3332
Breese, Kenneth, 4846
Breese, Kevin, 4117
Brehalter, Gregg, 7981
Breheny, Lisa, 3106
Breig, Jim, 6571
Breikjern, Eric, 8398, 8399, 8400
Breit, Jonathan, 2230
Breitner, Michael J., 5862
Breitzig, Glenn, 2010
Brekke, Gail, 6419
Breland, A. Barron, 2170
Bremer, Christopher, 3218, 3219
Bremer, Paulette, 3189
Brennan, Adam, 5466
Brennan, Ann, 6431
Brennan, Christopher P., 6592, 6593
Brennan, Doug, 6303
Brennan, Janet, 767
Brennan, John, 5177
Brennan, Megan, 6485
Brennan, Michael F., 7176, 7177, 7178
Brennan, Suzanne, 6430
Brennan, Thomas, 2866
Brennan, Tom, 8157
Brenneman, James E., 6878
Brenner, Bonnie, 2180
Brenner, Janis, 433
Brenner Brown, Debora, 581
Brennfoerder, Roxann, 1305
Brenninkmeijer, Titus, 803
Brenstuhl, Nancy, 538
Brent, Bill, 4715
Bresciani, L, 5281
Bresil, Witnie, 2766
Breske, Samantha, 2905
Breskin, Efrem, 5188
Breslau, Bela, 1196
Breslau, Howard L, 3137
Breslin, Marc, 4352
Breslow, Stephanie R., 7739
Breslow, Stephine R., 7738
Bresnahan, Carol.M, 6605, 6606
Bresnahan, Rich, 5799
Bresner, Carol, 3543
Bressler, Hallie, 3825, 3837
Brestoff, Richard, 2478
Bretall, Kristine, 6698
Brett, Bobby, 8609
Brett, Rita, 2022
Bretton, Leonard, 4410
Breuder, Robert L, 6789, 6790, 6791
Breuer, Lee, 3516
Breuer, Sue, 4186
Breuninger, Jarrett, 8244
Brew, Marc, 51
Brewe, Bret, 3770
Brewe, Crystal, 8155
Brewe, Merry, 3926
Brewer, Charles, 3878
Brewer, Denise, 4934
Brewer, Diana, 714
Brewer, John W., 4505
Brewer, Kenny, 6051
Brewer, Sheila, 3679
Brewer, Steven, 8624
Brewer, Teresa, 3456
Brewster, Cornelia, 1468, 1469
Brewster, David, 8581
Brewster, Edward, 8567
Brezer, Lawrence, 443

Executive Name Index

Brezer, Laz, 443
Brezik, Steve, 1726
Bria, Tom, 847, 4299
Brian Alley, David, 3904
Brice, Daniel J., 1828
Brick, Jan Ramsey, 6486
Brickell, Tara, 4366
Bricker, J. Denton, 8360
Brickler, Emily, 7438
Brickson, Dick, 2157
Brictson, Hanna, 211
Bridenstine, Art, 4082
Bridge, Rob, 5209
Bridgeforth, Pamela, 7548
Bridgeland, Steven, 3721
Bridger, Josh, 4790
Bridger, Penny, 8336
Bridges, George, 2062, 2063, 6847
Bridges, Mike, 7462
Bridges, Scott A, 8757
Bridges, Theresa, 1144
Bridich, Jeff, 5999
Brieanna, Thao, 6921, 6922, 6923, 6924, 6925
Briell, Scott, 6648, 6649
Brien, Kyle O, 5418
Brienza, Gleneen, 122
Brienza, Jill, 485
Brienzi, Jessi, 8222
Brierre, Guy P., 246
Brigben, Tracy, 3841
Briggs, Charlin, 5305
Briggs, David, 7893
Briggs, Donna, 3780, 5414, 8083
Briggs, Dr. Robert, 1767
Briggs, Joan, 4264
Briggs, Julie, 2507
Briggs, Kriston, 4977
Briggs, Lisa, 1909
Briggs, Liz, 1866
Briggs, Mary M, 1682
Briggs, Norma, 698
Briggs, Patricia, 2539
Briggs Roberts, Jeremy, 1796
Brigham, Elladean, 2098
Brigham, Mandy, 1885
Bright, Brad, 6899
Bright, Elizabeth, 506
Bright, Ron, 2381
Brightman, Thomas W., 4962
Briley, Brantley, 5272
Briley Strand, Gwendolyn, 3130
Brill, Dr. Byron, 4042
Brill, Linda, 1560
Brillhart, Jeffrey, 2314
Brim, Martha, 5537
Brimhall, Jeremy, 1749
Brincefield, John, 3678
Brinda, Connie, 3848
Brinda, Wayne, 3848
Brindisi, Michael, 3223
Brindley, Christey, 1135
Briner, Donna, 4764
Bring, Murray, 2011
Bringola, Tom, 3346
Brink, Bro. Edward, 6676
Brink, Todd, 3886, 3888
Brinker, Thomas H, 525
Brinkley, Michele, 4001
Brinkley, Vickie, 5629
Brinkley III, Arthur S., 1785
Briody, John, 3820
Briody, Katheleen, 3820
Briones, Shelia, 3988
Briscar, Don, 7912
Briscoe, Doris, 7413
Briscoe, Rodney, 2182
Brisk, Barry, 830
Briskin, Michael, 5188
Brisky, Jerre, 4475, 6580
Bristol, Brynn, 3972
Bristol, Denise, 3074
Bristow, Alice, 2802
Bristrow, Alexandra, 6182
Brito, Shelly, 3890
Britt, Brian, 1581
Britting, Darrin T., 1647
Britton, Anton J., 4563
Britton, Barbara, 3661

Britton, Charlotte, 8886
Britton, Ernest, 6894
Britton, Harold, 1365
Britton, Julie, 6596
Britton, Larua, 934
Britton, Mary Lou, 7264, 7569
Britton, Susan, 769
Britton, Terry, 8036
Brladhust, Susan, 8169
Broad, Lynn, 5901, 5902, 5903, 5904
Broad White, Joanna, 4147
Broadhead, Paul, 4117
Broadhurst, Jamie, 1683
Broadwater, Jane, 3870
Brock, Ann, 1286
Brock, Brad, 2589
Brock, Carol, 4672
Brock, Jay D, 1998
Brock, Kathy, 7440, 7442
Brock, Lee, 3470
Brock, McKenzie, 8077
Brock, Patricia, 1821
Brock, Robert, 3063
Brockette, Jr., Marion L., 3959
Brockley, Debbie, 7139
Brockman, Beate, 5479
Brockman, Bruce, 2431
Brockman, Charles, 2888
Brockpahler, Jennifer, 5833
Brockway, Adrienne, 3540
Brockway, Amie, 3454, 3540
Brockway, Patsy, 5609, 5611
Broderick, Jasmine, 1874
Broderick, John R, 666
Broderick, Kate, 3442
Brodfuehrer, Gordon, 6246
Brodsky, Gisela, 4435
Brodsky, Giselle, 964
Brodsky, Jack, 964, 4435
Brodsky, Julian A., 1645
Brody, Jean, 1653
Brody, Jeffrey, 2119, 2124
Brody, Kim, 4356
Broecker, Leslie, 3071
Broege, Marilyn, 3384
Brogan, Kate, 229
Brogan, Patrick, 5429
Brogden, Stephen R., 6314
Brohan, Paul, 4759, 7203
Broido, Irving, 1911
Broido, Karen, 1911
Brokamp, Nolan, 3014
Brokaw, Colin, 8413
Brokaw, Norman, 8727, 8862, 8900
Brokenshire, Alyson, 142
Brokke, Vickie, 3049
Bromacki, GP, 7659
Broman, John, 4513
Brombacher, Kathy, 6319
Bromley, Lynn, 4071
Brondyke, Amy, 5005
Bronnenberg, Joshua, 8301
Bronner, Gwethalyn, 4579
Bronson, Laurel, 1087
Bronstein, Fred, 2343, 5610
Brook, Andrea, 4248
Brook, Hal, 3545
Brooke, Karen, 1104, 1105
Brooke, Mary, 730
Brookey, Lauren, 8059
Brookhart, Ph.D., Susan, 1299
Brookman, Geordie, 3933
Brookman, Rob, 3933
Brooks, Alfred, 2655
Brooks, Bonnie, 202, 6736
Brooks, Christopher, 4889
Brooks, David, 865
Brooks, Debra, 3029
Brooks, Delina P., 96
Brooks, Diana, 551
Brooks, Dr. Randy, 6767, 6768
Brooks, Faith, 6559
Brooks, Gail E., 6317
Brooks, Geoffrey, 4290, 6136
Brooks, Glen O, 3966
Brooks, Jack, 6132
Brooks, Kermitt, 3464
Brooks, Linda, 2902

Brooks, Marae, 5597
Brooks, Marianne, 172
Brooks, Melody, 3533
Brooks, Mike, 3071, 3088
Brooks, Ray, 8067, 8069
Brooks, Raymond, 7404
Brooks, Roger, 3266, 3267
Brooks, Rosetta, 148
Brooks, Russell, 2405
Brooks, Ruth, 5819
Brooks, Susan, 4138
Brooks, Sylvester, 4206, 5425
Brooks, Tina, 6085
Brooks, Tyrone, 172
Brooks Hopkins, Karen, 5053
Brooks, Jr., John, 591
Brooks, Jr., William M., 1491, 5242
Brooks-Bruzzese, James, 968
Broschart, Elizabeth E, 1561
Broschart, Tania, 1389
Brose, Alexander, 1944, 6328
Brose, Dr. .William P., 1774
Brose, Mike, 4159
Brosemer, Rebecca, 4525
Brosie, Vanessa, 8027
Brosier, Jerry a M, 4371
Brosius, Peter C, 3237
Brosius, Peter C., 4121
Brosnan, Deane, 3593
Brosnan, Tim, 6055, 8178
Brosowsky, Bert, 2401
Bross, Bridget, 3373
Bross, Matt, 317
Brosvik, Steven, 1731
Broth, Ray, 4685
Brothers, Leslie, 8023, 8024
Brothers Smith, Ann, 5817
Brotherton, Jon, 2265
Broth, Ray, 4447
Brotman, Joel, 1533
Brotons, Salvador, 1811
Brott, Boris, 885
Brougher, W. Dale, 4470
Broughton, Charles, 3316
Broughton, Chuck, 6340
Broun, Kenneth, 3643
Broussard, Julia, 3927
Broussard, Lisa, 244
Broussard, Mike, 7124
Broussard, Nic, 7677
Brouwer, Kimberly, 33
Browand, John, 1686
Browder, Kory, 225
Brower, Eric, 2306, 5200
Brower, Robert, 4289
Brown, Abena J., 208
Brown, Abena Joan, 2929
Brown, Abena Joan P, 2929
Brown, Alan, 1787
Brown, Alfreda, 7995
Brown, Amy, 7991
Brown, Andrea, 5129
Brown, Andrew, 6005, 6006, 6007, 6008
Brown, Angela, 5198
Brown, Angela M., 578
Brown, Anjeanette, 8067, 8069
Brown, Anne Marie C, 1124
Brown, Beatrice H., 4276
Brown, Becky, 439, 1787, 5635
Brown, Bob, 6247
Brown, Bobbie, 1836, 5370
Brown, Byron, 7653
Brown, Carlyle, 3252
Brown, Carmela, 1473
Brown, Carol, 1526, 3804
Brown, Carolina, 102
Brown, Carolyn, 750
Brown, Carrie, 489
Brown, Cassidy, 6089
Brown, Catherine, 2445
Brown, Charles, 1069
Brown, Chris, 7653
Brown, Christal, 354
Brown, Cindy, 7095
Brown, Corey, 6386
Brown, Craig, 531, 7250
Brown, Craig M., 5317
Brown, Daisy, 3111

Brown, Darlene, 6472
Brown, Dave, 5953
Brown, David, 682, 1984, 2199
Brown, David L., 1360
Brown, Deborah, 712, 1717
Brown, Dennis, 2436
Brown, Derk, 2851
Brown, Dr. Bruce, 5088
Brown, Dr. Janice M., 1244
Brown, Duncan, 7245
Brown, Dusty, 4504
Brown, Elizabeth, 1318, 1557
Brown, Elliot, 3540
Brown, Eric J, 7956
Brown, Erin, 3284
Brown, F Reed, 3296
Brown, Frances, 661
Brown, Gary, 5355
Brown, Genevieve, 2233
Brown, George H, 6815, 6816
Brown, Giles, 5614
Brown, Glenda, 633
Brown, Greg, 5643
Brown, Gregory M., 6494, 6495
Brown, Heather, 2464
Brown, Hope, 8463
Brown, Howie, 3793
Brown, Jack, 2123
Brown, Janet, 310, 4913
Brown, Janice M., 4854
Brown, Jason, 7462, 8141
Brown, Jeanette, 3688
Brown, Jeff, 2048, 3225, 6034, 6146
Brown, Jerry, 2764
Brown, Jerry Lee, 2043
Brown, Jim, 5335, 5878, 7992, 8043
Brown, Joel, 5201
Brown, John, 6589
Brown, Julia, 3252
Brown, Julie, 4368
Brown, Kara, 3070
Brown, Karen, 308, 3447, 4777, 5756, 8047
Brown, Katherine E., 466
Brown, Kathy, 2376
Brown, Kellie D., 1692
Brown, Kelly, 605
Brown, Kenneth, 5254
Brown, Kim, 4541
Brown, Kimberly, 6580
Brown, Kyler, 5510
Brown, Larry, 3914
Brown, Laura E., 5688
Brown, Lauren, 854
Brown, Leanna, 3370
Brown, Leslie, 1079
Brown, Ila, 2008
Brown, Lila, 5197
Brown, Lindie K, 5885
Brown, Marc L., 5497
Brown, Marcus, 1986
Brown, Marilyn K, 7963, 7964, 7965, 7966
Brown, Melissa, 3621, 6027
Brown, Meredith, 1245
Brown, Michael G, 2824, 6585
Brown, Michele, 2370
Brown, Mike, 7956
Brown, Morley, 768
Brown, Nanci, 264
Brown, Nicci, 5276
Brown, Owen, 874
Brown, Paige, 47
Brown, Pamela, 4090, 4092
Brown, Paul, 6174, 7956
Brown, Paula, 4525
Brown, Paulette, 4810
Brown, Peggy, 7293
Brown, Pete, 7956
Brown, Philip, 2125
Brown, Ralph, 1199
Brown, Randy, 6876
Brown, Ray, 499
Brown, Richard, 1669, 1907, 5062
Brown, Ricklin, 695
Brown, Robbie, 1737
Brown, Robert, 6048
Brown, Roberta, 3292
Brown, Robin, 5007
Brown, Roger H, 7219

1145

Executive Name Index

Brown, Ronald, 7207
Brown, Ronnie, 4053
Brown, Rory, 6304
Brown, Ryan, 4430
Brown, Sabrina, 5721
Brown, Sandra, 122
Brown, Sarah, 4709
Brown, Sashi, 7960
Brown, Sean, 8297
Brown, Sharon, 4942
Brown, Shaunna, 252
Brown, Shawn, 6977
Brown, Shelley, 3801, 8121
Brown, Stacey, 802
Brown, Stacy A, 6866
Brown, Stella, 1897
Brown, Stephen, 6586
Brown, Stephen D., 4135
Brown, Stephen L., 4493, 6602
Brown, Steven, 7948
Brown, Susan, 2691
Brown, Susan E, 1916
Brown, Susan M., 3460
Brown, Tamara, 3830
Brown, Taylor, 2708
Brown, Terry, 4257
Brown, Thomas, 6300
Brown, Thomas A, 6300
Brown, Thomas L., 6720, 6721
Brown, Tim, 4212
Brown, Tom, 3207
Brown, Tony, 3245
Brown, Tricia, 489
Brown, Trisha, 489
Brown, Vanessa, 633
Brown Ceres, Brittany, 6262
Brown Elliot, Jennifer, 6328
Brown Shepherd, Lauren, 5558
Brown Sinclair, Paula, 1028
Brown-Thompson, Debbie, 6771, 6772
Browne, Doug, 5575
Browne, Pete, 3287
Brownell, Tom, 1778
Brownfield, Eleanor, 184
Brownfiled, Sara, 2261
Browning, April, 2940, 4557
Browning, Barbara, 3059
Browning, Douglas D., 4763
Browning, Helene, 491
Browning, Robert H, 491
Browning, Tami, 4065
Brownlee-Sager, Elizabeth, 580
Brownson, Gwen, 3466
Brownstein, Barry S., 3833
Brownstein, Esquire, Andrew R., 5483
Brown, James, 6706
Brown, Tanisha, 4455
Broyles, Adrienne, 2164
Broyles, Beverly, 1064
Broyles, Chuck, 7056, 7058
Brozek, Nancy, 3203
Brubacher, Paul W., 6217
Brubakar, Sue, 222
Brubaker, LeAnn, 6371
Brubaker, Lynn, 1145
Brubaker, Thomas, 8134, 8135
Bruce, Angie, 223, 311
Bruce, Christopher, 638
Bruce, Greg, 5535
Bruce, Stephen, 1969
Bruce Jr, James W, 2294
Bruch Bucki, Deborah, 1474
Bruckner, Stephen, 2169
Bruder Munafo, Mj, 3177
Brue, Sonja, 1838
Brueckner, Deedee, 152
Brueckner, Richard F., 1437
Bruek, Sonja, 1841
Bruell, David, 1791
Bruemmer, Bob, 4976
Bruening, Richard, 1281
Bruening, Richard P., 2160
Bruer, Sheila, 7914
Bruffy, Charles, 1854, 2158, 2161
Bruggeman, Michael, 4362
Bruice, Ann, 2612
Bruker, Gordon, 2026
Brule, Steve, 549, 550

Brumet, Travis, 8098
Brumfield, DJ, 5164
Brumit, Scott, 2119
Brummel, Sara, 7466
Brummett, Bob, 4386
Brummett, Tom, 6343
Brundage, Dr Robert, 8011
Brundage, CBC, Dick, 1940, 1941
Brunel, David, 4356
Brunelle, Philip, 2147, 4873
Bruneman, Cindy, 71
Bruner, Sara, 5320
Brunet, Robert, 7149
Bruning, Linda, 3238
Brunk, Jennifer, 4851
Brunner, David, 985
Brunner, Karen, 3921
Brunner, Paul, 6855, 6857, 6858, 6859, 6920
Brunner, Rhea, 6230
Bruno, Carol, 4277
Bruno, Natalie, 291
Bruno, Nick J., 7135
Bruno, Pam, 4156
Bruno, Theresa H., 5887
Bruns, Dr. Brenda, 2387
Brunschmid, Robert, 3430
Brunson, Micheal, 2328
Brunswick, Tim, 8297
Brunt, Raymond, 4999
Brunton, Barb, 3774
Brush, Michael, 1251
Bruss, Ph.D., Dan R., 4869
Bruton, Ashley, 6438
Brutsche, Juliana, 735
Bruza, Daniel, 2083, 4713
Bruzina, Mikelle, 243
Bryan, Carol, 6434, 6435
Bryan, Dave, 8153
Bryan, David, 3994
Bryan, Diane, 7183
Bryan, Joan, 4058
Bryan, John, 6338
Bryan, Martin, 4025, 4968
Bryan, Miranda, 1263
Bryan, Nancy, 3994
Bryan, Paul, 1649
Bryan, Rich, 2060
Bryan, Richard B., 1694
Bryan, Sarah, 1403
Bryan, Steve, 7998
Bryan, Wayne, 3051
Bryan, Jr., Joseph M., 2200
Bryan-Ployer, Dori, 3152
Bryant, Anne, 1087
Bryant, David, 8032
Bryant, Dr. William, 1498
Bryant, Dwight E, 7891
Bryant, Lindsay, 6530
Bryant, Martha, 1750
Bryant, Paul A, 5731
Bryant, Rick, 5507
Bryant, Robert, 1487
Bryant, Tom, 4679
Bryant Johnson, Michelle, 4512
Bryant, Jr., Robert W., 5266
Bryce, Alan, 4069
Bryce, Mark, 5991, 5992
Bryce, J.D., Mark, 738
Brydon, Thomas, 507
Brye, Peter, 1661
Brymer, Christopher, 1419
Bubalo, Julie M, 7466
Bubesi, Aimira, 382
Bubniak, Laureen, 4791
Buccino, Cheri, 3978
Buch, Bart, 3242
Buch, Rene, 1043, 3556
Buch, Samantha, 1819
Buchacker, Todd, 3034
Buchalter, Gregory, 1848, 1989
Buchanan, Barbara, 4540
Buchanan, Bill, 190, 4152
Buchanan, Carol, 6584
Buchanan, Joceyln, 190
Buchanan, Paul, 5909, 6555, 6556
Buchanan, Scott, 4342
Buchanan, Tom, 8720
Bucheit, Karen Niemic, 5434

Buches, Joseph J, 2312
Buchholtz, Matthew, 2504
Buchholz, Dr. Horst, 4920
Buchholz, Ted, 740
Buchmann, Molly, 244
Buchwalter, Charles, 4939
Buck, Dawn, 3276
Buck, Evan, 2391
Buck, Joann, 5302
Buck, Robin, 2478
Buck, Rueben, 3915
Buck, Shauna, 59
Buck, William, 8527, 8528
Buck, Ph. D., Judysharon, 4606
Buck-Ahrens, Sharon, 1167
Buckalew, Laura, 8626
Bucker, Robert, 5420
Buckholz, Lee, 3004
Buckingham, Tim, 1770
Buckles, Monique, 1171, 1172
Buckles, Randy, 5559
Buckley, Brent M, 5314
Buckley, Brent M., 7961
Buckley, Brian, 4321
Buckley, Jackie, 3278
Buckley, Leticia Rhi, 6157
Buckley, Lewis J, 929
Buckley, Mary, 2740
Buckley, Natalie, 4102
Buckley, Richard, 2336, 2339
Buckley, Sue, 4682
Buckley, William F., 1571
Buckley-Ball, Megan, 3200
Buckman, Matthew, 1890
Buckner, Alex, 140
Buckner, Bill, 4756
Buckner, Nathan, 7489
Buckner, Thomas, 1373
Buczek, Andrzej, 370
Budd, Anna, 6320
Budd, Jeff, 4163
Buddeke, Kate, 2906
Buddendorf, Bill, 2305
Buddenhagen, Jennifer, 6678
Budding, Carrie, 8488
Budig Jr, Otto M, 515
Budish, Dustin, 1315
Budnick, Shannon B., 2079
Buechmann, Sara, 1261
Buehler, Dennis, 703
Buehler, Ken, 7345
Buehler, Kim, 1570
Buehner, Stacy, 8241
Buery, Jr., Richard R., 2224
Buettner, Alfred P, 903
Bufalino, Brenda, 387
Buff, Gary, 2197
Buffett, Susie, 3334
Buffington, Monica, 1634
Buffington, Robert E, 2673
Buffman, Zev, 7104
Buffum, Brad, 3327
Buffum, James, 1324, 1345
Buford, Shannon, 7414
Bufter, David F., 4763
Bugg, Tom, 3906, 8273
Bugg, Tom, 8269
Bugher, David, 539
Bugli, David C., 1311
Bugli, Elinor, 1311
Buglisi, Jacqulyn, 400
Buhl, Bill, 4066
Buhl, Patti, 3768
Buhl, Patti D, 3768, 5391
Buhr, William, 2054
Buhrman, Jeff, 1986
Buhrman, Esq., John, 1453
Buikstra, Dr. Jane, 6459
Buitrago, Kerrie, 7849
Bujeaud, Mark, 4075
Bujnoski, Joanne, 3812
Bukovac, Dan, 4903
Bukowski, Tracy, 3852
Bukstein, Roy, 800
Bulgari, Anna, 2251
Bulkley, Hannah, 557
Bull, Christoph, 4240
Bull, Dr. Christoph, 802

Bull, Jennifer, 5161
Bullard, Clyde, 5073
Bullard, Ryan, 876
Bullard, Steve, 7462
Bullard, Terry, 287
Bullard, Therese, 287
Bullin, Christine, 1912
Bullion, Jim, 1002
Bullitt, Julian, 1173
Bullitt, William C, 5382
Bullock, Beth, 6729
Bullock, Brad, 1743
Bullock, Dr Emily, 1666
Bullock, Jared, 7853
Bullock, Steve, 1864
Bullock, William, 6640
Bulos, Liza, 3421
Bultman, James E, 1241
Bumby, Brian D, 5123
Bumby, Brian D., 5172
Bump, Charles, 2373
Bumstedd, John, 1213
Bunano, Diane, 7579
Bunce, Linda, 1773
Bundy, Alfred, 3379
Bundy, James, 2699, 2700, 6427
Bunker, B, 8002
Bunker, Gail, 5696
Bunker, Paul R, 1519
Bunn, Andrew, 1020
Bunn, Brian, 1100
Bunn, Jenny, 3636
Bunnell, Colin, 1367
Buonasera, Russell, 8407
Buoy, Jean, 1
Buoy, Larry, 2705
Burach, Marcy, 7599
Buratto, Alan, 2348
Buratto, Sue, 8382
Burawa, Christopher, 8257
Burbach, Mason, 7502
Burbach, Sarah, 6652
Burch, Barbara, 1406
Burch Gordon, Sarah, 4088
Burch Sr., B. Angeloe, 508
Burchfield, Janelle, 4046
Burchfield, Patricia, 1705
Burchinal, Kenneth H, 4669
Burchmore, John, 4376
Burciaga, Oscar, 65
Burck, Christina, 2513
Burd, Nancy, 3827
Burden, Zach, 4909
Burdett, Patricia, 2756
Burdette, Susan, 1164
Burdick, Brad, 4062, 4063, 8572
Burdick, Cathie, 5210
Burdick, Mickey, 6345
Burdick, Shelby, 5965
Burfeind, Kristine, 8107
Burford, Robin, 1615, 5424
Burgeson, Marty, 6815, 6816
Burgess, Amy, 4102
Burgess, Barry, 1818
Burgess, Dana Tai Soon, 142, 2740
Burgess, Hunter, 7431
Burgess, Kevin, 6522, 8215
Burgett, Vanessa, 4601, 6843, 6844, 6845
Burggren, Dr. Warren, 8369
Burghart, Rita, 1113
Burgin, Janis, 4901
Burgon, Kathy, 1284
Burgoyne, Andrea, 2101
Burgreen, Andrew, 3153
Burgus, Shelby, 3034
Burian, Lawrence, 6192, 6753
Burich, Tiffany, 4183
Burish, Thomas G., 6927, 6931, 6932, 6933, 6934, 6935
Burk, Mark, 8500
Burk, Sue, 4629
Burk Vickery, Diana, 126
Burke, Adam, 3648
Burke, Billy, 6656
Burke, Brendan, 3438
Burke, Charles, 7283
Burke, Dr Leon, 1029
Burke, Greg, 3193, 7138

Executive Name Index

Burke, Irene, 1502
Burke, Jason, 2014
Burke, John J, 3394
Burke, John J., 7560
Burke, Justin, 297
Burke, Ken, 2535
Burke, Kevin, 6424
Burke, Lori, 6831
Burke, Lorna, 4275
Burke, Maureen, 2452
Burke, Morgan, 6950, 6952
Burke, Richard, 1480
Burke, Robert, 5038
Burke, Sara, 1924
Burke, Spencer B., 2163
Burke, Tom, 679
Burke III, Leon, 1053
Burkett, Andrew, 3390, 7592
Burkett, Genie, 1499
Burkette, D. Wayne, 5278
Burkhardt, John, 1601
Burkharht, Allison, 2992
Burkhart, Andrea, 1812
Burkhart, Catherine, 3436
Burkhart, Laura, 246
Burkhart Reddick, Sherri, 717
Burkle, Jess, 3545
Burkot, Kay, 3850
Burkot, Louis, 2173
Burks, David, 4192
Burks, Kathy, 3945, 3951
Burks, Keith W., 6888
Burks, Pam, 3131
Burleigh, Betsy, 2317
Burleson, D Cal, 6903
Burleson, Debra, 1756
Burleson, Ed, 264
Burley, Patrick J, 230
Burlin, Philip M, 960
Burline-Roser, Lisa, 504
Burman, Howard, 2485, 2486
Burman, Sarah, 1688
Burman-Hall, Linda, 873, 4328
Burn, Malcolm, 670
Burnaby, Laurie, 4325
Burneikis, Alexa, 491, 5171
Burnell, Diana, 2633
Burnes, Mike, 2802
Burness, Judy, 4331
Burnett, Andrew, 4278, 4279
Burnett, Annette M., 5049, 5120
Burnett, Anthony, 4419
Burnett, Carol, 1027
Burnett, Chris, 4904
Burnett, Dr. Tod A., 4252
Burnett, Ellen, 2705
Burnett, Kathleen, 33
Burnett, Marc, 4594, 6817
Burnett, Marty, 2625
Burnett, Roger, 6608
Burnett, Tammy, 1599
Burnett Ed.D, Henry J, 6298
Burnett, Jr, Zaron W, 2857
Burnett, Jr., Zaron, 2857
Burnette, Sonny, 4690
Burnettl, Mark, 6818
Burnham, Dianne, 2690
Burnham, Rika, 5133
Burnham, Tina, 6577
Burns, Andrew, 7396
Burns, Brian, 1342
Burns, Charlie, 3770
Burns, Claire, 1890
Burns, Danny, 7423
Burns, Daren, 4174
Burns, Gary W, 1036
Burns, George, 4739, 4744
Burns, Jerry, 3641
Burns, John, 3009
Burns, Karen, 2680
Burns, Michael, 3844
Burns, Miriam, 1782
Burns, R Jameson, 5038
Burns, Reg, 8413
Burns, Rita, 789
Burns Coogan, Cynthia, 3119
Burns Houck, Deborah, 3430
Buroojy, Karen, 7560

Burpee, Chuck, 3203
Burr, Charles, 2133
Burr, Robert, 371
Burrage, Anna, 514
Burress, Jim, 2324
Burress, Richard, 5835
Burrey, Felicia A, 1176
Burrill, Chris, 6134
Burrill, Christopher, 6134
Burrill, Mike, 8083
Burrill Jr, Mike, 1598
Burris, John, 5829
Burroughs, Donna, 7152
Burroughs, Fe, 5387
Burroughs, Joan duB., 4421
Burrow, M. Bryan, 757
Burrowes, Keith, 1316
Burrows, Bill, 6050
Burrows, Bruce, 716
Burrows, Gay, 716
Burrows, Thomas B., 7658
Burrows, SC, Ph.D., Joanne M., 4652
Burrus, John, 1128
Burt, David, 6635
Burti, Joyce, 3898
Burtis, Susan, 1367
Burtless, Chris, 2011
Burton, Cathy, 6891
Burton, J Bryan, 1666
Burton, Jan, 4356
Burton, LaVern, 931, 4395
Burton, Louise, 7159
Burton, Mrs. Marsha, 7954
Burwell, Elizabeth, 4260
Burzynski, Michael, 4126
Busa, Steve, 3253
Busackijno, Barbara, 3498
Busby, Arthur, 1579
Buscetti, Anthony, 3370
Busch, Dennis, 654
Busch, Robin, 7472
Buschlen, Eric, 4863
Buschman, Jason, 1579
Buser, Zac, 5551
Busfield, Buck, 2552
Bush, Bonita J, 1162
Bush, Ellen, 2782
Bush, Estelle, 2532
Bush, Gus, 6325
Bush, Ilsa, 264
Bush, Scott, 7373
Bush, TJ, 1092
Bush Helzberg, Shirley, 1283, 4903
Bush-Morris, Kathy, 8627
Bushell Jr, Robert G, 4020
Bushey, Valerie, 204
Bushlow, Lisa, 3446
Bushman, Kris, 8477, 8478, 8480, 8481
Bushnel, Robert, 5710
Busk, Don, 5386
Buskirk, Brian, 4065
Buskirk, Thomas, 4156
Buson, Daniela, 554
Buss, Al, 2141
Busse, Madelyn, 4070
Busse, Walter, 977
Bussell, Julie, 6110, 6111, 6114
Bussey, Amy, 3893
Bussiki, Marcelo, 1705
Bussing, Ellen E., 5997, 6000
Busterud, Jim, 2222
Bustow, Treva, 7211
Buswellk, Richard, 3048
Butcher, Carolyn, 2611
Butcher, Dan, 6375
Butera, Kathleen, 2910
Butiu, Precious, 4082
Butkevich, Keri, 1896
Butler, Candace, 4631
Butler, Carol, 6461
Butler, Chris, 6089
Butler, Chuck, 5400
Butler, Dick, 2974
Butler, Elizabeth, 5285
Butler, Frank, 3239, 7351
Butler, Gretchen, 2878
Butler, Isrea, 1510
Butler, Jack, 2306

Butler, James E., 3303
Butler, Louetta, 6800
Butler, Louise, 1342
Butler, Marcy, 141
Butler, N. Marie, 2330
Butler, Patricia, 899
Butler, Rachel, 3
Butler, Rebecca, 5500
Butler, Robert, 1746
Butler, Ronal, 1773
Butler, Sandra, 1228
Butler, Sarah, 621
Butler, Susan L, 2750
Butler, Terry, 8192
Butorac, Darko, 1300
Butsic, Bill, 4118
Butt, Laura, 802
Butt, Randy, 8513, 8514
Buttars, Jack A., 4009
Buttenwieser, Lawrence, 3548
Butterbaugh, Brian, 1625
Butterman, Michael, 899, 1144
Butterworth, Lynne, 8079
Buttram, Jan, 3460
Buttram, Joan, 177
Butts, Barbara, 6779, 6780, 6781, 6782, 6783
Butz, Carole, 4642
Butz, Ellen, 5081
Buxton, Barry M., 5221
Buxton, Donald C, 4762
Buxton, Dr Barry M, 7855
Buxton, Dr. Barry M, 3640
Buyan, Elizabeth, 2156
Buzynski, Brenda, 6961, 6963, 6964, 6965
Buzza, David T., 7582
Buzza, Jim, 2070
Byard, Barney, 7067, 7068, 7069
Byer, Alyssa, 4078
Byerly, Alison R, 5445
Byers, Dane, 1488
Byers, Diana, 467
Byers, Jay, 7000, 7001, 7002
Byers, Sara, 8504
Byers, Vicki, 4285
Byers-Pevitts, Beverley, 7436
Byess, Steven, 1278
Bykov, Vladimir, 162
Byler, Hannah, 4764
Bylsma, Karen, 2138
Bylsma, Megan, 7303
Bylsma, Tom, 1241
Bynum, Amanda, 7270
Bynum, Jennifer, 1489
Byokawski, Marsha, 186
Byokawski-Gordon, Jennifer, 186
Byrd, Aaron, 499
Byrd, David B., 3904
Byrd, Donald, 686
Byrd, Fracena, 2872
Byrd, Joann, 4080
Byrd, Jr., P. Carrigan, 5635
Byrne, Cherie, 8015
Byrne, Dan, 621
Byrne, Frank, 1283
Byrne, James, 2100
Byrne, Paul, 2680
Byrne, Ron, 8716
Byrne, Teresa, 1919
Byrnes, Joseph, 4728
Byrnes, Katie, 3864
Byrnes, Mollie, 1208, 4800
Byron, Dr. John, 1515
Byron, Richard, 3928

C

C. Eschels, Philip, 3069
C. Ewers, Anne, 8155
C. Grieshaber, Robert, 2087
C. Hudgins, Carter, 8207
C. MARSHALL, ELIZABETH, 2821
C. Martin, Thomas, 6899, 6901, 6902
C. Nicola, James, 3536
C. Webster, Steven, 3239
C. White, George, 2714, 2715
C.Prichard, David, 8151
C.Stillman, Bradley, 1171, 1172
Caan, Michael, 109

Cabalka, Scott K., 3270
Caballero, Lenny, 8329, 8331, 8332
Caball,-Domenech, Josep, 903
Cabanatan, Precy, 4337
Cabaniss, Boyce, 5589
Cabaong, Macario, 4272
Cabe, Crista, 5760
Cable, Bob, 4337
Cable, David, 182
Cable, Robert, 4337
Cabllero, Jorge, 4178
Cabot, Raymond, 4995
Cabral, Brian D, 3184, 4814
Cabral, Eva, 6321
Cabral, Manuel, 6682
Cabrales, Enrique, 8439
Cabrera, Donato, 1313
Cabrera, Nico, 6069
Cabrera, Robert, 1563
Cabrera-Nieves, Brenda, 138
Cabuta, Froylon, 2495
Cacas, Ron, 2558
Caccam, Juanita, 29
Cacciottoli, Anne, 1053
Caciopto, Robert, 2779
Cackovich, James, 5483
Cada, Suzanne, 3902
Cade Holmes, Sally, 3184
Cadieux, Ron, 1560
Cadigan, Cornelius, 5109
Cadley, Carola, 3143
Cadwallader, Trish, 525
Cadwell, Jeffrey, 1258, 1259
Cady, Jeffrey, 7430
Caemmerer, Michael, 5783
Cafarella, Doreen, 323
Cafarelli, Margaret, 4323
Cafer, Jayne, 1123, 2076
Caffery, Steven J, 8621, 8653
Cagan, Charlotte, 6238, 6243
Cagan, Ray, 6067
Cage, Dan, 8306
Cager, Barbara, 3974
Cagle, Benny, 6040
Cagle, Jenny, 5609, 5611
Cahan, Cora, 7767
Cahill, Keri Ellis, 3153
Cahill, Mary, 2723
Cahn, Marcia, 2967
Cai, Lily, 82, 97
Caiarelli, Dawn, 3804
Cain, Allison, 2937
Cain, Angela, 3262
Cain, Dawn, 727
Cain, Dr Jerry, 1046
Cain, John, 8036
Cain, John M, 1093
Cain, Nancy B., 8279
Cain, Susan, 3771, 8062, 8063
Cain, Tom, 2369
Cain, W.S., 5539
Caine, Robert, 6194
Caine, Sunny, 6194
Caines, Christopher, 401, 406
Caines, Shonda, 611
Caiola, Rose, 7768
Cairns, Whitney, 2164
Cairo, Shelley I., 6585
Caisley, Robert, 2900
Caisley, Robert C., 6699, 6701, 6702
Cakar, Eve, 6127, 6157
Calabrese, Charles, 4105
Calabro, Rita, 679, 8608
Calamia, Jay, 7142, 7144
Calaway, Terry A., 7055
Caldeira, Michelle, 278
Calder, Tom, 7192
Calderon, Keisha, 172
Caldwell, Bruce, 651
Caldwell, David, 4614
Caldwell, Dr. Agnes, 7263
Caldwell, Gary, 1767
Caldwell, Gayle, 6186
Caldwell, George, 4077
Caldwell, Lauren, 6519
Caldwell, Lori, 2447
Caldwell, Mary Ann, 1717
Caldwell, Raymond, 3993, 5649

1147

Executive Name Index

Caldwell, Thomas, 4967
Caldwell, Tim, 2165
Caldwell, Wendy, 1885
Caldwell III, Charles, 5574
Cale, Douglas, 1253
Calentine, Chanda, 3636
Calerdine, Don, 6298
Calhoon, Patrick M, 6583
Calhoun, Charles, 1916
Calhoun, Eva, 6511
Calhoun, M Grace, 8161
Calhoun, Sam, 5787
Calhoun, Tysha, 3995
Caliendo, Kathleen, 3794
Calkin, Wes, 4042
Calkins, Ashley, 8506
Calkins, Chris, 6164
Calkins, Christopher C, 6179, 6182
Calkins, Jeffrey E, 7811
Calkins, Katherine Charl, 4346
Call, Chris, 6280
Call, Curtis, 249
Call, Joseph R, 1026
Callaghan, Barb, 3318
Callaghan, David, 2411
Callaghan, Mary, 6732
Callahan, Constance, 2866
Callahan, Deirdre, 2263
Callahan, Margie, 1781
Callahan, Ryan, 2505
Callan, Gene, 2817
Callas, Ellen, 2590
Callaway, Cathy, 4147
Callaway, Evelyn, 3942
Callaway, Terry, 4165
Callery Jr., Thomas J., 6415
Calli, Jr., William S., 5213
Callihan II, C. F., 243
Calmer, Charles, 1605
Calmer, Joseph, 1548
Calocerinos, Nancy, 3410
Caltvedt, Sonia, 852, 6254
Caluori, Jeanne, 2123
Calvaruso, Joseph S., 4817
Calvert Kappel, Victoria, 5174
Calvin, Darrell, 4436
Calvin, Dennis, 1792
Calvin, Sandra, 4297
Camano, Jennifer, 4182
Camargo, Rick, 3988
Cambron, J. Edward, 8155
Camel, Marelle, 43
Cameli, Mark, 2398
Camera, Rev Kathleen L, 3539
Cameron, Clark, 3512
Cameron, Dennis, 554
Cameron, Erin, 3717
Cameron, Greg, 199, 205
Cameron, Gretchen, 1629
Cameron, Jamie, 2872
Cameron, Jim, 6536
Cameron, John, 3036, 7003, 7006, 7007, 7008
Cameron, Sue, 5402
Cameron Ph.D, Tom, 1789
Cameron-Webb, Gavin, 3429
Camille Hersh, Anne, 160
Camillus, John C., 5493
Camin, Pete, 4582
Caminiti, June, 6277
Camino, Marty, 5884
Camlin, Jo, 3875
Camm, Laurie, 739
Cammack, John, 2628
Camp, John, 6640
Camp, Philip, 5651
Campagna, Jerry, 5003
Campanelli, Joe, 870, 871
Campanero, Connie, 3650
Campanie, Sue, 7661
Campbell, Alan, 8503
Campbell, Amy, 1489
Campbell, Ann S, 1909
Campbell, Bridgett, 7183
Campbell, C. Dealey, 1715
Campbell, Chad, 8029
Campbell, Chris, 4882
Campbell, Colin, 2589
Campbell, Daniel, 2995, 6851

Campbell, Darsen, 4182
Campbell, Diane, 2033
Campbell, Dianne, 4640, 6962
Campbell, Dr. Heather, 5276, 8221
Campbell, Duane, 2694
Campbell, Gary, 4894
Campbell, Iain, 3840
Campbell, Ian D, 1909
Campbell, J. Kermit, 1256
Campbell, James, 4762
Campbell, Jeffery, 4180
Campbell, Joan, 752
Campbell, Karen, 704
Campbell, Kelly, 2224
Campbell, Kim J, 1714
Campbell, Laura, 4069
Campbell, Lynn, 4862
Campbell, Mary C., 4742
Campbell, Michael A, 6196
Campbell, Neil, 8604
Campbell, Patrick, 775
Campbell, Patrick M, 7832
Campbell, Philip D, 8654
Campbell, Sandra, 1324
Campbell, Scott, 2425
Campbell, Susan, 6831
Campbell, Suzy, 2427
Campbell, Thomas, 7371
Campbell, Tim, 4004, 6634
Campbell, Tom, 2669, 8568
Campbell, William, 7212
Campbell, William I., 5053
Campbell Carey, Charlene, 315
Campbell Davis, Barbara, 5269
Campbell Dempsey, Paul, 1814
Campbell Disher, Jacque, 3927, 8321
Campbell-White, Annette, 4207
Campbell, JoLane, 7986
Campell, Alan, 1327
Camper, Robert, 2634
Campione, Anthony, 1332
Campo, Crayn, 7705
Campo, Dr. Todd, 8531, 8532
Campo, Steve, 2688
Campos, Leslie, 4172
Campos, Naiha, 5659
Canada, Tonya, 3574
Canan, Laurel, 5838
Canarina, John, 1108
Canatella, Donna, 8346
Candler, John, 7861
Canellakis, Nicholas, 4174
Canepa, Tiffine, 8712
Canfield, James, 319, 6204
Canfield, Joan, 4527
Cangahuala, Gloria, 773
Canino, Bob, 3987
Caniparoli, Val, 554
Canlas, Marlene, 6469
Cann, Kimberly, 1478
Cannady, Gregg, 897
Cannaits, Phil, 8025
Cannan, Margarita, 6129
Canning, Kathie, 6569
Cannistraci, Jerrod, 1633
Cannizzaro, Rosina, 1770
Cannizzo, Roseanna, 1820
Cannon, Jasson, 3296
Cannon, Kristine, 3222
Cannon, Margarita, 6129
Cannon, Pat, 502
Cannon, Sarah, 4613
Cannon, Tim, 153
Canny, Kathryn, 1067
Cano, Andrea, 1254
Canon, Charles, 4143
Cansfield, Michael, 4576
Cantarella Culpo, Madeline, 280
Canter, Judi, 3120
Canter, Ph.D Nancy J, 6093
Cantey, Kayla, 1740
Cantey, Paul, 811, 4256
Cantler Fulwiler, Anne, 3118
Cantlo-Cockfield, Tonya L., 7691
Cantoni, Linda, 2206
Cantoni, Marie L., 2206
Cantor, Margalit, 1409, 5117
Cantor, Nancy, 1467

Cantrell, Brent, 5571
Cantrell, Carol, 1705
Cantrell, Ruth, 7613
Cantu, Tony, 6106
Cantwell, Domonique, 4060
Cantwell, Paul, 5103
Canty, Dean R PhD, 5655
Canty, Ned, 2332
Caoile, Nikolas, 1614, 1813
Caotes, Jon, 4164
Capasso, Michael, 2250
Capell, Peter, 3235
Capella, Giusi, 6291, 6293, 6294, 6296
Capellupo, Shannon, 1656
Capen, CJ, 2376
Caperton y Montoya, Will, 4236
Capetillo, Carla, 633
Capi, Sherill, 968
Capitanini, Pamella, 6760
Caplan, Susan, 1184
Caple, Blair, 1997
Caples, Richard, 418
Caples, Richard J, 446
Caplin, Toni, 5696
Capo, Laurrence, 5015
Caporale, Anthony C, 5237
Cappala, Anna, 6442
Capparella, Donald, 3917, 5581
Capparrella, Donald, 5581
Cappelletti, Corinne, 445
Cappelli, Andy, 402
Cappello, Dana, 6247
Capps, Josh, 3877
Capps, Kris, 4159
Capri, Nicole, 2439
Caprio, Nicholas, 6155
Carabajal Hunt, Elisa, 3409
Caraballo Dorfman, Sherry, 1939
Carabelli, Carl, 1340
Caraco, Candace, 7195
Carafelli, GA, 3831
Caraher, James, 2065
Carano, Vince, 1352
Carbon, John, 5462
Carbone, Casey, 574
Carbone, Marie, 1598, 5414, 8083
Carbone, Vincent, 2047
Carbonell Smith, Laura, 3595
Carchidi, Paul J, 1184
Card, Cory, 5177
Card, Deborah, 2042
Card, Deborah R., 1035, 1038
Cardaci, Michael, 1782
Cardelli, Gioia, 125
Carden, William, 3490, 7727
Cardenas Herrera, Camilo, 6
Cardenes, Andres, 918
Carder, Dale, 4928
Cardibali, Julie, 7832
Cardinal, Vincent J., 6495
Cardinali, Tashi, 4239
Cardo, Tom, 3742
Cardona, Cora, 3956
Cardoni, John, 8181
Cardoza, Cathy, 3777
Cardoza, Karen, 4173
Cardoza, Luisa, 766
Cardwell, Evan, 5924, 5925
Cardwell, James Jay, 2658
Cardwell, Leanne, 4173
Cardwell, Neil, 2019
Care, Carrie, 6372, 6375
Carey, Alison, 2498
Carey, Annie, 1008
Carey, Diana K., 5800
Carey, Donald, 315
Carey, Erin, 1594
Carey, James, 2494
Carey, Jared T, 1454
Carey, Jared T., 5189
Carey, Jon, 8085
Carey, Katie, 2960
Carey, Mary, 4164
Carey Joullian IV, Mr. E., 8454
Carey Louden, Katie, 2960
Cargile, Jennifer, 717
Cargill, Clinton, 3487
Cargill, Dr. Jack, 1742

Cargle, Scott, 111
Carhart, Deborah, 5177
Carhart, Ralph, 3440
Cariaga, Luisa, 2495
Carignan, Steve, 4640
Carioti, Sam, 3161
Carl, Jane, 4907
Carl, Jim, 3650
Carl Bromberg, Lee, 1173
Carless, Tim, 1925
Carleton, Matthew, 2502
Carleton, Paul, 7975, 7976, 7977
Carleton, Paul H, 5292
Carleton, Paul H., 1521
Carlgren, Daniel, 2418
Carlile, Amy, 1742
Carlile, Heather, 1718
Carlile, Ragen, 5265
Carlin, Sharon, 2427
Carlisle, Steve, 4254
Carlon, Pete, 8319
Carlos, Juan, 3499
Carlos Gonzalez, Juan, 2833
Carlotto, Lynn, 6392
Carlow, Heidi, 7174
Carlsen, Allan, 138
Carlsen, Beth, 2552
Carlsen, Jill, 696
Carlson, Alan, 766, 4211
Carlson, Clint, 5905, 5906
Carlson, Doug, 6246
Carlson, Elisa, 6646
Carlson, Eric, 6303
Carlson, Eric A, 3719
Carlson, Jeffrey, 2264
Carlson, Ken Carlson, 3235
Carlson, Kendra, 3226, 3227
Carlson, Kurt, 5255
Carlson, Lindsey, 4026
Carlson, Margaret, 541
Carlson, Marian, 1590
Carlson, Marilyn, 1618
Carlson, Max, 4883, 4884
Carlson, Nancy, 1356
Carlson, Rick, 8570
Carlson, Steve, 6430
Carlson, Tamsin, 44
Carlson, Trevor, 456
Carlson, Wendy, 2072
Carlson Nelson, Marilyn, 1265
Carlson-Brown, Sarah, 4949
Carlson-Brown, Vincent, 4949
Carlton, Cindy, 1992
Carlton, Steve, 800
Carlucci, Carl, 8402, 8408
Carlyn, Annie, 7462
Carmack, Lesa, 6051
Carmack, Teresa, 7160
Carmichael, Hoagy B, 387
Carmichael, Lynne, 3771
Carmichael, Steve, 4584
Carnahan, Craig, 7361
Carne, Margaret, 5865
Carnero, Veronica, 363
Carnes, Justin, 3645
Carnesale, Albert, 2518
Carnew-Megginson, Maegan, 3937
Carney, Chrissy, 2443
Carney, David C., 747
Carney, Devon, 515
Carney, Greg, 6351
Carney, Jack, 1712
Carney, Jeff, 2165
Carney, Jon, 1155
Carney, Jonathan, 1153
Carney, Julianne, 7645
Carney, Laura, 8154
Carney, Margaret, 7824
Carney, Matt, 64
Carney, Shawn P., 1827
Carno, Ellen, 3138
Carole, Barr, 7052
Carollo, Daren A.C., 6068
Caron, Jim, 3318
Caropepe, Karen, 5794
Carpenter, Carol L., 4206
Carpenter, Christopher, 4118
Carpenter, Chuck, 3791

Executive Name Index

Carpenter, Dean, 3565
Carpenter, Deborah, 2775
Carpenter, Emma Lee, 2827
Carpenter, Gery, 7477, 7478
Carpenter, Gregory, 1954
Carpenter, Jack, 117, 4307, 4316
Carpenter, JD, 5813
Carpenter, Jennifer, 8431
Carpenter, Kristy, 6710, 6711, 6712, 6715, 6716
Carpenter, Rich, 4666
Carpenter, Sarah, 6271
Carpenter, Steve, 3494
Carpenter Sylvester, Julie, 3416
Carpenter, Jack, 90, 94
Carpentier-Alting, Neil, 6320
Carpentieri, Teresa, 2377
Carpio, Cece, 6069
Carr, Bernadette, 432
Carr, David, 2566
Carr, Deana, 4880
Carr, Donnagail, 304
Carr, Dr. Tessa, 3640
Carr, Eileen, 5337
Carr, Emily, 6274
Carr, George H, 3712
Carr, John F., 6412, 6413, 6414
Carr, Joseph R., 1076
Carr, Joshua, 2466
Carr, Kevin, 6557
Carr, Lucy, 2980
Carr, Michael, 216
Carr, Stephanie, 3392
Carr, Steve, 6697
Carr, Tim, 8570
Carr, Vincent, 1335
Carreno, Karen, 315
Carreon-Robledo, Enrique, 2356
Carrettin, Zachary, 4353
Carrico, Paula, 439
Carrieri, Mary, 6078
Carrigg, Tonja, 8051
Carrington, Simon, 1970
Carriom, Xochitl, 2576
Carrol, Denny, 3700
Carrolan, Greg, 6268
Carroll, Arlene, 1721
Carroll, Charles, 3618
Carroll, Dennis, 6674
Carroll, Donna M, 6820, 6821
Carroll, Donna M., 4596
Carroll, Elaine C, 940
Carroll, Gregory A., 4904
Carroll, James, 5461
Carroll, James FL, 5461
Carroll, Jeanne, 496
Carroll, Joanne P., 5461
Carroll, Joy, 1623
Carroll, Kathleen, 1571
Carroll, Laura, 1933
Carroll, Michael, 4997, 7945
Carroll, Pat, 4771
Carroll, Patricia, 5946
Carroll, Robert, 6680
Carroll, Shannon, 3859
Carroll, Sisi, 1299
Carroll, Sue, 5560
Carroll, Teri L, 4844
Carroll, Thomas, 3385
Carroll, William, 8009
Carroll, William J, 6836
Carroll, Zachary, 560
Carroll Bosler, Kim, 4365
Carros, Elke, 4162
Carry, Bob, 5159
Carski, Ruth, 7211
Carson, Barbara, 7705
Carson, Phillip, 1986
Carson, Susan, 836
Carson, Tracey, 4128
Carson-Dwyer, Amy, 8824
Carstens, Lena, 2851
Carswell, Cathy T., 6720, 6721
Carte, Mary, 8334
Carten, Jane, 4062, 4063, 8572
Carter, Aaron, 2952
Carter, Brenda, 6551
Carter, Brenda A., 7953
Carter, Chris, 4084, 7867

Carter, Cindy, 4655
Carter, Cornelius, 5927, 5930, 8482
Carter, Deanna, 221
Carter, Elizabeth, 2582
Carter, Gary, 6119
Carter, Geoffrey, 3021
Carter, Hazo, 8625
Carter, Helen, 1024
Carter, JC, 4014
Carter, Jean, 3911
Carter, Joel M., 3881
Carter, Larry, 8261
Carter, Lois, 2791
Carter, Luther F, 5540
Carter, Margaret, 7761, 7771
Carter, Matthew, 316
Carter, Megan E, 3593
Carter, Opal, 765
Carter, Pam, 1585, 1634
Carter, Robert, 2853
Carter, Sally, 984
Carter, Selina, 2273
Carter, Sharol, 4221, 6116
Carter, Stephen, 4084
Carter, Steve, 249
Carter, Stewart, 1508, 5138
Carter, Susan, 4188
Carter, Travis, 5220
Carter, Walter F, 1203
Carter, Warrick L, 6743
Carter, Warrick L., 6754
Carter Jr, Hazo W, 8641
Carter Austin, Robert, 1726, 1735
Carter Beane, Douglas, 3487
Carter Jr, Hazo, 5817
Carter, Esq., Kirk A., 4815
Carter, Jr., Kenneth F., 6660
Carter, PhD, Lolita D, 29
Cartmill, Joyce, 3327
Carto, Dr. Thomas J, 3742
Carto, Thomas, 3742
Cartona, Michael, 6438
Cartwright, Ben, 1908
Cartwright, Carol, 7950
Carty, Denise, 3338
Carucci, Frank, 3510
Caruso, Robert, 3812
Caruso, Shea, 6660
Caruso Haviland, Linda, 5436
Carvajal, Carlos, 90, 94, 100, 101, 4307, 4315, 4316
Carver, Petra, 6690, 6691, 6692, 6693, 6694
Carver, Sue, 900, 901, 4361
Carvlin, Richard, 1005, 1006
Cary, Richard, 3162
Casau, Michele, 4310
Casazza, Chris, 3703
Cascione, Gregory, 7290
Cascor, Bruce, 3388
Case, Deborah, 644
Case, Del, 4200
Case, Donna, 939
Case, Peggy, 4702
Case King, Barbara, 6377, 6378, 6380
Casey, Brain W., 6879, 6880, 6881
Casey, Courtenay, 2223
Casey, Deborah, 2702
Casey, Eubank, 3052
Casey, Jim, 610
Casey, Joyce, 3718
Casey, Linda M., 1523, 1524
Casey, Madison, 4369
Casey, Martha, 1826
Casey, Michele, 1992
Casey, Mrs. Eugene B, 1997
Casey, Nate, 1013
Casey, Stephen, 3822
Cash, Colton, 2812
Cash, Marsha, 3074
Cash, Vickie, 3025
Cashman, Brian, 7640
Cashman, Colleen, 470
Caskey, Doug, 6878
Cason, Katie, 6632
Cason, Tony, 808
Casper, George, 6710, 6711, 6712, 6715, 6716, 8472
Casper, Rebecca, 6696

Caspers, Rod, 3929
Casperson, Patricia, 1952
Casquilho, Chris, 5773
Cass, James, 2831
Cass, Lynn, 4516
Cassanajor, Jane, 2743
Cassano, Ron, 775
Cassanova, Dinora, 977
Cassanova, Marcia, 3090
Cassel, James G., 3819
Cassel, Keisha, 1205
Cassell, Jim, 8725
Cassidy, James R, 1133
Cassidy, Jeanne, 632
Cassidy, Kim, 5436
Cassidy, Liz, 3436
Cassidy, Sean, 8126
Cassidy, Sharon, 4062, 4063
Cassidy, Sharon, 8572
Cassidy, Stephen K., 1912
Cassidy, Timothy J., 4592
Cassidy, Tina, 323
Casso, Alan, 2126
Castagna, Bobby, 6281
Castagna, Dr John, 768
Castaneda, Shelly, 5957
Castellani, David, 2475
Castellano, Maria, 345
Castellano, Orlando, 6547
Castille, Michael, 4709
Castillo, Myriam, 3556, 3570
Castillo, Philip, 5663, 8450, 8451
Castillo, Tami, 3336
Castillo, Valarie, 2665, 6355
Castle, John K., 5162
Castle, Thomas, 935
Castleman, Charles, 1461
Casto, Shelly, 7987
Castro, Alpha, 2705
Castro, Douglas, 7149
Castro, Mauricio, 6078
Castrodale, Richard, 3880
Castronovo, Frank, 8023, 8024
Caswell, Rosa L., 1234
Cataladi, Matthew, 1065, 1066
Catalani, John, 2352
Catalfano, Joseph, 4790
Catapano-Friedman, Lisa, 4017
Catazaro Hayward, Jennifer, 513
Cate, Cindy, 6937
Cate, Michael, 1735
Cates, Anna, 733, 4174
Cates, Gilbert, 2502
Cates, Hunter, 3769
Cates, Lou Ann, 6719
Cathey, Stephanie, 343
Cathy, James, 756
Catingub, Matt, 1021
Catlett, Richard M., 6528
Catmull, Katherine, 3930
Cato, Marcus, 2616
Caton-Noble, Svetlana, 7847
Catrillo, Guy, 331
Catron, Sue, 5391
Catron, Sue S, 3768
Catron, Susan, 4520
Cattanach, John, 3281, 7464
Cattanach, Robert, 7375
Catton, Jack, 117
Cattran, Diane, 2283
Caudill, W.Lowry, 7866
Caudle, Rose, 185
Cauldwell, Susan, 1334
Caulker, Ferne, 702
Caulkins, Ellie, 1954
Caulkins, Joseph, 2010
Cauthen, Caroline, 7889
Cauthen, Samantha Test, 6262
Cauthen, Sheila, 1493
Cavalieri, Robert, 8180
Cavallaro, David, 3457
Cavallaro Rongere, Carm, 222
Cavalli, Paul, 252, 4746
Cavanagh, Dan, 5998
Cavanaugh, Genevieve S., 1355
Cavanaugh, Jan, 3812
Cavanaugh, Megan, 7987
Cavanaugh, Terrence, 8123

Cavano, Tom, 3740
Cavazos, Elias, 626
Cavenaugh, Corey, 4806
Cavenaugh, Dr. Jennifer, 2842
Cavender, Annie, 8292
Cavendish, Dr Thomas, 2003
Cavendish, Mike, 4096
Caverson, Jenni A., 4841
Caves, Alan, 4465
Caves, Jonathan, 8605
Cavileer, Craig, 319
Cawvey, Jan, 717
Cays, Diane, 6383
Caywood, Larry, 1014
Caywood, Scott, 379
Cazan, Ken, 1889
Cazeaux, Lena, 126
Ceasare, Denise, 8190
Cebula, Paula, 2055
Cebull, Brian, 7469
Ceceri, Mike, 3134
Cech, Kyle, 3326
Cecil, Bill, 1006
Cecile, Stanzione, 2710, 2711
Cecsarini, David, 4126
Cedar, Cussin, 2418
Cedillo, Jennifer, 2345
Celaya, Al, 3975
Celedonia, Cherie, 8020
Celeste, Morgiana, 329
Celeste Varricchio, Morgiana, 329
Celestin, Denise A, 240
Cella, Louis A., 7454
Centers, Ken, 8077
Centers, Zachary, 8077
Centilli, Charles, 7611
Cento Munoz, Rafaela, 241
Centrella, Maria, 6299
CEO, Becker, 8134, 8135
Cepeda, Breanne, 1299
Ceragioli, Erin M, 689
Cerar, Matt, 3254
Cerato, Sara A, 2310
Cerceo, Danielle, 5382
Ceresa, Richard, 2628
Cermack, Jim, 3260
Cernek, Steven, 2023
Cernik, Christopher, 2255
Cerny, Keith, 2342
Cerny, Keithy, 1922, 1923
Cerone, David, 1539
Cerri, Marc, 1407
Cerrudo, Alejandro, 203
Certain, Phillip, 2395
Ceruillo, Richard, 2218
Cervantes, Enedina G, 2431
Cesar, Kamala, 450, 5146
Cesar Rodriguez, Carlos, 257
Cesaretti, Charles, 1367
Cesario, Liz, 3395
Cetera, Zona, 3060
Cetiz, Mahir, 1415
Cetnar, Kathleen, 7820
CFO, Steiner, 869
Cfoke, Melissa, 4562
Chabalowski, Molly, 3207
Chace-Larson, Donna, 1671
Chacko, Joyce, 4550
Chaddick, Cheryl, 622
Chadwell, Erik, 2419
Chadwick, Jeffre, 5254
Chadwin, Rachel, 7556
Chaenler, Roger, 4715
Chafe, Eric, 1214, 1215
Chaffee, Arden, 8029
Chaffee, Don, 6424
Chaffin, Janie, 3912, 8292
Chaffin, John, 3912, 8292
Chafin, Jim, 712
Chafin, Peggy, 549, 550
Chafin, Richard, 373
Chaganos, Jane, 1820
Chagnard, Christophe, 1799
Chagnon, Kathleen A., 7198
Chai, Haw Bin, 1456
Chai, Sung, 1419
Chaifetz, David, 2011
Chaikin, Jeri, 541

Executive Name Index

Chaimson, Judie, 3131
Chain, Herbert M., 1389
Chair, Wendy, 3239
Chait, Matt, 2505, 6125
Chalfant, Margaret, 5616
Chalk, Phoebe, 6001
Challacombe, Tamra, 220
Challener, Elisbeth, 3935
Challey, Robert, 91
Challinor, David, 850
Chalmers, Susan, 4797
Chalupa, Leo M., 6462
Chamard, John, 3603
Chamber, Tony, 3662
Chamber S, Gerald, 2026
Chamberlain, Jeanne, 5869
Chamberlain, Patrick, 7193
Chamberlain, Richard C, 5444
Chamberlin, Betsy, 5796
Chamberlin, Chris, 3915
Chambers, Alan, 2955
Chambers, Allan, 6729
Chambers, Bret E., 1488
Chambers, Chris, 470
Chambers, Christopher, 339
Chambers, Ed, 2654
Chambers, Kay, 2654
Chambers, Laura, 2048
Chambers, Liz, 6202
Chambers, Mary Jane, 6013
Chambers, Philip, 1195
Chambers, Raymond G., 7574
Chambers, Sheree, 4307, 4315, 4316
Chambers, Susan, 3036
Chambers, Thea, 5618
Chamblee, James, 1495
Chambord, Jacqueline, 5132
Champagne, Heidi, 7125
Champagne, Mario, 879, 6306, 6307, 6309
Champie, Bruce, 6219
Champion, Elizabeth D., 774
Chan, Darlene, 4209
Chan, Ida, 6124
Chan, Judy, 820
Chan, Kenyon S., 6164
Chan, Kim, 471
Chan, Oiman, 1413
Chan, Scott, 6670
Chance, Angela, 3686
Chancey, Tina, 1776
Chander, Jagriti, 210
Chandier-Marshall, Diana, 4556
Chandler, Barbara, 496
Chandler, C, 1484
Chandler, Dave, 2599
Chandler, Fielding, 630
Chandler, John, 1210, 1211
Chandler, Julie, 4362
CHANDLER, KIM, 3209
Chandler, Kim, 7312
Chandler, Paul, 5566
Chandler, Ray, 7377
Chandler, Rosanne, 4077
Chandler, Roy W, 8042, 8045
Chandler, Susan T, 3235
Chandler, Susan T., 3235
Chandler, Tamara, 4087
Chandler, Wayne, 8301
Chandler-White, Lis‰, 1787
Chandley, Dr. Paul, 5270
Chaney, George, 6972
Chaney, Laura, 252, 2090, 4746
Chaney, Lecia, 3939, 8336
Chang, Andrew, 2851
Chang, Ann, 4945
Chang, Anna, 7491
Chang, Caroline, 6289, 6290
Chang, Jennifer, 854
Chang, Laura, 677
Chang, Marie, 87
Chang, Mi-Hwa, 1419
Chang, Michelle, 2112
Chang, Mona, 1216
Chang, Peggy.H, 414
Chang, Rina, 861
Chang, Tisa, 3541
Chang, Wei-Lin, 883
Chang, Wendy, 2030

Chang, Ya-Ting, 5453
Chang, Yu-Hui, 1179, 1214, 1215
Chang-Barnea, Anne, 1304
Chang-Calderon, Maria, 1934
Chanoff, Rachel, 3459
Chansler, Robert J., 4311
Chao, Mei-yuan, 1446
Chao, Myrna, 5135
Chapaloney, Michael, 8129
Chaparro, Javier, 1705
Chapel, Michell, 1479
Chapin, Theodore S., 7768
Chaplin, Diane, 4993
Chaplin, Gwen, 1814
Chaplow, Kathryn, 3204
Chapman, Andy, 428
Chapman, Ariane, 3050, 7065
Chapman, Chris, 5277
Chapman, Colin, 4078
Chapman, Duane, 5815
Chapman, George L., 8017
Chapman, Jim, 6949
Chapman, Joe, 4513
Chapman, Keith, 2356
Chapman, Linda, 3416
Chapman, Linda S., 3536
Chapman, Mary, 2157
Chapman, Randy, 2152
Chapman, Sandra, 1819
Chapman, Scott, 817
Chapman, William, 2107, 2873
Chappell, Drew, 2598
Chappell, Karisa, 4095
Chappell, Sue, 6652
Chappell, Sylvia, 1556, 5350
Chappell Hicks, Deborah, 5921, 5922
Chappelle, Cheri, 1034
Chapple, Bernadette, 5918
Chapter, Carrie, 3836
Chapuis, Clayton, 4183
Chard, Jennifah, 2616
Chardwick, Chandler, 7545
Charig, Peter, 4783
Charles, David, 6605, 6606
Charles, Gerard, 199, 205, 525
Charles, Laura, 5065
Charles, Sheryle, 1459
Charles Levin, Richard, 2700
Charlesworth-Miller, Kate, 3737
Charloff, Ruth, 773
Charlop, Vivian, 5072, 7673
Charlton, Amanda, 3184, 4814
Charlton, Lori T., 6434, 6435
Charnas, Charles, 855, 4312
Charno, Melody, 5787
Charnow, Carole, 2107, 3143
Charon, Daniel, 654
Charry, Yoni, 4043
Chase, David, 6310
Chase, Diane, 6565, 6568, 6573
Chase, Mark, 122
Chase, Michael E, 1903
Chase, Murray, 2835
Chase, Rachelle D., 2144
Chase, Richard, 925
Chase, Valerie, 6298
Chase Bryer, Kathryn, 3120
Chase PhD, Ken, 6848
Chase, Kaitlyn, 8559
Chasitz, Robbie, 3153
Chasse, Janet, 13
Chasse, Lindsay, 5194
Chastain, Bettina, 5
Chastain, Steve, 8223
Chatal, Ed, 8418
Chatfield, Andrew R., 6412, 6413, 6414
Chatlain, Salina, 3319
Chatterjea, Ananya, 390
Chatterton, Bryan, 6231
Chaussee, Andrea, 4580
Chaves, Frank, 211
Chavez, Becky, 6014
Chavez, E J, 1911
Chavez, Freddy, 8424, 8425, 8426, 8427, 8428
Chavez, Pat, 830
Chavez, Raul, 2558
Chaya, Masazumi, 381, 385
Chayat, Juliet, 304

Chazanovitz, Gail, 4970
Chazen, David, 4352
Cheatham, Ann, 3449
Cheatham, Joel, 2011
Cheatham, Rich, 6323, 6324
Cheatwood, Sharon, 3759
Checchia, Anthony, 1645, 5480
Checchia, Anthony P, 1643, 5480
Checketts, Max L, 6681
Cheek, Don, 8445
Cheek, Jimmy G., 5572
Cheeks III, James, 2498
Cheever, Gene, 2552
Cheever, Jean, 3545
Chekow Lusignan, Susan, 5194
Chelesvig, Jeff, 6984
Cheli, Dave, 1288
Cheline OFB, Rev Paschal, 5423
Chelminski, Sarah Jane, 2702
Chelsen, Paul, 6848, 6849
Chema, Thomas V, 5346
Chema, Tom, 5346
Chemaly, Ed, 3520
Chembers, Audley, 4146
Chemerow, Doreen C., 5865
Chen, Bernice K., 4783
Chen, Chantel, 794, 4229
Chen, Chiung Chi, 821
Chen, Emily, 1672
Chen, H.T., 404, 429
Chen, HT, 429
Chen, Huifang, 977
Chen, Janet, 1548
Chen, Mei-Ann, 1034, 1695
Chen, Nai-Ni, 328
Chen, Richard, 804
Chen, Robert, 1035, 1038
Chen, Sidney, 846
Chen, Wei, 5575
Chen, Xiaolun, 2008
Chen, Yan, 163
Chenault, Marilyn, 2836
Chene, Douglas, 4743
Chenette, Jonathan, 4656
Cheney, Amy, 3706
Cheney, Dianne, 6079
Cheng, Gilbert, 834
Cheng, Jennifer, 39
Cheng, Mariette, 5085
Chenier, Tamika, 6249
Chenoweth, Ellen, 266
Chepp, Mark, 8006
Chereskin, Alvin, 456
Cherly, Pearce, 3052
Cherniak, Renee, 6165
Cherniavsky, Fyodor, 1015
Chemin, Megan, 4282
Chernof, David, 871
Cherry, Marlon, 351
Cherryholmes, Diana, 5089
Cherryholmes, Diana J, 5090
Chertock, Michael, 5313
Cherwien, David, 2145
Chesak, Kristen, 7264, 7312
Chesak, Kristen, 7569
Chesbrough, Herbert A, 3619, 7819
Chesebro, Dr. Robert, 1680
Cheshire, Carol, 6576
Cheshire, Nancy, 4116
Cheshire, Robyn, 4338
Cheslock, Elizabeth, 2252
Chesnut, Reagan, 7305
Chess, Robert B, 6207
Chess, Susan, 527
Chesser, Andrew, 6977
Chesser, Roger, 1127
Chester, Ivan, 4641
Chester, Karen, 5129
Chester, Ron, 7384
Chestnut, Madge, 4695
Chetel, Daniel, 1126
Cheung, Teresa, 1617
Chevreux, Shawn, 5995
Chi, Dr. Jacob, 917
Chi, Jacob, 917
Chiang, Andrew, 328
Chiao-Ping, Li, 696, 706
Chiapetta, Ric, 4512

Chiappetta, Al, 6431
Chiarelli, Randall G., 682
Chiarolanzio, Thomas, 6469
Chiasson, Marcy, 1281
Chichmanian, Tania J, 265
Chick, Kathleen, 4790
Chick, Steve, 4903
Chick Marquardt, Rickey, 5581
Chickery, Steven, 1455, 7695
Chieh Hsu, Pang, 6658, 6659
Chihoski, Phil, 6833
Child, Lucinda, 364
Childers, Martin, 3075
Childs, Donald, 8042, 8045
Childs, Jennifer, 3823
Childs, Kendall, 1110
Childs, Louise, 1735
Chille, Alan, 8199
Chilton, Carol, 7456
Chilton, Katrina, 7136
Chin, Candice, 5796
Chin, Deanne, 936, 4402
Chin, John, 2615
Chin, Paul, 6069
Chin, Pearl, 5171
Chin-Parker, Melissa J., 2558
Ching, Robin, 50
Ching, Selena, 1019
Ching-ming, Ciu, 1446
Chinn, Debbie, 4211
Chinn, Tom, 603
Chinn, Wesley, 2211
Chinyere, Hubbard, 4419
Chiolino, Jim, 4116
Chiong, Ruby Pearl B, 29
Chiosso-Glass, Judy, 8084
Chipman, John, 1054
Chipman, Robert E., 6793
Chipman, Shleby, 998
Chirco-Coontz, Sue, 1814
Chisessi, Massimo, 860
Chishti, Muzaffar, 3541
Chism Wright, Jan, 4947
Chistian, Barbara, 904
Chitresh Das, Pandit, 75
Chitwood, Charlie, 1004
Chiu, Leslie, 4808
Cho, Ahran, 1419
Cho, Angela, 896
Cho, David, 1741
Cho Wagner, Anna, 4262
Choate, David, 514
Choate, Roxie, 1366
Choate, Timothy, 6068
Choate-Pettit, Gail, 289
Chod, Andrew, 1171, 1172
Chohan, Prital, 381, 385
Choi-Dalton, Lucia, 71
Choksi, Armeane, 149
Cholerton, Clive, 2756
Chomo, Alicia, 2729
Chong, Emma, 8115
Chong, Ping, 2591, 3492, 3547
Chong Kee, Kevin, 6670
Choo, Kean-San, 6690, 6691, 6692, 6693, 6694
Chookasian, John, 31, 784, 786
Chopp, Rebecca, 5085
Chopp, Rebecca, 7680
Choquette, Anne, 8202
Chorale, Philharmonic, 1029
Chotard, Ann, 6040
Chotiner, Melissa, 5762
Chou, Lucinda, 5008, 5009
Chou, Sophy, 873
Chow, Dr. Allan, 4717
Chow, Elaine, 4269
Chow, Lisa R, 12
Chow, Martha, 3940
Choy, Colleen, 4546
Chris, Qualls, 2400
Chrisfield, Carla, 4783
Chrisman, Vicki, 4709
Chrisnan, Elaine, 8466
Chrispell, Sandy, 1240
Chriss, Joel, 8838
Christ, Al, 5513
Christ, Carol T, 7247
Christ, Kati, 5386

Executive Name Index

Christ, Maggie, 394
Christ, Maurine, 4331
Christel, Chris, 6173
Christen, Tim, 4115
Christensen, Brad, 2427
Christensen, Carrie, 4945
Christensen, Carrie, 7491
Christensen, David A., 1852, 1857
Christensen, Dr Carl, 768
Christensen, Elisabeth, 1187
Christensen, Heinrich, 4779
Christensen, Jim, 6200
Christensen, June, 5049, 5643
Christensen, June M, 1367
Christensen, Kelli, 1348
Christensen, Lee, 4190
Christensen, Les, 6034
Christensen, Lisette, 1863
Christensen, Lynda, 8499
Christensen, Russ, 8082
Christensen, Thordal, 42
Christenson, Barbara, 3892
Christenson, Chris, 100, 101
Christenson, Ellen, 650
Christenson, Patrick J, 7513
Christian, Gail, 43
Christian, Harry Patrick, 3392
Christian, Maria, 4848
Christian, Robert, 1557
Christiano, Mary, 2165
Christiansen, Jill, 1855
Christiansen, Kai, 4210
Christiansen, Paul, 1811
Christiansen, Tia, 4536
Christianson, Bonnie, 1795
Christie, Alfred, 3345
Christie, Bryan, 6876
Christie, Carlene, 5037
Christie, Eva, 53
Christie, Joni, 290
Christie, Keith, 6973
Christie, Kell, 8286
Christie, Michael, 2144, 4356
Christiel, Kelly, 4563
Christilles, Dennis, 3045
Christison, John, 8570
Christman, Kathy, 913
Christman, Mary Anne, 5333
Christman, Tom, 1932
Christmas, Gary, 61
Christopher, Amy, 668
Christopher, Bostin, 2419
Christopher, Dave, 5492
Christopher, Gregory, 7949, 7950
Christopher, Ron, 1811
Christopher, Virginia, 5594
Christophers, Harry, 1181, 2106
Christy, Gregory, 7015
Christy, Jon, 6980, 6981, 6982, 6983
Chromow, Charles, 2237
Chu, Arnold, 405
Chu, Chen, 1409, 5117
Chu, Elizabeth, 149
Chu, Ellin, 8778
Chu, Ken, 820
Chua, Carmina, 820
Chuckerman, Jill, 2946
Chulick, Ben, 6373
Chuma, Yoshiko, 492
Chumbler, Bert, 6206
Chun, Duane, 5982
Church, Ahkim, 5915, 5916
Church, Diane, 7454
Church, Jeff, 3286
Church, Julia, 5191
Churchill, Angeline, 1712
Churchill, Brittany K, 5997, 6000
Churchill, Holly, 1905
Churchill, Mark, 1182, 1197
Churchill, Natalie, 1918
Chute, Karen L., 6424
Chwalisz, John, 6530
Ciabattari, Becky, 1668
Cianchetta, Anthony, 7832
Ciancia, Carol, 2190
Ciani-Dausch, Jessica, 6469
Ciaravino, Asia, 4003
Ciarlillo, Marjorie Ann, 5315

Cibler, Stephanie, 213
Ciccitto, Frank, 1622
Ciccolella, Ann, 5589
Ciccone, Ted, 5979
Ciccone, Vito, 1493, 4361
Cichomska, Grace, 6820, 6821
Cichon, Ron, 6557
Cicolani, Angelo, 4421
Cieply, Jeff, 8667
Ciesla, Maria, 206, 2044, 2045
Cifuentes, PhD, Ines, 266
Cihlar, Meagan, 5854
Cika Heschmeyer, Aundrea, 546
Cilley, Brock, 4214
Cillo, Paul, 8845
Cilman, Wendy, 762
Cimaglia, Sharon, 3110
Ciminelli, Louis P., 1376
Cimprich, Ronnie, 4989, 7556
Cimyotte, Nick, 6327
Cinati, Michael, 3974
Cincone, Marc, 5084
Cioffi, Michael A., 1527
Cioffi,, Michael, 3454
Cion, Shira, 1894
Cioruttoli, Robert, 8190
Ciphers, Judith, 4257
Cipolla, Laurie, 1622
Cipolla, Vin, 393
Cipollini, Craig, 1986
Cipriano, Allen, 2713
Ciraldo, Desiree, 5343
Cirillo, Tom, 1606
Ciss, Idy, 208
Citron, Bea, 4467
Ciulla, Carol, 1208
Ciulla, John, 6269, 6270
Ciulla, Peter, 6115
Cizon, Frank A., 206, 2044, 2045
Claar, Kristina, 6099
Clabaugh, John, 1343
Clabby, Kathleen, 4362
Claflin, Megan, 5788, 5789, 5790
Clagett, Kay, 918
Clair, Jeffrey.T, 63
Clair, Whitney, 7961
Claire, Fred, 6210
Clancy, Adrienne, 264
Clancy, Jennifer, 264
Clanton, Byron, 5901, 5902, 5903, 5904
Clapham, John, 1261
Clapham, Nate, 6961, 6963, 6964, 6965
Clapp, Deb, 2697
Clapp, Sarah, 1244
Clarac, Jean-Philippe, 2231
Clare Allen, Anna, 2266
Claridge, Jon, 5725
Claridge, Jon Palmer, 5724
Clark, Andrew, 843
Clark, Annie, 14
Clark, Barbara, 651
Clark, Bill, 2235
Clark, Brandi, 6690, 6691, 6692, 6693, 6694
Clark, Bruce, 2360
Clark, C Jordan, 8226
Clark, Carolyn, 334
Clark, Casey, 7095
Clark, Chris, 1669
Clark, Constance, 1196
Clark, Darryl K., 7466
Clark, Dave, 5397
Clark, David, 2370
Clark, Dennis, 2969
Clark, Donna, 384
Clark, Dr. Leroy, 2797
Clark, Dwight, 8416
Clark, Ernest, 1217, 4813
Clark, Harry, 741
Clark, Jason, 8475
Clark, Jerald, 3480
Clark, Jessica, 263
Clark, Jocelyn, 722, 4160
Clark, John C, 4822
Clark, John C., 4770
Clark, John R, 8108
Clark, Judy, 3973
Clark, Karen, 1587
Clark, Kathy, 687, 4081

Clark, Katy, 1436, 1441
Clark, Lara D., 5797
Clark, Laurel, 2808
Clark, Lauren, 1273
Clark, Leroy, 2797
Clark, Lisa, 3706
Clark, Marilyn, 5607, 8364
Clark, Mark E, 2360
Clark, Marybeth, 8206
Clark, Matthew Cameron, 2894
Clark, Molly, 844
Clark, Mr. Laron, 8525
Clark, Natalie, 6581
Clark, Nate, 7262
Clark, Phyllis, 2224
Clark, Rendl, 6332
Clark, Richard Auldon, 1082
Clark, Richard, 6349
Clark, Robert W, 6189
Clark, Rod, 1156, 4113
Clark, Rodrigo Durte, 2577
Clark, Ron, 3028, 3038
Clark, Rusty, 1115, 1116
Clark, Sabrina, 4046
Clark, Sandi, 7171
Clark, Sandra, 6110, 6111, 6114
Clark, Stephen, 6158
Clark, Thomas, 1541
Clark, Tom, 8039, 8040
Clark, Tracy, 1008
Clark, Walter, 4281
Clark, Wayne, 6717
Clark, William, 1477
Clark Helzer, Katherine, 3491
Clark Ph.D, Donald, 5487
Clark-Carpenter, Karen, 3730
Clark-Getzin, Wendy, 1789
Clarke, Ashley, 6520
Clarke, Beth, 235
Clarke, Bill, 7879
Clarke, Carolyn, 35
Clarke, Donna, 7611
Clarke, Jerrie, 2421
Clarke, Melanie, 1341
Clarkin, Jared, 4120
Clarkson, Jackie, 3083, 7141
Clarkson, MD, Sarah B., 4046
Clary, Jennifer, 6372, 6375
Clary, Melissa, 127
Claus, Robert E, 393
Claus, Nathan K., 393
Clausen, Kyle, 2616, 6297
Claussen, Diane, 2965, 4577
Clautero Soto, Sarah, 51
Clavelli, Chris, 2779
Clavio, Laura, 4635
Clawson, Todd, 7515
Clay,, 824, 825
Clay, Carl, 3474
Clay, Derrick, 1545, 1546, 5326
Clay Love, Maggie, 1489
Clay Luedloff, Brian, 1958
Clayton, Dr. Jan, 8059
Clayton, Ellen, 2092
Clayton, J. Kerry, 3081, 7738, 7739
Clayton, Meaghan, 2953
Clayton, Sharon, 6567
Clayton Jr, John, 4379
Claytor, Nelson, 3967, 3975
Clazelle, Peter, 8503
Cleage, Pearl, 2857
Cleage, Pearle, 2857
Clear, Annette, 4270
Clear-Forest, Ivy, 248
Clearfield, Andrew, 406
Cleary, Pamela, 1309, 1310
Cleary, Robert E, 697
Cleary Griffiths, Sally, 1544
Cleary-Hague, Rosemary, 124
Clegg, Tim, 7434
Cleland, Carl, 1226
Cleman, Thomas, 4174
Clemens, Karyl, 1449
Clemens, Keith, 2851
Clemens, Stephanie, 219
Clement, Barbara, 1218
Clement, Leanne P., 2082
Clement, Nikki, 5343

Clement, Robert, 1504
Clement, Tamara, 755, 1784
Clements, Chelle, 812
Clements, Mark, 4124
Clements, Melaine A., 4995
Clements, Rene, 5081
Clements, Renie, 1026
Clements, Roger, 4905
Clemmens, Lisa, 1451
Clemmens, Thomas, 1451
Clemmer, Greg, 7872
Clemmer, Sid, 2360
Clemmons, Bennye H., 756
Clemmons, Laura, 1690
Clemmons, Tom, 1451
Clemons, Tiffany, 1698
Clephane, Connie, 4409
Clephane, Thoams, 4409
Clesse, Michelle, 4756
Cleve, George, 847, 4299
Cleveland, Carol, 5166, 7790
Clewell, Fred, 6203
Click, Blaine, 172
Clifford, Ed, 753, 3288
Clifford, Marie, 228
Clifford, Mike, 3437
Clifford, Steven A., 2387
Clift, Ryan, 1753
Clift George, Jeannette, 3980
Clifton, David, 5324
Cline, Caradee, 630
Cline, Caroline, 3058
Cline, Jesse, 3816
Cline, Judith, 5758
Cline, Keith, 678
Cline, Linda, 3770
Cline, Lt. Cmdr.Walt, 960, 961, 962, 963
Cline, Michael, 4906
Cline, Rob, 7004
Cline, Shannon, 1651
Cline, Susan, 5131
Clinger, Cliff, 7513
Clinkenbeard, Donna, 4634
Clinton, Angeline, 7867
Clinton, Holly, 1743
Clinton, Tom, 3204
Clissold, Joan, 2368
Clogg, Carrie, 4649
Clore, Cynthia, 6886
Close, Bill, 1226
Close, Don, 1359
Close, Jamie, 3284
Close, William, 4248
Cloud, John, 4183
Clough, John, 1849
Cloughly, Dr. Cecilia, 773
Clouse, Mike, 3870
Clow, Heather J., 7536
Clower, Thom, 633
Clowes, Kevin, 6076
Clubb, Sandy, 6986, 6987, 6988, 6989
Cluckerman, Jill, 2946
Cluff, Cheryln Ann, 4011
Clutter, William B, 5249
Clymer, Julia, 5941
Co Mather, Christina, 4434
Coakley, Brian, 334
Coakley, Jane, 1212
Coalmer, Lynn, 1733
Coan, Sandra, 8559
Coar, Constance, 5516
Coash, Tom, 4034
Coates, Bob, 1795
Coates, Elena, 3929
Coates, George, 2579
Coates, Tom, 4859
Coatsworth, John H, 1415
Cobb, Dana, 3960
Cobb, Dr. Gary, 808
Cobb, Elizabeth, 3269
Cobb, Joe, 1786
Cobb, Jon, 6841, 6842
Cobb, Katie, 729
Cobb, Kristin, 8205
Cobb, Rita, 6625
Cobb, Steve, 5937
Cobb, Susan, 3456
Cobbett,, Yasmine, 2812

Executive Name Index

Cobble, Julie, 333
Cobbs, Dr. Loma L, 1810
Cobbs, Dr. Paul-Elliot, 1810, 5809
Coble, Christine, 7277
Cobrda, Pauline, 3660
Coburn, Bob, 8037
Coburn, Jeff, 3143
Cobus, Tamara, 179
Cocciarelli, Leo, 7280
Cocco, Cathy, 5591
Cochran, Catherine, 1447
Cochran, Dr. Grant, 1844
Cochran, Dr. Jerry, 1504
Cochran, Dr. Teri, 3768
Cochran, Elle, 6680
Cochran, George, 428
Cochran, Harry, 6864
Cochran, Judy, 4675, 7041
Cochran, Kevin, 2454
Cochran, Lisa, 6687
Cochran, Michael, 3074
Cochran, Misty, 8302
Cochran, MUCM Mark C, 961
Cochran, Nancy, 6273
Cochran, Steve, 3582
Cock, Christopher M, 2068
Cockburn, Marilyn, 910
Cockburn, Mrs. Harold, 5665
Cocke, Dudley, 4047
Cockerham, Ann, 1609
Cockey, Jim, 2033
Cockrell, Maxine, 4166
Cockrell, Thomas, 4186
Cockriel, Torie, 7078, 7079
Cockrill, Chris, 6576
Cocuzza, Peter, 6771, 6772
Coddington, Dr.Jonathan A., 6459
Coddington, Jonathan A., 6461
Cody, Dr. Karen, 1747
Cody, Jeff, 3903
Cody, Raymond, 180
Coe, John G, 5879
Coe, NancyBell, 4323
Coelho Baisa, Gladys, 6680
Coen, Jeanne, 513
Coen, Stephanie, 3384
Cofer, Dr R Shayne, 6748, 6750
Cofer Sr, James E, 7134
Coffey, Ashley, 5643
Coffey, Diane M, 7729
Coffey, Erin, 4777
Coffey, Mary Ruth, 2905
Coffey, Richard, 1966
Coffey, Suzanne, 7216
Coffin, David, 4783
Coffin, Don, 3756
Coffin, G Christopher, 1056
Coffin, Jed, 4256
Coffman, David, 4309, 6262
Coffman, Peter, 4504
Cogan, Brian, 7645
Cogdill, Sharon, 1269
Coggin, Steve, 7913
Coggins, APR, Nancy, 3760
Coglan, Michael, 3184, 3473
Cogmann, Don, 4173
Cogswell, Ann, 2168
Cohan, Art, 6073
Cohan, Mattie, 952
Cohan, Muriel, 237
Cohen, Aaron, 1325
Cohen, Andrew, 3866, 4248
Cohen, Barrie, 4085
Cohen, Becky, 1858
Cohen, Benjamin, 104
Cohen, Bruce, 2848
Cohen, Dr. Erik, 2603
Cohen, Francine Garber, 2206
Cohen, Gary, 3363
Cohen, Herbert A, 1174
Cohen, Howard, 3291
Cohen, Ira, 757
Cohen, Irwin, 1294
Cohen, Jeremy, 3252
Cohen, Jerry, 6039
Cohen, Joel, 2104, 5093
Cohen, Judith, 5795
Cohen, Kate, 5204

Cohen, Lillian Z., 5167
Cohen, Lily, 414
Cohen, Louis R., 2736, 2737, 6467
Cohen, Marc, 2397
Cohen, Marcy, 7211
Cohen, Miles, 1645, 5480
Cohen, Rachel, 379
Cohen, Richard, 6329
Cohen, Richie, 1945
Cohen, Saul, 4729
Cohen, Sissie, 1200
Cohen, Steve, 1408
Cohen, Sue, 3705
Cohen, Victor, 5908
Cohen, Warren, 1856
Cohen,, EJ, 3343
Cohen-Cruz, Jan, 4047
Cohn, Alan D, 7729
Cohn, Diana, 6267
Cohn, Donald, 2565
Cohn, Donna, 4178
Cohn, Fred, 1411
Cohn, George L, 3177
Cohn, James, 1381
Cohn, Lois, 5096, 5097
Cohn, Sally, 3151
Cohn, Tara, 7733
Coil, Scott, 679
Coker, Alan, 8233
Coker, Tim, 2401
Colacci, David, 3206
Colaccino, Frank, 7250
Colahan, Nancy, 2612
Colamarino, Rob, 8297
Colbert, Brandi, 5957
Colbert, Clint, 5957
Colbert, John, 941
Colbert, MM, 699
Colbert, Soyica, 6479
Colby, Michael, 8686
Colclough, Tracy, 293
Cole, C. Kenneth, 3021
Cole, Carol, 4101
Cole, Colleen, 2336, 2339
Cole, Darlene, 8253
Cole, Doug, 5355
Cole, Elizabeth, 2251
Cole, J T, 1856
Cole, Joan B, 8107
Cole, Kathy, 6254
Cole, Margi, 202
Cole, Mark, 2430
Cole, Mica, 2932
Cole, Monty, 6760
Cole, Morgan, 2009
Cole, Rachel, 5954
Cole, Rhodes M., 2853
Cole, Richard, 2579
Cole, Robert, 759, 761, 4205, 4207
Cole, Robert W, 4203
Cole, Robin, 349
Cole, Sara K., 8083
Cole, Skip, 3098
Cole, Susan, 7596
Cole, Susan A., 3391
Cole, Suzanne, 1096
Cole, Thomas H, 6194
Cole, William, 2273, 2280
Cole Dostie, Marilyn, 1217
Colegrove, Kathryn, 3916
Colehower, Beth, 112
Coleman, Alice, 822
Coleman, Barbara, 2976
Coleman, Brenda, 4342
Coleman, Bud, 2647, 4363
Coleman, Chris, 3885
Coleman, Darrell, 1708
Coleman, Eric, 3496
Coleman, FR, 2976
Coleman, Freddie, 2386
Coleman, Jackie, 6415, 6416
Coleman, Jim, 2628
Coleman, Karen, 7686
Coleman, Kevin, 5002
Coleman, Marjorie, 2740
Coleman, Mary, 4709
Coleman, Mary Sue, 7265, 7266, 7267, 7269
Coleman, Michael, 1207

Coleman, Randall, 4155, 5926, 5928
Coleman, Rashida, 954
Coleman, RJ, 2914
Coleman, Ronald, 5575
Coleman, Roquita, 5575
Coleman, Stacey, 2896
Coleman, Terry, 4182
Coleman, Ed.D., Ruthe, 2199
Coleman-Heppler, Jason, 4091
Coler, Douglas, 2491
Coles, Diana, 3627
Colett, Shae, 78
Coley, Al, 3606
Coley, Melissa, 5139, 5170
Colf, Howard, 4330
Colfer, David, 3178, 4808
Colglazier, Dr. R Scott, 802
Colglazier, Phillip, 3009
Coll, Margy, 3373
Collard, Beverly, 1903
Colleary, Eric, 3728
Colledge, Jacqueline P, 650
Colleen, Metzger, 2418
Collesano, Leona, 6585
Collet, Jim, 1682
Collett-O'Brien, Debbie, 5048
Collette, Rochelle, 4662
Colletti, Ned, 6156
Colley, Lynn A, 3307
Collier, David, 8301
Collier, E M, 5920
Collier, J. Allen, 273
Collier, Jeff, 2642
Collier, Jeffery, 1621
Collier, Katherine, 918
Collier, Mark, 5292
Collier, Miles C., 6592, 6593
Collier, Richard, 1952
Collier, Winston, 1522
Collier III, William H., 3438
Colligan, Kelly, 6558
Collings, Richard, 7504
Collings, W. Zane, 6529
Collins, Bill, 1247, 1248, 1739, 4856, 7317
Collins, Brooke, 2932
Collins, Camara, 3688
Collins, Deb, 6298
Collins, Dennis, 8611
Collins, Dick, 5221
Collins, Don, 8405
Collins, Eilizabeth, 2522
Collins, Elsbeth M., 2519
Collins, Greg, 5648
Collins, Hilda, 5079
Collins, James, 895
Collins, James L, 6839
Collins, James L., 4600
Collins, Jennifer, 2225
Collins, Jim, 3021
Collins, Jody, 7074
Collins, John, 6481
Collins, John W, 5732
Collins, Judy, 7057
Collins, Justine, 2431
Collins, Kevin, 8322
Collins, Laurie, 3753
Collins, Leon, 2033
Collins, Lyman, 7864
Collins, Noreen, 7644
Collins, Philip, 1718
Collins, Rachel, 6025
Collins, Rives, 4577
Collins, Roger B., 8058
Collins, Russ, 7270
Collins, Russell, 7270
Collins, Sheila, 581
Collins, Steve, 944, 1890, 6753
Collins, Susan, 973
Collins, Walter, 889
Collins PhD, Mary Ella, 8904
Collinson, Lynne, 3865, 4043
Collmann, Fran, 2338
Collver, Larry, 8082
Colman, Bruce, 2583
Colman, AIA, David L., 3836
Colom, Alejandro, 3988
Colon, Gretchen, 1556
Colon, Jackie, 6415

Colon Lespier, Alvan, 3415
Colon Valle, Miriam, 3553
Colonna, Tom, 3115
Colopy, Brian, 7275
Colosa Lucas, Stacey, 2855
Colosi, Michael, 2237
Colpitts, Phyllis, 8717
Colson, Darrel, 4667, 7026, 7027
Colson, David J, 6083
Colson, William, 8389
Columbus, Curt, 3864
Colvin, Sandy, 4137
Colwell, Denis, 5489
Colwell, Nevada, 7515
Colwill, Dana, 7162, 7163, 7164
Comalli Dillon, Kathleen, 887
Combar, Natalie T., 1473
Combopiano, Charles, 2287
Combs, Ann, 8026
Combs, Cory, 4309, 4312
Combs, Jayna, 5934
Combs, Ken, 5416
Combs, Linda, 342
Combs, Marlon, 7573
Combs, Mary E, 886
Combs, Mike, 8618
CombsCannaday, Syreeta, 3796
Comeau, L Renee, 1909
Comer, George, 6395
Comer, Lisa, 3788
Comess, Linda, 3944
Comet, Jeff, 3632
Companioni, Lisbet, 11
Compson, Robert, 3733
Compton, Carol, 2369, 5704
Compton, Casey, 3617
Compton, Jenny, 1695
Compton, Mary, 1750
Compton, Nancy, 5521
Compton, Salli, 2170
Compton, Taylor, 6358
Comstock, Allan, 1118
Conant, Dawn, 2477
Conant, Nancy, 1392
Conant, Robert, 1392, 5083
Conard, Jon, 8113
Conaty, Donna, 4291
Conaway, Robert, 8655
Conboy, Roy, 2589
Concilla, Scott Skip, 2312
Concra, Joseph, 2256
Condeluci, Annette, 1637
Condemi, Jose Maria, 1931
Condit, David, 959, 1994
Condon, Andrew, 1119
Condon, Karl, 618
Condrey, John, 7915
Cone, Margaret, 2167
Coners, Daniel, 5084
Confessore, Christopher, 975
Conforti, Michael, 7259
Congo, Andrea, 5382
Congress, Sarah, 4997
Conjura, Vivienne, 3639
Conklin, Chaunce, 2971
Conklin, Elizabeth, 2031
Conklin, Jacqui, 8141
Conley, Claire, 2934
Conley, Julie, 1815
Conley, Kim, 3700, 7082
Conley, Marnie, 5459
Conley, Patrick, 6303
Conley, Tim, 3121
Conlin, Cathleen, 5682
Conlon, James, 4243, 4581, 5304
Conlon, Julia, 1257
Conlon, Timothy J., 4652
Conn, Paul, 5562
Connard, Jennie, 2621
Conneely, Natalie, 2498
Connell, Donna, 3994
Connell, Elaine, 4307, 4315, 4316
Connell, Kelley, 601
Connell, Lynn, 2025
Connell, Mitch, 3994
Conneley, Maureen, 8116
Connelly, Bill, 7956
Connelly, Edward, 4017

Executive Name Index

Connelly, Larry, 3935
Connelly, Laura, 792
Connelly, Michelle, 5174
Conner, Carol, 984
Conner, Chris, 3716
Conner, Christiana, 2059
Conner, Jeanine, 2508
Conner, Kaye Ellen, 1078
Conner, Lynne, 7182
Conner, Margie, 5885
Conner, W. D., 5539
Conner, William B, 5325
Conner Jr, Cecil C, 638
Conner, Jr., William B., 2282, 2283
Conners, Jeanne, 1566
Connnolly, Mike, 7166
Connolly, Craig, 4004
Connolly, Janet, 7474
Connor, Catherine M, 2262
Connor, Shane, 519
Connor, Shane, 7968
Connor, Sue, 626
Connor, Zenobia, 3421
Connor-Linton, Jeffery, 6469
Connors, Austin, 3816
Connors, Kevin, 2718
Connors, Price, 1576
Conoley Taberiou, Curby, 2339
Conoley Tableriou, Curby, 2336
Conors Jr, Martin J., 4140
Conover, Patricia, 686
Conquist, Robert, 1567
Conquist, Robert L, 1556
Conrad, Beth, 1080
Conrad, Cecilia, 6086
Conrad, Colette, 6870
Conrad, Eric, 6717
Conrad, Gordon, 1213
Conrad, Lois V, 2380
Conrad, Richard, 2679
Conrad, Rodney, 7952
Conran, Donna, 3088
Conrick, Sharon, 5081
Conroy, Annemarie, 6249
Conroy, Dorothy, 7839
Conroy, Nick, 6560
Conry, Randal, 5671, 8464
Consolazio, Joseph, 7554
Consolo, Frank, 5513
Consort, Folger, 2736
Consort, Pierrot, 5055
Constable, Robert C, 4481
Constance, Danielle, 3370
Constantine, Andrew, 1080, 1661
Contavesprie, Leon, 3083, 7141
Conte, Anthony, 7656
Conte, John, 2696
Conti, Laura, 5718
Conti, Louis, 5145
Conti, William, 8025
Contino, Bobbie, 5243
Contino, Fiora, 2057
Contos, Laura, 8015
Contos, Paul, 4255
Contreni, John J., 6948, 6951
Conver, Rita, 7500
Convey, Bridget, 2087
Conville, William, 2315
Conway, Chip, 6351
Conway, Eileen, 3905
Conway, Ellena, 1807
Conway, Gerald, 1253
Conway, Lois, 2225
Conway, Michael K., 5099
Conway, Mikka Gee, 6158
Conway, Paul B, 3676
Conway, Scott, 5661
Conway, Terry, 90, 94
Conway, Vicki J, 5674
Conyers, Chris, 6985
Cooangelo, Jerry, 5976
Coogan, Anna, 1076
Coogan, Janice, 4999
Coogan, Sean, 2466
Coogan, Susan, 670
Cook, Al, 4179
Cook, Alisa, 3622, 5205
Cook, Allison, 765

Cook, Antoinette, 975
Cook, Brian, 2420
Cook, Bridget A, 3836
Cook, Carol, 4942
Cook, Cindy, 434
Cook, Clide, 6145
Cook, Colleen, 1558
Cook, Connie G, 4369
Cook, Cynthia, 1794
Cook, Dave, 7043
Cook, David, 4783
Cook, Debra M, 1014
Cook, Elaine, 1128
Cook, Erin, 2952
Cook, Gale, 7330
Cook, Glade, 504
Cook, H Richard, 1028
Cook, H. Richard, 1028
Cook, HR, 7061
Cook, Jennifer, 4374, 6944
Cook, Jon, 6281
Cook, Julia, 2261
Cook, Lakin, 8627
Cook, Larry E., 6646
Cook, Lin, 1658
Cook, Lisa, 1680
Cook, Nancy, 3461, 7630
Cook, Patty, 4138
Cook, Peter C., 339
Cook, Rachel, 8404
Cook, Richard, 5468
Cook, Sally, 971
Cook, Stephen, 4349
Cook, Steven, 6410
Cook, Tamara, 724
Cook, Terri, 4317
Cook, Terry, 1799
Cook, Thomas, 1227
Cook Glover, Rosemarie, 765
Cooke, Ann, 2686
Cooke, Brendan, 1980
Cooke, Debbie, 1779
Cooke, Samuel A., 6673
Cooksey, William, 7158
Cook, Dr. Carey, 6704, 6707
Cool, Andrea, 2554
Cool, Michael, 7582
Coolen, Richard, 2381
Cooley, Beatrice, 726
Cooley, Pamela, 5179
Coolich, Stephanie, 6247
Coombs, Chris, 4061
Coombs, Jackie, 3284
Coombs, Rene,, 5087
Coombs, Steven, 7217
Coon, Susan, 5236
Coonc, Aliana, 1788
Coonet, Christopher, 6700
Cooney Frelinghuysen, Alice, 8509
Cooney O'Hara, Theresa, 4779
Coons, Carol, 5173
Coons, Edgar E, 5110
Coons, William, 5173
Coope, Helen, 131, 132
Cooper, Amanda, 3498
Cooper, Beverly, 2877
Cooper, Bruce, 2320
Cooper, Connie, 5800
Cooper, David, 576
Cooper, David J., 2105
Cooper, Elizabeth, 2339
Cooper, Farobaghomi, 4560
Cooper, Frank, 4621
Cooper, Grant, 1468, 1469
Cooper, Hal, 6049
Cooper, Jeffrey A., 6635
Cooper, Jennifer, 1916
Cooper, Jill, 6853
Cooper, Joeseph, 3988
Cooper, John, 4013, 4015, 4468
Cooper, Jon, 5374
Cooper, Kate, 4883, 4884
Cooper, Krista, 1256
Cooper, Lonnie, 478
Cooper, Lorraine, 394
Cooper, Maggie, 533
Cooper, Marlene, 6471
Cooper, Martha, 7739

Cooper, Paula, 1373
Cooper, Philip, 5271
Cooper, Roger, 3488
Cooper, S. Harry, 2085
Cooper, Simone, 411
Cooper, Steve, 3426, 4089
Cooper, Steven, 2612
Cooper, Suzanne, 8326
Cooper, Teresa, 1584
Cooper, William, 8555
Cooper Albright, Ann, 539
Cooper Holmes, Janice, 166
Coors, Dabney, 8286
Copaken, Bunni, 3289
Cope, Kathy A., 7994
Cope, Kevin, 1154
Cope, Shirley, 5545
Copeland, Joanne, 2166
Copeland, Nathan, 4500
Copeland, Rene, 3915, 3919
Copeland, Scot, 3916
Copeland, Tatiana, 949
Copenhaver, Ida, 1548
Copland, Andrea, 6356, 6364
Copley, Bob, 2709
Copley, Tom, 1300
Copp, Carolyn, 1202
Copp, David, 873
Coppel, Claude, 4220
Copper, Andrew, 5167
Copper, Don, 2930
Copperman, Jack, 1812
Copple, Barry, 8122
Coppleson, Joan, 2923, 6734
Coppock, Ada, 3836
Coppock, Bruce, 1272, 1535
Coppock, Paula, 3766, 8047
Coppola, Anton, 1629
Coppola, Camille, 2213
Coppola, Louis J., 3825, 3837, 5474
Coquilette, Kenneth, 6879, 6880, 6881
Coranado, Vince, 6288
Corbett, Jeffrey A., 1500
Corbett, Robb, 8088
Corbett, Sally, 4507, 6620
Corbin, Heather A., 8008
Corbin, Les, 770
Corbin, Paula, 6710
Corbin, Paula, 6711, 6712, 6715, 6716
Corbin, R Richard, 5095
Corbin, Richard, 1396, 5095
Corbin, Ron, 8303, 8304
Corboy, Alix, 1470
Corcoran, Francine, 3256
Corcoran, Megan, 229
Corcoran, Rosemary, 3739
Cordell, Janet, 1578
Cordell Avis, Pamela, 2327
Cordes, Lisa, 4903
Cordice, Keisha, 5957
Cordick, Stephanie, 5244
Cordick, Stephanie B., 5244
Cordier, Gloria, 5957
Cordini, Salvatore, 2003
Cordova, Al, 6122
Cordova, Chris, 5027
Cordova, Tish, 660
Core, Gary, 5244
Coretti, Lola, 1877
Corey, April, 4848
Corey, Carl, 2126
Corey, Dean, 794, 4229
Corey, Winthrop, 4
Corfman, Patty, 2277
Corham, Albert C, 3417
Corkran, Dee, 3058
Corkwell, Patty, 4833, 7280
Corl, Chris, 7853
Corley, Dr. Sheila, 5967
Corley, Kathleen, 1682
Corley, Richard, 4115
Corman, Joel, 1203
Cormier, Giselle, 7125
Cornacchia, John, 6186
Cornachio, Anthony, 5076
Corneil, Mary, 1122
Cornejo, Abel, 2797
Cornejo, Gisselle, 6164, 6179

Cornejo, Sam, 6064
Cornelison, Gayle, 2633
Cornelius, Emily, 1543
Cornelius, Marti, 6942
Cornelius, Rita, 4900
Cornelius, Sigmund L., 3990
Cornelius-Ochs, Cheryl, 1585
Cornell, Allen D, 2836, 6600
Cornell, Anne, 7988
Cornell, Dennis, 6154, 6171, 6176
Cornell, Heather, 505
Cornell, Julie, 2113
Corner, William, 1905
Cornet, Jennifer, 319
Cornez, Gerry, 3461
Corning, Beth, 579, 3842
Cornwell, Ed, 3664
Cornwell, Grant, 2290
Cornwell, John M., 3986
Cornwell, Karen, 1026
Corpus, Conrad, 2575
Corr, Melissa, 127
Corral, Teresita, 1720
Corrao, Kathy, 8508
Corren, Talia, 3568
Corrente, Judith-Anne, 2234
Corrick, Jeffery, 3591
Corrie, John, 1147, 2087
Corrigan, Robert, 2589
Corrigan, Nick, 4335
Corriveau, MA, MFA, Jeff, 4045
Corroa, Anthony, 1703
Corry, Betsy, 4120
Corry, Britton, 6590, 6591
Corsett, Bob, 3629
Corsi, Fred, 7456
Corsi, Rich, 5325
Cort, Susan, 1629
Cortelyou, Don, 2908
Cortes Jr, Pedro, 300
Cortese, Federico, 1180
Cortese, Glen, 913
Cortese, Phyllis, 6396
Corlez, Dave, 4002
Corti, Jim, 6719
Cortis, Jack, 2573
Cortner, Hann, 726
Cortot, Diana, 2215
Cortright, Joanna, 7357
Corvino, Andra, 422
Corvino, Ernesta, 422
Corwin, Aarone, 8036
Corwin, JoBeth, 1640
Corwin, Kara, 7335
Cosby, Dawn, 7462
Cosby, Susan, 551
Coscia, Carlos, 1724
Cosenza, Lucia, 6549
Cosgrove, Sue, 79
Cosgroze, Patricia, 7559
Cosley, Jeanette, 3984
Cosman, Denise, 6730
Cosnow, Iris, 1052
Cossa, Joanne, 5164
Costa, Collin, 5129
Costa, Cynthia, 6658, 6659
Costa, Jorge, 6251
Costa, Michael, 850
Costantini, Cathy, 4122
Costantino, Jenny, 185
Costanza, Christine, 6085
Costanza, Kristin, 8572
Costello, Alison, 3601
Costello, Ann, 3446
Costello, Jackie, 6698
Costello, Josh, 2447
Costello, Kathleen, 2609
Costello, Mark, 2843, 6611
Costello, Stephen, 8687
Costello, Suzanne, 298
Costello, Wanell, 4171, 5962
Cota, Joe, 7172, 7173
Cothran, Laurie, 1549, 1550
Cotner, Michele, 3699
Cotnoir, Tracy, 8907
Cotter, Ardice, 4719, 7150, 7151
Cotter, Donna, 5584
Cotter, Patti, 4637

1153

Executive Name Index

Cottingham, Jennifer, 380
Cottingham, Michael, 1275, 1276
Cottingham, Tura, 6850
Cottle, Megan, 1
Cotton, Bill, 2415
Cotton, Jilissa, 8345
Cottongim, Paul, 6621
Cottrell-Adkins, Leone, 2381
Couch, Guy, 15
Couch, Suzanne, 3301
Couch, Taylor, 3850
Coughenour, Rebecca, 138
Coughlan, Pauline, 2974
Coughlin, Cynthia, 47, 753
Coughlin, Dennis, 7185
Coughlin, Kathleen, 1371
Coulam Addison, Michelle, 1764
Coulson, Amanda, 322
Coulter, Flossie, 4249
Coulter, Ken, 4249
Coulter, Martha, 3048
Coulter, Todd, 7182
Coulthard, Anita, 5733
Countermine, Terry, 5569
Countryman, John, 2802
Counts, Dr. Michael L., 2432
Counts, Jackie, 5542
Counts, Michael L, 2432
Counts, Paulett S., 5056
Counts, Paulette S., 374, 3423
Counts, Wynnifred, 8289
Couret, Keiron, 4704
Courneen, Sister JoAnne K, 8123
Court, Joe, 6915, 6916, 6917, 6918
Courtade, Marc, 5084, 7678
Courtney, Courtney, 4716
Courtney, Janice, 4881
Courtney, Michael, 6960
Courtney Connolly, Evonne, 3120
Courtway, Tom, 4185, 6018, 6019, 6020
Coussens, Jeffrey L, 6825, 6827
Couture, Raymond, 2547
Couturiaux, Clay, 1745
Covach, John, 1462
Covan, Ellie, 3483
Covault, Jim, 3967, 3968, 3975
Coven, Richard, 4615
Coverdale, Thad, 1174
Covey, David, 527
Covington, Coline, 3859
Covington, Douglas, 5751, 8546
Covington, Joan, 1267
Covington, Robert A., 4280
Covington, Jr, Howard E, 1495
Covitz, Aviva, 2639
Covollmer, Erich, 2198
Covrest, Keiron, 4704
Cowan, Linda, 8568
Cowan, Ricard, 53
Coward, Charles, 6464, 6466, 6470
Cowart, Melanie, 5663, 8450, 8451
Cowart, Steed, 4260, 6198
Cowden, Richard R, 2671
Cowden, Richard R., 6377, 6378, 6380
Cowee, Bill, 3336
Cowell, Sylvia, 6450
Cowin, Sylvia, 2337
Cowling, Judy, 1092
Cowperthwaite, Janet, 846
Cox, Adam W., 3239
Cox, Barbara J., 4751
Cox, Barbara.J, 1156
Cox, Benjamin, 6490
Cox, Bruce, 1788
Cox, Bud, 1556
Cox, Carrie, 527
Cox, Cathy, 6667, 6668
Cox, David M., 6377, 6378, 6380
Cox, Donnie, 7138
Cox, Douglas, 5716
Cox, Douglas D., 2099
Cox, Helene, 690
Cox, Jane, 6953, 6954, 6955, 6956, 6957, 6958, 6959
Cox, Jasper, 7208
Cox, John, 5335, 7992
Cox, Julia D, 1181
Cox, Julia D., 2106
Cox, Julie, 3269
Cox, Katherine, 8634
Cox, Katie, 6528
Cox, Lori, 7474
Cox, Matt, 6520
Cox, Misty, 5335, 7992
Cox, Putter, 7666
Cox, Robert, 4442
Cox, Sherry, 4407
Cox, Tom, 1365
Cox, Tommy, 2869
Cox Dunwody, Eugene, 1012
Coxey, Clare D, 230
Coxwell, Margi, 1956
Coykendall, John, 7046
Coyle, Ashley, 6254
Coyle, Peter, 5235
Coyne, Alexa, 5126
Coyne, Butch, 6289, 6290
Coyne Katayama, Alyce, 5856
Coyote, Peter, 2591
Cozine, Sabrina, 1313
Crabb, Theodore, 4117
Crabill, Casey, 3380
Crabtree, Dawn, 3066
Crabtree, Dr Kacy, 7855
Crabtree, Jim, 3895
Crabtree, LeAnne, 6528
Crade, Kathy, 32
Craft, Chris, 5353
Craft, Chris, 6516
Craft, Mart K., 5806
Craft. Jr., Randal R., 466
Crafton, Donald, 3021
Crager, Adora, 2181
Crager, Heidi, 8127
Cragin Day, Chris, 3512
Crai, Nicki, 6430
Craig, Alonzo, 4502
Craig, Anthony, 354
Craig, Arnold, 1106
Craig, Cari, 813
Craig, Carol, 3027
Craig, Marilyn, 3767
Craig, Mimi, 3503
Craig, Ronda, 8187
Craig, JoAnne, 6644
Crain, Cathy, 5305
Crain, Rob, 8142
Craioveanu, Mihai, 1239
Cramer, Alexandra, 2185
Cramer, Alexandra H., 2185
Cramer, Anne E., 7545
Cramer, Brany, 8014
Cramer, Cassia N., 528
Cramer, Chris, 6245, 6248
Cramer, Dan, 7353, 7354
Cramer, John, 4136
Cramer, John F., 5800
Cramer, Karen, 1749
Cramer, Lauren B, 497
Cramer, Oneida, 1713
Cramer, Terry, 2419
Cramer, Trevor, 4482
Cramer, Zach, 2589
Crandall, Jillian, 899
Crandall, Leo, 5208
Crandall, Lucas, 203
Crandall, Rachel, 2612
Crandell, Kelly, 2185
Crane, Gene C., 4148, 5915, 5916
Crane, Steve, 7175
Crane, Tony, 112
Cranford, Ereka, 7871
Cranmer, Terri, 4177, 5986
Cranson, Todd, 4189
Crary, Laura M, 3164
Craton, Marie, 4937
Craven, Jerard-James, 3093
Craven, Jr, COL Grover O, 8529
Cravens, John, 3950
Cravey, Claudia, 174
Cravota, Jeff, 506
Crawford, Bill, 8287
Crawford, Brett Ashley, 3122
Crawford, Bruce, 715
Crawford, Carol I, 2297
Crawford, Christina L., 5927, 5930
Crawford, Delores, 8021
Crawford, Eddie, 7858
Crawford, Ereka, 7870
Crawford, Jeri, 1313
Crawford, Jonnell, 4545
Crawford, Joy, 7290
Crawford, Lauren, 2427
Crawford, Lisa, 1493
Crawford, Paul, 1795
Crawford, Remmie, 1537
Crawford, Sally, 1745
Crawford, Shawn, 4045
Crawford, Sonni, 6942
Crawford, Suzanne, 866, 867
Crawford, Teresa, 6456, 6457
Crawford, Thomas, 924
Crawford III, William, 5947
Crawl, Chris, 4613
Crawley, Dr Vernon O, 6813
Crayton, Kenny, 5887
Creach, Terry, 408
Creamer III, Anthony B., 1406
Crecelius, Kathryn J., 7191, 7192
Cree, Christopher, 1797
Creech, Nancy, 4058
Creed Barros, Margaret, 5718
Creed Maxey, Michael, 5759
Cregan, Erin, 1453
Creighton, Margaret, 3762
Creighton, Robert C., 1401
Creighton, Scott, 2995
Crellin, Justin, 4278, 4279, 6219
Cremata, Alfonso, 2798
Crenca, Umberto, 8195
Cress, Donald, 5858
Cress, Donald A., 4122
Creveling, John, 996
Crew, Shirly, 601
Crews, Cynthia, 238
Crews, Emily, 143, 144
Crews, Lionel, 5573
Crews, Robin, 7886
Crickard, Lewis, 4965
Crider, Cheryl, 2304
Criggs, Dave, 3278
Crilly, Taunya, 3397, 3398
Cripps, David, 2356
Cripps, Lori, 4207
Criscuolo, Lou, 3684
Crisman, Bob, 6706
Criss, Kelly, 4032
Crist, Lou, 8074
Crist, Mary, 8091
Crist, Shane, 1242
Cristofer, Michael, 3412
Criswell, Amaya, 196
Criswell, Cathy, 6541, 6542
Criswell, Rick, 6595
Critchley Pittman, Ellen, 1571
Crittell, Dr. Margaret, 247
Crittenden, Alan, 2320
Crneckiy, Marty, 8704
Crnko, Joseph, 2384
Croak, Robert, 8036
Crocco, Italo, 7520
Crock, Stefanie, 3929
Crockard III, James E., 582
Crocker, Bill, 1026
Crocker, Carol, 64, 2271
Crocker, Deborah, 576
Crocker, Dr. Ron, 1302
Crocker, Patty, 4517
Crocker, Therese, 1737
Crocker, Warner, 4042
Crockett, Julie, 6825, 6826, 6827
Crockett, Vicki, 750
Crockett, Ph. D, Susan J., 2147, 4873
Croen, Evan, 2246
Crofford, Danny-Joe, 6039
Crofoot-Ritchey, Tjasa, 568
Crofton, Susan, 8679
Croft, Jim, 7258
Croghan, Jack, 7458
Croiter, Jeff, 434
Croken, Pete, 6026
Croll, Emily, 4991
Cromarty, Peter, 2239
Cromin, Timothy, 8620
Cromley, Robert, 606, 610
Crompton, Peter, 50
Cromwell, Esq., Bbrian S., 1485
Croner, Harry, 885
Cronin, David, 4783
Cronin, Judy, 2352
Cronin, Karl, 51
Cronin, Robert Jay, 3491
Cronk, Dan, 4828
Cronk, Daniel, 4828
Croog, Elizabeth A., 4416, 4429
Crook, David, 3678
Crook, Terri, 2563
Cropp, Hal, 3232
Cropper, Dennis, 4038, 4039
Crosbie, Kate, 5826
Crosby, Denise, 47
Crosby, Emily, 8508
Crosby, Heidi, 743
Crosby, Helen, 790
Crosby, Julie, 3593
Crosby, Pamela, 3915
Crosby, S, 5041
Crosby, Shareen, 2415
Cross, Angie, 6991
Cross, Loretta, 1732
Cross, Maureen, 1701, 5588
Cross, Mike, 6204
Cross, Nancy, 6952
Cross, Robert W, 5749
Cross, Ruth, 1729
Cross, Samantha, 6887
Crossland, Merle, 4595
Crothers, Nina, 921
Crothers, Shannon M., 6332
Crotty, Amanda, 2377
Crouch, Dollie, 4705
Crouch, Jordan, 2778
Crouch, Julie, 5669
Crouse, Dan, 6201
Crouse, Karen, 1030
Crouter, Jan, 1812
Crow, Genevia, 5654
Crow, Laura, 2711
Crow, Michael M, 736, 737
Crow, Micheal, 4177
Crow, Todd, 4737
Crow, Tom, 5644
Crow, Wanda, 5609, 5611
Crowder, Ryan, 3931
Crowe, Becky, 1311
Crowe, Brian B., 4998
Crowe, George, 2581
Crowe, Jim, 488
Crowe, Stefanie, 612
Crowell, Cindy, 6201
Crowell, Jen, 4814
Crowell, Stuart, 4976
Crowell, Stuart, 7581
Crowell Sawyer, Cathey, 4100
Crowley, Barb, 3855
Crowley, Cassandra, 513
Crowley, Chris, 8494, 8495
Crowley, Elecia, 2020
Crowley, Kayle, 6441
Crowley, Michael, 6197
Crowley, Peter, 7225
Crowley, Robert, 3855
Crowley, Terry, 4689
Crown, a Steven, 217
Crownover, Desha, 2567
Crowson, Marcella, 3786
Crowson, Patrick, 394
Croy, Scott, 3996
Cruise, David, 6146
Crum, Jane Ann, 3593
Crum, Michael E, 7870, 7871
Crumb, Cynthia, 1778
Crumb, Jake, 7165
Crumb, Michael, 8051
Crumbo, Kevin, 1696
Crump, Robert, 2217
Cruse, Mark, 8233
Cruser, Sally, 6703
Cruser, Sally J., 4537
Cruszewski, Jeff, 3738
Crutcher, Jennifer, 7095
Cruz, David, 977

Executive Name Index

Cruz, Miguel, 2178
Cruz, Pat, 4756
Cruz, Patricia, 7707
Cruz, Rosaura, 3950
Cruz, Terru, 6456
Cruz De Jesus, Enrique, 384
Csepel, Lenore de, 925
Csoboth, Gail, 249
Cuatto, Dianna, 253
Cubbage, Linda, 1576
Cuccaro, Christine, 7261
Cucurello, Edward R., 149
Cucuzzella, Tony, 2567
Cudahy, Michael, 8690, 8692
Cuddy, Mark, 3609
Cuepara, Laura, 2666
Cuesta, Carlo, 3971
Cueva, Roberto, 1907
Cueva, Ryan, 4222
Cughbert, Jim, 5195
Cukken, Kim, 356
Culbersom, Pam, 2879
Culbert, John, 2924
Culbertson, James, 902
Culbertson, Myrna, 4667
Culhane, Danielle, 818
Culhane, Sandra, 2166
Culick, Fritzie, 826
Culick, Liza, 4327
Cull, Christopher, 2717
Cullar, John, 1756
Cullem, Catherine, 2296
Cullen, James D., 2387
Cullen, Kelli, 6446
Cullen, Sean, 96
Culler, Lori, 6886
Culler, Ted, 3131
Culley, Jane, 3467
Culley, Joe, 3005
Cullin, Richard, 8226
Cullinan, Deborah M., 6267
Cullinan, Mary, 8061, 8064
Cullinane, Dennis, 6900
Cullison, Stacy, 4293
Cullum, Bonnie, 3934
Culmo, Meg, 6438
Culp, Thomas, 4303
Culp, Jr., H. Lawrence, 4758
Culpepper, J.Pamela, 634
Culshaw, Denise, 296
Culton, Jim, 2812
Culver, Daniel, 1063
Culver, Dr. Daniel, 2059
Culver, Sherry, 715
Cumbaa, Charlie, 1678
Cumbo, Willie A, 7926
Cumming, Don, 2520
Cumming, Edward, 928, 4390
Cumming, Joan, 841
Cumming, Richard, 1956
Cummings, Brian, 7941
Cummings, Cary, 7462
Cummings, Don, 2520
Cummings, Dorothea, 891
Cummings, Elissa, 324
Cummings, Kay, 371
Cummings, Kaye, 4905
Cummings, Kelly A., 4592
Cummings, Lindsay, 2711
Cummins, Doug, 753
Cummins, Sharon, 4641, 6967, 6969, 6971
Cummins, Stephen, 2055, 6789, 6790, 6791
Cummiskey PhD, Raymond V, 6792
Cunha, Tony, 4688
Cuningham, Joesph, 1461
Cunnigham, Bill, 1942
Cunningham, Alissa, 6388
Cunningham, Art, 2905
Cunningham, Ben, 3923
Cunningham, Bill, 3152, 7235
Cunningham, Florence, 1285
Cunningham, Gary, 6281
Cunningham, Hannah, 2083, 4713
Cunningham, Hannah J, 4713
Cunningham, Jackie, 546
Cunningham, Jamie, 8271
Cunningham, Jay, 2061
Cunningham, Jennifer, 4960

Cunningham, Jon, 2961
Cunningham, Laura, 1606
Cunningham, Lesley, 6286
Cunningham, Michelle, 2961
Cunningham, Rham, 2437, 6029
Cunningham, Ron, 63
Cunningham, Trista, 4293
Cunningham IV, Russell M., 5887
Cuno, James, 6158
Cupersmith, Neal, 3836
Cupp, D. Tristan, 3734
Cupp, Micheal, 4112
Curatolo, Caroline, 1437
Curatolo, Katherine, 7283
Curchin, Alexander B., 4902
Cure, Clint, 6500
Cureton, Beverley, 7867
Curl, Bill, 7143
Curns, Jon, 131, 132
Curran, Dr. Daniel J., 5337
Curran, Leah, 53
Curran, Shelley, 5201
Curran, Susan M, 984
Curren, Randall, 5196
Currie, Doug, 6410
Currier, Robert, 2608
Currier, Summer, 1840
Curris, Constantine W., 7099, 7100, 7101, 7102
Curry, Brandon, 7623
Curry, Charlotte, 2297
Curry, Eddie, 3010
Curry, Joseph, 506
Curry, Michael D., 4033
Curry, Michael P, 5737
Curry, Richard, 3704
Curry, Steve, 1586
Curtin, Carole, 6301
Curtin, Karen, 3643
Curtis, Barbara, 1788
Curtis, Bonaventure, 3813
Curtis, Cheri, 1908
Curtis, Chris, 2675
Curtis, Doug, 8349
Curtis, Dr Steven, 1581
Curtis, Elyse, 3476
Curtis, Julie, 5626
Curtis, Kim, 147
Curtis, Linda, 2167
Curtis, Michael A., 1999, 2000, 2001
Curtis, Mike, 7621
Curtis, Norman, 3476
Curtis, Patti, 7563
Curtis, Paul J, 488
Curtis PhD, Elyse, 3476
Curtiss, Brain, 2675
Curtwright, Derrick, 6246
Cury, Craig, 6043
Cusano, Tom, 1317
Cushing, David, 6257, 6259, 6263
Cushman, Lauren, 6605, 6606
Cusimano, Carey, 2367
Cussins, Cedar, 5936
Custanza, Kathy, 2598
Cutchall, Davin, 3804
Cutietta, Robert, 1889
Cutler, Brian, 6603
Cutler, John, 809
Cutler, Sarah S, 5316, 7962
Cutler, Sarah S., 7962
Cutler, Sean, 2453, 2776
Cutrone, Signe, 1273
Cutter MD, Phillip D, 1208, 4800
Cutz, Dave, 8106
Cynkar, Jeremy, 6522
Cynthia Darling, Cynthia Darling, 2048
Cypher, Diane, 112
Cyphers Benson, Laura, 6214
Cyr, Deb, 1214, 1215
Cyrus, Ed, 3160
Cyrus, Edgar, 3160
Cyrus, Jim, 5111
Czaplinski, Lane, 5799
Czelusniak, Richard, 4806

D

D'Acosta, Chris, 2077
D'Addio, Dan, 945

D'Agostino, Bill, 3793
D'Agostino, David, 4979
D'Agostino, Sharon, 3382
D'Agostino, Tina, 4805, 7252
D'Agostino, Esq., Clare, 3840
D'Aiutolo, Jacy, 3131
D'Alimonte, Nancia, 955
D'Amato, Joanne, 6398
d'Amboise, Christopher, 305
d'Amboise, Jacques, 403, 463
D'Amico, Julian, 3670
D'Amore, Joe, 1932
D'Angelo, John, 1137, 7067, 7068, 7069
D'Angelo, Patrick J, 6270
D'Aniello, Daniel A., 5762
D'Aniello, Michael J, 5433
D'Anna, Dorothy, 3017
D'Aquino, Roger, 5191
D'Arcangelo, Inez, 1204, 4796, 4797
D'Arcy, Mike, 3363
D'Argenio, Nick, 2729
D'Avella, Jr., Bernard J., 2184
D'Eugenio, Joseph, 1965
D'Montebello, Philippe, 5149
D'Onofrio, Jennifer, 5352
D'Orleans Juste, Roxane, 439
D'Rivera, Paquito, 1331
D'Vanzo, Rob, 2186
D. Ballantine, Frank, 2917
D. Dosedlo, Ricky, 3099
D. Gilbert, Dr. Katheryn, 702
D. Hammond, Troy, 6803, 6804
D. Paul, John, 3234
D. Prusha, Tammy, 6997, 6998, 6999
D.Bartlet, Parnell, 7910
D.Chiang, Darrel, 2575
Da Costa, David, 6132
da Cruz, Catherine, 939
da Frota, Bryan, 153
Daab, James, 4052
Daahgren, Keith, 4068
Daarstad, Erik, 2901
Dabbs, Mike, 7319, 7321
Dabney, Lisa, 179
Dabnpork, H M, 3943
Dabon, Richard, 5636
Daboval, Jeanne, 7129, 7130
Dabroski, Michael, 4757
Dabrowska Huling, Joanna, 1782
Dabrowski, Anne, 682
Dabrowski, Dr. Peter, 1719
Dachenhaus, Terry, 8014
Dachs, Alan M, 2692
Dack, Nikole, 5286
Dackow, Dr. Sandra, 1629
Dacosta, Ismay, 6457
Dadian, Susan, 1411
Dadone, David, 6332
Daehler, Carl, 8007
Dagenais, Don, 4907
Dagenais, Don F., 4186
Daher Hodgson, Denise, 3839
Dahl, Adam, 7370
Dahl, Dan, 5289, 7942
Dahl, Matt, 5703
Dahlberg, Molly, 2082
Dahle, Tammy, 4539
Dahlquist, Peggy, 1996
Dahlstrom, Tom, 2385
Dahma, Alfred, 4314
Dahmus, Jennifer, 1899
Dahnke, Paul, 5365
Daia, Pete, 1741
Daich, Jon, 653
Daigle, Dr. Ronnie, 4709
Daigle, Kay, 5627
Daigle, Steven, 2290
Daigneault, Paul, 3142
Dail, Heather, 5250
Daily, Dawn, 3937
Dakin, Kae, 1987
Dalal, Yogen, 3771
Dalambakis, Judy, 515
Dalba, Richard, 3370
Dale, Catherine, 1382, 5071
Dale, Diane, 2567
Dale, Ellen, 4204

Dale, Gloria, 3762
Dale, Jennifer, 3791, 8106
Dale, Larry, 8244
Dale Sands, Bobby, 3991
Dale Weary, Marca, 569
Daley, Erin, 3471
Daley, Kristen, 2549
Daley, Lauren, 7920
Daley, Pamela, 440
Daley, Philip, 1911
Daley, Richard M, 6747, 6749
Daley, Scott, 791
Dalis, Irene, 1929
Dalla, Lynne D, 5409
Dallas, Barnaby, 6272
Dallas, David, 7385
Dallas, Dionna, 4171
Dallas, Sheree, 702
Dallas, Tony, 6846
Dallin, Heidi J, 3153
Dallinger, Barb, 4590, 6805
Dally, Lynn, 41
Dalrymple, James, 4419
Dalrymple, Mark, 879, 6306
Dalrymple Frye, Tam, 6352, 6360, 6367, 6368, 6369, 6370
Dalton, Claire, 280
Dalton, Cody, 3367
Dalton, Dale, 6972
Dalton, J Truman, 2391
Dalton, Jaime, 7056, 7059
Dalton, Karen, 6236, 6237
Dalton, Richard, 1170
Dalton, Valory, 8044
Dalton Dickinson, Janet, 2262
Daly, Dr. Adrian, 5314
Daly, Gloria, 1682
Daly, Maureen, 3062
Daly, Susan, 668
Dalzell, David, 1819
Dalzell, Drew, 2500
Damasco, Gabrielle, 2315
Damasco, Leandro, 39
Dambra, Deborah, 6876
Dame, Benjamin, 7921, 7923, 7924, 7927
Dameron, Bill, 1600, 5417
Dameron, George, 5706, 8505
Dameron Phipps, Amy, 1750
Damiani, Alexandra, 402, 467
Damiani, Tracy, 8107
Damkroger, Courtney, 6256
Damman, Mike, 297
Damschroder, Michael, 1252
Dan, Diedriech, 7421
Dan, Kayoko, 1689, 2329
Dan Ain, Rabbi, 5109
Dan Zausner, Dan Zausner, 7670
Dancy, Jr., James M., 5473
Danello, Ed.D., Rebecca, 5735
Danenhauer, Bob, 7495
Dang, Tim, 2499
Danhauer, Jeff, 7104
Daniel, Brigitte F., 3836
Daniel, Carlgren, 2418
Daniel, Carol, 2872
Daniel, Courtney, 3871
Daniel, E. Randy, 1127
Daniel, Jeff, 4559
Daniel, Jerry, 1724
Daniel, Justin, 2872
Daniel, Marty, 1726
Daniel, Meg, 5137
Daniel, Sarah N, 7920
Daniel, T, 212, 2993, 2994
Daniel Tatum, Dr Beverly, 4509
Daniel, Jr, Issac, 963
Danielle, Brittany, 1939
Daniels, Beth, 4870
Daniels, Cathie, 4155, 5926, 5928
Daniels, Charles, 1577
Daniels, David, 2155
Daniels, Don, 2135
Daniels, Erica, 2952
Daniels, Genevieve, 2945
Daniels, Jeff, 3195
Daniels, Lewis A, 5007
Daniels, Priscilla, 1820
Daniels, Richard, 8696

1155

Executive Name Index

Daniels, Rick, 62
Daniels, Ronald W., 1474
Daniels, Shiela, 4081
Daniels, Susan E., 2139
Daniels, Wayne, 361
Daniels Jr, Mitchell E., 6949, 6950
Daniels Lister, Dorothytte, 152
Daniels Nowells, Julie, 5256
Danielson, Alan, 439
Danielson, Jody, 929
Danielson, Neil, 1271
Daniels, Angela, 6501
Danihel, Mari.L, 805
Danis, Ann, 1673
Danis, Susan T., 2004
Danko, James, 6888
Danko, James M, 1082
Dannemiller, Jerry, 7987
Danner, Katie, 4136
Danner, Tyson, 3032
Danovich, Helena, 6134
Dant, Angela, 1896
Dantchik, Cathy, 3459
Dante, Sharon, 133
Danysh, Terrence I., 4085
Danzis, Alan L., 1336, 1337, 5005
Danzmayr, David, 1548
Dar, Arianne, 96
Darby, Lorrin, 2168
Darby, Melanie E., 6654
Darby, Susan, 5886
Darckett, William, 8199
Darcy, Bill, 7624
Darden, Kim, 1722
Darden Medina, Donna, 2227
Darius, Jennifer, 6436, 6437
Darius, Rick, 6202
Darkovich, Brenda, 519
Darkovich, Brenda, 7968
Darland, Carmen, 4587, 4597
Darling, Eric, 4785
Darling, Martha, 2130
Darling Lillie, Margaret, 3787
Darlington, Kara, 1625
Darlington, Madge, 3932
Darna, Sandy, 6581
Darnall, Danny, 3058
Darno, Jeanetta, 1547
Daroca, Jodee, 2085
Darr, Patt, 6475
Darring, Rainn, 4565
Darroca, Roberto J A, 1092
Darroch, Donna, 2848
Darrow, Robert K, 3090
Darrow, Susan, 8779
Darst, Janelle, 6962
Darst, Nanci, 2803
Dart, Stan, 3325
Dartin, John, 5614
Darwin, Dave, 1905
Darwin, Donna, 8285
Das, Sandeep, 2905
Dasher, Sarah, 2866
DaSilva, Cheryl, 1199
Dasinger, Norman.R, 709
Daspit, Paul, 4292
Dassenko, Pam, 864
Dasti, Jerry, 5020
Datema, Luanne, 7303
Dathe, Carlotta, 889
Dattilo, Michael, 1338
Daubney, Rebecca, 7185
Daugherty, David, 1558
Daughtey, Michael, 5253
Daukayev, Marat, 36
Daukss, Martins, 1541
Daum, Bryan, 740, 4181
Daum, Shana, 6251
Dauphinais, Michael, 4186
Dave, Kamlesh N., 671
Daveluy, Rene, 47
Davenny Wyner, Susan, 1213, 2291
Davenport, Cindy, 3310, 4927
Davenport, Richard, 3234
Davenport, Sarah, 6656
Davey, Chuck, 1620
Davey, Jeff, 7328
Davey Limarzi, Megan, 3128

David, Andy, 4513
David, Barrett, 7052
David, Edgecombe, 2418
David, Judy, 101
David, Michael, 8827
David Gier, Delta, 1688
David Wood, Ira, 3677
Davidman, Aaron, 2596
Davidoff, Judith, 1428
Davidson, Ashley, 8052
Davidson, Aviva, 413
Davidson, Barry, 1343
Davidson, David, 2507
Davidson, Gabrielle, 4128
Davidson, George, 5135
Davidson, Jamie, 3176
Davidson, Jean, 397
Davidson, Jenny, 608
Davidson, Kenneth S., 5119
Davidson, Larry, 4212
Davidson, Madeleine, 7671
Davidson, Niza, 576
Davidson, Randall, 2145
Davidson, Richard, 4086
Davidson, Sandra, 2603
Davidson, Sarah, 3209
Davidson, Suzanne, 1412
Davidson, Thomas, 2084
Davidson, Tippen, 4442
Davidson, Virginia, 2242
Davies, Catherine, 1985
Davies, Dan, 7166
Davies, Hugh, 1911
Davies, John, 7039
Davies, Katherine, 6520
Davies, Mari, 545
Davies, Molly, 456
Davies, Rick, 4851
Davies, Ron, 6308
Davies, Sandra, 3727
Davies, Walter, 812
DaVigo, Donna, 4254
Davila, Brigitte, 2576
Davis, Adam, 6127, 6157
Davis, Al, 3157
Davis, Alan, 1077, 1849
Davis, Allen, 3553
Davis, Allyson, 778
Davis, Andrew, 2046
Davis, April, 1714
Davis, Art, 8281
Davis, Aubrey, 5688
Davis, Barbara, 3252
Davis, Belva, 6258
Davis, Betty J., 4948
Davis, Bill A, 5277
Davis, Bronson, 3967, 3975
Davis, Carl, 754, 1134, 5626
Davis, Carol Prud'homm, 3566
Davis, Catherine, 7459
Davis, Christin, 8117
Davis, Chuch, 508
Davis, Chuck, 508
Davis, Clarence, 618
Davis, Connie, 1012
Davis, Craig, 204
Davis, David, 762
Davis, Dawn, 8112
Davis, Denis, 2557
Davis, Donna, 756
Davis, Doralene, 2313
Davis, Elizabeth, 8469
Davis, Elliot, 5441
Davis, Elwood B., 6419
Davis, Evett, 4510
Davis, Fran, 3237, 4121
Davis, Frederic H, 3068
Davis, George, 4182
Davis, Ivor, 4344
Davis, J.O., 6283
Davis, Jack, 2430
Davis, Jadd, 2897
Davis, Jake, 4870
Davis, James, 2244
Davis, Jane, 1669
Davis, Janet, 249
Davis, Jenny, 3994
Davis, Jerome, 1415, 3674

Davis, Jerry, 7437
Davis, Jessica, 716
Davis, Jillian, 3712
Davis, Jim, 2964
Davis, Joe, 6853
Davis, John, 3832, 5531
Davis, Julie, 223, 311
Davis, Karen, 5958, 5959, 6313
Davis, Karla, 7601
Davis, Katie, 315
Davis, Keith, 1557
Davis, Kelly, 6048
Davis, Lawrence, 5117
Davis, Lenore Fishman, 1350
Davis, Lisa, 1683
Davis, Lonnie, 309
Davis, Marilyn, 6767, 6768
Davis, Mary, 1268, 2151
Davis, Mary K, 6456
Davis, Matt, 4139
Davis, Matthew, 983
Davis, Megan, 4035
Davis, Michael, 1131, 2066
Davis, Milton, 2929
Davis, Mindy, 2087
Davis, Molly, 7743
Davis, Patricia, 26, 1586
Davis, Paul, 1684, 6972
Davis, Paula J, 6093
Davis, Peggy, 8545
Davis, Pete, 6663
Davis, Priscilla, 2453
Davis, Raquel, 6683, 6684, 6686, 6688
Davis, Renee, 12
Davis, Richard, 5734
Davis, Rick, 2210, 2504
Davis, Sandra, 139, 1667, 5122
Davis, Sarah K, 5570
Davis, Scottie, 3563
Davis, Sharon, 2326, 7611
Davis, Shyvonne, 3197
Davis, Sterling, 6195
Davis, Steve, 2336, 5280
Davis, Sue, 1327
Davis, Sue Ellen, 2291
Davis, Susan, 2005, 5204
Davis, Ted, 4073
Davis, Terry, 7606
Davis, Therese, 2081
Davis, Tom, 4860, 6432
Davis, Toni Marie, 3498
Davis, Vanessa, 2261
Davis, Victoria, 4212
Davis, Wes, 4061
Davis, William Temple, 6356
Davis, Winter, 6340
Davis Brame, Renee, 3898
Davis III, Allen, 3553
Davis Jones, Lori, 7121
Davis Jr/Ph.D, Lawrence, 6043
Davis Rabkin, Marilyn, 2336, 2339
Davis Taylor, Linda, 6085
Davis, Jr., Bert, 2266
Davis-Jeffers, Christine, 6698
Davis-Singh, Tracy, 2160
Davis-Tucker, Joyce, 5631
Davison, Barbara, 6078
Davison, Brian, 8222
Davison, Patricia, 4903
Davis, Ron, 1062
Davonport, Ashley, 7961
Davoren, Sally, 8170, 8171
Dawe, Dr. Lloyd A, 548
Dawes, Carol, 8502
Dawes, Robert, 4276, 6216, 6217
Dawkins, Allyson, 1748
Dawling, Joe, 3239
Daws, Russell S., 4491
Dawson, Barbara, 6202
Dawson, Chelsey, 7031
Dawson, David, 4630
Dawson, Frances, 2098
Dawson, Gail, 6110, 6111
Dawson, George, 2974
Dawson, Gregory, 126
Dawson, Jason, 3158
Dawson, Kimberly, 3768
Dawson, Kitty, 4356

Dawson, Shirley, 2281
Dawson, Suzy, 1778
Dawson, Verlina, 3829
Dawson, Will, 3027
Dawson, Wynne, 5080
Day, Candice, 6302
Day, Dan, 3952
Day, Devon, 5026
Day, Fifi, 1315
Day, H Corbin, 707
Day, James, 5037
Day, Kate, 3674
Day, Lindsay, 3409
Day, Mary, 5947
Day, Michael, 3737
Day, Pam, 4321
Day, Randy, 1669
Day, Sandra, 2308
Day, Stephanie, 6537
Day-Brown, Wendy, 6135
Daykin, Judith E., 5053
Daynard, Richard, 3138
De Bernard, Johnnie, 3194
De Briel, Sydney, 610
De Cormier, Robert, 1769, 2237
De Falla, Emily M, 1952
De Feis, Frederic, 3431
de Figols, Anne, 5744
De Franco Browne, Diane, 57
De Guzman, Rene, 6267
de Haro, Stuart A., 1044
De Jesus, Margareth, 2184
De La Cruz, Luis, 2461, 6091
De La Nuez, Mario, 517
De La Torre, Deborah, 907
De Laura, Kaity, 5001
De Laurentis, Semina, 2713
De Laurentis, Teresa, 2713
De Leon, Chris, 8382
de Leon, Sylvia A., 149
De Leon, Tomas, 1721
De Leon De Vega, Sonia Marie, 806
De Lorenzo, John, 4218
De Melo, Carolyn, 3431
De Mesa, Alycia, 727
De Palma, Samuel, 2191
de Quadros, Andra, 1175
De Saa, Margarita, 573
de Saa White, Margarita, 573
De Santo, Jen, 402
de Vinna, Cynthia, 4452
de Vries, Kathleen, 4256
De Walle, Thomas, 1034
De Wayne, Dan, 6083
Dea Glodt, Marita O', 3169
Deal, Chris, 7431
Deal, Paul, 2083
Deal, Tanya, 4472
Dean, Debbie, 6197
Dean, Dr. Jay, 1274
Dean, Dusti, 5057
Dean, Eva, 366
Dean, James, 1998
Dean, Jay, 2156, 4892
Dean, Jean, 701
Dean, Kathy, 4448
Dean, Kevin, 3980
Dean, Margo, 630
Dean, Marilyn, 6987, 6988
Dean, Molly, 5637
Dean, Robert, 3893
Dean, Stan, 6578
Dean, Tim L, 6051
Dean, Tina, 8221
Dean, Tom, 1895
Dean, Webster, 630
Dean Singleton, William, 6352, 6360, 6367, 6368, 6369, 6370
Deane, Diane, 5369
Deaner, Carol, 4541
Deaner, Nancy, 4957, 7512
Deangelis, Elena, 2266
Dearborn, Gloria, 1061
Dearborn, Lindsay, 1318
Dearing, Dancer, 3406
Dearing, Ted, 7276
Dearling, Kevin, 8337
Dearth, Janice, 3686

Executive Name Index

DeAtley, Kathleen, 4281, 6221, 6222, 6223, 6226
DeAtley, Kathy, 6221, 6222, 6223, 6226
Deaton, Joel L., 654
Deats, Wayn, 757
Deaver, Susan, 5055
DeBeauvais, Leslie, 4350
DeBenedetto, Patricia, 1595
DeBerry, Robert, 597
DeBlack Ph.D, Thomas, 6048
DeBoer, Kathleen, 7089
DeBoer, Sid, 3771, 8062, 8063
DeBow, Charley, 5507
DeBoy, Lori, 1160
DeBree, Lynn, 3848
DeBriyn, Norm, 6024
DeBunda, Esq., Salvatore M., 1644
Decaprio, Gene, 5471
DeCarlo, Chris, 2618
DeCarmo, Mary, 4472
December, June, 373
DeCesaris, Mark, 5511
deChalus Lee, CCTE, Colette, 578
DeChant, Jennifer, 4728
DeChello, Sheila, 6417, 6425, 6426
DeCherney, Nancy, 4161
Decima, Karlee, 4237
DeCinque, Jennifer, 5172
Deck, Kate, 698
Deck, Tim, 6687
Deck, Warren, 907
Deckard, Corinne, 2821
Decker, Chip, 3646
Decker, Ed, 2586
Decker, Matthew, 3827
Deckman, Paula, 7837
Deckter, Cookie, 895
Declert, Alain G, 5658, 8443
Decottignes, Becky, 6206
DeCroix, Gina, 311
DeCroix Russell, Gina, 223
DeCrona, Bruce, 6302
Dedrick, Cameron, 1515
Dee, Richard.M, 310
Deedee, Ted, 8679
DeeDee Flores, Lydia, 1710
Deegan, Patrick, 5076
Deely, Pat, 4179
Deem, Bobbi, 581
Deem, Dick, 1509, 2273, 2274
Deen, Tracey, 1712
Deener, Larry, 1128
Deer-Owens, Ann Marie, 3917
Deering, Lynn, 3113
Deering, Sidney, 684
Deering, Tom, 684
Deets, Julie, 5844
DeFanti, Elizabeth, 312
DeFazi, Dr. Joseph, 5017
DeFazio, Joseph, 2189
Defelice, Fr Jonathan, 4969
Deffenbaugh, Jordan, 3328
Deffner, Sunshine, 1940, 1941
Defillippo, Gene, 7232
DeFrancesco, Joyce, 1656
DeFries-D'Albert, Beverly, 4551
DeGarmo, Mark, 452
DeGarmo, Penny, 1224
DeGarmo, Phd, Mark, 452
DeGeneste, Stephanie, 5012
Degerness, Marv, 1267
Degioia, Jack, 6469
DeGiusti, Elaine, 552
Degnan, Tim, 3292
DeGrace, John, 5076
Degrace, Karen L, 928
DeGrace, Lou, 2373
DeGraff, Deborah S, 6785, 6787, 6788
DeGrandpre, Audrey, 7426
DeGregoria, Angela, 1436
DeGregorie, Frank, 5155
DeGroff, Anne, 918
Dehart, Deborah, 2728
DeHayes, Donald H., 8193
Dehn, Janice, 2721
Dehn Van Dessel, Mary, 735
Dehne, Tanuja M., 5015
Dehner, Ann, 2895
DeHollander, Kevin, 5194

Dehoney, Catherine, 1985
DeHope, Edward K., 3370
Deichman, Nancy, 5389
Deiss-Costanzo, Susanne, 4256
Deissler, Mary, 1181, 6558
Deitemeyer, Dr. Kandi W., 7882
Deiterman, Maretta, 1754
Deitrick, David, 1568
DeJong, Jim, 4556
DeKeyser, Hal, 4176
Dekker Davidson, Beverly, 4212
Dekolletti, David, 4632
Del Bello Spencer, Delphine, 570
Del Colletti, David, 3024
Del Colletti, David G., 3023, 6943, 6945
Del Gobbo, George, 1010
Del Guercio, Fernando, 3394
Del Monaco, Giancarlo, 2191
Del Monte, Elaine, 499
Del Negro, Dr. Albert, 253
Del Prado, Serfio, 6156
Del Rosario, Roger, 688
Del Valle, Miguel, 6747
Del Vecchio, Glenn, 285
Del Vecchio, Lucia, 506
Delahunty, Mary, 8587
Delaino, Tom, 6578
deLambart, Chris, 3679
Delaney, Andrea, 1184
DeLaney, Anne, 557
Delaney, Christine, 2133
Delaney, Janice, 2736
Delano, Wendy, 8561
Delaronde, Joe, 5909, 5911, 6555, 6556
DeLaurier, Roger, 2617
Delbrouck, Allen, 62
Delbyck, Kipp, 2526
Delduke, Lisa, 3360
Deleault, Joe, 4969
Delecki, Michelle, 7296
Delekta, Kelly, 278
Deleon, Judi, 5664
DeLeone, Carmon, 515, 1060, 1559
Delgadillo, Efren, 6195
Delgado, Andrew, 6939, 6940
Delgado, Yvonne, 736, 737
Delgiudice, Andrea, 2250
DeLillo, Jennifer, 225
DeLio, Bart, 6150
Dell'Omo, Dawn, 339
Della Sala, Tom, 2256
DelLago, Randolph, 2773
Dellaira, Michael, 2222
Dellaporta, John, 1998
Dellenback, Erik, 6528
Dellheim, Richard, 2092
Delli Bovi, Eric, 4563
Delliger, Todd, 2490
Dellinger, Rachel, 1694, 3905
Dellins, Marc, 6169, 6174
Delman, Dita, 2192
Delmenico, Lesley, 6997, 6998, 6999
Delmhorst, John, 2327
Delmhorst, John R., 2327
Delmhorst, Michele J,, 2327
Delmhorst, Michele J., 1974, 2327
Deloach, Katherine, 2026
Deloeuil, Olivier, 2231
DeLon, Richard M., 531
Delong, Jeff, 6729
DeLong, Ted, 8062, 8063
DeLorenzo, Ann, 1143
Delp, Jennah, 1891
Deluca, Alyssa, 8170, 8171
Deluca, Bernie, 6475
DeLuca, Diane, 326
DeLuca Stephens, MA, Karen, 452
DeMain, John, 2395
DeMaio, Lou, 3354
Demarco Goor, Anita, 4830
Demas, Terrance, 3626
Demaso, Mary, 272
Dember, Larry, 7573
Dembinski, Mary, 4136
Dembler, Stuart, 2180
Dembrow, Beth, 3471
Dembrow, Jon, 7783
DeMella, Jonathan, 1801

Demellweek, Jennifer, 7998
Demes Maydew, Catherine, 3333
Demes Maydew, Catherine, 3333
Demeter, Ellen, 1175
Demeter, George, 1175
DeMeyere, Gail, 4857
Deminster, Larry, 5048
Demko, Lynda, 3699
Demko, Steve, 3699
Demling, Dr. Ann, 6646
DeMoss, Virginia, 2487
Dempset, Ronald, 2755
Dempsey, Kadie, 5001
Dempsey, Seth, 4101
Dempski, Scott, 675
Demsey, Kim, 6438
Demski, Michele, 1227
Demski, Regina, 7327
Demson, Martha, 2475
Denardo, Judith, 543
Denaut, Joanne, 2461
DeNaut, Joanne, 6091
DeNeff, Steve, 6909, 6910, 6911
Denenberg, Carol, 2308
Denevan, Dion, 3887
Deneve, Stephane, 4795
Deng, Helen, 1969
Denhard, August, 1798, 5793
DenHerder, Darla, 8084
Denis, Jude-Laure, 5171
Denis, Peter, 4060
Denk, Todd, 6864, 6867
Denman, Matthew, 6155
Dennen, Kathryn, 944
Denney, Karen, 3969, 8384
Dennin, Steve, 6410
Denning, Deb, 6899
Denning, Ed, 5215
Dennis, Allan, 1054
Dennis, Dr. Allan, 1054
Dennis, John, 509
Dennis, Joseph L., 6644
Dennis, Karen, 1054
Dennis, Kim, 5646
Dennis, Pat, 4637
Dennis, Patricia, 3226, 3227
Dennis, Reid W., 1922
Dennis, Robin, 4129
Dennis, Will, 3836
Dennis, Jr., Joseph, 6644
Dennis, Ph.D., Martha, 796, 4233
Dennison, Nathan, 6876
Denniston, G. H., 7727
Denniston, Jr., G. H., 3490
Denny, Frederick, 897
Denny, Kelly, 6094
Denny, Paige, 1838
Denove, Robert C., 2321
Densa, Steve, 8297
Densmore, Ginny, 998
Dent, Clarence, 4280
Dent, Jennifer, 3211
Dent, Kevin, 4041
Denton, Abbie, 4166
Denton, Andrea, 8088
Denton, Brenda, 3999
Denton, Dean, 5411
Denton, Michele, 1384
Denton, Nina, 695
Dentzel, Paul, 4259
Dentzel, Paul A., 4259
dePasquale, Gloria, 1649
Depew, John, 7039
Depler, Irina, 164
DePonte, Niel, 564
DePoy, D.M., Dr. Bryan, 8023, 8024
Deppen, Andrew, 3798
DePreist, James, 824, 825
DeQuasie, Art, 1770
der Hoeven, Bill van, 1477, 5218
Derby, Ann, 59
Derderian, Pat, 1250
Derecho, Edwin, 4777
Derecho, Jan, 874
Derheim, Donald, 4309, 4312
Derivan, Miriam, 5188
Derloshon, Jerry, 6185
DeRobbio, Dr Robert, 2325

DeRobbio, Nanci, 2325
DeRosa, Mary, 1436, 1441
DeRose, Robert C., 6832
Derousseau, Sarah, 5645
Derr, Carla, 7952
Derr, Frederick, 4483
Derr, Michael, 4703, 7110, 7111, 7112, 7117
Derrick, John M, 2732
Derry, Dr Lisa, 4534
Derusha, Allison, 8837
Dervisa, Ashia, 3526
Derybowski, Stephanie, 2066
Desai, Viktor, 3770
Desai, Vishakha N, 5114
DeSalvo, Dr. Nancy, 8146
Desalvo, Nancy, 8146
Desalvo, Steve, 8225
Desanctis, Paul, 2315
DeSantis, Deborah, 1951
DeSantis, Kyle, 2982
Desautels, Michael L., 1401
Desazio, Joseph, 7588
Deschamps, Vincent, 1996
Deschenes, Linda, 1464, 5200
Deschere, Karen, 5859
DeScherer, Jennie L., 596, 1679, 3869
Descoteau, Christopher, 4962
Desens, Joan, 2169
DeSerio, Michaelangelo, 3505
DeShelter, George, 3848
DeShetler, George, 3844
DeShields, April, 4254
Desiderio, Christine, 1383
deSimone, Joanne, 6839
DeSimone, Sheryl, 574
Desio, Alfred, 45
DeSio, Robert, 2254, 2255
Desisto, Lisa, 4784
Desjardins, Gary, 8044
Desmond, Stacy, 6239
Desper, Michael, 4109
DeSpirito, Carolyn, 2325
Desroches, Jack, 3150
Desrosiers, Ted E, 3177
Dessens, Scott, 245
Desser, Ronald J., 5448
Dessureau, Sara, 2837
Destefano, Frank, 5457
DeStefano, Johanna, 2283
Destefano, Todd, 6167
Detamore, Betty, 2804
Deterding, Peyton, 6806, 6809
Detesco, Gloria, 1575
Detmer, Chris, 1390
Detmer, Kim, 4139
Detroit, Michael, 3908, 3910
Detroy, Christopher, 3629
DeTroy, Douglas, 3629
Detsie, Fran, 975
Dettmann, Michelle, 2154
Dettra, Scott, 959
Deturk, Mary, 4964
Deuel, Carolyn, 5878
Deuel, Raymond, 4066
Deuren, Denise Van, 6227
Deuschle, Connie, 3001
Deutch, Philip J., 2736, 2737, 6467
Deutsch, Gail, 253
Deutsch, Lauren, 4556
Deutsch, Margery, 1831
Deutsch, Paul, 7369
Deva, Alek, 3471
Devan, David B, 2311
Devan, David B., 2311
Devanney, Gigi, 261
Deveau, David, 1208, 4786, 4800
deVeaux, Riddick, 668
DeVelder, Derek, 5034
Develin Coley, Joan, 7195
Deveney, Karen, 1600, 5417
DeVere, Rollin, 3701
Deverman, Benjamin, 6207
Devey, Trey, 1528, 1529
DeVille, Pam, 7125
DeVine, Jeff, 6283
DeVine, Jesse, 3320
Devine, John, 6428
Devine, Maryann, 2305

1157

Executive Name Index

DeVine, Scott, 4020
Devine, Tammy, 6500
Devine, Val, 6719
DeVito, Jeannie, 4346
Devlin, Mallory, 2567
Devon, Rosalind, 5129
DeVore, Ai, 1587
DeVore, Chris, 4537, 6703
Devost, Don, 2370
Devous, Julia, 5972
Dew, Emily, 3791
Dewar, Cynthia, 601
Dewar, Janet L, 2750
Dewayne, Dan, 2458
Dewey, Jeremy, 4843, 4868
Dewey, Jim, 6281
Dewey, Linda, 4264
DeWine, Sue, 4618, 6883, 6884
DeWitt, Adam, 199, 205
DeWitt, James, 2534
Dewyngaert, Rachel, 5533
Deyoung, Ruth, 8704
DeYoung Kohler, Ruth, 5867
Dhand, Sanjeev K., 65
Di Palma, Susana, 300
Di Piazza Jr., Samuel A., 5162
Di Santo, Christopher, 1325
Di Trolio, Michael, 2274
Diacon, Todd A., 7995
Diaguardi, Sara, 1067
Diamant, Michelle, 3328
Diamond, Becky, 1977
Diamond, Betty, 4116
Diamond, James, 1230, 1237
Diamond, Mark, 507
Diamond, Tamara, 3209
Diana, Rebecca M, 3817
DiAndrea, Aimee, 582
Dianne, Darwin, 7455
Dias, John, 3384
Diaz, Al, 6949, 6950
Diaz, Alex M, 6546
Diaz, Andrea, 50, 100, 101
Diaz, Arthur, 4155
Diaz, Damien, 61
Diaz, Erik, 2704
Diaz, Kathy, 1788
Diaz, Kelly, 6527
Diaz, Lester, 1126
Diaz, Miguel, 2615
Diaz, Oscar, 1737
Diaz, Rita, 4467
Diaz, Tony, 6150
Dib, Roland, 3488
Dibble, Jerry, 2847
Dibble, Susan, 3178, 7254
DiBello, Courtney, 552
DiBello, Lucille, 1400
DiBernardo, Ann C., 5708
DiBlasi, Gesielle, 190
Dibrell, Glenna, 4882
DiCamillo, Joyce, 941
DiCarlo, John, 799
DiCesare, Daniel, 4555
DiCesare, Giuseppa, 6737
Dichiera, David, 2134
Dichoza, Karen, 1245
DiCiaccio, Evie, 6124
DiCicco, Stan, 461
Dicikinson, Jeff, 3061
Dick, James, 5658
Dick, James C., 8443
Dicke, Chris, 6897
Dickens, Pierce, 4518
Dickens, Stef, 3232
Dicker, Patricia, 4090, 4092
Dickerson, Charles, 765
Dickerson, Frank, 2272
Dickerson, Lynn, 6187
Dickerson, Stacy, 7160
Dickerson, Wes, 8233
Dickey, Jessica, 8010
Dickey, Jim, 1152
Dickey, Kris, 1838
Dickey, Marc R., 6110, 6111, 6114
Dickinson, Beth, 915
Dickinson, Jeff, 3061
Dickinson, Joe, 3954

Dickinson, Margaret, 2080
Dickinson, Melvin, 1129, 2080
Dickinson, Mike, 1584
Dickinson, Richard, 541
Dickmeyer, Tim, 7496, 7499
Dickney, Jessica, 3751
Dickson, Donna, 3756
Dickson, Douglas, 1968
Dickson, Jeff, 3065
Dickson, Karen, 588
Dickson, Kate, 588
Dickson, Sally, 6891
Dickson, Susan, 204
Dickson-Lewis, Nancy, 55
Dicky, Jerry, 2781
DiCristofaro, David, 6209
Dicus, Chuck, 6024
Dicus, Woody, 5260, 5261
Dieffenbach, Penny, 3618
Diegel, Skip, 967
Diehl, Dr. Carol, 1846
Diehl, Elena, 243
Diehl, Richard, 3705
Diehr, Jim, 5561
Dieker, Joe, 7013, 7014
Diekroeger, Greg, 8707
Diemecke, Enrique, 799, 1232, 1233
Diemer, Judy, 2969
Diener, Melissa, 5850
Dienes, David, 5609, 5611
Dienstag, Marion, 7724
Dienstfrey, Sherri R, 6714, 6715, 6716
Diep, Van, 686
Diera, Dennis, 2833
Diesch, Lauren, 3231
Diestel, David, 834
Dieter-Robinson, Susan, 8077
Dietlein, Mark, 4016
Dietlein, Quinn, 4016
Dietlein, Sally, 4016
Dietrich, Aaron, 8072
Dietrich, Dr. Wilfred, 5598
Dietrich, Nancy, 6488
Dietrich Yockey, Sarah, 223, 311
Dietrick, David, 1568
Dietsch, James, 2191
Dietz, Cindy, 1813
Dietz, Duane, 4998
Dietz, Kathy, 4635
Dietz, Larry, 6805, 6807, 6808, 6809, 6810, 6811
Dietzler, Beth, 3793
Dietzler, Harry, 3800, 8120
DiEugenio, Nicholas, 900, 901
Diez, Oliver, 977
Difabio Raffield, Gale, 334
Diffley, Ray, 6443
DiGabriele, Linda, 2821
Digabriele, Linda M, 4480
DiGenti, Vic, 4455
Digel, Jeffrey, 6407
Diggs, Andrea, 1992
Diggs, Crystal, 6558
Diggs, Kevin, 8361
DiGuglielmo, Paula, 6456, 6457
Dijkstra, Paul, 1039
Dike-Hughes, Cynthia A., 4272
Dikes-Larsen, Lindsey, 4193
Dilbeck, Sandy, 6026
Dildine, Rick, 3054
Dileno, Susan, 5292
DiLeo, Nick, 1680
Dilger, Patrick, 6418
Dilks, Edward, 2809
Dill, Brian, 5609, 5611
Dillard, Carmen, 188
Dillard, Denise, 4044
Dillard, Sidney, 208
Dillard Lidell, Maya, 4179
Dille, Mason, 801
Dillehay, Andy, 3326
Dilley, Jane, 4414
Dillingham, Charles, 2463, 2493, 2509, 6170
Dillingham, Charles A., 2109
Dillingham, Eve, 1849
Dillion, Terri, 2894
Dillman, Sabrina, 711
Dillon, C.J., 6730
Dillon, Charles, 4860

Dillon, Cynthia, 68
Dillon, George, 4796
Dillon, James E., 3302
Dillon, Joseph, 8155
Dillon, Joseph G., 2970
Dillon, Lorraine, 2445
Dillon, Ray, 6040
Dillon Jauken, Allison, 4147
Dilworth, Robert E, 950
Dilworth, Rollo, 1985
Dimascio, Marianne, 4023
DiMattia, Ernest A., 6434, 6435
Dimengo, Michael, 4584
DiMenno, Joey, 2330
Dimmerman, Jeffery, 8816
Dimond, Kimberly, 1247, 1248
Dimston, Charles, 5129
Dimun, Lori, 6738
Dineals, Andy, 7393
Dineen, Alicia, 6336
Dineen, Bradley, 213
Dingle, Michael, 2581
Dingle, Mike, 4306
Dingledein, Tom, 1541
Dingman, Richel, 8140
DiNicola, Ed, 3183
Dinin, Sarah, 1441
Dinizulu, Alice, 377
Dinizulu, Kiamati, 377
Dinkin, Joel, 5640
Dinur, Esty, 8675, 8681, 8683
Dinur, Yaniv, 999
Dinwiddie, Elizabeth, 1183
Dinwiddie, Mike, 2812
Dioeosio, Ron, 2676
Dion, Doug, 7033, 7034
Dion, Kari, 4822
Dionne, Robert, 8507
DiPalma, Michael, 6685
DiPaolo, Lauren, 428
Dipeolu, Vivienne, 2526
DiPetro, David, 8167
DiPietra, Eloise, 8001
DiPietro, Michael, 414
Dir, Drew, 2923
Director, Kathy, 8458
Director Emeritus, Anderson, 5038
Director Performing/, Hassig, 8698
DiSabatino, Brian, 1979
DiSabatino, L Jeffrey, 2725
DiSalle, Kate, 4108
DiSalvo, Anthony, 686
Disandro, Anthony, 5433
Disano, Cynthia, 6420
Discenza, Gregg, 7837
Dischinger, Lynn, 1562
Dischinger, Sally, 297, 4872, 7358
Disharoon, Elizabeth, 432
Disharoon Prickett, Betty, 177
Disner, Joyce, 7644
Disney, Glenn, 4283, 5130
Dissette, Alyce, 474
DiStasio-Waddell, Elizabeth, 7651
Distler, Bruce, 8082
Ditchey, Allyson, 3298
Dittman, Gloria S., 4988
Dittmer, Cindy, 6545
Dittmer, Sue, 3034
Dittrich, Darren, 3955, 5612
Dittus, Heather, 2023
Ditzler, Dr Mauri, 6802
Divelbiss, Doug, 1576
Divelbiss, Maggie, 2676
Diver, Colin, 8101
Divine, Elizabeth G., 6154, 6171, 6176
Dixon, Albert, 2582
Dixon, Alisa, 1864
Dixon, Christina, 8031
Dixon, Christopher P., 5164
Dixon, Dale, 6044, 6046
Dixon, Dave, 4366
Dixon, Delores, 3496
Dixon, Ed, 1812
Dixon, Georgette, 2262
Dixon, Jane, 3399
Dixon, Julie, 6943, 6945
Dixon, Keith, 3077, 4091
Dixon, Lee S., 1681

Dixon, Mary, 4207
Dixon, Pamela, 3832
Dixon, Roger, 7501
Dixon, Sally, 1669
Dixon, Sam, 6654
Dixon, Shelby, 1831
Dixon, Terri, 6315
Dixon-Olson, Donna, 1342
Djuric, Milhailo, 593
Dlouhy, Paul, 727
Doan, Jim, 2774
Doan, Myron, 3059
Doan, Sandra, 1722
Doar III, Tom, 6850
Dobbins, Daniel C., 4585
Dobbins, Steve, 6250
Dobbs, Kimberly, 2399
Dobbs, Rodney, 3954
Dobbs, Rruth, 1578
Dobbs Mackenzie, Barbar, 1404
Dobell, Robert J, 8272
Doblin, Dr. Stephen, 8333
Dobos, Al, 4004, 8463
Dobrin, Tory, 448
Dobrowoiski, Jennifer, 6527
Dobrowolski, Jennifer, 4452
Dobrzynski, Jessie, 7636
Dobson, Tarry, 3959
Dobson, Terry, 3959
Dockery, Ceola, 6032
Docking PhD, Jeffrey R, 7263
Dockstader, J.D., 5958, 5959
Dockter, Caryl, 783
Doctor, Polly, 7322
Dodd, Anne, 5001
Dodd, John, 3993, 5649
Dodd, Julia, 908
Dodd, Liz, 4160
Dodds, DeLoss, 8322
Dodds, Nancy B, 7741
Dodds III, Charles, 1720, 5619
Dodge, Tom, 7346
Dodson, Brooks, 5836
Dodson, Ken, 725
Dodson, Mark, 1515
Dodson, R. Scott, 1036
Dodson, Scott, 1785
Doenges, Rob, 6883, 6884
Doepkens, William, 1992
Doer, Tiffany, 969
Doerfler, Jennifer, 4703
Doering, Pat, 4264
Doerner, Brian, 3814
Doerner, David, 1254
Doerner, Melanie, 3675
Doggett, Walter, 1982
Doheny, Phil, 32
Doherty, Alison, 1197, 4793
Doherty, Charles, 5483
Doherty, Danielle, 3536
Doherty, Jennifer, 2405
Doherty, Lisa, 839
Doherty, Mary Jane, 7256
Doherty, Maureen, 7256
Dohry, Nancy, 3425
Dohtery, Dennis, 5421
Doig, Alan, 6133, 6135
Doike, Ann, 1019
Doike, Joan, 1019
Dolan, Bob, 2777
Dolan, James L, 7752
Dolan, James L., 6192, 6753
Dolan, Larry, 7991
Dolan, Marianne, 6112
Dolan, William, 1602, 1603
Dolan Jr., Daniel D., 6795
Dolan-Neill, Rose, 5832
Dolbashian, Edward, 1287
Dolbeare, Kristy, 956
Dolden, Ginger, 1440
Dolenga, Katrina, 4282
Dolese, Peter, 5386
Dolezal, Joe, 8579
Dolgallo, Valery, 219
Dolgen, Susan, 4282
Dolich, Cory, 8097
Dolid, Paul, 876
Dolinksy, Serena, 2618

1158

Executive Name Index

Dolkas, Peggy, 319
Doll, Cynthia, 4270
Doll, William, 4971
Dollar, June, 2013
Dollar, Terri, 5260, 5261
Dolling, Ulf, 2195
Dolphin, John, 6496
Domann, Beth, 7462
Domask, Asanga, 141
Dombroski, Lee, 4526, 6669
Dombrow, Debbie, 6114
Domes, Chris E., 5850
Domine, James Elza, 893
Domingo, Placido, 1887, 1997, 2315, 7773
Dominguez, Luis, 242
Dominguez, Monique, 647
Dominguez, Nancy, 242
Dominguez, Robert, 3119
Domini, Timothy, 2190
Dominick, Daniel, 1752
Dominie, Jason L., 5189
Domm, Jason, 3967, 3968, 3975
Domme, Michael, 3803
Domond, Francois, 6523
Domoracki, Jim, 4995
Domue, Barbara, 448
Don, Kay, 7829
Don Bahr, Michael, 4006, 5682
Don Siratt, Colby, 3969
Donabauer, Jill, 3204
Donahoe, Tom, 7804
Donahue, Christine, 1864
Donahue, Lenny, 2150
Donahue, Michael, 1340
Donahue, Nancy, 4257
Donahue, Victile, 280
Donahue III Esq, Michael, 2180
Donald, Herbe, 3749
Donald, William, 4387
Donald Edwards, Michael, 4480
Donaldson, Candice, 2227
Donaldson, Charles, 4191
Donaldson, Dennis, 2989
Donaldson, Jody, 4004, 8463
Donaldson, Joyce, 6094
Donaldson, Keir, 5183
Donaldson, Maria, 8548
Donalson, David, 8080
Donato, Michael A., 3827
Doncaster, Elizabeth, 5711
Doncaster, Sarah, 5711
Dondero Meyer, Ellen, 3359
Donegan, Sharon, 3295
Donelly, Brian, 1336, 1337
Doner, Everett L, 848
Dong, Dian, 429
Donini, Marilynn, 5052
Donley, Miranda, 310
Donlon, Claudette, 4426
Donnarumma, Maureen, 944
Donne Gunter, Terry, 694
Donnell Budd, Susan, 5001
Donnelley, Bev, 910
Donnelly, Brian, 5005
Donnelly, Jennifer, 3837
Donnelly, Paula, 2498
Donnelly, Richard E., 3021
Donner, Marda, 8508
Donner, Marvin, 6594
Donoghue, Emma, 2107
Donoghue, Winnie, 2820
Donohoe, Alica, 8285
Donohoe, Kathleen, 723
Donohue, Jim, 6438
Donohue, Joseph, 2102
Donohue, Kevin T., 5162
Donohue Templeton, Beth, 1376
Donovan, Alex, 5419
Donovan, Anna, 632
Donovan, Eve, 2577
Donovan, Lynn H, 1494, 2265
Donovan, Stacy, 3503
Dooley, David, 1838
Dooley, David M., 8193
Dooley, Matthew, 2316
Dooley, Patrick, 2451
Doolin, Bill, 158
Doolin, Thomas, 5448, 8122

Doolittle, Phillip, 829
Doppelt, Ava, 163
Doran, Donna, 5312, 5313
Doran, Elizabeth, 6209, 7623
Doran, Richard A, 2310
Dorawala, Dr. Tansukh, 3606
Doren, Jared, 3705
Dorethy, James, 2963
Dorf, Michael, 1407
Dorf, Sandy, 6344
Dorfman, Carolyn, 343
Dorfmann, Tracey E., 7211
Dorhout, Bret, 4921
Doris, Assistant, 8721
Dorman, Jon, 6567, 6571
Dorman, Michelle, 3778, 5411, 8081
Dorn, Tanja, 5112
Dorney, Diane, 4487
Dornicik, Joseph, 1383
Dorning, Jan, 4147
Doroba, Ron, 4248
Dorr, Douglas, 2389
Dorrell, David, 8033
Dorrity, Sharon, 4859
Dorsey, Jeff, 4900
Dorsey, John, 6094, 6095, 6096, 6098, 8011
Dorsey, Sam, 1783
Dorsey, Stuart, 8461
Dortch, Sterling, 5965
Doser, Scott, 6391
Doser, Sue, 218
Dosh, Fran, 1260
Doss, Chris, 4255
Doss, Cynthia, 6079
Doss, Jennifer, 711
Doss, Suzanne, 2520, 2523
Dossett, Laura, 3769
Dossett, Traci L., 6860
Dotson, Shelley, 7439
Doty, Bryan, 3034
Doty, Merline Batiste, 3271
Doty, Philip E., 1951
Doty, Rachel, 2369
Dotz, Abby, 7268
Dougherty, David, 1578, 5498
Dougherty, Dennis F., 6154, 6171, 6176
Dougherty, Jim, 6283
Dougherty, Lee, 4685
Dougherty, Rick, 8163, 8164, 8165, 8166
Dougherty, Tim, 8241
Dougherty Brunzell, Julie, 4851
Dougherty Ross , Lee, 4447
Dougherty, Ph.D., Charles J., 8167
Doughty, Brian, 4010
Doughty, Nate, 8557
Douglas, Amy, 6510
Douglas, David W., 2356
Douglas, Hazel, 4504
Douglas, Karen, 1583
Douglas, Mary, 8009
Douglas, Michele, 7060
Douglas, Rodney K, 3606
Douglas, Shea, 3531, 3535
Douglas, Thomas W, 1121, 2316
Douglas Morrow, Scott, 5045
Douglas Roberts, Susan, 631
Douglass, David, 4558
Douglass, Frank, 4743
Doulin CSA, Jack, 3536
Douple, Tom, 7120, 8474
Doura, Daniel, 7773
Douthat, Ellen, 2429
Douthat, James, 3856
Douthit, Susanna, 84
Dovala, Bud, 8712
Dove, Kristal, 8268
Dover, Dan, 7853
Doviak, George, 1516
Dowd, Shaun, 3092
Dowdy, Dr. Eugene, 1736
Dowell, Karen, 3331
Dower, David, 7223
Dowling, Diana, 1112
Dowling, Fred, 7261
Dowling, Gary, 6597
Dowling, Joe, 3239, 7351
Dowling, Marina, 4478
Dowling, Shannon, 4060

Downall, Bradley, 7097
Downey, Bob, 6525
Downey, Brittany, 1305
Downey, Elliot, 5099
Downey, Linda, 2836, 3038, 6600
Downey, Matthew, 288
Downey, Vicki, 1424
Downey, Vonnie, 3999
Downing, Holly, 3890
Downing, Robert, 1492, 6525
Downing, Sara, 3077
Downing, Shawna, 4906
Downing, Trent, 4958, 7516
Downs, Chris, 7659
Downs, Steve, 6947
Dows, Yvonne, 6212
Dowse, Sean, 3212
Doyan, Suzette, 2813
Doyle, Alec, 7534
Doyle, Caitlin, 6401
Doyle, David, 2967
Doyle, Edward, 2174
Doyle, James N., 8008
Doyle, John, 4319, 4320
Doyle, Kathy, 5375
Doyle, Kerry, 659
Doyle, Linda, 1352
Doyle, Marlana, 639
Doyle, Patricia, 2067
Doyle, Roger, 5422
Doyle Berk, Maureen, 149
Dozzi, CPA, Victor, 5493
DP Sheridan, Daniel, 3032
Drackley, Scott, 2304
Drago, Alejandro, 1511
Dragon, Joan, 4461
Dragone, Diane, 331
Dragun, Kathryn, 4210
Draizin, Mitchell, 3624
Drake, Bill, 1024
Drake, Dannye, 3
Drake, James, 8422
Drake, Kay, 4257
Drake, Kerry, 1086
Drake, Kimberly, 23
Drake, Robert, 2847, 6635
Drake, Robert M, 1002
Drake, Sylvie, 6352
Drake, Tim, 8796
Drake, Tom, 1054
Drake, Virginia, 2599
Dramaturg, Bass, 3627
Drapal Kluver, Jodie, 2326
Draper, Loretta, 5993
Draper, Mary Jean, 8489
Draper, Michael G., 1454
Drapes, Michael, 2345
Drapkin Vanaver, Livia, 380
Drasner, Courtney, 428
Drastal, Heather, 3528
Draudt, Wayne, 6832
Dray, Deena, 2884
Dray, Scott, 2960
Dreger, Chris, 6621
Dreiske, John, 2926
Dreiske, Nicole, 2926
Drennan, Kim, 6386
Drennon, Amanda, 6032, 6033
Dresden, Danielle, 700
Dresher, Paul, 849
Dresken, Rhoda, 5256
Dresner, Marty Dr. Jazz, 745
Dresser, Bruce, 1588
Dressner, Courtney, 6
Dretzka, Kevin, 801
Dreves, Jeffrey E, 5371
Drew, DeeAnn, 4649
Drew, Zenetta S, 628
Drews, Donna, 7367, 7368
Drews Hanlon, Karen, 6134
Drexel, Pamela, 5136
Dreyer, Darlene A, 1250
Dreyer, Leslie, 2591
Dreyfus Smith, Pamela, 4792
Driese, Clark, 5787
Driggers, Jeff, 4451
Drill, Amy, 8094
Drinan, Ann L., 1966

Driscoll, Joann, 4307
Driscoll, John, 1300
Driscoll, K C, 197
Driscoll, KC, 194
Driscoll, Michael, 3386
Driscoll, Patricia, 1180
Driskell, Stacey, 1842
Drislane, John P, 3134
Drive, Russ, 8593
Driver, Mary, 3771
Driver, Robert B, 2310, 2311
Driver, Russ, 4076
Droessler, Elizabeth, 508
Droessler, Elizabeth Grime, 5265
Droetemueller, Jill, 6382
Drog, Elizabeth, 6830
Drogalis, Kevin, 3798
Droge, Michael, 7436
Drogus, Carol, 7662
Drongowski, Mary, 5349
Droppa, Laura, 1779
Drosd, Nancy, 7792
Drown, Darin, 1946
Drowne, Carol, 8197
Drucker, Arnold W., 5076
Drudge, Mike, 8898
Drustrup, Barbara, 2071
Dryden, Sherrill, 4072
Duane Warren, Jr., Jack, 4433
Dubault, Cathleen M., 1249
Dubie, Marsette, 4820
Dubinsky, John, 3181
Dubno, Julia, 392
Dubois, Marilyn, 8197
Dubois, Philip, 8720
DuBose, Bruce, 3960
DuBose, Foye, 5
Dubose, Kevin, 3986
Dubrovskaya, Zhanna, 224
Ducayet, Wally, 900, 901, 4361
Ducey, Seth, 854, 4293
Ducharme, Michael, 2636, 5526
Duchrow, Steven A, 6773
Ducich, Cindy, 4069
Duck, John M., 246
Duckett, Mary E, 967
Duckey, Kathleen, 201
Duckler, Heidi, 38
Duckworth, Karrah, 1294
Duckworth, Michael, 1933
Duckworth, Tony, 5391
Duda, Amy, 346
Duda, Karen, 1336, 1337, 5005
Duddy, Joan, 406, 3577
Dudevoir, Kayleigh, 2037
Dudley, Bruce K, 3068
Dudley, Daniel, 1556, 5350
Dudley, Earleen Ferguso, 839
Dudley, Jesse, 498
Dudzik, Lorraine, 5940
Duell, Daniel, 198
Duensing, Dale, 1301
Duer, Fred M., 6855, 6857, 6858, 6859
Duerk, Carrie, 5982
Duerr OSB, Abbot Gregory, 5423
Duerst, Jeanne, 4257
Duff, Chris, 8609
Duff, Reenie, 5804
Duff, Tammy, 4691
Duff, Tom, 4348
Duffee, Josh, 4646
Duffey, Ally, 402
Duffin, Larry R, 8489
Duffner, Tassi, 2504
Duffy, B, 4593
Duffy, Katherine P, 4650
Duffy, Robyn, 592
Duffy, Shauna, 592
Duffy, Sue, 8913
Duffy, Susan, 3071
Duffy, Terry, 2062, 2063
Duffy, Terry, 6847
Duffy, William, 1253
Dufrene, Rachel, 7161
Dufty, Barbara, 489
Dugal, Dimitra, 4139
Dugan, Aileen, 4979

Executive Name Index

Dugan, Heidi, 3393
Dugan, Tim, 4317
Dugan, Emily, 6732
Dugas, Matt, 4709
Dugay, A. J., 4246
Duggal, Elizabeth, 6459, 6461
Duggan, Ervin S., 4470
Duggan, Rob, 3153
Duggan, Scott, 1493
Dugger, Vicki, 5027
Dugser, Dr. Richard, 1142
Duhaime, Becca, 8397
Duhigg, Jeff, 2947
Duhon, Christine, 166
Duhon, Denise, 4709
Duitman, Henry, 1114
Duke, Cherry, 2211
Duke, Stuart, 4026
Duke, Todd, 8228
Dukes, Julie, 4856
Dukes, Pete, 8599, 8600, 8602, 8603
Dulik, John, 1653
Dumais, Ryan, 3099
Dumas Albert, Jacqueline, 343
Dumez, Steve, 7139
Dumkelberg, Kermit, 3132
Dumm, Chris, 261
Dumont, Nancy M, 7162
Dumphrey, Chad, 7442
Dun, Cheryl, 2794
Dunagan, Tiffany, 3669
Dunayer, Laurel, 8519
Dunbar, Elizabeth, 8404
Dunbar, Jeff, 5410
Duncan, Annett, 1609
Duncan, Betty, 949
Duncan, Bill, 4979
Duncan, Cameron, 4836
Duncan, Cameron B., 2134
Duncan, Dawn, 3689
Duncan, Dell, 1518
Duncan, Gerry, 7921, 7923, 7924, 7927
Duncan, Griff, 1880, 6113
Duncan, Ilesa, 2942
Duncan, Jacob, 4004, 8463
Duncan, Jan, 1880, 6113
Duncan, Jeanie, 5247
Duncan, Kevin, 905
Duncan, Lewis.M, 6605, 6606
Duncan, Michel, 1577, 5379
Duncan, Natalia, 4138
Duncan, Robert, 2797
Duncan, Roger, 7459
Duncan, Sally, 304
Duncan, Shawn, 6298
Duncan, Stephen, 1291
Duncan, Travis, 6962
Dunfee, Norman, 5150
Dungan, Cheryl, 5430
Dungan, John, 8335
Dunham, Deborah, 2326
Dunham, Siobhan, 1464, 5200
Dunham Jr, Royal, 4776
Dunigan, Doris, 3369
Dunker, Steffany, 285
Dunkle, Amanda, 4635
Dunlap, Mike, 4846
Dunleavy, Rosemary, 466
Dunleavy, Willa, 1724
Dunlevy, J. Thomas, 3819
Dunlevy, Patty, 1819
Dunmyer, Tracey, 8182
Dunn, Alan, 2331
Dunn, Alex, 2341
Dunn, Chris, 5267
Dunn, Dale, 8271
Dunn, Dann, 3441
Dunn, Darryl, 6210
Dunn, David R, 3611
Dunn, Dorsey C., 4430
Dunn, Douglas, 419
Dunn, Gerald, 4904
Dunn, Julie, 311
Dunn, Lorianne, 7462
Dunn, Michael, 4897
Dunn, Mike, 6831
Dunn, Mildred Geckler, 2853
Dunn, Mr. Michael, 7954

Dunn, Randy, 6667, 6668
Dunn, Sandy, 4001
Dunn, Sean, 4041
Dunn, Susan, 8581
Dunn Hamrick, Kathy, 624
Dunnahoo, Jay B., 1736
Dunne, carol, 7541
Dunne, John, 1799
Dunning, Becky, 2886
Dunning, Gary, 4777
Dunning, Peter, 5750
Dunsby, John, 2593
Dunscomb, Richard, 6743
Dunstan, Kirstein, 2858
Dunsworth, Richard, 4185
Dupin, Charles, 2084
Duplantis, Shannon, 7142, 7144
Dupler, Mitchell S., 3121
Duplessis, Susan, 8205
DuPont, Jennifer, 5835
Dupont, Lisaann, 8301
Dupont, Tiffany, 3066
Dupre,, Cheryl, 2523
DuPree, Mary, 4535
Dupree, Steve, 3905
Dupuis, Carol, 8014
Dupuis, Jordan, 8404
Duque, Alejandra, 96
Duran, Hon. John, 1942
Duran, Laura, 4587
Duran, Patricia, 1707
Durant, Brenda, 4510
Durant, Linda S., 8118
Durante, Tom, 55
Duree, Ashley, 20
Duren, Mary, 1284
Durgin, Peter, 3176
Durham, Karen, 7996
Durham, Leslie, 6683, 6684, 6686, 6688
Durham, Lynn, 6619
Durham, Paul M., 4009
Durham, Rebecca, 2368
Durham, Sarah, 520
Durham, Tim, 8016
Durham, William H, 5276
Durieux, Anne, 691
Duritsch, Chuck, 2284
Durkin-Drga, Rachel, 8326
Duro, Dan, 2108
Durocher, Chris, 7318
Duron, Mario A, 3965
Durrence, Larry, 4495
Durrett, Cecily, 3650
Durso, John, 2306
Durso, Lois, 2306
Dusman, Linda, 1158
Dussek, Josy, 5121
Dustin, Bill, 5213
Duston, Jennifer, 815
Duston, Rich, 896
Dutcher, Bill, 7469
Dutcher, Dan, 2222
Dutka, Mike, 219
Dutkiewicz, Patricia, 3202
Dutson, Lyn, 5960
Dutton, Alice, 801
Dutton, Maryann, 2427
Dutton-Swain, Lisa, 4815
Duttweiler, Norman, 3441
Duval, David, 2275
Duval, Ginger, 8047
Duvall, Beth, 4094
Dworin, Judy, 2689
Dworkin, Hanna, 2930
Dwyer, Carolyn, 1341
Dwyer, Christopher, 972
Dwyer, Kara, 2014
Dwyer, Patricia, 100, 101
Dwyer, Paul, 2673
Dwyer, Ruth, 1078
Dwyer, Terrence W., 6090
Dwyer, Terry, 2481
Dwyer Seaburg, Dyan, 5958, 5959
Dyce, Erik, 6366
Dycks, Tony, 4220
Dye, Ron, 4617
Dyer, Jackie, 496
Dyer, Mary, 6900

Dyer, Pamela, 2468, 6109
Dyer, Sharon L., 2202
Dyer, CFE, Courtney, 8564
Dyer, Pamela, 2468
Dyess, Jerry, 8441
Dyke, Phillip, 3832
Dykes, Gordon, 5901, 5902, 5903, 5904
Dykhouse, Amanda, 1240
Dykstra, Diana, 1982
Dyner, Jeannine, 3437
Dynicki, Tony, 4125, 8694
Dysinger, Sean, 3073
Dyson, Chris, 2443
Dziedzic, Laura, 900, 901, 4361
Dzierwinski, Pat, 3118
Dziolo, June, 2209
Djaz, Roberto, 8149

E

E. Gold, Alan, 3353
E. Hamilton, Heather, 3234
E. Lawhead, Lawrence, 1077
E. Lee III, Robert, 2205
E. Moran, Jr., Michael, 6434, 6435
E. Nagrodzk, Glenda, 2401
E. Smith, Joseph, 6516
E. Taylor, David, 6476
E. Wankel, Robert, 2472
E. Young, Jared, 2727
E.Grubb, George, 3234
Eagleson, Craig, 376
Eaken, John, 1669
Eakle, Curt, 2051
Ealy, Sara, 1851
Eames, Karin, 1940, 1941
Eames, Kim, 2420
Eanes, Christopher, 2277
Earehart, Seay, 6
Earhart, Jeanne, 3719
Earhart, Lucie, 1139
Earick, Rhonda, 55
Earl, Jimmy, 5590
Earl, CFE, Jimmy, 8323
Earle, Jim, 8176
Earle, Peter, 3168, 7248
Earley, Andromeda, 5439
Earley, Melissa, 5548
Earls, John G., 5313
Early, Angela, 1394
Early, Richard L, 1107
Earnest, Steve, 3880
Easler, Eileen, 3872
Easley, David, 1834
Easley, John, 4921
Easley, Kathryn, 4156
Easley, Rosemary, 5775
Easom, Chris, 5961
East, Alexander, 4907
East, James, 1385, 1955
East, Kathy, 4319, 4320
East, Tim, 8514
Eastbourne, Lee, 2326
Eastbrook, Norman S., 7410
Eastep, Patricia, 2010
Easter, Quentin, 2582
Eastham, Wayne, 4692
Eastman, David, 450
Eastman, Roger, 7988
Eastman, III, Donald R., 6592, 6593
Easton, Martha, 341
Easton, Susan, 2773
Eastwood, Patricia B., 620
Eastwood, Vicky, 3452
Eastwood, Victoria, 7696
Eaton, Amanda, 4129
Eaton, Chad, 1558
Eaton, David, 1427
Eaton, Harvill, 8276
Eaton, Helen S., 5485
Eaton, Jeffrey, 1594
Eaton, Jonathan, 2322
Eaton, Joyce, 5245
Eaton, Linda M., 3745
Eaton, Marielle, 2727
Eaton Johnson, Vickie, 7972
Eaton-Johnson, Vickie, 7973, 7974
Ebann, Linnea, 5831

Ebdon, Carol, 4948
Ebel, Charles, 6575
Ebelhar, Jeff, 7104
Ebenhoch, Mark, 1902
Eberhart, Eileen, 7171
Eberl, Carl, 4542
Eberle, Samantha, 3960
Eberly, Gwen, 3732
Eberly, Jodi, 4645
Ebersole, Susan, 1430
Ebert, Gary, 4136
Ebert, John, 3696
Ebinger, Phil, 6625
Ebner, Billy, 5600
Ebner, Robert, 7320
eBow-Sachs, Lainy, 7198
Eccles, Autumn, 7693
Eccles, Mary, 142
Eccles, Tom, 1853
Echeveste, John, 2495
Echols, Sherry, 6654
Eck, Daniel, 5868
Eck, Leigh, 3898
Eckardt, Jason, 1417
Eckardt, Jill, 6487
Eckenrode, Bryan, 1664
Ecker, Kevin, 3115
Eckerberg, Eric, 4845
Eckern, Scott, 2553
Eckerson, Earnest, 2419
Eckert, John, 3438
Eckert, Jon N., 7560
Eckert, Patricia, 6310
Eckert, Todd, 83
Eckford, Karen, 8205
Eckhardt, Mark, 5627
Eckholdt, John, 2084
Eckroth, Julius, 1633
Eckstrom, John, 2134
Ecliff, D Scott, 1708
Edberg, Allison, 1089
Eddlemon, Scott, 1697
Eddy, Abby, 4635
Eddy, Alexandra, 4353
Eddy, Margaret, 2381
Eddy, Mark, 7175
Eddy, Tianna, 3777
Edelberg, David, 2926
Edelberg, Joseph, 878
Edelman, David, 3720
Edelman, Sheldon, 7048
Edelstein, Alan, 2308
Edelstein, Gerardo, 5508
Edelstein, Gordon, 2697, 6419
Edelstein, Linda, 1831
Edelston, Robin, 941
Eden, Erika, 7044
Edenfield, Holly, 172
Edenson, Alan, 6234
Edge-O'Bergfell, John, 4280
Edgecomb, David, 5936
Edgecombe, David, 2418
Edgell, Neil, 3131
Edgerton, Glenn, 203
Edgerton, William H, 1961
Edholm, Jacob, 292
Edington, Cheryl, 1279
Edler, Madeleine, 8188
Edlinger, Carole, 1939
Edlund, Kristin, 1792
Edmonds, Bobby, 6021
Edmonds, Daven, 3061
Edmonds, Larry, 4173
Edmondson, Charles, 5041, 7628
Edmons, Jeff, 844
Edmunds, Kristy, 6181
Edmunds, Mark, 855, 4309, 4312
Edrington, Carol, 5655
Edrington, Janett, 816
Eduardo Gonz lez, Jos,, 3785
Edward, Diane, 8205
Edward, Justin, 8022
Edward Hughes, Ralph, 1901
Edward Niles, John, 2372
Edwards, Amanda, 6645
Edwards, Andrew, 3778, 5411, 8081
Edwards, Angie, 4414
Edwards, Bruce, 8515

Executive Name Index

Edwards, Cathy, 7724
Edwards, David, 1777
Edwards, Dawn, 608
Edwards, Don, 5616
Edwards, Dr James L, 6853
Edwards, Dr. Scott, 6459
Edwards, Emily, 340
Edwards, Gail, 816
Edwards, Hanna, 363
Edwards, Harve, 4253, 6189
Edwards, Haw, 1794
Edwards, Huw, 1608
Edwards, JoLynn, 1798, 5793
Edwards, Justin, 8023, 8024
Edwards, Katie, 4470
Edwards, Linda, 1781, 7090, 7091
Edwards, Lisa, 1886
Edwards, Marla, 15
Edwards, Maurice, 379
Edwards, Melissa M., 5244
Edwards, Michael, 2821, 7722
Edwards, Mike, 1695
Edwards, Peter L, 2125
Edwards, Richards L, 1202
Edwards, Steven, 2085
Edwards, Sue, 4299
Edwards, Tara, 8201
Edwards, PhD, Carol D., 8573, 8574, 8575, 8576
Edy, Treasurer, 874
Eeckhout, Ed Van, 2197
Effron, Blair W., 5151
Effron, David, 7861
Egan, Claudia, 1832
Egan, Grete, 1939
Egan, Matthew, 4091
Egan, Tim, 4321
Egar, Joseph, 1490
Egbert, Kathleen, 891
Egel, Michael, 2072
Eggar, Beth Jennings, 5068
Eggar, Dave, 477
Eggeman, Natalie, 4616
Egger, Llinda, 1308
Egger McKern, Chandra, 2009
Eggert, Karl, 6333, 6337
Eggington, Paul, 2460
Eggleston, Lenore, 1393
Egins, Paul, 6348
Egler, Fran, 8168
Ehle, Heidi, 613
Ehler, Sylvia, 5490
Ehlinger, Bruce, 4117, 8675, 8681, 8683
Ehnebuske, Kathy, 30
Ehrenberg, Joyce, 6211
Ehret, Mary, 11
Ehrhardt, Ralf, 1527
Ehrich, Denise K, 2766
Ehrlich, David, 6365
Ehmstrum, Peter, 3613
Eibeck, JW, 6800
Eibeck, Pamela, 4338
Eichar, William J, 4604
Eichbauer, Mary, 887
Eichenberger, Sharon, 6041
Eicher, MFA, Chris, 2446
Eichhorn, Erich, 1534
Eichinger, Bill, 7662
Eichmann, Marla, 4109
Eickelberg, Jenni, 2393
Eickhacker, Bruce, 6996
Eiden, Jeremy, 4579
Eidson, Deborah, 6689
Eifert, Eunice R, 6819, 6822
Eihorn, Cathy, 356
Eikner, Edward, 4516
Eiland, Sharlotte, 4812
Eilber, Janet, 454
Eilers, Justin, 3770
Eilers, Laura, 2985
Einach, Judith, 3180
Einhorn, Nancy, 197
Einhouse, Lucinda B, 7997
Eischeid, Nancy, 1668
Eisdorfer, Jessi, 1201
Eiseman, F Lee, 4778
Eisemann, Marisa, 1361
Eisemann, MD, Marisa, 5039
Eisenbarth, Jeffrey.G, 6605, 6606

Eisenberg, David M, 1281
Eisenberg, Lee, 4115
Eisenberg, Marc, 1994
Eisendrath, Dr Craig, 2315
Eisenhart, Blake H., 5473
Eisenhart, Sylvia, 5185
Eisenhower, Laurie, 291
Eisenmann, Harold, 635
Eisenmenger, Eleanor C, 5036
Eisenreich, Ted, 8667
Eisenstat, Melissa B., 1433
Eiser, Michael, 3812
Eisler, David L, 7278
Eisler, Davis, 4828
Eisner, David, 2100
Eisner, Michael, 6539
Eitel, Don, 3248
Eitze, Chester, 3936, 8328
Ek, Karen, 5847
Ekholm, Tricia, 179
Ekker, Kelsey, 5716, 8507
Ekmalian, Mary, 1439
Ekstrand, Laura, 3387
Ekstrand, Norma, 4356
El Dabh, Halim, 2281
El-Hage, Elias, 491
Elby, Janet, 1351
Elderkin, Ann L., 2089
Eldridge, Rick, 4334
Eleas, Suzanne, 3893
Eledlestein, Gordan, 2697
Elegant Huff, Linda, 4592
Elena Megret, Maria, 8377
Elia, Elizabeth, 930
Elias, Byron W., 504
Elias, Carlos, 912
Elias, Ralph, 2819
Elias, Shannon, 7383
Elicks, Lauren, 363
Elienberger-Ubell, Cathy, 2579
Elihu Kramer, Daniel, 3149
Elieabeth Swerz, Mary, 4777
Elitzer, Donald B., 4814
Elizabeth,, 4903
Elizabeth Campeau, CM Sgt, 951
Elizabeth Carey, Mary, 4447, 4685
Elizabeth Rice, Laura, 3240
Elizondo, Malu, 6322
Elkhouse, Guillermo, 336
Elkin, Saul, 3428
Elkington, Susan, 1079
Elkins, Doug, 417
Elkins, Gregory, 5652
Elkins, Tamara, 3957
Elkinton, Eleanor M., 2310
Elkiss, Dale, 1669, 5515
Ell, Frank, 5268
Ellebracht, Mark, 1285
Ellen Consolver, Kay, 5052
Ellen Harder, Lee, 4478
Ellen McCall, Jo, 4164
Ellen Parker, Jo, 8562
Ellenberger, Jr, Carl, 5447
Ellenberg, Dolly, 8170, 8171
Ellenoff, Neil, 3176
Eller, David, 8203
Ellerbee, Carmen, 4522
Ellersick, Joan, 4775
Ellestein, David, 2625
Ellia, Michelle, 8123
Ellie Choi, Wooyoung, 2024
Ellingson, Craig, 4876
Ellingson, Craig A, 3261
Ellingsworth, Patrick, 1315
Ellington, Mercedes, 387
Ellington, Theo, 6252
Elliot, Becky, 2280
Elliot, John, 1817, 2392
Elliot, Judy, 1938
Elliot, Lisa, 6267
Elliot, Richard, 6089
Elliot, Scott, 3529
Elliott, Anthony, 1223
Elliott, Britney, 707
Elliott, Cynthia, 5164
Elliott, Cynthia, 7787
Elliott, Geoff, 2490
Elliott, J. Cari, 4430

Elliott, Kay Arden, 3143
Elliott, Mark, 479
Elliott, Michael, 1251
Elliott, Peggy, 878
Elliott, Richard, 2363
Elliott, Scott, 3576
Elliott, Vincent, 5046
Elliott, Vincent G., 6800
Elliott Rich, Susan, 2329
Elliott Williams, Jean, 1097
Ellis, Adrian, 5142, 7729
Ellis, Brenda, 5353
Ellis, Charles, 1170
Ellis, Cheryl, 5001
Ellis, Dave, 6887
Ellis, David, 1041
Ellis, Denise, 5920
Ellis, Grant, 1786
Ellis, Jeff, 2011
Ellis, Jennifer, 2082
Ellis, Jerry, 903
Ellis, Joan, 2197
Ellis, Joe, 6351
Ellis, John, 1223, 3638, 7854
Ellis, Justin, 1784
Ellis, Kate, 2422, 5951, 5955
Ellis, Manty, 4918
Ellis, Margaret, 2059
Ellis, Michael, 1234
Ellis, Nancy, 1729
Ellis, Peter, 4967
Ellis, Rick, 2381
Ellis, Robert, 8005
Ellis, Rodney, 1134
Ellis, Steve, 4855
Ellis, Susan, 4708
Ellison, Gerald, 3656
Ellison, Martha, 1993
Ellison, Patricia S, 8539
Ellison, Scott P, 7363
Ellison, Soyia, 4504
Ellman, Stuart J., 5109, 7788
Ellsworth, David, 8044
Ellsworth, Emily, 2054
Ellsworth, Laura E., 5506
Ellsworth, Liz, 4074
Ellsworth, Michelle, 2647, 4363
Ellwood, Jeffrey, 4346
Ellwood, Stan, 2983
Ellwood, William R, 2698
Ellzy, Leatrice, 4505
Elman, Phillip, 3444
Elman, Shelly, 2869
Elmasri Buchholz, Marianne, 4352
Elmendorf, Becky, 1788
Elmore, John, 6411, 6412, 6413, 6414
Elmore, L. Franklin, 5540
Elmore, Lee, 1680
Elo, Jorma, 271
Eloiffer, Edonard A, 7566
Elowitch, Jennifer, 4743
Elrod, James, 7157
Elsbury, Anjo, 7128
Elson, Phil, 6036
Elston, Ken, 8519
Elston, Tish, 6588
Elwood, Charlie, 7690
Elwood, Damien, 1889
Ely, Dr. Eileen, 8568
Elyse Carleton, Lucy, 4457
Elzey, Thomas J., 8211
Emanuel, David, 2296, 5393
Embry, Kathy, 6864, 6867, 6869
Emerman, Janet, 4157
Emerson, Bill, 7483
Emerson, Derek, 4847
Emerson, Fran, 1640
Emerson, Jan, 2167
Emerson, John B, 4243
Emert, Lyndal, 2360
Emery, Jo, 690
Emery, Joan, 224
Emery, Stephani, 1390
Emge, Jeffrey D, 5674
Emily,, 1266
Emlen, George, 2126
Emmanuel, Karen, 7119
Emmes, David, 2461, 6091

Emmons, Melanie, 3109
Emmons, Zette, 491, 5171
Emory, Thomasina, 7311
Empey, John, 1806
Emrick, William T, 7628
Ende, Rebecca, 6478
Enders, Morrie, 3326
Enders, Murvin, 6901, 6902
Endo, Keith, 6169
Endres, Dr. Donald, 1845
Endres, Peg, 3265
Endress, Cathy, 774
Endrizzi, Susan, 8743
Endsley, Ann, 47
Endsley, Gerald, 906
Enfinger, Stanley, 5920
Eng, Calvin D., 6066, 6070, 6071, 6072
Engebretson, Stan, 1169
Engel, Eric, 3153
Engel, Kim, 6609, 7627
Engel, Kristina, 6132
Engelhardt, Kimberly, 4439
Engelhardt, Paul, 2980
Engelhardt, Suzanne, 2163
Engelhart, Cecilia, 855
Engelman, Arnold, 7796
Engelman, Bob, 875
Enger, Linda,, 3216
England, Charles, 1449
England, Leslie, 3061
Englander, Marlene, 1543
Englander, Jr., Robert P., 5753
Engle, Dale, 1870
Engle, Tyler, 5799
Engler, Kyle, 1665
Engler, Rich, 8175
Engler, Rick, 4998
English, Bonnie, 4801
English, Gary, 2711, 6439
English, Gary M, 2709
English, Geof, 2527
English, Martin, 4906
English, Teri, 127
Englund, Jim, 1791
Engstrom, Royce, 8248
Enicoine, Susan, 2568
Enloe, Sarah, 4056
Enlow, Todd, 3768
Ennabe, Sureya, 4976
Ennals, Rebecca, 4311
Ennis, Claire, 2725
Ennis, Michael, 4860
Ennis, Stephanie, 8580
Enns, Gordon, 5399
Enns, Richard, 6104
Enos, Jerald, 2613
Enos, Mike, 3286
Enrich, Jeff, 2964
Enright, Keely, 3872
Enright, Tim, 6732
Enright, William, 6256
Enriquez, Veronica, 8377
Enriquez, Wilson, 4494
Enslen, Pamela, 1244
Enslen, Sonny, 1488
Ensor, Diane, 7184
Ensz, Brette, 3325
Enzinger, Juli, 1076
Enzmam, Brian, 2778
Enzor, Scott, 6022
Epling, Garth, 4278, 4279, 6219
Epperson, Eugenia L, 1519
Epperson, Sandra, 3667
Eppler Colvin, Marcia, 5109, 7788
Epplett, Shannon, 202
Epps, Arnie A., 2859
Epps, Sheldon, 2542, 6209
Epstein, Eileen, 2039
Epstein, Ira, 2625
Epstein, Joel, 3556, 3570
Epstein, Katie, 278
Epstein, Mark, 4560
Epstein, Melvin, 5592
Epstein, Victoria A., 564
Epsteis, Howard, 5345
Epsztein Bedel, Jude, 4775
Epting, James B, 5551
Epting, Reverend Bobbie, 4141

Executive Name Index

Erb, Steve, 8084
Erdberg, Lisa, 1922, 1923
Erdman, Harley, 3149
Erdman, Jean, 3540
Erdmann, Karl, 3738
Erdmann, Larry, 1962
Ereckson, Judy, 5940
Erhardt, Pat, 2723
Erhart, Mildred, 5655
Ericksen, Jackie, 5032
Ericksen, Ph.D., Julia, 3836
Erickson, Julia, 7375
Erickson, Lee, 1830
Erickson, Linda G., 6481
Erickson, M Joy, 3690
Erickson, Paul, 7340
Erickson, Raymond, 922, 4383
Erickson, Rick, 897, 2217, 2351
Erickson, Robert, 4669
Ericson, Karen, 485
Erienbush, Robin, 2167
Erik A, Moses, 4419
Eriksen, Amy, 6275
Erlick, Janet, 2776
Ermer, Margaret, 7194
Ernesto, John, 5501
Ernst, Diane, 5364
Ernst, Katie, 4556
Ernst, Steve, 3750
Eroe, Geof, 5977
Errante, Steven, 1506
Erreca, Sarah, 5891, 5892
Errichetti, Thomas, 6395
Ersek, Andy, 6112
Ertsgaard, Kathy, 499
Ervice, Jenna, 889
Ervin, John D., 7182
Ervin, Mike, 6760
Erwin, Ingrid, 3878
Erwin, James, 4469
Erwin, John, 1863, 4572
Erwin, Linda, 5545
Erwin, Sandy, 7586
Erwin, Terri, 2438
Esasky, Elise, 7869
Esau, John, 7063
Esau, Larry, 5421
Esau, Matt, 7367
Escalada, John, 3292
Escandon, Homero, 1908
Esch, Sarajo, 2627
Eschenbach, Christoph, 956, 958, 1997, 4424, 4795, 6471
Eschentacher, Herman, 2323
Escobar, Camila, 170
Escobar, Jesus, 6403
Escoda, Cristina, 386
Escola, Suzanne, 939
Eshkenazy, Maxim, 868
Eshleman, Dennis, 5994
Eske, Dave, 7210
Eskenazi, Leah, 4246
Eskola, Crystal, 4510
Esparza, Ce Ce, 4162
Esparza, Daniel, 6322
Espinosa, Leandro, 1597
Espinoza, Albertossy, 34
Espinoza, Arthur, 149
Esplin, Fred, 4009
Esposito, Jeff, 5448
Esposito, Jeff, 8122
Esquivel, Cecilia, 3130
Esser, Frank, 6961, 6962, 6963, 6964, 6965
Esser, Maureen, 8084
Esserman, Ron, 160
Essner, Erica, 365
Estabrook, Ashlee, 6769
Estabrook, Todd, 2106
Este, Geovanni, 362
Esteban, Sergio, 3609
Estep, Randee, 3725
Ester, Lawrence, 1563
Estes, Maggie, 1722
Estes, Mimi, 2704
Esther Schmidt, Amy, 527
Estrada, Aide, 13
Estrada, Ed, 798
Estrada, Mary, 4176

Estrada, Sam, 3937
Estrella, Tony, 3859
Estrin, Gabriel, 2252
Esvang, Richard, 4668
Etchings, Vicki, 3346, 7538
Etemad, Mario, 7273
Etgen, Ann, 629
Ethens, James, 5800
Etheridge, Marti, 3956
Etherly, Don, 4188
Ethridge, Alan, 5541
Ethridge, Mark, 7129
Etminan, Kaweh, 4937
Etro, Sarah, 662
Ettenbazh, Lelah, 4986
Ettenger, Mark D., 5103
Etter, Orval, 1591
Etzel, Greg, 1061
Eubank, Ronie, 3650
Eubanks, Jaye, 4522
Eubanks, Ray, 1547
Eugenio, Sammy, 6639
Eukel, Linus, 4195
Euler, Megan, 2663
Eure, Margaret, 4058
Eure, Van, 3677
Eustance, Lynn, 1956
Eustis, Oskar, 3552, 7710, 7749, 7757, 7769, 7781
Evancho, Mark, 8506
Evano, George, 5405
Evans, Alicia, 5533
Evans, Allen, 3877
Evans, Anita, 2932
Evans, Ann, 4569
Evans, Anne, 4569
Evans, Barb, 3883
Evans, Becky, 2835
Evans, Beth, 139
Evans, Bill, 353
Evans, Bob, 4085
Evans, Brian, 4690
Evans, Carlos E., 1679, 3869, 5534
Evans, Carlos.E, 596
Evans, Christine, 6479
Evans, Chuck, 5887
Evans, Clay, 4363
Evans, Corey, 7222
Evans, Deborah L., 8113
Evans, Douglas H., 5168
Evans, Dr Cory, 2035
Evans, Dr. Kenneth, 8333
Evans, Dr. Rebecca, 14, 6032, 6033
Evans, Emily (Penny), 7185
Evans, Erin, 5952
Evans, George, 1481
Evans, Gregory D., 1406
Evans, Holly, 478
Evans, Jane, 5375
Evans, John, 5405
Evans, John H, 1624
Evans, John R, 6091
Evans, Joseph, 7123
Evans, Kristin, 6052
Evans, Laura, 4309, 4312
Evans, Lauren, 3986
Evans, Laurence, 3897
Evans, Lydia, 1385
Evans, Lyn, 4211
Evans, Lynn, 766
Evans, Margaret L., 1431
Evans, Maria, 3381
Evans, Noel, 1788
Evans, Pete, 4110
Evans, Robert, 1444
Evans, Sarah, 4970
Evans, Sharon, 2938
Evans, Sheila, 1616, 8107
Evans, Susan, 1954
Evans, Thomas, 3447
Evans, Timothy J., 2986
Evans, Tracy, 4016, 6525
Evans Waldron, Heide, 983
Evans, CPA, Scott, 33
Evans, Jr, Terry L., 2312
Evans, M.P.A., Beth M., 7692
Evanson, Mary, 4171, 5962
Evenden, Michael, 6629

Evens, Craige, 7545
Evenson, Grant, 6327
Everet, Clay, 2635
Everett, Beverly, 1510
Everett, David J., 3204
Everett, Dr Beverly, 1257
Everett, Dr Mark A, 1582
Everett, Dr. H Dean, 1582
Everist, Juliet, 1115, 1116
Everitt, Bob, 3326
Everitt, John, 2296, 5393
Everly, Jack, 1083, 1084, 1155
Everly Klassen, Laurie, 6325
Evershed, Jeffrey, 2300
Eversole, Henry O, 823
Everson, James, 911
Evert, Tom, 521
Evins, Jennifer, 5548
Evleshin, Catherine, 3785
Ewald, Jeffrey, 6199
Ewalt, Ginger, 4264
Ewalt, James B Ewalt, 6957
Ewalt, Mark E, 6957
Ewan-Kroeger, Joanne, 6101
Ewanus, Donald S, 8640
Ewell, Maryo, 4367
Ewen, John G, 1964
Ewen, Malcolm, 4026
Ewers, Anne, 2366
Ewers, Mathew, 1807
Ewing, Dr. Ray G, 4896
Ewing, Lawrence, 77, 103
Ewing, Maria H., 1500
Ewing, Rene', 1791
Ewing Allen, Jenny, 4104, 5822
Executive Vice Presi,, 6632
Exler, Tony, 8302
Exner, Molly, 7334
Eyck Swackhamer, Ten, 3982
Eyink, Pam, 2284
Eylar, Leo, 820
Eyre McDonald, Jane, 1592
Ezell, David, 2014
Ezhokino, Oksana, 5783

F

F. Dalton, Brain, 8140
F. Fisher, John, 6424
F. Fry, Stephen F., 6902
F. Leahy, Dr. Patrick, 8189
F. Neidorff, Michael, 6471
F.Cornell, Michelle, 3753
Faber, Brandon, 1226
Faber, Cameron, 6155
Faber, Peter L., 4783
Fabian, Katherine, 163
Fabre, Guy, 4258
Fabrizi, Michele, 2321
Fabrizio, Dominic, 3751
Factor, Lori, 8023, 8024
Fadem, Kimmie, 764
Fadler, Melissa, 8418
Faegre, Aron, 1606
Fagan, Garth, 498
Fagan, John, 3878
Fagerstrom, Jamie, 2870
Fagg, Connie, 3969, 8384
Fagin, Gary S, 1342
Fahey, James M, 6752
Fahim, Yvette, 6085
Fahringer, Dr James, 773
Faiella, Ida, 5040
Fail, Joseph, 4886
Fair, Douglas J., 1704
Fairbank, Elmer, 376
Fairbanks, Ann, 1730
Fairbend, Karen, 2334
Fairchild, Jeannine, 2510
Fairchild, Mary, 1476, 5217
Faircloth, Janice, 4523
Faircloth, Wander, 3066
Fairfield, Scot, 220
Fairlie, Thomas, 1754
Fairservis, Teviot, 2680
Fairweather, Jane, 3120
Faison, Ade, 3525
Faison, Shirley, 3525

Fajans, Pepper, 467
Fajardo, Jose, 163
Faker, Brian, 5801
Falb, Robert E., 2747
Falco, Art, 3716
Falco, Art J., 7975, 7976, 7977
Falco, Theresa, 3094
Falcone, Lorrie, 642
Falcone, Robert, 5324
Falcone Vedric, Jill, 5189
Falconer, Beth, 7244
Fale, Debra, 5868
Falene, Kalley, 1517
Fales, Priscilla, 3143
Falese, Joseph T., 6832
Falgiano, Rob, 7658
Falk, Elizabeth, 2249
Falk, Larry, 8322
Falk, Susie, 2538
Falkowski, Phil, 654
Fallete, Joanne, 2375
Falletta, Maestro JoAnn, 1021
Fallis, Jim, 5953
Fallock, John, 3795, 8115
Fallon, Dan, 3933
Fallon, Shirley, 2125
Fallon, Skye, 2425
Fallow, Tom, 6315
Falls, Robert, 2933
Familian, David, 6133, 6135
Fan, Cindy, 821
Fan, Sylvie H, 3541
Fane, Lisa, 3593
Fanelli, Genevieve, 140
Faneuff, Ken, 6667, 6668
Fanger, David, 414
Fanik, Blanche, 5873
Fank, Cathy, 8708
Fank, Sandra Q., 246
Fankhauser, Teresa, 4915
Fann, Drew, 8306
Fannin Baker, Cliff, 6040
Fanning, Christine, 3194
Fanning, Wendy, 5880
Fant, Deborah, 5797
Fantasia, Louis, 804
Fantl, Sharon, 7535
Fantova, Marketa, 5041
Fantozzi, Tony, 7326
Faraone, Cheryl, 4021
Farber, Dave, 4263
Fardiany, Nana, 766
Farer, David B, 1204
Farer, David B., 4796, 4797
Farer, Lian, 5003
Farfan, Juana, 185
Farger Clark, Michelle, 6373
Faricy, Kate, 4364, 6340
Faridany, Lucy, 4212
Faridy, Jim, 2180
Farley, Barbara A., 6793
Farley, Bill, 4209
Farley, D. Michael, 3393
Farley, Drew, 4337
Farley, Jery, 7062
Farley, Jillian, 2727
Farley, Jim, 6278
Farley, Katherine, 5151
Farley, Robert J., 2878
Farlow, Lesley, 2689
Farlow-Cornell, Jeffrey, 1031
Farm, Pete, 1271
Farmer, Carol, 1464
Farmer, Erin, 3236
Farmer, Lesley, 3066
Farmer, Peter, 821
Farmer, Richard, 1979
Farmer Hall, Kristen, 5888
Farnham, Cindy, 1220
Farnks, CE Bud, 1910, 2571
Farno, Meaghan, 4756
Farnsley, Steve, 8276
Faron, Sally, 4483
Faron, Sally R, 4483
Farquhar, Thomas, 997
Farrell, Carol, 3096
Farrell, Christina, 2322
Farrell, Cindy, 7529

Executive Name Index

Farrell, Freda, 5706
Farrell, James, 3444
Farrell, John, 1745, 3096
Farrell, Joseph, 2201
Farrell, Katie, 3612
Farrell, Patricia, 5752
Farrell, Tina, 634
Farrell, Wayne, 2827
Farrell Murray, Sheila, 789
Farrelly, Paddy, 8558
Farrer, John, 757, 1357
Farrer, Lian, 5003, 7573
Farrington, Kate, 3545
Farris, Sandra, 8256
Farrow Raines, Wendy, 2732
Farry, Mike, 3594
Fartas, Adil, 6267
Farve Hayes, Charlie, 5919
Farwell, Shaina, 2038
Fasl, Tom, 7446
Fass, Richard, 6086
Fassberg, Edith, 403, 463
Fassett, Melissa, 6283
Fassett, Priscilla, 1815
Fassler, Kylee, 499
Faszholz, James, 5710
Fath, Harry, 5305
Fathman, M.D., Anthony, 4920
Fator, Gertrude, 4328
Fatt Vitale, Marilyn, 2923
Fatt Vitale, Marilyn, 6734
Faucett, Bill, 2014
Faucette, Charlotte, 6024
Faue, Larry, 7090, 7091
Faulk, Ellen, 2060
Faulkner, Andrew, 491
Faulkner, Barbara, 4251
Faulkner, Craig J., 3353
Faulkner, Curtis, 4918
Faulkner, Jerome, 3788
Faulkner, Larry, 8326
Faulkner, Marilyn, 3989
Faulkner, Scott, 1315
Faulkner Jr, Grady L, 2691
Faure, Laura, 250, 4735
Fausaut, John, 7843
Fauska, Brian, 4087
Faust, Gail, 599
Faust, Lisa, 8186
Faustino, Lovelie, 81
Favara, Annette, 4099
Favara, Vinnie, 4099
Favero, Peter, 870
Favreau, Laurelle, 8780
Fay, David, 4390, 6406, 6409
Fay, Kathleen, 4774, 4783
Fay, Laura, 8091
Fay, Lori, 754
Fazenbaker, Alexa, 4099
Fazio, Daryl, 4504
Fazio Lynch, Beth, 5289
Fazzini, Pamela, 733, 4174
Fazzini, Susan, 2134
Fazzino, Joe, 133
Fearing, Don, 5626
Fearnow, Mark, 4618
Fearon, Richard H., 7975, 7976, 7977
Feasel, Gregory D, 6348
Featherly, Walter, 717
Featherman, David, 4825
Feathers, Vicky, 5196
Feazel Meiki, Kendra, 247
Feazell, Trey, 6625
Fechter, Andrea, 2197
Fecth, Bob, 1837
Feder, Joshua, 7541
Feder, Larry, 4062, 4063
Feder, Mike, 6009
Feder, Phyllis, 5129
Federico, Agostini, 7812
Federico, Michael, 2679
Federico, Robert, 3556, 3570
Fedie, Dan, 243
Fedore, Max, 1633
Fedrick, Joe, 2686
Fee, Charles, 2895, 4533, 5320
Feehan, Scott, 4707
Fees, Douglas, 710

Fefe, Jesse, 8174
Feher, Robyn, 8587
Fehr, Cinnie, 1984
Fehr, Deborah, 4814
Feibelman, Laura, 1565
Feigelman, Jacalyn, 6164, 6179
Feigenbaum, Phyllis, 231
Feighan, Nadine H, 8005
Feighan, Nadine H., 8005
Feil, Jonathan, 1792
Fein, Oliver, 359
Feiner, Barbara, 3303
Feiner, Cipora, 3149
Feiner, Scott, 4113
Feinerman, Frances, 7249
Feingold, Daniel, 920
Feingold, Ed, 1180
Feingold, Edmund, 769, 1060
Feingold, Mary, 5382
Feinour, Ted, 4055
Feinsod, Arthur, 3023, 3024
Feinstein, Michael, 824, 825, 6860, 7211
Feinstein, Michael, 7211
Feintuch, Richard, 5483
Feit, Richard, 869, 4323
Feith, Dan, 418
Feitzinger, Polly, 1477
Feld, Barbara, 5288
Feld, Bonnie, 4033
Feld, Eliot, 394
Feld, Steve, 5948
Feldblum, Miriam, 6086
Felder, Carrie, 5289
Felder, David, 5057
Felder, Eileen, 5057
Feldheim, Mark, 4030
Feldman, Alan, 3396, 7599
Feldman, Candace, 5051
Feldman, Danny, 3511
Feldman, Greg S, 7743
Feldman, Heidi, 2943
Feldman, Josh, 6673
Foldman, Marc, 836
Feldman, Richard, 5544
Feldman, Susan, 1031, 5052
Felix, Jessica, 4224
Felix, Peggy, 6948, 6951
Felker, Craig, 1135
Fellenstein, Lynn, 668
Feller, Bob, 7273
Feller, Brandon, 7994
Fellers, Stacey, 3929
Felling, Gene, 6192
Fellner, Micheal, 3886
Fellows, Catherine J., 6415, 6416
Fellows, David, 3134
Fellows, Steve, 686
Felmet, Steve, 2843, 6611
Felt, Kelli Shana, 5545
Felt, Ruth A, 4310
Felt, Ruth A., 4310
Felter, Ann, 4354
Feltman, Ronald, 4813
Felton, Carolyn, 1483
Feltsman, Vladimir, 5108
Femling, Roxanne, 2464
Fenandez, Robert I, 3971
Fender, George, 3809
Fendley, Curtis, 8440
Fengler, Corty, 1911
Fenley, Molissa, 459
Fenlon, Gigi, 6879, 6880, 6881
Fennelly, Brian, 5169
Fennelly, Patrick, 4122
Fenneman, Craig E., 6888
Fenske, Hannah, 4064
Fenton, Dan, 6270
Fenton, Jane, 5141
Fenton, Kevin G, 6348
Fentress, Duke, 3675
Fenwick, Lisa, 1394
Feo, Pamela, 1187
Ferasat, Anahita, 4237, 6175
Ferdland, Elliot, 2908
Fergus-Jean, Christin, 4379
Fergusen, R Neil, 1739
Fergusen, Warren, 1736
Ferguson, Brad, 1582

Ferguson, Cecily, 5542
Ferguson, Christel, 3470
Ferguson, Erick, 4267
Ferguson, Esther B., 5172, 8866
Ferguson, Jennifer, 6346
Ferguson, Joan, 7291
Ferguson, Joseph W., 1786
Ferguson, Marilyn, 1977
Ferguson, Mary, 648
Ferguson, Michael, 6432
Ferguson, Paul W., 7173, 7174
Ferguson, Rebecca C., 7949
Ferguson, Richard, 3013
Ferguson, Stanley L., 2047
Ferguson, Stuart, 4334
Ferguson, Terrence J., 2169
Ferguson-Webb, Sheila, 65
Fergusson, Sheila, 1812
Ferlo, Joseph A, 8697
Ferlo, Patrick, 6609, 7627
Fermaglich, Ken, 8811
Ferman, Polly, 7773
Fernadez, Soledad, 7706
Fernald, Sarah, 2589
Fernand, Enrique, 8350
Fernandes, Manny, 3376, 7571
Fernandez, Arturo, 71
Fernandez, Darleen, 717
Fernandez, Jennifer, 3916
Fernandez, Patricia, 979
Fernandez, Raul, 6475
Fernandez, Ricardo, 3988
Fernandez, Soledad, 5103
Ferr, Naomi, 6814
Ferra, Max, 3502
Ferrandis, Bruno, 878, 4332
Ferrante, Deanna K.G., 4995
Ferrantino, John, 352
Ferrara, David, 1525
Ferrara, Simona, 454
Ferrari, Andea, 499
Ferraro, Debbie, 5121
Ferraro, Peter, 6423
Ferre, Loren, 7062
Ferrell, Edward, 1482
Ferrer, Dr Joseph, 2003
Ferrer, William, 4277
Ferrie, Vincent, 6421
Ferrier, Stephanie, 4999
Ferriera, Linda, 5199
Ferris, Christopher, 678
Ferris, Diane, 4793
Ferris, Harris N, 582
Ferris, Ruth, 4920
Ferrucci, Darryl, 21
Ferry, Patrick, 5853
Ferstead, Nora, 6732
Ferziger, Susan, 3577
Fesenmey, Thomas, 6969
Fessenden, Mary, 3445
Fete, Suzan, 4128
Fether, Harriet, 5672
Fethke, Gary C., 7003, 7006, 7007, 7008
Fetler, David, 1460, 1462
Fett, Jessi, 7352
Fetta, Frank, 763, 777
Fetter, Beverly, 2755
Fetter, Steve, 5790
Fetter, Thompson, 6238, 6243
Fetterman, Bob, 2771
Fetterplace, Gary, 4066
Fettkether, Louis, 1101
Feucht, Katherine, 2958
Feuerstein, Marjorie, 5161
Feustel, Joe, 4134
Fey, Lorenne, 2847, 6635
Ficca, Ray, 3803
Ficca, Raymond, 2744
Fick, Joel, 6054
Ficklin, Edward, 2247
Ficklin, Linda, 4955
Ficks, Leo, 923
Fiebig, Jeremy, 3656
Fiechtner, Margaret, 1510
Field, Crystal, 3578
Field, Doug, 7104
Field, Drew, 2342
Field, Robert E., 6720, 6721

Fielder, Pamela, 3466
Fielding, Tamara, 3599, 3600
Fields, Barbara, 59
Fields, Brad, 386
Fields, Chris, 2500
Fields, Craig, 2153
Fields, Jack, 5889, 5890
Fields, Kevin, 7518
Fields, Lynne, 1834
Fields, Mark, 6456, 6457, 7558
Fields, Michael, 2452
Fields, Michael D, 1283
Fields, Richard, 3767
Fields-Gold, Anita, 3080, 7128
Fieldsend, Kent, 4649
Fiet, Joyce, 4193
Fife, Barbara J., 3517
Fife, Bernadette, 6190
Fife, Dr. Phyllis, 3768
Fifield, Nathan, 554, 620
Figaro, Lori, 8465
Figaro, Tyrone, 5990
Figgins, Barbara, 2947
Figgins, Nicola, 6249
Figo, Laura, 999
Figols, Alberto, 5744
Figueredo, Marie, 1331
Figueroa, Ernest, 2619
Figueroa, Guillermo, 4368
Figueros, Guillermo, 1354
Fijolo, Alberto, 5744
Fike, Jennifer, 4770
Fike, Laura, 1549, 1550
Fiksenbaum, Jordan, 8155
Filagina, Marina, 116
Filbin, Johnmike, 3073
Filer, Barbara, 2074
Filer, Edward, 2939
Filer, Felicia, 4236, 6168, 6172
Filer, Randall, 3140
Fili-Krushel, Pat, 7781
Filipo, Sam, 3207
Filippo, Sam, 7308
Fillmer, Les, 709
Fillmore, Kristen, 7161
Filstrup, Ph.D., Alvin W., 2321
Finch, Cory, 5750
Finch, Jim, 6581
Finch, Kristine, 1802
Fine, Arlene, 5694
Fine, Bernard J, 4812
Fine, Emily, 346
Fine, Isabel, 3144
Fine, Lew, 5694
Fine, Lindsay, 303
Fine, Stacy, 4028
Fineburg, Elizabeth, 5473
Fineman, Carol, 5013
Finer, Lisa, 810
Finger, Anne, 51
Finger, Dr. Ellis, 5445
Fingerhut, Lois, 6478
Fingerote, Paul S, 4255
Fink, Jamie, 1916
Fink, Karen, 7584
Fink, Myrna, 3806
Finke, Anya, 6056
Finkel, Alan, 2639
Finkelberg, Jessica, 4990, 7557
Finkelstein, Allison, 3721
Finkelstein, Paul, 1272
Finkelstein, Stuart, 1448
Finkelstein, Susan, 3128
Finkler, John, 6203
Finlaw, Jack, 6366
Finlay, Adrien C., 4815
Finlayson, Victoria, 6280
Finley, Angie, 5905, 5906
Finley, Barry L., 1706
Finley, Marsha, 2210
Finley, Michael, 1726
Finn, Deborah, 1481
Finn, Ellen B., 2079
Finn, Hayley, 3252
Finn, Jerry M., 2822
Finn, Jim, 3485
Finn, Stephen D., 7953
Finne, Chrix, 1189

1163

Executive Name Index

Finnegan, Joe, 4814
Finnegan, Mick, 2675
Finnegan, Peter, 2315
Finnell, Ray, 6065
Finneran, John G., 6592, 6593
Finnerty, Mary, 3269
Finnerty, Patricia, 2254, 2255
Finney, John, 2106
Finney, Lee, 2091
Finney, Shannon, 4907
Finney, Terrell, 7955, 7958
Finton, Paula, 6926
Fioccola, Joe, 3639
Fiore, Michael, 1000
Fiore Hirsch, Julie, 215
Fiorello, Sally, 3945
Fiori Blanchfield, Joan, 1473
Fiorini, Phillip, 1089
Fioroni, Alexa, 552
Firedman, Jerry, 6264
Firestine, Morgan, 8127
Firestone, Roy, 1869
Firnstahl, Amelia, 823
First, Deborah S., 2106
Fiscella, Edward P, 3341
Fischelis, Mea, 5797
Fischer, Amanda, 1336, 1337
Fischer, Daniel M., 1475
Fischer, Daryl, 3204
Fischer, David, 1808, 5808
Fischer, Elsa, 1058
Fischer, Ethan, 3039
Fischer, Jeffery A., 6154, 6171, 6176
Fischer, John, 3014
Fischer, Karen A, 6677
Fischer, Katharine, 3608
Fischer, Kenneth C., 4825
Fischer, Kenny, 2347
Fischer, L. Sue, 2299
Fischer, Linda, 1721
Fischer, Mark, 984
Fischer, Steve, 7625
Fischer, Thierry, 1766, 2366, 2367
Fischler, Carol, 1589
Fish, Alan, 7191, 7192
Fish, Diane, 7697
Fish, Jamie, 6501
Fish, Julie, 1005, 1006
Fish, Maria, 5719
Fishback, Rachel, 2997
Fisher, a Arthur, 6279
Fisher, Adam, 8538
Fisher, Bill, 7468
Fisher, Brent, 6740
Fisher, Cindy, 8718, 8719
Fisher, Claudie, 2300
Fisher, Corey, 2596
Fisher, Curtis L., 3916
Fisher, David, 2344, 8350
Fisher, Dennis, 5459, 8137
Fisher, Douglas, 2013
Fisher, Edward B., 1474
Fisher, Ellen, 8033
Fisher, Emily L, 1097
Fisher, Eve, 5556
Fisher, Fran, 4327
Fisher, Gary, 7999
Fisher, Ginny, 4976
Fisher, Ginny, 7581
Fisher, Howard, 766, 4211
Fisher, Jeanne Donovan, 7630
Fisher, Joe, 7889
Fisher, John, 2593
Fisher, John L, 962, 963
Fisher, Ken, 2130, 4825
Fisher, Kevin, 3980
Fisher, Lawrence L, 5325
Fisher, Lawrence L., 7986
Fisher, Lynda, 1951
Fisher, Marc, 6281
Fisher, Pete, 8296
Fisher, Randy, 4467
Fisher, Rick, 2159
Fisher, Sanford H., 2017
Fisher, Steve, 2314
Fisher, William, 6895
Fisherman, Jay, 466
Fishman, Alan H., 5053

Fishman, Carol, 3548
Fishman, Jay, 1266
Fishman, Karen, 2047
Fishman, Raphael, 1266
Fishman, Robert, 4288
Fishman-Klopman, Susan, 1368
Fisk, Andrew, 269
Fisk, David J. L., 1785
Fisk, David J.L., 1785
Fiske, Dave, 1589
Fister, Terrence, 380
Fistos, John, 7760
Fitch, Brandon, 1537
Fitch, Dorothy, 742
Fitch, Kerry, 3005
Fitch, Lori, 1602, 1603
Fitchuk, Kathy, 5842
Fiterstein, Alexander, 4174
Fithian, David B., 7258
Fitsch, Tony, 5072
Fitz-Simons, Haskell, 7908
Fitzgerald, Adele, 5050
Fitzgerald, Betsy, 2027
Fitzgerald, Cindy, 6994, 6995
Fitzgerald, Claire, 2112
Fitzgerald, Clyde, 2272
FitzGerald, Curt, 3947
FitzGerald, Gayla, 4841
Fitzgerald, Ivan, 2730
Fitzgerald, John S., 5003
Fitzgerald, John S., 7573
Fitzgerald, Marc, 2745
Fitzgerald, Megan, 6406
Fitzgerald, Ryan, 6572
Fitzgerald, Shanna, 5850
Fitzgerald, Suzanne, 138
Fitzgerald, Virginia, 2118
Fitzgerald, William A., 1309, 1310
Fitzmaurice, Daniel, 2696
Fitzmorris, Brian, 6164
Fitzpatrick, Barclay, 3819
Fitzpatrick, Bridget, 5503
Fitzpatrick, Cassidy, 2005
Fitzpatrick, Dennis, 3787
Fitzpatrick, Gretchen, 262
Fitzpatrick, James L., 1909
Fitzpatrick, Joe, 2563
Fitzpatrick, Patti, 6794
Fitzpatrick, Robert, 8732
Fitzpatrick, Susan, 4859
Fitzsimmons, Beth, 4386
Fitzsimmons, Brendan, 1167
Fitzsimmons, Lori, 742
Fitzsimons, Connie, 6315
Fitzwater, Lu, 974
Fitzwater, Patrick, 2758
Flack, Amy, 5189
Flack, Claire P., 485
Flack, Jean-Marc, 485
Flack, Stephanie, 1782
Flad-Jesion, Ann, 5868
Flagg, Aaron, 136
Flagg, Aaron A., 4410
Flaherty, Beth, 1820
Flaherty, Drew, 6124
Flake, Sandra, 2813
Flam, Karen, 3843
Flanagan, Edward C, 2213
Flanagan, Joe, 7251
Flanagan, John, 4129
Flanagan, Laura, 2475
Flanahan, Don, 7610
Flanders, Kellee, 6211
Flandreau, Tara, 795
Flanigan, Colleen, 2041, 6730
Flannagan, Ford, 4053
Flannery, Teresa, 6476
Flaster, Nancy, 2961
Flatness, Dennis, 4920
Flatt, Robyn, 3945
Flatt, Steven, 3914
Flaum, Jackie, 3898
Flavin, Jim, 8617
Flax, John, 3201
Flax, Steven, 359
Fleck, Alan, 1735
Fleck, Wanda, 1370
Fleck Kavic, Patricia, 2291

Fleisch, Marsha, 7599
Fleischer, Mark, 3442, 5080
Fleischer, Mary, 3583
Fleischer, Randall Craig, 717, 1455, 8022
Fleischmann Owen, Marla, 8387
Fleisher, Jan, 1656
Fleisher, Leon, 1419
Fleitz, Deborah L, 5296
Fleming, Angela, 2337
Fleming, Celeste, 4284
Fleming, Christopher, 177
Fleming, Cynthia, 4012
Fleming, Dr Timothy, 913
Fleming, G Bryan, 3229
Fleming, Irving A, 732
Fleming, Joanne, 2957
Fleming, Julie Ann, 4140
Fleming, Lucy, 1693
Fleming, Mark, 1180, 3937
Fleming, Morgan, 613
Fleming, Pauline, 379
Fleming, Ren,e, 2046, 6740
Fleming, Richard, 7815
Flesch, Edward, 4224
Flesher, David J., 3761
Flesher, Gina, 5380
Fleshler, Clementina, 1375
Fletcher, Alan, 1944, 6328
Fletcher, Bernadette, 231
Fletcher, Donna, 1753
Fletcher, Georgia, 7534
Fletcher, Heidi, 7195
Fletcher, John, 3278, 7412
Fletcher, Kathleen, 5523
Fletcher, Liz, 3912, 8292
Fletcher, Mark, 8518
Fletcher, Michelle, 83
Fletcher, Rebecca, 3947
Fletcher, Richard L, 5292
Fletcher, Robert, 710
Fletcher, Shiela, 7878
Fletcher, Todd J, 5157
Fletcher, W.L., 1009
Fletcher, MBA, Richard L., 1521
Flexner, Jillian, 1433
Flexner, Lynne, 924
Fliagnina, Marina, 104
Flickinger, Rob, 1716
Flinchum, Doug, 4055
Flinger, Benjamin, 5342
Flinn, Grier, 2727
Flint, Jere, 1006, 1007, 4503
Flint, Karen, 948
Flint, Mark, 2026
Flint, Terry, 4046
Flint Ballenger, Robin, 8051
Flint, Jr., Peter, 5154
Flintom, Blair, 8113
Flippo, Dianna, 6018, 6019, 6020
Flockhart, Kay, 3911
Flockhart, Key, 8287
Flom, Leslie, 3655
Flood, Matthew E, 1401
Floodin, Lucinda, 6834
Flora, Don, 4060
Floranz Kennedy, Rozella, 853
Florenz, Paul A, 5430
Flores, Abe, 6055
Flores, Gloria, 1738
Flores, Goyo, 2560
Flores, Jessica, 554
Flores, Joseph, 2191
Flores, Ramon A, 3401
Flores PhD, Roy, 6002
Florescu, William, 2398
Flores, Robin, 8107
Florian, Sonia, 199, 205
Florin-Weiss, Dana, 436
Florio, Ermanno, 638
Floto, Jennifer, 830
Flower, Ann, 767
Flower, Deborah, 4391
Flower, Kristine K., 3442, 5080
Flowers, Cynthia, 3468, 3568, 7783
Flowers, Dave, 6423
Flowers, Ed, 1384
Flowers, Henry, 8443
Flowers, James, 1754

Flowers, Jordan, 2856, 4504
Flowers, June, 4240
Flowers, Leana B., 208
Flowers, Michael, 5891, 5892
Floyd, Dorinda, 703
Floyd, Dorothy, 616
Floyd, Elson S., 5791
Floyd, Gregg S., 7995
Floyd, Kirsten D., 3877
Floyd, Nancy J, 3150
Floyd, Shirley, 7872
Floyd-Archibald, Robbye, 3986
Fluck, Jonathan, 3503
Flucker, Turry M., 4889
Flugrath, Nancy, 1692
Flugum, Ron, 718
Fluhrer, Roy, 3878
Flummerfelt, Joseph, 596, 3869, 5534
Flunker, Tom, 4869
Flusser, Beth, 5165
Fly, Dr. Pamela, 3768
Flygt, Charlene, 4106, 5828
Flynn, Brigid, 1041, 4559
Flynn, Daniel A, 1124
Flynn, Denny, 6030
Flynn, Eileen, 874
Flynn, Elizabeth, 351
Flynn, Eyvette, 2417
Flynn, Joan, 7200
Flynn, Julie, 1843
Flynn, Patricia, 4846
Flynn, Patrick, 832, 2004
Flynn, Vivian, 3990
Flynt,, Juliet, 3184
Flyr, Diane, 811
Flythe, Kara, 8125
Fochi, Amber, 6353
Fockler, Emily, 5013
Foehringer, Mark, 84
Foerster, Wendy Marie, 6062
Fofonoff, Meg, 3167
Fogal, Wendy, 1383
Fogarty, Christine, 6590, 6591
Fogarty, Sharon, 3516
Fogarty, Esq., Edward M., 593
Fogderud, Iris, 2275
Fogel, Bonnie, 3120
Fogel, Henry, 4549
Fogel Mykles, Vicki, 1958
Fogell, Steven, 4060
Fogelman, Peggy, 6158
Fogg, Anthony, 1177, 1178, 7227
Fogger, Danny, 7160
Fogle, Vincent W., 1868
Foglia, Sophie, 7633
Folcomer, Charlene, 86
Folding, John, 1273
Foley, Bob, 8556
Foley, Brad, 8071
Foley, Delia, 504
Foley, Dennis, 4846
Foley, Don, 546
Foley, Jack, 8114
Foley, Patricia, 2062, 2063
Foley, Jr, Gene E., 1609
Folger, Marvin, 3681
Folin, Paul, 4874
Folio, Sam, 7523
Folk, Jim, 7971
Folk, Susie, 4204
Folkerth-Jett, Brooke, 7990
Folkerts, Cheryl, 4133
Folkes, Mark, 1731
Follett, Kristine, 733, 4174
Folmer, John, 3435
Folse, Bart, 2085
Folse, Dick, 2979, 4589
Folsom Smith, Anne, 989, 991, 992, 993, 994, 995
Folta, Carl D., 5162
Folta, Rand, 1202
Foltz, Kyla, 8713
Foltz, Paul, 3806
Foltz, Sarah, 5343
Fomin, Arkady, 4368
Fong, Adam, 4305
Fong, Dr Bobby, 6889
Fong, Dr. Bobby, 6890

Executive Name Index

Fonnegra, David, 100, 101
Fonseca, Bryan, 3014
Fontaine, John C, 957
Fontaine, Megan, 152
Fontaine, Paul, 2312
Fontayne, Cynthia, 4250
Fonte, Addyson, 170
Fonte, Henry, 2768, 6495
Fontenot, Jason, 4707
Foody, Jan, 241
Foord, Ellen, 4979
Foorman, Jackie, 1948, 1949
Foot, William, 3212
Foote, Orland, 6100
Foote, Stan, 3786
Foppe, Ed, 3244
Forbes, Amy R., 6170
Forbes, Jerry, 8028
Forbes, Jimmy, 3718, 7980
Forbes, Liam, 719
Forbes, Malcolm H, 944
Forbes, Natalie, 932
Forbess, Greg, 6227
Forbrich, Joe, 2949
Forbush, Lindsey, 4041
Forcher, Jerry, 642
Ford, Adam, 2973
Ford, Alice, 1735
Ford, Alissa, 1722, 5625
Ford, Ben, 8000
Ford, Bev, 3744
Ford, Brayn W., 8286
Ford, David B., 3466
Ford, Foy, 3875
Ford, Gail, 213
Ford, Jeff, 940
Ford, Kelly, 2439
Ford, Linda Marie, 3949
Ford, Matthew, 5455
Ford, Michael T., 243
Ford, Rachel, 1101, 1694
Ford, Rebecca, 6418
Ford, Rosanne P., 4382
Ford, Sara, 198
Ford, Tanner, 5900
Ford, Teresa, 8471
Ford, III, Lafayette J., 2160
Forde, Kevin, 3780
Fordham, Kayla, 8085, 8086
Forehand, Corey, 3988
Forehead, Greg, 6569
Forehilich, Mark A., 4140
Foreht, Stephen, 3533
Foreman, Adam J., 8031
Foreman, George, 4689, 7081
Foreman, George C., 6612, 6613, 6616
Foreman, Hank, 5223
Foreman, Jeff, 7105, 7106
Foreman, Judy, 873
Foreman, Kelly, 3885
Foreman, Lilly Ann, 3773
Foreman, Margaret, 4846
Foreman, Richard, 3538
Foreman, Ronlin, 2452
Forenger, Nancy J., 3761
Foresman, Judy, 3410
Forette, Kim M, 7839
Forgiano, Martha, 1449
Forlenza PhD, Michael J, 580
Fornander, Vera, 2969
Forney, Pamela, 4222
Forrest, Jacque, 1748
Forrest, Pat, 730
Forrest Brock, Andrea, 1769
Forrest Helmuth, Paula, 1099
Forrest Kelly, Thomas, 4354
Forrestal, Maureen E., 8125
Forrester, Christy, 6502
Forrester, Ellard, 5239
Forrester, Juliet H, 940
Forsberg, Cecile L., 4362
Forsch, Ken, 6055
Forsell, Shannon, 3011
Forshaw, Stacey, 687
Forst, Edward C., 5818, 7719
Forster, Julia, 596, 1679, 3869, 5534
Forstner, Melissa, 5079
Forsyte, John E, 868

Forsyth, Lisa, 305
Forsyth, Mark K., 7171
Forsythe, Eric, 3036, 7003, 7006, 7007, 7008
Forsythe Koritala, Jill, 1856
Forszt, Gregg, 4179
Fort, Ellen, 1500
Fort, Frankie, 4520
Fort, Tim, 4026
Fort, Zan, 5550
Forte, A. Charles, 347
Forte, Christina, 1744
Forte, Dan, 5089
Forte, James, 4771
Fortier, Francis, 4727
Fortier, Leigh McLeod, 2474
Fortier, Sandy, 723
Fortin, Maurice, 8444
Fortney, Dr. Pat, 1303
Fortuna, Dave, 3170
Fortune, Susan, 5409
Fos, Peter J., 7152
Fosdick, Susan, 5831
Foshee, Bethany, 8334
Foss, Jim, 6064
Foss, Lukas, 5042
Foss, Margaret, 5847
Fosse, Stephanie, 1312
Fost, Ruth, 3392
Foster, Angella, 176
Foster, Bill, 6588
Foster, Brian, 4563
Foster, Britta, 6187
Foster, Charlotte, 189
Foster, Deborah, 5194
Foster, Edward, 1812
Foster, Elizabeth, 1784, 2375
Foster, Gay, 2369, 5704
Foster, Jessica, 1862
Foster, Karen, 64
Foster, Lee, 117
Foster, Mark, 1886
Foster, Randy, 4046
Foster, Rebecca M., 7009, 7010
Foster, Ronald, 1862
Foster, Stacie, 4085
Foster, Tim, 2671, 6377, 6378, 6380
Foster, Tracie, 510
Foster Weya, Mary, 2885
Fotis, Mike, 3236
Foulds, Michael, 2425
Foulk, Robert, 7425
Fountain, Leslie, 735
Fountain, Robin, 1252, 1668
Fountaine, Paul, 6108
Fournie, Raymond R., 7454
Fournier, Serge, 5583
Fousekis, Sara, 2519, 2522
Foust, Amanda, 2297
Foust, Ameri, 7808
Fouts, Andrew, 959
Fowle, Bruce, 4428
Fowle, Catherine, 352
Fowleks, Andre, 5575
Fowler, Deedy, 7277
Fowler, Dorothea, 3435
Fowler, Dr Gregory, 1587
Fowler, Faith E., 4817
Fowler, G William, 3998
Fowler, Jeanine, 3906
Fowler, Jeanine, 8269
Fowler, Llalan, 1558
Fowler, Lori, 2586
Fowler, Mike, 1802
Fowler, Shannon, 4906
Fowler, Stephanie, 5567
Fowler, Susan R., 3807
Fowler, Terry, 5256
Fowler, Tom, 1706
Fowler, Vivia, 6650
Fowler Slade, Frances, 2187
Fowlkes, H. Lee, 5280
Fox, Adam, 4589
Fox, Andrew, 4033
Fox, Barry, 8674, 8677
Fox, Becky, 3190
Fox, Bill, 7105, 7106
Fox, Cynthia, 4166
Fox, Dick, 1763

Fox, Donald, 2021
Fox, Elizabeth, 368
Fox, Elliot, 3549
Fox, Herbert A, 1202
Fox, Jennifer, 3804
Fox, Jerold, 8689
Fox, Jonathan, 2610
Fox, Julie, 4263
Fox, Kevin, 1897
Fox, Mark, 8268
Fox, Marye Anne, 6137, 6138, 6139, 6140, 6141, 6143
Fox, Michael, 1194
Fox, Micheal A, 6900
Fox, Michele, 5155
Fox, Nancy, 3726
Fox, Pamela, 5760
Fox, Patricia, 530, 534
Fox, Peter, 4263
Fox, Richard, 7997
Fox, Robert A., 3825, 3837, 5474
Fox, Steve, 8283
Fox, Steven, 2189, 2259
Fox, Stu, 5492
Fox, Virginia, 4860
Fox, William, 7413
Fox Hillard, Claire, 1002
Fox Marceau, Shana, 589
Fox, Jr., William H., 756
Foy, America, 53
Frackenpohl, Steven, 1364
Fradler, Kerry, 6590, 6591
Fraher, David, 3235
Fraher, Lorraine, 3409
Fraider, Steven, 4228
Fraioli, John, 2213
Fraker, Weldon, 4005, 4027
Fraley, Robert, 4973
Framill, Stephen, 1665
Frampton, Dennis R, 5446
Frampton, Mac, 4143
Francais, Beatrice, 4400, 4730, 4731, 4732, 4733
France, Hal, 2169
Frances Cooper, Mary, 8169
Franceschelli, Anthony D., 3410
Francesco, Jerry, 2306
Francia, Sharon, 3929, 3933, 8325
Francis, Anne, 5706, 8505
Francis, Bob, 4091
Francis, Dennis, 2884
Francis, Katharine, 1061
Francis, Kathleen, 7554
Francis, Mark, 1782
Francis, Michael, 2482
Francis, Michael D., 6137, 6138, 6139, 6140, 6141, 6142, 6143
Francis, Vickie, 3706
Francis, Wayne, 4263
Francis Donovan, Donald, 3479
Francis PhD, Christina, 3796
Francisco, Susan, 8583
Franck, Alison, 7567
Franck, Samantha, 11
Franco, Fabrizio, 1646
Franco, John, 5132
Franco, Miltrerd, 3288
Francolini, Lisa, 8106
Francos, Jose Maria, 6267
Francuz, Liliane, 5879
Frandina, Joe, 7804
Frandsen, Nancy, 2314
Frangos, Maria, 2616, 6297
Frank, David, 4135, 5034
Frank, Emily, 821
Frank, Jeff, 4120
Frank, Jonathan, 3218, 3219
Frank, Mark, 3043
Frank, Michael, 8763
Frank, Paul A., 1782
Frank, Peter B., 2200
Frank, Sarah, 467
Frank, Scott, 1592
Frank Fernandez, Eddy, 163
Frank Madera, Mary, 6558
Frank, J.D., Gary A., 1644
Frankart, Nick, 781
Franke, David, 7225

Franke, Jason, 8298
Frankel, Stanley, 1229
Frankey, Cindy, 1979
Frankish, Matt, 4406
Frankl, Marika, 894
Franklin, Amy, 8329, 8331, 8332
Franklin, Cary John, 1262
Franklin, Cindy, 2331
Franklin, Grady, 7915
Franklin, Jane, 659
Franklin, Joseph, 1653
Franklin, Julian, 5252
Franklin, Paul, 2256
Franklin-Sewell, Shaun, 4958
Franklyn, Aimee Gwynne, 7621
Franks, Becky, 6013
Franks, Randy, 4325
Frans, Robert, 3742
Fransen, Emily, 2085
Fransto, Hector, 4000
Frantz, Meg, 5002
Frantz, Patrick, 26
Frantz, Susan P, 8559
Franulovic Petrish, Maria, 674
Franz, Brad, 6384
Franz, Robert, 1024, 2033
Franzen, Dale, 2619
Franzese, Jeff, 376
Frary, Kalsa Thuresson, 6202
Frascatore, Kathleen, 5181
Frasch, Georgia, 1436, 1441
Fraschilla, Fran, 7610
Fraser, Bob, 8030
Fraser, Bridget, 1828
Fraser, John, 5934
Fraser, Kristin, 4406
Fraser, Scott, 278
Fraser Wilson, Dr Elisa, 2345
Fratar, Kate, 53
Frates, Thomas, 2113
Frattare, Christine, 2317
Frattare, Tom, 1541
Fratti, Mario, 3539
Frautschi, John, 4135
Frautschi, Laura, 1437
Frawley, Amy Roberts, 5123
Frawley, Kathy, 1164
Frazee, Shellee, 6732
Frazier, Brian, 762
Frazier, Elizabeth, 820
Frazier, Ian, 4033
Frazier, John, 3957
Frazier, Lynn, 2439
Frazier, Maryann, 8
Fred, Nicole, 8245
Fredeman, Chris, 5899
Frederic, Alan P, 4370
Frederick, James, 4156
Frederick, Larry, 3327
Frederick, Nicholas, 4713
Frederick, Steve, 7502
Frederick, Victoria, 5029
Frederick, Wayne, 6464, 6466, 6470
Fredericks, Jim, 8083
Fredericks, Stephen L, 7571
Fredericks, Tom, 4327
Frederickson, Alan P, 4370
Frederickson, Jeri, 2947
Fredler, Robert, 7421
Fredricks, Rita, 2717
Fredricksen, Erik, 3191
Fredrickson, Ivor, 711
Fredrickson, Karen, 4845
Fredrik, Burry, 2717
Freed, Jennifer, 4010
Freedberg, Richard, 3180
Freede, Josephine, 8042, 8045
Freedland, Kathy, 822, 4268
Freedman, Robert, 394, 3154
Freeh, Penelope, 295
Freeman, Alexander, 5483
Freeman, Allen, 6179
Freeman, Brian, 2835
Freeman, Claudia, 2062, 2063
Freeman, Isadore, 4992
Freeman, Joann, 4829
Freeman, John W, 1368

1165

Executive Name Index

Freeman, Judy, 188
Freeman, Mac, 6351
Freeman, Nancy, 1045
Freeman, Robert, 5815
Freeman, Roxanne, 7138
Freeman, Tonya, 3274
Freeman, Ruth, 8203
Freeman, CPRP, Claudia, 6847
Freemanzon, June, 1432
Freer, Amanda, 2022
Freese, Leon, 7363
Freestone, Jessica V., 127
Freet, Jackie, 4069
Freeze, Gary, 7913
Frei, Susan, 554
Freiberg, Richard, 8691, 8695
Freidag, Carin, 2721
Freiman, Barbara, 1497
Freimuth, Stacia, 4366
Freitag, Linda, 1228
Freitas,, Felicia, 2523
Freking, Debra, 7456
Frellick, Paul, 3643
Fremiotti, Jo Ann, 8181
Fremont-Smith, Anne, 1201
French, Arthur, 3474
French, Brian, 2274
French, Cheryl, 3487
French, Donna, 5879
French, Gregory, 667
French, Heidi, 5713
French, John, 2310
French, Nancy, 4362
French, Pam, 1235
French, Paul, 2050
French, Ruthann, 4831
French, Shery, 7365
French, Stephanie, 470
French, Thomas H., 5052
French, Van, 3757
Frenkel, Feliks, 3493
Frenock, Larry, 3819
Frentz, Dr. Johnette, 1754
Frere, Jill, 446
Frerichs, Beth, 4692
Freshwater, Richard, 1528, 1529
Fresiello, Mariann, 1398
Fresquez, Adam, 6103
Fretz, Amanda, 6662
Fretz, Bruce, 1945
Freud, Anthony, 2046, 2353, 6740
Frey, Adam L, 853
Frey, Cristin, 918
Frey, Dave, 3007
Frey, Jeff, 293
Frey, Jill, 8000
Frey, Lukas, 8010
Frey, Mary, 5829
Frey, Victoria, 8100
Frey '79, P. Gregory, 6676
Friar, Tati, 1738
Fricca, Nan, 2744
Frick, Christy, 7264
Frick, Jim, 7545
Frick, Phillip S, 1124
Fricke, Heinz, 956
Fricker, Paula, 4525
Fricklas, Michael D, 7729
Frick, Christy, 7569
Friday, Jeanie, 7409
Fridy, Scott, 5723
Frieben, Jeanne, 4102
Fried, Jody, 4025, 4968
Fried, Lawrence J., 5039
Fried, Linda, 245
Fried, Richard, 1542
Fried, William C., 1246
Friedell, Ellen S., 5485
Friedeman, John, 725
Friedl, Christina, 659
Friedl, Jim, 4342
Friedlaender, Stephen, 4778
Friedland, Bernice, 1166
Friedland, Ethan, 2813
Friedlander, Steve, 5884
Friedli, Deidre, 6706
Friedman, Beatrice, 4482
Friedman, Bennett, 877

Friedman, Cheri E, 2675
Friedman, Dan, 3477
Friedman, Debra, 3793
Friedman, Dr Ellis, 4182
Friedman, Jay, 1059
Friedman, Josh, 7687
Friedman, Julie, 7980
Friedman, Leslie, 92
Friedman, Mary, 5223
Friedman, Matt, 4044
Friedman, Peggy, 5168
Friedman, Robert, 88, 8746
Friedman, Scott, 4565
Friedman White, Jean, 7168
Friedmann, Laura, 3081
Friedrich, Elizabeth, 4085
Friedrich, Larry, 2792
Friedson Garrett, Barbara, 2766
Friel, John P., 3846
Friel, Mark, 3786
Friend, David, 1173
Friend, Virginia, 197
Fries, Ava, 2463, 2493, 2509, 6170
Fries, Patrick, 2964
Friesen, Jane M., 8573, 8574, 8575, 8576
Friesen-Carper, Dennis, 1098
Frinzi, Julie, 5867
Frisby Byers, Dawn, 5483
Frisch, Bill, 2265
Fritsch, Greg, 4202
Fritsche, Donna, 6150
Fritz, Christine, 7593
Fritz, Joanie, 3515
Fritz, Melinda, 587
Fritz, Michael D., 7298
Fritz Blank, Chef, 2313
Fritz-Logrea, Beth, 496
Fritze, Mia, 1770
Fritze, Teri, 532
Frizzell, Mitchell, 4730, 4731, 4732, 4733
Froehlich, Melissa, 823
Froehlich, Rose, 2598
Froehlich, Steven, 5997, 6000
Froehlich PhD, Thomas J, 543
Froehlick, Mark, 5382
Frohamayer, Dave, 8070
Frohlich, Phil, 8051
Frohnmayer, Dave, 558
Frome, Robin, 6431
Fromm, Emily, 1222
Fromson, Michele, 849
Fron, Richard, 1456
Froncek, Michael C, 2603
Fronzaglia, Brian, 4902
Frosaker, Dave, 1593
Frost, Camilla C, 6207
Frost, Delphine, 2634
Frost, Jim, 6560
Frost, Karen, 895, 1067
Frost, Peter, 2224
Frost, Sue, 4384
Frost, Tonya, 4682
Frucci, Jim, 127
Fruchter, Mickey, 1874
Frueh, Andy, 3058
Frugoli, Donna, 1207
Fruits, Gary, 1343
Fry, Keener, 8718, 8719
Fry, Stephen F., 6899, 6901
Fryar, Maridell, 1743
Frydel Kim, Irene, 2218
Frye, Andrea, 2859
Frye, Candice, 5081
Frye, Jessica, 4327
Frye, Linnea, 2851
Fryling, Mike, 8538
Fryman, Hubert, 3821
Fryman, Louis, 3839
Fu Jun, Jiang, 4271
Fuchs, Adriaan, 1412
Fuchs, Elissa, 509
Fuchs, F John, 1396, 5095
Fuchs, Jeff, 7938
Fuchsberg, Larry, 2143
Fudge, Chuck, 6805
Fuehrer, Kris, 4935
Fuente, Malena de la, 5013
Fuentes, Lupe, 6011

Fugate, Judith, 497
Fugatt, Eddie, 6018, 6019, 6020
Fugnitti, Briana, 4599
Fuguitt, Graham, 1828
Fugura, Joshua, 5067
Fuhrer, Jeffrey, 1199
Fuhrman, Carolyn, 947
Fuhrman, Michael, 8123
Fuhrman, Philip, 947
Fujihara Anderson, Wendy, 2499
Fujimoto, Michael, 1916
Fukuhara Arthurs, Lynn, 2499
Fulghum, Kipper, 1948, 1949
Fulkerson, Roxanne, 6099
Fullbright, Alicia, 890
Fullen, Ruth, 3730
Fuller, Cailin, 7500
Fuller, Charles, 6016
Fuller, Conrad, 2623
Fuller, David, 3507
Fuller, Elizabeth, 2623
Fuller, James, 5707
Fuller, Jennifer, 3286
Fuller, Jim, 5905, 5906
Fuller, Joe, 5559
Fuller, John, 4257
Fuller, Johnny, 1716
Fuller, Katherine, 5259
Fuller, Kathryn S., 6459, 6461
Fuller, Kristi, 3832
Fuller, Lewis, 1008
Fuller, Randolph, 2107
Fuller, Rex, 1954
Fuller, Robert S., 1232, 1233
Fuller, Sarah D., 3068
Fullerton, Michael, 2482
Fullerton, Dr. Fred, 6704, 6707
Fulliwider, John, 3956
Fullman, Aimee, 146
Fully, Jim, 4094
Fulmer, Dina, 3844
Fulton, Bill, 1963
Fulton, Justine, 8424, 8425, 8426, 8427, 8428
Fulton, Rozalynn, 3660
Fulton, Steve, 5182
Fulton, Tom, 8003
Fulton, Wanda, 246
Fulweiler, Dan, 2037
Fumbanks Mathis, Paige, 2022
Funderburk, Liz, 8239
Funderburk, Lucas, 7140
Fungeld, Greg, 5430
Funicello, Ralph, 6240, 6241
Funk, Jennifer, 1527
Funk, Lori, 3514
Funking, Bob, 7669
Furano, Kim, 2720
Furbish, Melissa, 4976, 7581
Furiga, Paul, 1659
Furland, Robert, 7336
Furlong, Jim, 3500
Furlong, Paul, 1450
Furman, Ty, 3818
Furphy, Theresa, 8350
Furr, Rick, 1786
Furr, Tracy, 4999, 5003
Furr, William P, 3126
Furshpan, Roy, 6057, 6058, 6059, 6060, 6061
Furtado, Mike, 5590
Furumoto, David, 8680
Furumoto, Kimo, 1818
Furusa, Ph.D., Munashe, 771
Furusho, Craig, 4289
Fusaris, Kurt, 2679
Fusaro, Ruby, 1790
Fusco, Benedetto, 2220, 2243
Fusco, Linda, 2220, 2243
Fusco, Michael, 3737
Fushi, Geoffrey, 1419
Fushille, Celia, 91
Fusillo, Lisa, 177
Fuson, Rick, 6896
Fuss, Alicia, 3916
Fussaro, Dianne, 2304
Fuster, Daren, 1545, 1546
Futral, Joseph, 182
Futrell, Patti, 6619
Futterman, Alan, 675, 1789

Fyfe, Scott, 4072
Fyodorov, Deborah, 7212

G

G. Reis, Paul, 1077
G. Stroman, Gerry, 6906
Gabb, Carolyn S, 2844
Gabb, Jill S., 3587
Gabbard, Tom, 7874
Gabbart, Tom, 7869
Gabbert, John, 8520
Gabel, Audrey, 7011
Gabel, John S, 1338
Gabel, Sarah, 2940, 4557
Gabel, Theresa, 758
Gabel PhD, Sarah, 6751
Gabella, Dominique, 691
Gabhard, Tom, 8513, 8514
Gabka, Larry, 3207
Gaboury, Marieke, 3081, 3087
Gabrian, Craig, 373
Gabriel, Stephen J, 6321
Gabriels, Jane, 355
Gabrielson Deckard, Corinne, 4480
Gachignard, Norene, 3172
Gacioch, Jim, 5048
Gadda, Jennifer, 2526, 6734
Gaddis, Bernard H., 320
Gaddis, Carole, 8507
Gaddis, Kristen, 6887
Gaddy, Bob, 752
Gadly, Mason, 4498
Gadzinski, Josefina, 61
Gaeddert, John, 6698
Gaenslen, Anneke, 4210
Gaertner, Gregory, 5018
Gaertner, Katy, 4856
Gaffin, Barbara, 2120
Gaffney, Floyd, 2570
Gaffney, Michael, 3747
Gaffney, Paul, 5630
Gaffney, Tom, 3971
Gaffney FSC, Br James, 6832
Gagaglio, James, 3186
Gage, Richard, 1054
Gage, Robert, 4892
Gagliano, Patrick, 3881
Gagne, Roland, 5623
Gagnon, Sandra, 6441
Gague, Jay, 8408
Gahagan, Frances, 1002
Gahan, Joan, 8202
Gaharan, Deanna, 4703
Gail Kessler, Karen, 3866
Gaillard, Jeff, 6332
Gailmann, Greg, 8499
Gaines, Barbara, 2917
Gaines, Bob, 2412
Gaines, Cassandra, 8037
Gaines, Norman, 1114
Gaines, Robert A, 2412
Gaines, Terry, 5529
Gaines, Weaver, 153
Gajewski, Piotr, 1169
Galamba-Pierce, Marie, 1002
Galante, Marco, 449
Galazzi, Marcia, 3168
Galban, Margarita, 2495
Galbraith, Bruce, 969
Galbraith, Scott, 3969
Galbraith, Yvette, 4157
Galbreath, Woody, 8531, 8532
Gale, Doug, 2167
Gale, John, 6047
Galeana, Anita, 4210
Galek, Tom, 6040
Gales, Elizabeth, 7012
Galesi, Francesca, 5134
Galey, Ramona, 2101
Galgano, Olivia, 342
Galib, Michael, 2324
Galichia MD, Joseph, 2077
Galinson, Brad, 4970
Galinson, Shannon, 4970
Galitzer, Steve, 7048
Galizio, Dr. Lawrence, 8065
Gall, Joanna, 7329

Executive Name Index

Galla, Trisha, 4065
Gallacher, Jennifer, 106
Gallagher, Bridget, 5697
Gallagher, Casey William, 5437
Gallagher, Jean, 5774
Gallagher, Jerry, 7836
Gallagher, Makalina, 450
Gallagher, Marie, 5483, 8148
Gallagher, Nikki, 1977
Gallagher, Stephanie, 529
Gallagher, Thomas, 1982
Gallagher, Tim, 6066, 6070, 6071, 6072
Galland, Ann, 3991, 5645
Gallant, Doris, 1046
Gallant, Thomas, 5009
Gallas, Stephanie, 3617
Gallavan, Deanna, 3764
Gallavan, Rob, 3764
Gallay, Dina, 217
Galle, Pamela, 3871
Gallegos, Deborah E, 4313
Gallegos, Debra, 2665
Gallegos, Geoggrey, 1934
Galles, Cynthia, 2487
Galli Esq, Nicole D, 575
Gallin, Valerie, 3105
Gallo, Marie D, 6187
Gallo, Robert, 1198
Gallo, Steve, 7544
Gallogly, John, 2517
Gallon, Dennis P, 6484
Gallot, Freddie, 5918
Galloway, Deane, 5860
Galloway Kellogg, Cindy, 6351
Gallucci, Victor, 7831
Galt, Jack, 8504
Galvin, Rachel, 870
Gamage Tucker, Meg, 3013
Gamba, Stephen, 3409
Gambee, Judy, 8084
Gambill, Larry, 3670
Gamble, Jeffery, 7471
Gamble, Robert, 1240
Gamble, Sharon, 3014
Gamble, Steven, 5033
Gamble, Suzan Z., 3299
Gamble, Tom, 7682
Gamble, Wendy, 1
Gamble, Ph.D., Thomas J., 8123
Gamboa, Norman, 1838, 1877
Gambone, Jim, 3231, 3265
Gambone, Ralph, 963
Gambony, Gina, 5274
Gambs, John, 1928
Gamell, Mark, 3507
Gamer, Jack, 8571
Gammons, Eric, 4707
Gampel, Abigail, 3490
Gamso, Nancy, 5341
Gamst, Nicole, 8715
Gandara, Babil, 5618
Gandy, Tasha, 5196, 1679
Gandy, Taylor, 3969, 3970, 8384
Ganeshan, MD, MPH, Shakthi, 78
Gang, David, 1210, 1211
Gang, Sylvia, 809
Gangemi, Marie, 2248
Gangloff, Kim, 668
Gannar, Chris, 8288
Gannarelli, Daniel, 7939
Gans, Diane, 2077
Gansky, Gary, 2310, 2311
Gansky, Gary H, 2311
Gant, David, 176
Gant, Katherine, 176
Gant, Jr., Thomas, 570
Ganter, Jeremy, 6095, 6096, 6098
Ganter, Vallejo, 7774
Gantt, Karen, 6407
Gantvoort, Leif, 6130
Gantz, Amy I., 7211
Ganun, Alan, 5012
Ganun, Allan, 5012
Gapasin, Krystel, 2499
Gaples, Richard, 371
Gappa, Judith, 4332
Garanzini SJ, Michael J, 6739, 6751
Garay, Mary Beth, 2361

Garay, Olga, 4236
Garback, Douglas M., 5003
Garbee, Richard, 1786
Garber, Donald B., 4049, 4053, 4054
Garber, Seneca, 5800
Garber, William, 3972
Garberson, Jeffrey B, 4235
Garbo, Bernard, 2918
Garcia, Alexandra, 4596, 6820, 6821
Garcia, Anthony J, 2665
Garcia, Brittney, 8459
Garcia, Cecilia, 2495
Garcia, David, 2791
Garcia, Felice, 4001
Garcia, Fernando, 646
Garcia, Hector, 5373
Garcia, Juliet, 5599
Garcia, Katherine, 6612, 6613, 6616
Garcia, Kelliann, 3786
Garcia, Kim, 7508
Garcia, Leticia, 6318
Garcia, Lorrie, 621
Garcia, Marika, 4250
Garcia, Mike, 6159
Garcia, Miki, 6286
Garcia, Mildred, 771
Garcia, Oscar, 6275
Garcia, Petra, 4182
Garcia, Rocio, 5073
Garcia, Sandra, 4182
Garcia, Timothy, 4995
Garcia, Tony, 2665, 6355
Garcia, Victor, 4852
Garcia de Benavidez, Mica, 2665, 6355
Garcin, Jane, 789
Garcja, Monica, 8175
Garcja Oliva, Manolo, 3499
Garden, Joanne, 6152
Gardener, Michelle, 3603
Gardenhire, Andrea, 6653
Gardiner, Gayle, 338
Gardiner, Matthew, 4033
Gardiner, Pamela, 160
Gardinier, Lynn, 5838
Gardino, Vincent A, 924
Gardner, Alston, 7866
Gardner, Annette, 8123
Gardner, Dick, 2894
Gardner, Elaine, 501
Gardner, Gary C., 2354
Gardner, Grey, 2899
Gardner, James, 1764
Gardner, Jeannette, 8832
Gardner, Jennifer, 8404
Gardner, John, 656, 6455
Gardner, Keith, 3685
Gardner, Kurt, 7754
Gardner, Loren, 3216
Gardner, Mark, 3796
Gardner, Michael, 2472
Gardner, Nancy, 2296
Gardner, Pam, 8405
Gardner, Robert, 293
Gardner, Sarah, 5265
Gardner, Sue, 697
Gardner, Tim, 3746
Gardner, Valia, 2165
Gardner, Vanessa, 4786
Gardyn, Jorge, 5076
Garey, Phyllis, 3991, 5645
Garfield, Jed H., 1433
Garfield, Leslie J, 1433
Gargaro, Ken V., 3845
Gargus, Dalton, 5900
Garg, Sunil (Sonny), 7258
Garibaldi, Ph.D., Antoine M., 7290
Garin, Ross, 5489
Garland, David, 5678
Garland, Timothy W, 580
Garlando, J., 1531
Garlando, Jenne, 5288
Garling, Shana, 587
Garlington, Nina, 4806
Garman, Leslie, 2072
Garner, Brad, 558
Garner, Carol P., 8465
Garner, Deborah, 6622
Garner, Heather, 1560

Garner, James, 8040
Garner, John, 1560
Garner, Kate, 4182
Garner, Richard, 2855, 4504
Garner, Sadie B., 4770
Garner, Sandra, 3594
Garnes, Lori, 7616
Garnett, Jane, 5065
Garnett, Joe, 6752
Garnett, Tim, 231
Garnham, David, 4130
Garonzik, Sara, 3836
Garrard, Mimi, 458
Garrett, David A, 4621
Garrett, Gordon, 990
Garrett, Jan, 51
Garrett, Josh, 8897
Garrett, Margo, 1204
Garrett, Marshall, 2034
Garrett, Mike, 376
Garrett, Sidonie, 4903
Garrett, Tim, 5380
Garrett, Tre, 2974
Garrett, Walter, 5894
Garrick, Skot, 597
Garrigues, Alexis, 4085
Garrin, Richard, 2194
Garriott, Holly, 5250
Garrison, Carol, 5897
Garrison, Kelly, 4242
Garrison, Lissy, 4357, 4360
Garrison, Tom, 752
Garrison Esq, Paul E, 815
Garrity, Alicia, 39
Garrity, Michelle, 3333
Garrone, James, 4921
Garruba, Peter, 3601
Garry Aliperta, Amanda, 2394
Garside, Edwin, 4977
Garst, Peter, 7785
Gartin, Stanton, 6390
Gartner, James, 8419, 8420
Garton, Nancy, 63
Garton Edie, Diane, 2396
Garvan, Steve, 2901
Garvey, Jim, 7991
Garvey, Kevin, 1084
Garvey, Pamela, 7658
Garvey, William, 2065
Garvey-Blackewell, Jennifer, 3587
Garvin, Dr. James, 2181
Garwood, Laurie, 199, 205
Gary, Executive Direc, 8486
Gary, Janice, 5949, 5950
Gary Kaplowitz, Risa, 341
Gary Sheldon, Maestro, 160
Garza, Rene De La, 2325
Gasand, Ferdinand, 4233
Gasang, Ferdinand, 4233
Gasbarre, Roberta, 2734
Gasea, Manny, 1724
Gasenica, Kim, 4542
Gasewicz, Jim, 1734, 1744
Gash, Brittany, 4242
Gaskill, Julia, 764
Gaskin Nemschoff, Anne, 4846
Gaspardo, Cynthia, 6773
Gasparinetti, Ron, 2599
Gasparini, Marilyn, 7818
Gasper, Nina, 7229
Gass-Youmans, Lavene, 1349
Gassner, Michael, 2528
Gast, Alice P, 8114
Gasteyer, Karl, 6395
Gastineau, Emily, 294
Gastler, Diane, 803
Gaston, Bill, 7160
Gaston, Brian, 3861
Gaston, Finus, 5924, 5925
Gately, Timothy F, 4374
Gates, J. Robert, 1222
Gates, Kelly, 227
Gates, Paula, 3156
Gates, Rebecca, 3738
Gates, Rebeccath, 3738
Gates, Robert, 8343
Gates, Stephen, 1119

Gates, Tiffanny, 1983, 1984
Gates, Tiffany, 1983
Gatesmith, Jeff, 4870
Gatewood, Barbara, 7049
Gather, Greg, 3352
Gatlin, Jerry, 2339
Gatti, Janice, 1806, 5803
Gattis, Courtney, 711
Gatto, Angelo, 1165
Gatto, Margaret, 1165
Gatto, Michael, 7983
Gatton, Terri, 166
Gatton, Tommy, 3064
Gatz, Jill, 1121
Gatzke, Gary, 1256
Gau, Victoria, 952
Gaub, Eugene, 5069
Gaub, Nancy, 5069
Gaubatz, Kathryn B, 966
Gaubatz, Kathryn B., 4440
Gaudreau, Alison, 1253
Gaudry, Frank, 1012
Gaul, Dr. Gerald, 1511
Gaul, Patricia, 3716
Gaupp, Natalie, 3968
Gause, Julie, 3906
Gauthier, Bethany, 7311
Gautney, Will, 4042
Gauvin, Carolyn, 7682
Gauvin, J. Paul H, 1198
Gavezzoli, Marco, 470
Gavica, Alaina, 196
Gavin, Ellen, 2576
Gavin, Kim, 1689, 2329
Gavitte, Don, 6075
Gavriel, Beth, 1059
Gawlak, Mark, 6412, 6413, 6414
Gawlik, John, 2985
Gay, Erin, 7978
Gay, Jason, 1560
Gay Anderson, Donna, 3079
Gaydos, Gary, 3283
Gayer, Julie, 391
Gaylard, Timothy, 1780
Gaylin, David, 1173
Gaylin, Jed, 1325
Gaylor, Michael, 5538
Gaylord, Hugh, 5368
Gaynor Murray, Lesly, 1275, 1276
Gazsi, John, 1629
Gear, Dr.Bill, 8268
Gearhart, Dave, 6025
Gearhart, Patrick, 2077
Gearin, Dan, 7165
Geary, Robert, 1927, 1952, 4270
Geballe, Tom, 4526
Gebara, Marsha, 6216
Gebb, Paul, 551
Gebhardt, Dave, 8615, 8616
Gebhart, Kara, 8821
Geddes, Lila, 2362
Gedeon, David, 1533
Gedeon, Jean, 572
Gee, Cheryl, 5907, 5909, 5911, 6555, 6556
Gee, Gordon, 8305
Gee, Shaleane, 1766
Gee, Shirley, 3898
Geehan, Deahna, 6371
Geelan, John, 3252
Geer, Deborah, 1364
Geer, Ellen, 2634
Geer, Karan, 7645, 7671
Geery-Zink, Stephanie, 3326
Geeslin, Keith B., 1922, 1923
Geeting, Daniel, 4341
Geffen, Jeremy, 1291
Gegner, Jeffrey, 6906
Gehl, Amanda, 6876
Gehl, Carol, 4120
Gehlar, Paul, 1614
Gehler. Ed.D., Jan L., 5980
Gehley, Jordan, 421
Gehring, David, 6966, 6968, 6970
Gehring, Joseph, 1630
Geib, Cynthia, 1659
Geier, Eric, 7370
Geiersbach, Rik, 4556
Geiger, Darby, 6996

1167

Executive Name Index

Geiger, Elizabeth, 185, 418
Geiger, Hal, 723
Geiger, Kira, 4945
Geiger, Mary C., 283
Geiger, S Kay, 8004
Geile, Cindy, 2033
Geiogamah, Hanay, 2574
Geiser, David, 6848, 6849
Geisler, Barry H, 8520
Geisler, David, 4845
Geiss-Robbins, Suzanne, 4409
Geitner, Robert, 6549
Gelb, Peter, 2234
Gelbart, Norman, 1894
Gelblum, Seth, 3530, 7766
Geldert, Den, 2148, 2149
Geldin, Sherri, 7987
Gelfand, Amy, 546
Gelfand, Michael, 1516, 1624
Gelfand, Michael D, 5376
Gelinas, Karen, 6558
Gellar, Marc, 3495
Gelleerd, Judith, 1058
Geller, Michael, 1406
Gellert, Ronald, 2228
Gellert, Susan, 4365
Gelman, Alexander, 6764, 6765, 6766
Gelman, Linda, 3478
Gelman, Sam, 5013
Gelormino, Lynn, 6441
Geltner, Beverley, 4825
Gelvin, Constance, 903
Gemmell, Kathleen, 5091
Gempesaw, Ph.D., Conrado, 7692
Gencarelli, Dana, 5549
Gendler, Steven, 3957
Generous, Laura, 1497
Genesky, Marsha, 1924
Geneso, Suny, 1388
Genevie, Kathy, 8203
Genevie, Micheal, 8203
Genise, Livia, 3790
Gennaro, Michael, 3864, 7567
Genne, Beth, 406
Genochio, Jerry, 3289
Genser, Andi, 3143
Genshaft, Judy, 2834
Gent, Chris, 200
Genter, Jeremy, 6094
Gentile, Rebecca, 3729
Gentry, Jennifer, 509
Gentry, Norma, 4182
Gentry, Susan, 7882
Genung, Jeff, 5174
Geoffery, Rae, 3638
George, Alexander, 907
George, Bill, 3795, 7464, 8115
George, Brad, 1634
George, Bridget, 5430
George, David, 1758, 7193
George, Dr. Marle, 5499
George, Jeffry, 3181
George, Jessica, 3760
George, Maggie, 5993
George, Mark, 4604
George, Mark A, 8654
George, Scott, 8755
George, Steve, 6429
George, Tara, 570
George, Tesse, 677
George, Wayne, 2827
Georger, Frobes, 7748
Georgiadis, John, 1119
Georgiev, Peter, 8458
Geotis, Loretta, 2795
Gerard, Greg, 1821
Gerardot, Alison, 229
Gerasin, Elisa, 324
Gerber, Barbara, 2573
Gerber, Cheryl, 5471
Gerberding, William P., 2387
Gerdenich, Laura, 8011
Gerdes, David F., 1249
Gerdes, Kirsten, 6332
Gerdes Becnel, Julie, 141
Gerdts, Dan, 4869
Geres, Lenard, 1935
Gerhardt, Christine, 967

Gerhardt, Julie, 7214, 7215
Gerhardt, Rick, 7199
Gerhart, Kieta, 2351
Gerig, Vern, 3133
Geringer, Janice, 6175
Geringer Fogelman, Janice W., 4237
Gerken, Michael, 4904
Gerland, Dr Oliver, 2647
Gerleit, Steven, 373
Gerlitz, Mary, 1938
Gerlough, Kate, 5133
Gerlt, Michelle, 3310
Germack, Victor, 924
Germain, Kelly, 3703
Germaine, Steve, 6438
Germond, Mark, 3381
Gerould, Robert, 62
Gerould, Rosemarie, 62, 2550, 2551
Gerrard, Alice, 1403
Gerrish, Don, 7167
Gerritson, Shasha, 2043
Gersen, Joshua, 1433
Gershenfeld, Mitch, 6202
Gershon, Grant, 1886, 1887, 4243
Gerson, Jonathon, 5026
Gerst, Gilbert, 628
Gersten, Bernard, 7746
Gersten, Fredrick, 5881
Gersten, Jenny, 4814
Gertner, Paul, 1440
Gertz, Tanya M B, 4648
Gervais, Michael, 61
Gerwig, Larry, 4438
Gesling, Anne, 6300
Gesling, Larry, 6300
Gesmer, Ellen, 413
Gessert, Chuck, 6919
Gessner, Patty, 855, 4309, 4312
Getchel, Dee, 6356, 6364
Geter, Angela, 5548
Gets, Lispbeth, 970
Getto, Judith P., 4323
Getty, Barbara, 5177
Getty, Carrie, 2899
Getty, Gordon, 889
Getty, Gordon P, 848
Getty, Sarah, 2118
Gettys, William L., 1478
Getzof, Israel, 750
Geuther, Ronald C., 1471
Gevertz, Allyson, 1015
Geyer, Dave, 1556, 5350
Geyer, Richard A, 4125, 8691, 8694
Geyer, Richards A, 8695
Gezairlian Grib, Sonia, 1399
Ghaznavi, Roshan, 4350
Gherty, Mark J, 8670
Gheslin, Paul, 448
Ghin, Vadim, 457
Ghitelman, Seth, 3131
Ghrist, Dr. John, 1107
Giacchetti, Cindy, 2958
Giacobbe, Georgia, 5940
Giacobbe, Joseph, 245
Giacobbe, Maria, 245
Giacummo, Beth, 5071
Giaimo, Kathryn A, 3624
Giamalis, Stacey, 1927
Giametta, Jessica, 8822
Giammatteo, Adrianne, 6433
Giampapa, Heather S., 3825, 3837, 5474
Giancola, Barbara, 5718
Gianelis, Olga, 2125
Gianetti, Marilyn, 6113
Giangiullio, Richard C., 1699
Giannascol, Lisa, 3378
Giannini, Christina, 131, 132
Gianniny, Amy, 4038, 4039
Giannis, Brenda, 5819
Giannni, A. Christina, 104
Giannone, Larry, 8133
Gianopoulos, Nick, 6124
Gianopulos, George, 787
Giantonio, John, 6582
Giardina, David, 927
Giardini, Kay, 1563
Giarraputo, Deanne, 1991
Giarusso, Richard, 2376

Giasson, Marie, 1722, 5625
Gibbons, Chuck, 3804
Gibbons, Mike, 3867
Gibbons, Patrick, 744
Gibbons, Pete, 2357
Gibbons Brown, Karen, 228
Gibbs, Anthony, 261
Gibbs, Barclay, 261
Gibbs, Brent, 2431
Gibbs, Christopher, 5044
Gibbs, D Andrew, 2435
Gibbs, Derek, 6763
Gibbs, Dr. Andrew, 2435
Gibbs, Jane, 3442, 5080
Gibbs, Jolana R, 7385
Gibbs, Lawrence, 7154
Gibbs, Phyllis M., 6590, 6591
Giblin, Elizabeth, 2254
Gibney, Gina, 428
Gibralter, Dr. Jonathan C., 259
Gibson, Anthony, 7382
Gibson, Berdie, 8440
Gibson, Brooke, 3769
Gibson, Camille, 2057
Gibson, Cynthia, 4163
Gibson, David, 8845
Gibson, Don, 999, 2013
Gibson, Doug, 7601
Gibson, Eric, 2296, 5393
Gibson, Frances, 5627
Gibson, Gail, 2122
Gibson, Gerald, 8278
Gibson, Jacob, 1548
Gibson, Jannes, 143, 144
Gibson, Jim, 2523
Gibson, Joe, 4342
Gibson, John, 1791
Gibson, Jon, 468
Gibson, Judy, 2357
Gibson, Kate, 4759
Gibson, Marty, 3038
Gibson, Matt, 8615, 8616
Gibson, Melissa, 2464
Gibson, Mike, 749, 4566
Gibson, Paul, 682
Gibson, Rob, 4521
Gibson, Robert, 1160
Gibson-Woolbright, Normadien, 508
Giddings, Jean, 5704
Gideons, Rod, 1903
Gidley, Margaret, 2323
Gidron, Danny, 3810
Gidwitz, John, 4750
Gier, Delta David, 2260
Gierchak, Karen, 4055
Gierke, Rob, 8585
Gierke, Roni, 8585
Gies, Ken, 7423
Giese, Astrid, 4770
Giese, David, 1099
Gieser, Dr. David K., 4603
Giesler, Ann, 1885
Giffen, Linda, 5600
Giffin, Brian, 6639
Gifford, Emily, 7262
Giglinto, Kevin, 6752
Giglio, Michael J, 129
Gignilliat, Paul C., 1035, 1038
Gilad, Yehuda, 1321
Gilbert, David, 925, 1344
Gilbert, Doug, 2265
Gilbert, Edes, 252, 4746
Gilbert, Laura, 4974
Gilbert, Mary K., 1572
Gilbert, Sally, 5620
Gilbert, Stanley, 3629
Gilbert, Susan, 3121
Gilbert, Suzanne, 4469
Gilbertson, Carole, 881
Gilbertson, Eric, 7332
Gilbreath, John, 5794
Gilcrease, Lynn, 3055, 3063
Gildan, Laurie, 2792
Gildden, Sara, 3138
Gildor, Catherine, 461
Giles, Charlotte, 5817
Giles, Dylan, 593
Giles, Jacquelyn, 2389

Giles, Korja, 4075
Giles, Matt, 4087
Giles, Nancy, 608
Giles, Priscilla, 1317
Giles, Sonsheree, 51
Giles, Steve, 1200
Gilfus, John, 3612
Gilg, Kerstin, 4740, 4741
Gilgore, Laurence, 1972
Gilgore, Lawrence, 1972
Gilkes, Jarbean, 361
Gill, Amy, 1535
Gill, Diane, 4854
Gill, Edward B, 843
Gill, Rosemary, 7243
Gill, Temple, 3137
Gill Jr, Thomas D, 2108
Gillan, Eugenia, 4666
Gillan, Maria M, 5011
Gillen, Pete, 8518
Gillese, Kevin, 2851
Gillespe, Dan, 7851
Gillespie, Don, 1373
Gillespie, Dr. Diane, 1796
Gillespie, Kathleen, 4584
Gillespie, Susan, 8002
Gillespie, William, 2771
Gillett, Dedra, 6621
Gillette, Brenna, 1365
Gillette, Timothy, 2107
Gilley, J Wade, 5816
Gilliam, Joshua M, 5256
Gilliam, Judy, 1572
Gilliam, Ryan, 1885
Gilligan, Jan, 6794
Gilliland, Laura, 2152
Gilliland, Rich, 3660
Gillim, Linda G., 1463
Gillinson, Clive, 5818, 7719, 8642
Gillis, Chester, 6469
Gillis, Graeme, 7727
Gillis, Patricia, 1801
Gillispie, Charley, 4633
Gillmor, Lisa, 5768, 5769
Gillmore, Lisa, 2380
Gillner, Joan, 5510
Gillooley, JoEllen, 352
Gilman, Gail, 3152, 7235
Gilman, Irvin E, 1362
Gilman, Kevin, 2081
Gilmer, Kim, 8080
Gilmer, Kirkland, 7699
Gilmore, Dulcie, 6728
Gilmore, John, 3994
Gilmore, LeAnn, 1811
Gilmore, Leslie, 3994
Gilmour, Matt, 7441
Gilmour Smyth, Deborah, 2460
Gilooley, Jennifer, 352
Gilreath, Nena, 180
Gilstrap, Dave, 1779
Gilstrap, Kenneth, 4929
Gilstrap, Kennith, 4929
Gimbel, Anne, 2639
Gimenez, Jana, 1176
Gimpel, Joel, 2891
Gindele, Jerry, 1657
Ginder, RuthAnn, 1075
Gindler, David, 1886
Ginkauf, Kaitlin, 1744
Ginless, Siiri, 7438
Ginnis, Richard, 1798, 5793
Ginnow, Jonathan, 7566
Ginsberg, Debra, 2787
Ginsberg, Michael, 461, 3846
Ginsburg, Hana, 412
Ginsburg, Kathryn, 7283
Ginther, Kristen, 706
Giordano, Chris, 7157
Giordano, Frank, 1644, 1649
Giordano, Gus, 217
Giordano, John, 1640
Giordano, Nan, 217
Giordano, Philip, 1972
Giordono, John, 1708
Giovannetti, Claire, 1919
Giovanni, Greg, 3828
Girard, Geoff, 2616, 6297

Executive Name Index

Girod, Doug, 7043
Girotto, John R., 6966, 6968, 6970
Giroux, Avery, 7677
Giroux, Leigh, 3488
Giroux, Mrs. Pamela O., 5520
Girton, Irene, 4245
Gische, David, 1782
Gishey, Laurence, 5993
Gisler, Ellie, 5096, 5097
Gissi, Mark, 1644
Gistelinck, Peter H., 1244
Gitchell, David D, 7052
Gitler, Janette, 71
Gitlitz, Lynn, 428
Gittleman, Neal, 1549, 1550
Giudicessi, Joy, 6990
Giuliani, Leslie, 931, 4395
Giunta, Joseph, 1107
Giuntini, Trey, 8284
Giuranna, Bruno, 4483
Giurleo, Miranda, 4808
Giusti, Tom, 3730
Given, Matthew, 3799, 5437
Givens, Bill, 5990
Giza, Tom, 2882
Gizzi, Vincent, 6507
Gjovig, Bruce, 5282
Glace, Alice, 1450
Gladden, Dean, 8397
Gladden, Dean R., 3982, 8398, 8399, 8400
Gladden, Heather, 1246
Gladhill, Bethany, 3268
Gladieux, Elizabeth, 8015
Gladish, Kendal, 1702
Gladstein, Mimi, 8380, 8381
Gladstone, Becky, 4790
Gladstone, Josh, 3437
Glandon, Bert, 915
Glandon, Debbie, 8308
Glandorf, Matthew C., 1639, 2307, 5475
Glann, Klm, 6157
Glantz, Bob, 7503
Glasenhardt, Andrew, 198
Glaser, Amy, 4016
Glaser, Robert, 6004
Glaser, Scott, 6599
Glasgal, Linda, 2185
Glasgow, Michael J., 1503
Glasner, David, 6760
Glasoe, Carolyn, 6286
Glasoe, Jim, 7342
Glass, Brandi, 122
Glass, Garret, 6356, 6364
Glass, Jenna, 86
Glass, Lilian, 5887
Glass, Philip, 7743
Glass, Phillip, 2035
Glassberg, David, 1196
Glassbrook, Daryn, 2409
Glasscok, Tom, 4839
Glasscox, Kathi, 5886
Glasser, Joanne K, 6815, 6816
Glassick, Charles, 6664
Glassmeyer, Diane, 5354
Glassner, Barry, 8094
Glasson, Robert, 809
Glatz, Adrienne, 6083
Glauberman, Nancy, 5135
Glaudini, Steven A, 2547
Glauser, Mary, 1533
Glavich, Mary, 30
Glaza, Marg, 2137
Glaze, Kathy, 2600
Glaze, Richard, 4475
Glazer, Bruce, 6365
Glazer, Jordana, 7497
Glazer, Norma, 1519
Glazier, Terri, 1223
Gleasner, Gregg, 856
Gleason, Dennis, 4134
Gleason, Jenny, 1614
Gleason, Jessica, 3783
Gleason, Joe, 7536
Gleason, Julia, 7464
Gleason, Kathy, 3097, 3552
Gleason, Larry, 235
Gleason, Todd, 7261
Gledsoe, Gene, 507

Gleicher, Vicki, 1400
Glenn, Casey, 8007
Glenn, Cynthia, 4282
Glenn, Devon M., 4009
Glenn, Victor, 1700
Glennon, Maureen, 344
Glew, Paul, 1899
Gleysteen, Nicholas, 1181, 2106
Glick-Anderson, Jeri, 4412
Glicker, James, 4750
Glickman, Dr Morton, 1418
Glickman, Elissa, 6115
Glickman, Mitch, 6166
Glickman, Pauline, 1748
Glickman, Randolph, 1748
Glidewell, Rae, 6037
Gliebe, Don, 1552
Glien, Yvonne, 756
Gliman, Phil, 3444
Glines, John, 3494
Glist, Kothi, 2783
Globenfelt, Jack, 5084
Glodfelter, Carolyn, 3075
Glogovsky, Jim, 2062, 2063
Glogovsky, CPRP, Jim, 6847
Gloo, Jo, 7703
Glore, John, 2461
Glose, Karen, 5430
Glossman, James, 3370
Glotzbach, Philip A., 5201
Glouner, Kevin, 5901, 5902, 5903, 5904
Glover, Constance, 6618, 6628
Glover, Danny, 2515
Glover, Jane, 2047
Glover, Kaye, 972
Glover, Laura, 231
Glover, Marcene, 8132
Glover, Merrilee, 2167
Gluck, David, 2583
Glucklich, Rebecca, 3158
Gluckstern, Judy, 3460
Gluecker, Joseph, 4557
Gluesing, Laurie, 3231
Glymph, Joseph, 1037
Glynn, Penelope, 7256
Gnage, Marie, 3385, 5821
Gnagy, Katie, 541
Gockel, Janice, 1801
Gockley, David, 1922, 1923, 1926
Gockley, David M., 1922, 1923
Gockowski, Suzanne, 8125
Goddard, Bob, 4525
Goddard, Jim, 6268
Goddard, Tony, 7369
Godec, Dan, 4378
Godfrey, Ellen, 379
Godfrey, Ken, 7315
Godfrey, Margaret, 3048
Godfrey, Rayna, 907
Godfrey, Robert, 876
Godfrey, Virginia, 2782
Godlock, Jacqueline, 7915
Godsey, Kirby, 4517
Godsey, Sally, 2377
Goel, David E., 7222
Goerger, Carole, 4305
Goerlitz, Amanda, 215
Goerrich, Marilyn, 1024
Goers, Abbey, 4118
Goertemoeller, Cynthia, 1449
Goesel, Brian W, 5671
Goesl, Brian, 8464
Goestch, Lara, 2958
Goettle IV, Richard J., 2126
Goetz, Jenny, 6931
Goetz, Rick, 7000, 7001, 7002
Goetz, Tracy, 1223
Goff, Becky, 305
GoForth, Dana, 1904
Gogal, Gary, 2727
Gogol, Peter, 5524
Gohman, Melissa, 7369
Gohn, Kay, 6949
Goida, Robert, 7678
Goilden Drake, Clare, 3818
Golan, Lawrence, 1814
Golay, Ardis, 3889
Gold, Andrew, 4305

Gold, Gene, 2883
Gold, Michele, 3482
Gold, Rob, 3213
Goldbar, Judy, 6231, 6232
Goldberg, Allan, 5039
Goldberg, Bernel, 1805
Goldberg, Camille, 213
Goldberg, Jane, 8567
Goldberg, Robert, 3459
Goldberg, Roberta, 5191
Goldberg Aronson, Martha, 3239
Golden, Anne, 811, 4256
Golden, Cara, 912
Golden, Carol, 4175
Golden, Carolyn C., 2412
Golden, Elisa, 3878
Golden, Eugene, 4244
Golden, Jennifer, 4491
Golden, Joe, 6690, 6691, 6692, 6693, 6694
Golden, Judy, 3973
Golden, Leslie, 6040
Golden, Nancy, 1588, 1931
Golden, Steven, 6732
Goldenberg, Helyn, 1041
Goldenberg, Jeffery B, 1447
Goldensohn, Ellen, 1411
Goldfarb, Alvin, 6797, 6798, 6799
Goldhirsch, Sheri, 3598
Golding, Ella, 5039
Goldkamp, Joseph A., 2323
Goldklang, Jeff, 7373
Goldman, David, 1046
Goldman, Derek, 6479
Goldman, Douglas E., 4313
Goldman, Dr. Fran, 2202
Goldman, Fran, 1513, 1514, 5286
Goldman, Frances H, 969
Goldman, John D, 856, 857
Goldman, Margaret, 7703
Goldman, Renee, 2308
Goldman, Richard, 5015
Goldman, Robert T, 3461
Goldman, Scott, 3378
Goldman, Sherwin M., 2209
Goldman, Stephen, 866, 867
Goldman, William A., 7982
Goldring, Jeffrey, 4718
Goldschmid, Joyce, 2489
Goldseker, Ana, 3129
Goldsmith, Jeff, 1109
Goldsmith, Kelsey, 7181
Goldsmith, Richard, 1410
Goldsmith, Robert, 5133
Goldsmith, William, 3721
Goldspiel, Alan, 4720
Goldstein, Andrew, 944
Goldstein, Barbara, 2002
Goldstein, Barry, 4752
Goldstein, Bert, 7294
Goldstein, Constance, 4783
Goldstein, David Ira, 2430
Goldstein, Dr. Gary, 3935
Goldstein, Elizabeth, 4313
Goldstein, Eric, 8295
Goldstein, Francine, 2246, 2251
Goldstein, Harold, 564
Goldstein, Jess, 2699
Goldstein, Jon, 2879
Goldstein, Lynn, 2583
Goldstein, Michael, 1447, 5109
Goldstein, Sandra, 6434, 6435
Goldstein, Stuart, 507
Goldston, Valerie, 6771, 6772
Goldthwait, Marilyn, 3622
Goldthwaite, Chuck, 4164
Goldthwaite, Kay, 1724
Goldwaite, Mary, 4164
Goldwater, Bobby, 6178
Goldweber, Mark, 651
Golik, Valerie, 5826
Golka, Tomasz, 832
Gollihar, Mandy, 1698
Golomb, Joie, 359
Golstein, Jo, 7599
Goltz, Jennifer, 7268
Golub, Jerel, 1361, 5039
Golub, Peter, 4013, 4015
Golub, Spencer, 3861

Gomes, Angela, 7515
Gomes, Matt, 7243
Gomes Jr., Edward, 508
Gomez, Carmen, 6221, 6222, 6223, 6226
Gomez, Ileana, 6552
Gomez, Isaac, 6760
Gomez, Teresa, 5130
Gomez, Vicki, 3999
Gonce, Nancy C, 4144
Gonda, Louis L., 3466
Goner, Brian, 1820
Gong, Jasper, 6103
Gongora, Anthony, 146
Gonthier, Stephanie, 997
Gonzales, Alexander, 2554
Gonzales, Debra, 7148
Gonzales, James, 880, 4338, 6310
Gonzales, Maggie, 3415
Gonzales, Myredith, 179
Gonzales, Ray, 6102
Gonzalez, Alex, 439
Gonzalez, Amelia, 6069
Gonzalez, Annabella, 388
Gonzalez, Carla, 6132
Gonzalez, Dan, 646
Gonzalez, Gil, 6323, 6324
Gonzalez, Gio, 2932
Gonzalez, Gus, 6321
Gonzalez, Jennifer, 5663, 8450, 8451
Gonzalez, Jonathan, 3986
Gonzalez, Juan Carlos, 2015
Gonzalez, Julia, 8424, 8425, 8426, 8427, 8428
Gonzalez, Leddy, 3991
Gonzalez, Lois, 5032
Gonzalez, Luis, 8216
Gonzalez, Lutecia, 388
Gonzalez, Maria, 6103
Gonzalez, Maria E., 3785
Gonzalez, Michael, 6304, 6308
Gonzalez, Michael L., 1830, 5856
Gonzalez, Penelope, 478
Gonzalez, Rene, 2015, 2833
Gonzalez, Rene J, 2833
Gonzalez, Robert, 2345
Gooch, Anthony C., 1412
Good, Art, 4266
Good, Jay, 4164
Good, Mary, 4191
Good, Rick, 533
Good-Morgan, Kelly, 4299
Goodall, John W., 5656
Goode, Glennette, 645
Goode, Joe, 79
Goode, Katheleen, 7988
Goode, Rusty, 6985
Goode, Susan, 1784, 2375
Goodemotte, Ed, 6541, 6542
Gooden, LaDonna, 4906
Goodhart, Saul, 5075
Goodkind, E. Robert, 2472
Goodloe, Mark, 3410
Goodman, Allen S., 3408
Goodman, Cheryl T., 255
Goodman, Darryl, 2929
Goodman, David S., 7975, 7976, 7977
Goodman, Eve, 1657
Goodman, Gillian, 2970
Goodman, Jane, 1719
Goodman, Lawrence, 5342
Goodman, Leonard, 5129, 7759
Goodman, Michael, 2445
Goodman, Peggy, 3060, 3064
Goodman, Richard, 4352
Goodman, Stormy, 6530
Goodman, Todd, 1637
Goodnight, Ann B., 5246
Goodpaster, Larry, 7997
Goodrich, Bruce, 6114
Goodrich, Edward A., 1696
Goodrich, Linda, 2554
Goodrich, Rose, 6196
Goodrick, Victoria, 938
Goodsell, Claudia, 6064
Goodson, Dr. Leigh, 8059
Goodwater, Dan, 6231, 6232
Goodwin, Davd, 2593
Goodwin, Dot, 3002
Goodwin, James K., 6434, 6435

1169

Executive Name Index

Goodwin, Jonathan, 1070
Goodwin, Larry, 4867
Goodwin, Myrna, 4292
Goodwin, Jr., Russell C., 7982
Goodwin-Lightfoot, Stacy, 611
Goodyear Wisser, Jessica, 1773
Goold, Robert, 3773
Gooley, Tom, 3669
Goor, Anita, 4830
Gopal, Dr. Arvin, 1340
Gora, Jo Ann M., 6915, 6916, 6917, 6918
Gorboulev, Oleg, 676
Gorchynsky, Natalie, 4110
Gordley, Deb, 1110
Gordley, Rich, 1110
Gordon, Ain, 474
Gordon, Alice, 3313
Gordon, Andrea, 2578
Gordon, Andrew Brandon, 6166
Gordon, Catherine, 1832
Gordon, Charlotte, 8006
Gordon, Christopher, 1078
Gordon, David, 474
Gordon, Derek, 4424
Gordon, Eve, 4207
Gordon, Frank, 8295
Gordon, Ginna, 4212
Gordon, Glen, 2102
Gordon, Greg, 714
Gordon, James, 4389
Gordon, Joan, 4293
Gordon, Joanne, 2485, 2486
Gordon, Joel, 1499
Gordon, John A, 6762
Gordon, Judith, 5197
Gordon, Kelli, 750
Gordon, Laura J., 454
Gordon, Leila, 5752, 8547
Gordon, Leslie, 6626
Gordon, Lisa, 2980
Gordon, M, 2002
Gordon, Marjorie, 2002
Gordon, Mark Robert, 3484
Gordon, Michael, 5115
Gordon, Michael S, 6091
Gordon, Milton A., 6110, 6111, 6114
Gordon, Nicholas, 4392
Gordon, Nina, 4209
Gordon, Roger, 2941
Gordon, Samuel, 3625
Gordon, Sheryl, 7261
Gordon, Skip, 1680
Gordon, Valerie, 4562
Gordon, Van, 2627
Gordon Ross, John, 1497
Gore, Jacqui, 1743
Gore, Jeannie, 4101
Gorecki, Kate, 1168
Gorelick, Christine, 3686
Gorelick, Ellen, 888
Goren, Neal, 2228
Gorewitz, Steve, 5963
Gorham, Nate, 3369
Gorichev, Alexei, 8837
Gorke, Sarah, 1825
Gorman, David, 2690
Gorman, Father Richard, 7639
Gorman, Mark, 3882
Gorman, Michael, 5742
Gorman, Rachel, 434, 3081
Gormley-Chapman, Margaret, 5268
Gorneault, Peter, 368
Goronkin, JuliAnn, 373
Gorter, Wieneke, 1918
Gortmaker, Jeff, 8245, 8246
Gortner, David, 1613
Gosack-Fleming, Elizabeth, 668
Gose Clemens, Karen, 5788, 5789, 5790
Gose Enghauser, Rebecca, 177
Goss, Karen, 2027
Gossard, Jeni, 5588
Gossard, Jenni, 1701
Gossett, Summer, 4693, 4694
Gotesman, Victor, 86, 6262, 6432
Gotlieb, Julie, 7353, 7354
Gotsch, Juliea, 13
Gotsch, Susan D., 6323, 6324
Gottfried, Bradley, 7207

Gottlie, John, 2637
Gottlieb, Geordan, 2797
Gottlieb, Jane, 440
Gottlieb, Marc, 1585
Gottlieb Beckerman, Susan, 5201
Gottschalk, John, 7496, 7500
Gottschalk, Susan, 1191
Gottwald, Donald, 6860
Gottwald, Nancy, 676
Gotwald, Mercedes, 3434
Goudimiak, Oleg, 571
Goudreau, Trace, 5697
Gough, Jimmy, 6635
Gouillart, Laura, 2113
Gould, Aaron, 1630
Gould, Barbara, 4110
Gould, Betty, 3732
Gould, Cindy, 726
Gould, Dr. Charlene, 7425
Gould, Karen L., 7644
Gould, Marnie, 3885
Gould, Mary, 3882
Gould, Rebecca, 7048
Gould, Rodney, 6775, 6776, 6777, 6778
Gould, Sally, 5207
Gould, Susan S., 1645
Gould Sugden, Alisa, 4205
Gould, Esq., Ross, 5191
Gould-Aaron, Nancy, 5252
Goulding, Emily, 2739
Goulet, James F, 3187
Goulstone, Robert, 4164
Gourlay, James, 1659
Gouwens, Thomas, 4553
Govan, Michael, 6166
Govanucci, Renee, 8174
Govatos, Barbara, 4414
Govatos, Ruth, 4414
Govea, Rodger M, 5318, 5351
Gow, Joe, 8672
Gow, John, 5637
Grabarkewitz, David, 2345
Grabau, Chris, 7445
Grabel, Naomi, 418
Grabenstein, Ann, 7194
Graber, Matthew, 2473, 2998
Grabin, Elizabeth.A, 222
Grabowski, Donald, 2044, 2045
Grabowski, John, 3462
Grace, J, 1192
Grace, Matthew D, 2131
Gracey, Cynthia, 4826
Graci, Sharon, 3868
Gracia, Rauli, 1731
Gracia, Rodrigo, 2606
Gracieux, Vincent, 3255
Gradl Seitz, Christine, 3225
Gradone, J.P., 5007
Grady, Cade, 7697
Grady, Harve, 4166
Grady, Jeff, 6132
Grady, Julie, 4166
Grady, Lisa, 632
Graeter, Harold, 8282
Graf, Buddy, 2826
Graf, Carol, 2826
Graf, Howard, 5073
Grafe, Fallon, 1360
Grafe, Tamara, 2140
Grafman, Laura R., 5979
Grafos, Tania, 57
Grafton, Ken, 5281
Gragg, Wendy, 4242
Graham, Brad, 3302
Graham, Buzz, 5508
Graham, David, 4625
Graham, Debbie, 1144
Graham, Gina, 2610
Graham, Jason, 2547
Graham, Jerri, 4276, 6217
Graham, John, 729, 788, 1021, 8051
Graham, John M, 5590
Graham, John M., 8323
Graham, Jon, 6347, 6353, 6357
Graham, Karen, 8346
Graham, Kathryn T., 91
Graham, Kelly, 3880
Graham, Micael J, 5307, 5308, 5310, 5311

Graham, Michael, 1720, 5308
Graham, Michael J, 5311
Graham, Michelle, 1633
Graham, Mike, 5609, 5611
Graham, Patty, 601
Graham, Robert, 3856, 4873
Graham, Sarah, 2230, 5172
Graham, Seong-Kyung, 1820
Graham, Stephen, 3540
Graham, Steve, 7571
Graham, Steven, 3459
Graham, Wallace A, 7819
Graham Harrison, Susan, 4207, 6066, 6070, 6071, 6072
Graham Hughes, Jeffrey, 512
Graham Ryken, Dr Philip, 6848, 6849
Grahl, Michele, 2789, 6535
Grahn-Howard, Chris, 305
Grainger, Clive, 2107
Grainger, H. Frank, 5246
Gralbey, Jerry W, 8156
Gram, Jesse, 2048
Gramer, Lori, 1240, 4846
Granados, Arthur, 6163
Granados, Claudia, 3379
Granados, Dr Patricia, 6823, 6824
Granados, Gabriela, 378
Granados, Michael, 8091
Granata, Eric, 8174
Grandberry, Walter, 384
Grandbois, Peggy, 5343
Grande-Weiss, Robert, 2610
Grandis, David, 952
Grandy, Linda, 1681
Graney, Pat, 683
Granger, Amie, 6719
Granger, Eric, 7984
Granger, Heather, 5343
Granger, John Larry, 874
Granger, Sara, 1267
Granholm, John, 1612
Grannan, Riley, 557
Grannemann, Hannah, 3645
Granold, John, 8210
Granquist, Charles, 8509
Granquist, Jo Anne, 4600
Granquist, JoAnne, 6839
Grant, Barbara, 6089
Grant, Brid, 6436, 6437
Grant, Debbie, 5225
Grant, Emily, 5103
Grant, Holly, 2207
Grant, Jamie, 5850
Grant, Lindsey, 1836
Grant, LT Michael S, 961
Grant, Nick, 843
Grant, Patrice, 1959
Grant, Rachel, 4810
Grant, Richard, 1870
Grant, Robert, 4085
Grant, Steven, 964, 4435
Grant, Suzy, 200, 207
Grant, Taunee, 1986
Grant Burdick, Lindsey, 1365
Grant,, Elizabeth, 3252
Grantham, Dr Greg, 4473
Granucci, Tom, 6239
Granville, Patty, 5629
Grapey, Marc, 2930
Gras, Deanna, 1464, 5200
Grassby, Betse, 918
Grassieux, Jean Paul, 4204
Grasso, Alicia, 3361
Gratch, Susan, 2512
Grau, Evelyn, 5763, 5764, 5765
Graumann, Keith, 1640
Grava, Karen, 943
Graveline, Dr Michelle, 2127
Graven, Stacy, 8570
Gravenor, Alan, 7213
Graver, Monica M., 1632
Graves, Betsi, 274
Graves, Kelli, 8047
Graves, Linda, 4221, 6116
Graves, Michael, 4347
Graves, Nicholas M, 2449
Graves, Robert, 4602
Graves, Thomas, 3932

Graves, William T., 7135
Gravison, Michael, 8201
Gravitz, Charles, 266
Gravley, Bert, 2357
Grawe, Denice, 947
Grawemeyer, Christine, 6349
Gray, Acia, 625
Gray, Barbara L., 117
Gray, Beverly, 1735
Gray, Brian, 7885
Gray, Catherine, 3901
Gray, Christopher, 462
Gray, Cindy, 5660
Gray, Dan, 3723
Gray, Don, 4159
Gray, Gary, 872
Gray, Jeanne, 5196
Gray, Joan, 208
Gray, Kathleen A., 4124
Gray, Krissy, 1939
Gray, Margaret, 548
Gray, Marlena, 3790
Gray, Matt, 3172
Gray, Matthew, 2205
Gray, Melanie, 5643
Gray, Michael, 844, 2726
Gray, Nancy, 5758
Gray, Patricia, 1168
Gray, Perien, 5218
Gray, Peter, 2010
Gray, Peter C, 3196
Gray, Rachel D., 1341
Gray, Rick, 2958, 5256
Gray, Roger, 548
Gray, Samantha, 3893
Gray, Terry, 6455
Gray, William Jon, 766
Gray, William P., 1999, 2000, 2001
Gray, Winifred Perkin, 2107
Gray Covington, Conner, 1695
Gray Hildenbrand, Saul, 6286
Gray-Little, Bernadette, 7043
Grayson, David, 2199
Grazi, Leslie, 1384
Greason, Kathy, 3095
Greaver, Rick, 2534
Grecki, Barbara, 3488
Greco, Domarino, 4989
Greco, Guy, 2504
Greco, Loretta, 2583, 3593
Greco, Mitchell, 3987, 8416
Greco, Phil, 6846
Greefield, Beck, 1905
Greeley, Mike, 3744
Greemayer, Judith, 1630
Green, Andrew, 5193, 7812
Green, Ann, 4851
Green, Aspen, 5996, 6010
Green, Barbara, 6909, 6910, 6911
Green, Barry, 1717
Green, Bill, 3948, 6303
Green, Brenda, 3916
Green, Bryan, 6536
Green, Chad, 8298
Green, Charity, 4278, 4279
Green, Dan, 1497
Green, David, 1027, 2366
Green, Dr Hal, 4662
Green, Gretchen, 3510
Green, J Ernest, 1152
Green, Jack, 2283
Green, James, 2610
Green, Janet, 728
Green, Jay, 5969, 5970, 5971, 5975
Green, Jean-Pierre, 4087
Green, Jen, 2967
Green, Jennifer, 1887, 2967
Green, Jim, 4473
Green, Joanne, 1513, 1514, 5286
Green, John, 2166
Green, Juanita P, 4370
Green, Judie, 2907
Green, Judie Moore, 6730
Green, Kayla, 5324
Green, Laura Gayle, 8686
Green, Lauren, 1576, 1845
Green, Lia, 3886, 3888
Green, Lisa, 2939

Executive Name Index

Green, Mary, 2302
Green, Mary Tush, 3052
Green, Mary W, 1634
Green, Mary Woodmansee, 2302
Green, Melinda, 4812
Green, Melorra, 6249
Green, Mike, 5578, 6036
Green, Randall, 6794
Green, Robert, 1493
Green, RuthAnn, 4563
Green, Shel, 1226
Green, Stephanie E., 7986
Green, Steve, 1943
Green, Susan, 1904
Green, Tiffany, 5965
Green, Tod, 2582
Green, Tom, 4172
Green Chace Collins, Eliza, 3859
Green Edison, Carol, 1992
Green, PhD, John C., 6890
Green-Moneta, Jennifer, 5612
Greenberg, Daniel B, 8101
Greenberg, Hon Mel, 3187
Greenberg, Laura, 3302
Greenberg, Matthew, 2038
Greenberg, Shira, 345
Greenberg, Steve, 6396
Greenberg, Sue, 3300, 7454
Greenberg, Yvan, 485
Greenburg, Martin, 4520
Greenburg, Meredith, 2497
Greendale, Dr. Robert, 2064
Greene, Allison, 2482
Greene, Arleen, 1218
Greene, Dave, 4900
Greene, Denise, 152
Greene, John, 4124
Greene, Kathleen, 3509
Greene, Kevin, 152
Greene, Lesley, 3447
Greene, Linda, 6349
Greene, M. Dwaine, 4690
Greene, Manna Jo, 5191
Greene, Molly, 890
Greene Udden, Rebecca, 3986
Greene,, Marcus, 6488
Greene, Jr, Frank S, 6270
Greenek, Gino, 485
Greenfield, Gordon, 989, 991, 992, 993, 994, 995, 4486
Greenfield, Hope, 478
Greenfield, Sally, 1365
Greenfield, Stuart, 2251
Greenfield, Taylor, 7303
Greenham, David, 3099
Greenhill, Bruce, 3207
Greenhill, Manuel, 8748
Greenhill, Matthew, 8748
Greenhill, Mitchell, 8748
Greenhut, Ph.D, Deborah S., 434
Greenland, Amy, 5359
Greenleaf, Mark, 2995, 6851
Greenough, Kathleen, 1779
Greenspun, Martin, 6156
Greenstein, Adra, 3582
Greenwald, Laura, 2177
Greenwald, Leslie, 2095
Greenwald, Robert, 329
Greenwood, Jean, 5875
Greenwood, John, 3576
Greenwood, Juanita P, 4370
Greenwood, Mary Ann, 753
Greenwood, Nan, 1455, 7695
Greenwood, Reed, 753
Greenwood, Robin, 1606
Greenwood, Terriann, 8201
Greeny, Adam H., 2181
Green, Jessica, 7206
Greep, Larry, 1601
Greer, Ginger, 1680
Greer, Skip, 3609
Greer-Sikora, Heather, 520
Greeting, Daniel M, 4340
Grefe, Tamara, 2140
Grega-Pikul, Alicia, 3139
Gregerson, Greg, 3037
Gregg, Bill, 3668
Gregg, Margaret G., 2314

Gregg, P.D., 5826
Gregg, Randy A., 1715
Gregg, William, 3668
Gregis, Denise, 2195
Grego, Peter, 2534
Gregoire, Chris, 1285
Gregorczyk, Michelle, 541
Gregorio, Mark, 6400, 6401, 6402, 6403
Gregory, Amanda, 4696
Gregory, Cristen, 1664
Gregory, Helen, 2668
Gregory, Jeni, 1263
Gregory, John, 3092
Gregory, Karen, 2446
Gregory, Lisa, 3180
Gregory, Mark, 5838
Gregory, Michael, 1210, 1211
Gregory, Ted, 4926
Gregory Ruiz, Cookie, 621
Greif, Geoffrey L., 4755
Greig, Brandie, 7374
Greig, Rick E, 5659
Greigo, Darlene, 7620
Greil, Steven J., 5901, 5902, 5903, 5904
Grein, Catherine E, 2108
Greiner, Ken, 3587
Greiser, Kathy, 2281
Greiss, Terry, 3420, 3505
Grele Barrie, Lisa, 3675
Grell, D'Ann, 1497
Gremel, Lori, 6238, 6243
Gren, Jason, 4156
Grenell, Tom, 8133
Grenfell, Robert, 140
Grenfell, Robert, 140
Grenz, Garrett, 5830
Gresham, Quin, 7412
Gresham, Quinn, 3278
Greskovich, Lisa, 166
Grether, Susan, 822, 4268
Grether Marion, Sheila, 6209
Grewe, Karen, 4624
Grgas, Elayne, 102
Grice, Michael, 4693, 4694, 7088
Griepentrog, Tedd, 1163
Griepp, Marvel, 2257
Grier, Anita, 7617
Grier, Ed, 1795
Grier, Kelly, 4581
Grier, Kim, 480
Gries, Rachel, 1077
Griesen, James, 1305
Grieshaber, Annette, 6236, 6237
Griesmer, Denis M., 7967
Griesmer, Dennis, 3712
Griessel, Erica, 7154
Grieve, Erin, 4682
Griff, Kaatri, 1912
Griffen, Ginger, 5379
Griffen, Joe, 4647
Griffeth, Bruce, 2848
Griffey, Linda Boyd, 6209
Griffie, Dave, 5238
Griffin, Bill, 8114
Griffin, Carolyn, 4030
Griffin, Charlotte, 7167
Griffin, Craig, 3980
Griffin, Dr. Jackie, 5551
Griffin, Eileen, 907
Griffin, Elizabeth, 4088
Griffin, G. Chris, 71
Griffin, Gabrielle, 6760
Griffin, Jeff, 3479
Griffin, Jennifer, 1739
Griffin, John C., 2139
Griffin, Jonnie, 4140
Griffin, Judson, 1392
Griffin, Julia, 4089
Griffin, Kenneth J., 1473
Griffin, Kevin, 6605, 6606
Griffin, Lee T, 3408
Griffin, Linda, 5176
Griffin, Lois D, 999
Griffin, Paul, 1758
Griffin, Peter, 4400, 4730, 4731, 4732, 4733
Griffin, Robert, 2166
Griffin, Sean M., 2779
Griffin, Steve, 4145

Griffinger, Esq., Michael R., 7574
Griffins, Greg, 4643
Griffith, Dick, 1804
Griffith, Jim, 3837, 4479
Griffith, Kelley, 2265
Griffith, Kris, 4592
Griffith, Larry, 6861, 6862, 6863
Griffith, Nancy, 2264
Griffith, Prescott F, 3695, 7618
Griffith, Shelley, 5558
Grigal, Helen M., 3112
Griggs, Michael, 5419
Griggs-Janower, David, 2201
Grigsby, Bryon L., 8113
GrillerMitchell, Pauline, 3131
Grillet, Grace, 3814
Grim, Vicki, 4102, 8644, 8645
Grimaldi, F Michael, 6990
Grimaldi, Joe, 1180
Grimaldi, Stacy, 1966
Grimes, Angela, 2040
Grimes, Janet, 8291
Grimes, Petra, 2347
Grimes, Rebekah, 1851
Grimes, Ron, 5901, 5902, 5903, 5904
Grimes Hudson '76, Lea Ann, 6642, 6643
Grimes,, Alison, 2829
Grimm, Richard, 388
Grimm, Shea, 4283
Grindle, Cathy, 1792
Grine, Geraldine, 1833
Grine, James, 1833
Griner, Christopher, 1168
Grinnell, Lori, 8696
Grinspan, Jen, 7593
Grinter, Kay, 2763
Grisanti, Lisa, 7656
Grisham, Nancy, 1152
Grishman, Kurt, 1458
Grissom, Doug, 4034
Griswold, William M., 7962
Grittner, Curtiss, 3222
Grive, Michael, 6261
Grix, Heidi, 4770
Grlfinkel, Tom, 5964
Grobe, Fritz, 7181
Grocki, Alma, 2031
Grode, Desiree, 4552
Groetsch, Amelia, 1126
Groff, Wally, 8341
Grogan, Carrie, 4562
Grogan, Jeffrey, 1420
Groggett, Christy, 6703
Groggett, Scotta, 6703
Grohs, Ben, 5951, 5955
Grohs, Benjamin W., 2422
Grokowsky, Shelly, 4108
Gronau, Gary, 1288, 4919
Gronbeck, Lori, 673
Gronningen, Stuart, 758
Gropman, Saul, 4300
Grose, Lynn, 5280
Grosman, Diane, 65
Gross, Allen, 876, 4245
Gross, Amy, 7048
Gross, Austin, 1666
Gross, Chad, 6714
Gross, Dan, 3468
Gross, David, 1749
Gross, Iris, 4140
Gross, Jaime, 525
Gross, Leslie, 2764
Gross, Liz, 4065
Gross, Murray, 1221
Gross, Peter A., 5191
Gross, Susan, 1625
Gross, Thomas, 1848
Gross, William, 1651
Grossenbacher, Nancy, 5661
Grosser, Jeff, 6774
Grosser, Robert, 7462
Grossman, Adam, 2118
Grossman, Daniel, 7573
Grossman, Daniel B., 8302
Grossman, David, 871
Grossman, Debbie, 952
Grossman, Ellen, 279
Grossman, Gary, 6073

Grossman, Ian, 1998
Grossman, Ian M., 2097
Grossman, Kathy, 6718, 8611
Grossman, Lois, 200
Grossman, Sheila, 6400, 6402, 6403
Grossman, Esquire, Elin, 635
Grossq, Hank, 4140
Grosz, Charles, 1834
Grothe, Kevin, 5575
Grothe Cullen, Judith, 3281
GrothOlson, Lee, 1576
Grotke, Colleen, 1164
Grotpeter, Peggy, 4920
Grouse, Rebecca, 4939
Grove, Barry, 3517, 7754
Grove, Richard, 5229
Grover, Dana, 2600
Grover, Darcie, 2600
Grover, Olivia, 4361
Grover, Philip, 4410, 6445
Grover, Robinson A, 4390
Groves, J Randall, 4828
Groves, Siobhan, 8159
Groves, Xandie, 6939, 6940
Grubb, Carolyn, 6455
Grubb, Clifford, 3133
Grubb, Elizabeth, 8068
Grube, Bruce, 6664
Gruber, Amy, 1837
Gruber, Duane, 4290
Gruber, Glenn W., 7139
Gruber, Judy, 1996
Gruca, Ronald, 8170, 8171
Gruel, Don, 2760
Grueneberger, Art, 3277
Gruenler, Eric, 6217
Gruenler, Georgia, 7500
Gruessing, James W, 834, 6227
Grueter, Erich, 6328
Grueter, Fritz, 1944, 6328
Grueter, Ingrid, 6328
Grufik, Terry, 5395
Grumbach Jr, George J, 2225
Grumet, Diane, 486
Grundmann, Anya, 2101
Grundy, Lilia, 5783
Grunenwald, Joe, 8119
Grunko, Lenore, 4407
Grunwell, Brad, 5374
Grupe, Steven, 1955
Gruppman, Igor, 1762
Grusmark, R Glen, 2683
Gruzin, David, 4958
Gryuruch, Andrew, 3194
Gualitieri, Marco, 2251
Guardino, Geri, 4776
Guarino, Christine, 7281
Guarino, Gil, 2378, 5762
Guatieri, Erica, 593
Gubala, Lori, 5749
Gubelmann, William S., 4470
Guberman, Laura, 7505
Gubits, David, 1476, 5217
Guc, Bill, 1823
Gudenius, Carl, 2740
Guelfi, James D, 5434, 8117
Guenther, Barbara, 2036
Guenther, Bonnie, 3032
Guenther, Peter, 921
Gueraiero, James, 5825
Guercio, Benjamin, 4233
Guerra, Jesus, 6533
Guerra, Michael, 6106
Guerrera, Anthony, 6013
Guerrero, Daniel G, 6174
Guerrero, Daniel G., 6169
Guerrero, Giancarlo, 1696
Guerrero Buckley, Lee Ann, 4321
Guerriero, James C, 5825
Guerriero, William, 5947
Guerrisi, Teri, 5452
Guertin, Pierre H, 928
Guevara, Miguel, 4117
Guggenheim, Regina, 6257, 6259, 6263
Guibao, Paul K., 2332
Guibbory, Shem, 5106
Guibeaux, Gerald, 4708
Guice, Bret, 6528

1171

Executive Name Index

Guidice, Michael, 7703
Guidroz, Greg, 4708
Guidry, Maj. Scott, 951
Guidry, Randy, 4707
Guiher, Catharine, 3533
Guijarro, Jesus, 889
Guillermo,, 1048
Guillory, Bennet, 2515
Guillory, Don, 7109
Guin, Catherine, 2280
Guin, Dan, 150
Guin Kittner, Hattie, 4384
Guinn, Dave, 3766
Guinn, Mark, 7154
Guiraud, Rose Marie, 354
Guisinger, Michelle, 8
Gula, Denise, 538
Gularte, Stephanie, 2555
Guldin, Adrienne, 201
Gulia, Gregory, 351
Gulick, Katherine, 2246, 2251
Gullans, Andrew, 2708
Gullickson, Andrea, 1082
Gullickson, Gunther, 3266
Gullickson, Lynn, 8686
Gulling, Rebecca, 3032
Gulyaeva, Luba, 334
Gum Jr, John, 3077
Gund, Ann, 7231
Gundersen, Glenn, 3836
Gunderson, Paul, 4841
Gunderson, Richard, 4164
Gundlach, Karen, 3241
Gunin, Dave, 8047
Gunn, Dennis, 2365
Gunn, John A., 1922, 1923
Gunn, Rachel, 6784
Gunning, Greg, 3374
Gunter, Kate, 673
Gunter, Norma J, 694
Gunter, Paul, 4540
Gunter, Suzy, 694
Gunther, John, 1319
Gunther, Paul, 1265
Gunther Pugh, Dorothy, 618
Gunzburg, Nathalie de, 5127
Gunzenhauser, Gerard R, 2272
Guo, Qianping, 5929, 5931
Gupte, Rebecca, 371
Gura, Rebecca, 3471
Gural, Ron, 3086
Gurd, David, 1697
Guriel, Darci, 3706
Gurnow, Jomarie, 7326
Gurol, Erol, 2230
Gussman, Roy D, 1347
Gustafson, Bruce, 5462
Gustafson, Karen Jo, 686
Gustafson, Kelli, 4723
Gustafson, Kirk, 912
Gustafson, Lisa, 3220
Gustafson, Rodney, 104
Gustavson, Penny B, 3804
Gustek, Greg, 6044, 6045, 6046
Gustin, Dan, 4854
Guston, Debra, 3175
Gutelius, Chris, 1364
Guterman, Neil B., 7258
Gutermuth, Bob, 2969
Guthier, Mark, 4117
Guthier, Mark, 4117
Guthrie, Carol, 3680
Guthrie, Debbi, 6224
Guthrie, Duke, 2880
Guthrie, H Duke, 6665, 6666
Guthrie, H. Duke, 4524
Guthrie, John, 1183
Guthrie, Richard, 2077
Gutierrez, Gina, 4262
Gutierrez, Olfary, 1335
Gutierrez, Teresa, 2389
Gutmann, Dr. Amy, 8154
Gutoff, Olivia W, 1159
Gutt, Christian, 6278
Gutter, Robert, 1494
Guttman, Richard, 5497
Guttmann, James, 1190, 2110
Guttmann, Jim, 1190

Guy, Daniel X., 3833
Guy, David, 1594
Guy, Don, 305
Guy, Dr. Todd, 1091
Guy, Marilyn, 7933
Guy, Patricia, 6841, 6842
Guy, Rusty, 7956
Guy, Shirley, 6150
Guyaux, Joseph C., 2319
Guyer, Shari, 1210, 1211
Guyer, Steven, 3729
Guyeskey, Will, 3202
Guyett, Robert, 1898
Guyette, Dan, 2672
Guyver, Russell, 914
Guzielek, Scott, 2017
Guzman, Alex Alejandro, 2206
Guzman, Hector, 1734, 1744, 1747, 2359
Gwin, Robert G., 3990
Gwinn, Anne, 7106
Gwinn, Elizabeth, 4496
Gwinn, Kit, 1732
Gwock Silton, Kristen, 2856
Gwozdz, Lee, 1737, 5602
Gwynne, Susan, 869, 4323
Gyetvai, Alayne, 883

H

H. Bostian II, Dr. Carey, 1112
H. Buckman, Robert, 8226
H. Byrnes Jr, William, 3376
H. Dorman, Dr. Richard, 8146
H. Horowitz, Alfred, 7789
H. Lenchus, Gilbert, 2814
H. Shaheen, Yvonne, 6899, 6901, 6902
H.Brodsky, Heidi, 1171, 1172
Haack, Kaytina, 597
Haack, Randy, 7489
Haag, Gordon, 1880
Haag, MD, Gordon, 6113
Haak, Eric, 6592, 6593
Haarstad, Ken, 7616
Haas, Cindy, 4129
Haas, Joel, 6346
Haas, Karen, 2333
Haas, M, 541
Haas, Mike, 6330
Haas, Patty, 6386
Haas, Paul, 753
Haas, Phil J, 2386
Haas, Steven N., 5485
Haas, Susan, 3249
Haase, Diego Sanchez, 1121
Haase, Thomas, 1256
Habben, Ph.D., Dorothy E., 7692
Habecker, Elizabeth H, 2303
Habeger, Tim, 2873
Haberman, Ian S., 3747
Habermann, Joshua, 2343, 8362
Habermann, Tom, 3065
Habermann, D.M., Joshua, 2198
Habetz, Nancy, 6403
Habina, Esq. Louis K., 1644
Hachmeister, Fred, 2911
Hackem, Diane, 2354
Hackenmiller, Molly, 4640, 6962
Hackett, Ben, 1750
Hackett, Patricia, 6433
Hackney, III, Edward J, 7632
Haddock, Regina, 8504
Haddock, Ruth Triplett, 5329
Hadersbeck, Patti, 4843, 4868
Hadler, Jessica, 5123
Hadley, David, 682
Hadley, Kerry, 7168
Hadley, Mary, 714
Hadley, Susan, 65
Hadley, Suzanne, 6344
Hadley, Tamara, 577
Hadlock, David, 3974
Hadlock, Deirdre, 4060
Hadlow, Fred, 1318
Hadrick, Mack, 2846, 2862
Haeberle, Mary, 3325
Haefner, Dale, 7349
Haenni, Sabine, 3445
Hafen, Eric, 7568

Hafen, Jonathan O., 8493
Haferkamp, Deberah, 1053
Haffey, Kenneth M., 7963, 7964, 7965, 7966
Haffly, Amanda, 8130
Haffner, Barbara, 1048
Hagaman, Jerry, 5558
Hagan, Lynn, 5441
Hagan, Margaret, 7961
Hagan, Sandee, 3263
Hagan, Siobhan, 575
Hagardt, Debbi, 2381
Hagberg, Marilyn, 1115, 1116
Hage, Lindsay, 7253, 7254
Hageboeck, Charles R., 1817
Hagedorn, Karm, 8073
Hagedorn, Meredith, 2546
Hageman, Carol, 538
Hageman, Donald C, 1551, 5336
Hageman, Paul, 1737
Hageman, Schatzi, 8901
Hagemann, Karen, 3207
Hagemeier, Julie, 3327
Hagen, David, 1843
Hagen, Dr. Gary, 5283
Hagen, Eric, 3886, 3888
Hagen, Katie, 759, 761, 4205
Hagen, R. Andrew, 2258
Hagen, Sara, 2891
Hagenah, Elizabeth A, 1206
Hager, Kenneth V., 2160
Hager, Nancy, 491, 1425
Hagerman, Douglas M., 1830
Hagerty, John B., 596, 1679, 3869
Hagerty, Patrick, 2312
Haggard, Robbie, 4692
Haggard, PhD, Carrol, 7035, 7036, 7037, 7038
Haggerty, Dave, 3381
Haggerty, Emily, 659
Haggerty, Jim, 1932
Haghighat, Sheila, 4757
Hagino, Pauline, 35
Hagloch, Jonathan, 2946
Hagy, David, 1504
Hagy, Dr. David, 1508
Hagymassy, Cheryl, 1496
Hagymassy, Jules, 1496
Hahm, Anna, 8679
Hahn, Audrey, 6909, 6910, 6911
Hahn, Christopher, 2321
Hahn, Chuck, 697
Hahn, Craig, 1703
Hahn, David, 2036
Hahn, Ernie, 6247
Hahn, Glen, 3970
Hahn, Hillary, 1766
Hahn, Jenna, 1068
Hahn, Jennifer, 6719
Hahn, Julie, 1939
Hahn, Leigh Ann, 6175
Hahn, Marian, 4174
Hahn, Marjorie, 979
Hahn, Pamela, 725
Hahn, Ralph, 4070
Hahn, Ron, 6247
Hahs, Sharon K, 6748, 6750
Hai, Helen, 4271
Hai, Ken, 4271
Hai, Melinda, 4271
Hai, Steven, 4271
Haidostian, Alice, 1230, 1237
Haigh, Margi, 1541
Haigler, Michael, 2204
Haigler-Robles, Susan, 5537
Haigood, Joanna, 96, 2591
Haile, Evans, 970
Hailes, Brian, 1004
Haimes, Todd, 3561
Haimor, Fawzi, 1656, 1657
Haines, Angela, 5096, 5097
Haines, Kevin, 1744
Haines, Marty, 1788
Haines, Sarah, 1433
Haines, Steven P, 4313
Hair, Donald, 1744
Hair, Ray, 5615
Haire, James, 2573
Hairston, Jay, 5293, 7948

Haislet, Jascenna, 6961, 6963, 6964, 6965
Haislip, Douglas, 1326
Haist, Dean, 1307
Haist, Dean W, 1303
Haj, Joseph, 3645
Hajduk, Patrick, 6256
Hajewski, Vicky, 5866
Hakoda, Ken, 2077
Hakoshima, Yass, 3375
Halama, Dave, 4118
Halberstam, Michael, 2970
Halboupis, John, 3608
Halbreich, Kathy, 3258
Halbritter, Judy, 1617
Halbruner, Aimee, 1785
Halcomb, Daniel, 711
Halcrow, Jennifer, 3255
Hale, Carey, 4110
Hale, Gene, 6119
Hale, John, 7067, 7068, 7069
Hale, Kim, 3280
Hale, Marie, 174
Hale, Ruth J, 4372
Hale, Shane, 8493
Hale, Susan M., 3281
Hale, Tamara, 2336
Hale, Ted, 2358
Halen, David, 1291
Halerz, Allison, 7268
Haley, Catherine, 53
Haley, Daniel, 3671
Haley, Jennifer, 1383
Haley, Laima, 4357, 4360, 4363
Haley, M. Ed., Mark, 3356
Halfen, Chuck, 139
Halkyard, Kari, 319
Hall, Adam, 1985
Hall, Adele, 3291
Hall, Alex, 8281
Hall, Betty, 190, 4941
Hall, Billy, 8468
Hall, Brittany, 1367
Hall, C. Wells, 2262
Hall, Carl, 7084
Hall, Charls, 6155
Hall, Craig, 4468
Hall, Daniel, 7991
Hall, David C., 4448
Hall, Derrick, 5964
Hall, Dianne, 5917
Hall, Donald J., 3289
Hall, Dr. William D, 1876, 1898
Hall, Em, 2903
Hall, Eric, 4355
Hall, Frank, 4472
Hall, Gretchen, 6038
Hall, James, 5154
Hall, Janet L., 3266
Hall, Joel, 204
Hall, John, 1637
Hall, Jordan, 574
Hall, Justin, 6319
Hall, Kelly, 1740, 2217
Hall, Kevin, 6695
Hall, Lili, 3237, 4121
Hall, Liz, 2327
Hall, Maureen, 7045
Hall, Miche, 2590
Hall, Nancy, 1802
Hall, Rob, 1986
Hall, Roger, 888
Hall, Ron, 6185
Hall, Sann, 4087
Hall, Sherri, 4491
Hall, Steve, 6949
Hall, Susan, 3846
Hall, Tom, 1214, 1215, 2092
Hall, William, 1898
Hall Coombs, Joanne, 1672, 5518
Hall III, John E, 778
Hallen, Mark, 3831
Hallford, Donald K, 5920
Hallford, Donald K., 5920
Hallick, Lesley M., 8076, 8078
Halliday, Janis, 3983
Halligan, David, 2148, 2149
Halligan, Sherry, 5397
Hallinan, Hugh, 6394

Executive Name Index

Hallman, Linda, 220
Hallman, Susan, 2469
Hallmen, Thomas, 5527
Halloran, Catherine, 695
Halloran, Dan, 4257
Halloran, Pat, 8285
Hallowell, Tom, 1648
Halls, Matthew, 1593
Halls, Matthew, 5405
Halls, Mike, 3241
Hallsten, Dawn R., 6828
Halperin, Bryan, 3349
Halperin, Jan, 6906
Halpern, Gerald, 402
Halpern, Harley, 7582
Halpern, Sonya M., 4505
Halpert, Dr Marcella, 1418
Halsan, Stuart, 8579
Halstead, David, 4783
Halstead, John, 5466
Halstead, Mark, 923
Halter, Carol, 3429
Halter, Cyndi, 513
Halter, Peter, 5037
Haltkamp, Dan, 6991
Halton-Subkis, Barbara, 5219
Ham, Carol, 3097
Ham, Karen, 8052
Hambey, Chris, 2425
Hamblin, Wes, 8493
Hamborsky, Jane, 1489
Hambrick, Matt, 2848
Hamburger, David, 2095
Hamburger, Susan, 372
Hamburger, Victor, 4177
Hamburger, M.D., Jerome, 822, 4268
Hamby, Doug, 256
Hamby, Lee, 3906
Hamel, Emily, 7640
Hamel, Ernest, 1993
Hamel, Lou, 1349
Hamel, Matthew, 2079
Hamel, Robert A., 7009, 7010
Hamer, Harriet, 1096
Hamernik, Audra, 4570
Hamernik, Tom, 4571
Hamey, Adele, 5934
Hamil, Jake, 1821
Hamilton, Andrea, 2030
Hamilton, Aya, 682
Hamilton, Charles H., 1412
Hamilton, Cynthia, 1749
Hamilton, Dave, 2266
Hamilton, David, 2275, 7128
Hamilton, Ed, 3966
Hamilton, Frankie, 6028
Hamilton, Gabrielle M., 5073
Hamilton, Jeffrey, 1711
Hamilton, Jenny R, 246
Hamilton, Jerry, 7325
Hamilton, John, 5037
Hamilton, Kathy, 3902
Hamilton, Kathy, 6790, 6791, 6792
Hamilton, Kim, 6031
Hamilton, Lee, 7670
Hamilton, Lisa, 236
Hamilton, Michael, 1481, 3281
Hamilton, Mike, 883
Hamilton, Monica, 8050
Hamilton, Nan, 4319, 4320
Hamilton, Noel, 794
Hamilton, Rachael, 220
Hamilton, Sally, 223, 311
Hamilton, Susan, 1204, 4796, 4797
Hamilton, Tom, 6079
Hamilton, Del, 6627
Hamingson, Andrew D, 7710, 7757, 7769
Hamingson, Andrew D., 5052
Hamington, Andrew D, 7749
Hamley, Vickie, 1731
Hamlin, Erica, 5800
Hamlin, Jeff, 3588, 7746
Hamlin, Larry Leon, 3687
Hamlin, Lindsey, 7152
Hamlin, Valerie, 1953
Hamlyn, Debbie, 5621
Hamm, Zachary, 5041
Hamman, Ralph, 3183

Hammann, Ralph, 3183
Hammel, Laura R, 3715
Hammerli, Angela, 4725
Hammerstrom, Ashley, 5953
Hammon, Norman H, 5385
Hammon, Norman H., 1580
Hammond, Carrie, 928, 4390
Hammond, Edward H., 7035, 7036, 7038
Hammond, Greg, 8732
Hammond, Holly, 6527
Hammond, Holly E., 4452
Hammond, Jared, 3928
Hammond, Jim, 6646
Hammond, Lou Rena, 596
Hammond, Michael, 7235
Hammond, Paul, 5389
Hammrich, Jenny, 8242
Hamner, Cindy, 1785
Hamor, Jane, 4975
Hampton, Barbara, 4257
Hampton, Jamey, 560
Hampton, Joey, 4562
Hampton, Nan, 5591
Hampton, Neal, 1214, 1215
Hamrah, George, 4469
Hamrick, Claudia, 4468
Hamson, Susie, 8587
Han, Derek, 4483
Han, Juliana, 1422
Han, Linda, 1865
Hanani, Yehunda, 4792
Hanani,, Hannah, 4792
Hanauer, Gerald L., 2387
Hanauer, Joe, 2484
Hance, Kent, 8424
Hancock, Becky, 3906
Hancock, Becky, 8273
Hancock, Cristine, 770
Hancock, James T., 4592
Hancock, Jory, 5997, 6000
Hancock, Larry, 1929
Hancock, Mariko, 5707
Hancock, Nika, 1705
Hancock Griffith, Nancy, 7963, 7964, 7965, 7966
Hancy, Tim, 3754
Hand, Douglas A, 7743
Hand, Mary, 91
Handforth, Dwight, 8545
Handis, Eric, 968
Handlan, Robin R, 6570
Handley, Lawrence M, 1204
Handley, Lawrence M., 4796, 4797
Handley, Thomas, 7375
Handman, Wynn, 3466, 7709
Handorf, Jerry, 3706
Handzo, Cassie, 3645
Hanes, Kent, 4708
Hanes, Lara, 506
Hanes PhD, Michael L, 8129
Hanex, Taylor, 1423
Haney, Lisa, 3773
Haney, Liz, 6321
Haney, Michelle, 911
Hanford, Marcia, 6115
Hangen, Bruce, 1199
Hanger, Howard, 1479
Hanifin, Dan, 7820
Hanisee, Robert M., 1886
Hank, Steve, 8322
Hanka, Stephen, 1765
Hankins, Robert, 4078
Hankinson, Holbrook, 6901, 6902
Hanle, Kristie, 3942
Hanley, Mary, 8558
Hanley, Ray, 5324
Hanley, Terri, 887
Hanna, Hugh, 1273
Hanna, Wes, 4162
Hannabass, Gary, 8560
Hannah, Chris, 8460
Hannah, Phil, 3601
Hannahan, Sharon, 2083
Hannan, Dottye, 6
Hannan, Erin, 6340
Hanney, Bill, 3134
Hanning, Dr Christopher, 1666
Hannom, Bruce, 8010
Hannon, Sharon, 952

Hanono, Cecilia, 111
Hanrahan, Robert, 870
Hans, Peter D., 5246
Hansen, Alfred, 195
Hansen, Beatrice, 5449
Hansen, Carol, 8493
Hansen, David B., 2368
Hansen, Duane, 4683
Hansen, Gary, 2279
Hansen, Heather, 7322
Hansen, John (Mark), 7258
Hansen, Joseph, 6234
Hansen, Judy, 4124
Hansen, Krista, 6820, 6821
Hansen, Lindsay, 6543
Hansen, Margaret, 1111
Hansen, Mark R, 1025
Hansen, Michael, 2468, 6109
Hansen, Neil, 5882
Hansen, Paul, 231
Hansen, Peter H., 7574
Hansen, Richard, 1957
Hansen, Rick, 1026
Hansen, Robin, 847, 4299
Hansen, Stephanie, 1797
Hansen, Tina, 1951
Hansen, Torben, 1184
Hansen, Trevor, 6289, 6290
Hansen Mecklenburg, Janis, 639
Hansen-Murray, Jamia, 1798, 5793
Hanson, Amanda, 1847
Hanson, Barbara, 6984
Hanson, Carolyn, 4088
Hanson, Christine, 1268
Hanson, Gary, 1535, 7978
Hanson, Helen, 1588
Hanson, Jacqueline, 1908
Hanson, Josef, 1462
Hanson, Les, 2520
Hanson, Linda, 6497
Hanson, Lori, 896
Hanson, Mark C., 1731
Hanson, Michael, 903
Hanson, Paul, 4882
Hanson, Robert, 1046
Hanson, Sarah, 1829
Hanson, Steve, 1888
Hanson, Susie, 1940, 1941
Hanson PhD, Richard A, 4655
Hanstein-Hanlan, Dana, 2488
Hanthorn, Dennis, 2020
Hanvelt, Randy, 4201
Hanz, Patty, 1831
Hao, Ping, 4246
Hapaz, Clay, 3594
Harada, Koichiro, 1419
Harada, Ricki, 2662
Harano Adams, Elizabeth, 236
Harbaugh, Ross, 977
Harbert, Norman, 1541
Harbinson, Joe, 7213
Harbour, Nancy, 5934
Harcar, Jenis, 3747
Harcke, Virginia, 140
Harclerode, Bert, 733, 4174
Harcombe, Elizabeth, 1358
Harcourt, Chris, 6207
Hardcastle, Mr. Ben, 3768
Hardee, Kellie, 6527
Harder, James H, 5294
Harder, Lillian U, 8212, 8213
Harder, Steve, 4637
Hardin, Jane, 2155
Hardin, Ryan, 4222
Harding, Kristin, 3769
Harding, Micheal, 3022
Harding, Taylor, 1016
Hardison, Cathy, 5250
Hardison, Carolyn S, 1083, 1084
Hardman, Chris, 2622
Hardman, Molly, 4353
Hardman, Robert, 5815
Hardt, Daniel, 1584
Hardward, Bernerd, 8163, 8164, 8165, 8166
Hardwick, Gwendolen, 3481
Hardy, John, 4028
Hardy, Lona, 811, 4256
Hardy, Michael C, 6553

Hardy, Peter, 2852, 3672
Hardy Jr, Lonza, 8525
Hardy-Lucas, Atty. Faye, 8525
Hare, Dan, 4709
Hare, Mark, 4120
Hare, William, 781
Harfst, Sherry, 2156
Hargens, Dr. Mark H., 4911
Hargis, Danielle, 175
Hargis, Ellen, 2049, 4558
Hargis, Jeremy, 3896
Hargrave, John R., 8028
Hargreaves, D. Keith, 3830
Hargrove, Gwen, 5607
Hargrove, Kristi, 904
Hargrove, Kristi, 6344
Haring, Betty, 3875
Haris Jr., Marion, 7882
Haritgan Connelly, Elizabeth, 6738
Harkaway, Alex, 7373
Harker, Patrick, 6451, 6452, 6453, 6454
Harkin, Alane, 3318
Harkins, Ann, 4104, 5822
Harkins, Jeffrey, 5837
Harkness, Jenny, 1835
Harkness, Laura, 3455
Harks, Ted, 8675, 8683
Harlan, Greg, 1065, 1066
Harland, Robert, 8667
Harless, Winston N., 3916
Harley, Gabriel, 1086
Harley, Margot, 3461
Harlow, Russell, 5690, 5691, 5692, 5693
Harman, David, 1453, 1462
Harman, Robert L. B., 3839
Harmatz, Kate, 6175
Harmelin, Alison, 3542
Harmon, Alex, 4905
Harmon, Dr. David, 5196
Harmon, Jim, 6513
Harmon, John, 1365
Harmon, Lisa, 7469
Harmon, Mary Elizabeth, 4501
Harmon, Peggy, 2893
Harmon, Scott, 3650
Harmon, Tiffany, 1808, 1809, 5808
Harmon Gardner, Kathleen, 8499
Harms, Helmuth, 1030
Harms, Mary Lynn, 6286
Harms, Tim, 6903
Harney, Jon, 2167
Harnick, Jay, 3582
Harnish, Jim, 2361
Haro, Delane, 879
Harold, Jacob, 3831, 4441
Harold W.,, 2565
Harowitz, Mark, 269
Harp, James, 2093
Harp, Morgan, 3280
Harper, Ben, 714
Harper, C. Gregory, 3990
Harper, Chuck, 3298
Harper, Cindy, 8430
Harper, Cynthia, 1839
Harper, Jill, 890
Harper, Joann, 7533
Harper, Kathleen, 2419
Harper, Kurt A, 1124
Harper, Kyle, 8039, 8040
Harper, Mary, 3685, 7597
Harper, Sandy, 2416
Harper, Selena, 4502
Harper, Steve, 8599, 8600
Harper, Susan, 3636
Harper, Tamara, 3182
Harper, Tanya, 4693, 4694, 7088
Harper Bonham, Meredith, 7661
Harrah, Meghann O, 5390
Harrell, Erin, 3932
Harrell, Lynn, 1419
Harrell, Richard, 1957
Harrell, William E, 5372
Harriamn, Suzie, 3928
Harrier, Anna, 8452
Harrigan, Ann, 1296
Harrigan, Anne, 1224, 1225
Harrigan, Anne L., 3864

1173

Executive Name Index

Harrill, Stephen, 5257
Harriman, Danielle, 4729
Harrington, Andrew, 7192
Harrington, Andrew D., 3552
Harrington, Christopher, 2774
Harrington, Frank, 1693
Harrington, Jerry, 794
Harrington, Josephine, 6460
Harrington, Lauren A., 3839
Harrington, Steven, 3679
Harrington, Tina, 1918
Harris, Al, 1795
Harris, Albert, 3555
Harris, Alex, 7636
Harris, Ali, 4172
Harris, Alison, 2720
Harris, Allen, 4696
Harris, Anna, 1732, 7193
Harris, Anthony, 6541
Harris, Ben, 753
Harris, Caryn, 6738
Harris, Celia D., 7253, 7254
Harris, Chan, 3810
Harris, Chuck, 4945
Harris, Coralee, 597
Harris, Craig, 3249
Harris, David, 6660
Harris, David M, 1501
Harris, Deborah, 1755
Harris, Dewey, 6490
Harris, Dewey L, 6544
Harris, Diane, 4707
Harris, Don, 1593
Harris, Ed, 8338
Harris, Falls, 5226
Harris, Henry, 6160, 6161, 6162
Harris, J B, 4602
Harris, James, 4077
Harris, Janet, 1668
Harris, Jason, 7425
Harris, Jay, 3589
Harris, Jonathan, 759, 4205
Harris, Julie, 3181
Harris, Lizzie, 3356
Harris, Marcia, 931, 3867, 4395
Harris, Marlon, 8011
Harris, Marsha, 603
Harris, Matthew C., 4814
Harris, Michael, 243
Harris, Monroe E., 4049
Harris, Nancy, 4251
Harris, Olivia, 3475
Harris, Patricia, 4957
Harris, Patricia L, 1312
Harris, Paulette, 3423
Harris, Paulette D, 374, 5056
Harris, Paulette.D, 374
Harris, Raven, 6042
Harris, Ray, 7284
Harris, Robert, 4285
Harris, Russ, 4217
Harris, Samuel D., 1541
Harris, Sheryl, 765
Harris, Stephanie, 1707
Harris, Tim, 1732
Harris, Tom, 5964
Harris Flynn, Rebecca, 3367
Harris Holmes, Abby, 414
Harris III, James T, 8118
Harris Jr., Dr. Monroe E., 4053
Harris Jr., Monroe E., 4054
Harris-Cannizzo, Angela, 3986
Harris-Kistner, Colleen, 1354
Harrison, Amy, 478
Harrison, Bill, 5946
Harrison, David, 470
Harrison, Debra, 1778
Harrison, Jack F., 8605
Harrison, Jan, 5029
Harrison, Joyce, 4473
Harrison, Kim, 3063
Harrison, Marylin, 4467
Harrison, Micheal, 2093
Harrison, Robert, 2256
Harrison, Stennis, 7409
Harrison, Wade C, 4607
Harrison, Shanqua, 7691
Harriss, Cynthia, 2484

Harrod, Beth Miller, 4369
Harrold, Sally, 5402
Harry-Spencer, Debora, 4026
Harsha, Kathryn, 1555
Harski, Nicole, 1842
Harson, Christy, 4709
Hart, Alex, 3034
Hart, Caroline, 7855
Hart, Celeste, 2007
Hart, Chris, 2893
Hart, Daniel, 1376, 5326
Hart, Ed, 4058
Hart, Edward, 1678
Hart, Hillary J, 3947
Hart, J Erik, 4452
Hart, Jarin, 229
Hart, Jennifer, 1274
Hart, Katonya, 4097
Hart, Lizanne, 5129
Hart, Lori, 7040
Hart, Louisa, 7890
Hart, Mark, 4440
Hart, Mary, 121
Hart, Nicky, 6389
Hart, Steven, 840, 1296
Hart, Tom, 6199
Hart, Velerie, 4713
Hart Baker, Dr Robert, 1669
Hart Baker, Robert, 1290
Hart, Jr., Robert, 756
Hartel, Austin, 549
Harten, Dean, 5434, 8117
Hartenstein, David, 117
Hartert, Sunny, 3264
Hartge, David, 2042
Hartgraves, Jeffrey, 2593
Hartgrove, Lillian, 1690
Hartken, Dave, 7573
Hartkern, Dave, 5003
Hartkern, David, 5003
Hartley, Carol, 4839
Hartley, Cynthia, 1678
Hartley, David, 5896
Hartley, Erinn, 3654
Hartley, Greg, 3798
Hartley, Heather, 202
Hartley, Nita, 4065
Hartline, Craig, 3743
Hartlove, Regina, 7193
Hartman, Bruce, 4043
Hartman, Christy, 723
Hartman, Kelly, 3728
Hartman, Marisa, 1802
Hartman, Michelle, 233
Hartman, Mike, 6978
Hartman, Scott, 883
Hartman, Virginia, 546
Hartman, William, 1669
Hartmann, David, 8212, 8213
Hartmann, Nancy, 334
Hartmann, Terry, 3609
Hartnell, Bryan C., 4276
Harton, Flavia, 1681
Hartung, Paul J., 4135
Hartvigsen, Forrest, 1024
Hartwell, Mary Lynn, 1026
Hartwell, Samuel, 5320
Harty Gray, Kathy, 4029
Hartzell, Lance, 7366
Hartzell, Linda, 4085
Hartzell, Louise, 2723
Hartzell, Susan, 853
Hartzler, Jarrod, 5288
Hartzog, Joe, 1903
Hartzog, Scott, 33
Harvard, Bernard, 3839
Harvey, Ann, 3559
Harvey, Christina, 8258
Harvey, Fran, 5606
Harvey, Gertrude, 5806
Harvey, Janet, 2359
Harvey, Kathryn, 6152
Harvey, Maggie, 5966
Harvey, Mark, 3226, 3227
Harvey, Patricia A., 4035
Harvey, Raymond, 1244
Harvey, Robin, 4058
Harveycutter, Carey, 8561

Harward, Alice, 1279
Harwitz, Libby S., 5485
Harwood, Elizabeth, 3081
Harwood, Ian, 747
Harwood, James C., 8836
Harwood, Kathy, 2600
Harwood, Tom, 6433
Haschke, Nicki, 2983
Hase, Michael K., 4085
Hase Kojima, Yuriko, 4160
Hasekoester, Penelope A., 8419
Haselbock, Martin, 1933
Haselwood, Joanne, 4065
Hashani, Besnick, 977
Hashimoto, Gail, 461
Hashimoto, Helen, 6163
Haskell, Becky, 3853
Haskell, C Conrad, 2391
Haskell, Peter, 6130
Haskell, Wyatt R, 1839
Haskew, Chris, 1144
Haskin, Ryan, 1115, 1116
Haskins, James, 3840
Haslam, Jimmy, 7960
Haslett, Justin, 7224
Haslow, Jo, 7502
Haslun, Robert A, 2114, 2288
Haslun, Ursula R, 2114, 2288
Hass, Marjorie, 5668
Hassard, David, 4771
Hasse, Marie, 4458
Hassel, Beverly, 5861
Hassett, Timothy D, 7553, 7554, 7555
Hassevoort, Darrin, 2329
Hassey, Stephen W., 1999, 2000, 2001
Hasshill, Denise, 1250
Hassig, John, 8689, 8698, 8699, 8700
Hassle, John, 482
Hassler, Jessica, 3231
Hassler, Joanne T., 1426
Hastings, Deward, 4299
Hastings, Janel, 6085
Hastings, Ryan, 6725, 6726
Hastings, Shalon, 7479
Hastings, Susanne, 4976
Hasty, Carolyn, 3009
Hasty, Kay, 3740
Hasty, Laurie, 3108
Hasty, Robert G., 1825
Hasty Jr, Stephen, 507
Haswell, Rob, 1866
Hatathlie, Theresa, 5993
Hatch, Dick, 3168
Hatch, Nathan O., 1508
Hatcher, Bill, 6557
Hatcher, Jimmy, 714
Hatcher, Rob, 7077, 7078, 7079
Hatcher-White, Kimberly, 6410
Hatfield, Anne, 1983
Hatfield, Mathilda, 4913
Hathaway, James, 8192
Hathaway, Sylvia, 2586
Hathorn Penick, Meredith, 2084
Hattemer, Sally, 2031
Hattner, David, 1609
Hatton, Betsy, 1608
Hatton, Jana, 7084, 7085
Haub, Walter, 6255
Hauber, Rosi, 6333
Haug, Shelby, 7039
Haug, Sue, 5507, 5508
Hauge, Kevin R, 2598, 2601
Hauge, Peter, 2259
Haugen, David, 1269
Haugen, Gretchen, 4292
Haugen, Mitchell, 5726
Haugen, Nancy, 1257
Hauger, Michael, 347
Haught, Jeff, 4097
Haughton, Sandra, 3830
Haughton, Sandra N, 578
Hauptmann, Shawn, 8413
Hausam, Wiley, 7810
Hauschildt, Craig, 5635
Hauschildt, John, 4978
Hauser, Anthony, 6322
Hauser, Elaine, 6322

Hauser, Robert M., 4417
Hauser Jasmin, Heidi, 294
Hauser Jr, Ralph, 6322
Hauser, CCE, David, 3774
Hausfather, Ph.D., Sam H, 3299
Hausman, Kathy, 1635
Hausman, William, 1208, 4800
Hausmann, Dr Charles, 2355
Hautala, Melinda, 4693, 4694
Hautala, Nancy, 679
Hava-Robbins, Nadia, 60
Haven, Barbara, 8827
Havener, Jaqueline, 1991
Havens, Ted, 3679
Havens-Hasty, Nancy, 386
Havens-Parker, Robin, 4031
Haver, Karen, 5501
Haver, Michael.J, 582
Haver, Steven J, 8633
Haverkamp, Phyllis, 3325
Haverman Jr, James K, 7278
Haverty, Michael, 2846, 2862
Havey, Kathryn, 6151
Haviaras, Steve, 2134
Haviken, Griffin, 3377
Havlena, Jim, 4251
Havlicek, Michael, 2136
Havlicek, Tedd, 5135
Havwood, Amy, 4776
Hawes-Saunders, Ro Nita, 532
Hawk, Kathy, 3794
Hawkanson, David, 2952
Hawkes, Meghan, 5923
Hawkey, Thil, 2483
Hawkhaw, Paul, 4402
Hawkins, Brent, 4657, 4658, 4659, 4660, 4661
Hawkins, Deborah, 1735
Hawkins, Dr. David, 1735
Hawkins, Erin, 4613
Hawkins, Josh, 201
Hawkins, Kevin, 8454
Hawkins, Kim, 6159
Hawkins, Steven, 7431
Hawkins-Smith, Dr. Anastacia, 6490
Hawks, Richard, 4545
Hawkshaw, Paul, 936
Hawley, Kevin, 1557
Haworth South, Sandy, 2650
Hawpt, Paulette, 2715
Hawryliw, Neil, 7324
Hawryluk, Alan, 2124
Hawthorne, Kelly, 121
Hawthorne, Mr. Douglas D., 8454
Hawthorne, Randolph, 3176
Hawthorne, Susan, 4056
Hay, Frank, 612
Hay, Janice, 1647
Hay, Michael, 4870
Hay Lanners, Buncie, 4512
Haya, Antoinette, 7256
Hayden, Carol, 8689
Hayden, Ethan, 5057
Hayden, Jim, 4472
Hayden, Jonna, 2298
Hayden, Lynne, 3432
Hayden, Robert, 4331
Hayden, Steve, 286, 7306, 7307
Hayden, Susan, 3303
Hayden Findlay, Lynne, 2223
Hayden, Jr., Gerard M., 620
Hayden-Findlay, Lynne, 2223
Haydon, Jeffrey, 5096, 5097
Hayen-Miller, Julie, 278
Hayes, Aimee, 3081, 3087
Hayes, Aim,e, 3087
Hayes, Alison, 2856
Hayes, Barbara, 5242
Hayes, Betty, 6043
Hayes, Bryan, 379
Hayes, David, 2237, 2313, 2337
Hayes, John M, 8060
Hayes, Kimberly, 6249
Hayes, Letitia, 141
Hayes, Lisa, 8286
Hayes, Marcus, 613
Hayes, Michael, 3651, 4856, 7317
Hayes, Michelle H, 4466
Hayes, Mike, 1247, 1248

Executive Name Index

Hayes, Monica, 1605
Hayes, Nora, 4797
Hayes, Rainey, 241
Hayes, Rob, 6246
Hayes, Scott, 3735
Hayes, Stephen R, 4036
Hayes, Theresa, 2472
Hayes, Tom, 6584
Haylock, Anna, 4156
Hayman, Mark, 5172
Hayman-Loa, Denise, 4989, 7556
Hayne, Jennifer, 5645
Haynes, Beth, 2867
Haynes, Cassundra, 6042
Haynes, David, 1266
Haynes, Darrell, 5196
Haynie, Todd, 738, 5991, 5992
Haynson, Richard, 2397
Hays, Carol, 8588
Hays, Cheryl, 6527
Hays, James, 5635
Haysbert, Dr. JoAnn W., 8525
Hayward, Mindy, 8001
Hazangeles, Monica Jeffries, 7208
Hazelbaker, Billie, 3730
Hazelbaker, Randall, 2133
Hazelton, Sandy, 7281
Hazen-Diehm, Keith, 2034
Hazewinkel, Jeff, 2068
Hazlet, Carolee, 3294
Hazlett, Jenna, 850
Hazzard, Wayne, 78
Hcapma, Jefferson, 3902
Head, Donald L., 2089
Head, Dr Robert, 6828, 6830
Head, Martha S., 266
Headrick, Hollis, 3420
Headrick, Mack, 2846, 2862, 6627
Headrick, Samuel, 1175
Heakey, Maureen, 3140
Healey, Brandi, 1163
Healey, Roberta, 5085
Healy, Christopher, 3564
Healy, Mike, 8121
Heang, Reasey, 4281, 6221, 6222, 6223, 6226
Heaphy, Joseph, 3200
Heard, Alex, 2289
Heard, Guy Jordin, 2745
Heard, John, 4002
Hearno, Garbo, 3288
Heartlein, Kathleen, 6785, 6787, 6788
Heatherington, Alan, 1056
Heatherington, Gayle, 1056
Heatherly, Danika, 6318
Heaton Brown, Christine, 7240
Heavner Baker, Jennifer, 3760
Heavrin, Frances, 6892
Hebach, Susan, 387
Hebda, Johnny, 4014
Hebein, Rose, 4129
Heberling, Dan, 8016
Heberling, Scott, 8031
Hebert, Carolynn, 6406
Hebert, Sandie, 8297
Heble, Matthew, 4166
Hebner, Michael, 4067
Hecht, Dr. Donald, 6193
Hecht, Ethan, 4356
Hecht, Laurel, 8875
Hecht, Michael, 489
Hecht, Richard, 8689
Heck, Brian J., 1407
Heck, Sandra, 7949
Heck, Ph.D., James B., 2014
Heckathorn, Peter, 166
Heckel, Tara, 5869
Heckler, Dr. Mark, 4633
Heckler, Laura, 3854
Heckler, Mark A, 6946
Heckler, Mark A., 6885
Heckman, Dave, 3099
Heckman, Kevin, 2950
Heckman, Kyle, 899
Heckman, Sarah, 690
Hedblom, CW4 Bruce J, 1270
Hedding, Dale, 2094
Hedge, Randy, 8697
Hedgecock, Ashley, 3665

Hedgecock, Ms. Ashley, 5251
Hedges, Don, 4568
Hedges, John, 3747
Hedges-Peerman, Kelly, 2788
Hedlin, Lawrence K, 1107
Hedstrom, Cynthia, 3594, 4396
Hedtke, Jackie, 7481
Hee Kim, Rang, 999
Heejeong Kim, Cecelia, 4160
Heeke, Dave, 7319, 7321
Heen, Ph.D., Carol, 4882
Heerlein, Nicole, 4920
Heet, Tess, 228
Heffernn, Maureen, 5015
Heffner, Richard, 3017
Heffner, Virginia E, 5298
Hefler, Stephen, 4594
Hefley, Leonie, 1691
Hefner, Hugh, 4209
Hegdahl, David, 3777
Hege, Daniel, 1124, 1468, 1469
Hegedus, Joyce, 3794
Hegmann, Jessica, 6460
Hehn, Logan, 2633
Heidger, Kim, 4848
Heidt, Jack, 2705
Heidt, W Daniel, 682
Heidtbrink, Barry, 3994
Heidtbrink, Summer, 3994
Heidtke, Brian, 3545
Heidtke, Brian J., 386
Heike, Lee, 4108
Heilbut, Francis L, 5112
Heilenbrond, Harry, 4317
Heilman, Kari H., 757
Heilman, Paul, 1658
Heim, Father Jack, 5310
Heim, Jack, 5307, 5308
Heim, Jacques, 39
Heim S J, John P, 5307
Heiman, Peter, 2204
Hein, Janice, 5437
Hein, Janice S., 3799
Heinbaugh, Chris, 8349
Heinecke Krumhus, Leah, 6744
Heinks, Matt, 6105
Heinlein, Anne, 4233
Heins, Tim, 3253
Heinz, James A, 972
Heinze, Cameron, 2036
Heinze, John J, 3797
Heirr, Jeff, 2146
Heise, Martha, 3804
Heisel, John, 3727
Heisinger, Jim, 2807
Heitmann, Cheryl, 4344
Heitmeier, Don, 7848
Heitmiller, Scott E., 4961
Heitsch, Tracy, 8244
Heitzman, Robert, 6775, 6776, 6777, 6778
Hejmanowski, David, 1552
Helander, Danelle, 118
Helaney, Dianne, 513
Held, Joy, 694
Heldreth, Victoria, 175
Helf, Peter, 5588
Helfrich, Paul, 531, 1549, 1550, 1817
Hellam, Judith A., 1294
Hellard, Ellen, 3067
Heller, Brian, 4106, 5828, 8658
Heller, Francie, 8226
Heller, Frank, 1404, 1405
Heller, Jack, 965
Heller, John, 849
Heller, Rosalie, 5031, 7615
Heller, Ryan, 2337
Hellerich, Chuck, 6246
Hellige, Kristan, 7003, 7006, 7007, 7008
Helligso, Katie, 4162
Hellman, Sheila, 5025
Hellmann, Mary, 5239
Hellstern, Elizabeth, 2422
Hellstrand, Christer, 4081
Hellyer, Peter, 907
Helman, Jason, 8181
Helmboldt, Andy, 7274
Helmeke, Mary Jo, 2035
Helmer, Dave, 7570

Helmer, Robert, 8009
Helmer, Robert C, 5292
Helmer, Ph.D., J.D., Robert C., 1521
Helmick Jr, Carl N, 4280
Helmner, Drew, 1732
Helms, Randall, 5427
Helppie, Dennis, 1792
Helprin, Jennifer, 7599
Helse, Gerry, 913
Helser, D Corey, 8678
Helsinger, Jim, 4469
Heltman, Gregory, 1360
Heltman, Gregory W., 1360, 2199
Heltne, Dan, 4933
Helton, Anna, 3338
Helton, Jessica, 5612
Helton, Reggie, 1497
Helton, Richard, 4634
Helveston, Suzanne, 7403
Helvey, Steve, 2642
Helweg, Richard, 2915
Helwick, Christine, 6317
Hemans, Chris, 5230
Hembree, Larry, 3874
Hemenway, Anne, 3480
Hemenway, Robert, 7042
Hemingway, Margaret, 1992
Hemink, Jack, 5095
Heminover, Lillian, 2928
Hemiston, Connie, 4904
Hemley, Gene, 7605
Hemmann, Marlies, 1568
Hemmendinger, Dennis, 7048
Hemmer, Paul, 3035
Hemmings, Mary, 7039
Hemphill, Michael, 7156
Hemy, Sigal, 4824
Henberg, Marvin, 6690
Henckens, Johan, 368
Hendckson, Marlene, 4936
Hendel, Jerry, 2969
Henderson, Allan, 1513, 1514
Henderson, Anno, 150
Henderson, Barbara, 1167
Henderson, Chad, 3874
Henderson, Criss, 2917
Henderson, Dempsey, 8290
Henderson, Doug, 5884
Henderson, Gene, 6966, 6968, 6970
Henderson, Gregg, 5632
Henderson, Heather, 3460
Henderson, Jason, 8333
Henderson, Jerry, 5303
Henderson, Lu H., 4035
Henderson, Mark, 4724
Henderson, Martha, 2502
Henderson, Marvette, 1408
Henderson, Raymond, 730
Henderson, Terrance, 602
Henderson Jr, Leon, 7707
Hendersot, Pati, 4201
Hendra, Carla, 1418
Hendrick, Bill, 7656
Hendrick, Jacque, 1956
Hendricks, Judy, 4348
Hendricks, Karen, 5635
Hendricks, Matt, 6289, 6290
Hendricks, Misty, 287
Hendricks, Richard, 1222
Hendricks, Sande J., 1623
Hendrickson, Chris, 3211
Hendrickson, Dr Peter, 2142
Hendrickson, Jeanne J., 131, 132
Hendrickson, Lisa, 231
Hendrickson Svvzency, Tari, 1305
Hengst, Jim, 6775, 6776, 6777, 6778
Henke, Robert L, 1554, 1562
Henkel, Rich, 6005, 6006, 6007, 6008
Henley, Doy B., 817
Henley, Hank, 2344
Henley, Jennifer, 5652
Henley, Jessica, 6632
Henley, Larry, 4958, 7516
Henley, Laura, 2997
Hennager, Dave, 832
Hennessey, David, 3232
Hennessey, Debbie, 6897
Hennessey, Terry, 6897

Hennessy, Dr. Andrea M., 5175
Hennessy, John, 6304
Hennessy, Susan, 6360, 6367, 6368, 6369, 6370
Henniger, Rai, 6342
Henning, Daniel, 2473
Henning, Jacqueline, 1904
Henning, Marcus, 1748
Henningsen, Charlie, 7971
Henrich, Richard, 2749
Henrich, William, 7945
Henriques, Malika, 373
Henry, Barbara, 4977
Henry, Becky, 5595
Henry, Ben, 3144
Henry, Carol F., 1887
Henry, Chris, 6518
Henry, Dave, 6527
Henry, Gregg, 2742, 2752, 4415
Henry, Jason, 6057, 6058, 6060, 6061
Henry, Jerry, 1103
Henry, Marci, 6390
Henry, Mary Pat, 309
Henry, Matt, 6297
Henry, Mila, 2205
Henry, Patricia, 5468
Henry, Reid, 1795
Henry, Ruth S, 5891, 5892
Henry, Susan, 834, 6227
Henry Curry, William, 1488, 1500
Henry McDonald, John, 1702
Henry Stokes, Karen, 1234
Henschel, Kathleen G., 1912
Hensel, Tommy, 6813
Hensley, Bonnie, 1607
Hensley, Michael, 3297, 7448
Henson, Barry, 6625
Henson, Brandon, 1750
Henson, Charlotte, 3057
Henson, Cherly, 5137
Henson, Holly, 3057
Henson, Jason, 6034
Henson, John, 6169
Henson, Judy, 4989
Henson, Michael, 1265
Henson, Michele, 2879
Henson, Rob, 8618
Henson, Sandy, 8236, 8237
Henson, Jr., Robert W., 5051
Hepburn, Charles, 3621
Hepburn, Muriel, 4505
Hepler, Melissa, 4017
Hepner, Virginia, 6631
Hepple, David, 1154
Her-ron, Paul D., 1325
Herald, Marjorie, 3013
Herasingh, Trevor, 6123
Herber, Dan, 3242
Herbers, Joan, 1548
Herbert, Adam, 4610
Herbert, F John, 4644
Herbert, Kathy, 6276
Herbert, Marilynne, 1477
Herbert, Minde, 1007, 4503
Herbert, Stephen, 5475
Herbold, Barry M., 3444
Herbst, Cynthia B, 8802
Herbst, Edward, 3584
Herbst, George, 2840
Herbst, Jeffrey, 4110
Herbst, Susan, 6436
Herche, David, 8004
Herczog, Rich, 6174
Herd, Lily, 7160
Hereford, Earle J., 4087
Hereford, Nancy, 6173
Herendeen, Ed, 4104, 5822
Herendeen, Stevie, 3849
Herg Sisler, Elaine, 263
Hergenhahn-Zhao, Glenn, 4061
Hergert, Erin, 4374
Herigstad, Jeremy, 912
Hering, J. Clayton, 1605, 8091
Hering, Paul, 843
Herman, Ken, 1906
Herman, Marvin, 2940
Herman, Richard, 4602
Herman, Todd, 3384
Herman, Vatea, 3786

1175

Executive Name Index

Hermansen, Philip W., 4006
Hermanson, Ruslyn, 3766, 8047
Hermes, Jerry, 845
Hermetz, PhD., Robert, 1277
Hermiller, Anne, 3735
Herminjard, Patrizia, 4363
Hermodson, Mark, 6908
Hernandez, Alex, 3988
Hernandez, Blanca, 6769
Hernandez, Bryant, 2560
Hernandez, Cathie, 305
Hernandez, Chris, 3292
Hernandez, Jesse, 6269, 6270
Hernandez, Kin, 5132
Hernandez, Lacey, 8377
Hernandez, Lorrie, 5373
Hernandez, Monica, 1801
Hernandez, Ricky, 4002
Hernandez, Rusty, 2908
Hernandez, Sandra, 8454
Hernandez, Tricia, 1093
Hernandez, Wilfredo, 343, 6065
Herndon, Jonathan, 4350
Herndon, Karen, 5355
Herndon, Lynda, 1389
Herod, Vincent, 2339
Herold, Jordi, 7246
Heroux, Barbara, 1952
Herr, Diane, 2061
Herr, Eric M, 3269
Herr, Linda, 2701, 6429
Herr, Stanley, 2284
Herren, K Wood, 707
Herrera, Cathy, 5508
Herrera, Gilbert, 7062
Herrera, Laura, 233
Herrera, Mary, 4267
Herrera, Richard, 58
Herrick, Andrew, 7532
Herrick, Ken, 1602, 1603
Herriges, Norbert, 682
Herriman, Jack, 725
Herrin, Marry, 7071, 7072, 7073
Herring, Carol P, 5114
Herring, Howard, 980, 5096, 7694
Herring, J Daniel, 2464, 3071
Herring, Joyce, 478
Herring, Linda, 5166, 7790
Herring, Patrick, 1715
Herrington, Alisa, 1406
Herrman, Dave, 249
Herrmann, Jeffrey, 2754
Herro, Alan, 6066, 6070, 6071, 6072
Herro, Susan, 4136
Herron, Andy, 5374
Herron, Clifford, 6561
Herron, Ken, 6102
Herron, Laurence, 5800
Herron, Mark R., 6085
Herron, Sandra, 6921, 6922, 6923, 6924, 6925
Herron, Steve, 4094
Herron Robb, Katie, 3250
Herschensohn, Michael, 5797
Hersey, Marilyn, 2717, 3078
Hershberger, Amy, 870
Hershenson, Karen, 4310
Hershey, Dale, 1654
Hershey, Jason, 2385
Hershfield, Steven, 2262
Herskovits, David, 3574
Hersman, Greg, 3236
Hertel, Jerry, 1607
Herts, George, 6043
Herwald Zitelli, Margi, 3718, 7980
Herzig, David, 1512, 2130
Herzog, Chad, 5456
Herzog, Floyd, 7635
Hesik, Richard, 4078
Heskel, Mitchell, 2619
Heslop, Tuesday, 6341
Hess, Andrea, 1606
Hess, Brad, 2312
Hess, Craig, 3958
Hess, Dan, 561
Hess, David, 4483
Hess, Dr. Jay B., 4465
Hess, Jeremiah, 1229
Hess, Rhonda, 7993

Hess, William, 4629
Hesse, Joe, 4646
Hesse, Keith, 4469
Hesse, Lynn, 184
Hesse, Marian, 1641
Hesse Zumoff, Michael P., 1425
Hest, Rachel, 1262
Hester, Tom, 5260, 5261
Hester, Tracy, 6027
Heston, Frank, 8107
Hetherington, Julie, 6602
Hettwer, Kami, 1614
Hettwer, Mike, 1614
Hetz, Matthew, 777
Hetzel, Bob, 8672
Hetzel, Dr. Marilyn, 2663
Heu, Bri, 3248
Heumann, Fred, 888
Heuser, Thomas, 1026
Hewell, Joe, 5677
Hewes, Tyler, 841
Hewett, Laurie, 2351
Hewis, Kristina, 5318, 5351
Hewitt, Lauren, 6068
Hewitt, Rebekah, 4079, 8598
Hewlett, Gayle, 4457
Heyde, Stephen, 1756
Heyer, Erica, 1329
Heyl, Esq, Dorothy, 2241
Heyman, Richard, 1682, 3334
Hhamilton, Craig, 1647
Hiatt, Courtney M., 8573, 8574, 8575, 8576
Hibberd, Tom, 3816
Hibbs, Joyce, 8029
Hibshman, Dan, 2636
Hick, Joe, 5614
Hick, Ken, 564
Hickambottom, Ann Marie, 6210
Hicken, Leslie W, 1680
Hickernell, Larry, 8181
Hickernell, Linda, 2301
Hickerson, Judy, 5627
Hickes, Denice, 3917
Hickey, Jack, 2980
Hickey, Jim, 3384
Hickey, Michael, 2854
Hickey, Michael E, 2854
Hickey, Nichole J., 4761
Hickey, Robert W., 4977
Hickey, Teresa, 2628
Hickle, Nathan, 1958
Hicklin, Kate, 2484
Hickman, Holly, 4353
Hickman, Jeff, 2485
Hickman, Timothy L, 7415, 7416
Hickok, Molly, 357
Hicks, Ann, 4201
Hicks, Cara, 243
Hicks, Denice, 5581
Hicks, Jimmy, 8372
Hicks, Joe, 5668
Hicks, Kirsten, 716
Hicks, Lesa, 1752
Hicks, Lisa, 417
Hicks, Michael, 648
Hicks, Robert B, 2014
Hicks, Robert D, 1231
Hicks, Terry, 753
Hicklin, Kat, 2484
Hidalgo, Michael, 2879
Hiddlestone, John, 2706
Hiendlmayr, Jackie, 2830
Hiendlmayr, Richard, 921
Hierholzer, John, 7298
Hieronymus, Theodore, 5356
Higbee, Brad, 2899, 6697
Higbie, Zander, 347
Higby, Lawrence M., 6090
Higby, Sha Sha, 25
Higdon, Michael, 3921
Higginbotham, John, 1584, 4675, 7041
Higgins, Barbara, 2219
Higgins, Fifi, 2085
Higgins, Jane E., 3373
Higgins, Joseph, 4999
Higgins, Kelly, 8248
Higgins, Kris, 3144
Higgins, Melissa L, 5912, 5913, 5914

Higgins, Mike, 3027
Higgins, Ronald W., 4962
Higgins Clark, Mary, 3539
Higgins Pechter, Lisa, 3799
Higginson, Lyn, 6105
Higgons, Doug, 8538
Higgs, Michael, 1316
Higgs, Michelle, 2517
Highsmith, Carol, 233
Highsmith, Sheryl, 6375
Highstone, Sarah, 4584
Highstrete, Liz, 42
Highstrete, CFRE, Kathy, 42
Hightower, Peggy, 1579
Higley, Al, 4587
Hilburger, Jimmy, 2018
Hildabrant, Rebecca, 2084
Hildahl, David, 3039
Hildebrand, Fran, 852
Hildebrand, Paul, 6883, 6884
Hilinski, Richard, 8119
Hill, Alan, 2239
Hill, Andy, 1792
Hill, Bredyn, 6960
Hill, Carla, 1249
Hill, Cherie, 263
Hill, Daniel, 6921, 6922, 6923, 6924, 6925
Hill, Daniel C., 4596
Hill, David, 5187
Hill, Dick, 7511
Hill, Donna, 2261
Hill, Elisa L, 1170
Hill, Elizabeth A, 7647
Hill, Eric, 3178, 4808
Hill, Gayle, 1053
Hill, J Tomlinson, 7746
Hill, J. Cindy, 6651
Hill, James, 545
Hill, Jane, 836
Hill, Jenifer, 7160
Hill, Jessi D, 2950
Hill, Jessica, 3859
Hill, John, 2747
Hill, K K, 7411
Hill, Kathi, 1504
Hill, Kevin, 5970, 5971, 5975
Hill, Larry, 1191
Hill, Laurie, 977
Hill, Linda, 3055
Hill, Lisa, 5200
Hill, Loretta, 4207, 6088
Hill, Mars, 3407
Hill, Meg, 5187
Hill, Melissa, 6099
Hill, Mike, 2464
Hill, Patty, 6184
Hill, Peggy, 7818
Hill, Phill, 6394
Hill, Rhonda, 549
Hill, Robbie, 4670
Hill, Robert, 163, 4141
Hill, Sharaon, 8455
Hill, Sharon, 8300
Hill, Sue R, 3677
Hill, Timothy A., 1999, 2000, 2001
Hill, Wilbur, 715
Hill, Wyndel E., 3303
Hill Jr, Dr Willie L, 7217
Hill, Esq., William K., 2004
Hill-Protos, Kara, 187
Hillecke, Ruth, 781
Hiller, Kira, 1785
Hilliard, Alex, 4708
Hilliker, Wendy, 1802
Hillis, Rich, 6256
Hillman, Jan, 5616
Hillmer, Sarah, 179
Hillner, Paul, 7955, 7958
Hills, Christopher, 3138
Hills, Ernie, 4283, 5130
Hills, Joe, 3163
Hills, Marian, 1506
Hills, Rod, 2642
Hillson, Janet, 863, 4319, 4320
Hilmy, Steve, 146
Hilovsky, Richard T., 2603
Hilsmier, William, 2287
Hilson, Paul, 2788

Hilt, Angela, 1911
Hilton, Katherine, 1152
Hilton, Lawrence, 872
Hilton, Sharon, 3093
Hilton, Stephen, 3761
Himberg, Phillip, 4013
Hime, Dave, 3932
Himebaugh, Liqia, 6736
Himes, A.C. Buddy, 5656
Himes, Ron, 3303
Himle, Karen, 1265, 7359
Himmelheber, David, 1438, 5156
Himmelreich, David, 2594
Himmelreich, Ellen, 7668
Himmelstein, Amos, 6179, 6182
Himmelstrup, Julie, 4883, 4884
Hinckley, Diane, 997
Hinckley, Greg, 2300
Hinde Stewart, Joan, 7661
Hinderer, John, 5359
Hinderks, Tim, 4637
Hindle, John, 8309
Hinds, Andrew, 1957
Hinds, John A., 3377
Hine, Jane, 996
Hine, Roy, 3027
Hineline, Alan, 569
Hines, Greg, 1691
Hines, James E., 3825, 3837, 5474
Hines, Laura, 6340
Hines, Leslie, 1134
Hines, Tom, 8620
Hines, Jr., Ph.D, Samuel M., 8211
Hines-Jones, Angelina, 450
Hines-Pham, Cara, 1089
Hing, Brent, 8303, 8304
Hinkel, Debbie, 8113
Hinkel, Harry, 7092, 7093
Hinken, Michele, 6277
Hinkle, Allan, 1539
Hinkle, Amanda, 3505
Hinkle, Cate, 1855
Hinkle, Harry, 7096
Hinkle, Milton, 1938
Hinkley, Rhonda, 5658
Hinojosa, Greg, 4002
Hinsch, Lowell, 5673
Hinsdale-Knisel, Ann, 1220
Hinsley, Matthew, 1702
Hinson, Oliver, 2749
Hinton, Cindy, 152
Hinton, James, 878, 4332
Hinton, Toby, 6648, 6649
Hinton, Wayne, 832
Hinz, Julie E, 6819, 6822
Hipp, William, 880
Hippert, Amelia, 6122
Hippolite Wright, Debbie, 6681
Hipps, Barry, 3672
Hirche, Jerry, 5948
Hird, Thomas, 4223, 6118
Hird, Tom, 6120, 6121
Hirokawa, Marla A., 362
Hiroshima, Janet, 40
Hirsch, Barbara, 4262
Hirsch, Diana, 3017
Hirsch, Ellen, 3545
Hirsch, Greg, 2017
Hirsch, Jim, 1034
Hirsch, Joyce, 2395
Hirsch, Justin, 5757
Hirsch, Melissa, 3999
Hirsch, Mira, 6635
Hirsch, Wayne, 3313
Hirsh, Jonathan, 1205, 2121
Hirshman, Karl, 5048
Hirsig, Nancy, 3827
Hirst, R Dennis, 5685
Hirst, M.U.P., Martha K., 7692
Hisek, Derek, 6953, 6954, 6955, 6956, 6957, 6958, 6959
Hisey, Christopher, 923
Hissong, Terry, 7262
Hitaffer, Taylor, 2742, 2752
Hitchcock, Dennis, 2984
Hitchcock, Erik, 1076
Hitchcock, Karen, 2201
Hitchings, Carolyn, 7440, 7442

Executive Name Index

Hite, Andy, 2973
Hite, Jane, 8109
Hites, Andy, 2973
Hiteshew, Dan, 5513
Hitesman, Sara, 2165
Hitt, David, 5594
Hitt, Steven, 7705
Hittle, Jr., Max W., 6903
Hittner, Kathleen C., 5500
Hittner, Shelly, 4901
Hixenbaugh, Brian, 6572, 6573
Hixon, Sarah, 526
Hixson, Christina, 7044
Hixson, Tyler, 6769
Hoag, Shanon, 2953
Hoang, Huong, 368
Hoart, Tracy, 6697
Hobaica, Tom, 6429
Hoban, Deb, 2038
Hobart, Jim, 2953
Hobart, Max, 1216
Hobbs, Clinton G., 6667, 6668
Hobbs, Eric E., 1830, 5856
Hobbs, Franklin W., 5133
Hobbs, Karen, 6028
Hobbs, Patty, 5905, 5906
Hoberman, Joanne, 8141
Hobgood, Gail, 4525
Hobin, Tom, 125
Hobson, Ian, 1070
Hobson, Pamela M., 5474
Hoch, Joanna, 3220
Hoch, Robert, 1959
Hoch, Tom, 7353, 7354
Hochberg, Stephan, 7647
Hochoy, David, 231
Hochstedler, Darren, 2576
Hockenyos, Jon, 3930
Hockman, Jean, 5952
Hodder, John, 689
Hodes, Linda, 351
Hodge, David, 8004
Hodge, Doug, 3161
Hodge, Howard, 7080
Hodge, Joseph, 929
Hodge, Kathy, 3911
Hodge, Kelly, 3161
Hodgen, Barbara, 2472, 2586
Hodges, Daine, 7994
Hodges, David, 654
Hodges, Jason, 4156
Hodges, Joe, 8043
Hodges, Meredith (Max), 367
Hodges, Ralph, 7994
Hodges, Seena, 3254
Hodges, Thomas, 2970
Hodges Smith, Anna, 1491, 5242
Hodgin, Ric, 3980
Hodgkins, Robin, 4955
Hodgkinson, Shon, 8329, 8331, 8332
Hodgson, David C., 3517
Hodgson, Jan, 6
Hodgson, Jen, 3106
Hodgson, Jody, 8618
Hodgson, Paul, 3106
Hodney, Ed, 5396, 5398
Hodson, Brian, 2133
Hodson, Tom, 6947
Hodzman, Thomas, 4816
Hoebee, Mark S, 3373, 7567
Hoefer Jr., Bruce R., 3083
Hoeffler, Angela, 4002
Hoefnagel, Ali, 2903
Hoeft, Steven H., 6803, 6804
Hoehl, Lockwood, 1153
Hoehn, Natasha, 1920, 1921
Hoekstra, Erik, 7018, 7020, 7021
Hoel, Donna, 2148, 2149
Hoel, Roger S, 2148, 2149
Hoelscher, Nita, 2341
Hoener, Ann, 2195
Hoenigsberg, Jennifer, 2596
Hoerman, Carmela, 224
Hoesly, Cody, 3338
Hoey, Donna, 1298
Hoey, John, 577
Hoezee, Melissa, 7302
Hofer, Calvin, 6379

Hofer, Meret, 7732
Hofer, Shelby, 2873
Hoff, Christina, 2853
Hoff, Evelyn, 2853
Hoff, Pat, 4843, 4868
Hoff, Shannon, 2261
Hoff, Steven, 174
Hoffer, Robin, 3689
Hofflund, Mark, 2895
Hoffman, Andrew, 6685
Hoffman, Arnold, 989, 991, 992, 993, 994, 995
Hoffman, Ashley, 1955
Hoffman, Avi Ber, 3534
Hoffman, Barbara, 325, 4467
Hoffman, Brian, 7634
Hoffman, Carl, 3369, 4997
Hoffman, Clare, 4169
Hoffman, Cory, 8282
Hoffman, Cy, 3397, 3398
Hoffman, David, 577
Hoffman, Diane, 1625
Hoffman, Doug, 770
Hoffman, Douglas, 7997
Hoffman, Gabrielle, 395
Hoffman, Greg, 4913
Hoffman, Irwin, 4167
Hoffman, Jay, 924
Hoffman, Jeffrey S., 4384, 6398
Hoffman, Mike, 5353
Hoffman, Roberta, 893
Hoffman, Ron, 2504
Hoffman, Scott, 7504
Hoffman, Susan, 1061, 2018
Hoffman, Terry, 4065
Hoffman, Tim, 4065
Hoffmann, Andrew, 3022
Hoffmann, Evan, 4037
Hoffmann, Sarah, 4124
Hoffmann, Tamara, 618
Hoffmann-Robertson, Sheila, 662
Hoffmeister, Jane B., 1078
Hoffmire, Sylvia B., 3663
Hoffstein, Judy, 2239
Hoffstot, Jr., Henry P., 2322
Hofilena, Ron, 8570
Hofland, John, 8612
Hofman, Matilda, 775
Hofmeister, Ed, 2460
Hofrichter, Thom, 3008
Hofscher, Patricia, 1632
Hogan, Beth, 2513
Hogan, Carolyn, 3399
Hogan, Dan, 7522
Hogan, Jim, 820
Hogan, Lee, 7256
Hogan, Marie, 1911
Hogan, Randall, 7351
Hogan, Steve, 2366
Hogan, Jr., T. Michael, 6676
Hoge, Chuck, 5281
Hogeboom, Richard, 6671
Hogen, Jon, 4262
Hogenmiller, Rudy, 2064
Hogenson, Donna, 1271
Hogg, Heather, 8553
Hogg, Paula, 661
Hogg, Thomas, 8549
Hoggard, Jim, 1757
Hoggard, Lee, 6874
Hogland, Jane, 345
Hogle, Paul W., 7283
Hoglund, Robert, 1412
Hogwood, Christopher, 1181, 2106
Hohman, Jessica, 4354
Hoiness, Teak, 1299
Hoing, Ms. Samantha, 4184
Hoit, Eric, 2536
Hokanson, Natalie, 1272
Hoke, Shawn, 5439
Hoke '83, Darrel R., 6676
Holan,, Jennifer, 3038
Holbrook, Catherine, 1236
Holbrook, David D., 7739
Holbrook, Gerald, 1958
Holbrook, Gerald W., 1958
Holbrook, Mike, 6024
Holbrook, Paul E., 241
Holcomb, Alixe, 5995

Holcomb, Betsy, 293
Holcomb, J Mark, 5304
Holcomb, Kay, 4451
Holcomb, Michele, 1329
Holden, Alys, 6128
Holden, Bob, 6201
Holden, Connie, 4356
Holden, Fran, 4364
Holden, Luktann, 5562
Holden, Stanley, 315
Holden, Theresa, 3082
Holder, LaWanza, 931
Holderby, Katie, 233
Holderle, Ed, 6775, 6776, 6777, 6778
Holding, Phil, 3622, 5205
Holdt, Mathew, 6340
Holefelder, Jack, 3816
Holehan, Tom, 2712
Holets, David, 1087
Holeva, Megan, 4421
Holihan, Mark D, 2043
Holland, Beth, 968
Holland, Brad, 1756
Holland, Dick, 1135
Holland, Doris, 4150
Holland, Dorothy J., 8553
Holland, Greg, 6257, 6259, 6263
Holland, M Terry, 8517
Holland, Madeleine, 4356
Holland, Noel, 2760
Holland, Ouida, 2156
Holland, Richard D, 7496
Holland, Richard D., 7500
Holland, Robert, 1281
Holland, Steve, 1868
Holland, Terri, 8467
Holland Lundberg, Teresa, 1693
Hollander, Jonathan, 395
Hollander, Katie, 5126
Hollander, Matt, 7251
Hollander, Nicole, 142
Holleman, James A, 1238
Hollembaek, Linda, 242
Hollenbeck, Ann T., 1222
Hollenbeck, Margeret, 7739
Hollerith, Charles, 3524
Holley, Caroline, 5616
Holley, Cheri, 7160
Holley, Thomas, 245
Holliday, Corey, 8008
Holliday, Katie, 562
Holliday, Steve, 5766
Hollingshead, David, 2897
Hollingsworth, Christa, 3346, 7538
Hollins, Brian E., 855, 4309, 4312
Hollinsed, W. Christopher, 143, 144
Hollis, Cynthia, 7942
Hollis, Cynthia A., 5289
Hollis, Mark, 7293
Hollis, Tom, 3647
Hollister, Charlotte, 659
Hollister, Lynn, 113
Holloway, Ivor, 4336
Holloway, Kay, 4448
Holloway, Michele, 8129
Holloway, Peter, 3070, 3071
Holloway, Raven, 166
Hollsman, Jon, 5695
Holly, John, 3990
Holly, John Peter, 1346
Holly, Vicky, 2425
Holman, Kathleen, 670
Holmberg, Todd, 4676, 7049, 7050, 7051
Holmbo, Davey, 3194, 7279
Holmen, Linda, 2145
Holmes, Abby, 1355
Holmes, April, 8326
Holmes, Bill, 1721, 5998
Holmes, Bob, 2859
Holmes, Denis, 2774
Holmes, Dr. Ruth, 5651
Holmes, Harriette, 2686
Holmes, Jack, 837
Holmes, Jay Judith, 2628
Holmes, Jennifer, 6323, 6324
Holmes, Jenny, 7074
Holmes, Lauren, 299
Holmes, Loretta, 1252

Holmes, Nicole, 3207
Holmes, Rick, 4590, 6805
Holmes, Ronia, 2395
Holmes, Susan, 3296
Holmes, Wally, 4247
Holmgren, Janet L., 4260
Holmquist, Joe, 1306
Holmquist, Ward, 2160
Holnan, Torra, 8548
Holodak, Lawrence, 452
Holp, Karen, 5385
Holp, Kay E, 2294
Holscher, Dave, 8233
Holsclaw, Scott, 4183, 6015, 6016, 6017
Holst, Corey, 2485
Holst, Laura, 4873
Holst, Robert, 2053
Holste, Steve, 2154
Holstein, Michael P., 6899, 6901, 6902
Holston, Julie, 5973, 5974
Holt, Gary, 1908
Holt, James L., 5575
Holt, Joseph, 1984
Holt, Kristy, 8500
Holt, Mary Margaret, 549, 550
Holt, Robin, 2802
Holt, Simon, 2327
Holt, Simon D., 1974
Holt, Susan L., 4342
Holt, Tondra, 7955, 7958
Holtberg, Laveda, 3220
Holte, Virginia, 193
Holth, Henry, 349
Holton, Anne, 2036
Holtschneider CM, Rev Dennis H, 6741
Holtz, Andrew, 2430, 6089
Holtz, Heidi, 3627
Holtzclaw, Barbara, 4894
Holtzman, Steve, 700
Holub, Dennis, 3235
Holvick-Thomas, Carl, 4311
Holzapfel, Bernie, 2196
Holzer, Candy, 1296, 2166
Homan, Gail, 1885
Homan, Kieth, 3332
Homan, Ralph, 4067
Homan, Tensie, 905
Homann, Felice, 4751
Home, William, 809
Homick, Paul, 2316
Homoelle, Cathy, 1926, 1927
Honbach, Melissa, 2851
Hone, Mary, 4629
Honea, Dex, 169
Honebrink, Allie, 515
Honeck, Manfred, 1656, 8173
Honegger, Lois, 7244
Honegger PhD, Dr. Greta, 2733
Honeycutt, Cindy, 3927, 8321
Honeycutt, Debbie, 6051
Hong, Ethan, 552
Hong, Thomas, 1558, 2343
Honig, Peter, 1403
Honka, Rita, 558
Honke, Jerre, 1053
Honold, Greta, 2952
Honorof, Debbi, 5089, 5090
Honorof, Debbie, 1398
Honowitz, James, 4352
Honsel, Jason, 4995
Honsen, Susan, 1104, 1105
Hontz, Rick, 6388
Hontzas, Stacy, 7309
Honzawa, Masahiro, 8298
Hood, Frankie, 2649, 6336
Hood, Katherine, 440
Hood, Lam, 8187
Hood, Lynn, 2381
Hood, Rob, 8384
Hood, Robert, 1245
Hood, Woody, 7913
Hoogestraat, Linda, 6122
Hook, Don, 317
Hooker, Jane, 3200
Hooks, Cassandra, 2631
Hooks, Gayle, 41
Hooks, Leighland, 6068
Hoomes, John, 2333

Executive Name Index

Hooper, Allison, 5034
Hooper, Cindy, 6850
Hooper, Jane, 5402
Hooper, Jeff, 3753
Hoops, H Ray, 6865
Hoose, David, 2105
Hoover, Brian, 5439
Hoover, Charles H., 1523, 1524
Hoover, Darla, 569
Hoover, Elinor L., 1412
Hoover, Jeffery, 4572
Hoover, Jodi, 3804
Hoover, Robert, 6691, 6692, 6693, 6694
Hoover, Wanda, 2439
Hoover Gibson, Frankie, 197
Hoovler, Drew, 5637
Hope, Jr, Walter, 2323
Hopes, David B, 3637
Hopewell, Michael, 3350
Hopkin, Rachel, 4959
Hopkins, Bruce, 1198
Hopkins, Carron, 7641
Hopkins, D.J., 2569, 6240, 6241
Hopkins, Jesse E, 5727
Hopkins, Laurie, 5537
Hopkins, Mark, 6056
Hopkins, Melanie, 4559
Hopkins, Michael, 3396
Hopkins, P, 5727
Hopkins, Paulette, 5609, 5611
Hopkins, Rebecca, 6584
Hopkins, Richard, 998, 2823, 6584
Hopkins,, Mychelle, 3216
Hoppe, Cherry, 5561
Hoppe, Susan, 8581
Hoppenstedt, Robert, 2691
Hopper, Alan T., 1137
Hopper, David, 143, 144
Hopper, Dee, 5835
Hopper, Dr. Jack, 8333
Hopper, Lois, 5062
Hopson, Dan, 4161
Hopson, Pamela, 807
Hopson, Terri, 6273
Hopwood, Christine, 788
Horab, Kim, 3689
Horan, John E, 5446
Horan, Susan, 6825, 6826, 6827
Horbal, Jason, 7832
Horgan, Bernadette, 1177, 1178
Horgend, Garen, 5417
Horgon, Theresa, 8299
Hori, Robert, 6163
Horiuchi, Gen, 305
Horn, Andrew, 3623
Horn, Donald I, 5421
Horn, John, 2327, 3507
Horn, Julie, 4740, 4741
Horn, Mark, 4187, 6027
Horn, Mary, 3853
Horn, Mary G., 1348
Horn, Olivia, 2842, 6605, 6606
Hornaday, Cole, 4079, 8598
Horne, Angela, 6658, 6659
Horne, Rex M., 6015, 6016, 6017
Horne, Sarah, 368
Horne, William, 809
Horneff, Don, 1625
Horner, Ned, 1294
Horner, Rebecca J., 1785
Horner, Ross, 7932
Horner, Ross D., 6639
Horner, Jr., Edward W., 4604
Hornstein, Dr. Daniel, 1512
Horny, Karen, 2165
Horovitz, Dr. Len, 1423
Horovitz, Israel, 3153
Horowitz, Fred, 3819
Horowitz, Gigi, 2454
Horowitz, James, 4352
Horowitz, Jay, 7672
Horowitz, Jeffrey, 3580
Horrocks, Tom, 5694
Horsely, Brian, 8561
Horsley, Alison, 2481
Horsley, Leigh, 2949
Horsman, Robert B, 1909
Horst, Dana, 2910

Horst Reyen, Dawn, 1892
Horto, Joseph M, 4969
Horton, Alan, 4083
Horton, David, 3911
Horton, Evelyn, 8203
Horton, Mary B, 5912, 5913, 5914
Horton, Sarah, 3338, 3783
Horton, Sean, 2622
Horton, Vivian, 2125
Horton-Stewart, Carly, 1843
Horvath, Amanda, 4549
Horvath, Dr. Kathleen, 1540
Horvath, Ginny, 7674
Horvath, Jim, 3747
Horvath, Ken, 7292
Horvath, Mary Beth, 5757
Horvath, Meghan, 7457
Horvath, Phillip, 488
Horvath, Susan, 5079
Horvitz, Michael J., 5133
Horwitz, Jeffrey A., 3511
Hosack, Dianna, 1983
Hosale, Cindy, 2398
Hosey, Joan, 729
Hosier, C J, 6363
Hosking, Eileen, 3316
Hosking, John, 3316
Hoskinson, Tim, 970
Hosler, Charles, 1734
Hosogi, Ron, 2387
Hosslund, Mark, 4533
Hoste, Ann, 2900
Hoste, Ann, 6699, 6701, 6702
Hostetler, Brian, 2066
Hostetler, Pat, 1279
Hostetler, Tim, 5564
Hostetter, Mark, 3494
Hotchkin, Brian, 1931
Hotchkiss, Brianna, 5832
Hotes, Andrea, 6444
Hotman, Bernice, 8334
Hottendorf, Diane, 145
Houby, Ida, 797
Houck, Elise, 1064
Houden, Dr Guido, 1639
Hough, James, 5631
Hough, Katherine, 6203
Hough, Richard, 2813
Houghton, Brian, 2526
Houghton, Bruce, 8559, 8786
Houghton, Charles, 4475, 6580
Houghton, James, 3567
Houghton, John R., 760
Houghton, Kris, 1210, 1211
Houghton, Quincy, 6158
Houihan, Mahlon, 6870
Houk, Elissa, 574
Houk, Lorree, 574
Houk, Phillip, 8088
Houlahan, Gary, 2387, 8605
Houlihan, Gerri, 5233
Houlihan, Laura, 3621
Houlihan, Mahlon, 3009
Houlton, Lise, 296
Housby, Kathy, 1755
Householder, Amanda, 381, 385
Houser, David, 5858
Houssels, Nancy, 319
Houston, Arnold, 5932
Houston, CiCi, 304
Houston, Paul, 1133
Houston, Sherri, 3846
Houston, Vinson, 5905, 5906
Houston, Wesley A., 3335, 4949
Hovick, Larry, 7423
Hovland, Jody, 3038
Howard, Abby, 4682
Howard, Abby, 7063
Howard, Angela, 6545
Howard, B Michael, 5919
Howard, Bob, 8185
Howard, Carrie, 4357
Howard, Dave, 7672
Howard, David, 3991, 5645
Howard, Derrick, 8452
Howard, Heidi S., 2846, 2862
Howard, Jared, 5028
Howard, Kevin T, 2098

Howard, Len, 8471
Howard, Lois, 8752
Howard, Maria, 6238, 6243
Howard, Mark, 216
Howard, Monroe, 3974
Howard, Robert, 1029, 2222
Howard, Tammy M., 5857
Howard, Valarie, 2707
Howare, Aryaane, 5254
Howatt, Nadine, 2724
Howe, Jay, 3789
Howe, Lisa, 304
Howe, Marion B, 5175
Howe, Richard, 4017
Howe, Richard R, 1438, 5156
Howell, Andrew, 2326
Howell, Ann, 1026
Howell, Blair, 4014
Howell, James, 8036
Howell, Jay, 4041
Howell, Jeff, 3900
Howell, Lowry, 1695
Howell, Matt, 1744
Howerton, Cheryl, 4226
Howerton, Martin, 1586
Howerton, Trish, 7190
Howes, Janet, 3153
Howett, Michael, 3483
Howett, Nadine, 6452
Howland, Kris, 3223
Hoy, Sandy, 1480
Hoye, Cindy, 6887
Hoying, Deanna, 2079
Hoyt, Mike, 3251
Hoyt Chapman, Megan, 193
Hrabowski,III, Freeman A, 256
Hradil, Susan, 592
Hrebec, Heather, 8438
Hrebik, Ron, 2186
Hren, Katharina, 4123
Hricik, Ray, 1658
Hrobsky, Donna, 8694
Hrubetz, JC, 8452
Hruska, Dennis, 3587
Hsu, Dolores M, 4322
Hsu, John, 4383, 4791
Hsu, Johson, 1073
Hsu, Sam, 4882
Hu, Ching Yee, 1928
Huang, June, 1446
Huang, Lily, 820
Huang, Renee, 1766
Huang, Tina, 814
Huang, Wen, 1185
Hubbard, Amy, 3901
Hubbard, Anne, 135
Hubbard, Caitlin M., 6612, 6613, 6616
Hubbard, Chinyere, 6481
Hubbard, Cindi, 850
Hubbard, Eric, 4911
Hubbard, Gregory A., 2160
Hubbard, Joel, 6013
Hubbard, John T, 4722
Hubbard, Kathy, 5129
Hubbard, Mr. Philip G., 4603
Hubbard, Susan, 7372
Hubbard, Toni, 5725
Hubbard, Zachary, 4319, 4320
Hubbart, Dean, 7433
Hubbell, Todd, 1606
Huber, David R., 1336, 1337, 5005
Huber, Hope, 228
Huber, Jane E., 3369, 4999
Huber, Steve, 326, 5629
Huber Weber, Roxanne, 983
Hubert, Daniel, 2233
Hubert, Linda, 1799
Hubley, Patrick, 4013
Hubman, Martin, 8698, 8699, 8700
Hubner, Carla, 4423
Huckabay, Bandi, 4955
Huckabone, Cort, 6150
Hucko, Stephen, 2217
Huckstep, Brenn, 4029
Hudacs, Chris, 371
Hudak, Holly H., 1036
Huddleston, Mark, 5341
Huddleston, Robb, 4313

Huddleston, Robert, 8490, 8491, 8492
Huddleston, Sara, 2583
Huddleston, Will, 2633
Hudgins, Charlene, 3689
Hudgins, Mark, 4058
Hudman, Debbie, 3924
Hudnell, Melissa Y., 411
Hudson, Bannus, 855, 4309, 4312
Hudson, Chirs, 7300
Hudson, David L., 2354
Hudson, Dr. Jerry, 5413
Hudson, Frank M., 1774
Hudson, Gregg, 4266
Hudson, Hank, 2877
Hudson, Jan, 4276, 6216
Hudson, John, 969
Hudson, Michael, 7359
Hudson, Phyllis, 822, 4268
Hudson, Richard, 1275, 1276
Hudson-Stowe, Shanna E., 4718
Huebner, Libby, 6173
Hueg, Kurt, 6153
Huelsing, Jeremy, 7677
Huesman, William, 1507
Hueston, Eddie, 8355
Huey, Liana, 8722
Huff, Joseph H., 1009
Huff, Mae, 8560
Huff, Maurice, 4275
Huff, Monica, 1682
Huff, Richard, 641
Huff, Richard E, 8420
Huffer, Chuck, 4342
Huffman, Cynthia, 4082
Huffman, Frances K., 711
Hug, Butch, 7492
Huger, George, 4038, 4039
Huger, Stephanie, 7139
Huggett, Monica, 1606
Huggins, Brenda, 3144
Huggins, Cynthia, 3098
Huggins, Cynthia E., 7170
Huggins, Patti, 186
Hugh, Elisabeth, 1554
Hugh, Jen, 947
Hugh, Jennifer, 947
Hugh McWilliams, Ryan, 3490
Hughes, Ava J., 5548
Hughes, Bob, 6652
Hughes, Brain, 4654
Hughes, Brian, 4654
Hughes, Carolyn, 883
Hughes, Christian W., 2126
Hughes, David, 1779, 2022
Hughes, Don, 4271
Hughes, Earl, 3847, 5494
Hughes, Jason, 7566
Hughes, Joyce, 4163
Hughes, Judy, 1101
Hughes, Linda, 2335
Hughes, Maura L., 5317
Hughes, Michael, 1954
Hughes, Mr. Joey, 4184
Hughes, Nicholas D, 3805
Hughes, Nick, 5575
Hughes, Owen, 5052
Hughes, Robert L., 8058
Hughes, Robin, 6718
Hughes, Sandra, 2854
Hughes, Scott, 2314
Hughes, Sheila, 5783
Hughes, Stephen, 6062
Hughes, Thomas, 2262
Hughes, III, MD, R Condon, 1277
Hughett, Julie, 2455
Hughett, Richard, 4254
Hughson, Barry, 271
Hugo, John, 1786
Hugo Martinez, Albert, 1905
Hugo Martinez, Gay, 841
Huie, Michael, 3665
Huizinga, Scott, 1236
Hui, Molly, 6678
Hukill, Betty, 6358
Hula, Kuma, 4530
Hulbert, Gail, 3859
Hulbert, Mariclare, 4772
Hulburt, Jane, 2041

Executive Name Index

Hull, Annie, 7479
Hull, Charles, 3582
Hull, Harry, 6115
Hullette, Suzette, 3088
Hulsman, Gerald R., 1605
Humble, Phillip, 8033
Hume, David, 1578
Hume, John C., 3479
Hume, Karen, 7077, 7078, 7079
Hume, Pattie, 91
Humes, James, 4091
Humiston, Marilyn K, 1290
Humleker, William, 1496
Hummel, Dave, 6887
Hummel, Patricia, 5500
Humpage, Corey, 6408
Humpherys, Douglas, 1760, 5699
Humphrey, Andrew, 1404, 1405
Humphrey, Joe, 3448
Humphreys, Emily, 6746
Humphreys, Liz, 3188
Humphreys, Tracy, 1691
Humphries, Joel, 8395
Humphries Breeskin, Gail, 2731
Hunciag, Maria, 7281
Hundrieser, Karen, 2051
Hung, Cathy, 405, 7691
Hungate, Galen, 6001
Hungerford, Carol, 1838
Hungerford, Fannie, 3036
Hunkapiller, Johnny, 5901, 5902, 5903, 5904
Hunkins, Marcia, 2124
Hunley, Marina, 4096
Hunnicutt, James, 3114
Hunsan, Paign, 1479
Hunsberger, Donald, 1463
Hunsinger, Jeff, 729
Hunstien, DeeAnne, 4405
Hunt, Bill, 1604
Hunt, Calvin, 381, 385
Hunt, Deborah, 7353, 7354
Hunt, Edward, 3651
Hunt, Harold, 55
Hunt, Jeff, 2061
Hunt, Jeffrey, 1069
Hunt, Jennifer, 2061, 7095
Hunt, Jeremy, 55
Hunt, Lawrence J., 1321
Hunt, Linda, 729
Hunt, Mary, 55
Hunt, Robb, 4072
Hunt, Robert, 4068
Hunt, Rosanna, 5008, 5009
Hunt, Sheila, 525
Hunt, Stacey, 2345
Hunt, Steve, 3632
Hunt, Susan, 6517
Hunt, Sylvia, 4534
Hunt, Todd, 7404, 7409
Hunt, Tom, 6228
Hunt, William Todd, 1851
Hunt Marion, Loretta, 3590
Hunt, Ph.D, Linda, 8076, 8078
Hunte, Cliff, 4767
Hunter, Art, 3815
Hunter, Bill, 6156
Hunter, Brian, 7270
Hunter, Christine F., 2234
Hunter, Frances, 1905
Hunter, Greg, 146
Hunter, Jane E, 1096
Hunter, Jeff, 2464, 8293
Hunter, Jim, 8207
Hunter, Jonas, 4179
Hunter, Larry, 6199
Hunter, Malina, 8710
Hunter, Mark, 7013, 7014
Hunter, Mary, 6536
Hunter, Mrs. Cristine F, 1997
Hunter, Pam, 1681
Hunter, Susette, 5889
Hunter, Terri, 1243, 4853, 4854
Hunter, Todd, 4977, 7543
Hunter, Will, 868
Hunter, Esquire, David, 1554
Hunterfields, Emilye, 2926
Huntington, Dorri, 2584
Huntington, Dr. Tammie, 1091

Huntley, Christopher, 2034
Huntley, Jim, 4204
Huntley, Lance, 100, 101
Huntley, Walter R, 2857
Huntoon, Ann, 1835
Huntoon, Terence, 4242
Huntowski, Kasha, 8665, 8666, 8669
Huntsman, Pamela, 5062
Huntsman, Scott M., 651
Huntzinger, Sherene, 691
Hunzelman, Amy, 4640, 6962
Huotari, Amanda, 7181
Hupp, Charles, 3746
Hupp, Robert, 2439, 2441, 6035
Hupp, William, 2054
Hupper, John R., 2209
Hupperts, Bernie, 5831
Hurcum, Rob, 4543
Hurd, Ed, 7496, 7499
Hurd, Sandra, 2258
Hurdle, Terra, 1614
Hurley, Cristine, 6156
Hurley, Jack, 5064
Hurley, Kathleen, 236
Hurley, Linda, 1207
Hurley, Mary, 2709
Hurley, Ms Diane S, 5520
Hurley, Patricia, 2327
Hurley, Stephen, 2395
Hurley, Thomas, 1207
Hurov, Jessica, 6519
Hurst, Berry, 347
Hurst, Brian, 2952
Hurst, Jeff, 3956
Hurst, Michael, 3384, 7725
Hurst, Sheldon, 1456
Hurt, Martha R, 2305
Hurty, Anna, 6825, 6827
Hurty, Dr. Jon, 2059
Hurty, Jon, 1063, 2059
Hurwitz, Dr. T. Alan, 145
Hurwitz, Eric M., 1332
Huscroft, Sue, 1903
Huseby, Michael, 1953
Huseman, Sue, 3098
Huseth, Solveig, 3223
Huskey, Lloyd, 4159
Hussein, Samir, 5135
Hussey, Hawley, 452
Hussey, Michael S., 7169
Hussie-Taylor, Judy, 414
Hussong, Jennifer, 2889
Hustis, Greg, 4368
Hustoles, Paul J, 3234
Huston, Cathy, 5331
Huston, Robin, 3762
Huston, Roger, 4089
Huston, Wayne, 6942
Huston Drudge, Susan, 8898
Hutchcraft, Brice, 2989
Hutcheson, Philip, 5578
Hutchings, Matt, 6365
Hutchings, Owen, 7815
Hutchinson, Chisa, 3416
Hutchinson, Jenny, 5081
Hutchinson, Leland E, 2047
Hutchinson, Loura, 5275
Hutchinson, Owen, 4379
Hutchison, Jay, 7336, 7337
Hutheesing, Ajit, 4409
Hutsell, Marcus, 8324
Hutson, Dr Don, 1707
Hutton, Heidi, 4755
Huwiler, Macie, 2905, 7697
Huxford, Camilla, 716
Huyck, Janet, 7375
Hval, Kathy, 4985
Hval, Palmer, 4985
Hwang, Cindy S., 5123
Hwang, Erica, 262
Hwang, Kirsten, 271
Hwang, Sora, 1419
Hwang-Williams, Yumi, 905
Hyatt, M Michael, 3639
Hyatt Mazon, Gina, 187
Hyatt-Mazon, Gina, 187
Hyde, Bob, 8497
Hyde, Bruce, 3220

Hyde, Eric, 3247
Hyde, Nancy, 552
Hyer, Warren W, 1552
Hyers, Stephen D., 3659
Hygom, Gary, 3615
Hyland, Jim, 2397
Hyland, Louise, 2178
Hyler, Linda, 2722
Hylton, Gary, 4101
Hyman, Dick, 5143
Hyman, Eric, 8381
Hyman, Michael, 7947
Hyman, Ralph, 2440
Hyman, Steve, 8015
Hymel, Larry M, 7121
Hymes, Gerald, 8109
Hymes, Wendy, 4190
Hynson, Michelle, 2397
Hyssong, Mark, 3896

I

I. Katz, Isador, 1104, 1105
I. Scheer, David, 6419
Iacopino, Jennifer L., 4962
Iafrate, Tommy, 3030
Iams, David, 1325
Ianco, Garry, 2223
Iannacito, Lisa, 412
Ianniciello, Bill, 7672
Iannone, Ron, 4103
Iaropoli, Vincent, 4452
Ibister, Jim, 7372
Ibrahim, Michael, 4810
Icasas, Jonathan, 1804
Icenhower, Donna, 1906
Ichinohe, Saeko, 481
Ichmond, Sandy, 7196
Iddi, Adam, 5851
Idhe, Albert, 3412
Idmes, Karen, 829
Ietto, Domenick, 6134
Ifewande Olowe, Jeaunita, 514
Iger, Arnold, 2587
Iglitzin, Alan, 1648, 5798
Ignagni, Linda J., 1246
Ihde, Albert, 2610
Iida, Gary, 773
Ike, Lynne, 7301
Ikeda, Virginia, 727
Ikegami, Julienne, 1634
Ikemiya, Masanobu, 1146
Iler, Heather, 305
Iler, Susan, 7961
Iles, Delma, 151
Ilinskaya, Marina, 170
Illic, Mike, 62
Illick, Joe, 2347
Illingwarth, Scott, 2992
Ilumin, Rena, 5796
Im, Dr Mi-Jung, 7795
Ima, Kim, 3564
Imadiyi, Felix, 5958, 5959
Imamoto, Meg, 2499
Imasogie, Osagie, 8151
Imboden, Elis, 6304
Imbriaco, Joe, 7165
Imel, Gary, 5977
Imley, Eric, 2485, 2486
Immediato, Aaron, 3840
Immel, Deanna, 4542
Immink, Tinna, 7296
Imper, Keith, 5419
Imperial, Franco, 861
Ims, Chris, 5082
Imscher, Mark, 5412
Indenbaum, Tina, 5075
Indrutz, Janice, 6949, 6950
Infanate, Carla, 2291
Infinger, Russell, 8221
Ing, Richard, 1019
Ingalz, Tom, 862
Ingber, Rabbi Abie, 5309
Inger, Ivan, 1600, 5417
Ingersoll, John, 6620
Ingle, Brandon, 7214, 7215
Inglima, Donna, 6147
Inglin, Kate, 1794

Inglis, Andrew, 5574
Inglis, Martin, 1545, 1546, 2282, 5326
Ingraham, Bruce, 6947
Ingraham, Edward, 733, 4174
Ingraham, Ken, 815
Ingram, David, 228
Ingram, John M, 7490, 7492
Ingram, Judith, 1207
Ingram, Judy, 4738
Ingram, Kate, 6565, 6568
Ingram, Randy, 7352
Ingram McDowell, Molly, 6850
Inigo, Maxie, 5952
Inkel, Ran, 4006, 5682
Inkel, Ray, 4006
Inkles, Alan, 5206
Inman, Arlon, 730, 731
Inman, Fran, 6215
Inman, Marcie, 8420
Innaurato, Arthur, 2306
Innocenti, Celeste, 2560
Insco, Michael, 1286
Inteeworn, Oliver, 1407
Interim Artistic Dir, Wochner, 2510
Interrante, Rosie, 3456
Intraub, Neil, 3554, 3581
Intres, Heather, 6033
Intres, Jackie, 2931
Intriligator, William, 1109, 1837
Inungaray, Isela, 8377
Ioannides, Sarah, 1809
Iovanne, Thomas, 8592
Ip, Mary, 2163
Ippel, Larry, 219
Ira Goldstein, David, 2430, 6004
Irby, Jerry, 5286
Irby, Randi, 5784
Ireland, Chris, 5669
Ireland, Doug, 7137
Ireland, Jock, 406
Ireland, Linda, 5595
Ireland, R. Todd, 3839
Ireland Robinson, Heather, 6732
Ireland, Jr., James D., 2007
Irmscher, Krista, 5359
Irons, Heather G, 4359
Irons, Heather G., 4359
Irons, Jason, 3297
Irvin, Jim, 7879
Irvin, Lauri, 4522
Irvine, Nobert, 7853
Irvine II, Horace H, 2108
Irving, Don, 3778, 5411, 8081
Irving, John, 3933
Irving, Kevin, 564
Irving, Rino, 2358
Irwing, Rino, 1743
Isaac, Frederick J., 760
Isaac, Frederick M., 2282
Isaac, Karen, 5103
Isaac, Marivi, 1720, 5619
Isaacs, Charlotte, 4483
Isaacs, Jean, 69
Isaacs, John, 4669
Isaacson, Margie, 6719
Isaacson, Mike, 3300, 7454
Isacke, Beth, 6332
Isacke, Edith, 1617
Isadiar, Eman, 783
Isadore, Jennifer, 1728
Isban, Sharon, 1419
Isbell, David, 5949, 5950
Isbell, Tom, 3226, 3227
Isdaner, Bart, 3825, 3837
Isenberg, Alice, 4954
Isenberg, JoAnne, 5456
Isensee, Paul, 5463
Ishee, Suzanne, 2183
Ishibashi, Gerald, 40
Ishida, Neil, 2030
Ishii, Wendy, 2669
Ishii-Eto, Kimbo, 1394
Ishikawa, Iris, 5947
Isidoro-Mills, Edith, 1311
Israel, Richard, 2520
Israel, Tom, 5799
Issaev, Vladimir, 159
Issen, Stacy, 6977

1179

Executive Name Index

Issersohn, Amy, 6550
Istvanick, Wendy, 2950
Isunza-Rodriguez, Delia I., 5662
IT Manager, Ames, 761
Itkin, David, 1698
Ito, Leslie A., 40
Ivanov, Lana, 5161
Ivany, Robert, 5644
Ivers, David, 5682
Ivers, Polly, 8087
Iverson, Charles, 8122
Iveson, Ciera, 4068, 4072
Iveson, Clea, 5079
Ivester, Jim, 7376
Ivin, Jerry, 8441
Iwakawa, Tomoko, 833
Iwanski, Linda, 3996
Iwasaki, Yurie, 1715
Ixcamey, Leo, 6133, 6135
Izraelevitz, Terry, 5031
Izumi, Cathy, 192
Izzo, Gary, 3622

J

J. Aibel, Howard, 2720
J. Daniels, Ronald, 7191, 7192
J. Denolf, Marry, 3203
J. Gale, Thomas, 6559
J. Hartman, John, 2940
J. Hribar, Dr.Frank, 7263
J. Kelly, Patrick, 2940
J. Lukas, Henry, 3135
J. Mascara, Ken, 6516
J. O'Connor, Patrick, 6921, 6922, 6923, 6924, 6925
J. Sammler, Bronislaw, 2699
J. Seel,, Kenneth, 2720
J. Solomon, Steven, 2917
J.Hanneke, Mandi, 1196
J.Moore, Victoria, 1068
Jabara, Douglas, 2212
Jabbour, Chuck, 8282
Jabbour, Hind, 1668
Jaber, Thomas, 2354
Jablonsky, Kyra, 89
Jabobsen, Jon, 8498
Jack, Jim, 3378
Jack, Secretary, 6921, 6922, 6923, 6924, 6925
Jackman, JJ, 2520
Jackman, Lois, 7281
Jackoboice-Lesneski, Karin, 5285
Jackson, Anna, 3130
Jackson, Barbara, 7512
Jackson, Barry, 333
Jackson, Bob, 4957
Jackson, Candace, 8845
Jackson, Clayton F, 1005
Jackson, Dael, 3799
Jackson, Darren, 2141
Jackson, David, 1579
Jackson, Dr. Eugene R, 2410
Jackson, Earl, 1842
Jackson, Ernest, 5935
Jackson, Fiona, 333
Jackson, Greg, 6598
Jackson, Gregory, 4466
Jackson, Heather, 560, 729
Jackson, Herman F., 5920
Jackson, Jack, 7987
Jackson, Jeannette, 2128
Jackson,, Jessica, 6343
Jackson, Jim, 3006
Jackson, John, 4198
Jackson, Karen, 4649
Jackson, Katie, 6530
Jackson, Keith, 8644, 8645
Jackson, Kenneth W., 5540
Jackson, Laura, 1316
Jackson, Linda, 1964, 2209
Jackson, Lynnaa, 2651
Jackson, Mark, 3991
Jackson, Mary Jo, 3310
Jackson, Mary K, 1840
Jackson, Meredith, 7459
Jackson, Molly, 1565
Jackson, Mr. Hunter, 4184
Jackson, Myra, 4360

Jackson, Nathaniel, 886
Jackson, Nicole, 6465
Jackson, PennyMaria, 381, 385
Jackson, Pope, 3566
Jackson, Richard, 2458
Jackson, Robert H, 1519
Jackson, Ron, 6644
Jackson, Ronald, 235
Jackson, Roz, 5371
Jackson, Sara, 3243
Jackson, Scott, 3021
Jackson, Sherly, 7839
Jackson, Sherry, 3971
Jackson, Susan, 235
Jackson, Tim, 4255, 6292
Jackson, Tom, 1099, 1100
Jackson, Wanda, 5076
Jackson, Wes, 3803
Jackson, Willda S., 3984
Jackson, Zac, 7960
Jackson Bradley, Eric, 477
Jackson Chihuly, Leslie, 1805
Jackson Jr, Stanley, 3714
Jackson Scott, Geoffrey, 2959
Jackson-Forsyth, Elena, 2297
Jackson-Lee, Barbara, 208
Jacob, Charlie, 7228
Jacob, Chris, 5057
Jacob, Howard J., 5855
Jacob, Jerry, 7228
Jacob, Karen Hite, 1482
Jacob, Lou, 7228
Jacob, Mariellen, 2153
Jacob, Sue, 3744
Jacobey, Linda, 2780
Jacobowitz, Diane, 363
Jacobs, Brooke E, 869
Jacobs, Carin, 6323, 6324
Jacobs, Chris, 5057
Jacobs, David, 3108
Jacobs, Dr. Alice Marie, 1044
Jacobs, Eleanor, 4311
Jacobs, Ellen, 3570
Jacobs, Frank, 1571
Jacobs, Ilene B., 4777
Jacobs, Jake, 3979
Jacobs, Jeremy, 7228
Jacobs, Nichol Julia, 2023
Jacobs, Nina S, 7567
Jacobs, Raymond, 8295
Jacobs, Rea, 5075
Jacobs, Roy, 7438
Jacobs, Sandy, 1769
Jacobs, Stephen, 1425
Jacobs, Trey, 2344
Jacobs Esq, Jeffrey, 2306
Jacobsen, Jon A., 4948
Jacobsen, Marian, 4012
Jacobsen, Sheila, 4626
Jacobsohn, Stephen, 4755
Jacobson, Alan, 2793
Jacobson, Benjamin, 4174
Jacobson, Catherine, 113
Jacobson, Denny P, 1448
Jacobson, Donald, 1659
Jacobson, Jay, 2248
Jacobson, Joshua, 2120
Jacobson, Joshua R., 2120
Jacobson, Leslie B, 2740, 4032
Jacobson, Nancy, 1015
Jacobson, Ruth Ellen, 1721
Jacobson, Shannyn, 3689
Jacobson, Sharon, 292
Jacobson, Susan, 6424
Jacobson, Ph.D., Judy, 1327
Jacobus, Arturo, 179
Jacoby, Dr. Peter, 6423
Jacoby, Ginny, 1159
Jacoby, Kristen, 944
Jacoby, Mike, 5994
Jacoby, Mlke, 7587
Jacoby, Pat, 2566
Jacques, Holly, 7900, 7903, 7904, 7905
Jacques, Margaret, 7521
Jacumin, Johnny, 8220
Jaeger, Lois, 4869
Jafari, Hedi, 2482, 6137, 6138, 6139, 6140, 6141, 6142, 6143

Jaffe, Bob, 3490, 7727
Jaffe, David B, 2715
Jaffe, Denise, 1336, 1337, 5005
Jaffe, Doug, 2639
Jaffe, Elise, 471
Jaffe, Jeff, 1570
Jaffe, Jerry, 3578
Jaffe, Maestro Peter, 1866
Jaffe, Peter, 882
Jaffe, Robert M, 4282
Jaffe, Walter, 565
Jaffee, Michael, 1452
Jagoditz, Joe, 5303
Jagoditz, Joseph F, 5303
Jahi, Runako, 2929
Jahn, Chris, 2764
Jahn, Kerry, 4046
Jahnke, Joel, 3314
Jaime, Bridget, 3764
Jaissle, Rick, 1256
Jaklitsch, Elizabeth, 1383
Jakobson, Ellen, 3545
Jakolat, Kathy, 1315
Jakoulov, Jakov, 275
Jakovac, Brett, 7479
Jalonen, Nancy, 4210
Jamason, Corey, 1917
Jamerson, Richard, 2944
James, Amanda, 5156
James, Andrea, 7105, 7106
James, Argentina M., 3984
James, Benjamin, 2900
James, Brock, 8294
James, Coran, 384
James, Daryl, 4360
James, David F, 5160
James, Dobson, 1157
James, Doug, 3313
James, Eugene, 424
James, Frederic B, 730
James, Harold, 730
James, Harry, 4619
James, Heather, 6372
James, Holly, 1789
James, Jan, 4095
James, Jefferson, 516
James, Jeffery, 1475
James, Jeffrey, 8800
James, Jennifer, 4947
James, John, 8424, 8425, 8426, 8427, 8428
James, Julianne, 4240
James, Kate, 6550
James, Kevin, 1376, 1406
James, Lana, 3310
James, Lance C, 2448
James, Lori, 4958
James, Mandy, 1556
James, Matt, 6672
James, Michael, 7691
James, Michelle, 2356, 4100
James, Muffi, 2065
James, Paul, 3765
James, R Lee, 8119
James, Randy, 330
James, Richard L, 8498
James, Ruby, 4724
James, Sarah, 2919
James, Scott, 1879
James, Terry E, 2973
James, Timothy, 3474
James, Travis, 8897
James, Valerie, 5979
James Bey, Kim, 6466, 6470
James Brandau, Ryan, 2187
James Malagiere, Kenneth, 1345
James Miller, Anna, 1791
Jameson, Cory, 4368
Jamieson, Bill, 3116
Jamieson, Brad, 4970
Jamison, Greg, 6268
Jamison, John, 1812
Jamison, Matt, 2271
Janco Daniels, Myra, 981
Jane,, 8148
Jane, Tanner, 3052
Jane Armacost, Mary, 4542
Jane Chase, Mary, 3355
Jane DeHoff, Sara, 8017

Jane Plummer, Mary, 4764
Jane Saunders, Mary, 6487
Jane Smith, Mary, 1757
Janeczko, Ron, 6687
Janes, Jeanne, 8452
Janes, Sasha, 507
Janes, Sr, David A., 817
Janeway, Whitney, 1962
Jang, Ignace, 1021
Janiro, Rocky, 719
Janisch, Joseph, 2392
Janka, Frederick, 6286
Jankowaski, John, 7825, 7826
Janks, Leo, 414
Janners, Dr. Sigurds, 4845
Jannise, Stacie, 5595
Janow, Marilyn, 1476
Jansen Jurczyk, Annie, 4126
Janson, Eric, 7536
Janssen, Joan, 2057
Jantzi, John, 2298
Janucsh, Barry, 5774
Janus, Alana, 7654
Janz, Deborah, 8705
Jao, D Bryan, 7294
Jaoui, Laura, 773
Jaquay, Cheryl, 6936
JaQuay, Joe, 201
Jaquet, Jill, 6502
Jaraba, Betty, 5621
Jaramillo, Eric, 8346
Jaramillo, John C., 7609
Jaray, Istvan, 1632
Jarchow, Mary, 4360
Jarden, Charles, 2205
Jardin, Maureen, 1184
Jarecki, Doug, 4136
Jares, Terry, 8761
Jarjisian, Catherine, 5292
Jarman, Mary, 1253
Jaros, MBA, Allegra, 3430
Jaroslow, Risa, 479
Jarowski, Paula, 467
Jarrell Urbanek, Emily, 2262
Jarret, Ron, 1762
Jarrett, Lonnie, 7601
Jarrett, Lori, 8877
Jarrett, Paul, 5286
Jarrett, Ron, 2363
Jarrod Stackhouse, Gary, 8445
Jarvi, Neeme, 1337, 5005
Jarvie, Greg, 7995
Jarvis, Anne M, 1147
Jarvis, Anne M., 2087
Jarvis, Annette W., 1766
Jarvis, Christina, 739
Jarvis, Cynthia, 4196
Jarvis, Jeffery, 750
Jarvis, Jim, 6719
Jarvis, Theresa, 4233
Jasany, Robert, 3679
Jasper, Daniel, 8113
Jasper, Stuart, 5483
Jaudon, Jon, 8513, 8514
Jauregui, Art, 19
Jaus, Bonnie, 5994
Jaworski, Alexis, 211
Jaworski, Jim, 6500
Jay, Ben, 7985
Jay Smith, Don, 343
Jazczak, Chris, 7295
Jean Heller, Carol, 1549, 1550
Jean Morris, Betty, 6115
Jean Wei, Dr. Laurie, 5915, 5916
Jean Weil, Dr Laurie, 4148
Jean-Louis, Judene, 459
Jean-Philippe, Pharah, 3421
Jeanette, Gertrude, 3496
Jeanette, Gertrude, 3496
Jeannotte, Sandra, 2132, 4833
Jecklin, Lois, 8769
Jedyniak, Theresa, 4385
Jeenan, Kathleen, 4022
Jeenkins, Dr. Robert, 2604
Jeffcoat, Harold, 6768
Jeffcoat, Joe, 3492
Jeffe, Chris, 1525
Jefferies, Kathy, 6075

Executive Name Index

Jeffers, Tinay, 2273
Jefferson, Leigh, 4689
Jefferson, Michael, 1558
Jeffery, Diane, 4976
Jeffery, Rev, 2684
Jeffords, Jr, Walter M., 3619
Jeffrey, Dean, 5233
Jeffrey, Diane, 7581
Jeffries, Bob, 6345
Jeffries, Chris, 5801
Jeffries, Cindy, 3291
Jeffries, Jackie, 7868
Jeffries, Mike, 1158
Jeffries Hazangeles, Monica, 7208
Jekowsky, Barry, 889
Jelinek, Dr. Mark, 1355
Jelks, Mark, 694
Jelle, Selbey, 1795
Jelley, Celia, 1485
Jellum, Dick, 4856
Jemson, Scott, 8487
Jenik, Adriene, 736, 737
Jenkins, Andrea, 4870
Jenkins, Arland, 8256
Jenkins, Bill, 4596, 6915, 6916, 6917, 6918
Jenkins, Cara M., 1478
Jenkins, Charles E., 1405
Jenkins, Chloe, 876
Jenkins, David A., 7960
Jenkins, DeVida, 8158
Jenkins, Donald P, 1949
Jenkins, Donald P., 1948
Jenkins, Gregory K, 1128
Jenkins, J. Stephen, 154
Jenkins, Janice, 3496
Jenkins, Jennifer, 6638
Jenkins, Jim, 4250, 6551
Jenkins, Jynx, 195
Jenkins, Karla, 5288
Jenkins, Kate, 7653
Jenkins, Linda, 154
Jenkins, Margaret, 83
Jenkins, Michael, 5611
Jenkins, Michael A, 5609
Jenkins, Michael A., 8360
Jenkins, Newell, 5064
Jenkins, Ronald J, 2282
Jenkins, Sidney O, 7566
Jenkins, Speight, 2387, 8605
Jenkins, Suzan, 4766
Jenkins, Suzanne, 154
Jenkins, Vantony, 7587
Jenkins, Willard, 4766, 5321
Jenkins McFadden, Elizabeth, 1998
Jenkins, CSC, Rev. John I., 6927, 6929, 6931, 6932, 6933, 6934, 6935
Jenks, Kat, 1364
Jenneman, Eugene, 7330
Jenness, Julie, 1901
Jennifer,, 1086, 8721
Jennings, Chris, 2747, 6477
Jennings, Christina, 1522
Jennings, Craig, 531, 1549, 1550, 2284
Jennings, Elyse, 1785
Jennings, James, 3467
Jennings, Janet, 8266
Jennings, John, 4278, 4279, 6219
Jennings, Judy, 8560
Jennings, Lisa, 1683
Jennings, Llisa, 1683
Jennings, Marc, 1744
Jennings, Markus, 6946
Jennings, Robert, 6636
Jennings, Stacy, 4520
Jennings, Tim, 3237, 4121
Jennings Cullen, Sherre, 4563
Jennings-Roggensack, Colleen, 4177, 5986
Jenoure, Jasmin, 369
Jenschke, Laurie, 1751
Jensen, Alexis, 1870
Jensen, Amy S., 4129
Jensen, Beth, 5775
Jensen, Christina, 1406
Jensen, Daniel L., 1544
Jensen, Donna, 3220
Jensen, Eric, 3483, 4008
Jensen, Hans, 4132
Jensen, James, 4860

Jensen, Janet, 4264
Jensen, Joelle, 1789
Jensen, JoLynne, 3960
Jensen, Judy, 7563
Jensen, Linda, 4066
Jensen, Randy, 5684
Jensen, Rebecca, 3390, 7592
Jensen, Rob, 3269, 5948
Jensen, Ronnamarie, 753
Jensen, Sandy, 4008
Jensen, PhD, Dr. Bryon, 1301
Jenson, Amy E., 1309, 1310
Jenson, Gary, 1761
Jepson, Kathy, 6391
Jeremy King, OSB, Fr., 6866
Jeremy Stevens, Samuel, 3769
Jerger, Dori, 4133
Jerkins, Nathan, 3931
Jerome, Phyllis, 1599
Jerome, M.D., E. Heidi, 1368
Jerry, Philip, 280
Jesch, Sue, 1311
Jeske, Charles, 7935
Jessee, John, 4055
Jessen, Christian A, 4310
Jessop, Craig, 4007
Jessop, Dr Craig, 2035
Jeter, John, 754
Jeter, Karon, 553
Jett, Rachel, 2715
Jette, Steven, 6577
Jewell, Shane, 552
Jewett, Sandra, 2606
Jewison, Ghlee, 6938
Jews, Brenda, 7195
Jex, Jori, 3752, 8016
Jeziorski, Jeremy, 3855
Jhonson, Anita, 6077
Jhunjhunwala, Maneesh, 3048
Jiayan Yong, Jessie, 405
Jiguor, Robin, 2614
Jimenez, Alexander, 999
Jimenez, Gracie, 5663, 8450, 8451
Jimenez, Laura, 2482, 6137, 6138, 6139, 6140, 6141, 6143
Jimison, Kevin, 8318
Jinbo, Michael, 1662
Jirak, Dr. James, 1024
Jiranek, David, 3507
Jischke, Martin C., 6948, 6951
Jivoff, Ray, 4129
JM, Garrone, 7455
Jo, Whitney, 3908
Jo Bergstrom, Mary, 1588
Jo Hornaday, Mary, 1286
Jo Hudgel, Mary, 4206
Jo Peloquin, Mary, 295
Jo Snider, Nancy, 4430
Jo Walker, Mary, 6292
Jo Williams, Ruby, 5614
Joaquin, Nicholai, 1432
Jobe-Ishman, Gina, 5918
Jobel, George, 1319
Jobin, David, 1986
Jobin, Sara, 780
Jockers, Ken, 3500
Jocketty, Walt, 7444
Jody, Interim Directo, 1526
Joe, Glenda, 5638
Joe, Supervisor, 1526
JOFFRED, ELLEN, 3818
Joffred,, Ellen, 3471
Johanek, Michael, 8207
Johannesen, April, 910
Johanningermeier, Elizabeth, 461
Johansen, Dave, 8715
Johanson, Charles, 2454
John, Easley, 7455
John, Katherine, 5698
John, Katherine St, 5698
John, Rice, 5991, 5992
John Chabotar, Kent, 5245
John Stanbery, Paul, 1553
Johnathan, Baldo, 7812
Johngren, Jane, 5062
Johns, Angelee, 6824
Johns, Denise, 7249
Johns, Janet, 6879, 6880, 6881

Johns, Peter, 7377
Johns, Tammy, 594
Johns, Vertira, 6076
Johnsen, Curt, 1065, 1066
Johnsen, David, 706
Johnson, A. Richard, 1694
Johnson, A. Robert, 1431
Johnson, Alex, 8005
Johnson, Alford, 5037
Johnson, Aline, 3645
Johnson, Allan, 6567, 6570
Johnson, Allen, 6571
Johnson, Allyson, 6708, 6709
Johnson, Amy, 4590
Johnson, Anna, 4050
Johnson, Annette, 48, 49
Johnson, Arabella, 4418
Johnson, Arlene, 1744
Johnson, B J, 2151
Johnson, Barbara, 2824
Johnson, Becky, 1808, 1809, 5808, 7159
Johnson, Ben, 297, 4825
Johnson, Ben, 6796
Johnson, Bert, 197
Johnson, Beth, 1781, 5232
Johnson, Bj, 4879
Johnson, Blair, 6605, 6606
Johnson, Bobae, 1865
Johnson, Brett, 4012
Johnson, Brian, 4010, 4011, 4065
Johnson, Bruce, 2377
Johnson, Bryan, 3326
Johnson, C Nicholas, 240
Johnson, Candace, 6465
Johnson, Carl, 1110
Johnson, Carole H., 2209
Johnson, Charles, 6901, 6902
Johnson, Charles A., 1727
Johnson, Charles E., 1806, 5803
Johnson, Charmaine, 5847
Johnson, Cheri, 6230
Johnson, Chris, 7677
Johnson, Christina, 197
Johnson, Christopher, 5155
Johnson, Craig, 1657
Johnson, Dale, 1810, 2144
Johnson, Darla, 623
Johnson, Dave, 2654, 4397
Johnson, David, 1309, 1310, 5266
Johnson, Denise, 3060
Johnson, Derrick, 1269
Johnson, Dwight, 8554
Johnson, E. Scott, 4756
Johnson, Elizabeth, 1793
Johnson, Eric, 2886, 4134
Johnson, Erika, 117
Johnson, Ester, 7080
Johnson, Fedrick, 3847
Johnson, Feleesha, 5561
Johnson, Felicity, 2889
Johnson, Fred B., 3881
Johnson, Gail, 5607
Johnson, Galen, 628
Johnson, George, 5932
Johnson, Glenda, 4680
Johnson, Gordon, 4939
Johnson, Gordon J, 1298
Johnson, Greg, 970, 3256, 6036, 7362, 7379
Johnson, Harryette, 121
Johnson, Howard, 2287
Johnson, James, 2144
Johnson, James A, 4425
Johnson, James M, 1309, 1310
Johnson, Jan, 120, 2187
Johnson, Janet, 6220, 6466, 6470
Johnson, Jaquelyn, 6669
Johnson, Jean, 1957, 3916
Johnson, Jeff, 2788, 3269, 6896
Johnson, Jeffrey, 4814, 5250
Johnson, Jill, 5869
Johnson, John, 1302
Johnson, Joia M., 1509
Johnson, Joyce, 4904
Johnson, Judi, 5946
Johnson, Julia, 2138
Johnson, Karen, 1252, 8221
Johnson, Kathie, 1036
Johnson, Kathy, 5678

Johnson, Kathy, 8552
Johnson, Kelli, 6661
Johnson, Ken, 1496
Johnson, Kevin, 4509
Johnson, Kimberly, 3974
Johnson, Kirk, 6459, 6461
Johnson, Kittrell, 4
Johnson, Kristen, 3147
Johnson, Kristin, 5616
Johnson, Lance, 621
Johnson, Lani, 2693, 6416
Johnson, Larry, 6110, 6111
Johnson, Laurie, 7369
Johnson, Lillie, 2291
Johnson, Lisa, 5788, 5789, 5790
Johnson, Lori, 1269
Johnson, Lynda, 2126
Johnson, Lynne, 4793
Johnson, Margaret, 257
Johnson, Maria, 2384
Johnson, Marilyn, 4046
Johnson, Marisha, 444
Johnson, Mark, 3473
Johnson, Marlys, 7417
Johnson, Matthew, 6685
Johnson, Michael, 5228, 6080, 6081, 6082, 6084
Johnson, Michael L., 6080, 6081, 6082, 6084
Johnson, Mike, 4327, 7379
Johnson, Miles, 260
Johnson, Mimi, 459, 3538
Johnson, Misty, 3986
Johnson, Monica, 7951
Johnson, Mr. Mark L, 8386
Johnson, Nancy, 2794, 3891
Johnson, Neal, 6382
Johnson, Nick, 8722
Johnson, Nina, 3472
Johnson, North, 7892
Johnson, Orin, 2157
Johnson, Pam, 1061
Johnson, Patricia, 2144
Johnson, Patrick, 2129
Johnson, Paul E, 960, 961, 962, 963
Johnson, Pete, 3679
Johnson, Peter, 252, 1940, 1941, 2090
Johnson, Priscilla, 7268
Johnson, Ray, 1932
Johnson, Raymond, 4400
Johnson, Rich, 4646
Johnson, Rita Gail, 429
Johnson, Robert, 4571
Johnson, Roger, 618
Johnson, Ron, 8697
Johnson, Ronald G, 6214
Johnson, Rosemary, 2436
Johnson, Roy, 1765, 3133, 4611
Johnson, Russel, 3212
Johnson, Ruth, 5744
Johnson, Sally C., 1500
Johnson, Sam, 7882
Johnson, Sandy, 3222
Johnson, Sarah, 6356, 6364, 8006
Johnson, Scott, 7886
Johnson, Seah, 347
Johnson, Sheri, 8407
Johnson, Sigrid, 2147
Johnson, Stephen, 5161
Johnson, Stephen P, 8389
Johnson, Steve, 4147
Johnson, Steven, 7231
Johnson, Steven G., 6464
Johnson, Susan, 293, 2778, 3286
Johnson, Susie, 1277
Johnson, Tamiko, 6249
Johnson, Ted, 4812
Johnson, Thomas P, 6996
Johnson, Tom, 1053, 6212
Johnson, Veronica, 2369
Johnson, Vicki, 6632
Johnson, Virgina, 1348
Johnson, Virginia, 471, 430
Johnson, Walter, 7659
Johnson III, William H, 5917
Johnson Jr., Willie, 4123
Johnson Sr., Robert L, 4592
Johnson, Jr, Joseph S, 5579
Johnson, MD, Cecil, 1277
Johnson-Brooks, Mekeda, 4556

1181

Executive Name Index

Johnson-Hamilton, Joyce, 775
Johnson, Barbara, 6585
Johnson, Lyn, 8587
Johnson, Nicolas, 3885
Johnston, Alex, 1430
Johnston, Andrew, 6177
Johnston, Brenda, 8000
Johnston, Camille, 6156
Johnston, Casey, 4487
Johnston, Cathy, 7697
Johnston, Craig, 1608
Johnston, David, 2893
Johnston, David C, 2893
Johnston, Jennifer, 1944, 6328
Johnston, Joanna, 653
Johnston, Lynn, 2895, 4533
Johnston, Margaret A., 6040
Johnston, Rick, 213
Johnston, Stephanie, 6619
Johnston, Steve, 6197
Johnston, Suzanne M., 346
Johnston, Tamara, 81
Johnston Green, Milly, 1742
Johntz, Jr., John H., 3289
Joiner, Dr. Thomas, 1496
Joiner, Eric, 5386
Joiner, Yvonne, 8282
Jolicouer, Pamela, 4875
Jolivet, David, 2036
Jolley, Jeremy, 5800
Jolly, Beryl, 7236
Jolly, Linda Lee, 8019
Jolly, Todd, 1924
Joly, Maureen S, 8107
Jonas, Lauren, 117
Jonas, Valerie, 812
Jonason, Susan, 1145
Jones, Alan, 4295
Jones, Alison, 175
Jones, Alonzo T., 3863
Jones, Amy, 2408
Jones, Anthony, 40
Jones, Barbara H., 6506
Jones, Barry, 4091
Jones, Betty, 7119
Jones, Bill, 309
Jones, Bill T, 397
Jones, BJ, 2986
Jones, Brain, 3809
Jones, Brett, 2727
Jones, Bryan, 5887
Jones, Carol, 4815
Jones, Cathy, 4752
Jones, Christopher, 270, 2679
Jones, Courtney, 4904
Jones, Daphne, 4510
Jones, Darryl V, 6118
Jones, Darryl V., 1895
Jones, David, 2259
Jones, De Ann S, 3675
Jones, Deborah, 8079
Jones, Deneese, 6986, 6987, 6988, 6989
Jones, Dennis, 2626, 6303
Jones, Dianne, 8711
Jones, Dr Stephen, 8224
Jones, Dr. Martin, 4896
Jones, Dr. Roger, 1140
Jones, Dr. Russell, 4679
Jones, E Bradley, 3038
Jones, E. Stewart, 5200
Jones, Ed, 4342
Jones, Ellen, 1700, 3877
Jones, Evan, 3209
Jones, Gary, 1916, 6362
Jones, Guy, 3187
Jones, Gwyneth, 7167
Jones, Heather, 2896
Jones, Jana L., 6488
Jones, Jane, 4080
Jones, Janet R., 5768, 5769
Jones, Jeff, 2582
Jones, Jennifer, 2189, 4472, 6576
Jones, Joan, 3632
Jones, Joela, 2279
Jones, John D, 1840
Jones, John D., 1840
Jones, Jonathan, 4371
Jones, Joseph R., 1717

Jones, Katherine, 100, 6473
Jones, Kathleen M., 6698
Jones, Ken, 5651
Jones, Kevin A, 295
Jones, LaDawn, 244
Jones, Lary, 2627
Jones, Laurel, 6056
Jones, Lial, 6230
Jones, Linda, 1504
Jones, Linda K., 1577
Jones, Linzy, 5965
Jones, Lisa, 5543, 5589
Jones, Loisdawn, 5380
Jones, Maceo, 6481
Jones, Maren, 8098
Jones, Marion K, 12
Jones, Mark W., 5003
Jones, Mary, 6652
Jones, Mary Margaret, 6262
Jones, Marya, 8197
Jones, Maureen, 4188
Jones, Max, 8394, 8395
Jones, Meghan, 3834
Jones, Michael, 4624, 6905
Jones, Mike, 6303, 7920
Jones, Monty, 6633
Jones, Ms. Meredith L., 8028
Jones, Neal, 3504
Jones, Nina M., 2397
Jones, Norma, 1880, 6113
Jones, Ozzie, 7548
Jones, Patty, 3669
Jones, Paul, 5033
Jones, Phillip A, 8587
Jones, Rachel, 3780
Jones, Ralph, 2195, 5614
Jones, Renet, 6636
Jones, Rhett S, 3863
Jones, Rick, 1309, 1310
Jones, Ris,, 1755
Jones, Robert, 799
Jones, Robert L., 2813
Jones, Ron, 2834, 4348
Jones, Roy, 7970
Jones, Russ, 3028
Jones, Sabra, 3522
Jones, Sandra, 2989
Jones, Sara, 2626, 6303
Jones, Shawn, 2141
Jones, Sheri, 2911
Jones, Spencer B., 5039
Jones, Stacey, 4187
Jones, Stephen C., 7454
Jones, Steve, 3945, 8236, 8237
Jones, Steven, 3070, 4498
Jones, Sue, 5324
Jones, Susan, 386
Jones, Susie, 1596, 5418
Jones, Terrence, 8563
Jones, Terrence D., 2378
Jones, Terry, 4082
Jones, Thom, 7423
Jones, Tim, 2341
Jones, Tom, 4519
Jones, Tracy, 6747
Jones, Ty, 3575
Jones, Wally, 3970
Jones, Walt, 6375
Jones, William, 3675
Jones Evans, Dr Charles, 1683
Jones III, Clyde B., 2321
Jones III, DeWitt C, 2114, 2288
Jones Jr, Conway B, 816
Jones Levenson, Rev Russell, 4474
Jones Smalley, Candance, 547
Jones'Pomatto, Alison, 2529
Jones, III, Marshall, 3377
Jonestrask, Becky, 2567
Jones, Rachel, 3780
Jonker-Burke, Sarah, 3448
Jonna, Robertson, 7455
Jonnes, Audrey J, 1210, 1211
Jonson, Michael, 2065
Jopke, LeAnn, 4867
Joranger, Amanda, 4563
Jorda, Aisha, 3130
Jordan, Andrea, 5355
Jordan, Bruce, 2941

Jordan, Caitlin, 662
Jordan, Carol, 380
Jordan, Damien M., 6091
Jordan, Daniel, 989, 991, 992, 993, 994, 995
Jordan, Darrell, 8360
Jordan, David, 2067
Jordan, Gregory B., 5812
Jordan, Irece, 8434
Jordan, Jackie, 2586
Jordan, James, 308
Jordan, James M., 638
Jordan, James P, 8115
Jordan, James P., 3795
Jordan, Jeff, 4675
Jordan, Jennifer, 89
Jordan, Jennifer E., 8159
Jordan, Jonathan, 265
Jordan, Lisa, 3795, 8115
Jordan, Maica, 3929, 3933
Jordan, Nichole, 6249
Jordan, Ryan, 1773
Jorden, Cule, 5018
Jordon, Bill, 210
Jordon, Damien, 2461
Jordon, Jeff, 7041
Jorgen, Bengt, 5079
Jorgensen, Erin, 5799
Jorgensen, Jackie, 4912
Jorgensen-Finley, Kathy, 1528, 1529
Jorgenser, Kathy, 4941
Jorgenson, Jerry, 7616
Jorgenson Sundquist, Rebecca, 2145
Jose, Brian, 7370
Jose, Renne, 5303
Josefson, Mary, 1262
Joseph, Cassandre, 356
Joseph, Cassondra, 2205
Joseph, Jerald, 6252
Joseph, Jim, 7754
Joseph, Rowan, 8124
Joseph, Russell C., 638
Joseph, Steeve, 6523
Joseph, Tony, 1655
Joseph, Esq., Thomas, 1655
Josephson, Gregg, 63
Josephson, Karen, 263
Joslyn, Patricia, 992, 993, 994, 995
Jost, Jack, 4482
Josue, Rebecca, 470
Joy, Robert J., 3442, 5080
Joy, Stephany, 2452
Joy Bell-Gouthiere,, Amanda, 2086
Joy-Fisk, Erin, 6711, 6712, 6715, 6716
Joyal, Debbie, 4507
Joyce, Jeffrey J., 5500
Joyce, Jennifer, 4309
Joyce, Julie, 5753
Joyce, Michael, 3812
Joyce, Patricia, 5081
Joyce, Susan, 592
Joyce, William, 1332
Joyce Wright, Pamela, 1782
Joyner, Quinton, 3830
Joyner, Sidney.B, 388
Joynt-Borger, Sarah, 2485
Jozoff, Malcolm, 729
Jr. Robert, Copley, 2711
Juan Han, Kee, 149
Jubelirer, Dr. Steve, 5814
Jubin, Jessica, 8334
Juchelka, Marie, 2024
Judd, James, 1422, 4444
Judd, Nancy, 930
Judge, Hugh, 4743
Judge, Joseph, 2267
Judice, Sandy, 5637
Judin, Joy, 5655
Judson, Bright M, 1426
Judson, Horece, 7119
Judson, Stephen, 65
Judy, George, 4006, 5682
Judy, Paul, 1048
Jue, Geoff, 3237
Jukes, Cheryl, 1159
Jul Hansen, Henrik, 63
Julian, Audrey, 1608
Julian, Donna P, 7190
Juliano, Frank, 3475

Julien, Rick, 2981
Jun, Ula, 677
Jundt, Jake, 8622
Juneau, Dr. Thomas, 2194
Jungels, Aaron, 592
Jungels, Dorothy, 592
Jungels, Rachael, 592
Junkert, Mark, 2034
Junkin, Jerry, 1714
Junphi, John, 5509
Jupin, a Alexandra, 8756
Juresich, Virginia, 3202
Jurgens, Denise, 347
Jurgens, Travis, 899
Jurney, Peter, 3778, 8081
Jurowski, Michail, 2191
Jusell, Chris, 913
Justice, Debra, 8424, 8425, 8426, 8427, 8428
Justo, Hernan, 606, 610
Justus, Craig, 3636
Justus, Glenda, 3280
Justus Murphy, Fionnegan, 2519
Jutagir, Hattie K, 3588

K

K. Auman, Elizabeth, 2958
Ka'ai Barrett, Malia, 2030
Kaats, Rod, 7803
Kaatz, Jeffry, 832
Kabalin, Pamela, 7502
Kabateck, Jack, 789
Kabo, Yaya, 544
Kacenjar, Leonard, 1742
Kacergis, Matthew, 1998, 2097
Kachnowski, Rose, 1246
Kacinski, Kathi, 3095
Kaczmarek, Pam, 290
Kadar, Dwight, 733, 4174
Kadavy, Heather, 3328
Kadel, Susan, 3805
Kaduri, Arie, 4450
Kaferly, Jenna, 2036
Kafkalas, E A, 7789
Kagan, Mark, 1214, 1215
Kagan, Martin, 471
Kagan, Martin I., 7760
Kahalehoe, Kawika, 1340
Kahan, James, 1058
Kahan, Jeffery, 2631
Kahan, Marvin, 3464
Kahane, Jeffrey, 803, 878, 905
Kahle, Bronna, 1220
Kahle, Linda, 4624
Kahler, Jim, 7970
Kahler, Ray, 8584
Kahlert, Helmut, 1271
Kahn, Hannah, 123
Kahn, Jenette, 7707
Kahn, Leigh, 1947
Kahn, Michael, 2747, 6477
Kahn, Sandra, 326
Kahne, Roberta, 2019
Kahns, Kristie, 201
Kai, Njia, 4835
Kaikkonen, Gus, 3351, 3559
Kail, Emma, 1283
Kaine, Kim, 194
Kaine, Paul, 194
Kaiser, Allison, 1128
Kaiser, Amy, 1291, 1945, 6329
Kaiser, Chris, 8052
Kaiser, Geoffrey, 1992
Kaiser, James F, 4745
Kaiser, Jill, 1258, 1259
Kaiser, Keith, 101
Kaiser, Kevin, 678
Kaiser, Marian, 1308
Kaiser, Michael, 956, 2742, 2752, 4425
Kaiser, Michael M, 958
Kaiser, Michael M., 1997, 4424, 4426, 6471
Kaiser, Roy, 577
Kaiser, Russell, 271
Kaissar, Amy, 3798
Kaizer, Brandan, 7202
Kajiwana, Lauriey, 6079
Kakos, Michael, 4496

1182

Executive Name Index

Kakuk, Charles, 4126
Kalaf, Jerry, 41
Kalbfleisch, Jon, 1579
Kale, Alex, 1372
Kale, Jim, 5653
Kalenda, Robert, 7369
Kaler, Ilya, 1056
Kaletta, Mary, 939
Kalfus, Donald, 325
Kalia, Megha, 469
Kalin, Catharine L, 852
Kalin, Catharine L., 6254
Kalina, Paul, 3036
Kalkor, Dr. Alan, 1499
Kall, Scott, 1299
Kallen, Tom, 6754
Kallish, Jan, 2959
Kallman, Robert A., 1455, 7695
Kallunki Gotham, Deb, 7308
Kalman, Susan, 1927
Kalmar, Carlos, 4554
Kalogeras, Alexandros, 1175
Kalos, Kiki, 513
Kalson, Dorothy, 5071
Kalstein, Jerry, 2180
Kalver, Gail, 211
Kam, Roxanne, 5005
Kamalani, Alva, 6678
Kambalov, Kristina, 140
Kambalov, Pasha, 140
Kamin, Carol L., 2322
Kamin, Hester, 3169
Kamine, Marjorie, 2422
Kaminski, Linda, 6428
Kaminsky, Laura, 5792
Kamis, Bro. Joseph, 6676
Kamlay, Kristine, 7328
Kammendiener, Kathi, 2455
Kammerer, Laura, 1062
Kamp, Mary, 263
Kampa, Bonnie, 747
Kamrath, Carolyn, 143, 144
Kamrath, Jon, 1799
Kanaga, Sarah R, 2122
Kanazawa, Chris, 2884
Kancianic, Phil, 1160
Kane, Angela, 282
Kane, Franny, 5419
Kane, Jeff, 4649
Kane, Jodi, 7701
Kane, Margaret L., 2553
Kane, Sandra, 1779
Kane, Scott, 6257, 6259, 6263
Kanengiser, William, 2550, 2551
Kaneten, Norval, 5275
Kang, Grace, 970
Kang, Hahn, 1419
Kang, Hyo, 1419
Kang, Kyung, 1419
Kang, Woosung, 4180
Kanner, Catherine, 42
Kano, Dr Thea, 1986
Kanoff, Scott, 3933
Kansas, George P, 7625
Kansau, Jimmy, 1916
Kantar, Ned, 8782
Kanter, Mark, 7849
Kanter, Stephen A, 823
Kantor, Herbert C, 3509
Kantrowitz, Stephen, 7568
Kao, Peling, 459
Kapask, Dick, 2543
Kapella, Karen, 753
Kaplan, Anne, 199, 205
Kaplan, Carolyn, 6478
Kaplan, Christian, 6400, 6402, 6403
Kaplan, Elizabeth, 513
Kaplan, Jodi, 477
Kaplan, Lewis, 1405, 4400, 4730, 4731, 4732
Kaplan, Melvin, 8907
Kaplan, Richard, 3610
Kaplan, Sheri, 6424, 7986
Kaplan, Steven, 4434
Kaplan, Thomas S, 1447
Kaplan, Thomas S., 5109, 7788
Kaplan, Ph.D., Julius, 2196
Kaplin, Lewis, 4733
Kaplin, Van, 2319

Kaplin Reider, Kara, 546
Kaplunas, Dr. Daniel, 1117
Kapp, Barbara, 1448
Kapp, David, 4428
Kapp, Rich, 6896
Kapp, Richard, 1448
Kappas, Mike, 8747
Kappaz, Phillip, 1718
Kappel, Jim, 6831
Kappel, Mark, 8846
Kappus, Sheryl, 5633
Kaptur, Terese, 4159
Karacson, Annamaria, 897
Karakantas, Susan, 1651
Karakas, Fred, 2381
Karalus, Carol, 677
Karapetian, Patrick, 6115
Karas, Sr Linda, 3802
Karasik, Dr. Stuart, 845
Karbhari, Vistasp M., 5587
Karcher, Jim, 3848
Karel, Rob, 3202
Karen, Woddy, 8071
Karian, D.D.S., Dr. Bernard K., 785
Karidoyanes, Steven, 1207, 2111
Karinski, Edna, 789
Karius, Diane, 1285
Karl, Teressa, 1685, 1686
Karlin, Andrew, 3904
Karlin, Jan, 826
Karmanos, Peter, 7909
Karnap, Kathy, 2283
Karnes, Kevin, 1008
Karnopp, Adam, 5553
Karoub, Carl, 1246
Karoui, Faycal, 466
Karp, Karen, 5114
Karp, Nancy, 85
Karp, Steve, 1014, 2707, 2710, 2711
Karpanty, Kimberly, 542
Karpinski, Kathy, 5129
Karr, Steve, 1509
Karra, Ashok, 4041
Karrenbauer, Julia, 6623
Kartcheske, Paul, 2909
Karter, Jerome, 1219
Karteron, Philippa L., 7691
Karush, Karen, 5172
Karuskopf, Fred, 3007
Karutz, Peter, 304
Kasel, Barb, 3221
Kasenow, Susan, 1938
Kashkin, MD, Kenneth B., 2184
Kasper, Lee, 8007
Kasper, Lewis, 1575
Kasperek, Ellen, 2334
Kass, Artha, 5776
Kass, Randy, 5521
Kass, Roger E., 3468
Kassa, Michael, 6408
Kassa, Tefera, 296
Kasses, Ed, 3825
Kassoy, Caryl F., 4356
Kast, Christina, 2392
Kastelic, Patty, 4159
Kastla, Margaret, 2309
Kastle, Margaret, 2309
Kastner, G Ronald, 2377
Kastner, Simmie, 3674
Katcher, Kyle, 8460
Kate Joshi, Amanda, 3460
Katherine, Kramer, 2418
Kathka, David, 8721
Kathryn Collins, Mary, 3991
Katlin, Stephen, 3453
Katona, Cathy, 2748
Katona Pille, Krista, 3703
Katschke, Richard, 4109
Katselas, Milton, 6073
Katt, Anna Marie, 5377
Katt, Sandy, 7298
Katz, Abigail, 3468
Katz, Bill, 397
Katz, Cheryl, 3395
Katz, Danny, 3039
Katz, Donalee, 351
Katz, Gerry, 2115
Katz, Helene, 1382, 5071

Katz, Irwin, 4467
Katz, Joel, 8548
Katz, Louis H., 6462
Katz, Saul, 7672
Katz, Sherman, 2748
Katz, Sondra R., 7224
Katz,, David, 2905
Katzenmeyer, John, 5320
Katzenstein, Lawrence P., 4921
Katzman, Julee, 7497
Katzman, Marnie, 352
Kauffman, David, 4511
Kauffman, Ellen, 8140
Kauffman, Julia I., 308
Kauffman, Laura, 1781
Kauffman, Rhona S, 819
Kauffman, Scott, 6729
Kauffman, Welz, 4581
Kaufman, Bill, 2190
Kaufman, Elaine, 4988, 7759
Kaufman, Jake, 3803
Kaufman, Judy, 8124
Kaufman, Julie, 2541
Kaufman, Lon S., 6757
Kaufman, Millicent, 1393
Kaufman, Richard, 868, 8362
Kaufman, Steven, 129
Kaufman, Sylvia C., 3235
Kaufman Ilstrup, Christopher, 4019
Kaufman,, Marlin, 3343
Kaufmann, Charles, 379
Kaufmann, Effie, 2034
Kaufmann, Kathy, 414
Kaufmann, Marcia, 900, 901, 4361
Kaufmann Baum, Ann, 1283
Kauk, Cindy, 4940
Kaul, Steve, 8811
kaups, Caty, 7344
Kaus, Stephen, 3184
Kaushagen, Ingrid Joy, 4931
Kautsky, Natasha, 3786
Kauvar, Joanne, 6363
Kauzlaric, Robert, 2937
Kavatian, Ida, 1358
Kavanagh, Eileen, 5050
Kavanagh, Patricia, 2209
Kavanaugh, Dr Patrick, 4636
Kawaguchi, Gary, 6163
Kawahara, Robert M., 2499
Kawakami, Ed, 998
Kawamura, Naomi, 6243
Kawamura, Naomi Ostwald, 6238
Kawano, Hirofumi, 34
Kawaoka, Gerald R., 6674
Kawashima, Kimi, 5699
Kay, Bruce, 8523
Kay, David, 6036
Kay, Kenneth, 3641
Kay, Valerie, 3459
Kay Dixon, Mary, 2357
Kay Hanson, Lisa, 2398
Kay Pelt, Nora, 215
Kay Zimmerman, Ima, 1625
Kaye, Gordon, 6831
Kaye, Marvin, 3539
Kaye, Michael, 2346
Kaye, Robert, 7560
Kayes, Carla, 7693
Kayler, Kyle, 1377
Kaylor, Hugh, 8841
Kays, Daniel, 6319
Kayser, Denise, 4765
Kazanjian, John, 4083
Kazee, Sharon, 1079
Kazee, Tom, 8226
Kazer, Meredith, 6400, 6402, 6403
Kazez, Dr. Daniel, 1569
Kazis, Earle, 2251
Kazis, Eearle W, 2246
Kazmierczak, Thomas T., 3750
Kazmierczak III, Thomas T., 7837
Keagle, Karen, 3593
Keal, Chris, 5979
Kean, Jeff, 6325
Kean, Thomas H., 4998
Kearney, Leigh, 351
Kearney, Patty, 5948
Kearns, Gene, 3059

Kearns, Karen, 4258
Kearns, Patrick Alan, 2673
Kearns, Paul, 4544
Kearns, Robbi, 1433
Keary, David, 302
Keates, Esq., Charles, 1644
Keating, Thomas P., 2015
Keating-Sladic, Clare, 1165
Keaton, Charles, 3069
Keay, Sumiko, 4565
Keches, George, 1180
Kechley, David, 4813
Keck, Jell, 3035
Keck, Michael, 4047
Keck, Robert T., 3382
Kecskemethy, Joe, 1620
Keech, Leo, 769
Keedy, Paige, 2064
Keefe, Annie, 2720
Keefe, Brittany, 222
Keefe, Katherine, 1163
keefe, Kristi, 7220
Keefe, Matthew, 222
Keefe, Quentin W, 7539
Keefer, Betsy, 1669
Keefer, Karen, 5511
Keegstra, Jaime, 3878
Keel, Eric, 65
Keelan, Brenda, 4855
Keeler, Donna, 3945
Keeley, Dawn, 2885
Keeley, Kamala, 5065
Keeley, Steve, 6181
Keeling, Kenneth, 5489
Keeling, Tabitha, 3336
Keeling, Trudy, 1700
Keen, David, 1832
Keenan, Allen, 1585
Keenan, Cheryl, 1383
Keenan, John, 3878
Keenan, Nick, 4111
Keene, John, 2005
Keene, Karin, 5216
Keene Cooper, Kara, 6626
Keene III, James H., 4947
Keeney, Sally J., 1478
Keens, Kathleen, 7426, 7427
Keeter, Skip, 2138
Keeton, Leslie, 4822
Keevil, Jeff, 7418
Keffer, Lindsay, 8369
Kegler, Angela, 1683
Kegler, PhD, Angela, 1683
Kegley, Elizabeth, 3160
Keglovits, David, 8058
Kehoe, Bobbie, 5007
Keicher, Roger, 3428
Keifer, Ed, 7988
Keiffer-Rinkerman, Vicki, 6394
Keigwin, Larry, 444
Keil, Amanda, 5134
Keilbach, Kurt, 2675
Keilitz, Douglas, 2194
Keimach, Brad, 790
Keiser, Anne, 1983, 1984
Keith, Brian, 1646
Keith, Daryle, 6903
Keith, Kenneth, 131, 132
Keith, RuAnn, 6384
Keith, Sue, 2264
Kekas, Dennis, 7906
Keleman, Karen, 1813
Kell, Barbara, 6457
Kellachan, Dan, 5215
Kelleher, Barbara, 6504
Kelleher, Leslie, 869
Kelleher, Michael, 5072, 7673
Kelleher, Neil J., 5211
Kellenher, Kenneth, 4311
Keller, Barrie, 3165
Keller, Dave, 7335
Keller, Eileen, 1634
Keller, Emily, 6076
Keller, Kathleen, 8129
Keller, Kevin, 351
Keller, Linda, 1577
Keller, Melanie, 887
Keller, Michelle, 1571

1183

Executive Name Index

Keller, Patrick, 6186
Keller, R. Scott, 3202
Keller, Rodney, 6481
Keller, Susan, 184
Keller Moon, Heidi, 3864
Kellerman, Keri, 4082
Kellerman, Keri, 3252
Kelley, Andrew, 278
Kelley, Audrey, 5772
Kelley, Betty, 3054, 7075
Kelley, Cameron, 4032
Kelley, Dana, 14, 6032, 6033
Kelley, Heidi, 969
Kelley, Heidi J., 1367
Kelley, Joe, 4960
Kelley, Karen, 2894
Kelley, Karla, 249
Kelley, Kathy, 3984
Kelley, Priscilla, 4740, 4741
Kelley, Robert, 112, 2525, 2541
Kelley, Stephanie, 5584
Kelley, Steve, 2079, 2353
Kelley, Susan, 4270
Kelley, Tim, 790
Kelley, Wade, 2358
Kelley, Warren, 3558
Kelley Sammis, Erin, 2009
Kellogg, Jan, 8693
Kellogg, Nia, 152
Kellogg, Sue, 1252
Kellogg, Tonia, 5389
Kelly, Ann, 658
Kelly, Barbara, 1979
Kelly, Barbara, 7193
Kelly, Brenda E., 2960
Kelly, Brendan, 4475
Kelly, Bridget, 1605
Kelly, Christine, 4257
Kelly, Cynthia, 242
Kelly, Dave, 1853
Kelly, Emerson, 4970
Kelly, Franklin, 4416, 4429
Kelly, GloriBelle, 1753
Kelly, Jackie, 3037
Kelly, Jana, 6227
Kelly, Jim, 7990
Kelly, Jo-Ann S, 5437
Kelly, Jo-Ann S., 3799
Kelly, Julianne, 5068
Kelly, Kathleen, 2116, 4246
Kelly, Laura, 726, 5887
Kelly, Mara, 790
Kelly, Michael T, 6748, 6750
Kelly, Monica, 252, 1151, 2090, 4746
Kelly, Nancy, 1965
Kelly, Patrick, 8315
Kelly, Peter, 7244
Kelly, Rebecca, 476
Kelly, Ryan, 985
Kelly, Sara, 2960
Kelly, Sean, 8362
Kelly, Sue, 790
Kelly, Susan, 1773, 2315
Kelly, Tony, 2595
Kelly, M.D., Pamela, 4616
Kelner, Russell, 1323
Kelsch, Nicole, 253
Kelsch, Tyler, 6390
Kelsheimer, Jerry L., 8005
Kelso, Amy S., 1478
Keltner, Karen, 1909
Kelty, Dr Mary, 4898
Kely, Erica, 1436
Kemble, Ray, 4357
Kemerling, Alice, 4854
Kemmerer, Cindy, 8121
Kemp, Jenny, 6389
Kemp, Judy, 2964
Kemp, Nancy, 5943
Kemp Thompson, Carla, 1722
Kemper, Alene, 4270
Kempskie, Jeff, 148
Kempton, Barry, 4883, 4884
Kemson, J, 1192
Kenaley, Debra, 947
Kenar, Talin, 598
Kenchen, Armeei, 508
Kend, Peter, 5096, 5097

Kendall, Christopher, 1160, 1223
Kendall, Greg, 6386
Kendall, Haley, 1525
Kendall, Henry, 8057
Kendall, Janet, 8051
Kendall, Jonathan, 2680
Kendall, Kay, 141, 2061
Kendall, Kelley, 6746
Kendall, Paulette, 2470
Kendall, Sara, 1808, 1809, 5808
Kendall, Suzanne, 3134
Kenderdine, Henry, 5447
Kenderdine, Suzanne, 5447
Kendrick, Cheryl, 6245, 6248
Kendrick, Donald, 1879
Kendrick, James M., 7712
Kendrick, Matt, 1284
Kendziorsk, Clint, 4820
Kener, David, 3466, 7709
Kenerson, Gayle, 7248
Kenig, Leseley, 4026
Kenin, Jean, 1358
Keninll, Rohana, 5159
Kenleigh, Alexis, 4641
Kennard, John, 2130, 4825
Kennebeck, John, 4247
Kennebeck, Scott, 4920
Kennedy, Bill, 7121
Kennedy, Brian P, 8017
Kennedy, Brian P., 8017
Kennedy, Bryan, 8378
Kennedy, Charry, 7506
Kennedy, Christopher, 5161
Kennedy, Courtney, 188
Kennedy, David, 860, 6449
Kennedy, Deborah, 3373
Kennedy, Debralee L., 4801
Kennedy, Diane, 5912, 5913, 5914
Kennedy, Elizabeth, 4243
Kennedy, Ellen, 7249
Kennedy, Floy, 5948
Kennedy, James W., 428
Kennedy, Jerry, 6729
Kennedy, John W, 3291
Kennedy, Karen, 4, 1021
Kennedy, Kevin W., 2234
Kennedy, Leslie, 4487
Kennedy, Lynn, 1002
Kennedy, Mary, 3288
Kennedy, Megan, 371
Kennedy, Patrick, 7614
Kennedy, Richard, 7790
Kennedy, Robert M, 7260
Kennedy, Sarah, 93, 2594
Kennedy, Seth, 3409
Kennedy, Steve, 3284
Kennedy, Susanne G., 3455
Kennedy, Willie B., 6252
Kennedy Clark, Kristin, 466
Kennedy Smith, Jean, 956, 958
Kennell, Carly, 540
Kenner, Doug, 1290
Kenneth Morell, George, 680
Kenney, Brad, 3187
Kenney, Bradford T, 7171
Kenney, Crane, 6761
Kenney, David, 3355
Kenney, Jessica, 2091
Kenney, Wes, 909, 910
Kenney, Will, 4594, 6817, 6818
Kenny, Emily, 3105
Kenny, Fionnuala, 2609
Kenny, Jack, 1877
Kenny, Sheila, 7084, 7085
Kenny, Wes, 1958
Kenny-Urban, Anne, 1785
Kensok, Jim, 1807
Kent, David, 1972
Kent, Emily, 5052
Kent, George A, 715
Kent, Jill, 959
Kent, Judy, 4069
Kent, Matt, 135
Kent, Terri, 3738
Kent, Thad, 1577
Kent, Esq., Thomas L., 131, 132
Kent,, Drew, 2903
Kenworthy, Jane E, 882

Kenyan, Thomas, 4409
Kenyon, Matt, 4113
Keogh, Andy, 5851
Keolanui, Dayva, 6678
Keough, Michael, 2020
Kepa, Judy, 6148
Kepl, Daniel, 870
Kepler, David, 1247, 1248
Kepley, Laura, 7963, 7964, 7965, 7966
Kepley, Scott, 879, 6307, 6309
Kepple Jr, Thomas R, 5456
Kerber, Jenifer, 315
Kerbs, Amy K, 5469
Kerby, Rick, 2759
Kerchoff, Steve, 1821
Kerekes, Zoltan, 8151
Kereny, Kelli, 5963
Kerins, Kelly, 1035, 1038, 2042
Kerkhof, Lynn, 3
Kerley, Cathy, 5616
Kerley, Jean, 2183
Kerley, Mimi, 6678
Kerlin, Bill, 2625
Kern, Ann, 325
Kern, Dennis, 8547
Kern, Doug, 6908
Kern, Jerome H, 905
Kern, Marty S, 8215
Kern, Molly, 3262
Kern Anderson, Linda, 3886, 3888
Kern DC PhC, Donald, 6976
Kern Paste, Gail, 2736
Kernaghan, Maryellen, 8818
Kernahan, Dennis A., 1995
Kerney, John, 1622
Kerney-Quillen, Suzanne, 1693
Kernodle, Jr, John R, 1495
Kerr, Alexander, 8362
Kerr, Allan, 618
Kerr, Anne, 6541
Kerr, Anne B., 6541, 6542
Kerr, Bryan, 3827
Kerr, Nanne, 4459
Kerr, Patrick, 2991
Kerr-Berry, Julie, 3234
Kerrick, Wallace Glenn, 977
Kerry, Kris, 6052
Kerry Boyles, Adam, 1861, 4186
Kerschbaum, Rob, 3209
Kersey, Don, 3826
Kersey, James, 6520
Kersey, Wade, 2886
Kersh, Nunally, 596, 3869, 5534
Kersh, Rogan, 1508
Kershaw, Stewart, 682
Kersy, Don, 3824
Kerwin, Cornelius M., 6476
Kerwin, Patrick, 8127
Keshishian, Moira, 3314
Kessel, Courtney, 7943
Kessel, Patrick, 1256
Kessel, Robert, 865
Kessen, John, 1183, 1185
Kessick, Steve, 8631
Kessler, Allan, 2594
Kessler, Andjela, 2846, 2862
Kessler, Andjela, 6627
Kessler, Ann, 6885
Kessler, Chad, 3503
Kessler, David, 2619
Kessler, Jennifer, 1436, 1441
Kessler, Kristin, 1588
Kessler, Laura, 220
Kessler, Lawrence, 2764
Kessler, Martin, 1520
Kessler, Melvin P, 963
Kessler, Michael, 5461
Kessler, Patricia, 5372
Kessler, Richard, 5159
Kessler, Sean, 5324
Kestner, R. Steven, 5316
Kestner, R. Steven, 7962
Ketcham, Sara, 1010
Ketchum, Allegra, 3854
Ketchum, John A., 7234, 7255
Ketner, Robert C., 1495
Kettelle, Steve, 5065
Ketterer, James P, 1392

Ketterer, Marty, 5831
Kettler, Kim, 6644
Keuchle, Lauralynn, 4866
Kevis, Tom, 7605
Key, Tom, 2867
Keyes, Jeffrey, 4787
Keyes, Kendal, 1801
Keyes, Stephen, 1548
Keyes, Trevor, 3193
Keyser, LaShawn, 3447
Keyser Phillips, Leigh, 8504
Keyt, Aaron, 8598
Khajinova, Rada, 4160
Khalifa, Jayne, 3270
Khalili, Mariam, 2356
Khan, Ricardo, 3377
Khanna, Prema, 6333
Kharatian, Roudolf, 265
Khasawneh, Rami, 6832
Khattar, Renu, 8402, 8408
Khele, Linda, 6905
Khimm, Christina, 5188
Khosrovi, Behzad, 847
Khoury, Colleen, 1150
Khuner, Jonathan, 1868
Ki Lau, Woon, 4284
Kibelsbeck, Erik, 1365
Kibelsheck, Erik, 5092
Kibort, Charles, 4742
Kickel, Mary, 3512
Kickles PhD, Mary Kay, 5972
Kicklighter, Deborah, 6661
Kidd, Chris, 7136
Kidd, James, 5736
Kidd, Onallee, 3065
Kidd, Steve, 3859
Kido, Marshall, 4204
Kidwell, Dave, 6725, 6726
Kidwell, Jacqueline, 2102
Kidwell, Linda, 2425
Kiedrowski, Jay, 7351
Kieffer, Paul B., 7629
Kiefhaber, Kathryn, 4159
Kielsing, Bruce, 888
Kielty, Linda, 7348
Kiely III, W. Leo, 6352, 6360, 6367, 6368, 6369, 6370
Kienow, Heather, 1150
Kientz, Tom, 3286
Kieran, Mark, 3378
Kiermaier, Daniel, 1902
Kies Folpe, Emily, 5168
Kiesel, David, 3077
Kieser, Bob, 4935
Kieser, John, 1925
Kiesewetter, Erica, 1401
Kiesler, Kenneth, 1223
Kiester, Kenneth, 1320
Kiger, Jennifer, 2699, 2700, 6427
Kiggins, Lona, 785
Kiker, Kim, 5595
Kilbourn, Jennifer, 7617
Kilburn, Tonya, 553
Kiley, Clare, 8535
Kiley, Paul, 1207
Kilgore, Stephen, 4809
Kilgus, James F., 1680
Kilian, Charles, 4148
Kilkelly, Janet E., 2062, 2063, 6847
Killacky, John R., 8504
Kille, Ruth, 8016
Kille, Rutte, 8016
Killebrew, Chelsey, 4179
Killian, Erin, 6500
Killick, Linda, 835
Killingsworth, Karen, 6279
Killion, Jennifer, 3297, 7448
Killips, Kevin M., 4596
Kilmartin, Tim, 3209
Kilmer, R, 5836
Kilpane, Dan, 3712
Kilpatrick, Annette, 1629
Kim, David, 1647
Kim, Deborah, 875
Kim, Hee-Jung, 910
Kim, Jeff, 6281
Kim, Jihyun, 1141
Kim, Jiyoung, 5073

Executive Name Index

Kim, John, 2218
Kim, Julie, 1535, 1609
Kim, K. Dennis, 2143
Kim, Kyu-Young, 1272
Kim, Maureen, 1419
Kim, Minji, 4559
Kim, Paula, 5994
Kim, Scott, 107
Kimaszewski, Maria, 5966
Kimball, Allan, 6792
Kimball, Chris, 6313
Kimball, Joan, 1651
Kimbell, John, 3134
Kimbell, Jon, 3134
Kimbrell, Marketa, 3450
Kimmel Meyers, Patti, 2776
Kimmelman, Douglas W., 7545
Kimpel, Tom, 690
Kimpton, Jeffrey, 286, 4850
Kimsey, Kevin, 2896
Kimura, Wakana, 40, 6163
Kin, Jeffery, 6585
Kinavey, Kelsey, 1614
Kincaias, Tess, 2878
Kincaid, Jack, 3332
Kincart, R. Jeffrey, 974
Kindall, Kara V, 3915
Kindell, Ron, 7991
Kinder, Bethany, 1817
Kinder, Charles, 1383
Kindred, Don, 1874
King, Alan, 3788
King, Alex, 4060
King, Alonzo, 71
King, Arnold, 2665
King, Ben, 7683
King, Brian, 3739
King, Carlyn, 8722
King, Cathleen, 2603
King, Christie, 2425, 2541
King, Curtis, 5607
King, Cynthia, 1973
King, Don, 969
King, Ellen, 634
King, Evangel, 78
King, Harriet, 6642
King, James, 7707
King, Jayne, 28
King, Jeff, 1722
King, Jennifer, 1133
King, John, 615
King, Julie, 1531
King, Katherine, 1600, 5417
King, Kathy, 284
King, Kenny, 8411
King, Kevin, 1637
King, Lucas, 1062
King, Martha, 4689
King, Mertedith, 2600
King, Patricia, 3433, 5061
King, Paul, 565
King, Randall, 2603
King, Russell, 68
King, Rusty, 1699
King, Stephen, 4171
King, Stephen P, 4100
King, Suzanne, 2536
King, Teena, 1690
King, Teresa, 1723
King, Theresa, 5687
King, Valarie, 7894
King, Victoria, 1253
King Cole, Sara, 1598, 3780, 5414
King Jr, Woodie, 3526, 3531, 3535
King Ruggaber, Amy, 3705
King Shepherd, Doris, 1128
King, Jr., Eugene, 553
Kingdom, Robert, 1607
Kingery, Craig, 1307
Kingsbury, David, 1940, 1941
Kingston, Nancy, 1430
Kington, Raynard, 6997, 6998, 6999
Kinkade, Laura, 2349
Kinkade, Niki, 4689
Kinnaird, Helen, 6238, 6243
Kinne, Mary, 7846
Kinnear, Connie M., 4770
Kinnery, Mary, 1491

Kinney, Amber, 8349
Kinney, Charles, 959, 1994
Kinney, Mary, 5242
Kinney, Melinda, 3770
Kinney, Ryan, 1104, 1105
Kinney Frost, Douglas, 2258
Kinnison, Sharon, 3070
Kinser, Holly, 3827
Kinsey, Kari, 6938
Kinsey III, James W, 4350
Kinsman, Chad, 6449
Kinsman, Pat, 4180
Kinstle, Bob, 3067
Kinstle, Jimi, 3129
Kintz, Liz, 5884
Kinzey, Virginia, 446
Kipe, Andres, 730
Kipp, Lisa, 564
Kipp, Robert A, 1283
Kippenberger, Terry, 8784
Kipper, Joel, 3866
Kipper, Olivia, 1609
Kipris, Lois, 1398
Kiraly, Frank, 3874
Kirazian, Lisa, 2566
Kirby, Carolyn, 3110
Kirby, Eileen, 6375
Kirby, Elizabeth, 488
Kirby, Liz, 4
Kirby, Lori, 8684
Kirby, Mary, 1091
Kirby, William J, 1042
Kirchdoerffer, Ed, 4990, 7557
Kirchner, Jennifer, 4689
Kirchner, Shawn, 1886
Kirchner, Wendy, 678
Kirimica, Irfan, 7640
Kirinovic, Tom, 7278
Kirk, Denise, 7221
Kirk, James, 856, 857
Kirk, Joe, 8033
Kirk, Joe L., 4902
Kirk, John R., 1411
Kirk, Kara, 2337
Kirk, Kim, 3971
Kirk, Lee, 1243, 4853
Kirk, Paul, 7687
Kirk, Sean, 1739
Kirkendall, Jeff, 6386
Kirkendall, Joe, 3986
Kirkendall, Linda, 4537, 6703
Kirkham, Karen, 3618
Kirkpatric, Brad, 2375
Kirkpatrick, Brad, 1784
Kirkpatrick, Jim, 626
Kirkpatrick, Kevan, 7409
Kirkwood, James, 1388
Kirlcham, Carol, 5675
Kirmser, Fran, 406
Kim, Emily, 66
Kirschbaum, Donald, 943
Kirschman, Alfred, 5494
Kirschner, Lisa, 3867
Kirshner, Howard, 8295
Kirsner, Steve, 6268
Kirstein, Lincoln, 466
Kirtland, John, 2032
Kirwan, Roger T., 6090
Kisanga, Christian, 3788
Kiser, Walt, 7128
Kish, Eva, 301
Kishlock, Lori, 8132
Kisling, Amie, 3066
Kisling, Jeremy, 3066
Kiss, Elizabeth, 6642, 6643
Kissek, John, 1736
Kisselle, Amanda, 1752
Kissler, John, 3622, 5205
Kisslo, Kitty, 1481
Kistler, David, 3332
Kistler, Julie, 2978
Kitayama, Michiko, 6494, 6495
Kitchell, Elizabeth, 514
Kitchen, Gail, 3621
Kitchen, Heather M., 3947
Kitelinger, Becca, 4129
Kitner, Clifford, 8136
Kitsman, Charles B., 1700

Kitsopoulos, Constantine, 1389, 1577, 5379
Kittelberger, Kathleen, 499
Kitterman, Susan, 1086
Kittner, Harriett, 6398
Kittrell, Francis, 2352
Kitts, Brian, 6353, 6360, 6367, 6368, 6369, 6370
Kittsley, Julie, 3427
Kitzmiller, Shirley, 1221
Klaase, Ray, 972
Kladja, Connie, 7285
Kladzyk, Sarah, 4848
Klapper, David, 3013
Klareich, Beth, 845
Klaris, Edward, 135
Klaskin, Lisa, 2077
Klassen, Damon, 5037
Klaus, Bob, 7880
Klausner, Florence, 2173
Klautsch, Richard, 6683, 6684, 6686, 6688, 6689
Klecanda, Patricia, 2189
Kleefeld, Megan, 3393
Kleeman, Laura, 3591
Kleiman, Rose, 3012
Klein, Alex, 310
Klein, Alycia, 5963
Klein, Bob, 5934
Klein, Carole, 783
Klein, Doretta, 8684
Klein, Doug, 1300
Klein, Dr. Lonnie, 1356
Klein, Emmy, 3927
Klein, James M., 8061, 8064
Klein, Julie, 3729
Klein, Kathleen, 536
Klein, Lisa, 1036
Klein, Margaret, 5982
Klein, Mary Anne, 4595
Klein, Michael R., 2747
Klein, Patrick, 2540
Klein, Rick, 5982
Klein, Sarah, 1588
Klein, Scott Richard, 3758
Klein, Teresa, 186
Klein-Brown, Jacquelyn, 6286
Kleinbub, Angelina, 796
Kleinerman, Kay, 6254
Kleinfeld, Lauren, 4488, 6588
Kleinhans, Becky, 6325
Kleinknecht, Daniel, 2069
Kleinmann, Kurt, 3953
Kleinsasser, Alan, 790
Kleinsasser, Jerry, 757
Kleinschmidt, Alan, 1927
Kleinschmidt, Volker, 2036
Kleinstiver, Wayne, 2016
Kleiser, David, 5053
Klem, Alan, 3335, 4949
Klementz, Nicholas, 1665
Klemme, Katie, 2966
Klemmt, Lyle, 6529, 6532
Klenjoski, Regina, 34
Klessig, Karl, 885
Klevan, Dr. Rob, 4255
Klevan, Rob, 6317
Klick, Susan, 1627
Kliger, Jack, 1407
Klima, Roman, 3363
Klimpel, Jonathan, 4920
Klimplova, Petra, 8525
Kline, Amy, 8174
Kline, Brand, 4122
Kline, Joan, 3971
Kline, Lindsey, 616
Kline, Randal, 4309, 4312
Kline, Randall, 855, 4309, 4312
Kline, Wayne, 616
Kline Ugaz, Shalisa, 5154
Kline,, Lisa, 3229
Kling, Hannes, 796
Kling, Michael P., 285
Kling, J.D. Joyce, 2386
Klinga, Gunnar, 1623, 2322
Klinger, Kristen, 207
Klinger, Lori, 529
Klinger, Mia, 529
Klinger Welch, Mia, 529
Klingher, Michael, 2720
Klink, Jeanne, 4971

Klinke, Louise H, 498
Klitze, Rege, 7028
Kloc, Floyd P., 1251
Klopchin, Heather, 298
Klopfenstein, Kailey, 162
Klos, Fran, 2395
Klosky, Linda, 5034
Kloss, Cindy, 8289
Klotz, John, 714
Klotz, Kevin M., 2355
Klotz, Kurt M, 965
Klotz, Paul, 1841
Kluender, Janet, 3895
Klug, Eric, 7505
Klug, Lynn, 48, 49
Klug, Misty, 5826
Klugherz, Laura, 5085
Klunk, Clare, 1625
Klushmire, Robin, 3321, 7485
Kluttig, Roland, 904
Kment, Margie, 2522
Knabe, Faith, 2178
Knapp, Andrew, 2281
Knapp, Arianna, 3134
Knapp, Barry, 4355
Knapp, Dana M., 3288
Knapp, Eric Dale, 1971
Knapp, Gunnar, 4157
Knapp, Maggie, 3967, 3975
Knapp, Maria, 3420, 3505
Knapp, Mary, 4056
Knapp, Patti, 3845
Knaus, Peter, 930
Kneeland, Jennifer L., 3128
Knerly Jr, Stephen J, 7962
Knickerbocker, Calvin, 4971
Knickrehm, Glenn, 7230
Knierim, LeeAnn, 14, 6032
Knigge, Larry, 6113
Knight, Cynthia, 7600
Knight, Gloria, 5239
Knight, Hyperion, 5070
Knight, Joann, 7031
Knight, John F., 5918
Knight, Mary-Jo P, 2248
Knight, Mike, 1683
Knight, Tricia, 704
Knight - Jaffrey, Amy, 4974
Knighton, Bit, 498
Knippel, Mark, 3780, 8083
Knipple, Mark, 5414
Knobel, Tom, 3435
Knobloch, Karen, 1779
Knodi, Kevin, 7370
Knoepfel, Gerald, 5873
Knoles, Amy, 772
Knopf, Robert, 7657
Knopp, Cindy, 3004
Knopp, Seth, 5716, 8507
Knott, Carol, 4704
Knott, Don, 6944
Knott, Paula, 1134
Knotts, Martha, 2354
Knouse, Frank, 4198
Knowles, Jack, 1687
Knowles, Katherine, 7243
Knowles, Lawrence J, 7205
Knowles, Sharon, 2168
Knowles, Terry, 1886
Knowles, Vanessa, 2488
knowlton, Alex, 7737
Knowlton, Gwen, 708
Knox, James B, 3192
Knox, Kenny, 2969
Knox, Ruth A, 6650
Knox, Steve, 8081
Knox, Steve, 3778
Knuckles, Jill, 6377, 6378, 6380
Knudsen, Maiken, 2334
Knutson, Katie, 8243
Kober, Dieter, 1033
Kobler, Raymond, 868
Koch, Arend-Julius, 1713
Koch, Dick, 3887
Koch, Douglas D., 2351
Koch, Eric, 7459
Koch, Paul, 3750
Kochan, Alex, 8569

1185

Executive Name Index

Kochan, Michael, 3376
Kochan, Michael, 7571
Kocher, Amber, 3794
Kocher, Kevin, 3794
Kocher, Stephanie, 1750
Kochmann, Chris, 4179
Kocivar, Ira, 1383
Kodadek, Ellen, 5073, 7827
Kodeih, Allison, 544
Koe, Jonathan, 1439
Koebley, Jennifer, 3855
Koehler, Jim, 6758
Koehler, Joel, 1560
Koehler, Steven, 3064
Koehn, David, 5391
Koehn, Mr. David, 3768
Koelsch, Christopher, 1887
Koen, Genie, 3770
Koenig, Dr Laura, 4157
Koenig, Robert, 545
Koenig, Steve, 5350
Koenig, Victoria, 48, 49
Koening, Steve, 1556
Koeninger, Dr. Mary, 1705
Koenning, Vick, 8718, 8719
Koep, Ph.D., Jeffrey, 4958
Koepke, Bob, 725
Koepke, Kathy, 725
Koeppel, Linnea, 4122
Koeppel-Taylor, Liana, 2488
Koerner, Debby, 4894
Koerner, Kirsten, 254
Koerper, Ronn, 3748
Koesten, Stewart S., 3287
Koester, Jolene, 6195
Kofahl, Tim, 3615
Koffin, Mike, 2706
Koffin, Nancy, 2706
Koffler, Abby, 6486
Koffman, David, 6638
Koffskey, Dawn, 606, 610
Kogan, Anne, 6473
Kogan, Deen, 3838, 8160
Kogan Weinreb, Alice, 1774
Kogod, Bonnie, 142
Koh, Milly, 1456
Koh, Vincent, 1456
Kohberger, Ken, 5876, 8710
Kohl, Lawrence, 812
Kohl, Rhonda, 3901
Kohler, Cathy, 3316
Kohler, David R., 2304
Kohler, Ruth, 5841
Kohler-Hall, Kristine, 1043
Kohlhaas, Seth, 6722, 6723
Kohlhepp, Robert J, 5307, 5308, 5310, 5311
Kohlstedt, Marian, 1868
Kohn, Dixie, 7464
Kohn, Gloria, 4923
Kohnhorst, Bridgette, 5582
Kohr, C. Byron, 1359
Koijane, Ed, 70
Koinzan, Ron, 6961, 6963, 6964, 6965
Koivoigue, Hamidou, 514
Kojovic, Anna, 1834
Kokolus, Greg, 5460
Kokoskie, Douglas S, 7580
Kolack, Greg, 2036
Kolasinski, Johnny, 2599
Kolb, Leah, 4166
Kolb, Margaret, 2272
Kolchanova, Tatiana, 1811
Koldenhoven, James, 1114
Kole, Tange, 6961, 6962, 6963, 6964, 6965
Kolek, John, 6239
Koleske, Josh, 8665, 8669
Koleski, Josh, 8666
Kolkhurst Ruddy, Kathy, 723
Kollar, Allan, 2835
Kollra, Ernie, 2774
Kolman, Barry, 1780
Kolman, T L, 2494
Kolodge, Christine, 4081
Kolodziej, Joseph, 4801
Kolokoff, Jeannette, 1743
Kolquist, Ken, 293
Kolson, Rob, 6727
Kolstad, Mike, 4108

Koltak, Ronald J., 7982
Komaiko, Libby, 2928
Komassa, Roy, 6203
Komlesk, Gabrielle, 3363
Konar, Sandra, 4291
Kondak, Ann, 1230, 1237
Kondziolka, Michael, 2130, 4825
Konecky, Isobel Robins, 7766
Kongsgaard, John, 838, 4286
Kongsgaard, Maggy, 838, 4286
Konik, David, 8025
Konkel, Richard, 1669
Konkle, Robert, 827
Konowitz, Suzanne, 400
Kontos, Lydia, 5129, 7759
Konyak, Kris, 1455
Konz, John, 2150
Koon, Janice, 6625
Koonce, Lee, 393
Koonin, Steeve, 6625
Koons, Natalie, 129
Koontz, David, 794
Koop, Nancy, 1515
Koop, Sarah, 1420
Koosman, Tolby, 5571
Kopac, Sarah, 569
Kopani, Gvozden, 2757
Kopans, Matthew, 2201
Kopelman, Roberta, 1218
Kopf, John Gross, 4462
Kopielski, Camille, 2044, 2045
Kopp, Bryan, 6415, 6416
Kopp, Jarrod, 3769
Kopp, Lee, 99
Kopp, Mara, 6255
Kopp, Meagan, 7885
Kopp, Phil, 6336
Koppel, Allison, 2679, 2680
Koppel, Lenore P., 1542
Koppel, Tina, 3173
Kopper, Beverly, 8711
Koralewicz, Peter, 6513
Koran, Janet M, 6785, 6787, 6788
Koran, Noel, 2389
Korbel, Josh, 4321
Korbell, Mr. John C., 8454
Korbitz, Ron, 2054
Korbrs, Kristi, 4913
Korchin, Season, 2590
Korchynsky, Casey, 5049, 5120
Kordes, Gesa, 1097, 4609
Korelitz, Ruthy, 5304
Koresh, Alon, 576
Koresh, Ronen, 576
Korf, Anthony, 1439
Korinko, Matthew, 2758
Korkmas, Marguerite, 1734
Korkos, Melody, 6292
Korman, Jerry, 403
Kormberger, Tim, 7196
Korn, Donna, 3718, 7980
Korn, Sheila, 845
Kornbluh, Walter, 109
Korney, Cornelia, 1893
Koropeckyj-Cox, Matt, 4451
Korot, Judy, 1456
Korslien, Renae, 7940
Korstange, Patrick, 139
Kort, Stephen, 1122
Korth, Jonathan, 4527
Korza, Pam, 4367
Korzec, Melissa, 6856
Korz, Carl, 4117
Kos, Kristen, 3882
Kosaka, Hirokagu, 6163
Kosaka, Hirokazu, 40
Kosar, Jennifer, 1439
Koscso, Michae, 1524
Koscso, Mike, 900, 901
Koshgarian, Richard, 1120
Kosinski, Doroth, 4431
Koski Janners, Candace E., 4845
Koslow Hines, Pamela, 387
Koslowski, Andre, 584
Kosmatka, James, 3712, 7967
Kosoff, Susan, 3143
Kossler, Deborah, 3585
Koster, Diane, 221

Koster, Emlyn, 7562
Kostreva, Jenny, 4124
Kostusiak, Thomas, 7650
Kotch, Trent, 3705
Kothman, Mary, 1092
Kotik, Peter, 1373
Kotis, Constance, 2264
Kotler, David A, 2316
Kotsanis, Kia, 5079
Kottyan, Tim, 3665
Kotval, Tom, 1260
Kotze, Mike, 2064
Kough, Kelly, 6887
Koulman, Bryan, 573
Kouma, Cecelia, 2566
Kouting, Don, 5944
Koutrakos, Vivian, 3605
Kovac, Kim Peter, 6471
Kovac, Larry, 5986
Kovach, Bob, 7991
Kovach, Sarah, 1541
Kovacs, Kim, 1875
Kovacs, Scott, 2383
Koval, Volga, 6058, 6059, 6060, 6061
Kovala, Irene, 5956
Kovalesky, Kelly, 1488
Kovcic, Zoran, 3815
Kovitz, Bob, 742
Kowalik, Thomas F., 5048
Kowalke, Kim, 1462
Kowalski, Peggy, 8153
Kowatch, Justin, 4841
Kowski, James A, 5120
Koykkar, Joseph N, 696
Koza, John, 1904
Kozadayev, Sergey, 224
Kozera, Mark, 2802
Kozerski, Patti, 2722
Koziol, Linda, 7699
Kozloff, Jessica, 5432
Kozlowski, Dolores, 4833, 7280
Kozlowski, Eugene, 6797, 6798, 6799
Krabach, Larry, 7325
Kradel, Suzanne, 1629
Kraeger, Amy, 1728
Kraemer, Jayne, 8244
Kraemer, Jennifer, 4115
Kraemer, Matthew, 1620
Krafft-Bellsky, Kristi, 2140
Kraft, Anne, 2827
Kraft, Debra, 1983, 1984
Kraft, Dr James, 4636
Kraft, John, 5018
Kraft, Leigh 4068, 4072
Kraft, Meryl, 8295
Kraft, Michelle, 5651
Kraft, Nettie, 3917, 5581
Kraft, Rachel, 2939
Krafthofer, Shaun, 6446
Kraine, Cynthia, 1047
Krajewski, Michael, 1007, 1354, 1644, 2018, 4503
Krajniak, Miranda, 7303
Krajsa, Fusie, 4445
Krak, Jean, 5120
Kraklio, Michael, 3885
Kraklow, Kristen, 4109
Kral, Marty, 1515
Kralicek, Jason, 3292, 7430
Krall, Dr. Jim, 4193
Kramer, Cristy S., 2079
Kramer, Donald, 386
Kramer, Elissa, 5135
Kramer, Eric, 1451
Kramer, Judy, 1948, 1949
Kramer, Kim, 5333
Kramer, Patricia, 1983, 1984
Kramer, Randall, 7629
Kramer, Rebecca, 4094
Kramer-Fitzgerald, Michelle, 2726, 8184
Kramme, Marilyn, 6985
Kranak, Jamie, 2208
Krane, Victoria, 2641
Kranenburg, Philip, 795
Kranich, Denise, 8523
Kranicke, Michelle, 214
Krantz, Roberta F, 5020
Kranzberg, Ken, 310

Krasco, KJ, 7166
Krashan, Matthew, 8608
Krasny, Peter, 3524
Krasser, Jerry, 8033
Krassovska, Nathalie, 218
Kratochwill, Carol, 4106, 5828
Kratochwill, Jenn, 319
Kratt, Laura, 7841
Kratzer, Jodi, 2164
Kratzer, Patricia, 3120
Kraus, Andrew, 6066, 6070, 6071, 6072
Kraus, Joe, 1304
Kraus, Lisa, 5436
Kraus, Theresa, 6105
Krause, Cathryn, 4262
Krause, Darrell, 3989
Krause, Leigh Flippin, 5278
Krause, Sandra, 6183
Krauskopf, Fred, 3007
Krauss, Donna, 2343
Krausz, Jeanne, 2827
Kravchak PhD, Richard, 771
Kravchuk, Scott, 8297
Kravec, Mike, 6408
Krebs, Eric, 3534
Krebs, Jonathan, 560
Krebs, S. Warren, 3163
Krebs, Tom, 6375
Kreeger, Julian H, 976
Krehbiel, Lee, 6027
Krehbiel, Lee E., 4187
Kreider, Lisa, 8129
Kreider, Paul, 1314
Kreider, Steven P., 1244
Kreig, Tyler, 2897
Kreigh, Billy, 4611
Kreilick, Susanna, 498
Kreiman, Kerry, 631
Kreinberg, Steven, 8150
Kreinces, Matthew, 5075
Kreitler, John, 1964
Kreitz, Jennifer, 1309, 1310
Krekhofer, Catherine, 2398
Krelis, George, 8655
Krell, Roberto, 7773
Kreloff, Dr. Herschel, 742
Kremen, David, 3844
Kremer, Chris, 4640
Kremer, Elizabeth, 5543
Kremer, Susan, 8019
Krendl, Kathy A, 5372
Kress, Bille, 1823
Kress, Joel, 7645, 7671
Kressaty, Sarah, 2373
Kreuger, Timothy, 898
Kreulen, Colonel Douglas, 6338
Kreuter, Shellee, 4281
Kreutz, Charlotte, 3524
Kreutzer Barber, Leah, 340
Krevitt, Shelly, 6728
Krey, Peggy, 8684
Kriaski, Susan, 3900
Kridler, Douglas F, 5325
Kriebs, John, 6104
Kriegel, I. Stanley, 5053
Krieger, David, 5188
Krieger, Hillary, 602
Krieger, Stuart, 6221, 6222, 6223, 6226
Krieger, Yoni, 5188
Kriegler, Keri, 6598
Krienke, Joe, 2452
Kriha Dye, Peggy, 2283
Krikawa, Andrew, 2390
Krikawa, Jennifer, 2390
Krinksy, Susan, 3081
Krinsky, Robert D., 403, 463
Krippel, Nancy, 6648, 6649
Krishnan, Mini, 1340
Krishnan MD, Geeta, 3796
Krispinsky, Todd, 5320
Krist, Andrea, 3739
Kristensen, Doug, 7488, 7489
Kristof Moy, Patricia, 4210
Kriston, Julie, 7667
Kriv, Arlene, 7645
Krivin, Dr. Martin, 5024
Krivinchuk, Jeremiah, 6537
Krizan, Renee T, 3819

Executive Name Index

Kroening, Chris, 4125, 5697
Kroenke, E Stanley, 6365
Kroenke, Josh, 6365
Kroeze-Visser, Angela, 4663
Kroger, Pat, 2837
Krogh, David G., 1115, 1116
Krogstad, Andy, 7367, 7368
Kroh, Loren H., 5515, 8191
Krohley, Anne, 335
Krol, Patricia, 4775
Kronauer, Steven, 1885
Kronfeld, Beth L., 2970
Kronfeld, Maria, 2766
Kronick, Susan D., 160
Kroninger Knerr, Karen, 568
Kroon, Herb, 1261
Kropa, Ed, 1111
Kroth, Richard, 4991
Kroth, Richard A., 4991
Krotseng, Marsha V., 5813
Krott, Joel, 1333
Krous, Mary, 2177
Krubsack, Kathryn, 1825
Krueger, Baird, 3746
Krueger, Dr Michael T, 1957
Krueger, Kate, 1823
Krueger, Megan, 5874
Krueger, Michael, 1821
Krueger, Steven L, 2235
Krueger, Timothy, 1955
Kruempel, Julie, 310
Kruger, Kristin, 8108
Krugman, Josh, 2324
Krugman, Neil B., 620
Krull, Hannah, 6769
Krull, Michael, 6841, 6842
Krumbine, Rovbert, 5230
Kruml, Dr. Susan, 6767, 6768
Krumwiede, Keith, 6770
Krumwiede, Sara, 6334
Krupa, Roger, 7907
Krupka, Maggie, 1368
Krupski, Ann, 5161
Kruse, J. Joseph, 8199
Kruse, Lora, 7994
Kruse, William S, 5425
Kruse, William S., 4206
Kruszka, Kamala, 2446
Kruzas, Mark, 1877
Krystal, Veronica, 2902
Krywosz, Ben, 3268
Kryzanowski, Steve, 2749
Krzyzanowski, Sharyn, 5007
Kuba, Samuel, 3806
Kubas, Linda, 8126
Kuberka, Kathleen, 941
Kubiak, Greg, 1986
Kubly, Joe, 6977
Kubovy, Itamar, 135
Kuchar, Theodore, 785, 1315
Kuchle, Marcus, 2278
Kuchmaner, Ryan, 3700
Kuchner, Robet, 7766
Kudick, Martha, 5874
Kudo, Elaine, 149
Kudravetz, Doug, 6476
Kudravy, Christine, 921
Kudysch, Bernice, 1399
Kuechler, Henry, 6255
Kuehl, Sheri, 71
Kuehn, Renee, 1792
Kuehn, Woody, 2196
Kuehne, Bruce, 1163
Kuehnlein, Tim, 4820
Kuepper, Jeff, 5852
Kuftinec, Sasha, 2174
Kugelmas, Jennifer, 1393
Kugler, Trent, 5822
Kuharsky, Andrew, 607
Kuharsky, Merry, 607
Kuhlman, Kevin, 3633
Kuhlmann, Kent, 895
Kuhn, Bill, 4078
Kuhn, Darlene, 5893, 5896
Kuhn, Jeff, 8192
Kuhn, Jill Dubbeldee, 7370
Kuhn, John, 3719
Kuhn, Judy, 3587

Kuhn, Keith, 1300
Kuhn, Reginald S., 1305
Kuhn, Sharon, 6086, 6087
Kuhns, Thomas O, 2047
Kujawsky, Eric, 831
Kukier, Donald, 2137
Kukuk, Jack, 4172
Kulas, Nikki, 8671
Kulick, Brian, 3479
Kulik, Jackie, 7570
Kulik, Rosa, 2
Kulkarni, Subhash, 4713
Kull, Dr. Arthur, 1026
Kulle, Joan, 252, 2090, 4746
Kulnicki, Travis, 1305
Kulp Wahamaki, Sheila, 7323
Kumar, Mythili, 98
Kumataka, Jeff, 4246
Kumery, Jerri, 670
Kumi, Cyd, 4636
Kumin, Jan, 8003
Kumin, Ron, 8003
Kun, Tina, 809
Kun Wan, Shao, 4271
Kuna, Lizzy, 1667
Kuncl, Dr. Ralph W, 6215
Kund Nolan, Kathleen, 3799
Kunda, Donna, 8181
Kundell,, Linda, 3454
Kung, Jacquelyn, 4246
Kunin, Claudia, 2965
Kunitomi, Darrell, 2510
Kunkel, David S, 1787
Kunkel, John, 1561
Kunkel, Myke, 4201
Kunsch, Joan, 133
Kunz, C. Thomas, 2268
Kunze, Kathryn, 3189
Kuppler, Karl, 2057
Kupsco, Beth, 1503, 2270
Kuraishi, Mari, 3831, 4441, 4569
Kuranda, Richard, 7845
Kuras, Jeffrey, 3191
Kuras, Roz, 1400
Kurdi, Krystle, 8698, 8699, 8700
Kurdziel-Formato, Lynne, 7657
Kurent, Molly K., 4019
Kurka Reimer, Jeanie, 2393
Kurland, Phyllis, 5076
Kurlas, Anthony, 1137
Kurtz, Andrew M, 2306
Kurtz, Dr Harold, 2306
Kurtz, Jan, 8101
Kurtz, Joy, 2306
Kurtz, Richard, 8138
Kurylo, Shandai, 3241
Kurz, Cathy, 3329
Kurz, Janet, 5940
Kurz, Sandy, 2616
Kushigian, Elise J, 6889, 6893
Kushner, Wendi, 2336, 2339
Kushner, William, 1136
Kusinitz, Esq., Alan R., 467
Kutler, Ken, 7689
Kutner, Shiela, 3815
Kutrow, Blair, 197
Kutschied, Benjamin, 3256
Kuttner, Eric, 1426
Kutz, Raymond, 4311
Kuwabara, Anna, 4921
Kuwahara, Shizuo, 1009
Kuzma, Samuel, 3787
Kvancz, Jack, 6462
Kvistad, Gregg, 1953
Kwak, Kyudong, 318
Kwame Johnson, Paul, 384
Kwan, Kurt, 3251
Kwan, Paul, 2587
Kwitsky, Chris, 8039, 8040
Kwok, Glen, 1085
Kye, Joseph, 4563
Kyle, Barry, 3078
Kyle, Robert, 2453
Kyle, J.D Penelope W., 8547
Kyler, Tricia, 3048
Kyler Bowling, Tricia, 1281
Kyme, Katherine, 820
Kyser, Julia, 4269

Kyzmir, Anne K., 3428

L

L'Roy, Diann, 3950
L. Appert, Dr. Donald, 1601
L. Cato, Dr. Tom, 6658, 6659
L. Goldman, Arlene, 3549
L. Hall, Timothy, 8258
L. Kane, Margaret, 2553
L. Martin, Mindy, 1860
L. McGovern, wILLIAM, 1167
L. Medd, Gary, 1104, 1105
L. Pemberton, Gregory, 1086
L. Stevens, Roger, 6471
L. Thayer, David, 7003
L. Wauls, David, 8138
La Bonne, Pamela L, 3503
La Fever, Susan, 2177
La Gamma, Theresa, 4977
La Mee, Maurice, 2651
La Rocca, Sr., John M., 591
La Rock, John, 6218
La Rosa, Ricard de, 5158
La Rose, Anne, 2542
La Rue, Rita, 2354
La Selva, Vincent, 2240
Laarman, Linda, 5835
Laas, Virginia J., 4902
Labadie, Bruce, 860
Labbate, Kim, 2440
Labbe, E Randolph, 8101
Labbe, Travis, 4536
Labedz, Jr, Chester S, 2323
Labella, Frank, 7844
LaBella, Stephanie, 6517
LaBelle, Dean, 6852
LaBelle, Dorothea S, 4401
Labiner, Howie, 3669
Labishak, Micah, 1819
Laboda, Dr Gerald, 2779
Labombard, Chad, 4805
LaBonte, Renee, 968
Laborie, Dawn, 4713
LaBrake, Randolph W, 7659
LaBran, Ronald M, 824, 825
LaBranche, Dr Mark, 5255
LaBranche, Sheri, 1143, 4718
LaBruyere, Dr. Louise, 2083
Labruyere, Louise, 2083
LaBumbard, Chad, 7252
Lacamera, Lisa, 5762
LaCario, Eileen, 2913, 6731
Lacasse, Adam, 7532
LaCause, Elizabeth, 1465, 7827
Lacey, Cassandra, 5745
Lacey, Erica, 8247
Lacey, Susan, 4682
Lach, Barabara B, 5325
Lach, Barbara B., 7986
LaChance, Peggy, 6543
Lachenbruch, Zac, 7479
Lacher, Lisa, 6987, 6988
Lachman, David, 436
Lachmann, Richard, 1020
Lachtman, Susan, 4321
Lack, Phil, 6343
Lackie, Joe, 8286
Lacko Kelley, Pamela, 535
Lacombe, Jacques, 1336
LaComfora, Lynne, 2127
Lacorte, Jerome, 5348
LaCount, Shawn, 3136
LaCourse, Donald, 301
Lacroix, Christine, 969
Lacy, Brent, 6044
Lacy, Judy, 6490
Lacy, Nancy, 6475
Laczynski, Tim, 3359
Lada, Edward, 2077
Ladd, Neil, 7340
Ladd, Tom, 1249
LaDeau, Justin, 5172
LaDew, Lisa, 593
Ladewig, Cathy, 4490
Ladish Selander, Mary, 6740
Ladner, Benjamin, 6458, 6460, 6474, 6476
Ladouceur, Cheryl, 5176

Ladrigan, Kathay, 1854
Ladrigan Cobb, Laura, 1854
Ladwig, Carol, 5303
Ladwig, Paul, 6104
Ladzekipo, CK, 4315, 4316
Ladzekpo, CK, 90, 94, 4307
Laemmli Orth, Cornelia, 1693
Lafe, William, 581, 1654
LaFerle Gergely, Carrie, 2504
Lafferty, Allison, 2628
Laffoon, Don, 2609
LaFlair Nieves, Nicole, 2688
Lafler, Donald, 870
Lafond, Charles, 3865, 4043
Laforce, Gail, 6390
LaForge, Bonnie, 2023
LaForge, John, 2023
LaFountain, Weston, 7529
LaFreniere, Jamie, 1820
Lagakos, Matina, 4989
Lage, Theresa, 1068
Lageveen, David, 6948, 6951
Lagomarcino, Suzanne, 2157
Lagos, Marta, 4834
Lagrone, Betty, 6047
LaGruth, Anthony, 1324, 1345
LaGuardia, Tracy, 915
LaGuardia, Vincent C, 915
Laguni, Andrea, 803
Lahaie, Lawrence, 7498
Lahti, Andrew, 554
Laidler, Eileen, 8378, 8379
Laifer, Matthew, 8847
Laing, Ronald T, 1246
Laird, Christine, 1966
Laird, Jim, 6134
Lairsen, John, 3995
Lake, J Bryan, 5606
Lake, Jody, 8484
Lake, Jody G, 8484
Lake, Martha, 2557
Lake, Michael, 2775
Lake, Octavia, 6546
Lake, Sara, 50
Lake, SSG Robert A, 1270
Lakeru-Rivers, Titi, 1159
Lakey, Arnold, 7917
Lakey, Denise, 908
Lakosil, Robert, 6212
Lakus, Frank, 2832
Lakus, Priscilla, 2832
Lalitha, Grace, 2315
Lalias, Demetrios, 706
Lallement, Stephanie, 529
Lalli, Alexia, 922
Lally, Peter, 7239
Lam, Dale, 598
Lam, George, 2235
Lam, Ken, 1678
Lamadore, Lily, 8072
Laman, Greg, 7271
Lamandia, Paul, 47
Lamar, Jamey, 1024
LaMarca, Stephen, 1455
Lamarca, Stephen, 2808
Lamarca-Kandel, Priscilla, 1937
Lamb, Barbara, 4397
Lamb, Becky, 7991
Lamb, David, 3426
Lamb, Jenni, 6545
Lamb, Jim, 4165
Lamb, Maggie, 3189
Lamb, Robert, 701
Lamberson, Rodney, 2291
Lambert, Beth, 2827
Lambert, Beverly, 841, 1905
Lambert, Cliff, 6944
Lambert, Debra, 1915, 4202
Lambert, Ian, 5858
Lambert, Jane, 2633
Lambert, John Henry, 1418
Lambert, Karen, 2027
Lambert, La Doyce, 3998
Lambert, LaDoyce, 1743
Lambert, Len, 2415
Lambert, Leo, 5240
Lambert, Michael, 3811
Lambert, Michael W., 2303

1187

Executive Name Index

Lambert, Richard, 473
Lambert, Robyn, 2430, 6004
Lambert, William M., 2319
Lamberto, Tony, 6433
Lamboley, Virginia, 970
Lambros, Jason, 3399
Lamette, William, 7423
Lamey, Chris, 3660
Lamkin, Dr. Fletcher M, 7420
Lamm, Robert, 3278
Lammers, Cassandra, 6473
Lamn, Robert, 7412
Lamon, Suzanne, 1613
LaMonaca, Mary, 1297
LaMondue, Tracy, 6459, 6461
Lamontagne, Raymond A., 7768
Lamort, Robert, 1617
Lamorte, Dan, 2914
Lamos, Mark, 6449
Lamoureux, Kelly, 48, 49
Lampe, Tim, 8557
Lampert, Rachel, 310, 3447
Lampert-Hopkins, Frank, 2194
Lamphere, Carla, 1256
Lamping, Mark, 7444
Lampitelli, Jude, 2885
Lamprecht, David, 3262
Lamprey, Jo, 4977
Lamse, Eileen W., 6004
Lamson, Charles K., 8058
LaMuro, Leslie, 5876, 8710
Lamy, Whitnaey, 5718
Lan, Kyle, 1678
Lana, Caitlyn, 1565
Lanahan, Jim, 3482
Lanane, Cindy, 1075, 1677
Lancaster, Christopher, 397
Lancaster, Karen, 2128
Lancaster, Linda, 4697
Lancaster, Sharon, 531
Lancaster, Stacey, 5129
Lance, Miller, 8071
Lanciano, Pat, 4994
Lancisi, Vincent M., 3116
Land, Charlie, 5647, 8421
Land, Liz, 5590, 8323
Land, Marie, 3869
Land, Pat, 3685
Land, Ronald, 1972
Landaich, Pierre, 8282
Landau, Ellen, 7908
Landau, Ellis, 1313
Landau, Kathy, 403, 463
Lande, Aaron, 913
Landeen, Mike, 7672
Landen, Serena, 1753
Lander, John, 8300
Lander, Kim, 7474
Lander, Nancy, 5941
Landeros Valle, Zindy, 4237
Landers, Colby, 3399
Landers, Vernon, 3984
Landes, Heather, 736, 737, 738
Landey, Sena, 6853
Landgren, Peter, 1521, 7948
Landgren, Peter, 7955, 7958
Landino, Robert, 4384, 6398
Landis, Carolyn, 2187
Landis, Dave, 3908, 3910
Landis, Diana, 1885
Landis, Gary, 2489
Landis, George, 1745
Landis, Ryan, 716
Landis, Sharon, 1857
Landman, Alan H, 6544
Landmesser, Drew, 6740
Landon, John, 8340
Landon, Mark, 1053
Landon, Stuart, 3805
Landow, Brett, 2079, 3049
Landrelle, James N, 2503
Landrigan, Jim, 5501
Landry, Janie, 7159
Landry, Joan, 1021, 1219
Landsman, Dennis, 239
Landsman, Kathy, 239
Landstreet, Susan, 5061
Lane, Andrew, 983

Lane, Bruce S., 3121
Lane, Dr Michael R, 7032
Lane, Jack, 3281
Lane, John, 2305
Lane, Marcia, 2863
Lane, Nicole, 3783
Lane, Peter B, 8156
Lane, Peter B., 6026
Lane Christilles, Karen, 7044
Lane Rawlins, Dr. V., 8369
Lane, CMP, Sandi, 8470
Laney, Donald, 692
Laney, Michael, 5081
Laney, Rachel, 7857
Laney, Walter, 3660
Lang, Amanda, 8693
Lang, Brien, 5524
Lang, David, 5115
Lang, Gayle, 1682
Lang, Kathy, 1082
Lang, Kim, 127
Lang, Mark E, 3495
Lang, Michael, 545
Lang, Tom, 1975
Lang Kosloff, Doris, 1976
Lang Sollinger, Mary, 1826
Lang, Jr., Conrad H., 5211
Langbehn, Marilyn, 4204
Langdon, Robert B, 2863
Lange, Brent, 4016
Lange, David, 8697
Lange, Eric J., 5109
Lange, George M., 4342
Lange, Michael, 6196
Lange, Michelle, 769
Lange, Sandra A, 8691, 8695
Langel, Greg, 5490
Langel, Leighann, 4178
Langer, Michael J, 8126
Langer, Patricia, 3542
Langford, David, 2872
Langford, Rebecca, 2823
Langham, Michael, 1311
Langill, Mark, 6156
Langill, Norman, 5804
Langley, Carole, 4186
Langley, Duane D., 4186
Langley, Jeff, 2549
Langley, Jim, 4422
Langley, Ken, 6852
Langley, William, 1600, 5417
Langlitz, Harold N., 3619
Langlois, Joel, 7300
Langlois, John, 4058
Langlois, Sandia, 96
Langmyer, Patricia, 1450
Langrock, Joann, 2370
Langrock, Kathy, 4321
Langr,e, Louis, 1528, 1529
Langstraff, Kay, 4375
Langway, Nicole, 6473
Langworthy, Dr. Bill, 1793
Langzel, Susan, 1887
Lanham, Lou Ann, 8629
Lanham, Tadd, 1701, 5588
Lani, Elizabeth, 89
Lani Fiedelman, Rosie, 434
Lanier, Greg, 2813
Lanier, Kym, 647
Lanier, Michelle, 5263
Lankay, Cristina, 3385
Lann, Nonie, 2453
Lannerd, Andrew, 2066
Lanni, Terry, 7511
Lannoye, Sheril, 4132
Lans, Scott, 1821
Lansberry, Rod A., 6327
Lansbury, Edgar, 3461
Lansdowne, Catherine, 1698
Lansford, Me Lissa, 5380
Lansing, Carol, 3244
Lansing, Laura, 253
Lansky, David G., 386
Lantaff, Kent, 6494, 6495
Lanter Blank, Susan, 1409, 5117
Lantz, Ashlea, 3034
Lantz, Jere, 2152
Lantz, Ronald, 4739, 4744

Lanz, Arianna, 5013
Lanza, Ruth, 330
Lanzillo, Richard A., 8123
Lanzilotti, Louise, 2886
LaPan, Mike, 4460, 6543
LaPart, Gary, 3172
Lapedes, Richard, 532
Lapenieks Rosenberg, Sarma, 20
LaPenna, Tom, 5988
LaPenta, Emilia, 3382
Lapidus, Dr. Ira, 3184, 4814
Lapidus, Ira, 4814
Lapin, Matvey, 1097
Lapine, Edward, 2657
LaPointe, Michelle, 2160
Lapore, Larry, 8198
Lappalainen, Eilana, 5150
Lappin, Jon, 1001
Lappin, Robert, 1001
Lapsley, Shannon, 8298
Laqua, Lori, 6262
Lara, Carmen Z., 1719
Lara, Luis, 6829
Laredo, Jaime, 1393, 1530, 5312, 5313
Laredo, Jamie, 1769
Larew, Donald, 3690
Large, Jim, 6588
Largess, Bill, 2753
Laribee, Nancy, 3444
Larimore, David, 8258
Larimore, James, 7533
Larish, Melissa, 504
Larison, Tamara, 561
Lariviere, Eric, 4441
Lariviere, John, 2793
Larivivere, Eric, 4442
Larmore, Stephen, 1290
Larner, Daniel, 4062, 4063
LaRocco, Claire, 4100
LaRocco, Jon-Paul, 2688
LaRocco, Michael C., 582
Larochelle, Michael, 3715
LaRosa Montez, Alison, 1186
LaRowe, Bruce, 3648
Larrimer, Marilyn, 1654
Larsen, Georganne, 1159
Larsen, Honey, 2820
Larsen, Jarrod, 8477, 8478, 8480, 8481
Larsen, Jeanne, 718
Larsen, Kristin, 6755
Larsen, Lawrence B., 650
Larsen, LeeAnne, 63
Larsen, Meryl, 90, 94
Larsen, Nicole, 5027
Larsen, Rick, 874
Larsen, Steven, 1031, 1065, 1066
Larsen, Thomas A., 1922
Larsen, TJ, 3339
Larsen Brown, Micaela, 1955
Larsen Engmyr, Renee, 39
Larsh, Marcio, 979
Larsh, Susy, 979
Larson, Andre, 8249
Larson, Ann, 7518
Larson, Beth, 3796
Larson, Bill, 3297, 7448
Larson, Daniel, 2258
Larson, Darrell, 5282
Larson, David, 5528
Larson, Don, 1813
Larson, Dr. Brook, 1853
Larson, Emely, 2686
Larson, Fred, 1271
Larson, Heather, 1945
Larson, Jack, 7377
Larson, James, 3334
Larson, Jennifer, 6724
Larson, Julie, 1885
Larson, Karin D., 2368
Larson, Kenneth A, 1967
Larson, Kim, 3890
Larson, Leslie Ann, 47
Larson, Lowell, 4875
Larson, Lynne, 653
Larson, Maree, 8241
Larson, Melanie, 4179
Larson, Nicki, 2166
Larson, Priscilla, 5643

Larson, Rob, 6980, 6981, 6982, 6983
Larson, Scott, 4843, 4868
Larson, Steffan, 5884
Larson, Tiffany, 4841
LaRue, Barry, 7265
LaRue, Jaclyn, 557
Lasansky, Enrique, 744
LaSante, Jeff, 8554
Lascar, Anna, 434
Lasch McNamee, Kathleen, 3408
Lash, Nicole, 2194
Lasher, Robert W, 856
Lashof, Donna, 2092
Laskey, Kim, 4062, 4063, 8572
Laskey, Richard, 3345
Laskey, Tom, 6300
Lasley, Henny, 122
Lasley, Susan, 1552
Lasorda, Tommy, 6156
Lassell, Pamela, 1996
Lasser, Stephen, 3396
Lassinger, Allen, 4434
Lassiter, Tina S, 4418
Lastrapes, David, 1702
Laszlo, Charles, 7978
Lata, Matthew, 2013
Latham, Den, 8230
Latham, Joan, 160
Lathan, Laurie, 3721
Lathrop, George, 4090, 4092
LaTorella, Anthony, 3588
Latshaw, Charles, 1076
Latson, Frank, 4003
Latta, Deb, 8186
Lattarulo, Craig, 515
Lattea, Charlene, 4102
Lattimer, Marvin, 4155
Lattin, Shean, 5410
Laturno Bojanic, Nancy, 840
Lau, Clara, 902
Lau, Diana, 675
Lau, Irene, 1441
Lau, JoAnna, 686
Lau, Louise, 1433
Lau, Tina, 1019
Laub, JR, 6500
Lauber, John, 4947
Lauber, Pat, 4137
Lauer, Kelsey, 1256
Lauffer, Bruce, 1637
Laughlin, Tim, 1746
Laughton, John C, 4991
Laun, Michael, 2557
Launer, Leland C, 6215
Laurenceau, Melissa R., 4502
Laurent, Jan, 4670
Laurent, Sabrina, 7161
Laurent O'Neil, Andr., 1362
Laurent-Ottomane, Charlotte, 1001
Lauridsen, Diane, 113
Laurino, Pasquale, 1834
Lauritzen, Sharon, 6314
Laurrell, Patti, 6151
Lautenbach, Ned C., 6558
Lauterbach, Dennis, 3216
Lauterbach, Gregg, 1363
Laux, Kelly, 8697
LaVallee, Corky, 2583
LaValleur, June, 3250
Lave, Roy, 2489
Lavelle, Jim, 2820
Laven, Pete, 6036
Laverty, Marie, 2127
Lavery, James G, 7907
Lavery, Sharon, 781
Lavey, Martha, 2952
Lavin, Michael, 6752
Lavin, Steven D, 4343
Lavin, Tim, 4065
Lavoie, Patricia, 323
Law, Bob, 3474
Law, Don, 1794
Law, Harold, 3924
Law, Reggie, 3921
Law, Ron, 3649, 5229
Law Dake, Susan, 1464
Lawie, Tracey, 7311
Lawler, Jon R., 1694

Executive Name Index

Lawless, Debbie, 5946
Lawlor, Charlie, 8527, 8528
Lawlor, Deborah, 2501
Lawlor, Lee, 4237, 6175
Lawlor, Natalie, 6423
Lawrence, Abigail, 58
Lawrence, Anne, 1688
Lawrence, Beth, 8220
Lawrence, Blake, 3488
Lawrence, Bob, 2745
Lawrence, Carrie, 2900
Lawrence, Craig, 8072
Lawrence, Daniel L, 2467
Lawrence, Fredrick M., 7253, 7254
Lawrence, Grace, 1739
Lawrence, Helen, 3746
Lawrence, Jack, 1255
Lawrence, Jan, 1708
Lawrence, Jeffery, 7820
Lawrence, Jeffery A., 3620
Lawrence, Joane, 3665
Lawrence, John, 2904
Lawrence, Josie, 3577
Lawrence, Margaret, 4965
Lawrence, Megan, 1835
Lawrence, Michael, 5119
Lawrence, Nathaniel, 4587
Lawrence, Pat, 1127
Lawrence, Sally, 8100
Lawrence, Scott, 1562, 1688
Lawrence, Shannon, 1343
Lawrence, Tiffani, 3746
Lawrence, Tory, 207
Lawrence Rivera, Jon, 2514
Lawrey, Cathy, 1280
Laws, Karen, 1820
Lawson, Anne, 4452
Lawson, Bob, 3990
Lawson, Dr Darren, 3876, 8224
Lawson, Fred, 2178
Lawson, H Ray, 3114
Lawson, Holbrook, 1583
Lawson, Jeffory, 3468
Lawson, Jennifer, 2547
Lawson, Joanne W, 2237
Lawson, John, 2237
Lawson, Kim, 3927
Lawson, Martha, 677
Lawson, Michael, 1331
Lawson, Mick, 1112
Lawson, Opha, 3746
Lawson, Sheeler, 5277
Lawson, Stephanie, 2430
Lawson, Tracey, 6293, 6294, 6296
Lawther, Josh, 6500
Lawton, Bill, 3359
Lawton, Dana, 78
Lawton, Maryi, 2778
Lawton, Patricia, 2583
Lawton, Pattie, 2583
Lawton Brown, Katharine, 4923
Lawyer, Alecia, 1732
Law, Bob, 6706
Laxalt, Mrs. Paul, 2738
Lay, Lee, 5570
Layendecker, Col Dennis M, 951, 1981
Layman, Jane, 4514
Layman, Rhonda, 1747, 2359
Layne, Helene, 4467
Layne, Margaret, 4078
Layne, Margaret Mary, 8634
Lazar, Elie, 221
Lazar, Joel, 1171, 1172
Lazar, Paul, 357
Lazar, Jr, Zachary D., 199, 205
Lazaro, Rosa, 8345
Lazaros, Sruly, 5115
Lazenberg, William, 5426
Lazin, Steve, 576
Lazo, Christina, 2585
Lazorcik, David, 5451
Lazzara, Teri, 4089
Lazzari, OSB, Boniface V, 5782
Lazzerini, Diane, 5285
Le Barbier, Christophe, 1560
Le Beau, Bryan, 7045
Le Coque, Louise, 4606
Le Houillier, Paul, 3660

Le Sorte, Jana, 372
Lea Albers, Sandra, 4077
Leach, Christiane, 5493
Leach, Curtis, 3321, 7485
Leach, Dale, 3541
Leach, Kate, 5517
Leach, Renaye, 4131
Leader Stoeber, Denise, 4317
Leahey, Jamey, 7081
Leahy, Carol, 3124
Leahy, Jim, 6197
Leahy, Mary, 703
Leahy, Sharon, 533
Leahy, Shayna, 2077
Leahy Duckworth, Rosilan, 988
Leake, Tracy, 3754
Leal, Andrea M., 1896
Leal, Anna, 6069
Leaming, Jim, 2906
Leamon, Irene, 1174
Leamy, Matthew, 2627
Lear, Cindy, 7462
Lear, Kate B., 393
Learmonth, Brad, 7707
Learner, Jay, 2062, 2063
Leary, Jeannie, 5274
Leary, Ms. Susan, 802
Leary, Pam, 5752
Leary, Susan, 4240
Leas, Catherine, 735
Leass, Richard, 4927
Leath, steven, 6954, 6955, 6956, 6957, 6958, 6959
Leatherberry, Wendy, 520
Leatherman, Brian Patrick, 1947
Leavit, Dr. Edward, 1476
Leavitt, Dr. Edward, 5217
Leavitt, Mark A., 270
Leavitt, Roy, 5135
Leavitt, Toby, 4311
Leavitt, Tony, 4675, 7041
Leaycraft, Matthew, 7849
LeBarre, Ruth, 4820
Lebauer, Dr. Samuel M., 5244
Lebdetter, Jason, 6247
Lebeau, Jim, 7813
Leberman, Pam, 3843
Leblanc, Marianne, 496
Leblanc, Sarah, 7619
LeBlance Burley, Jelynne, 8450, 8451
Lebo, Shirley, 1506
LeBow, Lainy, 1155
LeBreton, Cynthia, 246
LeCain, Elaine, 757
Lecce-Chong, Francesco, 1830
Lechner, Doreen, 4624
Lecompte, Elizabeth, 3594
Ledbetter, A. Wayne, 2271
Ledbetter, A.Wayne, 2271
Ledbetter, Joe, 1912
Ledbetter, Kristy, 6197
Ledbetter, Lark, 1002
Ledbetter, Tommy, 3274
Lederkramer, Ron, 6167
Ledford, Brad, 6806, 6809
Ledford, Laura, 6769
Ledford, Laura, 6767, 6768
Ledford, Woody, 6238, 6243
Ledgewood, Kevin, 4152, 5923
Ledingham, Allan, 2755
Ledingham, Joyce, 2755
Ledney, Gerald, 5513
LeDoux, Sgt. Craig, 951
Ledri-Aguilar, Lisa, 2460
Ledyard, John, 1888
Lee, Bruce, 4006, 5682
Lee, Charlene, 1415
Lee, Charlotte C, 3858
Lee, Christopher, 1661
Lee, Dan, 6149
Lee, Darren, 3887
Lee, Dennis, 2073
Lee, Diane, 82, 97
Lee, Doc, 3886
Lee, Doug, 6579
Lee, Dr Hae Jong, 2291
Lee, Dr. Yuan-Yuan, 1072
Lee, Elaine, 6269, 6270

Lee, Gary, 5177
Lee, Genevieve, 6087
Lee, Greg W., 6026
Lee, Gregory, 7458
Lee, Howard C., 3980
Lee, Irene S, 183
Lee, James, 875
Lee, James E., 2078
Lee, James L, 8334
Lee, Jay, 6390
Lee, Jeanette L., 1523, 1524
Lee, Jeff, 910, 2235
Lee, Jeffrey, 405, 4159
Lee, Jenny, 758
Lee, Joe, 711
Lee, John, 4552
Lee, Jonathan, 6167
Lee, Joseph, 712
Lee, Josephine, 2039
Lee, Katy, 6852
Lee, Keith, 663
Lee, Leeheng, 1446
Lee, Lisa, 2885, 6672
Lee, Lynda, 4452
Lee, Lynnette, 3410
Lee, Mark, 988
Lee, Marlene, 40, 6163
Lee, Matthew, 1811
Lee, Mike, 5988
Lee, Patricia Taylor, 852
Lee, Rachel, 463
Lee, Ralph, 3617
Lee, Rev. Daniel, 6819, 6822
Lee, Richard Diebold, 853
Lee, Robert, 390, 768, 2144
Lee, Ronald, 1673
Lee, Ruth, 221
Lee, Ryan, 799
Lee, Sarah, 2196
Lee, Song, 491
Lee, Stephanie, 6621
Lee, Suzanne, 1021
Lee, Tamara, 6647
Lee, Terri, 4676, 7049, 7050, 7051
Lee, Tom, 1491, 2745, 5242
Lee Clark, Peggy, 5433
Lee Conti, Laura, 3443
Lee Fischer, Laura, 2098
Lee Henderson, Helen, 6471
Lee Hope, Mary, 1612
Lee III, Robert E., 2205
Lee Kathan, Nancy, 3825, 5474
Lee Katz, Lucinda, 848
Lee Kemper, Nancy, 1281
Lee Mann, Mary, 4448
Lee Mathis, Richard, 3081
Lee Morrow, Ms. Emma, 4184
Lee Rogers, Rodney, 3868
Lee Smith, Amanda, 4070
Lee Stantley, James, 2550, 2551
Lee Warner, Mary, 4174
Lee, IV, John C., 2378
Lee, MD, Myles, 805
Lee-Painter, David, 6699, 6701, 6702
Leech, Perryn, 2353
Leeestma, Heidi Holst, 3204
Leehey, David, 1059
Leemon, Dick, 3173
leeper, Anna, 7549
Leeper, Robert, 5164
Leepman, Karen, 3858
Lees, Brian E., 7185
Leet, Lisa.P, 243
Leeth, Arthur, 656
Leevers, Carol, 3693, 7606
Lefaive, Patty, 299
Lefebvre, Bill, 1194
Lefever, Jim, 6272
LeFevour, Tim, 6749
LeFevre, Camille, 299
LeFevre, Suzanne, 1732
Leff, Judy, 2566
Leffler, Lacey, 5808
Leffler, Marvin, 7789
Lefler, Brian J., 1245
Lefton Esq, Ira S, 575
Leftwich, Ronald W, 7413
Legarza, Tracy, 7522

Legassik, Autrey, 6077
Legge, Dori, 7243
Legow, Elliot, 2291
Lehan Siegel, Pamela, 556
Lehan-Siegel, Pamela, 556
Lehl, Debra, 1956
Lehman, Anne, 1164
Lehman, David, 5453
Lehman, Jean, 1358
Lehman, Karen H, 3805
Lehman, Katherine, 5584
Lehman, Kathy, 5438
Lehman, Terry, 8129
Lehmann, Carter, 3133
Lehmann, Jay, 814
Lehmann, Kathryn, 2088
Lehmann, Klaus-Dieter, 7732
Lehmann, Robert, 1174
Lehna, Wayne, 3353
Lehnert, Charles, 8012, 8013
Lehning, Steven, 1911
Lehr, Dr.Les, 770
Lehr, Les, 770
Lehr, Lester E, 770
Lehr, Linda, 2206
Lehr, Jr., William, 1627, 1628
Lehto, Michael, 6696
Lehwalder, Heidi, 5735
Leiblinger-Hedderson, Carole, 3715
Leibundgut, Dan, 1533
Leifer, Mel, 410
Leigh, Barbara, 4123
Leigh, Karon, 5994
Leighton, Lesley, 1886, 1935
Leighton, Public Relation, 6228
Leiken, David, 8090
Leikvoll, Vanessa, 4792
Leinbach, Tyler, 4046, 8545
Leinen, John, 4960
Leiniger, John, 915
Leininger, Alexis, 6926
Leininger, John, 915
Leinwell, Checkle, 5248
Leipold, Louisa, 1977
Leiser, Randy, 2343, 8362
Leisner, Sue, 2511
Leitao, Sandy, 6115
Leiter, Martha, 4484
Leivick, Joel, 6304
Leiweke, Tim, 6178
Leiweke, Tod, 8095, 8102
Leja, Jim, 2130
Lekrone, Erik, 55
Leland, Mary, 4285
LeMay, Tina, 8215
Lemberger, Julie, 371
Lemcke, Paul, 1017
Lemecha, Brenda, 1228
LeMelle, Debbie, 5366, 5367
Lemire, Martha, 324
Lemke, Chuck, 720, 5939
Lemke, Connie, 1685, 1686
Lemler, Sharon, 1963
Lemmer, Betty, 4724
Lemmo, Angelo, 513
Lemoi, Kyle, 6860
Lemoine, Chris, 2124
Lemons, James, 7697
Lemons, Jay, 5504
Lemos, Jurgen de, 907
Lenaburg, Becky, 4087
Lenaghan, Michael, 2688
Lendaro, Melody, 6253, 6265
Lendermon, David L., 7140
Leniado-Chira, Joseph, 926
Lenix-Hooker, Catherine, 3379
Lenk, Sarah, 8003
Lennen, Michael, 1123, 2076
Lennon, Barbara, 1088
LeNoire, Rosetta, 3464
Lent, James, 1943
Lent, Michael, 450
Lent, Richard, 4857
Lent, Stan, 2651
Lenti, Amanda, 4998
Lentz, Lamar, 5658, 8443
Lentz, Matt, 8016
Lenz, Ron, 4894

1189

Executive Name Index

Lenzen, Maria, 642
Lenzner, Emily, 141
Leo, James, 7175
Leo, Peter, 2261
Leogite, Carol, 450
Leon, Alexis, 3795, 8115
Leon, Mechele, 3045, 7043
Leonard, Ame, 915
Leonard, Angela Jo, 3125
Leonard, Anne, 8140
Leonard, Anne Marie, 7241
Leonard, Arlene, 4645
Leonard, Barbara, 6173
Leonard, Beth, 7419
Leonard, Brian, 6031
Leonard, Connie, 2510
Leonard, Daniel, 4363
Leonard, Gayle, 7456
Leonard, Ian, 1939
Leonard, Jami, 2222
Leonard, Katye, 810
Leonard, Kelly, 2948
Leonard, Rachael, 161
Leonard, Reid, 3678
Leonard III, Edward, 7046
Leone, Stephan R., 5020
Leones, Kathleen, 1926, 1927
Leonetti, Mario, 1872
Leonetti, Mario E, 1872
Leong, Randy, 6675
Leonsis, Ted, 6475
Leoreti, Douglas, 4724
Leos, Linda, 7507
Leporati, Douglas, 4724
Lepore-Hagan, Michele, 8023, 8024
Leppert-Largent, Anna, 1251
Leppman, John, 8507
Leppo, John, 5757
Lerbs, Christopher, 1998
Lerch, Natalie, 2383
Lerette, Lindsay, 7276
Lerian, Steve, 4317
Lerman, Mark, 8197
Lerman, Steven, 6462
Lerner, Jenny, 418
Lerner, Karen, 2228
Lerner, Linus, 743
Lerner, CPRP, CPP, Jay, 6847
LeSage, Amber, 5350
Lesage, Jasper, 7015
Lesage, Stephanie, 4841
Lesartre, Stacy, 910
Lescinski, Joan, 6974, 6975, 6979
Lese, Sahra T., 5172, 8866
Lesemann, Heidi, 826
Lesenger, Jay, 2252
Lesho, Christopher, 7952
Lesinski, Christie, 4237
Leskin, Katherine, 1753
Leskowitz, Ali, 7224
Lesley, Lana, 3932
Leslie, Carol, 7590
Leslie, Charles, 6371, 8326
Leslie, Christine, 100, 101
Leslie, Diane, 3830
Leslie, Dottie, 5062
Leslie, Matthew, 6112
Leslie, Toby, 8523
Lesniak, Magdalena, 896
Lesniak PhD, Melissa, 977
Lesnick, Peter, 6152
Lesnik, Peter, 39
Leson, Rick, 6204
Less, Christopher, 3428
Lessenger, Neal, 1814
Lesser, Felice, 425
Lesser, Henry, 1892
Lesser, Peter, 7624
Lessig, Tim, 6506
Lester, Diane, 1348
Lester, G Ron, 2598
Lester, Joel, 5147
Lester, Johanna M, 498
Lester, Mark, 842, 4290
Lester, Silvia M H, 6094, 6095
Lester, Tennie, 7385
Lester, William J, 7356
Lestz, Loryn, 1792

LeSuer, Karyn, 368
Leszczewicz, Cher, 1469
Letourneau, DeAnn, 1313
Lett, Daniel J., 4585
Letz, Stan, 6343
Leube, Jr., Joseph J., 1639, 2307, 5475
Leung, Daniel, 2030
LeVan, Leila, 154
Levan, Steve, 8205
Levasseur, Ali, 6991
LeVelle, Teresa, 4349
Leven, Terri, 8117
Levenfus, Mark, 3461
Levengood, Barney, 6900
Levenson, Leon, 3131
Leventhal, Judy, 7584
Leventhal, Max, 2849
Leventhal, Steven, 1475
Leverett, Jamey, 499
Leveridge, Cindy, 1128
Leveriny, Cynthia, 2095
Leverock, Robert, 6528
Leverton, Millie, 3741
Levett Zody, Suzannah, 3020
Levigne, Marianne, 2271
Levin, Allen J, 5465
Levin, Ann, 541
Levin, Cynthia, 3292, 7430
Levin, Ira, 2191
Levin, James, 3712
Levin, John, 4055
Levin, Ken, 6068
Levin, Lorraine, 1725
Levin, Michael, 1725
Levin, Mollie, 3725
Levin, Morton Q., 519
Levin, Robert, 4486
Levin, Susan, 3721
Levin, Vicky N., 7253, 7254
Levine, Dena, 4743
Levine, Georgi, 6315
Levine, James, 1177, 1178, 1179, 2234, 4795, 7238
Levine, Joel, 1584
Levine, Joshua D., 3364
Levine, Leigh, 4554
Levine, Marcia, 7967
Levine, Maureen, 2722
Levine, Richard J., 1341
Levine, Ricki L., 1236
Levine, Soll, 930
Levine, Stephen, 1365
Levine, Sue, 898
Levinson, Gary, 8362
Levinson, Leslie, 65
Levinton, Michael, 369
Levioff, Arielle, 1363
Levitman, David, 1426
Leviton, Averill, 6754
Levitt, Charlotte, 7740
Levitz, Richard, 1381
Levy, Barbara R., 747
Levy, Chad, 351
Levy, Dr Philip, 330
Levy, Elsi, 1389
Levy, Francie, 888
Levy, Jim, 715
Levy, Karen E, 5748
Levy, Karen S., 2106
Levy, Marc, 8071
Levy, Marc D, 1102
Levy, Michael, 3338
Levy, Michele, 2345
Levy, Paul, 5109, 7788
Levy, Sally S., 2163
Levy, Sarah, 141
Levy, Simon, 2501
Levy, Ursala, 1619
Levy-Page, Laurie, 3120
Lewanbowski, Sara, 4866
Lewanda, Sheryl, 4342
Lewandowski, Randy, 6903
Lewckyj, Taras, 571
Lewey, David, 2974
Lewi, Edward J., 5200
Lewicki, Stephan, 6236
Lewins, Caitlin, 7967
Lewis, Andrew, 2037

Lewis, Barbara, 686, 4058
Lewis, Bill, 2901
Lewis, Blanche, 8764
Lewis, Brian, 7913
Lewis, Cari, 5835
Lewis, Charles, 5905, 5906
Lewis, Christian, 6123
Lewis, Dale, 5167
Lewis, Dave, 8617
Lewis, David A., 6681
Lewis, Deborah, 1885, 6275
Lewis, Denise, 1891
Lewis, Diane, 767
Lewis, Dr. John, 4683
Lewis, Dr. Terry, 8345
Lewis, Edward, 3168
Lewis, Edward J., 4759, 7203
Lewis, Ellie, 5508
Lewis, Gary, 2358
Lewis, Glenn, 3292
Lewis, Irene, 3113
Lewis, J Reilly, 959, 1982, 1994
Lewis, Jason, 4092
Lewis, Jennifer, 3685
Lewis, Joanna, 603
Lewis, June, 410
Lewis, Kathleen, 2300
Lewis, Krista, 8366
Lewis, Larry, 781
Lewis, Laureen, 4326
Lewis, Loyd, 456
Lewis, Marc, 3539
Lewis, Mark A, 3980
Lewis, Mary E, 6675
Lewis, Meg, 4148
Lewis, Owen, 6181
Lewis, P M, 926
Lewis, Patricia, 4176
Lewis, Peter, 7171
Lewis, Philip, 5029
Lewis, Phillip, 1711
Lewis, Ralph, 3546
Lewis, Richard, 2553
Lewis, Robert A, 3630
Lewis, Scott, 562
Lewis, Skip, 2826
Lewis, Tony, 7548
Lewis, Valerie, 5154
Lewis, Willard, 7915
Lewis, William, 5264
Lewis-Finein, Erica, 2590
Lewit, Louanne, 2172
Lewit, Louanne, 7524
Lewitin, Margot, 3592
Ley Hamilton, Esq., David, 1979
Leyba Kramer, Lori, 8089, 8092, 8096, 8099
Leyerle, James, 2137
Leykam, Scott, 8093
Leynse, Andrew, 3549
Li, Ester, 4316
Li, Esther, 4307, 4315
Li, Millie, 356
Li, Nico, 405
LI, Sue, 1885
Li Che, Meng, 1808, 1809, 5808
Li-Ming Wong, Michael, 4311
Liachowitz, Irvin R, 5505
Liakus-Pilcher, Sandra, 5027
Liao, Joyce, 3416
Liao, Martha, 4284
Lias, Margaret, 1200
Libbrecht, Tanguy, 718
Libby, Elizabeth, 6795
Libby, Susan, 5039
Libby Komaiko, Dame, 6737
Libenson, Sara, 2105
Liberatore, Ed, 7219
Liberatore, Marianne, 4411
Liberatore, Patti, 5362
Liberatore, William, 2541
Liberatori, Victoria, 3383
Libin, Paul, 7721
Libman, April, 1593
Libonati, Christian, 2931
Libonati, Daren, 7513
Libretti, Lauren, 454
Licensing Director, Lent, 456
Licha, Marian, 3130

Lichenstein, Elly, 2543
Lichtman, Suzanne, 7333
Licklider, Joey, 6015, 6016, 6017
Lickteig, Steve, 3113
Liddel, Alan, 3380
Liddell, Alan, 3385, 7576
Liddell, Catherine, 4383, 4791
Liddy, Edward M, 6833
Lidgett, J.R., 3047
Lidvall, Christine, 635
Lieber, Pam, 8058
Lieberman, Donna, 3596
Lieberman, Moira, 1316
Lieberman, Sol, 1424
Liebert, Erica, 1600
Liebman, Stuart D., 3374, 8791
Liebmann, Wilhelm E., 5662
Lief, Charles G., 6335
Lienau, Ellie, 712
Lienau, Rudy, 8679
Lierle, Pam, 2369, 5704
Liese, Ted, 730
Lifchitz, Max, 1435
Liffick, Cynde, 5755
Lifland, Amy, 2112
Lightfoot, Kay, 3909
Light, Elena, 428
Light, John, 2558, 4055
Lightfoot, William, 3674
Lignelli, Ron, 6469
Lignitz-Hahn, Kellie, 1737
Ligon, Claude M, 4760
Ligon, Jack, 8538
Likens, Peter, 5995
Likness, Joan, 5557
Liles, Henry, 372
Liles, Susan, 4889
Liljeberg, Robert, 3663
Lilley, Jean, 2030
Lilley, Richard, 2010
Lillibridge, Tom, 8249
Lillie, Bob, 6339
Lillie, Jana, 4017
Lillie, Robert, 2070
Lillis, Linda, 5260, 5261
Lilly, Dr. Claude C., 5535
Lilly, Susan, 4185
Lilyhorn, Ranita, 3332
Lim, Bernadette, 8025
Lim, Shelley, 7329
Lim, Susan, 4921
Lima, Ilona, 3488
Lima, Tori, 649
Limb, Amber, 8104
Limbacher, Jon, 1535
Limberg, Wendy, 2208
Limeberry, Lora, 243
Limoncelli, Gary, 352
Limondjian, Hilde Annik, 5149
Limonoff, Steve, 2445
Lin, Anita S, 546
Lin, Ann, 82, 97
Lin, Cho-Liang, 796, 4233
Lin, Ellie, 2349
Lin, Kun-Yang, 455
Lin, Yi-Ching, 2224
Lin Fink-Hammack, Connie, 142
lin Hornbaker, Jade, 4240
Linchon, Victoria, 3578
Lincoln, Deborah C., 1317
Lincoln, Eric, 2086
Lincoln, Howard, 8604
Lincoln, Merideth, 5670
Lincoln, Priscilla, 1794
Lind, Carol, 1978
Lind, Dr. Robin, 8146
Lind, Gayle, 5927, 5930
Lind, Mary Joyce, 236
Lind, Sophia, 1441
Lind, Steven J, 1302
Linda, Bell, 2400
Lindahl, Nancy, 1265
Lindall, Christine, 635
Lindauer, Erik D., 5154
Lindberg, John, 4038, 4039
Lindberg, Prof. Jeffrey, 1573
Linde, Ed, 7227
Lindeke, Terence, 2415

Executive Name Index

Linden, Dr. Patt, 1751
Lindenauer, Paul, 4274
Lindenmayer, Kathy, 686
Lindenmeyr, Louise, 4403
Linder, Martha, 974
Linder, Steven A., 801
Linder, Ulrich, 7732
Lindgren, Mark, 310
Lindholm, Eric, 774
Lindner, Dan, 1771, 1772
Lindner, Hollie, 6704, 6707
Lindner, Richard, 5188
Lindorff, Joyce, 5467
Lindquist, Carol, 1080
Lindquist, David, 1481
Lindsay, Gary, 84
Lindsay, Karen, 329
Lindsay, Kris, 2347
Lindsay, Lynn, 682
Lindsay, Shaylor, 2118
Lindsay Jr., George N., 5084
Lindsay, Jr., George N., 7678
Lindsay, Robert, 8587
Lindsen, Bruce, 769
Lindsey, Bonnie, 5430
Lindsey, Kristen, 4156
Lindsey, Paula H, 7385
Lindsey-McCintock, Jennifer, 8043
Lindsley, Stephanie, 7991
Lindstrom, Amy, 2152
Line, Rita, 2285
Lineaweaver, Kim, 6336
Lineaweaver, Mark, 2649
Linenko, Lori, 684
Linfante, Kristen, 1541, 1654
Ling, Chris, 4004, 8463
Ling, Christopher H, 8726
Ling, Jahja, 843
Ling, Lauren, 506
Ling, Virginia, 2022
Lingas, Alexander, 2299
Lingenfelter, Joshua, 6889, 6893
Lingle, Ronald, 5253
Linguanti, Thomas V., 2953
Link, Geoffrey, 4308
Link, Jim, 4147
Link, John, 432
Link, Mimi, 140
Links, Richard, 4210
Linksz, James, 5473
Linn, Hjordis, 387
Linn, Irena, 616
Linn, Joelle, 1
Linnane, SJ, Fr Brian, 7197
Linnell, Sherry, 2459
Linnens, Kelly, 4683
Linnerson, Raina, 3241
Linnes, Jeanne, 489
Lino, Chris, 4009
Lins, Mary, 8141
Linssen, Daniel, 1823
Linster, Debbie, 6340
Lint, Rosemary, 1612
Linton, Judith, 885
Linton, Leonard, 885
Linville, Dwayne, 364
Linville, Penny, 4142, 5898
Linville, Tim, 8044
Lionberger, Justine, 2070
Liou, Benjamin, 6158
Lipari, Peter, 1055
Liphart, Toni, 4683
Lipkin, Seymour, 4729
Lipkis, Larry, 8113
Lipman, Alan, 5640
Lipman, Blayne, 8295
Lipman, Susan, 1041, 2943, 4559
Lipowsky, Brenda, 262
Lipp, Robert, 466
Lipper, Anni, 844
Lipper, Ruth C., 1336, 1337
Lippert, Anne, 5284
Lippetz, Gregory L, 4313
Lipshie, Jean, 1382, 5071
Lipsitt, Steven, 1202
Lipsky, Arie, 1222, 1515
Lipsky, Jon, 3177
Lipstein, Amy, 1995

Liptak, Rose, 5441
Lipton, Elaine, 1204
Lipton, Lini, 5109
Lipuma, Kathryn M., 2970
Lisa, Jeanine, 3928, 3933
Lisbeth Navarrete, Rosa, 78
Lisbon, Crystal, 324
Lischick, Dorothea, 6341
Lisenby, Shannon, 2401
Lish, Herd, 8169
Lisi, Judith, 6596
Liskh, Matt, 6756
Lisle, Liz, 2451
Lisle, Susan, 3658
Lisner, Pam, 1755
Lisowski, Dan, 8676, 8680
Liss, Brooke, 2379
Lister, Robin, 3761
Lister-Sink, Barbara, 5278
Liston, Betty, 1280
Lit, Mark A, 7333
Litch, Debbi, 8286
Litch, Debbie, 8286
Litch, John, 1262
Litecky, Larry, 3273
Litfin, Duane, 4603
Litfin, Micheal, 2539
Litinas, Kathleen, 1699
Litle, Bob, 1285
Litoff, Mel, 5086
Litrell, Dave, 8596
Litt, Robin, 4379
Littauer, Ernest L., 4210
Littaur, Ernest, 4210
Little, Brad, 5567
Little, Carol, 1734
Little, Elden, 2339
Little, Jacey, 3982
Little, Laura, 2897
Little, Linda, 1768
Little, Merry, 5874
Little, Michelle, 1672, 5518
Little, Roderick, 1222
Little, Stacy, 1224, 1225
Little, Stephen, 6673
Little, Wendy, 4631
Littlefield, Durwood, 2222
Littlejohn, Christina, 755
Littlejohn, Laura, 8071
Littlepage, Craig, 8518
Littleton, Joe, 5558
Littleton, Renee, 2730
Littlewood, Lucky, 2489
Littlewood, Peter B., 4544
Littman, Tom, 5642
litton, Andrew, 905
Litton, James, 2186
Litvack, Mike, 6156
Litvin, Mark, 7725
Liu, Christine, 1832
Liu, Helen, 900, 901
Liu, Julia, 50
Liu, Lei, 996
Liva, Dr. Victor, 1537
Lively, Dr. Judy, 5967
Livengood, Jim, 5995, 6001
Livesay, Stephen, 5564
Livingston, Derek, 2566
Livingston, Derek Charles, 2640
Livingston, Jesse, 2306
Livingston, John, 6292
Livingston, Mike, 7106
Livingston, Nancy, 2573
Livingston, Richard, 4308
Livingston, W. Curtis, 5154
Livingstone, Pamela, 3662
Livingstone, Sherrill, 2895
Livington, Amy, 5379
Livollen, Kathleen, 7183
Lizenbery, Gregg, 107, 6674
Llafet, Park, 1811
Lldow, Alexander, 6207
Llewellyn, Grant, 1181, 1500, 2106
Llinas, Emilio, 1520
Lloveras, Sonia, 2476
Lloyd, B. Michl, 1314
Lloyd, David, 3176
Lloyd, Derek, 7774

Lloyd, Evan, 1613
Lloyd, Hannah, 5900
Lloyd, J.D., 4089
Lloyd, Joe, 5967
Lloyd, Justin, 8605
Lloyd, Steven, 3682
Lloyd Olson, David, 2746
Lloyd, Jr., David L., 4806
LIveris, Andrew N, 6207
Lo, Daniel, 53
Lobanova-Heasley, Inna, 1639
Lobdell, Barbara, 4982
Lobel, Dan, 1422
Lobel, Meriam, 7595
Lobel, Steven, 5039
Lobsinger, Lori, 6870
LoBue, Louis, 3077
Lochow, Michael, 3691
Lochra, Julia, 900, 901, 4361
Lochtefeld, Maureen, 1906
Locke, Nancy, 564
Locke, Robert J, 3817
Locker, Kelli, 7991
Lockett, Bonnie, 1868
Lockhart, Foye S., 5280
Lockhart, John, 1778
Lockhart, Keith, 1176, 5226
Lockhart, Sarah, 849
Lockington, David, 810, 1234
Locklear, Chad, 7899
Lockwood, Rich, 3916
Lockwood, Ruth, 5799
Lockwood, William W, 3382
Lockwood Blais, Patti, 7666
Lococo, Mark, 6739, 6751
Loder, David E., 3840
Lodes, Mike, 2297
Lodico, Vincent, 1547
Lodico Welshons, Andrea, 444
Loeb, Ben, 6518
Loeb, Benjamin, 1329
Loeb, Eve, 4148, 5915, 5916
Loeb Carroll, Tina, 7953
Loeble, Jeff, 8309
Loeffler, Barbara, 5458
Loehman, TJ, 8581
Loesch, Dr. Cliffton, 4683
Loevner, Brian, 2916
Loewen, Debra, 704
Loewenberg, Alvin A., 5662
Loewenthal, Norm, 2263
Loewy, Peter, 3372
Lofdahl, Will, 5030, 7614
Lofgren, Martha, 2552
Loftin, Christy, 8208
Loftin, Dennis, 1104, 1105
Loftin, Stephen A, 5301
Loftin, Stephen A., 7953
Loftus, James P., 5857
Lofvall, Gabriel, 1975
Lofy, Heidi, 8689
Logan, Dennis, 6211
Logan, Kathryn, 1654
Logan, P Bradley, 7339
Logan, Scoot, 141
Logan Barton, Nancy, 5289, 7942
Logan III, Joseph, 2377
Loghry, Laura, 7603
Logowitz, Steve, 4810
Logrea, Jean, 496
Loh, Lawrence, 1657, 1667
Lohman, Barbara, 832
Lohman, Crystal, 988
Lohr, Laura, 7099, 7100, 7101, 7102
Lohr, Lawrence, 8779
Lohr Ph.D, Steven, 6321
Lohse, Nancy, 6325
Loigman, Mark D, 8073
Lomas, Jenny, 1119
Lombard, Mary Frances, 1991
Lombard Todd, Zo‰, 4
Lombardi, Hugh, 8294
Lombardi, Joanne, 2727
Lombardo, Dan, 3181
Lombardo, Justin J., 2344
Lombardo, Rick, 2602, 3164
Lombardo, Robert, 8844
Lombardozzi, Quimby, 3791

Lombardy, Lisa, 1297
Lommen, Dana, 8077
LoMonaco, Dr. Martha, 2684
Lomonaco, Peter, 1339
Lonardo, Mike, 371
Loncasty, Don, 2158
Loncle, David, 7825, 7826
Loncto, Nancy, 6314
London, Amy, 91
London, Leonard, 3427
London, Todd, 3530, 7706
Lonegran, Richard, 848
Lonergan, Michael, 397
Long, Andrew, 623
Long, Andy, 6990
Long, April, 1702
Long, Carolyn, 1839
Long, Curtis, 707
Long, Daniel, 2361
Long, Flo, 7390
Long, Janet A., 5812
Long, Joan, 246
Long, Joe R., 1703
Long, Kathy, 6122
Long, Laura, 6272
Long, Michelle, 3648
Long, Nikisha, 2735
Long, Robert, 2185
Long, Rocky, 7610
Long, Shara, 1581
Long, Stephanie, 3256
Long, Stephen, 8047
Long, Tim, 3971
Long, Tracy, 3442
Long, Trish, 3945
Long, William J, 5371
Long, Ph.D., Eva, 795
Long-Voelkner, Ann, 1257
Longenberger, Andy, 8130
Longey, Mary, 2370
Longfield, Ross, 1321
Longley, Chet, 5527
Longlois, Marc, 6221, 6222, 6223, 6226
Longlois, Mark, 2548
Longman, Stanley V, 2845
Longmire, Molly, 1698
Longo, Lou, 3215
Longo, Vince, 3156
Longrey, Louis, 5151
Longshore, John, 5900
Longstreth, Clara, 2236
Longto, Jodi, 7695
Lonick, Deb, 4133
Lonsbury, Eric, 6876
Lonsdorf, Richard, 1925
Lonshein, Alison, 5133
Loo, Violet S.W., 6673
Looker, Wendy, 2271
Loomis, John H., 2745
Loomis, Sue, 1586
Loomis, Warren, 4178
Looney, Deane H., 2162
Looney, Dr. Gail, 1819
Looney, Sean M., 7185
Looper, Dr. Doris, 8032
Loos, Alicia, 8089, 8092, 8096, 8099
Loos, Jon, 8247
Loos, Sky, 3780
Loper Bloch, Shar, 1858
Lopera, Andres, 1254
Lopes, Bernadette, 6250
Lopes, Gail, 3771, 8062, 8063
Lopes, Stacey, 7537
Lopez, Abel, 2739
Lopez, Deirdre A., 6359
Lopez, George, 6321
Lopez, Gladys Yvette, 6748, 6750
Lopez, J.A., 6520
Lopez, Lourdes, 160, 461
Lopez, Marina, 380
Lopez, Soledad, 3624
Lopez, Starr, 6144
Lopiccolo, Kim, 8721
Lopinsky, Lisa, 1817
Lopresti, Joseph, 5320
LoPresto, Tony, 5386
Lord, Connie, 1789
Lord, Heidi, 1258, 1259

Executive Name Index

Lord, John S., 4469
Lord, Lindsey, 6894
Lord, Ruth, 6419
Lord, Stephen, 2163
Lorde, Carolyn, 401
Lorello, Christine, 7603
Loren, Bonnie, 3550
Loren, Nicholas, 2138
Lorenz, Blake, 1170
Lorenz, Elizabeth, 1750
Lorenz, Thomas, 7493
Lorenzen, Sherry, 3061
Lorick, Steve, 6096, 6098
Lorimer, Valerie, 6431
Lorimore, David, 8259
Lorincz, Joey, 7485
Lorino, Anthony, 7150, 7151
Loris, Susan, 1830
Lorraine, Ted, 859
Lorraine, Vince, 1232, 1233
Loscheider, Paul, 6803, 6804
Loscuito, John, 4130
Losey, Ryan, 1180
Lotman, Herbert, 3837, 5474
Lott, Allison, 5643
Lott, Kathryn, 5643
Lotter, Marcia, 4251
Lotz, Joshua, 6662
Lotze, Gary, 5996, 6010
Lou Aleskie, Mary, 4559
Lou Brown, Mary, 1806
Lou Henson, Mary, 6388
Lou Heran, Mary, 3345
Lou Madden, Mary, 724
Lou Stricklin, Mary, 1518
Lou Weingart, Mary, 8023, 8024
Lou Weingart, Mrs. Mary, 8022
Lou Winnick, Mary, 2821
Louder, Michael, 5261
Loudermilk, Sarah, 5635
Loudermilk, Wanda, 4194
Loughman, Henry, 2539
Loughran, Una, 560
Louis Coco, Samuel, 1632
Louise, Jean, 783
Louise Burke, Mary, 1951
Louise Montgomery, Mary, 8507
Louise Perot, Mary, 2202
Louise Stoughton, Mary, 3810, 8132
Loula, Chris, 6825, 6826, 6827
Loula, Rick, 3036
Loungway, Stuart, 221
Lourenso, Frank, 7647
Lourie, Mark, 8786
Loux, Jennifer, 1643, 5480
Lovaglia, Toni, 5637
Lovan, Tracy, 1126
Lovano, Joe, 5097
Love, Candace, 6
Love, Cynthia, 1305
Love, David, 8119
Love, Debbie, 4541
Love, Ed, 1307
Love, Jason, 1163
Love, John, 4527
Love, Kathy, 6763
Love, Lisa, 234, 5990
Love, Reve, 7605
Lovejoy, Jennifer, 1021
Lovejoy, Philip, 7220
Lovejoy Goldman, Melissa, 689
Lovelace, Byron, 8462
Lovell, Ryan, 3323
Loverin, Benjamin, 3361, 6303
Lovering, Earle, 5583
Lovero, Elizabeth, 6286
Loving, Cathy, 1705
Loving, Ronald A., 3903
Loving, Sharon, 5459
Lovinggood, David, 2673
Lovoy Koch, Denise, 5895
Lovtang, Prudy, 863
Low, David, 850
Lowchow, Michael, 3689
Lowden Norman, Nancy, 6560
Lowder, Michael, 5260
Lowdon, TJ, 8104
Lowe, Heather, 2904

Lowe, Helen, 5162
Lowe, Jamie, 4510
Lowe, Kathleen, 4201
Lowe, Leah, 2701
Lowe, Michele, 5167
Lowe, Pam, 820
Lowe, Phillip, 5633
Lowe, Ryan, 1254
Lowe, Sonja, 4088
Lowell, Jim, 3194
Lowenstein, Amy, 4034
Lowentritt, Tonya, 3079
Lower, Frank, 5653
Lower-Shirey, Anne, 3755
Lowery II, BS, MA, Charles W., 5027
Lowndes, Rita, 4469
Lowne, Carol, 1453
Lowrie, Gerald M, 2738
Lowrie, Kate, 1179
Lowry, Audrey, 363
Lowry, Douglas, 1459, 1526
Lowry, Glenn, 5163
Lowry, Rose, 3356
Lowry, William A., 6795
Lowry III, L. Randolph, 5578, 8291
Loyd, Ryan C., 6062
Lozano, Danilo, 892, 4349
Lozano, Fran, 766, 4211
Lozano, Raul, 2605
Lozier, Jim, 2261
Lozier, Steve, 2506, 2507
Lu, Chris, 2542
Lubaroff, Scott, 1295
Lubin, Susan, 2336
Lubkeman, Brian, 1778
Lubner, Sonya, 2779
Lubovitch, Lar, 446
Luca, Sergiu, 5412
Lucas, Amy, 1088
Lucas, Bob, 3753
Lucas, Cynthia, 103
Lucas, Darren, 7866
Lucas, Katie, 5324
Lucas, Kay, 5401
Lucas, Kiki, 639
Lucas, Marilyn, 1647
Lucas, Natalie, 2557
Lucas, Pamela, 1585
Lucas, Waverly, 180
Lucchesi, Melinda S., 222
Luce, Becky, 5355
Luce, Michael, 3443
Luce, Priscilla M., 3836
Luce West, Lanni, 3443
Luce-Aurilio, Amity, 3443
Lucero, David, 4531
Lucero, Dennis, 6341
Luchsinger, Ron, 2115, 2173
Luciano, Karen, 8142
Lucibello, Arlene, 6421
Lucier, David, 6522
Lucier, John, 6104
Lucier, Susan, 3163
Lucio, Jaime, 3939, 8336
Lucio, Jessie, 6201
Lucio, Saul, 4452
Luck, Oliver, 8648
Lucks, Barbara J., 4574
Lucoff, Don, 5419
Lucy, Cecil, 5932
Ludwa, Chris, 4827
Ludwick, Julie, 426
Ludwig, Carolyn, 3844
Ludwig, David, 1769, 8149
Ludwig, David R., 1254
Ludwig, Jeffrey, 5776
Ludwig, Linda, 3176
Ludwig, Lisa, 3428
Ludwig, Richard, 7550
Ludwig, Stephanie, 1309, 1310
Lueben, Becky, 3222
Lueder, Michael, 4129
Lueers, Cathy, 1657
Lueking, Arthur L., 7451
Luening Long, Esq., Elizabeth, 577
Luessen, Lawrence, 2380, 5768, 5769
Luft, Andy, 7375
Luger, Alan, 2081

Lugo, Carolina, 27
Lugo, Jim, 3601
Luhdorff, Mark, 835
Luisi, Fabio, 2234
Luisotti, Nicola, 1922, 1923, 1926
Luisser, Henry, 3138
Lujan, Linda, 5947
Luka, MD, Norman, 1352
Lukach, Terri, 1775
Lukas, Alisha, 7174
Luke, Doug, 3996
Luke, Kathleen, 670
Lukefahr, Brenda, 1737
Lukinovich, Phillip, 7126
Luley, Gail, 2318
Luley, Gail M., 1658
Lum, Eileen, 2028
Lum, Ryan, 1021
Lumia, David, 4997
Lumpkin, Bruce, 3990
Luna, Carlos, 1738
Luna, CPA, CFE, Natalie, 4003
Lunceford, Darby I, 2747
Lunch, David, 2425
Lund, Arlene, 6212
Lund, Karen, 4088
Lund, Kjristine, 1805
Lund, Mark, 4088
Lund, Susan, 4637
Lund, Tom, 7468
Lundahl, Steven, 5138
Lundberg, David, 2615
Lundberg, Mary, 2615
Lundberg, Susan, 1510
Lundegard, John, 4322
Lundell, Albert, 897
Lundell, Diana, 4657, 4658, 4659, 4660, 4661
Lundervold, Barbara, 2143
Lundgren, Kari, 4163
Lundquist, Keith, 975
Lundquist, Patricia, 5773
Lundy, Anne, 8401
Lundy, Larry, 700
Luneau, Anni, 7739
Lunke, Candy, 8579
Lunser, Leo, 3109
Lunsford, Christie, 7095
Lunsford, John, 2268
Lunsford, Martha, 8631
Lunt, Pamela, 5945
Luntz, Justin, 3700
Luo, Rolland, 82, 97
Luongo, David, 8201
Lupercio, Celeste, 3292
Luper, Fred, 4662
Lupi, Ginnie, 5065
Lupo, Ellie, 590
Lupone, Robert, 3519
Luppescu, Naomi, 468
Luquire, Wilson, 710
Luria, Donald, 8179
Luria Caplan, Paula, 1368
Lurie, Karie, 4177, 5986
Lurie, Steve, 5191
Luse, Don, 5228
Lusk, Joan, 1675
Lusk, Kelly, 2328
Lussier, Christine M, 575
Luster, Cliff, 7644
Lustig, Graham, 53
Luton, Hank, 8561
Luttenberger, C.M., Rev. Gerard, 7692
Lutwak, Mark, 2886
Lutz, Angela, 1738
Lutz, Greta, 5439
Lutz, Joseph, 4113
Lutz, Linda, 7283
Lutz, Marilyn, 1630
Lutz, Nina, 1016
Lutz, Paula, 7439
Lutz, Paula M, 7438
Lutz, Tony, 4901
Lutzke, Myron, 1399
Luukko, Peter, 5478, 8162
Luxner, Michael, 1045
Luy, Peggy S., 2052
Luzicka Reinschmidt, Laura, 307
Lvenla, Randy, 6603

Lyall, Katharine C, 8672
Lyall, Robert, 2084, 2136
Lybeck, Greg, 8682
Lyddon-Hattan, Lana, 236
Lydecker, Dr. Kent, 4489
Lydum, Chip, 8599, 8600
Lykins, Ron, 1572
Lyle, Janice, 6203
Lyle, Nancy, 1796
Lyle, Shawn F, 3403
Lyle, Vivian S, 2401
Lyles, Katy, 2334
Lyles, Ronald, 920
Lyles, Susan, 2653
Lyman, Burt, 7350
Lyman, Dave, 2140
Lyman, Janet, 1351
Lyman, Sue, 6724
Lyman Geotz, Jean, 5168
Lyn Avey, Meredith, 391
Lynch, Brian, 4588
Lynch, Brian T, 6803, 6804
Lynch, Clellie, 1405
Lynch, Dennis M, 5770
Lynch, Jane, 2263, 6146
Lynch, Jeffrey, 3695
Lynch, Kathleen, 2737
Lynch, Kelly, 7601
Lynch, Lisa, 3908, 3910
Lynch, Mary, 6193
Lynch, Michelle, 78
Lynch, Mike, 1291
Lynch, Mitzi, 3058
Lynch, Patricia, 4977, 7543, 8201
Lynch, Patrick J, 6167
Lynch, Robert, 5772
Lynch, Shane, 1780
Lynch, Susan, 1753
Lynes, James J., 3580
Lyng, Nora Mae, 7760
Lyngstad, Gail, 5557
Lynn, Fred A, 5323
Lynn, Joseph, 6718, 8611
Lynn, Michaele, 1564
Lynn, Nancy R, 4322
lynn, Robin, 7766
Lynn Cooper Hilton, Donna, 6398
Lynn Mann, Joey, 163
Lynn Petersen, Rebecca, 1258, 1259
Lynn Plier, Tammy, 5912, 5913, 5914
Lynn Wiley, Diana, 2540
Lynn Willingham, Karen, 5912, 5913, 5914
Lynne, Jessica, 5051
Lynne, Michael, 3437
Lynne Bolda, Sheila, 6662
Lynner, Susan A., 4430
Lynskey, Susan, 6479
Lyon, Courtney, 221
Lyon, David, 1290
Lyon, Kathy, 987
Lyons, Andrea, 895, 2209
Lyons, Brad, 2977
Lyons, David, 6430
Lyons, Jean, 4971
Lyons, Jenny, 6328
Lyons, Kit, 3017
Lyons, Rachel, 4718
Lyons, Robert, 3537
Lyons, Shane, 5924, 5925
Lyss, Sherri, 1288, 4919
Lytart, Sylvie, 691
Lyttle, John, 4137

M

M Horne Jr, Dr Rex, 4183
M. Baker, Eleanor, 1150
M. Cahill, Catherine, 8156
M. Crampton, Susanna, 3158
M. Dickson, Lisa, 1150
M. Djaz, Carlos, 6550
M. Macosko, Gregory, 3549
M. Mullen, Regina, 1204
M. Papada, James, 8151
M. Wirtshafter, Tom, 7789
M.Thomas, Carl, 3071
M. Feldman, Ruth, 6427
Ma, Kathryn, 3771, 8062, 8063

Executive Name Index

Ma, Xina, 6671
Ma, Yo-Yo, 1035, 1038
Maag, Kathy, 1123
Maas, Lisa, 2553
Maaskant, Robert, 7981
Maass, Jeanne, 1348
Mabe, Tim, 3665
Mabins, Tondrea, 6394
Mabley, Frank, 7380
Mably, Mary, 227
Maby, Marion, 733
Mac Ewan, Peter, 8005
Macaluso, Emily, 6738
Macarthur, Eva, 268
MacArthur Miele, Linda, 249
Macatsoris, Christofer, 2305
Macchiarini, Marianella, 2582
MacDavis, William, 8389
MacDonald, David L, 3472
MacDonald, Douglas, 7234, 7255
MacDonald, Greg, 4025, 4968
MacDonald, Jerry, 8465
MacDonald, Kathryn, 3126
Macdonald, Katie, 3113
MacDonald, Kenneth, 325
MacDonald, Martine, 4862
MacDonald, Rae, 1943
Macdonald, Robert, 4459
MacDonald, Robert, 6541
MacDonald, Stephen C., 1627, 1628
MacDougall, Kristin, 3158
Mace, Mary Jo, 2230
Macek, Robert C., 2130
Macel Theys, Emily, 266
Macewicz, Diane, 1800
Macferran, Fran, 8407
MacGregor, Lowell, 8090
Mach, Steven P., 1731
Machac, Lisa, 53
Machacek, R J, 8351
Machado, Eduardo, 3502
Machado, Paul, 4376
Macheel, Jeff, 8675, 8683
Machlin, Steven D., 5049, 5120
Machtinger, Steven, 866, 867
Machuta, Chris, 7301
Macias, Mike, 4196
Macier, Karen, 1364
Macintosh, Hyacinth, 5373
Macioce, Leah, 7462
Mack, Eric, 6291, 6293, 6294, 6296
Mack, Frank, 2709
Mack, Fredric, 1447
Mack, Kevin L, 929
Mack, Linda, 1956, 2198
Mack, Liz, 4412
Mack, Mary, 7635
Mack, Rory, 4137
Mack, Stephen, 2098
Mack, Tamara, 5998
MacKay, Charles, 2200
Mackay, Greg, 8271
Mackay, Lynn, 762, 814
Mackay, Susan P., 3247
MacKay-Galbraith, Janet, 4546
MacKeigan, Richard, 7301, 7304
Mackenzie, Estelle, 944
MacKenzie Miller, Lauren, 717
Mackes, Gary, 7213
Mackesey, Brandom, 8698, 8699, 8700
Mackey, Eileen, 2124
Mackey, Janice, 2298
Mackey, Jennifer, 1979
Mackie, Richard H., 1826
Mackin, Jodi, 1301
MacKinnon, J Allan, 1850
MacKinnon, Steve, 2806
Macklin, Diane, 3130
Mackus, Boyd, 8860
MacLachlan, Julie, 4662
MacLaughlin, Debbie, 3290
Maclay, John, 2229
MacLean, Cal, 3904
Maclean, Lyla, 4579
MacLeod, Amy, 6283
MacLeod, Debbie, 4060
MacLeod, Kim, 8050
MacMillan, Scooter, 2870

Macnab, Rowena, 4141
MacNamee, Rebecca, 1654
MacNaughton, Luther, 4947
MacNish, Linda, 3432
Macon, Linda, 755
Macor, Chris, 2662
Macoun, Scott, 2952
MacPhearson, Iain, 3896
MacPherson, Bruce, 8442
MacPherson, Chris, 3897
MacPherson-Evans, Jennifer, 3897
MacQueen, Steve, 1768, 7859
MacRae, Katherine, 5267
Macri, Richard A., 1342
Macris, Nicoletta, 7199
Macris, Peter, 3603
MacRitchie, Andrew, 5413
MacRoberts, Brenda, 3791
Macy, Becky, 2870
Macy, James, 8697
Macy, Jo Ann, 904, 6344
Madalinski, Sarah, 6967, 6971
Madcharo, Cynthia, 1464
Madden, Brian M., 3121
Madden, Charles, 7158
Madden, J. Robert, 5594
Madden, Sandra, 6575
Maddock, Leah, 814
Maddox, Doug, 1932
Maddox, George, 2006
Maddox Peterson, Jeanne, 566
Madgin, Angela, 5474
Madia, Joey, 4098
Madigan, Leslie, 3685, 7597
Madison, Beth, 2353
Madkour, Christopher, 5712
Madlem, Peter, 871
Madlom, James, 4123
Madoni, Pat, 4132
Madore, Paul, 2124
Madover, Arielle Tepper, 7781
Madsen, Susie, 6044, 6045, 6046
Madson, Heidi, 2389
Mae Frederick, Erla, 8141
Maedel, Ouida, 266
Maestas, Michelle, 807
Magara, Albert, 8324
Magee, Irma A, 7838
Magee, Joyce, 927
Magee, Sean, 3442, 5080
Magendanz, Dr. Jon, 1473
Mager, Stephen, 2162
Magerer, Lisa, 4967
Mages, William, 2956
Maggard, Dave, 8408
Maggio, Robert, 1666
Maggs, Patricia, 1874
Maghsoudi, Paymaneh, 2642
Magida, Lennie, 3131
Magidson, Joshua, 6488
Magin, Marilyn, 3721
Maginnis, Tara, 2420
Magnani, Peter, 7691
Magner, Jamie, 5839
Magnesen, Larry S., 1527
Magnus, Eric, 3048
Magnus, Michael, 3926
Magnus, Robert, 7167
Magnuson, Jana, 4739, 4744
Magoon, Kurt, 4136
Magowan, Peter A, 6251
Magruder, Dennis R, 8654
Magruder, Kate, 2636
Maguda, John, 1450
Maguire, Dan, 5787
Maguire, Kate, 3176, 4806
Maguire, Matthew, 3480
Maguire, Nancy, 7547
Maguire, Siobhan, 4060
Mahaffey, Courtney, 1747, 2359
Mahaffey, Michael, 1545, 1546, 2282, 5326
Mahan, Liz, 4814
Mahan, Michael A, 1198
Mahdi, Nadia, 6479
Mahe, Kathy, 2076
Maher, Colleen, 2600
Mahler, Richard J., 5001
Mahli, Dan, 1267

Mahon, Maxine, 65
Mahoney, Andy, 5884
Mahoney, Bill, 6281
Mahoney, Duncan, 2519, 2522
Mahoney, Eva, 3527
Mahoney, Joyce, 1763
Mahoney, Leanne, 4890
Mahoney, Sharyn, 620
Mahoney, Thomas, 3840
Mahoney, Tim, 4276, 6217
Mahony, Jim, 7263
Mahony, Maggie, 4970
Mahraun, Daniel, 4674
Mahrdt, Margie, 3170
Maier, Dave, 4110
Maier, Melissa, 1970
Maiers, Ashley, 2071
Maimon PhD, Elaine P, 6841, 6842
Main, Alice L, 6331
Main, Nancy, 2615
Mainolfi, Massimiliano, 5188
Mains, Dr. Ronda, 6025
Maiorano, Julie, 64
Maiorano, Robert, 2702
Mairs, David, 1751
Maisch, Chuck, 1131
Maisel, Garry, 6230
Maisel, Garry P., 6096, 6098
Maisel, Seth, 6386
Maisonet, Elba, 2928
Maissen, Jean, 2427
Maister, Nigel, 3612
Maitland, Al, 814
Maiulloni, David, 2184
Majkut, Martin, 1588
Major, Glenn, 8554
Major, James E., 4589
Major, Joshua, 4845
Major, Leon, 2280
Major, Naomi, 2228
Maker Palmieri, Michele, 8194
Maki, Patricia, 4344
Makino, Ben, 2332
Makino, Yuri, 2431
Makowski, Stan, 7652, 7655
Maksym, Gwen, 691
Malagiere, Kenneth J., 1324
Malan, Danielle, 3785
Malan, Roy, 889, 919, 4375
Malashock, John, 68
Malatesta, John, 5166
Malaty, Jean-Philippe, 347, 349
Malburg, Gary, 3202
Malcolm, Bill, 830
Malcolm, Rasheda, 515
Malcolm, III, D.H., 2874
Malcolm-Naib, Rebecca, 542
Malcom, Blake, 6496
Maldonado, Ken, 417
Maldonado, Ricardo, 1447
Maldonado, Viri, 3988
Male, Phillip, 2848
Malecki, Karen, 2092
Maleczech, Ruth, 3516
Malenka, Richard, 5818, 7719, 8642
Malet, Ryan, 6465
Maletta, Wendy, 3845
Maley, Susan, 3636
Maley, Teresa, 4670
Malfitano, Frank, 4836, 4837
Malhotra, Sandhya, 491
Malhotra Degenemark, Simmi, 450
Malicki, Jessica, 4053
Malik, Meena, 1191
Malikowski, Paul, 7521
Malin, Cathy, 4029
Malina, Arnie, 1768, 5705, 8505
Malina, Judith, 3515
Malina, Stuart, 1627, 1628
Malinger, Andi, 3731
Malinkine, Denis, 703
Malinoski, Sarah, 2208
Malinoski-Umberger, Sarah, 2208
Malinova, Margarita, 5063
Malinowski, Barbara, 2580
Malinowski, Emily, 1372
Malis, David, 904
Malis Kincaid, Tess, 2878

Malisch, Brenda, 8679
Maliske, Brian, 8245
Malitas, Gail, 1318
Malitz, Morton, 4829
Malizia, Lester, 2771
Malkovich IV, Mark P, 5520
Malkowski, Christopher, 7948
Mallady, Dr. Shawn, 1044
Mallare Acton, Suzanne, 2137
Mallernee, Judith, 3989
Mallery, Mike, 8076, 8078
Mallet, John, 1576
Mallette, Lisa, 2599, 2633
Malley, Fred, 1352
Mallin, Erika, 3567
Mallin, Heidi, 6900
Mallinson, J Stephen, 911
Mallory, Desiree, 4230
Mallory, Mark, 4271
Malloy, Harvey, 759, 761, 4205
Malloy, Jeff, 2586
Malloy, Jeffrey P., 2573
Malloy, Sue, 6936
Mallquist, Carol, 4409
Malm, Cathy, 6774
Malmuth-Onn, Ann, 98
Maloff Esq, Peter, 334
Malon, Dick, 3278, 7412
Malone, Doug, 8220
Malone, Fran, 4132
Malone, Giles, 6489
Malone, Kent, 1061
Malone, Larissa, 529
Malone, Phyllis, 1750
Malone, Raymond M, 3711
Malone, Raymond M., 7963, 7964, 7965, 7966
Malone, Ryan, 5382
Malone, Terry W, 1252
Malone-Gray, Terrance, 1036
Maloney, Devon, 4755
Maloney, Elaine, 1450
Maloney, Kathy, 7180
Maloney, Mariah, 202
Maloney, Patty, 3623
Maloy, Heather, 506
Malozzi, Rosalba, 1400
Maltbia, Anita, 4904
Maltby, Joyce, 6679
Maltby, Mark, 2482
Maltby, Randy, 2132, 4833
Malucelli, Ken, 8730
Malvar'Ruiz, Fernando, 2186
Malvar-Ruiz, Fernando, 2186
Mam-Luft, Jeannes.S, 516
Manager, Marketing, 3169
Managing Director, Lozier, 2510
Manahan, George, 2238
Manasse, Jon, 1204, 4796, 4797
Mance, Robert, 2075
Mancill, Brenda, 5545
Mancinelli-Cahill, Margaret, 7623
Mancini, Rae, 4043
Mancuso, Jim, 1021
Mancuso, Kim, 3132
Mandel, David, 3868
Mandel, Peter, 801
Mandel, Rene, 758
Mandel, Susan, 5123
Mandell, Mark, 4390
Mandell, Peter, 826
Manders, Kelsey, 706
Mandery, Sharon, 7493
Mandicott, Bill, 4764
Mandicott, William, 4764
Mandile, Michael, 1196
Mandl, Alexander, 1834
Mandler, Susan, 135
Maneca, Fernando, 359
Manetta, Edward J, 7690
Maneval, Philip, 1643, 1645, 5480
Manfield, Lisa, 3747
Manfred, Rob, 6055
Manfredi, Heather, 4976
Manfred, Rob, 8178
Mangan, Carol, 2300
Mangan, F Lee, 1622
Mangan, Jacki, 2650
Mangan, Patricia, 2369, 5704

Executive Name Index

Mange, Dave, 1244
Mangelsdorf, Margaret, 2056
Mangeng, Carolyn, 5031
Manger, Susan, 4764
Mangers, Dennis H., 2553
Manghum, John, 1925
Mangiantini, Marc, 1908
Mangili, Jan, 2626
Mangino, Bob, 5800
Manhart, Mark, 3332
Maniaci, Dr. Vincent, 7250
Maniaci, Nicole, 1360
Manich, Crystal, 2211
Manifold, James, 6085
Manin, Lois, 6670
Manin, Molly, 6088
Manion, Diane, 5715
Manley, Ben, 1440
Manley, Kelly, 712
Manley, Natasha, 639
Manly, Dorothy, 759, 761, 4205
Mann, Alan, 1185
Mann, Anna, 2225
Mann, Ed, 5220
Mann, Emily, 3382
Mann, Mark, 3721
Mann, Molly, 8821
Mann, Philip, 755
Mann, Ross, 1646
Mann, Susan, 5277
Mann, Theodore, 2215, 7721
Mann Baehr, Celia, 714
Mannelli, Chris, 6760
Manning, Alison, 3151
Manning, Allison, 3151
Manning, Guy, 3967, 3968
Manning, Jacky, 1577
Manning, Jessica, 8444
Manning, Jessica A., 8445
Manning, Leslie, 5238
Manning, Michael, 4784
Manning, Roger, 2997
Manning, Thurston, 897
Mannion, Dennis, 7273
Mannshardt, Steve, 4311
Manocha, Arvind, 4227, 5762
Manoney, Gordon, 6031
Manos, Christopher B, 2865
Manos, George, 957, 4416, 4429
Manos, Nicholas F, 2865
Manrique, Anthony S, 1875
Manrique, Javier, 93, 2594
Mansbridge, Anna, 685
Manselle, Leslie, 920
Mansfield, Donna, 1792
Mansfield, Jennifer, 2786
Manta Meyer, Jessica, 1896
Manteau, Nicole M., 4962
Mantegna, John, 1770
Mantell, Mark, 1389
Manteris, Carol, 2316
Mantey, Erma, 899
Mantner, Fred, 2513
Mantzke, Marilyn, 2381
Manu, Costin, 3153
Manuel, David, 7118
Manuel, David E., 6636
Manuel, Robert, 6899, 6901, 6902
Manus, Dr. Betty, 5276
Manus, Mara, 7725
Manus, Ms. Betty, 8221
Manvicott, Bill, 4764
Manwaring, Barb, 5182
ManWaring, Glenda, 3877
Manwarr, Matthew, 5539
Manwell, Penny, 2816
Manzanales, Michelle, 393
Manzo, Kai, 6710
Mao, Michael, 457
Mao, Ruotao, 1325
Maple, Charles, 32
Maples, Steve, 5901, 5902, 5903, 5904
Maplethorpe, Kristi, 8619
Maraffi, Matt, 921
Maraldi, Lisa, 2919
Marano, Mario A., 1324, 1345
Maraviglia-Manalo, Jamie, 6062
Marc Chaves, Jr, Aurelius, 7699

Marc Torre, Jean, 71
Marcanio, Jerry, 3154
Marcante, Mark, 3578
Marcelletti, Jr., Lanfranco, 1394
March, Barney, 5910
March, Gary, 1875
Marchant, Beth, 496
Marchant, Susan, 4679
Marchbank, Adell, 8202
Marchell, Carla, 1733
Marchese Sidoti, Catherine, 8810
Marchesi, Josh, 2461
Marchesi, Joshua, 6091
Marchetta, Ralph, 5966
Marchsano, Jamie, 8051
Marcial, Adriana, 79
Marciano, Kathy, 7198
Marck, David, 403, 463
Marck, Neil, 4060
Marcoccia, Lou, 3627
Marcom, John, 1927
Marcon, Alison, 7562
Marconi, Donna, 6441
Marcozzi, Rudy, 4549, 6746
Marcucci, Sheree, 6423
Marcum, Ryan, 6972
Marcum, Travis, 1702
Marcus, Abby, 5052
Marcus, Ann, 3785
Marcus, Courtney, 632
Marcus, Ellen, 5172, 8866
Marcus, Gail, 5072
Marcus, Greg, 7947
Marcus, James S., 1406
Marcus, Jana, 6056
Marcus, Leslie, 3548
Marcus, Steve, 4126
Marcuse, Yvonne, 1341
Marcussen, Jack, 6575
Marcy, Mary B, 6277
Marden, David, 1418
Marder, Ellen, 1712
Marder, Meredith K., 747
Mardsen Fox, Ana, 589
Mareck Grundy, Karen, 306
Marecle, Rachel, 8617
Marek, Kim, 4156
Marek, Melonea, 3870
Marek, Reverend Walter, 3217
Marek, Wayne, 4108
Maren, James T., 8122
Marengo, Maury, 882
Margo, Dan, 4843, 4868
Margolf, Claire, 122
Margolis, Craig, 271
Margolis, Karl, 3245
Margolis, Laura, 3444
Margulies, Vicki, 5172
Marguth, Dave, 7522
Maria Alfonso, Sebrina, 973
Maria Kish, Eva, 301
Marian, Paula, 8207
Mariani, Angela, 4354
Mariani, Linda, 2714, 2715
Maricle, Dr. Sherrie, 1432
Marie Adams, Anne, 6784
Marie Baker, Ann, 1345
Marie Buck, Beth, 2094
Marie Codina Barlick, Ana, 160
Marie Deer-Owens, Ann, 5581
Marie Fernandez, Jean, 149
Marie Folkins, Kate, 2656
Marie Gewirtz, Anna, 5003
Marie Horton, Lisa, 3769
Marie Keenan, Ann, 7587
Marie Rauscher, Ann, 1700
Marie Ross, Dawn, 4124
Marie Shouse, Rose, 7082
Marietti, Maurice, 2311
Marigza, Robert, 3917, 5581
Marilyn,, 8490, 8491, 8492
Marina, Lorrain, 2260
Marina Alvarado, Elissa, 2606
Marina Mote, Tanya, 6355
Marincic, Jean, 3699
Marine, Eleanor, 1080
Mariner, Elaine, 4367
Mariner, Jonathan, 6055

Marinescu, Ovidiu, 1630
Marini, Donna, 1516
Marini, Vincent, 3657
Marino, J. F., 2312
Marino, James J., 3382
Marino, Peter, 1663, 5509
Marion, Cyndy A., 3590
Marita, Mina, 2449
Mark, Curtis, 5026
Mark, Dean, 8650
Mark, Jack, 4009
Mark, Peter, 2374
Mark, Susan, 5203
Marke, Philip, 1875
Markert, Wayne, 5758
Markes, Kris, 1584
Markevitch, Pat, 1899
Markewell, Suzanne, 1640
Markey, David, 3120
Markey, Micheal, 3335
Markham, C.W., 1786
Markham, Jay, 4068, 4072
Markham, Judith, 1314
Markham, Peggy, 510
Markham, Sharon, 6581
Markiewicz, Chris, 4810
Markinson, Martin, 6183
Markle, Debra, 1625
Markle, Marsha, 3017
MARKLE, NANCY, 2821
Markle, Patrick, 1922, 1923, 1926
Markou, Kypros, 1228
Markowitz, Andrew, 3605
Markowitz, John, 4475, 6580
Marks, Deborah, 2758
Marks, Dick, 8217
Marks, Jeffery A., 2377
Marks, Kristin, 2702
Marks, Lucky, 1779
Markus,, 8164, 8165, 8166
Markus, Joel, 3839, 8163
Markush, Robert, 708
Markuson, Cira P, 5180
Markwalter, Zoe, 5109
Markward, Dr. Edward, 1676
Markward, Edward, 1670, 2323
Markyna, Alicia, 1009
Marlatt, Rick, 3325
Marley, Ann, 1633
Marloff, Marilyn, 666
Marlowe, Ina, 2966
Marlyn Singer, Audrey, 2530
Marmor, Martin, 5694
Marmor, Seth A., 150
Marmora, Sharon, 3446
Marnell, Kristi, 4276, 6217
Marnen, James T, 5448
Maroney, Kevin, 3113, 7188
Maroney, Sharon, 3791, 8106
Marosi, Abi, 1565
Marquardt, Tami, 4010, 4011
Marquette, Ron, 7695
Marquez, Anthony E., 6135
Marquez, Kate, 4179
Marquis, Aldee, 752
Marquis, Bruce, 4545, 7074
Marquis, Jacques, 1722, 5625
Marquis, Marilyn, 759, 761, 4205
Marquis, Trent, 8622
Marr, Doug, 3331
Marr, Laura, 3331
Marra, Jr, Robert, 1174
Marraccini, Mike, 169
Marraccini, William J., 3384
Marrama, Elizabeth, 53
Marreel, Heather, 3037
Marrero, Kyle, 2009
Marrero, Michael, 4457
Marrero, Miguel, 3956
Marret, Greg, 3906
Marri, Richard A., 1342
Marriner Maull, George, 1348
Marriott, J W, 2973
Marriott, Nada, 2031
Marriott, Susan, 3428
Marriott, Wendi, 5942
Marro, Peter, 326
Marroquin, Rogelio, 3988

Marsalis, Wynton, 1421, 5142, 7729
Marsden, Barbara Ann, 589
Marsden, Herci, 589
Marsden, Mark, 589
Marsden Fox, Ana, 589
Marsh, Christopher J., 11
Marsh, James, 7241
Marsh, Lara, 317
Marsh, Paul, 3160
Marsh, Ryan, 6135
Marsh, Stephen L., 797
Marsha, Jeff, 7650
Marshal, Lowry, 3860
Marshall, Amy, 351
Marshall, Ann, 4838
Marshall, Carol P., 4971
Marshall, Dennis, 636
Marshall, Diane, 5805
Marshall, Don, 1143, 4718
Marshall, Frederick, 3012
Marshall, Galen, 2111
Marshall, Hearther, 5541
Marshall, Kari, 1265
Marshall, Katherine, 2642
Marshall, Kelli, 1642
Marshall, Kevin, 2781
Marshall, Laura, 4031
Marshall, Lea, 671
Marshall, Linda, 1124
Marshall, Margo, 636
Marshall, Rev. Paul, 6676
Marshall, Richard, 2222
Marshall, Scott, 6244
Marshall, Terry, 747
Marshall, Tom, 2725
Marshall , Ashley, 4703
Marsted, Garrison, 3435
Marta, Charles, 5565
Martel, Leslie, 5361
Martel, Robert, 4790
Martell, Fredrick, 2241
Martell, Rodney, 1784
Martelli, Ruth, 3852
Marten, Ethan, 4043
Marten, Richard, 4043
Martens, Jordan, 3047
Martin, Biddy, 7216
Martin, BJ, 227
Martin, Brete, 23
Martin, Bud, 2727
Martin, Carol, 2677
Martin, Carter, 8673
Martin, Courtney A., 3859
Martin, Craig, 2579
Martin, David, 8001
Martin, Debbie, 4649
Martin, Douglas, 339
Martin, Dr Alice, 2950
Martin, Edward F., 2084, 4719
Martin, Eff W., 1925
Martin, Elisa, 3154
Martin, Frank, 4472
Martin, Geoffery, 3719
Martin, Glenn, 5586
Martin, Gordon G., 4148, 5915, 5916
Martin, Harolt, 7922
Martin, Iiona, 2484
Martin, Jason Keith, 227
Martin, Jennifer, 4318
Martin, Jesse, 3158
Martin, Jill, 4545
Martin, Jill Cary, 2470
Martin, Jim, 6365
Martin, John, 2779, 5195
Martin, Jonathan, 2343, 8362
Martin, Jorge, 6156
Martin, Kari, 8721
Martin, Karla L, 4313
Martin, Keith J, 227
Martin, Kerry, 6697
Martin, Kevin, 4756
Martin, Kim, 3847, 5494
Martin, Laurie, 4801
Martin, Leah, 201
Martin, Linda, 308, 7387
Martin, Lusha, 4801
Martin, Maggie, 1136
Martin, Martha, 1890

Executive Name Index

Martin, Mary, 4675
Martin, Marya, 5119
Martin, Meghan, 6560
Martin, Michael, 7613
Martin, Michelle, 621
Martin, Myron G., 7514
Martin, Nels, 3806
Martin, Olivia, 8058
Martin, Pamela, 112
Martin, Peter, 8509
Martin, Philip K. , 1317
Martin, Rebecca, 1283
Martin, Richard, 4676
Martin, Rick, 2595
Martin, Robert, 3527, 5044, 7619
Martin, Robin, 14, 6032, 6033
Martin, Sandy, 3359
Martin, Sharon, 1143
Martin, Shelley, 2549
Martin, Stacey, 7122
Martin, Stephen, 1065, 1066, 8104
Martin, Steve, 2429
Martin, Susan, 1875, 7335
Martin, Terry, 3923
Martin, Trevor, 3498
Martin, Wayne, 5263
Martin, Wesley, 1875
Martin, William, 2687
Martin, William C, 7266
Martin, William C., 3359
Martin Blackwell, Angela, 667
Martin Comstock, Pam, 4035
Martin Hayduk, Rosemary, 6394
Martin Mintz, Deborah, 1491, 5242
Martin-Caughey, Ananda, 2112
Martin-Palmo, Kathy, 673
Martin-Wilkins, Danita, 2437
Martindale, Diane, 2250
Martindale, Tonya, 7277
Martineau, Laura, 6344
Martinell, Nicole A., 267
Martinell, Paul M., 267
Martinez, Adriana, 1708
Martinez, Diana, 2987
Martinez, Dr. George A., 1854
Martinez, Eduardo, 1933
Martinez, Francisco, 115
Martinez, Hector, 6115
Martinez, Ivan, 7774
Martinez, Joseph, 3318
Martinez, Leroy, 4000
Martinez, Margarita, 6129
Martinez, Mark, 6052
Martinez, Shauna, 39
Martinez Rivera, Isabel, 448
Marting, Kristen, 3498
Marting, Kristin, 371
Martini, Philip, 207
Martino, Gail L., 1523, 1524
Martins, Jesse, 2011
Martins, Peter, 466
Martinsek, Tamara, 4109
Martinson, Jody, 2154
Martinson, Leslie, 2525, 2541, 4020
Martire, Frank R., 6399
Martone, Elaine, 4262
Martorano, Joseph F, 1475
Martula, Susan, 1217
Martus, Ketty, 2897
Marty,, 8486
Marty, David, 4843, 4868
Marty, Sarah, 4114
Martynuk, Nusha, 539
Martz, Earl, 3796
Marumoto, Karen, 6156
Marus, Linda, 845
Marvel, Kenneth R., 5034
Marvel Loskot, Chris, 648
Marvit, Betsy, 1916
Marx, Frances, 1463, 1464
Marx, Dr. Anthony W., 8724
Mary, Davis, 8590, 8591
Mary Tosh, Green, 3052
Maryanov, Eric, 1942
Maryman, Carol, 7208
Maschino, Janine, 280
Mascio, Sherry, 572
Mash, Fraizer, 3068

Mashburn, Victor, 3970
Mashuta, Anthony J., 3620
Masini, Jim, 2946
Mason, Ardeth, 3766, 8047
Mason, Barbara, 1795
Mason, Christina M., 5129
Mason, Ed, 6869
Mason, Erica, 1284
Mason, J. Scott, 739
Mason, Kirsten, 1231
Mason, Lacy, 5962
Mason, Maria, 3092
Mason, Martha, 279
Mason, Riss, 8546
Mason, Shay S., 1390
Mason, Suzy, 6001
Mason, V. Peter V.R., 5174
Mason, William, 2046
Mason Gregg, Lynette, 634
Mason III, Cory, 1834
Mason Jr, David, 1101
Masone, David, 1898
Massa, Gary, 5307, 5308, 5310, 5311
Massa, Michelle, 3363
Massaro, Chris, 8289
Massaro, John, 1852
Masselli, Mark, 4384, 6398
Massenkoff, Nikolai, 4297
Masserini, John, 4168
Massey, Brandon, 7832
Massey, Janet L., 3945
Massey, Robert, 4641
Massey, Rufus, 2802
Massey, Jr., Paul J., 1432
Massie, Ray, 7469
Massimiano, Tracy, 4276
Massman, Martin, 2463, 2493, 2509
Massmann, Martin, 6170
Massod, Al, 1617
Massolia, William, 2934
Massoudi, Barry, 5785
Massry, Morris, 7820
Mast, Brian, 6878
Mastako, Rodger, 803
Mastalski, Beverly, 1657
Mastalski, Elaine, 3802
Masten, John, 1431
Mastenbrook, Ellen, 277
Masterson, John, 5667
Masterson, Marc, 3068, 6091
Masterson, Michael, 3284
Masterson, Veronica, 2581
Mastick, Mary, 1688
Mastro, Michael, 2727
Mastrocola, Arlene, 339
Masubuchi, Aiko, 5141
Maswick, James, 7697
Mata, Ray, 8622
Matan, Debbie, 3719
Matchett, Bobby, 3759
Matczynski, Leonard, 1318
Mateo, Jose, 278
Mathay, Fran, 1486
Mathena, Lori, 3761
Matheny, Jane, 4100
Matheny, Kenneth, 5371
Mather, Carol, 117
Mather, Jill, 6151
Matherne, Michael, 7161
Mathes, Leon, 7142, 7144
Mathew, Prakash C, 5281
Mathews, Blair, 706
Mathews, Emily, 7270
Mathews, M. Marguerite, 3352
Mathews, Melanie, 4081
Mathews, Paul, 8689
Mathews, Sharon, 244
Mathias, Dick, 8518
Mathias, Jane, 2207
Mathieu, Jeff, 6075
Mathis, Caren, 717
Mathis, David, 5213
Mathis, James, 1390
Mathis, Melanie, 242
Mathis, Paul, 1058
Mathwich, Lowell A, 531
Matine, Katherine A, 3226, 3227
Matkins, Cliff, 5280

Matlock, Ph.D., Kathy S, 5272
Matlrack, Katherine, 2567
Mato, Nancy, 4470
Matpaliano, Christopher, 2300
Matson, Bonnie C., 3231
Matson, L, 1192
Matson, Mary, 5282
Matson, Paulette, 799
Matsui, Nancy, 40, 6163
Matsurra, Taks, 6092
Matt, Director of Ope, 4903
Matter, Charles E, 7819
Mattes, Jennifer, 1831
Matteson, Jim, 4107
Matteson, Steve, 2361
Matthes, Sina, 5975
Matthew,, 4393, 4394
Matthew, Charlie, 8402
Matthews, Benjamin, 2244
Matthews, Ingrid, 1798, 1803
Matthews, John, 1228, 3924
Matthews, Michael, 2640, 6155
Matthews, Nancy, 315
Matthews, Pam, 1918, 1919
Matthews, Virginia, 751
Matthews Hill, Mary, 1904
Matthies, David, 779
Matthieson, Megan, 4325
Mattice, Richard W., 738, 5991, 5992
Mattiello, Brian, 6441
Mattingly, Kate, 2740
Mattison, Donald C, 1051
Mattison, Mike, 3037
Mattocks, Bobbi, 5242
Mattoon, Bill, 2677
Mattson, Brian, 4662
Mattson, Steve, 7360
Mattson, Wendi C, 6797, 6798, 6799
Matula, Mike, 1727
Matula, Sherrie, 1727
Mauceri, John, 4227
Mauer, Amanda, 2516
Maughan, Kent, 3290
Mauk, Shelley A, 3742
Mauldin, Sarah, 2846, 2862
maull, Chester, 7084
Maultsby, Vance, 1715
Maurer, Lisa, 1845
Maurer, Ron, 3190
Maurier, MD, Cheryl, 1788
Mauriocourt, Jeanne, 5350
Mauro, Roberto, 2134
Mauroff, David, 2576
Maury, Albert, 6548
Mauss, Steven.K, 778
Mauzy Nemir, Claudia, 1939
Mavity, Robert, 6651
Mavity, Robert Mavity, 2027
Max, Adam E., 5053
Max, Bethany, 2420
Max, Darla, 3831
Max, Doug, 6373
Maxedon, David, 3274
Maxfield, Adam, 3645
Maxson, Stan, 3044
Maxwell, Carla, 439
Maxwell, Clair, 2024
Maxwell, Dan, 4586
Maxwell, Dr. David, 6986, 6987, 6988, 6989
Maxwell, Elliot, 266
Maxwell, Jennifer, 4561
Maxwell, Mihael D, 2409
Maxwell, Mitchell, 2658
Maxwell, Mitzi, 2805
Maxwell, Rhoni, 8007
Maxwell, Susie, 6891
Maxwell Greig, Ph.D., Judith, 4202
Maxwell Zagel, Margaret, 6734
May, Alfred T., 2012
May, Bobby, 8414
May, Brian, 8424
May, Debbie, 3621
May, Denise, 4937
May, Dr. Brian J., 8444
May, Eileen, 297
May, John, 1367
May, Jonathan P, 1447
May, Keith W., 2101

May, Lauren, 3256
May, Linda, 4941
May, Lisa, 1911
May, Nancy, 6347, 6353, 6357, 6360, 6367, 6368, 6369, 6370
May, Robin, 760
May, Susan, 6119
May, Thomas, 7227
May, Thomas D, 1176
May Damen, Margaret, 6602
May Flowers, Rebecca, 3793
May Krebs, Eileen, 6375
Mayans, Steve, 4494
Mayberry, Kent, 8052
Mayee, Kimberly, 8391
Mayer, Adam, 5536
Mayer, C. Andrew, 3101
Mayer, Daniel, 8586
Mayer, Diane, 3077
Mayer, Hanna, 1308
Mayer, Holly, 2342
Mayer, Janice, 8839
Mayer, Leslie, 3793
Mayer, Lisa, 545
Mayer, Marc O., 1437
Mayer, Rick, 4397
Mayer, Sally, 7609
Mayer, Scott, 7353, 7354
Mayers, Shannon, 7535
Mayes, Joseph, 1646
Mayes, Thom, 1788
Mayes, Tony, 387
Mayes, Ty, 1735
Mayes-Smith, Susan, 3340
Mayfield, Amy, 4147
Mayfield, Maryhelen, 509
Maygard, Jan, 4691
Mayhew, Jamie, 4577
Mayleas, William, 1907
Maynard, Daniella, 6634
Mayner, John, 6038
Mayo, Anna Y, 4284
Mayo, Erik, 6267
Mayo, James, 7131, 7132, 7133
Mayo, Paula M., 5155
Mayone, Michael, 940
Mayor, Mara, 4432
Mayor, the Lord, 1250
Mayotte, David, 4815
Mays, Jeffrey, 6398
Mays, Julia, 6586
Mays, Kelly, 4959
Mays, Roger, 3322
Mays Boyd, Stephanie, 578
Mayse, Val, 691
Mayshark, Myriam, 3633
Mayson, William S, 2148, 2149
Mayta, Dave, 1280
Mazdra, Janet, 3404
Mazern, Leonard, 4829
Mazey, Mary Ellen, 5295, 5296
Mazmanian, Nancy, 6055
Mazon, Janusz, 187
Mazuca, Roland, 4001
Mazur, Catherine A, 7529
Mazur, Richard, 370
Mazza, Lynne S, 1358
Mazzarella, Susan, 4070
Mazzella, Christina, 8108
Mazzocco, Lisa, 807
Mazzola, Michael, 396, 564
Mazzola, Vincent, 5023
Mazzolini, Tom, 4306
Mazzonelli, Joan, 2955
Mc Cullough, Mike, 7988
McAdams, Beverly, 5254
McAdams, Lorraine, 338
McAdams-Connor, Kenna, 338
McAdams-Graham, Lizanne, 126
McAdon, Matthew, 356
McAfee, Charles, 2696
McAfee, Charlie, 2691
McAfee, Matthew, 972
McAfee-Gundrum, Spencer, 706
Mcahon, Steven, 618
McAleese, Helene, 5177
McAlister, Kevin, 6867
McAlister, Meredith, 5650

1195

Executive Name Index

McAllister, Kari, 6119
McAllister, Katie, 4152
McAllister, Meredith, 5650
McAllister, Robert, 898
McAlpine, Jeanie, 7185
McAmis, Craig, 866, 867
McAnany Jr., John W., 6490
McAndrew, Marty, 6749
McAndrews, Bart, 3990
McAndrews, Dawn, 3099
McAndrews, Peter, 1104, 1105
McAnuff, Des, 2481
McArdle, Brian, 3391
McArthur, Stuart, 4406
McAteer, Rita, 7223
McAuliffe, Nancy, 590
McAuliffe, Warren, 590
McBeth, Christopher, 2366, 2367
McBeth, Rachel, 3536
McBride, Cindy, 5788, 5789, 5790
McBride, Daivd, 7493
McBride, Don, 3739
McBride, Donna, 6596
McBride, Howard, 3192
McBride, Jerry L., 8686
McBride, Karen, 7289
McBride, Kevin A., 6410
McBride, Mary, 3489
McBride, Patricia, 507
McBrien, Joanie, 2451
McBurney, Christine, 5318, 5351
McCabe, Andrea V., 1622
McCabe, Chris, 1093
McCabe, Michael, 4948
McCabe, Nuala, 8558
McCabe, Patrick R., 4310
McCabe, Rosanne, 4482
McCabe, Rose Ann, 989, 991, 992, 993
McCabe, RoseAnne, 4486
McCabe, Terry, 2919
McCaffrey, Terry, 3007
McCaffrey MD, Brian, 810
McCain, James, 1409
McCaleb, Geri, 7298
McCall, Angela, 6549
McCall, Jackie, 3029
McCall, Jonathan, 4716
McCall, Sean, 3029, 6996
McCallie, Spencer, 1689, 2329
McCallum, Allen, 7198
McCandless, Stephen, 8084
McCandless, Tom, 2012
McCann, Betsy, 1814, 1815
McCann, Bruce, 3935
McCann, Christina, 7256
McCann, Chuck, 4903
McCann, Margo, 632
McCann, Robert J., 5812
McCarthy, Bill, 1963
McCarthy, Cindy, 2167
McCarthy, Devin, 3783
McCarthy, Edward F., 4755
McCarthy, Heather Keller, 2517
McCarthy, Joseph E., 4792
McCarthy, Michael, 1985
McCarthy, Mike, 2147, 4873, 6459
McCarthy, Mitchell, 1420
McCarthy, Ryan, 7423
McCarthy, Stephen, 2195
McCarthy, Tim, 3170, 5172
McCarthy-Brown, Nyama, 7167
McCarty, Steve, 8435, 8436
McCarty, Tina, 6232
McCarty III, Bill, 3276
Mccarver, Viva, 7949
McCasland, Debbie, 5978
McCauley, Frank, 8238
McCauley, Shirley, 4590, 6805
McCaw, Connie, 5459
McChesney, Dr. David, 1503
McChristian, Priscilla, 4191
McClain, David, 4528, 6671
McClain, Emily, 997
McClain, Ronald R., 6199
McClain, Steve, 8718, 8719
McClatchy, Kevin, 8178
McCleary, Marilyn, 7044
McClellan, Cathie, 2630

McClellan, Darlene, 3815
McClellan, James, 546
McClellan, Robert, 1739
McClellan, Roberta, 835
McClellan, Terrence, 6766
McClements, Nancy, 698
McClenan, Julie, 4388
McClendon, Beverly L., 6027
McClenny, Kevin Trip, 8652
McClintock, Thomas, 5407
McClintock, Thomas C, 5404
McCloskey, Carolyn, 3779
McCloskey, Sharon, 8513, 8514
McClosky, Midge, 3853
McCloy, Hugh, 8642
McClure, Deirdre, 1895
McClure, Jay, 4056
McClure, Priscilla, 824, 825
McClure, Renee, 7644
McClure, Sara, 1308
McClure, Shannon, 2284
McClure, Tom, 5079
McClure, William W., 4416, 4429
McClure Mahood, Sandra, 8347
McClure Mautinko, Victoria, 4049
McCluremahood, Sandra, 3943
McClurkan, Carolyn, 1789
McClusky, Lynette, 1079
McCollam, Neal, 6757
McCollum, David, 117
McCollum, Sarah, 3211
McCollum, Timothy, 1829
McColm, Reed, 4090, 4092
McComb, Barry, 6115
McComb, Sharon, 5586
McConnaughey, Shelly, 6908
McConnell, Bill, 6529, 6532
McConnell, John, 3804
McConnell, Kathy, 5949, 5950
McConnell, Mark, 2020
McConnell, Michele, 3364
McConnell, Robert, 1111
McCook, Andrea, 6590, 6591
McCord, Micki, 4707
McCorkle, Michael W, 2735
McCorkle, Monica S, 2735
McCorkle, Patricia, 3512
McCorkle, Sharon, 1929
McCormack, Amy, 6820, 6821
McCormack, Mark, 327
McCormack, Vince, 6527
McCormick, Cecilia M, 8118
McCormick, James, 1879
McCormick, John, 3490
McCormick, Julie, 2449
McCormick, Marilyn, 2467
McCormick, Mary, 4854
McCormick, Michael, 912
McCormick, Richard, 7578
McCormick, Todd, 5529
McCorvey, Everett, 2078
McCourt, Frank, 6156
McCourt, Jamie, 6156
McCowan, Mark, 2332
McCoy, David, 3597
McCoy, Dr. Jerry, 2348
McCoy, Fred, 7493
McCoy, James F., 393
McCoy, Janelle, 2310
McCoy, Jerry, 2348
McCoy, Larry, 326
McCoy, Lynn, 1745
McCoy, Patti, 1739
McCoy, Robb, 6511
McCoy, Susan, 668
McCoy, Yvonne, 2034
McCracken, Jed, 8560
McCracken, Larry, 1813
McCracken, Marva Lee, 1813
McCrary, Curtis, 6052
McCrary, Mike, 1101
McCrary, MBA, CAE, Mark R., 8079
McCrea, Ashley, 8070
McCready, P. J., 4478
McCreanor, Trudy, 114
McCreath, Brian, 8917
Mccrimmon, Melissa, 5639
McCrocklin, Mark, 2086

McCrohan, Betty, 5679
McCrory, Rollin J., 1495
McCrory, Wendy, 5281
McCue, Donna, 983
McCue, Edward, 4353
McCue, Ellen, 7066
McCue, Jennie, 4252
McCullaugh, Pam, 6325
McCullers, Mark, 7981
McCulloch, Gavin, 3818
McCulloch, Karen, 7994
McCullogh, Aileen, 3818
McCullogh, Gavin, 3818
McCullough, David, 2407
McCullough, Diana, 5970
McCullough, Diane, 5971, 5975
McCullough, John, 5825
McCullough, Kevin, 6302
McCullough, Laura, 8625
McCullough, Richard, 2527
McCullough, Sean C, 6056
McCullough, Shannon, 6615
McCully, James K, 1990
McCumber, Kathryn, 3839
McCune, Jeff, 3898
Mccune, Richard, 3587
McCune, Tony, 913
McCunn, James, 2593
McCunney-Thomas, Tricia, 1332
McCurdy, Michael, 2439
McCurry, Sharon, 8104
McCurry, Stephen, 823
McCusker, Beverly, 7024
McCutcheon, Janet, 758
McCutcheon, Jim, 1525
McDade, Eric, 6573
McDadeny, Hon. Joseph, 2738
McDanial, Pam, 2681
McDaniel, Bronwyn, 2927
McDaniel, Diane, 6909, 6910, 6911
McDaniel, Donald, 1701, 5588
McDaniel, Dr Tom J, 8042, 8045
McDaniel, Erik, 3638
McDaniel, George W, 8207
McDaniel, Janet, 769
McDaniel, Joe, 1166
McDaniel, Randy, 3283
McDaniel, Sharon, 4493
McDaniel, Stacie, 6663
McDaniel, Tom J., 2295
McDavis, Roderick J., 7944
McDavis, Rodney, 5290
McDermott, Anne-Marie, 4378
McDermott, Casey, 2300
McDermott, Frankie, 63
McDermott, Greg, 7504
Mcdermott, John, 3514
McDermott, Kathleen, 1368
McDermott, Michael, 3140
McDermott, Terry Y, 4996
McDevitt, Lisa, 6575
McDiarmid, Robert B., 4280
McDonalad, Linda, 1513, 1514
McDonald, Barb, 4843, 4868
McDonald, Brian J., 3382
McDonald, Charlie, 7653
McDonald, Christine, 2254, 2255
McDonald, Debbie, 6245
McDonald, Elizabeth, 2257
McDonald, Emmett O, 354
McDonald, Geoffrey, 1407
McDonald, Heather, 1708
McDonald, John, 3894, 5121
McDonald, John C, 3461
McDonald, Kathy, 1811
McDonald, Linda, 5286
McDonald, Lyndell, 5929, 5931
McDonald, Marilyn, 1927
McDonald, Maryanna, 3679
McDonald, Michael, 6186
McDonald, Mimi, 2789, 6535
McDonald, Rebecca, 2
McDonald, Rod, 3627
McDonald, Sean, 929
McDonald, Sharon, 6596
McDonald, Stephanie, 1712
McDonald, Suzanne, 1719
McDonald, Tamara, 5773

McDonald, Teri, 4434
McDonald, Tom, 6251
McDonell, Michael, 2579
McDonell, Sally, 153
McDonnell, Margot, 557
McDonnell, Sean, 4751
McDonough, Allison, 7224
McDonough, Briget, 2064
McDonough, Deb, 4912
McDonough, Molly S, 3390, 7592
McDorman, Mike, 8008
McDormand, Frances, 3459
McDougal, Pat, 3862
McDougle, Eugene, 448
McDowell, Arlyne, 5732
McDowell, David, 720, 5939
McDowell, K James, 2305
McDowell, K. James, 2305
McDowell, Kim, 5998
McDuffie, Susan T, 1012
McDufford, John, 5335
McEachran, Cheryl, 911
McElfresh, Phil, 5996, 6010
McElhinney, Kevin, 4974
McElhinny, Wilson, 4542
McElliot, John, 8879
McElrath, Athena, 3787
McElrath, Bill, 6984
McElrath, KJ, 3787
McElroy, Mary Lynne, 1993
McElroy, Todd, 4705
McEnergy, Martie, 2412
McEniry, Dr. Deborah, 2838
McEnrue, Carolyn, 5660
McEvoy, Annette, 1406
McEvoy, Scotty, 1565
McEwan, Danielle, 1608
McFadden, Dale, 3020, 6855, 6857, 6858, 6859, 6920
McFadden, Harry, 7810
McFadden, Nancy, 3681
McFadeen, Sherry, 6943, 6945
McFall, John, 179
McFarland, Dave, 2763
McFarlane, Edwin, 8101
McFate, Patricia A., 2200
McFatrich, Patti, 3306
McFatridge, Bill, 5614
McGarrigan, Tim, 2314
McGarry, Michael, 2923
McGarry, Michael, 6734
McGarvey, Tim, 7015
McGaskey Jr, Oscar, 7426, 7427
McGee, Daniel, 1251
McGee, DeNae, 5779
McGee, Dr. Jerry E, 5276
McGee, Dr. Jerry E., 8221
McGeever, Kathleen M, 5951, 5955
McGeever, Kathleen M., 2422
McGhee, Cindy, 1817, 2392
McGhee, Terri, 8494
McGhee, Twyla, 702
McGhee Stinson, Anne, 2650
Mcgill, Katherine, 3612
McGill, Kathryn, 3764
McGill, Michael, 3318
McGillicuddy, Denise, 2965
McGillicuddy, Dennis, 6584
McGillivray, Karla, 113
McGinley, Helen, 4214
McGinley Papas, Linda, 1404
McGinn, Arlo, 1760
McGinn, Josy, 5207
McGinnis, Cathy, 5569
McGinnis, Sue, 58
McGinniss, Michael J., 8157
McGlasson, Paula, 8193
McGloin, Gale, 3844
McGloin, Tim, 508
McGlone, Jen, 6155
McGlothlin, Meredythe, 2359
McGlumphy, Chris, 1655
McGlynn, Kervin, 4302
McGoire, Melissa, 3063
McGonigle, Robert, 5511
McGovern, Annie, 3371
McGovern, Carey, 1194
McGovern, Frank, 1782

1196

Executive Name Index

McGovern, Joe, 4041
McGovern, Kathleen, 3752
McGovern, Margaret, 3371
McGovern, Meg, 2409, 5911
McGovern, Michelle, 4494
McGovern, Pat, 7672
McGovern, Terece, 1729
McGovern, William, 1756
McGovern-Stevens, Ellen, 3371
McGowan, Esther, 5113
McGowan, Larry, 3911, 8287
McGowan, Molly, 15
McGowen, Grant, 2861
McGrann, Loretta, 7647
McGrath, Bob, 3557
McGrath, David, 6169
McGrath, Robert, 1528, 1529, 7455
McGrath, Russ, 8594
McGrath, Will, 4552
McGraw, David, 7003, 7006, 7007, 7008
McGregor, Arianna, 4406
McGregor, Kate, 6749
McGregor, Keli S, 6348
McGrory, Jack, 840
McGuan, Hope, 7997
McGuffin, Kyle, 4676, 7049, 7050, 7051
McGuigan, Michael, 3475
McGuiness, Dana, 4177
McGuire, Alison, 8603, 8607
McGuire, Cheri L, 2960
McGuire, Courtney, 376
McGuire, Cyndee, 3618
McGuire, Elizabeth, 1837
McGuire, Jason, 95
McGuire, Kevin, 1031
Mcguire, Michael, 5033
McGuire, Nicole, 1563
McGuire, Paul, 2827
McHale, Kevin, 7360
McHale Jr., John, 6055
McHancy, Roger, 2154
McHenry, Bart, 4252, 6063
McHodgkins, Jim, 4705
McHugh, Damhnait, 7662
McHugh, Ilona, 24
McHugh, James, 6313
McHugh, Jamie, 8126
McHugh, Jim, 1984
McHugh, Karen, 3685
Mclalwain, Joseph, 8581
McIlraith, Ian, 876
McInally, David, 6966
McIntoch, Jason, 5393
McIntosh, Amy, 3548
McIntosh, Eulaine, 1640
McIntosh, Greg, 5031
McIntosh, Justin, 3896
McIntyre, Alan, 940
McIntyre, Chris, 5171
McIntyre, Darren, 6
McIntyre, Dr. Eric, 1112
McIntyre, Eric L, 1100
McIntyre, George C., 5540
McIntyre, Seth, 5826
McIntyre, Steve, 3387
McIntyre, Trey, 197
McIver, Jean, 7148, 8459
McIvor, June, 864
McKallor, MaryLisa, 2429
McKay, Britney, 1821
McKay, Iain B, 5700
McKay, Kent, 440
McKay, Robert, 1008, 4507
McKay, Thomas, 7239
McKayle, Donald, 43
McKee, Ann, 8563
McKee, Dainn E., 6943, 6945
McKee, Eileen, 1718
McKee, Katherine, 1924
McKee, Ruth, 3598
McKee Ridgway, James, 2305
McKee, Ross, 3786
McKeever, Melissa, 3629
McKeller, Rusty, 2879
McKenna, Fay, 3305
McKenna, Jen, 3471
McKenna, Joe, 989, 991, 993, 994, 995

McKenna, Joseph, 991, 992, 993, 994, 995, 4482, 4486
McKenna, Kevin, 7495
McKenna, Theresa, 3500
McKenna,, Fay, 3305
McKeno, Michael, 321
McKenzie, Alena, 1092
Mckenzie, Gary, 104
McKenzie, James B, 2780
McKenzie, Joanne, 4131
McKenzie, Kevin, 386
McKenzie, Peter, 1300
McKenzie, Scott, 2261
McKenzie, Ty, 2588
McKeon, Patrick, 7464
McKeown, Xandra, 5413
McKernan, Ryan, 6965
McKey, James, 4630
McKibbon, Penny, 5935
McKim, Don, 7573
McKim, Scott, 6195
McKinley, Cam, 6854
McKinley, Kathleen, 2468
McKinley, Lainey, 1915
McKinley, Margie, 2130
McKinley, Ronald, 3247
McKinley, William, 249
Mckinney, Aaron, 5051
McKinney, Ameita, 640
McKinney, Brian, 1053
McKinney, Dave, 5149
McKinney, Jennifer, 229
McKinney, John S, 5815
McKinney, Kathleen C., 1681
McKinney, Kevin, 8720
McKinney, Larry, 4443
McKinney, Lee, 628
McKinney, Sheila, 8205
McKinney, Sue, 670
McKinnon, Elizabeth, 1856
McKinstry, Pamela, 2447
MoKinzie, Deborah, 7668
McKitish, Michael, 4995
McKittrick, Margie, 2219
McKlosky, Patricia, 1823
McKnight, Sara, 6358
McKowen, Peggy, 4104
McKoy, Elizabeth, 6068
McKvay, Gary, 3523
McLacken, Christine, 3866
McLamore, Gena, 6690, 6691, 6692, 6693, 6694
McLane, Tegan, 2601
McLaren, Gayle, 3320
McLaren, James I., 5053
McLaren, Scotty, 3320
McLarnon, M.D., Mary, 467
McLauchlan, Stewart, 1745
McLaughlin, Ann, 6455
McLaughlin, Ed, 6458, 6460, 6474, 6476
McLaughlin, Elizabeth J., 1485
McLaughlin, Gary, 791
McLaughlin, Jeff, 4190, 6034
McLaughlin, Karen, 5136
McLaughlin, Kenn, 3987, 8416
McLaughlin, Kirk, 1741
McLaughlin, Steve, 1834
McLaws, Scott, 3761
McLean, Anne, 4427
McLean, Deborah, 5037
Mclean, Dollie, 2685
McLean, Elizabeth, 254
McLean, Florence, 7193
McLean, Jackie, 2685
McLean, Kimmary, 254
McLean, Leigh, 3908
McLean, Peg, 5490
McLean Braun, Joan, 4360
McLellan, Mark A., 3270
McLemore, Laura, 1144
McLeod, Christopher K., 6399
McLeod, Judy, 1746
McLeod, Mark, 1778
Mcleod, Martha, 3346
McLntyre, Ed, 6514
McLornan, Sarah, 5663, 8450, 8451
McLucas, Barbara, 4814
McLuckey, G W, 7588
McLuckey, Gw, 5017

McIver, Brandon, 3874
McMahan, C Page, 3168
McMahon, Becky, 612
McMahon, Charles, 3834
McMahon, Diane, 108
McMahon, Emily, 4657, 4658, 4659, 4660, 4661
McMahon, J Kevin, 583
McMahon, Jennifer, 4179
McMahon, Kevin, 1051, 8168
McMahon, Louise, 8035
McMahon, Nancy, 1691
McManus, Priscilla D, 4385
McManus, Vicki, 6678
McManus, Willy, 293
McMaster, Mendy, 2446
McMeekin, Becky, 8508
McMeekin, Rebecca B, 5717
McMenaman, Jackie, 126
McMichael, Judith, 2108
McMicken, Donna, 3821
McMillan, Allison, 2324
McMillan, Brent, 8256
McMillan, George DH, 5895
McMillan, Greg, 1693
McMillan, Jeff, 1911
McMillan Mannelly, Elvira, 8562
McMillen, Eileen, 7154
McMillian, Laura, 333
McMillian, Thomas N., 5001
McMillin, Stephanie, 6012
McMillion, Donald C., 5244
McMullan, Sarah, 3997
McMullen, Christopher, 2325
McMullen, Emily, 3160
McMullen, Fran, 8181, 8190
McMullin, Cara, 4122
McMunn, Brent, 1889
McMurtray, Sue, 3803, 8124
McNab, Cheryl, 6386
McNair, Ph. D., Dennis, 1632
McNamara, Frank, 1602, 1603
Mcnamara, Judy, 3269
McNamara, Karen, 4988
McNamara, Marilyn, 742
McNamara, Mary Sue, 2557
McNamara, Meghan, 6738
McNamara, Michaela, 5726
McNamee, June, 735
McNaughton, Maurey, 5716
McNeel, James, 4104
Mcneel, James, 5822
McNeil, Albert, 1881
McNeil, Dona, 4740, 4741
McNeil, Gretchen, 1869
McNeil, Heather, 2702
McNeill, Lloyd, 44
McNicholl, B.T., 6434, 6435
McNiece, Evie, 1014
McNulty, Barry, 7232
McNulty, Dale, 986
McNulty, Joy, 3170
McNulty, Lisa, 3593
McNulty, Sally P, 6256
McNutt, Charlotte, 253
McNutt, Darron, 946
McOmie, Diane, 5642
McPartlan, Bryan, 5103, 7706
McPartlin, Kenneth, 5099
McPeak, Brian, 3798
McPeek, Beth, 4062, 4063
McPhee, Jonathan, 271
Mcpherson, Jannina, 6640
McPherson, Scott, 3699
McQueen, Andrew, 7390
McQueen, Angus, 5760
McQueen, Brett, 6337
McQueen, Candice, 5578
McQueen, Gordo, 1959
McQuere, Gordon, 2076
McQuern, Marcia, 832
McQuillan, Kevin, 8132
McRae, Paul Hilliard, 334
McRobbie, Michael A, 6854
McRobbie, Michael A, 6877
McRoberts, Barbara, 4639
McShane, David R., 1649
McShane, Debra, 2901

McSherry, Vita, 47
McStraw, Michael, 217
McSweeney, Jennifer, 4176
McSweeney, Mike, 6244
McSweeney, Ryan, 1930
McTague, Keith, 6173
McVay, Marcelle, 2959
McVeigh, Beth, 3880
McVicker, Charmaine, 6586
McVicker, Katherine, 1194
Mcvicker, Marry, 4894
McVicker, Maryellen H, 4895
McWhirter, Hays, 8302
McWhirter,, Hays, 1696
McWhorter, Odari, 4113
McWhorter, Shawn, 3262
McWilliams, Kitty, 520
McWilliams, Patric, 3089
McWoods, Stephanie, 7673
Meacham, Kate, 7410
Meachum, Grant, 928
Mead, Doug, 5751
Mead, Jaylee M, 2750
Mead, Monique, 918
Mead, Sandy, 7048
Mead, Tim, 6055
Meade, James, 2013
Meade, Karen, 7993
Meade, Michelle, 4668
Meador, Cassie, 266
Meador, Christine, 1541
Meadors, Alan, 2434
Meadow, Lynne, 3517, 7754
Meadows, Charlotte, 6
Meadows, Chris, 2360
Meadows, Edward, 6578
Meadows, Kay Perdue, 2699
Meadows, Steve, 7951
Meads, Fred, 2186
Meads, Kerry, 2460
Meads, Rachael, 5823
Meagher, Dan, 117
Meagher, Denise, 4136
Meahl, Bruce, 3877
Meak, Don, 4225
Means, Colleen, 6022
Means, Dr. David, 1719
Means, Jennifer G., 4400, 4730, 4731, 4732, 4733
Means, Kathie, 1838
Means, Molly, 3777
Means, Peter, 4177
Mear, David, 1453
Mears, Cliff, 3741
Mears, Dave, 4220
Mears, Rachael, 140
Measelle, Barbara, 70
Measley, Sarah, 8130
Mecca, Joseph, 5524
Mecene, Virginie, 454
Mechlin, David, 135
Meckel, Peter, 1873
Meckley, David, 1669
Medak, Susan, 2449
Medas, Glenn, 7510
Medford, Kay, 8334
Medford, Marie, 881
Medford, Mary Beth, 7952
Medich, William G., 3869
Medina, Adriane, 489
Medina, Derek, 2631
Medina, George, 2227
Medina, Joe, 4003
Medina, Omega, 764
Medina, Rhiana, 5688
Medina, Rita, 4994
Medley, Gaius, 1273
Medley, Susan, 2317, 2320
Medoff Marks, Debra, 1356
Medrano, Hugo, 2739
Medrono, Hugo, 2739
Medvec, Lucy, 247
Medved, Danita, 4121
Medved, Paul, 4121
Meecham, Paul, 2094, 7198
Meegan, Kevin, 5073
Meeham, Bill, 5905, 5906
Meehan, Kathleen, 7690

Executive Name Index

Meehan Ph D, Mary, 5855
Meehan, Ph.D, Mary J., 8693
Meehen, Conor, 1217
Meek, Vicki, 8364
Meeker, Coludine, 4196
Meeker, M David, 5983
Meeks, Mike, 8581
Meena, James, 2262
Meess, Mark, 1318
Meeuwsen, Jeff, 3204
Megginson, Dr Julie, 1003
Megginson, Julie, 4499
Megliola, Michael, 2223
Megna, Debbie, 6224
Megna, Scott, 6224
Mehan, Tom, 319
Meharg, Stephanie, 5755
Mehlan, Matthew, 1440
Mehler, Leilane G, 1991
Mehner, JC, 1706
Mehr, Alison, 4716
Mehta, Mervon, 8155
Mehta, Nuvi, 4344
Mehta, Zarin, 1430
Meier, Connor, 8052
Meier, Gustav, 921
Meier, Johanna, 3888
Meier, Tim, 7004
Meikkejohn, Stuart, 4262
Meineke, Donald, 2217
Meiners, Patti, 3937
Meinhardt, Luanne, 1516
Meinhold, Genia, 2721
Meirose, Leo, 996
Meisner Smit, Carrisa, 4089
Meister, Kara A., 3281
Meixner, Rebekkah, 6921, 6922, 6923, 6924, 6925
Mejia, Marco, 1874
Melady, Timothy, 133
Melancon, Denise, 1138
Melancon, Julia, 851
Melcher, John, 1795
Melchior, Tyler, 3823
Melcon, Margot, 2526
Mele, Karhy, 403, 463
Mele, Steven, 1942
Melear, Eric, 2353
Meleck, Amy, 3795
Melendez, Danielle, 7636
Melikian, Trisha, 5515
Melilo, Joseph V., 5053
Melina, Gajger, 1157
Melisi, Sara, 8110, 8111
Mella, Leanne, 3594
Melland, Brad, 7960
Melle, Veronique Le, 7220
Mellinger, Stephanie, 499
Mello, Carolyn, 4123
Mello, Deb, 4542
Mellon, Cynthia, 1966
Mellor, Ann, 5191
Mellow, Gale, 7705
Melnick, Dan, 5148
Melnick, Jacqueline, 1209
Melnick, Peter, 8326
Melo, Jean, 1612
Meloccaro, Lynne, 1407
Melody, Michael E., 1360, 2199
Melone, Paul, 3142
Melone, Roger, 1354
Melrose, Sue, 3242
Melton, Melissa, 5961
Melvin, Bill, 7473
Melvin, Dr. Cruse, 8333
Melvin, Susan, 7172, 7173
Melzer, Robert T., 5868
Menard, Glenn, 7143, 7147
Menchaca, Belinda, 646
Menchaca, Louis A, 5853
Mencher, Cynthia, 1420
Menchey, Joel, 5515, 8191
Mendel, Diana, 4105
Mendel, Lisa, 1695
Mendelowitz, Kade, 2420
Mendelsohn, Asher, 7981
Mendelsohn, Joann, 1803
Mendelson, Arlene H., 2004

Mendelson, Julianna, 4596
Mendelson, Victor H., 2004
Mendes, William, 6255
Mendez, Lisa, 13
Mendez, Nancy, 2642
Mendez, Susana, 896
Mendoza, Agnes, 4406
Mendoza, Cathy, 810
Mendoza, Connie, 4945
Mendoza, Jennifer, 977
Mendoza, Jole, 798
Mendoza, Sandy, 1560
Meneeli, Brian, 5509
Meneer, Christine, 537
Menefee, Brian, 8079
Menefee, Ken, 3009
Menekseoglu, Anna W., 2925
Menekseoglu, Jeremy, 2925
Menendian, Michael, 2944
Meng, Rosie, 641, 8420
Menger, James E., 1535
Menges, Christina, 5259
Mengwasser, Frank, 3339
Menichino Parou, Debbie, 574
Menino, M T, 4962
Menner, Vera, 5304
Mennino, Mary-Therese, 7525
Mennino, MT, 4962
Menschel, Robert, 5163
Ment, Ted De, 326
Menta, Ed, 7313
Menz, Evan, 1244
Menzies, Steven, 1922, 1923
Mercadante Marple, Kiyomi, 598
Mercadel, Demetric, 4718
Merced, Jorge, 3415
Mercer, Brian, 6063
Mercer, Debra, 120
Mercer, Gwenn, 5594
Merchant, Elaine, 3744, 5354
Merckens, Meg, 3029, 6996
Mercurio, Steven, 2077
Meredith, Jeff, 4058
Meredith, Kent, 8430
Meredith, Leda, 412
Meredith, Mary Ellen, 3767
Merer, Robert L, 1853
Meresman, Stan, 6078
Merilatt, Douglas, 980
Merkel, Donna, 333
Merkel, Tom, 2060
Merkeley, Ally, 1934
Merkley, Marty, 1378
Merkt, Mary, 3700
Merlino, Donna, 2594
Merlo, Dan, 7536
Merluzzi, Paul, 1634
Mermel, Marcy, 4189
Mern, Heather, 8679
Merola, Deborah, 6624
Merrell, Marion, 3
Merriam, Burton, 5498
Merriam, Linda, 523
Merrick, Bruce C, 3068
Merrien, Jeannine, 986
Merrifield Papp, Gail, 7781
Merrill, Dee, 7867
Merrill, Helen, 7693
Merrill, Jim, 2391
Merrill, Shirley, 3059
Merrill-Buttzak, Lisa B, 3160
Merrins, James, 1385
Merritt, Nicole, 4559
Merritt, Robert, 1976
Merriweather, Malcolm, 2237
Merson, Rebecca, 2381
Merten, Doris, 3989
Mertens, Allan, 5734
Mertz, Annelise, 310
Mertzlufft, Sharon Cognac, 7453
Merwin, Bill, 6510
Mery, James G, 8456
Mery, Jim, 8447
Merz, Jesse, 4095
Merz, Laurel, 4095
Merz, Stephen P., 6631
Mesa, Natalia, 395
Mesbah, Davood, 835

Mesce, Jennifer, 343
Mescher, Gary, 3483
Mescon, Richard, 3159
Mesenbrink, Catherine, 1879
Meservey, Mike, 2303
Mesic, Kathy, 1879
Messerschmidt, Lydia, 929
Messerschmidt, Peggy, 6415, 6416
Messian, Erica, 923
Messing, Carla, 1236
Messinger, Joyce, 2127
Messitte, Zach, 5865
Messmer, Abbey, 4173
Messmer, Barbara, 6229
Messmer, Michael, 6229
Messner, Peter, 3609
Mester, Jorge, 825, 1131
Mestichelli, Mario, 1647
Metlicka, Scott, 1064
Metnick, Carolyn, 198
Metoxen, Mallory, 4128
Mets, Dr. Lisa A., 6592, 6593
Metteauer, Michael, 2339
Metz, Gerald, 2230
Metz, Thomas J., 8156
Metz, M.D., W. Peter, 4815
Metzdorf, Michael, 8407
Metzgar, Rae, 5124
Metzger, Andy, 2008
Metzger, Charlie, 7273
Metzger, Colleen, 2418
Metzger, Jeff, 2670
Metzger, Kathy, 5402
Metzger, Steven C., 5609, 5611
Metzger, Walter, 1351
Metzler, Thomas, 790
Metzler, Tom, 790
Metzroth, Andrew, 4360
Meu, Robert, 7359
Meunier, Deb, 588
Mewha, Jennifer, 89
Meye, Michael L, 2263
Meyer, Alex, 6755
Meyer, Allen, 1589
Meyer, Betsy, 3706
Meyer, Bronson, 1030
Meyer, Dafna, 1640
Meyer, Daniel, 1478, 1621, 1623
Meyer, Dirk, 1258, 1259
Meyer, Frank, 2035
Meyer, Greg, 4065, 4582
Meyer, Jack, 6218
Meyer, Jack R., 271, 277
Meyer, Jeffrey, 6848, 6849
Meyer, Jocelyn, 3705
Meyer, Jon, 2427
Meyer, Joseph, 2150
Meyer, Judy, 1240
Meyer, Karen, 4533
Meyer, Karl A, 3796
Meyer, Kristin, 3032
Meyer, Kurt, 4113
Meyer, Mary, 1823
Meyer, Matt, 8051
Meyer, MW, 4545
Meyer, Nancy, 2541
Meyer, Patty, 5606
Meyer, Rev. William, 6676
Meyer, Terry, 5194
Meyer, Twyla, 1885
Meyer, William A., 4493
Meyer, M.D., Daniel K., 2311
Meyers, Andy, 6210
Meyers, D Lynn, 3705
Meyers, Marie, 1795
Meyers, Mark, 8203
Meyers, Mary, 1706
Meyers, Michael A, 8552
Meyers, Miriam, 8415
Meyers, Susan, 356
Meyers, Vicki, 2074
Meyers Heibeck, Kalena, 1236
Meyer, William A., 6602
Meyrose, Tom, 7946
Mfume, Kweisi, 3111
Mgebroff, Andrea, 1254
Miccolis Jr., Anthony F., 3866
Miceli, Joanne, 7571

Micha, Rebecca, 970
Michael, Bruce, 5248
Michael, Hermann, 5971
Michael, John, 3632
Michael, R Keith, 3020
Michael, Rusty, 8899
Michael, Shawn, 2530
Michael Myatt, MajGen J., 6260, 6266
Michaels, Cary, 5666
Michaels, Kenneth, 1409, 5117
Michaels, Norman M, 2116
Michaels, Scott, 3027
Michaelsen, Jonathan, 6855, 6857, 6858, 6859
Michaelson, Jonathan, 3020
Michaelson, Jonathan R., 6920
Michalicek, Virginia, 2069
Michalowski, Phil, 6428
Michalson, Jay, 5399
Michaud, Laura, 6755
Micheals, Jay, 2204
Michel, Aimee K, 4719
Michel, Demer, 2711
Michel, Roberta, 5161
Michel, Robin W., 4313
Michel,, William, 2903
Michell, David, 5774
Michell, Lisa, 2155
Michell-Leon, Carol, 2859
Michelon, Mike, 4822
Michels, Tony, 5479
Michelson, Sarah V, 5366, 5367
Michener, Cindy, 2380
Michener, Cyndi, 5768, 5769
Michero, Robert, 824, 825
Michka, Shirley, 5606
Mick, Jame, 998
Mickan, Carlos F., 246
Micke, Nanci, 2393
Mickelson, Joan, 3259
Mickelson, Kameron, 1767
Mickiewicz, John, 2056
Mickler-Konz, Carla, 282
Mickletz, Catie, 7214, 7215
Miclot, Kathleen, 582
Micotto, Steve, 2957
Midciff, Patty, 1855
Middaugh, Laurie, 2411
Middleman, Karl, 1650
Middleton, Charles, 4549
Middleton, Charles R, 1042
Middleton, Chuck, 6746
Middleton, Dr. Betty, 1504
Middleton, Mike, 7207
Middleton, Sarisa, 2515
Middleton, Sharon, 4122
Midkiff, Kittie, 6486
Midkiff, Robert, 2885
Midori Goto, Mary Ann, 4082
Mielke, Joyce, 4126
Mieseala, Philip, 4280
Migala, Lucyna, 206, 1039, 2044, 2045
Migdal Gee, Michelle, 53
Mihelick, Kathryn, 543
Mijares, Marianne, 4439
Mikalonis, Ruth, 5012
Mike,, 8406
Mike, Chuck, 8553
Mikel, Tim, 104
Miksa, Cindy, 6190
Mikula, Deborah E, 4823
Milano, Albert, 8349
Milanov, Rosen, 1341
Milanov, Rossen, 1329
Milanovich, Donna, 1048
Milarch, Carla, 3190
Milauskas, Brian, 3185
Milbauer, M.B.A, Barbara S., 7290
Milberg, Frances, 414
Milbrandt, Dr. Lanny, 4524
Milburn, Diana, 949
Milder, Larry, 1535
Mile, Martha, 236
Milenski, Michael, 1882
Miler, Paul, 7431
Miles, Christian, 2215
Miles, Dr Michael, 4887, 7392
Miles, Dr. Michael D., 3898
Miles, Dwayne, 6207

Executive Name Index

Miles, Heiko, 1793
Miles, Patrick, 1835
Miles, Rosemary, 179
Miles, Vicky, 6352
Milewski, Paulette, 3029
Miley, Sally, 2395
Milhan, Andrew, 44
Milhorn, Brian, 5990
Miliato, Francesco, 1067
Milicevic, Zeljko, 1255
Milik, Christian, 6412, 6413, 6414
Mill, Neil, 2627
Millan, Bruce, 3197
Millan, Tahra, 5097
Millard, Bethany, 3517, 7759
Millard, Carolina, 3793
Millard, Stephen, 5608
Millay, Mike, 6539
Millay, Peggy, 7502
Millbrook, Courtney, 1245
Millen, Christine M, 3567
Miller, A. Ridgeway, 1077
Miller, Adam, 129, 6064
Miller, Alex, 2939
Miller, Ali, 3119
Miller, Amy, 428
Miller, Andrea, 367
Miller, Ann, 3011
Miller, Anna, 163
Miller, Anne, 3011
Miller, Anne G., 5888
Miller, Barbara, 930
Miller, Barry, 2317
Miller, Bebe, 396
Miller, Bradley, 564
Miller, Bruce, 1165, 2720, 3076, 4049, 4054, 6449, 8549
Miller, Bruce J, 2768
Miller, Carolyn, 13, 2585
Miller, Cathy, 4278, 4279
Miller, Charles A., 4421
Miller, Chris, 8316
Miller, Christine, 7682
Miller, Clayton, 3670
Miller, Colin, 4709
Miller, David, 1414, 4309, 4312
Miller, David Alan, 1361, 5039
Miller, Denise, 530
Miller, Dennis, 221
Miller, Denny, 2759, 7318
Miller, Don Z, 4170
Miller, Doug, 7294
Miller, Dr. E. Darlene, 1677
Miller, Drew, 6292
Miller, Duane K, 6214
Miller, Dustin, 6977
Miller, E.P., 7145
Miller, Elizabeth, 6347, 6353, 6357
Miller, Eric, 1746
Miller, Everett, 3044
Miller, Gary, 2658, 5474
Miller, Glen, 4314
Miller, Greg, 3264, 5363
Miller, Jane, 4857
Miller, Janet, 1599
Miller, Jason E., 8132
Miller, Jean, 4020
Miller, Jeff, 7429
Miller, Jeffrey, 5141
Miller, Jerry, 1667
Miller, Jessica, 1683
Miller, Jill, 4013, 4015
Miller, Jim, 8555
Miller, Joan, 435
Miller, JoEllen, 3010
Miller, John, 4843, 4868, 8076, 8078
Miller, John A., 1639, 2307
Miller, John J, 1335, 5004
Miller, Jonathan, 2038
Miller, Jonathan S., 7223
Miller, Jonathan Seth, 3146
Miller, Joshua, 6018, 6019, 6020
Miller, Justin, 1932
Miller, Kara L, 3719
Miller, Katie, 3580
Miller, Kay, 1450
Miller, Kelly L., 6091
Miller, Ken Elston, 8519

Miller, Kris, 3940
Miller, Lance, 8569
Miller, Laura, 3194, 7279
Miller, Lauren, 1845
Miller, Lawrence, 305
Miller, Linda, 7106
Miller, Lisa, 1332
Miller, Llewellyn, 2301
Miller, Lloyd, 1759, 5698, 5702
Miller, Mac, 4781
Miller, Malcolm, 1839
Miller, Marcia, 263
Miller, Marie, 1118
Miller, Marilyn, 3522
Miller, Mark, 8432
Miller, Mary, 581, 1174, 1316
Miller, Mary K., 1593
Miller, Matt, 2557
Miller, Maureen, 662
Miller, Melvin, 5894
Miller, Michael, 288, 876, 2601
Miller, Michael W, 7497
Miller, Mike, 4173
Miller, Mindy, 1085
Miller, Monica M, 5367
Miller, Nat, 3935
Miller, Nicole, 6
Miller, NonaMarie, 1767
Miller, Omari, 5051
Miller, Pat, 2259
Miller, Patricia, 597
Miller, Paul, 4995
Miller, Paulette, 1497
Miller, Peggy, 5601, 8240
Miller, Ralph, 3822, 8144
Miller, Randy, 891
Miller, Rebecca, 3769
Miller, Regine, 2502
Miller, Rhonda, 8360
Miller, Rob, 3668
Miller, Robert, 2255, 3641
Miller, Robert C, 2254
Miller, Ron, 8087
Miller, Ronnie, 7402
Miller, Rosalie, 7355
Miller, Russel, 2214
Miller, Russell, 2216
Miller, Sam, 414
Miller, Sarah, 939
Miller, Scott D., 1633, 5812
Miller, Shayne, 3373
Miller, Sheryl, 4662
Miller, Sophie, 4252
Miller, Stephen, 3361
Miller, Steve, 8014
Miller, Steven N., 6760
Miller, Sue, 1095, 1903
Miller, Susan, 3774, 5089, 5090
Miller, Suzi, 7174
Miller, Tracy Liz, 4023
Miller, Tricia, 5402, 8093
Miller, Vance, 5957
Miller, William, 944, 5834
Miller Casey, Donna, 4282
Miller Coulson, Sarah, 1647
Miller Hull, Deborah, 4630
Miller Saunders, Rebecca, 1482
Miller White, LaNeshe, 8159
Miller, Jr., Craig S., 1773
Miller, MBA, CMP, Bryan, 8564
Miller-Chapman, Diane, 392
Miller-Stephany, John, 7351
Millet, Francisco, 1718
Millheiser, Daniel F., 1383
Milligan, Amy K., 4770
Milligan, Katy, 5029
Milligan, Sharon, 2465
Milligan Sheaffer, Caitlin, 3247
Milling, Darrin C., 5099
Millington, Eric, 1464
Millington, Julie, 5934
Million, Lisa, 2835
Million, Sharon, 1226
Milliren, Gregory, 6166
Millner, Kai'li, 8516
Millner, Larry, 2113
Millow, Mare, 5194
Mills, Alicia, 1984

Mills, Alvin, 875
Mills, Barry, 7166
Mills, Bart, 5353
Mills, Bernadette, 4176
Mills, Carmen, 8712
Mills, Crystal, 4031
Mills, David, 3965
Mills, Eric, 6282, 6285, 6287
Mills, Gail, 4963
Mills, Grant, 1311
Mills, Harry, 693
Mills, Joanna, 7241
Mills, Karl O., 1914
Mills, Leslie, 7185
Mills, Lisa, 4096
Mills, Michael M., 2313
Mills, Miriam, 7564
Mills, Norma, 5256
Mills, Robert, 552
Mills, Stephen, 621
Mills, Steve, 6230
Mills, Tiffany, 371
Mills Jr, A. Slade, 1433
Milne, Dorothy, 2937
Milner, Julie E, 7430
Milnes, David, 853
Milnes, Dwane, 881
Milnes, Sara milnes, 881
Milom, Chad, 3917, 5581
Milstead, Haney, 4947
Milstein, Harvey, 2180
Mimm, Ethan M, 3840
Mims, Jane, 1695
Mims, Jeremy, 1812
Mims, Shannon, 6377, 6378, 6380
Min, Meredith, 6209
Mina, Manelo, 2767
Minadakis, Andrea, 2856
Minadakis, Jasson, 2526
Minahan, Dr John P, 5415
Minamoto, Kazuko, 5141
Minasi, Mark, 5212
Minchala, Alexandra, 3553
Minde, Stefan, 1611
Minderman, Dean, 3301
Mindich, Eric M, 7746
Mindich, Stacey, 7768
Mindlin, Debra, 5015
Mindy,, 8474
Mindy, Event Coordinat, 8495
Miner, Chad, 1933
Mines, Robert, 1749
Ming, Adron, 1739
Minges, Valery, 4152
Mingo, Theresa, 3423
Minibayeva, Natalia, 1665
Minkins, Tommie, 8329, 8331, 8332
Minner, D C, 5388
Minner, Dr. Sam, 8547
Minner, Selby, 5388
Minnick, Craig, 4707
Minskoff Breede, Patricia, 6430
Minteer, Kellen, 6271
Minton, Elizabeth, 1863
Mintz, Beverly, 1746
Mintz, Gary, 6314
Mintz, Richard, 1733
Minyard, Gary, 7993
Minyard, Michelle, 4707
Miozza, Tennina, 4846
Mirabello, Barbara, 660
Mirabello, Robert, 660
Mirabello, Esq., Francis J., 3839
Mirageas, Evans, 1005, 2278
Miraglia, Kasey, 6197
Mirahver, Laura, 1723
Mirakian, Robert, 2289
Miralles, Diego, 875
Miranda, Connie, 785
Miranda, Mariclare, 597
Miranda, Michael, 4239
Miranda, Regina, 445
Miranda Wedig, Rachel, 5998
Mircea-Trotz, Alina, 1930
Mirek, Lori, 1891
Mirenda, Rosalie, 8110

Mirenda PhD, Rosalie, 8111
Mirich-Spear, Helene, 777
Miritell, Penny, 6904
Miron, George, 1444
Miropolsky, Michael, 1790
Mirrione, Jim, 3481
Mische, Erich, 7376
Mischel, Hal L, 7103
Mischler, Nicholas, 1826
Misenheiner, Christa, 5260
Mishell, Kathryn, 5591
Mishler, Brian, 1661
Miskavige, Sally, 5282
Miskell, Jerome, 1513, 1514
Miskimins, Jacki, 8243
Miskinis, Mark, 5462
Misner, Tom, 7183
Mistick, Dr Barbara K, 5438
Mistri, Jeffrey, 794
Mistrot, Kyle, 1712
Mital, Brian, 5705
Mitchell, Andrew, 4092
Mitchell, Andy, 1154
Mitchell, Brett, 1251, 1536
Mitchell, Brian, 1672, 5464
Mitchell, Bryan, 5518
Mitchell, Cheri, 525
Mitchell, CJ, 1041
Mitchell, David, 1097
Mitchell, David D., 7187
Mitchell, Deborah, 325
Mitchell, Henry, 3126
Mitchell, Jack, 2557
Mitchell, James J, 1042
Mitchell, Jane M., 4493
Mitchell, Jessica, 83
Mitchell, Judith A., 4493, 6602
Mitchell, Katheleen, 2097
Mitchell, Kevin, 1147
Mitchell, Luke, 1091
Mitchell, Lydia, 180
Mitchell, Marcus, 5126
Mitchell, Mariana, 6102
Mitchell, Mark, 1580
Mitchell, Mary, 529
Mitchell, Mike, 3083
Mitchell, Neil, 6196
Mitchell, Nicole M., 160
Mitchell, Pat, 4013, 4015
Mitchell, Patricia, 7375
Mitchell, Robert, 3128
Mitchell, Roy, 7061
Mitchell, Rusty, 4133
Mitchell, Ruth, 188
Mitchell, Sara, 4332
Mitchell, Scott, 6174
Mitchell, Stephanie, 751
Mitchell, Steve, 5897
Mitchell, Ted, 6179
Mitchell, Terrill, 639
Mitchell, Todd, 7423
Mitchell, Tom, 4851
Mitchell, Jane M., 6602
Mitchell Hood, Dr. Marcia, 6609
Mitchell, Barbara, 1062
Mitchell, Patricia J., 7195
Mitchell, Teresa, 6501
Mitchell, Tracy, 3615
Mitchelson, Bill, 3595
Mitchko, Eric, 2020, 2268
Mitchko, Janet, 3097
Mitchum, Cindy, 6571
Mitisek, Andreas, 2041
Mittelstadt, Paul, 4920
Mitts, Brandon, 5390
Mitze, Teri Solomon, 4121
Miura, Naoyuki, 5153
Mivillie, Susan, 1703
Mixon, A. Malachi, 5314, 7961
Mixon, Emily, 4886
Mixsell, Maggie, 2611
Mixter, H Perry, 5548
Miyamoto, George, 6675
Miyamoto-Mills, Jarred, 1867
Miyamura, Henry, 1019
Miyoshi, Shin R, 5114
Mizanin, John, 4600, 6839
Mize, Ranney, 4716

1199

Executive Name Index

Mizens, Ph. D., Maija, 4606
Mizerany, Michael, 68
Mizrachi, Eli, 7508
Mizrahi, Isaac, 368
Mlady, Patrick, 6763
Mlotek, Mark, 3493
Mlotek, Zalmen, 3493
Moak, Jr., James A., 4690
Moats, Ellen, 3114
Moberly, Phyllis, 6173
Mobley, Sherwood, 1681
Mocek, Rita, 3299
Moch, David, 43
Moch, Jennifer, 3359
Mock, Aspen, 5513
Mock, Elsie, 5513
Mock, Joey, 602
Mockli, Shannon, 558
Modjeski, Ivy, 2008
Modugno, Mike, 7314
Moe, Elaine, 5980
Moe, Joan, 834
Moe, Karen, 3222
Moe, Mechelle, 2944
Moe, Nina, 1191
Moebius, Jim, 1726
Moehlenkamp, Betty Sue, 5743
Moehring, Albert E, 1484
Moehring, Patricia, 1484
Moellenberg, Charles, 3844
Moeller, Barbara, 1579
Moeller, Gary, 4624, 6905
Moeller, Jocelyn, 4640, 6962
Moench, Mark C., 5682
Moenich, Candice, 91
Moenter, Tina, 7998
Moeri, Paul, 1682
Moerman, LeeAnn, 7018, 7020, 7021
Moffat, Jean, 4186
Moffat, John, 5772
Moffatt, Marcia, 2086
Moffatt, Michael, 3012
Moffett, Micheeal R., 7121
Moffitt, Christian, 3854
Moffitt, James, 1017
Mogle, Melanie, 8467
Mohamed, Joe, 6718
Mohammed, Hussain, 4041
Mohatt, Jayson, 2445
Mohebbizadeh, Henriette, 1758
Mohnani, Christopher, 619
Mohney, William, 2303
Mohoney, Ruth, 1385
Mohr, Erin, 6537
Mohr, Jamie, 5716, 8507
Mohr, Matt, 6831
Mohrmann, Peter, 2555
Mohror-Hill, Elizabeth, 3220
Mohylsky, Katherine, 1526
Moiola, Leigh, 347
Moir, Bob, 1656
Molden, Jennifer, 6949
Moldenhauer, Judith A., 7291
Molesky, Todd, 3987
Molina, Carlos, 978
Molina, Marisol, 733, 4174
Molina, Russell, 4378
Molinaro-Blonigan, Bryan, 7024
Moline, John, 5667
Molino, Christine, 6456, 6457
Molis, Sigmund, 7600
Moll, Al, 4616
Moll, AL, 6871
Moll, Ted, 1278
Moller, John, 6450
Molleson, Karen, 4237, 6175
Molloy, Andrew, 919
Molloy, Honour, 3595
Molnar, Jane, 2911
Momani, Lisa, 1517
Momich, Bruce, 6052
Momkus, Edward J., 4574
Mona, David, 2147
Monaco-Angell, Nada, 2489
Monagas, Enrique, 2586
Monaghan, Kate, 2729
Monahan, Arleene, 258
Monahan, Jim, 154

Monahan, Mark, 7335
Monahan Bremer, Cris, 6106
Monarch, Donna, 8043
Monas, Anna, 2121
Monasterio, Ben, 196
Monasterio, Frank, 4537, 6703
Monasterio, Marie, 196
Moncrief, Clare, 3086, 4719, 7150, 7151
Monday, Travis, 8273
Mondestin, Paul, 4255
Monestere, Noralee, 866, 867
Monetza, Robert, 7298
Money, Chris, 4960
Monfort, Charles K, 5999, 6348
Monfort, Richard L, 5999, 6348
Monfre, Brian, 5839
Mongeau, Gilles, 4247
Mongold, Mark, 7768
Moniz, Calvin, 5393
Monk, Robert, 6210
Monnier, Liz, 229
Monroe, James, 2127
Monroe, Jensen, 7667
Monroe, Jim, 6941
Monroe, Kendyl K, 3512
Monroe, Kimberly, 508
Monroe, Parker E, 848
Monroe, Robert, 3675
Monroy, Rosalinda, 4269
Monsman, Nancy, 4181
Monson, Anna, 1717
Montalvo, Lina, 2495
Montalvo, Mary, 8387
Montanari, John, 4802
Montanaro, Kavi, 7181
Montano Gianetta, Jeanne, 3357
Monte, Bonnie J, 4998
Monte, Elisa, 421
Montejano, Vivian, 5641
Montemurro, JoAnn, 2944
Monter, Marilyn, 5075
Montera, Melissa, 5096, 7694
Monterosso, Melissa, 8642
Montes, Michael, 1721
Montez, Miguel, 2891
Montgomery, Andy, 1754
Montgomery, Bill, 7157
Montgomery, Bob, 7384
Montgomery, Bruce, 6352, 6360, 6367, 6368, 6369, 6370
Montgomery, Chris, 5976
Montgomery, Dave, 5688
Montgomery, Davis, 4122
Montgomery, Howell, 6485
Montgomery, J Sherwood, 1907
Montgomery, Janet, 1160, 2189
Montgomery, Julie, 5312, 5313
Montgomery, Kathleen, 1064
Montgomery, Kerri, 4335
Montgomery, Liz, 428
Montgomery, Meredith, 762
Montgomery, Nicole, 640
Montgomery, Paula, 5267
Montgomery, Robb, 2320
Montgomery, Scott, 6633
Montgomery, Tabitha, 3247
Montgomery, Jr., Edward A., 1645
Montilino, John, 3229
Montpetit, Christopher, 5929, 5931
Montpetit, Christopher M, 5046
Monts, Lester, 4825
Moody, Carolyn K., 2304
Moody, Dwain, 2406
Moody, Emily, 1634
Moody, Gloria N, 707
Moody, Joan, 4449
Moody, Michael, 1678
Moody, Robert, 1509, 2273, 2274, 4164
Moody, Sherie M., 2817
Moody, Travis, 8261
Moomey, Adam, 4078
Moon, Emma, 4305
Moon, Jonni, 3336
Moon, Lee, 8718, 8719
Moon, Marjorie, 3418
Moon, Nulson, 3053
Mooney, Carol Ann, 4628
Mooney, Kenneth, 4017

Mooney, Kevin, 2819
Mooney, Madison, 6150
Mooney, Patti, 6092
Mooney, Paul, 5492
Mooney, Phyllis, 1627, 1628
Mooney, Robert, 3559, 3591
Mooney, Stacey, 6706
Moore, Al, 6639
Moore, Amy, 5513
Moore, Barb, 1562
Moore, Becky, 103
Moore, Ben, 8606
Moore, Benjamin, 4087
Moore, Beth, 3791
Moore, Charles, 361, 1365
Moore, Charlie, 3247
Moore, Chris, 5366
Moore, Christopher, 7122
Moore, Chuck, 1715
Moore, Dave, 6348
Moore, Denise, 3438
Moore, Dick, 4386
Moore, Doug, 4472, 7418
Moore, Douglas B, 1217
Moore, Ezekial J, 4724
Moore, Franklin, 4989
Moore, Fred, 4664
Moore, Gary, 1863
Moore, Griff, 1699
Moore, Heather, 6450
Moore, Helen, 254
Moore, J Chris, 5367
Moore, Jack, 1618
Moore, James, 1688
Moore, Jeff, 3055, 8583
Moore, Jeffrey, 985
Moore, Jennifer, 6626
Moore, Jill, 3919
Moore, Jo, 8429
Moore, Kathleen, 339, 687, 1431
Moore, Ken, 3779
Moore, Kevin, 3733, 7963, 7964, 7965, 7966
Moore, Kimberly, 798
Moore, Laree, 7460
Moore, Larry, 1870
Moore, Lee, 8893
Moore, Linda, 1724
Moore, Lou, 6074
Moore, Mal, 5924, 5925
Moore, Marilyn, 1305
Moore, Mark, 6523
Moore, Mary, 757
Moore, Melanie, 4764
Moore, Melissa, 289
Moore, Michael, 1804, 1845
Moore, Pamela, 254
Moore, Patrick, 6637, 7808
Moore, Paul, 680
Moore, Peter, 2951
Moore, Rachel, 386
Moore, Rhonda, 550
Moore, Richard, 4386
Moore, Rita, 1201
Moore, Ross, 1905
Moore, Roy, 6076
Moore, Sharon, 5259
Moore, Shirley, 1924, 8310
Moore, Sonia, 3465
Moore, S,an W., 4382
Moore, Tammy, 6654
Moore, Thomas A., 4110
Moore, Thurston, 3907
Moore, Walter, 1804
Moore, Wiley, 2929
Moore, Zac, 1222
Moore Green, Judie, 2907
Moore Jr, Eddie N, 8545
Moore Jr, Michael, 6057, 6058, 6059, 6060, 6061
Moore Morton, Amy, 617
Moore, Esq, Franklin, 7556
Moorer, Stephen, 2455
Moorhead, Tom, 236
Moorman, Frank, 3655
Moorman, Lisa, 8560
Moorman, Mark, 4365
Moorman, Priscilla, 822
Moors, Cat, 229
Moquin, Andrew, 5772

Mor, Anne, 4244
Mora, Raffaela, 448
Morabito, Sam, 6180
Morain, Michael, 7009, 7010
Moraitakis, Ann Marie, 6618, 6628
Morales, Cesar, 8046
Morales, Jazmin N., 4233
Morales, Joe, 3874
Morales, John, 1924
Morales, Lisa, 6316
Morales, Mitchell, 6554
Morales, Phoebe, 1580
Morales, Yvette, 373
Morales Matos, Jamie, 1552
Moran, Andy, 1721
Moran, Eve, 2918
Moran, Gina, 5001
Moran, Jim, 3196
Moran, Kendall, 1972
Moran, Lynda A., 1382, 5071
Moran Jr, Charles, 7228
Morander, Jeff, 6228
Morden, Max, 1418
Mordine, Shirley, 207
Mordo, Jean, 2489
More, Jeff, 985
More Glagov, Jennifer, 2047
Moree, Adeena, 5921, 5922
Morel, Michael J., 1478
Morelli, Jian Paul, 8684
Moreno, Bernardo F., 519
Moreno, Rene, 5612
Moreno, Rolando, 2767
Moreno, Vanessa, 6730
Morenoff, Jerry, 3120
Morer, Paul, 2502
Moretto Spencer, Kathleen, 4354
Morey, Herbert, 3548
Morey, Jason, 6603
Morey, Melissa, 2143
Morfesis, Andrew, 3656
Morfin, Anthony, 6318
Morgan, Bennett, 8803
Morgan, Cheryl, 7998
Morgan, David L., 3013
Morgan, David M, 6054
Morgan, Deborah A., 7953
Morgan, Ed, 6696
Morgan, Elijah, 6196
Morgan, Emily, 3483
Morgan, Howard, 3825, 3837, 5474
Morgan, Ian, 3529
Morgan, James, 3597
Morgan, James T., 4400, 4730, 4731, 4732, 4733
Morgan, Jim, 3597
Morgan, John S, 7809
Morgan, Julie, 2225, 2727
Morgan, Kathleen, 4332
Morgan, Lea, 552
Morgan, Marsha, 7436
Morgan, Merilyn, 1933
Morgan, Michael, 815, 816, 836, 1940, 1941, 5893, 5896
Morgan, Miles, 966, 4440
Morgan, Nathan, 1760
Morgan, Richard, 3668
Morgan, Sharron, 1714
Morgan, Steve, 2483
Morgan, Tammy, 4016
Morgan, Thomas, 7229
Morgan, Victoria, 515
Morgan, William, 3713
Morgan Coggin, Abigail, 4512
Morgan Riggs, Janet, 8125
Morgan-Lewellyn, Risa, 680
Morgan-Weeisberg, Carmel, 1826
Morgenstein, Barbara R., 5244
Morgenstern, Shirley, 1518
Morgon, Larry, 6213
Moriarty, Elvin, 3989
Moriarty, John, 1950
Moriarty, Kevin, 3947
Moriarty, Suzan, 3007
Morimoto, Dennis, 6383
Morin, Joseph, 1158
Morin, Mark, 593
Morin, Phil, 5941
Morineau, Gastin, 2563

Executive Name Index

Morisi, Michael, 667
Morison, Kathy, 2464
Morison, Patricia L., 4417
Moritsugu, Jim, 1275, 1276
Morley, Dave, 820
Morley, James T., 6399
Morlock, David R., 8012, 8013
Morman, Andrea, 8034
Morman, Stavis, 8034
Moroney, Ross, 5646
Moross, Matthew, 7624
Morr, Alex, 921
Morr, Garry, 4616
Morr, Judy, 6090
Morre, D Greg Kehl, 5872
Morrell, John, 4173
Morrell, Wendy, 263
Morrelli, Marietta, 2707, 2710, 2711
Morreo, Tracy, 3859
Morrill, Cynthia, 4397
Morrill, Peter, 4088
Morris, Adia, 299
Morris, Amanda, 4680
Morris, B Matt, 5545
Morris, Bonnie, 3241
Morris, Brad, 6903
Morris, Chip, 268
Morris, Clark, 4910
Morris, Curtis, 865
Morris, David, 3628
Morris, Dylan, 5261
Morris, Eileen J., 3984
Morris, Eric, 3066
Morris, Gary, 6049
Morris, Ginger, 3928
Morris, Goffrey, 3392
Morris, Jean, 4841
Morris, Jeannine, 5371
Morris, Jeremiah, 6194
Morris, Jeremy M, 3208
Morris, Jim, 4807
Morris, Justine, 5879
Morris, Lauren, 2855, 6150
Morris, Linda, 1804, 1867
Morris, Magena, 5244
Morris, Marah, 6127
Morris, Mark, 368, 1340
Morris, Marley, 2633
Morris, Matthew, 4269
Morris, Michael, 1754
Morris, Nancy, 2010
Morris, Philip, 3620, 7820
Morris, Samantha, 900, 901
Morris, Stacey, 1563
Morris, Steven, 470
Morris, Susan F., 2200
Morris, Susan Waring, 3592
Morris, Thomas W., 4262
Morris, Tom, 6700, 7607
Morris, William, 3041, 3438
Morris, William C., 2234
Morris, Zhana, 4977
Morris-Smith, James, 8635, 8636, 8639
Morrisey, Larry, 4889
Morrisey, Linda, 1401
Morrisey, Llinda M., 1401
Morrison, Bill, 3557
Morrison, Chris, 1315
Morrison, Darrell, 4187, 6027
Morrison, Dave, 3818
Morrison, David, 6648, 6649
Morrison, Duncan, 3621
Morrison, Gene, 3940
Morrison, Gillian, 2107, 4777
Morrison, Josh, 3987, 8416
Morrison, Lawan, 675
Morrison, Mallory, 675
Morrison, Marcia, 5434, 8117
Morrison, Margaret, 387
Morrison, Richard, 2567
Morrison, Sandy, 4467
Morrison, Sarah, 524
Morrison, Scott, 4102
Morrison, Tim, 6086
Morrison-Hrbek, Stephanie, 3715
Morrison, Mike, 6438
Morrissey, Charles, 2320
Morrissey, Greg, 7374

Morrissey, Kara, 1995
Morrissey, Maggie, 1112
Morrissey, Michael, 5876
Morrow, Amy, 5559
Morrow, Christopher, 1093
Morrow, Dr Lynne, 1870
Morrow, Jeffrey, 1658
Morrow, Jew, 2796
Morrow, Kate, 3982
Morrow, Marcelyn, 716, 4152
Morrow, Prosser, 1934
Morrow, Jr., Gregory V., 4280
Morrs, Karl, 5371
Morsberger, Michael J., 6462
Morsching, Gene, 5552
Morse, Alison, 11
Morse, Allan, 2260
Morse, Bill, 6211
Morse, Cinda, 4017
Morse, Donald, 4666
Morse, Margaret, 7331
Morse, Merna, 783
Morse, Naomi, 5134
Morse, William, 911
Morss, Anthony, 2181
Morten, Ivonne, 2783
Mortensen, Beth, 7539
Mortensen, Brenda, 3291
Mortensen, Robert E, 2313
Mortensen, Rod, 1934
Mortimore, Curtis, 6915, 6916, 6917, 6918
Mortis, Robert, 5214
Morton, Dr. Paul, 4710
Morton, Mae, 2974
Morton, Paul, 4711
Morton, Renee, 5998
Morton, Wyant, 4340, 4341
Mosakowski, Susan, 3480
Mosbacher, Merry L., 3281
Moscato, Robin, 339
Mosce, Diane, 2465
Moschner, Karl, 1471
Mosco, Marlene D., 8123
Moscone, Jonathan, 2538, 4204
Moscovich, Jose Luis, 1899
Mose, Franz, 2279
Mosel, Steve, 5015
Moseley, Charles, 7591
Moseley, Chuck, 3681
Moseley, James, 6875
Moseley, Lee, 1277
Moser, Chris, 2854
Moser, John, 3741
Moser, Marian, 558
Moser, Mel, 6345
Moser, Rich, 6725, 6726
Moser, Ted, 1897
Moses, Cathey, 5966
Moses, Diane, 2465
Moses, Erik A., 6465, 6481
Moses, Jack C., 5679
Moses, John, 2836
Moses, Jon, 6600
Moses, Jon R., 2836
Mosey, Sue, 4835
Mosey, Susan, 4835
Mosher, Bob, 1955
Mosher, Chris, 5449
Mosher, Mala Yee, 3588
Mosier, Chris, 5449
Mosier, Diane K, 17
Moskalenko, Tania C, 6860
Moskowitz, Janey, 1994
Mosler, Diane K, 4219
Mosley, Alta, 6562
Mosley, Dr. Loma, 5809
Mosley, George, 1110
Mosley, CPA, Henry W., 6481
Moss, Arthur H., 7019
Moss, Barbara, 1856
Moss, Deborah, 24
Moss, Gerald F., 5089, 5090
Moss, Jane, 5151
Moss, Sandy, 2427
Moss, Sarah, 4707
Moss, Vanessa, 6745
Moss Kincaid, Jennifer, 4033
Moss Moore, Annie, 5776
Moss Southall, Kelly, 142

Mossbrucker, Tom, 347, 349
Mostaroy, Marc, 5458
Mostellar, Rhea, 4
Mostovoy, Marc, 1642
Mosur, Gloria, 5375
Mote, Tanya, 2665
Moten, Gwen, 3379
Motes, David R, 836
Motherwell, Emily, 8824
Motley, Barbara, 4719
Mott, Ray, 745
Motta, Nathan, 7980
Motts, Warren E., 7982
Motyca Dawson, Frances, 2098
Moughalian, Sato, 2228
Moules, Todd C., 2319
Moulin, Mark, 1506
Moulopoulos, Gloria, 3752
Moulton, Charles, 309
Moulton, Gordon, 713, 2410
Mountford, Sharon, 1943
Mounts, Chris, 4906
Mourning, Dan, 7609
Mouser, Elizabeth, 3867
Mouser, Kimberly, 4897
Mousin, Philip A., 1408
Mousseau, Jeff, 5166
Mousset, Caroline, 4431
Mouton, Camille, 8333
Mouwad, Jerry, 3604
Movic, Amy, 1637
Mowbray, Maria, 1034
Mowery Bolton, Marti, 616
Mowry, Kerry, 5001
Mowry, Tonya, 1626
Mox, Gregory, 8663
Moxley, Cynthia, 1694
Moxley, Linda, 2092
Moxness, Kay, 8087
Moy, Eric, 2065
Moye, Darrell, 3167
Moye, Stacie, 3167
Moyer, Dale, 6186
Moyer, Joshua, 2273, 2274
Moyer, Lavinia, 3196
Moyer, Nicole, 3799
Moynihan, Bess, 3298
Moynihan, John, 4979
Mozer, Clark, 1957
Mozzoni, Annette, 1671
Mraz, Laura, 5483
Mroch, Mike, 2953
Mruk, Laura.D, 222
Mszanski, Lorraine, 3794
Muast Jr, Walter, 1625
Mucci, Barbara, 1523, 1524
Mucci, Michael, 1182
Muchnick, Amy, 2165
Muckleroy, George, 2348
Mudd, Patti, 2171
Mudgett, Jane, 1585
Mudre, Roger, 931, 4395
Muehleisen, Lynn, 5796
Muela, David, 6190
Mueller, Anne, 564
Mueller, Audrey, 1866
Mueller, Christopher, 4356
Mueller, Dale, 1594
Mueller, Jeffrey, 931
Mueller, Karen, 3266
Mueller, Michael L., 4854
Mueller, Midge, 5404, 5407
Mueller, Nancy, 798
Mueller, Paul F, 1963
Mueller, Paula J., 1437
Mueller, Scott C, 5316
Muenzer, Frances, 4262
Muffitt, Dr. Timothy W, 1137
Mufson, Dr. Maurice, 1818
Mugar Eveillard, Elizabeth, 7247
Muggia Stuff, Paola, 91
Muh, Berit S., 4310
Muir, Steven P., 5317
Muir, Terence, 970
Muir, M.D., W. Angus, 5735
Muirhead, Aalan, 1651
Mukherjee, Dipankar, 3250
Mulcahy, Bob, 7578

Mulcahy, Kathleen, 5493
Mulcahy, Patrick, 3799, 5437
Mulcahy, Sallyann, 313
Muldin, Sarah, 6627
Mulhern, Brian C, 1895
Mullaly, Michelle, 1523, 1524
Mullane, Susan, 5735
Mullangi, Sundeep V., 6720, 6721
Mullany, Janet, 1994
Mulle, Nancy, 2722
Mullen, Charlie, 1087
Mullen, Dennis, 105
Mullen, Jackie, 4891
Mullen, John W., 5812
Mullen, Kathleen, 2109
Mullen, Scott, 6801, 7842
Mullen, Shirley A., 7683
Mullen, William, 5035
Muliens, Rob, 8070
Muller, Annette, 71
Muller, Cathy, 1599
Muller, David, 6169
Muller, David J., 4349
Muller, Debra, 8485
Muller, Erin L., 6660
Muller, Gene, 8159
Muller, George, 1644
Muller, Irene, 2257
Muller, James, 7047
Muller, Jennifer, 434
Muller, John, 2722
Muller, Nancy, 4335
Muller-Kimball, Ed.D, Dominee, 2628
Mullet, Janet, 2986
Mullet, Steven, 1802
Mulligan, David A, 4082
Mulligan, Stephanie, 3338
Mullikin, Nick, 149, 651
Mullin, Debbie, 8553
Mullin, Maureen L, 7548
Mullins, Carol, 414
Mullins, Cindy, 5886
Mullins, Denise, 632, 3969
Mullins, John, 2175
Mullins, Loren, 1440
Mullins, Steve, 6048
Mullone, Tina N., 631
Mulloy, Anne, 4958
Mulver, Esq, Timothy, 3626
Mulvey, Kirsten, 704, 4122
Mulvill, William, 7945
Mumbauer, Stephanie, 570
Mumma, Kenneth, 3814
Mumme, Teri, 679
Mummey, Sara, 1089
Mumpton, Lisa, 6330, 6331
Munch-Dittmar, Jessica, 1509
Munchak, Mike, 8290
Mundell, Matt, 6537
Munds, Rose, 6854
Munger, Molly, 5949, 5950
Munier, John, 742
Muniz, Lorenzo, 6496
Munkittrick, Alain, 2691
Munley, Charlene, 7212
Muno, Crystal, 8079
Munoz, Adrian, 6239
Munoz, Jo-Ann, 339
Munro, Deborah, 2447
Munro, Don, 3288
Munro, Jo, 233
Munroe, Katy, 4504
Munsell, Robert, 948
Munselle, Ted, 5609, 5611
Munson, Dana, 7352
Munson, Derek R, 393
Munson, William G, 7804
Munt, Maxine, 2655
Munyan, John, 5177
Munzer, Al, 6478
Muolo, David, 7837
Mura, Debbie, 3369
Murakami, Kiri, 1341
Murata, Les, 1019
Murchison, Pamela, 1655
Murdo, David, 7526
Murdoch, Colin, 854, 4293
Murdock, Christine, 5570

Executive Name Index

Murdock, Colleen, 4822
Murdock, Lindsay, 4930
Murdock, Moira, 6304
Murdock, Noreen, 1600
Murdock, Suzanne, 2891
Murdough, Toni, 1394
Murnick, Elliot, 8631
Murphey, Tracy, 1752
Murphrey, Donna, 312
Murphy, Amy L, 3827
Murphy, Bill, 7215
Murphy, Brad, 7470, 7471
Murphy, Carmella, 2127
Murphy, Cason, 2427
Murphy, Cheryl, 2818
Murphy, Christopher, 1785
Murphy, Culley, 7216
Murphy, Dan, 3791
Murphy, David, 2442
Murphy, Donn B., 2745
Murphy, Donna, 2124
Murphy, Ed, 2473
Murphy, Edward Leo, 8635, 8636, 8639
Murphy, Elizabeth, 3370
Murphy, George, 2208
Murphy, Hugh, 389
Murphy, Jan, 6397
Murphy, Joseph, 1389
Murphy, Karen, 89
Murphy, Kathryn, 1855
Murphy, LeAnn, 647
Murphy, Leonard, 1622
Murphy, Margaret Anne, 1278
Murphy, Mark, 5863, 7679
Murphy, Matt, 350
Murphy, Michael, 2565
Murphy, Nicholas, 2818
Murphy, Pam, 3660
Murphy, Peggy, 3203
Murphy, Phil, 3216
Murphy, Rick, 1070
Murphy, Robert, 1069
Murphy, Russell, 394
Murphy, Ryan, 1762
Murphy, Seth, 4693, 4694
Murphy, Shannon, 6258
Murphy, Stephanie, 2401
Murphy, Tim, 8318
Murphy, Vincent, 2864
Murphy Douglas, Anne, 8549
Murray, Andrea, 7759
Murray, Ann, 4552
Murray, Ashley, 373
Murray, Barbara, 2614
Murray, Bob, 6550
Murray, David, 4255
Murray, Ed, 4242
Murray, Elizabeth, 6260, 6266
Murray, Finnie, 7489
Murray, Gibbs, 3355
Murray, Greg, 7369
Murray, James, 1280
Murray, Jason, 4202
Murray, John, 7417
Murray, Jon, 2721
Murray, Karen, 8105
Murray, Kent, 2100
Murray, Liz, 3381
Murray, Melissa, 3793
Murray, Michael, 1627, 5447
Murray, Nancy, 1367
Murray, Natalie, 2347
Murray, Pia, 372
Murray, Rich, 8518
Murray, Robert, 4698
Murray, Robin, 626
Murray, Ryan, 4257
Murray, Sean, 2561
Murray, Sherrie, 8288
Murray, Tom, 643
Murray, William, 364
Murray III, James, 1284
Murrell, Carol, 3552
Murrietta, Jeannette, 6366
Murrin, Mary, 3849
Murrow, Gene, 5134
Murtaugh, Gina, 7662
Muse, David, 2750

Muse, Mary, 7481
Musgrave, Bryan N., 1294
Musher, Daniel, 1730
Mushet, Julie, 90, 94, 4307, 4315, 4316
Musholt, Janine, 903
Musial, Mark, 8
Musick, Mike, 3893
Muska, Scott, 7999
Muskin, Sharon, 1542
Muspratt, Kirk, 1050, 1093, 2055, 6789, 6790, 6791
Mussafer, Joe, 715
Musselman-Cox, Sherry, 8030
Musselwhite, Nancy, 1006
Musser, Betty, 809
Musser, Margaret, 4851
Musser III, Robert D., 4817
Musso, Michellei, 4073
Musson, Renee, 6522
Must, Miriam, 3253
Musto, Pat, 2722
Muti, Lorenzo, 1481
Muti, Riccardo, 1035, 1038, 6733
Muze, Barbara, 964, 4435
Muzeni, Barbara, 4469
Muzio, Donna L., 586
Muñoz, Billy, 4001
Mwanger, Mary, 2465
Myatt, Katie, 3923
Myer, Anna, 275
Myer, Linda, 3180
Myers, Alyse, 5109
Myers, Ashley, 5269
Myers, Barbara, 402
Myers, Byron D, 1286
Myers, Charles, 863, 4319, 4320
Myers, Cheryl, 5230
Myers, Chris, 6825, 6826, 6827
Myers, Christine, 4959
Myers, Curtis J., 3811
Myers, Don L, 5086
Myers, Dr. Eugene, 2322
Myers, Dwight, 3890
Myers, Evies, 5281
Myers, George, 4088
Myers, Ginny, 4184
Myers, Holly I, 2966
Myers, Janelle, 1572
Myers, Jeffrey C, 963
Myers, Joel, 689
Myers, Jonathan, 1217
Myers, Karen, 5285
Myers, Kevin A, 48, 49
Myers, Lois, 3000
Myers, Martha, 371
Myers, Marty, 6674
Myers, Pam, 2267
Myers, Robert, 4627, 6316
Myers, Thomas A., 5857
Myers, Timothy, 2268
Myers, Vicki, 4901
Myers, Willie, 8711
Myers, Yvonne, 3641
Myers Brown, Joan, 578
Myers CFRE, Eileen K, 1329
Myers-Morgan, Pam, 3949
Myhre, Barbara, 2033
Myhre, Keven, 4012
Myhre, Mona, 735
Myhrum, Roxanna, 3144
Myhrum, Roxie, 3144
Mykles, Vicki Fogel, 1957
Mylett, Chelsea, 5534
Myllykoski, Theresa, 1555
Mylson, Denyce, 5015
Mynatt, Kevin, 2004, 2005
Myrick, Kathy, 908
Myrick, Robin, 4824
Myslewski, Lee Anne, 2378
M ller-Stosch, Johannes, 1240

N

N. Nanon, Patricia, 3151
N. Pierce, Gregory, 2846, 2862, 6627
Naas, Dennis, 6212
Nable, Majo, 2619
Nachajski, Mark, 662

Nachamie, Stephen, 3464
Nachman II, A. Robert, 1681
Nachtrab, Kandace, 5037
Nadalin, JoAnne, 911
Nadeau, Eric, 1024
Nadeau, Joseph, 2159
Nadeau, Rachel, 3865
Nadeau, Sandy, 1269
Nadel, Jim, 4336
Nadel, Sybel, 3541
Nadel, Sybil, 3541
Nadelman, Maddy, 2204
Nadler, Dr. Dan, 6725, 6726
Nafe, Rick, 6589
Naff, Gretchen, 4579
Nafziger, Kenneth, 5740
Naganathan, Nagi, 8012, 8013
Nagano, Jerry, 6199
Nagano, Kent, 758
Nagata, Naoko, 468
Nagelberg, Dr Steven, 2463, 2509, 6170
Nagelhout, Molly, 8242
Naggar, Alan, 6130
Nagle, John, 4023
Nagle, Will, 1622
Nagy, Debra, 4354
Nagy, Glen, 2445
Nagy, Jill, 1471
Nagy, Julie, 4999
Nagy, Martin W, 5368
Nagy, Mary, 7297
Nagy, Wayne, 1031
Nagy Ph.D, Rebecca M, 6521
Nahagian, Angela, 1369
Nahat, Dennis, 99, 5167
Nahulu, Nola A, 2030
Naiditch, Beverley, 2273
Naiditch, Beverly, 5244
Naidu, Laveen, 411, 430
Nail, Nancy, 3290
Naillon, Jane, 197
Nailor, Steven, 1065, 1066
Naishtat, Sandy, 557
Najarian, Mark, 6347, 6353, 6357, 6360, 6367, 6368, 6369, 6370
Nakajama, Ichiko, 382
Nakasone, Michael, 1019
Nakasue, Cory, 34
Nakazawa, Roger, 1779
Nalivka Hancock, Sharon, 1298
Naluai Jr, Carl, 1902
Namesnik, Dave, 6388
Nance, Beverlee, 5272
Nancy, Beer, 7748
Nanna, Marylouise, 1374, 5058
Nantais, Clyde, 276
Nantell, Ronald, 4806
Napier, Debra, 3377
Napier, Tommy, 1817
Napier, Ph.D., William J., 519
Naplan, Allan, 4164
Naple, Jerry, 3606
Napoli, August A, 5316
Napoli, Mary, 1140
Naquin, Nicole, 244
Nardi, Caron, 7244
Nardo, Michael C., 1439
Nardo, Rachel Lee, 6317
Narramore Moody, Gloria, 8839
Narver, Allison, 4081
Nasatir, Robin, 78
Nascimento, Claudia, 2692
Nash, Claudine, 954
Nash, David, 569
Nash, Jon, 2339
Nash, Ron, 3441
Nash, Sean, 1808, 5808
Nash, Steve, 2665
Nash Ambler, Michael, 5172, 8866
Nash, M.D., Clyde L., 1541
Nasif, William J., 6283
Nason, Brad, 1668
Nassal, Bill, 982
Nassimbene, Nancy, 6227
Nassivera, John, 4020
Nastaskin, Natalia, 8811
Natale, Alexjo, 371
Natale, Vittoria, 336

Natalicio, Diana, 8373
Natalicio, Dr. Diana, 8380
Nath, John W, 7064
Nathan, Angel, 8289
Nathan, Robert, 5103
Nathan, Rodney, 8415
Nathan Golias, Allison, 5595
Nations, Anne W., 6443
Natker, Leon, 1907
Natoli, Esq., Lisa A., 5174
Natrajan, Meena, 3250
Natyam, Bharatha, 664, 665
Naulot, Philippe, 279
Naumoff, Paul, 1560
Nause, Allen, 3783
Navarra, Elizabeth, 4693, 4694, 7088
Navarre, Tricia, 2669
Navarro, a Cappella Chor, 1924
Navias, Geoffrey, 3625
Navin, Erika, 4109
Navis, Jr, Bob, 3715
Navratil, Paul, 942
Nazarenko, John, 1217
Nazarenko, Larissa, 108
Nazworth, Mark, 8422
Nchege, Nnena U, 4502
Neal, Corinne, 2903
Neal, Dustin, 1698
Neal, Gwendolyn, 3423, 5056
Neal, Justin, 7743
Neal, Marquise, 2051
Neal Beasley, David, 6080, 6081, 6082, 6084
Neale, Alasdair, 866, 4542
Nealy, Sara, 1940, 1941
Near, John, 4575
Nearing, Elizabeth, 6419
Neary, Colleen, 42
Nebistinsky, Joseph P., 5485
Neblett, Carol, 2315
Neblett, Will, 2567
Neckels, Josh, 2298
Neckles, Josh, 557
Neckles, Natasha, 2797
Necphee, Sidney A, 5577
Necrason, Adam, 4023
Necrason, Jena, 4023
Nederland, James L, 6159
Nederland, James M, 6159
Nederlander, James, 7778
Nedved, Linda, 4682, 7063
Needham, Mary, 4906
Needle, Lynn, 342
Neeleman, John, 1806, 5803
Neeley, Linda, 1026
Neely, Bonnie, 2452
Nees, David, 5876
Neese, Linda, 7024
Nef, Virginia, 8371
Neff, Laurence, 846
Negley, Marvin, 4645
Negrete, Kim, 4226
Negri, Lisa, 890, 4348
Nehring, Larry, 5318, 5351
Neidich, Brooke Garber, 7746
Neier, Yvette, 394
Neikrug, Marc, 5034
Neil, Terri, 4494
Neill, Jeannette, 273
Neill, Laura, 2290
Neill Ridgley, Katherine, 4433
Neilly, Adam, 1497
Neilsen-Steinhardt, Therry, 4974
Neilson, Leanne, 6313
Neilson, Margaret, 1292
Neilson, Sally, 1917
Neilson, Tara, 3262
Neisser, Judy, 1041
Neisser, Judys, 2943
Neitzel, Kate, 1827
Neitzer, Dave, 7273
Nell Martin, La, 1896
Nelleman, Lynne, 2061
Nellis, Andrea, 2238, 7710, 7749, 7769, 7781
Nellis, Andrew, 7757
Nelson, Ann, 775
Nelson, Bob, 6245
Nelson, Cory Elizabeth, 3164
Nelson, David, 4073

Executive Name Index

Nelson, Don, 1754
Nelson, Donald, 1807
Nelson, Elizabeth L., 5753
Nelson, Emily, 217
Nelson, Eric, 1897
Nelson, Esther, 2108
Nelson, Geoffrey, 3720
Nelson, James, 638, 936, 4402
Nelson, Janice, 3090
Nelson, Jeffery R., 5682
Nelson, Jerry, 2197
Nelson, KellyAnn, 2277
Nelson, Ken, 224
Nelson, Lisa, 8159
Nelson, Madeline, 2043
Nelson, Margaret, 198
Nelson, Mary Ann, 2198
Nelson, Mitchell, 1156, 4751
Nelson, Pamela J, 7779
Nelson, Paul, 5714
Nelson, Paul E., 4656
Nelson, Pauline, 1640
Nelson, Philip, 8442
Nelson, Philip B., 8559
Nelson, Robert, 1837
Nelson, Ryan T., 2965
Nelson, Sandie, 4056
Nelson, Scott, 3151, 6761
Nelson, Shannon, 1792
Nelson, Susan, 6383
Nelson, Timothy, 7330
Nelson, William C., 3289
Nelson, William H., 1766
Nelson Nash, Denise, 4267
Nelson Walker, Adam, 639
Nemac, Lucy, 4284
Nemanich, Ann Marie, 71
Nemec, Chris, 2331
Nemeroff, Brian, 975
Nemhauser, Frank, 4801
Nemiroff, Steve, 4990, 7557
Nerad, Alex, 6763
Nerenhausen, Mark, 6506
Nerguizian, Micaela A., 90, 94
Neri, Debi, 4478
Nerr, Linda, 2701
Nesbit, Sarah R., 8442
Nesbitt, Amy, 4822
Nesbitt, Bill, 1294
Nesholm, John F., 8605
Nesholm, Laurel, 1805
Nesler, Clay, 2398
Ness, Corinne, 5840
Ness, Paul, 1409, 5117
Ness, Ted, 4065
Nessenoff, Goldie, 1400
Nestle, Rebecca, 4295
Nestor, Argy, 4740, 4741
Nestvold, Karen, 1803
Netherton, Shane, 8059
Netsky, Hankus, 1190, 2110
Netter, D Terence, 4453
Nettesheim, Joel, 4120
Nettles, John, 66
Netzley, Ben, 7355
Neu, Georgia, 3338
Neu, Robert, 1265
Neubauer, Brenda, 4891
Neubeck, Jack, 1860
Neuberger, Emily, 2967
Neubert, Otto, 682
Neuen, Donald, 1943
Neuenswander, Joyce, 4901
Neuert, Natalie, 5706
Neufeld, Keith, 1121
Neufeld, Ken, 3429, 7993
Neugebauer, Cedric, 401
Neuman, Daniel, 6180
Neuman, David J, 852
Neuman, David J., 6254
Neuman, Michael, 4845
Neumann, Amber, 4368
Neumann, Frederick, 3516
Neumann, Kenda, 6149
Neumann, Laura, 6339
Neumann, Mary, 1393
Neumann, Michael, 837
Neumann, Sam, 6333

Neuner, Jim, 3783
Neustadter, Kathryn, 4261
Nevarez, Glenda, 3966
Neve, John, 1859
Nevenschwander, Janet, 4003
Neverman, Brock, 8665, 8666, 8669
Neves, Matt, 2547
Neville, Cody, 5079
Neville, Susan, 6107
Neville, Thomas M., 1703
Nevin, Doug, 3549
Nevins, Patrick, 4582
Nevins, Polly, 4012
Nevins, Rhoda, 4291
Nevola, Gabriel, 1323
New, Lea, 3779
Newberg, Joan, 4282
Newberry, Bill, 3971
Newberry, Susan, 5264
Newbrough, Nathan, 903
Newcastle, Mimi, 4421
Newcomb, Garlan, 5449
Newcomb, Kenneth, 7591
Newcomb, Mike, 7515
Newcomb, Vickie, 5449
Newcombe, Don, 6156
Newcomer, Carole, 222
Newell, Beck, 3317
Newell, Charles, 2923, 6734
Newell, Douglas, 1578
Newell, Rachel, 1121, 1779
Newell, Sarah, 4087
Newenhisen, Stephan, 512
Newhouse, Ron, 6100
Newkirk, John, 767
Newland, Lee Ann, 1418
Newlin, Helen, 1280
Newman, Adrrenne, 8300
Newman, Andrea, 5135
Newman, Carrie, 910
Newman, Charlotte, 4354
Newman, Dan, 3242
Newman, David, 801
Newman, Gretchen, 2376
Newman, Heather, 2654
Newman, J. Leroy, 1584
Newman, James, 2620
Newman, Jim, 4305
Newman, John, 1288, 2169, 4919
Newman, Kurt, 1847
Newman, Lisa, 1847
Newman, Maria, 1649
Newman, Michael, 5008
Newman, Nancy, 8156
Newman, Naomi, 2596
Newman, Patrice, 2324
Newport, Bari, 3092
Newsom, Deborah, 6986, 6987, 6988, 6989
Newsom, Eli, 2678
Newsom, Jon, 4427
Newson, Perry, 1249
Newton, Roger, 8223, 8225
Newville, Meg, 3760
Neyman, Rob, 5984
Ng, Julia, 7812
Ng, Kok-Koon, 1072
Ng, Ming, 6173
Ng, Stella, 139
Ngenda, Crispin, 8049
Nguyen, Anh-Tuyet, 7738, 7739
Nice, Carter, 4201
Nice, Jamie, 6529, 6532
Nicely, Rita, 5805
Nicholas, Christine, 194
Nicholas, Christopher P., 2239
Nicholas Jr, Frederick, 2327
Nicholls-Smith, Jennie, 4012
Nichols, Alexandra C., 6738
Nichols, Ann, 4692
Nichols, Jackie, 3908, 3910
Nichols, Jason, 5531
Nichols, Jeff, 4173
Nichols, Julie, 829
Nichols, Kay, 972
Nichols, Kimberly, 6203
Nichols, Lorenzo, 3991
Nichols, Lynn, 4357
Nichols, Mary, 4097

Nichols, Mary B., 5589
Nichols, Nick, 2602
Nichols, Norma, 1017
Nichols, Pam, 1977
Nichols, Ricky, 8378, 8379
Nichols, Trey, 2507
Nichols, Wade, 3461
Nichols-Lawrence, Donna, 2184
Nicholson, James B, 7283
Nicholson, Marty, 6092
Nichter, Sarah, 4616
Nickel, Caroline, 810
Nickel, Jerri, 3998
Nickel, Russell, 1801
Nickerson, Kati, 4068
Nickerson, Madge, 4982
Nickie Levy, Nitzan, 413
Nicolaisen, Dan, 4757
Nicole, Nicole, 6519
Nicolosi, Sonja, 247
Nicolson, James, 4785
Niebauer, Joyce, 5443
Nieberlein, Debbie, 4142, 5898
Niebuhr, Judi, 2190
Niebulski, M.D., Harvey, 5797
Niece, Dr Rick, 4184
Niederberg, Richard, 2632
Niederberger, Kristin, 1284
Niedziela, Andrew, 8131
Niehaus, Mark, 1830
Niehoff, Rachel, 1995
Niejadli, Walter, 3339
Niekrasz-Laurent, Virginia, 30
Niell, Dana, 2429
Nielsen, Andrew, 703
Nielsen, Glenn, 684
Nielsen, Joel, 7995
Nielsen, John T., 2368
Nielsen, Larry, 7569
Nielsen, Mark, 868
Nielsen, Susan, 1605, 8091
Nielsen, Larry, 7264
Nielson, Emily, 1719
Nielson, Mindy, 8494
Nielson, Pete, 122
Nielson, Tammie, 6645
Nieman, Jamie, 1100
Nieman, Patricia, 4070
Nieman, Tom, 4826
Niemann, Donna, 5155
Niemann, Jimmy, 3923
Niemczyk, Benjamin, 2257
Niemi, Erika, 1968
Niemi, Loren, 3242
Nienhouse, Brenda, 1807
Nies, Bryan, 815
Niesen, Jim, 3420, 3505
Niess, Christopher, 2811
Nieto, Sammy, 646
Nietzel, John F., 3373
Nieves, Nicole LaFlair, 2688
Niezen, Richard, 896
Nightengale, Ruth, 3564
Nigrelli, Antonina, 1400
Nigro, Joseph, 2380
Nikias, C. L. Max, 6154, 6171, 6176
Nill, Mellisa, 5941
Nilsen, Andrea, 8674
Nilson, Amy, 6303
Nilssen, Liv, 1912
Nimerichter, Jodee, 5233
Nina, Hand, 4988
Nir, Hila, 4666
Nisbet, Wyck, 2439
Nissen, Pat, 1056
Nissenbaum, Richard, 6192
Nissien, Mikko, 271
Nist, Thomas J., 1659
Nitchun, Alyssa, 5126
Nitsch, Paul, 1486, 5231
Nitter, Susanne, 3140
Nittoli, Christopher, 2182
Nivelle, Serge, 3576
Niven, Doug, 3095
Nivison, William F., 6398
Nix, Dr. Brad, 4681
Nix, William, 7403
Nixon, Grant, 4540

Nixon, Kathy, 2634
Noack, Lori, 4299
Noack, Kelly, 6825, 6826, 6827
Noah, Libby, 3685
Noah, Mike, 7209
Noah Uldall, Ivan, 2903
Nobel, Brooke, 2764
Nobis, Ricklen, 653
Noble, Diane, 6313
Noble, Mark, 169
Noble, Mike, 1770
Noble, Seth, 707
Noble, Weston, 2070
Nobles, Sr., Eric, 1491, 5242
Noblin, Kathleen, 116
Nobusawa, Kiko, 5091
Nocera Godbout, Mia, 589
Nocero, Paul, 1926, 1927
Nocks, Nancy S, 3730
Nocks, Ronald E., 3730
Noe, Kevin, 1655
Noel, Christine, 2324
Noel, Craig, 2565
Noel, Michelle, 2679, 2680
Noerr, Beverly, 4276, 6216, 6217
Noffsinger, Lynn, 970
Noffsinger, Steven, 1799
Noguchi, Valena, 833
Noguera, Marta, 1381
Nolan, Beth, 6462
Nolan, Katherine, 1888
Nolan, Kathleen, 3382
Nolan, Kathleen Kund, 5437
Nolan, Kevin, 4647
Nolan, Victoria, 2699, 6427
Noland, Lynn, 3077
Noland, Tara, 5274
Noldy, Cindy, 2428
Noldy, Cynthia, 5985, 5987, 5989
Nolen, Roy, 2352
Nolen, Terrence J, 3827
Noles, Julie, 711
Nolin, Dovid, 1523, 1524
Nolin, Heather, 3169
Noll, Phill, 8018
Nolte, Carol, 409
Nolte, Scott, 4088
Noltemy, Kim, 1176
Nomura Clark, Margaret, 1916
Nonken, Marilyn, 1417
Noodele, Noucha, 2661
Noofhazar, Katie, 5398
Noon, Molly, 6973
Noonan, Claire, 4596, 6820, 6821
Noonan, Ed, 7479
Noonan, Lily, 4250
Noonan, Peggy, 8008
Nordahl, Sandy, 4640, 6962
Nordberg, Edward P., 4758
Nordeen, Kate, 4841
Nordgren, Carol, 4395
Nordin, Bill, 7609
Nordstrom, Burt, 6058, 6059, 6060, 6061
Nordstrom, Harry, 4878
Nordyke, Peter, 6240, 6241
Noren, Jay, 7291
Norfleet, Rachel, 620
Norian, Bruce, 1218
Noriega, Dorothy, 5660
Norlander, Angela, 2613
Norman, Julyen, 1166
Normand, Polly, 244
Norpel, Haley, 8698, 8699, 8700
Norrington, Kelley, 43
Norris, Christine, 4740, 4741
Norris, Daniel, 4504
Norris, Emily, 4756
Norris, James, 2440
Norris, Jennifer E., 6260, 6266
Norris, Jim, 4447, 4685
Norris, Jonathan, 8302
Norris, Kay Allison, 2262
Norris, Marilyn, 3020
Norris, Rosanne, 5049, 5120
Norris, Virginia, 4344
Norris Pattan, Ann, 4559
Norskey, Gail, 7247
North, Carol, 3299

Executive Name Index

North, John E., 3153
North, Mark, 4637
North, Moira, 431
North, Rosie, 3094
North, Timothy, 8477, 8478, 8480, 8481
Northam, Betsy, 4289
Northburg, Tim, 127
Northcutt, Diana, 1740
Northcutt, Dr. Jamil, 7960
Northrup, Pam, 4049
Northway, MD, J.D., 785
Norton, Ann, 2753
Norton, Anne, 7220
Norton, Cherly, 5506
Norton, Cheryl, 2698
Norton, Cheryl J., 6418, 6421
Norton, David, 1765
Norton, Janet, 4224
Norton, Laura, 721
Norton, Mary, 8239
Norton, Peter, 3567
Norton, Sarah, 8286
Norton, Scott, 6064
Norton, Tom, 6528
Norway, Dawn, 8337
Norwood, Marie, 1797
Norwood, Norris, 2271
Nose, Kimi, 524
Noser, Brett, 1303
Nossaman, Kathy, 1751
Nostrala, Jennifer, 3034
Notara, Darrell, 585
Notara, Sally, 585
Notingburd, Mark, 5496
Nott, Andrea, 1834
Nottage, James, 6891
Notter, Penelope, 3203
Nottingham, Sue, 4938
Notz, Joanne, 2956
Nova, Giuseppe, 4274
Novak, Dan, 2048
Novak, Jason, 4140
Novak, John, 8079
Novak, Linda L., 5020
Novak, Walter, 6130
Novice, Ken, 2502
Novo, Celia, 8801
Novo, Jose-Luis, 1367, 1565
Novotney, Laurence, 1151, 2090
Nowak, Larry, 3428
Nowak, Michael, 864
Nowakowski, Alexa, 141
Nowell, Catherine, 725
Nowell, Frank, 4359
Nowell, Jeff, 1770
Nowell, Sean, 3475
Nowlen, Pete, 4257
Nowlin, Kent, 6332
Nowlin, Richard, 6302
Nowlin, Teresa, 3769
Nowotny, Patrick, 8470
Noyes, Andrew, 7538
Noyes, Sylvia, 1781
Nuckolls, Ellen, 756
Nugara, Mario, 61
Nugent, Martin, 2299
Nuhfer, D., 8002
Null, Brian, 2550, 2551
Null, Derek, 6913, 6914
Null, Lisa, 1740
Numedahl, Brandi, 4356
Nunemacher, Andrew, 2425
Nunley, Jennifer, 5558
Nunley, Stephen, 3447
Nunnally, Marvin, 6615
Nunnally, Tracy, 6766
Nunnelley, William, 5893
Nurdin, Mark G., 1723
Nurse, Wilma, 1348
Nusbaum, Alan, 3585
Nusbaum, Alan S, 3285, 3585
Nuss, Patty, 1708
Nussbaum, Jeff, 5138
Nuttall, Geoff, 596, 3869, 5534
Nutter, Bill, 3390, 7592
Nutter, Michael, 2023
Nuzum, Laura, 3402
Nuzzaci Park, Tamara, 4361

Nuzzolo, Laura, 5215
Nvari Vartanian, Melissa, 4124
Nyberg, Marilyn, 8249
Nygren, Dave, 4540
Nygren, Kim, 8292
Nyheim, John A, 2305
Nyman, Brent, 2362
Nyman, Thomas W., 4003
Nyquist, Andrea, 6341
Nyquist, Janet, 799
NyQuist, Kristen, 1805
Nystedt, Julie, 1234
Nystrom, David K., 836
Nytch, Jeffery, 1655
N,zet-S,guin,, Yannick, 1647

O

O'Berski, Jay, 3651
O'Berst, Norma, 3070
O'Blak, John B, 4202
O'Boyle, Kelly, 8014
O'Brian, Elizabeth, 6672
O'Briant, Diana, 4101
O'Brien, Betsy, 413
O'Brien, Cynthia, 6497
O'Brien, Dana, 359
O'Brien, Ellen, 3099, 6477, 8108
O'Brien, Eugenia L., 251
O'Brien, Hayes, 4101
O'Brien, Helen, 1260
O'Brien, Jack, 2565
O'Brien, Jessica, 3359
O'Brien, Kacy, 3389
O'Brien, Kevin J, 6264
O'Brien, Liz, 5977
O'Brien, Marcy, 3855
O'Brien, Nancy, 1203
O'Brien, Randall, 5568
O'Brien, Rosemary, 6325
O'Brien, Stephanie, 795
O'Brien, Terrence, 3433, 5061
O'Brien, Ph.D., J. Patrick, 8340
O'Bryant, Daniel, 1269
O'Callaghan, Colleen, 116
O'Cana, Tess, 3642
O'Connell, Brenda, 7460
O'Connell, Craig, 4397
O'Connell, Dennis, 3696
O'Connell, Jim, 5874
O'Connell, John, 6874
O'Connell, Tiffany, 6057
O'Connell Esq, Daniel, 2241
O'Conner, David M, 2733
O'Conner, Linda, 1980
O'Conner, Pat, 8297
O'Connor, Chris, 3366, 6897
O'Connor, Cindy, 1579
O'Connor, Jacquie, 4051
O'Connor, Jim, 3028
O'Connor, John, 988
O'Connor, Leon, 5513
O'Connor, Michael, 6184
O'Connor, Molly, 1583
O'Connor, Susan, 4991
O'Connor, Tom, 749, 1359
O'Daniel, Kent, 6033
O'Day, Rey, 2547
O'Dea, Eileen, 7195
O'Dell, David, 2335
O'Dell, Gregory A., 6481
O'Dell, James, 1192
O'Dell, Susan, 1430
O'Dette, Paul, 4783
O'Donnell, Allison, 6790, 6791, 6792
O'Donnell, Bill, 7625
O'Donnell, James, 4953, 6395
O'Donnell, James F, 3301
O'Donnell, Jim, 3279
O'Donnell, Maureen, 886
O'Donnell, Mimi, 3511
O'Donnell, Peter, 7664
O'Donnell, Rich, 1288, 4919
O'Donoghue, Sean, 6192, 6753
O'Donohue, Kevin, 230
O'Dowd, Daniel J, 5999, 6348
O'Fallon, David, 4882
O'Farrell, Rita, 2347

O'Finn, Kevin, 6756
O'Flinn, Chris W., 4430
O'Geen, Roni, 5048
O'Gorman, Tom, 7501
O'Hagan, Janet, 7426
O'Hagan, Patrick, 4999
O'Halloran, KerryAnn, 1596, 5418
O'Halloran, Sue, 5418
O'Halloran, Susie, 1596
O'Hara, Michael, 6155
O'Hara Walker, Elizabeth, 6005, 6006, 6007, 6008
O'Hare, George, 4137
O'Harrah, Meghann, 5390
O'Hearn, Dr. Christopher, 4346
O'Henley, Connie, 6062
O'Keefe, Catie, 3708
O'Keefe, Tim, 632
O'Kelly, Katie, 4087
O'Kelly, Morris, 765
O'Konek, Cindy, 7369
O'Leary, E Colin, 7721
O'Leary, Gregory, 2041
O'Leary, Harold, 5826
O'Leary, Susan, 7663
O'Leary, Timothy, 2163
O'Linger, Colleen, 6873
O'Loughlin, Carol, 4542
O'Malley, Barbara, 6732
O'Malley, Brian, 3170
O'Malley, Cathleen, 3795
O'Mara, Heather, 308
O'Mara, Michele, 403, 463
O'Muircheartaigh, Colm A., 7258
O'Neal, John, 3082
O'Neal, Judi, 4139
O'Neal, Melinda, 2095
O'Neal, Steve, 7440
O'Neal, Susan, 6664
O'Neil, Brian, 1945, 6329
O'Neil, C.J., 5839
O'Neil, James, 4738
O'Neil, Jennifer, 6417, 6425, 6426
O'Neil, Pam, 6336
O'Neil, Scott, 905
O'Neil, Sean, 1690
O'Neill, Bob, 7561
O'Neill, Cheri, 6528
O'Neill, Eileen, 897
O'Neill, Jan, 6087
O'Neill, Jeso, 363
O'Neill, Kittson, 3833
O'Neill, Vincent, 3425
O'Neill, Zoura, 59
O'Neill Arose, Jsssie, 7963, 7964, 7965, 7966
O'Neill Louden, Molly, 6407
O'Neill-Butler, Marjorie, 4024
O'Neill-Butler, Robert, 4024
O'Rear, Dr Randy, 5596
O'Reilly, Aidan, 4026
O'Reilly, Allen, 2855, 4504
O'Reilly, Gavin, 8811
O'Reilly, Gery, 6504
O'Reilly, Thom, 3724
O'Rielly, Kate, 6009
O'Rourke, Emily, 576
O'Rourke, Kim, 2542
O'Rourke, Thomas, 6718
O'Rourke-Smith, BJ, 2477
O'Shaughnessy, Ferris, 1034
O'Shaughnessy, Harry, 7672
O'Shaughnessy, James P., 1412
O'Sullivan, Mike, 1935
O'Sullivan, Mort, 2813, 6580
O'Toole, Amanda, 2131
O'Toole, Kara, 5776
O'Wyatt, Jane, 1425
O. Morrison '66, Portia, 6642, 6643
Oagasapian, Nancy, 7244
Oakes, Michael, 3542
Oakes, Vincent, 2328
Oakley, Eleonor H, 5265
Oakley, Eraina, 5241
Oakley, Gail, 2447
Oates Charles, Mrs. Marion, 5520
Oatmen, Ben, 1407
Obala, Apiyo, 4707
Obara, Paige, 140

Obel, Susan B., 4383, 4791
Ober, Gayle M., 1985
Oberbling, Lynn, 7247
Oberfelder, Jody, 436
Oberg, David, 1353
Oberhausen, Leslie K., 243
Oberjat, Kate, 1389
Oberkfell, Esq., Keith F., 1485
Oberlag, Lee, 5312, 5313
Oberlander, Michael, 3302
Oberlin, Matt, 7332
Oberman, Gabriel, 2890
Oberman, I. Allan, 4350
Obermueller, Karola, 4160
Oberstein, Mathew, 1332
Obuchowski, Sara, 878
Ochart, Louise M., 606, 610
Ochoa, Dr Reynaldo, 1733
Ochs, Carol, 3459
Ochs, Sara, 3248
Octera, John, 7179
Odell Catlett, Elizabeth, 262
Oden, Alice, 757
Odhner, Bryonna, 264
Odle-Scott, Brenda, 3887
Odom, Dr. Gale, 4721
Oduntunde A. Kerr, Neffer, 208
Odza, Randall, 1376
Oelker, Kity, 6542
Oelkers, Casey, 1826
Oerman, Wyatt, 8191
Oesch, Michael, 91
Oetgen, Susan, 940, 2231
Oettinger, Rebecca, 4106, 5828
Office Manager, Donohue, 982
Ogle, Jonnah, 8049
Oglesby, Donald, 966, 4440
Oglesby, Wendy, 7869
Oh, Julii, 1430
Ohlandt, D, 6795
Ohlemeyer Esq, William S, 1422
Ohlsen, Miki, 591
Ohyama, Heiichiro, 870
Oien, Fred, 8240
OJ Parson, Ron, 2923
Okashiro, Chitose, 5158
Okun, Maury, 291, 1253, 4861
Okunseinde, Ayodamola, 146
Okura-Youtsey, Jaz, 4061
Olafsson, Olaf, 3468
Olaisen, Artie, 3945
Olan, Ben, 2513
Olans, Steven A, 1319
Olazaba, Javier, 6088
Olcott, Dallen, 8475
Oldenburg, Fritz, 3092
Oldfield, Madie, 3536
Oldham, Barbara, 1381
Oldham, Susanne, 6468
Oldham, Jr., Kenneth, 1169
Olds, Diane, 2977
Oldt, Thomas, 4458
Oldt, Tom, 4458
Olechno, Judee, 6732
Oleno, Erin, 841, 1905
Olim, Dorothy, 3416
Olin, Dr. Robert F., 5927, 5930
Olinder, Laurie, 3557
Olinger, Scott, 7013, 7014
Oliss, Philip, 7967
Olivares, Miranda, 4211
Oliveira, Felipe, 6493
Oliver, Cathy, 6325
Oliver, Cheryl, 4525
Oliver, Katie, 4162
Oliver, Laurie, 4289
Oliver, Mike, 8182
Oliver, Ruth, 6853
Oliver, Thomas, 4080
Oliverio, Nettie, 7521
Oliverson, Cathy, 4326
Olivieri, Denise, 1784
Olivieri, Diane, 1948, 1949
Olmos, Kim, 32, 55
Olmstead, Richard, 4223
Olmstead, Jr, Dale, 7175
Olmsted, Daniel H, 1321
Olowe Sr, Adebola T, 514

Executive Name Index

Olsaver, Michael, 1220
Olsen, Cody, 4064
Olsen, Heather, 5216
Olsen, Kathleen, 5190
Olsen, Katie, 499
Olsen, Merritt, 3885, 4070
Olsen, Paul, 7536
Olsen, Rowena, 7052
Olsen Lamden, Evelyn, 843
Olshan, Alan, 471
Olson, Carl, 1306
Olson, Cheryl, 3092
Olson, David, 3405
Olson, Denise, 4092
Olson, Douglas, 6823, 6824
Olson, Jeremy, 487
Olson, Jim, 8497
Olson, Jon, 4871
Olson, Joseph, 7846
Olson, Ken, 4173
Olson, Kris, 3338
Olson, Lynette J., 7056, 7059
Olson, Mary, 6313
Olson, Michael, 4067
Olson, Nathan, 4361
Olson, Paul D., 4883, 4884
Olson, Paula, 3405
Olson, Robert, 916, 4355
Olson, Robert W, 5305
Olson, Shari L., 5973, 5974
Olson, Shirley, 7616
Olsson, Milton, 1242
Olstein, Sheri, 3097
Olthaus, Kevin, 7959
Oltmann, Eric, 1931, 4344
Olzerowicz, Paul, 4982
Oman, Daphne, 593
Omar-Makram, Mohamed, 6052
Omardien, Hisham, 525
Omilami, Afemo, 2860
Omilami, Elizabeth, 2860
Omori, Roy K, 591
Omotalade, Jacquelyn, 2576
Onaga, Carolyn, 40
Oneppo, Vincent P., 4387
Oney, Kayla, 3050, 7065
Ong, Kathryn, 2386
Ongaro, Giulio M., 4338, 6310, 6311
Onishi, Deidre, 3758
Onnen, Steve, 4193
Onorato, Dan, 5488
Onstad, Pat, 7981
Ontko, Raymond, 4630
Oosterwaal, Amber, 1715
Opel, Justine M., 2196
Operman Cash, Amy, 376
Ophime, Jeffery, 6655
Oppelaar, Carol, 2094, 5515, 8191
Oppenheim, Ellen, 7522
Oppenheimer, Martin A., 2120
Orakpo, Tracy, 718
Orange, Catherine, 3111
Orange, Catherine, 7187
Orange, Rodney, 7187
Orange Jr, Rodney, 3111
Orazi, Nondi, 2054
Orbach, Evelyn, 3218, 3219
Orbach, Pearl, 3218, 3219
Orchard, Joseph, 922, 4383, 4791
Orchard, Lee F, 6946
Orchard, Lee F., 6885
Orchard, Robert J, 3146
Orcutt, Jim, 1394
Ordoñez, Jenaro, 6291
Orduno, Candice, 13
Orellana Wheeler, Noemy, 1874
Orent, James, 1184
Oreschnick, Robert, 1390
Oreskovich, Mark, 4102, 8644, 8645, 8651
Oreskovich, Mark S., 8643, 8646, 8647, 8649
Organ Solis, Sandra, 640
Organisak, Paul, 583
Orgel, Frank, 6610
Oriel, Jane, 791
Orlandi, Janice, 3383
Orlando, JeannieRae, 2600
Orlando, Richard T, 2600
Orlando, Thomas, 4323

Orlofsky, Debo, 5027
Ormai, Ted, 5461
Orme, Charles, 730
Ormes, Vance, 3896
Ormsby, Gloria, 8504
Ormsby Hargis, Gayle, 3938
Orndorff, Vivian, 3050
Oroian, Paul, 1750
Oroson, Ron, 6705
Orr, Bob, 862
Orr, Terrence S, 582
Orr, Timothy, 4357
Orrall, Karl, 3864
Orrios, Angel Gil, 3624
Orseske, Melanie, 4144
Orsillo, Michael, 3688
Orsua, Sally, 6281
Ort, Don, 1713
Ort, Eric D., 6398
Ort, June, 1713
Ortega, Ann, 5446
Ortega, Frank, 1932
Ortega, Gregory, 2213
Ortega Cowan, Roman, 2016
Orth, Ruth, 2009
Orthmann, Trevor, 1068, 1329
Orthwein, Mrs. Ruth, 5520
Ortiz, Tony, 8093
Ortiz-Barreto, Ricardo, 6129
Ortman, Michael, 6749
Ortmayer, Amanda, 4308
Ortmeier, Thomas, 2275
Ortner, Richard, 4773
Ortolano, David, 6335
Orts, Daryl, 4068, 4072
Orum, Daniel, 6271
Orza, Stephanie, 48
Orzaureux, Stephanie, 49
Orzeck, Lida, 418
Orzello, Mary, 1667
Osajima, Amy, 6855, 6857, 6858, 6859, 6920
Osborn, Ed, 758
Osborn, Eliot, 4403
Osborn, George D, 5100
Osborn, Jack D, 3704
Osborn, Megan, 1785
Osborn, William A, 6733
Osborn, William A., 1035, 1038
Osborne, Allan, 3683
Osborne, David, 2134
Osborne, Denise Simpson-, 8232
Osborne, Doug, 1317
Osborne, Ethan, 8519
Osborne, George, 5100, 7700
Osborne, George D, 7700
Osborne, Jason, 8232
Osborne, Jeremy, 1702
Osborne, Julie, 5612
Osborne, Lynda, 1929
Oschman, Shane, 8117
Oselinsky, Katrina, 5507
Osetek, Bill, 2982
Osgood, Diane, 8109
Osgood, Steven, 2205
Osiecki, Harry, 5449
Osika, Geoffrey, 832
Osmus, Patti, 8048
Osnes, JP, 6334
Osorio, Arturo, 4636
Osrow, BA, Jes, 452
Ossadnik, Alex, 194
Ossello, Lauren, 7078, 7079
Ossian, Amy, 3328
Ossian, Angela, 4637
Ossipoff, Valerie, 2031
Ossit, Sheila, 1394
Ossmann, Kathy, 1901
Ossowski, Tom, 3322
Ostapiuk, Marta, 4798
Ostberg, Ed, 1397, 5098
Osterburg, Jack, 1496
Ostermeir, Vidette, 3263
Ostertag, Tricia, 3700
Ostheimer, John, 1958
Ostler, Bill, 5696
Ostling, Jr, Dr. Acton, 1130
Ostroff, Marc, 6300

Ostrowski, Andrew, 1655
Osuba, Yulita, 6569
Ota, Diane, 1179
Ota, Henry Y, 6163
Ota, Henry Y., 40
Otake, Eiko, 420
Otake, Koma, 420
Otake, Miko, 475
Otero, Jennifer, 3114
Ott, Andrew, 5943
Ott, Carole, 1509
Ott, Jeremie, 4125, 5697
Ott, Kate, 3144
Ott, Mike, 1604
Ott, Sharon, 8606
Otten Leverone, Elece, 6078
Ottens, Amy, 4606
Ottmers, Carlton, 5627
Otto, Brigitte, 2191
Otto, Patricia J., 2303
Otto, Phillip, 3
Otto, Roberta J, 1207
Ounanian, Harding, 2119
Ouosterwaal, Barry, 1715
Outlaw Atchison, Karen, 714
Ouweleen, Fred, 6112
Ovens, Douglas, 5427
Overbeck, Mr. David, 7954
Overfelt, William, 6105
Overhoff, Thomas G, 889
Overland, Doug, 1262
Overman, Devin, 5612
Overstreet, Audrey, 1807
Overstreet, Rodney, 1786
Overton, Cindy Lee, 2820
Overton, David, 4855
Overton, Miriam, 1137
Overturff, Erika, 316
Ovitsky, Steven, 1411, 5034
Owecki, Karen, 4109
Owen, Bill, 7085
Owen, Donald, 3111
Owen, Jessica, 5901, 5902, 5903, 5904
Owen, Lauren, 172
Owen, Moris, 4946
Owen, Rebecca, 2893
Owen, Richard, 2218, 2303
Owen, William B, 7084
Owen Jr, Richard, 1398
Owens, Charles, 4390, 5196
Owens, Christopher, 4059, 5766
Owens, Donald, 7187
Owens, Judson H, 2448
Owens, Katherine, 3960
Owens, Mitchell, 1809
Owens, Richard, 5825
Owens, Sean, 118
Owens, Shaun, 6094, 6095
Owens, Susan, 8560
Oxtoby, David, 2459, 6087
Oxtoby, David W., 6086
Oyarzun Moltedo, Felipe, 142
Oyloe, Peter, 2931
Ozawa, Seiji, 1176, 1177, 1178
Ozbilgin, Handan, 7705
Ozello, Kenneth, 4155
Ozment, Dustin, 4004, 8463
Ozuzu, Onye, 2647

P

P'An, Jessica, 364
P. Heaton, Murray, 7676
P. Pheneger, Richard, 2712, 6394
P. Rose, Jonathan F., 1421
P. Saar, David, 2429
P. Scarbrough, William, 3203
Pabros, Marcella, 81
Pacana, Nicolas, 190
Paccione, Michael, 5133
Pace, David, 653
Pace, Jacqueline, 3467
Pace, Marco, 2191
Pace, Richard A, 2248
Pacey, Jane, 1030
Pachecano, Sophia, 383

Paci, Christopher, 2519
Pacifici, Robert, 833
Pacileo, Christian, 2708
Pacis Meservey, Sister, 5855
Packard, Charles, 6330, 6331
Packard, Danielle, 2901
Packer, Alexis, 1587
Packer, Jefferson, 857
Packer, Tina, 3159
Packer, Whitney, 5952
Packman, Joyce, 4468
Pacylowski Justo, Anita Sun, 606, 610
Padilla, Clarence, 1108
Padilla, Kathy, 6247
Padron, Eduardo, 4466
Padula, Roberta, 2323
Paez, Deborah, 1995
Pagano, Michael J, 6173
Pagano, Michael J., 4243
Page, G Troy, 3677
Page, Janice, 7639
Page, John, 5478
Page, Karen, 661
Page, Nancy, 586
Page, Thom, 3830
Pagella, Heather, 2748
Pagenkopf, Lauren, 4120
Pag n, Edwin, 3499
Paige, Alvin, 4804
Paige, Warner, 919
Paine, Allison, 3105
Paine, Cassandra, 7150, 7151
Paine, Rebekah, 3536
Paine, Stanley, 4816
Painter, David Lee, 2900
Painter, Scott, 5808
Painter, Stephen, 1372
Paiz, Veronica A., 4834
Pak, Jing-Ho, 1905
PAK, JUNG-HO, 1219
Pakendorf, Rudi, 5827
Pal, Tridib, 6856
Palade Syrotiak, Mariana, 4018
Palant, Bill, 8837
Palant, Roberta, 3387
Palao, Sally, 3602, 5176
Palefsky, Vicki, 2849
Palermo, James, 4378
Palermo, James W, 4554
Palin, Meredith, 3574
Palincsar, Danielle, 2128
Palker, Reba, 432
Palleja-Vissicchio, Evelyn, 580
Pallotta, Nick, 7837
Palm, Melody, 4590
Palmer, Angela, 8075
Palmer, Brian, 694, 6023
Palmer, Chad, 8001
Palmer, Charles L., 6506
Palmer, Coco, 3638
Palmer, David, 149, 6053
Palmer, John, 8604
Palmer, Juanita, 5527
Palmer, Michael, 5386
Palmer, Micheal, 5772
Palmer, Nicholas, 1134
Palmer, Nick, 1089
Palmer, Paul, 491, 5171
Palmer, Perry, 2009
Palmer, Rick, 673
Palmer, Stephen, 4857
Palmer, Steve, 4857
Palmer, Susan, 8017, 8353
Palmer, Theodore, 1594
Palmer Todd, Andrew, 5884
Palmieri, Christopher, 6433
Palmisano, Ralph, 7941
Palmo, Kathy, 673
Palmquist, Jason D., 203
Palms, John.M, 596
Palocz, Henry, 1467
Palreiro, Donna, 8202
Paltauf, Julie, 6430
Palumbo, Evan, 4190, 6034
Pamela,, 870
Panacciulli, Louis, 1472
Pancrazi, Dana, 2472
Pandian, R. Devadoss, 6803, 6804

Executive Name Index

Pandora, Betsy, 3728
Pangman, Marylee, 3622, 5205
PanGriff, Gabin, 2454
Pani, Eric, 7135
Panico, Michael, 6199
Panico, Stephanie, 6392, 6422
Panis, Alleluia, 81
Panitz, Harriet, 4755
Pankhurst, Neil, 3349
Pannullo, Joe, 3361
Panoff, Kathleen, 5754
Panoff, Kathy, 8326
Panofsky, Margaret, 1425
Pantages, Lisa, 6251
Pantaleo, Jackie, 4278, 4279
Pantano, Mary, 3188
Pantazelos, Janice, 4550
Pantell, Pam, 4244
Pantely, Harold J, 2703
Pantely, Harold J., 2703
Pantely, Susan P, 2703
Pantely, Susan P., 2703
Pantos, Pamela A., 2173
Panttaja, Dean, 6699, 6701, 6702
Panttaja, Dean, 6699, 6701, 6702
Pantzer, Holly M, 1083, 1084
Pantzer, Mairee, 2101
Pantzlaff Curry, Kelly, 2468, 6109
Panvini, Michael, 11
Panzella, Jennifer, 6537
Pao, Melody, 4777
Paoli, Juliana, 6271
Paones, Dr. Irwin, 4208
Papa, Phyllis, 326, 327
Papadimitriou, Dimitri B., 1407
Papale, David, 801
Papamichael, Haris, 2118
Paparella, Lynn, 5720
Paparelli, P J, 2905
Pape, Robert, 2105
Papel, Elizabeth, 2333
Papp, Tim, 3696
Pappas, Debbie, 7629
Pappas, Ida, 4790
Pappas, Katrina, 5946
Pappas, Ted, 3846
Pappin, Diana, 1095
Pappin, Diiana, 1095
Paprzycki, Joseph M., 3360
Paquette, Nancy, 4967
Paquin, Marc H., 1361, 5039
Para, Dave, 4894
Paradowski, Kristy, 7699
Parady, James R, 965
Paragary, Randy, 2552
Paranay, Alfred, 1342
Paras, Chris, 6599
Parbhoo, Sami, 4707
Parcel, Kathreen, 7393
Parch, Jerry, 4015
Pardo, Jr., James A., 5059
Pareja, Mariana, 2797
Parekh, Deven, 4428
Parent, Frances, 5177
Parfet, Donald, 4854
Parga, Alyssa, 6389
Pargac, Eric, 3587
Pargmann, Kathy, 4616
Parham, Misty, 6636
Parhizkar, Maryam, 1425
Parige, Lakshmi, 2601
Parillo, Joseph, 2325
Paris, David A., 4122
Paris, Jeff, 654
Paris, Leah, 4400, 4730, 4731, 4732, 4733
Parish, Jean, 1272
Parish, RJ, 3284
Parisi, Barbara, 3422
Parisi, Diane, 4009
Parisi, Mark, 137
Parisi, Michelle, 137
Park, Bob, 6174
Park, Carol, 5924, 5925
Park, Jeannie, 5154
Park, Jung-Ho, 7234, 7255
Parkard, Joni, 8593
Parke, Bert, 6036
Parke, David, 7108

Parke, Hank, 8182
Parker, Addison, 2645
Parker, Alyce, 1325
Parker, Amy, 7331
Parker, Annette, 6794
Parker, Bob, 7480
Parker, Carrie, 3221
Parker, Dale, 4029
Parker, Dave, 6078
Parker, David, 414, 1709
Parker, Dori, 2806
Parker, Gentry, 3274
Parker, Jason, 4848, 6625, 7858
Parker, Joshua, 3190
Parker, Kathy, 4848
Parker, Keith, 2748
Parker, Leska, 1740
Parker, Liz, 2434
Parker, Margaret, 2440
Parker, Marianne, 42
Parker, Mark Edward, 3763
Parker, Marsha, 4926
Parker, Matthew, 1688
Parker, Melissa J Chin, 2558
Parker, Michael A, 2650
Parker, Nancy S., 1953
Parker, Robert, 6396
Parker, Scott J, 3644
Parker, Tina, 3952
Parker Robinson, Cleo, 121
Parker, Esq., Eleanor, 1299
Parkerson, Lynn, 360
Parker, Carol, 4662
Parkhill, Sam, 1150
Parkhill, Tom, 3905
Parkhurst, Angie, 6240, 6241
Parkhurst, Bob, 1061
Parkhurst, Carol, 1315
Parkin, CPA, Hope J., 8180
Parkins, Barbara, 8134, 8135
Parkins, Derek, 6537
Parkins, Sam, 4677
Parkinson, Coleridge, 1040
Parkinson, John, 1962
Parkinson, Kaori, 4541
Parkinson, Pam, 222
Parkinson, Robin, 1376
Parkinson, W Michael, 7944
Parks, Demetrice, 6642, 6643
Parks, Jeffrey, 5429
Parks, Jo Vincent, 1895
Parks, Loretta J, 7612
Parks, Michael, 983
Parks, Monica, 1430
Parks, Steve, 7274
Parlee, Patty, 222
Parman, Ben, 4119
Parmelee, Bill, 3677
Parnell, Joe, 5940
Parolari, Kim, 6250
Parr, Howard, 7941
Parr, Nancy, 5951, 5955
Parr, Phil, 1659
Parra, Angelo, 3623
Parran, Teeko, 2498
Parrella, Ellen K, 4401
Parrini, Naho, 1409
Parrino, Stephanie, 7140
Parris, Liz, 8293
Parris-Bailey, Linda, 3903
Parrish, Connie, 1493
Parrish, Jason, 2779
Parrish, Jonathan, 1017
Parrish, Paul, 1705
Parrish, Robyne, 3656
Parrish, Tom, 3609
Parrish,, Kristin, 3229
Parrott, Bob, 3904
Parrott, Harvey, 6206
Parrott, Steve, 4657, 4658, 4659, 4660, 4661
Parry, Jude, 2800
Parry, Raphael, 3955, 5612
Parry, Scott, 2260
Parson, Annie B, 357
Parson, Ron OJ, 6734
Parsonnet, Dr. Victor, 1336, 1337, 5005
Parsons, Anne, 7283
Parsons, Bill, 8594

Parsons, Buddy, 4141
Parsons, Chris, 7959
Parsons, Dana, 2110
Parsons, David, 309
Parsons, Donna, 6113
Parsons, Estelle, 3285
Parsons, Joan, 4946
Parsons, Julia, 3852
Parsons, Kathy, 2194
Parsons, Pamela, 5015
Parsons, Priscilla, 8333
Parssinen, Stephanie, 6122
Partington, Rex, 4028
Partis, Jeanette, 1366
Partlan, William, 7355
Partridge, Allen, 2845
Parulski, Steve, 1667
Pasanowic, Margaret, 370
Pascale, Laurie, 6042
Paschich, Kelsey, 345
Paschka, Alexander, 7303
Paschke-Wood, Missy, 4707
Pascual, DMA, Jennifer, 5162
Pascucci, Molly, 6192
Pashigan, Kathy, 2421
Pasion, Rodney, 1894
Pasquinelli, Elizabeth, 766, 4211
Passariello, Laura, 7273
Passarro, Joan, 7664
Pastel, Judith, 3446, 7687
Pasternack, Barbara, 3582
Pasternack, Gary, 3118
Pasternak, Anne, 5126
Pasterneck, Michael, 3422
Pasteur, Lynda, 201
Pastor, Brian, 2919
Pastor, Katie, 8721
Pastori, Joe, 5946
Pastrana, Jose, 7563
Pastreich, Michael, 997, 4444
Pastrick, Nora Ann, 5470
Pastwik Minter, Lauren, 6640
Pat Foley, Patricia, 6847
Pat Thuma, Mary, 5772
Patch, Kristin, 1309, 1310
Patchen, Richard V., 2283
Patchin, Jill, 7264, 7569
Pate, Andy, 5646
Pate, Maldwyn, 443
Pate, Travis, 8485
Patel, Hiten, 3935
Patel, Jitendra, 6523
Patel, Tanveer, 4140
Paterno, April M, 928
Paterson, Jon, 1351
Paterson-Mills, Grusha, 875
Patmon, Jr. Charles W, 2465
Patmor, Roxanne, 6150
Patmore, Linda, 5994
Patrakis, Suzanne, 7543
Patramanis, Christina, 2069
Patrauski, Claudia, 2990
Patregnani, Christopher A., 2255
Patrelle, Francis, 280, 412
Patricia, Patricia, 4581
Patrick, Ben, 5067
Patrick, David, 2975, 6797, 6798, 6799
Patrick, David E, 6797, 6798, 6799
Patrick, Denita, 6451
Patrick, Dick, 6475
Patrick, James, 6689
Patrick, Jehra, 294
Patrick, Joan, 245
Patrick, John, 6116
Patrick, Julie, 1859
Patrick, Mark, 707, 964
Patrick, Michelle, 4277
Patrick, Pamela, 4796
Patrick, Pat, 3919
Patrick, Sharon, 386
Patrick, Suzanne, 862
Patrick Rice, John, 4959
Patrik, Janaki, 441
Patrone, Brian, 8886
Patt, Dave, 5944
Pattee, Gordon B, 466
Patten, Matt, 8083
Patten, Sybil, 2086

Pattern, Matt, 1598, 8083
Patterson, Bernie L., 8707
Patterson, Bob, 8467
Patterson, Cam, 8209
Patterson, Camille, 3677
Patterson, Carrick, 750
Patterson, Carrie, 213
Patterson, Chad, 3205
Patterson, Elizabeth, 7290
Patterson, Elizabeth C, 2122
Patterson, Greg, 4904, 6147
Patterson, Katheryn.C, 440
Patterson, Kevin, 1845
Patterson, Keyana K., 411
Patterson, Kraig, 5118
Patterson, Marilyn, 754
Patterson, Millie, 2563
Patterson, Miriam, 4186
Patterson, Paige, 8389
Patterson, Pat, 8030
Patterson, Patti, 647
Patterson, Richard, 2201, 4304
Patterson, Rory, 3901
Patterson, Steve, 8322
Patterson, Susan, 133
Patterson, Tafee, 2023
Patterson, Victoria G, 965
Patterson, Wayne, 2405
Patterson, Dr. Paige, 8390
Patterson-Shaw, Kay, 2105
Patti, Joe, 2892, 6682
Patton, Donna, 6792
Patton, Glenda, 4350
Patton, Jan, 1956
Patton, John, 5921, 5922
Patton, Lauren, 2988
Patton, Linda, 2923
Patton, Linda, 6734
Patton, Maureen M, 5628
Patton, Maureen M, 8391
Patton, Steven, 3791
Patton, TaRon, 2921
Patton, Tom, 7981
Pauken, Michael, 1067, 6835
Paul, Alan, 6477
Paul, Andrew S, 3844
Paul, Deepa, 2932
Paul, Diane, 1629
Paul, Diane B., 792, 4227
Paul, Dick, 1805
Paul, Elena, 406
Paul, Frank, 1626
Paul, George, 5413
Paul, James, 5402
Paul, Michelle S., 4590, 6805
Paul, Pamela, 4100
Paul, Sharon, 1592
Paul, Tom, 724
Paul, Vincent, 7289
Paul Morelli, Gian, 4073
Paul Nolte, Eric, 1451
Paul Wong, Jean, 308
Paul Wood, Jr., John, 1724
Paulek, Megan, 7355
Paulette, Carolyn, 4049, 4053
Pauletto, Randy, 6390
Pauley, Kim R, 693
Pauli, Linda, 3003
Paulin, Dorothy, 3606
Paulin, W M, 4259
Paulin, William, 4259
Paull, Dee, 1866
Paulsen, Melissa, 4521
Paulson, John, 1612
Paulson, Krisse L, 6819, 6822
Paulson, Merritt, 8097
Paulson, Shawn S., 8593
Paulus, Diane, 3145, 3146
Paulus, Dianne, 7231
Pauly, Susan, 5278
Pauly, Susan E, 5278
Pavao Jones, Hoku, 2893
Pavel, Robin, 2669
Pavell, Andrea, 3969
Pavey, Matt, 6087
Pavlacka, Ron, 218
Pawar, Ph.D., Sheela, 771
Pawlik, Matthew, 8201

Executive Name Index

Pawlyshynor, Peter, 557
Paxos, Georgia, 7952
Paxton, Laurence, 1022
Paxton, Sarah T., 5753
Payette, Lynn, 4189
Payling, Catherine, 4421
Paymer, Michele, 164
Payn, Dr. William A, 1501
Payne, Amaniyea, 208
Payne, Gary, 3927, 6134, 8321
Payne, Jenni, 6
Payne, Keely, 1249
Payne, Maggi, 6198
Payne, Patrick, 4381
Payne, Sylvia, 742
Payne, Thomas, 7026, 7027
Payne, Tony, 4603
Payne Symmons, Clare, 4138
Payne, Jr, Philip D., 243
Payton, Christopher, 1782
Paz, Coya, 2932
Paz, Lyn, 38
Peace, Kathy, 5434, 8117
Peace, Paula, 1004
Peach, Rebecca, 7329
Peacock, Linda, 1294
Peacock, Margaret, 2437
Peacock-Young, Rachel, 7462
Peak, Christopher, 6807, 6808, 6810, 6811
Pearce, Joe, 5112
Pearce, Joseph R., 5112
Pearce, Mark, 3563
Pearce, Pelham G, 1950
Pearce, Sarah, 4013, 4015
Pearce, Vera, 1250
Pearce, William, 1510
Pearce, Jr., Pelham G., 1953
Pearl Cane, Laurie, 220
Pearlman, Marilyn, 3369, 4997
Pearlman, Martin, 1173
Pearlman, Sondra, 3786
Pearlman, Stephen, 4383, 4791
Pearlson, Tom, 2449
Pearlson, Vicki, 2639
Pearlstein, Brian, 1171, 1172
Pearlstein, Corey, 3545
Pearsall, Erika, 4138
Pearson, Alexander, 840, 4288
Pearson, Alexandra, 6042
Pearson, Barbara, 6034
Pearson, Betsey, 766, 4211
Pearson, Carolyn, 1578
Pearson, Dr. Tom, 4889
Pearson, Eric, 1702
Pearson, L. Wayne, 3881
Pearson, Larry, 7432
Pearson, Molly, 3544
Pearson, Norris A, 7839
Pearson, Paula, 2569
Pearson, Ralph, 8167
Pearson, Ron, 5538
Pearson, Rose, 3971
Pearson, Sarah R., 7169
Pearson, Shannon, 7940
Pearson, Corey, 8585
Pease, James, 4174
Pease, Karry, 8580
Pease, Michael, 3269
Pease, CFRE, C. Michael-jon, 3269
Peavy, Mimi, 346, 2196
Peay, J Binford, 8530
Peay, Sue, 520
Peay, III, J H Binford, 8529
Pecceu, Gill, 2891
Pecina, Greg, 8445
Peck, Carolyn, 139
Peck, James, 8315
Peck, Mary, 1451
Peck, Michele, 7456
Peck, Norman, 112
Peck, Scott, 8351
Peck, Steve, 8786
Peck, Vaune, 7598
Peckar, Pam, 4031
Peckett, Donna, 700
Pecsok, Michael, 6682
Pectol, Elaine, 1692
Pedaci, Brian, 5318, 5351

Pedersen, Heather, 673
Pedersen, Lloyd, 2531
Pedersen, Marianne, 3369, 4997
Pedersen, N. Thomas, 2097
Pederson, Gail, 6333
Pederson, N Thomas, 1998
Pederson, Steve, 8172, 8176
Peditto, Chris, 3501
Peditto, Paul, 3501
Pedlow, John, 4062, 4063, 8572
Pedraza, Jennifer, 2776
Pedraza-Cumba, Miguel, 3500
Pedretti, Michael, 3857
Pedro, Gary, 5049, 5120
Pedroso, Dr. Angelina, 2928
Pedrotty, Kate, 247
Pedroza, Natasha, 6289, 6290
Peebles, Gregory, 1912
Peek, John, 2432
Peeler, Katie, 5233
Peeling, Dianne, 1668
Peeples, Wiliam, 3674
Peer, Charles, 2556
Peers, Max, 7883
Peet, Nancy, 5194
Pegg, Valerie, 4849
Pegi,, 874
Peimann, Chris, 3298
Peiperl, Julia, 5013
Peiser, Robert A., 1731
Peister, Valerie, 4276
Pelkey, Melissa L., 1432
Pell, Jonathan, 2342
Pellegrino, Vanessa, 6314
Pelletier, Trudy, 4976, 7581
Pellon, Karen, 5729
Pellow, Patti, 7340
Peloro, Filomena, 1323
Pelster, Jolette M, 3286
Peltier, Meg, 2812
Pelto, WIlliam L., 5223
Pelton, Darla, 7932
Peltz, Charles, 1390
Peluso, Ron, 3266
Pembrook, Randall, 4908
Pena, Debi, 2343, 8362
Pena, Leticia, 6269, 6270
Pena, Mario, 3513
Penberthy, Beverly, 3539
Pence, Ann-Carol, 2874
Pence, Lisa, 5669
Pender, James R., 7975, 7976, 7977
Pendergraft, CMP, Carla, 8470
Pendleton, Curtis, 863
Pendleton, H. Alexander, 7963, 7964, 7965, 7966
Pendleton, Melinda, 573
Pendleton, Moses, 7, 134, 460
Penfield, Jennifer, 710
Penhallegon, Marge, 7193
Penick, Pam, 5926, 5928
Penland, Dr. Penelope, 1360
Penland, Quelani, 887
Penland, Ed.D., Penelope, 2199
Penley, Larry, 6372
Penn, Thom, 3880
Penn Lewis, John, 3395
Pennant, Sandie, 8584
Penner, Gerald, 6759
Penner, Mike, 7985
Penner-Johnson, Karen, 1315
Pennewell, Karen, 3211
Pennewell, Norwood, 498
Penney, Henry, 5934
Pennington, Cyndee, 6577
Pennington, John, 44
Pennington, Joy, 3288
Pennington, Mark, 6587
Pennock, Rob, 7311
Penny, Anne, 3012
Penny, Mary, 1931
Penrod Kronk, Laura, 3850
Penrose, Kyle, 2339
Pensinger Witman, Kim, 2378
Pent, Margaret Ann, 2077
Penterman, Carol, 2333
Penuela, Juan-Carlos, 393
Penza, Marie, 1465

Penzkover, Angela, 4136
Peotter, Craig, 1831
Pepe, Neil, 3468
Pepis, Susanne, 3623
Peplowski, Ken, 8074
Pepmueller, Calla Ann, 5026
Pepper, Amy, 3760
Pequignot, Nadine, 514
Perantoni, Elena, 5325
Perantoni, Elena, 7986
Perazzo, Roz, 53
Percival, Jon, 8222
Percival, Stephen, 4069
Percy Rockefeller, Sharon, 4416, 4429
Perdicaris, Stephen, 880, 4338
Perdicaris, Stephens, 6310
Perdue, Greg, 4951
Pereira, Linda, 6271
Pereira, Toni, 8604
Perez, Adam, 797
Perez, Araceli, 8366, 8367
Perez, David, 393
Perez, Earle, 1096
Perez, Fernando, 3988
Perez, Javier, 3988
Perez, Jorge, 6737, 6748
Perez, Marco A., 7140
Perez, Peter M., 1234
Perez, Rudy, 44
Perez, Sixto, 7595
Perez Webster, Kris, 7128
Perfitt, John, 4237
Pergament, Lori, 587
Pergament, Steve, 587
Pergolizzi, Frank, 7121
Perhulste, Frederica, 4950
Perillo, James E, 6422
Perkin, Steve, 1860
Perkins, Amber Ann, 309
Perkins, Daniel, 2174
Perkins, David, 2911
Perkins, Hilary, 2447
Perkins, John, 7222
Perkins, Lew, 7042
Perkins, Stephanie, 653
Perkinson, Sterling, 2268
Perkovich, Lori, 6262
Perlich, Linda, 11
Perlis, Susan, 244
Perlman, Fran, 2187
Perlman, Lee, 3176, 4806
Perlman, Marc, 3864
Perlo, Carla, 143, 144
Perloff, Carey, 2573
Perlotto, Joel, 133
Perlow, Ken, 4558
Perman, Gerald, 1993
Pernell, Robert, 920
Pemerewski, Paul, 6423
Perney, Jill, 1243, 4853
Perotti, Janey, 1338
Perra, Dr. Lenette, 616
Perra, Lenette, 616
Perreault, Dana, 4082
Perreault, Joe, 7636
Perregaux, Beth, 7541
Perrella, J. Michael, 7539
Perrelli, Jozee, 6088
Perreovlt, Mark, 1203
Perri, Dr Geraldine, 6116
Perrin, Ralph, 828
Perrin Flynn, John, 2516
Perro, Amelia, 1318
Perro, Vincent C., 5154
Perrone, Sophia, 6202
Perry, Al, 208
Perry, Anthony, 7055
Perry, Charles, 707
Perry, Cheryl A, 7535
Perry, Dan, 2780
Perry, Debbie, 6815, 6816
Perry, Igal, 472
Perry, Jason, 7540
Perry, Jordan, 4912
Perry, Martha, 4609
Perry, Martina, 1373
Perry, Mary, 6204
Perry, Nathan, 3819

Perry, Paul, 4257
Perry, Randall, 5458
Perry, Sean, 343
Perry, Shaunielle, 3526
Perry, Shawn, 6576
Perry, Sheila, 7011
Perry, Tara, 6631
Perry, William L, 6725, 6726
Persico, Mary, 4482, 4486
Persinger, Dan, 1236
Persoff, Deb, 2645
Person, Garth, 2908
Persson, Helen K., 2017
Persson, James, 5050
Pertalion, Albert, 2912
Perterson, Jeff, 3266
Perttu, Dr.Daniel, 8146
Peruyera, Celso, 2797
Pesavento, Ellen, 889
Pescatello, Michael, 2526
Pesch, Fran, 7991
Peskanov, Mark, 1074, 1369, 4606
Peska, Nancy, 7569
Peska, Nancy, 7264
Peskin, Bob, 2143
Peskoe, Anne, 2578
Pesner, Steven M., 7738, 7739
Peter, Bob, 5910
Peter, Buffi, 5910
Peter, Carmela, 23
Peter, Steve, 6971
Peter, Zoltan, 23
Peterkin, Caitlin, 5794
Peterlin, Brian, 6755
Peters, Brisa, 3791
Peters, Darrilyn, 4019
Peters, Dr. John G., 6766
Peters, Gerald E, 4625
Peters, Jean, 1000
Peters, John G, 6762
Peters, Kevin, 1725
Peters, Laura, 3300
Peters, Mark, 4544
Peters, Randall L., 2391
Peters, Steve, 6967
Peters, Tracy, 2680
Peters, Ward, 3331
Petersen, Cheryl, 1886
Petersen, Daniel, 1806
Petersen, David A., 1766
Petersen, Derek, 1825
Petersen, Dick, 7932
Petersen, Jean, 5441
Petersen, Jim, 4327
Petersen, Lance, 5941
Petersen, Mark, 2088
Petersen, Richard L, 7932
Petersen, Scott, 8247
Peterson, Anna, 4848
Peterson, Bruce D, 1229
Peterson, Catherine, 1985
Peterson, Chelsa, 1054
Peterson, David, 1269
Peterson, Dean, 1300
Peterson, Derron, 4075
Peterson, Dianne, 1995
Peterson, Don, 2361
Peterson, Drew, 1853
Peterson, Eric, 4017
Peterson, G. P. Bud, 6619
Peterson, Gregg, 2556
Peterson, Helene, 2894
Peterson, James, 4885, 7378
Peterson, Janet, 4119
Peterson, Jeff, 3267
Peterson, Jennifer, 2247
Peterson, John, 5783, 7608
Peterson, Jon, 5572
Peterson, Kandice, 6382
Peterson, Kathryn, 6560
Peterson, Kim, 8032
Peterson, Kwin, 4009
Peterson, Leslie, 218, 2366, 2367
Peterson, M. Denis, 8266
Peterson, Mike, 4929
Peterson, Nina, 2997
Peterson, Paige, 5966, 5976
Peterson, Pam, 1683

1207

Executive Name Index

Peterson, Paul, 2081
Peterson, Pete, 1586
Peterson, Randy, 4119
Peterson, Ray, 2141
Peterson, Reynold, 8679
Peterson, Robert L, 830
Peterson, Ronald R., 5865
Peterson, Steven, 1877
Peterson, Steven C, 3095
Peterson, Susan, 1327, 4648
Peterson, Suzie, 887
Peterson, Tom, 2141, 6228
Peterson, Will, 4905
Peterson, Yolonde, 6800
Peterson Jenks, Vicki, 1828
Petersons, Erik, 1645
Petiet, Patricia, 2129
Petiet, Thomas, 2129
Petit, Kim, 4848
Petitmaire, Carol, 6386
Petitt, Gordon, 1518
Petkewicz, Jeannie, 4584
Petkun, Janet, 1218
Petlin, Alan, 4002
Petlock, Marty, 6517
Petno, Lisa, 938
Petosa, James, 4021
Petosa, Jim, 4021
Petraglia, Philip G., 1659
Petrecca, Michael, 5325
Petrecca, Michael, 7986
Petrick, Gwyn W., 4350
Petrik, Beth, 7326
Petrillose, Lindsay, 7668
Petrini Lynch, Paula, 211
Petroni, Louis A., 8157
Petroni, Renata Petroni, 5113
Petronio, Stephen, 485
Petrosky, Val, 4166
Petrov, Ventzislav, 7847
Petrovich, Dushan, 6786
Petrovick, Michael, 4974
Petrucci, C David, 3125
Petrucci, Colleen, 3845
Petrullo, Dennis, 7456
Petrutiu, Vasile, 162
Petry, Greg, 2062, 2063
Petry, CPRE, Greg, 6847
Petsche, Carolyn, 2071
Petsche, Jim, 3737
Petska, Dean, 3693, 7606
Pett, Michelle, 3249
Pettaway, Marc, 3080
Pettersen, Dan, 5803
Pettibone, Jennifer, 1547
Pettit, Atlee, 8236, 8237
Pettit, Jim, 869
Pettit, Sam, 1357
Pettit Sr., Dr Stephen D., 3876
Pettry, Michael, 2066
Petttan, Pat, 4093
Petty, Beverly, 3510
Petty Jones, Lesley, 1799
Pettyjohn, Susan, 5223
Petzold, Tony, 8579
Pevitts, Beverly Byer, 7435
Pevzner, Michael, 4782
Pew Wolters, Kate, 1234
Pezzella, Tony, 1783
Pfaelzer, Johanna, 3607
Pfaelzer, Lorna S., 6795
Pfaffmann, Lindsay, 1944
Pfanstiehl, Eliot, 7208
Pfeffer, Allie, 428
Pfeffer, Mike, 5943
Pfeifer, Karen, 1560
Pfeifer, Patricia, 1783
Pfeiffer, Connie, 1732
Pfeiffer, Heather, 3404
Pfeiffer, Joe, 3404
Pfeil, Peter, 4704
Pfeil, Roy, 1963
Pfingsten, Chris, 3118
Pfleger, Tabitha, 7193
Pfluger, Candyce, 1747, 2359
Pforzheimer, Zelie, 2721
Pham, Ly, 6128
Pheil, William, 3114

Phelan, Richard J, 1103
Phelps, Blake, 4145
Phelps, Chris, 7659
Phelps, Donna, 1944
Phelps, John, 967, 6831
Phelps, Kris, 639
Phelps, Richard, 2139
Phelps West, Jessica, 2876, 6653
Phenix, Linda, 635
Philand, Tom, 6365
Philbin, Gail, 3204
Philip,, 8100
Philip Davis, Micheal, 2244
Philipp, Megan, 104
Philipp, Michael, 912
Philippidis, Nicole, 478
Philips, Mark, 369
Philips, Mel, 6026
Philipson, Adam, 7587
Phillabaum, Robbie, 244
Phillip, John, 5144
Phillip, Kim, 4924
Phillipe, David, 6326
Phillips, Adam, 2708
Phillips, Arden, 2730
Phillips, Beau, 3877
Phillips, Brad, 6980, 6981, 6982, 6983
Phillips, Bradley, 4648
Phillips, Brooks, 7470
Phillips, Bruce, 4180
Phillips, Bryan I, 5306
Phillips, Candace, 1635
Phillips, Clayton, 3354
Phillips, Cynthia, 1661
Phillips, David, 2359
Phillips, Doug, 1244
Phillips, Dr. Morgan, 5272
Phillips, E Gail, 2272
Phillips, Erika, 2566
Phillips, Jack, 2992
Phillips, Jackie, 3984
Phillips, Jeff, 850
Phillips, Jessie, 3040
Phillips, Jim, 6784
Phillips, John, 759, 761, 4205
Phillips, Jon, 2166
Phillips, Katherine, 5057
Phillips, Kristin M, 928
Phillips, Leslie, 6189
Phillips, Lisa, 2235
Phillips, Marissa, 758
Phillips, Michael, 3342
Phillips, Paul, 1196, 1674
Phillips, Piper, 4507
Phillips, R Scott, 5682
Phillips, the Honorable M, 3855
Phillips, Tommy, 843
Phillips, Tony, 6209
Phillips, Tracie, 33
Phillips, Ty, 8526
Phillips, Wendy, 2389
Phillips, Wonda, 3044
Phillips Read, Hon. Susan, 1464
Phillips Thornburgh, Maurita, 1938
Phillips,, Scott, 3730
Phillips-Sandy, Joan, 7183
Philpot, Meg, 1731
Philps, Eric, 8100
Phinney, Raymond, 4734
Phipps, Greg, 5353
Phipps, Ph.D, Kim S., 1628
Phipps, Ph.D., Kim S., 1627
Phoenix, Sara, 3769
Piantanida, Greg, 4079, 8598
Piantini, Daisy, 1734
Piatigorsky, Gregor, 764
Piatt-Eckert, Kate, 211
Piatt-Eckert, Katie, 2951
Piazza, Joseph, 1913
Piazza, Kim, 3424
Picards, Robert P, 8202
Picciotto, Gil, 6281
Pichard, Janet, 172
Pichardo, Diana, 2178
Pichini, Guido M., 5506
Picinich-Byrd, Laurie, 154
Pickard, Billy, 8342
Pickard, Kathleen, 816

Pickard, Paul, 7314
Pickard, Porter, 3470
Picke, Leslie W, 4487
Pickel, James, 1583
Pickens, Jeff, 5548
Pickens, Linda, 1578
Pickerill, Karen, 3464
Picket, Elle, 8717
Pickett, John, 2065
Pickett Steele, Cynthia, 958
Pickles, Kyle, 386
Pickron-Davis, Marcine, 8118
Picone, Rick, 7513, 7515
Pictor, Bill, 5069
Piechocinski, Ted, 1097
Piecuch, Martin, 2249
Piehl, George F., 3347
Piekarski, Lauren, 1376
Piekarski, Lisa, 4132
Piela, Andrew, 323
Pielaet, Dina, 4263
Piele, Philip, 2298
Pieper, Andrew, 2148, 2149
Pieper Fink, Patricia, 1313
Pierce, Amy G., 3990
Pierce, Art, 3613, 7817
Pierce, Bob, 7392
Pierce, Brigid, 454
Pierce, Carl G, 8118
Pierce, David, 5080
Pierce, Earl, 5041
Pierce, Jerry, 7137, 7138
Pierce, June G., 5471
Pierce, Kelly, 179
Pierce, Ken, 8506
Pierce, Lauren, 1945, 6329
Pierce, Mallory, 8062, 8063
Pierce, Melanie, 5907
Pierce, Paul R, 2870
Pierce, Paul R., 2870
Pierce, Rick, 6062
Pierce, Steven C., 1222
Pierce, Wendy, 1860
Pierce-Winters, Candace, 2131
Piercefield, Anthony, 545
Pierle, Thomas, 3095
Piern, James G, 1167
Pieroni, Alexandria, 326, 327
Pierpont, Richard H, 972
Pierre, Danielle, 578
Pierre, Suzanne La, 8
Pierre Green, Jean, 8606
Pierro, Frances, 1475
Pierson, Gordon, 1064
Pierson, Greg, 1371
Pierson, Stephen, 1961
Piersontorre, Davin, 4839
Pietkiewicz, Steve, 783
Pietrowski, John, 3370
Pietrzak, Elizabeth, 2483
Pietz, Brad, 6051
Pifko, David, 3003
Pigman, Stephen, 6050
Pignanelli, Roxy, 4374
Piitz, Willie, 4942
Pike, Gail, 8208
Pike, Kate, 8031
Pike, Ken, 1366
Pikel, Johannes, 6607
Pikler, Charles, 1033
Pilak, Jeanette, 4329
Piland, Jack, 5220
Pilat, Ben, 42
Pilbrow, Richard, 6432
Pilch, Jerry, 8722
Pilcher, George, 1572
Pile, Stephanie, 54
Pileckis, Rob, 6834
Pileggi, Annamaria, 3298
Pilgrim, Neva, 5209
Pili Pang, Michael, 4530
Pillow, Gary, 5730
Pillow, Vicki, 6032, 6033
Piluk, Megan, 141
Pimble, Toni, 557
Pimental, Penny, 7243
Pimsler, Stuart, 298
Pina, Jorge, 3988

Pina, Julio, 6239
Pinales, Harold, 2002
Pinckney, Joanna, 882
Pincus, Barry, 8837
Pine, Ava, 1640
Pine, Joanna, 7636
Pine, Rachel B, 4803
Pineault,, Wally, 3343
Pines, Paul, 1397, 5098
Pinguelo, Leann, 321
Pinholster, Jacob, 2428
Pink, Michael, 703
Pink,, Sidney, 3118
Pinkham, Linda, 3350
Pinkhasov, PhD, Elizabeth, 1408
Pinner, Leigh, 1783
Pinsky, Renee, 5285
Pinson, Robert, 5242
Pinsoneault, Jee, 1220
Pintar Obenauf, Melissa, 535
Pinzke, Ilona, 4116
Pinzler, Johanna, 3491
Piotrowska, Ilona, 39
Piotrowski, Donna, 8691, 8695
Piper, Mitchell, 8864
Piper Ph.D., Jonathan, 4233
Pipert, Cherilynne, 662
Pipitone, Renee, 1513, 1514
Pipitone, Renne, 5286
Piplits, Martin, 2297
Pippin, Donald, 1915
Pipta, Rita M., 1875
Piquard, Scott, 4641
Pirazzini, Meredith, 5832, 5864
Pirolo, Mark, 3686
Pisano, Jane, 2736, 2737
Pisano, Jennifer, 5460
Pisarro-Grant, Judy, 26
Pisaturo, Joseph, 2325
Pischke, Fred, 7334
Pisciotta, Esq., Aileen A., 1782
Piscopo, Albert E, 2310
Pisha, David, 7853
Piskel, James, 3762
Pistole, Brittan, 4400, 4729, 4730, 4731, 4732, 4733
Pitcairn, Elizabeth, 885, 5099
Pitcairn, Laren, 2305
Pitcher, Cynthia, 4815
Pitchford, Bart, 4911
Pitchford, Jeff, 4185
Pitchford, Nicola, 71
Pitman, Ashley, 381, 385
Pitman, Carolyn, 3320
Pitman, Jared L., 198
Pitman, Leslie, 3313
Pitone, Dorothy, 982
Pitt, David, 2141
Pittman, Carolyn, 1683
Pittman, Guy, 677
Pittman, Jason, 7099, 7100, 7101, 7102
Pittman, Jenni, 5612
Pittman, Richard, 1183, 1186, 1193
Pittman, Toni, 1359, 5034
Pittman-DeLancey, Adah, 6473
Pittmant, Will, 7695
Pitts, Jonathan, 8236, 8237
Pitts, Kim, 5450
Pitt, David, 8587
Pivar, Phyllis, 4220
Piven, Byrne, 2967
Piven, Joyce, 2967
Pizzingrilli, Bev, 4131
Pizzo, Stephanie, 291
Pizzorno, Jim, 1698
Plackis-Cheng, Paksy, 871
Pladera, Lucretia, 4090, 4092
Plambeck, Vernon, 1302
Planchon, Laurent, 842, 4290
Plancich, Bernie, 690
Plangere, III, Jules L., 3357
Planich, Alma, 674
Planich Kesovija, Maria, 674
Plapp, Tom, 2354
Plasch, Harvey, 293
Plasencio, Lucinda, 5269
Plaskiewicz, Kathie, 4409
Plasson, Emmanuel, 2370

Executive Name Index

Plaster, Wendy, 319
Plastino, Toni, 4092
Plate, Stephen, 5562
Plate, Stephen W, 5562
Plath, Eric, 1261
Platt, Alexander, 1091, 1476, 1511, 5217
Platt, Craig, 7673
Platt, George I., 6506
Platt, Jack, 6311
Platt, Karen Kay, 6173
Platt, Myra, 4080
Platt, Reg, 3945
Platt, Ronald S., 2202
Platts, Lauren, 7869
Platz, Thomas H, 3097, 3552
Platznzie, Charles, 1980
Playstead, Keith, 1794
Plaza, Albert M, 6196
Pleasec, Steve, 7824
Pledger, Dianna, 5234
Pledger, Dianne, 7881
Plemmons, Ron, 8229
Plesent, Mark, 3595
Pless, Kellie, 6612, 6613, 6616
Pletcher, Richard, 3019
Plewe, Stan, 8490, 8491, 8492
Pfleger, Lila, 3902
Pline, Beth, 1786
Plondke, Dr J, 1016
Ploss, Skip, 2721
Plott, Glenn, 2278
Plowman, Julie A., 7457
Plozizka, Dennis, 2974
Plucknett, Janet, 2248
Plumbar, Elnora, 7126
Plumlee, Traci, 4675
Plumley, Mary Ann, 789
Plummer, Dan, 2396
Plummer, Jody, 1160
Plummer, Maxine, 5347
Plummer, Rick, 4860
Plunk, Patrick, 3990
Plunkett, John, 2175
Plunkett, Kathryn, 6065
Plunkett, Steve, 3963
Plunkett Letner, Jenny, 5
Plunkett Muenster, Karen, 2398
Pluntz, Pat, 5870
Plutz, Eric, 2187
Poce, Pat, 8485
Podagrosi, June, 2918
Podcasy, Melissa, 511
Podell, Tamar C, 5109
Podkulski, Stan, 1683
Poe, Matthew, 6169, 6181
Poe, Phillip, 7104
Poe, Vicki, 1624
Pofcher, Greta, 4409
Pofsky, Judi, 6202
Pogas, Kiley, 143, 144
Pogin, Kenneth, 293
Pogue, Frank G., 7119
Pohl, Donna, 7636
Pohl, Lesley, 1587
Pohle, Marianne, 1722
Pohlmann Duffy, Dr. Katherine, 4651
Poindexter, Alan, 3648
Poindexter, Wendell, 4763
Pointer, Martha, 1692
Pointi Jr, Carlo, 839
Poisson, Amy, 4081
Polakoff, Ph.D., Keith, 2485
Poland, John, 4445
Polaski, Danny, 2394
Polemis, Michael, 8509
Poler-Buzali, Gabriela, 439
Polese, James K, 3134
Poley, Scott, 8297
Polgar, Michelle, 3933
Polimeno, Maureen, 7538
Poling, Kermit, 751
Poling, Scott, 4613
Polinski, Teresa, 1982
Poliquit, Raymond, 4724
Polisky, Mike, 6784
Polite, Kyle J., 4337
Polizzi, Kristin, 161
Polk, Sherry, 3

Polk, Susie, 5839
Polkinhorn, Scott, 7886
Polko, Richard A, 5371
Poll, Melvyn, 2035
Pollack, Allan, 835, 4251
Pollack, Elizabeth, 1157
Pollack, Gloria, 893
Pollack, Howard, 8046
Pollak, Lucy, 2501
Pollak, Maxine, 446
Pollara, Barry, 4046
Pollard, Dr. Leslie, 4146
Pollard, Jack, 8728
Pollard, Jamie, 8677
Pollard, Jolie, 8728
Polleck, Frank, 1286
Pollei, Paul C, 5699
Pollert, Bruce, 1078
Pollet, Jane, 1062
Pollichino, Robert, 6192
Pollichino, Robert M, 7752
Pollini, Michelina, 3850
Pollino, Jim, 3802
Pollman, Howard, 8128
Pollock, Carol, 8447
Pollock, Jeffrey, 1571
Pollock, Jenny, 6607
Pollock, Kelly, 7447
Polo, Mike, 2722
Polochick, Edward, 1156, 1305, 4751
Polott, Arthur, 1171, 1172
Polsky, Maya, 1041
Polster, Keith, 7947
Polucha, Jeffrey, 8202
Polutanovich, Cynthia, 364
Polutnik, Sue, 4604
Polvado, Jennifer, 551
Polver, Jennifer, 8098
Polvinale, Ann G., 4417
Pomerance, Robin, 4207, 8780
Pomerantzeff, Suzanne, 171
Pomeroy, Ann, 263
Pomeroy, Jim, 4225
Pomfrey, Robert, 3627
Pominville, Roberta, 8670
Ponasik, Jill Anna, 2394
Ponce, Jose, 5027
Ponce, Ubaldo, 4220
Ponder, Ann, 4972
Ponder, Pier, 6044
Pone, Zinta, 301
Ponikvar, Dale L., 446
Ponomarenko, Larissa, 271
Pons-Gunther, Cherie, 1141
Pont, Tanya, 5935
Pontecorvo, Barbara, 324
Ponti, Raffaele, 1135, 1366
Ponticelli, Max, 3865
Ponto, Thomas, 5865
Poohachoff, Marianne, 4335
Poole, Clayton J., 4523
Poole, Ginger, 4055
Poole, James, 2258
Poole, John, 6807, 6808, 6810, 6811
Poole, Kristin, 6698
Poole, Mary Ellen, 854
Poole, Natalie, 826
Poole, Richard L., 7022
Poole, Robert, 5255
Poole Baker, Beverly, 4148
Pooler, Mark, 2292
Poor, Don, 6501
Pope, Carol, 5787
Pope, Jeffery, 3111
Pope, Kip, 1031
Pope, Kit, 5963
Pope, Kristen, 3428
Pope, Martha A, 8264
Pope, Patrick, 3887
Popolizio, Jill, 2598
Popov, Mikhail, 525
Popovich, Marko, 6132
Popovich, Mira, 5891, 5892
Popp, Tom, 1827
Poppers, Ari, 2576
Porat, Ami, 776, 793
Porco, Robert, 5304
Porten, Mike, 1690

Porter, Bradley, 143, 144
Porter, Brenda, 6635
Porter, Brenda Porter, 2847
Porter, Catherine, 3483, 3546
Porter, Charles E., 2004
Porter, David, 632, 1366
Porter, Dean, 6175
Porter, Gregg, 7139
Porter, Jackie, 4371
Porter, Janice, 1862
Porter, Julian, 4035
Porter, Lynne, 6401
Porter, Marian, 1012
Porter, Mark, 3933
Porter, Sam, 6344
Porter, Susan, 525, 1438, 5156
Porter, Tara, 6261
Porter, Tim, 6942
Porterfield, Donna, 4047
Porth Blackwell, Deborah, 5606
Portillo, Esther, 8376
Portner, Richard, 3355
Portnoy, Ian K., 4421
Portnoy, Esq., Ian K., 4422
Porto, Michael, 6477
Ports, Ruth, 7029
Posen, Brian, 6755
Posey, Elsa, 494
Posey, Paige, 3657
Poshard, Glenn, 6722, 6723
Posner, Debra, 7947
Posner, Lawrence, 1476, 5217
Posnikoff, Judy, 6193
Posnock, Jason, 1637, 5226
Possinger, Clive, 2260
Post, Arthur, 908
Post, Laura, 6332
Post, Mike, 4504
Postema, Beth, 2275
Poster, Robert L, 1433
Postoian, Diane, 3862
Poevar, Mildred, 2322
Potasnik, Amanda, 1633
Poteet, Brenda, 3900
Potenza, Ellen, 394
Poter, Ben, 4008
Potozkin, Amy, 2449
Potter, Becky, 6089
Potter, Brian, 1643, 5480
Potter, Clark, 1306
Potter, Dennis, 3400
Potter, DJ, 3356
Potter, Joe, 4899, 7421
Potter, John H, 8670
Potter, Joseph, 3298
Potter, Larry, 4855
Potter, Lauren, 1854
Potter, Linda, 141
Potter, Lynn, 2836
Potter, Rollin R., 6018, 6019, 6020
Potter, Stephanie, 4106, 5828
Potter, Tom, 5994
Potter Hayes, Jennifer, 5177
Pottinger, Kristine, 1437
Potts, Don, 2156
Potts, Jeff, 8697
Potts, Kimberly, 7385
Potts, Joe, 8585
Potucek, Kevin, 4991
Potvin, Portia, 5554
Pouli Sosnowski, Mary, 1474
Poulin, Jari, 1394
Poulson, Rebekah, 1813
Poulus, Al, 6187
Pounds, Paul, 7387
Pov, Dr. David, 3090
Pov, Jan, 3090
Powazek, Jack, 6180
Powell, Corey, 2356
Powell, David D., 8080
Powell, Dr Patricia, 1666
Powell, Gail, 616
Powell, Jack, 8249
Powell, Jan, 4051
Powell, Jill, 5259
Powell, Lori, 6543
Powell, Mark, 1606, 2299, 8497
Powell, Mary, 1892

Powell, Molly, 8694
Powell, Sandy, 1692
Powell, Todd, 7035, 7036, 7037, 7038
Powell, Zakiya, 4556
Powell III, Earl A., 4416, 4429
Powell, III, Daniel B., 1703
Powell, Sherry, 997
Powelson, Matt, 118
Power, Bill, 1932
Power, Debbie, 6025
Power, Katharine, 2689
Power, Mark R., 3841
Power, Ross, 2359
Powers, Charlotte, 2603
Powers, Daniel, 1097
Powers, Earl E, 963
Powers, Edward W., 5076
Powers, James, 2373
Powers, Marc, 2834
Powers, Margaret, 1078
Powers, Paul C, 1092
Powers, PJ, 2958
Pradere, Oswaldo, 3485
Prager, Annabelle F., 1420
Prairie, Sue, 4805, 7252
Prance, Cathy, 6597
Prange, Stephen E, 568
Prater, Jerry, 5629
Prather, Tharyle, 7564
Prather, Will, 2778
Pratt, Art, 6800
Pratt, Barbara, 8007
Pratt, Dick, 1797
Pratt, Gray, 3623
Pratt, Neal, 7175
Pratt, Noni, 1373
Pratt, Susan L., 6793
Pratt, Suzanne, 7191
Pratt Johnson, Jennifer, 3834
Pratt-Stokes, Cindy, 4903
Pratt, Nancy, 8079
Praxell, Trink, 6293, 6294, 6296
Preast, Kevin, 6625
Prechtel, Herta, 1848
Precourt, Anthony, 7981
Preddy, Kathy, 5632
Predmore, Roger, 6518
Pree, Cindi, 4063
Preheim, Doyle, 2197
Premeau, Chad P, 5854
Prenatt, Susan L, 1083, 1084
Prenetta, Bill, 4407
Prentice, Daniel, 3879
Prentice, Martin, 4998
Prentiss, Sherri, 1528, 1529
Prescia, Karen, 7511
Prescott, Carol, 1955
Prescott, Gary, 4705
Presher, Darren, 4303
President, A.Burkert, 8134, 8135
President, Hunt, 8588
Presley, Annika, 51
Pressentin Wright, Carol von, 932
Pressman, Elijah S., 113
Presti, Geralyn M., 5317
Preston, Joshua, 393
Preston, Marvin, 339
Preston, Micelle, 3564
Preston, Michelle, 3564
Preston, Mr. Steven C., 4603
Presutti, Corina, 68
Preu, Eckart, 1807
Prevette, Thom, 667
Pribbenow, Ph.D., Paul, 2147, 4873
Price, Allan, 2944
Price, Beth, 647
Price, Bill, 1134
Price, Brent, 900, 901
Price, Calvin S, 1964
Price, Chuck, 6840
Price, Deborah, 5373
Price, Faye, 3251
Price, Glenda D, 1229
Price, James, 3462
Price, Jill, 4258
Price, Joyce, 3303
Price, Judy, 6944
Price, Julian, 1002

1209

Executive Name Index

Price, Karen, 3378
Price, Kass, 8420
Price, Kent, 3074
Price, Laura, 954
Price, Lisbet, 4985
Price, Michael P, 6398
Price, Michel, 2683
Price, Nancy, 6656
Price, Sonya, 4193
Price, Tarrance, 7278
Price, Taylor, 5659
Price, Tim, 2974
Price, Vincent, 8154
Price Becker, Alison, 434
Price Lea, Patricia, 5280
Price Meyers, MacKenzie, 614
Price Moss, Kara, 614
Prickett, Karla, 4680
Pridal, Ph.D., Cathryn G., 4913
Priddy, S. Bryan, 2349
Pride, Bibi B., 710
Pride, David, 5718
Pride, Paul, 1520
Prieshoff, Matt, 6261
Priest, Heather, 6762
Priest, Robert, 3855
Priest, Tree, 6391
Prieto, Rafael, 1989
Prim, Margaret, 4692
Primack, Ellen M, 4327
Primoff, Mark, 7630
Prince, Bobby, 4485
Prince, Charles, 1339
Prince, Jamie, 606, 610
Prince, Judith, 3582
Prince, Linda, 1068
Prince, Liz, 397
Prince, Nathan, 4276, 6217
Prince, Robert, 2420
Prince, Ryan, 6343
Princiotti, Anthony, 1769
Pringle, Shannon, 6317
Pringle, Tamia, 8167
Prins, Jamie, 4173
Prior, Mary Ann, 3762
Prior, Richard, 1008
Priore, Leonarda, 2223
Pritchard, Arlen, 2171
Pritchard, Celeste, 1205
Pritchard, David M, 2673
Pritchard, Rod, 4642
Pritner, Calvin, 2452
Privette, Whit, 7539
Privon, Chris, 194
Prnoeis, Eileen, 7817
Probst, Tom, 5999
Procaccini, John, 7505
Prochaska, Bonnie, 1834
Prochazka, Dr. James, 787
Prochazka, Maria, 787
Procise, Jennifer, 4035
Proctor, Rev. Bill, 1747
Proctor, Travis, 975
Prodger, Jim, 6147
Productions, Micocci, 5118
Proett, Michael, 907
Proffitt, Michael, 4104, 5822
Proffitt, Mr. James N., 8279
Proia, Alexandre, 133
Pronesti, Laura, 341
Prosek, Denise, 3254
Pross, Kimberly, 4337
Prostein, Zac, 2454
Protopap, Kostis, 1861
Protopapas, Kostis, 2297
Protti, Michel, 4327
Proud, Linda, 4322
Prough, Dr. Gene, 4463
Prout, Elissa R., 1471
Provonca, Joe, 5216
Provost, Robert, 3379
Prows, Mark W., 7511
Prud'homme Davis, Carol, 3566
Prud'homme, Margaret, 630
Prue, Kyle, 3116
Pruett, Mark, 4977
Pruett, Millie, 1220
Pruitt, Alison, 2794

Pruitt, Hannah, 4696
Pruitt, Jonah, 160
Pruitt, Ken, 6516
Pruitt, Laura S., 1983, 1984
Pruitt, Dawn, 3229
Pruitt, III, Jonah, 160
Pruittg, Barbara K, 3359
Pruner, Linda, 4028
Prusa, Mike, 6894
Pruzek, Kate, 2201
Pryer, Lynn, 3656
Pryma, Paul, 6812
Prymas, Ashley, 5103
Przybyl, Susan, 7704
Publications Editor, Harris, 761
Puc, Iowna, 1039
Puc, Iwona, 206, 2044, 2045
Pucci, B.J., 2761
Pucciatti, Joseph, 2180
Puccio, Ben, 5204
Puchalski, Philip J., 3610
Puckett, Carine, 173, 175
Puckett, Ken, 8097
Pudil, Brian, 2949
Puente, Ricardo, 3553
Puerte, Ronald, 7843
Pugh, Gaylen, 4147
Pugh, Gloria, 1549, 1550
Pugh, Lee, 3662
Pugh, Megan, 6521
Pugh, Teresa, 1793
Pugh Gratton, Gaile, 2401
Puglieli, Adam, 50, 6089
Puglielli, Adam, 3979
Pugliese, AC, 2309
Pugliese, Matthew J., 2691
Pugliese, Ronald, 6423
Pugmire, Rance, 8479
Puleo, Michael, 940
Puliafito, Loual, 5162
Pulice, David, 2135
Pulice, John A, 5446
Pulito, Joe, 7587
Pulk, Mary Ann, 2147, 4873
Pullen, Emma, 43
Pullen, Robert, 954
Pullia, Nick, 4581
Pulliam, Kristi, 14, 2437
Pulliam, Leisa, 6038
Pullinsi, William, 6919
Pulvermacher, Neta, 464
Puma, Jr., Nicholas J., 3159
Punty, Brad, 3488
Punzi, Debra, 500
Pupanek, Nicole, 5839
Puphal, Shannon, 6109
Purcell, Judy, 1788
Purcell, Keith, 2974
Purcell, Nancy, 575
Purcell, Ryan, 2583
Purcell Welch, Maranne, 3843
Purdie, Doris, 1049
Purdin, Rebecca, 2601
Purington, Emily, 4079
Purinton, Juniper, 5037
Purpura, Dawn, 4119
Purser, Becky, 6530
Purves, Susie, 686
Purvis, Bob, 6045
Puryear, Mike, 8397, 8398, 8399
Puryear, Molly, 68
Pusateri, Frank, 2255
Pusateri, Joe, 1131
Putnam, Keri, 4013, 4015
Putnam, Leslie, 4042
Putnam, Robert, 3789
Putnam Paquette, Ellen, 3855
Putney, Carolyn, 8017
Putney, Charles, 4017
Putney, Jim, 1615, 5424
Putzke, Jon A, 4492
Puyau, Susan, 244
Puyau Stelzer, Renee, 244
Puzo, Madeline, 2519, 6154, 6171, 6176
Pybus, Alison, 8837
Pyke, Pat, 1023
Pyle, Fred, 4943
Pyles, Kristin, 1565

Pyles, Taylor, 6300
Pyne, Sara, 1608
Pyper, Carol, 3158
Pyron, Megan, 6261
Pyrzynski, Vicky, 2132
P*f*quette, Marc, 2582

Q

Qayoumi, Mo, 6120, 6121
Qayoumi, Mohammad, 4223
Qi, Jiang, 405
Quackenbush, Bets, 498, 5194
Quadar, Glen, 1778
Quaife, Evelyn, 2181
Quaintance, Tom, 3655
Quam, Erik, 1753
Quan, Jackie, 405
Quartuccio, Anthony, 788, 883
Quastler, Shirley, 4907
Quattrocchi, Laura, 332
Quattrucci, Donald R., 3864
Queen, Linda, 8644, 8645, 8646, 8647, 8649
Queen, Rachel, 7464
Queen, Todd, 6375
Queen, James, 4703
Queler, Eve, 2246
Quensenberry, Jim, 3893
Query, Devin, 7086, 7087
Quibell, Jeff, 1280
Quick, Angela, 319
Quick, Julie, 1126
Quick, Monique, 974
Quick, Wendy, 2436
Quick-Warner, Brittany, 3774
Quick-Wright, Adrienne, 7880
Quigley, Dawn, 534
Quigley, John, 4469
Quijano, Jose, 6310
Quill, Shauna, 1433
Quillen, Karen S, 2380
Quillen, Karen S, 5768, 5769
Quilleux, Irene, 971
Quillian, Benjamin F., 6317
Quillinan, Nancy, 5081
Quilling, Cindy, 4118
Quimby, Charlie, 3252
Quinley, John, 3047
Quinn, Angela, 842, 4290
Quinn, Chad, 4041
Quinn, Connie, 2272
Quinn, Cynthia, 7, 134, 460
Quinn, Daniel P, 4984
Quinn, Jeffrey, 3107
Quinn, Jennie, 7556
Quinn, John, 4034
Quinn, Kay, 4680
Quinn, Kelli, 141
Quinn, Marta, 836
Quinn, Martin, 4310
Quinn, Maureen, 810
Quinn, Meg, 3430
Quinn, Moira, 5230
Quinn, Patrick, 1731
Quinn, Peter, 4995
Quinn, Steve, 8180
Quinn, Thomas, 3854, 7326
Quinn, Thomas P., 3839, 8163, 8164, 8165, 8166
Quinn, Tom, 6129
Quinnett, Kelly, 2900
Quinnett, Kelly, 6699, 6701, 6702
Quinones, Barbara, 8825
Quintas, Thomas, 6920
Quinto, Joan, 826
Quintom, Dan, 2627
Quirin, Meredith, 1639, 2307, 5475
Quirk, Alison A., 271
Quirk, Alison.A, 277
Quishenberry, Lissie, 1885
Quistgaard, Jon, 7339

R

R. Adams, Anne M., 5735
R. Anfenson, Carl, 6718
R. Hageboeck, Charles, 2392
R. Hoefer, Bruce, 7141
R. Jones, Janet, 2380

R. Jones, Jr., Franklin D., 3990
R. Kimbell, Alan, 6903
R. Schuh, Steven, 7198
R.MacNalley, Elizabeth, 3251
R.Schuh, Steven, 1155
R.Snipes, Vivian, 3066
R. Goundie, Tedd, 7169
Raab-Snyder, Delia, 1649
Raabe, Kass, 1835
Raasch, Randy, 2263
Rabbiner, Stan, 5181
Raben, Norman, 2246, 2251
Rabens, Lynda E., 1324, 1345
Rabin, Deb, 4131
Rabin, Sol, 2513
Rabinovici, Pamela, 924
Rabinowitz, Anna, 2205
Rabinowitz, Elite, 364
Rabon, Stacy, 3875
Racanelli, Janine, 352
Rachele, Gary, 7614
Rachele Bayles, Allison, 4806
Rachelle, Tamar, 572
Rachev, Daniel, 1592
Rachleff, Larry, 1048
Rackey, David A., 4387
Raczka, Laurel, 8159
Radatz, Joel, 5251
Radcliffe, Mary J, 925
Rademacher, Lisa, 6289, 6290
Rademaker, Dana, 4572
Rader, Paul, 4701
Radice, Neal, 3424, 3427
Raditz, Edward, 1330
Radke, Kirk, 489
Radke, Scott, 524
Radke Brown, Sara, 724
Radler, Bruce D., 5102
Radley, Bruce, 7682
Radley, Katherine, 1201
Radley, Kathy, 1201
Radosh, Sondra, 3154
Radr, Steve, 2320
Radtke, Mark, 1823
Raduenz, Les, 8664, 8668
Rafael Bairos, Jacomo, 1700
Raff, Michael, 7396
Raffel, Lori, 3014, 3015
Raffel, Roland, 1050, 6789, 6790, 6791
Raffetto, Richard A., 1438, 5156
Raffield, Chris, 4501
Rafinski, Mark, 3801, 8121
Rafter, Kate, 1608
Rag, Maya, 6469
Ragan, Edward, 7156
Ragan, Joe, 1168
Ragan, Ronald K., 8089
Ragatz, Missy, 1309, 1310
Ragen, Ronald K, 8092, 8096, 8099
Raggio, Paula, 4387
Ragir, John, 2938
Raglin Cecola, Shannon, 213
Ragni, Angela, 800
Ragogini, Dr. Ernest, 4753
Ragogini, Ernest, 4753
Ragotzy, Brendan, 3192
Ragotzy, Jack P, 3192
Ragsdale, Amy, 314
Ragsdale, Kelly, 4073
Ragsdale, Linell, 6068
Ragsdale, Jr, Oliver, 4823
Rague, Suzanne, 1602, 1603
Rahm, Nivi, 845
Rahn, Frank, 800
Rai, Susan S, 1433
Raifsnider, Christopher J, 960, 961, 962, 963
Raiguel, Faith, 987
Railsback, Teresa, 7053
Raim, Ethel, 7720
Raimondi, Matthew, 4737
Raimondi, Natalie, 4737
Raimondi, Richard, 197
Raine, Scott, 8493
Rainer, Robert, 5549
Raines, Susan, 4675
Rainey, Gini, 5673
Rainey, Jeannette, 4044
Rainey, Selina, 670

Executive Name Index

Rainie, Dr. Robert C, 4962
Rainone, Nanette, 5054
Rains, Susan, 7041
Rainwater, Nellie, 360
Raisebrough, Doug, 7377
Raish, Don, 2197
Raizin, Lou, 2913, 6731
Rajagopalan, Hema, 210
Rajagopalan, Krithika, 210
Rajeckas, Paul, 3554, 3581
Rajotte, Jennifer, 491
Rakestraw, Jennifer, 2968
Rakoski, Joseph G., 1609
Raleigh, Elaine, 2072
Ralenkotter, Rossi, 7509
Raley, Jane, 1316
Ralls Forcher, Jacquelyn, 642
Ralon, Marketing, 507
Ralph, David, 2237, 2248
Ralph, James, 5406
Ralph, Jim, 5406
Ralph, Trevor, 6088
Ralston, Kelly, 8552
Ralston, Pamela, 4318
Ramach, Kevin, 2144
Ramadanoff, David, 762, 887
Ramage, Fred, 8573, 8574, 8575, 8576
Ramagli, Susan, 1834
Ramaker, David, 4856, 7317
Ramaker, Tammy, 4842
Ramanan, V R, 5265
Rambaud, Laurie, 6336
Rambo, John, 3662
Ramirez, Alex, 4171
Ramirez, Ericka, 1905
Ramirez, Jose, 5958, 5959
Ramirez, Luis, 910
Ramirez, Paul, 7503
Ramirez, Rogelio, 6160, 6161, 6162
Ramirez, Thom, 5590, 8323
Ramm, Martie, 6131
Ramos, Alan, 6250
Ramos, Dana, 1930
Ramos, Rosa, 1382, 5071
Rampage, John, 2884
Rampton, Hadley, 653
Ramsay, David, 2202
Ramsey, Betty Jo, 5272
Ramsey, Carolyn, 1451
Ramsey, Elmer, 884
Ramsey, Sandy M, 5221
Ramsey, Thomas R, 1083, 1084
Ramsey, Tom, 2154
Ramshaw, Karen, 506
Ranaghan, Jr, Richard, 7175
Ranck, Christopher, 984
Rand, Tyson Douglas, 5318
Randall, Brenda, 4152, 5923
Randall, Howard, 4404
Randall, Meridith, 828
Randall, Nathan A, 5014
Randall, Torri, 2578
Randall, Victoria, 2578
Randalls, Dave, 7350
Randazzo, Anthony, 271
Randazzo, Susan, 1199
Randazzo M.S., Leslie, 7171
Randels, Ben, 7276
Randles, Lucy J., 3747
Raneri, George J., 5211
Raney, Dr. Linda, 1360
Raney, Linda, 2199
Rangel, Gena, 5112
Rangel, John F., 5112
Rankin, Abram, 8442
Rankin, Alfred M, 7962
Rankin, Cree, 6734
Rankin, David, 2442
Rankin, Douglas B, 6802
Rankin, Douglas C., 6134
Rankin, Larry, 7028
Rankin, Renee, 3803, 8124
Rankin, Sandy, 2539
Rankin, Tiffany, 7994
Ranney, Don, 2892, 6682
Ranney, Emily, 4116
Ranney, Tim, 3483
Ranscht, Michael, 5846, 8673

Ransdell, Gary A., 7078, 7079
Ransley, Shari, 2292
Ransom, Sherry, 1757
Ransom, William, 5252
Ransone, Donna, 670
Ranton, Judi, 3785
Rao, Michael, 7319, 7320, 7321
Rao, Susan, 677
Rapach, Mark, 4759
Rapchak, Lawrence, 1058
Raphael, Brett, 131, 132
Raphael, Dr Jay, 2441
Raphael, John P., 7982
Raphael Ph.D, Jay, 6035
Raphel, Andr,, 1819
Raphel, David, 7150, 7151
Rapier, Jerry, 4010, 4011
Rapier, Nicky, 3054
Raposa, Dan, 7530
Rapp, Ed, 6191
Rappaport, Dr. Irwin, 1423
Rappaport, Toby, 5129
Raptis, Step, 12
Raschiatore, Jeffrey, 34
RaschMcDonald, Margaret, 3299
Raskey, Michelle, 62
Rasmussen, Anne, 4412
Rasmussen, Doug, 1240
Rasmussen, Lisa, 4128
Rasmussen, Patrick, 7337
Rasmussen, Randy, 4010, 8499
Rasmussen, Teri, 4161
Rasmussen, Victor, 6201
Rassussman, Ann, 3883
Ratchford, Sandra, 188
Rateaver, Jane, 1868
Rater, Tim, 6719
Rath, Lutz, 5168
Rath, Patrick, 1831
Rathbun, Jamin, 8200
Rathbun, Tanya, 8200
Rathburn, Debbie, 1144
Rathers, Clarice, 319
Rathgeber, John, 4998
Rathje, Karen, 3783
Rathje, Vic, 6996
Rathrop, Philippe, 1840
Ratner, Hank, 6192, 6753
Ratner, Hank J, 7752
Ratner, James, 3716
Ratner, James A, 5316
Rattay, Bohuslav, 1247, 1248, 1721
Ratterree, Charles, 5541
Rattigan, Elizabeth, 2173
Rattliff, Howard, 630
Ratz, Julie, 223
Rau, Jude, 8168
Rau, Sarah J., 4824
Rauch, Bill, 3771, 4047, 8062, 8063
Rauch, Kim, 1633
Rauch, Michael, 3567
Rauf, Wendeth, 14
Raughton, Jim, 4364, 6340
Raum, Shannon, 1164
Rausch, Carol, 2252
Rauschenberg, Robert, 489
Rauschkolb, Tiffany, 7121
Rauss, Alan, 3711
Rautmann, Eric J., 4112
Ravelo, Giovanni, 333
Raven, Peter H, 7453
Raver, Jim, 8300, 8455
Raviolo, Dino, 8075
Ravndal III, Eric, 4496
Rawitch, Josh, 6156
Rawlings, Keith, 7059
Rawlins, Keith, 5355
Rawls, Matthew, 6536
Rawls, Wendy, 1493
Rawson, Anne, 1491, 5242
Rawson, Brendan, 860
Rawson, Jr., Robert H., 519
Ray, Barry D., 5528
Ray, Catherine, 1451
Ray, Chris, 597
Ray, Dr Edward, 8068
Ray, Jack, 5584
Ray, James B., 2569

Ray, Jenna, 4877
Ray, Judith, 7530
Ray, Marilyn, 2412
Ray, Michael, 2804
Ray, Rachel, 3066
Ray, S. Alan, 4574
Ray, Sandy, 2014
Ray, Vicki, 772
Ray, W Irwin, 4506
Ray Jr, Dr W Irwin, 6624
Ray, Jr., Marcus, 5027
Raybuck, Lynnie, 3127
Rayburn, Larry, 163
Rayfield, Rudd, 3238
Raymer, Tim, 1236
Raymond, Abby, 905
Raymond, John, 5103
Raymond, John J., 2017
Raymond, Kelli, 5205
Raymond, Melanie, 2362
Raymond, Noel, 3251
Raymond, No‰l, 3251
Raymond, Shay, 626
Raymond, V., 2163
Raymond, Wayne, 996
Raymonde, Michelle, 4111
Raytkwich, Doris, 2098
Raywrtch, Cynthia, 4258
Re, Yugo, 1323
Rea, Eric, 1123, 2076
Rea Fisher, Tiffany, 421
Read, Chris, 2579
Read, David, 4250
Read, James A., 1432
Read, Jesse, 766
Read, Marvin, 2625
Read, Russell, 8349
Read Medrano, Rebecca, 2739
Readding, Joan, 2003
Reade, Cyril, 7547
Reade, Ned, 5183
Reader, Rachel, 2447
Reader, Whitney, 5772
Readey, John, 4904
Reading, Teresa, 1753
Reagan, Dennis, 7454
Reagan, Dennis M, 3300
Reagins, Tony, 6055
Reagle, Patti, 7077, 7078, 7079
Reahm, Jean, 3700
Real, Hal, 3814
Realduto, Thrish, 4781
Reale, Mary, 4258
Realista, Kate, 4252
Realmuto, Richard, 8855
Ream, Jim, 6899
Reardon, Dan, 2849
Reardon, James, 276
Reaves, Cindy, 711
Reaves, Graham, 1795
Reaves, Hal, 1480
Reaves, Sharon, 5316
Reay, Andrea, 8605
Rebarchak, Joe, 3806
Rebbeck, Kristy, 3933
Rebecca, Crigler, 7748
Rebman, Kenneth J, 4523
Rebman, Susan, 7609
Recalde, Diego, 7773
Recher, Florence, 2788
Rechler, Mitchell, 1398
Rechnitz, Robert M., 3384
Rechtfertig, John, 84
Reckelhoff, Donnajean, 5015
Rector, Anne, 1773
Rector, Melissa, 576
Reda, Neil, 6282, 6285, 6287
Redd, Marisa, 103
Redden, Nigel, 596, 3869, 5534
Redder, Esq.,, Bonnie A., 3430
Reddin, Peter N., 5868
Redding, Gwen, 1137
Redding, Lydia, 4993
Redfern, Jane Forrest, 7943
Redfern, Jenny, 788
Redfield, Cynthia, 4281
Redford, Robert, 4013, 4015
Redl, Lillian, 1451

Redlinger, Wendy, 5134
Redman, Paul B, 5459
Redman, Paul B., 8137
Redmon, Mary, 4907
Redmond, Dr. Warren, 3883
Redmond, Elizabeth, 4800
Redmond, Scott, 4306
Redwine, Rob, 4374
Reece, Wade, 3126
Reed, Adam, 3955, 5612
Reed, Ann, 4910
Reed, Brian Allan, 6323, 6324
Reed, Camille, 1911
Reed, Charles B, 6317
Reed, Charles B., 6317
Reed, Debbie, 1139
Reed, Dixie, 6371
Reed, Donna, 5999
Reed, Jacob, 526
Reed, Jared, 3815
Reed, Jenica, 2324
Reed, Jess, 2709
Reed, Jim, 1352
Reed, Jonathan, 2699
Reed, Justin, 7677
Reed, Kathie, 1604
Reed, Kathy, 1549, 1550
Reed, Kathy H., 616
Reed, Kevin, 6180
Reed, Larry, 2591
Reed, Mark C., 6401
Reed, Michael, 4177
Reed, Penelope, 3815
Reed, Robert A., 1708
Reed, Scott, 869
Reed, Shannon, 6687
Reed, Stacy, 2473
Reed, Steve, 7315
Reed, Tim, 4127, 5081
Reed, Timothy, 5757
Reed, Virginia, 445
Reed Weaver, Suzan, 4430
Reed, Esq., Cynthia E., 2304
Rooder, Beverly, 8006
Reeder, Scott, 2806
Reeder, Susan, 2461
Reeder, Susan C., 6091
Reeder, Vicki, 2489
Reeder, William, 5734
Reenstierna, Karin, 47
Rees, Johanna, 792, 805
Rees, Mandy, 2446
Rees, Mark, 7176, 7177, 7178
Rees, Tanya, 5258
Reese, Anita, 2969
Reese, Bonnie, 3932
Reese, Carole, 8113
Reese, Norma, 6118
Reese, T Terrance, 8126
Reese, Ted, 1627, 1628
Reese, Tim, 8272
Reese, Timothy L, 8274
Reese Waag, William, 718
Reeve, Carolyn, 1874
Reeves, Darcy, 5380
Reeves, Jessica, 7534
Reeves, Jessica, 7534
Reeves, Joanne, 5104
Reeves, John, 7800
Reeves, Katy, 2017
Reeves, Nancy, 3051
Reeves, Nora, 6763
Reeves, Rebecca, 648
Reeves, Sharlene, 7682
Reeves, Susan, 169
Regal, David, 3213
Regan, Dave, 764
Regan, George, 1320
Regan, Gerry, 6497
Regan, Kari, 799
Regan, Tara, 373
Regine DDS, Anthony, 2325
Regish, Anita, 2115
Regler, Ron, 6273
Regner, Elizabeth, 5650
Rehard, Phil, 7654
Rehard, Philip, 5057
Rehearsal Director/C, Contreras, 12

1211

Executive Name Index

Rehkemper, Jarod, 1723
Rehl, George, 5068
Rehm, Pat, 524
Rehrmann, Alexis, 3487
Rehse, Dick, 1858
Reich, Bob, 63
Reich, Margo, 684
Reich, Nicholas, 421
Reich, Robert, 4218
Reicher, Thomas Z., 758
Reichlin, Louise, 45
Reichman, Eric, 6144
Reichman, Ted, 364
Reid, Alice, 376
Reid, Ashley, 179
Reid, Cindy, 376
Reid, Denise, 4793
Reid, Donna, 8552
Reid, Jean, 5032
Reid, Jim, 8556
Reid, Larry, 4167
Reid, Martha, 1619
Reid, Nick, 6240, 6241
Reid, Rufus, 5024
Reid, Rusfus, 1411
Reid, Stephen, 5106
Reid, Victor L, 954
Reid, W Nick, 2569
Reid-Kane, Sharon, 6488
Reidy, Bart, 1177, 1178, 3184, 7227
Reifel, Charles, 959, 1994
Reiff, Katherine, 59
Reiffer, Melissa, 7299
Reifler, Katherine, 2112
Reigel, Ernie, 5230
Reilly, Audrey, 3542
Reilly, Colleen, 3813
Reilly, Courtney, 5274
Reilly, Elizabeth, 2474
Reilly, Kimberly, 2256
Reilly, Lisa, 5103, 7825, 7826
Reilly, Michael J, 1989
Reilly, Nicola, 4211
Reilly, Robert, 982
Reilly, Shannon, 7061
Reilly, Teresa, 2993
Reim, Dick, 1793
Reiman, Sue Ellen, 3764
Reimer, Treva, 7016, 7017
Reimonenq, Ph.D, Alden, 6118
Rein, Carol, 769
Rein, Catherine, 3361
Reinach, Richard, 8285
Reineccius, Richard, 2581
Reiner, Greg, 3479
Reiner, Gregg, 2462
Reinert, Matt, 3609
Reines, M Seth, 2988
Reinfeldt, Mike, 8290
Reinhard, Johnny, 5110
Reinhardt, Brandy, 315
Reinhart, Charles L, 5233
Reinhart, Floyd, 1877
Reinhart, Julia C., 1423
Reinhart, Lynda, 6522
Reinharz, Jehuda, 3178
Reinhold, Don, 1124
Reinschmidt, Mathew, 307
Reinschmidt, Matthew, 307
Reinsdorf, Jerry, 6759
Reinwald, David, 3872
Reise, Amy, 4118
Reiser, David, 7943
Reiser-Memmer, Michelle, 5060
Reiss, Anne, 5013
Reiss, Elizabeth, 5495
Reiss, Scott, 1776
Reissig, Shirley, 7052
Reitenbach, Janine, 4225
Reiter, Ashley, 3360
Reiter, Brad, 3360
Reiter, Linda, 2949
Reitter, Tom, 798
Reitz, Casey, 3565
Rejali, Pama, 651
Rejman-Staufenbeil, Stephanie, 4109
Rejto, Peter, 748, 4181
Reklis, Heidi, 3645

Remenschneider, Michele, 6876
Remington, Greg, 7610
Remington, Steven, 4536
Remis, James S, 928
Remis, James S., 4390
Remmel, Lee, 8667
Ren, David, 1657
Ren Zhao, Jimmy, 452
Rena Hammond, Lou, 3869
Renbarger, Grace F., 3929, 3933, 8325
Rendek, Carl, 983
Rendek, Sandy, 984
Rendina, Rhonda, 323
Reneau, Dan, 4720
Renedette, Todd, 7695
Renee Wilson, Amy, 616
Renehan, M Smokey, 5984
Renfrow, Tracie, 7862
Renick, Kyle, 3596
Reniff, William M, 5292
Renken, Heather, 4113
Rennell, Dean, 11
Renner, Bradley, 179
Renner, Daniel, 2657, 2664
Renner, Steven, 3069, 4696
Rennerfeldt, Noel, 6828, 6830
Rennie, Bruce, 4049
Rennie, Eleanor, 668
Rennie, Michael, 6212
Reno, Jim, 7469
Reno, Kim, 1167
Reno, Rick, 7883
Reno, Stella, 8138
Renoe, Greg, 2484
Renshaw, Jordan, 4064
Renton, Jim, 8067, 8069
Renz, Frederick, 1416, 5128
Renz, Fredrick, 2226
Repasi, Joanne, 7215
Repper, Mike, 4757
Resch, Carol, 1335
Rescigno, Joseph, 2398
Resnick, Jeff, 3469
Resnicow, David, 368
Ressel, Teresa, 6399
Retchless, Kevin, 6496
Retenbach, Paul R., 3196
Retrum, JoJean, 705
Retterath Jones, Tessa, 4883, 4884
Rettew, Jr., Robert H., 4961
Rettman, Zeke, 2474
Reuing, Johnathan, 3488
Reuler, Jack, 3247
Reuter, Ingrid K., 3886
Reuter, Ingrid K. J., 3888
Reuter, Jason, 3886, 3888
Reuter, Laurel, 5282
Reuter, Paul, 7457
Reuter, Yong, 830
Reuther, Barbara, 5001
Reveles, Nicolas M, 1909
Revels, Jeff, 2810
Reverand, Cedric, 5880
Revzen, Joel, 1385, 1852, 1857
Rexford, Heidi, 1617
Reyen, Dawn, 1960
Reyer, Jim, 5048
Reyes, Benjamin, 105
Reyes, Jose, 4240
Reyes, Julie, 4647
Reyes, Kathy, 1710
Reyes, Kristine, 2583
Reyes, Randy, 3248
Reykers, Bob, 6028
Reynders, John C., 7019
Reynes, Roberta, 5204
Reynold, R. Louis, 8050
Reynolds, Ann, 6536
Reynolds, Brett, 3598
Reynolds, Brigette, 4145
Reynolds, Claire, 5726
Reynolds, David, 1685
Reynolds, David T, 1134
Reynolds, Donna, 6406
Reynolds, Elaine, 1740
Reynolds, Francine Thomas, 3276
Reynolds, H. Robert, 1253
Reynolds, Howard Lang, 8635, 8636, 8639

Reynolds, Jeff, 8220
Reynolds, Jeremy, 5786
Reynolds, Julie Moe, 6227
Reynolds, Kevin, 4841
Reynolds, Laura, 4293
Reynolds, Linda, 3648
Reynolds, Lynda, 1383
Reynolds, Mark, 2298
Reynolds, Michael, 5735
Reynolds, Nancy, 406
Reynolds, Pamela, 1716
Reynolds, Phil, 202, 6736
Reynolds, Phillip A., 2207
Reynolds, Sheila, 4120
Reynolds, Stephen, 1348
Rezak, Bob, 775
Rezeven, Joel, 1852
Reznik, Todd, 43
Reznikov, Hanon, 3515
Rhakar, Markand, 1153
Rham Cunningham, Nick, 2436
Rhamstine, John, 8536, 8537, 8540, 8541, 8543, 8544, 8601, 8603
Rhea, Matthew, 1086
Rhee, Byung-Hyun, 1696
Rhi Buckley, Leticia, 6127
Rhiger, Genevieve, 6283
Rhine, Anthony, 6284
Rhinehart, Lori, 4172
Rhoad, Paris, 2425
Rhoades, Gordon, 912
Rhoads, Bill, 1436, 1441
Rhoads, Robert, 1144
Rhoads, Thomas, 6158
Rhoden, Dwight, 507
Rhoderick, David, 1212
Rhodes, Curtis, 4240
Rhodes, Dan, 3027
Rhodes, David W, 4673
Rhodes, Kevin, 1191, 1210, 1211, 1256, 8075
Rhodes, Lawrence, 440
Rhodes, Lisa, 5981
Rhodes, Marian, 7444
Rhodes, Michael, 1245
Rhodes, Sean, 6685
Rhodius, Sheri, 2631
Rhodovi, Marilyn, 1152
Rholdon, Richard, 245
Rhoton, Nick, 2847
Rhymer, Valerie, 3648
Rhyner, Lara, 3609
Riall, Ron, 243
Ribant, Alan, 3195
Ribbens, Jirina, 431
Ribble, Kristin, 2759
Ribeau, Sidney, 5296
Ribeau, Sidney A., 2741
Ribeiro, Liliane, 40, 6163
Ricca, Janel, 7122
Ricca, Peter, 1845
Riccardi, Don, 4334
Ricci, Chrisena, 3064
Ricci, Steve, 4666
Ricciardi, Gene, 6435
Ricciardi, Karen J., 6428
Rice, Alexandra, 1415
Rice, Carl, 6761
Rice, Clint, 4016
Rice, David, 4591
Rice, Ed, 1616
Rice, Ellis, 1312
Rice, Eric, 4399
Rice, Gordon, 3612
Rice, Janice, 3017
Rice, Jim, 6038
Rice, Karen, 4104, 5822
Rice, Kathryn, 2066
Rice, Kent, 6353, 6360, 6367, 6368, 6369, 6370
Rice, Lora, 2436, 2437, 6029
Rice, Pat, 68
Rice, Paul G, 8562
Rice, Paul G., 8562
Rice, Philip O, 1014
Rice, Rob, 1278
Rice, Rory, 6728
Rice, Shannon, 7265, 7267, 7269, 7271
Rice, Thomas H, 6180
Rice, Todd, 15

Rich, Andrea, 4241
Rich, Darren, 1296
Rich, Geoffrey, 3529
Rich, Karen, 5775
Rich, Kevin, 2979, 4589
Rich, Millie, 1201
Rich, Mimi, 2691
Rich, Nancy, 3673
Rich, Sammy, 6657
Richard,, 8240
Richard, Ellen, 2573, 3533, 3565
Richard, Erin, 4636
Richard, Joseph, 3138
Richard, Julie A., 4740, 4741
Richard, Sarah, 2885
Richard, Stephen, 2732
Richard, Verna, 714
Richard E., Richard E., 5168
Richards, Amy, 2316
Richards, Barbara, 935
Richards, Catherine, 6855, 6857, 6858, 6859
Richards, David, 2043
Richards, Dr. John K, 1604
Richards, Gwyn, 6856
Richards, Jeff, 4071
Richards, Jessica, 4204
Richards, Kim, 8732
Richards, Patricia A, 1766
Richards, Sarah M, 6672
Richards, Scott, 8167
Richards, Shawn, 736, 737
Richards, Stephen, 2743
Richards, Vicki, 4071
Richardson, Ambrose, 1423
Richardson, David, 2100
Richardson, Ernest, 1309, 1310
Richardson, Jenny, 7141
Richardson, John, 6346
Richardson, Jon, 1570
Richardson, Kyle, 4362
Richardson, Mark, 7868
Richardson, Mary Ann, 3804
Richardson, Michael, 2436, 5797
Richardson, Paul, 6221, 6222, 6223, 6226
Richardson, Priscilla J., 1623
Richardson, Steve, 3255
Richardson, Susan, 6957
Richardson, Tracey, 3035
Richardson, William, 6559
Richardson-Melech, Joyce, 2178
Richardson-Newton, Tracey, 4739, 4744
Richerson, Jim, 4374
RICHERSON, JIM, 6389
Riches, John, 8104
Richey, Eva, 1811
Richey, James H, 6544
Richey, Jeremy, 6028
Richgruber, Ben, 5832
Richman, James, 1712
Richman, Valerie, 1877
Richmond, Barry Alan, 3579
Richmond, Gail, 1785
Richmond, Grady Lee, 2491
Richmond, Rollin, 6057
Richmond, Rollin C., 6058, 6059, 6060, 6061
Richmond, Rosemary, 5111
Richmond, Sandy, 7199
Richmond, PhD, John W., 7494
Richner, Judy, 523
Richter, Al, 2780
Richter, Charles, 5427
Richter, Elena, 2014
Richter, Jaralee, 5845
Richter, Julia, 4270
Richter, Martha, 2780
Richter, Robert A, 4398
Richter, Tom, 8242
Rick, Matthew, 7327
Rickbone, Catherine, 8087
Rickcreek, Kelly, 4250
Ricke, Alan, 6524
Ricket, Logan, 3190
Rickets, Stephanie, 220
Rickett, Ann, 4081
Rickey, David, 4302
Rickman, Victor S., 651
Ricks, Shaun, 2366
Riddle, Eileen, 116

Executive Name Index

Riddle, Mary Ann, 3319
Riddle, Sheri, 7099, 7100, 7101, 7102
Ridenour, Donna, 5343
Ridenour, Greg, 6260
Ridenour, Stacy, 972
Rideout, Ernie, 4336
Rider, Cynthia, 3289, 3771, 8062, 8063
Rider, Jaron, 8418
Ridgeway, Carly, 3868
Ridgley, Jay, 1746
Ridley, Anthony, 3998
Ridley, Cynthia.K, 572
Ridley, Gordon, 1827
Ridley, Megan Ridley, 5587
Riebau, Kathy, 1956
Riebe, Alan, 1080
Rieben, Greg, 588
Riedel, David T., 2323
Riedel, John, 1372
Riedell, Keith, 2555
Rieder, Greg, 8104
Riedinger, Kirk, 6698
Riegel, Megan, 8227
Riegel Jr., George W., 4049, 4053
Riegelman, John, 5616
Rieger, Drew, 4751
Riegle, Dale, 2008
Riehle, Bettyalice, 2207
Riehle, Brad, 6876
Riekse, Jonathan, 1245
Rierdon, Sean, 4126
Riffe, Keith, 8621, 8653
Riffey, Ginny, 4257
Rifilato, Annie, 1633
Rifkin, Monte, 201
Rigas, Kas, 467
Rigby, Helen, 2526
Rigby, Randy, 8497
Rigdon, Kevin, 3982
Rigdon, Trish, 8406
Riger, Helen, 6502
Rigerman, Marilyn, 2763
Riggi, Ronald, 1464, 5200
Riggins, Dr. J. Wayne, 5242
Riggs, Ben, 2146
Riggs, Clare, 6581
Riggs, Dr. Robert, 4893
Riggs, Dudley, 3236
Riggs, Mike, 5073
Riggs, Nancy, 2872
Riggs, Ashley, 6619
Righter, Jere, 7262
Rightmire, Karen A., 5500
Riker, Kathleen, 61
Rile, Joanne, 1631, 8884
Riles-Robinson, Valerie, 6553
Rilette, Ryan, 3121
Rilettech, Ryan, 2526
Riley, Bill, 1576
Riley, Christina, 4806
Riley, Christopher A., 2064
Riley, Clint, 2349
Riley, Dale, 641
Riley, Darrin, 6022
Riley, Deborah, 144
Riley, Emily, 2074
Riley, Jim, 7984
Riley, Kate, 8706
Riley, Moreen, 4835
Riley, Rebecca Hill, 1070
Riley, Sean, 90, 94
Riley, Timothy, 5844
Riley, Tonya, 5965
Riley, Jr, Joseph P., 8210
Riley-Tepie, Yvonne, 7644
Riley, Kay, 6763
Rilley, Michael, 5325, 8459
Rilling, Helmuth, 1593, 5405
Rimes, Jen, 2272
Rimmer, Paula, 2385
Rimovsky, Paul, 3044
Rinaldi, Denise, 4324
Rinaldi, Michele, 4324
Rincon, Jose, 1436, 1441
Rinderknecht, Margrit, 6274
Rindfleisch, Greg, 5851
Rindt, Brooke, 3051, 7065
Rinehart, Cheryl, 8595

Rinehart, Dave, 3741
Rinehart, John, 6228
Rinehart, Richard, 541, 1531
Rinehart Yeager, Timothy, 506, 620
Rinere, Patricia, 6302
Riney, Cecil J, 4683
Ring, Paul, 7998
Ringer, Cheryl, 1838
Ringer, Enid, 379
Ringer, Jennifer, 412
Ringger, Amanda, 7707
Ringle, Jennifer, 843
Ringler, Denise, 5223, 5224
Ringler, Martha, 1633
Rinier, Joshua M., 2304
Rink, Bennett, 381, 385
Rink, Jeffrey, 1203
Rinker, J. T., 5057
Rinker, Jill, 8000
Rinn, Susan, 5667
Rinsema, Joe, 1854
Rinsema, Joel, 1854
Riordan, Jay, 6212
Riordan, Rose, 3788
Riorden, George T, 5577
Rios, Jasmine, 64
Rioult, Pascal, 478
Ripke, Tim, 6239
Ripley, James, 1824
Ripper, Jan, 3841
Ripplinger, Mary Ann, 4172
Rippon, Clif, 2035
Ririe, Rhees, 654
Risberg, Del W., 7188
Risch, Kenneth, 4007
Risco, Norbe, 241
Risco, Ralph, 4117
Riser, Barbara, 6315
Riser, Sandy, 745
Risher, Rene, 3102
Rishi, Arthur, 2117
Risho, Susie, 315
Risinger, Andrew, 2334
Riso, Stephanie, 3844
Rissing, Nancie, 1734
Rissman, Steven B., 5052
Rist, John, 4096
Ritchey, Greg, 2017
Ritchey, Julie, 2931
Ritchie, Daniel L., 6352
Ritchie, Marilyn, 8462
Ritchie, Michael, 2463, 2493, 2509, 4243, 4814, 6170
Ritsch, Joseph, 3122
Ritschel, Debbie, 6817, 6818
Ritsema, Jenna, 3203
Ritsema, Robert, 1241
Rittell, James, 4302
Rittenhouse, Jacob, 4673
Ritter, Ann, 184
Ritter, Brian, 1183
Ritter, Gretchen, 5091
Ritter, Kim, 6450
Ritter, Mathew, 1180
Ritter, Nancy, 1501
Ritter, Paul, 1298
Ritter, Rosemary, 4269
Ritts, Jim, 3929
Ritvo Hughes, Jennifer, 2105
Ritz, Debbie, 4934
Ritz, Fran, 5441
Ritzo, Joe, 6271
Riva, Denis, 4050
Rivas, Sylvia, 5162
Rivas, Tlaloc, 3036
Rivel, David, 5121
Rivenbark, Tony, 7920
Rivera, Carol, 5983
Rivera, Craig, 3400, 7604
Rivera, Emma, 359
Rivera, Jessica, 6382
Rivera, Rachel, 5155
Rivera, Rita, 6428
Rivera, Virginia, 2606
Rivers, Brian, 4960
Rivers, Elisabeth, 7986
Rivers, Karen, 180
Rivers, Voza, 3560

Rives, Bryan L, 6722, 6723
Rives, Harold, 1966
Rivkin, Dan, 2930
Rixen, Jacqueline, 1702
Rixon, Katherine, 6698
Rizer, Lola, 4096
Rizzo, Bob, 5521, 5525
Rizzo, John, 7617
Rizzo, Joseph J, 4497
Rizzo, Karen, 6394
Rizzo, Lynette P., 381, 385
Rizzugo, Jim, 6384
Roach, AJ, 1
Roach, David, 8196
Roach, Victoria, 7129, 7130
Roark, Margaret, 1568
Robards, ?Kim, 124
Robards, Kim, 124
Robatty, Alessandra, 1791
Robb, Elizabeth, 4920
Robb, James, 5482
Robb, Rachel, 2296
Robbert, Brad, 3086
Robbert, Millie, 1240
Robbins, Amy, 7474
Robbins, Hollie, 5965
Robbins, Jeannie, 823
Robbins, Jerome, 466
Robbins, John, 5786
Robbins, Kenneth, 4720
Robbins, Liz, 47
Robbins, Patrick, 711
Robbins, Pete, 7645, 7671
Robbins, Peter S., 60
Robbins, Royal, 47
Robbins, Sandra, 3566
Robbins, Sanford, 2724
Robbins, Serena, 1437
Robbins, Staci, 8539
Robbins, Sue, 6512
Robbins, Susan, 1680
Robbins, Tim, 2462
Robbinson, Wade, 7071, 7072, 7073
Robbins, Staci, 5026
Roberge, Bethany, 4742
Roberge, Michele, 6151
Roberson, David, 5915, 5916
Roberson, Emily, 5669
Roberson, Jim, 890
Roberson, Melynda, 1357
Roberson, Ralph, 2268
Roberson, Samuel, 2921
Roberson, Stephanie, 6273
Roberson, Wanda, 3945
Robert, Andy, 3820
Robert, Bob, 8441
Robert, Debbie, 6784
Robert, Paul, 8583
Robert Beres, Leslie, 736, 737
Robert Young, Honorable, 6450
Roberto, Catherine, 4102
Roberts, Barclay, 8286
Roberts, Bobby, 8897
Roberts, Brian, 8621, 8653
Roberts, Chris, 3270
Roberts, Christopher, 7092, 7093, 7096
Roberts, Cynthia, 1917
Roberts, Dana, 4999
Roberts, David, 3545, 3575
Roberts, Deborah, 7590
Roberts, Dr. John, 4517
Roberts, Glenn, 1079
Roberts, H. Parker, 3354
Roberts, Heather, 197
Roberts, Hector, 7355
Roberts, Jay, 8177
Roberts, Jeff, 7416
Roberts, Jennifer, 2686
Roberts, Jim, 3774
Roberts, John, 3746, 4517, 6687
Roberts, Karey, 8121
Roberts, Kathryn, 4873
Roberts, Kendra, 5374
Roberts, Kevin, 972
Roberts, Kimberley, 288
Roberts, Kris, 180
Roberts, Kyle, 4031
Roberts, Lance, 8897

Roberts, Lincoln, 6512, 6513
Roberts, Linda, 6632, 6633
Roberts, Louise, 443
Roberts, Mark, 2904, 3986
Roberts, Mary, 7154
Roberts, Mary Ellen, 4621
Roberts, Melissa, 1693
Roberts, Michele, 6190
Roberts, Pamela, 6117
Roberts, Parker, 3354
Roberts, Randall, 4686
Roberts, Robin, 6875
Roberts, Sandra, 2774
Roberts, Sharon, 4031
Roberts, Shawn, 686
Roberts, Wayne A, 5330
Roberts Frawley, Amy, 5123
Roberts Jr, T Atkins, 4140
Robertson, Andrea, 1061
Robertson, Barbara, 869
Robertson, Barbara J, 4323
Robertson, Carole, 5868
Robertson, Cathy, 1278
Robertson, Charles, 2287
Robertson, Dan, 4670
Robertson, David, 1291, 1292, 1293, 4916
Robertson, Diane M., 5233
Robertson, Elaine, 856, 857, 1925
Robertson, Elise, 4599
Robertson, Greg, 2353, 4707
Robertson, Ian, 1916, 1924
Robertson, Janet, 177
Robertson, John D, 8626
Robertson, Jon, 829
Robertson, Jonna, 4921
Robertson, Julia, 4211
Robertson, Kirk, 4956
Robertson, Leah, 1150
Robertson, Lynn, 4687
Robertson, Monique, 4550
Robertson, Sally, 4592
Robertson, Scott, 2553
Robertson, Stacey, 4191
Robertson, Susan, 1722, 5625
Robertson, Syndi L., 1926, 1927
Robertson Dennis, Brenda, 5
Roberts, J. William, 6720, 6721
Robertz, Roger, 1736
Robey, David, 4176
Robicaille, Michel, 7776
Robin, Allan, 2553
Robin, Charles E, 3297
Robin, Charlie, 7448
Robin, Diane, 4708
Robin, Jaffe, 2400
Robin, Marc, 2303, 3811
Robin, Toni, 69
Robin Macmillan, L., 326
Robins, Daina, 7305
Robins, Irwin, 7712
Robins, Larry, 610
Robins, Michael, 3241
Robins, Tiffany, 3241
Robins Koneccy, Isobel, 3530
Robinson, Annette, 5523
Robinson, Becky, 5658
Robinson, Brian, 934
Robinson, Bryan, 7627
Robinson, Carla, 3027
Robinson, Carol, 1811
Robinson, Carolanne, 6949
Robinson, Clifton, 208
Robinson, Curtis W., 1730
Robinson, Cynthia, 4975
Robinson, David, 1992, 2848, 3869
Robinson, Davis, 7181
Robinson, Debbie, 2271
Robinson, Dennis, 2322
Robinson, Dr Susan, 996
Robinson, Dr. Kathryn, 5391
Robinson, Earl, 5221
Robinson, Eloise, 3377
Robinson, Faye, 6113
Robinson, Frank, 6065
Robinson, Gail, 7107
Robinson, Gerry, 5303
Robinson, Greg, 2284
Robinson, Guin, 2401

1213

Executive Name Index

Robinson, James, 1954, 2163
Robinson, Jane A., 2004
Robinson, Jimmie, 6372
Robinson, John, 5799, 6254
Robinson, Josh, 4100
Robinson, Joyce, 5507
Robinson, Judy, 616
Robinson, Kashara, 2449
Robinson, Kia, 4718
Robinson, Lai-Lin, 372
Robinson, Les, 7910, 8210
Robinson, Lois, 1144
Robinson, Malik, 121
Robinson, Marcia, 1954
Robinson, Margaret B, 2279
Robinson, Martha, 1009
Robinson, Mary, 8606
Robinson, Maryann, 6655
Robinson, Melanie, 5662
Robinson, Michael, 3946
Robinson, Mitchell, 3476
Robinson, Neil, 4610
Robinson, Pam, 6092
Robinson, Pamela, 381, 385
Robinson, Pete, 5303
Robinson, Ray, 986
Robinson, Rhonda, 1357
Robinson, Robby, 2981
Robinson, Robin, 1506
Robinson, Sandy, 241
Robinson, Sara, 4777
Robinson, Sharon, 1530, 5312, 5313
Robinson, Sherry, 1411
Robinson, Shirley, 4080
Robinson, Stewart, 2004
Robinson, Wolly, 8255
Robinson Esq, Donald A, 334
Robinson Hill, Joanne, 7739
Robinson Hollander, Pamela, 2502
Robinson Rogers, Ph., Judy, 4913
Robinson, Dr. P.H., Robert R., 2086
Robinson, Esq, Toni M, 1131
Robinson-Harris, Pamela, 651
Robinson-Prater, Danielle, 299
Robinson-Watkins, Gaynell, 7150, 7151
Robison, Beth, 3008
Robison, De Etta, 6973
Robitshek, Heidi, 673
Robkin, David, 6115
Robson, Geoffrey, 755
Roca, Cesar, 1842
Rocco, Deborah, 2254
Rocha, Linda, 153
Rochaix, Francois, 3146
Roche, Dr.Edward (Ted), 3321
Roche, Edward, 7485
Rochester, Chris, 1589
Rochester, Terry, 5843
Rochford Figgs, Sheri, 908
Rochon, Ph.D., MPH, Gilbert L., 5932
Roch,, Richard, 1749
Rock, Neen, 4110
Rock, Peggy, 1870
Rock, Rod, 6439
Rock, Rodney, 6436, 6437
Rockefeller, Janet, 5394, 5395, 8053, 8054, 8055, 8056
Rockmaker, Jody, 738
Rockoff, Gayle, 5640
Rocks, Lawrence, 4556
Rockwell, Noralee, 4204
Rodale Houghton, Nina, 4758
Rodarte, John, 3785
Rodaz, John, 2765
Rodd, Abby, 2209
Rodd, Stephen T, 3572
Rodde, Dr James, 2071
Roddy, Patrick, 3902
Rodeheffer, Stephen, 8007
Rodenbaugh, Connie, 1699
Rodenbeck, Rick, 4088
Rodenhizer, Carl S, 943
Rodet, Laird, 846
Rodgers, Barry, 557
Rodgers, Brain, 7317
Rodgers, Brian, 1247, 1248, 4856
Rodgers, Chip, 3568
Rodgers, David, 887

Rodgers, Monica, 4509
Rodgers, Rod, 480
Rodgers, Thomas, 5078
Rodman, Katherine, 715
Rodrigue, Morris, 6214
Rodrigues, Lisa, 5656
Rodriguez, Amanda, 7277
Rodriguez, Ana, 3939, 8336
Rodriguez, Andrea, 2591
Rodriguez, Anthony, 2874
Rodriguez, Darlene, 6742
Rodriguez, D maso, 3783
Rodriguez, Isabel A., 8459
Rodriguez, Julie, 5034
Rodriguez, Laurie, 6230
Rodriguez, Leslie, 4596, 6820, 6821
Rodriguez, Miguel A, 1186
Rodriguez, Raul, 2629
Rodriguez-Hodory, Rebecca, 525
Rodriquez, Julia, 2490
Rody, Bob, 3716
Rody, Marje, 3749
Roe, Alex, 3520
Roe, James, 5005, 5136
ROE, Jane, 2132
Roe, Jane, 4833, 7280
Roe, Randall, 1989
Roe, Susan, 2846, 2862, 6627
Roeben, Wally, 4345, 6318
Roebuck, Chris, 3276
Roeder, Scott, 1719
Roedig, Alissa, 873
Roedl, Sherry M, 1013
Roehrenbeck, Patrick, 3720
Roelofs, Jessie, 4870
Roemer, Elizabeth, 613
Roeper, Karen, 1095
Roer, Sara, 359
Roesler, George M, 3273
Roesslein, Charles J., 1703
Roest, Michael, 1563
Roettger, Walter, 2432
Rogachevskaya, Lana, 6841, 6842
Rogala, Katherine, 499
Rogan, Mike, 6937
Rogen, Melysa, 1688
Roger, James, 3655
Roger-Cropper, Natalie, 498
Rogers, Andrea, 1768, 5705, 8505
Rogers, Bruce, 4346
Rogers, Carole, 2436
Rogers, Conant Scott, 2305
Rogers, David, 997
Rogers, Deborah, 5433
Rogers, Don, 6092
Rogers, Donald, 8235
Rogers, Donald M, 5547
Rogers, Eric R., 4629
Rogers, Geoffrey M., 4758
Rogers, Jen, 1854
Rogers, Jesse, 1757
Rogers, Jessy, 5680
Rogers, Joel P, 2457
Rogers, John R, 7462
Rogers, June A, 6187
Rogers, Laurie, 2254, 2255
Rogers, Lesley, 1339
Rogers, Lynn, 4220
Rogers, Mike, 2409, 5911
Rogers, Mollie, 3769
Rogers, Richard, 1015
Rogers, Richard L., 5609, 5611
Rogers, Richards, 4511
Rogers, Ruth, 4220, 5775
Rogers, Scott, 2887
Rogers, Teresa, 1732
Rogers, Victoria, 980
Rogers, William, 4733
Rogers Ard, Rachelle, 1896
Rogers Branstrom, Robin, 5263
Rogers Radcliffe, Stephen, 5803
Rogers, Jr.,, William, 4400
Rogers, Jr., Esq., William, 4730, 4731, 4732, 4733
Rogers-Walker, Dorothy, 148
Rogerson, Gus, 3459
Rogge, Leolive, 5676
Rogoff, Marie, 1733

Rogosin, Eileen, 3353
Rogosin, Roy, 3103
Rogow, Andy, 2783
Rogozienski, Frank, 6246
Rohde, Joshua, 2127
Rohla, Dru A, 8714
Rohlfs, Charles, 4430
Rohne, Dirk, 8065
Rohr, Jenni, 7998
Rohr, Myrna, 6122
Rohr, Nicole, 2918
Rohrbaugh, David, 1929
Rohrer, Richard, 4604
Rohrig, Becky, 1224, 1225
Roistacher, Dick, 2596
Roizin, Irina, 358
Rokus, Mary Beth, 5877
Roland, Ashley, 560
Rolandi, Gianna, 2048
Rolek, Timm, 1903
Roles, Linda, 3220
Rolett, Virginia, 2173
Rolf, Shelly, 2902
Rollene, Donna, 4193
Rollett, Rebecca, 2318
Rolley, Bill, 3950
Rollins, Jackie, 6024
Rollins, John, 1980
Rollins III, John W, 1980
Rollison, Randy, 3498, 3712
Roloff, John, 1107
Roloff, Toni, 3023
Rolon, Rosalba, 3415
Rom, Brittany, 1308
Romagnoli, Richard, 4021
Roman, Bertha, 53
Roman, Marcelo, 182
Roman, Mary, 572
Romanin, Thomas, 1101
Romano, Dominick J., 7545
Romano, Jay, 582
Romano, Joseph, 4637
Romano, Peola, 5155
Romanoff, Vanessa, 4742
Romanstein, Stanley E, 1005, 1006
Romberg, Roberta V., 2596
Romeo, R.J., 3849
Romero, Deborah, 6381
Romero, Giga, 915
Romero, Margaret, 4356
Romero, Victoria, 6085
Romero Wolf, Margie, 12
Romig, Kenneth, 5471
Rominger, Anna, 233
Rominger, Nancy, 4148, 5915, 5916
Rominger, Signe, 1385
Rommel, Heather Know, 6391
Rommereim, John, 4656
Romney, Bonnie, 655
Romoser, W. David, 4135
Ron, Yuval, 44
Ronai, Anne, 4365
Ronberg, Kerry, 4453
Rondeau, Jean, 8202
Ronen, Yarden, 472
Roney, Regina, 4323
Roney, Sondra, 8364
Ronus, Robert, 1887
Ronzi, Anthony, 2315
Ronzi, Mrs Anthony, 2315
Rooney, Flo, 4157
Rooney, Gordon, 5533
Rooney, Jim, 4157
Roos, Jerry, 8062, 8063
Roos-Brown, Erinn, 6411
Roose Pullin, Marion, 1852
Roosevelt, Oliver, 708
Roosevelt, Franklin D., 8128
Root, Jerry, 886, 6315
Root, Robert T, 2425
Roots, Shamika, 7297
Roper, Cara, 8581
Ropp, Kristen, 7959
Rorick, Suzanne, 2289
Ros, Sokeo, 592
Rosa, Adriana, 329
Rosa, Alex, 1787
Rosa, Thomas, 1199

Rosado, Jos,, 8108
Rosal, Maia, 79
Rosario, Editha, 3502
Rosati, Anthony, 6408
Rose, Celeste, 3776
Rose, Charlie, 3493
Rose, Diemet, 842, 4290
Rose, Douglas, 1542
Rose, Dr. Michael J, 8148
Rose, Ed, 3650
Rose, Frank, 1067, 6835
Rose, Gayle S., 1695
Rose, Gil, 1200, 2107, 4974
Rose, Jayne, 3889
Rose, Jeanne, 7955, 7958
Rose, Jerome, 5147
Rose, Joe, 2123
Rose, John, 2227
Rose, Kathy, 442
Rose, Kevin, 8082
Rose, Lee, 1247, 1248
Rose, Leslie, 986
Rose, Linwood, 8526
Rose, Lois, 1542
Rose, Michael, 4552
Rose, Michael J, 5483
Rose, Peggy, 2590
Rose, Philip, 380
Rose, Phyllis, 473
Rose, Ric, 158
Rose, Richard, 4028
Rose, Shawn, 6390
Rose, Steven, 5011
Rose, Whitney, 8031
Rose, Zoe, 2171
Rose Dunning, Lily, 5750
Rosean, Christopher, 218
Roseland, Chad, 1097
Roselius, Alice, 7412
Roseman, Kim, 5994
Roseman, Phyllis, 1708
Rosen, Eric, 3289
Rosen, Ilene, 3487
Rosen, Lee E., 769
Rosen, Marcy, 4762
Rosen, Michael, 803
Rosen, Robert, 3255
Rosen, Rosemarie, 2255
Rosen, Rosemarie V., 2254
Rosen, Ruth, 809
Rosen, Stuart, 3493
Rosen, Todd, 3471
Rosenbaum, Beth, 5935
Rosenbaum, Dennis, 1463
Rosenbaum, Dr. Arthur, 1468, 1469
Rosenbaum, Edith R., 2220, 2243
Rosenbaum, Eli, 1185
Rosenbaum, Faye, 454
Rosenbaum, Glen A., 2353
Rosenbaum, Harold, 2243, 2257
Rosenbaum, Robert A, 7351
Rosenbaum, Thomas F, 6207
Rosenbaun, Allan, 1470
Rosenberg, Audrey, 1107
Rosenberg, Douglas, 706
Rosenberg, Jeff, 2120
Rosenberg, Lana Kay, 540
Rosenberg, Lawrence, 20
Rosenberg, Lon, 6156
Rosenberg, Maidie O., 2280
Rosenberg, Michael S, 3487
Rosenberg, Robert J., 3576
Rosenberg, Sheli Z., 2917
Rosenberg, Steve, 5331, 5352
Rosenberg,, Martha, 1939
Rosenberg, Craig, 3216
Rosenblatt, Steven R., 7463
Rosenblum, Ann, 8795
Rosenblum, Mark C, 1321
Rosenblum, Paul, 5096, 5097, 7694
Rosenbluth, Susan, 2503
Rosenboom, David, 4343
Rosenbuam, Harold, 2220
Rosenfeld, Fay, 3493
Rosenfeld Margulis, Elaine, 213
Rosenfield, Jack, 3290
Rosenholtz, Ellen, 8159
Rosenmayer, David, 2248

Executive Name Index

Rosenstein, Deborah, 1214, 1215
Rosenstiel, Jeffrey, 1133
Rosenthal, Debbie, 4467
Rosenthal, Leah Z, 4233
Rosenthal, Linda, 723
Rosenthal, Nan, 1156, 4751
Rosenthal, Regina, 3929
Rosenthal, Pruuueu, 4825
Rosentrater, Jill, 6382
Rosenwasser, Robert, 71
Rosenzweig, David C., 7766
Rosenzweig, Richard, 4209
Roses, MD, Allen D., 5233
Rosette, Vicki, 3780
Rosevear, Esta, 4090, 4092
Rosh, John, 7081
Rosica, Bill, 1932
Rosipal, David, 8445
Roskelly, Jim, 7885
Roslonski, Erica, 8132
Rosmarin, Annalisa, 2737
Rosner, Kathy, 7314
Rosnock, Joseph, 6565, 6568, 6573
Ross, Alice, 1399
Ross, Andy, 2878
Ross, Ann-Marie, 4220
Ross, Barry, 1244
Ross, Bertam, 455
Ross, Brad, 65
Ross, Brian, 4234
Ross, Chris, 1400, 1732
Ross, Cindy, 5384
Ross, David, 7414
Ross, Dr. Jerrold, 5167
Ross, Ellen, 3163
Ross, Glenn, 898, 899, 4353
Ross, Jack, 2889
Ross, James, 1160
Ross, Jane, 1420
Ross, Janine, 1596, 5418
Ross, Jeanette, 1010
Ross, Jennifer, 96
Ross, Jerry, 8780
Ross, Jim, 7273
Ross, Kathleen T., 4033
Ross, Kay, 3982
Ross, Kendra, 3416
Ross, Linda Mason, 7746
Ross, Lisa, 590
Ross, Lou, 5352
Ross, Michael, 3113, 6150, 6208, 6449
Ross, Mike, 1823, 4601
Ross, Murray, 6492
Ross, Olivia, 8345
Ross, Ora, 4549
Ross, Paul, 1148, 4739, 4744, 5134
Ross, Paula, 262
Ross, Robert J., 3984
Ross, Sara, 7464
Ross, Tom, 2447, 3571, 5623
Ross III, Arthur, 1009
Ross III, Hugh, 47
Ross Thomas, Marth, 1275, 1276
Rossall, Gina, 33
Rossanese Jr, Judge Maurino J, 1622
Rossant, Tomas J., 439
Rosselet, Stu, 1257
Rosser, William, 6313
Rossi, Amy, 63
Rossi, Armand, 4388
Rossi, Deborah C., 4451
Rossi, Fran, 290
Rossi, Joseph, 3128
Rossi, Joseph A., 3124
Rossi, Julie, 3396
Rossi, Renee, 466
Rossi, Richard Robert, 1032
Rossi-Copeland, Carolyn, 3512
Rossick Kern, Mary, 905
Rossie, Lisa, 2552
Rossin, Eric, 878
Rossiter, Dr. James, 1115, 1116
Rossman, Candace, 4261
Rossotti, Barbara M., 1983, 1984
Rossow, Eileen, 3886, 3888
Rosswurm, Glenn, 4102
Rostan, Mark, 3681
Rote, Carey, 8345

Roth, Ari, 6478
Roth, Brittan, 7985
Roth, Cynthia L., 2317
Roth, Daryl, 7746
Roth, David M, 928
Roth, Deborah, 2079
Roth, Diana, 125
Roth, Don, 1928, 4351, 6095
Roth, Harold R, 5999, 6348
Roth, Henry, 4202
Roth, James.A., 363
Roth, Jim, 6212
Roth, Mary, 138
Roth, Maya E., 6479
Roth, Mayda, 5497
Roth, Paul, 2713
Roth, Rebecca, 1817, 2392
Roth, Virginia, 1769
Roth Ph.D, Don, 6094
Roth, PhD, Don, 6096, 6098
Rothamer, Jill, 4562
Rothbard, Michael, 7684
Rothchild, Ken, 3420
Rothenberg, Eedee, 5107
Rothenberg, Michael G, 5107
Rothenberg, Micheal, 5107
Rothenberg, Ned, 1440
Rothenberg, Sarah, 5635
Rothman, Carole, 3565
Rothman, Don, 2616
Rothman, George, 1439
Rothman, Jeremy, 1647
Rothman, Neal, 4621
Rothman, Rebecca, 4152
Rothman, Stephen, 2497
Rothmann, Lola, 1554, 5287
Rothmann, MD, Bruce F, 1554
Rothschild, Arnie, 3610
Rothstein, Peter, 3254
Rothstein, Roberta, 147
Rothwell, Carol, 1343
Rothwell, Rick, 4073
Rotman, Christy, 51
Rotman, Dr. Harold, 5218
Rottenberg, Herman, 383
Rotton, Bryan, 6067
Roudebush, Kathy, 228
Rouen, Deborah B., 4713
Rouen, Deborah R., 2083
Rougeau, Weldon, 1034
Rouille, Jan, 1640
Roullier, A., 350
Roullier, Alain, 350
Roundtree, Stephen D, 4243
Rounsavall, Elizabeth, 3069
Rountree, Paula, 5250
Rountree, Stephen D, 6173
Rous, Benjamin, 2375
Rouse, Charles, 4983
Rouse, Lee, 4856, 7317
Rouse, Turner, 1496
Roush, Edmund, 7852
Roush, Erika, 743
Roush, Philip S., 3281
Rousse, Sally, 295
Rousseau, Charles R, 7213
Rousso, Suzanne, 1489
Routh, Paloma, 1852
Routhier, Christina, 6662
Rowan, Jean, 3592
Rowan, Jo, 551
Rowe, Alan, 2371
Rowe, Carl, 195
Rowe, David, 7156
Rowe, H. C., 7510
Rowe, John W, 7746
Rowe, Ken, 5607
Rowe, Ray, 7023
Rowe, Tim, 5366, 5367
Rowe, J.D., Jack, 308
Rowell, Barry, 3546
Rowen, Carol, 6194
Rowitz, Scott, 6267
Rowland, Ann, 6166
Rowland, Dan, 6353
Rowland, James, 1339, 1732
Rowland, Joanne, 1760
Rowland, Justin, 3160

Rowland, Lisa, 7867
Rowland, Tom, 6607
Rowlett, Ann, 7967
Rowlette, Jeanne, 4822
Rowley, Eric, 8298
Rowley, Jackie, 6550
Rowley, Jill, 1024
Rowley, Wesley, 7902
Rowser, Della, 7878
Rowsey, R I, 2898
Roxey, Mark, 333
Roxey, Melissa, 333
Roxey - Jone, Nilda, 333
Roy, Cathy, 4990, 7557
Roy, Marcia, 1897
Roy, Phyllis, 3154
Roy, Thomas, 5442
Roy, Tonya, 1760
Roy White, Stephen, 4111
Royal, Billy, 5965
Royal, Richard, 5658
Royal, Richard R., 8443
Royall, Inda, 2859
Royals, Deb, 7864
Royce, Liz, 778
Royce, Matthew, 2585
Royer, Dale, 7094
Royer, Vivian, 6520
Roysdan, Christine, 1619
Royston, George, 3472
Royt, Melody, 7055
Rozanski, Emily, 4019
Rozelle, Dave, 1243, 4853
Rozema, David, 3325
Rozendaal, Susan, 2944
Rozin, Seth, 3833
Rozman, Beth, 4106, 5828
Roznski, Mordechai, 2188
Rozsa, Scott, 3957
Rpsenthal, Leah Z, 796
Rrivers, Michael, 1366
Ruark, Joel, 7766
Rub, Timothy, 7962
Rubanenko, Gil, 7947
Rubardt, Peter, 988
Rubardt, PhD., Peter, 1277
Rubarth, Clara Jane, 2436
Rubenfeld, Louis, 7244
Rubenstein, David M, 956, 958
Rubenstein, David M., 1997, 4424, 6471
Rubenstein, Ed, 8223
Rubenstein, Eliza, 1883
Rubenstein, Eric, 2967
Rubenstein, Harriet, 8159
Rubenstein, Jerry G., 1645
Rubenstein, Joyce, 4128
Rubenstein, Michael, 3464
Rubeo, David, 2228
Ruberg, Alan, 50
Rubienstien, Kim, 2697
Rubin, Anne K., 4822
Rubin, Bobbie, 6330
Rubin, David, 5039
Rubin, Holli, 2830
Rubin, Jack, 2953
Rubin, Jim, 4029
Rubin, Joseph, 2239
Rubin, Judith, 3548
Rubin, Paul, 7805
Rubin, Peter, 2280
Rubin, Scott, 6903
Rubinfeld, Gail, 4207, 6066, 6070, 6071, 6072
Rubino, Caroline, 5216
Rubino, Paige, 6406
Rubins, Harry, 878, 4332
Rubinsky, Jane, 1381
Rubinstein, Matan, 706
Rubinstein, Suzanne, 706
Rubio, Domingo, 221
Rubio, Jill, 1454
Rubsam, Henning, 483
Rucco, Deborah, 2255
Rucinski, Robert, 3186
Rucker, Melissa, 242
Ruckwardt, Mark, 8070
Ruda, Anthony J., 4718
Rudd, Wiss, 1725
Rudderow, Bryan, 1334

Rudenko, Michele, 2590
Rudenstine, Neil L, 6158
Ruderman, Marcia, 3134
Rudge, Dr David, 1450
Rudge, Dr. David, 1385
Rudie, Evelyn, 2618
Rudisill, Abra, 16
Rudiskov, Ariel, 5713
Rudley, Carolyn, 4100
Rudnick, Matthew, 4236, 6168, 6172
Rudolph, Andrea, 1626
Rudolph, Ellen, 7786
Rudolph, Marleen, 4864
Rudolph, Pate, 5362
Rudolph, Steven, 1626
Rudolph, Teresa, 6213
Rudow, Vivian A, 4754
Rudowski, Sharon, 4152
Rudowski, Sharron, 5923
Rudsill, Guy, 2272
Rudy, Kippy, 4400, 4730, 4731, 4732, 4733
Rueff, Rusty, 2573
Ruegger, Christy, 8079
Ruehl, Sheri, 4134
Ruemping, Denise, 3264
Ruen, David, 3232
Ruetten, Amy, 4913
Ruettiger, Diana, 393
Rugen, Richard, 5432
Ruggiera, Wanda, 388
Ruggiero, Dom, 3413
Ruggiero, Marianne, 277
Ruggiero, Rob, 2688
Ruggirello, Kelly, 1930
Ruhberg, Regina, 8247
Ruhe, Pierre, 707
Ruhle, Jeannette, 1673
Ruhlin, Peggy M, 5372
Ruigomez, Christopher W, 1176
Ruiz, Donna, 6228
Ruiz, Irma Suarez, 6737
Ruiz, Jessica, 7283
Ruiz, Rosa, 5161
Ruiz, Suzanne, 1021
Rukark, Joel K, 3530
Rukowski, Rich, 8568
Rule, David, 7323
Rulison, Mark, 2042
Rumley, Patrick, 718
Rundberg, Julina, 4779
Runfola, Anthony, 2429
Runft, Courtney, 387
Runice, Linda, 3330
Runk, Karen, 2590
Runnels, Brian, 1728
Runnicles, Donald, 1007, 2018, 4503, 5884
Runnion III, C. S., 4904
Rupert, Jeff, 985
Rupnow, Susan, 5874
Rupp, Kelly, 706
Rupp, Mark, 3009
Rupp, Naomi, 3404
Ruppel, David, 4438
Ruppenthal, Stephen, 831
Ruprecht-Belt, Sean, 3305
Rusch, Gretchen, 1257
Ruscic, Dr. Branko, 4544
Ruscitti, Nico, 6382
Rush, Ben, 3471
Rush, David, 7064
Rush, Margaret, 6406
Rush, Sam, 3166
Rush, Terry, 1306
Rushdi, Lawrence, 1728
Rushefsky, Peter, 7720
Rushing, Matthew, 381, 385
Rushmore, Mt., 8597
Rushton, Kori, 3503
Rusinko, Michael E., 7676
Ruskin, Lewis J., 728
Rusnak, Jeff, 897
Rusnock, Joseph, 2811
Russ, Steve, 2789
Russel, Dan, 7344
Russel, Eric, 4669
Russel, Jerry, 3975
Russell, Amy, 3184, 4814
Russell, Andrew, 4082

1215

Executive Name Index

Russell, Ann, 647
Russell, Barry A, 4347
Russell, Ben, 7848
Russell, Bill, 3055
Russell, Bob, 3283
Russell, Carol, 1510
Russell, Caroline, 5260, 5261
Russell, Craig, 7409
Russell, Elona, 4333
Russell, Eric, 5704
Russell, Jeff, 8539
Russell, Jerry, 3967
Russell, Jill, 5131, 5140
Russell, John Morris, 1682
Russell, John T., 1401
Russell, Martin, 5131, 5140
Russell, Michael, 1904
Russell, Paul, 2465, 6099
Russell, Peter, 1993
Russell, Robert, 4072
Russell, Sheryl, 2465
Russell, Stephanie M., 4505
Russell, Steve, 1841
Russell, Tal, 4167
Russell, Timothy, 2161
Russell, Tony, 4038, 4039
Russell Smith, Mark, 1104, 1105, 1263
Russenberger, Sally, 5401
Russianoff, Gene, 359
Russo, Cheryle, 5324
Russo, Chris, 3803, 8124
Russo, Evelyn, 3601
Russo, John, 3799, 5437
Russo, Joseph, 946
Russo, Philip N., 5485
Russo, Ralph, 8675, 8681, 8683
Russo Burke, Karen, 531
Russomanno, Betsy, 3237, 4121
Russo, Carrie, 3774
Rust, Catherine, 3365, 4994
Rust, Martin, 8548
Rust, Richard, 3182
Rutenberg, Peter, 1884
Ruter, Margo, 198
Ruth, Cathie, 2061
Ruth, Sean, 4520
Ruth Edge, Laura, 1134
Ruth Marotte, Mary, 2433
Rutherford, Angie, 8253
Rutherford, David, 6346
Rutherford, Jim, 7909
Rutherford, Kurtis, 402
Rutherford, Leslie, 6386
Rutherford, Mary J, 1582
Rutherford, Norman, 93
Ruthfield, Mark, 4666
Ruthven, Andrew, 3986
Rutkowski, Beth, 522
Rutkowski, Joan, 1931
Rutkowski, Rebecca, 830
Rutland, Jim, 6640
Rutland, John, 1295
Rutland, Patty-Jo, 6249
Rutledge, Don, 1730
Rutter, Deborah, 6745, 6752
Rutter, Deborah F, 6733
Rutter, Hank, 5688
Rutter, Martha, 658
Ruzevich, Peter, 7479
Ruzzamenti, LeAnne, 6230
Ryabova, Elena, 1411
Ryabova, Elena, 395
Ryan, Arthur E., 7574
Ryan, Benita, 1635
Ryan, Crista, 4365
Ryan, Debbie, 8518
Ryan, Denise, 1077
Ryan, Dorothy, 3580
Ryan, G Jeremiah, 3385
Ryan, Henry, 7241
Ryan, Jan, 5333
Ryan, Jim, 2484, 6147
Ryan, Judy, 3693, 7606
Ryan, Kelly, 5439
Ryan, Marcia, 6112
Ryan, Mark T., 8199
Ryan, Mo, 3726
Ryan, Natalie Kate, 6359

Ryan, Pat, 5434, 8117
Ryan, Rev. John, 5511
Ryan, Sue, 3393
Ryan, Tobin, 5838
Ryan, William N, 4495
Ryder, Hal, 4086
Ryder, Linda, 2157
Ryder, Tim, 668
Rydlinski, George, 720, 5939
Rydum, Bill, 6192
Ryerson, Debra, 2445
Ryherd, Mike, 1794
Ryker, Rebecca, 5783
Ryle, John, 2190
Rylyk, Andrew, 658
Ryman, Kelly, 3378
Ryno, W Douglas, 8812
Ryvkin, Valery, 2266
R"nmark, Erik, 7283

S

S Novak, Jodie, 8134, 8135
S. Grabow, Bradford, 1077
S. Howard, Heidi, 6627
S. Kwan, Derek, 7044
S. Mankoff, Joy, 2342
S. Pfaff, Christopher, 2970
S. Semmler, Shelley, 7687
S.Fields, Patricia, 7899
Saal, Jeff vom, 866, 867
Saar, David P., 2429
Saathoff, Mary, 1741
Saatkamp, Herman, 7582
Saavedra, Waundell, 2227
Saavendra, Rod, 8222
Saba, Zoe, 2446
Sabah, C J, 1302
Saban, Alan, 5177
Sabater, Marianna, 3556, 3570
Sabatini, Kathryn, 3864
Sabato, Pat, 3793
Sabean, Brian R, 6251
Sabel, Shannon, 6908
Sabin, Phyllis B, 4856
Sablan, Janet, 6672
Sabo, Cindy, 4708
Sabo, Erin, 3190
Sabol, Lesley, 1731
Sacaratis, Deborah, 8116
Saccomano, Jim, 6351
Sach, Marty, 3086
Sachs, Ann, 3490, 7727
Sachs, George, 4041
Sachs, Martin, 4719
Sachs, Stephen, 2501
Sachse, Todd, 7333
Sack, September, 6344
Sackett, Linda, 3739
Sackett, Pam, 3209
Sackowitz, Izzy, 7587
Sackstein, Rosalina G., 4465
Sadd, Martin, 1672, 5518
Saddoris, Tawny, 5379
Sadeg, Eitan, 790
Sadler, Chelsea, 3190
Sadler, Danielle, 540
Sadler, Hal, 6238, 6243
Sadler, Janet, 2115, 4803
Sadler, Kerrie, 885
Sadler, Suzanne, 6412, 6413, 6414
Sadlock, Linda, 3345
Saeger, Becky, 6262
Saenger, Kathryn, 3937
Saenger, Ketherine, 1451
Saenz de Viteri, Robbie, 7783
Saetta, Mary Lou, 1362
Saeverud, Trond, 1145
Saferstein, Robert, 2223
Saffirstein, Dr Benjamin H, 1418
Safford, Ken, 4728
Saffos, Giovanna, 140
Saffron, Jennifer, 5493
Safin, Melissa, 1842
Safonovs, Jurijs, 667
Sagawa, Susan, 5771
Sage, Carl L., 3350
Sage, Robert, 773

Sagerty, Sharon, 1355
Saget, Lenore, 4
Sagisselman, Margo, 3244
Sagman, A.J., 8785
Sahakian, Annabella, 3985
Sahakian, Maria, 6115
Saibel, Natalie, 2590
Saidpour, Massoud, 5316
Saiget, Jan, 6209
Sailer, Carol, 735
Sailer, Fred, 3862
Sain, Robert L., 2409
Saine, Jaime, 3156
Sainscein, Norman, 6429
Saint, David, 3378
Saintpeter, Richard, 3064
Saisselin, Numa, 4452
Saisselin, Numa C., 6527
Sakai Hazzard, Claire, 1021
Sakamoto, Kristen, 796, 4233
Sakurai, Motoatsu, 5141
Sal, Louie, 8441
Saladino, Judy, 2722
Saladow, Saul, 6300
Saladrigas, Stephen, 7024
Salamone, Sal, 764
Salamone, Vincent, 7648
Salamun, Betty, 701
Salamunovich, Paul, 1886
Salanitro, Cathie r, 6109
Salanski, Charles, 1286
Salazar, Bob, 7297
Salazar, Hector, 6315
Salazar, Ken, 7609
Salce, Karen, 6164
Salcher, Jennifer, 8052
Salchow, William, 5082
Salcido, David, 5029
Sald, Wes, 4676
Saldana, John, 2428
Salem, Chuck, 8629
Salem, Emad, 395
Saler, Ed, 3841
Salerno, Christina, 224
Salerno, Gina, 4075
Sales, Graca, 199, 205
Saleski, Gale, 7534
Salesky, Brian, 2330
Salganek, Maya, 2420
Salim, Luqman, 6466, 6470
Salimpour, Jamila, 18
Salimpour, Suhaila, 18
Salinas, Dr. Veronica, 1737
Salinas, Vicki, 1746
Salisbury, Diane, 797
Salisbury, Robert, 6330
Salistean, Rob, 1303
Salkind, Mark, 848
Sall, Louise, 632
Sallee, Dave, 4910
Salling, Rusty, 6519
Salm, Lori, 5850
Salmon, Nancy, 250, 1166, 4735
Salmonsen, Robert, 935
Salomon, Christie C, 2225
Salomon, Dan, 3355
Salomon, Frank, 1438, 5156, 8831
Salonen, Esa-Pekka, 805, 4227, 4243
Salovey, Todd, 6242
Salsbery, Wendy, 3060
Salterini, Diego, 157
Saltoun, Andre, 4322
Saltzman, H Royce, 5405
Saltzman, Julie, 2447
Saltzman, Royce, 5405
Saltzman Romey, Kathy, 1593
Salute, Lou, 745
Salva, Larry, 1247, 1248, 4856, 7317
Salveson, Nora, 1510
Salzman, Eric, 2222
Salzman, Jaquee, 4133
Salzman, Jeanne, 5002
Salzman, Wilma, 2345
Salzone, Joe, 1364
Sam PhD JD, David, 6773
Samaniego-Lira, Mik, 5659
Samano, L. Sam, 4067
Samat, Vincent, 388

Samborn, Josh, 5025
Samek, Richard, 4616
Samimi, Sean, 794
Sammarco, Adele, 4997
Sammis, Erin, 2009
Samoff, Marjorie, 3837
Sampson, Bonnie, 3847
Sampson, Carol, 5334
Sampson, Cornelia, 290
Samson, Suzanne, 1321
Samuel, Gail, 6124
Samuel, Tunde, 3525
Samuel-Siegel, Tamar, 5065
Samuels, Janie, 1144
Samuels, Sara, 6737
Samuelson, Cecil O., 8489
Samule, Reene, 1476
San Soucie, Beth, 4967
Sanborn, Cheryl R, 4165
Sanborn, Ellen, 7176, 7177, 7178
Sanchez, Gail, 1710
Sanchez, Grace, 4550
SanChez, Janet, 7745
Sanchez, Mario Ernesto, 2767
Sanchez, Olda, 3785
Sanchez, Rick, 1710, 5605
Sandberg, Dr. Hershel, 1230, 1237
Sanddik, Katrina, 7024
Sandefur, Beth, 1868
Sandefur, Judy, 163
Sander, Jennifer, 1866
Sander, Karen, 5171
Sanderling, Stefan, 997, 1571
Sanders, Abby, 1814
Sanders, Adam, 1855
Sanders, Chris, 8382
Sanders, Donald T, 4798
Sanders, Dr. Sandi, 754
Sanders, Dudley, 2871
Sanders, Dudley W, 2871
Sanders, Jeffri, 739, 4180
Sanders, Jerry, 6346
Sanders, Jim, 7515
Sanders, John, 6247
Sanders, Nan, 4889
Sanders, Stefan, 1746
Sanders, Thomas, 1750
Sanders, Wayne, 2244
Sanders Evans, Stacie, 4756
Sanders Haupert, Carolyn, 4652
Sanderson, Brian, 7371
Sanderson, Dedra, 7899
Sanderson, Gary, 8029
Sanderson, Julianna, 3905
Sanderson, Kirsten, 2473
Sanderson, William, 1875
Sandifer, Ombra, 2589
Sandin, Christine, 6078
Sandkamp, Anthony, 3550
Sandler, Deborah, 2160
Sandler, Luke, 6155
Sandley, Dr Don, 5893
Sandmaier, Christy, 228
Sandman, James F, 4434
Sandorfi, Joanne, 306
Sandoval, Gema, 56
Sandoval, Robbie, 8271
Sandquist, Thomas, 1065, 1066
Sandretto Hull, Jennifer, 2598, 2601
Sandridge, Laura, 3678
Sands, Alayna, 8156
Sands, Sean, 6481
Sands, Stephen, 2176
Sands, Jr Resita M, 1040
Sandstedt, Phyllis, 913
Sandstrom, Jane, 1848
Sandvik, Katrina, 3039
Sandy, Heather, 1027
Sandy, Sherrick, 5910
Sandys, Nick, 2945
Sanferrare, Bob, 1213
Sanford, Julia, 611
Sanford, Sara, 5
Sanford, Tim, 3548
Sang, Barry, 7913
Sang, Fred, 4852
Sanger, James R., 5829
Sanie, Michael, 1899

Executive Name Index

Sankovich, Dennis, 7403
Sankowich, Lee, 2522
Sankowski, Carol, 5706
Sanman, Lisa, 3788
Sanner, Laura, 5646
Sanning, Erik, 6997, 6998, 6999
Sannuto, John, 3422
Sano, Stephen M, 879, 6306, 6307, 6309
Sansone, Laurie, 5010
Sant, Geoffrey R., 405
Sant, Roger W., 6459
Sant, Victoria P, 957
Sant, Victoria P., 4416, 4429
Santa, Staci, 4182, 5996, 6010
Santana, Wilhelmina, 6105
Santanam, Ramesh, 3847
Santaniello, Chris, 4967
Santarelli, Marilyn, 8190
Santelli, Francesco, 2177
Santiago, Donna, 4718
Santiago, Tara, 3282
Santiago, Tiffany, 3638, 7854
Santini, Trish, 3239
Santo, Amen, 72
Santopadre, Greg, 3367
Santora, Phil, 2541, 4020
Santora, Philip, 2986
Santorelli, Rachel, 1245
Santori, Jim, 1261
Santoro, Angelo, 1517
Santoro, Lucie G., 362
Santoro, Pasquale, 362
Santoro-Au, Lynette, 5369
Santos, Ana, 3553
Santos, Charles, 3957
Santos, Loelia, 7787
Santos, Marivel, 6164, 6179
Santourian, Asadour, 1944, 4351, 6328
Santy, Robert, 932
Sanville, Guy, 3195
Sanzel, Jeffrey, 3605
Saperston, Bruce, 5685
Sapinski, Paula, 220
Saponaro, Jessica, 540
Sapora, Joseph K., 2237
Sappington, Tucker, 4707
Sapunor, Jeanne, 6232
Sapunor-Davis, Caitlin, 63
Saquicela, Fabricio, 3624
Sara, Elizabeth C, 1991
Sara, Spicer, 8071
Sarah, Interim Directo, 848
Saran, Wendy, 2122
Sarasvati, Bala, 178
Sarate, Jason, 5935
Sarber, John, 6906
Sarberg, Robert, 3789
Sarch, Kenneth, 5466
Sardelli, Giovanna, 2541
Sardone, Frank J., 4854
Sardou Klein, Mitchell, 800
Sare, Curt, 8722
Sarette, Marlies, 712
Sargent, Anthony, 4559
Sargent, Leona, 8019
Sargent, Matt, 2371
Sarnoff, Rosita, 3169
Sarocka, William, 2062, 2063
Sarrgeri, Jacqueline, 872
Sartori, Joe, 4077
Sarvis, Paul, 7167
Sasaki, Kenny, 7515
Sasaki, Robert, 8599, 8600, 8602, 8603
Sasenbury, Scott, 7218
Saskowski, Paul, 1366
Saslav, Ann, 5657
Sass, Molly, 6891
Sasse, Molly, 1689, 2329
Sasser, Chris, 7809
Sasser, John, 2043
Sassi, Rebekah, 3839, 8163, 8164, 8165, 8166
Sasso, Ann, 588
Sather, Sonja, 5773
Sathre, Rock, 8722
Satisky, Grahan, 5265
Satkunaratnam, Pushpa, 210
Sato, Nonoko, 2575
Sato Ambush, Benny, 2578

Sattelberger, Alfred P., 4544
Satter, Carolyn, 6245, 6248
Satterburg, Joanne, 830
Satterfield, April, 1007
Sattler, Suzanne, 3200
Satton, June, 1888
Satz, David, 2223
Satz, Linda, 840, 4288
Satzger, Bruce, 829
Sauer, Sharon, 2189
Sauer, Sheri, 1030
Sauers, Tim, 4563
Sauerwein, Jonathan, 1811
Sauerwein, Robin, 297, 7358
Saul, Maureen, 6894
Sauls, Miriam, 3652
Saunders, Anne, 4404
Saunders, Eleni, 5230
Saunders, Jeffrey N., 3270
Saunders, Jennifer, 1866
Saunders, John, 8561
Saunders, Keith, 411
Saunders, Kelly, 4193
Saunders, Melissa, 1740
Saunders, Nicholas, 440
Saunders, Robert, 810
Saunders, Ryan, 2326
Saunders, Sharon, 1165
Saunders, Steve, 4747
Saunders, Tom, 6392
Saunders Thompson, Denise, 6464, 6466, 6470
Sauro, Alice, 1229, 7283
Sausner, Karen, 5057
Sauter, Ava, 3889
Sautter, William R., 8157
Savage, Donna, 2721
Savage, Laura Q, 1097
Savage, Timothy, 1454
Savage, William U, 101
Savard, Suzette, 113
Savarise, Terry, 6758
Savathphoun, Friday, 2579
Savelson, Kenny, 5115
Savery, Matthew, 1836
Savia, Laura, 3184
Savidge, Dr. Dale, 5551
Savit, Michael, 8216
Savitch, Dorothy, 1383
Savitsky, Ava, 351
Savitz, Allison, 494
Savod, Bob, 7866
Savona, Tim, 6388
Savoy, Susan, 273
Savoye, Rojana, 6334
Sawada, M. Jeffrey, 6154, 6171, 6176
Sawka, Ilyana, 1969
Sawyer, John, 7956
Sawyer, Suzanne, 4143
Sawyers, Amy, 5259
Sax, Leslie M., 8295
Saxon, Ellen, 5002
Saxton, Susan, 733
Saya Henderson, Vicky, 3874
Sayer, Laurel, 6697
Saygers, David, 545
Saykaly, Ronald, 1128
Sayler, Diana, 4757
Sayles, Ed, 3410
Saylor, Brian, 2415
Sayre, Mary E., 4971
Sayre, Matty, 2291
Sayyad, Banafsheh, 110
Sbrega, John J, 7233
Sbrogna, Kristen, 6069
Scaduto, LeeAnn, 3500
Scaglione, Case, 764
Scaglione, Louis, 1644, 1649
Scaife, Georgia, 628
Scala Wilson, Nancy, 3649
Scalamoni, Sam, 3364
Scales, Briana, 983
Scales, David, 3901
Scales, Robert, 6154, 6171, 6176
Scallen, Thomas K, 3223
Scallet, Rebekah, 2433
Scally, Ken, 4805
Scandiuzzi, Gian-Carlo, 4078
Scanlon, Hugn, 6482

Scanlon, Mike, 8095, 8102
Scannell, Cheryl, 658
Scannella, Susan, 153
Scaoom, James, 7441
Scarboro, Kim, 4462
Scarlata, Estela, 2495
Scarlata, Susan, 5884
Scarlato, Amy, 1069
Scarlett-Johnson, Rana, 1308
Scarpino, Dina, 4354
Scarpone, Theresa, 3376, 7571
Scarpulla, Paul, 152
Scarrow, Susan, 2355
Scartelli, Dr. Joe, 5751
Scartelli, Joe, 5751
Scarvie, Kerry, 4071
Scatterday, Mark David, 1459
Scavullo, Charles, 6634
Scerbo, Richard, 1160
Schaaf, Bud, 6866
Schaafs, Katharine, 3991, 5645
Schaake Jr, Fred, 7532
Schaal, Kaneza, 3594
Schadegg, Tom, 8046
Schaefer, Al, 1349
Schaefer, Alice, 3144
Schaefer, Carol D, 1422
Schaefer, Catherine, 8642
Schaefer, Diane, 1983, 1984
Schaefer, Donn, 1764
Schaefer, Gary, 3077
Schaefer, Gretchen, 4046
Schaefer, Helen, 4169
Schaefer, Kelly, 6953, 6954, 6955, 6956, 6957, 6958, 6959
Schaefer, Steve, 6652
Schaeffer, Astrida, 7529
Schaeffer, Debbie, 3381
Schaeffer, Eric, 4033
Schaeffer, Jim, 2222
Schaeffer, Nancy, 3945
Schaeffer, Scot, 6980, 6981, 6982, 6983
Schaetzle, Tricia, 2511
Schafer, Mary, 3206
Schafer, Mike, 5921, 5922
Schaffel, Nancy, 5223
Schaffer, Barbara, 2696, 4367
Schaffer, Candler, 1757
Schaffer, Jeremy, 7785
Schaffer, Karl, 107
Schaffer, Mita M., 6478
Schaffhausen, Dick, 6936
Schaffler, Charles D., 2332
Schaffner, Eleanor, 7885
Schaiper, Greg, 3706
Schall, Lawrence, 4506, 6624
Schaller, Douglas, 1653
Schallern, Sarah N, 1171, 1172
Schambelan, Ike, 3577
Schandler, Hymann, 1567
Schantz, Alison, 5704
Schantz, Ellen, 1083, 1084
Schantz, Lowell, 1351
Schantz, Marcella, 783
Schanwald, Steve, 6758
Schap, Julie, 5574
Schapiro PhD, Morton Owen, 7259
Schapp, Reggie, 723
Scharbauer III, Mr. Clarence, 8386
Schardt, Donna, 2357
Scharff, David, 4942
Scharfman, Daniel D., 2105
Scharine, Richard, 4277
Schario, Christopher, 3097
Scharr, George, 7234, 7255
Scharrer, Steve, 4134
Scharres, John, 6851
Scharres, John H, 2995
Schasch, Linda, 33
Schattschneider, Adam, 5294
Schattschneider, Dr. Adam J, 5294
Schatz, Leon, 4139
Schatzlein, Dale, 4872, 7358
Schaub, Owen, 6895
Schauman, Martha, 7893
Schaus, Susie, 3741
Schaut, Becky, 4626
Schay, Dan, 2425, 2541

Schechter, Dorothy Elliott, 4340
Scheckner, Lucia, 359
Scheele, Marian, 2389
Scheer, Greg, 317
Scheer, Tracey, 932
Scheffer, Brian, 3927
Schehr, Kevin, 3310
Scheibe, Myron, 4587
Scheible, William, 1338
Scheidegger, Mary, 7688
Scheidemantle, David, 1885
Scheidemantle, Lori, 574
Scheider, Eric, 1496
Scheidt, Kerry, 7743
Schein, David, 5094
Scheiner, Alec, 7960
Scheirle, Alexander, 904, 4365
Schelhammer, Robert, 2820
Schelkopf, Mary M, 4941
Schelkopf, Mary M., 4941
Schell, Steve, 4451
Schemmel, Shane, 4657, 4658, 4659, 4660, 4661
Schempf, Kevin, 1522
Schenck, Stephen, 983
Schendel, Kaye, 5866
Schenkel, Sharon, 1616
Schenkman, Bryon, 1803
Schenkman, Byron, 1798
Schenly, Paul, 5070
Schepers, Donna, 4624
Scherer, Anne, 6506
Schert, John Michael, 197
Schertz, Jessamyn, 743
Schertz, Josh, 8261
Schesiuk, Volodymyr, 1246
Scheuerman, Debra, 1877
Scheuermann, Chris, 8673
Scheuermann, Robby, 8271
Schezer, Sarah, 4087
Schick, Steven, 797
Schief, Margaret, 5366
Schiefelbein, Scott, 3791, 8106
Schioffer, Kevin V., 8249
Schields, Jacque, 4671
Schieman, Sue, 1543
Schienbein, Ryun, 1437
Schiff, Edward L., 1439
Schiff, Gunther, 764
Schiff, Lisa, 7729
Schiff Soros, Melissa, 7743
Schiffer, Mark, 4606
Schiffman, Lance, 649
Schilansky, Jennifer, 3444
Schilb, Brian, 3007
Schilke, Melissa Z, 2691
Schiller, Rick, 3929
Schillhammer, David, 984
Schilling, Blake, 7951
Schilling, Darren, 4228
Schilling, Jim, 2718
Schilling, Mike, 7147
Schindeler, Robert Eugene, 4699
Schindler, Aldo, 2642
Schindler, Sarah, 471
Schinhofen, Lisa, 4728
Schirato, Caroline, 4201
Schirato, Patrick, 4242
Schireson, Clifford, 796, 4233
Schirle, Joan, 2452
Schirm, Ted, 2780
Schirmer, Marcia, 897, 4353
Schisgall Currier, Lesley, 2608
Schisler, Erica, 6758
Schkeeper, Amanda, 5475
Schlabach, Teresa, 5933
Schlachter, Rosemary, 1527
Schlaker, Tom, 7458
Schlegel, Jane, 3013
Schlegel, Tim, 6840
Schleicher, Marissa, 895
Schleifer, Mike, 3129
Schlenker, John, 2536
Schleuning, Maria, 1718
Schloner, Karl, 7353, 7354
Schlosberg, Dr. Ted, 1351
Schlosberg, Dr. Theodore K., 1351
Schlosser, Leo, 8007

1217

Executive Name Index

Schlossman, Paul, 1664
Schlouch, Sam, 2059
Schlough, Bill, 6251, 6271
Schmad, Tim, 317, 3333
Schmalzel, Jerusha, 747
Schmelzer, Roger, 3011
Schmerge, Stephen, 1837
Schmertz, Amelia, 5485
Schmidt, Bernard, 407, 465, 490
Schmidt, Bill, 2561, 6348
Schmidt, Casey, 5251
Schmidt, Catherine, 1516
Schmidt, Cathy, 1263
Schmidt, Christiane, 5479
Schmidt, Danielle, 23
Schmidt, Joan, 1298
Schmidt, Jody, 1587
Schmidt, Lawrence, 4989
Schmidt, Lois, 2195
Schmidt, Maggie, 3841
Schmidt, Marlene, 2677
Schmidt, Mary, 2393
Schmidt, Meagan, 2010
Schmidt, Stephen, 34
Schmidt, Steven J, 4880
Schmidt, Terry, 3321
Schmidt, Todd, 3373, 4111
Schmidt-Nowara, Betsy Ebert, 5026
Schmidtling, Dr. Ron, 1273
Schmitt, Connie, 7040
Schmitz, Bill, 524
Schmitz, David, 5600
Schmitz, David M., 2952
Schmitz, Linda Marty, 5848
Schmocker, Kelly, 6227
Schmotter, James, 6397
Schmoyer, Dara, 576
Schmuck, Tobin, 2217
Schmutte, Lara, 3014
Schnabel, Tom, 4227
Schnack, Paul, 6972
Schnake, Allison, 8206
Schnake, Ken, 5327
Schnall, Rose, 3836
Schnede Grusecki, Brenda, 2945
Schneider, Aleena, 4075
Schneider, Bekki Jo, 3004
Schneider, Bret, 3341
Schneider, Charles, 1449
Schneider, David, 3995, 4125
Schneider, Jack, 1929
Schneider, John, 4130
Schneider, Laura, 1281
Schneider, Lynna, 552
Schneider, Maria, 4854
Schneider, Mark, 2040
Schneider, Michael P., 7052
Schneider, Mike, 6903
Schneider, Nancy, 882
Schneider, Paul, 720, 5939
Schneider, Pauline, 2747
Schneider, Peggy, 1031
Schneider, Scott, 2204, 6430
Schnell, Elizabeth, 2054
Schnell, Will, 6210
Schneps, Joshua, 7644
Schnippert, Cheryl, 8168
Schnobrick, Eric, 2209
Schnuck, Connie, 310
Schnur, Alan, 4204
Schnur, Joel, 2974
Schnur, Wendy W., 4399
Schoeder, Collen, 1314
Schoeffler-Warren, Diane, 531
Schoelwer, Edward, 5146
Schoemaker, Tiffany, 869
Schoemehl, Jr, Vincent, 7450
Schoen, Susan, 6997, 6998, 6999
Schoenecker, Jeannine, 8117
Schoenhals, Rick, 6351
Schoenike, Scott, 6869
Schoening, Amy, 71
Schoening, Donald, 6011
Schoepf, Susie, 5642
Schofield, Patricia, 1751
Schofield, Scott, 2417
Schoh, Eric, 7504
Scholl, Elizabeth, 2775

Scholl, Greg, 1421
Scholl, Sarah, 3835
Schollars, David, 1510
Scholtemeyer, Tracey J, 4281
Scholten, Lisa, 8241
Scholze, Elizabeth, 2705
Schonberg, William, 7947
Schondel, Chris, 5015
Schoonmaker, Nancy, 6909, 6910, 6911
Schoonover, Shaun, 6817
Schork, Peter F., 4770
Schorle, Robbie, 2138
Schott, Randy, 2411
Schotten, Yizhak, 918
Schotz, Laurie, 3019
Schrade, Randolph RA, 5160
Schrade, Robert W, 5160
Schrade, Rolande Y, 5160
Schrade, Rorianne C, 5160
Schrade-James, Robelyn, 5160
Schrader, Ed, 6648, 6649
Schrader, Linda, 6557
Schrader, Mary, 8315
Schrader, Stefani, 4676, 7049, 7050, 7051
Schraff, Paul, 2885
Schrag, Michael, 2596
Schrager, Dan, 1193
Schrager, Seth, 6605, 6606
Schram, Andrew, 1969
Schramm, Lynn, 6131
Schrank, Barbara, 2396
Schray, Alison Y, 5339
Schreck, Matthew, 1966
Schreiber, John, 7574
Schrey, Liz, 4211
Schrickel, William, 1264
Schrift, Rachel, 6603
Schrodi, David, 7993
Schroedeer, Thomas, 3298
Schroeder, Bil, 2461, 3429
Schroeder, Bill, 6091
Schroeder, Charlotte, 8824
Schroeder, Jolie, 6585
Schroeder, Keith, 7040
Schroeder, Scott, 6203
Schroeder, Steve, 8679
Schroeder, Sue, 185
Schroeder, Tim, 6262
Schroeder, Todd, 3264
Schroer, Dee, 743
Schroeter, Rudolf, 4212
Schroeter, Steve, 1906
Schrum, Jake, 5630, 5733
Schubert, Barbara, 1043, 1049
Schubert, Leo, 4646
Schubert, Linda, 1835
Schubert, Michelle, 4928
Schubert, Warren, 252, 1151, 2090, 4746
Schubert, OSFS, Gerard J, 5437
Schuerholz, John, 6630
Schuessler, Nina, 3182
Schuette, Lynn, 70
Schuh, Ms. Patti, 4184
Schuldmann, Sanda, 741
Schuldt, Laura, 1782
Schuler, Roche, 2933
Schuler, Wendy, 8685
Schuler Hint, Kristin, 1907
Schuller, Gunther, 5806
Schultes, Dana, 3967, 3968, 3975
Schultheis, Lisa, 5007
Schultz, Amy, 2945
Schultz, Bernard, 8651
Schultz, Brian T., 3883
Schultz, Caron, 1297
Schultz, Dr. Pamela, 979
Schultz, Elliot, 2281
Schultz, J Bernard, 8643, 8646, 8647, 8649
Schultz, Jeanne, 301
Schultz, Jill, 1572
Schultz, John, 3519
Schultz, Katherine, 1607
Schultz, Kimberley, 1948, 1949
Schultz, Laura, 6317
Schultz, Michele, 6486
Schultz, Rita, 301
Schultz, Ryan, 7301
Schultz, Shaun, 5966

Schultz, Todd, 1909
Schultz Kilduff, Pat, 6256
Schultz-Ithier, Joanne, 6874
Schulz, Joshua, 6300
Schulz, Steven, 7012
Schulz, Tom, 7471
Schulz, Wesley, 4060
Schulze, Elizabeth, 726, 1167
Schulzetenberg, Jane, 1269
Schumacher, Bruce, 6903
Schumacher, Dr. Guy, 6796
Schumacher, Max B, 6903
Schumacher, Paul, 3274
Schumaker, Adam, 4854
Schuman, Daniel, 142
Schuman Silver, Jo, 2592
Schumann, Dr. Michelle, 1701
Schumann, Laura E, 1561
Schumann, Michelle, 5588
Schupiro, Morton, 4813
Schurulst, Carolyn, 1858
Schuster, Karen, 4360
Schutt, Stephen D, 6795
Schutts, Patricia H., 8382
Schuyler, Lynden, 1053
Schwab, Chris, 7373
Schwab, Fred, 3397, 3398
Schwab, Philip R., 4585
Schwabe, Sara, 3220
Schwait, Julie A., 4755
Schwalb, Joel, 6575
Schwallie, Ruth, 1527
Schwartz, Bernard, 1447
Schwartz, Beth, 2758
Schwartz, Bob, 8162
Schwartz, Daniel, 8201
Schwartz, Donald, 4472
Schwartz, Ethan, 8822
Schwartz, Frederic W, 4559
Schwartz, Gerard, 2035
Schwartz, Jennifer, 4309
Schwartz, Joel, 3378
Schwartz, Joshua, 5433
Schwartz, Lauren, 126
Schwartz, Lilly, 855
Schwartz, Margie, 1736
Schwartz, Melissa, 5984
Schwartz, Roger, 4251
Schwartz, Susan, 1493, 7653
Schwartz, Susan M, 1532
Schwartz, Tiffany, 4155
Schwartz, William, 5366
Schwartz Geller, Sara, 2596
Schwartzberg, Harvey, 1137
Schwartz, Scott, 3615
Schwarz, Eric, 4776
Schwarz, Gerard, 5244
Schwarz, Mary, 5332
Schwarz, Mary, 5207
Schweitzer, Catherine, 7653
Schweitzer, Catherine F., 2207
Schweizer, Mark, 2161
Schweizer II, Al, 2373
Schwem, Marti, 5844
Schwendimann, Chau, 794
Schwenk-Berman, Laura, 285
Schwent, Michael, 2482
Schweppe, Bebe, 347
Schweppe, Mark, 8152
Schwerin, Michael, 5616
Schwerin, Tami, 1263
Schwizer, Paul, 5214
Sciame-Giesecke, Susan, 6906
Scianna, Dominic, 7690
Sciannameo, Lousie, 1656
Sciarratta, Patrick, 3475
Sciarrio, Jamie, 4092
Scilla, Anthony, 6424
Scinto, Christopher, 5972
Sciola, Michael, 2691
Scippione, Don, 2280
Sciro, Cherrie, 4720
Scisio, Brain, 8052
Scmitz, Chris, 3035
Scobee, Tim, 6512
Scobey, David, 5578
Scofield, Elizabeth, 8116
Scoggins, Diana, 1254

Scoggins, Gene, 1758
Scolamiero, Michael, 577
Scollon, Alex, 2848, 6319
Scotland, Jeffrey, 1858
Scott, Allan R, 1622
Scott, Allan R., 1299
Scott, Ben, 6502
Scott, Bert, 2811
Scott, Camille, 640
Scott, Cliff, 3486
Scott, Debbie, 661
Scott, Dennis, 7298
Scott, Douglas, 182
Scott, Edd, 5421
Scott, Eric, 7871
Scott, Gwen, 8477, 8478, 8480, 8481
Scott, James, 1713
Scott, Jamie, 1624
Scott, Jennifer, 596, 1679, 3869, 5534
Scott, Jerome T., 5242
Scott, Joe, 2383
Scott, John E, 5394, 8053, 8054, 8055, 8056
Scott, John T., 3082
Scott, Jon, 6742
Scott, Joya, 5985, 5987, 5989
Scott, Kathleen, 351, 2140
Scott, Kay, 3352
Scott, L Brett, 2207
Scott, Linda, 6386
Scott, Lois, 1326, 8787
Scott, Megan, 6786
Scott, Melissa, 1528, 1529
Scott, Phillips M, 2400
Scott, R Joseph, 1792
Scott, Ray, 4625
Scott, Rebecca L, 3285
Scott, Richard, 1306
Scott, Robert, 1708
Scott, Ryan, 1579
Scott, Sean Vaughn, 2450
Scott, Stefanie, 3485
Scott, Steve, 2933, 4289, 7056, 7059
Scott, Stuart, 7661
Scott, Susan, 1931
Scott, Tara, 1678
Scott, Thomas, 428
Scott, Tianna, 8525
Scott, Tracey, 5975
Scott, Troy, 6465
Scott Hobbs, Patricia, 3830
Scott-Wiley, Dewey, 3874
Scotto, Lisa.M, 387
Scoville, Mary Lee, 5416
Scowden, Bonnie, 754
Scribner, Norman, 1983, 1984
Scribner, William, 1368
Scrivens, Connie O, 8220
Scrofani, Aldo, 3523
Scrofani, Robert, 1972
Scroggs, William, 7866
Scruggs, Richard, 5568
Scruggs, Tammy S, 5730
Scudder, June, 3909
Scudese, Joseph, 3582
Scully, Rebecca, 1918, 1919
Sculz, Kathleen, 2893
Scutero, Kim, 8288
Swartz, Ellen, 6149
Seacord, Alana, 2033
Seacoumb, John, 2667
Seal, Eric, 3064
Seale, Kitty, 5
Seale,, Tricia, 2829
Seals, James, 180
Seaman, Jennifer, 854
Seaman, Jerry, 5837
Seaman, Mark, 5593
Seamans, Caroline, 2090
Seamons, Darla, 2362
Seamster, Jennifer, 1782
Searcy, Joe, 7105, 7106
Searfoorce, Geeda, 1768, 5705
Searles, Joann, 1390
Sears, Anne, 2188
Seaton, David D, 4961
Seaver, Richard, 4343
Seawell, Angela, 1495

Executive Name Index

Seawell, Donald R., 6360, 6367, 6368, 6369, 6370
Sebastian, Jim, 518
Sebeika, Jeff, 1080
Sebena, Jane, 2421
Sebens, Mark, 2421
Sebens, Tod, 2421
Seber, Jason, 1132
Secomb, Tim, 743
Secoy, Reid, 7943
Secretary, Cogan, 7671
Secretary, Gray, 8588
Secretary, Kathryn B., 7195
Secrist, Alice, 2487
Sedek, Martin, 2195
Sedgeman, Willian J., 4482
Sedgwick, Dan, 7810
Sedlachek, Buffy, 3231
Sedley, Aimee, 4789
Seebacher, Robert J., 1692
Seebacher, Robert. J., 714
Seeback, John, 217
Seeber, Elaine, 8470
Seeberg, Mary, 4110
Seeberg, Tim, 6028
Seefeld, Donna, 4945
Seefeldt, Chris, 5871
Seeger, Matthew W., 7291
Seely, Chad, 6972
Seeman, Bob, 2129
Seery, Florie, 3517, 7754
Seese, Robert, 5513
Seevak, Elinor A, 3461
Sefton, David, 6169, 6174
Segal, David F., 1476, 5217
Segall, Aviva, 1308
Segall, Cissy, 3990
Segall Davis, Cissy, 8413
Segalla, Greg, 6039
Segan, Marc, 3535, 3607
Segel, Kenneth T., 5497
Seger, Christine, 3186
Seger, Dan, 897, 4353, 4359
Segundo, Shakira, 149
Segura, Justin, 8445
Seibel, Brian, 7653
Seiber, Heather, 8273
Seibert, Peter, 1798, 5793
Seidel, Kathryn, 2810
Seiden, Michael, 6004
Seiden, Sharon, 3396
Seidenfeld, Miriam, 4412
Seifert, Stephen, 6359
Seifert, Stephen W, 6364
seigel, Adam, 3588
Seigel, Daniel, 1840
Seigle, Jennifer, 4095
Seigle, Joe, 211
Seiler, Patsy, 5277
Seiler, Thomas, 1243, 4853
Seilheimer, Donna, 917
Seim, Ruth, 1111
Seinturier, Pam, 6224
Seiter, Susan, 2348
Seither, Beth, 540
Seitz, Beverly, 2261
Seitz, Robert, 7063
Seitz, Jr., James R., 2200
Sekhran, Ajay, 7360
Selak, Joy H., 3935
Selby, Denise, 3211
Selby, Margaret, 7, 134
Selby, Sally, 3292
Self, Bette, 5256
Self, Reid, 3942
Self, Sandra, 1009
Self, Sharee, 5907, 5909, 5911
Seliger PhD, Bryce, 8076, 8078
Selinger, Mark, 368
Selinske, Robert, 1915
Selissen, Aaron, 433
Selker, Kathy, 515
Seller, John, 7009, 7010
Sellers, Laura, 7879
Sellers, Linda, 1815
Sellers, M. Edward, 1679, 3869, 5534
Sellers, M.Edward, 596
Sellers, Marc, 154

Sellers, Nancy, 811, 4256
Sells, Brian, 7956
Selmon, Joe, 2741
Selover, Jon, 2558
Seltzer, Bow, 1598, 3780, 5414
Seltzer, Nicole, 8282
Seltzer, Norm, 3131
Selvey, Alta, 5392
Selvey, Jeremiah, 2051
Semel, Alan, 7947
Semel, Eric, 3444
Semel, Terry, 6166
Semmes, Mr. Thomas R., 8454
Semmler, Shelley S., 3446
Sena, Jacob, 5027
Sena, Jim, 1948, 1949
Sene, Daniel, 1135
Seneca, Matthew, 2313
Senediak, Mary Ann, 2291
Seneviratne, Jit, 428
Senft, Deborah, 1448
Senften, Penny, 7048
Sengstacke, Diane, 1164
Sennett, Alana, 1205
Sensat, Roger, 7131, 7132, 7133
Sensi Sellner, Maria, 1513, 1514
Sentell, Julie, 3991, 5645
Seo, Veri, 2112
Separovich, David, 6230
Seppala, Joan K, 798
September, Al, 6441
Sepulveda, Ernesto, 1719
Sepulveda, Rachel, 1309, 1310
Sequeira, Susan, 4276
Sequeria, Susan, 6216
Serafica-Stermer, Maria, 36
Sergel, Madelyn, 2991
Serling, Sarah, 3353
Serluco, Michael, 3367
Serotsky, Shirley, 6478
Serpa, Valerie J, 4956
Serpanchy, Susan, 6260
Serpe, Michael, 5835
Serra, Luca, 6749
Serrand, Dominique, 3255
Serrano, Maryory, 1779
Serrell, Robert, 3470
Sessions, Ann, 4107
Setlow, Marcie, 4792
Settle, Samuel, 1817
Settles, Susan, 3377
Setzer, Doug, 7591
Setzer, Elizabeth, 1894
Setzer, Marc, 1484
Seurkamp, Dr James, 4753
Sever, Micki, 2598
Severance, Michael O., 7171
Severance, Scott H., 3346, 7538
Severtson, Paul, 864
Sevier-Monsey, Renee, 3305
Sevy, Bruce K, 2657
Seward, Jeff, 7469
Seward, Peter, 5216
Seward, Philip, 1039
Sewell, Andrew, 1827
Sewell, James, 295
Sewell, Michael J, 515
Sewell, Ronald F, 1078
Sexson, Bud, 8030
Sexton, Elizabeth, 1252
Sexton, Eric L., 7070, 7071, 7072, 7073
Sexton, Sarah, 3121
Seyer, Dave, 3732
Seymour, Anne, 6224
Seymour, Gayle, 6018, 6019, 6020
Seymour, Marie, 131, 132
Seymour, Stephanie, 4365
Seymour, Tara, 333
Seymour, Jr., Thom, 3877
Sgarlat, Susan, 3904
Shackelford, Cynthia K, 5912, 5913, 5914
Shackelford, John, 2702
Shackelford, Lee, 3887
Shackell, Margaret, 3446
Shackell, Margaret, 7687
Shackford, Andrea, 4801
Shaddock, Pamela, 352
Shade, Alex, 3795, 8115

Shade, David, 1075, 1677
Shade, Wendy, 1273
Shadid, George, 3289
Shadid, Lisa, 3286
Shadier, Bob, 4099
Shadler, Sandy, 4099
Shadley, Sherry, 3689
Shaefer, Linda, 223, 311
Shafer, John J, 7108
Shafer, Judy, 1547
Shafer, Robert, 1992
Shaff, Richard, 6253, 6265
Shaffer, Greg, 6001
Shaffer, Kate, 8109
Shaffer, Katherine, 8109
Shaffer, Susan, 2742, 2752
Shaffer, Teren, 818
Shaffer, Vee, 4640, 6962
Shaffer, Travis, 6763
Shaffner, Anna, 343
Shafman, Arthur, 8815
Shah, Chirag, 2499
Shah, Jeffrey, 5188
Shah, Payal, 210
Shaheen, Gerald L, 6815, 6816
Shahijanian, Patrick, 789
Shaiman, Steven D, 5123
Shakarian, Roupen, 1793
Shakespeare, Marge, 1767
Shakespeare, William, 2369, 5704
Shakhman, Igor, 1811
Shalala, Donna E., 6493, 6494
Shalam, Jane, 1401
Shalett, Merit, 7513
Shallcross, Brian, 7202
Shaller, John, 4070
Shallue, Shana, 5827
Shalwitz, Howard, 2754
Shama, Debbie, 3747
Shames, Jeff, 7219
Shames, Jonathan, 1581
Shamos, Jeremy, 2656
Shampnois, Sarah, 3136
Shamsie, Mohamed, 7157
Shanahan, Alanna, 8161
Shanahan, Bill, 8216
Shand, Howard S., 1232, 1233
Shane, David, 3455
Shane, Lana, 3773
Shane, Rebecca, 4944
Shangkuan, Pearl, 1234
Shangrow, George, 2385
Shank, Carolyn, 5761
Shank, Cheryl, 225
Shank, Dr Jennifer, 4887, 7392
Shank, Ginny, 5943
Shankar, Rupal, 450
Shankles, Allen, 3925
Shanklin, Cathy, 5334
Shanley, Douglas, 989, 991, 992, 993, 994, 995, 4486
Shanley, Kelley, 6506
Shannon, Donna Sue, 3910
Shannon, Greg, 7261
Shannon, Hayley, 686
Shannon, Heather, 7462
Shannon, Jenny, 191
Shannon, Peter, 1691
Shannon, Rob, 3094
Shannon, Susan, 7474
Shannon-Auel, Erin, 3844
Shannoni, Jerome, 1841
Shantzek, Cece, 345
Shao, Hong, 4693, 4694
Shaomian, Dr. Armen, 4465
Shapiro, Aaron, 4771
Shapiro, Bonnie, 4789
Shapiro, Daavid, 1748
Shapiro, Jeffrey, 39
Shapiro, Madeline, 891
Shapiro, Mark, 2221, 2230
Shapiro, Marvin S., 1887
Shapiro, Matthew, 1592
Shapiro, Stanton J, 1015
Shapiro, Wendy, 143, 144
Shapiro PhD, Stephen R, 852
Shapovalov, Dimitri, 1825
Share, Alison, 50

Sharif, Hana, 7188
Sharkey, Jeffrey, 1157
Sharkey, Pat, 8558
Sharkova, Elena, 1891
Sharlow, Denise, 4967
Sharnoff, Mark, 4414
Sharon, Jenn, 3846
Sharp, Beth, 4915
Sharp, Beverly, 6030
Sharp, Brain P., 7991
Sharp, Dale, 2259
Sharp, Debbie, 3067
Sharp, Debra, 14, 6032, 6033
Sharp, Eric, 3248
Sharp, John, 4472
Sharp, Julia, 4994
Sharp, Kim T., 3460
Sharp, LeAnna, 1924
Sharp, Liz, 199, 205
Sharp, Pam, 5388
Sharp, Randy, 3469
Sharp, Tami, 4613
Sharp, Tom, 1054
Sharp Wooten, Harvey, 5250
Sharpan, Susan, 3095
Sharpe, Bruce, 5265
Sharpe, Kevin, 7785
Sharpe, Larry, 5778
Sharpe, Melissa, 7612
Sharpe, Michael, 3970
Sharpe, Nicole P, 7792
Sharpe, Ruth, 3829
Sharpe, Steven, 1931
Sharpstone, Lewis, 4282
Sharpton, Blake, 1012
Sharp, Judith, 65
Sharrett, Charles R, 8018
Sharror, Jack, 2573
Shartin, Anastasia, 8670
Sharum, Paula, 2436, 2437, 6029
Shastri, Laurel, 611
Shattuck, Mary Ann, 1952
Shauf, Karen, 1617
Shaver, Barrett, 4309, 4312
Shaver, Christie, 7502
Shaver, Deb, 7247
Shaver, Debrah, 257
Shaver, John, 3922
Shaver, Judson, 3583
Shaver PhD, Judson, 7758
Shavitz, Peter, 1422
Shaw, Andy, 3793
Shaw, Art, 2100
Shaw, Brian, 671
Shaw, Courtney, 5244
Shaw, David, 8661
Shaw, Deborah, 2575
Shaw, Erika, 602
Shaw, Gina, 773
Shaw, Jim, 8043
Shaw, John, 3098
Shaw, Kevin, 7438
Shaw, Nathaniel, 3350
Shaw, Stacy, 2657
Shaw, Teresa, 6087
Shaw, Terry, 8484
Shaw, Theron, 54
Shay, Christopher, 1971
Shay, Mike, 5879
Shay, Ora, 1701, 5588
Shaylor, Linda, 8205
Shdeed, William F, 8042, 8045
Shea, Bob, 4969
Shea, Ed, 3865, 4043
Shea, Joan, 7256
Shea, Kari, 1152
Shea, Maggie, 7653
Shea, Melinda, 824, 825
Shea, Patrick, 2707
Shea, Richard.P, 278
Shea, Veronica, 3562
Shead, Rhetta, 6349
Sheaffer, Charles, 1890
Sheaffer, Karen, 1626
Sheakley, Rhonda, 515
Shealy, Laura, 5535
Shean, Kay, 4011
Shearer, Charles, 7086, 7087

Executive Name Index

Sheehan, Dan, 7820
Sheehan, Jason, 3158
Sheehan, Jeffrey B., 1500
Sheehy, John, 3459
Sheen, Kay, 4010
Sheeran, Robert, 5307, 5308, 5310, 5311
Sheeran, Sarah, 1612
Sheets, Dr. Thomas, 1876
Sheets, Harriet, 3164
Sheets, Lanova, 5029
Sheffer,, Ann, 2720
Sheffield, Bill, 621
Sheffield, Edward, 166
Sheffield, Lin, 6655
Sheffield, Simone, 4265
Shehee, Virginia, 1144
Sheheen, Fred, 597
Sheila, Emery, 8590, 8591
Sheilds, Mary, 1258, 1259
Sheinen, Drew, 1630
Sheing, Tina M., 2725
Sheingild, David, 7724
Sheingold, Rick, 2912
Sheir, Rebecca, 3598
Shekhter, Jean, 4233
Shelburne, Michael M., 1999, 2000, 2001
Shelby, Bryan, 3211
Shelby Arditi, Robin, 3433, 5061
Sheldon, Bill, 4176
Sheldon, Edwin O., 1826
Sheldon, Gary, 5352
Sheldon, Ingrid, 4822
Sheldon, William C., 5868
Sheley, Christopher, 6340
Shelin, Ken, 2824
Sheline, Carl, 2087
Shell, Gary, 7919
Shelley, Melanie, 551
Shelley, Michael, 755
Shelley Evans, Muriel, 661
Shellhammer, Angela, 6325
Shelt, Christopher, 4888, 7395
Shelton, Chris, 4093
Shelton, John, 3336
Shelton, Kay, 6763
Shelton, Lara, 2437
Shelton, Leslie, 2296
Shelton, Lillian, 5279
Shelton, Linda, 7739
Shelton, Mike, 7472
Shelton, Norma, 6537
Shelton, Robert, 2431
Shelton, Russ, 515
Shelton, Sandy, 7885
Shelton, Scott, 1808, 1809
Shelton Tabor, Valerie, 627
Sheltra, Tabatha, 6130
Shelver, Bradley, 486
Shemper Schwartz, Rachel, 4889
Shen, Dr. Sin-yan, 1072, 1073
Shenton, Bill, 4525
Shepard, Bob, 7479
Shepard, David, 103
Shepard, Joan, 3558
Shepard, Noel C, 3719
Shepard, Lorrin, 6596
Sheperd, Sheri, 1876
Shephard, Eric, 3994
Shepherd, Craig, 8066
Shepherd, Louise, 2213
Shepherd, Tim, 5366, 5367
Sheppard, C A, 48, 49
Sheppard, Dawn, 3829
Sheppard, Leslie, 716
Sheppard, Stephanie, 2338
Sheppard, W. Anthony, 4813
Sheppard,, Gregory, 2244
Shepperd, Teresa, 2401
Shepsle, Seth, 3384
Sher, Daniel, 3473
Sheran, Nancy Idaka, 699
Sherber, Aaron, 2096
Sherck, Timothy, 211
Sherer, John W W, 4553
Sherer, Paul, 5439
Sherertz Morgan, Robin, 64
Shergy, Donna, 711
Sheridan, Connor, 4999

Sheridan, Daniel, 3032
Sheridan, Hans, 6873
Sheridan, Julia, 2300
Sheridan, Lindsay, 5362
Sheridan, Michael, 577
Sherman, Colleen, 1533
Sherman, Colleen G., 2280
Sherman, David, 2783
Sherman, Donna, 4756
Sherman, Geoffrey, 4148, 5915, 5916
Sherman, Howard, 4243
Sherman, Jack, 3405
Sherman, Joan, 7240
Sherman, Joanna, 3475
Sherman, Mark, 4085
Sherman, Rich, 4197, 4222
Sherman, Robert, 1408
Sherman, Sylvia, 6254
Sherman, Val, 3528
Sherman-Cisler, Patti, 5867
Shernan, Kim, 3616
Sherr, Elizabeth, 3454
Sherr, Rebecca, 4082
Sherr,, Elizabeth, 3454
Sherrell Norwood, Gigi, 1714
Sherrill, Robert A., 3511
Sherrill, Sarah, 5706
Sherry, Bree, 3160
Sherwood, David, 8220
Sherwood, John, 5325
Sherwood, John, 7986
Sherwood, Kimberley, 4364, 6340
Sherwood, Lisa, 1152
Sherwood, Virginia, 2762
Shetler, Stephen, 8511
Shetler, Terry, 1958
Shi, David E, 8226
Shields, Cathy, 4843, 4868
Shields, Dale, 179
Shields, Geoff, 3367
Shields, Lindsay, 6186
Shields, Margaret, 4716
Shields, Timothy, 3382
Shields, Todd, 6025
Shields, Tom, 1497
Shiffin, David, 2732
Shiffman, Carol, 5792
Shifrin, David, 1600, 5417
Shifs, Masha, 4321
Shilling, Kyna, 4079
Shilvock, Matthew, 1922, 1923
Shimada, Toshiyuki, 934, 935
Shimi, S T, 4001
Shimkin, Mary, 7787
Shimotakahara, David, 522
Shindelman, Damien, 729
Shindle, Elaine, 2124
Shine, Stephanie, 5802
Shine, Susan, 5096, 7694
Shineflug, Nana, 200
Shinn, Jeff, 2643, 6326
Shintani La, Miki, 386
Shioya, Yoko, 5141
Shiozaki, Keith, 40
Shipkowitz, Vicki, 6267
Shipley, Kent, 2066
Shipley, Rachel, 3032
Shipp, Bill, 253
Shipton, Robyn, 5952
Shiraishi, Iris, 3248
Shiraishi, Poppo, 475
Shirey, Don, 3755
Shirhall, Jean, 2372
Shirley, Harriet, 8295
Shirley, Pag, 6130
Shirvani, Hamid, 2635
Shishkov, Patricia, 6441
Shisko, Emily, 1916
Shively, Brian, 2849
Shkolnick, Lisa, 7497
Shmidt, Denis, 2631
Shmigelsky, Sara, 8072
Shockley, Edgar, 5476
Shockley, Theresa, 5476
Shoemake, Anna, 6623
Shoemaker, Dan, 3646
Shoemaker, Kris, 6569
Shoemaker, Michelle, 4810

Shofner, Carol, 5352
Shohet, Robert L, 4401
Sholar, Cathey, 2086
Sholeen, Jeffery, 446
Shollenberger, Marissa J., 569
Sholly, Kim, 5541
Sholze, Betsy, 6431
Shomaker, Diana, 5032
Shonnard, Parker, 7518
Shonrock, Michael, 7034
Shonrock, Michael, 7033
Shook, Forrest, 7873
Shook, Jeanne B., 3795
Shook, Jeanne B., 8115
Shook, Leslie, 6741
Shook, Scott, 8014
Shoor, Louis B., 6428
Shope, Katrina, 5507
Shoptaw, Carrie, 4905
Shor, Corinne, 2517
Shore, James, 2666
Shorenstein Hays, Carole, 6257, 6259, 6263
Shores, Gary, 1757
Shorrock, Thomas, 2756
Short, Carol, 5615
Short, Dave, 2071
Short, Donald J, 3134
Short, Jack, 6755
Short, Kari, 3991, 5645
Short, Patti, 779
Short, Rick A., 4921
Short, Steve, 4368
Short, Tracey, 5971
Shostak, Karen, 5559
Shostek, Tara, 4042
Shotwell, David, 7577
Shoults, Lenore, 6042
Shoup, John, 3001
Shoup, Robert, 2375
Shoven, Jimmy, 6289, 6290
Shows, John S, 4925
Shrader, Steven, 5585
Shreeve, Nathan, 7783
Shrieves, Natasha, 2619
Shrift, Rraymond G., 1632
Shrock, Darryl, 1171, 1172
Shrode, G. Karen, 4613
Shron, Director Studen, 8474
Shropshire, Robin, 7479
Shryock, Andrew, 2104
Shtein, Tanya, 3731
Shubic Weiner, Kelly, 253
Shuck, Kevin, 899
Shue, Abby, 7092, 7093, 7096
Shuff, Anne, 3834
Shukairy, Khaled, 7297
Shuler, Arlene, 7768
Shuler, Don, 1456
Shuler, Ellen M, 2397
Shuler, Jyl L., 4006
Shull, Stephen, 3939, 8336
Shullenberger, John, 4019
Shulman, Ivan, 804
Shuman, Allan, 6126
Shumate, Al, 4048
Shumate, Daren, 1782
Shumate, Megan, 1439
Shumway, Beth, 553
Shupping, Sallie, 7866
Shure, Jaime, 4089
Shurkin, Melissa, 363
Shurr, Buff, 5629
Shurs, Brad, 3144
Shuster, Dianna, 1915
Shutte, Rick, 1525
Shutte, Thomas, 7646
Shuttz, Brenda, 6908
Shwab, Robert M, 541
Shwartz, Benjamin, 857
Shymanovitz, Karl, 2345
Sias, Jeannette, 1583
Sibbring, Kevin, 1556, 5350
Sibert, Randy, 1629
Sibery, Paula, 4629
Sibilski, Nicole, 3917
Sibley, Roger, 3447
Sibley, Thomas E, 2269
Sibley, Jr., D. J., 1703

Sichak, Jr., Stephen, 1336, 1337
Sicilia, Domenick, 6451
Sicilian, Peter, 2202
Siciliano, Debbie, 4635
Sickle, Dolly R, 3677
Sickles, Mary Beth, 4103
Sidgreaves, Ivan, 1250
Sidlan, Murry, 5401
Sidoti, David, 4334
Sieber, Tara, 4362
Sieberling, David, 1480
Siebert, Cynthia, 1281
Siebert, Dr. Lynn L., 5001
Siebert, Lynne, 783
Siebert, Muriel, 3437
Siedenburg, Charlie, 3359
Siefkas, Linda J., 1547
Siegal, Adam, 3588
Siegal, Adam, 7746
Siegel, David, 6156
Siegel, Marc, 556
Siegel, Mark S, 6158
Siegroth, Debbie, 1517
Siek, Matt, 1929
Sielschott, Tim, 1557
Siemers, Jennifer, 6352, 6360, 6367, 6368, 6369, 6370
Siems, Eric, 6320
Siena, Jane, 1168
Siergiej, Berne, 3793
Sierichs, Lt Col Alan C, 951
Sieveking, Michael, 7464
Siff, Ira, 2232
Sigel, Jeanne, 6428
Sigel, Steve, 6428
Sigler, J. Michael, 2160
Sigler, Stephanie, 6619
Sigmon, Susan, 4511
Sigurdson, Patricia, 224
Siipola, Rosemary, 4073
Sikora, Robert, 1533
Silber, Jerry, 1509, 2274
Silber, Merry, 2002
Silbergleit, Nina, 7294
Silbert, Scott A., 1999, 2000, 2001
Siler, Daniel, 3761
Siler, Ken, 8018
Siliven, Tom, 6645
Silker, David, 7367, 7368
Sillery, Jan, 4337
Sills, Morgan, 3671
Sills, Sam, 369
Silow, Alan, 878, 4332
Silva, Chris, 1455, 7808
Silva, Fernando, 264
Silva, Gail, 2591
Silva, Heather, 4326
Silva, Hendryx, 436
Silva, Linda, 4176
Silva, Pedro, 3665, 5251
Silver, Dena, 5265
Silver, Jeff, 2851
Silver, Joseph H., 5918
Silver, Kevin, 5937
Silver, Nancy, 5242
Silver, Nate, 2936
Silver, Regina, 326
Silver, Steven, 2345
Silveria, Amy, 4069
Silverman, Bill, 3318
Silverman, Lizzie, 2566
Silverman, Matthew, 6589
Silverman, Mike, 7497
Silverman, Robert, 5408
Silverman, Ron, 8084
Silverman, Stephen, 70
Silvers, Laurie S., 6602
Silverthorn III, Rob, 4696
Silverton, Seth, 3106
Sim, Claudia, 905
Simanskey, Mara, 4856
Simcox, Damian, 7005
Simeone, George M, 1398
Simeone, Jeanne, 8025
Simerson, Brian, 133
Simkins, Paula, 7430
Simmet, Karla, 1353

Executive Name Index

Simmon, Ruth, 3861
Simmonds, Jr., Scafford, 5051
Simmons, Beverly, 1414
Simmons, Bill, 3012
Simmons, Carter, 1831
Simmons, Chip, 3980
Simmons, Dianne, 2120
Simmons, Doug, 8271
Simmons, Emily, 38
Simmons, Heather, 3926
Simmons, J. Brett, 6440
Simmons, Jay, 7000, 7001, 7002
Simmons, Joe, 2835
Simmons, Leslie, 2299
Simmons, Nina, 7873
Simmons, Peter, 4400, 4730, 4731, 4732, 4733
Simmons, Phil, 7509
Simmons, Robert, 3410
Simmons, Scott, 1264
Simmons, Shawn A., 6349
Simmons, Timothy Todd, 2084
Simmons, William, 1069
Simmons Jr, C W, 5383
Simms, Becca, 2897
Simms, III, J. Thomas, 2086
Simoens, Mary, 113
Simolij, Mariusz, 1635
Simon, Barbara, 8822
Simon, Benjamin, 760
Simon, Brad, 8822
Simon, Dale, 4991
Simon, David, 2513
Simon, Dennis, 1351
Simon, Eli, 2478
Simon, Eve, 4949
Simon, Fred, 4949
Simon, Herbert, 4619
Simon, John, 169
Simon, Lehua, 2892
Simon, Mary, 2971
Simon, Mary D., 3984
Simon, Melvin, 4619
Simon, Nancy, 8620
Simon, Pamela, 4527
Simon, William A., 5136
Simoncic, Tara, 925
Simonds, Joshua, 954
Simone, Denise, 2898
Simone, Elaine, 5476
Simone, Giovanni, 2181
Simone, John, 7831
Simone, Tex, 7831
Simonetti, Maria, 11
Simoniello, Patrick, 211
Simonis, Bert, 6303
Simons, Bardon, 1843
Simons, Diana, 3973
Simons, Diane, 8388
Simons, Jen, 1200
Simons, Johnny, 3973, 8388
Simons III, E Gray, 3176, 4806
Simonson, Lisa, 4078
Simotes, Tony, 3159, 8676
Simpkins, Al, 3829
Simpkins, John, 2704
Simpkins, Kya, 3829
Simpson, Bruce, 243
Simpson, Donna, 1690, 2369, 5704
Simpson, Doug, 1947
Simpson, Jane, 6655
Simpson, Jean, 4204
Simpson, Jeanmarie, 4959
Simpson, Jesse B., 1852
Simpson, Jim, 3471
Simpson, John, 2593
Simpson, Karen, 4393, 4394
Simpson, Larry, 1644
Simpson, Lawrence, 5321
Simpson, Michele, 904
Simpson, Mike, 7589
Simpson, Robert, 2352
Simpson, Stephen, 6384
Sims, Alan, 6038
Sims, David, 2704
Sims, John, 4533
Sims, Larry, 1011
Sin-yan, Shen, 1072
Sinaguglia, Gloria, 941

Sinatra, Kim, 7514
Sinclair, J. Walter, 4533
Sinclair, James, 933, 946
Sinclair, John V, 4496
Sinclair, Sean, 4743
Sinclaire, Murray, 5305
Sindelar, Gail, 915
Sines Mayer, Jerri, 7645, 7671
Singer, Amy, 3837
Singer, Debra, 7743
Singer, Isabelle G, 935
Singer, Ken, 557
Singer, Matt, 2600
Singer, Pam, 4335
Singer, Paulette, 2214, 2216
Singer, Richard, 6005, 6006, 6007, 6008
Singer, Sally, 5783
Singer, Valerie, 2600
Singer, Vicki Marie, 3402
Singer Kelley, Staci, 2954
Singh, Violet, 1743
Singleton, Doug, 507
Singleton, Gwendolyn, 6196
Singleton, Jacki, 2950
Singleton, Kathryne, 3384
Singleton, Mark, 4391
Singleton, Sean, 999
Siniard, Lydia, 303
Sink, Christopher, 4974
Sink, Mark, 2373
Sinniger, Elisabeth, 1398
Sinniger, Elisabeth, 6434, 6435
Sinquefield, Shane, 2
Sinser, Gene, 871
Sipe, Brian R., 8631
Sipe, Don, 1831
Siple, Julia, 2951
Siples, David, 3007
Sipusic, Grace, 7978
Siragusaal, Sheila, 2693
Siratt, Colby, 3969, 3970
Sircar, Mary, 4605
Sirio, Terry, 4703
Sirochman, Brandon, 5965
Siroka Hilton, Kat, 538
Sirotin, Peter, 1628, 5453
Sirovatka, Stephanie, 8671
Sischo, Brian, 3627
Sisemore, Tommy, 7153, 7155
Siska, John, 8043
Siskron, Elizabeth, 1144
Sisler, Ben, 6384
Sission, Rhaondas, 4603
Sisson, Benjamin, 83
Sisson, Karen, 6086, 6087
Sistek, Linda, 3221
Sites, Robert, 1783
Sitkin, Charles, 4078
Sitkovetsky, Dmitry, 1493
Sitt, Jerry, 7914
Sitton, Michael, 7807
Situ, Gang, 82, 97
Sitz, Michelle, 1599
Sitzer, Kathleen, 3282, 7452
Siuda, Aaron, 6088
Siuda, Chester, 7661
Sjamsu, Andi, 1340
Sjoerdsma, Dr. RD, 1824
Sjullie, Greg, 224
SKAGGS, DONA, 6389
Skaggs, Marissa, 1677
Skala, Gary, 2908
Skalicky, LaRana, 124
Skavronski, Robert, 5489
Skeeman, Sean, 8397
Skelton, Bevera, 6201
Skelton, Patrick, 6190
Skerrett, Dennis, 7126
Skewis-Arnett, Bette, 7019
Skey, Carol M, 965
Skiffington, Thomas, 5473
Skiles, Christa, 3704
Skiles, David, 8687
Skilton, W. Matthew, 1649
Skinascous, Plato, 249
Skinner, Anita Sims, 1557
Skinner, Beth, 3584
Skinner, Corby, 3313, 7468

Skinner, Cristina, 3274
Skinner, Darlene, 1480
Skinner, David, 7145, 7148
Skinner, Eric, 560
Skinner, Halcyon E, 972
Skinner, Judy, 153
Skinner, Melissa, 8536, 8537, 8540, 8541, 8543, 8544
Skinner, Terra, 225
Skinner SPHR, Ashley, 8302
Skip" Pennella
   Chair, Francis J., 1979
Skipper, Sharon, 5929, 5931
Skipper, Sharron, 5927
Skirvin, Don, 2383
Skj"ldebrand, Max, 1212
Sklarz, Andrew, 7593
Sklute, Adam, 651
Skolits, Adele, 4042
Skolnick, Frances, 2079
Skoney, Bob, 8300, 8455
Skore, Tom T, 5936
Skore, Tom T., 2418
Skorton, David, 7005
Skouras, George, 461
Skov, Kent, 2624
Skovholt, Katie, 2388
Skow, Marilyn R., 2797
Skrabalak, Duane, 2202
Skrebutenas, Barbara, 1725
Skrocki, Kait, 3818
Skundrich, Joseph, 5174
Skurdal, Clay, 2298
Slaby, Mary, 1683
Slack, Amy, 5189
Slack, Janet, 5377
Slack, Lueretha, 3950
Sladek, John, 4340
Sladic, Gary, 1165
Slager, W. Gregg, 3517
Slagle, Jill, 1625
Slagle, Richard J, 925
Slanigan, Cheri, 2529
Slater, Deana, 1087
Slater, Robert A, 5297
Slater, Robert W, 6343
Slater, Rpbert, 2651
Slater, Stewart, 6270
Slatkin, Leonard, 1229, 1292, 1657, 4425, 4426
Slaton, Gram, 1945, 6329
Slaton, Pam, 1011
Slattery, Kathy, 7533
Slaughter, Staci A, 6251
Slaughter, Thomas, 3038, 6600
Slaughter, Tim, 1022
Slaughter, Timothy, 4527
Slaughter, Tom, 6985
Slavin, Barbara, 6455
Slavin, Dan, 3443
Slavin, Dwayne, 837
Slavin, Richard, 2720
Slayden, Roxanne, 910
Slayton, Dr. Deborah, 6767, 6768
Slechta, Lisa, 1860
Slee, Paul A., 3490, 7727
Sleeman, Anita, 606, 610
Sleeper, Chuck, 7293
Sleeper, John, 1909
Sleeper, Mike, 4510
Sleeper, Susan, 3585
Sleight, Joan, 3959
Slein, Scott, 2036
Slemp, Jeff, 4662
Slimko, Gabe, 1249
Slipper, Sarah, 562
Slipski, Cheryl, 2314
Slivinski, Mark P., 745
Sloan, Amy, 7809
Sloan, Charles, 1400
Sloan, Chris, 999
Sloan, Jack, 4713
Sloan, Jeff, 6292
Sloan, Joan K., 8159
Sloan, Sandy, 6292
Sloan, Sarah, 3932
Sloan Jr, Robert B, 8469
Sloan, CFP, Jack, 2083
Sloane-Boekbinder, Karel, 4713

Slobodin, Karen, 1347
Slocomb, Teresa.N, 569
Slocum, Lauren, 228
Slocum, William, 1537
Sloin, Charlie, 3737
Sloman, Scott, 4460, 6543
Slonski, Michael, 1805
Slosarek, Kat Harrell, 7161
Slosberg, Michael, 3468
Slosky, Robert S., 6360, 6367, 6368, 6369, 6370
Slough, Mika, 5616
Slowik, Kenneth, 1392, 1564, 5360
Slozar, Richard, 3713
Slugg, Ramsay, 3969
Smaczny, Carrie A, 46
Smail, Ed, 4138
Small, Norman, 2839
Smalling, Curtis, 5225
Smallwood, Dale, 3545
Smallwood, Paul, 1819
Smallwood, Sarah, 5952
Smarelli, David, 1517
Smart, Roger, 2949
Smart, Scott, 5033
Smeester, Chuck, 3203
Smelser, Charlotte, 4889, 5671
Smeltzer, James, 1627, 1628
Smerud, Jennifer, 797
Smey, Melissa, 7740
Smice, Di, 6383
Smiglewski, Larry, 3441
Smiley, Sarah, 3645
Smillie, Cameron, 5079
Smith, Melissa, 2573
Smirnoff, Joel, 1532, 5314, 7961
Smith, Aaron, 1416, 2226, 3204, 5128
Smith, Aaron Nigel, 1881
Smith, Adam, 4376
Smith, Alan, 1352
Smith, Alayne D, 2162
Smith, Alfred J., 1700
Smith, Alicia, 292
Smith, Amanda, 658
Smith, Amy M., 1999, 2000, 2001
Smith, Andrew, 2573, 6441
Smith, Anelia, 7972, 7973, 7974
Smith, Angela, 1021
Smith, Anna McCoy, 5278
Smith, Annette, 2421, 5940
Smith, April, 4981, 8346
Smith, Arks, 1203
Smith, Arthur, 4613
Smith, Ashley, 1536, 6042
Smith, Barbara E., 519
Smith, Barbara E., 7968
Smith, Bea, 7412
Smith, Ben, 1700
Smith, Bev, 724
Smith, Billy, 5883
Smith, Brian, 7640
Smith, Bruce C., 4860
Smith, Cameron, 4800
Smith, Camilla, 4310
Smith, Carolyn, 2030
Smith, Chad, 792, 805
Smith, Charlotte, 1275, 1276
Smith, Cherlyn, 432
Smith, Christian, 2474
Smith, Christina, 4104, 8624
Smith, Christine, 1377, 3155, 7237
Smith, Christopher, 3527
Smith, Cindy, 5079, 7994
Smith, Clinton, 1269
Smith, Colleen, 165
Smith, Craig, 3176, 6193
Smith, Curtis, 846, 4305
Smith, Dale, 4088
Smith, Daley, 4064
Smith, Dalouge, 844
Smith, Darren, 2653
Smith, Daryl D., 1408
Smith, Dave, 3356
Smith, David, 243
Smith, David A., 1756
Smith, David R, 4518
Smith, Deborah, 6650
Smith, Debra, 8232
Smith, Del, 1307

Executive Name Index

Smith, DeLancey, 3301
Smith, Denise, 8121
Smith, Derrell, 6608
Smith, Desiree, 1232, 1233
Smith, Diana, 2515
Smith, Don, 8000
Smith, Donald, 5956
Smith, Donna E., 6346
Smith, Dorothy, 1802, 5058
Smith, Doug, 7316
Smith, Douglas H., 794
Smith, Dr Richard, 4662
Smith, Dr. David, 1811
Smith, Dr. J Arlen, 1484
Smith, Dr. John, 8041
Smith, Dr. Robert, 6444
Smith, Dr. Rodney D., 8525
Smith, Earl, 374
Smith, Earle, 4065
Smith, Edward, 3111
Smith, Edward, 7187
Smith, Elaine, 2484
Smith, Emily, 8459
Smith, Emily P., 1485
Smith, Ephraim P., 6317
Smith, Eric, 7840
Smith, Erin, 7447
Smith, Ernie, 844
Smith, Eve, 6050
Smith, F. Brian, 6796
Smith, Freda, 3641
Smith, Fritz, 6475
Smith, Gail, 4005, 4027
Smith, Gary, 5642
Smith, Gilbert, 6129
Smith, Gilbert A., 6129
Smith, Gordon, 2071
Smith, Grant, 4092
Smith, Gray, 3634
Smith, Greg, 1668
Smith, Gregg, 5199
Smith, Gregory, 63
Smith, Gregory A., 5856
Smith, Hal, 4292
Smith, Hannah, 3980
Smith, Harley, 2162
Smith, Henry, 484
Smith, Hyrum W., 8493
Smith, Ingrid, 1791
Smith, Jack, 6062
Smith, Jackie, 1906
Smith, Jacob, 1643, 1645, 5480
Smith, James, 3946, 8377
Smith, James D, 8049
Smith, James R, 1828
Smith, Jason, 6422
Smith, Jeff, 4687
Smith, Jeffrey, 3725
Smith, Jennifer, 372
Smith, Jenny, 1693
Smith, Jeremy, 3549
Smith, Jim, 2092, 4920
Smith, John Gettys, 5530
Smith, Joi, 1755
Smith, Joseph A, 471
Smith, Joseph B., 5493
Smith, Juanita, 6663
Smith, Judith, 51
Smith, Judith O, 5026
Smith, Justin, 2109
Smith, Karen, 1256
Smith, Karl, 1605, 8091
Smith, Kathryn, 2389, 2395
Smith, Kathy, 794
Smith, Kenyard, 2168
Smith, Kevin, 2722, 5847, 8293
Smith, Kevin W, 2292
Smith, Kimberley, 673
Smith, Kirsten, 312
Smith, Kitty, 3750
Smith, Kortney, 2392
Smith, Kristen, 333
Smith, Larry, 3103
Smith, Larry Alan, 2380
Smith, Laura, 4085, 6328
Smith, Laura E., 3864
Smith, Lavar, 6573
Smith, Lee, 1899

Smith, Leland, 5298
Smith, Linda, 239, 1064
Smith, Linda C, 653
Smith, Lisa, 4906
Smith, Liz, 278
Smith, Lois, 1832
Smith, Louise K., 1411
Smith, Lucy, 668
Smith, Lukas, 4930
Smith, Lyn, 7943
Smith, Lynda, 3741
Smith, Madeleine, 3933
Smith, Mandy R., 1485
Smith, Manuel, 8034
Smith, Marc, 3115
Smith, Marie, 5386
Smith, Marilyn, 5031
Smith, Marjorie, 3316
Smith, Mark A., 1689
Smith, Mark D, 6839
Smith, Mark D., 4600
Smith, Mary, 2603
Smith, Mary Ellen, 6941
Smith, Matthew, 934
Smith, Melanie, 1920, 1921, 4310
Smith, Michael, 1678, 1860, 1955, 4366, 5230
Smith, Michelle, 639
Smith, Molly, 2732, 2743
Smith, Nathan, 229
Smith, Nicholas R., 1983, 1984
Smith, Nicole M., 4870
Smith, Nikki, 689
Smith, Noelle, 2713
Smith, Orcenith, 1081, 1087
Smith, Owen M., 3408
Smith, Pamela, 653
Smith, Patricia, 2053
Smith, Paul, 1588, 1649
Smith, Peggy, 1509
Smith, Philip, 8152
Smith, Pix, 3946
Smith, Pompea, 2476
Smith, Rand, 1558
Smith, Randee, 3490, 7727
Smith, Rebecca, 1885
Smith, Reed, 2202
Smith, Richard, 4978, 5485
Smith, Rita, 1249
Smith, Rob, 201
Smith, Robert, 546
Smith, Robert E., 8108
Smith, Roger, 1878
Smith, Sandy, 2312
Smith, Sarah, 4182
Smith, Scott, 8242
Smith, Shannon, 4599
Smith, Sharon, 5286
Smith, Sheila A., 4584
Smith, Shelia, 1430
Smith, Shirley, 4889
Smith, Steph, 7619
Smith, Stephanie, 4539, 4907, 6266
Smith, Stephen, 4069
Smith, Steve, 2126
Smith, Steven, 1531, 2199, 3234, 6390
Smith, Stuart, 7815
Smith, Susan, 4567
Smith, Susan Sheridan, 5366, 5367
Smith, Susannah, 919
Smith, Suzanne, 1014
Smith, Tad, 6753
Smith, Tamara Lyn, 4414
Smith, Ted, 4611
Smith, Terry, 1453
Smith, Thomas R., 5511
Smith, Thomas S, 2072
Smith, Timothy, 6118
Smith, Tony, 4366
Smith, Tracy Ann, 4414
Smith, Trentonn, 2379
Smith, Tyler, 196, 4124
Smith, Tyson, 6488
Smith, Valerie, 2829
Smith, Valerie W., 2829
Smith, Vanita Rae, 2882
Smith, Warren, 384
Smith, William E, 3013
Smith, Wilma, 1599

Smith, Zeph, 1763
Smith Jr, AW, 4434
Smith Jr, J Kellum, 5198
Smith R.N., Sally, 4938
Smith Thomas, Margot, 764
Smith, III, George G., 2310
Smith, J.D., Angi, 6667, 6668
Smith, Ph.D., Bea, 3278
Smith-Porter, Phoebe, 1275, 1276
Smith-Stedman, LeAnne, 5666
Smitherman, Carla, 2292
Smitherman, Mike, 6555, 6556
Smithgall, Thurmond, 1407
Smithwick, Sheila, 5648
Smithyman, Megan, 6186
Smithyman, Paul, 3588
Smith, Virginia, 3327
Smogoleski, Sarah, 2396
Smoke, Charles, 1841
Smoke, Joe, 4236, 6168, 6172
Smolak, Jan, 3410
Smolarz, Karl, 7672
Smolen, Michael, 6949
Smoley, Sandra R, 836
Smolij, Mariusz, 1138
Smolnik, Carric, 1853
Smoot, Barry, 6358
Smoot, Dennis R, 4432
Smoot, PJ, 3908
Smorol, Jason, 7832
Smuda, Karen, 5834
Smuin, Michael, 315
Smyth, Carol, 1095
Smyth, Deborah, 2460
Smyth, Robert, 2460
Smyth, Tim, 1493
Smyth, W Robert, 2460
Snaith, Kellie, 7935
Snapp, David, 5230
Snarr, Joanne, 4339
Snarry, Kathleen, 2124
Snavely, Don, 4675, 7041
Snavely, Sharon, 1300
Snead, Charles, 4155, 5926, 5928
Snead, Jennifer, 4074
Snead, Peggy, 971
Snead, Skip, 716
Sneden, Curtis, 4682
Sneed, Diann, 4003
Sneed, Philip, 6327
Sneed, Philip Charles, 2529
Sneed, Terry, 3805
Snel, Sharon, 1795
Snell, Jill, 587
Snider, Diana, 2373
Snider, Eric, 7025
Snider, Steve, 1895
Snider, Tad, 5890
Snipes, Larry, 3066
Snodgrass, Jacob, 198, 200
Snodgrass, Jennifer, 1183
Snow, Gina, 2582
Snow, Gordon, 3189
Snow, James S., 707
Snow, Mark, 1779
Snow, Todd, 8201
Snowden, Michael, 7129, 7130
Snowdon, Chuck, 698
Snowdy, Sterling, 3088
Snukals, Beverly, 8270
Snuttjer, Jackie, 2952
Snyder, Aileen, 4004
Snyder, Barbara R., 1540
Snyder, Betty, 2320
Snyder, Cheryl, 5359
Snyder, Clarise, 4786
Snyder, David, 843, 6738, 8694, 8695
Snyder, Donald D, 7514
Snyder, Eve, 1488
Snyder, Gil, 1562
Snyder, Guy, 1601
Snyder, Janie, 231
Snyder, Jerry, 862
Snyder, Lee, 5294
Snyder, Lorrie P., 6181
Snyder, Matt, 4193
Snyder, Phil, 1820

Snyder, Rhett, 6334
Snyder, Robert, 2120, 4413
Snyder, Robert A, 6058, 6059, 6060, 6061
Snyder, Teri, 1813
Snyder, Tracy, 3428
Snyder Etters, Pamela J., 1617
Snyder Marr, Jill, 4089
Snyder-Logan, Bekah, 225
So, Clement, 1447
Sobat, Kim, 5267
Sobel, Edward, 3827
Sobel, Shepard, 3545
Sobera, Mary Jane, 1085
Soberg, Ryan, 5844
Sobey, Sarah, 6066, 6070, 6071, 6072
Sobieraj, Mike, 6408
Sobieska, Dorota, 2281
Sobieski, Jacek, 2281
Sobin, Carole, 403, 463
Sobrato, John Michael, 2602
Sockwell, Jamila, 3421
Sodd, Mary Jo, 7016, 7017
Sodeman, Kelby, 545
Soderberg, Steve, 953
Soderling, Dinah, 6039
Soderlund, Theron, 5776
Soderstrom, Erik, 4581
Sodomka, Dennis, 2026, 4510
Soell, Emily, 2704
Soencksen, Benjamin, 3483
Soffel, Andy, 3196
Soffer, Sheldon, 5172
Soffian, Robert, 6214
Soffin, Paulette, 2213
Sofley, John, 3678
Sofranko, Vicki, 4489
Sogge, Pamela, 4311
Sohl-Ellison, Linda, 35
Sohniki, Arnie, 7211
Soich, Sheri, 236
Sokoloff, Philip, 2517
Sokolow, Anna, 309
Solace, Caty, 197
Solano, Jaime, 2345
Solari, Sue, 1743
Soleau, William, 104
Solice, Mary, 2606
Solice, Rachel, 2429
Solidarios, Serni, 5811, 8619
Solin Lee, David, 2499
Solino, Paul, 6090
Solis, Felipa, 1720, 5619
Solis, Lisa, 8159
Solis, Mark, 8344
Soll, Amy, 305
Soll, Beverly, 5833
Sollecito, Victoria, 3364
Sollender, Joel, 844
Sollers, Kathie, 760
Solley, Ray, 6316
Solley EdD, Anna, 5977
Solma, Rev. Martin, 6676
Solomon, Cori, 4989, 7556
Solomon, Lori, 4467
Solomon, Magen, 1918
Solomon, Michael, 6173
Solomon, Tracy, 2
Solomon, Will, 5191
Solomonov, Sasha, 4012
Solounias, Jason, 1998
Soltow, Rosalind, 1563
Soltz, Christi, 6496
Solyan, Nancy, 6117
Somary, Johannes, 1962
Someone, Amanda, 2174
Somerfield, Mark, 104
Sommer, Bruce, 7458
Sommer, Don, 3244
Sommer, Katy, 4123
Sommers, Charlotte, 3120
Sommers, Mitchel, 3660
Song, Daniel, 1944, 6328
Song, Tom, 8389
Songer, Lewis, 1692
Sonnen, Daniel W., 5049, 5120
Sonnenberg, Nadja Salemo, 848
Sonnentag, Carolyn, 2803
Sonnet, Beth, 797

Executive Name Index

Sonzogi, Robby, 4116
Soolman, Harvey, 278
Soorian, Robert, 1186
Sope, Donald, 8917
Soper, George, 1096
Sopp, Nancy, 718
Sorani, Giorgio, 760
Soraparu, Peter, 3035
Sorensen, Andrew, 8207
Sorensen, Colleen, 4012
Sorensen, Don, 4012
Sorensen, Dunny, 1592
Sorensen, H C, 8486
Sorensen, Mardie, 5587
Sorensen, Margaret, 3618
Sorensen, Randall, 7154
Sorenson, Karen, 4283, 5130
Sorenson, Steven, 5837
Sorge, Robert, 1827
Soriano, Cecilia, 6236, 6237
Soroca, Barbara J, 940
Soroczynski, Anastasia, 478
Sorokin, Cheryl, 2573
Soros, Annaliese, 5172
Sorrell, Bruce, 1282, 1585
Sorrell, Jeannette, 1541
Sorrells, Michael, 4422
Sorrels, Diane, 5673
Sorrin, Ellen, 466
Sosa, Robyn, 6346
Soscia, Lois, 6511
Sosenko, Roma, 160
Sosinsky, E, 1342
Sosnowski, Mike, 1474
Soso, Melissa, 2531
Sossi, Ron, 2513
Sotelo, Rich, 6268
Soto, Merian, 355
Sotolongo, Joao, 6548
Sottile, Lauren, 4792
Sotzing, Andrea, 3840
Soucie, Laura, 912
Soukup, Gregory J, 803
Soule, Debra, 8721
Soulis, Tim, 7086, 7087
Sours, Abbey, 4119
Sousa, Tracy, 7522
Sousley, Mary, 1285
South, Dave, 8342
South, Myrna, 1026
Southall, Mark, 6022
Southard, AnneMarie, 1194
Southard, Scott, 1194
Southard-Dean, Kate, 1795
Southern, William A., 545
Southwell, Teresa B., 1732
Southworth III, Press, 1547
Souwapawong, Reka, 1426
Souza, Craig, 2593
Sowers, Richard, 1075, 1677
Sowinski, Richard, 1474
Spafford, Susan, 1394
Spahn, Jeff, 200
Spahr, John, 3751
Spain, Anthony, 1800
Spain, Bonnie, 2277
Spain, Bruce, 886, 6315
Spain, Grace, 1769
Spak, Allison, 3892
Spalding, Jennifer, 1560
Spallina, Joe, 2257
Spallone, Elaine, 1483
Spalter, Benjamin, 1647
Spangenberg, Gail, 467
Spangler, Brett, 1075, 1677
Spangler, Christopher, 5485
Spangler, James, 1232, 1233
Spanhauer, Charles, 5873
Spaniola, Joseph, 4475, 6580
Spann-Swallwood, Carolyn, 5017
Spano, Robert, 1005, 1006, 1007, 1445, 2018, 2021, 4503
Sparacino, Tamara, 3636
Sparger, Dr a Dennis, 2162
Sparger, Lori, 3028
Sparhawk, Don, 4538
Sparks, Barbara, 1208, 4800
Sparks, Becky, 5335, 7992

Sparks, Casey, 6577
Sparks, Cory, 333
Sparks, Deborah, 5776
Sparks, John, 2955
Sparks, Kevin, 4701
Sparks, Mary, 4514
Sparks, Susan, 579, 3842
Sparks-Petraits, Catherine, 225
Sparling, Vanessa, 3564
Sparrow, Erica, 5039
Sparrow, John, 2021
Sparso, Jacob, 552
Sparti, Dr. Patricia, 5222
Spaseff, Steve, 662
Spath-Mercado, Evelyn, 5017, 7588
Spatucci, Dan, 1646
Spatz, Jolie, 3286
Spatz-Omburn, Stephanie, 3287
Spatz-Omburn, Stephanie, 7424
Spaulding, Mike, 7836
Spaulding, Jr., Josiah A., 7222
Spaulding-Gaston, Aubra, 2430
Spear, Amanda, 4805, 7252
Spear, Rob, 6700
Spearhawk, Don, 6695
Spearing, Billie Jo, 868
Spearman, Delores, 6490
Spears, April, 1742
Spears, Trenton, 2713
Specht, Lisa, 4243, 6173
Spechts, Fran, 7171
Speck, Frederick C, 1132
Speck, Justin, 3885
Speck, Scott, 149, 199, 205, 714
Speckhart, Heidi, 4998
Specter, Evan, 2596
Specter, Joseph, 2336, 2339
Spector, Laraine, 2927
Speed, Greg, 4724
Speer, Sandy, 3068
Speert, Arnold, 5023
Speights, Dr Pam, 5679
Speirs, Jim, 2897
Speiss, Timothy P., 3460
Spejewski, Gene, 3921
Spelling, Karen, 3204
Spellins, Dan, 6149
Spellman, David, 6117
Spells, Doretha J., 8525
Spence, Chenault, 481
Spence, Darlene, 1756
Spence, Mike, 8373, 8378, 8379
Spence, Scott, 3739, 7997
Spence, Susan, 5805
Spence Coffey, Dr. Darla, 8188
Spencer, A. Clayton, 7169
Spencer, Cindy, 4040
Spencer, Dave, 1023
Spencer, Deirdre, 51
Spencer, Eric, 4066
Spencer, Jennifer, 2430
Spencer, John, 3280
Spencer, Jonathan, 6089
Spencer, Kay, 788
Spencer, Kerry, 3870
Spencer, Kevin, 4040
Spencer, Nancy, 829
Spencer, Rob, 2437, 6032
Spencer, Ron, 3015
Spencer, Sonya, 628
Spencer, Sue, 3855
Spencer, Tammy, 6027
Spendelow, Howard, 952
Spensieri, Kristine, 1437
Sperber, Jeffrey, 7625
Sperber, Michael A., 146
Sperber, Mikko, 2634
Sperling, Ted, 1393
Sperry, Christine, 5123
Sperry, Paula, 2667
Sperry, Sandra, 1465
Spetzler, Nancy, 1857
Spevak, Shron, 8473
Speyer, Sharon, 8012, 8013
Sphar, Kate, 2316
Spice, Graham, 1780
Spicer, Kit, 5773
Spicer, Michael, 3047

Spicer, Mike, 3047
Spicuzza, Lizzy, 96
Spidle, Gail, 3397, 3398
Spiegel, Noah E., 2333
Spiegler, Lorraine, 141
Spielberg, Genevieve, 8795
Spielberger, Christine, 1929
Spieler, Sandy, 3242
Spierman, Ben, 2204
Spierman, Michael, 2204
Spieth, Brendan, 470
Spieth, Cathy, 821
Spieth, Donald, 1636
Spikes, Pamela, 2450
Spiller, W. Terrance, 4317
Spillman, Robert, 4353
Spina, Joanie, 4040
Spindler, Jeremy, 1179
Spinella, Katie, 591
Spink, Katherine, 686
Spinner, Michael, 373
Spino, Laura, 1933
Spiotto, Bob, 5192
Spira, Robert, 3772
Spires, H Edward, 2719
Spisto, Louis G, 2565
Spitz Greenleaf, Andrea, 3131
Spitzer, Daniel, 6132
Spitzer, Kirsten, 4334
Spivack, Kacy, 1721
Spivey, Matthew, 2094
Splike, John F., 1681
Spoehr, Christy, 287, 1236
Spokes, Judy, 1372
Sponseller, Dianne, 6558
Spoone, Rochelle, 4374
Spooner, Brad, 6329
Spooner, Jenny, 292
Spooner, Rebecca, 2905
Spott, Patrick, 1258, 1259
Sprabery, Peggy, 4889
Spradley, Carol, 4374
Spradlin, Sarah, 48
Spraggins, Mark, 4340
Sprague, Carol, 8176
Sprague, Daryl, 452
Sprague, Jid, 3184
Sprague, Stephen, 2177
Spreen, Kristofer, 7967
Sprenger, Gordon M., 1265, 7359
Sprick, Andrea, 349
Spriggs, Elise, 8008
Spring, Rob, 3094
Springer, Craig, 6288
Springer, Mark, 1269
Springer, Marlene, 7825, 7826
Springer, Martha, 720, 5939
Springfield, Catherine, 5308
Springs, Alex, 418
Sprinkle, Jim, 6358
Sprinkle, Tony, 1489
Sprinkles, Kirk, 412
Spritzer, S.J., Fr. Robert J., 8612
Sprokkereef, Michelle, 6152
Sproul, Robert, 1629
Sproule, Ann, 1560
Spruell, Michelle, 2022
Spruiell, Marc, 4740
Spruill, Niki, 1341
Sprunger, Benjamin, 2903
Spurgeon, Thomas, 6949, 6950
Spurlock, Daniel, 2081
Spurlock, Lez, 4101
Spurlock, Liz, 4101
Spurrier, PhD, James J, 3026
Squillante, Michael, 5050
Squire, Ana W., 1864
Squire, Emma, 4101
Squire, Gilda, 411
Squires, Catherine, 1069
Squires, Diane, 1869
Squires, Joan, 7496, 7499
Squires, Kathleen, 5029
Squires, Stephen, 1046, 1064, 1069
Squires, Steven, 1042
Srb, Paula, 1306
Srb, Thomas, 1306
Srinivas, Bob, 820

Srirama, Malini, 664
Sroka, Elliott, 5084
Sroka, Elliott, 5084, 7678
Sroka, Linda, 7656
St Clair, Carl, 868
St Clair, James, 1818
St Clair, Neil, 3668
St John, Brian, 916
St John, Katherine, 652
St. Aubin, Jean de, 2932
St. Claire, Jason, 2603
St. Hilaire, Gary D., 8129
St. John, Anita, 5331
St. John, Katherine, 1759
St.Germain, Danielle, 3239
Staab, Jane, 3143
Staats, Marilyn J, 6189
Staats, Raymond W., 5900
Staats, Terri, 1852
Staber, Judy, 5204
Stacey, Sharone, 3454
Stack, Ken, 3100, 3101
Stackhouse, Holly, 1636
Stacy, Donald, 5858
Stacy, Kathleen, 4123
Stacy, Patti, 8617
Stadleman, Bob, 1126
Stadler, Jeffrey T., 3990
Stadsklev, Joan, 4463
Stadtner, Deborah, 4321
Stadulis PhD, Robert, 543
Staeter, Doug, 5257
Stafford, Feb, 6975
Stafford, Jan, 6974, 6975, 6979
Stafford, Leslie, 4303
Stafford, Lisa, 4707
Stafford, Thomas G, 5320
Stafford Wilson, Peter, 1545, 1546, 1568, 1572
Stafura, Paul G, 1660
Stagger, Paul, 3327
Staggs, Charlie, 6039
Stahara, Ron, 756
Staheli, Sara, 4016
Stahl, Charles, 8266
Stahl, Charlie, 8266
Stahl, Elisabeth R., 5317
Stahl, Murray, 1393
Stahler, Lisa A., 4089
Stahmer, Ann, 1992
Stahr, Jason, 7464
Staib, Rosalind, 6620, 6629
Staiger, Ron, 7932
Staiman Vosk, Cynthia, 5512
Stair, Mary, 3109
Staiv, Rosalind, 2864
Staley, Doug, 4089
Staley, Dr. Grant B, 5532
Staley, Jim S., 1440
Stalheim, Kevin, 1832
Stalkell, Joe, 3516
Stallings, Anna, 5255
Stallings, Lisa, 1723
Stallworth, Steve, 7513
Stalsberg, Michael, 5838
Stalvey, Dorrance, 4241, 4246
Stamatin, Andy, 6177
Stamberger, Jim, 4905
Stamer, Rick, 4168
Stamoulis, Lorraine, 2625
Stamper, Robin, 2007, 2171
Stampley, Travis, 8454
Stamps, David, 4967
Stanaland, Dr Eugene, 4148
Stanaland, Eugene, 5915, 5916
Stanberry, Marty, 3298
Stanbery, Paul, 2285
Stanco, Holly, 6310
Stander, Scott, 8749
Standish, Christine, 1361
Standish, Thomas K, 1964
Standring, Elaine, 841
Staneva, Natalia, 885
Stanford, Alan, 3844
Stanford, Gregory, 2098
Stanford, Janet, 3120
Stanford, Kim, 1431
Stangel, John, 2393
Stangel, Karen, 2393

1223

Executive Name Index / S

Stangleberger, George, 1855
Stanhope, Linnea, 1300
Stanier, Graham, 8185
Staniloff, Fran, 2181
Staniloff, Stan, 2181
Stanke, Ann, 2395
Stanke, CPA, William, 1796
Stanko, Holly, 4338
Stanko, Tracy, 3334
Stanley, Christine, 4033
Stanley, Dr. James, 2130
Stanley, J, 3856
Stanley, Jean, 5615
Stanley, Jonathan, 14
Stanley, Parker, 1121
Stanley, William, 1856
Stann, Jimmy, 4097
Stanner, Cathie, 6099
Stansbury, Beanie, 4704
Stansell, Fritz, 3217
Stanton, Alex, 4657, 4658, 4659, 4660, 4661
Stanton, Don, 2477
Stanton, Janet, 2044, 2045
Stanton, Jeffrey, 564
Stanton, Juile, 2953
Stanton, Oliver, 1447
Stanton, Todd, 8797
Stanwood, David, 1212
Stanworth, Libby, 269
Stanzione, Cecile, 2709
Stapin, Scott, 7530
Staples, Lisa, 6913, 6914
Staples, Marsha, 1784
Stapleton, Jennifer, 3718
Stapleton, Jennifer, 7980
Stapp, Taunya, 6219
Stapp, Trish, 8291
Stare, Ward, 1012
Starin, Donna, 7061
Stark, Barbara, 8249
Stark, Douglas, 3010
Stark, Edward J., 1773
Stark, Eric, 2066
Stark, Jim, 6883, 6884
Stark, Kathe, 5029
Stark, Ray, 1024
Stark, Richard, 3038, 6600
Stark, Roberta, 1834
Stark, Sharon, 3263
Stark,, Daniel, 3234
Starkey, Craig, 4250
Starkey, David Craig, 2260
Starkey, David, 6421
Starkey, J Shane, 5304
Starkins, Ashley, 936
Starkman, Stephen, 1457
Starks, Rosie, 6948, 6951
Starling, Kimberly, 3103
Starman, Kurt, 6213
Starnes, Rhonda, 152
Starnes, T.W., 6466, 6470
Starr, Edward C, 6189
Starr, Frederick B., 5244
Starr, John, 3473, 8820
Starr, Josephine, 4790
Starr, Kenn, 8469
Starr, Patrick, 4076, 8593
Starrett, Jon, 7971
Starrett, Mary, 5671, 8464
Starrett, William, 504, 597
Starrus, Melville, 3437
Startzman, Lorna, 6898
Stary, Shirley, 5350
Stash, Edward, 2312
Stasolla, Debbie, 2188
Staton, Chris, 7563
Staton, Dennis, 2275
Staton, Jennifer, 1781
Staton, Maurice, 1632
Statucka, Marta, 370
Staub, Bobby, 7134, 7135
Staub, Mary, 432
Staubitz, Linda, 1852, 1857
Staudenmaier, S.J,, John, 7290
Stauffer, George, 5002
Stauffer, Laura A., 4742
Stava, Keith, 4046
Stavnes, Diane, 7477, 7478

Stavrianidis, Peter, 5003
Stavropoulos, Franci, 5844
Stavropoulos, Ted, 6446
Stavrou, Gregory, 3264
Stawiasz, Suzanne, 938
Stayduhar, Marla N, 580
Stead, Meredith, 194
Steadham, Charles, 8753
Steakley, Dave, 3935
Steans, Jennifer W., 4581
Stearns, David, 2410
Stearns, Hartt, 8324
Stearns, Jill, 6188
Stearns, Nada, 8324
Stebbins, Carla, 2327
Stebbins, Carla M., 1974
Stebbins, Michael, 3122
Steck, Bob, 3824
Steck Worley, Cassie, 3083, 7141
Steckel-Monique, Marie, 5132
Stedsand, Lindsey, 4959
Steeber, Donald E., 670
Steedman, Chuck, 6408
Steel, Diane, 7045
Steel, George, 2238
Steel, James, 8670
Steele, Allie, 2727
Steele, Barry, 395
Steele, David, 8032
Steele, George, 747
Steele, Heather, 634
Steele, Hillary, 169
Steele, James, 2895
Steele, Jan, 5381
Steele, Jonathan E, 4490
Steele, Karen, 6889, 6893
Steele, Pamela, 4620, 4794
Steele, Thomas W., 2380, 5768, 5769
Steele, Toren, 180
Steelman, Christi, 4586
Steelman, Trent, 2453
Steen, David, 247
Steenland, Douglas M, 7351
Steenport, Dyan, 698
Steere, Rob, 3186
Stefanou, Maria, 1879
Steffan, Joanna, 8805
Steffee, John, 569
Steffee MD, William, 1519
Steffek Blaske, Mary, 1222
Steffen, Jim, 4163
Steffy, Don, 6898
Stefiuk, Mike, 1545, 1546
Stegeman, Charles, 885
Steger, Charles, 8513, 8514
Stegman, Laura, 2490
Stegmeir, Johann, 8553
Stehlik, Brent, 7960
Stehlik, Milos, 2926
Steichen, Gerald, 932, 939, 2367
Steigelman, Alan, 1062
Steigler, Lou R, 4799
Steigmeyer, C.J., 6876
Stein, Avi, 2211, 5136
Stein, Barbara S, 2764
Stein, Bonnie, 492
Stein, Dean, 4739, 4744
Stein, Dr. Harvey J., 1408
Stein, Emily, 214
Stein, Erik, 2617
Stein, Jane, 2189
Stein, Jane B., 1349
Stein, Joan, 3540
Stein, Lawrence, 2764
Stein, Lawrence E, 2764
Stein, Lester, 6183
Stein, Maggie, 1456
Stein, Mary, 3885
Stein, Richard, 2484
Stein, Rick, 5173
Stein, Robert, 6225
Stein, Thomas H., 5471
Stein Skafft, Thea, 4310
Steinacher, Robert M, 6214
Steinacker, Nancy, 2160
Steinberg, Andrews, 6625
Steinberg, Brenda, 4217
Steinberg, Jim, 7781

Steinberg, Joseph S., 5052
Steinberg, Lewis, 446
Steinberg, Richard, 831
Steinberg, Roy, 3361
Steinberg, Saundra, 3957
Steinberg, Virginia, 2257
Steinborn, P, 926
Steinbrecher, Marcia, 7635
Steinbrenner, Jan, 5204
Steinbrunner, John, 733, 4174
Steineker, Helen, 715
Steiner, Christian, 1404
Steiner, Don, 938
Steiner, Frances, 834
Steiner, Kristen, 760
Steiner, Paula, 1133
Steiner, Randall, 3009
Steiner, Steve, 3358
Steiner, William, 8142
Steinert, Richard, 166
Steinhauer, Debra, 1089
Steinhauser, Jan, 4284
Steinkamp, Lorraine, 2995
Steinke, Ramona, 1260
Steinman, CPA, Sara, 1609
Steinmetz, Arnie, 4468
Steinzor, Curt, 501
Steitler, Dr. Wallace, 8190
Steitz, Meg J., 1951
Stellmann, Dennis, 4926
Stelluto, George, 1061
Stelson, Audrey, 1697
Stelzer, Alexandrea, 5350
Stem, N David, 1816
Stembler-Smith, Anna, 5294
Stemen, Adrienne, 1533
Stemen, Cara, 4267, 6207
Stemerman, Jerald M, 7667
Stemmler, Brandy, 2895
Stemmler, Julie, 7359
Stenberg, Tricia, 1261
Stenborg, Tom, 1835
Stende, Dave, 3689
Stender, Ryan, 597
Stenftenagel, Erin, 4624
Stengel, Dianne, 1453
Stengel, Jack, 8241
Stengle, Diane, 246, 2199
Stenn, Rebecca, 477
Stenske, David, 876
Stensrud, William R, 1909
Stepanova, Liza, 4269
Stephan, Bill, 4945, 7491
Stephan, Catherine, 5716, 8507
Stephani, Bill, 6348
Stephen, Amy, 8538
Stephens, Alice, 1039
Stephens, Beth, 217
Stephens, Bonnie, 1971
Stephens, Darlene, 672
Stephens, Dennis, 719
Stephens, Doris, 5523
Stephens, Gary, 5960
Stephens, Grethen L, 5290
Stephens, Jason, 2396
Stephens, Jessica, 8077
Stephens, John, 2866, 2988
Stephens, Margie, 1583
Stephens, Mark R, 6823, 6824
Stephens, Sarah, 1371
Stephens, Steve, 719
Stephens, Thomas, 1345
Stephens, Thomas L., 1324
Stephens, Tim, 8335
Stephens, MA, Karen, 452
Stephenson, Arthur, 7178
Stephenson, Christopher, 8020
Stephenson, Father Alphonse, 1322
Stephenson, Monica, 3848
Stephenson, Robert, 6097
Stepner, Daniel, 922, 4383, 4791
Stepowany, Michael C., 6464, 6466, 6470
Stepowany, Michael, 6466, 6470
Stepper, Marka G., 5485
Steptoe, Eugene, 6252
Sterenfeld, MD, Elliot, 3811
Sterenfeld, MD, Elliot B., 2303
Stern, Adam, 1795, 1804

Stern, Bob, 6219
Stern, Diane, 5689
Stern, Ed, 3704
Stern, Erik, 107
Stern, Jessica, 1254
Stern, Joe, 2492
Stern, John, 1267
Stern, Jolyon F., 2472
Stern, Karl S., 638
Stern, Liz, 4179
Stern, Marc I, 1887
Stern, Michael, 1283
Stern, Sarah, 3587
Stern, Stephen, 6478
Stern, Yonatan, 4665, 4666
Sternberg, Donna, 109
Sternberg, Stuart, 6589
Sterner, Scott, 2638
Sternfeld, Fred, 8003
Sterrett, Joe, 8114
Stessel, Larry, 8303, 8304
Stetson Rebollo, Amy, 4025, 4968
Stettler, Steve, 4026
Stettner, Enid, 5105
Stetzik, Pavana, 1545, 1546
Steurbaut, Margo, 6154, 6171, 6176
Steven, Norman, 4437
Steven Wiley, Jon, 3890
Stevens, Aaron, 1808, 1809
Stevens, Bill, 3270
Stevens, Byam, 3149
Stevens, Calvin, 62
Stevens, Cheryl, 659
Stevens, Christine, 1732
Stevens, Christopher D, 924
Stevens, Darryl, 1298
Stevens, Delores, 764, 1212
Stevens, Erik Joe, 6376
Stevens, Fern M, 2863
Stevens, Greg, 2859
Stevens, Jeanne, 6027
Stevens, Joanna, 3754
Stevens, John, 2077
Stevens, John H, 2863
Stevens, Jonn H, 2863
Stevens, Keith, 1777, 3351
Stevens, Laurel, 4220
Stevens, Les, 2603
Stevens, Libby, 8519
Stevens, Lisa, 5838
Stevens, Mark A., 2027
Stevens, Michael J, 8433
Stevens, Richard, 6607
Stevens, Rick, 4544
Stevens, Robbie, 6520
Stevens, Robert L, 958
Stevens, Robin Bender, 3833
Stevens, Roger L, 956
Stevens, Roger L, 4425
Stevens, Roger L., 1997
Stevens, Shannon, 2620
Stevens, Sue, 678
Stevens, Thomas, 3716
Stevenson, Gina, 6697
Stevenson, Hunter, 2454
Stevenson, Joseph, 5487
Stevenson, Mark, 5660
Stevenson, W Jerome, 3756
Stevenson, W. Jerome, 3757
Stevenson, O.B.E., Ben, 632, 638
Steward, Campbell, 2107
Steward, David, 1291, 1292, 4921
Steward, Harold, 8364
Stewart, Anita, 3105
Stewart, Ann, 1527
Stewart, Carol, 4666
Stewart, Carolee, 1157
Stewart, Carolyn, 6678
Stewart, Cathie, 3193
Stewart, Daniel, 2237
Stewart, David, 8676
Stewart, Dr. Rowena, 1652, 5484
Stewart, Duff M., 3929, 3933, 8325
Stewart, Ellen, 3510
Stewart, Gary, 5363
Stewart, Greg, 8622
Stewart, Jacques, 3355
Stewart, James, 8462

Executive Name Index / S

Stewart, Janet J., 5407
Stewart, John, 3061
Stewart, Jon, 7055
Stewart, Leslee, 6199
Stewart, Mary E, 4987
Stewart, Meisha, 6026
Stewart, Rev, 657
Stewart, Scott, 2398, 3085
Stewart, Shani, 4178
Stewart, Shannon, 6105
Stewart, Shelley, 1992
Stewart Kellogg, Cal, 727
Stewart Wiley, David, 1786
Stewart-Ackers, Elizabeth, 7150, 7151
Sthrner Traum, Lynda, 3524
Stich, Jennifer, 7655
Stichler, Ann, 6574
Sticka, Michael S., 3734
Stickel, Peter, 1213
Stickey, Terre, 7493
Stickler, Lee, 1942
Stickler, Robert L., 1485
Stickley, Susanna, 7678
Stickney, Allie, 4019
Stickney, Ann, 1798, 5793
Stickrod, Rodney, 6148
Stidfole, Arthur, 1653
Stidham, Lisa, 1885
Stidham, Troy, 3927, 8321
Stiegler, Harvey, 1718
Stiehl, Cynthia, 4110
Stiehm, Robin, 555
Stielstra, Darcy, 4162
Stieneker, Stephen, 6365
Stiffler, Karen, 2140
Stikeleather, Donald, 6335
Stiles, Diane, 3477
Stiles, Rodney, 7083
Stilings, Cynthia, 3738
Still, Chuck, 3038
Still, Pamela, 6149
Stilley, Randall D., 3990
Stillman, Bradley C., 7211
Stilson, Joyce, 3424
Stilson, Marni, 8052
Stilwell, Gill, 6374
Stilwell, Verna, 587
Stilwill, Charles, 3039, 7024
Stimac, Coral, 6521
Stimler, Nick, 6434, 6435
Stimpson, John, 2704
Stimson, Susan, 5100, 7700
StinchComb, Donna, 6389
Stinson, Donald, 43
Stinson, Martha, 6800
Stinson, William, 6887
Stinstone, Christine, 3662
Stirling Munro, Cristina, 626
Stirrett, Rebecca, 6465
Stites, Fred, 4237, 6175
Stith, Barbara, 6913, 6914
Stith, W Mead, 1783
Stitt, Charlie, 1620
Stitt, Katea, 4420
Stitt, Shonda, 4677, 7054
Stivers, Caroline, 4539
Stobbe, Karen, 4123
Stock, David J, 2598
Stock, Jacque, 7426
Stock, Rosen, 2282
Stockel, Allison, 6430
Stocker, Kate, 1372
Stockman, James, 8119
Stockmann, Colleen, 660
Stocks, Kevin, 1268
Stocks, Melanie, 7470, 7471
Stockton, David, 2816
Stockwell, Dan, 6057
Stoddard, Bill, 6155
Stoddard, R. Sanford, 6419
Stoddart, Amy Lynn, 312
Stoddart, Lynette, 7938
Stoecklein, Denny, 7040
Stoessinger, Caroline, 5084
Stoffel, Zabrina, 3366
Stokes, Dr. Kelly, 224
Stokes, Harry, 374
Stokes, Hary, 3423

Stokes, Karen, 542
Stokes Bott, Laurie, 1426
Stokes-Pena, Lynn, 104
Stolberg, Carolyn M, 1356
Stolfa, Jeremy, 8435, 8436, 8460
Stoll, Carl, 413
Stoll, Mike, 6328
Stoll, Sherideen S, 7949
Stolle, Kara, 1089
Stolte, Adam, 6327
Stolz, Don, 3228
Stolzel, Ingrid, 1122
Stolzfus, Susan, 2384
Stone, Amy, 8581
Stone, Bonnie, 1478
Stone, Carol, 4986
Stone, Chris, 2690
Stone, Dana, 1075
Stone, Dana E., 1677
Stone, Dorothy, 772
Stone, Elizabeth, 809
Stone, Eric, 7003, 7006, 7007, 7008
Stone, George, 4318
Stone, Howard L, 4379
Stone, Jan, 4289
Stone, Jason, 2058, 5215
Stone, Jeremy, 1699
Stone, Joel, 243
Stone, John, 707, 1669
Stone, Joyce, 3284
Stone, Judy, 1917
Stone, Karin, 1532, 5314, 7961
Stone, Kevin, 4722
Stone, Klara, 227
Stone, Marcia, 6202
Stone, Mark, 6228
Stone, Michael, 1250
Stone, Philip, 3417
Stone, Phillip, 5727
Stone, Rebecca, 5706
Stone, Rebecca J., 8505
Stone, Shawn D, 577
Stone, Sue, 5834
Stone, Susan, 5321
Stone, Terry, 2052
Stone, Tim, 3455
Stone, III, C F, 471
Stoneman, Bill, 6055
Stoner, Andrea, 864
Stoner, Gyda, 4545
Stonerock, Sarah, 8033
Stonnell, Chris, 1485
Stool, Ann, 5613
Stoops, Bob, 7084, 7085
Stopa, Jean, 5100, 7700
Stope, Dan, 8030
Storer, Jeff, 3651
Storer, Shawn, 1170
Storey, Raelin, 6523
Storey, Rebecca, 1541
Storie, Sheri, 6044, 6045, 6046
Storm, Barbara, 308
Stortz Branch, Lindsey, 1723
Story, Sharon, 179
Story IV, Christopher, 872
Story VI, Christopher, 872
Stotler, Dan, 4675
Stott, Elizabeth, 4017
Stotts, Michael, 2686, 2697
Stotzer, Jan, 4255
Stoughton Marafino, Teresa, 3810
Stout, Dr Karen A, 5433
Stoven, Annette, 3587
Stover, Darrell, 7881
Stover, Michael, 953
Stover, Paula, 3761
Stowe, Shannon, 2489
Stows, Tanya, 6148
Strachan, Stephen M., 1951
Strachman, Jesse, 3179
Strachman, PJ, 3179
Stracka, Karen, 823
Strader, Jamie, 7636
Strader, Laura, 7952
Straf, Miron L., 4417
Strahl, Eric, 8084
Strahm, Kerry, 3898
Straight, Adam, 6623

Strain Smythe, Karen, 1455
Strait, Margie, 7659
Straley, Forrest A, 6011
Strand, Deirdre, 625
Strand, Heather, 59
Strange, Adam, 3769
Strange, Laurie, 1789
Strange, Marilyn, 2297
Strange, Richard, 952
Strange, Susan, 1682
Strange, Tom, 3878
Strangis, Jerry, 2603
Stranix, John, 6475
Strasberg, Anna, 2641
Strasberg, David, 2641
Strasser Dixon, Julie, 3771
Strassler, Robert B, 922
Strassler, Robert S., 4383, 4791
Strater, Sam, 1528, 1529
Stratton, Heather, 1224, 1225
Stratton, Laura, 6085
Straub, Janneke, 4262
Strauch, Michael, 6908
Straughn Pratt, Suzanne, 3117
Straus, Tracy, 403, 463
Strause, Phil, 2596
Strauss, Debra, 3732
Strauss, Fred E, 5194
Strauss, Iris Lynn, 1909
Strauss, John, 2070
Strauss, Marilyn, 4903
Strauss, Matthew, 6245
Straw, James B, 2310
Straw, Marcy, 847
Strazza, Preston, 4542
Streb, Elizabth, 356
Strebel, Roberta, 1662
Strebig, Margo, 1253
Strebig, Margo, 291
Street, Cathy, 3918
Street, Mary, 899
Street, Tearanny, 1274
Streels, Sally, 24, 117
Strege, John, 1602, 1603
Strehlow, Taimi, 468
Strein, Bill, 3131
Streit, Edward L., 1074
Streshinsky, Mark, 1868
Stretz, Matthew, 2159
Stricka, Michael, 3754
Strickland, Barbour, 5250
Strickland, Carol, 471
Strickland, Eric Q., 2917
Strickland, Kelli, 2944
Strickland, Steve, 2439
Strickland Jr, William E, 8174
Strickland, Jr, William E., 5491
Strickler, Allen, 4220
Strickler, Beulah, 4220
Strickler, John, 1123, 2076
Strickler, Pam, 8008
Stricks, Debbie, 3088
Stried, David, 6993
Stried, Robert, 6509
Stringer, Michelle, 568
Strip, Wendy, 7333
Stripling, Bryon, 1547
Stripling, Byron, 1737
Strobel, Greg, 8114
Strobel-Lopez, Bernadette, 6132
Strock, Cara, 572
Strode, Scott K., 6926
Strode, Thomas, 2128
Stroebel, Paul, 1496
Strohl, Curtis, 2219
Strohl, Darryl, 1902
Strohl, Glenn, 2264
Strohmaier, Sharon, 2071
Strohmeyer, Donna, 5670
Strollo, Ron, 8021
Stroman, Guy, 3810
Stroman, Jay T., 6667, 6668
Stromgren, Richard L, 2115
Stromquist, Lee, 566
Strone, Michael, 2239
Strong, Craig, 7621
Strong, David, 1500, 8660
Strong, John, 1397, 5098

Strong, Kira, 8148
Strong, Lisa, 6102
Strong, Michael, 3751, 8010
Strongren, Richard, 2115
Strope, John L., 1842
Strother, Alexandria, 2131
Strother, Lauren, 15
Stroud, Buzz, 8093
Stroud, Eric A, 580
Stroud, Julie, 1100
Stroud, Maureen, 6319
Stroud, Natalie, 4945
Stroud, Natalie, 7491
Stroup, Daniel, 5161
Strubbe, Sandra, 2259
Strubhart, Lita, 2357
Struble, George, 1613
Struck, Robin M., 3099
Strul, Hellene, 4467
Strumpf, Dan, 1372
Strunsky, Jean, 2449
Struthers, Kevin A., 4426
Struve, Millie, 7556
Struyk, Pieter, 7261
Stryker, Tina, 8581
Stuart, Adam, 6
Stuart, Brian R., 4783
Stuart, Claudia, 3582
Stuart, Gregory, 393
Stuart, Jon R., 8039, 8040
Stuart, Robert A., 2829
Stubbs, David, 7057
Stubbs, John, 65
Stubbs, Stephen, 4783
Stuber, Karen, 8662
Stuberg, Lois, 4482
Stubner, Heidi, 5077
Stuchiner, Kathy, 3552
Stuck, Kathy, 3883
Stuck, Les, 4260, 6198
Stuckenbruck, Dale, 5055
Stucker, Susan, 5005
Stuckey, Sara, 2523
Stuokoy, Sara J., 2520
Stuckey, Wesley, 4751
Stucki, Steve, 2153
Stuckwisch, Marianne, 1232, 1233
Stucky, Steve, 6908
Studard, Leslie, 8355
Studebaker, Katelvn, 4334
Studt, Teddy, 4131
Stueve, Client, 7065
Stueve, Clint, 3051
Stuhlreyer, Michelle, 290
Stuhlreyer, Paul A, 2374
Stulberg, Lois, 989, 991, 992, 993, 994, 995
Stulen, Scott, 294
Stum, Tanya, 1916
Stump, Herb, 6482
Stumpf, Thomas, 2117
Sturbois, Lou, 5038
Sturdevant, Maggie, 4542
Sturgell, James F, 2770
Sturges, Jan, 1859
Sturgill, Mike, 1598
Sturgill, Mike, 3780
Sturgis, Alfred E., 2270
Sturgis, Dr. Alfred E., 1503
Sturk, Karl C., 5052
Sturk, Stephen, 4290
Sturm, Anne, 5515
Sturm, Maria, 5479
Stutler, Bill, 7669
Stutts, Will, 3819
Styche, Dan, 3848
Stynchula, Renee, 6343
Styring, Chris, 3256
Suarez, Ada, 3624
Suarez, Marsha, 166
Suarez, Sheryl, 6132
Subbaraman, Viswa, 4129
Sublett, Barry, 2408
Sublette, George, 7459
Subotic, Goran, 130
Subramanian, Karthik, 3136
Succoso, Marian, 3567
Suchland, Robert, 7993
Suczek, Alexander, 1230, 1237

1225

Executive Name Index / T

Sudavicius MacCallum, Nellie, 3335, 4949
Sudbury, Lynn, 630
Sudhakar, Rama, 6400, 6402, 6403
Sudimack, Wendy, 1720, 5619
Sudmeier, Greg, 117
Sudol, Andrew T., 4255
Sudol, Ryszard, 370
Sue Arnsdorff, Clara, 3321
Sue Greiner, Mary, 1694
Sue McNamara, Mary, 2557
Sue Rogers, Carol, 4065
Suegi, Hans, 5694
Sueko, Seema, 6209
Sueoka, Ryan, 2885
Suess, Kristin, 7955, 7958
Suetanoff, Rick, 1093
Sueyoshi, Dan, 861
Sufi, Rehmah, 210
Sugar, Richard, 1054
Sugarman, Jackie, 1126
Sugg, Allan, 2435
Suggs, Donald, 4921
Sukenik, Phil, 1617
Sukraw, Janet, 8599, 8600, 8602, 8603
Sulinski, Nina, 4386
Sulla, Michael J., 1368
Sullivan, Aimee, 3869
Sullivan, Alison, 5640
Sullivan, Amy, 7845
Sullivan, Bill, 3610
Sullivan, Bob, 2796
Sullivan, Brian, 1930, 7206
Sullivan, Bridget, 4026
Sullivan, Charles Q, 5858
Sullivan, Danni, 4461
Sullivan, Denise, 6927, 6932, 6933, 6934, 6935
Sullivan, Erin, 4211
Sullivan, Jane, 96
Sullivan, Jim, 4461
Sullivan, John, 2594
Sullivan, JR, 4006
Sullivan, Kerri, 4989, 7556
Sullivan, Laura, 8186
Sullivan, Linda S., 5723
Sullivan, Michele, 1183, 1185, 1899
Sullivan, Mike, 4491
Sullivan, Msgr. Kevin, 5152
Sullivan, Nancy, 4364
Sullivan, Pamela, 4313
Sullivan, Sean, 2306
Sullivan, Taimur, 5130
Sullivan, Tim, 5767
Sullivan, Timothy J, 8565, 8566
Sullivan, Todd, 4168
Sullivan Sachs, Leslie, 4404
Sullivan, M.Ed, Melissa, 4045
Sullivan-Blum, Ph.D., Constance R., 5065
Sultz, Jen, 2967
Sumberg, Craig, 5998
Sumey, Doug, 4696
Summar, Jan, 3996
Summerlin, Dr Tim, 1736
Summers, Barbara, 5347
Summers, Greg, 8707
Summers, Jeremy, 7918
Summers, Liz, 5247
Summers, Mike, 3978
Summers, Patrick, 1926, 2353
Summers, Rebecca, 6094, 6095
Summerville, Suzanne, 1846
Sumner, Anne-Marie W., 5168
Sumner, Any, 359
Sumner, Brent, 1491, 5242
Sumnicht, Liz, 2393
Sumrall, Whitney, 1273
Sun, Chris, 7165
Sunday, Rob, 8177
Sunde, Sarah C, 3532
Sunderman, Steven, 5304
Sundet-Schoenwald, Rebecca, 1267
Sundin, Jacqueline, 3777
Sundquist, Cindy, 5401
Sundquist, Michael, 6188
Sundquist, Ted, 6351
Sundstrom, Mary, 4846
Sung, Heidi, 257
Sung, Vicki, 1917
Sunkin, Howard, 6156

Sunshine Malleck, Kailee, 8445
SunSpiral, Claire, 6267
Supelak, Dave, 1513, 1514, 5286
Surdi, Deborah, 2246, 2251
Surmacz, Jonathan, 3847
Surowitz, Molly, 2980
Surslen, Sera, 1395, 5093
Surtasky, David, 8131
Susan, Tolis, 2710, 2711
Susan Fulghum, Mary, 1500
Susman, Matthew, 6424
Susman, Thomas, 5817
Susskind, Peter, 847
Sussman, Paul, 852, 6254
Susswein, Harvey, 5161
Susswein, Jane, 5161
Suszynski, Maria, 288
Suter, Ann, 5797
Sutherland, Doug, 5203
Sutherland, L Frederick, 3814
Sutherland, Melanie, 3416
Sutherland, Robin, 4375
Sutphin, Eric N, 5326
Sutphin, Eric N., 1545, 1546, 2282
Sutten, Aaron, 670
Sutter, Laurence, 5134
Sutter, Michael F., 3833
Sutton, Alex, 2128
Sutton, Angela, 1439
Sutton, David, 814
Sutton, Debora A., 1478
Sutton, Elizabeth, 2007
Sutton, George, 295
Sutton, John, 1943, 2347
Sutton, Scott, 7908
Sutton, Sean, 868
Sutton, Susan, 3244
Sutton, Vern, 1861
Sutton Jr MD, David R, 155
Sutton,, Bob, 3008
Sutton-Simballa, Jolly, 346
Suydam, John, 7130
Suydam, Matt, 8155
Suzeau, Patrick, 237
Suzuki, Masaaki, 1970
Suzuki, Ira, 979
Svalander, Judith, 215
Svanda, Kyle, 6123
Svedlow, Andrew Jay, 914
Svengalis, David, 2505
Sveum, Jay, 7938
Svingos, Christen, 1998
Svoboda, Stephen, 7636
Svorinich, Christa, 6150
Svyatlovskaya, Lydia, 903
Swagerty, Ray, 5533
Swaha, Leslie, 21
Swain, Margaret, 2057
Swain, Marisa, 1915
Swain, Mark, 5493
Swain, Tim, 8216
Swain, William, 2057
Swalley, Arthur, 871
Swan, Barbara, 4135
Swan, Mark, 112
Swan, Phillip A., 2393
Swanborn, Edwin, 2120
Swanglier, Tom, 7936
Swango, Carol, 5378
Swann, Kyle, 1968
Swanson, Anne M, 1432
Swanson, Betsy, 3433, 5061
Swanson, Charles, 7004
Swanson, Dana, 3183
Swanson, Dwight, 3977
Swanson, Hilary, 1802
Swanson, Karen, 2094
Swanson, Patrick, 2126
Swanson, Roberta, 4670
Swap, Walter, 4181
Swartwout, Glen, 2883
Swartz, Bob, 4025
Swartz, F Randolph, 575
Swartz, F. Randolph, 575
Swartz, Micheal, 1306
Swartz, Nita, 1356
Swartzentruber, Loren, 5740
Swatek, E Paul, 850

Swatnik, Karen, 2918
Swatt, Steve, 6394
Swayne, Sherry, 6302
Swayze, Donna, 822
Swearingen, Joel, 4873
Swedberg, Robert, 1861, 2007, 4186
Swedin, Tori, 413
Sweek, Kathee, 4067
Sweek, Kathleen, 4067
Sweeney, Adrienne, 3232
Sweeney, Cynthia, 8231
Sweeney, Dan, 1197
Sweeney, Dennis, 5133
Sweeney, Don, 4350
Sweeney, John, 2079
Sweeney, Maureen, 3836
Sweeney, Polly, 824, 825
Sweet, Laura, 6984
Sweet, Mary Beth, 1327
Sweet, Michele, 350
Sweetbaum, Selma, 7211
Sweeter, Janice, 2426
Sweetland, Theresa, 4870
Sweetman-LeClair, Jennifer, 4670
Sweetser, Kelly, 5029
Sweetser, Sandy, 7360
Sweezey, C Otis, 2963
Sweitzer, Rod, 3590
Swensen, Laren, 5686
Swenson, Gordon, 1024
Swenson, Robert, 5043
Swenson, Sarah, 44
Swenson, Theresa, 1629
Swenson Petras, Julie, 4128
Swerling, Jeremy, 1044
Swett Robinson, Marion, 1448
Swezey, Vicky, 2829
Swiergosz, Roseann, 6651
Swift, Karie, 1317
Swift, Ron, 6991
Swift, Sasha, 6078
Swift, Stephen, 1376
Swift, Tricia, 758
Swift-Matton, Carol, 1353
Swift, Lydia P., 2958
Swigger, Bettina, 863, 4319, 4320
Swiggum, Randal, 1046
Swindell, Archie C., 4399
Swindle, Tyler, 1691
Swingle, Sharon, 6320
Swinney, R. Andrew, 5382
Swinston, Robert, 456
Swint, Charles, 6627
Swirka, Dr Joyce, 2325
Swirsky, Marvin, 3674
Swisher, Iris, 6062
Swiss, Timothy, 6155
Switaj, Dan, 249
Switzler, Jonne-Marie, 4209
Swofford, Patti Hannan, 5362
Swoope, Janice, 1491
Swyer, Edward P., 7819
Syak, Patricia A, 1575
Sycks, Adam, 723
Sygielski, John J., 5452
Sykes, Becky R., 5668
Sykes, Dr. David, 773
Sylves, Beth, 8618
Sylvester, Mark D., 3839, 8163, 8164, 8165, 8166
Symanski, Julia, 122
Symcox, Lee, 8043
Symczak, Paul E., 797
Symington, Jennifer, 3175
Symons, Meridith, 3779
Synder, Elena, 2606
Synder, Lauren, 2589
Syrotiak, David A., 4018
Syrotiak, David J., 4018
Syrotiak, Peter, 4018
Syssoyeva, Kathryn, 7167
Syth, Donna, 8036
Szablewski, Laurie, 1173
Szabo, Elizabeth, 6389
Szabo, Marcy, 7335
Szafranski, J.P., 3769
Szaj, Kathleen C, 3539
Szalay, Kathleen, 2023

Szawan, Annette, 1163
Szczepkowski, Michael, 7222
Szuberla, Micahael, 8011
Szucs, Melanie, 7997
Szulc, Joel, 3990
Szura, John, 2494

T

T. Anderson, Edward, 2541
T. Ford, Henry, 7849
T. Miltenberg, Andrew, 7789
T. Murphy, Dr. Bruce, 7161
T. Wright, Merry Ann, 6463
Tabaczka, Chris, 7270
Tabarrok, Rey, 163
Tabath, Willie, 6112
Tabbitas, Julie, 5177
Taber, Adam, 5726
Taber, John, 6117
Tabereaux Ph.D, Charlotte, 7403
Tabizon, Renee, 19
Tabnick, Michelle, 467, 2228
Tabor, Penny, 4856
Tackett, Chris, 1858
Tackett, Elizabeth, 1812
Tackett, Joe, 1817
Tackett, Joseph, 1661
Tada, Steve, 724
Taddeucci, Katie, 3326
Taetzsch, Cindra, 6848, 6849
Tafel, Donna, 6398
Taff, Leah, 689
Tafoya, Alicia, 4003
Tai Soon Burgess, Dana, 2740
Tait, Nancy, 5400
Takahashi, Drew, 2591
Takei, Kei, 443
Takushi, Alicia, 2048
Talasek, J D, 4428
Talberg, Dr. Jonathan, 4240
Talberg, Jonathan, 802
Talbert, Terrie, 8253
Talbot-Stanaway, Susan, 8027
Talbott, Jeff, 6215
Talbott, Lauren, 141
Talbut, Greg, 7414
Talcott, Cathy, 1751
Talegaonkar, Vinita, 2081
Tali, Anu, 4482, 4486
Taliaferro, Casandra, 4278, 4279
Taliaferro, Shannon, 1741
Taliaferro, Trudy, 6274
Taliferro, Marisa, 3389
Tall, Erin Pike, 2365
Tallchief, Maria, 218
Tallent, Kathy, 3921
Talley, Alicia, 4069
Talley, Sara, 4180
Tallis, Gale, 3287, 7424
Tallman, Brooke, 3603
Tallman, David, 5417
Taloff, Chris, 6325
Talvi, Ilkka, 1802
Tam, Angela, 405
Tam, Sherman, 5421
Tamasi, Michael, 5026
Tamburri, Lawrence, 8173
Tammen, Brad, 8298
Tammi, John, 7305
Tamura, Randall, 833
Tan, Aimee, 1806, 5803
Tan, Joel, 6267
Tan, Rana, 4066
Tan-Cohen, Madelyn, 2051
Tanaka, George, 6163
Tanaka, Peter, 4528
Tanaka, Yuko, 759, 761, 4205
Tandoc, Bonnie, 1121
Taney, Nicole, 1679
Tang, John, 5985, 5987, 5989
Tang, Jordan, 1135
Tang, Rrichard, 1339
Tang, Yun, 833
Tani, Ann, 7180
Tania Becerra, PhD, Maria, 2446
Tanikawa, Darryl W, 833
Tankersley, Dr. Bruce, 1742

Executive Name Index / T

Tanmen, Bruce, 2040
Tanner, Douglas, 850
Tanner, Jessica, 1180
Tanner, John, 3193
Tanner, Judy, 5924, 5925
Tanner, Linda, 3356
Tanner, Lloyd, 2619
Tanner, Mary, 6148
Tanner, Mehgan, 2610
Tanner, Richard, 466
Tannous, John, 5952
Tanous, Peter, 4033
Tanury, Thomas A., 8199
Tanya, Tanya, 8244
Taormina, Michael, 6607
Taphorn, Peggy, 3679
Tapia, John, 2982
Tapick, Nancy, 819
Taplin, Anthony, 4206, 5425
Taplin, Bonnie, 7346
Tarble, Sherrie, 3272
Tarconish, Christy, 581
Tardibuono, Jennifer, 3369, 4997
Taribassi, Maria, 3501
Tarler, Gene, 3408
Tarlow, David, 2640, 6155
Tarnay, Linda, 3151
Tarnopolsky, Mat¡as, 4207, 6066, 6070, 6071, 6072
Tarpley, Sue, 2802
Tarr Hart, Nancy, 3122
Tarrant, David, 6704, 6707
Tarshis, Jay, 2950
Tarson, Derek, 3601
Tartaglione, Simeone, 947
Tarter, Diane, 5415
Tartt, Nancy, 141, 146
Tarver, Christa, 1299
Tarver, Helga, 2732
Tasak, Alexandra, 3149
Tashiro, Satoru, 1806, 5803
Tashjian, Donald, 1359
Tassi, Nanci, 2001
Tatarowski, Stefan, 6112
Tate, Becky S., 4
Tate, Harold, 5932
Tate, Johnny, 1137
Tate, Marci, 2855
Tate, Tom, 1356
Tatge, Pamela, 6411, 6412, 6413, 6414
Tatman, Neil, 4257
Tatom, Katherine, 7045
Tattersall, Jillian, 201
Tatum, Douglas, 6860
Tatum, Erin E., 6612, 6613, 6616
Tatum, Judy, 1888
Tatum, Milton, 628
Tatum, Richard, 2631
Tatum, Stephanie, 5574
Taube, Dan, 2981
Taubert, Tony, 6278
Taubert, Uwe, 3571
Taubman, William, 5869
Taucher, Kate, 4362
Taul, Jim, 2586
Taulbee, Karen, 4221
Taulu, Norman, 4369
Tavaglione, Eunice, 2357
Tavares, Teri, 6240, 6241
Tavarres, Fabio, 356
Taveau, Daniella Y., 4422
Tavernier, David M, 5543
Tavitian, Aso O., 5133
Taxman, Barbara, 4950
Taykalo, Christopher, 2146
Taylo Lee, Patricia, 6254
Taylor, Amy, 308
Taylor, Anne, 1168
Taylor, Ben, 878, 5492
Taylor, Bob, 5320
Taylor, Brew, 8190
Taylor, Bryan, 4472
Taylor, Carl, 726
Taylor, Cathy, 837
Taylor, Christopher, 4091
Taylor, Dallas, 5981
Taylor, Damon, 5952
Taylor, Danny H., 5578

Taylor, Darlene, 3742
Taylor, Dave, 3811
Taylor, David, 6386
Taylor, Delia, 2748, 6478
Taylor, Dr. Carol, 4925
Taylor, Elaine, 8387
Taylor, Elizabeth A., 8470
Taylor, Ellen, 112
Taylor, Fred W, 809
Taylor, George, 2024
Taylor, Gwendolyne D., 771
Taylor, Holly, 5952
Taylor, Houston, 6041
Taylor, Issac, 6549
Taylor, J. Thomas, 2320
Taylor, Jackie, 2909
Taylor, James, 2459
Taylor, James I., 1473
Taylor, James P, 6085
Taylor, Jan, 5398
Taylor, Janet L, 5301
Taylor, Jason, 1847
Taylor, Johy, 3677
Taylor, Jonathan, 1401
Taylor, Jordan, 5367
Taylor, Josh, 2105
Taylor, Kevin, 6264
Taylor, Keyona, 2376
Taylor, Lisa, 4510
Taylor, Louise, 8440
Taylor, Marcellus, 6149
Taylor, Michelle, 3916
Taylor, Molly, 6055
Taylor, Nan, 587
Taylor, Norita, 3284
Taylor, Pamela, 870
Taylor, Paul, 471
Taylor, Robert, 379, 4307, 5023
Taylor, Roger, 6785, 6787, 6788
Taylor, Ryaniam, 2116
Taylor, Sara, 654
Taylor, Sean, 2694
Taylor, Seth, 1552
Taylor, Sharon, 1220
Taylor, Stacy, 1694
Taylor, Susan, 1756
Taylor, Thomas, 3066
Taylor, Thomas T, 5366, 5367
Taylor, Todd, 2997
Taylor, Tom, 2997, 6009
Taylor, Vivian, 6530
Taylor, William, 2534, 6195
Taylor, William B., 1283
Taylor, Winston, 6047
Taylor Baker, Newman, 391
Taylor Esq, E Dwight, 896
Taylor Kindle, Jo Ann, 4921
Taylor Lange, Ali, 24
Taylor Love, Shelby, 4055
Taylor Neal, Sara, 139
Taylor-Corbett, Lynne, 511, 610
Taylor-Richardson, Karen H., 4696
Taylor, Paul, 471
Tazlaf, Dieter, 1811
Tcherkassky, Marianna, 582
Tchernichov, Alexei, 133
Tchernychev, Maxim, 64
Tchivzhel, Edvard, 1681
Teachey, Sarah, 6104
Teague, Mark, 1008
Teague, William, 5927, 5929, 5930, 5931, 8482
Teahen, Peter R., 3029
Teal, Terri, 2125
Tebar, Ramon, 986, 2005
Teberg, Jack, 776
Tecklenburg, Don, 5306
Tecza Shearer, Andrea, 543
Tedesco, Art, 3399
Tedesco, Diane, 406
Tedesco, Marjorie, 131, 132
Tedesco, Michael, 2625
Tedford, Berrien, 310
Tedford, Chris, 4808
Teeple, Mitch, 5911
Teer, Barbara Ann, 3525
Teer, Craig, 1782
Teer, Craig B., 1773
Teer, Kelly, 7220

Teeter, Kyle, 4629
Tehrani, Roxanna, 1749
Tei, Paul, 2801
Teich, Leonard, 2351
Teich, Tracy, 3193
Teicholz, Leslie, 1404, 1405
Teie, David, 1774
Teig, Stephen, 3804
Teig-Torres, Kristin, 7024
Tein, Ken, 8325
Teinowitz, Nancy, 204
Teis, Dr. Larry, 8460
Teisinger, Jennifer, 4542
Teixeria, Ann, 1185
Teixeria, Kristen, 1194
Tejada, Clayton, 3840
Tejada, Kate, 3823
Telesco, Linda, 263
Telford, Donald M., 6245, 6248
Tellalian, Robert S, 921
Teller, Deborah, 3528
Tellock, Don, 411
Temirkanov, Yuri, 1155, 4750
Temm, Pat, 2872
Tempest, Bill, 1744
Temple, Carla, 5023
Temple, Nancy, 3539
Temple, Reggi, 6036
Temple, Riley K, 2732
Templeton, Annetta, 2357
Templeton, Heidi, 4909
Tench, Mary, 6282, 6285, 6287
Tenenbaum, Alexandr, 1448
Tenenbaum, Arnold, 5034
Tenenbaum, Mela, 1448
TenErck, Steve, 7688
Teng, Yu-chiung, 1413
Tennant, Georgia, 5763, 5764, 5765
TenNapel, Roger, 1708
Tennes, Charles, 4182, 5996, 6010
Tenzer, David, 8559
Tenzin, Lobsang, 183
Teplitz, Ron, 1877
Tepper, Frances, 7682
Tepper, Janson, 7645
Ter Haar, Teresa, 7018, 7020, 7021
Ter-Jung, Heather, 818
Teraspulsky, Leopold, 1209
Terenzi, Kimberly, 175
Teresa Soltis, Esq., Mary, 1649
Terford, Sandi, 1062
Terhune, Laura, 8337
Teri, Washington, 4419
Terleckyi, Ramon, 2742, 2752
Ternes, Barbara, 7032, 7033, 7034
Terrell, Ann, 702
Terrell, Julian, 8306
Terrell, Mike, 6573
Terrell, Scott, 1128
Terri,, 8495
Terrill, Steve, 1403
Terris, Brenda, 169
Terry, Cheryl, 8018
Terry, Cori, 288
Terry, Duffy, 8366, 8367
Terry, Ed, 3111
Terry, Matthew, 6662
Terry, Michael, 4828
Terry, Paula, 171
Terry, Phillip, 2761
Terry, Pinkie, 769
Terry Paul, Kami, 4006, 5682
Terry, Jr, Daniel, 882
Terry-Morgan, Elmo, 3863
Terwilliger, Carol, 7202
Terwilliger, Rodney, 2932
Terwilliger, William, 897, 1683
Teschner, Mimi, 6328
Teske, Deborah J, 1948, 1949
Tesmer, Ashler, 215
Tessitore, Antonio, 2232
Test, Anne Marie, 3036
Test, Stephen G., 1784, 2375
Tester, Cathy, 8506
Teter, Dane, 886
Teter, Samantha, 1689, 6873
Teter, Jr, Harry, 2745
Tetreault, Paul, 2738, 8397

Tetreault, Paul R., 2738
Tetting, Dan, 1853
Teves Sedayao, Frances Gay, 87
Teymourtache, Karim, 6175
Tezuka, Miwako, 5141
Thadani, Anisha, 5726
Thadani, Rahul, 5887
Thaggard, David, 7899
Thake, Shanta, 7737
Thaler, Emily, 345
Tharaldson, Bruce, 6268
Tharkur, Sharon, 262
Tharp-Bernard, Lisa, 3867
Thatcher, Evelyn, 691
Thatcher, Kristine, 2919
Thatcher, Michael, 691
Thatcher, Sue, 6898
Thatcher, Tom E., 7016, 7017
Thaut, Michael H, 909
Thaut, Michaelh, 909
Thaxton, Melissa, 7136
Thayer, David L., 7006, 7007, 7008
Thayer, Jeff, 843
Thayer, Marc C, 7455
Thayer, Pat, 8015
Thayer, Ronald, 5012
Thayer, Tom, 3894
Thea Beck, Ann, 1450
Theall, Cathy, 5594
Theatre has allowed, the Dor, 6065
Thede, Jeff, 2300
Theige Hascall, Larae, 682
Theile, David, 8155
Thein, Dr. Anthony, 5283
Theo, George, 6770
Theriault, Candy, 7513
Therriault, Steven, 7536
Theryoung, Richard, 5017
Thiagarajan, Krishna, 1437
Thibeault, April, 1200
Thiede, Conrad, 3706
Thielen, Aaron, 2973
Thiolon, Mork, 074
Thielking, Erik, 1451
Thielman, James, 8014
Thieme, John, 1089
Thies, Terry, 4691
Thiesen, Yukari, 4219
Thiessen, John, 1917
Thigpen, Kay, 3874
Thiroux, Isabel, 801
Thoburn, Christina, 4825
Thodeson, Paul, 4504
Thodos, Melissa, 213
Thoma, Kurt, 3205
Thoma, Mark, 4062, 4063, 8572
Thoma, Melissa, 6040
Thoma, Rich, 6876
Thoma, Tracy, 5891, 5892
Thomae-Morphew, Susan, 8395
Thomas, Alvin, 1728
Thomas, Amy, 4234
Thomas, Andrew, 3556
Thomas, Anita, 343
Thomas, Anna, 1747
Thomas, Barbara S., 3549
Thomas, Bill, 5580, 8226, 8307
Thomas, Blair, 2910
Thomas, Bob, 3788
Thomas, Brigette, 2586
Thomas, Candyce, 4377
Thomas, Casey, 3603
Thomas, Charles E, 7047
Thomas, Cheryl, 186
Thomas, Cheryl M., 5932
Thomas, CM Sgt Jerry, 951
Thomas, Crist P., 4226
Thomas, Dan, 4882
Thomas, Darryl, 559
Thomas, David, 1119, 2879
Thomas, Debi, 186
Thomas, Devin, 803
Thomas, Dr. Wanda, 247
Thomas, Ed, 6199
Thomas, Erica C, 2292
Thomas, Gary, 893
Thomas, Gordon, 4368
Thomas, Harriet, 6623

Executive Name Index / T

Thomas, James, 3198
Thomas, Jay, 6128
Thomas, Jedd, 1027
Thomas, Jeffrey, 1911
Thomas, Joelle, 1506
Thomas, John, 6228
Thomas, Jonna, 2154
Thomas, Juames, 2202
Thomas, Julie, 1065, 1066
Thomas, Karen, 141
Thomas, Karen P., 2388
Thomas, Katherine, 3567
Thomas, Keith, 1626
Thomas, Kristina, 5809
Thomas, Kurt, 5835
Thomas, Larry, 5841
Thomas, Laurie, 4780
Thomas, Lee, 1521, 5292
Thomas, Leslie, 4236, 6168, 6172
Thomas, Linda, 3181
Thomas, Lori, 6153
Thomas, M. Denise, 3303
Thomas, Margaret, 204
Thomas, Mark, 2966, 8190
Thomas, Matt, 6648, 6649
Thomas, Michael, 1558
Thomas, Mike, 4687, 8518
Thomas, Nancy, 1841
Thomas, Nicholas, 6813
Thomas, Patricia, 8568
Thomas, Philip, 5562
Thomas, Regina, 5796
Thomas, Robbie, 3872
Thomas, Roger, 7937
Thomas, Ronald, 1185, 4387
Thomas, Rony, 1784, 2375
Thomas, Saundra, 363
Thomas, Steven, 1474, 2301
Thomas, Suzanne, 2437, 3960
Thomas, Tara, 6340
Thomas, Tim, 5115
Thomas, Valarie, 6619
Thomas, Wayne, 1587
Thomas, Wesley, 4513
Thomas, William, 7234, 7255
Thomas Dodson, John, 1220, 1226
Thomas Rideout, Glen, 2140
Thomas, CPA, Cynthia A., 1504
Thomas, Esq, Kenneth, 1381
Thomas, Jr., Samuel R., 6481
Thomas-Cutts, Lisa, 6639
Thomas-Morphew, Susan, 8467
Thomas-Smith, Vanessa, 578
Thomason, Dr John, 4458
Thomason, Jessica, 6191
Thomason, Qiana, 4906
Thomas, Andrew, 3570
Thomforde, Christopher, 4879
Thomley, Sandy, 7294
Thompkins, Geoff M, 7951
Thompsom, Lisa, 6191
Thompson, Andrew, 6513
Thompson, Anna M., 6927, 6929, 6930, 6931, 6932, 6933, 6934, 6935
Thompson, Barb, 580
Thompson, Barbara, 4530
Thompson, Briana, 1741
Thompson, Buddy, 2319
Thompson, Carol, 6663
Thompson, Charles, 1127
Thompson, Chelsie, 1558
Thompson, Connie, 1732
Thompson, Darin, 7340
Thompson, Dave, 3007
Thompson, Deane, 2157
Thompson, Diana, 5805
Thompson, Dr. Jim, 1761
Thompson, Dr. Norma, 1206
Thompson, Dr. Randy, 1577
Thompson, Ellen, 4497
Thompson, Emily Anne, 3893
Thompson, George, 867
Thompson, Glenda, 3974
Thompson, Herbert, 5458
Thompson, J Lynn, 2863
Thompson, Jane, 8043
Thompson, Jennifer, 1047
Thompson, Joe, 6980, 6981, 6982, 6983

Thompson, John, 673, 4918
Thompson, Joseph C, 7245
Thompson, Judy, 4210
Thompson, Kathy, 6499
Thompson, Kendall, 4648
Thompson, Kent, 2657, 6352
Thompson, Kerby, 3435
Thompson, Larry, 2837
Thompson, Lauri, 319
Thompson, Lee, 7852
Thompson, Lennis, 1135
Thompson, Lisa, 6191
Thompson, Lynn, 1588
Thompson, Maria, 4137
Thompson, Mary, 278
Thompson, Matt, 2598
Thompson, Maxine, 3903
Thompson, Megan, 4064
Thompson, Michael, 4616, 6570
Thompson, Michele M, 6757
Thompson, Nadia, 703
Thompson, Nathan, 2666
Thompson, Pam, 8722
Thompson, Pamela, 4
Thompson, Paul, 7369
Thompson, Peggy, 4335
Thompson, Phil, 7061
Thompson, Phillippa, 5115
Thompson, Richard L., 2738
Thompson, Robert, 6445
Thompson, Robin, 2374
Thompson, Roger, 104
Thompson, Scott, 3928
Thompson, Stephanie, 2452
Thompson, T.T. Tyler, 1863
Thompson, Terri, 2722
Thompson, Thomas M., 3846
Thompson, Virginia M, 2022
Thompson, Waddy, 1420
Thompson, William, 5979
Thompson Jr, Charles, 6210
Thompson Kretschmer, Dr. Joan, 1423
Thompson-Cantu, Katya, 2361
Thompson-Moore, Ella, 361
Thompston, Dennis M, 3851
Thomsen, Johanna H., 5164, 7787
Thomsen, Nancy, 5557
Thomson, Brach, 3312
Thomson, Don, 3312
Thomson, Donna, 5062
Thomson, Jude, 3312
Thomson, Judith, 2966
Thomson, Kenneth, 4785
Thomson, Robert B., 6793
Thomson Jr, William E, 6210
Thomson Kretschmer, Dr. Joan, 1423
Thonvold, Dennis D., 1263
Thoreson, Glen, 6890
Thoreson, Larry, 5835
Thorn, George, 565
Thorn, Nancy, 565
Thornburgh, John R, 1083, 1084
Thorndike, Dan, 5400
Thorne, Creon, 3788
Thorne, Jeffrey, 6937
Thorne, Jon, 1698
Thorne, Ken, 4356
Thorne, Larry, 8029
Thorne, Phebe, 2035
Thorne, III, John W., 5172, 8866
Thornley, Anthony, 2565
Thornton, Debbie, 1767
Thornton, Eric, 5918
Thornton, Kay, 6153
Thornton, Lucas, 1786
thornton, Matthew, 8553
Thornton, Mike, 4912
Thornton, Nicole, 8155
Thornton, Patricia, 648
Thorp, Anne, 4212
Thorp, Jean, 8462
Thorpe, Jim, 3777
Thorsson , Bryn, 3536
Thrall, Jesse, 1859
Thrall, Rosanne, 3991, 5645
Threewitt, Don, 4137
Thresher, Mark R, 5372
Thriffiley, Cherie, 4705

Throckmorton, James, 1004
Throndill, Margaret, 5811
Throne, Tracy, 2245
Thrumon, Patti, 7134
Thulin, Jr., Carl V., 5020
Thumin, Irma, 5999
Thummel, Ellen, 2438
Thur, Paul, 8659
Thurber, Patricia, 6439
Thuresson Frary, Kajsa, 6202
Thurman, Keith, 3279
Thurman, Lynne, 8060
Thurman, Mickey, 8584
Thurman, Robert, 7982
Thurrell, Lisa Andrea, 697
Thurston, Rosemary, 887
Thuzar, Zahni, 6530
Thysen, Janel, 4336
Th,venot, Maxine, 2197
Tiberi, Paola, 1408
Tiboris, Peter, 5150
Tiboris, Petern, 5150
Tick, Carolyn, 5523
Tick, Michael, 3078
Tickler, Mike, 2436
Tidball, Colette, 8084
Tidwell, Janet, 1012
Tidwell, Trent, 5669
Tiebout, Bobbie, 2705
Tiede, David, 6980, 6981, 6982, 6983
Tiemeyer, Christian, 1102
Tiencken, Charlotte M., 4080
Tierney, Abby, 3805
Tierney, Jane, 1506
Tierney, Marianne, 5480
Tierney, Martin, 2397
Tierno, David A., 1341
Tietz, Jerry, 2041
Tietz, Lori, 3110
Tievsky, Jan, 142
Tiffany, Edwin P, 4776
Tiffany, Tracy, 7264
Tigner, Gary, 1420, 1421
Tigner, Latanya D, 52
Tilford, Marcia, 6277
Tilghman, Shirley, 7583
Tiller, Karen, 2029
Tilley, Carree, 8240
Tilley, Melissa, 1704
Tillman, Melissa, 3276
Tillman, Richard, 5934
Tilmon, Samuel, 1251
Tilson Thomas, Michael, 856, 980
Tilton, Carly, 3381
Tilton, Mary, 4609
Timm, Scott, 2322
Timmel, William C, 4401
Timmerman, Diane, 6890
Timmerman-Epperson, Karla, 1810
Timmins, John, 8002
Timmons, Eugene, 977
Timmons, Jackie, 3649
Timmons, Rick, 8227
Timmons, Sean, 4989
Timms, Henry, 5109
Tinberg, Elaine, 2970
Tindall, Karen, 4449
Ting, Eric, 2697
Tingley, Michael, 8100
Tini, Dennis J., 7291
Tinianow, Jennifer, 2727
Tinker, Bruce, 3203
TinkerLee, Lee, 5662
Tinkham, Allen, 1036
Tinklenberg, Mark, 6388
Tinny, Bitty, 8626
Tinsch, Carolyn, 2365
Tinsley, Melissa, 6915, 6916, 6917, 6918
Tinsley, Tiffany, 120
Tinsley, Tom, 3831, 4441, 4569
Tippel, Mathew, 2065
Tippett, Norma, 5207
Tipton, Betty, 3904
Tipton, John, 7518
Tipton, Ray, 8337
Tirado, Norma, 1252
Tirney, Tom, 3833
Tischhauser, D.M., Andreas, 2198

Tisdale, Preston, 921
Tiser, Autum, 3716
Tish, Laurie, 8570
Tishkoff, Eric, 1802
Titens, Michael, 3957
Titus, Perry, 7271
Tjaden, Karen, 2134
Tkach, Tom, 7606
Tobias, Nina, 4865
Tobias, Scott, 985
Tobiassen, Kathy, 3603
Tobin, Becky, 2352
Tobisch, Kathryn, 4328
Tobish, Kathryn, 873
Tocco, James, 4861
Tod Smith, Sarah, 3597
Todaro, Bobbi, 6292
Todd, Dina, 4983
Todd, Karin A, 1342
Todd, Lee, 7083
Todd, Raymond, 3566
Todd, Tim, 2745
Todd, Tracey, 8208
Todd Jr, Lee T, 7089
Todd Osborn, Anne, 5191
Todorinov, Nikolay, 228
Tofte, Roger, 3792
Tofteland, Curt, 3069
Togawa, Jill, 87
Toggenburger, Joan, 4078
Tognoli, Era, 2175
Toirac, Margarita, 3513
Toizer, Eric, 4321
Tokuda, Marilyn, 2499
Tolan, Rj, 7727
Toland, Nancy, 6039
Tolbert, Cathy, 2286
Tolbert, Lee, 3825, 3837, 5474
Tolden, Derrien, 1137
Toledo, David, 2619
Toledo, Robert, 4323
Toler, Acie, 4096
Toles, Lynne, 6204
Tolia, Sam, 6823, 6824
Toliver, Linda, 2522
Toll, Larry, 8247
Tollefson, Kristina, 2811
Tolles, Beth, 2395
Tolleson, Natasha, 4004, 8463
Tollett, Gerald J, 5641
Tolliver, Joseph, 740, 4181
Tolliver, Tricia, 418
Tolokan, Anthony, 1766
Tom,, 848
Tom Bogart, Dr. William T., 8279
Tom Miller, Canon, 5120
Tomaro, Robert, 1821
Tomas, Charles, 7136
Tomascak, Larry, 6421
Tomasetti, Alan J., 729
Tomashek, Anthony, 3785
Tomassi, Noreen, 5113
Tomasson, Helgi, 89
Tomaszek, Michael, 1852
Tomaszewski, Peggy, 3189
Tomei, Paula, 2461, 6091
Tomeromce, Robin, 4207
Tomhave, Dan, 4869
Tomkins, Leslie, 5688
Tomkins, Steve, 4068, 4072
Tomlinson, Anne, 1885
Tomlinson, Charlie, 288, 1243, 4853
Tomlinson, Janis, 4417
Tomlinson, John, 471
Tomlinson, Karen M., 1647
Tomlinson, Kathie, 288
Tomlinson, Linda, 4839
Tomlinson, Tom, 1005, 6553
Tompkins, David, 11
Tompkins, Fred, 1288, 4919
Tompkins, Glenn, 6952
Tompkins, Roger, 4275
Tona, Mike, 2812
Tondu, Sarah, 5233
Toney, Dennis, 8530
Tonget, Alan, 5972
Toni, Claudia, 4559
Tonkin, Richard, 27

Executive Name Index / T

Tonry, Reggie, 2298
Toohey, Bill, 8267
Toohey, Jennifer, 8864
Toohey, John A., 5662
Tooley, Karen, 1752
Toomes, Janni, 1749
Toomey, Helen, 1991
Toor, Sarah, 565
Tootell, Tracy, 1316
Toothman, Tim, 2430, 6004
Topilow, Carl, 1518, 4362
Toplansky, Howard, 1351
Topoleski, Jan, 4999
Topper, Matson, 1002
Topper, Paul, 1495
Toppin, C. Thomas, 2134
Topping, Jim, 4353
Topping, Karin, 5994
Torano, Michael J., 2330
Torbert, Max, 8712
Torchia, Kathleen, 1878
Torgelson, Nathan, 2384
Torgerson, Jeff, 4118
Torgesen, Rachel, 1621
Torget, Sandy, 2173
Torkelson, Barbara, 292
Torkildson, Terry, 8245, 8246
Tormela, Anne, 2212
Tornow, Ted, 6972
Torok, Jeanne, 7335
Torok, Leslie, 3001
Torrano, Sharon, 100, 101
Torre, Paul, 1232, 1233, 4839, 7296
Torres, Christina, 3900
Torres, Jesse, 7028
Torres, Jim, 3142
Torres, Jose, 6122
Torres, Mark, 3092
Torres, Robert, 8034
Torres, Walter, 1470
Torres-Perez, Betty, 1710
Torresen, Emma, 1249
Torri, Erika, 6136
Torruella, Mariama, 4549
Tortolano, Dr. William, 5709
Toscan, Richard E, 671
Tosch, Mary, 4565
Toth, Eleanor, 4812
Toth, Gabor, 602
Toth, Stephan, 2775
Totten, Cynthia, 2825, 6592, 6593
Touchi-Peters, Karen M., 2143
Touchstone, Robert, 3646
Toultant, William, 4258
Toups, Joe, 7131, 7132, 7133
Toups, Stephen, 3077
Tourangeau, Frank, 2911
Tourangeau, Melia P, 2367
Tourangeau, Melia P., 1766, 2366
Tourigny, Roxana, 5519
Tousant Milligan, Florine, 749
Toutant, Jenny, 4124
Tovar, Colleen, 2985
Tovar, Francisco, 3978
Towe, Darrell, 8288
Tower, Darryl, 3029
Tower, Libby, 8073
Towers, Charles, 3160
Towers, Sheryl, 1012
Town, Allison, 6112
Townsend, Angeline, 1738
Townsend, Arnold, 6249
Townsend, Brendan, 1738
Townsend, Chelly, 7344
Townsend, David, 6230
Townsend, Don, 2330
Townsend, Erika, 1890
Townsend, Sueann, 269
Townsend, T. Peter, 2342
Towson II, G. Edward, 1478
Toy, Dina D., 89
Toy, Lucinda, 846
Tozzi, Giorgio, 2315
Traband, Michele, 8676
Trabichoff, Geoffrey, 1024
Tracey, Fred, 6319
Tracey, Ms. Megan, 7954
Trachtenberg, Matthew J, 1426

Tracy, Barbara, 835
Tracy, Barbara B., 1420
Tracy, Jeff, 7998
Tracy, Jerry, 2891
Tracy, Michael, 135
Tracy, Michaela, 2112
Tracy, Michelle, 1296
Tracy Carris, William, 5718
Traester, Carolyn M., 6443
Train, Simon, 6562
Trambley, Megan, 574
Tramm, Jason C., 2184
Trammel, Jeff, 7455
Trammell, Edward J, 1002
Tramp, Gus, 1735
Trampe, Catherine, 1135
Tran, Duc Joie, 4302
Trankel, Chris, 4881
Tranquada, Warren, 7574
Trapani, Sal, 2681
Trapanovski, Katherine, 7658
Trapp, Eric, 6685
Trapp, Franklin, 3441
Trapp, Micah, 4088
Trapp, Phillip R, 2449
Trask, Randy, 345
Trask, Susan F., 2087
Trask, Susan.F, 1147
Trask IV, Frederick K., 1951
Trask PhD, Franklin, 7257
Traupman-Carr, Carol, 5431
Trautwein, Sharon, 1796
Travaglia, Lorita, 122
Travaglini, Michael, 3135
Travaline, Barbara, 1332
Travers, Kerry, 1813, 5775
Traverso, Mark, 2758
Travis, Barry, 6038
Traxler, Dee, 8678
Traxler, Sharon, 7136
Trayer, Tom, 2238
Traynor, Jane, 3693, 7606
Traynor, Michael C., 4520
Trayte, Ryan, 6052
Trayte Peters, Leslie, 3916
Treacy, Mike, 6255
Treacy Beyer, John, 135
Treadaway, Jim, 3770
Treadway, John, 3274
Treadway, Scott, 3657
Treasurer, Mark, 6775, 6776, 6777, 6778
Treasurer, Roodzant, 8588
Treasurer, Tepper, 7671
Treat, Tyler, 3244
Trebour, Todd, 3149
Trebus, Danielle, 7045
Trecker, Barbara, 6677
Tredent, Joesph, 1516
Treebee, Carolyn, 230
Trefz, Curtis L., 7953
Treganza, James, 2628
Tregg, Mike, 2062, 2063
Trego, Adrienne, 5242
Trego, Jim, 8469
Trehar, Jennifer, 3844
Trejo, Mical, 3930
Trekell, Kirk, 8029
Trela, Christopher, 6193
Trela, Eugene, 2281
Trella, Mary T, 3361
Trembley, Gary, 7899
Treney, Jeff, 7498
Trenney, Tom, 4944
Trent, Layne, 2350
Trepton, Jessica, 7281
Treptow, Amelia, 4891
Trerice, Lauren, 304
Tresansky, F. Victoria, 1991
Tresnjak, Darko, 2686
Tresnowski, Bernard, 1039
Tressett, Ian, 3116
Treuer, Mary, 3224
Treuhaft, Joanne, 1570
Trevens, Janine Nina, 3572
Trevino, Ernie, 91
Trevino, Esther, 5675
Trevino, Victor, 447
Trexell, Brad, 1926, 1954

Trezza, Frank, 3457
Tribbey, Stuart N., 1833
Tribert, Margaret, 3867
Triboulet, DeAnn, 3041
Trice, Markus, 4207
Trich, Teresa, 3849
Trificana, Nicole, 504
Trifle, Carol, 3604
Trigg, Mary, 2187
Trigg, CPRP, Mike, 6847
Trimble, Pat, 2836
Trimingham, Barrie, 5485
Trimmer, Carol, 4629
Trinchero, Brisa, 8106
Trinh, Khanh, 1198
Trinki, John, 8233
Trinkle, Steven, 1499
Trinkoff, Donna, 3464
Triplett, Greg, 7355
Tripp, Jennifer, 5250
Tripvoi, Andrea, 7894
Trisler, Jeff, 8596
Tritle, Kent, 2248
Tritt, Jenny, 3288
Trivella, Marc, 133
Trivette, Susan, 1504
Trivilino, Brenda, 5176
Trizila, Jo, 5646
Trnobis, Eileen, 3613
Trocchia, Robert, 2286
Trofimenko, Peter, 1775
Troiano, Toni, 7154
Trojanowsky, John, 7699
Troll, Shane, 1891
Trombetta, Teal, 175
Trombold, Martha, 3848
Tromler, Nicole, 7500
Trompeter, Craig, 2049
Tropea, Rich, 1226
Trosko, Mariella, 8130
Tross Esq, Scott T, 334
Trotman, Bert, 5886
Trotter, Casey, 5697
Trotter, Jessica, 603
Trotter, Porrin, 2870
Trotter, Thomas, 8298
Troup, BP, 1192
Troup, David, 3106
Trout, Mark, 6041
Troutt, William, 5576
Trovillion, Nancy, 5263
Trowbridge, Marcella, 2691
Troxel, Nedra, 4669
Troxler, George, 5240
Troy, Carol, 8043
Truax, Katie, 1753
Truax, Nan, 3948
Truax, Selena, 7704
Truckenbrod, Phillip, 8751
Truckey, Amy, 7271
Trudeau, George, 8186
Trudelle, Tammy, 4862
Trueblood, Mark, 4322
Truelove, Michael, 1136
Truelove, Mike, 8403
Truesdell, Crystal, 46
Truex, Kathi, 5672
Trugdeau, John, 5545
Truhett, Meghan, 4152
Truilo, Julia, 2771
Truitt, Roger, 1135
Trujillo-Lucero, Jeanette, 128
Trulson, Kathie, 2365
Truman, Don, 5676
Truman, Rick, 3290
Trumble, Kyle, 3346, 7538
Trupiano, Greg, 2011
Trussell, Dana, 2735
Trussell Stanton, Ted, 2228
Trussler, Susan, 5503
Truvillion, Vanessa, 204
Truyell, Diana, 1554
Tryer, Mary, 1737
Tryon, William J., 122
Tsafoyanni, John, 3246, 3257
Tsai, Elbert, 900, 901
Tsai, Stella, 4516
Tsamous, Louis, 1547

Tsang, Dr. Chui, 2619
Tsang, Judy, 4313
Tsao, Andrew, 2035
Tsao, David, 2575
Tsao, Joe, 5738, 8524
Tschamler, Melissa, 1823
Tschernisch, Sergei, 5792
Tschida, Christine, 7358
Tseitli, Michael, 4272
Tseitlin, Irina, 4272
Tseitlin, Michael, 4272, 4273, 4274
Tseng, Muna, 462
Tseng, Ray, 462
Tsong, Rachael, 821
Tsou, Jason C, 7774
Tsui, Olivia, 789
Tsukamoto, Jean, 1019
Tu, Chi-Tsao, 1446
Tuan, Leon, 4270
Tubb, Billy, 7606
Tubman-Reichhoff, Denise, 5839
Tubre, Kimmie, 7148
Tucci, Al, 2431
Tucciarone, Christine, 7836
Tuceling, Barbara, 4432
Tuck, Mary, 5292
Tucker, Anita, 1101
Tucker, Billie, 2213
Tucker, Charlotte, 1311
Tucker, Cindi, 2
Tucker, Claire, 8303, 8304
Tucker, Curtis, 2254, 2255, 2287
Tucker, David, 4066
Tucker, Earl, 1434
Tucker, Eleesha, 4433
Tucker, Evan, 4082
Tucker, Gary, 7920
Tucker, Jean, 1109
Tucker, Jeffrey L., 1258, 1259
Tucker, JoAnne, 391
Tucker, Laurence, 1696, 8302
Tucker, Lawrence, 2334
Tucker, Michael, 4977
Tucker, Michelle, 4109
Tucker, Mike, 8610, 8613, 8614
Tucker, Scott, 1983, 1984
Tucker, William E., 2020
Tucker, Zack, 829
Tuckerman, Jan, 3328
Tucker, Andre, 7960
Tuckness, Amber, 1761
Tufte, Heidi, 4136
Tufts, Robert R, 856, 857
Tufts, Robert R., 1925
Tuggle, Clyde C., 6642, 6643
Tukloff, Scott, 2603
Tulley, Becky, 693
Tullidge, Jr, Thomas H., 8549
Tullos, Chaney, 4719
Tully, Jaclyn, 6185
Tuma, Dorothy, 4948
Tuma, Gary, 4123
Tuminella, Carolyn, 1659
Tumlinson, Christa, 4270
Tunbridge, Erin, 264
Tunie, Tamara, 7707
Tuntland, Lori, 1316
Tuohy, Gloria, 233
Tuomey-DePiro, Ann, 414
Tuomi PhD, Scott, 8076, 8078
Turbenson, Mitch, 4179
Turbyville, Eva, 613
Turek, Mark, 3864
Turgeon, Brianne, 2022
Turk, Dr. David F., 5175
Turkenkopf, Howard, 3156
Turlington, Maggie, 184
Turnbo, Marcus, 2927
Turnbull, Patricia, 2380
Turnbull, Ramona, 1297
Turner, Aimee, 3866
Turner, Allen M, 6754
Turner, Becky, 509
Turner, Brad, 5065
Turner, Carole, 293
Turner, Carolyn, 3126
Turner, Cary, 632
Turner, Christian, 2460

1229

Executive Name Index / U

Turner, Dr Greg, 713
Turner, Dr Steve, 5391
Turner, Erin, 4536, 5541
Turner, Heather, 3361
Turner, James, 4852
Turner, Janay, 5723
Turner, Jennifer, 2907
Turner, Joseph, 7882
Turner, Joyce, 5269
Turner, Kathleen, 4718
Turner, Krina, 686
Turner, Lindsey, 4393, 4394
Turner, Margaret, 4975
Turner, Mark, 4129
Turner, Nick, 3326
Turner, Nicole, 592
Turner, Paul, 2
Turner, Paulette, 628
Turner, Rebecca, 5905, 5906
Turner, Richard, 450, 5878
Turner, Ryan, 4775
Turner, Scott, 3067
Turner, Stephanie, 5084
Turner, Trent R., 1999, 2000, 2001
Turner, Valencia, 702
Turner, Vicky, 7815
Turner, Wendy, 4178
Turner, Wesley R., 1722
Turner, Jr., James F., 620
Turner, Ph.D., Dr. Steve, 3768
Turnham, Diane, 8289
Turning, Katie, 1517
Turpin, Bonnie, 1263
Turteltaub, Rhea, 6180
Turtle, Hillary, 1802
Turton, Neil, 7796
Turville, Gigi, 1316
Tuskan, Dennis, 207
Tutera, Cynthia J., 3846
Tuthill, Robert, 5050
Tuthill, William, 2201
Tutor, Jesse B., 1731
Tutt, Cheri, 4510
Tutterow, Russ, 2916
Tuttle, Dr. Siri, 1846
Tuttle, JB, 8326
Tuttle, Katie, 1680
Tuttle, Kim, 153
Tuttle, Michael R., 8504
Tuttle, Mo, 5637
Tuzicka,, 6962
Tuzicka, William, 4640
Tweeddale, Kelly, 8605
Twiss, Margaret, 2127
Twist, Basil, 3498
Twohig, Kevin, 8613
Twohig, Kevin J, 8615, 8616
Twomey, Jr., Thomas A., 3437
Tygeson, Sue, 6986, 6987, 6988, 6989
Tygett, Tom, 5964
Tykocki, Abbie, 1768
Tyler, Betsy, 826
Tyler, Cheever, 2696
Tyler, Edward, 4391
Tyler, Jennifer, 1236
Tyler, Lydia, 6655
Tyler, Maggie B., 2126
Tyler, Sally, 5643
Tyler, Sundi, 6026
Tymon, Deborah, 7640
Tynek, Dusan, 364
Tyner, Gaylon, 6033
Tyree, Fara, 4702
Tyree, Jane, 150
Tyrrell, Louis, 2792, 2794
Tyson, Hilary, 5497
Tyson, Susan, 658
Tyson, II, George E., 4121
Tyson,II, George E., 3237
Tyzik, Jeff, 8362

U

U'Prichard, PhD, David, 3840
U. Parfet, William, 6795
Ubbing, Mina, 5352
Ubell, Shirley, 429
Uberuaga, Lael, 196

Uchibori, Rochelle, 1017
Uchida, Christy, 1041, 2943, 4559
Uchida, Mitsuko, 5480
Uchizono, Donna, 416
Udagawa, Yoichi, 1195, 1201, 1218
Udeagha, Samantha, 3994
Udine, Laurie, 150
Udlock, Vicki, 1615, 5424
Udval, Bat Erdene, 254
Udy, Leo, 5791
Udy, Leo A., 4076, 8593
Uebele, Mark, 1654
Uebelhor, Heidi, 6928
Uecke, Ryan, 198
Uecker, Mark B., 2145
Ueckert, Allen, 8415
Ueefe, Anne, 2717
Uemura, Wisa, 861
Ugarte, Salvador, 2798
Uhl, Benjy, 5352
Uhl, Bud, 2137
Uhl, Dustin, 4134
Uhlemann, Barbara, 2157
Uhlhorn, Decker, 8161
Uhlmann, Heather, 139
Ujiiye, Ron, 6689
Ukura, Roberta, 6014
Uliasz, Lisa, 3852
Ulibarri, Linda, 7608
Ullberg, Heather, 4068, 4072
Ullestad, Kevin, 4547, 6724
Ullested, Kevin, 6854
Ullrich, Dawn, 8411
Ullrich, Down, 8409
Ulman, Barry, 1793
Ulmer, Jamie, 3323, 7484
Ulrich, Charles, 1515
Ulrich, Larry, 8009
Ulrich, Melanie, 3256
Ulrich, Sally, 1396, 5095
Ulvested, Glen, 5555
Umanoff, Nancy, 368
Umansky, David J., 4422
Umberger, Steve, 3665
Underdahl, Karla, 3691
Underhill, Catherine, 4356
Underhill, Michael, 736, 737
Underkoffler, Rod, 8130
Underwood, Cindy, 7456
Underwood, Denny, 2997
Underwood, Jill, 3232
Underwood, John, 1948, 1949
Underwood, Julia, 2089
Underwood, Julie K, 696
Underwood, Kim A, 7338
Underwood, Stephen, 3104
Underwood, William D., 4517
Undgren, Jodi, 8241
Unger, Lora, 824, 825
Unger, Matt, 6926
Uniatowski, Dr Joanne, 5314
Unkefer, Linda, 1830
Unrein, Cory, 1285
Unruh, Eric, 8713
Upbin, Brian, 1409, 5117
Upchurch, Jennifer, 3419
Upchurch, Lynn, 6230
Upchurch, Robert, 1489
Updegraff, Bill, 2238
Updegraff, Samantha, 345
Upham, Dr Steadman, 8057
Upper, Holly, 4352
Uprichard, Laurie, 485
Upsher, Kim, 7352
Upton, Barb, 923
Upton, Tracy, 8229
Upton Hill, Linda, 3903
Urban, Al, 4908
Urban, Sheri, 704
Urbanowski, Alexandra, 2602, 3356
Urbanski, Krzysztof, 1083, 1084
Urbis, Richard, 5599
Urion, Steve, 1110
Uroff, Dan, 6089
Urrutia, Moore, 1981
Urrutia, Oscar, 6238, 6243
Urwin, Ray, 1938
Usahacharoenporn, Proud, 55

Uscher, Nancy, 4882
Usdan, John, 5167
Usdan, Suzanne, 5167
Usherwood, Ron, 3406
Ussery, Norman, 3927, 8321
Uthoff, Michael, 310
Uwe Kern, Harald, 243
Uzdawinnis, Jeannie, 207

V

V. Ciccone, Gene, 3370
V. Romano, Dominick, 3376
Vacca, Michele L, 2920
Vaccaro, Sal, 5096, 7694
Vachon, Ann, 439
Vaden, Betsy, 343
Vadia, Roxana, 360
Vadnal, Michael, 2787
Vail, Jimmy, 5927, 5930
Vail, Martha, 1519
Vail, Mary, 4540
Vail, Robin, 1489
Vail, Sue, 4625
Vail, Tony, 6408
Vailas, Arthur C, 6711
Vailas, Arthur C., 6708, 6709, 6710, 6713
Vailes, Jomal, 2859
Vaillant, Caroline, 2173
Vajda, Gregory, 711
Valacich, Carolyn, 1298
Valcarcel, Carlos, 11
Valcke, Cathy, 6906
Valdes, Julian E., 8378, 8379
Valdes-Vargas, Maria, 4552
Valdez, Alfy, 4003
Valdez, Kinan, 2606
Valdez, Luis, 2606
Vale, Denise, 454
Vale, E. Merritt, 1509
Vale, Merrit, 2274
Vale, Merritt, 2273
Valencia, Jos,, 1088
Valenta, George, 2129
Valentin, Saul, 3988
Valentine, Alan D., 1696, 2334, 8302
Valentine, Bill, 6036
Valentine, Jill, 6755
Valentine, Joanne, 1866
Valentine, Rayna, 1027
Valentine, Richard D, 7413
Valentine, Whitney, 854
Valenzano Pampe, Vicki, 1140
Valiensi, Rachel, 6195
Valk, Chad E, 6433
Valk, Kate, 3594
Valkonen, Jukka, 4270
Valla, Sagine, 3377
Valle, Bree, 4318
Valle, Laura, 1110
Vallee, Dave, 1978
Vallee, Steve, 703
Valles, Judith, 839
Valles, Kirk, 2621
Valleto, Lisa, 1659
Valliere, Robby, 2900
Valoris, Henry, 4430
Valverde, Tim, 4906
Van, Dave, 4936
Van Alstyne, Annie, 649
Van Arsdale, Anneliese, 3833
van Baale, Christa, 2944
Van Becker, Antonia, 1870
Van Bergen, Christopher, 949
van Bergen, Kathleen, 981, 4882
Van Bergen, Kathleen, 6558
Van Beurden, Cle, 864
van Bever, Ann, 1608
Van Boxtel, Faye, 2603
Van Brandeghen, Claire, 1234
Van Buskirk, Christy, 7998
Van Cott, Claire, 3354
van de Christopher, Desiree, 4176
Van den Berg, Hank, 1307
van den Dorpel, Jan-Willem, 5135
Van den Hende, Jan H., 1748
Van Den Hoogen, Ingrid, 8
van der Hoeven, Bernard, 1359

Van Der Salm, Ruud, 2299
Van Derveer, Linda, 5003
Van Dewalli, Kathy, 8391
Van Dreser, Mike, 4126
Van Duvall, Una, 702
Van Duyne, Paul, 221
Van Dyke, Jan, 510
Van Dyke, Jeanna, 8077
Van Ersvelde, Ivy, 4656
Van Ess, Jan, 1477
Van Ess, Neal, 5836
van Eyck, Anthony, 3119
Van Eyck, Selma, 2396
Van Fleet, Vicki, 723
Van Fleteren, Roger, 1
Van Gelder, Phyllis, 4663
Van Gilder, Doug, 1313
Van Gilder, Lisa, 2789
Van Gilder, Lisa, 6535
Van Gomple, Megan, 1787
Van Gordon, Elizabeth, 6906
Van Hagan, Katherine, 1940, 1941
Van Handel, Michael, 1831
Van Hermert, Lettie, 5306
Van Heyde, Cindy, 982
Van Horn, Bill, 3099
Van Horn, Eric, 3048
Van Horn, Kathlee Favrot, 3083
Van Horn, Kathleen, 7141
Van Houten, Sallie, 2023
van Kalken, Maria, 4783
Van Kirk, Amy, 2258
Van Kleeck, Marty, 3979, 8394
Van Lee, Reginald, 4434
Van Leeuwen, Janene, 4176
Van Loo, Scott, 5299
Van Meter, Daivd, 7703
van Mook, Davida, 3850
Van Natta, Andrea, 1835
Van Nest, Deborah, 4207, 6066, 6070, 6071, 6072
Van Ommeren, Ryan, 6313
Van Osselaer, Andrew, 8324
Van Patten, Mauriel, 4477
Van Pelt, Carter, 7745
Van Pelt, Nita, 1604
Van Pelt, Peter, 4845
Van Pelt Petry, Susan, 527
Van Putten, Lisa, 411
van Rensburg, Desiree, 487
Van Rysdam, Jennifer, 7652
Van Scoy, Emily, 2686
Van Sickle, Dan, 2393
Van Sudmeier, Gregory, 782, 783
Van Tine, Kelsey, 241
Van Vrancken, Jessica D., 245
van Wageningen, Edith Wittig, 5768, 5769
Van Winkle, Ken, 11
van Zweden, Jaap, 2343, 5610
Vanasdale, Karen, 3286
VanAssche, Jack, 1246
Vanausdall, John, 6891
Vanaver, Bill, 380
Vanaver, Livia, 380
Vanberger, Kathleen, 4916
Vance, Aimee, 3916
Vance, Debra, 6282, 6285, 6287
Vance, Grace R., 1426
Vance, Mark, 4257
Vance, Mindy, 223, 311
Vance, Sonia, 325
Vance, Tom, 3647
VanCura, Barry, 611
Vandaveer, Kristen, 6040
Vanden Wyngaard, Julianne, 4818
VanDenBerg, Cindy, 4854
Vandenberg-Suju, Christina, 677
Vander Heyden, Cheryl, 293
Vander Leek, Scott, 7303
Vanderbilt, Thomas, 180
VanderBroek, Liese, 6954, 6955, 6956, 6957, 6958, 6959
Vanderburg, Judy, 8085, 8086
Vandergrift, Deborah, 6477
Vanderhoof, Winston, 4909
VanderLinden, Ed, 1111
Vandermaten, Ann, 3260
Vanderslice, Dr Ronna, 5384

Executive Name Index / W

Vanderyacht, Darcie, 8082
Vandeveen, Ron, 7553
Vanham, Lee, 8269
VanHarn, Chris, 4076, 8593
Vanison-Blakely, Dolores, 384
VanLandingham, Nancy, 8187
VanLandingham, Natalie, 3136
VanLent, Anne, 3381
VanLoon, Chelsea, 4881
Vanloon, Cheri, 3686
VanMoorsel, Mindi, 4352
Vann, Chris, 4376
Vann, Marvin, 8533
Vann, Robert, 837
Vanrenterghem, Craig, 5343
VanRy, Arvin, 6343
VanRy, Arvinene, 2651
Vanschaak, Tom, 8142
VanSpronsen, Norm, 1890
Vant Hof, Sandie, 4663
Vanzant, Cherie, 3808
Vapnek, Daniel, 4325
Vapnek, Dianne, 4325
Varadarajan, Ram, 98
Varano, Tom, 8799
Varde, Lisa, 6677
Vardigans, Sarah, 4210
Vareika, Allison, 3864
Vargas, Melissa, 898
Vargas, Rebeca, 439
Vargas, Vivian V., 1719
Vargas-Vetter, Rima, 421
Varghese, Annie, 7825, 7826
Vari, John, 3345
Varin, Charles, 2657
Varineau, John, 1235
Varnadore, Jamey, 3669
Varner, Elisabeth P., 1478
Varner, John, 2400
Varner, Marilee, 242
Varner, Robert, 1334
Varney, Jeana, 1294
Varney, Raye, 2876, 6653
Varnhagen, Frances, 1927
Voron, Neil, 1459
Varone, Doug, 418
Varricchio, Celeste, 329
Vasley, Susan, 3792
Vasquez, Alden, 4111
Vasquez, Daniel, 2576
Vasterling, Paul, 620
Vaughan, Casey, 5
Vaughan, David, 942
Vaughan, Deborah B, 52
Vaughan, Edee, 5572
Vaughan, John, 4221, 6116
Vaughan, Mary K, 1748
Vaughn, Bob, 4599, 6837
Vaughn, Katie, 4512
Vaughn, Merrill, 3562
Vaughn, Michael, 7867
Vaughn, Nanna G, 1086
Vaughn, Robert, 6838
Vaughn, Susan, 1079
Vaughn, Zena, 3931
Vaughn Scott, Dr. Mona, 2450
Vaugn Scott, Mona, 2450
Vaughn-Howard, Marion, 1786
Vaupel, Kathy, 1846
Vaupel, Tatjana, 8621, 8653
Vaupotich, Miran, 2227
Vautar, James, 8133
Vayna, Helena, 2631
Vazquez, Brandon, 1409
Vazquez, Cecilia, 8214
Vazquez, Islara, 1
Vazquez, Jorge, 8378, 8379
Vazquez, Silvio, 6280
Veal, Rodney, 530
Veater, Claire, 966, 4440
Vecchione, Tony, 8161
Veech, Lex, 6569
Veenhuis, David, 2139
Veenstra, Darlene, 7305
Vega, Dianne, 2605, 2606
Vega, Kay, 3778, 8081
Veidemanis, Gladys, 5837
Veitch, Jonathan, 6164, 6179, 6182

Vela, Luis, 2495
Velasco, Javier, 64
Velasco, Jerry G, 6129
Velasco, Zoot, 6112
Velasquez, Carol, 695
Velasquez, James, 5919
Velasquez, Mariah, 6280
Velasquez, Tom, 6065
Velkuer, Melody, 4568
Vella, Allan C., 6622
Vellaon, Jenna, 5306
Velli, Susan, 1158
Veloudos, Spiro, 3138
Veloz, Frank, 1929
Velthuisen, Riet, 292
Veltkamp, Vic, 1793
Veltri, Carrie, 7700
Vener, Victor, 865
Venis, Brent, 4682
Venizelos, Cindi, 3381
Venker, Teri, 1826
Venman, Bill, 2102
Vennerbeck, Eric, 2504
Vens, Kyrstin, 4092
Vento, Art, 6677
Ventre, Philip T, 943
Ventura, Vivian, 977
Venzago, Mario, 4750
Vera, Eric A., 3939, 8336
Verbsky, Franklin, 1384
Verburg, Carol, 4302
Verdeyen, Jacqueline, 3017
Verdier, Paul, 2476
Verdugo, Chris, 1942
Verenezi, Claire, 5204
Verept, Dotty, 5646
Vergara, Joy, 4562
Vergilio, Rosie, 8156
Vergin, Kelly, 7637
Verhoogen, Robert, 1589
Verhoogen, Sandra, 1589
Vermillion, Judd, 3758
Vermuele, Joel, 3892
Vernick, Clifford, 5035
Vernon, Mark, 2312
Veronesi, Alberto, 2251
Veronneau, Patrick, 6445
Verrastro, Elisabeth, 6424
Verrastro, Philip, 6615
Verschoor, Lynn, 8241
Vershbow, Ben, 3503
Verville, Timothy, 1581
Verzatt, Marc, 1968
Vesely, Alison, 4591
Vesely, Alison C, 4591
Vest, Suzanne, 2026
Vestal, Bill, 6166
Vestal, Lisa, 6304
Vestal, Robby, 5650
Vetsch-Sandoval, Theresa, 8098
Vetter, Valerie M, 4656
Vetters, Judy, 6119
Vezdos, Scott, 1547
Viallet, Marie, 8137
Viamontes, Orlando, 241
Viana, Kyle, 1234
Vianello, Lili, 1279
Vibe, Karen, 1315
Vicari, Matt, 3203
Vicens, Julienne, 432
Vick, Connie, 6025
Vick, Jackie, 2167
Vickers, Erin, 1690
Vickers, Frances, 7150, 7151
Vickrey, Robert, 582
Victor, Selah, 3901
Vidalakis, Zoe, 57
Vidmar, Alec, 8897
Viebrock, Lois, 3310
Vieceli, Ami, 7251
Viegas, Stephanie, 8089, 8092, 8096, 8099
Vieira, Matthew, 3503
Vienneau, Irene, 3178
Vierck, Judy, 1019
Vierk, Richard, 4945
Viertel, Tom, 2714, 2715
Viets, Scott, 6303
Vigessa, Delores, 1297

Vigil, Todd, 729
Vigilant, Michael, 4148, 4836, 5915, 5916
Vigna, Courtney, 6214
Vignati, Ruth, 2065
Vignola, Leonard, 131, 132
Vilaro, Eduardo, 393
Vilas, Doug, 6187
Villa-Strack, Wendy, 61
Villagomez, Luther, 8411
Villalobos, Cesar, 277
Villanueva, Josefa, 105
Villarreal, Teresa, 6318
Villarreal, Rick, 8369
Villaume, Emmanuel, 2342
Villeda, Archie, 2665, 6355
Villedsen, Alice, 5622
Villegas, Amanda, 2108
Villella, Edward, 160
Villeneuve, Anya, 7697
Villines, Jeremy, 3066
Villiot, Kristine, 4080
Vilsmeier, Beth, 1622
Vilter, Dan, 4221, 6116
Vincens, Danny, 7143
Vincent, Michael, 2422
Vincent, Nikki, 6651
Vine, Chris, 3481
Vines, Georgiana, 3904
Vinscon, Banitha, 2067
Vinsk, Lorene, 8168
Vinski, David, 3847, 5494
Vinson, Amy, 2405
Vinson, Mara, 676
Vinyard, George A., 6720, 6721
Vinzant, Douglas, 7392
Vinzant, Dr. Douglas, 4887
Violand-Jones, Shirley, 1488
Vipperman, Dick, 4055
Virgili, Gail, 5402
Virgin, Janice, 231
Viricel, Dr. Anne L., 839
Virtue, Tom, 6194
Visceglia Rodgers, Nicole, 4988
Visconti, dan, 953
Visel, Alexae J., 2447
Visel, Nikki, 4088
Visintainer-Armstron, Nancy, 4109
Viski Mestas, Nicholas A, 6160, 6161, 6162
Visuano, Denise, 8085, 8086
Vita Ganley, Damara, 79
Vitacca, Kelly Ann, 638
Vitale, Lori, 5260, 5261
Vitale, Ted, 3170
Vitalis, Ernese, 315
Vitello, Linda M, 8511
Vitter, Jeffrey S., 7043
Vittone, Anthony, 4046
Vitucci, Susan, 3490, 7727
Viverito, Diane, 6823, 6824
Vivero, H, 927
Vivirito, August, 2494
Vivolo, Nancy, 5787
Vizolis, Andris, 1203
Vizulis, Anda, 285
Vizzini, Tony, 7071, 7072, 7073
Vjailand, Leis, 4482
Vlassis, Dennis, 2792
Vo, Natalie, 6128
Vocatura, Nicholas, 4360
Voegelie, Laura, 7446
Voeltz, Suzanne, 697
Vogel, Debra, 968
Vogel, Jacob, 818
Vogel, Laura, 7796
Vogel, Monica, 4920
Vogelgesang, Denise, 6557
Vogelzang, Alexa, 1741
Vogt, Dolly, 8180
Vogt, Dolly, 8554
Vogt, Sean, 2141
Voight, Jerry, 848
Vokolek, Dana, 8827
Volckhausen, Sharon L., 1422
Volgenau, Lew, 5479
Volikir, Erica, 7346
Volk, Gregory, 5827
Volke, Jim, 7480

Volkers, Mark, 4663
Volkert, Susan, 6654
Volkoff, Andrew, 2903
Volkwein, Fred, 1963
Vollmer, Erich, 5096, 7694
Vollom-Matturro, Tammy, 721
Volpe, Karen, 8109
Volpe, Mark, 1177, 1178, 4795, 7227, 7238
Volpert, Michael, 1437
Voltaire, Keiko, 434
Voly, Carina, 4369
von Arx, Emmanuel, 8864
von Arx SJ, Rev Jeffrey P, 6400, 6401, 6402
Von Arx, S.J., Rev. Jeffrey P, 6403
von Bernuth, Marietta, 1473
von Brandt-Siemers, Barbara, 3991, 5645
von der Schmidt, Jeff, 826
Von Ells, Randi, 2294
Von Eschen, Lynn A., 7352
von Frank, Jane, 1796
Von Heidecke, Kenneth, 218
Von Hoffmann, Betty, 3281
Von Kloha, Geneen, 2162
Von Klug, Theresa, 3580
Von Rains Jr, Roy, 3790
von Reichbauer, William, 1732
von Stade Downing, Frances, 8509
Von Tempsky, Frances A, 2893
Von Wald, Robin, 1247, 1248
von Wurtzler, Dr. Aristid, 1429
Vonderheid, Barbara, 4362
Vonderschmitt, Andrew, 6150
Vonfrankemberg, Carlos, 6225
Vooren, R Scott, 1104, 1105
Voos, Angela, 6997, 6998, 6999
Vorbeck, Dave, 6908
Vorburger, Jane, 552
Voreyer, Matthew, 6231
Voreyer, Matthew W., 6232
Voris, Joe, 2997
Vorrasi, John, 2050
Vorsanger, Fred, 6024
Vosburgh, David, 2291
Vose, Erik, 6187
Voss, Gary, 6375
Voss, Kelly, 6936
Voss, Randy, 6062
Voss, Ray, 4646
Voss Howard, Peg, 3172
Voth, Pam, 3310
Votypka, Judi, 7997
Vourvoulas, Cheryl, 3115
VP, Horak, 8588
VP for Institutional, Bishop, 869
Vrebalov, Aleksandra, 364
Vredeveld, Carol, 4846
Vreugdenhil, Karen, 7018, 7020, 7021
Vroom II, Jacques, 3957
Vsarek, Alicija, 1002
Vulgamore, Allison, 1007, 1647, 2021, 4503
Vuocolo, Michael, 1668
V„nsk„, Osmo, 1265

W

W. Allen,, Susan, 3229
W. Belluck, Joseph, 7849
W. Cone, Elizabeth , 7885
W. Davis, Elizabeth, 3069
W. Risberg, Del, 3113
W. Rosa, John, 8211
W. Satterlee, Anne, 6517
Waag, Tony, 387
Waart, Edo de, 1830
Waaser, Carol, 7669
Waber, Art, 8872
Wachenheimer, Neal, 1384
Wachner, Julian, 1995
Wacholder, Linda, 4025, 4968
Wacholz, JC, 1058
Wachtel, Jeff, 883
Wachtel, Linda, 1058
Wacker, Dr. Jonathan, 1503
Wada, Francis, 1198
Wada, Toshimasa, 1198
Waddell, Blair, 612
Waddell, Dona, 4381
Waddell, Ginna, 3870

1231

Executive Name Index / W

Waddell, Grady, 1698
Waddell, Greg, 5303
Waddell, Rachel L., 1523, 1524
Waddell, Vivian, 4465
Waddill, Russ, 1704
Wadding, Ed, 1620
Wade, Ann, 4409
Wade, Becky, 2341
Wade, Bill, 523
Wade, Dawn, 780
Wade, Eugene, 6347, 6353, 6357
Wade, Jacob, 1605, 8091
Wade, Mark, 8222
Wade, Martha, 8860
Wade, Rachel, 829
Wade, Rebekka K., 4491
Wade, Robert, 2383
Wade, Tim, 1778, 4850
Wade, Mike, 6800
Wadhams, John, 1976
Wadler, Michael, 2453
Wadley, Marlyn, 2833
Wadsworth, Kim, 3520
Wadsworth, Pebbles, 8326
Wadsworth, Susan, 5172
Wadsworth, Tom, 1688
Waetzman, Ronald, 2905
Wafer, Shay, 5051
Wagar, Jeannine, 752
Wagenfeld, Sandra, 2246
Wager, Kimberly M., 494
Wager, Susan, 5742
Wager, Timothy, 2173
Waggoner, Mark, 6365
Wagler, Erin, 4626
Wagman, Laurie, 2310
Wagner, Allen, 1137
Wagner, Andrea, 5801
Wagner, Barbara, 1128
Wagner, Bill, 4255
Wagner, James W., 6620
Wagner, Jeannine, 1936
Wagner, Jerry, 5557
Wagner, JL, 6597
Wagner, John, 7981
Wagner, Joylene, 6115
Wagner, Kaye, 8663
Wagner, Kevin, 1661
Wagner, Lisa, 4664, 7993
Wagner, Maria, 4743
Wagner, Michael, 1655
Wagner, Pat, 3029, 6996
Wagner, Rick, 1586
Wagner, Roger, 1936
Wagner, Shirley, 3048
Wagner, Sr. Marella, 5850, 8685
Wagner, Suzanne L., 2041
Wagner, Thomas, 3716
Wagner, Thomas C., 7997
Wagner, Tony, 3251
Wagner, Tracy, 6364
Wah, Amanda, 4237
Wahl, David, 5547
Wahl, Diana, 4540
Wahlberg, Sonja, 3244
Wahr, David, 7569
Wahr, David, 7264
Waickman, Kit, 3255
Waicul, Ron, 7523
Wain-Becker, Roberta, 1934
Wainstein, Michael, 3049
Waipio Werner, Lisa, 5788, 5789, 5790
Wait, Charles V, 3619
Wait, Gregory, 1892
Waiters, Jess, 6210
Waitt, Rebecca, 324
Wakefield, Will, 2384
Wakely, Judith, 4526
Walaitis, Gregory, 6104
Walbolt, Margo, 2761
Walborn, Dr. Ronald, 5175
Walden, Captain Brian O, 960, 961, 962, 963
Walden, Nathan, 2997
Walden-Dixson, Bruce, 3777
Waldi, Susan, 3341
Waldman, Alison, 659
Waldman, Jen, 7687
Waldman, Mara, 2181

Waldo-Dentzel, Elisabeth, 4259
Waldron, Archie, 4525
Waldron, Jeffrey L, 6216
Waldron, Jeffrey L., 4276
Waldrop, Jane, 2376
Walerysiak, Beverly, 8134
Walerysiak, Beverlyh, 8135
Wales, Gena, 1789
Wales, Lorraine, 5344
Walizer, Amy, 1626
Walk, David, 5707
Walk, Margaretha, 5884
Walkar, Anita, 7040
Walke, Suzanne, 3744
Walker, Al, 121
Walker, Andress, 43
Walker, Anthony, 1996
Walker, Antony, 2321
Walker, Arlene, 4904
Walker, Audrey, 2554
Walker, Barb, 8298
Walker, Bill, 4191, 7141
Walker, Bruce, 1814, 1815
Walker, Charles D, 2219
Walker, Chet, 4772
Walker, Christina, 7978
Walker, Cindy, 1355
Walker, Craig, 6112
Walker, Dan, 2642
Walker, David, 2268, 6133, 6135
Walker, Debbie J, 6146
Walker, Dorothy, 8315
Walker, Dr. Billy, 6460
Walker, Dr. J. Patrick, 5606
Walker, Dr. Janice, 5307, 5308, 5310, 5311
Walker, Eddie, 1584
Walker, Erik, 365
Walker, Ethel Pitts, 2572
Walker, Fred, 7938
Walker, James, 1386, 1387
Walker, James L., 3883
Walker, Jeffrey, 6405
Walker, Jennifer, 7662
Walker, Jim, 3883
Walker, Joan, 4959
Walker, John, 1685, 1828, 5976, 8202
Walker, Joseph, 1440
Walker, Judith H, 5728
Walker, Juli, 2982
Walker, Karen, 1483
Walker, Katheryn, 3524
Walker, Kimberly, 6177
Walker, Marsha, 296
Walker, Mary, 1685, 1686
Walker, John Powel, 4922
Walker, Philip, 5218
Walker, Phillip E, 2572
Walker, Ray, 3984
Walker, Robert C, 3208
Walker, Robin, 4041
Walker, Scott, 4790
Walker, Shaquan A, 5446
Walker, Stacy, 3877
Walker, Stephanie, 8048
Walker, Sue, 891
Walker, Tyrone C., 262
Walker, Walter, 1863
Walker, Willa R., 1231
Walker Jr., Alexander J, 7539
Walker-Wilkens, Sheila, 209
Walkoczy, Deborah, 3373
Wall, Becky, 2267
Wall, Betty, 1727
Wall, Bob, 1727
Wall, Charles R., 2238
Wall, David, 1264
Wall, Emma, 1500
Wall, John, 1213
Wall, Katelyn, 1767
Wall, Kendell, 8221
Wall, Larry, 1752
Wall, Mike, 4162, 5943
Wallac, Patrick, 5823
Wallace, Abigail, 659
Wallace, Amy, 4089
Wallace, Angela, 5071
Wallace, Ashley, 8444
Wallace, Bill, 1758
Wallace, Brad, 8268

Wallace, Bruce, 4263
Wallace, Charly, 5590, 8323
Wallace, Claud, 5648
Wallace, Emily, 194
Wallace, Heather, 328
Wallace, Jerry, 3055
Wallace, Josiah, 7018, 7020, 7021
Wallace, Kadie, 6083
Wallace, Leslie, 262
Wallace, Marilyn, 4263
Wallace, Matt, 4696
Wallace, Mike, 6289, 6290
Wallace, Nancy E., 1474
Wallace, Patrick, 4104
Wallace, Patrick H., 4104, 5822
Wallace, Ray, 6027
Wallace, Reed M, 1506
Wallace, Robin, 6639
Wallace, Rosemarie, 4331
Wallace, Shawn, 8195
Wallace, Steven, 2828
Wallach, Daria L., 381, 385
Wallenmeyer-Krahman, Ann, 4164
Waller, Dameka, 2848
Waller, Mark, 4870
Waller, Richard, 5312
Waller, Richard H, 1002
Waller, Rosemarie, 4331
Waller, Winifred, 3924
Wallerstein, David S, 1017
Wallfisch, Elizabeth, 766
Wallick, Michael, 725
Wallin, Dr. Nicholas L., 1797
Wallin, Erik, 5052
Wallin, Katy, 6077
Walling, Ardis, 879
Walling, Tim, 7584
Wallington, Joy, 5306
Wallis, Jessica, 518
Wallis, Kathryn, 4456
Wallmeyer, Katrina, 4873
Wallnau, Carl, 3365, 4994
Walls, George, 4125
Walls, Jody, 4472
Walls, II,, Fredric T., 3120
Walp, Robert, 1728
Walsh, Brad, 6846
Walsh, Debi, 1201
Walsh, Diane, 5203
Walsh, Dominic, 221
Walsh, Donnie, 4619
Walsh, Freda, 6447
Walsh, Goeff, 4871
Walsh, Jack, 5054
Walsh, John Powel, 4922
Walsh, Joseph, 2374, 2379
Walsh, Joseph W., 8199
Walsh, Kathy, 4751
Walsh, Kristi, 4171, 5962
Walsh, Kyle, 6735
Walsh, Liz, 3840
Walsh, Margaret, 2907
Walsh, Meredith, 7253, 7254
Walsh, Michele, 7825, 7826
Walsh, Mike, 6829
Walsh, Pamela, 1430
Walsh, Robert, 4970
Walsh, Sharon, 5200
Walsh, Shasti, 5799
Walsh, Susan, 8061, 8064
Walsh, Terrance, 660
Walt, Peggy, 5079
Walter, Debra, 3799
Walter, Elaine, 742
Walter, Elaine R, 1991
Walter, Hank, 4117
Walter, Sherry, 7867
Walter, U. William, 1557
Walter, Zach, 6271
Walters, Barry, 1726
Walters, Carole, 3204
Walters, Charles, 8563
Walters, Chris, 5065
Walters, Dr. Teresa, 5000
Walters, Gary D, 7583
Walters, Jaclyn, 8295
Walters, Jennifer, 5352
Walters, Kathryn, 1609
Walters, Randall, 525

Walters, Rudolph, 4892
Walters Goddard, April, 1764
Walter, Hank, 4117
Walther, Joe, 7522
Waltman, David, 1802
Walton, Chip, 2656
Walton, Jerry, 6026
Walton, William, 2681
Walworth, Candace, 3097
Walz, Robin Walz, 2419
Wampler, Karen, 7990
Wampler, Kimberly, 7990
Wanderman, Ken, 767
Wandling, Mary, 1474
Wandstrat, Scott, 2851
Wanenchak, Leo, 2092
Wang, Annie, 2575
Wang, Dana, 7288
Wang, Henry, 860
Wang, Jocelyn R., 2499
Wang, Lorraine C., 7222
Wang, Shou-lai, 1446
Wangen, Doug, 1028
Wangh, Jo-Ann, 1199
Wankel, Edward E., 1382, 5071
Wanlass, Megan, 3564
Wanlass Szalla, Megan, 3564
Wannemacher, Greg, 7998
Wannen, David, 2239, 8780
Wanner, Dan, 5145
Wanserski, Emily, 38
Want, Hsu, 1446
Wanta, Bruce, 4068, 4072
Wanvig, Barbara, 6255
Warburg, Joan M, 3461
Ward, Andrew, 4839, 7296
Ward, Ann, 1163
Ward, Anne, 1163
Ward, Beverly, 4234
Ward, Bonnie, 1910, 2571
Ward, Bonnie J, 2570
Ward, Butch, 6345
Ward, Buzz, 3704
Ward, Charles, 6267
Ward, Charmaine, 4505
Ward, Christoper, 1943
Ward, Don, 1910, 2571, 4539
Ward, Donna, 3522
Ward, Elizabeth, 1810
Ward, Frank, 8298
Ward, Glenn, 1908
Ward, Jacqueline, 1018
Ward, James K., 729
Ward, Jimmy, 3879
Ward, Laura, 2883
Ward, Lauren C., 6282, 6285, 6287
Ward, Marianne, 1488
Ward, Marybeth, 6137, 6138, 6139, 6140, 6141, 6142, 6143
Ward, Matthew, 6313
Ward, Patrick, 3816
Ward, Rachel, 1934
Ward, Randall, 7500
Ward, Roger, 865
Ward, Roger Allen, 865
Ward, Scott, 7271
Ward, Sharon, 3904
Ward, Sherry, 3945
Ward, Shirlene, 8760
Ward, Thomas, 418
Ward, Thomas L., 5752
Ward, Warren, 4613
Ward, Wayne, 2119
Ward, William, 2518
Ward Ruffner, Lester, 730
Wardell, Matthew, 982
Wardlaw Bailey, James, 4159
Wardle, Sarah, 1786
Wardropper, Ian, 5133
Wardwell, Maria, 3158
Ware, AJ, 2936
Ware, Chris, 3430
Ware, Dennert O., 1749
Ware, Eugenia, 1191
Ware, Tom, 2542
Wareham, Ann E., 2484, 6147
Wares, Robbie, 6680
Warf, Fred, 3320

Executive Name Index / W

Warfield, Neill, 4079
Warfield, Todd, 3424
Warfield, Neill, 8598
Warford, Lindsey, 1432
Warg, Dana, 3199, 7282, 7286, 7287
Warhol, Kay, 635
Warhol, Mark, 1264
Warmflash, Stuart, 3495
Warmington, Flynn, 1188
Warne, Katherine M, 5319
Warner, Becki, 5386
Warner, Bruce, 3804
Warner, Buddy, 4204
Warner, Carol, 2284
Warner, Charles C., 1544, 2283
Warner, Douglas, 2523
Warner, Ethan, 4407
Warner, Irene, 4467
Warner, Kathy, 5355
Warner, Lorrie A., 372
Warner, Maria, 3660
Warner, Mark, 7175
Warner, Mark D., 2953
Warner, Mary Lee, 733
Warner, Mike, 860
Warner, Ron, 4061
Warner Esq, Ken, 129
Warner Limoli, Denise, 133
Warnick, Kevin, 8493
Warnock, Bettye, 643
Warran, Sarah, 1832
Warre, John, 5539
Warrell, Bill, 4420
Warren, Angela, 1598, 5414
Warren, Beverly, 7995
Warren, Don, 2677
Warren, Gina, 8277
Warren, Janet, 4026
Warren, Jean S, 2408
Warren, Jenni, 720, 5939
Warren, Jennifer, 305
Warren, Jim, 4056
Warren, Joel, 7803
Warren, Laurielle, 1724
Warren, Lee, 1691
Warren, Robert, 4838, 6586
Warren, Scott, 8536, 8537, 8540, 8541, 8543, 8544
Warren, Wendy, 1786
Warren-Green, Christopher, 1485
Warrenton, Virginia, 4057
Warrick, Cynthia, 8235
Warrick, Douglas, 4207
Warrick, Liz, 2035
Warshaw, Marvin, 5772
Warshaw, Marya, 359
Warshawsky, Evy, 4770, 4822
Warshawsky, Adam, 1340
Warstler, Deidra, 5965
Wartella, Brad, 4096
Wartella, Nicholas, 1382, 5071
Warwick, Helen, 414
Warwick, Teri, 1549, 1550
Warzyn, Janet, 4206
Washburn, Daniel, 3969, 8384
Washburn, Drew, 3737
Washburn, Nan, 1250
Washington, Erwin, 43
Washington, Jennifer J, 4548
Washington, Lula, 43
Washington, Pat, 2039
Washington, Terence, 640
Washington, Teri, 6465
Washington, Valerie, 7639
Washington Mayhew, Ruth, 1197
Washington-Miller, Tamica, 43
Washton, Martin C, 2463, 2493, 2509
Wasser, Steven, 3138
Wassergord, Dale, 3290
Wasserman, Bryna, 3493
Wasserman, Elliot H, 6865, 6866
Wasserman, Mark D, 1005, 1006
Wasserman, Rena, 2521
Wassermann, Brittney, 100, 101
Wasserstrom, Chuck, 6761
Waszczak, John, 4180
Wat, John, 2887
Watanabe, Derek, 4072

Watanabe, Kensho, 934
Waterhouse, Tamsyn, 1924
Waterman, Glennis, 6301
Waters, Ashley, 356
Waters, James, 3947
Waters, Neville, 4419
Waters, Shirley, 2702
Waters, Willie, 1964
Waters Broe, Dr Carolyn, 1865
Watkins, David, 5031
Watkins, Heidi, 6984
Watkins, James, 5900
Watkins, Jeffery, 2858
Watkins, Karin, 7236
Watkins, Kendra, 4042
Watkins, Mark, 7941
Watkins, Penny, 5816
Watkins, Robert, 668
Watkins, Russ, 1694
Watkins, Salena M., 444
Watkins, Sandy, 5541
Watkins, Sara, 938
Watkins, Scott, 751
Watkins, Thaddeus, 6265
Watkins, Timothy R, 1010
Watley, Matt, 7397
Watson, Alison, 506
Watson, Barbara, 3113
Watson, Clare, 6
Watson, Dan, 8570
Watson, David, 1933
Watson, Debbie, 1744, 4152, 5923
Watson, Dolores, 5277
Watson, Doris, 1705
Watson, Eugenie, 2540
Watson, Frank, 4491
Watson, Gail, 1451
Watson, Jennifer, 3898
Watson, Karen, 8238
Watson, Libby, 1220
Watson, Lisa, 2859
Watson, Lisa Dickerson, 5366, 5367
Watson, Lisa L, 2859
Watson, Mary Jane, 1454
Watson, Mike, 7332
Watson, Nancy, 708
Watson, Paula, 5671
Watson, Rebecca, 8595
Watson, Scott, 5533
Watson, Steve, 5507
Watson, Tom, 1698
Watson, Walter, 1554
Watt, Jim, 7304, 8205
Watters, Robert, 1325
Watterson, Ralph, 3973
Watton, Janet, 5717, 8508
Wattrick, Lou Anne, 4844
Watts, Edward Q, 2193
Watts, Rob, 6448
Watts, Robbin, 2760
Watts, Sue, 7469
Watts, Terry Ann, 6354
Waugh, Bill, 7429
Waugh, Christopher, 6087
Waugh, Michael, 8127
Wawrukiewicz, Mary, 1601
Wax, David M., 3859
Way, Brenda, 86, 6262
Way, Jim, 1682
Waye, Avril, 1193
Waye, Avril K, 4815
Wayne, Jill, 126
Wayne, Nick, 3234
Wayns, Kevin E., 5474
Wayte, Alan, 792, 4227, 6124, 6157
Waz Jr., Joseph, 5489
Wead, Carol, 1321
Weakland, Christina, 8504
Weakland, Steve, 6104
Wealthy, John, 2468
Wears, William O, 1993
Weast, Wade, 1507
Weatherburn-Thiemet, Jennifer, 225
Weatherington, Jim, 6817
Weatherly, Tom, 2246, 2251
Weathers, Danny x, 2788
Weathwax, Alyson, 7249
Weaver, Arden, 3226, 3227

Weaver, Coutland, 8
Weaver, Earl D, 3304
Weaver, Jessica, 3973
Weaver, Jim, 7418, 8513, 8514
Weaver, Justin, 4322
Weaver, Lawrence, 2019
Weaver, Mack, 5575
Weaver, Martha, 4629
Weaver, Mathew, 5462
Weaver, Rollie, 6078
Weaver, Stephanie, 7234, 7255
Webb, Anne Hopper, 1218
Webb, Daphne, 6349
Webb, Darin, 413
Webb, David, 6095
Webb, Donald A, 1144
Webb, Iain, 169
Webb, Jimmy, 7712
Webb, Judson, 6332
Webb, Judy, 8391
Webb, Paul, 6262
Webb, Roger, 988
Webb, Suzannne, 7459
Webb, Tela, 6022
Webb, Terry, 5353
Webber, Christine, 1119
Webber, David, 1436
Webber, Len, 5404, 5407
Webbs, David, 6094
Weber, Beverly D., 3847
Weber, Bill, 1905
Weber, David, 4999
Weber, Donna, 2855
Weber, Eugene, 5300
Weber, Hal, 837
Weber, Kaitlin, 261
Weber, Kathleen A, 6774
Weber, Mark R, 4844
Weber, Mary, 1266
Weber, Mellissa, 4877
Weber, Michael, 3018
Weber, Paul, 5221
Weber, Paula, 309
Weber, Ronald B, 4476
Weber, Stephen, 2569
Weber, Susan, 24
Weber, Virginia, 5628, 8391
Weber Federico, Robert, 1043
Webre, Septime, 149
Webster, Ken, 3930
Webster, Lynn, 231
Webster, Martin, 1667
Webster, Obie, 8256
Webster, Richard R, 4576
Webster, Theresa, 1515
Webster, Wayne, 5865
Webster Latshaw, Sunshine, 138
Wecht, Dr. Cary, 8023, 8024
Weck, Fred, 953
Weckesser, John, 7617
Weckesser, Josh, 211
Weckesser Hall, Kelly, 267
Weddle, Christopher, 4097
Wedekindt, David, 7658
Wedin, Sharon, 4264
Wedington, Bonnie, 4549
Wedseltoft, Jorgen, 6205
Weeber, Rod, 7301, 7304
Weed, Jim, 1164
Weeda, Linn, 718
Weeden, Mary, 1396, 5095
Weekley, Dallas, 967
Weekly, Joyce, 5653
Weeks, Dr Douglas, 1684
Weeks, Jason, 4657, 4658, 4659, 4660, 4661
Weeks, Ralph, 3839, 8163, 8164, 8165, 8166
Weeks, Randy, 2657, 6352, 6360, 6367, 6368, 6369, 6370
Weems, Ron, 7160
Weesley, Tom, 3895
Wefald, Jon, 7050, 7051
Wefelmeyer, Kimberly, 8138
Wegener, Kim, 194
Wegmann, Linda, 7141
Wegner, Kenneth, 3373
Wehman, Rollin, 4036
Wehman, Rollin E, 4036
Wehr, Gail, 3280

Wehrle, Kate, 3632
Wehrman, Robert, 4529
Wei, Crystal, 1441
Weidemann, Julie, 6122
Weidemann, Thomas, 7667
Weidenborner, Stephanie, 217
Weidner, Bill, 5868
Weidner, Catherine, 7688
Weidner, Lucy, 4118
Weidner, Marcia, 5355
Weigand, Connor, 567
Weigandt, Chris, 3887
Weigel, Ellen, 1807
Weigel, Jane, 4155
Weigel, Jay, 7139
Weigle, Deborah, 2380
Weihert, Glenn, 8679
Weil, Ben, 4020
Weil, Bradley, 1286
Weil, Bruno, 766
Weil, Joan, 5969
Weil, John, 3299
Weil, John D., 3299
Weil, Richard, 552
Weilbaecher, Danial, 4717
Weiler, Ernest, 5479
Weiler, Linda, 125
Weiler, Susan, 4788
Weill, Bruno, 4211
Weill, Joan H., 381, 385
Weill, Sanford I., 5818, 7719
Wein, George, 1421, 4209, 5144
Wein, Stephanie, 1445
Weinberg, Gary, 7639
Weinberg, Matthew, 1171, 1172
Weinberger, Barbara, 3953
Weinberger, Jason, 1101
Weinberger, Rachel, 1348
Weinberger, Thomas R, 6173
Weinberger, Thomas R., 4243
Weiner, Earl, 3461
Weiner, Earl D, 3461
Weiner, James, 7589
Weiner, Melanie, 3588
Weiner, Sydell, 2456
Weiner, Toby F., 6135
Weinert, Kirk, 1730
Weinert, Richard, 5123
Weinert MS DC, Daniel, 6976
Weinflash, Alison, 7835
Weingarten, Susana, 521
Weinkle, Susan, 4482
Weinlein, Alfonso, 375
Weinlein, Estelle, 375
Weinstein, David, 1440
Weinstein, Ellen, 403, 463
Weinstein, Mark, 2321, 5226
Weinstein, Stanley, 8789
Weinstein Gary, Kaye, 669
Weintraub, Aviva, 7736
Weintraub, Jason, 1378
Weir, Debi, 2350, 5624
Weir, James, 3977
Weir, Todd, 1681
Weirich, Keith, 4970
Weirick, Joel, 3409
Weisenburger, Leigh A., 7169
Weisfield, Jodi, 1656
Weising, Jennifer, 4850
Weisinger, Shannon, 8098
Weiskel, Catherine, 1180
Weiskittel, Ford, 5079
Weisman, Arthur A., 7947
Weisman, Walter, 4015
Weisman, Walter L., 4013, 4015
Weiss, Al, 6539
Weiss, Arthur A, 1229
Weiss, Atty. Ronald, 1210, 1211
Weiss, Bob, 7218
Weiss, David, 764
Weiss, Debra, 495
Weiss, Dr. John, 3721
Weiss, Gerri, 3846
Weiss, Harriet, 3836
Weiss, Joe, 6291, 6293, 6294, 6296
Weiss, Jurgen, 279
Weiss, Kathy, 5076
Weiss, Mark, 5874

1233

Executive Name Index / W

Weiss, Mark D., 8085, 8086
Weiss, Raymond, 8816
Weiss, Rhonda, 379
Weiss, RJ, 4457
Weiss, Robert, 511
Weiss, Sande, 8308
Weiss, Sandra, 1052
Weiss, Steven Marc, 6966, 6968, 6970
Weiss, CPA, JD, Dan, 1547
Weissman, Allie, 91
Weissman, Jay, 477
Weissman, Neile, 3569
Weit, Frances, 1039
Weitzman, Ron A, 768
Welborn, David, 6023
Welch, Cecil, 4143
Welch, Doris Fritz, 1180
Welch, Jim, 3296
Welch, Karen, 4107
Welch, Kip, 1584
Welch, Lisa, 5136
Welch, Nina, 4252
Welch, Richard, 6996
Welch, Stanton, 638
Welcher, Christine, 1916
Welde, Constance, 6450
Weldon, Jane, 4623
Welker, Darren, 5515, 8191
Well, Ashley, 3761
Wellbaum, Ray F, 1177, 1178
Wellborn, Michael, 4085
Wellbourne, Jr, Dr. Sullivan, 5246
Welle, Megan, 4877
Weller, Elissa, 4873
Weller, Harry, 1531
Weller, Kathleen, 575
Weller, Patricia, 3161
Welles, Jr., David K., 8017
Wellington, Imelda, 2774
Wellington, Ph.D., Judith L., 8627
Welliver, Cassie, 8590, 8591
Wellman, Alan, 2051
Wellman, Ron, 7925
Wells, Alan, 2331
Wells, Barbara, 5756
Wells, Barbara C, 2804
Wells, Biz, 2903
Wells, Bob, 2654
Wells, Brian, 6236, 6237
Wells, Christine, 1207
Wells, Dr James R, 4840
Wells, Emily, 726
Wells, J. Michael, 6407
Wells, Jeff, 4545
Wells, Jennifer, 2376
Wells, Jeremy, 8298
Wells, John A, 5448
Wells, John a Casey, 8122
Wells, Katie, 6633
Wells, Kermit, 2056
Wells, Larry, 1604
Wells, Palmer, 2876, 6653
Wells, Pat, 1644
Wells, Shaler, 1703
Wells, Steve, 4358, 6337
Wells, Taylor, 1998
Wells, Travis, 1647
Wels, Elly, 3638
Welser-M"st, Franz, 1535
Welsh, Carliegh, 7774
welsh, Caroline, 7697
Welsh, Christine, 7300
Welsh, George, 8518
Welsh, Greta, 6057, 6058, 6059, 6060, 6061
Welsh, Meghan, 4029
Welsh, Melody, 1132
Welsh, Susan, 6650
Welsh, Thomas, 5316
Welter, Linda, 1877
Welty, Peg, 6511
Wenckus, Tracy, 2300
Wendeborn, Mark, 1795
Wendt Lasota, Kay, 200
Wengrzynek, Fred, 942
Weninger, Jill, 8223
Wenta, Stefan, 36
Wente, Philip R, 798
Wentworth, Kenneth, 8806

Wenzel, Pete, 8631
Werch, Shifra, 2043
Werder, Tom, 5001
Werdmuller, Dana, 767
Weres, Kurt, 5439
Werkmeister, Christina, 7825, 7826
Werle, Dr. Kathy, 4252
Werlinich, Lucille, 1448
Werner, Ellen, 4729
Werner, Jessica, 3424
Werner, Warren, 2800
Werstler, Greg, 2950
Wert, Steve, 285
Werth, Ernest, 3211
Wertheim, Frederick, 1438, 5156
Wertheim, James, 5131
Wertheimer Esq, Spencer, 578
Wertzer, Carla, 3063
Werz, Andreas, 787
Weskamp, Birgit, 4327
Weske, Anne, 1851
Wesler, Ken, 1642, 1669, 5515, 8191
Wesley, Barbara, 1890
Wesley, Dawn, 4687
Wesley Strickler, Dr. John, 1273
Wesp, E Joel, 3730
Wesp, Patricia, 5766
Wessel, Michael, 2123
Wesselhoft, Betsy, 3207, 7308
Wesselowski, Nathan, 2394
Wesson, Ed, 5917
West, Claire, 4169
West, Cyd, 3994
West, Don, 4171, 4932, 5962
West, Erin, 6050
West, Jonathan, 4109
West, Judy, 4631
West, Katie, 5481
West, Lance, 8632
West, Lance A, 8638
West, Lee, 3679
West, Morgayne, 473
West, Philip, 618
West, Sallie, 4510
West, Shannon, 306
West, Shirley, 1089
West Muir, Vita, 4393, 4394
West-McCombs, Traci, 8627
Westbrooke, Paul, 5391
Westemeier, Tim, 6969
Wester, Jeanie J., 4739, 4744
Westerbeek, Glynda, 5260, 5261
Westerdoll, Jennifer, 6685
Westergaard, Cynthia, 4163
Westerman, Kit, 463
Western, John, 4311
Western, Thomas F., 242
Westhoff, Christopher, 3753
Westlake, Adrienne, 253
Westland, Martha, 1917
Westmoreland, Andrew, 5893, 5896
Westmoreland, Andy, 6016
Westmoreland, Brian, 131, 132
Weston, Wade, 7939
Weston Bell, Heather, 7092, 7093, 7096
Westover, Pam, 4833, 7280
Westover, Pamela, 2132
Westveer, J R, 7218
Westwood, Donald, 2245
Westwood, Jefferson, 7674
Wetherall, T K, 2828
Wetherbee, Charles, 5340
Wetherbee, Mary Ann, 4641
Wetherber, Charles, 5340
Wetherington, Jim, 4594
Wethers, Shane, 7371
Wethrill, Wendy, 1630
Wetli, Peg, 3231, 3265
Wettach, Michael, 7682
Wettach Esquire, Thomas, 3848
Wetter, Margaret, 8601, 8602
Wetz, Coni, 8038
Wetz, Gary, 8082
Wetzel, James D., 1963
Wetzel, Richard, 7944
Wetzel, Todd E, 4635
Wetzell, Nicole, 6730
Wexchler, Malcolm, 3494

Wexler, Larry, 2851
Wexner, Leslie H, 7987
Weyand, Doug, 7629
Weyer, Brandi, 6866
Weyerhaeuser, William T., 2387, 8605
Weyler, Walter E., 1605, 8091
Weyrauch, Clark, 2275
Whalen, Anita, 1074
Whaley, Danielle, 201
Whaley, Olivia, 8049
Whaley, Ron, 918
Whaley, Tom, 7373
Whang, Josephine, 5196
Wharton, Beverly A., 7022
Whatley, Thurmond, 3867
Wheat, Gary, 896
Wheater, Ashley C, 199
Wheater, Ashley.C., 205
Wheatley, Samantha, 5536
Wheeldon, Howard, 4478
Wheeler, Bruce, 1819
Wheeler, Dana, 7104
Wheeler, Dann, 3786
Wheeler, Dick, 2691
Wheeler, Emily, 8329, 8331, 8332
Wheeler, Harmony, 6303
Wheeler, Jack, 7461
Wheeler, Jacque, 2880, 4524, 6665, 6666
Wheeler, Mark, 177
Wheeler, Phil, 6023
Wheeler, Ronald, 1586
Wheelock, Pat, 5220
Wheelwright, Martin, 2187
Wheelwright, Steven C., 6681
Whelan, Anita, 4606
Whelan, Franklin, 2066
Whelan, Joanna, 5079
Whelan, Kelly, 1128
Whelan, Patrick, 3767
Whelchel, Anna, 6887
Wheldom, Sue, 2261
Whidden, Shannon, 1852
Whimper, Carl, 6043
Whipkey, Dana, 3122
Whipp, Billie A., 8034
Whipple, Dr. Shederick, 1091
Whipple, Jane, 7955, 7958
Whipple, Robert, 1103
Whisenant, Joyce, 6618, 6628
Whisler, W. Scott, 6190
Whisted, Don, 3123
Whitacre, Pamela, 179
Whitaker, Don, 1092
Whitaker, Dr. Evans P., 5528
Whitaker, John, 5229
Whitaker, Johnny, 6338
Whitaker, Lisa, 6889, 6893
Whitaker, Rita, 8288
Whitco, Dana, 396
White, Allie, 126
White, Andrew, 2939, 3904
White, Arthur, 8762
White, B Carger, 3176
White, B Joseph, 6724, 6756, 6757, 6838, 6843, 6844, 6845
White, Bob, 1343
White, Bryan, 5966
White, Burton, 2885, 6672
White, C. Julian, 2545
White, Carmen, 4308
White, Chris, 1395, 5093, 6130
White, Claiborne, 185
White, Coral, 1687
White, Cynthia, 1630
White, D Patton, 184
White, D. Patton, 185
White, David, 2019
White, David R, 3151
White, David R., 3151
White, Deborah, 6207
White, Diane, 7955, 7958
White, Donny, 8530
White, Dr Leslie, 8511
White, Dr. Frances L., 866, 867
White, Dr. Patrick, 6767
White, Elizabeth, 545
White, Eve, 141
White, Ginger, 6360, 6367, 6368, 6369, 6370

White, Gwendolyn, 8122
White, Gwendolyn, 5448
White, Heather, 4805
White, Holly, 5037
White, James A., 2047
White, Janessa, 2034
White, Jessica, 1617
White, Jill Sharon, 977
White, John, 573, 2435
White, Josh, 6332
White, Joyce, 6991
White, Judith, 3770
White, Karen, 5797
White, L Keith, 4714
White, Lance, 3050, 7065
White, Lauren, 89
White, Leslie, 3481
White, Linda, 3977
White, Lyam, 4078
White, Lyla L, 2542
White, Manami, 1527
White, Marcia, 5200
White, Marcia J., 1464, 5200
White, Mark, 1576
White, Marla, 4692
White, Mary T, 1574
White, Matthew, 5594
White, Michael, 2900
White, Michelle, 1332
White, Millette, 246
White, Pat, 3531, 3535, 4812
White, Patrick, 6861, 6862, 6863
White, Paul, 2360
White, Randy, 2179
White, Reid, 4792
White, Rick, 5774
White, Robert, 6673
White, Robert A., 3816, 4496
White, Roger, 705
White, Sandy, 1818
White, Sheila, 726
White, Steven, 1840, 2377
White, Susan, 1700, 1791
White, Teresa, 3984
White, Thalia E., 6602
White, Tim, 4536
White, Wendy, 3833
White, Wendy D., 1957
White, Wil, 4494
White Chapin, Frances, 5777
White O'Rourke, Cathy, 5129
White Thomson, Ian, 807
White, III, David A, 7418
White-Brunetti, Ginger, 6353
White-Spunner, Jon, 3796
White-Spunner, Merv, 1841
Whitefield, William, 4999
Whitehair, Bruce Q, 5448, 8122
Whitehall, James, 656
Whitehead, Cynthia, 1868
Whitehead, Janae L, 5606
Whitehead, Kathy, 5077, 5252
Whitehead, Sarah, 2892
Whitehead, Tammy, 3930
Whitehill, David N., 1478
Whitehill, Joanne, 656
Whitehill III, N. James, 386
Whiteleather, Carole, 4533, 6689
Whiteman, Erlyne, 6280
Whiteman, Ray, 8210
Whitener, Gae, 2342
Whitener, Kim, 3498, 5052
Whitener, William, 308
Whites, Kent, 3979
Whitescarver, Martha, 1739
Whitesell, Lavonna, 4186
Whiteway, Phil, 3076, 4049, 4054
Whiteway, Preston, 2714, 2715
Whitfield, Suan, 237
Whitford, Thomas K, 579, 3842
Whitley, Ran, 5227
Whitlock, Bobbi, 1095
Whitlock, David, 5389
Whitlock, Dr. Keith, 5967
Whitlock, Karen, 5643
Whitlock, Laurie, 4247
Whitlock, Mary, 1833
Whitlock, R David, 3889

Whitlow, Todd, 4646
Whitlow, Victoria, 4060
Whitlum, Maggie, 3433
Whitman, Robert F., 8779
Whitmer, Lou, 1512
Whitmore, Erin, 8315
Whitmore, James, 5652
Whitmore, Tyler, 3124
Whitney, Anita, 2386, 5783
Whitney, Bill, 1596
Whitney, Catherine, 1729
Whitney, Cornelius, 3619
Whitney, Edward, 1416
Whitney, John, 4055
Whitney, Linda, 4075
Whitney, Lisa, 4243
Whitney, Marylou, 5200
Whitney, Rebecca, 2397
Whitney, Scot, 4075
Whiton, Matt, 3138
Whitson, Caroline, 5537
Whitson, Gwen, 58
Whitt, Vincent, 3685
Whitt-Lambert, Connie, 3962
Whittaker, Jetta, 724
Whittaker, Julie, 42
Whittaker, Nicole, 4578
Whitten, Cathy, 1697
Whitten, Kay, 785
Whittman, Loretta, 8562
Whittry, Diane M, 1616
Whitver, Josh, 1110
Whitworth, Bruce, 6109
Wholey, Lois, 582
Wholf, Brian, 7423
Whysong, Van, 4074
Wiatt, James A., 8727, 8862, 8900
Wible, Tom, 2104
Wibrew, Tara, 3775
Wichern, Lynn, 456
Wick, Carl, 6035
Wick, Chad, 5312, 5313
Wick, Rebecca, 1818
Wick, Stephen, 5177
Wicker, Russell J, 7915
Wickersham, Mark, 1785
Wickham, Josh, 2589
Wickham, Katherine, 428
Wickline, Jason, 6767, 6768
Wicklund, Faith, 7311
Wicks, Elisa, 1620
Wickstrom, Clif, 745
Widdall, Russ, 3835
Widdelow, Jim, 1502
Widdifield, Terra, 1268
Widdinton, Cheddy, 15
Wideman, Ron, 4439
Widener, Tom, 7587
Widland, Michael L., 6434, 6435
Widoff, David, 8330
Width, Tom, 4035
Wiebe, Shurrell, 647
Wiedenmayer, Rosemary G., 1951
Wiedenmeier, Brian, 86
Wiedermann, John, 3385
Wiegers, Betsy, 4378
Wiegmann, Kirstin, 3242
Wiegraffe, Merrell, 7450
Wiemken, Robert, 1651
Wiener, James, 5999
Wiener, Matthew, 2426
Wiensch, Adam, 2398
Wier, Christopher, 4288
Wier, Judyth, 4913
Wier, Richard, 2912
Wierzel, Robert, 397
Wiese, Rochelle, 5403
Wiesen, Ruth, 170
Wiesenfeld, Jeffrey S., 3493
Wiesle, Laura, 7199
Wiess, Marjorie, 3739
Wietfeldt, Cory, 3209
Wietzke, Phoebea, 4857
Wigby, Lorentz E., 4210
Wigger, Debby, 7474
Wiggin, Renate, 1584
Wiggins, Barbara, 4682
Wiggins, Judy H, 1839

Wiggs, Steve, 1755
Wight, Chales A., 8487
Wight, Nathan, 5967
Wight, Roger, 1647
Wightman, Alec, 5372
Wightman, Penny, 1449
Wiglesworth, Anita, 6302
Wigmore, Heather, 489
Wihite, Lauren, 7457
Wijayratne, Ramona, 684
Wikander, Karen, 4959
Wikler-Luker, Ruth, 3475
Wilber, Mitchell, 7676
Wilberg, Mack, 1762
Wilberg, Mark, 2363
Wilbourne, Sara, 112
Wilbrecht, Dick, 2150
Wilcock, Paul, 6302
Wilcosky, James E., 1519
Wilcox, Agnes, 3301
Wilcox, Andy, 3326
Wilcox, Ericka, 8776
Wilcox, Gina, 1779
Wilcox, Linda, 4637
Wilcox, Paul S., 2415
Wilcox-Smith, Tamara, 3527
Wilczak, Anne, 1229, 7283
Wild, William, 3017
Wildenthal, Kern, 2342
Wilder, Glenn, 5744
Wilder, Jim, 2702
Wilder, Kit, 2599
Wilder Joslin, Pam, 7855
Wilder Joslin, Pamela, 3640
Wildermuth, Catherine, 1701, 5588, 5589
Wildermuth, Dan, 4224
Wildes, Kevin, 7142, 7144
Wildman, Esquire, Thomas R, 4390
Wildonger, David M., 8108
Wilenius, Heidi, 5137
Wiles, Amy, 1313
Wiles, Julian, 8206
Wiley, Bert, 1498
Wiley, David, 1401
Wiley, Ella, 2450
Wiley, Hannah C, 679
Wiley, Lyn, 6585
Wiley, Mike, 2190
Wiley, Russell L, 5383
Wiley, Scott Jackson, 2206
Wiley Pickett, Kyle, 724, 1294
Wilford, Ronald A, 8825
Wilgendusch, Nancy, 5413
Wilhelm, Curtis, 2586
Wilhelm, Elizabeth, 4936
Wilhelm, Jan, 1080
Wilhelm, Jonathan, 7980
Wilhelm, Roberta, 3334
Wilhelmus, Tom, 6866
Wilhite, Stephen C., 8118
Wilimek, MaryAnne, 1257
Wilk, Chris, 6446
Wilk, Woody, 6106
Wilke, Dr David, 5357
Wilke, Sarah, 5799
Wilkenson, Scott, 1745
Wilker, Laurence J, 4425
Wilker, Lawrence J., 3825
Wilkerson, David, 3919
Wilkes, Dan, 7058
Wilkes, John, 6517
Wilkes, Pegi, 8006
Wilkey, Patricia M., 268
Wilkie, Alan, 725
Wilkiins, Joel, 7292
WILKIN, JENNIFER, 3818
Wilkins, Christopher, 984, 1513, 1514
Wilkins, Corey, 1878
Wilkins, Dwight, 3833
Wilkins, Gary, 8401
Wilkins, Grover, 1717
Wilkins, Helen, 676
Wilkins, John, 676
Wilkins, Karel, 1622
Wilkins, Thomas, 1309, 1310
Wilkins, Wayne, 1671
Wilkinson, Amy, 1164
Wilkinson, Ann, 7016, 7017

Wilkinson, Dan, 6866
Wilkinson, Donna, 1291, 1292, 4921
Wilkinson, James, 1656, 5493
Wilkinson, John, 4859
Wilkinson, Kimm, 7244
Wilkinson, Martha, 3912, 8292
Wilkinson, Scott, 3963
Wilkinson, Toni, 5034
Wilkos, Robert, 4472
Will, Jack, 721
Will, Mona, 7350
Willaman, Dennis, 2138
Willams, Biff, 6943, 6945
Willard, Christopher, 2649, 6336
WILLARD, DARRYL, 3075
Willard, Dean, 1806, 5803
Willard-Bevans, Ann, 4344
Willcox, Diane E., 7294
Willcutt, Brian, 1741
Wille, Miriam, 885
Willeke, Linda, 7011
Willems, Stephen, 3519
Willems, Tristan, 8800
Willemsen, Chris, 7662
Willen, Claudia, 6256
Willet, Susan, 1374, 5058
Willets, Laurie, 212, 2993, 2994
Willett, Greg, 4348
Willett, Lance O, 1104, 1105
Willett, Shawn Z., 8856
Willey, J.Fletcher, 7882
Willey, Katherine, 2115
Willey, Marty, 4765
Willhelm, Noreen, 533
William, Maxwell, 2686
William Gallagher, Casey, 3799, 5437
Williama, Jimmy, 8717
Williams, Aaron D., 2904
Williams, Alex, 4038, 4039
Williams, Alison, 2539
Williams, Amy, 6796
Williams, Anita, 2877
Williams, Ann M, 628
Williams, Anthony H, 5487
Williams, Audrey, 5099
Williams, Barry F., 4751
Williams, Barry.F, 1156
Williams, Becky, 3274
Williams, Betty, 4971
Williams, Bob, 4971
Williams, Brant, 8080
Williams, Brian, 4906
Williams, Caitlin, 246
Williams, Cameron, 2621
Williams, Carol, 1589
Williams, Charles E., 5932
Williams, Christina, 3103
Williams, Christopher, 5763, 5764, 5765
Williams, Coe, 1828
Williams, Cristina F., 2829
Williams, Cynthia L., 4906
Williams, D. Joeff, 5278
Williams, David, 8305
Williams, Delores, 1034
Williams, Denise, 3060, 6192
Williams, Dennis, 2017, 2729
Williams, Diane, 1449, 4889
Williams, Don, 5651
Williams, Donald, 3983
Williams, Donna, 850, 4545
Williams, Dr. Edwin, 5284
Williams, Edwin H., 4062, 4063, 8572
Williams, Elaine, 2409
Williams, Eloise, 1839
Williams, Emelyne, 184
Williams, Eric, 4053
Williams, Fred, 4376
Williams, Gail, 4142, 5898
Williams, Ginger, 3779
Williams, Gloria, 2782
Williams, Greg, 6539
Williams, Harry A., 6775, 6776, 6777, 6778
Williams, Heather, 1701
Williams, Jakie, 1479
Williams, James M, 6158
Williams, Jamie, 7837
Williams, Jeremy, 2131
Williams, JoAnn, 2730

Williams, John, 1135
Williams, Jonathan, 2555
Williams, Judy, 4191
Williams, Julie, 2268
Williams, Kate, 2415, 7496, 7499
Williams, Kris, 7082
Williams, Kristin, 3074
Williams, L. Vincent, 5817
Williams, Larry, 8093
Williams, Laura, 8270
Williams, Loreda, 6586
Williams, Lorraine E, 7591
Williams, Lucinda, 949
Williams, Luther, 5932
Williams, Malvin, 4892
Williams, Marc, 6661
Williams, Mark, 270, 1034
Williams, Matt, 4979
Williams, Matthew, 4810
Williams, Melva, 7156
Williams, Pamela M., 246
Williams, Paul, 7712
Williams, Peggy, 7689
Williams, Peter, 6191
Williams, Philip, 7129, 7130
Williams, Philip C, 5912, 5913, 5914
Williams, R. Jamison, 2134
Williams, R. Owen, 7086, 7087
Williams, Reggie, 6539
Williams, Rhonda, 186, 4264
Williams, Rhys, 1679, 5534
Williams, Richard, 424
Williams, Robyn, 8089, 8092, 8096, 8099
Williams, Rosemary, 1522
Williams, Ross, 6308
Williams, Ruth, 5677
Williams, Sally, 8296
Williams, Sandi, 8087
Williams, Scott, 4138
Williams, Shelly, 4172
Williams, Simon, 1931
Williams, Smith, 707
Williams, Stanley, 2582
Williams, Susan, 4070
Williams, Teneese, 2785
Williams, Tina, 2829
Williams, Todd, 5463
Williams, Todd A., 5668
Williams, Tom, 3207, 7308
Williams, Valerie, 235
Williams, Velda, 879, 6306, 6307, 6309
Williams, Walter, 5334
Williams, William Shane, 1053
Williams, Zsuzsa, 249
Williams Freestone, Lorma, 4846
Williams Jr, James S, 3632
Williams Niles, Renae, 4243
Williams Reagoso, Leslie, 3386
Williams, Ph.D., Luther S., 5932
Williams-Ness, Shane, 5141
Williamsch,, 1155
Williamson, Alana, 717
Williamson, Angela, 1133
Williamson, Becky, 4692
Williamson, Charlene, 7187
Williamson, Cheryl, 780
Williamson, Elizabeth, 2686, 3721
Williamson, Joni, 5472
Williamson, Kimb, 5980
Williamson, Meleia, 1583
Williamson, Robert, 1078
Williamson, Sharon, 4972
Williamson, Tanja, 4070
Williamson, Thomas, 5471
Williamson, Trina, 4066
Williamson, Vel, 1755
Williamson, Wade, 4070
Williamson Urbis, Sue Zanne, 5599
Williamson, D.M.A, Scott, 2377
Williams, Daniel, 7172, 7173
Williams, Lyn, 8587
Willian J., Secretary, 4486
Willie, Bob, 612
Willing, Richard, 4736
Willingham, Jeanne M, 645
Willingham, John, 3688
Willingham, Patrick, 7781
Willingham, William, 1606

Executive Name Index / W

Williott, Richard, 3310
Willis, Allistair, 997
Willis, Cheryl, 3101
Willis, Craig, 3775
Willis, Debbie, 4291
Willis, Dwyne, 863
Willis, Erin, 7412
Willis, Judy, 5616
Willis, Mervyn, 3612
Willis, Rusell A, 1287
Willis, Sachiko, 2591
Willis, Sandra, 6336
Willis,, Betsy, 3216
Willison, Patrick, 6
Willmann, Melinda, 1751
Willmon, Andrew, 2408
Willmott, Georgina, 2759
Willms, Jim, 5879
Willoughby, Warren, 1808, 1809, 5808
Wills, Betsy, 1696
Wills, Teresa, 3073
Wilson, Darrell, 4416, 4429
Wilmers, Robert G., 5132
Wilmot, Mike, 4255
Wilmott, Leymis Bolanos, 168
Wilner, Jon, 3642
Wilpon, Fred, 7672
Wilsey, Diane B., 6258
Wilson, Amy, 5164
Wilson, Anita, 1034
Wilson, Ann, 3998
Wilson, Anne, 2095
Wilson, Bettye, 734, 4175
Wilson, Bill, 230
Wilson, Bobby, 4639
Wilson, Bob, 8266
Wilson, Charles D, 5227
Wilson, Cheri, 8722
Wilson, Chris, 3981
Wilson, Christopher, 7505
Wilson, Chuck, 5878
Wilson, Daniel P., 2489
Wilson, Darryl, 4556
Wilson, David, 4328
Wilson, Dawn, 6738
Wilson, Dixie, 8214
Wilson, Don, 3202
Wilson, Donald, 873
Wilson, Dr. Carolyn, 4473
Wilson, Dr. Joanne, 8698, 8699, 8700
Wilson, Dr. Melinda, 2554
Wilson, Eileen, 4173
Wilson, Elizabeth, 4025, 4968
Wilson, Eska, 5777
Wilson, Gerald, 6481
Wilson, Grant, 7179
Wilson, J Nicole, 579, 3842
Wilson, Jack, 6022
Wilson, James, 3680
Wilson, Jane, 7343
Wilson, Janet, 4589
Wilson, Jeff, 4836
Wilson, Jennifer, 2610
Wilson, Joey, 648
Wilson, John C., 3118
Wilson, Katherine, 832
Wilson, Kathy, 8401
Wilson, Laura, 262
Wilson, Lauren, 179
Wilson, Laurens, 3868
Wilson, Linda, 616, 3935
Wilson, Lisa, 1537
Wilson, Lois, 5380
Wilson, Lynette, 2070
Wilson, M Faye, 6245, 6248
Wilson, Mark, 6271, 8467
Wilson, Marolyn, 3630
Wilson, Michelle, 8479
Wilson, Nancy, 1414
Wilson, Rachel, 5013
Wilson, Rhys T., 2020
Wilson, Richard, 1407
Wilson, Richard F, 6720, 6721
Wilson, Robert A, 1972
Wilson, Roger G, 1034
Wilson, Ron, 7969
Wilson, Rusty, 2898
Wilson, Sallie, 467

Wilson, Sandy, 2791
Wilson, Scott, 1805
Wilson, Stephen, 785
Wilson, Steve, 6363
Wilson, Sylvia, 1262
Wilson, Terry, 1264
Wilson, Thomas, 903
Wilson, Tristan, 2651, 3169
Wilson, Velma, 2929
Wilson, Vivian C, 3714
Wilson, William, 2703
Wilson Grant, Adrienne, 3091
Wilson III, John W, 7896
Wilson, III, Cassidy, 7082
Wilson, Jr., Richard M., 4860
Wilt, Mike, 1577
Wimmer, Kim, 8044
Wimsatt, Patty, 8310
Winbourne, Ann, 6
Winbush, Sigele, 179
Winchester, Jeremy, 1232, 1233
Wind, Dina, 1653
Windham, Daniel, 4906, 5317
Windham, Verne, 5806
Windle, Kaitlin, 347
Windle, Sally, 5353
Windover, Fred A, 3184
Windsor, Melissa, 4670
Windstein, Mary, 3848
Wineland, Vicki, 6647
Winemiller, John, 3901
Wing, Shea, 22
Wing, Steve, 3319
Wing Hamilton, Anne, 704
Wingard, Maurinda C, 569
Wingard, Patrick, 8065
Wingert, Lori, 7281
Winges, Mark, 1952
Winget, Carol, 4540
Wingfield, Russell, 751
Winke, Mara, 299
Winkler, David, 1475
Winn, Bud, 1562
Winn, Calvin, 911
Winn, Donna, 6440
Winn, Jim, 8334
Winn, Mandi, 650
Winn, Melanie, 1562
Winner, Jim, 2169
Winograd, Dana, 1360, 2199
Winship, Shelley, 5034
Winslett, Stoner, 670
Winslow, Ann, 4364, 6340
Winslow, Ellie, 2194
Winslow, Kandace, 3945
Winslow Gabriel, Norma, 304
Winslow Sherwood, Sandra, 1191
Winsor, William, 8643, 8646, 8647, 8649
Winston, Adrelle K., 6835
Winston, Carol, 1888
Winston, Joel M, 3719
Winston, Joni, 1005
Winter, Gary, 3471
Winter, Josie, 2296
Winter, Lyn Osborne, 3355
Winter, Renee, 2616
Winter, Robert, 822
Winter Skerritt, Joan, 2376
Winterfeld, Mary, 1814
Winters, Alan P, 7792
Winters, Brent, 8043
Winters, Doris, 6113
Winters, Linda, 4156
Winters, Michael, 3938
Winters, Tony, 8049
Winters-Morris, Cecilia, 639
Wintersteen, Carrie, 3692
Wintersteen, Wendy, 6735
Winthrop, Nina, 468
Winton-Henry, Cynthia, 54
Winzer, Monya, 2771
Wioskowski, Alan, 1454
Wipple, Jonathan, 2636
Wippmann, Jane, 4199
Wire, Jan, 4206
Wirth, Jason, 2230
Wirthlin, Robin, 4302
Wirtschafter, David, 8727, 8862, 8900

Wische, Jerry, 5640
Wisdom, James, 1213
Wise, Adrienne, 3603
Wise, Chuck, 3563
Wise, Jason, 8382
Wise, Michael, 595, 7613
Wise, Olga, 595
Wise, Thom, 2644
Wiseman, Elizabeth, 3201
Wiseman, Holly, 3081
Wiseman, Mark, 1792
Wiseman, Mr. Shaun, 4184
Wiseman, Pamela, 5753
Wiser, Karen, 5330
Wishchnia, Janet, 8151
Wishnia, J, 4408
Wisk, Andy, 7213
Wisneski, Frank, 2108
Wisniewski, Clark, 7502
Wissler, John, 3355
Wistrich, Elizabeth, 66
Wistrich, Steven, 66
Witecki, Jill, 6597
Witham, Janene, 2759
Withers, David, 8337
Withers, Laurel, 2566
Withers, Maida, 146
Withers, W. Andrew, 5735
Witherspoon, Brenda, 235
Witherspoon, David, 1711
Witkin, Judy, 605
Witmore, Michael, 2736, 2737, 6467, 6468
Witmore, Michael, 6467
Witt, Dana, 3803, 8124
Witt, Gary, 8690, 8692
Witt, Michelle, 8608
Witt, Paul, 4365
Witt, Roxi, 7104
Witt Ellis, Thomas, 2464
Witt-Callahan, Rachel, 4031
Witte, Bob, 4540
Witten, Cora, 6601
Wittenauer, Douglas, 8025
Witter, Inger K., 454
Wittig, Edith, 2380
Wittig, Jace, 1912
Wittig, Mark, 5663, 8450, 8451
Wittiq, Matt, 8052
Wittman, Loretta, 4057
Wittmann, Jane G, 4199
Wittow, Frank, 2847
Wittreich, Charles, 7822
Wittwer, Cassandra, 7955, 7958
Witzel, Stephanie, 2452
Wladis, Beth, 8860
Wobensmith, Erica, 2622
Wochner, Lee, 2506, 2507
Wodecki, Cheryl, 5448
Woeger, William, 4948
Woehlke, Erin M., 1832
Woehrle, Paul, 980
Woelpper, Craig, 1349
Wofford, Darrell, 2875
Wofford, Shirley, 4253, 6189
Wogaman, Stephen, 1231
Wohleber, Marlene, 5441
Wohlers, William R, 5563
Wohlers, Tricia, 33
Wohlford-Metallo, Dawn, 4597
Wohlgemuth, Sonja, 1891
Wohlleber, Sandra, 5067
Wohlman, Susan, 4597
Wohlust, Derek, 6520
Woish, Betsy, 7844
Woitach, Richard, 2249
Wojslawowicz, Barbara, 4776
Wolak, John, 577
Wolber, David, 3190
Wolcott, Nicole, 444
Wold, Greg, 1963
Woldseth, Hayley, 1798, 5793
Wolesworth, Mark, 8698, 8699, 8700
Wolf, Al, 1510
Wolf, Christine, 3037
Wolf, David, 762
Wolf, Dr Scott, 3224
Wolf, Dr. Judith, 1857
Wolf, Erika, 276

Wolf, Hans, 2389
Wolf, Isabel, 8864
Wolf, Jackie, 319
Wolf, James, 5777
Wolf, Paige, 1979
Wolf, Sigrid, 6131
Wolf, Thomas, 7180
Wolf Fogel, Alexandra, 252, 4746
Wolf, Ph.D., Judith G., 1852
Wolfanger, Deborah, 1449
Wolfe, Al, 4174
Wolfe, Duain, 905, 6733
Wolfe, Duane, 2042
Wolfe, Fletcher, 2019
Wolfe, George C, 7725
Wolfe, Johnny, 7430
Wolfe, Julia, 5115
Wolfe, Katherine, 5328
Wolfe, Keith, 2347
Wolfe, Kimberly C., 715
Wolfe, Lorin, 319
Wolfe, Meredith, 5333
Wolfe, Michael, 6079
Wolfe, Patricia, 1981
Wolfe, Randall, 2277
Wolfe, Roberta, 2019
Wolfe, Sandra, 4152, 5923
Wolfensohn, Adam, 5115
Wolff, Catherine, 2258
Wolff, Holly, 1962
Wolff, June, 1724
Wolff, Karen, 3191
Wolff, Paul Martin, 4434
Wolff, Richard, 2167
Wolff-Bolton, Judy, 4321
Wolfgang, Tom, 4219
Wolfinger, Harold, 730
Wolford, Deb, 7370
Wolford, Serena, 6340
Wolfsohn, Eve S, 476
Wolfson, Hannah, 5891, 5892
Wolfson, Scott, 3442
Wolhers, Bill, 5563
Woking, Chris, 1079
Woll, Cary, 863
Woll, Kathy, 3850
Wollan, Curtis N, 3246, 3257
Wollan, Jane, 3257
Wollen, Cort, 3246, 3257
Wollenberger, JB, 5824
Wollesen, Martin, 4234, 4759
Wollman, Dr Julie E, 5446
Wolpert, Harold, 3561
Wolpert, Jacqueline, 8129
Wolsey, Lynn, 6212
Wolter, John, 4384
Wolverton, David, 1783
Wolverton, Susan, 6966, 6968, 6970
Wolynec, Gregory, 8258
Womac, Amanda, 3906
Womac, Amanda, 8269
Womack, Steve, 6064
Won, Alisa, 1928
Won, Glen, 1929
Wonchala, Stephanie, 9
Wondisford, Diane, 2235, 3524
Wong, Audrey, 1919
Wong, Baldwin, 5130
Wong, Deborarh, 921
Wong, Francis, 81
Wong, Janet, 397
Wong, Janie, 405
Wong, JoAnn, 411
Wong, Les, 7315
Wong, M.K., 7225
Wong, Paula, 4210
Wong, Pearl, 2575
Wong, Randal P., 4303
Wong, Randy, 1019
Wong, Samuel, 1021
Wong, Shirley, 686, 691
Wong, Steve, 5548
Wong, Wileen, 6185
Wong III, Harry, 2887
Wong, CPA, Derick, 1934
Wong, Esq, Mary, 2030
Wonham, Fred, 6600
Woo, Cynthia, 7220

Executive Name Index / X

Woo Ho, Doreen, 1914
Wood, Anthony C., 4026
Wood, Benjamin, 2898
Wood, Beth, 7967
Wood, Cindy, 7998
Wood, Cynthia, 4815
Wood, Darcy, 4627
Wood, David, 5447
Wood, Doris, 1012
Wood, Dr. David, 4539
Wood, Dr. Donna, 8059
Wood, Erica, 221
Wood, Frank, 6536
Wood, Jane, 5471
Wood, Karen, 2484, 6147, 6242
Wood, Lindsey, 2367
Wood, Mary, 4161
Wood, Mason, 3085
Wood, Nancy L, 4322
Wood, Paul L, 1088
Wood, Pennie, 2408
Wood, Rick, 6345
Wood, Sally, 1614, 3099
Wood, Shannon, 3913
Wood, Spencer, 198
Wood, Thom, 1770
Wood, Thomas J, 6054
Wood, Wade P, 6354
Wood, Wendell P, 3134
Wood, William, 4850
Wood, William R., 3313
Wood Schwartz, Debbra, 816
Wood-Holmes, Margaret, 5713
Woodall, Dan, 3292
Woodard, Pam, 5926, 5928
Woodard, Sarah, 1489
Woodard, Steve, 3154
Woodbridge, Gregory, 1628
Woodbury, Jena, 654
Woodbury, Joan, 654
Woodbury, John, 1318
Woodbury, Richard, 202
Woodbury, Pat, 3128
Woodcockne, Jim, 7456
Wooden, Joe, 5935
Woodfield, Sara, 4332
Woodgate, Steven, 638
Woodham, Leigh, 6483, 6484
Woodham, Susan, 351
Woodhams, Erica, 1229
Woodhouse, Sam, 2568, 4287, 6242
Woodhouse Boston, Kelly, 1805
Woodke, Chalayane, 1608
Woodland, Woody, 4986
Woodland, Jr, Naaman J, 5594
Woodrell, Christopher, 406
Woodriff, Barbara, 8696
Woodroff, Beth, 3896
Woodruff, Carol, 5249
Woodruff, Dr. Ernest, 7433
Woodruff, Jeff, 1627, 1628
Woodruff, Louise, 1207
Woodruff, Robert, 1325, 3146
Woods, Aaron, 6239
Woods, Cecelia, 2437
Woods, Charlotte, 1828
Woods, Darren, 2347
Woods, Darren K., 2347
Woods, David, 5837
Woods, Erin, 3765
WoodS, Eunice, 2965
Woods, Harry, 904, 6344
Woods, Judy, 2065
Woods, Martha, 8806
Woods, Michael, 1789
Woods, Mitzi, 6308
Woods, Norbert, 2254
Woods, Shauna, 4087
Woods, Simon, 1805
Woods, Stacy, 785
Woods, Tyler, 3765
Woods-McDonald, Cecelia, 6029
Woodward, Ervin L, 4235
Woodward, Jeffery, 3627
Woodward, Sandy, 1617
Woodward Page, Asmira, 1445
Woodworth, Mary Ann, 2026
Woodworth, Zo‰, 7004

Woody, Richard, 2531
Woody, Tonya, 1164
Woolbright, Brad, 2200
Wooldridge, Dave, 62
Woolery, Sam, 7088
Woolery, Wendy, 4079, 8598
Wooley, Larry, 1841, 4091
Woolley, Brandon, 3788
Woolverton, Katherine, 4089
Woolwever, Scott, 4738
Woosnam, Richard E., 3839
Wooster, Phyllis L., 3391
Wooten, Harry, 2357
Wooten, Jim, 4141
Worboys, Billy, 3900
Worby, Joshua, 1393
Worby, Rachael, 824
Worcel, Michael, 225
Word, Christopher, 709
Word, Cynthia, 257
Word, Jim, 7141
Word, Linda, 4903
Worden, Alicia, 333
Work, Dianne, 1661
Working, Thomas, 1239
Workman, Dan, 3886, 3888
Workman, Ginger, 4097
Workman, Harold, 7090, 7091
Workman, Jane, 1888
Workman, Kenny, 2723
Workman, Rikkee, 2436
Works, Kim, 2789, 6535
Worland, Len, 2675
Worley, Butch, 8322
Worley, Cindy, 4096
Worley, Colin, 4469
Worley, Elena, 6219
Worley, Ernestine, 3685
Worley, Kathleen, 8101
Worley, Richard B., 1647
Wormley, Sam, 1100
Wornick, Deborah, 4073
Woronka, Joe, 1575
Worst, Laura, 2265
Worth, Robert, 878
Wortham, Tyese, 4315
Wortham, Tyese M., 87
Worthing, Marcia L., 428
Worthington, Donald, 2011
Worthington, Wendy E, 3814
Wortman, Charles J., 393
Wortman, Dawn C., 362
Woske, Lisa, 4317
Wotta, Craig, 7272
Wozniak, Amy, 3824
Wozniak, Joseph C., 6790, 6791, 6792
Wratchford, Amy, 4056
Wray, Patti, 4044
Wreen, Peg, 5164, 7787
Wreen, Peggy, 5164
Wren, Bill, 6193
Wren, Jody, 2832
Wrenn, Ella, 3105
Wrenn, Nancy B., 1755
Wrentmore, Stephen, 2430, 6004
Wride, Valerie, 1779
Wright, Anthony M, 507
Wright, Ardis, 8431
Wright, Arleen, 4166
Wright, Bob, 3294
Wright, C. Michael, 4122
Wright, Carolyn, 2893
Wright, Charles, 1594
Wright, Chatt G, 6679
Wright, Christina, 7055
Wright, Cliff, 1728
Wright, Cortney, 7418
Wright, David, 6909, 6910, 6911, 8125
Wright, Deb, 5402
Wright, Denise, 8407
Wright, Diana, 4068
Wright, Diane, 4072
Wright, Elizabeth, 8306
Wright, Emilie L. S., 4159
Wright, Helenann, 1218
Wright, Jack, 2011, 4777
Wright, James, 7533
Wright, Jerry, 7263

Wright, Jonas, 854
Wright, Josie, 817
Wright, Latonya, 1509, 2274
Wright, Lori, 7961
Wright, Margaret, 2198
Wright, Mark, 2786
Wright, Mark J., 5865
Wright, Mary, 647, 6122, 8115
Wright, Michael, 6102
Wright, Nancy, 1739
Wright, Nicole, 6967, 6971
Wright, Rebecca, 3641
Wright, Roberta, 7175
Wright, Sandra, 2447
Wright, Sarah, 1841
Wright, Scott, 1842
Wright, Shanna, 2341
Wright, Steve, 2061
Wright, Ten., 2143
Wright, Virginia, 874
Wright, William, 1774
Wright, William (Bill), 8138
Wright Maurer, Holly, 1482
Wrighthouse, Mike, 4607
Wrigley, John, 1385
Wroath, Tami, 6521
Wroe, David, 1352
Wronker, Lynn, 6445
Wrye, Phil, 7202
Wszolek, Matthew, 6761
Wu, Eva, 3686
Wu, Hsing-Kuo, 1446
Wu, Jing-jyi, 1446
Wu, Nancy, 5125
Wu, Pamela, 2575
Wu, Sandra, 1711
Wubbena, Terri, 4193
Wuellner, Andrew V., 2162
Wuepper, Ken, 4858
Wuerffel, Charis, 2040
Wulfe, Ed, 1731
Wun, Yvonne, 4210
Wurdack, Hope, 3304
Wurst, Christopher, 1796
Wyant, Clyde, 4365
Wyant, Gladys, 4515
Wyant, Todd, 8289
Wyatt, Cathy, 7952
Wyatt, Charles, 5529, 8204
Wyatt, Denise M., 1491, 5242
Wyatt, Doug, 1919
Wyatt, Elizabeth H.S., 4057
Wyatt, Lynn, 2353
Wyatt, Staci, 3940
Wyatt '69, M.B.A., Elizabeth H.S., 8562
Wyatt III, Dr Les, 749
Wyatt, Elizabeth H.S, 8562
Wyckoff, Laurel, 1653
Wyer, Dr. Peter, 5184
Wyk, Ella Van, 2989
Wyle, Noah, 2473
Wylie, Bruce, 4086
Wylie, Eric, 2341
Wylliams, Leni, 309
Wyman, Rae, 6275
Wynkoop, Gerda, 1794
Wynkoop, Rodney, 2263
Wynn, J. H., 5218
Wynn, Jeff, 6717
Wynn, Vanessa, 3912, 8292
Wynne, Stephen, 4374, 6389
Wynstra, Carole, 1939
Wypych, Julie, 743
Wyse, Cynthia, 5233
Wyse, Joe, 828

X

Xander, Betty, 4044
Xu, Meina, 4299

Y

Y Montoya, Will Caperton, 6168, 6172
Y.C. Pepe, Melanie, 3747
Yaeger, Douglas H., 7454
Yaffe, Michael, 4410
Yager, David, 3346, 7538

Yagura, Terry, 4339
Yakstis, Gary, 6436, 6439
Yamada, Dori, 4526
Yamada, Jay, 4204
Yamaguchi, Chisa, 39
Yamaguchi, Honnako, 5151
Yamaguchi, Soyou, 58
Yamane, Derrick, 1019
Yampolsky, Victor, 5834
Yancey, Connie, 1733
Yancey, Lisa, 8845
Yancey, Victoria, 3833
Yanci, Ricardo, 2032
Yanez, Vonda, 228
Yang, Shirley, 820
Yangyeitie Caulker, Ferne, 702
Yankee, Brian, 7226
Yankee, Megan, 1224, 1225
Yankwitt, Stephanie, 3446
Yannatos, Dr. James, 1189
Yanofsky, Jon, 7644, 7805
Yanowitz, Sally, 169
Yarborough, Joe, 8548
Yarbroug, Laurie, 8617
Yarbrough, Emma, 6629
Yarbrough, Kathy, 5927, 5930
Yarbrough Guttman, Ann, 1407
Yarchin, Ann, 6131
Yardbrough, John, 6514
Yarenhuk, Marcella, 5819
Yarick Cross, Doris, 1968
Yarnell, Ashley, 1571
Yarrington, Sadie, 38
Yarrow, Jacob, 5764, 5765, 7004
Yarrow, Jacod, 5763
Yates, Becky, 754
Yates, Bill, 3675
Yates, Cindi, 47
Yates, Dan, 2177
Yates, Johnathan, 937
Yates, Linelle, 605
Yates, Susan, 6106
Yates Jr, Charles R, 2020
Yavnel, Inessa, 186
Yawitz, Mitchell, 4305
Yawn, Mary, 0521
Ycaza, Mitch, 4066
Yeadon, Nanci, 7292
Yeager, Derryl, 649
Yeager, Elizabeth, 1757
Yeager, Richard, 1286
Yeager, Sylvia, 1858
Yeamans, Nancy, 561
Yeanoplos, Kevin, 5998
Yeardie, Webley J, 3817
Yearley, Graham, 3117
Yearwood, Valencia, 5051
Yeatman, Sandra P., 1634
Yebra, David, 8418
Yee, Jen, 4171
Yee, John F, 6251
Yee, Michael, 40
Yee, Thomas, 1022
Yegen, Chris, 470
Yeh, John Bruce, 2993
Yeh, Terence, 1794
Yeh, Tsung, 1096
Yelle, Heather, 4989
Yelvington, Steve, 4520
Yen, Cristina, 1607
Yencha, Tom, 5821
Yeo, Cynthia, 653
Yeoman, Jacque, 6608
Yerger, Jenae, 3968
Yerman, Margo, 6206
Yeshiwas, Dag, 5726
Yetter, Erich, 220
Yew, Chay, 2959, 6760
Yianilos, Bea, 2783
Yinak, David, 3940
Ying Hai, Mei, 4271
Ying Pang, Ching, 820
Yocca, Mohylyn, 572
Yockel, Peter, 5331
Yockey, Denton, 3291, 3969
Yocom, Anders, 1826
Yoder, Lonelle, 3724
Yoder, Stephanie, 3001

1237

Executive Name Index / Z

Yoder, Timothy, 3001
Yoeng, Alan, 2869
Yogi Holman, Lamont, 6661
Yohalem, Ira, 3169
Yoho, Terri, 5841
Yonally, Jennifer, 201
Yonally, Mark, 201
Yoo, Donna, 4402
Yoo, Esther S., 2031
Yoo, Jay S, 8812
Yoo, Scott, 863, 4319, 4320
York, Casey, 3548
York, Catherine, 4979
York, Will, 2403
Yoshida, Naho, 1920, 1921
Yoshida, Ryan, 861
Yoshidome, Marie, 861
Yost, Caroline, 421
Yost, David, 1531
Yost, Emily, 6077
Yost, Jamie, 8301
Yost Olson, Nancy, 2010
You, Kaiwen, 74
Youmans, Sabrina, 6169
Younan, Anne, 2599
Young, Aaron, 2303
Young, Aaron A., 3811
Young, Barbara Sellers, 2464
Young, Becky, 1010
Young, Betty, 1311
Young, Bill, 398
Young, Cindi, 2443
Young, Cynthia, 58, 1933
Young, Dave, 4819, 8531
Young, David, 6264
Young, Emily, 43
Young, Eric, 8490, 8491, 8492
Young, Frank M, 3990
Young, Georgiana, 6596
Young, Gerald, 3622
Young, Jamie, 5883
Young, Jim, 6197
Young, Joanna, 1711
Young, John G., 4630
Young, John P., 7099, 7100, 7101, 7102
Young, Julia, 1926, 1927
Young, Karen, 454, 2721
Young, Karey, 8907
Young, LouAnn, 225
Young, Margot, 1982
Young, Marla, 4224
Young, Melissa M, 628
Young, Michael, 7707
Young, Nancy, 256
Young, Pam, 520
Young, Pat, 745
Young, Paul, 6438
Young, Richard W., 7256
Young, Sian, 3889, 3890
Young, Sue, 5644, 6183
Young, Suella, 1454
Young, Susan, 5393
Young, Tami, 3994
Young, Tim, 1316
Young, Vicky, 8588
Young, Victoria, 1769
Young, Virginia, 3622
Young, Wallace, 3082
Young, Welborn, 2264, 2265
Young, Wendy T, 1787
Young III, H G, 5821
Young Schrade, Rolande, 5160
Young Switzer, Jo, 6926
Young, Jr., CPA (Bil, William A., 4035
Youngdoff, Beth, 6306, 6307, 6309
Younger, Kay, 4671
Younghans-Haug, Samantha, 6133, 6135
Youngren, Lynn, 1935
Young, Jeff, 8465
Youtsey, Phil, 7868
Yowell, Robert, 5951, 5955
Ypma, Dr. Nancy, 4585
Ysaguiree, Trevor, 2474
Yu, Jin-Wen, 696
Yu, Lonny, 1753
Yu, Stacy, 257
Yu Fong, Kuang, 3453
Yuen, Chris, 1019

Yukevich, Gerald, 3177
Yun, Henry, 2895
Yund, George, 8297
Yung, Eleanor, 390
Yuritic, Alice, 1097
Yurkanin, Mark, 5486
Yuska, Brandon, 3029

Z

Zaback, Jerry, 3614
Zabala, Eli, 6273
Zabelle, Robert, 169
Zabie Nields, Erika, 13
Zabinski, Daniel, 3186
Zabokrtsky, Connie, 103
Zaborski, Mark, 6685
Zaccagnino, Rebecca, 3367
Zacek, Dennis, 2959
Zach, Barbara, 1305
Zach, Jane, 4942
Zachary, Luccio, 2175
Zachary, Michael, 1802
Zachary, Nedra, 763, 1871
Zack, Gaile, 1506
Zackheim, Ali, 7479
Zagelow, Pat, 1602, 1603, 5420
Zager, James, 2394
Zager, Katherine, 1459
Zaharias, Alexandra, 304
Zaharias, Irina, 358
Zahler, Clara, 5084
Zahour, Annie, 213
Zahrobsky, Laurell, 1041, 4559
Zaiger, Mark, 4657, 4658, 4659, 4660, 4661
Zajac, Kathryn, 7955, 7958
Zak, David, 2908
Zaklynsky, Dr. Orest V., 5520
Zakreski, Ed, 2747, 6477
Zaldivar, Gilbert, 3570
Zaldivar, Gilberto, 1043, 3556
Zaldıvar, Chayo, 4001
Zaleski, Peter, 863, 4319, 4320
Zalewski, Ruth, 6345
Zambello, Francesca, 2209
Zamboni, Helen, 3609
Zamiska, Dragica, 2276
Zamora, Dr. Debbie, 1746
Zamorski, Allison, 620
Zamos, Willow, 4156
Zana, Colleen, 3025
Zana, Steve, 3025
Zancanella, Tony, 2196
Zanchuk, Walter, 1319
Zander, Benjamin, 1187
Zander, Leslie, 1260
Zandman, Ronnie, 2848
Zandol, Tony, 3789
Zangari, Mario, 932
Zanichkowsky, Jane, 1216
Zannucci, David, 3921
Zanon, Duane, 4264
Zaparanick, Carl, 6408
Zapletal, Jarmila, 3277
Zapletal, Peter, 3277
Zappala, Kathy, 3627
Zaremberg, Allan, 2552
Zaremski, Robin, 5460
Zarkadas, Aggie, 2043
Zarkowski, J.D., M.P, Pamela, 7290
Zartman, Denny, 2856
Zastrow, Ann, 2964
Zastrow, Anna, 3475
Zavala, Fidencio, 3939
Zavelle, Charles, 5103
Zavoina, Jean, 5623
Zawada, Jackie, 3313
Zawoysky, Rob, 4088
Zayas, Doreen, 2450
Zbella, Emil, 4552
Zbikowski, Lawrence, 1043
Zbornik, John, 4118
Zdunek, Paul Jan, 810, 824, 825
Zearfoss, Susan, 242
Zecher-Ross, Joshua, 2988
Zedlacher, Irene, 5044
Zee Steinberg, Judith, 347
Zehnacker, Serge, 1507

Zehr, Robert, 3010
Zehring, Tyler, 3266, 3267
Zeides, Melissa, 7549
Zeidman, Martin, 1058
Zeitlin, Jide J, 7216
Zeitouni, Jean - Marie, 5326
Zeitouni, Jean-Marie, 1545, 1546, 2282
Zelenak, Christine A., 2188
Zeliff Kearney, Jennifer, 4388
Zell, Jason, 8734
Zellers, Linda, 1625
Zellmer, Emilia, 7355
Zellner, Dick, 6099
Zellner, Jennifer, 6663
Zellner, Susan, 4126
Zelnis, Edward, 2047
Zemke, Douglas E, 6769
Zemke, Douglas E., 2052
Zendora, Nancy, 493
Zendzian, Alexander, 79
Zenger, Dr Sheahon, 6806, 6809
Zenk, Dee, 4166
Zenk, Elizabeth, 1053
Zenni, Liza, 3902
Zerangue, Matt, 7410
Zerbe, David, 1221
Zerbe Hurford, Carol, 394
Zerbey, Joseph H., 8012, 8013
Zeren, Corby, 1152
Zern, Michelle, 7706
Zervan, Carlie, 7300
Zeschin, Walter, 1528, 1529
Zgoda, James, 2780
Zhang, Helen, 821
Zhang, Xian, 1526
Zhang, Yan, 4284
Zheng, Alex Xiaozhong, 725
Zhou, Aiping, 74
Zhou, Frank, 82, 97
Zhu, Natalie, 1672, 5518
Ziaks Halperin, Gayle, 3957
Ziaukas, Tim, 5434, 8117
Ziccardi, Sheri, 136
Ziccardi, Sheri A., 4410
Zick, Kim, 2394
Zieg, Patricia, 113
Ziegenfuss, Randy, 1619
Ziegler, Kathy, 1793
Ziegler, Terry L, 5512
Zielke, Philip, 8386
Ziemann-Devos, Michele, 187
Ziemer, Paul, 3567
Zientarski, Ben, 7999
Ziess, Tony, 7877
Ziff, Ann, 2234
Zigler, Denise, 6941
Zigler, Scott, 7231
Zigmund, Steve, 3741
Zigun, Dick, 3419
Zikos, Greg, 6227
Zikri, Mina, 206, 1039, 2044, 2045
Zilavy, Jack, 5834
Zilberkant, Eduard, 720
Ziller, Jammie, 15
Zillman, Richard, 697
Zimbric, Dana Mambourg, 1905
Zimmann, Robyn, 1568
Zimmer, Constance S., 4421
Zimmer, Ingrid, 257
Zimmer, Ronna, 7920
Zimmer Cox, Wendy, 1231
Zimmerly, Lauralee, 6714
Zimmerman, Cathy, 417
Zimmerman, Don, 7131, 7132, 7133
Zimmerman, Dr J, 326
Zimmerman, Gail, 23
Zimmerman, Gigi, 4473
Zimmerman, Ima Kay, 1625
Zimmerman, Jeanne, 5267
Zimmerman, Jeff, 8077
Zimmerman, Kathryn, 194
Zimmerman, Lawrence, 2043
Zimmerman, Lynda, 3481
Zimmerman, Mark, 2069
Zimmerman, Mary, 4907
Zimmerman, Robyn, 3877
Zimmerman, Steve, 1778
Zimmerman, Timothy K., 2319

Zimmerman, Warren, 7573
Zimmerman, Warren R., 5003
Zimmermann, Gerhard, 1523
Zimmermann, Gerhardt, 4361
Zimmermann, Philip, 4134
Zimmermann, Gerhardt, 900, 901
Zimmern, Johann, 6267
Zinc, Christopher, 7913
Zinet, Paul, 3573
Zingg, Paul, 2458, 6080, 6081, 6082, 6083, 6084
Zingler, Gregory B, 7186
Zingula, Lonnie, 4642
Zink, Abbey, 1737
Zinman, David, 1944, 4351, 6328
Zinman, Sandra, 5068
Zinn, Jeff, 3181
Zinnes, Allen, 1619
Zinni, Elizabeth, 143, 144
Zinoman, Joy, 2750
Zinser, Virginia, 4859
Zipoy, Lanie, 3416
Zippert, Anita, 4989, 7556
Zirkare, Anne, 8184
Zisholtz, Ellen, 5530
Zisser PhD, Michael H, 7792
Zitnay, Sarah, 391
Zito, Christopher M, 5292
Zito, Christopher M., 1521
Zitzelberger, Tammy, 1010
Zizka, Blanka, 3840
Zlupko, Kristina M., 567
Zoback, Mykle, 4178
Zock, Annie, 2659
Zoehrer, Jim, 8572
Zoehrer, John, 4062
Zoffinger, George, 7553, 7554, 7555
Zola, Diane, 2353
Zolan, Ness, 1592
Zoll, Corrie, 3251
Zoller, Alfred, 1399
Zolty, Merediph, 3507
Zona, Joshua, 1136
Zonder, Adam, 7687
Zonola, Brenda, 7453
Zook, Chris, 6246
Zook, Gemma, 7426
Zook, Lori, 1895
Zopfi, Dr Steven, 2088
Zorach, Deb, 4730, 4731, 4732, 4733
Zorn, John, 1918, 1919
Zorn, Sheila, 1232, 1233, 7296
Zoromski, Hannah, 4131
Zotnowski, Kathy, 4263
Zoufaly, Howard, 1955
Zsolnay, Carol, 2944
Zubiria, Alexi, 50
Zubrod, Stephen, 3334
Zucker, Barry, 1352
Zucker, Lawrence C, 7789
Zuckerman, Ed, 1
Zuckerman, Kris, 7318
Zuckerman, Michael, 7549
Zuckerman, Paul, 3478
Zucosky, Marlyn, 3381
Zueger, Karl, 7316
Zuehlke, Elizabeth, 4290
Zulager, Becky, 228
Zulfiqar, Judy, 4225
Zummo, Joyce C., 5174
Zumoff, Barnett, 3493
Zuniga, Noe, 6939, 6940
Zuniga, Virgil, 817
Zupan, Lori, 1222
Zupaniotis, Melinda, 2678
Zupko, Arthur, 2779
Zureich, Melissa, 908
Zust, Genie, 3171
Zwaan, Bob, 1579
Zwahlen, Ryan, 6166
Zwail, Leslie, 2625
Zweden, Jaap van, 8362
Zwierankin, David, 3618
Zygmonski, Aimee, 6137, 6138, 6139, 6140, 6141, 6143
Zygowicz, John, 843
Zynsky, Toots, 593

Facilities Index / A

A

A Contemporary Theatre, 8597
A.J. Fletcher Opera Theater, 7900
A.J. Palumbo Center, 8167
Abbeville Opera House, 8203
Abilene Civic Center: Exhibit Hall, 8312
Abilene Civic Center: Theater, 8311
Abravanel Hall, 8494
Abravanel Symphony Hall, 8495
Academy of Music: Main Auditorium, 8147
Academy Playhouse, 7248
Academy Theatre, 6635
Adams Event Center, 7481
Adelphia Stadium, 8290
Adirondack Lakes Center for the Arts, 7636
African American Art and Culture Complex, 6249
African-American Cultural Center: Paul Robeson Hall, 7649
Afro-American Cultural Center, 7867
Agassiz Theatre, 7229
Agnes Scott College, 6642
Aia Actor's Studio, 6077
Aillet Stadium, 7153
Akron Civic Theatre, 7941
Al Caniglia Stadium, 7495
Al Ringling Theatre, 8658
Alabama Shakespeare Festival - Festival Stage, 5915
Alabama Shakespeare Festival - Octagon, 5916
Alabama Theatre, 5886
Alamodome, 8447
Alaska Center for the Performing Arts, 5934
Alaskaland Civic Center & Theatre, 5938
Albano Ballet and Performing Arts Center, 6404
Albany James H Gray Sr Civic Center, 6608
Albany Performing Arts Center, 7622
Albert Lea City Arena, 7336
Albert Lea Community Theatre, 7337
Albert Taylor Hall, 7032
Albert Taylor Theatre, 6767
Alberta Bair Theatre for the Performing Arts, 7468
Albuquerque Convention Center, 7602
Alcazar Theatre, 6250
Alden Theatre at Mclean Community Center, 8535
Alerus Center, 7935
Alex Box Stadium, 7110
Alex Theatre, 6115
Alice Statler Hall, 7685
All Seasons Arena, 7940
Allaert Auditorium, 6974
Allan Carr Theatre, 6795
Allen Arena, 8291
Allen County War Memorial Coliseum, 6876
Allen Fieldhouse, 7042
Allen Theatre, 8422
Allentown Symphony Hall, 8107
Alley Theatre, 8398
Alley Theatre: Hugo V Neuhaus Arena Stage, 8397
Alley Theatre: Large Stage, 8399
Alliance Bank Stadium, 7831
Allstate Arena, 6833
Alma Performing Arts Center, 5933
Aloha Stadium, 6670
Alpine Valley Music Theatre, 8661
Alumni Auditorium, 8118
Alumni Hall Gymnasium, 7690
Alumni Memorial Field, 8529
Alva Public Library Auditorium, 8029
Alys Robinson Stephens Performing Arts Center, 5887
Aman Arena, 8264
Amarillo Civic Center: Arena, 8317
Amarillo Civic Center: Music Hall, 8316
Ambassador Theatre, 7708
American Airlines Arena, 6546
American Bank Center, 8346
American Place Theatre, 7709
American Royal Center Kemper Arena, 7423
American Southwest Center, 7613
American Theatre, 7443
American University - Mcdonald Recital Hall, 6458
Ames City Auditorium, 6953
Amherst College Lefrak Gym, 7216
Amoin G Carter Stadium, 8381
Amphitheatre, 6690, 6921
Amway Arena, 6571
Anaheim Convention Center - Arena, 6054
Anderson Arena, 7949
Anderson Sports Center, 8204
Andrews Outdoor Theatre, 6671
Andy Kerr Stadium, 7679
Angelo State University Auditorium, 8444
Angels Gate Cultural Center, 6275
Annenberg Auditorium, 6304
Annenberg Center, 8148
Annenberg Theater, 6203
Annie Russell Theatre, 6605
Anniston Museum of Natural History, 5885
Anpsacher Stage, 7710
Antoinette E. Falbo Theatre, 8643
Apollo Theater, 6727
Apollo Theatre, 7711
Appel Farm Arts and Music Center, 7556
Apsu Concert Hall, 8257
Apu Theater, 6063
Arco Arena, 6228
Arden Playhouse, 6229
Ardrey Auditorium, 5949
Arena at Harbor Yard, 6392
Arena Players Playhouse, 7187
Arena Theater, 6848
Arie Crown Theatre, 6728
Arizona Stadium, 5995
Arizona Veterans Memorial Coliseum, 5962
Arizona Western College Amphitheatre, 6011
Arkansas River Valley Arts Center, 6047
Arlene Schnitzer Concert Hall, 8089
Arlington Center for the Performing Arts, 6279
Armstrong Hipkins Center for the Arts, 7545
Armstrong State College Fine Arts Auditorium, 6658
Arneson River Theatre, 8448
Arnold Hall Theater United States Air Force, 6338
Arthur Ashe Stadium, 7670
Arthur Miller Theatre, 7265
Arthur R Outlaw Mobile Convention Center, 5907
Artists Civic Theatre and Studio, 7128
Artpark, 7700
Arts and Science Center for Southeast Arkansas, 6042
Arts Center, 6561
Arts Center of the Ozarks, 6050
Arts Guild at Neumann College, 8110
Arts in The Parks Portable Stage, 7341
Arts Performance Lab, 6221
Arvada Center for the Arts and Humanities, 6327
As220, 8195
Ascap, 7712
Asheville Civic Center, 7853
Ashurst Auditorium, 5950
Aspen Music Festival and School, 6328
Assembly Hall, 6724, 6854
Astrodome, 8400
At&T Park, 6251
At&T Peronrming Arts Center, 8349
Athenaeum Music & Arts Library, 6136
Athenaeum Theatre, 6729
Atkinson Auditorium, 8623
Atlanta Civic Center, 6618
Atlantic Center for the Arts, 6560
Attucks Theatre, 8536
Auditorium Theatre, 6730
Augsbury Center, 7659
Augusta Civic Center Arena Center Stage, 7163
Augusta Civic Center Half House Concert Stage, 7164
Augusta Civic Center North Stage, 7162
Augusta Entertainment Complex, 6632
Augustana Arts, 6346
Augustana Theatre, 6825
Aurora Fox Arts Center, 6330
Austin Arts Center, 6405
Autzen Stadium, 8070
Avista Stadium, 8609
Aycock Auditorium, 7884
Aztec, 8313

B

B & a Warehouse, 5888
B C Playhouse, 6855
B.J. Haan Auditorium, 7018
Babcock Auditorium, 8562
Bailey Concert Hall, 6505
Baird Auditorium, 6459
Baker Field, 7713
Balboa Park Recital Hall, 6236
Balboa Park Starlight Theater, 6237
Balboa Performing Arts Theater, 6193
Ball Theater, 6861
Ballpark in Arlington, 8318
Bama Theatre Performing Arts Center, 5923
Bancorpsouth Arena and Conference Center, 7409
Bangor Civic Center & Auditorium, 7165
Bank of America Stadium, 7868
Bank of America Theatre, 6731
Bank United Center, 6496
Barbara B Mann Performing Arts Hall, 6511
Barbara K & W Turrentine Jackson Hall, 6094
Barbara Pfeiffer Memorial Hall, 6803
Bardavon 1869 Opera House, 7808
Barn Theatre, 6222
Barnum Studio Theatre, 7000
Barre Opera House, 8502
Barron Arts Center, 7600
Barrus Auditorium- Concert Hall, 6695
Barter Playhouse/Theatre House, 8510
Bartlesville Community Center, 8030
Bass Performance Hall, 8382
Bath House Cultural Center, 8350
Bathhouse Theatre, 8598
Battle Creek Civic Theatre, 7274
Bayfront Plaza Convention Center: Auditorium, 8344
Bayonne Veterans Memorial Stadium, 7544
Bayview Opera House, 6252
Beach-Schmidt Performing Arts Center, 7035
Beall Concert Hall, 8071
Beasley Performing Arts Coliseum, 8593
Beau Rivage Theatre, 7382
Beaumont Civic Center Complex: Julie Rogers Theatre, 8329
Beaver Stadium, 8184
Becker Auditorium, 6775
Beeghly Gym, 8021
Beeghly Theater, 8145
Beethoven Hall: San Jose Convention Center, 8449
Belhaven College Center for the Arts, 7395
Belk Theater, 7869
Bell County Expo Center, 8335
Bellevue Little Theatre, 7485
Bemidji State University Thompson Recital Hall, 7339
Ben Light Gym, 7686
Bender Arena, 6460
Benedicta Arts Center, 7370
Benedum Center, 8168
Benjiman Ide Wheeler Auditorium, 6066
Benton Auditorium, 6954
Bergman Theatre, 6819
Berkeley Community Theatre, 6067
Berklee Performance Center, 7219
Bernard B Jacobs Theatre, 7714
Bernard G Johnson Coliseum, 8418
Bernhard Center, 6393
Berrie Center for Performing and Visual Arts, 7566
Berry Events Center, 7315
Bertha Martin Theatre, 6961
Bethel Woods Center for the Arts, 7701
Beverly Center, 6732
Beverly B. Bistline Thrust Theatre, 6710
Beverly Hills Playhouse, 6073
Bi-Lo Center, 8223
Biblical Arts Center, 8351
Bickford Theatre at the Morris Museum, 7568
Big Bear Lake Performing Arts Center, 6075
Big Sandy Super Store Arena, 8631
Bigfork Center for the Performing Arts, 7467
Bijou Theatre, 8269
Bijou Theatre Center, 8270
Bill Graham Civic Auditorium, 6253
Bilyeu Theatre, 6708
Bing Concert Hall, 6305
Bing Theatre, 6154
Bininger Theatre, 6593
Biola University, 6145
Birch Creek Music Performance Center, 8663
Birmingham-Jefferson Convention Complex Arena, 5889
Birmingham-Jefferson Convention Complex Concert Hall, 5890
Birmingham-Southern College Theatre, 5891, 5892
Bishop Center for Performing Arts, 8567
Bismark Civic Center, 7932
Bistline Family Theatre, 6709
Black Box, 6565, 8590
Black Box Theater, 6566
Black Box Theatre, 6415, 6494
Black Hawk Children's Theatre, 7024
Black Liberated Arts Center, 8041
Blackham Coliseum, 7123
Bladen Opera House, 7486
Blanche M. Touhill Performing Arts Center, 7464
Bloch Learning and Performance Hall, 8644
Blossom Music Center, 7989
Blue Cross Arena, 7811
Bob Carpenter Center, 6451
Bob Carr Performing Arts Center, 6567
Bob Devaney Sports Center, 7490
Bob Hope Theatre, 8352
Bob Jones University, 8224
Bobby Dodd Stadium at Grant Field, 6619
Bologna Performing Arts Center, 7385
Booth Theatre, 7715
Boston Center for the Arts Plaza Theatre, 7220
Boston College Alumni Field Stadium, 7232
Boston Opera House, 7221
Boulder Museum of Contemporary Art Galleries and Theater, 6332
Bowie State University Martin Luther King Jr. Center, 7201
Bowlus Fine Arts Center, 7041
Bowman Gray Stadium, 7921
Bowne Theatre, 7565
Braden Auditorium, 6805
Bradford Creative & Performing Arts Center, 8117
Bradley Center, 8687
Dranscomb Memorial Auditorium, 6541
Bratton Recital Hall, 7527
Breckenridge Backstage Theatre, 6336
Breedlove Auditorium Westark Community College, 6027
Breenden Field House/Worthington Arena, 7470
Bren Events Center, 6132
Brewery Arts Center, 7505
Briar Cliff Theatre, 7022
Bridgeforth Stadium, 8526
Bridgestone Arena, 8294
Britt Pavilion, 8083
Broadhurst Theatre, 7716
Broadway Rose Theatre, 8106
Broadway Theatre, 7717
Broken Arrow Performing Arts Center, 8031
Bronco Arena, 8353
Brooklyn Academy of Music: Carey Playhouse, 7641, 7642
Brooklyn Academy of Music: Opera House, 7643
Brooklyn Center Community Center, 7342
Brooklyn Center for the Performing Arts, 7644
Brooklyn Conservatory of Music, 7645, 7671
Brooks Atkinson Theatre, 7718
Brooks Center for the Performing Arts, 8212
Broome County Veterans Memorial Arena, 7634
Broward Center for the Performing Arts, 6506
Brown Auditorium, 7052
Brown County Arena, 8664
Brown County Playhouse, 6920
Brown Stadium, 8196
Brownwood Area Chamber of Commerce, 8337
Bryant Denny Stadium, 5924
Bryce Jordan Center, 8185
Buckner Theatre, 6542
Bucks County Playhouse, 8144
Bud Walton Arena, 6024
Budweiser Events Center, 6388
Buena Performing Arts Center, 5982
Buffalo State College Performing Arts Center, 7650
Bulldogs Stadium, 6104
Burg Theatre, 8042

1239

Facilities Index / C

Burlington Memorial Auditorium, 6960, 8503
Burnett Theatre, 7046
Burning Hills Amphitheatre, 7939
Burruss Auditorium, 8512
Burton Coliseum, 7129
Busch Stadium, 7444
Busch Student Center, 7445
Bushnell Center for the Performing Arts, 6406
Butler University, 6888
Butte Center for the Performing Arts, 7472
Butte Civic Center, 7473

C

Cabrillo Crocker Theater, 6056
Caesars Palace, 7506
Cafe Del Rey Moro, 6238
Cahn Auditorium, 6779
Cain Park Theatre, 7979
Caine Lyric Theatre, 8477
Cajun Stadium, 7124
Cajundome and Convention Center, 7125
Cal Poly State University Performing Arts Center, 6273
Caldwell College Student Union Building, 7546
Calico Theatre, 7945
California Center for the Arts-Escondido, 6101
California Institute of Technology Performing Arts Center, 6207
California Polytechnic University Theatre, 6211
California State University Stanislaus Performing Arts Center, 6317
California State University-Hayward - Main Theatre, 6118
California Theatre of Performing Arts, 6234
Calumet Theatre Company, 7279
Calvin College Fine Arts Center, 7299
Calvin Theatre and Performance Arts Center, 7246
Cam Henderson Center, 8632
Cam-Plex Heritage Center, 8717
Cambria County War Memorial Arena, 8133
Camden Opera House, 7168
Cameron Hall, 8530
Camille Playhouse, 8336
Camp Randall Stadium, 8674
Camp Theater, 7863
Campbell Recital Hall, 6306
Canton Memorial Civic Center, 7951
Cape Cod Conservatory of Music & Arts, 7255
Capital Baseball Stadium, 8395
Capital Repertory Theatre, 7623
Capitol Arts Center, 7077
Capitol Center, 8625
Capitol Center for the Arts, 7525
Capitol City Stadium, 8216
Capitol Civic Centre, 8684
Capitol Music Hall & Jamboree Usa, 8653
Capitol Theatre, 7817, 8496, 8621
Caramoor Center for Music and The Arts Venetian Theatre, 7694
Caravan of Dreams, 8383
Cardinal Stadium, 7090, 8330
Carl Wooten Stadium, 8032
Carlson Center, 6023
Carmichael Auditorium, 6461
Carnegie Hall, 8642
Carnegie Hall Corporation, 7719
Carnegie: Lecture Hall, 8169
Carnegie: Museum of Art Theatre, 8170
Carnegie: Music Hall, 8171
Carnie Smith Stadium, 7056
Carole and Gordon Mallett Theatre, 6948
Carolina Coliseum, 8217
Carolina Theatre, 7885
Carpenter Center for the Performing Arts, 8548
Carrier Dome, 7832
Carroll College Theatre, 7476
Carson Center, 7105
Carter Finley Stadium, 7901
Caruth Auditorium, 8354
Carver Community Cultural Center, 8450
Carver Complex, 8451
Cary Field, 8565
Casa Manana Theatre, 8384
Casell Coliseum, 8513
Casper Events Center, 8712
Caswell County Civic Center, 7931

Catawba College Community Center Theatre, 7913
Cathedral of Saint Louis, 7446
Cave Theatre, 6915
Ce Gaines Complex, 7922
Cedarburg Performing Arts Center, 8659
Cedartown Civic Auditorium, 6637
Celebration Barn Theater, 7181
Celebration Theatre, 6155
Celebrity Theatre, 5963
Centenary College Recital Hall, 7156
Centennial Hall, 5996, 6826
Centennial Hall Convention Center, 5942
Center for the Arts, 6411
Center for the Arts Lecture Hall, 7826
Center for the Arts Recital Hall, 7825
Center for the Creative & Performing Arts, 6650
Center for Traditional Music & Dance, 7720
Center for Visual and Performing Arts, 6919
Center of Creative Arts, 7447
Center Stage, 7188, 8547
Center Theater, 8230
Center Theater Company of Tampa Bay, 6595
Centerarts, 6057
Centre Stage, 6018
Centrum Arena, 8473
Century Center Convention Hall, 6940
Century Center Recital Hall, 6939
Century II Civic Center Exhibition Hall, 7067
Century II Civic Center Mary Jane Teall Theatre, 7068
Century II Performing Arts & Convention Center, 7069
Century Link Arena Boise, 6685
Century Village Theaters, 6486
Centurylink Center Omaha, 7501
Cerritos Center for the Performing Arts, 6079
Cfa Studio, 6452
Cfa Theater, 6412
Cfa Thompson Theatre, 6453
Chabot College Performing Arts Center, 6119
Chadron State College Memorial Hall, 7487
Chaffin's Barn Dinner Theatre, 8292
Chamizal National Memorial: Theater, 8371
Chandler Center for the Arts, 5946
Chandler Music Hall and Cultural Center, 8508
Chaparral Center, 8433
Chapin Hall, 7258
Charles E Smith Center, 6462
Charles H Macnider Art Museum, 7011
Charles Ives Center Pavilion, 6396
Charles Koch Arena, 7028
Charles M Murphy Athletic Center, 8288
Charles W Davis Concert Hall, 5939
Charles W. Eisemann Center for Performing Arts & Corporate Presentations, 8442
Charleston Civic Center, 8626
Charleston Heights Arts Center, 7507
Charlotte Coliseum, 7870
Charlotte Harbor Event and Conference Center, 6581
Charlotte Knights Baseball Stadium, 8222
Charter Oak Cultural Center, 6407
Chase Field, 5964
Chase Fine Arts Center, 8478
Cheboygan Opera House, 7280
Cheek Theatre, 6828
Cheney Stadium, 8617
Chester Fritz Auditorium, 7936
Cheyenne Civic Center, 8714
Chicago Symphony Orchestra Association, 6733
Chichester Black Box Theatre, 5912
Chilkat Center for the Arts, 5940
Choral Recital Hall, 8645
Chris and Anne Reyes Organ and Choral Hall, 6927
Christian Arts Auditorium, 6852
Chrysler Hall, 8537
Church of Fine Arts, 7517
Cincinnati Music Hall, 7953
Cintas Center, 7954
Circle in The Square Theater School, 7721
Citi Field, 7672
Citi Performing Art Center Wang Theatre, 7222
City Center of Music and Drama, 7722
City of Bellingham Facilities, 8571
City of Grand Haven Community Center, 7298
City of Jamestown North Dakota, 7938

City of Morganton Municipal Auditorium, 7896
Civic Auditorium, 6696
Civic Center Complex, 8331
Civic Center Music Hall, 8043
Civic Center of Greater Des Moines, 6984
Civic Center of Onondaga County Carrier Theatre, 7834
Civic Center of Onondaga County Crouse-Hind Hall, 7833
Civic Hall Performing Arts Center, 6937
Claire Trevor School of the Arts, 6133, 6135
Claremont Opera House, 7524
Clarice Smith Performing Arts Center, 7203
Clark Center for the Perorming Arts, 6062
Clark State Performing Arts Center, 8008
Clatsop Community College Performing Arts Center, 8065
Claudia Crosby Theatre, 5921
Clay Center for the Arts & Sciences, 8627
Clemens Center, 7667
Clemson Memorial Stadium, 8213
Cleve L Abbott Memorial Alumni Stadium, 5932
Cleveland Browns Stadium, 7960
Cleveland Institute of Music, 7961
Cleveland Museum of Art: Gartner Auditorium, 7962
Cleveland Play House, 7963
Cleveland Play House Bolton Theatre, 7964
Cleveland Play House Brooks Theatre, 7965
Cleveland Play House Drury Theatre, 7966
Cleveland Public Theatre, 7967
Cleveland State University: Convocation Center, 7968
Clifford E White Theatre, 5951
Clowes Memorial Hall, 6889
Co Brown Stadium, 7275
Coa Community Auditorium, 7882
Coaster Theatre, 8066
Cobb Energy Performing Arts Centre, 6607
Cobo Arena, 7282
Cocoa Expo Sports Center, 6489
Coconino Center for the Arts, 5952
Coe Park Civic Center, 6440
Cofrin Family Hall, 8665
Coger Theatre, 7466
Cohen Stadium, 8372
Colden Center for the Performing Arts, 7673
Coleman Coliseum, 5925
Coliseum Civic Center, 7389
College of Southern Maryland Fine Arts Center, 7207
College of the Siskiyous Theatre, 6320
Collingwood Arts Center, 8011
Collins Center for the Arts, 7172
Colonial Theatre, 6697, 7534
Colorado Springs City Auditorium, 6339
Colorado State University Theatre, 6372
Colquitt County Arts Center, 6655
Columbia Exposition Center, 7387
Columbia Meadows, 8090
Columbian Theatre: Museum & Art Center, 7065
Columbus Civic Center, 6639
Commonwealth Stadium, 7083
Communication Arts Theatre, 8671
Community Center for the Performing Arts, 8072
Community Fine Arts Center, 8721
Community Music Center, 6254, 8091, 8401
Community Players Theater, 7484
Community Theatre, 7569
Community Theatre Association of Michigan, 7264
Community Theatre of Terre Haute, 6942
Concord City Auditorium, 7526
Constant Convocation Center, 8538
Constellationcenter, 7230
Constitution Hall, 6463
Contemporary Arts Center, 7139
Continental Airlines Arena, 7553
Convocation Center, 6762
Cooley Auditorium, 8688
Coors Amphitheatre, 6123
Coors Events Conference Center, 6337
Coors Field, 6348
Coral Springs Center for the Arts, 6497
Corbet Theatre, 8579
Corbett Auditorium, 7955
Cordier Auditorium, 6926
Cordiner Hall, 8620

Corn Palace, 8243
Coronado Performing Arts Center, 6829
Cort Theatre, 7723
Cotton Bowl/Fair Park, 8355
Coughlin Alumni Stadium, 8240
Count Basie Theatre, 7587
Court Theatre, 6734
Coussoulis Arena, 6233
Cow Palace, 6255
Cowan Fine & Performing Arts Center, 8467
Cowboy Stadium, 7130
Cowell Theater, 6256
Cox Arena at Aztec Bowl, 6239
Cox Convention Center, 8044
Crafton-Preyer Theatre, 7043
Cramton Auditorium, 6464
Cranford Dramatic Club Theatre, 7551
Craterian Ginger Rogers Theater, 8084
Creede Repertory Theatre, 6343
Crested Butte Mountain Theatre, 6344
Crew Stadium, 7981
Cricket Arena, 7871
Cricket Pavilion, 5965
Crisler Arena, 7266
Crocker Art Museum Ballroom, 6230
Crowder Hall, 5997
Crowell Concert, 6413
Cullen Performance Hall, 8402
Cultural Activities Center, 8462
Culver-Stockton College Performing Arts Hall, 7413
Cumberland County Civic Center, 7175
Cumberland County Coliseum Complex, 7883
Cumberland University Auditorium, 8276
Curb Event Center, 8293
Curran Theatre, 6257
Curtis Institute of Music, 8149
Curtis Theatre, 6076
Curtiss Hall, 6735
Cutler Majestic Theatre at Emerson College, 7223
Cuyahoga Community College: Western Campus Theatre, 8005
Cynthia Woods Mitchell Pavilion, 8465

D

D Glen Smith Spectrum, 8479
Dade County Auditorium, 6547
Dairy Barn Cultural Arts Center, 7943
Dakota Dome, 8248
Dallas Theater Center: Kalita Humphreys Theatre, 8358
Dana Arts Center University Theatre, 7680
Dana Fine Arts Building, 6643
Dance Center, 6736
Dance Studio 3, 6137
Dance Studio Theatre, 6223
Dance Theater Workshop, 7724
Daniel-Meyer Coliseum, 8385
Danny Peterson Theatre, 6683
Darien Lake Performing Arts Center, 7664
Darrell K Royal-Texas Memorial Stadium, 8322
David Adler Music and Arts Center, 6796
David O Mckay Auditorium, 6681
David Thayer Theatre, 7003
Dawson Auditorium, 7263
Dayton Hara Arena, 7990
Dayton Playhouse, 7991
Daytona Beach Community College Theatre Center, 6498
Daytona Playhouse, 6499
Dc Armory, 6465
Deane E Smith Center, 7865
Decatur Civic Center - Venue, 8367
Decatur Civic Center Theatre, 8366
Dee Events Center, 8484
Deer Valley Resort Amphitheatre, 8488
Delacorte Theater in Central Park, 7725
Delaware County Cultural Arts Center, 7994
Delmar Stadium Complex, 8403
Delray Beach Playhouse, 6503
Delta Classic Chastain Park Amphitheatre, 6620
Deltaplex Arena & Conference Center, 7300
Demmer Recital Hall, 8702
Dennos Museum Center Milliken Auditorium, 7330
Denver Botanic Gardens, 6349

Facilities Index / E

Denver Broncos, 6362
Denver Broncos Football Club, 6351
Denver Center for the Performing Arts, 6352
Denver Performing Arts Complex, 6347, 6353
Denver Victorian Playhouse, 6354
Department of Fine Arts, 6609
Department of Theatre and Dance, 8506
Department of Theatre Arts, 6466
Depot Theatre, 7381
Derthick Theatre, 8265
Des Moines Women's Club, 6985
Desert Sun Stadium, 6012
Detroit Symphony Orchestra Hall, 7283
Devos Performance Hall, 7301
Dewitt Theatre Arts Center, 7015
Deyor Performing Arts Center, 8022
Diana Wortham Theatre at Pack Place, 7854
Dickens Opera House, 6387
Diddle Arena, 7078
Diller Street Theater, 6850
Dillingham Center for the Performing Arts, 7688
Dine College, 5993
Dinkelspiel Auditorium, 6307
Discover Houston County Visitors Center: Museum, 8348
Diverseworks, 8404
Dixie Classic Fairgrounds, 7923
Dixie College Arena Theatre, 8491
Dixie College Fine Arts Center, 8490
Dixie College Proscenium Theatre, 8492
Dobama Theatre, 7980
Dobbs Theatre, 6667
Dock Street Theatre, 8206
Dodge City Festivals, 7031
Dodge Theatre, 5966
Dodger Stadium, 6156
Dolly Hands Cultural Arts Center, 6483
Dolores Winningstad Theatre, 8092
Dominican College Auditorium, 6277
Don Haskins Center, 8373
Don Powell Theatre, 6240
Donald W. Reynolds Auditorium, 6019
Dore Theatre/Madigan Gallery, 6065
Dorothy Dickson Darte Center, 8189
Dorothy I Summers Auditorium, 8028
Dothan Civic Center, 5899
Dover Little Theatre, 7552
Dow Theatre, 6966
Downtown Cabaret Theatre, 6394
Doyt L Perry Field, 7950
Drake Stadium, 6986
Drayton Hall, 8207
Dreiser Theatre, 6943
Duane Smith Auditorium, 7615
Duluth Entertainment Convention Center, 7344
Dunbar Performing Arts Center, 7189
Duncan Theatre, 6540
Dunham Hall Theater, 6771
Dunn Center for the Performing Arts, 7912
Dupont Theatre, 6455
Durham Hall, 8713
Durham Performing Arts Center, 7880

E

Earle a Chiles Center, 8093
Earlville Opera House, 7666
East County Performing Arts Center - Theatre, 6099
East Gymnasium, 6058
Eastern Howard Performing Arts Society, 6882
Eastern Michigan University Convocation Center, 7335
Eastern Slope Inn Playhouse, 7542
Eastman Theatre, 7812
Eatsern Kentucky University Alumni Coliseum, 7108
Eccles Coliseum, 8474
Eccles Community Art Center, 8485
Ed Cabell Theatre, 6646
Ed Landreth Auditorium, 8386
Ed Smith Stadium Sports Complex, 6583
Eden's Expressway, 7726
Edgerton Center for the Performing Arts, 6399
Edison International Field of Anaheim, 6055
Edison Theatre, 7448
Edman Chapel, 6849
Edmonds Center for the Arts, 8581

Edmund P. Joyce Athletic & Convocation Center, 6928
Edward S. Strother Theatre, 6916
Egg-Empire State Performing Arts Center, 7624
Egyptian Theatre, 6763
Eidson-Duckwall Recital Hall, 6890
Eisenhower Auditorium, 8186
Eiteljorg Museum, 6891
Ej Thomas Performing Arts Hall, 7942
El Camino College Center for the Arts, 6315
El Centro Su Teatro, 6355
El Dorado Municipal Auditorium, 6021
El Paso Civic Center: Exhibition Hall, 8374
El Paso Civic Center: Theatre, 8375
El Paso Convention & Performing Arts Center, 8376
El Paso County Coliseum, 8377
El Portal Theatre, 6194
Eldred Hall, 7969
Elgin Community College Visual & Performing Arts Center, 6773
Elias J Halling Recital Hall, 7349
Eliza R Snow Performing Arts Center, 6717
Elizabeth Eriksen Byron Theatre, 6356
Elizabeth T Champ Auditorium, 7420
Ellen Porter Hall, 6280
Ellie Caulkins Opera House, 6357
Elliott Hall of Music, 6949
Eloise Martin Recital Hall, 6820
Embassy Centre, 6870
Emelin Theatre for the Performing Arts, 7706
Emens Auditorium, 6917
Empire Theatre Complex, 8549
Empire Theatre Complex: Empire Stage, 8550
Empire Theatre Complex: Little Theatre, 8551
Energy Solutions Arena, 8497
Enron Field, 8405
Ensemble Espanol, 6737
Ensemble Studio Theatre, 7727
Erie Civic Center: Lj Tullio Arena, 8122
Ernie Shore Field, 7924
Eros Theatre, 6691
Esther Boyer Performing Arts Center, 8150
Ethel Barrymore Theatre, 7728
Ethel M Barber Theatre, 6780
Ethington Auditorium, 5967
Eugene O'neill Theater Center, 7845
Eunice Players Theatre, 7118
Evans Auditorium, 8094
Evansville Auditorium and Convention Centre, 6864
Everbank Field, 6525
Everest-Rohrer Auditorium, 6913
Everett Civic Auditorium, 8582
Everett Parks and Recreation Department, 8583
Ewing Children's Theatre, 8280
Ewu Pavilion, 8580
Experiemntal Theater, 6862
Experimental Theater, 6291
Experimental Theatre, 6241, 8527

F

Fabulous Fox Theatre, 7449
Fair & Expo Center, 7682
Fairmont Opera House, 7346
Fairmount Center for the Creative and Performing Arts, 8003
Fallon House Theatre, 6303
Family Arena, 7463
Fant-Ewing Coliseum, 7134
Fargodome, 7933
Farm Show Complex and Expo Center, 8127
Farmington Civic Center, 7612
Farrel Stadium, 8188
Farthing Auditorium, 7856
Faurot Fieldhouse, 7415
Faye Spanos Concert and Recital Halls, 6310
Fclo Music Theatre, 6113
Felten-Start Theatre, 7036
Felton Center, 7037
Ferrel Center, 8469
Ferst Center for the Arts, 6621
Fess Parker Studio Theatre, 6289
Festival Concert Hall, 7934

1

1515 Broadway Performance Venue, 7295

F

Fine Arts Center Auditorium, 5991
Fine Arts Center Colorado Springs, 6340
Fine Arts Center of Kershaw County, 8205
Fine Arts Theatre, 8703
Firehouse Center for the Arts, 7244
First Mariner Arena, 7190
First Niagara Center, 7652
Fisher Audtorium, 8131
Fisher Theatre, 6955, 7284
Fitzgerald Fieldhouse, 8172
Fitzgerald Theater, 7371
Fitzgibbon Recital Hall, 6883
Five Flags Center - Theatre, 6992
Five Flags Center Arena, 6991
Flagler Auditorium, 6575
Flickinger Center for Performing Arts, 7601
Flint Center for the Performing Arts, 6093
Flint Institute of Music, 7296
Floral Hall, 7030
Florence Civic Center, 8221
Florence Events Center, 8075
Florence Gould Theatre, 6258
Florida National Pavilion, 6526
Florida Studio Theatre, 6584
Florida Theatre, 6527
Flynn Center for the Performing Arts, 8504
Fm Kirby Center for the Performing Arts, 8190
Foellinger Theater in Franke Park, 6871
Folger Consort, 6467
Folkife Center of International House, 8151
Folly Theater, 7424
Folsom Field/Coors Events Conference Center/Stadium Club, 6333
Fontana Performing Arts Center, 6102
Footlight Players Theatre, 8208
Ford Amphitheatre, 6157
Ford Field, 7285
Ford Theatre, 8023
Forrest Theatre, 8152
Fort Eustis Music and Video Center - Jacobs Theatre, 8521
Fort Griffin Fandangle Outdoor Theatre, 8314
Fort Howard Hall, 8666
Fort Lauderdale Stadium, 6507
Fort Lewis College Community Concert Hall, 6371
Fort Myers Harborside, 6512
Fort Smith Convention Center, 6028
Fort Smith Little Theatre, 6029
Fort Worth Community Arts Center, 8387
Forum, 6032
Foundation of Arts, 6033
Fountain Street Church, 7302
Four Rivers Center for the Performing Arts, 7106
Four Seasons Arena, 7474

1

14th Street Playhouse, 6617

F

Fowler Center at Arkansas University, 6034
Fox Cities Performing Arts Center, 8656
Fox Theatre, 6622, 7039, 7286
Fox Tucson Theatre, 5998
Francis Scott Key Auditorium, 7184
Franciscan Center of Lourdes University, 8009
Frank Erwin Center, 8323
Frank Moody Music Building, 5926
Franklin County Veterans Memorial, 7982
Franklin Field, 8153
Frauenthal Center for the Performing Arts, 7322
Fraze Pavilion for the Performing Arts, 7996
Frazier Hall, 6381
Fred Bramlage Coliseum, 7047
Fred P Meagher Theatre, 8111
Fred Stone Theatre, 6606
Frederick Brown Jr Amphitheater, 6656
Frederick P Rose Hall, 7729
Fredric March Play Circle, 8675
Freedom Hall Arena, 7091

Freedom Hall Civic Center, 8266
Freedom Hall: Nathan Manilow Theatre, 6814
Freedom Hill Amphitheatre, 7328
Freeman Coliseum, 8452
Fresno Convention & Entertainment Center, 6105
Frontier Field, 7813
Frontier Park, 8715
Fulkerson Recital Hall, 6059
Fulton Chapel, 7405

G

G Rollie White Coliseum, 8341
Gaillard Municipal Auditorium, 8209
Galbraith Hall Studio Theatre 157, 6138
Gallagher Bluedorn Performing Arts Center, 6962
Gallaway Theatre, 5927
Gallo Center for the Arts, 6187
Galvin Fine Arts Center, 6975
Galvin Playhouse, 5985
Gammage Auditorium, 5986
Garde Arts Center, 6428
Garland Granville Arts Center, 8393
Garret Coliseum, 5917
Garrison Theatre, 6085
Gary Soren Smith Center for the Fine and Performing Arts, 6103
Gaston Hall, 6468
Gatlinburg Convention Center, 8260
Gator Bowl, 6528
Gcc Performing Arts Center, 5956
Geary Auditorium, 8628
Generic Theater, 8539
George M Sullivan Sports Arena, 5935
George Mason University Department of Theater, 8519
Georgetown University Department of Performing Arts, 6479
Georgetown University Performing Arts Center, 6469
Georgia Dome, 6623
Georgia Mountains Center, 6647
Georgia Southern University Performing Arts Center, 6663
Gerald Schoenfeld Theatre, 7730
Gershwin Theatre, 7731
Gertrude C. Ford Center for the Performing Arts, 7410
Gertrude Russell Jones Auditorium, 8334
Getty Center, 6158
Giants Stadium, 7554
Gibson Theatre, 7668
Gilbert V. Hemsley Theatre, 8676
Gildenhorn/Speisman Center for the Arts, 7211
Gill Coliseum, 8067
Givens Performing Arts Center, 7899
Gladys G. Davis Theatre, 8646
Glass Bowl Stadium, 8012
Glassboro Center for the Arts, 7558
Glema Mahr Center for the Arts, 7097
Glenn Wallichs Theatre, 6215
Glens Falls Civic Center, 7677
Goethe-Institut New York/German Cultural Center, 7732
Golden Gate Theatre, 6259
Golden Hurricane Club, 8052
Golden Lion Stadium, 6043
Golden Panther Sportsplex, 6548
Golden West College Mainstage Theatre, 6131
Goldstein Auditorium, 7835
Goodspeed Opera House, 6398
Goppert Theatre, 7425
Goranson Hall, 6711
Gordon Center for Performing Arts, 7210
Gordon Jewish Community Center, 8295
Gorge Amphitheatre, 8594
Gosman Sports & Convocation Center, 7253
Grady Cole Center, 7872
Graham Tyler Memorial Chapel, 7435
Grainer Stadium, 7892
Grambling University Memorial Gymnasium, 7119
Granbury Opera House, 8394
Grand 1894 Opera House, 8391
Grand Casino Hinckley Amphitheater, 7347
Grand Center Grandel Theatre, 7450
Grand Lobby, 6704

1241

Facilities Index / H

Grand Ole Opry House, 8296
Grand Opera House, 6456, 6457, 8697
Great Auditorium, 7577
Great Falls Civic Center Theater, 7475
Great Plains Coliseum, 8033
Great Western Forum, 6192
Greater Buffalo Youth Ballet Theater, 7651
Greater Richmond Convocation Center, 8552
Greek Theatre, 6159
Greensboro Coliseum: War Memorial Auditorium, 7886
Greenville Municipal Stadium, 8225
Greenwood Civic Center, 8229
Greer Garson Theatre Center, 7617
Greer Stadium, 8297
Griswold Theatre, 7250
Grover C. Maxwell Performing Arts Theatre, 6633
Groves Stadium, 7925
Guadalupe Historic Foundation (Santuario De Guadalupe) Dinner Theater, 7618
Gund Arena, 7970
Gusman Center for the Performing Arts, 6549
Gusman Concert Hall, 6493
Guthrie Theater, 7351
Gwinnett Center, 6644

H

Hadlock Field, 7176
Haislip Arena Theatre, 6035
Hal Palmer Recital Hall, 7038
Hallberg Theatre, 6110
Hallie B. Flanagan Studio Theatre, 6997
Halton Arena, 7873
Hamilton College: Minor Theatre, 7661
Hamman Hall, 8406
Hammerstein Ballroom, 7733
Hammons Student Center, 7460
Hampton Beach Casino Ballroom, 7532
Hampton Coliseum, 8524
Hampton Playhouse Theatre Arts Workshop, 7531
Hampton University, 8525
Hancher Auditorium, 7004
Hancock Stadium, 6806
Hangar Theatre, 7687
Harbach Theater, 6785
Harbor Park Stadium, 8540
Harborside Event Center, 6513
Harder Stadium, 6281
Harlem Stage, 7707
Harlen Adams Theatre, 6080
Harley Outdoor Amphitheatre, 7383
Harlingen Cultural Arts Center: Auditorium, 8396
Harmon Fine Arts Center, 6987
Harold and Charlotte Smtih Theatre, 6994
Harriet & Charles Luckman Fine Arts Complex, 6160
Harriet and Charles Luckman Fine Arts Complex, 6161
Harriet S. Jorgensen Theatre, 6436
Harrigan Cantenno Hall, 5944
Harris Theater for Music and Dance, 6738
Harrison Opera House, 8541
Harrison Theatre, 5893
Hartford Civic Center, 6408
Hartshorn Theater, 6454
Hartung Theatre, 6699
Hatlen Theatre, 6282
Haugh Performing Arts Center, 6116
Havens Auditorium, 6906
Hawaii Theatre Centre, 6672
Hayes Auditorium, 7855
Hb Playwrights Foundation Theatre House, 7734
Hearnes Center, 7416
Hec Edmundson Pavilion, 8599
Heininger Auditorium, 6804
Heinz Hall for the Performing Arts, 8173
Helen Hayes Performing Arts Center, 7803
Helen M. Hosmer Concert Hall, 7807
Helen Mallette Studio Theatre, 6865
Helen Schoeni Theater, 6186
Helena Civic Center, 7477
Helena Civic Center Auditorium, 7478
Henderson Fine Arts Center, 7082
Hendrix Theatre, 7887
Hennepin Center for the Arts, 7352

Hennessy Center, 7528
Henry B. Gonzalez Convention Center & Lila Cockrell Theatre, 8453
Henry J Kaiser Convention Center, 6196
Henry Levitt Arena, 7070
Herbest Theatre, 6260
Heritage Center, 8475
Heritage Theater, 7327
Herman Baker Recital Hall, 6909
Herschel Greer Stadium, 8298
Hershell Carrousel Factory Museum, 7802
Hershey Theatre, 8130
Hestand Stadium, 6044
Heymann Performing Arts Convention Center, 7126
Hi Corbett Field, 5999
Hickox Field, 7648
High Point Theatre and Exhibition Center, 7890
Highfield Theatre, 7234
Highlands Playhouse, 7891
Hilbert Center Theatre, 6892
Hilda D Glenn Auditorium, 6668
Hill Auditorium, 7267
Hilton Center for the Arts, 7451
Hilton Coliseum, 6956
Hingham High School Auditorium, 7237
Hinkle Fieldhouse, 6893
Hip Pocket Theatre, 8388
Hippodrome State Theatre, Inc., 6519
Hirsch Memorial Coliseum, 7157
Historic Elsinore Theatre, 8104
Historic Orpheum Theatre, 7353
Historic Palace Theatre, 7571
Historic State Theatre, 7354
Hobart Arena, 8018
Hobby Center for the Performing Arts, 8407
Hoffman Auditorium, 6444
Hofheinz Pavilion, 8408
Hofstra University Stadium & Arena, 7681
Holland Performing Center-Orpheum Theater, 7496
Hollywood Bowl, 6124
Hollywood Complex Theatre, 6125
Hollywood Palladium, 6126
Holsclaw Recital Hall, 6000
Holt Arena, 6712
Homer Bryce Stadium, 8435
Homestead Sports Complex, 6524
Honeywell Center, 6947
Honolulu Academy of Arts, 6673
Hooper Eblen Center, 8258
Hope College Theatre, 7305
Horace Bushnell Memorial Hall, 6409
Horrabin Hall Theatre, 6797
Horton Grand Theatre, 7355
Hosch Theatre, 6648
Hot Springs Convention Summit Center, 6031
Houma Terrebonne Civic Center, 7122
Houston Civic Center: George R Brown Convention Center, 8411
Houston Civic Center: Gus Wortham Theater, 8409
Houston Civic Center: Jesse H Jones Hall for the Performing Arts, 8410
Houston Fine Arts Center, 6359
Houston Harte University Center, 8445
Howard Center for Performing Arts, 7154
Hp Pavilion at San Jose, 6268
Hubert H Humphrey Metrodome, 7356
Hudson River Museum, 7851
Huey Recital Hall, 5928
Hugh Hodgson Concert Hall, 6612
Hugh Mills Memorial Stadium, 6610
Hughes Stadium, 6373
Hulman Center, 6944
Hult Center for the Performing Arts, 8073
Humphrey Coliseum, 7404
Huntington Civic Arena, 8633
Huntington Museum of Art Auditorium, 8634
Huntington Playhouse, 7946
Huntington Theatre Company, 7224
Huntridge Theatre, 7508
Hunziker Black Box Theater, 7597
Husky Stadium, 8600
Hyslop Sports Center, 7937

I

I Wireless Center, 6801
I-90 Expo Center, 7379
Idaho Center, 6705
Idaho State University, 6713
Imperial Theatre, 6634, 7735
Inb Performing Arts Center, 8610
Indianapolis Arts Garden, 6894
Indianola Little Theatre, 7393
Ingalls Rink, 6417
Innsbrook Pavilion, 8523
Inter-Media Art Center, 7684
Interlochen Center for the Arts Dendrinos Center, 7307
Interlochen Center for the Arts Kresge Auditorium, 7306
Interurban Center for the Arts, 8568
Intimate Theatre, 6162
Iowa State Center, 6957
Ira Aldridge Theater, 6470
Ironwood Theatre, 7308
Irvin L. Young Auditorium, 8710
Irvine Auditorium, 8154
Irvine Barclay Theatre, 6134
Irving Arts Center, 8420
Isabella Stewart Gardner Museum, 7225
Isothermal Community College Performing Arts Center, 7915
Iudons, 6877

J

J Birney Crum Stadium, 8108
J Lawrence Walk-Up Skydome, 5953
J. Clyde Turner Auditorium, 7862
Jack Benny Center for the Arts, 6847
Jack Breslin Student Events Center, 7292
Jackie Gleason Theater, 6554
Jackie Robinson Ball Park, 6500
Jackson Academy Performing Arts Center, 7309
Jackson Auditorium, 8461
Jackson Civic Center, 8262
Jackson Municipal Auditorium Thalia Mara Hall, 7396
Jacobs Field, 7971
Jadwin Gymnasium, 7583
Jamaica Center for the Performing & Visual Arts, 7691
James E O'neil Jr Arena, 7332
James E. and Rogers Black Box Theatre, 6715
James F Byrnes Auditorium, 8235
James F Metcalf Student Experimental Theater, 6772
James L Camp Memorial, 8553
James L Knight Center, 6550
James R Armstrong Theatre, 6316
James W Miller Auditorium, 7311
Japanese American Cultural & Community Center, 6163
Jaqua Concert Hall, 8074
Jasper Arts Center, 6905
Jayne Stadium, 7098
Je Broyhill Civic Center, 7893
Jeanne B. Mccoy Community Center for the Arts, 8001
Jefferson Community College Mcvean Student Center, 7846
Jefferson Theatre Center, 8559
Jenkins Theatre, 6659
Jerome Schottenstein Center, 7983
Jerry Herman Ring Theatre, 6495
Jesse Auditorium, 7417
Jesse H. Jones Hall for the Performing Arts, 8412
Jewel Theatre, 6980
Jewett Auditorium, 6692
Jewish Community Center of Metropolitan Detroit, 7333
Jewish Community Center of Omaha, 7497
Jewish Community Center of Saint Louis, 7452
Jewish Museum, 7736
Jiffy Lube Live, 8515
Jim Butterfield Stadium, 7689
Joan C Edwards Playhouse, 8635
Joan C Edwards Stadium, 8638
Joan C. Edwards Performing Arts Center, 8636
Jobing.Com Arena, 5968

Joe L Reed Acadome, 5918
Joe Louis Arena, 7287
Joe's Pub at the Public Theater, 7737
John a Walker Community Center, 7917
John Addison Concert Hall, 7205
John Anson Ford Theatres, 6127
John E Tucker Coliseum, 6048
John F Savage Hall, 8013
John Golden Theatre, 7738
John Harms Center for the Arts, 7557
John Lane's Ogunquit Playhouse, 7171
John Lyman Center for the Performing Arts, 6420
John M Greene Hall, 7247
John Michael Kohler Arts Center, 8704
John Paul Theatre, 5977
John S. Umble Center, 6878
John Van Duzer Theatre, 6060
Johnny 'red' Floyd Stadium, 8289
Johns Hopkins, 7191
Johns Hopkins University Homewood Field, 7192
Johnson Hagood Stadium, 8210
Jon M Huntsman Center, 8498
Jones At&T Stadium, 8423
Jones Auditorium, 7437
Jones Performing Arts Center, 6015
Jones Theatre, 6360
Jordan Hall at New England Conservatory, 7226
Jordan Stage, 6988
Jorgensen Center for the Performing Arts, 6437
Joseph Meyerhoff Symphony Hall, 7193
Josephine Louis Theater, 6781
Journal Pavilion, 7603
Joyce Theater, 7739
Js Dortin Arena, 7902
Juanita K Hammons Hall, 7461
Judd and Mary Lou Leighton Concert Hall, 6929
Julia Morgan Center for the Arts, 6068
June Company, 7632

K

K.R. Williams Auditorium, 7926
Kahilu Theatre Foundation, 6678
Kalamazoo Civic Auditorium, 7312
Kansas City Municipal Auditorium, 7427
Kansas City Municipal Auditorium Music Hall, 7426
Kansas Coliseum, 7064
Kansas Expocentre, 7061
Kansas State Fair - Grandstand, 7040
Kaplan Jcc on The Palisades, 7590
Karamu House Performing Arts Theatre: Amphitheatre, 7973
Karamu House Performing Arts Theatre: Arena, 7974
Karamu House Performing Arts Theatre: Prosce Hall, 7972
Karl C. Bruder Theatre, 7033
Kate Buchanan Room, 6061
Kathleen Mullady Memorial Theatre, 6739
Kathryn Bache Miller Theatre, 7740
Kauffman Stadium, 7428
Kay Bailey Hutchison Convention Center, 8356, 8357
Kay Rogers Park, 6030
Kaye Playhouse at Hunter College, 7741
Kazuko Hirabayashi Dance Theatre, 7742
Keck Theatre, 6164
Keith-Albee Theatre, 8637
Kellogg Arena, 7276
Kelly Shorts Stadium, 7319
Kenan Center, 7704
Kenan Memorial Auditorium, 7918
Kenan Stadium, 7866
Kendall Drama Lab, 6418
Kennedy Theatre, 6674, 7903
Kenneth C Beck Center for the Performing Arts, 7997
Kent Concert Hall, 8480
Kentucky Center for the Arts Bomhard Theatre, 7093
Kentucky Center for the Arts Robert S Whitney Hall, 7092
Kerrville Outdoor Theatre, 8421
Kerrytown Concert House, 7268
Keyarena at Seattle Center, 8601
Kibbie-Asui Activity Center, 6700
Kidd Brewer Stadium, 7857

1242

Facilities Index / L

Kiefer Uno Lakefront Arena, 7140
Kimbrough Memorial Stadium, 8338
Kimmel Center for the Performing Arts, 8155
Kimmel Theatre, 7013
Kimo Theatre, 7604
King Center for the Performing Arts, 6544
Kings Point Theatre at the Clubhouse, 6594
Kingsbury Hall, 8499
Kinnick Stadium, 7005
Kirkland Art Center, 7662
Kirkland Fine Arts Center, 6768
Kirkland Performance Center, 8586
Kirkpatrick Auditorium, 8045
Kirtland Center for the Performing Arts, 7326
Kiva Theatre, 6701
Klein Memorial Auditorium, 6395
Kleinert/James Arts Center, 7849
Kleinhans Music Hall, 7653
Klinger-Neal Theatre, 7019
Knickerbacker Recreational Facility and Ice Arena, 7838
Knox College, 6786
Knoxville Civic Auditorium and Coliseum-Auditorium, 8271
Kodak Theatre, 6128
Kodiak Arts Council, 5943
Koger Center for the Arts, 8218
Kohl Center, 8677
Koussevitzky Performing Arts Center, 7249
Krannert Center for the Performing Arts - Studio, 6844
Krannert Center for the Performing Arts - Theatre 2, 6845
Krannert Center for the Performing Arts - Theatre 3, 6843
Kraushaar Auditorium, 7194
Kravis Center for the Performing Arts, 6602
Kresge Auditorium, 6879
Kresge Recital Hall, 6787
Kulas Musical Arts, 7948
Kuumbwa Jazz Center, 6292
Kyle Field, 8342

L

L'ermitage Foundation Stage, 6165
L. E. and Thelma E. Stephens Performing Arts Center, 6716
L.C Walker Arena, 7324
La Mirada Theatre for the Performing Arts, 6146
La Pena Cultural Center, 6069
La Porte Civic Auditorium, 6907
Lab Theatre, 6815
Lackawanna County Stadium, 8142
Lafayette Community Theatre, 7127
Lagoon Entertainment Division, 8476
Laguardia Performing Arts Center, 7705
Laguna Playhouse, 6147
Lahaina Civic Center, 6680
Laidley Field Athletic Recreational Center, 8629
Lake Charles Civic Center - Exhibition Hall, 7132
Lake Charles Civic Center - James E Sudduth Coliseum, 7131
Lake Charles Civic Center - Rosa Hart Theatre, 7133
Lake George Dinner Theatre, 7696
Lake Oswego Parks & Rec, 8080
Lake Placid Center for the Arts Theater, 7697
Lakeland Center, 6543
Lakeshore Playhouse, 7380
Lakeview Arena, 7316
Lakewood Center for the Arts, 8081
Lamar University Studio Theatre, 8332
Lamb's Theatre, 7744
Lambeau Field, 8667
Lambuth Theatre, 8263
Lancaster New York Opera House, 7699
Landcaster Performing Arts Center, 6148
Lane Stadium, 8514
Lantz Arena, 6725
Larry Wismer Theatre, 6081
Las Vegas Convention and Visitors Authority, 7509
Lasells Stewart Center, 8068
Latimer-Shaeffer Theatre, 8528
Laurel Arts/The Philip Dressler Center, 8182
Laurie Auditorium, 8454
Lawlor Events Center, 7518

Lawrence Joel Veterans Memorial Coliseum, 7927
Lawrence University Music-Drama Center, 8657
Laxson Auditorium, 6082
Le Petit Theatre Du Vieux Carre, 7141
Leach Theatre, 7438
Lebanon Opera House, 7536
Leclerc Auditorium, 7195
Lee Arena, 7062
Lee Civic Center, 6562
Lee Civic Center - Small Theater, 6563
Lee Little Theatre, 5992
Leflore County Civic Center, 7390
Legendary Roy Wilkins Auditorium at Saint Paul Rivercentre, 7372
Legion Field Stadium, 5894
Legion Stadium, 7919
Lehman Center for the Performing Arts, 7639, 7745
Lenoir - Rhyne College Facilities, 7889
Lensic Performing Arts Center, 7619
Levitt Pavilion for the Performing Arts, 6447
Lewis Auditorium, 5969
Lexington Center, 7084
Lexington Opera House, 7085
Liberty Bowl Memorial Stadium, 8281
Liberty Performing Arts Theatre, 7431
Liberty Science Center, 7562
Lied Center for Performing Arts, 7491
Lied Center of Kansas, 7044
Lilly Hall Studio Theatre, 6895
Lincoln Amphitheatre: Musical Outdoor Drama, 6866
Lincoln Center, 6374
Lincoln Center Theater, 7746
Lincoln Cultural Center, 7894
Lincoln Memorial Stadium, 7492
Lincoln Park Stocker Stadium, 6376
Lincoln Theatre, 6445, 6472
Lincoln Theatre Center, 8588
Lippes Concert Hall in Slee Hall, 7654
Lisner Auditorium, 6473
Little Theatre of Norfolk, 8542
Littlejohn Coliseum, 8214
Littman Theater & Conference Center, 6564
Llyod Noble Center, 8039
Lobero Theatre Foundation, 6283
Loeb Drama Center, 7231
Long Beach Convention and Entertainment Center, 6149
Long Beach Playhouse, 6150
Long Center for the Performing Arts, 6908
Long Island University: Fine Arts Theatre, 7823
Long Theatre, 6311
Long Wharf Theatre Stage II, 6419
Long's Park Amphitheatre, 8138
Longacre Theatre, 7747
Longstreet Theatre, 8219
Longwood Gardens, 8137
Loon Mountain, 7537
Los Angeles County Museum of Art, 6166
Los Angeles Memorial Coliseum & Sports Arena, 6167
Los Angeles Performing Arts Theatres, 6168
Los Angeles Tennis Center, 6169
Louis B. Mayer Theatre, 6290
Louis Brown Athletic Center, 7578
Louis J. Roussel Performance Center, 7142
Louise Mandrell Theater, 8308
Louisiana Superdome, 7143
Louisville Memorial Auditorium, 7094
Louisville Palace Theatre, 7095
Lowell Memorial Auditorium, 7239
Loyola University Theatre, 7144
Lsu Union Theater, 7111
Lt Smith Stadium, 7079
Lubbock Memorial Civic Center Banquet Hall, 8425
Lubbock Memorial Civic Center Coliseum, 8426
Lubbock Memorial Civic Center Exhibit Hall, 8427
Lubbock Memorial Civic Center Municipal Auditorium, 8428
Lubbock Memorial Civic Center Theater, 8424
Lucas Theatre for the Arts, 6660
Lucille Ball Little Theatre of Jamestown, 7693
Lucille C Little Theater, 7086
Lucille Lortel Theatre, 7748

Lucille Tack Center for the Arts, 8705
Luesther Hall, 7749
Lumiere Ballet, 7847
Lund Auditorium, 6821
Lunt-Fontanne Theatre, 7750
Lutcher Theater, 8437
Luther College, 6981
Lyceum Hall, 6976
Lyceum Theatre, 5987, 7412, 7751
Lyceum Theatres Complex, 6242
Lydia Mendelssohn Theatre, 7269
Lyell B Clay Concert Theatre, 8647
Lyric Opera House, 7196
Lyric Opera of Chicago, 6740

M

Mabee Center Arena, 8049
Mabel Claire Allen Theatre, 6807
Mabel Shaw Bridges Auditorium, 6086
Mabie Theatre, 7006
Mackey Arena, 6950
Mackey Stadium, 7519
Macky Auditorium Concert Hall, 6334
Macomb Center for the Performing Arts, 7281
Macphail Center for the Arts, 7357
Maddox Theatre, 6830
Madison Morgan Cultural Center, 6652
Madison Square Garden, 7752
Madison Theater, 7080
Maggie Allesee Department of Theatre and Dance, 7291
Magoffin Auditorium, 8378
Mahaffey Theatre/Duke Energy Center for the Arts, 6588
Mahalia Jackson Theatre of Performing Arts, 7145
Maharishi University Performing Arts Center, 6993
Main Stage, 6421, 6568, 8591
Main Stage Theatre, 7016
Maine Center for the Arts at the University of Maine, 7173
Mainstage, 6841
Mainstage Theater, 6293
Mainstage Theatre, 6590
Majestic Theatre, 7753, 8359
Majestic Valley Arena, 7480
Malone Stadium, 7135
Manchester Craftsmen's Guild, 8174
Mandalay Bay Events Center, 7510
Mandel Jewish Community Center of Cleveland, 7947
Mandell Weiss Forum, 6140
Mandell Weiss Forum Studio, 6139
Mandell Weiss Theatre, 6141
Mandeville Theatre, 6142
Manhattan Arts Center, 7048
Manhattan Theatre Club, 7754
Manion Theatre, 8708
Mann Center for the Performing Arts, 8156
Manon Caine Russell Kathryn Caine Wanlass Performance Hall, 8481
Manti Temple Grounds Amphitheatre, 8483
Marcus Center for the Performing Arts, 8689
Margaret L Jackson Arts Center, 7233
Marian Gallaway Theatre, 5929
Marie P. Debartolo Center for the Performing Arts, 6930
Marin Center Showcase Theatre, 6278
Marina Civic Center, 6576
Marine Midland Arena, 7655
Marion Cultural and Civic Center, 6800
Marion Palace Theatre, 8000
Marjorie Ward Marshall Dance Center, 6782
Mark Taper Forum, 6170
Markey Square Arena, 6896
Marquee Theatre, 5988
Marquis, 7755
Marriott Center/Cougar Stadium, 8489
Marshall Civic Center, 8431
Martin Beck Theater, 7756
Martin Luther College Lyceum, 7366
Martin Massman Theatre, 6171
Martinson Theatre, 7757
Marvin Cole Auditorium, 6638
Marwick Boyd Auditorium, 8119
Mary D'angelo Performing Arts Center, 8123

Mary Emery Hall, 7958
Mary Linn Performing Arts Center, 7433
Maryland Hall for the Creative Arts, 7185
Maryland Theatre, 7206
Marymoor Amphitheatre, 8596
Marymount Manhattan College, 7758
Maryville College, 8278
Mashantucket Pequot Museum & Research Center, 6410
Masonic Temple Theatre, 7288
Massachusetts Museum of Contemporary Art, 7245
Massmutual Center, 7251
Mateel Community Center, 6219
Maui Arts & Cultural Center, 6677
Maurice Levin Theater, 7599
Maverick Concert Hall, 7850
Maverick Stadium, 8319
May Bonfils Stanton Center for the Performing Arts, 6361
Mayo Civic Center Arena, 7367
Mayo Civic Center Auditorium Theatre, 7368
Mcafee Coliseum, 6197
Mcalister Auditorium, 8226
Mcalister Fieldhouse, 8211
Mcaninch Arts Center Mainstage, 6790
Mcaninch Arts Center Studio Theatre, 6791
Mcaninch Arts Center Theater 2, 6789
Mcarthur Sports Field, 8085
Mcc Performing Arts Center, 5957
Mccahon Memorial Auditorium, 8034
Mccain Auditorium, 7049
Mccallum Theatre for the Performing Arts, 6202
Mccarter Theatre, 7584
Mccarthy Stadium, 8157
Mccaskey Lyceum, 7026
Mcelvey Center of York, 8239
Mcclelland Arts Center, 8587
Mcdonald Recital Hall, 6474
Mcdowell Columns Auditorium, 7898
Mcfarlin Memorial, 8360
Mckale Memorial Center, 6001
Mcmahon Memorial Auditorium, 8035
Mcmanus Theater, 7197
Mcmorran Place Theatre, 7325
Mophorcon Theatre, 6720
Meadowlands Theater, 7555
Mechanics Hall, 7260
Meek Auditorium, 7406
Melbourne Auditorium, 6545
Mellon Arena, 8175
Memorial Athletic & Convocation Center, 7995
Memorial Auditorium, 6308, 7029, 7904, 8472
Memorial Auditorium and Convention Center, 7057
Memorial Coliseum, 8095
Memorial Stadium, 7533
Memphis Cook Convention Center Complex, 8282
Mendel Center, 7277
Meng Concert Hall, 6111
Mercer Arena at Seattle Center, 8602
Mercy College: Lecture Hall, 7665
Meridian Community College Theatre, 7402
Merkin Concert Hall at Kaufman Center, 7759
Merriam Theater, 8158
Merrill Auditorium, 7177
Merrill Field, 7628
Merton Wray Theatre, 6321
Mesa Convention Center, 5958
Mesa Convention Center-Mesa Amphitheatre, 5959
Mesa Experimental Theatre, 6377
Mesa Park Arena, 6504
Mesa Recital Hall, 6378
Metrapark, 7469
Metropolis Performing Arts Centre, 6718
Metropolitan Performing Arts Center, 8611
Meyer Jacobs Theatre, 6816
Meyerhoff Symphony Hall, 7198
Meymandi Concert Hall, 7905
Mfa Directing Studio, 6808
Mgm Grand Garden Arena, 7511
Miami Arena, 6551
Michael Browning Family Cinema, 6931
Michael C Rockefeller Arts Center, 7674
Michael D. Palm Theatre, 6391
Michael Schimmel Center for the Arts, 7760

1243

Facilities Index / N

Michigan Theater, 7270
Mid-Atlantic Center for the Arts & Humanities, 7549
Mid-Hudson Civic Center, 7809
Mid-South Coliseum, 8283
Middle Township Performing Arts Center, 7550
Midland Center, 8434
Midland Center for the Arts, 7317
Midway Stadium, 7373
Midwest Wireless Civic Center, 7350
Milan Stadium, 8060
Millbrook Playhouse, 8141
Millenium Park, 6742
Miller Concert Hall, 7071
Miller Outdoor Theatre, 8413
Millett Hall, 8004
Mills College Concert Hall, 6198
Mills Experimental Theatre, 6968
Milwaukee Riverside Theater, 8690
Milwaukee Theatre, 8691
Minetta Lane Theatre, 7761
Mini Dome, 8267
Minskoff Theatre, 7762
Mishler Theatre, 8109
Mississippi Veterans Memorial Stadium, 7397
Missouri Botanical Garden Amphitheatre, 7453
Missouri Theater, 7440
Missouri Theatre, 7418
Missouri Western State College Fine Arts Theatre, 7441
Mitchell Center, 5908
Mitchell Fine Arts Center, 7087
Mitchell Hall Gymnasium, 8672
Mizel Arts & Culture Center, 6363
Mk Brown Memorial Auditorium & Civic Center, 8439
Mobile Civic Center, 5909
Mobile Civic Center - Exposition Hall, 6555
Mobile Civic Center - Theatre, 6556
Mobile Theatre Guild, 5910
Modell Performing Center at the Lyric, 7199
Modesto Junior College Performing Arts Center, 6188
Mohawk Park, 8050
Mohawk Valley Center for the Arts, 7703
Monroe Arts Center, 8696
Monroe Civic Center, 7136
Montagne Center, 8333
Montaineer Field, 8648
Montclair State College Memorial Auditorium, 7596
Montgomery College Robert E Parilla Performing Arts Center, 7212
Montgomery Theatre, 6269
Monticello Opera House, Inc., 6557
Moody Civic Center: Exhibition Hall, 8392
Moody Coliseum, 8361
Moonlight Amphitheatre, 6319
Moore Auditorium, 7895
Moore Theater, 6880
Moraine Valley Community College Fine & Performing Arts Center, 6813
Moravian College: Music Institute, 8113
Morgan Auditorium, 5930
Morgan Theatre, 8482
Morgan-Wixson Theatre, 6300
Morrell Gym, 7166
Morris Fx Jeff Sr Municipal Auditorium, 7146
Morris Performing Arts Center, 6941
Morrison Center for the Performing Arts, 6684
Morton H Meyerson Symphony Center, 8362
Mount Airy Fine Arts Center, 7897
Mount Baker Theatre, 8572
Mountain Home Arts Council, 6703
Mountain Laurel Center for Performing Arts, 8183
Mountain Playhouse, 8132
Mountain View Center for the Performing Arts, 6190
Msu Riley Center, 7403
Mud Island River Amphitheatre, 8284
Mule Barn Theatre, 7465
Mulroy Civic Center, 7836
Municipal Art Gallery Theater, 6172
Municipal Auditorium, 8455
Muny Amphitheatre, 7454
Murray State University Lovett Auditorium, 7099
Music Box, 7763

Music Center Recital Hall, 6294
Music Center/ Performing Arts Center of Los Angeles County, 6173
Music Hall, 6836, 7543
Music Hall at Fair Park, 8363
Music Hall Center for the Performing Arts, 7289
Music Library Association, 8686
Music Mill Amphitheatre, 8320
Music Recital Hall, 6002
Music Theater of Santa Barbara, 6284
Musical Arts Center, 6856
Musical Fare Theatre, 7629
Muskogee Civic Center, 8037
Muskogee Little Theatre, 8038
Musselman Stadium, 8125
Myrna Loy Center, 7479

N

Nampa Civic Center, 6706
Nancy T. Hansen Theatre, 6951
Napa Valley Opera House, 6191
Naples Philharmonic, 6558
Naropa University Performing Arts Center, 6335
Nashville Convention Center, 8299
Nashville Municipal Auditorium, 8300
Nassau Veterans Memorial Coliseum, 7842
National Hispanic Cultural Center of New Mexico, 7605
National Music Museum, 8249
National Sports Center, 7340
Nationwide Arena, 7984
Nazareth Arts Center, 7814
Ncca Papermill Theatre, 7538
Neal S Blaisdell Center, 6675
Nederlander Theatre, 7764
Neil Simon Theatre, 7765
Nelda K Balch Playhouse, 7313
Nelson W Wolff Municipal Stadium, 8456
Neodesha Arts Association, 7053
Nesholm Family Leature Hall, 8603
Neumann Auditorium, 7027
New Dramatists, 7766
New Haven Veterans Memorial Coliseum, 6422
New Hope Outdoor Theatre, 7365
New Jersey Performing Arts Center, 7574
New Jersey State Museum Auditorium, 7591
New Lecture Hall, 6476
New London Barn Playhouse, 7541
New Studio Theatre, 6743
New Theater, 6945
New Victory Theater, 7767
New World Theatre, 7020
New York City Center, 7768
Newark Symphony Hall, 7575
Newberry Opera House, 8232
Newman Stage, 7769
Newmark Theatre, 8096
Newport Performing Arts Center, 8087
Newport Yachting Center, 8194
Neyland Stadium, 8272
Nicholls State University Gym, 7161
Nichols Theatre, 7050
Nob Hill Masonic Center, 6261
Norfolk Scope Arena, 8543
Norman Mitby Theater, 8678
Norris Center for the Performing Arts, 6227
Norris Cultural Arts Center, 6839
North Carolina Blumenthal Performing Arts Center, 7874
North Carolina School of the Arts - Roger, 7928
North Carolina State University Center Stage, 7906
North Charleston Performing Arts Center, 8233
North Hennepin Community College Theater, 7343
North Iowa Community Auditorium, 7012
Northeastern Junior College Theatre, 6390
Northern Star Arena, 7561
Northland Pines High School, 8660
Northrop Auditorium, 7358
Northshore Center for the Performing Arts, 6835
Norton Center for the Arts, 7081
Norton Hall, 7660
Notre Dame Stadium, 6932

O

O'brien Field, 6726
O'connell Theatre, 6764
O'neill Center, 6397
O'rourke Center for the Performing Arts, 6744
O'shaughnessy Theatre, 7374
Oakdale Theatre, 6442
Ocean Center, 6501
Octorium, 6914
Odc Theatre, 6262
Odeum Sports & Expo Center, 6846
Oglethorpe University Theatre, 6624
Ohio Stadium, 7985
Ohio Theatre, 7986
Ohio University: School of Music Center, 7944
Oklahoma City Zoo Amphitheatre, 8046
Okoboji Summer Theatre, 7419
Old Bastrop Opera House, 8328
Old Creamery Theatre, 6996
Old Jail Art Center, 8315
Old Main Theater, 8573
Old National Centre, 6897
Old Opera House Theatre Company, 8624
Old Tucson Studios, 6003
Ole Olsen Memorial Theatre, 6936
Olin Arts Center, 7169
Oliver C Dawson Stadium, 8234
Olympic Center, 7698
Omaha Civic Auditorium, 7498
Omni Auditorium, 6491

1

171 Cedar Arts Center, 7663

O

One World Performing Arts, 8061
One World Theatre, 8324
Open Eye: New Stagings, 7770
Orange Bowl Stadium, 6552
Orange County Convention Center, 6569
Orchestra Hall, 6745, 7359
Ordway Center for the Performing Arts, 7375
Oregon Shakespeare Festival, 8062
Oregon Shakespeare Festival: Black Swan Theater, 8063
Orlando Centroplex, 6570
Oroville State Theater, 6200
Orpheum Theater, 7499
Orpheum Theatre, 6263, 7235, 7500, 7771, 8285
Orrie De Nooyer Auditorium, 7559
Osceloa County Stadium & Sports Complex, 6538
Osceola Center for the Arts, 6537
Ottawa Municipal Auditorium, 7054
Ouachita Baptist University Harvey & Bernice Jones Performing Arts Center, 6016
Ovens Auditorium, 7875
Overbrook Theater, 7323
Overture Center for the Arts, 8679
Owensboro Sports, 7103
Oxnard Civic Auditorium, 6201
Ozark Civic Center, 5920

P

P Brown County Arena, 8668
Pabst Theatre, 8692
Pac Auditorium, 5947
Pac Concert Hall, 8574
Pac Mainstage Theater, 8575
Pacific Conservatory of the Performing Arts, 6299
Paducah Community College Fine Arts Center, 7107
Painted Bride Art Center, 8159
Palace at Auburn Hills, 7273
Palace Civic Center, 7999
Palace of Fine Arts Theatre, 6264
Palace Performing Arts Center, 7625
Palace Theatre, 6423, 7539, 7772, 8126
Palestine Civic Center Complex, 8438
Palm Beach Community College Performing Arts Center, 6484
Palm Springs Convention Center, 6204
Palmer Auditorium, 6429

Palmer Theatre, 5913
Pan American Center, 7614
Pan American Musical Art Research, 7773
Panola Playhouse, 7408
Paper Mill Playhouse, 7567
Paradise Performing Arts Center, 6206
Paramount Arts Center, 7074
Paramount Center for the Arts, 7805
Paramount Theater for the Performing Arts, 8325
Paramount Theater Visuals & Arts Center, 7369
Paramount Theatre, 6199, 6719, 6969
Paris Junior College, 8440
Park College Alumni Hall Theatre, 7436
Park Place Hotel, 7331
Park Theatre Performing Arts Centre, 7595
Parker Auditorium, 6884
Parker Playhouse, 6508
Pasadena Civic Auditorium, 6208
Pasadena Playhouse - Mainstage Theatre, 6209
Pasco Schools Center for the Arts at River Ridge, 6559
Pasquerilla Performing Arts Center, 8134, 8135
Patricia George Decio Theatre, 6933
Patrick L O'malley Theatre, 6746
Patriot Center, 8520
Patriots Theater at the War Memorial, 7592
Paul and Vi Loo Theatre, 6679
Paul Brown Stadium, 7956
Paul Creative Arts Center, 7529
Paul G. Robinson Theater, 6922
Paul Mellon Arts Center, 6443
Paul Snow Memorial Stadium, 5905
Paul W Ogle Cultural & Community Center, 6923
Pauley Pavilion, 6174
Pavilion & Events Center Inc., 7503
Peabody Auditorium, 6502
Peace Center for the Performing Arts, 8227
Pearce Auditorium, 6649
Pearson Auditorium, 7616
Peery's Egyptian Theatre, 8486
Peforming Arts Center, 8345
Pendleton Convention Center, 8088
Pennsylvania Centre Stage, 8187
Pensacola Bay Center, 6577
Pensacola Junior College Performing Arts Center, 6578
Peoria Civic Center, 6817, 6818
Peoria Sports Complex, 5961
Pepperdine University Smothers Theatre, 6185
Pepsi Arena, 7626
Pepsi Center, 6365
Pepsi Coliseum, 6887
Pepsico Theatre, 6401
Perani Arena and Event Center, 7297
Performance Space 122, 7774
Performing Arts Center, 6872
Performing Arts Center of Greater Miami Foundation, 6553
Performing Arts School of Worcester, 7261
Performing Arts Series, 7055
Performing Arts Theatre, 6285
Perishable Theatre, 8197
Perot Theatre, 8464
Pershing Center, 7493
Pete Maravich Assembly Center, 7112
Pete Mathews Coliseum, 5906
Petrillo Music Shell, 6747
Pge Park, 8097
Phelps-Stokes Auditorium at Berea College, 7076
Philip Lynch Theatre, 6832
Philips Arena, 6625
Phillippe Auditorium, 6910
Phillips Center, 6520
Phipps Center for the Arts, 8670
Phoenix Convention Center - Ballrooms, 5970
Phoenix Convention Center - Symphony Hall, 5975
Phoenix Stages, 5971
Pick-Staiger Concert Hall, 6783
Pickard Theatre, 7167
Picketwire Players, 6385
Pico Rivera Sports Arena, 6322
Pier One Theatre, 5941
Pike Performing Arts Center, 6898
Pikes Peak Center, 6341
Pine Bluff Convention Center Arena, 6046
Pine Bluff Convention Center Auditorium, 6045

Facilities Index / Q

Pioneer Amphitheatre, 8339
Pioneer Center for the Performing Arts, 7520
Pioneer Courthouse Square, 8098
Pioneer Field, 8698
Pipe Dreams Studio Theatre, 6769
Piper's Opera House, 7523
Pitman Theatre, 8693
Pitt Stadium, 8176
Pittsburgh Civic Arena, 8177
Plachta Auditorium, 7320
Players Theatre, 6765
Playhouse Square Center: Ohio Theatre, 7975
Playhouse Square Center: Palace Theatre, 7976
Playhouse Square Center: State Theatre, 7977
Plaza Del Sol Performance Hall, 6195
Plaza Grand Performances, 6175
Plum Fleming Studio Theatre, 7014
Pnc Park, 8178
Pocono Playhouse, 8143
Point Stadium, 8136
Pollak Theatre, 7598
Pomerene Center for the Arts, 7988
Pompano Beach Amphitheatre, 6603
Ponca Playhouse, 8047
Popejoy Hall, 7606
Porter Center for Performing Arts, 7859
Portland Center for the Performing Arts, 8099
Portland Exposition Building, 7178
Portland Institute for Contemporary Art, 8100
Pote Theatre, 7001
Potter Center, 7310
Poway Center for the Performing Arts, 6212
Powell Little Theatre, 6714
Powell Symphony Hall, 7455
Power Center for the Performing Arts, 7271
Prado at Balboa Park, 6243
Prairie Arts Center, 7348
Prairie Center for the Arts, 6834
Prather Coliseum, 7137
Pratt Institute: Auditorium, 7646
Preus-Brandt Forum, 6313
Price Cutter Park, 7434
Prince George's Stadium, 7202
Prince William County Stadium, 8533
Princess Theatre, 7388
Princess Theatre Center for the Performing Arts, 5898
Priscilla Beach Theatre, 7257
Prism Theatre, 5989
Pritchard Theater, 6776
Prochnow Auditorium, 5954
Proctor's Theatre, 7820
Promenade Theatre, 7775
Providence Dunkin Donuts Center, 8198
Providence Performing Arts Center, 8199
Purchase College Performing Arts Center, 7810
Purple Masque, 7051
Pvcc Center for the Performing Arts, 5972
Pyramid Arts Center, 7815

Q

Quad City River Bandits Baseball Stadium, 6977
Qualcomm Stadium, 6244
Quandt Fieldhouse, 8707
Quebec Government House, 7776
Queensborough Community College Theater, 7633
Quick Center for the Arts, 6402

R

Rabobank Arena, Theater and Convention Center, 6064
Racer Arena, 7100
Rachel M. Schlesinger Concert Hall and Arts Center, 8511
Racine Civic Center- Festival Hall & Park &Memorial Hall, 8701
Radford University Theatre, 8546
Radio City Music Hall, 7777
Rahner-Gibbs Second Stage Theatre, 6591
Rajah Theatre, 8179
Raleigh Civic Center Complex, 7907
Raleigh Little Theatre, 7908
Ralph Wilson Stadium, 7804
Ramona Bowl Amphitheatre, 6122
Ramsey Concert Hall, 6613

Ramsey Regional Activity Center, 7879
Ransburg Auditorium, 6899
Rapides Coliseum, 7109
Ratcliffe Stadium, 6106
Rawhide Pavilion & Rodeo Arena, 5948
Ray Kroc Baseball Complex, 6013
Ray Winder Field, 6036
Raymond F Mccallister Hall, 6777
Raymond Theater, 8595
Rbc Center, 7909
Rca Black Box Theatre, 6911
Rca Dome, 6900
Reardon Auditorium, 6853
Recital Hall, 6693, 6748, 6924, 6982, 6995
Red Barn Theatre, 6535
Red Rocks Amphitheatre & Visitor Center, 6366
Redbird Arena, 6809
Redbud Theatre, 8368
Redding Civic Auditorium, 6213
Redfern Arts Center on Brickyard Pond, 7535
Redlands Bowl Amphitheatre, 6216
Redlands Community Music Association, 6217
Redondo Beach Performing Arts Center, 6218
Reed Theatre, 8101
Reed Whipple Cultural Arts Center, 7512
Regina A. Quick Center for the Arts, 6400
Regional Arts Center, 8466
Regional Special Events Center, 7101
Regis College Fine Arts Center, 7256
Regis Philbin Studio Theatre, 6934
Reilly Center Arena, 7824
Reitz Arena, 7200
Reno H Sales Stadium, 7471
Reno Little Theater, 7521
Reno Sparks Convention Centennial Coliseum, 7522
Rensselaer Newman Foundation Chapel and Cultural Center, 7840
Rensselaer Polytechnic Institute: Houston Field House, 7839
Reser Stadium, 8069
Resistol Arena/Rodeo Center Exhibit Hall, 8432
Reynolds Coliseum, 7910
Reynolds Memorial Auditorium, 7929
Reynolds Studio Theatre, 5914
Rialto Center for the Arts, 6626
Rialto Square Theatre, 6794
Ricardo Montalban Theater, 6129
Rice Auditorium, 8086
Rice Stadium, 8414
Rice-Eccles Stadium, 8500
Richard & Helen Brodbeck Concert Hall, 8699
Richard & Karen Carpenter Performing Arts Center, 6151
Richard and Karen Carpenter Performing Arts Center, 6152
Richard B Fisher Center for the Performing Arts at Bard College, 7630
Richard K. Stem Concert Hall, 6925
Richard L Swig Arts Center, 7560
Richard Rogers Theatre, 7778
Richardson Auditorium, 7585
Richmond Civic Theatre, 6938
Richmond Coliseum, 8554
Richmond Memorial Convention Center, 6220
Richmond Stadium, 8555
Ricketson Theatre, 6367
Rinker Outdoor Amphitheatre, 6778
Ritz Civic Center, 6037
River Center Arena, 7113
River Center Exhibition Hall, 7114
River Center Grand Ballroom, 7115
River Center Theatre for Performing Arts, 7116
River Center/Adler Theatre, 6978
River Parks Amphitheatre, 8051
River Raisin Centre for the Arts, 7318
Riverbend Music Center, 7957
Rivercenter, 7376
Rivercenter for the Performing Arts, 6640
Riverpark Center, 7104
Riverside Arena, 7338
Riverside Center Dinner Theater and Conference Facility, 8522
Riverside Convention Center, 6224
Riverside Municipal Auditorium, 6225
Riverside Theatre, 6600
Riverview Hall & Theater, 7158
Riverview Stadium, 6972

Roanoke Civic Center, 8560
Robert & Margrit Mondavi Center for the Performing Arts, 6095
Robert C Smithwick Theatre, 6153
Robert M Collins Center, 6823
Roberts Municipal Stadium, 6867
Roberts Stadium, 7023
Roberts Theatre, 6998
Robertson Stadium, 8415
Robins Center, 8556
Robinson Center Music Hall, 6038
Robinson Theatre, 6323
Rockford Metrocentre, 6831
Rockport Opera House, 7180
Rogers Stadium, 8545
Roland E Powell Convention Center, 7209
Roland Hayes Concert Hall, 8254
Roland Taylor Theatre, 6083
Rome City Auditorium, 6657
Ronald E. Mitchell Theatre, 8680
Ronald Q. Frederickson Theatre, 7034
Rose and Alfred Miniaci Performing Arts Center on The Nova Southeastern University, 6518
Rose Arena, 7321
Rose Bowl Stadium, 6210
Rose Quarter, 8102
Rose State College Performing Arts Theatre, 8036
Rosemont Theatre, 6770
Ross Ragland Theater & Cultural Center, 8079
Ross-Ade Stadium, 6952
Round Top Festival Institute, 8443
Rowland-Taylor Recital Hall, 6084
Roy Stewart Stadium, 7102
Rushmore Plaza Civic Center, 8244
Russell Theatre, 8612
Rutgers Arts Center, 7572
Rutgers Athletic Center, 7579
Rutgers Stadium, 7580
Rutgers-Camden Center for the Arts Gordon Theater, 7547
Ruth Eckerd Hall, 6488
Ruth Lilly Performance Hall, 6901
Ruth N Halls Theatre, 6857
Ryan Center, 8192
Ryan Field, 6784
Rye Arts Center, 7818
Ryman Auditorium, 8301

S

Sacramento Community Center Theatre, 6231
Sacramento Convention Center, 6232
Saenger Theatre, 6579, 7148, 7391
Saenger Theatre of the Performing Arts, 7384
Safeco Field, 8604
Saint Anne's-Belfield School Summer Music Academy, 8516
Saint Clement's Church, 7779
Saint James Theater, 7780
Saint Joseph Civic Arena, 7442
Saint Joseph's College Center for the Arts, 7647
Saint Louis Center for the Performing Arts, 6676
Saint Lucie County, 6516
Salem Civic Center, 8561
Salina Bicentennial Center, 7059
Salt Lake County Center for the Arts, 8501
Salter Concert Hall, 6863
Sam Boyd Stadium, 7513
Sam Houston State University Theatre, 8419
Samuel P Harn Museum of Art, 6521
San Angelo City Auditorium, 8446
San Antonio Convention Center   Lila Cockrell Hall, 8457
San Diego Civic Theatre, 6245
San Diego Museum of Art Auditorium, 6246
San Diego Sports Arena, 6247
San Diego Theatres/Balboa & Civic Theatres, 6248
San Francisco County Fair Arena, 6265
San Francisco War Memorial and Performing Arts Center, 6266
San Jose Center for the Performing Arts, 6270
San Jose Municipal Stadium, 6271
San Jose State University Theatre, 6272
San Mateo Performing Arts Center, 6274
Sanford Stadium, 6614
Sangamon Auditorium, 6837

Sangre De Cristo Arts and Conference Center, 6389
Santa Barbara Contemporary Arts Forum, 6286
Santa Cruz Civic Auditorium, 6295
Santa Fe Convention and Visitors Bureau Sweeney Center, 7620
Santa Fe Opera House, 7607
Santa Fe Stages, 7621
Santa Monica Civic Auditorium, 6301
Saratoga Performing Arts Center, 7819
Savannah Civic Center, 6661
Sawyer Theatre, 6665
Scene Dock Theatre, 6176
Schaeffer Fine Arts Center, 7378
Schenectady Civic Players Theater, 7821
Schermerhorn Symphony Center, 8302
School of Theatre and Dance, 6766
Schwartz Center for the Arts, 6450
Scott Stadium, 8517
Scottish Rite Center, 6873
Scottrade Center, 7456
Scottsdale Center for the Performing Arts, 5979
Scottsdale Community College Performing Arts Center, 5980
Scranton Cultural Center at the Masonic Temple, 8181
Seagate Convention Centre, 8014
Seaside Civic and Convention Center, 8105
Seattle Center Opera House, 8605
Seattle Repertory Theatre, 8606
Second Stage, 6296
Secrest Auditorium, 8026
Sedona Cultural Park, 5981
Seeger Chapel Concert Hall, 8268
Segerstrom Center for the Arts, 6090
Seminole County Government, 6582

7

7th Street Theatre, 8584

S

7 Stages Theatre, 6627
Severance Hall, 7978
Shafer Auditorium, 8140
Shakespeare Theatre Company, 6477
Shasta College Fine Arts Theatre, 6214
Shaw Center Auditorium, 7009
Shea Theatre, 7822
Shea's Performing Arts Center, 7656
Sheely Center for the Performing Arts, 6812
Sheila & Hughes Potiker Theatre, 6143
Sheldon Concert Hall and Ballroom, 7457
Sherwood Auditorium, 6144
Sheslow Auditorium in Old Main, 6989
Shiva Theatre, 7781
Show Me Center, 7414
Shreveport Municipal Auditorium, 7159
Shrine Auditorium and Exposition Center, 6177
Shryock Auditorium and Arena Promotions, 6722
Shubert Theater, 6424
Shubert Theatre, 7782
Sibert Theatre, 6793
Sierra Vista Theatre Hall, 5983
Silver Center for the Arts, 7581
Silver Lake College, 8685
Simpkins Theatre, 6798
Sinclair Auditorium, 6970
Singletary Center for the Arts, 7088
Sioux Falls Arena, 8245
Sioux Falls Community Playhouse, 8246
Sioux Falls Stadium, 8309
Siu Arena, 6723
Sky Sox Stadium, 6342
Skyhawk Arena, 8277
Slagle Auditorium, 8250
Sleep Train Pavillion at Concord, 6088
Slocomb Auditorium, 8441
Sloss Furnaces National Historic Theater, 5895
Smcc Performing Arts Center, 5973
Smcc Studio Theatre, 5974
Smith Opera House, 7676
Smith Recital Hall, 8639
Smoothie King Center, 7147
Snug Harbor Cultural Center, 7827
Society Hill Playhouse, 8160
Soho Rep, 7783

1245

Facilities Index / T

Soka Performing Art Center, 6053
Soldier Field, 6749
Soldiers & Sailors Memorial Coliseum, 6868
South Arkansas Arts Center, 6022
South Broadway Cultural Center, 7608
South Coast Repertory Segerstrom Auditorium, 6091
South Dakota Art Museum, 8241
South Dallas Cultural Center, 8364
South Florida Center for the Arts, 6534
South Jackson Civic Center, 8310
Southeastern Illinois College Visual & Performing Arts Center, 6792
Southeastern Louisiana University Center, 7121
Southeastern Louisiana University Strawberry Stadium, 7120
Southern Ohio Museum & Cultural Center, 8006
Southern Oregon University, 8064
Southington Community Theatre Inc., 6433
Southwest Performing Arts Theatre, 6100
Southwestern Baptist Theological Seminary, 8389
Sovereign Center, 8180
Space Theatre, 6368
Spangenburg Theatre, 6205
Spartan Stadium, 7293
Spartanburg Memorial Auditorium: Arena, 8237
Spartanburg Memorial Auditorium: Theatre, 8236
Special Olympics Stadium, 7637
Spencer Theater for the Performing Arts, 7611
Spingold Theater Center, 7254
Spirit Square Center for the Arts, 7876
Spivey Hall, 6654
Spokane Convention Center, 8613
Spokane Opera House, 8614
Spokane Veterans Memorial Arena, 8615
Sports Complex, 7829
Spotlight Arena, 8024
Springfield Little Theatre at the Landers, 7462
Springfield Symphony Hall, 7252
Springstead Theatre, 6587
Squitieri Studio Theatre, 6510
St Louis County Heritage and Arts Center, 7345
St. Croix Festival Theatre, 8706
St. John's University, 7692
St. Joseph's Historic Foundation/Hayti Heritage Center, 7881
Stabler Arena, 8114
Stadium Theatre Performing Arts Center, 8202
Stage 773, 6755
Stage Center Theatre, 6750
Stage Theatre, 6369
Stages Repertory Theatre, 8416
Staller Center for the Arts, 7830
Stambaugh Auditorium, 8025
Stamford Center for the Arts, 6435
Stanford University Department of Music, 6309
Stanley Performing Arts Center, 7843
Stanley-Sinsheimer Festival Glen, 6297
Stanly County Agri-Civic Center, 7852
Staples Center, 6178
Star Plaza Theatre, 6912
Star Theatre, 8616
Starlight Theatre, 7429
Starlite Patio Theatre, 6189
State Museum of Pennsylvania, 8128
State Palace Theatre, 7149
State Theatre, 7179, 7573
State Theatre Center for the Arts, 8121
State University of New York-Binghampton: Anderson Center for the Arts, 7635
Stella Boyle Smith Concert Hall, 6025
Stephen C O'connell Center, 6522
Stephen Foster Productions, 7075
Stephen Foster State Folk Culture Center, 6604
Stephens Auditorium, 6958, 6959, 7214
Sterling & Francine Clark Art Institute, 7259
Sterling Centennial Auditorium, 6840
Stevens Center, 7930
Stiefel Theatre for the Performing Arts, 7060
Stillwater Community Center, 8048
Stockton Performing Arts Center, 7582
Strahan Coliseum, 8460
Stranahan Theater Great Hall, 8015
Strand Theatre, 7160, 7563
Strand-Capitol Performing Arts Center, 8191
Strathmore, 7208
Straus Auditorium, 7860

Strayer-Wood Theatre, 6963, 6964
Strider Theater, 7182
Strong Theatre, 7816
Stuart C. Siegel Center, 8557
Student Union Special Events Center, 6686
Studio One, 8669
Studio Theatre, 5955, 6020, 6096, 6120, 6287, 6324, 6592, 6694, 6751, 6788, 6827, 6838, 6902, 6946, 6979, 7007, 7010, 7017, 7702
Sturges Center for Fine Arts, 6235
Sullivan Street Playhouse, 7784
Summer Theatre, 7877
Sumter Country Gallery of Art, 8238
Sun Bowl, 8379
Sun Devil Stadium, 5990
Sun National Bank Center, 7593
Sun Valley Center for the Arts, 6698
Sundome Center, 5984
Sunken Garden Amphitheatre, 8458
Sunrise Theatre, 6517
Sunset Cultural Center, 6078
Sunshine Daydreams Campground, 8652
Suny Center for the Arts, 7657
Supper Club Theater, 7785
Surdna Foundation, 7786
Susan Brotman Auditorium, 8607
Sven and Mildred Lekberg Recital Hall, 7002
Swayne Auditorium, 6707
Swiftel Center, 8242
Symphony Center, 6752
Symphony Hall, 7227
Symphony Space, 7787
Syracuse Area Landmark Theatre, 7837

T

Taco Bell Arena, 6687
Tacoma Dome, 8618
Tampa Bay Performing Arts Center, 6596
Tampa Theatre, 6597
Tanglewood Music Center, 7238
Target Center, 7360
Taylor-Meade Performing Arts Center, 8076
Td Bank Amphitheater, 8112
Td Bank Arts Centre, 7589
Td Banknorth Garden, 7228
Te Paske Theatre, 7021
Tecumseh Center for the Arts, 7329
Ted Mann Concert Hall, 7361
Temple Civic Theatre, 8463
Temple Hoyne Buell Theatre, 6370
Temple of Music & Art, 6004
Temple Theatre Company, 7914
Tennessee Performing Arts Center, 8303
Tennessee Performing Arts Center: Andrew Jackson Hall, 8304
Tennessee Theater, 8273
Tennessee Williams Theatre, 6536
Tennis Center at Crandon Park, 6533
Tex Turner Arena, 8261
Texas Tech University Performing Arts Center, 8429
Texas Wesleyan College: Fine Arts, 8390
Thaddeus Torp Theatre, 6416
Thalia Mara Hall, 7398
Thalian Hall Center for the Performing Arts, 7920
Thanksgiving Square: Courtyard at Thanksgiving, 8365
Thatcher Music Building, 6087
The Allen Bales Theatre, 5931
The Arts Center, 6973
The Boisefeuillet Jones Atlanta Civic Center, 6628
The Butter Theater, 6345
The Carton Palace Theatre Association, 7952
The Center for the Arts, 6117
The Center for the Performing Arts, 6842
The Center for the Peorming Arts, 6860
The Chicago Theatre, 6753
The Classic Center, 6615
The Convocation Center, 6051
The Croswell Opera House & Fine Arts Association, 7262
The Denver Brass, 6350
The Granada, 6288
The Grand Opera House, 6651
The Green at Shelburne Museum, 8509
The Hemmens Cultural Center, 6774

The Historic Cocoa Village Playhouse, 6490
The Historic Paramount Theatre, 6358
The Holmes Center, 7858
The Ikon Center, 8716
The Island Players Theatre, 6482
The John F Kennedy Center for the Performing Arts, 6471
The Kitchen, 7743
The Leeward Theatre, 6682
The Leslie Wright Center, 5896
The Lynn Auditorium., 7241
The Mahaiwe Performing Arts Center Theatre, 7236
The Majestic and Charline Mcombs Empire Theatres, 8459
The Merle Reskin Theatre, 6741
The Muckenthaler Cultural Center, 6112
The Music Center, 6754
The Otero Players, 6384
The Palace, 6434
The Palace Theatre, 8231
The Palestra, 8161
The Paramount Center for the Arts, 8252
The Players Theatre, 6585
The Rialto Theatre, 6052
The Ridgefield Playhouse, 6430
The Ritz Theatre, 8010
The Robert and Judi Newman Center for the Performing Arts, 6364
The Sherman Playhouse, 6431
The Smith Center for the Performing Arts, 7514
Theater, 8700
Theater at Emory, 6629
Theater J, 6478
Theatre Albany, 6611
Theatre Arlington, 8321
Theatre at Ewing, 6810
Theatre at Meydenbauer, 8570
Theatre at Raritan Valley Community College, 7576
Theatre B, 7008
Theatre East, 6130
Theatre Guild, 8287
Theatre in The Grove, 8077
Theatre in The Park, 7911
Theatre in The Round Players, 7362
Theatre in The Square, 6653
Theatre Margot, 6875
Theatre Memphis, 8286
Theatre Outback, 5960
Theatre Project Consultants, 6432
Theatre Suburbia, 8417
Theatre Three Productions Second Stage, 7806
Theatrevirginia, 8558
Thomas & Mack Center, 7515
Thomas Assembly Center, 7155
Thomasville Center for the Arts, 6664
Thompson Recital Hall, 6881
Thompson-Boling Arena, 8274
Thorne Hall, 6179
Thousand Oaks Civic Arts Plaza, 6314
Three Arts Theatre, 6641
Tiger Stadium, 7117
Tilles Center for the Performing Arts, 7678
Tillman Auditorium, 8215
Times-Union Center for the Performing Arts, 6529
Timmons Arena, 8228
Tingley Coliseum, 7609
Tisch Center for the Arts, 7788
Tivoli Theatre, 8255
Toby's Dinner Theatre, 7204
Toledo Cultural Arts Center Valentine Theatre, 8016
Toledo Museum of Art, 8017
Tom Bradley International Hall, 6180
Tom Miles Theatre, 8078
Topeka Performing Arts Center, 7063
Totem Pole Playhouse, 8124
Touchstone Theatre, 8115
Tower Fine Arts Center and Hartwell Hall, 7638
Tower Theater for the Peforming Arts, 6107
Town Hall Arts Center, 6386
Town Hall Concert Hall, 7789
Town of Cary Cultural Arts Division, 7864
Townsend Center for the Performing Arts, 6636
Towson Center Arena, 7215
Transworld Dome at Americas' Center, 7458

Tri-Cities Coliseum, 8585
Triangle Cultural Center, 7411
Tribeca Performing Arts Center, 7790
Trinity Arts Center, 8200
Trinity Mother Frances Rose Stadium, 8468
Triton College Performing Arts Center, 6824
Trojan/Adams Center Performing Arts Theatre, 5922
Tropicana Field, 6589
Troy Hayner Cultural Center, 8019
Troy Savings Bank Music Hall, 7841
Trumbull New Theatre, 8002
Trustees Theater, 6662
Tryon Fine Arts Center, 7916
Tuacahn Amphitheatre, 8493
Tubac Center of the Arts, 5994
Tucson Convention Center - Arena, 6005
Tucson Convention Center - Exhibition Hall, 6006
Tucson Convention Center - Leo Rich Theatre, 6007
Tucson Convention Center - Music Hall, 6008
Tucson Electric Park, 6009
Tulane University, 8259
Tulane University Albert Lupin Experimental Theatre, 7150
Tulane University Department of Theatre and Dance, 7151
Tulane University Newcomb Department of Music, 5919
Tulsa Community College Performing Arts Center for Education, 8059
Tulsa Performing Arts Center, 8053
Tulsa Performing Arts Center: Doenges Theater, 8055
Tulsa Performing Arts Center: John H William Hall, 8054
Tulsa Performing Arts Center: Studio II, 8056
Tultex Corporation, 8534
Turner Field, 6630
Turpin Stadium, 7138
Tweeter Center for the Performing Arts, 7242
Tyrrell Hall, 8057

U

U S Airways Center, 5976
U.S. Cellular Arena, 8694
Uaa Recital Hall, 5936
Uab Arena, 5897
Uapresents Centennial Hall, 6010
Ucf Arena, 6572
Ucla Performing Arts, 6181
Uhh Theatre, 6669
Uic Pavilion, 6756
Uic Theatre, 6757
Ulster Performing Arts Center, 7695
Umb Bank Pavilion, 7432
Underground Theatre, 8576
Unf Arena, 6530
Uni-Dome, 6965
Unicorn Theatre, 7430
Union Avenue Opera Theatre, 7459
Union Colony Civic Center, 6382
Union County Arts Center, 7586
Union Square Theatre, 7791
Union Theater, 8681
United Center, 6758
United Supermarkets Arena, 8430
University at Albany Performing Arts Center (Pac), 7627
University at Buffalo Center for the Arts, 7658
University Center Auditorium, 6487
University Center for the Arts, 6375
University Center Theatre Complex and Conference Center, 8343
University of California Santa Cruz Performing Arts Center, 6298
University of Connecticut Sports Complex - Harry a Gampel Pavilion, 6438
University of Detroit Mercy Calihan Hall, 7290
University of Georgia Performing Arts Center, 6616
University of Hartford Sports Center, 6446
University of Idaho Theatre Arts, 6702
University of Kentucky Memorial Coliseum, 7089
University of Maine Alumni Stadium, 7174
University of Maine Performing Arts Center, 7170

Facilities Index / V

University of Massachusetts Center for the Arts, 7240
University of Massachusetts Fine Arts Center, 7217
University of Minnesota Sports Pavillion, 7363
University of Mississippi Studio Theatre, 7407
University of Missouri Performing Arts Series, 7439
University of Montana Theatre, 7482
University of Nebraska Theatre, 7488
University of Nebraska-Lincoln: Kimball Recital Hall, 7494
University of Nevada-Las Vegas Performing Arts Center Artemus Ham Concert Hall, 7516
University of New Mexico Stadium, 7610
University of New Orleans Performing Arts Center, 7152
University of North Florida Fine Arts Center, 6531
University of North Texas Performing Arts Center, 8369
University of Northern Colorado, 6383
University of Rhode Island Fine Arts Center, 8193
University of Southern California, 6182
University of Southern Mississippi School of Music, 7392
University of Tennessee Music Hall, 8275
University of Texas at Austin Performing Arts Center, 8326
University of Texas at Austin: Theatre Room, 8327
University of Texas at El Paso: Main Playhouse, 8380
University of Texas-Pan American: Theater, 8370
University of Vermont: Recital Hall, 8505
University of Virginia Hall, 8518
University of West Florida Center for Fine & Performing Arts, 6580
University of Wisconsin Fieldhouse, 8682
University of Wyoming: Arts and Sciences Auditorium, 8718
University of Wyoming: Fine Arts Concert Hall, 8719
University Settlement, 7792
University Theatre, 6121, 6226, 6573, 6885, 6918, 8040
Unk Sports Center, 7489
Upper Darby Performing Arts Center, 8120
Ups Fieldhouse, 8619
Urban Institute for Contemporary Arts, 7303
Us Bank Arena, 7959
Us Cellular Arena, 8695
Us Cellular Center, 6971
Us Cellular Field, 6759
Us Military Academy, 7631
Us Military Academy Michie Stadium, 7848
Us Naval Academy Alumni Hall, 7186
Us Sailors Center, 6967
Usa Saenger Theatre, 5911
Usf Special Events Center, 6598
Usf Sun Dome, 6599
Utc Mckenzie Arena, 8256
Utica Memorial Auditorium, 7844
Uw World Series, 8608

V

Val a Browning Center for the Performing Arts, 8487
Valdez Convention and Civic Center, 5945
Valencia College Performing Arts Center, 6574
Van Andel Arena, 7304
Van Wezel Performing Arts Hall, 6586
Vanderbilt Stadium, 8305
Vanderbilt University: Memorial Gym, 8306
Velma V. Morrison Center for the Performing Arts, 6688, 6689
Verizon Center, 6475
Verizon Wireless Amphitheatre, 7878
Verizon Wireless Arena, 7540
Vern Riffe Center for the Arts, 8007
Vero Beach Concert Association, 6601
Verser Theater, 6017
Veteran's Memorial Complex, 6092
Veterans Memorial Arena, 6532
Veterans Memorial Auditorium, 6990, 8201
Veterans Memorial Civic and Convention Center, 7998
Veterans Memorial Field House, 8640
Veterans Memorial Hall, 7828
Veterans Wadsworth Theatre, 6183
Veterans' Memorial Theatre, 6097
Victoria Theatre Association, 7993
Victory Field: Indianapolis Baseball Club, 6903
Victory Gardens Theater, 6760
Victory Theatre, 6869
Viking Hall Civic Center, 8253
Vines Center, 8531
Virginia Beach Pavilion Convention Center, 8564
Virginia Theater, 7793
Visalia Convention Center Rotary Theatre, 6318
Viterbo University Fine Arts Center, 8673
Vivian Davis Michael Laboratory Theatre, 8649
Von Braun Civic Center Arena, 5902
Von Braun Civic Center Concert Hall, 5903
Von Braun Civic Center Exhibit Hall, 5904
Von Braun Civic Center Playhouse, 5901
Von Der Mehden Recital Hall, 6439

W

W L Lyons Brown Theatre, 7096
W. Turrentine and Barbara K. Jackson Hall, 6098
W.D. Packard Music Hall, 8020
W.J. Hale Stadium, 8307
Wachovia Spectrum, 8162
Waco Convention Center Chisholm Hall, 8470
Waco Hippodrome, 8471
Wadsworth Auditorium, 7675
Walker Art Center, 7364
Wall Performance Lab, 6999
Wallace Hall Fine Arts Center, 5900
Wallis Annenberg Center for the Performing Arts, 6074
Walnut Street Theatre, 8163
Walnut Street Theatre: Mainstage, 8164
Walnut Street Theatre: Studio 3, 8165
Walnut Street Theatre: Studio 5, 8166
Walt Disney Wide World of Sports Stadium, 6539
Walt Whitman Cultural Arts Center, 7548
Walter Arts Center, 8058
Walter E. Washington Convention Center, 6481
Walter Kerr Theatre, 7794
Walter Walker Auditorium, 6379
Walton Arts Center, 6026
War Memorial Auditorium, 6509
War Memorial Stadium, 6039
War Memorial Stadium (Wy), 8720
Warehouse Living Arts Center, 8347
Warhawk Stadium, 8711
Warner Grand Theatre, 6276
Warner Theatre, 6441, 6480
Warnor's Theater, 6108
Warren Atherton Auditorium, 6312
Warren M Lee Center, 8251
Warren Performing Arts Center, 6904
Washington Center for the Performing Arts, 8592
Washington Hall Auditorium, 6935
Washington Pavilion of Arts & Science, 8247
Waterloo Riverfront Stadium, 7025
Waterville Opera House, 7183
Watt Powell Stadium, 8630
Waukesha Civic Theatre, 8709
Wayne State College Arena, 7504
Web Concert Hall, 7795
Weede Arena, 7058
Weis Center for the Performing Arts, 8139
Wellington Memorial Auditorium, 7066
Wells Fargo Center for the Arts, 6302
Wells Fargo Sports Complex, 5937
Wells Theater, 6802
Wells Theatre, 8544
Wells-Metz Theatre, 6858
Werner Auditorium, 6822
Wesley Chapel, 7683
West Nebraska Arts Center, 7502
West Virginia State College Theatre, 8641
West Virginia University Coliseum, 8650
West Virginia University Creative Arts Center, 8651
Westbeth Studio Theatre, 7796
Westbeth Theatre Center, 7797
Westbrook Auditorium, 6721
Westchester Broadway Theatre, 7669
Western Illinois University Theatre and Dance Department, 6799
Western Washington University Main Stage, 8577
Western Washington University Old Main Theatre, 8578
Westhoff Experimental Theatre, 6811
Weston H. Noble Recital Hall, 6983
Westport Community Theatre, 6448
Westport Country Playhouse, 6449
Westside Theatre, 7798
Wexner Center for the Arts, 7987
Whalberg Recital Hall, 6109
Wharton Center for Performing Arts, 7294
Wheeler Opera House, 6329
Wheeling Civic Center, 8654
Wheeling Island Stadium, 8655
Whidbey Playhouse, 8589
Whistle Stop Playhouse, 7386
Whitaker Center for Science and The Arts, 8129
White River Amphitheatre, 8569
Whitehead Auditorium, 6666
Whitney Museum of Art Theater, 7799
Whittemore Center, 7530
Whittington-Pfohl Auditorium, 7861
Wicomico Civic Center, 7213
Wiedemann Recital Hall, 7072
Wien Experimental Theatre, 6403
Wien Stadium, 7800
Wild Bill's Atlanta, 6645
Wildwood Park for the Performing Arts, 6040
Wilkens Theatre, 7594
Wilkins Stadium, 6041
Will W Orr Auditorium, 8146
William & Mary Hall, 8566
William D Mullins Memorial Center, 7218
William G Mennen Sports Arena, 7570
William H Hammond Stadium, 6514
William R Frizzell Cultural Centre Claiborne & Ned Foulds Theatre, 6515
William R Johnson Coliseum, 8436
William Randolph Hearst Greek Theatre, 6070
William S. Robinson Theatre, 6380
William Stadium, 8532
William Woods College Campus Center Dulany Auditorium, 7421
Williams Center for the Arts Newman Theatre, 7588
Williams Theatre, 6874
Williams-Brice Stadium, 8220
Willows Theatre, 6089
Wilma Theatre, 7483
Wilner Auditorium, 7073
Wilshire Ebell Theatre, 6184
Wilson Center for the Performing Arts, 8103
Wilson Chapel Complex, 8279
Wings Stadium, 7314
Wink Arena, 7278
Winston Churchill Memorial Hall, 7422
Winter Garden Theatre, 7801
Wisconsin Union Theatre, 8683
Witherspoon Arts Center, 6049
WI Zorn Arena, 8662
Wolf Trap Farm Park for the Performing Arts, 8563
Wood College Theatre, 7399
Woodland Opera House, 6325
Woodruff Arts Center, 6631
Woodstock Opera House, 6851
Workshop Theatre, 6859
World Music Hall, 6414
Wright Auditorium, 7888
Wright State University's Nutter Center, 7992
Wrigley Field, 6761
Wt Neal Civic Center, 6485
Wtamu Theatre, 8340
Wynmoor Recital Hall, 6492
Wyo Theater, 8722

X

Xavier Hall Theatre, 7045
Xcel Energy Center, 7377

Y

Yaok Arena, 7334
Yakima Valley Sundome, 8622
Yale Baseball Stadium, 6425
Yale Bowl, 6426
Yale Repertory Theatre, 6427
Yamhill County Fairgrounds, 8082
Yankee Stadium, 7640
Yavapai College Performance Hall, 5978
Yellow Barn, 8507
Yerba Buena Center for the Arts, 6267
Yost Ice Arena, 7272
Young Circle Park and Bandshell, 6523
Young Theatre, 6114
Yreka Community Theatre Center, 6326
Yuma Civic Center, 6014
Yvonne Theater, 7564

Z

Zanesville Art Center, 8027
Zeiterion Theatre, 7243
Zellerbach Auditorium, 6071
Zellerbach Playhouse, 6072
Zoellner Arts Center, 8116
Zurcher Auditorium, 6886

1247

Specialized Field Index / Dance

Dance

African
- Najwa Dance Corps, 209

African American Dance
- African American Dance Ensemble, Inc., 508

African Dance
- African American Dance Ensemble, Inc., 508
- African-American Cultural Center, 374
- Cleo Parker Robinson Dance, 121
- Dimensions Dance Theater, 52
- Dinizulu African Dancers, Drummers and Singers, 377
- Ocheami African Dance Company, 681
- Salia Ni Seydou, 482
- the Charles Moore Dance Theatre, 361
- Wofa! Percussion and Dance From Guinea, West Africa, 490

African Traditional
- Les Guirivoires Dance Company, 354

American Sign Language
- Gallaudet Dance Company, 145

American Vernacular Dance
- National Tap Ensemble, 260

Anatomy & Kinesiology
- Laban/Bartenieff Institute of Movement Studies, 445

Apeja Dance
- Bi-Okoto Cultural Institute, 514

Apepe
- Bi-Okoto Cultural Institute, 514

Appalachian Clogging
- Pat Cannon's Foot & Fiddle Dance Company, 502

Asian American Dance
- H.T. Chen Dance Company, Inc., 429

Ballet
- Allan Hancock College Dance Program, 108
- Alonzo King Lines Ballet, 71
- Alpha Omega Theatrical Dance Company, 384
- Alvin Ailey American Dance Theater, 385
- Amherst Ballet Theatre Company Inc, 269
- Anaheim Ballet, 20
- Appalachian Youth Jazz-Ballet Company, 695
- Aria Dance Company, 677
- Arlington Dance Theatre, 658
- Ballet Excel Ohio, 529
- Ballet Florida, 174
- Ballet Idaho, 194
- Ballet Western Reserve, 546
- Beacon Dance Company, 184
- Boca Ballet Theatre, 150
- Brandywine Ballet, 586
- Breatriz Rodriguez, 199
- Bullard School of Dance, 287
- Burklyn Ballet Theatre, 656
- California Riverside Ballet, 61
- Celebration Team, 403
- Central Pennsylvania Youth Ballet, 569
- Charlotte Ballet, 507
- City Ballet, 615
- Civic Dance Company, 67
- Cleo Parker Robinson Dance, 121
- Connecticut Ballet, 131
- Contemporary Dance Theater, 516
- Dance Affiliates, 575
- Dance Center of Columbia College, 202
- Dance Program, 680
- Dayton Ballet, 531
- Delaware Dance Company, 138
- Desert Dance Theatre, 12
- Doug Hamby Dance, 256
- Evansville Dance Theatre, 227
- Felice Lesser Dance Theater, 425
- Firethorn Dance Academy, 173
- Fort Wayne Ballet, 228
- Frostburg State University Dance Company, 259
- Georgia Dance Conservatory, 188
- Huntsville Ballet Company, 3
- Interlochen Center for the Arts, 286
- Iowa Dance Theatre, 236
- Irving Ballet Company, 641
- Joan Miller Dance Players, 435
- Joel Hall Dancer Center, 204
- Johnson/Long Dance Company, 623
- Kentucky Ballet Theatre, 241
- Marjorie Liebert, 451
- Maryland Ballet Theatre, 258
- Metro Dancers, 561
- Metropolitan Ballet Theatre Inc., 262
- Miami University Dance Theatre, 540
- Mid Ohio Valley Ballet Company, 694
- Minnesota Ballet, 293
- Mm Colbert, 699
- Molissa Fenley and Dancers, 459
- Momentum Dance Company, 151
- Music in Motion, 672
- Neta Dance Company, 464
- New Castle Regional Ballet, 574
- New York Theatre Ballet/Ballet School of Ny, 467
- Northeast Atlantic Ballet, 186
- Notara Dance Theatre, 585
- Odyssey Dance Theatre, 649
- Oklahoma City Ballet, 552
- Oregon Ballet Theatre, 564
- Pasadena Civic Ballet, Inc., 57
- Pdac/Arts for All, 125
- Pittsburgh Dance Council, 583
- Posey Dance Company, 494
- Redwood Concert Ballet, 30
- Regina Klenjoski Dance Company, 34
- Rio Grande Valley Ballet, 644
- Robert Ivey Ballet, 595
- Rockford Dance Company, 222
- Sacred Dance Guild, 263
- San Diego Dance Theater, 69
- Sinclair Dance, 534
- St. Mark's Dance Studio, 148
- Tacoma Performing Dance Company, 690
- Tapestry Dance Company, 625
- Tennessee Association of Dance, 613
- Texas Ballet Theater, 632
- the Charleston Ballet, 693
- the Springfield Ballet Company, 223
- Theatre Arts Dance Program, 666
- Thomas Armour Youth Ballet, 170
- Uga Core Concert Dance Company, 178
- Vladimir Issaev's School of Classical Ballet, 159
- Wichita Contemporary Dance Theatre, 240
- Wichita Falls Ballet Theatre, 648
- Young Dancers in Repertory, 373
- Zephyr Dance, 214

Ballroom
- Dance Saint Louis, 310

Bartenieff Fundamentals
- Laban/Bartenieff Institute of Movement Studies, 445

Bartenieff X-Class for Fitness
- Laban/Bartenieff Institute of Movement Studies, 445

Belly Dance
- Aisha Ali Dance Company, 37
- Fort Wayne Dance Collective, 229
- Suhaila Dance Company & Suhaila Salimpour School of Dance, 18

Bolero
- American Bolero Dance Company, 378

Break Dancing
- Cleo Parker Robinson Dance, 121

Caribbean
- the Charles Moore Dance Theatre, 361

Carribean
- Najwa Dance Corps, 209

Character Dance
- Aria Dance Company, 677
- Fort Wayne Ballet, 228
- Metro Dancers, 561
- Pasadena Civic Ballet, Inc., 57

Chinese Classic
- China Dance School & Theatre, 74

Classic
- Les Ballets Grandiva, 447

Classical
- Albany Berkshire Ballet, 280
- Allegro Ballet of Houston, 633
- Ballet Hispanico of New York, 393
- Bullard School of Dance, 287
- Eglevsky Ballet, 352
- Eugene Ballet Company, 557
- Ithaca Ballet, 376
- Metro Dancers, 561
- Ohio Dance Theatre, 538
- Peninsula Dance Theatre, 675
- Saint Louis Ballet, 305
- the Concert Ballet of Virginia, 668
- the Springfield Ballet Company, 311

Classical Ballet
- Alabama Ballet, 1
- Alabama Dance Theatre, 5
- Ballet Tennessee, 611
- Brighton Ballet Theatre Company, Inc., 358
- Carolina Ballet Theatre, 606
- Commonwealth Ballet Company, 268
- Dance Alive National Ballet, 153
- Dance Saint Louis, 310
- Pennsylvania Youth Ballet, 568
- Pioneer Dance Arts, 687
- Voloshky Ukrainian Dance Ensembles, 571

Clogging
- Leahy Good, 533

Collaborative Dance
- Crossroads Performance Group, 10
- Nancy Karp & Dancers, 85

Comedy
- Les Ballets Grandiva, 447

Concert
- Ballet Hispanico of New York, 393

Contemporary
- Albany Berkshire Ballet, 280
- Allegro Ballet of Houston, 633
- Ballet Hispanico of New York, 393
- Brandywine Ballet, 586
- Carolina Ballet Theatre, 606
- Eglevsky Ballet, 352
- Eugene Ballet Company, 557
- Ithaca Ballet, 376
- Janis Brenner and Dancers, 433
- K Dance, 669
- Les Ballets Grandiva, 447
- Les Guirivoires Dance Company, 354
- Nai-Ni Chen Dance Company, 328
- Neta Dance Company, 464
- Saint Louis Ballet, 305
- Snappy Dance Theater, 279
- the Charleston Ballet, 693
- the Springfield Ballet Company, 311

Contemporary Ballet
- Alabama Ballet, 1
- Ballet Florida, 174
- Ballet Tennessee, 611
- Commonwealth Ballet Company, 268
- Dance Saint Louis, 310
- Metro Dancers, 561
- Milwaukee Ballet Company, 703

Contemporary Dance
- Battery Dance Company, 395
- Bernard Schmidt Productions, Inc, 407
- Bill Evans Dance Company, 353
- Cohan/Suzeau Dance Company, 237
- Creach/Company, 408
- Dance Alive National Ballet, 153
- Dance June Lewis and Company, 410
- Dance Kaleidoscope, 231
- Dayton Ballet, 531
- Dayton Contemporary Dance Company, 532
- Donald Williams, 415
- Ethan Brown, 423
- Fort Wayne Ballet, 228
- Giordano Dance Chicago, 217
- Minnesota Dance Theatre & Dance Institute, 296
- Momenta, 219
- Ohio Dance Theatre, 538
- Parsons Dance Company, 470
- Peninsula Dance Theatre, 675
- Pennsylvania Dance Theatre, 584
- Philadelphia Dance Company, 578
- River North Chicago Dance Company, 211
- the Concert Ballet of Virginia, 668
- Wofa! Percussion and Dance From Guinea, West Africa, 490

Contemporary Jazz
- Pioneer Dance Arts, 687

Contemporary Persian Dance
- Banafsheh Sayyad and Namah, 110

Contemporary Photography
- Muna Tseng Dance Projects, 462

Contemporary/Indian Fusion
- Cohan/Suzeau Dance Company, 237

Contemporary/Modern
- Miami University Dance Theatre, 540

Creative Movement
- Amherst Ballet Theatre Company Inc, 269
- Desert Dance Theatre, 12
- Huntsville Ballet Company, 3
- Zephyr Dance, 214

Dance
- Bates Dance Festival, 250
- Burklyn Ballet Theatre, 656
- Columbia Community Arts Centre, 599
- Muna Tseng Dance Projects, 462

Designing
- Frostburg State University Dance Company, 259

Directing
- Frostburg State University Dance Company, 259

Drama
- Columbia Community Arts Centre, 599

Dramatic Dance
- Blanco Performing Arts Foundation, 399
- China Dance School & Theatre, 74
- Rev. J. Bruce Stewart, 657

East Indian Classical Dance
- Cohan/Suzeau Dance Company, 237

Eastern Europe Dance
- the Radost Folk Ensemble, 684

Edo Dance
- Bi-Okoto Cultural Institute, 514

Educational Dance
- Brooklyn Arts Exchange, 359
- Chamber Dance Company, 679
- Debra Weiss Dance Company, 495
- Isadora Duncan Dance Foundation, 432
- Jane Franklin Dance, 659
- Joel Hall Dancer Center, 204
- Kathy Rose, 442
- Marjorie Liebert, 451
- Nebraska Theatre Caravan, 317
- Ohio State University of Dance, 527
- Virginia School of the Arts, 671

Egyptian Dance
- Joel Hall Dancer Center, 204

Ethnic Dance
- African-American Cultural Center, 374
- Alvin Ailey American Dance Theater, 385
- Annabella Gonzalez Dance Theater, 388
- Asian American Arts Centre, 390
- China Dance School & Theatre, 74
- Dallas Black Dance Theatre, 628
- Dance Affiliates, 575
- Dance Center of Columbia College, 202
- Dance Place, 143
- Dance Saint Louis, 310
- Dinizulu African Dancers, Drummers and Singers, 377
- Eugene James Dance Company, 424
- Garth Fagan Dance, 498
- Into Salsa Studio, 232
- Joan Miller Dance Players, 435
- Merian Soto Dance & Performance, 355
- Oinkari Basque Dancers, 196
- Phyllis Rose Dance Company, 473
- Prairie Dance Theatre, 553
- Rio Grande Valley Ballet, 644
- Solaris Dance Theatre & Video, 484
- the Radost Folk Ensemble, 684
- Vanaver Caravan, 380
- World Music Institute, 491
- Young Dancers in Repertory, 373

Experimental Dance
- Danspace Project, 414
- Leaven Dance Company, 543

Flamenco
- American Bolero Dance Company, 378
- Banafsheh Sayyad and Namah, 110
- Clarita & the Arte Flamenco Dance Theatre, 19
- Guadalupe Dance Academy, 646
- Pdac/Arts for All, 125
- Yaelisa and Caminos Flamencos, 95

Folk Dance
- Asian American Arts Centre, 390
- Brighton Ballet Theatre Company, Inc., 358
- Dance Affiliates, 575
- Oinkari Basque Dancers, 196
- Phyllis Rose Dance Company, 473
- Prairie Dance Theatre, 553
- Rio Grande Valley Ballet, 644
- Solaris Dance Theatre & Video, 484
- the Springfield Ballet Company, 223
- Vanaver Caravan, 380
- World Music Institute, 491

Folkloric Dance
- Carmel Dance Arts-Indy Latin Dance, 226
- Guadalupe Dance Academy, 646

1249

Specialized Field Index / Dance

German Dance
   Neuer Tanz, 465
Ghana Dance
   Obo Addy Master Drummer, 563
Ghana Music
   Obo Addy Master Drummer, 563
Hip Hop
   Alabama Dance Theatre, 5
   Anaheim Ballet, 20
   Central Pennsylvania Youth Ballet, 569
   Cleo Parker Robinson Dance, 121
   Contemporary Dance Theater, 516
   Dance Saint Louis, 310
   Firethorn Dance Academy, 173
   Jeannette Neill Dance Studio, 273
   Joel Hall Dancer Center, 204
   Pasadena Civic Ballet, Inc., 57
   Pdac/Arts for All, 125
   Sacred Dance Guild, 263
Historical Dance
   Momenta, 219
   Ocheami African Dance Company, 681
Improv
   Frostburg State University Dance Company, 259
Improvisation
   Contemporary Dance Theater, 516
   Dance Center of Columbia College, 202
   Interplayce, 54
Indigenous
   Sacred Dance Guild, 263
Interdisciplinary
   Crossroads Performance Group, 10
   Nancy Karp & Dancers, 85
Irish Dance
   Pat Cannon's Foot & Fiddle Dance Company, 502
Jameba
   Bi-Okoto Cultural Institute, 514
Japanese Arts
   Japanese American Cultural and Community Center, 40
Japanese Dance
   Japanese American Cultural and Community Center, 40
Jazz
   Alabama Dance Theatre, 5
   Allan Hancock College Dance Program, 108
   Alpha Omega Theatrical Dance Company, 384
   Alvin Ailey American Dance Theater, 385
   American Tap Dance Foundation, 387
   Amherst Ballet Theatre Company Inc, 269
   Anaheim Ballet, 20
   Ann Lacey School of American Dance and Arts Management, 551
   Appalachian Youth Jazz-Ballet Company, 695
   Arlington Dance Theatre, 658
   Ballet Western Reserve, 546
   Beacon Dance Company, 184
   Bill Evans Dance Company, 353
   Boca Ballet Theatre, 150
   Celebration Team, 403
   Central Pennsylvania Youth Ballet, 569
   City Ballet, 615
   Civic Dance Company, 67
   Cleo Parker Robinson Dance, 121
   Contemporary Dance Theater, 516
   Dallas Black Dance Theatre, 628
   Dance Affiliates, 575
   Dance Center of Columbia College, 202
   Dance Saint Louis, 310
   Dayton Contemporary Dance Company, 532
   Desert Dance Theatre, 12
   Dimensions Dance Theater, 52
   Firethorn Dance Academy, 173
   Fort Wayne Ballet, 228
   Fort Wayne Dance Collective, 229
   Frostburg State University Dance Company, 259
   Gallaudet Dance Company, 145
   Georgia Dance Conservatory, 188
   Giordano Dance Chicago, 217
   Huntsville Ballet Company, 3
   Iowa Dance Theatre, 236
   Irving Ballet Company, 641
   Jazz Tap Ensemble, 41
   Jeannette Neill Dance Studio, 273
   Joan Miller Dance Players, 435
   Joel Hall Dancer Center, 204
   Kanopy Dance Company, 697
   Les Guirivoires Dance Company, 354
   Metro Dancers, 561
   Metropolitan Ballet Theatre Inc., 262
   Miami University Dance Theatre, 540
   Minnesota Ballet, 293
   Mm Colbert, 699
   Momentum Dance Company, 151
   Music in Motion, 672
   Najwa Dance Corps, 209
   National Dance Institute, 463
   National Tap Ensemble, 260
   New Castle Regional Ballet, 574
   Northeast Atlantic Ballet, 186
   Notara Dance Theatre, 585
   Odyssey Dance Theatre, 649
   Oklahoma City Ballet, 552
   Oregon Ballet Theatre, 564
   Pasadena Civic Ballet, Inc., 57
   Pdac/Arts for All, 125
   Phyllis Rose Dance Company, 473
   Posey Dance Company, 494
   Redwood Concert Ballet, 30
   Rio Grande Valley Ballet, 644
   River North Chicago Dance Company, 211
   Robert Ivey Ballet, 595
   Rockford Dance Company, 222
   Sacred Dance Guild, 263
   Southeast Alabama Dance Company, 2
   Spoleto Festival Usa, 596
   St. Mark's Dance Studio, 148
   Tacoma Performing Dance Company, 690
   Tapestry Dance Company, 625
   Tennessee Association of Dance, 613
   the Springfield Ballet Company, 223
   Theatre Arts Dance Program, 666
   Vladimir Issaev's School of Classical Ballet, 159
   Wichita Contemporary Dance Theatre, 240
   Zenon Dance Company and School, 299
Jazz, Folk
   Aria Dance Company, 677
Koroso
   Bi-Okoto Cultural Institute, 514
Laban Movement Analyis
   Laban/Bartenieff Institute of Movement Studies, 445
Latin
   Ballet Hispanico of New York, 393
   Carmel Dance Arts-Indy Latin Dance, 226
Liturgical Dance
   Leaven Dance Company, 543
Martial Arts
   Solaris Dance Theatre & Video, 484
Mediterranean Dance
   Mosaic Dance Theater Company, 329
Middle Eastern
   Mosaic Dance Theater Company, 329
Middle Eastern Dance
   Suhaila Dance Company & Suhaila Salimpour School of Dance, 18
Middle-Eastern
   Aisha Ali Dance Company, 37
Mime
   Rev. J. Bruce Stewart, 657
Modern
   Alpha Omega Theatrical Dance Company, 384
   Alvin Ailey American Dance Theater, 385
   Amherst Ballet Theatre Company Inc, 269
   Annabella Gonzalez Dance Theater, 388
   Aria Dance Company, 677
   Asian American Arts Centre, 390
   Ballet Excel Ohio, 529
   Ballet Idaho, 194
   Ballet Western Reserve, 546
   Battery Dance Company, 395
   Beacon Dance Company, 184
   Boca Ballet Theatre, 150
   California Riverside Ballet, 61
   Celebration Team, 403
   Charlotte Ballet, 507
   Chrysalis Repertory Dance Company, 635
   City Ballet, 615
   Connecticut Ballet, 131
   Contemporary Dance Theater, 516
   Dallas Black Dance Theatre, 628
   Dance Affiliates, 575
   Dance Center of Columbia College, 202
   Dance June Lewis and Company, 410
   Dance Kaleidoscope, 231
   Dance Place, 143
   Dance Program, 680
   Dance Saint Louis, 310
   Danspace Project, 414
   Dayton Contemporary Dance Company, 532
   Delaware Dance Company, 138
   Desert Dance Theatre, 12
   Dimensions Dance Theater, 52
   Doug Elkins Dance Company, 417
   Doug Hamby Dance, 256
   Eugene James Dance Company, 424
   Felice Lesser Dance Theater, 425
   Firethorn Dance Academy, 173
   Fort Wayne Dance Collective, 229
   Frostburg State University Dance Company, 259
   Gallaudet Dance Company, 145
   Garth Fagan Dance, 498
   Georgia Dance Conservatory, 188
   H.T. Chen Dance Company, Inc., 429
   Huntsville Ballet Company, 3
   Interlochen Center for the Arts, 286
   Interplayce, 54
   Iowa Dance Theatre, 236
   Janis Brenner and Dancers, 433
   Joan Miller Dance Players, 435
   Joel Hall Dancer Center, 204
   Johnson/Long Dance Company, 623
   K Dance, 669
   Kanopy Dance Company, 697
   Les Guirivoires Dance Company, 354
   Metro Dancers, 561
   Mid Ohio Valley Ballet Company, 694
   Minnesota Ballet, 293
   Mm Colbert, 699
   Molissa Fenley and Dancers, 459
   Momenta, 219
   Momentum Dance Company, 151
   Music in Motion, 672
   National Dance Institute, 463
   Neta Dance Company, 464
   Neuer Tanz, 465
   Notara Dance Theatre, 585
   Oregon Ballet Theatre, 564
   Parsons Dance Company, 470
   Pasadena Civic Ballet, Inc., 57
   Pdac/Arts for All, 125
   Pennsylvania Dance Theatre, 584
   Philadelphia Dance Company, 578
   Phyllis Rose Dance Company, 473
   Pick Up Performance Company, 474
   Pioneer Dance Arts, 687
   Pittsburgh Dance Council, 583
   Posey Dance Company, 494
   Prairie Dance Theatre, 553
   Redwood Concert Ballet, 30
   Regina Klenjoski Dance Company, 34
   Robert Ivey Ballet, 595
   Rockford Dance Company, 222
   Rod Rodgers Dance Company & Studios, 480
   Sacred Dance Guild, 263
   San Diego Dance Theater, 69
   Sinclair Dance, 534
   Snappy Dance Theater, 279
   Solaris Dance Theatre & Video, 484
   Southeast Alabama Dance Company, 2
   Tacoma Performing Dance Company, 690
   Tapestry Dance Company, 625
   Tennessee Association of Dance, 613
   Texas Ballet Theater, 632
   the Charleston Ballet, 693
   the Springfield Ballet Company, 223
   Theatre Arts Dance Program, 666
   Uga Ceco Concert Dance Company, 178
   Vanaver Caravan, 380
   Wichita Contemporary Dance Theatre, 240
   Wichita Falls Ballet Theatre, 648
   Young Dancers in Repertory, 373
   Zenon Dance Company and School, 299
   Zephyr Dance, 214
Modern Ballet
   Alabama Dance Theatre, 5
   Alonzo King Lines Ballet, 71
Modern Dance
   Najwa Dance Corps, 209
Moorish Dance
   Bernard Schmidt Productions, Inc, 407
Movement
   Jane Franklin Dance, 659
Multi-Disciplinary Work
   Tapit/New Works Ensemble Theater, 700
Multi-Media Dance
   Maida Withers Dance Construction Company, 146
Multidisciplinary Collaboration Dance
   the Purple Moon Dance Project, 87
Music
   Bates Dance Festival, 250
   Columbia Community Arts Centre, 599
Musical Theater
   Pasadena Civic Ballet, Inc., 57
Musical Theater Dance
   Ann Lacey School of American Dance and Arts Management, 551
Musical Theatre
   Frostburg State University Dance Company, 259
New Media
   Maida Withers Dance Construction Company, 146
Non-Western
   the Purple Moon Dance Project, 87
North African Dance
   Aisha Ali Dance Company, 37
Novelty Dance
   Phyllis Rose Dance Company, 473
Pilates
   Boca Ballet Theatre, 150
Playwriting
   Frostburg State University Dance Company, 259
Pointe
   Huntsville Ballet Company, 3
   Vladimir Issaev's School of Classical Ballet, 159
Post-Modern Dance
   Chrysalis Repertory Dance Company, 635
   Danspace Project, 414
   Maida Withers Dance Construction Company, 146
Residencies
   Tapit/New Works Ensemble Theater, 700
Rhythm Tap and Ballet
   Ann Lacey School of American Dance and Arts Management, 551
Russian Classical
   Maryland Ballet Theatre, 258
Salsa
   Carmel Dance Arts-Indy Latin Dance, 226
   Into Salsa Dance Studio, 232
Shakespeare
   Frostburg State University Dance Company, 259
Singing
   Frostburg State University Dance Company, 259
Spanish
   American Bolero Dance Company, 378
   Clarita & the Arte Flamenco Dance Theatre, 19
   Yaelisa and Caminos Flamencos, 95
Spanish Dance
   Bernard Schmidt Productions, Inc, 407
Square Dance
   Pat Cannon's Foot & Fiddle Dance Company, 502
Stage Combat
   Frostburg State University Dance Company, 259
Storytelling
   Debra Weiss Dance Company, 495
   Rev. J. Bruce Stewart, 657
Street Theatre
   Dance Theatre Etcetera, 369
   Doug Elkins Dance Company, 417
Sufi Whirling
   Banafsheh Sayyad and Namah, 110
Swing Dance
   Leahy Good, 533
   Pat Cannon's Foot & Fiddle Dance Company, 502
Tap
   Alabama Dance Theatre, 5
   American Tap Dance Foundation, 387
   Anaheim Ballet, 20
   Ann Lacey School of American Dance and Arts Management, 551
   Arlington Dance Theatre, 658
   Central Pennsylvania Youth Ballet, 569

Specialized Field Index / Instrumental Music

Civic Dance Company, 67
Contemporary Dance Theater, 516
Dance Saint Louis, 310
Delaware Dance Company, 138
Firethorn Dance Academy, 173
Frostburg State University Dance Company, 259
Gallaudet Dance Company, 145
Huntsville Ballet Company, 3
Jazz Tap Ensemble, 41
Joel Hall Dancer Center, 204
Leahy Good, 533
Miami University Dance Theatre, 540
Minnesota Ballet, 293
Najwa Dance Corps, 209
National Dance Institute, 463
National Tap Ensemble, 260
New Castle Regional Ballet, 574
Northeast Atlantic Ballet, 186
Notara Dance Theatre, 585
Pasadena Civic Ballet, Inc., 57
Pat Cannon's Foot & Fiddle Dance Company, 502
Pdac/Arts for All, 125
Pioneer Dance Arts, 687
Sacred Dance Guild, 263
Sinclair Dance, 534
Tapestry Dance Company, 625
Tapit/New Works Ensemble Theater, 700
Tennessee Association of Dance, 613
the Springfield Ballet Company, 311
Thomas Armour Youth Ballet, 170
Vladimir Issaev's School of Classical Ballet, 159
Wichita Contemporary Dance Theatre, 240

Theatre Dance
Blanco Performing Arts Foundation, 399
Delaware Dance Company, 138
Jeannette Neill Dance Studio, 273
Ohio Dance Theatre, 538
Pennsylvania Youth Ballet, 568
San Diego Dance Theater, 69
Tapit/New Works Ensemble Theater, 700
the Springfield Ballet Company, 311

Theatrical Dance
Brooklyn Arts Exchange, 359
Chamber Dance Company, 679
China Dance School & Theatre, 74
Dance Place, 143
Dance Theatre Etcetera, 369
Dancing on Common Ground, 181
Evansville Dance Theatre, 227
Interplayce, 54
Kathy Rose, 442
Kentucky Ballet Theatre, 241
Minnesota Dance Theatre & Dance Institute, 296
Nebraska Theatre Caravan, 317
New York Theatre Ballet/Ballet School of Ny, 467
Odyssey Dance Theatre, 649
Phyllis Rose Dance Company, 473
Pick Up Performance Company, 474
Rod Rodgers Dance Company & Studios, 480
Spoleto Festival Usa, 596
Virginia School of the Arts, 671

Traditional Ballet
Bullard School of Dance, 287
Milwaukee Ballet Company, 703
Nai-Ni Chen Dance Company, 328

Traditional Dance
Breatriz Rodriguez, 199
Creach/Company, 408
Dancing on Common Ground, 181
Donald Williams, 415
Ethan Brown, 423
Isadora Duncan Dance Foundation, 432
Jane Franklin Dance, 659
Merian Soto Dance & Performance, 355
Minnesota Dance Theatre & Dance Institute, 296
Ohio State University of Dance, 527

Ukrainian Dance
Voloshky Ukrainian Dance Ensembles, 571

Visual Art
Muna Tseng Dance Projects, 462

Visual Arts
Rev. J. Bruce Stewart, 657

West African Dance
Salia Ni Seydou, 482

Western
the Purple Moon Dance Project, 87

Workshops
Tapit/New Works Ensemble Theater, 700

World Music
World Music Institute, 491

Yoga
Fort Wayne Dance Collective, 229

Instrumental Music

Youth Symphony
Pittsburgh Youth Symphony Orchestra Association, 1657

Art
University of Southern Mississippi Symphony, 1274

Arts
New Jersey Workshop for the Arts, 1351

Avant Garde
New Music Circle, 1288

Bach
Bach Festival of Philadelphia, 1639
Boulder Bach Festival, 897
Carmel Bach Festival, 766
Whittier College Bach Festival, 892

Bag Pipes and Drums
Fairbanks Red Hackle Pipe Band, 719

Ballet
Anchorage Symphony Orchestra, 717

Band
451st Army Band, 1270
Alma Symphony Orchestra, 1221
Augustana Symphony Orchestra, 1063
Austin Symphony Orchestra Society, 1703
Cleveland Jazz Orchestra, 1533
Denver Municipal Band, 906
Depauw University Chamber Symphony, 1081
Grand Junction Musical Arts Association, 912
Highland British Brass Band Association, 1492
Jamestown Concert Association, 1396
Klezmer Conservatory Band, 1190
Massachusetts Youth Wind Ensemble, 1182
Minnesota State Band, 1271
Music Society: Midland Center for the Arts, 1248
New Orleans Concert Band, 1142
New Orleans Jazz and Heritage Foundation, 1143
Paddywhack, 1505
River City Brass Band, 1659
Roulette Intermedium, 1440
Saratoga Performing Arts Center, 1464
Smoky Mountain British Brass, 1498
Tar River Choral & Orchestral Society, 1503
Toledo Jazz Society, 1570
United States Air Force Band, 951

Baroque
All Seasons Chamber Players, 1328
Arizona Early Music Society, 739
Boston Baroque, 1173
Carolina Pro Musica, 1482
Early Music New York (Em/Ny), 1416
Foundation for Baroque Music, 1392
Go for Baroque, 1583
Long Island Baroque Ensemble, 1399
Oberlin Baroque Ensemble, 1564
Portland Baroque Orchestra, 1606
Renaissance and Baroque Society of Pittsburgh, 1658
Santa Cruz Baroque Festival, 873
Seattle Baroque, 1803

Bluegrass
Britt Festivals, 1598

Blues
Cruisers, 962
Juneau Jazz and Classics, 723

Brass Ensemble
Chestnut Brass Company, 1641
Classical Quartet, 1414
Highland British Brass Band Association, 1492
River City Brass Band, 1659
Saturday Brass Quintet, 1442
Smoky Mountain British Brass, 1498
Solid Brass, 1326
Trinkle Brass Works, 1499

Broadway
Cleveland Pops Orchestra, 1518

Celtic
Nomadics, 1402

Ceremonial Music
United States Navy Band, 963

Chamber
Adrian Symphony Orchestra, 1220
Alea III, 1175
Amarillo Symphony, 1700
Ames Town and Gown Chamber Music Association, 1099
Annapolis Chamber Orchestra, 1152
Apple Hill Center for Chamber Music, 1318
Ars Nova Musicians Chamber Orchestra, 1374
Asheville Chamber Music Series, 1477
Ashtabula Chamber Orchestra, 1516
Aston Magna Foundation, 922
Atlanta Symphony Orchestra, 1005
Augustana Symphony Orchestra, 1063
Austin Symphony Orchestra Society, 1703
Bach Festival of Philadelphia, 1639
Bachanalia Chamber Orchestra, 1408
Baltimore Consort, 1631
Bangor Symphony Orchestra, 1145
Baton Rouge Symphony Orchestra, 1137
Battle Creek Symphony Orchestra, 1224
Bloomingdale School of Music, 1409
Boston Classical Orchestra, 1202
Boston Musica Viva, 1186
Boston Symphony Chamber Players, 1177
Boston Symphony Orchestra, 1178
Bowling Green-Western Symphony Orchestra, 1125
Brandeis University Department of Music, 1215
Brazos Valley Symphony Orchestra, 1705
Bronx Arts Ensemble, 1368
Brookings Chamber Music Society, 1685
Brooklyn Philharmonic Orchestra, 1371
Brooklyn Symphony Orchestra, 1372
Cambridge Society for Early Music: Chamber Music Series, 1188
Candlelight Concert Society, 1162
Canton Symphony Orchestra, 1523
Carnegie Chamber Players, 1410
Carthage Chamber Music Series, 1824
Cascade Symphony Orchestra, 1790
Cathedral Basilica of the Sacred Heart Concert Series, 1335
Cayuga Chamber Orchestra, 1394
Ccm Philharmonia & Concert Orchestra, 1526
Cedar Rapids Symphony Orchestra, 1102
Cedarhurst Chamber Music, 1057
Chamber Music Hawaii, 1017
Chamber Music Houston, 1730
Chamber Music Northwest, 1600
Chamber Music Society of Lincoln Center, 1412
Chamber Music Society of Oregon, 1601
Chamber Orchestra of Albuquerque, 1353
Chamber Players International, 1475
Charleston Chamber Music Society, 1816
Charleston Symphony Orchestra, 1678
Chestnut Brass Company, 1641
Cheyenne Symphony Orchestra, 1837
Chinese Classical Orchestra and Educational Program, 1072
Cincinnati Chamber Orchestra, 1527
Classical Quartet, 1414
Cleveland Chamber Symphony, 1531
Cleveland Octet, 1534
Clinton Symphony Orchestra, 1103
Colorado Springs Philharmonic, 903
Columbus Symphony Orchestra, 1545
Columbus Symphony Youth Orchestras, 1546
Concert Artists of Baltimore, 1156
Concerto Soloists, 1642
Conejo Pops Orchestra, 884
Dallas Bach Society, 1712
Danville Symphony Orchestra, 1044
Dayton Philharmonic Orchestra Association, 1549
Daytona Beach Symphony Society, 967
Dc Youth Orchestra Program, 954
Delaware Symphony Orchestra, 949
Des Moines Symphony, 1107
Detroit Chamber Winds & Strings, 1253
Dinosaur Annex Music Ensemble, 1179
Dubuque Symphony Orchestra, 1109
Duluth-Superior Symphony Orchestra, 1258

Duluth-Superior Youth Orchestras & Sinfonia, 1259
Dupage Symphony, 1049
Early Music Guild of Seattle, 1798
Eastern Arizona College- Community Orchestra, 738
El Camino Youth Symphony, 821
El Paso Pro-Musica, 1720
Emerald Chamber Players, 1591
Emory Symphony Orchestra, 1008
Evansville Philharmonic Orchestra, 1079
Fairbanks Symphony Association, 720
Fairfax Symphony Orchestra, 1778
Fontana Chamber Arts, 1243
Fort Worth Symphony Orchestra, 1723
Friends of Chamber Music of Troy, 1470
Go for Baroque, 1583
Goliard Chamber Soloists, 1363
Grand Rapids Symphony, 1234
Great Falls Symphony Association, 1298
Greater Boston Youth Symphony Orchestras, 1180
Greater Grand Forks Symphony Orchestra, 1511
Greater Twin Cities Youth Symphonies, 1263
Green Bay Symphony Orchestra, 1823
Greenville Symphony Orchestra, 1681
Handel and Haydn Society, 1181
Hawaii Chamber Orchestra Society, 1018
Helena Symphony Society, 1299
Hesperus, 1776
Hope College Orchestra, 1241
Houston Civic Symphony Orchestra, 1728
Houston Early Music, 1729
Hudson Valley Philharmonic, 1455
Huntington Symphony Orchestra, 1818
Illinois Chamber Symphony, 1069
Indianapolis Symphony Orchestra, 1084
International Violin Competition of Indianapolis, 1085
Interschool Orchestras of New York, 1420
Islip Arts Council Chamber Music Series, 1382
Johnstown Symphony Orchestra, 1632
Kalamazoo Symphony Orchestra, 1244
Kansas City Chamber Orchestra, 1282
Kenosha Symphony Association, 1825
Kingston Chamber Music Festival at the University of Rhode Island, 1672
Kokomo Symphony, 1088
La Jolla Music Society, 796
Lakeside Symphony, 1556
Lansing Symphony Orchestra, 1245
Laredo Philharmonic Orchestra, 1738
Lark Society for Chamber Music, 1148
Lehigh Valley Chamber Orchestra, 1636
Lexington Philharmonic Society, 1128
Lima Symphony Orchestra, 1557
Lincoln Friends of Chamber Music, 1304
Long Island Baroque Ensemble, 1399
Long Island Philharmonic, 1401
Louisville Orchestra, 1131
Lubbock Symphony Orchestra, 1741
Maine Music Society, 1147
Marlboro School of Music, 1643
Massachusetts Youth Wind Ensemble, 1182
Memphis Symphony Orchestra and Youth Symphony Orchestra, 1695
Miami Wind Quintet, 1566
Midland Symphony Orchestra, 1247
Midland-Odessa Symphony and Chorale, 1743
Midwest Young Artists, 1054
Mill Valley Chamber Music Society, 809
Milwaukee Youth Symphony Orchestra, 1831
Mississippi Symphony Orchestra, 1275
Missouri Symphony Society, 1279
Montclaire String Quartet, 1817
Montgomery County Youth Orchestra, 1159
Mozart Classical Orchestra, 793
Music Academy of the West, 869
Music at Manoa/University of Hawaii at Manoa Outreach College, 1022
Music Before 1800, 1425
Music Society: Midland Center for the Arts, 1248
Nashville Symphony, 1696
National Gallery Orchestra, 957
National Musical Arts, 1168
National Orchestral Association, 1426

1251

Specialized Field Index / Instrumental Music

National Symphony Orchestra Association, 958
New Black Music Repertory Ensemble, 1040
New Jersey Symphony Orchestra, 1336
New West Symphony Association, 885
New World Symphony, 980
New World Youth Symphony Orchestra, 1086
New York City Symphony Orchestra, 1427
New York Philharmonic, 1430
New York Philomusica Chamber Ensemble, 1431
New York Youth Symphony, 1433
Norfolk Chamber Music Festival, 936
North Carolina Symphony, 1500
North/South Consonance, 1435
Northwest Indiana Symphony Orchestra and Society, 1093
Oberlin Baroque Ensemble, 1564
Ohio Chamber Orchestra, 1519
Oklahoma Mozart International Festival, 1577
Omaha Area Youth Orchestras, 1308
Omaha Symphony, 1309
Oregon Mozart Players, 1594
Orpheus Chamber Orchestra, 1437
Pacific University Community Wind Ensemble, 1595
Peoples' Symphony Concerts, 1438
Philadelphia Classical Guitar Society, 1646
Philadelphia String Quartet, 1648
Philadelphia Youth Orchestra, 1649
Philharmonia Virtuosi Corporation, 1448
Philharmonic Orchestra of Indianapolis, 1087
Piffaro: the Renaissance Band, 1651
Pittsburgh New Music Ensemble, 1655
Pittsburgh Symphony Orchestra, 1656
Pittsburgh Youth Symphony Orchestra Association, 1657
Plymouth Philharmonic Orchestra, 1207
Portland Chamber Orchestra Association, 1607
Portland String Quartet Concert Series/Workshop, 1149
Present Music, 1832
Pro Arte Chamber Orchestra, 1191
Pro Musica Chamber Orchestra of Columbus, 1548
Quad City Youth String Ensemble, 1105
Quincy Symphony Orchestra, 1062
Quintet of the Americas, 1381
Relache Ensemble, 1653
Renaissance and Baroque Society of Pittsburgh, 1658
Reno Chamber Orchestra, 1315
Richmond Symphony Orchestra, 1785
Rochester Chamber Orchestra, 1462
Rose City Chamber Orchestra, 1610
Rosewood Chamber Ensemble, 1466
Roulette Intermedium, 1440
Saint Louis Symphony Youth Orchestra, 1292
Saint Lukes Chamber Ensemble, 1441
Saint Paul Chamber Orchestra, 1272
Salem Chamber Orchestra, 1614
San Antonio Chamber Music Society, 1748
San Diego Chamber Orchestra, 841
San Francisco Conservatory of Music, 854
San Francisco Contemporary Music Players, 853
San Francisco Early Music Society, 759
Santa Barbara Chamber Orchestra, 870
Santa Fe Pro Musica, 1359
Santa Fe Symphony, 1360
Santa Rosa Junior College Chamber Concert Series, 877
Santa Rosa Symphony, 878
Saturday Brass Quintet, 1442
Seattle Symphony Orchestra, 1805
Sem Ensemble, 1373
Shreveport Symphony Orchestra, 1144
Silk and Bamboo Ensemble, 1073
Sinfonia Concertante Orchestra, 1611
Smoky Mountain British Brass, 1498
Solid Brass, 1326
South Dakota Symphony, 1688
South Texas Symphony Association, 1719
Spokane Symphony Orchestra, 1807
Springfield Symphony Orchestra, 1211
St. Patrick's Cathedral Chamber Music Series, 1444
Stockbridge Chamber Concerts at Searles Castle, 1206
Summer Strings on The Meherrin, 1495
Sunriver Music Festival, 1615
Symphony of the Mountains, 1693
Syracuse Symphony Orchestra, 1468
Tacoma Youth Symphony, 1810
Tannery Pond Concerts, 1404
the National Philharmonic, 1169
Tisch Center for the Arts, 1447
Toledo Symphony, 1571
Traverse Symphony Orchestra, 1256
Tremont String Quartet, 1388
Trinkle Brass Works, 1499
Troy Chromatics Concerts, 1471
Tulsa Youth Symphony, 1586
Umpqua Symphony Association, 1612
United States Air Force Band, 951
University Circle Chamber Orchestra, 1540
University of Central Florida Orchestra, 985
Venti Da Camera, 1522
Voices of Change, 1718
Washington and Lee University Concert Guild, 1780
Waterloo-Cedar Falls Symphony Orchestra, 1101
West Coast Chamber Orchestra, 872
West Jersey Chamber Music Symphony & Society, 1333
West Michigan Symphony, 1249
Western New York Chamber Orchestra, 1385
Wichita Symphony, 1124
Winston-Salem Symphony, 1509
Wisconsin Chamber Orchestra, 1827
Wittenberg University Department of Music, 1569
Yakima Youth Orchestra, 1815
Yellowstone Chamber Players, 1297
Young Musicians Foundation Debut Orchestra, 764
Young People's Symphony Orchestra, 762
Youth Symphony Association of Kansas, 1122

Chamber Music
Chamber Music Society of Detroit, 1231
Raleigh Symphony Orchestra, 1502

Chamber Orchestra
Chicago Chamber Orchestra, 1033

Children's Chamber Music
Strings in The Mountains, 918

Children's Concerts
Candlelight Concert Society, 1162
San Luis Obispo Mozart Festival, 863

Chinese Music
Chinese Music Ensemble of New York, 1413

Chorus
Carson City Symphony Association, 1311
Manchester Symphony Orchestra/Chorale, 929
United States Air Force Band, 951
Washington Bach Consort, 959

Classic Repertory
Chicago Chamber Orchestra, 1033

Classical
Arkansas Symphony Orchestra, 755
Bakersfield Symphony Orchestra, 757
Beach Cities Symphony Association, 830
Britt Festivals, 1598
Chicago Sinfonietta, 1034
Delaware Symphony Orchestra, 949
Early Music New York (Em/Ny), 1416
Fairbanks Symphony Association, 720
Fort Smith Symphony, 754
Friends of Chamber Music of Troy, 1470
Juneau Jazz and Classics, 723
Kingston Chamber Music Festival at the University of Rhode Island, 1672
Montgomery Symphony Orchestra, 715
Music Academy of the West, 869
New England String Ensemble, 1213
Northbrook Symphony Orchestra, 1058
Oakland East Bay Symphony, 815
Orlando Philharmonic Orchestra, 984
Portland Chamber Orchestra Association, 1607
Salem Chamber Orchestra, 1614
Santa Rosa Junior College Chamber Concert Series, 877
Scottsdale Symphony Orchestra, 732
Seattle Baroque, 1803
Staten Island Symphony, 1465
University Chamber Orchestra, 736
University Symphony Orchestra, 737
Washington Bach Consort, 959
Waterbury Symphony Orchestra, 944
West Valley Symphony, 735
Young Musicians Foundation Debut Orchestra, 764

Classical Guitar
Philadelphia Classical Guitar Society, 1646

Classical Music
Anchorage Symphony Orchestra, 717
Arcady Music Society, 1146
Beethoven Festival, 1398
Chamber Music Northwest, 1600
Chamber Music Society of Lincoln Center, 1412
Cleveland Institute of Music, 1532
El Paso Pro-Musica, 1720
Hesperus, 1776
Huntsville Youth Orchestra, 712
Nomadics, 1402
Noonday Concerts, 1434
Pro Musica of Detroit, 1237
Santa Fe Pro Musica, 1359
Saratoga Performing Arts Center, 1464
St. Cecilia Music Society, 1236
Tannery Pond Concerts, 1404

Classical Rock
United States Navy Band, 963

Classical on Period Instruments
Portland Baroque Orchestra, 1606

Colonial
Nomadics, 1402

Concert Band
Interschool Orchestras of New York, 1420
Music Center of South Central Michigan, 1225

Contemporary
All Seasons Chamber Players, 1328
Berkeley Symphony Orchestra, 758
Cruisers, 962
Pittsburgh New Music Ensemble, 1655
Relache Ensemble, 1653

Country
Britt Festivals, 1598
United States Navy Band, 963

Crafts
New Jersey Workshop for the Arts, 1351

Dance
New Jersey Workshop for the Arts, 1351
University of Southern Mississippi Symphony, 1274

Dance & Music Drama
Early Music New York (Em/Ny), 1416

Early Music
Aston Magna Foundation, 922
Cambridge Society for Early Music: Chamber Music Series, 1188
Carolina Pro Musica, 1482
Early Music Guild of Seattle, 1798
Early Music New York (Em/Ny), 1416
Hesperus, 1776
Music Before 1800, 1425
Piffaro: the Renaissance Band, 1651
Renaissance and Baroque Society of Pittsburgh, 1658

Educational
Atlanta Symphony Youth Orchestra, 1006
Breckenridge Music Festival Orchestra, 901
Breckenridge Music Institute Orchestra, 900
Carmel Bach Festival, 766
Carolina Pro Musica, 1482
Carson City Symphony Association, 1311
Cleveland Institute of Music, 1532
Fort Wayne Philharmonic Orchestra, 1080
Fremont Symphony Orchestra, 783
Marlboro School of Music, 1643
Metropolitan Youth Symphony, 1604
New World Symphony, 980
Norfolk Chamber Music Festival, 936
Northbrook Symphony Orchestra, 1058
Rhode Island Philharmonic Orchestra and Music School, 1671
Rockford Area Youth Symphony Orchestra, 1065
San Luis Obispo Mozart Festival, 863
St. Cecilia Music Society, 1236
Youngstown Symphony Orchestra, 1575

Electronic
Alea III, 1175
Bloomingdale School of Music, 1409
Brandeis University Department of Music, 1215
Chinese Classical Orchestra and Educational Program, 1072
Dinosaur Annex Music Ensemble, 1179
Howard Hanger Jazz Fantasy, 1479
New Music Circle, 1288
North/South Consonance, 1435
Relache Ensemble, 1653
Roulette Intermedium, 1440
San Francisco Conservatory of Music, 854
University of Maryland Baltimore County Symphony, 1158

Ensemble
451st Army Band, 1270
Adrian Symphony Orchestra, 1220
Akron Symphony Orchestra, 1513
Albany Symphony Orchestra, 1361
Alea III, 1175
Alma Symphony Orchestra, 1221
Amarillo Symphony, 1700
American Symphony Orchestra, 1407
Ames Town and Gown Chamber Music Association, 1099
Apple Hill Center for Chamber Music, 1318
Arcady Music Society, 1146
Asheville Chamber Music Series, 1477
Augustana Symphony Orchestra, 1063
Austin Symphony Orchestra Society, 1703
Bach Festival of Philadelphia, 1639
Bachanalia Chamber Orchestra, 1408
Baltimore Consort, 1631
Bangor Symphony Orchestra, 1145
Baton Rouge Symphony Orchestra, 1137
Beethoven Festival, 1398
Birmingham-Bloomfield Symphony, 1226
Bismarck-Mandan Symphony Orchestra, 1510
Bloomingdale School of Music, 1409
Boston Symphony Chamber Players, 1177
Boston Symphony Orchestra, 1178
Boulder Bach Festival, 897
Brandeis University Department of Music, 1215
Bremerton Symphony Orchestra, 1789
Brookings Chamber Music Society, 1685
Brooklyn Philharmonic Orchestra, 1371
Butler University Symphony Orchestra, 1082
Candlelight Concert Society, 1162
Canton Symphony Orchestra, 1523
Carmel Bach Festival, 766
Carnegie Chamber Players, 1410
Carthage Chamber Music Series, 1824
Cascade Symphony Orchestra, 1790
Cathedral Basilica of the Sacred Heart Concert Series, 1335
Cedar Rapids Symphony Orchestra, 1102
Cedarhurst Chamber Music, 1057
Central College Community Orchestra, 1113
Chamber Music Hawaii, 1017
Chamber Music Houston, 1730
Chamber Music Northwest, 1600
Chamber Music Society of Lincoln Center, 1412
Chamber Music Society of Oregon, 1601
Chamber Players International, 1475
Charleston Chamber Music Society, 1816
Charleston Symphony Orchestra, 1678
Charlotte Symphony, 1485
Chinese Classical Orchestra and Educational Program, 1072
Chinese Music Ensemble of New York, 1413
Cincinnati Orchestra, 1528
Cleveland Octet, 1534
Cleveland Orchestra, 1535
Columbus Symphony Orchestra, 1545
Concerto Soloists, 1642
Crested Butte Music Festival, 904
Des Moines Symphony, 1107
Dinosaur Annex Music Ensemble, 1179
Drake Symphony Orchestra, 1108
Dubuque Symphony Orchestra, 1109
Duluth-Superior Symphony Orchestra, 1258
Duluth-Superior Youth Orchestras & Sinfonia, 1259
Dupage Symphony, 1049
Eastern Connecticut Symphony, 935
Eastman Philharmonia, 1459
Emerald Chamber Players, 1591
Evansville Philharmonic Orchestra, 1079
Fairfax Symphony Orchestra, 1778
Fontana Chamber Arts, 1243
Foundation for Baroque Music, 1392

Specialized Field Index / Instrumental Music

Fremont Symphony Orchestra, 783
Go for Baroque, 1583
Grand Rapids Symphony, 1234
Greater Dallas Youth Orchestra Association, 1715
Greater Grand Forks Symphony Orchestra, 1511
Greater Twin Cities Youth Symphonies, 1263
Greenville Symphony Orchestra, 1681
Handel and Haydn Society, 1181
Hawaii Chamber Orchestra Society, 1018
Hillsdale College Community Orchestra, 1238
Houston Early Music, 1729
Howard Hanger Jazz Fantasy, 1479
Indianapolis Symphony Orchestra, 1084
Islip Arts Council Chamber Music Series, 1382
Jamestown Concert Association, 1396
Jazz in June, 1580
Jefferson Symphony Orchestra, 911
Kalamazoo Symphony Orchestra, 1244
Kansas City Chamber Orchestra, 1282
La Jolla Music Society, 796
Lake George Jazz Weekend, 1397
Lansing Symphony Orchestra, 1245
Lark Society for Chamber Music, 1148
Lexington Philharmonic Society, 1128
Lincoln Friends of Chamber Music, 1304
Long Island Baroque Ensemble, 1399
Lubbock Symphony Orchestra, 1741
Luther College Symphony Orchestra, 1106
Maine Music Society, 1147
Massachusetts Youth Wind Ensemble, 1182
Midland Symphony Orchestra, 1247
Midland-Odessa Symphony and Chorale, 1743
Midsummer Mozart Festival, 847
Midwest Young Artists, 1054
Mill Valley Chamber Music Society, 809
Milwaukee Youth Symphony Orchestra, 1831
Minnesota State Band, 1271
Montclaire String Quartet, 1817
Music at Manoa/University of Hawaii at Manoa Outreach College, 1022
Music Society: Midland Center for the Arts, 1248
National Gallery Orchestra, 957
National Musical Arts, 1168
Nevada Symphony Orchestra, 1314
New Black Music Repertory Ensemble, 1040
New Jersey City University Orchestra, 1330
New Jersey Symphony Orchestra, 1336
New West Symphony Association, 885
New World Symphony, 980
New World Youth Symphony Orchestra, 1086
New York Philomusica Chamber Ensemble, 1431
Noonday Concerts, 1434
North Carolina Symphony, 1500
North/South Consonance, 1435
Northwest Indiana Symphony Orchestra and Society, 1093
Oberlin Baroque Ensemble, 1564
Ohio Chamber Orchestra, 1519
Oklahoma Mozart International Festival, 1577
Omaha Area Youth Orchestras, 1308
Omaha Symphony, 1309
Orchestra of St. Peter by The Sea, 1322
Paddywhack, 1505
Peoples' Symphony Concerts, 1438
Philadelphia Youth Orchestra, 1649
Piffaro: the Renaissance Band, 1651
Pinellas Youth Symphony, 996
Pittsburgh New Music Ensemble, 1655
Pittsburgh Youth Symphony Orchestra Association, 1657
Plainfield Symphony, 1339
Plymouth Philharmonic Orchestra, 1207
Portland Youth Philharmonic Association, 1609
Present Music, 1832
Pro Musica of Detroit, 1237
Quad City Youth String Ensemble, 1105
Relache Ensemble, 1653
Richland Performing Arts, 1633
Richmond Symphony Orchestra, 1785
Rosewood Chamber Ensemble, 1466
Roulette Intermedium, 1440
Saint Olaf College Orchestra, 1268
Saint Paul Chamber Orchestra, 1272
San Antonio Chamber Music Society, 1748
San Francisco Conservatory of Music, 854
San Francisco Contemporary Music Players, 853
San Francisco Early Music Society, 759
San Francisco Jazz Organization, 855
San Luis Obispo Mozart Festival, 863
Santa Cruz Baroque Festival, 873
Santa Rosa Symphony, 878
Saratoga Performing Arts Center, 1464
Seattle Symphony Orchestra, 1805
Shreveport Symphony Orchestra, 1144
Silk and Bamboo Ensemble, 1073
Sioux City Symphony Orchestra, 1115
South Dakota Symphony, 1688
South Florida Youth Symphony, 979
Springfield Symphony Orchestra, 1211
St. Patrick's Cathedral Chamber Music Series, 1444
Stamford Symphony Orchestra, 940
Stockbridge Chamber Concerts at Searles Castle, 1206
Symphony of the Mountains, 1693
Tacoma Youth Symphony, 1810
Tamburitzans Folk Ensemble, 1660
Tannery Pond Concerts, 1404
Tisch Center for the Arts, 1447
Toledo Symphony, 1571
Troy Chromatics Concerts, 1471
Umpqua Symphony Association, 1612
United States Air Force Band, 951
University Chamber Orchestra, 736
University Circle Chamber Orchestra, 1540
University of Central Florida Orchestra, 985
University of Oklahoma Symphony Orchestra, 1581
University Symphony Orchestra, 737
Vermont Symphony Orchestra, 1769
Voices of Change, 1718
Washington Idaho Symphony, 1796
Waterloo-Cedar Falls Symphony Orchestra, 1101
Westerville Symphony, 1572
Westmoreland Symphony Orchestra, 1623
Whittier College Bach Festival, 892
Winston-Salem Symphony, 1509
Yellowstone Chamber Players, 1297
Youth Symphony Association of Kansas, 1122

Entertainment
Putnam Symphony Orchestra, 1377

Ethnic Music
451st Army Band, 1270
American Balalaika Symphony, 1775
Austin Symphony Orchestra Society, 1703
Bloomingdale School of Music, 1409
Brooklyn Philharmonic Orchestra, 1371
Cedarhurst Chamber Music, 1057
Chinese Classical Orchestra and Educational Program, 1072
Chinese Music Ensemble of New York, 1413
Crested Butte Music Festival, 904
Helena Symphony Society, 1299
Houston Early Music, 1729
Klezmer Conservatory Band, 1190
Mamadou Diabate, 1379
Minnesota State Band, 1271
Music at Manoa/University of Hawaii at Manoa Outreach College, 1022
New Black Music Repertory Ensemble, 1040
Paddywhack, 1505
Presidential Jazz Weekend, 1652
Quintet of the Americas, 1381
Roulette Intermedium, 1440
Silk and Bamboo Ensemble, 1073
Tamburitzans Folk Ensemble, 1660

Family Programming
La Jolla Music Society, 796

Flute and Jazz Ensemble
Stamford Young Artists Philharmonic, 941

Folk Music
451st Army Band, 1270
Austin Symphony Orchestra Society, 1703
Baltimore Consort, 1631
Bloomingdale School of Music, 1409
Breckenridge Music Institute Orchestra, 900
Britt Festivals, 1598
Chinese Classical Orchestra and Educational Program, 1072
Chinese Music Ensemble of New York, 1413
Crested Butte Music Festival, 904
Denver Municipal Band, 906
Hesperus, 1776
Houston Early Music, 1729
Interschool Orchestras of New York, 1420
Klezmer Conservatory Band, 1190
Music Center of South Central Michigan, 1225
Music Society: Midland Center for the Arts, 1248
Nomadics, 1402
Norfolk Chamber Music Festival, 936
Oakland East Bay Symphony, 815
Paddywhack, 1505
Roulette Intermedium, 1440
Tamburitzans Folk Ensemble, 1660
Wittenberg University Department of Music, 1569

Highland Dance
Fairbanks Red Hackle Pipe Band, 719

Historical Music
New Orleans Jazz and Heritage Foundation, 1143

Instrumental Music
Cliburn Concerts, 1722

International
International Music Network, 1194
International Violin Competition of Indianapolis, 1085

Jazz
Breckenridge Music Institute Orchestra, 900
Britt Festivals, 1598
Butler University Symphony Orchestra, 1082
Chestnut Brass Company, 1641
Chicago Sinfonietta, 1034
Cleveland Pops Orchestra, 1518
Depauw University Chamber Symphony, 1081
Drake Symphony Orchestra, 1108
Howard Hanger Jazz Fantasy, 1479
Illinois Philharmonic Orchestra, 1060
International Music Network, 1194
Jazz in June, 1580
Juneau Jazz and Classics, 723
La Jolla Music Society, 796
Lake George Jazz Weekend, 1397
Luther College Symphony Orchestra, 1106
Midwest Young Artists, 1054
New Orleans Jazz and Heritage Foundation, 1143
Noonday Concerts, 1434
San Francisco Jazz Organization, 855
San Luis Obispo Mozart Festival, 863
Spoleto Festival Usa, 1679
Strings in The Mountains, 918
Tisch Center for the Arts, 1447
United States Navy Band, 963
Wittenberg University Department of Music, 1569

Jazz Ensemble
Cleveland Jazz Orchestra, 1533
New York Youth Symphony, 1433
Presidential Jazz Weekend, 1652
Toledo Jazz Society, 1570

Jazz, Folk Music
Breckenridge Music Festival Orchestra, 901

Korean Music
Jocelyn Clark, 722

Live Electronic
Alea III, 1175
Bloomingdale School of Music, 1409
Brandeis University Department of Music, 1215
Chinese Classical Orchestra and Educational Program, 1072
Dinosaur Annex Music Ensemble, 1179
Howard Hanger Jazz Fantasy, 1479
New Music Circle, 1288
North/South Consonance, 1435
Relache Ensemble, 1653
Roulette Intermedium, 1440
San Francisco Conservatory of Music, 854

Medieval
Arizona Early Music Society, 739
Carolina Pro Musica, 1482
Early Music New York (Em/Ny), 1416

Middle-Eastern Music
John Chookasian International Folk Ensemble, 786

Movie Themes
Cleveland Pops Orchestra, 1518

Mozart
Midsummer Mozart Festival, 847
Oklahoma Mozart International Festival, 1577
Oregon Mozart Players, 1594
San Luis Obispo Mozart Festival, 863

Music
New Jersey Workshop for the Arts, 1351
Putnam Symphony Orchestra, 1377
Symphony Orchestra of Augusta, 1009
University of Southern Mississippi Symphony, 1274

Near-East Music
John Chookasian International Folk Ensemble, 786

New Music
Boston Musica Viva, 1186
Chicago Chamber Orchestra, 1033
New Music Circle, 1288
North/South Consonance, 1435
Pro Musica of Detroit, 1237

Non-Western Music
Jocelyn Clark, 722

Opera
Music Academy of the West, 869

Orchestra
Abilene Philharmonic Association, 1698
Adrian Symphony Orchestra, 1220
Alabama Symphony Orchestra, 707
Albany Symphony Orchestra, 1002
Allentown Symphony Association, 1616
Alma Symphony Orchestra, 1221
Amarillo Symphony, 1700
American Balalaika Symphony, 1775
American Composers Orchestra, 1406
American Symphony Orchestra, 1407
Anchorage Youth Symphony, 718
Ann Arbor Symphony Orchestra, 1222
Annapolis Chamber Orchestra, 1152
Ars Nova Musicians Chamber Orchestra, 1374
Ashland Symphony Orchestra, 1515
Ashtabula Chamber Orchestra, 1516
Atlanta Symphony Orchestra, 1005
Augustana Symphony Orchestra, 1063
Austin Symphony Orchestra Society, 1703
Bangor Symphony Orchestra, 1145
Bartlesville Symphony Orchestra, 1576
Baton Rouge Symphony Orchestra, 1137
Battle Creek Symphony Orchestra, 1224
Belleville Philharmonic Orchestra, 1020
Berkeley Youth Orchestra, 814
Billings Symphony Society, 1296
Binghamton Philharmonic Orchestra, 1367
Birmingham-Bloomfield Symphony, 1226
Bismarck-Mandan Symphony Orchestra, 1510
Black Hills Symphony Orchestra, 1687
Bloomingdale School of Music, 1409
Boston Baroque, 1173
Boston Classical Orchestra, 1202
Boston Philharmonic Orchestra, 1187
Boston Pops Orchestra, 1176
Boston Symphony Orchestra, 1178
Bowling Green-Western Symphony Orchestra, 1125
Brandeis University Department of Music, 1215
Brazos Valley Symphony Orchestra, 1705
Bremerton Symphony Orchestra, 1789
Brookings Chamber Music Society, 1685
Brooklyn Philharmonic Orchestra, 1371
Brooklyn Symphony Orchestra, 1372
Butler University Symphony Orchestra, 1082
Canton Symphony Orchestra, 1523
Cascade Symphony Orchestra, 1790
Cathedral Basilica of the Sacred Heart Concert Series, 1335
Catskill Symphony Orchestra, 1449
Cayuga Chamber Orchestra, 1394
Ccm Philharmonia & Concert Orchestra, 1526
Cedar Rapids Symphony Orchestra, 1102
Cedarhurst Chamber Music, 1057
Central College Community Orchestra, 1113
Centralia Philharmonic Orchestra, 1030
Chamber Music Society of Oregon, 1601
Chamber Orchestra of Albuquerque, 1353
Charleston Symphony Orchestra, 1678
Charlotte Symphony, 1485
Cheyenne Symphony Orchestra, 1837
Chicago Symphony Orchestra, 1035
Chinese Classical Orchestra and Educational Program, 1072
Cincinnati Chamber Orchestra, 1527

1253

Specialized Field Index / Instrumental Music

Cincinnati Orchestra, 1528
Clear Lake Symphony, 1727
Cleveland Orchestra, 1535
Cleveland Philharmonic Orchestra, 1537
Cleveland Pops Orchestra, 1518
Clinton Symphony Orchestra, 1103
Colorado Springs Philharmonic, 903
Colorado Symphony Orchestra, 905
Columbus Symphony Orchestra, 1545
Concert Artists of Baltimore, 1156
Concerto Soloists, 1642
Concord Orchestra, 1193
Culver City Symphony Orchestra, 777
Dallas Bach Society, 1712
Dallas Wind Symphony, 1714
Danville Symphony Orchestra, 1044
Dayton Philharmonic Orchestra Association, 1549
Daytona Beach Symphony Society, 967
Dc Youth Orchestra Program, 954
Delaware Symphony Orchestra, 949
Depauw University Chamber Symphony, 1081
Des Moines Symphony, 1107
Dinosaur Annex Music Ensemble, 1179
Drake Symphony Orchestra, 1108
Dubuque Symphony Orchestra, 1109
Duluth-Superior Symphony Orchestra, 1258
Dupage Symphony, 1049
East Texas Symphony Orchestra, 1755
Eastern Connecticut Symphony, 935
Eastman Philharmonia, 1459
El Camino Youth Symphony, 821
El Paso Symphony Orchestra, 1721
Elgin Symphony Orchestra, 1046
Elmhurst Symphony Orchestra, 1047
Emerald Chamber Players, 1591
Enid-Phillips Symphony Orchestra, 1578
Erie Philharmonic, 1621
Eugene Symphony Association, 1592
Evansville Philharmonic Orchestra, 1079
Fairbanks Symphony Association, 720
Fairfax Symphony Orchestra, 1778
Flagstaff Symphony Orchestra, 726
Flint School of Performing Arts: Youth Ensembles, 1232
Flint Symphony Orchestra, 1233
Florida Orchestra, 997
Fort Wayne Philharmonic Orchestra, 1080
Fort Worth Symphony Orchestra, 1723
Fremont Symphony Orchestra, 783
Fresno Philharmonic, 785
Garden State Philharmonic Symphony Orchestra, 1345
Garland Symphony Orchestra, 1726
Glendale Symphony Orchestra Association, 789
Grand Junction Musical Arts Association, 912
Grand Rapids Symphony, 1234
Grand Rapids Youth Symphony, 1235
Great Falls Symphony Association, 1298
Greater Bridgeport Symphony Youth Orchestra, 923
Greater Grand Forks Symphony Orchestra, 1511
Greater Trenton Symphony Orchestra, 1346
Greeley Philharmonic Orchestra, 913
Green Bay Symphony Orchestra, 1823
Greensboro Symphony Orchestra/Carolina Pops, 1493
Greenville Symphony Society, 1624
Haddonfield Symphony, 1329
Harrisburg Symphony Association, 1627
Hastings Symphony Orchestra, 1301
Hays Symphony Orchestra, 1119
Heights Chamber Orchestra, 1543
Helena Symphony Society, 1299
Hillsdale College Community Orchestra, 1238
Hope College Orchestra, 1241
Houston Civic Symphony Orchestra, 1728
Hudson Valley Philharmonic, 1455
Huntington Symphony Orchestra, 1818
Idaho Falls Symphony, 1026
Illinois Chamber Symphony, 1069
Illinois Philharmonic Orchestra, 1060
Imperial Symphony Orchestra, 974
Imperial Valley Symphony, 782
Indianapolis Symphony Orchestra, 1084
Interschool Orchestras of New York, 1420
Irving Symphony Orchestra Association, 1734
Jackson Symphony Association, 1691

Jacksonville Symphony Orchestra, 972
Jamestown Concert Association, 1396
Jefferson Symphony Orchestra, 911
Johnstown Symphony Orchestra, 1632
Kalamazoo Symphony Orchestra, 1244
Kenosha Symphony Association, 1825
Knoxville Symphony Orchestra, 1694
Kokomo Symphony, 1088
Lafayette Symphony, 1089
Lake Charles Symphony, 1139
Lake Forest Symphony, 1056
Lake St. Clair Symphony Orchestra, 1255
Lakeside Symphony, 1556
Lansing Symphony Orchestra, 1245
Laredo Philharmonic Orchestra, 1738
Lawton Philharmonic Orchestra, 1579
Lehigh Valley Chamber Orchestra, 1636
Lima Symphony Orchestra, 1557
Lincoln Symphony Orchestra, 1305
Long Beach Symphony Orchestra, 799
Long Island Philharmonic, 1401
Longview Symphony Orchestra, 1740
Louisiana Philharmonic Orchestra, 1141
Louisville Orchestra, 1131
Lubbock Symphony Orchestra, 1741
Luther College Symphony Orchestra, 1106
Magic Valley Symphony, 1028
Manchester Symphony Orchestra/Chorale, 929
Mankato Symphony Orchestra, 1261
Marshall Symphony Orchestra, 1742
Marshfield-Wood Community Symphony, 1829
Melrose Symphony Orchestra, 1201
Mid-Columbia Symphony, 1797
Midland Symphony Orchestra, 1247
Midland-Odessa Symphony and Chorale, 1743
Midwest Young Artists, 1054
Milwaukee Symphony Orchestra, 1830
Minot Symphony Association, 1512
Mississippi Symphony Orchestra, 1275
Missouri Symphony Society, 1279
Monroe Symphony Orchestra, 1140
Monterey Symphony, 769
Montgomery Symphony Orchestra, 715
Mozart Classical Orchestra, 793
Mt Hood Jazz Festival, 1596
Music Academy of the West, 869
Music Center of South Central Michigan, 1225
Music Society: Midland Center for the Arts, 1248
Nashville Symphony, 1696
National Gallery Orchestra, 957
National Orchestral Association, 1426
National Symphony Orchestra Association, 958
Nevada Symphony Orchestra, 1314
New Hampshire Philharmonic Orchestra, 1319
New Hampshire Symphony Orchestra, 1320
New Jersey City University Orchestra, 1330
New Jersey Symphony Orchestra, 1336
New Mexico Symphony Orchestra, 1354
New World Symphony, 980
New World Youth Symphony Orchestra, 1086
New York Philharmonic, 1430
Newton Symphony Orchestra, 1203
North Carolina Symphony, 1500
North Shore Philharmonic Orchestra, 1174
Northbrook Symphony Orchestra, 1058
Northwest Indiana Symphony Orchestra and Society, 1093
Oak Ridge Civic Music Association, 1697
Ocean City Pops, 1338
Ohio Chamber Orchestra, 1519
Oklahoma City Philharmonic Orchestra, 1584
Oklahoma Mozart International Festival, 1577
Olympia Symphony Orchestra, 1794
Omaha Symphony, 1309
Orchestra of St. Peter by The Sea, 1322
Oregon Mozart Players, 1594
Orlando Philharmonic Orchestra, 984
Orpheus Chamber Orchestra, 1437
Oshkosh Symphony Orchestra, 1833
Owensboro Symphony Orchestra, 1134
Pacific University Community Wind Ensemble, 1595
Palm Beach Pops, 1001
Peter Nero and The Philly Pops, 1644
Philadelphia Orchestra, 1647

Philharmonia Virtuosi Corporation, 1448
Philharmonic Center for the Arts, 981
Philharmonic Orchestra of Indianapolis, 1087
Pine Bluff Symphony Orchestra, 756
Pinellas Youth Symphony, 996
Pittsburgh Symphony Orchestra, 1656
Plymouth Philharmonic Orchestra, 1207
Portland Baroque Orchestra, 1606
Portland Symphony Orchestra, 1150
Pro Arte Chamber Orchestra, 1191
Pro Musica Chamber Orchestra of Columbus, 1548
Quad City Symphony Orchestra Association, 1104
Quincy Symphony Orchestra, 1062
Raleigh Symphony Orchestra, 1502
Renaissance and Baroque Society of Pittsburgh, 1658
Reno Chamber Orchestra, 1315
Richland Performing Arts, 1633
Richmond Symphony Orchestra, 1785
Ridgewood Symphony Orchestra, 1342
Rio Hondo Symphony Association, 891
Riverside Symphony, 1439
Rochester Chamber Orchestra, 1462
Rose City Chamber Orchestra, 1610
Roswell Symphony Orchestra, 1357
Saint Lukes Chamber Ensemble, 1441
Saint Olaf College Orchestra, 1268
Saint Paul Chamber Orchestra, 1272
Salisbury Symphony Orchestra, 1504
San Antonio Symphony, 1749
San Diego Chamber Orchestra, 841
San Diego Symphony Orchestra, 843
San Francisco Conservatory of Music, 854
San Juan Symphony, 908
Santa Barbara Chamber Orchestra, 870
Santa Fe Pro Musica, 1359
Santa Fe Symphony, 1360
Santa Rosa Symphony, 878
Seattle Symphony Orchestra, 1805
Sem Ensemble, 1373
Sherman Symphony Orchestra, 1752
Shreveport Symphony Orchestra, 1144
Sinfonia Concertante Orchestra, 1611
Sioux City Symphony Orchestra, 1115
South Bend Symphony Orchestra, 1096
South Dakota State University Civic Symphony, 1686
South Dakota Symphony, 1688
South Florida Youth Symphony, 979
Southeast Iowa Symphony Orchestra, 1111
Southwest Michigan Symphony Orchestra, 1252
Spokane Symphony Orchestra, 1807
Springfield Symphony Orchestra, 1211
Stamford Symphony Orchestra, 940
Stamford Young Artists Philharmonic, 941
Suburban Symphony Orchestra, 1520
Sunriver Music Festival, 1615
Symphony of Southeast Texas, 1704
Symphony of the Mountains, 1693
Symphony Orchestra of Augusta, 1009
Syracuse Symphony Orchestra, 1468
Tacoma Symphony Orchestra, 1809
Tar River Choral & Orchestral Society, 1503
Tassajara Symphony Orchestra, 780
the National Philharmonic, 1169
Tisch Center for the Arts, 1447
Toledo Jazz Society, 1570
Toledo Symphony, 1571
Traverse Symphony Orchestra, 1256
Tulare County Symphony, 888
Tupelo Symphony Orchestra Association, 1278
Tuscarawas Philharmonic, 1562
Umpqua Symphony Association, 1612
United States Air Force Band, 951
University Chamber Orchestra, 736
University Circle Chamber Orchestra, 1540
University of Maryland Baltimore County Symphony, 1158
University of Oklahoma Symphony Orchestra, 1581
University Symphony Orchestra, 737
Vallejo Symphony Association, 887
Walla Walla Symphony, 1812
Wallingford Symphony Orchestra, 943
Wartburg Community Symphony Orchestra, 1117

Waterloo-Cedar Falls Symphony Orchestra, 1101
West Coast Chamber Orchestra, 872
West Jersey Chamber Music Symphony & Society, 1333
West Michigan Symphony, 1249
Western New York Chamber Orchestra, 1385
Westerville Symphony, 1572
Westmoreland Symphony Orchestra, 1623
Wheeling Symphony, 1819
Wichita Falls Symphony Orchestra, 1757
Wichita Symphony, 1124
Winston-Salem Symphony, 1509
Wisconsin Chamber Orchestra, 1827
Wooster Symphony Orchestra, 1573
Wyoming Symphony Orchestra, 1836
Yakima Symphony Orchestra, 1814
Yale Symphony Orchestra, 934
Youngstown Symphony Orchestra, 1575

Patriotic
Cleveland Pops Orchestra, 1518

Patriotic Orchestral Music
Monterey Bay Symphony, 768

Piano
La Jolla Music Society, 796
Soirees Musicales Piano Series, 1551

Pops
Arkansas Symphony Orchestra, 755
Binghamton Philharmonic Orchestra, 1367
Boston Pops Orchestra, 1176
Britt Festivals, 1598
Civic Orchestra of Tucson, 742
Delaware Symphony Orchestra, 949
Greensboro Symphony Orchestra/Carolina Pops, 1493
Greenville Symphony Orchestra, 1681
Mississippi Symphony Orchestra, 1275
Monterey Bay Symphony, 768
Montgomery Symphony Orchestra, 715
Mt Hood Jazz Festival, 1596
New York Pops, 1432
Ocean City Pops, 1338
Orlando Philharmonic Orchestra, 984
Palm Beach Pops, 1001
Peter Nero and The Philly Pops, 1644
Saratoga Performing Arts Center, 1464
Scottsdale Symphony Orchestra, 732
Tisch Center for the Arts, 1447
Waterbury Symphony Orchestra, 944

Recitals
Chamber Music Society of Detroit, 1231

Renaissance
Arizona Early Music Society, 739
Piffaro: the Renaissance Band, 1651

Renassiance
Early Music New York (Em/Ny), 1416

Rock
Cruisers, 962

Rythym
Cruisers, 962

Scottish Music
Fairbanks Red Hackle Pipe Band, 719

Series & Festivals
Cliburn Concerts, 1722

Show Tunes
Britt Festivals, 1598
Centralia Philharmonic Orchestra, 1030
Margot Astrachan Music, 1424
Philharmonic Center for the Arts, 981
Saratoga Performing Arts Center, 1464

Soloists
Concerto Soloists, 1642
Goliard Chamber Soloists, 1363
Music at Manoa/University of Hawaii at Manoa Outreach College, 1022
Soirees Musicales Piano Series, 1551
Troy Chromatics Concerts, 1471
Washington and Lee University Concert Guild, 1780

String Ensemble
Detroit Chamber Winds & Strings, 1253
New England String Ensemble, 1213
Philadelphia String Quartet, 1648
Portland String Quartet Concert Series/Workshop, 1149
Sarasota Youth Orchestras, 989
Strings in The Mountains, 918
Summer Strings on The Meherrin, 1495
Tremont String Quartet, 1388

Summer Jazz Workshop

Specialized Field Index / Theatre

Stamford Young Artists Philharmonic, 941
Swing
　Tar River Choral & Orchestral Society, 1503
Symphony
　Abilene Philharmonic Association, 1698
　Adrian Symphony Orchestra, 1220
　Akron Symphony Orchestra, 1513
　Alabama Symphony Orchestra, 707
　Albany Symphony Orchestra, 1002
　Allentown Symphony Association, 1616
　Amarillo Symphony, 1700
　American Composers Orchestra, 1406
　American Symphony Orchestra, 1407
　Anchorage Youth Symphony, 718
　Ann Arbor Symphony Orchestra, 1222
　Arkansas Symphony Orchestra, 755
　Ashland Symphony Orchestra, 1515
　Atlanta Symphony Orchestra, 1005
　Austin Symphony Orchestra Society, 1703
　Bakersfield Symphony Orchestra, 757
　Bangor Symphony Orchestra, 1145
　Bartlesville Symphony Orchestra, 1576
　Baton Rouge Symphony Orchestra, 1137
　Battle Creek Symphony Orchestra, 1224
　Beach Cities Symphony Association, 830
　Belleville Philharmonic Orchestra, 1029
　Berkeley Symphony Orchestra, 758
　Berkeley Youth Orchestra, 814
　Billings Symphony Society, 1296
　Birmingham-Bloomfield Symphony, 1226
　Bismarck-Mandan Symphony Orchestra, 1510
　Black Hills Symphony Orchestra, 1687
　Boston Classical Orchestra, 1202
　Boston Philharmonic Orchestra, 1187
　Boston Symphony Orchestra, 1178
　Bowling Green-Western Symphony Orchestra, 1125
　Brazos Valley Symphony Orchestra, 1705
　Bremerton Symphony Orchestra, 1789
　Bronx Arts Ensemble, 1368
　Brooklyn Philharmonic Orchestra, 1371
　Canton Symphony Orchestra, 1523
　Carson City Symphony Association, 1311
　Cascade Symphony Orchestra, 1790
　Cathedral Basilica of the Sacred Heart Concert Series, 1335
　Catskill Symphony Orchestra, 1449
　Cedar Rapids Symphony Orchestra, 1102
　Charleston Symphony Orchestra, 1678
　Charlotte Symphony, 1485
　Cheyenne Symphony Orchestra, 1837
　Chicago Symphony Orchestra, 1035
　Chinese Classical Orchestra and Educational Program, 1072
　Civic Orchestra of Tucson, 742
　Clear Lake Symphony, 1727
　Cleveland Chamber Symphony, 1531
　Cleveland Orchestra, 1535
　Cleveland Philharmonic Orchestra, 1537
　Colorado Springs Philharmonic, 903
　Colorado Symphony Orchestra, 905
　Columbus Symphony Orchestra, 1545
　Concord Orchestra, 1193
　Conejo Pops Orchestra, 884
　Culver City Symphony Orchestra, 777
　Danville Symphony Orchestra, 1044
　Dayton Philharmonic Orchestra Association, 1549
　Daytona Beach Symphony Society, 967
　Dc Youth Orchestra Program, 954
　Delaware Symphony Orchestra, 949
　Des Moines Symphony, 1107
　Dubuque Symphony Orchestra, 1109
　Duluth-Superior Symphony Orchestra, 1258
　Dupage Symphony, 1049
　East Texas Symphony Orchestra, 1755
　Eastern Arizona College- Community Orchestra, 738
　Eastern Connecticut Symphony, 935
　El Paso Symphony Orchestra, 1721
　Elgin Symphony Orchestra, 1046
　Elmhurst Symphony Orchestra, 1047
　Emory Symphony Orchestra, 1008
　Enid-Phillips Symphony Orchestra, 1578
　Erie Philharmonic, 1621
　Eugene Symphony Association, 1592
　Evansville Philharmonic Orchestra, 1079
　Fairbanks Symphony Association, 720
　Fairfax Symphony Orchestra, 1778
　Flagstaff Symphony Orchestra, 726
　Flint Symphony Orchestra, 1233
　Florida Orchestra, 997
　Fort Smith Symphony, 754
　Fort Worth Symphony Orchestra, 1723
　Fremont Symphony Orchestra, 783
　Fresno Philharmonic, 785
　Garden State Philharmonic Symphony Orchestra, 1345
　Garland Symphony Orchestra, 1726
　Glendale Symphony Orchestra Association, 789
　Grand Junction Musical Arts Association, 912
　Grand Rapids Symphony, 1234
　Great Falls Symphony Association, 1298
　Greater Bridgeport Symphony Youth Orchestra, 923
　Greater Trenton Symphony Orchestra, 1346
　Greeley Philharmonic Orchestra, 913
　Green Bay Symphony Orchestra, 1823
　Greenville Symphony Orchestra, 1681
　Greenville Symphony Society, 1624
　Haddonfield Symphony, 1329
　Harrisburg Symphony Association, 1627
　Hastings Symphony Orchestra, 1301
　Hays Symphony Orchestra, 1119
　Heights Chamber Orchestra, 1543
　Helena Symphony Society, 1299
　Houston Civic Symphony Orchestra, 1728
　Hudson Valley Philharmonic, 1455
　Idaho Falls Symphony, 1026
　Imperial Symphony Orchestra, 974
　Imperial Valley Symphony, 782
　Indianapolis Symphony Orchestra, 1084
　Interschool Orchestras of New York, 1420
　Irving Symphony Orchestra Association, 1734
　Jackson Symphony Association, 1691
　Jacksonville Symphony Orchestra, 972
　Jefferson Symphony Orchestra, 911
　Johnstown Symphony Orchestra, 1632
　Kalamazoo Symphony Orchestra, 1244
　Kenosha Symphony Association, 1825
　Knoxville Symphony Orchestra, 1694
　Kokomo Symphony, 1088
　La Jolla Music Society, 796
　Lafayette Symphony, 1089
　Lake Charles Symphony, 1139
　Lake Forest Symphony, 1056
　Lake St. Clair Symphony Orchestra, 1255
　Lakeside Symphony, 1556
　Lansing Symphony Orchestra, 1245
　Laredo Philharmonic Orchestra, 1738
　Lawton Philharmonic Orchestra, 1579
　Lexington Philharmonic Society, 1128
　Lima Symphony Orchestra, 1557
　Lincoln Symphony Orchestra, 1305
　Long Beach Symphony Orchestra, 799
　Long Island Philharmonic, 1401
　Longview Symphony Orchestra, 1740
　Louisiana Symphony Orchestra, 1141
　Louisville Orchestra, 1131
　Lubbock Symphony Orchestra, 1741
　Magic Valley Symphony, 1028
　Manchester Symphony Orchestra/Chorale, 929
　Mankato Symphony Orchestra, 1261
　Marshall Symphony Orchestra, 1742
　Marshfield-Wood Community Symphony, 1829
　Melrose Symphony Orchestra, 1201
　Mid-Columbia Symphony, 1797
　Midland Symphony Orchestra, 1247
　Midland-Odessa Symphony and Chorale, 1743
　Milwaukee Symphony Orchestra, 1830
　Minot Symphony Association, 1512
　Mississippi Symphony Orchestra, 1275
　Missouri Symphony Society, 1279
　Monroe Symphony Orchestra, 1140
　Montclaire String Quartet, 1817
　Monterey Symphony, 769
　Montgomery Symphony Orchestra, 715
　Nashville Symphony, 1696
　National Gallery Orchestra, 957
　National Symphony Orchestra Association, 958
　New Hampshire Philharmonic Orchestra, 1319
　New Hampshire Symphony Orchestra, 1320
　New Jersey Symphony Orchestra, 1336
　New Mexico Symphony Orchestra, 1354
　New West Symphony Association, 885
　New World Symphony, 980
　New York City Symphony Orchestra, 1427
　New York Philharmonic, 1430
　New York Pops, 1432
　Newton Symphony Orchestra, 1203
　North Carolina Symphony, 1500
　North Shore Philharmonic Orchestra, 1174
　Northbrook Symphony Orchestra, 1058
　Northwest Indiana Symphony Orchestra and Society, 1093
　Oak Ridge Civic Music Association, 1697
　Ohio Chamber Orchestra, 1519
　Oklahoma City Philharmonic Orchestra, 1584
　Olympia Symphony Orchestra, 1794
　Omaha Symphony, 1309
　Oshkosh Symphony Orchestra, 1833
　Owensboro Symphony Orchestra, 1134
　Palm Beach Pops, 1001
　Peoples' Symphony Concerts, 1438
　Philadelphia Orchestra, 1647
　Philharmonic Orchestra of Indianapolis, 1087
　Pine Bluff Symphony Orchestra, 756
　Pittsburgh Symphony Orchestra, 1656
　Plainfield Symphony, 1339
　Plymouth Philharmonic Orchestra, 1207
　Portland Symphony Orchestra, 1150
　Pro Musica Chamber Orchestra of Columbus, 1548
　Quad City Symphony Orchestra Association, 1104
　Quincy Symphony Orchestra, 1062
　Raleigh Symphony Orchestra, 1502
　Rhode Island Philharmonic Orchestra and Music School, 1671
　Richland Performing Arts, 1633
　Richmond Symphony Orchestra, 1785
　Ridgewood Symphony Orchestra, 1342
　Rio Hondo Symphony Association, 891
　Riverside Symphony, 1439
　Roswell Symphony Orchestra, 1357
　Salisbury Symphony Orchestra, 1504
　San Antonio Symphony, 1749
　San Diego Chamber Orchestra, 841
　San Diego Symphony Orchestra, 843
　San Juan Symphony, 908
　Santa Fe Pro Musica, 1359
　Santa Fe Symphony, 1360
　Santa Rosa Symphony, 878
　Scottsdale Symphony Orchestra, 732
　Seattle Symphony Orchestra, 1805
　Sherman Symphony Orchestra, 1752
　Shreveport Symphony Orchestra, 1144
　Sioux City Symphony Orchestra, 1115
　South Bend Symphony Orchestra, 1096
　South Dakota State University Civic Symphony, 1686
　South Dakota Symphony, 1688
　South Texas Symphony Association, 1719
　Southeast Iowa Symphony Orchestra, 1111
　Southwest Michigan Symphony Orchestra, 1252
　Spokane Symphony Orchestra, 1807
　Springfield Symphony Orchestra, 1211
　Stamford Symphony Orchestra, 940
　Staten Island Symphony, 1465
　Suburban Symphony Orchestra, 1520
　Symphony of Southeast Texas, 1704
　Symphony of the Mountains, 1693
　Syracuse Symphony Orchestra, 1468
　Tacoma Symphony Orchestra, 1809
　Tassajara Symphony Orchestra, 780
　Toledo Symphony, 1571
　Traverse Symphony Orchestra, 1256
　Troy Chromatics Concerts, 1471
　Tulare County Symphony, 888
　Tupelo Symphony Orchestra Association, 1278
　Tuscarawas Philharmonic, 1562
　Umpqua Symphony Association, 1612
　United States Air Force Band, 951
　University Circle Chamber Orchestra, 1540
　Vallejo Symphony Association, 887
　Vermont Symphony Orchestra, 1769
　Walla Walla Symphony, 1812
　Wallingford Symphony Orchestra, 943
　Wartburg Community Symphony Orchestra, 1117
　Washington Idaho Symphony, 1796
　Waterloo-Cedar Falls Symphony Orchestra, 1101
　West Coast Chamber Orchestra, 872
　West Valley Symphony, 735
　Westerville Symphony, 1572
　Westmoreland Symphony Orchestra, 1623
　Wheeling Symphony, 1819
　Wichita Falls Symphony Orchestra, 1757
　Wichita Symphony, 1124
　Winston-Salem Symphony, 1509
　Wittenberg University Department of Music, 1569
　Wooster Symphony Orchestra, 1573
　Wyoming Symphony Orchestra, 1836
　Yakima Symphony Orchestra, 1814
　Yale Symphony Orchestra, 934
　Young People's Symphony Orchestra, 762
Theatre
　University of Southern Mississippi Symphony, 1274
Theatrical Dance
　Spoleto Festival Usa, 1679
Traditional Classics
　Margot Astrachan Music, 1424
Vocal Ensemble
　Concert Artists of Baltimore, 1156
Vocal Music
　Cliburn Concerts, 1722
Wind Ensemble
　Dallas Wind Symphony, 1714
　Detroit Chamber Winds & Strings, 1253
　Miami Wind Quintet, 1566
　New Orleans Concert Band, 1142
　Pacific University Community Wind Ensemble, 1595
　Venti Da Camera, 1522
World Music
　Britt Festivals, 1598
　Chicago Sinfonietta, 1034
　Cleveland Institute of Music, 1532
　International Music Network, 1194
　Mamadou Diabate, 1379
　Nomadics, 1402
　Pro Musica of Detroit, 1237
　San Francisco Jazz Organization, 855
Youth Orchestra
　Atlanta Symphony Youth Orchestra, 1006
　Columbus Symphony Youth Orchestras, 1546
　Duluth-Superior Youth Orchestras & Sinfonia, 1259
　Flint School of Performing Arts: Youth Ensembles, 1232
　Great Falls Symphony Association, 1298
　Greater Dallas Youth Orchestra Association, 1715
　Hawaii Youth Symphony Association, 1019
　Huntsville Youth Orchestra, 712
　Massachusetts Youth Wind Ensemble, 1182
　Memphis Symphony Orchestra and Youth Symphony Orchestra, 1695
　Milwaukee Youth Symphony Orchestra, 1831
　Montgomery County Youth Orchestra, 1159
　Omaha Area Youth Orchestras, 1308
　Philadelphia Youth Orchestra, 1649
　Quad City Youth String Ensemble, 1105
　Saint Louis Symphony Youth Orchestra, 1292
　Yakima Youth Orchestra, 1815
　Youth Symphony Association of Kansas, 1122
Youth Philharmonic
　Portland Youth Philharmonic Association, 1609
　Sarasota Youth Orchestras, 989
Youth Strings
　Carson City Symphony Association, 1311
Youth Symphony
　Grand Rapids Youth Symphony, 1235
　Greater Boston Youth Symphony Orchestras, 1180
　Greater Twin Cities Youth Symphonies, 1263
　Hawaii Youth Symphony Association, 1019
　Metropolitan Youth Symphony, 1604
　New York Youth Symphony, 1433
　Rockford Area Youth Symphony Orchestra, 1065
　Sarasota Youth Orchestras, 989
　Tacoma Youth Symphony, 1810
　Tulsa Youth Symphony, 1586
　West Michigan Symphony, 1249

Theatre

AEA LOA Prodctions

Specialized Field Index / Theatre

John Drew Theater at Guild Hall, 3437
Acting
  University of California-Irvine: Department of Drama, 2478
Acting Course of Study
  American Academy of Dramatic Arts/Hollywood, 2472
African American
  African American Cultural Centre, 3423
  African American Drama Company, 2572
  African Continuum Theatre Company (Actco), 2730
  Black Experience Ensemble, 3407
  Black Spectrum, 3474
  Crossroads Theatre Company, 3377
  Harlem Artists Development League, 3496
  Junebug Productions, 3082
  Karamu House, 3714
  National Black Touring Circuit, 3526
  Negro Ensemble Company, 3529
  North Carolina Black Repertory Company, 3687
  Rites and Reason, 3863
  Robey Theatre Company, 2515
  Roger Furman Theatre, 3560
  Saint Louis Black Repertory Company, 3303
Alternative
  Brava! for Women in The Arts, 2576
  Cleveland Signstage Theatre, 3713
  Darkhorse Theater, 3913
  Lambda Players, 2556
  National Theatre of the Deaf, 2687
  Theatre Du Grand-Guignol De Paris, 3579
  Vsa Arts, 2752
Arts Education
  Paper Mill Playhouse, 3373
Asian American
  Asian American Theater Company, 2575
  Pan Asian Repertory Theatre, 3541
Asian Pacific Islander
  Asian American Theater Company, 2575
Avant-garde
  Hudson Theatre, 2474
Bilingual Theatre
  Thalia Spanish Theatre, 3624
Broadway Musical Revivals
  Broadway Theatre League of Pueblo, 2676
  Broadway Theatre League of South Bend, 3022
  Broadway Theatre League of Utica, 3630
  Playhouse on The Square, 3910
  Rochester Broadway Theatre League, 3610
  State Theatre Center for the Arts, 3801
Cabaret
  Actors Cabaret/Mainstage Theatre Company, 3774
  Carousel Music Theatre, 3094
  Forestburgh Playhouse, 3441
  Quality Hill Playhouse, 3290
  Shadowbox Cabaret, 3729
Children's Crafts
  Afrikan Poetry Theatre, 3449
Children's Theater
  Academy Theatre, 2847
  Acting Up Theatre Company, 3205
  Actors Theatre of Nantucket, 3162
  American Theater Arts for Youth, 3826
  Andy's Summer Playhouse, 3356
  Aurora Fox Children's Theatre Company, 2644
  Broadhollow Players Limited, 3614
  Cabbages and Kings, 3944
  Casa Manana Playhouse, 3970
  Children's Musical Theater-San Jose, 2598
  Children's Theater Company, 3237
  Children's Theatre of Eden, 3653
  City Arts Drama Center, 3659
  Creative Arts Theatre and School, 3926
  Das Puppenspiel Puppet Theater, 3633
  Delray Beach Playhouse, 2773
  Depaul University Merle Reskin Theatre, 2924
  Don Quixote Children's Theatre, 3485
  First Stage Children's Theater, 4120
  Forestburgh Playhouse, 3441
  Fort Lauderdale Children's Theatre, 2776
  Gateway Playhouse, 3413
  Gooseberry Park Players, 3260
  Greenbrier Valley Theatre, 4100
  Greensboro Children's Theatre, 3661
  Hershey Theatre, 3807
  Honolulu Theatre for Youth, 2886
  Imagination Stage, 3120
  Irish Arts Centre Theatre, 3504
  J Howard Wood Theatre, 2820
  Junior Players, 3950
  Junior Theatre, 3032
  Kids 4 Broadway, 2480
  Kids on Broadway, 2615
  Kidstock Creative Theater Education Center, 3185
  Laguna Playhouse, 2484
  Lexington Children's Theatre, 3066
  Looking Glass Theatre, 3862
  Los Angeles Theatre Works, 2639
  Matthews Playhouse, 3669
  Missoula Children's Theatre, 3318
  Mount Vernon Community Children's Theatre, 4031
  Nine O'clock Players, 2511
  Oklahoma Children's Theatre, 3762
  Oregon Children's Theatre, 3786
  Palo Alto Children's Theatre, 2539
  Pensacola Little Theatre, 2812
  Pittsburgh International Children's Theater, 3843
  Puppet Arts Theatre, 3277
  Puppet Showplace Theatre, 3144
  Riverside Center Dinner Theater, 4036
  Salt and Pepper Mime Company, 3563
  San Jose Children's Musical Theater, 2601
  Seattle Children's Theatre, 4085
  Sesame Place, 3812
  Shawnee Playhouse, 3853
  State Theatre Center for the Arts, 3801
  Surfside Players, 2763
  Theatre of Western Springs, 2992
  Vagabond Acting Troupe, 3818
  Vive Les Arts Theatre, 3994
  Weathervane Playhouse, 3747
  Young Artists Theatre, 3126
  Youtheatre, 3215
Classic
  52nd Street Project, 3459
  A.D. Players, 3980
  Aai Productions, 3416
  Academy of Performing Arts, 3168
  Acting Company, 3461
  Acting Company of Riverside Theatre, 2836
  Actor's Express Theatre, 2848
  Actors Cabaret/Mainstage Theatre Company, 3774
  Alden Theatre Series, 4041
  Allenberry Resort Inn and Playhouse, 3797
  Alliance Theatre Company, 2849
  Allied Theatre Group/Stage West, 3967
  Amas Musical Theatre, 3464
  American Conservatory Theatre, 2573
  American Family Theater, 3824
  American Music Theater Festival/Prince Music Theater, 3825
  American Theater Company, 2905
  American Theatre, 2906
  Antenna Theater, 2622
  Arden Theatre Company, 3827
  Arena Players Repertory Theatre Company of Long Island, 3431
  Arizona Theatre Company, 2430
  Arkansas Repertory Theatre, 2439
  Art Station Theatre, 2879
  Artists Repertory Theatre, 3783
  Artreach: a Division of the Children's Theatre of Cincinnati, 3703
  Auburn University Montgomery Theatre, 2412
  Augusta Arts Council/Augusta Historic Theatre, 3041
  Barnstormers, 3354
  Barrow Group, 3470
  Barter Theatre - State Theatre of Virginia, 4028
  Beasley Performing Arts Coliseum, 4076
  Belmont Playhouse, 3414
  Berkshire Public Theatre, 3176
  Berry College Theatre Company, 2802
  Big Mess Theatre, 3828
  Bilingual Foundation of the Arts, 2495
  Black Hills Passion Play, 3888
  Black Repertory Group, 2450
  Black Swan Theatre, 3637
  Blackfriars Theatre, 3608
  Blank Theatre Company, 2473
  Boston Children's Theatre, 3135
  Bowen Park Theatre & Opera, 2990
  Britt Festivals, 3780
  Broad Stage, 2619
  Broadway Live at the Opera House, 3065
  Broadway Theatre League of Pueblo, 2676
  Broadway Theatre League of South Bend, 3022
  Broadway Theatre League of Utica, 3630
  California Institute of the Arts: School of Theater, 2637
  California State University, Fresno: Theatre Arts Department, 2468
  California State University, Fullerton: Department of Theatre and Dance, 2469
  California State University, Sacramento: Department of Theatre and Dance, 2554
  Calumet Theatre Company, 3194
  Camille Players, 3939
  Cape Cod Melody Tent, 3156
  Carrollwood Players Community Theater, 2831
  Castillo Theatre, 3477
  Catholic University of America: Drama Department, 2733
  Celebration Theatre, 2640
  Center Stage, 3113
  Central Connecticut State University: Department of Theatre, 2693
  Chicago Shakespeare Theater on Navy Pier, 2917
  Children's Theatre Board, 3685
  Cincinnati Playhouse in The Park, 3704
  Cinnabar Theater, 2543
  Circle Theatre, 3202
  City of Albuquerque Kimo Theatre, 3400
  Clarence Brown Theatre Company, 3904
  Classics on Stage!, 2920
  Cleveland Play House, 3711
  Columbia Theatre/Fanfare, 3079
  Commonweal Theatre Company, 3232
  Company of Fools, 2898
  Creative Arts Team, 3481
  Creede Repertory Theatre, 2651
  Cumberland Theatre, 3123
  Cutter Theatre, 4074
  Dallas Theater Center, 3947
  Darkhorse Theater, 3913
  Daytona Playhouse, 2770
  Detroit Repertory Theatre, 3197
  Diamond Circle Melodrama, 2668
  Diana Wortham Theatre at Pack Place, 3638
  Drama Department, 3487
  Ensemble Theatre Company of Santa Barbara, 2610
  Everett Theatre, 4067
  Famous Door Theatre, 2930
  Fargo-Moorhead Community Theatre, 3689
  Florissant Civic Center Theater, 3283
  Foothill Theatre Company, 2529
  Foothills Theatre Company, 3187
  Ford's Theatre Society, 2738
  Forum Theatre, 3372
  Georgia Shakespeare, 2855
  Gilbert Theater, 3656
  Golden Thespians, 2782
  Goodman Theatre, 2933
  Granbury Opera House Theatre, 3979
  Greenbrier Valley Theatre, 4100
  Gretna Productions, 3819
  Group at the Strasberg Acting Studio, 2641
  Guthrie Theater, 3239
  Hangar Theatre, 3446
  Hartford Stage Company, 2686
  Harwich Junior Theatre, 3182
  Hedgerow Theatre, 3815
  Hershey Theatre, 3807
  Hickory Community Theatre, 3662
  Hip Pocket Theatre, 3973
  Horse Cave Theatre, 3063
  Houston Shakespeare Festival, 3985
  Hudson Valley Shakespeare Festival, 3433
  Illinois Shakespeare Festival, 2979
  Impulse Theater, 2661
  Indian River Theatre of the Performing Arts, 3832
  Indiana Repertory Theatre, 3013
  Irish Classical Theatre Company, 3425
  Irondale Ensemble Project, 3505
  Jean Cocteau Repertory, 3507
  Jewish Ensemble Theatre, 3219
  John Drew Theater at Guild Hall, 3437
  Kalamazoo Civic Players, 3209
  Kavinoky Theatre, 3426
  Kennedy Center American College Theatre, 2742
  Kitchen Dog Theater, 3952
  Knutzen Family Theatre - City of Federal Way, 4069
  Le Centre Du Silence Mime School, 2646
  Lewis & Clark Theatre Company, 3892
  Lifeline Theatre, 2937
  Limelight Theatre, 2827
  Lincoln Community Playhouse, 3326
  Little Theater of Gastonia, 3658
  Lookingglass Theatre Company, 2939
  Los Angeles Designers' Theatre, 2632
  Lyric Stage Company of Boston, 3138
  Mabel Tainter Memorial Theater, 4118
  Mabou Mines, 3516
  Madcap Productions Puppet Theatre, 3706
  Magical Theatre Company, 3696
  Main Street Theater, 3986
  Mainstage Center for the Arts, 3341
  Marin Theatre Company, 2526
  Maui Academy of Performing Arts, 2893
  Meadow Brook Theatre, 3213
  Milwaukee Chamber Theatre, 4122
  Miracle Theatre Group, 3785
  Mirror Repertory Company, 3522
  Montana Shakespeare in The Parks, 3314
  Mountain Playhouse, 3810
  Nautilus Music-Theater, 3268
  New Conservatory Center Theatre, 2586
  New Day Repertory Company, 3606
  New Federal Theatre, 3531
  New Jersey Repertory Company, 3369
  New Repertory Theatre, 3164
  New Stage Theatre, 3276
  Next Theatre Company, 2964
  North Carolina Shakespeare Festival, 3665
  North Coast Repertory Theatre, 2625
  Northwestern University Theatre and Interpretation Center, 2965
  Ogdensburg Command Performances, 3602
  Oklahoma Shakespeare in The Park, 3764
  Old Lyric Repertory Company, 4007
  Old Town Playhouse, 3216
  Oregon Shakespearean Festival Association, 3771
  Orpheum Theatre, 2968
  Palace Theatre, 3744
  Pangea World Theater, 3250
  Park Square Theatre Company, 3269
  Pasadena Playhouse, 2542
  Pearl Theatre Company, 3545
  Pegasus Players, 2942
  Pegasus Theatre, 3953
  Penguin Repertory Company, 3623
  Pennsylvania Shakespeare Festival, 3799
  Peoria Players Theatre, 2983
  Performance Network of Ann Arbor, 3190
  Philadelphia Theatre Company, 3836
  Piedmont Players Theatre, 3678
  Pioneer Theatre Company, 4009
  Pittsburgh Public Theater, 3846
  Piven Theatre Workshop, 2967
  Players Guild of Canton, 3700
  Playhouse Square Foundation, 3716
  Playwrights' Center, 3252
  Pollard Theatre, 3756
  Pomona College Department of Theatre and Dance, 2459
  Portland Center Stage, 3788
  Pregones Theater, 3415
  Princeton Rep Company/Princeton Rep Shakespeare Festival, 3383
  Proctor's Theatre, 3620
  Public Theatre, 3552
  Purple Rose Theatre Company, 3195
  Redhouse Arts Center, 3626
  Renaissance Theatre, 3742
  Rep Stage, 3122
  Ritz Theatre, 3751
  Ritz Theatre and La Villa Museum, 2785
  River Rep Theatre Company, 3558
  Rochester Civic Theatre, 3264
  Rosebriar Shakespeare Company, 3727
  Roundabout Theatre Company, 3561
  Saddleback College, 2527

Specialized Field Index / Theatre

Saint Louis Black Repertory Company, 3303
Saint Sebastian Players, 2946
Salt Lake Acting Company, 4012
San Francisco Mime Troupe, 2590
San Jose Repertory Theatre, 2602
San Jose Stage Company, 2603
Sandusky State Theatre, 3750
Saratoga Performing Arts Center, 3619
Seattle Repertory Theatre, 4087
Shakespeare Festival at Tulane, 3086
Shakespeare in Delaware Park, 3428
Sheldon Theatre, 3212
Signature Theatre, 4033
Snow Camp Historical Drama Society, 3680
Society Hill Playhouse, 3838
Sooner Theatre of Norman, 3760
Southern Arkansas University Theatre & Mass Communications Department, 2442
Southern Connecticut State University: Department of Theatre, 2698
Spencers: Theater of Illusion, 4040
Springer Opera House, 2870
Starlight Musical Theatre, 2571
Stephen Foster-Musical, 3054
Sterling Renaissance Festival, 3622
Stockton Civic Theatre, 2628
Straw Hat Players, 3261
Strawberry Productions, 3150
Struthers Library Theatre, 3855
Studio Theatre, 2750
Summer Repertory Theatre, 2620
Swamp Fox Players, 3875
Temple Theatre Company, 3679
Tennessee Players, 3907
Tennessee Repertory Theatre, 3919
Tennessee Stage Company, 3905
Texas Shakespeare Festival, 3993
the Round Barn Theatre at Amish Acres, 3019
Theater Coalition/The Lear Theater, 3340
Theater Emory, 2864
Theater Schmeater, 4089
Theaterworks, 2688
Theatre Albany, 2843
Theatre Arlington, 3927
Theatre at Monmouth, 3099
Theatre Previews at Duke, 3652
Theatre Three, 3959
Theatre West, 2517
Theatre Winter Haven, 2839
Theresa Lang Theatre, 3583
Thick Description, 2595
Touchstone Theatre, 3795
Two River Theater Company, 3384
Ukiah Players Theatre, 2636
University of Arkansas at Fayetteville: Department of Drama, 2435
University of Arkansas at Little Rock: Department of Theatre and Dance, 2441
University of California-Riverside: Department of Theatre, 2548
University of California-San Diego: Department of Theatre and Dance, 2482
University of Colorado at Boulder: Department of Theatre and Dance, 2647
University of Colorado at Denver: Department of Performing Arts, 2666
University of Denver Department of Theatre, 2667
University of Florida: School, Theater and Dance, 2781
University Theatre: Summer Show Biz, 2963
Urban Institute for Contemporary Arts, 3204
Vanguard Theatre Ensemble, 2470
Venice Theatre, 2835
Veronica's Veil Players, 3851
Village Players Theater, 2981
Virginia Stage Company, 4046
Vortex Repertory Company, 3934
Vsa Arts, 2752
Walnut Street Theatre, 3839
Warehouse Theatre, 3878
Waterloo Community Playhouse & Black Hawk Childrens Theatre, 3039
Watertower Theatre, 3923
Westport Country Playhouse, 2720
Whittier Junior Theatre, 2642
Wichita Falls Backdoor Players, 4027
Williamstown Theatre Festival, 3184
Woodstock Opera House, 2995
Wwu Summer Stock, 4064

Zachary Scott Theatre Center, 3935

Classic Fairy Tales
Nine O'clock Players, 2511

Classical
South Coast Repertory, 2461

Classics
Playmakers Repertory Company, 3645

Classics by the Phoenix & Other Nomadic Theatre Co
Phoenix Arts Association Theatre/Westcoast Playwrights Alliance, 2588

Comedy
7 Stages, 2846
a Noise Within, 2490
A.D. Players, 3980
Aai Productions, 3416
Aberdeen Community Theatre, 3883
About Face Theatre, 2903
Academy of Performing Arts, 3168
Act II Playhouse, 3793
Acting Company, 3461
Actors Cabaret/Mainstage Theatre Company, 3774
Actors Co-Op, 3901
Actors Forum Theatre, 2530
Actors Theatre of Houston, 3981
Actors' Guild of Lexington, 3064
Adobe Theater, 3397
Ahmanson Theatre, 2493
Al Ringling Theatre Lively Arts Series, 4106
Alden Theatre Series, 4041
Allenberry Resort Inn and Playhouse, 3797
Alley Theatre, 3982
Alliance Theatre Company, 2849
Allied Theatre Group/Stage West, 3967
American Theater Company, 2905
Antenna Theater, 2622
Arden Theatre Company, 3827
Arena Stage, 2732
Arizona Theatre Company, 2430
Arkansas Arts Center Children's Theater, 2438
Arkansas Repertory Theatre, 2439
Art Station Theatre, 2879
Artists Repertory Theatre, 3783
Artreach: a Division of the Children's Theatre of Cincinnati, 3703
Atlantic Theater Company, 3468
Auburn University Montgomery Theatre, 2412
Auburn University Theatre, 2400
Auditorium Theatre of Roosevelt University, 2907
Augusta Arts Council/Augusta Historic Theatre, 3041
Aurora Theatre Company, 2447
Avenue Theater, 2654
Bainbridge Performing Arts, 4060
Barrow Group, 3470
Barter Theatre - State Theatre of Virginia, 4028
Bat Theatre Company, 3471
Beasley Performing Arts Coliseum, 4076
Bellevue Little Theatre, 3321
Berkeley Repertory Theatre, 2449
Berry College Theatre Company, 2802
Black Hills Playhouse, 3886
Black Repertory Group, 2450
Blackfriars Theatre, 3608
Blank Theatre Company, 2473
Blowing Rock Stage Company, 3641
Bond Street Theatre Coalition, 3475
Boston Children's Theatre, 3135
Bristol Riverside Theatre, 3798
Bristol Valley Theater, 3455
Britt Festivals, 3780
Broadway Live at the Opera House, 3065
Broadway Palm Dinner Theatre, 2778
Broadway Theatre, 2408
Brown County Playhouse, 3020
Burning Coal Theatre Company, 3674
California Institute of the Arts: School of Theater, 2637
California State University, Fresno: Theatre Arts Department, 2468
California State University, Fullerton: Department of Theatre and Dance, 2469
California State University, Sacramento: Department of Theatre and Dance, 2554
Calumet Theatre Company, 3194
Cape Cod Melody Tent, 3156

Cape May Stage, 3361
Casa Manana Musicals, 3969
Castillo Theatre, 3477
Center Stage, 3113
Central Connecticut State University: Department of Theatre, 2693
Chanhassen Dinner Theatre, 3223
Chicago Shakespeare Theater on Navy Pier, 2917
Children's Theatre Board, 3685
Chippewa Valley Theatre Guild, 4107
Cincinnati Playhouse in The Park, 3704
Cinnabar Theater, 2543
Circle Theatre, 3202
Circuit Playhouse, 3908
City Lights Theatre Company, 2599
City Theatre Company, 3841
Clarence Brown Theatre Company, 3904
Cleveland Play House, 3711
Clinton Area Showboat Theatre, 3030
Clockwork Repertory Theatre, 2703
Colony Theatre Company, 2453
Commedia Theater Company, 3238
Commonweal Theatre Company, 3232
Country Dinner Playhouse, 2673
Creative Arts Team, 3481
Creede Repertory Theatre, 2651
Cumberland County Playhouse, 3895
Cumberland Players, 3393
Cumberland Theatre, 3123
Cutter Theatre, 4074
Cyrano's Theatre Company, 2416
Dad's Garage Theatre Company, 2851
Dallas Children's Theater, 3945
Daytona Playhouse, 2770
Denver Civic Theatre, 2658
Derby Dinner Playhouse, 3004
Diamond Head Theatre, 2884
Dundalk Community Theatre, 3115
Elmwood Playhouse, 3601
Enchanted Forest Summer Theatre, 3792
Ensemble Theatre Company of Santa Barbara, 2610
Everett Theatre, 4067
Fargo-Moorhead Community Theatre, 3689
Filament Theatre, 2931
Flat Rock Playhouse, 3657
Fleetwood Stage, 3458
Florida Atlantic University: Department of Theatre, 2757
Florida Stage, 2792
Florissant Civic Center Theater, 3283
Foothill Theatre Company, 2529
Foothills Theatre Company, 3187
Ford's Theatre Society, 2738
Fort Salem Theatre, 3616
Fort Smith Little Theatre, 2436
Fort Wayne Civic Theatre, 3009
Forum Theatre, 3372
Found Theatre, 2487
Foundation of Arts, 2437
Gallery Theatre of Oregon, 3779
Geffen Playhouse, 2502
Generic Theater, 4044
Gold Coast Theatre, 2800
Goodman Theatre, 2933
Great American Melodrama and Vaudeville, 2536
Groundling Theatre, 2504
Group at the Strasberg Acting Studio, 2641
Grove Theatre Center, 2454
Guthrie Theater, 3239
Hale Centre Theatre at Harman Hall, 4016
Hangar Theatre, 3446
Hardin County Playhouse, 3058
Harlequin Productions, 4075
Harwich Junior Theatre, 3182
Hickory Community Theatre, 3662
Highland Summer Theatre, 3234
Hip Pocket Theatre, 3973
Hollywood Complex Theatre, 2505
Holmdel Theatre Company, 3367
Horizon Theatre Company, 2856
Horse Cave Theatre, 3063
Hot City Theatre, 3298
Humbolt State University: Department of Theatre, Film and Dance, 2445
Huntington Beach Playhouse, 2477
Icehouse Theatre, 2803
Illusion Theater, 3241

Impulse Theater, 2661
Indiana Repertory Theatre, 3013
Iowa Summer Repertory, 3036
Irondale Ensemble Project, 3505
Irving Community Theater, 3992
Jackson Theatre Guild, 3900
Jean Cocteau Repertory, 3507
Jewish Ensemble Theatre, 3219
John Drew Theater at Guild Hall, 3437
Kalamazoo Civic Players, 3209
Kent County Theatre Guild, 2722
Kirk Douglas Theatre, 2463
Kitchen Dog Theater, 3952
La Connection Comedy Theatre, 2624
La Jolla Playhouse, 2481
Laguna Playhouse, 2484
Lakewood Theater, 3107
Lamb's Players Theatre, 2460
Le Centre Du Silence Mime School, 2646
Leatherstocking Theatre Company, 3434
Leeward Community College Theatre, 2892
Lewis & Clark Theatre Company, 3892
Licking County Players, 3746
Lincoln Community Playhouse, 3326
Little Theater of Gastonia, 3658
Little Theatre of Winston-Salem, 3686
Little Theatre on The Square, 2988
Live Bait Theatrical Company, 2938
Long Wharf Theatre, 2697
Looney's Tavern Productions, 2406
Los Angeles Designers' Theatre, 2632
Lynn Canal Community Players, 2421
Madison Repertory Theatre, 4115
Magic Circle Theater, 2550
Magic Theatre, 2583
Magical Theatre Company, 3696
Manhattan Theatre Club, 3517
Mark Taper Forum, 2509
Marriott's Theatre in Lincolnshire, 2973
Mary L Welch Theatre, 3856
Maui Academy of Performing Arts, 2893
Medora Musical, 3246
Mendocino Theatre Company, 2523
Menlo Players Guild, 2524
Metro Theater Company, 3299
Metropolitan Playhouse, 3520
Metrostage, 4030
Milwaukee Chamber Theatre, 4122
Miracle Theatre Group, 3785
Mirror Repertory Company, 3522
Montana Shakespeare in The Parks, 3314
Mooresville Community Theatre, 3670
Mount Baker Theatre, 4063
Mountain Playhouse, 3810
Mu Performing Arts, 3248
Music Theatre Louisville, 3070
Mystery Dinner Playhouse, 4052
New Century Theatre, 3166
New Conservatory Center Theatre, 2586
New Federal Theatre, 3531
New Jomandi Productions, 2859
New Repertory Theatre, 3164
New Stage Theatre, 3276
Next Act Theatre, 4126
Next Theatre Company, 2964
North Coast Repertory Theatre, 2625
North Shore Music Theatre, 3134
Northeastern Theatre, 3139
Northlight Theatre, 2986
Northwestern University Theatre and Interpretation Center, 2965
Off Broadway Theatre, 4008
Oklahoma Shakespeare in The Park, 3764
Old Creamery Theatre Company, 3029
Old Lyric Repertory Company, 4007
Old Town Playhouse, 3216
Open Fist Theatre Company, 2475
Orpheum Theatre, 2968
Palace Theatre, 3744
Pangea World Theater, 3250
Park Square Theatre Company, 3269
Peninsula Players, 4111
Penobscot Theatre Company, 3092
Peoria Players Theatre, 2983
Performance Riverside, 2547
Perseverance Theatre, 2419
Philadelphia Theatre Company, 3836
Phoenix Theatre, 3014
Piedmont Players Theatre, 3678
Pirate Playhouse, 2819

Specialized Field Index / Theatre

Pittsburgh Public Theater, 3846
Piven Theatre Workshop, 2967
Plan - B Theatre Company, 4010
Players Guild of Canton, 3700
Playhouse Square Foundation, 3716
Playwrights Horizons, 3548
Playwrights' Center, 3252
Pocket Sandwich Theatre, 3954
Pollard Theatre, 3756
Pomona College Department of Theatre and Dance, 2459
Ponca Playhouse, 3766
Portland Center Stage, 3788
Pregones Theater, 3415
Princeton Rep Company/Princeton Rep Shakespeare Festival, 3383
Purple Rose Theatre Company, 3195
Red Barn Playhouse, 3214
Redhouse Arts Center, 3626
River Rep Theatre Company, 3558
Rochester Civic Theatre, 3264
Rosebriar Shakespeare Company, 3727
Round House Theatre, 3121
Roundabout Theatre Company, 3561
Saddleback College, 2527
Salt Lake Acting Company, 4012
San Francisco Mime Troupe, 2590
San Jose Repertory Theatre, 2602
San Pedro Playhouse, 4003
Sandusky State Theatre, 3750
Sanford Maine Stage Company, 3109
Saratoga Performing Arts Center, 3619
Seacoast Repertory Theatre, 3353
Seanachai Theatre Company, 2947
Seattle Mime Theatre, 4086
Seattle Repertory Theatre, 4087
Second Stage Theatre, 3565
Seven Angels Theatre, 2713
Shadowbox Cabaret, 3729
Sheboygan Theatre Company, 4134
Showboat Becky Thatcher, 3743
Showboat Majestic, 3709
Signature Theatre Company, 3567
Silver Spring Stage, 3131
Sioux City Community Theatre, 3037
Sleuths Mystery Dinner Shows, 2808
Smallbeer Theatre Company, 3127
Soho Repertory Theatre, 3568
Sooner Theatre of Norman, 3760
South Park Theatre, 3794
Southeast Alabama Community Theatre, 2405
Southern Appalachian Repertory Theatre, 3668
Southern Arkansas University Theatre & Mass Communications Department, 2442
Southern Connecticut State University: Department of Theatre, 2698
Spokane Interplayers Ensemble, 4092
Sro Theatre Company, 3730
Stage 3 Theatre Company, 2627
Stage One: the Louisville Children's Theatre, 3071
Stages St. Louis, 3281
Stageworks, 3444
Stephen Foster-Musical, 3054
Sterling Renaissance Festival, 3622
Steve Silver Productions, 2592
Studio Arena Theatre, 3429
Studio Arts, 3067
Studio Theatre, 2750
Su Teatro, 2665
Summer Repertory Theatre, 2620
Sundance Institute, 4013
Swamp Fox Players, 3875
Swift Creek Mill Playhouse, 4035
Teatro Vision, 2605
Temple Theatre Company, 3679
the Actors' Gang Theater, 2462
the Round Barn Theatre at Amish Acres, 3019
Theater Barn, 3456
Theater Coalition/The Lear Theater, 3340
Theater Emory, 2864
Theater Works, 2425
Theaterworks, 2688
Theatre Albany, 2843
Theatre Arlington, 3927
Theatre at Monmouth, 3099
Theatre De La Jeune Lune, 3255
Theatre Du Grand-Guignol De Paris, 3579
Theatre L'homme Dieu, 3220

Theatre on The Square, 3015
Theatre Previews at Duke, 3652
Theatre Three, 3959
Theatre West, 2517
Theatre Workshop of Owensboro, 3073
Theatreworks Usa, 3582
Theresa Lang Theatre, 3583
Timber Lake Playhouse, 2977
Touchstone Theatre, 3795
Troupe America, 3257
Trumpet in The Land, 3745
Trustus, 3874
Ukiah Players Theatre, 2636
Unicorn Theatre, 3292
University of Arkansas at Fayetteville: Department of Drama, 2435
University of Arkansas at Little Rock: Department of Theatre and Dance, 2441
University of California-Riverside: Department of Theatre, 2548
University of California-San Diego: Department of Theatre and Dance, 2482
University of Denver Department of Theatre, 2667
University of Florida: School, Theater and Dance, 2781
University Theatre: Summer Show Biz, 2963
Urban Institute for Contemporary Arts, 3204
Vanguard Theatre Ensemble, 2470
Venice Theatre, 2835
Victory Gardens Theater at the Biograph, 2959
Vigilante Theatre Company, 3316
Village Players Theater, 2981
Virginia Stage Company, 4046
Walnut Street Theatre, 3839
Waterloo Community Playhouse & Black Hawk Childrens Theatre, 3039
Watertower Theatre, 3923
Waukesha Civic Theatre, 4136
Wayside Theatre, 4042
Weathervane Playhouse, 3747
Weathervane Theatre, 3355
Wellfleet Harbor Actors Theater, 3181
West Coast Ensemble, 2520
Weston Playhouse, 4026
Westport Country Playhouse, 2720
Whittier Junior Theatre, 2642
Wichita Falls Backdoor Players, 4027
Wilma Theater, 3840
Woodstock Opera House, 2995
Working Theatre Company, 3595
Wwu Summer Stock, 4064
Yale Repertory Theatre, 2699
Zachary Scott Theatre Center, 3935

Community Theater

Aberdeen Community Theatre, 3883
About Face Theatre, 2903
Actors' Guild of Lexington, 3064
Adobe Theater, 3397
African American Cultural Centre, 3423
Albuquerque Little Theatre, 3399
Antenna Theater, 2622
Arena Dinner Theatre, 3007
Arena Players Repertory Theatre Company of Long Island, 3431
Arizona Theatre Company, 2430
Arkansas Repertory Theatre, 2439
Army Entertainment Program, 2882
Artists Theatre Association, 2725
Artists' Civic Theatre and Studio, 3080
Arts & Culture Alliance of Greater Knoxville, 3902
Arts Midwest, 3235
Artscenter, 3682
Augusta Arts Council/Augusta Historic Theatre, 3041
Aurora Fox Children's Theatre Company, 2644
Bay City Players, 3193
Bellevue Little Theatre, 3321
Bermerton Community Theatre, 4066
Berry College Theatre Company, 2802
Black Experience Ensemble, 3407
Black Repertory Group, 2450
Blackfriars Theatre, 3608
Bond Street Theatre Coalition, 3475
Brava! for Women in The Arts, 2576
Bread and Circus Theatre, 3962
Brecksville Little Theatre, 3698

Broad Stage, 2619
Broadhollow Players Limited, 3614
Broadway Palm Dinner Theatre, 2778
Brown Grand Theatre, 3044
California State University, Fresno: Theatre Arts Department, 2468
California State University, Sacramento: Department of Theatre and Dance, 2554
Calumet Theatre Company, 3194
Cape Cod Melody Tent, 3156
Cape Fear Regional Theatre, 3655
Carolina Theatre of Durham, 3650
Carrollwood Players Community Theater, 2831
Castillo Theatre, 3477
Castle Rock Players, 2650
Central Piedmont Community Theatre, 3647
Chanute Community Theatre, 3042
Charlestown Working Theater, 3147
Cheshire Community Theatre, 2679
Cheyenne Little Theatre Players, 4137
Chinese Theatre Works, 3453
Christian Community Theater, 2465
Cincinnati Playhouse in The Park, 3704
Circle Theatre, 3202
Circuit Playhouse, 3908
City Lights Theatre Company, 2599
Civic Theatre & School of Theatre, 3203
Clockwork Repertory Theatre, 2703
Coach House Players, 3451
Coffeyville Community Theatre, 3043
Columbia Theatre for the Performing Arts, 4073
Community Theatre of Clay County, 3000
Community Theatre of Greensboro, 3660
Creative Arts Team, 3481
Cumberland Players, 3393
Dayton Playhouse, 3732
Daytona Playhouse, 2770
Delray Beach Playhouse, 2773
Diamond Head Theatre, 2884
Dolphin Players, 3782
Dundalk Community Theatre, 3115
Eau Claire Children's Theatre, 4108
Edison Theatre, 3297
Elmwood Playhouse, 3601
Encore Players, 2974
Fargo-Moorhead Community Theatre, 3689
Fiddlehead Theatre Company, 3167
Florida Atlantic University: Department of Theatre, 2757
Florissant Civic Center Theater, 3283
Foothill Theatre Company, 2529
Footlight Players, Inc., 3017
Ford's Theatre Society, 2738
Fort Totten Little Theatre, 3693
Fort Wayne Civic Theatre, 3009
Fostoria Footlighters, 3736
Foundation of Arts, 2437
Free Street Programs, 2932
Garland Civic Theatre, 3977
Germantown Theatre Guild, 3831
Globe of the Great Southwest Theatre, 3998
Golden Thespians, 2782
Grand Opera House, 3035
Green Earth Players, 3233
Greensboro Children's Theatre, 3661
Group at the Strasberg Acting Studio, 2641
Hale Centre Theatre at Harman Hall, 4016
Hangar Theatre, 3446
Hardin County Playhouse, 3058
Harwich Junior Theatre, 3182
Hersheypark Entertainment, 3808
Hickory Community Theatre, 3662
Hilo Community Players, 2883
Hole in The Wall Theatre, 2695
Huntington Theatre, 3697
Imago, the Theatre Mask Ensemble, 3604
Impulse Theatre, 2661
Irving Community Theater, 3992
Jackson County Community Theatre, 3002
Jackson Community Theatre Guild, 3900
John Drew Theater at Guild Hall, 3437
Junior Theatre, 3032
Kalamazoo Civic Players, 3209
Kaleidoscope Theatre, 2791
Kearney Community Theatre, 3325
Kent County Theatre Guild, 2722
Kitchen Theatre Company, 3447
Lakewood Center for the Arts, 3778

Lamp-Lite Theater, 3997
Las Vegas Little Theatre, 3339
Le Centre Du Silence Mime School, 2646
Liberty Center, 3306
Licking County Players, 3746
Lincoln Community Playhouse, 3326
Little Theater of Gastonia, 3658
Little Theatre of Bedford, 2997
Little Theatre of Owatonna, 3263
Little Theatre of Winston-Salem, 3686
Little Theatre on The Square, 2988
Los Angeles Designers' Theatre, 2632
Lynn Canal Community Players, 2421
Lyric Theatre Warehouse, 2613
Magic Circle Theater, 2550
Make a Circus: Arco Sports, 2584
Mansfield Playhouse, 3741
Marathon Community Theatre, 2795
Martin Community Players, 3683
Matchbox Children's Theatre, 3221
Memphis Community Players, 3293
Mendocino Theatre Company, 2523
Menlo Players Guild, 2524
Mixed Blood Theatre Company, 3247
Mohawk Players, 3411
Mooresville Community Theatre, 3670
Morristown Theatre Guild, 3911
Muhlenberg Community Theatre, 3061
Municipal Theater Association of Saint Louis, 3300
Music Theatre Louisville, 3070
National Theatre, 2745
Near West Theatre, 3715
New Conservatory Center Theatre, 2586
New Federal Theatre, 3531
New York Street Theatre Caravan, 3450
Newark Performing Arts Corporation/Newark Symphony Hall, 3379
Northwestern University Theatre and Interpretation Center, 2965
Off-Broadway Musical Theatre, 3262
Oklahoma Children's Theatre, 3762
Old Creamery Theatre Company, 3029
Old Town Playhouse, 3216
Olney Theatre Center, 3128
Orange Park Community Theatre, 2804
Oregon Fantasy Theatre, 3776
Orlando Broadway Dinner Theatre, 2806
Orpheum Theatre, 2968
Out North - Vsa Alaska, 2417
Peninsula Players, 2780
Pensacola Little Theatre, 2812
Peoria Players Theatre, 2983
Performance Riverside, 2547
Perry Players, 2877
Piccadilly Puppets Company, 2872
Piedmont Players Theatre, 3678
Plantation Theatre Company, 2815
Players Guild of Canton, 3700
Plays-In-The-Park, 3363
Pompano Players, 2816
Ponca Playhouse, 3766
Possum Point Players, 2723
Prairie Players Civic Theatre, 2969
Pregones Theater, 3415
Puppet House Theatre, 2708
Rainbo Children's Theatre Company, 3271
Rajeckas and Intraub - Movement Theatre, 3581
Reading Community Players, 3852
Renaissance Theatre, 3742
Repertory People of Evansville, 3006
Richmond Children's Theatre, 3076
Ritz Theatre, 3751
Rochester Civic Theatre, 3264
Rosebriar Shakespeare Company, 3727
Roxy Theater, 3894
Royal Arts Council, 3310
Saddleback College, 2527
Saint Louis Black Repertory Company, 3303
Salina Community Theatre, 3047
San Francisco Mime Troupe, 2590
San Jose Children's Musical Theater, 2601
Scarlet Mask Society, 3728
Seven Angels Theatre, 2713
Shawano County Arts Council, 4133
Sheboygan Theatre Company, 4134
Sheridan Civic Theatre Guild, 4139
Sherman Players, 2705
Side by Side, 3676

1258

Specialized Field Index / Theatre

Sikeston Little Theatre, 3307
Silver Spring Stage, 3131
Six Flags Magic Mountain, 2638
Slocum House Theatre Company, 4094
Soho Repertory Theatre, 3568
Sooner Theatre of Norman, 3760
Southeast Alabama Community Theatre, 2405
Southern Arkansas University Theatre & Mass Communications Department, 2442
Southwest Repertory Organization, 3966
Spanish Theatre Repertory Company, 3570
St. John Theatre, 3088
Stages St. Louis, 3281
Sterling Renaissance Festival, 3622
Stockton Civic Theatre, 2628
Struthers Library Theatre, 3855
Studio Theatre, 2750
Su Teatro, 2665
Teatro Vision, 2605
Thalia Spanish Theatre, 3624
Theater Emory, 2864
Theater Works, 2425
Theaterworks, 2688
Theatre Albany, 2843
Theatre Bristol, 3893
Theatre Club of the Palm Beaches, 2794
Theatre De La Jeune Lune, 3255
Theatre El Dorado, 2544
Theatre Harrisburg, 3806
Theatre in The Park, 3677
Theatre L'homme Dieu, 3220
Theatre of Western Springs, 2992
Theatre on The Ridge, 3611
Theatre West, 2517
Theatreworks Usa, 3582
Topeka Civic Theatre & Academy, 3049
Town Players, 3891
Towne and Country Players, 3748
Trilakes Community Theatre, 3280
Ucf Civic Theatre, 2810
Ukiah Players Theatre, 2636
University of California-San Diego: Department of Theatre and Dance, 2482
University of Colorado at Boulder: Department of Theatre and Dance, 2647
University of Denver Department of Theatre, 2007
University Theatre: Summer Show Biz, 2963
Urban Institute for Contemporary Arts, 3204
Vanguard Theatre Ensemble, 2470
Venice Theatre, 2835
Village Players Theater, 2981
Vive Les Arts Theatre, 3994
Vsa Arts, 2752
Waimea Community Theatre, 2889
Waterloo Community Playhouse & Black Hawk Childrens Theatre, 3039
Watertown Lyric Theater Productions, 3632
Weathervane Playhouse, 3747
Whittier Junior Theatre, 2642
Wilmington Drama League, 2729
Windward Theatre Guild, 2888
Woodstock Opera House, 2995
Yale Repertory Theatre, 2699
Yard, 3151
Young Actors Theatre, 2829
Youtheatre, 3663

Contemporary
52nd Street Project, 3459
7 Stages, 2846
A.D. Players, 3980
Aai Productions, 3416
About Face Theatre, 2903
Academy of Performing Arts, 3168
Acting Company, 3461
Acting Company of Riverside Theatre, 2836
Actor's Express Theatre, 2848
Actor's Theatre of Charlotte, 3646
Actors Cabaret/Mainstage Theatre Company, 3774
Actors Theatre of Phoenix, 2426
Actors' Guild of Lexington, 3064
Alberta Bair Theatre, 3313
Alden Theatre Series, 4041
Alley Theatre, 3982
Alliance Theatre Company, 2849
Allied Theatre Group/Stage West, 3967
Amas Musical Theatre, 3464
American Conservatory Theatre, 2573
American Family Theater, 3824

American Theater Company, 2905
Antenna Theater, 2622
Arden Theatre Company, 3827
Arena Players Repertory Theatre Company of Long Island, 3431
Arizona Theatre Company, 2430
Ark Theatre Company, 2631
Arkansas Repertory Theatre, 2439
Art Station Theatre, 2879
Artists Collective, 2685
Artists Repertory Theatre, 3783
Artreach: a Division of the Children's Theatre of Cincinnati, 3703
Atlantic Theater Company, 3468
Auburn University Montgomery Theatre, 2412
Barrow Group, 3470
Barter Theatre - State Theatre of Virginia, 4028
Bat Theatre Company, 3471
Beasley Performing Arts Coliseum, 4076
Bellevue Little Theatre, 3321
Berkshire Theatre Festival, 3176
Berry College Theatre Company, 2802
Black Repertory Group, 2450
Black Swan Theater, 3637
Blackfriars Theatre, 3608
Blank Theatre Company, 2473
Blind Parrot Productions, 2911
Bond Street Theatre Coalition, 3475
Boston Children's Theatre, 3135
Brave New Workshop, 3236
Bristol Valley Theater, 3455
Britt Festivals, 3780
Broad Stage, 2619
Broadway Palm Dinner Theatre, 2778
Broadway Theatre League of South Bend, 3022
Brooke Hills Playhouse, 4105
Broom Street Theater, 4113
Brown County Playhouse, 3020
Brown Summer Theatre, 3860
Bullshed Theatre Project, 3755
California Institute of the Arts: School of Theater, 2637
California State University, Fresno: Theatre Arts Department, 2468
California State University, Fullerton: Department of Theatre and Dance, 2469
California State University, Sacramento: Department of Theatre and Dance, 2554
Calumet Theatre Company, 3194
Camille Players, 3939
Carrollwood Players Community Theater, 2831
Casa Manana Musicals, 3969
Castillo Theatre, 3477
Catamount Film and Arts Company, 4025
Catholic University of America: Drama Department, 2733
Cedar Point Live Entertainment, 3749
Celebration Theatre, 2640
Center Stage, 3113
Central Connecticut State University: Department of Theatre, 2693
Changing Scene Theater, 2655
Chicago Shakespeare Theater on Navy Pier, 2917
Childsplay, 2429
Cincinnati Playhouse in The Park, 3704
Cinnabar Theater, 2543
Circle Theatre, 3202
City Lights Theatre Company, 2599
City of Albuquerque Kimo Theatre, 3400
City Theatre Company, 3841
Clarence Brown Theatre Company, 3904
Cleveland Play House, 3711
Clockwork Repertory Theatre, 2703
Commonweal Theatre Company, 3232
Company of Fools, 2898
Cornerstone Theater Company, 2498
Country Dinner Playhouse, 2673
Creation Production Company, 3480
Creative Arts Team, 3481
Creede Repertory Theatre, 2651
Cumberland County Playhouse, 3895
Cumberland Theatre, 3123
Cutter Theatre, 4074
Dallas Theater Center, 3947
Darkhorse Theater, 3913
Daytona Playhouse, 2770

Detroit Repertory Theatre, 3197
Diana Wortham Theatre at Pack Place, 3638
Dixon Place, 3483
Dobama Theatre, 3718
Dundalk Community Theatre, 3115
Enchanted Forest Summer Theatre, 3792
Ensemble Theatre Company of Santa Barbara, 2610
Essential Theatre, 2852
Everett Theatre, 4067
Fairfield County Stage Company, 2717
Famous Door Theatre, 2930
Fargo-Moorhead Community Theatre, 3689
Figures of Speech Theatre, 3096
Flat Rock Playhouse, 3657
Florissant Civic Center Theater, 3283
Foothill Theatre Company, 2529
Foothills Performing Arts Company, 3187
Forum Theatre, 3372
Free Street Programs, 2932
Gallery Theatre of Oregon, 3779
Generic Theater, 4044
George Street Playhouse, 3378
Germinal Stage Inc, 2660
Gilbert Theater, 3656
Gold Coast Theatre, 2800
Goodman Theatre, 2933
Greenbrier Valley Theatre, 4100
Group at the Strasberg Acting Studio, 2641
Guthrie Theater, 3239
Hangar Theatre, 3446
Harbor Theatre, 3495
Hardin County Playhouse, 3058
Harlequin Productions, 4075
Hartford Stage Company, 2686
Harwich Junior Theatre, 3182
Hawaii Theatre, 2885
Hickory Community Theatre, 3662
Hip Pocket Theatre, 3973
History Making Productions, 3180
Horizon Theatre Company, 2856
Horse Cave Theatre, 3063
Humbolt State University: Department of Theatre, Film and Dance, 2445
Illusion Theater, 3241
Illustrated Stage Company, 2580
Impulse Theater, 2661
Indian River Theatre of the Performing Arts, 3832
Indiana Repertory Theatre, 3013
Iowa Summer Repertory, 3036
Irondale Ensemble Project, 3505
J Howard Wood Theatre, 2820
Jackson Theatre Guild, 3900
Jafrika, 2662
Jam and Company, 3506
Jean Cocteau Repertory, 3507
Jewish Ensemble Theatre, 3219
John Drew Theater at Guild Hall, 3437
Just Us Theater Company, 2857
Kalamazoo Civic Players, 3209
Key West Players, 2788
Kitchen Dog Theater, 3952
Laguna Playhouse, 2484
Lambda Players, 2556
Le Centre Du Silence Mime School, 2646
Lewis & Clark Theatre Company, 3892
Lincoln Community Playhouse, 3326
Little Theater of Gastonia, 3658
Little Theatre of Winston-Salem, 3686
Little Theatre on The Square, 2988
Live Bait Theatrical Company, 2938
Lookingglass Theatre Company, 2939
Lorraine Hansberry Theatre, 2582
Los Angeles Designers' Theatre, 2632
Lynn Canal Community Players, 2421
Mabou Mines, 3516
Magic Circle Theater, 2550
Magic Theatre, 2583
Magical Theatre Company, 3696
Main Street Theater, 3986
Make a Circus: Arco Sports, 2584
Manhattan Theatre Club, 3517
Maui Academy of Performing Arts, 2893
Mayfair Theatre/Shear Madness, 2941
Meadow Brook Theatre, 3213
Medora Musical, 3246
Mendocino Theatre Company, 2523
Merrimack Repertory Theatre, 3160
Metro Theater Company, 3299

Metrostage, 4030
Milwaukee Chamber Theatre, 4122
Miracle Theatre Group, 3785
Mirror Repertory Company, 3522
Missouri Repertory Theatre, 3289
Mixed Blood Theatre Company, 3247
Mooresville Community Theatre, 3670
Mu Performing Arts, 3248
Music Theatre Associates, 3523
National Theater Institute, 2715
Nautilus Music-Theater, 3268
Nebraska Repertory Theatre, 3327
New Century Theatre, 3166
New Conservatory Center Theatre, 2586
New Day Repertory Company, 3606
New Federal Theatre, 3531
New Repertory Theatre, 3164
New Stage Theatre, 3276
New Theatre, 3301
Next Theatre Company, 2964
North Coast Repertory Theatre, 2625
North Shore Music Theatre, 3134
Northside Theatre Company, 2600
Northwestern University Theatre and Interpretation Center, 2965
Offstage Theatre, 4034
Oklahoma Children's Theatre, 3762
Old Creamery Theatre Company, 3029
Old Globe, 2565
Old Lyric Repertory Company, 4007
Old Town Playhouse, 3216
Ontological-Hysteric Theater, 3538
Open Stage of Harrisburg, 3805
Openstage Theatre and Company, 2670
Oregon Children's Theatre, 3786
Oregon Shakespearean Festival Association, 3771
Orpheum Theatre, 2968
Out North - Vsa Alaska, 2417
Palace Theatre, 3744
Pangea World Theater, 3250
Park Avenue Theatrical Group, 3543
Park Square Theatre Company, 3269
Peoria Players Theatre, 2983
Performance Network of Ann Arbor, 3190
Philadelphia Theatre Company, 3836
Piccadilly Puppets Company, 2872
Piedmont Players Theatre, 3678
Pilgram Theater Research & Performance Collaboration, 3132
Pillsbury House Theatre, 3251
Ping Chong & Company, 3547
Pioneer Theatre Company, 4009
Pittsburgh Public Theater, 3846
Piven Theatre Workshop, 2967
Players Guild of Canton, 3700
Plays-In-The-Park, 3363
Playwrights Horizons, 3548
Playwrights' Center, 3252
Pollard Theatre, 3756
Pomona College Department of Theatre and Dance, 2459
Pontine Theatre, 3352
Pregones Theater, 3415
Princeton Rep Company/Princeton Rep Shakespeare Festival, 3383
Proctor's Theatre, 3620
Purple Rose Theatre Company, 3195
Raven Theatre Company, 2944
Red Barn Theatre, 2789
Redhouse Arts Center, 3626
Renaissance Theaterworks, 4128
Repertory Theatre of Saint Louis, 3302
Ridge Theater, 3557
Ritz Theatre, 3751
Rochester Civic Theatre, 3264
Round House Theatre, 3121
Roundabout Theatre Company, 3561
Saddleback College, 2527
Saint Louis Black Repertory Company, 3303
Salt Lake Acting Company, 4012
San Diego Repertory Theatre, 2568
San Francisco Mime Troupe, 2590
San Jose Repertory Theatre, 2602
San Jose Stage Company, 2603
Sandusky State Theatre, 3750
Seattle Mime Theatre, 4086
Seattle Repertory Theatre, 4087
Second Stage Theatre, 3565
Seven Angels Theatre, 2713

1259

Specialized Field Index / Theatre

Shakespeare & Company, 3159
Shakespeare Festival at Tulane, 3086
Smallbeer Theatre Company, 3127
Soho Repertory Theatre, 3568
Sooner Theatre of Norman, 3760
Soupstone Project, 3569
South Coast Repertory, 2461
Southeast Alabama Community Theatre, 2405
Southern Appalachian Repertory Theatre, 3668
Southern Arkansas University Theatre & Mass Communications Department, 2442
Southern Connecticut State University: Department of Theatre, 2698
Spokane Interplayers Ensemble, 4092
Sro Theatre Company, 3730
Stage 3 Theatre Company, 2627
Stage One: the Louisville Children's Theatre, 3071
Stamford Theatre Works, 2707
Stephen Foster-Musical, 3054
Stop-Gap, 2609
Studio Theatre, 2750
Summer Repertory Theatre, 2620
Sundance Institute, 4013
Swamp Fox Players, 3875
Swift Creek Mill Playhouse, 4035
Teatro Vision, 2605
Texas Shakespeare Festival, 3993
the Round Barn Theatre at Amish Acres, 3019
Theater Barn, 3456
Theater Emory, 2864
Theater Grottesco, 3201
Theater Rhinoceros, 2593
Theater Schmeater, 4089
Theaterworks, 2688
Theatre Albany, 2843
Theatre Arlington, 3927
Theatre Artaud, 2594
Theatre Club of the Palm Beaches, 2794
Theatre De La Jeune Lune, 3255
Theatre II Company, 2957
Theatre L'homme Dieu, 3220
Theatre Previews at Duke, 3652
Theatre West, 2517
Theatre-In-The-Works, 2809
Theatreworks Usa, 3582
Theatrical Outfit, 2867
Theresa Lang Theatre, 3583
Thick Description, 2595
Thunder Bay Ensemble, 3584
Timber Lake Playhouse, 2977
Touchstone Theatre, 3795
Triarts Sharon Playhouse, 2704
Troupe America, 3257
Trumpet in The Land, 3745
Two River Theater Company, 3384
Ukiah Players Theatre, 2636
Unicorn Theatre, 3292
University of Arkansas at Fayetteville: Department of Drama, 2435
University of Arkansas at Little Rock: Department of Theatre and Dance, 2441
University of California-Riverside: Department of Theatre, 2548
University of California-San Diego: Department of Theatre and Dance, 2482
University of Colorado at Boulder: Department of Theatre and Dance, 2647
University of Colorado at Denver: Department of Performing Arts, 2666
University of Denver Department of Theatre, 2667
University of Florida: School, Theater and Dance, 2781
University Theatre: Summer Show Biz, 2963
Urban Institute for Contemporary Arts, 3204
Vanguard Theatre Ensemble, 2470
Venice Theatre, 2835
Vermont Stage Company, 4019
Victory Gardens Theater at the Biograph, 2959
Vigilante Theatre Company, 3316
Village Players Theater, 2981
Virginia Stage Company, 4046
Vortex Repertory Company, 3934
Vsa Arts, 2752
Walker Art Center, 3258
Walnut Street Theatre, 3839

Waterloo Community Playhouse & Black Hawk Childrens Theatre, 3039
Watertower Theatre, 3923
Weathervane Theatre, 3355
Westport Country Playhouse, 2720
Whittier Junior Theatre, 2642
Wichita Falls Backdoor Players, 4027
Williamstown Theatre Festival, 3184
Wiltern Theatre, 2521
Wilton Playshop, 2721
Woodstock Opera House, 2995
Wwu Summer Stock, 4064
Yale Repertory Theatre, 2699
Yard, 3151
York Theatre Company, 3597
Zachary Scott Theatre Center, 3935

Contemporary & Original New Plays
Phoenix Arts Association Theatre/Westcoast Playwrights Alliance, 2588

Contemporary Works
Playmakers Repertory Company, 3645

Contemporary and classic plays and musicals
the Human Race Theatre Company, 3733

Dance
Afrikan Poetry Theatre, 3449
Fountain Theatre, 2501
Theatre Project, 3118

Dance Series
Whitefish Theatre Company, 3320

Design
Rollins College: Department of Theatre and Dance, 2842

Design (Costume, Lighting, Scene, Sound), Directin
University of California-Irvine: Department of Drama, 2478

Dinner Theater
Actors Cabaret/Mainstage Theatre Company, 3774
Amas Musical Theatre, 3464
Antenna Theater, 2622
Arena Dinner Theatre, 3007
Arkansas Arts Center Children's Theater, 2438
Arkansas Repertory Theatre, 2439
Augusta Arts Council/Augusta Historic Theatre, 3041
Bastrop Opera House, 3936
Black Repertory Group, 2450
Black Spectrum, 3474
Broadway Palm Dinner Theatre, 2778
California State University, Sacramento: Department of Theatre and Dance, 2554
Chaffin's Barn Dinner Theatre, 3912
Chanhassen Dinner Theatre, 3223
Chanute Community Theatre, 3042
Cheyenne Little Theatre Players, 4137
Coffeyville Community Theatre, 3043
Community Theatre of Clay County, 3000
Country Dinner Playhouse, 2673
Derby Dinner Playhouse, 3004
Dolphin Players, 3782
Drury Lane Oakbrook Terrace, 2982
Encore Players, 2974
Florida Atlantic University: Department of Theatre, 2757
Foothill Theatre Company, 2529
Goldenrod Showboat Dinner Theatre, 3308
Hardin County Playhouse, 3058
Impulse Theater, 2661
Iowa Summer Repertory, 3036
Jackson County Community Theatre, 3002
Kaleidoscope Theatre, 2791
Kauai International Theatre, 2890
Lake George Dinner Theatre, 3452
Le Centre Du Silence Mime School, 2646
Lynn Canal Community Players, 2421
Magic Circle Theater, 2550
Marathon Community Theatre, 2795
Marriott's Theatre in Lincolnshire, 2973
Morristown Theatre Guild, 3911
Mountain Playhouse, 3810
Muhlenberg Community Theatre, 3061
Mystery Dinner Playhouse, 4052
New Conservatory Center Theatre, 2586
North Shore Music Theatre, 3134
Orlando Broadway Dinner Theatre, 2806
Orpheum Theatre, 2968
Peninsula Players, 2780

Pioneer Playhouse of Kentucky, 3057
Pocket Sandwich Theatre, 3954
Possum Point Players, 2723
Prairie Players Civic Theatre, 2969
Renaissance Theaterworks, 4128
Side by Side, 3676
Stages St. Louis, 3281
Studio Theatre, 2750
the Round Barn Theatre at Amish Acres, 3019
Theaterworks, 2688
Theatre Albany, 2843
Theatre at Monmouth, 3099
Theatre on The Ridge, 3611
Timbers Dinner Theatre, 3820
Topeka Civic Theatre & Academy, 3049
Towne and Country Players, 3748
University of Colorado at Boulder: Department of Theatre and Dance, 2647
University of Denver Department of Theatre, 2667
University Theatre: Summer Show Biz, 2963
Vaudeville Palace, 2826
Village Players, 3157
Waimea Community Theatre, 2889
Windward Theatre Guild, 2888

Disney Theater
Disney Theatrical Productions, 3482

Drama
Act II Playhouse, 3793
Acting Company of Riverside Theatre, 2836
Actor's Express Theatre, 2848
Actor's Theatre of Charlotte, 3646
Actors Co-Op, 3901
Actors for Themselves, 2492
Actors Forum Theatre, 2530
Actors Theatre of Houston, 3981
Admiral Theatre Foundation, 4065
Adobe Theater, 3397
African American Drama Company, 2572
Ahmanson Theatre, 2493
Alberta Bair Theater, 3313
Allied Theatre Group/Stage West, 3968
American Center for Stanislavski Theatre Art, 3465
Arena Stage, 2732
Ark Theatre Company, 2631
Arrow Rock Lyceum Theatre, 3278
Arundel Barn Playhouse, 3091
Astors Beechwood Mansion, 3858
Auburn University Theatre, 2400
Aurora Theatre Company, 2447
Bainbridge Performing Arts, 4060
Barrow-Civic Theatre, 3804
Bay Street Theatre, 3615
Beck Center for the Cultural Arts, 3739
Belmont Dramatic Club, 3133
Berkeley Repertory Theatre, 2449
Berkshire Theatre Festival, 3176
Black Hills Passion Play, 3888
Blind Parrot Productions, 2911
Bloomsburg Theatre Ensemble, 3796
Bob Jones University Concert, Opera & Drama Series, 3876
Body Politic Theatre, 2912
Brave New Workshop, 3236
Brewery Arts Center, 3336
Bristol Riverside Theatre, 3798
Britt Festivals, 3780
Broadway Theatre, 2408
Broom Street Theater, 4113
Bullshed Theatre Project, 3755
Burning Coal Theatre Company, 3674
Bus Barn Stage Company, 2489
Caldwell Theatre Company, 2756
Cape Fear Regional Theatre, 3655
Cape May Stage, 3361
Catholic University of America: Drama Department, 2733
Celebration Theatre, 2640
Centre Stage-South Carolina, 3877
Changing Scene Theater, 2655
Circle Theatre, 3971
Circuit Playhouse, 3908
City Arts Drama Center, 3659
City Lit Theater Company, 2919
City of Albuquerque Kimo Theatre, 3400
City Theatre Company, 3841
Clinton Area Showboat Theatre, 3030
Colony Theatre Company, 2453
Columbia Theatre/Fanfare, 3079

Columbian Theatre: Museum & Art Center, 3050
Cornerstone Theater Company, 2498
Cumberland Players, 3393
Cyrano's Theatre Company, 2416
Diamond Circle Melodrama, 2668
Dobama Theatre, 3718
Dreiske Performance Company, 2926
East West Players, 2499
Essential Theatre, 2852
Eureka Theatre Company, 2578
Fairfield County Stage Company, 2717
Famous Door Theatre, 2930
Filament Theatre, 2931
Florida Repertory Theatre, 2779
Florida Stage, 2792
Florida Studio Theatre, 2823
Footlight Players, Inc., 3017
Fort Smith Little Theatre, 2436
Found Theatre, 2487
Foundation of Arts, 2437
Freedom Repertory Theatre, 3830
Frontera, 3930
Gablestage, 2766
Gallery Theatre of Oregon, 3779
Geffen Playhouse, 2502
Generic Theater, 4044
Georgia Ensemble Theatre, 2878
Germinal Stage Inc, 2660
Geva Theatre, 3609
Grande Olde Players Theatre Company, 3332
Great American Melodrama and Vaudeville, 2536
Group Repertory Theatre, 2531
Grove Theatre Center, 2454
Hackmatack Playhouse, 3093
Harbor Theatre, 3495
Hawaii Theatre, 2885
Hedgerow Theatre, 3815
Hershey Theatre, 3807
Hill Country Arts Foundation/Point Theatre, 3991
History Making Productions, 3180
Hollywood Complex Theatre, 2505
Hollywood Playhouse, 2783
Holmdel Theatre Company, 3367
Hot City Theatre, 3298
Hudson Theatre, 2474
Huntington Beach Playhouse, 2477
Icehouse Theatre, 2803
Idaho Falls Arts Council Colonial Theater, 2899
Illustrated Stage Company, 2580
Independent Eye, 2623
Institute of Outdoor Drama, 3644
Intiman Theatre Company, 4082
Ironwood Theatre, 3207
Jafrika, 2662
Jam and Company, 3506
Julian Theatre, 2581
Just Us Theater Company, 2857
Karamu House, 3714
Kent County Theatre Guild, 2722
Key West Players, 2788
Kirk Douglas Theatre, 2463
Knutzen Family Theatre - City of Federal Way, 4069
La Jolla Playhouse, 2481
Lakewood Center for the Arts, 3778
Lakewood Theatre, 3107
Lamb's Players Theatre, 2460
Leatherstocking Theatre Company, 3434
Licking County Players, 3746
Lifeline Theatre, 2937
Limelight Theatre, 2827
Little Country Theatre, 3690
Little Theatre of Owatonna, 3263
Live Bait Theatrical Company, 2938
Long Way Home, 4048
Long Wharf Theatre, 2697
Looney's Tavern Productions, 2406
Los Angeles Theatre Center: Moving Arts, 2507
Lost Nation Theater, 4022
Lyon College Theatre Department, 2432
Lyric Stage Company of Boston, 3138
Madison Repertory Theatre, 4115
Magic Circle Theater, 2551
Mainstage Center for the Arts, 3341
Mark Taper Forum, 2509

Specialized Field Index / Theatre

Mary L Welch Theatre, 3856
Maurice Levin Theater Season, 3396
Mayfair Theatre/Shear Madness, 2941
Mcc Theater, 3519
Mccarter Theatre, 3382
Menlo Players Guild, 2524
Merrimack Repertory Theatre, 3160
Metropolitan Playhouse, 3520
Mid-America Arts Alliance, 3288
Montana Repertory Theatre, 3319
Mountain Playhouse, 3810
National Theater Institute, 2715
New Jomandi Productions, 2859
New Phoenix, 3183
New York State Theatre Institute, 3628
Newberry College Theatre, 3881
Northeastern Theatre, 3139
Northern Lights Playhouse, 4112
Northlight Theatre, 2986
Northside Theatre Company, 2600
Ogdensburg Command Performances, 3602
Old Globe, 2565
Olney Theatre Center, 3128
Open Eye Theater, 3454
Open Fist Theatre Company, 2475
Openstage Theatre and Company, 2670
Park Avenue Theatrical Group, 3543
Patriots Theater at the War Memorial, 3390
Pegasus Players, 2942
Penobscot Theatre Company, 3092
Performing Arts Chicago, 2943
Perseverance Theatre, 2419
Peterborough Players, 3351
Phoenix Theatre, 3014
Pirate Playhouse, 2819
Playhouse on The Square, 3910
Playhouse Square Foundation, 3716
Portland Center Stage, 3788
Queens College Summer Theatre, 3440
Red Barn Playhouse, 3214
Red Barn Theatre, 2789
Rep Stage, 3122
Repertory Theatre of Saint Louis, 3302
Ritz Theatre and La Villa Museum, 2785
River Rep Theatre Company, 3558
Riverside Theatre, 3038
Roadside Theater, 4047
Rosebriar Shakespeare Company, 3727
Saenger Theatre, 2409
Saint Vincent Summer Theatre, 3813
Salt and Pepper Mime Company, 3563
Sanford Maine Stage Company, 3109
Saratoga Performing Arts Center, 3619
Seacoast Repertory Theatre, 3353
Seanachai Theatre Company, 2947
Seattle Children's Theatre, 4085
Shadowland Artists, 3438
Sheldon Theatre, 3212
Sierra Repertory Theatre at East Sonora, 2626
Signature Theatre Company, 3567
Silver Spring Stage, 3131
Sioux City Community Theatre, 3037
Sleuths Mystery Dinner Shows, 2808
Snow Camp Historical Drama Society, 3680
Source Theatre Company, 2748
South Park Theatre, 3794
Southern Appalachian Stages, 2881
Speaking of Stories, 2611
Spencers: Theater of Illusion, 4040
Stage West, 3975
Stages Repertory Theatre, 3987
Stageworks, 3444
Stamford Theatre Works, 2707
State Theater Company, 3933
Strawberry Productions, 3150
Strawdog Theatre Company, 2953
Studio Arena Theatre, 3429
Studio Players, 3067
Sundance Institute, 4013
Sunset Playhouse, 4109
Sweet Fanny Adams Theatre & Music Hall, 3897
Synthaxis Theatre Company, 2532
Syracuse Stage, 3627
Tacoma Actors Guild, 4093
Teatro Shalom, 2528
Tecumseh!, 3702
Temple Theatre Company, 3679
Tennessee Repertory Theatre, 3919

Texas International Theatrical Arts Society, 3957
the Actors' Gang Theater, 2462
Theater Coalition/The Lear Theater, 3340
Theater Rhinoceros, 2593
Theater Works, 2425
Theatre Artaud, 2594
Theatre Club of the Palm Beaches, 2794
Theatre Du Grand-Guignol De Paris, 3579
Theatre in The Round, 3256
Theatre on The Square, 3015
Theatre Suburbia, 3989
Theatre Winter Haven, 2839
Theatre-In-The-Works, 2809
Theatrical Outfit, 2867
Thick Description, 2595
Toledo Repertoire Theatre, 3752
Town Players, 3891
Triarts Sharon Playhouse, 2704
Trinity Repertory Company, 3864
Trustus, 3874
University of California-Irvine: Department of Drama, 2478
University Productions: University of Michigan, 3191
Unto These Hills, 3672
Vermont Stage Company, 4019
Vineyard Playhouse, 3177
Vivian Beaumont Theater, 3588
Walker Art Center, 3258
Walnut Street Theatre, 3839
Warehouse Theatre, 3878
Washington Stage Guild, 2753
Waukesha Civic Theatre, 4136
Weathervane Playhouse, 3747
Wellfleet Harbor Actors Theater, 3181
West Coast Ensemble, 2520
West Virginia Public Theatre, 4103
Western Stage, 2558
Weston Playhouse, 4026
Williamstown Theatre Festival, 3184
Wilma Theater, 3840
Wilton Playshop, 2721
Working Theatre Company, 3595
Writers' Theatre Chicago, 2970

Drama, Comedy
Performance Network of Ann Arbor, 3190

Dramaturgy
Rollins College: Department of Theatre and Dance, 2842

Educational
Actors Repertory Theatre, 3338
Actors Studio, 3285
Agnes Scott College: Department of Theatre and Dance, 2871
American Academy of Dramatic Arts/Hollywood, 2472
American Repertory Theatre, 3146
American University Theatre Program, 2731
Andy's Summer Playhouse, 3356
Arena Stage, 2732
Arizona State University Theatre, 2428
Ark Theatre Company, 2631
Arts Midwest, 3235
Asolo Repertory Theatre, 2821
Auburn University Theatre, 2400
Auditorium Theatre of Roosevelt University, 2907
Babcock Season, 4057
Bailiwick Repertory, 2908
Baltimore Actors' Theatre, 3112
Berkeley Repertory Theatre, 2449
Bloomington County Playhouse, 2999
Bob Jones University Concert, Opera & Drama Series, 3876
Broadhollow Players Limited, 3614
Brown University Theatre, 3861
California Repertory Company, 2485
California State Polytechnic University: Department of Theatre and Dance, 2545
California State University, Bakersfield: Theatre Program, 2446
California State University, Dominguez Hills: Department of Theatre, 2456
California State University, Long Beach: Department of Theatre, 2486
California State University, Northridge: Department of Theatre, 2534
California State University, Stanislaus, 2635

California State University-Los Angeles - Players, 2497
Cameron University: Theatre Arts Department, 3758
Cape May Stage, 3361
Center Theater and The Training Center, 2914
Central Connecticut State University: Department of Theatre, 2693
Chicago Dramatists, 2916
City Lit Theater Company, 2919
Civic Theatre & School of Theatre, 3203
Climb Theatre - Creative Learning Ideas, 3265
Connecticut College Department of Theatre, 2701
Connecticut Conservatory of the Performing Arts, 2702
Connecticut Repertory Theatre, 2709
Cornell University Theatre, Film & Dance Department, 3445
Dallas Children's Theater, 3945
Depaul University Merle Reskin Theatre, 2924
Diamond Head Theatre, 2884
Downriver Theatre Company, 3098
Eckerd College Theatre Department, 2825
Edyvean Repertory Theatre, 3012
El Paso Association for the Performing Arts/Viva El Paso!, 3965
Ensemble Espanol Spanish Dance Theater, 2928
Fairfield University: Department of Visual & Performing Arts, 2684
Florida Atlantic University: Department of Theatre, 2757
Florida International University: Department of Theatre and Dance, 2797
Florida Repertory Theatre, 2779
Florida Southern College: Department of Theatre Arts, 2790
Florida State University: School of Theatre, 2828
Fort Lauderdale Children's Theatre, 2776
Freedom Repertory Theatre, 3830
George Washington University: Department of Theatre and Dance, 2740
Georgia Repertory Theatre, 2845
Greenbrier Valley Theatre, 4100
Hilberry Theatre, Wayne State University, 3198
Hilo Community Players, 2883
Honolulu Theatre for Youth, 2886
Hope Summer Repertory Theatre, 3206
Horsefeathers & Applesauce Summer Dinner Theatre, 3053
Howard University Department of Theatre Arts, 2741
Idaho Repertory Theatre Company, 2900
Indiana State University Summer Stage, 3024
Junior Players, 3950
Kennedy Center American College Theatre, 2742
Kids 4 Broadway, 2480
Kidstock Creative Theater Education Center, 3185
Kumu Kahua Theatre, 2887
Leeward Community College Theatre, 2892
Little Theatre of the Rockies, 2672
Loyola Marymount University Theatre Arts Department, 2508
Loyola University Department of Theatre, 2940
Lyon College Theatre Department, 2432
Matthews Playhouse, 3669
Metropolitan State College of Denver: Department of Theatre, 2663
Mills College Department of Dramatic Arts & Communications, 2535
Missouri Repertory Theatre, 3289
Montclair State University, 3391
Mule Barn Theatre of Tarkio College, 3309
Myart, 2488
National Conservatory of Dramatic Arts, 2744
National Theater Institute, 2715
National Theatre Conservatory, 2664
New Orleans Recreation Department Theatre, 3084
New Paltz Summer Repertory Theatre, 3457
New York Theatre Workshop, 3536
Northern Arizona University: Theatre Division, School of Performing Arts, 2422
Northlight Theatre, 2986

Occidental College Department of Theatre, 2512
Ohio State University-Department of Theatre, 3723
Oklahoma Opera & Musical Theater Company, 3763
Old Lyric Repertory Company, 4007
Open Eye Theater, 3454
Organic Theater Company, 2966
Palm Beach Atlantic College: Department of Theatre, 2838
Point Park University's Pittsburgh Playhouse, 3847
Pullman Summer Palace, 4077
Purdue Professional Summer Theatre, 3028
Pushcart Players, 3392
Repertory People of Evansville, 3006
Rogue Music Theatre, 3777
Rollins College: Department of Theatre and Dance, 2842
Sacramento Theatre Company, 2557
Saint Bart's Players, 3562
Saltworks Theatre Company, 3850
San Diego Repertory Theatre, 2568
San Diego State University: Department of Theatre, 2569
San Francisco State University: Department of Theatre Arts, 2589
San Jose Children's Musical Theater, 2601
San Jose State University: Department of Theatre Arts, 2604
Santa Clara University Theatre and Dance Department, 2614
School of Theatre Arts, 2431
Shakespeare & Company, 3273
Shakespeare on The Green, 3335
Shakespeare Orange County, 2537
Sierra Repertory Theatre at East Sonora, 2626
Sonoma State University Theater Department, 2549
Street Theater, 3634
Surfside Players, 2763
Swine Palace Productions, 3078
Theatre at Raritan Valley Community College, 3380
Theatre El Dorado, 2544
Theatre in The Round, 3256
Theatre Previews at Duke, 3652
Theatre West Virginia, 4096
Theatreworks, 2525
Trinity College Theatre and Dance Department, 2689
Two River Theater Company, 3384
University of Alabama, Birmingham: Department of Theatre, 2403
University of Alaska, Anchorage: Department of Theatre and Dance, 2418
University of Alaska, Fairbanks: Theatre Department, 2420
University of California, Davis: Department of Dramatic Art, 2464
University of California-Los Angeles: Department of Theater, 2518
University of California-Santa Barbara: Department of Dramatic Art, 2612
University of Central Florida: Department of Theatre, 2811
University of Connecticut: Department of Dramatic Arts, 2711
University of Hartford: Department of Art History, Cinema, Drama, 2716
University of Laverne, 2483
University of Miami: Department of Theatre Arts, 2768
University of Minnesota Duluth: Department of Theatre, 3226
University of Montevallo: Division of Theatre, 2411
University of Notre Dame Department of Film, Television & Theatre, 3021
University of Rochester Theatre Program, 3612
University of South Alabama, 2410
University of South Florida: School of Theatre, 2834
University of Southern California: School of Theatre, 2519
University of the Pacific: Department of Theatre Arts, 2630

Specialized Field Index / Theatre

University of West Florida, 2813
University Productions: University of Michigan, 3191
Vagabond Acting Troupe, 3818
Village Theatre, 4068
Vsa Arts, 2752
Weathervane Playhouse, 3747
Wesleyan University Theater Department, 2692
West Georgia Theatre Company Summer Classic, 2869
Western Connecticut State University: Theatre Arts Department, 2681
Yale School of Drama, 2700
Young Artists Theatre, 3126

Ensembles
52nd Street Project, 3459
Actors Art Theatre, 2491
American Ensemble Company, 3119
Artists Collective, 2685
Attic / New Center Theatre, 3196
Attic Theatre Centre, 2494
Bilingual Foundation of the Arts, 2495
Black Ensemble Theater, 2909
Bloomsburg Theatre Ensemble, 3796
Carpetbag Theatre, 3903
City Arts Drama Center, 3659
Cornerstone Theater Company, 2498
Dad's Garage Theatre Company, 2851
Delaware Theatre Company, 2727
Dixon Place, 3483
Dreiske Performance Company, 2926
Ensemble Studio Theatre, 3490
Ensemble Theatre of Cincinnati, 3705
Florida Studio Theatre, 2823
Georgia Ensemble Theatre, 2878
Group Repertory Theatre, 2531
Inventions, 2993
Julian Theatre, 2581
Just Us Theater Company, 2857
Kincaid Regional Theatre, 3059
Lorraine Hansberry Theatre, 2582
Magic Theatre, 2583
Magical Theatre Company, 3696
Musical Theatre Works, 2585
Nebraska Repertory Theatre, 3327
New Phoenix, 3183
Nine O'clock Players, 2511
Odyssey Theatre Ensemble, 2513
One Way Puppets, 2777
Open Fist Theatre Company, 2475
Palace Theatre of the Arts, 2706
Pearl Theatre Company, 3545
Performance Riverside, 2547
Persona Grata Productions, 2587
Peterborough Players, 3351
Playwrights' Center, 3252
Pocono Playhouse, 3821
Publick Theatre, 3140
Rattlestick Theatre, 3555
Red Herring Theatre Ensemble, 3726
Saint Sebastian Players, 2946
San Jose Repertory Theatre, 2602
Seanachai Theatre Company, 2947
Sherman Players, 2705
Shoestring Productions Limited, 2728
Smoky Mountain Repertory Theatre, 3639
Source Theatre Company, 2748
Southern Appalachian Repertory Theatre, 3668
Speaking of Stories, 2611
Spokane Interplayers Ensemble, 4092
Stage 3 Theatre Company, 2627
Stop-Gap, 2609
Theatre II Company, 2957
Theatreworks, 2541
Thunder Bay Ensemble, 3584
Thunder Bay Theatre, 3189
Touchstone Theatre, 3795
Vineyard Playhouse, 3177
Wilmington Drama League, 2729
Wilton Playshop, 2721
Women's Theatre Alliance, 2960
Wooster Group, 3594

Ethnic Theater
7 Stages, 2846
Academy of Performing Arts, 3168
Actors' Guild of Lexington, 3064
African American Cultural Centre, 3423

African Continuum Theatre Company (Actco), 2730
Alliance Theatre Company, 2849
Amas Musical Theatre, 3464
American Folklore Theatre, 4110
Antenna Theater, 2622
Arena Players Repertory Theatre Company of Long Island, 3431
Arizona Theatre Company, 2430
Asian American Theater Company, 2575
Augusta Arts Council/Augusta Historic Theatre, 3041
Barrow Group, 3470
Bellevue Little Theatre, 3321
Belmont Playhouse, 3414
Black Repertory Group, 2450
Brava! for Women in The Arts, 2576
Britt Festivals, 3780
Broad Stage, 2619
Broadway Live at the Opera House, 3065
Broadway Palm Dinner Theatre, 2778
Brown Grand Theatre, 3044
California State University, Fresno: Theatre Arts Department, 2468
California State University, Sacramento: Department of Theatre and Dance, 2554
Calumet Theatre Company, 3194
Carpetbag Theatre, 3903
Center Stage, 3113
Children's Theatre of Eden, 3653
Chinese Theatre Works, 3453
Clarence Brown Theatre Company, 3904
Crossroads Theatre Company, 3377
El Teatro Campesino, 2606
Ensemble Espanol Spanish Dance Theater, 2928
Florida Atlantic University: Department of Theatre, 2757
Foothill Theatre Company, 2529
Gala Hispanic Theatre, 2739
Gold Coast Theatre, 2800
Golden Thespians, 2782
Goodman Theatre, 2933
Greek Theatre, 2503
Hardin County Playhouse, 3058
Harwich Junior Theatre, 3182
Horizon Theatre Company, 2856
Humbolt State University: Department of Theatre, Film and Dance, 2445
Impulse Theater, 2661
Irish Classical Theatre Company, 3425
Jet Theatre, 3218
Jewish Theatre of New England, 3165
La Compania De Teatro De Albuquerque, 3401
Laguna Playhouse, 2484
Le Centre Du Silence Mime School, 2646
Lime Kiln Theater, 4038
Lorraine Hansberry Theatre, 2582
Los Angeles Designers' Theatre, 2632
Magic Theatre, 2583
Manhattan Theatre Club, 3517
Maui Academy of Performing Arts, 2893
Mettawee Theatre Company, 3617
Mirror Repertory Company, 3522
Mixed Blood Theatre Company, 3247
Mu Performing Arts, 3248
National Theatre, 2745
New Century Theatre, 3166
New Conservatory Center Theatre, 2586
New Stage Theatre, 3276
Northwestern University Theatre and Interpretation Center, 2965
Odyssey Theatre Ensemble, 2513
Orpheum Theatre, 2968
Out North - Vsa Alaska, 2417
Pangea World Theater, 3250
Penumbra Theatre Company, 3270
Piedmont Players Theatre, 3678
Pillsbury House Theatre, 3251
Piven Theatre Workshop, 2967
Pomona College Department of Theatre and Dance, 2459
Puppet House Theatre, 2708
Puppet Theatre: Dance and Music From Indonesia, 3599
Rainbo Children's Theatre Company, 3271
San Francisco Mime Troupe, 2590
Shadow Box Theatre, 3566
Side by Side, 3676

Smallbeer Theatre Company, 3127
Smoky Mountain Repertory Theatre, 3639
Southern Arkansas University Theatre & Mass Communications Department, 2442
Southern Connecticut State University: Department of Theatre, 2698
Stages St. Louis, 3281
Studio Theatre, 2750
Su Teatro, 2665
Talento Bilingue De Houston, 3988
Tamara and The Shadow Theatre of Java, 3600
Teatro Shalom, 2528
Teatro Vision, 2605
the Round Barn Theatre at Amish Acres, 3019
Theater Emory, 2864
Theaterworks, 2688
Theatre Albany, 2843
Theatre L'homme Dieu, 3220
Theatre Workshop of Owensboro, 3073
Traveling Jewish Theatre, 2596
Ukiah Players Theatre, 2636
University of Arkansas at Fayetteville: Department of Drama, 2435
University of Arkansas at Little Rock: Department of Theatre and Dance, 2441
University of California-Riverside: Department of Theatre, 2548
University of California-San Diego: Department of Theatre and Dance, 2482
University of Colorado at Boulder: Department of Theatre and Dance, 2647
University of Denver Department of Theatre, 2667
University of Florida: School, Theater and Dance, 2781
University Theatre: Summer Show Biz, 2963
Urban Institute for Contemporary Arts, 3204
Vanguard Theatre Ensemble, 2470
Venice Theatre, 2835
Victory Gardens Theater at the Biograph, 2959
Village Players Theater, 2981
Vsa Arts, 2752
Woodstock Opera House, 2995
Yale Repertory Theatre, 2699
Yueh Lung Shadow Theatre, 3448

Experimental
52nd Street Project, 3459
Attic Theatre Centre, 2494
Big Mess Theatre, 3828
Body Politic Theatre, 2912
Changing Scene Theater, 2655
Creation Production Company, 3480
En Garde Arts, 3489
Latin American Theatre Experiment & Associates, 3513
Lightning Strikes Theatre Company, 3514
Mayfair Theatre/Shear Madness, 2941
Openstage Theatre and Company, 2670
Performing Arts Chicago, 2943
Pilgram Theater Research & Performance Collaboration, 3132
Reality Theatre, 3725
Red Eye, 3253
Ridge Theater, 3557
Sundance Institute, 4013
Synthaxis Theatre Company, 2532
Theater for the New City, 3578
Theatreworks, 2525
Undermain Theatre, 3960
Vagabond Acting Troupe, 3818

Film
Whitefish Theatre Company, 3320

Hellenic Drama
Target Margin Theater, 3574

Historical
American Magic-Lantern Theater, 2682
American Theatre, 2906
Astors Beechwood Mansion, 3858
Augusta Arts Council/Augusta Historic Theatre, 3041
Black Hills Passion Play, 3888
Cabbages and Kings, 3944
Cherokee National Historical Society, 3767
City Lit Theater Company, 2919
Columbian Theatre: Museum & Art Center, 3050
Folger Shakespeare Library, 2736
Fort Griffin Fandangle Association, 3924

Great American History Theatre, 3266
History Making Productions, 3180
Interborough Repertory Theater, 3503
Long Way Home, 4048
Lost Nation Theater, 4022
Maritime Productions, 3102
Montana Repertory Theatre, 3319
Old Colony Players, 3681
Patriots Theater at the War Memorial, 3390
Rites and Reason, 3863
Ritz Theatre and La Villa Museum, 2785
Shepherd of the Hills, 3279
Showboat Becky Thatcher, 3743
Tecumseh!, 3702
Texas Panhandle Heritage Foundation, 3940
Unto These Hills, 3672
Veronica's Veil Players, 3851

Improvisation
Commedia Theater Company, 3238
Dad's Garage Theatre Company, 2851
Essential Theatre, 2852
Groundling Theatre, 2504
Imagination Theater, 2935
Performing Arts Chicago, 2943

Interactive Theatre
Reduxion Theatre Company, 3765

International
East-West Fusion Theatre, 2680
Pittsburgh International Children's Theater, 3843
Society Hill Playhouse, 3838

Jazz
Spoleto Festival Usa, 3869

Jewish
Jet Theatre, 3218
Jewish Ensemble Theatre, 3219
Jewish Theatre of New England, 3165
Traveling Jewish Theatre, 2596

Light Theater
Bowen Park Theatre & Opera, 2990
Broadway Live at the Opera House, 3065
Fulton Opera House/Actor's Company of Pennsylvania, 3811
Hershey Theatre, 3807
Lyric Theatre Warehouse, 2613
Matthews Opera House Society, 3889
People's Light and Theatre Company, 3814
Springer Opera House, 2870
Theatre Suburbia, 3989

Live Theatre (Contemporary
Marin Theatre Company, 2526

Marionettes
Theatre West Virginia, 4096

Mask Theater
Imago, the Theatre Mask Ensemble, 3604
in The Heart of the Beast Puppet and Mask Theatre, 3242

Meisner Technique
Acting Studio, 3462

Mime
Catamount Film and Arts Company, 4025
Gold Coast Theatre, 2800
Le Centre Du Silence Mime School, 2646
Salt and Pepper Mime Company, 3563

Mostly Contemporary Plays
Public Theatre, 3097

Movement
Phoenix Arts Association Theatre/Westcoast Playwrights Alliance, 2588

Movement Theater
Actors for Themselves, 2492
Idaho Falls Arts Council Colonial Theater, 2899
Kathy Harty Gray Dance Theatre, 4029
Los Angeles Theatre Center: Moving Arts, 2507
Margolis Brown Theatre Company, 3245
Rajeckas and Intraub - Movement Theatre, 3581

Multi-Cultural
African American Cultural Centre, 3423
Beck Center for the Cultural Arts, 3739
Carpetbag Theatre, 3903
Chinese Theatre Works, 3453
Cornerstone Theater Company, 2498
East-West Fusion Theatre, 2680
Karamu House, 3714
La Compania De Teatro De Albuquerque, 3401
Negro Ensemble Company, 3529

Specialized Field Index / Theatre

New York State Theatre Institute, 3628
Pan Asian Repertory Theatre, 3541
People's Light and Theatre Company, 3814
Ping Chong & Company, 3547
Puerto Rican Traveling Theatre Company, 3553
Puppet Theatre: Dance and Music From Indonesia, 3599
Repertorio Espanol, 3556
Robey Theatre Company, 2515
Roger Furman Theatre, 3560
Soupstone Project, 3569
Talento Bilingue De Houston, 3988
Tamara and The Shadow Theatre of Java, 3600
Teatro Avante, 2767
Teatro Shalom, 2528
Theatre Du Grand-Guignol De Paris, 3579
Unto These Hills, 3672
Yueh Lung Shadow Theatre, 3448

Multi-Media
Astors Beechwood Mansion, 3858
Lakewood Center for the Arts, 3778
Margolis Brown Theatre Company, 3245
Peculiar Works Project, 3546
Red Eye, 3253
Tennessee Players, 3907
Theatre Building Chicago, 2955
Walker Art Center, 3258

Multicultural
South Coast Repertory, 2461

Music
Afrikan Poetry Theatre, 3449
Theatre Project, 3118
Whitefish Theatre Company, 3320

Music Theater
University of California-Irvine: Department of Drama, 2478

Musical
A.D. Players, 3980
Aberdeen Community Theatre, 3883
About Face Theatre, 2903
Academy of Performing Arts, 3168
Act II Playhouse, 3793
Actors Cabaret/Mainstage Theatre Company, 3774
Actors Forum Theatre, 2530
Actors Theatre of Nantucket, 3162
Actors' Guild of Lexington, 3064
Admiral Theatre Foundation, 4065
Ahmanson Theatre, 2493
Al Ringling Theatre Lively Arts Series, 4106
Alberta Bair Theater, 3313
Alden Theatre Series, 4041
Allenberry Resort Inn and Playhouse, 3797
Alliance Theatre Company, 2849
Allied Theatre Group/Stage West, 3967
Amas Musical Theatre, 3464
American Ensemble Company, 3119
American Folklore Theatre, 4110
American Music Theater Festival/Prince Music Theater, 3825
American Theater Company, 2905
Annapolis Summer Garden Theatre, 3110
Antenna Theater, 2622
Aracoma Story, 4101
Arden Theatre Company, 3827
Arena Stage, 2732
Arizona Theatre Company, 2430
Arkansas Arts Center Children's Theater, 2438
Arkansas Repertory Theatre, 2439
Army Entertainment Program, 2882
Arrow Rock Lyceum Theatre, 3278
Art Station Theatre, 2879
Artists Repertory Theatre, 3783
Artists Theatre Association, 2725
Artreach: a Division of the Children's Theatre of Cincinnati, 3703
Arts & Culture Alliance of Greater Knoxville, 3902
Arundel Barn Playhouse, 3091
Attic / New Center Theatre, 3196
Auburn University Theatre, 2400
Auditorium Theatre of Roosevelt University, 2907
Augusta Arts Council/Augusta Historic Theatre, 3041
Aurora Theatre Company, 2447
Austin Musical Theatre, 3928

Bainbridge Performing Arts, 4060
Baltimore Actors' Theatre, 3112
Barn Theatre, 3192
Barrow Group, 3470
Barrow-Civic Theatre, 3804
Barter Theatre - State Theatre of Virginia, 4028
Bastrop Opera House, 3936
Bay City Players, 3193
Bay Street Theatre, 3615
Beasley Performing Arts Coliseum, 4076
Beck Center for the Cultural Arts, 3739
Bellevue Little Theatre, 3321
Berkeley Repertory Theatre, 2449
Berkshire Theatre Festival, 3176
Bermerton Community Theatre, 4066
Berry College Theatre Company, 2802
Bigfork Summer Playhouse, 3312
Black Ensemble Theater, 2909
Black Hills Playhouse, 3886
Black Repertory Group, 2450
Black Spectrum, 3474
Blackfriars Theatre, 3608
Blank Theatre Company, 2473
Blind Parrot Productions, 2911
Blowing Rock Stage Company, 3641
Blue Lake Repertory Theatre, 3217
Boston Children's Theatre, 3135
Brave New Workshop, 3236
Bread and Circus Theatre, 3962
Brecksville Little Theatre, 3698
Brewery Arts Center, 3336
Bristol Riverside Theatre, 3798
Bristol Valley Theater, 3455
Broad Stage, 2619
Broadway Live at the Opera House, 3065
Broadway Palm Dinner Theatre, 2778
Broadway Theatre, 2408
Broadway Tomorrow, 3476
Brooke Hills Playhouse, 4105
Brown Grand Theatre, 3044
Burning Coal Theatre Company, 3674
Bus Barn Stage Company, 2489
Caldwell Theatre Company, 2756
California State University, Fresno: Theatre Arts Department, 2468
California State University, Fullerton: Department of Theatre and Dance, 2469
California State University, Sacramento: Department of Theatre and Dance, 2554
Calumet Theatre Company, 3194
Camille Players, 3939
Cape Cod Melody Tent, 3156
Cape Fear Regional Theatre, 3655
Capitol Theatre Summerstage, 3613
Carolina Theatre of Durham, 3650
Carousel Music Theatre, 3094
Casa Manana Musicals, 3969
Casa Manana Playhouse, 3970
Castillo Theatre, 3477
Catamount Film and Arts Company, 4025
Cedar Point Live Entertainment, 3749
Center Stage, 3113
Central Connecticut State University: Department of Theatre, 2693
Central Piedmont Community Theatre, 3647
Centre Stage-South Carolina, 3877
Chaffin's Barn Dinner Theatre, 3912
Chanhassen Dinner Theatres, 3223
Chanute Community Theatre, 3042
Cheshire Community Theatre, 2679
Cheyenne Little Theatre Players, 4137
Chicago Shakespeare Theater on Navy Pier, 2917
Children's Musical Theater-San Jose, 2598
Children's Theatre Board, 3685
Children's Theatre of Eden, 3653
Chinese Theatre Works, 3453
Chippewa Valley Theatre Guild, 4107
Christian Community Theater, 2465
Cincinnati Playhouse in The Park, 3704
Cinnabar Theater, 2543
Circle Theatre, 2920
Circuit Playhouse, 3908
City Arts Drama Center, 3659
City Lights Theatre Company, 2599
City Lit Theater Company, 2919
Clarence Brown Theatre Company, 3904
Classics on Stage!, 2920
Cleveland Play House, 3711

Clinton Area Showboat Theatre, 3030
Coach House Players, 3451
Coffeyville Community Theatre, 3043
Colony Theatre Company, 2453
Columbia Theatre for the Performing Arts, 4073
Columbia Theatre/Fanfare, 3079
Commonweal Theatre Company, 3232
Community Theatre of Clay County, 3000
Community Theatre of Greensboro, 3660
Company of Fools, 2898
Coney Island Usa, 3419
Country Dinner Playhouse, 2673
Creative Arts Team, 3481
Creede Repertory Theatre, 2651
Cumberland County Playhouse, 3895
Cumberland Players, 3393
Cumberland Theatre, 3123
Cutter Theatre, 4074
Cyrano's Theatre Company, 2416
Dallas Children's Theater, 3945
Darkhorse Theatre, 3913
Dayton Playhouse, 3732
Daytona Playhouse, 2770
Delaware Theatre Company, 2727
Delray Beach Playhouse, 2773
Denver Civic Theatre, 2658
Derby Dinner Playhouse, 3004
Diamond Head Theatre, 2884
Dolphin Players, 3782
Don Quixote Children's Theatre, 3485
Drury Lane Oakbrook Terrace, 2982
Dundalk Community Theatre, 3115
East West Players, 2499
Edison Theatre, 3297
El Paso Association for the Performing Arts/Viva El Paso!, 3965
Elmwood Playhouse, 3601
Enchanted Forest Summer Theatre, 3792
Encore Players, 2974
Ensemble Espanol Spanish Dance Theater, 2928
Eureka Theatre Company, 2578
Everett Theatre, 4067
Fairfield County Stage Company, 2717
Famous Door Theatre, 2930
Fargo-Moorhead Community Theatre, 3689
Fiddlehead Theatre Company, 3167
First Stage Children's Theater, 4120
Flat Rock Playhouse, 3657
Fleetwood Stage, 3458
Florida Atlantic University: Department of Theatre, 2757
Florida Stage, 2792
Florida State University: School of Theatre, 2828
Florissant Civic Center Theater, 3283
Folger Shakespeare Library, 2736
Foothill Theatre Company, 2529
Foothills Theatre Company, 3187
Ford's Theatre Society, 2738
Fort Salem Theatre, 3616
Fort Smith Little Theatre, 2436
Fort Totten Little Theatre, 3693
Fort Wayne Civic Theatre, 3009
Forum Theatre, 3372
Fostoria Footlighters, 3736
Found Theatre, 2487
Foundation of Arts, 2437
Freedom Repertory Theatre, 3830
Frontera, 3930
Fulton Opera House/Actor's Company of Pennsylvania, 3811
Gablestage, 2766
Gallery Theatre of Oregon, 3779
Galveston Outdoor Musicals, 3976
Garland Civic Theatre, 3977
Gateway Playhouse, 3413
Geffen Playhouse, 2502
George Coates Performance Works, 2579
George Street Playhouse, 3378
Georgia Ensemble Theatre, 2878
Gold Coast Theatre, 2800
Golden Thespians, 2782
Goodman Theatre, 2933
Granbury Opera House Theatre, 3979
Grand Opera House, 3035
Great American History Theatre, 3266
Great American Melodrama and Vaudeville, 2536

Greek Theatre, 2503
Green Earth Players, 3233
Green Mountain Guild, 4024
Greenbrier Valley Theatre, 4100
Greensboro Children's Theatre, 3661
Gretna Productions, 3819
Grove Theatre Center, 2454
Guthrie Theater, 3239
Hale Centre Theatre at Harman Hall, 4016
Hampton Playhouse, 3345
Hangar Theatre, 3446
Hardin County Playhouse, 3058
Harlequin Productions, 4075
Harwich Junior Theatre, 3182
Hawaii Theatre, 2885
Hedgerow Theatre, 3815
Hershey Theatre, 3807
Hersheypark Entertainment, 3808
Hickory Community Theatre, 3662
Highland Summer Theatre, 3234
Hill Country Arts Foundation/Point Theatre, 3991
Hip Pocket Theatre, 3973
Hole in The Wall Theatre, 2695
Hollywood Playhouse, 2783
Holmdel Theatre Company, 3367
Horizon Theatre Company, 2856
Humbolt State University: Department of Theatre, Film and Dance, 2445
Huntington Beach Playhouse, 2477
Huntington Theatre, 3697
Icehouse Theatre, 2803
Idaho Falls Arts Council Colonial Theater, 2899
Igloo, the Theatrical Group, 3501
Illusion Theater, 3241
Illustrated Stage Company, 2580
Impulse Theater, 2661
Indian River Theatre of the Performing Arts, 3832
Indiana Repertory Theatre, 3013
Interborough Repertory Theater, 3503
Inventions, 2993
Ironwood Theatre, 3207
Irving Community Theater, 3992
J Howard Wood Theatre, 2820
Jean Cocteau Repertory, 3507
John Drew Theater at Guild Hall, 3437
Junebug Productions, 3082
Junior Theatre, 3032
Kalamazoo Civic Players, 3209
Kaleidoscope Theatre, 2791
Karamu House, 3714
Kathy Harty Gray Dance Theatre, 4029
Kavinoky Theatre, 3426
Kearney Community Theatre, 3325
Key West Players, 2788
Kincaid Regional Theatre, 3059
Kirk Douglas Theatre, 2463
La Jolla Playhouse, 2481
Laguna Playhouse, 2484
Lakewood Center for the Arts, 3778
Lamp-Lite Theater, 3997
Las Mascaras Theatre, 2798
Las Vegas Little Theatre, 3339
Le Centre Du Silence Mime School, 2646
Leeward Community College Theatre, 2892
Lewis & Clark Theatre Company, 3892
Liberty Center, 3306
Licking County Players, 3746
Lime Kiln Theater, 4038
Lincoln Community Playhouse, 3326
Little Country Theatre, 3690
Little Theater of Gastonia, 3658
Little Theatre of Bedford, 2997
Little Theatre of Winston-Salem, 3686
Little Theatre on The Square, 2988
Live Bait Theatrical Company, 2938
Long Wharf Theatre, 2697
Looney's Tavern Productions, 2406
Los Angeles Designers' Theatre, 2632
Lynn Canal Community Players, 2421
Lyric Theatre Warehouse, 2613
Mabel Tainter Memorial Theater, 4118
Mac-Haydn Theatre, 3432
Magic Circle Theater, 2550
Magic Theatre, 2583
Magical Theatre Company, 3696
Maine State Music Theatre, 3095
Manhattan Theatre Club, 3517

1263

Specialized Field Index / Theatre

Mansfield Playhouse, 3741
Marathon Community Theatre, 2795
Mark Taper Forum, 2509
Marriott's Theatre in Lincolnshire, 2973
Martin Community Players, 3683
Mary L Welch Theatre, 3856
Matchbox Children's Theatre, 3221
Matthews Opera House Society, 3889
Matthews Playhouse, 3669
Mcc Theater, 3519
Mccarter Theatre, 3382
Meadow Brook Theatre, 3213
Medora Musical, 3246
Memphis Community Players, 3293
Metropolitan Playhouse, 3520
Metrostage, 4030
Mid-America Arts Alliance, 3288
Milwaukee Public Theatre, 4123
Miracle Theatre Group, 3785
Mirror Repertory Company, 3522
Missoula Children's Theatre, 3318
Montana Shakespeare in The Parks, 3314
Mooresville Community Theatre, 3670
Morristown Theatre Guild, 3911
Mount Baker Theatre, 4063
Mount Washington Valley Theatre Company, 3350
Mountain Playhouse, 3810
Mu Performing Arts, 3248
Muhlenberg Community Theatre, 3061
Music Theatre Associates, 3523
Music Theatre Group at Lenox Arts Center, 3524
Music Theatre Louisville, 3070
Musical Theatre Works, 2585
Myart, 2488
National Theatre, 2745
Nautilus Music-Theater, 3268
Near West Theatre, 3715
New Conservatory Center Theatre, 2586
New Federal Theatre, 3531
New Jomandi Productions, 2859
New Raft Theater Company, 3534
New Repertory Theatre, 3164
New Stage Theatre, 3276
Newark Performing Arts Corporation/Newark Symphony Hall, 3379
Newberry College Theatre, 3881
Next Act Theatre, 4126
Nine O'clock Players, 2511
North Carolina Black Repertory Company, 3687
North Coast Repertory Theatre, 2625
Northern Lights Playhouse, 4112
Northside Theatre Company, 2600
Northwestern University Theatre and Interpretation Center, 2965
Off Broadway Theatre, 4008
Off-Broadway Musical Theatre, 3262
Oklahoma Children's Theatre, 3762
Oklahoma Opera & Musical Theater Company, 3763
Old Creamery Theatre Company, 3029
Old Globe, 2565
Old Lyric Repertory Company, 4007
Old Town Playhouse, 3216
Olney Theatre Center, 3128
Opera House Theatre Company, 3684
Orange Park Community Theatre, 2804
Oregon Fantasy Theatre, 3776
Orlando Broadway Dinner Theatre, 2806
Orpheum Theatre, 2968
Orpheus Theatre, 3603
Ozark Actors Theatre, 3296
Palace Theatre, 3744
Palace Theatre of the Arts, 2706
Palo Alto Children's Theatre, 2539
Pasadena Playhouse, 2542
Paul Bunyan Playhouse, 3222
Peach State Summer Theatre, 2880
Pegasus Theatre, 3953
Peninsula Players, 4111
Penobscot Theatre Company, 3092
Penumbra Theatre Company, 3270
Peoria Players Theatre, 2983
Performance Riverside, 2547
Performing Arts Chicago, 2943
Perry Players, 2877
Perseverance Theatre, 2419
Philadelphia Theatre Company, 3836

Piccadilly Puppets Company, 2872
Piedmont Players Theatre, 3678
Pioneer Playhouse of Kentucky, 3057
Pioneer Theatre Company, 4009
Pittsburgh International Children's Theater, 3843
Pittsburgh Public Theater, 3846
Plantation Theatre Company, 2815
Players Guild of Canton, 3700
Playhouse Square Foundation, 3716
Plays-In-The-Park, 3363
Playwrights Horizons, 3548
Playwrights' Center, 3252
Pocono Playhouse, 3821
Pollard Theatre, 3756
Pomona College Department of Theatre and Dance, 2459
Pompano Players, 2816
Ponca Playhouse, 3766
Portland Center Stage, 3788
Possum Point Players, 2723
Pregones Theater, 3415
Process Studio Theatre, 3550
Proctor's Theatre, 3620
Publick Theatre, 3140
Puerto Rican Traveling Theatre Company, 3553
Purple Rose Theatre Company, 3195
Pushcart Players, 3392
Quality Hill Playhouse, 3290
Rattlestick Theatre, 3555
Reading Community Players, 3852
Red Barn Playhouse, 3214
Red Barn Theatre, 2789
Red Herring Theatre Ensemble, 3726
Redhouse Arts Center, 3626
Richmond Children's Theatre, 3076
Ritz Theatre, 3751
Ritz Theatre and La Villa Museum, 2785
River Rep Theatre Company, 3558
Riverside Center Dinner Theater, 4036
Riverside Theatre, 3038
Rochester Civic Theatre, 3264
Rogue Music Theatre, 3777
Round House Theatre, 3121
Roundabout Theatre Company, 3561
Roxy Theater, 3894
Royal Arts Council, 3310
Ryan Repertory Company at Harry Warren Theatre, 3422
Saddleback College, 2527
Saenger Theatre, 2409
Saint Bart's Players, 3562
Saint Louis Black Repertory Company, 3303
Saint Vincent Summer Theatre, 3813
Salina Community Theatre, 3047
Salt and Pepper Mime Company, 3563
Salt Lake Acting Company, 4012
San Francisco Mime Troupe, 2590
San Jose Children's Musical Theater, 2601
San Pedro Playhouse, 4003
Sandstone Productions, 3403
Sandusky State Theatre, 3750
Sanford Maine Stage Company, 3109
Saratoga Performing Arts Center, 3619
Scarlet Mask Society, 3728
Seacoast Repertory Theatre, 3353
Seattle Repertory Theatre, 4087
Second Stage Theatre, 3565
Seven Angels Theatre, 2713
Shadow Box Theatre, 3566
Shadow Lawn Summer Stage, 3394
Shadowland Artists, 3438
Shawano County Arts Council, 4133
Shawnee Playhouse, 3853
Sheboygan Theatre Company, 4134
Sheldon Theatre, 3212
Sheridan Civic Theatre Guild, 4139
Sherman Players, 2705
Shoestring Productions Limited, 2728
Showboat Becky Thatcher, 3743
Showboat Majestic, 3709
Side by Side, 3676
Signature Theatre Company, 3567
Sikeston Little Theatre, 3307
Sioux City Community Theatre, 3037
Slocum House Theatre Company, 4094
Smallbeer Theatre Company, 3127
Somervell County Expo Center, 3978
Sooner Theatre of Norman, 3760

Source Theatre Company, 2748
South Park Theatre, 3794
Southeast Alabama Community Theatre, 2405
Southern Appalachian Stages, 2881
Southern Connecticut State University: Department of Theatre, 2698
Southwest Repertory Organization, 3966
Spanish Lyric Theatre, 2833
Spanish Theatre Repertory Company, 3570
Spokane Interplayers Ensemble, 4092
Springer Opera House, 2870
Sro Theatre Company, 3730
St. John Theatre, 3088
Stage One: the Louisville Children's Theatre, 3071
Stage West, 3975
Stages St. Louis, 3281
Stamford Theatre Works, 2707
Starlight Musical Theatre, 2571
State Theater Company, 3933
Stephen Foster-Musical, 3054
Sterling Renaissance Festival, 3622
Steve Silver Productions, 2592
Straw Hat Players, 3261
Studio Arena Theatre, 3429
Su Teatro, 2665
Summer Music Theatre, 2975
Summer Repertory Theatre, 2620
Sundance Institute, 4013
Swamp Fox Players, 3875
Sweet Fanny Adams Theatre & Music Hall, 3897
Swift Creek Mill Playhouse, 4035
Syracuse Stage, 3627
Tamara and The Shadow Theatre of Java, 3600
Temple Theatre Company, 3679
Tennessee Repertory Theatre, 3919
Texas International Theatrical Arts Society, 3957
Texas Panhandle Heritage Foundation, 3940
Texas Shakespeare Festival, 3993
Thalia Spanish Theatre, 3624
the Round Barn Theatre at Amish Acres, 3019
Theater Barn, 3456
Theater Coalition/The Lear Theater, 3340
Theater Rhinoceros, 2593
Theaterworks, 2688
Theatre Albany, 2843
Theatre Arlington, 3927
Theatre Artaud, 2594
Theatre Bristol, 3893
Theatre Building Chicago, 2955
Theatre Club of the Palm Beaches, 2794
Theatre De La Jeune Lune, 3255
Theatre Harrisburg, 3806
Theatre in The Park, 3677
Theatre L'homme Dieu, 3220
Theatre on The Ridge, 3611
Theatre on The Square, 3699
Theatre Previews at Duke, 3652
Theatre Three, 3959
Theatre West, 2517
Theatre Winter Haven, 2839
Theatre Workshop of Owensboro, 3073
Theatreworks, 2541
Theatreworks Usa, 3582
Theatrical Outfit, 2867
Theresa Lang Theatre, 3583
Thunder Bay Theatre, 3189
Timber Lake Playhouse, 2977
Timbers Dinner Theatre, 3820
Toledo Repertoire Theatre, 3752
Topeka Civic Theatre & Academy, 3049
Towne and Country Players, 3748
Trilakes Community Theatre, 3280
Troupe America, 3257
Tvi Actors Studio, 3585
Ukiah Players Theatre, 2636
Unicorn Theatre, 3292
University of Arkansas at Fayetteville: Department of Drama, 2435
University of Arkansas at Little Rock: Department of Theatre and Dance, 2441
University of Colorado at Boulder: Department of Theatre and Dance, 2647
University of Denver Department of Theatre, 2667
University of Florida: School, Theater and Dance, 2781

University of Minnesota Duluth: Department of Theatre, 3226
University Theatre: Summer Show Biz, 2963
Upper Darby Summer Stage, 3800
Venice Theatre, 2835
Victory Gardens Theater at the Biograph, 2959
Vigilante Theatre Company, 3316
Village Players, 3157
Village Players Theater, 2981
Village Theatre, 4068
Vincennes University Summer Theatre, 3026
Vineyard Theatre, 3587
Virginia Stage Company, 4046
Vive Les Arts Theatre, 3994
Vivian Beaumont Theater, 3588
Vsa Arts, 2752
Waimea Community Theatre, 2889
Walnut Street Theatre, 3839
Warehouse Theatre, 3878
Washington Stage Guild, 2753
Waterloo Community Playhouse & Black Hawk Childrens Theatre, 3039
Watertower Theatre, 3923
Watertown Lyric Theater Productions, 3632
Waukesha Civic Theatre, 4136
Wayside Theatre, 4042
Weathervane Playhouse, 3747
Weathervane Theatre, 3355
West Coast Ensemble, 2520
West Virginia Public Theatre, 4103
Western Stage, 2558
Weston Playhouse, 4026
Westport Country Playhouse, 2720
Whittier Junior Theatre, 2642
Wichita Falls Backdoor Players, 4027
Williamstown Theatre Festival, 3184
Windward Theatre Guild, 2888
Woodstock Opera House, 2995
Wwu Summer Stock, 4064
York Theatre Company, 3597
Young Actors Theatre, 2829
Zachary Scott Theatre Center, 3935
Musical Theatre
Paper Mill Playhouse, 3373
Tada!, 3572
Young Artists Theatre, 3126
Musicals
Cortland Repertory Theatre, 3435
Geva Theatre, 3609
Musicals)
Marin Theatre Company, 2526
Mystery
Goldenrod Showboat Dinner Theatre, 3308
New American Works
American Theatre, 2906
Society Hill Playhouse, 3838
New Plays
Actors & Playwrights' Initiative, 3208
Adobe Theatre Company, 3398
Asian American Theater Company, 2575
Barnstormers, 3354
Belmont Dramatic Club, 3133
Belmont Playhouse, 3414
Big Mess Theatre, 3828
Black Swan Theater, 3637
Brava! for Women in The Arts, 2576
Bristol Valley Theater, 3455
Broadway Tomorrow, 3476
Brown Summer Theatre, 3860
Bullshed Theatre Project, 3755
Circuit Playhouse, 3908
Columbia Gorge Repertory Theatre, 4095
Dobama Theatre, 3718
Drama Department, 3487
Emerging Artists Theatre Company, 3488
Ensemble Studio Theatre, 3490
Ensemble Theatre of Cincinnati, 3705
Geffen Playhouse, 2502
George Coates Performance Works, 2579
Geva Theatre, 3609
Harlem Artists Development League, 3496
Hollywood Playhouse, 2783
Igloo, the Theatrical Group, 3501
Intar Theatre, 3502
Interact Theatre Company, 3833
J Howard Wood Theatre, 2820
Jafrika, 2662
Kauai International Theatre, 2890
Kavinoky Theatre, 3426

Specialized Field Index / Theatre

Kitchen Theatre Company, 3447
Lightning Strikes Theatre Company, 3514
Mettawee Theatre Company, 3617
Mooresville Community Theatre, 3670
Music Theatre Associates, 3523
Music Theatre Group at Lenox Arts Center, 3524
New Dramatists, 3530
New Jersey Repertory Company, 3369
New Raft Theater Company, 3534
New Theatre, 3301
Offstage Theatre, 4034
Ontological-Hysteric Theater, 3538
Open Stage of Harrisburg, 3805
Pasadena Playhouse, 2542
Peculiar Works Project, 3546
Penguin Repertory Company, 3623
Performing Arts Chicago, 2943
Playwrights Project, 2566
Playwrights Theatre of New Jersey, 3370
Potomac Theatre Project, 4021
Process Studio Theatre, 3550
Quartz Theatre, 3772
Rattlestick Theatre, 3555
Reality Theatre, 3725
Ryan Repertory Company at Harry Warren Theatre, 3422
Saratoga International Theater Institute, 3564
Shadowland Artists, 3438
Shakespeare & Company, 3159
Shakespeare Festival at Tulane, 3086
Sierra Repertory Theatre at East Sonora, 2626
Signature Theatre, 4033
Soho Repertory Theatre, 3568
Soupstone Project, 3569
Sro Theatre Company, 3730
Stages Repertory Theatre, 3987
Stagewrights, 3571
Sundance Institute, 4013
Theater Grottesco, 3201
Theatre on The Square, 3699
Theatre-In-The-Works, 2809
Undermain Theatre, 3960
Vagabond Acting Troupe, 3818
Vineyard Theatre, 3587
Vortex Repertory Company, 3934
Women's Interart Center, 3592
Women's Project & Productions, 3593
Wooster Group, 3594

New Works of Social Importance
Body Politic Theatre, 2912
Climb Theatre - Creative Learning Ideas, 3265
Interact Theatre Company, 3833
Intiman Theatre Company, 4082
Jet Theatre, 3218
Playmakers Repertory Company, 3645
Saltworks Theatre Company, 3850
Syracuse Stage, 3627

New York
South Coast Repertory, 2461

New works of social importance
the Human Race Theatre Company, 3733

Non Musicals
Cortland Repertory Theatre, 3435

Opera
Theatre Project, 3118

Original Work
Dream Theatre Company, 2925

Outdoor Theater
Annapolis Summer Garden Theatre, 3110
Cain Park Theatre, 3717
Cherokee National Historical Society, 3767
El Paso Association for the Performing Arts/Viva El Paso!, 3965
Galveston Outdoor Musicals, 3976
Garden Variety Shakespeare, 2402
Illinois Shakespeare Festival, 2979
Institute of Outdoor Drama, 3644
Long Way Home, 4048
Nashville Shakespeare Festival, 3917
New York Street Theatre Caravan, 3450
Old Colony Players, 3681
Portland Actors Ensemble, 3787
Snow Camp Historical Drama Society, 3680
Somervell County Expo Center, 3978
Tecumseh!, 3702

Performance
Rollins College: Department of Theatre and Dance, 2842

Performing Arts
Theatre Project, 3118
Whitefish Theatre Company, 3320

Poetry
Afrikan Poetry Theatre, 3449

Political Comedy
Actors Theatre of Phoenix, 2426

Psychological
Dream Theatre Company, 2925

Puppet
Aai Productions, 3416
Al Ringling Theatre Lively Arts Series, 4106
Antenna Theater, 2622
Aracoma Story, 4101
Artscenter, 3642
Augusta Arts Council/Augusta Historic Theatre, 3041
Bat Theatre Company, 3471
Bond Street Theatre Coalition, 3475
Brown Grand Theatre, 3044
California Institute of the Arts: School of Theater, 2637
California State University, Sacramento: Department of Theatre and Dance, 2554
Cape Fear Regional Theatre, 3655
Castillo Theatre, 3477
Charlestown Working Theater, 3147
Children's Theatre Board, 3685
Children's Theatre of Eden, 3653
Childsplay, 2429
Chinese Theatre Works, 3453
Circle Theatre, 3202
Creative Arts Team, 3481
Creede Repertory Theatre, 2651
Dallas Children's Theater, 3945
Das Puppenspiel Puppet Theater, 3633
Denver Puppet Theatre, 2659
Diana Wortham Theatre at Pack Place, 3638
Don Quixote Children's Theatre, 3485
Florida Atlantic University: Department of Theatre, 2757
Florissant Civic Center Theater, 3283
Gold Coast Theatre, 2800
Goodman Theatre, 2933
Hangar Theatre, 3446
Hip Pocket Theatre, 3973
Impulse Theatre, 2661
in The Heart of the Beast Puppet and Mask Theatre, 3242
John Drew Theater at Guild Hall, 3437
Le Centre Du Silence Mime School, 2646
Liberty Center, 3306
Lincoln Community Playhouse, 3326
Live Bait Theatrical Company, 2938
Los Angeles Designers' Theatre, 2632
Madcap Productions Puppet Theatre, 3706
Marathon Community Theatre, 2795
Milwaukee Public Theatre, 4123
Mu Performing Arts, 3248
National Theatre, 2745
New Conservatory Center Theatre, 2586
Next Theatre Company, 2964
North Shore Music Theatre, 3134
Northwestern University Theatre and Interpretation Center, 2965
One Way Puppets, 2777
Oregon Fantasy Theatre, 3776
Orlando Broadway Dinner Theatre, 2806
Orpheum Theatre, 2968
Peoria Players Theatre, 2983
Performance Riverside, 2547
Persona Grata Productions, 2587
Piccadilly Puppets Company, 2872
Plan - B Theatre Company, 4010
Pontine Theatre, 3352
Prairie Players Civic Theatre, 2969
Puppet Arts Theatre, 3277
Puppet House Theatre, 2708
Puppet Showplace Theatre, 3144
Puppet Theatre: Dance and Music From Indonesia, 3599
River Arts Repertory, 3412
Rochester Civic Theatre, 3264
San Jose Children's Musical Theater, 2601
Shadow Box Theatre, 3566
Smallbeer Theatre Company, 3127
Southern Connecticut State University: Department of Theatre, 2698
Stages St. Louis, 3281
Theaterworks, 2688
Theatre Albany, 2843
Theatre De La Jeune Lune, 3255
University of Denver Department of Theatre, 2667
University Theatre: Summer Show Biz, 2963
Vigilante Theatre Company, 3316
Vsa Arts, 2752
Woodstock Opera House, 2995
Yale Repertory Theatre, 2699
Yueh Lung Shadow Theatre, 3448

Radio Performances
Independent Eye, 2623
Los Angeles Theatre Works, 2639
Plan - B Theatre Company, 4010

Renaissance
Renaissance Theatre, 3742
Roundabout Theatre Company, 3561
Sterling Renaissance Festival, 3622

Scriptwriting
Phoenix Arts Association Theatre/Westcoast Playwrights Alliance, 2588

Shadow Theater
Shadow Box Theatre, 3566
Shadowlight Productions, 2591
Tamara and The Shadow Theatre of Java, 3600

Shakespeare
Folger Shakespeare Library, 2736
Garden Variety Shakespeare, 2402
Georgia Shakespeare, 2855
Globe of the Great Southwest Theatre, 3998
Houston Shakespeare Festival, 3985
Hudson Valley Shakespeare Festival, 3433
Illinois Shakespeare Festival, 2979
Nashville Shakespeare Festival, 3917
National Shakespeare Company, 3528
Oklahoma Shakespeare in The Park, 3764
Oregon Shakespearean Festival Association, 3771
Pennsylvania Shakespeare Festival, 3799
Portland Actors Ensemble, 3787
Public Theatre, 3552
Reduxion Theatre Company, 3765
Rosebriar Shakespeare Company, 3727
Shakespeare & Company, 3159
Shakespeare Festival at Tulane, 3086
Shakespeare in Delaware Park, 3428
Tennessee Stage Company, 3905

Spanish Language Company
Bilingual Foundation of the Arts, 2495
El Teatro Campesino, 2606
Ensemble Espanol Spanish Dance Theater, 2928
Gala Hispanic Theatre, 2739
Intar Theatre, 3502
La Compania De Teatro De Albuquerque, 3401
Latin American Theatre Experiment & Associates, 3513
Puerto Rican Traveling Theatre Company, 3553
Repertorio Espanol, 3556
Spanish Lyric Theatre, 2833
Spanish Theatre Repertory Company, 3570
Talento Bilingue De Houston, 3988

Specialty Acts
American Magic-Lantern Theater, 2682
Columbian Theatre: Museum & Art Center, 3050
Coney Island Usa, 3419
Folger Shakespeare Library, 2736
Gablestage, 2766
Goldenrod Showboat Dinner Theatre, 3308
Grande Olde Players Theatre Company, 3332
Independent Eye, 2623
La Connection Comedy Theatre, 2624
Maurice Levin Theater Season, 3396
National Theatre of the Deaf, 2687
Sesame Place, 3812
Target Margin Theater, 3574
Vaudeville Palace, 2826
Wiltern Theatre, 2521
Women's Theatre Alliance, 2960

Staged Readings
Abingdon Theatre Company, 3460
Ergo Theatre Company, 3491
Figures of Speech Theatre, 3096
Fort Griffin Fandangle Association, 3924
Hole in The Wall Theatre, 2695
Shawnee Playhouse, 3853

Strawdog Theatre Company, 2953

Stanislavski Technique
American Center for Stanislavski Theatre Art, 3465

Storytelling
Junebug Productions, 3082
Long Way Home, 4048
Mettawee Theatre Company, 3617
Shadowlight Productions, 2591
Speaking of Stories, 2611

Student/Youth Programs
South Coast Repertory, 2461

Studio Productions
Abingdon Theatre Company, 3460

Summer Stock
Acting Up Theatre Company, 3205
Andy's Summer Playhouse, 3356
Barn Theatre, 3192
Bastrop Opera House, 3936
Bigfork Summer Playhouse, 3312
Black Hills Playhouse, 3886
Blowing Rock Stage Company, 3641
Blue Lake Repertory Theatre, 3217
Bread and Circus Theatre, 3962
Brown Summer Theatre, 3860
Cain Park Theatre, 3717
Cape Cod Melody Tent, 3156
Capitol Theatre Summerstage, 3613
Charlestown Working Theater, 3147
Clinton Area Showboat Theatre, 3030
Columbia Gorge Repertory Theatre, 4095
Enchanted Forest Summer Theatre, 3792
Forestburgh Playhouse, 3441
Gooseberry Park Players, 3260
Green Mountain Guild, 4024
Hackmatack Playhouse, 3093
Hampton Playhouse, 3345
Highland Summer Theatre, 3234
Hope Summer Repertory Theatre, 3206
Horsefeathers & Applesauce Summer Dinner Theatre, 3053
Imago, the Theatre Mask Ensemble, 3604
Junior Players, 3950
Lake George Dinner Theatre, 3452
Lakewood Theater, 3107
Las Mascaras Theatre, 2798
Leatherstocking Theatre Company, 3434
Lime Kiln Theater, 4038
Long Way Home, 4048
Mac-Haydn Theatre, 3432
Maine State Music Theatre, 3095
Maurice Levin Theater Season, 3396
Mount Washington Valley Theatre Company, 3350
Municipal Theater Association of Saint Louis, 3300
New Paltz Summer Repertory Theatre, 3457
Opera House Theatre Company, 3684
Orlando Broadway Dinner Theatre, 2806
Ozark Actors Theatre, 3296
Paul Bunyan Playhouse, 3222
Peach State Summer Theatre, 2880
Peninsula Players, 4111
Pioneer Playhouse of Kentucky, 3057
Public Theatre, 3552
Puppet House Theatre, 2708
Queens College Summer Theatre, 3440
Red Barn Playhouse, 3214
River Arts Repertory, 3412
Rochester Broadway Theatre League, 3610
Sandstone Productions, 3403
Shadow Lawn Summer Stage, 3394
Shepherd of the Hills, 3279
Showboat Majestic, 3709
Summer Music Theatre, 2975
Sunset Playhouse, 4109
Teatro Avante, 2767
Thunder Bay Theatre, 3189
Timber Lake Playhouse, 2977
Triarts Sharon Playhouse, 2704
Upper Darby Summer Stage, 3800
Village Players, 3157
Vincennes University Summer Theatre, 3026
Vineyard Playhouse, 3177

Summer Stock Theatre
Cortland Repertory Theatre, 3435

Tech
Rollins College: Department of Theatre and Dance, 2842

Tech Theater

1265

Specialized Field Index / Theatre

California State Polytechnic University: Department of Theatre and Dance, 2545
University of Minnesota Duluth: Department of Theatre, 3226

Theater
Detroit Repertory Theatre, 3197
Roadside Theater, 4047

Theater Cruise
Maritime Productions, 3102

Theater Workshops
Academy Theatre, 2847
Acting Company of Riverside Theatre, 2836
Acting Studio, 3462
Actors & Playwrights' Initiative, 3208
Actors Art Theatre, 2491
Actors Co-Op, 3901
Actors for Themselves, 2492
Actors Forum Theatre, 2530
Actors Repertory Theatre, 3338
Actors Studio, 3285
Actors Theatre of Houston, 3981
Adobe Theatre Company, 3398
Agnes Scott College: Department of Theatre and Dance, 2871
Albuquerque Little Theatre, 3399
American Center for Stanislavski Theatre Art, 3465
American Repertory Theatre, 3146
American University Theatre Program, 2731
Annapolis Summer Garden Theatre, 3110
Arena Stage, 2732
Arizona State University Theatre, 2428
Ark Theatre Company, 2631
Asolo Repertory Theatre, 2821
Attic Theatre Centre, 2494
Austin Musical Theatre, 3928
Avenue Theater, 2654
Babcock Season, 4057
Bailiwick Repertory, 2908
Black Hills Playhouse, 3886
Bloomington County Playhouse, 2999
Bob Jones University Concert, Opera & Drama Series, 3876
Broad Stage, 2619
Brown University Theatre, 3861
California Repertory Company, 2485
California State Polytechnic University: Department of Theatre and Dance, 2545
California State University, Bakersfield: Theatre Program, 2446
California State University, Dominguez Hills: Department of Theatre, 2456
California State University, Long Beach: Department of Theatre, 2486
California State University, Northridge: Department of Theatre, 2534
California State University, Stanislaus, 2635
California State University-Los Angeles - Players, 2497
Cameron University: Theatre Arts Department, 3758
Castle Rock Players, 2650
Center Theater and The Training Center, 2914
Civic Theatre & School of Theatre, 3203
Connecticut College Department of Theatre, 2701
Connecticut Conservatory of the Performing Arts, 2702
Connecticut Repertory Theatre, 2709
Cornell University Theatre, Film & Dance Department, 3445
Creative Arts Theatre and School, 3926
Delray Beach Playhouse, 2773
Depaul University Merle Reskin Theatre, 2924
Downriver Theatre Company, 3098
Eau Claire Children's Theatre, 4108
Eckerd College Theatre Department, 2825
Edyvean Repertory Theatre, 3012
Ergo Theatre Company, 3491
Fairfield University: Department of Visual & Performing Arts, 2684
Flashpoint Studios, 2735
Flat Rock Playhouse, 3657
Florida Atlantic University: Department of Theatre, 2757
Florida International University: Department of Theatre and Dance, 2797
Florida Repertory Theatre, 2779
Florida Southern College: Department of Theatre Arts, 2790
Florida State University: School of Theatre, 2828
Florida Studio Theatre, 2823
Fort Lauderdale Children's Theatre, 2776
Gateway Playhouse, 3413
George Washington University: Department of Theatre and Dance, 2740
Georgia Repertory Theatre, 2845
Germantown Theatre Guild, 3831
Group Repertory Theatre, 2531
Grove Theatre Center, 2454
Hackmatack Playhouse, 3093
Harlem Artists Development League, 3496
Hilberry Theatre, Wayne State University, 3198
Hope Summer Repertory Theatre, 3206
Horsefeathers & Applesauce Summer Dinner Theatre, 3053
Howard University Department of Theatre Arts, 2741
Idaho Repertory Theatre Company, 2900
Imagination Stage, 3120
Indiana State University Summer Stage, 3024
Interact Story Theatre, 3130
Irish Arts Centre Theatre, 3504
J Howard Wood Theatre, 2820
Kennedy Center American College Theatre, 2742
Little Theatre of the Rockies, 2672
Loyola Marymount University Theatre Arts Department, 2508
Loyola University Department of Theatre, 2940
Lyon College Theatre Department, 2432
Metropolitan State College of Denver: Department of Theatre, 2663
Mills College Department of Dramatic Arts & Communications, 2535
Montclair State University, 3391
Mount Vernon Community Children's Theatre, 4031
Mule Barn Theatre of Tarkio College, 3309
National Conservatory of Dramatic Arts, 2744
National Theater Institute, 2715
National Theatre Conservatory, 2664
New Orleans Recreation Department Theatre, 3084
New Paltz Summer Repertory Theatre, 3457
New York Theatre Workshop, 3536
Newberry College Theatre, 3881
Northeastern Theatre, 3139
Northern Arizona University: Theatre Division, School of Performing Arts, 2422
Occidental College Department of Theatre, 2512
Oddfellows Playhouse, 2691
Ohio State University-Department of Theatre, 3723
Old Colony Players, 3681
Organic Theater Company, 2966
Orpheus Theatre, 3603
Palm Beach Atlantic College: Department of Theatre, 2838
Penobscot Theatre Company, 3092
Phoenix Theatre, 3014
Point Park University's Pittsburgh Playhouse, 3847
Potomac Theatre Project, 4021
Pullman Summer Palace, 4077
Purdue Professional Summer Theatre, 3028
Repertory Theatre of Saint Louis, 3302
Sacramento Theatre Company, 2557
Saint Bart's Players, 3562
San Diego Junior Theatre, 2567
San Diego Repertory Theatre, 2568
San Diego State University: Department of Theatre, 2569
San Francisco State University: Department of Theatre Arts, 2589
San Jose State University: Department of Theatre Arts, 2604
Santa Clara University Theatre and Dance Department, 2614
School of Theatre Arts, 2431
Shakespeare on The Green, 3335
Shakespeare Orange County, 2537
Sierra Repertory Theatre at East Sonora, 2626
Sonoma State University Theater Department, 2549
State Theater Company, 3933
Street Theater, 3634
Swine Palace Productions, 3078
Synthaxis Theatre Company, 2532
Tacoma Actors Guild, 4093
Theater Grottesco, 3201
Theatre at Raritan Valley Community College, 3380
Theatre Workshop of Owensboro, 3073
Theatreworks, 2525
Trinity College Theatre and Dance Department, 2689
Trinity Repertory Company, 3864
University of Alabama, Birmingham: Department of Theatre, 2403
University of Alaska, Anchorage: Department of Theatre and Dance, 2418
University of Alaska, Fairbanks: Theatre Department, 2420
University of California, Davis: Department of Dramatic Art, 2464
University of California-Los Angeles: Department of Theater, 2518
University of California-Santa Barbara: Department of Dramatic Art, 2612
University of Central Florida: Department of Theatre, 2811
University at Connecticut: Department of Dramatic Arts, 2711
University of Hartford: Department of Art History, Cinema, Drama, 2716
University of Laverne, 2483
University of Miami: Department of Theatre Arts, 2768
University of Minnesota Duluth: Department of Theatre, 3227
University of Montevallo: Division of Theatre, 2411
University of Notre Dame Department of Film, Television & Theatre, 3021
University of Rochester Theatre Program, 3612
University of South Alabama, 2410
University of South Florida: School of Theatre, 2834
University of Southern California: School of Theatre, 2519
University of the Pacific: Department of Theatre Arts, 2630
University of West Florida, 2813
University Productions: University of Michigan, 3191
Wesleyan University Theater Department, 2692
West Georgia Theatre Company Summer Classic, 2869
Western Connecticut State University: Theatre Arts Department, 2681
Wilma Theater, 3840
Women's Theatre Alliance, 2960
Yale School of Drama, 2700
Young Playwrights, 3598

Theater in the Round
Magic Circle Theater, 2551

Theatre
Fountain Theatre, 2501
Theatre Project, 3118
Whitefish Theatre Company, 3320

Theatre Workshops in Acting
Phoenix Arts Association Theatre/Westcoast Playwrights Alliance, 2588

Theatre for Deaf
Cleveland Signstage Theatre, 3713

Theatre for Young Audiences
South Coast Repertory, 2461

Theatrical
Sleuths Mystery Dinner Shows, 2808

Theatrical Dance
Spoleto Festival Usa, 3869

Thenic Theater
Actors Theatre of Phoenix, 2426

Thought Provoking
Dream Theatre Company, 2925

Touring Company
Acting Up Theatre Company, 3205
American Magic-Lantern Theater, 2682
American Theater Arts for Youth, 3826
Artspower National Touring Theatre, 3374
Broadway Theatre League of Utica, 3630
Das Puppenspiel Puppet Theater, 3633
Disney Theatrical Productions, 3482
En Garde Arts, 3489
Imagination Theater, 2935
Lime Kiln Theater, 4039
Looking Glass Theatre, 3862
Mohawk Players, 3411
National Black Touring Circuit, 3526
National Shakespeare Company, 3528
New Phoenix, 3183
New York Street Theatre Caravan, 3450
Oklahoma Children's Theatre, 3762
Peculiar Works Project, 3546
Piccadilly Puppets Company, 2872
Ping Chong & Company, 3547
Playhouse Square Foundation, 3716
Puerto Rican Traveling Theatre Company, 3553
Pushcart Players, 3392
Rochester Broadway Theatre League, 3610
Saint Vincent Summer Theatre, 3813
Saratoga International Theater Institute, 3564
Swine Palace Productions, 3078
Theatre West Virginia, 4096
Traveling Jewish Theatre, 2596

Women's Theater
Women's Interart Center, 3592
Women's Project & Productions, 3593

World Classics
Geva Theatre, 3609

Young Playwrights
Actors & Playwrights' Initiative, 3208
Artscenter, 3642
Chicago Dramatists, 2916
Dobama Theatre, 3718
Emerging Artists Theatre Company, 3488
J Howard Wood Theatre, 2820
Kumu Kahua Theatre, 2887
New Dramatists, 3530
Omaha Theatre Company for Young People, 3334
Playwrights Project, 2566
Playwrights Theatre of New Jersey, 3370
Playwrights' Center, 3252
Prime Stage, 3848
Quartz Theatre, 3772
Stagewrights, 3571
Sundance Institute, 4013
Theater for the New City, 3578
Working Theatre Company, 3595
Writers' Theatre Chicago, 2970
Young Playwrights, 3598

Youth
Tada!, 3572

Youth Theater
7 Stages, 2846
a Noise Within, 2490
About Face Theatre, 2903
Academy of Performing Arts, 3168
Acting Company, 3461
African American Cultural Centre, 3423
Alliance Theatre Company, 2849
American Conservatory Theatre, 2573
American Family Theater, 3824
Annapolis Summer Garden Theatre, 3110
Antenna Theater, 2622
Arena Players Repertory Theatre Company of Long Island, 3431
Arizona Theatre Company, 2430
Arkansas Arts Center Children's Theater, 2438
Arkansas Repertory Theatre, 2439
Artists' Civic Theatre and Studio, 3080
Artreach: a Division of the Children's Theatre of Cincinnati, 3703
Artscenter, 3642
Artspower National Touring Theatre, 3374
Atlantic Theater Company, 3468
Augusta Arts Council/Augusta Historic Theatre, 3041
Berry College Theatre Company, 2802
Black Repertory Group, 2450
Blank Theatre Company, 2473
Bond Street Theatre Coalition, 3475
Boston Children's Theatre, 3135
Broad Stage, 2619
Broadway Live at the Opera House, 3065
Broadway Palm Dinner Theatre, 2778
Broadway Theatre League of South Bend, 3022

Specialized Field Index / Vocal Music

California Institute of the Arts: School of Theater, 2637
California State University, Fresno: Theatre Arts Department, 2468
California State University, Fullerton: Department of Theatre and Dance, 2469
California State University, Sacramento: Department of Theatre and Dance, 2554
Casa Manana Musicals, 3969
Center Stage, 3113
Children's Theater Company, 3237
Children's Theatre Board, 3685
Childsplay, 2429
Christian Community Theater, 2465
Cinnabar Theater, 2543
Creede Repertory Theatre, 2651
Cumberland Theatre, 3123
Dallas Children's Theater, 3945
Denver Puppet Theatre, 2659
Derby Dinner Playhouse, 3004
Diana Wortham Theatre at Pack Place, 3638
Ensemble Theatre Company of Santa Barbara, 2610
Flashpoint Studios, 2735
Flat Rock Playhouse, 3657
Fleetwood Stage, 3458
Florida Atlantic University: Department of Theatre, 2757
Foothill Theatre Company, 2529
Ford's Theatre Society, 2738
Fort Salem Theatre, 3616
Fort Wayne Civic Theatre, 3009
Free Street Programs, 2932
Geffen Playhouse, 2502
Gold Coast Theatre, 2800
Goodman Theatre, 2933
Green Mountain Guild, 4024
Group at the Strasberg Acting Studio, 2641
Horse Cave Theatre, 3063
Humbolt State University: Department of Theatre, Film and Dance, 2445
Illusion Theater, 3241
Impulse Theater, 2661
Indiana Repertory Theatre, 3013
Interact Story Theatre, 3130
Irondale Ensemble Project, 3505
Jackson Theatre Guild, 3900
Junior Theatre, 3032
Kids on Broadway, 2615
Knutzen Family Theatre - City of Federal Way, 4069
Laguna Playhouse, 2484
Lakewood Theater, 3107
Le Centre Du Silence Mime School, 2646
Lexington Children's Theatre, 3066
Little Theatre on The Square, 2988
Lookingglass Theatre Company, 2939
Lorraine Hansberry Theatre, 2582
Lynn Canal Community Players, 2421
Madcap Productions Puppet Theatre, 3706
Madison Repertory Theatre, 4115
Magic Circle Theater, 2550
Magic Theatre, 2583
Mainstage Center for the Arts, 3341
Make a Circus: Arco Sports, 2584
Marriott's Theatre in Lincolnshire, 2973
Maui Academy of Performing Arts, 2893
Mendocino Theatre Company, 2523
Metro Theater Company, 3299
Mirror Repertory Company, 3522
Missoula Children's Theatre, 3318
Myart, 2488
New Century Theatre, 3166
New Conservatory Center Theatre, 2586
North Carolina Shakespeare Festival, 3665
North Shore Music Theatre, 3134
Northwestern University Theatre and Interpretation Center, 2965
Oddfellows Playhouse, 2691
Old Creamery Theatre Company, 3029
Omaha Theatre Company for Young People, 3334
Open Eye Theater, 3454
Orpheum Theatre, 2968
Out North - Vsa Alaska, 2417
Palo Alto Children's Theatre, 2539
Penobscot Theatre Company, 3092
Peoria Players Theatre, 2983
Performance Network of Ann Arbor, 3190
Piccadilly Puppets Company, 2872
Piedmont Players Theatre, 3678
Pillsbury House Theatre, 3251
Piven Theatre Workshop, 2967
Pontine Theatre, 3352
Prime Stage, 3848
Princeton Rep Company/Princeton Rep Shakespeare Festival, 3383
Public Theatre, 3097
Pushcart Players, 3392
Raven Theatre Company, 2944
Round House Theatre, 3121
Saddleback College, 2527
Saltworks Theatre Company, 3850
San Diego Junior Theatre, 2567
San Francisco Mime Troupe, 2590
San Jose Repertory Theatre, 2602
Seven Angels Theatre, 2713
Six Flags Magic Mountain, 2638
Southern Arkansas University Theatre & Mass Communications Department, 2442
Spencers: Theater of Illusion, 4040
Stage One: the Louisville Children's Theatre, 3071
Stages St. Louis, 3281
Stephen Foster-Musical, 3054
Steve Silver Productions, 2592
Street Theater, 3634
Studio Theatre, 2750
Su Teatro, 2665
Summer Repertory Theatre, 2620
Teatro Vision, 2605
the Round Barn Theatre at Amish Acres, 3019
Theaterworks, 2688
Theatre Albany, 2843
Theatre at Monmouth, 3099
Theatre West, 2517
Theatre Workshop of Owensboro, 3073
Theatreworks Usa, 3582
Timber Lake Playhouse, 2977
Tvi Actors Studio, 3585
Ucf Civic Theatre, 2810
Ukiah Players Theatre, 2636
University of California-San Diego: Department of Theatre and Dance, 2482
University of Colorado at Boulder: Department of Theatre and Dance, 2647
University of Denver Department of Theatre, 2667
University Theatre: Summer Show Biz, 2963
Urban Institute for Contemporary Arts, 3204
Vanguard Theatre Ensemble, 2470
Venice Theatre, 2835
Village Players Theater, 2981
Vsa Arts, 2752
Waterloo Community Playhouse & Black Hawk Childrens Theatre, 3039
Weathervane Theatre, 3355
Westport Country Playhouse, 2720
Whittier Junior Theatre, 2642
Woodstock Opera House, 2995
Yard, 3151
York Theatre Company, 3597
Youtheatre, 3215

Vocal Music

20th Century Operas
Chicago Opera Theater, 2041
a Cappella
Augustana Choir, 2059
Chicago a Cappella, 2038
Sound of the Rockies, 1946
Alternative
Philadelphia Gay Men's Chorus, 2312
Arias
Atlanta Symphony Orchestra Chorus, 2021
Band
Klezmer Conservatory Band, 2110
Barbershop
Sound of the Rockies, 1946
Baroque
Bach Vespers at Holy Trinity, 2217
Chicago Opera Theater, 2041
Early Music New York (Em/Ny), 2226
Music of the Baroque Chorus & Orchestra, 2047
Broadway Musicals
Schenectady Light Opera Company, 2256
Sea Chanters, 2000
Chamber
the Long Beach Chorale and Chamber Orchestra, 1883
Voce Chamber Singers, 2376
Chamber Music
Arkansas Chamber Singers, 1863
Chamber Opera
Houston Chamber Choir, 2352
Summer Fest, 2322
Choral
American Boychoir, 2186
American Opera Music Theater, 2215
Anima Singers, 2054
Arch-Opera House of Sandwich, 2060
Arizona Opera, 1857
Arkansas Chamber Singers, 1863
Aspen Opera Theater Center, 1944
Augusta Opera Association, 2026
Augustana Choir, 2059
Austin Lyric Opera, 2336
Bach Choir of Pittsburgh, 2316
Bach Society Houston, 2351
Bach Vespers at Holy Trinity, 2217
Baltimore Opera Company, 2093
Bel Canto Chorus, 2397
Bella Voce, 2037
Berkshire Lyric Theatre, 2123
Boston Camerata, 2104
Boychoir of Ann Arbor, 2128
Braintree Choral Society, 2109
Brattleboro Music Center, 2369
Canterbury Choral Society, 2219
Canticum Novum Singers, 2220
Carolina Voices, 2261
Cathedral Choral Society, 1982
Cecilia Chorus of New York, 2221
Chamber Singers of the Colorado Springs Chorale, 1948
Charleston Civic Chorus, 2391
Chicago Children's Choir, 2039
Children's Aid Society Chorus, 2224
Children's Opera Theater, 2346
Choral Society of Greensboro, 2265
Cimarron Circuit Opera Company, 2292
Cincinnati Boychoir, 2277
Cleveland Orchestra Chorus, 2279
Colorado Children's Chorale, 1951
Columbus Symphony Chorus, 2282
Connecticut Choral Artists, 1966
Dallas Opera, 2342
Dallas Symphony Chorus, 2343
Des Moines Choral Society, 2071
Fairfield County Chorale, 1962
Gloriae Dei Artes Foundation, 2122
Greensboro Opera Company, 2266
Gulf Coast Opera Theatre, 2155
Handel and Haydn Society, 2106
Handel Choir of Baltimore, 2095
Hawaii Ecumenical Chorale, 2028
Hidden Valley Music Seminar, 1873
Holland Chorale, 2138
Honolulu Children's Opera Chorus, 2030
Houston Chamber Choir, 2352
Houston Masterworks Chorus, 2354
Indianapolis Opera, 2065
Kentucky Opera, 2079
Kitka Women's Vocal Ensemble, 1894
Knoxville Opera Company, 2330
Lindenwood Concerts, 2331
Lira Chamber Chorus, 2044
Lyric Opera of Kansas City, 2160
Maine Music Society, 2087
Master Singers, 2118
Mendelssohn Choir of Pittsburgh, 2317
Mendelssohn Club of Philadelphia, 2310
Millikin University Opera Theatre, 2052
Minnesota Chorale, 2143
Minnetonka Chamber Choir, 2148
Moline Boys Choir, 2056
Mormon Tabernacle Choir, 2363
Music of the Baroque Chorus & Orchestra, 2047
National Lutheran Choir, 2145
Nevada Opera, 2171
New Jersey Association of Verismo Opera, 2181
New Rochelle Opera, 2213
Oakland Youth Chorus, 1896
Oklahoma Opera and Music Theater Company, 2295
Opera Ebony, 2244
Opera Lite, 2135
Opera Omaha, 2169
Opera Theatre of Saint Louis, 2163
Orchestra Seattle & Seattle Chamber Singers, 2385
Orpheus Male Chorus of Phoenix, 1853
Paul Madore Chorale, 2124
Philomusica Choir, 2178
Piedmont Chamber Singers, 2271
Princeton Pro Musica Chorus & Orchestra, 2187
Radcliffe Choral Society, 2112
Regina Opera Company, 2206
Rochester Symphony Orchestra & Chorale, 2152
Saint Louis Symphony Children's Choir, 2164
San Diego Children's Choir, 1906
San Francisco Girls Chorus, 1920
Santa Fe Desert Chorale, 2198
Sarasota Opera Association, 2011
Smith College Glee Club & Choirs, 2121
St Olaf Choir, 2151
Symphony Chorus of New Orleans, 2085
Tar River Choral & Orchestral Society, 2270
Texas A&M University Opera & Performing Arts, 2341
Texas Bach Choir, 2361
Texas Girls' Choir, 2350
the Long Beach Chorale and Chamber Orchestra, 1883
the New York Virtuoso Singers, 2243
Townsend Opera Players, 1890
Utah Chamber Artists, 2368
Valparaiso University Chorale, 2068
Virginia Opera, 2374
Vocal Arts Society, 1993
Vocalessence, 2147
Voce Chamber Singers, 2376
Washington Bach Consort, 1994
Westchester Oratorio Society, 2257
Westminster Choir College, 2188
Windy City Performing Arts, 2051
Zamir Chorale of Boston, 2120
Classical
Academy of Vocal Arts Opera Theatre, 2305
American Opera Music Theater, 2215
Anchorage Opera Company, 1845
Arch-Opera House of Sandwich, 2060
Aspen Opera Theater Center, 1944
Austin Lyric Opera, 2336
Bach Choir of Pittsburgh, 2316
Bach Society Houston, 2351
Baltimore Opera Company, 2093
Bel Canto Chorus, 2397
Bella Voce, 2037
Berkshire-Hudson Valley Festival of Opera, 2203
Birmingham Music Club, 1839
Boston Camerata, 2104
Boychoir of Ann Arbor, 2128
Braintree Choral Society, 2109
Brattleboro Music Center, 2369
Carolina Voices, 2261
Cathedral Choral Society, 1982
Cecilia Chorus of New York, 2221
Chamber Singers of the Colorado Springs Chorale, 1948
Charleston Civic Chorus, 2391
Chautauqua Opera, 2275
Chicago Children's Choir, 2039
Chicago Opera Theater, 2041
Children's Aid Society Chorus, 2224
Choral Society of Greensboro, 2265
Cimarron Circuit Opera Company, 2292
Cincinnati Boychoir, 2277
Colorado Children's Chorale, 1951
Columbus Symphony Chorus, 2282
Comic Opera Guild, 2129
Community Opera, 2193
Connecticut Choral Artists, 1966
Dallas Opera, 2342
Dayton Opera Association, 2284
Early Music New York (Em/Ny), 2226
Fairbanks Choral Society, 1846
Fairfield County Chorale, 1962
Gloriae Dei Artes Foundation, 2122
Grand Youth Chorus, 1979
Gulf Coast Opera Theatre, 2155
Handel and Haydn Society, 2106
Handel Choir of Baltimore, 2095

1267

Specialized Field Index / Vocal Music

Holland Chorale, 2138
Houston Masterworks Chorus, 2354
Indianapolis Opera, 2065
Kentucky Opera, 2079
Kitka Women's Vocal Ensemble, 1894
Knoxville Opera Company, 2330
Lindenwood Concerts, 2331
Lyric Opera of Kansas City, 2160
Maine Music Society, 2087
Master Singers, 2118
Mendelssohn Choir of Pittsburgh, 2317
Mendelssohn Club of Philadelphia, 2310
Millikin University Opera Theatre, 2052
Minnesota Chorale, 2143
Minnetonka Chamber Choir, 2148
Moline Boys Choir, 2056
Nashville Opera Association, 2333
Nevada Opera, 2171
New Jersey Association of Verismo Opera, 2181
New Rochelle Opera, 2213
Oakland Youth Chorus, 1896
Ohio Light Opera, 2290
Opera Birmingham, 1840
Opera Ebony, 2244
Opera Illinois, 2057
Opera Lite, 2135
Opera Omaha, 2169
Opera San Jose, 1929
Opera Theatre of Saint Louis, 2163
Orchestra Seattle & Seattle Chamber Singers, 2385
Orlando Opera, 2007
Philomusica Choir, 2178
Piedmont Chamber Singers, 2271
Portland Opera, 2300
Princeton Pro Musica Chorus & Orchestra, 2187
Radcliffe Choral Society, 2112
Saint Louis Symphony Children's Choir, 2164
Santa Fe Desert Chorale, 2198
Sarasota Opera Association, 2011
Smith College Glee Club & Choirs, 2121
Spanish Lyric Theater, 2015
St Olaf Choir, 2151
Symphony Chorus of New Orleans, 2085
Tar River Choral & Orchestral Society, 2270
Texas A&M University Opera & Performing Arts, 2341
Texas Bach Choir, 2361
Texas Girls' Choir, 2350
the New York Virtuoso Singers, 2243
Townsend Opera Players, 1890
Valparaiso University Chorale, 2068
Virginia Opera, 2374
Vocal Arts Society, 1993
Vocalessence, 2147
Washington Bach Consort, 1994
West Bay Opera, 1899
Westminster Choir College, 2188

Classical for Young Audiences
Grand Youth Chorus, 1979
Opera in The Ozarks at Inspiration Point, 1861
Opera Northeast/Children's Opera Theatre, 2245

Concerts
Conspirare, Craig Hella Johnson & Company of Voices, 2338

Contemporary
American Opera Music Theater, 2215
Arch-Opera House of Sandwich, 2060
Aspen Opera Theater Center, 1944
Baltimore Opera Company, 2093
Bella Voce, 2037
Berkshire-Hudson Valley Festival of Opera, 2203
Birmingham Music Club, 1839
Brattleboro Music Center, 2369
Carolina Voices, 2261
Cathedral Choral Society, 1982
Chamber Singers of the Colorado Springs Chorale, 1948
Charleston Civic Chorus, 2391
Chautauqua Opera, 2252
Chicago Children's Choir, 2039
Children's Aid Society Chorus, 2224
Choral Society of Greensboro, 2265
Claremont Opera House, 2172
Cleveland Orchestra Chorus, 2279

Community Opera, 2193
Connecticut Choral Artists, 1966
Dayton Opera Association, 2284
Fairbanks Choral Society, 1846
Fairfield County Chorale, 1962
Gloriae Dei Artes Foundation, 2122
Holland Chorale, 2138
Indianapolis Opera, 2065
Kentucky Opera, 2079
Kitka Women's Vocal Ensemble, 1894
Master Singers, 2118
Minnetonka Chamber Choir, 2148
Moline Boys Choir, 2056
Nashville Opera Association, 2333
New Jersey Association of Verismo Opera, 2181
Oakland Youth Chorus, 1896
Opera Birmingham, 1840
Opera Ebony, 2244
Opera Omaha, 2169
Opera Theatre of Saint Louis, 2163
Philomusica Choir, 2178
Piedmont Chamber Singers, 2271
Portland Opera, 2300
Radcliffe Choral Society, 2112
Smith College Glee Club & Choirs, 2121
Spanish Lyric Theater, 2015
St Olaf Choir, 2151
Texas A&M University Opera & Performing Arts, 2341
Texas Girls' Choir, 2350
the New York Virtuoso Singers, 2243
Vocalessence, 2147
Westminster Choir College, 2188

Dance
Revels, 2126

Drama & Dance
Early Music New York (Em/Ny), 2226

Early Music
Early Music New York (Em/Ny), 2226

Educational
Broadway Center Stage, 2183
Des Moines Choral Society, 2071
Hidden Valley Music Seminar, 1873
Lyric Opera Theatre Street, 2309
Opera in The Ozarks at Inspiration Point, 1861
San Diego Children's Choir, 1906

English Operetta
San Diego Comic Opera/Lyric Opera San Diego, 1907

Ensemble
Utah Chamber Artists, 2368

Entertainment Chorus
All American Boys Youth Chorus, 1875
Grand Youth Chorus, 1979

Ethnic Music
American Opera Music Theater, 2215
Arch-Opera House of Sandwich, 2060
Aspen Opera Theater Center, 1944
Baltimore Opera Company, 2093
Biotzetik Basque Choir, 2032
Birmingham Music Club, 1839
Boston Camerata, 2104
Carolina Voices, 2261
Chamber Singers of the Colorado Springs Chorale, 1948
Chicago Children's Choir, 2039
Children's Aid Society Chorus, 2224
Choral Society of Greensboro, 2265
Cimarron Circuit Opera Company, 2292
Cincinnati Boychoir, 2277
Colorado Children's Chorale, 1951
Columbus Symphony Chorus, 2282
Dallas Opera, 2342
Dallas Symphony Chorus, 2343
Hawaii Ecumenical Chorale, 2028
Holland Chorale, 2138
Honolulu Children's Opera Chorus, 2030
Indianapolis Opera, 2065
Kentucky Opera, 2079
Kitka Women's Vocal Ensemble, 1894
Klezmer Conservatory Band, 2110
Matapat, 2253
Millikin University Opera Theatre, 2052
Minnesota Chorale, 2143
Minnetonka Chamber Choir, 2148
Moline Boys Choir, 2056
New Jersey Association of Verismo Opera, 2181

Oakland Youth Chorus, 1896
Opera Ebony, 2244
Opera Theatre of Saint Louis, 2163
Philomusica Choir, 2178
Radcliffe Choral Society, 2112
Saint Louis Symphony Children's Choir, 2164
Saint Sava Free Serbian Orthodox Church, 2276
Smith College Glee Club & Choirs, 2121
Spanish Lyric Theater, 2015
St Olaf Choir, 2151
Texas A&M University Opera & Performing Arts, 2341
Westminster Choir College, 2188
Zamir Chorale of Boston, 2120

Folk Music
Biotzetik Basque Choir, 2032
Colorado Children's Chorale, 1951
Dallas Symphony Chorus, 2343
Hawaii Ecumenical Chorale, 2028
Klezmer Conservatory Band, 2110
Matapat, 2253
Saint Sava Free Serbian Orthodox Church, 2276
Wheeler Opera House, 1945

Gilbert and Sullivan
New York Gilbert and Sullivan Players, 2239
Opera a La Carte, 1888
Washington Savoyards, 2097

Grand Opera
Adrian Symphony Orchestra, 2018
Anchorage Opera Company, 1845
Arizona Opera, 1857
Aspen Opera Theater Center, 1944
Atlanta Symphony Orchestra Chorus, 2021
Augusta Opera Association, 2026
Austin Lyric Opera, 2336
Baltimore Opera Company, 2093
Beaumont Civic Opera, 2340
Berkshire-Hudson Valley Festival of Opera, 2203
Chattanooga Symphony and Opera Association, 2329
Chautauqua Opera, 2252
Chicago Children's Choir, 2039
Cimarron Circuit Opera Company, 2292
Cincinnati Opera, 2278
Commonwealth Opera, 2115
Connecticut Opera, 1964
Dallas Opera, 2342
Dayton Opera Association, 2284
Eugene Opera, 2298
Florida State Opera at Florida State University, 2013
Greensboro Opera Company, 2266
Gulf Coast Opera Theatre, 2155
Hawaii Ecumenical Chorale, 2028
Honolulu Children's Opera Chorus, 2030
Houston Grand Opera, 2353
Indianapolis Opera, 2065
Kentucky Opera, 2079
Knoxville Opera Company, 2330
Long Beach Opera, 1882
Lyric Opera of Kansas City, 2160
Master Singers, 2118
Merola Opera Program, 1914
Metro Lyric Opera, 2175
Michigan Opera Theatre, 2134
Millikin University Opera Theatre, 2052
Mississippi Opera, 2156
Mobile Opera, 1842
Nashville Opera Association, 2333
Nevada Opera, 2171
New Jersey Association of Verismo Opera, 2181
New Rochelle Opera, 2213
Oklahoma Opera and Music Theater Company, 2295
Opera Birmingham, 1840
Opera Ebony, 2244
Opera Lite, 2135
Opera Omaha, 2169
Opera San Jose, 1929
Opera Southwest, 2196
Opera Theatre of No Virginia, 2372
Opera Theatre of Saint Louis, 2163
Orlando Opera, 2007
Pala Opera Association, 2249
Philomusica Choir, 2178
Piedmont Opera Theatre, 2272

Pocket Opera, 1915
Portland Opera, 2300
San Francisco Opera Center, 1922
Sarasota Opera Association, 2011
Smith College Glee Club & Choirs, 2121
Sro - a Lyric Theatre Company, 2165
Summer Fest, 2322
Syracuse Opera, 2258
Texas A&M University Opera & Performing Arts, 2341
Townsend Opera Players, 1890
Tulsa Opera, 2297
University of Southern California Thornton Opera, 1889
Utah Festival Opera Company, 2362
Utah Opera Company, 2366
Virginia Opera, 2374
Westminster Choir College, 2188
Wolf Trap Opera Company, 2378

Light Opera
Anchorage Opera Company, 1845
Arch-Opera House of Sandwich, 2060
Arizona Opera, 1857
Aspen Opera Theater Center, 1944
Augusta Opera Association, 2026
Austin Lyric Opera, 2336
Baltimore Opera Company, 2093
Beaumont Civic Opera, 2340
Berkshire Lyric Theatre, 2123
Chattanooga Symphony and Opera Association, 2329
Chautauqua Opera, 2252
Chicago Children's Choir, 2039
Children's Opera Theater, 2346
Cimarron Circuit Opera Company, 2292
College Light Opera Company, 2114
Columbus Symphony Chorus, 2282
Comic Opera Guild, 2129
Community Opera, 2193
Connecticut Opera, 1964
Dallas Opera, 2342
Dallas Symphony Chorus, 2343
Dayton Opera Association, 2284
Diablo Light Opera Company, 1939
Dupage Opera Theater, 2055
Eugene Opera, 2298
Gulf Coast Opera Theatre, 2155
Honolulu Children's Opera Chorus, 2030
Houston Grand Opera, 2353
Indianapolis Opera, 2065
Kentucky Opera, 2079
Knoxville Opera Company, 2330
Light Opera Oklahoma - Look, 2296
Lyric Opera of Kansas City, 2160
Millikin University Opera Theatre, 2052
Mississippi Opera, 2156
Moline Boys Choir, 2056
Nashville Opera Association, 2333
Nevada Opera, 2171
New England Lyric Operetta, 1961
New Jersey Association of Verismo Opera, 2181
New Rochelle Opera, 2213
North Star Opera, 2153
Ohio Light Opera, 2290
Oklahoma Opera and Music Theater Company, 2295
Opera Ebony, 2244
Opera Lite, 2135
Opera New England, 2108
Opera Omaha, 2169
Opera Southwest, 2196
Opera Theatre of No Virginia, 2372
Opera Theatre of Saint Louis, 2163
Orlando Opera, 2007
Philomusica Choir, 2178
Piedmont Opera Theatre, 2272
Pittsburgh Civic Light Opera, 2319
Pocket Opera, 1915
San Francisco Opera Center, 1922
Sarasota Opera Association, 2011
Schenectady Light Opera Company, 2256
Smith College Glee Club & Choirs, 2121
Spanish Lyric Theater, 2015
Sro - a Lyric Theatre Company, 2165
Starlight Musical Theatre, 1910
Syracuse Opera, 2258
Texas A&M University Opera & Performing Arts, 2341
Townsend Opera Players, 1890

Specialized Field Index / Vocal Music

University of Southern California Thornton Opera, 1889
Utah Festival Opera Company, 2362
Utah Opera Company, 2366
Virginia Opera, 2374
Washington Savoyards, 2097
Westminster Choir College, 2188

Lyric Opera
Academy of Vocal Arts Opera Theatre, 2305
Adrian Symphony Orchestra, 2018
American Opera Music Theater, 2215
American-International Lyric Theatre, 2216
Anchorage Opera Company, 1845
Arch-Opera House of Sandwich, 2060
Arizona Opera, 1857
Aspen Opera Theater Center, 1944
Augusta Opera Association, 2026
Austin Lyric Opera, 2336
Baltimore Opera Company, 2093
Berkshire-Hudson Valley Festival of Opera, 2203
Boston Camerata, 2104
Chamber Singers of the Colorado Springs Chorale, 1948
Chattanooga Symphony and Opera Association, 2329
Chautauqua Opera, 2252
Chicago Children's Choir, 2039
Cimarron Circuit Opera Company, 2292
Cincinnati Opera, 2278
Columbus Symphony Chorus, 2282
Commonwealth Opera, 2115
Community Opera, 2193
Dallas Opera, 2342
Dallas Symphony Chorus, 2343
Dayton Opera Association, 2284
Dupage Opera Theater, 2055
Eugene Opera, 2298
Florida State Opera at Florida State University, 2013
Gulf Coast Opera Theatre, 2155
Houston Grand Opera, 2353
Indianapolis Opera, 2065
Kentucky Opera, 2079
Knoxville Opera Company, 2330
Long Beach Opera, 1882
Lyric Opera of Kansas City, 2160
Merola Opera Program, 1914
Millikin University Opera Theatre, 2052
Mississippi Opera, 2156
Nashville Opera Association, 2333
Nevada Opera, 2171
New Jersey Association of Verismo Opera, 2181
New Rochelle Opera, 2213
North Star Opera, 2153
Ohio Light Opera, 2290
Oklahoma Opera and Music Theater Company, 2295
Opera Birmingham, 1840
Opera Ebony, 2244
Opera Lite, 2135
Opera New England, 2108
Opera Omaha, 2169
Opera Southwest, 2196
Opera Theatre of Saint Louis, 2163
Philomusica Choir, 2178
Piedmont Opera Theatre, 2272
Pocket Opera, 1915
San Francisco Opera Center, 1922
Sarasota Opera Association, 2011
Smith College Glee Club & Choirs, 2121
Spanish Lyric Theater, 2015
Sro - a Lyric Theatre Company, 2165
Syracuse Opera, 2258
University of Southern California Thornton Opera, 1889
Virginia Opera, 2374
Westminster Choir College, 2188

Medieval
Early Music New York (Em/Ny), 2226

Men's Chorus
Orpheus Male Chorus of Phoenix, 1853
Philadelphia Gay Men's Chorus, 2312

Multi-Disciplinary
Dorian Music Festivals, 2070

Music
Revels, 2126

Musical Performance
University Musical Society Choral Union, 2130

Musical Theatre
American Opera Music Theater, 2215
American-International Lyric Theatre, 2216
Arch-Opera House of Sandwich, 2060
Aspen Opera Theater Center, 1944
Augusta Opera Association, 2026
Austin Lyric Opera, 2336
Baltimore Opera Company, 2093
Boston Camerata, 2104
Chamber Singers of the Colorado Springs Chorale, 1948
Chautauqua Opera, 2252
Chicago Children's Choir, 2039
College Light Opera Company, 2114
Colorado Children's Chorale, 1951
Columbus Symphony Chorus, 2282
Comic Opera Guild, 2129
Community Opera, 2193
Dallas Opera, 2342
Dayton Opera Association, 2284
Diablo Light Opera Company, 1939
Dorian Music Festivals, 2070
Florida State Opera at Florida State University, 2013
Fulton Opera House, 2303
Gloriae Dei Artes Foundation, 2122
Grand Opera House Season at the Grand, 2027
Greensboro Opera Company, 2266
Gulf Coast Opera Theatre, 2155
Indianapolis Opera, 2065
Jpas Children's Chorus/Youth Chorale, 2083
Kentucky Opera, 2079
Knoxville Opera Company, 2330
Light Opera Oklahoma - Look, 2296
Lyric Opera of Cleveland, 2280
Lyric Opera of Kansas City, 2160
Lyric Opera Theatre Street, 2309
Michigan Opera Theatre, 2134
Millikin University Opera Theatre, 2052
Mississippi Opera, 2156
Moline Boys Choir, 2056
New England Lyric Operetta, 1961
New Jersey Association of Verismo Opera, 2181
New Rochelle Opera, 2213
New York Gilbert and Sullivan Players, 2239
Ohio Light Opera, 2290
Opera a La Carte, 1888
Opera Ebony, 2244
Opera Illinois, 2057
Opera Lite, 2135
Opera Music Theater International, 1990
Opera Omaha, 2169
Opera San Jose, 1929
Opera Theatre of Saint Louis, 2163
Pala Opera Association, 2249
Pella Opera House, 2074
Philomusica Choir, 2178
Pittsburgh Civic Light Opera, 2319
Regina Opera Company, 2206
Sarasota Opera Association, 2011
Smith College Glee Club & Choirs, 2121
Spanish Lyric Theater, 2015
Starlight Musical Theatre, 1910
Summer Fest, 2322
Summer Opera Theatre Company, 1991
Texas A&M University Opera & Performing Arts, 2341
Utah Festival Opera Company, 2362
Vocalessence, 2147
West Bay Opera, 1899
Western Opera Theater, 1928
Westminster Choir College, 2188
Windy City Performing Arts, 2051

Opera
Claremont Opera House, 2172
Cleveland Orchestra Chorus, 2279
Fulton Opera House, 2303
Grand Opera House Season at the Grand, 2027
Grand Youth Chorus, 1979
Jpas Children's Chorus/Youth Chorale, 2083
Lyric Opera of Cleveland, 2280
Oakland Youth Chorus, 1896
Opera a La Carte, 1888
Opera Camerata of Washington, 1989
Opera Illinois, 2057
Opera in The Ozarks at Inspiration Point, 1861
Opera Music Theater International, 1990
Opera Northeast/Children's Opera Theatre, 2245
Paul Madore Chorale, 2124
Pella Opera House, 2074
Regina Opera Company, 2206
San Diego Comic Opera/Lyric Opera San Diego, 1907
Summer Opera Theatre Company, 1991
West Bay Opera, 1899
Western Opera Theater, 1928
Wheeler Opera House, 1945
Wolf Trap Opera Company, 2378

Operetta
Adrian Symphony Orchestra, 2018
Atlanta Symphony Orchestra Chorus, 2021
Beaumont Civic Opera, 2340
Chattanooga Symphony and Opera Association, 2329
Cincinnati Opera, 2278
College Light Opera Company, 2114
Dallas Symphony Chorus, 2343
Diablo Light Opera Company, 1939
Eugene Opera, 2298
Florida State Opera at Florida State University, 2013
Houston Grand Opera, 2353
Indianapolis Opera, 2065
Los Angeles Concert Opera Association, 1871
Lyric Opera of Kansas City, 2160
Metro Lyric Opera, 2175
Michigan Opera Theatre, 2134
Millikin University Opera Theatre, 2052
Mississippi Opera, 2156
Mobile Opera, 1842
New York Gilbert and Sullivan Players, 2239
North Star Opera, 2153
Oklahoma Opera and Music Theater Company, 2295
Opera Camerata of Washington, 1989
Opera Southwest, 2196
Piedmont Opera Theatre, 2272
Pocket Opera, 1915
San Francisco Opera Center, 1922
Sro - a Lyric Theatre Company, 2165
Syracuse Opera, 2258
University of Southern California Thornton Opera, 1889
Utah Festival Opera Company, 2362
Washington Savoyards, 2097

Orchestra
Rochester Symphony Orchestra & Chorale, 2152

Period Instruments
Bach Vespers at Holy Trinity, 2217

Religious
Arch-Opera House of Sandwich, 2060
Baltimore Opera Company, 2093
Bel Canto Chorus, 2397
Bella Voce, 2037
Canterbury Choral Society, 2219
Carolina Voices, 2261
Cathedral Choral Society, 1982
Chamber Singers of the Colorado Springs Chorale, 1948
Chicago Children's Choir, 2039
Choral Society of Greensboro, 2265
Cimarron Circuit Opera Company, 2292
Cincinnati Boychoir, 2277
Connecticut Choral Artists, 1966
Fairbanks Choral Society, 1846
Fairfield County Chorale, 1962
Gloriae Dei Artes Foundation, 2122
Gulf Coast Opera Theatre, 2155
Holland Chorale, 2138
Kentucky Opera, 2079
Lindenwood Concerts, 2331
Maine Music Society, 2087
Master Singers, 2118
Minnetonka Chamber Choir, 2148
Moline Boys Choir, 2056
Mormon Tabernacle Choir, 2363
National Lutheran Choir, 2145
New Jersey Association of Verismo Opera, 2181
New Rochelle Opera, 2213
Opera Ebony, 2244
Opera Lite, 2135
Philomusica Choir, 2178
Radcliffe Choral Society, 2112
Saint Sava Free Serbian Orthodox Church, 2276
Santa Fe Desert Chorale, 2198
Smith College Glee Club & Choirs, 2121
St Olaf Choir, 2151
Symphony Chorus of New Orleans, 2085
Texas Girls' Choir, 2350
the New York Virtuoso Singers, 2243
Valparaiso University Chorale, 2068
Vocalessence, 2147
Westminster Choir College, 2188

Renaissance
Early Music New York (Em/Ny), 2226

Sea Chanteys
Sea Chanters, 2000

Series & Festivals
Conspirare, Craig Hella Johnson & Company of Voices, 2338
University Musical Society Choral Union, 2130

Theatre
Revels, 2126

Theatrical Dance
American International Lyric Theatre, 2214
Broadway Center Stage, 2183

Traditional Choral Music
Canticum Novum Singers, 2220
Chicago a Cappella, 2038
Sea Chanters, 2000
Texas Bach Choir, 2361
Westchester Oratorio Society, 2257

Vocal Music
Conspirare, Craig Hella Johnson & Company of Voices, 2338
Los Angeles Concert Opera Association, 1871

World Music
American International Lyric Theatre, 2214

Youth Chorus
All American Boys Youth Chorus, 1875
American Boychoir, 2186
American Opera Music Theater, 2215
Anima Singers, 2054
Austin Lyric Opera, 2336
Baltimore Opera Company, 2093
Berkshire-Hudson Valley Festival of Opera, 2203
Boychoir of Ann Arbor, 2128
Chicago Children's Choir, 2039
Children's Aid Society Chorus, 2224
Cimarron Circuit Opera Company, 2292
Cincinnati Boychoir, 2277
Colorado Children's Chorale, 1951
Columbus Symphony Chorus, 2282
Dallas Opera, 2342
Greensboro Opera Company, 2266
Gulf Coast Opera Theatre, 2155
Handel Choir of Baltimore, 2095
Jpas Children's Chorus/Youth Chorale, 2083
Kentucky Opera, 2079
Lindenwood Concerts, 2331
Lira Chamber Chorus, 2044
Minnetonka Chamber Choir, 2148
Moline Boys Choir, 2056
New Jersey Association of Verismo Opera, 2181
New Rochelle Opera, 2213
Oakland Youth Chorus, 1896
Opera Birmingham, 1840
Opera in The Ozarks at Inspiration Point, 1861
Opera Lite, 2135
Opera Northeast/Children's Opera Theatre, 2245
Opera Omaha, 2169
Opera Theatre of Saint Louis, 2163
Orlando Opera, 2007
Radcliffe Choral Society, 2112
Saint Louis Symphony Children's Choir, 2164
San Diego Children's Choir, 1906
San Francisco Girls Chorus, 1920
Santa Fe Desert Chorale, 2198
Sarasota Opera Association, 2011
Smith College Glee Club & Choirs, 2121
Summer Fest, 2322
Tar River Choral & Orchestral Society, 2270
Texas A&M University Opera & Performing Arts, 2341
Texas Girls' Choir, 2350
Townsend Opera Players, 1890
Tulsa Opera, 2297
Westminster Choir College, 2188

Geographic Index / Alabama

Alabama

Alabama Ballet, 1
Alabama Dance Theatre, 5
Alabama Shakespeare Festival, 4148
Alabama Shakespeare Festival - Festival Stage, 5915
Alabama Shakespeare Festival - Octagon, 5916
Alabama Symphony Orchestra, 707
Alabama Theatre, 5886
Alys Robinson Stephens Performing Arts Center, 5887
Anniston Museum of Natural History, 5885
Art Association of East Alabama, 4149
Arthur R Outlaw Mobile Convention Center, 5907
Arts Council of Tuscaloosa Fanfare, 4152
Auburn University Montgomery Theatre, 2412
Auburn University Theatre, 2400
B & a Warehouse, 5888
Bama Theatre Performing Arts Center, 5923
Birmingham Children's Theatre, 2401
Birmingham International Center, 4140
Birmingham Music Club, 1839
Birmingham-Jefferson Convention Complex Arena, 5889
Birmingham-Jefferson Convention Complex Concert Hall, 5890
Birmingham-Southern College Theatre, 5891, 5892
Broadway Theatre, 2408
Bryant Denny Stadium, 5924
Chichester Black Box Theatre, 5912
City of Gulf Shores Entertainment Series, 4145
Claudia Crosby Theatre, 5921
Cleve L Abbott Memorial Alumni Stadium, 5932
Coffee County Arts Alliance, 4143
Coleman Coliseum, 5925
Community Actors' Studio Theatre Inc., 2399
Dothan Civic Center, 5899
Frank Moody Music Building, 5926
Gadsden Symphony Orchestra, 709
Gallaway Theatre, 5927
Garden Variety Shakespeare, 2402
Garret Coliseum, 5917
Harrison Theatre, 5893
Huey Recital Hall, 5928
Huntsville Ballet Company, 3
Huntsville Chamber Music Guild, 710
Huntsville Opera Theater, 1841
Huntsville Symphony Orchestra, 711
Huntsville Youth Orchestra, 712
Independent Presbyterian Church-November Organ Recital Series, 4141
Joe L Reed Acadome, 5918
Legion Field Stadium, 5894
Looney's Tavern Productions, 2406
Marian Gallaway Theatre, 5929
Mitchell Center, 5908
Mobile Ballet Inc, 4
Mobile Chamber Music Society, 713
Mobile Civic Center, 5909
Mobile Opera, 1842
Mobile Symphony, 714
Mobile Theatre Guild, 5910
Momix, 7
Montgomery Ballet, 6
Montgomery Symphony Orchestra, 715
Morgan Auditorium, 5930
Oakwood College Arts & Lectures, 4146
Opera Birmingham, 1840
Ozark Civic Center, 5920
Palmer Theatre, 5913
Panoply Arts Festival, 4147
Paul Snow Memorial Stadium, 5905
Pete Mathews Coliseum, 5906
Princess Theatre Center for the Performing Arts, 2404, 5898
Princess Theatre Professional Series, 4142
Red Mountain Chamber Orchestra, 708
Reynolds Studio Theatre, 5914
Saenger Theatre, 2409
Selma Community Concert Association, 4150
Sloss Furnaces National Historic Theater, 5895
Southeast Alabama Community Theatre, 2405
Southeast Alabama Dance Company, 2
The Allen Bales Theatre, 5931
The Leslie Wright Center, 5896
Theatre Tuscaloosa, 2414
Trojan/Adams Center Performing Arts Theatre, 5922
Tulane University Newcomb Department of Music, 5919
Tuscaloosa Symphony Orchestra, 716
Uab Arena, 5897
University of Alabama School of Music Celebrity Series, 4155
University of Alabama, Birmingham: Department of Theatre, 2403
University of Montevallo: Division of Theatre, 2411
University of North Alabama: Department of Music & Theatre, 2407
University of South Alabama, 2410
Usa Saenger Theatre, 5911
Virginia Samford Theatre, 2413
Von Braun Civic Center Arena, 5902
Von Braun Civic Center Concert Hall, 5903
Von Braun Civic Center Exhibit Hall, 5904
Von Braun Civic Center Playhouse, 5901
Wallace Hall Fine Arts Center, 5900
Wc Handy Music Festival, 4144

Alaska

Alaska Center for the Performing Arts, 5934
Alaska Chamber Singers, 1843
Alaska Dance Theatre, 8
Alaskaland Civic Center & Theatre, 5938
Alma Performing Arts Center, 5933
Anchorage Community Theatre, 2415
Anchorage Concert Association, 4156
Anchorage Concert Chorus, 1844
Anchorage Festival of Music, 4157
Anchorage Opera Company, 1845
Anchorage Symphony Orchestra, 717
Anchorage Youth Symphony, 718
Centennial Hall Convention Center, 5942
Charles W Davis Concert Hall, 5939
Chilkat Center for the Arts, 5940
Crosssound, 4160
Cyrano's Theatre Company, 2416
Fairbanks Choral Society, 1846
Fairbanks Concert Association Master Series, 4158
Fairbanks Light Opera Theatre, 1847
Fairbanks Red Hackle Pipe Band, 719
Fairbanks Summer Arts Festival, 4159
Fairbanks Symphony Association, 720
George M Sullivan Sports Arena, 5935
Harrigan Cantenno Hall, 5944
Jocelyn Clark, 722
Juneau Arts & Humanities Council, 4161
Juneau Jazz and Classics, 723
Juneau Lyric Opera, 1849
Juneau Oratorio Choir, 1850
Juneau Symphony, 724
Kenai Peninsula Orchestra, 721
Kodiak Arts Council, 4162, 5943
Lynn Canal Community Players, 2421
Opera Fairbanks, 1848
Opera to Go, 1851
Out North - Vsa Alaska, 2417
Perseverance Theatre, 2419
Pier One Theatre, 5941
Pulse Dance Company, 9
Sitka Summer Music Festival, 4163
Uaa Recital Hall, 5936
University of Alaska, Anchorage: Department of Theatre and Dance, 2418
University of Alaska, Fairbanks: Theatre Department, 2420
Valdez Convention and Civic Center, 5945
Wells Fargo Sports Complex, 5937

Arizona

Actors Theatre of Phoenix, 2426
Ardrey Auditorium, 5949
Arizona Broadway Theatre, 2424
Arizona Early Music Society, 739
Arizona Exposition & State Fair, 4171
Arizona Friends of Chamber Music, 740
Arizona Jazz Festival, 734
Arizona Opera, 1852, 1857
Arizona Stadium, 5995
Arizona State University Public Events, 4177
Arizona State University Theatre, 2428
Arizona Theatre Company, 2430
Arizona Veterans Memorial Coliseum, 5962
Arizona Western College Amphitheatre, 6011
Ashurst Auditorium, 5950
Ballet Arizona, 11
Buena Performing Arts Center, 5982
Celebrity Theatre, 5963
Centennial Hall, 5996
Chamber Music Plus Southwest, 741
Chamber Music Sedona, 733, 4174
Chandler Center for the Arts, 5946
Chandler Symphony Orchestra, 725
Chase Field, 5964
Childsplay, 2429
Civic Orchestra of Tucson, 742
Clifford E White Theatre, 5951
Coconino Center for the Arts, 5952
Cricket Pavilion, 5965
Crossroads Performance Group, 10
Crowder Hall, 5997
Desert Dance Theatre, 12
Desert Foothills Musicfest, 4164
Desert Sun Stadium, 6012
Desert Voices, 1858
Dine College, 5993
Dodge Theatre, 5966
Eastern Arizona College- Community Orchestra, 738
Ethington Auditorium, 5967
Fine Arts Center Auditorium, 5991
Flagstaff Festival of the Arts, 4167
Flagstaff Symphony Orchestra, 726
Fox Tucson Theatre, 5998
Galvin Playhouse, 5985
Gammage Auditorium, 5986
Gcc Performing Arts Center, 5956
Gila Valley Arts Council, 4172
Grand Canyon Music Festival, 4169
Hale Centre Theatre, 2423
Hi Corbett Field, 5999
Holsclaw Recital Hall, 6000
J Lawrence Walk-Up Skydome, 5953
Jobing.Com Arena, 5968
John Paul Theatre, 5977
Lee Little Theatre, 5992
Lowis Auditorium, 5969
Lyceum Theatre, 5987
Marquee Theatre, 5988
Mcc Performing Arts Center, 5957
Mckale Memorial Center, 6001
Mesa Convention Center, 5958
Mesa Convention Center-Mesa Amphitheatre, 5959
Music Recital Hall, 6002
Musicanova, 1856
Northern Arizona University Jazz Madrigal Festival, 4168
Northern Arizona University: Theatre Division, School of Performing Arts, 2422
Old Tucson Studios, 6003
Orpheus Male Chorus of Phoenix, 1853
Pac Auditorium, 5947
Paradise Valley Jazz Party, 4170
Peoria Sports Complex, 5961
Phoenix Bach Choir, 1854
Phoenix Boys Choir, 1855
Phoenix Chamber Music Society, 728
Phoenix Convention Center - Ballrooms, 5970
Phoenix Convention Center - Symphony Hall, 5975
Phoenix Stages, 5971
Phoenix Symphony, 729
Pima Community College for the Arts, 4178
Pinal County Fine Arts Council: Arts in The Desert, 4165
Prescott Fine Arts, 2427
Prism Theatre, 5989
Prochnow Auditorium, 5954
Pvcc Center for the Performing Arts, 5972
Rawhide Pavilion & Rodeo Arena, 5948
Ray Kroc Baseball Complex, 6013
School of Theatre Arts, 2431
Scottsdale Arts Festival, 4173
Scottsdale Center for the Performing Arts, 5979
Scottsdale Community College Performing Arts Center, 5980
Scottsdale Symphony Orchestra, 732
Sedona Cultural Park, 5981
Sedona Jazz on The Rocks, 4175
Sierra Vista Theatre Hall, 5983
Smcc Performing Arts Center, 5973
Smcc Studio Theatre, 5974
Southern Arizona Arts and Cultural Alliance, 4179
Southern Arizona Symphony Orchestra, 743
St. Philip's in The Hills Friends of Music, 4180
Studio Theatre, 5955
Sun Devil Stadium, 5990
Sundome Center, 5984
Symphony of the Southwest, 727
Temple of Music & Art, 6004
The Arizona Repertory Singers, 1859
The Tucson Jazz Soceity, 745
Theater Works, 2425
Theatre Outback, 5960
Tubac Center of the Arts, 5994
Tucson Arizona Boys Chorus, 1860
Tucson Chamber Orchestra, 744
Tucson Convention Center - Arena, 6005
Tucson Convention Center - Exhibition Hall, 6006
Tucson Convention Center - Leo Rich Theatre, 6007
Tucson Convention Center - Music Hall, 6008
Tucson Electric Park, 6009
Tucson Philharmonia Youth Orchestra, 746
Tucson Symphony Orchestra, 747
Tucson Winter Chamber Music Festival, 748, 4181
U S Airways Center, 5976
Ua Presents, 4182
Uapresents Centennial Hall, 6010
University Chamber Orchestra, 736
University Symphony Orchestra, 737
Verde Valley Concert Association, 4166
West Valley Arts Council, 4176
West Valley Symphony, 735
Yavapai College Performance Hall, 5978
Yavapai Symphony Association, 730
Yuma Ballet Theatre & Performing Arts Company, 13
Yuma Civic Center, 6014

Arkansas

Arkansas Arts Center Children's Theater, 2438
Arkansas Chamber Singers, 1863
Arkansas Repertory Theatre, 2439
Arkansas River Valley Arts Center, 6047
Arkansas Shakespeare Theatre, 2433
Arkansas State Music Programs, 749
Arkansas Symphony Orchestra, 755
Arts and Science Center for Southeast Arkansas, 6042
Arts Center of the Ozarks, 6050
Artspree, 4191
Ballet Arkansas, Inc., 15
Breedlove Auditorium Westark Community College, 6027
Bud Walton Arena, 6024
Carlson Center, 6023
Centre Stage, 6018
Conway Symphony Orchestra, 750
Delta Symphony Orchestra, 1862
Donald W. Reynolds Auditorium, 6019
El Dorado Municipal Auditorium, 6021
Fort Smith Convention Center, 6028
Fort Smith Little Theatre, 2436, 6029
Fort Smith Symphony, 754
Forum, 6032
Foundation of Arts, 2437, 6033
Four Seasons Orchestra, 1865
Fowler Center at Arkansas State University, 4190
Fowler Center at Arkansas University, 6034
Golden Lion Stadium, 6043
Grand Prairie Festival of the Arts, 4194
Haislip Arena Theatre, 6035
Harding University Concert & Lyceum Series, 4192
Hestand Stadium, 6044
Hot Springs Convention Summit Center, 6031
Hot Springs Music Festival Chamber Orchestra, 4189
Inspiration Point Fine Arts Colony, 4186
John Brown University Lyceum Concert Series, 4193

1271

Geographic Index / California

John E Tucker Coliseum, 6048
Jones Performing Arts Center, 6015
Kay Rogers Park, 6030
Lyon College Theatre Department, 2432
North Arkansas Symphony Society, 752
Opera in The Ozarks at Inspiration Point, 1861
Opera in The Rock, 1864
Ouachita Baptist University Harvey & Bernice Jones Performing Arts Center, 6016
Ouachita Baptist University: Artists Series, 4183
Pine Bluff Convention Center Arena, 6046
Pine Bluff Convention Center Auditorium, 6045
Pine Bluff Symphony Orchestra, 756
Ray Winder Field, 6036
Ritz Civic Center, 6037
Robinson Center Music Hall, 6038
Rogers Little Theater, 2444
Season of Entertainment, 4187
South Arkansas Arts Center, 6022
South Arkansas Symphony, 751
Southern Arkansas University Theatre & Mass Communications Department, 2442
Stella Boyle Smith Concert Hall, 6025
Studio Theatre, 6020
Symphony of Northwest Arkansas, 753
The Convocation Center, 6051
The Foundation of Arts, 14
The Rialto Theatre, 6052
The Weekend Theater, 2440
Twin Lakes Playhouse, 2443
University of Arkansas at Fayetteville: Department of Drama, 2435
University of Arkansas at Little Rock: Department of Theatre and Dance, 2441
University of Central Arkansas Public Appearances, 4185
University of Central Arkansas Theatre Program, 2434
Verser Theater, 6017
Walton Arts and Ideas, 4184
Walton Arts Center, 6026
War Memorial Stadium, 6039
Warfield Concerts, 4188
Wildwood Park for the Performing Arts, 6040
Wilkins Stadium, 6041
Witherspoon Arts Arena, 6049

California

A Noise Within, 2490
Abhinaya Dance Company, 98
Actors Art Theatre, 2491
Actors for Themselves, 2492
Actors Forum Theatre, 2530
Actors Repertory Theatre at Santa Monica Playhouse, 2618
Aeolian Ballet Theatre, 36
African American Art and Culture Complex, 6249
African American Drama Company, 2572
Ahmanson Theatre, 2493
Aia Actor's Studio, 6077
Aisha Ali Dance Company, 37
Alameda Civic Ballet, 16
Albert Mcneil Jubilee Singers of Los Angeles, 1881
Alcazar Theatre, 6250
Alex Theatre, 6115
Alhambra Performing Arts, 4196
All American Boys Youth Chorus, 1875
Allan Hancock College Dance Program, 108
Alonzo King Lines Ballet, 71
American Academy of Dramatic Arts/Hollywood, 2472
American Bach Soloist, 1911
American Conservatory Theatre, 2573
American Indian Dance Theatre, 2574
American Philharmonic - Sonoma County, 1877
American Youth Symphony, 801
Anaheim Ballet, 20
Anaheim Convention Center - Arena, 6054
Angeles Chorale, 1943
Angels Gate Cultural Center, 6275
Annenberg Auditorium, 6304
Annenberg Theater, 6203
Antenna Theatre, 2622
Apu Theater, 6063
Arco Arena, 6228
Arden Playhouse, 6229

Ark Theatre Company, 2631
Arlington Center for the Performing Arts, 6279
Arts for the Schools, 4339
Arts Performance Lab, 6221
Asia America Symphony Orchestra, 833
Asian American Theater Company, 2575
At&T Park, 6251
Athenaeum Music & Arts Library, 6136
Attic Theatre Centre, 2494
Auburn Symphony, 1866
Aurora Theatre Company, 2447
Axis Dance Company, 51
B Street Theater, 2552
Backhausdance, 55
Bakersfield Symphony Orchestra, 757
Balboa Park Recital Hall, 6236
Balboa Park Starlight Theater, 6237
Balboa Performing Arts Theater, 6193
Ballet Folclorico Do Brasil, 72
Ballet San Jose, 99
Banafsheh Sayyad and Namah, 110
Barbara K & W Turrentine Jackson Hall, 6094
Barn Theatre, 6222
Bayview Opera House, 6252
Beach Cities Symphony Association, 830
Bear Valley Music Festival, 4201
Benjiman Ide Wheeler Auditorium, 6066
Berkeley Ballet Theater, 24
Berkeley Community Chorus and Orchestra, 1867
Berkeley Community Theatre, 2448, 6067
Berkeley Festival & Exhibition, 4203
Berkeley Opera, 1868
Berkeley Repertory Theatre, 2449
Berkeley Symphony Orchestra, 758
Berkeley Youth Orchestra, 814
Beverly Hills Playhouse, 6073
Big Bear Lake Performing Arts Center, 6075
Bilingual Foundation of the Arts, 2495
Bill Graham Civic Auditorium, 6253
Bing Concert Hall, 6305
Bing Theatre, 6154
Biola University, 6145
Black Repertory Group, 2450
Blank Theatre Company, 2473
Bob Baker Marionette Theatre, 2496
Brava! for Women in The Arts, 2576
Bren Events Center, 6132
Brenda Angiel Aerial Dance Company, 73
Brentwood-Westwood Symphony Orchestra, 875
Broad Stage, 2619
Broadway San Diego, 2559
Bulldogs Stadium, 6104
Bus Barn Stage Company, 2489
Cabrillo Crocker Theater, 6056
Cabrillo Festival of Contemporary Music, 4327
Cafe Del Rey Moro, 6238
Cal Poly Arts Presents & Great Performances, 4317
Cal Poly State University Performing Arts Center, 6273
California Ballet Company, 65
California Center for the Arts-Escondido, 6101
California Chamber Orchestra & Chamber Opera, 1869
California E.A.R. Unit, 772
California Institute of Music, 4272
California Institute of Technology Performing Arts Center, 6207
California Institute of the Arts: School of Theater, 2637
California Lutheran University Music Series, 4340, 4341
California Musical Theatre, 2553
California Philharmonic Orchestra, 865
California Polytechnic University Theatre, 6211
California Repertory Company, 2485
California Riverside Ballet, 61
California Shakespeare Theater, 2538, 4204
California State Polytechnic University: Department of Theatre and Dance, 2545
California State Summer School for the Arts, 4282
California State University East Bay, 4223
California State University Stanislaus Performing Arts Center, 6317
California State University, Bakersfield: Theatre Program, 2446

California State University, Dominguez Hills: Department of Theatre, 2456
California State University, Fresno: Theatre Arts Department, 2468
California State University, Fullerton: Department of Theatre and Dance, 2469
California State University, Long Beach: Department of Theatre, 2486
California State University, Northridge: Department of Theatre, 2534
California State University, Sacramento: Department of Theatre and Dance, 2554
California State University, Stanislaus, 2635
California State University-Hayward - Main Theatre, 6118
California State University-Los Angeles - Players, 2497
California Symphony, 889
California Theatre Company, 2633
California Theatre of Performing Arts, 6234
California Youth Symphony, 820
Caltech Public Events Series, 4267
Camellia Symphony Orchestra, 835
Cameratas Singers of Monterey County, 1904
Campbell Recital Hall, 6306
Cantabile Youth Singers, 1891
Cantori Domino, 1938
Canyon Industries, 4265
Capistrano Valley Symphony, 779
Capital Stage Company, 2555
Capitol Opera Sacramento, 1878
Carmel Bach Festival, 766, 4211
Carmel Music Society, 4212
Carmel Valley Library Concert Series, 4273
Carolina Lugo's & Carole Acuna's Ballet Flamenco & Dance Center, 27
Carson-Dominguez Hills Symphony, 771
Casa Italiana Opera Company, 1872
Catalina Island Jazztrax Festival, 4266
Celebration Theatre, 2640, 6155
Celebrity Presentations, 4232
Center for the Visual and Performing Arts, 4258
Centerarts, 6057
Centerstage, Osher Marin Jewish Community Center, 4321
Central California Ballet, 17
Central West Ballet, 47
Cerritos Center for the Performing Arts, 6079
Chabot College Performing Arts Center, 6119
Chamber Music in Napa Valley, 838, 4286
Chamber Music Masters, 4293
Chamber Music Monterey Bay, 767
Chamber Orchestra of the South Bay, 834
Chanticleer, 1912
Chapman University Symphony Orchestra & Chamber Orchestra, 817
Chico Performances, 2458
Children's Musical Theater-San Jose, 2598
China Dance School & Theatre, 74
Chitresh Das Dance Company, 75
Chookasian Armenian Concert Ensemble, 31, 784
Christian Community Theater, 2465
Chronos Theatre Group, 2560
Cinnabar Theater, 2543
Citrus College Haugh Performing Arts Center, 4221
City Ballet San Diego, 66
City Lights Theatre Company, 2599
City of Los Angeles Cultural Affairs Department, 4236
Civic Dance Company, 67
Claire Trevor School of the Arts, 6133, 6135
Claremont Symphony Orchestra, 773
Clarita & the Arte Flamenco Dance Theatre, 19
Clark Center for the Perorming Arts, 6062
Coleman Chamber Concerts, 4268
Coleman Chamber Music Association, 822
College of Marin, 795
College of the Siskiyous Performing Arts Series, 4347
College of the Siskiyous Theatre, 6320
Colony Theatre Company, 2453
Community Arts and Music Association of Santa Barbara-Cama, 4322
Community Music Center, 6254
Concerts West, 4330
Conejo Pops Orchestra, 884

Conejo Recreation & Park District Summer Concert Series, 4342
Conservatory of Music, 880
Coors Amphitheatre, 6123
Cornerstone Theater Company, 2498
Corona Symphony Orchestra, 1874
Corpus Acrobatic Theatre, 4294
Coussoulis Arena, 6233
Cow Palace, 6255
Cowell Theater, 6256
Cox Arena at Aztec Bowl, 6239
Crash, Burn and Die Dance Company, 21
Crocker Art Museum Ballroom, 6230
Csun Youth Orchestras, 813
Cuesta College Performing Arts, 4318
Culver City Symphony Orchestra, 777
Curran Theatre, 6257
Curtis Theatre, 6076
Cygnet Theatre, 2561
Cypress Pops Orchestra, 778
Dance Brigade, 76
Dance Studio 3, 6137
Dance Studio Theatre, 6223
Dance Through Time, 77
Dancers' Group, 78
Dancing Cat Productions, Inc, 106
Danza Floricanto/Usa, 56
Del Norte Association for Cultural Awareness, 4215
Del Valle Fine Arts Concert Series, 4235
Dell'arte International School of Physical Theatre, 2452
Desert Symphony, 819
Diablo Ballet, 117
Diablo Light Opera Company, 1939
Diablo Symphony Association, 775
Diavolo, 39
Dimensions Dance Theater, 52
Dinkelspiel Auditorium, 6307
Dixieland Monterey, 4254
Dodger Stadium, 6156
Dominican College Auditorium, 6277
Don Powell Theatre, 6240
Donna Sternberg & Dancers, 109
Dore Theatre/Madigan Gallery, 6065
Downey Symphony Orchestra, 781
Dr. Schaffer and Mr. Stern Dance Ensemble, 107
Dragon Productions, 2546
Early Music in Marin, 4205
East County Performing Arts Center - Theatre, 6099
East Gymnasium, 6058
East West Music and Dance, 858
East West Players, 2499
Echo Theater Company, 2500
Eclectic Orange Festival, 4229
Edison International Field of Anaheim, 6055
El Camino College Center for the Arts, 6315
El Camino Youth Symphony, 821
El Portal Theatre, 6194
El Teatro Campesino, 2606
El Teatro De La Esperanza, 2577
Ellen Porter Hall, 6280
Ensemble Theatre Company of Santa Barbara, 2610
Eureka Theatre Company, 2578
Experimental Theater, 6291
Experimental Theatre, 6241
Fairfield City Arts, 4218
Fallon House Theatre, 6303
Family Caregiver Alliance, 4246
Faye Spanos Concert and Recital Halls, 6310
Fclo Music Theatre, 6113
Ferndale Repertory Theatre, 2467
Fess Parker Studio Theatre, 6289
Festival Mozaic, 4319
Festival of New American Music, 4283
Festival Opera, 1940
Finest Asian Performing Arts, 4284
Flint Center for the Performing Arts, 6093
Florence Gould Theatre, 6258
Fontana Performing Arts Center, 6102
Foothill Theatre Company, 2529
Ford Amphitheatre, 6157
Found Theatre, 2487
Fountain Theatre, 2501
Four Seasons Concerts, 4206

Geographic Index

Francisco Martinez Dance Theatre, 115
Fremont Symphony Orchestra, 783
Fresno Convention & Entertainment Center, 6105
Fresno Philharmonic, 785
Friends of Chamber Music, 881
Fujitsu-Concord Jazz Festival, 4213
Fulkerson Recital Hall, 6059
Fullerton Civic Light Opera, 1880
Fullerton Friends of Music, 4220
Galbraith Hall Studio Theatre 157, 6138
Gallo Center for the Arts, 6187
Garrison Theatre, 6085
Gary Soren Smith Center for the Fine and Performing Arts, 6103
Gay Men's Chorus of Los Angeles, 1942
Geffen Playhouse, 2502
George Coates Performance Works, 2579
Getty Center, 6158
Glendale Centre Theatre, 2471
Glendale Symphony Orchestra Association, 789
Glendale Youth Orchestra, 790
Glenn Wallichs Theatre, 6215
Golden Gate International Children's Choral Festival, 4270
Golden Gate Men's Chorus, 1913
Golden Gate Opera, 1934
Golden Gate Theatre, 6259
Golden West College Mainstage Theatre, 6131
Grace Cathedral Concerts, 4295
Grand Performances, 4237
Great American Melodrama and Vaudeville, 2536
Great Western Forum, 6192
Greek Theatre, 2503, 6159
Grounding Point Dance Company, 46
Groundling Theatre, 2504
Group at the Strasberg Acting Studio, 2641
Group Repertory Theatre, 2531
Grove Theatre Center, 2454
Hallberg Theatre, 6110
Harder Stadium, 6281
Harlen Adams Theatre, 6080
Harmonia Baroque Players, 894
Harriet & Charles Luckman Fine Arts Complex, 6160
Harriet and Charles Luckman Fine Arts Complex, 6161
Hatlen Theatre, 6282
Haugh Performing Arts Center, 6116
Healdsburg Jazz Festival, 4224
Heidi Duckler Dance Theatre, 38
Helen Schoeni Theater, 6186
Henry J Kaiser Convention Center, 6196
Herbest Theatre, 6260
Hidden Valley Music Seminar, 1873
Hollywood Bowl, 6124
Hollywood Bowl Orchestra, 792
Hollywood Bowl Summer Festival, 4227
Hollywood Complex Theatres, 2505, 6125
Hollywood Palladium, 6126
Horton Grand Theatre, 2562
Hp Pavilion at San Jose, 6268
Hudson Theatre, 2474
Hughes Stadium, 4285
Humbolt State University: Department of Theatre, Film and Dance, 2445
Huntington Beach Playhouse, 2477
Iai Presentations, 4271
Idyllwild Arts-Academy & Summer Program, 4228
Illustrated Stage Company, 2580
Imperial Valley Symphony, 782
Independent Eye, 2623
Indian Wells Valley Concert Association, 4280
Inland Pacific Ballet, 48, 49
International Concerts Exchange, 4208
International Institute of Music Festival, 4274
Interplayce, 54
Intimate Theatre, 6162
Irina Dvorovenko, 4296
Irvine Barclay Theatre, 6134
James R Armstrong Theatre, 6316
Janlyn Dance Company, 28
Japanese American Cultural & Community Center, 6163
Japanese American Cultural and Community Center, 40

Jazz at Drew Legacy Music & Cultural Marketplace, 4238
Jazz on The Lake: People Productions, 4277
Jazz Tap Ensemble, 41
Joe Goode Performance Group, 79
John Anson Ford Theatres, 6127
John Chookasian International Folk Ensemble, 786
John Van Duzer Theatre, 6060
Jose Greco II Flamenco Dance Company, 80
Julia Morgan Center for the Arts, 6068
Julian Theatre, 2581
Kate Buchanan Room, 6061
Keck Theatre, 6164
Kelsonarts Performances, 4195
Keshet Chaim Dance Ensemble, 111
Kids 4 Broadway, 2480
Kids on Broadway, 2615
Kirk Douglas Theatre, 2463
Kitka Women's Vocal Ensemble, 1894
Kodak Theatre, 6128
Kronos Quartet, 846
Kularts, 81
Kuumbwa Jazz Center, 6292
L'ermitage Foundation Stage, 6165
La Connection Comedy Theatre, 2624
La Danserie, 26
La Jolla Music Society, 796
La Jolla Music Society Summerfest, 4233
La Jolla Playhouse, 2481
La Jolla Symphony & Chorus, 797
La Marca American Variety Chorus Singers, 1937
La Mirada Theatre for the Performing Arts, 6146
La Pena Cultural Center, 6069
Lacma Monday Evening Concerts, 4241
Laguna Playhouse, 2484, 6147
Lamb's Players Theatre, 2460
Lambda Players, 2556
Landcaster Performing Arts Center, 6148
Larry Wismer Theatre, 6081
Laxson Auditorium, 6082
Light Opera Theatre of Sacramento, 1900
Lily Cai Chinese Dance Company, 82, 97
Lipinsky Family San Diego Jewish Arts Festival, 4287
Lively Arts Foundation, 4219
Livermore Amador Symphony, 798
Lmu Guitar Concert & Masterclass Series, 4239
Lobero Theatre Foundation, 6283
Long Beach Convention and Entertainment Center, 6149
Long Beach Opera, 1882
Long Beach Playhouse, 6150
Long Beach Symphony Orchestra, 799
Long Theatre, 6311
Loren L Zachary Society for the Performing Arts, 763
Lorraine Hansberry Theatre, 2582
Los Angeles Bach Festival, 802, 4240
Los Angeles Ballet, 42
Los Angeles Chamber Orchestra, 803
Los Angeles Chamber Singers & Cappella, 1884
Los Angeles Children's Chorus, 1885
Los Angeles Choreographers and Dancers - Zapped Taps, 45
Los Angeles Concert Opera Association, 1871
Los Angeles County Museum of Art, 6166
Los Angeles Designers' Theatre, 2632
Los Angeles Doctors Symphony Orchestra, 804
Los Angeles Master Chorale, 1886
Los Angeles Memorial Coliseum & Sports Arena, 6167
Los Angeles Opera, 1887
Los Angeles Performing Arts Theatres, 6168
Los Angeles Philharmonic Association, 805
Los Angeles Tennis Center, 6169
Los Angeles Theatre Center: Moving Arts, 2507
Los Angeles Theatre Works, 2639
Los Robles Master Chorale, 1935
Louis B. Mayer Theatre, 6290
Loyola Marymount University Theatre Arts Department, 2508
Lula Washington Dance Theatre, 43
Lyceum Theatres Complex, 6242
Lyric Theatre Warehouse, 2613
Mabel Shaw Bridges Auditorium, 6086
Magic Circle Theater, 62, 2550, 2551

Magic Theatre, 2583
Mainly Mozart, 840
Mainly Mozart Festival, 4288
Mainstage Theater, 6293
Make a Circus: Arco Sports, 2584
Malashock Dance, 68
Mammoth Lakes Jazz Jubilee, 4249
Mandell Weiss Forum, 6140
Mandell Weiss Forum Studio, 6139
Mandell Weiss Theatre, 6141
Mandeville Theatre, 6142
Margaret Jenkins Dance Company, 83
Marie Hitchcock Puppet Theatre in Balboa, 2563
Marin Ballet/Center for Dance, 103
Marin Center Showcase Theatre, 6278
Marin Shakespeare Company, 2608
Marin Symphony Orchestra, 866
Marin Symphony Youth Orchestra, 867
Marin Theatre Company, 2526
Mark Foehringer Dance Project, 84
Mark Taper Forum, 2509, 6170
Martin Massman Theatre, 6171
Mass Ensemble, 4248
Massenkoff Russian Folk Festival, 4297
Master Chorale of Orange County, 1876
Masters of Harmony, 1932
Mateel Community Center, 6219
Maxim Belotserkovsky, 4298
Mcafee Coliseum, 6197
Mccallum Theatre for the Performing Arts, 6202
Memorial Auditorium, 6308
Mendocino Ballet, 114
Mendocino Music Festival, 4251
Mendocino Theatre Company, 2523
Meng Concert Hall, 6111
Menlo Players Guild, 2524
Merola Opera Program, 1914
Merton Wray Theatre, 6321
Midsummer Mozart Festival, 847, 4299
Mill Valley Chamber Music Society, 809
Mills College Concert Hall, 6198
Mills College Department of Dramatic Arts & Communications, 2535
Mills College Music Department, 4260
Modesto Junior College Performing Arts Center, 6188
Modesto Symphony Orchestra, 810
Monterey Bay Symphony, 768
Monterey Jazz Festival, 4255
Monterey Symphony, 769
Montgomery Theatre, 6269
Moonlight Amphitheatre, 6319
Morgan-Wixson Theatre, 6300
Morrison Artist Series, 4300
Mount Saint Mary's College - the Da Camera Society, 4242
Mount San Antonio College Performing Arts Center, 4346
Mountain View Center for the Performing Arts, 6190
Mountain Winery, 4334
Mozart Classical Orchestra, 776, 793
Multi-Cultural Music and Art Foundation of Northridge (Mcmafn), 4259
Municipal Art Gallery Theater, 6172
Music Academy of the West, 869
Music Academy of the West Festival, 4323
Music at Kohl Mansion, 4210
Music Center of Los Angeles County, 4243
Music Center Recital Hall, 6294
Music Center/ Performing Arts Center of Los Angeles County, 6173
Music Guild, 4244
Music in The Mountains, 4257
Music in The Vineyards, 811, 4256
Music Theater of Santa Barbara, 6284
Musica Angelica, 1933
Musical America, 1893
Musical Theatre Works, 2585
Myart, 2488
Mystery Cafe, 2564
Nancy Karp & Dancers, 85
Napa Valley Opera House, 6191
Napa Valley Symphony, 895
National Song and Dance Company of Mozambique, 4301
New Century Chamber Orchestra, 848
New Conservatory Center Theatre, 2586

New West Symphony Association, 885
Nine O'clock Players, 2511
Nob Hill Masonic Center, 6261
Noontime Concerts-San Francisco's Musical Lunch Break, 4302
Norris Center for the Performing Arts, 6227
North Coast Repertory Theatre, 2625
North Orange County Community Concerts Association, 4198
Northside Theatre Company, 2600
Notre Dame De Namur Ralston Concert Series, 4202
Nova Vista Symphony, 883
Oakland Ballet, 53
Oakland East Bay Symphony, 815
Oakland Opera Theater, 1895
Oakland Youth Chorus, 1896
Oakland Youth Orchestra, 816
Oakmont Concert Series, 4331
Occidental College Artist Series, 4245
Occidental College Department of Theatre, 2512
Odc Theater, 86
Odc Theatre, 6262
Odyssey Theatre Ensemble, 2513
Ojai Music Festival, 4262
Ojai Shakespeare Festival, 4263
Old First Concerts, 4303
Old Globe, 2565
Old Pasadena Jazz Festival - Jazzfest West, 4197
Omni Foundation for the Performing Arts, 4304
Open Fist Theatre Company, 2475
Opera a La Carte, 1888
Opera San Jose, 1929
Opera Santa Barbara, 1931
Orange Coast College Community Education, 4214
Orange County Youth Symphony Orchestra, 818
Orchestra Nova (San Diego), 1905
Oroville Concert Association, 4264
Oroville State Theater, 6200
Orpheum Theatre, 6263
Other Minds Music Festival, 4305
Oxnard Civic Auditorium, 6201
Pacific Boychoir Academy, 1897
Pacific Chamber Symphony, 812
Pacific Chorale, 1930
Pacific Conservatory of the Performing Arts, 6299
Pacific Repertory Theatre/Carmel Shakespeare Festival, 2455
Pacific Symphony, 868
Pacific Union College Fine Arts Series, 4200
Palace of Fine Arts Theatre, 6264
Palm Springs Convention Center, 6204
Palo Alto Children's Theatre, 2539
Palo Alto Players, 2540
Paradise Performing Arts Center, 6206
Paramount Theatre, 6199
Pasadena Civic Auditorium, 6208
Pasadena Civic Ballet, Inc., 57
Pasadena Conservatory of Music, 823
Pasadena Dance Theatre, 58
Pasadena Playhouse, 2542
Pasadena Playhouse - Mainstage Theatre, 6209
Pasadena Pops Orchestra, 824
Pasadena Symphony, 825
Paul Dresher Ensemble, 849
Pauley Pavilion, 6167
Pcpa Theaterfest, 2617
Peninsula Ballet Theatre, 100
Peninsula Symphony Orchestra, 800
Pepperdine University Orchestra, 808
Pepperdine University Smothers Theatre, 6185
Performance Riverside, 2547
Performing Arts Presentations, 4281
Performing Arts Theatre, 6285
Persona Grata Productions, 2587
Perspective Dance Theatre/Reno Ballet, 101
Petaluma City Ballet, 59
Philharmonia Baroque Orchestra, 850
Philharmonic Society of Orange County, 794
Philip Lorenz Memorial Keyboard Concerts, 787
Phoenix Arts Association Theatre/Westcoast Playwrights Alliance, 2588
Pickwick Players, 2621
Pico Rivera Sports Arena, 6322
Pine Hills Lodge and Dinner Theatre, 2479

1273

Geographic Index

Placer Theatre Ballet, 22
Playboy Jazz Festival, 4209
Playwrights Project, 2566
Playwrights' Arena, 2514
Plaza Del Sol Performance Hall, 6195
Plaza Grand Performances, 6175
Pocket Opera, 1915
Point Loma Nazarene University Cultural Events Series, 4289
Pomona College Department of Theatre and Dance, 2459
Pomona College Orchestra, 774
Poway Center for the Performing Arts, 6212
Prado at Balboa Park, 6243
Preus-Brandt Forum, 6313
Professional Ballet School, 23
Project Artaud, 93
Qualcomm Stadium, 6244
Rabobank Arena, Theater and Convention Center, 6064
Ramona Bowl Amphitheatre, 4225, 6122
Ramona Hillside Players, 4226
Ratcliffe Stadium, 6106
Redding Civic Auditorium, 6213
Redlands Bowl Amphitheatre, 6216
Redlands Bowl Summer Music Festival, 4276
Redlands Community Music Association, 6217
Redlands Symphony Association, 829
Redondo Beach Performing Arts Center, 6218
Redwood Art Council, 4261
Redwood Coast Dixieland Jazz Festival, 4217
Redwood Concert Ballet, 30
Redwood Symphony, 831
Regina Klenjoski Dance Company, 34
Rhapsody in Taps, 35
Ricardo Montalban Theater, 6129
Richard & Karen Carpenter Performing Arts Center, 6151
Richard and Karen Carpenter Performing Arts Center, 6152
Richmond Memorial Convention Center, 6220
Rio Hondo Symphony Association, 891
Rivercity Jazz Festival, 4275
Riverside Convention Center, 6224
Riverside County Philharmonic, 832
Riverside Municipal Auditorium, 6225
Robert & Margrit Mondavi Center for the Performing Arts, 6095
Robert C Smithwick Theatre, 6153
Robert Friedman Presents, 88
Robey Theatre Company, 2515
Robinson Theatre, 6323
Roger Wagner Chorale, 1936
Rogue Machine Theatre, 2516
Roland Taylor Theatre, 6083
Rose Bowl Stadium, 6210
Rova Saxaphone Quartet, 851
Rowland-Taylor Recital Hall, 6084
Russian River Blues Festival, 4222
Russian River Chamber Music, 791
Sacramento Ballet, 63
Sacramento Choral Society and Orchestra, 1879
Sacramento Community Center Theatre, 6231
Sacramento Convention Center, 6232
Sacramento Jazz Jubilee, 890, 4348
Sacramento Master Singers, 1901
Sacramento Men's Chorus, 1902
Sacramento Opera Company, 1903
Sacramento Philharmonic Orchestra, 836
Sacramento Symphonic Winds, 770
Sacramento Theatre Company, 2557
Sacramento Youth Symphony & Academy of Music, 837
Saddleback College, 2527
Saddleback College Guest Artists Series, 4252
Samahan Filipino American Performing Arts, 29
San Bernardino Symphony Orchestra, 839
San Diego Ballet Company, 64
San Diego Chamber Orchestra, 841
San Diego Children's Choir, 1906
San Diego Civic Theatre, 6245
San Diego Comic Opera/Lyric Opera San Diego, 1907
San Diego Dance Theater, 69
San Diego Early Music Society, 842, 4290
San Diego Junior Theatre, 2567
San Diego Men's Chorus, 1908
San Diego Museum of Art Auditorium, 6246

San Diego Opera, 1909
San Diego Repertory Theatre, 2568
San Diego Sports Arena, 6247
San Diego State University-School of Music and Dance, 4291
San Diego State University: Department of Theatre, 2569
San Diego Symphony Orchestra, 843
San Diego Thanksgiving, Dixieland Jazz Festival, 4292
San Diego Theatres/Balboa & Civic Theatres, 6248
San Diego Youth Symphony, 844
San Fernando Valley Symphony Orchestra, 893
San Francisco Bach Choir, 1917
San Francisco Ballet, 89
San Francisco Blues Festival, 4306
San Francisco Boys Chorus, 1916
San Francisco Chamber Orchestra, 760
San Francisco Choral Artists, 1918, 1919
San Francisco Community Music Center, 852
San Francisco Conservatory of Music, 854
San Francisco Contemporary Music Players, 853
San Francisco County Fair Arena, 6265
San Francisco Early Music Society, 759, 761
San Francisco Ethnic Dance Festival, 90, 4307
San Francisco Fringe Festival, 4308
San Francisco Girls Chorus, 1920
San Francisco Girls Chorus and Association, 1921
San Francisco Jazz Organization, 855
San Francisco Jazz Spring Season, 4309
San Francisco Mime Troupe, 2590
San Francisco Opera, 1926
San Francisco Opera Center, 1922, 1923
San Francisco Performances, 4310
San Francisco Renaissance Voices, 1924
San Francisco Shakespeare Festival, 4311
San Francisco State University: Department of Theatre Arts, 2589
San Francisco Symphony, 856
San Francisco Symphony Chorus, 1925
San Francisco Symphony Youth Orchestra, 857
San Francisco War Memorial and Performing Arts Center, 6266
San Jose Center for the Performing Arts, 6270
San Jose Chamber Music Society, 859
San Jose Children's Musical Theater, 2601
San Jose Jazz Society, 860
San Jose Municipal Stadium, 6271
San Jose Repertory Theatre, 2602
San Jose Stage Company, 2603
San Jose State University Theatre, 6272
San Jose State University: Department of Theatre Arts, 2604
San Jose Taiko Group, 861
San Luis Obispo Mozart Festival, 863, 4320
San Luis Obispo Symphony, 864
San Mateo Performing Arts Center, 6274
San Pedro City Ballet, 102
Santa Barbara Chamber Orchestra, 870
Santa Barbara Contemporary Arts Forum, 6286
Santa Barbara Festival Ballet, 4324
Santa Barbara Symphony Association, 871
Santa Cecilia Orchestra, 806
Santa Clara Ballet, 105
Santa Clara University Theatre and Dance Department, 2614
Santa Cruz Ballet Theatre, 112
Santa Cruz Baroque Festival, 873, 4328
Santa Cruz Civic Auditorium, 6295
Santa Cruz County Symphony, 874
Santa Monica Civic Auditorium, 6301
Santa Monica Symphony Orchestra, 876
Santa Rosa Concert Association, 4332
Santa Rosa Junior College Chamber Concert Series, 877
Santa Rosa Junior College Chamber Music Series, 4333
Santa Rosa Symphony, 878
Scene Dock Theatre, 6176
Schola Cantorum, 1892
Second Stage, 6296
Segerstrom Center for the Arts, 6090
Sfjazz, 4312
Sha Sha Higby, 25
Shadowlight Productions, 2591
Shakespeare Orange County, 2537

Shakespeare Santa Cruz, 2616
Shasta College Fine Arts Theatre, 6214
Shasta Community Concert Association, 4199
Shasta Symphony Orchestra, 828
Sheila & Hughes Potiker Theatre, 6143
Sherwood Auditorium, 6144
Shotgun Players, 2451
Shrine Auditorium and Exposition Center, 6177
Sierra Repertory Theatre at East Sonora, 2626
Six Flags Magic Mountain, 2638
Sleep Train Pavillion at Concord, 6088
Smuin Ballet, 91
Soka Performing Art Center, 6053
Songfest, 4269
Sonoma State University Theater Department, 2549
South Bay Ballet, 113
South Bay Guitar Society, 862
South Coast Repertory, 2461
South Coast Repertory Segerstrom Auditorium, 6091
South Orange County Community Theatre, 2607
South Valley Symphony, 788
Southeast Community Theatre, 2570
Southeast Symphony, 765
Southwest Chamber Music, 826
Southwest Performing Arts Theatre, 6100
Spangenburg Theatre, 6205
Speaking of Stories, 2611
Spring Music Festival: California University of Arts, 4343
Stage 3 Theatre Company, 2627
Stages Theatre Center, 2476
Stanford Jazz Festival & Workshop, 4336
Stanford Lively Arts, 4337
Stanford Symphony Orchestra, 879
Stanford University Department of Music, 6309
Stanley-Sinsheimer Festival Glen, 6297
Staples Center, 6178
Starlight Musical Theatre, 1910, 2571
Starlite Patio Theater Summer Series, 4253
Starlite Patio Theatre, 6189
State Street Ballet, 104
Stern Grove Festival Association, 4313
Steve Silver Productions, 2592
Stockton Civic Theatre, 2628
Stockton Symphony Association, 882
Stop-Gap, 2609
Studio Theatre, 6096, 6120, 6287, 6324
Sturges Center for Fine Arts, 6235
Suhaila Dance Company & Suhaila Salimpour School of Dance, 18
Summer Arts & Music Festival, 4278
Summer Repertory Theatre, 2620
Summerdance Santa Barbara, 4325
Sunset Cultural Center, 6078
Sushi Performance & Visual Art, 70
Sweet & Hot Summer Music Festival, 4247
Swingdance America, 4314
Symphony Orchestra, 886
Synthaxis Theatre Company, 2532
Tahoe Arts Project, 4335
Tahoe Jazz Festival, 4231
Tassajara Symphony Orchestra, 780
Teatro Shalom, 2528
Teatro Vision, 2605
Thatcher Music Building, 6087
The Actors' Gang Theater, 2462
The Antelope Valley Ballet, 33
The Center for the Arts, 6117
The Festival Opera Association Inc, 1941
The Granada, 6288
The Lively Foundation, 92
The Long Beach Chorale and Chamber Orchestra, 1883
The Maple Conservatory of Dance, 32
The Muckenthaler Cultural Center, 6112
The Pacific Mozart Ensemble, 1870
The Purple Moon Dance Project, 87
The Road Theatre Company, 2533
The San Francisco Choral Society, 1927
The Traveling Bohemians, 60
The Ventura County Ballet Company, 116
Theater Rhinoceros, 2593
Theatre Artaud, 2594
Theatre East, 6130
Theatre El Dorado, 2544
Theatre West, 2517

Theatreworks, 2525, 2541
Thick Description, 2595
Thorne Hall, 6179
Thornton Symphony, 807
Thousand Oaks Civic Arts Plaza, 6314
Tifereth Israel Community Orchestra, 845
Tillie Lewis Theater, 2629
Tom Bradley International Hall, 6180
Tower Theater for the Peforming Arts, 6107
Townsend Opera Players, 1890
Traveling Jewish Theatre, 2596
Tulare County Symphony, 888
Uc Davis Presents, 4216
Uc Santa Cruz Arts & Lectures, 4329
Ucla Performing Arts, 6181
Ucsb Arts & Lectures, 4326
Ukiah Players Theatre, 2636
Un-Scripted Theater Company, 2597
University Events Office, 4234
University of California Irvine Cultural Events, 4230
University of California Santa Cruz Performing Arts Center, 6298
University of California, Davis: Department of Dramatic Art, 2464
University of California-Berkeley California, 4207
University of California-Irvine: Department of Drama, 2478
University of California-Los Angeles: Department of Theater, 2518
University of California-Riverside: Department of Theatre, 2548
University of California-San Diego: Department of Theatre and Dance, 2482
University of California-Santa Barbara: Department of Dramatic Art, 2612
University of Laverne, 2483
University of Southern California, 6182
University of Southern California Thornton Opera, 1889
University of Southern California: School of Theatre, 2519
University of the Pacific Conservatory of Music - Resident Artist Series, 4338
University of the Pacific: Department of Theatre Arts, 2630
University Theatre, 6121, 6226
Vallejo Symphony Association, 887
Valley Cultural Center Concerts in The Park, 4350
Vanguard Theatre Ensemble, 2470
Ventura Music Festival, 4344
Veteran's Memorial Complex, 6092
Veterans Wadsworth Theatre, 6183
Veterans' Memorial Theatre, 6097
Village Center for the Arts, 827
Visalia Convention Center Rotary Theatre, 6318
Visalia Cultural Programs-On Stage Visalia, 4345
Vox Dance Theater Inc, 44
W. Turrentine and Barbara K. Jackson Hall, 6098
Wallis Annenberg Center for the Performing Arts, 6074
Warner Grand Theatre, 6276
Warnor's Theater, 6108
Warren Atherton Auditorium, 6312
Welk Resort San Diego Theatre, 2466
Wells Fargo Center for the Arts, 6302
West Bay Opera, 1899
West Coast Chamber Orchestra, 872
West Coast Ensemble, 2520
Western Ballet, 50
Western Opera Theater, 1928
Western Stage, 2558
Whalberg Recital Hall, 6109
Whittier College Bach Festival, 892, 4349
Whittier Junior Theatre, 2642
Will Geer Theatricum Botanicum, 2634
William Hall Chorale, 1898
William Randolph Hearst Greek Theatre, 6070
Willows Theatre, 6089
Wilshire Ebell Theatre, 6184
Wiltern Theatre, 2521
Winter Arts Faire, 4279
Woodland Opera House, 6325
World Arts Ethnic Festival: West, 4315
World Arts West, 94, 4316
Yaelisa and Caminos Flamencos, 95
Yerba Buena Center for the Arts, 6267

Geographic Index

Young Musicians Foundation Debut Orchestra, 764
Young People's Symphony Orchestra, 762
Young Theatre, 6114
Yreka Community Theatre, 2643
Yreka Community Theatre Center, 6326
Yuba County-Sutter County Regional Arts Council Touring/Presenting Program, 4250
Zaccho Dance Theatre, 96
Zellerbach Auditorium, 6071
Zellerbach Playhouse, 6072
Zephyr Theatre, 2522

Colorado

Academy Concerts, 4377
Adams Mystery Playhouse, 2652
And Toto Too Theatre Company, 2653
Arapahoe Philharmonic, 915
Arnold Hall Theater United States Air Force, 6338
Arvada Center for the Arts and Humanities, 6327
Aspen Music Festival and School, 4351, 6328
Aspen Opera Theater Center, 1944
Augustana Arts, 6346
Aurora Fox Arts Center, 6330
Aurora Fox Children's Theatre Company, 2644
Aurora Singers, 1960
Aurora Symphony Orchestra, 896
Avenue Theater, 2654
Bas Bleu Theatre Company, 2669
Bicentennial Art Center, 2650
Boulder Bach Festival, 897, 4353
Boulder International Music Festival for Young Performers, 4354
Boulder Museum of Contemporary Art Galleries and Theater, 6332
Boulder Philharmonic Orchestra, 898, 899
Bravo! Vail Valley Music Festival, 4378
Breckenridge Backstage Theatre, 2649, 6336
Breckenridge Music Festival Orchestra, 901, 4361
Breckenridge Music Institute Orchestra, 900
Broadway Theatre League of Pueblo, 2676
Budweiser Events Center, 6388
Canyon Concert Ballet, 127
Castle Rock Players, 2650
Central City Opera, 1950, 1953
Chamber Singers of the Colorado Springs Chorale, 1948
Changing Scene Theater, 2655
Cherry Creek Arts Festival, 4366
Cleo Parker Robinson Dance, 121
Colorado Ballet, 122
Colorado Children's Chorale, 1951
Colorado College Dance Festival, 4363
Colorado Council on The Arts, 4367
Colorado Mahlerfest, 4355
Colorado Music Festival & Rocky Mountain Center for Musical Arts, 4356
Colorado Shakespeare Festival, 4357
Colorado Springs Chorale, 1949
Colorado Springs City Auditorium, 6339
Colorado Springs Fine Arts Center Performing Arts Series, 4364
Colorado Springs Philharmonic, 903
Colorado State University Orchestra, 909
Colorado State University Theatre, 6372
Colorado Symphony Orchestra, 905
Columbine Chorale, 1952
Coors Events Conference Center, 6337
Coors Field, 6348
Country Dinner Playhouse, 2673
Creede Repertory Theatre, 2651, 6343
Crested Butte Chamber Music Festival, 4365
Crested Butte Mountain Theatre, 6344
Crested Butte Music Festival, 904
Cu Coors Events, 4358
Curious Theatre Company, 2656
Dawson Wallace Dance Project, 126
Denver Botanic Gardens, 6349
Denver Broncos, 6362
Denver Broncos Football Club, 6351
Denver Center for the Performing Arts, 6352
Denver Center Theater Company, 2657
Denver Civic Theatre, 2658
Denver Municipal Band, 906
Denver Performing Arts Complex, 6347, 6353
Denver Puppet Theatre, 2659
Denver Victorian Playhouse, 6354
Denver Young Artists Orchestra, 907
Diamond Circle Melodrama, 2668
Dickens Opera House, 6387
Durango Choral Society, 1956
Early Music Colorado Fall Festival of Early Music, 4359
El Centro Su Teatro, 6355
Elizabeth Eriksen Byron Theatre, 6356
Ellie Caulkins Opera House, 6357
Fiesta Colorado Dance Company, 128
Fine Arts Center Colorado Springs, 6340
Folsom Field/Coors Events Conference Center/Stadium Club, 6333
Fort Collins Symphony Orchestra, 910
Fort Lewis College Community Concert Hall, 6371
Frazier Hall, 6381
Germinal Stage Inc, 2660
Grand Junction Musical Arts Association, 912
Greeley Philharmonic Orchestra, 913
Hannah Kahn Dance Company, 123
Helander Dance Theater, 118
Houston Fine Arts Center, 6359
Hughes Stadium, 6373
Impossible Players, 2677
Impulse Theater, 2661
Jafrika, 2662
Jazz Aspen Snowmass, 4352
Jazz in The Sangres, 4380
Jefferson Symphony Orchestra, 911
Jones Theatre, 6360
Kim Robards Dance, 124
Larimer Chorale, 1957
Le Centre Du Silence Mime School, 119, 2646
Lincoln Center, 6374
Lincoln Park Stocker Stadium, 6376
Little Theatre of the Rockies, 2672
Longmont Symphony Orchestra, 916
Longmont Theatre Company, 2675
Loveland Friends of Chamber Music, 4372
Lovland Opera Theatre, 1959
Macky Auditorium Concert Hall, 6334
May Bonfils Stanton Center for the Performing Arts, 6361
Mesa County Community Concert Association, 4371
Mesa Experimental Theatre, 6377
Mesa Recital Hall, 6378
Mesa State College Theatre Department, 2671
Metropolitan State College of Denver: Department of Theatre, 2663
Michael D. Palm Theatre, 6391
Mizel Arts & Culture Center, 6363
Music in Ouray, 4373
Music in The Mountains Classical Music Festival, 4368
Naropa University Performing Arts Center, 6335
National Repertory Orchestra, 4362
National Theatre Conservatory, 2664
Northeastern Junior College Theatre, 6390
Openstage Theatre and Company, 2670
Opera Colorado, 1954
Opera Fort Collins, 1958
Ormao Dance Company, 120
Pdac/Arts for All, 125
Pepsi Center, 6365
Picketwire Players, 2674, 6385
Pikes Peak Center, 6341
Pueblo Symphony, 917
Red Rocks Amphitheatre & Visitor Center, 6366
Ricketson Theatre, 6367
Rocky Ridge Music Center, 4369
San Juan Symphony, 908
Sangre De Cristo Arts and Conference Center, 4374, 6389
Sky Sox Stadium, 6342
Sound of the Rockies, 1946
Space Theatre, 6368
St Martin's Chamber Choir, 1955
Stage Theatre, 6369
Strings in The Mountains, 918
Su Teatro, 6365
Summit Jazz Swinging Jazz Concerts, 4370
Symphony Orchestra, 914
Telluride Chamber Music Festival, 919, 4375
Telluride Jazz Celebration, 4376
Temple Hoyne Buell Theatre, 6370
The Butter Theater, 6345
The Cherry Creek Chorale, 1947
The Denver Brass, 6350
The Historic Paramount Theatre, 6358
The Otero Players, 6384
The Robert and Judi Newman Center for the Performing Arts, 6364
Town Hall Arts Center, 6386
Union Colony Civic Center, 6382
University Center for the Arts, 6375
University of Colorado at Boulder: Department of Theatre and Dance, 2647
University of Colorado at Denver: Department of Performing Arts, 2666
University of Colorado Concerts, 4360
University of Denver Department of Theatre, 2667
University of Northern Colorado, 6383
Upstart Crow Theatre Company, 2648
Vail Jazz Festival, 4379
Vintage Theatre Productions, 2645
Walden Piano Quartet/Walden Chamber Music Society, 902
Walter Walker Auditorium, 6379
Westminster Community Artist Series, 4381
Wheeler Opera House, 1945, 6329
William S. Robinson Theatre, 6380

Connecticut

Adam Miller Dance Project, 129
Albano Ballet and Performing Arts Center, 6404
American Classical Orchestra, 924
American Magic-Lantern Theater, 2682
Arena at Harbor Yard, 6392
Armstrong Chamber Concerts, 4409
Artists Collective, 2685
Aston Magna Foundation, 922, 4383
Austin Arts Center, 6405
Bernhard Center, 6393
Black Box Theatre, 6415
Bridgeport Theatre Company, 2678
Bushnell Center for the Performing Arts, 6406
Centennial Theater Festival, 4406
Center for the Arts, 6411
Central Connecticut State University: Department of Theatre, 2693
Cfa Theater, 6412
Charles Ives Center Pavilion, 6396
Charter Oak Cultural Center, 6407
Cheshire Community Theatre, 2679
Chestnut Hill Concerts, 4387
Clockwork Repertory Theatre, 2703
Coe Park Civic Center, 6440
Connecticut Ballet, 131
Connecticut Choral Artists, 1966
Connecticut Choral Society, 1971
Connecticut Classical Guitar Society, 927
Connecticut College Department of Theatre, 2701
Connecticut College: on Stage, 4398
Connecticut Concert Opera, 1976
Connecticut Conservatory of the Performing Arts, 2702
Connecticut Early Music Festival, 4399
Connecticut Grand Opera and Orchestra, 1972
Connecticut Opera, 1964
Connecticut Repertory Theatre, 2709
Connecticut Theater Festival, 4407
Connecticut Theatre Company, 2694
Connecticut Youth Symphony, 945
Crowell Concert, 6413
Downtown Cabaret Theatre, 6394
East-West Fusion Theatre, 2680
Eastern Connecticut Symphony, 935
Edgerton Center for the Performing Arts, 6399
Elm Shakespeare Company, 2696
Enfield Cultural Arts Commission, 4385
Fairfield County Chorale, 1962
Fairfield County Stage Company, 2717
Fairfield University: Department of Visual & Performing Arts, 2684
Falcon Ridge Folk Festival, 4404
First Night Hartford, 4389
Garde Arts Center, 6428
Goodspeed Musicals, 2683
Goodspeed Opera House, 4384, 6398
Great Connecticut Jazz Fest, 4382
Greater Bridgeport Symphony Orchestra, 921
Greater Bridgeport Symphony Youth Orchestra, 923
Greater New Britain Opera Association, 1967
Greenwich Choral Society, 1963
Greenwich Symphony Orchestra, 925
Harriet S. Jorgensen Theatre, 6436
Hartford Civic Center, 6408
Hartford Jazz Society, 920
Hartford Stage Company, 2686
Hartford Symphony Orchestra, 928
Hartt School Concert Series, 4410
Hoffman Auditorium, 6444
Hole in The Wall Theatre, 2695
Horace Bushnell Memorial Hall, 6409
Hot Steamed Jazz Festival, 4386
Ingalls Rink, 6417
International Festival of Arts & Ideas, 4396
John Lyman Center for the Performing Arts, 6420
Jorgensen Center for the Performing Arts, 6437
Joyful Noise, 1975
Kendall Drama Lab, 6418
Klein Memorial Auditorium, 6395
Levitt Pavilion for the Performing Arts, 6447
Lincoln Theatre, 6445
Litchfield Jazz Festival, 4393
Litchfield Performing Arts Series, 4394
Long Wharf Theatre, 2697
Long Wharf Theatre Stage II, 6419
Main Stage, 6421
Manchester Musical Players, 2690
Manchester Symphony Orchestra/Chorale, 929
Mashantucket Pequot Museum & Research Center, 6410
Momix, 134
Music Mountain, 4392
Music Theatre of Connecticut, 2718
Mystic Ballet, 130
National Theater Institute, 2715
National Theatre of the Deaf, 2687
New Britain Symphony Orchestra, 930
New England Lyric Operetta, 1961
New Haven Jazz Festival, 4397
New Haven Symphony Orchestra, 932
New Haven Veterans Memorial Coliseum, 6422
Newtown Friends of Music, 4401
Norfolk Chamber Music Festival, 938
Norfolk Chamber Music Festival/Yale Summer School of Music, 4402
Northwest Corner Young Artists Series, 4405
Norwalk Symphony Orchestra, 937
Norwalk Youth Symphony, 938
Nutmeg Ballet, 133
O'neill Center, 6397
Oakdale Theatre, 6442
Oddfellows Playhouse, 2691
Orchestra New England, 933, 946
Palace Theatre, 6423
Palace Theatre of the Arts, 2706
Palmer Auditorium, 6429
Paul Mellon Arts Center, 6443
Pepsico Theatre, 6401
Pilobolus Dance Theatre, 135
Pro Arte Chamber Singers of Connecticut, 1973
Project Troubador, 4403
Puppet House Theatre, 2708
Quick Center for the Arts, 6402
Regina A. Quick Center for the Arts, 6400
Ridgefield Symphony Orchestra, 939
Salt Marsh Opera, 1974
Seven Angels Theatre, 2713
Sherman Players, 2705
Shoreline Arts Alliance, 4388
Shubert Theater, 6424
Silvermine Guild Art Center Series, 4395
Silvermine Guild Summer Music Series, 931
South Shore Music, 4411
Southern Connecticut State University: Department of Theatre, 2698
Southington Community Theatre Inc., 6433
Square One Theatre Company, 2712
Stamford Center for the Arts, 6435
Stamford Symphony Orchestra, 940
Stamford Theatre Works, 2707
Stamford Young Artists Philharmonic, 941
Stratford Festival Theater, 4408
Summer Music, 4400

1275

Geographic Index

Symphony on The Sound, 926
Talcott Mountain Music Festival, Summer Series, 4390
Temple Israel, 4412
Thaddeus Torp Theatre, 6416
The Greater Middletown Chorale, 1965
The Hartt School, 136
The Palace, 6434
The Ridgefield Playhouse, 6430
The Sherman Playhouse, 6431
Theaterworks, 2688
Theatre Project Consultants, 6432
Triarts Sharon Playhouse, 2704
Trinity College Theatre and Dance Department, 2689
University of Connecticut Sports Complex - Harry a Gampel Pavilion, 6438
University of Connecticut: Department of Dramatic Arts, 2711
University of Hartford Sports Center, 6446
University of Hartford: Department of Art History, Cinema, Drama, 2716
Von Der Mehden Recital Hall, 6439
Wallingford Symphony Orchestra, 943
Warner Theatre, 6441
Waterbury Symphony Orchestra, 944
Wesleyan University Theater Department, 2692
Western Connecticut State University: Theatre Arts Department, 2681
Westport Community Theatre, 2719, 6448
Westport Country Playhouse, 2720, 6449
Wien Experimental Theatre, 6403
Willimantic Orchestra, 942
Wilton Playshop, 2721
Woodland Concert Series, 4391
World Music Hall, 6414
Yale Baseball Stadium, 6425
Yale Bowl, 6426
Yale Opera, 1968
Yale Repertory Theatre, 2699, 6427
Yale Russian Chorus, 1969
Yale Schola Cantorum, 1970
Yale School of Drama, 2700
Yale Symphony Orchestra, 934
Zig Zag Ballet, 132

Delaware

Artists Theatre Association, 2725
Belle Voix, 1978
Bob Carpenter Center, 6451
Brandywine Baroque, 948
Cfa Studio, 6452
Cfa Thompson Theatre, 6453
City Theater Company, 2726
Delaware Chamber Music Festival, 4414
Delaware Dance Company, 138
Delaware Symphony Orchestra, 949
Delaware Theatre Company, 2727
Deleware Dance Alliance, Llc, 137
Diamond State Chorus of Sweet Adelines, 1977
Dickinson Theatre Organ Society, 950
Dupont Theatre, 6455
First State Ballet Theatre, 140
Grand Opera House, 6456, 6457
Grand Youth Chorus, 1979
Hartshorn Theater, 6454
Kent County Theatre Guild, 2722
Mid-Atlantic Ballet, 139
Newark Symphony Orchestra, 947
Opera Delaware, 1980
Possum Point Players, 2723
Resident Ensemble Players, 2724
Schwartz Center for the Arts, 6450
Shoestring Productions Limited, 2728
University of Delaware Performing Arts Series, 4413
Wilmington Drama League, 2729

District of Columbia

African Continuum Theatre Company (Actco), 2730
American College Theater Festival, 4415
American Music Festival, 4416
American University - Mcdonald Recital Hall, 6458
American University Theatre Program, 2731

Arena Stage, 2732
Arts in The Academy, National Academy of Sciences, 4417
Baird Auditorium, 6459
Bender Arena, 6460
Capital City Symphony, 952
Carmichael Auditorium, 6461
Cathedral Choral Society, 1982
Catholic University of America: Drama Department, 2733
Charles E Smith Center, 6462
Children's National Medical Center, New Horizons Program, 4418
Choral Arts Society of Washington, 1984
Chorus America, 1985
Citydance Ensemble, 141
Commodores, 960
Constitution Hall, 6463
Contemporary Music Forum, 953
Country Current/Us Navy Band, 961
Cramton Auditorium, 6464
Cruisers, 962, 1999
Dana Tai Soon Burgess & Company, 142
Dance Place, 143
Dc Armory, 6465
Dc Sports & Entertainment Commission, 4419
Dc Youth Orchestra Program, 954
Deborah Riley Dance Projects, 144
Department of Theatre Arts, 6466
Discovery Theater, 2734
District Curators, 4420
Dumbarton Concert, 4421
Embassy Series, 4422
Flashpoint Studios, 2735
Folger Consort, 6467
Folger Shakespeare Library, 2736
Folger Theatre, 2737
Ford's Theatre Society, 2738
Gala Hispanic Theatre, 2739
Gallaudet Dance Company, 145
Gaston Hall, 6468
Gay Men's Chorus of Washington, 1986
George Washington University Symphony Orchestra, 955
George Washington University: Department of Theatre and Dance, 2740
George Washington's Series at Mount Vernon College, 4423
Georgetown University Department of Performing Arts, 6479
Georgetown University Performing Arts Center, 6469
Howard University Department of Theatre Arts, 2741
Imagination Celebration - Kennedy Center Performances for Young People, 4424
Ira Aldridge Theater, 6470
Kennedy Center American College Theatre, 2742
Kennedy Center Annual Open House Arts Festival, 4425
Kennedy Center Opera House Orchestra, 956
Kennedy Center/Mary Lou Williams Women in Jazz Festival, 4426
Library of Congress Chamber Music Concert Series, 4427
Lincoln Theatre, 6472
Lisner Auditorium, 6473
Living Stage, 2743
Maida Withers Dance Construction Company, 146
Mcdonald Recital Hall, 6474
Momentum Dance Theatre, 147
National Academy of Sciences Concerts, 4428
National Conservatory of Dramatic Arts, 2744
National Gallery of Art/Concert Series, 4429
National Gallery Orchestra, 957
National Symphony Orchestra Association, 958
National Theatre, 2745
New Lecture Hall, 6476
Opera Camerata of Washington, 1989
Opera Lafayette, 4430
Opera Music Theater International, 1990
Phillips Collection Sunday Concerts, 4431
Pointless Theatre, 2746
Sea Chanters, 2000
Shakespeare Theatre Company, 2747, 6477

Smithsonian Institution: the Smithsonian Associates, 4432
Society of the Cincinnati Concerts at Anderson House, 4433
Source Theatre Company, 2748
Spooky Action Theatre, 2749
St. Mark's Dance Studio, 148
Studio Theatre, 2750
Summer Opera Theatre Company, 1991
Taffety Punk Theatre Company, 2751
The Choral Arts Society of Washington, 1983
The City Choir of Washington, 1992
The John F Kennedy Center for the Performing Arts, 6471
Theater J, 6478
United States Air Force Band, 951
United States Air Force Singing Sergeants, 1981
United States Navy Band, 963
Us Navy Band, 2001
Verizon Center, 6475
Vocal Arts Society, 1993
Vsa Arts, 2752
Walter E. Washington Convention Center, 6481
Warner Theatre, 6480
Washington Bach Consort, 959, 1994
Washington Ballet, 149
Washington Chorus, 1995
Washington Concert Opera, 1996
Washington National Opera, 1997
Washington Performing Arts Society, 4434
Washington Savoyards, 1998
Washington Stage Guild, 2753
Woolly Mammoth Theatre Company, 2754

Florida

Acting Company of Riverside Theatre, 2836
Actors' Playhouse at the Miracle Theatre, 2764
Alhambra Dinner Theatre, 2784
American Airlines Arena, 6546
Amway Arena, 6571
Annie Russell Theatre, 6605
Area Stage Company, 2765
Arts Center, 6561
Asolo Repertory Theatre, 2821
Asolo Theatre Festival, 4480
Athens Theatre, 2772
Atlantic Center for the Arts, 6560
Atlantic Coast Theatre, 2760
Atlantic Shakespeare Festival, 4492
Bach Festival of Central Florida, 4458
Bachs Festival Society of Winter Park, 4496
Bailey Concert Hall, 6505
Ballet Florida, 174
Ballet Palm Beach, 165
Ballet Pensacola, 166
Bank United Center, 6496
Banyan Theater Company, 2822
Barbara B Mann Performing Arts Hall, 6511
Bay Arts Alliance, 4472
Bay Street Players, 2775
Beaches Fine Arts Series, 4456
Beethoven by The Beach, 4444
Berry College Theatre Company, 2802
Big Arts: Great Performers Series, 4478
Big Bend Community Orchestra, 998
Bininger Theatre, 6593
Bits 'n Pieces Giant Puppet Theatre, 2830
Black Box, 6565
Black Box Theater, 6566
Black Box Theatre, 6494
Bob Carr Performing Arts Center, 6567
Boca Ballet Theatre, 150
Bonk Festival of New Music, 4481
Branscomb Memorial Auditorium, 6541
Breakthrough Theatre, 2841
Brevard Symphony Orchestra, 975
Broadway in Fort Lauderdale, 4445
Broadway Palm Dinner Theatre, 2778
Broward Center for the Performing Arts, 6506
Buckner Theatre, 6542
Caldwell Theatre Company, 2756
Carrollwood Players Community Theater, 2831
Center Theater Company of Tampa Bay, 6595
Central Florida Ballet, 162
Central Florida Cultural Endeavors, 4441
Century Village Theaters, 6486

Charlotte Harbor Event and Conference Center, 6581
Charlotte Players, 2817
Chipola College Artist Series, 4463
Choral Society of Pensacola, 2008
City Players, 2761
Classicfest: Pensacola Summer Music Festival, 4474
Clearwater Jazz Holiday, 4438
Cocoa Expo Sports Center, 6489
Concert Association of Florida, 4468
Coral Ridge Presbyterian Church Concert Series, 4446
Coral Springs Center for the Arts, 6497
Cornerstone Theatre Company, 2818
Dade County Auditorium, 6547
Dance Alive National Ballet, 153
Dance Nowl Miami, 157
Daytona Beach Community College Theatre Center, 6498
Daytona Beach International Festival, 4442
Daytona Beach Symphony Society, 967
Daytona Playhouse, 2770, 6499
Delius Festival, 4451
Delray Beach Playhouse, 2773, 6503
Dolly Hands Cultural Arts Center, 6483
Down in Front Theater, 2814
Duncan Theatre, 6540
Eckerd College Theatre Department, 2825
Ed Smith Stadium Sports Complex, 6583
Everbank Field, 6525
Festival Miami, 4439
Festival of Orchestras, 4497
Firethorn Dance Academy, 173, 175
First Arts Series, 4449
Flagler Auditorium, 6575
Florida Arts Concert Series, 4447
Florida Atlantic University: Department of Theatre, 2757
Florida Ballet at Jacksonville, 154
Florida Dance Association, 158
Florida Grand Opera, 2005
Florida International Festival Featuring the London Symphony Orchestra, 4443
Florida International University: Department of Theatre and Dance, 2797
Florida National Pavilion, 6526
Florida Orchestra, 997
Florida Repertory Theatre, 2779
Florida Southern College, 4459
Florida Southern College: Department of Theatre Arts, 2790
Florida Stage, 2792
Florida State Opera at Florida State University, 2013
Florida State University: School of Theatre, 2828
Florida Studio Theatre, 2823, 6584
Florida Suncoast Puppet Guild, 2832
Florida Symphony Youth Orchestra, 983
Florida Theatre, 6527
Florida Theatre Performing Arts Series, 4452
Florida West Coast Symphony Series, 4482
Fort Lauderdale Children's Theatre, 2776
Fort Lauderdale Stadium, 6507
Fort Myers Community Concert Association Series, 4448
Fort Myers Harborside, 6512
Fred Stone Theatre, 6606
Freddick Bratcher & Company, 167
Friends of Chamber Music of Miami, 976
Friends of Music of Charlotte County Concert Series, 4477
Fuzion Dance Artists Inc., 168
Gablestage, 2766
Gainesville Chamber Orchestra, 970
Gator Bowl, 6528
Ginsberg Productions, 2787
Gold Coast Opera, 2003
Gold Coast Theatre, 2800
Golden Panther Sportsplex, 6548
Golden Thespians, 2782
Greater Miami Youth Symphony, 977
Gusman Center for the Performing Arts, 6549
Gusman Concert Hall, 6493
Harborside Event Center, 6513
Hippodrome State Theatre, Inc., 6519
Hispanic-American Lyrical Theatre, Inc, 2006
Hollywood Playhouse, 2783

Geographic Index

Homestead Sports Complex, 6524
Icehouse Theatre, 2803
Imperial Symphony Orchestra, 974
Irish Theatre of Florida, 2774
Island Players, 2755
J Howard Wood Theatre, 2820
Jackie Gleason Theater, 6554
Jackie Robinson Ball Park, 6500
Jacksonville Ballet Theatre, 155
Jacksonville Symphony Orchestra, 972
Jacksonville University Master-Class & Artists Series, 4453
James L Knight Center, 6550
Jazz Club of Sarasota, 990
Jazz Society of Pensacola, 987
Jerry Herman Ring Theatre, 6495
Kaleidoscope Theatre, 2791
Key Chorale, 2010
Key West Contemporary Dance Company, 156
Key West Council on The Arts Series, 4457
Key West Music Festival, 4464
Key West Players, 2788
Key West Symphony, 973
King Center for the Performing Arts, 6544
Kings Point Theatre at the Clubhouse, 6594
Kravis Center for the Performing Arts, 6602
Kuumba Fest, 4454
La Musica Festival, 4483
Lakeland Center, 4460, 6543
Las Mascaras Theatre, 2798
Lee Civic Center, 6562
Lee Civic Center - Small Theater, 6563
Limelight Theatre, 2827
Littman Theater & Conference Center, 6564
Mad Cat Theatre Company, 2801
Mad Cow Theatre, 2805
Mahaffey Theater, 4488
Mahaffey Theatre/Duke Energy Center for the Arts, 6588
Main Stage, 6568
Mainstage Theatre, 6590
Manatee Players/Riverfront Theatre, 2759
Marathon Community Theatre, 2795
Marina Civic Center, 6576
Master Chorale of Tampa Bay, 2014
Melbourne Auditorium, 6545
Melbourne Chamber Music Society, 971
Melbourne Civic Theatre, 2796
Mesa Park Arena, 6504
Miami Arena, 6551
Miami Bach Society/Tropical Baroque Music Festival, 966, 4440
Miami City Ballet, 160
Miami Civic Music Association Series, 4465
Miami Classical Guitar Society, 978
Miami Dade Community College, 4466
Miami International Piano Festival, 964, 4435
Mobile Civic Center - Exposition Hall, 6555
Mobile Civic Center - Theatre, 6556
Momentum Dance Company, 151
Monticello Opera House, Inc., 6557
Museum of Fine Arts Series, 4489
Music Hall Artist Series, 4475
Naples Philharmonic, 6558
New World Symphony, 980
North Florida Community College, 4462
Northwest Florida Ballet, 152
Nyk Productions, 4450
Ocala Symphony Orchestra, 982
Ocean Center, 6501
Omni Auditorium, 6491
One Way Puppets, 2777
Opera Guild, 2004
Orange Bowl Stadium, 6552
Orange County Convention Center, 6569
Orange Park Community Theatre, 2804
Orlando Ballet, 163
Orlando Broadway Dinner Theatre, 2806
Orlando Centroplex, 6570
Orlando Opera, 2007
Orlando Philharmonic Orchestra, 984
Orlando Shakespeare Theater, 2807
Orlando-Ucf Shakespeare Festival, 4469
Osceloa County Stadium & Sports Complex, 6538
Osceola Center for the Arts, 6537
Palm Beach Atlantic College: Department of Theatre, 2838
Palm Beach Community College Performing Arts Center, 6484
Palm Beach Opera, 2017
Palm Beach Pops, 1001
Palm Beach Symphony, 986
Panama City Music Association Series, 4473
Parker Playhouse, 6508
Pasco Schools Center for the Arts at River Ridge, 6559
Peabody Auditorium, 6502
Peninsula Players, 2780
Pensacola Bay Center, 6577
Pensacola Junior College Performing Arts Center, 6578
Pensacola Little Theatre, 2812
Pensacola Opera, 2009
Pensacola Symphony Orchestra, 988
Performing Arts Center of Greater Miami Foundation, 6553
Performing Arts Society of South Florida, 4436
Philharmonic Center for the Arts, 981
Phillips Center, 6520
Piccolo Opera Company, 2002
Pinellas Youth Symphony, 996
Pirate Playhouse, 2819
Plantation Theatre Company, 2815
Players Theatre, 2824
Polk Community College Special Performance Series, 4495
Pompano Beach Amphitheatre, 6603
Pompano Players, 2816
Rahner-Gibbs Second Stage Theatre, 6591
Red Barn Theatre, 2789, 6535
Regional Arts Music at the Kravis Center for the Performing Arts, 4493
Ritz Theatre and La Villa Museum, 2785
Riverside Theatre, 6600
Rollins College: Department of Theatre and Dance, 2842
Rose and Alfred Miniaci Performing Arts Center on The Nova Southeastern University, 6518
Russian Ballet of Orlando, 164
Ruth Eckerd Hall, 6488
Saenger Theatre, 6579
Saint Lucie County, 6516
Samuel P Harn Museum of Art, 6521
Sanibel Music Festival, 4470
Sarasota Ballet of Florida, 169
Sarasota Concert, 4484
Sarasota Jazz Festival, 4485
Sarasota Music Festival, 4486
Sarasota Opera Association, 2011
Sarasota Orchestra, 992
Sarasota Orchestra Brass Quintet, 995
Sarasota Orchestra New Artists Piano Quartet, 993
Sarasota Orchestra String Quartet, 991
Sarasota Orchestra Wind Quintet, 994
Sarasota Youth Orchestras, 989
Seaside Institute Series, 4487
Seaside Music Theater, 2771
Seminole County Government, 6582
Showboat Dinner Theatre, 2762
Sleuths Mystery Dinner Shows, 2808
Slow Burn Theatre Co., 2758
Society of the Four Arts, 4470
South Florida Center for the Arts, 6534
South Florida Community College Cultural Series, 4437
South Florida Jazz, 4476
South Florida Youth Symphony, 979
Southwest Florida Symphony Orchestra & Chorus Association, 969
Spanish Lyric Theater, 2015
Spanish Lyric Theatre, 2833
Springstead Theatre, 6587
Squitieri Studio Theatre, 6510
St Petersburg College, 4490
St.Petersburg Opera Company, 2012
Stephen C O'connell Center, 6522
Stephen Foster State Park Folk Culture Center, 6604
Studio Theatre, 6592
Suncoast Dixieland Jazz Classic, 4461
Sunfest of Palm Beach County, 4494
Sunrise Theatre, 6517
Surfscape Contemporary Dance Theatre, 161
Surfside Players, 2763
Symphony of the Americas, 968
Tallahassee Museum, 4491
Tallahassee Symphony Orchestra, 999
Tampa Bay Performing Arts Center, 6596
Tampa Bay Symphony, 965
Tampa Theatre, 6597
Teatro Avante, 2767
Temple Beth Am Series, 4467
Tennessee Williams Theatre, 6536
Tennis Center at Crandon Park, 6533
The Academy of Ballet Arts, 171
The Historic Cocoa Village Playhouse, 6490
The Island Players Theatre, 6482
The M Ensemble Inc., 2799
The Players Theatre, 6585
The Plaza Theatre, 2793
The Stage Door Theatre, 2769
The Tallahassee Ballet, 172
Theatre Club of the Palm Beaches, 2794
Theatre Jacksonville, 2786
Theatre Winter Haven, 2839
Theatre-In-The-Works, 2809
Thomas Armour Youth Ballet, 170
Times-Union Center for the Performing Arts, 6529
Treasure Coast Concert Association, 4471
Tropicana Field, 6589
Ucf Arena, 6572
Ucf Civic Theatre, 2810
Unf Arena, 6530
University Center Auditorium, 6487
University of Central Florida Orchestra, 985
University of Central Florida: Department of Theatre, 2811
University of Florida: School, Theater and Dance, 2781
University of Miami: Department of Theatre Arts, 2768
University of North Florida Fine Arts Center, 6531
University of South Florida: School of Theatre, 2834
University of West Florida, 2813
University of West Florida Center for Fine & Performing Arts, 6580
University Theatre, 6573
Usf Special Events Center, 6598
Usf Sun Dome, 6599
Valencia College Performing Arts Center, 6574
Van Wezel Performing Arts Hall, 6586
Vaudeville Palace, 2826
Venice Symphony, 1000
Venice Theatre, 2835
Vero Beach Concert Association, 6601
Vero Beach Opera Inc, 2016
Vero Beach Theatre Guild, 2837
Veterans Memorial Arena, 6532
Vladimir Issaev's School of Classical Ballet, 159
Walt Disney Wide World of Sports Stadium, 6539
War Memorial Auditorium, 6509
William H Hammond Stadium, 6514
William R Frizzell Cultural Centre Claiborne & Ned Foulds Theatre, 6515
Wjct Jacksonville Jazz Festival, 4455
Wt Neal Civic Center, 6485
Wynmoor Recital Hall, 6492
Young Actors Theatre, 2829
Young Circle Park and Bandshell, 6523

Georgia

Academy Theatre, 2847, 6635
Actor's Express Theatre, 2848
Adrian Symphony Orchestra, 2018
Agnes Scott College, 6642
Agnes Scott College: Department of Theatre and Dance, 2871
Albany James H Gray Sr Civic Center, 6608
Albany Symphony Orchestra, 1002
Alliance Theatre Company, 2849
Armstrong Atlantic State University, 4519
Armstrong State College Fine Arts Auditorium, 6658
Art Station Theatre, 2879
Arts Association in Newton County, 4512
Arts Council, 4515
Atlanta Ballet, 179
Atlanta Boy Choir, 2019
Atlanta Chamber Players, 1004
Atlanta Civic Center, 6618
Atlanta Downtown Festival and Tour, 4501
Atlanta Festival Ballet Company and School, 190
Atlanta Jazz Festival, 4502
Atlanta Opera, 2020
Atlanta Symphony Orchestra, 1005
Atlanta Symphony Orchestra Chorus, 2021
Atlanta Symphony Youth Orchestra, 1006
Atlanta Young Singers of Callanwolde, 2022
Augusta Entertainment Complex, 6632
Augusta Opera Association, 2026
Augusta Players, 2868
Aurora Theatre, 2874
Ballethnic Dance Company, 180
Beacon Dance Company, 184
Bobby Dodd Stadium at Grant Field, 6619
Brewton-Parker College Fine Arts Council, 4518
Capitol City Opera, 2023
Cedartown Civic Auditorium, 6637
Center for Puppetry Arts, 2850
Center for the Creative & Performing Arts, 6650
Chastian Park Amphitheatre Atlanta Symphony Orchestra Festival Pops, 1007, 4503
Choral Guild of Atlanta, 2024
Cobb Energy Performing Arts Centre, 6607
Cobb Symphony Orchestra, 1013
Colquitt County Arts Center, 6655
Columbus Civic Center, 6639
Columbus Symphony Orchestra, 1010
Core Performance Company, 185
Dad's Garage Theatre Company, 2851
Dana Fine Arts Building, 6643
Dancing on Common Ground, 181
Dekalb Symphony Orchestra, 1015
Delta Classic Chastain Park Amphitheatre, 6620
Department of Fine Arts, 6609
Dobbs Theatre, 6667
Ed Cabell Theatre, 6646
Emory Symphony Orchestra, 1008
Essential Theatre, 2852
Fabrefaction Theatre Conservatory, 2853
Ferst Center for the Arts, 6621
Forte: the University Union Performing Arts Series, 4500
14th Street Playhouse, 6617
Fox Theatre, 6622
Frederick Brown Jr Amphitheater, 6656
Full Radius Dance, 102
Gabbies Puppets, 2844
Gainesville Symphony Orchestra, 1011
Gateway Performance Productions, 2854
Georgia Ballet, 187
Georgia Dance Conservatory, 188
Georgia Dome, 6623
Georgia Ensemble Theatre, 2878
Georgia Mountains Center, 6647
Georgia Perimeter College Guest Artist Series, 4511
Georgia Repertory Theatre, 2845
Georgia Shakespeare, 2855
Georgia Shakespeare Festival, 4504
Georgia Southern University Performing Arts Center, 6663
Georgia Southwestern State University Chamber Concert Series, 1003, 4499
Gilmer Arts & Heritage Association Series, 4514
Grand Opera House Season at the Grand, 2027
Greater Augusta Arts Council, 4510
Grover C. Maxwell Performing Arts Theatre, 6633
Gwinnett Center, 6644
Hilda D Glenn Auditorium, 6668
Horizon Theatre Company, 2856
Hosch Theatre, 6648
Hugh Hodgson Concert Hall, 6612
Hugh Mills Memorial Stadium, 6610
Imperial Theatre, 6634
Jekyll Island Musical Theatre Festival, 4524
Jenkins Theatre, 6659
Just Us Theater Company, 2857
Lowndes/Valdosta Arts Commission, 4525
Lucas Theatre for the Arts, 6660
Macon Concert Association, 4516
Macon Symphony Orchestra, 1012
Madison Morgan Cultural Center, 6652
Marvin Cole Auditorium, 6638
Music Mercer Series, 4517
National Black Arts Festival, 4505

1277

Geographic Index

New American Shakespeare Tavern, 2858
New Jomandi Productions, 2859
North Georgia College & State University Music Series, 4513
Northeast Atlantic Ballet, 186
Oglethorpe University Theatre, 6624
Oglethorpe University-Arts and Ideas at Oglethorpe, 4506
Omilami Productions/People's Survival Theatre, 2860
Parenthesis Theatre Club, 2875
Peach State Summer Theatre, 2880
Pearce Auditorium, 6649
Perry Players, 2877
Philips Arena, 6625
Piccadilly Puppets Company, 2872
Pinch N' Ouch Theatre, 2861
Porterfield Memorial United Methodist Church - Distinguished Artist Series, 4498
Pushpush Theater, 2873
Ramsey Concert Hall, 6613
Refuge Dance Company, 176
Rialto Center for the Arts, 6626
Rivercenter for the Performing Arts, 6640
Rome City Auditorium, 6657
Rome Symphony Orchestra, 1014
Sanford Stadium, 6614
Savannah Civic Center, 6661
Savannah Concert Association, 4520
Savannah Music Festival, 4521
Sawyer Theatre, 6665
Schwartz Center for Performing Arts at Emory, 4507
7 Stages, 2846, 6627
Seven Stages Theatre, 2862
Sideways Contemporary Dance Company, 189
Six Flags Over Georgia, 4508
Southeastern Savoyards, 2863
Southern Appalachian Stages, 2881
Spelman College Fresh Images Chamber Music Series, 4509
Spivey Hall, 6654
Springer Opera House, 2870
Symphony Orchestra of Augusta, 1009
The Boisefeuillet Jones Atlanta Civic Center, 6628
The Classic Center, 6615
The Grand Opera House, 6651
The Mystical Arts of Tibet, 183
Theater at Emory, 6629
Theater Emory, 2864
Theater of the Stars, 2865
Theatre Albany, 2843, 6611
Theatre Gael, 2866
Theatre in The Square, 2876, 6653
Theatrical Outfit, 2867
Thomaston-Upson Arts Council Performing Series, 4522
Thomasville Center for the Arts, 6664
Thomasville Entertainment Foundation, 4523
Three Rivers Theatre, 6641
Townsend Center for the Performing Arts, 6636
Troika Balalaikes World Artists, 2025
Trustees Theater, 6662
Turner Field, 6630
Uga Ballet Ensemble, 177
Uga Core Concert Dance Company, 178
University of Georgia Performing Arts Center, 6616
Valdosta Symphony Orchestra, 1016
West Georgia Theatre Company Summer Classic, 2869
Whitehead Auditorium, 6666
Wild Bill's Atlanta, 6645
Woodruff Arts Center, 6631

Hawaii

Aloha Performing Arts Company, 2891
Aloha Stadium, 6670
Andrews Outdoor Theatre, 6671
Army Entertainment Program, 2882
Brigham Young University: Hawaii Performance Series, 4531
Chamber Music Hawaii, 1017
Convergence Dance Theatre, 191
David O Mckay Auditorium, 6681
Diamond Head Theatre, 2884
Halau Hula Ka No'eau, 4530
Hawaii Chamber Orchestra Society, 1018
Hawaii Concert Society, 4526
Hawaii Ecumenical Chorale, 2028
Hawaii Opera Theatre, 2029
Hawaii Theatre, 2885
Hawaii Theatre Centre, 6672
Hawaii Youth Symphony Association, 1019
Hilo Community Players, 2883
Honolulu Academy of Arts, 6673
Honolulu Chamber Music Series, 1020, 4527
Honolulu Children's Opera Chorus, 2030
Honolulu Dance Studio, 192
Honolulu Symphony Orchestra, 1021
Honolulu Theatre for Youth, 2886
Kahilu Theatre Foundation, 6678
Kauai International Theatre, 2890
Kennedy Theatre, 6674
Kumu Kahua Theatre, 2887
Lahaina Civic Center, 6680
Leeward Community College Theatre, 2892
Maui Academy of Performing Arts, 2893
Maui Arts & Cultural Center, 6677
Maui Community College Series, 4529
Music at Manoa/University of Hawaii at Manoa Outreach College, 1022
Neal S Blaisdell Center, 6675
Oahu Choral Society, 2031
Paul and Vi Loo Theatre, 6679
Saint Louis Center for the Performing Arts, 6676
The Leeward Theatre, 6682
Uhh Theatre, 6669
University of Hawaii Series, 4528
Waimea Community Theatre, 2889
West Hawaii Dance Theatre, 193
Windward Theatre Guild, 2888

Idaho

Amphitheatre, 6690
Arts on Tour Series, 4543
Auditorium Chamber Music Series, 4535
Ballet Idaho, 194
Barrus Auditorium- Concert Hall, 6695
Beverly B. Bistline Thrust Theatre, 6710
Bilyeu Theatre, 6708
Biotzetik Basque Choir, 2032
Bistline Family Theatre, 6709
Boise Chamber Music Series, 1023, 4532
Boise Contemporary Theater, 2894
Boise Master Chorale, 2033
Boise Philharmonic Association, 1024
Boise State University Classical Guitar Society, 1025
Brigham Young University, 4538
Caldwell Fine Arts Series, 4534
Century Link Arena Boise, 6685
Civic Auditorium, 6696
Coeur D'alene Summer Theatre/Carousel Players, 2897
Colonial Theatre, 6697
Company of Fools, 2898
Danny Peterson Theatre, 6683
Eliza R Snow Performing Arts Center, 6717
Eros Theatre, 6691
Festival at Sandpoint, 4540
Goranson Hall, 6711
Grand Lobby, 6704
Hartung Theatre, 6699
Holt Arena, 6712
Idaho Center, 6705
Idaho Dance Theatre, 195
Idaho Falls Arts Council Colonial Theater, 2899
Idaho Falls Symphony, 1026
Idaho Repertory Theatre Company, 2900
Idaho Shakespeare Festival, 2895
Idaho State Civic Symphony, 1027
Idaho State University, 6713
James E. and Rogers Black Box Theatre, 6715
Jewett Auditorium, 4692
Kibbie-Asui Activity Center, 6700
Kiva Theatre, 6701
L. E. and Thelma E. Stephens Performing Arts Center, 6716
Lionel Hampton Jazz Festival, 4536
Magic Valley Symphony, 1028
Morrison Center for the Performing Arts, 6684
Mountain Home Arts Council, 4537, 6703
Nampa Civic Center, 6706
Oinkari Basque Dancers, 196
Opera Idaho, 2034
Panida Theatre, 2901
Pend Oreille Arts Council, 4541
Powell Little Theatre, 6714
Recital Hall, 6693
Salmon Arts Council, 4539
Shakespeare Festival, 4533
Stage Coach Theatre, 2896
Student Union Special Events Center, 6686
Studio Theatre, 6694
Sun Valley Center for the Arts, 6698
Sun Valley Opera, 2035
Sun Valley Summer Symphony, 4542
Swayne Auditorium, 6707
Taco Bell Arena, 6687
Trey Mcintyre Project, 197
University of Idaho Theatre Arts, 6702
Velma V. Morrison Center for the Performing Arts, 6688, 6689

Illinois

About Face Theatre, 2903
Albert Taylor Theatre, 6767
Allan Carr Theatre, 6795
Allstate Arena, 6833
Alton Symphony Orchestra, 1053
American Theater Company, 2905
American Theatre, 2906
Anima Singers, 2054
Annual Chicago Jazz Festival, 4548
Apollo Chorus of Chicago, 2036
Apollo Theater, 6727
Arch-Opera House of Sandwich, 2060
Arena Theater, 6848
Arie Crown Theatre, 6728
Artist Series at Wheaton College, 4603
Artists Showcase West, 4570
Arts at Argonne Music Series, 4544
Assembly Hall, 6724
Athenaeum Theatre, 6729
Auditorium Theatre, 6730
Auditorium Theatre of Roosevelt University, 2907
Augustana Choir, 2059
Augustana Symphony Orchestra, 1063
Augustana Theatre, 6825
Bach Week Festival in Evanston, 4576
Bailiwick Repertory, 2908
Ballet Chicago, 198
Ballet Quad Cities, 221
Bank of America Theatre, 6731
Barat College Performing Arts Center Season, 4584
Barbara Pfeiffer Memorial Hall, 6803
Becker Auditorium, 6775
Bella Voce, 2037
Belleville Philharmonic Orchestra, 1029
Bergman Theatre, 6819
Beverly Arts Center, 6732
Big Noise Theatre Company, 2961
Black Ensemble Theater, 2909
Blair Thomas & Co., 2910
Blind Parrot Productions, 2911
Body Politic Theatre, 2912
Bowen Park Theatre & Opera, 2990
Braden Auditorium, 4590, 6805
Breatriz Rodriguez, 199
Broadway in Chicago, 2913
Cahn Auditorium, 6779
Cedarhurst Chamber Music, 1057
Centennial Hall, 6826
Center Theater and The Training Center, 2914
Centralia Philharmonic Orchestra, 1030
Chamber Music Society of the North Shore, 1052
Champaign Urbana Theatre Company, 2989
Champaign-Urbana Symphony Orchestra, 1031
Cheek Theatre, 6828
Chicago a Cappella, 2038
Chicago Actors Ensemble, 2915
Chicago Chamber Orchestra, 1033
Chicago Children's Choir, 2039
Chicago Chorale, 2040
Chicago College of Performing Arts Music Conservatory Series, 4549
Chicago Dramatists, 2916
Chicago Festival Ballet, 218
Chicago Opera Theater, 2041
Chicago Philharmonic, 1048
Chicago Shakespeare Theater on Navy Pier, 2917
Chicago Sinfonietta, 1034
Chicago Studio of Professional Singing Performance Series, 4550
Chicago Symphony Chorus, 2042
Chicago Symphony Orchestra, 1035
Chicago Symphony Orchestra Association, 6733
Chicago Tap Theatre, 201
Chicago Youth Symphony Orchestra, 1036
Child's Play Touring Theatre, 2918
Chinese Classical Orchestra and Educational Program, 1072
Christian Arts Auditorium, 6852
Circa '21 Dinner Playhouse, 2984
Citadel Theatre Company, 2972
City Lit Theater Company, 2919
Classical Symphony Orchestra & the Protege Philharmonic, 1037
Classics on Stage!, 2920
Clockwise Theatre, 2991
Coleman Puppet Theatre, 2976
College of Lake County - Performing Arts Building, 4579
Community Children's Theatre of Peoria Park District, 4592
Congo Square Theatre Company, 2921
Conklin's Barn 2 Dinner Theatre, 2971
Convocation Center, 6762
Corn Productions at Conservatory, 2922
Coronado Performing Arts Center, 6829
Court Theatre, 2923, 6734
Crystal Ballroom Concert Association Series, 4551
Cso Presents, 1038
Curtiss Hall, 6735
Dame Myra Hess Memorial Concert Series, 4552
Dance Center, 6736
Dance Center of Columbia College, 202
Danville Symphony Orchestra, 1044
David Adler Music and Arts Center, 6796
Depaul University Merle Reskin Theatre, 2924
Des Plaines Theatre Guild, 2962
Diller Street Theater, 6850
Dominican University Performing Arts Center, 4596
Downers Grove Choral Society, 2053
Downers Grove Concert Association Series, 4571
Dream Theatre Company, 2925
Dreiske Performance Company, 2926
Drury Lane Oakbrook Terrace, 2982
Dunham Hall Theater, 6771
Dupage Opera Theater, 2055
Dupage Symphony, 1049
Eastern Symphony Orchestra, 1032
Eclipse Theatre Company, 2927
Edman Chapel, 6849
Egyptian Theatre, 6763
Elgin Community College Visual & Performing Arts Center, 6773
Elgin Symphony Orchestra, 1046
Elmhurst College Jazz Festival, 4574
Elmhurst Symphony Orchestra, 1047
Eloise Martin Recital Hall, 6820
Encore Players, 2974
Ensemble Espanol, 6737
Ensemble Espanol Spanish Dance Theater, 2928
Eta Creative Arts Foundation, 2929
Ethel M Barber Theatre, 6780
Famous Door Theatre, 2930
Fermilab Arts Series, 4546
Filament Theatre, 2931
First Folio Shakespeare Festival, 4591
Fox Valley Repertory, 2985
Free Street Programs, 2932
Freedom Hall: Nathan Manilow Theatre, 6814
Friday Noon Concert Series, 4553
Giordano Dance Chicago, 217
Goodman Theatre, 2933
Grant Park Music Festival, 4554
Greenville College Guest Artist Series, 4580
Griffin Theatre Company, 2934
Hancock Stadium, 6806
Harbach Theater, 6785
Harris Theater for Music and Dance, 6738

Geographic Index

Heartland Theatre Company, 2978
Heininger Auditorium, 6804
Horrabin Hall Theatre, 6797
Hubbard Street Dance Chicago, 203
I Wireless Center, 6801
Illinois Central College Subscription Series, 4572
Illinois Chamber Symphony, 1069
Illinois Institute of Technology, Union Board Concerts, 4555
Illinois Philharmonic Orchestra, 1060
Illinois Shakespeare Festival, 2979, 4589
Illinois Symphony Orchestra, 1068
Imagination Theater, 2935
Inventions, 2993
Jack Benny Center for the Arts, 6847
Jackalope Theatre Company, 2936
James F Metcalf Student Experimental Theater, 6772
Jazz Institute of Chicago, 4556
Joel Hall Dancer Center, 204
Joffrey Ballet, 205
Josephine Louis Theater, 6781
Judith Svalander School Ballet, 215
Kathleen Mullady Memorial Theatre, 6739
Kirkland Fine Arts Center, 6768
Knox College, 6786
Knox-Rootabaga Jamm Jazz Festival, 4578
Krannert Center for the Performing Arts - Studio, 6844
Krannert Center for the Performing Arts - Theatre 3, 6843
Krannert Center for the Performing Arts - Theatre 2, 6845
Krannert Center Marquee Series, University of Illinois, 4601
Kresge Recital Hall, 6787
L'opera Piccola, 2043
Lab Theatre, 6815
Lake Forest Symphony, 1056
Lantz Arena, 6725
Lifeline Theatre, 2937
Light Opera Works, 2064
Lira Chamber Chorus, 2044
Lira Dancers of the Lira Ensemble, 1039
Lira Singers, 2045
Little Theatre on The Square, 2988
Live Bait Theatrical Company, 2938
Lookingglass Theatre Company, 2939
Loyola University Department of Theatre, 2940
Loyola University of Chicago Season Subscription Series, 4557
Lund Auditorium, 6821
Lyric Opera of Chicago, 2046, 6740
Mabel Claire Allen Theatre, 6807
Maddox Theatre, 6830
Maine Township Community Concert Association, 4569
Mainstage, 6841
Marion Cultural and Civic Center, 6800
Marjorie Ward Marshall Dance Center, 6782
Marriott's Theatre in Lincolnshire, 2973
Mayfair Theatre/Shear Madness, 2941
Mcaninch Arts Center Mainstage, 6790
Mcaninch Arts Center Studio Theatre, 6791
Mcaninch Arts Center Theater 2, 6789
Mckendree College Fine Arts Series, 4585
Mcpherson Theatre, 6720
Mendelssohn Club, 1064
Metropolis Performing Arts Centre, 6718
Meyer Jacobs Theatre, 6816
Mfa Directing Studio, 6808
Midwest Jazz Heritage Festival, 4593
Midwest Young Artists, 1054
Millenium Park, 6742
Millikin University Opera Theatre, 2052
Millikin-Decatur Symphony Orchestra, 1045
Moline Boys Choir, 2056
Momenta, 219
Moraine Valley Community College Fine & Performing Arts Center, 6813
Mordine and Company Dance Theatre, 207
Muddy River Opera Company, 2058
Muntu Dance Theatre of Chicago, 208
Music Hall, 6836
Music Institute of Chicago Series, 4604
Music of the Baroque Chorus & Orchestra, 2047
Mystery Cafe Series, 4583
Najwa Dance Corps, 209

Naperville-North Central College Performing Arts Series, 4588
Natya Dance Theater, 210
New Black Music Repertory Ensemble, 1040
New Philharmonic, 1050
New Studio Theatre, 6743
Newberry Consort, 4558
Next Theatre Company, 2964
Norris Cultural Arts Center, 6839
Northbrook Symphony Orchestra, 1058
Northern Illinois University Fine Arts Series, 4565
Northlight Theatre, 2986
Northshore Center for the Performing Arts, 6835
Northwestern University Summer Drama Festival, 4577
Northwestern University Theatre and Interpretation Center, 2965
O'brien Field, 6726
O'connell Theatre, 6764
O'rourke Center for the Performing Arts, 6744
Oak Park Festival Theatre, 2980
Odeum Sports & Expo Center, 6846
Opera Illinois, 2057
Orchestra Hall, 6745
Organic Theater Company, 2966
Orpheum Theatre, 2968
Paramount Arts Centre Performing Arts Series, 4545
Paramount Theatre, 6719
Patrick G and Shirley W Ryan Opera Center, 2048
Patrick L O'malley Theatre, 6746
Pegasus Players, 2942
Peoria Ballet, 220
Peoria Civic Center, 4594, 6817, 6818
Peoria Players Theatre, 2983
Peoria Symphony Orchestra, 1061
Performing Arts Association, 4559
Performing Arts Chicago, 1041, 2943
Performing Arts Series for Students, 4566, 4567
Petrillo Music Shell, 6747
Pheasant Run Theatre, 2987
Philip Lynch Theatre, 6832
Pick-Staiger Concert Hall, 6783
Pipe Dreams Studio Theatre, 6769
Piven Theatre Workshop, 2967
Players Theatre, 6765
Prairie Center for the Arts, 6834
Prairie Players Civic Theatre, 2969
Principia College Concert Series, 4575
Pritchard Theater, 6776
Quad City Arts, 4597
Quad-Cities Jazz Festival, 4587
Quincy Civic Music Association, 4595
Quincy Symphony Orchestra, 1062
Raven Theatre Company, 2944
Ravinia Festival, 4581
Raymond F Mccallister Hall, 6777
Recital Hall, 6748
Redbird Arena, 6809
Remy Bumppo Theatre Company, 2945
Rialto Square Theatre, 6794
Rinker Outdoor Amphitheatre, 6778
River North Chicago Dance Company, 211
Robert M Collins Center, 6823
Rock Valley College Lecture/Concert Series, 4598
Rockford Area Youth Symphony Orchestra, 1065
Rockford Dance Company, 222
Rockford Metrocentre, 6831
Rockford Smyphony Orchestra, 1066
Roosevelt University Orchestra: Chicago College of Performing Arts, 1042
Rosemont Theatre, 6770
Ryan Field, 6784
Saint Sebastian Players, 2946
Salt Creek Ballet, 224
Sangamon Auditorium, 6837
School of Theatre and Dance, 6766
Seanachai Theatre Company, 2947
Second City, 2948
Shattered Globe Theater, 2949
Sheely Center for the Performing Arts, 6812
Shryock Auditorium and Arena Promotions, 6722
Sibert Theatre, 6793
Silk and Bamboo Ensemble, 1073
Simpkins Theatre, 6798
Sinfonia Da Camera, 1070

Siu Arena, 6723
Skokie Valley Symphony Orchestra, 1067
Soldier Field, 6749
Southeastern Illinois College Visual & Performing Arts Center, 6792
Southern Illinois University Edwardsville Series, 4573
St Charles Art & Music Festival, 4600
St Charles Singers, 2061
Stage 773, 6755
Stage Center Theatre, 6750
Stage Left Theatre, 2950
Starry Nights Summer Concert Series, 4582
Steep Theatre Company, 2951
Steppenwolf Theatre Company, 2952
Sterling Centennial Auditorium, 6840
Strawdog Theatre Company, 2953
Studio Theatre, 6751, 6788, 6827, 6838
Summer Music Theatre, 2975
Symphony Center, 6752
Symphony of Oak Park & River Forest, 1059
T Daniel & Laurie Willets, 212
T Daniel Productions, 2994
The Albright Theatre Company, 2902
The Center for the Performing Arts, 6842
The Chicago Moving Company, 200
The Chicago Theatre, 6753
The Haymarket Opera Company, 2049
The Hemmens Cultural Center, 6774
The Lira Ensemble, 206
The Merle Reskin Theatre, 6741
The Music Center, 6754
The Rising Stars Theatre Company, 2954
The Springfield Ballet Company, 223
Theatre at Ewing, 6810
Theatre Building Chicago, 2955
Theatre First, 2956
Theatre II Company, 2957
Theatre of Western Springs, 2992
Thodos Dance Chicago, 213
Timber Lake Playhouse, 2977
Timeline Theatre Company, 2958
Trinity College School of Music, 4568
Trinity Irish Dance Company, 216
Triton College Performing Arts Center, 6824
Uic Pavilion, 6756
Uic Theatre, 6757
United Center, 6758
University of Chicago Professional Instrumental Music Series, 4560, 4561
University of Chicago Symphony Orchestra, 1043
University of Illinois at Chicago Fine Arts Series, 4562
University of Illinois at Springfield Sangamon Performing Arts Series, 4599
University of Illinois: Assembly Hall, 4547
University of Illinois: Summerfest, 4602
University Theatre: Summer Show Biz, 2963
Urban Gateways Series: Center for Arts Education, 4563
Us Cellular Field, 6759
Victory Gardens Theater, 6760
Victory Gardens Theater at the Biograph, 2959
Village Players Theater, 2981
Waukegan Concert Chorus, 2062
Waukegan Symphony Orchestra & Concert Chorus, 1071, 2063
Wells Theater, 6802
Werner Auditorium, 6822
West Suburban Symphony, 1055
Westbrook Auditorium, 6721
Western Illinois University Bca Performing Artist Series, 4586
Western Illinois University Theatre and Dance Department, 6799
Westhoff Experimental Theatre, 6811
Wheaton Symphony Orchestra, 1051
Wilbur College Cultural Events Series, 4564
William Ferris Chorale, 2050
Windy City Performing Arts, 2051
Women's Theatre Alliance, 2960
Woodstock Fine Arts Association - Music for A Sunday Afternoon Series, 4605
Woodstock Mozart Festival, 1074, 4606
Woodstock Opera House, 2995, 6851
Wrigley Field, 6761
Writers' Theatre Chicago, 2970

Zephyr Dance, 214
Zion Passion Play, 2996

Indiana

4th Street Theater, 3003
Allen County War Memorial Coliseum, 6876
Amphitheatre, 6921
Anderson Symphony Orchestra Association, 1075
Anderson Young Ballet Theatre, 225
Arena Dinner Theatre, 3007
Arts Place, Inc., 4629
Assembly Hall, 6854
B C Playhouse, 6855
Ball Theater, 6861
Ballet Internationale, 230
Beef and Boards Dinner Theatre, 3010
Bethel College Fine Arts Series, 4626
Bloomington County Playhouse, 2999
Bloomington Early Music Festival, 4609
Bloomington Symphony Orchestra, 1076
Broadway Series: Indianapolis, 4612
Broadway Theatre League of South Bend, 3022
Brown County Playhouse, 3020, 6920
Butler University, 6888
Butler University Symphony Orchestra, 1082
Cabaret at the Columbia Club, 3011
Canterbury Summer Theatre/The Festival Players Guild, 4625
Carmel Dance Arts-Indy Latin Dance, 226
Carmel Symphony Orchestra, 1077
Carole and Gordon Mallett Theatre, 6948
Cave Theatre, 6915
Center for Visual and Performing Arts, 6919
Century Center Convention Hall, 6940
Century Center Recital Hall, 6939
Chanticleer String Quartet, 1094
Chris and Anne Reyes Organ and Choral Hall, 6927
Civic Hall Performing Arts Center, 6937
Clowes Memorial Hall, 6889
Columbus Area Arts Council, 4613
Columbus Indiana Philharmonic, 1078
Community Theatre of Clay County, 3000
Community Theatre of Terre Haute, 6942
Concesco Fieldhouse, 4619
Connersville Area Artists Series, 4614
Cordier Auditorium, 6926
Crossroads Repertory Theatre, 3023
Crown Point Community Theatre, 3005
Culver Military Academy Concert Series, 4615
Dance Kaleidoscope, 231
Dearborn Highlands Arts Council Series, 4608
Depauw University Chamber Symphony, 1081
Depauw University Performing Arts Series, 4617
Derby Dinner Playhouse, 3004
Dreiser Theatre, 6943
Earlham College Guest Artist Series, 4630
Eastern Howard Performing Arts Society, 6882
Edmund P. Joyce Athletic & Convocation Center, 6928
Edward S. Strother Theatre, 6916
Edyvean Repertory Theatre, 3012
Eidson-Duckwall Recital Hall, 6890
Eiteljorg Museum, 6891
Elkhart Civic Theatre, 3001
Elliott Hall of Music, 6949
Embassy Centre, 6870
Emens Auditorium, 4627, 6917
Ensemble Music Society of Indianapolis Series, 4620
Evansville Auditorium and Convention Centre, 6864
Evansville Dance Theatre, 227
Evansville Philharmonic Orchestra, 1079
Everest-Rohrer Auditorium, 6913
Experiemntal Theater, 6862
Festival Music Society of Indiana, 4621
Firefly Festival for the Performing Arts, 4631
First Presbyterian Theater, 3008
Fitzgibbon Recital Hall, 6883
Foellinger Theater in Franke Park, 6871
Footlight Players, Inc., 3017
Fort Wayne Ballet, 228
Fort Wayne Civic Theatre, 3009
Fort Wayne Dance Collective, 229
Fort Wayne Parks & Recreation Festival, 4616

1279

Geographic Index

Fort Wayne Philharmonic Orchestra, 1080
Fountain/Warren Musical Arts Series, 4607
Hanover College Community Artist Series, 4618
Havens Auditorium, 6906
Helen Mallette Studio Theatre, 6865
Herman Baker Recital Hall, 6909
Hilbert Center Theatre, 6892
Hinkle Fieldhouse, 6893
Honeywell Center, 6947
Hulman Center, 6944
Indiana Ballet Company, 233
Indiana Repertory Theatre, 3013
Indiana State University Summer Stage, 3024
Indiana University Summer Music Festival, 4610
Indianapolis Arts Garden, 6894
Indianapolis Chamber Orchestra, 1083
Indianapolis Opera, 2065
Indianapolis Symphonic Choir, 2066
Indianapolis Symphony Orchestra, 1084
Indy Jazz Festival, 4622
International Violin Competition of Indianapolis, 1085
Into Salsa Dance Studio, 232
Iudons, 6877
Jackson County Community Theatre, 3002
Jasper Arts Center, 6905
Jasper Community Arts, 4624
John S. Umble Center, 6878
Judd and Mary Lou Leighton Concert Hall, 6929
Kokomo Symphony, 1088
Kresge Auditorium, 6879
La Porte Civic Auditorium, 6907
Lafayette Symphony, 1089
Lilly Hall Studio Theatre, 6895
Lincoln Amphitheatre: Musical Outdoor Drama, 6866
Little Theatre of Bedford, 2997
Long Center for the Performing Arts, 6908
Mackey Arena, 6950
Marie P. Debartolo Center for the Performing Arts, 6930
Marion Philharmonic Orchestra, 1091
Markey Square Arena, 6896
Masterworks Festival, 4636
Michael Browning Family Cinema, 6931
Moore Theater, 6880
Morris Performing Arts Center, 6941
Muncie Ballet Studio, 234
Muncie Symphony Orchestra, 1092
Musical Arts Center, 6856
Nancy T. Hansen Theatre, 6951
National Women's Music Festival, 4623
New Theater, 6945
New World Youth Symphony Orchestra, 1086
Northwest Indiana Symphony Orchestra and Society, 1093
Notre Dame Stadium, 6932
Octorium, 6914
Old National Centre, 6897
Ole Olsen Memorial Theatre, 6936
Parker Auditorium, 6884
Patricia George Decio Theatre, 6933
Paul G. Robinson Theater, 6922
Paul W Ogle Cultural & Community Center, 6923
Pepsi Coliseum, 6887
Performing Arts Center, 6872
Performing Arts Series of Indiana State University, 4632
Philharmonic Orchestra of Indianapolis, 1087
Phillippe Auditorium, 6910
Phoenix Theatre, 3014
Pike Performing Arts Center, 6898
Purdue Professional Summer Theatre, 3028
Purdue University Convocations & Lectures, 4635
Ransburg Auditorium, 6899
Rca Black Box Theatre, 6911
Rca Dome, 6900
Reardon Auditorium, 6853
Recital Hall, 6924
Regis Philbin Studio Theatre, 6934
Repertory People of Evansville, 3006
Richard K. Stem Concert Hall, 6925
Richmond Civic Theatre, 6938
Richmond Symphony Orchestra, 1095
Ridgewood Arts Foundation: Theatre at the Center, 3018
Roberts Municipal Stadium, 6867

Ross-Ade Stadium, 6952
Ruth Lilly Performance Hall, 6901
Ruth N Halls Theatre, 6857
Saint Mary's College Cultural Arts Season, 4628
Salter Concert Hall, 6863
Scottish Rite Center, 6873
Shawnee Theatre of Greene County, 2998
Soldiers & Sailors Memorial Coliseum, 6868
South Bend Symphony Orchestra, 1096
Star Plaza Theatre, 3016, 6912
Studio Theatre, 6902, 6946
Terre Haute Symphony Orchestra, 1097
The Center for the Peroming Arts, 6860
The Round Barn Theatre at Amish Acres, 3019
Theatre Margot, 6875
Theatre on The Square, 3015
Thompson Recital Hall, 6881
Tippecanoe Chamber Music Society, 1090
University of Notre Dame Department of Film, Television & Theatre, 3021
University Theatre, 6885, 6918
Valparaiso Theatrical Company, 3025
Valparaiso University Chorale, 2068
Valparaiso University Guest Artists Series, 4633
Valparaiso University Symphony Orchestra, 1098
Vesper Chorale, 2067
Victory Field: Indianapolis Baseball Club, 6903
Victory Theatre, 6869
Vincennes University Community Series, 4634
Vincennes University Summer Theatre, 3026
Wagon Wheel Theatre, 3027
Warren Performing Arts Center, 6904
Washington Hall Auditorium, 6935
Wells-Metz Theatre, 6858
Williams Theatre, 6874
Workshop Theatre, 6859
Zurcher Auditorium, 6886

Iowa

Allaert Auditorium, 6974
Alliance World Festival of Women Singing, 4666
Ames City Auditorium, 6953
Ames Town and Gown Chamber Music Association, 1099
B.J. Haan Auditorium, 7018
Barnum Studio Theatre, 7000
Benton Auditorium, 6954
Bertha Martin Theatre, 6961
Bix Biederbecke Memorial Jazz Festival, 4646
Black Hawk Children's Theatre, 7024
Briar Cliff Theatre, 7022
Broadway Theatre League of the Quad-Cities, 3031
Buena Vista University Academic & Cultural Events Series, 4664
Burlington Civic Music Association, 4639
Burlington Memorial Auditorium, 6960
Cass County Arts Council, 4638
Cedar Rapids Community Concerts Association, 4641
Cedar Rapids Opera Theatre, 2069
Cedar Rapids Symphony Orchestra, 1102
Central College Community Orchestra, 1113
Central Iowa Symphony, 1100
Charles H Macnider Art Museum, 7011
Charles Koch Arena, 7028
Civic Center of Greater Des Moines, 6984
Civic Music Association of Des Moines, 4649
Clarke College Cultural Events Series, 4652
Clinton Area Showboat Theatre, 3030
Clinton Symphony Orchestra, 1103
Co' Motion Dance Theater, 235
Coe College Jazz Summit, 4642
Coe College Marquis Series, 4643
David Thayer Theatre, 7003
Des Moines Choral Society, 2071
Des Moines Community Orchestra, 1110
Des Moines Metro Opera, 2072
Des Moines Symphony, 1107
Des Moines Women's Club, 6985
Dewitt Theatre Arts Center, 7015
Dorian Music Festivals, 2070
Dow Theatre, 6966
Drake Stadium, 6986
Drake Symphony Orchestra, 1108
Dubuque Symphony Orchestra, 1109
Fisher Theatre, 6955

Five Flags Center - Theatre, 6992
Five Flags Center Arena, 6991
Friday Night Concert Series, 4657
Gallagher Bluedorn Performing Arts Center, 6962
Galvin Fine Arts Center, 6975
Glenn Miller Festival, 4645
Grand Opera House, 3035
Grand View College-Nielsen Concert Series, 4650, 4651
Grinnell College Music Department Concert Series, 4656
Hallie B. Flanagan Studio Theatre, 6997
Hancher Auditorium, 7004
Harmon Fine Arts Center, 6987
Harold and Charlotte Smtih Theatre, 6994
Hilton Coliseum, 6956
Iowa Arts Festival, 4658
Iowa City Jazz Festival, 4659
Iowa Dance Theatre, 236
Iowa Picture Show, 4660
Iowa State Center, 6957
Iowa State University Performing Arts Council Series, 4637
Iowa Summer Repertory, 3036
Jackson Concert Series, 4662
Jewel Theatre, 6980
Jordan Stage, 6988
Junior Theatre, 3032
Kimmel Theatre, 7013
Kinnick Stadium, 7005
Klinger-Neal Theatre, 7019
Legion Arts, 4644
Loras College Arts & Lecture Series, 4654
Luther College, 6981
Luther College Center Stage Series, 4648
Luther College Symphony Orchestra, 1106
Lyceum Hall, 6976
Mabie Theatre, 7006
Maharishi University Performing Arts Center, 6993
Main Stage Theatre, 7016
Mccaskey Lyceum, 7026
Mills Experimental Theatre, 6968
Mississippi Valley Blues Festival, 4647
Neumann Auditorium, 7027
New World Theatre, 7020
North Iowa Community Auditorium, 7012
Northwest Iowa Symphony Orchestra, 1114
Old Creamery Theatre, 6996
Old Creamery Theatre Company, 3029
Orange City Arts Council, 4663
Ottumwa Symphony Orchestra, 1112
Paramount Theatre, 6969
Pella Opera House, 2074
Plum Fleming Studio Theatre, 7014
Pote Theatre, 7001
Quad City River Bandits Baseball Stadium, 6977
Quad City Symphony Orchestra Association, 1104
Quad City Youth String Ensemble, 1105
Recital Hall, 6982, 6995
River Center/Adler Theatre, 6978
Riverside Theatre, 3038
Riverview Stadium, 6972
Roberts Stadium, 7023
Roberts Theatre, 6998
Sand in The City, 4661
Shaw Center Auditorium, 7009
Sheslow Auditorium in Old Main, 6989
Sinclair Auditorium, 6970
Sioux City Community Theatre, 3037
Sioux City Symphony Orchestra, 1115
Siouxland Youth Symphony Orchestra, 1116
Southeast Iowa Symphony Orchestra, 1111
Stagewest Theater Company, 3034
Stephens Auditorium, 6958, 6959
Strayer-Wood Theatre, 6963, 6964
Studio Theatre, 6979, 7007, 7010, 7017
Sven and Mildred Lekberg Recital Hall, 7002
Tallgrass Theatre Company, 3040
Te Paske Theatre, 7021
The Arts Center, 6973
The Curtainbox Theatre Company, 3033
Theatre B, 7008
Una Vocis Choral Ensemble, 2073
Uni-Dome, 6965
University of Northern Iowa Artists Series, 4640
Us Cellular Center, 6971

Us Sailors Center, 6967
Veterans Memorial Auditorium, 6990
Waldorf Community Artists Series, 4655
Wall Performance Lab, 6999
Wartburg College Artists Series, 4667
Wartburg Community Symphony Orchestra, 1117
Waterloo Community Playhouse & Black Hawk Childrens Theatre, 3039
Waterloo Riverfront Stadium, 7025
Waterloo-Cedar Falls Symphony Orchestra, 1101
Weston H. Noble Recital Hall, 6983

Kansas

Albert Taylor Hall, 7032
Allen Fieldhouse, 7042
Augusta Arts Council/Augusta Historic Theatre, 3041
Bam Players Theatre, 7048
Beach-Schmidt Performing Arts Center, 7035
Bowlus Cultural Attractions Series, 4675
Bowlus Fine Arts Center, 7041
Brown Auditorium, 7052
Brown Grand Theatre, 3044
Burnett Theatre, 7046
Carnie Smith Stadium, 7056
Central Standard, 2075
Century II Civic Center Exhibition Hall, 7067
Century II Civic Center Mary Jane Teall Theatre, 7068
Century II Performing Arts & Convention Center, 7069
Chanute Community Theatre, 3042
Coffeyville Community Theatre, 3043
Coffeyville Cultural Arts Council Inc, 4669
Cohan/Suzeau Dance Company, 237
Columbian Theatre: Museum & Art Center, 3050, 7065
Crafton-Preyer Theatre, 7043
Dodge City Festivals, 7031
Emporia Arts Council Performing Arts/Concert/Children's Series, 4670
Emporia Symphony Orchestra, 1118
Felten-Start Theatre, 7036
Felton Center, 7037
Floral Hall, 7030
Fort Hays State University Encore Series, 4672
Fox Theatre, 7039
Fred Bramlage Coliseum, 7047
Friends University Miller Fine Arts Series, 4683
Goodland Arts Council, 4671
Great Plains Theatre Festival, 4668
Hal Palmer Recital Hall, 7038
Hays Symphony Orchestra, 1119
Henry Levitt Arena, 7070
Hesston/Bethel Performing Arts Series, 4673
Horsefeathers & Applesauce Summer Dinner Theatre, 3053
Hutchinson Symphony Association, 1120
Kansas Coliseum, 7064
Kansas Expocentre, 7061
Kansas Regional Ballet, 239
Kansas State Fair - Grandstand, 7040
Kansas State University Mccain Performance Series, 4676
Kansas University Theatre, 3045
Karl C. Bruder Theatre, 7033
Lawrence Ballet Theatre, 238
Lee Arena, 7062
Lied Center of Kansas, 7044
Manhattan Arts Center, 7048
Mccain Auditorium, 7049
Memorial Auditorium, 7029
Memorial Auditorium and Convention Center, 7057
Messiah Festival of Music, 4674
Miller Concert Hall, 7071
Music Theatre of Wichita, 3051
Neodesha Arts Association, 7053
Newton Mid-Kansas Symphony Orchestra, 1121
Nichols Theatre, 7050
Ottawa Municipal Auditorium, 7054
Ottawa Municipal Auditorium Entertainment Series, 4677
Overland Park Arts Commission, 4678
Performing Arts Series, 7055
Pittsburg State University Solo & Chamber Music Series, 4679

Geographic Index

Purple Masque, 7051
Ronald Q. Frederickson Theatre, 7034
Salina Arts & Humanities Commission, 4680
Salina Bicentennial Center, 7059
Salina Community Theatre, 3047
Sterling College Artist Series, 4681
Stiefel Theatre for the Performing Arts, 7060
The Martin City Melodrama & Vaudeville Company Ltd., 3046
Topeka Civic Theatre & Academy, 3049
Topeka Performing Arts Center, 4682, 7063
Topeka Symphony, 1123
Topeka Symphony Chorus, 2076
Weede Arena, 7058
Wellington Memorial Auditorium, 7066
Wichita Community Theatre, 3052
Wichita Contemporary Dance Theatre, 240
Wichita Grand Opera, 2077
Wichita State University Connoisseur Series, 4684
Wichita Symphony, 1124
Wiedemann Recital Hall, 7072
Wilner Auditorium, 7073
Xavier Hall Theatre, 7045
Youth Symphony Association of Kansas, 1122

Kentucky

Actors Theatre of Louisville, 3068
Actors' Guild of Lexington, 3064
Alice Lloyd College Caney Convocation Series, 4700
American Spiritual Ensemble, 2078
Artists in Concert Series, 4685
Asbury College Artist Series, 4701
Berea College Convocation Series, 4686
Bowling Green-Western Symphony Orchestra, 1125
Broadway Live at the Opera House, 3065
Capitol Arts Alliance, 4687
Capitol Arts Center, 7077
Cardinal Stadium, 7090
Carson Center, 7105
Central Kentucky Arts Series, 4688
Central Kentucky Youth Orchestras, 1126
Chamber Music Society of Central Kentucky, 1127
Commonwealth Stadium, 7083
Diddle Arena, 7078
Eastern Kentucky University Alumni Coliseum, 7108
Far-Off Broadway Players, 3060
Fountain Square Players, 3055
Four Rivers Center for the Performing Arts, 7106
Foust Artist Series, 4690
Freedom Hall Arena, 7091
Glema Mahr Center for the Arts, 7097
Great American Brass Band Festival, 4689
Greater Hazard Area Performing Arts Series, 4691
Hardin County Playhouse, 3058
Henderson Fine Arts Center, 7082
Horse Cave Theatre, 3063
Jayne Stadium, 7098
Jenny Wiley Theatre, 3075
Kentucky Ballet Theatre, 241
Kentucky Center for the Arts Bomhard Theatre, 7093
Kentucky Center for the Arts Robert S Whitney Hall, 7092
Kentucky Opera, 2079
Kentucky Shakespeare Festival, 3069, 4696
Kentucky Symphony Orchestra, 1133
Kincaid Regional Theatre, 3059
Legend of Daniel Boone/James Harrod Amphitheatre, 3062
Lexington Center, 7084
Lexington Children's Theatre, 3066
Lexington Opera House, 7085
Lexington Philharmonic Society, 1128
Louisville Bach, 1129
Louisville Bach Society, 2080
Louisville Ballet, 243
Louisville Chamber Music Society, 1130
Louisville Chorus, 2081
Louisville Memorial Auditorium, 7094
Louisville Orchestra, 1131
Louisville Palace Theatre, 7095

Louisville Youth Orchestra, 1132
Lt Smith Stadium, 7079
Lucille C Little Theater, 7086
Madison Theater, 7080
Market House Theatre, 3074
Mitchell Fine Arts Center, 7087
Muhlenberg Community Theatre, 3061
Murray Civic Music Association Series, 4698
Murray State University Lovett Auditorium, 7099
Music Theatre Louisville, 3070
Norton Center for the Arts, 7081
Owensboro Sports, 7103
Owensboro Symphony Orchestra, 1134
Paducah Community College Fine Arts Center, 7107
Paducah Symphony Orchestra, 1135
Paramount Arts Center, 7074
Pennyroyal Arts Council Series, 4692
Phelps-Stokes Auditorium at Berea College, 7076
Pikeville Concert Association Series, 4699
Pine Knob Theatre, 3056
Pioneer Playhouse of Kentucky, 3057
Racer Arena, 7100
Regional Special Events Center, 7101
Richmond Children's Theatre, 3076
Riverpark Center, 7104
Roy Stewart Stadium, 7102
Singletary Center for the Arts, 7088
Stage One: the Louisville Children's Theatre, 3071
Stephen Foster Productions, 7075
Stephen Foster-Musical, 3054
Studio Players, 3067
Sue Bennett College, Appalachian Folk Festival, 4695
The Lexington Ballet, 242
Theatre Workshop of Owensboro, 3073
Twilight Cabaret Productions, 3072
University of Kentucky Artists Series, 4694
University of Kentucky Memorial Coliseum, 7089
University of Kentucky Singletary Center for the Arts, 4693
W L Lyons Brown Theatre, 7096
Winchester Council for the Arts Series, 4702

Louisiana

Acadiana Symphony Orchestra, 1138
Aillet Stadium, 7153
Alex Box Stadium, 7110
Artists Civic Theatre and Studio, 7128
Artists' Civic Theatre and Studio, 3080
Baton Rouge Ballet Theater, 244
Baton Rouge Little Theater, 3077
Baton Rouge Symphony Orchestra, 1137
Blackham Coliseum, 7123
Burton Coliseum, 7129
Cajun Stadium, 7124
Cajundome and Convention Center, 7125
Centenary College Recital Hall, 7156
Columbia Theatre/Fanfare, 3079
Contemporary Arts Center, 7139
Cowboy Stadium, 7130
Delta Festival Ballet, 245
Eunice Players Theatre, 7118
Fanfare Festival, 4704
Fant-Ewing Coliseum, 7134
Festival International De Louisiane, 4707
Friends of Music Series, 4721
Grambling University Memorial Gymnasium, 7119
Heymann Performing Arts Convention Center, 7126
Hirsch Memorial Coliseum, 7157
Houma Terrebonne Civic Center, 7122
Howard Center for Performing Arts, 7154
Impresario's Choice-The Broadway Series at the Monroe Civic Theatre, 4724
Jeff Davis Arts Council, 4706
Jefferson Performing Arts Society, 4713
Jpas Children's Chorus/Youth Chorale, 2083
Junebug Productions, 3082
Kiefer Uno Lakefront Arena, 7140
Lafayette Community Concerts Series, 4708
Lafayette Community Theatre, 7127
Lake Charles Civic Center - Exhibition Hall, 7132

Lake Charles Civic Center - James E Sudduth Coliseum, 7131
Lake Charles Civic Center - Rosa Hart Theatre, 7133
Lake Charles Symphony, 1139
Le Petit Theatre Du Vieux Carre, 3083, 7141
Louis J. Roussel Performance Center, 7142
Louisiana Philharmonic Orchestra, 1141
Louisiana Superdome, 7143
Louisiana Tech Concert Association Series, 4720
Loyola University Theatre, 7144
Lsu Union Great Performances Theater Series, 4703
Lsu Union Theater, 7111
Mahalia Jackson Theatre of Performing Arts, 7145
Malone Stadium, 7135
Mamou Cajun Music Festival, 4712
Monroe Civic Center, 7136
Monroe Symphony Orchestra, 1140
Morris Fx Jeff Sr Municipal Auditorium, 7146
New Orleans Ballet Association, 246
New Orleans Concert Band, 1142
New Orleans Friends of Music Series, 4716
New Orleans International Piano Competition & Keyboard Festival, 4717
New Orleans Jazz and Heritage Foundation, 1143
New Orleans Opera Association, 2084
New Orleans Recreation Department Theatre, 3084
Nicholls State University Artists & Lecture Series, 4725
Nicholls State University Gym, 7161
Northwestern State University Concert Series, 4715
Opera Louisiane, 2082
Performing Arts Society of Acadiana Series, 4709
Pete Maravich Assembly Center, 7112
Prather Coliseum, 7137
Rapides Coliseum, 7109
Rapides Symphony Orchestra, 1136
Red River Revel Arts Festival, 4722
River Center Arena, 7113
River Center Exhibition Hall, 7114
River Center Grand Ballroom, 7115
River Center Theatre for Performing Arts, 7116
River City Repertory Theatre, 3089
Riverview Hall & Theater, 7158
Saenger Theatre, 3085, 7148
Shakespeare Festival at Tulane, 3086, 4719
Shreveport Little Theatre, 3090
Shreveport Metropolitan Ballet, 247
Shreveport Municipal Auditorium, 7159
Shreveport Opera, 2086
Shreveport Symphony Orchestra, 1144
Slidell Department of Cultural Affairs, 4723
Smoothie King Center, 7147
Southeastern Louisiana University Arts & Lectures Series, 4705
Southeastern Louisiana University Center, 7121
Southeastern Louisiana University Strawberry Stadium, 7120
Southern Rep, 3087
Southern Rep Theatre, 3081
St. John Theatre, 3088
State Palace Theatre, 7149
Strand Theatre, 7160
Swine Palace Productions, 3078
Symphony Chorus of New Orleans, 2085
The New Orleans Jazz & Heritage Festival and Foundation, Inc., 4718
Thomas Assembly Center, 7155
Tiger Stadium, 7117
Tulane University Albert Lupin Experimental Theatre, 7150
Tulane University Department of Theatre and Dance, 7151
Turpin Stadium, 7138
University of Louisiana at Lafayette Concert Series, 4710
University of Louisiana at Monroe Performing Arts Series, 4714
University of New Orleans Performing Arts Center, 7152
University of Southwestern Louisiana Concert Series, 4711

Maine

Acadia Repertory Theatre, 3100, 3101
Arcady Music Society, 1146
Arundel Barn Playhouse, 3091
Augusta Civic Center Arena Center Stage, 7163
Augusta Civic Center Half House Concert Stage, 7164
Augusta Civic Center North Stage, 7162
Bangor Ballet, 248
Bangor Civic Center & Auditorium, 7165
Bangor Symphony Orchestra, 1145
Bar Harbor Music Festival, 4727
Bates Dance Festival, 250, 4735
Bay Chamber Concerts, 252, 1151, 2090, 4746
Bowdoin College Concert Series, 4730
Bowdoin International Music Festival, 4731
Bowdoin Summer Music Festival, 4732
Camden Opera House, 7168
Carousel Music Theatre, 3094
Celebration Barn Theater, 7181
Chocolate Church Arts Center Festival, 4728
Colby Music Series, 4747
Collins Center for the Arts, 7172
Cumberland County Civic Center, 7175
Downriver Theatre Company, 3098
Figures of Speech Theatre, 3096
Forum Series, 4745
Gamper Festival of Contemporary Music, 4733
Good Theater, 3104
Hackmatack Playhouse, 3093
Hadlock Field, 7176
John Lane's Ogunquit Playhouse, 7171
Kneisel Hall Chamber Music Festival, 4729
L/A Arts, 4736
Lakewood Theater, 3107
Lark Society for Chamber Music, 1148, 4739
Mad Horse Theatre Company, 3108
Maine Arts Series, 4740
Maine Center for the Arts at the University of Maine, 7173
Maine Festival, 4741
Maine Music Society, 1147, 2087
Maine State Ballet, 249
Maine State Music Theatre, 3095
Maritime Productions, 3102
Merrill Auditorium, 7177
Morrell Gym, 7100
Mt Desert Festival of Chamber Music, 4737
New Musik Directions Series, 4726
Ogunquit Playhouse, 3103
Olin Arts Center, 7169
Pca Great Performances, 4742
Penobscot Theatre Company, 3092
Pickard Theatre, 7167
Portland Ballet Company, 251
Portland Chamber Music Festival, 4743
Portland Exposition Building, 7178
Portland Stage Company, 3105
Portland String Quartet Concert Series/Workshop, 1149, 4744
Portland Symphonic Choir, 2088
Portland Symphony Orchestra, 1150
Portopera, 2089
Public Theatre, 3097
Rockport Opera House, 7180
Saco River Festival, 4738
Sanford Maine Stage Company, 3109
State Theatre, 7179
Strider Theater, 7182
The Everyman Repertory Theatre, 3106
Theatre at Monmouth, 3099
University of Maine Alumni Stadium, 7174
University of Maine at Fort Kent, International Performers Series, 4734
University of Maine Performing Arts Center, 7170
Waterville Opera House, 7183

Maryland

Adventure Theatre: Glen Echo Park, 3124
American Ensemble Company, 3119
Annapolis Chamber Orchestra, 1152
Annapolis Opera, 2091
Annapolis Summer Garden Theatre, 3110
Arena Players, 3111
Arena Players Playhouse, 7187
Arka Ballet, 265

1281

Geographic Index

Artscape-Baltimore's Festival of the Arts, 4749
Ballet Theatre of Maryland, 253
Baltimore Actors' Theatre, 3112
Baltimore Chamber Orchestra, 1153
Baltimore Choral Arts Society, 2092
Baltimore Classical Guitar Society, 1154
Baltimore Opera Company, 2093
Baltimore Symphony Chorus, 2094
Baltimore Symphony Orchestra, 1155
Baltimore Symphony Orchestra Summer Music Fest: Oregon Ridge Concert Series, 4750
Baltimore-Washington Jazzfest, 4760
Bowie State University Martin Luther King Jr. Center, 7201
Candlelight Concert Society, 1162
Capital Jazz Festival, 4767
Center Stage, 3113, 7188
Children's Chorus of Maryland & School of Music, 2101
City of Gaithersburg Cultural Arts Division, 4765
Clancyworks Dance Company, 264
Clarice Smith Performing Arts Center, 7203
Cockpit in Court Summer Theatre, 3114
College of Southern Maryland Fine Arts Center, 7207
Columbia Festival of the Arts, 4761
Columbia Orchestra, 1163
Columbia Pro Cantare, 2098
Concert Artists of Baltimore, 1156, 4751
Cumberland Theatre, 3123
Dance Baltimore, 255
Dance Exchange, 266
Deep Vision Dance Company, 267
Doug Hamby Dance, 256
Dunbar Performing Arts Center, 7189
Dundalk Community Theatre, 3115
Eastern Shore Chamber Music Festival, 4762
Everyman Theatre, 3116
First Mariner Arena, 7190
Francis Scott Key Auditorium, 7184
Frederick Chorale, 2099
Frederick Community College Arts Series, 4763
Frostburg State University Cultural Events Series, 4764
Frostburg State University Dance Company, 259
Gildenhorn/Speisman Center for the Arts, 7211
Gordon Center for Performing Arts, 7210
Handel Choir of Baltimore, 2095
Harford Ballet Company, 261
Imagination Stage, 3120
Institute of Musical Traditions, 2100
Interact Story Theatre, 3130
Jewish Community Center Symphony, 1171
John Addison Concert Hall, 7205
Johns Hopkins, 7191
Johns Hopkins University Homewood Field, 7192
Joseph Meyerhoff Symphony Hall, 7193
Kraushaar Auditorium, 7194
Leclerc Auditorium, 7195
Lyric Opera House, 7196
Maryland Ballet Theatre, 258
Maryland Hall for the Creative Arts, 7185
Maryland International Chamber Music Festival, 4752
Maryland Symphony Orchestra, 1167
Maryland Theatre, 7206
Maryland Youth Symphony Orchestra, 1165
Mcmanus Theater, 7197
Metropolitan Ballet Theatre Inc., 262
Meyerhoff Symphony Hall, 7198
Modell Performing Center at the Lyric, 7199
Montgomery College Robert E Parilla Performing Arts Center, 7212
Montgomery County Youth Orchestra, 1159
Music at Penn Alps, 1166
Music in The Great Hall Series, 4757
National Ballet Company, 254
National Musical Arts, 1168
National Orchestral Institute, 1160
National Tap Ensemble, 260
Notre Dame of Maryland University, 4753
Olney Theatre Center, 3128
Open Sky, 4766
Opera Vivente, 2096
Peabody Conservatory of Music, 1157
Petrucci's Dinner Theatre, 3125
Prince George's Philharmonic, 1170
Prince George's Stadium, 7202

Pumpkin Theatre, 3129
Reitz Arena, 7200
Rep Stage, 3122
Res Musicamerica Series, 4754
Roland E Powell Convention Center, 7209
Round House Theatre, 3121
Sacred Dance Guild, 263
Shriver Hall Concert Series, 4755
Silver Spring Stage, 3131
Smallbeer Theatre Company, 3127
St. John's College Concert Series, 4748
Stephens Auditorium, 7214
Strathmore, 7208
Susquehanna Symphony Orchestra, 1164
The National Philharmonic, 1169
Theatre Hopkins, 3117
Theatre Project, 3118
Toby's Dinner Theatre, 7204
Towson Center Arena, 7215
University of Maryland Baltimore County Symphony, 1158
University of Maryland International William Kapell Piano Competition & Festival, 4759
University of Maryland: International William Kapell Piano Competition & Festival, 1161
Us Naval Academy Alumni Hall, 7186
Washington College Concert Series, 4758
Washington Jewish Theatre, 1172
Washington Savoyards, 2097
Wicomico Civic Center, 7213
Word Dance Theater, 257
Young Artists Theatre, 3126
Young Audiences of Maryland, 4756

Massachusetts

Academy of Performing Arts, 3168
Academy Playhouse, 7248
Actors Theatre of Nantucket, 3162
Agassiz Theatre, 7229
Albany Berkshire Ballet, 280
Alea III, 1175
All Newton Music School, the Andrew Wolf Concert Series, 4810
American International College Series, 4804
American Repertory Theatre, 3146
Amherst Ballet Theatre Company Inc, 269
Amherst College Lefrak Gym, 7216
Ann Arbor Summer Festival, 4770
Anna Myer and Dancers, 275
Apollinaire Theatre Company, 3148
Arena Civic Theatre, 3154
Aston Magna Festival, 4791
Back Bay Chorale, 2103
Barrington Stage Company, 3169
Bay Colony Productions, 3152
Belmont Dramatic Club, 3133
Bentley College Bowles Performance Series, 4807
Berklee Performance Center, 7219
Berkshire Choral Festival, 4801
Berkshire Lyric Theatre, 2123
Berkshire Opera Company, 2116
Berkshire Theatre Festival, 3176, 4806
Blue Spruce Theatre, 3179
Booth Productions, 3186
Boston Ballet, 271
Boston Baroque, 1173
Boston Camerata, 2104
Boston Center for the Arts Plaza Theatre, 7220
Boston Chamber Music Society, 1185
Boston Children's Theatre, 3135
Boston Civic Symphony Orchestra of Boston, 1216
Boston Classical Orchestra, 1202
Boston College Alumni Field Stadium, 7232
Boston Conservatory, 4773
Boston Dance Company, 276
Boston Early Music Festival, 4783
Boston Globe Jazz & Blues Festival, 4784
Boston Modern Orchestra Project, 1200
Boston Musica Viva, 1186
Boston Opera House, 7221
Boston Philharmonic Orchestra, 1187
Boston Pops Orchestra, 1176
Boston Symphony Chamber Players, 1177
Boston Symphony Orchestra, 1178
Braintree Choral Society, 2109

Brandeis Symphony Orchestra, 1214
Brandeis University Department of Music, 1215
Brandeis University Spingold Theater Center Series, 4808
Bridgewater State College Program Committee, 4781
Brockton Symphony Orchestra, 1184
Calvin Theatre and Performance Arts Center, 7246
Cambridge Society for Early Music: Chamber Music Series, 1188, 4785
Cantata Singers, 2105
Cape & Islands Chamber Music Festival, 4796
Cape Ann Symphony Orchestra, 1195
Cape Cod Chamber Music Festival, 1204, 4797
Cape Cod Conservatory of Music & Arts, 7255
Cape Cod Melody Tent, 3156
Cape Cod Symphony Orchestra, 1219
Chapin Hall, 7258
Charles River Concert Series, 4774
Charlestown Working Theater, 3147
Chester Theatre Company, 3149
Citi Performing Art Center Wang Theatre, 7222
Close Encounters With Music Series, 4792
College Light Opera Company, 2114
Commonwealth Ballet Company, 268
Commonwealth Opera, 2115
Company One, 3136
Concerts-At-The-Common, 4812
Concord Band, 1192
Concord Orchestra, 1193
Constellationcenter, 7230
Cutler Majestic Theatre at Emerson College, 7223
Dance Prism, 272
Dinosaur Annex Music Ensemble, 1179
Electric Symphony Festival, 4771
Emmanuel Music Bach Cantata Series, 4775
Ensemble Music Society of Indianapolis Series, 4794
Fiddlehead Theatre Company, 3167
Fine Arts Chorale, 2125
Firehouse Center for the Arts, 7244
First Night Boston, 4776
Fleetboston Celebrity Series, 4777
Foothills Theatre Company, 3187
Footlight Club, 3158
Friends of the Performing Arts, 4790
Gloriae Dei Artes Foundation, 2122
Gloucester Stage Company, 3153
Gosman Sports & Convocation Center, 7253
Greater Boston Youth Symphony Orchestras, 1180
Griswold Theatre, 7250
Handel and Haydn Society, 1181, 2106
Harvard Musical Association in Boston, 4778
Harvard-Radcliffe Orchestra, 1189
Harwich Junior Theatre, 3182
Highfield Theatre, 7234
Hingham High School Auditorium, 3155, 7237
History Making Productions, 3180
Hudson Community Arts Series, 4793
Huntington Theatre Company, 3137, 7224
Inca Son: Music and Dance of the Andes, 277
Indian Hill Symphony, 1199
International Music Network, 1194
Isabella Stewart Gardner Museum, 7225
Jacob's Pillow Dance, 270
Jacob's Pillow Dance Festival, 4772
Jeannette Neill Dance Studio, 273
Jewish Theatre of New England, 3165
John M Greene Hall, 7247
Jordan Hall at New England Conservatory, 7226
Jose Mateo Ballet Theatre, 278
Kidstock Creative Theater Education Center, 3185
King Richard's Faire, 4789
King's Chapel Concert Series, 4779
Klezmer Conservatory Band, 1190, 2110
Koussevitzky Performing Arts Center, 7249
Loeb Drama Center, 7231
Longwood Opera, 2119
Lowell Memorial Auditorium, 7239
Lyric Stage Company of Boston, 3138
Margaret L Jackson Arts Center, 7233
Martha's Vineyard Chamber Music Society, 1212
Massachusetts International Festival of the Arts, 4798

Massachusetts Museum of Contemporary Art, 7245
Massachusetts Youth Wind Ensemble, 1182
Massasoit Community College Buckley Arts Center Performance Series, 4782
Massmutual Center, 7251
Master Singers, 2118
Masterworks Chorale, 2111
Mechanics Hall, 7260
Melrose Symphony Orchestra, 1201
Merrimack Repertory Theatre, 3160
Mit Guest Artists Series, 4786
Mohawk Trail Concerts/Music in Deerfield, 4802
Museum of Fine Arts Concerts & Performances, 4780
Music at Amherst Series, 4769
Musicorda Festival & Summer String Program, 1209
Musicorda Summer Festival, 4803
New Century Theatre, 3166
New England Philharmonic, 1183
New England String Ensemble, 1213
New Phoenix, 3183
New Repertory Theatre, 3164
Newton Symphony Orchestra, 1203
North Shore Music Theatre, 3134
North Shore Philharmonic Orchestra, 1174
Northeastern Theatre, 3139
Opera Boston, 2107
Opera New England, 2108
Orpheum Theatre, 7235
Paul Madore Chorale, 2124
Performing Arts School of Worcester, 7261
Pilgrim Theater Research & Performance Collaboration, 3132
Pioneer Valley Symphony, 1196
Plymouth Philharmonic Orchestra, 1207
Priscilla Beach Theatre, 7257
Prism Opera, 2117
Pro Arte Chamber Orchestra, 1191
Provincetown Repertory Theatre, 3170
Publick Theatre, 3140
Puppet Showplace Theatre, 3144
Quincy Symphony Orchestra, 1218
Radcliffe Choral Society, 2112
Regattabar Jazz Festival at the Charles Hotel, 4787
Regis College Fine Arts Center, 7256
Revels, 2126
Robbins-Zust Family Marionettes, 3171
Rockport Chamber Music Festival, 1208, 4800
Salem Theatre, 3172
Salisbury Singers, 2127
Savoyard Light Opera Company, 2113
Science Fiction Theatre Company, 3141
Shakespeare & Company, 3159
Sharon Community Theatre, 3173
Smith College Glee Club & Choirs, 2121
Smith College Orchestra, 1205
Snappy Dance Theater, 279
South Mountain Concerts, 4799
Speakeasy Stage Company, 3142
Spingold Theater Center, 3178, 7254
Springfield Orchestra Association, 1210
Springfield Performing Arts Development Corporation, 4805
Springfield Symphony Hall, 7252
Springfield Symphony Orchestra, 1211
Sterling & Francine Clark Art Institute, 7259
Stockbridge Chamber Concerts at Searles Castle, 1206
Strawberry Productions, 3150
Summer Theatre at Mt. Holyoke College, 3175
Symphony Hall, 7227
Symphony Pro Musica, 1197
Tanglewood Festival, 4795
Tanglewood Music Center, 7238
Td Banknorth Garden, 7228
Thayer Symphony Orchestra, 1198
The Art of Black Dance and Music, 281
The Dinner Detective, 3174
The Lynn Auditorium., 7241
The Mahaiwe Performing Arts Center Theatre, 7236
Theatre Workshop of Nantucket, 3163
Tweeter Center for the Performing Arts, 7242
University of Massachusetts Center for the Arts, 7240

Geographic Index

University of Massachusetts Fine Arts Center, 7217
Urbanity Dance, 274
Valley Light Opera, 2102
Village Players, 3157
Vineyard Playhouse, 3177
Waltham Community Concert Series, 4809
Wellfleet Harbor Actors Theater, 3181
Westfield State College Music & More Performing Arts Series, 4811
Wheelock Family Theatre, 3143
William D Mullins Memorial Center, 7218
Williams Chamber Players, 1217
Williams College Series, 4813
Williamstown Theatre Festival, 3184, 4814
Woodland Theatre Company, 3161
Worcester Children's Theatre, 3188
Worcester Music Festival, 4815
World Music Festival, 4788
Yard, 3151
Zamir Chorale of Boston, 2120
Zeiterion Theatre, 7243

Michigan

Acting Up Theatre Company, 3205
Actors & Playwrights' Initiative, 3208
Adrian College Events Series, 4816
Adrian Symphony Orchestra, 1220
Albion Performing Artist & Lecture Series, 4817
Alma College Performing Arts Series, 4819
Alma Symphony Orchestra, 1221
American Artists Series, 4829
Ann Arbor Blues & Jazz Festival, 4821
Ann Arbor Dance Works, 282
Ann Arbor Summer Festival, 4822
Ann Arbor Symphony Orchestra, 1222
Arthur Miller Theatre, 7265
Attic / New Center Theatre, 3196
Bach Festival Society of Kalamazoo, 4852
Barn Theatre, 3192
Battle Creek Civic Theatre, 7274
Battle Creek Symphony Orchestra, 1224
Bay Arts Council, 4826
Bay City Players, 3193
Bay View Music Festival, 4827
Berry Events Center, 7315
Birmingham-Bloomfield Symphony, 1226
Blue Lake Repertory Theatre, 3217
Boychoir of Ann Arbor, 2128
Bullard School of Dance, 287
Calumet Theatre Company, 3194, 7279
Calvin College Fine Arts Center, 7299
Casa De Unidas Series, 4834
Chamber Music Society of Detroit, 1231
Cheboygan Area Arts Council/Opera House, 2132, 4833
Cheboygan Opera House, 7280
Circle Theatre, 3202
City of Grand Haven Community Center, 7298
Civic Theatre & School of Theatre, 3203
Co Brown Stadium, 7275
Cobo Arena, 7282
Comic Opera Guild, 2129
Community Theatre Association of Michigan, 7264
Cranbrook Music Guild Concert Series, 4830
Crisler Arena, 7266
Crooked Tree Arts Council, 4857
Dawson Auditorium, 7263
Dearborn Orchestral Society / Dearborn Symphony, 1228
Deltaplex Arena & Conference Center, 7300
Dennos Museum Center Milliken Auditorium, 7330
Detroit Chamber Winds & Strings, 1253
Detroit Festival of the Arts, 4835
Detroit Repertory Theatre, 3197
Detroit Symphony Orchestra, 1229
Detroit Symphony Orchestra Hall, 7283
Devos Performance Hall, 7301
Downriver Council for the Arts, 4862
Eastern Michigan University Convocation Center, 7335
Eisenhower Dance Ensemble, 291
Ferris State University-Arts & Lectures Series, 4828
Festival of the Arts, 4842
1515 Broadway Performance Venue, 7295
Fisher Theatre, 7284
Flint Institute of Music, 4839, 7296
Flint School of Performing Arts: Youth Ensembles, 1232
Flint Symphony Orchestra, 1233
Fontana Chamber Arts, 1243
Fontana Festival of Music & Art, 4853
Ford Detroit International Jazz Festival, 4836
Ford Field, 7285
Fountain Street Church, 7302
Fox Theatre, 7286
Frauenthal Center for the Performing Arts, 7322
Freedom Hill Amphitheatre, 7328
Gaylord Area Council for the Arts, 4841
Gopherwood Concert Series, 4831
Grand Rapids Ballet Company, 285
Grand Rapids Symphony, 1234
Grand Rapids Youth Symphony, 1235
Grand Valley State University Arts at Noon Series, 4818
Great Lakes Chamber Music Festival, 4861
Grosse Pointe War Memorial, 4844
Heritage Theater, 7327
Hilberry Theatre, Wayne State University, 3198
Hill Auditorium, 7267
Hillsdale College Community Orchestra, 1238
Holland Area Arts Council, 4846
Holland Chamber Orchestra, 1239
Holland Chorale, 2138
Holland Symphony Orchestra, 1240
Hope College Great Performance Series, 4847
Hope College Orchestra, 1241
Hope College Theatre, 7305
Hope Summer Repertory Theatre, 3206
Interlochen Center for Arts, 4850
Interlochen Center for the Arts, 286
Interlochen Center for the Arts Dendrinos Center, 7307
Interlochen Center for the Arts Kresge Auditorium, 7306
Ironwood Theatre, 3207, 7308
Irving S Gilmore International Keyboard Festival, 4854
Jack Breslin Student Events Center, 7292
Jackson Academy Performing Arts Center, 7309
James E O'neil Jr Arena, 7332
James W Miller Auditorium, 7311
Jet Theatre, 3218
Jewish Community Center of Metropolitan Detroit, 7333
Jewish Ensemble Theatre, 3219
Joe Louis Arena, 7287
Kalamazoo Civic Auditorium, 7312
Kalamazoo Civic Players, 3209
Kalamazoo Singers, 2139
Kalamazoo Symphony Orchestra, 1244
Kellogg Arena, 7276
Kelly Shorts Stadium, 7319
Kerrytown Concert House, 7268
Keweenaw Symphony Orchestra of Michigan Technological University, 1242
Kirtland Center for the Performing Arts, 7326
L.C Walker Arena, 7324
Lake St. Clair Symphony Orchestra, 1255
Lake Superior State University Cultural Events Series, 4859
Lakeview Arena, 7316
Lansing Symphony Orchestra, 1245
Livonia Symphony Orchestra, 1246
Lydia Mendelssohn Theatre, 7269
Macomb Center for the Performing Arts, 7281
Macomb Symphony Orchestra, 1227
Maggie Allesee Department of Theatre and Dance, 7291
Masonic Temple Theatre, 7288
Matrix Theatre Company, 3200
Matrix: Midland Festival-Celebration of the Arts, Sciences & Humanities, 4856
Mcmorran Place Theatre, 7325
Meadow Brook Theatre, 3213
Mendel Center, 7277
Metropolitan Youth Symphony, 1254
Michigan Association of Community Arts Agencies, 4823
Michigan Ballet Theatre, 290
Michigan Classic Ballet Company, 283
Michigan Opera Theatre, 2134
Michigan Renaissance Festival, 4848
Michigan Shakespeare Festival, 4851
Michigan Theater, 7270
Midland Center for the Arts, 7317
Midland Symphony Orchestra, 1247
Mpulse Ann Arbor, 4824
Mtu/Great Events Series, 4849
Music Center of South Central Michigan, 1225
Music Hall Center for the Performing Arts, 7289
Music in The Parks, 4840
Music Society: Midland Center for the Arts, 1248
Musical Society of the University Series, 4825
Nelda K Balch Playhouse, 7313
New Year's Fest, 4855
Old Town Playhouse, 3216
Opera Grand Rapids, 2136
Opera Lite, 2135
Overbrook Theater, 7323
Palace at Auburn Hills, 7273
Park Place Hotel, 7331
Perani Arena and Event Center, 7297
Performance Network of Ann Arbor, 3190
Pine Mountain Music Festival, 4845
Plachta Auditorium, 7320
Plymouth Symphony, 1250
Port Huron Civic Theatre, 3211
Potter Center, 7310
Power Center for the Performing Arts, 7271
Pro Musica of Detroit, 1230, 1237
Purple Rose Theatre Company, 3195
Rackham Symphony Choir, 2137
Red Barn Playhouse, 3214
Reif Arts Center, 4843
River Raisin Ballet Company, 289
River Raisin Centre for the Arts, 7318
Rose Arena, 7321
Saginaw Bay Symphony Orchestra, 1251
Saginaw Choral Society, 2140
Saginaw Valley State University Concert: Lecture Series, 4863
Sheldon Theatre, 3212
Southwest Michigan Symphony Orchestra, 1252
Spartan Stadium, 7293
St. Cecilia Music Society, 1236
Syracuse Jazz Festival, 4837
Tecumseh Center for the Arts, 7329
Temple Theatre Organ Club, 4858
The Croswell Opera House & Fine Arts Association, 7262
The Michigan Dance Project, 284
Theater Grottesco, 3201
Thunder Bay Arts Council, 4820
Thunder Bay Theatre, 3189
Tibbits Opera Foundation and Arts Council, 2133
Traverse Symphony Orchestra, 1256
United Black Artists: Usa Series, 4838
University Musical Society Choral Union, 2130
University of Detroit Mercy Calihan Hall, 7290
University of Michigan Gilbert and Sullivan, 2131
University of Michigan Symphony Orchestras, 1223
University Productions: University of Michigan, 3191
Urban Institute for Contemporary Arts, 3204, 7303
Van Andel Arena, 7304
Village Bach Festival, 4832
Waterford Cultural Council, 4864
Wellspring/Cori Terry & Dancers, 288
West Michigan Symphony, 1249
West Shore Community College Cultural Series, 4860
Wharton Center for Performing Arts, 7294
Wings Stadium, 7314
Wink Arena, 7278
Yack Arena, 7334
Yost Ice Arena, 7272
Youtheatre, 3215

Minnesota

Albert Lea City Arena, 7336
Albert Lea Community Theatre, 7337
Alexandria Festival of the Lakes, 4865
Allied Concert Services, 4874
Arts in The Parks Portable Stage, 7341
Arts Midwest, 3235
Augsburg Choir, 2142
Bemidji State University Thompson Recital Hall, 7339
Bemidji Symphony Orchestra, 1257
Benedicta Arts Center, 7370
Bethany Lutheran College Concerts & Lectures, 4869
Brave New Workshop, 3236
Brooklyn Center Community Center, 7342
Carleton College Concert Series, 4878
Chanhassen Dinner Theatre, 3223
Children's Theater Company, 3237
Civic Orchestra of Minneapolis, 1262
Climb Theatre, 3231
Climb Theatre - Creative Learning Ideas, 3265
Colder by The Lake Comedy Theatre, 3224
College of St. Scholastica Mitchell Auditorium, 4867
Commedia Theater Company, 3238
Commonweal Theatre Company, 3232
Concord Singers of New Ulm, 2150
Concordia College Cultural Events Series, 4875
Continental Ballet Company, 292
Duluth Entertainment Convention Center, 7344
Duluth-Superior Symphony Orchestra, 1258
Duluth-Superior Youth Orchestras & Sinfonia, 1259
Elias J Halling Recital Hall, 7349
Ethnic Dance Theatre, 301
Fairmont Opera House, 7346
Fargo-Moorhead Symphony Orchestra, 1267
Fitzgerald Theater, 7371
451st Army Band, 1270
Gooseberry Park Players, 3260
Grand Casino Hinckley Amphitheater, 7347
Great American History Theatre, 3266
Greater Twin Cities Youth Symphonies, 1263
Green Earth Players, 3233
Gustavus Adolphus College Artist Series, 4885
Guthrie Theater, 3239, 7351
Hauser Dance Company, 294
Heartland Symphony Orchestra, 1260
Hennepin Center for the Arts, 7352
Hidden Theatre, 3240
Highland Summer Theatre, 3234
Historic Orpheum Theatre, 7353
Historic State Theatre, 7354
Hobson Union Programing Board Performing Artists Series, 4866
Horton Grand Theatre, 7355
Hubert H Humphrey Metrodome, 7356
I-90 Expo Center, 7379
Illusion Theater, 3241
In the Heart of the Beast Puppet and Mask Theatre, 3242
Intermedia Arts, 4870
Jackson Marionette Productions, 3243
James Sewell Ballet, 295
Jungle Theater, 3244
Lakeshore Players, 3272
Lakeshore Playhouse, 7380
Legendary Roy Wilkins Auditorium at Saint Paul Rivercentre, 7372
Little Theatre of Owatonna, 3263
Long Lake Theater, 3230
Macphail Center for the Arts, 7357
Mankato Symphony Orchestra, 1261
Margolis Brown Theatre Company, 3245
Martin Luther College Lyceum, 7366
Matchbox Children's Theatre, 3221
Mayo Civic Center Arena, 7367
Mayo Civic Center Auditorium Theatre, 7368
Medora Musical, 3246
Metropolitan Symphony Orchestra, 1264
Midway Stadium, 7373
Midwest Wireless Civic Center, 7350
Minneapolis Park & Recreation Board-Summer Music in The Parks, 4871
Minnesota Ballet, 293
Minnesota Center Chorale, 2154
Minnesota Chorale, 2143
Minnesota Dance Theatre & Dance Institute, 296
Minnesota Opera, 2144
Minnesota Orchestra, 1265
Minnesota Sinfonia, 1266
Minnesota State Band, 1271
Minnesota State University Moorhead Series, 4876
Minnetonka Chamber Choir, 2148

1283

Geographic Index

Minnetonka Symphony Chorus, 2149
Mixed Blood Theatre Company, 3247
Mu Performing Arts, 3248
National Lutheran Choir, 2145
National Sports Center, 7340
Nautilus Music-Theater, 3268
New Hope Outdoor Theatre, 7365
North Hennepin Community College Theater, 7343
North Star Opera, 2153
Northrop Auditorium, 7358
Northrop Dance Season, 297
O'shaughnessy Theatre, 7374
Off-Broadway Musical Theatre, 3262
Old Log Theater, 3228
Open Eye Figure Theatre, 3249
Orchestra Hall, 7359
Ordway Center for the Performing Arts, 7375
Pacific Composers Forum, 4882
Pangea World Theater, 3250
Paramount Theater Visuals & Arts Center, 7369
Park Square Theatre Company, 3269
Paul Bunyan Playhouse, 3222
Penumbra Theatre Company, 3270
Pillsbury House Theatre, 3251
Playwrights' Center, 3252
Prairie Arts Center, 7348
Rainbo Children's Theatre Company, 3271
Red Eye, 3253
Reif Greenway Series, 4868
Rivercenter, 7376
Riverside Arena, 7338
Rochester Civic Music, 4880
Rochester Civic Theatre, 3264
Rochester Symphony Orchestra & Chorale, 2152
Saint Olaf College Orchestra, 1268
Saint Paul Chamber Orchestra, 1272
Schaeffer Fine Arts Center, 7378
Schubert Club International Artist Series, 4883, 4884
Shakespeare & Company, 3273
St Cloud State University Program Board Performing Arts Series, 4881
St Louis County Heritage and Arts Center, 7345
St Olaf Choir, 2151
St. Cloud Symphony Orchestra, 1269
St. Olaf College Artist Series, 4879
Stages Theatre Company, 3229
Straw Hat Players, 3261
Stuart Pimsler Dance & Theater, 298
Target Center, 7360
Ted Mann Concert Hall, 7361
The Apollo Club, 2141
The Duluth Playhouse, 3225
Theater Latte Da, 3254
Theatre De La Jeune Lune, 3255
Theatre in The Round, 3256
Theatre in The Round Players, 7362
Theatre L'homme Dieu, 3220
Troupe America, 3257
Twin Cities Gay Men's Chorus, 2146
University of Minnesota at Minneapolis Series, 4872
University of Minnesota Duluth: Department of Theatre, 3226, 3227
University of Minnesota Morris Cac Performing Arts Series, 4877
University of Minnesota Sports Pavillion, 7363
Vocalessence, 2147, 4873
Walker Art Center, 3258, 7364
World Tree Puppet Theater, 3259
Xcel Energy Center, 7377
Zenon Dance Company and School, 299
Zoronco Famenco Dance Theater and School, 300

Mississippi

, 7394, 7400, 7401
Ballet Mississippi, 302
Bancorpsouth Arena and Conference Center, 7409
Beau Rivage Theatre, 7382
Belhaven College Center for the Arts, 7395
Belhaven College Preston Memorial Series, 4888
Bologna Performing Arts Center, 7385
Coliseum Civic Center, 7389
Columbia Exposition Center, 7387
Corinth Theatre-Arts, 3274
Delta Center Stage, 3275
Depot Theatre, 7381
Fulton Chapel, 7405
Gertrude C. Ford Center for the Performing Arts, 7410
Gulf Coast Opera Theatre, 2155
Gulf Coast Symphony, 1273
Harley Outdoor Amphitheatre, 7383
Hinge Dance Company, 303
Humphrey Coliseum, 7404
Indianola Little Theatre, 7393
Jackson Municipal Auditorium Thalia Mara Hall, 7396
Jazz in The Grove, 4886
Leflore County Civic Center, 7390
Meek Auditorium, 7406
Meridian Community College Theatre, 7402
Meridian Symphony Orchestra, 1277
Mississippi Arts Commission, 4889
Mississippi Opera, 2156
Mississippi State University Lyceum Series, 4891
Mississippi Symphony Orchestra, 1275
Mississippi Veterans Memorial Stadium, 7397
Mississippi Youth Symphony Orchestra, 1276
Msu Riley Center, 7403
Natchez Festival of Music, 4892
New Stage Theatre, 3276
Panola Playhouse, 7408
Princess Theatre, 7388
Puppet Arts Theatre, 3277
Saenger Theatre, 7391
Saenger Theatre of the Performing Arts, 7384
Thalia Mara Hall, 7398
Triangle Cultural Center, 7411
Tupelo Symphony Orchestra Association, 1278
University of Mississippi Artist Series, 4893
University of Mississippi Studio Theatre, 7407
University of Southern Mississippi School of Music, 4887, 7392
University of Southern Mississippi Symphony, 1274
Whistle Stop Playhouse, 7386
Wood College Theatre, 7399
World Performance Series: Thalia Mara Foundation, 4890

Missouri

Actors Studio, 3285
Alexandra Ballet, 304
American Royal Center Kemper Arena, 7423
American Theatre, 7443
Arrow Rock Lyceum Theatre, 3278
Bach Society of Saint Louis, 2162
Ballet North, 307
Blanche M. Touhill Performing Arts Center, 7464
Busch Stadium, 7444
Busch Student Center, 7445
Capital City Council on The Arts, 4901
Cathedral of Saint Louis, 7446
Center of Creative Arts, 7447
Central Methodist College Convocations, 4898
Central Missouri State University Symphony Orchestra, 1295
Citicorp Summerfest, 4916
City Theatre of Independence, 3284
Coger Theatre, 7466
Coterie Theatre, 3286
Cottey Lecturers & Artists Super Series, 4913
Culver-Stockton College Performing Arts Hall, 7413
Dance Saint Louis, 310
Edison Theatre, 3297, 7448
Elizabeth T Champ Auditorium, 7420
Evangel University Artists & Lectureship Series, 4925
Fabulous Fox Theatre, 7449
Family Arena, 7463
Faurot Fieldhouse, 7415
Florissant Civic Center Theater, 3283
Folly Theater, 3287, 7424
Fox Associates, 4917
Friends of Chamber Music, 1281
Friends of Historic Boonville Performing Arts, 4894
Goldenrod Showboat Dinner Theatre, 3308
Goppert Theatre, 7425
Graham Tyler Memorial Chapel, 7435
Grand Center Grandel Theatre, 7450
Hammons Student Center, 7460
Hannibal Concert Association, 4900
Harriman-Jewell College, 4910
Hearnes Center, 7416
Heart of America Shakespeare Festival, 4903
Heartland Men's Chorus, 2159
Hilton Center for the Arts, 7451
Hot City Theatre, 3298
Independence Symphony Orchestra, 1280
Insight Theatre Company, 3311
Jesse Auditorium, 7417
Jewish Community Center of Saint Louis, 7452
Jones Auditorium, 7437
Juanita K Hammons Hall, 7461
Juneteenth Heritage & Jazz Festival, 4918
Kansas City Ballet, 308
Kansas City Blues & Jazz Festival, 4904
Kansas City Chamber Orchestra, 1282
Kansas City Municipal Auditorium, 7427
Kansas City Municipal Auditorium Music Hall, 7426
Kansas City Renaissance Festival, 4905
Kansas City Symphony, 1283
Kansas City Symphony Chorus, 2161
Kansas City Young Audiences Series, 4906
Kansas City Youth Symphony Association of Kansas, 1293
Kauffman Stadium, 7428
Kirkwood Symphony Orchestra, 1287
Leach Theatre, 7438
Liberty Center, 3306
Liberty Performing Arts Theatre, 7431
Liberty Symphony Orchestra, 1285
Lindenwood College Mainstage Season, 4926
Lyceum Theatre, 7412
Lyric Opera of Kansas City, 2160
Mark Twain Outdoor Theatre, 3295
Mary Linn Performing Arts Center, 7433
Memphis Community Players, 3293
Metro Theater Company, 3299
Mid-America Arts Alliance, 3288
Missouri Botanical Garden Amphitheatre, 7453
Missouri Contemporary Ballet, 306
Missouri Repertory Theatre, 3289
Missouri River Festival of the Arts, 4895
Missouri Symphony Society, 1279
Missouri Theater, 7440
Missouri Theatre, 7418
Missouri Western State College Fine Arts Theatre, 7441
Moberly Area Council on The Arts, 4912
Moberly Community Theatre, 3294
Mule Barn Theatre, 7465
Mule Barn Theatre of Tarkio College, 3309
Municipal Theater Association of Saint Louis, 3300
Muny Amphitheatre, 7454
New Jewish Theatre, 3282
New Music Circle, 1288
New Music Circle Series, 4919
New Theatre, 3301
Northland Symphony Orchestra, 1284
Northwest Missouri State University Performing Arts Series, 4911
Okoboji Summer Theatre, 7419
Opera Theatre of Saint Louis, 2163
Ozark Actors Theatre, 3296
Park College Alumni Hall Theatre, 7436
Performing Arts Association of Saint Joseph, 4915
Powell Symphony Hall, 7455
Price Cutter Park, 7434
Pro Musica, 4902
Quality Hill Playhouse, 3290
Repertory Theatre of Saint Louis, 3302
Royal Arts Council, 3310, 4927
Saint Joseph Civic Arena, 7442
Saint Joseph Symphony Society, 1286
Saint Louis Ballet, 305
Saint Louis Black Repertory Company, 3303
Saint Louis Cathedral Concerts, 4920
Saint Louis Chamber Chorus, 2157
Saint Louis Classical Guitar Society, 1289
Saint Louis Hills Arts Council, 4922
Saint Louis Philharmonic Orchestra, 1290
Saint Louis Symphony Children's Choir, 2164
Saint Louis Symphony Orchestra, 1291
Saint Louis Symphony Youth Orchestra, 1292
Saint Louis Symphony: Classics in The Loop Festival, 4921
Scott Joplin Ragtime Festival, 4924
Scottrade Center, 7456
Sheldon Concert Hall and Ballroom, 7457
Shepherd of the Hills, 3279
Show Me Center, 7414
Sikeston Little Theatre, 3307
Southeast Missouri State University: Cultural Series, 4896
Springfield Little Theatre at the Landers, 7462
Springfield Symphony Orchestra, 1294
Sro - a Lyric Theatre Company, 2165
Stages St. Louis, 3281
Starlight Theatre, 3291, 7429
Summerfest Concerts, 4907
The Kansas City Chorale, 2158
The Springfield Ballet Company, 311
Theater Factory Saint Louis, 3304
Theron C Bennet Ragtime & Early Jazz Festival, 4914
Transworld Dome at Americas' Center, 7458
Trilakes Community Theatre, 3280
Truman State University Lyceum Series, 4909
Umb Bank Pavilion, 7432
Unicorn Theatre, 3292, 7430
Union Avenue Opera Theatre, 7459
University of Central Missouri, 4928
University of Missouri Performing Arts Series, 7439
University of Missouri-Kansas City Conservatory Series, 4908
University of Missouri: Columbia Concert Series, 4897
University of Missouri: Saint Louis Premier Performances, 4923
West End Players Guild, 3305
William Woods College Campus Center Dulany Auditorium, 7421
William Woods University Concert & Lecture Series, 4899
Winston Churchill Memorial Hall, 7422
Wyliams/Henry Contemporary Dance Company (Whcdc), 309

Montana

Adams Event Center, 7481
Alberta Bair Theater, 3313
Alberta Bair Theatre for the Performing Arts, 7468
Aleph Movement Theatre, 3317
Associated Students of Montana State University, 4930
Ballet Montana, 313
Bigfork Center for the Performing Arts, 7467
Bigfork Summer Playhouse, 3312
Billings Symphony Orchestra & Chorale, 2166
Billings Symphony Society, 1296
Breenden Field House/Worthington Arena, 7470
Butte Center for the Performing Arts, 7472
Butte Civic Center, 7473
Carroll College Theatre, 7476
Dillon Community Concert Association, 4931
Flathead Festival of the Arts, 4939
Flathead Valley Festival, 4935
Four Seasons Arena, 7474
Great Falls Civic Center Theater, 7475
Great Falls Symphony Association, 1298
Havre Community Concert Association, 4933
Headwaters Dance Company, 314
Helena Civic Center, 7477
Helena Civic Center Auditorium, 7478
Helena Symphony Society, 1299
Intermountain Opera Bozeman, 2167
Majestic Valley Arena, 7480
Metrapark, 7469
Missoula Children's Theatre, 3318
Missoula Symphony Association, 1300
Montana Chorale, 2168
Montana Repertory Theatre, 3319
Montana Shakespeare in The Parks, 3314
Montana Traditional Jazz Festival, 4932
Myrna Loy Center, 7479
Northern Showcase Concert Association, 4934
Old Timers Concert Series, 4938

Geographic Index

Red Lodge Music Festival, 4929
Reno H Sales Stadium, 7471
Rocky Mountain Ballet Theatre, 315
The Montana Ballet Company, 312
University of Montana Performing Arts Series, 4936
University of Montana Theatre, 7482
Verge Theater, 3315
Vigilante Theatre Company, 3316
Whitefish Theatre Company, 3320
Wilma Theatre, 7483
Yellowstone Chamber Players, 1297

Nebraska

Abendmusik Series, 4944
Al Caniglia Stadium, 7495
Ballet Nebraska, 316
Bassett Arts Council, 4941
Bellevue Little Theatre, 3321, 7485
Bladen Opera House, 7486
Bob Devaney Sports Center, 7490
Brigit Saint Brigit Theatre Company, 3329
Brownville Concert Series, 4947
Cathedral Arts Project Series, 4948
Center Stage, 3330
Centurylink Center Omaha, 7501
Chadron State College Memorial Hall, 7487
Circle Theatre, 3331
Columbus Friends of Music Association, 4942
Community Players Theater, 7484
Concordia University Concert Series, 4952
Crane River Theater Company, 3324
Gothenburg Community Playhouse, 3323
Grande Olde Players Theatre Company, 3332
Harlan County Arts Council, 4940
Hastings Symphony Orchestra, 1301
Heritage Days Festival, 4946
Holland Performing Center-Orpheum Theater, 7496
Jewish Community Center of Omaha, 7497
Kearney Area Symphony Orchestra, 1302
Kearney Community Theatre, 3325
Lied Center for Performing Arts, 4945, 7491
Lincoln Civic Orchestra, 1303
Lincoln Community Playhouse, 3326
Lincoln Friends of Chamber Music, 1304
Lincoln Memorial Stadium, 7492
Lincoln Symphony Orchestra, 1305
Lincoln Youth Symphony, 1306
Midland Lutheran College Concert: Lecture Series, 4943
Nebraska Jazz Orchestra, 1307
Nebraska Repertory Theatre, 3327
Nebraska Shakespeare Festival, 4949
Nebraska Theatre Caravan, 317
Omaha Area Youth Orchestras, 1308
Omaha Civic Auditorium, 7498
Omaha Community Playhouse, 3333
Omaha Symphony, 1309
Omaha Symphony Chamber Orchestra, 1310
Omaha Theatre Company for Young People, 3334
Opera Omaha, 2169
Orpheum Theater, 7499
Orpheum Theatre, 7500
Pavilion & Events Center Inc., 7503
Pershing Center, 7493
Post Playhouse Incorporated, 3322
River City Mixed Chorus, 2170
Shakespeare on The Green, 3335
The Haymarket Theatre, 3328
Tuesday Musical Concert Series, 4950
University of Nebraska at Omaha Music Series, 4951
University of Nebraska Theatre, 7488
University of Nebraska-Lincoln: Kimball Recital Hall, 7494
Unk Sports Center, 7489
Wayne State College Arena, 7504
Wayne State College Special Programs Black & Gold Series, 4953
West Nebraska Arts Center, 7502

Nevada

Actors Repertory Theatre, 3338
Boulder City Arts Council, 4954
Brewery Arts Center, 3336, 7505
Caesars Palace, 7506
Carson City Symphony Association, 1311
Charleston Heights Arts Center, 7507
Church of Fine Arts, 7517
Churchill Arts Council, 4956
Huntridge Theatre, 7508
Las Vegas Ballet Company, 318
Las Vegas Civic Symphony, 1312
Las Vegas Convention and Visitors Authority, 7509
Las Vegas Little Theatre, 3339
Las Vegas Philharmonic, 1313
Lawlor Events Center, 7518
Mackey Stadium, 7519
Mandalay Bay Events Center, 7510
Mgm Grand Garden Arena, 7511
Nevada Arts Council, 4955
Nevada Ballet Theatre, 319
Nevada Festival Ballet, 321
Nevada Opera, 2171
Nevada Shakespeare Festival, 4959
Nevada Symphony Orchestra, 1314
Pioneer Center for the Performing Arts, 7520
Piper's Opera House, 7523
Reed Whipple Cultural Arts Center, 4957, 7512
Reno Chamber Orchestra, 1315
Reno Little Theater, 7521
Reno Philharmonic, 1316
Reno Sparks Convention Centennial Coliseum, 7522
Sam Boyd Stadium, 7513
The Las Vegas Contemporary Dance Theater, 320
The Reno Irish Dance Company, 322
The Smith Center for the Performing Arts, 7514
Theater Coalition/The Lear Theater, 3340
Thomas & Mack Center, 7515
University of Nevada Performing Arts Center, 4958
University of Nevada-Las Vegas Performing Arts Center Artemus Ham Concert Hall, 7516
University of Nevada: Reno Performing Arts Series, 4960
Western Nevada Musical Theatre Company, 3337

New Hampshire

American Stage Festival Peacock Players, 4970
Andy's Summer Playhouse, 3356
Apple Hill Center for Chamber Music, 1318
Barnstormers, 3354
Belknap Mill Society, 4967
Bratton Recital Hall, 7527
Capitol Center for the Arts, 7525
Claremont Opera House, 2172, 7524
Colby-Sawyer College, 4972
Colonial Theatre, 7534
Community Players of Concord, 3343
Concord City Auditorium, 7526
Dartmouth College Hopkins Center Performing Series, 4965
Eastern Slope Inn Playhouse, 7542
Franklin Pierce College Crimson-Grey Cultural Series, 4980
Friends of the Arts Regional Art Council, 4975
Friends of the Music Hall Concert Series, 4977
Great Bay Academy of Dance, 324
Great Waters Music Festival, 4982
Hampton Beach Casino Ballroom, 7532
Hampton Playhouse, 3345
Hampton Playhouse Theatre Arts Workshop, 7531
Harbor Arts Jazz Night: Portsmouth Jazz Festival, 4978
Hennessy Center, 7528
Keiser Concert Series, 4961
Lakes Region Summer Theatre, 3348
Lebanon Opera House, 7536
Loon Mountain, 7537
Mainstage Center for the Arts, 3341
Manchester Choral Society, 2174
Memorial Stadium, 7533
Monadnock Music, 4974
Mount Washington Valley Theatre Company, 3350
Music Hall, 7543
Nashua Community Concert Association, 4971
Ncca Papermill Theatre, 7538
Nevers' 2nd Regiment Band, 1317
New England College Cultural Events Series, 4966
New Hampshire Philharmonic Orchestra, 1319
New Hampshire Shakespeare Festival, 4963
New Hampshire Symphony Orchestra, 1320
New London Barn Playhouse, 7541
North Country Chamber Players Summer Festival: Music in The White Mountains, 4968
Northern Ballet Theatre Dance Center, 323
Opera North, 2173
Palace Theatre, 7539
Papermill Theatre/North County Center for the Arts, 3346
Paul Creative Arts Center, 7529
Peterborough Players, 3351
Plymouth State University, 4976
Pontine Theatre, 3352
Prescott Park Arts Festival, 4979
Rb Productions, 3344
Redfern Arts Center on Brickyard Pond, 7535
Saint Anselm College Performing Arts Series, 4969
Seacoast Repertory Theatre, 3353
Stageone Productions, 3347
Summer Music Associates Series, 4973
The Hampstead Stage Company, 3342
The Winnipesaukee Playhouse, 3349
University of New Hampshire Celebrity Series, 4964
Verizon Wireless Arena, 7540
Waterville Valley Foundation Summer Festival, 4981
Weathervane Theatre, 3355
Whittemore Center, 7530
William H Gile Trust Fund Concert Series, 4962

New Jersey

Academy of Saint Elizabeth Performing Arts Series, 5000
Algonquin Arts, 4999
All Seasons Chamber Players, 1328
Alliance Repertory Theatre Company, 3386
Am Productions Series, 4996
American Atlantic Chorale, 2179
American Boychoir, 2186
American Repertory Ballet, 339
Annual Ocean Grove Choir Festival, 5007
Appel Farm Arts and Music Center, 4989, 7556
Arbor Chamber Music Society, 1350
Argen Tango Dancers, 336
Armstrong Hipkins Center for the Arts, 7545
Ars Musical Chorale & Orchestra, 2185
Art of Motion Inc., 342
Arts Council of the Morris Area, 5001
Artspower National Touring Theatre, 3374
Asbury Park Jazz Festival, 4983
Atlantic City Ballet, 326
Atlantic Contemporary Ballet, 327
Attic Ensemble, 3368
Barron Arts Center, 7600
Bay-Atlantic Symphony, 1325
Bayonne Veterans Memorial Stadium, 7544
Bergen Philharmonic Orchestra, 1344
Berrie Center for Performing and Visual Arts, 7566
Bickford Theatre at the Morris Museum, 7568
Bloomfield Mandolin Orchestra, 1323
Boheme Opera, 2180
Bowne Theatre, 7565
Broadway Center Stage, 2183
Caldwell College Student Union Building, 7546
Cape May Jazz Festival, 4986
Cape May Music Festival, 4987
Cape May Stage, 3361
Carolyn Dorfman Dance Company, 343
Cathedral Basilica of the Sacred Heart Concert Series, 1335, 5004
Centenary Stage Company, 3365
Centenary Stage Company and Performing Arts Guild, 4994
Central Presbyterian Church, 5019
Choral Arts Society of New Jersey, 2195
College of New Jersey Center for the Arts, 4991
Colonial Symphony, 1321
Community Arts Partnership Series With Peddie School, 4995
Community Opera, 2193
Community Theatre, 7569
Continental Airlines Arena, 7553
Count Basie Theatre, 7587
Cranford Dramatic Club, 3362
Cranford Dramatic Club Theatre, 7551
Creative Theatre, 3381
Crescent Concerts, 5012
Crossroads Theatre Company, 3377
Cumberland Players, 3393
Dancevision Inc., 341
Dietsch Artists International, 2191
Discovery Orchestra, 1348
Dover Little Theatre, 7552
Dreamcatcher Repertory Theatre, 3387
Edison Arts Society, 4988
Fair Lawn Summer Festival, 4992
Forum Theatre, 3372
Garden State Philharmonic Symphony Orchestra, 1345
Garden State Philharmonic Symphony Youth Orchestra, 1324
George Street Playhouse, 3378
Giants Stadium, 7554
Glassboro Center for the Arts, 7558
Great Auditorium, 7577
Great Gorge Festival, 4984
Greater Princeton Youth Orchestra, 1340
Greater Trenton Symphony Orchestra, 1346
Growing Stage Theatre Company, 3376
Haddonfield Symphony, 1329
Historic Palace Theatre, 7571
Holmdel Theatre Company, 3367
Hunziker Black Box Theater, 7597
Jadwin Gymnasium, 7583
Jazz It Up Festival, 5022
Jette Performance Company, 5021
John Harms Center for the Arts, 4990, 7557
Julius Forstmann Library Second Sunday Series, 5010
Kaplan Jcc on The Palisades, 7590
Liberty Science Center, 7562
Lkb Dance, 340
Louis Brown Athletic Center, 7578
Luna Stage, 3395
Maurice Levin Theater, 7599
Maurice Levin Theater Season, 3396
Mccarter Theatre, 3382, 7584
Meadowlands Theater, 7555
Metro Lyric Opera, 2175
Mid-Atlantic Center for the Arts & Humanities, 7549
Middle Township Performing Arts Center, 7550
Mile Square Theatre, 3366
Moe-Tion Dance Theatre, 344
Monmouth Symphony Orchestra, 1347
Montclair State College Memorial Auditorium, 7596
Montclair State University, 3391
Mosaic Dance Theater Company, 329
Music in The Somerset Hills, 2176
Nai-Ni Chen Dance Company, 328
National Ballet of New Jersey, 338
New Jersey Association of Verismo Opera, 2181
New Jersey Ballet Company, 334
New Jersey City University Orchestra, 1330
New Jersey Dance Center, 335
New Jersey Festival Orchestra, 1352
New Jersey Intergenerational Orchestra, 1327
New Jersey Music Society, 1331
New Jersey Performing Arts Center, 7574
New Jersey Repertory Company, 3369, 4997
New Jersey State Museum Auditorium, 7591
New Jersey State Opera, 2184
New Jersey State Repertory Opera, 2192
New Jersey Symphony Orchestra, 1336, 1337
New Jersey Symphony Orchestra Amadeus Festival, 5005
New Jersey Tap Ensemble, 325
New Jersey Workshop for the Arts, 1351
New Jersey Youth Symphony, 1334
Newark Museum Association, 5006
Newark Performing Arts Corporation/Newark Symphony Hall, 3379
Newark Symphony Hall, 7575
Northern Star Arena, 7561

Geographic Index

Ocean City Pops, 1338
Ocean County College Fine & Performing Arts Select-A-Series, 5020
Ocean Professional Theatre Company, 3358
Orchestra of St. Peter by The Sea, 1322
Orrie De Nooyer Auditorium, 7559
Paper Mill Playhouse, 3373, 7567
Park Theatre Performing Arts Centre, 7595
Passage Theatre Company, 3389
Passaic County Community College Series, 5011
Patriots Theater at the War Memorial, 3390, 7592
Philharmonic of Southern New Jersey, 1332
Philomusica Choir, 2178
Plainfield Symphony, 1339
Plays-In-The-Park, 3363
Playwrights Theatre of New Jersey, 3370
Pollak Theatre, 7598
Princeton Pro Musica Chorus & Orchestra, 2187
Princeton Rep Company/Princeton Rep Shakespeare Festival, 3383
Princeton Shakespeare Festival, 5013
Princeton Symphony Orchestra, 1341
Princeton University Concerts, 5014
Pro Arte Chorale, 2189
Pushcart Players, 3392
Randy James Dance Works, 330
Raritan River Music, 5008, 5009
Raritan Valley Chorus, 2182
Revision Theatre, 3357
Richard L Swig Arts Center, 7560
Richardson Auditorium, 7585
Ridgewood Gilbert and Sullivan Opera Company, 2190
Ridgewood Symphony Orchestra, 1342
Ringwood Friends of Music Series, 5016
Roxey Ballet, 333
Rutgers Arts Center, 7572
Rutgers Athletic Center, 7579
Rutgers Stadium, 7580
Rutgers University Concert Series, 5002
Rutgers-Camden Center for the Arts Gordon Theater, 7547
Scandinavian Fest, 4985
Shadow Lawn Summer Stage, 3394
Shakespeare Theater of New Jersey, 4998
Shua Group, 332
Silver Center for the Arts, 7581
Simulations, 3371
Skyline Theatre Company, 3364
Solid Brass, 1326
Soundfest Chamber Music Festival, Colorado Quartet, 4993
South Camden Theatre Company, 3360
St. John's Renaissance Dancers, 337
State Theatre, 7573
State Theatre Regional Arts Center at New Brunswick, 5003
Stockton Performing Arts Center, 7582
Strand Theatre, 7563
Summit Chorale, 2194
Summit Symphony, 1343
Sun National Bank Center, 7593
Surflight Theatre, 3359
Td Bank Arts Centre, 7589
Teaneck New Theatre, 3388
The Garden State Opera, 2177
The Kennedy Dancers, 331
Theatre at Raritan Valley Community College, 3380, 3385, 7576
Two River Theater Company, 3384
Union County Arts Center, 7586
Walt Whitman Cultural Arts Center, 7548
Waterloo Foundation for the Arts Series, 5018
West Jersey Chamber Music Symphony & Society, 1333
Westminster Choir College, 2188
Wilkens Theatre, 7594
William G Mennen Sports Arena, 7570
William Paterson College: the Jazz Room Series, 5023
William Paterson University Performing & Visual Arts, 1349
Williams Center for the Arts, 5017
Williams Center for the Arts Newman Theatre, 7588
Willowbrook Jazz Festival, 5024
Yass Hakoshima Mime Theatre, 3375

Ym-Ywha of North Jersey Cultural Arts Series, 5025
Young Audiences of New Jersey, 5015
Yvonne Theater, 7564

New Mexico

Adobe Theater, 3397
Adobe Theatre Company, 3398
Albuquerque Convention Center, 7602
Albuquerque Little Theatre, 3399
American Southwest Center, 7613
Aspen Santa Fe Ballet, 347
Carlsbad Community Concert Association, 5028
Chamber Music Albuquerque Presents the June Music Festival, 5026
Chamber Orchestra of Albuquerque, 1353
City of Albuquerque Kimo Theatre, 3400
Dona Ana Arts Council, 5029
Duane Smith Auditorium, 7615
Eastern New Mexico University, 5033
Farmington Civic Center, 7612
Flickinger Center for Performing Arts, 7601
Greer Garson Theatre Center, 7617
Guadalupe Historic Foundation (Santuario De Guadalupe) Dinner Theater, 7618
Journal Pavilion, 7603
Keshet Dance Company, 345
Kimo Theatre, 7604
La Compania De Teatro De Albuquerque, 3401
Las Cruces Community Theatre, 3404
Las Cruces Symphony Orchestra, 1356
Lensic Performing Arts Center, 7619
Los Alamos Concert Association, 5031
Maria Benitez Teatro Flamenco, 348
Music From Angel Fire, 1358
Musical Theatre Southwest, 3402
National Hispanic Cultural Center of New Mexico, 7605
New Mexico Ballet Company, 346
New Mexico Jazz Workshop, 5027
New Mexico Symphony Orchestra, 1354
Opera Southwest, 2196
Pan American Center, 5030, 7614
Pearson Auditorium, 7616
Placitas Artists Series, 5032
Popejoy Hall, 7606
Roswell Symphony Orchestra, 1357
Sandstone Productions, 3403
Sangre De Cristo Chorale, 2197
Santa Fe Chamber Music Festival, 5034
Santa Fe Concert Association, 5035
Santa Fe Convention and Visitors Bureau Sweeney Center, 7620
Santa Fe Desert Chorale, 2198
Santa Fe Festival Ballet, 349
Santa Fe Opera House, 7607
Santa Fe Pro Musica, 1359
Santa Fe Stages, 7621
Santa Fe Symphony, 1360
Santa Fe Symphony Orchestra and Chorus, 2199
South Broadway Cultural Center, 7608
Southwest Symphony, 1355
Spencer Theater for the Performing Arts, 7611
Taos Art Association, 5037
Taos School of Music, 5038
The Santa Fe Opera, 2200
Theaterwork, 3405
Tingley Coliseum, 7609
Twentieth Century Unlimited Series, 5036
University of New Mexico Stadium, 7610
Working Class Theatre, 3406

New York

A Festival of Art, 5065
A Good Old Summer Time's Genesee Street Festival, 5212
Aai Productions, 3416
Abingdon Theatre Company, 3460
Acting Company, 3461
Acting Studio, 3462
Adelphian Players, 3417
Adirondack Festival of American Music, 5199
Adirondack Lakes Center for the Arts, 7636
Adirondack Theatre Festival, 3442, 5080
Aeolian Chamber Players, 1405

African American Cultural Centre, 3423
African-American Cultural Center, 374, 5056
African-American Cultural Center: Paul Robeson Hall, 7649
Afrikan Poetry Theatre, 3449
Ailey II, 381
Ajkun Ballet Theatre, 382
Albany Performing Arts Center, 7622
Albany Pro Musica, 2201
Albany Symphony Orchestra, 1361
Albany Symphony Orchestra American Fesitval, 5039
Alfred University Performing Arts, 5041
Alice Statler Hall, 7685
Alleyway Theatre, 3424
Alliance Bank Stadium, 7831
Allnations Dance Company, 383
Alpha Omega Theatrical Dance Company, 384
Alumni Hall Gymnasium, 7690
Alvin Ailey American Dance Theater, 385
Amas Musical Theatre, 3464
Ambassador Theatre, 7708
American Ballet Theatre, 386
American Bolero Dance Company, 378
American Center for Stanislavski Theatre Art, 3465
American Composers Orchestra, 1406
American Festival of Microtonal Music, 5110
American Indian Community House Series, 5111
American International Lyric Theatre, 2214
American Landmark Festivals, 5112
American Opera Music Theater, 2215
American Opera Projects Inc, 2205
American Place Theatre, 3466, 7709
American Symphony Orchestra, 1407
American Tap Dance Foundation, 387
American Theatre of Actors, 3467
American-International Lyric Theatre, 2216
Amherst Symphony Orchestra, 1474
Amsterdam Area Community Concert Association, 5043
Amy Marshall Dance Company, 351
Andy Kerr Stadium, 7679
Annabella Gonzalez Dance Theater, 388
Anpsacher Stage, 7710
Apollo Theatre, 7711
Apollo's Banquet, 389
Arena Players Repertory Theatre Company of Long Island, 3431
Ars Nova Musicians Chamber Orchestra, 1374
Arthur Ashe Stadium, 7670
Artpark, 5100, 7700
Arts at St. Ann's, 5052
Arts Center/Old Forge, 5177
Arts Council for Chautaugua County, 5094
Arts Council for the Northern Adirondacks, 5216
Arts International, 5113
Ascap, 7712
Asia Society, 5114
Asian American Arts Centre, 390
Atlantic Theater Company, 3468
Auburn Chamber Orchestra, 1364
Auburn Players Community Theatre, 3409
Augsbury Center, 7659
Aurora Players, 3436
Avodah Dance Ensemble, 391
Axis Company, 3469
Bach Vespers at Holy Trinity, 2217
Bachanalia Chamber Orchestra, 1408
Baker Field, 7713
Ballet Academy East, 392
Ballet Hispanico of New York, 393
Ballet Long Island, 500
Ballet Ny, 497
Ballet Tech, 394
Bang on A Can, 5115
Bard Music Festival, 5044
Bardavon 1869 Opera House, 7808
Bargemusic, 1369
Barrow Group, 3470
Basketball City, 5102
Bat Theatre Company, 3471
Battery Dance Company, 395
Bay Shore-Brightwaters Library Performing Arts Series, 5050
Bay Street Theatre, 3615
Bebe Miller Company, 396
Beethoven Festival, 1398, 5101

Bell Atlantic Jazz Festival, 5116
Belleayre Music Festival, 5086
Belmont Playhouse, 3414
Ben Light Gym, 7686
Berkshire-Hudson Valley Festival of Opera, 2203
Bernard B Jacobs Theatre, 7714
Bernard Schmidt Productions, Inc, 407
Best of Broadway, 3472
Bethel Woods Center for the Arts, 7701
Big Dance Theater Inc, 357
Big League Theatricals, Inc., 3473
Bill Evans Dance Company, 353
Bill T Jones/Arnie Zane Dance Company, 397
Bill Young/Colleen Thomas and Dancers, 398
Billie Holiday Theatre, 3418
Binghamton Philharmonic Orchestra, 1367
Binghamton Summer Music Festival, 5048
Black Experience Ensemble, 3407
Black Spectrum, 3474
Blackfriars Theatre, 3608
Blanco Performing Arts Foundation, 399
Bleecker Street Opera, 2218
Bloomingdale School of Music, 1409
Bloomingdale School of Music Concert Series, 5117
Blue Cross Arena, 7811
Bond Street Theatre Coalition, 3475
Booth Theatre, 7715
Bopi's Black Sheep/Dance by Kraig Patterson, 5118
Bridgehampton Chamber Music Festival, 5119
Brighton Ballet Theatre Company, Inc., 358
Bristol Valley Theater, 3455
Broadhollow Players Limited, 3614
Broadhurst Theatre, 7716
Broadway Theatre, 7717
Broadway Theatre League of Utica, 3630
Broadway Tomorrow, 3476
Bronx Arts Ensemble, 1368
Brooklyn Academy of Music, 5053
Brooklyn Academy of Music: Carey Playhouse, 7641, 7642
Brooklyn Academy of Music: Opera House, 7643
Brooklyn Arts Exchange, 359
Brooklyn Ballet, 360
Brooklyn Center for the Performing Arts, 7644
Brooklyn Conservatory of Music, 7645, 7671
Brooklyn Friends of Chamber Music, 1370
Brooklyn Philharmonic Orchestra, 1371
Brooklyn Symphony Orchestra, 1372
Brooks Atkinson Theatre, 7718
Broome County Veterans Memorial Arena, 7634
Buffalo Chamber Music Society, 1375
Buffalo Philharmonic Chorus & Chamber Singers, 2207
Buffalo Philharmonic Orchestra, 1376
Buffalo State College Performing Arts Center, 7650
Buglisi Dance Theatre, 400
Canterbury Choral Society, 2219
Canticum Novum Singers, 2220
Capital Repertory Theatre, 7623
Capitol Chamber Artists, 1362
Capitol Theatre, 7817
Capitol Theatre Summerstage, 3613
Caramoor Center for Music and The Arts, 5096
Caramoor Center for Music and The Arts Venetian Theatre, 7694
Caramoor International Music Festival, 5097
Carnegie Chamber Players, 1410
Carnegie Hall Corporation, 7719
Carolyn Lord and Company, 401
Carrier Dome, 7832
Castillo Theatre, 3477
Castleman Quartet Programs, 1461
Cathedral Arts, 5120
Catskill Symphony Orchestra, 1449
Cayuga Chamber Orchestra, 1394
Cecilia Chorus of New York, 2221
Cedar Lake Dance, 402
Celebrate Brooklyn Festival, 5054
Celebration Team, 403
Center for Contemporary Opera, 2222
Center for the Arts Lecture Hall, 7826
Center for the Arts Recital Hall, 7825
Center for Traditional Music & Dance, 7720
Central Park Summerstage, 5121
Chamber Music America, 1411

Geographic Index

Chamber Music at Rodef Shalom With Stephen Starkman & Friends, 1457
Chamber Music Festival of the East, 5106
Chamber Music Society of Lincoln Center, 1412
Chamber Music Society of Utica, 1473
Chamber Players International, 1475
Chautauqua Institution, 5059
Chautauqua Opera, 2252
Chautauqua Summer Schools of Fine and Performing Arts, 2208
Chautauqua Symphony Orchestra, 1378
Chelsea Opera, 2223
Chen Dance Center, 404
Chenango County Council for the Arts, 5174
Chicago City Limits, 3478
Children's Aid Society Chorus, 2224
Chinese Folk Dance Company, 405
Chinese Music Ensemble of New York, 1413
Chinese Theatre Works, 3453
Christopher Caines Dance Company, 406
Circle in The Square Theater School, 7721
Citi Field, 7672
City Center of Music and Drama, 7722
Civic Center of Onondaga County Carrier Theatre, 7834
Civic Center of Onondaga County Crouse-Hind Hall, 7833
Civic Morning Musicals, 5207
Clarion Concerts in Columbia County, 5064
Clarion Music Society, 5122
Classic Stage Company, 3479
Classical Frontiers, 5184
Classical Quartet, 1414
Clearwater's Great Hudson River Revival, 5191
Clemens Center, 7667
Coach House Players, 3451
Colden Center for the Performing Arts, 7673
Colden Center Performances, 5072
Colgate University Concert Series, 5085
Collegiate Chorale, 2225
Collegium Westchester, 1451
Columbia University Orchestra, 1415
Common Stage Theatre Company, 3635
Community Performance Series, 5189
Concert Artists Guild New York Recital Series, 5123
Concert Socials, 5124
Concerts at the Cloisters, 5125
Coney Island Usa, 3419
Cooperstown Concert Series, 5062
Cooperstown Theatre & Music Festival, 5063
Cornell Concert Series, 5091
Cornell University Theatre, Film & Dance Department, 3445
Corning-Painted Post Civic Music Association, 5066
Cort Theatre, 7723
Cortland Repertory Theatre, 3435
Covenant Ballet Theatre of Brooklyn, 362
Crane School of Music Annual Spring Festival of the Arts, 5190
Creach/Company, 408
Creation Production Company, 3480
Creative Arts Team, 3481
Creative Time Series, 5126
Cultural Resources Council of Syracuse, 5208
Cw Post Chamber Music Festival, 5055
Dana Arts Center University Theatre, 7680
Dance Collective New York, 409
Dance June Lewis and Company, 410
Dance Theater Workshop, 7724
Dance Theatre Etcetera, 369
Dance Theatre of Harlem, 411, 430
Dances Patrelle, 412
Dancewave, 363
Dancing in The Streets, 413
Danspace Project, 414
Darien Lake Performing Arts Center, 7664
Das Puppenspiel Puppet Theater, 3633
Debra Weiss Dance Company, 495
Del-Se-Nango Olde Tyme Fiddlers Association, 1403
Delacorte Theater in Central Park, 7725
Dillingham Center for the Performing Arts, 7688
Dinizulu African Dancers, Drummers and Singers, 377
Disney Theatrical Productions, 3482
Dixon Place, 3483

Do Gooder Productions, 3484
Don Quixote Children's Theatre, 3485
Donald Williams, 415
Donna Uchizono Company, 416
Dorothy Taubman Seminar at Lincoln Center, 5105
Doug Elkins Dance Company, 417
Doug Varone and Dancers, 418
Douglas Dunn and Dancers, 419
Downtown Art Company, 3486
Drama Department, 3487
Duson Tynek Dance Theatre, 364
Earlville Opera House, 7666
Early Music New York (Em/Ny), 1416, 2226, 5128
Eastman Philharmonia, 1459
Eastman School of Music, 5193
Eastman Theatre, 7812
Eden's Expressway, 7726
Egg-Empire State Performing Arts Center, 7624
Eglevsky Ballet, 352
1891 Fredonia Opera House, 2210
Eiko and Koma, 420
Elaine Kaufman Cultural Center Presentations, 5129
Elisa Monte Dance, 421
Elmwood Playhouse, 3601
Emelin Theatre for the Performing Arts, 5103, 7706
Emerging Artists Theatre Company, 3488
Empire Opera Inc, 2227
En Garde Arts, 3489
Ensemble 21 Artists, 1417
Ensemble Studio Theatre, 3490, 7727
Ergo Theatre Company, 3491
Erica Essner Performance Co-Op, 365
Ernesta Corvino's Dance Circle Company, 422
Ethan Brown, 423
Ethel Barrymore Theatre, 7728
Eugene James Dance Company, 424
Eugene O'neill Theater Center, 7845
Eva Dean Dance Company, 366
Fair & Expo Center, 7682
Felice Lesser Dance Theater, 425
Festival of Baroque Music, 5083
Festival of New Music, 5130
Festival of the Arts, 5179
52nd Street Project, 3459
Fiji Company, 3492
First Niagara Center, 7652
Fleetwood Stage, 3458
Flushing Council on Culture & the Arts, 5073
Fly-By-Night Dance Theater, 426
Folksbiene Yiddish Theatre, 3493
Fools Company, 5131
Forest Hills Symphony Orchestra, 1384
Forestburgh Playhouse, 3441
Fort Salem Theatre, 3616
Foundation for Baroque Music, 1392
Frederick P Rose Hall, 7729
French Institute Alliance Francaise, 5132
Frick Collection Concert Series, 5133
Friends of Chamber Music of Troy, 1470
Friends of Good Music, 5178
Friends of Music Orchestra, 1386
Frontier Field, 7813
Gallim Dance, 367
Garth Fagan Dance, 498
Gateway Playhouse, 3413
Genesee Community College, 5046
Genesee Symphony Orchestra, 1366
Geneseo Symphony Orchestra, 1387
Geneva Concerts, 5079
Gerald Schoenfeld Theatre, 7730
Gershwin Theatre, 7731
Geva Theatre, 3609
Gibson Theatre, 7668
Gilma Bustillo, 427
Gina Gibney Dance, 428
Glens Falls Civic Center, 7677
Glens Falls Symphony Orchestra, 1390
Glimmerglass Opera, 2209
Glines, 3494
Glyde Recitals: New York Viola Society, 5082
Goethe-Institut New York/German Cultural Center, 7732
Goldstein Auditorium, 7835
Goliard Chamber Soloists, 1363

Gotham Chamber Opera, 2228
Gotham Early Music Scene, 5134
Grace Church Choral Society, 2229
Gramercy Brass Orchestra of New York, 1418
Great Neck Philharmonic, 1391
Great Performers in Westchester Series, 5068
Greater Buffalo Youth Ballet Theater, 7651
Greece Performing Arts Society Series, 5173
Greece Symphony Orchestra, 1460
Greenwich House Arts: North River Music, 5135
H.T. Chen Dance Company, Inc., 429
Hamilton College: Minor Theatre, 7661
Hammerstein Ballroom, 7733
Hangar Theatre, 3446, 7687
Harbor Theatre, 3495
Harlem Artists Development League, 3496
Harlem Stage, 7707
Hartwick College Foreman Creative & Performing Arts Series, 5180
Hb Playwrights Foundation Theatre House, 7734
Helen Hayes Performing Arts Center, 7803
Helen M. Hosmer Concert Hall, 7807
Helicon Foundation, 5136
Henson International Festival of Puppet Theatre, 5137
Here Arts Center, 3498
Hershell Carrousel Factory Museum, 7802
Hickox Field, 7648
Hill & Hollow Music, 5198
Hispanic Organization of Latin Actors, 3499
Historic Brass Society - Early Brass Festival, 5138
Hofstra University Stadium & Arena, 7681
Hornell Area Arts Council, 5087
Houghton College Artist Series, 5088
Hudson Guild Theatre, 3500
Hudson Highlands Music Festival, 5077
Hudson River Festival, 5139
Hudson River Museum, 7851
Hudson Valley Community College Cultural Affairs Program, 5211
Hudson Valley Philharmonic, 1455
Hudson Valley Shakespeare Festival, 3433, 5061
Huntington Arts Council, 5089
Huntington Summer Arts Festival, 5090
I Cantori Di New York, 2230
Ice Theatre of New York, 431
Igloo, the Theatrical Group, 3501
Imago, the Theatre Mask Ensemble, 3604
Imperial Theatre, 7735
Intar Theatre, 3502
Inter-Media Art Center, 7684
Interborough Repertory Theater, 3503
International Offestival, 5140
International Seejong Soloists, 1419
Interschool Orchestras of New York, 1420
Irish Arts Centre Theatre, 3504
Irish Classical Theatre Company, 3425
Irondale Ensemble Project, 3420, 3505
Isadora Duncan Dance Foundation, 432
Islip Arts Council Chamber Music Series, 1382, 5071
Ithaca Ballet, 376
Ithaca College Concerts, 5092
Jam and Company, 3506
Jamaica Center for the Performing & Visual Arts, 7691
Jamestown Concert Association, 1396, 5095
Janis Brenner and Dancers, 433
Japan Society Performing Arts Series, 5141
Jazz at Lincoln Center's Essentially Ellington Jazz Festival, 1421
Jazz at Lincoln Center: Essentially Ellington Jazz Festival, 5142
Jazz in July, 5143
Jean Cocteau Repertory, 3507
Jefferson Community College Mcvean Student Center, 7846
Jennifer Muller: the Works, 434
Jewish Museum, 7736
Jim Butterfield Stadium, 7689
Joan Miller Dance Players, 435
Jody Oberfelder Dance Projects, 436
Joe's Pub at the Public Theater, 7737
John Drew Theater at Guild Hall, 3437
John Gardner, 437
John Golden Theatre, 7738
Jolinda Menendez, 438

Joyce Theater, 7739
Juilliard School, 440
June Company, 7632
June in Buffalo, 5057
Jvc Jazz Festival New York, 5144
Kathak Ensemble & Friends/Caravan, 441
Kathryn Bache Miller Theatre, 7740
Kathy Rose, 442
Kavinoky Theatre, 3426
Kaye Playhouse at Hunter College, 7741
Kazuko Hirabayashi Dance Theatre, 7742
Kei Takei's Moving Earth, 443
Keigwin + Company, 444
Kenan Center, 7704
Kirkland Art Center, 7662
Kitchen Theatre Company, 3447
Kleinert/James Arts Center, 7849
Kleinhans Music Hall, 7653
Knickerbacker Recreational Facility and Ice Arena, 7838
Kohav Theatre Foundation, 3509
L'ensemble Chamber Music, 5040
L'opera Francais De New York, 2231
La Gran Scena Opera Company, 2232
La Mama Experimental Theatre, 3510
Laban/Bartenieff Institute of Movement Studies, 445
Labyrinth Theater Company, 3511
Laguardia Performing Arts Center, 7705
Lake George Chamber Orchestra, 1456
Lake George Dinner Theatre, 3452, 7696
Lake George Jazz Weekend, 1397, 5098
Lake George Opera at Saratoga, 2254
Lake Placid Center for the Arts Theater, 7697
Lamb's Theatre, 7744
Lamb's Theatre Company, 3512
Lancaster New York Opera House, 7699
Lar Lubovitch Dance Company, 446
Latin American Theatre Experiment & Associates, 3513
League of Composers-Iscm New York Season, 5145
Leatherstocking Theatre Company, 3434
Lehman Center for the Performing Arts, 7639, 7745
Les Ballets Grandiva, 447
Les Ballets Trockadero De Monte Carlo, 448
Les Grands Ballets De Loony, 449
Les Guirivoires Dance Company, 354
Lightning Strikes Theatre Company, 3514
Lincoln Center Theater, 7746
Lippes Concert Hall in Slee Hall, 7654
Little Orchestra Society of New York, 1422
Living Theatre, 3515
Long Island Baroque Ensemble, 1399
Long Island Opera, 2233
Long Island Philharmonic, 1401
Long Island University/Tilles Center, 5084
Long Island University: Fine Arts Theatre, 7823
Longacre Theatre, 7747
Longisland Mandolin & Guitar Orchestra, 1400
Lorraine Productions: East/West, 5045
Lotus Fine Arts Productions, 5146
Lotus Music & Dance, 450
Lower Adirondack Regional Arts Council, 5081
Lucille Ball Little Theatre of Jamestown, 7693
Lucille Lortel Theatre, 7748
Luesther Hall, 7749
Lumiere Ballet, 7847
Lunt-Fontanne Theatre, 7750
Luzerne Chamber Music Festival, 5099
Lyceum Theatre, 7751
Lyric Chamber Music Society of New York, 1423
Mabou Mines, 3516
Mac-Haydn Theatre, 3432
Madison Square Garden, 7752
Majestic Theatre, 7753
Mamadou Diabate, 1379
Manhattan Lyric Opera, 2212
Manhattan Tap, 505
Manhattan Theatre Club, 3517, 7754
Mannes College of Music International Keyboard Institute and Festival, 5147
Marcel Marceau Mime Theater, 3518
Margot Astrachan Music, 1424
Marine Midland Arena, 7655
Marjorie Liebert, 451
Mark Degarmo and Dancers, 452

1287

Geographic Index

Mark Kappel, 453
Mark Morris Dance Group, 368
Marquis, 7755
Martha Graham Dance Company, 454
Martin Beck Theater, 7756
Martinson Theatre, 7757
Mary Anthony Dance Theatre, 455
Marymount Manhattan College, 7758
Matapat, 1380, 2253
Maverick Concert Hall, 7850
Maverick Concerts, 1476, 5217
Mcc Theater, 3519
Mellon Jazz in Philadelphia, 5148
Merce Cunningham Dance Company, 456
Mercy College: Lecture Hall, 7665
Merian Soto Dance & Performance, 355
Merkin Concert Hall at Kaufman Center, 7759
Merrill Field, 7628
Merry-Go-Round Playhouse, 3410
Metropolitan Museum Concerts and Lectures, 5149
Metropolitan Opera, 2234
Metropolitan Playhouse, 3520
Mettawee Theatre Company, 3617
Michael C Rockefeller Arts Center, 7674
Michael Mao Dance, 457
Michael Schimmel Center for the Arts, 7760
Mid-Hudson Ballet Company, 375
Mid-Hudson Civic Center, 7809
Midamerica Productions, 5150
Mimi Garrard Dance Company, 458
Minetta Lane Theatre, 7761
Minskoff Theatre, 7762
Mint Theater Company, 3521
Mirror Repertory Company, 3522
Modern-Day Griot Theatre Company, 3421
Mohawk Players, 3411
Mohawk Valley Center for the Arts, 7703
Mohawk Valley Community College Cultural Series, 5213
Molissa Fenley and Dancers, 459
Momix, 460
Morphoses Ltd, 461
Mostly Mozart Festival, 5151
Mount Kisco Concert Association, 5107
Mowhawk Valley Ballet, 504
Mulroy Civic Center, 7836
Muna Tseng Dance Projects, 462
Munson-Williams-Proctor Arts Institute, 5214
Music at Port Milford, 5187
Music Before 1800, 1425, 5152
Music Box, 7763
Music Festival of the Hamptons, 5042
Music From Japan, 5153
Music From Salem, 5197
Music in The Park: Third Street Music School Settlement, 5154
Music Theatre Associates, 3523
Music Theatre Group at Lenox Arts Center, 3524
Music-Theatre Group, 2235
Musical Concerts at the Burlingham Inn, 5186
Musical Fare Theatre, 7629
Nassau Community College Cultural Program, 5076
Nassau Symphony Society, 1472
Nassau Veterans Memorial Coliseum, 7842
National Black Theatre, 3525
National Black Touring Circuit, 3526
National Dance Institute, 463
National Improvisational Theatre, 3527
National Orchestral Association, 1426
National Shakespeare Company, 3528
Nazareth Arts Center, 7814
Nazareth College Arts Center Series, 5194
Nederlander Theatre, 7764
Negro Ensemble Company, 3529
Neil Simon Theatre, 7765
Neta Dance Company, 464
Neuer Tanz, 465
New Amsterdam Singers, 2236
New Day Repertory Company, 3606
New Directions Cello Festival, 1395, 5093
New Dramatists, 3530, 7766
New Federal Theatre, 3531
New Georges, 3532
New Paltz Summer Repertory Theatre, 3457
New Perspectives Theatre Company, 3533
New Raft Theater Company, 3534

New Rochelle Opera, 2213
New Victory Theater, 7767
New York Choral Society, 2237
New York City Ballet, 466
New York City Center, 7768
New York City Opera, 2238
New York City Symphony Orchestra, 1427
New York Consort of Viols, 1428
New York Gilbert and Sullivan Players, 2239
New York Grand Opera Company, 2240
New York Harp Ensemble, 1429
New York Opera Project, 2241
New York Philharmonic, 1430
New York Philomusica Chamber Ensemble, 1431
New York Pops, 1432
New York Renaissance Faire, 3629
New York Stage & Film, 3535
New York State Theatre Institute, 3628
New York Street Theatre Caravan, 3450
New York Theatre Ballet/Ballet School of Ny, 467
New York Theatre Workshop, 3536
New York Treble Singers, 2242
New York Youth Symphony, 1433
Newman Stage, 7769
Nina Winthrop and Dancers, 468
92nd Street Y, 5109
Nomadics, 1402
Noonday Concerts, 1434
Noonday Concerts at One, 5155
North/South Consonance, 1435
Norton Hall, 7660
Nyack College Program of Cultural Events, 5175
Nyc Bhangra Dance Company, 469
Ogdensburg Command Performances, 3602, 5176
Ohio Theatre, 3537
Olympic Center, 7698
171 Cedar Arts Center, 7663
Onondaga Civic Symphony Orchestra, 1365
Ontological-Hysteric Theater, 3538
Open Book, 3539
Open Eye Theater, 3454
Open Eye: New Stagings, 3540, 7770
Open Hand Theater, 3625
Opera Ebony, 2244
Opera Northeast/Children's Opera Theatre, 2245
Opera Omnia, 2211
Opera Orchestra of New York, 2246
Opera Saratoga, 2255
Operamission, 2247
Oratorio Society of New York, 2248
Orchard Park Symphony, 1450
Orchestra of Northern New York, 1454
Orchestra of St. Luke's, 1436
Orpheum Theatre, 7771
Orpheus Chamber Orchestra, 1437
Orpheus Theatre, 3603
Oswego Harbor Festivals, 5182
Oyster Bay Arts Council, 5104
Pala Opera Association, 2249
Palace Performing Arts Center, 7625
Palace Theatre, 7772
Pan American Musical Art Research, 7773
Pan Asian Repertory Theatre, 3541
Pandora's Box Theatre Company, 3427
Paper Bag Players, 3542
Paramount Center for the Arts, 7805
Park Avenue Theatrical Group, 3543
Park Playhouse Incorporated, 3408
Parsons Dance Company, 470
Partial Comfort Productions, 3544
Pat Cannon's Foot & Fiddle Dance Company, 502
Paul Taylor Dance Company, 471
Pawling Concert Series, 5183
Pearl Theatre Company, 3545
Peculiar Works Project, 3546
Pendragon Theatre, 3618
Penfield Smyphony Orchestra, 1453
Penguin Repertory Company, 3623
Peoples' Symphony Concerts, 1438, 5156
Pepsi Arena, 7626
Performance Space 122, 7774
Performing Arts at Hamilton, 5060
Peridance Contemporary Dance Company, 472
Petronio, 485
Philharmonia Virtuosi Corporation, 1448
Phyllis Rose Dance Company, 473

Piano Summer at New Paltz, 5108
Pianofest, 5070
Pick of the Crop Dance, 501
Pick Up Performance Company, 474
Ping Chong & Company, 3547
Players of Utica, 3631
Playwrights Horizons, 3548
Plural Arts International, 5157
Polish American Folk Dance Company, 370
Poppo & the Gogo Boys, 475
Posey Dance Company, 494
Powerhouse Theater at Vassar, 3607
Pratt Institute: Auditorium, 7646
Pregones Theater, 3415
Primary Stages Company, 3549
Pro Piano New York Recital Series, 5158
Process Studio Theatre, 3550
Proctor's Theatre, 3620, 7820
Professional Performing Arts Series, 5047
Promenade Theatre, 7775
Public Theatre, 3552
Puerto Rican Traveling Theatre Company, 3553
Puppet Theatre: Dance and Music From Indonesia, 3599
Purchase College Performing Arts Center, 7810
Putnam Symphony Orchestra, 1377
Pyramid Arts Center, 7815
Quebec Government House, 7776
Queens College Summer Theatre, 3440
Queens Symphony Orchestra, 1389
Queensborough Community College Theater, 7633
Quintet of the Americas, 1381
Radio City Music Hall, 7777
Rajeckas and Intraub - Movement Theatre, 3581
Rajeckas and Intraub Movement Theatre, 3554
Ralph Wilson Stadium, 7804
Rattlestick Theatre, 3555
Rebecca Kelly Ballet, 476
Rebecca Stenn Company, 477
Redhouse Arts Center, 3626
Regina Opera Company, 2206
Reilly Center Arena, 7824
Rensselaer Newman Foundation Chapel and Cultural Center, 7840
Rensselaer Polytechnic Institute: Houston Field House, 7839
Repertorio Espanol, 3556
Rhinebeck Chamber Music Society, 1458
Richard B Fisher Center for the Performing Arts at Bard College, 7630
Richard Rogers Theatre, 7778
Ridge Theater, 3557
Rioult, 478
Risa Jaroslow and Dancers, 479
River Arts Repertory, 3412
River Rep Theatre Company, 3558
Riverside Shakespeare Company, 3559
Riverside Symphony, 1439
Roberts Wesleyan College, 5195
Rochester Broadway Theatre League, 3610
Rochester Chamber Orchestra, 1462
Rochester City Ballet, 499
Rochester Philharmonic Orchestra, 5196
Rockaway Theatre Company, 3439
Rod Rodgers Dance Company & Studios, 480
Roger Furman Theatre, 3560
Rosewood Chamber Ensemble, 1466
Roulette Intermedium, 1440
Roundabout Theatre Company, 3561
Roycroft Chamber Music Festival, 5069
Ryan Repertory Company at Harry Warren Theatre, 3422
Rye Arts Center, 7818
Saeko Ichinohe Dance Company, 481
Saint Bart's Players, 3562
Saint Clement's Church, 7779
Saint James Theater, 7780
Saint Joseph's College Center for Arts, 7647
Saint Lukes Chamber Ensemble, 1441
Salia Ni Seydou, 482
Salt and Pepper Mime Company, 3563
Saratoga International Theater Institute, 3564
Saratoga Performing Arts Center, 1464, 3619, 7819
Saratoga Performing Arts Festival Series, 5200
Saturday Brass Quintet, 1442
Schenectady Civic Players, 3621

Schenectady Civic Players Theater, 7821
Schenectady Light Opera Company, 2256
Schenectady Museum: Union College Concert Series, 5202
Schneider Concerts at the New School, 5159
Second Stage Theatre, 3565
Sem Ensemble, 1373
Sensedance, 483
Sevenars Concerts Music Festival, 5160
Shadow Box Theatre, 3566
Shadowland Artists, 3438
Shakespeare in Delaware Park, 3428
Shandelee Music Festival, 5161
Shea Theatre, 7822
Shea's Performing Arts Center, 7656
Sheila-Na-Gig Music, 1443
Shiva Theatre, 7781
Shubert Theatre, 7782
Signature Theatre Company, 3567
651 Arts, 5051
Skaneateles Festival, 5203
Skidmore Music Department, 5201
Smith Opera House, 7676
Snug Harbor Cultural Center, 7827
Society for Chamber Music in Rochester, 1463
Soho Rep, 7783
Soho Repertory Theatre, 3568
Solaris Dance Theatre & Video, 484
Sound Symphony Orchestra, 1383
Soupstone Project, 3569
Spanish Theatre Repertory Company, 3570
Special Olympics Stadium, 7637
Spencertown Academy Performing Series, 5204
Sports Complex, 7829
St. John's University, 7692
St. Patrick's Cathedral Chamber Music Series, 1444, 5162
Stageworks, 3444
Stagewrights, 3571
Staller Center for the Arts, 7830
Stanley Performing Arts Center, 7843
State University of New York at Binghamton Performing Arts Series, 5049
State University of New York at Cortland: Campus Artist & Lecture Series, 5067
State University of New York at Stony Brook Concert Series, 5206
State University of New York-Binghampton: Anderson Center for the Arts, 7635
Staten Island Ballet, 503
Staten Island Symphony, 1465
Steps Beyond, 486
Sterling Renaissance Festival, 3622, 5205
Streb Laboratory for Action Mechanics (Slam), 356
Street Theater, 3634
String Orchestra of New York City, 1445
Strong Theatre, 7816
Studio Arena Theatre, 3429
Studio Theatre, 7702
Suffolk Theater, 5192
Suffolk Y Jcc International Jewish Arts Festival & the Celebration Series, 5075
Sullivan Street Playhouse, 7784
Summergarden, 5163
Summit Music Festival, 5188
Suny Center for the Arts, 7657
Suny College at Geneseo Limelight Artist Series, 5078
Supper Club Theater, 7785
Surdna Foundation, 7786
Susan Marshall and Company, 487
Symphony Spaces, 5164, 7787
Syracuse Area Landmark Theatre, 7837
Syracuse Friends of Chamber Music, 1467
Syracuse Opera, 2258
Syracuse Society for New Music, 5209
Syracuse Stage, 3627
Syracuse Symphony Orchestra, 1468
Syracuse Symphony Youth Orchestra, 1469
Tadal, 3572
Taghkanic Chorale, 2259
Taipei Theater of Chinese Information & Culture, 1446
Talking Band, 3573
Tamara and The Shadow Theatre of Java, 3600
Tannery Pond Concerts, 1404
Target Margin Theater, 3574

Geographic Index

Thalia Spanish Theatre, 3624
The American Mime Theatre, 488
The Bronx Opera Company, 2204
The Charles Moore Dance Theatre, 361
The Classical Theatre of Harlem, 3575
The Construction Company, 379
The Dicapo Opera Theatre, 2250
The Eba Theatre, 350
The Jose Limon Dance Foundation, 439
The Kitchen, 7743
The New Group, 3576
The New York Virtuoso Singers, 2243
The Opera Orchestra of New York, 2251
The Westchester Ballet Company, 496
Theater Barn, 3456
Theater by The Blind, 3577
Theater for the New City, 3578
Theatre Du Grand-Guignol De Paris, 3579
Theatre for A New Audience, 3580
Theatre of Youth Company, 3430
Theatre on The Ridge, 3611
Theatre Three Productions, 3605
Theatre Three Productions Second Stage, 7806
Theatreworks Usa, 3582
Theresa Lang Theatre, 3583
Third Street Music School Settlement Faculty Artists Series, 5165
Thunder Bay Ensemble, 3584
Ticonderoga Festival Guild, 5210
Tiffany Mills Company, 371
Tilles Center for the Performing Arts, 7678
Tisch Center for the Arts, 1447, 7788
Tower Fine Arts Center and Hartwell Hall, 7638
Town Hall Concert Hall, 7789
Tremont String Quartet, 1388
Tri-Cities Opera Company, 2202
Tribeca Performing Arts Center, 5166, 7790
Trisha Brown Dance Company, 489
Troy Chromatics Concerts, 1471
Troy Savings Bank Music Hall, 7841
Tvi Actors Studio, 3585
Ulster Performing Arts Center, 7695
Union Square Theatre, 7791
University at Albany Performing Arts Center (Pac), 7627
University at Buffalo Center for the Arts, 7658
University of Rochester Theatre Program, 3612
Univercity Sottlement, 7792
Upper Catskill Community Council of the Arts, 5181
Urban Bush Women, 372
Us Military Academy, 7631
Us Military Academy Michie Stadium, 7848
Usdan Center for the Creative & Performing Arts: Festival Concerts, 5167
Utica Memorial Auditorium, 7844
Vanaver Caravan, 380
Veterans Memorial Hall, 7828
Vineyard Theatre, 3587
Virginia Theater, 7793
Viva Vivaldi Festival Xxiii, 5058
Vivian Beaumont Theater, 3588
Wadsworth Auditorium, 7675
Walter Kerr Theatre, 7794
Washington Square Contemporary Music Society, 5169
Washington Square Music Festival, 5168
Watertown Lyric Theater Productions, 3632
Waverly Consort, 1452
Web Concert Hall, 7795
Weissberger Theater Group, 3589
Wesley Chapel, 7683
Westbeth Studio Theatre, 7796
Westbeth Theatre Center, 7797
Westbury Music Fair, 5215
Westchester Broadway Theatre, 7669
Westchester Oratorio Society, 2257
Westchester Philharmonic, 1393
Western New York Chamber Orchestra, 1385
Westside Theatre, 7798
White Horse Theatre Company, 3590
Whitney Museum of Art Theater, 7799
Wien Stadium, 7800
Wings Theatre Company, 3591
Winter Garden Theatre, 7801
Wofa! Percussion and Dance From Guinea, West Africa, 490
Women's Interart Center, 3592

Women's Project & Productions, 3593
Wooster Group, 3594
Working Theatre Company, 3595
World Financial Center Arts & Events Program, 5170
World Music Institute, 491, 5171
Wpa Theatre, 3596
Yankee Stadium, 7640
Yates Performing Arts Series, 5185
York Theatre Company, 3597
Yoshiko Chuma and The School of Hard Knocks, 492
Young Concert Artists Series, 5172
Young Dancers in Repertory, 373
Young Playwrights, 3598
Youtheatre, 3443
Yueh Lung Shadow Theatre, 3448
Zendora Dance Company, 493

North Carolina

A.J. Fletcher Opera Theater, 7900
Actor's Theatre of Charlotte, 3646
Actors Comedy Lab, 3673
African American Dance Ensemble, Inc., 508
Afro-American Cultural Center, 7867
American Dance Festival, 5233
An Appalachian Summer Festival, 5223
Anam Cara Theatre Company, 3654
Appalachian State University Performing Arts & Forum Series, 5224
Arts Council of Fayetteville/Cumberland County, 5242
Arts Council of Macon County, 5243
Arts Council of Moore County, 5267
Arts Ncstate, 5259
Artscenter, 3642
Artsplosure: 2003 Spring Jazz & Art Festival, 5260
Asheville Chamber Music Series, 1477, 5218
Asheville Civic Center, 7853
Asheville Community Theatre, 3636
Asheville Lyric Opera, 2260
Asheville Symphony Orchestra, 1478
Aycock Auditorium, 7884
Bank of America Stadium, 7868
Barton International, 5275
Beaufort County Community Concerts Association, 5220
Bel Canto Company, 2264
Belk Theater, 7869
Black Swan Theater, 3637
Blowing Rock Stage Company, 3641
Bowman Gray Stadium, 7921
Brevard Music Festival, 5226
Bull Durham Blues Festival, 5234
Burning Coal Theatre Company, 3674
Camp Theater, 7863
Campbell University Community Concert Series, 5227
Cape Fear Regional Theatre, 3655
Carolina Ballet, 511
Carolina Pro Musica, 1482
Carolina Theatre, 7885
Carolina Theatre of Durham, 3650
Carolina Union Performing Arts Series, 5228
Carolina Voices, 2261
Carolinas Concert Association, 5229
Carter Finley Stadium, 7901
Caswell Council for the Arts, 5280
Caswell County Civic Center, 7931
Catawba College Community Center Theatre, 7913
Ce Gaines Complex, 7922
Central Piedmont Community Theatre, 3647
Chamber Arts Society, 1487
Chamber Music of Charlotte, 1483
Chamber Orchestra of the Triangle, 1481
Charlotte Ballet, 507
Charlotte Center City Partners, 5230
Charlotte Coliseum, 7870
Charlotte Philharmonic Orchestra and Chorus, 1484
Charlotte Symphony, 1485
Children's Theatre Board, 3685
Children's Theatre of Charlotte, 3648
Children's Theatre of Eden, 3653
Choral Society of Greensboro, 2265

City Arts Drama Center, 3659
City of Morganton Municipal Auditorium, 7896
Coa Community Auditorium, 7882
Coa Community Center Auditorium, 5238
Coastal Carolina Community College, 5253
Community Theatre of Greensboro, 3660
Cricket Arena, 7871
Cumberland County Coliseum Complex, 7883
Cumberland County Friends of the Orchestra, 1491
Deane E Smith Center, 7865
Deep Dish Theater Company, 3643
Diana Wortham Theatre at Pack Place, 3638, 7854
Dixie Classic Fairgrounds, 7923
Duke University Union Broadway Committee / on Stage Committee, 5235
Dunn Center for the Performing Arts, 7912
Durham Civic Choral Society, 2263
Durham Performing Arts Center, 7880
Durham Symphony Orchestra, 1488
East Carolina University Rudolph Alexander Performing Art Series, 5249
Eastern Music Festival & School, 5244
Edgecombe County Arts Council, 5269
Elizabeth City State University Lyceum Series, 5239
Elon University Lyceum Committee, 5240
Ernie Shore Field, 7924
Farmville Community Arts Council, 5241
Farthing Auditorium, 7856
First Night Raleigh, 5261
Flat Rock Playhouse, 3657
Foothills Community Theatre, 3667
Gallery of Art & Design, 5262
Gardner-Webb University Distinguished Artist Series, 5222
Gilbert Theater, 3656
Givens Performing Arts Center, 7899
Grady Cole Center, 7872
Grainer Stadium, 7892
Greensboro Ballet, 509
Greensboro Children's Theatre, 3661
Greensboro Coliseum: War Memorial Auditorium, 7886
Greensboro Opera Company, 2266
Greensboro Symphony Orchestra/Carolina Pops, 1493
Groves Stadium, 7925
Guilford College Arts, 5245
Halton Arena, 7873
Hayes Auditorium, 7855
Haywood Arts Regional Theatre, 3682
Hendersonville Symphony Orchestra, 1496
Hendrix Theatre, 7887
Hickory Community Theatre, 3662
High Point Community Theatre, 3664
High Point Theatre and Exhibition Center, 7890
Highland British Brass Band Association, 1492
Highlands Cashiers Chamber Music Festival, 5252
Highlands Playhouse, 7891
Horn in The West, 5225
Howard Hanger Jazz Fantasy, 1479
Institute of Outdoor Drama, 3644
Isothermal Community College Performing Arts Center, 7915
J. Clyde Turner Auditorium, 7862
Jan Van Dyke Dance Group, 510
Je Broyhill Civic Center, 7893
John a Walker Community Center, 7917
Johnston Community College on Stage Concert Series, 7906
Js Dortin Arena, 7902
Judson Theatre, 3671
K.R. Williams Auditorium, 7926
Kenan Memorial Auditorium, 7918
Kenan Stadium, 7866
Kennedy Theatre, 7903
Kidd Brewer Stadium, 7857
Lawrence Joel Veterans Memorial Coliseum, 7927
Lees-Mcrae College, 3640
Lees-Mcrae College Forum, 5221
Legion Stadium, 7919
Lenoir - Rhyne College Facilities, 7889
Lincoln Art Council, 5254
Lincoln Cultural Center, 7894

Little Theater of Gastonia, 3658
Little Theatre of Winston-Salem, 3686
Lost Colony, 3666
Louisburg College Concert Series, 5255
Mallarme Chamber Players, 1489
Manbites Dog Theater, 3651
Martin Community Players, 3683
Matthews Playhouse, 3669
Mcdowell Columns Auditorium, 7898
Memorial Auditorium, 7904
Messiah 2000, 5270
Meymandi Concert Hall, 7905
Moore Auditorium, 7895
Moore Community Band, 1480
Mooresville Community Theatre, 3670
Mount Airy Fine Arts Center, 7897
North Carolina A&T State University Lyceum Series, 5246
North Carolina Arts Council, 5263
North Carolina Black Repertory Company, 3687
North Carolina Blumenthal Performing Arts Center, 7874
North Carolina Opera Company, 2268
North Carolina School of the Arts - Roger, 7928
North Carolina School of the Arts Symphony Orchestra, 1507
North Carolina School of the Arts: School of Music Performance Series, 5277
North Carolina Shakespeare Festival, 3665, 5251
North Carolina State University Center Stage, 7906
North Carolina Symphony, 1500
North Carolina Theatre, 3675
Old Colony Players, 3681
Opera Carolina, 2262
Opera House Theatre Company, 3684
Ovens Auditorium, 7875
Paddywhack, 1505
Pfeiffer University Artist Series, 5257
Philharmonia of Greensboro, 1494
Piedmont Chamber Singers, 2271
Piedmont Opera Theatre, 2272
Piedmont Players Theatre, 3678
Pine Cone-Piedmont Council of Traditional Music, 5264
Pitt County Arts Council, 5250
Playmakers Repertory Company, 3645
Porter Center for Performing Arts, 7859
Queens University: Queens Friends of Music Chamber Series, 1486, 5231
Raleigh Boychoir, 2269
Raleigh Civic Center Complex, 7907
Raleigh Little Theatre, 7908
Raleigh Ringers, 1501
Raleigh Symphony Orchestra, 1502
Ramsey Regional Activity Center, 7879
Rbc Center, 7909
Reynolds Coliseum, 7910
Reynolds Memorial Auditorium, 7929
Roanoke Island Historical Association, 5256
Salem College, 5278
Salisbury Symphony Orchestra, 1504
Side by Side, 3676
Smoky Mountain British Brass, 1498
Smoky Mountain Repertory Theatre, 3639
Snow Camp Historical Drama Society, 3680
Southeastern Community College Performing Arts Series, 5272
Southern Appalachian Repertory Theatre, 3668
Spirit Square Center for the Arts, 7876
St. Joseph's Historic Foundation/Hayti Heritage Center, 7881
Stanly County Agri-Civic Center, 7852
Stanly County Chorale, 2267
Stevens Center, 7930
Straus Auditorium, 7860
Summer Festival of Chamber Music at Duke University, 5236
Summer Strings on The Meherrin, 1495
Summer Theatre, 7877
Surry Arts Council, 5258
Swannanoa Chamber Music Festival, 5268
Symphony for United Nations, 1490
Tar River Choral & Orchestral Society, 1503, 2270
Temple Theatre Company, 3679, 7914
Terpsicorps Theatre of Dance, 506

1289

Geographic Index

Thalian Hall Center for the Performing Arts, 7920
The Holmes Center, 7858
Theatre Charlotte, 3649
Theatre in The Park, 3677, 7911
Theatre Previews at Duke, 3652
Town of Cary Cultural Arts Division, 7864
Triangle Theatre Festival, 5237
Trinkle Brass Works, 1499
Tryon Concert Association Subscription Series, 5271
Tryon Fine Arts Center, 7916
United Arts Council of Greensboro, 5247
United Arts Council of Raleigh and Wake County, 5265
University of North Carolina at Asheville Cultural & Special Events, 5219
University of North Carolina at Greensboro Concert/Lecture Series, 5248
University of North Carolina at Wilmington, 5274
Unto These Hills, 3672
Verizon Wireless Amphitheatre, 7878
Wake Forest University, 5279
Wake Forest University Symphony Orchestra, 1508
Western Carolina University Lectures, Concerts & Exhibitions, 5232
Western Piedmont Symphony, 1497
Whittington-Pfohl Auditorium, 7861
Wilmington Symphony Orchestra, 1506
Wingate University, 5276
Winston-Salem Piedmont Triad Symphony Association, 2273
Winston-Salem Symphony, 1509, 2274
Wright Auditorium, 7888
Yadkin Players, 3688
Youtheatre, 3663

North Dakota

Alerus Center, 7935
All Seasons Arena, 7940
Bismarck-Mandan Symphony Orchestra, 1510
Bismark Civic Center, 7932
Burning Hills Amphitheatre, 7939
Chester Fritz Auditorium, 7936
City of Jamestown North Dakota, 7938
Empire Theatre Company, 3694
Fargo-Moorhead Community Theatre, 3689
Fargo-Moorhead Opera Company, 2275
Fargodome, 7933
Festival Concert Hall, 7934
Fort Totten Little Theatre, 3693
Greater Grand Forks Symphony Orchestra, 1511
Hyslop Sports Center, 7937
Little Country Theatre, 3690
Mayville State University (Nd) Fine Arts Series, 5283
Minot Symphony Association, 1512
North Dakota Museum of Art, 5282
North Dakota State University Lively Arts Series, 5281
The Tin Roof Theatre Company, 3691
Theatre B, 3692

Ohio

Actors' Theatre Company, 3719
Akron Civic Theatre, 7941
Akron Symphony Orchestra, 1513
Akron Youth Symphony Orchestra, 1514
Alma Dance Experience, 544
Anderson Arena, 7949
Apollo's Fire: the Cleveland Baroque Orchestra, 1541
Art Song Festival, 5314
Artreach: a Division of the Children's Theatre of Cincinnati, 3703
Arts Council Lake Erie West, 5368
Arts Partnership of Greater Hancock County, 5343
Ashland Symphony Orchestra, 1515
Ashtabula Chamber Orchestra, 1516
Baldwin-Wallace College Academic & Cultural Events Series, 5293
Baldwin-Wallace College Symphony Orchestra, 1521
Baldwin-Wallace University, 5292
Ballet Excel Ohio, 529
Ballet in Cleveland, 518
Ballet Theatre of Ohio, 537
Ballet Western Reserve, 546
Balletmet Dance Centre, 525
Beck Center for the Cultural Arts, 3739
Beeghly Gym, 8021
Bi-Okoto Cultural Institute, 514
Blossom Music Center, 7989
Blue Jacket, First Frontier, 3754
Bluffton University Artist Series, 5294
Bowling Green State University Festival Series, 5296
Bowling Green State University: New Music & Art Festival, 5295
Brecksville Little Theatre, 3698
Cain Park Theatre, 3717, 7979
Calico Theatre, 7945
Canton Ballet, 513
Canton Memorial Civic Center, 7951
Canton Symphony Orchestra, 1523
Canton Youth Symphony, 1524
Carousel Dinner Theatre, 3695
Catco (Contemporary American Theatre Company), 3720
Ccm Philharmonia & Concert Orchestra, 1526
Cedar Point Live Entertainment, 3749
Cedarville University Artist Series, 5299
Central Ohio Symphony Orchestra, 1552
Central Ohio Technical College, 5359
Chagrin Valley Little Theatre, 3701
Chamber Music Columbus, 1544
Chamber Music Connection, 5373
Chamber Music Yellow Springs, 1574
Children's Concert Society of Akron, 5285
China Music Project, 5315
Cincinnati Arts Association: Aronoff Center for the Arts, 5301
Cincinnati Ballet, 515
Cincinnati Boychoir, 2277
Cincinnati Chamber Orchestra, 1527
Cincinnati Folk Life Series, 5302
Cincinnati Gardens, 5303
Cincinnati May Festival, 5304
Cincinnati Music Hall, 7953
Cincinnati Opera, 2278
Cincinnati Opera Association Summer Festival, 5305
Cincinnati Orchestra, 1528
Cincinnati Playhouse in The Park, 3704
Cincinnati Shakespeare Festival, 5306
Cincinnati Symphony Youth Orchestra, 1529
Cintas Center, 7954
Clark State Performing Arts Center, 8008
Classical Guitar Series, 5307
Classical Piano Series, 5308
Clermont Philharmonic Orchestra, 1517
Cleveland Browns Stadium, 7960
Cleveland Chamber Music Society, 1542
Cleveland Chamber Symphony, 1531
Cleveland Institute of Music, 1532, 7961
Cleveland Jazz Orchestra, 1533
Cleveland Museum of Art Performing Arts Series, 5316
Cleveland Museum of Art: Gartner Auditorium, 7962
Cleveland Music School Settlement Artists Concert Series, 5317
Cleveland Octet, 1534
Cleveland Orchestra, 1535
Cleveland Orchestra Chorus, 2279
Cleveland Orchestra Youth Orchestra, 1536
Cleveland Philharmonic Orchestra, 1537
Cleveland Play House, 3711, 7963
Cleveland Play House Bolton Theatre, 7964
Cleveland Play House Brooks Theatre, 7965
Cleveland Play House Drury Theatre, 7966
Cleveland Pops Orchestra, 1518
Cleveland Public Theatre, 3712, 7967
Cleveland Shakespeare Festival, 5318, 5351
Cleveland Signstage Theatre, 3713
Cleveland State University Dance Company, 519
Cleveland State University: Convocation Center, 7968
Cleveland Women's Orchestra, 1567
College Light Opera Company, 2288
College-Community Arts Council, 5300
Collingwood Arts Center, 8011
Columbiana Summer Concert Association, 5323
Columbus Arts Festival, 5324
Columbus Association for the Performing Arts: Signature Series, 5325
Columbus Children's Theatre, 3721
Columbus Symphony Chorus, 2282
Columbus Symphony Orchestra, 1545
Columbus Symphony Orchestra: Picnic With the Pops, 5326
Columbus Symphony Youth Orchestras, 1546
Contemporary Dance of Sinclair, 530
Contemporary Dance Theater, 516
Cooper Stadium, 5327
Corbett Auditorium, 7955
Council for the Arts of Greater Lima, 5353
Crawford County Community Concert Association, 5297
Crew Stadium, 7981
Curtain Players, 3737
Cuyahoga Community College: Western Campus Theatre, 8005
Dairy Barn Cultural Arts Center, 7943
Dancecleveland, 520
Dancevert, 521
Darius Milhaud Society, 5319
Dayton Ballet, 531
Dayton Classical Guitar Society, 1525
Dayton Contemporary Dance Company, 532
Dayton Hara Arena, 7990
Dayton Opera Association, 2284
Dayton Philharmonic Orchestra Association, 1549
Dayton Philharmonic Youth Orchestra, 1550
Dayton Playhouse, 3732, 7991
Dayton's Jazz at the Bend Festival, 5334
De La Dance Company, 517
Delaware County Cultural Arts Center, 7994
Demetrius Klein Dance Company, 536
Denison University Vail Series, 5344
Deyor Performing Arts Center, 8022
Dobama Theatre, 3718, 7980
Doyt L Perry Field, 7950
Drake County Center for the Arts, 5355
Early Music in Columbus, 5328
Ej Thomas Performing Arts Hall, 7942
Eldred Hall, 7969
Ensemble Theatre of Cincinnati, 3705
Fairmount Center for the Creative and Performing Arts, 8003
Fall Arts Festival/Jewish Folk Festival, 5309
Fine Arts Council of Trumbull County, 5370
Foothills Art Festival, Southern Hills Arts Council, 5347
Ford Theatre, 8023
Fostoria Footlighters, 3736
Franciscan Center of Lourdes University, 8009
Franklin County Veterans Memorial, 7982
Fraze Pavilion for the Performing Arts, 7996
Glass Bowl Stadium, 8012
Great Lakes Theater, 5320
Greater Akron Musical Association, 5286
Groundworks Dance Theater, 522
Gund Arena, 7970
Hamilton-Fairfield Symphony & Chorale, 2285
Hamilton-Fairfield Symphony Orchestra, 1553
Heights Chamber Orchestra, 1543
Hiram College Concert & Artist Series, 5346
Hixon Dance, 526
Hobart Arena, 8018
Huntington Playhouse, 7946
Huntington Theatre, 3697
Inlet Dance Theatre, 523
Jacobs Field, 7971
Jazz Arts Group of Columbus, 1547
Jazz Guitar Series, 5310
Jazz Piano Series, 5311
Jeanne B. Mccoy Community Center for the Arts, 8001
Jefferson Academy of Music, 5329
Jerome Schottenstein Center, 7983
John F Savage Hall, 8013
Karamu House, 3714
Karamu House Performing Arts Theatre: Amphitheatre, 7973
Karamu House Performing Arts Theatre: Arena, 7974
Karamu House Performing Arts Theatre: Prosce Hall, 7972
Kenneth C Beck Center for the Performing Arts, 7997
Kent/Blossom Music, Kent State University, 5348
Kentfest, 5349
Kulas Musical Arts, 7948
Lakeland Civic Orchestra, 1555
Lakeside Chatauqua, 5350
Lakeside Symphony, 1556
Lancaster Chorale, 2286
Lancaster Festival, 5352
Lange Trust, 5364
Leahy Good, 533
Leaven Dance Company, 543
Licking County Players, 3746
Lima Symphony Orchestra, 1557
Linton Chamber Music Series/Encore, 5312
Linton Chamber Music Series/Encore! Linton, 1530
Linton's Peanut Butter & Jam Sessions, 5313
Lithopolis Performing Artists Series, 5298
Lively Arts Series: Palace Cultural Arts Association, 5354
Logan County Community Concerts, 5291
Lorain County Community College: Stocker Arts Center Programming, 5342
Loveland Stage Company, 3740
Lyric Opera of Cleveland, 2280
Mad River Theater Works, 3753
Madcap Productions Puppet Theatre, 3706
Madlab, 3722
Magical Theatre Company, 3696
Mandel Jewish Community Center of Cleveland, 7947
Mansfield Playhouse, 3741
Mansfield Symphony Orchestra, 1558
Mariemont Players, 3707
Marion Palace Theatre, 8000
Mary Emery Hall, 7958
Memorial Athletic & Convocation Center, 7995
Mentor Performing Artists Concert Series, 5356
Miami University Dance Theatre, 540
Miami University Performing Arts Series, 5362
Miami University Symphony Orchestra, 1565
Miami University: Hamilton Artist Series, 5345
Miami Wind Quintet, 1566
Midamerica Chamber Music Festival, 5340
Middletown Symphony Orchestra, 1559
Millett Hall, 8004
Monday Musical Club of Youngstown, Ohio, 5375
Morrisondance, 524
Mount Vernon Nazarene College: Lecture Artist Series, 5357
Music From Stan Hywet, 5287
Music From the Western Reserve, 1554
Music in The Air, 5330
Nationwide Arena, 7984
Near West Theatre, 3715
New Albany Symphony, 1560
Northeast Ohio Jazz Society, 1538
Northern Ohio Youth Orchestras, 1563
Oberlin Baroque Ensemble, 1564
Oberlin Baroque Performance Institute & Festival, 5360
Oberlin College Conservatory of Music Artist: Recital Series, 5361
Oberlin Theater and Dance Program, 539
Ohio Ballet, 512
Ohio Chamber Orchestra, 1519
Ohio Dance Theatre, 538
Ohio Light Opera, 2290
Ohio Northern University Artist Series, 5284
Ohio Outdoor Historical Drama Association, 5358
Ohio Stadium, 7985
Ohio State University of Dance, 527
Ohio State University-Department of Theatre, 3723
Ohio Theatre, 7986
Ohio University Performing Arts Series, 5290
Ohio University: School of Music Center, 7944
Ohio Wesleyan University Performing Arts Series, 5341
Opera Circle, 2281
Opera Columbus, 2283
Opera Western Reserve, 2291
Otterbein University, 5372
Palace Civic Center, 7999
Palace Theatre, 3744
Paul Brown Stadium, 7956

Geographic Index

Phoenix Theatre for Children, 3724
Players Guild of Canton, 3700
Playhouse Square Center: Ohio Theatre, 7975
Playhouse Square Center: Palace Theatre, 7976
Playhouse Square Center: State Theatre, 7977
Playhouse Square Foundation, 3716
Pomerene Center for the Arts, 7988
Porthouse Theatre Company, 3738
Pro Musica Chamber Orchestra of Columbus, 1548
Reality Theatre, 3725
Red Herring Theatre Ensemble, 3726
Renaissance Theatre, 3742
Ritz Theatre, 3751
Riverbend Music Center, 7957
Rosebriar Shakespeare Company, 3727
Saint Sava Free Serbian Orthodox Church, 2276
Sandusky Concert Association, 5365
Sandusky State Theatre, 3750
Scarlet Mask Society, 3728
Seagate Convention Centre, 8014
Secrest Auditorium, 8026
Seven Dance Company, 528
Severance Hall, 7978
Shadowbox Cabaret, 3729
Shaker Symphony Orchestra, 1539
Shalhavet Festival, 5322
Shark Eat Muffin Theatre Company, 3708
Short North Performing Arts Association, 5331
Showboat Becky Thatcher, 3743
Showboat Majestic, 3709
Sinclair Dance, 534
Soirees Musicales Piano Series, 1551, 5336
Sorg Opera Company, 2287
Southeastern Ohio Symphony Orchestra, 1561
Southern Ohio Museum & Cultural Center, 8006
Spotlight Arena, 8024
Springfield Arts Council, 5366, 5367
Springfield Symphony Orchestra, 1568
Sro Theatre Company, 3730
Stagecrafters, 3710
Stambaugh Auditorium, 8025
Star Players Theatre, 3731
Stranahan Theater Great Hall, 8015
Suburban Symphony Orchestra, 1520
Summer Stock at the University of Findlay, 3735
Tecumseh!, 3702
The Carton Palace Theatre Association, 7952
The Human Race Theatre Company, 3733
The Ritz Theatre, 8010
The Wright State University Nutter Center, 5335
The Zoot Theatre Company Inc., 3734
Theatre on The Square, 3699
Toledo Ballet Association, 545
Toledo Cultural Arts Center Valentine Theatre, 8016
Toledo Jazz Society, 1570
Toledo Museum of Art, 8017
Toledo Opera, 2289
Toledo Repertoire Theatre, 3752
Toledo Symphony, 1571
Towne and Country Players, 3748
Travesty Dance Group Cleveland, 542
Tri-C Jazzfest, 5321
Triune Concert Series, 5332
Troy Hayner Cultural Center, 8019
Trumbull New Theatre, 8002
Trumpet in The Land, 3745
Tuesday Musical Association, 5288
Tuscarawas Philharmonic, 1562
University Circle Chamber Orchestra, 1540
University of Akron: Ej Thomas Hall Series, 5289
University of Dayton Arts Series, 5337
Upper Arlington Cultural Arts Commission, 5369
Us Bank Arena, 7959
Valley Artists Series, 5363
Vanguard Concerts, 5338
Venti Da Camera, 1522
Verb Ballets, 541
Vern Riffe Center for the Arts, 8007
Veterans Memorial Civic and Convention Center, 7998
Victoria Theatre Association, 7993
W.D. Packard Music Hall, 8020
Warren Civic Music Association, 5371
Weathervane Playhouse, 3747
Westerville Symphony, 1572
Wexner Center for the Arts, 7987
Wittenberg University Department of Music, 1569
Women in Music: Columbus, 5333
Wooster Symphony Orchestra, 1573
Worthington Arts Council, 5374
Wright State University Artist Series, 5339
Wright State University's Nutter Center, 7992
Youngstown State University: Dana Concert Series, 5376
Youngstown Symphony Orchestra, 1575
Zanesville Art Center, 8027
Zanesville Concert Association, 5377
Zivili Dance Company, 535

Oklahoma

Alva Public Library Auditorium, 8029
Ann Lacey School of American Dance and Arts Management, 551
Arts Council of Oklahoma City, 5386
Bartlesville Community Center, 8030
Bartlesville Symphony Orchestra, 1576
Black Liberated Arts Center, 8041
Broken Arrow Performing Arts Center, 8031
Bullshed Theatre Project, 3755
Burg Theatre, 8042
Cameron University: Lecture & Concert Series, 5384
Cameron University: Theatre Arts Department, 3758
Canterbury Choral Society, 2294
Carl Wooten Stadium, 8032
Central Oklahoma Concert Series, 5381
Chamber Music in Oklahoma, 1582
Chamber Music Tulsa, 1585
Charlie Christian International Jazz Festival, 5387
Cherokee National Historical Society, 3767
Chisholm Trail Arts Council, 5380
Cimarron Circuit Opera Company, 2292
Cimarron Opera, 2293
Civic Center Music Hall, 8043
Community Concerts of Bartlesville, 5378
Concertime, 5392
Contemporary Dance Oklahoma, 549
Cox Convention Center, 8044
Dorothy I Summers Auditorium, 8028
Duncan Lawton City Ballet, 548
Dusk Till Dawn Blues Festival, 5388
Enid-Phillips Symphony Orchestra, 1578
Go for Baroque, 1583
Golden Hurricane Club, 8052
Great Plains Coliseum, 8033
Jazz in June, 1580, 5385
Kirkpatrick Auditorium, 8045
Lawton Arts & Humanities Theater, 3759
Lawton Philharmonic Orchestra, 1579
Light Opera Oklahoma - Look, 2296, 5393
Llyod Noble Center, 8039
Lyric Theatre of Oklahoma, 3761
Mabee Center Arena, 8049
Mccahon Memorial Auditorium, 8034
Mcmahon Memorial Auditorium, 8035
Milan Stadium, 8060
Mohawk Park, 8050
Muskogee Civic Center, 8037
Muskogee Little Theatre, 8038
Northeastern Oklahoma State University Allied Arts Series, 5391
Northeastern State University Sizzlin' Summer Showcase, 3768
Oklahoma Baptist University Artist Series, 5389
Oklahoma Children's Theatre, 3762
Oklahoma City Ballet, 552
Oklahoma City Philharmonic Orchestra, 1584
Oklahoma City Zoo Amphitheatre, 8046
Oklahoma Festival Ballet, 550
Oklahoma Mozart International Festival, 1577, 5379
Oklahoma Opera & Musical Theater Company, 3763
Oklahoma Opera and Music Theater Company, 2295
Oklahoma Shakespeare in The Park, 3764
Oklahoma State University Allied Arts, 5390
Philadelphia Foundation, 5382
Pollard Theatre, 3756
Ponca Playhouse, 3766, 8047
Prairie Dance Theatre, 553
Reduxion Theatre Company, 3765
River Parks Amphitheatre, 8051
Rose State College Performing Arts Theatre, 8036
Sooner Theatre of Norman, 3760
Stillwater Community Center, 8048
The Pollard Theatre, 3757
Theatre Tulsa, 3769
Tri-State Music Festival, 5383
Tulsa Ballet, 554
Tulsa Community College Performing Arts Center for Education, 8059
Tulsa Opera, 2297
Tulsa Performing Arts Center, 8053
Tulsa Performing Arts Center Trust, 5394, 5395
Tulsa Performing Arts Center: Doenges Theater, 8055
Tulsa Performing Arts Center: John H William Hall, 8054
Tulsa Performing Arts Center: Studio II, 8056
Tulsa Youth Symphony, 1586
Tyrrell Hall, 8057
University of Oklahoma Symphony Orchestra, 1581
University Theatre, 8040
Walter Arts Center, 8058
Western Oklahoma Ballet Theatre, 547
Woodward Arts and Theatre Council, 3770

Oregon

Abbey Bach Festival, 5423
Actors Cabaret/Mainstage Theatre Company, 3774
Arlene Schnitzer Concert Hall, 8089
Artists Repertory Theatre, 3783
Ashland Folk Music Club, 5399
Autzen Stadium, 8070
Beall Concert Hall, 8071
Bodyvox, 560
Britt Festivals, 1598, 3780, 5414
Britt Pavilion, 8083
Broadway Rose Theatre, 8106
Broadway Rose Theatre Company, 3791
Brody Theater, 3784
Camelot Theatre Company, 3790
Camerata Musica, 1613
Cappella Romana, 2299
Cascade Festival of Music, 5401
Cascade Head Music Festival, 5412
Cascades Theatrical Company, 3773
Chamber Music Concerts, 1587
Chamber Music Corvallis, 1589
Chamber Music Northwest, 1600, 5417
Chamber Music Society of Oregon, 1601
Children's Performing Arts Series, 5396
City of Albany Parks and Recreation Department, 5397
Clatsop Community College Performing Arts Center, 8065
Coaster Theatre, 8066
Columbia Meadows, 8090
Community Center for the Performing Arts, 8072
Community Music Center, 8091
Coquille Performing Arts, 5403
Corvallis-Oregon State University Music Association, 5404
Craterian Ginger Rogers Theater, 8084
Dance Theatre of Oregon, 556
Dancing People Company, 555
Dolores Winningstad Theatre, 8092
Dolphin Players, 3782
Earle A Chiles Center, 8093
Eastern Oregon State College Performing Arts Program, 5410
Emerald Chamber Players, 1591
Enchanted Forest Summer Theatre, 3792
Ernest Bloch Music Festival at Newport, 5416
Eugene Ballet Company, 557
Eugene Opera, 2298
Eugene Symphony Association, 1592
Evans Auditorium, 8094
Florence Events Center, 8075
Friends of Chamber Music, 1602, 1603
Gallery Theatre of Oregon, 3779
Gill Coliseum, 8067
Grande Ronde Symphony Orchestra, 1597
Historic Elsinore Theatre, 8104
Hult Center for the Performing Arts, 8073
Jaqua Concert Hall, 8074
Klamath Community Concerts, 5409
Lake Oswego Festival of the Arts, 5411
Lake Oswego Parks & Rec, 8080
Lakewood Center for the Arts, 3778, 8081
Lasells Stewart Center, 8068
Little Ballet Theatre, 566
Marylhurst University Music Department, 5413
Mcarthur Sports Field, 8085
Memorial Coliseum, 8095
Metro Dancers, 561
Metropolitan Youth Symphony, 1604
Miracle Theatre Group, 3785
Mount Hood Festival of Jazz: the Governor Building, 5418
Mt Hood Jazz Festival, 1596
Mt. Hood Community College, 5408
Newmark Theatre, 8096
Newport Performing Arts Center, 8087
Northwest Dance Project, 562
Obo Addy Master Drummer, 563
One World Performing Arts, 8061
Oregon Bach Festival, 1593, 5405
Oregon Ballet Theatre, 564
Oregon Children's Theatre, 3786
Oregon Coast Music Festival, 5402
Oregon Contemporary Theatre, 3775
Oregon East Symphony, 1599
Oregon Fantasy Theatre, 3776
Oregon Festival of American Music, 5406
Oregon Mozart Players, 1594
Oregon Shakespeare Festival, 8062
Oregon Shakespeare Festival: Black Swan Theater, 8063
Oregon Shakespearean Festival Association, 3771, 5400
Oregon Symphony, 1605
Osu-Corvallis Symphony Orchestra, 1590
Pacific University Community Wind Ensemble, 1595
Pendleton Convention Center, 8088
Pentacle Theatre, 3789
Pge Park, 8097
Pioneer Courthouse Square, 8098
Portland Actors Ensemble, 3787
Portland Baroque Orchestra, 1606
Portland Center for the Performing Arts, 8099
Portland Center Stage, 3788
Portland Chamber Orchestra Association, 1607
Portland Columbia Symphony, 1608
Portland Institute for Contemporary Art, 8100
Portland Opera, 2300
Portland State University Piano Recital Series, 5420
Portland University Portland International: Performance Festival, 5419
Portland Youth Philharmonic Association, 1609
Quartz Theatre, 3772
Rainbow Dance Theatre, 559
Red Octopus Theatre Company, 3781
Reed Theatre, 8101
Reser Stadium, 8069
Rice Auditorium, 8086
River Rhythms, 5398
Rogue Music Theatre, 3777
Rogue Valley Symphony, 1588
Rose City Chamber Orchestra, 1610
Rose Quarter, 8102
Ross Ragland Theater & Cultural Center, 8079
Salem Chamber Orchestra, 1614
Seaside Civic and Convention Center, 8105
Sinfonia Concertante Orchestra, 1611
Southern Oregon University, 8064
Sunriver Music Festival, 1615, 5424
Taylor-Meade Performing Arts Center, 8076
Theatre in The Grove, 8077
Tom Miles Theatre, 8078
Triangle Productions, 5421
Umpqua Symphony Association, 1612
University of Oregon Chamber Music Series, 5407
University of Oregon Department of Dance, 558
University of Portland Music at Midweek, 5422
Western Oregon University Edgar H Smith Fine Arts Series, 5415
White Bird, 565
Wilson Center for the Performing Arts, 8103

1291

Geographic Index

Yachats Music Festival, 5425
Yamhill County Fairgrounds, 8082

Pennsylvania

1812 Productions, 3823
A.J. Palumbo Center, 8167
Academy of Music: Main Auditorium, 8147
Academy of Vocal Arts Opera Theatre, 2305
Act II Playhouse, 3793
Albright College Concert Series, 5500
Allegheny Ballet Company, 567
Allegheny Civic Symphony, 1638
Allegheny College Public Events Series, 5468
Allegheny County Summer Concert Series, 5488
Allegheny Valley Concert Association, 5470
Allenberry Resort Inn and Playhouse, 3797
Allentown Community Concerts, 5426
Allentown Symphony Association, 1616
Allentown Symphony Hall, 8107
Altoona Symphony Orchestra, 1617
Alumni Auditorium, 8118
Ambler Symphony, 1618
American Family Theater, 3824
American Music Theater Festival/Prince Music Theater, 3825, 5474
American Theater Arts for Youth, 3826
Annenberg Center, 8148
Annenberg Center for the Performing Arts, 5483
Arcadia Theater, 5513
Arden Theatre Company, 3827
Arts Guild at Neumann College, 8110
Artsquest, 5429
Bach Choir of Pittsburgh, 2316
Bach Festival of Philadelphia, 1639
Baltimore Consort, 1631
Barrow-Civic Theatre, 3804
Beaver Stadium, 8184
Beaver Valley Community Concert Association, 5428
Beeghly Theater, 8145
Benedum Center, 8168
Berks Jazz Festival, 5501
Bethlehem Bach Festival, 5430
Big Mess Theatre, 3828
Big Spring Symphony Orchestra, 1640
Bloomsburg Theatre Ensemble, 3796
Bloomsburg University Artist-Celebrity Series, 5432
Bradford Creative & Performing Arts Center, 5434, 8117
Brandywine Ballet, 586
Bristol Riverside Theatre, 3798
Brodhead Cultural Center Summer Series, 5469
Bryce Jordan Center, 8185
Bryn Mawr College Performing Arts Series, 5436
Bucknell University: Weis Center Performance Series, 5464
Bucks County Community College Cultural Programming, 5473
Bucks County Performing Arts Series, 5514
Bucks County Playhouse, 3822, 8144
Bushfire Theatre of Performing Arts, 3829
Butler County Symphony, 1620
Cabrini College, 5499
Cambria County War Memorial Arena, 8133
Camerata Philadelphia Inc, 1665
Carin University, 5463
Carnegie-Mellon School of Music, 5489
Carnegie: Lecture Hall, 8169
Carnegie: Museum of Art Theatre, 8170
Carnegie: Music Hall, 8171
Center City Opera Theater, 2306
Central Community Concerts, 5505
Central Pennsylvania Festival of the Arts, 5507
Central Pennsylvania Friends of Jazz, 1626
Central Pennsylvania Youth Ballet, 569
Chamber Music Society of Bethlehem, 1619
Chestnut Brass Company, 1641
Choral Arts Philadelphia, 5475
Choral Arts Society of Philadelphia, 2307
City Theatre Company, 3841
Clarion University Activities Board Arts, 5439
Community Education Center, 5476, 5477
Concerto Soloists, 1642
Cresson Lake Playhouse, 3802
Crs National Festival for the Performing Arts, 5435

Curtis Institute of Music, 8149
Dance Affiliates, 575
Dance Alloy Theater, 579, 3842
Dance Delbello, 570
Delaware Valley Opera Company, 2308
Delaware Water Gap Celebration of the Arts, 5444
Dorothy Dickson Darte Center, 8189
Edinboro University of Pennsylvania Performing Arts Series, 5446
Eisenhower Auditorium, 8186
Erie Civic Center/ Warner Theatre, 5448
Erie Civic Center: Lj Tullio Arena, 8122
Erie Civic Music Association, 5449
Erie Philharmonic, 1621
Esther Boyer Performing Arts Center, 8150
Farm Show Complex and Expo Center, 8127
Farrel Stadium, 8188
First Friday at the Frick Concert Series, 5490
Fisher Auditorium, 8131
Fitzgerald Fieldhouse, 8172
Fm Kirby Center for the Performing Arts, 8190
Folklife Center of International House, 8151
Forrest Theatre, 8152
Franklin & Marshall College Sound Horizons Concert Series, 5462
Franklin Field, 8153
Fred P Meagher Theatre, 8111
Freedom Repertory Theatre, 3830
Fulton Opera House, 2303
Fulton Opera House/Actor's Company of Pennsylvania, 3811
Germantown Theatre Guild, 3831
Greater York Youth Ballet, 587
Greenville Symphony Society, 1624
Gretna Productions, 3819
Hanover Symphony Orchestra, 1625
Harrisburg Area Community College, 5452
Harrisburg Symphony Association, 1627
Harrisburg Symphony Orchestra, 1628
Hedgerow Theatre, 3815
Heinz Hall for the Performing Arts, 8173
Hershey Symphony Orchestra, 1629
Hershey Theatre, 3807, 8130
Hersheypark Arena/Stadium, 5455
Hersheypark Entertainment, 3808
Hill School Center for the Arts Lively Arts Series, 5498
Immaculata Symphony, 1630
Indian River Theatre of the Performing Arts, 3832
Indiana University of Pennsylvania Onstage: Arts and Entertainment, 5457
Interact Theatre Company, 3833
Irvine Auditorium, 8154
J Birney Crum Stadium, 8108
Johnstown Symphony Orchestra, 1632
Juniata Presents, 5456
Kennett Symphony, 1634
Keystone Repertory Theater, 3809
Kimmel Center for the Performing Arts, 8155
King's College Experiencing the Arts Series, 5511
Koresh Dance Company, 576
Kutztown University Performing Artists Series, 5460
Labco Dance, 580
Lackawanna County Stadium, 8142
Lafayette College Concert Series, 5445
Lancaster Opera Company, 2304
Lantern Theater Company, 3834
Laurel Arts/The Philip Dressler Center, 8182
Laurel Festival of the Arts, 5458
Lehigh Valley Blues & Jazz Festival, 5440
Lehigh Valley Chamber Orchestra, 1636
Long's Park Amphitheatre, 8138
Longwood Gardens, 8137
Longwood Gardens Performing Arts, 5459
Lyric Opera Theatre Street, 2309
Manchester Craftsmen's Guild, 8174
Mann Center for the Performing Arts, 8156
Mansfield University Fine Arts Series, 5466
Market Square Concerts, 5453
Marlboro Music, 5480
Marlboro School of Music, 1643
Marwick Boyd Auditorium, 8119
Mary D'angelo Performing Arts Center, 8123
Mary Green Singers, 2302

Mary L Welch Theatre, 3856
Mary Miller Dance Company, 581
Mccarthy Stadium, 8157
Mcjazz Jugend Bigband, 5491
Mckeesport Symphony Orchestra, 1637
Media Theatre for the Performing Arts, 3816
Mellon Arena, 8175
Mendelssohn Choir of Pittsburgh, 2317
Mendelssohn Club of Philadelphia, 2310
Merriam Theater, 8158
Messiah College Cultural Series, 5450
Midatlantic Arts Foundation Pennsylvania Performing Arts on Tour, 5481
Millbrook Playhouse, 8141
Mishler Theatre, 8109
Montgomery County Community College Lively Arts Series, 5433
Montgomery Theater, 3854
Moravian College: Music Institute, 8113
Mount Aloysius College Performing Arts Series, 5443
Mountain Laurel Center for Performing Arts, 8183
Mountain Playhouse, 3810, 8132
Movement Theatre International, 3857
Muhlenberg College Concert Series, 5427
Music at Fishs Eddy, 5467
Music at Gretna, 5447
Music at Penn's Woods, 5508
Music for Mt. Lebanon, 5492
Music for Mt.Lebanon, 5441
Musselman Stadium, 8125
New Arts Program, 5461
New Castle Regional Ballet, 574
New City Stage Company, 3835
Next Generation Festival, 5454
Nittany Valley Symphony, 1662
Northeast Philadelphia Cultural Council, 5482
Northeastern Pennsylvania Philharmonic ., 1667
Notara Dance Theatre, 585
Open Stage of Harrisburg, 3805
Opera Company of Philadelphia, 2311
Painted Bride Art Center, 8159
Palace Theatre, 8126
Pasquerilla Performing Arts Center, 8134, 8135
Pcca Festival at Little Buffalo, 5472
Pennsylvania Academy of Ballet, 573
Pennsylvania Ballet, 577
Pennsylvania Centre Stage, 8187
Pennsylvania Dance Theatre, 584
Pennsylvania Renaissance Faire, 5442
Pennsylvania Shakespeare Festival, 3799, 5437
Pennsylvania Youth Ballet, 568
People's Light and Theatre Company, 3814
Peter Nero and The Philly Pops, 1644
Philadelphia Chamber Music Society, 1645
Philadelphia Classical Guitar Society, 1646
Philadelphia Classical Symphony, 1650
Philadelphia Dance Company, 578
Philadelphia Gay Men's Chorus, 2312
Philadelphia Orchestra, 1647
Philadelphia Singers, 2313
Philadelphia String Quartet, 1648
Philadelphia Theatre Company, 3836
Philadelphia Youth Orchestra, 1649
Piffaro: the Renaissance Band, 1651
Pitt Stadium, 8176
Pittsburgh Arts Council, 5493
Pittsburgh Ballet Theatre, 582
Pittsburgh Camerata, 2318
Pittsburgh Chamber Music Society, 1654
Pittsburgh Civic Arena, 8177
Pittsburgh Civic Light Opera, 2319
Pittsburgh Concert Chorale, 2320
Pittsburgh Dance Council, 583
Pittsburgh International Children's Theater, 3843
Pittsburgh Irish & Classical Theatre, 3844
Pittsburgh Musical Theater, 3845
Pittsburgh New Music Ensemble, 1655
Pittsburgh Opera, 2321
Pittsburgh Playhouse, 5494
Pittsburgh Public Theater, 3846
Pittsburgh Symphony Orchestra, 1656
Pittsburgh Youth Ballet Company & School, 572
Pittsburgh Youth Symphony Orchestra Association, 1657
Pnc Park, 8178

Pocono Playhouse, 3821, 8143
Point Park University's Pittsburgh Playhouse, 3847
Point Stadium, 8136
Presidential Jazz Weekend, 1652, 5484
Prime Stage, 3848
Prince Music Theater, 3837
Quantum Theatre, 3849
Rajah Theatre, 8179
Reading Community Players, 3852
Reading Symphony Orchestra, 1661
Relache Ensemble, 1653
Renaissance and Baroque Society of Pittsburgh, 1658
Richland Performing Arts, 1633
River City Brass Band, 1659
Riverside Symphonia, 1635
Robert Morris University Colonial Theatre, 3817
Saint Vincent Summer Theatre, 3813
Saltworks Theatre Company, 3850
Scranton Community Concerts, 5503
Scranton Cultural Center at the Masonic Temple, 8181
Sesame Place, 3812
Settlement Music School, 5485
Shafer Auditorium, 8140
Shawnee Playhouse, 3853
Singing City, 2314
Slippery Rock University - Performing Arts Series, 5506
Society Hill Playhouse, 3838, 8160
South Park Theatre, 3794
Southeastern Pennsylvania Symphony Orchestra, 1622
Sovereign Center, 8180
St. Stephen's, 5486
Stabler Arena, 8114
Star Series Association, 5502
State Museum of Pennsylvania, 8128
State Theatre Center for the Arts, 3801, 8121
Strand-Capitol Performing Arts Center, 8191
Strand-Capitol Performing Arts Center Series, 5515
Struthers Library Theatre, 3855
Summer Fest, 2322
Susquehanna University Artist Series, 5504
Tamburitzans Folk Ensemble, 1660
Td Bank Amphitheater, 8112
The Arcadia Chorale, 2301
The Atlantic Coast Opera Festival, 2315
The German Society of Pennsylvania, 5479
The Mifflin-Juniata Concert Association, 5465
The Palestra, 8161
Theatre Harrisburg, 3806
Three Rivers Arts Festival, 5495
Timbers Dinner Theatre, 3820
Tony Williams Scholarship Jazz Festival, 5487
Totem Pole Playhouse, 3803, 8124
Touchstone Theatre, 3795, 8115
27th Annual Central Pa Commerce Bank Jazz Festival, 5451
University of Pittsburgh Concert Series, 5496
Upper Darby Performing Arts Center, 8120
Upper Darby Summer Stage, 3800
Vagabond Acting Troupe, 3818
Veronica's Veil Players, 3851
Villanova University Chamber Series, 1663, 5509
Voloshky Ukrainian Dance Ensembles, 571
Wachovia Spectrum, 8162
Walnut Street Theatre, 3839, 8163
Walnut Street Theatre: Mainstage, 8164
Walnut Street Theatre: Studio 3, 8165
Walnut Street Theatre: Studio 5, 8166
Warren Civic Orchestra, 1664
Weis Center for the Performing Arts, 8139
Wells Fargo Center, 5478
West Chester University of Pennsylvania School of Music, 1666
Westminster College Celebrity Series, 5471
Westmoreland Symphony Orchestra, 1623
Whitaker Center for Science and The Arts, 8129
Wildflower Music Festival, 5510
Will W Orr Auditorium, 8146
Williamsport Community Concert Association, 5512
Williamsport Symphony Orchestra, 1668
Wilma Theater, 3840
Wilson College Performing Arts Series, 5438

Geographic Index

Y Music Society of the Jewish Community Center, 5497
York Symphony Orchestra, 1669
Zoellner Arts Center, 8116

Rhode Island

2nd Story Theatre, 3865
As220, 8195
Astors Beechwood Mansion, 3858
Brown Stadium, 8196
Brown Summer Theatre, 3860
Brown University Orchestra, 1674
Brown University Theatre, 3861
Capitolarts Providence Cultural Affairs, 5521
Chorus of Westerly, 2326
Concerts by The Bay, 5516
Convergence Arts Festival, 5522
Cultural Organization of the Arts, 5517
Everett Dance Theatre, 592
Festival Ballet Providence and School, 593
First Night Providence, 5523
Fusionworks Dance Company, 588
Island Moving Company, 591
Kingston Chamber Music Festival at the University of Rhode Island, 1672
Kingston Chamber Music Festival at Uri, 5518
Looking Glass Theatre, 3862
New England Presenters: University of Rhode Island Great Performances, 5519
Newgate Theater, 5524
Newport Music Festival, 5520
Newport Yachting Center, 8194
Ocean State Theatre, 3866
Opera Providence, 2325
Perishable Theatre, 8197
Providence Division of Public Programming Departments, 5525
Providence Dunkin Donuts Center, 8198
Providence Performing Arts Center, 8199
Rhode Island Chamber Music Concerts, 1675
Rhode Island Civic Chorale & Orchestra, 1670
Rhode Island Civic Chorale and Orchestra, 2323
Rhode Island College Symphony Orchestra, 1676
Rhode Island College: Performing Arts Series, 5526
Rhode Island Philharmonic Orchestra and Music School, 1671
Rhode Island's Ballet Theatre, 590
Rites and Reason, 3863
Ryan Center, 8192
Salt Marsh Opera Company, 2327
Sandra Feinstein-Gamm Theatre, 3859
Stadium Theatre Performing Arts Center, 8202
State Ballet of Rhode Island, 589
The Providence Singers Inc., 2324
Trinity Arts Center, 8200
Trinity Repertory Company, 3864
University of Rhode Island Fine Arts Center, 8193
University of Rhode Island Symphony Orchestra, 1673
Veterans Memorial Auditorium, 8201

South Carolina

Abbeville Opera House, 8203
Aiken Community Playhouse, 3867
Anderson Sports Center, 8204
Anderson Symphony Orchestra, 1677
Anderson University, 5528
Arts Center of Coastal Carolina, 5544
Arts Etc, 5546
Arts Partnership of Greater Spartanburg, 5548
Atlantic Stage, 3880
Bi-Lo Center, 8223
Bob Jones University, 8224
Bob Jones University Concert, Opera & Drama Series, 3876
Brooks Center for the Performing Arts, 8212
Capitol City Stadium, 8216
Carolina Ballet Theatre, 606, 610
Carolina Coliseum, 8217
Carolina Productions, Performing Arts Commission, 5536
Carolina Youth Symphony, 1680
Center Theater, 8230
Centre Stage-South Carolina, 3877
Charleston Concert Association, 5531
Charleston Symphony Orchestra, 1678
Charlotte Knights Baseball Stadium, 8222
Citadel Fine Arts Series, 5532
Civic Center of Anderson, 5529
Clemson Memorial Stadium, 8213
Coastal Concert Association, 5545
Columbia City Ballet, 597
Columbia College Power Company Series, 5537
Columbia Community Arts Centre, 599
Columbia Stage Society at Town Theatre, 3873
Columbia's Ballroom Company, 600
Converse Symphony Orchestra, 1684
Crabpot Players, 3879
Dance 1 Studio, 609
Dance Station, 594
Dock Street Theatre, 8206
Drayton Hall, 8207
Erskinarts (The Fine & Performing Arts at Erskine College), 5539
Fine Arts Center of Kershaw County, 8205
Fine Arts Council of Sumter Performing Arts Series, 5550
Florence Civic Center, 8221
Footlight Players Theatre, 8208
Francis Marion University Artists Series, 5540
Gaillard Municipal Auditorium, 8209
Gilbert Studio of Dance Arts, 605
Greenville Ballet School and Company, 607
Greenville Municipal Stadium, 8225
Greenville Symphony Orchestra, 1681
Greenwood Civic Center, 8229
Greenwood-Lander Performing Arts, 5542
Hartsville Community Concert Association, 5543
Hilton Head Symphony Orchestra, 1682
James F Byrnes Auditorium, 8235
Johnson Hagood Stadium, 8210
Koger Center for the Arts, 5538, 8218
Littlejohn Coliseum, 8214
Long Bay Symphony Orchestra, 1683
Longstreet Theatre, 8219
Mcalister Auditorium, 8226
Mcalister Fieldhouse, 8211
Mcelvey Center of York, 8239
Metropolitan Arts Council, 5541
Music Foundation of Spartanburg Concert Series, 5549
Newberry College Theatre, 3881
Newberry Opera House, 8232
North Charleston Performing Arts Center, 8233
North Greenville University: Fine Arts Series, 5551
Oliver C Dawson Stadium, 8234
Peace Center for the Performing Arts, 8227
Piccolo Spoleto Festival, 5533
Presbyterian College, 5535
Pure Theatre, 3868
Robert Ivey Ballet, 595
Sc Christian Dance Theater, 601
South of Broadway Theatre Company, 3882
Southeastern School of Ballet, 602
Spartanburg Memorial Auditorium: Arena, 8237
Spartanburg Memorial Auditorium: Theatre, 8236
Spoleto Festival Usa, 596, 1679, 3869, 5534
Sumter Country Gallery of Art, 8238
Swamp Fox Players, 3875
The Columbia City Jazz Dance Company & School, 598
The Footlight Players, 3870
The Palace Theatre, 8231
The Southern Strutt Studio, 608
Threshold Repertory Theatre, 3871
Tillman Auditorium, 8215
Timmons Arena, 8228
Trustus, 3874
Unbound Dance Company, 603
University of South Carolina-Beaufort, 5530
University of South Carolina: Aiken Etherredge Center, 5527
Village Repertory Company, 3872
Vista Ballroom, 604
Warehouse Theatre, 3878
Williams-Brice Stadium, 8220
Winthrop University College of Visual & Performing Arts, 5547

South Dakota

Aberdeen Community Concert Association, 5552
Aberdeen Community Theatre, 3883
Black Hills Community Theatre, 3885
Black Hills Passion Play, 3888
Black Hills Playhouse, 3886
Black Hills Symphony Orchestra, 1687
Brookings Chamber Music Society, 1685
Corn Palace, 8243
Coughlin Alumni Stadium, 8240
Dakota Dome, 8248
Huron Arena, 5555
Lewis & Clark Theatre Company, 3892
Madison Area Arts Council, 5556
Matthews Opera House Society, 3889
National Music Museum, 8249
Pierre Community Concerts Association, 5557
Prairie Repertory, 3884
Rushmore Plaza Civic Center, 8244
Sioux Falls Arena, 8245
Sioux Falls Community Playhouse, 3887, 8246
Slagle Auditorium, 8250
South Dakota Art Museum, 8241
South Dakota State University Civic Symphony, 1686
South Dakota State University Student Activities, 5553
South Dakota Symphony, 1688
Spearfish Center for the Arts, 3890
Swiftel Center, 8242
The Laura Ingalls Wilder Pageant Society, 5554
Town Players, 3891
Warren M Lee Center, 8251
Washington Pavilion of Arts & Science, 8247

Tennessee

Actors Co-Op, 3901
Adelphia Stadium, 8290
Allen Arena, 8291
Aman Arena, 8264
Appalachian Ballet Company, 617
Apsu Concert Hall, 8257
Arts & Culture Alliance of Greater Knoxville, 3902
Athens Area Council for the Arts, 5558
Austin Peay State University, 5561
Ballet Memphis, 618
Ballet Tennessee, 611
Bijou Theatre, 8269
Bijou Theatre Center, 8270
Bridgestone Arena, 8294
Bryan College Department of Music, 5564
Bryan Symphony Orchestra, 1690
Carpetbag Theatre, 3903
Carson-Newman College Concert-Lecture Series, 5568
Chaffin's Barn Dinner Theatre, 3912, 8292
Charles M Murphy Athletic Center, 8288
Chattanooga Ballet, 612
Chattanooga Boys Choir, 2328
Chattanooga Symphony and Opera, 1689
Chattanooga Symphony and Opera Association, 2329
Circuit Playhouse, 3908
City Ballet, 615
Clarence Brown Theatre Company, 3904
Concerts International, 5574
Cumberland County Playhouse, 3895
Cumberland University Auditorium, 8276
Curb Event Center, 8293
Dance Theatre of Tennessee, 619
Darkhorse Theater, 3913
David Lipscomb University Theater, 3914
David Lipscomb University: Music Department, 5578
Derthick Theatre, 8265
Dixie Stampede, 3922
East Tennessee Fine and Performing Arts Scholars, 5569
Etowah Arts Commission, 5565
Ewing Children's Theatre, 3909, 8280
Freedom Hall Civic Center, 8266
Friends of Music, 5579
Gatlinburg Convention Center, 8260
Germantown Community Theatre, 3898
Germantown Performing Arts Centre, 5566
Gordon Jewish Community Center, 8295
Grand Ole Opry House, 8296
Greer Stadium, 8297
Herschel Greer Stadium, 8298
Hooper Eblen Center, 8258
Howard C Gentry Complex, 5580
Jackson Civic Center, 8262
Jackson Symphony Association, 1691
Jackson Theatre Guild, 3900
Johnny 'red' Floyd Stadium, 8289
Johnson City Area Arts Council, 5570
Johnson City Symphony Orchestra, 1692
Jubilee Community Arts, 5571
Knoxville Civic Auditorium and Coliseum-Auditorium, 8271
Knoxville Opera Company, 2330
Knoxville Symphony Orchestra, 1694
Lambuth Theatre, 8263
Lee University Presidential Concert Series, 5562
Liberty Bowl Memorial Stadium, 8281
Lindenwood Concerts, 2331
Louise Mandrell Theater, 8308
Maryville College, 8278
Memphis Cook Convention Center Complex, 8282
Memphis in May International Festival, 5575
Memphis Symphony Orchestra and Youth Symphony Orchestra, 1695
Mid-South Coliseum, 8283
Middle Tennessee State University, 5577
Mini Dome, 8267
Mockingbird Public Theatre, 3915
Morristown Theatre Guild, 3911
Mud Island River Amphitheatre, 8284
Nashville Ballet, 620
Nashville Children's Theatre, 3916
Nashville Convention Center, 8299
Nashville Municipal Auditorium, 8300
Nashville Opera Association, 2333
Nashville Shakespeare Festival, 3917
Nashville Symphony, 1696
Nashville Symphony Chorus, 2334
Neyland Stadium, 8272
Oak Ridge Civic Music Association, 1697, 5583
Oak Ridge Playhouse, 3921
Opera Memphis, 2332
Orpheum Theatre, 8285
Playhouse on The Square, 3910
Poplar Pike Playhouse, 3899
Pull-Tight Players, 3896
Rhodes College: Mccoy Visiting Artist Series, 5576
Riverbend Festival, 5559
Roland Hayes Concert Hall, 8254
Roxy Theater, 3894
Ryman Auditorium, 8301
Schermerhorn Symphony Center, 8302
Seeger Chapel Concert Hall, 8268
Sewanee Festival Orchestras / Sewanee Music Festival, 5585
Sewanee Summer Music Festival, 5584
Sioux Falls Stadium, 8309
Skyhawk Arena, 8277
South Jackson Civic Center, 8310
Southern Adventist University, 5563
Street Theatre Company, 3918
Sweet Fanny Adams Theatre & Music Hall, 3897
Symphony of the Mountains, 1693
Tennessee Association of Dance, 613
Tennessee Children's Dance Ensemble, 616
Tennessee Performing Arts Center, 8303
Tennessee Performing Arts Center: Andrew Jackson Hall, 8304
Tennessee Players, 3907
Tennessee Repertory Theatre, 3919
Tennessee Stage Company, 3905
Tennessee Theater, 8273
Tennessee Theatre Company, 3920
Tex Turner Arena, 8261
The Nashville Shakespeare Festival, 5581
The Paramount Center for the Arts, 8252
Theater Knoxville, 3906
Theatre Bristol, 3893
Theatre Guild, 8287
Theatre Memphis, 8286
Thompson-Boling Arena, 8274
Tivoli Theatre, 8255
Tulane University, 8259
University of Tennessee at Chattanooga, 5560

1293

Geographic Index

University of Tennessee at Knoxville: Cultural Arts, 5572
University of Tennessee at Martin Arts Council, 5573
University of Tennessee Music Hall, 8275
Utc Mckenzie Arena, 8256
Vanderbilt Stadium, 8305
Vanderbilt University: Great Performances, 5582
Vanderbilt University: Memorial Gym, 8306
Viking Hall Civic Center, 8253
W.J. Hale Stadium, 8307
Watertown Jazz Festival, 5586
Wilson Chapel Complex, 8279
Zion Dance Company, 614

Texas

A.D. Players, 3980
Abilene Civic Center: Exhibit Hall, 8312
Abilene Civic Center: Theater, 8311
Abilene Philharmonic Association, 1698
Actors Theatre of Houston, 3981
Adventures With the Arts, 5657
Alamo City Performing Arts Association, 5661
Alamodome, 8447
Allegro Ballet of Houston, 633
Allen Philharmonic, 1699
Allen Theatre, 8422
Alley Theatre, 3982, 8398
Alley Theatre: Hugo V Neuhaus Arena Stage, 8397
Alley Theatre: Large Stage, 8399
Allied Theatre Group/Stage West, 3967, 3968
Amarillo Civic Center: Arena, 8317
Amarillo Civic Center: Music Hall, 8316
Amarillo Little Theatre, 3925
Amarillo Opera, 2335
Amarillo Symphony, 1700
American Bank Center, 8346
Amoin G Carter Stadium, 8381
Angelo State University, 5659
Angelo State University Auditorium, 8444
Arneson River Theatre, 8448
Arts Council of Washington County, 5598
Arts San Antonio, 5662
Astrodome, 8400
At&T Perorming Arts Center, 8349
Austin Chamber Music Center, 1701
Austin Chamber Music Festival, 5588
Austin Classical Guitar Society, 1702
Austin College Community Series, 5668
Austin Lyric Opera, 2336
Austin Musical Theatre, 3928
Austin Shakespeare Festival, 5589
Austin Symphony Orchestra Society, 1703
Austin Theatre for Youth, 3929
Aztec, 8313
Bach Society Houston, 2351
Ballet Austin, 621
Ballet Concerto, 630
Ballpark in Arlington, 8318
Bass Performance Hall, 8382
Bastrop Opera House, 3936
Bath House Cultural Center, 8350
Bay Area Harbour Playhouse, 3964
Bay Area Houston Ballet & Theatre, 634
Bay City Festival Arts Association, 5592
Bayfront Plaza Convention Center: Auditorium, 8344
Baylor University Distinguished Artist Series, 5678
Baytown Little Theater, 3937
Beaumont Civic Center Complex: Julie Rogers Theatre, 8329
Beaumont Civic Opera, 2340
Beaumont Music Commission, 5594
Beethoven Hall: San Jose Convention Center, 8449
Bell County Expo Center, 8335
Bernard G Johnson Coliseum, 8418
Biblical Arts Center, 8351
Big Spring Cultural Affairs Council, 5597
Bob Hope Theatre, 8352
Brazos Valley Symphony Orchestra, 1705
Brazosport Symphony Orchestra, 1706
Bread and Circus Theatre, 3962
Bronco Arena, 8353
Brookhaven College Center for the Arts, 5622

Brownwood Area Chamber of Commerce, 8337
Cabbages and Kings, 3944
Cactus Jazz & Blues Festival, 5660
Camille Players, 3939
Camille Playhouse, 8336
Capital Baseball Stadium, 8395
Caravan of Dreams, 8383
Cardinal Stadium, 8330
Caruth Auditorium, 8354
Carver Community Cultural Center, 8450
Carver Complex, 8451
Casa Manana Musicals, 3969
Casa Manana Playhouse, 3970
Casa Manana Theatre, 8384
Cathedral Concert Series, 5602
Chaddick Dance Theater, 622
Chamber Music Houston, 1730
Chamber Music International, 1711
Chamizal National Memorial: Theater, 8371
Channing Players, 3983
Chaparral Center, 8433
Charles W. Eiseman Center for Performing Arts & Corporate Presentations, 8442
Children's Opera Theater, 2346
Children's Theatre Festival, 5634
Chorus Austin, 2337
Chrysalis Repertory Dance Company, 635
Circle Theatre, 3971
City Ballet of Houston, 636
City of Bryan Parks and Recreation, 5600
Civic Center Complex, 8331
Clear Lake Symphony, 1727
Cliburn Concerts, 1722, 5625
Cohen Stadium, 8338
Community Music Center, 8401
Conroe Symphony Orchestra, 1707
Conspirare, Craig Hella Johnson & Company of Voices, 2338
Contemporary Ballet Dallas, 627
Contemporary Dance/Fort Worth, 631
Corpus Christi Ballet, 626
Corpus Christi Chamber Music Society, 1709
Corpus Christi Live, 5603
Corpus Christi Symphony Orchestra, 1708
Corsicana Community Playhouse, 3943
Cotton Bowl/Fair Park, 8355
Cowan Fine & Performing Arts Center, 8467
Creative Arts Theatre and School, 3926
Cross Timbers Fine Arts Council, 5669
Cullen Performance Hall, 8402
Cultural Activities Center, 8462
Cultural Council of Victoria, 5676
Cynthia Woods Mitchell Pavilion, 8465
Da Camera of Houston, 5635
Dallas Bach Society, 1712
Dallas Black Dance Theatre, 628
Dallas Brass, 1725
Dallas Chamber Music Society, 1713
Dallas Children's Theater, 3945
Dallas Metropolitan Ballet, 629
Dallas Opera, 2342
Dallas Puppet Theater, 3946
Dallas Summer Musicals, Inc., 5609, 5611
Dallas Symphony Chorus, 2343
Dallas Symphony Orchestra, 5610
Dallas Theater Center, 3947
Dallas Theater Center: Kalita Humphreys Theatre, 8358
Dallas Wind Symphony, 1714
Daniel-Meyer Coliseum, 8385
Darrell K Royal-Texas Memorial Stadium, 8322
Decatur Civic Center - Venue, 8367
Decatur Civic Center Theatre, 8366
Deep Ellum Arts Festival, 5608
Del Mar College Student Cultural Programs, 5604
Delmar Stadium Complex, 8403
Denton Arts & Jazz Festival, 5615
Denton Community Campus Theatre, 3963
Discover Houston County Visitors Center: Museum, 8348
Diverseworks, 8404
Dominic Walsh Dance Theater, 637
Don Haskins Center, 8373
Drama Circle Theatre, 3948
Earthen Vessels, 640
East Texas Symphony Orchestra, 1755
Eastland Fine Arts Association, 5617

Echo Theatre, 3949
Ed Landreth Auditorium, 8386
El Paso Association for the Performing Arts, 5618
El Paso Association for the Performing Arts/Viva El Paso!, 3965
El Paso Chamber Pro-Musica Festival, 5619
El Paso Civic Center: Exhibition Hall, 8374
El Paso Civic Center: Theatre, 8375
El Paso Convention & Performing Arts Center, 8376
El Paso County Coliseum, 8377
El Paso Opera, 2345
El Paso Pro-Musica, 1720
El Paso Symphony Orchestra, 1721
Enron Field, 8405
Ensemble Theatre, 3984
Entertainment Series of Irving, 5646
Evelyn Rubenstein Jewish Community Center, 5640
Ferrel Center, 8469
Festival Arts Association, 5593
Firehouse Arts Center, 5613
Fort Bend Symphony Orchestra, 1753
Fort Griffin Fandangle Association, 3924
Fort Griffin Fandangle Outdoor Theatre, 8314
Fort Hood Community Music and Theater, 5623
Fort Worth Community Arts Center, 8387
Fort Worth Opera Association, 2347
Fort Worth Symphony Orchestra, 1723
Fort Worth Theatre, 3972
Frank Erwin Center, 8323
Frank Erwin Center/ University of Texas-Austin, 5590
Fredericksburg Music Club, Inc., 5627
Freeman Coliseum, 8452
Frontera, 3930
G Rollie White Coliseum, 8341
Galveston Outdoor Musicals, 3976
Garland Civic Theatre, 3977
Garland Granville Arts Center, 8393
Garland Summer Musicals, 5629
Garland Symphony Orchestra, 1726
Gaslight Baker Theatre, 3995
Gertrude Russell Jones Auditorium, 8334
Globe of the Great Southwest Theatre, 3998
Granbury Opera House, 8394
Granbury Opera House Theatre, 3979
Grand 1894 Opera House, 5628, 8391
Grayson County College Humanities, 5614
Greater Dallas Youth Orchestra Association, 1715
Greater Denton Arts Council, 5616
Guadalupe Cultural Arts Center, 4000
Guadalupe Dance Academy, 646
Hamman Hall, 8406
Harlingen Community Concert Association, 5631
Harlingen Cultural Arts Center: Auditorium, 8396
Henry B. Gonzalez Convention Center & Lila Cockrell Theatre, 8453
Hill College, 5633
Hill Country Arts Foundation, 5645
Hill Country Arts Foundation/Point Theatre, 3991
Hip Pocket Theatre, 3973, 8388
Hobby Center for the Performing Arts, 8407
Hofheinz Pavilion, 8408
Homer Bryce Stadium, 8435
Houston Ballet, 638
Houston Chamber Choir, 2352
Houston Civic Center: George R Brown Convention Center, 8411
Houston Civic Center: Gus Wortham Theater, 8409
Houston Civic Center: Jesse H Jones Hall for the Performing Arts, 8410
Houston Civic Symphony Orchestra, 1728
Houston Early Music, 1729
Houston Grand Opera, 2353
Houston Harte University Center, 8445
Houston Masterworks Chorus, 2354
Houston Shakespeare Festival, 3985, 5637
Houston Symphony, 1731
Houston Symphony Chorus, 2355
Houston's Annual Asian-American Festival, 5638
Impact: Programs of Excellence, 5620
Irving Arts Center, 8420
Irving Ballet Company, 641
Irving Chorale, 2357

Irving Community Theater, 3992
Irving Symphony Orchestra Association, 1734
Jackson Auditorium, 8461
Jazz Education Inc., 5636
Jesse H. Jones Hall, 5643
Jesse H. Jones Hall for the Performing Arts, 8412
Johnson/Long Dance Company, 623
Jones At&T Stadium, 8423
Jones Hall for the Performing Arts, 5641
Jubilee Theatre, 3974
Jump-Start Performance Company, 4001
Junior Players, 3950
Kathy Burks Theatre of Puppetry Arts, 3951
Kathy Dunn Hamrick Dance Company, 624
Kay Bailey Hutchison Convention Center, 8356, 8357
Kerrville Folk Festival, 5647
Kerrville Outdoor Theatre, 8421
Kerrville Performing Arts Society, 643
Kilgore Community Concert Association, 5648
Kimbrough Memorial Stadium, 8338
Kingsville Symphony Orchestra, 1737
Kitchen Dog Theater, 3952
Kyle Field, 8342
Lamar University Studio Theatre, 8332
Lamp-Lite Theater, 3997
Laredo Philharmonic Orchestra, 1738
Las Colinas Symphony Orchestra, 1735
Laurie Auditorium, 8454
Lewisville Lake Symphony Orchestra, 1739
Longview Symphony Orchestra, 1740
Lubbock Arts Alliance, 5650
Lubbock Christian University, 5651
Lubbock Memorial Civic Center Banquet Hall, 8425
Lubbock Memorial Civic Center Coliseum, 8426
Lubbock Memorial Civic Center Exhibit Hall, 8427
Lubbock Memorial Civic Center Municipal Auditorium, 8428
Lubbock Memorial Civic Center Theater, 8424
Lubbock Symphony Orchestra, 1741
Lutcher Theater, 8437
Magik Theatre, 4002
Magoffin Auditorium, 8378
Main Street Theater, 3986
Majestic Theatre, 8359
Marshall Civic Center, 8431
Marshall Regional Arts Council, 5653
Marshall Symphony Orchestra, 1742
Maverick Stadium, 8319
Mcallen Performing Arts, 5654
Mcfarlin Memorial, 8360
Memorial Auditorium, 8472
Mesquite Community Theatre, 3996
Metdance, 639
Mid-Texas Symphony Orchestra, 1751
Midland Center, 8434
Midland-Odessa Symphony and Chorale, 1743, 2358
Midwestern State University: Artist Lecture Series, 5680
Miller Outdoor Theatre, 8413
Mk Brown Memorial Auditorium & Civic Center, 8439
Momentum Dance Company, 642
Montagne Center, 8333
Montgomery County Performing Arts Series, 5601
Moody Civic Center: Exhibition Hall, 8392
Moody Coliseum, 8361
Morton H Meyerson Symphony Center, 8362
Municipal Auditorium, 8455
Museums & Cultural Affairs Department, 5621
Music Hall at Fair Park, 8363
Music Mill Amphitheatre, 8320
Nelson W Wolff Municipal Stadium, 8456
New Life Symphony Orchestra, 1716
Old Bastrop Opera House, 8328
Old Jail Art Center, 8315
One World Theatre, 8324
Onstage in Bedford, 3938
Opera in The Heights, 2356
Orchestra of New Spain, 1717
Palestine Civic Center Complex, 8438
Pampa Civic Ballet, 645
Paramount Theater for the Performing Arts, 8325

Geographic Index

Paris Junior College, 8440
Peforming Arts Center, 8345
Pegasus Theatre, 3953
Penfold Theatre, 3931
Performing Arts Fort Worth, Inc, 5626
Permian Playhouse of Odessa, 3999
Perot Theatre, 8464
Piney Woods Fine Arts Association, 5606
Pioneer Amphitheatre, 8339
Plano Symphony Orchestra, 1744
Plaza Theatre Company, 3941
Pocket Sandwich Theatre, 3954
Redbud Theatre, 8368
Regional Arts Center, 8466
Resistol Arena/Rodeo Center Exhibit Hall, 8432
Rice Stadium, 8414
Rio Grande Valley Ballet, 644
Rio Grande Valley International Music Festival, 5655
Riofest: a Blending of the Arts and Entertainment, 5632
River Oaks Chamber Orchestra (Roco), 1732
Robertson Stadium, 8415
Round Rock Symphony Inc, 1746
Round Top Festival Institute, 5658, 8443
Rude Mechanicals, 3932
Salon Concerts, Inc., 5591
Sam Houston State University Theatre, 8419
San Angelo City Auditorium, 8446
San Angelo Symphony Orchestra and Chorale, 1747, 2359
San Antonio Chamber Music Society, 1748
San Antonio Convention Center Lila Cockrell Hall, 8457
San Antonio Parks Foundation, 5664
San Antonio Symphony, 1749
San Pedro Playhouse, 4003
Schola Cantorum of Texas, 2348
Shakespeare Dallas, 3955, 5612
Sherman Symphony Orchestra, 1752
Slocomb Auditorium, 8441
Somervell County Expo Center, 3978
South Dallas Cultural Center, 8364
South Texas Symphony Association, 1719
Southwest Repertory Organization, 3966
Southwest Texas State University Arts Series, 5666
Southwestern Baptist Theological Seminary, 8389
Southwestern University Artist Series, 5630
Stage West, 3975
Stagecenter, 3942
Stages Repertory Theatre, 3987, 8416
State Theatre Company, 3933
Stephen F Austin University Visual & Performing Arts, 5656
Strahan Coliseum, 8460
Sun Bowl, 8379
Sunken Garden Amphitheatre, 8458
Symphony North of Houston, 1733
Symphony of Southeast Texas, 1704
Symphony of the Hills, 1736
Talento Bilingue De Houston, 3988
Tapestry Dance Company, 625
Tarleton State University Student Programming, 5670
Teatro Hispano De Dallas, 3956
Temple Civic Theatre, 4004, 8463
Temple Symphony Orchestra, 1754
Texarkana Regional Arts & Humanities Council, 5671
Texas A&M University Opera & Performing Arts, 2341
Texas Bach Choir, 2361
Texas Ballet Theater, 632
Texas Boys Choir, 2349
Texas Girl's Choir, 5624
Texas Girls' Choir, 2350
Texas International Theatrical Arts Society, 3957
Texas Jazz Festival Society, 1710, 5605
Texas Lutheran University Cultural Arts Events, 5667
Texas Panhandle Heritage Foundation, 3940
Texas Shakespeare Festival, 3993, 5649
Texas Tech University Artists & Speakers, 5652
Texas Tech University Performing Arts Center, 8429
Texas Wesleyan College: Fine Arts, 8390
Thanksgiving Square: Courtyard at Thanksgiving, 8365
The Austin Lyric Opera, 2339
The Black Academy of Arts and Letters Series, 5607
The Carver Community Cultural Center, 5663
The Immanuel & Helen Olshan Texas Music Festival, 5639
The Majestic and Charline Mcombs Empire Theatres, 8459
The Richard Symphony, 1745
The Shepherd School of Music, 5642
Theatre Arlington, 3927, 8321
Theatre Gemini, 3958
Theatre Suburbia, 3989, 8417
Theatre Three, 3959
Theatre Under the Stars, 3990
Tomball Regional Arts Council, 5672
Trinity Mother Frances Rose Stadium, 8468
Tuesday Musical Club Artist Series, 5665
Turtle Creek Chorale, 2344
Twin Mountain Tonesmen, 2360
Tyler Civic Ballet, 647
Tyler Community Concert Association, 5673
Undermain Theatre, 3960
United Supermarkets Arena, 8430
University Center Theatre Complex and Conference Center, 8343
University of Mary Hardin: Baylor, 5596
University of North Texas Performing Arts Center, 8369
University of St. Thomas, 5644
University of Texas at Arlington, 5587
University of Texas at Austin Performing Arts Center, 8326
University of Texas at Austin: Theatre Room, 8327
University of Texas at Brownsville, 5599
University of Texas at El Paso: Main Playhouse, 8380
University of Texas at Tyler, 5674
University of Texas-Pan American: Theater, 8370
Uptown Players, 3961
Uvalde Arts Council, 5675
Victoria Fine Arts Association, 5677
Vive Les Arts Theatre, 3994
Voices of Change, 1718
Vortex Repertory Company, 3034
Waco Convention Center Chisholm Hall, 8470
Waco Hippodrome, 8471
Waco Symphony Orchestra, 1756
Warehouse Living Arts Center, 8347
Watertower Theatre, 3923
Wharton County Junior College the Center for the Arts Series, 5679
Wichita Falls Backdoor Players, 4005
Wichita Falls Ballet Theatre, 648
Wichita Falls Symphony Orchestra, 1757
William R Johnson Coliseum, 8436
Wtamu Theatre, 8340
Young Audiences of Southeast Texas, Inc., 5595
Youth Orchestra of Greater Fort Worth, 1724
Youth Orchestras of San Antonio, 1750
Zachary Scott Theatre Center, 3935

Utah

Abravanel Hall, 8494
Abravanel Symphony Hall, 8495
American West Heritage Center, 5703
Autumn Classic Music Festival, 5690
Ballet West, 651
Brigham Young University Performing Arts Series, 5695
Cache Valley Center for the Arts, 5683
Caine Lyric Theatre, 8477
Canyonlands Arts Council, 5687
Capitol Theatre, 8496
Celebrity Concert Series Office, 5696
Centrum Arena, 8473
Chamber Music Society of Salt Lake City, 1758
Chase Fine Arts Center, 8478
Clog America, 655
Contemporary Music Consortium, 5691
D Glen Smith Spectrum, 8479
Dee Events Center, 8484
Deer Valley Resort Amphitheatre, 8488
Dixie College Arena Theatre, 8491
Dixie College Fine Arts Center, 8490
Dixie College Proscenium Theatre, 8492
Eastern Arts International Dance Theater, 1759, 5698
Eccles Coliseum, 8474
Eccles Community Art Center, 8485
Energy Solutions Arena, 8497
Gina Bachauer International Piano Competition & Festival, 5699
Gina Bachauer International Piano Foundation, 1760
Granite Youth Symphony, 1761
Hale Centre Theatre at Harman Hall, 4016
Heritage Center, 8475
International Dance Theater, 652
Jon M Huntsman Center, 8498
Kent Concert Hall, 8480
Kingsbury Hall, 8499
Lagoon Entertainment Division, 8476
Manon Caine Russell Kathryn Caine Wanlass Performance Hall, 8481
Manti Temple Grounds Amphitheatre, 8483
Marriott Center/Cougar Stadium, 8489
Moab Music Festival, 5688
Morgan Theatre, 8482
Mormon Miracle Pageant, 5686
Mormon Tabernacle Choir, 2363
Odyssey Dance Theatre, 649
Off Broadway Theatre, 4008
Old Lyric Repertory Company, 4007
Oratorio Society of Utah, 2364
Orchestra at Temple Square, 1762
Park City & Salt Lake Music Festival, 5692
Park City Film Music Festival, 5693
Park City Jazz Festival, 5694
Peery's Egyptian Theatre, 8486
Pioneer Theatre Company, 4009
Plan - B Theatre Company, 4010
Plan-B Theatre Company, 4011
Repertory Dance Theatre, 653
Rice-Eccles Stadium, 8500
Ririe Woodbury Dance Company, 654
Salt Lake Acting Company, 4012
Salt Lake County Center for the Arts, 8501
Salt Lake Symphonic Choir, 2365
Salt Lake Symphony, 1763
Southwest Symphony Orchestra, 1767
Sundance Children's Theatre, 4015
Sundance Institute, 4013
Temple Square Concert Series, 5700
The Wisconsin Center District, 5697
Tuacahn Amphitheatre, 8493
University of Utah: School of Music, 1764
Utah Chamber Artists, 2368
Utah Classical Guitar Society, 1765
Utah Festival Opera Company, 2362
Utah Opera Company, 2366
Utah Regional Ballet, 650
Utah Repertory Theater Company, 4014
Utah Shakespearean Festival, 4006, 5682
Utah State University Performing Arts Series, 5684
Utah Symphony, 1766, 2367
Val a Browning Center for the Performing Arts, 8487
Wassermann Piano Festival, 5685
Weber State University Cultural Affairs, 5689
Westminster College, 5701
World Arts/Noon Concerts Series, 5702

Vermont

American Theatre Works, 4020
Banjo Dan and The Mid-Nite Plowboys, 1771
Barre Opera House, 8502
Brattleboro Music Center, 2369, 5704
Burklyn Ballet Theatre, 656
Burlington Discover Jazz Festival, 1768, 5705
Burlington Memorial Auditorium, 8503
Castleton State College Performing Arts Series, 5707
Catamount Film and Arts Company, 4025
Chaffee Art Center, 5718
Chandler Music Hall and Cultural Center, 8508
Department of Theatre and Dance, 8506
Dorset Theatre Festival, 5710
Festival of the Arts, 5712
Flynn Center for the Performing Arts, 8504
Green Mountain Festival Series, 5708
Green Mountain Guild, 4024
Killington Music Festival, 5719
Lost Nation Theater, 4022
Manchester Music Festival, 5713
Middlebury College Concert Series, 5714
National Marionette Theatre, 4018
North Country Chorus, 2371
Oldcastle Theatre Company, 4017
Onion River Arts Council: Celebration Series, 5715
Opera Company of Middlebury, 2370
Pentangle Council on The Arts and The Woodstock Town Hall Theatre, 5721
Potomac Theatre Project, 4021
Sky Blue Boys, 1772
St. Michael's College Concerts, 5709
Stowe Performing Arts, 5720
The Green at Shelburne Museum, 8509
University of Vermont: George Bishop Lane Series, 5706
University of Vermont: Recital Hall, 8505
Vermont Shakespeare Company, 4023
Vermont Stage Company, 4019
Vermont Symphony Orchestra, 1769
Vermont Youth Orchestra Association, 1770
Warebrook Contemporary Music Festival, 5711
Weston Playhouse, 4026
White River Valley Chamber of Commerce, 5717
Wichita Falls Backdoor Players, 4027
Yellow Barn, 8507
Yellow Barn Music Festival, 5716

Virginia

Alden Theatre at Mclean Community Center, 8535
Alden Theatre Series, 4041
Alexandria Recital Series, 5722
Alexandria Symphony Orchestra, 1773
Alleghany Highlands Arts Council/Performing Arts, 5730
Alumni Memorial Field, 8529
American Balalaika Symphony, 1775
Arlington Cultural Affairs Division, 5724
Arlington Dance Theatre, 658
Arlington's Arts Al Fresco & the Innovators, 5725
Ashlawn-Highland Summer Festival, 5728
Attucks Theatre, 8536
Averett University Concert-Lecture Series, 5731
Babcock Auditorium, 8562
Babcock Season, 4057
Barksdale Theatre, 4049
Barter Playhouse/Theatre House, 8510
Barter Theatre - State Theatre of Virginia, 4028
Bluemont Concert Series, 5750
Bridgeforth Stadium, 8526
Bridgewater College Lyceum Series, 5727
Burruss Auditorium, 8512
Cadence Theatre Company, 4050
Cameron Hall, 8530
Carl Broman Concerts, 5760
Carpenter Center for the Performing Arts, 8548
Cary Field, 8565
Casell Coliseum, 8513
Center Stage, 8547
Charlottesville Classical Guitar Society, 1777
Christopher Newport University, 5746
Chrysler Hall, 8537
Citycelebrations Musicfest, 5753
College of Visual and Performing Arts, 5734
Constant Convocation Center, 8538
Dance Theatre of Lynchburg, 663
Danville Area Association for the Arts & Humanities, 5732
Eclipse Chamber Orchestra, 1774
Emory & Henry College Concert Series, 5733
Empire Theatre Complex, 8549
Empire Theatre Complex: Empire Stage, 8550
Empire Theatre Complex: Little Theatre, 8551
Experimental Theatre, 8527
Fairfax Symphony Orchestra, 1778
Fort Eustis Music and Video Center - Jacobs Theatre, 8521
Fredericksburg Music Festival, 5735
Garth Newel Music Center, 5763
Generic Theater, 4044, 8539

1295

Geographic Index

George Mason University Department of Theater, 8519
Greater Richmond Convocation Center, 8552
Hampden-Sydney Music Festival, 5736
Hampton Arts Commission, 5737
Hampton Coliseum, 8524
Hampton Jazz Festival, 5738
Hampton Roads Civic Ballet, 661
Hampton University, 8525
Harbor Park Stadium, 8540
Harrison Opera House, 8541
Henley Street Theatre, 4051
Hesperus, 1776
Hollins University Performing Arts Series, 5758
Horizons Theatre, 4032
Innsbrook Pavilion, 8523
International Children's Festival, 5723
James L Camp Memorial, 8553
James Madison University Encore Series, 5739
Jane Franklin Dance, 659
Jefferson Theatre Center, 8559
Jiffy Lube Live, 8515
K Dance, 669
Kathy Harty Gray Dance Theatre, 4029
Lane Stadium, 8514
Latimer-Shaeffer Theatre, 8528
Lime Kiln Theater, 4038, 4039
Little Theatre of Norfolk, 4045, 8542
Long Way Home, 4048
Loudoun Ballet Company, 662
Loudoun Symphony, 1779
Lynchburg Community Concert Association, 5743
Lynchburg Symphony Orchestra, 1781
Lyric Opera Virginia, 2379
Malini's Dances of India, 665
Malini's Dances of India Troupe, 664
Mclean Orchestra, 1782
Metrostage, 4030
Middle Peninsula Community Concert Association, 5761
Mill Mountain Theatre, 4055
Modlin Center for the Arts, 5754
Mount Vernon Community Children's Theatre, 4031
Music in Motion, 672
Mystery Dinner Playhouse, 4052
Nextstop Theatre Company, 4037
Norfolk Festevents, 5747
Norfolk Scope Arena, 8543
Offstage Theatre, 4034
Opera Roanoke, 2377
Opera Theatre of No Virginia, 2372
Patriot Center, 8520
Prince William County Stadium, 8533
Rachel M. Schlesinger Concert Hall and Arts Center, 8511
Radford University Performing Arts Series, 5751
Radford University Theatre, 8546
Reston Community Center Hunters Woods, 5752
Rev. J. Bruce Stewart, 657
Richmond Ballet, 670
Richmond Coliseum, 8554
Richmond Shakespeare Festival, 5755
Richmond Stadium, 8555
Richmond Symphony Orchestra, 1785
Riverside Center Dinner Theater, 4036
Riverside Center Dinner Theater and Conference Facility, 8522
Roadside Theater, 4047
Roanoke Civic Center, 8560
Roanoke College Performing Arts Series, 5759
Roanoke Symphony Orchestra, 1786
Robins Center, 8556
Rogers Stadium, 8545
Saint Anne's-Belfield School Summer Music Academy, 8516
Salem Civic Center, 8561
Scott Stadium, 8517
2nd Story Theatre Company, 4043
Shenandoah Shakespeare, 4056
Shenandoah Valley Bach Festival, 5740
Shenandoah Valley Music Festival, 5770
Signature Theatre, 4033
Special Music Holidays, 5764
Spencers: Theater of Illusion, 4040
Stuart C. Siegel Center, 8557
Summer Chamber Music Festival, 5765
Swift Creek Academy of the Performing Arts, 5745
Swift Creek Mill Playhouse, 4035
Symphonicity, 1787
The Concert Ballet of Virginia, 668
Theatre Arts Dance Program, 666
Theatre IV, 4053
Theatrevirginia, 5756, 8558
Tidewater Classical Guitar Society, 1783
Tidewater Performing Arts Society, 5748
Touring Concert Opera Company: Martinsville-Henry County Festival of Opera, 5744
Town of Herndon, 5741
Tuesday Evening Concert Series, 5729
Tultex Corporation, 8534
University of Virginia Hall, 8518
Vines Center, 8531
Virginia Arts Festival, 5749
Virginia Ballet Company, 660
Virginia Ballet Theatre, 667
Virginia Beach Pavilion Convention Center, 8564
Virginia Choral Society, 2373
Virginia Commonwealth University Commons College, 5757
Virginia Musical Theatre, 4058
Virginia Opera, 2374
Virginia Repertory Theatre, 4054
Virginia School of the Arts, 671
Virginia Shakespeare Festival, 4059, 5766
Virginia Stage Company, 4046
Virginia Symphony, 1784
Virginia Symphony Chorus, 2375
Virginia Tech Union Lively Arts Season, 5726
Voce Chamber Singers, 2376
Washington & Lee University Lenfest Series, 5742
Washington and Lee University Concert Guild, 1780
Wayside Theatre, 4042
Wells Theatre, 8544
William & Mary Concert Series, 5767
William & Mary Hall, 8566
William Stadium, 8532
Williamsburg Ballet Theatre, 673
Wintergreen Performing Arts, 2380, 5768
Wintergreen Summer Music Festival, 5769
Wolf Trap Farm Park for the Performing Arts, 8563
Wolf Trap Foundation for the Performing Arts, 5762
Wolf Trap Opera Company, 2378

Washington

A Contemporary Theatre, 8597
Abbey Church Events, 5782
Act Theatre, 4078
Admiral Theatre Foundation, 4065
Aria Dance Company, 677
Auburn Arts Commission, 5771
Avista Stadium, 8609
Bainbridge Performing Arts, 4060
Bathhouse Theatre, 4079, 8598
Beasley Performing Arts Coliseum, 4076, 8593
Bellingham Festival of Music, 5772
Bermerton Community Theatre, 4066
Bishop Center for Performing Arts, 8567
Black Box, 8590
Book-It Repertory Theatre, 4080
Bremerton Symphony Orchestra, 1789
Broadway Center for the Performing Arts, 5808
Capitol Theatre, 8621
Cascade Symphony Orchestra, 1790
Chamber Dance Company, 679
Cheney Stadium, 8617
City of Bellingham Facilities, 8571
Columbia Gorge Repertory Theatre, 4095
Columbia Theatre for the Performing Arts, 4073
Connoisseur Concerts Association, 5806
Corbet Theatre, 8579
Cordiner Hall, 8620
Cornish College: Cornish Series, 5792
Cutter Theatre, 4074
Dance Festival: Centrum Festival, 5788
Dance Program, 680
Early Music Guild International Series/Recitals, 5793
Early Music Guild of Seattle, 1798
Earshot Jazz Festival, 5794
Edmonds Arts Commission, 5777
Edmonds Center for the Arts, 8581
Empty Space Theatre, 4081
Enumclaw Arts Commission, 5779
Esoterics, 2383
Everett Civic Auditorium, 8582
Everett Parks and Recreation Department, 8583
Everett Theatre, 4067
Evergreen City Ballet, 678
Evergreen Music Festival: Tacoma Youth Symphony Association, 5809
Evergreen State College Evergreen Expressions, 5786
Ewu Pavilion, 8580
Federal Way Symphony, 1791
Filipiniana Dance Company, 688
Gorge Amphitheatre, 8594
Governors Chamber Music Series, 5795
Harlequin Productions, 4075
Hec Edmundson Pavilion, 8599
Husky Stadium, 8600
Icicle Creek Music Center, 5783
Idiom Theater, 4061
Inb Performing Arts Center, 8610
Interplayers Ensemble Theatre, 4090
Interurban Center for the Arts, 8568
Intiman Theatre Company, 4082
Jazz in The Valley, 5778
Jazz Port Townsend: Centrum Festival, 5789
Juan De Fuca Festival of the Arts, 5787
Kent Arts Commission, 5781
Keyarena at Seattle Center, 8601
Kirkland Performance Center, 8586
Kitsap Opera, 2381
Knutzen Family Theatre - City of Federal Way, 4069
Ladies Musical Club, 5796
Lake Chelan Bach Festival, 5775
Lake Union Civic Orchestra, 1799
Lincoln Theatre Center, 8588
Lynnwood Jazz Festival at Edmonds Community College, 5784
Main Stage, 8591
Marymoor Amphitheatre, 8596
Mbt Studio Theatre, 4062
Mcclelland Arts Center, 8587
Mercer Arena at Seattle Center, 8602
Mercer Island Arts Council, 5785
Metropolitan Performing Arts Center, 8611
Mid-Columbia Symphony, 1797
Mount Baker Theatre, 4063, 8572
Music Center of the Northwest, 1801
Nesholm Family Leature Hall, 8603
New City Theater, 4083
Next Stage Dance Theatre, 691
Northwest Choirs, 2384
Northwest Folklife Festival, 5797
Northwest Puppet, 4084
Northwest Symphony Orchestra, 1800
Ocheami African Dance Company, 681
Old Main Theater, 8573
Olympia Symphony Orchestra, 1794
Olympic Ballet Theatre, 676
Olympic College, 5774
Olympic Music Festival, 5798
On the Boards, 5799
Orcas Theater & Community Center, 5776
Orchestra Seattle & Seattle Chamber Singers, 2385
Pac Concert Hall, 8574
Pac Mainstage Theater, 8575
Pacific Lutheran University Program Board, 5810
Pacific Northwest Ballet, 682
Paradise Theatre, 4071
Peninsula Dance Theatre, 675
Pioneer Dance Arts, 687
Port Angeles Symphony, 1795
Port Townsend Blues Heritage Festival: Centrum Festival, 5790
Pullman Summer Palace, 4077
Rainier Symphony, 1802
Raymond Theater, 8595
Russell Theatre, 8612
Safeco Field, 8604
Sammamish Symphony Orchestra Association, 1792
San Juan Community Theatre and Arts Center, 4070
Seattle Baroque, 1803
Seattle Center Opera House, 8605
Seattle Chamber Music Festival, 5800
Seattle Children's Theatre, 4085
Seattle Choral Company, 2386
Seattle Early Dance, 685
Seattle International Children's Festival, 5801
Seattle Mime Theatre, 4086
Seattle Opera, 2387
Seattle Philharmonic Orchestra, 1804
Seattle Pro Musica, 2388
Seattle Repertory Theatre, 4087, 8606
Seattle Shakespeare Festival, 5802
Seattle Symphony Orchestra, 1805
Seattle Youth Symphony Orchestra, 1806
Seattle Youth Symphony Orchestra's Marrowstone Music Festival, 5803
7th Street Theatre, 8584
Skagit Opera, 2382
Skagit Symphony, 1793
Slocum House Theatre Company, 4094
Spectrum Dance Theater, 686
Spokane Civic Theatre, 4091
Spokane Convention Center, 8613
Spokane Interplayers Ensemble, 4092
Spokane Opera House, 8614
Spokane Symphony Orchestra, 1807
Spokane Veterans Memorial Arena, 8615
Star Theatre, 8616
Susan Brotman Auditorium, 8607
Tacoma Actors Guild, 4093
Tacoma City Ballet, 689
Tacoma Dome, 8618
Tacoma Opera Association, 2389
Tacoma Performing Dance Company, 690
Tacoma Philharmonic, 1808
Tacoma Symphony Orchestra, 1809
Tacoma Youth Symphony, 1810
Taproot Theatre Company, 4088
Teatro Zinzanni, 5804
The Pat Graney Company, 683
The Radost Folk Ensemble, 684
Theater Schmeater, 4089
Theatre at Meydenbauer, 8570
Tri-Cities Coliseum, 8585
Underground Theatre, 8576
University of Puget Sound Cultural Events, 5811
Ups Fieldhouse, 8619
Uw World Series, 8608
Vancouver Symphony Orchestra, 1811
Vashon Opera, 2390
Vela Luka Croatian Dance Ensemble, 674
Village Theatre, 4068, 4072
Walla Walla Symphony, 1812
Washington Center for the Performing Arts, 8592
Washington Idaho Symphony, 1796
Washington State University, 5791
Water Music Festival, 5805
Weatchee Valley Symphony Orchestra, 1813
Western Washington University Main Stage, 8577
Western Washington University Old Main Theatre, 8578
Western Washington University Performing Arts Center Series, 5773
Whatcom Symphony Orchestra, 1788
Whidbey Playhouse, 8589
White River Amphitheatre, 8569
Wwu Summer Stock, 4064
Yakima Symphony Orchestra, 1814
Yakima Valley Sundome, 8622
Yakima Youth Orchestra, 1815

West Virginia

Antoinette E. Falbo Theatre, 8643
Appalachian Youth Jazz-Ballet Company, 695
Apple Alley Players, 4099
Aracoma Story, 4101
Atkinson Auditorium, 8623
Bethany College, 5812
Big Sandy Super Store Arena, 8631
Bloch Learning and Performance Hall, 8644
Bluefield State College, 5813
Brooke Hills Playhouse, 4105
Cam Henderson Center, 8632

Geographic Index

Capitol Center, 8625
Capitol Music Hall & Jamboree Usa, 8653
Carnegie Hall, 5818, 8642
Charleston Chamber Music Society, 1816
Charleston Civic Center, 8626
Charleston Civic Chorus, 2391
Charleston Community Music Association, 5824
Choral Recital Hall, 8645
Clay Center for the Arts & Sciences, 8627
College of Creative Arts, 4102
Contemporary American Theater Festival, 4104, 5822
Fairmont Chamber Music Society, 5819
Geary Auditorium, 8628
Gladys G. Davis Theatre, 8646
Glenville State College Cultural Affairs Commission, 5815
Greenbrier Valley Theatre, 4100
Huntington Civic Arena, 8633
Huntington Museum of Art Auditorium, 8634
Huntington Symphony Orchestra, 1818
Jewish Cultural Series, 5814
Joan C Edwards Playhouse, 8635
Joan C Edwards Stadium, 8638
Joan C. Edwards Performing Arts Center, 8636
Kanawha Players, 4097
Keith-Albee Theatre, 8637
Laidley Field Athletic Recreational Center, 8629
Lyell B Clay Concert Theatre, 8647
Marshall Artists Series, 5816
Mid Ohio Valley Ballet Company, 694
Montaineer Field, 8648
Montclaire String Quartet, 1817
Oglebay Institute, 5826
Old Opera House Theatre Company, 8624
Performing Arts Series at Shepherd, 5823
Seven Stories Theatre Company, 4098
Smith Recital Hall, 8639
Sunshine Daydreams Campground, 8652
The Charleston Ballet, 693
Theatre West Virginia, 4096
Veterans Memorial Field House, 8640
Vivian Davis Michael Laboratory Theatre, 8649
Watt Powell Stadium, 8630
West Liberty College Concert Series, 5825
West Virginia Dance Company, 692
West Virginia Public Theatre, 4103
West Virginia State College Theatre, 8641
West Virginia State Univertisy Music Series, 5817
West Virginia Symphony Chorus, 2392
West Virginia University at Parkersburg, 5821
West Virginia University Coliseum, 8650
West Virginia University Creative Arts Center, 8651
Wheeling Civic Center, 8654
Wheeling Island Stadium, 8655
Wheeling Symphony, 1819
Wvu Arts Series, 5820

Wisconsin

Acacia Theatre, 4119
Al Ringling Theatre, 8658
Al Ringling Theatre Lively Arts Series, 4106
Al Ringling Theatre: Lively Arts Series, 5828
Alpine Valley Music Theatre, 8661
Alverno College, 5855
American Folklore Theatre, 4110
American Players Theatre, 4135
Arts Council of South Wood County, 5877
Bel Canto Chorus, 2397
Beloit College Performing Arts Series, 5829
Beloit Janesville Symphony Orchestra, 1821
Birch Creek Music Performance Center, 8663
Bradley Center, 8687
Broom Street Theater, 4113
Brown County Arena, 8664
Brown County Civic Music Association, 5836
Camp Randall Stadium, 8674
Capitol Civic Centre, 8684
Cardinal Stritch University School of Visual and Performing Arts, 5857
Carthage Chamber Music Series, 1824
Carthage College Chamber Music & Lecture Series, 5840
Cedarburg Performing Arts Center, 8659
Central Wisconsin Symphony Orchestra, 1835
Chippewa Valley Theatre Guild, 4107
Cofrin Family Hall, 8665
Communication Arts Theatre, 8671
Concordia University Wisconsin, 5853
Cooley Auditorium, 8688
Council for the Performing Arts, 5839
Dance Program, 696
Dance Wisconsin, 705
Dancecircus, 701
Demmer Recital Hall, 8702
Door Community Auditorium Series, 5835
Early Music Now, 5858
Eau Claire Children's Theatre, 4108
Eau Claire Regional Arts Center, 5832
Fine Arts Theatre, 8703
First Stage Children's Theater, 4120
Flambeau Valley Arts Association, 5847
Florentine Opera Company, 2398
Fond Du Lac Symphonic Band, 1822
Fort Howard Hall, 8666
Four Seasons Theatre, 4114
Fox Cities Performing Arts Center, 8656
Fox Valley Symphony, 1820
Fredric March Play Circle, 8675
Gilbert V. Hemsley Theatre, 8676
Grand Opera House, 8697
Great American Children's Theatre Company, 4121
Great River Festival of Arts, 5842
Great River Jazz Fest, 5843
Green Bay Symphony Orchestra, 1823
Green Lake Festival of Music, 5837
Headwaters Council for the Performing Arts, 5831
Irvin L. Young Auditorium, 8710
Janesville Performing Arts Center, 5838
John Michael Kohler Arts Center, 8704
John Michael Kohler Arts Center: Footlights, 5867
Kanopy Dance Company, 697
Kenosha Symphony Association, 1825
Ko-Thi Dance Company, 702
Kohl Center, 8677
Kohler Foundation, 5841
Lakeland College Krueger Fine Arts Series, 5868
Lakeland Performing Arts Association, 5860
Lambeau Field, 8667
Lawrence University Music-Drama Center, 8657
Li Chiao-Ping Dance, 706
Lucille Tack Center for the Arts, 8705
Lucius Woods Performing Arts Center: Music in The Park, 5870
Mabel Tainter Memorial Theater, 4118
Madison Blues Festival, 5849
Madison Jazz Society, 5848
Madison Opera, 2395
Madison Repertory Theatre, 4115
Madison Scottish Country Dancers, 698
Madison Symphony Orchestra, 1826
Madison Theatre Guild, 4116
Manion Theatre, 8708
Marcus Center for the Performing Arts, 8689
Marshfield-Wood Community Symphony, 1829
Merrill Area Concert Association, 5854
Milwaukee Ballet Company, 703
Milwaukee Chamber Theatre, 4122
Milwaukee Opera Theatre, 2394
Milwaukee Public Theatre, 4123
Milwaukee Repertory Theater, 4124
Milwaukee Riverside Theater, 8690
Milwaukee Symphony Orchestra, 1830
Milwaukee Theatre, 4125, 8691
Milwaukee Youth Symphony Orchestra, 1831
Mitchell Hall Gymnasium, 8672
Mm Colbert, 699
Monroe Arts Center, 8696
Music Library Association, 8686
Newvoices, 2393
Next Act Theatre, 4126
Norman Mitby Theater, 8678
Northern Lights Playhouse, 4112
Northland Pines High School, 8660
Northwoods Concert Association, 5864
Opera for the Young, 2396
Oshkosh Symphony Orchestra, 1833
Overture Center for the Arts, 8679
P Brown County Arena, 8668
Pabst Theatre, 8692
Peninsula Players, 4111
Performing Arts at Lawrence, 5827
Performing Arts Foundation, 5874
Phipps Center for the Arts, 8670
Pioneer Field, 8698
Pitman Theatre, 8693
Playtime Productions, 4131
Portage Area Community Theatre, 4132
Prairie Performing Arts Center, 5863
Present Music, 1832
Pump House Regional Arts, 5844
Quandt Fieldhouse, 8707
Racine Civic Center- Festival Hall & Park &Memorial Hall, 8701
Racine Symphony Orchestra, 1834
Reed Marionettes, 4127
Renaissance Theaterworks, 4128
Richard & Helen Brodbeck Concert Hall, 8699
Ripon College: Caestecker Fine Arts Series, 5865
Ronald E. Mitchell Theatre, 8680
Shawano County Arts Council, 4133
Sheboygan Theatre Company, 4134
Shell Lake Arts Center, 5869
Silver Lake College, 8685
Silver Lake College Guest Artist Series, 5850
Skylight Opera Theatre, 4129
St. Croix Festival Theatre, 8706
St. Norbert College Performing Arts, 5830
Studio One, 8669
Sunset Playhouse, 4109
Tapit/New Works Ensemble Theater, 700
The Peninsula Music Festival, 5834
Theater, 8700
Theatre X, 4130
U.S. Cellular Arena, 8694
Union Theater, 8681
University of Wisconsin at Eau Claire Artists Series, 5833
University of Wisconsin at La Crosse Lectures, 5845
University of Wisconsin at Oshkosh Chamber Arts Series, 5861
University of Wisconsin at Stevens Point Performing Arts, 5871
University of Wisconsin at Whitewater, 5876
University of Wisconsin Center - Fox Valley, 5852
University of Wisconsin Fieldhouse, 8682
University of Wisconsin Lectures and Fine Arts, 5851
University of Wisconsin Marathon County, 5875
University of Wisconsin River Falls: Wyman Concerts & Lectures Series, 5866
University of Wisconsin-Platteville, 5862
University of Wisconsin: Superior University, 5872
Us Cellular Arena, 8695
Viterbo University Bright Star Season, 5846
Viterbo University Fine Arts Center, 8673
Warhawk Stadium, 8711
Waukesha Civic Theatre, 4136, 8709
Waupaca Fine Arts Festival, 5873
Wild Space Dance Company, 704
Wisconsin Chamber Orchestra, 1827
Wisconsin Conservatory of Music, 5859
Wisconsin Union Theater, 4117
Wisconsin Union Theatre, 8683
Wisconsin Youth Symphony Orchestras, 1828
WI Zorn Arena, 8662

Wyoming

Artcore, 5878
Cam-Plex Heritage Center, 8717
Casper Events Center, 8712
Cheyenne Civic Center, 8714
Cheyenne Little Theatre Players, 4137
Cheyenne Symphony Orchestra, 1837
Community Fine Arts Center, 8721
Durham Hall, 8713
Frontier Park, 8715
Grand Teton Music Festival, 5884
Northwest College, 5882
Off Square Theatre Company, 4138
Powder River Symphony Orchestra, 1838
Sheridan Civic Theatre Guild, 4139
The Ikon Center, 8716
University of Wyoming Cultural Programs, 5880
University of Wyoming: Arts and Sciences Auditorium, 8718
University of Wyoming: Fine Arts Concert Hall, 8719
War Memorial Stadium (Wy), 8720
Western Arts Music Festival, 5881
Western Wyoming College, 5883
Wyo Theater, 8722
Wyoming Arts Council, 5879
Wyoming Symphony Orchestra, 1836

Information Resources Index

A

Academy of Country Music, 8723
Academy of Motion Picture Arts and Sciences, 8724
Academy of Science Fiction Fantasy and Horror Films, 8725
Academy Players Directory, 9173
Accordian Federation of North America, 8726
Accordion Teachers Guild, 8727
Acoustical Society of America, 8728
Actors Equity Association, 8729
Advanstar, 8959
AfterTouch: New Music Discoveries, 8960
American Academy of Arts & Sciences Bulletin, 8903
American Alliance for Theatre and Education, 8730
American Association of Community Theatre, 8731
American Association of Community Theatre Membership Directory, 9174
American Choral Directors Association, 8732
American Choral Directors Association National Conference, 9115
American Cinema Editors, 8733
American Cinematographer, 8961
American College of Musicians, 8734
American Dance, 8904
American Dance Therapy Association, 8735
American Dancer, 8962
American Disc Jockey Association, 8736
American Federation of Musicians of the United States and Canada, 8737
American Federation of Violin and Bow Makers, 8738
American Film Institute Festival: AFI Fest, 9116
American Guild Associate News Newsletter, 8905
American Guild of Music, 8739
American Guild of Musical Artists, 8740
American Guild of Organists, 8741
American Guild of Organists, National Conference, 9117
American Harp Society, 8742
American Harp Society National Conference, 9118
American Indian Registry for the Performing Arts, 8743
American Institute of Organ Builders, 8744
American Institute of Organbuilders Annual Convention, 9119
American Music, 8963
American Music Center Directory, 9175
American Music Center Opportunity Update, 8906
American Music Teacher, 8964
American Music Therapy Association, 8745
American Music Therapy Conference, 9120
American Musical Instrument Society, 8746, 9121
American Musical Instrument Society Newsletter, 8907
American Musicological Society, 8747
American Musicological Society Annual Meeting, 9122
American Musicological Society Inc, 8908
American Orff-Schulwerk Association, 8748
American Orff-Schulwerk Association National Conference, 9123
American Organist, 8965
American School Band Directors Association, 8749
American School Band Directors Association Newsletter, 8909
American Society of Cinematographers, 8750
American Society of Composers, Authors and Publishers, 9176
American Society of Composers, Authors and Publishers (ASCAP), 8751
American Society of Music Arrangers and Composers, 8752
American String Teachers Association, 8753
American String Teachers Journal, 8966
American Symphony Orchestra League National Conference, 9124
American Theatre Magazine, 8967

American Viola Society, 8754
American Viola Society Journal, 8968
American Viola Society Newsletter, 8910
Americans for the Arts Field Directory, 9177
Animation Magazine, 8969
Annual Index to Motion Picture Credits, 9178
Applause Magazine, 8970
Art Directors Guild, 8755
Artsearch, 8911
Asian Pacific American Journal, 8971
Assistant Directors Training Program, 8756
Associated Pipe Organ Builders of America, 8757
Association for Theatre in Higher Education, 8758
Association of Arts Administration Educators, 8759
Association of Cinema and Video Laboratories, 8760
Association of Concert Bands, 8761
Association of Hispanic Arts, 8762
Association of Performing Arts Presenters, 8763
Association of Performing Arts Presenters Membership Directory, 9179
Association of Talent Agents, 8764
ASTA National Conference, 9114
AudArena International Guide, 9180

B

Back Stage, 8973
Banjo Newsletter, 8912
Billboard Magazine, 8974
Billboard Subscriber File, 9181
Blu-Book Production Directory, 9182
Bluegrass Music Profiles, 8913
Bluegrass Now, 8914
Bluegrass Resource Directory, 9183
Bluegrass Unlimited, 8915
Blues Foundation, 8765
BMI Musicworld, 8972
Bomb Magazine, 8975
BoxOffice Magazine, 8976
Boxoffice: Circuit Giants, 9184
Boxoffice: Distributor Directory, 9185
Broadcast Music Incorporated BMI, 8766
Broadside, 8916
Brooklyn Institute for Studies in American Music, 8917

C

Callaloo, 8978
Callboard, 8979
Canadian Theatre Review, 8980
Casting Society of America, 8767
CCM Magazine, 8977
Celebrity Service, 8981
Chamber Music America, 8768
Chamber Music America National Conference, 9126
Chamber Music Magazine, 8982
Children in Film, 8769
Chinese Music Society of North America, 8770
Choral Journal, 8983
Chorus America, 8771
Chorus America Annual Conference, 9127
Cineaste, 8984
Cinefantastique, 8985
Cinefex, 8986
Cinema Journal, 8987
CinemaCon, 9128
Clarinet Journal, 8988
Classical Action, 8772
Clavier, 8989
Close Up Magazine, 8990
CMS National Conference, 9125
CMS Newsletter, 8918
College Music Society, 8773
Complete Catalogue of Plays, 9186
Conductors Guild, 8774
Confrontation, 8991
Congress on Research in Dance, 8775
Contact Quarterly Journal of Dance and Improvisation, 8992
Contemporary Record Society, 8776
Costume Designers Guild Directory, 9187
Country Dance & Song Society, 8777

Country Dance and Song Society News, 8919
Country Music Association, 8778
Country Radio Broadcasters, 8779
Country Radio Seminar, 9129
Country Weekly Magazine, 8993
Creative Musicians Coalition, 8780
Cue Magazine, 8994

D

Daily Variety/Gotham, 8996
Daily Variety/LA, 8997
Dance Annual Directory, 9188
Dance Chronicle, 8998
Dance Critics Association, 8781
Dance Educators of America, 8782
Dance Films Association, 8783
Dance Magazine, 8999
Dance Magazine College Guide, 9189
Dance Magazine: Summer Dance Calendar Issue, 9190
Dance Masters of America, 8784
Dance on Camera Journal, 9003
Dance Research Journal, 9000
Dance Spirit, 9001
Dance Teacher Magazine, 9002
Dance USA, 8785
Dance/USA Annual Directory and List-Serv, 9191
Dance/USA Journal, 9004
Dancedrill, 8921
Descant, 9005
Diapason, 9006
Directors Guild of America, 8786
Directors Guild of America Directory of Members, 9192
Directory of Theatre Training Programs, 9193
Dirty Linen, 8922
Discoveries, 9007
DJ Times, 8995
DNBulletin, 8920
Downbeat, 9008
Drama Review, 9009
Dramatics College Theatre Directory, 9194
Dramatics Magazine, 9010
Dramatics Magazine: Summer Theatre Directory, 9195
Dramatist's Sourcebook, 9196
Dramatists Guild Annual Resource Directory, 9197
Dramatists Guild Newsletter, 8923
Dramatists Guild of America, 8787

E

Early Music Newsletter, 8924
East-2-West Marketing & Promotion, 8788
Editors Guild Directory, 9198
EdTA Thespian Festival, 9131
Educational Theatre Association, 8789
Educational Theatre Association Conference, 9132
Electronic Musician, 9011
Encore Performance Publishing, 9012
Encyclopedia of Exhibition, 9199
Esperanza Performing Arts Association, 8790
EXPO, 9130

F

Fame Index, 9200
Feedback Theatrebooks and Prospero Press, 9201
Festival Rag, 8925
Film & History, 9013
Film & Video Magazine, 9014
Film Advisory Board Monthly, 8926
Film Journal International, 9015
Film Journal: Distribution Guide Issue, 9202
Film Journal: Equipment Guide, 9203
Film Journal: Exhibition Guide, 9204
Film Society of Lincoln Center, 8791
Film Superlist: Motion Pictures in the Public Domain, 9205
Film Threat, 9016
Flatpicking Guitar, 8927
Flute Talk, 9017
Folk Alliance, 8792
Folk Alliance Annual Meeting, 9133

Folklife Center of International House, 8793
Fritz and Lavinia Jensen Foundation, 8794

G

Gina Bachauer International Piano Foundation, 8795
Girl Groups Gazette, 8930
GMA Update, 8928
GMAil, 8929
Goldmine, 9018
Gospel Music Association, 8796
Gospel Music Industry Directory, 9206
Gospel Music Week, 9134
Gospel Music Workshop America, 9135
Gospel Today, 9019
Greek Americans in the Arts and Entertainment, 8797
Grey House Performing Arts Directory, 9207
Grey House Performing Arts Directory - Online Database, 9208
Guild of American Luthiers, 8798
Guitar Accessory and Marketing Association (GAMA), 8799
Guitar Foundation of America, 8800
Guitar One, 9020
Guitar Review, 9021

H

HipHop Weekly, 9022
Hispanic Arts News, 9023
Historians Film Committee, 8801
Hollywood Arts Council, 8802, 8931
Hollywood Life, 9024
Hollywood Reporter, 9025
Horns Over the Sea, 9136
http://gold.greyhouse.com, 9246

I

In Focus, 8933
In the Groove, 8935
In Theater, 8934
Independent Film & Television Alliance, 8803
InLEAGUE, 8936
Instrumentalist, 9026
International Animated Film Society, 8804
International Association of Electronic Keyboard Manufacturers, 8805
International Association of Jazz Education, 8806
International Association of Jazz Educators Conference, 9137
International Association of Round Dance Teachers, 8807
International Association of Venue Managers, 9138
International Bluegrass Music Association, 8808, 8937
International Buyers Guide, 9209
International Cinema Equipment (ICECO) Showest, 9139
International Cinema Equipment Company ICECO Show East, 9140
International Cinematographers Guild, 8809
International Cinematographers Guild Magazine, 9027
International Clarinet Association, 8810
International Computer Music Association, 8811
International Computer Music Conference, 9141
International Documentary Association, 8812
International Documentary Magazine, 9028
International Festivals and Events Association, 8813
International Horn Competition of America, 9142
International Horn Society, 8814
International Motion Picture Alamanc, 9210
International Music Products Association NAMM, 8815
International Musician, 9029
International Piano Guild, 8816
International Planned Music Association, 8817
International Polka Association, 8818
International Society for the Performing Arts, 8819
International Society of Folk Harpers and Craftsmen, 8820
International Steel Guitar Convention, 9143

1299

Information Resources Index

International Stunt Association, 8821
International Talent and Touring Guide, 9211
International Television and Video Almanac, 9212
International Theatre Equipment Association, 8822
International Ticketing Association, 8823
INTIX Bulletin, 8932

J

JAMIA, 9030
Jazz Education, 8824
Jazz Education Journal, 9031
JazzTimes, 9032
Job Contact Bulletin, 8938
Journal of American Organbuilding, 9033
Journal of Arts Management, Law, Society, 9034
Journal of Dance Education, 9035
Journal of Film and Video, 9036
Journal of Music Theory, 9037
Journal of Music Therapy, 9038
Journal of Popular Film and Television, 9039
Journal of Research in Music Education, 9040
Journal of Singing, 9041
Journal of the American Musicological Society, 9042
Jukebox Collector Magazine, 9043

K

Keyboard Teachers Association International, 8825, 9213
Keyframe Magazine, 9044

L

League of American Ochestras, 8826
League of American Theatres and Producers, 8827
League of Historic American Theatres, 8828
Lighting Dimensions, 9045
Literary Managers and Dramaturgs of the Americas, 8829
Live Sound International, 9046

M

Metropolitan Opera Guild, 8830
Mid-Atlantic Arts Foundation, 8831
Mid-Atlantic Events Magazine, 9047
Mid-South Horn Conference, 9144
Midland Center for the Arts Midland Music and Concert Series, 8832
Midwest International Band & Orchestra Clinic, 9145
Millimeter Magazine, 9048
Mini Reviews, 9215
Mix, 9049
MLA Membership Handbook, 9214
Modern Drummer, 9050
Money for Film and Video Artists, 9216
Money for International Exchange in the Arts, 9217
Money for Performing Artists, 9218
Money for Visual Arts, 9219
Moondance Film Festival, 9146
Motion Picture Association of America, 8833
Motion Picture Editors Guild, 8834
Motion Picture Pilots Association, 8835
Motion Picture TV and Theatre Directory, 9220
Movie Collectors World, 9051
Movie World Almanac, 9221
MovieMaker, 9052
Music, 9053
Music & Sound Retailer, 9054
Music and Sound Journal, 9057
Music Distributors Association, 8836
Music for All Foundation, 8841
Music for the Love of It, 8939
Music Library Association, 8837
Music Library Association Membership Directory, 9222
Music Performance Fund, 8838
Music Publishers Association, 8839
Music Row, 9055
Music Teachers National Association, 8840
Music Teachers National Association Convention, 9147

Music Trades Magazine, 9056
Musical America Directory, 9223
Musical America International Directory of the Performing Arts, 9224
Musical Box Society International, 8842
Musical Merchandise Review, 9058
Musician's Guide, 9225
Musicians Foundation, 8843

N

NAMM: International Music Products Association, 9148
National Association for Drama Therapy, 8844
National Association for Music Education Conference, 9151
National Association for Music Education MENC, 8845
National Association of Band Instrument Manufacturers, 8846
National Association of College Wind and Percussion Instructor, 8847
National Association of Negro Musicians Inc, 8848
National Association of Pastoral Musicians, 8849
National Association of Pastoral Musicians Convention, 9152
National Association of Professional Band Instrument Repair Technicians, 8850
National Association of Recording Merchandisers, 8851
National Association of Recording Merchandising Trade Show, 9153
National Association of Schools of Music, 8852
National Association of Schools of Music Annual Meeting, 9154
National Association of Teachers of Singing, 8853
National Ballroom and Entertainment Association, 8854
National Band Association, 8855
National Black Theatre Festival, 9155
National Costumers Association, 8856
National Dance Association, 8857
National Dance Education Organization, 8858
National Endowment for the Arts, 8859
National Federation of Music Clubs, 8860
National Music Museum Newsletter, 8940
National Music Publishers Association, 8861
National Network for Artist Placement, 9227
National Opera Association, 8862
National Opera Association Conference, 9156
National Opera Association Membership Directory, 9228
National Piano Travelers Association, 8863
National Square Dance Convention, 9157
National Squares, 9059
NATS National Conference, 9149
NDEO National Conference, 9150
New England Theatre Conference, 8864, 9158
New England Theatre Journal, 9060
New on the Charts, 9061
New York Film Festival, 9159
No Depression, 8941
North American Performing Arts Managers and Agents, 8865
North Carolina Southeastern Theatre Conference, 9160
Northeast Horn Workshop, 9161
Notes, 9062
Notes a Tempo, 8942
Nouveau Magazine, 9063
NYC/On Stage, 9226

O

OffBeat, 9064
Old Time Herald, 8943
Opera America, 8866
Opera America Conference, 9162
Opera America Membership Directory, 9229
Opera America Newsline, 9065
Opera News, 9066
Oratorio Society of New York, 8867
Organization of American Kodaly Educators, 8868
Orion Blue Book: Guitars and Musical Instruments, 9230

Orion Blue Book: Professional Sound, 9231
Orion Blue Book: Vintage Guitar, 9232

P

Pedal Steel Guitar Association, 8869
Pedal Steel Newsletter, 8944
Percussion News, 8945
Percussive Arts Society, 8870
Percussive Notes, 9067
Performing Arts Association, 8871
Performing Arts Insider, 8946
Performing Arts Insider Magazine, 9068
Performing Arts Medicine Association, 8872
Performing Arts Resources, 9069
Piano Guild Notes, 9070
Piano Manufacturers Association, 8873
Piano Technicians Guild, 8874
Piano Technicians Guild Annual Convention, 9163
Piano Technicians Journal, 9071
Pitch Pipe, 9072
Playback, 9073
Playbill, 9074
Plays and Playwrights, 9233
Plays: Drama Magazine for Young People, 9075
Pointe Magazine, 9076
Pollstar: Concert Hotwire, 9077
Premiere Magazine, 9078
Prescott Park Arts Festival, 9164
Preview Family Movie & TV Review, 8947
Pro Audio Review, 9079
Pro Sound News, 9080
Produced By, 9081
Producer, 9082
Producers Guild of America, 8875
Production Music Library Association, 8876
Professional Women Singers Association, 8877

R

Record Retailing Directory, 9234
Reel Directory, 9235
Regional Theatre Directory, 9236
RePlay Magazine, 9083
Retail Print Music Dealers Association, 8878
Rhythm and Blues Foundation, 8879
Rolling Stone, 8948
Rolling Stone Magazine, 9084
Roots and Rhythm Newsletter, 8949

S

San Francisco Cinematheque, 9086
Screen Actors Guild, 8880
Script, 9087
SETC News, 8950
Shakespeare Bulletin, 9088
Sheet Music Magazine, 9089
Show Music, 9090
ShowBiz Bookkeeper, 9237
Sing Out!, 8951
SMPTE Journal, 9085
Society for Cinema & Media Studies, 8881
Society News, 9091
Society of American Magicians, 8882
Society of Camera Operators, 8883
Society of Motion Picture & Television Engineers, 8884
Society of Professional Audio Recording Services, 8885
Society of Stage Directors and Choreographers, 8886
Sondheim Review, 9092
Songwriters Guild of America, 8887
Source Directory of Books, Records and Tapes, 9238
Source Directory of Musical Instruments, 9239
Southern Arts Federation, 8888
Southern Theatre, 9093
Southwestern Musician, 9094
Spectrum, 9095
Spotlight, 8952
Stage of the Art, 9096
Stagebill, 9097
Stages, 9098
Starlog, 9099
Stars in Your Eyes...Feet on the Ground, 9240

Student's Guide to Playwriting Opportunities, 9241
Studio Report: Film Development, 9242
Stuntmen's Association of Motion Pictures, 8889
Stuntwomen's Association of Motion Pictures, 8890
Summer Theatre Directory, 9243
Sundance Film Festival, 9165
Sundance Institute, 8891
Sweet Adelines International, 8892
Sweet Adelines International Convention, 9166
Symphony Magazine, 9100
Symposium, 9101

T

TCG National Conference, 9167
TD & T: Theatre Design & Technology, 9102
Teaching Theatre Journal, 9103
Technical Brief, 8953, 9104
Telluride Film Festival, 9168
Tempo, 8954
The Voice, 8955
Theater Magazine, 9105
Theatre Authority, 8893
Theatre Bay Area, 8894
Theatre Bay Area Magazine, 9106
Theatre Bill, 9107
Theatre Communications Group, 8895
Theatre Development Fund, 8896
Theatre Journal, 9108
Theatre Profiles Database, 9244
Theatre Symposium, 9109
Theatre Topics, 9110
Toronto International Film Festival, 9169

U

University Film and Video Association, 8899
US Institute for Theatre Technology, 8897
US Institute for Theatre Technology Annual Conference & Stage Expo, 9170
USA Dance Inc, 8898

V

Variety, 9111
Vibe, 9112

W

Westfield Center, 8956
Whole Arts Directory, 9245
Winter Music Conference, 9171
Women in Bluegrass Newsletter, 8957
Women in Film, 8900
Women in the Arts Bulletin, 8958
Women in the Arts Foundation, 8901
World of Bluegrass, 9172
World Piano Competition/AMSA, 8902
www.aact.org, 9247
www.aahperd.org/nda, 9248
www.aate.com, 9249
www.absolutewrite.com, 9250
www.acdaonline.org, 9251
www.acmcountry.com, 9252
www.actioncutprint.com, 9253
www.actorsequity.org, 9254
www.actorsite.com, 9255
www.actorsource.com, 9256
www.actorstheatre.org, 9257
www.adta.org, 9258
www.afm.org, 9259
www.afvbm.com, 9260
www.agohq.org, 9261
www.aislesay.com, 9262
www.americandanceguild.org, 9263
www.americantheaterweb.com, 9264
www.answers4dancers.com, 9265
www.artdirectors.org, 9266
www.artsmed.org, 9267
www.artspresenters.org, 9268
www.artstabilization.org, 9269
www.asatalent.com, 9270
www.ascap.org, 9271
www.asmac.org, 9272
www.bachauer.com, 9273
www.backstage.com, 9274

Information Resources Index

www.backstagejobs.com, 9275
www.backstageworld.com, 9276
www.billboard.com, 9277
www.bmi.com, 9278
www.castingsociety.com, 9279
www.catf.org, 9280
www.chorusamerica.org, 9281
www.cincinnatiarts.org, 9282
www.clarinet.org, 9283
www.classicalaction.org, 9284
www.cmaworld.com, 9285
www.computermusic.org, 9286
www.conductorsguild.org, 9287
www.contactimprov.net, 9288
www.costume-con.org, 9289
www.costume.org, 9290
www.costumegallery.com, 9291
www.costumers.org, 9292
www.costumes.org, 9293
www.costumesocietyamerica.com, 9294
www.creativedir.com, 9295
www.creativemusicalcoalition.org, 9296
www.criticaldance.com, 9297
www.csulb.edu/~jvancamp/copyrigh.html, 9298
www.csusa.org/face/index.htm, 9299
www.cyberdance.org, 9300
www.danceart.com/edancing, 9301
www.dancenotation.org, 9302
www.dancepages.com, 9303
www.dancer.com/dance-links, 9304
www.danceusa.org, 9305
www.deadance.com, 9306
www.discoverhollywood.com, 9307
www.dma-national.org, 9308
www.documentary.org, 9309
www.dramaguild.com, 9310
www.dramaleague.org, 9311
www.dtw.org, 9312
www.edta.org, 9313
www.esperanzaarts.org, 9314
www.etecnyc.net, 9315
www.flmusiced.org, 9316
www.folkharpsociety.org, 9317
www.gmn.com, 9318
www.goldmime.com, 9319
www.gospelmusic.org, 9320

www.greyhouse.com, 9321
www.guitarfoundation.org, 9322
www.harada-sound.com/sound/handbook, 9323
www.harpsociety.org, 9324
www.hawaii.edu, 9325
www.heniford.net/1234, 9326
www.horndoggie.com/horn, 9327
www.iaekm.org, 9328
www.ibma.org, 9329
www.ifea.com, 9330
www.imeamusic.org, 9331
www.internationalpolka.com, 9332
www.intix.org, 9333
www.iqfilm.org, 9334
www.ispa.org, 9335
www.jensenfoundation.org, 9336
www.latinoarts.org, 9337
www.lib.colum.edu/costwais.html, 9338
www.light-link.com, 9339
www.livebroadway.com, 9340
www.lmda.org, 9341
www.luth.org, 9342
www.lycos.com, 9343
www.magicsam.com, 9344
www.makeupmag.com, 9345
www.members.aol.com/thegoop/gaff.html, 9346
www.metguild.org, 9347
www.midatlanticarts.org, 9348
www.milieux.com/costume, 9349
www.millimeter.com, 9350
www.mpa.org, 9351
www.mpaa.org, 9352
www.mtishows.com, 9353
www.mtna.org, 9354
www.music.org, 9355
www.musicalamerica.com, 9356
www.musicalartists.org, 9357
www.musicdistributors.org, 9358
www.musicianshealth.com, 9359
www.musiclibraryassoc.org, 9360
www.nacwpi.org, 9361
www.nadt.org, 9362
www.namm.org, 9363
www.napama.org, 9364
www.napbirt.org, 9365
www.narm.com, 9366

www.natoonline.org, 9367
www.nats.org, 9368
www.nbea.com, 9369
www.nbtf.org, 9370
www.netconline.org, 9371
www.netsword.com/stagecombat.html, 9372
www.newplaysforchildren.com, 9373
www.nmpa.org, 9374
www.noa.org, 9375
www.npm.org, 9376
www.ntcp.org, 9377
www.nyfa.com, 9378
www.nyfa.org, 9379
www.nypl.org/reseach/lpa/lpa.html, 9380
www.nyssma.org, 9381
www.nytimes.com, 9382
www.oobr.com, 9383
www.opencasting.com, 9384
www.oscars.org, 9385
www.paastjo.org, 9386
www.pas.org, 9387
www.pen.org, 9388
www.performingarts.net, 9389
www.pianoguild.com, 9390
www.pianonet.com, 9391
www.pipeorgan.org, 9392
www.plasa.org, 9393
www.playbill.com, 9394
www.playwrights.org, 9395
www.playwrightshorizons.org, 9396
www.playwrightsproject.com, 9397
www.press.jhu.edu/press/journals/paj, 9398
www.press.jhu.edu/press/journals/tj, 9399
www.press.jhu.edu/press/journals/tt, 9400
www.printmusic.org, 9401
www.producersguild.org, 9402
www.proppeople.com, 9403
www.ptg.org, 9404
www.renfaire.com/Language/index.html, 9405
www.resumegenie.com, 9406
www.rigging.net, 9407
www.roundalab.org, 9408
www.safd.org, 9409
www.sag.org, 9410
www.sapphireswan.com/dance, 9411
www.setc.org, 9412

www.sfballet.org, 9413
www.smpte.org, 9414
www.southarts.org, 9415
www.spars.com, 9416
www.spolin.com, 9417
www.ssdc.org, 9418
www.stage-directions.com, 9419
www.stageplays.com/markets.htm, 9420
www.stetson.edu/csata/thr_guid.html, 9421
www.stuntnet.com, 9422
www.stuntwomen.org, 9423
www.summertheater.com, 9424
www.sundance.org, 9425
www.symphony.org, 9426
www.talkinbroadway.com, 9427
www.tcg.org, 9428
www.tdf.org, 9429
www.teleport.com/~bjscript/index.htm, 9430
www.theatre-resource.com, 9431
www.theatrebayarea.org, 9432
www.theatrecrafts.com, 9433
www.theatrejobs.com, 9434
www.theatrelibrary.org/links, 9435
www.theatrelibrary.org/links/index.html, 9436
www.thecastingnetwork.com/webring.html, 9437
www.theplays.org, 9438
www.tmea.org, 9439
www.top20performingarts.com, 9440
www.towson.edu/worldmusiccongresses, 9441
www.unc.edu/depts/outdoor, 9442
www.ups.edu/professionalorgs/dramaturgy, 9443
www.urta.com, 9444
www.usabda.org, 9445
www.usitt.org, 9446
www.variety.org, 9447
www.vcu.edu/artweb/playwriting, 9448
www.vl-theatre.com, 9449
www.wif.org, 9450
www.writersguild.com, 9451
www.wwar.com, 9452
www2.sundance.org, 9453

Y

Youth Theatre Journal, 9113

2014 Title List

Visit www.GreyHouse.com for Product Information, Table of Contents and Sample Pages

General Reference
America's College Museums
American Environmental Leaders: From Colonial Times to the Present
An African Biographical Dictionary
An Encyclopedia of Human Rights in the United States
Constitutional Amendments
Encyclopedia of African-American Writing
Encyclopedia of the Continental Congress
Encyclopedia of Gun Control & Gun Rights
Encyclopedia of Invasions & Conquests
Encyclopedia of Prisoners of War & Internment
Encyclopedia of Religion & Law in America
Encyclopedia of Rural America
Encyclopedia of the United States Cabinet, 1789-2010
Encyclopedia of War Journalism
Encyclopedia of Warrior Peoples & Fighting Groups
From Suffrage to the Senate: America's Political Women
Nations of the World
Political Corruption in America
Speakers of the House of Representatives, 1789-2009
The Environmental Debate: A Documentary History
The Evolution Wars: A Guide to the Debates
The Religious Right: A Reference Handbook
The Value of a Dollar: 1860-2009
The Value of a Dollar: Colonial Era
This is Who We Were: A Companion to the 1940 Census
This is Who We Were: The 1920s
This is Who We Were: The 1950s
This is Who We Were: The 1960s
US Land & Natural Resource Policy
Working Americans 1770-1869 Vol. IX: Revolutionary War to the Civil War
Working Americans 1880-1999 Vol. I: The Working Class
Working Americans 1880-1999 Vol. II: The Middle Class
Working Americans 1880-1999 Vol. III: The Upper Class
Working Americans 1880-1999 Vol. IV: Their Children
Working Americans 1880-2003 Vol. V: At War
Working Americans 1880-2005 Vol. VI: Women at Work
Working Americans 1880-2006 Vol. VII: Social Movements
Working Americans 1880-2007 Vol. VIII: Immigrants
Working Americans 1880-2009 Vol. X: Sports & Recreation
Working Americans 1880-2010 Vol. XI: Inventors & Entrepreneurs
Working Americans 1880-2011 Vol. XII: Our History through Music
Working Americans 1880-2012 Vol. XIII: Education & Educators
World Cultural Leaders of the 20th & 21st Centuries

Business Information
Complete Television, Radio & Cable Industry Directory
Directory of Business Information Resources
Directory of Mail Order Catalogs
Directory of Venture Capital & Private Equity Firms
Environmental Resource Handbook
Food & Beverage Market Place
Grey House Homeland Security Directory
Grey House Performing Arts Directory
Hudson's Washington News Media Contacts Directory
New York State Directory
Sports Market Place Directory

Education Information
Charter School Movement
Comparative Guide to American Elementary & Secondary Schools
Complete Learning Disabilities Directory
Educators Resource Directory
Special Education

Health Information
Comparative Guide to American Hospitals
Complete Directory for Pediatric Disorders
Complete Directory for People with Chronic Illness
Complete Directory for People with Disabilities
Complete Mental Health Directory
Diabetes in America: A Geographic & Demographic Analysis
Directory of Health Care Group Purchasing Organizations
Directory of Hospital Personnel
HMO/PPO Directory
Medical Device Register
Older Americans Information Directory

Statistics & Demographics
America's Top-Rated Cities
America's Top-Rated Small Towns & Cities
America's Top-Rated Smaller Cities
American Tally
Ancestry & Ethnicity in America
Comparative Guide to American Hospitals
Comparative Guide to American Suburbs
Profiles of America
Profiles of… Series – State Handbooks
The Hispanic Databook
Weather America

Financial Ratings Series
TheStreet.com Ratings Guide to Bond & Money Market Mutual Funds
TheStreet.com Ratings Guide to Common Stocks
TheStreet.com Ratings Guide to Exchange-Traded Funds
TheStreet.com Ratings Guide to Stock Mutual Funds
TheStreet.com Ratings Ultimate Guided Tour of Stock Investing
Weiss Ratings Consumer Guides
Weiss Ratings Guide to Banks & Thrifts
Weiss Ratings Guide to Credit Unions
Weiss Ratings Guide to Health Insurers
Weiss Ratings Guide to Life & Annuity Insurers
Weiss Ratings Guide to Property & Casualty Insurers

Bowker's Books In Print®Titles
Books In Print®
Books In Print® Supplement
American Book Publishing Record® Annual
American Book Publishing Record® Monthly
Books Out Loud™
Bowker's Complete Video Directory™
Children's Books In Print®
El-Hi Textbooks & Serials In Print®
Forthcoming Books®
Law Books & Serials In Print™
Medical & Health Care Books In Print™
Publishers, Distributors & Wholesalers of the US™
Subject Guide to Books In Print®
Subject Guide to Children's Books In Print®

Canadian General Reference
Associations Canada
Canadian Almanac & Directory
Canadian Environmental Resource Guide
Canadian Parliamentary Guide
Financial Services Canada
Governments Canada
Health Services Canada
Libraries Canada
Major Canadian Cities
The History of Canada

Grey House Publishing | Salem Press | H.W. Wilson
4919 Route, 22 PO Box 56, Amenia NY 12501-0056

SALEM PRESS
2014 Title List
Visit **www.SalemPress.com** for Product Information, Table of Contents and Sample Pages

Literature
American Ethnic Writers
Critical Insights: Authors
Critical Insights: New Literary Collection Bundles
Critical Insights: Themes
Critical Insights: Works
Critical Survey of Drama
Critical Survey of Graphic Novels: Heroes & Super Heroes
Critical Survey of Graphic Novels: History, Theme & Technique
Critical Survey of Graphic Novels: Independents & Underground Classics
Critical Survey of Graphic Novels: Manga
Critical Survey of Long Fiction
Critical Survey of Mystery & Detective Fiction
Critical Survey of Mythology and Folklore: Heroes and Heroines
Critical Survey of Mythology and Folklore: Love, Sexuality & Desire
Critical Survey of Mythology and Folklore: World Mythology
Critical Survey of Poetry
Critical Survey of Poetry: American Poetry
Critical Survey of Poetry: British, Irish & Commonwealth Poets
Critical Survey of Poetry: European Poets
Critical Survey of Poetry: European Poets
Critical Survey of Poetry: Topical Essays
Critical Survey of Poetry: World Poets
Critical Survey of Science Fiction & Fantasy Literature
Critical Survey of Shakespeare's Sonnets
Critical Survey of Short Fiction
Critical Survey of Short Fiction: American Writers
Critical Survey of Short Fiction: British, Irish & Commonwealth Poets
Critical Survey of Short Fiction: European Writers
Critical Survey of Short Fiction: Topical Essays
Critical Survey of Short Fiction: World Writers
Cyclopedia of Literary Characters
Introduction to Literary Context: American Post-Modernist Novels
Introduction to Literary Context: American Short Fiction
Introduction to Literary Context: English Literature
Introduction to Literary Context: World Literature
Magill's Literary Annual 2014
Magill's Survey of American Literature
Magill's Survey of World Literature
Masterplots
Masterplots II: African American Literature
Masterplots II: Christian Literature
Masterplots II: Drama Series
Masterplots II: Short Story Series
Notable African American Writers
Notable American Novelists
Notable Playwrights
Short Story Writers

Science, Careers & Mathematics
Applied Science
Applied Science: Engineering & Mathematics
Applied Science: Science & Medicine
Applied Science: Technology
Biomes and Ecosystems
Careers in Chemistry
Careers in Communications & Media
Careers in Healthcare
Careers in Hospitality & Tourism
Careers in Law & Criminology
Careers in Physics
Computer Technology Inventors
Contemporary Biographies in Chemistry
Contemporary Biographies in Communications & Media
Contemporary Biographies in Healthcare
Contemporary Biographies in Hospitality & Tourism
Contemporary Biographies in Law & Criminology
Contemporary Biographies in Physics
Earth Science
Earth Science: Earth Materials & Resources
Earth Science: Earth's Surface and History
Earth Science: Physics & Chemistry of the Earth
Earth Science: Weather, Water & Atmosphere
Encyclopedia of Energy
Encyclopedia of Environmental Issues
Encyclopedia of Global Resources
Encyclopedia of Global Warming
Encyclopedia of Mathematics and Society
Encyclopedia of the Ancient World
Forensic Science
Internet Innovators
Introduction to Chemistry
Magill's Encyclopedia of Science: Animal Life
Magill's Encyclopedia of Science: Plant life
Magill's Medical Guide
Notable Natural Disasters
Solar System

Health
Addictions & Substance Abuse
Cancer
Complementary & Alternative Medicine
Genetics & Inherited Conditions
Infectious Diseases & Conditions
Magill's Medical Guide
Psychology & Mental Health
Psychology Basics

Grey House Publishing | Salem Press | H.W. Wilson
4919 Route, 22 PO Box 56, Amenia NY 12501-0056

SALEM PRESS

2014 Title List

Visit www.SalemPress.com for Product Information, Table of Contents and Sample Pages

History and Social Science

- A 2000s in America
- 50 States
- African American History
- Agriculture in History (check)
- American First Ladies
- American Heroes
- American Indian Tribes
- American Presidents
- American Villains
- Ancient Greece
- Bill of Rights, The
- Cold War, The
- Defining Documents: American Revolution 1754-1805
- Defining Documents: Civil War 1860-1865
- Defining Documents: Emergence of Modern America, 1868-1918
- Defining Documents: Exploration & Colonial America 1492-1755
- Defining Documents: Manifest Destiny 1803-1860
- Defining Documents: Reconstruction, 1865-1880
- Defining Documents: The 1920s
- Defining Documents: The 1930s
- Defining Documents: World War I
- Eighties in America
- Encyclopedia of American Immigration
- Fifties in America
- Forties in America
- Great Athletes
- Great Events from History: 17th Century
- Great Events from History: 18th Century
- Great Events from History: 19th Century
- Great Events from History: 20th Century, 1901-1940
- Great Events from History: 20th Century, 1941-1970
- Great Events from History: 20th Century, 1971-200
- Great Events from History: Ancient World
- Great Events from History: Middle Ages
- Great Events from History: Modern Scandals
- Great Events from History: Renaissance & Early Modern Era
- Great Lives from History: 17th Century
- Great Lives from History: 18th Century
- Great Lives from History: 19th Century
- Great Lives from History: 20th Century
- Great Lives from History: African Americans
- Great Lives from History: Ancient World
- Great Lives from History: Asian & Pacific Islander Americans
- Great Lives from History: Incredibly Wealthy
- Great Lives from History: Inventors & Inventions
- Great Lives from History: Jewish Americans
- Great Lives from History: Latinos
- Great Lives from History: Middle Ages
- Great Lives from History: Notorious Lives
- Great Lives from History: Renaissance & Early Modern Era
- Great Lives from History: Scientists & Science
- Historical Encyclopedia of American Business
- Immigration in U.S. History
- Magill's Guide to Military History
- Milestone Documents in African American History
- Milestone Documents in American History
- Milestone Documents in World History
- Milestone Documents of American Leaders
- Milestone Documents of World Religions
- Musicians & Composers 20th Century
- Nineties in America
- Seventies in America
- Sixties in America
- Survey of American Industry and Careers
- Thirties in America
- Twenties in America
- U.S. Court Cases
- U.S. Laws, Acts, and Treaties
- U.S. Legal System
- U.S. Supreme Court
- United States at War
- USA in Space
- Weapons and Warfare
- World Conflicts: Asia and the Middle East

2014 Title List

Visit www.HwWilsonInPrint.com for Product Information, Table of Contents and Sample Pages

Current Biography
Current Biography Cumulative Index 1946-2013
Current Biography Magazine
Current Biography Yearbook-2004
Current Biography Yearbook-2005
Current Biography Yearbook-2006
Current Biography Yearbook-2007
Current Biography Yearbook-2008
Current Biography Yearbook-2009
Current Biography Yearbook-2010
Current Biography Yearbook-2011
Current Biography Yearbook-2012
Current Biography Yearbook-2013
Current Biography Yearbook-2014

Core Collections
Senior High Core Collection
Middle & Junior High School Core
Children's Core Collection
Fiction Core Collection
Public Library Core Collection: Nonfiction

Sears List
Sears List of Subject Headings
Sears: Lista de Encabezamientos de Materia

The Reference Shelf
Aging in America
Revisiting Gender
The U.S. National Debate Topic, 2014/2015
Embracing New Paradigms in education
Marijuana Reform
Representative American Speeches 2013-2014
Reality Television
The Business of Food
The Future of U.S. Economic Relations: Mexico, Cuba, and Venezuela
Sports in America
Global Climate Change
Representative American Speeches, 2012-2013
Conspiracy Theories
The Arab Spring
U.S. National Debate Topic: Transportation Infrastructure
Families: Traditional and New Structures
Faith & Science
Representative American Speeches 2011-2012
Social Networking
Dinosaurs
Space Exploration & Development
U.S. Infrastructure
Politics of the Ocean
Representative American Speeches 2010-2011
Robotics
The News and its Future
American Military Presence Overseas
Russia
Graphic Novels and Comic Books
Representative American Speeches 2009-2010

Readers' Guide
Readers Guide to Periodicals Literature
Abridged Readers' Guide to Periodical Literature
Short Story Index

Indexes
Short Story Index
Index to Legal Periodicals & Books

Facts About Series
Facts About the Presidents, Eighth Edition
Facts About China
Facts About the 20th Century
Facts About American Immigration
Facts About World's Languages

Nobel Prize Winners
Nobel Prize Winners, 2002-2013

World Authors
World Authors 2000-2005
World Authors 2006-2013

Famous First Facts
Famous First Facts, Seventh Edition
Famous First Facts About American Politics
Famous First Facts About Sports
Famous First Facts About the Environment
Famous First Facts, International Edition

American Book of Days
The American Book of Days, Fifth Edition
The International Book of Days

Junior Authors & Illustrators
Tenth Book of Junior Authors & Illustrations

Monographs
The Barnhart Dictionary of Etymology
Celebrate the World
Indexing from A to Z
Radical Change: Books for Youth in a Digital Age
The Poetry Break
Guide to the Ancient World

Wilson Chronology
Wilson Chronology of Asia and the Pacific
Wilson Chronology of Human Rights
Wilson Chronology of Ideas
Wilson Chronology of the Arts
Wilson Chronology of the World's Religions
Wilson Chronology of Women's Achievements

Book Review Digest
Book Review Digest, 2014

Grey House Publishing | Salem Press | H.W. Wilson
4919 Route, 22 PO Box 56, Amenia NY 12501-0056